CAR MODELS

CHILTON'S IMPORT CAR MANUAL 1990-1994

Publisher and Editor-In-Chief	Kerry A. Freeman, S.A.E.
Managing Editors	Peter M. Conti, Jr., W. Calvin Settle, Jr., S.A.E.
Assistant Managing Editor	Nick D'Andrea
Senior Editors	Debra Gaffney, Ken Grabowski, A.S.E., S.A.E.
	Michael L. Grady, Richard J. Rivele, S.A.E.
	Richard T. Smith, Jim Taylor
	Ron Webb
Editorial Staff	Peter A. Bilotta, A.S.E., Lawrence C. Braun, S.A.E., A.S.C., Thomas P. Browne III, Hugh J. Brulliea, Dean G. Callahan, Michael M. Carroll, William C. Cottman, A.S.E., Robert B. Day, Jr., Paul DeGuiseppi, A.S.E., Robert F. Dougherty, Jr., Robert E. Doughten, Sam Fiorani, Andrew J. Folz, A.S.E., Edward J. Giacomucci, A.S.E., Jacques Gordon, Neil Leonard, Kevin Maher, Robert McAnally, Raymond K. Moore, Craig P. Nangle, A.S.E., Roy Ripple, A.S.E., John H. Rutter, Don Schnell, A.S.E., S.A.E., Larry E. Stiles, Anthony Tortorici, A.S.E., S.A.E., Thom Young
Assistant Production Manager	Andrea M. Steiger
Production Assistants	Marsha Park Herman, Monica Santa Maria, Margaret Stoner
Mechanical Artists	Lisa Gressen, Kim Hayes
Director of Manufacturing	Mike D'Imperio
OFFICERS	
President, Chilton Enterprises	David S. Loewith
Senior Vice President	Ronald A. Hoxter

CHILTON BOOK COMPANY

ONE OF THE **DIVERSIFIED PUBLISHING COMPANIES,**
A PART OF **CAPITAL CITIES/ABC,INC.**

Manufactured in
© 1993 Chilton Book Company
Chilton Way, Radnor, PA 19089
ISBN 0-8019-7913-7
ISSN 0271-3608

1234567890 2109876543

TABLE OF CONTENTS

Car Sections

HOW TO USE THIS MANUAL

Car Section

Car sections are grouped by manufacturer and arranged in alphabetical order. The text and illustrations that comprise the service procedures in each Car Section are arranged in the following order of systems and components: Engine Mechanical, Engine Lubrication, Engine Cooling, Engine Electrical, Emission Controls, Fuel System, Drive Axle, Manual Transmission/Transaxle, Clutch, Automatic Transmission/Transaxle, Front Suspension, Rear Suspension, Steering, Brakes, Chassis Electrical.

Specification charts are always located at the front of each section. All illustrations are located as close as possible to the pertinent text. Procedures are for all models in the particular section unless specifically noted otherwise.

Locating Information

The Table of Contents, at the front of the book, lists the beginning of each Car Section in the manual.

To find where a particular Car Section is located in the book, you need only look in the Table of Contents. Once you have found the proper section, you may wish to find where specific procedures are located in that section. Turn to the Index at the front of the section. At the upper left-hand side is a listing of the main topics within the section and the page number they will be found on. Following the main topics is an alphabetical listing of all the procedures within the section and their page numbers.

Safety Notice

Proper service and repair procedures are vital to the safe, reliable operation of all motor vehicles, as well as the personal safety of those performing repairs. This manual outlines procedures for servicing and repairing vehicles using safe effective methods. The procedures contain many NOTES and CAUTIONS which should be followed along with standard safety procedures to eliminate the possibility of personal injury or improper service which could damage the vehicle or compromise its safety.

It is important to note that repair procedures and techniques, tools and parts for servicing motor vehicles, as well as the skill and experience of the individual performing the work vary widely. It is not possible to anticipate all of the conceivable ways or conditions under which vehicles may be serviced, or to provide cautions as to all of the possible hazards that may result. Standard and accepted safety precautions and equipment should be used when handling toxic or flammable fluids, and safety goggles or other protection should be used during cutting, grinding, chiseling, prying, or any other process that can cause material removal or projectiles.

Some procedures require the use of tools specially designed for a specific purpose. Before substituting another tool or procedure, you must be completely satisfied that neither your personal safety, nor the performance of the vehicle will be endangered.

Part Numbers

Part numbers listed in this book are not recommendations by Chilton for any product by brand name. They are references that can be used with interchange manuals and aftermarket supplier catalogs to locate each brand supplier's discrete part number.

Although information in this manual is based on industry sources and is as complete as possible at the time of publication, the possibility exists that some car manufacturers made later changes which could not be included here. Information on very late models may not be available in some circumstances. While striving for total accuracy, Chilton Book Company cannot assume responsibility for any errors, changes, or omissions that may occur in the compilation of this data.

Copyright Notice

Acura 1

—Integra, Legend, Vigor

SPECIFICATIONS

ENGINE IDENTIFICATION

Year	Model	Engine Displacement Liters (cc)	Engine Series (ID/VIN)	Fuel System	No. of Cylinders	Engine Type
1990	Integra	1.8 (1834)	B18A1	PGM-FI	4	DOHC
	Legend	2.7 (2675)	C27A1	PGM-FI	6	SOHC
	Legend Coupe	2.7 (2675)	C27A1	PGM-FI	6	SOHC
	827	2.7 (2675)	C27A1	PGM-FI	6	SOHC
1991	Integra	1.8 (1834)	B18A1	PGM-FI	4	DOHC
	Legend	3.2 (3206)	C32A1	PGM-FI	6	SOHC
	Legend Coupe	3.2 (3206)	C32A1	PGM-FI	6	SOHC
	827	2.7 (2675)	C27A1	PGM-FI	6	SOHC
	NSX	3.0 (2977)	C30A1	PGM-FI	6	DOHC
1992	Integra	1.8 (1834)	B18A1	PGM-FI	4	DOHC
	Integra GSR	1.7 (1678)	B17A1	PGM-FI	4	DOHC
	Legend	3.2 (3206)	C32A1	PGM-FI	6	SOHC
	Legend Coupe	3.2 (3206)	C32A1	PGM-FI	6	SOHC
	Vigor	2.5 (2451)	G25A1	PGM-FI	5	SOHC
	NSX	3.0 (2977)	C30A1	PGM-FI	6	DOHC
1993	Integra	1.8 (1834)	B18A1	PGM-FI	4	DOHC
	Integra GSR	1.7 (1678)	B17A1	PGM-FI	4	DOHC
	Legend	3.2 (3206)	C32A1	PGM-FI	6	SOHC
	Legend Coupe	3.2 (3206)	C32A1	PGM-FI	6	SOHC
	Vigor	2.5 (2451)	G25A1	PGM-FI	5	SOHC
	NSX	3.0 (2977)	C30A1	PGM-FI	6	DOHC
1994	Integra	1.8 (1834)	B18A1	PGM-FI	4	DOHC
	Integra GSR	1.7 (1678)	B17A1	PGM-FI	4	DOHC
	Legend	3.2 (3206)	C32A1	PGM-FI	6	SOHC
	Legend Coupe	3.2 (3206)	C32A1	PGM-FI	6	SOHC
	Vigor	2.5 (2451)	G25A1	PGM-FI	5	SOHC
	NSX	3.0 (2977)	C30A1	PGM-FI	6	DOHC

DOHC—Double Overhead Camshaft
SOHC—Single Overhead Camshaft
PGM-FI—Programmed Fuel Injection

GENERAL ENGINE SPECIFICATIONS

Year	Engine ID/VIN	Engine Displacement Liters (cc)	Fuel System Type	Net Horsepower @ rpm	Net Torque @ rpm (ft. lbs.)	Bore × Stroke (in.)	Compression Ratio	Oil Pressure @ rpm
1990	B18A1	1.8 (1834)	PGM-FI	130 @ 6000	121 @ 5000	3.19 × 3.50	9.2:1	69–79 @ 3000
	C27A1	2.7 (2675)	PGM-FI	161 @ 5900	162 @ 4500	3.43 × 2.95	9.0:1	71–82 @ 3000
1991	B18A1	1.8 (1834)	PGM-FI	130 @ 6000	121 @ 5000	3.19 × 3.50	9.2:1	69–79 @ 3000
	C27A1	2.7 (2675)	PGM-FI	161 @ 5900	162 @ 4500	3.43 × 2.95	9.0:1	71–82 @ 3000
	C32A1	3.2 (3206)	PGM-FI	200 @ 5500	210 @ 4500	3.54 × 3.31	9.6:1	71–82 @ 3000
	C30A1	3.0 (2977)	PGM-FI	270 @ 7100①	210 @ 5300	3.54 × 3.07	10.2:1	50 @ 3000
1992	B18A1	1.8 (1834)	PGM-FI	140 @ 6300	126 @ 5000	3.19 × 3.50	9.2:1	50 @ 3000
	B17A1	1.7 (1678)	PGM-FI	160 @ 7600	117 @ 7000	3.19 × 3.20	9.7:1	50 @ 3000
	C32A1	3.2 (3206)	PGM-FI	200 @ 5500	210 @ 4500	3.54 × 3.31	9.6:1	50 @ 3000
	G25A1	2.5 (2451)	PGM-FI	176 @ 6300	170 @ 3900	3.35 × 3.40	9.0:1	50 @ 3000
	C30A1	3.0 (2977)	PGM-FI	270 @ 7100①	210 @ 5300	3.54 × 3.07	10.2:1	50 @ 3000
1993	B18A1	1.8 (1834)	PGM-FI	140 @ 6300	126 @ 5000	3.19 × 3.50	9.2:1	50 @ 3000
	B17A1	1.7 (1678)	PGM-FI	160 @ 7600	117 @ 7000	3.19 × 3.20	9.7:1	50 @ 3000
	C32A1	3.2 (3206)	PGM-FI	200 @ 5500	210 @ 4500	3.54 × 3.31	9.6:1	50 @ 3000
	G25A1	2.5 (2451)	PGM-FI	176 @ 6300	170 @ 3900	3.35 × 3.40	9.0:1	50 @ 3000
	C30A1	3.0 (2977)	PGM-FI	270 @ 7100①	210 @ 5300	3.54 × 3.07	10.2:1	50 @ 3000
1994	B18A1	1.8 (1834)	PGM-FI	140 @ 6300	126 @ 5000	3.19 × 3.50	9.2:1	50 @ 3000
	B17A1	1.7 (1678)	PGM-FI	160 @ 7600	117 @ 7000	3.19 × 3.20	9.7:1	50 @ 3000
	C32A1	3.2 (3206)	PGM-FI	200 @ 5500	210 @ 4500	3.54 × 3.31	9.6:1	50 @ 3000
	G25A1	2.5 (2451)	PGM-FI	176 @ 6300	170 @ 3900	3.35 × 3.40	9.0:1	50 @ 3000
	C30A1	3.0 (2977)	PGM-FI	270 @ 7100①	210 @ 5300	3.54 × 3.07	10.2:1	50 @ 3000

PGM-FI—Programmed Fuel Injection
① With manual transmission; 252 @ 6600 with automatic transmission

GASOLINE ENGINE TUNE-UP SPECIFICATIONS

Year	Engine ID/VIN	Engine Displacement Liters (cc)	Spark Plugs Gap (in.)	Ignition Timing (deg.)		Fuel Pump (psi)	Idle Speed (rpm)		Valve Clearance	
				MT	AT		MT	AT	In.	Ex.
1990	B18A1	1.8 (1834)	0.041	16B	16B	35–41①	700–800	700–800	0.006–0.008	0.006–0.008
	C27A1	2.7 (2675)	0.041	15B	15B	36–41①	630–730	630–730	Hyd.	Hyd.
1991	B18A1	1.8 (1834)	0.041	16B	16B	35–41①	700–800	700–800	0.006–0.008	0.006–0.008
	C27A1	2.7 (2675)	0.041	15B	15B	36–41①	630–730	630–730	Hyd.	Hyd.
	C32A1	3.2 (3206)	0.041	15B	15B	31–37①	600–700	650–750	Hyd.	Hyd.
	C30A1	3.0 (2977)	0.041	15B	15B	36–44①	750–850	650–750	0.006–0.007	0.007–0.008
1992	B18A1	1.8 (1834)	0.041	16B	16B	41–48①	700–800	700–800	0.003–0.005	0.006–0.008
	B17A1	1.7 (1678)	0.050	16B	16B	48–56①	700–800	700–800	0.006–0.007	0.007–0.008
	C32A1	3.2 (3206)	0.041	15B	15B	31–37①	600–700	650–750	Hyd.	Hyd.
	G25A1	2.5 (2451)	0.043	16B	16B	43–50①	650–750	650–750	0.009–0.011	0.011–0.013
	C30A1	3.0 (2977)	0.041	15B	15B	36–44①	750–850	650–750②	0.006–0.007	0.007–0.008
1993	B18A1	1.8 (1834)	0.041	16B	16B	41–48①	700–800	700–800	0.003–0.005	0.006–0.008
	B17A1	1.7 (1678)	0.050	16B	16B	48–56①	700–800	700–800	0.006–0.007	0.007–0.008
	C32A1	3.2 (3206)	0.041	15B	15B	31–37①	600–700	650–750	Hyd.	Hyd.
	G25A1	2.5 (2451)	0.043	16B	16B	43–50①	650–750	650–750	0.009–0.011	0.011–0.013
	C30A1	3.0 (2977)	0.041	15B	15B	36–44①	750–850	650–750②	0.006–0.007	0.007–0.008
1994	B18A1	1.8 (1834)	0.041	16B	16B	41–48①	700–800	700–800	0.003–0.005	0.006–0.008
	B17A1	1.7 (1678)	0.050	16B	16B	48–56①	700–800	700–800	0.006–0.007	0.007–0.008
	C32A1	3.2 (3206)	0.041	15B	15B	31–37①	600–700	650–750	Hyd.	Hyd.
	G25A1	2.5 (2451)	0.043	16B	16B	43–50①	650–750	650–750	0.009–0.011	0.011–0.013
	C30A1	3.0 (2977)	0.041	15B	15B	36–44①	750–850	650–750②	0.006–0.007	0.007–0.008

NOTE: The lowest cylinder pressure should be within 75% of the highest cylinder pressure reading. For example, if the highest cylinder is 134 psi, the lowest should be 101. Engine should be at normal operating temperature with throttle valve in the wide open position.

The underhood specifications sticker often reflects tune-up specification changes in production. Sticker figures must be used if they disagree with those in this chart.

B—Before Top Dead Center

Hyd.—Hydraulic

① At idle, pressure regulator vacuum hose disconnected

② Check idle speed in gear

FIRING ORDERS

NOTE: To avoid confusion, always replace spark plug wires one at a time.

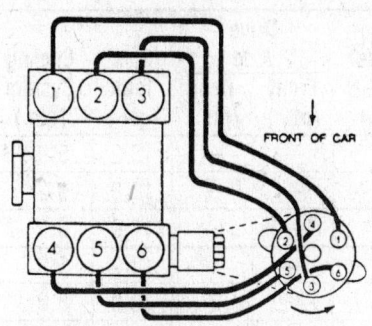

Legend 2.7L, 3.2L and 3.0L Engines
Engine Firing Order: 1-4-2-5-3-6
Distributor Rotation: Counterclockwise

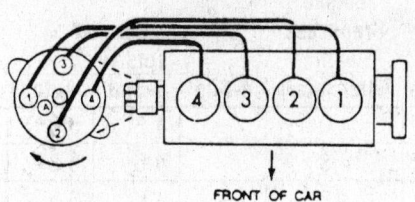

Integra 1.8L Engines
Engine Firing Order: 1-3-4-2
Distributor Rotation: Clockwise

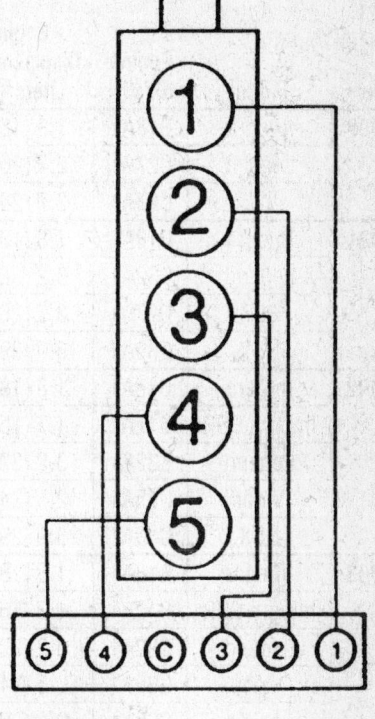

Vigor 2.5L Engine
Engine Firing Order: 1-2-4-5-3
Distributor Rotation: Counterclockwise

CAPACITIES

Year	Model	Engine ID/VIN	Engine Displacement Liters (cc)	Engine Crankcase with Filter (qts.)	Transmission (pts.) 4-Spd	5-Spd	Auto.	Transfer case (pts.)	Drive Axle Front (pts.)	Rear (pts.)	Fuel Tank (gal.)	Cooling System (qts.)
1990	Integra	B18A1	1.8 (1834)	4.0	—	4.8	6.4①	—	—	—	13.2	5.9④
	Legend	C27A1	2.7 (2675)	4.8	—	4.6	6.8①	—	—	—	18.0	9.2
	827	C27A1	2.7 (2675)	4.8	—	4.6	6.8①	—	—	—	17.0	9.2
1991	Integra	B18A1	1.8 (1834)	4.0	—	4.8	6.4①	—	—	—	13.2	5.9④
	Legend	C32A1	3.2 (3206)	5.0	—	5.2②	7.0①	—	2.2	—	18.0	8.0
	827	C27A1	2.7 (2675)	4.8	—	4.6	6.8①	—	—	—	17.0	9.8
	NSX	C30A1	3.0 (2977)	5.3	—	5.8	6.2①	—	—	—	18.5	③
1992	Integra	B18A1	1.8 (1834)	4.0	—	4.8	6.4①	—	—	—	13.2	5.9④
	Integra GSR	B17A1	1.7 (1678)	4.2	—	4.8	6.4①	—	—	—	13.2	6.0
	Legend	C32A1	3.2 (3206)	5.0	—	5.2②	7.0①	—	2.2	—	18.0	8.0
	Vigor	G25A1	2.5 (2451)	4.5	—	3.8①	5.2①	—	2.0	—	17.2	6.2
	NSX	C30A1	3.0 (2977)	5.3	—	5.8	6.2①	—	—	—	18.5	③
1993	Integra	B18A1	1.8 (1834)	4.0	—	4.8	6.4①	—	—	—	13.2	5.9④
	Integra GSR	B17A1	1.7 (1678)	4.2	—	4.8	6.4①	—	—	—	13.2	6.0
	Legend	C32A1	3.2 (3206)	5.0	—	5.2②	7.0①	—	2.2	—	18.0	8.0
	Vigor	G25A1	2.5 (2451)	4.5	—	3.8①	5.2①	—	2.0	—	17.2	6.2
	NSX	C30A1	3.0 (2977)	5.3	—	5.8	6.2①	—	—	—	18.5	③
1994	Integra	B18A1	1.8 (1834)	4.0	—	4.8	6.4①	—	—	—	13.2	5.9④
	Integra GSR	B17A1	1.7 (1678)	4.2	—	4.8	6.4①	—	—	—	13.2	6.0
	Legend	C32A1	3.2 (3206)	5.0	—	5.2②	7.0①	—	2.2	—	18.0	8.0
	Vigor	G25A1	2.5 (2451)	4.5	—	3.8①	5.2①	—	2.0	—	17.2	6.2
	NSX	C30A1	3.0 (2977)	5.3	—	5.8	6.2①	—	—	—	18.5	③

① Oil change capacity
② With cooler, 4.8 without cooler
③ Manual transmission, 17.0
   Automatic transmission, 17.4
④ One quart more for engine overhaul

CAMSHAFT SPECIFICATIONS

All measurements given in inches.

Year	Engine ID/VIN	Engine Displacement Liters (cc)	Journal Diameter					Elevation		Bearing Clearance	Camshaft End Play
			1	2	3	4	5	In.	Ex.		
1990	B18A1	1.8 (1834)	—	—	—	—	—	1.3160	1.5510	0.006	0.020
	C27A1	2.7 (2675)	—	—	—	—	—	1.5530	1.5510	0.004	0.020
1991	B18A1	1.8 (1834)	—	—	—	—	—	1.3160	1.3080	0.006	0.020
	C27A1	2.7 (2675)	—	—	—	—	—	1.5530	1.5510	0.004	0.020
	C32A1	3.2 (3206)	—	—	—	—	—	1.5750	1.4870	0.004	0.006
	C30A1	3.0 (2977)	—	—	—	—	—	①	①	0.006	0.020
1992	B18A1	1.8 (1834)	—	—	—	—	—	1.3274	1.3083	0.006	0.020
	B17A1	1.7 (1678)	—	—	—	—	—	②	②	0.006	0.020
	C32A1	3.2 (3206)	—	—	—	—	—	1.5750	1.4870	0.004	0.006
	G25A1	2.5 (2451)	—	—	—	—	—	1.5430	1.5300	0.006	0.020
	C30A1	3.0 (2977)	—	—	—	—	—	①	①	0.006	0.020
1993	B18A1	1.8 (1834)	—	—	—	—	—	1.3274	1.3083	0.006	0.020
	B17A1	1.7 (1678)	—	—	—	—	—	②	②	0.006	0.020
	C32A1	3.2 (3206)	—	—	—	—	—	1.5750	1.4870	0.004	0.006
	G25A1	2.5 (2451)	—	—	—	—	—	1.5430	1.5300	0.006	0.020
	C30A1	3.0 (2977)	—	—	—	—	—	①	①	0.006	0.020
1994	B18A1	1.8 (1834)	—	—	—	—	—	1.3274	1.3083	0.006	0.020
	B17A1	1.7 (1678)	—	—	—	—	—	②	②	0.006	0.020
	C32A1	3.2 (3206)	—	—	—	—	—	1.5750	1.4870	0.004	0.006
	G25A1	2.5 (2451)	—	—	—	—	—	1.5430	1.5300	0.006	0.020
	C30A1	3.0 (2977)	—	—	—	—	—	①	①	0.006	0.020

NOTE: All specifications are maximum ware limits.
① Manual transmission:
   In.: Primary—1.460, Mid.—1.497,
       Secondary—1.469
   Ex.: Primary—1.439, Mid.—1.472,
       Secondary—1.446
   Automatic transmission:
   In.: Primary—1.467, Mid.—1.482,
       Secondary—1.476
   Ex.: Primary—1.439, Mid.—1.472,
       Secondary—1.446
② In.: Primary—1.302, Mid.—1.434,
   Secondary—1.377
   Ex.: Primary—1.291, Mid.—1.406,
   Secondary—1.364

CRANKSHAFT AND CONNECTING ROD SPECIFICATIONS

All measurements are given in inches.

Year	Engine ID/VIN	Engine Displacement Liters (cc)	Crankshaft				Connecting Rod		
			Main Brg. Journal Dia.	Main Brg. Oil Clearance	Shaft End-play	Thrust on No.	Journal Diameter	Oil Clearance	Side Clearance
1990	B18A1	1.8 (1834)	2.1644–2.1654②	0.0009–0.0017③	0.004–0.014	3	1.7707–1.7717	0.0008–0.0015	0.0060–0.0120
	C27A1	2.7 (2675)	2.5187–2.5197	0.0009–0.0019	0.004–0.014	3	2.0463–2.0472	0.0010–0.0020	0.0060–0.0120
1991	B18A1	1.8 (1834)	2.1644–2.1654②	0.0009–0.0017③	0.004–0.014	3	1.7707–1.7717	0.0008–0.0015	0.0060–0.0120
	C32A1	3.2 (3206)	2.6762–2.6772	0.0008–0.0017	0.004–0.011	4	2.0866–2.1250	0.0008–0.0017	0.0060–0.0120
	C27A1	2.7 (2675)	2.5187–2.5197	0.0009–0.0019	0.004–0.014	3	2.0463–2.0472	0.0010–0.0020	0.0060–0.0120
	C30A1	3.0 (2977)	2.5187–2.5197	0.0009–0.0019	0.004–0.014	3	1.9676–1.9685	0.0016–0.0024	0.0060–0.0120
1992	B18A1	1.8 (1834)	2.1644–2.1654②	0.0009–0.0019③	0.004–0.014	3	1.7707–1.7717	0.0008–0.0015	0.0060–0.0120
	B17A1	1.7 (1678)	2.1644–2.1654②	0.0009–0.0019③	0.004–0.014	3	1.7707–1.7717	0.0013–0.0020	0.0060–0.0120
	C32A1	3.2 (3206)	2.6762–2.6772	0.0008–0.0017	0.004–0.011	4	2.0866–2.1250	0.0008–0.0017	0.0060–0.0120
	G25A1	2.5 (2451)	2.1644–2.1654	0.0007–0.0019	0.004–0.014	4	1.7707–1.7717	0.0006–0.0017	0.0060–0.0120
	C30A1	3.0 (2977)	2.5187–2.5197	0.0009–0.0019	0.004–0.014	3	1.9676–1.9685	0.0016–0.0024	0.0060–0.0120
1993	B18A1	1.8 (1834)	2.1644–2.1654②	0.0009–0.0019③	0.004–0.014	3	1.7707–1.7717	0.0008–0.0015	0.0060–0.0120
	B17A1	1.7 (1678)	2.1644–2.1654②	0.0009–0.0019③	0.004–0.014	3	1.7707–1.7717	0.0013–0.0020	0.0060–0.0120
	C32A1	3.2 (3206)	2.6762–2.6772	0.0008–0.0017	0.004–0.011	4	2.0866–2.1250	0.0008–0.0017	0.0060–0.0120
	G25A1	2.5 (2451)	2.1644–2.1654	0.0007–0.0019	0.004–0.014	4	1.7707–1.7717	0.0006–0.0017	0.0060–0.0120
	C30A1	3.0 (2977)	2.5187–2.5197	0.0009–0.0019	0.004–0.014	3	1.9676–1.9685	0.0016–0.0024	0.0060–0.0120
1994	B18A1	1.8 (1834)	2.1644–2.1654②	0.0009–0.0019③	0.004–0.014	3	1.7707–1.7717	0.0008–0.0015	0.0060–0.0120
	B17A1	1.7 (1678)	2.1644–2.1654②	0.0009–0.0019③	0.004–0.014	3	1.7707–1.7717	0.0013–0.0020	0.0060–0.0120
	C32A1	3.2 (3206)	2.6762–2.6772	0.0008–0.0017	0.004–0.011	4	2.0866–2.1250	0.0008–0.0017	0.0060–0.0120
	G25A1	2.5 (2451)	2.1644–2.1654	0.0007–0.0019	0.004–0.014	4	1.7707–1.7717	0.0006–0.0017	0.0060–0.0120
	C30A1	3.0 (2977)	2.5187–2.5197	0.0009–0.0019	0.004–0.014	3	1.9676–1.9685	0.0016–0.0024	0.0060–0.0120

① No. 1 oil clearance—0.0012–0.0190
② No. 3—2.1642–2.1651
③ No. 3—0.0012–0.0190

VALVE SPECIFICATIONS

Year	Engine ID/VIN	Engine Displacement Liters (cc)	Seat Angle (deg.)	Face Angle (deg.)	Spring Test Pressure (lbs. @ in.)	Spring Installed Height (in.)	Stem-to-Guide Clearance (in.)		Stem Diameter (in.)	
							Intake	Exhaust	Intake	Exhaust
1990	B18A1	1.8 (1834)	45	45	—	—	0.0010–0.0020	0.0020–0.0030	0.2591–0.2594	0.2579–0.2583
	C27A1	2.7 (2675)	45	45	—	—	0.0010–0.0020	0.0020–0.0030	0.2591–0.2594	0.2579–0.2583
1991	B18A1	1.8 (1834)	45	45	—	—	0.0010–0.0020	0.0020–0.0030	0.2591–0.2594	0.2579–0.2583
	C32A1	3.2 (3206)	45	45	—	—	0.0026–0.0035	0.0039–0.0046	0.2157–0.2161	0.2146–0.2150
	C27A1	2.7 (2675)	45	45	—	—	0.0010–0.0020	0.0020–0.0030	0.2591–0.2594	0.2579–0.2583
	C30A1	3.0 (2977)	45	45	—	—	0.0010–0.0020	0.0020–0.0030	0.2156–0.2159	0.2146–0.2150
1992	B18A1	1.8 (1834)	45	45	—	—	0.0010–0.0020	0.0020–0.0030	0.2590–0.2594	0.2578–0.2582
	B17A1	1.7 (1678)	45	45	—	—	0.0009–0.0022	0.0020–0.0030	0.2156–0.2159	0.2146–0.2150
	C32A1	3.2 (3206)	45	45	—	—	0.0026–0.0035	0.0039–0.0046	0.2157–0.2161	0.2146–0.2159
	G25A1	2.5 (2451)	45	45	—	—	0.0008–0.0018	0.0020–0.0030	0.2156–0.2159	0.2146–0.2150
	C30A1	3.0 (2977)	45	45	—	—	0.0010–0.0020	0.0020–0.0030	0.2156–0.2159	0.2146–0.2150
1993	B18A1	1.8 (1834)	45	45	—	—	0.0010–0.0020	0.0020–0.0030	0.2590–0.2594	0.2578–0.2582
	B17A1	1.7 (1678)	45	45	—	—	0.0009–0.0022	0.0020–0.0030	0.2156–0.2159	0.2146–0.2150
	C32A1	3.2 (3206)	45	45	—	—	0.0026–0.0035	0.0039–0.0046	0.2157–0.2161	0.2146–0.2159
	G25A1	2.5 (2451)	45	45	—	—	0.0008–0.0018	0.0020–0.0030	0.2156–0.2159	0.2146–0.2150
	C30A1	3.0 (2977)	45	45	—	—	0.0010–0.0020	0.0020–0.0030	0.2156–0.2159	0.2146–0.2150
1994	B18A1	1.8 (1834)	45	45	—	—	0.0010–0.0020	0.0020–0.0030	0.2590–0.2594	0.2578–0.2582
	B17A1	1.7 (1678)	45	45	—	—	0.0009–0.0022	0.0020–0.0030	0.2156–0.2159	0.2146–0.2150
	C32A1	3.2 (3206)	45	45	—	—	0.0026–0.0035	0.0039–0.0046	0.2157–0.2161	0.2146–0.2159
	G25A1	2.5 (2451)	45	45	—	—	0.0008–0.0018	0.0020–0.0030	0.2156–0.2159	0.2146–0.2150
	C30A1	3.0 (2977)	45	45	—	—	0.0010–0.0020	0.0020–0.0030	0.2156–0.2159	0.2146–0.2150

PISTON AND RING SPECIFICATIONS

All measurements are given in inches.

Year	Engine ID/VIN	Engine Displacement Liters (cc)	Piston Clearance	Ring Gap Top Compression	Ring Gap Bottom Compression	Ring Gap Oil Control	Ring Side Clearance Top Compression	Ring Side Clearance Bottom Compression	Ring Side Clearance Oil Control
1990	B18A1	1.8 (1834)	0.0004–0.0016	0.0080–0.0140	0.0160–0.0220	0.008–0.028	0.0018–0.0028	0.0018–0.0028	—
	C27A1	2.7 (2675)	0.0006–0.0015	0.0080–0.0140	0.0140–0.0190	0.008–0.028	0.0006–0.0018	0.0006–0.0018	—
1991	B18A1	1.8 (1834)	0.0004–0.0016	0.0080–0.0140	0.0160–0.0220	0.008–0.028	0.0018–0.0028	0.0018–0.0028	—
	C27A1	2.7 (2675)	0.0006–0.0015	0.0080–0.0140	0.0140–0.0190	0.008–0.028	0.0006–0.0018	0.0006–0.0018	—
	C32A1	3.2 (3206)	0.0010–0.0020	0.0100–0.0160	0.0160–0.0220	0.008–0.028	0.0014–0.0024	0.0012–0.0021	—
	C30A1	3.0 (2977)	—	0.0100–0.0160	0.0140–0.0200	0.008–0.028	0.0010–0.0020	0.0010–0.0020	—
1992	B18A1	1.8 (1834)	0.0004–0.0016	0.0080–0.0140	0.0160–0.0220	0.008–0.028	0.0018–0.0028	0.0018–0.0028	—
	B17A1	1.7 (1678)	0.0004–0.0016	0.0080–0.0140	0.0160–0.0220	0.008–0.028	0.0018–0.0028	0.0018–0.0028	—
	G25A1	2.5 (2451)	0.0004–0.0016	0.0080–0.0140	0.0160–0.0220	0.008–0.028	0.0010–0.0020	0.0010–0.0020	—
	C32A1	3.2 (3206)	0.0010–0.0020	0.0100–0.0160	0.0140–0.0200	0.008–0.028	0.0014–0.0024	0.0012–0.0021	—
	C30A1	3.0 (2977)	—	0.0100–0.0160	0.0140–0.0200	0.008–0.028	0.0010–0.0020	0.0010–0.0020	—
1993	B18A1	1.8 (1834)	0.0004–0.0016	0.0080–0.0140	0.0160–0.0220	0.008–0.028	0.0018–0.0028	0.0018–0.0028	—
	B17A1	1.7 (1678)	0.0004–0.0016	0.0080–0.0140	0.0160–0.0220	0.008–0.028	0.0018–0.0028	0.0018–0.0028	—
	G25A1	2.5 (2451)	0.0004–0.0016	0.0080–0.0140	0.0160–0.0220	0.008–0.028	0.0010–0.0020	0.0010–0.0020	—
	C32A1	3.2 (3206)	0.0010–0.0020	0.0100–0.0160	0.0140–0.0200	0.008–0.028	0.0014–0.0024	0.0012–0.0021	—
	C30A1	3.0 (2977)	—	0.0100–0.0160	0.0140–0.0200	0.008–0.028	0.0010–0.0020	0.0010–0.0020	—
1994	B18A1	1.8 (1834)	0.0004–0.0016	0.0080–0.0140	0.0160–0.0220	0.008–0.028	0.0018–0.0028	0.0018–0.0028	—
	B17A1	1.7 (1678)	0.0004–0.0016	0.0080–0.0140	0.0160–0.0220	0.008–0.028	0.0018–0.0028	0.0018–0.0028	—
	G25A1	2.5 (2451)	0.0004–0.0016	0.0080–0.0140	0.0160–0.0220	0.008–0.028	0.0010–0.0020	0.0010–0.0020	—
	C32A1	3.2 (3206)	0.0010–0.0020	0.0100–0.0160	0.0140–0.0200	0.008–0.028	0.0014–0.0024	0.0012–0.0021	—
	C30A1	3.0 (2977)	—	0.0100–0.0160	0.0140–0.0200	0.008–0.028	0.0010–0.0020	0.0010–0.0020	—

TORQUE SPECIFICATIONS

All readings in ft. lbs.

Year	Engine ID/VIN	Engine Displacement Liters (cc)	Cylinder Head Bolts	Main Bearing Bolts	Rod Bearing Bolts	Crankshaft Damper Bolts	Flywheel Bolts	Manifold Intake	Manifold Exhaust	Spark Plugs	Lug Nut
1990	B18A1	1.8 (1834)	⑤	56	30	87	③	17	23	13	80
	C27A1	2.7 (2675)	①	②	33	123	③	16	④	16	80
1991	B18A1	1.8 (1834)	⑤	56	30	87	③	17	23	13	80
	C27A1	2.7 (2675)	①	②	33	123	③	16	④	16	80
	C32A1	3.2 (3206)	①	⑨	33	174	③	16	25	16	80
	C30A1	3.0 (2977)	56	⑥	⑦	⑧	③	16	23	16	80
1992	B18A1	1.8 (1834)	⑤	56	30	87	③	17	23	13	80
	B17A1	1.7 (1678)	⑤	56	23	130	③	19	23	16	80
	G25A1	2.5 (2451)	72	49	24	181	③	16	23	16	80
	C32A1	3.2 (3206)	③	⑨	33	174	③	16	25	16	80
	C30A1	3.0 (2977)	56	⑥	⑦	⑧	③	16	23	16	80
1993	B18A1	1.8 (1834)	⑤	56	30	87	③	17	23	13	80
	B17A1	1.7 (1678)	⑤	56	23	130	③	19	23	16	80
	G25A1	2.5 (2451)	72	49	24	181	③	16	23	16	80
	C32A1	3.2 (3206)	①	⑨	33	174	③	16	25	16	80
	C30A1	3.0 (2977)	56	⑥	⑦	⑧	③	16	23	16	80
1994	B18A1	1.8 (1834)	⑤	56	30	87	③	17	23	13	80
	B17A1	1.7 (1678)	⑤	56	23	130	③	19	23	16	80
	G25A1	2.5 (2451)	72	49	24	181	③	16	23	16	80
	C32A1	3.2 (3206)	①	⑨	33	174	③	16	25	16	80
	C30A1	3.0 (2977)	56	⑥	⑦	⑧	③	16	23	16	80

① 1st step—29 ft. lbs.
　2nd step—56 ft. lbs.
② Cap bolt (9mm)—29 ft. lbs.
　Cap bridge bolt (11mm)—49 ft. lbs.
　Side bolt (10mm)—36 ft. lbs.
③ Manual transaxle—76 ft. lbs.
　Automatic transaxle—54 ft. lbs.
④ 8mm nuts—22 ft. lbs.
　10mm nuts—40 ft. lbs.
⑤ 1st step—22 ft. lbs.
　2nd step—61 ft. lbs.
⑥ Inner—48 ft. lbs.
　Outer—29 ft. lbs.
⑦ Torque to 14 ft. lbs. plus 95 degrees
⑧ Torque to 203 f.t lbs., loosen, then torque to
　181 ft. lbs.
⑨ Inner—57 ft. lbs.
　Outer—29 ft. lbs.

BRAKE SPECIFICATIONS

All measurements in inches unless noted

Year	Model	Master Cylinder Bore	Brake Disc Original Thickness	Brake Disc Minimum Thickness	Maximum Runout	Brake Drum Diameter Original Inside Diameter	Brake Drum Diameter Max. Wear Limit	Brake Drum Diameter Maximum Machine Diameter	Minimum Lining Thickness Front	Minimum Lining Thickness Rear
1990	Integra	—	F 0.830 R 0.540	F 0.750 R 0.315	0.004	—	—	—	0.60	0.60
	Legend	—	F 0.830 R 0.390	F 0.750 R 0.310	0.004	—	—	—	0.60	0.60
	Sterling	—	F 0.830 R 0.390	F 0.750 R 0.310	0.004	—	—	—	0.60	0.60
1991	Integra	—	F 0.830 R 0.540	F 0.750 R 0.315	0.004	—	—	—	0.60	0.60
	Legend	—	F 0.910 R 0.350	F 0.830 R 0.300	0.004	—	—	—	0.06	0.06
	Sterling	—	F 0.830 R 0.390	F 0.750 R 0.310	0.004	—	—	—	0.60	0.60
1992	Integra	—	F 0.830 R 0.545	F 0.750 R 0.315	0.004	—	—	—	0.60	0.60
	Legend	—	F 0.910 R 0.350	F 0.830 R 0.300	0.004	—	—	—	0.60	0.60
	Sterling	—	F 0.830 R 0.390	F 0.750 R 0.310	0.004	—	—	—	0.60	0.60
	Vigor	—	F 0.906 R 0.390	F 0.827 R 0.320	0.004	—	—	—	0.60	0.60
	NSX	—	F 1.100 R 0.830	F 1.020 R 0.750	0.004	—	—	—	0.60	0.60
1993	Integra	—	F 0.830 R 0.545	F 0.750 R 0.315	0.004	—	—	—	0.60	0.60
	Legend	—	F 0.910 R 0.350	F 0.830 R 0.300	0.004	—	—	—	0.60	0.60
	Sterling	—	F 0.830 R 0.390	F 0.750 R 0.310	0.004	—	—	—	0.60	0.60
	Vigor	—	F 0.906 R 0.390	F 0.827 R 0.320	0.004	—	—	—	0.60	0.60
	NSX	—	F 1.100 R 0.830	F 1.020 R 0.750	0.004	—	—	—	0.60	0.60
1994	Integra	—	F 0.830 R 0.545	F 0.750 R 0.315	0.004	—	—	—	0.60	0.60
	Legend	—	F 0.910 R 0.350	F 0.830 R 0.300	0.004	—	—	—	0.60	0.60
	Sterling	—	F 0.830 R 0.390	F 0.750 R 0.310	0.004	—	—	—	0.60	0.60
	Vigor	—	F 0.906 R 0.390	F 0.827 R 0.320	0.004	—	—	—	0.60	0.60
	NSX	—	F 1.100 R 0.830	F 1.020 R 0.750	0.004	—	—	—	0.60	0.60

F—Front
R—Rear

WHEEL ALIGNMENT

Year	Model	Caster Range (deg.)	Caster Preferred Setting (deg.)	Camber Range (deg.)	Camber Preferred Setting (deg.)	Toe-in (in.)	Steering Axis Inclination (deg.)
1990	Integra	1⅛P–3⅛P	2⅛P	1½N–½P	½N	1/32N	13
	Legend	11/16P–2 1/16P	1 11/16P	1N–1P	0	0	NA
	Sterling	11/16P–2 1/16P	1 11/16P	1N–1P	0	0	NA
1991	Integra	1⅛P–3⅛P	2⅛P	1½N–½P	½N	1/32N	13
	Legend	11/16P–2 1/16P	1 11/16P	1N–1P	0	0	NA
	Sterling	11/16P–2 1/16P	1 11/16P	1N–1P	0	0	NA
1992	Integra	1⅛P–3⅛P	2⅛P	1½N–½P	½N	1/32N	13
	Legend	11/16P–2 1/16P	1 11/16P	1N–1P	0	0	NA
	Sterling	11/16P–2 1/16P	1 11/16P	1N–1P	0	0	NA
	Vigor	3/16P–2 3/16P	1 3/16P	1N–1P	0	1/32P	NA
	NSX	¾N–¾P	0	½N–½P	7/16P	⅛N	NA
1993	Integra	1⅛P–3⅛P	2⅛P	1½N–½P	½N	1/32N	13
	Legend	11/16P–2 1/16P	1 11/16P	1N–1P	0	0	NA
	Sterling	11/16P–2 1/16P	1 11/16P	1N–1P	0	0	NA
	Vigor	3/16P–2 3/16P	1 3/16P	1N–1P	0	1/32P	NA
	NSX	¾N–¾P	0	½N–½P	7/16P	⅛N	NA
1994	Integra	1⅛P–3⅛P	2⅛P	1½N–½P	½N	1/32N	13
	Legend	11/16P–2 1/16P	1 11/16P	1N–1P	0	0	NA
	Sterling	11/16P–2 1/16P	1 11/16P	1N–1P	0	0	NA
	Vigor	3/16P–2 3/16P	1 3/16P	1N–1P	0	1/32P	NA
	NSX	¾N–¾P	0	½N–½P	7/16P	⅛N	NA

NA—Not available
N—Negative
P—Positive

ENGINE MECHANICAL

NOTE: Disconnecting the negative battery cable on some vehicles may interfere with the functions of the on-board computer or security systems and may require reprogramming when the battery cable is reconnected.

Engine Assembly

REMOVAL AND INSTALLATION

Integra

On these vehicles, the engine and transaxle are removed as a unit. The lower ball joints and the inner CV-joints will be separated but not removed.

1. Raise and safely support the vehicle. Remove the engine and wheel well splash shields.

2. Disconnect the battery cables from the battery, negative cable first. Remove the battery and the battery tray from the engine compartment.

3. It is not necessary to remove the hood. Raise it to a full vertical position and support it properly.

4. Drain the oil from the engine, the coolant from the radiator and the fluid from the transaxle.

5. Remove the intake air duct and air cleaner assembly.

6. Remove the fuel filler cap and loosen the service bolt on the fuel filter banjo bolt to relieve the fuel pressure. Disconnect the fuel feed hose from the fuel filter and the fuel return hose from the pressure regulator.

— CAUTION —
The fuel system may be under pressure and fuel will be sprayed. Be sure there is good ventilation and take the appropriate fire safety precautions.

7. Disconnect the charcoal canister hose from the throttle body. Vehicles with automatic transaxle have an emissions control equipment box on the firewall. Rather than disconnecting the vacuum hoses, it may be easier to unplug the connectors, remove the box from the firewall and lay it on the engine.

8. Remove the ground cable from the transaxle. Disconnect the 2 distributor electrical connectors, make

an alignment mark on the distributor body and the engine and remove the distributor.

9. Remove the throttle cable by loosening the locknut, then slip the cable end out of the throttle bracket and accelerator linkage. Take care not to bend the cable when removing it. Do not use pliers to remove the cable from the linkage.

10. Remove the mounting bolts and the V-belt for the power steering pump, then without disconnecting the hoses, secure the pump out of the way.

11. Near the brake booster, disconnect the engine wiring harness connectors and remove the wire from the clamp.

12. Remove the brake booster vacuum hose from the intake manifold. Disconnect the upper and lower radiator hoses and heater hoses.

13. Without disconnecting the hydraulic hoses or cable, remove the bolt to remove the speed sensor from the transaxle as an assembly.

14. Disconnect the transaxle cooling hoses, if equipped, and unplug the radiator fan connectors. Remove the radiator and fans as an assembly.

15. If not already removed, remove the driver's side splash shield at the wheel well.

16. If equipped with air conditioning, remove the belt. Remove the compressor with the hoses still attached and secure the compressor to the front beam.

NOTE: Do not loosen or disconnect the air conditioning freon lines. Do not vent freon into the air.

17. To disconnect the halfshafts, the lower damper fork and ball joint must be disconnected, allowing the steering knuckle to move away from the transaxle.

a. With the front wheels removed, remove the damper fork nut and pinch bolt. Remove the damper fork from the lower arm.

b. Remove the lower ball joint castle nut press the ball joint out of the lower arm using a suitable puller, with the puller jaws grasping the lower arm.

c. Carefully pry the inner CV-joint away from the transaxle to force the set ring at the inner end past the groove.

d. Pull the inboard CV-joint, not the halfshaft, and remove the CV-joint out of the intermediate shaft.

NOTE: Do not pull on the halfshaft, as the CV-joint may come apart. Use care when prying out the assembly and pull it straight to avoid damaging the intermediate shaft seals.

e. Support the halfshafts or hang them from the body with wire. Do not let them hang from the outer CV-joint or it will be damaged.

18. Disconnect the alternator wiring harness connector. Remove the alternator belt, the mount bolts, the alternator and the mounting bracket.

19. Remove the front exhaust pipe.

20. If equipped with a manual transaxle, perform the following procedures:

a. Disconnect the clutch cable. Avoid using pliers to remove the cable from the linkage.

b. To disconnect the shift linkage rod, push back the boot and drive out the pin securing the shift rod universal joint to the transaxle. Use a new pin when reassembling.

c. Remove the shift lever torque rod.

21. If equipped with an automatic transaxle, remove the torque converter cover. Remove the cable holder, cotter pin and control pin, then remove the shift control cable. Take care not to bend the cable when removing it. Avoid using pliers to remove the cable from the linkage.

22. Attach a suitable lifting device to the engine. Raise the engine slightly to remove all the slack from the lifting device.

23. Remove the rear transaxle mount and rear transaxle mounting bracket.

24. Remove the front transaxle mount. Remove the side transaxle mounting bracket. Remove the side engine mount.

25. Check that the engine/transaxle assembly is completely free of all vacuum hoses and electrical wires.

26. Slowly raise the engine approximately 6 inches and check again.

27. Raise the engine/transaxle assembly all the way and remove it from the vehicle. Place the engine on a suitable engine stand assembly.

To install:

28. Slowly lower the engine and transaxle assembly into the vehicle.

29. Check that the engine and transaxle are free from any hoses or electrical connectors.

30. Install the mounts and bolts. Some of the transaxle mount bolts are designed to be torqued only one time and must be replaced whenever the engine is removed. Be sure to torque all bolts in 2 steps in the sequence. This is important to help minimize engine vibrations.

31. If equipped with an automatic transaxle, reinstall the control pin, cotter pin, cable holder and cable. Install the torque converter cover.

32. If equipped with a manual transaxle, install the shift rod and the shift torque rod. Connect the clutch cable and check the clutch adjustment.

33. Install the front exhaust pipe with new self-locking nuts and torque to 40 ft. lbs. (55 Nm).

34. Reinstall the alternator assembly.

35. Install the halfshaft assemblies. Be sure to use new set rings.

36. Reinstall the air conditioning compressor and drive belts.

37. Install the speedometer drive.

38. Reinstall the radiator assembly, coolant hoses, heater hoses and oil cooler lines.

39. Reinstall the power steering pump and drive belts. Install the throttle cable bracket and throttle cable.

40. Reinstall the distributor assembly and ground cable to the transaxle.

41. Reinstall the control box brackets and control box connectors. Reconnect all disconnected vacuum lines and electrical connectors.

42. Reinstall the battery box, battery and battery cables.

43. Reinstall the wheel well and engine splash shields.

44. Carefully check to make sure all wires, hoses, belts and control cables are connected and properly adjusted.

45. Refill the coolant system, engine oil and transaxle fluid. Start the engine, bleed the cooling system and make all necessary adjustments.

Vigor

On these vehicles, the engine and differential are removed as a unit but the transmission remains in the vehicle. The lower ball joints and the inner CV-joints will be separated but not removed. The radio is equipped with a theft protection program. Be sure the 5-digit security code is available before disconnecting the battery.

1. Disconnect the negative battery cable. Raise and safely support the vehicle and remove the engine splash shield.

2. Drain the engine oil and coolant and the fluid from the transmission and differential.

3. It is not necessary to remove the hood. Raise it to a full vertical position and support it properly.

4. Label and disconnect the wiring from the ignition coil and from the ABS relay box.

5. Remove the ABS relay box and heatshield and remove the battery.

6. Remove the intake air duct and air cleaner assembly.

7. Remove the fuel filler cap and loosen the service bolt on the fuel filter banjo bolt to relieve the fuel system pressure. Remove the banjo bolt to remove the fuel feed hose from the fuel filter. Remove the fuel return hose from the pressure regulator.

CAUTION

The fuel system may be under pressure and fuel will be sprayed. Be sure there is good ventilation and take the appropriate fire safety precautions.

---

8. Remove the throttle cable by loosening the locknut, then slip the cable end out of the throttle bracket and accelerator linkage. Take care not to bend the cable when removing it. Unbolt the throttle cable clamp and move the cable aside.

9. Label and disconnect all the engine wiring harnesses.

10. Disconnect the charcoal canister hoses, fuel return hose, brake booster hose and the emission control vacuum hose.

11. Disconnect the heater hoses and the transmission wiring connector that is near the heater hoses.

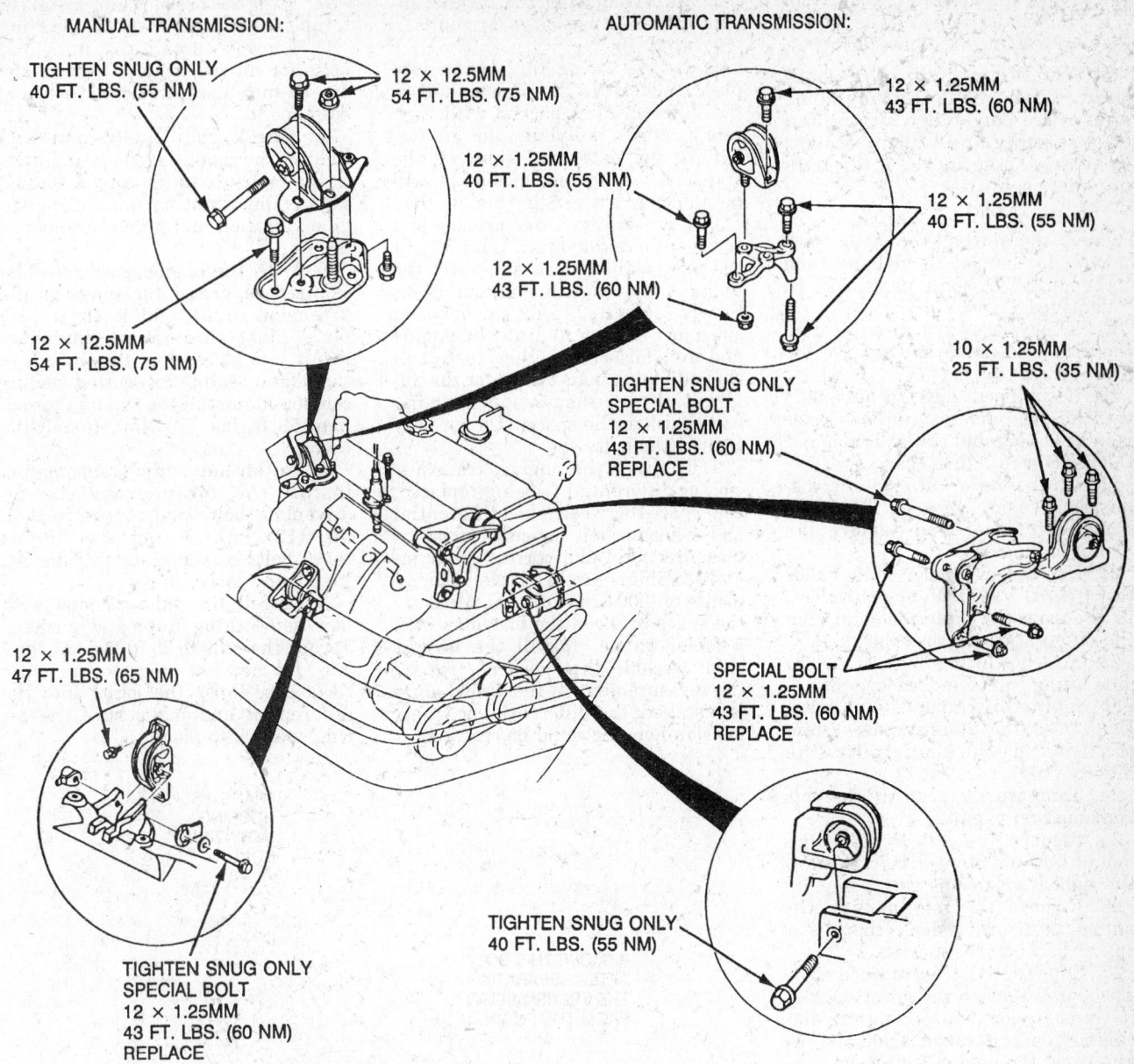

MANUAL TRANSMISSION:

TIGHTEN SNUG ONLY
40 FT. LBS. (55 NM)

12 × 12.5MM
54 FT. LBS. (75 NM)

12 × 12.5MM
54 FT. LBS. (75 NM)

AUTOMATIC TRANSMISSION:

12 × 1.25MM
43 FT. LBS. (60 NM)

12 × 1.25MM
40 FT. LBS. (55 NM)

12 × 1.25MM
40 FT. LBS. (55 NM)

12 × 1.25MM
43 FT. LBS. (60 NM)

10 × 1.25MM
25 FT. LBS. (35 NM)

TIGHTEN SNUG ONLY
SPECIAL BOLT
12 × 1.25MM
43 FT. LBS. (60 NM)
REPLACE

12 × 1.25MM
47 FT. LBS. (65 NM)

SPECIAL BOLT
12 × 1.25MM
43 FT. LBS. (60 NM)
REPLACE

TIGHTEN SNUG ONLY
SPECIAL BOLT
12 × 1.25MM
43 FT. LBS. (60 NM)
REPLACE

TIGHTEN SNUG ONLY
40 FT. LBS. (55 NM)

Engine mount torque specifications — Integra

12. Disconnect the wiring and remove the 2 bolts to remove the distributor. Be careful not to lose the collar that is behind the distributor.

13. Label and disconnect the wiring as required from the relay box under the hood. Disconnect the ground cables in the same area.

14. Without disconnecting the hoses, remove the power steering pump and the air conditioner compressor and secure them out of the way.

NOTE: Do not loosen or disconnect the air conditioning freon lines. Do not vent freon into the air.

15. On the transmission, remove the speed sensor without disconnecting the hydraulic hoses. Disconnect the wiring and secure the unit out of the way.

16. Disconnect the transmission cooler hoses, upper and lower radiator hoses and the fan wiring. Remove the 2 upper brackets to remove the radiator assembly.

17. If equipped with an automatic transmission, remove the small torque converter cover. Rotate the crankshaft as required to remove the torque converter-to-driveplate bolts.

18. To disconnect the halfshafts, the lower damper fork and ball joint must be disconnected, allowing the steering knuckle to move away from the transaxle.

a. With the front wheels removed, remove the damper fork nut and pinch bolt. Remove the damper fork from the lower arm.

b. Remove the lower ball joint castle nut press the ball joint out of the lower arm using a suitable puller, with the puller jaws grasping the lower arm.

c. Carefully pry the inner CV-joint away from the transaxle to force the set ring at the inner end past the groove.

d. Pull the inboard CV-joint, not the halfshaft. Remove the CV-joint out of the intermediate shaft.

NOTE: Do not pull on the half-shaft, as the CV-joint may come apart. Use care when prying out the assembly and pull it straight to avoid damaging the intermediate shaft seals.

e. Support the halfshafts or hang them from the body with wire. Do not let them hang from the outer CV-joint or it will be damaged.

19. Remove the oxygen sensor from the exhaust system and remove the front exhaust pipe.

20. If equipped with an automatic transmission, make sure the selector is in **P**. On manual transmission, put the selector into first gear.

21. On the lower left side of transmission housing, pry out the extension shaft cover and remove the 33mm sealing cap.

22. Use the extension shaft puller tool 07LAC PW50100 or equivalent, to disengage the extension shaft from the differential. Remove the shaft.

23. Attach a lifting hoist to the engine lifting points and remove the upper engine-to-transmission bolts. Don't lose the 26mm spacer shim that is on the bolt near the differential.

24. Temporarily remove the left transmission mount.

25. Remove the left front engine mount nut and stopper bolt. Remove the right front mount nut.

26. Remove the mid-mounts. On automatic transmissions, there is a spacer between the mounts.

27. Support the transmission with a jack and remove the lower engine-to-transmission bolts. Separate the engine from the transmission and begin lifting the engine out. Make sure all hoses, wires and cables are disconnected before raising the engine all the way out.

28. After removing the engine, install the transmission mid-mounts.

To install:

29. Before fitting the engine into place, make sure the pinion shaft in the differential is packed with high temperature molybdenum grease. Grease the extension shaft in the transmission and make sure it will not interfere with engine installation.

30. Support the transmission and remove the mid-mounts. Carefully fit the engine into place and start the upper engine-to-transmission bolts. Slowly tighten 2 bolts on opposite sides just enough to draw the engine and transmission together. Install all the remaining bolts except for the differential-to-transmission housing bolt that had the spacer. Do not fully tighten the bolts yet.

31. If either the engine, transmission or differential is being replaced, the space between the differential and transmission housings must be measured and the correct shim installed. Shims are available in increments of 0.004 in. (0.1mm). Measure the space between the housings with a feeler gauge. Install the largest shim possible that does not exceed the measurement. If the wrong shim is installed, the differential or transmission housing could be cracked.

32. With the proper shim installed, torque the bolts to 54 ft. lbs. (75 Nm).

33. Loosely install the nuts and bolts for all the mounts and set the engine into place. Remove the lifting equipment.

34. Check the illustration and tighten the mounting nuts and bolts in the sequence to the correct torque. This is important for minimizing engine vibration and premature mount failure.

35. With the engine and transmission secure, grease the spline on the extension shaft and push it into place. Make sure the set ring clicks firmly into place. Coat the threads of the 33mm sealing cap with a sealing compound, install the cap and torque it to 58 ft. lbs. (80 Nm). Install the cover.

36. On an automatic transmission, install the torque converter-to-driveplate bolts and torque to 9 ft. lbs. (12 Nm). Do not over torque these bolts or the plate will distort. Install the cover.

37. Install the exhaust pipe with new self-locking nuts and gaskets. Torque the nuts to 25 ft. lbs. (34 Nm).

38. Fit new set rings to the inner CV-joints. Press the joints into the differential and make sure the set ring snaps into place.

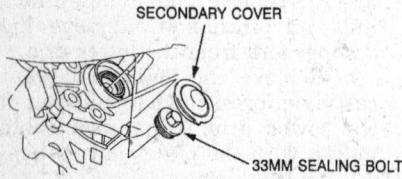

Extension shaft must be disengaged to separate the differential and transmission — Vigor

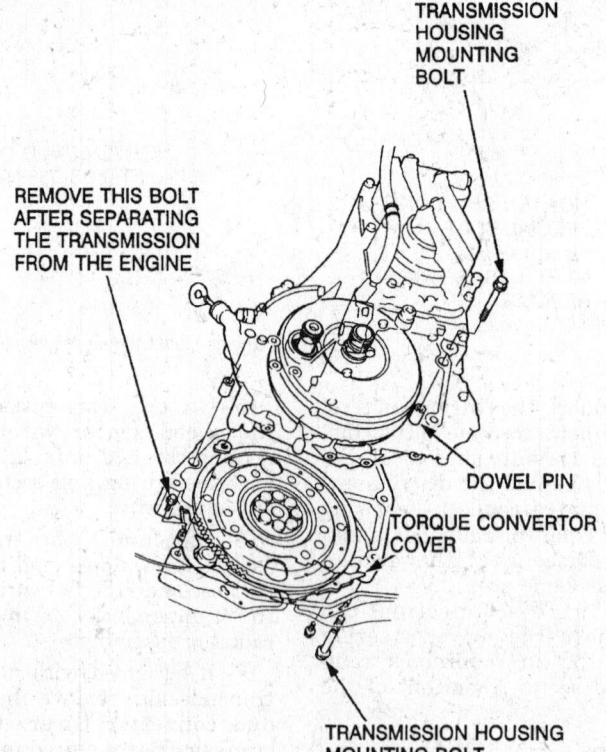

One of the torque converter cover bolts can only be reached after separating the engine and transmission — Vigor

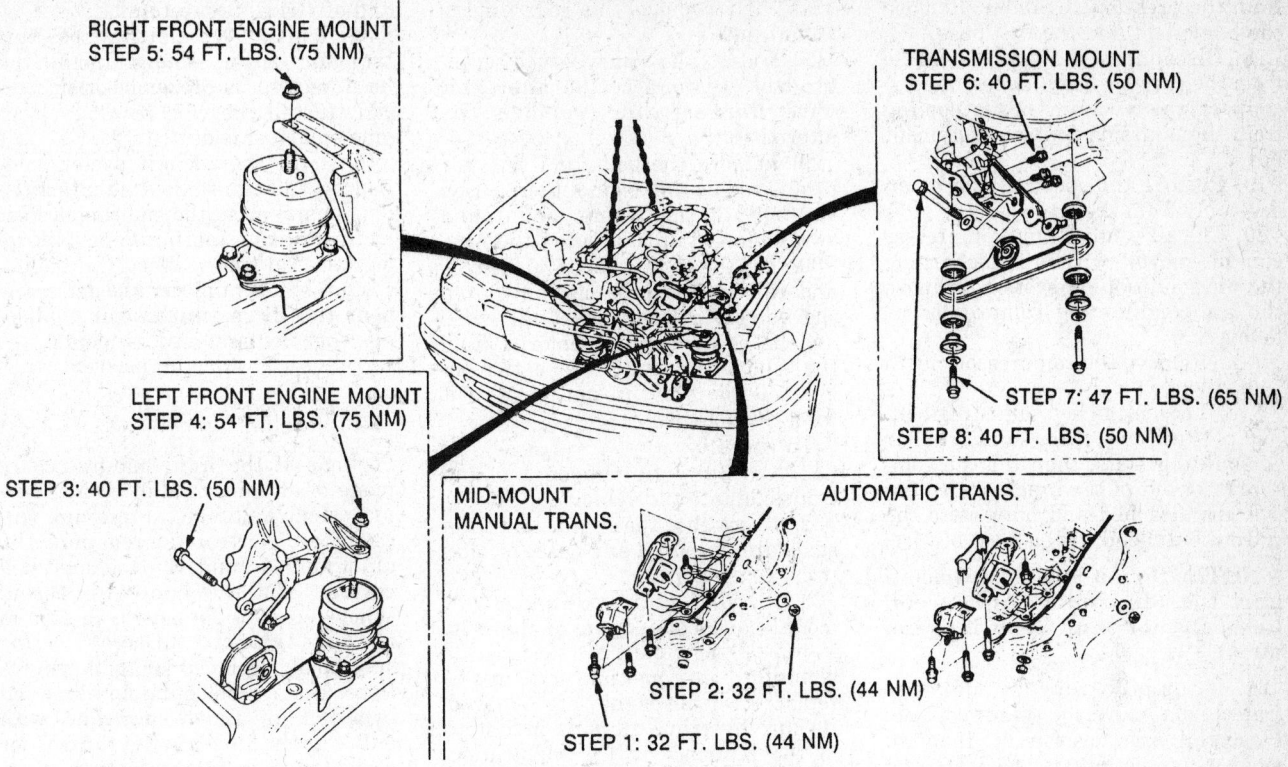

Engine mount torque sequence — Vigor

39. Connect the ball joint and damper fork. Torque the ball joint nut to 43 ft. lbs. (60 Nm) and install a new cotter pin.

40. Install the radiator assembly and connect the wiring and hoses.

41. Install the speed sensor, air conditioning compressor, power steering pump and alternator. Install and adjust the belts.

42. Before installing the distributor, check the condition of the O-rings on the collar.

43. Connect all remaining hoses, wires and control cables and adjust as required. Check the wiring carefully before connecting the battery.

44. After the engine is running, turn the heater control to full warm and bleed the cooling system.

1990 Legend

On these vehicles, the engine and transaxle are removed as a unit. The lower ball joints and the inner CV-joints will be separated but not removed.

1. Raise and safely support the vehicle.

2. Disconnect both battery cables from the battery. Remove the battery and the battery tray from the engine compartment.

3. Position the hood in the vertical position by removing the prop mounting bolt on the hood side and fitting it to the mounting hole near the hinge.

4. Remove the air intake tube, air cleaner and resonator tube as an assembly.

5. Remove the splash guard from under the engine.

6. Remove the oil filler cap and drain plug to drain the engine oil.

7. Remove the radiator cap, then open the radiator drain petcock and drain the coolant from the radiator. There are also block drain bolts on each side of the engine.

8. Remove the transaxle filler plug, then remove the drain plug and drain the transaxle.

9. Disconnect the pressure switch wire from the oil filter base.

10. Disconnect both water hoses from the engine oil cooler.

11. Remove the drain bolt from the oil filter base to drain the oil. Remove the oil filter base from the engine block.

12. Disconnect the upper and lower radiator hoses from the radiator.

13. If equipped with an automatic transaxle, disconnect cooler hose from the bottom of the radiator.

14. Disconnect the following engine sub-harness connectors from the body side:

  a. Four right side connectors and clamp

  b. Both left side main fuse connectors

  c. Coil wire, primary lead connectors and the condenser connector.

  d. Both ground cables from the cylinder head and the transaxle.

15. Disconnect the connector from the power steering pump and both hoses. Disconnect the hose from the cruise control actuator and the hose from the power brake booster.

16. To relieve the fuel system pressure, place a shop rag over the fuel filter to absorb any gasoline which may be sprayed on the engine while relieving the pressure. Slowly loosen the service bolt approximately one full turn. This will relieve any pressure in the system. Using a new sealing washer, tighten the service bolt.

CAUTION

The fuel system may be under pressure and fuel will be sprayed. Be sure there is good ventilation and take the appropriate fire safety precautions.

17. Disconnect the fuel return hose from the pressure regulator. Remove the banjo bolt and the fuel hose.

18. Disconnect the throttle cable from the throttle body. Label and disconnect the vacuum hoses coming from the emission control equipment box.

19. Remove the speed sensor as an assembly from the transaxle.

20. The air conditioning compressor can be moved without discharging the air conditioning system. Remove the air conditioning compressor as follows:

a. Remove the compressor clutch lead wire.

b. Loosen the belt adjusting bolt.

c. Remove the compressor mounting bolts, then lift the compressor out of the bracket with the hoses attached and hang it to the front bulkhead with a piece of wire.

NOTE: Do not loosen or disconnect the air conditioning freon lines. Do not vent freon into the air.

21. If equipped with an automatic transaxle, remove the center console. Place the shift lever in **R**, then remove the lock pin to separate the shift cable.

22. If equipped with a manual transaxle, at the shift rod universal joint, slide the pin retainer forward and drive out the spring pin. Separate the shift rod universal joint from the transaxle. Remove the banjo bolt to disconnect the clutch hydraulic hose from the clutch damper on the transmission. Catch and discard the hydraulic fluid that leaks out.

23. Remove the exhaust pipe from the front and rear manifolds.

24. Remove the halfshaft as follows:

a. Raise and safely support the vehicle and remove the front wheels.

b. Remove the ball joint bolt and separate the ball joint from lower control arm.

c. Using a small prybar, pry out the inboard CV-joint approximately 0.51 in. (13mm) in order to release the spring clip from the differential, then pull the halfshaft from the transaxle case.

d. Cover the inner CV-joints with a plastic bag and hang the halfshaft from the body with wire. Do not let the halfshafts hang by the outer CV-joint or it will be damaged.

25. Attach a suitable lifting chain to the engine and raise it enough to remove the slack.

26. Remove the engine side mount bracket bolts.

27. Remove the front engine mount nut, then remove the rear engine mount nut.

28. Loosen and remove the alternator belt. Disconnect the alternator wire harness and remove the alternator.

29. Remove the bolt from the rear torque rod at the engine, then loosen the bolt in the frame mount and swing the rod up and out of the way.

30. Tilt the engine about 30 degrees and raise the engine carefully from the vehicle checking that all wires and hoses have been removed from the engine/transaxle. Raise the engine all the way up and remove it from the vehicle.

To install:

31. Carefully fit the engine and transaxle into the vehicle.

32. Check that the engine and transaxle are free from any hoses or electrical connectors.

33. Install the transaxle and engine mounts and bolts. Some of the bolts in upper rear mount are designed to be torqued only one time and must be replaced whenever they are removed. Be sure to torque all bolts in 2 steps in the sequence in the illustration. This is important to help minimize engine vibrations.

34. If equipped with automatic transaxle, reinstall the control pin, cotter pin, cable holder and cable. Install the torque converter cover.

35. Reconnect the shift cable and reinstall the center console assembly.

36. If equipped with manual transaxle, connect the clutch hydraulic line, gear shift linkage and torque rod.

37. Install the front and rear exhaust pipes.

38. Reinstall the alternator assembly.

39. Install the halfshaft assemblies. Use new clips on the CV-joints and make sure they click firmly into place. Torque the lower ball joint nut to 72 ft. lbs. (100 Nm) and install a new cotter pin.

40. Reinstall the air conditioning compressor and drive belts.

41. Install the speedometer drive assembly.

42. Reinstall the radiator assembly, coolant hoses, heater hoses and oil cooler lines.

43. Reconnect the power steering hoses and refill the reservoir to the upper mark. Install the throttle cable bracket and throttle cable.

44. Install the distributor assembly and ground cable to the transaxle.

45. Install the control box brackets and control box connectors. Reconnect all disconnected vacuum lines and electrical connectors.

46. Reinstall the battery box, battery and battery cables. Install the hood back to its proper position.

47. Install the wheel well and engine splash shields.

48. Refill the coolant system, engine oil and transaxle fluid. Start the engine and bleed the steering system by turning the steering wheel lock-to-lock several times. Bleed the cooling system by opening the bleeder screw near the thermostat housing. Make all other necessary adjustments.

1991-94 Legend

Portions of the front sub-frame are made of aluminum alloy. Using normal steel bolts on aluminum will cause an electrolytic reaction: the aluminum around the fastener will corrode and the bolt will loosen. When replacing fasteners, be sure to use bolts that have a Dacro® coating specifically designed for such applications. Dacro® bolts can be identified by a dull grey finish, sometimes with a dull green finish on the threads for more accurate torque wrench readings. These parts should be available at the dealer.

On this vehicle, the engine and transaxle are lifted out as a unit. The battery will also be removed. Since the vehicle is equipped with a theft protected radio, it is important to have the security code before disconnecting the battery. After reconnecting power to the radio, the 5-digit code must be entered to restore operation.

1. Do not remove the hood. Disconnect the hood stay strut and reconnect it to hold the hood in a vertical position. Remove the battery and the battery box.

2. Remove the strut bar that runs across the engine compartment and the bracket. Working underneath the vehicle, remove the splash shield and drain the engine coolant and oil and the transaxle fluid.

3. Label and disconnect the starter and battery wiring from the main fuse/relay box. Remove the ground cable from the engine block and label and disconnect the main engine wiring harness.

4. Remove the throttle cable cover. Without turning the adjusting nut, loosen the locknut, which is closer to the throttle and disconnect the throttle cable from the throttle and bracket.

5. Remove the air cleaner assembly and ducting.

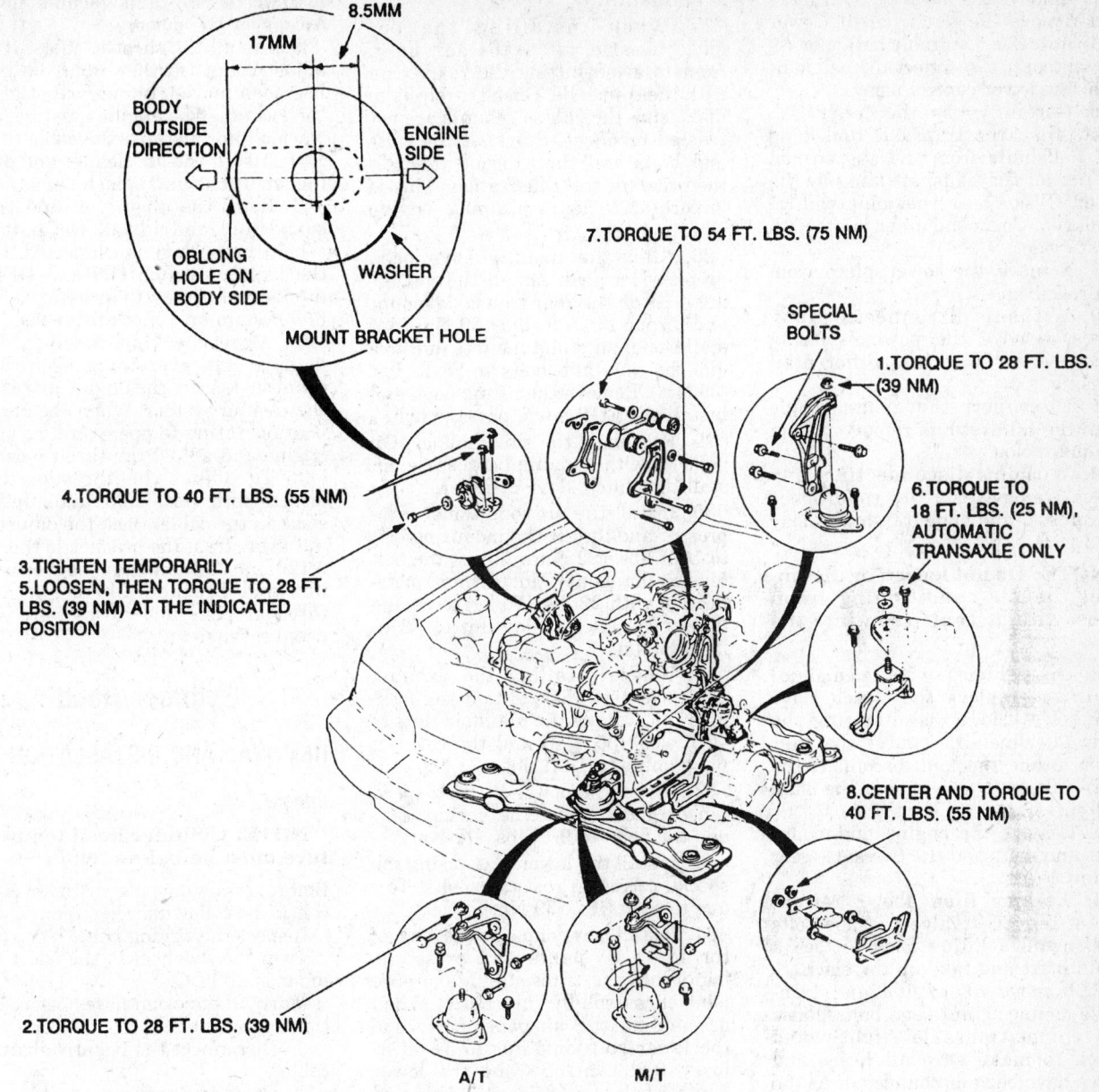

BODY OUTSIDE DIRECTION

OBLONG HOLE ON BODY SIDE

WASHER

MOUNT BRACKET HOLE

ENGINE SIDE

17MM

8.5MM

7.TORQUE TO 54 FT. LBS. (75 NM)

SPECIAL BOLTS

1.TORQUE TO 28 FT. LBS. (39 NM)

4.TORQUE TO 40 FT. LBS. (55 NM)

3.TIGHTEN TEMPORARILY
5.LOOSEN, THEN TORQUE TO 28 FT. LBS. (39 NM) AT THE INDICATED POSITION

6.TORQUE TO 18 FT. LBS. (25 NM), AUTOMATIC TRANSAXLE ONLY

8.CENTER AND TORQUE TO 40 FT. LBS. (55 NM)

2.TORQUE TO 28 FT. LBS. (39 NM)

A/T   M/T

Engine mount torque sequence — 1990 Legend

6. On the right shock tower, disconnect the igniter unit and remove the wiring harness clamp. Disconnect the engine ground cable.

7. On the firewall behind the right cylinder head is a control box containing emission control equipment. Without disconnecting any vacuum hoses, unplug the electrical connectors and remove the control box from the firewall. Lay the box on top of the engine.

8. Label and disconnect the main engine wiring harness connectors and remove the bracket.

9. On top of the fuel filter, relieve the fuel system pressure by slowly loosening the service bolt 1 turn.

CAUTION
The fuel system may be under pressure and fuel will be sprayed. Be sure there is good ventilation and take the appropriate fire safety precautions.

10. Remove the fuel supply hose and disconnect the return hose from the pressure regulator.

11. Disconnect the vacuum hose to the brake booster at the check valve.

12. At the left rear of the engine compartment, disconnect the transaxle wiring harness and remove the clamp.

13. Disconnect and plug the transaxle cooling hoses at the radiator. Disconnect the upper and lower hoses and the fan and sensor wiring. Remove the radiator and fans as an assembly.

14. Near the power steering fluid reservoir, remove the solenoid valve assembly, vacuum pipes and air tank.

15. Without disconnecting any hoses, remove the power steering pump and secure it out of the way.

16. Raise and safely support the vehicle and remove the front wheels.

17. Remove the lower damper forks and remove the nut from the lower ball joint. Use a suitable ball joint removal tool to disconnect the ball joint from the lower control arm.

18. Carefully pry the inner CV-joints from the transaxle and hang the halfshafts from the suspension. Do not let the halfshaft hang by the outer CV-joint or the joint will be damaged. Cover the inner joints with plastic bags.

19. Remove the lower plate from the rear beam.

20. Without disconnecting any hoses, remove the power steering speed sensor from the differential housing.

21. Disconnect the exhaust pipe from the catalyst and remove it from the manifolds.

22. Without disconnecting any hoses, remove the air conditioner compressor and hang it from the body with wire.

NOTE: Do not loosen or disconnect the air conditioning freon lines. Do not vent freon into the air.

23. On vehicles with a manual transaxle, remove the clutch slave cylinder without disconnecting the hydraulic line. Disconnect the shift lever torque rod and disconnect the shift linkage by driving out the 8mm roll pin.

24. Remove the engine mid-mount nuts and bolts and the transaxle rear mount.

25. Working from above, remove one of the EGR valve passage bolts and install a lifting hook. Attach a chain hoist and take up the slack.

26. Remove all engine and transaxle mounting nuts and bolts. Raise the engine/transaxle slightly and check to make sure all hoses and wires have been disconnected. As the unit is raised, allow it to tilt up in front to provide proper clearance past the rear beam.

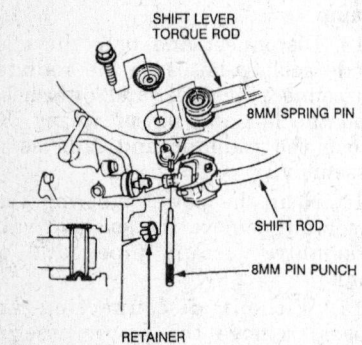

SHIFT LEVER TORQUE ROD

8MM SPRING PIN

SHIFT ROD

8MM PIN PUNCH

RETAINER

Manual shift linkage connection — 1991-94 Legend

To install:

27. When installing the engine/transaxle, rotate the unit up in front to avoid hitting the rear beam with the transaxle. Check carefully to make sure the rubber mounts are not twisted or offset. Start all the nuts and bolts and then torque them in the order in the illustration. This is important to help minimize engine vibrations.

28. After the mounts have been properly torqued, install the mounting bolts on the rear transaxle mount and torque to 28 ft. lbs. (39 Nm). Install the engine mid-mounts and torque the nuts and bolts to 28 ft. lbs. (39 Nm). Remove the lifting hook and install the EGR valve passage bolt.

29. Reconnect the shift linkage. On vehicles with a manual transaxle, install the clutch slave cylinder.

30. Install the air conditioner compressor and torque the mounting bolt to 16 ft. lbs. (22 Nm). Adjust the belt tension for about ¼ in. (6.4mm) of deflection with 22 lbs. (10 kg) force and torque the idler pulley nut to 33 ft. lbs. (45 Nm).

31. When installing the exhaust pipe, use new gaskets and self-locking nuts. Torque the manifold nuts to 40 ft. lbs. (55 Nm) and the catalyst flange nuts to 16 ft. lbs. (22 Nm).

32. Install the power steering speed sensor and connect the wiring. Torque the bolts to 9 ft. lbs. (12 Nm).

33. Install the lower plate using the special corrosion resistant bolts. Torque to 29 ft. lbs. (39 Nm).

34. Install new clips to the end of the inner CV-joints and press the joints into the transaxle. Make sure joint clicks solidly into place. When assembling the suspension, torque the lower ball joint nut to 51-58 ft. lbs. (70-80 Nm). Torque the lower damper bolt to 51 ft. lbs. (70 Nm) and the upper damper pinch bolt to 37 ft. lbs. (51 Nm).

35. Install the power steering pump and adjust the belt tension for about ½ in. (12.7mm) deflection with 22 lbs. (10 kg) force. Torque the mounting bolt to 33 ft. lbs. (45 Nm) and the nut to 16 ft. lbs. (22 Nm).

36. Install the radiator and connect the cooling hoses. When filling the system, open the bleeder where the upper hose connects to the engine.

37. Install the emission control equipment bracket and connect wiring and vacuum hoses.

38. Install the fuel supply pipe, using new gaskets. Connect the return hose and the brake booster vacuum hose. Finish connecting all the re-maining wiring and vacuum hoses, except for the battery.

39. Install the throttle cable. If the adjuster nut (farther from the boot) has been moved, temporarily tighten the locknut. The engine must be fully warmed up to adjust the cable.

40. Install the air cleaner and ducting, strut bar and splash shield.

41. Refill the engine oil and transaxle fluid and install the battery. When the battery is connected, turn the ignition switch **ON** and **OFF** a number of times to pressurize the fuel system and check for leaks.

42. After checking carefully and making sure everything is properly connected, start the engine and bleed the cooling system. When the engine is at operating temperature, stop the engine and adjust the throttle cable.

43. To adjust the throttle cable, loosen both nuts and take up the slack in the cable. Back the adjusting nut away from the bracket so there is 0.120 in. (3.0mm) gap between the nut and bracket. Make sure the throttle opens and closes fully with pedal movement.

Cylinder Head

REMOVAL AND INSTALLATION

Integra

NOTE: Cylinder head temperature must be below 100°F.

Before removing the cylinder head check the following:

Inspect the timing belt.

Turn the flywheel so the No. 1 cylinder is at TDC.

Mark all emission hoses before disconnecting them.

1. Disconnect the negative battery cable.

2. Drain the cooling system.

3. Remove the air cleaner:

   a. Remove the air cleaner cover and filter.

   b. Disconnect the hot/cold air intake ducts and remove the air chamber hose.

   c. Remove the air cleaner.

4. Relieve the fuel pressure by slowly loosening the service bolt on the top of the fuel filter about a turn.

—————— **CAUTION** ——————
The fuel system may be under pressure and fuel will be sprayed. Be sure to take the appropriate safety and fire precautions.
————————————————

5. Disconnect the fuel feed line. Remove the vacuum hose, breather hose and air intake hose.

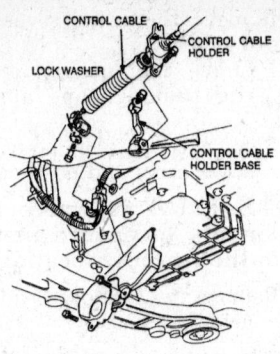

Automatic shift linkage connection — 1991-94 Legend

6. Remove the water bypass hose from cylinder head. Remove the charcoal canister hose from the throttle body.

7. Remove the brake booster vacuum hose from the intake manifold. Remove the fuel return hose. Remove the PCV hose.

8. Remove the throttle cable from the throttle body. Take care not to bend the cable when removing it. Do not use pliers to remove the cable from the linkage. Always replaced a kinked cable with a new one.

9. Disconnect the ignition coil connector, TDC and crankshaft/cylinder sensor connector from the distributor.

10. Remove and tag the spark plug wirers.

11. Remove the emission control equipment bracket, but do not disconnect the emission hoses.

12. Disconnect the 3 engine harness connectors on the left side of the engine compartment.

13. Disconnect the engine sub-harness connectors from the cylinder head and intake manifold. The connectors are as follows:

    a. Four injector connectors.

    b. TA sensor connector.

    c. Throttle angle sensor connector.

    d. EGR valve lift sensor; automatic transaxle only.

    e. Ground cable terminal.

    f. TW sensor ground.

    g. Coolant temperature gauge sender terminal.

    h. Oxygen sensor terminal.

    i. EACV connector.

14. Remove the upper radiator hose and heater inlet hose from the cylinder head.

15. Remove the power steering belt and power steering pump. Do not disconnect the hoses from the pump.

16. Raise and safely support the vehicle.

17. Remove the left front wheel and then remove the left splash shield.

18. Remove the intake manifold bracket bolts and remove the exhaust manifold upper shroud.

19. Remove the exhaust manifold bracket. Remove front exhaust pipe and remove the exhaust manifold.

20. Remove the valve cover and engine ground cable.

21. Remove the timing belt middle cover. Loosen, but do not remove the adjusting bolt and release the timing belt tension. Tighten the bolt to hold the tensioner in the released position.

22. Remove the timing belt from the driven pulleys. Be sure not to crimp or bend the timing belt more then 90 degrees in less then 1 in. (25mm) in diameter.

23. Remove the camshaft driven pulleys. Loosen all the camshaft holder bolts 1 full turn at a time to release valve spring pressure evenly. Remove the camshaft holder bolts, then remove the camshaft holders, camshafts and rocker arms.

24. Remove the cylinder head bolts and remove the cylinder head. To prevent warpage, unscrew all the cylinder head bolts in sequence $\frac{1}{3}$ turn at a time, repeat this sequence until all the bolts are loosened.

25. Remove the intake manifold from the cylinder head.

To install:

26. Use new gaskets and install the intake manifold onto the cylinder head and tighten the nuts in a criss-cross pattern in 2-3 steps, beginning in the middle. Torque the nuts to 17 ft. lbs. (23 Nm).

27. Install the cylinder head onto the engine block, after making sure the mating surface was cleaned and a new gasket was installed. Be sure to pay attention to the following points:

    a. Be sure the No. 1 cylinder is at TDC and the camshaft pulley UP mark is on the top before positioning the head in place.

    b. The cylinder head dowel pins and oil control jet must be aligned.

    c. Torque the cylinder head bolts, in 2 progressive steps: First to 22 ft. lbs. (30 Nm), in sequence, then to 61 ft. lbs. (85 Nm), in the same sequence. This sequence is the same as on earlier Integra engines.

    d. Apply engine oil to the cylinder head bolts and washers. Use the longer bolt in the No. 1 and No. 2 positions.

28. Make sure the keyways on the camshafts are facing up. The valve locknuts should be loosened and the

adjusting screw backed off before installation. Replace the rocker arms in their original position.

29. Place the rocker arms on the pivot bolts and the valve stems.

30. Install the camshafts and the camshaft seals with the open spring side facing in.

31. Be sure to note the **I** and **E** marks that are stamped on the camshaft holders. Do not apply oil to the seal mating surface of the camshaft holders.

32. Apply a liquid gasket to the head of the mating surfaces of the No. 1 and No. 6 camshaft holders then install them, along with No. 2, 3, 4 and 5. Tighten each bolt 1 turn at a time to insure that the rockers do not bind on the valves.

33. Torque the camshaft holder bolts and make sure the rocker arms are properly positioned on the valve stems. Start at the center holders and work out towards the ends, torque the bolts to 9 ft. lbs. (12 Nm).

34. Press in the camshaft seal securely with a suitable seal driver.

35. Install the keys into their grooves in the camshafts. To set the No. 1 piston at TDC, align the holes on the camshaft with the holes in the No. 1 camshaft holders and drive 0.197 in. (5.0mm) pin punches into the holes.

36. Push the camshaft pulleys onto the camshafts, then torque the retaining bolts to 27 ft. lbs. (38 Nm).

37. Install the timing belt and adjust the tension. Install the lower and middle timing belt covers and bolts.

38. Install the valve cover and engine ground cable.

39. Install the exhaust manifold and torque the nuts to 23 ft. lbs. (32 Nm). Install the bracket and upper shroud and attach the exhaust pipe.

40. Install the left front wheel splash shield and the left front wheel. Lower the vehicle.

41. Install the power steering pump and drive belt.

42. Reconnect all disconnected electrical connections and vacuum lines.

43. Reconnect the upper radiator hose and heater inlet hose.

44. Reinstall the spark plug wires to the spark plugs.

45. Install the engine ground wire to the valve cover. Reconnect the throttle cable from the throttle body.

46. Reinstall the air cleaner assembly and duct work that goes along with it. Reconnect the negative battery cable.

47. After installation, check to see that all hoses and wires are installed correctly.

NOTE: The engine oil should be changed after completing the cylinder head removal and installation.

48. Refill the coolant system.
49. Adjust the valve clearance. Make all other necessary adjustments

1990 Legend

Before removing the cylinder head check the following:
Inspect the timing belt.
Turn the flywheel so the No. 1 cylinder is at TDC.
Mark all wiring and emission hoses before disconnecting them.

1. Disconnect the battery ground cable.
2. Drain the cooling system.
3. Remove the vacuum hose from the brake booster.
4. Remove the secondary ground cable from the cylinder head and the transaxle housing.
5. Disconnect the radio noise condenser connector, ignition coil wire and the ignition primary connector.
6. Remove the air cleaner cover.
7. Relieve the fuel pressure by loosening the service bolt on the top of the fuel filter about a turn. Disconnect the fuel return hose from the pressure regulator. Remove the special nut and the fuel hose.

————— **CAUTION** —————
The fuel system may be under pressure and fuel will be sprayed. Be sure there is good ventilation and take the appropriate fire safety precautions.

8. Disconnect the throttle cable from the throttle valve.
9. Disconnect the charcoal canister hose from the throttle valve.
10. Disconnect the engine sub-harness connectors from the cylinder head and the intake manifold:
   a. The 6 injector connectors.
   b. The TA sensor connector.
   c. The temperature unit connector.
   d. The ground connector from the fuel pipe.
   e. The TW sensor connector.
   f. The throttle sensor connector.
   g. The crankshaft angle sensor connector.
   h. EGR valve connector.
   i. The 4 wire harness clamps.
11. Disconnect the oxygen sensor coupler.

12. Disconnect the cooling system hoses from the cylinder head. Remove the hose between the water passage and the intake manifold. Disconnect the connecting pipe to the valve body hose and bypass outlet hose.
13. Disconnect the spark plug wires from the spark plugs and remove the distributor assembly.
14. Remove the intake manifold cover from the intake manifold.
15. Remove the wire harness cover.
16. Remove the alternator pulley cover.
17. Remove the alternator and belt.
18. Remove the power steering pump and disconnect the pump hoses. Also, remove the hose clamp bolt on the body.
19. Disconnect the idle boost solenoid hoses.
20. Remove the cruise control actuator.
21. Remove the exhaust header pipe and pull it clear of the exhaust manifold.
22. Remove the air cleaner base mount bolts and disconnect the hose from the intake manifold to the breather chamber.
23. Remove the air cleaner base from the intake manifold.
24. Remove the EGR tube nuts from the cylinder head.
25. Remove the exhaust manifold cover nuts.
26. Remove the air suction tube nuts from the exhaust manifold and air suction valve.
27. Remove the intake manifold assembly from the cylinder head.
28. Remove the water passage assembly from the front and rear of the cylinder head.
29. Remove the timing belt upper covers.
30. Loosen the tensioner adjustment bolt and remove the timing belt.

NOTE: Advance the crankshaft by 15 degrees before removing the timing belt to prevent interference between the piston and the valve.

31. Remove the front and rear camshaft pulleys using the following procedure:
   a. Before removing the rear pulley, adjust the camshaft position so no valve is fully open.
   b. Remove the pulley mounting bolts with a universal holder and a double-end wrench. For the rear pulley, first, remove the top 2 bolts and then the remaining bolt.
32. Remove the upper cover back plates.

33. Remove the valve covers and the head side covers.
34. Remove the bearing cap oil pipes, the bearing caps and the camshaft.
35. Remove the intake and exhaust inside rocker arms and pushrods.

NOTE: Label all valve train components to ensure installation in their proper locations.

36. Remove the cylinder head bolts and remove the head.

NOTE: Unscrew the cylinder head bolts $\frac{1}{3}$ of a turn in the reverse order of the torque sequence until loose to prevent warpage to the cylinder head.

37. Clean the gasket mounting surfaces.
   To install:
38. Use new gaskets and install the exhaust manifold onto the cylinder head and tighten the bolts in a criss-cross pattern in 2-3 steps.
39. Install the cylinder head onto the engine block, after making sure the mating surface was cleaned and a new gasket was installed. Be sure to pay attention to the following points:
   a. Be sure the No. 1 cylinder is at TDC and the camshaft pulleys UP mark is on the top before positioning the head in place.
   b. The cylinder head dowel pins and oil control jet must be aligned.
   c. Torque the cylinder head bolts, in 2 progressive steps: First to 29 ft. lbs. (40 Nm), in sequence, then to 56 ft. lbs. (78 Nm), in the same sequence.
40. Pour engine oil into the cylinder head hydraulic tappet mounting hole, up to the level of the oil path.
41. Install the hydraulic tappet into the cylinder head. Do not rotate the hydraulic tappet while inserting it into the head.
42. Pour engine oil into the oil fillers on the cylinder head.
43. Install the pushrods and rocker arms. Be sure to install each part in its original position. Loosen the rocker arm adjusting screws and locknuts before installation.
44. Install the camshafts and camshaft oil seals. Be sure to take note of the locations of the camshafts; the front camshaft has a groove for driving the distributor.
   a. Make sure the camshaft is mounted parallel with the rocker arm slipper surface.
   b. Advance the crankshaft by 15 degrees from the No. 1 cylinder TDC of compression stroke to prevent interference between the piston and valve.

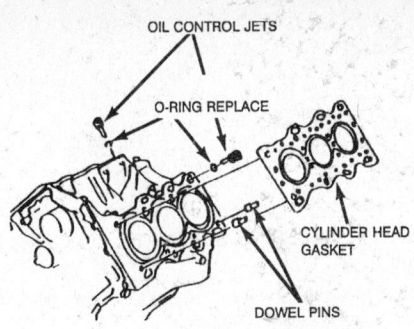

Dowel pin and oil jet control locations — 2.7L engine

c. Place the rear camshaft on the cylinder head at the position where the camshaft is not pushing the valve.

d. Preset the oil seal, with its spring side facing inward.

e. Install the rear camshaft sealing rubber. Do not apply oil to the camshaft holder side of the oil seal.

45. Apply liquid gasket to the camshaft oil seal mounting surface and on the head contact surface. Finger tighten the bearing caps.

46. Carefully fit the camshaft oil seal until it contacts the bearing cap. Torque the 8mm bolts to 20 ft. lbs.

(28 Nm) and the 6mm bolts to 9 ft. lbs. (12 Nm), in the sequence shown. Make sure the oil seal is properly positioned and torque those bolts last.

NOTE: Tighten the 6mm bolts last.

47. Install the upper timing cover plate. Install the camshaft pulley and torque the bolts to 23 ft. lbs. (32 Nm). Install the timing belt.

48. Install the water passage assembly from the front and rear of the cylinder head.

49. Install the intake manifold assembly and torque the bolts to 16 ft. lbs. (22 Nm).

50. Install the air suction tube nuts to the exhaust manifold and air suction valve.

51. Install the exhaust manifold cover nuts.

52. Install the EGR tube nuts to the cylinder head.

53. Install the air cleaner base to the intake manifold.

54. Install the air cleaner base mount bolts and reconnect the hose from the intake manifold to the breather chamber.

55. Install the exhaust header pipe to the exhaust manifold.

56. Install the cruise control actuator.

57. Reconnect the idle boost solenoid hoses.

58. Install the power steering pump and reconnect the pump hoses. Also, install the hose clamp bolt on the body.

59. Install the alternator and belt.

60. Install the alternator pulley cover.

61. Install the wire harness cover.

62. Install the intake manifold cover to the intake manifold.

63. Install the distributor assembly and reconnect the spark plug wires to the spark plugs.

64. Reconnect the cooling system hoses to the cylinder head. Install the hose between the water passage and the intake manifold. Reconnect the connecting pipe to the valve body hose and bypass outlet hose.

65. Reconnect the oxygen sensor and all disconnected electrical connections.

66. Reconnect the charcoal canister hose to the throttle valve.

67. Reconnect the throttle cable to the throttle valve.

68. Install all disconnected fuel lines. Install the air cleaner cover.

69. Install the secondary ground cable to the cylinder head and the transaxle housing.

70. Install the vacuum hose to the brake booster.

71. Refill the cooling system.

72. Reconnect the battery ground cable.

73. Readjust the exhaust valves:

a. With the engine at TDC on No. 1 cylinder, adjust cylinders 1, 2 and 4.

b. Turn the valve adjusting screw till it contacts the valve, then an additional 1½ turns.

c. Turn the engine to TDC on No. 5 cylinder and adjust cylinders 3, 5 and 6.

74. After the heads are reassembled, make sure the engine sits for approximately 5 minutes to allow the hydraulic tappets to reach the proper oil level.

75. Remove the spark plugs and crank the engine, feel for compression at each cylinder at the spark plug holes. It may be necessary to crank the engine through several cycles to confirm compression.

76. If any cylinder does not have compression, it may be necessary to disassemble the head and check the suspected tappet.

77. If all cylinders have compression, reinstall the plugs and start the engine.

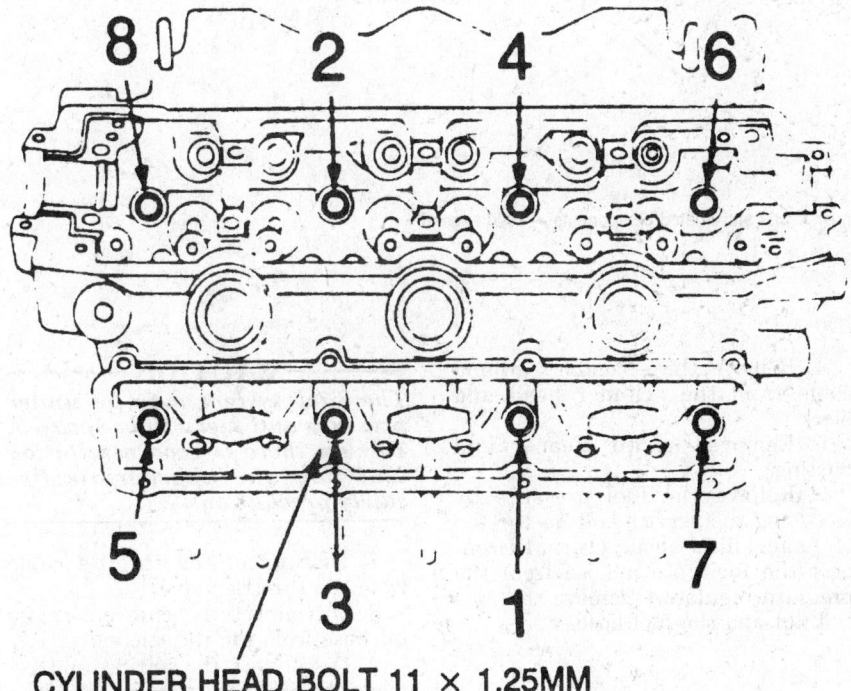

CYLINDER HEAD BOLT 11 × 1.25MM 56 FT. LBS. (78 NM)

Cylinder head bolt torque sequence — 1990 Legend

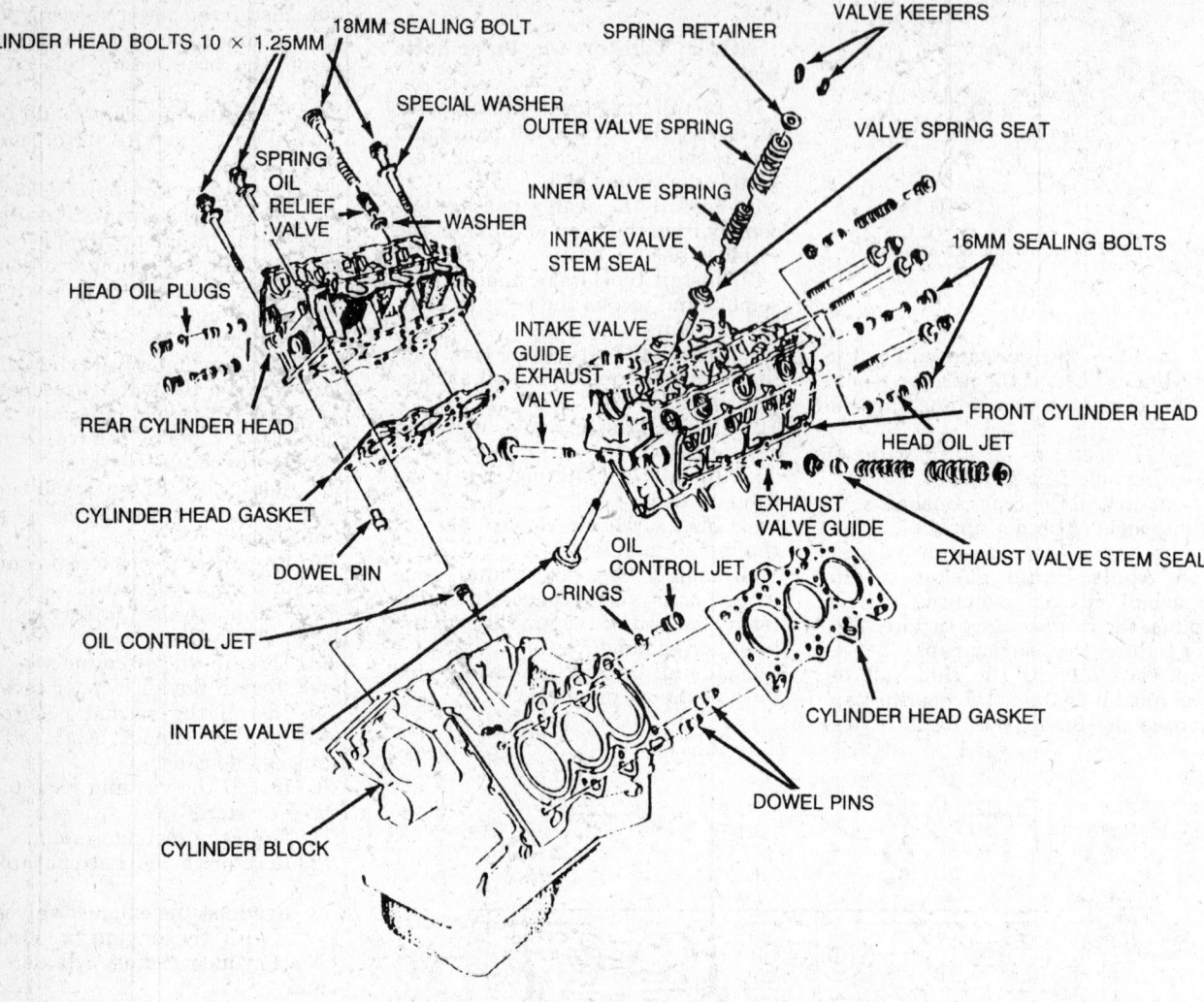

CYLINDER HEAD BOLTS 10 × 1.25MM
18MM SEALING BOLT
SPRING RETAINER
VALVE KEEPERS
SPECIAL WASHER
OUTER VALVE SPRING
VALVE SPRING SEAT
SPRING OIL RELIEF VALVE
INNER VALVE SPRING
16MM SEALING BOLTS
WASHER
INTAKE VALVE STEM SEAL
HEAD OIL PLUGS
INTAKE VALVE GUIDE
EXHAUST VALVE
REAR CYLINDER HEAD
FRONT CYLINDER HEAD
HEAD OIL JET
CYLINDER HEAD GASKET
EXHAUST VALVE GUIDE
DOWEL PIN
EXHAUST VALVE STEM SEAL
OIL CONTROL JET
O-RINGS
OIL CONTROL JET
INTAKE VALVE
CYLINDER HEAD GASKET
CYLINDER BLOCK
DOWEL PINS

Cylinder heads and related components — 1990 Legend

1991-94 Legend

NOTE: The cylinder head temperature must be below 100°F.

Before removing the cylinder head check the following:

Inspect the timing belt.

Turn the flywheel so the No. 1 cylinder is at TDC.

Mark all wiring and emission hoses before disconnecting them.

1. Remove the battery and battery box.
2. Drain the cooling system.
3. Remove the vacuum hose from the brake booster.
4. Remove the secondary ground cable from the cylinder head and block.
5. Remove the air cleaner and ducting.
6. Relieve the fuel pressure by loosening the service bolt on the top of the fuel filter about a turn. Disconnect the fuel return hose from the pressure regulator. Remove the special nut and the fuel hose.

CAUTION

The fuel system may be under pressure and fuel will be sprayed. Be sure there is good ventilation and take the appropriate fire safety precautions.

7. Disconnect the throttle cable from the throttle valve.
8. Disconnect the charcoal canister hose from the throttle valve.
9. Disconnect the wiring and remove the main fuse box.
10. Remove the injector resistor and the connector.
11. Unplug the connectors and remove the ignition coils.

12. Remove the engine wire harness covers and disconnect the following:

    a. The 6 injector connectors.

    b. The TA sensor connector.

    c. The temperature unit connector.

    d. The ground connector from the fuel pipe.

    e. The TW sensor connector.

    f. The EGR valve connector.

    g. The knock sensor.

    h. The crankshaft angle sensor connector.

13. Remove the air inlet pipe and vacuum pipes and hoses.

14. Disconnect the throttle sensor, oil pressure switch, oxygen sensors and engine ground terminals and remove the wiring harness.

15. Remove the intake manifold.

16. Remove the upper timing belt covers.

17. Do not remove the timing belt adjuster bolt. Loosen it ½ turn, relieve the belt tension and tighten the bolt.

18. Remove the camshaft timing belt and the camshaft pulleys.

19. Remove the timing belt cover plates from the heads and remove the crank angle sensor from the left head.

20. Remove the cylinder head covers.

21. Remove the bolts from the alternator and power steering pump brackets as required.

22. Remove the self-locking nuts from the exhaust manifolds and slip the manifolds off. If necessary, remove the camshafts.

23. Loosen each head bolt about ½ turn in the opposite of the installation sequence. This is important to prevent warping the heads. Repeat until all bolts are loose and the head can be removed.

To install:

24. It is easier to install the exhaust manifolds and their covers onto the heads before installing the heads to the engine. Use new gaskets and self-locking nuts and torque to 25 ft. lbs. (34 Nm).

25. Install the heads with new gaskets and O-rings, making sure the dowel pins and control orifices are properly positioned. Oil the threads and washers on the head bolts and torque in 2 steps in the sequence shown to 56 ft. lbs. (78 Nm).

26. Apply liquid gasket to the corners of the camshaft holders and install the cylinder head covers.

27. Install the crankshaft/cylinder sensor to the left cylinder head, then install both timing belt cover plates.

28. Install the camshaft pulleys and torque the bolts to 23 ft. lbs. (32 Nm). There is a left and right pulley; the left one goes with the crankshaft/cylinder sensor.

29. Align the timing marks on the crankshaft and camshaft pulleys, install the timing belt and adjust the belt tension. Install the timing belt covers.

30. Install the intake manifold with new gaskets. Torque the 6mm bolts to 9 ft. lbs. (12 Nm) and the 8mm bolts to 16 ft. lbs. (22 Nm). Connect the cooling system hoses.

31. Install the air suction, EGR, vacuum and air inlet pipes. Reconnect the vacuum and fuel system hoses, using new gaskets on the fuel supply hose.

32. Connect the sensor wiring and install the wiring harness for the injection and ignition systems.

33. Install the fuse box and connect the wiring.

34. Connect the throttle cable and refill the cooling system.

35. Make sure all other wires and hoses are properly connected and install the battery. Before starting the engine, turn the ignition switch **ON** and **OFF** a number of times to pressurize the fuel system. Check for leaks.

36. After starting the engine, bleed the cooling system.

Vigor

The radio is equipped with a theft protection program. Be sure the 5-digit security code is available before disconnecting the battery.

1. Disconnect the negative battery cable and drain the coolant.

2. Remove the fuel filler cap and loosen the service bolt on the fuel filter banjo bolt to relieve the fuel system pressure. Remove the banjo bolt to remove the fuel feed hose from the fuel filter. Remove the fuel return hose from the pressure regulator.

> ### CAUTION
> *The fuel system may be under pressure and fuel will be sprayed. Be sure there is good ventilation and take the appropriate fire safety precautions.*

3. Remove the intake air duct and air cleaner assembly.

4. Remove the throttle cable by loosening the locknut, then slip the cable end out of the throttle bracket and accelerator linkage. Take care not to bend the cable when removing it. Unbolt the throttle cable clamp and move the cable aside.

5. Label and disconnect the fuel and vacuum hoses from the intake manifold.

6. Disconnect the heater hoses and the brake booster hose.

7. Disconnect the wiring from the ignition coil and the ground wire.

8. Remove the ABS motor relay box and the battery heatshield.

9. Remove the 2 bolts to remove the distributor. Be careful not to drop the collar behind the distributor.

10. Label and disconnect all the wiring from the cylinder head.

11. Disconnect the remaining coolant hoses from the intake manifold.

12. Remove the intake manifold support brackets. The manifold will be removed after removing the cylinder head.

13. Remove the oxygen sensor.

14. Remove the exhaust manifold heatshields and disconnect the exhaust pipe from the manifold.

15. Remove the support bracket and remove the exhaust manifold.

16. Remove the cylinder head cover and the upper timing belt cover.

17. Rotate the crankshaft to bring No. 1 piston to TDC on the compression stroke. The camshaft sprocket is equipped with TDC marks that align with the edge of the cylinder head.

18. Inspect the condition of the belt. If it is not being replaced, use paint to matchmark the belt to the sprocket for reassembly.

19. Loosen the belt tension adjuster bolt and push the tensioner against the spring to release the tension on the camshaft belt, then tighten the bolt again. Carefully slide the belt off the camshaft sprocket.

20. Loosen each cylinder head bolt about ½ turn in the opposite of the installation sequence. This is important to prevent warping the head. Repeat until all bolts are loose and can be removed.

21. If the cylinder head is stuck to the block, there are pry points near the No. 9 and No. 11 cylinder head

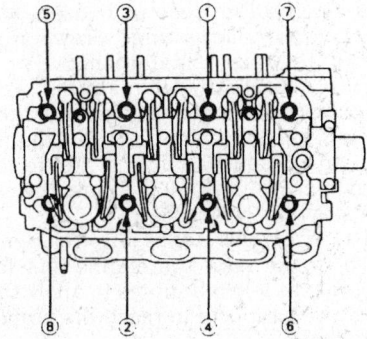

Cylinder head torque sequence — 1991-94 Legend

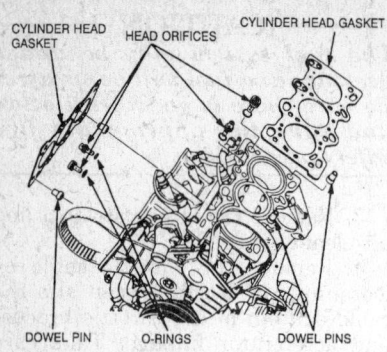

Control orifices and dowel pins — 1991-94 Legend

bolts. Do not pry against the gasket surfaces.

22. After removing the cylinder head, remove the intake manifold.

To install:

23. Make sure the cylinder head and the engine block sealing surfaces are flat. Repair or replace as required. Clean all gasket surfaces and run a tap through the bolt holes in the block to clean the threads.

24. Fit a new O-ring onto the oil control orifice and install the orifice and dowel pins onto the block. Lay the new head gasket in place.

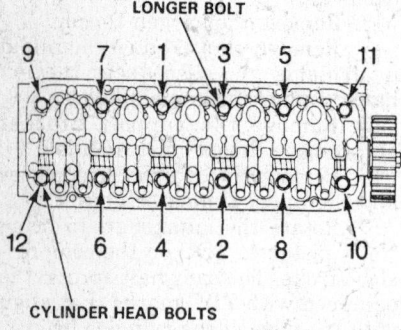

Cylinder head bolt torque sequence — Vigor

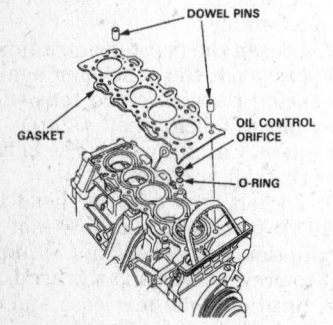

Be sure to replace the O-ring on the oil control orifice when installing a cylinder head gasket — Vigor

25. Install the intake manifold onto the cylinder head with a new gasket. Torque the nuts in a crisscross pattern in 2 steps to 16 ft. lbs. (22 Nm).

26. Make sure the crankshaft and camshaft are both at TDC for No. 1 piston and fit the cylinder head to the block. Make sure the oil control orifice is properly aligned.

27. Lightly oil the threads and washer surfaces of the cylinder head bolts and install them. Torque the bolts in 3 steps to 72 ft. lbs. (100 Nm) in the correct sequence.

28. Install the intake manifold brackets.

29. Loosely install the exhaust manifold bracket onto the manifold. Install the exhaust manifold with a new gasket and new self-locking nuts and torque the nuts to 23 ft. lbs. (32 Nm).

30. Connect the exhaust pipe and install the manifold shields.

31. Install the oxygen sensor.

32. If the crankshaft was not turned while the engine was apart and there is a matchmark on the timing belt and camshaft pulley, make sure the marks are aligned and slide the belt onto the camshaft sprocket. If the engine has been disturbed and the matchmark is not usable:

a. Align the white TDC mark on the crankshaft pulley with the pointer on the lower belt cover. Rotate the crankshaft slowly. If it stops, a piston is contacting the valves. Turn the camshaft to move the valves and try again.

b. On the camshaft sprocket, make sure the UP mark is up and align the TDC marks with the edge of the cylinder head.

c. Install the timing belt with no slack between the camshaft and crankshaft sprockets.

d. To adjust the belt tension, loosen the tensioner bolt, turn the crankshaft counterclockwise about ¼ turn, then tighten the bolt again. Rotate the crankshaft 2 full turns and make sure the timing marks and the TDC mark align properly.

33. Adjust the valves.

34. Apply silicone sealer to the ends of the cylinder head near the camshaft holders. Install the cylinder head cover with new rubber seals as required.

35. Install the timing belt covers.

36. Connect all wiring, hoses, vacuum lines and control cables. Adjust as required.

37. Change the oil and refill all fluids. Run the engine to bleed the cooling system and check for leaks.

Valve Lifters

REMOVAL AND INSTALLATION

1990 Legend

1. Remove the camshafts.

2. With the camshafts removed, remove the rocker arms and the pushrods.

3. Use a suitable valve lifter removal tool and remove the hydraulic tappet (lifter) from the cylinder head hydraulic tappet mounting hole.

4. Use the following steps to inspect the hydraulic tappet (lifter).

a. Inspect the hydraulic tappet for wear or damage or for a clogged oil hole.

b. Measure the free length of each hydraulic tappet by attaching the hydraulic tappet bleeder to the tappet. Then push and release the bleeder slowly while in a container filled with 10W-30W engine oil. Be sure to keep the hydraulic tappet upright and below the surface of the oil while pushing and release the bleeder.

c. Continue operating the bleeder until there are no air bubbles left in the hydraulic tappet.

d. Remove the hydraulic tappet and try to compress it quickly by hand. Measure the compression stroke with a dial indicator on a surface plate. The standard compression stroke measurement should be 0.0004-0.003 in. (0.01-0.08mm).

To install:

5. Pour engine oil into the cylinder head hydraulic tappet mounting hole, up to the level of the oil path.

6. Install the hydraulic tappet into the cylinder head. Do not rotate the hydraulic tappet while inserting it into the head.

7. Pour engine oil into the oil fillers on the cylinder head.

8. Install the pushrods and rocker arms. Be sure to install each part in its original position. Loosen the rocker arm adjusting screws and locknuts before installation.

9. Install the camshafts and camshaft oil seals. Be sure to take note of the locations of the camshafts; the front camshaft has a groove for driving the distributor. Adjust the exhaust valve clearance.

10. After the heads are reassembled, make sure the engine sits for approximately 5 minutes to allow the hydraulic tappets to reach the proper oil level.

11. Remove the spark plugs and crank the engine, feel for compres-

sion at each cylinder at the spark plug holes. It may be necessary to crank the engine through several cycles to confirm compression.

12. If any cylinder does not have compression, it may be necessary to disassemble the head and check the suspected tappet.

13. If all cylinders have compression, reinstall the plugs and start the engine.

1991-94 Legend

1. Remove the cylinder head cover.
2. The hydraulic lifters are in the rocker arms where they contact the valves. Each rocker arm has a letter **A** or **B** stamped into the side. Before disassembling the rocker arms, note the position of each letter so they can be reassembled the same way.
3. Remove the rocker arm assembly using the torque sequence of camshaft removal. This is important to avoid bending the rocker arm shafts.
4. Do not remove the hydraulic tappets unless they are to be replaced, they cannot be repaired or tested. Handle the rocker arms carefully so the oil does not drain out of the lifters. If replacing the lifters, also replace the O-ring.

To install:

5. Place a new camshaft seal on the end of the camshaft, lubricate the journals and set the camshaft in place on the head.
6. Apply liquid gasket to the mating surfaces of the end camshaft holders.
7. Set the rocker arm assemblies in place and start all the bolts. Make sure the rocker arms are properly positioned and turn each bolt in the correct sequence, 2 turns at a time until the holders are seated on the head. This is the only way to avoid damaging the valves or rocker assemblies.
8. When all the camshaft and rocker holders are seated, torque the bolts in the same sequence. Torque the 8mm bolts to 16 ft. lbs. (22 Nm) and the 6mm bolts to 9 ft. lbs. (12 Nm).

Valve Lash

ADJUSTMENT

Integra

NOTE: While all valve adjustments must be as accurate as possible, it is better to have the valve adjustment slightly loose than

tight, as burned valves may result from overly tight adjustments.

1. Make sure the engine is cold, cylinder head temperature below 100°F (38°C).
2. Remove the valve cover and the upper timing belt cover.
3. Set the No. 1 cylinder to TDC. The word UP should appear at the top and the TDC grooves on the pulley should align with the cylinder head surface.
4. With the No. 1 cylinder at TDC, adjust the valves of the No. 1 cylinder by performing the following procedures:
   a. Clearance should be 0.006-0.007 in. (0.15-0.19mm) on the intake valves and 0.007-0.008 in. (0.17-0.21mm) on the exhaust valves.
   b. Hold the rocker arm against the valve and place the feeler gauge between the rocker arm and the camshaft lobe. There should be a slight drag on the feeler gauge.
   c. If adjustment is required, loosen the valve adjusting the screw locknut.
   d. Turn the adjusting screw to obtain the proper clearance.
   e. Hold the adjusting screw and torque the locknut(s) to 18 ft. lbs. (24 Nm).
   f. Recheck the clearance.
5. Turn the crankshaft 180 degrees counterclockwise, the camshaft pulley will turn 90 degrees. With the No. 3 cylinder at TDC, the UP marks should be at the exhaust side, adjust the valves on the No. 3 cylinder.
6. Turn the crankshaft 180 degrees counterclockwise, the camshaft pulley will turn 90 degrees. With the No. 4 cylinder at TDC, both UP marks should be at the bottom. Adjust the valves on the No. 4 cylinder.
7. Turn the crankshaft 180 degrees counterclockwise. The No. 2 cylinder will now be on TDC and the

UP marks should be at the intake side. Adjust the valves on the No. 2 cylinder.

1990 Legend

This procedure is used to adjust the exhaust valves; the intake valves require no adjustment.

1. Make sure the engine is cold, cylinder head temperature below 100°F (38°C).
2. Remove the valve and side head covers.
3. Rotate the crankshaft to position the No. 1 piston on the TDC of its compression stroke; the camshaft sprockets should be in the upward position, aligned with the timing mark and the crankshaft pulley V-notch should be aligned with the timing pointer on the timing cover.
4. To adjust the exhaust valves, perform the following procedures:
   a. Loosen the exhaust valve locknuts on all of the cylinders.
   b. Tighten the adjusting screw of the No. 1 cylinder, until it contacts the valve, then an additional 1½ turns. Tighten the locknut firmly.
   c. Perform the same procedure for the exhaust valves No. 2 and 4.
   d. Rotate the crankshaft 360 degrees and align the crankshaft pulley's V-notch with the timing pointer on the timing cover; the No. 5 piston is at TDC of its compression stroke.
   e. Tighten the adjusting screw of the No. 5 cylinder, until it contacts the valve, then an additional 1½ turns. Tighten the locknut firmly.
   f. Perform the same procedure for the exhaust valves No. 3 and 6.
5. After adjustment, use new gaskets and install the valve and side head covers.

Vigor

1. Remove the cylinder head cover and the upper timing belt cover.

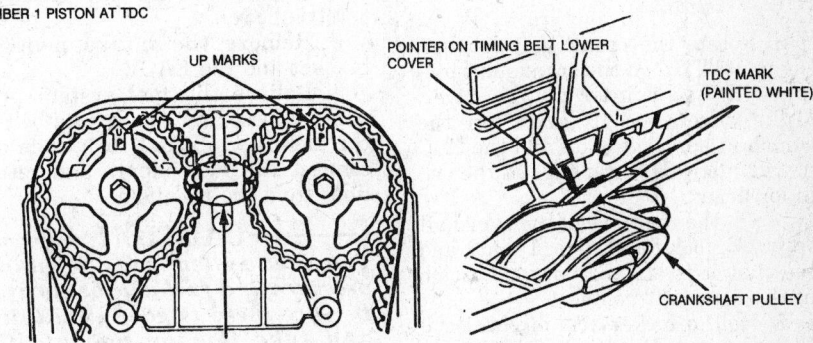

NUMBER 1 PISTON AT TDC

UP MARKS

POINTER ON TIMING BELT LOWER COVER

TDC MARK (PAINTED WHITE)

CRANKSHAFT PULLEY

Camshaft sprockets positioned for TDC No.1 cylinder at TDC — Integra

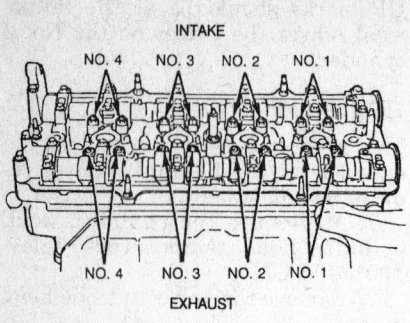

Valve locations — Integra with 1.8L engine

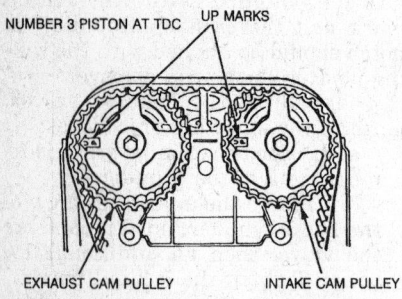

Number 3 piston at TDC — Integra

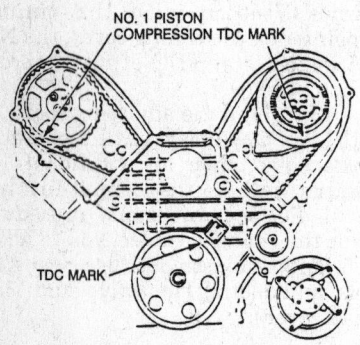

Camshaft sprockets and crankshaft pulley positioned for TDC No.5 — 1990 Legend

2. Rotate the crankshaft to align the white TDC on the crankshaft pulley with the pointer on the cover. Make sure the UP mark on the camshaft sprocket is up and the TDC marks align with the edge of the cylinder head.

3. On the rear face of the camshaft sprocket, look for the No. 1 mark and see that it is aligned with the notch in the camshaft holder.

4. Hold a rocker arm of No. 1 cylinder against the camshaft and use a feeler gauge to check the clearance at

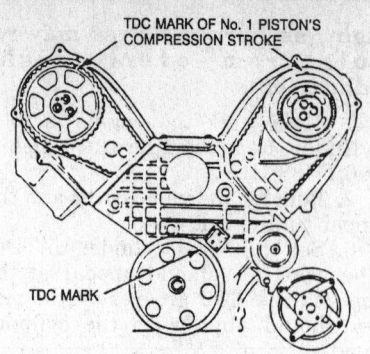

Camshaft sprockets and crankshaft pulley positioned for TDC No.1 — 1990 Legend

the valve stem. Intake valve clearance should be 0.010 in. (0.254mm), exhaust valve clearance should be 0.012 in. (0.30mm). Loosen the locknut to adjust as required.

5. Each cylinder is marked on the rear face of the camshaft sprocket. Rotate the crankshaft to align the next mark in the notch and adjust the valves. The order will be 1-2-4-5-3.

6. Install the cylinder head and timing belt covers.

Rocker Arms/Shafts

REMOVAL AND INSTALLATION

On all models, the rocker arms ride directly against the camshafts and are serviced with the camshaft. See the camshaft section for rocker arm service.

Intake Manifold

REMOVAL AND INSTALLATION

Integra

1. Disconnect the negative battery cable. Drain the cooling system.
2. Remove the air duct from the throttle body.
3. Remove the intake manifold bracket and the EACV.
4. Relieve the fuel system pressure by loosening the service bolt on the fuel filter about 1 turn, then disconnect the fuel supply and return lines from the manifold.

— **CAUTION** —
The fuel system may be under pressure and fuel will be sprayed. Be sure there is good ventilation and take the appropriate fire safety precautions.

5. Label and remove any electrical connectors running to the intake manifold.
6. Remove the intake manifold-to-cylinder head nuts, in a crisscross pattern, beginning from the center and moving out to both ends. Remove the manifold and the gasket.
7. Clean the gasket mounting surfaces. Inspect the manifold for cracks, flatness and/or damage; replace the parts, if necessary. If the intake manifold is to be replaced, transfer all the necessary components to the new manifold.

To install:

8. Use new gaskets and reverse the removal procedures. Torque the nuts/bolts, in a crisscross pattern, in 2-3 steps, starting with the inner nuts, to 16-17 ft. lbs. (22-23 Nm).
9. Start the engine, allow it to reach normal operating temperatures and check for leaks and engine operation.

Legend

1. Disconnect the negative battery cable. Drain the cooling system.
2. Remove the air duct from the throttle body.
3. Remove the EACV, the air suction valve and the EGR tube.
4. Label and remove any wires running to the intake manifold.
5. Relieve the fuel system pressure by loosening the service bolt on the fuel filter about 1 turn, then disconnect the fuel supply and return lines from the manifold.

— **CAUTION** —
The fuel system may be under pressure and fuel will be sprayed. Be sure there is good ventilation and take the appropriate fire safety precautions.

6. Remove the intake manifold nuts in a crisscross pattern, beginning from the center and moving out to both ends and the manifold.
7. Clean the gasket mounting surfaces. Inspect the manifold for cracks, flatness and/or damage; replace the parts as necessary. If the intake manifold is to be replaced, transfer all the necessary components to the new manifold.

To install:

8. Use new gaskets and reverse the removal procedures. Torque the nuts/bolts, in a crisscross pattern in 2-3 steps, starting with the inner nuts. Torque the 8mm bolts to 16 ft. lbs. (22 Nm) and the 6mm bolts to 9 ft. lbs. (12 Nm).

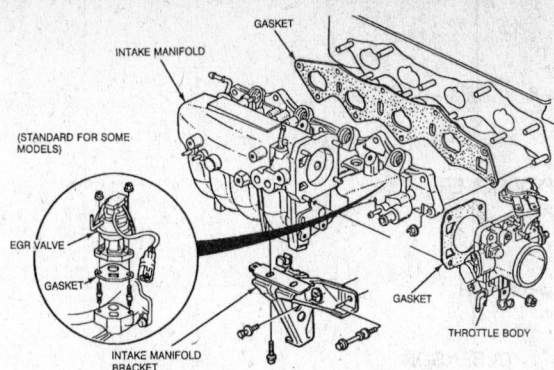

GASKET
INTAKE MANIFOLD
(STANDARD FOR SOME MODELS)
EGR VALVE
GASKET
INTAKE MANIFOLD BRACKET
GASKET
THROTTLE BODY

Intake manifold assembly — 1.8L engine

9. Start the engine, allow it to reach normal operating temperatures and check for leaks and engine operation.

Vigor

The radio is equipped with a theft protection program. Be sure the 5-digit security code is available before disconnecting the battery.

1. Disconnect the negative battery cable.

2. Remove the fuel filler cap and loosen the service bolt on the fuel filter banjo bolt to relieve the fuel system pressure. Remove the banjo bolt to remove the fuel feed hose from the fuel filter. Remove the fuel return hose from the pressure regulator.

────── CAUTION ──────
The fuel system may be under pressure and fuel will be sprayed. Be sure there is good ventilation and take the appropriate fire safety precautions.

3. Remove the intake air duct and air cleaner assembly.

4. Remove the throttle cable by loosening the locknut, then slip the cable end out of the throttle bracket and accelerator linkage. Take care not to bend the cable when removing it. Unbolt the throttle cable clamp and move the cable aside.

5. Label and disconnect the vacuum hoses and all wiring from the intake manifold.

6. To avoid having to drain the cooling system, remove the fast idle valve and the EACV without disconnecting the coolant hoses and lay them aside. Be careful not to lose the O-rings.

7. Remove the EGR pipe and the vacuum pipe.

8. Remove the intake manifold brackets.

9. Remove the nuts to remove the intake manifold from the engine.

To install:

10. Fit the manifold to the engine with a new gasket and torque the nuts to 16 ft. lbs. (22 Nm).

11. Install any components that were removed with new gaskets or O-rings as required. If the fuel injectors were removed, replace the seal rings and cushion rings to prevent noise and leakage.

12. Connect the wiring, vacuum hoses and fuel lines.

13. Connect and adjust the throttle cable as required.

14. Run the engine and check for leaks.

Exhaust Manifold

REMOVAL AND INSTALLATION

Integra

NOTE: Do not perform this operation on a warm or hot engine.

1. Disconnect the negative battery cable. Remove the exhaust manifold shroud.

2. Remove the exhaust pipe-to-exhaust manifold nuts.

3. Remove the oxygen sensor, if equipped.

4. Remove the exhaust manifold bracket bolt.

5. Remove the exhaust manifold-to-cylinder head nuts in a crisscross pattern starting from the center and the manifold.

6. Clean the gasket mounting surfaces. Inspect the manifold for cracks, flatness and/or damage; replace the parts if necessary.

To install:

7. Use new gaskets and reverse the removal procedures. Torque the manifold nuts in a crisscross pattern starting from the center, to 23 ft. lbs. (32 Nm) and the exhaust pipe-to-manifold nuts to 40 ft. lbs. (55 Nm).

8. Start the engine and check for leaks.

Vigor

1. Remove the heatshields.

2. Disconnect the wiring and remove the oxygen sensor.

3. Disconnect the exhaust pipe.

4. Remove the bracket and retaining nuts. Remove the manifold.

To install:

5. Install the bracket loosely and install the manifold with new gaskets and self-locking nuts. Torque the nuts to 23 ft. lbs. (32 Nm), then tighten the bracket bolts.

6. When installing the oxygen sensor, lightly coat the threads with an anti-seize compound. Be careful not to get any on the head of the sensor.

7. Use a new gasket and connect the exhaust pipe. Torque the nuts to 40 ft. lbs. (55 Nm). Install the heatshields.

Legend

1. Disconnect the negative battery cable. Remove the exhaust manifold shrouds.

2. Remove the exhaust pipe-to-exhaust manifold nuts.

3. Remove the oxygen sensors.

4. Remove the air suction tube.

5. Remove the exhaust pipe-to-exhaust manifold nuts.

6. Clean the gasket mounting surfaces. Inspect the manifold for cracks, flatness and/or damage; replace the parts, if necessary.

7. Remove the exhaust attaching nuts in a crass-cross pattern starting from the center of the manifold.

8. To install, use new gaskets and reverse the removal procedures. Torque the manifold nuts/bolts in a crisscross pattern starting from the center, to 16 ft. lbs. (22 Nm) on 2675cc engines or 22 ft. lbs. (31 Nm) on all other 6 cylinder engines.

9. Use new gaskets when installing the exhaust pipe to the manifold and torque the nuts to 40 ft. lbs. (55 Nm).

Timing Belt Front Cover

REMOVAL AND INSTALLATION

Integra

1. Disconnect the negative battery cable and remove the upper timing belt cover.

2. Rotate the crankshaft to the white timing mark on the pulley, indicating the No. 1 piston is at TDC. The camshaft sprockets **UP** mark

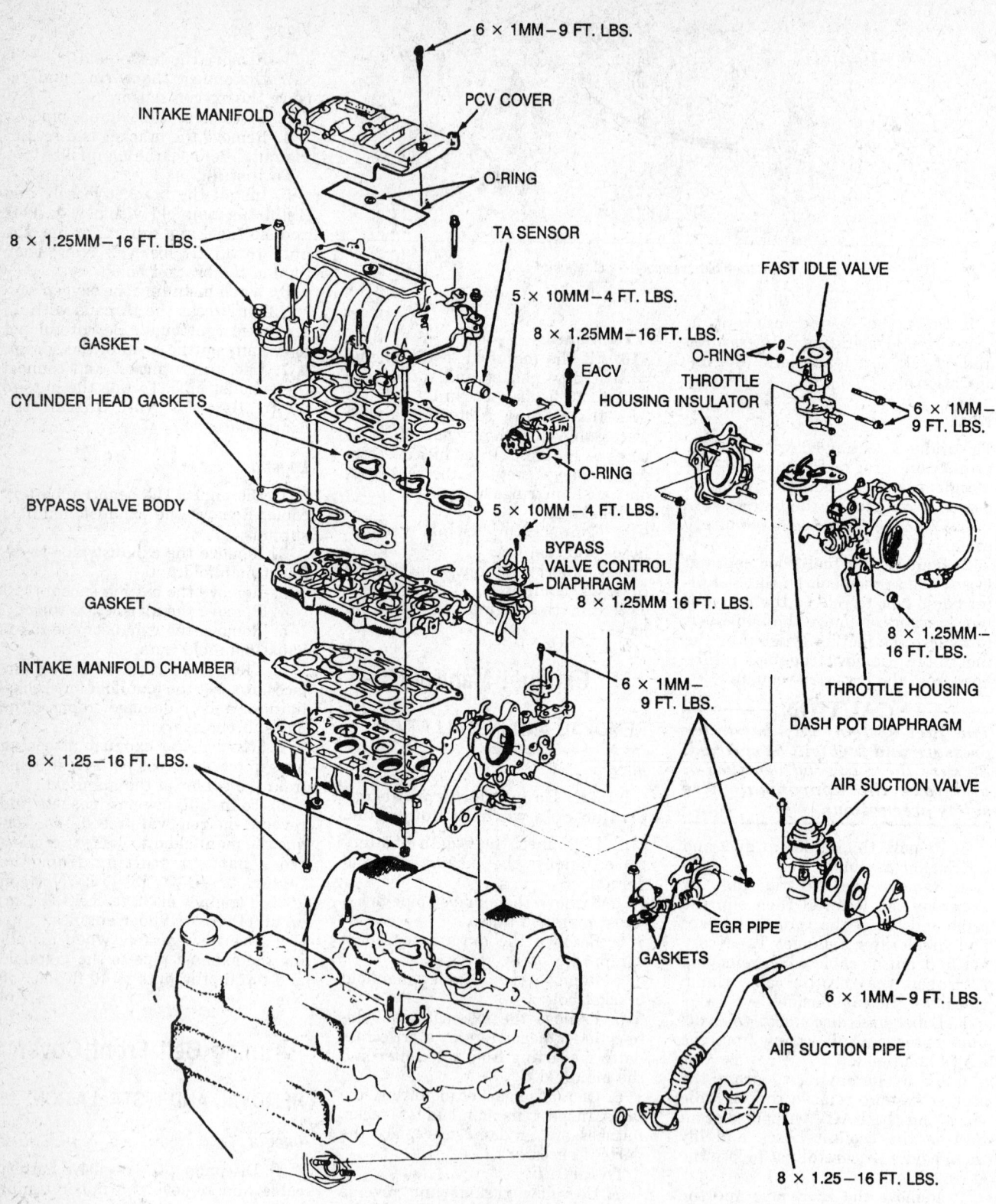

6 × 1MM — 9 FT. LBS.

PCV COVER

INTAKE MANIFOLD

O-RING

8 × 1.25MM — 16 FT. LBS.

TA SENSOR

FAST IDLE VALVE

5 × 10MM — 4 FT. LBS.

8 × 1.25MM — 16 FT. LBS.

O-RING

GASKET

EACV

THROTTLE
HOUSING INSULATOR

6 × 1MM —
9 FT. LBS.

CYLINDER HEAD GASKETS

O-RING

BYPASS VALVE BODY

5 × 10MM — 4 FT. LBS.

BYPASS
VALVE CONTROL
DIAPHRAGM

8 × 1.25MM 16 FT. LBS.

8 × 1.25MM —
16 FT. LBS.

GASKET

THROTTLE HOUSING

6 × 1MM —
9 FT. LBS.

DASH POT DIAPHRAGM

INTAKE MANIFOLD CHAMBER

AIR SUCTION VALVE

8 × 1.25 — 16 FT. LBS.

EGR PIPE

GASKETS

6 × 1MM — 9 FT. LBS.

AIR SUCTION PIPE

8 × 1.25 — 16 FT. LBS.

Intake manifold assembly — 2.7L engine

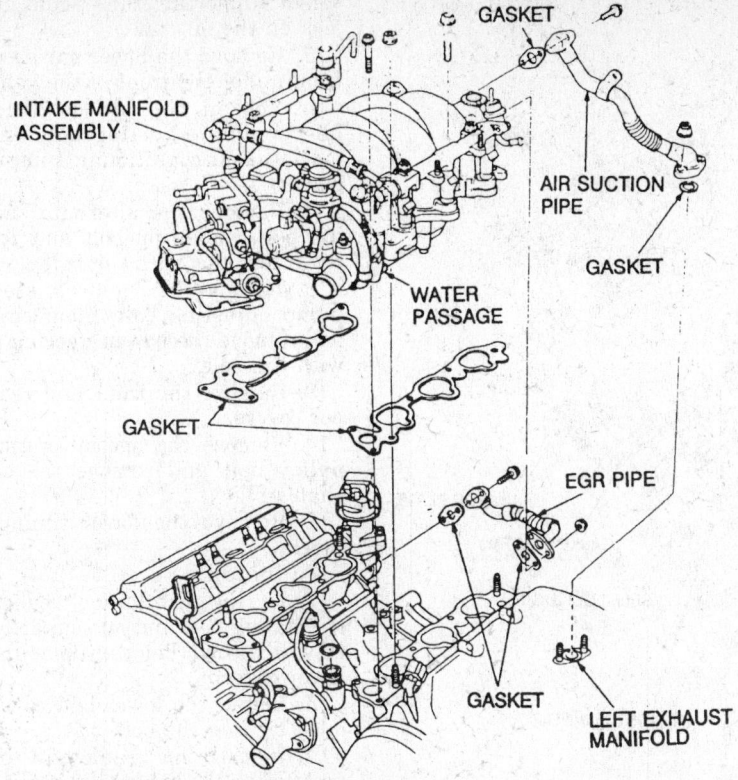

Intake manifold assembly — 3.2L engine

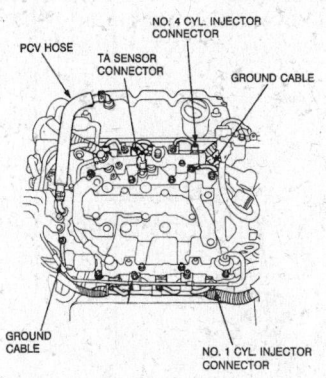

Intake manifold assembly — Vigor

8. Remove the middle timing cover.

9. Remove the special crankshaft pulley bolt and the crankshaft pulley.

10. Remove the lower timing belt cover.

To install:

11. Install the lower cover and crankshaft pulley. Carefully oil the threads of the pulley bolt without getting oil on the washer.

12. Torque the bolt, in 3 steps, to 145 ft. lbs. (200 Nm). Loosen it again, then retorque to 130 ft. lbs. (180 Nm).

13. The remaining installation is the reverse order of removal.

1990 Legend

1. Disconnect the negative battery cable. Rotate the crankshaft to align the crankshaft pulley or flywheel pointer, at TDC. The camshaft sprocket notches should align with the marks on the rear timing belt cover.

2. Remove the pulley cover and harness cover from above the timing belt upper cover.

3. Remove the engine sub harness clip.

4. Remove the engine support bolts. Loosen the side mount rubber and raise the side mount bracket.

should be facing upward with the alignment marks aligned with the top of the cylinder head.

3. Raise and safely support the vehicle and remove the left front wheel and splash shield.

4. Remove the power steering belt and power steering pump. Do not disconnect the power steering fluid lines.

5. Remove the air conditioning belt and the alternator belt.

6. Remove the engine support bolts and nut, then remove the side mount rubber.

7. Remove the valve cover.

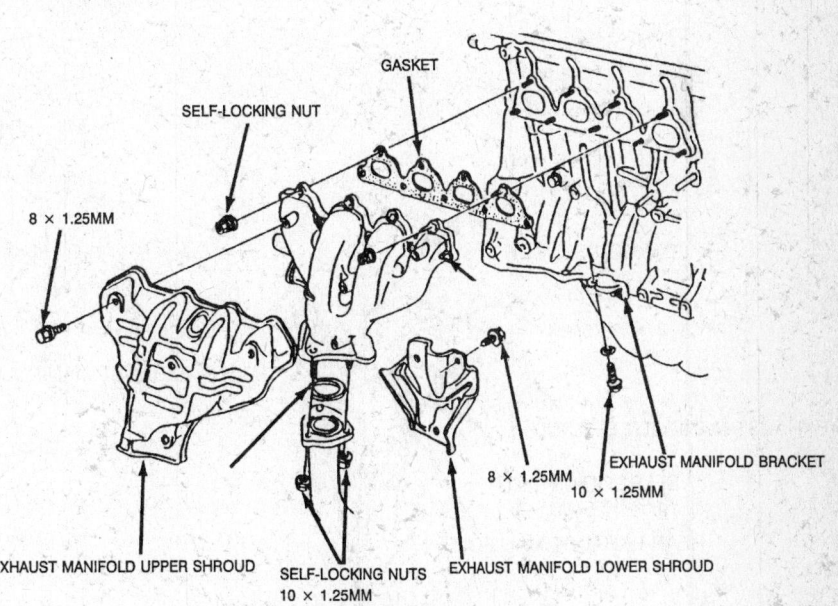

Exhaust manifold assembly — Integra

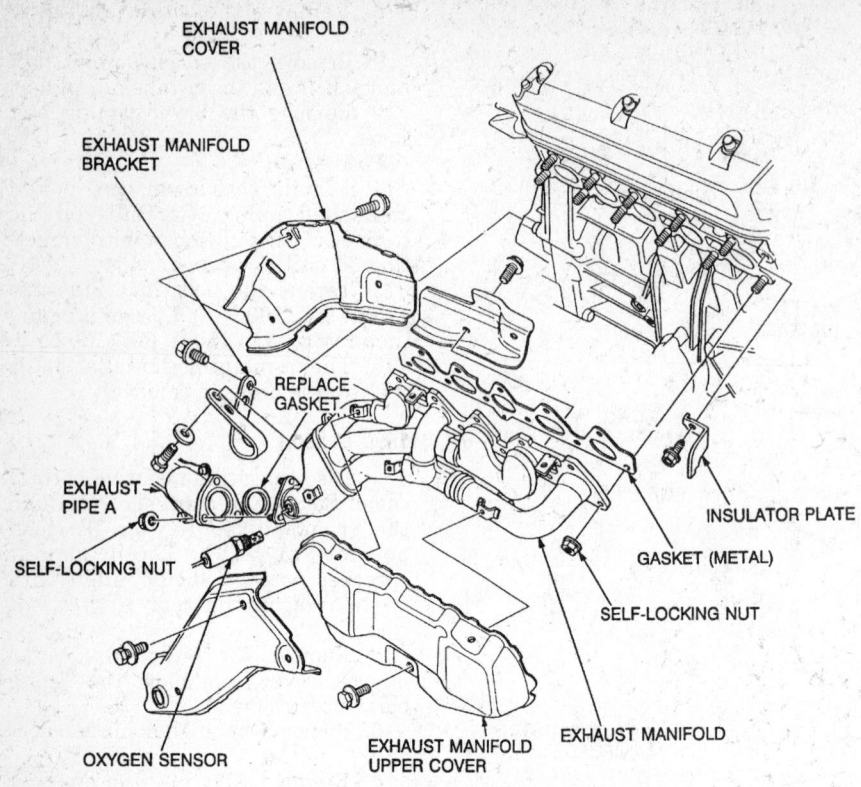

Exhaust manifold assembly — Vigor

When supporting the engine, do not jack on the oil pan.

5. Remove the lower splash guard from under the front of the vehicle.

6. Loosen the air conditioning idler pulley adjusting bolt and remove the air conditioning compressor belt.

7. Remove the alternator adjusting bolt, mounting bolt and remove the alternator with the belt.

8. Remove the power steering pump adjusting bolt, mounting bolt and remove the power steering pump with the belt.

9. Remove the front and rear upper covers.

10. Remove the special crankshaft pulley bolt and remove the crankshaft pulley.

11. Remove the lower timing belt cover.

To install:

12. During installation, make sure the timing belt and oil seal are properly installed before replacing the lower cover.

13. Install the lower belt cover but don't tighten the bolts yet.

14. Install the crankshaft pulley and torque the bolt to 123 ft. lbs. (170 Nm).

15. Install the remaining timing belt covers and tighten all bolts.

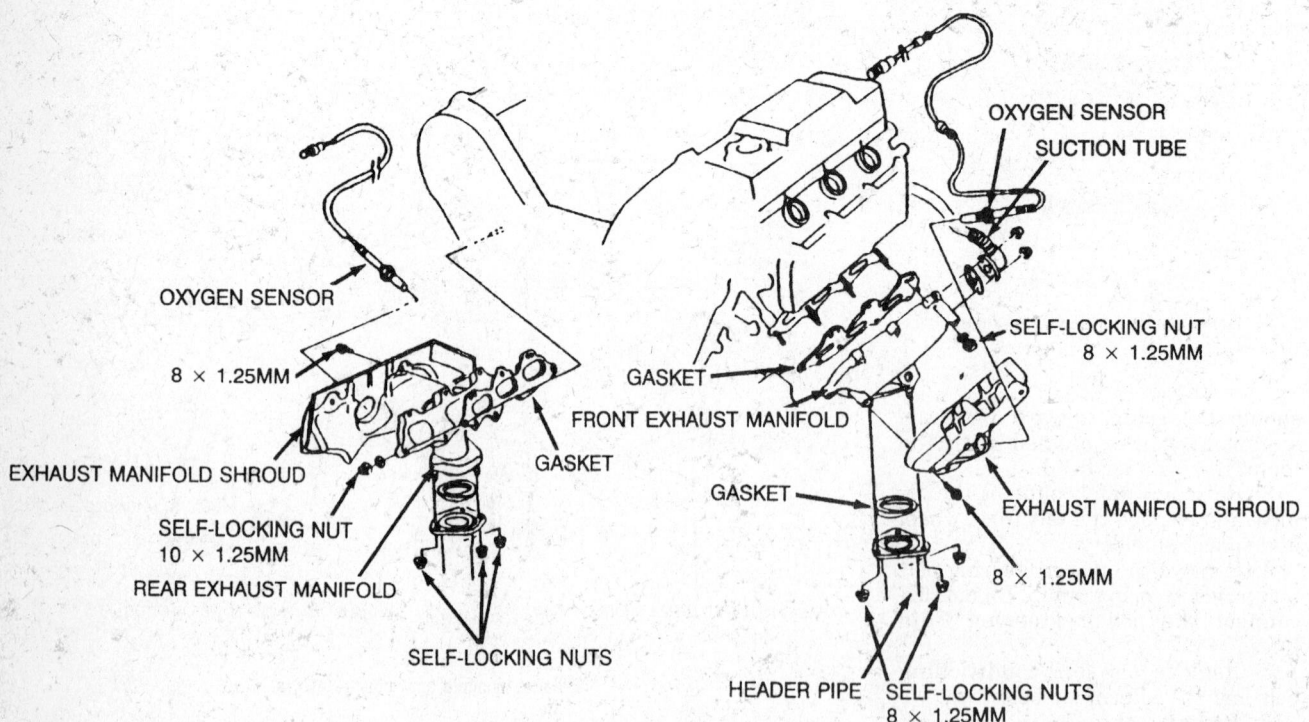

Exhaust manifold assembly — Legend

16. Install the power steering pump and alternator and properly tension the belts.

17. Install and tension the air conditioner belt.

18. Set the engine in place and install the engine side mount bracket bolts.

19. Secure the wiring in place and install the lower splash shield.

1991-94 Legend

1. Disconnect the negative battery cable.

2. Remove the engine wire harness covers at the front of the engine.

3. Label and disconnect the wiring harness.

4. Remove the breather pipe and vacuum pipe bracket.

5. Remove the alternator, air conditioning and power steering belts.

6. Remove the timing belt upper covers and turn the crankshaft pulley to the TDC No. 1 cylinder mark.

7. Remove the crankshaft pulley.

8. Remove the air conditioner belt tensioner pulley.

9. Remove the dipstick tube and the lower timing belt cover.

To install:

10. Make sure the rubber seals and cover are clean and dry and install the lower cover.

11. Carefully oil the threads of the pulley bolt without getting oil on the washer. Install the crankshaft pulley and torque the bolt to 174 ft. lbs. (240 Nm).

12. Use a new O-ring to install the dipstick tube.

13. Install and adjust the drive belts for the air conditioner, power steering and alternator.

14. Install the upper timing belt covers, breather pipe and the wiring harness.

Vigor

NOTE: The radio is equipped with a theft protection program. Be sure the 5-digit security code is available before disconnecting the battery.

1. Disconnect the negative battery cable.

2. Label and disconnect the engine wiring as required.

3. Loosen the adjusting bolts and remove the accessory drive belts.

4. Remove the cylinder head cover.

5. Remove the timing belt upper cover.

6. Rotate the crankshaft to align the white timing mark on the crankshaft pulley with the pointer on the lower cover. Make sure the **UP** mark

and the TDC marks on the camshaft sprocket are correctly positioned.

7. Remove the center bolt from the crankshaft and remove the crankshaft pulley.

8. Remove the lower timing belt cover.

To install:

9. Install the lower cover but do not fully tighten the bolts yet.

10. Install the crankshaft pulley and without getting oil on the washer, oil the threads on the bolt. Torque the bolt to 181 ft. lbs. (250 Nm).

11. Install the upper cover and tighten the bolts for both covers.

12. Install the cylinder head cover with new gaskets and O-rings as required.

13. Install and adjust the accessory drive belts.

14. After connecting the battery, enter the radio security code.

Front Cover Oil Seal

REPLACEMENT

If the proper seal driving tools are available, the front oil seal replacement can be done without removing the oil pump.

1. With camshaft drive belt removed, use a suitable seal removal tool and remove the front oil seal from the oil pump.

2. Apply a light coat of oil to the crankshaft and to the lip of the seal. Make sure the seal contact surface on the oil pump is clean and dry.

3. Using an oil seal driver tool deep enough to fit over the crankshaft, drive in the new seal into the pump until it just bottoms out.

Timing Belt And Tensioner

ADJUSTMENT

Integra and Vigor

NOTE: Always adjust the timing belt tension with the engine cold. The tensioner is spring-loaded to apply the proper tension to the belt automatically after making the following adjustments.

1. Turn the crankshaft pulley until the No. 1 piston is at TDC of the compression stroke.

2. Loosen the adjusting bolt on the tensioner pulley.

3. Rotate the crankshaft counterclockwise 3 teeth on the camshaft

pulley to create tension on the timing belt.

4. Torque the adjusting bolt on the tensioner pulley to 33 ft. lbs. (45 Nm).

5. If the crankshaft pulley bolt broke loose while turning the crank, torque it as follows:

Integra — 130 ft. lbs. (180 Nm)
Vigor — 181 ft. lbs. (250 Nm)

Legend

NOTE: Always adjust the timing belt tension with the engine cold. The tensioner is spring-loaded to apply the proper tension to the belt automatically after making the following adjustments.

1. Turn the crankshaft pulley until No. 1 is at TDC of the compression stroke.

2. Rotate the crankshaft clockwise 9 teeth on the camshaft pulley. The blue mark on the camshaft pulley should line up with the pointer on the lower cover.

3. Loosen the adjusting bolt about 1/2 turn. The spring will automatically provide the correct belt tension.

4. Torque the adjusting bolt to 31 ft. lbs. (43 Nm).

REMOVAL AND INSTALLATION

Integra

1. Raise and safely support the vehicle. Remove the left front wheel and remove the wheel well splash guard.

2. Remove the power steering belt and power steering pump. Do not disconnect the power steering fluid lines.

3. Remove the air conditioning belt and the alternator belt.

4. Remove the left side engine mount.

5. Remove the valve cover.

6. Remove the middle timing belt cover.

7. Set the crankshaft to TDC of the No. 1 piston. The white crankshaft pulley mark should be aligned with the pointer on the cover and the camshaft sprockets **UP** mark should be facing upward, sprocket timing marks aligned.

8. Remove the special crankshaft pulley bolt and the crankshaft pulley.

9. Remove the lower timing belt cover.

10. Loosen but do not remove the tensioner adjusting bolt, push the tensioner to slacken the timing belt, then retighten the bolt. If the timing belt is to be reinstalled, mark the di-

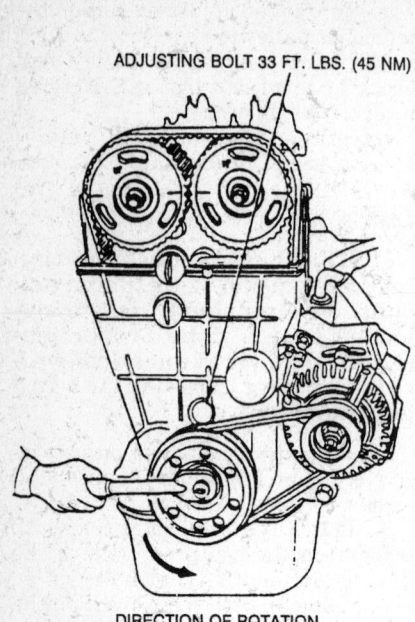

ADJUSTING BOLT 33 FT. LBS. (45 NM)

DIRECTION OF ROTATION

Timing belt tension adjustment — Integra — Vigor similar

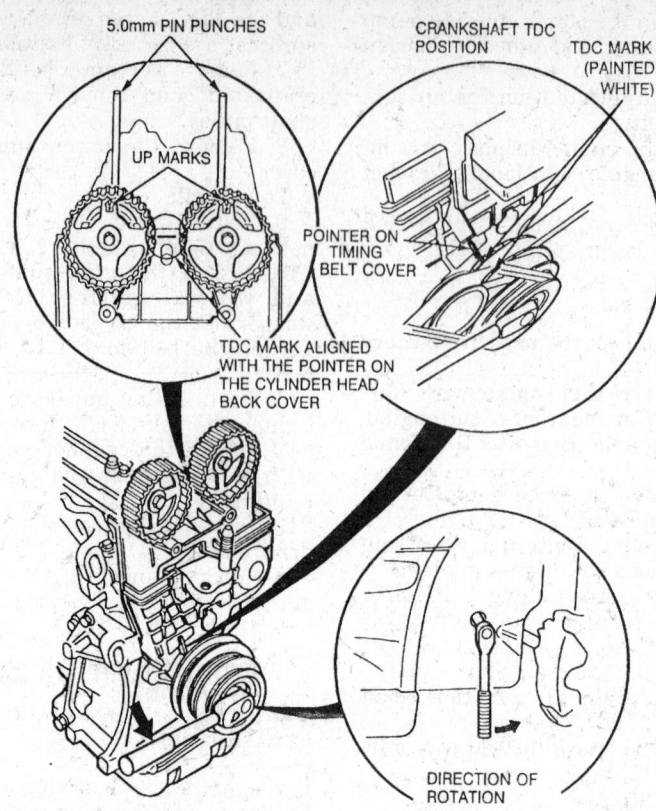

5.0mm PIN PUNCHES

UP MARKS

CRANKSHAFT TDC POSITION

TDC MARK (PAINTED WHITE)

POINTER ON TIMING BELT COVER

TDC MARK ALIGNED WITH THE POINTER ON THE CYLINDER HEAD BACK COVER

DIRECTION OF ROTATION

Timing belt and sprockets — Integra

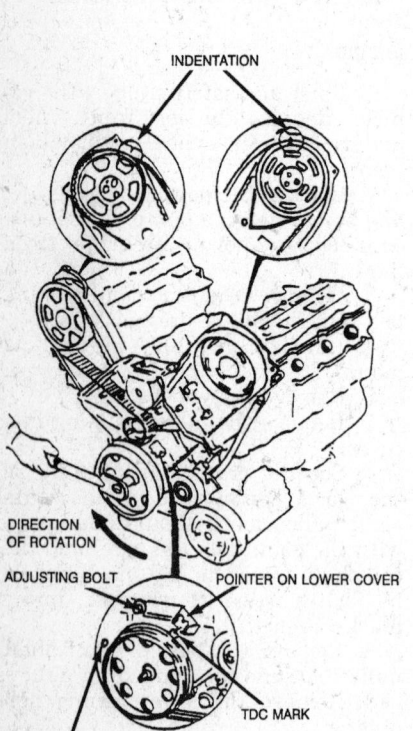

INDENTATION

DIRECTION OF ROTATION

ADJUSTING BOLT

POINTER ON LOWER COVER

TDC MARK

ADJUSTING MARK

Timing belt adjustment

rection of rotation. Remove the timing belt.

To install:

11. Install the timing belt with the No. 1 piston at TDC on its compression stroke. To set the camshafts to the TDC position for No. 1 cylinder, align the hole in the camshafts with the holes in the No. 1 camshaft holders and push a 0.197 in. (5.0mm) pin punches into the holes.

12. Install the timing belt. If installing the old belt, make sure it is turning the same direction.

13. Make sure the timing belt is properly installed on the crankshaft and that the front oil seal does not leak. Replace the cover and crankshaft pulley and carefully oil the threads of the pulley bolt without getting oil on the washer. Torque the bolt, in 3 steps, to 145 ft. lbs. (200 Nm). Loosen the bolt completely, then re-torque to 130 ft. lbs. (180 Nm).

14. Make sure the camshaft sprockets and crankshaft pulley are properly aligned with the timing marks. Loosen the tensioner bolt about ½ turn, then torque to 40 ft. lbs. (55 Nm). Tension adjustment is automatically accomplished with the spring on the tensioner. Check timing mark alignment again.

15. Install the remaining parts in reverse order. Torque the engine mount-to-engine bolt and nut to 54 ft. lbs. (75 Nm), torque the mount-to-body bolt to 40 ft. lbs. (55 Nm).

1990 Legend

1. Disconnect the negative battery cable. Remove the pulley cover and the harness cover from above the timing belt upper cover.

2. Remove the engine sub-harness clamp.

3. Remove the engine support bolts, loosen the side mount rubber and raise the side mount bracket.

NOTE: A suitable lifting device or chain hoist should be used to raise and support the engine. Do not jack on the oil pan.

4. Remove the lower splash guard.

5. Loosen the air conditioning idler pulley adjusting bolt and remove the compressor belt.

6. Remove the alternator adjusting bolt, the mounting bolt, the drive belt and the alternator.

7. Remove the power steering pump bolt, the mounting bolt, the drive belt and the power steering pump. It may be necessary to disconnect the hydraulic hoses.

8. Remove the front and rear upper covers.

9. Make sure the crankshaft is set to TDC No. 1 piston. Remove the special bolt and the crankshaft pulley.

10. Remove the lower cover.

11. Loosen but do not remove the tensioner adjusting bolt, push the tensioner to slacken the timing belt, then retighten the bolt. If the timing belt is to be reinstalled, mark the direction of rotation. Remove the timing belt.

NOTE: Do not rotate the crankshaft or camshafts with the belt removed. The pistons will contact the valves and cause engine damage.

12. Inspect the timing belt. Replace it if it is oil soaked or worn. Find and repair the source of the oil leak.

To install:

13. If the crankshaft or camshafts have been turned with the timing belt removed, remove the spark plugs and advance the crankshaft about 15 degrees beyond TDC of No. 1 cylinder. Make sure the camshaft sprockets are properly aligned with the marks and return the crankshaft to the TDC mark.

14. Install the belt in sequence on the crankshaft, the front camshaft, water pump and tensioner pulleys, then the rear camshaft.

15. To adjust the tension, loosen the tensioner pulley bolt about ½ turn. The spring will automatically set the proper tension. Torque the bolt to 31 ft. lbs. (43 Nm).

16. Rotate the crankshaft 6 turns clockwise and check that the timing marks on the crankshaft and camshafts align properly. Adjust the timing belt tension again by rotating the crankshaft to the align the blue mark on the pulley with the pointer. Loosen and retorque the tensioner pulley bolt.

17. Install the remaining parts in reverse order. Torque the crankshaft pulley bolt to 83 ft. lbs. (115 Nm). When installing the side mount bracket, torque the bolts to 40 ft. lbs. (55 Nm).

1991-94 Legend

1. Disconnect the negative battery cable.

2. Remove the engine wiring harness covers and the wiring harness from the front of the engine.

3. Remove the breather pipe and vacuum pipe bracket.

4. Remove the drive belts for the alternator, air conditioner and power steering pump.

5. Remove the upper timing belt covers.

6. Rotate the crankshaft to TDC No. 1 piston. The white mark on the crankshaft pulley will be aligned with the pointer on the lower cover, and the camshaft sprocket marks will be aligned with the yellow marks on the rear covers.

7. Remove the crankshaft pulley and the air conditioner belt tensioner pulley.

8. Remove the dipstick tube. Remove the lower timing belt cover.

9. Loosen the timing belt tensioner pulley bolt about ½ turn and push the pulley to slacken the belt tension. Tighten the bolt and remove the belt. If the belt is to be reinstalled, mark the direction of rotation.

NOTE: Do not rotate the crankshaft or camshafts with the belt removed. The pistons will contact the valves and cause engine damage.

To install:

10. If the belt is worn or oil soaked, it must be replaced. Find and repair the source of the oil leak before installing a new belt.

11. If the crankshaft or camshafts have been turned with the timing belt removed, remove the spark plugs and advance the crankshaft about 15 degrees beyond TDC of No. 1 cylinder. Make sure the camshaft sprockets are properly aligned with the marks and return the crankshaft to the TDC mark.

12. Install the belt in sequence on the crankshaft, adjuster pulley, the left camshaft, water pump, then the right camshaft.

13. To adjust the tension, loosen the tensioner pulley bolt about ½ turn. The spring will automatically set the proper tension. Torque the bolt to 31 ft. lbs. (43 Nm).

14. Rotate the crankshaft 6 turns clockwise and check that the timing marks on the crankshaft and camshafts align properly. Adjust the timing belt tension again by rotating the crankshaft to the align the blue mark on the pulley with the pointer. Loosen and retorque the tensioner pulley bolt.

15. When installing the crankshaft pulley, oil the threads of the bolt without getting oil on the washer. Torque the bolt to 174 ft. lbs. (240 Nm).

16. Installation of the remaining parts is the reverse of removal.

Vigor

NOTE: The radio is equipped with a theft protection program. Be sure the 5-digit security code is available before disconnecting the battery.

1. Disconnect the negative battery cable.

2. Label and disconnect the engine wiring as required.

3. Loosen the adjusting bolts and remove the accessory drive belts.

4. Remove the cylinder head cover.

5. Remove the timing belt upper cover.

6. Rotate the crankshaft to align the white timing mark on the crankshaft pulley with the pointer on the lower cover. Make sure the UP mark and the TDC marks on the camshaft sprocket are correctly positioned.

7. Remove the center bolt from the crankshaft and remove the crankshaft pulley.

8. Turn the crankshaft to align the white TDC mark with the pointer, then remove the lower timing belt cover. Make sure the UP mark on the camshaft sprocket is correctly positioned.

9. Mark the direction of rotation of the timing belt. Loosen the tensioner and remove the belt.

To install:

10. Install the belt on the crankshaft sprocket, tensioner, water pump, then the camshaft sprocket. If the old belt is being installed, make sure it will turn the same direction.

11. Loosen the tensioner bolt to allow the spring to set the tension, then tighten the bolt. Rotate the crankshaft 6 full turns to seat the belt and make sure the timing marks align properly.

12. Install the lower cover but do not fully tighten the bolts yet.

13. Install the crankshaft pulley and without getting oil on the washer, oil the threads on the bolt. Torque the bolt to 181 ft. lbs. (250 Nm).

14. Install the upper cover and tighten the bolts for both covers.

15. Install the cylinder head cover with new gaskets and O-rings as required.

16. Install and adjust the accessory drive belts.

17. After connecting the battery, enter the radio security code.

Timing Sprockets

REMOVAL AND INSTALLATION

Integra

1. Disconnect the negative battery cable. Set the No. 1 cylinder on the TDC of its compression stroke and remove the timing belt.

2. Align the holes in the No. 1 camshaft bearing holders with the holes in the camshafts. Insert a 0.197 in. (5.0mm) pin punches into the holes to secure the camshafts.

3. Remove the camshaft sprocket-to-camshaft bolts, the washers and the sprockets. Remove the sprocket with a pulley remover or a brass hammer.

NOTE: Be careful not to lose the Woodruff key.

4. The camshaft oil seal can be replaced without removing the camshaft holders. To check camshaft end-play, the rocker arm adjusting screws must be loosened.

5. Installation is the reverse of removal. Torque the camshaft sprocket-to-camshaft bolts to 27 ft. lbs. (38 Nm) and adjust the timing belt tension.

Vigor

1. Remove the timing belt cover and the cylinder head cover.

2. Rotate the crankshaft to align the white TDC mark on the pulley with the pointer on the lower cover. Make sure the UP mark on the camshaft sprocket is up.

3. Remove the cylinder sensor from below the camshaft sprocket.

4. Remove the bolt and slide the sprocket off the camshaft. Be careful not to drop the Woodruff key and secure the timing belt so it does not fall into the cover.

5. By removing the rear sprocket cover, the TDC/crank sensor and the front camshaft oil seal can be removed.

6. Installation is the reverse of removal. Torque the camshaft sprocket bolt to 54 ft. lbs. (75 Nm) and adjust the timing belt tension. Rotate the crankshaft 2 full turns and make sure the timing marks align properly.

Legend

1. Disconnect the negative battery cable. Remove the timing belt.

2. Using a camshaft holding tool or equivalent, secure the camshaft sprockets, remove the sprocket-to-camshaft bolts and the sprockets. On the rear camshaft, remove the bolt opposite the locating pin last.

3. On 1990 Legend, camshaft end-play can be checked without disturbing the valve adjustment. The seal can be replaced without removing the bearing caps.

4. Installation is the reverse of removal. Torque the camshaft sprocket-to-camshaft bolts to 23 ft. lbs. (32 Nm).

Camshaft

REMOVAL AND INSTALLATION

Integra

1. Disconnect the negative battery cable. Remove the timing belt cover and cylinder head cover.

2. Rotate the crankshaft to TDC of No. 1 piston and remove the timing belt.

3. Remove the camshaft sprockets.

4. To check camshaft end-play:

   a. Loosen the valve adjusters to remove as much spring tension as possible.

   b. Loosen the end bearing cap bolts 1 turn.

   c. Install the dial indicator.

   d. Push the camshaft fully towards the back of the head, zero the dial indicator and push the camshaft fully the other way to read end-play.

   e. End-play on a new camshaft should be 0.002-0.006 in. (0.05-0.15mm), 0.020 in. (0.5mm) is the service limit.

5. To remove the camshaft bearing caps, loosen each bolt 2 turns at a time in a crisscross pattern to avoid damage to the valves or rockers. Mark the caps so they can be replaced in their original position.

6. Lift the camshafts from the cylinder head, wipe them clean and inspect the lift ramps. Replace the camshafts and rockers if the lobes are pitted, scored or excessively worn.

7. Use Plasti-gauge ® to check bearing clearance: 0.002-0.004 in. (0.050-0.089mm) is standard clearance, 0.006 in. (0.15mm) service limit. If the clearance is too large and a new camshaft does not bring the clearance into specification, the cylinder head must be replaced.

   To install:

8. Check the following before installing the camshafts:

   a. Be certain the keyways on the camshafts are facing UP (No. 1 cylinder at TDC).

   b. The valve adjuster locknuts should be loosened and the adjusting screws backed off before installation.

   c. Replace the rocker arms in their original positions.

9. Place the rocker arms on the pivot bolts and the valve stems.

10. Install the camshafts with the seals part way on the camshaft, open side (spring) facing in. Lubricate the lip of the seal.

11. Do not apply oil to the holder mating surface of the camshaft seals.

12. Apply liquid gasket to the head mating surfaces of the No. 1 and No. 6 camshaft holders then install them along with the remaining holders.

13. Begin tightening the camshaft holder bolts, 2 turns at a time while making sure the rocker arms are positioned on the valve stems. Use a crisscross pattern when turning the bolts.

14. Using an oil seal driver tool 07947-SB00100 or equivalent, press new oil seals into the No. 1 camshaft holders.

15. Torque the bolts in the same pattern to 7 ft. lbs. (10 Nm). Check that the rockers do not bind on the valves.

16. Install the camshaft pulley keys onto the grooves in the camshafts.

17. Push the camshaft pulleys onto the camshafts, then torque the retaining bolts to 27 ft. lbs. (38 Nm).

18. Install the timing belt, adjust the valves and pour oil over the camshafts before finishing the assembly.

1990 Legend

1. Disconnect the negative battery cable. Remove the timing belt covers and cylinder head covers.

2. Rotate the crankshaft to TDC of No. 1 piston and remove the timing belt.

3. Remove the camshaft sprockets.

4. To check camshaft end-play:

   a. Loosen the valve adjusters to remove as much spring tension as possible.

   b. Loosen the end bearing cap bolts 1 turn.

   c. Install the dial indicator.

   d. Push the camshaft fully towards the back of the head, zero the dial indicator and push the camshaft fully the other way to read end-play.

   e. End-play on a new camshaft should be 0.002-0.006 in. (0.05-0.15mm), 0.020 in. (0.5mm) is the service limit.

5. To remove the camshaft bearing caps, loosen each bolt 2 turns at a time in a crisscross pattern to avoid damage to the valves or rockers.

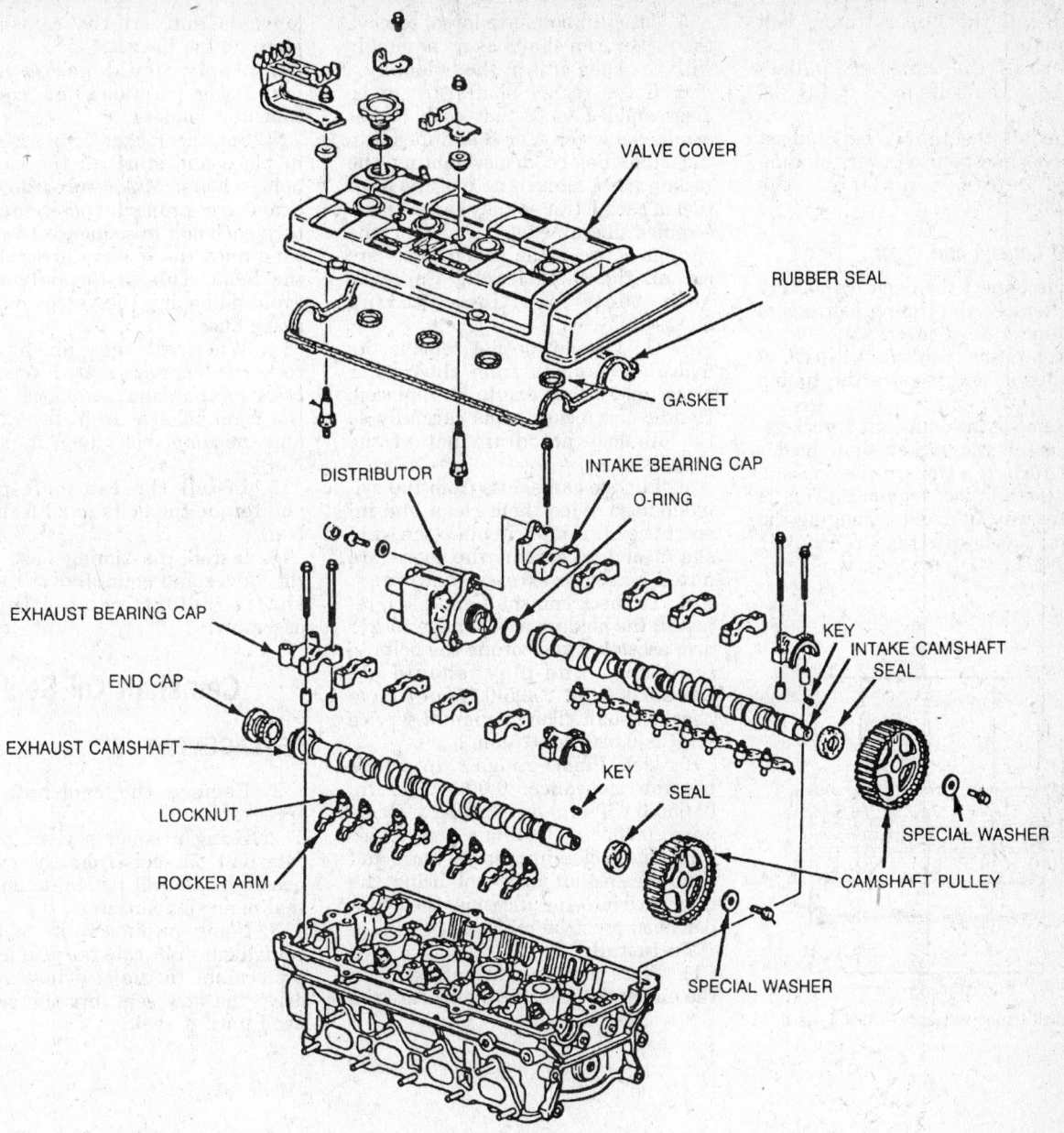

VALVE COVER

RUBBER SEAL

GASKET

DISTRIBUTOR

INTAKE BEARING CAP

O-RING

EXHAUST BEARING CAP

END CAP

EXHAUST CAMSHAFT

LOCKNUT

ROCKER ARM

KEY

KEY

SEAL

INTAKE CAMSHAFT

SEAL

SPECIAL WASHER

CAMSHAFT PULLEY

SPECIAL WASHER

Camshaft assembly — Integra

Mark the caps so they can be replaced in their original position.

6. Lift the camshafts from the cylinder head, wipe them clean and inspect the lift ramps. Replace the camshafts and rockers if the lobes are pitted, scored or excessively worn.

7. Use Plasti-gauge® to check bearing clearance: 0.002-0.004 in. (0.050-0.089mm) is standard clearance, 0.006 in. (0.15mm) is service limit. If the clearance is too large and a new camshaft does not bring the clearance into specification, the cylinder head must be replaced.

To install:

8. Fill the hydraulic lifter mounting holes with engine oil and install the lifters. Do not rotate the lifters while installing them. Also pour oil into the oil passages and fillers in the cylinder head.

9. With all the adjusting screws loose, install the pushrods and rocker arms in their original positions.

10. Advance the crankshaft 15 degrees, slip the camshaft seals onto the camshafts and lay the camshafts into the heads. Set the front camshaft so both valves on the No. 1 cylinder are be closed. Set the rear camshaft

to make sure the No. 4 cylinder exhaust valve is closed.

11. Apply liquid gasket sealer to the camshaft oil seal mounting surface and on the end bearing cap/cylinder head contact surface. Install the caps in their original position and tighten each cap bolt 2 turns at a time in the sequence shown to draw the camshaft down evenly against the valve springs.

12. Make sure the oil seal is properly positioned and torque the bolts in 2 steps in sequence to 20 ft. lbs. (28 Nm). Torque the 6mm bolts last to 9 ft. lbs. (12 Nm).

13. Install the upper timing belt cover plate.

14. Install the camshaft pulleys and torque the bolts to 23 ft. lbs. (32 Nm).

15. Install the timing belt, adjust the valves and pour oil over the camshafts before completing the assembly.

1991-94 Legend and Vigor

1. Disconnect the negative battery cable. Remove the timing belt covers and cylinder head covers.

2. Rotate the crankshaft to TDC of No. 1 piston and remove the timing belt.

3. Remove the camshaft sprockets.

4. Loosen the rocker shaft holder bolts 1 turn at a time in the opposite of the installation sequence. This is the only way to avoid damaging the valves, camshafts or rocker assemblies.

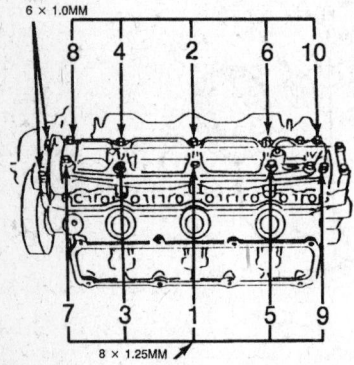

Camshaft torque sequence — 1990 Legend

5. After all bolts are loose, remove the rocker arm shafts as an assembly with the bolts still in the holders.

6. If the rocker shafts are to be disassembled, note that each rocker arm has a letter **A** or **B** stamped into the side. Before disassembling the rocker arms, make a note of the position of each letter so they can be reassembled the same way. On Vigor, the springs between the rocker arms are not all the same length. Carefully note their positions during disassembly.

7. On Legend, do not remove the hydraulic tappets from the rocker arms unless they are to be replaced. Handle the rocker arms carefully so the oil does not drain out of the tappets.

8. Lift the camshafts from the cylinder head, wipe them clean and inspect the lift ramps. Replace the camshafts and rockers if the lobes are pitted, scored or excessively worn.

9. To check camshaft end-play, reinstall the holders without the rocker arm assembly and torque the bolts in sequence. End-play should be 0.002-0.006 in. (0.05-0.15mm) on a new camshaft. The maximum service limit is 0.020 in. (0.5mm).

10. Use Plasti-gauge® to check bearing clearance: 0.002-0.004 in. (0.050-0.089mm) is standard clearance, 0.006 in. (0.15mm) is service limit. If the clearance is too large and a new camshaft does not bring the clearance into specification, the cylinder head must be replaced.

To install:

11. Place a new camshaft seal on the end of the camshaft, lubricate the

journals and set the camshaft in place on the head.

12. Apply liquid gasket to the mounting surfaces of the end camshaft holders.

13. Set the rocker arm assemblies in place and start all the camshaft holder bolts. Make sure the rocker arms are properly positioned and turn each bolt in sequence 1 turn at a time until the holders are seated on the head. This is the only way to avoid damaging the valves or rocker assemblies.

14. When all the camshaft and rocker holders are seated, torque the bolts in the same sequence. Torque the 8mm bolts to 16 ft. lbs. (22 Nm) and the 6mm bolts to 9 ft. lbs. (12 Nm).

15. Install the camshaft pulleys and torque the bolts to 23 ft. lbs. (32 Nm).

16. Install the timing belt, adjust the valves and pour oil over the camshafts before completing the assembly.

Camshaft Oil Seal

REPLACEMENT

1. Remove the camshaft drive sprockets.

2. Using a small prybar, pry the camshaft oil seals from the cylinder heads; be careful not to damage the seal mounting surfaces.

3. Using an oil seal driver tool or equivalent, lubricate the seal lips, apply sealant to the seal housing and drive the new seal into the cylinder head until it seats.

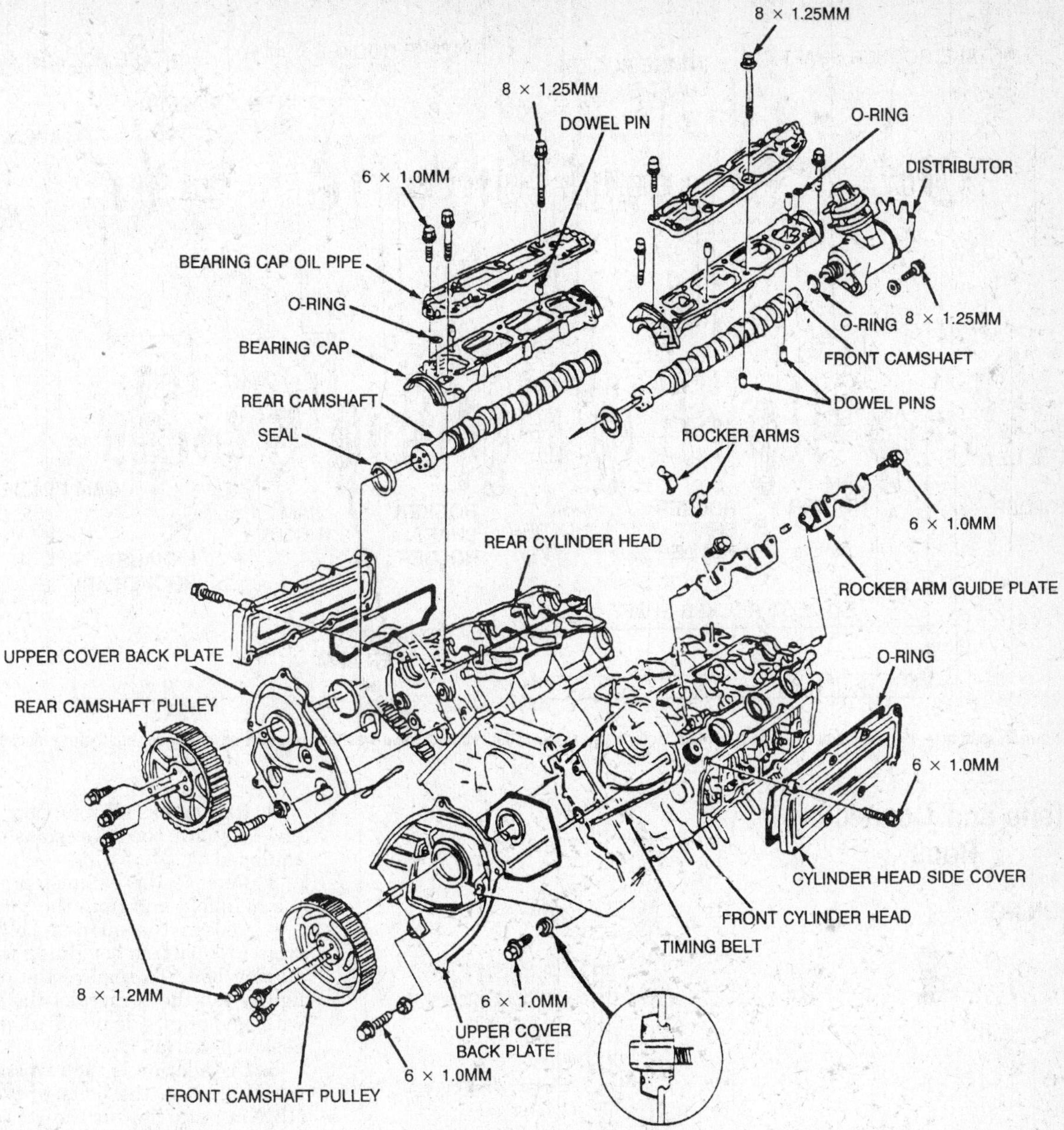

8 × 1.25MM

8 × 1.25MM

DOWEL PIN

O-RING

DISTRIBUTOR

6 × 1.0MM

BEARING CAP OIL PIPE

O-RING

BEARING CAP

REAR CAMSHAFT

SEAL

O-RING

8 × 1.25MM

FRONT CAMSHAFT

DOWEL PINS

ROCKER ARMS

6 × 1.0MM

REAR CYLINDER HEAD

ROCKER ARM GUIDE PLATE

UPPER COVER BACK PLATE

REAR CAMSHAFT PULLEY

O-RING

6 × 1.0MM

CYLINDER HEAD SIDE COVER

FRONT CYLINDER HEAD

TIMING BELT

8 × 1.2MM

6 × 1.0MM

UPPER COVER
BACK PLATE

6 × 1.0MM

FRONT CAMSHAFT PULLEY

Camshaft installation — 2.7L engine

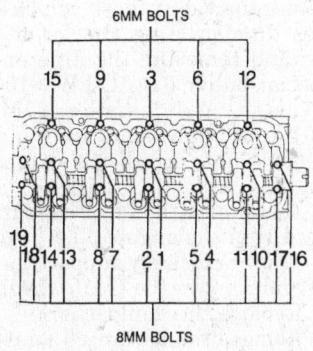

6MM BOLTS

15 9 3 6 12

19
18 14 13 8 7 2 1 5 4 11 10 17 16

8MM BOLTS

**Torque sequence for camshaft and rocker arm
holder assembly — Vigor**

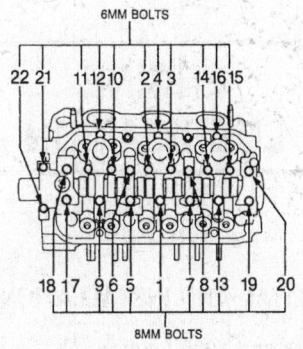

6MM BOLTS

22 21 11 12 10 2 4 3 14 16 15

18 17 9 6 5 1 7 8 13 19 20

8MM BOLTS

**Torque sequence for camshaft and rocker arm
holders — 1991-94 Legend**

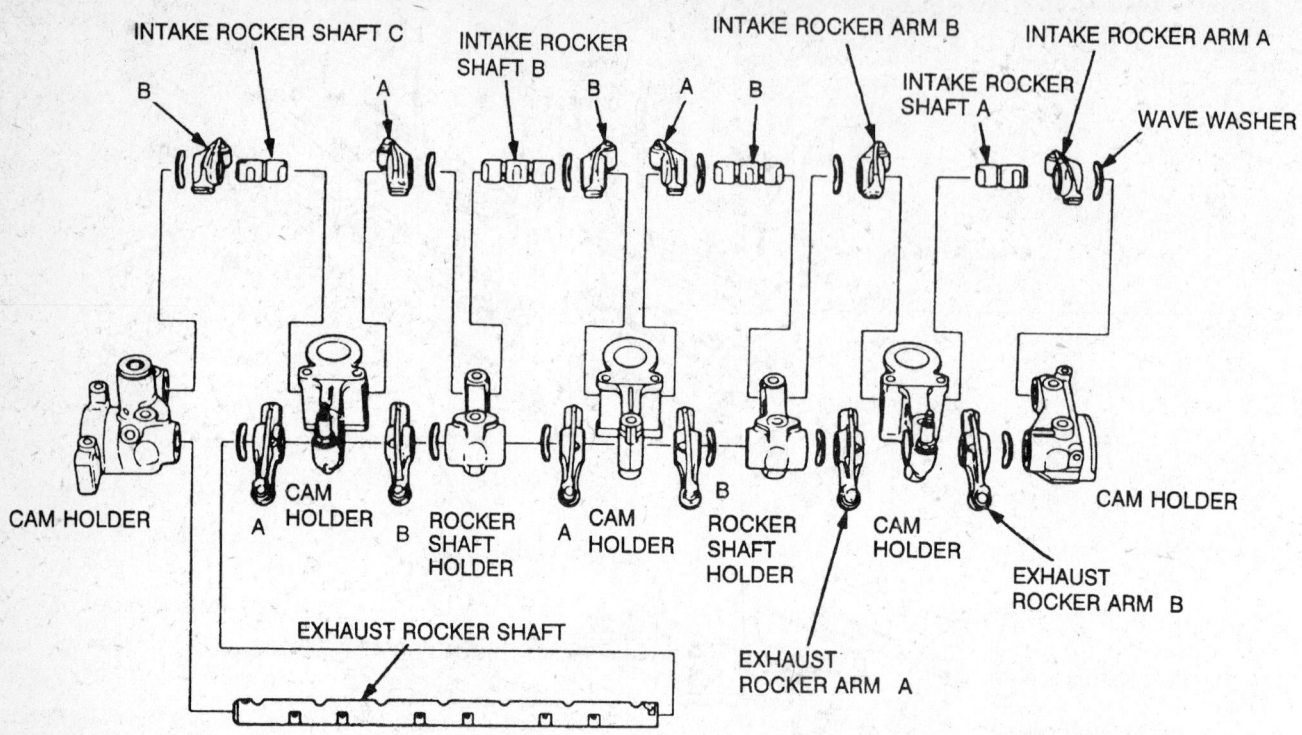

INTAKE ROCKER SHAFT C — INTAKE ROCKER SHAFT B — INTAKE ROCKER ARM B — INTAKE ROCKER ARM A — INTAKE ROCKER SHAFT A — WAVE WASHER

CAM HOLDER — CAM HOLDER — ROCKER SHAFT HOLDER — CAM HOLDER — ROCKER SHAFT HOLDER — CAM HOLDER — CAM HOLDER — EXHAUST ROCKER ARM B — EXHAUST ROCKER ARM A — EXHAUST ROCKER SHAFT

Rocker arm assembly — 1991-94 Legend — Vigor similar: note the position of letters and wave washers or short and long springs before disassembly

Pistons and Connecting Rods

POSITIONING

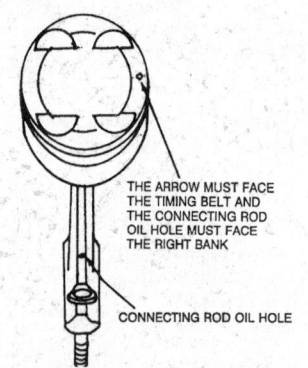

THE ARROW MUST FACE THE TIMING BELT AND THE CONNECTING ROD OIL HOLE MUST FACE THE RIGHT BANK

CONNECTING ROD OIL HOLE

Piston and rod positioning — Legend

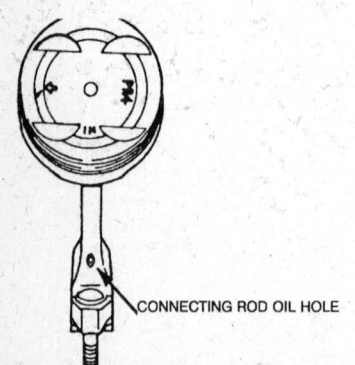

CONNECTING ROD OIL HOLE

Piston and rod positioning — Integra and Vigor

ENGINE LUBRICATION

Oil Pan

REMOVAL AND INSTALLATION

Integra and 1990 Legend

1. Disconnect the negative battery cable. Drain the engine oil.

2. Raise and safely support the vehicle. Remove the lower splash pan, if equipped.

3. Remove the exhaust pipe from the manifold and from the catalyst.

4. Loosen the oil pan bolts in a crisscross pattern beginning with the outside bolt. To remove the oil pan, lightly tap the corners of the oil pan with a mallet. Clean off all the old gasket material.

5. Installation is the reverse of removal. Torque the bolts to 9 ft. lbs. (12 Nm), starting in the center and working out.

Vigor and 1991-94 Legend

Oil pan removal in these vehicles requires disconnecting the lower ball joints and removing the differential. A special puller 07LAC-PW50100 or equivalent, and installer 07MAF-PY40100 or equivalent, are required to remove and install the extension shaft.

1. Disconnect the negative battery cable. Drain the engine oil.

2. Raise and safely support the vehicle and remove the front wheels.

3. Remove the damper forks.

4. Remove the lower ball joint nut and use a ball joint press tool to disconnect the ball joint from the control arm.

5. Carefully pry the inner CV-joints out of their sockets. Wrap them in plastic to keep them clean and do not let the drive shafts hang by the outer CV-joint.

6. Remove the engine splash shield and lower plate from the rear beam.

NOTE: On Legend, some of the bolts have a special coating for use in aluminum alloy. Do not substitute normal steel fasteners.

7. Drain the engine oil and coolant. On Vigor, remove the transmission mount and bracket.

8. Drain the oil from the differential.

9. Without disconnecting the hoses, remove the power steering speed sensor from the differential.

10. Disconnect the differential oil cooler hoses.

11. Shift the transmission into **1st** gear (manual) or **P** (automatic) and remove the secondary shaft cover and sealing bolt.

12. Install the puller and disengage the extension shaft from the differential.

13. On Vigor, remove the left front engine mount and bracket.

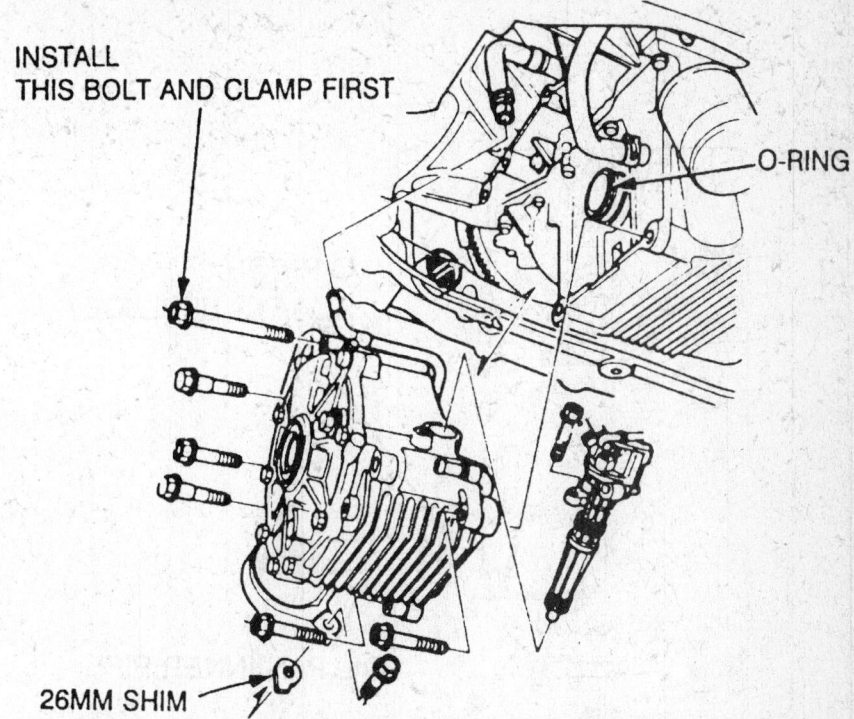

Removing the differential to remove the oil pan — 1991-94 Legend — Vigor similar

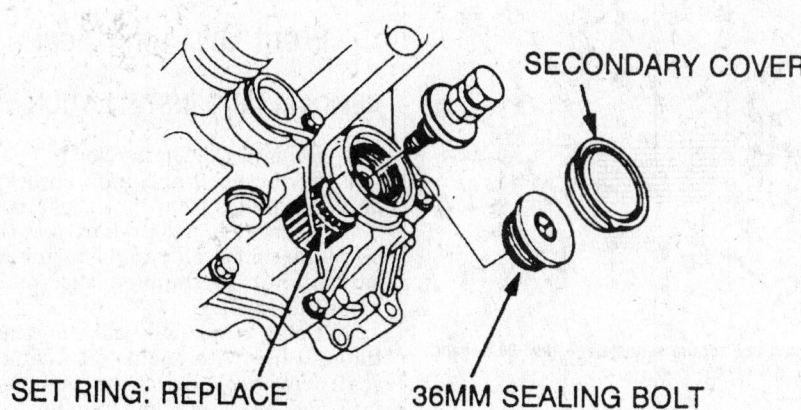

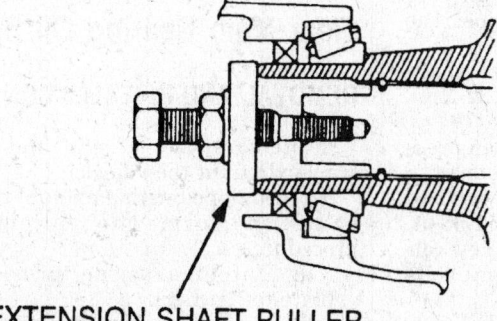

Use the puller at the bottom of the housing to disengage the extension shaft from the differential

14. Remove the mounting bolts and the 26mm shim and remove the differential.

15. On Legend, without disconnecting any hoses, remove the air conditioner compressor.

NOTE: Do not loosen or disconnect the air conditioning freon lines. Do not vent freon into the air.

16. Unbolt the intermediate shaft bearing housing from the oil pan and remove the intermediate shaft.

17. On Vigor, remove the set plate that holds the oil pan inner pipe from the right side of the engine.

18. Remove any brackets or covers and remove the oil pan.

To install:

19. Install new O-rings and apply liquid gasket evenly in a thin bead to the mating surface of the pan. Do not apply liquid gasket to the O-rings.

20. Install the oil pan and torque the bolts in the correct sequence to 16 ft. lbs. (22 Nm).

21. On Vigor, install the oil pan inner pipe with new O-rings and tighten the set plate in place. On Legend, install the flywheel cover and engine stiffener.

22. Install the differential, making sure the original shim is in the

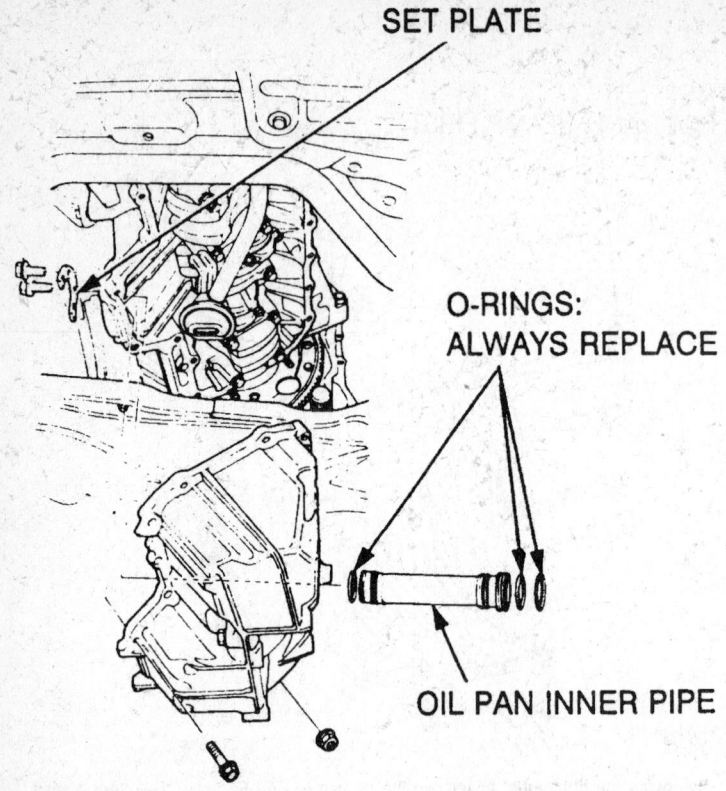

Replace the O-rings when installing the oil pan inner pipe — Vigor

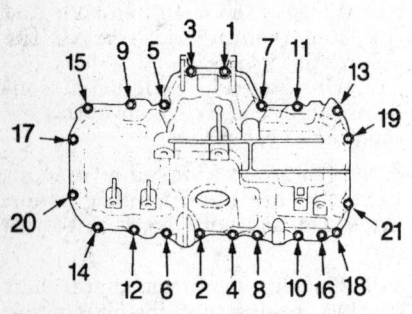

Oil pan bolt torque sequence — Vigor

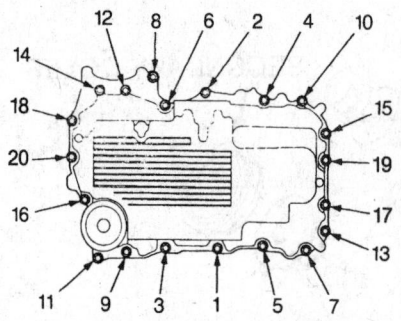

Oil pan bolt torque sequence — 1991-94 Legend

lower plate, torque the specially coated bolts to 29 ft. lbs. (39 Nm).

31. Install the remaining parts and refill the differential, engine oil and cooling system. Open the cooling system bleeder at the engine end of the upper radiator hose when filling the system.

Oil Pump

REMOVAL AND INSTALLATION

1. Disconnect the negative battery terminal. Raise and safely support the vehicle, drain the oil and remove the oil pan.
2. Make sure the crankshaft is at TDC on No. 1 cylinder and remove the timing belt cover and the timing belt.
3. Remove the oil pan and the pickup screen.
4. Remove the oil pump from the front of the engine. Any time the oil pump is removed, the front oil seal should be replaced.
5. Installation is the reverse of removal. Use new O-rings and apply liquid gasket to the pump mounting face. Torque the 6mm bolts to 9 ft. lbs. (12 Nm) and the 8mm bolts to 17 ft. lbs. (24 Nm).

Front Oil Pump Seal

REMOVAL AND INSTALLATION

1. Remove the timing belt.
2. Slide the crankshaft sprocket and belt guides from the crankshaft.
3. Using a small prybar, pry the oil seal from the oil pump housing; be careful not to damage the seal's mounting surface.
4. Using a new oil seal, lubricate the seal lips with engine oil. Using a seal drive tool, drive the new seal into the oil pump housing until it seats.

Rear Main Bearing Oil Seal

REMOVAL AND INSTALLATION

1. Remove the oil pan and the transaxle from the vehicle.
2. If equipped with a manual transaxle, perform the following procedures:
   a. Matchmark the pressure plate-to-flywheel.
   b. Insert the clutch alignment tool or equivalent, into the pilot bearing.

proper position. Torque the bolts to 47 ft. lbs. (65 Nm). Connect the cooling hoses.

23. Apply grease to the spline of the extension shaft and install a new set ring. Thread the special installation tool into the transmission case to install the extension shaft.

24. Pack the extension shaft cavity with special Honda grease, part number UM264 or equivalent, and install the sealing bolt. Torque the bolt to 58 ft. lbs. (80 Nm) and install the secondary cover.

25. On Legend, install the air conditioner compressor and adjust the belt tension.
26. Install the intermediate shaft, torque the bolts to 16 ft. lbs. (22 Nm).
27. Install the speed sensor.
28. Install new set rings, then press the CV-joints into their sockets.
29. When installing the lower ball joint nuts, torque them to 51-58 ft. lbs. (70-80 Nm) and install a new cotter pin. Torque the damper fork bolts to 51 ft. lbs. (70 Nm).
30. On Legend, install the rear beam and torque the bolts to 44 ft. lbs. (60 Nm). When installing the

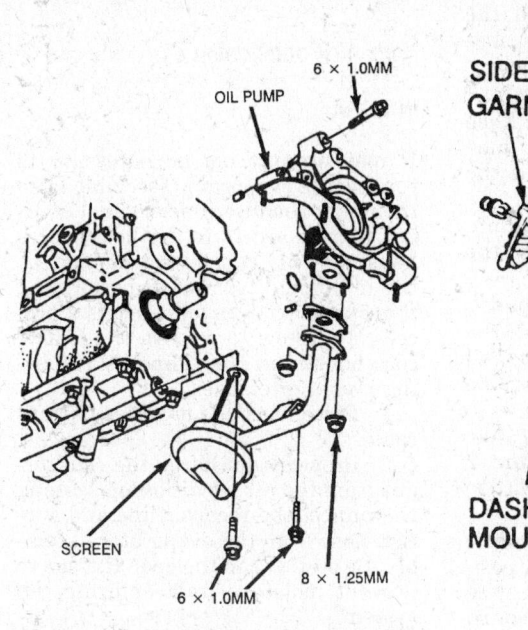

Oil pump mounting housing — Integra with 1.8L engines

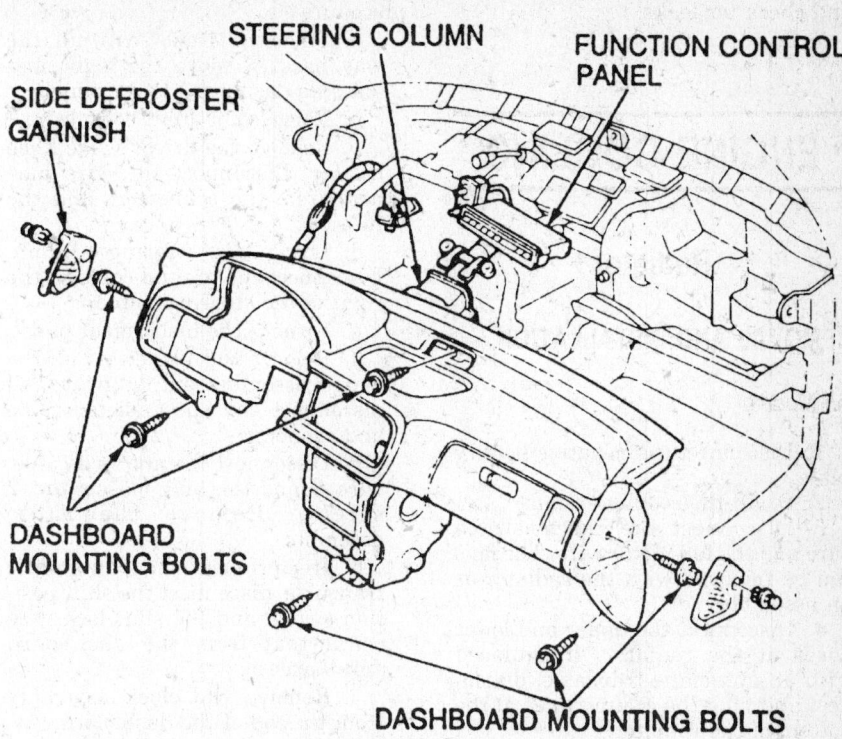

Heater core removal; dashboard must be removed — Integra shown — 1990 Legend similar

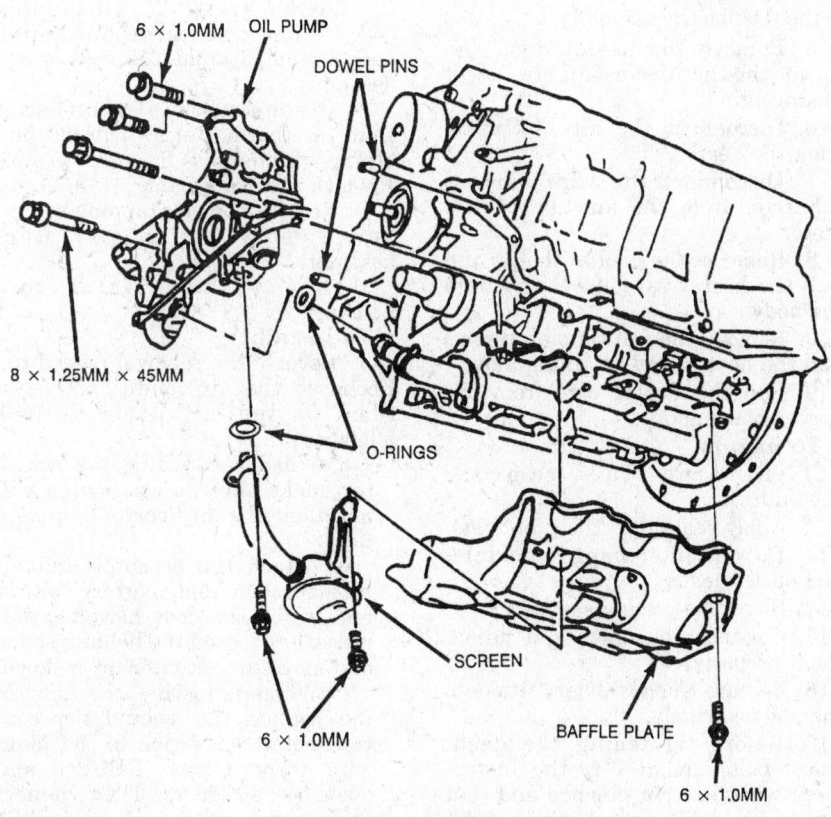

Oil pump mounting housing — 2.7L engine

c. Remove the pressure plate-to-flywheel bolts (gradually), the pressure and the clutch plate.

d. Remove the flywheel-to-crankshaft bolts and the flywheel.

3. If equipped with an automatic transaxle, remove the flexplate-to-flywheel bolts and the flexplate.

4. Remove the rear oil seal housing-to-engine bolts and the gasket.

5. Using a prybar, pry the oil seal from the housing.

To install:

6. Clean the gasket mounting surfaces. Check the flywheel or flexplate for cracks and/or damage; replace it, if necessary.

7. Using an oil seal installation tool or equivalent, drive the new oil seal into the rear oil seal housing until it seats.

8. Apply liquid gasket on the gasket mounting surface. Using oil, lubricate the oil seal lips.

9. Install the oil seal housing and torque the bolts to 9 ft. lbs. (12 Nm); be careful not to damage the oil seal lip.

10. To complete the installation, reverse the removal procedures. Torque the flywheel-to-crankshaft bolts in a cross pattern to 54 ft. lbs. (75 Nm) for automatic transaxles or 76 ft. lbs. (105 Nm) for manual transaxles. Re-

fill the crankcase, start the engine and check for leaks.

ENGINE COOLING

Radiator

REMOVAL AND INSTALLATION

All Models

1. Disconnect the negative battery cable.
2. Drain the cooling system.
3. Disconnect the thermoswitch wire and the fan motor wire. The fans can be removed with the radiator as an assembly.
4. Disconnect the upper and lower hoses at the radiator. If equipped with an automatic transaxle, disconnect and plug the cooling lines at the bottom of the radiator.
5. Remove the hoses to the coolant reservoir.
6. Remove the radiator bracket bolts and lift the assembly out.
   To install:
7. Install the fan to the radiator; then install the fan and radiator assembly into the vehicle.
8. Fill the cooling system. When filling the system, open the bleeder on the thermostat housing. On Vigor, there is a second bleeder near the fuel pressure regulator.
9. Connect the negative battery cable. Start the engine and watch the coolant level in the radiator. It will probably require more coolant as the engine warms up.

Heater Core

REMOVAL AND INSTALLATION

Without Air Conditioning

INTEGRA

1. Disconnect the negative battery cable. Drain the cooling system.
2. Place a suitable drain pan into position and disconnect the heater hoses at the firewall.
3. Disconnect the heater valve cable from the heater valve.
4. On Integra, it is necessary to remove the dashboard assembly. This

can be done by using the following procedure:
   a. Slide the front seats all the way back. Remove the right and left side dashboard lower panels.
   b. Remove the front console.
   c. Remove the driver's side knee bolster. Disconnect the wire harness from the connectors and the fuse box.
   d. Lower the steering column. Disconnect the ground cable to the right of the steering column.
   e. Remove the instrument panel.
   f. Remove the 4 screws. Pull the gauge assembly out halfway and disconnect the speedometer cable and connectors.
   g. Disconnect the antenna cable, wire connector and loosen the 2 screws. Remove the radio assembly.
   h. If equipped with automatic transaxle, disconnect the shift position switch and the shift lock wire connectors from the dashboard wire harness.
   i. Remove the clock assembly from the top of the dashboard.
   j. Remove the side defroster garnishes from both ends of the dashboard.
   k. Remove the dashboard mounting bolts. Lift and remove the dashboard assembly.
5. Remove the heater duct. Remove the heater assembly lower mounting nut.
6. Disconnect the air mix cable from the heater.
7. Disconnect the wire harness connector from the function control motor.
8. Remove the heater bolts and pull the heater assembly away from the body.
9. Remove the self tapping screws and the heater core retaining plate.
10. Pull the heater core from the heater housing.
    To install:
11. Reverse the removal procedures.
12. Apply sealant to the grommets.
13. Do not interchange the inlet and outlet hoses.
14. Bleed the cooling system.
15. Connect all cables and adjust them properly.
16. Be sure the dashboard fits onto the body correctly.
17. Before tightening the dashboard bolts, make sure the instrument wires are not pinched and that the dashboard is not interfering with the heater control cable. For ease of

installation, remove the gauge assembly from the dash.

With Air Conditioning

INTEGRA

It may or may not be necessary to remove the evaporator assembly from the under the instrument panel in order to gain access to the heater core housing. This can be determined by the individual technician performing this operation. The following is a procedure on how to remove the heater core housing if the evaporator housing must be removed.

1. Disconnect the negative battery cable.
2. Properly discharge the refrigerant from the air conditioning system. Disconnect the receiver line and suction hose from the evaporator assembly. Be sure to cap the open fittings to prevent moisture from entering the system.
3. Remove the passenger side lower dashboard cover.
4. Remove the glovebox assembly.
5. Remove the front console assembly.
6. Remove the passenger side knee bolster panel, located under the glovebox frame.
7. Remove the 2 self-tapping screws and the air conditioning bands from around the evaporator assembly.
8. Disconnect the wire connector from the thermostat switch and pull off the wire harness from the clamps. Remove the evaporator.
9. Remove the self-tapping screws and remove the heater duct assembly.
10. Remove the heater core housing.
    To install:
11. Reverse the removal procedure. Recharge the air conditioning system, paying attention to the following:
    a. When reattaching the actuator, make sure its positioning will not allow the air door to be pulled to far.
    b. Attach the actuator and all linkage, then apply battery voltage and watch the door movement. If necessary, loosen the holding screw and move the actuator up or down.
    c. When adjusting the control rod, connect the recirculation control motor connection to the main wire harness, push RECIRC and open the air doors. Then connect the control rod to the arm while holding the air doors open.

STERLING AND 1990 LEGEND

--------- **CAUTION** ---------

This vehicle is equipped with a driver side air bag. To avoid accidental deployment and serious personal injury, the system must be disarmed before beginning this repair procedure. See the disarming procedure in the Chassis Electrical section.

1. Disconnect the negative battery cable. Drain the cooling system.
2. Place a suitable drain pan into position and disconnect the heater hoses at the firewall.
3. Properly discharge the air conditioning system. Cap any open fittings to keep moisture out.
4. Remove the dashboard as follows:
   a. Disconnect the negative battery cable. Slide the seat all the way to the rear and remove the lower dashboard panel.
   b. Remove the knee bolster and the left air duct.
   c. Remove the hood opener and the center console.
   d. Disconnect the wire harness from the connector holder.
   e. Remove the dash harness ground bolt from the steering column.
   f. Remove the screws and radio panel assembly, then disconnect the wire connectors, antenna cables and wire tie.
   g. Remove the radio assembly, remove the center dash pocket.
   h. Lower the steering column. Be sure to remove the ignition key from the lock cylinder.
   i. Remove the dashboard mounting bolts.
   j. Pull the dashboard straight back and disconnect the speedometer. Remove the dashboard.
5. Disconnect the wire harness and the vacuum hoses.
6. Remove the heater mounting bolts and pull the heater assembly away from the body.
7. Remove the self-tapping screws and the heater core retaining plate.
8. Pull the heater core from the heater housing.
   To install:
9. Apply sealant to the grommets.
10. Do not interchange the inlet and outlet hoses.
11. Bleed the cooling system.
12. Connect all cables and adjust them properly.
13. Be sure the dashboard fits onto the body correctly.

14. Before tightening the dashboard bolts, make sure the instrument wires are not pinched and that the dashboard is not interfering with the heater control cable. For ease of installation, remove the gauge assembly from the dash.
15. Recharge the air conditioning system, paying attention to the following:
   a. When reattaching the actuator, make sure its positioning will not allow the air door to pulled to far.
   b. Attach the actuator and all linkage, then apply battery voltage and watch the door movement. If necessary, loosen the holding screw and move the actuator up or down.
   c. When adjusting the control rod, connect the recirculation control motor connection to the main wire harness, push the FRESH/RECIRC switch to FRESH and open the air doors. Then connect the control rod to the arm while holding the air doors open.

1991-94 LEGEND

--------- **CAUTION** ---------

This vehicle is equipped with a driver side air bag and, on LS models, a passenger side air bag. To avoid accidental deployment and serious personal injury, the system must be disarmed before beginning this repair procedure. See the disarming procedure in the Chassis Electrical section.

1. Disconnect the negative battery cable. Drain the cooling system.
2. Properly discharge the air conditioning refrigerant into recovery equipment.
3. Remove the dashboard:
   a. Remove the front seat track end covers and unbolt the seats. Unplug the connectors and remove the front seats.
   b. Unscrew the shift knob and remove the 2 screws directly in front of the shifter boot to remove the console panel.
   c. Remove the center armrest. Be careful not to damage the air bag control unit or wiring below the armrest.
   d. Remove the radio.
   e. Remove the glove compartment lower panel and the glove compartment.
   f. Remove the driver side lower dash panel.
   g. Remove the screws securing the center console to the dashboard and remove the center console.

h. Remove the mounting nuts and bolts and lower the steering column.
   i. On LS models, remove the passenger side air bag unit.
   j. Disconnect the hood release cable from the handle.
   k. Remove the side covers from the ends of the dashboard.
   l. Label and disconnect the wiring connectors.
   m. Remove the 2 bolts from each end and the 2 bolts from the center and lift the dashboard to remove it.
4. Remove the blower assembly.
5. Disconnect the heater hoses. Coolant will run out, be prepared with a drip pan.
6. Disconnect the heater valve cable from the heater valve.
7. At the firewall, disconnect the air conditioning hoses and cap all fittings to keep out moisture.
8. Remove the nuts and the evaporator seal plate from the firewall.
9. Disconnect the wiring and remove the nuts and screws to remove the heater/air conditioner assembly. To remove the heater core, remove the pipe clamps and lift the core out.
   To install:
10. Installation is the reverse of removal. Apply sealant to the grommets.
11. Do not interchange the inlet and outlet hoses.
12. Bleed the cooling system.
13. Connect all cables and adjust them properly.
14. Be sure the dashboard fits onto the body correctly.
15. Before tightening the dashboard bolts, make sure the instrument wires are not pinched and that the dashboard is not interfering with the control cable. For ease of installation, remove the gauge assembly from the dash.
16. Recharge the air conditioning system, paying attention to the following:
   a. When reattaching the actuator, make sure its positioning will not allow the air door to be pulled too far.
   b. Attach the actuator and all linkage, then apply battery voltage and watch the door movement. If necessary, loosen the holding screw and move the actuator up or down.
   c. When adjusting the control rod, connect the recirculation control motor connection to the main wire harness, push the FRESH/RECIR switch to FRESH and open the air doors. Connect the control rod to the arm while holding the air doors open.

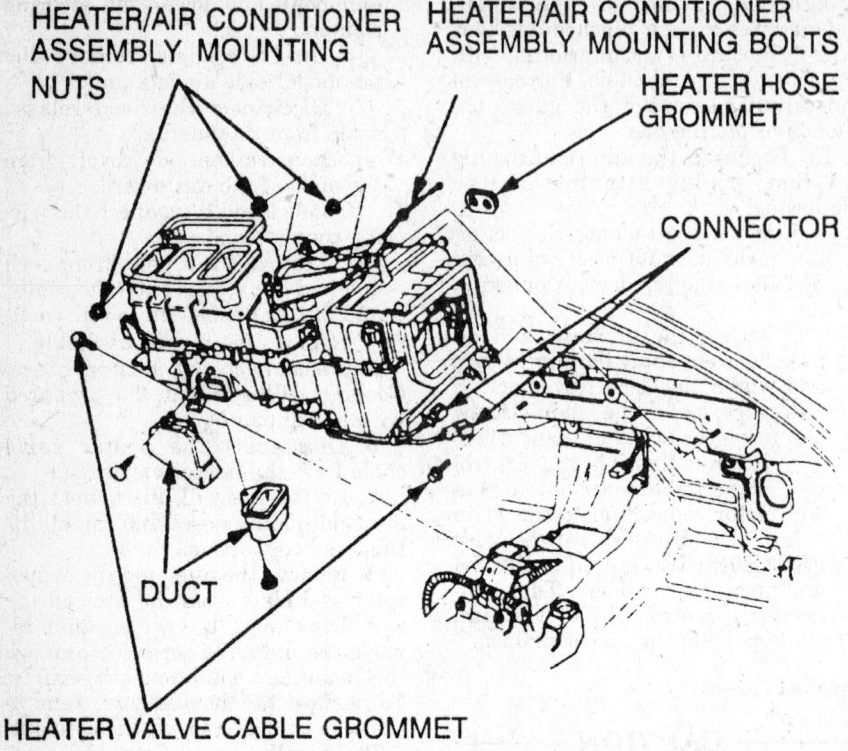

HEATER/AIR CONDITIONER ASSEMBLY MOUNTING NUTS

HEATER/AIR CONDITIONER ASSEMBLY MOUNTING BOLTS

HEATER HOSE GROMMET

CONNECTOR

DUCT

HEATER VALVE CABLE GROMMET

Heater/air conditioner removal — 1991-94 Legend

VIGOR

> **— CAUTION —**
>
> *This vehicle is equipped with a driver side air bag and, on LS models, a passenger side air bag. To avoid accidental deployment and serious personal injury, the system must be disarmed before beginning this repair procedure. See the disarming procedure in the Chassis Electrical section.*

1. The heater assembly must be removed to remove the heater core. Disconnect the negative battery cable. Drain the cooling system.

2. Properly discharge the air conditioning refrigerant into an approved recovery equipment.

3. Remove the dashboard:

   a. Remove the front seat track end covers and unbolt the seats. Unplug the connectors and remove the front seats.

   b. To remove the center console, remove the 2 screws at the lower front corners. Open the arm rest and lift the liner to remove the 2 screws at the rear. Be careful not to damage the air bag control unit or wiring.

   c. In the center of the heater control panel, remove the cap to remove the screw. Carefully pull the

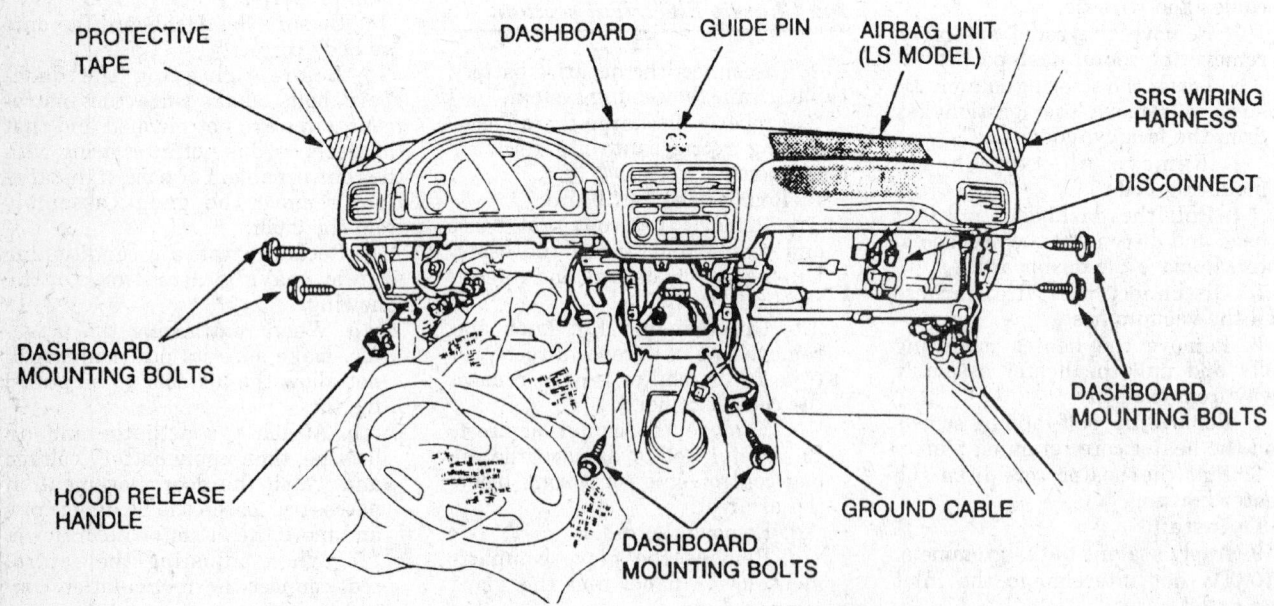

PROTECTIVE TAPE

DASHBOARD

GUIDE PIN

AIRBAG UNIT (LS MODEL)

SRS WIRING HARNESS

DISCONNECT

DASHBOARD MOUNTING BOLTS

DASHBOARD MOUNTING BOLTS

HOOD RELEASE HANDLE

DASHBOARD MOUNTING BOLTS

GROUND CABLE

Heater core removal; dashboard must be removed — Vigor and 1991-94 Legend

control panel out far enough to disconnect the wiring. There are clips at the rear of the panel.

    d. Remove the 2 screws behind the heater control panel and 2 more behind the ashtray. Pull the entire center console out far enough to disconnect the wiring.

    e. Remove the glove compartment door.

    f. Remove the driver side lower dash panel.

    g. Remove the 2 nuts and 2 bolts and lower the steering column.

    h. The trim panel with the air conditioning vents is held in place with clips and can be carefully pried out.

    i. The driver and passenger side kick panels are held in place with clips and can be pried out.

    j. Disconnect the hood release cable from the handle.

    k. Remove the side covers from the ends of the dashboard.

    l. Label and disconnect the wiring connectors.

    m. Remove the 3 bolts from each end and the 2 bolts from the center and lift the dashboard to remove it.

4. Disconnect the heater hoses. Coolant will run out, be prepared with a drip pan.

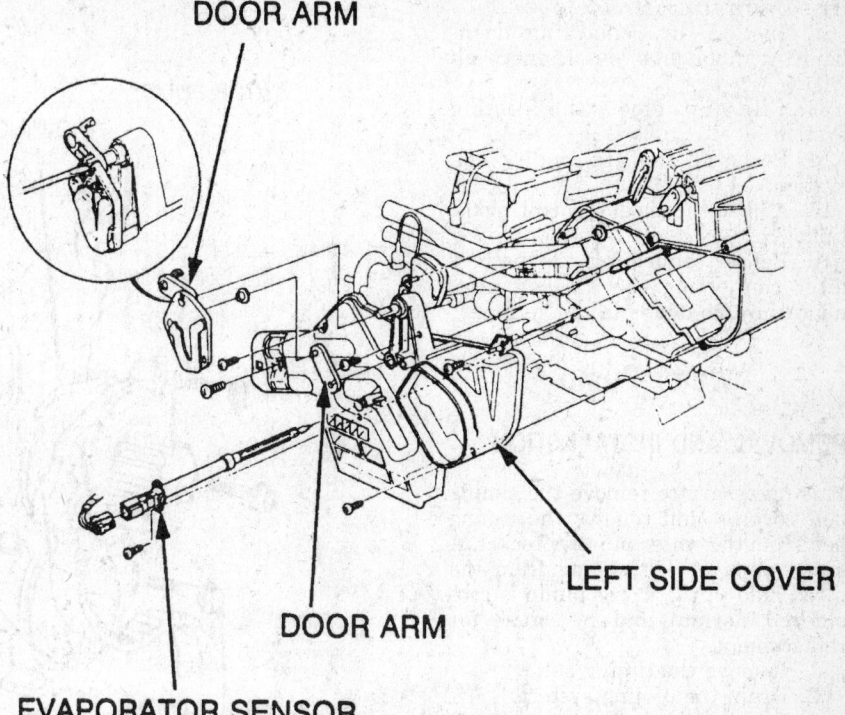

Remove the left side components and covers to remove the heater core

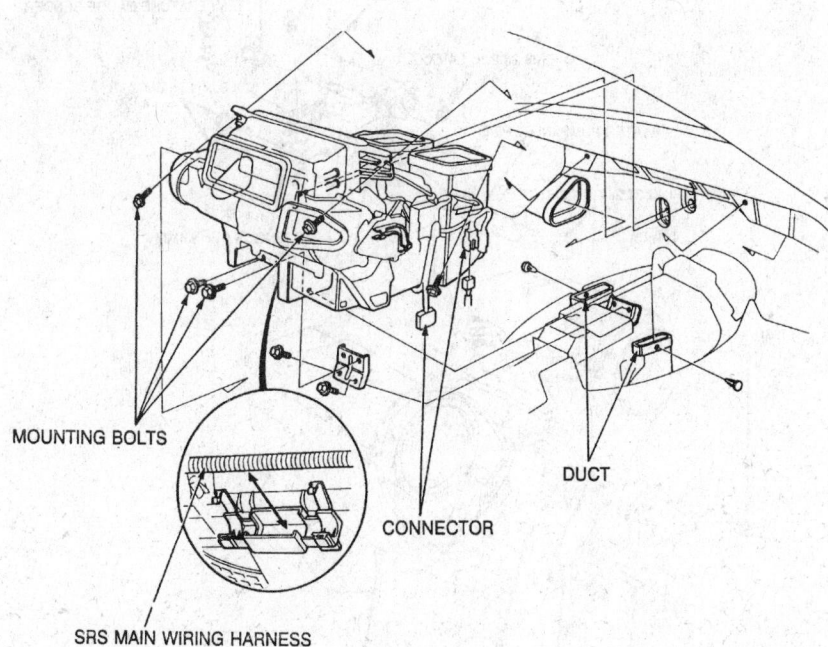

Be careful of the SRS wiring harness when removing the heater unit — Vigor

5. At the firewall, disconnect the air conditioning lines by removing the single nut that is between them. Cap all fittings to keep out moisture.

6. Near the heater hose connections is a single nut that holds the bottom of the heater assembly to the firewall. Remove the nut.

7. Remove the nuts and bolts as shown to remove the heater unit from the vehicle.

8. To remove the heater core:

    a. Remove the left side air duct and the pipe cover.

    b. Remove the pipe clamps.

    c. Remove the mode control motor assembly.

    d. Unplug the connector and remove the screw to slide the temperature sensor out.

    e. Remove the mode door arm assembly.

    f. Remove the left side covers and slide the heater core out of the housing.

To install:

9. Install the heater core and assembly the housing components.

10. Install the heater assembly and connect the water and freon lines.

11. Fit the dashboard into place and start the mounting bolts. Before tightening the bolts, make sure the instrument wires are not pinched

and that the dashboard is not interfering with the controls.

12. Install the remaining dashboard components and connect all wiring.

13. Fill and bleed the cooling system.

14. Recharge the air conditioning system.

15. Adjust the mode control motor linkage.

16. Before connecting the battery after connecting the air bag unit, make sure no one is in the vehicle.

Water Pump

REMOVAL AND INSTALLATION

It is necessary to remove the timing belt cover(s) and remove the timing belt from the water pump sprocket. A small amount of weeping from the bleed hole in the water pump is considered normal and no cause for replacement.

1. Remove the timing belt.
2. Drain the cooling system.
3. Remove the water pump-to-engine bolts and remove together with the drive sprocket.
4. To install, use a new O-ring and reverse the removal procedures. Torque the 6mm bolts to 9 ft. lbs. (12 Nm) and 8mm bolts to 16 ft. lbs. (22 Nm).
5. Refill and bleed the cooling system. Start the engine, allow it to reach normal operating temperatures and check for leaks. Check and/or adjust the engine timing.

Thermostat

REMOVAL AND INSTALLATION

1. Drain the cooling system and remove the lower radiator hose from the thermostat housing.
2. Remove the thermostat housing bolts, the housing and the thermostat.
3. Clean the gasket mounting surfaces.
4. To install, use new gaskets and reverse the removal procedures; install the thermostat's spring end toward the engine. Torque the housing bolts to 9 ft. lbs. (12 Nm). Refill and bleed the cooling system.

COOLING SYSTEM BLEEDING

When filling a cooling system, use a 50/50 mixture of antifreeze and clean

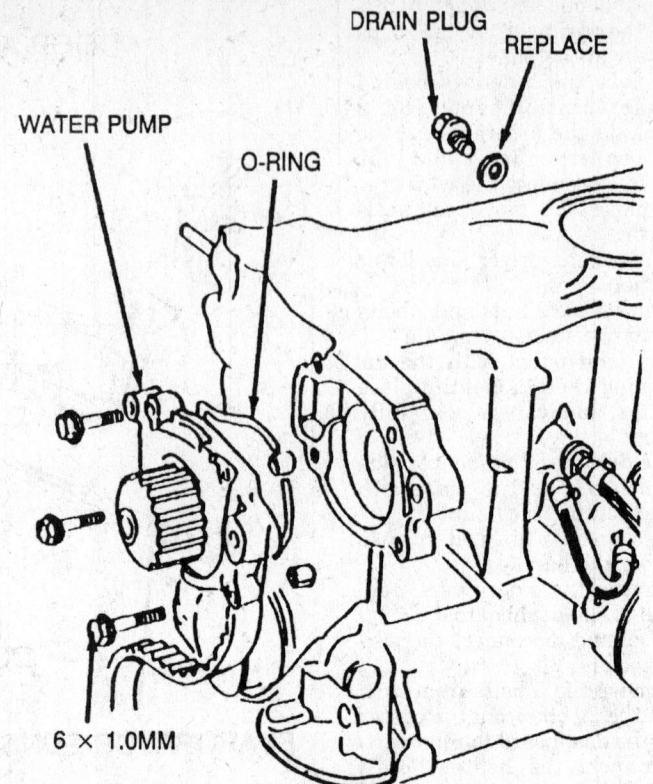

Water pump installation — Integra and Vigor

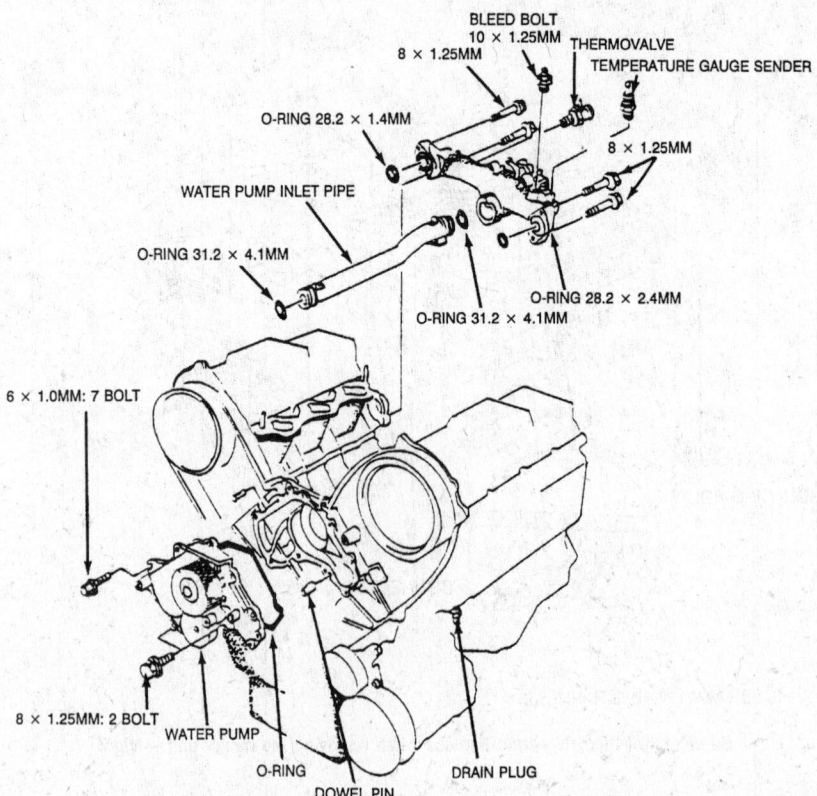

Water pump installation — 1990 Legend shown — 1991-94 Legend similar

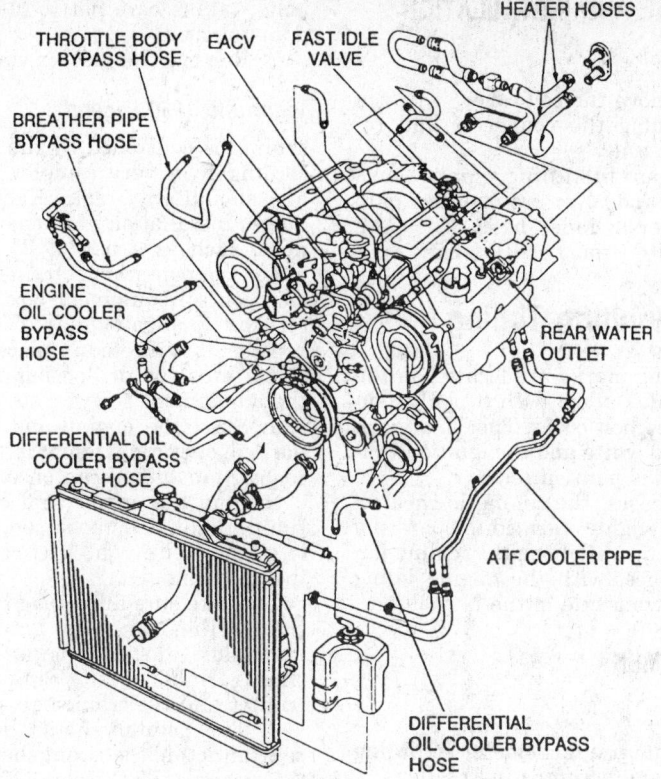

Cooling system components schematic — 1991-94 Legend

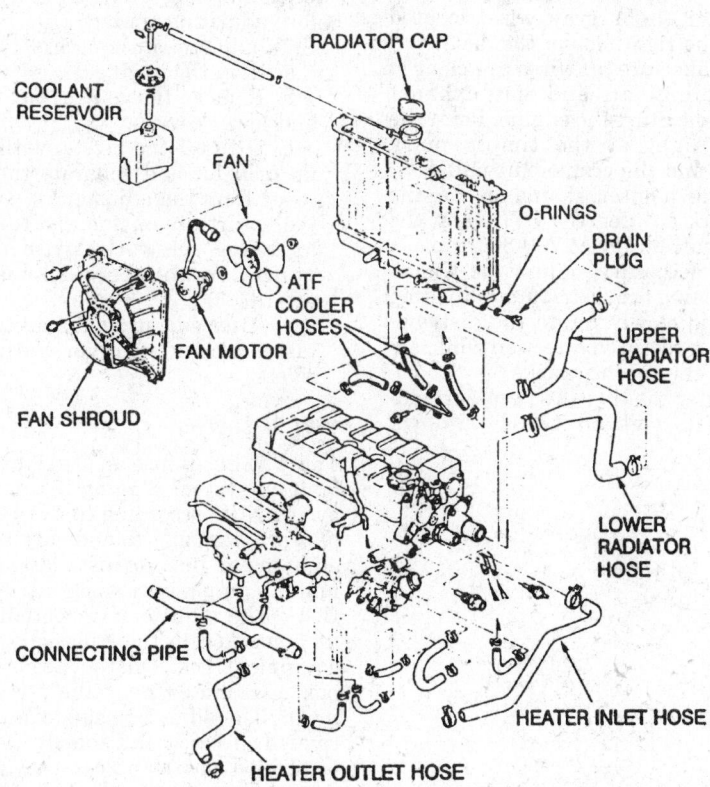

Cooling system components schematic — Integra

water. Make sure the antifreeze is suited for use in aluminum cooling system components. Do not mix brands of antifreeze.

All Models

1. Set the heater temperature selector for full heat.
2. Fill the coolant reservoir to the MAX mark.
3. Loosen the air bleed bolt at the engine end of the upper radiator hose. Fill the radiator to the bottom of the filler neck with the proper coolant mix. Tighten the bleed bolt as soon as the coolant starts to run out in a steady stream without any air bubbles in it.
4. With the radiator cap off, start the engine and allow it to warm; the cooling fan should go ON at least twice. Then, if necessary, add more antifreeze/coolant to bring the level back up to the bottom of the filler neck.
5. Put the radiator cap on, restart the engine and check for any leaks.

ENGINE ELECTRICAL

NOTE: Most vehicles are equipped with a theft protected radio. Before disconnecting the battery, obtain the owner's radio activation code. After reconnecting power to the radio, the 5 digit code must be entered to restore operation.

Distributor

REMOVAL

1. Make sure the ignition switch is **OFF**.
2. Remove the distributor cap. Label and disconnect the wires and vacuum lines from the distributor.
3. Mark the position of the distributor rotor in relation to the distributor housing and mark the position of the distributor housing in relation to the engine assembly.
4. Remove the distributor hold-down bolts and remove the distributor from the cylinder head.

INSTALLATION

Timing Not Disturbed

NOTE: The distributor drive is offset and fits into a slot in the camshaft. The distributor will drop into place when the drive is properly aligned.

1. Coat a new distributor O-ring with engine oil and install on the distributor. Insert the distributor into the engine and turn the rotor while gently pushing in on the shaft. Align the distributor housing and distributor rotor with the marks that were made during the removal procedure.
2. When the distributor is fully seated in the engine, install and tighten the distributor retaining bolts.
3. Install the distributor cap. Connect the wiring and vacuum hose.
4. Check the ignition timing.

Timing Disturbed

1. Disconnect the spark plug wire from the No. 1 cylinder spark plug and remove the spark plug.
2. Place a finger over the spark plug hole and turn the engine over slowly, by hand until compression is felt.
3. Align the timing mark on the crankshaft pulley with the timing pointer.
4. Coat a new distributor O-ring with engine oil and install on the distributor. Insert the distributor into the engine and turn the rotor while gently pushing in on the shaft. When the distributor is fully seated in the engine, install and tighten the distributor retaining bolts.
5. Install the distributor cap. Connect the wiring and vacuum hose.
6. Check the ignition timing.

Distributorless Ignition

The 1991-94 Legend uses a direct ignition system, one coil for each cylinder is mounted directly over each spark plug. They are controlled by an igniter unit, which is a solid state switching device that completes the ground circuit for each coil at the proper time. The igniter unit is controlled by the ECU, which determines ignition timing. To check the timing, a service loop is available that connects to the igniter unit and provides a trigger wire for connecting a standard timing light.

REMOVAL AND INSTALLATION

Coil

1. Remove the coil cover.
2. Unplug the connector and remove the coil.
3. When installing, make sure each coil and cover are installed onto the proper cylinder head. They are marked FF (front) or RR (rear).

Ignition Timing

The timing marks are located on the crankshaft pulley, with a pointer on the timing belt cover. The TDC mark is painted white and the ignition timing mark is painted red.

In all cases, the timing is checked with the engine warmed to operating temperature, allowing the cooling fan to run once, with the engine idling and the transaxle in the **N** position.

ADJUSTMENT

Integra

1. Connect a tachometer according to the manufacturer's instructions.
2. Using a suitable jumper wire, connect the green and brown terminals of the ignition timing adjusting connector (light gray wire) located under the right side of the dash.
3. Make sure all wires are clear of the cooling fan and hot exhaust manifolds. Start the engine. Point the timing light at the timing mark pointer and the crankshaft pulley.
4. The pointer should be on the red mark (16 degrees BTDC) on the crankshaft pulley at 700-800 rpm.
5. If necessary, adjust the timing by loosening the distributor adjusting bolts and slowly rotate the distributor in the required direction while observing the timing marks.
6. After making the necessary adjustment, tighten the hold-down

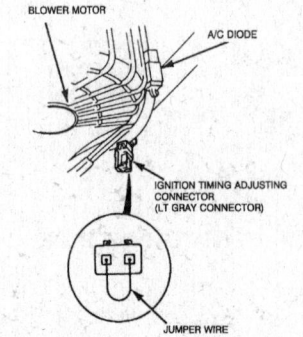

Jumper the timing connector near the blower motor — Integra

bolts, taking care not to disturb the adjustment.
7. Remove the jumper wire.

Vigor and 1990 Legend

Timing is controlled by the ECU according to a very complex program and should only require adjustment due to installation of a major component, such as a new ECU. The adjuster is a potentiometer, in the emission control equipment box mounted on the firewall near the brake booster. It is riveted in place and the rivets must be drilled out to access the adjustment screw.

1. Start the engine and warm to normal operating temperatures; the cooling fan should run once.
2. Stop the engine and connect a timing light and tachometer according to the manufacturer's instructions.
3. Make sure all wires are clear of the cooling fan and hot exhaust manifolds. Start the engine. Point the timing light at the timing mark pointer and the crankshaft pulley.
4. The pointer should be on the red mark on the crankshaft pulley (15 degrees BTDC) at 680 rpm. If timing is not correct, make sure all other possible faults (vacuum leak, bad connection, etc.) are corrected before adjusting timing.
5. If adjustment is necessary:
   a. Stop the engine.
   b. Remove the control box upper and lower cover.
   c. Drill off the rivets, with a 3/16 in. drill bit and separate the stay cover from the adjuster.
   d. Start the engine and turn the adjusting screw clockwise to advance or counterclockwise to retard.
   e. After adjusting, install the adjuster and stay cover with new rivets.

1991-94 Legend

These vehicles use a distributorless ignition system. Timing is controlled by the ECU according to a very complex program and should only require adjustment due to installation of a major component, such as a new ECU. The adjuster is a potentiometer, mounted in the emission control equipment box. On the Legend, the box is mounted near the left shock tower. The adjuster has a cap that is riveted in place and the rivets must be drilled out to access the adjustment screw.

1. Start the engine and warm to normal operating temperature; the cooling fan should run once.

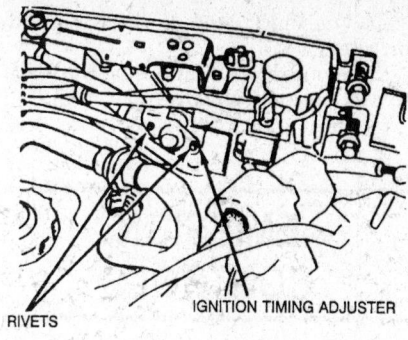

Ignition timing adjuster — Vigor and 1990 Legend

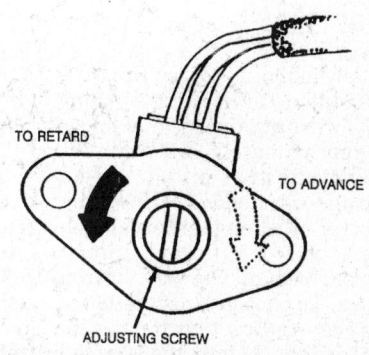

Ignition timing adjuster, exploded view — Vigor and 1990 Legend

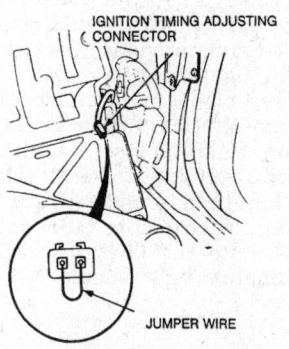

Timing adjuster connector, behind right side kick panel — 1991-94 Legend

2. Stop the engine and connect a service loop to the igniter unit and connect a timing light according to the manufacturer's instructions. On the Legend, the igniter unit is on the right shock tower.

3. On the Legend, locate the timing adjusting connector behind the passenger's side kick panel and jumper the black and white wire terminals.

4. Make sure all wires are clear and start the engine. Point the tim-

ing light at the timing mark pointer and the crankshaft pulley.

5. The pointer should be on the red mark on the crankshaft pulley:

Legend

Manual transaxle — 15 degrees BTDC at 650 rpm.

Automatic transaxle — 15 degrees BTDC at 600 rpm.

6. If timing or idle speed is not correct, make sure all other possible faults (vacuum leak, bad connection, etc.) are corrected before making any adjustments. Set idle speed first.

7. If adjustment is necessary:

a. Stop the engine.

b. Remove the control box cover.

c. Drill off the rivets with a 3/16 in. drill bit and separate the cover from the adjuster.

d. Start the engine and turn the adjusting screw clockwise to advance or counterclockwise to retard timing.

8. After adjusting, install the cover with new rivets.

Alternator

PRECAUTIONS

- Observe the proper polarity of the battery connections by making sure the positive (+) and negative (-) terminal connections are not reversed. Mis-connection will allow current to flow in the reverse direction, resulting in damaged diodes and an overheated wire harness.
- Never ground or short out an alternator or regulator terminals.
- Never operate the alternator unless all wiring is connected.
- Always remove the battery or disconnect the output lead while charging it.
- Always disconnect the ground cable when replacing any electrical components.
- Never subject the alternator to excessive heat or dampness if the engine is being steam cleaned.
- Never use arc welding equipment with the alternator connected.

BELT TENSION ADJUSTMENT

The initial inspection and adjustment to the alternator drive belt should be performed after the first 3000 miles or if the alternator has been moved for any reason; afterward, inspect the belt tension every 30,000 miles. Before adjusting, inspect the belt for

cracks or wear; be sure its surfaces are free of grease and oil.

1. Push down on the belt halfway between pulleys with a force of about 22 lbs. The belt should deflect:

Integra — 0.16-0.41 in. (4-11mm)

Legend

1990 — 0.43-0.77 in. (11-19.5mm)

1991-94 — 0.22-0.45 in. (5.5-11.5mm)

2. To adjust belt tension on Integra, loosen the adjustment lock bolt and move the alternator with a prybar positioned against the front of the alternator housing. Do not apply pressure to any other part of the alternator.

3. To adjust tension on all other models, loosen the adjustment lock bolt and turn the adjusting bolt as required.

4. After obtaining the proper tension, tighten the adjustment lock bolt.

NOTE: Do not over tighten the belt. Damage to the alternator bearings may result.

REMOVAL AND INSTALLATION

Integra

1. It is necessary to remove the halfshaft to remove the alternator. Disconnect the negative battery cable.

2. Raise the locking tab on the left front spindle nut and loosen the nut with a 1 7/16 socket.

3. Raise and safely support the vehicle and remove the left front wheel.

4. Remove the damper fork nut and damper pinch bolt. Remove the damper fork.

5. Remove the knuckle-to-lower arm castle nut and separate the lower ball joint using a suitable puller with the pawls applied to the lower arm.

6. Pull the knuckle outward and remove the halfshaft outboard CV-joint from the knuckle using a plastic mallet.

7. Carefully pry the inner CV-joint out of the intermediate shaft and remove the halfshaft.

NOTE: Do not pull on the driveshaft, as the CV-joint may come apart. Use care when prying out the assembly and pull it straight to avoid damaging the intermediate shaft seals.

8. Disconnect and tag the alternator wire connection from the alternator. Remove the terminal nut and the white wire from the **B** terminal.

9. Loosen the adjusting nut and remove the alternator nut. Remove the alternator belt from the alternator pulley. Remove the lower through bolt and raise the alternator.

10. Remove the 3 mounting bracket bolts and mounting brackets. Remove the adjusting nut and upper through bolt, pull out the alternator.

To install:

11. Position the alternator and install the through bolt and adjusting nut. Install the mounting brackets and mounting bracket bolts and torque to 33 ft. lbs. (45 Nm).

12. Lower the alternator and install the lower through bolt. Install the alternator belt and adjusting nut. Tension the belt and torque the adjusting nut to 17 ft. lbs. (24 Nm).

13. Reconnect all the wiring.

14. Use a new set ring on the end of the inner CV-joint and slide it into the intermediate shaft. Use the plastic mallet to tap in on the half-shaft and set the ring.

15. Slide the outer CV-joint into place and position the ball joint in the lower arm. Install the nut and torque to 40 ft. lbs. (55 Nm) and tighten as necessary to install a new cotter pin.

16. Install the damper fork, pinch bolt and fork nut. Torque the pinch bolt to 32 ft. lbs. (44 Nm) and the fork nut to 47 ft. lbs. (65 Nm).

17. Install a new self-locking spindle nut and wheel and place the vehicle on the ground before torquing the spindle nut. Attempting to torque the spindle nut while the vehicle is on jackstands or a lift may cause the vehicle to fall.

18. With the vehicle on the ground, torque the spindle nut to 134 ft. lbs. (185 Nm).

19. Reconnect the negative battery cable.

Vigor, and 1990 Legend

1. Disconnect the negative battery cable.

2. Remove the alternator belt and wire covers.

3. Disconnect the alternator wiring.

4. Loosen the through bolt and the adjuster bolt and remove the belt.

5. Remove the through bolt and alternator bolt and lift the alternator out.

6. Installation is the reverse of removal. Torque the through bolt to 33 ft. lbs. (45 Nm) and the nut to 16 ft. lbs. (22 Nm).

1991-94 Legend

1. Disconnect both battery cables and remove the battery and the battery base.

2. Remove the adjusting lock bolt and the lower mounting bolt and slip the belt off the pulley.

3. Rotate the alternator counterclockwise far enough to get the bolt hole past the bracket and pull the alternator straight forward.

4. Tilt the alternator down in front and disconnect the wiring to remove the alternator.

5. Installation is the reverse of removal. Torque the lower mounting bolt to 33 ft. lbs. (45 Nm) and the adjuster lock bolt to 16 ft. lbs. (22 Nm).

Starter

REMOVAL AND INSTALLATION

1. Disconnect the battery negative cable. On Vigor, remove the manifold bracket.

2. At the starter motor, label and disconnect the wiring.

3. Remove the starter-to-engine bolts and the starter.

To install:

4. Position the starter to the engine and torque the bolts 32 ft. lbs. (45 Nm). Connect the wiring to the starter.

5. On Vigor, install the manifold bracket.

6. Connect the cables to the battery. Check the starter operation.

EMISSION CONTROLS

Emission Warning Lamps

RESETTING

Some vehicles are equipped with a Scheduled Service Due warning light. This warning light is due to come ON at approximately 7500 mile intervals to indicate that an oil and oil filter change is needed. However, if a shorter oil change interval is desired, there are 7 different intervals to choose from all the way down to 1500 miles. To choose a new interval, push the Service Reset button (on the clock control panel) and the Arrow button for approximately 3 seconds, then push the Arrow button until the interval desired appears. Push the Set button again. After completing the necessary maintenance service, the warning light must be reset.

To reset the maintenance light, turn the ignition switch to the **ON** position. Hold the reset button in for at least 3 seconds. To verify that the reset has been completed, turn the ignition switch to the **OFF** position and back to the **ON** position. The maintenance light should not turn ON.

FUEL SYSTEM

Fuel System Service Precautions

• To avoid the possibility of fire and personal injury, always disconnect the negative battery cable unless the repair or test procedure requires that battery voltage be applied.

• Always relieve the fuel system pressure prior to disconnecting any fuel system component (injector, fuel rail, pressure regulator, etc.), fitting or fuel line connection. Exercise ex-

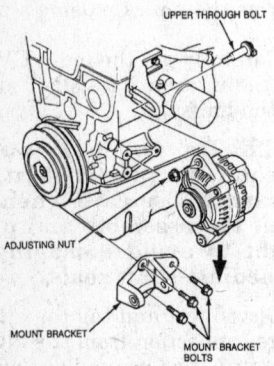

Alternator mounting — Integra

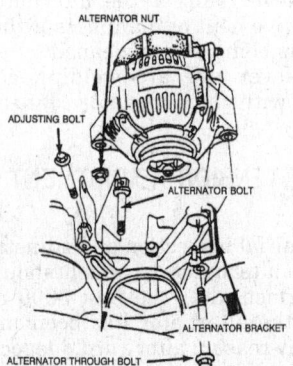

Alternator mounting — 1990 Legend

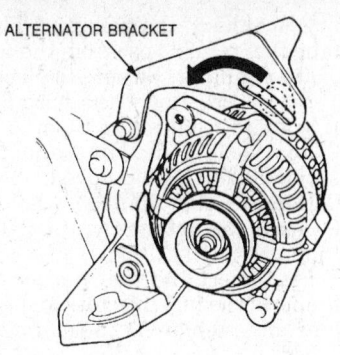

Rotate the alternator to remove it past the bracket

treme caution whenever relieving fuel system pressure to avoid exposing skin, face and eyes to fuel spray. Fuel under pressure may penetrate the skin or any part of the body that it contacts.

• Always place a shop towel or cloth around the fitting or connection prior to loosening to absorb any excess fuel spillage. Quickly remove any spilled fuel from engine and paint surfaces. Ensure that all fuel soaked cloths or towels are deposited into a suitable waste container.

• Always keep a dry chemical (Class B) fire extinguisher near the work area.

• Do not allow fuel spray or fuel vapors to come into contact with a spark or open flame.

• Always use a backup wrench when loosening and tightening fuel line connection fittings. This will prevent unnecessary stress and torsion to fuel line piping. Always follow the proper torque specifications.

• Always replace fuel fitting O-rings and gaskets with new ones. Do not substitute fuel hose where metal fuel pipe is installed.

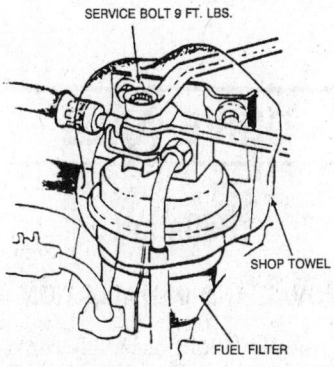

Relieving fuel system pressure

RELIEVING FUEL SYSTEM PRESSURE

— **CAUTION** —
The fuel system may be under pressure and fuel will be sprayed. Be sure there is good ventilation and take the appropriate fire safety precautions.

1. Place rag under the filter during this procedure to prevent fuel from spilling onto the engine.
2. Relieve the fuel pressure by slowly loosening the service bolt on the top of the fuel filter about a turn.
3. Always replace the washer between the service bolt and the banjo bolt whenever the service bolt has been loosened.

Fuel Tank

REMOVAL AND INSTALLATION

Vigor and Integra

1. Raise and safely support the vehicle and remove the rear wheels.
2. Remove the tank drain bolt and drain the fuel into an approved container.
3. Remove the rear seat and access panel and disconnect the gauge and pump wiring.
4. Remove the fuel hose protector and the 2-way valve. When disconnecting the hoses, twist and pull at the same time to work the hose off the tube.
5. Support the tank with a floor jack, remove the straps and lower the tank out of the vehicle. If it sticks on the undercoating, carefully pry it free.
6. Installation is the reverse of removal. Use a new sealing washer on the drain plug and torque to 36 ft. lbs. (50 Nm).

Legend

1. On 1990 Legend, remove the access panel from the floor of the trunk and disconnect the pump and gauge wiring.
2. On 1991-94 Legend, remove the rear seat and the access panel and disconnect the pump and gauge wiring.
3. Raise and safely support the vehicle and remove the rear wheels.
4. Remove the tank drain bolt and drain the fuel into an approved container.
5. Remove the fuel hose protector on 1991-94 models. When discon-

necting the hoses, twist and pull at the same time to work the hose off the tube.
6. Support the tank with a floor jack, remove the straps and lower the tank out of the vehicle. If it sticks on the undercoating, carefully pry it free.
7. Installation is the reverse of removal. Use a new sealing washer on the drain plug and torque to 36 ft. lbs. (50 Nm).

Fuel Filter

REMOVAL AND INSTALLATION

1. Disconnect the negative battery cable and remove the fuel filler cap.
2. Relieve the fuel pressure by slowly loosening the service bolt on the top of the fuel filter about a turn.

— **CAUTION** —
The fuel system may be under pressure and fuel will be sprayed. Be sure there is good ventilation and take the appropriate fire safety precautions.

3. Remove the fittings from the fuel filter, loosen the clamp and remove the filter.
4. Installation is the reverse of removal. Use new sealing washers on all fittings.

Electric Fuel Pump

PRESSURE TESTING

On all models, the fuel pump should run for about 2 seconds when the ignition is first turned **ON**. By removing the filler cap and listening at the filler, it should be possible to hear the pump run each time the ignition is switched **ON**. It will then stop again until the starter is activated.

1. Disconnect the negative battery cable and remove the fuel filler cap.
2. Relieve the fuel system pressure.
3. Remove the service bolt and attach a fuel pressure gauge to the top of the fuel filter.
4. Start the engine and measure the fuel pressure with the engine idling and vacuum hose from the pressure regulator disconnected:
Integra — 37-44 psi (255-304 kPa)
Legend
   1990 — 36-41 psi (250-279 kPa)
   1991-94 — 38-46 psi (265-314 kPa)
Vigor — 43-50 psi (300-350 kPa)

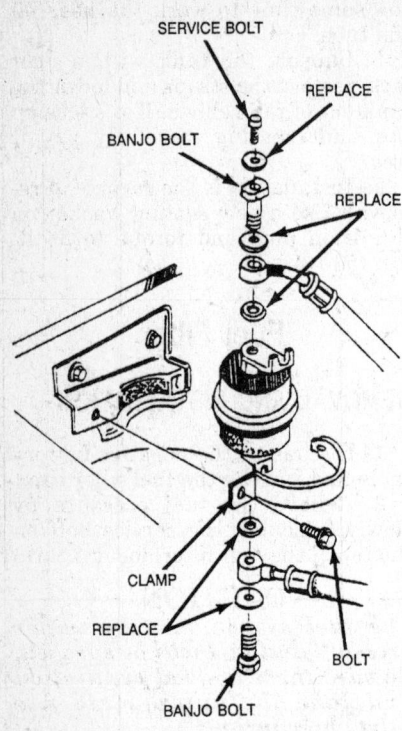

Fuel filter replacement — Integra shown

5. Check to see that the pressure decreases when the vacuum hose is connected.

6. If the pressure is higher than specifications, check for a pinched or clogged fuel return hose or faulty pressure regulator.

7. If the pressure is lower than specifications, check for a clogged filter, defective pressure regulator or leakage in the fuel line.

8. After inspection, remove the pressure gauge and install the service bolt with a new washer.

REMOVAL AND INSTALLATION

Vigor and Integra

1. On Integra, remove the rear seat and access panel and disconnect the wiring.

2. Remove the fuel tank.

3. Remove the pump flange mounting nuts and lift the pump out.

4. Installation is the reverse of removal. Use new sealing washers when connecting the fuel hoses. After the pump is installed, turn the ignition switch **ON** and **OFF** a number of times to pressurize the system and check for leaks.

Legend

1. Disconnect the negative battery cable.

2. Relieve the fuel system pressure.

3. Remove the maintenance access cover in the luggage area.

4. Disconnect the fuel lines and the electrical connectors.

5. Remove the fuel pump from the fuel tank.

6. Installation is the reverse of removal. Use new sealing washers when connecting the fuel hoses. After the pump is installed, turn the ignition switch **ON** and **OFF** a number of times to pressurize the system and check for leaks.

Fuel Injector

REMOVAL AND INSTALLATION

1. Disconnect the negative battery cable.

2. Relieve the fuel pressure from the fuel system.

3. On V6 engines, remove the wiring harness covers and intake manifold covers as required.

4. Disconnect the electrical connectors from the fuel injectors.

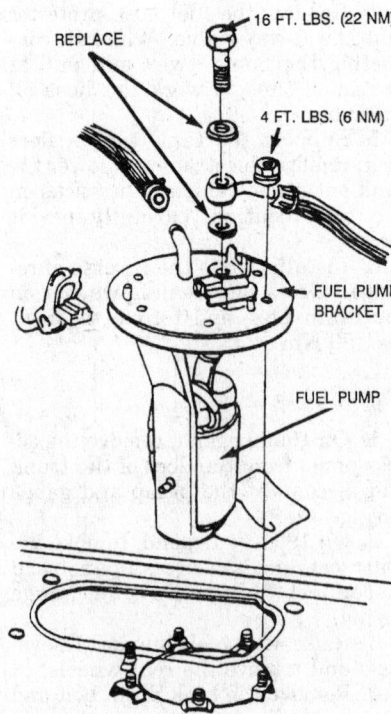

Fuel pump removal — Legend

5. Disconnect the vacuum hose and the fuel return hose from the fuel pressure regulator. Be sure to place a shop rag or towel over the hose and tube before disconnecting them.

6. Remove the fuel line and the pulsation damper, if equipped.

7. Remove the connector holder and loosen the retainer nuts of the fuel pipe assembly.

8. Disconnect the fuel pipe hoses and remove the fuel injectors and fuel pipe as an assembly from the intake manifold.

To install:

NOTE: When installing injectors, be sure to install new seal rings, sealing washers, O-rings and cushion rings. Using old parts may cause fuel or vacuum leaks and excessive injector noise.

9. Slide the new cushion rings onto the injectors. Be sure to coat the new O-rings with clean engine oil and put them onto the injectors.

10. Insert the injectors into the fuel pipe first. Coat the new seal rings with clean engine oil and press them into the intake manifold.

11. Install the injectors and fuel pipe assembly into the intake manifold. To prevent damage to the O-rings, install the injectors in the fuel pipe first then install them into the intake manifold.

12. Align the center line on the connector with the mark on the fuel pipe.

13. Install and tighten the retainer nuts. Connect the vacuum hose and the fuel return hose to the pressure regulator.

14. Install the electrical connectors on the fuel injectors.

15. Do not start the engine. Turn the ignition switch **ON** and **OFF** a number of times to pressurize the fuel system (the pump only runs for 2 seconds without the engine turning).

16. If there are no leaks, run the engine to test the injectors, then install the covers.

DRIVE AXLE

Halfshaft

REMOVAL AND INSTALLATION

The front halfshaft assembly consists of a sub-axleshaft and a halfshaft with 2 constant velocity (CV) joints.

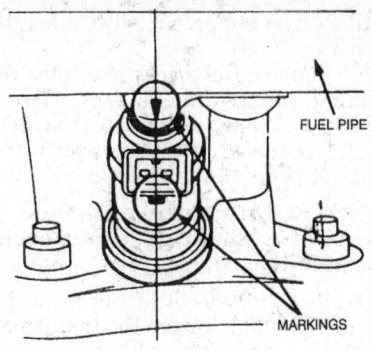

Align the marks on the injector and the fuel pipe

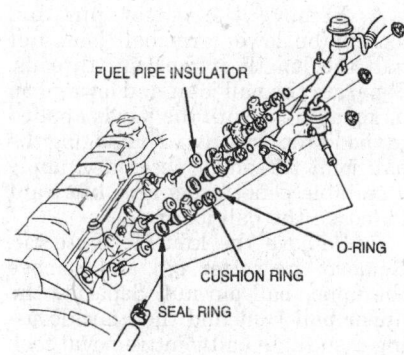

Injector assembly — Integra — Vigor similar

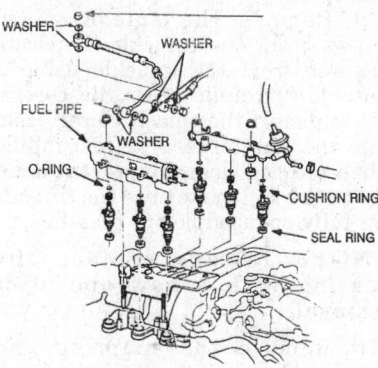

Injector assembly — V6 engines

The CV-joints are factory packed with special grease and enclosed in sealed rubber boots. The outer joint cannot be disassembled except for removal of the boot.

All Models

——— WARNING ———

The spindle nut torque is very high. Tighten or loosen the spindle nut only with the vehicle on the ground. Attempting to loosen

or torque the spindle nut while the vehicle is on jackstands or a lift may cause the vehicle to fall.

1. With the vehicle on the ground, raise the locking tab on the spindle nut and loosen it with a suitable socket.
2. Disconnect the negative battery cable.
3. Raise and safely support the vehicle and remove the spindle nut and front wheels.
4. If removing the right side halfshaft, drain the transaxle or differential oil.
5. Remove the damper fork nut and damper pinch bolt. Remove the damper fork.
6. Remove the lower ball joint nut and separate the lower ball joint using a suitable puller with the pawls applied to the lower arm.
7. Pull the knuckle outward and remove the halfshaft outboard CV-joint from the knuckle using a suitable plastic mallet.
8. Using a small prybar with a 3.5 x 7mm tip, carefully pry out the inboard CV-joint approximately ½ in. (13mm) in order to force the spring clip out of the groove in the differential side gears.

NOTE: Be careful not to damage the oil seal. Do not pull on the inboard CV-joint, it may come apart.

9. Pull the halfshaft out of the differential or the intermediate shaft.
10. To remove the intermediate shaft, remove the 3 bolts. Lower the bearing support close to the steering gearbox and remove the intermediate shaft from the differential. To prevent any damage from the differential oil seal, hold the intermediate shaft horizontal until it is clear of the differential.
    To install:
11. If either the inboard or outboard joint boot bands have been removed for inspection or disassembly of the joint (only the inboard joint can be disassembled), be sure to repack the joint with a sufficient amount of the correct CV-joint grease.
12. Always use a new set ring whenever the driveshaft is being installed. Be sure the driveshaft locks in the differential side gear groove and that the CV-joint sub-axle bottoms in the differential or the intermediate shaft.
13. Torque the ball joint nut to 40 ft. lbs. (55 Nm) on Integra, 43 ft. lbs. (60 Nm) on Vigor or 54 ft. lbs. (75

Nm) on Legend. Then tighten the nut as required to install a new cotter pin.
14. Torque the lower damper nut and bolt to 47 ft. lbs. (65 Nm) and the upper pinch bolt to 32 ft. lbs. (44 Nm).
15. With the vehicle on the ground, torque the spindle nut to the proper specification, then stake the nut:
    Vigor — 180 ft. lbs. (250 Nm)
    Legend
    1990 — 180 ft. lbs. (250 Nm)
    1991-94 — 242 ft. lbs. (335 Nm)
    Integra — 134 ft. lbs. (185 Nm)

Intermediate Shaft

REMOVAL AND INSTALLATION

All Models

1. Raise and safely support the vehicle and drain the oil from the transaxle.
2. Remove the halfshaft and the bearing heatshield, if equipped.
3. Remove the 3 bearing support bolts.
4. On Vigor and 1991-94 Legend, slide the shaft out of the oil pan. On all other models, lower the bearing support close to the steering gearbox and remove the intermediate shaft from the differential.

NOTE: To avoid damage to the differential oil seal, hold the intermediate shaft horizontal until it clears the differential.

5. To install, reverse the removal procedure. Torque the bearing support bolts to 16 ft. lbs. (22 Nm) for 8mm bolts, or 29 ft. lbs. (40 Nm) for 10mm bolts.

CV-Joint Boot

NOTE: The following procedures are for removing the CV-joint boot from the halfshaft once the halfshaft has been removed from the vehicle. If a quick seal boot is to be used, follow the instructions supplied with the part.

REMOVAL AND INSTALLATION

NOTE: Be sure to mark the roller grooves during disassembly to ensure proper positioning during reassembly. Before disassembly, mark the spider gear and the driveshaft so they can be installed in their original positions. The inboard joint must be removed to replace the boots.

1. Remove the halfshaft that requires the boot change.

2. Remove the front and rear boot retaining bands and slide the boots off the halfshaft.

To install:

3. Wrap the spline with vinyl tape to prevent damage to the boots. Install the outboard and inboard boots onto the halfshaft, then remove the vinyl tape.

4. Install the stopper ring onto the driveshaft groove. Also install the dynamic damper at this time, if equipped.

5. Install the spider gear onto the halfshaft by aligning the marks and install it in its original position.

6. Fit the snapring into the halfshaft groove.

7. Pack the outboard joint boot with CV-joint grease only. Do not use a substitute or mix types of grease.

8. Fit the rollers to the spider gear with their high shoulders facing outward. Reinstall the rollers in their original positions on the spider gear.

9. Pack the inboard joint boot with CV-joint grease.

10. Fit the inboard joint onto the halfshaft. Hold the halfshaft assembly so the inboard joint points up to prevent it from falling off.

11. With the boots installed, adjust the CV-joints in or out to place the inner boot ends in the original positions.

12. Install the new boot bands on the boots and bend both sets of locking tabs. Lightly tap on the locking tabs to ensure a good fit.

13. Reinstall the halfshaft.

Front Wheel Hub, Knuckle and Bearings

REMOVAL AND INSTALLATION

NOTE: The following procedures for hub and wheel bearing removal and installation necessitate the use of many special tools and a hydraulic press. Do not attempt this procedure without these special tools.

Integra

1. Pry the lock tab away and loosen the spindle nut. Slightly loosen the lug nuts.

2. Raise and safely support the vehicle. Remove the front wheel and spindle nut.

3. Remove the brake caliper bolts and the caliper from the knuckle. Do not allow the caliper to hang by the brake hose, support it with a length of wire.

4. Remove the disc brake rotor retaining screws, if equipped. Screw two 8 x 1.0mm bolts into the disc brake removal holes and turn the bolts to press the rotor from the hub.

NOTE: Only turn each bolt 2 turns at a time to prevent cocking the disc excessively.

5. Remove the cotter pin from the tie rod end and remove the castle nut. Break loose the tie rod ball joint using a suitable ball joint removal tool and lift the tie rod out the steering knuckle.

6. Remove the cotter pin and loosen the lower arm ball joint nut half the length of the joint threads. Separate the ball joint and lower arm using a puller with the pawls applied to the lower arm. Avoid damaging the ball joint thread. If necessary, apply a suitable penetrating type lubricant to loosen the ball joint.

7. Remove the knuckle protector. Remove the cotter pin and remove the upper ball pin nut. Separate the upper ball joint and the knuckle using a suitable ball joint removal tool.

8. Remove the steering knuckle and hub by sliding them off the halfshaft.

9. Remove the splash guard screws from the knuckle. Separate the hub from the knuckle using a suitable hydraulic press. Be careful not to distort the splash guard. Hold onto the hub to keep it from falling when pressed clear. To prevent damage to the tool make sure the threads are fully engaged before pressing.

NOTE: Always replace the bearing with a new one after removal.

10. Remove the snapring and knuckle ring from the knuckle. Press the wheel bearing out of the knuckle using suitable press tools and a hydraulic press.

11. Remove the outboard bearing inner race from the hub by using a suitable bearing puller.

To install:

12. Remove the old grease from the hub and knuckle and thoroughly dry and wipe clean all components. When pressing a new bearing into the hub, be sure to press only on the outer race or the bearing will be destroyed. Install the snapring securely in the knuckle groove.

13. Install the splash guard and tighten the screws.

14. Support the hub properly and press on the inner race of the bearing to install the knuckle onto the hub.

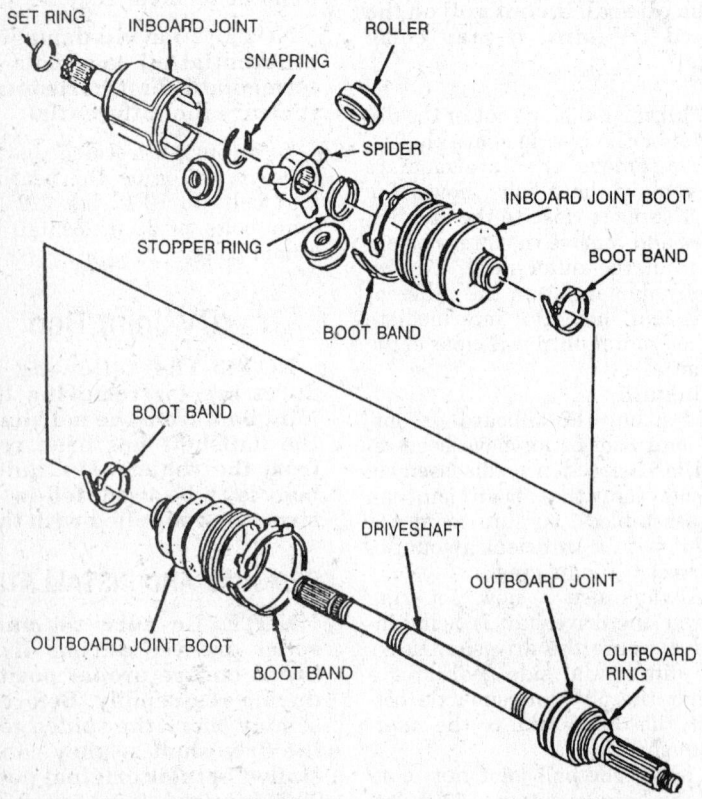

On all models, only the inner CV-joint can be disassembled

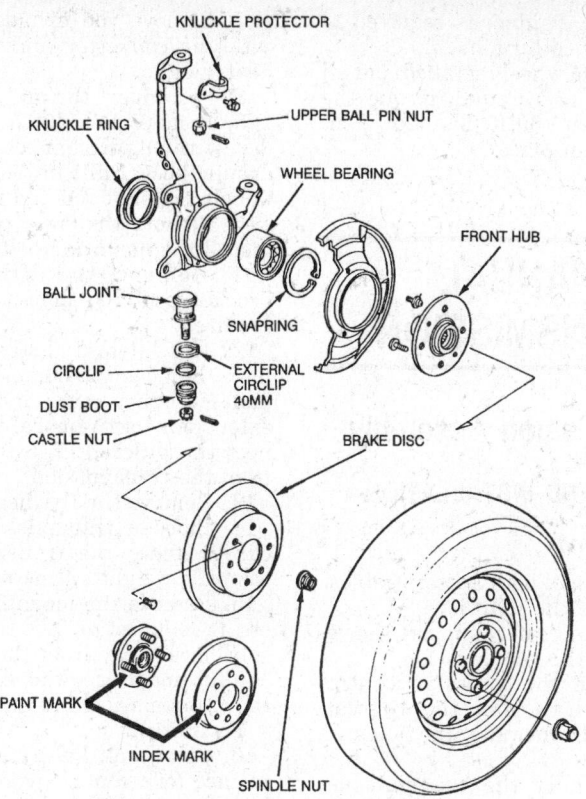

KNUCKLE PROTECTOR

KNUCKLE RING

UPPER BALL PIN NUT

WHEEL BEARING

FRONT HUB

BALL JOINT

SNAPRING

CIRCLIP

EXTERNAL CIRCLIP 40MM

DUST BOOT

CASTLE NUT

BRAKE DISC

PAINT MARK

INDEX MARK

SPINDLE NUT

Front steering knuckle, hub and bearing assembly — Integra

Do not press on the outer race or on the knuckle or the bearing will be destroyed. Install the front knuckle ring.

15. The remaining installation is the reverse of the removal procedure. Torque the upper ball joint and tie rod end nuts to 32 ft. lbs. (44 Nm). Torque the lower ball joint nut to 40 ft. lbs. (55 Nm). Install new cotter pins.

16. With the vehicle on its wheels, torque the spindle nut to 134 ft. lbs. (185 Nm). Use a new spindle nut and stake it after torquing.

Legend

1. Pry the lock tab away from the spindle and loosen the 36mm nut. Slightly loosen the lug nuts.

2. Raise and safely support the vehicle. Remove the front wheel and spindle nut.

3. Remove the bolts retaining the brake caliper and the caliper from the knuckle. Do not allow the caliper to hang by the brake hose, support it with a length of wire.

4. Remove the disc brake rotor retaining screws if equipped. Screw both 8 **x** 1.25 **x** 12mm bolts into the disc brake removal holes and turn the bolts to press the rotor from the hub.

NOTE: Only turn each bolt 2 turns at a time to prevent cocking the disc excessively.

5. Remove the tie rod from the knuckle using a tie rod end removal tool. Use care not to damage the ball joint seals.

6. Remove the cotter pin from the lower arm ball joint and the castle nut.

7. Remove the lower control arm from the knuckle using the ball joint remover.

8. Remove the cotter pin from the upper arm ball joint and the castle nut.

9. Remove the upper arm from the knuckle using the ball joint remover.

10. Remove the knuckle and hub by sliding the assembly off the halfshaft.

NOTE: Any time the hub is removed, the wheel bearing must be replaced with a new one.

11. On 1990 Legend, properly support the knuckle and press the hub out of the bearing.

12. On 1991-94 Legend, the hub can be removed with a slide hammer. Clamp the knuckle in a vise and secure the slide hammer to the wheel studs.

13. Remove the splash guard and snaprings.

14. Support the knuckle and press the bearing out towards the wheel side.

15. If the inner bearing race stayed on the hub, use a puller to remove it.

To install:

16. Clean all parts and examine for wear. A worn or damaged hub will cause premature bearing failure and should be replaced.

17. When pressing in a new bearing, install the inner snapring first and press the bearing in from the wheel side. Be sure to press only on the outer race or the bearing will be damaged.

18. Install the outer snapring and the splash guard.

19. Properly support the knuckle and press the hub into the bearing. Do not press on the wheel studs or they will press out of the hub. Be sure to support the knuckle by the inner race or the bearing will be damaged.

20. Install the knuckle in the reverse order of removal. Torque the lower ball joint nut to 54 ft. lbs. (75 Nm) and tighten as required to install a new cotter pin.

21. Torque the upper ball joint nut to 32 ft. lbs. (44 Nm) and tighten as required to install a new cotter pin. Torque the tie rod end to 36 ft. lbs. (50 Nm) and tighten as required to install a new cotter pin.

22. With the wheel installed and all 4 wheels on the ground, torque the spindle nut and stake it in place.
Legend
1990 — 180 ft. lbs. (250 Nm)
1991-94 — 242 ft. lbs. (335 Nm)

Vigor

The front wheel bearing and hub can be removed as an assembly, without removing the steering knuckle.

1. Pry the lock tab away from the spindle and loosen the 36mm nut. Slightly loosen the lug nuts.

2. Raise and safely support the vehicle. Remove the front wheel and spindle nut.

3. Remove the bolts retaining the brake caliper and remove the caliper from the knuckle. Do not allow the caliper to hang by the brake hose; support it with a length of wire.

4. Remove the ABS speed sensor from the knuckle.

5. Remove the tie rod from the knuckle using a properly sized ball joint pressing tool. Use care not to damage the joint seals.

6. Remove the cotter pin from the lower arm ball joint and the castle nut. Remove the lower control arm

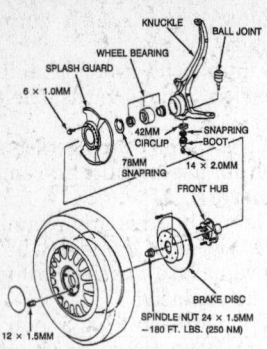

Front hub, bearing and knuckle assembly — 1990 Legend — later model similar

from the knuckle, using the ball joint pressing tool.

7. Remove the cotter pin from the upper arm ball joint and the castle nut. Remove the upper arm from the knuckle using the ball joint pressing tool.

8. Remove the knuckle and hub by sliding the assembly off the halfshaft.

9. To remove the hub from the knuckle, remove the 4 self-locking bolts from the back of the knuckle. Remove the 4 bolts from the hub to remove the brake disc.

NOTE: Any time the hub and bearings are separated, the wheel bearing must be replaced with a new one.

10. The bearing can be pressed off the hub with a hydraulic press. The inner race of the outer row will stay on the hub and can be removed with a bearing puller.

To install:

11. Clean all parts and examine for wear. A worn or damaged hub will cause premature bearing failure and should be replaced.

12. When pressing on a new bearing, be sure to press only on the inner race or the bearing will be damaged.

13. Install the brake disc and torque the bolts to 40 ft. lbs. (55 Nm). Do not over torque or the disc will warp.

14. Make sure the splash guard is installed on the knuckle. Install the hub assembly and torque the self-locking bolts to 33 ft. lbs. (45 Nm). Do not over torque or the hub will be distorted.

15. Install the knuckle in the reverse order of removal. Torque the lower ball joint nut to 40 ft. lbs. (54 Nm) and tighten as required to install a new cotter pin.

16. Torque the upper ball joint nut to 32 ft. lbs. (44 Nm) and tighten as required to install a new cotter pin. Torque the tie rod end to 36 ft. lbs.

(50 Nm) and tighten as required to install a new cotter pin.

17. With the wheel installed and all 4 wheels on the ground, torque the spindle nut to 180 ft. lbs. (250 Nm) and stake it in place.

MANUAL TRANSMISSION

Transmission Assembly

REMOVAL AND INSTALLATION

1991-94 Legend

1. Disconnect both battery cables.
2. Remove the strut bar.
3. Raise and safely support the vehicle. Drain the transmission.
4. Remove the emission control equipment box from the firewall without disconnecting the vacuum hoses.
5. Disconnect the transmission wiring.
6. Remove the upper transmission mounting bolts.

7. Remove the exhaust pipe and catalytic converter and remove the heatshield.

8. Disconnect the oil cooler hoses.

9. Remove the clutch slave cylinder without disconnecting the hydraulic hose. Shift into low gear and unbolt the shift rod and torque rod.

10. Remove the lower plate and reinstall the mounting bolts.

11. Remove the exhaust pipe bracket and the mount bracket as required.

12. The differential stays on the vehicle. Remove the 36mm sealing bolt and secondary cover and install the extension shaft removal tool. Disconnect the differential extension shaft from the transmission.

13. Remove the flywheel cover.

14. Place a transmission jack securely under the transmission and take the weight off the mounts.

15. Remove the mounts and brackets as required to slide the transmission back away from the engine. Be careful not to lose the shim between the transmission and differential.

To install:

16. Clean and lightly lubricate the release fork contact points with molybdenum grease and install the fork.

17. Install the dowel pins and set the extension shaft in place. Use a

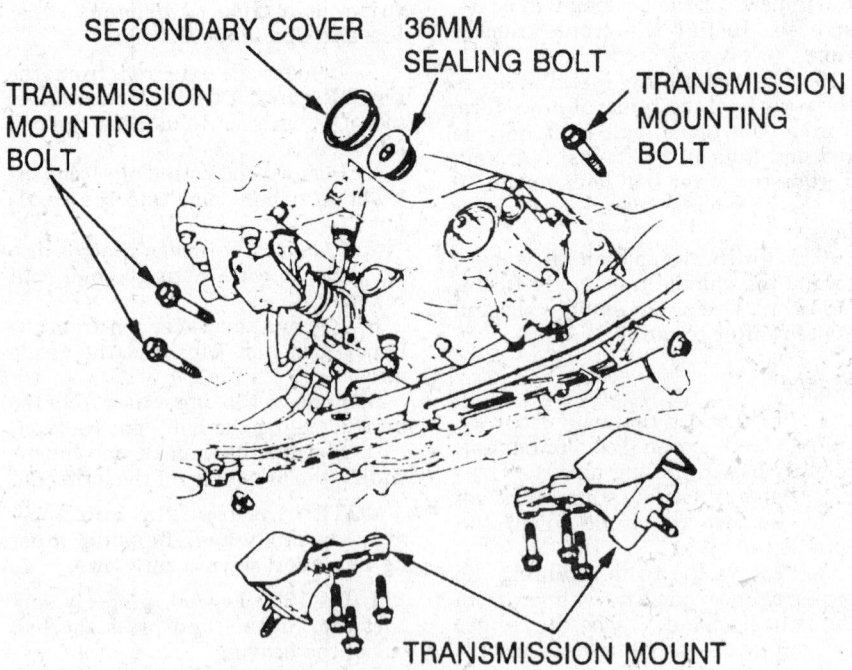

Transmission removal — 1991-94 Legend

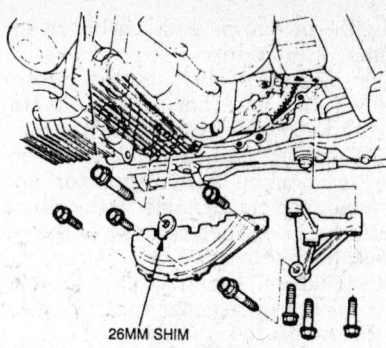

Install the 26mm shim when installing the transmission

new set ring on the shaft and lightly lubricate the splines with molybdenum grease.

18. Install the transmission and start all of the bolts. Don't forget the transmission-to-differential shim. Torque the 12mm bolts to 54 ft. lbs. (75 Nm).

19. Install all of the engine stiffener 8mm bolts, then torque to 16 ft. lbs. (22 Nm).

20. Install the mounts and brackets. Torque the 10mm bolts to 29 ft. lbs. (39 Nm), 10mm nuts to 36 ft. lbs. (49 Nm) and any remaining 12mm bolts to 54 ft. lbs. (75 Nm).

21. With the transmission in gear, install the extension shaft using the special tool. Make sure the shaft snaps into place on the set ring.

22. Pack the shaft area with molybdenum grease, but keep the thread area clean. Apply liquid gasket to the sealing bolt threads and install the bolt and cover.

23. Install the lower plate and torque the bolts to 28 ft. lbs. (39 Nm). These bolts thread into aluminum and must have the special Dacro® coating to avoid corrosion.

24. Install the slave cylinder and connect the shift linkage and torque rod.

25. Connect the oil cooler hoses, if equipped.

26. Install the heatshield and the exhaust pipe and catalytic converter. Use new locking nuts and gaskets. Torque the exhaust flange nuts to 40 ft. lbs. (55 Nm) and the catalyst flange nuts to 26 ft. lbs. (34 Nm).

27. Install the emission control equipment box and the strut bar.

28. Connect all the wiring and the battery cables and refill the transmission oil.

Vigor

1. Disconnect the battery cables and remove the battery and tray.

2. Without disconnecting the wiring, remove the ABS relay box.

3. Without disconnecting the wiring, remove the distributor.

4. Remove the emission control box from the firewall.

5. Disconnect the wiring from the transmission.

6. Without disconnecting the hydraulic line, remove the clutch slave cylinder and secure it out of the way.

7. Remove the upper transmission-to-engine bolts and the 26mm shim.

8. Shift the transmission into a low gear. Raise and safely support the vehicle and remove the transmission mounting beam and bracket.

9. The differential stays on the vehicle. Remove the 36mm sealing bolt and secondary cover and install the extension shaft removal tool. Disconnect the differential extension shaft from the transmission.

10. Remove the front exhaust pipe.

11. Remove the shift linkage extension rod.

12. To disconnect the shift linkage, remove the spring clip between the rubber boot and the linkage joint and push the roll pin out.

13. Support the transmission with a jack and remove the mounts and remaining transmission-to-engine bolts.

14. Carefully move the transmission away from the engine and lower it out of the vehicle.

To install:

15. Lubricate the release bearing, fork and guide with molybdenum grease and make sure the dowel pins are properly placed in the clutch housing.

16. While fitting the transmission to the engine, turn the release lever up and make sure the fork engages the release bearing on the clutch.

17. Make sure the transmission is properly fitted and install the lower

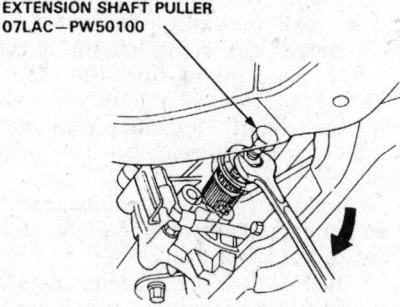

EXTENSION SHAFT PULLER 07LAC—PW50100

Extension shaft puller used — Vigor and 1991-94 Legend

transmission-to-engine bolts. Torque the bolts to 55 ft. lbs. (75 Nm).

18. If the transmission or differential is being replaced, measure the gap between them with a feeler gauge and select the correct 26mm shim.

19. Install the front transmission mounts.

20. Install a new set ring onto the extension shaft and lubricate the shaft with a high temperature molybdenum grease. Install the extension shaft.

21. Pack the shaft area with grease but keep the threads clean. Apply a liquid gasket compound to the threads and install the 33mm sealing bolt. Torque the bolt to 58 ft. lbs. (80 Nm) and install the secondary cover.

22. Connect the shift linkage and the extension rod.

23. Use new gaskets and install the exhaust pipe.

24. Install the rear transmission mount and bracket.

25. Install the 26mm shim and the remaining transmission-to-engine bolts. Torque the shim bolt to 55 ft. lbs. (75 Nm) and the rest to 47 ft. lbs. (65 Nm).

26. Install the remaining components and check the fluid level in the transmission before running the engine.

MANUAL TRANSAXLE

Transaxle Assembly

REMOVAL AND INSTALLATION

Integra

1. Disconnect the negative first and then the positive battery cables.

2. Remove the 4 battery mounting bolts and remove the battery.

3. Remove the air cleaner case complete with air intake tube. Disconnect the transaxle ground cable.

4. Loosen the clutch cable adjusting nut and disconnect the clutch cable at the release arm, then disconnect from the clutch cable bracket.

5. Disconnect the electrical connectors for the backup light switch, oxygen sensor and the starter motor cables and wire harness clamp from the starter.

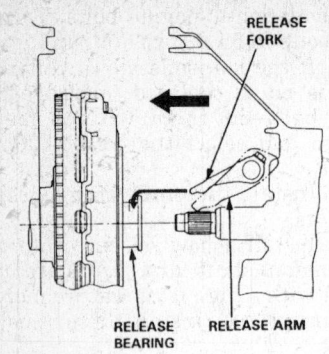

RELEASE FORK

RELEASE BEARING · RELEASE ARM

On Vigor, make sure release fork engages the bearing on the clutch

6. Remove the power steering speed sensor without disconnecting the sensor hose.

7. Disconnect the distributor connectors and remove the distributor mounting bolts. Before removing the distributor, be sure to make some alignment marks on the distributor housing and engine to aid in the installation procedure.

8. Raise and safely support the vehicle. Remove the starter.

9. Drain the transaxle oil into a suitable container.

10. Remove the right front splash shield and splash guard. Remove the center beam bolts and remove the center beam.

11. Remove the cotter pin from the lower right ball joint castle nut, remove the nut and using a ball joint separator, remove the ball joint from the lower arm.

12. Remove the right damper fork. Remove the right radius rod locknut, then the bolts and remove the right radius arm.

13. Remove the right halfshaft assembly.

14. Remove the cotter pin from the lower left ball joint castle nut, remove the nut and using a ball joint separator, remove the ball joint from the lower arm.

15. Remove the left halfshaft from the intermediate shaft. Remove the intermediate shaft bolts and remove the intermediate shaft.

16. Remove the shift rod and shift lever torque rod.

17. Remove the front engine stiffener and the rear engine stiffener. Remove the 4 bolts from the clutch housing cover and remove the cover.

18. Remove the 2 transaxle mount bolts from the engine side.

19. Remove the 2 transaxle mount bolts from the rear engine mount bracket.

20. Remove the side transaxle mount bolt from the underside. Remove the front transaxle mount bolts and mount.

21. Install the bolts into the cylinder head and attach a suitable lifting device or chain hoist to the bolts. Lift the engine slightly to take the load off the engine mounts.

22. Place a suitable transaxle jack under the transaxle and raise it enough to take the weight off of the transaxle mounts. Remove the bolts and nuts that attach the brackets to the side transaxle mounts.

23. Remove the 3 transaxle mount bolts from the transaxle side.

24. Pull the transaxle away from the clutch pressure plate until it clears the mainshaft, then remove the transaxle by lowering the jack.

To install:

25. Install the transaxle on a transaxle jack. Clean and lubricate the clutch release bearing surfaces.

26. Make sure both 14mm dowel pins are installed in the clutch housing.

27. Loosely install the transaxle mount bolts, then torque them to 49 ft. lbs. (68 Nm).

28. Secure the transaxle to the engine with the engine side mounting bolt and torque it to 50 ft. lbs. (68 Nm).

29. Install the transaxle to side transaxle mount. Install the transaxle to the front transaxle mount.

30. Install the transaxle to the rear engine mount bracket.

31. Loosely install the bolt in the front stiffener and then torque then to 17 ft. lbs. (24 Nm).

32. Loosely install the bolt in the rear stiffener and then torque then to 17 ft. lbs. (24 Nm).

33. Remove the transaxle jack. Remove the lifting device by removing the hoist bolts from the cylinder head.

34. Reconnect the shift linkage and torque rod.

35. Install the intermediate shaft.

36. Install the left halfshaft, then the left ball joint and lower arm.

37. Install the right halfshaft assembly. Be sure to turn the right steering knuckle fully outward and slide the axle into the differential until the spring clip engages the side gear.

38. Install the right radius arm, damper fork bolt and the right ball joint to the lower arm.

39. Install the center beam. Install the right front splash guard and splash shield.

40. Install the starter motor. Install the distributor, be sure to use the alignment marks made earlier in the removal procedure.

41. Connect the starter motor cables and wire harness clamp. Install the power steering speed sensor.

42. Connect the oxygen sensor connector, backup light connector and connect the clutch cable to the clutch cable bracket, then connect to the release arm.

43. Connect the transaxle ground. Install the air cleaner case complete with the air intake tube.

44. Install the battery base. Refill the transaxle with the recommended oil.

45. Install the battery and connect the battery cables.

46. Adjust the clutch free-play. Check the ignition timing and road test the vehicle to be sure the transaxle is operating properly.

1990 Legend

1. Disconnect the both battery cables from the battery.

2. Disconnect the starter and ground cables.

3. Disconnect the backup light wires from the engine harness.

4. Loosen the 6mm bolt attaching the harness holder at the side of the transaxle hanger and the release harness from the transaxle.

5. Loosen the 6mm bolts at the side of the battery base and the intake hose band.

6. Remove the air cleaner case assembly along with the intake hose.

7. Remove the 8mm bolts and the clutch slave cylinder with the clutch hose and the pushrod.

NOTE: Do not operate the clutch pedal once the slave cylinder has been removed.

8. Remove the 8mm bolts and clutch damper assembly from the transaxle hanger bracket.

9. Remove the power steering speed sensor without disconnecting the hose.

10. Drain the oil from the transaxle.

11. Remove the halfshafts from the vehicle.

12. Remove the bolts securing the intermediate shaft and remove the shaft.

13. Remove the shift rod and the shift extension.

14. Remove the bolts attaching the torque rod bracket to the clutch case.

NOTE: Replace the torque rod bolts whenever loosened or removed.

15. Place a transaxle jack securely beneath the transaxle.

16. Remove the sub-frame center beam.

17. Attach a support chain with two 10mm bolts to the engine block, 1 on each bank. Lift the engine slightly to take the weight off the mounts.

18. Remove the center stop bracket from the transaxle.

19. Remove the flywheel cover. On vehicles with automatic transaxle, unbolt the torque converter from the flywheel.

20. Remove both rear engine mounting bolts from the transaxle.

21. Remove both front engine mounting bolts from the transaxle housing.

22. Remove the starter mounting bolts and the starter assembly.

23. Remove the remaining transaxle mounting bolts.

24. Pull the transaxle away from the engine until it clears the 14mm dowel pins and lower on the transaxle jack.

To install:

25. Install the transaxle on a transaxle jack; clean and lubricate the clutch release bearing surfaces.

26. Make sure both 14mm dowel pins are installed in the clutch housing.

27. Raise the transaxle high enough to align the dowel pins with the matching holes in the block.

28. Roll the transaxle toward the engine and fit the mainshaft into the clutch disc splines.

29. Install the transaxle mounting bolts and torque to 55 ft. lbs. (75 Nm).

30. Install the starter and torque the mounting bolts.

31. Install the front engine mounting bolts and torque to 29 ft. lbs. (40 Nm).

32. Install the rear engine mounting bolts and torque to 29 ft. lbs. (40 Nm).

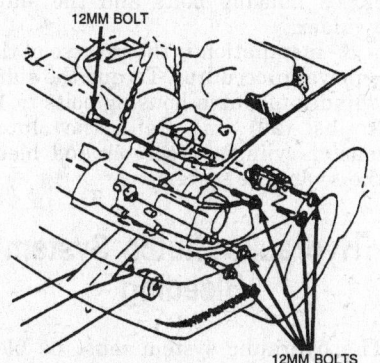

Transaxle removal — 1990 Legend

33. Install the center stopper bracket bolts and torque to 29 ft. lbs. (40 Nm).

34. Install the flywheel cover.

35. Install the center beam and remove the transaxle jack.

36. Install and torque the new torque rod bracket bolts to 29 ft. lbs. (40 Nm).

NOTE: Replace the torque rod bolts whenever loosened or removed.

37. Remove the engine support chain.

38. Connect the shift linkage or cable.

39. Install the intermediate shaft with the 8mm bolts. Torque the bolts to 29 ft. lbs. (40 Nm).

40. Install the right and left halfshaft.

41. Install the speed sensor.

42. Install the clutch slave cylinder with the 8mm bolts complete with the hose and pushrod. Torque the bolts to 16 ft. lbs. (22 Nm) and adjust.

43. Install the clutch damper assembly and the 8mm bolts to the transaxle hanger bracket. Torque the bolts to 16 ft. lbs. (22 Nm).

44. Install the air cleaner assembly and the air intake hose.

45. Install and torque both 6mm bolts at the side of the battery case and tighten the intake hose band.

46. Tighten the 6mm harness holder bolt at the side of the transaxle hanger.

47. Connect the backup light switch wire to the engine harness.

48. Connect the starter and ground cables.

49. Connect the both battery cables.

50. Refill the transaxle with the proper fluid.

51. Check the transaxle for smooth operation.

LINKAGE ADJUSTMENT

Manual shift linkage is not adjustable. If linkage problems are suspected, check the bushings and fastener torque on the shift rod and torque rod.

CLUTCH

All vehicles use a single dry disc with a diaphragm spring pressure plate. On Integra the clutch is cable operated. All other models use a hydraulic clutch release system with a master and slave cylinder.

Clutch Assembly

REMOVAL AND INSTALLATION

All Models

1. Disconnect the negative battery cable. Remove the transmission.

2. On Integra, remove the release shaft retaining bolt and remove the release shaft and release bearing assembly.

3. On the Legend, remove the slave cylinder with the hydraulic hose still connected. Remove the boot from the clutch case and remove the release fork with bearing.

4. Matchmark the flywheel and pressure plate for easy reassembly. Remove the pressure plate-to-flywheel bolts in a crisscross pattern 2 turns at a time to prevent warping the plate.

5. Inspect the flywheel for scoring and wear. Use a dial indicator to make sure it is flat and reface or replace, as necessary.

To install:

6. Reverse the removal procedure and pay attention to the following points:

a. Make sure the flywheel and the end of the crankshaft are clean before assembly. Torque the flywheel-to-crankshaft bolts to 76 ft. lbs. (105 Nm). Torque the bolts in a crisscross pattern.

b. When installing the pressure plate, align the mark on the outer edge of the flywheel with the alignment mark on the pressure plate. Failure to align these marks will result in imbalance.

c. When torquing the pressure plate bolts, use a pilot shaft to center the friction disc. After centering the disc, tighten the bolts 2 turns at a time, in a crisscross pattern to avoid warping the diaphragm springs; torque to 19 ft. lbs. (26 Nm).

d. When installing the transaxle, make sure the mainshaft is properly aligned with the disc spline and the aligning pins are in place, before torquing the case bolts.

PEDAL HEIGHT/FREE-PLAY ADJUSTMENT

Integra

1. Adjust the clutch free-play at the release lever by turning the adjusting nut (at the transaxle). The

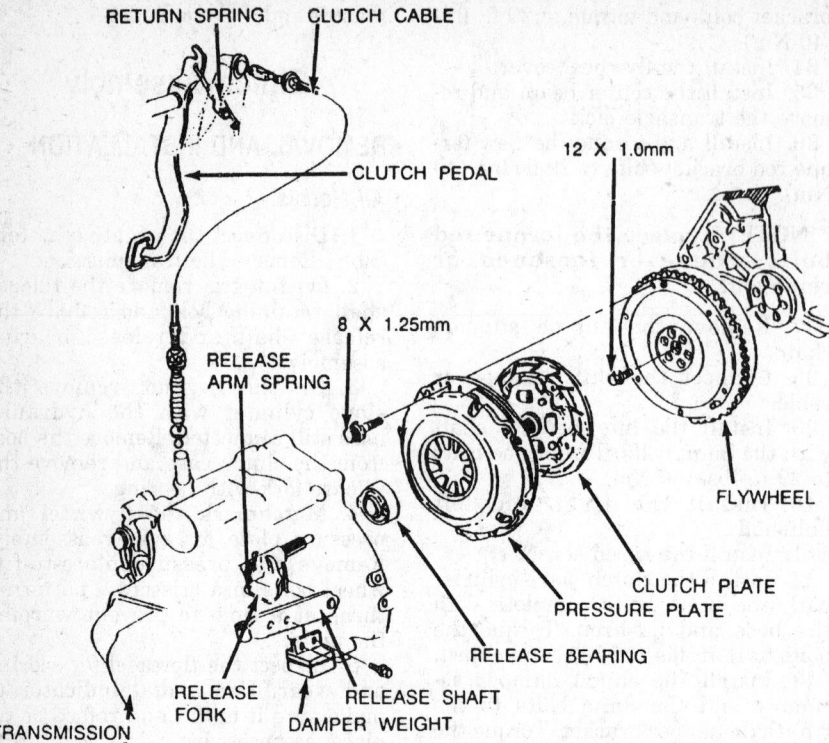

12 X 1.0mm

8 X 1.25mm

RETURN SPRING CLUTCH CABLE

CLUTCH PEDAL

RELEASE
ARM SPRING

RELEASE
FORK

TRANSMISSION

RELEASE SHAFT
DAMPER WEIGHT

RELEASE BEARING

CLUTCH PLATE
PRESSURE PLATE

FLYWHEEL

Clutch assembly, exploded view — Integra shown

clutch pedal height should be 6.97 (177mm)

2. Make sure there is 0.16-0.20 in. (4.0-5.0mm) of free-play at the tip of the release arm after the adjustment.

3. If equipped with cruise control, turn the adjuster (above the clutch pedal) until the clutch pedal stroke is 5.59-5.79 in. (142-147mm)

4. Tighten the locknut securely.

Legend, Vigor

1. Loosen the locknut on the clutch pedal switch and back off the switch until it does not touch the pedal.

2. Loosen the locknut on the clutch master cylinder pushrod. Turn the pushrod in or out to obtain the correct stroke and height at the clutch pedal.

Stroke at pedal — 5.7-5.8 in. (145-148mm)

Clutch pedal free-play — 0.040-0.280 in. (1.0-7.0mm)

3. Tighten the locknut on the clutch master cylinder pushrod.

4. Screw the clutch pedal switch until it contacts the pedal.

5. Turn the switch another ¼-½ turn. Tighten the locknut.

Clutch Cable

ADJUSTMENT

Integra

1. Measure the clutch pedal disengagement height.

2. Measure the clutch pedal free-play.

3. Adjust the clutch pedal free-play by turning the adjusting nut. Be sure there is 0.16-0.20 in. (4.0-5.0mm) free-play at the tip of the release arm after the adjustment.

4. Turn the adjusting nut right or left to bring the clutch pedal stroke to the proper specification and then tighten the locknut to 16 ft. lbs. (22 Nm).

REMOVAL AND INSTALLATION

1. Release the clutch cable from the release arm by loosening the adjusting nut to allow enough slack to enable the cable to be removed from the elongated hole in the release arm.

2. From under the dash panel and behind the clutch pedal, remove the clevis pin that retains the clutch cable to the clutch pedal.

3. Remove the clutch cable holder from the firewall. Push the clutch

cable through the grommet, if equipped, or squeeze the cable retaining clip and push or pull the cable through the firewall to remove it.

To install:

4. Install the cable through the firewall and seat the retaining clip, if equipped.

5. Connect the cable to the pedal.

6. Connect the cable to the release arm and adjust the free-play.

Clutch Master Cylinder

REMOVAL AND INSTALLATION

Vigor and Legend

The clutch master cylinder is located on the firewall in the engine compartment next to the brake master cylinder.

1. From the top of the clutch pedal, remove the cotter pin and pivot pin from the clutch pedal-to-pushrod junction.

2. Disconnect the hydraulic line from the clutch master cylinder. Do not allow brake fluid to contact paint.

3. Remove the master cylinder-to-firewall nuts and the master cylinder.

4. Disconnect the reservoir hose from the master cylinder.

5. Installation is the reverse of the removal procedures. Torque the master cylinder-to-firewall nuts to 16 ft. lbs. (22 Nm). Refill the clutch master cylinder reservoir and bleed the system.

Clutch Slave Cylinder

REMOVAL AND INSTALLATION

Vigor and Legend

1. Disconnect and plug the hydraulic line at the slave cylinder.

2. Remove the slave cylinder-to-clutch housing bolts and the slave cylinder.

3. Installation is the reverse of the removal procedures. Torque the slave cylinder-to-clutch housing bolts to 16 ft. lbs. (22 Nm). Refill the clutch master cylinder reservoir and bleed the hydraulic system.

Hydraulic Clutch System Bleeding

The hydraulic system must be bled whenever the system has been leaking or has been dismantled. The

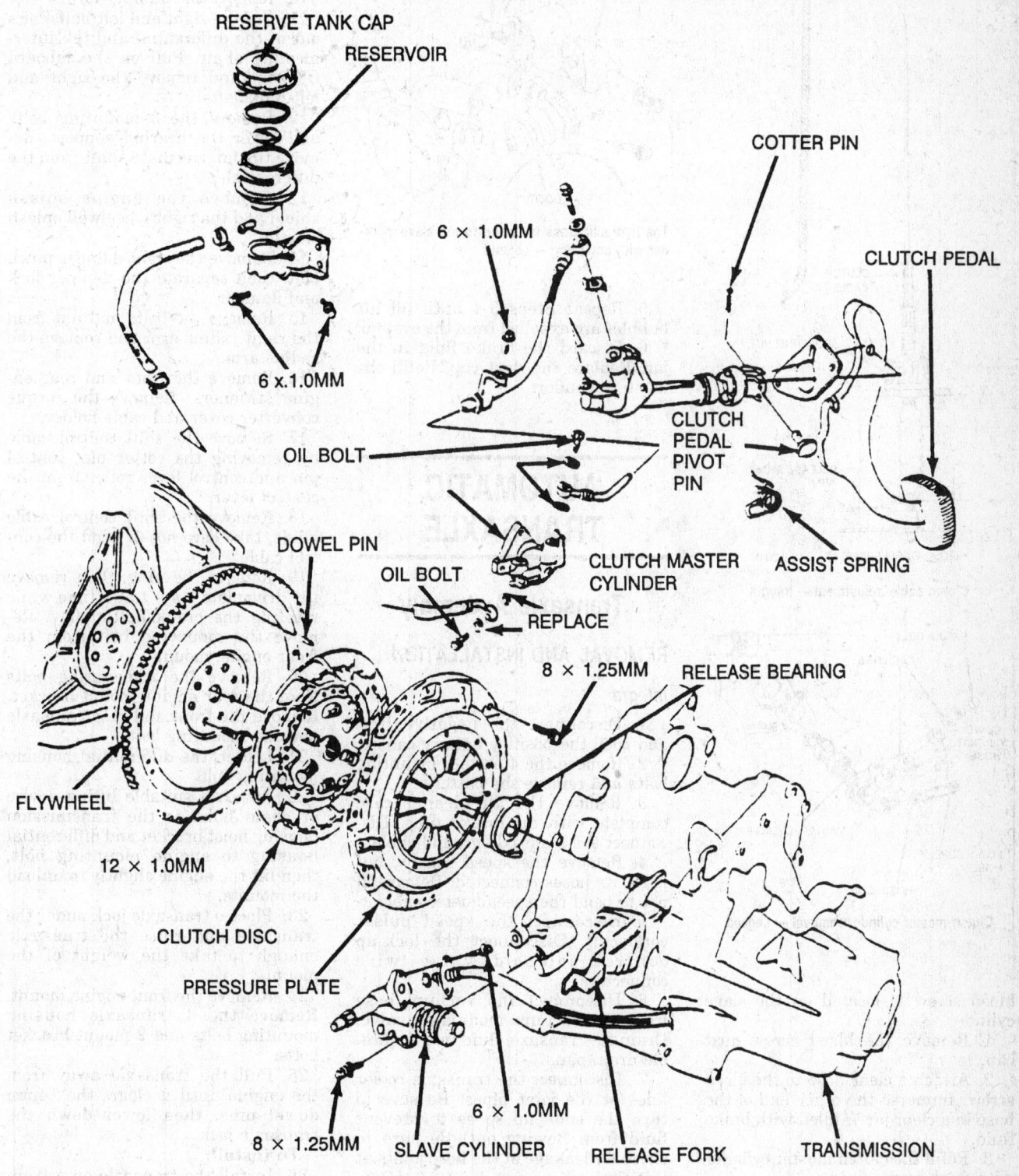

RESERVE TANK CAP

RESERVOIR

COTTER PIN

CLUTCH PEDAL

6 × 1.0MM

6 x.1.0MM

OIL BOLT

CLUTCH
PEDAL
PIVOT
PIN

CLUTCH MASTER
CYLINDER

ASSIST SPRING

DOWEL PIN

OIL BOLT

REPLACE

8 × 1.25MM

RELEASE BEARING

FLYWHEEL

12 × 1.0MM

CLUTCH DISC

PRESSURE PLATE

8 × 1.25MM

SLAVE CYLINDER

6 × 1.0MM

RELEASE FORK

TRANSMISSION

Clutch assembly, exploded view — Legend

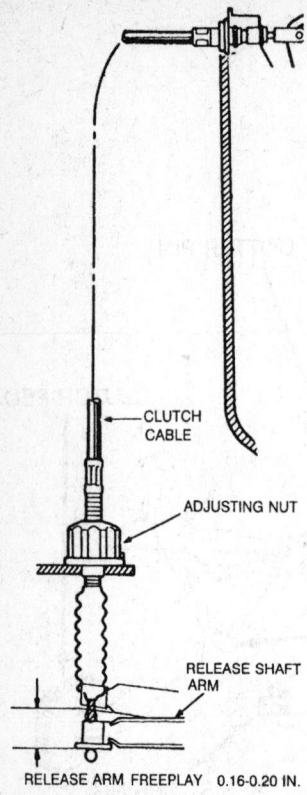

Clutch cable adjustment — Integra

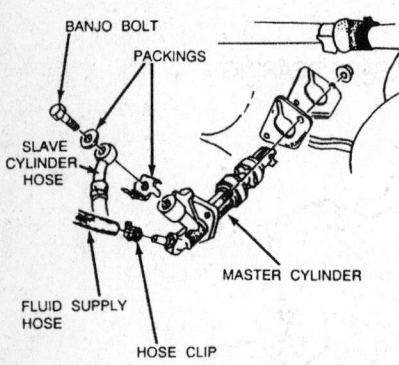

Clutch master cylinder removal — Legend

bleed screw is located on the slave cylinder.

1. Remove the bleed screw dust cap.

2. Attach a clear hose to the bleed screw. Immerse the other end of the hose in a clear jar ½ filled with brake fluid.

3. Refill the clutch master cylinder with fresh brake fluid.

4. Open the bleed screw slightly and have an assistant slowly depress the clutch pedal. Close the bleed screw when the pedal reaches the end of its travel. Allow the clutch pedal to return slowly.

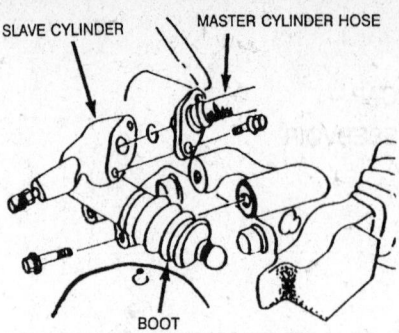

The hydraulic hose is sealed to the slave cylinder with an O-ring — Legend

5. Repeat Steps 3-4 until all air bubbles are expelled from the system.

6. Discard the brake fluid in the jar. Replace the dust cap. Refill the master cylinder.

AUTOMATIC TRANSAXLE

Transaxle Assembly

REMOVAL AND INSTALLATION

Integra

1. Disconnect the negative first and then the positive battery cables.

2. Remove the 4 battery mounting bolts and remove the battery.

3. Remove the air cleaner case complete with air intake tube. Disconnect the transaxle ground cable.

4. Remove the speed sensor, but leave its hoses connected. Be careful not to bend the speedometer cable.

5. Disconnect the speed pulser connector. Disconnect the lock-up control solenoid valve wire connectors.

6. Disconnect the vacuum hose from the vacuum modulator valve. Drain the transaxle fluid into a suitable drain pan.

7. Disconnect the transaxle cooler lines at the joint pipes. Be sure to turn the ends up so as to prevent fluid from flowing out. Be sure to check for leakage at the hose joints at this time.

8. Remove the center beam. Remove the header pipe.

9. Remove the cotter pins from the lower ball joint castle nuts and remove the lower ball joints nuts. Separate the ball joints from the lower

arms with a suitable ball joint separator tool.

10. Remove the damper fork.

11. Pry the right and left halfshafts out of the differential and the intermediate shaft. Pull on the inboard CV-joint and remove the right and left halfshafts.

12. Remove the 3 mounting bolts and lower the bearing support. Remove the intermediate shaft from the differential.

13. Remove the engine splash shield and the right wheelwell splash shield.

14. Remove the right damper pinch bolt, then separate the damper fork and damper.

15. Remove the bolts and nut from the right radius arm and remove the radius arm.

16. Remove the front and rear engine stiffeners. Remove the torque converter cover and cable holder.

17. Remove the shift control cable by removing the cotter pin, control pin and control lever roller from the control lever.

18. Remove the shift control cable guide, take care not to bend the control cable.

19. Remove the plug, then remove the driveplate bolts 1 at a time while rotating the crankshaft pulley. Remove the mounting bolt from the front engine mount.

20. Remove the 2 mounting bolts from the rear engine mount bracket. Remove the front and rear transaxle housing mounting bolt.

21. Loosen the differential housing mounting bolt.

22. Attach a suitable lifting device or chain hoist to the transmission housing hoist bracket and differential housing to engine mounting bolt, then lift the engine slightly to unload the mounts.

23. Place a transaxle jack under the transaxle and raise the transaxle enough to take the weight of the mounts.

24. Remove the front engine mount. Remove the 4 transaxle housing mounting bolts and 2 mount bracket bolts.

25. Pull the transaxle away from the engine until it clears the 14mm dowel pins, then lower down the transaxle jack.

To install:

26. Install the transaxle on a transaxle jack.

27. Make sure both 14mm dowel pins are installed in the torque converter housing.

28. Raise the transaxle high enough to align the dowel pins with

the matching holes in the block. Align the torque converter match-mark and the bolt heads with holes in the driveplate.

29. Install the 4 transaxle housing mounting bolts, then install the transaxle to the engine block.

30. Install the front engine mount to the front beam. Install the transaxle to the front engine mount.

31. Install the transaxle to the transaxle mount bracket. Remove the transaxle jack.

32. Install the 2 transaxle housing mounting bolts engine side and rear engine mount bracket bolts.

33. Attach the torque converter to driveplate with 8 (6 **x** 1 **x** 12mm) bolts and torque to 9 ft. lbs. (12 Nm). Rotate the crankshaft, as necessary, to tighten the bolts half torque, then the final torque in a crisscross pattern. Check for free rotation after tightening the last bolt.

34. Install the shift control cable and cable guide. Take care not to bend the control cable. Install the torque converter cover and engine stiffeners. Install all engine stiffener mounting bolts finger-tight, then tighten.

35. Remove the lifting device by removing the hanger plates.

36. Install the radius arm. Be sure to check for deterioration of the radius rod rubber bushings.

37. Install the intermediate shaft. Install a new set ring on the end of each halfshaft.

38. Install the right and left half-shafts. Be sure to turn the right and left steering knuckle fully outward and slide the axle into the differential until the spring clip engages in the side gear.

39. Install the damper fork. Install the splash shield.

40. Install the damper fork bolts and the ball joint nuts to the lower arms.

41. Install the header pipe and center beam.

42. Install the speed sensor and connect the speed pulser connector.

43. Connect the lockup control solenoid valve wire connectors. Connect the transaxle oil cooler lines to the joint pipes.

44. Connect the vacuum hose to the modulator. Install the transaxle ground cable.

45. Refill the transaxle with the proper transaxle fluid.

46. Connect the battery cables. Install the air intake hose.

47. Start the engine, set the parking brake and shift the transaxle through all gears 3 times. Check for proper control cable adjustment. Check the ignition timing.

48. Allow the engine to reach operating temperature with the transaxle in **N** or **P**, then turn it OFF and check the fluid level.

49. Road test the vehicle and make sure the transaxle is operating properly.

1990 Legend

1. Disconnect the negative and positive battery cables from the battery.

2. Disconnect the starter motor and ground cables.

3. Drain the transaxle fluid from the transaxle.

4. Remove both 6mm bolts located at the side of the battery base and the intake hose band at the throttle body.

5. Remove the air cleaner assembly along with the intake hose.

6. Remove the speedometer transmission complete with the power steering speed sensor hose.

7. Disconnect the throttle control cable from the transaxle housing.

8. Disconnect and plug the transaxle cooler hoses at the joint pipes; turn the ends up to prevent the transaxle fluid from flowing out.

9. Near the oil cooler pipe bracket, disconnect the lockup control solenoid valve wire connector and the automatic speed pulser wire connector for 1990 Legend.

10. Remove the center console, pry off the adjuster pin and disconnect the control cable.

11. Remove the control cable guide bolts and pull out the cable assembly; be careful not to bend the cable when removing it.

12. Remove both halfshafts and the intermediate shaft.

13. Remove the torque converter case mounting bolts from the torque rod bracket.

14. Attach a chain hoist to the engine at 2 points with bolts and raise

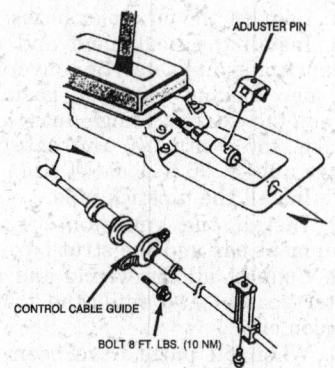

Shift control cable removal — 1990 Legend

the engine slightly to unload the mounts.

15. Remove the front engine mount bolts from the transaxle housing.

16. While holding the locknut, turn off the radius rod.

17. Remove the center beam.

18. Remove the center stopper bracket from the transaxle.

19. Remove the torque converter cover.

20. Place a transaxle jack under the transaxle and raise the transaxle just enough to take the weight off the mounts.

21. Remove both rear engine mount bolts from the transaxle.

22. Matchmark the torque converter-to-driveplate. Remove the plug and the driveplate bolts one at a time while rotating the crankshaft pulley.

23. Remove the starter-to-engine bolts and the starter.

24. Remove the remaining transaxle housing-to-engine bolts.

25. Pull the transaxle away from the engine and lower it from the vehicle.

To install:

26. Install the transaxle on a transaxle jack and raise to engine level.

27. Secure the transaxle to the engine with the mounting bolts.

28. Install the starter motor.

29. Align the matchmarks and install the torque converter-to-driveplate bolts; torque the bolts in 2 steps in a crisscross pattern to 9 ft. lbs. (12 Nm). Check for free rotation after torquing the last bolt.

30. Install the transaxle to the front engine mount bracket bolts and torque to 29 ft. lbs. (39 Nm).

31. Install the torque converter cover.

32. Install the center stopper bracket to the transaxle.

33. Install the center beam.

34. Connect the radius rod.

35. Remove the chain hoist from the engine.

36. Install the torque rod bracket and torque the bolts to 29 ft. lbs. (40 Nm).

NOTE: Always replace the torque rod bolts with new ones whenever they have been loosened or removed.

37. Remove the transaxle jack.

38. Connect the intermediate shaft, then install the right and left halfshafts.

39. Route the control cables to the center console through the cable guide and secure with the bolt; be careful not to bend the cables.

40. Connect the control cable with the lock pin and reinstall the center console.

41. Connect the lockup control solenoid valve wire connectors.

42. Connect the cooler hoses to the joint pipes.

43. Connect the control cable on the throttle body side.

44. Install the speedometer gearbox.

45. Install the air cleaner assembly and the air intake hose.

46. Install the battery base bolts and tighten the intake hose band on the throttle body.

47. Refill the transaxle with ATF.

48. Connect the starter and ground cables.

49. Connect the battery cables.

50. Start the engine, set the parking brake, then shift the transaxle through all gears 3 times. Check for proper control cable adjustment.

51. Allow the engine reach operating temperature with the transaxle in **N** or **P**, then turn it **OFF** and check the fluid level. Road test the vehicle.

1991-94 Legend

1. Disconnect both battery cables.

2. Remove the strut bar.

3. Drain the transmission.

4. Remove the emission control equipment box from the firewall without disconnecting the vacuum hoses.

5. Disconnect the transmission wiring and the dipstick pipe.

6. Remove the upper transmission mounting bolts.

7. Remove the exhaust pipe and catalytic converter and remove the heatshield.

8. Disconnect the oil cooler hoses.

9. Shift the transmission into **P**. Remove the center console and remove the lock pin to separate the shift cable from the selector lever. The lock pin is to the rear of the selector lever.

10. Remove the lower plate and reinstall the mounting bolts.

11. Remove the exhaust pipe bracket and the mount bracket as required.

12. The differential stays on the vehicle. Remove the secondary cover and the 36mm sealing bolt and install the extension shaft removal tool. Disconnect the differential extension shaft from the transmission.

13. Remove the torque converter cover and unbolt the torque converter from the flywheel. Turn the engine as required.

14. Place a transmission jack securely under the transmission and take the weight off the mounts.

15. Remove the mounts and brackets as required to slide the transmission back away from the engine. Be careful not to lose the shim between the transmission and differential.

To install:

16. Install the dowel pins and set the extension shaft in place. Use a new set ring on the shaft and lightly lubricate the splines with molybdenum grease. Make sure the secondary spring is in the differential side of the extension shaft.

17. Install the transmission and start all of the bolts. Don't forget the transmission-to-differential shim. Torque the 12mm bolts to 54 ft. lbs. (75 Nm).

18. Install all of the engine stiffener 8mm bolts, then torque to 16 ft. lbs. (22 Nm).

19. Install the mounts and brackets. Torque the 10mm bolts to 29 ft. lbs. (39 Nm), 10mm nuts to 36 ft. lbs. (49 Nm), and any remaining 12mm bolts to 54 ft. lbs. (75 Nm).

20. With the transmission in **P**, install the extension shaft using the special tool. Make sure the shaft snaps into place on the set ring.

21. Pack the shaft area with molybdenum grease, but keep the thread area clean. Apply liquid gasket to the sealing bolt threads and install the bolt and cover.

22. Install the torque converter-to-flywheel bolts and torque them in 2 steps in a crisscross pattern to 9 ft. lbs. (12 Nm). Install the torque converter cover.

23. Install the lower plate and torque the bolts to 28 ft. lbs. (39 Nm). These bolts thread into aluminum and must have the special Dacro® coating to avoid corrosion.

24. Connect the shift cable and install the holder and console cover. Make sure the selector lever moves easily.

25. Connect the oil cooler hoses.

26. Install the heatshield and the exhaust pipe and catalytic converter. Use new locking nuts and gaskets. Torque the exhaust flange nuts to 40 ft. lbs. (55 Nm) and the catalyst flange nuts to 26 ft. lbs. (34 Nm).

27. Install the dipstick pipe.

28. Install the emission control equipment box and the strut bar.

29. Connect all the wiring and the battery cables and refill the transmission oil.

30. When all parts have been installed, start the engine and shift through all the gears 3 times to fill all the passages with fluid and check the shift cable adjustment. When the engine is fully warmed up, stop the engine and check the fluid level.

31. Check the ignition timing.

Vigor

1. Make sure the transmission is in **P** Disconnect both battery cables and remove the battery and tray.

2. Without disconnecting the wires, remove the ABS relay box and set it aside.

3. Remove the distributor.

4. Remove the emission control equipment box from the firewall without disconnecting the vacuum hoses.

5. Remove the small torque converter cover and rotate the crankshaft as required to remove the 8 torque converter-to-driveplate bolts.

6. Disconnect the transmission wiring and the dipstick pipe.

7. Remove the upper transmission-to-engine bolts.

8. Remove the guard plate and remove the plug to drain the transmission fluid.

9. Disconnect the oil cooler hoses.

10. The differential stays on the vehicle. Remove the secondary cover and the 36mm sealing bolt and install the extension shaft removal tool. Disconnect the differential extension shaft from the transmission.

11. Remove the front exhaust pipe and the brackets as required.

12. Disconnect the shift cable from the transmission and remove the bracket and cable.

13. Place a transmission jack securely under the transmission and take the weight off the mounts.

14. Remove the mounts and the remaining transmission-to-engine bolts to slide the transmission back away from the engine. Do not remove the flywheel cover from the engine.

To install:

15. Install the dowel pins and set the extension shaft in place. Use a new set ring on the shaft, lightly lubricate the splines with molybdenum grease and pack the opening in the drive pinion with grease.

16. Install the transmission and start all of the bolts. Don't forget the transmission-to-differential shim. Torque the 12mm bolts to 54 ft. lbs. (75 Nm).

17. Install the mounts and brackets. Torque the bolts to 29 ft. lbs. (39 Nm) and the nuts to 32 ft. lbs. (44 Nm).

18. With the transmission in **P**, install the extension shaft using the

special tool. Make sure the shaft snaps into place on the set ring.

19. Pack the shaft area with molybdenum grease, but keep the thread area clean. Apply liquid gasket to the sealing bolt threads and torque the bolt to 58 ft. lbs. (80 Nm). Install the cover.

20. Install the rear mount and torque the bolts to 47 ft. lbs. (65 Nm).

21. Install the torque converter-to-flywheel bolts and torque them in 2 steps in a crisscross pattern to 9 ft. lbs. (12 Nm). Install the torque converter cover.

22. Connect the shift cable and wiring and make sure the selector lever moves easily.

23. Connect the oil cooler hoses.

24. Use new gaskets and install the exhaust pipe.

25. Install the dipstick pipe.

26. Install the emission control equipment box, the distributor and the ABS relay box.

27. Connect all the wiring and the battery cables and refill the transmission oil.

28. When all parts have been installed, start the engine and shift through all the gears 3 times to fill all the passages with fluid and check the shift cable adjustment. When the engine is fully warmed up, stop the engine and check the fluid level.

29. Check the ignition timing.

SHIFT LINKAGE ADJUSTMENT

All Models

1. Start the engine and shift into **R**. If the transaxle goes into gear, no adjustment is required.

2. If adjustment is required, stop the engine and remove the center console as required to access the cable lock pin. On Vigor and 1991-94 Legend, it is to the rear of the shift lever. On all other models it is in front of the lever.

3. Shift the transaxle into:
Integra — **N** or **R**
Legend
    1990 — **R**
    1991-94 — **N** or **R**
Vigor — **N**

4. Remove the locking pin from the cable and check the alignment of the hole in the adjuster with the hole in the cable end.

5. Loosen the locknut and turn the adjuster as required to align the holes perfectly. Install the lock pin and test again.

THROTTLE CABLE ADJUSTMENT

1. Perform the following checks:
    a. Make sure the throttle cable free-play is correct; it should be 0.39-0.47 in. (10-12mm).
    b. The engine is operating at normal operating temperatures; the cooling fan turns **ON**.
    c. The idle speed is correct.

2. While working the throttle cable by hand, remove the cable free-play.

3. Apply light thumb pressure to the throttle control lever and work the accelerator or throttle linkage; the lever should move as the engine speed increases above idle, if not, adjust the cable.

4. Loosen the control cable nuts at the transaxle, synchronize the control lever to the throttle and tighten the locknuts.

NOTE: To tailor the shift/lockup characteristics to the driving expectations, adjust the control cable up 0.12 in. (3mm) shorter than the synchronized point.

FRONT SUSPENSION

Shock Absorbers

REMOVAL AND INSTALLATION

Integra

1. Raise and safely support the vehicle and remove the front wheels.

2. Remove the damper pinch bolt.

3. Remove the fork bolt and disengage the fork.

4. Remove the upper mounting nuts and remove the damper unit. Mark the dampers left and right so they will not be installed wrong.

5. Installation is the reverse of removal. Use a new self locking nut on the fork bolt and torque to 47 ft. lbs. (65 Nm). Torque the upper mounting nuts to 29 ft. lbs. (40 Nm) and the pinch bolt to 32 ft. lbs. 44 Nm).

Vigor and Legend

1. Raise and safely support the vehicle and remove the front wheels.

2. Remove the brake hose clamps from the damper.

3. Remove the pinch bolt.

4. Remove the fork bolt and remove the fork.

LOCK PIN

LOCKNUT

ADJUSTER

SHIFT CABLE

Automatic transaxle shift cable adjustment: align the lock pin holes

5. Remove the upper mounting nuts and remove the damper. Mark the left and right sides so they will not be installed wrong.

To install:

6. Install the damper with the fork alignment tab facing out and loosely install the upper mount nuts.

7. Install the fork on the lower arm and the damper and loosely install the pinch bolt and fork bolt.

8. Place a floor jack under the lower ball joint and raise it just till the vehicle raises off the jack stand.

9. Torque the fork bolt to 47 ft. lbs. (65 Nm), the pinch bolt to 32 ft. lbs. (44 Nm) and the upper mount nuts to 28 ft. lbs. (39 Nm).

Coil Springs

REMOVAL AND INSTALLATION

1. Remove the damper unit and make a note of the spring seat and bracket positions for reassembly.

2. Install the damper into a spring compressor and tighten the compressor according to manufacturer's instructions.

3. Remove the locking nut from the top of the shock absorber and disassemble the damper and spring as required.

4. Installation is the reverse of removal. Be sure to properly position the spring seat and brackets.

Ball Joints

INSPECTION

Check ball joint play as follows:

1. Raise and safely support the vehicle.

2. Clamp a dial indicator onto the lower control arm and place the indicator tip on the knuckle, near the ball joint.

3. Place a prybar between the lower control arm and the knuckle. Replace the lower control arm if the play exceeds 0.020 in. (0.5mm).

REMOVAL AND INSTALLATION

Integra

1. Raise and support the vehicle safely. Remove the front wheel assemblies. Remove the steering knuckle.

2. Remove the boot by prying off the snapring. Remove the 40mm clip.

3. Install the special ball joint removal/installation tool 07965-SB00100 or equivalent, on the ball joint and tighten the ball joint nut.

4. Position the ball joint in this special tool and set this assembly in a vise. Press the ball joint out of the steering knuckle.

To install:

5. Place the ball joint in position by hand. Install the ball joint into the special tool and press in the new ball joint in the vise.

6. Install the 40mm circlip. Adjust the special tool with he adjusting bolt until the end of the tool aligns with the groove on the boot. Slide the clip over the tool and into position.

Vigor and Legend

NOTE: This procedure requires the use of a ball joint removal base (07GAF-SD40330), a ball joint installation base (07GAF-SD40320) and a clip guide (07GAG-SD40700) or their equivalent.

1. Raise and support the vehicle safely. Remove the front wheel assemblies. Remove the steering knuckle from the vehicle.

2. Position the ball joint removal tool base or equivalent, on the ball joint, position the assembly in a shop press and press the ball joint from the steering knuckle.

To install:

3. Position the new ball joint into the hole of the steering knuckle.

4. Install the ball joint installer tool or equivalent, with the small end facing outward.

5. Position the ball joint installation base tool or equivalent, on the ball joint, position the assembly in a shop press and press the ball joint into the steering knuckle.

6. Seat the snapring in the groove of the ball joint.

7. Install the boot and snapring using the clip guide tool.

Upper Control Arm

REMOVAL and INSTALLATION

Vigor and Legend

1. Raise and safely support the vehicle. Remove the front wheel.

2. Remove the cotter pin and the upper control arm-to-steering knuckle nut.

3. Using a ball joint removal tool or equivalent, separate the upper control arm from the steering knuckle.

4. Remove the upper control arm-to-chassis nuts, washers and the upper control arm from the vehicle.

To install:

5. Reverse the removal procedures. Torque the upper control arm-to-chassis nuts to 47 ft. lbs. (65 Nm) and the upper control arm ball joint-to-steering knuckle nut to 32 ft. lbs. (42 Nm).

Lower Control Arm

REMOVAL and INSTALLATION

Vigor and Legend

1. Raise and safely support the vehicle. Remove the front wheels.

2. Remove the lower damper fork bolt.

3. Disconnect the stabilizer bar from the arm.

4. Remove the lower arm ball joint-to-steering knuckle nut. Using a ball joint removal tool, separate the ball joint from the steering knuckle.

5. Disconnect the radius rod from the lower control arm and remove the arm.

To install:

6. Reverse the removal procedure. Torque the radius rod-to-control arm bolts to 76 ft. lbs. (105 Nm) and the chassis bolt to 39 ft. lbs. (55 Nm).

7. On 1990 Legend, torque ball joint nut to 72 ft. lbs. (100 Nm) and tighten as required to insert a new cotter pin.

8. On 1991-94 Legend, torque the ball joint nut to 54 ft. lbs. (75 Nm) and tighten as required to insert a new cotter pin.

9. On Vigor, torque the lower ball joint nut to 36 ft. lbs. (50 Nm) and tighten as required to install a new cotter pin.

Front Wheel Bearings

For information on the front wheel bearings, please refer to "Drive Axle" section.

REAR SUSPENSION

Shock Absorber

REMOVAL and INSTALLATION

Integra

1. Raise and safely support the vehicle and remove the rear wheels.
2. Remove the upper shock mount cover from the rear panel, just below the speaker.
3. Remove the upper mount nuts.
4. Remove the lower mount bolt and remove the damper assembly (shock and spring) as a unit.
5. Use a spring compressor to remove the spring from the shock absorber.
6. Installation is the reverse of the removal procedure. Torque the upper mount nuts to 29 ft. lbs. (40 Nm). Torque the lower mounting bolt with the weight of the vehicle on the wheels to 40 ft. lbs. (55 Nm).

1990 Legend

1. Raise and safely support the rear of the vehicle.
2. Remove the rear wheels.
3. Place a jack under the lower arm and raise slightly.
4. Remove the 8mm nuts from the top of the assembly.
5. Lower the jack.
6. Remove the lower shock pinch bolt.
7. Remove the shock absorber from the hub assembly.
8. Installation is the reverse of the removal procedure. Torque the upper 8mm bolts to 16 ft. lbs. (22 Nm) and the lower pinch bolt to 47 ft. lbs. (65 Nm).

Vigor and Legend

1. Raise and safely support the vehicle and remove the rear wheels.
2. Remove the rear speaker and the damper assembly cap.
3. Place a floor jack under the lower arm and slightly compress the spring.
4. Remove the upper mounting nuts and the lower mounting bolt.
5. Lower the jack to remove the damper unit.
6. Use a spring compressor to remove the spring from the shock absorber.
7. Installation is the reverse of the removal procedure. Loosely install the mounting nuts and bolt and lower

the vehicle onto the wheels to torque them. Torque the upper mounting nuts to 28 ft. lbs. (39 Nm) and the lower mounting bolt to 40 ft. lbs. (55 Nm) on Vigor or 76 ft. lbs. (105 Nm) on Legend.

Coil Springs

REMOVAL and INSTALLATION

1990 Legend

1. Raise and safely support the rear of the vehicle.
2. Place a floor jack under the lower arm.
3. Pull out the hub carrier lower bolt.
4. Loosen the lower arm outside bolt.
5. Pull out the lower arm inside bolt.
6. Lower the jack gradually and remove the rear spring.
7. Installation is the reverse of the removal procedure. Install the rear spring with the lower end of the spring outside.
8. Torque the lower arm-to-hub carrier nut/bolt to 54 ft. lbs. (75 Nm), with the weight of the vehicle on the ground.

Rear Wheel Hub Carrier and Bearing

REMOVAL and INSTALLATION

Integra

1. Raise and safely support the vehicle and remove the rear wheels.
2. Remove the brake caliper without disconnecting the hydraulic hose. Support the caliper so it does not hang by the hose.
3. Remove the brake disc.
4. Remove the hub cap and the nut and washer. The torque on the nut is very high, make sure the vehicle is firmly supported and will not fall.
5. Remove the hub/bearing unit from the spindle. The bearing is a sealed unit pressed into the hub.
6. Installation is the reverse of the removal procedure. Torque the hub nut to 134 ft. lbs. (185 Nm) and the caliper mounting bolts to 17 ft. lbs. (23 Nm).

1990 Legend

1. Raise and safely support the vehicle and remove the rear wheels.

2. Remove the caliper without disconnecting the hydraulic hose. Support the caliper so it does not hang by the hose.
3. Remove the disc by pressing it off with a pair of 8mm bolts threaded into the holes between the studs. Turn each bolt 2 turns at a time.
4. Place a floor jack under the lower arm and compress the spring slightly.
5. Remove the hub carrier lower bolt and separate the carrier from the lower arm.
6. Remove the damper assembly pinch bolt and slowly lower the floor jack to remove the hub carrier.
7. To remove the hub and bearing, remove the hub cap from the rear of the carrier and remove the nut. The torque on the nut is very high. Properly secure the hub in a holding fixture and be careful to not damage the hub studs when removing the nut.
8. The hub must be pressed out of the carrier. Be careful not to damage the spindle threads.
9. Remove the splash guard and the 68mm circlip.
10. Press the bearing out towards the outside of the carrier.
11. The inner race may stay with the hub. It can be removed with a bearing puller.
   To install:
12. Press a new bearing into the carrier. Make sure to press only on the outer race or the bearing will be destroyed.
13. Install the circlip and the splash shield.
14. Press the hub into the carrier. Make sure to support the inner race or the bearing will be destroyed.
15. Properly secure the hub in a holding fixture and install the spindle washer and nut. Torque the nut to 180 ft. lbs. (250 Nm). Install the O-ring and cap.
16. Install the carrier in the reverse order of removal. Torque the caliper bolts to 28 ft. lbs. (39 Nm), the lower bolt to 40 ft. lbs. (55 Nm) and the damper pinch bolt to 47 ft. lbs. (65 Nm).

Vigor and 1991-94 Legend

——————— **WARNING** ———————
The spindle nut torque is very high. Tighten or loosen the spindle nut only with the vehicle on the ground. Attempting to loosen or torque the spindle nut while the vehicle is on jackstands or a lift may cause the vehicle to fall.

1. With the vehicle on the ground, remove the hub cap and pry the spin-

dle nut lock tab away from the spindle. Loosen the nut.

2. Raise and safely support the vehicle and remove the rear wheels.

3. Remove the caliper without disconnecting the hydraulic hose. Support the caliper so it does not hang by the hose.

4. Remove the disc by pressing it off with a pair of 8mm bolts threaded into the holes between the studs. Turn each bolt 2 turns at a time.

5. Remove the spindle nut and remove the hub/bearing unit from the knuckle. The bearing is a sealed unit pressed into the hub.

6. Installation is the reverse of the removal procedure. Torque the caliper bolts to 28 ft. lbs. (39 Nm). With the vehicle on the ground, torque the spindle nut to 206 ft. lbs. (285 Nm) and stake the nut to the spindle.

STEERING

─── CAUTION ───

Some vehicles are equipped with a driver side air bag. To avoid accidental deployment and serious personal injury, the system must be disarmed before beginning any repair procedure. Review all safety precautions and disarming procedure under the Air Bag section.

Steering Wheel

REMOVAL and INSTALLATION

WITHOUT AIR BAG

1. Place the steering wheel in the straight-ahead position.

2. Disconnect the negative battery cable. Lift off the steering wheel pad.

3. Remove the steering wheel retaining nut and the horn pad.

4. If equipped with cruise control, remove or disconnect the cruise control set/resume switch.

5. Gently rock the steering wheel from side to side. Gently hit the back side of each of the steering wheel spokes with equal force from the palms of your hands. Pull the steering wheel off the shaft. Avoid hitting the wheel or the shaft with excessive force or the shaft will be damaged.

6. Installation is the reverse of the removal procedure. Torque the steering wheel nut to 36 ft. lbs. (50 Nm).

WITH AIR BAG

─── CAUTION ───

On vehicles equipped with an air bag, the negative battery cable must be disconnected before beginning work. Failure to do so may result in deployment of the air bag and possible injury.

1. Disconnect both the negative and positive battery cable from the battery.

2. Remove the lower maintenance lid below the air bag and then remove the short connector.

3. Disconnect the connector between the air bag and the cable reel.

4. Connect the short connector to the air bag side of the connector.

5. Remove the left side maintenance lid and the cruise control/set resume switch cover.

6. Insert a T30 Torx® bit and remove the Torx® bolts. Remove the air bag assembly.

NOTE: Be sure to store the air bag in a safe place with the pad side facing upwards.

7. Remove the steering wheel retaining nut. Gently hit the backside of each of the steering wheel spokes with equal force from the palms of the hands. Avoid hitting the wheel or the shaft with excessive force or the shaft will be damaged.

To install:

8. Before installing the steering wheel, the front wheels should be aligned straight forward.

9. Center the cable reel by rotating the cable reel clockwise until it stops. Then rotate it counterclockwise (approximately 2 turns) until the yellow gear tooth lines up with the mark on the cover. The arrow on the cable reel label points straight up.

10. Make sure the wires are not pinched or interfering with other parts when installing the wheel. Install the steering wheel and torque the nut to 36 ft. lbs. (50 Nm).

11. After reassembly confirm that the wheels are still straight ahead and that the steering wheel spoke angle is correct. If minor spoke angle adjustment is necessary, do so only by adjustment of the tie rods, not by removing and repositioning the steering wheel.

12. Using new Torx® screws, torque the air bag to 7 ft. lbs. (10 Nm). This torque is critical to proper operation of the air bag. Connect the air bag wiring harness and then the battery.

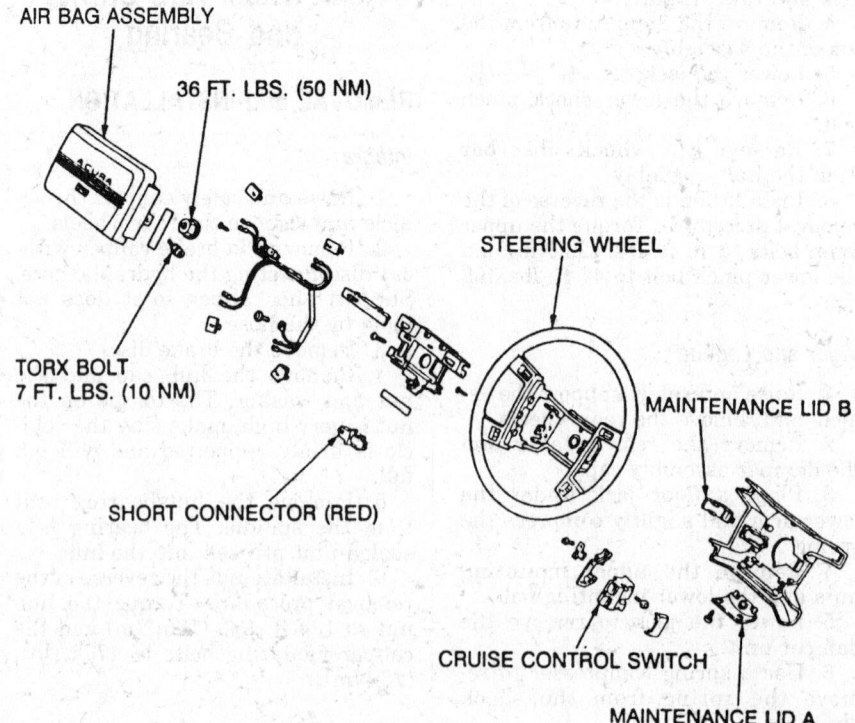

Steering wheel assembly with air bag

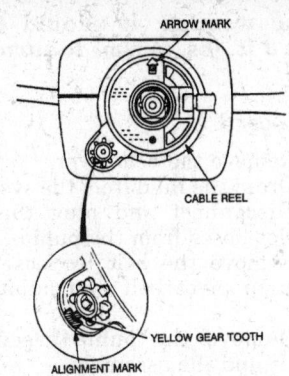

Cable reel alignment on vehicles with air bag

13. After installation, turn the ignition switch **ON**; the instrument panel SRS light should turn ON for about 8 seconds and turn OFF.

14. Check operation of the horn and the cruise control switches.

Manual Rack and Pinion

REMOVAL and INSTALLATION

Power Rack and Pinion

REMOVAL and INSTALLATION

Integra

1. Remove the steering joint cover, the steering shaft connector bolts and pull the connector up off the pinion shaft. Drain the power steering fluid and remove the gearbox shield.

2. Raise and safely support the vehicle.

3. Remove the front wheels.

4. Remove the cotter pins and unscrew the tie rod end ball joint nuts halfway.

5. Break the tie rod ball joints loose using a tie rod end removal tool or equivalent.

6. Remove the nuts and lift the tie rod ends out of the steering knuckles.

7. If equipped with a manual transaxle, perform the following procedures:

   a. Remove the shift extension from the transaxle case. Slide the boot at the connecting position of the gear shift rod.

   b. Slide the pin retainer out of the way, drive out the spring pin with a punch and disconnect the shift control rod. Note that on reassembly, install the pin retainer back into place after driving the spring pin in.

8. If equipped with an automatic transaxle, remove the shift cable guide from the floor and pull the shift cable down by hand. Remove the shift cable holder and cable from the transaxle case by removing the clamp.

9. Remove the exhaust header pipe from the catalyst.

10. Clean the fluid line connectors of all dirt and oils. Disconnect the fluid lines from the valve body.

11. Remove the center beam.

12. Remove the gearbox mounting bolts. Turn the pinion shaft so the tie rods are all the way to the right side.

13. Drop the gearbox far enough so the end of the pinion shaft comes out of its hole in the frame channel and rotate it forward until the shaft is pointing to the rear. Slide the gearbox to the right until the tie rod clears the rear beam, lower it from the vehicle to the left.

To install:

14. Install the power steering gear to the chassis and torque the bolts to 32 ft. lbs. (44 Nm). Torque the power steering gear clamp-to-chassis bolts to 29 ft. lbs. (40 Nm).

15. Connect the tie rod ends and torque the knuckle nuts to 40 ft. lbs. (55 Nm), then tighten the nuts just enough to install new cotter pins.

16. Connect the shift extension and torque the bolt to 7 ft. lbs. (10 Nm).

17. When everything is assembled, refill the reservoir with new power steering fluid. Start the engine and allow it run at fast idle, turn the steering wheel from lock-to-lock several times to bleed the air out.

18. Check the fluid again and add, if necessary. Check the system for leaks.

1990 Legend

1. Remove the steering joint cover and disconnect the steering shaft from the gearbox.

2. Drain the power steering fluid.

3. Remove the gearbox shield.

4. Using cleaning solvent and a brush, clean the control unit, its lines and the end of the gearbox. Blow dry with compressed air, if possible.

5. Raise and safely support the vehicle.

6. Remove the front wheels.

7. Remove the cotter pins and unscrew the tie rod end ball joint nuts halfway.

8. Break the tie rod ball joints loose, using a tie rod end removal tool or equivalent.

9. Remove the nuts and lift the tie rod ends from the steering knuckles.

10. If equipped with a manual transaxle, perform the following procedures:

   a. Remove the shift extension from the transaxle case.

   b. Disconnect the gearshift rod from the transaxle case by removing the 8mm spring pin.

11. If equipped with an automatic transaxle, remove the shift control cable from the clamp.

12. Remove the center beam bolts and the center beam. If the self-locking nuts are worn, replace them with new ones when installing the assembly.

13. Disconnect the exhaust header pipe from the manifold. Replace the exhaust gasket and the self-locking nuts when reinstalling the pipe.

14. Remove the header pipe joint nuts and the header pipe.

15. Disconnect the 4 lines from the control unit.

16. Slide the tie rod all the way to the right side.

17. Slide the gearbox right so the left tie rod clears the bottom of the rear beam and remove the gearbox.

To install:

18. Reverse the removal procedures. Torque the following items:

Power steering gear-to-chassis bolts to 28 ft. lbs. (39 Nm)

Exhaust pipe-to-exhaust manifold nuts to 40 ft. lbs. (55 Nm)

Exhaust pipe-to-muffler nuts to 25 ft. lbs.

Center beam-to-chassis bolts to 37 ft. lbs. (51 Nm)

Shift extension-to-transaxle bolt to 7 ft. lbs. (10 Nm)

Tie rod end-to-steering knuckle nut to 32 ft. lbs. (44 Nm).

19. Refill the reservoir with new power steering fluid. Start the engine and allow it to run at fast idle, turn the steering wheel from lock-to-lock several times to bled the air out.

20. Check the fluid again and add, if necessary. Check the system for leaks.

21. After installation, turn the ignition switch **ON**; the instrument panel SRS light should turn ON for about 8 seconds and turn OFF.

Vigor and 1991-94 Legend

1. Disconnect the fluid return hose from the rack and put the end in a container. Start the engine and turn the steering wheel lock-to-lock several times. When fluid stops coming out, stop the engine.

2. Raise and safely support the vehicle and remove the front wheels.

3. Remove the cotter pins and disconnect the tie rod ball joints using a

suitable press tool. Be careful to not damage the threads on the joints.

4. Loosen the steering joint bolt but do not remove it yet.

5. Remove the splash guard. The 2 long bolts also hold the rack in place, and the rack will now be partially hanging on the steering joint.

6. Carefully clean all the hydraulic fitting connections with solvent and a brush and blow them dry.

7. Disconnect the hydraulic fittings and hoses.

8. Remove the hydraulic line mounting clamps from the rack.

9. Place a jackstand under the rack and remove the steering joint bolt. Remove the rack assembly.

To install:

NOTE: On Legend, several bolts thread into aluminum. When replacing fasteners, be sure to use bolts that have a Dacro® coating specifically designed for such applications. Using normal steel bolts could cause corrosion and loosening of the bolt.

10. Fit the pinion into the steering joint and install the right side mounting rubber and bracket. Do not tighten the bolts yet.

11. Loosely connect the hydraulic lines. Install the hydraulic line cushions and clamps, then tighten the line connections.

12. Install the steering joint bolts, make sure the joint does not bind when turned, then torque the bolts to 16 ft. lbs. (22 Nm).

13. Torque the right side mount bolts to 28 ft. lbs. (39 Nm).

14. Install the splash guard and torque the short bolts to 28 ft. lbs. (39 Nm), the long bolts to 43 ft. lbs. (60 Nm) on Legend, 32 ft. lbs. (44 Nm) on Vigor.

15. Connect the tie rod ends and torque the nuts to 40 ft. lbs. (54 Nm), then tighten as necessary to install a new cotter pin.

16. When installation is complete, refill the hydraulic reservoir with new steering fluid, start the engine and turn the steering wheel lock-to-lock several times to bleed the system. Check fluid level again.

17. After installation, turn the ignition switch **ON**; the instrument panel SRS light should turn ON for about 8 seconds and turn OFF.

Power Steering Pump

REMOVAL and INSTALLATION

Integra

1. Drain the power steering fluid. Disconnect the inlet and outlet hoses from the power steering pump and plug them.

2. Remove the belt by loosening the adjusting bolts on the pump bracket.

3. Remove the power steering mounting bolts and remove the power steering pump.

To install:

4. Reverse the removal procedures. Torque the power steering pump-to-engine bolts to 17 ft. lbs. (24 Nm). Be sure to observe the following:

    a. Connect the hoses tightly.

    b. Adjust the belt tension.

    c. Check the fluid level and add, if necessary.

    d. Bleed the air from the system.

NOTE: When installing a new or rebuilt pump, check the power steering pump preload in a vise before installing it on the vehicle. Check the pump preload with a torque wrench: it should take about 3 ft. lbs. (4 Nm) to turn the pump.

1990 Legend

1. Remove the belt cover.

2. Drain the fluid from the system.

3. Disconnect and plug the inlet/outlet hoses from the pump.

4. Remove the belt by loosening the pump pivot bolt and adjusting nut.

5. Remove the pump assembly nut/bolt and the assembly.

To install:

6. Reverse the removal procedures. Torque the power steering pump-to-bracket bolt to 28 ft. lbs. (39 Nm) and the power steering pump-to-bracket nut to 16 ft. lbs. (22 Nm). Be sure to observe the following:

    a. Refill the reservoir with new fluid to the upper level on the reservoir.

    b. Connect the hoses tightly.

    c. Adjust the belt tension.

    d. Bleed the air from the system.

    e. Check the fluid level and add, if necessary.

Vigor and 1991-94 Legend

1. Disconnect the fluid return hose from the rack and put the end in a

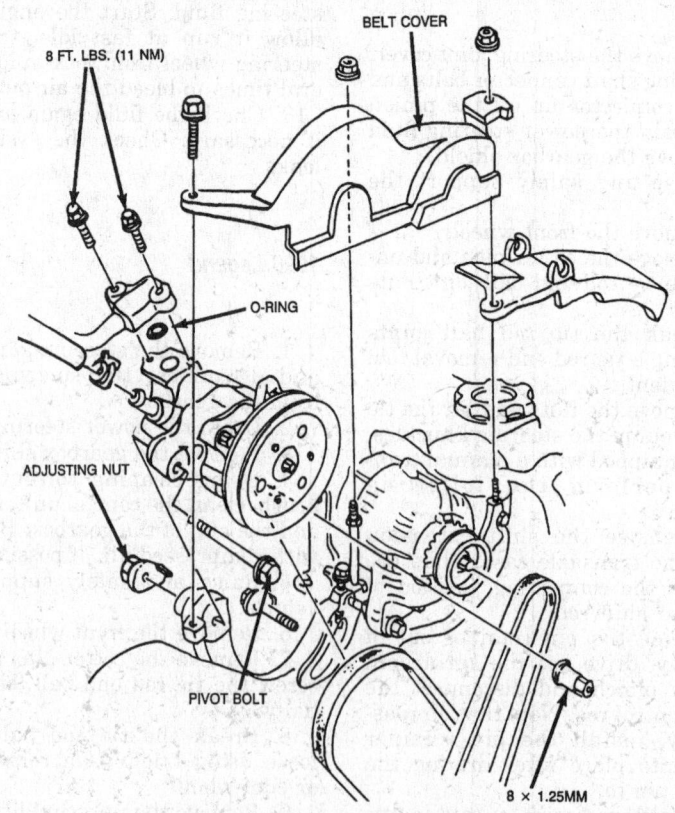

Power steering pump removal — 1990 Legend

container. Start the engine and turn the steering wheel lock-to-lock several times. When fluid stops coming out, stop the engine.

2. Remove the air cleaner cover and duct.

3. Disconnect the hydraulic lines from the pump.

4. Loosen the adjustment and remove the belt.

5. Remove the special bolt and nut and remove the pump.

To install:

6. Installation is the reverse of removal. Torque the special bolt to 33 ft. lbs. (45 Nm) and the nut to 16 ft. lbs. (22 Nm).

7. Connect the hydraulic lines, install and adjust the belt and refill the reservoir. To bleed the system, run the engine and turn the steering wheel lock-to-lock several times. Check the fluid level.

BELT ADJUSTMENT

1. Loosen the adjuster arm bolt.

2. Move the pump toward or away from the engine, until the belt can be depressed approximately 0.75-0.94 in. (19-24mm) at the mid-point between both pulleys under moderate thumb pressure. If the tension adjustment is being made on a new belt, the deflection should only be about 0.43 in. (11mm) to allow for the initial stretching of the belt.

3. Torque the bolt to 29 ft. lbs. (40 Nm) for Integra or 33 ft. lbs. (45 Nm) for Legend. Run the engine, then recheck the adjustment.

SYSTEM BLEEDING

1. Raise and safely support the vehicle.

2. Refill the power steering pump reservoir to the full level.

3. Start the engine and turn the steering wheel from lock-to-lock (several times).

4. After the air bubbles have been eliminated from the system, refill the reservoir and lower the vehicle.

Tie Rod Ends

REMOVAL and INSTALLATION

Integra

1. Raise and safely support the vehicle. Remove the front wheel.

2. Loosen the tie rod end-to-power steering gear jam nut.

3. Remove the tie rod end-to-steering knuckle cotter pin and nut.

4. Using a press type ball joint removal tool, separate the tie rod end from the steering knuckle. Take care to not damage the threads on the joint.

5. While supporting the power steering rod, remove the tie rod end, be sure to count revolutions required to remove the tie rod end.

To install:

6. Install the new tie rod end, turn it the same amount of revolutions necessary to remove it and tighten the jam nut to 42 ft. lbs. (58 Nm) and the tie rod end-to-steering knuckle nut to 29 ft. lbs. (40 Nm).

Except Integra

1. Raise and safely support the vehicle. Remove the front wheels.

2. Remove the cotter pin and the nut from the tie rod end. Use a press type ball joint remover tool, separate the tie rod from the steering knuckle. Be careful to not damage the threads on the joint.

3. Disconnect the air tube at the dust seal joint. Remove the tie rod dust seal bellows clamps and move the rubber bellows back on the tie rod rack joints.

4. Straighten the tie rod lockwasher tabs at the tie rod-to-rack joint and remove the tie rod by turning it with a wrench. On some models, the lock washer is staked.

To install:

5. Reverse the removal procedure. Always use a new tie rod lockwasher and cotter pin during reassembly.

6. Torque the tie rod end-to-power steering gear to 40 ft. lbs. (55 Nm) and the tie rod end-to-steering knuckle nut to 32 ft. lbs. (44 Nm). Install a new cotter pin.

7. Fit the locating lugs into the slots on the rack and bend the outer edge of the washer over the flat part of the rod, after the tie rod nut has been properly tightened.

BRAKES

Master Cylinder

REMOVAL and INSTALLATION

NOTE: Before removing the master cylinder, cover the body surfaces with fender covers and rags to prevent damage to painted surfaces by brake fluid.

1. Disconnect and plug the brake lines at the master cylinder.

2. Remove the master cylinder-to-power booster bolts and the master cylinder from the vehicle.

3. To install, reverse the removal procedure. Torque the master cylinder-to-power booster bolts to 11 ft. lbs. (15 Nm). Bleed the brake system.

Proportioning Valve

REMOVAL and INSTALLATION

1. Disconnect and plug the hydraulic lines from the dual proportioning valve.

2. Remove the proportioning valve-to-bracket bolts and the valve from the vehicle.

3. To install, reverse the removal procedures. Bleed the brake system.

Power Brake Booster

REMOVAL and INSTALLATION

1. Disconnect the vacuum hose from the booster.

2. Disconnect and plug the brake lines at the master cylinder.

3. Remove the brake pedal-to-booster link pin and the booster nuts; the pushrod and nuts are located inside the vehicle under the instrument panel.

4. Remove the booster with the master cylinder attached.

To install:

5. Reverse the removal procedure. Torque the power brake booster-to-firewall nuts to 9 ft. lbs. (13 Nm) and the master cylinder-to-power brake booster nuts to 11 ft. lbs. (15 Nm).

6. Check the vacuum booster pushrod-to-master cylinder piston clearance as outlined in the master cylinder removal procedure.

7. Bleed the brake system before operating the vehicle.

Brake Caliper

REMOVAL and INSTALLATION

Front

1. Raise and safely support the vehicle.

2. Remove the front wheel assembly.

3. Remove the banjo bolt and disconnect the brake hose from the caliper.

4. Remove the caliper slide mounting bolts and remove the caliper. Re-

move the pad spring from the caliper body.

To install:

5. Installation is the reverse of the removal procedure. Be sure to properly bleed the brake system after installation.

6. Torque the caliper slide mounting bolts:

Integra — 24 ft. lbs. (33 Nm)
Legend
1990 — 24 ft. lbs. (33 Nm)
1991-94 — 36 ft. lbs. (50 Nm)
Vigor — 36 ft. lbs. (50 Nm)

Rear

1. Raise and safely support the vehicle.

2. Remove the rear wheel assembly.

3. Remove the caliper shield.

4. Disconnect the parking brake cable from the lever on the caliper by removing the lock pin.

5. Remove the banjo bolt and disconnect the brake hose from the caliper.

6. Remove the 2 caliper slide mounting bolts and remove the caliper from the bracket.

To install:

7. Installation is the reverse of the removal procedure. Be sure to properly bleed the brake system after installation.

8. Torque the caliper slide mounting bolts:

Integram — 24 ft. lbs. (33 Nm)
Legend
1990 — 20 ft. lbs. (27 Nm)
1991-94 — 17 ft. lbs. (23 Nm)
Vigor — 17 ft. lbs. (23 Nm)

Disc Brake Pads

REMOVAL and INSTALLATION

Front

1. Raise and safely support the vehicle. Remove the front wheels.

2. Using a prybar between the outer brake pad and the caliper, carefully pry the brake caliper away from the disc as far as possible.

3. Remove the lower caliper slide mounting bolt and swing the caliper upward and away from the disc. If necessary, remove both caliper slide mounting bolts without disconnecting the hydraulic line and support the caliper so it does not hang on the line.

4. Remove the brake pad shim, the brake pad retainers and the pad.

5. Install new brake pads, the shims and retainers. Lightly coat the back of the pads with Molykote® M77, or equivalent.

6. Lower the calipers of the brake pad assemblies and install the caliper slide mounting bolt.

Rear

1. Raise and safely support the rear of the vehicle. Remove the rear wheels.

2. Using a prybar between the outer brake pad and the caliper, pry the brake caliper away from the disc as far as possible.

3. Remove both caliper slide mounting bolts without disconnecting the hydraulic line and support the caliper so it does not hang on the line.

4. Remove the brake pads and shims.

5. To install, use new brake pads and reverse the removal procedures. Install the caliper slide mounting bolts.

Brake Rotor

REMOVAL and INSTALLATION

1. Raise and safely support the vehicle. Remove the wheel.

2. Remove the brake caliper bolts and the caliper from the knuckle. Do not allow the caliper to hang by the brake hose, support it with a length of wire.

3. Remove the disc brake rotor retaining screws, if equipped. If the rotor will not easily pull off, screw two 8mm bolts into the disc brake removal holes and turn the bolts 2 turns at a time to press the rotor from the hub.

4. Installation is the reverse order of the removal procedure.

Brake System Bleeding

STANDARD BRAKES

NOTE: The master cylinder must be full at the start of the bleeding procedure and checked after bleeding each caliper. Add fluid as required. Use only DOT 3 or 4 brake fluid. If a pressure bleeder is not available it will be necessary to have the aid of an assistant to perform this brake bleeding operation.

1. Have an assistant slowly pump the brake pedal several times and then apply a steady pressure to the brake pedal.

2. Attach a bleed hose to the bleed screw and place it into a clear container. Loosen the brake bleed screw at the brake caliper furthest away from the master cylinder (passenger's rear) to allow the air to escape from the system.

3. Repeat this procedure for each brake caliper, until no air bubbles appear in the brake fluid. Use the following brake caliper sequence in order to bleed the brake system properly:

a. Right rear, passenger's side brake caliper.
b. Left front, driver's side brake caliper.
c. Left rear, driver's side brake caliper.
d. Right front, passenger's side brake caliper.

4. Check the fluid level in the master cylinder and add, if necessary. Road test the vehicle and check the brake performance.

Anti-Lock Brake System Service

PRECAUTIONS

• The anti-lock brake system accumulator contains a high pressure nitrogen gas. Do not puncture, expose to flame or attempt to disassemble the accumulator or it may explode and cause severe personal injury.

• The anti-lock brake system contains brake fluid under extremely high pressure within the power unit pump, accumulator and modulator assembly. Do not disconnect or loosen any lines, hoses, fittings or components without properly relieving the system pressure. Improper procedures or failure to discharge the system pressure may result in severe or fatal personal injury and/or property damage.

• Use only tool 07HAASG00100 or equivalent to relieve pressure.

RELIEVING ANTI-LOCK BRAKE SYSTEM PRESSURE

1. Insure the ignition switch is **OFF**.

2. Using a syringe or similar device, remove all the fluid from the master cylinder and modulator reservoirs.

3. Remove the red cover from the bleeder port on top of the power unit pump.

4. Install the bleeding tool onto the bleeder. Make certain the reservoir cap on the tool is secured.

5. Using the tool, turn the bleeder about 90 degrees to admit high pressure fluid into the reservoir. As the pressure drops, turn the bleeder open about 1 full turn to completely relieve the system.

6. Retighten the bleeder and remove the tool. Discard the captured brake fluid; do not reuse it. Install the red cap on the bleeder port.

Anti-Lock Brake Modulator

REMOVAL and INSTALLATION

1. Relieve the system pressure.
2. Disconnect and plug the lines from the hydraulic modulator.
3. Remove the mounting bolts and the modulator from the vehicle.
4. To install, reverse the removal procedures. Bleed the brake system.

Accumulator Pressure Switch

REMOVAL and INSTALLATION

———— **CAUTION** ————
The anti-lock brake system accumulator contains a high pressure nitrogen gas. Do not puncture, expose to flame or attempt to disassemble the accumulator or it may explode and cause severe personal injury.

1. Relieve the accumulator line pressure.

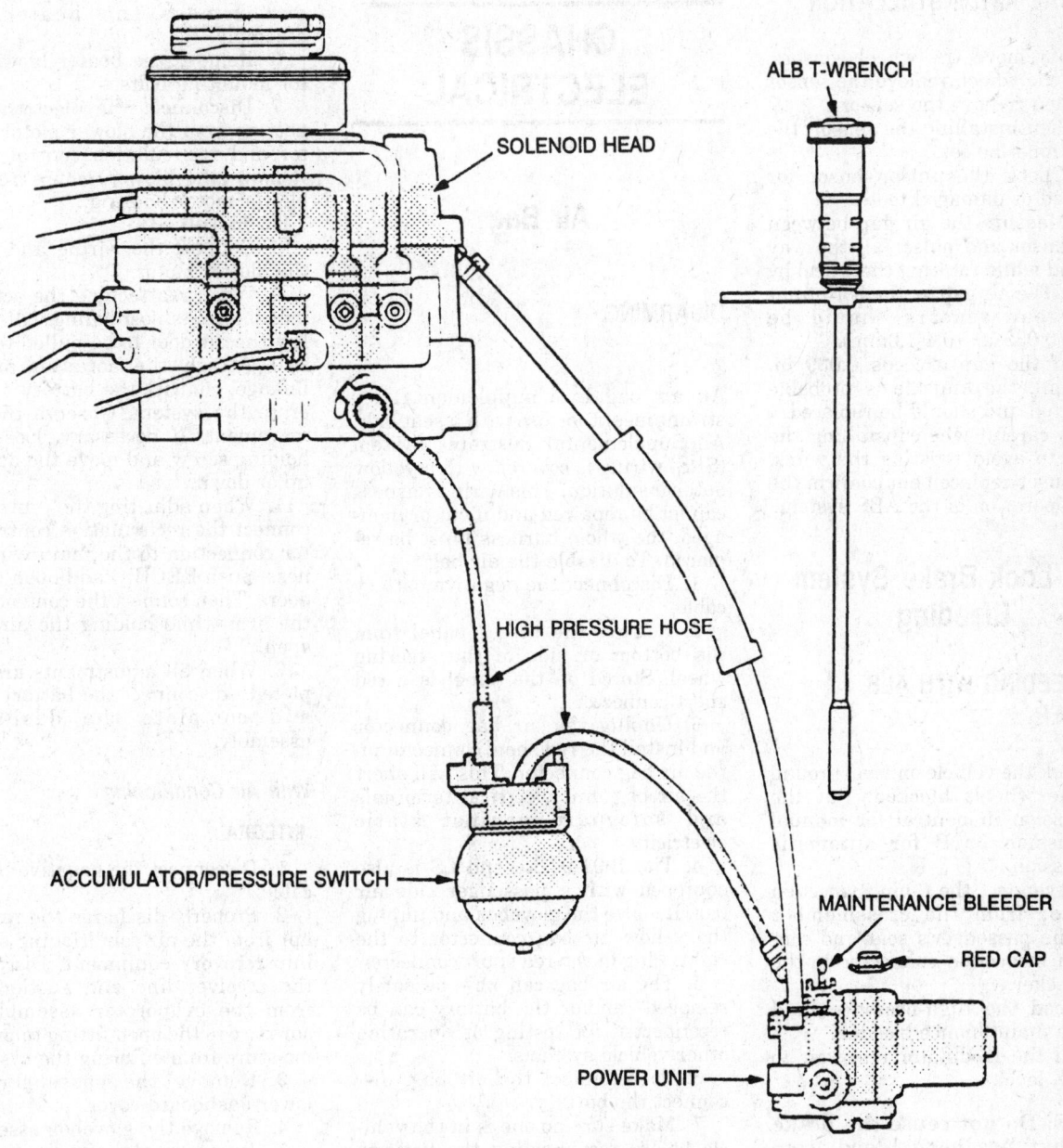

Bleeding the anti-lock brake high pressure system

2. Remove the 3 flange bolts, then remove the accumulator from the accumulator bracket.

3. Secure the accumulator in a suitable vise so the relief plug points straight up.

4. Slowly turn the plug 3½ turns and then wait 3 minutes for all pressure to escape.

5. Remove the plug completely and dispose of the accumulator unit.

6. To install, reverse the order of the removal procedure.

Pulsers/Sensors

REMOVAL AND INSTALLATION

1. To remove the wheel sensors, remove the wheel, remove the sensor bolts, then remove the sensor.

2. When installing the sensor, the air gap must be set:

   a. Check the pulser/sensor for chipped or damaged teeth.

   b. Measure the air gap between the sensor and pulser all the way around while rotating the wheel by hand. The air gap on the both front and rear sensors should be 0.016-0.039 in. (0.4-1.0mm).

   c. If the gap exceeds 0.039 in. (1.0mm), the knuckle is probable distorted and should be replaced.

3. Be careful when installing the sensors to avoid twisting the wires. After sensor replacement confirm the proper operation of the ABS system.

Anti-Lock Brake System Bleeding

AIR BLEEDING WITH ALB CHECKER

1. Park the vehicle on level ground with the wheels blocked. Put the transmission in neutral for manual transmission or **P** for automatic transmission.

2. Disconnect the 6-pin inspection connector from the crossmember under the passenger's seat and connect the inspection connector to the ALB checker.

3. Bleed the high-pressure fluid from the maintenance bleeder.

4. Fill the modulator reservoir to the MAX level.

NOTE: Do not reuse the brake fluid that has been bleed from the power unit.

5. Start the engine and release the parking brake.

6. Turn the mode selector to 2, 3, 4 and 5 and press the start button. Visually inspect the kickbacks of the brake pedal. There should be at least 2 kickbacks. If not, repeat Steps 3-6, as necessary.

7. Refill the modulator reservoir to the MAX level. Install the reservoir cap.

8. Check the anti-lock brake system function in all modes by using the ALB checker.

CHASSIS ELECTRICAL

Air Bag

DISARMING

An air bag is a supplemental restraint meant for use with a seat belt. All Supplemental Restraint System (SRS) wiring is covered with a yellow outer insulation. This wiring harness cannot be repaired and if cut or damaged, the whole harness must be replaced. To disable the air bag:

1. Disconnect the negative battery cable.

2. Remove the access panel from the bottom or side of the steering wheel. Stored on the panel is a red short connector.

3. Unplug the air bag connector and install the red short connector on the air bag connector. This will short the air bag unit electrical terminals and safeguard against static electricity.

4. The 1991-94 Legend LS is also equipped with a passenger side air bag. Remove the glovebox and unplug the yellow air bag connector to the right. Plug in the red short connector.

5. The air bag can now be safely removed and/or the battery can be reconnected for testing or operating other vehicle systems.

6. To reconnect the air bag, disconnect the battery.

7. Make sure no one is in the vehicle before reconnecting the battery. Connect the air bag wiring harness.

Heater Blower Motor

REMOVAL and INSTALLATION

Without Air Conditioning

INTEGRA

1. Disconnect the negative battery cable. Remove the passenger side lower dashboard cover.

2. Remove the glovebox assembly.

3. Remove the front console assembly.

4. Remove the passenger side knee bolster panel, located under the glovebox frame.

5. Remove the self tapping screws and remove the heater duct assembly.

6. Remove the heater blower motor mounting bolts.

7. Disconnect the electrical connectors from the blower motor, resistor and recirculation control motor. Remove the blower motor from the blower motor housing.

To install:

8. Connect the wiring and install the blower motor.

9. When reattaching the actuator, make sure its positioning will not allow the air door to be pulled to far.

10. Attach the actuator and all linkage, connect the battery and operate the system. Observe the door movement. If necessary, loosen the holding screw and move the actuator up or down.

11. When adjusting the control rod, connect the recirculation control motor connection to the main wire harness, push RECIRC and open the air doors. Then connect the control rod to the arm while holding the air doors open.

12. When all adjustments are completed, disconnect the battery again and complete the dashboard assembly.

With Air Conditioning

INTEGRA

1. Disconnect the negative battery cable.

2. Properly discharge the refrigerant from the air conditioning system into recovery equipment. Disconnect the receiver line and suction hose from the evaporator assembly. Be sure to cap the open fitting to prevent moisture from entering the system.

3. Remove the passenger side lower dashboard cover.

4. Remove the glovebox assembly.

5. Remove the front console assembly.

6. Remove the passenger side knee bolster panel, located under the glovebox frame.

7. Remove the 2 self tapping screws and the air conditioning bands from around the evaporator assembly.

8. Disconnect the wire connector from the thermostat switch and pull off the wire harness from the clamps. Remove the evaporator.

9. Remove the self-tapping screws and remove the heater duct assembly.

10. Remove the heater blower motor mounting bolts.

11. Disconnect the electrical connectors from the blower motor, resistor and recirculation control motor. Remove the blower motor from the blower motor housing.

To install:

12. Reverse the removal procedure.

13. When reattaching the actuator, make sure its positioning will not allow the air door to pulled to far.

14. Attach the actuator and all linkage, then apply battery voltage and watch the door movement. If necessary, loosen the holding screw and move the actuator up or down.

15. When adjusting the control rod, connect the recirculation control motor connection to the main wire harness, push RECIRC and open the air doors. Then connect the control rod to the arm while holding the air doors open.

1990 Legend

1. Disconnect the negative battery cable.

2. Remove the glovebox lower cover screws and the cover.

3. Remove the glovebox screws and the glovebox.

4. Remove the glovebox frame screws, the glovebox frame, the clips and the heater duct.

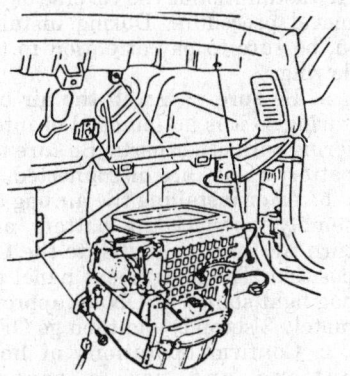

Blower motor removal — Integra

5. Properly discharge the refrigerant from the air conditioning system into recovery equipment.

6. Remove the evaporator as follows:

   a. Disconnect the receiver line and suction hose from the evaporator assembly.

   b. Be sure to cap the open fitting to prevent moisture from entering the system.

   c. Remove the self-tapping screws and the air conditioning bands from around the evaporator assembly.

   d. Disconnect the wire connector from the thermostat switch and pull off the wire harness from the clamps.

   e. Remove the evaporator.

7. Disconnect the wire connectors from the blower.

8. Remove the blower assembly bolts and the assembly.

To install:

9. Install the blower into the case and connect the wiring. Make sure all wiring is secure and temporarily connect the battery to test the blower and adjust the linkage. Check that there are no air leaks in the blower case.

10. When reattaching the actuator, make sure its positioning will not allow the air door to be pulled too far.

11. Attach the actuator and all linkage, then apply battery voltage and watch the door movement. If necessary, loosen the holding screw and move the actuator up or down.

12. When adjusting the control rod, connect the recirculation control motor connection to the main wire harness, push the FRESH/RECIRC switch to FRESH and open the air doors. Then connect the control rod to the arm while holding the air doors open.

13. After properly adjusting the linkage, disconnect the battery to complete the dashboard assembly.

1991-94 Legend

1. Disconnect the negative battery cable.

2. Remove the right side lower dashboard panel and unplug the connector.

3. Disconnect the glovebox light and remove the glovebox.

4. Remove both dashboard end caps.

5. Remove the glovebox frame.

6. Unplug the connectors, remove the screws and remove the blower assembly.

7. Installation is the reverse of removal. Make sure there are no air leads in the system.

Vigor

1. Remove the heater/evaporator assembly.

2. Remove the heater core and the door control motor.

3. Remove the screw to remove the left side air duct.

4. Remove the screws and clips to split the housing. Remove the screws to remove the motor from the lower housing.

5. Installation is the reverse of removal. Be sure to connect the hose to the motor when assembling the housing.

Windshield Wiper Motor

REMOVAL and INSTALLATION

Front

1. Remove the negative cable from the battery. Position the wiper arms in a positioned where they are not concealed. On the Integra, pull the lock tab with the wiper arm lifted away from the windshield to release the spring pressure.

2. Open the hood and remove the wiper arm nuts and the wiper arms.

3. Remove the front air scoop, windshield lower molding and hood seal, located over the wiper linkage by carefully prying off the trim clips and removing the retaining screws at the bottom of the windshield.

4. Remove the wiper maintenance grommet. Disconnect the linkage from the wiper motor.

5. Remove the wiper motor water seal cover clamp and the cover, if equipped.

6. Disconnect the wiper motor electrical connector, remove the motor mounting bolts and remove the motor.

To install:

7. Install the motor and connect the wiring. Connect the battery and run the motor in all speeds with the wiper switch to check operation. Turn the switch **OFF** to set the motor in its park position before turning the ignition switch **OFF**.

8. Lightly coat the linkage joints with grease and make sure the linkage moves smoothly, then connect the linkage.

9. When installing the wiper arms, be sure to position them on the bottom line of the stopper and then mount the cap nuts.

Rear

INTEGRA AND STERLING

1. Disconnect the negative battery cable. Remove the hatch trim panel.
2. Remove the nut cover, wiper arm nut, wiper arm, cap, special nut, special washer and the cushion rubber.
3. Disconnect the wiper motor electrical connector.
4. Remove the wiper motor mounting nuts with spacers and remove the wiper motor.
5. Installation is the reverse order of the removal procedure.

Windshield Wiper Switch

REMOVAL and INSTALLATION

Integra

1. Disconnect the negative battery cable and remove the steering wheel.
2. Remove the column covers and disconnect the wiring. If equipped with cruise control, remove the slip ring.
3. Remove the screws and slide the switch out to the side.
4. Installation is the reverse of removal.

Legend

WITHOUT AIR BAG

1. Remove the negative cable from the battery.
2. Remove the dashboard lower panel and disconnect the 6-pin and 8-pin connectors from the wiper control unit on the lower panel.
3. Disconnect the 10-pin connector from the wiper/washer switch.
4. Remove the steering wheel, the steering column lower cover and disconnect the 6-pin connector from the winter position switch.

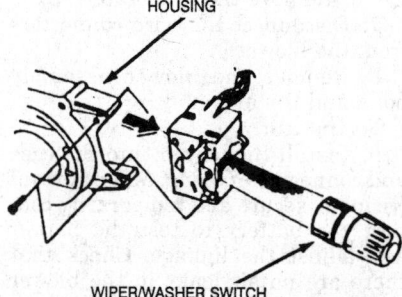

Wiper switch removal — Legend without air bag

5. Remove the upper cover from the steering column.
6. Remove the screws and slide the wiper/washer switch out of the housing.
7. To install, reverse the removal procedures.

With Air Bag

NOTE: Some vehicles are equipped with an air bag supplemental restraint system. It will be necessary to remove the air bag assembly in order to remove the combination switch. Read the precautions at the beginning of the Chassis Electrical section.

1. Disconnect both the negative and positive battery cables from the battery.
2. Remove the lower maintenance lid below the air bag and then remove the short connector.
3. Disconnect the connector between the air bag and the cable reel.
4. Connect the short connector to the air bag side of the connector.
5. Remove the left side maintenance lid and the cruise control/set resume switch cover.
6. Insert a T30 Torx® bit and remove the Torx® bolts. Remove the air bag assembly and place it in an out of the way area, such as the back seat, pad side up.
7. Remove the dashboard lower panel and disconnect the 6-pin connector from the wiper position switch and the 6-pin and 8-pin connectors from the wiper control unit on the lower panel.
8. Remove the left knee bolster. Disconnect the combination switch connectors.
9. Remove the upper and lower steering column covers.
10. Remove the lighting and wiper switch mounting screws and remove the switches.

To install:

11. Installation is the reverse of the removal procedure. During installation, be sure to pay attention to the following:

a. Be sure to install the air bag wiring so it is not pinched or interfering with other parts. Be sure the battery cables are disconnected.

b. After installing the air bag assembly, connect the battery and turn the ignition switch to the **ON** position. The instrument panel air bag light should go ON for approximately 8 seconds and then go OFF.

c. Confirm operations of horn buttons and cruise control set/resume switch.

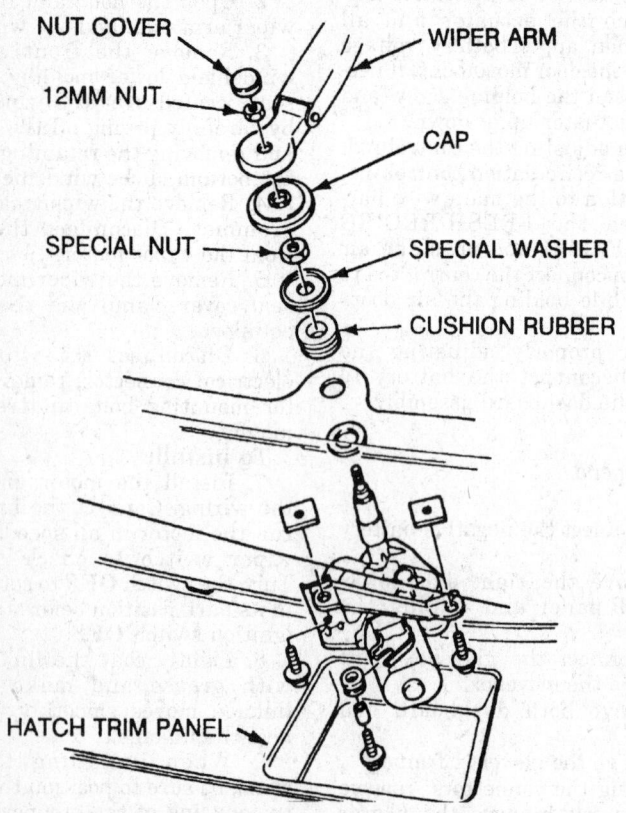

Rear wiper motor assembly — Integra shown

NUT COVER

12MM NUT

SPECIAL NUT

WIPER ARM

CAP

SPECIAL WASHER

CUSHION RUBBER

HATCH TRIM PANEL

3. Lay a clean cloth over the steering column and remove the 2 screws accessible through the switch openings.

4. Remove the 2 upper screws from the instrument panel and lay the panel on the cloth to disconnect the wiring.

5. Installation is the reverse of removal. Connect the wiring and test the instruments before installing all the covers.

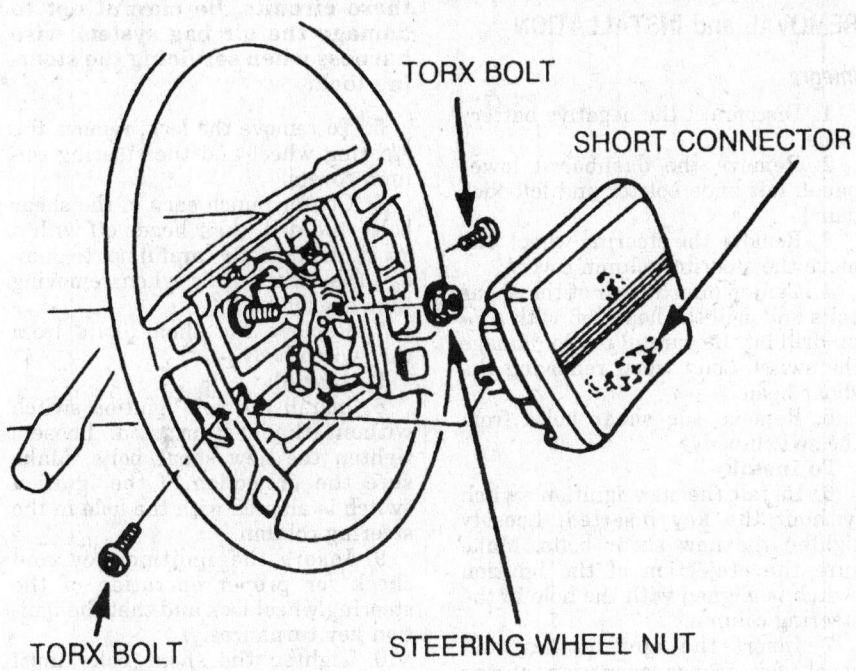

Removing air bag assembly — Legend

Instrument Cluster

REMOVAL and INSTALLATION

Integra

1. Remove the screws and instrument panel from the dashboard and disconnect the switches.

2. Remove the 4 screws to remove the gauge assembly enough to disconnect the wiring.

3. Installation is the reverse of removal.

1991-94 Legend

NOTE: This vehicle is equipped with an air bag system. It is not necessary to remove the air bag assembly in order to remove the instrument panel, but the system should be disarmed before starting work. Read the precautions at the beginning of the Chassis Electrical section.

1. Disconnect the battery cables and remove the lower dashboard panel.

2. Remove the upper and lower steering column covers.

3. Remove the 2 screws, unplug the switch connectors and remove the instrument panel.

4. Place a clean rag over the combination switch to prevent scratching the gauge assembly. Remove the 4 screws and lay the gauge assembly face down on the steering column.

5. Disconnect the wiring and rotate the gauge assembly out towards the right.

To install:

6. Fit the gauge assembly in place and connect the wiring. When installing the assembly, make sure the wiring is not pinched.

7. Install the switches and steering column covers. Connect the battery.

Vigor

NOTE: This vehicle is equipped with an air bag system. It is not necessary to remove the air bag assembly in order to remove the instrument panel, but the system should be disarmed before starting work. Read the precautions at the beginning of the Chassis Electrical section.

1. Remove the lower left dashboard panel and both steering column covers.

2. Carefully pry out the switches at the bottom of the instrument panel and disconnect the wiring.

Concealed Headlights

MANUAL OPERATION

The concealed headlights are controlled by 2 retractor motors which are in turn controlled by their respective relays. The relays are energized (UP) via the white/black lead, or the white/yellow lead (DOWN), through the slip ring on the retractor motors. The UP lead can be powered either by the headlight switch/control unit or by the retractor switch directly. The DOWN lead can be powered by the control unit by either the headlight switch or the retractor switch. The control unit also senses any abnormality in the way the retractor motors operate and warns the driver by illuminating the warning light in the dash assembly.

Each retractor motor has a knob on the motor housing. Turn the motor by hand to manually raise or lower the headlight.

Combination Switch

The headlight switch, dimmer switch, wiper/washer switch and the turn signal switch are all incorporated into the same assembly. On some vehicles, the individual switches can be removed from the combination switch. Otherwise the combination switch must be replaced as a complete unit.

REMOVAL and INSTALLATION

Integra

1. Disconnect the negative battery cable and remove the steering wheel.

2. Remove the column covers and disconnect the wiring. If equipped with cruise control, remove the slipring.

3. Remove the screws and slide the switch out to the side.

4. Installation is the reverse of removal.

Vigor and Legend

WITHOUT AIR BAG

1. Remove the negative cable from the battery.

2. Remove the dashboard lower panel and disconnect the 6-pin and 8-pin connectors from the wiper control unit on the lower panel.

3. Disconnect the 10-pin connector from the wiper/washer switch.

4. Remove the steering wheel, the steering column lower cover and disconnect the 6-pin connector from the winter position switch.

5. Remove the upper cover from the steering column.

6. Remove the screws and slide the wiper/washer switch out of the housing.

7. To install, reverse the removal procedures.

WITH AIR BAG

NOTE: Some vehicles are equipped with an air bag supplemental restraint system. It will be necessary to disable the system in order to remove the combination switch. Read the precautions at the beginning of the Chassis Electrical section.

1. Disconnect both the negative and positive battery cable from the battery.

2. Remove the lower maintenance lid below the air bag and then remove the short connector.

3. Disconnect the connector between the air bag and the cable reel.

4. Connect the short connector to the air bag side of the connector.

5. Remove the left knee bolster and the upper and lower steering column covers.

6. Disconnect the combination switch connectors.

7. Remove the switch mounting screws and remove the switch.

To install:

8. Install the switches and connect the wiring.

9. Install the steering column covers and temporarily connect the battery to test the switches.

10. Disconnect the battery again and assemble the remaining dashboard parts. Be sure the wiring is not pinched or interfering with other parts. Be sure the battery cables are disconnected.

11. After connecting the air bag wiring, connect the battery and turn the ignition switch to the **ON** position. The instrument panel air bag light should go ON for approximately 8 seconds and then go OFF.

Ignition Lock/Switch

REMOVAL and INSTALLATION

Integra

1. Disconnect the negative battery cable.

2. Remove the dashboard lower panel, left knee bolster and left kick panel.

3. Remove the steering wheel. Remove the steering column covers.

4. Center punch each of the shear bolts and drill the heads off with a $3/16$ in. drill bit. Be careful not to damage the switch body when removing the shear head.

5. Remove the shear bolts from the switch body.

To install:

6. Install the new ignition switch without the key inserted. Loosely tighten the new shear bolts. Make sure the projection of the ignition switch is aligned with the hole in the steering column.

7. Insert the ignition key and check for proper operation of the steering wheel lock and that the ignition key turns freely.

8. Tighten the shear bolts until the heads twist off.

1990 Legend

1. Disconnect the negative battery cable.

2. Remove the steering column lower cover. Disconnect the ignition switch wire connector from the dash fuse box.

3. Insert the key and place on the **O** position.

4. Remove the 2 screws and replace the base of the switch.

NOTE: The air bag system wire harness is routed near the steering lock assembly. All air bag system wire harness and connectors

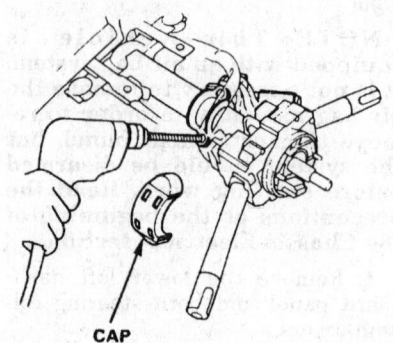

CAP

Ignition lock replacement; drill out shear bolts — Integra shown

are colored yellow. Do not use electrical test equipment on these circuits. Be careful not to damage the air bag system wire harness when servicing the steering lock.

5. To remove the lock, remove the steering wheel and the steering column covers.

6. Center punch each of the shear bolts and drill their heads off with a $3/16$ in. drill bit. Be careful not to damage the switch body when removing the shear head.

7. Remove the shear bolts from the switch body.

To install:

8. Install the new ignition switch without the key inserted. Loosely tighten the new shear bolts. Make sure the projection of the ignition switch is aligned with the hole in the steering column.

9. Insert the ignition key and check for proper operation of the steering wheel lock and that the ignition key turns freely.

10. Tighten the shear bolts until the heads twist off.

1991-94 Legend

1. Disconnect the negative battery cable.

2. On Legend, remove the switches from the lower dashboard panel and remove the panel.

3. Remove the steering column mounts and lower the column.

4. Disconnect the switch wiring and remove the 2 screws to remove the switch.

5. To remove the lock, grind a slot into the shear bolt head and use a chisel to unscrew and remove the bolt.

6. Insert the key and turn to the first position. Push in the lock pin in the service hole and pull the lock assembly out of the column.

To install:

7. Install the new lock and loosely install the shear bolt. Make sure the switch operates freely before twisting off the head.

8. Install the switch and connect the wiring.

9. Secure the column in place, install the dashboard panels and connect the battery.

Vigor

1. Disable the air bag system and remove the steering column covers.

2. Remove the instrument panel.

3. Disconnect the 7-pin connector from the dash fuse box.

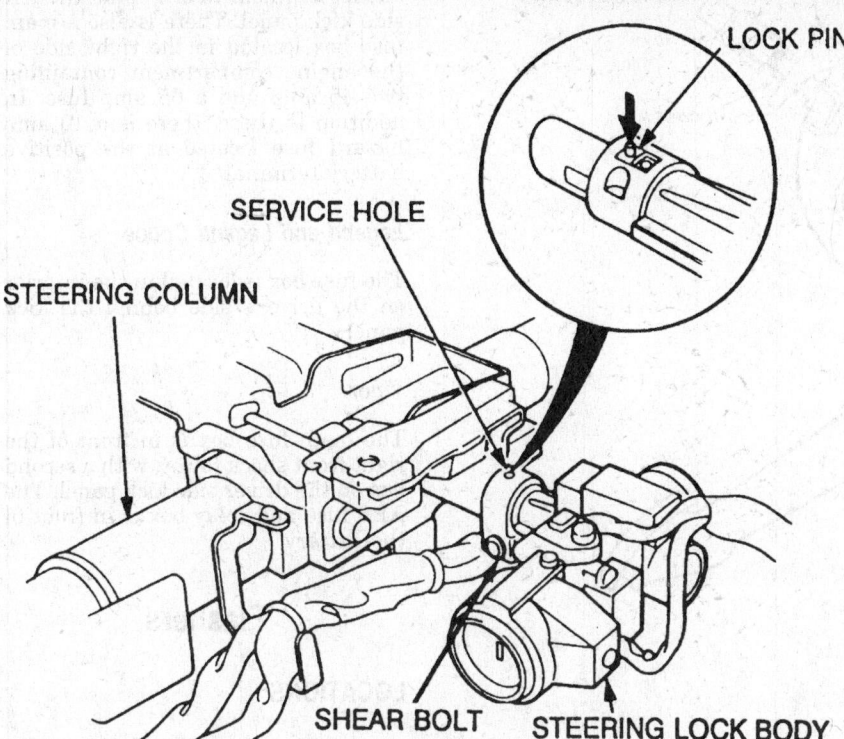

LOCK PIN

SERVICE HOLE

STEERING COLUMN

SHEAR BOLT   STEERING LOCK BODY

Ignition lock replacement; remove shear bolt and press the lock pin — 1991-94 Legend

4. If the ignition key is available, insert the key into the lock and turn to the **0** position.

5. Remove the 2 screws to remove the switch from the left side of the steering column.

6. To remove the lock with the key, turn the cover around the lock about 45 degrees and remove the screw. Pull the cover off the lock cylinder and remove the light from the cover.

7. Turn the ignition key to the **1** position and push the pin near the screw hole to release the lock cylinder from the steering column.

8. If the ignition key is not available, use a ³/₁₆ in. drill bit to drill out the shear bolts from the top and remove the lock body.

To install:

9. Install the lock body without the ignition key and loosely install the new shear bolts.

10. Check the operation of the steering lock, then tighten the shear bolts until the heads twist off.

11. To install the lock cylinder, turn the key to the **0** position and align the cylinder with the body.

12. Turn the key almost to the **1** position and insert the cylinder to let the pin click into place. Install the screw.

Stoplight Switch

ADJUSTMENT

1. Loosen the stoplight switch locknut and back off the stoplight switch until it does not touch the brake pedal.

2. If required, adjust the pedal height.

3. Screw in the stoplight switch until the plunger is fully depressed; threaded end touching the pad on the pedal arm.

4. Back off the switch half a turn and tighten the locknut.

REMOVAL and INSTALLATION

1. Disconnect the negative battery cable. Disconnect the stoplight switch electrical connectors.

2. Loosen the stoplight switch locknut and back off the stoplight switch until it is removed from the brake pedal.

3. Installation is the reverse order of the removal procedure.

Clutch Switch

ADJUSTMENT

NOTE: The clutch switch adjustment on the Integra is part of the clutch cable adjustment.

1. Loosen the locknut on the switch and back it off until it no longer touches the pedal.

2. If required, adjust the pedal height.

NOTE: The total clutch free-play is 0.35-0.59 in. (9-15mm). If there is no clearance between the master cylinder piston and the pushrod, the release bearing is held against the diaphragm spring, which can result in clutch slippage or other clutch problems.

3. Thread the pedal switch in until it contacts the pedal. Turn the switch in further ¼-½ of a turn.

4. Torque the pedal switch locknut to 8 ft. lbs. (10 Nm).

5. To adjust the clutch interlock (starter) switch, loosen the clutch interlock switch locknut. Measure the clearance between the floor board and the clutch pedal with the clutch pedal fully depressed.

6. Release the clutch pedal 0.59-0.79 in. (15-20mm) from the fully depressed position and hold it there. Adjust the position of the clutch interlock switch so the engine will start with the clutch in this position.

7. Thread the clutch interlock switch in further ¼-½ of a turn. Torque the clutch interlock locknut to 8 ft. lbs. (10 Nm).

REMOVAL and INSTALLATION

1. Disconnect the negative battery cable.

2. Remove the instrument panel lower cover and knee bolster, as required.

3. Disconnect the electrical connectors from the switch.

4. Loosen the switch locknut and unscrew the switch from the mounting.

5. To install, reverse the removal procedure and torque the switch locknut to 8 ft. lbs. (10 Nm).

Neutral Safety Switch

ADJUSTMENT

1. The switch is mounted at the base of the automatic transmission

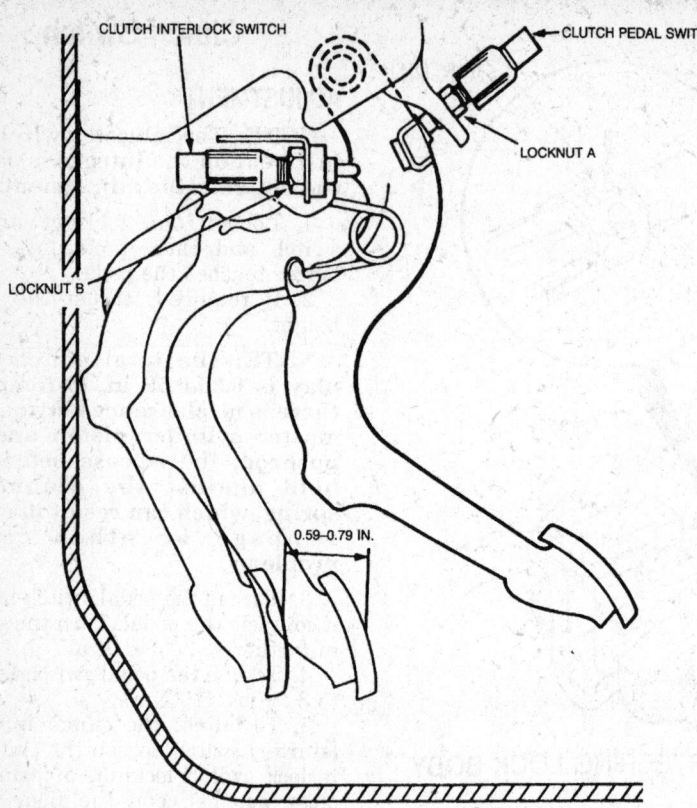

Clutch pedal switch adjustments

shift lever. Remove the console as required to access the switch.

2. Disable the ignition system so the engine will not start.

3. The switch is secured in place by 2 bolts in slotted holes. Place the lever in **N**, loosen the bolts and move the switch as required to allow starter operation in **P** and **N** only.

Fuses

LOCATION

Integra

The fuse/relay box is located in the interior on the drivers side below the dashboard, next to or behind the left side kick panel. There is also a main fuse box located in the right side of the engine compartment containing two 45 amp and a 65 amp fuse. In addition to these, there is a 10 amp hazard fuse located at the positive battery terminal.

Legend and Legend Coupe

The fuse box is located in the interior on the driver's side behind the kick panel.

Vigor

The main fuse box is in front of the right front shock tower, with a second box on the driver side kick panel. The ABS fuse and relay box is in front of the battery.

Flashers

LOCATIONS

Integra

The hazard/turn signal relay, is located either on the interior fuse/relay box or located up behind the left side of the instrument panel.

Except Integra

The hazard/turn signal relay, is located on the interior fuse/relay box, located under the left side of the instrument panel.

Audi 2

80, 90, 100, 200, Coupe, S4, V8

SPECIFICATIONS

ENGINE IDENTIFICATION

Year	Model	Engine Displacement Liters (cc)	Engine Series (ID/VIN)	Fuel System	No. of Cylinders	Engine Type
1990	80	2.0 (1983)	3A	CIS-Motronic	4	OHC
	80 Quattro	2.3 (2309)	NG	CIS-E III	5	OHC
	90	2.3 (2309)	NG	CIS-E III	5	OHC
	90 Quattro	2.3 (2309)	7A	MPI	5	OHC 20V
	Coupé Quattro	2.3 (2309)	7A	MPI	5	OHC 20V
	100	2.3 (2309)	NF	CIS-E III	5	OHC
	100 Quattro	2.3 (2309)	NF	CIS-E III	5	OHC
	200	2.2 (2226)	MC	CIS	5	Turbo
	200 Quattro	2.2 (2226)	MC	CIS	5	Turbo
	200 Quattro Wagon	2.2 (2226)	MC	CIS	5	Turbo
	V8 Quattro	3.6 (3562)	PT	Motronic	8	OHC 32V
1991	80	2.3 (2309)	NG	CIS-E III	5	OHC
	80 Quattro	2.3 (2309)	NG	CIS-E III	5	OHC
	90	2.3 (2309)	NG	CIS-E III	5	OHC
	90 Quattro	2.3 (2309)	7A	MPI	5	OHC 20V
	Coupé Quattro	2.3 (2309)	7A	MPI	5	OHC 20V
	100	2.3 (2309)	NF	CIS-E III	5	OHC
	100 Quattro	2.3 (2309)	NF	CIS-E III	5	OHC
	200	2.2 (2226)	MC	CIS	5	Turbo
	200 Quattro	2.2 (2226)	3B	Motronic	5	Turbo 20V
	200 Quattro Wagon	2.2 (2226)	3B	Motronic	5	Turbo 20V
	V8 Quattro	3.6 (3562)	PT	Motronic	8	OHC 32V
1992	80	2.3 (2309)	NG	CIS-E III	5	OHC
	80 Quattro	2.3 (2309)	NG	CIS-E III	5	OHC
	100	2.8 (2771)	AAH	MPI	6	OHC
	100S	2.8 (2771)	AAH	MPI	6	OHC
	100CS	2.8 (2771)	AAH	MPI	6	OHC
	100CS Quattro	2.8 (2771)	AAH	MPI	6	OHC
	100CS Quattro Wagon	2.8 (2771)	AAH	MPI	6	OHC
	S4 Quattro	2.2 (2226)	AAN	Motronic	5	Turbo 20V
	V8 Quattro	4.2 (4172)	ABH	Motronic	8	OHC 32V
1993	90S	2.8 (2771)	AAH	MPI	6	OHC
	90CS	2.8 (2771)	AAH	MPI	6	OHC
	90CS Quattro	2.8 (2771)	AAH	MPI	6	OHC
	100	2.8 (2771)	AAH	MPI	6	OHC
	100S	2.8 (2771)	AAH	MPI	6	OHC
	100CS	2.8 (2771)	AAH	MPI	6	OHC
	100CS Quattro	2.8 (2771)	AAH	MPI	6	OHC
	100CS Quattro Wagon	2.8 (2771)	AAH	MPI	6	OHC
	S4 Quattro	2.2 (2226)	AAN	Motronic	5	Turbo 20V
	V8 Quattro	4.2 (4172)	ABH	Motronic	8	OHC 32V

ENGINE IDENTIFICATION

Year	Model	Engine Displacement Liters (cc)	Engine Series (ID/VIN)	Fuel System	No. of Cylinders	Engine Type
1994	90S	2.8 (2771)	AAH	MPI	6	OHC
	90CS	2.8 (2771)	AAH	MPI	6	OHC
	90CS Quattro	2.8 (2771)	AAH	MPI	6	OHC
	100	2.8 (2771)	AAH	MPI	6	OHC
	100S	2.8 (2771)	AAH	MPI	6	OHC
	100CS	2.8 (2771)	AAH	MPI	6	OHC
	100CS Quattro	2.8 (2771)	AAH	MPI	6	OHC
	100CS Quattro Wagon	2.8 (2771)	AAH	MPI	6	OHC
	S4 Quattro	2.2 (2226)	AAN	Motronic	5	Turbo 20V
	V8 Quattro	4.2 (4172)	ABH	Motronic	8	OHC 32V

MPI—Multi Point Injection
CIS-E—Continuous Injection System-Electronic
OHC—Overhead Camshaft
V—Valve

GENERAL ENGINE SPECIFICATIONS

Year	Engine ID/VIN	Engine Displacement Liters (cc)	Fuel System Type	Net Horsepower @ rpm	Net Torque @ rpm (ft. lbs.)	Bore × Stroke (in.)	Compression Ratio	Oil Pressure @ rpm
1990	3A	2.0 (1983)	CIS-Motronic	108 @ 5300	121 @ 3200	3.25 × 3.65	10.5:1	29 @ 2000
	NG	2.3 (2309)	CIS-E III	130 @ 5700	140 @ 4500	3.25 × 3.40	10.0:1	29 @ 2000
	7A	2.3 (2309)	MPI	164 @ 6000	157 @ 4500	3.25 × 3.40	10.3:1	29 @ 2000
	NF	2.3 (2309)	CIS-E III	130 @ 5700	140 @ 4500	3.25 × 3.40	10.0:1	29 @ 2000
	MC	2.2 (2226)	CIS	162 @ 5500	177 @ 3000	3.19 × 3.40	8.4:1	29 @ 2000
	PT	3.6 (3562)	Motronic	240 @ 5800	245 @ 4000	3.19 × 3.40	10.6:1	29 @ 2000
1991	NG	2.3 (2309)	CIS-E III	130 @ 5700	140 @ 4500	3.25 × 3.40	10.0:1	29 @ 2000
	7A	2.3 (2309)	MPI	164 @ 6000	157 @ 4500	3.25 × 3.40	10.3:1	29 @ 2000
	NF	2.3 (2309)	CIS-E III	130 @ 5700	140 @ 4500	3.25 × 3.40	10.0:1	29 @ 2000
	MC	2.2 (2226)	CIS	162 @ 5500	177 @ 3000	3.19 × 3.40	8.4:1	29 @ 2000
	3B	2.2 (2226)	Motronic	217 @ 5700	228 @ 1950	3.19 × 3.40	9.3:1	29 @ 2000
	PT	3.6 (3562)	Motronic	240 @ 5800	245 @ 4000	3.19 × 3.40	10.6:1	29 @ 2000
1992	NG	2.3 (2309)	CIS-E III	130 @ 5700	140 @ 4500	3.25 × 3.40	10.0:1	29 @ 2000
	AAH	2.8 (2771)	MPI	172 @ 5500	184 @ 3000	3.25 × 3.40	10.3:2	29 @ 2000
	AAN	2.2 (2226)	Motronic	227 @ 5900	258 @ 1950	3.19 × 3.40	9.3:1	29 @ 2000
	ABH	4.2 (4172)	Motronic	276 @ 5800	295 @ 4000	3.33 × 3.65	10.6:2	29 @ 2000
1993	AAH	2.8 (2771)	MPI	172 @ 5500	184 @ 3000	3.25 × 3.40	10.3:2	29 @ 2000
	AAN	2.2 (2226)	Motronic	227 @ 5900	258 @ 1950	3.19 × 3.40	9.3:1	29 @ 2000
	ABH	4.2 (4172)	Motronic	276 @ 5800	295 @ 4000	3.33 × 3.65	10.6:2	29 @ 2000
1994	AAH	2.8 (2771)	MPI	172 @ 5500	184 @ 3000	3.25 × 3.40	10.3:2	29 @ 2000
	AAN	2.2 (2226)	Motronic	227 @ 5900	258 @ 1950	3.19 × 3.40	9.3:1	29 @ 2000
	ABH	4.2 (4172)	Motronic	276 @ 5800	295 @ 4000	3.33 × 3.65	10.6:2	29 @ 2000

MPI—Multi Port Injection
CIS—Continuous Injection System
CIS-E—Continuous Injection System-Electronic

GASOLINE ENGINE TUNE-UP SPECIFICATIONS

Year	Engine ID/VIN	Engine Displacement Liters (cc)	Spark Plugs Gap (in.)	Ignition Timing (deg.) MT	AT	Fuel Pump (psi)	Idle Speed (rpm) MT	AT	Valve Clearance In.	Ex.
1990	3A	2.0 (1983)	0.031	6B	6B	88–94	780–900	780–900	Hyd.	Hyd.
	NG	2.3 (2309)	0.031	15B	15B	88–94	720–860	720–860	Hyd.	Hyd.
	7A	2.3 (2309)	0.031	①	①	55–61	720–860	720–860	Hyd.	Hyd.
	NF	2.3 (2309)	0.031	15B	15B	88–94	670–770	670–770	Hyd.	Hyd.
	MC	2.2 (2226)	0.028	①	①	84–95	750–850	670–770	Hyd.	Hyd.
	PT	3.6 (3562)	0.032	①	①	58–62	700–760	700–760	Hyd.	Hyd.
1991	NG	2.3 (2309)	0.031	15B	15B	88–94	720–860	720–860	Hyd.	Hyd.
	7A	2.3 (2309)	0.031	①	①	55–61	720–860	720–860	Hyd.	Hyd.
	NF	2.3 (2309)	0.031	15B	15B	88–94	680–770	680–770	Hyd.	Hyd.
	MC	2.2 (2226)	0.028	①	①	84–95	700–740	700–740	Hyd.	Hyd.
	3B	2.2 (2226)	0.024	①	①	43–46	770–830	770–830	Hyd.	Hyd.
	PT	3.6 (3562)	0.032	①	①	58–62	700–760	700–760	Hyd.	Hyd.
1992	NG	2.3 (2309)	0.031	15B	15B	88–94	720–860	720–860	Hyd.	Hyd.
	AAH	2.8 (2771)	0.030	①	①	55–61	700–800	700–800	Hyd.	Hyd.
	AAN	2.2 (2226)	0.024	①	①	58–61	770–830	770–830	Hyd.	Hyd.
	ABH	4.2 (4172)	0.032	①	①	58–62	690–750	710–770	Hyd.	Hyd.
1993	AAH	2.8 (2771)	0.030	①	①	55–61	700–800	700–800	Hyd.	Hyd.
	AAN	2.2 (2226)	0.024	①	①	58–61	770–830	770–830	Hyd.	Hyd.
	ABH	4.2 (4172)	0.032	①	①	58–62	690–750	710–770	Hyd.	Hyd.
1994	AAH	2.8 (2771)	0.030	①	①	55–61	700–800	700–800	Hyd.	Hyd.
	AAN	2.2 (2226)	0.024	①	①	58–61	770–830	770–830	Hyd.	Hyd.
	ABH	4.2 (4172)	0.032	①	①	58–62	690–750	710–770	Hyd.	Hyd.

NOTE: The lowest cylinder pressure should be within 75% of the highest cylinder pressure reading. For example, if the highest cylinder is 134 psi, the lowest should be 101. Engine should be at normal operating temperature with throttle valve in the wide open position.

The underhood specifications sticker often reflects tune-up specification changes in production. Sticker figures must be used if they disagree with those in this chart.

Hyd.—Hydraulic

① Basic Setting TDC—Adjusted by ECU. Do not rotate distributor.

FIRING ORDERS

NOTE: To avoid confusion, always replace spark plug wires one at a time.

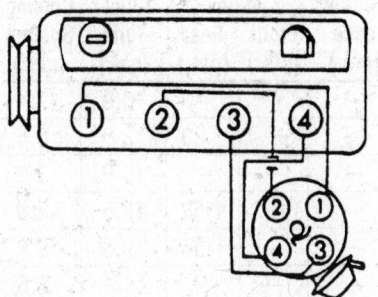

2.0L Engine
Engine Firing Order: 1-3-4-2
Distributor Rotation: Clockwise

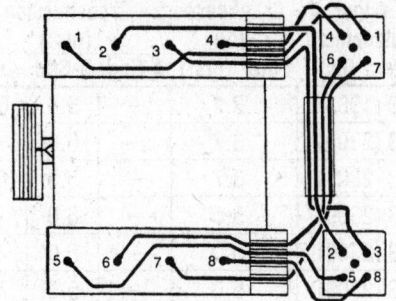

3.6L and 4.2L Engines
Engine Firing Order: 1-5-4-8-6-3-7-2
Distributor Rotation: Clockwise

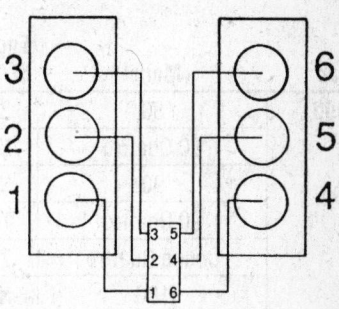

2.8L Engine
Engine Firing Order: 1-4-3-6-2-5
Distributorless Ignition

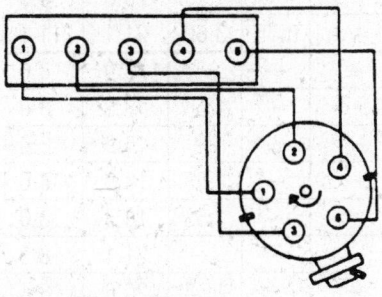

2.2L and 2.3L Engines
Engine Firing Order: 1-2-4-5-3
Distributor Rotation: Clockwise

CAPACITIES

Year	Model	Engine ID/VIN	Engine Displacement Liters (cc)	Engine Crankcase with Filter (qts.)	Transmission (pts.) 4-Spd	5-Spd	Auto.	Transfer case (pts.)	Drive Axle Front (pts.)	Rear (pts.)	Fuel Tank (gal.)	Cooling System (qts.)
1990	80	3A	2.0 (1983)	3.2	—	5.0	6.4	—	—	—	15.9	7.4
	80 Quattro	NG	2.3 (2309)	3.7	—	6.0	—	—	—	1.58	18.5	8.6
	90	NG	2.3 (2309)	3.7	—	5.0	6.4	—	—	—	15.9	8.6
	90 Quattro	7A	2.3 (2309)	5.0	—	6.0	—	—	—	1.58	18.5	8.6
	Coupé Quattro	7A	2.3 (2309)	5.0	—	6.0	①	—	—	1.58	18.5	8.6
	100	NF	2.3 (2309)	5.0	—	5.0	7.0	—	—	—	21.1	8.5
	100 Quattro	NF	2.3 (2309)	5.0	—	6.0	—	—	—	1.58	20.6	8.5
	200	MC	2.2 (2226)	5.0	—	5.0	7.0	—	—	—	21.1	8.5
	200 Quattro	MC	2.2 (2226)	5.0	—	6.0	—	—	—	1.58	20.6	8.5
	200 Quattro Wagon	MC	2.2 (2226)	5.0	—	6.0	—	—	—	1.58	20.6	8.5
	V8 Quattro	PT	3.6 (3562)	8.0	—	—	②	—	0.75	3.60	21.1	11.1
1991	80	NG	2.3 (2309)	3.7	—	5.0	①	—	—	—	15.9	8.6
	80 Quattro	NG	2.3 (2309)	3.7	—	6.0	—	—	—	1.58	18.5	8.6
	90	NG	2.3 (2309)	3.7	—	—	①	—	—	—	15.9	8.6
	90 Quattro	7A	2.3 (2309)	5.0	—	6.0	—	—	—	1.58	18.5	8.6
	Coupé Quattro	7A	2.3 (2309)	5.0	—	6.0	—	—	—	1.58	18.5	8.6
	100	NF	2.3 (2309)	5.0	—	—	③	—	—	—	21.1	8.5
	100 Quattro	NF	2.3 (2309)	5.0	—	6.0	—	—	—	1.58	20.6	8.5
	200	MC	2.2 (2226)	5.0	—	—	③	—	—	—	21.1	8.5
	200 Quattro	3B	2.2 (2226)	5.0	—	6.0	—	—	—	1.58	21.1	8.5
	200 Quattro Wagon	3B	2.2 (2226)	5.0	—	6.0	—	—	—	1.58	21.1	8.5
	V8 Quattro	PT	3.6 (3562)	8.0	—	—	②	—	0.75	3.60	21.1	11.1
1992	80	NG	2.3 (2309)	3.7	—	5.0	①	—	—	—	15.9	8.6
	80 Quattro	NG	2.3 (2309)	3.7	—	6.0	—	—	—	1.58	18.5	8.6
	100	AAH	2.8 (2771)	5.3	—	5.0	①	—	—	—	21.1	12.7
	100S	AAH	2.8 (2771)	5.3	—	5.0	①	—	—	—	21.1	12.7
	100CS	AAH	2.8 (2771)	5.3	—	5.0	①	—	—	—	21.1	12.7
	100CS Quattro	AAH	2.8 (2771)	5.3	—	5.0	—	—	—	2.00	21.1	12.7
	100CS Quattro Wagon	AAH	2.8 (2771)	5.3	—	5.0	—	—	—	2.00	21.1	12.7
	S4	AAN	2.2 (2226)	5.0	—	5.0	—	—	—	1.58	21.1	8.5
	V8 Quattro	ABH	4.2 (4172)	8.0	—	12.8	②	—	0.75	3.60	21.1	11.1
1993	90S	AAH	2.8 (2771)	5.3	—	5.0	①	—	—	—	17.4	11.6
	90CS	AAH	2.8 (2771)	5.3	—	5.0	①	—	—	—	17.4	11.6
	90CS Quattro	AAH	2.8 (2771)	5.3	—	5.0	①	—	—	2.00	16.9	11.6
	100	AAH	2.8 (2771)	5.3	—	5.0	①	—	—	—	21.1	12.7
	100S	AAH	2.8 (2771)	5.3	—	5.0	①	—	—	—	21.1	12.7
	100CS	AAH	2.8 (2771)	5.3	—	5.0	①	—	—	—	21.1	12.7
	100CS Quattro	AAH	2.8 (2771)	5.3	—	5.0	—	—	—	2.00	21.1	12.7
	100CS Quattro Wagon	AAH	2.8 (2771)	5.3	—	5.0	—	—	—	2.00	21.1	12.7
	S4	AAN	2.2 (2226)	5.0	—	5.0	—	—	—	1.58	21.1	8.5
	V8 Quattro	ABH	4.2 (4172)	8.0	—	12.8	②	—	0.75	3.60	21.1	11.1

CAPACITIES

Year	Model	Engine ID/VIN	Engine Displacement Liters (cc)	Engine Crankcase with Filter (qts.)	Transmission (pts.)			Transfer case (pts.)	Drive Axle		Fuel Tank (gal.)	Cooling System (qts.)
					4-Spd	5-Spd	Auto.		Front (pts.)	Rear (pts.)		
1994	90S	AAH	2.8 (2771)	5.3	—	5.0	①	—	—	—	17.4	11.6
	90CS	AAH	2.8 (2771)	5.3	—	5.0	①	—	—	—	17.4	11.6
	90CS Quattro	AAH	2.8 (2771)	5.3	—	5.0	①	—	—	2.00	16.9	11.6
	100	AAH	2.8 (2771)	5.3	—	5.0	①	—	—	—	21.1	12.7
	100S	AAH	2.8 (2771)	5.3	—	5.0	①	—	—	—	21.1	12.7
	100CS	AAH	2.8 (2771)	5.3	—	5.0	①	—	—	—	21.1	12.7
	100CS Quattro	AAH	2.8 (2771)	5.3	—	5.0	—	—	—	2.00	21.1	12.7
	100CS Quattro Wagon	AAH	2.8 (2771)	5.3	—	5.0	—	—	—	2.00	21.1	12.7
	S4	AAN	2.2 (2226)	5.0	—	5.0	—	—	—	1.58	21.1	8.5
	V8 Quattro	ABH	4.2 (4172)	8.0	—	12.8	②	—	0.75	3.60	21.1	11.1

NA—Not available
① Initial Fill—12.7 pts.
   Change—6.3 pts.
② Initial Fill—20.4 pts.
   Change—8.0 pts.
③ Initial Fill—11.4 pts.
   Change—6.3 pts.

CRANKSHAFT AND CONNECTING ROD SPECIFICATIONS

All measurements are given in inches.

Year	Engine ID/VIN	Engine Displacement Liters (cc)	Crankshaft Main Brg. Journal Dia.	Main Brg. Oil Clearance	Shaft End-play	Thrust on No.	Connecting Rod Journal Diameter	Oil Clearance	Side Clearance
1990	3A	2.0 (1983)	2.1268–2.1276	NA	NA	3	1.8827–1.8835	NA	NA
	NG	2.3 (2309)	2.2818–2.2825	0.0010–0.0020	0.003–0.009	4	1.8802–1.8810	0.0004–0.0020	0.016
	7A	2.3 (2309)	2.2818–2.2825	0.0010–0.0020	0.003–0.009	4	1.8802–1.8810	0.0004–0.0020	0.016
	NF	2.3 (2309)	2.2818–2.2825	0.0010–0.0020	0.003–0.009	4	1.8802–1.8810	0.0004–0.0020	0.016
	MC	2.2 (2226)	2.2818–2.2825	0.0006–0.0030	0.003–0.009	4	1.8487–1.8495	0.0004–0.0020	0.016
	PT	3.6 (3562)	NA	NA	NA	NA	NA	NA	NA
1991	NG	2.3 (2309)	2.2815–2.2825	0.0010–0.0020	0.003–0.009	4	1.8802–1.8810	0.0004–0.0020	0.016
	7A	2.3 (2309)	2.2818–2.2825	0.0010–0.0020	0.003–0.009	4	1.8802–1.8810	0.0004–0.0020	0.016
	NF	2.3 (2309)	2.2818–2.2825	0.0010–0.0020	0.003–0.009	4	1.8802–1.8810	0.0004–0.0020	0.016
	MC	2.2 (2226)	2.2814–2.2825	0.0006–0.0030	0.003–0.009	4	1.8487–1.8495	0.0004–0.0020	0.016
	3B	2.2 (2226)	2.2818–2.2825	0.0006–0.0030	0.003–0.009	4	1.8487–1.8495	0.0004–0.0020	0.016
	PT	3.6 (3562)	NA	NA	NA	NA	NA	NA	NA
1992	NG	2.3 (2309)	2.2815–2.2825	0.0010–0.0020	0.003–0.009	4	1.8802–1.8810	0.0004–0.0020	0.016
	AAH	2.8 (2771)	NA	NA	NA	NA	NA	NA	NA
	AAN	2.2 (2226)	2.2818–2.2825	0.0007–0.0023	0.003–0.009	4	1.8802–1.8810	0.0004–0.0020	0.016
	ABH	4.2 (4172)	NA	NA	NA	NA	NA	NA	NA
1993	AAH	2.8 (2771)	NA	NA	NA	NA	NA	NA	NA
	AAN	2.2 (2226)	2.2818–2.2825	0.0007–0.0023	0.003–0.009	4	1.8802–1.8810	0.0004–0.0020	0.016
	ABH	4.2 (4172)	NA	NA	NA	NA	NA	NA	NA
1994	AAH	2.8 (2771)	NA	NA	NA	NA	NA	NA	NA
	AAN	2.2 (2226)	2.2818–2.2825	0.0007–0.0023	0.003–0.009	4	1.8802–1.8810	0.0004–0.0020	0.016
	ABH	4.2 (4172)	NA	NA	NA	NA	NA	NA	NA

NA—Not available

VALVE SPECIFICATIONS

Year	Engine ID/VIN	Engine Displacement Liters (cc)	Seat Angle (deg.)	Face Angle (deg.)	Spring Test Pressure (lbs. @ in.)	Spring Installed Height (in.)	Stem-to-Guide Clearance (in.)		Stem Diameter (in.)	
							Intake	Exhaust	Intake	Exhaust
1990	3A	2.0 (1983)	45	45	—	—	0.039	0.051	0.3140	0.3130
	NG	2.3 (2309)	45	45	—	—	0.039	0.051	0.3140	0.3130
	7A	2.3 (2309)	45	45	—	—	0.039	0.051	0.2744	0.2732
	NF	2.3 (2309)	45	45	—	—	0.039	0.051	0.3140	0.3130
	MC	2.2 (2226)	45	45	—	—	0.039	0.051	0.3140	0.3130
	PT	3.6 (3562)	45	45	—	—	NA	NA	NA	NA
1991	NG	2.3 (2309)	45	45	—	—	0.039	0.051	0.3140	0.3130
	7A	2.3 (2309)	45	45	—	—	0.039	0.051	0.2744	0.2732
	NF	2.3 (2309)	45	45	—	—	0.039	0.051	0.3140	0.3130
	MC	2.2 (2226)	45	45	—	—	0.039	0.051	0.3140	0.3130
	3B	2.2 (2226)	45	45	—	—	0.039	0.051	0.2744	0.2732
	PT	3.6 (3562)	45	45	—	—	NA	NA	NA	NA
1992	NG	2.3 (2309)	45	45	—	—	0.039	0.051	0.3140	0.3130
	AAH	2.8 (2771)	NA	NA	—	—	NA	NA	NA	NA
	AAN	2.2 (2226)	45	45	—	—	0.039	0.051	0.2744	0.2732
	ABH	4.2 (4172)	45	45	—	—	NA	NA	NA	NA
1993	AAH	2.8 (2771)	NA	NA	—	—	NA	NA	NA	NA
	AAN	2.2 (2226)	45	45	—	—	0.039	0.051	0.2744	0.2732
	ABH	4.2 (4172)	45	45	—	—	NA	NA	NA	NA
1994	AAH	2.8 (2771)	NA	NA	—	—	NA	NA	NA	NA
	AAN	2.2 (2226)	45	45	—	—	0.039	0.051	0.2744	0.2732
	ABH	4.2 (4172)	45	45	—	—	NA	NA	NA	NA

NA—Not available

PISTON AND RING SPECIFICATIONS

All measurements are given in inches.

Year	Engine ID/VIN	Engine Displacement Liters (cc)	Piston Clearance	Ring Gap			Ring Side Clearance		
				Top Compression	Bottom Compression	Oil Control	Top Compression	Bottom Compression	Oil Control
1990	3A	2.0 (1983)	0.0012	0.012–0.018	0.012–0.018	0.010–0.018	0.0010–0.0020	0.0010–0.0020	0.0010–0.0020
	NG	2.3 (2309)	0.0012	0.008–0.016	0.008–0.016	0.010–0.020	0.0010–0.0030	0.0010–0.0030	0.0010–0.0020
	7A	2.3 (2309)	0.0012	0.006–0.014	0.006–0.014	0.006–0.014	0.0016–0.0028	0.0016–0.0024	0.0016–0.0028
	NF	2.3 (2309)	0.0012	0.008–0.016	0.008–0.016	0.010–0.020	0.0010–0.0030	0.0010–0.0030	0.0010–0.0020
	MC	2.2 (2226)	0.0012	0.008–0.020	0.008–0.020	0.010–0.020	0.0010–0.0030	0.0010–0.0030	0.0010–0.0030
	PT	3.6 (3562)	NA	NA	NA	NA	NA	NA	NA
1991	NG	2.3 (2309)	0.0012	0.008–0.016	0.008–0.016	0.010–0.020	0.0010–0.0030	0.0010–0.0030	0.0010–0.0020
	7A	2.3 (2309)	0.0012	0.006–0.014	0.006–0.014	0.006–0.014	0.0016–0.0028	0.0016–0.0028	0.0016–0.0028
	NF	2.3 (2309)	0.0012	0.008–0.016	0.008–0.016	0.010–0.020	0.0010–0.0030	0.0010–0.0030	0.0010–0.0020
	MC	2.2 (2226)	0.0012	0.008–0.020	0.008–0.020	0.010–0.020	0.0010–0.0030	0.0010–0.0030	0.0010–0.0030
	3B	2.2 (2226)	0.0012	0.006–0.014	0.006–0.014	0.006–0.014	0.0016–0.0028	0.0016–0.0028	0.0016–0.0028
	PT	3.6 (3562)	NA	NA	NA	NA	NA	NA	NA
1992	NG	2.3 (2309)	0.0012	0.008–0.016	0.008–0.016	0.010–0.020	0.0010–0.0030	0.0010–0.0030	0.0010–0.0020
	AAH	2.8 (2771)	NA	NA	NA	NA	NA	NA	NA
	AAN	2.2 (2226)	0.0012	0.006–0.014	0.006–0.014	0.006–0.014	0.0016–0.0028	0.0016–0.0028	0.0016–0.0028
	ABH	4.2 (4172)	NA	NA	NA	NA	NA	NA	NA
1993	AAH	2.8 (2771)	NA	NA	NA	NA	NA	NA	NA
	AAN	2.2 (2226)	0.0012	0.006–0.014	0.006–0.014	0.006–0.014	0.0016–0.0028	0.0016–0.0028	0.0016–0.0028
	ABH	4.2 (4172)	NA	NA	NA	NA	NA	NA	NA
1994	AAH	2.8 (2771)	NA	NA	NA	NA	NA	NA	NA
	AAN	2.2 (2226)	0.0012	0.006–0.014	0.006–0.014	0.006–0.014	0.0016–0.0028	0.0016–0.0028	0.0016–0.0028
	ABH	4.2 (4172)	NA	NA	NA	NA	NA	NA	NA

NA—Not available

TORQUE SPECIFICATIONS

All readings in ft. lbs.

Year	Engine ID/VIN	Engine Displacement Liters (cc)	Cylinder Head Bolts	Main Bearing Bolts	Rod Bearing Bolts	Crankshaft Pulley Bolts	Flywheel Bolts	Manifold Intake	Manifold Exhaust	Spark Plugs	Lug Nuts
1990	3A	2.0 (1983)	①	48	22③	④	74	15	18	15	81
	NG	2.3 (2309)	①	48	22③	258	74	22	26	14	81
	7A	2.3 (2309)	①	48	22③	258	74	22	26	14	81
	NF	2.3 (2309)	①	48	22③	258	74	22	26	14	81
	MC	2.2 (2226)	①	48	22③	258	74	22	26	14	81
	PT	3.6 (3562)	⑤	NA	NA	258	74	②	18	22	81
1991	NG	2.3 (2309)	①	48	22③	258	74	22	26	14	81
	7A	2.3 (2309)	①	48	22③	258	74	22	26	14	81
	NF	2.3 (2309)	①	48	22③	258	74	22	26	14	81
	MC	2.2 (2226)	①	48	22③	258	74	22	26	14	81
	3B	2.2 (2226)	①	48	22③	258	74	22	26	14	81
	PT	3.6 (3562)	⑤	NA	NA	258	74	②	18	22	81
1992	NG	2.3 (2309)	①	48	22③	258	74	22	26	14	81
	AAH	2.8 (2771)	⑤	NA	NA	258	74	15	15	14	81
	AAN	2.2 (2226)	①	48	22③	258	74	22	26	14	81
	ABH	4.2 (4172)	⑤	NA	NA	258	74	②	18	22	81
1993	AAH	2.8 (2771)	⑤	NA	NA	258	74	15	15	14	81
	AAN	2.2 (2226)	①	48	22③	258	74	22	26	14	81
	ABH	4.2 (4172)	⑤	NA	NA	258	74	②	18	22	81
1994	AAH	2.8 (2771)	⑤	NA	NA	258	74	15	15	14	81
	AAN	2.2 (2226)	①	48	22③	258	74	22	26	14	81
	ABH	4.2 (4172)	⑤	NA	NA	258	74	②	18	22	81

NOTE: Always use new rod bearing bolts.
NA—Not available
① In sequence 29 ft. lbs., 43 ft. lbs. and then tighten it a half turn more (180 degrees).
② Lower manifold to block—7 ft. lbs.
Lower manifold to upper manifold—11 ft. lbs.
③ Plus a quarter turn (90 degrees).
④ In sequence 66 ft. lbs., then a half turn more (180 degrees).
⑤ In sequence 30 ft. lbs., 44 ft. lbs., and then tighten it a half turn more (180 degrees). It is not necessary to retighten head bolts during maintenance service or after repairs.

BRAKE SPECIFICATIONS

All measurements in inches unless noted.

Year	Model	Master Cylinder Bore	Front Brake Disc			Rear Brake Disc			Minimum Lining Thickness	
			Original Thickness	Minimum Thickness	Maximum Runout	Original Thickness	Minimum Thickness	Maximum Runout	Front	Rear
1990	80	0.874	0.866	0.787	0.002	0.394	0.315	0.002	0.079	0.079
	80 Quattro	0.874	0.866	0.787	0.002	0.394	0.315	0.002	0.079	0.079
	90	0.874	0.866	0.787	0.002	0.394	0.315	0.002	0.079	0.079
	90 Quattro	0.874	0.866	0.787	0.002	0.394	0.315	0.002	0.079	0.079
	Coupé Quattro	1.000	0.984	0.906	0.002	0.394	0.315	0.002	0.079	0.079
	100	0.874	0.866	0.787	0.002	0.394	0.315	0.002	①	0.079
	100 Quattro	0.984	0.984	0.906	0.002	0.394	0.315	0.002	①	0.079
	200	0.984	0.984	0.906	0.002	0.394	0.315	0.002	①	0.079
	200 Quattro	0.984	0.984	0.906	0.002	0.394	0.315	0.002	①	0.079
	200 Quattro Wagon	0.984	0.984	0.906	0.002	0.394	0.315	0.002	①	0.079
	V8 Quattro	1.000	0.984	0.906	0.002	0.787	0.708	0.002	①	0.079
1991	80	0.874	0.866	0.787	0.002	0.394	0.315	0.002	0.079	0.079
	80 Quattro	0.874	0.866	0.787	0.002	0.394	0.315	0.002	0.079	0.079
	90	0.874	0.866	0.787	0.002	0.394	0.315	0.002	0.079	0.079
	90 Quattro	0.874	0.866	0.787	0.002	0.394	0.315	0.002	0.079	0.079
	Coupé Quattro	1.000	0.984	0.906	0.002	0.394	0.315	0.002	0.079	0.079
	100	0.874	0.866	0.787	0.002	0.394	0.315	0.002	①	0.079
	100 Quattro	0.984	0.984	0.906	0.002	0.394	0.315	0.002	①	0.079
	200	0.984	0.984	0.906	0.002	0.394	0.315	0.002	①	0.079
	200 Quattro	0.984	0.984	0.906	0.002	0.787	0.708	0.002	①	0.079
	200 Quattro Wagon	0.984	0.984	0.906	0.002	0.394	0.315	0.002	①	0.079
	V8 Quattro	1.000	0.984	0.906	0.002	0.787	0.708	0.002	①	0.079
1992	80	0.874	0.866	0.787	0.002	0.394	0.315	0.002	0.079	0.079
	80 Quattro	0.874	0.866	0.787	0.002	0.394	0.315	0.002	0.079	0.079
	100	0.984	0.984	0.906	0.002	0.394	0.315	0.002	①	0.079
	100S	0.984	0.984	0.906	0.002	0.394	0.315	0.002	①	0.079
	100CS	0.984	0.984	0.906	0.002	0.394	0.315	0.002	①	0.079
	100CS Quattro	0.984	0.984	0.906	0.002	0.394	0.315	0.002	①	0.079
	100CS Quattro Wagon	0.984	0.984	0.906	0.002	0.394	0.315	0.002	①	0.079
	S4	0.984	0.984	0.906	0.002	0.394	0.315	0.002	①	0.079
	V8 Quattro	1.000	0.984	0.906	0.002	0.787	0.709	0.002	①	0.079
1993	90S	0.874	0.866	0.787	0.002	0.394	0.315	0.002	0.079	0.079
	90CS	0.874	0.866	0.787	0.002	0.394	0.315	0.002	0.079	0.079
	90CS Quattro	0.874	0.866	0.787	0.002	0.394	0.315	0.002	0.079	0.079
	100	0.984	0.984	0.906	0.002	0.394	0.315	0.002	①	0.079
	100S	0.984	0.984	0.906	0.002	0.394	0.315	0.002	①	0.079
	100CS	0.984	0.984	0.906	0.002	0.394	0.315	0.002	①	0.079
	100CS Quattro	0.984	0.984	0.906	0.002	0.394	0.315	0.002	①	0.079
	100CS Quattro Wagon	0.984	0.984	0.906	0.002	0.394	0.315	0.002	①	0.079
	S4	0.984	0.984	0.906	0.002	0.394	0.315	0.002	①	0.079
	V8 Quattro	1.000	0.984	0.906	0.002	0.787	0.709	0.002	①	0.079

BRAKE SPECIFICATIONS

All measurements in inches unless noted.

Year	Model	Master Cylinder Bore	Front Brake Disc Original Thickness	Front Brake Disc Minimum Thickness	Front Brake Disc Maximum Runout	Rear Brake Disc Original Thickness	Rear Brake Disc Minimum Thickness	Rear Brake Disc Maximum Runout	Minimum Lining Thickness Front	Minimum Lining Thickness Rear
1994	90S	0.874	0.866	0.787	0.002	0.394	0.315	0.002	0.079	0.079
	90CS	0.874	0.866	0.787	0.002	0.394	0.315	0.002	0.079	0.079
	90CS Quattro	0.874	0.866	0.787	0.002	0.394	0.315	0.002	0.079	0.079
	100	0.984	0.984	0.906	0.002	0.394	0.315	0.002	①	0.079
	100S	0.984	0.984	0.906	0.002	0.394	0.315	0.002	①	0.079
	100CS	0.984	0.984	0.906	0.002	0.394	0.315	0.002	①	0.079
	100CS Quattro	0.984	0.984	0.906	0.002	0.394	0.315	0.002	①	0.079
	100CS Quattro Wagon	0.984	0.984	0.906	0.002	0.394	0.315	0.002	①	0.079
	S4	0.984	0.984	0.906	0.002	0.394	0.315	0.002	①	0.079
	V8 Quattro	1.000	0.984	0.906	0.002	0.787	0.709	0.002	①	0.079

① At 0.079 or when dash brake wear light illuminates

WHEEL ALIGNMENT

Year	Model	Caster Range (deg.)	Caster Preferred Setting (deg.)	Camber Range (deg.)	Camber Preferred Setting (deg.)	Toe-in (in.)	Steering Axis Inclination (deg.)
1990	80	$\frac{3}{4}$P–1$\frac{3}{4}$P	1$\frac{1}{4}$P	1$\frac{1}{4}$N–$\frac{1}{4}$N	$\frac{3}{4}$N	$\frac{5}{64}$	—
	80 Quattro	$\frac{3}{4}$P–1$\frac{3}{4}$P	1$\frac{1}{4}$P	1$\frac{11}{32}$N–$\frac{11}{32}$N	$\frac{27}{32}$N	$\frac{5}{64}$	—
	90	$\frac{3}{4}$P–1$\frac{3}{4}$P	1$\frac{1}{4}$P	1$\frac{1}{4}$N–$\frac{1}{4}$N	$\frac{3}{4}$N	$\frac{5}{64}$	—
	90 Quattro	$\frac{15}{16}$P–1$\frac{15}{16}$P	1$\frac{7}{16}$P	1$\frac{11}{32}$N–$\frac{11}{32}$N	$\frac{27}{32}$N	$\frac{5}{64}$	—
	Coupé Quattro	1$\frac{3}{4}$P–2$\frac{3}{4}$P	2$\frac{1}{4}$P	1$\frac{5}{16}$N–$\frac{5}{16}$N	$\frac{13}{16}$N	$\frac{5}{64}$	—
	100	$\frac{5}{16}$P–1$\frac{11}{16}$P	1P	1N–0	$\frac{1}{2}$N	$\frac{1}{16}$N	—
	100 Quattro	$\frac{5}{16}$P–1$\frac{11}{16}$P	1P	1N–0	$\frac{1}{2}$N	1$\frac{1}{16}$N	—
	200	$\frac{5}{16}$P–1$\frac{11}{16}$P	1P	1N–0	$\frac{1}{2}$N	1$\frac{1}{16}$N	—
	200 Quattro	$\frac{5}{16}$P–1$\frac{11}{16}$P	1P	1N–0	$\frac{1}{2}$N	1$\frac{1}{16}$N	—
	200 Quattro Wagon	$\frac{5}{16}$P–1$\frac{11}{16}$P	1P	1N–0	$\frac{1}{2}$N	1$\frac{1}{16}$N	—
	V8 Quattro	$\frac{5}{8}$P–1$\frac{7}{8}$P	1$\frac{1}{4}$P	1N–0	$\frac{1}{2}$N	$\frac{3}{16}$N	—
1991	80	$\frac{3}{4}$P–1$\frac{3}{4}$P	1$\frac{1}{4}$P	1$\frac{1}{4}$N–$\frac{1}{4}$N	$\frac{3}{4}$N	$\frac{5}{64}$	—
	80 Quattro	$\frac{3}{4}$P–1$\frac{3}{4}$P	1$\frac{1}{4}$P	1$\frac{11}{32}$N–$\frac{11}{32}$N	$\frac{27}{32}$N	$\frac{5}{64}$	—
	90	$\frac{3}{4}$P–1$\frac{3}{4}$P	1$\frac{1}{4}$P	1$\frac{1}{4}$N–$\frac{1}{4}$N	$\frac{3}{4}$N	$\frac{5}{64}$	—
	90 Quattro	$\frac{15}{16}$P–1$\frac{15}{16}$P	1$\frac{7}{16}$P	1$\frac{11}{32}$N–$\frac{11}{32}$N	$\frac{27}{32}$N	$\frac{5}{64}$	—
	Coupé Quattro	1$\frac{3}{4}$P–2$\frac{3}{4}$P	2$\frac{1}{4}$P	1$\frac{5}{16}$N–$\frac{5}{16}$N	$\frac{13}{16}$N	$\frac{5}{64}$	—
	100	$\frac{5}{16}$P–1$\frac{11}{16}$P	1P	1N–0	$\frac{1}{2}$N	$\frac{1}{16}$N	—
	100 Quattro	$\frac{5}{16}$P–1$\frac{11}{16}$P	1P	1N–0	$\frac{1}{2}$N	$\frac{1}{16}$N	—
	200	$\frac{5}{16}$P–1$\frac{11}{16}$P	1P	1N–0	$\frac{1}{2}$N	$\frac{1}{16}$N	—
	200 Quattro	$\frac{9}{16}$P–1$\frac{15}{16}$P	1$\frac{1}{4}$P	1N–0	$\frac{1}{2}$N	$\frac{1}{16}$N	—
	200 Quattro Wagon	$\frac{9}{16}$P–1$\frac{15}{16}$P	1$\frac{1}{4}$P	1N–0	$\frac{1}{2}$N	$\frac{1}{16}$N	—
	V8 Quattro	$\frac{5}{8}$P–1$\frac{7}{8}$P	1$\frac{1}{4}$P	1N–0	$\frac{1}{2}$N	$\frac{3}{16}$N	—
1992	80	$\frac{3}{4}$P–1$\frac{3}{4}$P	1$\frac{1}{4}$P	1$\frac{1}{4}$N–$\frac{1}{4}$N	$\frac{3}{4}$N	$\frac{5}{64}$	—
	80 Quattro	$\frac{3}{4}$P–1$\frac{3}{4}$P	1$\frac{1}{4}$P	1$\frac{11}{32}$N–$\frac{11}{32}$N	$\frac{27}{32}$N	$\frac{5}{64}$	—
	100	$\frac{1}{2}$P–1$\frac{7}{8}$P	1$\frac{3}{16}$P	1$\frac{1}{8}$N–$\frac{1}{8}$N ①	$\frac{11}{16}$N ②	$\frac{1}{16}$N	—
	100S	$\frac{1}{2}$P–1$\frac{7}{8}$P	1$\frac{3}{16}$P	1$\frac{1}{8}$N–$\frac{1}{8}$N ①	$\frac{11}{16}$N ②	$\frac{1}{16}$N	—
	100CS	$\frac{1}{2}$P–1$\frac{7}{8}$P	1$\frac{3}{16}$P	1$\frac{1}{8}$N–$\frac{1}{8}$N ①	$\frac{11}{16}$N ②	$\frac{1}{16}$N	—
	100CS Quattro	$\frac{1}{2}$P–1$\frac{7}{8}$P	1$\frac{3}{16}$P	1$\frac{1}{8}$N–$\frac{1}{8}$N ①	$\frac{11}{16}$N ②	$\frac{1}{16}$N	—
	100CS Quattro Wagon	$\frac{1}{2}$P–1$\frac{7}{8}$P	1$\frac{3}{16}$P	1$\frac{1}{8}$N–$\frac{1}{8}$N ①	$\frac{11}{16}$N ②	$\frac{1}{16}$N	—
	S4 Quattro	$\frac{9}{16}$P–1$\frac{15}{16}$P	1$\frac{1}{4}$P	1N–0	$\frac{1}{2}$N	$\frac{3}{16}$N	—
	V8 Quattro	$\frac{5}{8}$P–1$\frac{7}{8}$P	1P	1N–0	$\frac{1}{2}$N	$\frac{3}{16}$N	—
1993	90S	$\frac{3}{4}$P–1$\frac{3}{4}$P	1$\frac{1}{4}$P	1$\frac{1}{4}$N–$\frac{1}{4}$N	$\frac{3}{4}$N	$\frac{5}{64}$	—
	90CS	$\frac{3}{4}$P–1$\frac{3}{4}$P	1$\frac{1}{4}$P	1$\frac{11}{32}$N–$\frac{11}{32}$N	$\frac{27}{32}$N	$\frac{5}{64}$	—
	90CS Quattro	NA	NA	NA	NA	NA	—
	100	$\frac{1}{2}$P–1$\frac{7}{8}$P	1$\frac{3}{16}$P	1$\frac{1}{8}$N–$\frac{1}{8}$N ①	$\frac{11}{16}$N ②	$\frac{1}{16}$N	—
	100S	$\frac{1}{2}$P–1$\frac{7}{8}$P	1$\frac{3}{16}$P	1$\frac{1}{8}$N–$\frac{1}{8}$N ①	$\frac{11}{16}$N ②	$\frac{1}{16}$N	—
	100CS	$\frac{1}{2}$P–1$\frac{7}{8}$P	1$\frac{3}{16}$P	1$\frac{1}{8}$N–$\frac{1}{8}$N ①	$\frac{11}{16}$N ②	$\frac{1}{16}$N	—
	100CS Quattro	$\frac{1}{2}$P–1$\frac{7}{8}$P	1$\frac{3}{16}$P	1$\frac{1}{8}$N–$\frac{1}{8}$N ①	$\frac{11}{16}$N ②	$\frac{1}{16}$N	—
	100CS Quattro Wagon	$\frac{1}{2}$P–1$\frac{7}{8}$P	1$\frac{3}{16}$P	1$\frac{1}{8}$N–$\frac{1}{8}$N ①	$\frac{11}{16}$N ②	$\frac{1}{16}$N	—
	S4 Quattro	$\frac{9}{16}$P–1$\frac{15}{16}$P	1$\frac{1}{4}$P	1N–0	$\frac{1}{2}$N	$\frac{3}{16}$N	—
	V8 Quattro	$\frac{5}{8}$P–1$\frac{7}{8}$P	1P	1N–0	$\frac{1}{2}$N	$\frac{3}{16}$N	—

WHEEL ALIGNMENT

Year	Model	Caster Range (deg.)	Caster Preferred Setting (deg.)	Camber Range (deg.)	Camber Preferred Setting (deg.)	Toe-in (in.)	Steering Axis Inclination (deg.)
1994	90S	³⁄₄P–1³⁄₄P	1¹⁄₄P	1¹⁄₄N–¹⁄₄N	³⁄₄N	⁵⁄₆₄	—
	90CS	³⁄₄P–1³⁄₄P	1¹⁄₄P	1¹¹⁄₃₂N–¹¹⁄₃₂N	²⁷⁄₃₂N	⁵⁄₆₄	—
	90CS Quattro	NA	NA	NA	NA	NA	—
	100	¹⁄₂P–1⁷⁄₈P	1³⁄₁₆P	1¹⁄₈N–¹⁄₈N ①	¹¹⁄₁₆N ②	¹⁄₁₆N	—
	100S	¹⁄₂P–1⁷⁄₈P	1³⁄₁₆P	1¹⁄₈N–¹⁄₈N ①	¹¹⁄₁₆N ②	¹⁄₁₆N	—
	100CS	¹⁄₂P–1⁷⁄₈P	1³⁄₁₆P	1¹⁄₈N–¹⁄₈N ①	¹¹⁄₁₆N ②	¹⁄₁₆N	—
	100CS Quattro	¹⁄₂P–1⁷⁄₈P	1³⁄₁₆P	1¹⁄₈N–¹⁄₈N ①	¹¹⁄₁₆N ②	¹⁄₁₆N	—
	100CS Quattro Wagon	¹⁄₂P–1⁷⁄₈P	1³⁄₁₆P	1¹⁄₈N–¹⁄₈N ①	¹¹⁄₁₆N ②	¹⁄₁₆N	—
	S4 Quattro	⁹⁄₁₆P–1¹⁵⁄₁₆P	1¹⁄₄P	1N–0	¹⁄₂N	³⁄₁₆N	—
	V8 Quattro	⁵⁄₈P–1⁷⁄₈P	1P	1N–0	¹⁄₂N	³⁄₁₆N	—

NA—Not available
N—Negative
P—Positive
① w/manual transmission: 1¹⁄₄N–¹⁄₄N
② w/manual transmission: ¹³⁄₁₆N

SERIAL NUMBER IDENTIFICATION

Vehicle Identification Plate

The Vehicle Identification Number (VIN) is located on a plate on top of the instrument panel. The VIN number is visible from outside through the left side of the windshield. The VIN number is also stamped into the upper right corner of the firewall. The vehicle identification plate is mounted on the right front wheel housing.

Engine Number

4 and 5 Cylinder Engines

The engine serial number is stamped into the left rear side of the engine block. In addition to the serial number, an engine code number is stamped into the starter end of the engine block, below the cylinder head mounting surface. This number indicates the original cylinder bore size of the engine.

6 Cylinder Engine

The engine serial number is stamped on the right hand side inside of the engine block between the cylinder head and hydraulic pump.

8 Cylinder Engine

The engine serial number is stamped into the left side of the engine block, just above the power steering hydraulic pump.

Transaxle Number

To identify a transaxle there are 2 sets of numbers. The first set is located at the top of the bell housing. This set contains the transaxle code letters (first 3 digits or letters) and date of production. The second set is located at the side of the case. This set of numbers is the transaxle type.

NOTE: The transaxle code is also listed on the Vehicle Identification Label.

Model Data Sticker

On the inside of the luggage compartment lid is a sticker indicating the model type, chassis number, body type, paint number, engine and transaxle codes and the options package.

Body Panel Identification

The major body panels of all 1991 and later vehicles are marked with the complete VIN and the Audi logo. This is done in accordance with the Motor Vehicle Theft Law Enforcement Act to discourage theft and resale of the vehicle for parts. All authorized replacement parts will also have the Audi logo and a label with the "R DOT" designation in place of the VIN for that vehicle.

ENGINE MECHANICAL

NOTE: Disconnecting the negative battery cable on some vehicles may interfere with the functions of the on-board computer systems and may require the computer to undergo a relearning process, once the negative battery cable is disconnected. Most vehicles are equipped with theft protected radios, which cannot be operated if power to the radio is interrupted. Before disconnecting the battery cables, obtain the security code.

Engine Assembly

REMOVAL AND INSTALLATION

4 Cylinder Engine

1. Matchmark hood and hinges and remove hood. Relieve fuel pressure. Disconnect the negative battery cable.
2. Remove the 2 grille retaining clips on the top of the grille. Remove the screw on the bottom and remove the grille.
3. Loosen the right and left sides of the air conditioning condenser. Tie the condenser away from the radiator.
4. Remove the rubber air duct from the throttle valve housing.
5. Remove the hose from the air duct to the auxiliary air regulator.
6. Disconnect the fuel lines from the cold start valve and fuel injectors. Cap the end of the fuel lines. Remove the injectors from the cylinder head.
7. Remove the fuel distributor, air flow sensor, fuel injectors and the air cleaner from the vehicle, as an assembly.
8. Remove the front engine mount-to-chassis bolts and remove the mount.
9. Loosen the nuts on the outer half of the crankshaft pulley and remove the V-belt.

— **CAUTION** —
Compressed refrigerant used in the air conditioning system expands and evaporates into the atmosphere at a temperature of -21.7°F or less. This will freeze any surface it comes in contact with,

including eyes. In addition, the refrigerant decomposes into a poisonous gas in the presence of flame. To avoid injury, always wear eye protection and gloves when discharging the system.

10. Properly discharge the air conditioning system.
11. Remove all air conditioning lines from the compressor and plug the open connections.
12. Remove the crankcase ventilation hose from the valve cover.
13. Support the air conditioning hoses away from the engine.
14. Remove the air conditioning compressor mounting bolts and remove the compressor.
15. Open the heater control valve all the way.
16. Remove the cap on the expansion tank and drain the cooling system.
17. Remove the upper and lower radiator hoses from the radiator.
18. Disconnect and tag the radiator fan wiring and thermo-switch at the radiator. Remove the radiator with the fan and shroud as an assembly.
19. Remove the power steering pump, if equipped, with hoses attached, move aside and secure to body.
20. If equipped with a manual transaxle, disconnect the clutch cable at the release lever.
21. Disconnect and tag the engine wiring.
22. Remove the fuel control pressure regulator (above the oil filter) from the engine, leaving all the fuel lines connected. Support it aside.
23. Remove the air hose from the back of the alternator, if equipped.
24. Disconnect the blue wire from the alternator at the plug located between the battery and the rear of the engine, if equipped.
25. Remove the charcoal filter hose at the intake air duct.
26. Remove the heater hoses from the engine.
27. Remove the throttle cable from the engine.
28. Disconnect and tag all vacuum hoses at the engine.
29. Remove the hose from the auxiliary regulator to the air inlet duct.
30. Remove the 3 upper engine to transaxle mounting bolts.
31. Remove the right and left engine mount nuts.
32. Raise and support the vehicle safely. Disconnect the exhaust pipe from the exhaust manifold.

33. Remove the flywheel cover plate. If equipped with automatic transaxle, remove the torque converter-to-flywheel mounting bolts.

NOTE: Matchmark the converter to the flywheel for installation.

34. Remove the front engine mounting bolts and remove the mount.
35. Disconnect and tag the starter wiring and remove the starter.
36. Remove the 2 lower engine to transaxle mounting bolts.
37. Loosen the right and left engine mount nuts on the sub-frame.
38. Remove the bolt from the front exhaust pipe support.
39. Support the transaxle.
40. Lift the engine until the weight is taken off the engine mounts and carefully separate the engine and transaxle.
41. Remove the engine from the vehicle.

To install:
42. Guide the engine assembly into place and secure the engine mounts.
43. Connect the flexplate to the torque converter, then install the starter.
44. Connect the exhaust system using new gaskets if necessary.
45. Lower the vehicle and reconnect all electrical connections and vacuum lines.
46. Connect fresh air ducts, emission hoses, throttle cable and clutch cable, if equipped.
47. Install the fuel distributor and air flow sensor asembly.
48. Install the radiator, fan and shroud as an assembly.
49. Install the power steering pump, coolant hoses and air conditioning lines.
50. Install the fuel injectors into the cylinder head.
51. Install the accessory drive belts and connect all fuel lines.
52. Install air conditioning condenser and the grille.
53. Install and align hood.
54. Tighten the engine-to-transaxle bolts to 40 ft. lbs. (54 Nm), starter bolts to 14 ft. lbs. (19 Nm). Tighten the cold start valve, pressure control regulator and radiator mounting bolts to 7 ft. lbs. (10 Nm). Use a new gasket on the cold start valve when installing.
55. Evacuate and recharge the A/C system.
56. Refill and bleed the cooling system.

57. Road test the vehicle for proper operation.

NOTE: To minimize vibration, loosen all the engine and sub-frame mounting bolts, then tighten while the engine is running at idle. Tighten the front engine mount bolts to 18 ft. lbs. (25 Nm) and the right and left engine mount bolts to 25 ft. lbs. (34 Nm).

5 Cylinder Engine

WITH TURBOCHARGER

NOTE: Tag all hoses and wiring during removal, to use as reference during reassembly.

1. Disconnect the negative battery cable. Relieve fuel pressure.
2. Open the heater control valve all the way and drain the cooling system.
3. Remove the fuel injector cooling fan blower motor and intake hose from the engine.
4. On 80/90, remove the upper radiator cover, grille, bumper strip. Disconnect the wiring harness in bumper for turn signals and headlights. Remove the bumper.
5. Disconnect the electrical connector from the coolant fan. Remove the upper radiator hose from the engine. Remove the radiator-to-expansion tank hose from the tank and the bleeder hose from the auxiliary radiator.
6. Disconnect the wire from the thermo-switch. Remove the radiator mounting bolts, right-side radiator cover and bottom radiator cover.
7. Remove the windshield washer reservoir from the mount and support it aside.

--- **CAUTION** ---

The compressed refrigerant used in the air conditioning system expands and evaporates into the atmosphere at a temperature of -21.7°F or less. This will freeze any surface it comes in contact with, including eyes. In addition, the refrigerant decomposes into a poisonous gas in the presence of flame. To avoid injury, always wear eye protection and gloves when discharging the system.

8. Properly discharge the air conditioning system and disconnect the refrigerant hoses from the air conditioning condenser.
9. Remove the radiator and air conditioning condenser together. Remove the air conditioning compressor and mounting bracket from the engine.
10. Remove the power steering pump drive belt from the pump. Remove the pump from the mounts. Leaving the hoses attached, support it aside.
11. Disconnect the coolant hose from the thermostat housing and disconnect the wires from the oil pressure switch and temperature sender. Disconnect the wire plugs from the control pressure regulator.
12. Remove the control pressure regulator from the engine but leave the fuel lines connected. Support it aside.
13. Remove the throttle rod clips and remove the rod from the engine. Remove the injector line holder and remove the fuel injectors from the cylinder head.
14. Disconnect the electrical connector from the cold start valve and remove the valve from the intake manifold. Leave the fuel line connected.
15. At the throttle body, disconnect the electrical connectors from the throttle valve switches and intake air temperature switch.
16. Disconnect the air intake hose. Disconnect the wire from the auxiliary air regulator, pull off the vacuum hoses and disconnect the breaker hose from the engine.
17. At the 2-way valve, remove and tag the vacuum hoses. Remove the thermo-pneumatic valve. Leave the vacuum lines connected and remove the rpm sensor.
18. Disconnect the speedometer cable from the transaxle.
19. Remove the distributor from the engine.
20. Disconnect and tag the thermo-time switch and overheating warning lamp connectors. Disconnect the heater hoses from the engine.
21. At the left engine mount, disconnect the brake booster and reservoir from the firewall and leave the lines connected. On Quattro vehicles, disconnect the differential lock control lights connector. Disconnect the backup light switch wires.
22. Disconnect the tie rods from the steering rack. Disconnect the steering linkage.
23. If equipped with a manual transaxle, remove the clutch slave cylinder from the bell housing. Leave the line attached. Remove the bracket and pin under the transaxle bracket.
24. Disconnect the left engine mount ground strap. Disconnect the vacuum hose from the auxiliary air valve.
25. Remove the air duct from the intercooler and remove the intercooler.
26. Disconnect and tag the electrical connectors from the alternator. Remove the oil cooler. Leave the lines attached. Disconnect and tag the starter wiring.
27. Disconnect the exhaust pipe at the turbocharger. Remove the transaxle cover plates and the right side transaxle mount. Disconnect the halfshafts from the transaxle. On Quattro vehicles, disconnect the driveshaft from the rear of the transaxle.
28. On Quattro vehicles at the transaxle, disconnect the differential lock, remove the front and rear circlips and push back the boot. Disconnect the cable.
29. Remove the left-side transaxle mounting bolt and mounts from both sides.
30. At both front wheels, remove the ball joint pinch bolts. At the subframe, remove the mounting bolts and subframe. Separate the ball joints from the steering knuckle.
31. Install an engine lifting device on the engine. Raise the engine slightly and remove the left and right engine mounts. Lower the engine/transaxle assembly from the vehicle.
32. Raise the front of the vehicle and slide the engine/transaxle assembly from under the vehicle.
33. Separate the engine from the transaxle.

To install:
34. Install the engine assembly and temporarily secure the engine mounts.
35. Install the steering joints to the steering knuckles and torque to 22 ft. lbs. (30 Nm). Install the ball joints with the pinch bolts and torque to 44 ft. lbs. (65 Nm).
36. Install the exhaust and 4WD differential lock clips, if equipped.
37. Reconnect the exhaust pipe at the turbocharger.
38. Install the halfshafts to the transaxle.
39. Install the right side transaxle mount and transaxle cover plates.
40. On Quattro vehicles, reconnect the driveshaft to the rear of the transaxle.
41. Lower the vehicle and install all electrical connections.
42. Install the oil cooler.
43. Install the intercooler assembly and air duct.
44. Reconnect the left engine mount ground strap.

45. Install the clutch slave cylinder, if equipped.

46. Install the tie rods to the steering rack assembly.

47. Install the brake booster and reservoir. On Quattro vehicles, connect the differential lock control lights connector. Reconnect the backup light switch wires.

48. Install the heater hoses.

49. Install the distributor.

50. Install the speedometer cable and all vacuum lines.

51. Install the fuel injectors from the cylinder head.

52. Connect the throttle body connectors, throttle linkage and fuel injection pressure regulator.

53. Install the power steering pump and all drive belts.

54. Install the radiator and air conditioning condenser. Connect the hoses.

55. Install the windshield washer reservoir.

56. On 80/90, install the upper radiator cover and grille. Reconnect the wiring harness in bumper for turn signals and headlights. Install the bumper.

57. Install the cooling fan blower motor and intake hose to the engine.

58. Refill and bleed the cooling system. Connect the battery negative cable.

59. To minimize vibration, loosen all the engine and subframe mounting bolts, then torque to 25 ft. lbs. (34 Nm) while the engine is running at idle.

60. Check all fluid levels, road test for proper operation.

WITHOUT TURBOCHARGER

NOTE: Tag all hoses and wiring during removal to use as reference during reassembly.

1. Disconnect the negative battery cable. Relieve fuel pressure.

2. Drain the cooling system.

3. Disconnect the radiator and heater hoses from the engine.

4. Remove the control pressure regulator from the engine, without disconnecting the fuel lines.

5. Remove the cold start valve from the intake manifold, without disconnecting the fuel lines.

6. Pull out the fuel injectors from the cylinder head and support the injectors and fuel lines aside.

NOTE: Protect the fuel injectors and the cold start valve with caps.

7. Loosen the air duct and vacuum hoses from the throttle valve assembly.

8. Remove the air box cover and filter.

9. At the top of the grille, pull the hood latch cable guide off its bracket.

10. If equipped with air conditioning, perform the following procedures:

   a. Remove the 2 clips from the top of the grille and the screw from the bottom. Remove the grille.

   b. Remove the condenser mounting bolts.

   c. Remove the air duct to auxiliary air regulator hose and remove the air duct from the throttle valve housing.

   d. Remove the fuel distributor, air flow sensor, fuel injectors and air box, as a unit.

NOTE: When removing the fuel injectors, leave all of the lines connected and cover the fuel injectors with caps.

   e. Remove the accessory drive belts.

CAUTION

The compressed refrigerant used in the air conditioning system, expands and evaporates into the atmosphere at a temperature of -21.7°F or less. This will freeze any surface it comes in contact with, including eyes. In addition, the refrigerant decomposes into a poisonous gas in the presence of flame. To avoid injury, always wear eye protection and gloves when discharging the system.

---

   f. Properly discharge the refrigerant from the air conditioning system. Remove and plug the air conditioning hoses, move them away from the engine.

   g. Remove the upper/lower compressor mounting bolts and remove the compressor from the engine.

11. Remove the power steering pump from the engine, leaving the hoses connected.

12. Remove the vacuum amplifier.

13. Remove the EGR control valve.

14. Remove the windshield washer reservoir from its holder.

15. Remove the distributor cap and ignition wires. Remove the distributor vacuum hose(s).

NOTE: Tape the distributor dust cap on to prevent it from falling off.

16. Disconnect the throttle linkage from the engine.

17. If equipped with an automatic transaxle, remove the throttle pushrod.

18. Disconnect the oil pressure and water temperature sensor wiring.

19. Remove the exhaust pipe to manifold nuts.

20. Remove the exhaust pipe support bracket from the transaxle.

21. Remove the front engine mount bolts and remove the mount. Disconnect the ground strap on left engine mount, if equipped.

22. Tag and disconnect all wires from the starter and remove the starter.

23. Tag and disconnect all wires leading from the alternator and remove the alternator.

24. If equipped with an automatic transaxle, work through the starter mounting hole to remove the torque converter mounting bolts.

25. Remove the lower engine to transaxle mounting bolts.

26. Support the transaxle and lower the vehicle.

27. Remove the upper engine to transaxle mounting bolts.

28. Remove the left engine support bracket.

29. Loosen the right engine bracket from the right engine mount.

30. Lift the engine until the crankshaft V-belt pulley is behind the grille opening.

31. Carefully detach the engine from the transaxle.

32. Remove the engine assembly by turning it to the right while lifting it out.

To install:

33. Install the engine assembly and secure the mounts.

34. On vehicles with automatic transaxle, install the torque converter bolts. On 087 and 089 units, torque the bolts to 22 ft. lbs. (30 Nm). On 097 units, torque the bolts to 44 ft. lbs. (60 Nm).

35. Install the alternator and all wiring.

36. Install the starter and all necessary wiring.

37. Install the engine ground strap and engine mount.

38. Install the exhaust system and brackets.

39. Reconnect all engine compartment wiring including the oil pressure and water temperature sensor wiring.

40. Reconnect the throttle linkage.

41. Install the distributor cap and ignition wires.

42. Install the washer reservoir.

43. Install EGR valve and vacuum amplifier.

44. Install the power steering pump and all drive belts.

45. Install the air conditioning compressor and condenser.

46. Install the fuel injectors, control pressure regulator and cold start valve.

47. Install the hood latch cable guide onto the bracket.

48. Install the air box cover and all necessary hoses.

49. Install the radiator, refill and bleed the cooling system. Connect the battery negative cable.

50. Torque the engine-to-transaxle mounting bolts to 43 ft. lbs. (58 Nm), the starter bolts to 14 ft. lbs. (19 Nm), the air conditioner mounting bolts to 29 ft. lbs. (39 Nm) and the power steering pump and the control pressure regulator mounting bolts to 14 ft. lbs. (19 Nm).

51. Check all fluid levels, road test for proper operation.

NOTE: To minimize vibration, loosen all the engine and subframe mounting bolts, then tighten while the engine is running at idle. Tighten the engine and subframe mounting bolts to 32 ft. lbs. (43 Nm).

8 Cylinder Engine

The engine is taken out towards the front without the transaxle. All cable ties which have to be released or cut open when removing the engine must be replaced in the same position when the engine is installed.

1. Disconnect the battery negative cable. The battery is under the rear seat.

2. Under the dashboard, remove the retainers, remove left dashboard end cap and the knee protector.

3. Remove the heater duct for the driver-side area, under the dash panel, by removing the right-hand screw and loosening the left-hand clip.

4. Unclip the floor lamp and push it through the opening.

5. Remove the control units with brackets.

6. Open the locking mechanisms on the control unit connectors and disconnect the harness connectors. Lock the connectors so they don't become tangled when removing the cable harness. Pull off connectors 11, 13 and 15. The numbers are marked on the wiring harness.

7. Remove the connector panel by removing the lower screw, loosening the upper screw and pulling the panel downwards. Press the latch on the butterfly connector lock and slide it sideways to release the connector from the panel.

8. Under the hood, remove the plenum chamber cover and lift the rubber grommet on the middle wiring harness. Cut the cable tie and pull the wiring harness carefully out of the passenger compartment and plenum chamber. Open the expansion tank cap for coolant.

9. Raise and safely support vehicle. Remove the sound insulation or under pan.

10. Remove the bolts and nuts holding bumper and bracket, remove the electrical connectors and pull off the bumper towards the front.

11. Drain the coolant from the radiator. Also open the block drains on both sides.

12. Remove the oil cooler hoses from the oil filter housing and the hose from the bottom of the transaxle oil cooler. Remove the bracket for the line on the air conditioner and disconnect the engine ground cable at the engine.

13. Separate the harness for the headlight washing system and air conditioner harness. Disconnect the coolant temperature sensor harness, the cool air duct from the alternator, the coolant hose and hose for headlight washer system.

14. Disconnect the outer half of the air intake elbow for the alternator. Disconnect the wiring from the alternator and starter motor. Unscrew oil filter.

15. Remove the upper bolt on the starter by guiding a 10mm Allen® socket, with extension and flex fitting, through the opening on the transaxle housing over the final drive. Remove starter.

16. Locate and remove the bolts from the front of the subframe on left and right sides. Remove the bolts securing the exhaust system on the left and right sides.

17. Remove the 4 bolts connecting the bottom of the engine and transaxle.

18. Remove the bolts above and below the long member on the left and right sides.

19. Remove the harness connector from the temperature sensor at the front of the air conditioning condenser and disconnect the hood release cable.

20. Open the fuse box on the left side behind the hydraulic reservoir. Disconnect the wire to the fan and the ground wire at the top of the suspension strut. Expose the wiring.

21. Remove the air conditioning dryer with the bracket.

22. Remove the intake manifold bracket on the left and right. Pull out the exchanger. Remove the bar-shaped reinforcement strut.

23. Remove the air conditioning condenser bolts and swivel the condenser downward. Wiring should remain connected.

24. Remove the wiring bracket from the top of the transaxle cooler. Remove the water hose from both sides of the engine. Remove the bleeder hose from the expansion tank on the radiator. Remove the front apron.

25. Remove the screws securing the upper part of the air cleaner housing. There are 4 screws on the housing and 3 screws at the rear of the housing.

26. Remove the screws securing the lower part of the air cleaner housing. Press toward the rear and lift out. Remove the right-hand stud from the lower air cleaner housing.

27. Disconnect the carbon canister hose from the front of the engine. Cut both cable ties on the fuel injector. Remove the fuel supply and return lines.

28. Remove the coolant hose to expansion tank. Disconnect the high tension wire and connector on the ignition coil at the left and right. Remove the bolts holding the left coil, cable housing and retaining clip. Watch for the spacer sleeve.

29. Remove the left and right heatshields. Remove the housing for the ignition wire retainer. Disconnect the vacuum line.

30. Remove the screws securing the left and right distributor caps. Wiring remains connected. Using a cable tie, secure the 2 distributor caps aside against the PCV hose.

31. Disconnect the throttle cable by unclipping both retaining clips. Remove the screws securing the throttle cable support bracket. Unscrew both coolant hoses. Disconnect the supporting clamp.

32. Separate both harness connectors from the oxygen sensor. Disconnect the vacuum line to the cruise control system.

33. Remove the transaxle oil fill tube bolt from the engine. Pull the wiring harness through the contact plate and place on the engine.

34. Remove the 6 torque converter bolts through the starter opening.

35. Release the tension on the ribbed drive belt and remove the belt in a downward direction by placing a 13mm box wrench on the hexagon guide of tensioner and pressing wrench slowly upwards.

36. Remove the bolts holding the air conditioning compressor. Lift the

compressor over the strut. The lines remain connected.

37. Remove the bolts for the air conditioning compressor bracket and the hydraulic pump. Note the guide sleeves. Place the bracket with the hydraulic pump on the long member. The lines remain connected. At installation, fit the lower bolts with the guide sleeves in position and tighten lightly. Then the upper bolts can be installed.

38. Remove the nuts from the left and right engine mountings. Remove the bolts securing the engine support at the front. Take note of the shims. The same thickness shims must be used at installation.

39. Disconnect the engine and transaxle at the top by removing 3 of the 4 bolts. Loosen the 4th bolt but do not remove.

40. Install a suitable lifting sling to the front left-hand side and rear right-hand side.

41. Move in hoist, being careful of the air conditioning compressor. Lift engine carefully. Remove last bolt from the top of the engine and transaxle. Unscrew the engine mounting from the left and right sides and pull the engine out from the front. Lift carefully to prevent damage to the transaxle mainshaft, clutch and body.

42. Use care when selecting a suitable engine repair stand. Attaching to some types of stands could cause the engine block to distort and cause any cylinder bore measurements to be inaccurate.

To install:

43. Note that there are guide sleeves in the engine block for centering the engine and transaxle. Make sure they are installed.

44. Install the engine assembly and secure to the transaxle and engine mounts.

45. Install the 6 torque converter bolts.

46. Install the air conditioning compressor and hydraulic pump. Fit the lower bolts with the guide sleeves first. Tighten lightly and then install the top bolts.

47. Install and adjust the ribbed drive belt.

48. Install all electrical connectors, hoses and sheet metal hheatshields.

49. Reconnect the throttle cable.

50. Install the distributor caps.

51. Install the coolant hose to the expansion tank.

52. Reconnect all ignition coil wiring.

53. Install the fuel supply and return lines.

54. Install the air cleaner housing assembly.

55. Install the front apron.

56. Install the bleeder hose to the expansion tank on the radiator. Install all water hoses.

57. Install the radiator and air conditioning condenser and the small brackets that were removed.

58. Install the air conditioning dryer with bracket.

59. Install and route the hood release cable.

60. Install the starter and wiring.

61. Install a new oil filter. Reconnect all necessary wiring and hoses.

62. Install the engine ground cable.

63. Install the bumper bracket, bumper and all wiring.

64. Install the sound insulator or underpan.

65. Install the control units and interior parts removed. Reconnect all necessary wiring.

66. Connect battery negative cable.

67. Always replace all self-locking nuts. Make sure the exhaust system is installed free of strain. Check all fluid levels before starting the engine Check the fluid level in the automatic transaxle.

68. Road test the vehicle for proper operation.

Cylinder Head

NOTE: Before removing or installing the cylinder head, align the engine timing marks at TDC. Rotate the crankshaft mark away about ¼ turn (BTDC). This will prevent the valves from hitting the piston heads. Be sure to turn the crankshaft to the proper position after cylinder head installation.

REMOVAL AND INSTALLATION

NOTE: Cylinder head removal should not be attempted unless the engine is cold.

4 and 5 Cylinder Engines

1. Disconnect the negative battery cable.

2. Drain the cooling system.

3. Disconnect the air duct from the throttle valve assembly on all vehicles except the Turbo and Quattro. On the Turbo and Quattro, remove the hose which runs between the air duct and the turbocharger.

4. Disconnect the throttle cable from the throttle valve assembly.

5. Remove the air duct for the injector cooling fan on the Turbo and Quattro.

6. Clean and remove the fuel injectors and all other fuel lines.

NOTE: Protect the fuel injectors and the cold start valve with caps.

7. Tag and disconnect all vacuum and PCV lines.

8. Remove the hose which runs from the intake manifold to the turbocharger on the Turbo and Quattro.

9. Tag and disconnect all electrical lines leading to the cylinder head.

10. Remove the intake manifold.

11. Disconnect all radiator and heater hoses where they are attached to the cylinder head. Position them aside.

12. Tag and remove all spark plug wires.

13. Remove the distributor. To aid installation, scribe a mark on the body of the distributor and the cylinder head.

14. Separate the exhaust manifold from the exhaust pipe.

NOTE: Exhaust pipe detachment differs slightly on the Turbo and Quattro. First the exhaust pipe must be unbolted from the turbocharger. Second, it must be unbolted from the wastegate at the rear of the engine.

15. Disconnect the EGR valve and oxygen sensor from the exhaust manifold.

16. Remove the heat deflector shield.

17. Remove the oil lines (2) from the turbocharger.

18. Remove the exhaust manifold.

NOTE: When removing the exhaust manifold on the Turbo and Quattro, the manifold, turbocharger and wastegate should all be removed as a unit.

19. Remove the air hose cover from the back of the alternator.

20. Tag and disconnect all wires coming from the back of the alternator and remove the alternator from the engine.

21. Disconnect and plug the hoses coming from the power steering pump.

22. Remove the power steering pump and the V-belt.

23. Remove the timing belt cover and belt.

24. Remove the valve cover.

25. Loosen the cylinder head bolts in the reverse order of the tightening sequence.

26. Remove the bolts and lift the cylinder head off the engine.

To install:

27. Clean the cylinder head and engine block mating surfaces thoroughly and install the new gasket without any sealing compound. Make sure the words **TOP** or **OBEN** are facing up, when the gasket is installed.

28. Place the cylinder head on the engine block and install bolts No. 8 and 10 first. These holes are smaller and will properly locate the gasket and the head on the engine block.

29. Install the remaining bolts. Torque them in sequence in 3 stages as follows:
   Step 1 — 29 ft. lbs. (39 Nm)
   Step 2 — 43 ft. lbs. (58 Nm)
   Step 3 — Tighten ½ turn more (180 degrees).

30. Install the valve cover.

31. Install timing belt and timing belt cover.

32. Install the power steering pump and drive belt.

33. Install the alternator and all wiring.

34. Install the exhaust manifold.

35. Reconnect the 2 oil lines from the turbocharger assembly.

36. Install the heat deflector shield.

37. Reconnect the EGR valve and oxygen sensor to the exhaust manifold.

38. Reconnect the exhaust system.

39. Install the distributor and spark plug wires.

40. Install the intake manifold.

41. Install the radiator and heater hoses.

42. Install the fuel injectors. Reconnect the air duct.

43. Reconnect the throttle cable.

44. Connect the negative battery cable.

45. Refill and bleed the cooling system. Check all fluid levels.

46. Road test the vehicle check for proper operation.

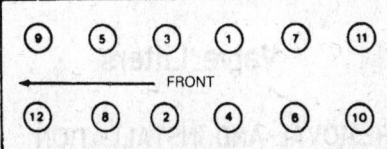

Cylinder head torque sequence — 5 cylinder engines

6 Cylinder Engine

This procedure is for the left cylinder head assembly with the engine installed in the vehicle. Modify the service procedure as necessary for the right side.

1. Disconnect the negative battery cable. Drain engine coolant. Relieve fuel pressure.

2. Remove the ribbed V-belt.

3. Remove the timing belt. The vibration damper should remain installed.

4. Remove the exhaust pipe from the manifold.

5. Remove the EGR valve hose at manifold.

6. Remove the air guide hose between air mass sensor and intake manifold.

7. Remove and tag all spark plug wires and injector connectors.

8. Remove the crankcase breathers on the left and right cylinder head covers.

9. Remove the fuel feed and return lines. Remove the silencer.

10. Remove the left side cover for fuel line.

11. Disconnect the throttle cable.

12. Mark and remove all vacuum hoses from vacuum pump and intake manifold.

13. Disconnect connectors on idling stabilization valve and throttle valve potentiometer.

14. Disconnect vacuum hose on vacuum control unit.

15. Disconnect connectors on oil pressure sender and oil pressure switch.

16. Disconnect connector for Hall sender sensor.

17. Remove the EGR valve from the intake manifold.

18. Remove the intake manifold assembly.

19. Remove the coolant pipe at the rear of the cylinder head.

20. Remove the oxygen sensor.

21. Remove the heatshield on the exhaust manifold.

22. Remove the cylinder head cover.

23. Remove the timing belt rear belt guard. Remove the hydraulic line from reservoir to pump.

24. Reverse the installation torque sequence and remove the cylinder head assembly from the engine.

To install:

25. Clean all sealing surfaces. Check cylinder head for distortion. Measure at several locations. The maximum permissible distortion is 0.1mm.

26. Install cylinder head gasket. The lettering must face upwards.

27. Install the cylinder head assembly, check centering pins in the cylinder block.

28. Install cylinder head bolts by hand.

29. Tighten the cylinder head bolts in sequence in 2 steps. Step 1 — 44 ft. lbs. and Step 2 — ½ turn (180 degrees). It is not necessary to retighten the cylinder head bolts after repairs or as part of inspection service.

30. Install the timing belt rear belt guard.

31. Install the cylinder head cover.

32. Install the oxygen sensor. Install the heatshield on the exhaust manifold.

33. Install the intake manifold assembly.

34. Install the EGR valve to the intake manifold.

35. Reconnect the hall sender sensor, oil pressure sender and oil pressure switch.

36. Reconnect connectors on idling stabilization valve and throttle valve potentiometer.

37. Install all vacuum hoses to vacuum pump and intake manifold.

38. Reconnect the throttle cable.

39. Reconnect the fuel feed and return lines. Install the silencer.

40. Install the crankcase breather on the cylinder head cover.

41. Install all spark plug wires and injector connectors.

42. Install the exhaust manifold.

43. Install the timing belt and V-belt.

44. Refill and bleed the cooling system.

45. Check all fluid levels. Operate the engine at normal operating temperatures and check for leaks.

46. Road test the vehicle for proper operation.

8 Cylinder Engine

1. Disconnect the negative battery cable. The battery is under the rear seat.

2. Remove the toothed cam drive belt. It should not be necessary to loosen or remove the vibration damper.

3. Open the left and right block drains.

4. Remove the bolts holding the exhaust pipe on both sides.

5. Remove the supply line at the fuel manifold. Remove the fuel return line. Remove the bolt holding the pressure regulator to the fuel manifold. At assembly, press the regulator directly into the seat of the O-ring seal. Do not pull in with bolts.

6. Disconnect the breather hose at the rear of the intake manifold, the

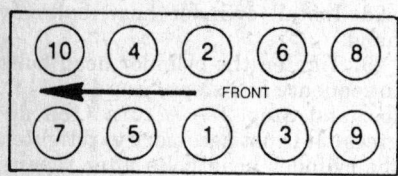

Cylinder head torque sequence — 4 cylinder engines

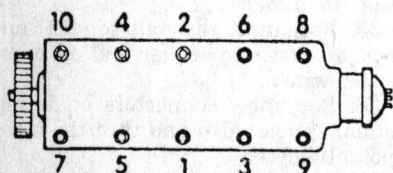

Cylinder head torque sequence — V8 engine

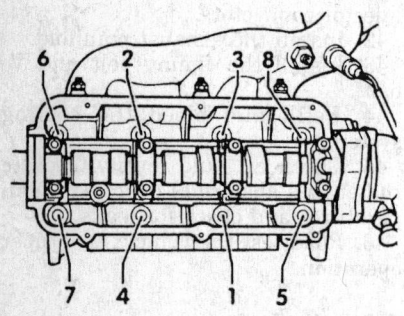

Cylinder head torque sequence — V6 engines

vacuum hose and the bolt holding the upper part of the supporting clamp for the engine wiring harness. Remove the mounting bracket for ignition wire holder.

7. Disconnect the linkage for the cruise control. Release the throttle cable by unclipping both retaining clips.

8. Disconnect the heater supply hose for coolant at the rear of the cylinder heads. Release the hose under the engine wiring harness clamp.

9. Remove the screws securing the 2 spark plug covers, disconnect the

spark plug connectors and remove the ignition cables complete with the distributor caps. Disconnect the harness connector for the left and right knock sensors. Disconnect the air mass sensor harness connector.

10. Disconnect the connector for the throttle valve harness connector potentiometer. Disconnect the idle stabilizer valve harness connector. Remove the idle stabilizer valve. Remove the hose from the carbon canister.

11. Remove the air temperature sensor. Remove the wiring holder behind the rear toothed belt guard at the right side and, if necessary, also on the left side.

12. Remove the bolts securing the coolant hose holder on the right rear cylinder head. Disconnect the heater supply hose from the cylinder heads by pulling towards the rear.

13. Disconnect the harness connector for the Hall sender on the right cylinder head. If the right cylinder head needs to be removed, disconnect the temperature sensor harness connector on the right cylinder head.

14. Remove the breather hose. Turn the hose with pliers until the retaining lug unlatches. Remove the breather hose on the cylinder head, on the left side at the rear.

15. Remove the bolts securing the fuel rails and lift out complete with injectors and place on plenum chamber. At installation, make sure the O-rings are not damaged. Moisten slightly with fuel.

16. Remove the bolts securing the intake manifold and lift out. Watch the front breather hose under the intake manifold.

17. If it is the left hand cylinder head being removed, unscrew the dipstick guide and pull out. Remove the transaxle oil filler tube bolt.

18. Remove the cylinder head cover. Note that the 2 center mounting bolts are different. The bolt with the longer hexagon fitting must be installed at the rear.

19. If the left cylinder head is being removed, remove the bolts securing the cruise control vacuum unit and bracket. Do not forget the deflector plate during installation.

20. Remove the cylinder head bolts in reverse sequence of tightening. Remove the cylinder head.

To install:

21. Observing the following during the installation. Check that the gasket surface is not distorted. Maximum permissible distortion is 0.004 in. (0.1mm).

22. Make sure the gasket surface is clean. Look for the word **OBEN** on the gasket. This is the top, facing the cylinder head. When installing the cylinder head, watch the centering dowels in the block.

23. Insert the cylinder head bolts hand-tight. Torque in sequence in 3 steps. First to 30 ft. lbs. (41 Nm), then to 44 ft. lbs. (60 Nm). The 3rd step is to give the bolts an additional 1/2 turn. Use a regular ratchet handle or breaker bar and turn in one smooth motion without stopping. It should not be necessary to retighten the cylinder head bolts during maintenance or after repairs.

24. Install the cylinder head cover.

25. Install the intake manifold assembly.

26. Install the fuel rails with fuel injectors. Make sure the O-rings are not damaged. Moisten slightly with fuel.

27. Install the breather hose.

28. Reconnect the coolant hose holder and install heater hose.

29. Install the air temperature sensor. Reconnect all wiring.

30. Reconnect the connector for the throttle valve harness connector potentiometer.

31. Install the idle stabilizer valve. Install the hose from the carbon canister.

32. Install spark plug wires, air mass sensor harness connector and distributor caps. Install the spark plug covers.

33. Reconnect the cruise control linkage and throttle cable.

34. Press the regulator directly into the seat of the O-ring seal. Install the bolt holding the pressure regulator to the fuel manifold.

35. Install the supply line and fuel return line.

36. Install the toothed cam drive belt.

37. Refill and bleed the cooling system.

38. Check all fluid levels. Operate the engine at normal operating temperatures and check for leaks.

39. Road test the vehicle for proper operation.

Valve Lifters

REMOVAL AND INSTALLATION

Use care when handling valve lifters. Always place a removed valve lifter on a clean surface with the contact surface or camshaft side facing downward. The camshaft bearing caps are marked at the top for correct installation.

1. Disconnect the negative battery cable. Remove the toothed camshaft drive belt.

2. Remove the cylinder head cover.

3. Remove the camshaft sprocket.

4. On the 8 cylinder engine, on the exhaust side, remove the intermediate flange and bearing cap for the distributor. Loosen the bearing cap in front of the chain, plus caps 2 and 3. Loosen bearing caps 1 and 4 alternately and in a diagonal sequence.

5. On the 8 cylinder engine, on the intake side, remove bearing caps 6 and 7. Loosen bearing caps 5 and 8 alternately and in a diagonal sequence.

6. Remove the cam and lift out the valve lifter. If it is to be reused, it must go in the bore from which it was removed.

To install:

7. Installation is the reverse of removal. Before assembly coat the moving parts with clean oil.

8. On the 8 cylinder engine, install the camshafts with the chain so the markings on the chain sprockets are in alignment. Install the bearing caps so the stamped-on numbers can be read from the intake side.

9. Make sure the bearing caps are installed properly. They will cause cam shaft failure if installed backwards. Tighten bearing caps alternately, in a diagonal sequence to 11 ft. lbs. (15 Nm).

Valve Lash

ADJUSTMENT

All engines are equipped with hydraulic valve lash adjusters that eliminate the need for routine valve lash adjustments. Intermittent valve noise is normal when the engine is cold. If valve noise persists, check the camshaft lobes and/or camshaft followers for wear. Replace if necessary. Do not attempt valve lifter repair. If worn or damaged, replace the complete assembly.

After working on the valve train, carefully turn the engine by hand at least 2 turns to make sure the valves do not strike the pistons when the engine is started. Do not start the engine for 30 minutes after installing new valve lifters or the valves may strike the pistons. The lifter must be allowed to bleed down to proper adjustment.

To check a suspect lifter, use the following procedure:

1. Warm the engine to operating temperature until the radiator fan comes ON at least once.

2. Bring the engine to approximately 2500 rpm for 2 minutes. If a lifter is still noisy, shut OFF engine and remove the cylinder head cover.

3. Turn the crankshaft pulley bolt clockwise until the cam lobes of the cylinder to be checked point upward.

4. Push down against the valve lifter with light pressure using a suitable tool. If the valve lifter can be pushed down more than 0.004 in. (0.1mm), replace the lifter.

5. Do not start the engine for 30 minutes after installing new valve lifters or the valves may strike the pistons. The lifter must be allowed to bleed down to proper adjustment.

Intake Manifold

REMOVAL AND INSTALLATION

4 Cylinder Engine

1. Disconnect the negative battery cable. Relieve the fuel pressure in the system.

2. Disconnect the throttle cable at the throttle valve housing.

3. Disconnect the wiring for the cold start valve and thermo-time switch.

4. Disconnect the ground wire from the intake manifold.

5. Remove the fuel line from the cold start valve. Cap the valve and line.

6. Remove the air boot from the throttle valve housing and sensor plate housing.

7. Disconnect and tag the vacuum hoses at the manifold.

8. Remove the fuel injectors from the cylinder head, without disconnecting the fuel lines from the injectors.

9. Remove the control pressure regulator line and move the regulator aside.

10. Remove the 2 straps that connect the intake and exhaust manifolds.

11. Disconnect the CO percentage check tube from the intake manifold.

12. Remove the intake manifold mounting nuts and remove the manifold from the engine.

NOTE: Before loosening the intake manifold mounting nuts, soak the nuts and studs with lu-

bricant. Studs are very difficult to replace with the cylinder head installed on the engine.

To install:

13. Clean the gasket mating surfaces of the engine and intake manifold.

14. Before installation, hold the intake manifold gasket up to the engine and check for proper fit. Trim, if necessary.

15. Install the intake manifold on the cylinder head. Tighten the 6mm nuts to 7 ft. lbs. (10 Nm) and the 8mm nuts to 18 ft. lbs. (24 Nm).

16. Install the check tube to the intake manifold.

17. Install the control pressure regulator and line.

18. Lubricate the fuel injector O-rings with a drop of engine oil, install the fuel injectors.

19. Reconnect all vacuum hoses at intake manifold.

20. Install the fuel line to the cold start valve. Reconnect the wiring for the cold start valve and thermo-time switch.

21. Reconnect the throttle cable at the throttle valve housing.

22. Check all fluid levels. Operate the engine at normal operating temperatures and check for leaks.

23. Road test the vehicle for proper operation.

5 Cylinder Engine

1. Disconnect the negative battery cable.

2. Relieve the fuel system pressure.

3. On non-turbocharged engines, disconnect the air duct from the throttle valve assembly. On turbocharged engines, remove the hose between the air duct and turbocharger.

4. Disconnect the throttle cable and rod from the throttle valve assembly.

5. On turbocharged engines, remove the air duct for the injector cooling fan.

6. Remove the fuel injectors from the cylinder head, with the fuel lines attached.

7. Disconnect the cold start valve wiring and remove the fuel line from the valve.

NOTE: Protect the fuel injectors and cold start valve with caps.

8. Tag and disconnect all vacuum and PCV lines.

9. Tag and disconnect all electrical lines leading to the cylinder head.

10. On turbocharged engines, remove the hose which runs from the intake manifold to the turbocharger. On the Quattro vehicle, remove the hose which runs from the intake manifold to the intercooler.

11. Remove the auxiliary air regulator. Remove the air box cover and filter element.

12. Remove the intake manifold mounting nuts and remove the manifold from the engine.

To install:

13. Clean the gasket mating surfaces on the manifold and engine.

14. Using a new gasket, install the manifold on the cylinder head and tighten the nuts to 15 ft. lbs. (20 Nm).

15. Install the auxiliary air regulator.

16. On turbocharged engines, install the hose which runs from the intake manifold to the turbocharger. On the Quattro vehicle, install the hose which runs from the intake manifold to the intercooler.

17. Reconnect all vacuum and electrical connections.

18. Install the fuel line to the cold start valve and reconnect the cold start valve wiring.

19. Install the fuel injectors.

20. Connect the throttle cable and rod to the throttle valve assembly. Install all air ducts.

21. Check all fluid levels. Operate the engine at normal operating temperatures and check for leaks.

22. Road test the vehicle for proper operation.

8 Cylinder Engine

1. Disconnect the negative battery cable.

2. Relieve the fuel system pressure.

3. Remove the 7 bolts retaining the upper part of the air cleaner housing and the 2 bolts securing the lower part. Press the housing towards the rear and lift out.

4. Remove the fuel supply and return lines. Remove the fuel pressure regulator from the fuel rail.

5. Remove the breather hose at the rear of the intake manifold, remove the vacuum hose and the bolt securing the upper part of the engine wiring harness clamp.

6. Disconnect the harness connectors for the left and right knock sensor, the air mass sensor, the potentiometer, the thermo-switch and idle stabilizer valve. Remove the idle stabilizer valve and disconnect the hose to the carbon canister.

7. Remove the air temperature sensor bolts. Remove the breather hose at the top of the cam cover by using pliers to turn the hose until the retaining lug unlatches. Remove the breather on the cylinder head at the left rear.

8. Remove the bolts securing the fuel rails and lift out the rails with the injectors. Place on the plenum chamber.

9. Remove the intake manifold bolts and lift out the manifold. Watch the front breather hose under the intake manifold. There are 2 oil retention valves that must be replaced if they sound noisy on short drives, although the noise may go away on longer drives. Replace these valves as follows:

   a. After the intake manifold has been removed, remove the right hand knock sensor and the bolts securing the engine breather cover.

   b. Lift out the cover along with the bulkhead panel. It may be easier to lift the right side first.

   c. Locate the oil retention valves and remove the circlips.

   d. Screw a M6 x times; 50mm bolt with a large washer into the oil retention valve. Remove the valve by prying evenly under the washer.

To install:

10. Use care when installing the intake manifold. First install the front breather hose to the engine under the intake manifold. Install the intake manifold assembly.

11. Install the fuel rails with fuel injectors. When reinstalling the fuel system parts, use care not to damage any O-rings.

12. Install the air temperature sensor, breather and hose.

13. Install the idle stabilizer valve and reconnect the hose to the carbon canister.

14. Reconnect the harness connectors for the left and right knock sensor, the air mass sensor, the potentiometer, the thermo-switch and idle stabilizer valve.

15. Install the fuel pressure regulator, by pressing it directly into the seat of the O-ring seal.

16. Install the fuel supply and return lines.

17. Check all fluid levels. Operate the engine at normal operating temperatures and check for leaks.

18. Road test the vehicle for proper operation.

Exhaust Manifold

REMOVAL AND INSTALLATION

Non-turbocharged Engines

EXCEPT 8 CYLINDER ENGINE

NOTE: Although not necessary, more working clearance will be found by removing the intake manifold before removing the exhaust manifold. Before beginning, soak the manifold studs with lubricant to aid in the removal.

1. Disconnect the negative battery cable. Raise and support the vehicle safely. Disconnect the exhaust pipe from the exhaust manifold.

2. Disconnect the EGR valve and oxygen sensor from the manifold.

3. Remove the heat deflector shield on 4 cylinder engines.

4. Disconnect the CO probe receptacle tube.

5. Remove the exhaust manifold mounting nuts and remove the manifold from the engine.

To install:

6. Clean the gasket mating surfaces of the manifold and engine.

7. Using a new gasket, install the manifold on the engine and tighten the nuts to 22 ft. lbs. (30 Nm).

NOTE: Always replace the old mounting nuts with new brass nuts. Check the condition of the studs before installation. The oxygen sensor, EGR tube, bolts and nuts exposed to high temperatures should receive a light coating of anti-seize compound on the threads before assembly.

8. Connect the exhaust pipe to the manifold, using a new gasket and tighten nuts to 26 ft. lbs. (35 Nm).

9. Install and tighten the CO measuring tube to 22 ft. lbs. (30 Nm).

10. Install EGR valve and oxygen sensor to the manifold.

11. Install the heat deflector shield, if equipped.

12. Reconnect the battery. Operate the engine at normal operating temperatures and check for leaks.

8 CYLINDER ENGINE

1. Disconnect negative battery cable.

2. Disconnect the front exhaust pipe at the manifolds.

3. For the left side manifold, unscrew the guide for the dipstick tube and remove.

4. For both the left and right manifolds, remove the bolts securing

the exhaust manifolds to the cylinder heads.

5. Remove the manifolds one at a time. Loosen the engine mounts. Lift the engine at the edge of the oil pan on the side of the manifold to be removed.

To install:

6. Clean the gasket mating surfaces of the manifolds and engine.

7. Using a new gasket, install the manifold on the engine and tighten the nuts to 18 ft. lbs. (24 Nm). Lower the engine.

8. Install the dipstick guide and replace the sealing ring, if necessary.

9. Reconnect the front exhaust pipe at the manifold.

10. Reconnect the battery. Operate the engine at normal operating temperatures and check for leaks.

Turbocharged Engine

1. Disconnect the negative battery cable. Remove the hose which runs between the air duct and the turbocharger.

2. If the intake manifold has not been removed, disconnect the hose which runs from the intake manifold to the turbocharger or intercooler.

3. Disconnect the exhaust pipe from the turbocharger.

4. Disconnect the exhaust pipe from the wastegate on the rear of the manifold.

5. Disconnect the EGR valve and the oxygen sensor, if necessary, from the manifold.

6. Remove the oil lines from the turbocharger.

7. Remove the line from the bottom of the turbocharger to the intercooler, if equipped.

NOTE: The manifold, turbocharger and wastegate are removed as a unit.

8. Remove the manifold assembly.

To install:

9. Clean the gasket mating surfaces of the manifolds and engine.

10. Install the exhaust manifold. Tighten the exhaust manifold mounting nuts to 26 ft. lbs. (35 Nm). Always use new gaskets and O-rings where necessary.

NOTE: The oxygen sensor, EGR tube, bolts and nuts exposed to high temperatures should receive a light coating of anti-seize compound on the threads before assembly.

11. Install the line from the bottom of the turbocharger to the intercooler, if equipped.

12. Reconnect the oil lines from the turbocharger.

13. Install the EGR valve and oxygen sensor, if necessary.

14. Install the exhaust system.

15. Install all hoses or air ducts.

16. Reconnect the battery. Operate the engine at normal operating temperatures and check for leaks.

Turbocharger

REMOVAL AND INSTALLATION

1. Disconnect the negative battery cable. Spray all mounting bolts with a lubricant.

2. Remove the vacuum tube between the intake air boot and turbocharger.

3. Remove the intake boot and crankcase ventilation hose. Remove the hose assembly between the intake manifold and throttle housing.

4. Remove the air box cover and remove the filter element.

5. Remove the right side engine mount heatshield.

6. Remove the oil supply pipe from the turbocharger. Remove the exhaust pipe from the corrugated pipe. Loosen the exhaust pipe at the transaxle mount and catalytic converter.

7. Remove the retaining clamp from the starter housing and sensor air hose.

8. Remove the exhaust pipe from the turbocharger.

9. Remove the alternator support bolt and position the alternator to the side.

10. Remove the oil return pipe from the turbocharger. Remove mounting bolts and turbocharger.

To install:

11. Install the turbocharger with new gaskets and torque the mounting nuts to 43 ft. lbs. (60 Nm).

12. Connect the oil supply and return lines using new gaskets.

13. Install the alternator assembly.

14. Connect the exhaust pipe and torque the nuts to 25 ft. lbs. (34 Nm). Install all exhaust brackets.

NOTE: Bolts and nuts exposed to high temperatures should receive a light coating of anti-seize compound on the threads before assembly. After servicing the turbocharger, always replace the engine oil along with the turbocharger filter and engine oil filter.

15. Connect the outlet air hose and breather hoses.

16. Install heatshield, filter element and air box cover.

17. Reconnect the battery. Operate the engine at normal operating temperatures and check for leaks.

Turbocharger Wastegate

REMOVAL AND INSTALLATION

NOTE: Although not necessary, more working clearance will be found by removing the intake manifold before removing the wastegate. Before starting, soak the studs with lubricant to aid in the removal.

1. Disconnect the negative battery cable. Remove the wastegate to exhaust pipe connecting tube. There are 3 bolts on the top and on the bottom.

2. Remove the mounting bolt for the tube leading from the wastegate to the exhaust manifold.

3. Remove the vacuum line from the end of the wastegate.

4. Remove the 4 mounting bolts and remove the wastegate from the exhaust manifold.

5. Installation is in the reverse order of removal. Torque the mounting nuts/bolts to 18 ft. lbs. (25 Nm).

NOTE: Bolts and nuts exposed to high temperatures should receive a light coating of anti-seize compound on the threads before assembly.

Timing Belt Front Cover

REMOVAL AND INSTALLATION

4 Cylinder

UPPER COVER

1. Disconnect the negative battery cable. Loosen the alternator adjusting bolts, pivot the alternator over and slip the drive belt off.

2. Loosen the air conditioning compressor mounting bolts and remove the drive belt.

3. Remove the valve cover nuts and remove the valve cover and retaining straps.

4. Remove the upper timing belt cover nuts. Note the position of the washers and spacers while removing the cover.

5. Installation is the reverse of the removal procedure.

6. Adjust the drive belt tension when finished.

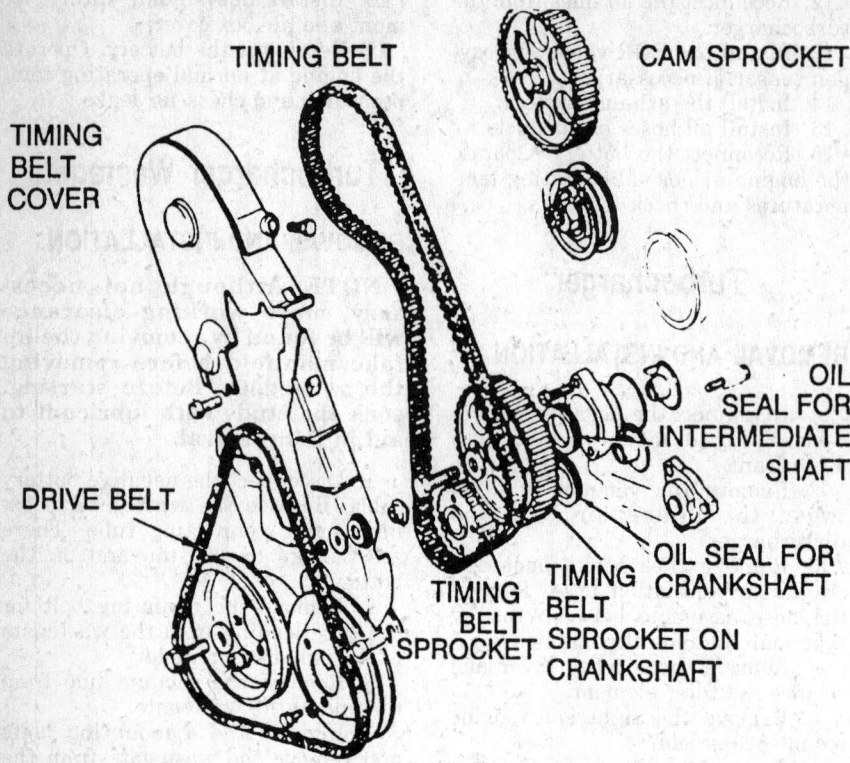

TIMING BELT

CAM SPROCKET

TIMING BELT COVER

OIL SEAL FOR INTERMEDIATE SHAFT

DRIVE BELT

OIL SEAL FOR CRANKSHAFT

TIMING BELT SPROCKET

TIMING BELT SPROCKET ON CRANKSHAFT

Timing belt — 4 cylinder engine

LOWER COVER

1. Disconnect the negative battery cable. Remove the upper timing belt cover.

2. Using the large bolt on the crankshaft sprocket, rotate the engine until the No. 1 cylinder is at TDC of the compression stroke. At this point, both valves for No. 1 cylinder will be closed and the **0** mark on the flywheel will be aligned with the pointer on the bell housing.

3. Remove the crankshaft pulley retaining bolts. If the sprocket or rear cover is to be serviced, loosen the crankshaft sprocket bolt.

NOTE: To remove the crankshaft sprocket bolt, on manual transaxle vehicles, place the vehicle in 5th gear and have an assistant apply the brake. The will stop the engine from rotating while loosening the bolt. On automatic transaxle vehicles, remove the starter and hold the flywheel from turning using a flywheel holding tool VW 10-201 or equivalent.

4. Remove the crankshaft pulley.

5. Remove the water pump pulley retaining bolts and remove the pulley.

6. Remove the lower cover retaining nuts and remove the cover. Take care not to lose any of the washers or spacers.

7. Installation is the reverse of removal procedure.

8. Tighten the crankshaft sprocket bolt to 66 ft. lbs. (89 Nm) plus ½ additional turn.

5 Cylinder Engine

UPPER COVER

1. Disconnect the negative battery cable. Loosen the alternator adjusting bolts and remove the drive belt.

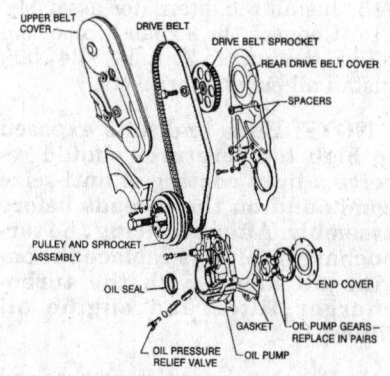

UPPER BELT COVER

DRIVE BELT

DRIVE BELT SPROCKET

REAR DRIVE BELT COVER

SPACERS

PULLEY AND SPROCKET ASSEMBLY

OIL SEAL

END COVER

GASKET

OIL PUMP GEARS— REPLACE IN PAIRS

OIL PRESSURE RELIEF VALVE

OIL PUMP

Timing belt — 5 cylinder engine

2. Loosen the power steering pump adjusting bolts and remove the drive belt.

3. Remove the retaining nuts and remove the timing belt cover. Take care not to lose any of the washers or spacers.

4. Installation is the reverse of the removal procedure.

5. Adjust the drive belt tension when finished.

LOWER COVER

1. Disconnect the negative battery cable. Remove the upper timing belt cover.

2. Loosen the air conditioning compressor mounting bolts and remove the drive belt.

3. Remove the crankshaft balancer center bolt.

NOTE: To remove the crankshaft balancer bolt, on manual transaxle vehicles, place the vehicle in 5th gear and have an assistant apply the brake. The will stop the engine from rotating while loosening the bolt. On automatic transaxle vehicles, remove the starter and hold the flywheel from turning, using a flywheel holding tool VW 10-201 or equivalent. This bolt is extremely tight.

4. Remove the lower timing belt cover bolts and remove the cover.
   To install:

5. Installation is the reverse of removal procedure.

6. Use the same procedure to install the crankshaft center bolt as when removing the bolt. Apply a locking compound on the bolt threads and tighten the bolt to 258 ft. lbs. (350 Nm) in several steps.

7. Adjust the drive belt tension when finished.

8 Cylinder Engine

1. Disconnect the negative battery cable. The battery is under the rear seat.

2. Remove the coolant expansion tank cap. Raise and safely support vehicle. Remove the sound insulator or lower pan. Drain coolant from radiator.

3. Remove the alternator cooling air duct. Loosen the clip and disconnect the coolant temperature sensor harness connector. Remove the coolant hose.

4. Disconnect the outer half of the air duct at the alternator. Remove the screws securing the wiring at the alternator. Note that the alternator wiring must be brought out at the

side, not downward. Otherwise, the alternator air duct cannot be mounted.

5. Release tension on the poly-ribbed drive belt and remove the belt in a downward direction. Place a 13mm box wrench on the hexagon guide of the tensioner and pressing the wrench slowly upwards.

6. Remove the alternator mounting bolts and remove the alternator.

7. Working from below, remove the 3 bolts for the toothed belt guard.

8. Remove the bolts securing the bracket for the air intake ducts on the left and right and remove the ducts. Remove the bar-shaped strut brace.

9. Remove the 7 screws securing the upper part of the air cleaner housing, then remove the bolts holding the lower part of the housing. Press towards the rear and lift out.

10. Remove the upper radiator hose and clips.

11. Disconnect the electric fan bolts, lift the fan assembly out and lay to one side, wiring still connected.

12. Remove the bolts securing the supporting clamp for the lower radiator hose and take off the upper part. Disconnect the radiator hose at the thermostat housing. Swing the radiator hose to right at rear.

13. Remove the fan shroud by unscrewing the bolts for the viscous fan at the top. Remove the bolts securing the viscous fan. A spanner wrench or equivalent may be needed to hold the fan hub. Note that this is a left hand thread. Turn to the right to loosen. Lift out the fan and shroud together.

14. Disconnect the engine support at the front. Note any shims. The same thickness shims must be used at installation. Remove the radiator hose. At installation, install the radiator hose first.

15. Loosen the center bolt of the vibration damper by one turn. A special tool may be needed to hold the damper from turning. This bolt was installed to over 250 ft. lbs. (340 Nm) torque and will be difficult to remove.

16. Remove the bolts securing the left side toothed belt cover or guard.

17. Remove the lower part of the supporting clamp for the lower radiator hose. Turn the tensioner for the poly-ribbed accessory drive belt in the loosening direction and insert an appropriate size holding pin in the hole provided.

18. Remove the bolts securing the right side toothed belt cover, with the exception of the top bolt. Remove the tensioner holding pin. Remove the belt cover top screw and remove the

cover or guard. Carefully lift the guard from the bottom to avoid damaging the radiator.

To install:

19. Install the right cover or guard.

20. Install tensioner holding pin. Install the left cover or guard.

21. Install crankshaft damper. The crankshaft damper center bolt must be torque to 258 ft. lbs. (350 Nm). A holding tool may be needed to keep the crankshaft from turning.

22. Install radiator hoses. Reconnect the engine support.

23. Install the viscous fan hub and shroud assembly. This uses a left hand thread. Turn right to loosen, left to tighten.

24. Install the electric fan and reconnect the wiring.

25. Install the alternator and wiring.

26. Install drive belt.

27. Install the sound insulator or lower pan.

28. Install the coolant expansion tank.

29. Refill and bleed the cooling system.

30. Install the air cleaner housing, air ducts and brace.

31. Check all fluid levels. Operate the engine at normal operating temperatures and check for leaks.

Oil Seal Replacement

Camshaft Seal

EXCEPT 8 CYLINDER ENGINE

1. Disconnect the negative battery cable. Set engine to TDC. Make sure crankshaft and cam timing marks are aligned.

2. Remove timing belt.

3. Hold camshaft from turning and remove cam drive sprocket by tapping from behind. Take care not to lose the cam drive key.

4. Pry out the old oil seal. In some cases it may be easier to remove the front camshaft bearing cap.

To install:

5. Installation is the reverse of the removal procedure. Lubricate the seal lip with clean engine oil. Reinstall the front bearing cap if removed. Torque hold-down nuts to 15 ft. lbs. (20 Nm).

6. Use a suitable driver and tap the new seal into position.

7. Install the cam drive sprocket with the drive key. Check the timing marks. Torque center bolt to 60 ft. lbs. (81 Nm).

8. Install cam belt and cover.

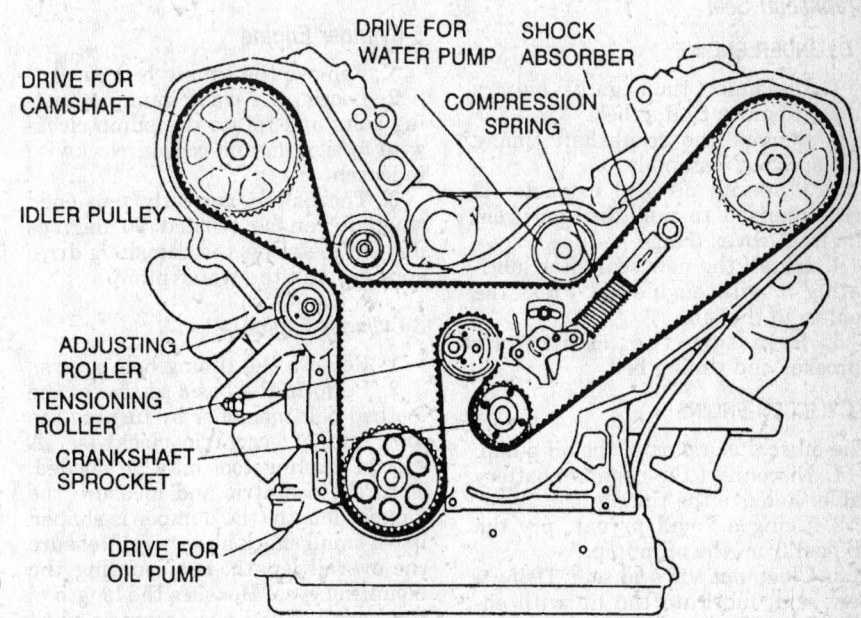

Timing belt layout — V8 engine

8 CYLINDER ENGINE

1. Disconnect the negative battery cable. Align timing marks cylinder No. 1 TDC of the compression stroke. Remove the toothed timing belt.

2. Remove the camshaft sprockets.

3. Remove the left and right belt guards.

NOTE: The toothed belt guard on the left-hand side contains 2 sealing rings and 1 shaft seal. The toothed belt guard on the right side contains 1 sealing ring and 1 shaft seal. If one shaft seal is leaking, the seals on both sides must be replaced.

4. Drive out the shaft seal.

To install:

5. When driving in the new seals, make sure the shaft seal is flush with the front edge of the belt guard. Replace the sealing rings.

6. Guide the camshaft sprocket into place.

7. Install the cam belt. Check timing marks on crankshaft and cam sprockets. Align timing marks cylinder No. 1 TDC of the compression stroke, if necessary.

8. Clean the sealing surface at the rear of the guard and on the cylinder head. After installing the new sealing rings, apply a thin coat of sealant to both surfaces. Install the rear toothed belt cover and torque the bolts to 7 ft. lbs. (10 Nm).

Crankshaft Seal

4 CYLINDER ENGINE

1. Disconnect the negative battery cable. Remove timing belt.

2. Remove the crankshaft timing belt sprocket assembly.

3. A special oil seal extractor is recommended to pull the seal from the front cover flange.

4. Install the new seal after lubricating it with engine oil. Press the seal in to the stop.

5. Reinstall the crankshaft sprocket and timing belt.

5 CYLINDER ENGINE

The oil seal is a part of the oil pump.

1. Disconnect the negative battery cable. Remove the timing belt.

2. Using a small prybar, pry the oil seal from the oil pump.

3. Clean out the seal seat. Using a new seal, lubricate the lip with engine oil. Using a suitable socket, drive the seal in to the seal seat.

NOTE: When installing a new seal, be careful not to damage the lip of the seal.

4. Reinstall the timing belt. Torque the crankshaft pulley bolt to 253 ft. lbs. (343 Nm).

8 CYLINDER ENGINE

1. Disconnect the negative battery cable. Remove the toothed cam drive belt.

2. Remove the vibration damper.

3. A special oil seal extractor is recommended to pull the seal from the front cover flange.

4. Install the new seal after lubricating it with engine oil. Press the seal in only until flush. Note that if the crankshaft shows signs of scoring, press the sealing ring in completely.

5. Reinstall the crankshaft sprocket and timing belt.

Timing Belt and Tensioner

Adjustment

4 Cylinder Engine

1. Remove the timing belt cover.

2. Holding the large bolt on the tensioner pulley, loosen the small nut and turn the tensioner clockwise to tighten and counterclockwise to loosen.

3. The belt is correctly tensioned when it can be twisted 90 degrees midway between the camshaft and the intermediate shaft drive sprockets.

5 Cylinder Engine

1. Remove the timing belt cover.

2. Loosen the water pump adjusting bolts and rotate the pump clockwise to tighten and counterclockwise to loosen.

3. The belt is correctly tensioned when it can be twisted 90 degrees midway between the camshaft drive sprocket and the water pump.

8 Cylinder Engine

1. Remove the timing belt covers.

2. Perform the basic setting of the toothed belt tensioner by turning the idler pulley eccentric clockwise. A special turning tool may be needed. Turn the eccentric and measure the damper length (the damper is shaped like a small shock absorber). Measure the overall length, not counting the mounting eyes. Measure the length of the barrel. Turn the eccentric until the damper length is 5.11-5.23 in. (130-133mm). Tighten the idler pulley eccentric to 18 ft. lbs. (24 Nm).

3. Remove any camshaft and crankshaft locking tool previously installed. Turn engine at least 2 turns. Tighten the vibration damper center bolt to 258 ft. lbs. (350 Nm). Check the damper length and if necessary, readjust the idler pulley.

4. Reinstall the timing belt covers.

REMOVAL AND INSTALLATION

4 Cylinder Engine

1. Disconnect the negative battery cable. Using the large bolt on the crankshaft sprocket, rotate the engine until the No. 1 cylinder is at TDC of the compression stroke. At this point, both valves will be closed and the **0** mark on the flywheel will be aligned with the pointer on the bell housing. If the belt hasn't jumped, the timing mark on the rear face of the camshaft sprocket should be aligned with the upper left edge of the valve cover.

2. Remove the upper and lower timing belt covers.

3. While holding the large hex nut on the tensioner pulley, loosen the smaller pulley locknut.

4. Turn the tensioner counterclockwise to relieve the tension on the timing belt.

5. Carefully slide the timing belt off the sprockets and remove the belt.

To install:

6. If the engine has moved or jumped timing, use the large bolt on the crankshaft sprocket to rotate the engine until the No. 1 cylinder is at TDC of the compression stroke. At this point, both valves will be closed and the **0** mark on the flywheel will be aligned with the pointer on the bell housing. Rotate the camshaft until the timing mark on the rear face of the camshaft sprocket is aligned with the upper left edge of the valve cover.

7. Install the crankshaft pulley and check that the notch on the pulley is aligned with the mark on the intermediate shaft sprocket. If not, rotate the intermediate shaft until they align.

NOTE: If the timing marks are not correctly aligned with the No. 1 piston at TDC of the compression stroke when the belt is installed, valve timing will be incorrect. Poor performance and possible engine damage can result from the improper valve timing.

8. Remove the crankshaft pulley. Note the pulley location on the crankshaft sprocket so it can be replaced in the same position. Hold the large nut on the tensioner pulley and loosen the smaller locknut. Turn the ten-

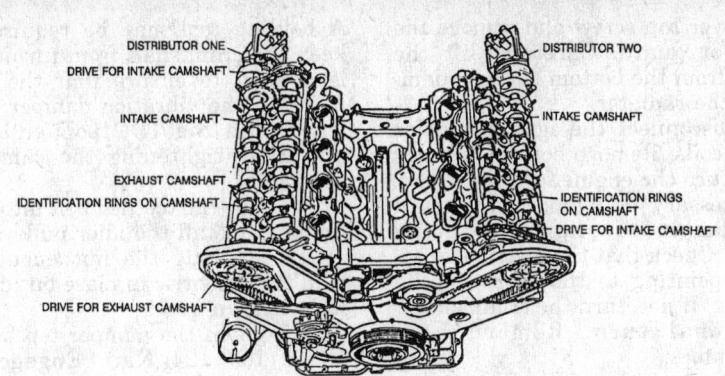

Camshaft layout train — V8 engine

Crankshaft pulley and intermediate sprocket alignment — 4 cylinder engine

Crankshaft pulley alignment marks — 5 cylinder engine

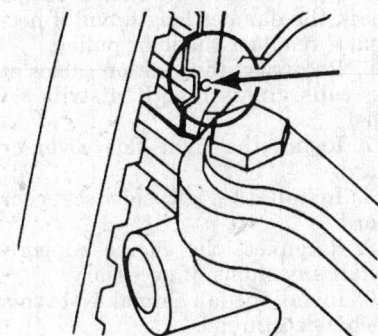

Camshaft sprocket alignment with cylinder head — 4 and 5 cylinder engines

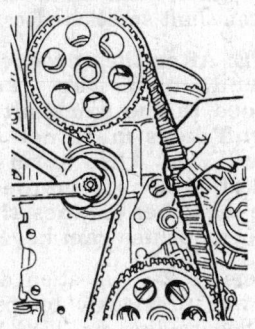

The timing belt on all models is correctly tensioned when the belt can be twisted 90° with thumb and 1 finger

sioner counterclockwise to loosen and install the timing belt.

9. Slide the timing belt onto the sprockets and adjust the belt tension. The timing belt tension is correct when the belt can be twisted 90 degrees midway between the camshaft and the intermediate shaft drive sprockets.

10. Install the crankshaft pulley. Torque the retaining bolts to 15 ft. lbs. (20 Nm).

11. Install the upper and lower timing belt covers.

12. Road test the vehicle for proper operation.

5 Cylinder Engine

1. Disconnect the negative battery cable. Using the large bolt on the crankshaft sprocket, rotate the engine until the No. 1 cylinder is at TDC of the compression stroke. Align the TDC mark **0** with the cast mark on the bell housing. If the belt hasn't jumped teeth, the timing mark on the rear face of the camshaft sprocket

should be aligned with the upper left edge of the valve cover.

2. Remove the alternator and air conditioner compressor drive belts.

3. Remove the upper and lower timing belt covers.

4. Loosen the water pump bolts only enough to turn the pump clockwise.

NOTE: By loosening the water pump bolts, the coolant may drain from the engine at the water pump. If necessary, drain the cooling system, remove the water pump and reinstall it with a new O-ring.

5. Slide the timing belt off the sprockets.

To install:

6. If necessary, turn the camshaft until the notch on the back of the sprocket is in line with the left side edge of the cylinder head gasket surface.

7. If necessary, align the TDC **0** mark with the with the lug cast on the bell housing.

8. Install the timing belt and turn the water pump counterclockwise to tighten the belt. Tighten the water pump bolts to 15 ft. lbs. (20 Nm).

NOTE: The timing belt is correctly tensioned when it can be twisted 90 degrees along the straight run between the camshaft sprocket and water pump. The belt must not be jammed between the oil pump and sprocket when installing the vibration damper.

9. Install the timing belt covers and tighten the bolts to 7 ft. lbs. (10 Nm).

10. Install the alternator and air conditioning compressor belts. These belts are correctly tensioned when they can be depressed ⅜ in. along their longest straight run.

8 Cylinder Engine

1. Disconnect the negative battery cable. The battery is under the rear seat.

2. Remove the coolant expansion tank cap. Raise and safely support vehicle. Remove the sound insulator or lower pan. Drain coolant from radiator.

3. Remove the alternator cooling air duct. Loosen the clip and disconnect the coolant temperature sensor harness connector. Remove the coolant hose.

4. Disconnect the outer half of the air duct at the alternator. Remove

the screws securing the wiring at the alternator.

5. Release tension on the poly-ribbed drive belt and remove the belt in a downward direction. Do this by placing a 13mm box wrench on the hexagon guide of the tensioner and pressing the wrench slowly upwards.

6. Remove the alternator mounting bolts and remove the alternator.

7. Working from below, remove the 3 bolts for the toothed belt guard.

8. Remove the bolts securing the bracket for the air intake ducts on the left and right and remove the ducts. Remove the bar-shaped strut brace.

9. Remove the 7 screws securing the upper part of the air cleaner housing, then remove the bolts holding the lower part of the housing. Press towards the rear and lift out.

10. Remove the upper radiator hose and clips.

11. Disconnect the electric fan bolts, lift the fan assembly out and lay to one side, wiring still connected.

12. Remove the bolts securing the supporting clamp for the lower radiator hose and take off the upper part. Disconnect the radiator hose at the thermostat housing. Swing the radiator hose to the right.

13. Remove the fan shroud by unscrewing the bolts for the viscous fan at the top. Remove the bolts securing the viscous fan. A spanner wrench or equivalent may be needed to hold the fan hub. Note that this is a left hand thread. Turn to the right to loosen. Lift out the fan and shroud together.

14. Disconnect the engine support at the front. Note any shims. The same thickness shims must be used at installation. Remove the radiator hose. At installation, install the radiator hose first.

15. Loosen the center bolt of the vibration damper by one turn. A special tool may be needed to hold the damper from turning. This bolt was installed to over 250 ft. lbs. (340 Nm) torque and will be difficult to remove.

16. Remove the bolts securing the left side toothed belt cover or guard.

17. Remove the lower part of the supporting clamp for the lower radiator hose. Turn the tensioner for the poly-ribbed accessory drive belt in the loosening direction and insert an appropriate size holding pin in the hole provided.

18. Remove the bolts securing the right side toothed belt cover, with the exception of the top bolt. Remove the tensioner holding pin. Remove the belt cover top screw and remove the cover or guard. Carefully lift the guard from the bottom to avoid damaging the radiator.

19. Disconnect the ignition cables at the coils. Remove both distributor caps. Turn the engine to TDC. It may be necessary to temporarily install the damper to align the timing marks. Check that the distributor rotor is pointing to the mark on the housing. If not, turn the crankshaft 1 additional turn. Remove both distributors.

20. Remove the stop plate at the toothed belt tensioner. Disconnect the shock-absorber shaped damper at the top bolt.

21. Remove the belt from the tensioning idler pulley (with eccentric). Pulley is on right side of engine. Take the belt off both camshaft sprockets.

22. A special holding tool is available that is installed on the back of the camshafts. It fits the locating pin on the distributor flanges. If necessary, use a special hook wrench tool to turn the camshaft until the pins latch into the special holding tool. Secure the special tool with the distributor mounting bolts.

23. At the camshaft sprocket end, loosen the mounting bolts 2 turns. Using a plastic hammer, tap the edge of the camshaft sprockets loose.

NOTE: After the sprockets are removed, note the grooves machined in the camshaft ends. Woodruff keys must not be installed in the camshaft sprocket/camshaft connection. Unlike the other engines, this engine does not use cam keys.

24. Remove the vibration damper which was previously temporarily reinstalled to line up TDC timing marks. A puller can be used. Unscrew 2 opposing bolts of the 4 bolts connecting the vibration damper and toothed belt sprocket. Use a puller in these holes.

25. Remove the toothed belt.

To install:

26. Before installing a new belt, the rollers and tensioners must be checked for dirt, rough running and ease of rotation. Clean or replace rollers and tensioners, as necessary.

27. Fit the toothed belt at the crankshaft and install the vibration damper with the belt on the crankshaft.

28. Apply thread locking compound to the center bolt and tighten to 332 ft. lbs. (450 Nm) using hand wrench.

A holding tool may be required to keep the crankshaft from turning. It is a must to ensure that the TDC mark on the vibration damper is aligned with the TDC pointer before and after tightening the camshaft sprockets.

29. Guide the toothed belt into position and install the idler pulley with eccentric. Snug the nut enough to hold the eccentric in place but do not fully tighten it yet.

30. Tighten the damper top bolt to 18 ft. lbs. (24 Nm). Engage the damper to the tensioner lever by pressing the lever downward.

31. Perform the basic setting of the toothed belt tensioner by turning the idler pulley eccentric clockwise.

32. A special turning tool may be needed. Turn the eccentric and measure the damper length. Measure the overall length of the barrel not counting the mounting eyes. Turn the eccentric until the damper barrel length is 5.11-5.23 in. (130-133mm).

33. Tighten the idler pulley eccentric to 18 ft. lbs. (24 Nm). Tighten the camshaft sprockets to 33 ft. lbs. (45 Nm).

34. Remove any camshaft and crankshaft locking tool previously installed.

35. Turn engine at least 2 turns. Check the damper length and if necessary, readjust the idler pulley.

36. Reconnect the ignition cables at the coils. Install both distributor caps.

37. Install the right side cover or guard.

38. Install the left side cover or guard.

39. Reconnect the engine support. Install any shims, if necessary.

40. Install the fan shroud. Note this left-handed thread.

41. Install all coolant hoses.

42. Install the electric fan.

43. Install the alternator and electrical wiring.

44. Install the drive belt and adjust.

45. Install the air filter housing. Install all air ducts. Install strut brace.

46. Install the coolant expansion tank.

47. Install the sound insulator or lower pan.

48. Refill and bleed the cooling system.

49. Check all fluid levels. Operate the engine at normal operating temperatures and check for leaks.

50. Road test the vehicle for proper operation.

Timing Sprockets

REMOVAL AND INSTALLATION

Except 8 Cylinder Engines

All timing belt sprockets, are located by keys on their respective shafts. Each sprocket is retained by a bolt. To remove any or all of the sprockets, first remove the timing belt cover(s) and timing belt.

1. Disconnect the negative battery cable. Remove the center retaining bolt for the sprocket.
2. Pull the sprocket off the shaft.
3. If the sprocket is sticking on the shaft, use a gear puller or tap lightly with a plastic mallet. Do not hammer on the sprocket or damage may occur.
4. Remove the sprocket, being careful not to lose the key.
5. Installation is in the reverse order of removal.

NOTE: Always check valve timing after removing the drive sprockets.

8 Cylinder Engines

1. Disconnect the negative battery cable. Remove timing cover, toothed timing belt and both distributors. Note that the timing belt drives the exhaust camshaft. A chain from the exhaust cam drives the intake cam.
2. A special holding tool is available that is installed on the back of the camshafts. It fits the locating pin on the distributor flanges. If necessary, use a special hook wrench to turn the camshaft until the pins latch into the special holding tool. Secure the special tool with the distributor mounting bolts.
3. At the camshaft sprocket end, loosen the mounting bolts 2 turns. Using a plastic hammer, tap the edge of the camshaft sprockets slightly loose.

NOTE: After the sprockets are removed, note the grooves machined in the camshaft ends. Woodruff keys must not be installed in the camshaft sprocket/camshaft connection.

4. When assembling the sprockets to the camshafts, make sure the timing marks found on the backside of the chain sprockets are still aligned. They should align next to each other at the 3 o'clock and 9 o'clock positions. Tighten the camshaft sprockets to 33 ft. lbs. (45 Nm).

Camshaft

REMOVAL AND INSTALLATION

4 Cylinder Engine

1. Disconnect the negative battery cable. Remove the upper drive belt, vacuum lines to valve cover and valve cover.
2. Using the large bolt on the crankshaft sprocket, rotate the engine until the No. 1 cylinder is at TDC of the compression stroke. At this point, both valves will be closed and the **0** mark on the flywheel will be aligned with the pointer on the bell housing. If the belt hasn't jumped, the timing mark on the rear face of the camshaft sprocket should be aligned with the upper left edge of the valve cover.
3. Remove the timing belt from the camshaft sprocket.
4. Remove the camshaft timing belt sprocket, take care not to lose Woodruff key.
5. First remove bearing caps No. 1 and 3. Bearing cap No. 1 is located at the sprocket. Next remove bearing caps No. 2 and 5, alternately and diagonally. Bearing cap No. 5 is on the opposite end from the cam sprocket. There is no bearing cap No. 4.
6. Remove the camshaft from the cylinder head.

To install:

7. Lubricate the camshaft journals, lobes and contact faces of the caps with assembly lube before reinstallation.
8. Replace the camshaft oil seal in the cylinder head.

NOTE: The bearing caps are offset. Before installing the camshaft, set the bearing caps into position. Check that they are facing in the correct direction. The numbers on the bearing caps are not always on the same side.

9. Install the bearing caps in the proper order, observing the off-center position.
10. Install bearing caps No. 2 and 5 and tighten to 15 ft. lbs. (20 Nm).
11. Install bearing caps No. 1 and 3 and tighten to 15 ft. lbs. (20 Nm).
12. Mount camshaft sprocket and tighten to 59 ft. lbs. (80 Nm).
13. Install the timing belt.
14. Install the valve cover and all vacuum lines.
15. Install the drive belt.

16. Reconnect the negative battery cable. Road test the vehicle for proper operation.

NOTE: Always recheck the valve timing and valve clearance after the camshaft has been removed.

5 Cylinder Engine

80 and 90

1. Disconnect the negative battery cable. Remove the upper drive belt cover, valve cover and upper part of intake manifold, if necessary.
2. Using the large bolt on the crankshaft sprocket, rotate the engine until the No. 1 cylinder is at TDC of the compression stroke. Align the TDC mark **0** with the cast mark on the bell housing. If the belt hasn't jumped the timing mark on the rear face of the camshaft sprocket should be aligned with the upper left edge of the valve cover.
3. Remove the timing belt from the camshaft sprocket. Remove the camshaft sprocket.
4. Remove bearing caps No. 1 and 3. Bearing caps are marked on the top.
5. Diagonally loosen bearing caps No. 2 and 4 and remove the bearing caps.
6. Lift the camshaft out of the cylinder head.

To install:

7. When installing, lightly oil the camshaft and bearing journals with clean engine oil.
8. Position the caps on the same journals from which they were removed.
9. Install bearing caps No. 2 and 4. Tighten alternately and diagonally to 15 ft. lbs. (20 Nm).
10. Install bearing caps No. 1 and 3 and tighten to 15 ft. lbs. (20 Nm).
11. Install the camshaft sprocket and timing belt. Install the valve cover. The camshaft sprocket bolt is tightened to 59 ft. lbs. (80 Nm).

100 and 200

1. Disconnect the negative battery cable. Remove the upper drive belt cover, valve cover and upper part of intake manifold, if necessary.
2. Using the large bolt on the crankshaft sprocket, rotate the engine until the No. 1 cylinder is at TDC of the compression stroke. Align the TDC mark **0** with the cast mark on the bell housing. If the belt hasn't jumped, the timing mark on the rear face of the camshaft sprocket should be aligned with the upper left edge of the valve cover.

3. Remove the timing belt from the camshaft sprocket. Remove the camshaft sprocket.

4. Diagonally loosen bearing caps No. 2 and 4 and remove the bearing caps. Bearing caps are marked on the top.

5. Diagonally loosen bearing caps No. 1 and 3 and remove the bearing caps.

6. Lift the camshaft out of the cylinder head.

To install:

7. When installing, lightly oil the camshaft and bearing journals with clean engine oil.

8. Position the caps on the same journals from which they were removed.

9. Tighten the nuts of caps 2 and 4 until snug.

10. Tighten all nuts to 15 ft. lbs. (20 Nm).

11. Install the camshaft sprocket and timing belt. Install the valve cover. The camshaft sprocket bolt is tightened to 58 ft. lbs. (79 Nm).

8 Cylinder Engine

1. Disconnect the negative battery cable. Remove the toothed camshaft drive belt.

2. Remove the cylinder head cover.

3. Remove the camshaft sprocket.

4. On the exhaust side, remove the intermediate flange and bearing cap for the distributor. All bearing caps that are removed should be marked or identified so they can be installed in the same position. Do not mix bearing caps or install then backwards. Loosen the bearing cap in front of the chain, plus caps No. 2 and 3. Loosen bearing caps No. 1 and 4 alternately and in a diagonal sequence. Bearing caps are marked on the top for correct installation.

5. On the intake side, remove bearing caps No. 6 and 7. Loosen

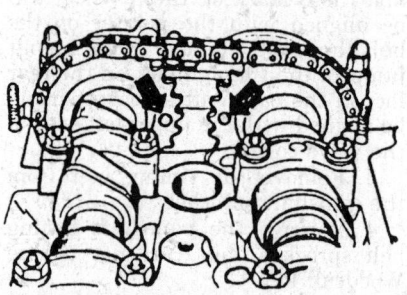

Cam gear alignment marks — V8 engine

bearing caps No. 5 and 8 alternately and in a diagonal sequence.

6. Remove the cam. If a lifter is removed and is to be reused, it must go in the bore from which it was removed.

To install:

7. Installation is the reverse of removal. Before assembly coat the moving parts with clean oil.

8. Install the camshafts with the chain so the markings on the chain sprockets are in alignment. The marks are on the back side of the chain sprocket. They should face each other at the 3 o'clock and 9 o'clock positions. Install the bearing caps so the stamped-on numbers can be read from the intake side.

9. Make sure the bearing caps are installed properly. They will cause parts failure if installed backwards. Torque the bearing caps to 11 ft. lbs. (15 Nm) in the following sequence:

Caps 5 and 8 in a diagonal sequence

Caps 1 and 4 in a diagonal sequence

Caps 2 and 3 in a diagonal sequence

Caps 6 and 7 in a diagonal sequence

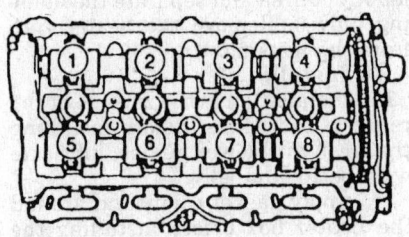

Cam bearing caps are numbered — V8 engine

Piston and Connecting Rod

Positioning

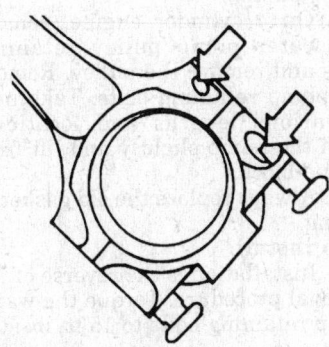

Align the forge marks when assembling the connecting rod caps

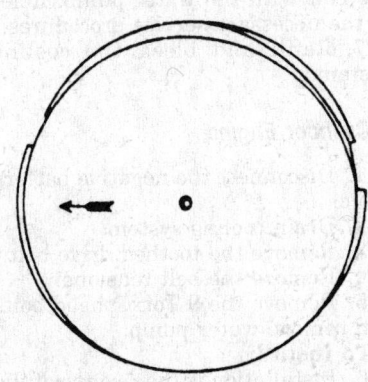

Arrow on piston faces front of vehicle

ENGINE LUBRICATION

Oil Pan

REMOVAL AND INSTALLATION

1. Disconnect the negative battery cable. Raise and support the vehicle safely.

2. Drain the oil from the crankcase. Remove the cover plate from under the engine, if equipped.

3. If necessary, remove the 4 bolts from the subframe and lower the subframe. Remove the oil pan bolts while supporting the pan.

4. Lower the pan from the engine. Discard the gasket. Note that the 8 cylinder engine uses a 2 piece oil pan as well as a honeycomb baffle insert. Both an upper and lower pan gasket will be required.

To install:

5. Coat both sides of a new gasket with sealer and install the gasket and oil pan.

6. Tighten the pan bolts to 7 ft. lbs. (10 Nm) on 4 cylinder engines or 15 ft. lbs. (20 Nm) on 5 cylinder engines. On 8 cylinder engines, tighten the lower pan-to-upper pan bolts to 14 ft. lbs. (19 Nm) and the upper pan-to-block bolts to 18 ft. lbs. (24 Nm).

Oil Pump

REMOVAL AND INSTALLATION

4 Cylinder Engine

1. Disconnect the negative battery cable. Raise and safely support vehicle. Drain the oil and remove the oil pan.

2. Remove the oil pump mounting bolts and pull the pump down and out of the engine.

3. Unscrew the 2 bolts and separate the pump halves.

4. Clean the lower half in solvent.

5. To remove the oil strainer for cleaning, bend out the metal rim of the oil strainer cover plate and remove it.

6. Examine the gears and the driveshaft for any wear or damage. Replace them, if necessary.

7. Reassemble the pump halves.

8. Prime the pump with oil and install in the reverse order of removal. Refill with oil to correct level.

5 Cylinder Engine

1. Disconnect the negative battery cable. Loosen and remove the crankshaft pulley bolt.

2. Remove the timing belt covers.

3. Loosen the water pump bolts and turn the pump body clockwise.

4. Remove the timing belt and V-belt pulley with the timing belt sprocket.

5. Remove the dipstick. Raise and safely support vehicle. Drain the engine oil.

6. Remove the front bolts on the subframe and remove the oil pan.

7. Remove the oil suction pipe from the base of the oil pump and bracket to the engine block.

8. Remove the oil pump bolts and remove the oil pump from the front of the engine.

9. Installation is the reverse of the removal procedure. Refill with oil to correct level.

8 Cylinder Engine

1. Disconnect the negative battery cable. Pull out dipstick. Raise and safely support vehicle.

2. Drain engine oil

3. Remove oil pan bolts and pull off pan assembly.

4. Remove bolts securing oil pump and pull out, disengaging from drive.

5. Installation is the reverse of the removal procedure. Refill with oil to the correct level.

Rear Main Bearing Oil Seal

REMOVAL AND INSTALLATION

The rear main oil seal is located at the rear of the engine block. It can be found in a housing or flange behind the flywheel/flexplate. To replace the seal, remove the transaxle or pull the engine.

1. Disconnect the negative battery cable. Remove the transaxle.

2. Remove the flywheel/flexplate.

3. Using a suitable tool, pry the old seal out of its housing.

4. To install, lightly oil the replacement seal and press it into place.

NOTE: Be careful not to damage the seal or score the crankshaft.

5. Install the flywheel/flexplate and the transaxle.

ENGINE COOLING

Radiator

REMOVAL AND INSTALLATION

Except 4 Cylinder Engine

1. Drain the cooling system.
2. Remove the 3 pieces of the radiator cowl and the fan motor assembly. Take care in removing the fan motor connectors to avoid bending them.
3. Remove the upper and lower radiator hoses and the coolant tank supply hose.
4. Disconnect the coolant temperature switch located on the lower right side of the radiator.
5. Remove the radiator mounting bolts and lift out the radiator.
6. Installation is the reverse of removal. Torque radiator mounting bolts to 14 ft. lbs. (19 Nm) and cowl bolts to 7 ft. lbs. (10 Nm). Refill and bleed the cooling system.

4 Cylinder Engine

NOTE: The 80 and 90 series vehicles use a dual fan electric/belt driven assembly. Replacement is similar to the other 4 cylinder engines.

1. Drain the cooling system.
2. If equipped with air conditioning, remove the grille and detach the condenser from the radiator. Leave refrigerant hoses attached, if possible. If not, properly discharge the air conditioning system.
3. Remove the upper and lower radiator hoses, the expansion tank supply hose and the expansion tank vent hose. Being careful not to crimp them, tie all hoses back aside.
4. Disconnect the wiring at the temperature switch (2 switches, if equipped with A/C) and the rear of the fan motor.
5. Unscrew the fan shroud retaining bolts and remove the fan, motor and shroud as an assembly.
6. Unscrew the radiator retaining bolts and remove the radiator.
7. Installation is in the reverse order of removal. Refill and bleed cooling system.

Heater Core

REMOVAL AND INSTALLATION

Except V8 Quattro

1. Disconnect the negative battery cable.
2. At the radiator, pull off the bottom hose and drain the coolant into a container for reuse.
3. Remove the heater hoses from the heat exchanger.
4. At the heater assembly control valve, disconnect the control wire.
5. Remove the console. Remove the left and the right heater covers from below the dashboard. On 80 and 90 model vehicles, remove the instrument panel.
6. Properly discharge the air conditioning system and remove the refrigerant lines from the evaporator.
7. At the heater control unit, pull off the control knobs.
8. Remove the trim plate from the heater control unit.
9. At the heater control unit, remove the retaining screws and the center cover.
10. Remove the heater air ducts and the heater assembly retaining springs.
11. Remove the air plenum from the cowl and the heater assembly from the vehicle.
12. Separate the heater unit and remove the heater core.
To install:
13. Install the heater core and reassemble the heater unit. Make sure the seals are in good condition.
14. Install the assembly into the vehicle and connect the ducts.
15. Connect the hoses and install the controls and instrument panel.
16. Refill the cooling system and evacuate and recharge the air conditioning system, if equipped.

V8 Quattro

1. Disconnect the negative battery cable.
2. Matchmark hood hinges and remove hood.
3. Remove the windshield wiper assembly.
4. Remove the cap from the engine coolant overflow bottle.
5. Remove the heater retaining band.
6. Remove the vacuum hoses from the vacuum servo motors.
7. Clamp the heater hoses and disconnect them from the heater core.
8. Remove the retainers between the body and heater and remove the heater box.

9. Remove the silicone rubber sealant from the heater core inlet/outlet area and separate the housing halves. Remove the heater core from the housing.
To install:
10. Installation is the reverse of the removal procedure. Before installing the fresh air blower guides, lubricate with petroleum jelly.
11. Apply gasket compound around the heater box before installing the heater core to seal box.
12. After installing the heater core, fill the opening between the heater core and the housing with silicone sealant.
13. When connecting the water hoses, make sure the lower connection on the heater core is connected to the hose going to the water pump.
14. Refill the cooling system.

Water Pump

REMOVAL AND INSTALLATION

4 and 5 Cylinder Engines

1. Drain the cooling system.
2. Remove the V-belts and the timing belt covers. On 5 cylinder engine, remove the timing belt from the water pump.
3. On 4 cylinder engine, remove the water pump pulley retaining bolts and remove the pulley. Remove the pump retaining bolts. Take note of various lengths and locations. Turn the pump slightly and lift from engine block.
4. Always replace the old gasket or O-ring.
To install:
5. Installation is the reverse of the removal procedure. Torque the water pump retaining bolts to 15 ft. lbs. (20 Nm).
6. Reinstall the timing belt on 5 cylinder engine and properly tension the belt with the water pump. Refer to the necessary service procedures.
7. Refill and bleed the cooling system.

8 Cylinder Engine

1. Disconnect the negative battery cable.
2. Drain cooling system.
3. Remove the toothed drive belt.
4. Remove the belt tensioner.
5. Remove the 9 Torx® head bolts and remove water pump.
To install:
6. Installation is the reverse of the removal process. Always use a new

gasket. Torque the water pump bolts to 7 ft. lbs. (10 Nm).

7. When refilling the cooling system, fill the expansion tank with new coolant to the maximum mark. Close the expansion tank and warm the engine until the radiator cooling fan cycles.

8. Check the coolant level and if necessary, top off. When the engine is at normal temperature, the level should be slightly over the maximum mark. When the engine is cold, the fluid should be between the maximum and minimum marks.

Thermostat

REMOVAL AND INSTALLATION

4 Cylinder Engine

The thermostat is located in the lower radiator hose neck on the bottom of the water pump housing. The cooling system is drained by removing the thermostat housing.

1. Loosen but do not remove the 2 thermostat housing bolts from the lower water pump neck. Have a large catch pan ready.

2. When the system is drained, remove the bolts.

3. Move the neck, with the hoses attached, aside.

4. Carefully, pry the thermostat out of the water pump housing.

To install:

5. Install the new O-ring and thermostat with the spring towards the engine. Do not use any gasket sealer on rubber gaskets or O-rings.

6. Install the housing, being careful to properly seat the thermostat and O-ring. Torque the bolts to 7 ft. lbs. (10 Nm).

7. Refill and bleed the cooling system.

5 Cylinder

The thermostat is located in the lower radiator hose neck, on the left side of the engine block, behind the water pump housing.

1. Drain the cooling system by removing the lower radiator hose.

2. Remove the 2 retaining bolts and remove the thermostat housing. Have a catch pan ready to catch the coolant that is still in the head.

3. Carefully pry the thermostat out of the head.

To install:

4. Install a new O-ring and thermostat with the spring towards the

engine. Do not use any gasket sealer on rubber gaskets or O-rings.

5. When installing the housing, be careful to properly seat the O-ring. Torque the bolts to 7 ft. lbs. (10 Nm).

6. Reconnect the hose. Refill and bleed the system.

6 Cylinder Engine

It is not necessary to remove the ribbed V-belt for access to thermostat and gasket.

1. Drain the cooling system.

2. Remove the drive (timing) belt cover.

3. Remove the thermostat housing from under the timing belt. Do not get coolant on timing belt.

4. Remove the thermostat and gasket.

5. Installation is the reverse of the removal procedure. Refill and bleed the cooling system.

8 Cylinder Engine

The thermostat is located at the front right-hand side of the engine below the intake manifold.

1. Drain the cooling system.

2. Remove the 2 retaining bolts from the thermostat housing.

NOTE: It is not necessary to disconnect the lower radiator hose. Removing the hose from the thermostat yoke may ease installation.

3. Remove the thermostat housing.

4. Carefully, pry the thermostat from the engine.

To install:

5. Install the new thermostat with the breather valve at the top or 12 o'clock position. Use a new gasket or O-ring.

6. Install the radiator hose, if removed. Refill and bleed the cooling system.

Cooling System Bleeding

After working on the cooling system, even to replace the thermostat, the system should be bled. Air trapped in the system will prevent proper filling and leave the radiator coolant level low, causing a risk of overheating.

1. To bleed the system, start with the system cool, the radiator cap off and the radiator filled to about an 1 in. below the filler neck.

2. Start the engine and run it at slightly above normal idle speed. This will insure adequate circulation.

If air bubbles appear and the coolant level drops, fill the system with an antifreeze/water mixture to bring the level back to the proper level.

3. Run the engine this way until the thermostat opens. When this happens, coolant will move abruptly across the top of the radiator and the temperature of the radiator will suddenly rise.

4. At this point, air is often expelled and the level may drop quite a bit. Keep refilling the system until the level is near the top of the radiator and remains constant.

5. Fill the radiator right up to the filler neck. Replace the radiator filler cap. Refill the overflow tank.

ENGINE ELECTRICAL

NOTE: Most vehicles are equipped with theft protected radios, which cannot be operated if power to the radio is interrupted. Before disconnecting the battery cables, obtain the security code. Never disconnect any electrical connector with the ignition key ON unless specified in the repair procedure, or damage to electronic components may result.

Distributor

REMOVAL

1. Disconnect the wiring harness connector from the distributor cap.

NOTE: V8 Quattro vehicles have 2 distributors, driven off the exhaust camshafts.

2. Unclip and remove the distributor cap and static shield with the spark plug wires still attached.

3. Disconnect and tag the vacuum lines at the distributor, if equipped.

4. Note the position of the rotor in relation to the distributor housing. Scribe a mark on the distributor and engine block or cylinder head for installation. Matchmark the tip of the rotor to the engine. Note the approximate position of the vacuum advance unit in relation to the engine.

5. Remove the distributor holddown bolt and clamp.

6. Lift the distributor assembly from the engine.

INSTALLATION

Timing Not Disturbed

1. With the rotor pointing in the same direction as when removed, insert the distributor into the engine.

2. Once the distributor is seated into the engine, line up the marks on the distributor and engine with the metal tip of the rotor.

3. Make sure the vacuum advance unit, if equipped, is pointed in the same direction as it was pointed originally. If the marks on the distributor and the engine are lined up properly, this will be done automatically.

4. Install the distributor hold-down clamp and bolt.

5. Install the distributor cap and static shield.

6. Install the vacuum lines, if equipped.

7. Install the distributor wiring harness connector.

8. Start the engine. Adjust the ignition timing.

Timing Disturbed

NOTE: If the engine has been turned or disturbed in any manner while the distributor was removed or if the marks were not

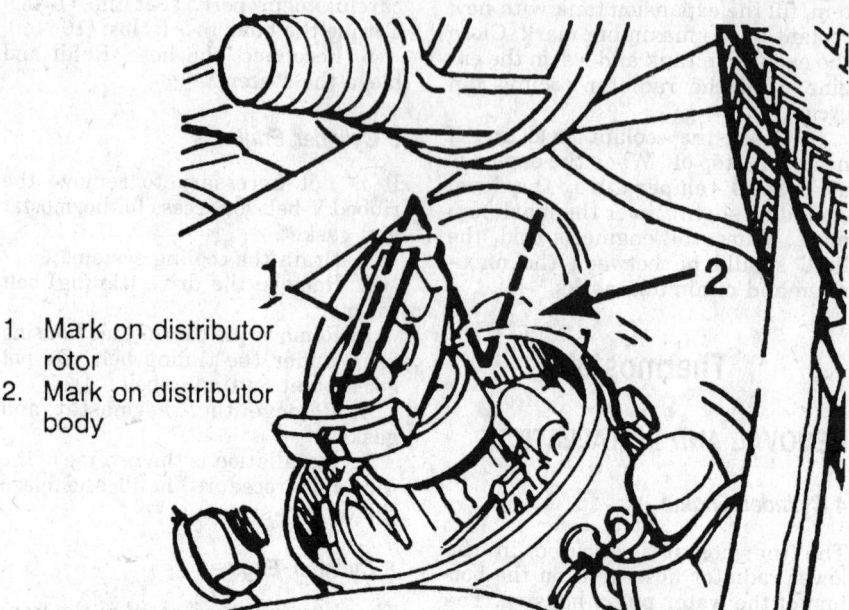

1. Mark on distributor rotor
2. Mark on distributor body

With the cap removed, turn the engine to align the rotor with the mark on the distributor body

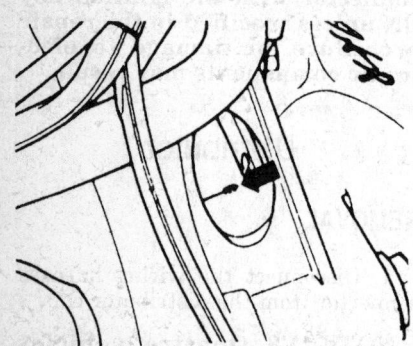

The timing mark is on the flywheel and aligns with a pointer on the bell housing

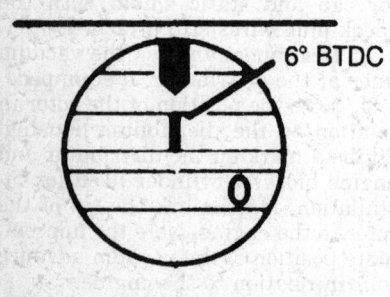

6° BTDC

Timing mark alignment on 4 cylinder engine

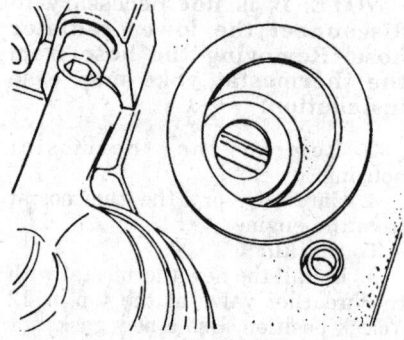

Oil pump driveshaft must be parallel to the crankshaft — 4 cylinder engine

drawn, it will be necessary to initially time the engine. Follow the procedure given below.

1. It is necessary to place the No. 1 cylinder in the firing position (TDC) to correctly install the distributor. To locate this position, the ignition timing marks on the flywheel and the clutch housing are used.

2. Remove the spark plug from the No. 1 cylinder. Turn the crankshaft until the piston in the No. 1 cylinder is moving up on the compression stroke. This can be determined by placing a finger over the spark plug

hole and feeling the air being forced out of the cylinder. Stop turning the engine when the timing mark on the flywheel is aligned with the lug on the flywheel housing.

3. Remove the timing belt cover.

4. Align the mark on the camshaft sprocket with the upper edge of the drive belt cover or with the upper edge of the valve cover gasket mounting surfaces.

5. On 4 cylinder engines, align the oil pump drive pinion lug on distributor so it aligns with the threaded bolt hole in the block.

6. Oil the distributor housing lightly where it bears on the cylinder block.

7. Install the distributor so the rotor tip points to the mark on the distributor housing for the No. 1 cylinder.

8. On 4 cylinder engines, when the distributor shaft has reached bottom, move the rotor back and forth slightly. The drive lug on the oil pump shaft should enter the slot cut into the end of the distributor shaft and the distributor assembly should slide down into place.

9. Clean the distributor cap and check for signs of cracking or carbon tracks. Install the cap and continue the installation procedure.

Ignition Timing

ADJUSTMENT

Some tachometers, dwell-meters and oscilloscopes will not work with these ignition systems. Some test equipment may be damaged. Consult the manufacturer of the test equipment if there is any doubt.

All engines are timed by aligning the distributor housing with reference marks, no dynamic adjustment is possible. The electronic control unit will retard or advance the timing for each cylinder as required.

NOTE: V8 Quattro vehicles have 2 ignition coils with power stages and 2 distributors. They are both controlled by the Motronic ECU. Each coil and distributor is responsible for providing spark to 4 cylinders. One distributor is mounted on the back of each cylinder head. Both distributors are driven by lugs on the exhaust camshafts. A Hall sender is installed in the distributor mounted on the right cylinder head. The signal from this Hall unit identifies cylinder No. 1 for the start of the sequential fuel injection and cylinder selective knock regulation. Ignition timing is determined by the electronic control unit and cannot be adjusted.

Alternator

PRECAUTIONS

Several precautions must be observed with alternator-equipped vehicles to avoid damage to the unit.

• If the battery is removed for any reason, make sure it is reconnected with the correct polarity. Reversing the battery connections may result in damage to the one-way rectifiers.

• When utilizing a booster battery as a starting aid, always connect the positive to positive terminals and the negative terminal from the booster battery to a good engine ground on the vehicle being started.

• Never use a fast charger as a booster to start vehicles.

• Disconnect the battery cables when charging the battery with a fast charger.

• Never attempt to polarize the alternator.

• Do not use test lamps of more than 12 volts when checking diode continuity.

• Do not short across or ground any of the alternator terminals.

• The polarity of the battery, alternator and regulator must be matched and considered before making any electrical connections within the system.

• Never separate the alternator as an open circuit. Make sure all connections within the circuit are clean and tight.

• Disconnect the battery ground terminal when performing any service on electrical components.

• Disconnect the battery if arc welding is to be done on the vehicle.

BELT TENSION ADJUSTMENT

The drive belts are correctly tensioned when the longest span of belt between pulleys can be depressed 1/8-1/2 in. (3-13mm) using moderate thumb pressure. To adjust, loosen the slotted adjusting bracket bolt on the alternator. If the alternator hinge bolts are very tight, it may be necessary to loosen them slightly to move the alternator. Move the alternator in or out to obtain the correct tension. Tighten the adjusting bolt when finished.

V-belts under 39 inches in length should deflect about 1/8 in. (3mm). Belts over 40 inches long should deflect about 1/2 in. (13mm).

Poly-ribbed belt alignment is especially important on 8 cylinder engines. Check that the poly-ribbed belt between the air conditioner compressor and the hydraulic pump is in alignment front-to-back to prevent damage to the belt. If the 2 pulleys are not in alignment, remove the bolts securing the ribbed belt pulley for the hydraulic pump. Using shims, available in sizes 0.020, 0.040 and 0.060 in. (0.5, 1.0 and 1.5mm) adjust the pulleys until they are in alignment. Note that the poly-ribbed belt

used on 8 cylinder engines is designed to last the life of the engine.

REMOVAL AND INSTALLATION

NOTE: If necessary, remove and install the alternator from below the vehicle.

1. Disconnect the negative battery cable.
2. Disconnect and tag the alternator wiring. On turbocharged engines, the cold air housing must be removed from the back of the alternator.
3. Remove the pivot bolt from the adjusting bracket.
4. Remove the drive belt.
5. Unbolt and remove the alternator.

NOTE: On some 4 cylinder engines, the top alternator mount has a bushing on the engine side of the mount. Check the condition of the bushing and replace if necessary before installing the alternator.

To install:

6. Hold the alternator in position and install the pivot bolts.
7. Install the drive belt and adjusting bolt.
8. Adjust the belt tension.
9. Connect the electrical connections, making sure they are installed in their original locations.
10. Connect the negative battery cable.

Starter

REMOVAL AND INSTALLATION

1. Disconnect both battery cables.
2. Raise and safely support the vehicle.
3. Disconnect and tag the starter wiring.
4. Remove the starter support bracket bolts. Remove the starter

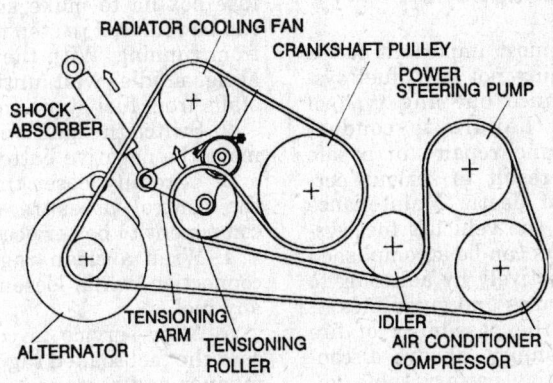

A single belt is used — V8 Quatro

mounting bolts from the rear of the starter.

5. On some engines, 1 bolt goes through the transaxle with a nut on the end of the bolt.

6. Remove the starter from the engine.

7. Installation is the reverse of the removal procedure. Check system for proper operation.

EMISSION CONTROLS

Emission Warning Lamps

RESETTING

Oxygen Sensor Reminder

Every 30,000 (60,000 miles on the 1990 100/200 vehicles) miles a maintenance reminder light in the dashboard will come ON. This is an indication that the emission system should be checked and that the oxygen sensor should be replaced.

1. To reset the non-turbocharged vehicles, remove the instrument panel cluster. Remove the switch cover near the **OXS** button. Push the switch to reset the light.

2. On turbocharged vehicles, lift the rear seat and push the button marked **OXS** on the reset box.

FUEL SYSTEM

Fuel System Service Precautions

Safety is the most important factor when performing not only fuel system maintenance but any type of maintenance. Failure to conduct maintenance and repairs in a safe manner may result in serious personal injury or death. Maintenance and testing of the vehicle's fuel system components can be accomplished safely and effectively by adhering to the following rules and guidelines.

• To avoid the possibility of fire and personal injury, always disconnect the negative battery cable unless the repair or test procedure re-

quires that battery voltage be applied.

• Always relieve the fuel system pressure prior to disconnecting any fuel system component (injector, fuel rail, pressure regulator, etc.), fitting or fuel line connection. Exercise extreme caution whenever relieving fuel system pressure to avoid exposing skin, face and eyes to fuel spray. Please be advised that fuel under pressure may penetrate the skin or any part of the body that it contacts.

• Always place a shop towel or cloth around the fitting or connection prior to loosening to absorb any excess fuel due to spillage. Ensure that all fuel spillage is quickly removed from engine surfaces. Ensure that all fuel soaked cloths or towels are deposited into a suitable waste container.

• Always keep a dry chemical (Class B) fire extinguisher near the work area.

• Do not allow fuel spray or fuel vapors to come into contact with a spark or open flame.

• Always use a backup wrench when loosening and tightening fuel line connection fittings. This will prevent unnecessary stress and torsion to fuel line piping. Always follow the proper torque specifications.

• Always replace worn fuel fitting O-rings with new. Do not substitute fuel hose or equivalent where fuel pipe is installed.

RELIEVING FUEL SYSTEM PRESSURE

Modern fuel injection systems operate under high pressure. This makes it necessary to first relieve the system of pressure before servicing. The pressurized fuel, when released, may ignite or cause personal injury.

1. Disconnect the power to the fuel pump by removing the relay or the fuel pump fuse. Check the list on the fuse box lid to make sure. The fuse can be removed to stop the fuel pump from running. With the engine operating at idle, wait until the engine stalls from fuel starvation.

2. Switch the ignition **OFF** and remove the negative battery cable.

3. Carefully loosen the fuel line on the control pressure regulator or component to be serviced.

4. Wrap a clean rag around the connection, while loosening, to catch any fuel.

5. After service is complete, discard the fuel soaked rag in the proper manner and reconnect negative battery cable, relay or fuses.

Fuel Tank

REMOVAL AND INSTALLATION

1. Disconnect the negative battery cable.

2. Relieve the fuel system pressure. Empty fuel tank and remove expansion tank if equipped.

3. Remove the rubber boot and overflow line from the body.

4. Remove the trunk panel and disconnect the harness connector from sending unit.

5. Remove all lines from the tank assembly. Loosen fuel tank straps or fuel tank retaining bolts and remove the fuel tank from the body.

6. Installation is the reverse of the removal procedure. Tighten fuel tank straps or retaining bolts evenly and install sound deadening strips in the the same position, as necessary.

Fuel Filter

REMOVAL AND INSTALLATION

Most vehicles use a fuel filter mounted under the vehicle, below the fuel tank. An arrow should be on the filter indicating fuel flow direction. Install with arrow pointing to engine. Use care not to mix up fuel supply or return lines. Fuel pressure applied to the return side of the system will cause damage.

In addition, some vehicles use a filter in the engine compartment near the fuel distributor. If equipped, use the following procedure:

1. Make certain to follow precautions and relieve fuel pressure.

2. Disconnect the fuel lines leading into and out of the fuel distributor.

3. Unscrew the filter retaining bracket and remove the filter.

4. Install a new filter in the bracket and reattach the bracket. Make sure the arrows are pointing in the direction of the fuel flow to the distributor.

5. Reconnect the fuel lines, start the engine and check for leaks.

Electric Fuel Pump

PRESSURE TESTING

NOTE: The fuel tank is pressurized. Open the filler cap carefully. Fuel system pressure is not adjustable.

CIS Systems

1. Using tool VW 1318 or an equivalent 0-100 psi (7 BAR) pressure gauge, connect the gauge in the line to the cold start valve. If using the special tool, position the lever so the valve is closed.

2. Remove the fuel pump relay from the main relay panel and plug a long jumper wire into terminal **52**. If special tool US 4480/3 or equivalent is available, connect it in place of the fuel pump relay with the switch OFF.

3. Remove the electrical connector from the differential pressure regulator, if equipped.

4. Apply 12 volts to the jumper wire or turn the special tool switch **ON** to run the fuel pump. The pressure should be 84-96 psi (5.8-6.6 Bar). If the pressure is low, check the fuel pump delivery quantity.

5. If the pressure is higher than specifications, disconnect the fuel tank return line from the diaphragm pressure regulator and repeat the test.

6. If the pressure is within specifications, check for a plugged fuel return line. If the pressure is not within specifications, replace the diaphragm pressure regulator.

MPI and Motronic Systems

1. The MPI and Motronic systems uses electric injectors. Using tool VW 1318 or an equivalent 0-100 psi (7 BAR) pressure gauge, connect the gauge in the system at a convenient place to read the pressure in the supply rail. This can be either at the inlet line or before the pressure regulator. If using the special tool, position the lever so the valve is open.

2. Disconnect the vacuum line to the pressure regulator.

3. Remove the fuel pump relay from the main relay panel and plug a long jumper wire into terminal **52**. If special tool US 4480/3 or equivalent is available, connect it in place of the fuel pump relay with the switch OFF.

4. Apply 12 volts to the jumper wire or turn the special tool switch **ON** to run the fuel pump. The pressure should be 55-61 psi (3.8-4.2 BAR). If the pressure is low, check the fuel pump delivery quantity.

5. If fuel comes out of the regulator at the vacuum hose connection, replace the regulator.

6. Install the fuel pump relay and start the engine. At idle with the engine warm, connect the vacuum line to the pressure regulator. The pressure should decrease by about 8 psi (0.6 BAR). If not, check for blockage

in the return lines, no vacuum to the pressure regulator or a bad regulator.

DELIVERY TESTING

1. Remove the fuel pump relay from the main relay panel and plug a long jumper wire into terminal **52**. If special tool US 4480/3 or equivalent is available, connect it in place of the fuel pump relay with the switch OFF.

2. Remove the fuel pump cover from the floor of the trunk. On 80 and 90 vehicles, raise and safely support vehicle to access the pump.

3. At the fuel pump connector, pull back the rubber cover to expose the terminals, leave the plug connected to the pump.

4. Using a voltmeter, connect the probes across the terminals and apply 12 volts to the jumper wire or turn the special tool switch ON to run the pump.

5. Check and note the voltage of the running pump, it should be at least 9.0 volts. Turn the pump OFF.

6. In the engine compartment, disconnect the fuel line return connection and place it into a graduated container.

7. On 4 cylinder and 10-valve, 5 cylinder engines, turn the fuel pump ON for 30 seconds and measure the quantity of fuel collected. Depending on the pump voltage, the delivered quantity should be approximately:

9 volts — 11 oz. (335cc)
10 volts — 15 oz. (450cc)
11 volts — 20 oz. (600cc)
12 volts — 26 oz. (760cc)

8. On turbocharged, V8 and 5 cylinder, 20-valve engines, run the pump for 15 seconds. Depending on the pump voltage, the delivered quantity should be approximately:

8 volts — 10 oz. (295cc)
9 volts — 12 oz. (355cc)
10 volts — 16 oz. (480cc)
11 volts — 19 oz. (560cc)
12 volts — 22 oz. (660cc)
13 volts — 25 oz. (750cc)
14 volts — 28 oz. (835cc)

REMOVAL AND INSTALLATION

All Except 80/90

1. Make certain to follow precautions and relieve fuel pressure. The fuel pump is located in the fuel tank. Remove the floor cover from the luggage compartment.

2. Disconnect the negative battery cable and the electrical connector from the fuel gauge sender.

3. Mark and remove the hoses from the fuel gauge sender.

4. Loosen the fuel gauge sender-to-fuel tank retaining ring. Pull out the fuel gauge/fuel pump assembly.

5. From inside the assembly housing, pull off the fuel hoses, detach the electrical connections and remove the gravity vent valve.

6. To install, reverse the removal procedures. Start the engine and check for leaks.

80 and 90

The fuel pump is located under the vehicle on a bracket in front of the fuel tank. The fuel pump assembly is located on the right side of front wheel drive vehicles and on the left side on Quattro vehicles. The 80 and 90 vehicles do not use a separate fuel pump filter. The filter is expected to be a lifetime unit unless the fuel was contaminated.

1. Make certain to follow precautions and relieve fuel pressure.

2. Disconnect the negative battery cable.

3. Raise and safely support vehicle.

4. Carefully loosen fuel line at fuel pump. Catch excess fuel in a container.

5. Remove fuel pump electrical connectors and remove the fuel pump.

To install:

6. Install fuel pump. Connect the fuel lines.

7. Connect the fuel pump electrical connectors.

8. Lower vehicle and connect the negative battery cable.

9. Replace any relays or fuses, that had been removed. Start engine and inspect for fuel leakage.

Fuel Injector

REMOVAL AND INSTALLATION

4 and 5 Cylinder Engines

1. Disconnect the battery negative cable. Relieve the fuel pressure.

2. Remove the wiring harness support clip attaching bolts and position the wiring harness aside.

3. Disconnect the fuel return and supply lines, then the pressure regulator vacuum hose.

4. Remove the fuel rail attaching bolts, then the fuel rail and injectors as an assembly.

To install:

5. Use new O-rings and make sure the injectors fit properly onto the fuel rail. Install them as an assembly and torque the bolts to 15 ft. lbs. (20 Nm).

6. Use new gaskets and connect the fuel supply and return lines. Torque the fittings to 18 ft. lbs. (25 Nm).

7. Reconnect all wiring. Install pressure regulator vacuum hose.

8. Start engine and check for fuel leaks.

6 and 8 Cylinder Engines

1. Disconnect the battery negative cable. Relieve the fuel pressure.

2. Remove the left and right support braces, then the intake air duct.

3. Remove the engine compartment support brace.

4. Remove the upper air cleaner attaching bolts, then the upper air cleaner.

5. Remove the lower air cleaner housing attaching bolts, then push the housing back and lift outward.

6. Remove the upper ventilation hose, then the right fuel rail cable tie.

NOTE: When assembling, install a new cable tie in the same position and location as the original.

7. Remove the engine wiring harness support clip attaching bolts and position the wiring harness aside.

8. Disconnect the throttle valve potentiometer, thermo-switch and idle stabilizer valve electrical connectors.

9. Remove the idle stabilizer valve, then disconnect the vacuum hoses to the carbon canister.

10. Remove the bolts attaching the intake air temperature sensor, then position aside.

11. Disconnect the air mass sensor electrical connectors, then the 2 knock sensor plug connections.

12. Disconnect the fuel return and supply lines, then the pressure regulator vacuum hose.

13. Remove the fuel rail attaching bolts, then the fuel rail and injectors as an assembly.

To install:

14. Use new O-rings and make sure the injectors fit properly onto the fuel rail. Install them as an assembly and torque the bolts to 7 ft. lbs. (10 Nm).

15. Use new gaskets and connect the fuel supply and return lines. Torque the fittings to 18 ft. lbs. (25 Nm).

16. Reconnect all wiring and vacuum hoses.

17. Install the air cleaner housing and ducting and properly secure the wires.

18. Install the support brace. Start engine and check for fuel leaks.

DRIVE AXLE

Front Halfshaft

REMOVAL AND INSTALLATION

Coupe, 80 and 90

NOTE: When loosening or tightening axle nut or bolt, make sure the vehicle is on the ground. Axle nut torque is high enough that attempting to loosen it may cause the vehicle to fall off the support.

1. Loosen the axle nut or bolt. Raise and safely support the vehicle.

2. Unbolt and remove the halfshaft-to-transaxle drive flange bolts.

3. Mark the position of the ball joint on the control arm, remove the 2 retaining nuts and disconnect the ball joint.

4. Remove the ball joint-to-steering knuckle bolt and separate the knuckle from the ball joint. Remove the mounting bolts for the control arm/stabilizer and push control arm downward, if necessary.

5. Pivot the strut outward and remove the halfshaft.

To install:

6. When installing the right halfshaft, take care not to damage the boot on the cover plate.

7. Tighten the ball joint-to-control arm/knuckle nuts/bolt to 47 ft. lbs. (64 Nm). Tighten the halfshaft flange bolts to 33 ft. lbs. (45 Nm).

8. Install the wheel and snug the axle nut or bolt. Place the vehicle on the ground and torque the axle nut or bolt to 200 ft. lbs. (270 Nm).

9. Check and adjust wheel alignment when finished.

100, 200 and V8

EXCEPT QUATTRO

NOTE: When loosening or tightening axle nuts, make sure the vehicle is on the ground. Axle nut torque is high enough that attempting to loosen it may cause the vehicle to fall off the support. A puller is required for this procedure.

1. Remove the halfshaft end nut.

2. Raise and support the vehicle safely and remove the wheels. If equipped with ABS, slide the speed sensor partly out of its mount.

3. On the right side, remove the halfshaft skid plate.

4. Disconnect the halfshaft from the transaxle. Using wire, support the halfshaft.

5. Using a 4-armed puller mounted on the wheel hub, press the halfshaft out of the hub.

6. Guide the inside end of the shaft up over the transaxle and out of the hub.

7. If equipped with an automatic transaxle, perform the following:

   a. Remove the stabilizer bar clamps.

   b. Remove the ball joint-to-hub bolt. Remove the ball joint from the hub.

   c. Press the halfshaft from the hub.

   d. Swing the suspension strut outward and press the halfshaft from the hub.

To install:

8. When installing, make certain that the splines are clean and free of grease. Apply a 1/4 in. (3mm) bead of RTV silicone sealant around the leading edge of the splines. Allow it to set at least 1 hour after installation.

9. Install the shaft-to-transaxle flange bolts and torque to 32 ft. lbs. (43 Nm).

10. Install the skid plate. If equipped with ABS, install the speed sensor.

11. With the wheels installed and the vehicle on the ground, torque the axle nut to 203 ft. lbs. (275 Nm).

QUATTRO

1. Remove the wheel cover and loosen the lug nuts. Remove the dust cover and the halfshaft nut or through bolt, if equipped.

2. Raise and support the vehicle safely. Remove the wheel. On vehicles equipped with ABS, slide the speed sensor partly out of its mount. Remove the right backing plate, if necessary.

3. Disconnect the halfshaft at the transaxle flange and position it aside.

4. Using a suitable puller, press out the stub axle from the hub. Use only a mechanical or hydraulic puller to remove the stub axle. Never use hot air blower or a flame to heat the stub axle.

To install:

5. Replace the gasket on the inner CV-joint.

6. Make sure the splines on the stub axle and the wheel hub are free of oil, grease and old locking compound. Apply a bead of suitable locking compound approximately 3/64 in. wide around the splines and install the stub halfshaft. Allow at least 1

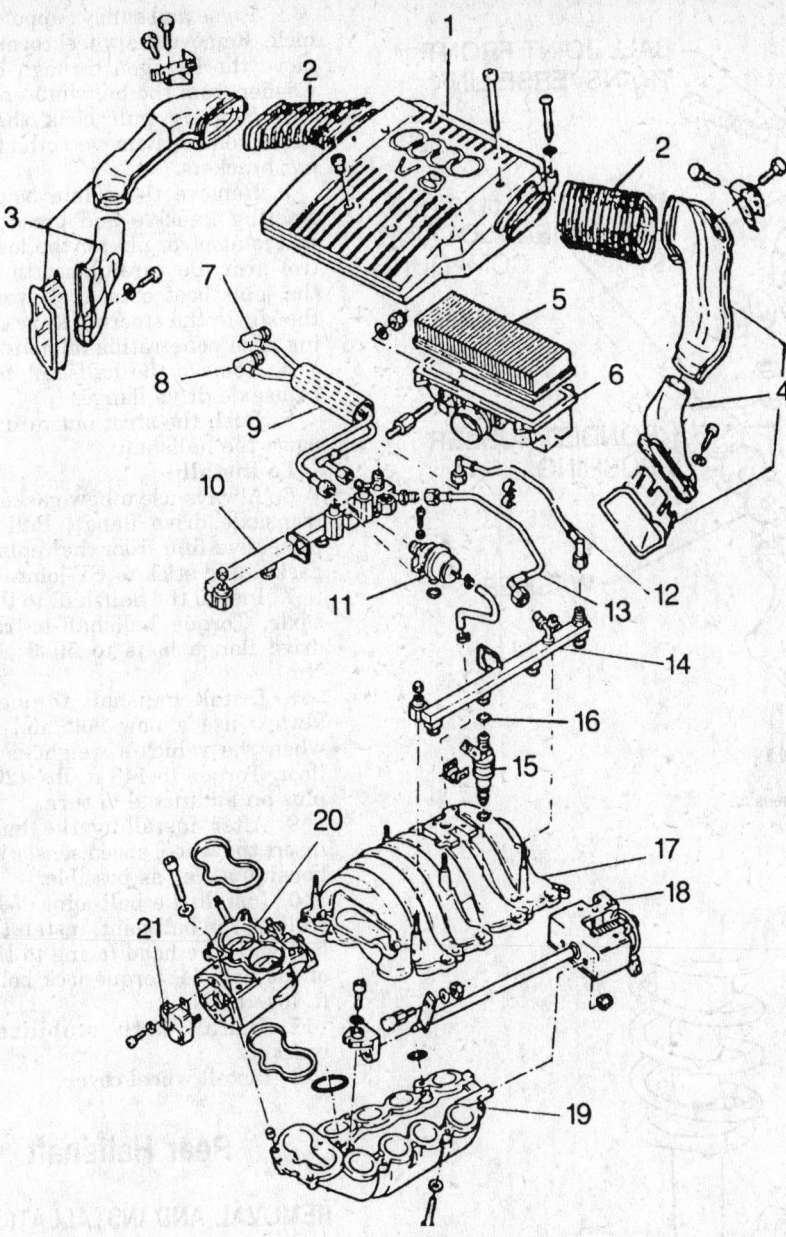

1. Upper air cleaner housing
2. Flexhose
3. Right air intake
4. Left air intake
5. Air cleaner filter element
6. Lower air cleaner housing
7. Return fuel line
8. Supply fuel line
9. Insulator
10. Right fuel manifold
11. Fuel pressure regulator
12. Supply line crossover
13. Return line crossover
14. Left fuel manifold
15. Fuel injector
16. O-ring
17. Upper intake manifold
18. Throttle shaft housing
19. Lower intake manifold
20. Throttle housing
21. Idle and full throttle switch

Injectors and intake system — V8 engine

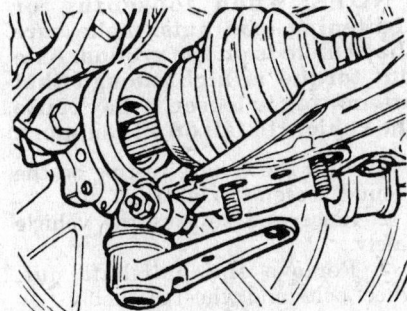

Remove the front halfshaft by pivoting the strut out from the bottom

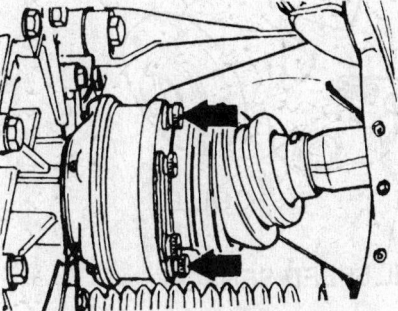

Halfshaft bolts at the transaxle drive flange

hour for the locking compound to harden after installtion.

7. Install and torque the halfshaft to transaxle bolts to 58 ft. lbs. (79 Nm) and install the wheel.

8. With the vehicle on the ground, torque the halfshaft end nut to 207 ft. lbs. (280 Nm).

V8 QUATTRO

NOTE: When loosening or tightening axle nuts, make sure the vehicle is on the ground. Axle nut torque is high enough that attempting to loosen it may cause the vehicle to fall off the support.

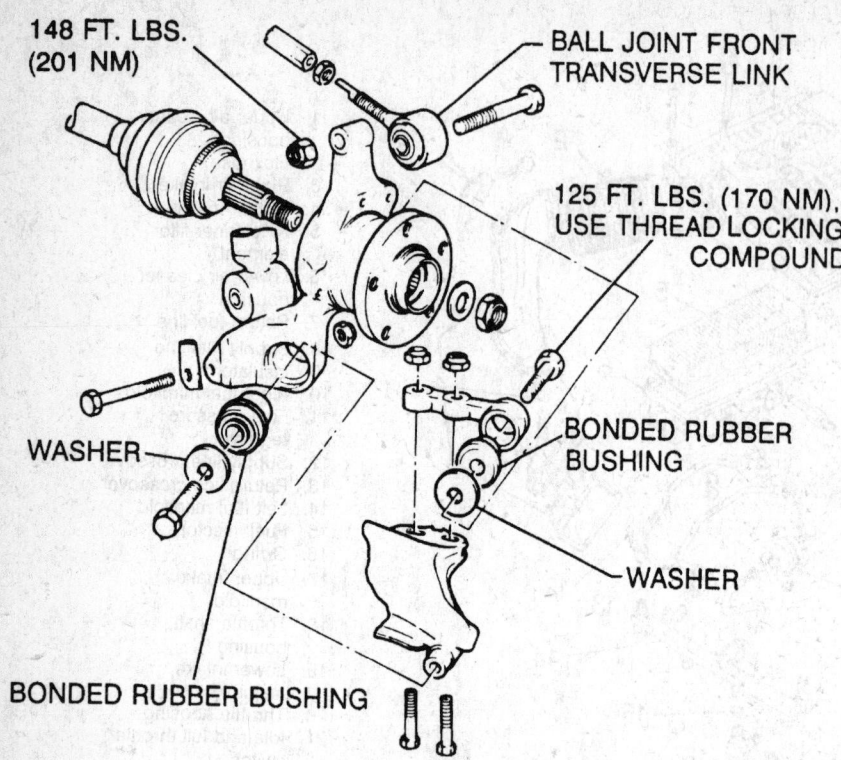

148 FT. LBS. (201 NM)

BALL JOINT FRONT TRANSVERSE LINK

125 FT. LBS. (170 NM), USE THREAD LOCKING COMPOUND

BONDED RUBBER BUSHING

WASHER

WASHER

BONDED RUBBER BUSHING

Rear suspension

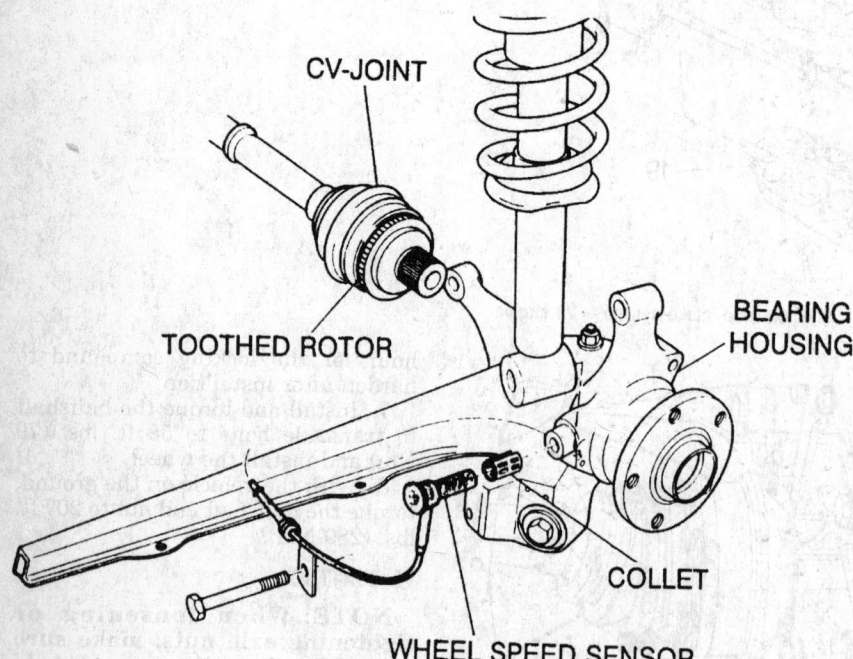

CV-JOINT

TOOTHED ROTOR

BEARING HOUSING

COLLET

WHEEL SPEED SENSOR

Rear axle speed sensor for ABS — 200 shown

1. Raise and safely support the vehicle. Remove the wheel cover and remove the hexagon through bolt and washer from the halfshaft end.

2. Slightly pull back the wheel speed sensor. Remove both stabilizer bar brackets.

3. Remove the clamp bolt at the steering knuckle and press out the ball joint pivot pin for the lower control arm. Be careful not to damage the joint boot or seal. Never widen the slit in the steering knuckle housing. Use penetrating oil as required.

4. Remove the halfshaft from the transaxle drive flange.

5. Push the strut outward and remove the halfshaft.

To install:

6. Always use a new gasket at the transaxle drive flange. Pull off the protective film from the replacement gasket and stick to CV-joint.

7. Install the halfshaft to the transaxle. Torque halfshaft-to-transaxle drive flange bolts to 59 ft. lbs. (80 Nm).

8. Install halfshaft through bolt, always use a new bolt and tighten when the vehicle's weight is on the floor. Torque to 148 ft. lbs. (200 Nm) plus an additional 1/4 turn.

9. After installing the halfshaft, insert the wheel speed sensor into the housing as far as possible.

10. Install the ball joint. When installing the ball joint, install the lock bolt with the head facing to the rear of the vehicle. torque lock bolt to 48 ft. lbs. (65 Nm).

11. Install both stabilizer bar brackets.

12. Install wheel cover.

Rear Halfshaft

REMOVAL AND INSTALLATION

80 and 90 Quattro

NOTE: When loosening or tightening axle nuts, make sure the vehicle is on the ground. Axle nut torque is high enough that attempting to loosen it may cause the vehicle to fall off the support.

1. With the vehicle resting on the ground, loosen the halfshaft nut.

2. Raise and support the vehicle safely.

3. Remove the halfshaft nut, wheel bolts and wheel assembly.

4. Remove the ball joint nut. Using a ball joint removal tool, separate the ball joint from the strut.

5. Using a suitable tool, pry downward on the lower control arm to re-

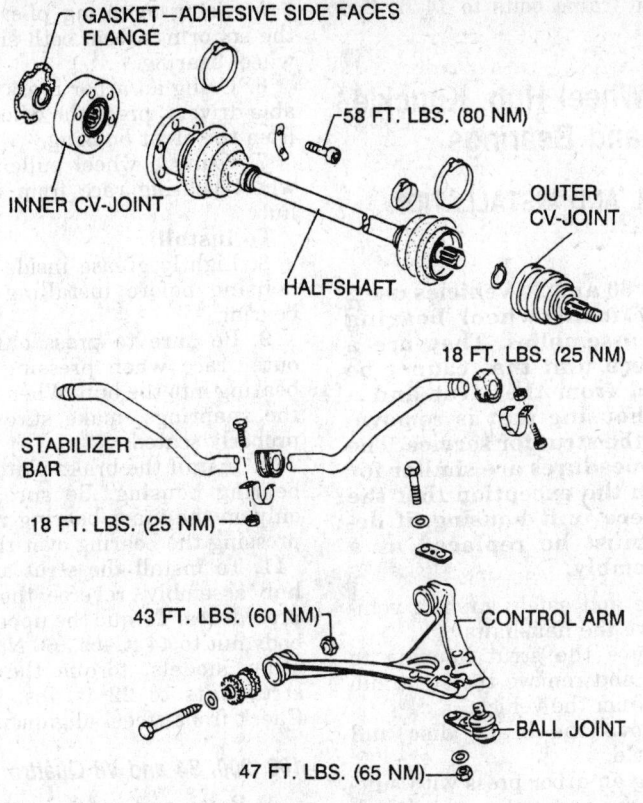

GASKET—ADHESIVE SIDE FACES FLANGE

58 FT. LBS. (80 NM)

INNER CV-JOINT

OUTER CV-JOINT

HALFSHAFT

18 FT. LBS. (25 NM)

STABILIZER BAR

18 FT. LBS. (25 NM)

43 FT. LBS. (60 NM)

CONTROL ARM

BALL JOINT

47 FT. LBS. (65 NM)

Rear drive axle — Quattro

move the ball joint from the control arm. If necessary, loosen lower control arm mounting bolts.

6. Pull the brake hose and parking brake cable, with grommets, from the holding fixture.

7. Remove the inner halfshaft flange bolts. Separate the shaft from the flange and support it.

8. Using a halfshaft pulling tool, attach it to the wheel hub and press the halfshaft out of the hub.

To install:

9. Clean the halfshaft splines of any grease, dirt or locking compound. Using the locking compound D-6, or equivalent, apply a ¼ in. (3mm) bead around the outer edge of the splines. Allow the locking compound to dry for an hour after installation.

10. When installing, use a new inner flange gasket and reverse the removal procedures. Torque the ball joint nut to 47 ft. lbs. (64 Nm).

11. Tighten the inner halfshaft flange bolts to 58 ft. lbs. (79 Nm) and install the wheel.

12. With the vehicle on the ground, torque the halfshaft to hub nut to 238 ft. lbs. (322 Nm).

100 and 200 Quattro

1. With the vehicle weight on the ground, loosen the halfshaft end nut.

2. Raise and support the vehicle safely.

3. Remove the halfshaft nut, wheel bolts and wheel assembly.

4. Remove the brake caliper to strut retaining bolts and remove the caliper, without disconnecting the hydraulic line. Using wire, support the caliper.

5. Remove the brake rotor. Remove the inner halfshaft flange bolts and support the halfshaft.

6. Remove the fuel tank cover plate, if necessary.

7. Remove the transverse link-to-wheel bearing housing nut and remove the link.

8. Remove the trapezoidal arm-to-crossmember nut and bolt. Pry the arm downward.

9. Remove the mounting bolt for suspension strut.

10. Before removing halfshaft, pull speed sensor out of the housing slightly.

11. Press down on wheel bearing housing and remove the halfshaft.

12. Clean the halfshaft splines of any grease, dirt or locking compound.

To install:

13. Use a new inner flange gasket and reverse the removal procedures.

14. Tighten the halfshaft flange bolts to 59 ft. lbs. (80 Nm).

15. Install caliper and torque the bolts to 48 ft. lbs. (65 Nm). Adjustment of parking brake may be necessary.

16. Install the halfshaft bolt and washer assembly, tighten until just snug.

17. Make certain speed sensor sleeve is in place and install speed sensor, by hand, until seated. Install wheels.

18. Lower vehicle and torque halfshaft bolts to 147 ft. lbs. (200 Nm) plus an additional ¼ turn.

V8 Quattro

NOTE: When loosening or tightening axle nuts, make sure the vehicle is on the ground. Axle nut torque is high enough that attempting to loosen it may cause the vehicle to fall off the support.

1. Remove the center cap from the wheel and remove the axle bolt and washer.

2. Raise and safely support the vehicle and remove the wheel.

3. Slide the speed sensor out of the holder and remove the brake caliper without disconnecting the hydraulic line. Hang the caliper with wire.

4. Remove the brake disc.

5. Disconnect the transverse link from the wheel bearing housing.

6. Remove the halfshaft bolts from the differential drive flange and support the axle.

7. Remove the lower strut mount bolt and push the suspension down to remove the halfshaft.

To install:

8. Always use a new gasket at the transaxle drive flange. Pull off the protective film from the replacement gasket and stick to CV-joint.

9. Install rear halfshaft to drive flange. Torque the halfshaft-to-drive flange bolts to 59 ft. lbs. (80 Nm).

10. Install halfshaft through bolt, always use a new bolt and tighten when the vehicle's weight is on the floor. Torque to 148 ft. lbs. (200 Nm) plus an additional ¼ turn.

11. Use a new self-locking nut on the lower strut mount bolt and torque to 66 ft. lbs. (90 Nm).

12. Install a new self-locking nut on the transverse link bolt and torque to 148 ft. lbs. (200 Nm).

13. Install the brake disc and caliper. Torque the bolts to 48 ft. lbs. (65 Nm) and return the speed sensor its normal position.

14. Install the wheel and center cap.

CV-Boot

REMOVAL AND INSTALLATION

NOTE: On some vehicles, the entire halfshaft must be replaced, not serviced. Always check parts availability before removing CV-boots. If boot kits are available, use the following procedure.

1. Raise and safely support the vehicle and remove the halfshaft. Always loosen the halfshaft end locking nut or through bolt with the vehicle on the floor.
2. On the inner joint, remove the circlip from the inner CV-joint stub shaft. On a shop press, support the ball hub and press out the shaft. Remove the boot.
3. On the outer joint, spread the circlip and drive the joint off the shaft by tapping lightly with a soft copper or brass drift against the hub.

To install:

4. Installation is the reverse of the removal process. Press the joint onto the shaft until the circlip can be pressed into the groove. The chamfer on the inside diameter of the ball hub splines must face the halfshaft.
5. After applying the correct amount of special lube, usually supplied with the replacement boots, install the new boot band and tighten it according to the instructions in the kit.

Driveshaft and U-Joints

REMOVAL AND INSTALLATION

Quattro

1. Raise and support the vehicle safely.
2. Using a scribing tool, mark the position of the driveshaft to the transaxle flange and the rear differential.
3. Remove the driveshaft flange mounting bolts from both ends and remove the driveshaft from the vehicle. Remove the center bearing bolts.

To install:

4. To install, reverse the removal procedures. Note that the universal joints are not replaceable. If a universal joint is damaged or worn out, replace the driveshaft assembly.
5. Align scribe marks and install driveshaft.
6. Tighten the driveshaft-to-transaxle/differential flange bolts to 39 ft. lbs. (53 Nm) on 80 and 90 Quattro, or 33 ft. lbs. (45 Nm) on 100, 200 and V8 Quattro. Torque the driveshaft center

bearing to frame bolts to 14 ft. lbs. (19 Nm).

Front Wheel Hub, Knuckle and Bearings

REMOVAL AND INSTALLATION

80 and 90

NOTE: 80 and 90 vehicles use 2 types of front wheel bearing housing assemblies. They are a single-piece unit that cannot be separated from the strut and a bearing housing that is removable from the strut for service. The repair procedures are similar for both with the exception that the single piece unit housing, if defective, must be replaced as a strut assembly.

1. Raise and safely support vehicle. Remove the halfshafts.
2. Remove the strut housing to body nuts and remove the strut/hub assembly from the vehicle.
3. Remove the brake disc and splash shield.
4. Using an arbor press with suitable drivers, press the wheel hub from the strut housing.

5. Using snapring pliers, remove the snaprings from both sides of the wheel bearing.
6. Using an arbor press with suitable drivers, press the wheel bearing from the strut housing.
7. Using a wheel puller, pull the wheel bearing race from the wheel hub.

To install:

8. Lightly grease inside the strut housing before installing the new bearing.
9. Be sure to press only on the outer race when pressing the new bearing into the hub. When installing the snaprings, make sure they are properly seated.
10. Install the brake plate onto the bearing housing. Be sure to press only on the inner bearing race when pressing the bearing over the hub.
11. To install the strut and wheel hub assembly, reverse the removal procedures. Torque the upper strut to body nut to 44 ft. lbs. (60 Nm). On all other models, torque the 3 upper strut nuts to 22 ft. lbs. (30 Nm). Check front wheel alignment.

100, 200, S4 and V8 Quattro

1. Raise and safely support vehicle. Remove the halfshafts.

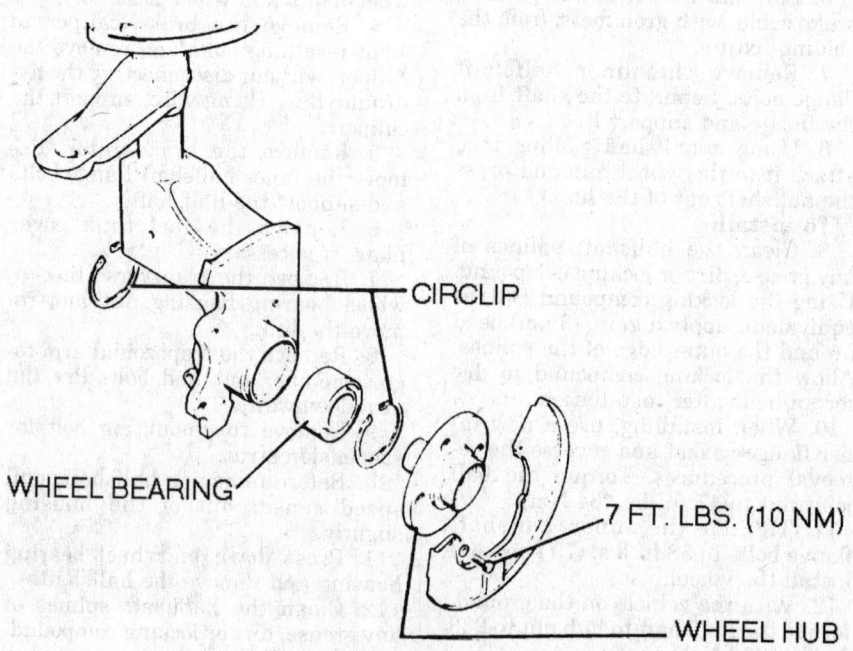

Front hub and bearing assembly

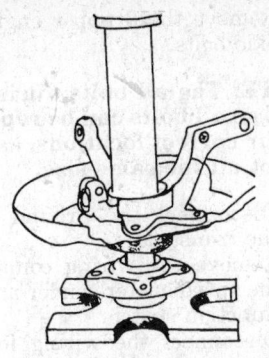

Be sure to press only on the inner race when pressing the bearing and housing onto the hub

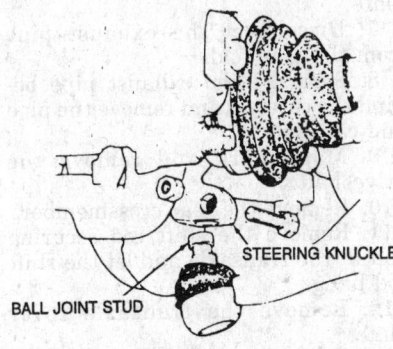

STEERING KNUCKLE

BALL JOINT STUD

Remove the bolt to separate the ball joint from the knuckle

2. Remove the strut to vehicle nuts and remove the strut from the vehicle.

3. Remove the disc brake rotor and splash shield.

4. Using an arbor press with suitable drivers, press the wheel hub from the strut housing.

5. Using snapring pliers, remove the snaprings from both sides of the wheel bearing.

6. Using an arbor press with suitable driver, press the wheel bearing from strut housing.

7. Using a suitable puller, remove the bearing race from the wheel hub.

To install:

8. Install the outer snapring into the strut housing.

9. Be sure to press only on the outer race when pressing the new bearing into the hub. When installing the snapring, make sure it is properly seated.

10. Install the brake plate onto the bearing housing. Be sure to press only on the inner bearing race when pressing the bearing over the hub.

11. To install the strut and wheel hub assembly, reverse the removal procedures. Tighten the strut to body nuts to 44 ft. lbs. (60 Nm). Check front wheel alignment.

Differential Carrier

REMOVAL AND INSTALLATION

80 and 90 Quattro

1. Raise and safely support the vehicle. Matchmark and disconnect the axle shafts from the flanges and disconnect the driveshaft. Hang them from the body with wire.

2. Remove the differential lock servo and bracket. Disconnect the wiring.

3. Remove the nut from the rear mount bushing.

4. Place a transaxle jack under the differential and take the weight of the unit off the mounts. Remove the right side and rear mounts.

5. Pull the differential slightly forward and lower it from the vehicle.

To install:

6. Installation is the reverse of removal. Torque the mount-to-subframe nuts or bolts to 18 ft. lbs. (25 Nm). Torque the differential-to-mount nuts or bolts to 33 ft. lbs. (45 Nm).

7. Torque the axle flange bolts to 33 ft. lbs. (45 Nm) and the driveshaft bolts to 40 ft. lbs. (55 Nm).

100 and 200 Quattro

1. Raise and safely support the vehicle and remove the cover plate.

2. Engage the differential lock and block a wheel or set the parking brake.

3. Matchmark and disconnect the axle shafts and driveshaft and hang them from the body with wire.

4. Release the parking brake and disconnect the cables at the caliper and at the front.

5. Unbolt the left parking brake retainer and remove the hheatshield.

6. Support the differential with a transaxle jack and take the weight off the mounts.

7. Remove the crossmember and the exhaust pipe.

8. Disconnect the mounts and lower the unit slightly.

9. Note the color coding of the vacuum hoses so they can be properly connected during installation. Disconnect the wiring and vacuum lines and carefully lower the unit out of the vehicle.

To install:

10. Installation is the reverse of removal. Make sure to properly connect the vacuum hoses.

11. Torque the crossmember-to-body bolts and the suspension-to-crossmember bolts to 33 ft. lbs. (45 Nm).

12. Torque the axleshaft 8mm bolts to 33 ft. lbs. (45 Nm) and the 10mm bolts to 60 ft. lbs. (80 Nm).

13. Torque the driveshaft bolts to 40 ft. lbs. (55 Nm).

V8 Quattro

NOTE: Any time the differential is removed from this vehicle, the driveshaft must be properly aligned. This requires the special alignment tool 3139 or equivalent.

1. Raise and safely support the vehicle and remove the rear wheels.

2. Remove the rear muffler system and remove the hheatshields, fuel tank shield and the axle shaft joint shield.

3. Disconnect the parking brake cables and the exhaust system support from the crossmember.

4. Matchmark the axle shafts and driveshaft and disconnect them from the differential. Hang them from the body with wire.

5. Detach the parking brake cables from the differential and disconnect them from the calipers.

6. Disconnect the brake hydraulic hoses from the distributor valve on the differential.

7. Use a 15mm socket to remove the mounting nut at the hole in the rear crossmember.

8. Support the rear crossmember and remove the crossmember mounting nuts.

9. At the front crossmember, loosen the left mounting bolt and remove the right mounting bolt to lower the crossmember slightly on the right side. Reposition the parking brake cables to the front.

10. Carefully support the differential with a transaxle jack. Separate the 2 halves of the front crossmember and unbolt the differential. Carefully lower the differential out of the vehicle.

To install:

11. Install the differential assembly to the vehicle with transmission jack.

12. Loosely install the differential and all crossmember bolts before torquing any of them. Torque the front crossmember bolts, front crossmember-to-body bolts and the differential-to-front and rear crossmember bolts to 33 ft. lbs. (45 Nm).

13. Install the rear crossmember. Torque the rear crossmember-to-suspension bolts to 37 ft. lbs. (50 Nm).

14. Reconnect the brake cables and hydraulic lines.

15. Clean the threads in the differential flanges and use new self sealing bolts when connecting the

driveshaft. Connect the axleshafts and driveshaft, making sure to align the matchmarks. Torque the axleshaft bolts to 60 ft. lbs. (80 Nm) and the driveshaft bolts to 40 ft. lbs. (55 Nm).

16. To align the driveshaft, install the driveshaft alignment tool and remove the bolts from the center support. Measure the gap between the support bolt holes and the body and install the proper spacers to make the gap even on both sides. Make sure the support is centered front to rear and install the bolts. Torque the bolts to 15 ft. lbs. (20 Nm) and remove the alignment tool.

17. Install the exhaust system. Install all hangers and align the exhaust components before tightening the clamps.

18. Install the heatshields, fuel tank shield and the axle shaft joint shield.

19. Install wheels. Bleed the brakes. Road test the vehicle.

MANUAL TRANSAXLE

Transaxle Assembly

REMOVAL AND INSTALLATION

NOTE: If the flywheel has been removed from the crankshaft for any reason, tighten the mounting bolts to: bolt without shoulder-72 ft. lbs. (98 Nm); bolt with shoulder — 54 ft. lbs. (73 Nm). Coat all threads with a locking compound.

80 and 90

EXCEPT QUATTRO

1. Disconnect the negative battery cable.
2. Unplug the 2 electrical connectors for the backup lights. They can be found between the ignition coil and the fuel distributor filter.
3. Remove the upper engine-to-transaxle bolts.
4. Detach the speedometer cable from the transaxle.
5. Detach the clutch cable from the clutch lever.
6. Unbolt the exhaust pipe from the exhaust manifold.

7. Unscrew the 3 mounting bolts and remove the center engine mount.
8. Unbolt the front exhaust pipe from the support bracket and unbolt it from the catalytic converter.
9. Unscrew the 6 screws and remove the left halfshaft from the transaxle. Wire the halfshaft up and aside. Repeat the procedure for the right halfshaft.
10. Remove the clutch cover plate.
11. Tag and disconnect all wires leading to the starter and remove the starter.
12. Remove the bolt from the shift rod coupling.
13. Pry off the linkage coupling with a small prybar.
14. Pull the shift rod coupling off the shift rod. Place a transaxle jack under the transaxle and support it by lifting slightly.
15. Loosen the left chassis bolt on the rear transaxle support. Remove the bolts from the right or transaxle side of the support and pivot the support aside.
16. Remove the rubber mounting block.
17. Unscrew 3 bolts and remove the front transaxle support.
18. Remove the lower engine-to-transaxle bolts.
19. Carefully pry the transaxle apart from the engine and remove it.

To install:
20. Carefully fit the transaxle to the engine and torque the bolts to 40 ft. lbs. (54 Nm).
21. Install the front transaxle support and torque the bolt to 18 ft. lbs. (24 Nm). Torque the rubber mount-to-body bolts to 80 ft. lbs. (108 Nm).
22. Install the subframe bolts and torque to 51 ft. lbs. (69 Nm). Install the rubber mount-to-transaxle bolts and torque to 40 ft. lbs. (54 Nm).
23. Connect the shift linkage and adjust as required. Secure the bolt with safety wire.
24. Install the starter and connect all electrical wiring. Install the clutch cover.
25. Install the halfshaft bolts and torque to 33 ft. lbs. (45 Nm).
26. Reassembly the exhaust system using new self-locking nuts. Torque to 25 ft. lbs. (34 Nm).
27. Connect the speedometer and clutch cables and adjust as required.
28. Road test the vehicle for proper operation.

QUATTRO

1. Disconnect the negative battery cable.

2. Remove the 3 upper engine-to-transaxle bolts.

NOTE: Tag all bolts during removal so all bolts can be replaced in their correct locations, as they are not all the same size.

3. Disconnect the ground strap from the transaxle.
4. Remove the wiring connectors from the speedometer sender and the multi-function switch.
5. Disconnect the wiring for the oxygen sensor and oxygen sensor heating element.
6. Remove the engine protection plate.
7. Disconnect the exhaust pipe from the manifold.
8. Separate the exhaust pipe behind the catalyst and remove the pipe and catalyst.
9. Matchmark and remove the driveshaft.
10. Remove the rear crossmember.
11. Remove the shift rod securing bolt at the transaxle and let the shift rod hang.
12. Remove the transaxle cover plate.
13. Remove the right halfshaft shield.
14. Disconnect the left and right halfshafts, turn the steering to the right lock and tie both shafts up.
15. Remove the clutch slave cylinder.
16. Remove the tie rod coupling from the steering rack and turn wheel to the left.
17. Support the engine.
18. Support the transaxle.
19. Remove the transaxle strut at the left rear and front engine mount.
20. Remove the heatshield from the bonded rubber bushing.
21. Remove the bonded rubber bushing support bracket from the transaxle.
22. Remove the bonded rubber bushing.
23. Remove the bolt from the seat belt tension in cable guide at the left rear of the transaxle. Position the cables and guide aside.
24. Lower the right rear subframe by loosening the mounting bolts.
25. Remove the remaining transaxle to engine bolts.
26. Remove the transaxle.

To install:
27. Install the transaxle, make certain that the alignment bushings are in the cylinder block before reassembly.
28. Tighten transaxle retaining bolts as follows: Torque the 8mm bolts to 18 ft. lbs. (24 Nm), the 10mm

bolts to 33 ft. lbs. (45 Nm) and the 12mm bolts to 48 ft. lbs. (65 Nm).

29. Install the subframe. Tighten subframe mounting bolts to 25 ft. lbs. (34 Nm), plus an additional 90 degree turn.

30. Install the seatbelt tension cables and guides.

31. Install transaxle mount and engine mount. Support engine and transaxle as necessary.

32. Install the tie rod to the steering rack assembly. Torque the tie rod coupling-to-steering rack to 33 ft. lbs. (45 Nm).

33. Install the clutch slave cylinder.

NOTE: A replacement bolt for mounting the clutch slave cylinder is available from Audi, with a pointed tip for easier installation.

34. Install the right and left halfshafts. Torque the halfshaft-to-flange bolts to 33 ft. lbs. (45 Nm).

35. Install shift rod.

36. Install rear crossmember.

37. Install the driveshaft. Torque the driveshaft to transaxle and final drive bolts to 40 ft. lbs. (54 Nm).

38. Install the exhaust system.

39. Install all necessary wiring, transaxle cover plate, halfshaft shield and engine protection plate.

40. Install ground strap to the transaxle.

41. Reconnect the battery. Bleed system. Road test the vehicle for proper operation.

100

1. Disconnect the negative battery cable.

2. Remove the upper engine-to-transaxle bolts.

NOTE: Tag all bolts during removal, so all bolts can be replaced in their correct locations, as they are not all the same size.

3. Disconnect the ground strap from the transaxle, if equipped.

4. Remove the wiring connectors from the speedometer sender and the multi-function switch.

5. Support the engine.

6. Disconnect the wiring for the oxygen sensor and oxygen sensor heating element.

7. Raise and safely support vehicle. Remove the splash shield, if equipped.

8. Disconnect the exhaust pipe from the manifold.

9. Separate the exhaust pipe behind the catalyst and remove the pipe and catalyst.

10. Remove the bolt for the shift rod at the transaxle and separate.

11. Remove the heatshield from the right inner CV-joint.

12. Remove the halfshafts from the flanges and tie aside.

13. Remove the heatshield for the bonded rubber bushing on the right side.

14. Support the transaxle, with a suitable holding fixture.

15. Remove the strut at the rear of the transaxle.

16. Remove the clutch slave cylinder. Do not remove the hydraulic line from the slave cylinder.

17. Remove the subframe assembly.

18. Remove the lower transaxle-to-engine bolts.

19. Pry transaxle back and lower assembly.

20. Remove the transaxle.

To install:

21. Install the transaxle, make certain alignment bushings are in the cylinder block before reassembly.

22. Tighten transaxle retaining bolts as follows: Torque the 8mm bolts to 18 ft. lbs. (24), the 10mm bolts to 33 ft. lbs. (45 Nm) and the 12mm bolts to 48 ft. lbs. (65 Nm).

23. Install the subframe.

24. Tighten subframe mounting bolts to 25 ft. lbs. (34 Nm), plus an additional 90 degree turn.

25. Install the strut at the rear of the transaxle. Support the transaxle as necessary.

26. Install the clutch slave cylinder.

NOTE: A replacement bolt for mounting the clutch slave cylinder is available from Audi, with a pointed tip for easier installation.

27. Install the halfshafts. Torque the halfshaft-to-flange bolts to 33 ft. lbs. (45 Nm) and the halfshaft-to-transaxle to 40 ft. lbs. (54 Nm).

28. Install the shift rod at the transaxle.

29. Install the exhaust system.

30. Install all necessary wiring, halfshaft shield and engine protection plate.

31. Install ground strap to the transaxle, if equipped.

32. Reconnect the battery. Bleed system. Road test the vehicle for proper operation.

200

1. Disconnect the negative battery cable.

2. Remove the upper engine to transaxle bolts.

3. Remove the connector for the speedometer sender by pressing in the clips.

4. Remove the clip from the clutch slave cylinder and drive out spring

pin, if equipped. Remove the bolt securing the clutch slave cylinder to the transaxle and remove the cylinder. Leave the hydraulic line connected.

5. Support the engine. Tie up coolant hoses and cables, as needed.

6. Remove the right side guard plate.

7. Disconnect the halfshafts from the flanges and rest both halfshafts on top of the subframe.

8. Tag and disconnect the wire from the backup light switch. Disconnect vacuum hoses at the servo if so equipped.

9. Pry off the shift and adjusting rods.

10. Remove the lower engine-to-transaxle bolts.

11. Remove the starter.

12. Remove the guard plate from the subframe.

13. With suitable jack, lift transaxle slightly.

14. Remove both rear subframe mounting bolts.

15. Remove both transaxle support bolts from the subframe.

16. Remove the bracket from the transaxle, push tension system cable and bracket off the retainer on transaxle. The retainer can only be removed with the transaxle out of the vehicle.

17. Remove the right side transaxle bracket.

18. Pull transaxle off dowel sleeves.

19. Lower transaxle and take out from below.

To install:

20. Installation is the reverse of the removal procedure. Before installing the transaxle, rest both halfshafts on top of the subframe.

21. Lubricate mainshaft splines.

22. Install transaxle onto dowels and install the lower bolts.

23. Install the tensioning system bracket and cable to the transaxle.

24. Tighten the transaxle bracket and subframe upper bolts to 29 ft. lbs. (39 Nm).

25. Check alignment of transaxle and torque transaxle-to-engine bolts to 40 ft. lbs. (54 Nm).

26. Torque subframe-to-body bolts to 80 ft. lbs. (108 Nm).

27. Torque halfshaft-to-drive flange bolts to 58 ft. lbs. (79 Nm).

V8 QUATTRO

NOTE: Any time the transaxle is removed from this vehicle, the driveshaft must be properly aligned. This requires the special alignment tool 3139 or equivalent.

1. Disconnect the negative battery cable, located under the rear seat.

2. Remove the strut between the front shock towers.

3. Remove the air cleaner assembly and the ducts.

4. Remove the bracket for the ignition wires. This is held with self-locking bolts, which should be replaced.

5. Remove the wiring harness bracket and the wiring retainers from the transaxle. Remove the 2 upper transaxle-to-engine bolts.

6. Remove the bolts for the right side engine mount.

7. Raise and safely support the vehicle and remove the front wheels.

8. Remove the splash shield under the engine and the body crossmember.

9. Remove the front exhaust pipe with the catalytic converter and the transaxle heatshield.

10. Install the driveshaft alignment tool. Matchmark the driveshaft and remove the driveshaft and heatshield.

11. Remove the transaxle mount-to-frame bolts.

12. Lower the vehicle and install an engine support bridge VAG 10-222A or equivalent across the inner fenders. Connect the bridge to the left engine mount and raise the engine just enough to take the weight off the mounts.

13. Remove the halfshaft shields and disconnect the halfshafts from the flanges. Support the shafts so they do not hang by the outer CV-joints.

14. Disconnect the hydraulic line from the clutch slave cylinder and plug the fittings to keep them clean.

15. Remove the clamp and lock sleeve to disconnect the shift linkage rods.

16. Disconnect the wiring for the backup lights and speedometer sensor and remove the wiring from the brackets.

Install the engine support bridge to take the weight off the mounts

17. Remove the cable guide for the seat belt tensioning system and position the cable/guide up out of the way.

18. At the left transaxle mount, pry the wire bracket open to release the oxygen sensor wire.

19. Disconnect the engine oil lines near the transaxle and plug the fittings.

20. Support the transaxle and subframe with a suitable transmission jack and remove the subframe mounting bolts. Lower the subframe to give clearance but make sure the radiator fan still turns freely; loosen the engine mounts if needed.

21. Tie the subframe in place so the jack can be removed. Secure the halfshafts to the subframe.

22. Disconnect the transaxle mounts and remove the engine-to-transaxle bolts. Move the unit back and carefully lower it out of the vehicle.

To install:

23. Check the condition of the dowel sleeves in the engine block and replace if necessary.

24. Install the transaxle assembly. Install all the mounting bolts loosely before torquing any of them. Observe the following engine-to-transaxle bolt torques:

    12mm — 48 ft. lbs. (65 Nm)
    10mm — 32 ft. lbs. (45 Nm)
    8mm — 18 ft. lbs. (20 Nm)

25. Install the subframe. Torque the subframe mounting bolts to 48 ft. lbs. (65 Nm) plus an additional ¼ turn. Reconnect the engine mounts if necessary.

26. Install the cable guide seat belt tensioning system. Torque the seat belt tensioning system bolts to 30 ft. lbs. (40 Nm).

27. Connect and adjust the shift linkage, if necessary.

28. Reconnect the line to the clutch slave cylinder.

29. Install the halfshafts. Torque the halfshaft flange bolts to 58 ft. lbs. (80 Nm). Install halfshaft shields.

30. Remove the engine support equipment or equivalent. Install transaxle mount.

31. Install the driveshaft with the matchmarks aligned and torque the flange bolts to 41 ft. lbs. (55 Nm). The shaft must be aligned.

32. To align the driveshaft, install the driveshaft with the alignment tool attached but do not install the bolts for the center support. Measure the gap between the support bolt holes and the body and install the proper spacers to make the gap even on both sides. Make sure the support

is centered front to rear and install the bolts. Torque the bolts to 15 ft. lbs. (20 Nm) and remove the alignment tool.

33. Install the exhaust system. When installing the exhaust, tighten the clamps after making sure everything is properly positioned to minimize vibration.

34. Install engine mount, body crossmember and strut between the front shock towers.

35. Install air cleaner and ducts.

36. Install all necessary wiring and engine protection plate.

37. Reconnect the battery. Bleed system. Road test the vehicle.

Linkage Adjustments

Except V8 Quattro, Quattro Turbo, Coupe 100 and 200

1. Place the shift lever into the **N** position.

2. Raise and safely support the vehicle and loosen the clamp nut on the shift rod. Be certain that the shift finger slides freely on the shift rod.

3. Working inside the vehicle, remove the gear shift lever knob and the boot.

4. Loosen the shifter base plate bolts slightly. Align the holes in the plate with the holes in the bearing housing and tighten the bolts.

5. Using the alignment tool 3057 or equivalent, slip it over the gearshift lever and make sure the locating pin is in the front centering hole.

6. Position the shift lever to the right detent cut-out for 5th and **R** and tighten the lower knurled nut of the tool.

7. At the top of the tool, move the slide with the gear shift lever to the right stop. Tighten the upper knurled nut of the tool.

8. Position the gear shift lever into the left cut-out of the slide. Adjust the shift rod and the shift finger with the transaxle in **N** and tighten the clamp nut.

9. Remove the tool and check the shifting of the gears for smoothness.

V8 Quattro, Quattro Turbo and Coupe

1. Place the shift lever in **N**. Adjust the length of the adjusting rod so the distance between the center point of the end holes is 5.275 in. (134mm).

2. Loosen the clamp nut, making sure the shift rod moves freely. Loosen the bolts slightly, align the centering holes of the gear shift lever housing and stop plate and tighten the bolts.

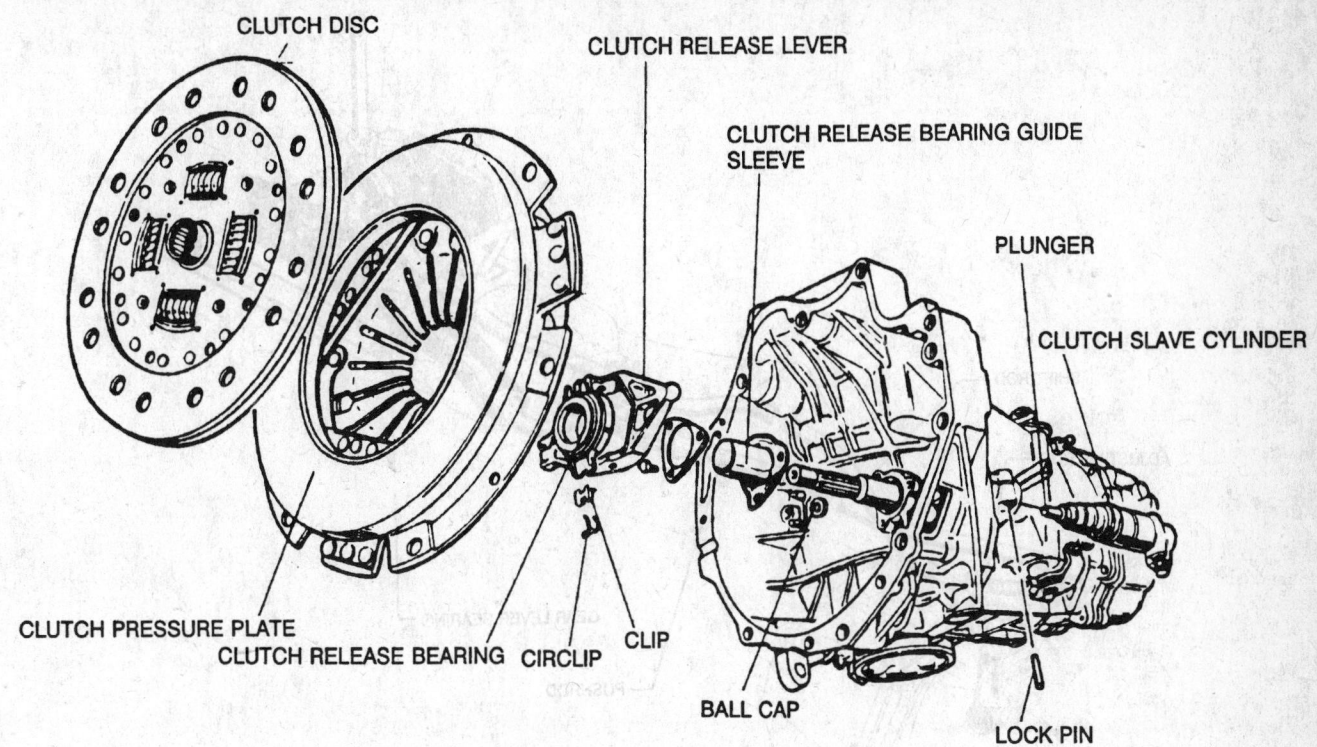

CLUTCH DISC

CLUTCH RELEASE LEVER

CLUTCH RELEASE BEARING GUIDE SLEEVE

PLUNGER

CLUTCH SLAVE CYLINDER

CLUTCH PRESSURE PLATE

CLUTCH RELEASE BEARING

CIRCLIP

CLIP

BALL CAP

LOCK PIN

Clutch assembly and hydraulic release system

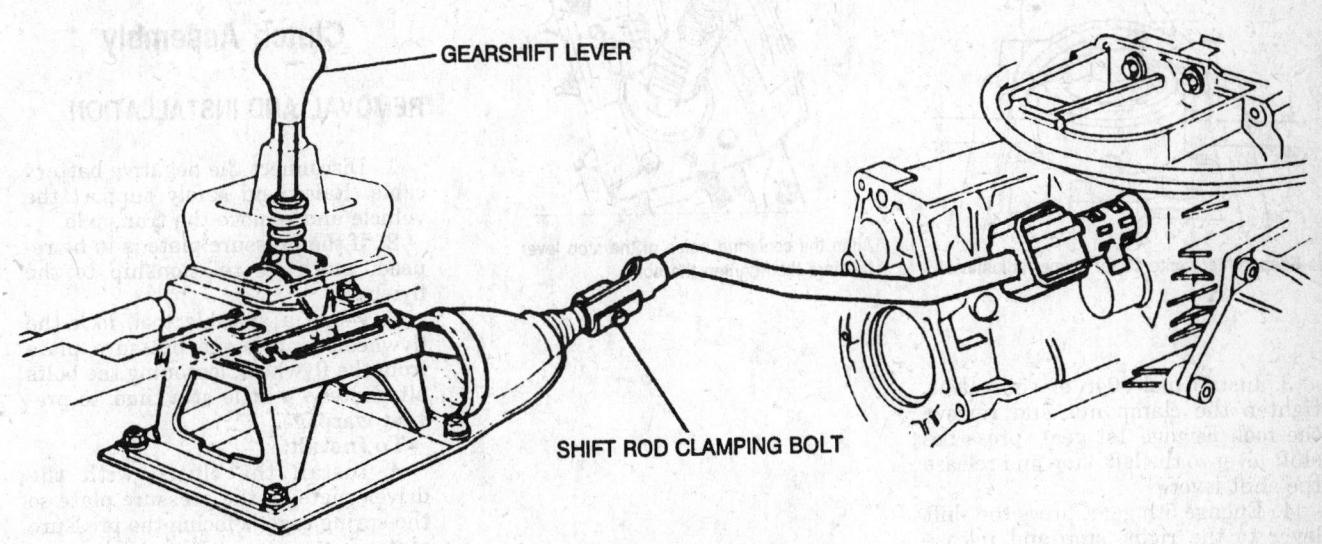

GEARSHIFT LEVER

SHIFT ROD CLAMPING BOLT

Manual shift linkage — 80/90 and 100

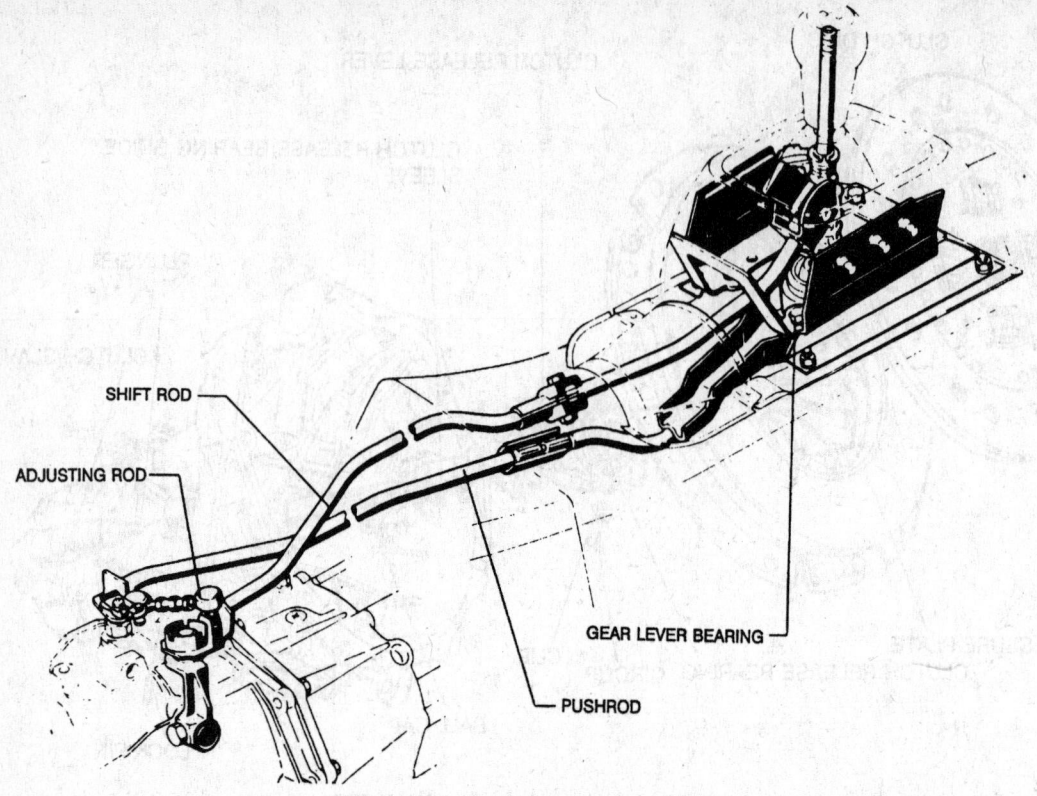

Manual shift linkage — 200 and V8 Quattro

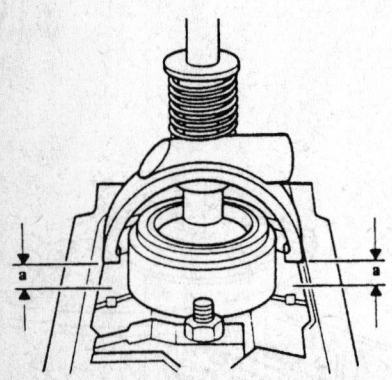

Keep shifter centered for proper adjustment

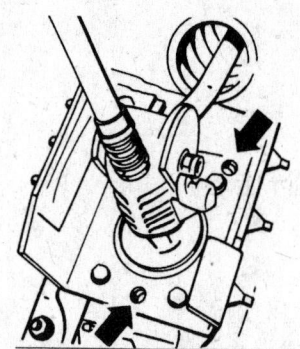

Align the centering holes of the stop lever bearing, then tighten the bolts

3. Install tool 3048 or equivalent, tighten the clamp nut and remove the tool. Engage 1st gear, press the shift lever to the left, stop and release the shift lever.

4. Engage 5th gear, press the shift lever to the right, stop and release the shift lever.

5. If the lever does not spring back approximately the same distance as in Steps 3 and 4, move the gear shift lever housing slightly in the slots sideward.

6. Make sure all gears engage easily without jamming.

100 and 200

1. Loosen the shift rod clamping bolt.

2. Place the gear shift in a vertical position so the dimensions are equal on both sides and retighten shift rod clamp bolt.

CLUTCH

Clutch Assembly

REMOVAL AND INSTALLATION

1. Disconnect the negative battery cable. Raise and safely support the vehicle and remove the transaxle.

2. If the pressure plate is to be re-used, mark its relationship to the flywheel.

3. Using a suitable tool, lock the flywheel. Unbolt the pressure plate from the flywheel, loosening the bolts alternately, a little at a time, to prevent warpage.

To install:

4. Install the clutch with the driven plate on the pressure plate so the spring cage is facing the pressure plate.

5. Hold the clutch assembly against the flywheel, aligning the marks made in Step 2 and the dowel pins on the flywheel with the pressure plate. Insert an alignment shaft tool through the pressure plate and the driven plate into the crankshaft pilot bearing.

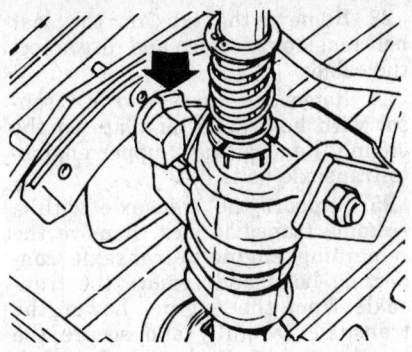

The plastic stop bracket should align with the curved stop plate

6. Install the pressure plate bolts finger tight. Tighten the bolts evenly, in a diagonal pattern, to avoid distortion. Torque the bolts to 18 ft. lbs. (24 Nm). Remove the alignment shaft.

7. The clutch release bearing in the front of the transaxle should be checked before reassembly. It is retained by 2 springs.

8. Replace the transaxle. Torque the engine-to-transaxle bolts to 40 ft. lbs. (54 Nm) and the halfshaft to 58 ft. lbs. (79 Nm).

FREE-PLAY ADJUSTMENTS

All vehicles use a hydraulic clutch release mechanisim. No free play adjustment is required or possible. If the clutch does not release or engage properly and pedal height is correct, try bleeding the system before moving on to more extensive repairs.

PEDAL HEIGHT ADJUSTMENTS

The clutch pedal should be about ⅜ in. (10mm) above the brake pedal. To adjust the pedal height, remove the cotter pin holding the clutch master cylinder clevis to the pedal, loosen the locknut on the clevis shaft and turn the shaft to give the required pedal height. Tighten the locknut and install the clevis on the pedal.

Clutch Master Cylinder

REMOVAL AND INSTALLATION

NOTE: The use of a pressure bleeder is necessary for this procedure. Before beginning, remove and plug the fluid line from the reservoir to the master cylinder. Empty the fluid in the line into a container.

1. Disconnect the negative battery cable. Locate the master cylinder

under the instrument panel, behind the clutch pedal.

2. Remove and plug the line leading to the slave cylinder from the end of the master cylinder.

3. Remove the circlip and the pin which attaches the clevis to the clutch pedal.

4. Remove the 2 master cylinder mounting bolts from the pedal mounting.

5. Remove and plug the reservoir line. Remove the master cylinder.

6. Installation is in the reverse order of removal. Tighten the master cylinder mounting bolts to 15 ft. lbs. (20 Nm).

7. Bleed the clutch system when finished.

Clutch Slave Cylinder

REMOVAL AND INSTALLATION

1. Disconnect the negative battery cable. Locate the slave cylinder on top of the transaxle housing.

2. Remove the retaining clip from the pin.

3. Drive out the slave cylinder lock pin, using a small punch.

4. Remove and plug the fluid line at the slave cylinder. This step is necessary only if the cylinder is being replaced.

5. Lightly grease the machined surfaces of the transaxle housing and the slave cylinder.

6. Install the fluid line on the slave cylinder. Install the slave cylinder in the transaxle. Install the retaining pin.

7. If the fluid line was removed, bleed the system.

Hydraulic Clutch System Bleeding

The clutch system should be bled using a pressure bleeder. Follow the instructions that come with the bleeder tank, for the proper bleeding procedure. The maximum line pressure must not exceed 36 psi. (248 kPa).

AUTOMATIC TRANSAXLE

Transaxle Assembly

REMOVAL AND INSTALLATION

Except V8 Quattro

1. Disconnect the negative battery cable.

2. Remove the upper engine-to-transaxle bolts. Raise and support the vehicle safely.

3. Using a suitable engine support tool, secure it to the engine and the vehicle.

4. At the front of the engine, remove both top bolts. Remove the starter.

5. Through the starter opening, remove the torque converter to drive plate bolts and remove torque converter cover plate.

6. Clamp off the coolant hoses at the ATF cooler and remove the hoses from the cooler.

7. Remove the speedometer cable from the transaxle.

8. Remove the inner halfshaft-to-transaxle bolts. Using a wire, tie up the halfshafts.

9. At the left control arm, mark the position of the ball joint and remove the ball joint and the support.

10. Place an oil catch pan under the transaxle, remove the oil filler tube from the oil pan and drain the fluid.

11. Remove the exhaust pipe-to-transaxle bracket.

12. Remove the selector cable bracket from the transaxle. At the transaxle shift lever, remove the selector cable circlip and the cable.

13. At the transaxle, remove the accelerator cable bracket and the cable from the operating lever.

14. Remove the center bolt, from the transaxle mount. Using the engine support tool, lift the engine slightly.

15. Remove the throttle cable bracket bolts and the bracket.

16. Support the transaxle and lift it slightly. Remove the lower transaxle-to-engine bolts.

17. Separate the engine from the transaxle and lower it from the vehicle. Be sure to secure the torque converter.

To install:

18. When installing the transaxle, should the torque converter slip off the one-way clutch support, the oil

pump shaft could be pulled from the oil pump. This may cause severe damage when bolting the transaxle to the engine. Make sure the torque converter is properly positioned before installing the bolts.

19. Torque the engine-to-transaxle bolts to 41 ft. lbs. (56 Nm), the subframe bolts to 52 ft. lbs. (71 Nm) and the transaxle mount center bolt to 30 ft. lbs. (40 Nm).

20. Install the torque converter-to-driveplate bolts and torque to 22 ft. lbs. (30 Nm). Install the cover plate.

21. Install the halfshaft-to-transaxle bolts and torque to 33 ft. lbs. (45 Nm).

22. Connect the ball joint to the control arm and torque the bolts to 48 ft. lbs. (65 Nm).

23. Install the exhaust system. When installing the exhaust, tighten the clamps after making sure everything is properly positioned to minimize vibration.

24. Connect the hoses to the oil cooler. Install the oil filler tube and refill the transaxle.

25. Connect and adjust the selector cable as required.

26. Connect and adjust the accelerator linkage and align the engine-to-transaxle mounts, if necessary.

V8 Quattro

1. Disconnect the negative battery cable. The battery is under the rear bench seat.

2. Raise and safely support vehicle. Remove the front wheels.

3. Remove the cross struts for the spring strut domes.

4. Remove the air cleaner housing and air cleaner assembly.

5. Remove the supports for the ignition cables and the left and right distributor caps. Remove the throttle cable and support.

6. Disconnect the oxygen sensor and probe heater. Remove the cable clamp for the electrical cables running alongside.

7. Disconnect the 2-pin plug connection at the transaxle bell housing. Disconnect the cable clamp for the wire harness next to the 2-pin plug.

8. Disconnect the retaining strap for the ventilation hose at the firewall.

9. Loosen the transaxle filler pipe on the cylinder head

10. Remove the radiator fan. The left fan can be set aside while still connected.

11. Remove the right engine mounting bolts on the body.

12. Raise and safely support vehicle. Remove the lower engine cover, the crossmember, the front exhaust pipe with catalytic converter and the heat deflector for the driveshaft.

13. Remove the driveshaft by loosening the driveshaft mounting bolts on the transaxle, rear final drive and body.

NOTE: A special driveshaft assembly device or aligning jig is required, tool 3213, or equivalent. This tool keeps the multi-piece driveshaft straight and in proper alignment. Attach this jig to the driveshaft and tighten the nuts. Remove the bolts on the transaxle and rear final drive. Support the driveshaft and alignment jig, remove the mounting bolts from the body and carefully lower the the driveshaft from the vehicle. Take note of any shims. Always move and store the driveshaft flat.

14. Detach the selector lever cable and support bracket at the transaxle and remove the oil filter. Remove the upper bolt on the starter by guiding a 10mm Allen socket with extension and flex fitting through the opening, on the transaxle housing, over the final drive. Remove the bolt and take out the starter.

15. Working through the starter opening, remove the 6 torque converter bolts.

16. Remove the mounting bolts on both sides of the transaxle mounting.

17. Attach a lifting hoist to the engine mounting on the left side and lift slighty.

18. Under the vehicle, support the subframe using a suitable transaxle jack. Remove the mounting bolts on the subframe and lower the subframe carefully until it hangs freely. Disconnect the halfshafts from the transaxle and tie up.

19. Drain the transaxle and remove the filler pipe. Unscrew the cooling lines, the retaining clip that holds both lines together and tie to the subframe, aside.

20. Remove the left and right transaxle mounts.

21. Disconnect the 8-pin electrical connector on the transaxle by turning counterclockwise.

22. Disconnect the plug on the speed sensor. Push the locking lever down and remove the plug from the multi-function transaxle switch. Remove the retainers for the electrical wires from the transaxle and unclamp the ventilation hose.

23. Remove the tabs on the seat belt tensioning cables and disconnect the cables.

24. Remove the speed and TDC sensor with heat deflector plate on the engine. Remove the 2 upper engine-to-transaxle bolts.

25. Support the transaxle with a suitable transaxle jack. Remove the remaining engine-to-transaxle connecting bolts and remove the transaxle from the engine. Lower the transaxle carefully and secure the torque converter to keep it from falling out. Use caution not to damage the halfshafts, bolt-on parts or the multi-function switch.

To install:

26. If a new replacement transaxle is being installed, the following must be carried out.

   a. Transfer the catalytic converter mountings on the left and right side of the housing.

   b. Transfer the pipes for the transaxle cooler and the support for the seat belt tensioning cables.

   c. Check that both guide sleeves are installed in the engine block at the 2 o'clock and 8 o'clock positions, viewed from the flywheel.

27. Make sure the torque converter is secured and install the transaxle. Note that if only the torque converter is replaced, it should be carefully positioned on the free-wheel support and should not be tilted. To engage the splines of the pump shaft, rotate the torque converter forward and backward slightly. The torque converter must be inserted onto the free-wheel support up to the stop.

28. Torque the converter-to-driveplate to 26 ft. lbs. (35 Nm).

29. Torque transaxle-to-engine to 44 ft. lbs. (60 Nm).

30. Install the halfshafts. Torque halfshaft-to-transaxle to 59 ft. lbs. (80 Nm).

31. Install the speed and TDC sensor with heat deflector.

32. Install the seat belt tensioning cables. Torque support for seat belt cables to 30 ft. lbs. (45 Nm).

33. Install the left and right transaxle mounts. Torque transaxle supports to 30 ft. lbs. (45 Nm).

34. Install automatic transaxle filler pipe.

35. Install the subframe assembly. Torque subframe-to-body to 48 ft. lbs. (65 Nm) plus ¼ turn.

36. Install the starter all necessary wiring.

37. Install oil filter, support bracket and selector lever cable.

38. Install and adjust the driveshaft. Align with care. Use the following procedure:

  a. With the alignment jig holding the driveshaft straight, set the driveshaft in place.

  b. Carefully, measure the distance between the body pan bolt holes and the mounting ears of the center support bracket. This distance should be the same left to right.

  c. Five different shims are available: 2, 4, 6, 8 and 10mm. Determine the thickness of the required shims.

  d. Push the driveshaft all the way to the rear up to the stop. Mark the position of the center mounting bracket on the floor pan.

  e. Push the driveshaft forward all the way and park the position of the center mounting bracket on the floor pan. The center mounting must be midway between these 2 marks.

  f. Insert the bolts and shims as determined beforehand and tighten to 15 ft. lbs. (20 Nm). Remove the alignment jig.

39. Install the heat deflector for the driveshaft.

40. Install the exhaust system. When installing the exhaust, tighten the clamps after making sure everything is properly positioned to minimize vibration.

41. Install the crossmember.

42. Install the radiator fan assembly.

43. Reconnect all necessary wiring and vacuum hoses.

44. Install throttle cable support and throttle cable.

45. Install the left and right distributor caps.

46. Install the air cleaner housing assembly.

47. Install the cross-strut support braces. Torque cross brace to suspension strut domes to 17 ft. lbs. (23 Nm).

48. Install front wheels.

49. Fill the unit with automatic transaxle fluid.

50. Adjust the selector cable. Check the throttle cable linkage and, if necessary, adjust.

51. Install and tighten all bolts for the lower engine cover.

52. Check engine oil level. Align front end. Road test the vehicle for proper operation.

Automatic Shift Linkage

All vehicles with automatic transaxle are equipped with the shiftlock transaxle control system. The system must be properly adjusted to make sure the transaxle is fully engaged in each shift position. If this is not done, the transaxle may be only partially engaged in a certain range position, causing severe damage due to slippage. Improper adjustment may also make it impossible to shift into or out of **P**.

The shiftlock system is designed to make it impossible to shift out of **P** or **N** unless certain parameters are met. The system depends on proper operation or condition of fuse S12, the brake light switch circuit, the interior light relay control unit, the driver's door switch circuit and vehicle speed signal.

SYSTEM FUNCTION

With ignition switch **ON**, the selector cannot be shifted out of **P** or **N** unless the brake pedal is depressed. At speeds under 3.7 mph, when shifted into **N** the shifter should lock in **N** after 1 second, unless the brake pedal is depressed. At speeds above 3.7 mph the shifter should not lock.

SYSTEM ADJUSTMENT

1. Adjust the solenoid switch, using a 1mm gauge between the selector lever and solenoid switch. With lever in **R**, push the solenoid against the gauge and tighten to 7 ft. lbs. (9 Nm).

2. Center the lower bore of fork piece and supply voltage to switch. The solenoid pin locks the fork piece.

3. Position the gear shift lever housing so selector lever is in the **N** position relative to the housing.

4. Position the shift arm with a 4mm aligning pin through the housing bore.

5. Shift the selector lever to the **N** position. Remove aligning pin.

6. Check for correct operation.

7. If shifter does not function properly, it may be necessary to check the electronic control systems.

KICKDOWN SWITCH ADJUSTMENT

087 Series

The accelerator control is to be adjusted so at closed throttle the operating lever on the transaxle is at the no-throttle position. If adjustment is incorrect, shift speeds will be too high

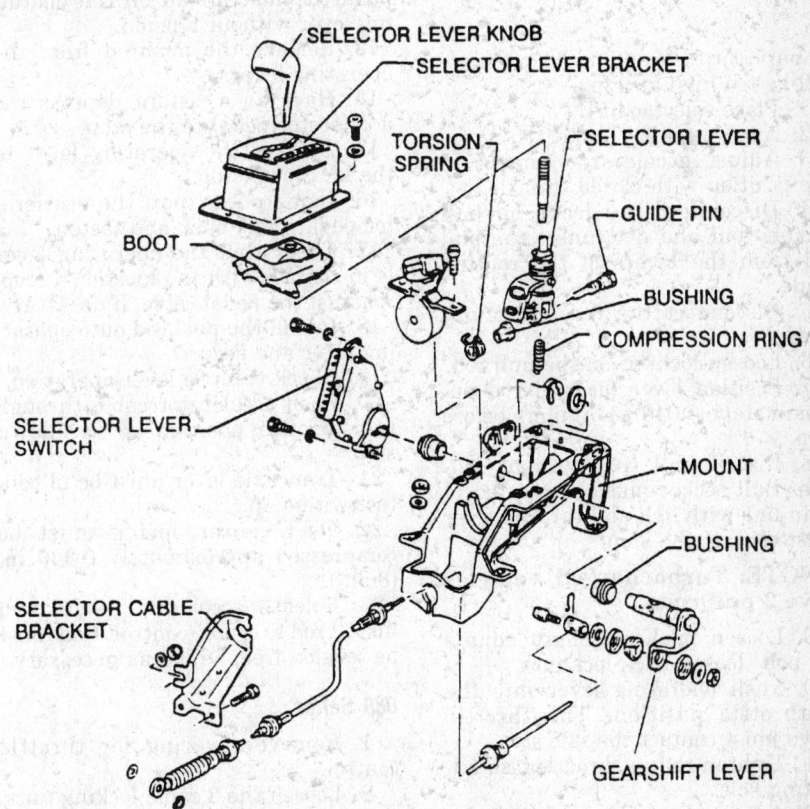

Shiftlock II automatic transaxle shifter assembly

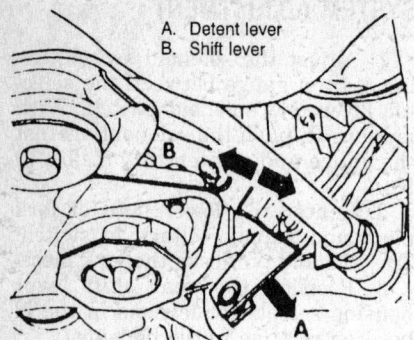

A. Detent lever
B. Shift lever

Adjusting transaxle pushrod

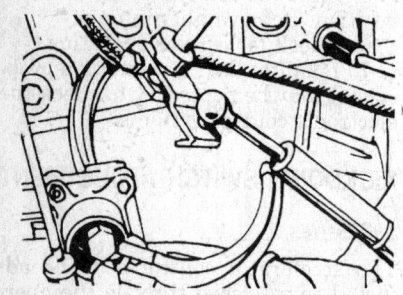

Kickdown detent linkage

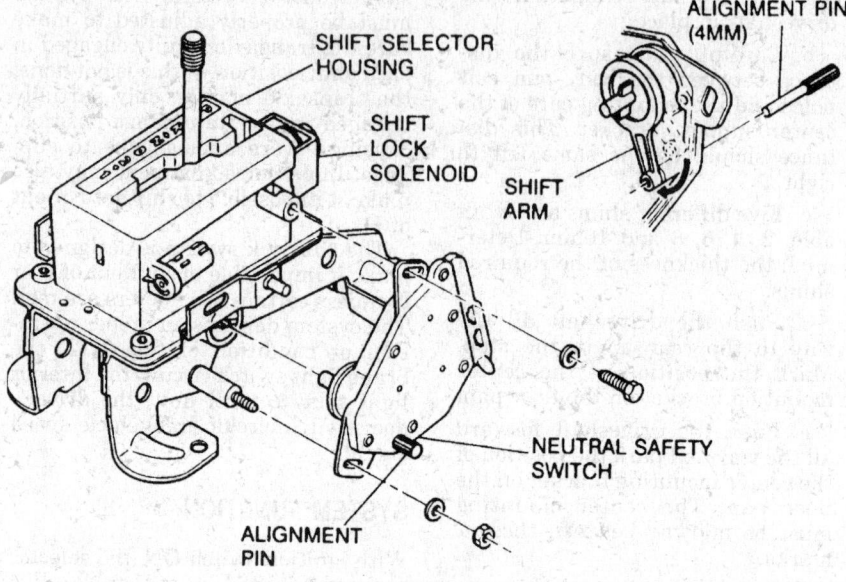

SHIFT SELECTOR HOUSING

SHIFT LOCK SOLENOID

ALIGNMENT PIN (4MM)

SHIFT ARM

NEUTRAL SAFETY SWITCH

ALIGNMENT PIN

Adjusting neutral safety switch

at part throttle and main pressure will be too high at idle.

1. Place selector in **P**.
2. Apply parking brake.
3. Adjust accelerator control in idle position with closed throttle.
4. Disconnect the locks on ball sockets and and disconnect the pull rod from the levers of the routing guide.
5. Disconnect the rods for cruise control.
6. Loosen locknut on the pull rod.
7. Position lever for pull rod approximately 0.040 in. (1mm) before stop.
8. Install pull rod, without tension. Ball socket must be twisted to be in line with ball and throttle lever must contact the stop.

NOTE: Turbocharged vehicles have 2 pull rods.

9. Loosen pushrod length adjusting bolt (loosen back locknut).
10. Push operating lever into the no-throttle position. The throttle valve must contact the idle stop.
11. Tighten the pushrod length adjusting bolt.
12. Adjust the pushrod length by shifting the adjusting plate. The

pushrod must install on the operating lever without tension.
13. Remove the pushrod from the operating lever.
14. Have an assistant depress the accelerator pedal to the stop.
15. Depress the operating lever to the kickdown stop.
16. Using pliers, pull the accelerator pedal cable back and fasten.
17. Check that the operating lever is in contact with the kickdown stop, readjust the pedal cable, if necessary.
18. Install the pushrod onto operating lever and secure.
19. Check throttle lever operation.
20. Push accelerator cable through full throttle position to kickdown stop.
21. Transaxle lever must be in contact with stop.
22. Over center spring must be compressed approximately 0.320 in. (8mm).
23. Release accelerator pedal and install rod to cruise control. Rod must be tension free, adjust as necessary.

089 Series

1. Remove covering for throttle control.
2. Loosen the 2 cable locking nuts.
3. Turn the throttle to the full throttle position and hold.

4. Using tool 3004 or equivalent, hold the throttle cable brackets at full open throttle. Attach tool end on the lever lower cable bracket and tool end on the end of the hood gas strut.
5. Insert a $^{11}/_{16}$ in. (17mm) spacer between the accelerator pedal and pedal stop.
6. An assistant is needed to push the pedal down to the stop.
7. Pull accelerator cable and install locking clip.
8. Pull cable until pressure from transaxle kickdown position is felt.
9. Tighten the nut on cable side against the bracket, next tighten the nut on pivot side against bracket.
10. Remove tool.
11. Throttle lever must rest against the idle stop when the accelerator is released.
12. Press accelerator to full throttle position, not kickdown.
13. The pressure point for full throttle position of the accelerator pedal must be approximately $^3/_4$ in. (19mm) away from the pedal stop.
14. Press the accelerator to the pedal (kickdown) stop.
15. Transaxle operating lever must contact the kickdown stop.
16. The spring between the cable brackets must be stressed.

17. For vehicles with cruise control, adjust the coupling rod by moving the ball end 0.039-0.059 in. (1-1.5mm).

18. For vehicles with cruise control, the air conditioning switch must only switch **ON** at kickdown and not at wide-open throttle. Approximately 5/64 in. (2mm) between the switch and cable bracket at wide-open throttle (not kickdown).

FRONT SUSPENSION

MacPherson Strut

REMOVAL AND INSTALLATION

1. Disconnect the negative battery cable. With the vehicle on the ground, remove the front axle nut or bolt and loosen the wheel bolts.

2. Raise and support the vehicle safely. Remove the wheel assembly.

3. Remove the brake caliper mounting bolts and disconnect the brake line from the bracket without disconnecting the line from the caliper. Remove speed sensor, if equipped.

4. Remove the brake caliper with the line still attached and support it aside.

5. Remove disc brake rotor.

6. Remove the ball joint clamp bolt and nut.

7. Remove the tie rod end nut and separate the tie rod end from the strut.

8. If equipped with a stabilizer bar, remove the retaining bolt and remove the stabilizer bar end clamps. Pivot the stabilizer bar downward.

9. Remove the 2 center stabilizer bar clamps and unbolt stabilizer bar from the lower control arm.

10. Remove the pinch bolt from the steering knuckle and separate the lower ball joint from the knuckle by pushing down on the control arm.

11. Using a suitable hub puller, press the halfshaft out of the hub.

12. On 80 and 90, support the strut assembly, hold the shock absorber piston rod with an internal socket wrench and remove the retaining nut. Remove the strut assembly from the vehicle.

13. On all other models, remove the upper strut cover, support the strut assembly and remove the 3 strut retaining nuts. Remove the strut assembly.

To install:

14. On 80 and 90 models, torque the upper strut retaining nut to 44 ft. lbs. (60 Nm). On other models, torque the 3 upper strut retaining nuts to 22 ft. lbs. (30 Nm).

15. When installing the stabilizer bar, the position is correct if the clamps are difficult to install in the rubber bushings. Attach the clamps loosely.

16. Tighten the ball joint bolt to 36 ft. lbs. (49 Nm) on 80 and 90 or 48 ft. lbs. (65 Nm), plus an additional 1/4 turn (90 degrees) on 100, 200 and V8 Quattro. Install and seat the speed sensor.

17. When installing the axle shaft, apply a bead of thread locking compound to the splines. When the vehicle is on the ground, torque the center nut or bolt to 195 ft. lbs. (265 Nm) on 80 and 90 or 148 ft. lbs. (200 Nm) plus 1/4 turn on all other models.

18. After test drive to seat stabilizer bushings in correct position tighten to 18 ft. lbs. (24 Nm).

Lower Ball Joint

REMOVAL AND INSTALLATION

Coupe, 80 and 90

1. Raise and safely support the vehicle. Remove the wheel assembly.

2. Remove the lower ball joint clamp nut and bolt and pry the control arm down to disengage the ball joint from the steering knuckle.

3. Remove the ball joint to control arm mounting bolts and remove the ball joint.

To install:

4. Install the new ball joint on the control arm and tighten the mounting bolts to 46 ft. lbs. (62 Nm).

5. Slowly allow the lower control arm and ball joint to fit into the strut assembly. Install the bolt and tighten to 48 ft. lbs. (65 Nm).

6. Install the wheel assembly and lower the vehicle.

7. Reset the front end alignment when finished.

All Other Models

The ball joint is permanently assembled to the lower control arm and cannot be replaced separately.

Lower Control Arms

REMOVAL AND INSTALLATION

1. Raise and support the vehicle safely. Remove the wheel assembly.

2. Remove the ball joint to strut bolt and nut. Pry and hold the control arm down. Remove the ball joint to control arm mounting bolts and nuts.

3. If equipped with a stabilizer bar, disconnect the end of the stabilizer bar and pull it down.

4. Remove the 2 control arm to subframe bolts and remove the control arm.

To install:

5. Installation is in the reverse order of removal. Check control arm bushings for cracking or undue wear. Tighten the control arm-to-subframe bolts to 43 ft. lbs. (58 Nm); the ball joint-to-strut bolt to 46 ft. lbs. (62 Nm) and the stabilizer bar bolts to 18 ft. lbs. (24 Nm).

Sway Bar

REMOVAL AND INSTALLATION

1. The sway bar or stabilizer bar is removed and installed with the vehicle standing on its wheels.

2. Remove both sway bar rubber bushing brackets.

3. Disconnect the ends of the sway bar where it goes through the lower control arm and remove.

4. Installation is the reverse of the removal procedure. Use new self-locking nuts and tighten to 80 ft. lbs. (108 Nm).

REAR SUSPENSION

MacPherson Struts

REMOVAL AND INSTALLATION

80 and 90

EXCEPT QUATTRO

NOTE: Always remove and install the suspension struts 1 at a time. Do not allow the rear axle to hang in place as this may cause damage to the brake lines.

1. With the vehicle at ground level, open the trunk and remove the trim from around the shock tower.

2. Remove the rubber cap.

3. Hold the strut rod and remove the strut mounting nut.

4. Raise and support the vehicle safely.

5. Remove the lower strut mounting bolt from the axle beam and remove the strut.

6. Installation is the reverse of removal. Torque the upper strut mounting bolt to 14 ft. lbs. (19 Nm) and the lower strut mounting bolt to 43 ft. lbs. (58 Nm).

80 AND 90 QUATTRO WITH SINGLE PIECE STRUT

1. With the vehicle on the ground, remove the axle nut.

2. Raise and safely support the vehicle and remove the rear wheels.

3. Unbolt the halfshaft from the differential flange.

4. Remove the self-locking lower ball joint nut and press the ball joint out of the wheel bearing housing. Use the nut to protect the threads.

5. Loosen the control arm mounting bolts and allow the arm to pivot down out of the way.

6. Remove the tie rod nut and press the tie rod joint out of the bearing housing arm. Use the nut to protect the threads.

7. Pull the parking brake cable out of the strut bracket. Remove the brake caliper with its bracket without disconnecting the hydraulic line. Hang the caliper from the body with wire.

8. Remove the brake disc and slide the wheel speed sensor out of its mounting, if equipped. Press the halfshaft out of the hub.

9. Support the strut from below. In the luggage compartment, remove the trim and the rubber cap at the top of the strut.

10. Hold the top of the strut with an Allen wrench and remove the self-locking nut. Lower the strut from the vehicle.

To install:

11. Replace all self-locking nuts. Install the strut into the upper mount and torque the new upper nut to 48 ft. lbs. (60 Nm).

12. Make sure the axle shaft splines are clean and apply a bead of threat locking compound to the outer end of the splines. Install the axle shaft but do not torque the center nut until the vehicle is on its wheels. Torque the axle flange bolts to 35 ft. lbs. (45 Nm).

13. Install the brake disc and caliper. Torque the caliper bracket mounting bolts to 92 ft. lbs. (125 Nm).

14. Attach the ball joint to the control arm and the tie rod to the bearing housing and install new self-locking nuts. Torque the tie rod nut to 29 ft. lbs. (40 Nm) and the ball joint nut to 54 ft. lbs. (75 Nm).

15. When installation is complete and the vehicle is on the ground, torque the center axle nut to 236 ft. lbs. (320 Nm).

80 AND 90 QUATTRO WITH 2-PIECE STRUT

1. In the luggage compartment, remove the trim and the cap from the top of the strut. With the vehicle on its wheels, hold the strut rod from turning and remove the upper strut nut.

2. Place a block of wood between the axle shaft and the frame. Carefully raise and safely support the vehicle and remove the rear wheels.

3. Remove the bolts securing the lower strut to the wheel bearing housing and remove the strut. These are stretch bolts that cannot be reused and must be replaced with the newer type.

To install:

4. Install the strut to the bearing housing with new bolts. Torque the new stretch bolts to 59 ft. lbs. (80 Nm), plus an additional ½ turn.

5. Install the wheel and lower the vehicle until the wood block can be removed. Be sure to carefully guide the strut into the upper mount.

6. Install a new self-locking upper strut mounting nut and torque to 44 ft. lbs. (60 Nm). Check the wheel alignment.

100 and 200

EXCEPT QUATTRO AND V8 QUATTRO

NOTE: The struts must be removed with the weight of the vehicle on the rear wheels. If not, a spring compressor must be used on the rear springs.

1. If the vehicle is not on its wheels, install the spring compressor and compress the spring. Do not attempt to remove the shock with the rear wheels raised without a compressor.

2. Remove the upper strut mounting nut.

3. Remove the lower strut mounting nut.

4. Remove the shock absorber.

5. Installation is the reverse of removal. Torque the lower mounts to 66 ft. lbs. (89 Nm) and the upper to 14 ft. lbs. (19 Nm).

QUATTRO AND V8 QUATTRO

1. Raise and support the vehicle safely. Remove the wheel assembly.

2. Open the trunk and remove the shock absorber covers, the remove the shock absorber-to-body nuts/bolts.

3. Remove the shock absorber-to-rear wheel knuckle assembly. Remove the shock absorber from the vehicle.

4. To install, reverse the removal procedures. Torque the shock absorber-to-body nuts/bolts to 15 ft. lbs. (20 Nm) and the shock absorber-to-rear wheel knuckle assembly bolt to 66 ft. lbs. (89 Nm).

Rear Control Arms

REMOVAL AND INSTALLATION

80 and 90 Quattro

1. Raise and support the vehicle safely, under the frame and differential.

2. Using a scribing tool, mark the position of the ball joint carrier with the control arm.

3. Remove the ball joint carrier-to-control arm nuts and the lock plate. Separate the ball joint carrier from the control arm.

4. Remove the control arm-to-subframe bolts and the control arm from the vehicle.

5. To install, reverse the removal procedures. Always use new replacement nuts. Torque the control arm-to-subframe bolts to 43 ft. lbs. (58 Nm) and the ball joint nut to 54 ft. lbs. (75 Nm). Check the rear wheel alignment.

100 and 200 Quattro

On these vehicles, the control arm is called the trapezoidal arm. It is connected to the wheel bearing housing and to 2 separate crossmembers. Always use new self-locking nuts on all applications.

1. Raise and support the vehicle safely, under the frame and differential.

2. Remove the wheel. Along the trapezoidal arm, remove the speed sensor wiring bracket nuts/bolts and the guide.

3. Remove the wheel bearing housing-to-trapezoidal arm front and rear bolts.

4. Remove the trapezoidal arm-to-rear crossmember bolt.

5. At the brake pressure regulator, disconnect the spring.

6. Remove the trapezoidal arm-to-front crossmember nut and the trapezoidal arm from the vehicle.

7. To install, reverse the removal procedures. Torque the trapezoidal arm-to-front crossmember nut to 44 ft. lbs. (60 Nm), the trapezoidal arm-to-rear crossmember bolt to 63 ft. lbs. (85 Nm), the trapezoidal arm-to-wheel bearing housing bolts to 125 ft. lbs. (169 Nm) and the speed sensor guide nut/bolts to 7 ft. lbs. (10 Nm). Adjust the rear wheel alignment.

NOTE: Before installing the trapezoidal arm, be sure to coat the fasteners with locking compound.

Rear Wheel Bearings

REMOVAL AND INSTALLATION

1. Raise and support the vehicle safely. Remove the wheel assembly.

2. Without disconnecting the hydraulic line, remove caliper assembly from rotor. Suspend caliper from the body with wire, do not let it hang by brake hose.

3. Pry off the grease cap and remove the cotter pin, nut and washer.

4. Remove the outer bearing.

5. Remove the brake rotor.

6. Remove the bearing inner bearing and seal from the rotor hub, using a soft drift or press.

7. Remove the bearing inner and outer race(s) from the rotor, using a soft drift or press.

To install:

8. Clean and inspect mating surfaces for bearing races.

9. Install new races, using soft drift or press.

10. Pack the new bearing with grease and set it into the inner race.

11. Install seal, making sure it is square in the rotor hub.

12. Install rotor, outer bearing, washer, nut and adjust bearing play.

13. Install cotter pin and dust cap.

14. Install caliper assembly.

15. If hydraulic lines had be removed, install and bleed brakes.

16. If parking brake cable has been remove, install and adjust as necessary.

17. Install the wheel assembly.

18. Lower vehicle and check brakes for proper operation.

ADJUSTMENT

1. Raise and support the vehicle safely.

2. Remove the grease cap.

3. Remove the cotter pin and the locking nut.

4. While turning the wheel, so the wheel bearing does not jam, tighten the adjusting nut firmly.

5. Back the nut off slightly. The nut is properly adjusted when it is possible to pry the thrust washer side to side with some drag but using light pressure on the tool.

6. Install the locking nut and a new cotter pin. When installing the cap, make sure it is securely in place.

Rear Axle Assembly

REMOVAL AND INSTALLATION

Front Wheel Drive

1. Raise and support the vehicle safely. Remove the wheel assembly. Detach the muffler hanger bands. Lower and support the muffler and tail pipe.

2. Remove the parking brake cable to equalizer nut. Pry the cable sleeve from the bracket. Remove both parking brake cables at the brackets and disconnect the brake hoses at the brake line brackets. Cap all hoses and lines. Vehicles equipped with anti-lock brakes, disconnect the speed sensor.

3. Remove the nuts from the bolts attaching the trailing arms to the body. Do not remove the bolts at this time. On the right side, disconnect the spring from the brake pressure regulator.

4. Remove the bolts attaching the diagonal arms to the axle and remove the bolts attaching the strut to the axle. Slide out the trailing arm to the body attaching bolts and carefully remove the axle from the vehicle.

NOTE: All bolts through rubber bushings should be tightened with the weight of the vehicle on its wheels. This is done to preset the bushings in a level, non-stressed position to avoid poor handling or tire wear.

To install:

5. After positioning the axle in the vehicle, install both trailing arm bolts finger tight. Attach the lower strut mounts and install the wheel and tire assemblies. Lower the vehicle to the ground.

6. Torque the trailing arm attaching bolts to 72 ft. lbs. (98 Nm) and the strut bolts to 66 ft. lbs. (90 Nm).

7. Install the diagonal arm and torque the bolt at the axle end to 70 ft. lbs. (95 Nm). Torque the bolt at the body end to 66 ft. lbs. (90 Nm).

Raise the vehicle again to install the remaining components.

8. After the installation procedure has been completed, install the speed sensor, if equipped, bleed the brake system and adjust the parking brake, as necessary.

STEERING

Steering Wheel

— **CAUTION** —

On vehicles equipped with an air bag, the negative battery cable and reserve power supply must both be disconnected before working on the vehicle. Failure to do so may result in deployment of the air bag and personal injury.

REMOVAL AND INSTALLATION

Without Air Bag

1. Center the steering wheel. Disconnect the negative battery cable.

2. Pull off the center horn pad and disconnect the wire. Mark the relationship of the steering wheel to the steering shaft.

3. Remove the steering wheel mounting nut and remove the steering wheel.

4. To install, align the matchmarks and tighten the nut to 30 ft. lbs. (41 Nm).

NOTE: Never strike or pound on the steering wheel. The collapsible steering column may be damaged.

With Air Bag

1. Center the steering wheel. Disconnect the negative battery cable.

2. Remove the side trim from center console, disconnect the red power supply connector to the air bag.

— **CAUTION** —

The reserve power supply can trigger the air bag even with the battery disconnected. The power connector to the air bag must be disconnected.

3. Remove the screws for the upper steering column trim and remove the upper trim.

4. Separate the connector for the air bag spiral spring.

5. Remove the air bag Torx® head retaining bolts.

6. Unhook the air bag unit, lift safety clamp and remove the air bag wiring at the terminal. Place the removed air bag unit face up in a safe place where it will not be disturbed.

7. Remove the steering wheel mounting nut and remove the steering wheel. A steering wheel puller may be necessary.

8. If removing spiral spring, wheel must be in the straight-ahead position. Do not twist spring after removing it.

To install:

9. To install, align the matchmarks and tighten the nut to 30 ft. lbs. (41 Nm).

NOTE: Never strike or pound on the steering wheel. The collapsible steering column may be damaged.

10. Reinstall air bag unit, air bag connector and Torx® head screws. Torque the Torx® head screws to 53 inch lbs. (6 Nm).

11. Install steering column upper trim.

12. Connect air bag system power connector.

13. Install the side trim on center console.

14. Connect the negative battery cable.

Power Steering Rack

REMOVAL AND INSTALLATION

80 and 90

1. Raise and safely support the vehicle.

2. Remove the lower left instrument panel cover, the steering column-to-steering rack clamp bolt and the steering column-to-dash bolts. Remove the steering column from the vehicle.

3. Using a pair of locking pliers, clamp off the fluid return line to the reservoir. Disconnect the fluid pressure line from the steering gear.

4. At the steering column boot, press in on the clips and remove the boot from the panel. From inside the vehicle, remove the fluid return line from the control valve body. On 5 cylinder vehicles, push off the dash panel boot and push the boot into the passenger compartment to access the pressure and return line.

5. At the left wheel housing, disconnect the steering rack from the frame.

6. At the steering rack, remove the tie rod coupling locknuts/bolts and the tie rods from the rack. Push the rack back into the steering housing.

7. Disconnect the steering assembly from the firewall. Turn the wheels to the right. Remove the assembly between the left wheel housing and the control arm.

To install:

8. Install the rack assembly and torque the left side bolts and nuts to 14 ft. lbs. (20 Nm). Use new self-locking nuts to secure the rack to the firewall and torque to 35 ft. lbs. (45 Nm).

9. Use new self-locking nuts and secure the tie rod coupling to the rack. Torque the nuts to 35 ft. lbs. (45 Nm).

10. Install the steering column, connect the hydraulic lines and bleed the system.

100, 200 and V8 Quattro

1. Raise and safely support the vehicle.

2. Pry off the lock plate and remove both tie rod mounting bolts from the steering rack, inside the engine compartment. Pry the tie rods out of the mounting pivot.

3. Remove the lower instrument panel trim.

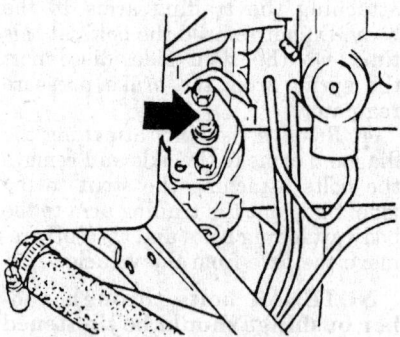

Steering rack adjustment bolt

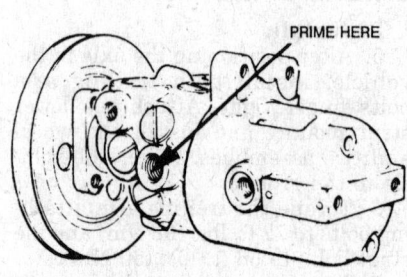

PRIME HERE

Prime the pump with fluid before installation

4. Remove the pressure and return lines from the steering rack control valve body.

5. Remove the shaft clamp bolt, pry off the clip and drive the shaft toward the inside of the vehicle with a brass drift.

6. Remove the steering gear mounting bolts at both ends. There is a single bolt at the right end.

7. Turn the wheels all the way to the right and remove the steering gear through the opening in the right wheel housing.

To install:

8. Temporarily install the tie rod mounting pivot to the rack with both mounting bolts. Remove 1 bolt, install the tie rod and replace the bolt. Do the same on the other tie rod. Make sure to install the lock plate.

9. Torque the following bolts:
Except the 100 and 200
Tie rod to 39 ft. lbs. (53 Nm)
Mounting pivot bolt to 15 ft. lbs. (20 Nm)
Steering gear-to-body mounting bolts to 15 ft. lbs. (20 Nm)
100 and 200
Tie rod to 44 ft. lbs. (60 Nm)
Pivot bolt to 30 ft. lbs. (41 Nm)
Gear-to-body bolts to 15 ft. lbs. (20 Nm)

10. Install hose lines with new O-rings and torque to 30 ft. lbs. (41 Nm).

11. Bleed the hydraulic system.

Power Steering Pump

REMOVAL AND INSTALLATION

Except V8 Quattro

1. Disconnect the negative battery cable. Remove the hoses from the pump. Plug the openings.

2. Remove the belt adjusting bolt or tensioner locknut, push the pump to 1 side and remove the belt.

3. Support the pump, remove the mounting bolts and lift out the pump.

4. Installation is the reverse of the removal. Torque the power stering mounting bolts to 14 ft. lbs. (20 Nm) and banjo bolts to 35 ft. lbs. (45 Nm). Adjust the belt, torque the tensioner locknut to 14 ft. lbs. (20 Nm). Be sure to fill the pump suction chamber with hydraulic fluid before attaching lines or the pump may be damaged.

V8 Quattro

1. Disconnect the battery negative cable.

2. Remove the air duct tube bolt near the engine oil dipstick.

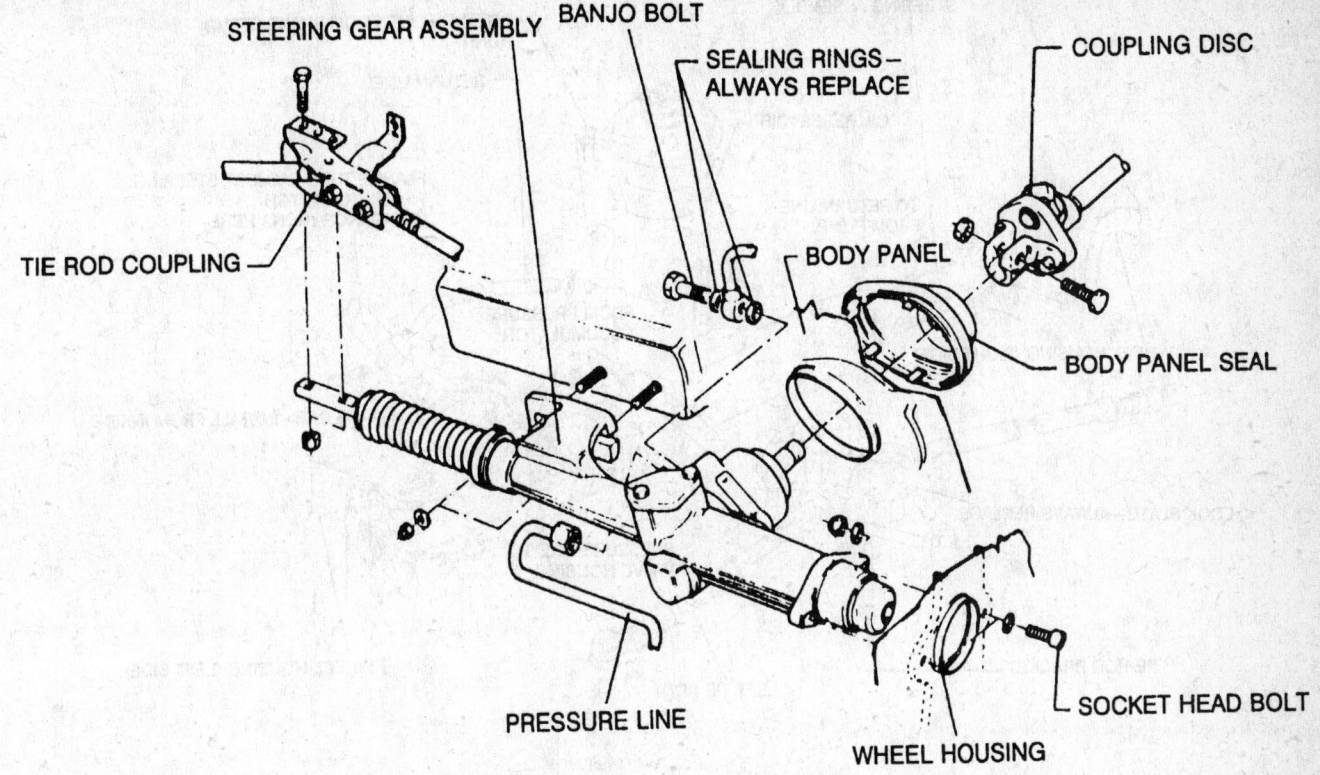

STEERING GEAR ASSEMBLY

BANJO BOLT

SEALING RINGS — ALWAYS REPLACE

COUPLING DISC

BODY PANEL

BODY PANEL SEAL

TIE ROD COUPLING

PRESSURE LINE

WHEEL HOUSING

SOCKET HEAD BOLT

Steering rack assembly removal — 80 and 90

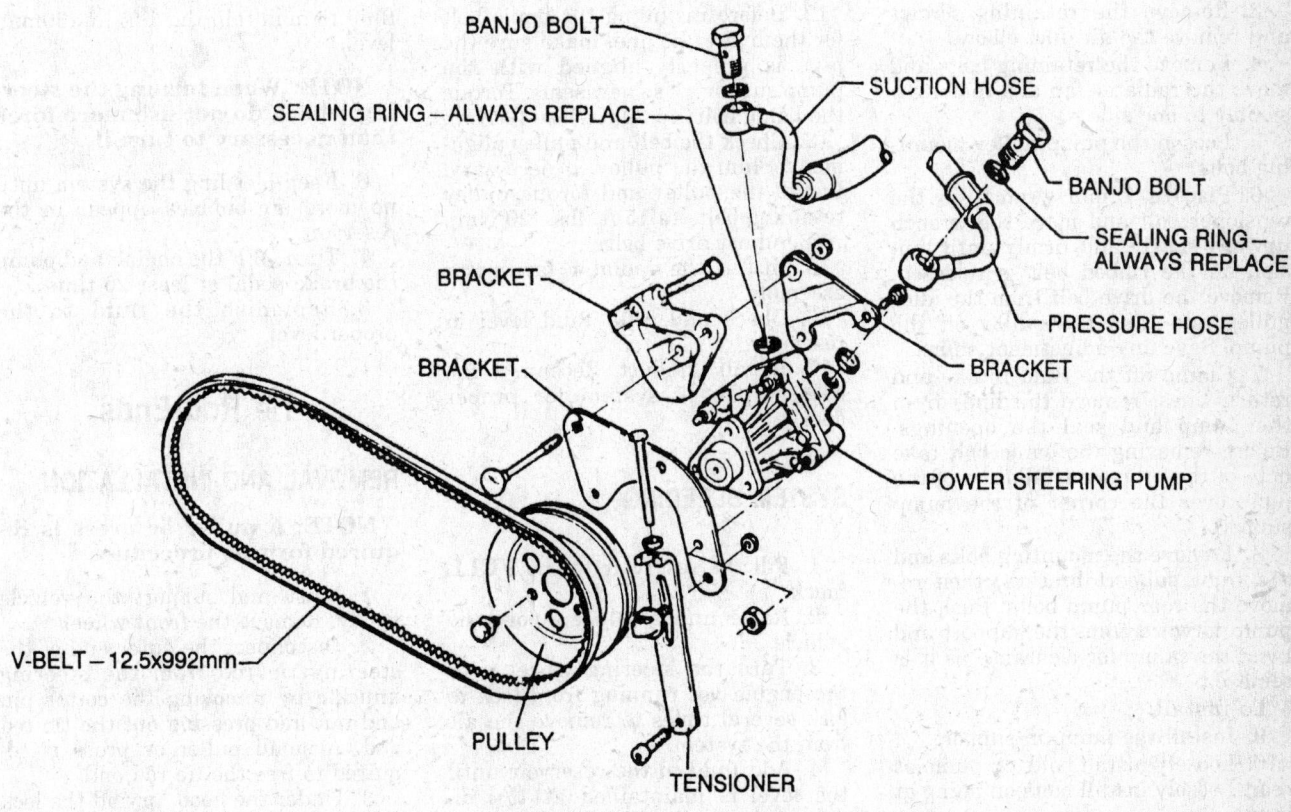

BANJO BOLT

SEALING RING — ALWAYS REPLACE

SUCTION HOSE

BANJO BOLT

SEALING RING — ALWAYS REPLACE

PRESSURE HOSE

BRACKET

BRACKET

BRACKET

POWER STEERING PUMP

V-BELT — 12.5x992mm

PULLEY

TENSIONER

Steering pump assembly — 80 and 90

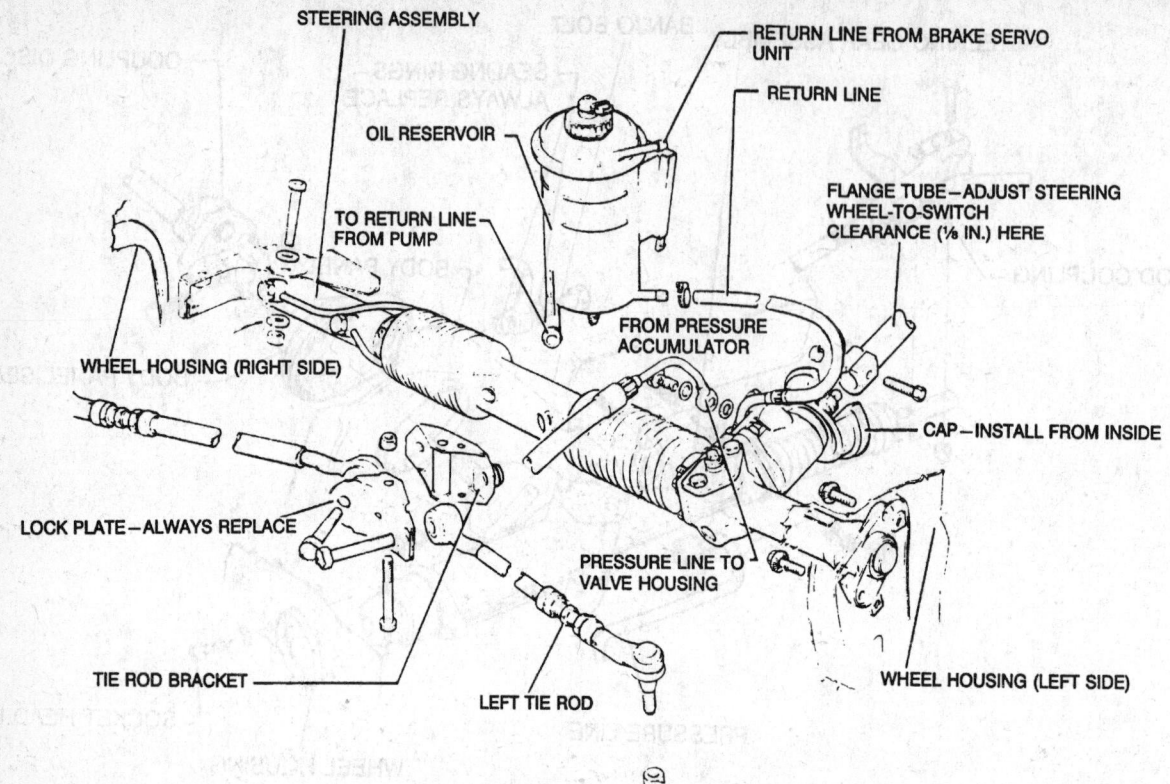

STEERING ASSEMBLY

RETURN LINE FROM BRAKE SERVO UNIT

RETURN LINE

OIL RESERVOIR

FLANGE TUBE—ADJUST STEERING WHEEL-TO-SWITCH CLEARANCE (⅛ IN.) HERE

TO RETURN LINE FROM PUMP

FROM PRESSURE ACCUMULATOR

WHEEL HOUSING (RIGHT SIDE)

CAP—INSTALL FROM INSIDE

LOCK PLATE—ALWAYS REPLACE

PRESSURE LINE TO VALVE HOUSING

TIE ROD BRACKET

LEFT TIE ROD

WHEEL HOUSING (LEFT SIDE)

Steering rack assembly — 100, 200 and V8 Quattro

3. Remove the retaining screws and remove the air duct elbow.

4. Remove the retaining bolts and move the radiator fan and motor assembly to one side.

5. Loosen the pump pulley mounting bolts.

6. Place a 13mm wrench on the tensioner bolt and move the wrench upward slowly and firmly until tension on the ribbed belt is released. Remove the drive belt from the idler pulley and take the pulley off the pump. Save any adjustment shims.

7. Clamp off the fluid intake and return lines, remove the lines from the pump and seal the openings. Before removing the banjo bolt take note of the proper installation of the pipe, over the corner of the pump support.

8. Remove the mounting bolts and the front support bracket, then remove the rear pump bolts. Push the pump forward from the support and twist the pump for clearance as it is removed.

To install:

9. Install the pump in support.

10. Loosely install bolts on pump at rear. Loosely install bolts on pump at front.

11. Torque all pump mounting bolts to 15 ft. lbs. (20 Nm).

12. Before installing the banjo bolt for the hydraulic line, make sure the pipe is properly aligned with the pump support. Use new seals. Torque the banjo bolts to 30 ft. lbs. (40 Nm).

13. Check the belt and pulley alignment. Shim the pulley, if necessary. Install the pulley and torque pulley retaining bolts to 15 ft. lbs. (20 Nm).

14. Adjust drive belt.

15. Install the radiator fan motor assembly.

16. Check and refill fluid level in reservoir.

17. Install air duct. Reconnect the battery. Check system for proper operation.

SYSTEM BLEEDING

1. Fill the reservoir to the **FULL** mark.

2. Raise and safely support the vehicle.

3. Turn the steering wheel with the engine not running from lock to lock several times to remove the air from the system.

4. Add fluid to the reservoir until the level is maintained at 1³/₁₆ in. (30mm) below the **FULL** mark.

5. Start the engine. As the fluid in the reservoir continues to drop, add fluid to maintain the 1³/₁₆ in. (30mm) level.

NOTE: When turning the steering wheel, do not use more force than necessary to turn it.

6. Keep bleeding the system until no more air bubbles appear in the reservoir.

7. Turn OFF the engine and pump the brake pedal at least 20 times.

8. Replenish the fluid to the proper level.

Tie Rod Ends

REMOVAL AND INSTALLATION

NOTE: A puller or press is required for this procedure.

1. Raise and support the vehicle safely. Remove the front wheels.

2. Disconnect the outer end of the steering tie rod from the steering knuckle by removing the cotter pin and nut and pressing out the tie rod end. A small puller or press is required to free the tie rod end.

3. Under the hood, pry off the lock plate and remove the mounting bolts from both tie rod inner ends. Pry the tie rod out of the mounting pivot.

4. Install the mounting pivot to the rack with both mounting bolts.

5. Remove 1 bolt, install the tie rod and replace the bolt. Do the same on the other tie rod.

6. Make sure to install the lock plate. The inner tie rod end bolts should be torqued to 44 ft. lbs. (60 Nm).

7. If replacing the adjustable left tie rod, adjust it to the same length as the old one. Check the toe-in.

8. Use new cotter pins or replace self-locking nuts when installing the outer tie rod end.

BRAKES

Master Cylinder

REMOVAL AND INSTALLATION

1. Disconnect the negative battery cable. Have an assistant hold the brake pedal down about 1½ in. Disconnect the brake lines nearest the firewall.

2. Hold a container under the fitting disconnected in Step 1 and have the assistant release the pedal. The contents of the reservoir will drain into the container. Discard the used fluid.

3. Disconnect the other brake line.

4. Disconnect the stoplight switch and any warning switches from the master cylinder.

5. Remove the master cylinder from the power brake unit. Be careful not to lose the sealing ring between the 2 units.

To install:

6. Install the new master cylinder and and torque the mounting bolts to 17 ft. lbs. (23 Nm). Install the switches.

7. Transfer the reservoir from the old master cylinder to the new unit.

NOTE: Bench bleeding master cylinder will speed the on-vehicle bleeding procedure. Raise the front or rear of the vehicle, if necessary, to maintain bleeding locations at the highest point in the hydraulic system.

8. Fill and bleed the system. There should be a pedal free-play of 0.2 in. (5mm). Free-play can be adjusted with the linkage, inside.

Proportioning Valve

REMOVAL AND INSTALLATION

This device is not used on vehicles with ABS.

1. Disconnect the negative battery cable. Remove and plug the 4 brake lines leading from the proportioning valve.

2. Disconnect the spring which is attached to the valve and the axle beam.

3. Remove the 2 mounting bolts and remove the valve.

NOTE: Do not disassemble the valve.

4. Installation is in the reverse order of removal.

5. Bleed the brake system when finished.

Power Brake Booster

REMOVAL AND INSTALLATION

1. Remove the master cylinder. Do not disconnect the brake lines.

2. Disconnect the vacuum hose from the power brake booster.

3. From under the dash, disconnect the pushrod from the brake pedal, remove the power brake booster-to-firewall nuts and remove the booster from the vehicle.

4. To install, reverse the removal procedures. Torque the master cylinder nuts to 17 ft. lbs. (23 Nm).

Brake Caliper

REMOVAL AND INSTALLATION

Front

DOUBLE PISTON CALIPER

1. Raise and safely support the vehicle.

2. Remove wheels.

3. Remove the lower caliper bolt, hold guide pin with an open end wrench while loosening. Disconnect the wear indicator, if equipped.

4. Swing brake caliper up and remove brake pads, taking note of spacer shims and heat-shield locations, if equipped.

5. Disconnect brake line and remove caliper.

To install:

6. Push pistons back into caliper. Place an old disc pad on piston side of caliper, using a C-clamp centered on old pad across both piston, push pistons back into bore. Make certain to

Girling rear brake caliper

SPRING CLIP

25 FT. LBS. (35 NM)

CALIPER HOUSING

PARKING BRAKE CALIPER

BRAKE PAD CARRIER

BRAKE PADS

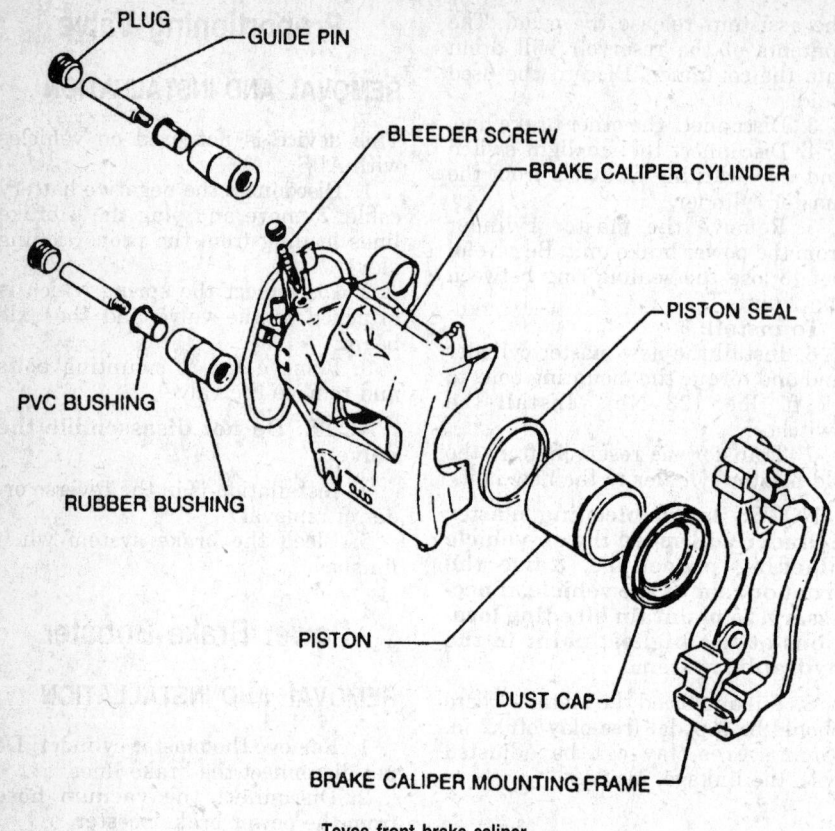

Teves front brake caliper

center C-clamp on pad and caliper to avoid cracking or jamming the pistons in their bores.

7. Install brake pads, shims and heatshield, if equipped. Install brake line.

8. Slide caliper over rotor and align pins. Make sure caliper moves freely on the pins.

9. Install guide pins and torque to 26 ft. lbs. (35 Nm).

10. Connect the wear indicator and install wheels.

11. Lower vehicle and fill master cylinder. Bleed brake system.

INTERNAL CALIPER

This type of brake system, used on the V8 Quattro, has the caliper mounted in the inside the rotor. The rotor is mounted with an external hat.

1. Raise and safely support the vehicle. Remove the wheels.

2. Press and unhook the brake pad retention spring to release the pads.

3. Press the piston back into its bore by pushing on the caliper housing. Once the piston is bottomed, push the entire housing towards the center of the vehicle to gain access for removal of the inside pad. Remove the pad.

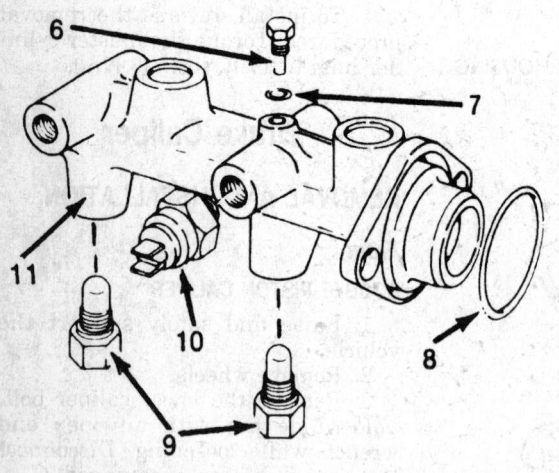

1. Reservoir Cap
2. Washer
3. Filter screen
4. Reservoir
5. Master cylinder plugs
6. Stop screw
7. Stop screw seal
8. Master cylinder seal
9. Residual pressure valves
10. Warning light sender unit
11. Brake master cylinder housing

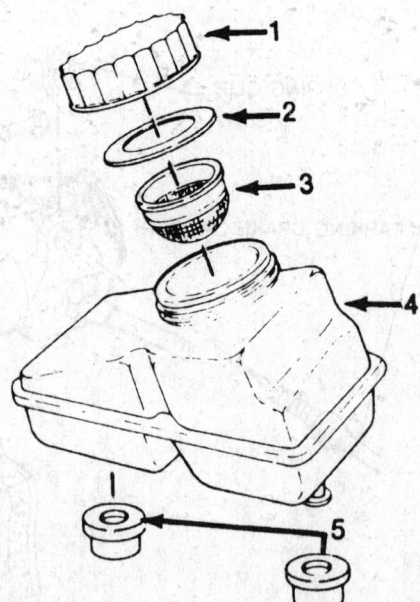

Master cylinder assembly

4. Remove the retaining bolt for the rotor. Remove the rotor by turning the rotor on an angle.

5. Disconnect the brake hose.

6. Remove the brake caliper from the wheel bearing housing. Brake caliper cannot be repaired, replace if necessary.

To install:

7. Install the brake caliper to the wheel bearing housing. Torque the retaining bolts to 92 ft. lbs. (125 Nm).

8. Install the brake hose.

9. Replace the rotor and torque the retaining or locating bolt to 44 inch lbs. (5 Nm). Install the inside pad and retaining spring.

10. Bleed the brakes.

11. Mount the wheels and depress the brake pedal to seat the pads before road test. Check brake fluid.

GIRLING CALIPER

1. Raise and safely support the vehicle.

2. Remove wheels.

3. Remove the lower caliper bolt, hold guide pin with open end wrench, while loosening. Disconnect the wear indicator, if equipped.

4. Swing brake caliper up and remove brake pads, taking note of spacer shims and heat-shield locations, if equipped. Remove brake line.

5. Remove the caliper.

To install:

6. Push piston back into caliper, using a C-clamp in bore of piston. Make certain to center C-clamp on piston and caliper to avoid cracking or jamming the piston in the bore.

7. Install brake pads, shims and heatshield, if equipped. Reconnect brake line.

8. Slide caliper over rotor and align pins.

9. Install guide pins and torque to 25 ft. lbs. (35 Nm).

10. Fill master cylinder and bleed brake system.

TEVES CALIPER

1. Raise and safely support the vehicle.

2. Remove wheels.

3. Remove guide pin caps and guide pins.

4. Remove brake hose retaining clip or bracket. Disconnect brake line.

5. Swing caliper up and remove. Remove brake pads, taking note of spacer shims and heat-shield locations. Disconnect the wear indicator, if equipped.

To install:

6. Installation is the reverse of the removal process. Push piston back into caliper, using a C-clamp in bore of piston. Make certain to center C-

clamp on piston and caliper to avoid cracking or jamming the piston in the bore.

7. Install brake pads, shims and heatshield, if equipped.

8. Slide caliper over rotor and align pins. Install guide pins and torque to 18 ft. lbs. (25 Nm).

9. Install brake hose and clip. Fill the master cylinder and bleed the brake system.

REAR

GIRLING CALIPER

1. Raise and safely support the vehicle.

2. Remove wheels.

3. Remove rear brake caliper housing, hold guide pin with open end wrench while loosening bolts. Disconnect the wear indicator, if equipped.

4. Remove brake pads, taking note of spacer shims and heat-shield locations. Disconnect brake line.

To install:

5. Screw piston into housing by turning it clockwise with a socket head wrench while pushing in firmly.

6. Install brake pads, shims and heatshield, if equipped.

7. Install brake line. Install caliper on housing. Install new bolts and torque to 25 ft. lbs. (35 Nm).

NOTE: The bolts are self-locking type; it is recommended to always use new bolts.

8. Make certain parking brake is free of tension.

9. Use a prybar to push caliper lever against stop on both sides of vehicle.

10. Parking brake is too tight if the lever of the opposite side caliper is pulled away from the stop.

11. Loosen parking brake adjusting nut and position, as necessary.

12. Push a tool of at least ¼ in. (6mm) diameter between rear hook of spring and roller.

13. Pump brake pedal slowly with moderate force about 40 times, with the engine OFF.

14. Check that both wheels rotate freely.

15. Remove spacer tool.

16. Install wheels. Lower vehicle and fill master cylinder. Bleed brake system.

TEVES CALIPER

1. Raise and safely support the vehicle.

2. Remove rear wheels.

3. Remove both protective caps. Loosen both guide pins but do not pull out of the rubber boots.

4. Pull caliper housing toward the outside of vehicle by hand. Disconnect brake line.

5. Swing the caliper housing to the rear and remove. Disconnect the wear indicator, if equipped.

6. Remove brake pads, taking note of spacer shims and heat-shield locations.

To install:

7. Push piston back into caliper, using a C-clamp in bore of piston. Make certain to center C-clamp on piston and caliper to avoid cracking or jamming the piston in the bore.

8. Install brake pads, shims and heatshield, if equipped.

9. Slide caliper over rotor and align pins. Install guide pins and torque to 18 ft. lbs. (25 Nm). Install the protective caps. Reconnect brake line.

10. Make certain parking brake is free of tension.

11. Use a prybar to push caliper lever against stop on both sides of vehicle.

12. Parking brake is too tight, if lever of opposite side caliper is pulled away from the stop.

13. Loosen parking brake adjusting nut and position, as necessary.

14. Push a tool of at least ¼ in. (6mm) diameter between rear hook of spring and roller.

15. Pump brake pedal slowly with moderate force about 40 times, with the engine OFF.

16. Check that both wheels rotate freely.

17. Remove the spacer tool.

18. Install wheels. Lower vehicle and fill master cylinder. Bleed brake system.

Disc Brake Pads

REMOVAL AND INSTALLATION

Front

DOUBLE PISTON CALIPER

1. Siphon a sufficient quantity of brake fluid from the master cylinder reservoir to prevent the brake fluid from overflowing the master cylinder when installing pads.

2. Raise and safely support the vehicle.

3. Remove wheels.

NOTE: Change the pads on 1 side at a time and use other side for reference. Do not disconnect the brake hoses, unless the caliper is to be serviced.

4. Remove the lower caliper bolt, hold guide pin with open end wrench,

while loosening. Disconnect the wear indicator, if equipped.

5. Swing brake caliper up and remove brake pads, taking note of spacer shims and heat-shield locations, if equipped.

6. Push pistons back into caliper. Place old disc pad on piston side of caliper, using a C-clamp centered on old pad across both piston, push pistons back into bore. Make certain to center C-clamp on pad and caliper to avoid cracking or jamming the pistons in their bores.

To install:

7. Install brake pads, shims and heatshield, if equipped.

8. Slide caliper over rotor and align pins.

9. Install guide pins and torque to 26 ft. lbs. (35 Nm).

10. Connect the wear indicator and install wheels.

11. Lower the vehicle and fill master cylinder.

12. Pump the brake pedal slowly several time to force pads against the rotors.

13. Check master cylinder level again and add new fluid, if needed.

INTERNAL CALIPER

This type of brake system, used on the V8 Quattro, has the caliper mounted in the rotor. The rotor is mounted with an external hat. This is a unique system, but poses no real difficulties in servicing.

1. Raise and safely support the vehicle. Remove the wheels.

2. Press and unhook the brake pad retention spring to release the pads.

3. Press the piston back into its bore by pushing on the caliper housing. Once the piston is bottomed, push the entire housing towards the center of the vehicle to gain access for removal of the inside pad. Remove the pad.

4. Remove the retaining bolt for the rotor. Remove the rotor by turning the rotor on an angle.

5. Remove the brake wear sensor wire from the holder. Remove the outer pad and wear sensor.

To install:

6. Install the outer pad and wear sensor. Clip the sensor wire into the holder.

7. Replace the rotor and torque the retaining bolt to 44 inch lbs. (5 Nm). Install the inside pad and retaining spring.

8. Mount the wheels and depress the brake pedal to seat the pads.

GIRLING CALIPER

1. Siphon a sufficient quantity of brake fluid from the master cylinder

reservoir to prevent the brake fluid from overflowing the master cylinder when installing pads.

2. Raise and safely support the vehicle.

3. Remove wheels.

NOTE: Change the pads on 1 side at a time and use other side for reference. Do not disconnect the brake hoses, unless the caliper is to be serviced.

4. Remove the lower caliper bolt, hold guide pin with open end wrench, while loosening. Disconnect the wear indicator, if equipped.

5. Swing brake caliper up and remove brake pads, taking note of spacer shims and heat-shield locations, if equipped.

6. Push piston back into caliper, using a C-clamp in bore of piston. Make certain to center C-clamp on piston and caliper to avoid cracking or jamming the piston in the bore.

To install:

7. Install brake pads, shims and heatshield, if equipped.

8. Slide caliper over rotor and align pins.

9. Install guide pins and torque to 25 ft. lbs. (35 Nm).

10. Install wheels.

11. Lower vehicle and fill master cylinder.

12. Pump the brake pedal slowly several time to force pads against the rotors.

13. Check master cylinder level again and add new fluid, if needed.

TEVES CALIPER

1. Siphon a sufficient quantity of brake fluid from the master cylinder reservoir to prevent the brake fluid from overflowing the master cylinder when installing pads.

2. Raise and safely support the vehicle.

3. Remove wheels.

NOTE: Change the pads on 1 side at a time and use other side for reference. Do not disconnect the brake hoses, unless the caliper is to be serviced.

4. Remove guide pin caps.

5. Remove guide pins.

6. Remove brake hose retaining clip or bracket.

7. Swing caliper up and secure in position, using a wire. Do not allow caliper to hang from brake hose.

8. Remove brake pads, taking note of spacer shims and heat-shield locations. Disconnect the wear indicator, if equipped.

9. Push piston back into caliper, using a C-clamp in bore of piston.

Make certain to center C-clamp on piston and caliper to avoid cracking or jamming the piston in the bore.

To install:

10. Install brake pads, shims and heatshield, if equipped.

11. Slide caliper over rotor and align pins.

12. Install guide pins and torque to 18 ft. lbs. (25 Nm).

13. Install brake hose clip.

14. Install wheels.

15. Lower vehicle and fill master cylinder.

16. Pump the brake pedal slowly several time to force pads against the rotors.

17. Check master cylinder level again and add new fluid if needed.

Rear

GIRLING CALIPER

1. Siphon a sufficient quantity of brake fluid from the master cylinder reservoir to prevent the brake fluid from overflowing the master cylinder when installing pads.

2. Raise and safely support the vehicle.

3. Remove wheels.

NOTE: Change the pads on 1 side at a time and use other side for reference. Do not disconnect the brake hoses, unless the caliper is to be serviced.

4. Remove brake caliper housing, hold guide pin with open end wrench while loosening bolts. Disconnect the wear indicator, if equipped.

5. Remove brake pads, taking note of spacer shims and heat-shield locations.

6. Screw piston into housing by turning it clockwise with a socket head wrench while pushing in firmly.

To install:

7. Install brake pads, shims and heatshield, if equipped.

8. Install caliper on housing.

NOTE: The bolts are self-locking type; it is recommended to always use new bolts.

9. Install new bolts and torque to 25 ft. lbs. (35 Nm).

10. Make certain parking brake is free of tension.

11. Use a prybar to push caliper lever against stop on both sides of vehicle.

12. Parking brake is too tight if lever of opposite side caliper is pulled away from the stop.

13. Loosen parking brake adjusting nut and position, as necessary.

14. Push a tool of at least ¼ in. (6mm) diameter between rear hook of spring and roller.

15. Pump brake pedal slowly with moderate force about 40 times, with the engine OFF.

16. Check that both wheels rotate freely.

17. Remove the spacer tool.

18. Install wheels.

19. Lower vehicle and fill master cylinder.

TEVES CALIPER

1. Siphon a sufficient quantity of brake fluid from the master cylinder reservoir to prevent the brake fluid from overflowing the master cylinder when installing pads.

2. Raise and safely support the vehicle.

3. Remove wheels.

NOTE: Change the pads on 1 side at a time and use other side for reference. Do not disconnect the brake hoses, unless the caliper is to be serviced.

4. Remove both protective caps.

5. Loosen both guide pins but do not pull out of the rubber boots.

6. Pull caliper housing toward the outside of vehicle by hand.

7. Swing the caliper housing to the rear and remove. Do not allow caliper to hang from brake hose. Disconnect the wear indicator, if equipped.

8. Remove brake pads, taking note of spacer shims and heat-shield locations.

9. Push piston back into caliper, using a C-clamp in bore of piston. Make certain to center C-clamp on piston and caliper to avoid cracking or jamming the piston in the bore.

To install:

10. Install brake pads, shims and heatshield, if equipped.

11. Slide caliper over rotor and align pins.

12. Install guide pins and torque to 18 ft. lbs. (25 Nm).

13. Install the protective caps.

14. Make certain parking brake is free of tension.

15. Use a prybar to push caliper lever against stop on both sides of vehicle.

16. Parking brake is too tight if lever of opposite side caliper is pulled away from the stop.

17. Loosen parking brake adjusting nut and position, as necessary.

18. Push a tool of at least ¼ in. (6mm) diameter between rear hook of spring and roller.

19. Pump brake pedal slowly with moderate force about 40 times, with the engine OFF.

20. Check that both wheels rotate freely.

21. Remove the spacer tool.

22. Install wheels. Refill master cylinder.

Brake Rotor

REMOVAL AND INSTALLATION

Except Internal Caliper Type

1. Raise and safely support vehicle.

2. Remove wheels.

3. Remove brake caliper.

4. Remove disc rotor.

5. When replacing rotors, always replace in pairs. If machining, watch wear limit. Always machine both sides, never one side only.

Internal Caliper Type

1. Raise and safely support vehicle.

2. Remove wheels.

3. Press and unhook the brake pad retention spring to release the pads.

4. Press the piston back into its bore by pushing on the caliper housing. Once the piston is bottomed, push the entire housing towards the center of the vehicle to gain access for removal of the inside pad. Remove the pad.

5. Remove the retaining bolt for the rotor. Remove the rotor by turning the rotor on an angle.

To install:

6. Replace the rotor and torque the retaining or locating bolt to 44 inch lbs. (5 Nm). Install the inside pad and retaining spring.

7. Mount the wheels and depress the brake pedal to seat the pads before road test. Check brake fluid.

Brake System Bleeding

To bleed the system, use a bottle with transparent hose attached so brake fluid can be checked for air bubbles. Do not re-use fluid removed from reservoir.

1. Raise and safely support vehicle. Start the engine.

2. Connect bleeder hose and bleed calipers. Have an assistant press the pedal. When in the down position, open the bleeder screw. Close the bleeder screw and press the pedal again. Open the bleeder screw and again allow the air to come out. Repeat at each wheel until the fluid in the container shows no sign of air bubbles.

3. Bleed in the following sequence:
a. Right rear caliper
b. Left rear caliper
c. Right front caliper
d. Left front caliper

4. After bleeding, refill brake fluid reservoir.

Anti-Lock Brake System Service

PRECAUTIONS

The following precautions should be observed when working on the Anti-lock Brake System (ABS).

• Electrical testing should be done using the factory LED tester. This tester must be used to check the hydraulic modulator, ABS control unit, wheel speed sensors and ABS wiring harness. It is also necessary to perform the test procedure if the brake lines or brake pressure regulators are replaced because of accident damage.

• Switch the ignition OFF before connecting or disconnecting the ABS control unit connector.

• Disconnect the ABS control unit connector before using electrical welding equipment on the vehicle.

• Disconnect the battery connections before charging the battery or replacing the hydraulic modulator.

• Remove the ABS control unit before drying paint repairs in an oven if the temperature will be more than 185°F. for more than 2 hours.

• Do not use mini-spare tires on vehicles equipped with ABS. Use wheels and tires of matching size on ABS equipped vehicles.

• Do not drive the vehicle with the anti-lock brake tester connected.

• Do not fabricate brake lines. Use only original equipment parts. Brake line flare nuts are to be tightened to 11 ft. lbs. (15 Nm).

• Do not repair the hydraulic modulator except when replacing relays. If the hydraulic modulator is defective, it must be replaced.

RELIEVING ANTI-LOCK BRAKE SYSTEM PRESSURE

A special factory tool is recommended for ABS system bleed-down. It is a set of high and low pressure gauges that is also used for system pressure testing. It is used as follows:

1. Raise and safely support vehicle. Remove one front wheel.

2. Make sure the ignition switch is **OFF**. Remove the bleeder screw from the caliper.

3. Connect the special tool and install a brake pedal depressor between the brake pedal and the driver's seat.

4. Press the brake pedal until the pressure gauge drops down indicating system pressure has been relieved.

SYSTEM TEST

The operational ABS system test must be performed after every repair to the service brake components. These repairs include replacement of linings and/or discs, hoses, booster or master cylinder, cables and parking brake components.

This short test insures that nothing within the ABS components was disturbed during the repair. To perform the test:

1. Turn the ignition switch **ON**; the ABS warning lamp should light.

2. Start the engine; the warning lamp should turn OFF.

3. While the engine is running, switch the ABS **OFF**; the warning lamp(s) should come ON.

4. Turn the ignition switch **OFF** and restart it; the ABS warning lamp should go out, showing that the manual switch position has been overridden and the system reset.

5. Drive the vehicle over 20 mph (30 kph); the ABS warning lamp should not come ON. The differential locks on Quattro vehicles must not be engaged during this test.

6. In a safe location and under controlled conditions, perform at least one test stop from about 20 mph which engages the anti-lock system. Check system function and vehicle stability.

Hydraulic Modulator

REMOVAL AND INSTALLATION

1. Disconnect negative battery cable.

2. Bleed down system pressure.

3. Remove the modulator cover.

4. Remove the harness retainer.

5. Disconnect the hydraulic modulator from the mounting.

6. Unclip the hydraulic fluid reservoir from the mounting.

7. Unscrew the brake lines. Mark the lines so they will be reinstalled in their proper locations. Seal any openings immediately with plugs.

To install:

8. Connect the hydraulic lines to the modulator but do not tighten them yet.

9. Install the modulator, then tighten the lines. Install the reservoir and connect the wiring.

10. Refill with DOT 4 brake fluid only. Bleed and test the system.

Wheel Speed Sensors

REMOVAL AND INSTALLATION

Front

The front wheel speed sensor is hand-pressed into the wheel bearing housing, also called a steering knuckle. A sleeve is inserted into a hole in the housing which retains the speed sensor.

1. Raise and safely support vehicle.

2. Remove wheel and tire assembly.

3. Locate the sensor in the side of the housing and pull out. Left and right are identical.

4. To disconnect the wiring, remove the engine lower cover.

5. Unclip the connector from its mount and disconnect sensor.

To install:

6. Installation is the reverse of the removal procedure. Before inserting the retainer sleeve, the opening in the wheel bearing housing should be greased.

7. Press the sleeve in as far as possible.

8. Push the sensor in to stop by hand.

Rear

The rear wheel speed sensor is hand pressed into the rear wheel bearing housing. A sleeve is inserted into a hole in the front side of the housing which retains the speed sensor.

1. Raise and safely support vehicle.

2. Remove wheel and tire assembly.

3. Locate the sensor in the front side of the rear wheel bearing housing and pull out. Left and right are identical. Unclip the connector and remove sensor.

To install:

4. Installation is the reverse of the removal process. Before inserting the retainer sleeve, the opening in the rear wheel bearing housing should be greased.

5. Press the sleeve in as far as possible.

6. Push the sensor in to stop by hand.

Acceleration Switch

REMOVAL AND INSTALLATION

4WD Vehicles

The ABS acceleration switch is located under the left rear seat bench. It is a mercury switch activated during deceleration. When braking with ABS the switch helps the braking system provide additional stabilization during braking.

1. Switch the ignition **OFF**.

2. Remove the mounting screws.

3. Disconnect the wiring.

4. At installation, note that the arrow on the cover must point forward, in the direction of driving.

Electronic Control Unit

REMOVAL AND INSTALLATION

The ABS electronic control unit is located under the left side of the rear passenger seat.

1. Switch ignition **OFF**.

2. Raise rear seat and locate ABS control unit. Remove hold-down nuts.

3. The ABS control unit plug has locks to secure it. Disconnect by pressing the spring on the narrow end of the plug. To connect, insert the lug of the connector into the adapter and push the connector against the spring. The connector should snap into the lock with a click.

4. Installation is the reverse of the removal process.

CHASSIS ELECTRICAL

─── **CAUTION** ───

On vehicles equipped with an air bag, the negative battery cable and reserve power supply must both be disconnected before working on the system. Failure to do so may result in deployment of the air bag and possible personal injury. Never disconnect any electrical connector with the ignition switch turned ON or damage to electronic controlling devices could occur.

NOTE: All vehicles are equipped with theft protected radios, which cannot be operated if power to the radio is interrupted. Before disconnecting the battery cables, obtain the security code.

Air Bag

DISARMING

1. Disconnect the battery and the red air bag power supply connector. This connector is labeled "Air bag". On 80 and 90, the connector is behind a panel under the driver side dashboard. On all other models, the connector is at the front of the center console.

2. Remove the screws for the upper steering column trim and remove the upper trim.

3. Separate the connector for the air bag spiral spring.

4. If required, a memory saver can now be safely used to preserve the radio code while the battery is disconnected.

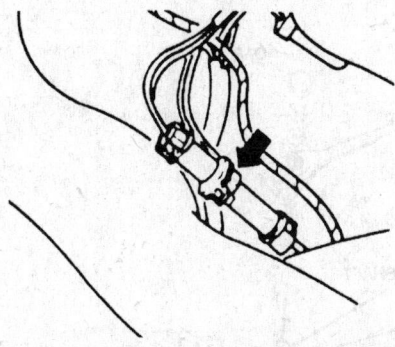

Power supply connector must be disconnected first

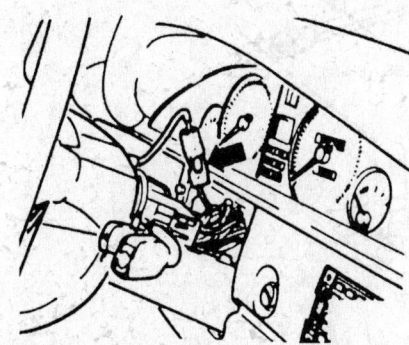

The air bag can be disconnected at the steering column

Heater Blower Motor

REMOVAL AND INSTALLATION

Coupe, 80 and 90

1. The blower is removed from under the hood. Disconnect the negative battery cable.

2. Remove the air plenum from the cowl.

3. Remove the ballast resistor.

4. At the blower motor, disconnect the electrical connector.

5. Remove the blower mounting bolts and the blower from the heater assembly.

6. To install, reverse the removal procedures.

100, S4 and 200

NOTE: Blower or core removal requires removal and disassembly of the heater/air conditioning unit.

1. Disconnect the negative battery cable.

2. Drain the cooling system.

NOTE: If equipped with air conditioning, the system must be discharged.

3. Properly discharge the air conditioning system.

4. Disconnect the following components:
   a. Temperature sensor connector
   b. Evaporator/heater connector clamp
   c. Temperature control cable
   d. Fresh air door vacuum hose

5. Disconnect the main harness connector.

6. Loosen the case retaining strap.

7. Remove the coolant hoses at the heater core tubes.

8. Label and remove the yellow, green and red vacuum hoses from the heater case.

9. Remove the air duct hoses.

10. Remove the heater case mounting screws, 2 in the passenger compartment, 1 in the engine compartment. Remove the 4 evaporator housing mounting screws in the passenger compartment.

11. Support the heater/evaporator unit and pull it away from the firewall.

12. Remove the control cable grommet to facilitate case removal.

13. The case halves may be separated by removing the clips at the top and bottom with a small prybar.

14. Remove the blower motor and the heater core from the unit.

To install:

15. Install the blower motor and heater core into the case. Make sure the case gasket is in good condition and assemble the case. Install the clips.

16. Position the case at the firewall, install the control cable grommet and secure the case in place with the screws.

17. Attach the ducts, wires, control cable, vacuum lines and coolant hoses.

18. Refill the cooling system and leak test. Recharge and leak test the air conditioner.

CAUTION

Refrigerant will freeze any surface it contacts, including skin and eyes. It also turns into a poisonous gas in the presence of an open flame. Wear eye protection and suitable gloves when working on or around the air conditioning system.

V8 Quattro

1. Disconnect the negative battery cable.

2. Matchmark hood hinges and remove hood.

3. Remove the windshield wiper assembly.

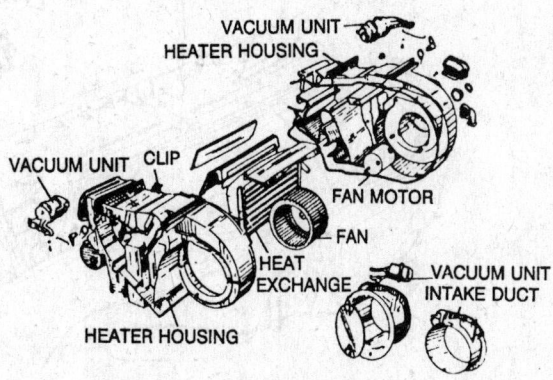

Heater assembly with blower motor

4. Remove the cap from the engine coolant overflow bottle.

5. Remove the heater retaining band.

6. Label and remove the vacuum hoses from the vacuum servo motors.

7. Clamp off the heater hoses to the heater core and remove the hoses.

8. Remove the retainers between the body and heater. Remove the heater box.

9. After removing the heater box, remove the blower cooling hose.

10. Remove the lockring, stop washer and grommet. Remove the blower from the housing.

To install:

11. Before installing the fresh air blower guides, lubricate with petroleum jelly. Install the blower motor using the black electrical connection area only.

12. Install the heater unit into the vehicle and connect the vacuum and coolant hoses. When connecting the water hoses, the lower connection on the heater core is connected to the hose going to the water pump.

13. Run the engine and check for leaks before completing the assembly.

Windshield Wiper Motor

REMOVAL AND INSTALLATION

1. Disconnect the negative battery cable and disconnect the wiring harness connector at the motor. Remove the wiper arm retaining nut. Pry off the wiper arms and remove the nuts from the studs in the cowl.

2. Remove the brace-to-body screws. While holding the crank, remove the nut securing the crank to the wiper motor and remove the crank.

3. Remove the bolts securing the wiper motor to the support and remove the motor.

4. Connect the new motor to the wiring harness, run the motor 2 revolutions and turn the wiper switch to the OFF position. The wiper motor should stop in the park position.

5. To install, reverse the removal procedures. Make sure the crank is installed in the proper position.

Instrument Cluster

——— CAUTION ———
On vehicles equipped with an air bag, the negative battery cable and reserve power supply must both be disconnected before working on the system. Failure to do so may result in deployment of the air bag and possible personal injury. Never disconnect any electrical connector with the ignition switch turned ON or damage to electronic controlling devices could occur.*

REMOVAL AND INSTALLATION

1. Disconnect the negative battery cable. Remove the steering wheel. On V8 Quattro vehicles, the instrument cluster is removed after first removing the instrument panel cover. The screws are under the speaker covers and behind the air conditioning outlets.

2. Loosen the clamp on the steering column switch.

3. Pull forward and remove electrical connector.

4. Remove steering column switches.

5. Tilt instrument cluster back and remove the connector retainers.

6. Remove the electrical connectors.

7. Remove the retaining screws for the instrument cluster and remove the instrument cluster.

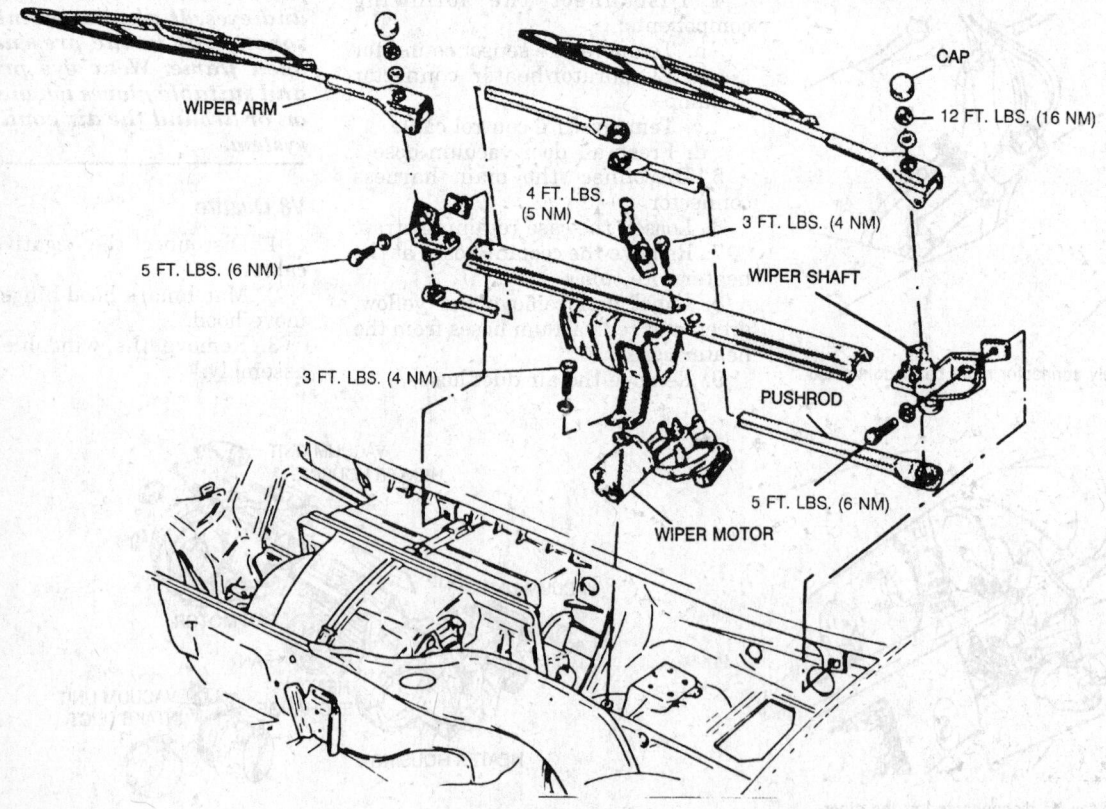

Wiper system assembly

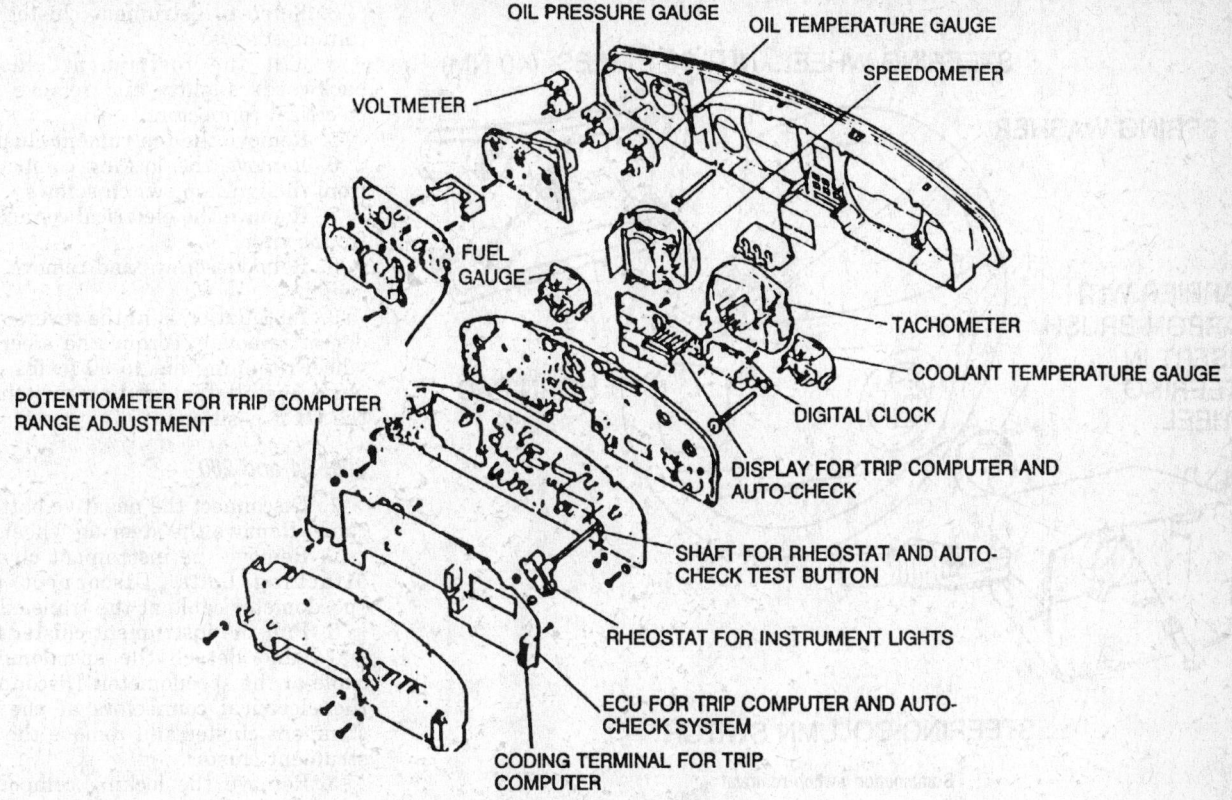

Instrument cluster assembly

8. Installation is in the reverse order of removal. Torque the steering wheel retaining nut to 30 ft. lbs. (40 Nm). Check all systems for proper operation.

Headlight Switch

REMOVAL AND INSTALLATION

Instrument Panel Mounted Type

1. Remove the instrument cluster cover.
2. Disconnect the wiring harness connector from the headlight switch.
3. Depress the clips on the headlight switch retainer and remove the switch from the instrument cluster.
4. Installation is the reverse order of the removal procedure. Check for proper operation.

NOTE: On some vehicles the headlight switch could be incorporated with the combination switch. This switch can contain the headlight switch, parking light switch, turn signal switch, low/high beam switch, headlight flasher switch and cruise control switch.

Combination Switch

CAUTION

On vehicles equipped with an air bag, the negative battery cable and reserve power supply must both be disconnected before working on the system. Failure to do so may result in deployment of the air bag and possible personal injury. Never disconnect any electrical connector with the ignition switch turned ON or damage to electronic controlling devices could occur.

REMOVAL AND INSTALLATION

The windshield wiper switch is incorporated with the combination switch, which includes the turn signal switch and dimmer switch, located on the steering column. On some vehicles, if the wiper switch has to be replaced, the combination switch must be replaced.

80 and 90

1. Disconnect the negative battery cable. Pull off the horn pad and remove the steering wheel.

2. Remove the steering column cover. Remove the 3 screws on the turn signal switch.
3. Pull the turn signal switch and the wiper switch from the column.
4. Installation is the reverse order of the removal procedure.

100, S4 and 200

1. Disconnect the negative battery cable. Remove the steering wheel.
2. Insert a tool into the slot at the bottom of the steering column cover and loosen the screw(s).
3. Pull the switch and the top of the cover assembly off the steering column. Remove the 2 screws inside the cover to remove the wiper switch from the cover.
4. Installation is the reverse order of the removal procedure. Torque the steering wheel retaining nut to 30 ft. lbs. (40 Nm).

V8 Quattro

The windshield wiper/washer switch, hazard flasher switch, intensive washer system switch, headlight wiper/washer switch and on-board computer function switch are built

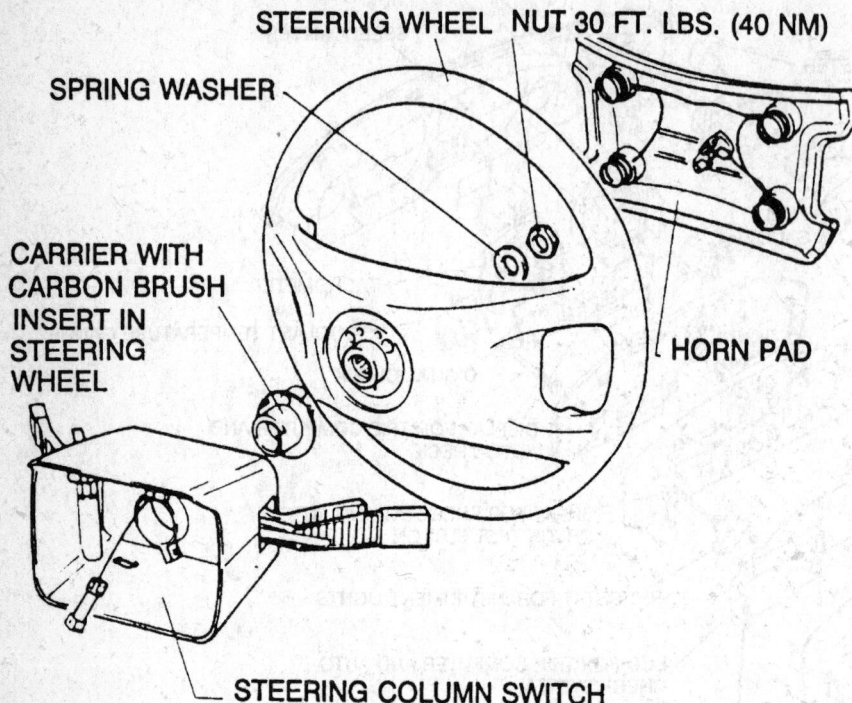

STEERING WHEEL NUT 30 FT. LBS. (40 NM)

SPRING WASHER

CARRIER WITH CARBON BRUSH INSERT IN STEERING WHEEL

HORN PAD

STEERING COLUMN SWITCH

Combination switch removal

into one steering column mounted combination switch.

1. Disconnect the negative battery cable.

NOTE: Most vehicles are equipped with theft protected radios, which cannot be operated if power to the radio is interrupted. Before disconnecting the battery cables, obtain the security code.

2. Remove the air bag unit or horn bar by removing the Torx® screws from behind the steering wheel.

3. Tilt the air bag unit down to remove the air bag connector retaining strap and remove the air bag assembly. Place the air bag assembly face up where it will not be disturbed.

4. Remove the upper steering column trim retaining screws and remove the trim.

5. Remove the air bag unit connector at top of column.

6. Make sure the front wheels are straight ahead and remove the steering wheel.

7. Loosen the steering column switch clamp and remove the steering column switches.

To install:

8. Install the switch and connect the wiring.

9. Install the steering wheel and the air bag connector assembly. Torque the steering wheel retaining nut to 30 ft. lbs. (40 Nm).

10. Install the air bag unit. Make sure no one is in the vehicle when power is connected to the unit.

Ignition Lock/Switch

CAUTION

On vehicles equipped with an air bag, the negative battery cable and reserve power supply must both be disconnected before working on the system. Failure to do so may result in deployment of the air bag and possible personal injury. Never disconnect any electrical connector with the ignition switch turned ON or damage to electronic controlling devices could occur.

REMOVAL AND INSTALLATION

80 and 90

1. Disconnect the negative battery cable.

2. Remove the steering wheel, the steering column covers and the steering column combination switches.

3. Remove instrument cluster retaining screws.

4. Tilt the instrument cluster backwards slightly and remove the electrical connectors.

5. Remove the instrument cluster.

6. Remove the locking compound from the ignition switch screws.

7. Remove the electrical connector from switch.

8. Remove screws and remove the switch.

9. Installation is in the reverse order of removal. Torque the steering wheel retaining nut to 30 ft. lbs. (40 Nm). Install the ignition switch in the **OFF** position.

100, S4 and 200

1. Disconnect the negative battery cable. Remove the steering wheel.

2. Remove the instrument cluster attaching bolts. Disconnect the speedometer cable at the transaxle.

3. Pull the instrument cluster forward and detach the speedometer cable at the speedometer. Disconnect the electrical connectors at the instrument cluster and remove the instrument cluster.

4. Remove the locking compound around the ignition switch and remove the switch. To remove the ignition lock cylinder use the following procedure.

   a. Support the steering column and drill out the 2 shear bolts using a ⅛ in. drill bit.

   b. Loosen the steering column bolts. Remove the left lower dash panel and the left air deflector.

   c. Slide the steering column tube with the steering column downward and remove the steering lock from the steering column clamp. Drill a hole in the center of the locking housing using a ⅛ in. drill bit.

   d. Push the retaining spring in with a suitable punch and remove the lock cylinder.

5. Installation is the reverse order of the removal procedure. Replace the locking compound and torque the steering wheel retaining nut to 30 ft. lbs. (40 Nm).

V8 Quattro

1. Disconnect the negative battery cable.

2. Remove the left and right air bag Torx® bolts from behind the steering wheel.

3. Tilt the air bag unit backward and lift the safety clamp. Disconnect the wiring from the air bag unit.

4. Remove the steering column trim top section.

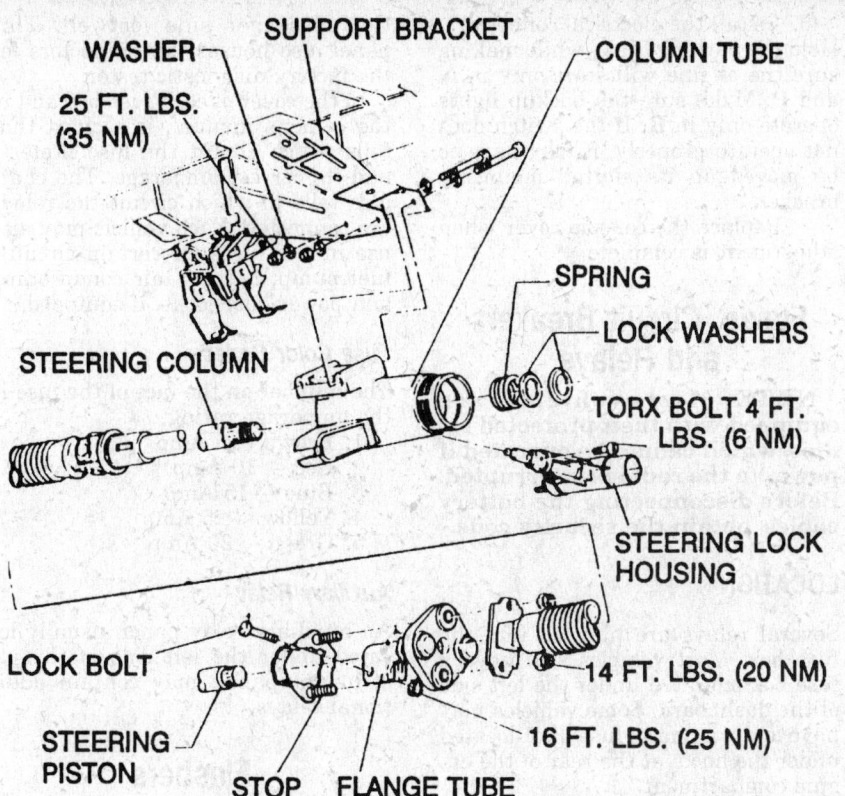

WASHER — SUPPORT BRACKET — COLUMN TUBE
25 FT. LBS. (35 NM)
STEERING COLUMN
SPRING
LOCK WASHERS
TORX BOLT 4 FT. LBS. (6 NM)
STEERING LOCK HOUSING
LOCK BOLT
14 FT. LBS. (20 NM)
STEERING PISTON
16 FT. LBS. (25 NM)
STOP   FLANGE TUBE

Steering column and lock assembly — 80 and 90 shown

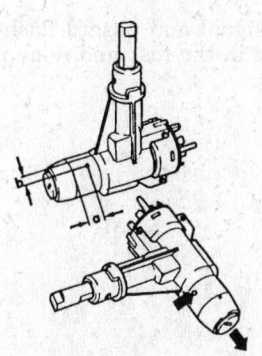

Drill lock housing to remove key cylinder: a=.5 in., b=0.125 in.

5. Separate the air bag connector.
6. Remove the steering wheel.
7. Loosen the steering column switch clamp and remove the column combination switches.
8. Remove the instrument cluster and trim under the left side of the instrument panel.
9. Remove the electrical connector from the ignition switch.
10. Remove the locking compound from the switch mounting screws, loosen the screws slightly and pull the ignition switch assembly from the

housing. To remove the ignition lock cylinder:

   a. Remove the glovebox.
   b. Remove instrument panel crossmember.
   c. Remove lock housing Torx® screw and remove steering lock housing.
   d. Drill one hole, approx. 1/8 in. (3mm) diameter in steering lock housing only 0.080 in. (2mm) deep, 0.50 in. (12.5mm) from the key end. Do not drill too deeply or the lock cylinder will be damaged.
   e. Remove the lock cylinder by pushing in on the retaining spring.
To install:
11. Install the lock cylinder, by pushing the cylinder into the steering lock housing until the retaining spring engages.
12. After installing the ignition switch, apply locking compound to switch mounting screws.
13. Install the glovebox.
14. Install the instrument panel crossmember.
15. Connect the ignition switch wiring and install the instrument cluster.
16. Install the steering column switches and connect all wiring.

17. Install the steering wheel. Torque the steering wheel retaining nut to 30 ft. lbs. (40 Nm).
18. Install the air bag module.
19. Check key switch for proper operation.

Stoplight Switch

REMOVAL AND INSTALLATION

1. Disconnect the negative battery cable.
2. Disconnect the stoplight switch wire connector from the switch.
3. If the stoplight switch is located behind the brake pedal, remove the hairpin retainer and outer nylon washer from the pedal pin. Slide the stoplight switch off the brake pedal pin just far enough for the outer side plate of the switch to clear the pin. Remove the switch. Quattro V8 vehicles will have 2 switches on the brake pedal. The stoplight switch is the top switch. It presses into clips on the pedal bracket.
4. If the stoplight switch is located in the master cylinder, use a suitable wrench and remove the switch from the master cylinder.
5. Installation is the reverse order of the removal procedure. If the switch was located in the master cylinder torque to 14 ft. lbs. (20 Nm), be sure to top off the master cylinder reservoir and bleed the brake circuit.

Neutral Safety Switch

The neutral safety switch prevents the engine from being started with the transaxle in any position other than **P** or **N**. It also activates the backup lights. The switch is at the base of the shift lever, inside the floorshift console except on the V8 Quattro.

On the V8 Quattro, a multi-function switch on the transaxle tells the transaxle ECU which selector lever position has been selected by the driver. It also energizes the backup light relay and sends a signal to the Automatic Shift Lock (ASL) control unit. This prevents the selector lever from being moved from the **P** or **N** positions unless the driver first steps on the foot brake.

ADJUSTMENT

1. Remove the 4 screws which hold the console to the floor.
2. Shift into **N**. Remove the 2 screws which hold the shift position

indicator plate to the console. Remove the shift knob and the console.

3. Disconnect the red/black electrical leads from the switch.

4. Loosen both switch retaining screws.

5. Using an ohmmeter, adjust the switch so the neutral safety switch contacts are together.

6. Install the electrical connectors. Hold the parking brake while making sure the engine will start only in **N** and **P**. Make sure the backup lights operate only in **R**. If the switch does not operate properly, it may have to be moved on its slotted mounting bracket.

7. Replace the console cover when adjustment is complete.

REMOVAL AND INSTALLATION

1. Remove the 4 screws which hold the console to the floor.

2. Shift into **N**. Remove the 2 screws which hold the shift position indicator plate to the console. Remove the shift knob and the console.

3. Disconnect the switch electrical leads.

4. Remove the 2 switch retaining screws. Remove the switch.

5. Install the new switch so the neutral safety switch contacts are together.

6. Install the electrical connectors. Hold the parking brake while making sure the engine will start only in **N** and **P**. Make sure the backup lights operate only in **R**. If the switch does not operate properly, it may have to be moved on its slotted mounting bracket.

7. Replace the console cover when adjustment is complete.

Fuses, Circuit Breakers and Relays

NOTE: Most vehicles are equipped with theft protected radios, which cannot be operated if power to the radio is interrupted. Before disconnecting the battery cables, obtain the security code.

LOCATION

Several relays are plugged into the fuse box. Most vehicles still have a fuse box mounted under the left side of the dashboard. Some vehicles may have only a main fuse box located under the hood, at the rear of the engine compartment.

V8 Quattro vehicles have the main fuse relay panel located behind the side kick panel cover in the front passenger footwell. An auxiliary relay panel is located under the carpet in the passenger side footwell. This panel also houses the connectors for the factory diagnostic tester.

In the cover of each fuse box and in the owner's manual, is a chart that tells which circuit the fuse protects and its correct amperage. The chart also tells to which circuit the relays are connected. Each vehicle may also use in-line fuses for certain circuits; fuel pump, battery, air conditioning and power door locks, if equipped.

Fuse Color Codes

The number on the face of the fuse is the amperage rating.
1. Brown — 5 Amp
2. Red — 10 Amp
3. Blue — 15 Amp
4. Yellow — 25 Amp
5. Green — 30 Amp

Auxiliary Relay

An auxiliary relay panel, usually located under the left side of the instrument panel, may contain additional relays.

Flashers

LOCATION

Turn signal and hazard flashers are located in the fuse and relay panels.

SERIAL NUMBER IDENTIFICATION

Vehicle Identification Plate

The manufacturer's plate is located in the engine compartment, on the right side inner fender panel or support.

Engine Number

The engine number is located on the left rear side of the engine, above the starter motor.

Vehicle Identification Number

The vehicle identification number is located on a plate, on the drivers side of the instrument panel.

Chassis Number

The chassis number can be found in the engine compartment on the right front inner fender support or facing forward on the right side of the bulkhead. A label is also attached to the upper steering column cover, inside the vehicle.

SPECIFICATIONS

ENGINE IDENTIFICATION

Year	Model	Engine Displacement Liters (cc)	Engine Series Identification	Fuel System ①	No. of Cylinders	Engine Type
1990	325i	2.5 (2494)	M20B25	M1.3	6	OHC
	325iC	2.5 (2494)	M20B25	M1.3	6	OHC
	325iX	2.5 (2494)	M20B25	M1.3	6	OHC
	M3	2.3 (2302)	S14B23	M1.2②	4	DOHC
	525i	2.5 (2494)	M20B25	M1.3	6	OHC
	535i	3.5 (3430)	M30B35	M1.3	6	OHC
	735i	3.5 (3430)	M30B35	M1.3	6	OHC
	735iL	3.5 (3430)	M30B35	M1.3	6	OHC
	750iL	5.0 (4988)	M70B50	M1.2	12	OHC
1991	318i	1.8 (1796)	M42B18	M1.7	4	DOHC
	318iC	1.8 (1796)	M42B18	M1.7	4	DOHC
	318iS	1.8 (1796)	M42B18	M1.7	4	DOHC
	325i	2.5 (2494)	M20B25	M1.3	6	OHC
	325iC	2.5 (2494)	M20B25	M1.3	6	OHC
	325iX	2.5 (2494)	M20B25	M1.3	6	OHC
	M3	2.3 (2302)	S14B23	M1.2②	4	DOHC
	525i	2.5 (2494)	M50B25	M3.1	6	DOHC
	535i	3.5 (3430)	M30B35	M1.3	6	OHC
	M5	3.6 (3535)	S38B36	M1.2②	6	DOHC
	735i	3.5 (3430)	M30B35	M1.3	6	OHC
	735iL	3.5 (3430)	M30B35	M1.3	6	OHC
	750iL	5.0 (4988)	M70B50	M1.7	12	OHC
	850i	5.0 (4988)	M70B50	M1.7	12	OHC
1992	318i	1.8 (1796)	M42B18	M1.7	4	DOHC
	318iC	1.8 (1796)	M42B18	M1.7	4	DOHC
	318iS	1.8 (1796)	M42B18	M1.7	4	DOHC
	325i	2.5 (2494)	M50B25	M3.1	6	OHC
	325iC	2.5 (2494)	M20B25	M1.3	6	OHC
	525i	2.5 (2494)	M50B25	M3.1	6	DOHC
	535i	3.5 (3430)	M30B35	M1.3	6	OHC
	M5	3.6 (3535)	S38B36	M1.2②	6	DOHC
	735i	3.5 (3430)	M30B35	M1.3	6	OHC
	735iL	3.5 (3430)	M30B35	M1.3	6	OHC
	750iL	5.0 (4988)	M70B50	M1.7	12	OHC
	850i	5.0 (4988)	M70B50	M1.7	12	OHC

ENGINE IDENTIFICATION

Year	Model	Engine Displacement Liters (cc)	Engine Series Identification	Fuel System ①	No. of Cylinders	Engine Type
1993	318i	1.8 (1796)	M42B18	M1.7	4	DOHC
	318iC	1.8 (1796)	M42B18	M1.7	4	DOHC
	325i	2.5 (2494)	M50B25	M3.1	6	OHC
	325iC	2.5 (2494)	M20B25	M1.3	6	OHC
	525i	2.5 (2494)	M50B25	M3.1	6	DOHC
	535i	3.5 (3430)	M30B35	M1.3	6	OHC
	M5	3.6 (3535)	S38B36	M1.2②	6	DOHC
	735i	3.5 (3430)	M30B35	M1.3	6	OHC
	735iL	3.5 (3430)	M30B35	M1.3	6	OHC
	750iL	5.0 (4988)	M70B50	M1.7	12	OHC
	850i	5.0 (4988)	M70B50	M1.7	12	OHC
1994	318i	1.8 (1796)	M42B18	M1.7	4	DOHC
	318iS	1.8 (1796)	M42B18	M1.7	4	DOHC
	325i	2.5 (2494)	M50B25	M3.1	6	OHC
	325iC	2.5 (2494)	M20B25	M1.3	6	OHC
	525i	2.5 (2494)	M50B25	M3.1	6	DOHC
	M5	3.6 (3535)	S38B36	M1.2②	6	DOHC
	750iL	5.0 (4988)	M70B50	M1.7	12	OHC
	850i	5.0 (4988)	M70B50	M1.7	12	OHC

OHC—Overhead Camshaft
DOHC—Double Overhead Camshaft
① Digital Motor Electronic Series
② Motorsport Electronics

GENERAL ENGINE SPECIFICATIONS

Year	Engine ID/VIN	Engine Displacement Liters (cc)	Fuel System Type	Net Horsepower @ rpm	Net Torque @ rpm (ft. lbs.)	Bore × Stroke (in.)	Compression Ratio	Oil Pressure @ rpm
1990	S14B23	2.3 (2302)	M1.2①	192 @ 6750	170 @ 4750	3.68 × 3.31	10.5:1	18 @ Idle
	M20B25	2.5 (2494)	M1.3	168 @ 5800	164 @ 4300	3.31 × 2.95	8.8:1	18 @ Idle
	M30B35	3.5 (3430)	M1.3	208 @ 5700	225 @ 4000	3.62 × 3.39	9.0:1	18 @ Idle
	M70B50	5.0 (4988)	M1.2	296 @ 5200	332 @ 4100	3.31 × 2.95	8.8:1	18 @ Idle
1991	M42B18	1.8 (1796)	M1.7	134 @ 6000	127 @ 4600	3.31 × 3.19	10.0:1	18 @ Idle
	S14B23	2.3 (2302)	M1.2①	192 @ 6750	170 @ 4750	3.68 × 3.31	10.5:1	18 @ Idle
	M20B25	2.5 (2494)	M1.3	168 @ 5800	164 @ 4300	3.31 × 2.95	8.8:1	18 @ Idle
	M50B25	2.5 (2494)	M3.1	189 @ 5900	181 @ 4700	3.31 × 2.95	10.0:1	28 @ Idle
	M30B35	3.5 (3430)	M1.3	208 @ 5700	225 @ 4000	3.62 × 3.39	9.0:1	18 @ Idle
	S38B36	3.6 (3535)	M1.2①	310 @ 6900	266 @ 4750	3.68 × 3.39	10.0:1	18 @ Idle
	M70B50	5.0 (4988)	M1.7	296 @ 5200	332 @ 4100	3.31 × 2.95	8.8:1	18 @ Idle
1992	M42B18	1.8 (1796)	M1.7	134 @ 6000	127 @ 4600	3.31 × 3.19	10.0:1	18 @ Idle
	M20B25	2.5 (2494)	M1.3	168 @ 5800	164 @ 4300	3.31 × 2.95	8.8:1	18 @ Idle
	M50B25	2.5 (2494)	M3.1	189 @ 5900	181 @ 4700	3.31 × 2.95	10.0:1	28 @ Idle
	M30B35	3.5 (3430)	M1.3	208 @ 5700	225 @ 4000	3.62 × 3.39	9.0:1	18 @ Idle
	S38B36	3.6 (3535)	M1.2①	310 @ 6900	266 @ 4750	3.68 × 3.39	10.0:1	18 @ Idle
	M70B50	5.0 (4988)	M1.7	296 @ 5200	332 @ 4100	3.31 × 2.95	8.8:1	18 @ Idle
1993	M42B18	1.8 (1796)	M1.7	134 @ 6000	127 @ 4600	3.31 × 3.19	10.0:1	18 @ Idle
	M20B25	2.5 (2494)	M1.3	168 @ 5800	164 @ 4300	3.31 × 2.95	8.8:1	18 @ Idle
	M50B25	2.5 (2494)	M3.1	189 @ 5900	181 @ 4700	3.31 × 2.95	10.0:1	28 @ Idle
	M30B35	3.5 (3430)	M1.3	208 @ 5700	225 @ 4000	3.62 × 3.39	9.0:1	18 @ Idle
	S38B36	3.6 (3535)	M1.2①	310 @ 6900	266 @ 4750	3.68 × 3.39	10.0:1	18 @ Idle
	M70B50	5.0 (4988)	M1.7	296 @ 5200	332 @ 4100	3.31 × 2.95	8.8:1	18 @ Idle
1994	M42B18	1.8 (1796)	M1.7	134 @ 6000	127 @ 4600	3.31 × 3.19	10.0:1	18 @ Idle
	M20B25	2.5 (2494)	M1.3	168 @ 5800	164 @ 4300	3.31 × 2.95	8.8:1	18 @ Idle
	M50B25	2.5 (2494)	M3.1	189 @ 5900	181 @ 4700	3.31 × 2.95	10.0:1	28 @ Idle
	M30B35	3.5 (3430)	M1.3	208 @ 5700	225 @ 4000	3.62 × 3.39	9.0:1	18 @ Idle
	S38B36	3.6 (3535)	M1.2①	310 @ 6900	266 @ 4750	3.68 × 3.39	10.0:1	18 @ Idle
	M70B50	5.0 (4988)	M1.7	296 @ 5200	332 @ 4100	3.31 × 2.95	8.8:1	18 @ Idle

① Motorsport Electronics

GASOLINE ENGINE TUNE-UP SPECIFICATIONS

Year	Engine ID/VIN	Engine Displacement Liters (cc)	Spark Plugs Gap (in.) ①	Ignition Timing (deg.) MT	AT	Fuel Pump (psi)	Idle Speed (rpm) MT	AT	Valve Clearance ③ In.	Ex.
1990	S14B23	2.3 (2302)	0.026	②	②	43	880	880	0.012	0.012
	M20B25	2.5 (2494)	0.030	②	②	43	760	760	0.010	0.010
	M30B35	3.5 (3430)	0.030	②	②	43	800	800	0.012	0.012
	M70B50	5.0 (4988)	0.030	②	②	43	800	800	Hyd.	Hyd.
1991	M42B18	1.8 (1796)	0.030	②	②	43	850	850	Hyd.	Hyd.
	S14B23	2.3 (2302)	0.026	②	②	43	760	760	0.012	0.012
	M20B25	2.5 (2494)	0.030	②	②	43	800	800	0.010	0.010
	M50B25	2.5 (2494)	0.030	②	②	50	700	700	Hyd.	Hyd.
	M30B35	3.5 (3430)	0.030	②	②	43	800	800	0.012	0.012
	S38B36	3.6 (3535)	0.026	②	②	43	970	970	0.012	0.012
	M70B50	5.0 (4988)	0.030	②	②	43	800	800	Hyd.	Hyd.
1992	M42B18	1.8 (1796)	0.030	②	②	43	850	850	Hyd.	Hyd.
	M20B25	2.5 (2494)	0.030	②	②	43	800	800	0.010	0.010
	M50B25	2.5 (2494)	0.030	②	②	50	700	700	Hyd.	Hyd.
	M30B35	3.5 (3430)	0.030	②	②	43	800	800	0.012	0.012
	S38B36	3.6 (3535)	0.026	②	②	43	970	970	0.012	0.012
	M70B50	5.0 (4988)	0.030	②	②	43	800	800	Hyd.	Hyd.
1993-94	REFER TO UNDERHOOD SPECIFICATIONS STICKER									

NOTE: The lowest cylinder pressure should be within 75% of the highest cylinder pressure reading. For example, if the highest cylinder is 134 psi, the lowest should be 101. Engine should be at normal operating temperature with throttle valve in the wide open position.
The underhood specifications sticker often reflects tune-up specification changes in production. Sticker figures must be used if they disagree with those in this chart.
Hyd.—Hydraulic
① With Triangle Ground Electrode—0.037 inch
② Motronic Injection System—Refer to Underhood Emission Decal
③ All Valve Specifications are with Engine Cold

FIRING ORDERS

NOTE: To avoid confusion, always replace spark plug wires one at a time.

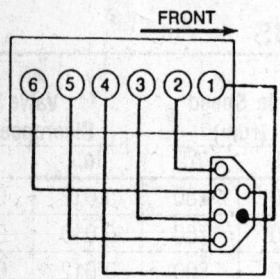

2.5L (M20B25), 3.5L and 3.6L Engines
Engine Firing Order: 1-5-3-6-2-4
Distributor Rotation: Clockwise

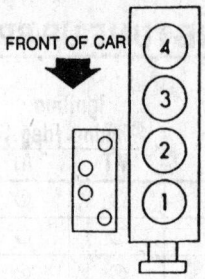

2.5L (M50B25) Engine
Engine Firing Order: 1-5-3-6-2-4
Distributorless Ignition System

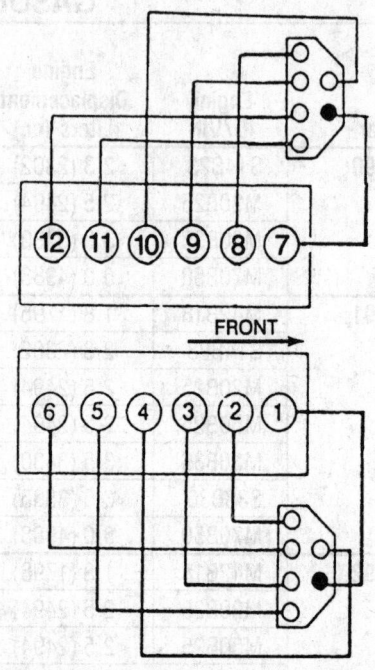

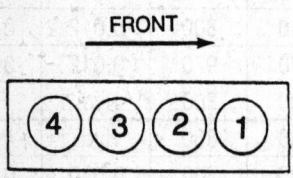

2.3L Engine
Engine Firing Order: 1-3-4-2
Distributor Rotation: Counterclockwise

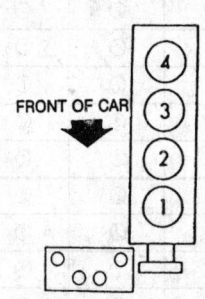

1.8L Engine
Engine Firing Order: 1-3-4-2
Distributorless Ignition System

5.0L Engine
Engine Firing Order: 1-7-5-11-3-9-6-12-2-8-4-10
Distributor Rotation: Clockwise

CAPACITIES

Year	Model	Engine ID/VIN	Engine Displacement Liters (cc)	Engine Crankcase with Filter (qts.)	Transmission (pts.)			Transfer Case (pts.)	Drive Axle (pts)		Fuel Tank (gal.)	Cooling System (qts.)
					4-Spd	5-Spd	Auto.		Front	Rear		
1990	325i	M20B25	2.5 (2494)	5.0	—	2.3	6.4	—	—	3.3	16.4	11.0
	325iC	M20B25	2.5 (2494)	5.0	—	2.6	6.4	—	—	3.3	16.4	11.0
	325iS	M20B25	2.5 (2494)	5.0	—	2.6	6.4	—	—	3.3	16.4	11.0
	325iX	M20B25	2.5 (2494)	5.0	—	2.6	6.4	2①	1.3	3.3	16.4	11.0
	M3	S14B23	2.3 (2302)	4.6	—	3.0	—	—	—	3.3	14.5	9.5
	525i	M20B25	2.5 (2494)	5.0	—	2.6	6.4	—	—	3.3	21.1	12.7
	535i	M30B35	3.5 (3430)	6.1	—	2.6	6.4	—	—	3.7	21.1	12.7
	735i	M30B35	3.5 (3430)	6.1	—	2.6	6.4	—	—	3.7	21.5	12.7
	735iL	M30B35	3.5 (3430)	6.1	—	2.6	6.4	—	—	3.7	24.0	12.7
	750iL	M70B50	5.0 (4988)	8.0	—	2.6	6.4	—	—	3.7	24.0	14.8
1991	318i	M42B18	1.8 (1796)	5.0	—	2.4	6.4	—	—	3.3	14.5	13.5
	318iC	M42B18	1.8 (1796)	5.0	—	2.6	Auto.	—	—	3.3	14.5	13.5
	318iS	M42B18	1.8 (1796)	5.0	—	2.6	6.4	—	—	3.3	14.5	13.5
	325i	M20B25	2.5 (2494)	5.0	—	2.6	6.4	—	—	3.3	16.4	11.0
	325iC	M20B25	2.5 (2494)	5.0	—	2.6	6.4	—	—	3.3	16.4	11.0
	325iX	M20B25	2.5 (2494)	5.0	—	2.6	6.4	2①	1.3	3.3	16.4	11.0
	M3	S14B23	2.3 (2302)	4.6	—	3.0	—	—	—	3.3	14.5	9.5
	525i	M50B25	2.5 (2494)	5.0	—	2.6	6.4	—	—	3.3	21.1	12.7
	535i	M30B35	3.5 (3430)	6.1	—	2.6	6.4	—	—	3.7	21.1	12.7
	M5	S38B36	3.6 (3535)	6.1	—	2.6	—	—	—	3.7	21.5	12.7
	735i	M30B35	3.5 (3430)	6.1	—	2.6	6.4	—	—	3.7	24.0	12.7
	735iL	M30B35	3.5 (3430)	6.1	—	2.6	6.4	—	—	3.7	24.0	12.7
	750iL	M70B50	5.0 (4988)	8.0	—	2.6	6.4	—	—	3.7	24.0	14.8
	850i	M70B50	5.0 (4988)	8.0	—	2.6	6.4	—	—	3.7	24.0	13.7
1992	318i	M42B18	1.8 (1796)	5.0	—	2.4	6.4	—	—	3.3	14.5	13.5
	318iC	M42B18	1.8 (1796)	5.0	—	2.4	—	—	—	3.3	14.5	13.5
	318iS	M42B18	1.8 (1796)	5.0	—	2.6	6.4	—	—	3.3	14.5	13.5
	325i	M50B25	2.5 (2494)	6.9	—	2.6	6.4	—	—	3.3	17.2	11.0
	325iC	M20B25	2.5 (2494)	5.0	—	2.6	6.4	—	—	3.3	16.4	11.0
	525i	M50B25	2.5 (2494)	6.9	—	2.6	6.4	—	—	3.3	21.1	12.7
	535i	M30B35	3.5 (3430)	6.1	—	2.6	6.4	—	—	3.7	21.1	12.7
	M5	S38B36	3.6 (3535)	6.1	—	2.6	—	—	—	3.7	21.1	12.7
	735i	M30B35	3.5 (3430)	6.1	—	2.6	6.4	—	—	3.7	21.5	12.7
	735iL	M30B35	3.5 (3430)	6.1	—	2.6	6.4	—	—	3.7	24.0	12.7
	750iL	M70B50	5.0 (4988)	8.0	—	2.6	6.4	—	—	3.7	24.0	14.8
	850i	M70B50	5.0 (4988)	8.0	—	2.6	6.4	—	—	3.7	24.0	13.7

CAPACITIES

Year	Model	Engine ID/VIN	Engine Displacement Liters (cc)	Engine Crankcase with Filter (qts.)	Transmission (pts.)			Transfer Case (pts.)	Drive Axle (pts)		Fuel Tank (gal.)	Cooling System (qts.)
					4-Spd	5-Spd	Auto.		Front	Rear		
1993	318i	M42B18	1.8 (1796)	5.0	—	2.4	6.4	—	—	3.3	14.5	13.5
	318iS	M42B18	1.8 (1796)	5.0	—	2.6	6.4	—	—	3.3	14.5	13.5
	325i	M50B25	2.5 (2494)	6.9	—	2.6	6.4	—	—	3.3	17.2	11.0
	325iC	M20B25	2.5 (2494)	5.0	—	2.6	6.4	—	—	3.3	16.4	11.0
	525i	M50B25	2.5 (2494)	6.9	—	2.6	6.4	—	—	3.3	21.1	12.7
	535i	M30B35	3.5 (3430)	6.1	—	2.6	6.4	—	—	3.7	21.1	12.7
	M5	S38B36	3.6 (3535)	6.1	—	2.6	—	—	—	3.7	21.1	12.7
	735i	M30B35	3.5 (3430)	6.1	—	2.6	6.4	—	—	3.7	21.5	12.7
	735iL	M30B35	3.5 (3430)	6.1	—	2.6	6.4	—	—	3.7	24.0	12.7
	750iL	M70B50	5.0 (4988)	8.0	—	2.6	6.4	—	—	3.7	24.0	14.8
	850i	M70B50	5.0 (4988)	8.0	—	2.6	6.4	—	—	3.7	24.0	13.7
1994	318i	M42B18	1.8 (1796)	5.0	—	2.4	6.4	—	—	3.3	14.5	13.5
	318iC	M42B18	1.8 (1796)	5.0	—	2.4	—	—	—	3.3	14.5	13.5
	318iS	M42B18	1.8 (1796)	5.0	—	2.6	6.4	—	—	3.3	14.5	13.5
	325i	M50B25	2.5 (2494)	6.9	—	2.6	6.4	—	—	3.3	17.2	11.0
	325iC	M20B25	2.5 (2494)	5.0	—	2.6	6.4	—	—	3.3	16.4	11.0
	525i	M50B25	2.5 (2494)	6.9	—	2.6	6.4	—	—	3.3	21.1	12.7
	M5	S38B36	3.6 (3535)	6.1	—	2.6	—	—	—	3.7	21.1	12.7
	750iL	M70B50	5.0 (4988)	8.0	—	2.6	6.4	—	—	3.7	24.0	14.8
	850i	M70B50	5.0 (4988)	8.0	—	2.6	6.4	—	—	3.7	24.0	13.7

① Use Approved Automatic Transmission Fluid

CAMSHAFT SPECIFICATIONS

All measurements given in inches.

Year	Engine ID/VIN	Engine Displacement Liters (cc)	Journal Diameter					Elevation		Bearing Clearance	Camshaft End Play
			1	2	3	4	5	In.	Ex.		
1990	S14B23	2.3 (2302)	—	—	—	—	—	1.721	—	0.0011–0.0021	0.0040–0.0060
	M20B25	2.5 (2494)	—	—	—	—	—	—	—	—	0.0008
	M30B35	3.5 (3430)	—	—	—	—	—	—	—	—	0.0012–0.0071
	M70B50	5.0 (4988)	—	—	—	—	—	—	—	0.0016–0.0029	0.0060–0.0130
1991	M42B18	1.8 (1796)	—	—	—	—	—	①	—	0.0060–0.0130	0.0008–0.0021
	S14B23	2.3 (2302)	—	—	—	—	—	1.721	—	0.0011–0.0021	0.0040–0.0060
	M20B25	2.5 (2494)	—	—	—	—	—	—	—	—	0.0008
	M30B35	3.5 (3430)	—	—	—	—	—	—	—	—	0.0012–0.0071
	S38B36	3.6 (3535)	—	—	—	—	—	—	—	0.0011–0.0021	0.0040–0.0060
	M70B50	5.0 (4988)	—	—	—	—	—	—	—	0.0016–0.0029	0.0060–0.0130
1992	M42B18	1.8 (1796)	—	—	—	—	—	①	—	0.0060–0.0130	0.0008–0.0021
	M20B25	2.5 (2494)	—	—	—	—	—	—	—	0.0060–0.0130	0.0008–0.0021
	M30B35	3.5 (3430)	—	—	—	—	—	—	—	—	0.0012–0.0071
	S38B36	3.6 (3535)	—	—	—	—	—	—	—	0.0011–0.0021	0.0040–0.0060
	M30B35	3.5 (3430)	—	—	—	—	—	—	—	—	0.0012–0.0071
	M70B50	5.0 (4988)	—	—	—	—	—	—	—	0.0016–0.0029	0.0060–0.0130
1993	M42B18	1.8 (1796)	—	—	—	—	—	①	—	0.0060–0.0130	0.0008–0.0021
	M20B25	2.5 (2494)	—	—	—	—	—	—	—	0.0060–0.0130	0.0008–0.0021
	M30B35	3.5 (3430)	—	—	—	—	—	—	—	—	0.0012–0.0071
	S38B36	3.6 (3535)	—	—	—	—	—	—	—	0.0011–0.0021	0.0040–0.0060
	M30B35	3.5 (3430)	—	—	—	—	—	—	—	—	0.0012–0.0071
	M70B50	5.0 (4988)	—	—	—	—	—	—	—	0.0016–0.0029	0.0060–0.0130

CAMSHAFT SPECIFICATIONS

All measurements given in inches.

Year	Engine ID/VIN	Engine Displacement Liters (cc)	Journal Diameter					Elevation		Bearing Clearance	Camshaft End Play
			1	2	3	4	5	In.	Ex.		
1994	M42B18	1.8 (1796)	—	—	—	—	—	①	—	0.0060–0.0130	0.0008–0.0021
	M20B25	2.5 (2494)	—	—	—	—	—	—	—	0.0060–0.0130	0.0008–0.0021
	M30B35	3.5 (3430)	—	—	—	—	—	—	—	—	0.0012–0.0071
	S38B36	3.6 (3535)	—	—	—	—	—	—	—	0.0011–0.0021	0.0040–0.0060
	M30B35	3.5 (3430)	—	—	—	—	—	—	—	—	0.0012–0.0071
	M70B50	5.0 (4988)	—	—	—	—	—	—	—	0.0016–0.0029	0.0060–0.0130

① 1.8780 ± 0.0024

CRANKSHAFT AND CONNECTING ROD SPECIFICATIONS

All measurements are given in inches.

Year	Engine ID/VIN	Engine Displacement Liters (cc)	Crankshaft				Connecting Rod		
			Main Brg. Journal Dia.	Main Brg. Oil Clearance	Shaft End-play	Thrust on No.	Journal Diameter	Oil Clearance	Side Clearance
1990	S14B23	2.3 (2302)	2.1653	0.0012–0.0027	0.0033–0.0068	3	1.8888–1.8894	0.0012–0.0027	0.0016
	M20B25	2.5 (2494)	2.3622	0.0012–0.0027	0.0031–0.0064	4	1.7707–1.7713	0.0008–0.0022	0.0016
	M30B35	3.5 (3430)	2.3616	0.0008–0.0018	0.0033–0.0068	4	1.8888–1.8894	0.0008–0.0022	0.0016
	M70B50	5.0 (4988)	2.9523	0.0010–0.0031	0.0033–0.0068	—	1.7707–1.7713	0.0006–0.0023	0.0016
1991	M42B18	1.8 (1796)	2.3616	0.0008–0.0018	0.0031–0.0064	—	1.7719–1.7726	0.0008–0.0022	0.0016
	S14B23	2.3 (2302)	2.1653	0.0012–0.0027	0.0033–0.0068	3	1.8888–1.8894	0.0012–0.0027	0.0016
	M20B25	2.5 (2494)	2.3622	0.0012–0.0027	0.0031–0.0064	4	1.7707–1.7713	0.0008–0.0022	0.0016
	M50B25	2.5 (2494)	2.3616	0.0008–0.0023	0.0031–0.0064	NA	1.7721–1.7727	0.0008–0.0022	0.0020
	M30B35	3.5 (3430)	2.3616	0.0008–0.0018	0.0033–0.0068	4	1.8888–1.8894	0.0008–0.0022	0.0016
	S38B36	3.6 (3535)	2.3622	0.0012–0.0027	0.0033–0.0068	4	1.8888–1.8894	0.0008–0.0022	0.0016
	M70B50	5.0 (4988)	2.9523	0.0010–0.0031	0.0033–0.0068	—	1.7707–1.7713	0.0006–0.0023	0.0016
1992	M42B18	1.8 (1796)	2.3616	0.0008–0.0018	0.0031–0.0064	—	1.7719–1.7726	0.0008–0.0022	0.0016
	M20B25	2.5 (2494)	2.3622	0.0012–0.0027	0.0031–0.0064	4	1.7707–1.7713	0.0008–0.0022	0.0016
	M50B25	2.5 (2494)	2.3616	0.0008–0.0023	0.0031–0.0064	NA	1.7721–1.7727	0.0008–0.0022	0.0020
	M30B35	3.5 (3430)	2.3616	0.0008–0.0018	0.0033–0.0068	4	1.8888–1.8894	0.0008–0.0022	0.0016
	S38B36	3.6 (3535)	2.3622	0.0012–0.0027	0.0033–0.0068	4	1.8888–1.8894	0.0008–0.0022	0.0016
	M70B50	5.0 (4988)	2.9523	0.0010–0.0031	0.0033–0.0068	—	1.7707–1.7713	0.0006–0.0023	0.0016
1993	M42B18	1.8 (1796)	2.3616	0.0008–0.0018	0.0031–0.0064	—	1.7719–1.7726	0.0008–0.0022	0.0016
	M20B25	2.5 (2494)	2.3622	0.0012–0.0027	0.0031–0.0064	4	1.7707–1.7713	0.0008–0.0022	0.0016
	M50B25	2.5 (2494)	2.3616	0.0008–0.0023	0.0031–0.0064	NA	1.7721–1.7727	0.0008–0.0022	0.0020
	M30B35	3.5 (3430)	2.3616	0.0008–0.0018	0.0033–0.0068	4	1.8888–1.8894	0.0008–0.0022	0.0016
	S38B36	3.6 (3535)	2.3622	0.0012–0.0027	0.0033–0.0068	4	1.8888–1.8894	0.0008–0.0022	0.0016
	M70B50	5.0 (4988)	2.9523	0.0010–0.0031	0.0033–0.0068	—	1.7707–1.7713	0.0006–0.0023	0.0016

CRANKSHAFT AND CONNECTING ROD SPECIFICATIONS
All measurements are given in inches.

Year	Engine ID/VIN	Engine Displacement Liters (cc)	Crankshaft				Connecting Rod		
			Main Brg. Journal Dia.	Main Brg. Oil Clearance	Shaft End-play	Thrust on No.	Journal Diameter	Oil Clearance	Side Clearance
1994	M42B18	1.8 (1796)	2.3616	0.0008–0.0018	0.0031–0.0064	—	1.7719–1.7726	0.0008–0.0022	0.0016
	M20B25	2.5 (2494)	2.3622	0.0012–0.0027	0.0031–0.0064	4	1.7707–1.7713	0.0008–0.0022	0.0016
	M50B25	2.5 (2494)	2.3616	0.0008–0.0023	0.0031–0.0064	NA	1.7721–1.7727	0.0008–0.0022	0.0020
	M30B35	3.5 (3430)	2.3616	0.0008–0.0018	0.0033–0.0068	4	1.8888–1.8894	0.0008–0.0022	0.0016
	S38B36	3.6 (3535)	2.3622	0.0012–0.0027	0.0033–0.0068	4	1.8888–1.8894	0.0008–0.0022	0.0016
	M70B50	5.0 (4988)	2.9523	0.0010–0.0031	0.0033–0.0068	—	1.7707–1.7713	0.0006–0.0023	0.0016

NA—Not available

VALVE SPECIFICATIONS

Year	Engine ID/VIN	Engine Displacement Liters (cc)	Seat Angle (deg.)	Face Angle (deg.)	Spring Test Pressure (lbs. @ in.)	Spring Installed Height (in.)	Stem-to-Guide Clearance (in.)		Stem Diameter (in.)	
							Intake	Exhaust	Intake	Exhaust
1990	S14B23	2.3 (2302)	45	NA	NA	NA	0.025	0.031	0.275	0.275
	M20B25	2.5 (2494)	45	NA	NA	NA	0.031	0.031	0.275	0.275
	M30B35	3.5 (3430)	45	NA	NA	NA	0.031	0.031	0.315	0.315
	M70B50	5.0 (4988)	45	NA	NA	NA	0.020	0.020	0.275	0.275
1991	M42B18	1.8 (1796)	45	NA	NA	NA	0.020	0.020	0.275	0.275
	S14B23	2.3 (2302)	45	NA	NA	NA	0.025	0.031	0.275	0.275
	M20B25	2.5 (2494)	45	NA	NA	NA	0.031	0.031	0.275	0.275
	M50B25	2.5 (2494)	45	NA	NA	NA	0.020	0.020	0.275	0.275
	M30B35	3.5 (3430)	45	NA	NA	NA	0.031	0.031	0.315	0.315
	S38B36	3.6 (3535)	45	NA	NA	NA	0.025	0.031	0.275	0.275
	M70B50	5.0 (4988)	45	NA	NA	NA	0.020	0.020	0.275	0.275
1992	M42B18	1.8 (1796)	45	NA	NA	NA	0.020	0.020	0.275	0.275
	M20B25	2.5 (2494)	45	NA	NA	NA	0.031	0.031	0.275	0.275
	M50B25	2.5 (2494)	45	NA	NA	NA	0.020	0.020	0.275	0.275
	M30B35	3.5 (3430)	45	NA	NA	NA	0.031	0.031	0.315	0.315
	S38B36	3.6 (3535)	45	NA	NA	NA	0.025	0.031	0.275	0.275
	M70B50	5.0 (4988)	45	NA	NA	NA	0.020	0.020	0.275	0.275
1993	M42B18	1.8 (1796)	45	NA	NA	NA	0.020	0.020	0.275	0.275
	M20B25	2.5 (2494)	45	NA	NA	NA	0.031	0.031	0.275	0.275
	M50B25	2.5 (2494)	45	NA	NA	NA	0.020	0.020	0.275	0.275
	M30B35	3.5 (3430)	45	NA	NA	NA	0.031	0.031	0.315	0.315
	S38B36	3.6 (3535)	45	NA	NA	NA	0.025	0.031	0.275	0.275
	M70B50	5.0 (4988)	45	NA	NA	NA	0.020	0.020	0.275	0.275
1994	M42B18	1.8 (1796)	45	NA	NA	NA	0.020	0.020	0.275	0.275
	M20B25	2.5 (2494)	45	NA	NA	NA	0.031	0.031	0.275	0.275
	M50B25	2.5 (2494)	45	NA	NA	NA	0.020	0.020	0.275	0.275
	M30B35	3.5 (3430)	45	NA	NA	NA	0.031	0.031	0.315	0.315
	S38B36	3.6 (3535)	45	NA	NA	NA	0.025	0.031	0.275	0.275
	M70B50	5.0 (4988)	45	NA	NA	NA	0.020	0.020	0.275	0.275

NA—Not available

PISTON AND RING SPECIFICATIONS

All measurements are given in inches.

Year	Engine ID/VIN	Engine Displacement Liters (cc)	Piston Clearance	Ring Gap			Ring Side Clearance		
				Top Compression	Bottom Compression	Oil Control	Top Compression	Bottom Compression	Oil Control
1990	S14B23	2.3 (2302)	0.0012–0.0024	0.0120–0.0220	0.0120–0.0220	0.0100–0.0200	0.0024–0.0035	0.0024–0.0035	0.0008–0.0020
	M20B25	2.5 (2494)	0.0004–0.0016	0.0080–0.0200	0.0080–0.0200	0.0080–0.0200	0.0016–0.0031	0.0012–0.0027	0.0008–0.0020
	M30B35	3.5 (3430)	0.0008–0.0020	0.0080–0.0180	0.0160–0.0250	0.0120–0.0240	0.0016–0.0028	0.0012–0.0024	0.0008–0.0022
	M70B50	5.0 (4988)	0.0004–0.0013	0.0080–0.0160	0.0080–0.0160	0.0100–0.0200	0.0016–0.0025	0.0012–0.0028	0.0008–0.0022
1991	M42B18	1.8 (1796)	0.0004–0.0016	0.0080–0.0160	0.0080–0.0160	0.0080–0.0180	0.0008–0.0020	0.0008–0.0020	0.0008–0.0022
	S14B23	2.3 (2302)	0.0012–0.0024	0.0120–0.0220	0.0120–0.0220	0.0100–0.0200	0.0024–0.0035	0.0024–0.0035	0.0008–0.0020
	M20B25	2.5 (2494)	0.0004–0.0016	0.0080–0.0160	0.0080–0.0160	0.0080–0.0180	0.0008–0.0020	0.0008–0.0020	0.0008–0.0022
	M50B25	2.5 (2494)	0.0004–0.0016	0.0080–0.0200	0.0080–0.0200	0.0080–0.0200	0.0016–0.0031	0.0012–0.0027	0.0008–0.0020
	M30B35	3.5 (3430)	0.0008–0.0020	0.0080–0.0180	0.0160–0.0250	0.0120–0.0240	0.0016–0.0028	0.0012–0.0024	0.0008–0.0022
	S38B36	3.6 (3535)	0.0012–0.0024	0.0120–0.0220	0.0120–0.0220	0.0100–0.0200	0.0024–0.0035	0.0024–0.0035	0.0008–0.0020
	M70B50	5.0 (4988)	0.0004–0.0013	0.0080–0.0160	0.0080–0.0160	0.0100–0.0200	0.0016–0.0025	0.0012–0.0028	0.0008–0.0022
1992	M42B18	1.8 (1796)	0.0004–0.0016	0.0080–0.0160	0.0080–0.0160	0.0080–0.0180	0.0008–0.0020	0.0008–0.0020	0.0008–0.0022
	M20B25	2.5 (2494)	0.0004–0.0016	0.0080–0.0160	0.0080–0.0160	0.0080–0.0180	0.0008–0.0020	0.0008–0.0020	0.0008–0.0022
	M50B25	2.5 (2494)	0.0004–0.0016	0.0080–0.0200	0.0080–0.0200	0.0080–0.0200	0.0016–0.0031	0.0012–0.0027	0.0008–0.0020
	M30B35	3.5 (3430)	0.0008–0.0020	0.0080–0.0180	0.0160–0.0250	0.0120–0.0240	0.0016–0.0028	0.0012–0.0024	0.0008–0.0022
	S38B36	3.6 (3535)	0.0012–0.0024	0.0120–0.0220	0.0120–0.0220	0.0100–0.0200	0.0024–0.0035	0.0024–0.0035	0.0008–0.0020
	M70B50	5.0 (4988)	0.0004–0.0013	0.0080–0.0160	0.0080–0.0160	0.0100–0.0200	0.0016–0.0025	0.0012–0.0028	0.0008–0.0022
1993	M42B18	1.8 (1796)	0.0004–0.0016	0.0080–0.0160	0.0080–0.0160	0.0080–0.0180	0.0008–0.0020	0.0008–0.0020	0.0008–0.0022
	M20B25	2.5 (2494)	0.0004–0.0016	0.0080–0.0160	0.0080–0.0160	0.0080–0.0180	0.0008–0.0020	0.0008–0.0020	0.0008–0.0022
	M50B25	2.5 (2494)	0.0004–0.0016	0.0080–0.0200	0.0080–0.0200	0.0080–0.0200	0.0016–0.0031	0.0012–0.0027	0.0008–0.0020
	M30B35	3.5 (3430)	0.0008–0.0020	0.0080–0.0180	0.0160–0.0250	0.0120–0.0240	0.0016–0.0028	0.0012–0.0024	0.0008–0.0022
	S38B36	3.6 (3535)	0.0012–0.0024	0.0120–0.0220	0.0120–0.0220	0.0100–0.0200	0.0024–0.0035	0.0024–0.0035	0.0008–0.0020
	M70B50	5.0 (4988)	0.0004–0.0013	0.0080–0.0160	0.0080–0.0160	0.0100–0.0200	0.0016–0.0025	0.0012–0.0028	0.0008–0.0022

PISTON AND RING SPECIFICATIONS

All measurements are given in inches.

Year	Engine ID/VIN	Engine Displacement Liters (cc)	Piston Clearance	Ring Gap			Ring Side Clearance		
				Top Compression	Bottom Compression	Oil Control	Top Compression	Bottom Compression	Oil Control
1994	M42B18	1.8 (1796)	0.0004–0.0016	0.0080–0.0160	0.0080–0.0160	0.0080–0.0180	0.0008–0.0020	0.0008–0.0020	0.0008–0.0022
	M20B25	2.5 (2494)	0.0004–0.0016	0.0080–0.0160	0.0080–0.0160	0.0080–0.0180	0.0008–0.0020	0.0008–0.0020	0.0008–0.0022
	M50B25	2.5 (2494)	0.0004–0.0016	0.0080–0.0200	0.0080–0.0200	0.0080–0.0200	0.0016–0.0031	0.0012–0.0027	0.0008–0.0020
	M30B35	3.5 (3430)	0.0008–0.0020	0.0080–0.0180	0.0160–0.0250	0.0120–0.0240	0.0016–0.0028	0.0012–0.0024	0.0008–0.0022
	S38B36	3.6 (3535)	0.0012–0.0024	0.0120–0.0220	0.0120–0.0220	0.0100–0.0200	0.0024–0.0035	0.0024–0.0035	0.0008–0.0020
	M70B50	5.0 (4988)	0.0004–0.0013	0.0080–0.0160	0.0080–0.0160	0.0100–0.0200	0.0016–0.0025	0.0012–0.0028	0.0008–0.0022

TORQUE SPECIFICATIONS

All readings in ft. lbs.

Year	Engine ID/VIN	Engine Displacement Liters (cc)	Cylinder Head Bolts	Main Bearing Bolts	Rod Bearing Bolts	Crankshaft Damper Bolts	Flywheel Bolts	Manifold Intake	Manifold Exhaust	Spark Plugs	Lug Nut
1990	S14B23	2.3 (2302)	①	⑤	⑨	311–325	82–94	6.5–8.0	6.5–8.0	14–22	65–79
	M20B25	2.5 (2494)	②	42–46	⑧	281–309	82–94	16–18	⑫	14–22	65–79
	M30B35	3.5 (3430)	③	42–46	38–41	311–325	82–94	16–18	⑫	14–22	65–79
	M70B50	5.0 (4988)	④	⑥	⑧	311–325	72	⑪	⑫	14–22	65–79
1991	M42B18	1.8 (1796)	⑦	⑤	⑧	217–231	82–94	10–12	17–18	14–22	65–79
	S14B23	2.3 (2302)	①	⑤	⑨	311–325	82–94	6.5–8.0	6.5–8.0	14–22	65–79
	M20B25	2.5 (2494)	②	42–46	⑧	281–309	82–94	16–18	⑫	14–22	65–79
	M50B25	2.5 (2494)	⑦	⑤	⑧	281–309	82–94	10–12	14	14–22	65–79
	M30B35	3.5 (3430)	③	42–46	38–41	311–325	82–94	16–18	⑫	14–22	65–79
	S38B36	3.6 (3535)	①	⑤	⑨	⑩	82–94	⑪	6.5–8.0	14–22	65–79
	M70B50	5.0 (4988)	④	⑥	⑧	311–325	72	⑪	⑫	14–22	65–79
1992	M42B18	1.8 (1796)	⑦	⑤	⑧	217–231	82–94	10–12	17–18	14–22	65–79
	M20B25	2.5 (2494)	②	42–46	⑧	281–309	82–94	16–18	⑫	14–22	65–79
	M50B25	2.5 (2494)	⑦	⑤	⑧	281–309	82–94	10–12	14	14–22	65–79
	M30B35	3.5 (3430)	③	42–46	38–41	311–325	82–94	16–18	⑫	14–22	65–79
	S38B36	3.6 (3535)	①	⑤	⑨	⑩	82–94	⑪	6.5–8.0	14–22	65–79
	M70B50	5.0 (4988)	④	⑥	⑧	311–325	72	⑪	⑫	14–22	65–79
1993	M42B18	1.8 (1796)	⑦	⑤	⑧	217–231	82–94	10–12	17–18	14–22	65–79
	M20B25	2.5 (2494)	②	42–46	⑧	281–309	82–94	16–18	⑫	14–22	65–79
	M50B25	2.5 (2494)	⑦	⑤	⑧	281–309	82–94	10–12	14	14–22	65–79
	M30B35	3.5 (3430)	③	42–46	38–41	311–325	82–94	16–18	⑫	14–22	65–79
	S38B36	3.6 (3535)	①	⑤	⑨	⑩	82–94	⑪	6.5–8.0	14–22	65–79
	M70B50	5.0 (4988)	④	⑥	⑧	311–325	72	⑪	⑫	14–22	65–79
1994	M42B18	1.8 (1796)	⑦	⑤	⑧	217–231	82–94	10–12	17–18	14–22	65–79
	M20B25	2.5 (2494)	②	42–46	⑧	281–309	82–94	16–18	⑫	14–22	65–79
	M50B25	2.5 (2494)	⑦	⑤	⑧	281–309	82–94	10–12	14	14–22	65–79
	M30B35	3.5 (3430)	③	42–46	38–41	311–325	82–94	16–18	⑫	14–22	65–79
	S38B36	3.6 (3535)	①	⑤	⑨	⑩	82–94	⑪	6.5–8.0	14–22	65–79
	M70B50	5.0 (4988)	④	⑥	⑧	311–325	72	⑪	⑫	14–22	65–79

① Step 1: 35–37 ft. lbs.
Step 2: 57–59 ft. lbs.
Step 3: wait 15 minutes
Step 4: 71–73 ft. lbs.

② Hex Head Bolts
Step 1: 29–33 ft. lbs.
Step 2: wait 15 minutes
Step 3: 43–47 ft. lbs.
Step 4: run engine 25 minutes
Step 5: +25–30 degree turn
Torx Head Bolts
Step 1: 22 ft. lbs.
Step 2: +90 degree turn
Step 3: +90 degree turn

③ Step 1: 42–44 ft. lbs.
Step 2: wait 20 minutes
Step 3: run engine 25 minutes
Step 4: +30–40 degree turn

④ Step 1: 22 ft. lbs.
Step 2: wait 15 minutes
Step 3: +120 degree turn

⑤ Step 1: 14–18 ft. lbs.
Step 2: +47–53 degree turn

⑥ Step 1: 14.5 ft. lbs.
Step 2: +47–53 degree turn

⑦ Step 1: 24 ft. lbs.
Step 2: +90–95 degree turn
Step 3: +90–95 degree turn

Note: M50B25 engine with 6mm torx:
7.2 ft. lbs. maximum

⑧ Step 1: 17 ft. lbs.
Step 2: +70 degree turn

⑨ Step 1: 7 ft. lbs.
Step 2: 22 ft. lbs.
Step 3: +60–62 ft. lbs.

⑩ Step 1: 43 ft. lbs.
Step 2: +60 degree turn
Step 3: +60 degree turn
Step 4: +30 degree turn

⑪ 6mm Bolts: 6.5–8.0 ft. lbs.
8mm Bolts: 14–17 ft. lbs.

⑫ Step 1: coat the upper row of bolts with thread sealer
Step 2: 16–18 ft. lbs.

BRAKE SPECIFICATIONS

All measurements in inches unless noted.

Year	Model	Master Cylinder Bore	Brake Disc Original Thickness	Brake Disc Minimum Thickness	Maximum Runout	Brake Drum Diameter Original Inside Diameter	Max. Wear Limit	Maximum Machine Diameter	Minimum Lining Thickness Front	Rear
1990	M3	—	—	①	0.008	—	—	—	0.079	0.079
	325i	—	—	①	0.008	—	—	—	0.079	0.079
	325iC	—	—	①	0.008	—	—	—	0.079	0.079
	325iS	—	—	①	0.008	—	—	—	0.079	0.079
	325iX	—	—	①	0.008	—	—	—	0.079	0.079
	525i	—	—	②	0.008	—	—	—	0.079	0.079
	535i	—	—	②	0.008	—	—	—	0.079	0.079
	M5	—	—	⑥	0.008	—	—	—	0.079	0.079
	735i	—	—	④	0.008	—	—	—	0.079	0.079
	735iL	—	—	④	0.008	—	—	—	0.079	0.079
	750iL	—	—	⑤	0.008	—	—	—	0.079	0.079
1991	318i	—	—	①	0.008	—	—	—	0.079	0.079
	318iC	—	—	①	0.008	—	—	—	0.079	0.079
	M3	—	—	①	0.008	—	—	—	0.079	0.079
	325i	—	—	①	0.008	—	—	—	0.079	0.079
	325iC	—	—	①	0.008	—	—	—	0.079	0.079
	325iX	—	—	①	0.008	—	—	—	0.079	0.079
	525i	—	—	②	0.008	—	—	—	0.079	0.079
	535i	—	—	②	0.008	—	—	—	0.079	0.079
	M5	—	—	⑥	0.008	—	—	—	0.079	0.079
	735i	—	—	④	0.008	—	—	—	0.079	0.079
	735iL	—	—	④	0.008	—	—	—	0.079	0.079
	750iL	—	—	④	0.008	—	—	—	0.079	0.079
	850i	—	—	⑤	0.008	—	—	—	0.079	0.079
1992	318iC	—	—	①	0.008	—	—	—	0.079	0.079
	325i	—	—	①	0.008	—	—	—	0.079	0.079
	325iC	—	—	①	0.008	—	—	—	0.079	0.079
	525i	—	—	②	0.008	—	—	—	0.079	0.079
	535i	—	—	②	0.008	—	—	—	0.079	0.079
	M5	—	—	⑥	0.008	—	—	—	0.079	0.079
	735i	—	—	④	0.008	—	—	—	0.079	0.079
	735iL	—	—	④	0.008	—	—	—	0.079	0.079
	750iL	—	—	④	0.008	—	—	—	0.079	0.079
	850i	—	—	⑤	0.008	—	—	—	0.079	0.079

BRAKE SPECIFICATIONS

All measurements in inches unless noted.

Year	Model	Master Cylinder Bore	Brake Disc Original Thickness	Brake Disc Minimum Thickness	Maximum Runout	Brake Drum Diameter Original Inside Diameter	Brake Drum Diameter Max. Wear Limit	Brake Drum Diameter Maximum Machine Diameter	Minimum Lining Thickness Front	Minimum Lining Thickness Rear
1993	318iC	—	—	①	0.008	—	—	—	0.079	0.079
	325i	—	—	①	0.008	—	—	—	0.079	0.079
	325iC	—	—	①	0.008	—	—	—	0.079	0.079
	525i	—	—	②	0.008	—	—	—	0.079	0.079
	535i	—	—	②	0.008	—	—	—	0.079	0.079
	M5	—	—	⑥	0.008	—	—	—	0.079	0.079
	735i	—	—	④	0.008	—	—	—	0.079	0.079
	735iL	—	—	④	0.008	—	—	—	0.079	0.079
	750iL	—	—	④	0.008	—	—	—	0.079	0.079
	850i	—	—	⑤	0.008	—	—	—	0.079	0.079
1994	318iC	—	—	①	0.008	—	—	—	0.079	0.079
	325i	—	—	①	0.008	—	—	—	0.079	0.079
	325iC	—	—	①	0.008	—	—	—	0.079	0.079
	525i	—	—	②	0.008	—	—	—	0.079	0.079
	535i	—	—	②	0.008	—	—	—	0.079	0.079
	M5	—	—	⑥	0.008	—	—	—	0.079	0.079
	735i	—	—	④	0.008	—	—	—	0.079	0.079
	735iL	—	—	④	0.008	—	—	—	0.079	0.079
	750iL	—	—	④	0.008	—	—	—	0.079	0.079
	850i	—	—	⑤	0.008	—	—	—	0.079	0.079

① Front: 0.906
  Rear: 0.315
② Front: 0.787
  Rear: 0.315
③ Front: 1.102
  Rear: 0.315
④ Front: 1.024
  Rear: 0.394
⑤ Front: 1.102
  Rear: 0.709
⑥ Front: 1.039
  Rear: 0.709

WHEEL ALIGNMENT

Year	Model		Caster Range (deg.)	Caster Preferred Setting (deg.)	Camber Range (deg.)	Camber Preferred Setting (deg.)	Toe-in (in.)	Steering Axis Inclination (deg.)
1990	325	Front	8P–9P	$8\frac{1}{2}$P	$\frac{3}{16}$N–$1\frac{3}{16}$N	$\frac{11}{16}$N	$\frac{5}{32}$P	$13\frac{7}{8}$
		Rear	—	—	$1\frac{13}{16}$N–$2\frac{13}{16}$N	$2\frac{5}{16}$N	$\frac{3}{16}$P	—
	325iC	Front	8P–9P	$8\frac{1}{2}$P	$\frac{3}{16}$N–$1\frac{3}{16}$N	$\frac{11}{16}$N	$\frac{5}{32}$P	$13\frac{7}{8}$
		Rear	—	—	$1\frac{13}{16}$N–$2\frac{13}{16}$N	$2\frac{5}{16}$N	$\frac{3}{16}$P	—
	325iX	Front	$1\frac{1}{16}$P–$2\frac{1}{16}$P	$1\frac{9}{16}$P	$\frac{1}{2}$N–$1\frac{1}{2}$N ①	1N ③	0	$12\frac{11}{16}$
		Rear	—	—	$1\frac{1}{2}$N–$2\frac{1}{2}$N ②	2N ④	$\frac{7}{32}$P ⑤	—
	M3	Front	$8\frac{1}{4}$P–$9\frac{1}{4}$P	$8\frac{3}{4}$P	$2\frac{1}{32}$N–$1\frac{21}{32}$N	$1\frac{5}{32}$N	$\frac{5}{32}$P	—
		Rear	—	—	2N–3N	$2\frac{1}{2}$N	$\frac{1}{4}$P	—
	525i	Front	$7\frac{3}{8}$P–$8\frac{3}{8}$P	$7\frac{7}{8}$P	$\frac{9}{32}$P–$\frac{23}{32}$N	$\frac{7}{32}$N	$\frac{5}{32}$P	$12\frac{1}{8}$
		Rear	—	—	$1\frac{13}{16}$N–$2\frac{13}{16}$N	$2\frac{5}{16}$N	$\frac{7}{32}$P	—
	535i	Front	$7\frac{3}{8}$P–$8\frac{3}{8}$P	$7\frac{7}{8}$P	$\frac{9}{32}$P–$\frac{23}{32}$N	$\frac{7}{32}$N	$\frac{5}{32}$P	$12\frac{1}{8}$
		Rear	—	—	$1\frac{13}{16}$N–$2\frac{13}{16}$N	$2\frac{5}{16}$N	$\frac{7}{32}$P	—
	735i	Front	$7\frac{1}{2}$P–$8\frac{1}{2}$P	8P	$\frac{9}{32}$P–$\frac{23}{32}$N	$\frac{7}{32}$N	$\frac{5}{32}$P	$12\frac{1}{8}$
		Rear	—	—	$1\frac{13}{16}$N–$2\frac{13}{16}$N	$2\frac{5}{16}$N	$\frac{7}{32}$P	—
	735iL	Front	$7\frac{1}{2}$P–$8\frac{1}{2}$P	8P	$\frac{9}{32}$P–$\frac{23}{32}$N	$\frac{7}{32}$N	$\frac{5}{32}$P	$12\frac{1}{8}$
		Rear	—	—	$1\frac{13}{16}$N–$2\frac{13}{16}$N	$2\frac{5}{16}$N	$\frac{7}{32}$P	—
	750iL	Front	$7\frac{1}{2}$P–$8\frac{1}{2}$P	8P	$\frac{9}{32}$P–$\frac{23}{32}$N	$\frac{7}{32}$N	$\frac{5}{32}$P	$12\frac{1}{8}$
		Rear	—	—	$1\frac{13}{16}$N–$2\frac{13}{16}$N	$2\frac{5}{16}$N	$\frac{7}{32}$P	—
1991	318i	Front	8P–9P	$8\frac{1}{2}$P	$\frac{3}{16}$N–$1\frac{3}{16}$N	$\frac{11}{16}$N	$\frac{5}{32}$P	$13\frac{7}{8}$
		Rear	—	—	$1\frac{13}{16}$N–$2\frac{13}{16}$N	$2\frac{5}{16}$N	$\frac{3}{16}$P	—
	318iC	Front	8P–9P	$8\frac{1}{2}$P	$\frac{3}{16}$N–$1\frac{3}{16}$N	$\frac{11}{16}$N	$\frac{5}{32}$P	$13\frac{7}{8}$
		Rear	—	—	$1\frac{13}{16}$N–$2\frac{13}{16}$N	$2\frac{5}{16}$N	$\frac{3}{16}$P	—
	318iS	Front	8P–9P	$8\frac{1}{2}$P	$\frac{3}{16}$N–$1\frac{3}{16}$N	$\frac{11}{16}$N	$\frac{5}{32}$P	$13\frac{7}{8}$
		Rear	—	—	$1\frac{13}{16}$N–$2\frac{13}{16}$N	$2\frac{5}{16}$N	$\frac{3}{16}$P	—
	325i	Front	8P–9P	$8\frac{1}{2}$P	$\frac{3}{16}$N–$1\frac{3}{16}$N	$\frac{11}{16}$N	$\frac{5}{32}$P	$13\frac{7}{8}$
		Rear	—	—	$1\frac{13}{16}$N–$2\frac{13}{16}$N	$2\frac{5}{16}$N	$\frac{3}{16}$P	—
	325iC	Front	8P–9P	$8\frac{1}{2}$P	$\frac{3}{16}$N–$1\frac{3}{16}$N	$\frac{11}{16}$N	$\frac{5}{32}$P	$13\frac{7}{8}$
		Rear	—	—	$1\frac{13}{16}$N–$2\frac{13}{16}$N	$2\frac{5}{16}$N	$\frac{3}{16}$P	—
	325iX	Front	$1\frac{1}{16}$P–$2\frac{1}{16}$P	$1\frac{9}{16}$P	$\frac{1}{2}$N–$1\frac{1}{2}$N ①	1N ③	0	$12\frac{11}{16}$
		Rear	—	—	$1\frac{1}{2}$N–$2\frac{1}{2}$N ②	2N ④	$\frac{7}{32}$P ⑤	—
	M3	Front	$8\frac{1}{4}$P–$9\frac{1}{4}$P	$8\frac{3}{4}$P	$2\frac{1}{32}$N–$1\frac{21}{32}$N	$1\frac{5}{32}$N	$\frac{5}{32}$P	—
		Rear	—	—	2N–3N	$2\frac{1}{2}$N	$\frac{1}{4}$P	—
	525i	Front	$7\frac{3}{8}$P–$8\frac{3}{8}$P	$7\frac{7}{8}$P	$\frac{9}{32}$P–$\frac{23}{32}$N	$\frac{7}{32}$N	$\frac{5}{32}$P	$12\frac{1}{8}$
		Rear	—	—	$1\frac{13}{16}$N–$2\frac{13}{16}$N	$2\frac{5}{16}$N	$\frac{7}{32}$P	—
	535i	Front	$7\frac{3}{8}$P–$8\frac{3}{8}$P	$7\frac{7}{8}$P	$\frac{9}{32}$P–$\frac{23}{32}$N	$\frac{7}{32}$N	$\frac{5}{32}$P	$12\frac{1}{8}$
		Rear	—	—	$1\frac{13}{16}$N–$2\frac{13}{16}$N	$2\frac{5}{16}$N	$\frac{7}{32}$P	—
	M5	Front	$7\frac{11}{16}$P–$8\frac{11}{16}$P	$8\frac{3}{16}$P	0–1N	$\frac{1}{2}$N	0	$12\frac{23}{32}$
		Rear	—	—	$1\frac{7}{16}$N–$2\frac{7}{16}$N	$1\frac{15}{16}$N	$\frac{1}{8}$P	—

WHEEL ALIGNMENT

Year	Model		Caster Range (deg.)	Caster Preferred Setting (deg.)	Camber Range (deg.)	Camber Preferred Setting (deg.)	Toe-in (in.)	Steering Axis Inclination (deg.)
	735i	Front	$7^1/_2$P–$8^1/_2$P	8P	$^9/_{32}$P–$^{23}/_{32}$N	$^7/_{32}$N	$^5/_{32}$P	$12^1/_8$
		Rear	—	—	$1^{13}/_{16}$N–$2^{13}/_{16}$N	$2^5/_{16}$N	$^7/_{32}$P	—
	735iL	Front	$7^1/_2$P–$8^1/_2$P	8P	$^9/_{32}$P–$^{23}/_{32}$N	$^7/_{32}$N	$^5/_{32}$P	$12^1/_8$
		Rear	—	—	$1^{13}/_{16}$N–$2^{13}/_{16}$N	$2^5/_{16}$N	$^7/_{32}$P	—
	750iL	Front	$7^1/_2$P–$8^1/_2$P	8P	$^9/_{32}$P–$^{23}/_{32}$N	$^7/_{32}$N	$^5/_{32}$P	$12^1/_8$
		Rear	—	—	$1^{13}/_{16}$N–$2^{13}/_{16}$N	$2^5/_{16}$N	$^7/_{32}$P	—
	850i	Front	$7^1/_2$P–$8^1/_2$P	8P	$^9/_{32}$P–$^{23}/_{32}$N	$^7/_{32}$N	$^5/_{32}$P	$12^1/_8$
		Rear	—	—	1N–$1^1/_2$N	$1^1/_4$N	$^5/_{32}$P	—
1992	318iC	Front	8P–9P	$8^1/_2$P	$^3/_{16}$N–$1^3/_{16}$N	$^{11}/_{16}$N	$^5/_{32}$P	$13^7/_8$
		Rear	—	—	$1^{13}/_{16}$N–$2^{13}/_{16}$N	$2^5/_{16}$N	$^3/_{16}$P	—
	325i	Front	8P–9P	$8^1/_2$P	$^3/_{16}$N–$1^3/_{16}$N	$^{11}/_{16}$N	$^5/_{32}$P	$13^7/_8$
		Rear	—	—	$1^{13}/_{16}$N–$2^{13}/_{16}$N	$2^5/_{16}$N	$^3/_{16}$P	—
	325iC	Front	8P–9P	$8^1/_2$P	$^3/_{16}$N–$1^3/_{16}$N	$^{11}/_{16}$N	$^5/_{32}$P	$13^7/_8$
		Rear	—	—	$1^{13}/_{16}$N–$2^{13}/_{16}$N	$2^5/_{16}$N	$^3/_{16}$P	—
	525i	Front	$7^3/_8$P–$8^3/_8$P	$7^7/_8$P	$^9/_{32}$P–$^{23}/_{32}$N	$^7/_{32}$N	$^5/_{32}$P	$12^1/_8$
		Rear	—	—	$1^{13}/_{16}$N–$2^{13}/_{16}$N	$2^5/_{16}$N	$^7/_{32}$P	—
	535i	Front	$7^3/_8$P–$8^3/_8$P	$7^7/_8$P	$^9/_{32}$P–$^{23}/_{32}$N	$^7/_{32}$N	$^5/_{32}$P	$12^1/_8$
		Rear	—	—	$1^{13}/_{16}$N–$2^{13}/_{16}$N	$2^5/_{16}$N	$^7/_{32}$P	—
	M5	Front	$7^{11}/_{16}$P–$8^{11}/_{16}$P	$8^3/_{16}$P	0–1N	$^1/_2$N	0	$12^{23}/_{32}$
		Rear	—	—	$1^7/_{16}$N–$2^7/_{16}$N	$1^{15}/_{16}$N	$^1/_8$P	—
	735i	Front	$7^1/_2$P–$8^1/_2$P	8P	$^9/_{32}$P–$^{23}/_{32}$N	$^7/_{32}$N	$^5/_{32}$P	$12^1/_8$
		Rear	—	—	$1^{13}/_{16}$N–$2^{13}/_{16}$N	$2^5/_{16}$N	$^7/_{32}$P	—
	735iL	Front	$7^1/_2$P–$8^1/_2$P	8P	$^9/_{32}$P–$^{23}/_{32}$N	$^7/_{32}$N	$^5/_{32}$P	$12^1/_8$
		Rear	—	—	$1^{13}/_{16}$N–$2^{13}/_{16}$N	$2^5/_{16}$N	$^7/_{32}$P	—
	750iL	Front	$7^1/_2$P–$8^1/_2$P	8P	$^9/_{32}$P–$^{23}/_{32}$N	$^7/_{32}$N	$^5/_{32}$P	$12^1/_8$
		Rear	—	—	$1^{13}/_{16}$N–$2^{13}/_{16}$N	$2^5/_{16}$N	$^7/_{32}$P	—
	850i	Front	$7^1/_2$P–$8^1/_2$P	8P	$^9/_{32}$P–$^{23}/_{32}$N	$^7/_{32}$N	$^5/_{32}$P	$12^1/_8$
		Rear	—	—	1N–$1^1/_2$N	$1^1/_4$N	$^5/_{32}$P	—
1993	318iC	Front	8P–9P	$8^1/_2$P	$^3/_{16}$N–$1^3/_{16}$N	$^{11}/_{16}$N	$^5/_{32}$P	$13^7/_8$
		Rear	—	—	$1^{13}/_{16}$N–$2^{13}/_{16}$N	$2^5/_{16}$N	$^3/_{16}$P	—
	325i	Front	8P–9P	$8^1/_2$P	$^3/_{16}$N–$1^3/_{16}$N	$^{11}/_{16}$N	$^5/_{32}$P	$13^7/_8$
		Rear	—	—	$1^{13}/_{16}$N–$2^{13}/_{16}$N	$2^5/_{16}$N	$^3/_{16}$P	—
	325iC	Front	8P–9P	$8^1/_2$P	$^3/_{16}$N–$1^3/_{16}$N	$^{11}/_{16}$N	$^5/_{32}$P	$13^7/_8$
		Rear	—	—	$1^{13}/_{16}$N–$2^{13}/_{16}$N	$2^5/_{16}$N	$^3/_{16}$P	—
	525i	Front	$7^3/_8$P–$8^3/_8$P	$7^7/_8$P	$^9/_{32}$P–$^{23}/_{32}$N	$^7/_{32}$N	$^5/_{32}$P	$12^1/_8$
		Rear	—	—	$1^{13}/_{16}$N–$2^{13}/_{16}$N	$2^5/_{16}$N	$^7/_{32}$P	—
	535i	Front	$7^3/_8$P–$8^3/_8$P	$7^7/_8$P	$^9/_{32}$P–$^{23}/_{32}$N	$^7/_{32}$N	$^5/_{32}$P	$12^1/_8$
		Rear	—	—	$1^{13}/_{16}$N–$2^{13}/_{16}$N	$2^5/_{16}$N	$^7/_{32}$P	—
	M5	Front	$7^{11}/_{16}$P–$8^{11}/_{16}$P	$8^3/_{16}$P	0–1N	$^1/_2$N	0	$12^{23}/_{32}$
		Rear	—	—	$1^7/_{16}$N–$2^7/_{16}$N	$1^{15}/_{16}$N	$^1/_8$P	—
	735i	Front	$7^1/_2$P–$8^1/_2$P	8P	$^9/_{32}$P–$^{23}/_{32}$N	$^7/_{32}$N	$^5/_{32}$P	$12^1/_8$
		Rear	—	—	$1^{13}/_{16}$N–$2^{13}/_{16}$N	$2^5/_{16}$N	$^7/_{32}$P	—
	735iL	Front	$7^1/_2$P–$8^1/_2$P	8P	$^9/_{32}$P–$^{23}/_{32}$N	$^7/_{32}$N	$^5/_{32}$P	$12^1/_8$
		Rear	—	—	$1^{13}/_{16}$N–$2^{13}/_{16}$N	$2^5/_{16}$N	$^7/_{32}$P	—

WHEEL ALIGNMENT

Year	Model		Caster Range (deg.)	Caster Preferred Setting (deg.)	Camber Range (deg.)	Camber Preferred Setting (deg.)	Toe-in (in.)	Steering Axis Inclination (deg.)
	750iL	Front	7½P-8½P	8P	9/32P-23/32N	1/32N	5/32P	12 1/8
		Rear	—	—	1 13/16N-2 13/16N	2 5/16N	7/32P	—
	850i	Front	7½P-8½P	8P	9/32P-23/32N	7/32N	5/32P	12 1/8
		Rear	—	—	1N-1½N	1¼N	5/32P	—
1994	318iC	Front	8P-9P	8½P	3/16N-1 3/16N	11/16N	5/32P	13 7/8
		Rear	—	—	1 13/16N-2 13/16N	2 5/16N	3/16P	—
	325i	Front	8P-9P	8½P	3/16N-1 3/16N	11/16N	5/32P	13 7/8
		Rear	—	—	1 13/16N-2 13/16N	2 5/16N	3/16P	—
	325iC	Front	8P-9P	8½P	3/16N-1 3/16N	11/16N	5/32P	13 7/8
		Rear	—	—	1 13/16N-2 13/16N	2 5/16N	3/16P	—
	525i	Front	7 3/8P-8 3/8P	7 7/8P	9/32P-23/32N	7/32N	5/32P	12 1/8
		Rear	—	—	1 13/16N-2 13/16N	2 5/16N	7/32P	—
	M5	Front	7 11/16P-8 11/16P	8 3/16P	0-1N	½N	0	12 23/32
		Rear	—	—	1 7/16N-2 7/16N	1 15/16N	1/8P	—
	750iL	Front	7½P-8½P	8P	9/32P-23/32N	7/32N	5/32P	12 1/8
		Rear	—	—	1 13/16N-2 13/16N	2 5/16N	7/32P	—
	850i	Front	7½P-8½P	8P	9/32P-23/32N	7/32N	5/32P	12 1/8
		Rear	—	—	1N-1½N	1¼N	5/32P	—

N—Negative
P—Positive
① M Suspension: 13/16N-1 13/16N
② M Suspension: 2N-3N
③ M Suspension: 15/16N
④ M Suspension: 2½N
⑤ M Suspension: ¼N

ENGINE MECHANICAL

NOTE: Disconnecting the negative battery cable on some vehicles may interfere with the functions of the on-board computer systems and may require the computer to undergo a relearning process.

Engine Assembly

REMOVAL AND INSTALLATION

3 Series

1.8L (M42B18) ENGINE

1. Disconnect the battery ground cable. Remove the transmission and remove the engine splash guard. Disconnect the gas spring and prop rod and support hood safely in the fully open position.

2. Remove the fan cowl by turning the expansion rivets on the left and right sides. Lift the cowl up and out of the engine compartment.

3. Hold the fan pulley while unscrewing the fan nut from the shaft.

The shaft uses left hand threads; turn the nut counterclockwise to unscrew.

4. Drain the coolant from the engine block. Disconnect the bottom hose from the radiator expansion tank, the engine coolant hoses and the heater hoses from the splash wall. Drain all coolant into clean containers for reuse or proper disposal.

5. Disconnect the air flow meter electrical plug and loosen the hose clamp and mounting screws. Lift the air sensor with the air cleaner up and out of the engine compartment.

6. Unclip the throttle cable and pull the cable out with the rubber holder.

7. Disconnect the fuel lines taking note of their positions. Pull off the vent hose to the filter for tank venting.

8. Disconnect the vacuum fitting at the brake booster.

9. Remove the ignition leads from the coil. Unscrew the connections at the alternator and starter. Disconnect the 2 plugs from the electrical duct. Remove the plug from the throttle valve potentiometer located at the throttle neck. Pull off the tank venting valve plug located next to the air cleaner. Disconnect the fuel injector plug located at the end of the electrical duct near to the fuel pipes. Pull

off the idle speed control connector at the rear of the intake manifold. Disconnect the oil pressure switch electrical connection.

10. Unscrew the front and rear intake manifold supports.

11. Remove the electrical duct from the engine. Disconnect the coolant temperature senders for the gauge and the DME.

12. Disconnect the electrical duct and wiring harness on the engine and lay it off to the side of the engine.

13. Use a suitable lifting yoke to attach to the engine lifting eyes. Unscrew the motor mounts and the engine ground strap. Lift out the engine.

To install:

14. Lower engine into engine compartment. Fasten the motor mounts and the ground strap.

15. Attach the engine wiring harness and electrical duct. Make sure the rubber grommets on the duct are clipped in correctly. Connect the leads to the 2 coolant sensors and the oil pressure switch.

16. Fasten the front and rear intake manifold supports.

17. Connect the idle speed control plug, the fuel injector plug, the tank venting valve plug, the throttle valve potentiometer plug and the electrical lead duct plugs.

18. Reconnect the starter and the alternator. Attach the ignition leads to the coil in the proper order.

19. Refit the vacuum connection to the brake booster. Reconnect the tank vent hose and the fuel hoses. The upper fuel hose is the return line and the bottom is the feed line.

20. Attach the throttle cable and its holder. Replace the air cleaner and air flow meter assembly. Attach the electrical connector to the air flow meter.

21. Connect the heater hoses, engine coolant hoses and the radiator expansion tank hose.

22. Install the fan using tool 11 5 040 or equivalent. Torque the nut to 29 ft. lbs. (40 Nm). If using the fan tool, set the torque wrench to 22 ft. lbs. (30 Nm); the additional length of the tool multiplies the torque to achieve 29 ft. lbs. (40 Nm) at the nut.

23. Replace the fan cowl taking care to engage the tabs at the right and left.

24. Replace the splash guard and the transmission. Reconnect the hood prop rod and gas spring.

25. Add the proper coolant mixture and bleed the cooling system.

26. Connect the battery leads and check all fluid levels before starting the engine.

2.3L (S14B23) ENGINE

1. Disconnect the negative battery cable. Remove the transmission.

2. Remove the splash guard from underneath the engine. Put a drain pan underneath and then drain coolant from both the radiator and block.

3. Loosen the hose clamps at either end of the air intake hose leading to the air intake sensor. Pull off the hose. Then, pull both electrical connectors off the air cleaner/air flow sensor unit. Remove both mounting nuts and remove the unit.

4. Disconnect the accelerator and cruise control cables. Unscrew the nuts mounting the cable housing mounting bracket and set the housings and bracket aside.

5. Loosen the clamp and disconnect the brake booster vacuum hose.

6. Loosen the clamp and disconnect the other end of the booster vacuum hose at the manifold. Remove the nut from the intake manifold brace.

7. Loosen the hose clamp and disconnect the air intake hose at the manifold. Then, remove all the nuts attaching the manifold assembly to the outer ends of the intake throttle necks and remove the assembly.

8. Put a drain pan underneath and then loosen the hose clamps and

disconnect the coolant expansion tank hoses. Disconnect the engine ground strap.

9. Disconnect the ignition coil high tension lead. Then, label and disconnect the plugs on the front of the block. Remove the nut fastening another lead farther forward of the plugs and move the lead aside so it will not interfere with engine removal.

10. Label and disconnect the plugs from the rear of the alternator. Label the additional leads and then remove the nuts and disconnect those leads. It's best to reinstall nuts once the leads are removed to keep them from being mixed up.

11. Remove the cover for the electrical connectors from the starter. Label the leads and then remove the attaching nuts and disconnect them. Reinstall the nuts.

12. There is a wire running to a connector on the oil pan to warn of low oil level. Pull off the connector, unscrew the carrier for the lead, and then pull the lead out from above. Pull off the connectors near where the lead for the low oil warning system ran and unclip the wires from the carrier.

13. Find the vacuum hose leading to the fuel pressure regulator. Pull it off. Label and then disconnect the plugs. Unscrew the mounting screw for the electrical lead connecting with the top of the block and remove the lead and its carrier.

14. There is a vacuum hose connecting with one of the throttle necks. Disconnect it and pull it out of the intake manifold bracket. Pull off the electrical connector. Pull out the rubber retainer, and then pull the idle speed control out and put it aside. The engine wiring harness is located nearby. Take it out of its carriers.

15. All the fuel injectors are plugged into a common plate. Carefully and evenly pull the plate off the injectors, pull it out past the pressure regulator and lay it aside.

16. Loosen the clamp and then disconnect the PCV hose. Label and then disconnect the fuel lines connecting the injector circuit. Put a drain pan underneath and then disconnect the heater hose from the cylinder head.

17. Loosen the clamp near the throttle necks and then pull the engine wiring harness out and put it aside. Put a drain pan underneath and then disconnect the heater hose that connects to the block.

18. Loosen the mounting clamp for the carbon canister, slide it out of the clamp and place it aside with the hoses still connected.

19. Note the routing of the oil cooler lines where they connect at the base of the oil filter. Label them if necessary. Put a drain pan underneath and then unscrew the flared connectors for the lines.

20. Unbolt and remove the fan. Store it in an upright position. Remove the radiator.

21. Support the power steering pump. Remove the adjusting bolt and disconnect and remove the belt. Then, remove the nuts and bolts on which the unit hinges. Pull the unit aside and hang it so there will not be strain on the hoses.

22. Remove the adjusting bolt for the air conditioning compressor and disconnect and remove the belt. Then, remove the nut at one end of the hinge bolt and pull the bolt out, suspending the compressor.

23. Remove the through bolts to disconnect the engine hood supports and then open the hood and support it securely.

24. Suspend the engine with a suitable lifting device. Then, remove the nuts for the engine mounting bolts. The mounts are on the axle carrier and the nut is at the top on the left and on the bottom on the right. Then, carefully lift the engine out of the compartment, avoiding contact between it and the components remaining in the vehicle.

To install:

25. Keep these points in mind during installation:

   a. Torque the engine mounting bolts to 32.5 ft. lbs. (44 Nm).

   b. Adjust the belt tension for the air conditioning compressor and power steering pump drive belts to give 1/2-3/4 in. deflection.

   c. Torque the oil cooler line flare nuts to 25 ft. lbs. (34 Nm).

   d. When reconnecting the intake manifold to the throttle necks, inspect and, if necessary, replace the O-rings. Torque the mounting nuts to 6.5 ft. lbs. (9 Nm).

26. Reverse the procedures used for removal and lower the engine into the engine compartment. When the engine is positioned, the guide pin must fit in the bore of the axle carrier. Torque the mounting bolts on the front axle carrier (small bolt) to 18-20 ft. lbs. (25-27 Nm) and the larger bolt to 31-35 ft. lbs. (40-47 Nm). The mount-to-bracket bolts are torqued to 31-35 ft. lbs. (40-47 Nm).

27. Install the intake manifold assembly and connect the fuel lines, use new hose clamps to connect the fuel lines to the fuel filter. Connect all of the multi-prong plugs and all vacuum hoses.

28. Connect the accelerator cable and cruise control cable to the throttle body and adjust the accelerator cable and cruise control cable.

29. Install the coolant recovery tank, use a new hose clamp on the coolant expansion tank.

30. Install the air cleaner and reconnect all electrical plugs. Connect and install the relays in the relay box.

31. Reconnect the wiring to the main control unit and install the idle control unit.

32. Install the air conditioning compressor and power steering pump, properly route the accessory drive belt. Adjust the belt tension.

33. Install the radiator and connect the hoses.

34. Install the transmission.

35. Install the hood support and lower the hood.

36. Make sure all fluid levels are correct before starting the engine. Bleed air from the cooling system.

2.5L (M20B25) ENGINE

1. Disconnect the negative battery cable. Remove the transmission.

2. Without disconnecting hoses, loosen and remove the power steering pump bolts and remove the pump and belts and support the pump out of the way.

3. Remove the drain plug and remove the coolant from the radiator. Then, remove the radiator. Unbolt and remove the fan from the engine. Store it in an upright position.

4. Without disconnecting hoses, remove the mounting bolts that run through the compressor body and remove the air conditioner compressor and drive belt and support the compressor out of the way.

5. Remove the through bolts to disconnect the engine hood supports and then open the hood and support it securely.

NOTE: The hood must be propped in a secure manner. If it falls during work serious injury could result.

6. Disconnect the accelerator cable. If equipped with cruise control, disconnect the cruise control cable. If equipped with an automatic transmission, disconnect the throttle cable leading to the transmission.

7. Pull the large, multi-prong plug off the air flow sensor (an integral part of the air cleaner). Loosen the clamp and disconnect the air intake hose at the air flow sensor. Remove the mounting nuts and remove the air cleaner/air flow sensor unit.

8. Disconnect the coolant expansion tank hose. Disconnect the large, multi-prong connector near the air intake hose.

9. The diagnosis plug is a large, screw-on connector located near the thermostat and associated hoses. Unscrew and disconnect this connector.

10. Disconnect the large coolant hoses connecting to the thermostat.

11. Make sure the engine is cold. Place a metal container under the connection to collect fuel; then, disconnect the fuel line at the connection right near the thermostat housing by unscrewing it. Unfasten the fuel line clip about a foot away from this connection.

12. Disconnect the electrical plugs near the diagnosis plug connector. Disconnect the bracket for the dipstick guide tube.

13. Remove the bolts which attach the water pipes going to the engine to mounting brackets.

14. Disconnect the heater hoses at the heater core (near the firewall). Remove the coolant hose running to the top of the block.

15. Place a metal container under the connection to collect fuel; then, disconnect the remaining fuel hose supplying the engine injectors. Disconnect the electrical connectors.

16. Remove the bolt from the mounting brace connecting with the cylinder head.

17. Mark and disconnect the electrical leads from the starter. Unbolt the starter and lift it out from above.

18. Place a metal container under the connection to collect fuel; then, disconnect the fuel pipe that runs right near the starter.

19. Label electrical connectors on the alternator. Then, pull off the rubber caps for the connectors which are attached with nuts and remove the nuts and any washers. Disconnect the plug-on connector.

20. Disconnect the electrical leads for the coil. Loosen the clips attaching the leads under the distributor and pull the harness away to the left. Disconnect the oil pressure sending unit.

21. Place a drain pan underneath the connections and then disconnect the oil cooler pipes at the crankcase by unscrewing the flarenut fittings.

22. Take the cover off the relay box. Then, lift out the relays and their mounting sockets. Place the relays and associated wiring on top of the engine so they will come out with it.

23. Loosen the mounting clamp and then remove the carbon canister. There is a plate to which a number of electrical leads are connected. Remove the mounting screws and move the plate aside so it will clear the dipstick guide tube when the engine is removed.

24. Remove the 2 bolts that fasten the wiring harness to the firewall. Then, disconnect the engine ground strap.

25. Remove both engine mount through bolts. Lift out the engine with a suitable hoist, using hooks at front and rear.

To install:

26. Lower the engine into the engine compartment. When the engine is positioned, the guide pin must fit in the bore of the axle carrier. Torque the mounting bolts on the front axle carrier small bolt to 18-20 ft. lbs. (25-27 Nm) and the larger bolt to 31-35 ft. lbs. (40-47 Nm). The mount-to-bracket bolts are torqued to 31-35 ft. lbs. (40-47 Nm). Engine-to-bracket mounts are torqued to (small bolt) 16-17 ft. lbs. (22-23 Nm) and large bolt to 31-35 ft. lbs. (40-47 Nm).

27. Connect the fuel lines, use new hose clamps to connect the fuel lines to the fuel filter. Connect all of the multi-prong plugs and all vacuum hoses.

28. Connect the accelerator cable and cruise control cable to the throttle body and adjust the accelerator cable and cruise control cable.

29. Install the coolant recovery tank, use a new hose clamp on the coolant expansion tank.

30. Install the air cleaner and reconnect all electrical plugs. Connect and install the relays in the relay box.

31. Reconnect the wiring to the main control unit and install the idle control unit.

32. Install the air conditioning compressor and power steering pump, properly route the accessory drive belt. Adjust the belt tension.

33. Install the radiator and connect the hoses.

34. Install the transmission.

35. Install the hood support.

36. Make sure all fluid levels are correct before starting the engine. Bleed air from the cooling system.

5 Series

2.5L (M20B25) AND 3.5L (M30B35) ENGINES

1. Disconnect both battery cables, negative first. There is a lead coming from the engine to the positive battery terminal. Disconnect it at the battery. On the 6 Series vehicles, disconnect the ground strap.

2. Unscrew the ground strap for the hood. Support the hood securely and then disconnect the gas props. Then, raise the hood until it is vertical and securely fasten it in place.

3. Remove the transmission. With the engine cool, place a clean container under the coolant drain plug in the side of the block. Remove the plug and drain all coolant from the block. Remove the fan and radiator.

4. Support the power steering pump. Remove the mounting bolts and then hang the pump out of the way in a position that will not put stress on the hoses.

5. Support the air conditioning compressor. Remove the mounting bolts and then hang the compressor out of the way in a position that will not put stress on the hoses.

6. Pull the wire leading to the oxygen sensor out of the clips under the floor. Disconnect the sensor at the exhaust pipe.

7. Pull off the plug at the air flow sensor and remove associated wiring. Remove the hoses and pipes connected to the air cleaner and air flow sensor. Remove the nuts and remove the airflow sensor and air cleaner as an assembly.

8. Pull the large, multi-prong plug off the DME box in the glove compartment. Disconnect the smaller plug that's connected to the same harness and plugged in. Then, run the entire harness back into the engine compartment.

9. Disconnect the engine ground wire located at the rear of the block. Unclip the harness for the DME from the firewall.

10. Disconnect both the low tension and the high tension wire from the coil. Disconnect the wires from the solenoid. Pull the wiring harness out of the holders.

11. Pull off the fuse box cover and the cap. Remove the relays (they have metal covers) on one side of the fuse box. Then, disconnect the wiring harness that leads into the fuse box. On the 635CSi, unclamp the harness where it is clamped to the fender well and remove the diagnosis socket, located right near the fuse box.

12. Disconnect the accelerator and cruise control cables.

13. Unclamp and remove the coolant hose that leads to the expansion tank. Disconnect the fuel return line, collecting any fuel in a metal container for safe disposal. Unclip the wiring harness clips on the wires that run through this area of the engine compartment.

14. Disconnect the fuel supply line, collecting any fuel in a metal container for safe disposal. Disconnect the heater hoses at connections.

15. Pull the main vacuum supply hose off at the intake manifold.

16. Disconnect the remaining coolant hose and plug it.

17. Install a lifting sling to the hooks on top of the engine. Unbolt the left side engine mount. Remove the main engine ground strap. Unbolt the right side engine mount. Carefully pull the engine out of the compartment.

To install:

18. Reverse the procedures used for removal and lower the engine into the engine compartment. When the engine is positioned, the guide pin must fit in the bore of the axle carrier. Torque the mounting bolts on the front axle carrier (small bolt) to 18-20 ft. lbs. (25-27 Nm); the larger bolt to 31-35 ft. lbs. (40-47 Nm). The mount-to-bracket bolts are torqued to 31-35 ft. lbs. (40-47 Nm).

19. Install the intake manifold assembly and connect the fuel lines, use new hose clamps to connect the fuel lines to the fuel filter. Connect all of the multi-prong plugs and all vacuum hoses.

20. Connect the accelerator cable and cruise control cable to the throttle body and adjust the accelerator cable and cruise control cable.

21. Install the coolant recovery tank, use a new hose clamp on the coolant expansion tank.

22. Install the air cleaner and reconnect all electrical plugs. Connect and install the relays in the relay box.

23. Reconnect the wiring to the main control unit and install the idle control unit.

24. Install the air conditioning compressor and power steering pump, properly route the accessory drive belt. Adjust the belt tension.

25. Install the radiator and connect the hoses.

26. Install the transmission.

27. Install the hood support and lower the hood.

28. Make sure all fluid levels are correct before starting the engine. Bleed air from the cooling system.

2.5L (M50B25) ENGINE

1. Disconnect the battery terminals, negative side first and remove the battery. Unscrew and remove the battery tray. Remove the transmission.

2. Loosen the clamp on the cooling duct to the alternator and remove the duct.

3. Disconnect the plug to the air flow meter and loosen the clamps to the air cleaner duct. Unscrew the mounting bolts and remove the air cleaner assembly.

4. Pull out the expansion rivets that hold the fan cowl. Remove the cowl by pulling up out of the engine compartment.

5. Hold the fan pulley while unscrewing the fan nut from the shaft. The shaft uses left hand threads; turn the nut counterclockwise to unscrew.

6. Drain the coolant from the block. The drain plug is located between the exhaust manifolds. Disconnect the coolant hoses from the radiator and remove the coolant level switch plug. On automatic transmission equipped vehicles, remove the oil lines to the radiator and plug.

7. Disconnect the bottom radiator hose and remove the trim panel from the right side of the engine compartment to expose the side of the radiator and the air conditioner condenser.

8. Pull the plug off of the air conditioner temperature switch.

9. Remove the radiator supporting clips by inserting a small prybar down from above into the slot and pulling back. Pull the radiator free from the clip. Remove the radiator from the vehicle.

10. Disconnect the heater hoses from the heater valve and the heater.

11. Unscrew the fastener from the throttle cable cover and pull the cover forward and off. Unclip the cable and pull the cable out with the rubber holder.

12. Pull the vacuum fitting from the brake booster and plug the openings.

13. Remove the engine and intake manifold covers. Unscrew the bolt holding the ground strap on the front lifting eye. Replace the bolt before lifting the engine.

14. Unscrew the 2 bolts holding the plug plate and pull off the plug plate. Be careful not to damage the rubber seals. Take off the ignition coil electrical plugs. Remove the plug plate complete with the electrical leads.

15. Remove the cylinder head vent hose and pull off the air temperature sensor plug. Remove the tank venting hose and the throttle heating hoses from the throttle body. Remove the throttle valve switch plug. Unclip the idle speed control valve mounted on the manifold. Disconnect the fuel hoses from the pipes.

16. Unscrew the hardware holding the intake manifold to the cylinder head. Remove the intake manifold taking care not to drop anything into the exposed ports.

17. Disconnect the plugs from the temperature sensor, temperature gauge, the oil pressure switch and the idle speed control valve. Disconnect the cylinder identifying sender plug (black) and the pulse sender plug (gray) for the DME. Unscrew the oxygen sensor plug in the holder.

18. Remove the electric leads from the alternator and the starter. Unscrew the electrical lead tray and place the engine wiring harness to the side.

19. Loosen the drive belt for the power steering pump and the air conditioner compressor by turning their respective tensioners clockwise. This will release the tension on the belt and allow the belt to be removed.

20. Unbolt the power steering pump and place to the side without disconnecting the hoses. Unbolt the air conditioner compressor and place to the side without disconnecting the lines.

21. Attach a lifting fixture to the engine lifting hooks. Unscrew the engine mounts and ground strap. Lift the engine out of the vehicle being careful of the front radiator mount.

To install:

22. Lower the engine into the vehicle and attach the motor mounts and ground strap.

23. Install the power steering pump and the air conditioner compressor. Install the drive belts.

24. Replace the wiring harness and electrical lead tray on the engine. Connect the leads to the starter and alternator. Screw in the plug for the oxygen sensor holder. Connect the leads for the cylinder identifying sender, the DME pulse sender, the temperature sensor, the temperature gauge sender, the oil pressure switch and the idle speed control valve.

25. Install the intake manifold making sure the intake seals are intact. Replace the intake seals if any signs of deterioration are evident.

26. Attach the fuel lines. The upper line is the return and the lower is the feed.

27. Attach the idle speed control valve hose located on the manifold.

28. Connect the throttle valve switch plug, the throttle valve heating lines and the tank vent line.

29. Connect the air temperature sensor plug and attach the cylinder head venting hoses.

30. Reconnect the plugs for the ignition coils and mount the plug plate. Attach the ground strap to the front lifting eye.

31. Replace the engine and manifold covers. Connect the line to the brake booster.

32. Reconnect the throttle cable and cover.

33. Connect the heater hoses to the valve and inlet. Remount the radiator by pressing down on the mounting clips to fasten. Check that the lower mounts are in place. Connect the temperature switch plug for the air conditioner and replace the trim panel. Connect the cooling system hoses and the automatic transmission lines.

34. Install the fan using tool 11 5 040 or equivalent. Torque the nut to 29 ft. lbs. (40 Nm). If using the fan tool, set the torque wrench to 22 ft. lbs. (30 Nm); the additional length of the tool multiplies the torque to achieve 29 ft. lbs. (40 Nm) at the nut. Replace the radiator cowling.

35. Replace the air cleaner assembly and connect the electrical plug. Install the transmission and fill and bleed the cooling system. Install the battery tray and battery. Check all fluids before starting engine.

3.6L (S38B36) ENGINE

1. Disconnect the battery negative cable. Then, disconnect the positive cable. Scribe matchmarks and then remove the hood.

2. Remove the fan. Remove the drain plugs in the block and radiator. Disconnect the hoses and remove the radiator.

3. Support the power steering pump. Remove the mounting bolts and then hang the pump out of the way in a position that will not put stress on the hoses.

4. Support the air conditioning compressor. Remove the mounting bolts and then hang the compressor out of the way in a position that will not put stress on the hoses.

5. Remove the transmission.

6. Remove the attaching bolt and, with an appropriate puller, remove the vibration damper from the front of the engine.

7. Remove the bolts at either end and remove the cross brace that runs under the engine. Remove the heatshield.

8. Disconnect the electrical connector going to the air flow sensor. Pull the electrical leads out of the wiring holders. Loosen the hose clamp for the air intake hose. Remove the mounting nut for the air cleaner. Then, remove the air cleaner and air flow sensor as an assembly.

9. Disconnect the large vacuum hose at the bottom of the intake manifold.

10. Disconnect the PCV hoses where they connect to the top of the manifold. Disconnect the throttle cable that runs across the top of the manifold and the hose running near the front. Remove the bolts fastening the manifold to the outer ends of the intake tubes and remove it.

11. Working inside the glove compartment, disconnect the plug that connects to the DME control. Then, guide the leads through and into the engine compartment. Disconnect the high tension lead and the low tension leads at the coil. Then, unfasten the wiring harness holders for the harness running to the coil where the harness runs along the fenderwell.

12. Disconnect the fuel hose connection at the rear of the fuel manifold on top of the engine. Disconnect the vacuum hose that runs along the firewall.

13. Disconnect the plugs for the reference mark and speed sensors. Disconnect the hoses on the coolant expansion tank.

14. Working on the fuse box, pull off the large electrical connector. Pull off the diagnosis socket. Disconnect the remaining leads.

15. Disconnect the heater hoses near the firewall. Using a backup wrench, disconnect the lines at the oil cooler. Disconnect the low pressure fuel line at the pressure regulator.

16. Disconnect the starter leads. Cut the straps and remove the solenoid heatshield.

17. Attach a lifting sling to the engine and support the assembly. Disconnect the ground lead. Then, disconnect the left side engine mount, removing the nut from underneath and then unscrewing the bolt out the top. Do the same for the right mount. Carefully lift the engine out of the compartment, tilting the front of the engine upward for clearance.

To install:

18. Keep these points in mind during installation:

   a. Torque the engine mounting bolts to 32.5 ft. lbs. (43 Nm).

b. Adjust the belt tension for the air conditioning compressor and power steering pump drive belts to give ½-¾ in. deflection.

c. Torque the oil cooler line flarenuts to 25 ft. lbs. (34 Nm).

d. When reconnecting the intake manifold to the throttle necks, inspect and, if necessary, replace the O-rings. Torque the mounting nuts to 6.5 ft. lbs. (8 Nm).

19. Lower the engine into the engine compartment. When the engine is positioned, the guide pin must fit in the bore of the axle carrier. Torque the mounting bolts on the front axle carrier (small bolt) to 18-20 ft. lbs. (25-27 Nm); the larger bolt to 31-35 ft. lbs. (40-47 Nm). The mount-to-bracket bolts are torqued to 31-35 ft. lbs. (40-47 Nm).

20. Install the intake manifold assembly and connect the fuel lines, use new hose clamps to connect the fuel lines to the fuel filter. Connect all of the multi-prong plugs and all vacuum hoses.

21. Connect the accelerator cable and cruise control cable to the throttle body and adjust the accelerator cable and cruise control cable.

22. Install the coolant recovery tank, use a new hose clamp on the coolant expansion tank.

23. Install the air cleaner and reconnect all electrical plugs. Connect and install the relays in the relay box.

24. Reconnect the wiring to the main control unit and install the idle control unit.

25. Install the air conditioning compressor and power steering pump, properly route the accessory drive belt. Adjust the belt tension.

26. Install the radiator and connect the hoses.

27. Install the transmission.

28. Install the hood support.

29. Make sure all fluid levels are correct before starting the engine. Bleed air from the cooling system.

6 Series

1. Disconnect the battery negative cable. Then, disconnect the positive cable. Scribe matchmarks and then remove the hood.

2. Remove the fan. Remove the drain plugs in the block and radiator. Disconnect the hoses and remove the radiator.

3. Support the power steering pump. Remove the mounting bolts and then hang the pump out of the way in a position that will not put stress on the hoses.

4. Support the air conditioning compressor. Remove the mounting bolts and then hang the compressor out of the way in a position that will not put stress on the hoses.

5. Remove the transmission.

6. Remove the attaching bolt and, with an appropriate puller, remove the vibration damper from the front of the engine.

7. Remove the bolts at either end and remove the cross brace that runs under the engine. Remove the heatshield.

8. Disconnect the electrical connector going to the air flow sensor. Pull the electrical leads out of the wiring holders. Loosen the hose clamp for the air intake hose. Remove the mounting nut for the air cleaner. Then, remove the air cleaner and air flow sensor as an assembly.

9. Disconnect the large vacuum hose at the bottom of the intake manifold.

10. Disconnect the PCV hoses where they connect to the top of the manifold. Disconnect the throttle cable that runs across the top of the manifold and the hose running near the front. Remove the bolts fastening the manifold to the outer ends of the intake tubes and remove it.

11. Working inside the glove compartment, disconnect the plug that connects to the DME control. Then, guide the leads through and into the engine compartment. Disconnect the high tension lead and the low tension leads at the coil. Then, unfasten the wiring harness holders for the harness running to the coil where the harness runs along the fender well.

12. Disconnect the fuel hose connection at the rear of the fuel manifold on top of the engine. Disconnect the vacuum hose that runs along the firewall.

13. Disconnect the plugs for the reference mark and speed sensors. Disconnect the hoses on the coolant expansion tank.

14. Working on the fuse box, pull off the large electrical connector. Pull off the diagnosis socket. Disconnect the remaining leads.

15. Disconnect the heater hoses near the firewall. Using a backup wrench, disconnect the lines at the oil cooler. Disconnect the low pressure fuel line at the pressure regulator.

16. Disconnect the starter leads. Cut the straps and remove the solenoid heatshield.

17. Attach a lifting sling to the engine and support the assembly. Disconnect the ground lead. Then, disconnect the left side engine mount,

removing the nut from underneath and then unscrewing the bolt out the top. Do the same for the right mount. Carefully lift the engine out of the compartment, tilting the front of the engine upward for clearance.

To install:

18. Keep these points in mind during installation:

a. Torque the engine mounting bolts to 32.5 ft. lbs. (43 Nm).

b. Adjust the belt tension for the air conditioning compressor and power steering pump drive belts to give ½-¾ in. deflection.

c. Torque the oil cooler line flarenuts to 25 ft. lbs. (34 Nm).

d. When reconnecting the intake manifold to the throttle necks, inspect and, if necessary, replace the O-rings. Torque the mounting nuts to 6.5 ft. lbs. (8 Nm).

19. Lower the engine into the engine compartment. When the engine is positioned, the guide pin must fit in the bore of the axle carrier. Torque the mounting bolts on the front axle carrier (small bolt) to 18-20 ft. lbs. (25-27 Nm); the larger bolt to 31-35 ft. lbs. (40-47 Nm). The mount-to-bracket bolts are torqued to 31-35 ft. lbs. (40-47 Nm).

20. Install the intake manifold assembly and connect the fuel lines, use new hose clamps to connect the fuel lines to the fuel filter. Connect all of the multi-prong plugs and all vacuum hoses.

21. Connect the accelerator cable and cruise control cable to the throttle body and adjust the accelerator cable and cruise control cable.

22. Install the coolant recovery tank, use a new hose clamp on the coolant expansion tank.

23. Install the air cleaner and reconnect all electrical plugs. Connect and install the relays in the relay box.

24. Reconnect the wiring to the main control unit and install the idle control unit.

25. Install the air conditioning compressor and power steering pump, properly route the accessory drive belt. Adjust the belt tension.

26. Install the radiator and connect the hoses.

27. Install the transmission.

28. Install the hood support.

29. Make sure all fluid levels are correct before starting the engine. Bleed air from the cooling system.

7 Series

1. Disconnect the negative battery cable and then the positive. Remove the transmission. Scribe hinge loca-

tions and remove the hood, or remove support struts and prop it securely all the way up.

2. Remove the splash guard from underneath the engine. Then, with the engine cool, remove the drain plugs in the radiator and block and drain the engine coolant.

3. Loosen the power steering pump bolts from underneath. Turn the adjusting pinion to loosen the belt and remove the belt. Then, remove the mounting bolts and remove the power steering pump without disconnecting the hoses. Support the pump out of the way so as to avoid stressing the hoses.

4. Do the same with the air conditioner compressor, this unit does not have the belt adjusting pinion — it is necessary only to loosen all the bolts and push the compressor toward the engine to remove the belt.

5. Loosen the air intake hose clamp and disconnect the hose. Remove the mounting nut and then remove the air cleaner(s).

6. Unscrew the oil filter cover bolt and disconnect the oil cooler lines and the plug from the oil pressure switch on 750iL.

7. The unit on the opposite side of the intake hose from the air cleaner contains the idle speed control valve, which must be removed next. Loosen the hose clamps and pull off the hoses. Disconnect the electrical connector. Remove the mounting nut and then pull the idle speed control out of the air intake hose.

8. Pull off the retainers for the air flow sensor, and then pull the unit off its mountings, disconnecting the vacuum hose from the PCV system at the same time.

9. Working on the coolant expansion tank, disconnect the electrical connector. Remove the nuts on both sides. Loosen their clamps and then disconnect the hoses and remove the tank.

10. Disconnect the heater hoses at both the control valve and at the heater core.

11. Disconnect the throttle and cruise control cables at the throttle lever. Unbolt the cable housing retainer and remove the housing and cables.

12. Pull off the low amperage starter connectors and disconnect the high amperage connector coming from the battery.

13. Loosen its clamp and then disconnect the coolant hose that runs to the alternator.

14. Disconnect the connecting plug for the oxygen sensor, as well as the other plugs.

15. Loosen the clamps and then disconnect the fuel supply and return pipes.

16. Disconnect the fuel pipe at the injector supply manifold. Disconnect the plug. Disconnect the electrical connector at the throttle body. Lift off the protective caps and then remove the attaching nuts for the protective cover for the wiring harness for the injectors and remove it.

17. Disconnect the ground strap at the block. Remove the engine mount nut from the top on both sides.

18. Attach a lifting sling to the engine and support the assembly. Disconnect the ground lead. Carefully lift the engine out of the compartment, tilting the front of the engine upward for clearance.

To install:

19. Keep these points in mind during installation:

a. Torque the engine mounting bolts to 32.5 ft. lbs. (43 Nm).

b. Adjust the belt tension for the air conditioning compressor and power steering pump drive belts to give 1/2-3/4 in. deflection.

c. Torque the oil cooler line flarenuts to 25 ft. lbs. (34 Nm).

d. When reconnecting the intake manifold to the throttle necks, inspect and, if necessary, replace the O-rings. Torque the mounting nuts to 6.5 ft. lbs. (8 Nm).

20. Lower the engine into the engine compartment. When the engine is positioned, the guide pin must fit in the bore of the axle carrier. Torque the mounting bolts on the front axle carrier (small bolt) to 18-20 ft. lbs. (25-27 Nm); the larger bolt to 31-35 ft. lbs. (40-47 Nm). The mount-to-bracket bolts are torqued to 31-35 ft. lbs. (40-47 Nm).

21. Connect the fuel lines, use new hose clamps to connect the fuel lines to the fuel filter. Connect all of the multi-prong plugs and all vacuum hoses.

22. Connect the accelerator cable and cruise control cable to the throttle body and adjust the accelerator cable and cruise control cable.

23. Install the coolant recovery tank, use a new hose clamp on the coolant expansion tank.

24. Install the air cleaner(s) and reconnect all electrical plugs. Connect and install the relays in the relay box.

25. Install the oil filter cover bolt and connect the oil cooler lines and

the plug to the oil pressure switch on the 750iL.

26. Reconnect the wiring to the main control unit and install the idle control unit.

27. Install the air conditioning compressor and power steering pump, properly route the accessory drive belt. Adjust the belt tension.

28. Install the radiator and connect the hoses.

29. Install the transmission.

30. Install the hood support and lower the hood.

31. Make sure all fluid levels are correct before starting the engine. Bleed air from the cooling system.

8 Series

1. Disconnect the negative battery cable and then the positive. Remove the transmission. Scribe hinge locations and remove the hood, or remove support struts and prop it securely all the way up.

2. Remove the mass air flow sensor from the engine. Remove the windshield washer tank.

3. Loosen the oil filter cap to permit the oil to drain back into the oil pan. Then, remove the oil filter lines.

4. Remove the radiator and expansion tank.

5. Unclip the diagnostic clip. Disconnect the wires at the left and right coils. Unscrew the right ignition coil.

6. Disconnect the D+ (thin lead) from the alternator. Disconnect the oil sender.

7. Disconnect the hoses and wire connections from the tank venting valves.

8. Remove the oil catching tray. Disconnect the wire connectors from the sensors, injectors and throttle body.

9. Disconnect the wiring cover at the rear of the engine.

10. Disconnect hoses at pressure regulator, noting there arrangement.

11. Disconnect the temperature sensors and remove the injector wiring harness.

12. Disconnect the alternator main feed wires, at the B+ connection point. Disconnect the starter wire connections.

13. Remove the air conditioning compressor, leaving the hoses connected.

14. Remove the cool air duct for the alternator.

15. Disconnect and plug the fuel lines.

16. Remove the heatshields located under the vehicle on the thrust struts.

17. Remove the heatshields on the right exhaust manifold and remove the right exhaust pipe from the manifold.

18. Drain the power steering fluid and remove the hose from the supply tank.

19. Remove the starter assembly. Disconnect any necessary connections.

20. Disconnect the heater hoses.

21. Attach a suitable lifting device to the engine and unscrew the ground strap and engine mounts.

22. Remove the guide tube for the oil dipstick.

23. Lift the engine slightly and remove the right engine bracket. Turn the rear of the engine to the right to clear the left exhaust pipe past the steering spindle.

24. Remove the engine and place on a suitable holding fixture.

To install:

25. Keep these points in mind during installation:

   a. Torque the engine mounting bolts to 32.5 ft. lbs. (43 Nm).

   b. Adjust the belt tension for the air conditioning compressor and power steering pump drive belts to give 1/2-3/4 in. deflection.

   c. Ensure all hose and wires are connected as prior to removal.

26. Lower the engine into the engine compartment. The mount-to-bracket bolts are torqued to 31-35 ft. lbs. (40-47 Nm).

27. Connect the fuel lines, use new hose clamps to connect the fuel lines to the fuel filter. Connect all of the multi-prong plugs and all vacuum hoses.

28. Install the coolant recovery tank and radiator, use a new hose clamps.

29. Reconnect all electrical plugs. Install the exhaust and starter motor.

30. Install the oil filter cover bolt and connect the oil cooler lines.

31. Install the air conditioning compressor and power steering pump, properly route the accessory drive belt. Adjust the belt tension.

32. Install the transmission.

33. Install the hood support and lower the hood.

34. Make sure all fluid levels are correct before starting the engine. Bleed air from the cooling system.

Engine Mounts

REMOVAL AND INSTALLATION

1. Raise and safely support the vehicle.

2. Support the engine using a suitable lifting device. Disconnect the mounting bolts.

3. Remove the ground strap, if equipped. Remove the engine mounts.

4. Install the mount onto the mounting bracket and replace the bolts.

5. Replace the ground strap, if equipped. Remove the lifting device.

6. Lower the vehicle.

Cylinder Head

REMOVAL AND INSTALLATION

1.8L (M42B18) Engine

1. Disconnect the negative battery cable.

2. Remove the ignition coil cover and pull off the spark plug connectors.

3. Remove the complete ignition tackle. Remove the cylinder head cover.

4. Disconnect the coolant hoses and unscrew the temperature sensor.

5. Remove the thermostat housing and thermostat. Unscrew the upper timing case cover.

6. Rotate the engine in the direction of the rotation until the camshaft peaks of the intake and exhaust camshafts for cylinder No. 1 face each other. The arrows on the sprocket face up.

7. Remove the chain tensioner. Remove the upper chain guide, chain guide bolt on the right side and the sprockets.

Cylinder head tightening sequence — 1.8L (M42B18) engine

8. Remove the cylinder head bolts from the outside to the inside in several steps using the proper tool.

9. Remove the cylinder head. Clean the sealing surfaces on the cylinder head and the crankcase.

10. The installation is the reverse of the removal procedure. Torque the cylinder head bolts in 3 steps in sequence as follows:

   a. Step 1 — 24 ft. lbs. (32.5 Nm)

   b. Step 2 — 90-95 degree turn

   c. Step 3 — plus an additional 90-95 degree turn.

2.3L (S14B23) Engine

1. Disconnect the negative battery cable. Remove the splash guard from under the engine. Put drain pans underneath and remove the drain plugs from both the radiator and block to drain all coolant.

2. Loosen the hose clamps for the air intake hose located next to the radiator and then remove the hose. Disconnect the electrical connectors for the air flow sensor. Then, remove the attaching nuts and remove the air cleaner/air flow sensor unit.

3. Disconnect the accelerator and cruise control cables. Unbolt the cable mounting bracket and move the cables and bracket aside.

4. Remove the attaching nut, pull off the clamp, and then detach the vacuum hose from the brake booster.

5. Loosen the hose clamp and remove the air intake hose from the intake manifold. Remove the nut from the manifold brace.

6. Loosen the clamp and disconnect the other end of the booster vacuum hose at the manifold. Remove the nut from the intake manifold brace.

7. Loosen the hose clamp and disconnect the air intake hose at the manifold. Then, remove the nuts attaching the manifold assembly to the outer ends of the intake throttle necks and remove the assembly.

8. Put a drain pan underneath and loosen the hose clamps and disconnect the coolant expansion tank hoses. Disconnect the engine ground strap.

9. Disconnect the ignition coil high tension lead. Label and then disconnect the plugs on the front of the block. Remove the nut fastening the lead farther forward of the plugs and move the lead aside so it will not interfere with cylinder head removal.

10. Find the vacuum hose leading to the fuel pressure regulator. Pull it off. Label and then disconnect the 2 plugs. Unscrew the mounting screw for the electrical lead connecting with

the top of the block and remove the lead and its carrier.

11. There is a vacuum hose connecting with one of the throttle necks. Disconnect it and pull it out of the intake manifold bracket. Pull off the electrical connector. Pull out the rubber retainer, and then pull the idle speed control out and put it aside. The engine wiring harness is located nearby. Take it out of its carriers.

12. All the fuel injectors are plugged into a common plate. Carefully and evenly pull the plate off the injectors, pull it out past the pressure regulator and lay it aside.

13. Loosen the clamp and then disconnect the PCV hose. Label and then disconnect the fuel lines connecting with the injector circuit. Put a drain pan underneath and then disconnect the heater hose from the cylinder head.

14. Loosen the clamp near the throttle necks and then pull the engine wiring harness out and put it aside. Put a drain pan underneath and then disconnect the heater hose that connects to the block.

15. Remove the bolts from the flanges connecting the exhaust pipes to the exhaust manifold. Provide new gaskets and self-locking nuts. Disconnect the oxygen sensor plug.

16. Put a drain pan underneath and then disconnect the radiator hoses from the pipe at the front of the block.

17. It is not necessary to remove the timing chain completely, but it is necessary to remove the camshaft cover, front covers for the camshaft drive sprockets, the upper guide rail for the timing chain and then turn the engine to TDC firing position for No. 1 cylinder. Remove the timing chain tensioner. Note the relationship between the chain and both the crankshaft and camshaft sprockets and then remove both camshaft drive sprockets. Leave the chain in a position that will not interfere with removal of the head and which will minimize disturbing its routing through the areas on the front of the block.

18. Remove the camshafts.

19. Remove the camshaft followers one at a time, keeping them in exact order for installation in the same positions.

20. Pull off the spark plug connectors. Remove the nuts from the camshaft cover, located just to one side of the row of spark plugs. Remove the ignition lead tube. Remove

the remaining nuts and remove the camshaft cover. Provide new gaskets.

21. Remove the bolts, some are accessible from below, that retain the timing case to the head at the front, the timing case houses the lifters and the camshaft lower bearing saddles. Note that one bolt, on the right side of the vehicle, is longer and retains the shaft for the upper timing chain tensioning rail.

22. Remove the coolant pipe that runs along the left/rear of the block. Remove one bolt at the left/front of the block that is located outside the camshaft cover. Then, go along in the area under the camshaft cover and remove all the remaining bolts for the timing case. Remove the timing case.

23. Remove the hex bolts fastening the head to the block at the front. These are located outside the camshaft cover and just behind the water pump drive belt. Then, remove the head bolts located under the camshaft cover in reverse order of the cylinder head torque sequence.

To install:

24. Make checks of the lower cylinder head and block deck surface to make sure they are true. Clean both cylinder head and block sealing surfaces thoroughly. Lubricate the head bolts with a light coating of engine oil. Make sure there is no oil or dirt in the bolt holes in the block. Install a new head gasket, making sure all bolt, oil and coolant holes line up. Install the bolts as follows:

   a. Torque them in the correct order to 35-37 ft. lbs. (47-50 Nm).

   b. Then torque them in order to 57-59 ft. lbs. (80-82 Nm).

   c. Wait 15 minutes.

   d. Torque them, in order, to 71-73 ft. lbs. (96-100 Nm).

   e. Remember to reinstall the bolts that go outside the cylinder head cover and fasten the front of the head to the block at front and rear.

Removing the timing case for the 2.3L engine. Remove all arrowed bolts

25. BMW recommends checking the fit of each tappet in the timing case, by performing the following procedure:

   a. Measure a tappet's outside diameter with a micrometer. Then, zero an inside micrometer at this exact dimension.

   b. Then, use the inside micrometer to measure the tappet bore that corresponds to this particular tappet. If the resulting measurement is 0.0001-0.0026 in. (0.00254-0.0660mm). The tappet may be reused. If it is worn past this dimension, replace it with a new one. If the tappet is being replaced, repeat steps a and b to make sure it will now meet specifications. If the bore were to be worn so much that even a new tappet would not restore clearance to specification, it would be necessary to replace the timing case.

   c. Repeat for all the remaining tappets. Make sure to measure each tappet and its corresponding bore only.

26. The remaining steps of installation are the reverse of the removal procedure. Note the following:

   a. Before remounting the timing case, replace the O-ring in the oil passage located at the left/front of the block. Also, check the O-rings in the tops of the spark plug bores and replace these as necessary.

   b. Install the timing case and torque the bolts in several stages. The smaller (M7) bolts are torqued to 10-12 ft. lbs. (14-16 Nm); the larger (M8) bolts are torqued to 14.5-15.5 ft. lbs. (19-21 Nm). Install each tappet back into the same bore.

   c. When bolting the exhaust pipes to the flange at the manifold, use new gaskets and self-locking nuts and torque the nuts to 36 ft. lbs. (48 Nm).

   d. When reinstalling the intake manifold, check and, if necessary, replace the O-rings where the manifold tubes connect to the throttle necks. Torque the nuts to 6.5 ft. lbs. (8 Nm).

   e. Make sure to refill the radiator and bleed the cooling system.

2.5L (M20B25) Engine

EXCEPT 525i

1. Disconnect the negative battery cable. Make sure the engine is cool. Disconnect the exhaust pipes at the manifold and at the transmission clamp. Remove the drain plug at the bottom of the radiator and drain the coolant. Drain the engine oil.

2. Disconnect the accelerator and cruise control cables. If equipped with automatic transmission, disconnect the throttle cable that goes to the transmission.

3. Working at the front of the block, disconnect the upper radiator hose, the bypass water hose and several smaller water hoses. Remove the diagnosis plug located at the front corner of the manifold. Remove the bracket located just underneath. Disconnect the fuel line and drain the contents into a metal container for safe disposal.

4. Working on the air cleaner/air flow sensor, disconnect the vacuum hoses, labeling them if necessary. Disconnect all electrical connectors and unclip and remove the wiring harness. There is a relay located in an L-shaped box near the strut tower. Disconnect and remove it. Unclamp and remove the air hose. Remove the mounting nuts and remove the assembly.

5. Disconnect the hose at the coolant overflow tank. Disconnect the idle speed positioner vacuum hose and then remove the positioner from the manifold.

6. If equipped with 4 wheel drive, disconnect the vacuum hose from the servo mounted on the manifold.

7. Place a drain pan underneath and then disconnect the water connections at the front of the intake manifold. Disconnect the electrical connector.

8. Disconnect the heater water hoses. Press down, in the arrowed direction, on the vent tube collar and install the special tool or a similar device to retain the collar in the unlocked position. Disconnect the vent tube and inspect its O-ring seal, replacing it, if necessary.

9. Unbolt the dipstick tube at the manifold. Remove the fuel hose bracket at the cylinder head. Make sure the engine is cold. Then, place a metal container under the connection and disconnect the fuel hose at the connection.

10. Disconnect the high tension lead from the coil. Disconnect and remove the coolant expansion tank.

11. If equipped with 4 wheel drive, disconnect the intake manifold vacuum hose leading the servo that engages 4 wheel drive.

12. Disconnect the fuel injector connectors at all 6 injectors, as well as the 2 additional electrical connectors to sensors on the head. Disconnect the oil pressure sending unit connector. Then, unfasten the carriers and

remove this wiring harness toward the left side of the vehicle.

13. Disconnect the coil high tension wire and disconnect the high tension wires at the plugs. Then, disconnect the tube in which the wires run at the camshaft cover. Disconnect the PCV hose. Then, remove the retaining nuts and remove the camshaft cover.

14. Turn the crankshaft so the TDC line is aligned with the indicator and the valves of No. 6 cylinder are in overlapping, slightly open position.

15. Remove the distributor cap. Then, unscrew and remove the rotor. Unscrew and remove the adapter just underneath the rotor. Remove the cover underneath the adapter. Check its O-ring and replace it, if necessary.

16. Remove the distributor mounting bolts and the protective cover.

17. These engines are equipped with a rubber drive and timing belt. Remove the belt covers. To loosen belt tension, loosen the tension roller bracket pivot bolt and adjusting slot bolt. Push the roller and bracket away from the belt to release the tension, hold the bracket in this position and tighten the adjusting slot bolt to retain the bracket it this position.

18. Remove the timing belt.

NOTE: Make sure to avoid rotating both the engine and camshaft from this point onward.

19. Remove the cylinder head mounting bolts in exact reverse order of the proper tightening sequence. Then, remove the cylinder head.

To install:

20. Clean both cylinder head and block sealing surfaces thoroughly with a hardwood scraper. Inspect the surfaces for flatness. Note that the M20B25 engine gasket is coded 2.5.

21. Install the head with a new gasket. Check that all passages line up with the gasket holes. Clean the threads on the head bolts and coat with a light coating of oil. Keep oil

out of the bolt cavities in the head or the head could be cracked or proper torquing affected.

22. Install the cylinder bolts and torque in steps, to correct specifications.

23. Engines with hex head bolts, tighten as follows:
   a. Step 1 to 29-33 ft. lbs. (39-45 Nm)
   b. Step 2 wait 15 minutes
   c. Step 3 to 43-47 ft. lbs. (58-64 Nm)
   d. Step 4 run engine 25 minutes
   e. Step 5 tighten to 25-30 degree turn

24. Engines with Torx head bolts, tighten as follows:
   a. Step 1 — 22 ft. lbs. (32.5 Nm)
   b. Step 2 — 90 degree turn
   c. Step 3 — plus an additional 90 degree turn

25. Adjust the valves.

26. Complete the installation by reversing all removal procedures. Make sure to refill the engine oil pan and cooling system with proper fluids and to bleed the cooling system.

27. Replace the gaskets for the exhaust system connections, if necessary. Coat the studs with the proper sealant. Note that the plugs for the DME reference mark and speed signals should be connected so the gray plug goes to the socket with a ring underneath.

NOTE: Align the timing marks when installing the timing belt. The crankshaft sprocket mark must point at the notch in the flange of the front engine cover. The camshaft sprocket arrow must point at the alignment mark on the cylinder head. Also, the No. 1 piston must be at TDC of the compression stroke. BMW recommends that the timing belt be replaced every time the cylinder head is removed and the belt is disturbed as a consequence. Tension the belt.

28. Start the engine and run it until it is hot. Stop the engine and again remove the camshaft cover. Using an angle gauge, retorque the head bolts to specification. Reinstall the camshaft cover.

525i

1. Unbolt the exhaust pipe connections at the manifold and at the transmission pipe clamp. Disconnect the negative battery cable.

2. Remove the splash shield from under the engine. With the engine cool, remove the drain plugs from the bottom of the radiator and block. Drain the engine oil.

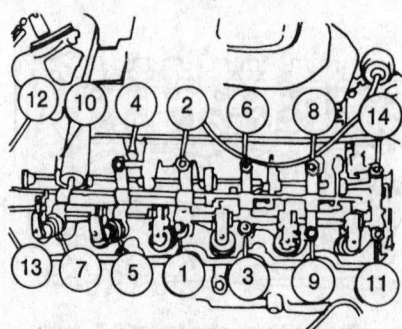

Cylinder head torque sequence — 2.5L (M20B25) engine

3. Remove the fan. Lift out the expansion rivets on either side and remove the fan shroud.

4. Loosen the hose clamp and disconnect the air inlet hose. Remove the mounting nut and remove the air cleaner.

5. The unit on the opposite side of the intake hose from the air cleaner contains the idle speed control valve, which must be removed next. Loosen the hose clamps and pull off the hoses. Disconnect the electrical connector. Remove the mounting nut and then pull the idle speed control out of the air intake hose.

6. Pull off the retainers for the air flow sensor, and then pull the unit off its mountings, disconnecting the vacuum hose from the PCV system at the same time.

7. Working on the coolant expansion tank, disconnect the electrical connector. Remove the nuts on both sides. Loosen their clamps and then disconnect all hoses and remove the tank.

8. Disconnect the heater hoses at both the control valve and at the heater core. Remove the valve, if needed.

9. Disconnect the throttle and cruise control cables at the throttle lever. Unbolt the cable housing retainer and remove the housing and cables.

10. Disconnect the plugs near the thermostat housing. Loosen the hose clamps and pull off the coolant hoses.

11. Disconnect the plug in the line leading to the oxygen sensor. Disconnect the other plugs.

12. Disconnect the fuel supply and return lines, collecting fuel in a metal container for safe disposal.

13. Disconnect the fuel pipe running along the cylinder head, near the manifold. Pull off the electrical connector at the throttle body. Remove the caps, then remove the attaching bolts and remove the wiring harness carrier and harness for the fuel injectors.

14. Disconnect the coil high tension lead. Disconnect the high tension wires at the plugs. Then, remove the mounting nuts and remove the carrier for the high tension wires from the head.

15. Remove the attaching nuts for the camshaft cover and remove it.

16. Turn the engine until the timing marks are at TDC and the No. 6 valves are at overlap, both slightly open.

17. Remove the upper timing case cover. Remove the timing chain tensioner piston.

18. Remove the upper timing chain sprocket bolts and pull the sprocket off, holding it upward and then supporting it securely so the relationship between the chain and sprockets top and bottom will not be lost.

19. Disconnect the upper radiator hose at the thermostat housing. Remove the bolts and remove the support for the intake manifold.

20. Remove the cylinder head bolts in the opposite of numbered order. Then, install 4 special pins part 11 1 063 or equivalent. This is necessary to keep the rocker arm shafts from moving. Then, lift off the head.

21. Make checks of the lower cylinder head and block deck surface to make sure they are true. Install a new head gasket, making sure all bolt, oil and coolant holes line up. Use a gasket marked M30B35. Use a 0.3mm thicker gasket, if the head has been machined.

To install:

22. Apply a very light coating of oil to the head bolts. Don't let oil get into the bolt holes or apply excessive amounts of oil, or torque could be incorrect and the block could crack. Use the type of bolt without a collar. Install the bolts, finger-tight.

23. Torque bolts 1-6 in the correct order to 42-44 ft. lbs. (57-61 Nm). Remove the pins holding the rocker shafts in place. Now, complete the first stage of torquing by torquing bolts 7-14 in the correct order, to the same specification. Adjust the valves after a 15 minute wait. Tighten the bolts, in the correct order, with a torque angle gauge 30-36 degrees, using special tool 11 2 110 or equivalent. Then, reassemble the engine as described below and run it until hot (25 minutes). Then, again remove the valve cover and turn the head bolts, in the correct order, 30-40 degrees.

24. Reinstall the timing sprocket to the camshaft. Make sure the camshaft is in proper time, that new lockplates are used and that nuts are properly torqued.

25. When reinstalling the timing cover, make sure to apply a liquid sealer to the joints between upper and lower timing covers. The remainder of installation is the reverse of removal. Note these points:

   a. Adjust throttle, speed control and accelerator cables. Inspect and if necessary, replace the exhaust manifold gasket.

   b. When reinstalling the cylinder block coolant plug, coat it with sealer. Make sure to refill the cooling system and bleed it. Make sure

to refill the oil pan with the correct amount of oil.

   c. Install the timing chain so the down pin on the camshaft sprocket is at the 8 o'clock when its tapped bores are at right angles to the engine. Torque the sprocket bolts to 6.5-7.5 ft. lbs. (8-10 Nm).

   d. Check the camshaft cover gasket, replacing, as necessary. Tighten camshaft cover bolts in the order shown. Torque the bolts to 6.5-7.5 ft. lbs. (8-10 Nm).

   e. When reinstalling the fan shroud, make sure all guides are located properly.

   f. Coat the tapered portion of the exhaust pipe connection flange with the proper sealant. Torque the attaching nuts to 4.5 ft. lbs. (6 Nm) and loosen 1½ turns.

2.5L (M50B25) Engine

1. If engine is not already removed from the vehicle, disconnect the negative battery cable and drain the engine coolant. Remove the intake manifold and throttle valve. Disconnect the exhaust pipes and the oxygen sensor wire. Remove the exhaust manifolds. Remove the thermostat housing and engine lifting eye.

2. Pull off the connectors for the ignition coils and remove the coils. Unscrew the cylinder heads cover and remove. Remove the sender from the head and the electrical lead duct.

3. Remove the upper timing case cover and the camshaft cover. Crank the engine in the direction of rotation so the intake and exhaust camshaft peaks for cylinder No. 1 face each other. Hold the camshafts in place with tool 11 3 240 or equivalent. With the camshafts in this alignment, the arrows on the sprockets will be facing up. Remove the valve cover mounting studs. Lock the flywheel in place to prevent movement of the crankshaft.

4. Unscrew the chain tensioner and carefully remove. There is a spring contained within the tensioner and may eject if care is not taken.

5. Press down on the upper chain tensioner and lock it into place using tool 11 3 290 or equivalent. Unscrew the transfer timing chain sprockets and pull the 2 off together with the chain. Remove the upper chain tensioner and the lower chain guide. Pull off the main timing chain sprocket along with the chain. Use a bent piece of wire to hold the chain from falling down into the engine. Do not rotate the engine after this point or the valve timing will be disturbed when the engine is reassembled.

6. Unscrew the bolts on the head at the ends of the cams. Using a proper sized Torx® bit or tool 11 2 250, loosen the cylinder head bolts in several steps. Use an outside to inside pattern to prevent warpage. On production heads the bolt washers are locked into place while on replacement heads the washers are loose. Keep track of the bolt washers.

To install:

7. If the camshafts have been removed and reinstalled a waiting period dependent on the ambient temperature is necessary before mounting the cylinder head on the engine. At room temperature wait 4 minutes to allow the lifters to compress fully. At temperatures down to 50°F (10°C) wait 11 minutes. At temperatures lower than 50°F (10°C) wait 30 minutes. This is to prevent contact between the valves and the piston tops. The engine may not be cranked under the same condition for a period of 10 minutes at room temperature; 30 minutes for temperatures down to 50°F (10°C); 75 minutes for temperatures below 50°F (10°C).

8. Clean all mounting surfaces and check the head for warpage. Take care not to drop any pieces of gasket or dirt into the oil or coolant passages. Check the condition of the head locating dowel sleeves.

9. Place a new head gasket on the engine block over the locating dowels and gently place the head on the engine. Align the head with the dowel sleeves and check that the head sits flat on the engine.

10. Cylinder head bolts may only be used once. Lightly oil the threads of the new cylinder head bolts. Check that the head bolt washers are in place and install the bolts. Torque the head bolts in 3 steps; Step 1 to 24 ft. lbs. (33 Nm), Step 2 and 3 to 93 degree torque angle. Torque the center bolts first and go out in a diagonal pattern.

11. Align main timing chain and sprocket on the can so the arrow faces up. The bolt holes in the camshaft should be on the left sides of the sprocket slots. This will allow the tensioner to take up the slack in the chain and rotate the gear to the counterclockwise position.

12. Install the upper chain tensioner and the lower chain guide. Install the transfer timing gears and chain on the camshafts with the arrows facing up. Make sure the pulse sender is installed on the intake cam. Do not tighten the sprocket bolts.

13. Install the lower timing chain tensioner with the groove in a vertical position. Use a new sealing ring and torque to 29 ft. lbs. (40 Nm).

14. Release the upper timing chain tensioner and torque the sprocket bolts to 16 ft. lbs. (22 Nm).

15. Install the valve cover mounting studs and remove the flywheel lock. Install the camshaft cover and the timing case covers using new gaskets. Install the lifting eye and the electrical lead duct. Install the camshaft sensor with a new seal if needed.

16. Install the valve cover using new gaskets if necessary. Check that the gasket seats correctly all the way around the seating area.

17. Install the ignition coils and connect the electrical leads to each coil.

18. Install the thermostat with the arrow or vent facing up with a new O-ring. Install the thermostat housing with a new gasket. Install the intake manifold and throttle valve. Install the exhaust manifolds.

3.5L (M30B35) and 5.0L (M70B50) Engines

1. Unbolt the exhaust pipe connections at the manifold and at the transmission pipe clamp. Disconnect the negative battery cable.

2. Remove the splash shield from under the engine. With the engine cool, remove the drain plugs from the bottom of the radiator and block. Drain the engine oil.

3. Remove the fan. Lift out the expansion rivets on either side and remove the fan shroud.

4. Loosen the hose clamp and disconnect the air inlet hose. Remove the mounting nut and remove the air cleaner.

5. The unit on the opposite side of the intake hose from the air cleaner contains the idle speed control valve,

which must be removed next. Loosen the hose clamps and pull off the hoses. Disconnect the electrical connector. Remove the mounting nut and then pull the idle speed control out of the air intake hose.

6. Pull off the retainers for the air flow sensor, and then pull the unit off its mountings, disconnecting the vacuum hose from the PCV system at the same time.

7. Working on the coolant expansion tank, disconnect the electrical connector. Remove the nuts on both sides. Loosen their clamps and then disconnect all hoses and remove the tank.

8. Disconnect the heater hoses at both the control valve and at the heater core. Remove the valve, if needed.

9. Disconnect the throttle and cruise control cables at the throttle lever. Unbolt the cable housing retainer and remove the housing and cables.

10. Disconnect the plugs near the thermostat housing. Loosen the hose clamps and pull off the coolant hoses.

11. Disconnect the plug in the line leading to the oxygen sensor. Disconnect the other plugs.

12. Disconnect the fuel supply and return lines, collecting fuel in a metal container for safe disposal.

13. Disconnect the fuel pipe running along the cylinder head, near the manifold. Pull off the electrical connector at the throttle body. Remove the caps, then remove the attaching bolts and remove the wiring harness carrier and harness for the fuel injectors.

14. Disconnect the coil high tension lead. Disconnect the high tension wires at the plugs. Then, remove the mounting nuts and remove the carrier for the high tension wires from the head.

15. Remove the attaching nuts for the camshaft cover and remove it.

16. Turn the engine until the timing marks are at TDC and the No. 6 valves are at overlap, both slightly open.

17. Remove the upper timing case cover. Remove the timing chain tensioner piston.

18. Remove the upper timing chain sprocket bolts and pull the sprocket off, holding it upward and then supporting it securely so the relationship between the chain and sprockets top and bottom will not be lost.

19. Disconnect the upper radiator hose at the thermostat housing. Remove the bolts and remove the support for the intake manifold.

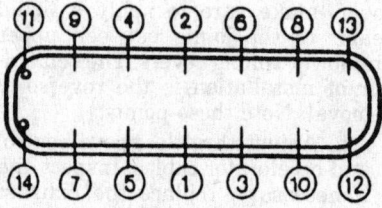

Cylinder head tightening sequence — 3.5L (M30B35) engine

20. Remove the cylinder head bolts in the opposite of numbered order. Then, install 4 special pins part 11 1 063 or equivalent. This is necessary to keep the rocker arm shafts from moving. Then, lift off the head.

To install:

21. Make checks of the lower cylinder head and block deck surface to make sure they are true. Install a new head gasket, making sure all bolt, oil and coolant holes line up. Use a gasket marked M30B35. Use a 0.3mm thicker gasket, if the head has been machined.

22. Apply a very light coating of oil to the head bolts. Don't let oil get into the bolt holes or apply excessive amounts of oil, or torque could be incorrect and the block could crack. Use the type of bolt without a collar. Install the bolts finger-tight.

23. Torque bolts 1-6 in the correct order to 42-44 ft. lbs. (57-60 Nm). Remove the pins holding the rocker shafts in place. Now, complete the first stage of torquing by torquing bolts 7-14 in the correct order, to the same specification. Adjust the valves after a 15 minute wait. Tighten the bolts, in the correct order, with a torque angle gauge 30-36 degrees, using special tool 11 2 110 or equivalent.

24. Reinstall the timing sprocket to the camshaft. Make sure the camshaft is in proper time, that new lockplates are used and that nuts are properly torqued.

25. When reinstalling the timing cover, make sure to apply a liquid sealer to the joints between upper and lower timing covers. The remainder of installation is the reverse of removal. Note these points:

a. Adjust throttle, speed control and accelerator cables. Inspect and if necessary replace the exhaust manifold gasket.

b. When reinstalling the cylinder block coolant plug, coat it with sealer. Make sure to refill the cooling system and bleed it. Make sure to refill the oil pan with the correct amount of oil.

c. Install the timing chain so the down pin on the camshaft sprocket is at the 8 o'clock when its tapped bores are at right angles to the engine. Torque the sprocket bolts to 6.5-7.5 ft. lbs. (8-10 Nm).

d. Check the camshaft cover gasket, replacing, as necessary. Tighten camshaft cover bolts in the order shown. Torque the bolts to 6.5-7.5 ft. lbs. (8-10 Nm).

e. When reinstalling the fan shroud, make sure all guides are located properly.

f. Coat the tapered portion of the exhaust pipe connection flange with the proper sealant. Torque the attaching nuts to 4.5 ft. lbs. (6 Nm) and loosen 1½ turns.

26. Start the engine and run it until hot (25 minutes). Then, again remove the valve cover and turn the head bolts, in the correct order, 30-40 degrees.

3.6L (S38B36) Engine

1. Disconnect the negative battery cable. Scribe matchmarks where the hood hinges attach to the hood. Then, disconnect the support struts, unbolt the hood at the hinges and remove it.

2. Disconnect the electrical connector at the air flow sensor. Loosen the hose clamp at the air intake hose going to the air cleaner, remove the air cleaner attaching nut and remove the air cleaner and air flow sensor.

3. Disconnect the large vacuum hose that connects to the bottom of the intake manifold. Disconnect the PCV hoses where they connect to the top of the manifold. Disconnect the throttle cable that runs across the top of the manifold and the hose running near the front. Remove the bolts fastening the manifold to the outer ends of the intake tubes and remove it.

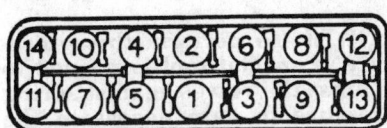

Cylinder head torque sequence — 3.6L (S38B36) engine

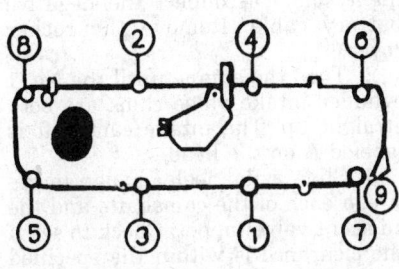

Torque the camshaft cover bolts in sequence — 3.5L (M30B35) engine

4. With the engine cool, drain the coolant from the block. Disconnect the exhaust pipe at the manifold.

5. Working underneath, remove the heatshields. Remove the cross brace and stabilizer bar where they connect to the engine carrier. Remove the exhaust manifold.

6. Disconnect the upper radiator hose. Pull the plugs off the water manifold that connects with the upper radiator hose. Pull off the plug coming from the same harness and connecting to the top of the engine. Then, unclip this harness and pull it out of the way.

7. Loosen the retaining straps and disconnect the electrical connector that runs directly across the front of the block. Disconnect the fuel pipe on the driver's side of the block, collecting fuel in a metal container for safe disposal.

8. Pull the electrical connector off the throttle bypass valve. Disconnect the water hose and remove the bypass valve. Disconnect the large hose just to the right of the throttle bypass valve. Remove the wiring harness clips just to the right.

9. At the rear of the engine, disconnect the fuel return line and collect fuel in a metal container for safe disposal. Disconnect both heater hoses. Remove the conduit for the injector wiring harness from the head. Remove the bolts in the front of the head which run down into the timing cover.

10. It is not necessary to remove the timing chain completely, but it will be necessary to remove the camshaft cover, front covers for the camshaft drive sprockets and the upper guide rail for the timing chain and then turn the engine to TDC firing position for No. 1 cylinder. Then, it will be necessary to remove the timing chain tensioner. Note the relationship between the chain and both the crankshaft and camshaft sprockets, and then remove both camshaft drive sprockets. Leave the chain in a position that will not interfere with removal of the head and which will minimize disturbing its routing through the areas on the front of the block.

11. Remove the camshafts as described below.

12. Remove the camshaft followers one at a time, keeping them in exact order for installation in the same positions.

13. Remove the coolant pipe that runs across the front of the block. Remove the bolts (some are accessible from below) that retain the timing

case to the head at the front, the timing case houses the lifters and the camshaft lower bearing saddles. Then, go along in the area under the camshaft cover and remove all the remaining bolts for the timing case. Remove the timing case.

14. Loosen the head bolts in reverse of the tightening sequence. Remove the cylinder head.

To install:

15. Make checks of the lower cylinder head and block deck surface to make sure they are true. Lubricate the head bolts with a light coating of engine oil. Make sure there is no oil or dirt in the bolt holes in the block. Install a new head gasket, making sure all bolt, oil and coolant holes line up. Use a gasket type M6 marked 3.5M 88.

16. Replace the O-ring in the head at the right/rear where the coolant pipe comes up from the block. Coat the pipe with a suitable sealer.

17. Install the head onto the block. Install the head bolts and tighten in the correct sequence.

18. When installing the timing case, replace the O-rings in the small oil passages in the ends of the head. Inspect the O-rings in the center of the block and replace them if necessary. Coat all sealing surfaces with a sealer. Tighten the bolts evenly, torquing the smaller (M7) bolts to 10-12 ft. lbs. (14-17 Nm) and the larger (M8) bolts to 14.5-15.5 ft. lbs. (19-21 Nm). Install all lifters back into the same bores.

19. Install the camshafts.

20. Reroute the timing chain, as necessary and remount the drive sprockets for the camshaft. Install the tensioning rail that goes at the top of the timing chain.

21. Install the front cover.

22. Continue to reverse the removal procedure. Note these points:

a. When reinstalling the intake manifold, inspect the O-rings and replace, as necessary.

b. Refill the cooling system with an appropriate anti-freeze/water mix and bleed the cooling system.

Valve Lash

ADJUSTMENT

Except M3 and M5

All engines except the M-Series, dual overhead camshaft designs, are equipped with a single overhead camshaft operating the intake and exhaust valves through rocker arm linkage.

NOTE: The valves must be adjusted cold.

1. Disconnect the negative battery cable. Remove the rocker cover.

2. Rotate the engine until the No. 1 cylinder is at TDC on the compression stroke.

NOTE: Locate No. 1 cylinder firing position by the distributor rotor-to-cap position, or by observing the valve action in the opposite cylinder.

3. Measure the valve clearance between the valve stem end and the rocker arm on the No. 1 cylinder.

4. Adjust the clearance by loosening the locknut on the rocker arm and turning the eccentric with a bent rod inserted through a hole provided on the surface of the eccentric.

5. When the proper clearance is obtained, tighten the locknut and recheck the valve clearance. Complete the adjustment on both valves.

6. Rotate the engine crankshaft to the next cylinder in the firing order, adjust the valves and repeat the procedures until all the valves are adjusted.

7. Replace the rocker cover, using a new gasket.

M3 and M5

NOTE: To perform this procedure, a special tool is needed to depress the valves against spring pressure to gain access to the valve adjusting discs. Use tool 11 3 170 or equivalent. Also needed are: compressed air to lift valve adjusting discs from the valve tappet; an assortment of adjusting discs of various thicknesses and a micrometer.

1. Make sure the engine is overnight cold. Disconnect the negative battery cable. Remove the rocker cover.

2. Turn the engine until the No. 1 cylinder intake valve cams are both straight up. The intake camshaft is labeled **A** on the head.

3. Slide a flat feeler gauge in between each of the camshafts and the adjacent valve tappet. Check to see if the clearance is within the specified range. If it is, proceed with checking the remaining clearances as described starting in Step 8. If not, switch gauges and measure the actual clearance. When actual clearance is achieved, proceed with Steps 4-7.

4. Turn the tappets so the grooves machined into their edges are aligned as shown. Looking at the valves from the center of the engine, the right hand tappet's groove should be at about 5 o'clock and the left hand tappet's groove should be at about 7 o'clock. Use the end of the special tool required for the camshaft involved— in this case the **A** or intake camshaft, the exhaust camshaft end is labeled **E** on the engine and tool. Slide the proper end of the tool, going from the center of the engine outward, under the cam, with the heel of the tool pivoting on the inner side of the camshaft valley. Force the handle downward until the handle rests on the protrusion on the center of the cylinder head.

5. Use compressed air to pop the disc out of the tappet. Read the thickness dimension on the disc.

6. Determine the thickness required as follows:

a. If the valve clearance is too tight, try the next thinner disc.

b. If the valve clearance is too loose, try the next thicker disc.

7. Slip the thinner or thicker disc into the tappet with the letter facing downward. Rock the valve spring depressing tool out and remove it. Then, recheck the clearance. Change the disc again, if necessary, until the clearance falls within the specified range.

8. Turn the engine in firing order sequence, turning the crankshaft forward $\frac{1}{3}$ of a turn each time to get the intake camshafts to the upward position for each cylinder. Measure the clearance as in Step 3 and, if it is outside the specified range, follow Steps 4-7 to adjust either or both valves. Repeat this for all the intakes, and then turn the engine until No. 1 cylinder exhaust valves are upward.

9. Follow the same sequence for all the exhaust valves, going through the firing order, checking clearance as described in Step 3 and adjusting the valves as in Steps 4-7. Note that it is necessary, however, to use the opposite end of the special tool, the end marked **E** to depress the exhaust valves.

10. When all the clearances are in the specified range, replace the camshaft cover, start the engine and check for leaks.

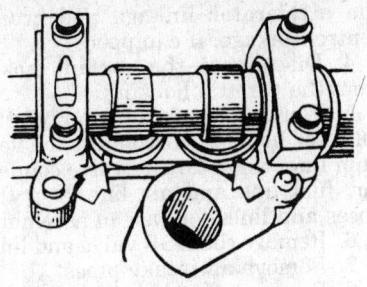

Rotate the valve tappets so the grooves machined in the tops are facing as shown before attempting to measure valve clearance — 3.6L (38B36) engine

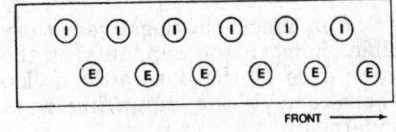

6 cylinder valve location

Rocker Arms/Shafts

REMOVAL AND INSTALLATION

Except 2.5L Engine

1. Disconnect the negative battery cable. Remove the cylinder head.
2. Remove the camshaft.
3. On 6 cylinder engines, remove the retaining bolts and remove the end cover from the rear of the cylinder head. Slide the thrust rings and rocker arms rearward and remove the snaprings from the rocker arm shafts.

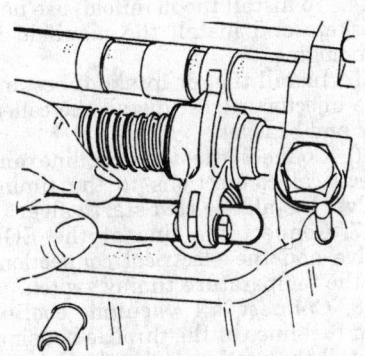

Checking the valve clearance with a flat feeler gauge

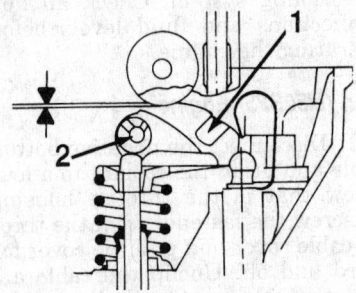

A backup wrench should be used at (1) when adjusting valves. The locknut that holds the adjusting eccentric is at (2). "V" shows the valve clearance

4. On 4 cylinder engines:
   a. Remove the distributor flange from the rear of the cylinder head.
   b. Using a long punch, drive the rocker arm shaft from the rear to the front of the cylinder head.

NOTE: Be sure all snaprings are off the shaft before attempting to drive the shaft from the cylinder head.

   c. The intake rocker shaft is not plugged at the rear, while the exhaust rocker shaft must be plugged. Replace the plug if necessary, during the installation.
5. On 6 cylinder engines:
   a. Install dowel pins part 11 1 063 or equivalent, to keep the rocker shafts from turning. Then, remove the rocker shaft retaining plugs from the front of the cylinder head. These require a hex head wrench. Then, push back the rocker arms against spring pressure and remove the snaprings retaining the shafts. Remove the dowel pins. If the rocker shafts have welded plugs, the shafts will have to be pressed out of the head with a tool such as 11 3 050 or equivalent.

CAUTION

There is considerable force on the springs positioning the rockers. They may pop out. Be cautious and wear safety glasses.

   b. Install a threaded slide hammer into the ends of the rear rocker shafts and remove.
   To install:
6. The rocker arms, springs, washers, thrust rings and shafts should be examined and worn parts replaced. Special attention should be given to the rocker arm camshaft followers. If these are loose, replace the arm assembly. The valves can be removed, repaired or replaced, as necessary,

while the shafts and rocker arms are out of the cylinder head.
7. Install the rocker arms in position, noting the following procedures:
   a. Design changes of the rocker arms and shafts have occurred with the installation of a bushing in the rocker arm and the use of 2 horizontal oil flow holes drilled into the rocker shaft for improved oil supply. Do not mix the previously designed parts with the later design.
   b. When installing the rocker arms and components to the rocker shafts, install locating pins in the cylinder head bolt bores to properly align the rocker arm shafts. Note that on 6 cylinder engines, the longer rocker shafts go on the chain end of the engine; the openings face the bores for the cylinder head bolts; and the plug threads face outward. The order of installation is: spring, washer, rocker arm, thrust washer, snapring. Note also that newer, short springs may be used with the older design.
   c. Install sealer on the rocker arm shaft retaining plugs and rear cover.
   d. On the 4 cylinder engines, position the rocker shafts so the camshaft retaining plate ends can be engaged in the slots of shafts during camshaft installation.
   e. Adjust the valve clearance.

2.5L Engine

The cylinder head must be removed before the rocker arm shafts can be removed.
1. Disconnect the negative battery cable. Remove the cylinder head.
2. Mount the head on a suitable holding fixture.
3. Remove the camshaft sprocket bolt and remove the camshaft distributor adapter and sprocket. Reinstall the adapter on the camshaft.
4. Adjust the valve clearance to the maximum allowable on all valves.
5. Remove the front and rear rocker shaft plugs and lift out the thrust plate.
6. Remove the spring-clips from the rocker arms by lifting them off.
7. Remove the exhaust side rocker arm shaft:
   a. Set the No. 6 cylinder rocker arms at the valve overlap position (rocker arms parallel), by rotating the camshaft through the firing order.
   b. Push in on the front cylinder rocker arm and then turn the camshaft in the direction of the intake rocker shaft, using a ½ in.

drive breaker bar and a deep well socket to fit over the camshaft adapter. Slide each rocker arm to one side as it develops sufficient clearance away from its actuating camshaft and the valve it actuates. Rotate the camshaft until all of the rocker arms are relaxed.

c. Remove the rocker arm shaft.

8. Remove the intake side rocker arm shaft:

a. Turn the camshaft in the direction of the exhaust rocker arm.

b. Use a deep well socket and ½ in. drive breaker bar on the camshaft adapter to turn the camshaft. Slide each rocker arm to one side as it develops sufficient clearance away from its actuating camshaft and the valve it actuates. Rotate the camshaft until all of the rocker arms are relaxed.

c. Remove the rocker arm shaft.

9. Install the rocker arm shafts by reversing the removal procedure. Keep the following points in mind:

a. The large oil bores in the rocker shafts must be installed downward, toward the valve guides and the small oil bores and grooves for the guide plate face inward toward the center of the head.

b. The straight sections of the spring clamps must fit into the grooves in the rocker arm shafts.

c. The guide plate must fit into the grooves in the rocker arm shafts.

d. Adjust the valve clearance.

Intake Manifold

REMOVAL AND INSTALLATION

318iS

1. Disconnect the negative battery cable. Unscrew the upper manifold section.

2. Disconnect the rear mounting bracket and remove the coolant hose.

3. Loosen the front mounting bracket and disconnect the holder for the preheater.

4. Remove the mounting bolts and lift off the upper manifold section. Pull the hose off the fuel pressure regulator at the same time.

5. Pull the plug plate off the fuel injectors and remove the wire holding clamp.

6. Remove the injection pipe with the fuel injectors attached and remove the lower manifold section.

7. The installation is the reverse of the removal procedure.

2.3L (S14B23) Engine

NOTE: A Torx® nut driver is needed to perform this operation.

1. Disconnect the negative battery cable. Remove the cap nuts at the outer ends of the 4 throttle necks. Then remove the mounting nuts underneath.

2. Make sure the engine has cooled off. Loosen the hose clamps for the air intake lines and for the fuel lines where they connect with the injection pipe. Collect fuel in a metal container.

3. Disconnect the throttle cable.

4. Pull off the intake manifold. Cut off the crankcase ventilation hose running to it from the crankcase. Then, remove the manifold and place it aside. Supply a new crankcase ventilation hose.

5. Pull off the throttle valve switch plug. Carefully pull the injector plug plate evenly off all 4 injectors.

6. Pull the fuel pressure regulator vacuum hose off the pressure regulator.

7. Remove the 2 mounting bolts for the injector pipe. Then, carefully lift off the pipe and injectors.

8. Unscrew the nut attaching the ball joint at the end of the throttle actuating rod to the throttle linkage. Supply a new self-locking nut.

9. Remove the nuts attaching the throttle necks to the cylinder head. Then, remove the 4 throttle necks as an assembly.

10. Separate the throttle neck assemblies by pulling them apart at the connecting pipe.

11. Inspect the O-rings in the connecting pipe and at the outer ends of the throttle necks. Replace as necessary.

12. Reverse the removal procedure to install. Use the new throttle linkage self-locking nut and the new crankcase ventilation hose.

13. Torque the nuts attaching the throttle necks to the head and the intake manifold to the throttle necks to 6.5 ft. lbs. (9 Nm). Adjust the throttle cable.

2.5L (M20B25) Engine

1. Disconnect the negative battery cable and drain the cooling system.

2. Disconnect the wire harness at the air flow sensor. Remove the air cleaner and sensor as an assembly. Disconnect the air intake hose running from the air cleaner to the manifold.

3. Remove and tag the vacuum hoses and electrical plugs. Disconnect

the accelerator linkage and cruise control linkage, if equipped.

4. Disconnect the coolant hoses from the throttle housing.

5. Working from the rear of the collector housing, disconnect the vacuum lines and starting valve connector, fuel line and air line. Tag the hoses and lines for ease of assembly.

6. Remove the EGR valve and line.

7. Remove all intake pipes.

8. Remove the air collector housing from the engine. On vehicles with a single intake manifold casting, remove the nuts and remove the throttle valve body.

9. Disconnect the plugs at the injector valves and remove the valves.

10. Disconnect the wire plugs at the coolant temperature sensor, the temperature time switch and the temperature switch.

11. Pull the wire loom upward through the opening in the intake manifold neck.

12. Remove the coolant hoses from the intake neck.

NOTE: Mark the heater hoses for proper reinstallation.

13. Remove the retaining bolts or nuts and remove either front, rear or both intake manifold necks. On some vehicles, remove the entire assembly.

To install:

14. To install the manifold, use new gaskets and install the manifold to the engine.

15. Install the air intake tubes and the injector valves. Install the collector and bracket.

16. Connect the vacuum line and electrical connections to the timing valve. Install the cold start valve.

17. Connect the line at the EGR valve and the electrical connections at the temperature timing switch.

18. Connect all vacuum, cooling and fuel lines at the throttle housing. Install the accelerator cable and vacuum hoses to the air collector.

19. Install the air cleaner and fill the cooling system. Check all hose connections and fluid levels before operating the engine.

2.5L (M50B25) Engine

1. Disconnect the negative battery cable and drain the coolant to a level below that of the throttle housing. Unscrew the fastener from the throttle cable cover and pull the cover forward and off. Unclip the cable and pull the cable out with the rubber holder.

2. Pull the vacuum fitting from the brake booster and plug the openings.

3. Remove the engine and intake manifold covers. Unscrew the bolt holding the ground strap on the front lifting eye. Replace the bolt before lifting the engine.

4. Unscrew the 2 bolts holding the plug plate and pull off the plug plate. Be careful not to damage the rubber seals. Take off the ignition coil electrical plugs. Remove the plug plate complete with the electrical leads.

5. Remove the cylinder head vent hose and pull off the air temperature sensor plug. Remove the tank venting hose and the throttle heating hoses from the throttle body. Remove the throttle valve switch plug. Unclip the idle speed control valve mounted on the manifold. Disconnect the fuel hoses from the pipes.

6. Unscrew the hardware holding the intake manifold to the cylinder head. Remove the intake manifold taking care not to drop anything into the exposed ports.

7. Installation is reverse of removal. Inspect the sealing rings at the intake port and replace as necessary.

3.6L (S38B36) Engine

The M5 uses a manifold chamber in combination with 6 throttle necks (one for each cylinder), each of which contains its own throttle. The throttle necks are divided into 3 assemblies each containing the necks for 2 adjacent cylinders.

1. Disconnect the negative battery cable. Remove the nuts at the outer ends of the throttle necks, these attach the manifold to the outer ends of the necks. Loosen the hose clamps for the crankcase ventilation hoses and for the air intake hose. Disconnect the accelerator cable.

2. Pull the intake manifold off the throttle necks. Check O-rings and replace any that are hard or cracked.

3. Disconnect the electrical connectors to the cold start valve, throttle bypass valve and throttle valve switch. Disconnect all the electrical connections going to the fuel injectors and remove the conduit for the injector wires from the throttle necks.

4. Disconnect the vacuum hoses for the fuel pressure regulator and the heater temperature sensor. Disconnect the fuel return pipe and collect the fuel in a metal container for safe disposal.

5. Remove the attaching nuts/bolts and remove the injection pipe and injectors.

NOTE: Clean the throttle shaft thoroughly and be sure not to use pliers on the shaft surface. Otherwise, needle bearings on which the shaft rides may be damaged.

6. Using a center punch, drive out the 4 pins locking the throttle shaft in place. Slide the shaft out of the bearings.

7. Unscrew its mounting nuts and remove the throttle bypass valve. Disconnect the air hoses from this valve.

8. Remove the nuts attaching the throttle valve necks to the head and remove them.

9. Remove the connecting pipes that run between the valve neck units. Replace O-rings, if necessary. Replace all gaskets and make sure gasket surfaces on the head and inner ends of valve necks are clean.

10. Install in reverse order, providing new pins for the throttle shaft and coating its bearing surfaces with a proper lubricant before assembly.

11. Replace the sleeves in the intake manifold, if necessary. Replace the crankcase ventilation hose connecting the intake manifold and crankcase.

5.0L (M70B50) Engine

1. Disconnect the negative battery cable. Loosen the clamps for the fuel lines.

2. Pull off the vacuum hoses for the pressure regulators. Lift out the injection pipes with the injectors attached.

3. Remove the distributor caps and the throttle valve necks on the manifolds.

4. Disconnect the spark plug wires and remove the ignition lead pipes.

5. Disconnect the crankcase breather hose and loosen the manifold support nuts.

6. Disconnect the nose guard and remove the intake manifold, using the proper tool.

7. The installation is the reverse of the removal procedure. Tighten the intake manifold mounting bolts to 14-17 ft. lbs. (19-23 Nm).

Exhaust Manifold

REMOVAL AND INSTALLATION

Except 2.3L (S14B23) and 3.6L (S38B36) Engines

The 4 cylinder manifold is a one piece, one outlet unit, while the 6 cylinder manifold assembly consists of a 2 piece, double outlet to the exhaust pipe. One piece can be replaced independently of the other.

1. Disconnect the negative battery cable. Remove the air volume control and if necessary, the air cleaner.

2. Disconnect the exhaust pipe at the reactor outlet(s).

3. Remove the guard plate from the reactor(s).

4. Disconnect the air injection pipe fitting, the EGR counter-pressure line, EGR pressure line and any supports.

NOTE: An exhaust filter is used between the reactor and the EGR valve and must be disconnected. Replace the filter if found to be defective.

5. Remove the retaining bolts or nuts at the reactor and remove it from the cylinder head.

To install:

6. Install the manifold, using new gaskets. Install the air injection fittings.

7. Connect the exhaust pipe at the reactor. Install the air cleaner.

2.3L (S14B23) Engine

1. Disconnect the negative battery cable. With the engine cool, remove the drain plug from the block. Remove the 3 electrical connectors from the front of the coolant manifold that runs along the left side of the engine. Disconnect the radiator hose from the front of this pipe. Then, remove all the mounting bolts for this pipe and remove it. Inspect the O-rings and replace any that are worn or damaged.

2. Disconnect the exhaust pipe at the manifold flange. Remove the heatshields from under the engine.

3. Remove the mounting nuts at the cylinder head and remove the manifold.

To install:

4. Clean all gasket material from the surfaces of the manifold and head and replace the gaskets.

5. Position the manifold on the head, torquing the manifold bolts to 7 ft. lbs. (9.5 Nm) and the coolant pipe mounting bolts to 8.5 ft. lbs. (11 Nm). Torque the bolts at the flange attaching manifold and exhaust pipe first to

22-25 ft. lbs. (30-34 Nm) and then to 36-40 ft. lbs. (48-54 Nm). Make sure to refill the cooling system with fresh anti-freeze/water mix and bleed the cooling system.

3.6L (S38B36) Engine

1. Disconnect the negative battery cable. With the engine cool, remove the drain plug from the block. Remove the 3 electrical connectors from the front of the coolant manifold that runs along the left side of the engine. Disconnect the radiator hose from the front of this pipe. Then, remove all the mounting bolts for this pipe and remove it. Inspect the O-rings (one for each cylinder, located in the block) and replace any that are worn or damaged.

2. Disconnect the exhaust pipe at the manifold. Remove the heatshields from under the engine.

3. Remove the cross brace that runs under the engine by removing the 2 bolts from either end and then removing it.

4. Disconnect the stabilizer bar near both ends where it is bushed to the engine carrier.

5. Attach a lifting sling to the engine. Remove the nut from the right side engine mount and lift the engine slightly for clearance.

6. Remove the mounting bolts and remove the manifold.

To install:

7. Clean all gasket material from the surfaces of the manifold and head and replace the gaskets.

8. Position the manifold, torquing the manifold bolts to 36-40 ft. lbs. (48-54 Nm) and the coolant pipe mounting bolts to 8.5 ft. lbs. (11 Nm). Make sure to refill the cooling system with fresh anti-freeze/water mix and bleed the cooling system.

Timing Chain Front Cover

REMOVAL AND INSTALLATION

1.8L (M42B18) and 2.5L (M50B25) Engines

1. Disconnect the negative battery cable. Drain the cooling system and remove the radiator and fan assembly.

2. Remove the drive belts and any accessories that block access to the timing cover. Remove the engine splash shield, if necessary.

3. Remove the vibration damper using the proper tool. Unscrew the central bolt and remove the vibration damper hub.

4. Remove the timing case cover bolts and remove the timing cover.

NOTE: The timing case cover can be removed without removing the water pump.

5. Reverse the removal procedure to install. Tighten the central hub bolt to 224 ft. lbs. (304 Nm) on the 1.8L engine or 295 ft. lbs. (400 Nm) on the 2.5L engine. Torque the vibration damper bolts to 17 ft. lbs. (24 Nm).

2.3L (S14B23) Engine

1. Disconnect the negative battery cable. Drain the cooling system through the bottom of the radiator. Remove the radiator and fan.

2. Disconnect all electrical plugs, remove the attaching nuts and remove the air cleaner and air flow sensor.

3. Note and, if necessary, mark the wiring connections. Then, disconnect all alternator wiring. Unbolt the alternator and remove it and the drive belt.

4. Unbolt the power steering pump. Remove the belt and then move the pump aside, supporting it out of the way but in a position where the hoses will not be stressed.

5. Remove the 3 bolts from the bottom of the bell housing and the 2 bolts below it which fasten the reinforcement plate in place.

6. Remove the drain plug and drain the oil from the lower oil pan. Then, remove the lower oil pan bolts and remove the lower pan.

7. Remove the 3 bolts fastening the bottom of the front cover to the front of the oil pan. Loosen all the remaining oil pan bolts so the pan may be shifted downward just slightly to separate the gasket surfaces.

8. Remove the water pump. Remove the center bolt and use a puller to remove the crankshaft pulley.

9. Remove the piston for the timing chain tensioner.

10. Remove the bolts attaching the top of the front cover to the cylinder head. Then, remove all the bolts fastening the cover to the block.

11. Run a sharp bladed tool carefully between the upper surface of the oil pan gasket and the lower surface of the front cover to separate them without tearing the gasket. If the gasket is damaged, remove the oil pan and replace it.

To install:

12. Before reinstalling the cover, use a file to break or file off flashing at the top/rear of the casting on ei-

ther side so the corner is smooth. Replace all gaskets, coating them with silicone sealer. Where gasket ends extend too far, trim them off. Apply sealer to the area where the oil pan gasket passes the front of the block.

13. Slide the cover straight on to avoid damaging the seal. Install all bolts in their proper positions. Coat the 3 bolts fastening the front cover to the upper oil pan with the proper sealant.

14. Tighten the bolts at the top, fastening the lower cover to the upper cover first. Then, tighten the remaining front cover bolts and, finally, the oil pan bolts to 7 ft. lbs. (9 Nm). Inspect the sealing O-rings and replace, as necessary. If it uses the DME distributor with the screw-off type rotor, make sure the bolt at the center of the rotor has its seal in place and that it is installed with a sealer designed to prevent the bolt from backing out.

15. Reverse the remaining portions of the removal procedures, making sure to fill and bleed the cooling system and to refill the oil pan with the correct oil.

16. Torque the oil drain plug to 24 ft. lbs. (32 Nm) and both upper and lower oil pan bolts to 7 ft. lbs. (10 Nm).

2.5L (M20B25) and 3.5L (M30B35) Engines

NOTE: The 3.5L engine requires the use of a special gauge.

1. Disconnect the negative battery cable. Remove the cylinder head cover. Remove the distributor.

2. Drain the coolant to below the level of the thermostat and remove the thermostat housing cover.

3. Remove the mounting bolts and remove the upper timing case cover.

4. Remove the piston which tensions the timing chain, working carefully because of very high spring pressure.

5. Remove the cooling fan and all drive belts. On 6 Series vehicles, the alternator must be swung aside by loosing the front bolt and removing the 2 side bolts. On all vehicles with the M30B35 engine, remove its attaching bolts and then remove the drive pulley from the water pump. The power steering pump must be removed, leaving the pump hoses connected and supporting the pump out of the way but so the hoses are not stressed.

6. Remove the flywheel housing cover and lock the flywheel in position with an appropriate tool.

7. Unscrew the nut from the center of the pulley and pull the pulley/vibration damper off the crankshaft.

8. Detach the TDC position transmitter on 635CSi and 7 Series.

9. Loosen all the oil pan bolts, and then unscrew all the bolts from the lower timing case cover, noting their lengths for reinstallation in the same positions. Carefully, use a sharp bladed tool to separate the gasket at the base of the lower timing cover. Then, remove the cover.

To install:

10. To install the lower cover, first coat the surfaces of the oil pan and block with sealer. Put it into position on the block, making sure the tensioning piston holding web (cast into the block) is in the oil pocket. Install all bolts; then tighten the lower front cover bolts evenly; finally, tighten the oil pan bolts evenly.

11. Inspect the hub of the vibration damper. If the hub is scored, install the radial seal so the sealing lip is in front of or to the rear of the scored area. Pack the seal with grease and install it with a sealer installer.

12. Install the pulley/damper and torque the bolt to specifications. When installing, make sure the key and keyway are properly aligned.

13. Remove the flywheel locking tool and reinstall the cover. Reinstall and tension all belts.

14. Before installing the upper cover, use sealer to seal the joint between the back of the lower timing cover and block at the top. On some vehicles, there are sealer wells which are to be filled with sealer. If these are present, fill them carefully. Check the cork seal at the distributor drive coupling and replace it, if necessary.

15. On all but M30B35 engines, tighten bolts 1 and 2 on 4 cylinder engines, the lower bolts, slightly. Then, tighten bolts 3-8. Finally, fully tighten the lower bolts.

16. On M30B35 engines, note that the top bolt on the driver's side and the bottom bolt on the passenger's side are longer. Tighten the 2 bolts that run down into the lower timing cover first; then tighten the remaining 6 bolts.

17. On the M30B35 engine, install the TDC transmitter and its mounting bracket. On remaining engines, install the TDC position transmitter loosely, if equipped. With the engine at exactly 0 degrees TDC, as shown by the marker on the front cover, adjust the position of the transmitter. It must fit the curve on the outside of the balancer and incorporate a notch (for the pin on the balancer) and a ridge against the transmitter. The straight line distance between the center of the notch and bottom of the ridge must be exactly 37.5mm. Then, tighten the transmitter mounting screw.

18. Just before installing the upper timing case cover, check the condition of that area of the head gasket. It will usually be in good condition. If it should show damage, it must be replaced.

19. Inspect the sealing O-rings and replace, as necessary. Make sure the bolt at the center of the rotor has its seal in place and that it is installed with a sealer designed to prevent the bolt from backing out.

20. Complete the installation, making sure to bleed the cooling system.

3.6L (S38B36) Engine

1. Disconnect the negative battery cable. Pull out the plug and remove the wiring leading to the air flow sensor. Loosen the hose clamp and disconnect the air intake hose. Remove the mounting nut and remove the air cleaner and air flow sensor as an assembly.

2. Remove the radiator and fan. Remove the flywheel housing cover and install a lock, to lock the position of the flywheel. Remove the mounting nut for the vibration damper with a deepwell socket. Pull the damper off with a puller.

3. Remove the pipe that runs across in front of the front cover. Remove the mounting bolts and remove the water pump pulley.

4. Loosen the top/front mounting bolt for the alternator. Remove the lower/front bolt. Loosen the 2 side bolts. Swing the alternator aside.

5. Remove the power steering pump mounting bolts. Make sure to retain the spacer that goes between the pump and oil pan. Swing the pump aside and support it so the hoses will not be under stress.

6. Remove the flywheel housing cover and lock the flywheel in position with an appropriate tool.

7. Unscrew the nut from the center of the pulley and pull the pulley/vibration damper off the crankshaft.

8. Remove the bolts at the top, fastening the lower front cover to the upper front cover. Remove the bolts at the bottom, fastening the lower cover to the oil pan. Loosen the remaining oil pan mounting bolts.

9. Run a sharp bladed tool carefully between the upper surface of the oil pan gasket and the lower surface of the front cover to separate them without tearing the gasket.

10. Loosen and remove the remaining front cover mounting bolts, noting the locations of the TDC sending unit on the upper/right side of the engine and the suspension position sending unit on the upper left. Also, keep track of the bolts that mount these accessories, as their lengths are slightly different. Remove the timing cover, pulling it off squarely.

To install:

11. Before reinstalling the cover, use a file to break or file off flashing at the top/rear of the casting on either side so the corner is smooth. Replace all gaskets, coating them with silicone sealer. Where gasket ends extend too far, trim them off. Apply sealer to the area where the oil pan gasket passes the front of the block.

12. Slide the cover straight on to avoid damaging the seal. Install all bolts in their proper positions. Tighten the bolts at the top, fastening the lower cover to the upper cover first. Then, tighten the remaining front cover bolts and, finally, the oil pan bolts. Inspect the sealing O-rings and replace as necessary. If it uses the DME distributor with the screw-off type rotor, make sure the bolt at the center of the rotor has its seal in place and that it is installed with a sealer designed to prevent the bolt from backing out.

13. Complete the installation procedure, making sure to refill and bleed the cooling system.

5.0L (M70B50) Engine

UPPER

1. Disconnect the negative battery cable. Drain the cooling system and remove the fan assembly.

2. Remove both intake manifolds and distributor housings.

3. Disconnect the round rubber mounts, bolts and nuts. Remove both cylinder head covers.

4. Remove the mounting bolts and lift out the timing cover.

5. To install, reverse the removal procedure.

LOWER

1. Disconnect the negative battery cable. Drain the cooling system and remove the fan assembly.

2. Remove the drive belts and the engine splash shield. Remove the tensioning bolt.

3. Unscrew the bolts but do not remove the vibration damper. Remove the central hub bolt with the proper tool.

4. Remove the vibration damper using the proper tool to pull the vibration damper hub from the crankshaft.

5. Drain the engine oil and remove the lower section of the oil pan. Remove the bottom mounting screws from the timing case cover and loosen the adjacent oil pan bolts on both sides.

6. Remove the timing belt tensioner and reference mark sender.

7. Remove the mounting screws and take off the timing case cover.

8. To install, reverse the removal procedure. Tighten the central hub bolt to 318 ft. lbs. (430 Nm) and the vibration damper mounting bolts to 17 ft. lbs. (25 Nm).

Front Cover Oil Seal

REPLACEMENT

2.5L (M20B25) and 3.5L (M30B35) Engines

1. Disconnect the negative battery cable. Position the No. 1 piston at TDC on the beginning of its compression stroke.

2. Remove the flywheel guard and lock the flywheel with a locking tool.

3. Remove the drive belts and the fan.

4. Remove the retaining nut and remove the vibration damper from the crankshaft.

NOTE: The Woodruff key should be at the 12 o'clock position on the crankshaft.

5. Remove the seal from the timing housing cover with a small prybar.

6. Using a special seal installer or equivalent, lubricate and install the seal in the cover. This tool is used to press the seal into the bore with even pressure around the entire perimeter.

NOTE: If the balancer hub has serious scoring on the sealing surface, position the seal in the cover so the sealing lip is in front of or behind the scored groove.

7. Lubricate the balancer hub and install it on the crankshaft, being careful not to damage the seal.

8. Complete the assembly, using the reverse of the removal procedure. Be sure to remove the flywheel locking tool before attempting to start the engine.

1.8L (M42B18), 2.5L (M50B25) and 5.0L (M70B50) Engines

1. Disconnect the negative battery cable.

2. Remove the vibration damper and hub assembly.

3. Press out the radial oil seal, using the proper tool.

4. Install the new seal flush in conjunction with the central bolt and washer, using the proper seal installer.

5. The remainder of the installation is the reverse of the removal procedure.

Timing Chain and Sprockets

REMOVAL AND INSTALLATION

1.8L (M42B18) Engine

1. Disconnect the negative battery cable. Remove the vibration damper and hub assembly.

2. Remove the lower timing case cover. Remove the timing chain tensioner.

3. Unscrew the upper chain guide and top bolt on the right chain guide.

4. Remove the timing chain sprockets and the lift out the chain. Remove the timing chain guide.

5. Remove the tensioning rail, if necessary. Remove the crankshaft sprocket with the proper tool and lift out the Woodruff key.

6. Remove the reversing roller, if needed.

NOTE: The reversing roller can only be replaced complete with bearings.

7. The installation is the reverse of the removal procedure.

2.3L (S14B23) Engine

1. Disconnect the negative battery cable. Remove the timing case cover.

2. Remove the camshafts and sprockets. It is not necessary to remove the cover from the rear of the head.

3. Make sure to catch the washer and lock washers which will be released at the front. Remove the 2 mounting bolts for the guide rail, which is located on the left (driver's) side of the engine. These are accessible from the rear.

4. Pull the guide rail forward and then turn it clockwise on its axis, looking at it from above, to free it from the chain.

5. Note the relationships between timing chain and sprocket marks. Remove the chain by separating it from the sprockets at top and bottom.

To install:

6. Engage the timing chain with the crankshaft sprocket so marks line up. Route the chain up through where the guide rail will go. Install the guide rail in reverse of the removal procedure.

7. Then engage the chain with the driver's side (E) sprocket with the marks aligned. Bolt this sprocket and the lockplate onto the front end of the intake camshaft. Use the adapter to keep the sprocket from turning and torque the bolts to 6-7 ft. lbs. (8.0-9.5 Nm). Turn this camshaft in the direction opposite to normal rotation to tension the timing chain on that side.

8. Engage the timing marks with the mark on the passenger's side (A) sprocket and install the sprocket and lockplate onto the front end of the exhaust camshaft. Again, use the adapter to keep the sprocket from turning and torque the bolts to 6-7 ft. lbs. (8.0-9.5 Nm). Make sure the timing chain has stayed in time.

9. Slide the chain tensioner piston into its cylinder. Install a new seal. Now install the spring with the conical end out. Install the cap which retains the spring and torque it to 29 ft. lbs. (40 Nm).

10. Turn the engine 1 revolution in the normal direction of rotation. Recheck the timing. With the crankshaft at TDC, one groove on each camshaft faces inward and another on each faces the cast boss on the bearing cap.

11. Install the camshaft and timing chain guides.

12. Install the timing case cover.

3.6L (S38B36) Engine

1. Disconnect the negative battery cable. Remove the fan shroud and the fan. Remove the cylinder head cover. Remove the timing cover.

2. Remove the camshaft. Remove the cover from the rear of the head.

3. Remove the water pump.

4. Remove the 2 mounting bolts for the guide rail, which is located on the left (driver's) side of the engine. These are accessible from the rear. Turn the guide rail counterclockwise on it's axis looking at it from above to clear the chain and block and remove it. Be careful to retain all washers.

5. Note the relationships between timing chain and sprocket marks. Remove the timing chain.

To install:

6. Install the timing chain with the marks on all 3 sprockets aligned with marked links on the chain. Make sure the chain runs on the inside of the guide sprocket on the left side of the engine and along the groove in the lower tensioning rail. Install the chain onto the camshaft drive sprockets and then install the sprockets onto the camshafts. Note that the exhaust side sprocket is marked **A** and the intake sprocket is marked **E**. Then, install the guide rail with all washers and lock washers by rotating it into position in reverse of the removal procedure.

7. Tighten the camshaft drive sprockets, install the chain tensioner and install the upper guide rail. Reverse the remaining removal steps to complete the procedure. Make sure to refill the cooling system with an appropriate anti-freeze/water mix and to bleed the cooling system.

3.5L (M30B35) Engine

1. Disconnect the negative battery cable. Rotate the crankshaft to set the No. 1 piston at TDC, at the beginning of its compression stroke.

2. Remove the distributor.

3. Remove the cylinder head cover, air injection pipe and guard plate.

4. Drain the cooling system and remove the thermostat housing.

5. Remove the upper timing housing cover.

6. Remove the timing chain tensioner piston by unscrewing the cap.

NOTE: The piston is under heavy spring tension.

7. Remove the drive belts and fan.

8. Remove the flywheel guard and lock the flywheel with a locking tool.

9. Remove the vibration damper assembly.

NOTE: The crankshaft Woodruff key should be in the 12 o'clock position.

10. Remove upper and lower timing covers.

11. Turn the crankshaft so the No. 1 cylinder is at firing position. Open the camshaft lockplates, if equipped, remove the bolts and remove the camshaft sprocket.

12. Remove the chain from the lower sprocket, swing the chain to the right front and out of the guide rail and remove the chain from the engine.

To install:

13. Install the chain in position.

14. Be sure No. 1 piston remains at the top of its firing stroke and the key on the crankshaft is in the 12 o'clock position.

15. Position the camshaft flange so the dowel pin bore is at the 7-8 o'clock position and the upper flange bolt hole is aligned with the cast tab on the cylinder head.

16. Position the chain on the guide rail and swing the chain inward and to the left.

17. Engage the chain on the crankshaft gear and install the camshaft sprocket into the chain.

18. Align the gear dowel pin to the camshaft flange and bolt and sprocket into place. Torque the sprocket bolts to 7.5 ft. lbs. (10 Nm).

19. Install the chain tensioner piston, spring and cap plug, but do not tighten.

20. To bleed the chain tensioner, fill the oil pocket, located on the upper timing housing cover, with engine oil and move the tensioner back and forth with a suitable prybar until oil is expelled at the cap plug. Tighten the cap plug securely.

21. Complete the assembly in the reverse order of removal. Check the ignition timing and the idle speed. Be sure the flywheel holder is removed before any attempt is made to start the engine.

2.5L (M50B25) Engine

1. Disconnect the negative battery cable. Remove the vibration damper and hub assembly.

2. Remove the upper and lower timing case covers. Compress and lock the upper timing chain tensioner. Unbolt the upper timing chain sprockets and remove from the camshafts along with the chain.

3. Unscrew the upper chain guide and top bolt on the right chain guide.

4. Remove the timing chain sprockets and the lift out the chain. Remove the timing chain guide.

5. Remove the tensioning rail, if necessary. Remove the crankshaft sprocket with the proper tool and lift out the Woodruff key.

6. Installation is the reverse of removal. Torque the camshaft sprocket bolts to 16 ft. lbs. (22 Nm), the lower timing cover bolts to 6.5-8.0 ft. lbs. (9-11 Nm) for M6 bolts and 16 ft. lbs. (22 Nm) for M8 bolts, the vibration damper hub bolt to 295 ft. lbs. (410 Nm) and the vibration damper bolts to 17 ft. lbs. (23 Nm). Use sealer at the intersections of the timing cover and the pan.

Timing Belt Front Cover

REMOVAL AND INSTALLATION

2.5L (M20B25) Engine

The 1990 3 Series is equipped with a neoprene timing belt and the distributor guard plate is actually the upper timing belt cover.

1. Disconnect the negative battery cable. Remove the distributor cap and rotor. Remove the inner distributor cover and seal.

2. Remove the 2 distributor guard plate attaching bolts and one nut. Remove the rubber guard and take out the guard plate (upper timing belt cover).

3. Rotate the crankshaft to set No. 1 piston at TDC of its compression stroke.

NOTE: At TDC of No. 1 piston compression stroke, the camshaft sprocket arrow should align directly with the mark on the cylinder head.

4. Remove the radiator.

5. Remove the lower splash guard and take off the alternator, power steering and air conditioning belts.

6. Remove the crankshaft pulley and vibration damper.

7. Hold the crankshaft hub from rotating with the proper tool. Remove the crankshaft hub bolt.

To install:

8. Install the hub bolt into the crankshaft about 3 turns and use the proper gear puller, to remove the crankshaft hub.

9. Remove the bolt from the engine end of the alternator bracket. Loosen the alternator adjusting bolt and swing the bracket out of the way.

10. Lift out the TDC transmitter and set it aside.

11. Remove the remaining bolt and lift off the lower timing belt cover.

12. The installation is the reverse of the removal procedure.

OIL SEAL REPLACEMENT

1. Disconnect the negative battery cable. Remove the front engine cover.

2. Press the 2 radial oil seals out of the front engine cover.

3. Install the oil seals flush with the front engine cover using the proper tools.

4. Install the front engine cover. Connect the negative battery cable.

Timing Belt and Tensioner

ADJUSTMENT

1. Disconnect the negative battery cable.
2. Remove the front engine cover.
3. Loosen the tensioner bolt. The spring force should be capable of moving the tensioner roller.
4. Rotate the crankshaft in the direction of the rotation to TDC mark. The mark on the camshaft sprocket with the mark on the cylinder head with the crankshaft at TDC mark.
5. Tighten the tensioner bolt and install the front engine cover.
6. Connect the negative battery cable.

REMOVAL AND INSTALLATION

1. Disconnect the negative battery cable. Remove the distributor cap and rotor. Remove the inner distributor cover and seal.
2. Remove the 2 distributor guard plate attaching bolts and 1 nut. Remove the rubber guard and take out the guard plate, upper timing belt cover.
3. Rotate the crankshaft to set No. 1 piston at TDC of its compression stroke.

NOTE: At TDC of No. 1 piston compression stroke, the camshaft sprocket arrow should align directly with the mark on the cylinder head.

4. Remove the radiator.
5. Remove the lower splash guard and take off the alternator, power steering and air conditioning belts.
6. Remove the crankshaft pulley and vibration damper.
7. Hold the crankshaft hub from rotating with tool 11 2 150 or equivalent. Remove the crankshaft hub bolt.
8. Install the hub bolt into the crankshaft about 3 turns and use the proper gear puller, to remove the crankshaft hub.
9. Remove the bolt from the engine end of the alternator bracket. Loosen the alternator adjusting bolt and swing the bracket out of the way.
10. Lift out the TDC transmitter and set it out of the way.
11. Remove the remaining bolt and lift off the lower timing belt cover.
12. Loosen the 2 tensioner pulley bolts and release the tension on the belt by pushing on the tensioner pulley bracket.

13. Mark the running direction of the timing belt and remove the belt.
14. Remove the 3 bolts across the front of the oil pan and loosen the remaining oil pan bolts. Try not to damage the oil pan gasket. Remove the 6 front engine cover bolts and remove the front engine cover.

To install:
15. Install the cover, noting the following:
   a. To tighten the timing belt, turn the engine in the direction of normal engine operation, with a ½ in. drive ratchet wrench on the crankshaft bolt. When the timing belt is tight, torque the 2 tensioner bolts.
   b. Align the hub centering pin through the hole in the vibration damper for proper installation.
   c. Align the timing marks when installing the timing belt. The crankshaft sprocket mark must point at the notch in the flange of the front engine cover. The camshaft sprocket arrow must point at the alignment mark on the cylinder head. Also, the No. 1 piston must be at TDC of the compression stroke.
   d. If the oil pan gasket is damaged, it must be replaced.
   e. Check and replace front cover oil seals, if needed.
   f. Use tools 11 2 211 (crankshaft seal aligner) and 11 2 212 (intermediate shaft seal aligner) or equivalent, to install the front engine cover without damaging the oil seals.
16. Check the engine oil level.
17. Install engine coolant and bleed the cooling system. Bring the engine up to operating temperature and loosen the bleed screw on top of the thermostat housing. Continue to bleed until escaping coolant is free of bubbles. Add coolant to the expansion tank if needed.

Timing Sprockets

REMOVAL AND INSTALLATION

1. Disconnect the negative battery cable. Remove the timing belt.
2. Hold the sprocket with the proper tool. Remove the bolt and take off the collar.
3. Remove the sprocket from the crankshaft with the proper tool.
4. Remove the sprocket from the intermediate shaft in the same way.
5. Reverse the removal procedure to install.

Camshaft

REMOVAL AND INSTALLATION

1.8L (M42B18) and 2.5L (M50B25) Engine

1. Disconnect the negative battery cable and strip the head of its covers and related items to expose the camshafts. Remove the timing chains and sprockets.

NOTE: Special tools are required to perform this operation. BMW tools 11 3 260, 11 3 270 and 11 3 250 or their equivalents are required for proper removal and installation of the camshafts and for retention of the valve lash compensators. Without these tools the camshafts will be damaged during removal or installation.

2. Remove the spark plugs and attach the 11 3 260 (plus addition 11 3 270) camshaft removal fixture. Torque the hold-down bolts in the spark plug bores to 17 ft. lbs. (23 Nm).
3. Apply load to the bearing caps by rotating the eccentric shaft. This relieves the tension on the bearing cap bolts. Loosen and remove the bearing cap bolts.
4. Remove the camshaft removal fixture after releasing the tension from the eccentric shaft.
5. Remove the camshafts and the bearing caps. Note that the intake camshaft is marked "E" and the exhaust camshaft is marked "A". The camshaft bearing are consecutively numbered with "A" or "E" to designate intake or exhaust side.
6. Hold the valve lash compensators in place using tool 11 3 250 and remove the bearing plate along with the valve plungers.

To install:
7. Inspect the camshafts and valve lash compensators for damage and wear and replace as necessary.
8. When the camshafts have been removed and reinstalled a waiting period dependent on the ambient temperature is necessary before mounting the cylinder head on the engine. At room temperature wait 4 minutes to allow the lifters to compress fully. At temperatures down to 50°F (10°C) wait 11 minutes. At temperatures lower than 50°F (10°C) wait 30 minutes. This is to prevent contact between the valves and the piston tops.
9. The engine may not be cranked under the same conditions as above for a period of 10 minutes at room

temperature; 30 minutes for temperatures down to 50°F (10°C); 75 minutes for temperatures below 50°F (10°C).

2.5L (M20B25) Engine

The cylinder head and the rocker arm shafts must be removed before the camshaft can be removed.

1. Disconnect the negative battery cable. Remove the cylinder head.
2. Mount the head on a stand. Secure the head to the stand with 1 head bolt.
3. Remove the camshaft sprocket bolt and remove the camshaft distributor adapter and sprocket. Reinstall the distributor adapter on the camshaft.
4. Adjust the valve clearance to the maximum allowable on all valves.
5. Remove the front and rear rocker shaft plugs and lift out the thrust plate.
6. Remove the clips from the rocker arms by lifting them off.
7. Remove the exhaust side rocker arm shaft:
    a. Set the No. 6 cylinder rocker arm to the valve overlap position, both rocker arms parallel.
    b. Push in on the rocker arm on the front cylinder and turn the camshaft in the direction of the intake rocker shaft, using a ½ in. breaker bar and a deep well socket to fit over the camshaft adapter. Rotate the camshaft until all of the rocker arms are relaxed.
    c. Remove the rocker arm shaft.
8. Remove the intake side rocker arm shaft:
    a. Turn the camshaft in the direction of the exhaust valves.
    b. Use a deep well socket and ½ in. drive breaker bar on the camshaft adapter to turn the camshaft until all of the rocker arms are relaxed.
    c. Pull out the rocker arm shaft.
9. Remove the camshaft thrust bearing cover. Check the radial oil seal and round cord seal and replace them if needed.
10. Pull out the camshaft.
    To install:
11. Install the camshaft, noting the following:
    a. Place the proper tool over the end of the camshaft during installation of the thrust bearing cover; this will protect the oil seals and guide the cover on.

b. The rocker arm thrust plate must be fit into the grooves in the rocker shafts.
    c. The straight side of the spring clip must be installed in the groove of the rocker arm shafts.
    d. The large oil bores in the rocker shafts must be installed down to the valve guides and the small oil bores must face inward toward the center of the head.
    e. Adjust the valve clearance.
12. To complete the installation, reverse the removal procedures.

3.5L (M30B35) Engine

1. Disconnect the negative battery cable. Remove the oil line from the top of the cylinder head.

NOTE: Observe the location of the seals when removing the hollow oil line studs. Install new seals in the same position.

2. Remove the cylinder head. Support the head in such a way that the valves can be opened during camshaft removal.
3. Adjust the valve clearance to the maximum clearance on all rocker arms.
4. A tool set 11 1 060 and 00 1 490 or its equivalent, is used to hold the rocker arms away from the camshaft lobes. When installing the tool, move the intake rocker arms of No. 2 and 4 cylinders forward approximately ¼ in. and tighten the intake side nuts to avoid contact between the valve heads. Turn the camshaft 15 degrees clockwise to install the tool. On these engines, to avoid contact between the valve heads, first tighten the tool mounting nuts on the exhaust side to the stop and then tighten the intake side nuts slightly. Reverse this exactly during removal.
5. Remove the camshaft by rotating the camshaft so the 2 cutout areas of the camshaft flange are horizontal and remove the retaining plate bolts.
6. Carefully, remove the camshaft from the cylinder head.
7. The flange and guide plate can be removed from the camshaft by removing the lockplate and nut from the camshaft end.
    To install:
8. Install the camshaft and associated components in the reverse order of removal.
9. After installing the camshaft guide plate, the camshaft should turn easily. Measure and correct the camshaft end-play.

10. The camshaft flange must be properly aligned with the cylinder head before the sprocket is installed.
11. Install the oil tube hollow stud washer seals properly, 1 above and 1 below the oil pipe. The arrow on the oil line must face forward.
12. Install the cylinder head. Adjust the valves.

2.3L (S14B23) and 3.6L (S38B36) Engines

NOTE: To perform this operation it is necessary to have a special tool 11 3 010 or equivalent. This is necessary to permit safe removal of the camshaft bearing caps and then safe release of the tension the valve springs put on the camshafts. The job also requires an adapter to keep the camshaft sprockets from turning while loosening and tightening their mounting bolts.

1. Disconnect the negative battery cable. Remove the cylinder head cover. Remove the fan cowl and the fan.
2. Remove the mounting bolts and remove the distributor cap. Remove the mounting screws and remove the rotor. Unscrew the distributor adapter and the protective cover underneath. Inspect the O-ring that runs around the protective cover and replace it, if necessary.
3. Remove the 2 bolts and remove the protective cover from in front of the right side (intake) camshaft. Remove the bolts and remove the distributor housing from in front of the left (exhaust) side cam. Inspect the O-rings and replace them, if necessary.
4. Remove the 6 mounting bolts from the cover at the rear end of the cylinder head and remove it. Replace the gasket. Note that on the M3, 2 of these bolts are longer. These fit into the 2 holes that are sleeved.
5. Remove the 2 nuts, located at the front of the head, which mount the upper timing chain guide rail. Then, remove the upper guide rail.
6. Turn the crankshaft to set the engine at No. 1 cylinder TDC. On the 6 cylinder engine, valves for No. 6 will be at overlap position — both valves just slightly open with timing marks at TDC.
7. Remove the cap for the timing chain tensioner, located on the right side of the front timing cover. Then, slide off the damper housing. Remove

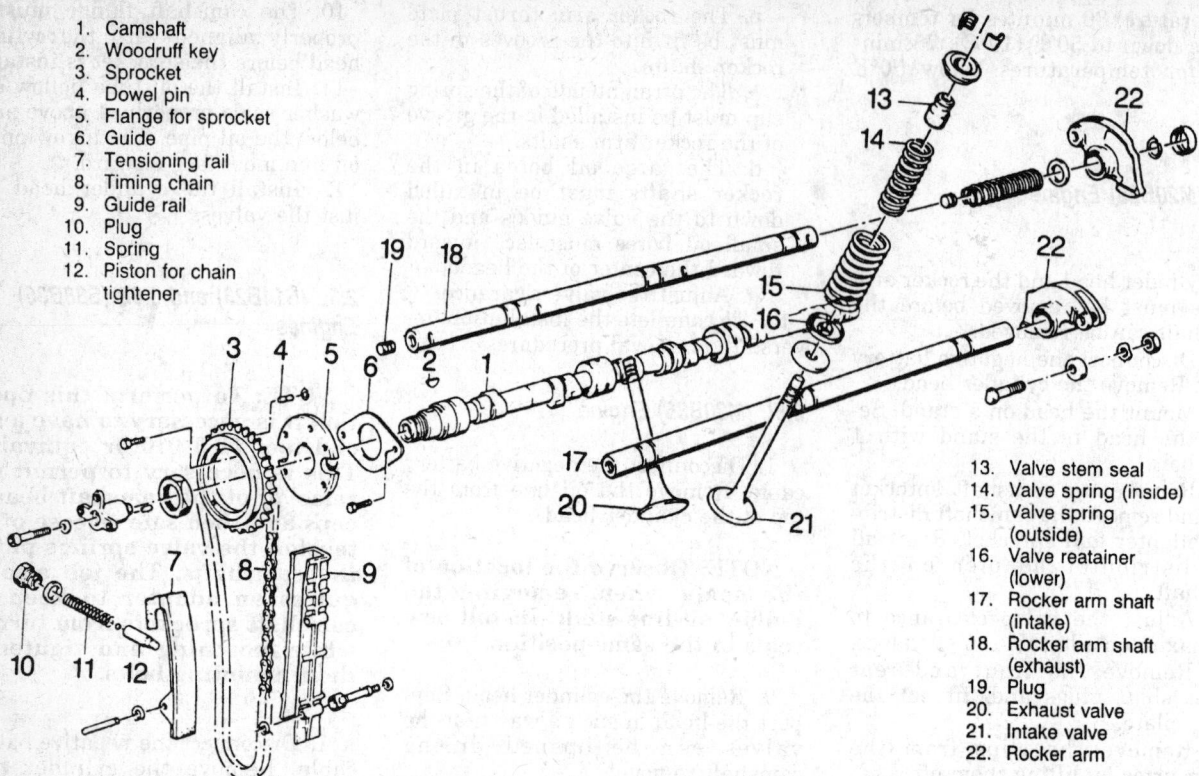

1. Camshaft
2. Woodruff key
3. Sprocket
4. Dowel pin
5. Flange for sprocket
6. Guide
7. Tensioning rail
8. Timing chain
9. Guide rail
10. Plug
11. Spring
12. Piston for chain tightener

13. Valve stem seal
14. Valve spring (inside)
15. Valve spring (outside)
16. Valve reatainer (lower)
17. Rocker arm shaft (intake)
18. Rocker arm shaft (exhaust)
19. Plug
20. Exhaust valve
21. Intake valve
22. Rocker arm

Exploded view of the camshaft assembly — 535i

Rear cover of the 2.3L engine, install the longer bolts into the 2 holes marked "1"

the seal, discard it and supply a new one for re-assembly.

NOTE: The next item to be removed is a plug which keeps the tensioner piston inside its hydraulic cylinder against considerable spring pressure. Use a socket wrench and keep pressure against the outer end of the plug, pushing inward, so spring pressure can be released very gradually once the plug's threads are free of the block.

8. Remove the plug from the tensioner piston and release spring tension. Remove the spring and then the piston. Check the length of the spring. It must be 6.240-6.280 in. (158.5-159.5mm) in length; otherwise, replace it to maintain stable timing chain tension.

NOTE: The timing chain should remain engaged with the crankshaft sprocket while removing the camshafts. Otherwise, it will be necessary to do additional work to restore proper timing. Keep the timing chain under slight tension by supporting it at the top while removing the camshaft sprockets.

9. Pry open the lockplates for the camshaft sprocket mounting bolts. Install an adapter to hold the sprockets still and remove the mounting bolts.

10. Using an adapter to keep the sprockets from turning and putting tension on the timing chain, loosen and remove the sprocket mounting bolts, keeping the chain supported.

11. Mount the special tool on the timing case, which mounts to the top of the head. Then, tighten the tool's shaft to the stop. This will hold both camshafts down against their lower bearings. Also, mark the camshafts as to which end faces forward.

12. Remove the mounting bolts and remove the camshaft bearing caps. It

is possible to save time by keeping the caps in order, although they are marked for installation in the same positions.

13. Once all bearing caps are removed, slowly crank backwards on the tool's shaft to gradually release the tension on the camshafts. Once all tension is released, remove the camshafts.

14. Carefully, remove the camshafts in such a way as to avoid nicking any bearing surfaces or cams.

To install:

15. Oil all bearing and camshaft surfaces with clean engine oil. Carefully, install the camshafts, marked **E** for intake and **A** for exhaust, to avoid nicking any wear surfaces. The camshafts should be turned so the groove between the front camshaft and sprocket mounting flange faces straight up. Install the special tool and tighten down on the shaft to seat the camshafts.

16. Install all bearing caps in order or as marked. Torque the attaching bolts to 15-17 ft. lbs. (20-23 Nm). Then, release the tension provided by the tool by turning the bolt and remove the tool.

17. Install the intake sprocket marked **E**, install the lockplate and install the mounting bolts. Use the adapter to keep the sprocket from

turning and torque the bolts to 7 ft. lbs. (10 Nm). Do the same for the exhaust side sprocket. Make sure the timing chain stays in time.

18. Slide the timing chain tensioner piston into the opening in the cylinder in the block. Install the spring with the conically wound end facing the plug. Install the plug into the end of the sprocket and then install it over the spring. Use the socket wrench to depress the spring until the plug's threads engage with those in the block. Start the threads in carefully and then torque the plug to 27-31 ft. lbs. (37-42 Nm). Install a new seal, connector, damper housing and the outside cap with a new cap seal. Torque the outside cap to 16-20 ft. lbs. (21-27 Nm) on the engine used in the M5 or 29 ft. lbs. (40 Nm) on the M3 engine.

19. Crank the engine forward just 1 turn in normal direction of rotation. Now, 1 camshaft groove on each side should face toward the center of the head and 1 on each side should face the case boss on the front bearing cap. Lock the sprocket mounting bolts with the tabs on the lockplates.

20. Reverse the remaining removal procedures to complete the installation. Before final tightening of the mounting nuts for the guide rail for the top of the timing chain, go back and forth, measuring the clearance between the sprockets and the center of the guide rail to center it. Then, tighten the mounting nuts.

Auxiliary/Silent Shaft

REMOVAL AND INSTALLATION

2.5L (M20B25) Engine

1. Disconnect the negative battery cable. Remove the front cover.
2. Remove the intermediate shaft sprocket.
3. Loosen and remove the 2 retaining screws and then remove the intermediate shaft guide plate.
4. Carefully, slide the intermediate shaft out of the block. Turn the crankshaft, if necessary, to remove it. Inspect the gear on the intermediate shaft and replace it, if necessary.

To install:
5. Install the intermediate shaft to the block. Install the guide plate.
6. Install the front cover. Connect the negative battery cable.

Piston and Connecting Rod

POSITIONING

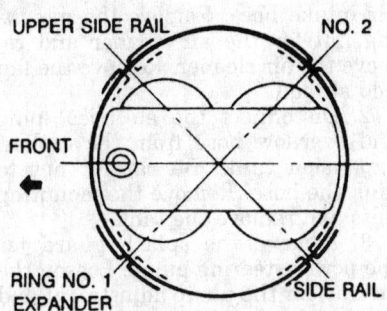

Location of piston in the the cylinder bore with ring gaps located 180 degrees apart

---

ENGINE LUBRICATION

Oil Pan

REMOVAL AND INSTALLATION

3 Series

1.8L (M42B18) ENGINE

1. Disconnect the negative battery cable. Raise and safely support the vehicle.
2. Drain the engine oil.
3. Disconnect the exhaust pipe, if necessary.
4. Remove the lower oil pan mounting bolts and take off the lower oil pan. Remove the upper section oil pan bolts and remove the upper oil pan.
5. Clean the mounting surfaces and install new gaskets.
6. The installation is the reverse of the removal procedure. Tighten the mounting bolts to 6.5 ft. lbs. (9 Nm).

2.5L (M20B25 AND M50B25) ENGINES

1. Disconnect the negative battery cable. Raise the vehicle and support it. Drain the engine oil.
2. Remove the front lower splash guard, if necessary.
3. Disconnect the electrical terminal from the oil sending unit.
4. Remove the power steering gear from the front axle carrier, if necessary.
5. Remove the flywheel cover.

6. Remove the oil pan bolts and lower the oil pan. Remove the oil pump bolts and take out the oil pump and oil pan.
7. Install the oil pan, paying attention to the following points:
   a. Clean the gasket surfaces and use a new gasket on the oil pan.
   b. Coat the joints on the ends of the front engine cover with a universal sealing compound.
   c. Install the sending unit wire and the engine oil. If the power steering gear was removed, make sure to refill and bleed this system.

2.3L (S14B23) ENGINE

1. Remove the dipstick. Remove the splash guard from underneath the engine. Raise and safely support the vehicle.
2. Remove the drain plug and drain the oil. Unscrew all the bolts for the lower oil pan and remove it.
3. Remove the oil pump.
4. Remove the lower flywheel housing cover by removing the 3 bolts at the bottom of the flywheel housing and the 2 bolts in the cover just ahead of the flywheel housing.
5. Disconnect the oil pressure sending unit plug. Unbolt the oil pan bracket. Disconnect the ground lead. Loosen its clamp and disconnect the crankcase ventilation hose.
6. Remove the oil pan bolts and remove the upper oil pan.

To install:
7. Clean all sealing surfaces. Supply a new gasket and the coat the joints where the timing case cover and block meet with a brush-on sealant. Install the pan and torque the bolts evenly to 7 ft. lbs. (10 Nm).
8. Install the oil pan drain plug, torquing to 24 ft. lbs. (33 Nm). Refill the oil pan with the required amount of approved oil.
9. Start the engine and check for leaks.

5 and 6 Series

EXCEPT 2.5L (M50B25) ENGINE

1. Disconnect the negative battery cable. Disconnect the electrical connector and separate the leads from the air cleaner/air flow sensor. Loosen the hose clamp and disconnect the air intake hose. Remove the mounting nut and remove the air cleaner and the air flow sensor as a unit. Remove the fan shroud.
2. Raise and safely support the vehicle. Drain the engine oil. Lower the vehicle.
3. Loosen the belt tension and remove the alternator drive belt. Loosen the upper/front mounting bolt

for the alternator and the 2 bolts on the side of the block that mount it at the rear. Remove the lower/front mounting bolt. Then, swing the alternator to the side.

4. Loosen the power steering pump mounts and remove the drive belt. Then, remove the mounting bolts and remove the pump and pump mounting bracket. Make sure to retain spacers. Remove the nuts and bolts that fasten the compressor to the hinge type mounting bracket. Make sure the compressor is suspended so there is no tension on the hoses. Unbolt the hinge type mounting bracket and remove it.

5. Remove the brace plate located under the oil pan. Remove those oil pan bolts that can be reached.

6. Remove the engine ground strap. Remove the engine mount through bolts. Attach a lifting sling to the hooks on top of the engine. Lift the engine slightly for clearance.

7. Shift the power steering pump out of the way and support it so no tension will be placed on the hoses.

8. Remove the remaining oil pan mounting bolts. Turn the crankshaft so the rods for cylinders 5 and 6 are as high as possible. Then, remove the pan.

To install:

9. Clean all sealing surfaces and supply a new gasket. Apply a liquid sealer to the joints between the block and the timing cover on the front and the rear main seal cover at the rear.

10. Install the oil pan in reverse order. Torque the pan bolts to 7 ft. lbs. (10 Nm). Make sure to refill the pan with the required amount of the correct oil. Mount all accessories securely and adjust the drive belts.

2.5L (M50B25) ENGINE

1. Disconnect the negative battery terminal and raise and safely support the vehicle. Drain the engine oil.

2. Loosen the holding bolt for the oil dipstick guide pipe and remove the clamp. Pull the guide tube free of the pan.

3. Remove all the oil pan bolts and remove the pan. Raise the engine slightly if needed for clearance.

To install:

4. Apply sealer to the joint between the pan, front cover and block.

5. Install new gaskets and install the pan. Torque mounting bolts to 6.5-8.0 ft. lbs. (9-11 Nm).

6. Install the dipstick guide tube using a new base seal and tighten the holding bolt.

7 Series

EXCEPT 5.0L (M70B50) ENGINE

1. Disconnect the negative battery cable. Loosen the hose clamp for the air intake hose. Remove the mounting nut for the air cleaner and remove the air cleaner. Remove the fan and shroud.

2. Disconnect the electrical plug and overflow hose from the coolant expansion tank. Be careful not to kink the hose. Remove the mounting nuts and remove the tank.

3. Remove the splash guard for the power steering pump. Loosen the locknut for the pump adjustment and remove the through bolt that mounts the pump lower bracket (which contains the adjustment mechanism) to the block. Swing the bracket aside. Unscrew the bolt attaching the power steering pump lines to the block and shift them aside too.

4. Disconnect the electrical plug for the suspension leveling switch on the left side engine mounting bracket. Raise and safely support the vehicle. Remove the oil pan drain plug and drain the oil.

5. Remove the bracket for the exhaust pipes located near the oil pan.

6. Disconnect the ground strap from the engine. Remove the nuts and washers attaching the engine to the mounts on both sides.

7. Attach an engine lifting sling to the hooks at either end of the cylinder head. Lift the engine as necessary for clearance.

8. Remove all oil pan mounting bolts and remove the pan.

To install:

9. Clean both sealing surfaces and supply a new gasket. Coat the 4 joints, between the block and timing case cover at the front and the block and rear main seal housing cover at the rear, with a proper sealer. Install the oil pan bolts and torque them to 7 ft. lbs. (10 Nm).

10. Reverse the remaining procedures to install the oil pan. Torque the engine mount nuts to 31-34 ft. lbs. (42-47 Nm). Refill the oil pan with the required amount and type of oil.

5.0L (M70B50) ENGINE

1. Disconnect the negative battery cable. Raise and safely support the vehicle.

2. Remove the transmission and the oil pump assembly. Lower the vehicle.

3. Disconnect and remove the windshield washer tank and the coolant expansion tank.

4. Remove the guide tube for the oil dipstick. Disconnect the oil pipe on the tandem pump. Remove the mounting bracket.

5. Unscrew the belt tensioner and remove the oil drain hose.

6. Crank the engine to TDC and unscrew the flywheel using the proper tool.

7. Disconnect the left and right engine mounts at the bottom. Pull off the pipe adapter for oil extraction.

8. Remove the oil pump consoles. Unscrew the oil pan bolts and remove the oil pan.

To install

9. Clean the mounting surfaces and install a new gasket.

10. Install the oil pan and tighten the mounting bolts to 7 ft. lbs. (11 Nm).

11. Connect the left and right engine mounts at the bottom and tighten to 32.5 ft. lbs. (43 Nm).

12. Replace the oil consoles and tighten to 25 ft. lbs. (34 Nm).

13. Install the flywheel and tighten the bolts to 72 ft. lbs. (97 Nm).

14. The remainder of the installation is the reverse of the removal procedure.

8 Series

1. Disconnect the negative battery cable. Raise and safely support the vehicle.

2. Remove the transmission and the oil pump assembly. Lower the vehicle.

3. Disconnect and remove the windshield washer tank and the coolant expansion tank.

4. Remove the guide tube for the oil dipstick. Disconnect the oil pipe on the tandem pump. Remove the mounting bracket.

5. Unscrew the belt tensioner and remove the oil drain hose.

6. Crank the engine to TDC and unscrew the flywheel using the proper tool.

7. Disconnect the left and right engine mounts at the bottom. Pull off the pipe adapter for oil extraction.

8. Remove the oil pump consoles. Unscrew the oil pan bolts and remove the oil pan.

To install

9. Clean the mounting surfaces and install a new gasket.

10. Install the oil pan and tighten the mounting bolts to 7 ft. lbs. (11 Nm).

11. Connect the left and right engine mounts at the bottom and tighten to 32.5 ft. lbs. (43 Nm).

12. Replace the oil consoles and tighten to 25 ft. lbs. (34 Nm).

13. Install the flywheel and tighten the bolts to 72 ft. lbs. (97 Nm).

14. The remainder of the installation is the reverse of the removal procedure.

Oil Pump

REMOVAL AND INSTALLATION

1.8L (M42B18) Engine

1. Disconnect the negative battery cable.

2. Raise and safely support the vehicle. Drain the engine oil.

3. Remove the timing case cover.

4. Disconnect the oil pump cover mounting bolts and remove the oil pump assembly.

5. Reverse the removal procedure for installation.

2.5L (M20B25), 3.5L (M30B35) and 5.0L (M70B50) Engines

EXCEPT 3 SERIES

1. Disconnect the negative battery cable and remove the oil pan.

2. Remove the bolts retaining the sprocket to the oil pump shaft and remove the sprocket.

3. Remove the oil pump retaining bolts and lower the oil pump from the engine block. On 6 cylinder engines other than the M30B35 engine, there are 3 bolts at the front and 2 bolts attaching the rear of the oil pickup to the lower end of a support bracket. It is necessary to remove all 5 bolts. On the M30B35 engine, there are only 3 bolts.

4. Do not loosen the chain adjusting shims from the 2 mounting locations.

5. Add or subtract shims between the oil pump body and the engine block to obtain a slight movement of the chain under light thumb pressure.

6. Install the oil pump in position.

NOTE: When used, the 2 shim thicknesses must be the same. Tighten the pump holder at the pickup end after shimming is completed to avoid stress on the pump.

7. On 6 cylinder engines, other than the M30B35, after the main pump mounting bolts are torqued, loosen the bolts at the bracket on the rear of the pickup, allowing the pickup to assume its most natural position. This will relieve tension on the bracket. Tighten the bolts. On the M30B35 engine, torque the oil pump mounting bolts to 16 ft. lbs. (21 Nm)

and the sprocket bolts to 19 ft. lbs. (26 Nm).

3 SERIES

1. Raise an safely support the vehicle. Drain the engine oil.

2. Remove the front lower splash guard.

3. Disconnect the electrical terminal from the oil sending unit.

4. Remove the flywheel cover.

5. Remove the oil pan bolts and lower the oil pan. Remove the oil pump bolts and take out the oil pump and oil pan.

To install:

6. Installation is the reverse of removal. Note the following:

a. Clean the gasket surfaces and use a new gasket on the oil pan.

b. Positioning the pump for installation of its mounting bolts, guide the pump driveshaft into the hole in the center of the drive gear.

c. Coat the joints on the ends of the front engine cover with a universal sealing compound.

d. Install the sending unit wire and the engine oil.

2.5L (M50B25) Engine

1. Raise and safely support vehicle. Disconnect the negative battery cable. Drain the oil from the engine. Remove the oil pan to access the oil pump drive sprocket.

2. Remove the oil pump drive sprocket nut. Note that it is a left hand thread. Remove the oil pump drive sprocket from the oil pump shaft. Check the shaft splines.

3. Unbolt the oil pump body from the block and remove. Check the condition of the dowel sleeves.

4. Installation is the reverse of removal. Torque the pump mounting bolts to 16 ft. lbs. (22 Nm) and the sprocket nut to 18 ft. lbs. (25 Nm).

Rear Main Bearing Oil Seal

REMOVAL AND INSTALLATION

The rear main bearing oil seal can be replaced after the transmission and clutch/flywheel or the converter/flywheel has been removed from the engine.

1. Raise and safely support the vehicle. Drain the engine oil and loosen the oil pan bolts. Carefully use a sharp bladed tool to separate the oil pan gasket from the lower surface of the end cover housing.

2. Remove the 2 rear oil pan bolts.

3. Remove the bolts around the outside of the cover housing and re-

move the end cover housing from the engine block. Remove the gasket from the block surface.

4. Remove the seal from the housing. Coat the sealing lips of the new seal with oil. Install a new seal into the end cover housing with a special seal installer tool. On the 6 cylinder engines, press the seal in until it is about 0.039-0.079 in. (0.991-2.070mm) deeper than the standard seal, which was installed flush.

5. While the cover is off, check the plug in the rear end of the main oil gallery. If the plug shows signs of leakage, replace it with another, coating it with the proper sealant to keep it in place.

NOTE: Fill the cavity between the sealing lips of the seal with grease before installing.

6. Coat the mating surface between the oil pan and end cover with sealer. Using a new gasket, install the end cover on the engine block and bolt it into place.

7. Complete the installation. If the oil pan gasket has been damaged, replace it. Install the transmission.

ENGINE COOLING

Radiator

REMOVAL AND INSTALLATION

1. Disconnect the negative battery cable. Drain the cooling system. On some engines, this requires removing the plug from the bottom radiator tank.

2. If equipped with a coolant expansion tank, remove the cap, disconnect the hose at the radiator and drain the coolant into a clean container. If equipped with a splash guard, remove it.

3. Remove the coolant hoses and disconnect the automatic transmission oil cooler lines and plug their openings as well as the openings in the cooler.

4. Disconnect any of the temperature switch wire connectors.

5. Remove the shroud from the radiator. On some vehicles, this is done by simply pressing plugs toward the rear of the vehicle. On others, there are metal slips that must be pulled upward and off to free the shroud from the radiator. The shroud will re-

main in the vehicle, resting on the fan on most vehicles. On the 735i and 735iL, remove the fan and shroud together. Make sure to store the fan in a vertical position. The fan must be held stationary with some sort of flat blade cut to fit over the hub and drilled to fit over 2 of the studs on the front of the pulley. Then, unscrew the retaining nut at the center of the fluid drive hub turning it clockwise to remove it because it has left hand threads.

6. If equipped with the M30B35 engine, remove the fan and shroud; then, spread the retaining clip and pull the oil cooler out to the right. Remove the radiator retaining bolt(s) and lift the radiator from the vehicle.

To install:

7. The radiator is installed in the reverse order of removal. Fill and bleed the cooling system.

NOTE: On the M3, there are rubber washers that go on either side of the mounting brackets at the top and that the bottom of the unit is suspended by rubber bushings into which prongs located on the bottom tank will fit. Make sure all parts fit right when the unit is installed.

8. Check that rubber mounts are located so as to effectively isolate the radiator from the chassis, as this will help ensure reliable radiator performance. Note that if the vehicle uses plastic upper and lower radiator tanks and has a radiator drain plug, be careful not to over torque the plugs.

9. Torque engine oil cooler pipes to 18-21 ft. lbs. (23-28 Nm) and transmission cooler pipes to 13-15 ft. lbs. (17-20 Nm).

10. Torque the thermostatic fan hub on the 735i and 735iL to 29-36 ft. lbs. (40-48 Nm).

Heater Core

REMOVAL AND INSTALLATION

325i, 325iC, 325iS, 325iX and M3

1. Disconnect the negative battery cable. Remove the package tray. Remove bolts and remove the left/lower dish trim panel.

2. Drain the coolant, loosen the bolt and remove the clamp bracing the 2 lines going to the heater core.

3. Remove the left side duct carrying air from the heater to the rear seat duct.

4. Unscrew the bolts and remove the lower heater discharge duct.

5. Unscrew the bolts fastening the water lines from the engine compartment to the lines coming down from the heater core. Remove and discard the O-ring seals.

6. Unscrew the bolts, separate the halves of the core housing and pull the core out of the housing.

7. Installation is the reverse of removal. Replace the O-ring seals for the water lines.

635CSi and M5

1. Disconnect the negative battery cable. Remove the instrument panel trim at bottom left. Remove the package tray.

2. Carefully, discharge the air conditioning system through the Schrader® valve and then cap the valve off.

3. Remove the bolts and remove the trim panel underneath the evaporator unit.

4. Remove the tape type insulation. Get caps for the refrigerant lines. Using a backup wrench, disconnect the low and high pressure lines and cap them.

5. Disconnect the electrical connector for the evaporator. Disconnect the temperature sensor plug, accessible from the outside of the evaporator housing.

6. Remove the bolts and then remove the bracket that braces the housing at the firewall. Remove the mounting bolt from either side of the housing.

7. Unclip both fasteners and remove the housing.

8. Move into the engine compartment and remove the rubber insulator from the cowl.

9. Remove the mounting bolts for the cover which is located under the windshield.

10. Remove the mounting nuts for the heater housing located on either side of the blower.

11. Drain the cooling system and disconnect the hoses at the core.

12. Working inside the vehicle, remove the 3 electrical connectors for the heater housing. Pull off the air ducts.

13. Remove the mounting nuts and remove the heater unit.

14. Remove the air duct connections from the housing. Push the retaining bar back and then split and remove the blower shells.

15. Remove the retaining clips from the housing halves and split the housing. Then, remove the core.

To install:

16. To install, reverse the removal procedure, noting the following points:

  a. Cement a new rubber seal on the core.

  b. Make sure when reassembling the halves of the housing, all the distributor door flap shafts pass through the holes in the housing.

  c. Before reconnecting the refrigerant lines, coat the threads with clean refrigerant oil.

  d. Refill the cooling system with clean coolant and bleed it.

  e. Properly, evacuate and recharge the air conditioning system.

525i, 535i, 735i, 735iL and 750iL

1. Disconnect the negative battery cable. Drain coolant from the cooling system. Remove the center console.

2. Remove the mounting bolts and remove the right core mounting bracket. Lift out the front blower motor on the 7 Series.

3. Remove the core cover screws. Loosen the wire straps and clips and remove the cover.

4. Disconnect the temperature sensor(s).

5. Unscrew the mounting bolts and lift out the heater pipes. Replace the O-rings. Then, lift out the core from the right side.

6. Install in reverse order. Refill and bleed the cooling system.

850i

1. Disconnect the negative battery cable. Drain coolant from the cooling system. Remove the instrument dashboard.

2. Remove the heater core hoses.

3. Disconnect the temperature sensors.

4. Remove the core cover screws. Loosen the wire straps and clips and remove the cover.

5. Unscrew the mounting bolts and lift out the heater pipes. Replace the O-rings. Then, lift out the core from the right side.

6. Install in reverse order. Refill and bleed the cooling system.

Water Pump

REMOVAL AND INSTALLATION

3 Series

EXCEPT 1.8L (M42B18) ENGINE

1. Disconnect the negative battery cable. Drain the cooling system.

2. Remove the distributor cap and rotor. Remove the inner distributor cap and rubber sealing ring.

3. The fan must be held stationary with some sort of flat blade cut to fit over the hub and drilled to fit over 2 of the studs on the front of the pulley or use the proper tool. Remove the fan coupling nut; left hand thread — turn clockwise to remove.

4. Remove the belt and pulley.

5. Remove the rubber guard and distributor and or upper timing belt cover.

6. Compress the timing tensioner spring and clamp pin with the proper tool.

NOTE: Observe the installed position of the tensioner spring pin on the water pump housing for reinstallation purposes.

7. Remove the water hoses, remove the 3 water pump bolts and remove the pump.

8. Clean the gasket surfaces and use a new gasket.

9. Install the water pump in position. Note the position of the tensioner spring pin. Torque the M8 bolts to 16 ft. lbs. (22 Nm) and the M6 bolts to 6.5 ft. lbs. (9 Nm).

10. Add coolant and bleed the cooling system.

1.8L (M42B18) ENGINE

1. Disconnect the negative battery cable. Drain the cooling system.

2. Remove the drive belt and the water pump pulley.

3. Remove the pump mounting bolts.

4. Screw 2 bolts into the tapped bores and press the water pump out of the cover uniformly.

5. Lubricate and install a new O-ring.

6. Install the water pump and tighten the bolts to 6.5 ft. lbs. (9 Nm).

7. The remainder of the installation is the reverse of the removal procedure.

5, 6, 7 and 8 Series

1. Disconnect the negative battery cable. Drain the cooling system.

2. Remove the fan cowl and fan, if necessary.

3. Remove the drive belt and the pulley. Disconnect the bracket, if necessary.

4. Remove the air cleaner with the air flow sensor, if needed.

5. Disconnect the cooling hoses and remove the water pump.

6. The installation is the reverse of the removal procedure. Torque the

M8 bolts to 16 ft. lbs. (22 Nm) and the M6 bolts to 6.5 ft. lbs. (9 Nm).

Thermostat

REMOVAL AND INSTALLATION

The thermostat is located near the water pump, either on the cylinder head or intake manifold on some vehicles and is located between 2 coolant hose sections on some vehicles.

Always drain some coolant out and save it in a clean container before removing the thermostat. On the M5 engine, the forward (removable) portion of the housing has a hose connected to it. The hose need not be disconnected to remove the housing. On the engine used in the M5, there is a large O-ring seal for the main portion of the housing and a small, O-ring located above it in a small passage. The M20B25 engines also use a large O-ring which must be replaced with the thermostat. Replace both these seals on all vehicles.

Note that thermostats for M30B35 engines carry an "A" designation. The thermostat for the M20B25 engines is smaller in diameter. On all vehicles, except M3, the thermostat is installed with the thermostatic sensing unit facing inward and the cross-band facing outward. Refill and bleed the cooling system.

On the M3, the thermostat is installed in a coolant lines with a 3rd connection that goes to the block. To replace it, first drain coolant and then note the routing of hoses. Loosen all 3 hose clamps and then replace the unit. Refill and bleed the system.

Cooling System Bleeding

WITH BLEEDER SCREW

Set the heat valve in the **WARM** position, start the engine and bring it to normal operating temperature. Run the engine at fast idle and open the venting screw on the thermostat housing until the coolant comes out free of air bubbles. Close the bleeder screw and refill the cooling system.

WITHOUT BLEEDER SCREW

Fill the cooling system, place the heater valve in the **WARM** position, close the pressure cap to the second (fully closed) position. Start the engine and bring to normal operating temperature. Carefully release the

pressure cap to the first position and squeeze the upper and lower radiator hoses in a pumping action to allow trapped air to escape through the radiator. Recheck the coolant level and close the pressure cap to its second position.

ENGINE ELECTRICAL

NOTE: Disconnecting the negative battery cable on some vehicles may interfere with the functions of the on board computer systems and may require the computer to undergo a relearning process.

Distributor

REMOVAL

NOTE: The 2.3L (S14B23) and 6 cylinder engines use a distributor which is contained within the engine. Other than distributor cap and rotor removal and installation, no service is possible.

1. Disconnect the negative battery cable. On all engines so equipped, remove the weather-proof rubber cap protecting the distributor cap and wires from moisture. Prior to removal, using paint, chalk or a sharp instrument, scribe alignment marks showing the relative position of the distributor body to its mount on the rear of the cylinder head.

2. Mark each spark plug wire with a dab of paint or chalk noting its respective cylinder. It will be easier and faster to install the distributor and get the firing order right if the plug wires are left in the cap.

3. Pull up and disconnect the secondary wire (high tension cable leading from the coil to the center of the distributor cap) and remove the spark plug loom retaining nut(s) from the cylinder head cover. Disconnect the vacuum line(s) from the vacuum advance unit.

4. Disconnect the primary wire (low tension wire running from one of the coil terminals to the side of the distributor) at the distributor. On electronic ignition distributors, disconnect the plug.

5. Disconnect the distributor retaining clasps and lift off the cap and wire assembly. On all engines

equipped with a dust cap under the rotor, remove the rotor, remove the dust cap and reinstall the rotor.

6. Now, with the aid of a remote starter switch, "bump" the starter a few times until the No. 1 piston is at TDC of its compression stroke. At this time, the notch scribed on the metal tip of the distributor rotor must be aligned with a corresponding notch scribed on the distributor case. Before removing the distributor, make sure these 2 marks coincide.

7. Loosen the clamp bolt at the base of the distributor (where it slides into its mount) and lift the distributor up and out. Notice that the rotor turns clockwise as the distributor is removed.

INSTALLATION

Timing Not Disturbed

1. To install the distributor, position it in the block. Remember to rotate the rotor approximately 1.4 in. counterclockwise from the notch scribed in the distributor body. This will ensure that when the distributor is fully seated in its mount, the marks will coincide. Adjust the ignition timing. Tighten the clamp bolt to 8.0 ft. lbs. (12 Nm).

2. Reinstall the cap and wires.

3. Connect the negative battery cable.

Timing Disturbed

1. Disconnect the spark plug wire and remove the spark plug from the No. 1 cylinder. Place a finger over the spark plug hole.

2. Turn the crankshaft pulley in the normal direction of rotation until compression is felt; the piston is approaching TDC on the compression stroke. Continue rotating the crankshaft pulley until the pulley mark aligns with the **T** mark on the timing belt cover.

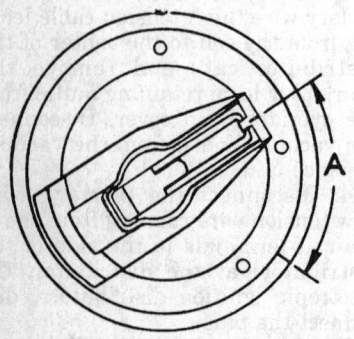

Distance (A) rotor from the housing mark during removal of the distributor

3. Apply clean engine oil to a new O-ring and install it on the distributor.

4. Install the distributor in the cylinder head. Make sure the distributor rotor is pointing toward the No. 1 spark plug tower position on the distributor cap.

5. Install the distributor mounting bolts. Align the marks made on the distributor housing and cylinder head during removal and loosely tighten the bolts.

6. Connect the distributor wiring and, if equipped, vacuum hoses.

7. Install the distributor cap and secure the screws.

8. Install the spark plug in the No. 1 cylinder and connect the spark plug wire.

9. Connect the spark plug wires to the distributor cap in their original locations.

10. Connect the negative battery cable. Check and adjust the ignition timing.

Distributorless Ignition

All ignition and fuel injection functions are controlled by the Digital Motor Electronics (DME) control unit. Ignition timing is fully electronically controlled; there is no vacuum advance or manual adjustment. Ignition functions are calculated from internal maps and from the same sensors used for the fuel injection system. Vehicles with an automatic transmission, the control unit will retard ignition timing briefly when the transmission is about to shift up or down. For this reason, there is a data link between the DME control unit and the transmission control unit.

Variations of this ignition system are used on different engines. The M42B18 engine uses distributorless ignition with a coil pack mounted on the inner fender. The M50B25 engine uses distributorless ignition with a coil pack mounted above each spark plug.

Ignition Timing

ADJUSTMENT

1. If equipped with the Motronic control unit, the timing can be checked; however, timing cannot be adjusted. The only cure for improper timing is to replace the control unit. Also, timing must be within a specified range, as the computer changes the timing slightly to allow for vari-

ous changes in operating condition. In other words, the timing does not have to be right on, but anywhere within the specified range.

2. The engine should be at normal operating temperature and the operation should be performed at normal room temperatures. The engine RPM should be within the specified range under the control of the computer.

3. Look up the control unit number on the unit itself. On 3, 5 and 6 Series vehicles, the unit is in the glove box; on the 7 and 8 Series, it is in the right side speaker cutout.

4. Connect a tachometer and a timing light to the engine (the latter to the No. 1 cylinder). Start the engine and check the rpm. If it is not correct, check the idle speed and reset it as necessary. Then, operate the timing light to see if timing is within range. If it is significantly outside the range, the Motronic control unit must be replaced.

Alternator

PRECAUTIONS

Several precautions must be observed with alternator equipped vehicles to avoid damaging the unit. They are as follows:

- If the battery is removed for any reason, make sure it is reconnected with the correct polarity. Reversing the battery connections may result in damage to the one-way rectifiers.
- When utilizing a booster battery as a starting aid, always connect it as follows: positive to positive, and negative (booster battery) to a good ground on the engine.
- Never use a fast charger as a booster to start vehicles with alternating-current (AC) circuits.
- When servicing the battery with a fast charger, always disconnect the battery cables.
- Never attempt to polarize an alternator.
- Avoid long soldering times when replacing diodes or transistors. Prolonged heat is damaging to alternators.
- Do not use test lamps of more than 12 volts for checking diode continuity.
- Do not short across or ground any of the terminals on the alternator.
- The polarity of the battery, alternator and regulator must be matched and considered before making any electrical connections within the system.

• Never operate the alternator on an open circuit. Make sure all connections within the circuit are clean and tight.

• Turn OFF the ignition switch and then disconnect the battery terminals when performing any service on the electrical system or charging the battery.

• Disconnect the battery ground cable if arc welding is to be done on any part of the vehicle.

BELT TENSION ADJUSTMENT

The fan belt tension is adjusted by moving the alternator on the slack adjuster bracket. The belt tension is adjusted to a deflection of approximately ½ in. under moderate thumb pressure in the middle of its longest span. On many engines, the position of the top of the alternator is adjusted via a bolt that is geared to the bracket. This bolt is turned to position the alternator and determine tension and then is locked in position with a lock bolt.

REMOVAL AND INSTALLATION

Except 750iL and 850i

1. Disconnect the negative battery cable.
2. Disconnect the wires from the rear of the alternator, marking them for installation. Note that there is a ground wire on some vehicles. Observe the following differences as applicable:
   a. On the 735i and 735iL, remove the cap and then disconnect the positive terminal at the junction box on the fender well.
   b. On the 325, M3, 635CSi, 735i and 735iL, it may be easier to remove the alternator mounting bolts, turn it, and then remove the wires.
   c. On the M5, unscrew the nut and loosen the hose clamp. Pull of the plug. Then, lift out the air cleaner and air flow sensor.
   d. Make sure the engine is cool. Place a pan under the radiator and disconnect the lower radiator hose.
   e. On the 325, 525 and M3, remove the air flow sensor and air cleaner, if necessary.
   f. On the 735i and 735iL, make sure the engine is cool. Place a pan under the radiator and disconnect the lower radiator hose.
3. Loosen the adjusting and pivot bolts and remove the belt on those vehicles with a standard mounting system. If the alternator has the ten-

sioning bolt described in Step 4, loosen the lock bolt, turn the tensioning bolt so as to eliminate belt tension and then remove the belt. Remove the bolts and remove the alternator. On the 635CSi, 735i and 735iL, it may be necessary to loosen the fan cowl to get at the mounting bolts. On the 535i and 525i, it may be necessary to disconnect a power steering line that runs near the alternator.

To install:
4. Install the alternator in position and install the retaining bolts.
5. Adjust the belt tension to approximately ⅜in., measured between the balancer and the alternator pulley.
6. The tensioning bolt on the front of the alternator must be turned so as to tension the belt, using a torque wrench, until the torque is approximately 5 ft. lbs. (7 Nm). Then, hold the adjustment with one wrench while tightening the locknut at the rear of the unit. Make sure, if the unit has a ground wire on the alternator, it has been reconnected. On the M5, 735i and 735iL, make sure to reconnect the radiator hose, refill and bleed the cooling system. On the M5, securely install the air cleaner and air flow sensor.

750iL and 850i

1. Disconnect the negative battery cables.
2. Loosen the oil filter cap.
3. Remove the air filter and mass air flow sensor.
4. Disconnect the ignition coil wires.
5. Remove the fan assembly.
6. Loosen clamp of air cooling hose on alternator.
7. Loosen the alternator drive belt tensioner and remove the drive belt.
8. Remove the under vehicle splash guard.
9. Disconnect oil level sender.
10. Unscrew the hydraulic pipe clamp on alternator.
11. Remove the tensioner and cooling hose from the alternator.
12. Remove the alternator pulley and mounting bolts.
13. Remove the upper hydraulic line clamp.
14. Remove the oil filter assembly including hoses.
15. Disconnect the alternator wires.
16. Remove the distributor cover and loosen the wire strap.
17. Remove the heatshield.
18. Remove the alternator assembly.

To install:
19. Install the alternator assembly.
20. Install the heatshield.
21. Install the distributor cover and tighten the wire strap.
22. Connect the alternator wires.
23. Install the oil filter assembly and hoses.
24. Install the upper hydraulic line clamp.
25. Install the alternator pulley and mounting bolts.
26. Install the tensioner and cooling hose onto the alternator.
27. Unscrew the hydraulic line clamp onto alternator.
28. Connect oil level sender.
29. Install the under vehicle splash guard.
30. Tighten the alternator drive belt tensioner and install the drive belt.
31. Tighten clamp of air cooling hose onto alternator.
32. Install the fan assembly.
33. Connect the ignition coil wires.
34. Install the air filter and mass air flow sensor.
35. Tighten the oil filter cap.
36. Connect the negative battery cables.

Starter

REMOVAL AND INSTALLATION

Except 750iL and 850i

1. Disconnect the negative battery cable.
2. On 6 cylinder engines with 6 identical intake tubes, it may be necessary to remove No. 6 intake tube for clearance. On 4 cylinder vehicles, remove the intake cowl from the mixture control unit.
3. On the 318, 325 and M3, remove the air cleaner and air flow sensor. Then, remove the mounting bolts for the bracket for the air collector and remove it.
4. On the 525i and 535i, make sure the engine is cool. Drain some coolant from the cooling system and then remove the expansion tank.
5. On the 635CSi, make sure the engine is cool and drain some coolant out. Disconnect the heater hose that is near the starter.
6. Operate the brake pedal hard 20 times. Disconnect the power steering line that would otherwise prevent access to the starter.
7. Cut off the straps and remove the solenoid switch insulating cover, located right near the solenoid.
8. On the M5, remove the exhaust manifold.

9. Cut off the straps and remove the solenoid switch insulating cover, located right near the solenoid.

10. Remove the starter solenoid wire leads, marking them for later installation, unless they have already been removed. On 4 cylinder vehicles, disconnect the mounting bracket at the block.

11. On the 325 and the M3, drain coolant out of the engine and then disconnect the heater hose located near the starter; also unscrew and remove the coolant pipe if necessary for clearance.

NOTE: Remove the accelerator cable holder on automatic transmission equipped vehicles.

12. Unbolt and remove the starter.

NOTE: On the 525i, 535i, 735i, it may be necessary to use a box wrench with an angled handle to unscrew the main starter mounting bolts. On the 635CSi, the final mounting bolt must be removed from underneath. On the 325 and M3, the starter must be pulled out from above. On the M3 remove the intake manifold, if necessary.

To install:

13. Install the starter and install the retaining bolts. Install all removed components on all vehicles.

14. Make sure to reconnect all hoses and refill and bleed the cooling system or power steering system.

15. Where the solenoid switch cover has been unstrapped, reinstall it with new straps to locate it properly for electrical safety.

750iL and 850i

1. Disconnect the negative battery cable.

2. Remove the exhaust system. Remove the heatshields on steering linkage.

3. Remove headlight washing tank and pump, position aside.

4. Remove the heatshields on the intake manifold. Unscrew the lines on the starter connection point.

5. Remove the exhaust manifolds, front manifold first.

6. Remove the starter mounting bolts. Remove the brackets and heatshields. Remove the starter assembly.

7. Installation is the reverse of the removal procedure.

EMISSION CONTROLS

Emission Warning Lamps

RESETTING

Service Interval Reminder Lights

The on-board computer is used to evaluate mileage, average engine speed and engine and coolant temperatures as well as other computer input factors that determine maintenance intervals. There are 5 green, a yellow and a red **LED** used to remind the driver of oil changes and other maintenance services.

The green LED'S will be illuminated when the ignition is in the **ON** position and the engine OFF. There will not be as many green LED'S illuminated when the maintenance time gets closer. A yellow LED that is illuminated when the engine is running, will indicate maintenance is now due. The red LED will be illuminated when the service interval has been exceeded by approximately 1000 miles. This is the computers way of saying this is your last warning.

There is a service interval reset tool manufactured by the Assenmacher Tool Company tool 62-1-100. This tool is used to reset BMW 6 cylinder and 4 cylinder vehicles with the aid of an additional adapter tool.

1. Locate the diagnostic connector near the thermostat housing.

2. Plug the special reset tool into the diagnostic connector and place the ignition switch in the **ON** position.

3. Depress the reset button on the tool until all 5 green LED'S are illuminated, showing that the reset has completed.

FUEL SYSTEM

Fuel System Service Precautions

Safety is the most important factor when performing not only fuel system maintenance but any type of maintenance. Failure to conduct maintenance and repairs in a safe manner may result in serious personal injury or death. Maintenance and testing of the vehicle's fuel system components can be accomplished safely and effectively by adhering to the following rules and guidelines.

• To avoid the possibility of fire and personal injury, always disconnect the negative battery cable unless the repair or test procedure requires that battery voltage be applied.

• Always relieve the fuel system pressure prior to disconnecting any fuel system component (injector, fuel rail, pressure regulator, etc.), fitting or fuel line connection. Exercise extreme caution whenever relieving fuel system pressure to avoid exposing skin, face and eyes to fuel spray. Fuel under pressure may penetrate the skin or any part of the body that it contacts.

• Always place a shop towel or cloth around the fitting or connection prior to loosening to absorb any excess fuel due to spillage. Ensure that all fuel spillage (should it occur) is quickly removed from engine surfaces. Ensure that all fuel soaked cloths or towels are deposited into a suitable waste container.

• Always keep a dry chemical (Class B) fire extinguisher near the work area.

• Do not allow fuel spray or fuel vapors to come into contact with a spark or open flame.

• Always use a backup wrench when loosening and tightening fuel line connection fittings. This will prevent unnecessary stress and torsion to fuel line piping. Always follow the proper torque specifications.

• Always replace worn fuel fitting O-rings with new. Do not substitute fuel hose or equivalent where fuel pipe is installed.

RELIEVING FUEL SYSTEM PRESSURE

To relieve the pressure in the system, first find the fuel pump relay plug, located on the cowl. Unplug the relay, leaving it in a safe position where the connections cannot ground. If necessary, tape the plug in place or tape over the connector prongs with electrical tape. Then, start the engine and operate it until it stalls. Crank the engine for 10 seconds after it stalls to remove any residual pressure.

Fuel Filter

REMOVAL AND INSTALLATION

Except M5

On filters that are located near the fuel tank, it is necessary to clamp the fuel lines closed before disconnecting them, or fuel will run out continuously.

1. Disconnect the negative battery cable. Relieve fuel system pressure. Clamp the lines closed if the filter is mounted low, near the fuel tank. Then, loosen the clamps and disconnect the inlet and outlet hoses. Remove the hose clamps or slide them back, well off the connections to make it easier to pull off the hoses, if necessary.

2. The filters will usually be attached to a frame, floor pan or wheel well by a bracket. Loosen the bracket and remove the filter. On the 735 with the M30B35 engine, remove the Phillips head screw clamping the filter inside the mounting band. Note the direction of flow and then remove the filter.

3. Observe the instructions on the inlet and outlet during installation.

M5

1. Relieve fuel system pressure. Disconnect the battery cables. Working under the fuel tank, pull back the protective caps and then unscrew the attaching nuts and pull off the electrical connections for the fuel pump.

2. Pinch off the inlet line to the fuel pump and the outlet from the filter. Then, loosen the clamps and disconnect these 2 hoses.

3. Remove the nut that clamps the fuel line near the pump. Then, remove the bolts which mount the pump and filter to the bottom of the body and remove the assembly.

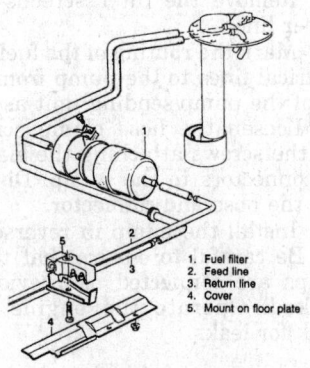

1. Fuel filter
2. Feed line
3. Return line
4. Cover
5. Mount on floor plate

Fuel filter location — 525i and 535i

4. Remove the bolt fastening the halves of the bracket together and remove the filter from the bracket. Loosen the clamp on the inlet side of the filter and disconnect the inlet line, noting the direction of flow (arrow). Remove the rubber bushing in which the filter is mounted and mount it on the new filter.

5. Install the filter in exact reverse order, making sure all clamps are securely tightened. Operate the engine and check for leaks.

Electric Fuel Pump

PRESSURE TESTING

Except 3 Series

1. Relieve fuel system pressure. Tee a pressure gauge into the fuel feed line in front of the pressure regulator on M5, tee in between the cold start valve and the fuel rail. Plug the fuel return hose.

2. Pull off the pump relay. Jumper terminals **87** and **30**. Measure the delivery pressure. It should be 43 psi on vehicles except the 735i and 735iL. On these vehicles, it should be 48 psi.

3 Series

EXCEPT M3

1. Relieve fuel system pressure. Tee a pressure gauge into the fuel feed line in front of the pressure regulator.

2. Disconnect the fuel pump relay.

3. Connect a remote starter switch between terminals **KL30** and **KL87** of the relay. Close the switch and check the pressure. It should be 43 psi. If not, the filter is severely clogged or the fuel pump is defective.

M3

1. Relieve fuel system pressure. Tee a pressure gauge into the fuel return line at the pressure regulator. Then, clamp off the return line so pressure builds up to the maximum level the pump can produce.

2. Remove the trim from the cowl on the right (passenger's side). Then, unplug the fuel pump relay. Connect a remote starter switch between terminals **30** and **87** (left side and top holding the male side of the connector). Energize the switch and check the pressure. It must be 43 psi. Check the filter for excessive clogging. If it is okay, the pump is defective.

REMOVAL AND INSTALLATION

325i, 325iS, 325iX and M3

1. Relieve fuel system pressure. Disconnect the negative battery cable. Going to the pump, which is under the vehicle and near the fuel tank, push back any protective caps, note the routing and disconnect the electrical connector(s).

2. Securely clamp the suction hose (coming from the tank) and plug the discharge hose so no fuel can escape.

3. Open the hose clamp connecting the suction hose to the pump and disconnect it.

4. Remove the attaching nuts which mount the pump and bracket to the floor pan and remove both as an assembly.

5. Remove the bolt passing through the 2 parts of the bracket and also mounting the hose attaching strap to the bracket. Then, pull the pump out of the bracket.

6. Loosen the hose clamp for the discharge hose and disconnect it at the pump. Pull the rubber ring off the pump.

7. Note the code number on the pump and make sure to replace it with one of the same number. Inspect all the rubber mounts on the pump mounting bracket and replace any that are cracked or crushed.

8. Install the pump in reverse order. Make sure to unclamp the hoses and then run the engine and check for leaks. Check the fuel system pressure.

525i and 535i

The fuel pump is an electrical unit, delivering fuel through a pressure regulator, to a fuel distributor or a ring-line for the injection valves. The fuel pump is mounted under the vehicle, in the fuel tank, or in the engine compartment.

1. Relieve fuel system pressure. Disconnect the negative battery connector. Push back any protective caps and disconnect the electrical connector(s).

2. If the fuel lines are flexible, pinch them closed with an appropriate tool. Disconnect the fuel lines and plug the ends.

3. Remove the retaining bolts and remove the pump and expansion tank as an assembly.

4. The pump can be separated from the expansion tank after removal.

To install:

5. Install the pump in the correct position, be sure to use similar types

of hose clamps, if any need replacing. The wrong type clamp can damage the pressure lines.

6. Run the engine and check the fuel lines for leakage. Check the fuel system pressure.

M5

1. Disconnect the negative battery cable. Relieve fuel system pressure. Clamp the lines closed if the filter is mounted low, near the fuel tank. Then, loosen the clamps and disconnect the inlet and outlet hoses. Remove the hose clamps or slide them back, well off the connections to make it easier to pull off the hoses, if necessary.

2. The filters will usually be attached to a frame, floor pan or wheel well by a bracket. Loosen the bracket and remove the filter. Note the direction of flow and then remove the filter.

3. Observe the instructions on the inlet and outlet during installation.

4. Remove the bolt fastening the halves of the bracket together and remove the filter from the bracket. Loosen the clamp on the outlet side of the fuel pump and disconnect the

line. Then, slide off the rubber bushing in which the pump is mounted.

5. Check the code number on the side of the pump and make sure the replacement unit carries the same code.

6. Install the pump in exact reverse order, making sure all clamps are securely tightened. Operate the engine and check for leaks.

635CSi, 735i, 735iL and 750iL

The pump on this vehicle is mounted in the top of the tank along with the fuel level sending unit.

1. Disconnect the negative battery cable. Drain the fuel tank, enough to prevent spillage when removing the pump.

2. Relieve fuel system pressure. Remove the trim panels from the trunk. Then, remove the screws from the cover for the pump/sending unit assembly.

3. Label the fuel hoses connecting at the top of the pump/sending unit assembly. Unclamp and disconnect the fuel hoses and then plug them.

4. Slide the collar for the electrical connector to one side and then unplug the connector.

5. Remove the mounting screws and remove the pump/sending unit assembly. Replace the gasket.

6. Press the retaining locks for the pump unit inward and slide the pump out of the pump/sending unit assembly.

7. Note the routing of the fuel and electrical lines to the pump from the top of the pump/sending unit assembly. Loosen the hose clamp screws and the screws attaching the electrical connectors to the pump. Disconnect the hose and connector.

8. Unscrew the pressure regulator from the top of the check valve. Then, unscrew the check valve from the top of the pump.

9. Pull the insulating sleeve off the pump. Then, loosen the retaining screw and slide the filter off the pump.

10. Install the pump in reverse order. Be careful to ensure that the 2 retaining locks fasten the pump in place in a secure manner. Operate the engine and check for leaks.

850i

The pump on this vehicle is mounted in the top of the tank along with the fuel level sending unit.

1. Disconnect the negative battery cable. Drain the fuel tank, enough to prevent spillage when removing the pump.

2. Relieve fuel system pressure. Remove the rear seat. Then, remove the screws from the cover for the pump/sending unit assembly.

3. Label the fuel hoses connecting at the top of the pump/sending unit assembly. Unclamp and disconnect the fuel hoses and then plug them.

4. Slide the collar for the electrical connector to one side and then unplug the connector.

5. Remove the coupling nut and remove the pump/sending unit assembly. Replace the gasket.

6. Remove the filter screens and rubber liner.

7. Mark the routing of the fuel and electrical lines to the pump from the top of the pump/sending unit assembly. Loosen the hose clamp screws and the screws attaching the electrical connectors to the pump. Disconnect the hose and connector.

8. Install the pump in reverse order. Be careful to ensure that the 2 pumps are connected as previously marked. Operate the engine and check for leaks.

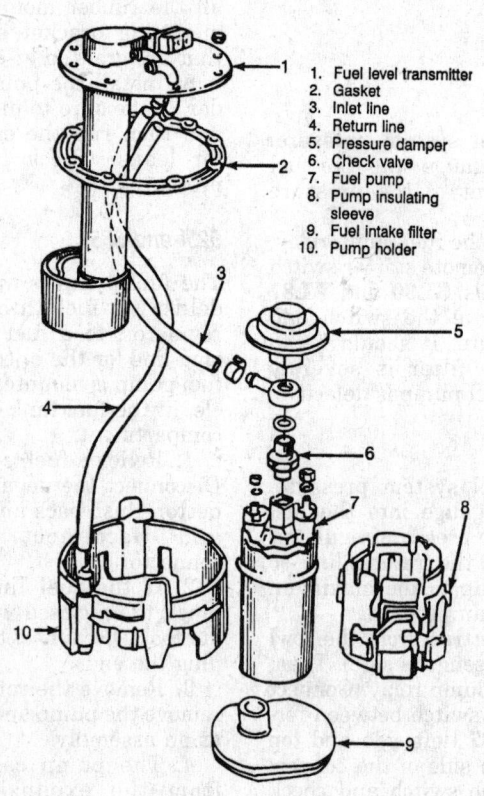

1. Fuel level transmitter
2. Gasket
3. Inlet line
4. Return line
5. Pressure damper
6. Check valve
7. Fuel pump
8. Pump insulating sleeve
9. Fuel intake filter
10. Pump holder

View of the in-tank fuel pump — 735i and 735iL

Fuel Injector

REMOVAL AND INSTALLATION

Except 1.8L (M42B18) and 2.5L (M50B25) Engines

1. Disconnect the negative battery cable. Remove the hose and plastic caps, if necessary.
2. Remove the plugs, plate and screws from the injector pipe.
3. Push up on the injector pipe until the injectors have cleared the guides on the intake manifold or the throttle valve housing.
4. Pull of the plugs and lift up the retainer. Remove the injectors.
5. Check the O-ring and replace, if necessary.
6. Install in the reverse order of the removal. Start the engine and check for leaks.

1.8L (M42B18) Engine

1. Disconnect the negative battery cable. Remove the upper section of the collector.
2. Disconnect the rear brace and remove the injector hose.
3. Remove the holder for the preheater.
4. Remove the screws and lift off the upper section of the intake manifold. Disconnect the hose from the fuel pressure regulator at the same time.
5. Remove the plug plate from the fuel injectors and unscrew the clamp.
6. Remove the injection pipe with the injectors attached. Lift off the retainer and remove the fuel injector.
7. Check the O-ring and replace, if necessary. Install in the reverse order of the removal. Start the engine and check for leaks.

2.5L (M50B25) Engine

1. Relieve the fuel pressure and disconnect the negative battery cable.
2. Remove the injector valley cover and disconnect and remove the plug plate.
3. Pull off the vacuum hose from the pressure regulator. Disconnect the fuel feed and return hoses from the fuel rail.
4. Unscrew the fasteners holding the fuel rail and remove the fuel rail along with the injectors.
5. Pull off the retainers and remove the injectors. If replacing an injector use the correct style and code number for the application.
6. Inspect the O-rings and replace as necessary. Replace the injectors on

the fuel rail and fit the retainers in place.
7. Lubricate the O-rings with Vaseline or gear oil prior to installation and replace the fuel rail. The remainder of the installation is reverse of removal.

DRIVE AXLE

Halfshaft

REMOVAL AND INSTALLATION

Front

325iX

1. Raise and safely support the vehicle. Remove the front wheels. Remove the drain plug and drain the lube oil from the front axle.
2. Lift out the lockplate in the center of the brake disc with a small prybar. Then, unscrew the collar nut.
3. Remove the attaching nut from each tie rod and then press the rod off the steering knuckle with the proper tool.
4. Remove the retaining nut and then press the control arm off the steering knuckle on either side.
5. Mount the proper tool to the brake disc with 2 wheel bolts. Press the output shaft out of the center of the steering knuckle on that side. Repeat on the other side.
6. To remove the drive axle from the differential on the left side: Install special tool by bolting it together around the axle so the ring on its inner diameter fits into the groove on the shaft. Install the tool onto the shaft so it will rest against the housing and the bolt heads of the tool will rest against it. Screw the 2 bolts in alternately in small increments to get even pressure on the shaft, pulling it out of the differential.
7. To remove the drive axle on the right side: Install the proper tool on the diameter of the shaft directly against the housing. Install the tool by bolting it together around the axle so the ring on its inner diameter fits into the groove on the shaft. Screw the 2 bolts in alternately in small increments to get even pressure on the shaft, pulling it out of the differential.

To install:

8. Install the halfshafts, bearing the following points in mind:
   a. Install the shafts into the housing until the circlip inside engages in the groove of the shaft. It may be necessary to install the removal tool and tap against it with a plastic-headed hammer to drive the shaft far enough into the housing.
   b. Before installing the shafts into the steering knuckle, coat the spline with light oil.
   c. When installing the control arms onto the steering knuckle, torque the nut to 61.5 ft. lbs. (84 Nm) and use a new cotter pin. When installing the tie rod onto the steering knuckle, torque to 61.5 ft. lbs. (84 Nm) and use a new self-locking nut.
   d. Drive a new lockplate into the brake disc with the proper tool. Torque the nut to 181 ft. lbs. (245 Nm).
   e. Replace the drain plug and refill the final drive unit with the required lubricant.

Rear

318iC, 318iS, 325i, 325iC, 325iS, 325iX AND M3

1. Raise and safely support the vehicle. Remove the rear tire and wheel assembly.
2. Lift out the lockplate and remove the retaining nut from the output flange. Remove the flange.
3. Disconnect the output shaft from the final drive by pressing out with the proper tool and suspend it.
4. Pull out the output shaft with a special tool.
5. Drive out the rear axleshaft with the proper tool.
6. Lift out the snapring. Then, pull out the wheel bearings, using the proper tool.
7. Pull out the seal with the proper tool.
8. If the inner bearing shell is damaged, pull it off with a puller and thrust pad.

To install:

9. Pull in the wheel bearing assembly, pull in the seal, insert the circlip and then pull in the rear axleshaft, all in reverse of the removal procedure. Install the axleshaft seal.
10. To install the output shaft, screw the threaded spindle into the shaft all the way and use the nut and washer against the outside of the bridge. Reconnect the output shaft to the final drive.

11. Lubricate the bearing surface of the outer nut with oil. Then install and torque the nut.

12. Using the proper installers or equivalent, knock in the lockplate. Use the following torque figures:

Output shaft to drive flange, 42-46 ft. lbs. (56-62 Nm).

Drive flange hub to output shaft, 140-152 ft. lbs. (190-206 Nm).

525i, 535i, M5, 635CSi, 735i, 735iL AND 750iL

1. Raise and safely support the vehicle.

2. Unscrew the output shaft on the rear drive assembly and the axleshaft end.

3. Remove the output shaft.

To install:

4. Install new washers on the rear drive assembly and the axleshaft end.

5. Install the output shaft and tighten to 42-46 ft. lbs. (56-62 Nm).

850i

1. Raise and safely support the vehicle. Remove the rear tire and wheel assembly.

2. Unscrew the hub collar nut.

3. Remove the final muffler assembly.

4. Compress the rear spring. Unscrew the output shaft bolts from the axle flange.

5. Remove the rear suspension trailing arm to leave sufficient room for the shaft to be pressed from the hub.

6. Using a suitable tool, press the axle from the hub assembly.

7. Installation is the reverse of the removal procedure.

CV-Boot

REMOVAL AND INSTALLATION

Front

325iX

1. Raise and safely support the vehicle. Remove the front wheel assembly.

2. Drain the gear lube and unscrew the collar nut.

3. Disconnect the tie rod ends and the control arm with the proper tool.

4. Remove the output shaft using the proper tool.

5. Loosen both clamps and pull the dust boot off the joint. Clean and remove grease from the joint. Add the required amount of the proper grease and install the boot and tighten the clamps.

6. The remainder of the installation is the reverse of the removal procedure.

Rear

1. Raise and safely support the vehicle.

2. Remove the output shaft and the snapring. Press off the cap and the dust cover.

3. Press the output shaft out of the CV-joint. Clean and remove the grease from the splines of the joint.

4. Install the dust cover with the inside cover on the output shaft.

5. Press on the joint with the cap and install the snapring. Pack the joint and dust cover with the proper grease.

6. Mount he dust cover and install new clamps.

7. Install the output shaft and lower the vehicle.

Driveshaft and U-Joints

REMOVAL AND INSTALLATION

318iC, 318iS, 325i, 325iC, 325iS and M3

1. Raise and safely support the vehicle. Remove the mufflers. Unscrew and remove the exhaust system heatshield near the fuel tank.

2. Unbolt and remove the cross brace that runs under the driveshaft.

3. Support the transmission. The automatic transmission must be supported by the case and not the pan. Loosen all transmission support bolts and remove. Remove the transmission rear support crossmember.

4. Lower the manual transmission for clearance. Remove the driveshaft bolts from the front coupling.

NOTE: Make sure the drive axle does not rest on the fuel line that runs across under it.

5. Unscrew and remove bolts at the coupling near the final drive.

6. Loosen the threaded sleeve on the driveshaft with a tool such as tool 26 1 040 or equivalent. Unbolt and remove the center mount.

7. Bend the driveshaft downward and remove it, being careful not to allow it to rest on the connecting line on the fuel tank.

To install:

8. Upon installation:

a. Mount the holder for the oxygen sensor plug.

b. Make sure the heatshield clears the fuel tank.

c. Wherever self-locking nuts are used, replace them. On the transmission-end flange, tighten the nuts/bolts only on the flange side, holding the other end stationary.

d. Preload the center mount to 0.157-0.236 in. (3.98-5.99mm) before tightening the bolts. Torque the mounting bolts to 16 ft. lbs. (21 Nm).

e. Lubricate the center bearing with the proper lubricant.

f. Make sure to reinstall the bracket for the oxygen sensor plug.

g. Make sure there is sufficient clearance between the rear heatshield and fuel tank.

325iX

NOTE: Never drive the vehicle with either driveshaft disconnected. This could damage the lockup mechanism in the transfer case.

1. Raise and safely support the vehicle. Remove the exhaust system. Remove both exhaust system heatshields.

2. Loosen the threaded sleeve near the front of the driveshaft with the proper tool. Turn the sleeve several turns outward, but do not disconnect it entirely.

3. Disconnect the driveshaft at the output flange of the transfer case by removing the nuts and the through bolts.

4. Disconnect the driveshaft at the final drive by removing the nuts and the through bolts.

NOTE: Make sure the drive axle does not rest on the fuel line that runs across under it.

5. Slide the sections of the driveshaft together and slide it out of the centering pin on the output flange of the transfer case. Remove it from the vehicle.

To install:

6. Install the driveshaft in reverse order, keeping these points in mind:

a. Whenever self-locking nuts are used, replace them.

b. Hold the nut or bolt in place where it runs through a U-joint and tighten at the opposite end, where the driveshaft flange is located.

c. Check the center bearing for lubrication and if it's dry, lubricate with the proper lubricant.

525i and 535i

1. Raise and safely support the vehicle.

2. Support the transmission from underneath with the special tools and a floor jack. Remove the nuts and washers from the transmission mounts on top of the rear transmission mounting crossmember. Loosen but do not remove the nuts located underneath which fasten the crossmember to the body. Then, slide this crossmember as far to the rear as it will go.

3. Unscrew the fastening nuts on the forward end of the CV-joint and then discard them.

4. Using a prybar to keep the driveshaft from turning, remove the self-locking nuts and bolts fastening the rear of the driveshaft to the final drive.

5. Remove the bolts fastening the center mount to the body. Bend the driveshaft down and pull the CV-joint off the transmission flange. Cover the joint to keep it clean.

To install:

6. Replace the gasket that fits between the joint bolts. Install in reverse order, keeping these points in mind:

    a. Replace the self-locking nuts used at either end of the shaft.

    b. Preload the center mount forward by forcing the bracket 0.157-0.197 in. (3.98-5.00mm) forward from the neutral position.

635CSi

1. Raise and safely support the vehicle. Remove the exhaust system.

2. Remove the heatshield near the fuel tank, if equipped.

3. Disconnect the driveshaft at the transmission by removing the nuts and bolts from the flexible coupling. If equipped with a vibration damper where the shaft connects to the transmission, turn the damper 60 degrees counterclockwise and remove it with the rubber coupling.

4. Loosen the center bearing bolts and remove them.

5. Disconnect the driveshaft at the final drive.

6. Bend the driveshaft down and pull out.

To install:

7. Installation is the reverse of removal.

8. The driveshaft is balanced as an assembly and must only be renewed as a complete assembly.

9. Preload the center bearing in the forward direction to 0.157-0.236 in. (3.98-5.99mm).

10. Wherever self-locking nuts are used, replace them. Hold the nut or bolt in place where it runs through a

U-joint and torque at the opposite end where the driveshaft flange is located. Check the center bearing for lubrication and if it's dry, lubricate with the proper lubricant.

735i, 735iL, 750iL and 850i

NOTE: If equipped with a front universal joint, use tools 24 0 120 and 00 2 020 or equivalent to support the transmission during this operation.

1. Raise and safely support the vehicle. Remove the exhaust system. Remove the heatshield from the floorpan. Remove the nuts and bolts fastening the driveshaft to the transmission at the flexible coupling. Replace the self-locking nuts.

2. If equipped with a front U-joint, support the transmission from underneath with the proper tools. When the transmission is securely supported, remove the 6 bolts and remove the rear transmission mounting crossmember.

3. Remove the self-locking nuts and then the bolts fastening the driveshaft to the final drive. Replace the self-locking nuts. Remove the driveshaft, taking care to keep it protected from dirt.

4. Remove the bolts from the crossbrace and remove the center driveshaft mount. Then, bend the shaft at the middle and remove it from the vehicle by pulling it off the centering pin on the forward end.

To install:

5. Install in reverse order, keeping the following points in mind:

    a. Repack the CV-joint with approved grease and replace the gasket, if necessary.

    b. Check the center bearing for lubrication and if it's dry, lubricate with the proper lubricant.

    c. If the vibration damper at the forward end of the driveshaft must be replaced, turn it 60 degrees to remove it.

    d. When remounting the center mount, preload it forward from its most natural position 0.157-0.236 in. (3.98-5.99mm).

    e. Torque U-joint bolts to 52 ft. lbs. (70 Nm) and CV-joint bolts to 51 ft. lbs. (69 Nm).

Front Wheel Hub, Knuckle and Bearings

REMOVAL AND INSTALLATION

Except 735i, 735iL, 750iL and 850i

1. Raise and safely support the vehicle. Remove the front tire and wheel assembly.

2. Disconnect and suspend the brake caliper from the body without disconnecting the brake line.

3. Remove the setscrew with an Allen® wrench. Pull off the brake disc and pry off the dust cover with a small prybar.

4. Using a chisel, knock the tab on the collar nut away from the shaft. Unscrew and discard the nut.

5. Pull off the bearing with the proper puller set and discard it. On the M3, use a puller set such as 31 2 102 105 106 or equivalent. On the M3, install the main bracket of the puller with wheel bolts.

6. If the inside bearing inner race remains on the stub axle, unbolt and remove the dust guard. Bend back the inner dust guard and pull the inner race off with a special tool capable of getting under the race. Reinstall the dust guard.

NOTE: Do not reuse the bearing unit if removed.

7. If the dust guard has been removed, install a new one. Install a special tool on M3, over the stub axle and screw it in for the entire length of the guide sleeve's threads. Press the bearing on.

8. Reverse the remaining removal procedures to install the disc and caliper. Torque the wheel hub collar nut to 188 ft. lbs. (255 Nm). Lock the collar nut by bending over the tab.

735i, 735iL, 750iL and 850i

1. Raise and safely support the vehicle. Remove the front tire and wheel assemblies. Remove the attaching bolts and remove and suspend the brake caliper, hanging it from the body so as to avoid putting stress on the brake line.

2. Remove the setscrew with an Allen® wrench. Pull off the brake disc and pry off the dust cover with a small prybar.

3. Using a chisel, knock the tab on the collar nut away from the shaft. Unscrew and discard the nut.

4. Install a puller collar such as 31 2 105 or equivalent to the bearing housing with 3 bolts. Install a puller such as 31 2 102 and 312 2 106 or

equivalent and pull off the bearing and discard it.

5. If the inside bearing inner race remains on the stub axle, unscrew and remove the dust guard, using a socket extension. Bend back the inner dust guard and pull the inner race off with a special tool capable of getting under the race. Reinstall the dust guard and install a new dust cover.

6. Then install a special tool over the stub axle and screw it in for the entire length of the guide sleeve's threads. Slide the bearing on and follow it with 31 2 100 or equivalent, and use this tool to press the bearing on.

7. Reverse the remaining removal procedures to install the disc and caliper. Torque the wheel hub collar nut to 210 ft. lbs. (285 Nm). Lock the collar nut by bending over the tab.

8. Install a new grease cap coated with the proper lubricant.

Rear Axle Shaft, Bearing and Seal

REMOVAL AND INSTALLATION

Except 318iC, 318iS, 325i, 325iC, 325iS, 325iX and M3

1. Raise and safely support the vehicle. Remove the rear tire and wheel assembly.

2. Lift out the lockplate and remove the retaining nut from the output flange. Remove the flange.

3. Disconnect the output shaft from the final drive by pressing out with the proper tool and suspend it.

4. Pull out the output shaft with a special tool.

5. Drive out the rear axleshaft with the proper tool.

6. Lift out the snapring. Then, pull out the wheel bearings, using the proper tool.

7. Pull out the seal with a tool such as 33 4 045 or equivalent.

8. If the inner bearing shell is damaged, pull it off with a puller and thrust pad.

To install:

9. Using an appropriate bearing installer, pull in the wheel bearing assembly, pull in the seal, insert the snapring and then pull in the rear axle shaft, all in reverse of the removal procedure. Install the axleshaft seal.

10. To install the output shaft, screw the threaded spindle into the shaft all the way and then use the

nut and washer against the outside of the bridge.

11. Reconnect the output shaft to the final drive.

12. Lubricate the bearing surface of the outer nut with oil. Then install and torque the nut.

13. Using the proper installers or equivalent, knock in the lockplate. Use the following torque figures:

Output shaft-to-drive flange to 42-46 ft. lbs. (56-62 Nm).

Drive flange hub-to-output shaft to 140-152 ft. lbs. (190 Nm).

318iC, 318iS, 325i, 325iC, 325iS, 325iX and M3

1. Raise and safely support the vehicle. Remove the rear tire and wheel assembly.

2. Disconnect the output shaft at the outer flange and suspend it with wire.

3. Unbolt the caliper and suspend it with the brake line connected. Unbolt and remove the rear disc.

4. Remove the large nut and remove the lockplate. If equipped with ABS, disconnect and then remove the ABS speed sensor by unscrewing it.

5. Unscrew the collar nut. Then, pull off the drive flange with the proper tool(s).

6. Screw on the collar nut until it is just flush with the end of the shaft and use a suitable hammer to knock out the shaft.

7. Remove the snapring. Pull out the wheel bearings, using the proper tool.

8. Pull the inner bearing race off the axleshaft with tool 00 7 500 or equivalent.

To install:

9. Install the new bearing assembly using the proper tools. Then, reinstall the snapring.

10. Install the rear axleshaft with special tools 23 1 300, 33 4 080 and 33 4 020 or equivalent.

11. Install the collar nut and drive in the lockplate with the proper tool(s).

12. Reconnect the output shaft. Remount the brake disc and caliper.

13. Lower the vehicle.

Axle Housing

REMOVAL AND INSTALLATION

1. Disconnect the negative battery cable.

2. Raise and safely support the vehicle. Disconnect and remove the rear exhaust.

3. Remove the heatshield, if equipped. Remove the driveshaft and disconnect the center support mount, if necessary.

4. Disconnect the parking brake lever cables. Disconnect and plug the rear brake lines.

5. Support the rear axle housing with a suitable jack device. Disconnect the thrust struts on both sides, if necessary.

6. Disconnect and plug the pulse senders and remove the rear seat cushion, if needed.

7. Remove the rear side trim panel on 3 Series convertible.

8. Disconnect the wires at the speedometer pulse sender. Unscrew the rear rubber mounting bolt.

9. Unplug the rear brake pad indicator and disconnect the wire connection.

10. Disconnect the switching valve for the ride control height and the plug on the camber warning sender on the 750iL.

11. Disconnect both rear shock absorbers at the trailing arms and move the brake cables out of the way.

12. Lower the rear axle assembly, using a suitable lifting device.

To install:

13. Install the rear axle assembly, lifting into position with a suitable lifting device.

14. Connect the shock absorbers to the trailing arms. Tighten the bolts when the vehicle is in the normal position to 52-63 ft. lbs. (70-85 Nm) on 3 Series or 90-144 ft. lbs. (122-195 Nm) on all vehicles except 3 Series.

15. Connect the switching valve for the ride control height and the plug on the camber warning sender on the 750iL.

16. Connect the rear brake pad indicator plug and the wire connection.

17. Connect the wires at the speedometer pulse sender. Replace the rear rubber mounting bolt and tighten to 31-35 ft. lbs. (42-47 Nm) except on the 7 Series or 36-38 ft. lbs. (48-52 Nm) on the 7 Series.

18. Replace the rear side trim panel on 3 Series convertible.

19. Connect and plug the pulse senders and replace the rear seat cushion, if needed.

20. Connect the thrust struts on both sides, if needed. Remove the lifting device from under the rear axle assembly.

21. Connect the parking brake cables and the brake lines.

22. Replace the heatshield, if equipped. Replace the driveshaft and connect the center support mount, if necessary.

23. Replace the rear exhaust. Lower the vehicle.

24. Connect the negative battery cable.

MANUAL TRANSMISSION

Transmission Assembly

REMOVAL AND INSTALLATION

318iC, 318iS, 325i, 325iC, 325iS, 325iX and M3

1. Disconnect the negative battery cable. Raise and safely support the vehicle. Remove the exhaust system. Remove the cross brace and heatshield. On the 325iX, remove the transfer case.

2. Hold the nuts on the front with one wrench and remove bolts from the rear with another to disconnect the flexible coupling at the front of the driveshaft. Some vehicles have a vibration damper at this point in the drivetrain. This damper is mounted on the transmission output flange with bolts that are pressed into the damper. On these vehicles, unscrew and remove the nuts located behind the damper.

3. Loosen the threaded sleeve on the driveshaft. Get a special tool to hold the splined portion of the shaft while turning the sleeve.

4. Remove its mounting bolts and remove the center driveshaft mount. Then, bend the driveshaft down at the center and pull it off the transmission output flange. Keep the sections of the driveshaft from pulling apart and suspend it from the vehicle with wire.

5. Remove the retainer and washer and pull out the shift selector rod.

6. Use a hex-head wrench to remove the self-locking bolts that retain the shift rod bracket at the rear of the transmission and then remove the bracket. If equipped with a shift arm, use a suitable prybar to pry the spring clip up off the boss on the transmission case and swing it upward. Then, pull out the shift shaft pin.

7. Unscrew and remove the clutch slave cylinder and support it so the hydraulic line can remain connected.

8. The transmission incorporates sending units for flywheel rotating speed and position. Remove the heatshield that protects these from exhaust heat and then remove the retaining bolt for each sending unit. Note that the speed sending unit, which has no identifying ring goes in the bore on the right, and that the reference mark sending unit, which has a marking ring, goes in the bore on the left. If the sending units are installed in reverse positions, the engine will not run at all. Pull these units out of the flywheel housing.

9. Disconnect the wiring connector going to the backup light switch and pull the wires out of the harness.

10. Support the transmission from underneath in a secure manner. Remove mounting bolts and remove the crossmember holding the rear of the transmission to the body. Then, lower the transmission onto the front axle carrier.

11. Using the proper tool, remove the bolts holding the transmission flywheel housing to the engine at the front. Make sure to retain the washers with the bolts. Pull the transmission rearward to slide the input shaft out of the clutch disc and then lower the transmission and remove from the vehicle.

To install:

12. Install the transmission in position under the vehicle. Align the input shaft and install the transmission, note the following points:

a. Coat the input shaft splines and flywheel housing guide pins with a light coating of suitable grease.

b. Make sure the front mounting bolts are installed with their washers. Torque them to 46-58 ft. lbs. (62-80 Nm).

c. Before reinstalling the sending units for flywheel position and speed, make sure their faces are free of either grease or dirt and then coat them with a light coating of a suitable lubricant. Inspect the O-rings and replace them if they are cut, cracked, crushed, or stretched.

d. When installing the shift rod bracket at the rear of the transmission, use new self-locking bolts and make sure the bracket is level before tightening them. Torque the shift rod bracket bolts to 16.5 ft. lbs. (22 Nm) except on the M3, which uses an aluminum bracket. On the M3, torque these bolts to 8 ft. lbs. (12 Nm).

e. Install the clutch slave cylinder with the bleed screw downward.

f. When installing the driveshaft center bearing, preload it forward 0.157-0.236 in. (3.98-5.99mm). Check the driveshaft alignment with an appropriate tool such. Replace the nuts and then torque the center mount bolts to 16-17 ft. lbs. (21-23 Nm).

g. Torque the flexible coupling bolts to 83-94 ft. lbs. (114-129 Nm).

525i, 535i, 635CSi and M5

1. Disconnect the negative battery cable. Raise and safely support the vehicle. Disconnect and lower the exhaust system to provide clearance for transmission removal. Remove the heatshield brace and transmission heatshield.

2. Support the driveshaft and then unscrew the driveshaft coupling at the rear of the transmission. Use a wrench on both the nut and the bolt.

3. Working at the front of the driveshaft center bearing, unscrew the screw-on ring type connector which attaches the driveshaft to the center bearing. Then, unbolt the center bearing mount. Bend the driveshaft down and pull it off the centering pin. If equipped with a vibration damper, turn it and pull it back over the output flange before pulling the driveshaft off the guide pin. Suspend it from the vehicle.

4. Pull off the wires for the backup light switch. Unscrew the passenger compartment console to disconnect it from the top of the transmission by removing the self-locking bolts. Discard and replace.

5. Pull out the locking clip and disconnect the shift rod at the rear of the transmission. Take care to keep all the washers.

6. If the transmission is linked to the shift lever with an arm, use a small prybar to lift the spring out of the holder on the bracket and then raise the arm. Pull out the shift shaft bolt.

7. If equipped with a flywheel housing cover (semi-circular in shape), remove the mounting bolts and remove the cover.

8. The speed sensor and reference mark sensor on the flywheel housing must be disconnected. Note their locations. The speed sensor goes in the upper bore, marked D. The reference mark sensor, which has a ring, goes in the lower bore, marked B. Check the O-rings for the sensors and install new ones if they are damaged.

9. Support the transmission securely. Then, unbolt and remove the rear transmission crossmember.

10. Remove the upper and lower attaching nuts and remove the clutch slave cylinder, supporting it so the hydraulic line need not be disconnected. Disconnect the reverse gear backup light switch and pull the wires out of the holders.

11. Unscrew the bolts fastening the transmission to the bell housing, using the proper tool. On some vehicles there are Torx® bolts used ; use a Torx® wrench for these. Pull the transmission rearward until the input shaft has disengaged from the clutch disc and then lower and remove it.

To install:

12. Place the transmission in gear. Insert the guide sleeve of the input shaft into the clutch pilot bearing carefully. Turn the output shaft to rotate the front of the input shaft until the splines line up and it engages the clutch disc.

13. Perform the remaining portions of the procedure in reverse of removal, observing the following points:

   a. Make sure the arrows on the rear crossmember point forward.

   b. Preload the center bearing mount forward of its most natural position 0.079-0.157 in. (2.07-3.99mm). On 7 Series vehicles with the M30B35 engine only and 6 Series vehicles with the 265/6 transmission (no integral clutch housing), preload the bearing 0.157-0.236 in. (3.99-5.99mm).

   c. In tightening the driveshaft screw on ring, use tool 26 1 040 or equivalent.

   d. When reconnecting the nuts and bolt at the transmission coupling, replace the nuts with new ones and turn only the nut, holding the bolts stationary.

   e. Make sure DME sensor faces are clean. Coat the sensor outside diameters with the proper lubricant.

   f. If equipped with a shift arm, lubricate the bolt with a light layer of a suitable lubricant.

   g. Observe these torque figures:
   Transmission-to-bell housing — 52-58 ft. lbs. (70-80 Nm).
   Rear/top transmission Torx® bolts — 46-58 ft. lbs. (62-80 Nm).
   Center mount-to-body — 16-17 ft. lbs. (21-23 Nm).
   Front joint-to-transmission — 83-94 ft. lbs. (114-129 Nm).

735i, 735iL, 750iL and 850iL

1. Disconnect the negative battery cable. Raise and safely support the vehicle. Remove the exhaust system. Remove the attaching bolts and remove the heatshield mounted just to the rear of the transmission on the floorpan.

2. Support the transmission securely from underneath. Then, remove the crossmember that supports it at the rear from the body by removing the mounting bolts on both sides.

3. Using wrenches on both the bolt heads and on the nuts, remove the bolts passing through the vibration damper and front universal joint at the front of the driveshaft.

4. Remove its mounting bolts and remove the center driveshaft mount. Then, bend the driveshaft down at the center and pull it off the transmission output flange. Keep the sections of the driveshaft from pulling apart and suspend it from the vehicle with wire.

5. Pull out the circlip, slide off the washer and then pull the shift selector rod off the transmission shift shaft. Disconnect the backup light switch.

6. Lower the transmission slightly for access. Then, use a small prybar to lift the spring out of the holder on the bracket and then raise the arm. Pull out the shift shaft bolt.

7. Remove the upper and lower attaching nuts and remove the clutch slave cylinder, supporting it so the hydraulic line need not be disconnected.

8. Unscrew the bolts fastening the transmission to the bell housing. Use a Torx® wrench to remove the bolts. Make sure to retain the washer with each bolt to ensure that they can be readily removed later, if necessary. Pull the transmission rearward until the input shaft has disengaged from the clutch disc and then lower and remove the transmission.

To install:

9. Install the transmission in position under the vehicle. Align the input shaft and install the transmission. Follow these procedures:

   a. Preload the center bearing mount forward of its most natural position 0.157-0.236 in. (3.98-5.99mm).

   b. When reconnecting the nuts and bolt at the transmission coupling, replace the nuts with new ones and turn only the nut, holding the bolts stationary.

   c. When reconnecting the shift arm, if equipped, lubricate the bolt with a light layer of a suitable lu-

bricant and check the O-ring for crushing, cracks or cuts, replacing it, if damaged.

   d. When installing the clutch slave cylinder, make sure the bleeder screw faces downward.

   e. Observe these torque figures:
   Center mount to body — 16-17 ft. lbs. (21-23 Nm).
   Front joint-to-transmission — 58.5 ft. lbs. (80 Nm).

CLUTCH

Clutch Assembly

REMOVAL AND INSTALLATION

1. Disconnect the negative battery cable. Raise and safely support the vehicle. Remove the heatshield and then the mounting bolts. Disconnect the speed and reference mark sensors at the flywheel housing. Mark the plugs for reinstallation.

2. Remove the transmission and clutch housing.

3. On vehicles with 6 cylinder engines, a Torx® socket is required. If equipped with a 265/6 transmission (without an integral clutch housing), remove the clutch housing.

4. Prevent the flywheel from turning, using a locking tool.

5. Loosen the mounting bolts one after another gradually, 1-1½ turns at a time, to relieve tension from the clutch.

6. Remove the mounting bolts, clutch and driveplate. Coat the splines of the transmission input shaft with Molykote® Long-term 2, Microlube® GL 2611 or equivalent. Make sure the clutch pilot bearing, located in the center of the crankshaft, turns easily.

7. Check the clutch driven disc for excess wear or cracks. Check the integral torsional damping springs, used with lighter flywheels only, for tight fit. Inspect the rivets to make sure they are all tight. Check the flywheel to make sure it is not scored, cracked, or burned, even at a small spot. Use a straightedge to make sure the contact surface is true. Replace any defective parts.

To install:

8. To install, fit the new clutch plate and disc in place and install the mounting bolts.

9. When installing the clutch retaining bolts turn them in gradually

to evenly tighten the clutch disc and to prevent warpage.

10. Install the transmission and the clutch housing.

11. If equipped, install the speed and reference mark sensors. Install the heatshield.

12. Note that on vehicles with 6 cylinder engines, the clutch pressure plate must fit over dowel pins. Torque the clutch mounting bolts to 16-19 ft. lbs. (21-26 Nm).

PEDAL HEIGHT/FREE-PLAY ADJUSTMENT

Measure the length of the over-center spring (Dimension "A") and, if necessary, loosen the locknut and rotate the shafts as necessary to get the proper clearance. Measure the distance (Dimension "B") from the firewall to the tip of the clutch pedal and move the pedal in or out, if necessary, by loosening the locknut and rotating the shaft.

Clutch Master Cylinder

REMOVAL AND INSTALLATION

1. Remove the necessary trim panel or carpet.

2. Disconnect the pushrod at the clutch pedal.

3. Remove the cap on the reservoir tank. On some vehicles, there is a clutch master cylinder reservoir, while on others there is a common reservoir shared with the brake master cylinder. Remove the float container, if equipped. Remove the screen and remove enough brake fluid from the tank until the level drops below the refill line or the connection for the filler pipe, if there is one.

4. Disconnect the coolant expansion tank without removing the hoses on the 735i and 735iL (vehicles with the M30 B35 engine do not require this).

5. Remove the lower/left instrument panel trim. Then, remove the retaining nut from the end of the master cylinder actuating rod where the bolt passes through the pedal mechanism.

6. Disconnect the line to the slave cylinder and the fluid fill line going to the top of the master cylinder. Remove the retaining bolts and remove the master cylinder from the firewall.

7. Install the clutch master cylinder in position. The piston rod bolt should be coated with the proper lubricant. Make sure all bushings re-

main in position. Bleed the system and adjust the pedal travel with the pushrod to 6 in.

Clutch Slave Cylinder

REMOVAL AND INSTALLATION

1. Remove enough brake fluid from the reservoir until the level drops below the refill line connection.

2. Remove the snapring or retaining bolts and pull the unit down.

3. Disconnect the line and remove the slave cylinder.

4. Install the slave cylinder on the transmission. On the 3 Series and M3, if the engine uses the 2-section flywheel, make sure a larger cylinder with a diameter of 0.874 in. (22.2mm) is used instead of the usual cylinder with a diameter of 0.809 in. (20.5mm). Make sure to install the cylinder with the bleed screw facing upward. When installing the front pushrod, coat it with the proper anti-seize compound. Bleed the system.

Hydraulic Clutch System Bleeding

1. Fill the reservoir.

2. Connect a bleeder hose from the bleeder screw to a container filled with brake fluid so air cannot be drawn in during bleeding procedures.

3. Pump the clutch pedal about 10 times and then hold it down.

4. Open the bleeder screw and watch the stream of escaping fluid. When no more bubbles escape, close the bleeder screw and tighten it.

5. Release the clutch pedal and repeat the above procedure until no more bubbles can be seen when the screw is opened.

6. If this procedure fails to produce a bubble-free stream:

   a. Pull the slave cylinder off the transmission without disconnecting the fluid line.

NOTE: Do not depress the clutch pedal while the slave cylinder is dismounted.

   b. Depress the pushrod in the cylinder until it hits the internal stop. Then, reinstall the cylinder.

AUTOMATIC TRANSMISSION

Transmission Assembly

REMOVAL AND INSTALLATION

Except 325i and 325iX

NOTE: To perform this operation, the following tools or equivalents are required. Special transmission support tools 24 0 120 and 00 2 020 and driveshaft locking ring tool 26 1 040 or equivalent. If equipped with the M30 B35 engine, a special socket, tool 24 1 110 or equivalent will be needed.

1. Disconnect the battery ground cable. Loosen the throttle cable adjusting nuts, release the cable tension and disconnect the cable at the throttle lever. Then, remove the nuts and pull the cable housing out of the bracket.

2. Disconnect the exhaust system at the manifold and hangers and lower it out of the way. Remove the hanger that runs across under the driveshaft. Remove the exhaust heatshield from under the center of the vehicle.

3. Support the transmission a suitable lifting device. Remove the crossmember that supports the transmission at the rear.

4. Remove the driveshaft coupling through bolts and nuts or the CV-joint through bolts and nuts. Either type is located right at the rear of the transmission. Discard used self-locking coupling nuts. Keep the CV-joint clean and replace its gasket.

5. Unscrew the transmission locking ring at the center mount, if equipped. Then, remove the bolts and remove the center mount. Bend the driveshaft downward and pull it off the centering pin. Suspend it with wire from the underside of the vehicle.

6. Drain the transmission oil and discard it. Remove the oil filler neck. Disconnect the oil cooler lines at the transmission by unscrewing the flarenuts and plug the open connections.

7. If equipped, remove the converter cover by removing the Torx® bolts from behind and the regular bolts from underneath. If equipped with a M30 B35 engine, pull the cover out of the bottom of the trans-

mission housing, just behind the oil pan.

8. Remove the bolts fastening the torque converter to the driveplate, turning the flywheel as necessary to gain access from below. Use a proper socket on vehicles with the M30 B35 engine.

9. If equipped, remove the guard for the speed and reference mark sensors. Remove the attaching bolt for each and remove each sensor. Keep the sensors clean.

10. Disconnect the shift cable by loosening the locknut fastening it to the shift lever and disconnecting the cable at the cable housing bracket.

11. If the transmission has an electrical connection, turn the bayonet fastener to the left to release the connection, disconnect it and pull the wire out of the ties.

12. Lower the transmission as far as possible. Then, remove all the Torx® or standard type bolts attaching the transmission to the engine.

13. Remove the small grill from the bottom of the transmission. Then press the converter off with a large prybar through this opening while sliding the transmission out.

To install:

14. Install the transmission under the vehicle and raise it into position. Observe the following points:

a. Make sure the converter is fully installed onto the transmission — so the ring on the front is inside the edge of the case.

b. When reinstalling the driveshaft, tighten the lockring with a special tool.

c. If the driveshaft has a simple coupling, rather than a CV-joint, make sure to replace the self-locking nuts and to hold the bolts still while tightening the nuts to keep from distorting the coupling.

d. When installing the center mount, preload it forward from its most natural position 0.157-0.236 in. (3.98-5.99mm).

e. Adjust the throttle cables.

325i and 325iX

NOTE: To perform this operation, a support for the transmission, BMW tool 24 0 120 and 00 2 020 or equivalent and a tool for tightening the driveshaft locking ring, BMW tool 26 1 040 or equivalent, are required. If the vehicle the M30 B35 engine, a special socket that retains bolts, will also be needed.

1. Disconnect the battery ground cable. Loosen the throttle cable ad-

justing nuts, release the cable tension and disconnect the cable at the throttle lever. Then, remove (and retain) the nuts and pull the cable housing out of the bracket.

2. Disconnect the exhaust system at the manifold and hangers and lower it aside. Remove the hanger that runs across under the driveshaft. Remove the exhaust heatshield from under the center of the vehicle.

3. On the 325iX, remove the transfer case from the rear of the transmission.

4. Drain the transmission oil and discard it. Remove the oil filler neck. Disconnect the oil cooler lines at the transmission by unscrewing the flarenuts and plug the open connections.

5. Support the transmission with the proper tools. Separate the torque converter housing from the transmission by removing the Torx® bolts with the proper tool from behind and the regular bolts from underneath. Retain the washers used with the Torx® bolts.

6. On the 325iX, disconnect the front driveshaft.

7. Remove bolts attaching the torque converter housing to the engine, making sure to retain the spacer used behind one of the bolts. Then, loosen the mounting bolts for the oil level switch just enough so the plate can be removed while pushing the switch mounting bracket to one side.

8. Remove the bolts attaching the torque converter to the driveplate. Turn the flywheel as necessary to gain access to each of the bolts, which are spaced at equal intervals around it. Make sure to re-use the same bolts and retain the washers.

9. To remove the speed and reference mark sensors, remove the attaching bolt for each and remove each sensor. Keep the sensors clean.

10. Turn the bayonet type electrical connector counterclockwise and then pull the plug out of the socket. Then, lift the wiring harness out of the harness bails.

11. Support the transmission using the proper jack. Then, remove the crossmember that supports the transmission at the rear.

12. Disconnect the transmission shift rod. Then, remove the nuts and then the through bolts from the damper-type U-joint at the front of the transmission.

13. Unscrew the transmission locking ring at the center mount, if equipped, using the special tool designed for this purpose. Then, remove

the bolts and remove the center mount. Bend the driveshaft downward and pull it off the centering pin. Suspend it with wire from the underside of the vehicle.

14. Lower the transmission as far as possible. Then, remove all the Torx® or standard type bolts attaching the transmission to the engine.

15. Remove the small grill from the bottom of the transmission. Then press the converter off with a large prybar passing through this opening while sliding the transmission out.

To install:

16. Install the transmission in position under the vehicle and raise it into position. Observe the following points:

a. Make sure the converter is fully installed onto the transmission — so the ring on the front is inside the edge of the case.

b. When reinstalling the driveshaft, tighten the lockring with the proper tool.

c. Make sure to replace the self-locking nuts on the driveshaft flexible joint and to hold the bolts still while tightening the nuts to keep from distorting it.

d. When installing the center mount, preload it forward from its most natural position 0.157-0.236 in. (3.98-5.99mm).

e. When reconnecting the bayonet type electrical connector, make sure the alignment marks are aligned after the plug it twisted into its final position.

f. When reinstalling the speed and reference mark sensors, inspect the O-rings used on the sensors and install new ones, if necessary. Make sure to install the speed sensor into the bore marked **D** and the reference mark sensor, which is marked with a ring, into the bore marked **B**.

g. Torque the crossmember mounting bolts to 16-17 ft. lbs. (21-23 Nm).

h. If O-rings are used with the transmission oil cooler connections, replace them.

i. Adjust the throttle cables.

SHIFT LINKAGE ADJUSTMENT

1. Move the selector lever to **P** position. Loosen the nut until the cable is free.

2. Push the transmission lever to the **D** or **P** position. Then push the cable rod in the opposite direction.

3. Clamp down the cable rod without tension.

4. Tighten the nut to 7.0-8.5 ft. lbs. (9-11 Nm).

NOTE: Do not bend the cable.

THROTTLE LINKAGE ADJUSTMENT

1. On the injection system throttle body, loosen the 2 locknuts at the end of the throttle cable and adjust the cable until there is a play of 0.010-0.030 in. (0.254-0.762mm).

2. Loosen the locknut and lower the kickdown stop under the accelerator pedal. Have someone depress the accelerator pedal until the transmission detent can be felt. Then, back the kickdown stop back out until it just touches the pedal.

3. Check that the distance from the seal at the throttle body end of the cable housing is at least 1.732 in. (43.9mm) from the rear end of the threaded sleeve. If this dimension checks out, tighten all the locknuts.

TRANSFER CASE

Transfer Case Assembly

REMOVAL AND INSTALLATION

With Manual Transmission

NOTE: To perform this procedure, a special, large wrench that locks onto flats on alternate sides of a section of the rear driveshaft is required. Use tool 26 1 060 or an equivalent.

1. Disconnect the negative battery cable. Raise and safely support the vehicle. Remove the exhaust system. Unbolt and remove the exhaust system heatshields located behind and below the transfer case.

2. Unscrew the rear section of the driveshaft at the sliding joint located behind the output flange of the transfer case.

3. Hold the through bolts stationary and remove the self-locking nuts from in front of the flexible coupling at the transfer case output flange. Discard all the self-locking nuts and replace them.

NOTE: During the next step, be careful not to let the driveshaft rest on the metal fuel line that crosses under it or the line could be damaged.

4. Slide the sections of the driveshaft together at the sliding joint and then pull the front of the driveshaft off the centering pin at the transmission output shaft.

5. Remove the nuts and through bolts from the flexible coupling linking the transmission output flange with the short driveshaft linking the transmission and the transfer case.

6. Support the transmission from underneath in a secure manner. Then, mark each of the 4 bolts fastening the crossmember that supports the transmission at the rear to the body, bolts are of different lengths. Remove the crossmember.

7. Lower the transmission/transfer case unit just enough to gain access to the bolts linking the 2 boxes together. Remove the 2 lower and 2 upper bolts. It is possible to gain access to the upper bolts using a socket wrench with a U-joint and extension.

8. There is a protective cap on the forward driveshaft where it links up with the transfer case. The cap is made of a brittle material, so it must be handled carefully. Gently slide the cap forward until is free of the transfer case.

9. Slide the transfer case to the rear so it can be separated from both the transmission and the forward driveshaft. When it is free, remove it.

To install:

10. Install the transfer case under the vehicle and raise it into position, bearing the following points in mind:

a. Inspect the dowel holes locating the transfer case with the transmission and the guide hole for the output shaft where it slides into the transfer case to make sure these parts will be properly located. Lubricate the guide pin and the splines of the front driveshaft section with grease.

b. When fitting the transfer case onto the transmission, check to make sure the output flange of the transmission is properly aligned with the flexible coupling. Put the through bolts through the flexible coupling and then install and torque the nuts to 65 ft. lbs. (88 Nm) while holding the bolts stationary.

c. When reconnecting the transfer case to the transmission, torque the bolts to 30 ft. lbs. (41 Nm).

d. Before fitting the driveshaft back onto the rear of the transmission, retain the seal in the protective cap by applying grease to it.

e. Torque the transmission crossmember bolts to 17 ft. lbs. (23 Nm).

f. Check the fluid level and fill with the recommended lubricant.

With Automatic Transmission

NOTE: To perform this procedure, a special, large wrench that locks onto flats on alternate sides of a section of the rear driveshaft is required. Use tool 26 1 060 or an equivalent.

1. Disconnect the negative battery cable. Raise and safely support the vehicle. Remove the exhaust system. Unbolt and remove the exhaust system heatshields located behind and below the transfer case.

2. Unscrew the rear section of the driveshaft at the sliding joint located behind the output flange of the transfer case.

3. Hold the through bolts stationary and remove the self-locking nuts from in front of the flexible coupling at the transfer case output flange. Discard all the self-locking nuts and replace them.

NOTE: During the next step, be careful not to let the driveshaft rest on the metal fuel line that crosses under it or the line could be damaged.

4. Slide the sections of the driveshaft together at the sliding joint and then pull the front of the driveshaft off the centering pin at the transmission output shaft.

5. Remove the nuts and through bolts from the flexible coupling linking the transmission output flange with the short driveshaft linking the transmission and the transfer case.

6. Note the locations of all the washers and then loosen the retaining nut and disconnect the range selector lever cable at the transmission by pulling out the pin. Be careful not to bend the cable in doing this. Then, loosen the nuts that position the cable housing onto the transmission and slide the cable housing backward so it can be separated from the bracket on the transmission housing.

7. There is a protective cap on the forward driveshaft where it links up with the transfer case. The cap is made of a brittle material, so it must be handled carefully. Gently slide the cap forward until is free of the transfer case.

8. Remove the drain plug in the bottom of the pan and drain the transmission fluid.

9. Support the transmission from underneath in a secure manner. Then, mark each of the 4 bolts fastening the crossmember that supports the transmission at the rear to the

body, bolts are of different lengths. Remove the crossmember.

10. Remove the 9 nuts fastening the transfer case to the transmission housing. Note the location of the wiring holder so it will be possible to re-install it on the same bolt.

11. Slide the transfer case to the rear and off the transmission.

To install:

12. Install the transfer case under the vehicle and raise it into position, bearing the following points in mind:

a. Inspect the sealing surfaces as well as the dowel holes in the transfer case to make sure they will seal and locate properly. Clean the sealing surfaces and replace the gasket.

b. When sliding the transfer case back onto the transmission, turn the front driveshaft section slightly to help make the splines mesh.

c. When reconnecting the shift cable, inspect the rubber mounts and replace any that are cut, crushed, or cracked. Adjust the shift cable.

d. Before fitting the driveshaft back onto the rear of the transmission, retain the seal in the protective cap by applying grease to it.

e. When fitting the transfer case onto the transmission, check to make sure the output flange of the transmission is properly aligned with the flexible coupling. Put the through bolts through the flexible coupling and then install and torque the nuts to 65 ft. lbs. (88 Nm) while holding the bolts stationary.

f. Torque the bolts holding the transfer case to the transmission to 65 ft. lbs. (88 Nm).

g. Torque the transmission crossmember bolts to 17 ft. lbs. (23 Nm).

h. Check the fluid level and fill with the recommended lubricant.

FRONT SUSPENSION

MacPherson Strut

REMOVAL AND INSTALLATION

318iC, 318iS, 325i, 325iC, 325iS and M3

1. Disconnect the negative battery cable.

2. Raise and safely support the vehicle. Remove the tire and wheel assembly.

3. Disconnect the brake pad wear indicator plug and ground wire. Pull the wires out of the holder on the strut. Remove the ABS pulse sender, if equipped.

4. Unbolt the caliper and pull it away from the strut, suspending it with a piece of wire from the body. Do not disconnect the brake line.

5. Remove the attaching nut and then detach the pushrod on the stabilizer bar at the strut.

6. Unscrew the attaching nut and press off the guide joint with the proper tool.

7. Unscrew the nut and press off the tie rod joint.

8. Press the bottom of the strut outward and push it over the guide joint pin, using the proper tool. Support the bottom of the strut.

9. Unscrew the nuts at the top of the strut, from inside the engine compartment, then remove the strut.

To install:

10. Install in reverse order, observing the following points:

a. Replace the self-locking nuts that fasten the top of the strut.

b. Tie rod and guide joints must have both pins and both bores clean for reassembly. Replace both self-locking nuts.

c. Torque the control arm to spring strut attaching nut to 43-51 ft. lbs. (59-69 Nm). Torque the spring strut to wheel well nuts to 16-17 ft. lbs. (21-23 Nm).

325iX

1. Disconnect the negative battery cable.

2. Raise and safely support the vehicle. Remove the front tire and wheel assembly. Unplug the ABS pulse transmitter.

3. Lift out the lockplate at the center of the brake disc with a small prybar. Unscrew the collar nut.

4. Disconnect the brake pad wear indicator plug and the ground wire. Pull the wires and brake hose out of the clip on the spring strut. Then, disconnect the small rod at the strut.

5. Remove the brake caliper mounting bolts and support the assembly with a piece of wire, keeping stress off the brake hose.

6. Remove the attaching nut from the tie rod end. Then press the stud off the knuckle with the proper tool.

7. Remove the attaching nut for the control arm and then press the

stud off the knuckle with an appropriate tool.

8. Mount the proper tool to the brake disc with 2 of the wheel bolts. Then, press the output shaft out of the center of the knuckle.

9. Support the spring strut from underneath. Remove the cap from the center of the wheel house. Remove the 3 bolts from the upper mount near the wheel housing. Remove the strut.

To install:

10. Install the strut, observing these points:

a. Torque the nuts attaching the strut to the wheel house to 16 ft. lbs. (21 Nm).

b. Lubricate the splines of the output shaft with oil before pressing it back into the center of the knuckle with the proper tool.

c. Keep grease off the studs for the control arm and tie rod end. Replace the cotter pin on the control arm and the self-locking nut on the tie rod end. Torque the control arm stud nut to 61.5 ft. lbs. (84 Nm). Torque the tie rod nut to 61.5 ft. lbs. (84 Nm) and then tighten it further to install the cotter pin, if necessary.

d. Replace the lockplate in the center of the disc with the proper tool.

e. Torque the bolts attaching the caliper to the steering knuckle to 63-79 ft. lbs. (87-109 Nm). Lower the vehicle.

f. Connect the negative battery cable.

525i, 535i, M5, 635CSi, 735i, 735iL, 750iL and 850i

1. Disconnect the negative battery cable.

2. Raise and safely support the vehicle. Remove the tire and wheel assembly.

3. Disconnect the brake pad wear indicator plug and ground wire. Pull the wires out of the holder on the strut. Remove the ABS pulse sender, if equipped.

4. Disconnect the stabilizer pushrod with the proper tool.

5. Disconnect the lower strut bolts at the control arm.

6. Support the bottom of the strut and unscrew the nuts at the top of the strut, from inside the engine compartment. Remove the strut.

7. The installation is the reverse of the removal procedure.

Lower Control Arms

REMOVAL AND INSTALLATION

318iC, 318iS, 325i, 325iC, 325iS and M3

1. Raise and safely support the vehicle. Remove the front tire and wheel assembly.

2. Disconnect the rear control arm bracket where it connects to the body by removing the bolts.

3. Remove the nut and disconnect the thrust rod on the front stabilizer bar where it connects to the center of the control arm.

4. Unscrew the nut which attaches the front of the stabilizer bar to the crossmember and remove the nut from above the crossmember. Then, use a plastic hammer to knock this support pin out of the crossmember.

5. Unscrew the nut and press off the guide joint where the control arm attaches to the lower end of the strut, using the proper tool.

To install:

6. Keep these points in mind:

a. Replace the self-locking nut that fastens the guide joint to the control arm.

b. Make sure the support pin and the bore in the crossmember are clean before inserting the pin through the crossmember. Replace the original nut with a replacement nut and washer.

c. Torque the control arm-to-spring strut nut to 43-51 ft. lbs. (58-69 Nm). Torque the control arm support to crossmember nut to 29-34 ft. lbs. (40-46 Nm). Torque the pushrod on the stabilizer bar to 29-34 ft. lbs. (40-46 Nm).

325iX

1. Raise and safely support the vehicle. Remove the tire and wheel assembly.

2. Disconnect the rear control arm bracket where it connects to the body by removing the bolts.

3. Remove the nut from the top of the stud that attaches to one corner of the control arm and runs through the crossmember.

4. Remove the cotter pin and then remove the nut from the ball joint stud where it passes through the steering knuckle. Then, press the ball joint stud out of the knuckle with the proper tool. Make sure to keep the stud and bore free of grease.

To install:

5. Keep these points in mind:

a. Make sure the support pin and the bore in the crossmember

are clean before inserting the pin through the crossmember. Replace the original nut with a replacement nut and washer equivalent.

b. Torque the control arm-to-spring strut nut to 61.5 ft. lbs. (84 Nm). Turn the nut farther, as necessary to align the cotter pin hole and install a new cotter pin. Torque the control arm support to crossmember nut to 30 ft. lbs. (41 Nm).

525i, 535i, M5, 635CSi, 735i, 735iL, 750iL and 850i

1. Raise and safely support the vehicle. Remove the tire and wheel assembly.

2. Remove the mounting bolts that fasten the bottom of the strut to the steering knuckle.

3. Remove the cotter pin and castellated nut. Use a suitable ball joint remover to press the ball joint end of the control arm off the steering knuckle.

4. Remove the self-locking nut. Then, remove the through bolt and the washers, slide the inner end of the strut and bushing out of the front suspension crossmember.

To install:

5. Note the following points:

a. Make sure both washers are replaced to cushion the bushing where it contacts the suspension crossmember.

b. Replace the bushing if it is worn or cracked.

c. Use a new self-locking nut on the bolt fastening the inner end of the strut.

d. Align the bottom of the strut with the steering knuckle so the tab on the arm fits into the notch on the bottom of the strut. Install the bolts with a locking type sealer.

e. When installing the arm ball joint onto the steering knuckle, tighten the nut until the cotter pin hole lines up and then use a new cotter pin in the nut.

f. Final tighten the through bolt for the inner end of the arm after the vehicle is on the ground at normal ride height.

Sway Bar

REMOVAL AND INSTALLATION

1. Raise and safely support the vehicle.

2. Disconnect the push/thrust rod on both sides.

3. Disconnect the left side control arm bracket on the 3 Series.

4. Disconnect the left and right stabilizer mounts. Remove the stabilizer bar.

5. The installation is the reverse of the removal procedure. Tighten the stabilizer mount bolts to 16 ft. lbs. (21 Nm).

Front Wheel Bearings

REMOVAL AND INSTALLATION

318iC, 318iS, 325i, 325iC, 325iS and M3

1. Raise and safely support the vehicle. Remove the tire and wheel assembly.

2. Remove the attaching bolts and remove and suspend the brake caliper, hanging it from the body so as to avoid putting stress on the brake line.

3. Remove the setscrew with an Allen® wrench. Pull off the brake disc and pry off the dust cover with a small prybar.

4. Using a chisel, knock the tab on the collar nut away from the shaft. Unscrew and discard the nut.

5. Pull off the bearing with a suitable bearing puller and discard it. On the M3, install the main bracket of the puller with 3 wheel bolts.

6. If the inside bearing inner race remains on the stub axle, unbolt and remove the dust guard. Bend back the inner dust guard and pull the inner race off with a special tool capable of getting under the race. Reinstall the dust guard.

To install:

7. If the dust guard has been removed, install a new one. Install a special tool over the stub axle and screw it in for the entire length of the guide sleeve's threads. Press the bearing on.

8. Reverse the remaining removal procedures to install the disc and caliper. Torque the wheel hub collar nut to 188 ft. lbs. (255 Nm). Lock the collar nut by bending over the tab.

525i, 535i, M5, 635CSi, 735i, 735iL, 750iL and 850i

1. Raise and safely support the vehicle. Remove the tire and wheel assembly.

2. Remove the attaching bolts and remove and suspend the brake caliper, hanging it from the body so as to avoid putting stress on the brake line.

3. Remove the setscrew with an Allen® wrench. Pull off the brake

disc and pry off the dust cover with a small prybar.

4. Using a chisel, knock the tab on the collar nut away from the shaft. Unscrew and discard the nut.

5. Using the proper tool, pull off the bearing and discard it.

To install:

6. If the inside bearing inner race remains on the stub axle, unscrew and remove the dust guard, using a socket extension. Bend back the inner dust guard and pull the inner race off with a special tool capable of getting under the race. Reinstall the dust guard and install a new dust cover.

7. Then install a special tool over the stub axle and screw it in for the entire length of the guide sleeve's threads. Slide the bearing on and follow it with the proper tool and use this tool to press the bearing on.

8. Reverse the remaining removal procedures to install the disc and caliper. Torque the wheel hub collar nut to 210 ft. lbs. (285 Nm). Lock the collar nut by bending over the tab.

9. Install a new grease cap coated with a suitable sealer.

REAR SUSPENSION

Shock Absorbers

REMOVAL AND INSTALLATION

318iS, 325, 325i, 325iS, 325iX and M3

1. Raise and safely support the vehicle. Support the control arms.

2. If equipped with ride level control, perform the following:

a. Disconnect the negative battery cable.

b. Remove the rear seat cushion. Disconnect the left or right plug under the insulation sheet and guide the electric wire through the hole in the floor plate.

c. Remove the rear tire and wheel assembly. Disconnect the electrical connection.

NOTE: The control arm must be securely supported throughout this procedure.

3. Remove the side backrest, seat belts and unscrew the centering shell on the wheel house.

4. Remove the lower shock retaining bolt.

5. Remove trim inside the trunk, if necessary, and disconnect the upper

strut retaining nuts at the wheel arch and remove the assembly.

6. Remove the shock absorber.

To install:

7. Install in reverse order, using new gaskets between the shock and the wheel arch, and new self-locking nuts on top of the strut.

8. Torque the shock-to-body nuts to 16-17 ft. lbs. (21-23 Nm); spring retainer-to-wheel house nuts — 6 cylinder engines to 16-17 ft. lbs. (21-23 Nm); lower bolt to 52-63 ft. lbs. (71-86 Nm) on 4 cylinder engines or 90-103 ft. lbs. (122-140 Nm) on 6 cylinder engines.

9. Final torquing of the lower strut bolt should be done with the vehicle in the normal riding position.

850i

1. Raise and safely support the vehicle.

2. Properly support the trailing arms.

3. Compress the coil springs safely, using a suitable tool.

4. Remove the trunk mat and remove upper shock mount bolts.

5. Remove the lower shock mount bolts and remove shock absorber.

6. Installation is the reverse of the removal procedure.

MacPherson Strut

REMOVAL AND INSTALLATION

525i, 535i, M5, 635CSi, 735i, 735iL and 750iL

1. Disconnect the negative battery cable. Remove the rear seat and back rest.

2. Raise and safely support the vehicle. Support the control arms.

NOTE: The coil spring, shock absorber assembly acts as a strap so the control arm should always be supported.

3. If equipped with automatic ride control perform the following:

a. Disconnect the low pressure switch electrical connection and turn on the ignition.

b. Disconnect the control rod nut, holding the collar with an 8mm wrench against torque. Don't disconnect the rod at the ball joint.

c. Operate the lever on the control switch in the "discharge" direction for about 20 seconds to discharge fluid from the lines.

d. Disconnect the hydraulic line on the shock absorber.

4. Remove the lower shock retaining bolt.

5. Remove trim if necessary and disconnect the upper strut retaining nuts at the wheel arch and remove the assembly.

To install:

6. Use new gaskets between the strut and the wheel arch and new self-locking nuts on top of the strut.

7. Torque the shock-to-body nuts to 16-17 ft. lbs. (21-23 Nm); spring retainer-to-wheel house nut to 16-17 ft. lbs. (21-23 Nm). Tighten the lower bolt to 52-63 ft. lbs. (70-86 Nm) on the M3 or 90-103 ft. lbs. (122-140 Nm), except on the M3.

8. Replace the gasket that goes between the top of the strut and the lower surface of the wheel well, if necessary

9. Final torquing of the lower strut bolt should be done with the vehicle in the normal riding position.

Coil Springs

REMOVAL AND INSTALLATION

318iC, 318iS, 325i, 325iS, 325iX and M3

1. Raise and safely support the vehicle.

2. Disconnect the rear portion of the exhaust system and hang it from the body.

3. Disconnect the final drive rubber mount, push it down, and hold it down with a wedge.

4. Remove the bolt that connects the rear stabilizer bar to the strut on the side being worked on. Be careful not to damage the brake line.

NOTE: Support the lower control arm securely with a jack or other device that will permit it to be lowered gradually, while maintaining secure support.

5. To prevent damage to the output shaft joints, lower the control arm only enough to slip the coil spring off the retainer.

6. Make sure, in replacing the spring, that the same part number, color code and proper rubber ring are used.

To install:

7. Make sure the spring is in proper position, keeping the control arm securely supported until the shock bolt is replaced. Tighten stabilizer bar and lower shock mount bolts with the control arm in the normal ride position.

8. Torque the stabilizer bolt to 22-24 ft. lbs. (30-34 Nm) and the

shock bolt to 52-63 ft. lbs. (70-86 Nm).

850i

1. Raise and safely support the vehicle.
2. Compress the coil spring using a suitable tool.
3. Properly support the trailing arm.
4. Remove the spring assembly.
5. Installation is the reverse of the removal procedure.

Trailing Arms

REMOVAL AND INSTALLATION

318iS, 325, 325i, 325iS, 325iX and M3

1. Raise and safely support the vehicle. Remove the tire and wheel assembly.
2. Apply the parking brake and disconnect the output shaft at the rear axle shaft, if necessary. Remove the parking brake lever.
3. Remove the brake fluid from the master cylinder reservoir. To do this, it will be necessary to remove the strainer at the top of the reservoir. Disconnect the brake line connection on the rear control arm. Plug the openings.
4. Support the trailing arm securely. Disconnect the shock absorber at the control arm.
5. Remove the nuts and then slide the bolts out of the mounts where the trailing arm is mounted to the axle carrier.
To install:
6. Install the bolt that goes into the inner bracket first.
7. Torque the bolts holding the trailing arm to the axle carrier to 48-54 ft. lbs. (65-74 Nm).
8. Make sure the spring is positioned properly top and bottom. Torque the strut bolt to 52-63 ft. lbs. (70-86 Nm).
9. Reinstall the hand brake or reconnect the cable and adjust. Then apply the brake and reconnect the output shaft.
10. Reconnect the brake line, replenish with the proper brake fluid and bleed the system.

525i, 535i, M5, 635CSi, 735i, 735iL and 750iL

1. Raise and safely support the vehicle. Remove the tire and wheel assembly.

2. Apply the parking brake to hold the driveshaft stationary. Disconnect the output shaft at the drive flange. Hang the shaft from the body by a piece of wire.
3. Disconnect the parking brake cable at the lever.
4. Remove the float housing from the brake fluid reservoir and then remove as much fluid as possible from the reservoir.
5. Pull the brake cable housing out of the mounting bracket near the control arm. Disconnect the brake line.
6. Pull down and disconnect the plug for the pulse sender, do not damage the rubber grommet. On the 750iL, remove the rear seat to gain access to the pulse sender.
7. Remove the rear pushrod and disconnect the camber warning sender on the rear axle carrier on the 750iL.
8. Support the trailing arm from underneath in a secure manner.
9. Remove the nuts and then remove the bolts to disconnect the control arm from the rear axle carrier.
10. If equipped with a stabilizer bar, remove the bolts and remove the attaching bracket for the stabilizer bar.
11. Disconnect the shock absorber and remove the control arm.
To install:
12. When reattaching the control arm, insert the bolt on the inner bracket first.
13. Attach the shock absorber and the stabilizer bar bracket. On the 750iL, attach the camber warning sensor and the pushrod.
14. Connect the pulse sender, the brake line and the brake cable. Connect the drive axle.
15. Tighten all mounting bolts with the vehicle resting on its wheels. Torque the bolts attaching the control arm to the axle carrier to 49-54 ft. lbs. (67-74 Nm). Refill and bleed the brake system.

850i

1. Raise and safely support the vehicle.
2. Remove the tire and wheel assembly.
3. Properly secure coil spring.
4. Remove integral arm top bolts.
5. Remove trailing arm front bolts.
6. Remove rear nuts and remove assembly from vehicle.
7. Press integral arm from trailing arm.
8. Installation is the reverse of the removal procedure.

STEERING

Steering Wheel

——— CAUTION ———
On vehicles equipped with an air bag, the negative battery cable must be disconnected, before working on the system. Failure to do so may result in deployment of the air bag and possible personal injury.

REMOVAL AND INSTALLATION

1. Disconnect the negative battery cable. Remove steering wheel pad or BMW emblem. Mark the relationship between the steering wheel and shaft for installation in the same position. Unlock the steering wheel lock with the key. Otherwise, the wheel cannot be removed.
2. Unscrew retaining nut and remove the wheel.

NOTE: Be careful not to damage the direction signal canceling cam, which is right under the steering wheel, in performing this operation. If equipped with an air bag, it is important to avoid banging on the wheel in any way.

3. Installation is the reverse of removal. Lubricate the direction signal canceling cam. Replace the self-locking nut on all models and torque it to 58 ft. lbs. (80 Nm).

Power Steering Rack

REMOVAL AND INSTALLATION

318iS, 325, 325i, 325iS and M3

1. Raise and safely support the vehicle and remove front wheels. Remove the pinch bolt and loosen bolt. Press the spindle off the steering gear.
2. Use a syringe to empty the power steering fluid reservoir. Loosen the clamp and pull off the hydraulic fluid return line from the power steering unit. Discard drained fluid.
3. Disconnect and plug the pressure line.
4. Unscrew left and right side nuts and press off the tie rods where they connect to the spring struts.

5. Remove the bolts attaching the steering unit to the front axle carrier and remove it.

To install:

6. Install in reverse order, keeping the following points in mind:

a. The steering unit bolts to the rear holes of the axle carrier. Use new self-locking nuts and torque them to 29-34 ft. lbs. (40-46 Nm).

b. When reconnecting tie rods to the spring struts, make sure tie rod pins and strut bores are clean. Replace self-locking nut and torque to 40-48 ft. lbs. (54-66 Nm).

c. Replace the seals on the power steering pump connection and torque the bolt to 29-32 ft. lbs. (40-43 Nm).

7. Refill the fluid reservoir with specified fluid. Idle the engine and turn the steering wheel back and forth until it has reached right and left lock 2 times each. Then, turn OFF the engine and refill the reservoir.

325iX

NOTE: To remove the steering gear on 4WD vehicles, use a special tool to support the engine via the body. It is also advisable to use a special tool to support the front axle carrier without damaging it. It is necessary to remove the entire front axle carrier to gain access to the mounting bolts for the steering gear on this vehicle.

1. Raise the vehicle and support it securely. Remove the splash guard. Remove the front wheels.

2. Remove the air cleaner. Use a clean syringe to remove the power steering fluid from the pump reservoir.

3. Attach the support tool and connect it to the engine hooks to be sure the engine is securely supported.

4. Remove the through bolts from the right and left engine mounts.

5. Disconnect both the hydraulic lines running from the power steering pump to the steering gear and then plug the openings.

6. Loosen both the retaining bolts and then disconnect the steering column spindle off the steering gear.

7. Remove the retaining nuts on both sides and then press the tie rod ends off the steering knuckles with the proper tools. Be careful to keep grease out of the bores and off the tie rod ball studs.

8. Remove the cotter pins, remove the retaining nuts on both sides and then use the proper tool to press the control arm ball joint studs out of the

steering knuckles. Be careful to keep grease out of the bores and off the control arm ball studs.

9. Remove the bolts on either side attaching the control arm brackets to the body.

10. Remove the bolts and remove the stabilizer bar mounting brackets from the front axle carrier on both sides.

11. Support the front axle carrier with a suitable lifting device. Then, remove the mounting bolts on either side and remove the axle carrier. Remove the mounting bolts and remove the steering gear from the axle carrier.

To install:

12. Install in reverse order, noting these points:

a. Clean the bores into which the axle carrier bolts are mounted. Use some sort of locking sealer and torque the bolts to 30 ft. lbs. (41 Nm).

b. Torque the mounting bolts holding the steering gear to front axle carrier to 30 ft. lbs. (41 Nm).

c. Install new cotter pins on the retaining nuts for the control arm ball studs. Torque to 61.5 ft. lbs. (84 Nm).

d. Replace the self-locking nuts on the tie rod end ball studs and connecting the steering column spindle to the steering box. Torque tie rod ball stud nuts to 24-29 ft. lbs. (33-40 Nm).

e. Replace the gaskets on power steering hydraulic lines.

13. Refill the fluid reservoir with specified fluid. Idle the engine and turn the steering wheel back and forth until it has reached right and left lock 2 times each. Then, turn off the engine and refill the reservoir.

Power Steering Gear

REMOVAL AND INSTALLATION

525i, 535i, M5, 635CSi, 735i, 735iL, 750iL and 850i

1. Disconnect the negative battery cable.

2. Remove the steering wheel, if equipped with an air bag (SRS).

3. Discharge the pressure reservoir by pushing in on the brake pedal about 10 times. Draw off hydraulic fluid in the supply tank.

4. Unscrew the bolt and press the tie rod off the steering drop arm with the proper tool.

5. Remove the heatshield on the steering gear and disconnect the ride level height control pipes on the 750iL.

6. Remove the bolt and push the U-joint from the steering gear. Disconnect and plug the hydraulic lines.

7. Unscrew the steering gear mounting bolts and remove the steering gear.

NOTE: If necessary, move the steering drop arm by turning the steering stub to enable the removal of the gear assembly.

To install:

8. Install the steering gear and tighten the mounting bolts.

9. Connect the hydraulic lines, using new seals.

10. Turn the steering wheel counterclockwise or clockwise against the stop and then back about 1.7 turns until the marks are aligned.

11. Connect the U-joint to the steering gear making sure the bolt is in the locking groove of the steering stub.

12. Install the tie rod to the steering drop arm and replace the self locking nut.

13. Replace the heatshield on the steering gear and connect the ride level height control pipes on the 750iL.

14. Refill the hydraulic fluid and replace the steering wheel, if equipped with an air bag (SRS).

15. Connect the negative battery cable.

Power Steering Pump

REMOVAL AND INSTALLATION

1. Disconnect the negative battery cable. Release the pressure from the reservoir.

2. Draw the hydraulic fluid from the pump reservoir. Disconnect and plug the hydraulic lines.

3. Disconnect and plug the hydraulic lines. Remove the bolts and loosen the nuts to turn the adjusting pinion.

4. Remove the drive belt.

5. Remove the bolts from the brackets holding the pump and remove the pump assembly.

6. Reverse the removal procedure for installation. Tighten the adjusting pinion to 6 ft. lbs. (8 Nm).

7. If equipped with a tandem pump, the removal and installation procedure is the same.

BELT ADJUSTMENT

Tighten the drive belt so when pressure is applied to the belt, the distance between both belt pulleys is 0.2-0.4 in. (5-10mm) of deflection.

1. Disconnect the negative battery cable. Loosen the nuts on the adjusting pinion.

2. Tighten the belt to the recommended specification and tighten the adjusting pinion nuts.

3. Connect the negative battery cable.

SYSTEM BLEEDING

1. Fill the reservoir to the **MAX** mark on the oil stick.

2. Rotate the steering in both directions fully, to each stop, until all the air is removed from the fluid.

3. Check the oil level and fill to the specified mark, if necessary.

Tie Rod Ends

REMOVAL AND INSTALLATION

1. Raise and safely support the vehicle. Loosen the clamping bolt that retains the toe-in adjustment by keeping the tie rod end from turning in relation to the tie rod.

2. Remove the cotter pin and castellated or self-locking nut from the bottom of the tie rod end. Then, press the tie rod end out of the steering knuckle with the proper tool. Then, unscrew the tie rod end from the tie rod and remove it, counting the number of turns required.

To install:

3. Install in reverse order, using a new cotter pin or castellated nut. Recheck the front alignment and reset the toe-in, if necessary.

4. Torque the castellated or self-locking nut to 26.5 ft. lbs. (36 Nm) and the clamping screw to 10 ft. lbs. (14 Nm). Final torque the clamping bolt with the vehicle resting on its wheels.

BRAKES

Master Cylinder

REMOVAL AND INSTALLATION

1. Disconnect the negative battery cable. Draw off the brake fluid from the reservoir.

2. Remove the plug and disconnect the hydraulic lines. Remove the hose for the hydraulic clutch, if needed.

3. Remove the reservoir. Remove the mounting bolts and lift out the master cylinder.

4. Install the master cylinder, making sure the rubber ring is making a good seal.

5. The remainder of the installation is the reverse of the removal procedure. Bleed the brake system and connect the negative battery cable.

Proportioning Valve

REMOVAL AND INSTALLATION

1. Disconnect the negative battery cable. Draw off hydraulic fluid from the master cylinder with a syringe or hose used only with clean brake fluid.

2. Disconnect the brake lines at the top and bottom of the proportioning valve.

3. Remove the clamp from the valve and disconnect the pressure connection at the union.

4. Check day/year codes, reduction factor and switch-over pressure to make sure the new valve is identical.

5. Install in reverse order. Bleed the system.

Power Brake Booster

REMOVAL AND INSTALLATION

1. Disconnect the negative battery cable. Draw off brake fluid in the reservoir and discard.

2. Remove the reservoir and disconnect the clutch hydraulic hose.

3. Disconnect all brake lines from the master cylinder.

4. Remove the instrument panel trim from the bottom/left inside the passenger compartment.

5. Remove the return spring from the brake pedal. Press off the clip and remove the pin which connects the booster rod to the brake pedal.

6. Remove the 4 nuts and pull the booster and master cylinder off in the engine compartment.

7. If the filter in the brake booster is clogged, it will have to be cleaned. To do this, remove the dust boot, retainer, damper and filter, and clean the damper and filter. Make sure when reinstalling that the slots in the damper and filter are offset 180 degrees.

8. Install in reverse order. Adjust the stoplight switch for a clearance of 0.197-0.236 in. (5.00-5.99mm).

9. Inspect the rubber seal between the master cylinder and booster and replace it, if necessary.

Brake Caliper

REMOVAL AND INSTALLATION

Front

1. Disconnect the negative battery cable. Draw off brake fluid with a suitable syringe.

2. Disconnect the hydraulic brake lines.

3. Raise and safely support the vehicle. Remove the front tire and wheel assembly.

4. Remove the caliper mounting bolts and disconnect the brake pad wear indicator plug.

5. Remove the caliper assembly.

6. The installation is the reverse of the removal procedure. Bleed the brake system. Tighten the caliper mounting bolts to 63-79 ft. lbs. (85-108 Nm) on the 3 Series or 80-89 ft. lbs. (109-121 Nm) except on the 3 Series. Tighten the guide bolts to 22-25 ft. lbs. (30-34 Nm).

NOTE: Make sure the brake wear indicator wire is held in the correct position by the tab of the dust cap.

Rear

1. Disconnect the negative battery cable. Draw off brake fluid with a suitable syringe.

2. Disconnect the hydraulic brake lines.

3. Raise and safely support the vehicle. Remove the rear tire and wheel assembly.

4. Remove the caliper mounting bolts and disconnect the brake pad wear indicator plug.

5. Remove the caliper assembly by pulling to the rear.

6. The installation is the reverse of the removal procedure. Bleed the brake system. Tighten the mounting bolts to 42-48 ft. lbs. (56-66 Nm) and the guide bolts to 22-25 ft. lbs. (30-34 Nm).

Disc Brake Pads

REMOVAL AND INSTALLATION

Front

1. Raise and safely support the vehicle.

2. Remove the tire and wheel assembly.

3. Disconnect the plug for the brake pad wear indicator

4. Remove the caliper guide bolts and the spring clamp.

5. Turn up the caliper and remove the brake pads. The inner pad is located with a spring in the piston.

NOTE: The brake pads on both calipers on 1 axle should be replaced at the same time.

6. Lubricate the mounting pads with a suitable grease.

7. The installation is the reverse of the removal procedure. Bleed the brake system.

Rear

1. Raise and safely support the vehicle.

2. Remove the tire and wheel assembly.

3. Disconnect the plug for the brake pad wear indicator

4. Remove the caliper guide bolts and the spring clamp.

5. Turn up the caliper and remove the brake pads. The inner pad is located with a spring in the piston.

NOTE: The brake pads on both calipers on 1 axle should be replaced at the same time.

6. Lubricate the mounting pads with a suitable grease.

7. The installation is the reverse of the removal procedure. Bleed the brake system.

Brake Rotor

REMOVAL AND INSTALLATION

Front

1. Raise and safely support the vehicle. Remove the front tire and wheel assembly.

2. Disconnect the rubber grommet from the bracket, if equipped.

3. Disconnect the plug for the brake pad indicator, if necessary.

4. Disconnect and support the caliper, using a piece of wire.

5. Remove the mounting bolts and remove the brake rotor with the proper tool.

NOTE: The inboard vented discs are balanced. Never remove or reposition the balance clamps.

6. The installation is the reverse of the removal procedure.

Rear

1. Raise and safely support the vehicle. Remove the tire and wheel assembly.

2. Disconnect and support the caliper, using a piece of wire.

3. Remove the mounting bolts and remove the brake rotor with the proper tool.

4. Always replace both discs of the same axle.

To install:

5. The installation is the reverse of the removal procedure. Adjust the parking brake.

6. The parking brake must be broken in after replacing the rear brake discs. This is done in the following steps:

    a. Step 1 — 5 complete stops from 30 mph

    b. Step 2 — Allow the brakes to cool off

    c. Step 3 — 5 complete stops from 30 mph

Brake System Bleeding

NOTE: This procedure is valid for both ABS and non-ABS braking systems. Always use clean, factory approved brake fluid.

1. Fill the master cylinder to the maximum level with the proper brake fluid.

2. Raise and safely support the vehicle. Remove the protective caps from the bleeder screws.

3. The proper bleeding sequence always start with the brake unit farthest from the master cylinder. The proper bleeding sequence is: right rear, left rear, right front and left front.

4. Insert a tight fitting plastic tube over the bleeder screw on the caliper and the other end of the tube in a transparent container partially filled with clean brake fluid.

5. Depress the brake pedal and loosen the bleeder screw to release the brake fluid. Pump the brake pedal to the stop 12 times. Tighten the bleeder screw when the escaping brake fluid is free of air bubbles.

6. Repeat this step on all 4 wheels. Lower the vehicle.

Anti-Lock Brake System Service

PRECAUTIONS

• Remove the plugs from the electronic control unit and turn off the ignition when using an electric welder.

• If the battery has been removed, the battery terminals must be tightened on the end poles perfectly after the reinstallation of the battery.

• After the replacement of the hydraulic unit, the control unit, the speed sensors or the wire harness, the entire ABS system has to be checked with the proper tester.

• The brake system must be bled after each repair procedure on the brake system.

ABS Electronic Control Unit

REMOVAL AND INSTALLATION

1. Disconnect the negative battery cable.

2. Remove the cover in the engine compartment on the right side.

3. Push back the clamp. Pull off the right side then disengage the left side of the multiple plug.

4. Remove the mounting bolts and lift out the control unit.

5. The installation is the reverse of the removal procedure.

Hydraulic Unit

REMOVAL AND INSTALLATION

1. Disconnect the negative battery cable.

2. Disconnect and plug the hydraulic brake lines at the unit. Do not mix up the brake lines. The lines are marked as follows:

    a. VL — LF Brake Caliper

    b. VR — RF Brake Caliper

    c. HL — LR Brake Caliper

    d. HR — RR Brake Caliper

3. Remove the cover mounting bolts and lift off the cover.

4. Disconnect the electrical connections and plugs.

5. Loosen the mounting nuts, pull up and remove the hydraulic control unit.

6. The installation is the reverse of the removal procedure. Bleed the brake system.

CHASSIS ELECTRICAL

──── CAUTION ────

On vehicles equipped with an air bag, the negative battery cable must be disconnected, before working on the system. Failure to do so may result in deployment of the air bag and possible personal injury.

Windshield Wiper Motor

The electric wiper motor assembly is located under the engine hood, at the top of the cowl panel. A few vehicles have covers over the wiper motor assembly, while others have the motors exposed. Link rods operate the left and right wiper pivot assemblies from a drive crank bolted to the wiper motor output shaft.

REMOVAL AND INSTALLATION

318iC, 318iS, 325i, 325iC, 325iS, 325iX and M3

1. Disconnect the negative battery cable. Remove the heater motor, as described above. Remove the bracket bracing the windshield wiper motor, which is now visible.
2. Disconnect the electrical connector for the motor.
3. Lift out the grill located at the top of the cowl and disconnect the linkages to both wiper arms at the left side shaft mounts.
4. Disconnect both wiper arms from their shafts by lifting the cover, unscrewing the nut and pulling the arm off. Then, remove the cover, nut and washer surrounding the shafts and holding the console in place. Now remove the entire console.
5. With the motor still mounted, remove the nut retaining the linkage to the motor shaft. Then, unbolt and remove the motor from the console.
6. Installation is the reverse of the removal procedure.

525i, 535i, 635CSi and M5

1. Disconnect the negative battery cable. Remove the cowl cover to expose the wiper motor, if equipped.
2. Disconnect the wiper motor crank arm from the motor output shaft by removing the nut and pulling off the crank arm.

3. Remove the motor retaining screws and disconnect the electrical connector.
4. Remove the wiper motor from the vehicle.
5. Reverse the procedure to install the motor.

735i, 735iL, 750iL and 850i

1. Disconnect the negative battery cable. Make sure the wipers are in the parked position. Remove the heater blower. Take off the cover near the blower.
2. Disconnect the heater cable and lift out the linkage. Disconnect the temperature sensor.
3. Disconnect the clips, lift the cowl cover slightly and then remove the fresh air inlet cowls on either side. Then, remove the cover.
4. Unscrew bolts and remove the mounting bracket for the wiper housing. Remove the left wiper arm by pulling up the cover, loosening the pinch bolt and removing it. Remove the right wiper by pulling up the cover, removing the through bolt and then pulling it off.
5. Lift out the clips and remove the cover for the linkage.
6. Unscrew and remove the nuts fastening the linkage to the cowl. Pull the linkage arms downward and out of the cowl.
7. Mark the relationship between the linkage lever and the motor. Remove the nut and disconnect the linkage at the motor shaft. Disconnect the electrical connector and remove the linkage.
8. Remove the mounting bolts and remove the wiper motor. If installing a new motor, connect the motor and operate it until it reaches parked position; then install the linkage so the shaft lever and linkage link are in a straight line.

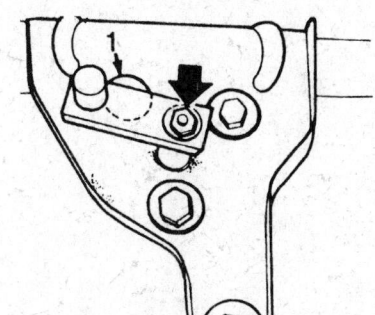

On the 735i and 735iL, install the motor crank in the position shown, with the bolt (1) half hidden by the upper edge of the crank

To install:
9. Perform the remaining portions of the installation in reverse order, noting these points:
   a. Make sure the wiper arms are pressed all the way onto the linkage shafts so the contact pressure control will work.
   b. Make sure the inlet cowling is installed in proper relation to the blower housing and fresh air flap.

Windshield Wiper Switch

REMOVAL AND INSTALLATION

1. Disconnect the negative battery cable. Remove the steering wheel. Remove the lower/left instrument panel trim.
2. Remove the screws and remove the lower steering column cover.
3. Push the locking hook for the flasher back and remove the relay, socket facing downward.
4. Take off the upper steering column cover. If equipped with air bags, drive out the pins and lift out the expansion rivet first.
5. Press the retaining hooks inward on both sides, pull the switch out, and then disconnect the electrical connector.
6. Installation is the reverse of removal.

Instrument Cluster

REMOVAL AND INSTALLATION

1. Disconnect the negative battery cable. Remove the attaching screws and remove the lower instrument panel trim from under the steering column.
2. Remove the mounting nuts for the trim just under the instrument carrier and remove it.
3. Unscrew the 4 screws underneath and 2 above the instrument carrier and remove trim that surrounds the instrument carrier.
4. Remove the 2 screws at the top of the carrier, lift it out of the instrument panel, and then disconnect the plugs. To disconnect the combination plug, first pull the sliding clamp off the center.
5. To replace the speedometer, pull the speedometer from the instrument carrier.
6. Installation is the reverse of removal.

Headlight Switch

REMOVAL AND INSTALLATION

1. Disconnect the negative battery cable. Remove the lower/left trim panel screws and remove the panel.
2. Unscrew the knob from the switch.
3. Pull off the connector plug from behind the dash panel. Pull out the switch from behind and remove it.
4. Install in reverse order.

Combination Switch

REMOVAL AND INSTALLATION

———— CAUTION ————
On vehicles equipped with an air bag, the negative battery cable must be disconnected, before working on the system. Failure to do so may result in deployment of the air bag and possible personal injury.

1. Disconnect the negative battery cable. Remove the steering wheel.
2. Remove the lower instrument panel on the left side.
3. Remove the steering column casing lower section.
4. If equipped with an air bag, drive out the pins and lift out the expansion rivet. Remove the upper section of the steering column casing.
5. Remove the plug and disconnect the electrical connectors.
6. Push in the retaining hooks on both sides and pull out the switch.
7. The installation is the reverse of the removal procedure.

Ignition Switch

REMOVAL AND INSTALLATION

1. Disconnect the negative battery cable. Remove the steering wheel.
2. Remove the trim panel on the lower left side.
3. Remove the steering column casing lower section.
4. Press in the retaining hooks on both sides and remove the switch.
5. The installation is the reverse of the removal procedure. Check the position of the ignition switch to the steering wheel lock.

Stoplight Switch

ADJUSTMENT

1. Disconnect the negative battery cable. Disconnect the electrical connector to the switch.
2. Loosen the locknut and then turn the switch outward to remove it.
3. Screw the new switch in. Adjust the gap between the pedal and actuator on the switch to 0.197-0.236 in. on the 3 Series and 0.236-0.020 in. except 3 Series.
4. Tighten the locknut.

REMOVAL AND INSTALLATION

1. Disconnect the negative battery cable.
2. Remove the lower left side trim panel and disconnect the plug.
3. Press down the brake pedal and pull the plunger and sleeve down completely.
4. Press in the retainers and pull back on the switch.
5. The installation is the reverse of the removal procedure

Neutral Safety Switch

ADJUSTMENT

1. Disconnect the leads at the switch terminal.
2. Ground the negative terminal and connect a proper test light to the positive terminal.
3. The test light should light when the gear selector is placed on **P** or **N**.
4. If the switch needs adjusting, unscrew the switch and place thicker shims behind the switch and the transmission housing.

REMOVAL AND INSTALLATION

1. Disconnect the negative battery cable. Raise and safely support the vehicle.
2. Disconnect the electrical connection at the switch.
3. Remove the switch using the proper tool.
4. The installation is the reverse of the removal procedure.

Fuses And Relays

LOCATION

The fuse box is located under the engine hood on the left side, near the upper strut housing or near the battery.
Various relays are also mounted on the fuse box for easy accessibility.

Flashers

LOCATION

The flashers are located behind the bottom center of the lower instrument trim panel.

Chrysler Corp. Imports 4
—Colt, Colt Wagon, Colt Vista

SERIAL NUMBER IDENTIFICATION

Vehicle Identification Number

The vehicle identification plate is mounted on the left side instrument panel, adjacent to the lower corner of the windshield on the driver's side and is visible through the windshield. A standardized 17 digit Vehicle Identification Number (VIN) is used. The 8th digit designates the engine code and 10th designates model year.

Vehicle Information Code Plate

The Vehicle Information Code Plate is attached to the bulkhead on the firewall, in the engine compartment. The plate shows model code, engine model, transaxle model and body color code.

Chassis Number

The chassis number plate is stamped on the top center of the firewall, located in the engine compartment.

Engine Number

The engine number is stamped at the right or front side, on the top edge of the cylinder block and contains the engine model number and engine serial number.

Vehicle Safety Certification Label

The label is located on the driver's door or the driver's door jamb. The label indicates the month and year of manufacture, gross vehicle weight and VIN number.

SPECIFICATIONS

VEHICLE IDENTIFICATION CHART

It is important for servicing and ordering parts to be certain of the vehicle and engine identification. The VIN (vehicle identification number) is a 17 digit number visible through the windshield on the driver's side of the dash and contains the vehicle and engine identification codes. The tenth digit indicates model year and the eighth digit indicates engine code. It can be interpreted as follows:

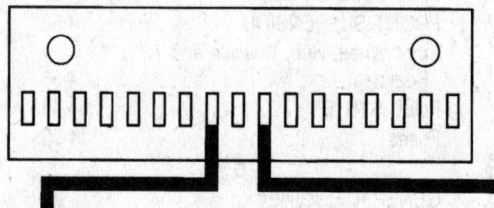

Engine Code						Model Year		
Code	Cu. In.	Liters	Cyl.	Fuel Sys.	Eng. Mfg.	Code		Year
A	89.6	1.5 (1468)	4	MPI	Mitsubishi	L		1990
C	111.9	1.8 (1834)	4	MPI	Mitsubishi	M		1991
D	111.9	1.8 (1834)	4	MPI	Mitsubishi	N		1992
G	146	2.4 (2350)	4	MPI	Mitsubishi	P		1993
T	107.1	1.8 (1755)	4	MPI	Mitsubishi	Q		1994
V	121.9	2.0 (1997)	4	MPI	Mitsubishi			
W	146	2.4 (2350)	4	MPI	Mitsubishi			
X	89.6	1.5 (1468)	4	MPI	Mitsubishi			
Y	97.3	1.6 (1595)	4	MPI	Mitsubishi			
Z	97.3	1.6 (1595)	4	MPI/TBO	Mitsubishi			

MPI—Multi-Port Fuel Injection
EFI—Electronic Fuel Injection
TBO—Turbocharged

ENGINE IDENTIFICATION

Year	Model	Engine Displacement Liters (cc)	Engine Series (ID/VIN)	Fuel System	No. of Cylinders	Engine Type
1990	Colt	1.5 (1468)	4G15 (X)	MPI	4	SOHC
	Colt	1.6 (1595)	4G61 (Y)	MPI	4	DOHC
	Colt Wagon	1.5 (1468)	4G15 (X)	MPI	4	SOHC
	Colt Wagon	1.8 (1755)	4G37 (T)	MPI	4	SOHC
	Colt Vista	2.0 (1997)	G63B (V)	MPI	4	SOHC
1991	Colt	1.5 (1468)	4G15① (A)	MPI	4	SOHC
	Colt Vista	2.0 (1997)	G63B (V)	MPI	4	SOHC
1992	Colt	1.5 (1468)	4G15① (A)	MPI	4	SOHC
	Colt Vista	1.8 (1834)	4G93 (D)	MPI	4	SOHC
	Colt Vista	2.4 (2350)	4G64 (W)	MPI	4	SOHC
1993	Colt	1.5 (1468)	4G15① (A)	MPI	4	SOHC
	Colt	1.8 (1834)	4G93② (C)	MPI	4	SOHC
	Colt Vista	1.8 (1834)	4G93② (C)	MPI	4	SOHC
	Colt Vista	2.4 (2350)	4G64 (G)	MPI	4	SOHC
1994	Colt	1.5 (1468)	4G15① (A)	MPI	4	SOHC
	Colt	1.8 (1834)	4G93② (C)	MPI	4	SOHC
	Colt Vista	1.8 (1834)	4G93② (C)	MPI	4	SOHC
	Colt Vista	2.4 (2350)	4G64 (G)	MPI	4	SOHC

EFI—Electronic Fuel Injection
MPI—Multi-Port Fuel Injection
DOHC—Dual Overhead Cam
SOHC—Single Overhead Cam
TBO—Turbocharged
① 3 valves per cyl.
   2—Intake
   1—Exhaust
② 4 valves per cyl.
   2—Intake
   2—Exhaust

GENERAL ENGINE SPECIFICATIONS

Year	Engine ID (VIN)	Engine Displacement Liters (cc)	Fuel System Type	Net Horsepower @ rpm	Net Torque @ rpm (ft. lbs.)	Bore × Stroke (in.)	Compression Ratio	Oil Pressure @ rpm
1990	4G15 (X)	1.5 (1468)	MPI	68 @ 5000	84 @ 3000	2.97 × 3.23	9.4:1	11.4 @ 850
	4G61 (Y)	1.6 (1595)	MPI	92 @ 6500	134 @ 5000	3.24 × 2.95	9.2:1	11.4 @ 850
	4G37 (T)	1.8 (1755)	MPI	87 @ 5000	102 @ 5000	3.17 × 3.39	9.0:1	11.4 @ 850
	G63B (V)	2.0 (1997)	MPI	120 @ 5000	108 @ 3500	3.35 × 3.46	8.5:1	11.4 @ 900
1991	4G15 (A)	1.5 (1468)	MPI	92 @ 6000	93 @ 3000	2.97 × 3.23	9.2:1	11.4 @ 850
	G63B (V)	2.0 (1997)	MPI	120 @ 5000	108 @ 3500	3.35 × 3.46	8.5:1	11.4 @ 900
1992	4G15 (A)	1.5 (1468)	MPI	92 @ 6000	93 @ 3000	2.97 × 3.23	9.2:1	11.4 @ 850
	4G93 (D)	1.8 (1834)	MPI	113 @ 6000	116 @ 4500	3.19 × 3.50	8.5:1	11.4 @ 830
	4G64 (W)	2.4 (2350)	MPI	136 @ 5500	145 @ 4250	3.41 × 3.94	9.5:1	11.4 @ 850
1993	4G15 (A)	1.5 (1468)	MPI	92 @ 6000	93 @ 3000	2.97 × 3.23	9.2:1	11.4 @ 850
	4G93 (C)	1.8 (1834)	MPI	113 @ 6000	116 @ 4500	3.19 × 3.50	9.5:1	11.4 @ 830
	4G64 (G)	2.4 (2350)	MPI	136 @ 5500	145 @ 4250	3.41 × 3.94	9.5:1	11.4 @ 850
1994	4G15 (A)	1.5 (1468)	MPI	92 @ 6000	93 @ 3000	2.97 × 3.23	9.2:1	11.4 @ 850
	4G93 (C)	1.8 (1834)	MPI	113 @ 6000	116 @ 4500	3.19 × 3.50	9.5:1	11.4 @ 830
	4G64 (G)	2.4 (2350)	MPI	136 @ 5500	145 @ 4250	3.41 × 3.94	9.5:1	11.4 @ 850

NOTE: Horsepower and torque are SAE net figures. They are measured at the rear of the transmission with all accessories installed and operating. Since the figures vary when a given engine is installed in different models, some are representative rather than exact.
EFI—Electronic Fuel Injection
MPI—Multi-Port Fuel Injection
TBO—Turbocharged

GASOLINE ENGINE TUNE-UP SPECIFICATIONS

Year	Engine ID (VIN)	Engine Displacement Liters (cc)	Spark Plugs Gap (in.)	Ignition Timing (deg.) MT	Ignition Timing (deg.) AT	Fuel Pump (psi)	Idle Speed (rpm) MT	Idle Speed (rpm) AT	Valve Clearance In.	Valve Clearance Ex.
1990	4G15 (X)	1.5 (1468)	0.039–0.043	5B	5B	47.6	750	700	0.006	0.010
	4G61 (Y)	1.6 (1595)	0.028–0.031	5B	5B	47.6	750	700	Hyd.	Hyd.
	4G15 (X)	1.5 (1468)	0.039–0.043	5B	5B	47.6	750	700	0.006	0.010
	4G37 (T)	1.8 (1755)	0.039–0.043	5B	5B	47.6	700	650	Hyd.	Hyd.
	G63B (V)	2.0 (1997)	0.039–0.043	5B	5B	47.6	700	650	Hyd.	Hyd.
1991	4G15 (A)	1.5 (1468)	0.039–0.043	5B	5B	47.6	750	700	0.006	0.010
	G63B (V)	2.0 (1997)	0.039–0.043	5B	5B	47.6	700	650	Hyd.	Hyd.
1992	4G15 (A)	1.5 (1468)	0.039–0.043	5B	5B	47.6	750	700	0.006	0.010
	4G93 (D)	1.8 (1834)	0.039–0.043	5B	5B	47.6	750	700	0.008	0.012
	4G64 (W)	2.4 (2350)	0.039–0.043	5B	5B	47.6	750	700	Hyd.	Hyd.
1993	4G15 (A)	1.5 (1468)	0.039–0.043	5B	5B	47.6	750	700	0.006	0.010
	4G93 (C)	1.8 (1834)	0.039–0.043	5B	5B	47.6	750	700	0.008	0.012
	4G64 (G)	2.4 (2350)	0.039–0.043	5B	5B	47.6	750	700	Hyd.	Hyd.
1994	4G15 (A)	1.5 (1468)	0.039–0.043	5B	5B	47.6	750	700	0.006	0.010
	4G93 (C)	1.8 (1834)	0.039–0.043	5B	5B	47.6	750	700	0.008	0.012
	4G64 (G)	2.4 (2350)	0.039–0.043	5B	5B	47.6	750	700	Hyd.	Hyd.

NOTE: The lowest cylinder pressure should be within 75% of the highest cylinder pressure reading. For example, if the highest cylinder is 134 psi, the lowest should be 101. Engine should be at normal operating temperature with throttle valve in the wide open position.
The underhood specifications sticker often reflects tune-up specification changes in production. Sticker figures must be used if they disagree with those in this chart.
Hyd.—Hydraulic
① Jet valve clearance: .010 (in.)

FIRING ORDERS

NOTE: To avoid confusion, always replace spark plug wires one at a time.

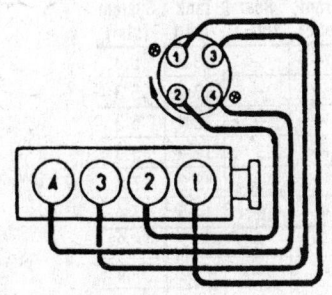

1468cc engine 1990, 1755cc and 1997cc Engines
Engine Firing Order: 1-3-4-2
Distributor Rotation: Clockwise

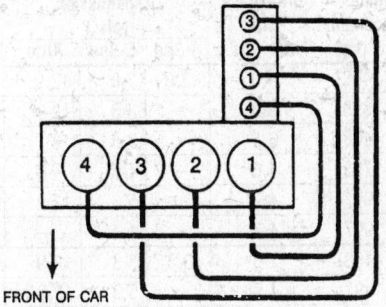

FRONT OF CAR

1595cc DOHC Engine
Engine Firing Order: 1-3-4-2
Distributorless Ignition System

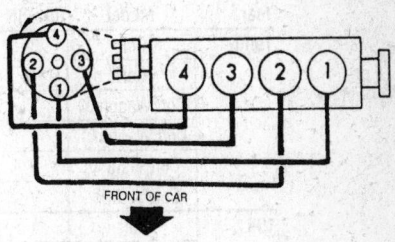

FRONT OF CAR

1834cc Engine
Engine Firing Order: 1-3-4-2
Distributor Rotation: Counterclockwise

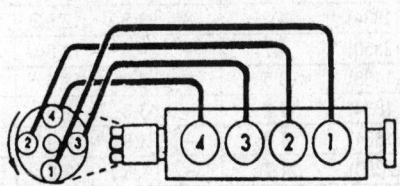

1468cc Engine 1991-94
Engine Firing Order: 1-3-4-2
Distributor Rotation: Counterclockwise

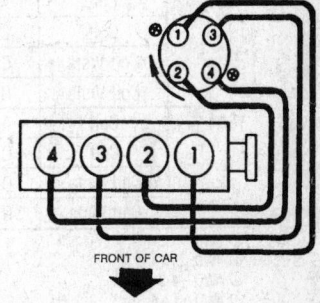

FRONT OF CAR

2350cc Engine
Engine Firing Order: 1-3-4-2
Distributor Rotation: Clockwise

CAPACITIES

Year	Model	Engine ID/VIN	Engine Displacement Liters (cc)	Engine Crankcase with Filter (qts.)	Transmission (pts.) 4-Spd	5-Spd	Auto.	Transfer Case (pts.)	Drive Axle Front (pts.)	Rear (pts.)	Fuel Tank (gal.)	Cooling System (qts.)
1990	Colt	X	1.5 (1468)	4.0	3.6	3.8	12.9	—	—	—	13.2	5.3
	Colt	Y	1.6 (1595)	5.0	—	3.8	12.9	—	—	—	13.2	5.3
	Colt Wagon ①	X	1.5 (1468)	3.5	—	3.8	12.2	—	—	—	12.4	5.3
	Colt Wagon ②	T	1.8 (1755)	4.0	—	4.7	—	1.3	—	2.3	12.4	5.3
	Colt Vista ①	V	2.0 (1997)	4.7	—	5.3	12.2	—	—	—	13.2	7.4
	Colt Vista ②	V	2.0 (1997)	4.7	—	4.4	—	1.5	—	1.5	14.5	7.4
1991	Colt	A	1.5 (1468)	4.0	3.6	3.8	12.9	—	—	—	13.2	5.3
	Colt Vista ①	V	2.0 (1997)	4.7	—	5.3	12.2	—	—	—	13.2	7.4
	Colt Vista ②	V	2.0 (1997)	4.7	—	4.4	—	1.5	—	1.5	14.5	7.4
1992	Colt	A	1.5 (1468)	4.0	3.6	3.8	12.9	—	—	—	13.2	5.3
	Colt Vista	D	1.8 (1834)	4.0	—	3.8③	12.9④	1.2②	—	1.5②	14.5	6.3
	Colt Vista	W	2.4 (2350)	4.1	—	4.8	12.9④	1.2②	—	1.5②	15.9	6.8
1993	Colt	A	1.5 (1468)	3.5	—	3.8	12.6	—	—	—	13.2	5.3
	Colt	C	1.8 (1834)	4.2	—	3.8	12.6	—	—	—	13.2	6.3
	Colt Vista	C	1.8 (1834)	4.2	—	3.8③	12.9④	1.2②	—	1.5②	14.5	6.3
	Colt Vista	G	2.4 (2350)	4.7	—	4.8	12.8④	1.2②	—	1.5②	14.5	6.8
1994	Colt	A	1.5 (1468)	3.5	—	3.8	12.6	—	—	—	13.2	5.3
	Colt	C	1.8 (1834)	4.2	—	3.8	12.6	—	—	—	13.2	6.3
	Colt Vista	C	1.8 (1834)	4.2	—	3.8③	12.9④	1.2②	—	1.5②	14.5	6.3
	Colt Vista	G	2.4 (2350)	4.7	—	4.8	12.8④	1.2②	—	1.5②	14.5	6.8

① 2WD
② 4WD
③ AWD—4.8
④ AWD—13.8

CAMSHAFT SPECIFICATIONS

All measurements given in inches.

| Year | Engine ID (VIN) | Engine Displacement Liters (cc) | Journal Diameter | | | | | Elevation | | Bearing Clearance | Camshaft End Play |
			1	2	3	4	5	In.	Ex.		
1990	4G15 (X)	1.5 (1468)	1.811	1.811	1.811	—	—	1.532	1.534	0.0015–0.0031	0.002–0.008
	4G61 (Y)	1.6 (1595)	1.020	1.020	1.020	1.020	1.020	1.386	1.374	0.0020–0.0035	0.004–0.008
	4G37 (T)	1.8 (1755)	1.336	1.336	1.336	1.336	1.336	1.414	1.414	0.0020–0.0035	0.002–0.006
	G63B (V)	2.0 (1997)	1.340	1.340	1.340	1.340	1.340	1.657	1.657	0.0020–0.0035	0.004–0.008
1991	4G15 (A)	1.5 (1468)	1.811	1.811	1.811	1.811	1.811	1.526	1.539	0.0024–0.0039	0.004–0.008
	G63B (V)	2.0 (1997)	1.340	1.340	1.340	1.340	1.340	1.657	1.657	0.0020–0.0039	0.004–0.008
1992	4G15 (A)	1.5 (1468)	1.811	1.811	1.811	1.811	1.811	1.526	1.539	0.0024–0.0039	0.004–0.008
	4G93 (D)	1.8 (1834)	1.769	1.769	1.769	1.769	1.769	1.488	1.500	0.0020–0.0039	0.004–0.008
	4G64 (W)	2.4 (2350)	1.336	1.336	1.336	1.336	1.336	1.753	1.753	0.0020–0.0039	0.004–0.008
1993	4G15 (A)	1.5 (1468)	1.811	1.811	1.811	1.811	1.811	1.526	1.539	0.0024–0.0039	0.004–0.008
	4G93 (C)	1.8 (1834)	1.769	1.769	1.769	1.769	1.769	1.488	1.500	0.0020–0.0035	0.004–0.008
	4G64 (G)	2.4 (2350)	1.769	1.769	1.769	1.769	1.769	1.472	1.475	0.0020–0.0035	0.004–0.008
1994	4G15 (A)	1.5 (1468)	1.811	1.811	1.811	1.811	1.811	1.526	1.539	0.0024–0.0039	0.004–0.008
	4G93 (C)	1.8 (1834)	1.769	1.769	1.769	1.769	1.769	1.488	1.500	0.0020–0.0035	0.004–0.008
	4G64 (G)	2.4 (2350)	1.769	1.769	1.769	1.769	1.769	1.472	1.475	0.0020–0.0035	0.004–0.008

CRANKSHAFT AND CONNECTING ROD SPECIFICATIONS

All measurements are given in inches.

Year	Engine ID/VIN	Engine Displacement Liters (cc)	Crankshaft				Connecting Rod		
			Main Brg. Journal Dia.	Main Brg. Oil Clearance	Shaft End-play	Thrust on No.	Journal Diameter	Oil Clearance	Side Clearance
1990	4G15 (X)	1.5 (1468)	1.890	0.0008–0.0018	0.002–0.007	3	1.650	0.0006–0.0017	0.004–0.010
	4G71 (Y)	1.6 (1595)	2.240	0.0008–0.0020	0.002–0.007	3	1.770	0.0008–0.0020	0.004–0.010
	4G37 (T)	1.8 (1755)	2.240	0.0008–0.0020	0.002–0.007	3	1.770	0.0008–0.0020	0.004–0.010
	G63B (V)	2.0 (1997)	2.240	0.0008–0.0020	0.002–0.007	3	1.770	0.0006–0.0020	0.004–0.010
1991	4G15 (A)	1.5 (1468)	1.890	0.0008–0.0028	0.002–0.007	3	1.650	0.0008–0.0024	0.004–0.010
	G63B (V)	2.0 (1997)	2.240	0.0008–0.0020	0.002–0.007	3	1.770	0.0006–0.0020	0.004–0.010
1992	4G15 (A)	1.5 (1468)	1.890	0.0008–0.0028	0.002–0.007	3	1.650	0.0008–0.0024	0.004–0.010
	4G93 (D)	1.8 (1834)	1.968	0.0008–0.0016	0.002–0.007	3	1.771	0.0008–0.0020	0.004–0.010
	4G64 (W)	2.4 (2350)	2.240	0.0008–0.0020	0.002–0.007	3	1.770	0.0008–0.0020	0.004–0.010
1993	4G15 (A)	1.5 (1468)	1.890	0.0008–0.0020	0.002–0.007	3	1.650	0.0008–0.0020	0.004–0.010
	4G93 (C)	1.8 (1834)	1.968	0.0008–0.0016	0.002–0.007	3	1.771	0.0008–0.0020	0.004–0.010
	4G64 (G)	2.4 (2350)	2.240	0.0008–0.0020	0.002–0.007	3	1.770	0.0008–0.0020	0.004–0.010
1994	4G15 (A)	1.5 (1468)	1.890	0.0008–0.0020	0.002–0.007	3	1.650	0.0008–0.0020	0.004–0.010
	4G93 (C)	1.8 (1834)	1.968	0.0008–0.0016	0.002–0.007	3	1.771	0.0008–0.0020	0.004–0.010
	4G64 (G)	2.4 (2350)	2.240	0.0008–0.0020	0.002–0.007	3	1.770	0.0008–0.0020	0.004–0.010

VALVE SPECIFICATIONS

Year	Engine ID (VIN)	Engine Displacement Liters (cc)	Seat Angle (deg.)	Face Angle (deg.)	Spring Test Pressure (lbs. @ in.)	Spring Installed Height (in.)	Stem-to-Guide Clearance (in.)		Stem Diameter (in.)	
							Intake	Exhaust	Intake	Exhaust
1990	4G15 (X)	1.5 (1468)	44–44.5	45–45.5	53 @ 1.469	1.469	0.0008–0.0020	0.0020–0.0035	0.260	0.260
	4G61 (Y)	1.6 (1595)	44–44.5	45–45.5	66 ①	1.902 ②	0.0008–0.0019	0.0020–0.0033	0.258	0.258
	4G37 (T)	1.8 (1755)	45	45–45.5	62 @ 1.469	1.469	0.0012–0.0024	0.0020–0.0035	0.320	0.320
	G63B (V)	2.0 (1997)	45	45–45.5	73 @ 1.591	1.591	0.0012–0.0024	0.0020–0.0035	0.310	0.310
1991	4G15 (A)	1.5 (1468)	44	45–45.5	51 @ 1.57 ③	1.570	0.0008–0.0020	0.0020–0.0035	0.258–0.259	0.257–0.258
	G63B (V)	2.0 (1997)	45	45–45.5	73 @ 1.591	1.591	0.0012–0.0024	0.0020–0.0035	0.310	0.310
1992	4G15 (A)	1.5 (1468)	44	45–45.5	51 @ 1.57 ③	1.570	0.0008–0.0020	0.0020–0.0035	0.258–0.259	0.257–0.258
	4G93 (D)	1.8 (1834)	43.5–44	45–45.5	132 ①	2.004 ④	0.0008–0.0016	0.0012–0.0024	0.235	0.235
	4G64 (W)	2.4 (2350)	44–44.5	45–45.5	73 @ 1.591	1.591	0.0012–0.0024	0.0020–0.0035	0.310	0.310
1993	4G15 (A)	1.5 (1468)	44	45–45.5	51 @ 1.57 ③	1.570	0.0008–0.0020	0.0020–0.0035	0.258–0.259	0.257–0.258
	4G93 (C)	1.8 (1834)	43.5–44	45–45.5	132 ①	2.004 ④	0.0008–0.0016	0.0012–0.0024	0.235	0.235
	4G64 (G)	2.4 (2350)	43.5–44	45–45.5	60 @ 1.74	1.740	0.0008–0.0020	0.0012–0.0028	0.235	0.235
1994	4G15 (A)	1.5 (1468)	44	45–45.5	51 @ 1.57 ③	1.570	0.0008–0.0020	0.0020–0.0035	0.258–0.259	0.257–0.258
	4G93 (C)	1.8 (1834)	43.5–44	45–45.5	132 ①	2.004 ④	0.0008–0.0016	0.0012–0.0024	0.235	0.235
	4G64 (G)	2.4 (2350)	43.5–44	45–45.5	60 @ 1.74	1.740	0.0008–0.0020	0.0012–0.0028	0.235	0.235

① At installed height.
② Free height, not installed height. Use limit = 1.768.
③ Exhaust valve = 64 @ 1.57.
④ Free height, not installed height. Use limit = 1.965.

PISTON AND RING SPECIFICATIONS

All measurements are given in inches.

Year	Engine ID/VIN	Engine Displacement Liters (cc)	Piston Clearance	Ring Gap			Ring Side Clearance		Oil Control
				Top Compression	Bottom Compression	Oil Control	Top Compression	Bottom Compression	
1990	4G15 (X)	1.5 (1468)	0.0008–0.0016	0.0079–0.0138	0.0079–0.0138	0.0079–0.0276	0.0012–0.0028	0.0008–0.0024	Snug
	4G61 (Y)	1.6 (1595)	0.0008–0.0016	0.0098–0.0157	0.0138–0.0199	0.0079–0.0276	0.0012–0.0028	0.0012–0.0028	Snug
	4G37 (T)	1.8 (1755)	0.0008–0.0016	0.0118–0.0177	0.0079–0.0138	0.0080–0.0280	0.0018–0.0033	0.0008–0.0024	Snug
	G63B (V)	2.0 (1997)	0.0004–0.0012	0.0098–0.0157	0.0079–0.0138	0.0079–0.0276	0.0012–0.0028	0.0008–0.0024	Snug
1991	4G15 (A)	1.5 (1468)	0.0008–0.0016	0.0079–0.0157	0.0079–0.0138	0.0079–0.0276	0.0012–0.0028	0.0008–0.0024	Snug
	G63B (V)	2.0 (1997)	0.0004–0.0012	0.0098–0.0157	0.0079–0.0138	0.0079–0.0276	0.0012–0.0028	0.0008–0.0024	Snug
1992	4G15 (A)	1.5 (1468)	0.0008–0.0016	0.0079–0.0157	0.0079–0.0138	0.0079–0.0276	0.0012–0.0028	0.0008–0.0024	Snug
	4G93 (D)	1.8 (1834)	0.0008–0.0016	0.0098–0.0157	0.0157–0.0217	0.0079–0.0236	0.0012–0.0028	0.0008–0.0024	Snug
	4G64 (W)	2.4 (2350)	0.0004–0.0012	0.0098–0.0157	0.0079–0.0157	0.0079–0.0276	0.0012–0.0028	0.0008–0.0024	Snug
1993	4G15 (A)	1.5 (1468)	0.0008–0.0016	0.0079–0.0157	0.0079–0.0138	0.0079–0.0276	0.0012–0.0028	0.0008–0.0024	Snug
	4G93 (C)	1.8 (1834)	0.0008–0.0016	0.0098–0.0157	0.0157–0.0217	0.0079–0.0236	0.0012–0.0028	0.0008–0.0024	Snug
	4G64 (G)	2.4 (2350)	0.0004–0.0012	0.0098–0.0138	0.0157–0.0217	0.0039–0.0157	0.0012–0.0028	0.0012–0.0028	Snug
1994	4G15 (A)	1.5 (1468)	0.0008–0.0016	0.0079–0.0157	0.0079–0.0138	0.0079–0.0276	0.0012–0.0028	0.0008–0.0024	Snug
	4G93 (C)	1.8 (1834)	0.0008–0.0016	0.0098–0.0157	0.0157–0.0217	0.0079–0.0236	0.0012–0.0028	0.0008–0.0024	Snug
	4G64 (G)	2.4 (2350)	0.0004–0.0012	0.0098–0.0138	0.0157–0.0217	0.0039–0.0157	0.0012–0.0028	0.0012–0.0028	Snug

TORQUE SPECIFICATIONS

All readings in ft. lbs.

Year	Engine ID/VIN	Engine Displacement Liters (cc)	Cylinder Head Bolts	Main Bearing Bolts	Rod Bearing Bolts	Crankshaft Damper Bolts	Flywheel Bolts	Manifold Intake	Manifold Exhaust	Spark Plugs	Lug Nut
1990	(X)	1.5 (1468)	51–54	36–40	14 ①	47–54	94–101	11–14	11–14	15–21	65–80
	(Y)	1.6 (1595)	65–72	47–51	36–38	80–94	94–101	18–22	18–22	15–21	65–80
	(T)	1.8 (1755)	51–54	37–39	24–25	80–94	94–101	11–14	11–14	15–21	65–80
	(V)	2.0 (1997)	65–72	37–39	37–38	80–94	94–101	11–14	11–15	15–21	65–80
1991	(A)	1.5 (1468)	51–54	36–40	14.5 ②	51–72	94–101	11–14	11–14	15–21	65–80
	(V)	2.0 (1997)	65–72	37–39	37–38	80–94	94–101	11–15	11–15	15–21	65–80
1992	(A)	1.5 (1468)	51–54	36–40	14.5 ②	51–72	94–101	11–14	11–14	15–21	65–80
	(D)	1.8 (1834)	③	14	14.5 ②	134	72	13	13	15–21	65–80
	(V)	2.4 (2350)	69	38	38	80–94	98	13	13	15–21	65–80
1993	(A)	1.5 (1468)	53	38	14.5 ②	62	98	13	14	15–21	65–80
	(C)	1.8 (1834)	③	18 ②	14.5 ②	134	72	13	11–14 ④	15–21	65–80
	(G)	2.4 (2350)	③	18 ②	14.5 ②	80–94	98	13	18–22	15–21	65–80
1994	(A)	1.5 (1468)	53	38	14.5 ②	62	98	13	14	15–21	65–80
	(C)	1.8 (1834)	③	18 ②	14.5 ②	134	72	13	11–14 ④	15–21	65–80
	(G)	2.4 (2350)	③	18 ②	14.5 ②	80–94	98	13	18–22	15–21	65–80

① Step 1: Torque to 14 ft. lbs.
   Step 2: Back off
   Step 3: Torque to 14.5 ft. bls.
   Step 4: Tighten an additional ¼ turn
② Plus ¼ turn
③ Step 1: Check all head bolt shank length limit
   (limit = 3.795 in.)
   Step 2: Torque bolts to 54 ft. lbs.
   Step 3: Loosen all bolts completely
   Step 4: Torque bolts to 14.5 ft. lbs.
   Step 5: Tighten bolts ¼ turn (90°)
   Step 6: Tighten bolts 1 final ¼ turn (90°)
④ The exhaust to cyl. head lower flange nuts are
   torqued to 22 ft. lbs.

BRAKE SPECIFICATIONS

All measurements in inches unless noted.

Year	Model		Master Cylinder Bore	Brake Disc Original Thickness	Brake Disc Minimum Thickness	Brake Disc Maximum Runout	Brake Drum Diameter Original Inside Diameter	Brake Drum Diameter Max. Wear Limit	Brake Drum Diameter Maximum Machine Diameter	Minimum Lining Thickness Front	Minimum Lining Thickness Rear
1990	Colt ①	—	0.812	0.510	0.449	0.006	7.1	7.2	NA	0.080	0.040
	Colt ②	front	0.875	0.940	0.882	0.006	—	—	—	0.080	0.080
		rear	—	0.390	0.331	0.006	—	—	—	0.080	0.080
	Colt Wagon ①④	—	0.870	0.512	0.450	0.006	8.0	8.1	NA	0.080	0.040
	Colt Wagon ③⑤	—	0.870	0.709	0.650	0.006	8.0	8.1	NA	0.080	0.040
	Colt Vista ④	—	0.870	0.710	0.650	0.006	8.0	8.1	NA	0.080	0.040
	Colt Vista ⑤	—	0.870	0.940	0.880	0.004	9.0	9.1	NA	0.080	0.040
1991	Colt ⑥	—	0.812	0.510	0.449	0.006	7.1	7.2	NA	0.080	0.040
	Colt ⑦	—	0.875	0.710	0.646	0.006	7.1	7.2	NA	0.080	0.040
	Colt Vista ④	—	0.875	0.710	0.650	0.006	8.0	8.1	NA	0.080	0.040
	Colt Vista ⑤	—	0.875	0.940	0.880	0.004	9.0	9.1	NA	0.080	0.040
1992	Colt ⑥	—	0.812	0.510	0.449	0.006	7.1	7.2	NA	0.080	0.040
	Colt ⑦	—	0.875	0.710	0.646	0.006	7.1	7.2	NA	0.080	0.040
	Colt Vista	front	⑩	0.945	0.882	0.003	—	—	—	0.080	0.040
		rear	—	0.394	0.331	0.003	⑪	⑫	—	0.080	0.040
1993	Colt ⑥	—	0.812	0.512	0.450	0.003	7.0	7.2	NA	0.080	0.040
	Colt ⑦	front ⑧	0.812	0.710	0.650	0.003	8.0	8.1	NA	0.080	0.040
		rear ⑨	0.937 ⑨	0.394	0.331	0.003	—	—	—	0.080	—
	Colt Vista	front	⑩	0.945	0.882	0.003	—	—	—	0.080	0.040
		rear	—	0.394	0.331	0.003	⑪	⑫	—	0.080	0.040
1994	Colt ⑥	—	0.812	0.512	0.450	0.003	7.0	7.2	NA	0.080	0.040
	Colt ⑦	front ⑧	0.812	0.710	0.650	0.003	8.0	8.1	NA	0.080	0.040
		rear ⑨	0.937 ⑨	0.394	0.331	0.003	—	—	—	0.080	—
	Colt Vista	front	⑩	0.945	0.882	0.003	—	—	—	0.080	0.040
		rear	—	0.394	0.331	0.003	⑪	⑫	—	0.080	0.040

NA—Not available
① 1.5L engine
② 1.6L engine
③ 1.8L engine
④ 2WD
⑤ 4WD
⑥ Hatchback
⑦ Sedan
⑧ Withuot ABS
⑨ With ABS
⑩ Without ABS: 0.9375
   With ABS: 1.0
⑪ 8 in. drum: 7.992
   9 in. drum: 9.0
⑫ 8 in. drum: 8.071
   9 in. drum: 9.079

WHEEL ALIGNMENT

Year	Model		Caster Range (deg.)	Caster Preferred Setting (deg.)	Camber Range (deg.)	Camber Preferred Setting (deg.)	Toe-in (in.)	Steering Axis Inclination (deg.)
1990	Colt	front	$1\frac{13}{16}$P–$2\frac{13}{16}$P	$2\frac{5}{16}$P	$\frac{1}{2}$N–$\frac{1}{2}$P	0	0	NA
		rear	—	—	$1\frac{3}{16}$N–$\frac{3}{16}$N	$\frac{11}{16}$N	0	
	Colt Wagon	front	$\frac{3}{16}$P–$1\frac{3}{16}$P	$\frac{11}{16}$P②	$\frac{1}{2}$N–$\frac{1}{2}$P	0	0	NA
		rear	—	—	$\frac{5}{8}$N–$\frac{5}{8}$P	0	0	
	Colt Wagon 4x4	front	$\frac{1}{2}$p–$1\frac{1}{2}$P	1P	$\frac{1}{2}$N–$\frac{1}{2}$P	0	0	NA
		rear	—	—	$\frac{5}{8}$N–$\frac{5}{8}$P	0	0	
	Colt Vista	front	$\frac{5}{16}$P–$1\frac{5}{16}$P	$\frac{13}{16}$P	$\frac{1}{16}$N–$1\frac{5}{16}$P	$\frac{7}{16}$P	0	NA
		rear	—	—	$1\frac{1}{4}$N–0	$\frac{5}{8}$N	$\frac{1}{16}$P	
	Colt Vista 4x4	front	$\frac{5}{16}$P–$1\frac{5}{16}$P	$\frac{13}{16}$P	$\frac{5}{16}$P–$1\frac{5}{16}$P	$\frac{13}{16}$P	0	NA
		rear	—	—	$\frac{1}{2}$N–$\frac{1}{2}$P	0	0	
1991	Colt	front	$1\frac{13}{16}$P–$2\frac{13}{16}$P	$2\frac{5}{16}$P	$\frac{1}{2}$N–$\frac{1}{2}$P	0	0	NA
		rear	—	—	$1\frac{3}{16}$N–$\frac{3}{16}$N	$\frac{11}{16}$N	0	
	Colt Vista 4x2	front	$\frac{5}{16}$P–$1\frac{5}{16}$P	$\frac{13}{16}$P	$\frac{1}{16}$N–$1\frac{5}{16}$P	$\frac{7}{16}$P	0	NA
		rear	—	—	$1\frac{1}{4}$N–0	$\frac{5}{8}$N	$\frac{1}{16}$P	
	Colt Vista 4x4	front	$\frac{5}{16}$P–$1\frac{5}{16}$P	$\frac{13}{16}$P	$\frac{5}{16}$P–$1\frac{5}{16}$P	$\frac{13}{16}$P	0	NA
		rear	—	—	$\frac{1}{2}$N–$\frac{1}{2}$P	0	0	
1992	Colt	front	$1\frac{13}{16}$P–$2\frac{13}{16}$P	$2\frac{5}{16}$P	$\frac{1}{2}$N–$\frac{1}{2}$P	0	0	NA
		rear	—	—	$1\frac{3}{16}$N–$\frac{3}{16}$N	$\frac{11}{16}$N	0	
	Colt Vista FWD	front	$1\frac{1}{2}$P–$2\frac{7}{8}$P	$2\frac{3}{16}$P	$\frac{5}{32}$N–$\frac{27}{32}$P	$\frac{11}{32}$P	0	NA
		rear	—	—	1N–0	$\frac{1}{2}$N	$\frac{3}{32}$P	
	Colt Vista AWD	front	$1\frac{3}{8}$P–$2\frac{3}{4}$P	$2\frac{1}{16}$P	$\frac{3}{16}$P–$1\frac{3}{16}$P	$\frac{11}{16}$P	0	NA
		rear	—	—	1N–0	$\frac{1}{2}$N	$\frac{3}{32}$P	
1993	Colt	front	$1\frac{13}{16}$P–$2\frac{13}{16}$P	$2\frac{5}{16}$P	$\frac{1}{2}$N–$\frac{1}{2}$P	0	0	NA
		rear	—	—	$1\frac{3}{16}$N–$\frac{3}{16}$N	$\frac{11}{16}$N	0	
	Colt Vista FWD	front	$1\frac{1}{2}$P–$2\frac{7}{8}$P	$2\frac{3}{16}$P	$\frac{5}{32}$N–$\frac{27}{32}$P	$\frac{11}{32}$P	0	NA
		rear	—	—	1N–0	$\frac{1}{2}$N	$\frac{3}{32}$P	
	Colt Vista AWD	front	$1\frac{3}{8}$P–$2\frac{3}{4}$P	$2\frac{1}{16}$P	$\frac{3}{16}$P–$1\frac{3}{16}$P	$\frac{11}{16}$P	0	NA
		rear	—	—	1N–0	$\frac{1}{2}$N	$\frac{3}{32}$P	
1994	Colt	front	$1\frac{13}{16}$P–$2\frac{13}{16}$P	$2\frac{5}{16}$P	$\frac{1}{2}$N–$\frac{1}{2}$P	0	0	NA
		rear	—	—	$1\frac{3}{16}$N–$\frac{3}{16}$N	$\frac{11}{16}$N	0	
	Colt Vista FWD	front	$1\frac{1}{2}$P–$2\frac{7}{8}$P	$2\frac{3}{16}$P	$\frac{5}{32}$N–$\frac{27}{32}$P	$\frac{11}{32}$P	0	NA
		rear	—	—	1N–0	$\frac{1}{2}$N	$\frac{3}{32}$P	
	Colt Vista AWD	front	$1\frac{3}{8}$P–$2\frac{3}{4}$P	$2\frac{1}{16}$P	$\frac{3}{16}$P–$1\frac{3}{16}$P	$\frac{11}{16}$P	0	NA
		rear	—	—	1N–0	$\frac{1}{2}$N	$\frac{3}{32}$P	

NA—Not available
N—Negative
P—Positive
① Caster w/power steering
  Range: $1\frac{13}{16}$P–$1\frac{13}{16}$P
  Preferred: $1\frac{5}{16}$P

ENGINE MECHANICAL

NOTE: Disconnecting the negative battery cable on some vehicles may interfere with the functions of the on board computer systems and may require the computer to undergo a relearning process, once the negative battery cable is reconnected.

Engine Assembly

REMOVAL AND INSTALLATION

1468cc Engine

The factory recommends that the engine and transaxle be removed as a unit.

1. Disconnect the battery cables, negative cable first. Remove the battery and the tray.
2. Remove the air cleaner assembly. Disconnect the purge control valve. Remove the purge control valve mounting bracket. Remove the windshield washer reservoir, radiator tank and carbon canister.
3. Drain the coolant from the radiator. Remove the radiator assembly with the electric cooling fan attached. Be sure to disconnect the fan wiring harness and the transaxle cooler lines, if equipped.
4. Disconnect the following cables, hoses and wires from the engine and transaxle: clutch, accelerator, speedometer, heater hose, fuel lines, PCV vacuum line, high altitude compensator vacuum hose (California vehicles), bowl vent valve purge hose (U.S.A. vehicles), inhibitor switch (automatic transaxle), control cable (automatic transaxle), starter, engine ground cable, alternator, water temperature gauge, ignition coil, temperature sensor, backup light (manual transaxle), oil pressure wires and the ISC cable on fuel injected vehicles.

NOTE: On fuel injected vehicles, release fuel system pressure before disconnecting any fuel lines.

5. Remove the ignition coil. Be sure all wires and hoses are disconnected.
6. Raise the vehicle and support safely. Remove the splash shield, if equipped.
7. Drain the lubricant out of the transaxle.

8. Remove the right and left half-shafts from the transaxle and support them with wire. Plug the transaxle case holes so dirt cannot enter.

NOTE: The halfshaft retainer ring should be replaced whenever the shaft is removed.

9. Disconnect the assist rod and the control rod from the transaxle. If equipped with a range selector, disconnect the selector cable.
10. Remove the mounting bolts from the front and rear roll control rods.
11. Disconnect the exhaust pipe from the engine and secure it with wire.
12. Loosen the engine and transaxle mounting bracket nuts. On turbocharged engines, disconnect the oil cooler tube.
13. Lower the vehicle.
14. Attach a lifting device to the engine. Apply slight lifting pressure to the engine. Remove the engine and transaxle mounting nuts and bolts.
15. Make sure the rear roll control rod is disconnected. Lift the engine and transaxle from the vehicle.

NOTE: Make sure the transaxle does not hit the battery bracket when the engine and transaxle are lifted.

To install:

16. Lower the engine and transaxle carefully into position and loosely install the mounting bolts.
17. Temporarily tighten the front and rear roll control rod mounting bolts.
18. Lower the full weight of the engine and transaxle onto the mounts, torque the nuts and bolts to 25 ft. lbs. (34 Nm).
19. Loosen and retighten the roll control rods.
20. Complete the rest of the installation in the reverse order of the removal procedures.
21. Make sure all cables, hoses and wires are connected.
22. Fill the radiator with coolant, the transaxle with lubricant.
23. Adjust the clutch cable and accelerator cable. Adjust the transaxle control rod.
24. Connect the negative battery cable. Start the engine and check for leaks.

1595cc DOHC Engine

1. Disconnect the battery cables, negative cable first. Remove the battery.

2. Raise the vehicle and support it safely. Relieve the fuel system pressure.
3. Drain the cooling system and the engine oil.
4. Disconnect the exhaust pipe from the turbocharger after removing the heat shields.
5. Remove the radiator. Remove the transaxle.
6. Remove the air cleaner. Disconnect the accelerator cable, the vacuum hose from the brake booster and all vacuum hoses. Label the hoses for correct installation.
7. Disconnect the high pressure fuel line and the fuel return hose. Remove their respective mounting O-rings.
8. Disconnect the heater hoses, the oxygen sensor, the coolant temperature sensor and the connection for the engine coolant temperature gauge unit.
9. Disconnect the engine coolant switch for the air conditioner. Disconnect the fuel injector wiring connection, the ignition coil, the power transistor, vacuum lines and the ISC motor.
10. On California vehicles, disconnect the EGR temperature sensor.
11. Disconnect the detonation sensor, the throttle position sensor, the crankshaft angle sensor and the control wiring harness connectors.
12. Disconnect the oil pressure switch for the power steering. Disconnect the alternator wiring. Remove the wiring harness mounting clamps. Disconnect the engine oil pressure switch.
13. Remove the air conditioning compressor, with lines attached and safely wire the assembly out of the way.
14. Remove the power steering pump, with hoses attached and safely wire it out of the way.
15. Connect a chain hoist to the engine with a suitable lifting bracket. Take up slack on the engine. Check to be sure all cables, hoses, harness connectors and vacuum hoses have been disconnected.
16. Remove the engine mounting bracket. Disconnect the front engine roll stopper and the rear roll stopper. Carefully raise and remove the engine assembly.

To install:

17. Installation is the reverse order of the removal procedure.
18. Make sure all cables, vacuum lines, hose and wire connectors are installed or attached.

19. Fill the radiator with the proper coolant mix. Fill the engine with the proper oil.

20. Adjust the clutch and accelerator cables.

21. Connect the negative battery cable. Start the engine and check for leaks.

22. Torque the lower engine mounts to 22-29 ft. lbs. (30-40 Nm), transaxle mount to 29-36 ft. lbs. (40-50 Nm), cylinder head mount to 43-58 ft. lbs. (60-80 Nm) and the exhaust pipe nuts to 14-22 ft. lbs. (20-30 Nm).

1834cc and 2350cc Engines

1. Relieve fuel system pressure.

2. Disconnect the negative battery cable. Remove the under cover if equipped.

3. Matchmark the hood and hinges and remove the hood assembly. Remove the air cleaner assembly and all adjoining air intake duct work.

4. Drain the engine coolant and remove the radiator assembly, coolant reservoir and intercooler.

5. Remove the transaxle and transfer case if equipped with 4WD.

6. Disconnect and tag for assembly reference the connections for the accelerator cable, heater hoses, brake vacuum hose, connection for vacuum hoses, high pressure fuel line, fuel return line, oxygen sensor connection, coolant temperature gauge connection, coolant temperature sensor connector, connection for thermo switch sensor, if equipped with automatic transaxle, the connection for the idle speed control, the motor position sensor connector, the throttle position sensor connector, the EGR temperature sensor connection (California vehicles), the fuel injector connectors, the power transistor connector, the ignition coil connector, the condenser and noise filter connector, the distributor and control harness, the connections for the alternator and oil pressure switch wires.

7. Remove the air conditioner drive belt and the air conditioning compressor. Leave the hoses attached. Do not discharge the system. Wire the compressor aside.

8. Remove the power steering pump and wire aside.

9. Remove the exhaust manifold to head pipe nuts. Discard the gasket.

10. Attach a hoist to the engine and take up the engine weight. Remove the engine mount bracket. Remove any torque control brackets (roll stoppers). Note that some engine mount pieces have arrows on them for

proper assembly. Double check that all cables, hoses, harness connectors, etc., are disconnected from the engine. Lift the engine slowly from the engine compartment.

To install:

11. Install the engine and secure all control brackets.

12. Install the exhaust pipe, power steering pump and air conditioning compressor.

13. Checking the tags installed during removal, reconnect all electrical and vacuum connections.

14. Install the transaxle.

15. Install the radiator assembly and intercooler.

16. Install the air cleaner assembly.

17. Fill the engine with the proper amount of engine oil. Connect the negative battery cable.

18. Refill the cooling system. Start the engine, allow it to reach normal operating temperature. Check for leaks.

19. Check the ignition timing and adjust if necessary.

20. Install the hood.

21. Road test the vehicle and check all functions for proper operation.

1997cc Engine

1. Disconnect the battery cables, negative battery cable first. Remove the battery, battery tray and bracket.

2. Disconnect the engine oil pressure switch and power steering pump connectors.

3. Disconnect the alternator harness.

4. Remove the air cleaner.

5. Remove the high tension cable from the distributor.

6. Disconnect the engine ground wire at the firewall.

7. Remove the windshield washer bottle.

8. Disconnect the brake booster vacuum hose.

9. Disconnect and tag all other vacuum lines connected to the engine.

10. Drain the coolant.

11. Remove the coolant reservoir tank.

12. Remove the radiator.

13. Disconnect the heater hoses at the engine.

14. Disconnect the accelerator cable from the carburetor.

15. Disconnect the speed control cable at the carburetor.

16. Disconnect the speedometer cable at the transaxle.

17. If equipped with air conditioning, the system must be evacuated.

18. Disconnect the hose at the air conditioning compressor and cap all openings immediately.

19. Disconnect the hoses at the power steering pump.

20. Disconnect the fuel return hose, then the fuel inlet hose, at the carburetor.

21. Disconnect the shift control cables at the transaxle.

22. Raise the vehicle and support it safely.

23. Remove the lower cover and skid plate.

24. Drain the transaxle and transfer case.

25. Disconnect the exhaust pipe from the manifold.

26. Remove the clutch slave cylinder.

27. Disconnect the halfshafts at the transaxle.

28. Remove the transfer case extension stopper bracket.

NOTE: The 2 top stopper bracket bolts are easier to get at from the engine compartment, using a T-type box wrench.

29. Lower the vehicle to the ground.

30. Remove the nuts only, from the engine mount-to-body bracket.

31. Remove the range select control valves from the transaxle insulator bracket.

32. Remove the nut only, from the transaxle mounting insulator.

33. Remove the front roll insulator nut.

34. Remove the rear insulator-to-engine nut.

35. Remove the grille and valance panel.

36. Remove the air conditioning condenser.

37. Take up the weight of the engine with a lifting device attached to the lifting eyes.

38. Remove all the mounting bolts.

39. Double check that all wiring, hoses and cables are disconnected from the engine, transaxle and transfer case have been disconnected. Move the assembly forward slightly, to a point at which it will clear the floor pan and lift the whole assembly clear of the vehicle.

To install:

40. Secure the engine to a suitable lifting device.

41. Carefully lower the engine and transaxle into position and loosely install the mounting bolts.

42. Temporarily tighten the front and rear roll control rod mounting bolts.

43. Lower the full weight of the engine and transaxle onto the mounts, tighten the nuts and bolts.

44. Loosen and retighten the roll control rods.

45. Complete the rest of the installation in the reverse order of the removal procedures.

46. Make sure all cables, hoses and wires are connected.

47. Fill the radiator with coolant, the transaxle with lubricant.

48. Adjust the clutch cable and accelerator cable. Adjust the transaxle control rod.

49. Observe the following torques:

Transaxle stopper — 58 ft. lbs. (79 Nm).

Engine-to-body bracket bolts — 47 ft. lbs. (64 Nm).

Rear insulator — 29 ft. lbs. (39 Nm).

Transaxle mount nuts — 58 ft. lbs. (79 Nm).

Heat shield — 7 ft. lbs. (9.5 Nm).

Front roll bracket nuts — 36 ft. lbs. (49 Nm).

50. Connect the negative battery cable. Start the engine and check for leaks.

Engine Mounts

REMOVAL AND INSTALLATION

Colt and 1990-91 Colt Vista

1. Disconnect the negative battery cable.

2. Using an engine support fixture tool, center it on the cowl and attach it to the engine. Raise the engine slightly to take the weight off the engine mounts.

3. From the front of the engine, remove the engine mount bolts and the mount.

4. Inspect the engine mount for deterioration and replace it, if necessary.

To install:

5. To install, support the engine using a engine support fixture tool.

6. Install the engine mounts and the retaining bolts to the engine.

7. Torque the engine mount-to-bracket bolts to 36-47 ft. lbs. (50-65 Nm) and the mount through bolt to 65-80 ft. lbs. (90-110 Nm).

8. Connect the negative battery cable.

1992-94 Colt Vista

1. Insert a piece of wood between a jack and oil pan. Place a jack against

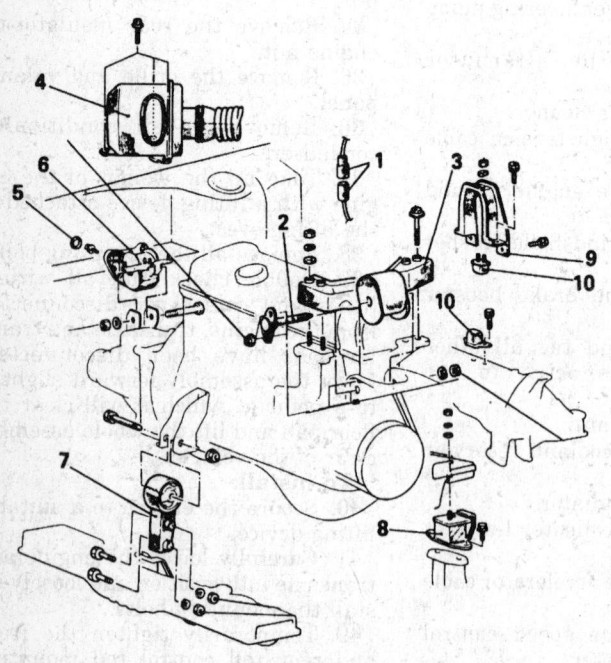

1. Oxygen sensor connector
2. Bolt assembly
3. Engine mount bracket
4. Air filter case
5. Cap
6. Transaxle mount bracket
7. Front roll stopper bracket
8. Rear insulator
9. Transfer extension stopper bracket
10. Transfer extension stopper

Exploded view of engine mounts

the oil pan to support the engine assembly.

2. Disconnect the power steering pressure and return hoses. Catch the fluid with a drain pan.

3. Remove the engine mount insulator bolt.

4. Remove the engine mount bracket and stopper.

To install:

5. Install the engine mount stopper and bracket so the arrow faces the center part of the engine.

6. Torque the mounting bolt to 25 ft. lbs. (35 Nm) and the bracket nuts to 42 ft. lbs. (58 Nm).

7. Install the power steering pump pressure and return hoses.

8. Install the remaining components, start the engine and check for leaks and proper operation.

Cylinder Head

REMOVAL AND INSTALLATION

NOTE: Never remove the cylinder head unless the engine is absolutely cold; the cylinder head could warp.

1468cc 1990

1. Disconnect the negative battery cable and drain the engine coolant.

2. Disconnect the accelerator cable, breather hose, air intake hose and radiator hoses.

3. Label and disconnect the brake booster hose, EGR vacuum hoses and spark plug cables.

4. Relieve the fuel pressure. Disconnect the fuel hoses.

5. Disconnect the distributor connector, oxygen sensor, condenser connector, coolant temperature connectors, motor position sensor connector, idle speed control connector, TPS connector, injector connectors, EGR temperature sensor connector and control harness.

6. Remove the distributor, where necessary.

7. Disconnect the exhaust pipe from the exhaust manifold flange.

8. Remove the exhaust manifold assembly.

9. Remove the intake manifold.

10. Turn the crankshaft to No. 1 piston at TDC on the compression stroke.

NOTE: During the following procedure, do not turn the crankshaft after locating TDC.

11. Remove the upper timing belt cover. Rotate the crankshaft clockwise and align the timing marks. Re-

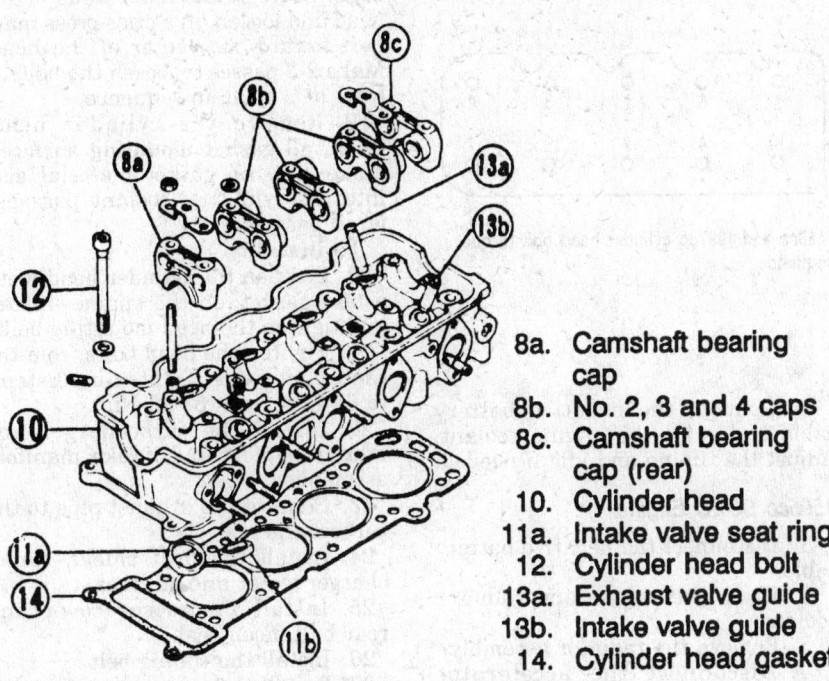

8a. **Camshaft bearing cap**
8b. **No. 2, 3 and 4 caps**
8c. **Camshaft bearing cap (rear)**
10. **Cylinder head**
11a. **Intake valve seat ring**
12. **Cylinder head bolt**
13a. **Exhaust valve guide**
13b. **Intake valve guide**
14. **Cylinder head gasket**

Exploded view of the cylinder head

move the camshaft sprocket and hold the sprocket and timing belt with a piece of wire. Remove the rocker cover and gasket.

12. Loosen and remove the cylinder head bolts in sequence, 2-3 stages to avoid cylinder head warpage.

13. Remove the cylinder head from the engine block.

To install:

14. Clean the cylinder head and block mating surfaces and install a new cylinder head gasket.

15. Position the cylinder head on the engine block, engage the dowel pins front and rear and install the cylinder head bolts.

16. Tighten the head bolts, in 3 steps, to 50-54 ft. lbs. (68-73 Nm).

17. Locate the camshaft in original position. Pull the camshaft sprocket and belt or chain upward and install on the camshaft.

NOTE: If the dowel pin and the dowel pin hole does not align between the sprocket and the spacer or camshaft, move the camshaft by bumping either of the 2 projections provided at the rear of the No. 2 cylinder exhaust cam of the camshaft, with a light hammer or other tool, until the hole and pin align. Be certain the crankshaft does not turn.

18. Install the camshaft sprocket bolt and the distributor gear and tighten.

19. Install the timing belt upper front cover and spark plug cable support.

20. Apply sealant to the intake manifold gasket on both sides. Position the gasket and install the intake manifold.

NOTE: Be sure no sealant enters the jet air passages when equipped.

21. Install the exhaust manifold gaskets and the manifold assembly.

22. Connect the exhaust pipe to the exhaust manifold and install the purge valve.

23. Install the water temperature gauge wire, heater hoses and the upper radiator hose.

24. Connect the fuel lines, accelerator linkage, vacuum hoses and the spark plug wires, air intake hose, hoses, purge valve hose and any other removed unit.

25. Fill the cooling system and connect the battery ground cable. Install the distributor.

26. Temporarily adjust the valve clearance to the cold engine specifications.

27. Install the gasket on the rocker arm cover and temporarily install the cover on the engine.

28. Connect the negative battery cable.

29. Start the engine and bring it to normal operating temperature. Stop the engine and remove the rocker arm cover.

30. Adjust the valves to hot engine specifications.

31. Install the rocker arm cover and tighten securely.

1468cc 12-Valve 1991-94

1. Disconnect the negative battery cable and drain the engine coolant.

2. Disconnect the accelerator cable, breather hose, air intake hose and radiator hoses.

3. Label and disconnect the brake booster hose, EGR vacuum hoses and spark plug cables.

4. Relieve the fuel pressure. Disconnect the fuel hoses.

5. Disconnect the distributor connector, oxygen sensor, condenser connector, coolant temperature connectors, motor position sensor connector, idle speed control connector, TPS connector, injector connectors, EGR temperature sensor connector and control harness.

6. Remove the upper timing belt cover. Rotate the crankshaft clockwise and align the timing marks. Remove the camshaft sprocket and hold the sprocket and timing belt with a piece of wire. Remove the rocker cover and gasket.

7. Remove the exhaust manifold-to-pipe nuts.

8. Remove the cylinder head bolts using a special socket TW-10B or equivalent. Remove the cylinder head and gasket.

To install:

9. Clean the gasket mating surfaces and check for warpage.

10. Match the old gasket with the new and install the gasket with the identification mark facing upward and to the front of the engine.

11. Install the cylinder head and bolts. Using the special head bolt tool TW-10B and torque the bolts in 3 steps and in sequence. 1st step to 20 ft. lbs. (27 Nm), 2nd step to 40 ft. lbs. (54 Nm) and the 3rd step to 51-54 ft. lbs. (70-75 Nm) Cold.

12. Install the exhaust manifold-to-pipe nuts and torque to 34 ft. lbs. (46 Nm).

13. Install the rocker cover, camshaft sprocket and upper timing belt cover.

14. Connect the distributor connector, oxygen sensor, condenser connec-

COLD ENGINE SPECIFICATIONS

	Inch	mm
Jet valve, if equipped	0.003	0.07
Intake valve	0.003	0.07
Exhaust valve	0.007	0.17

Cold engine specifications

HOT ENGINE SPECIFICATIONS

	Inch	mm
Jet valve, if equipped	0.006	0.15
Intake valve	0.006	0.15
Exhaust valve	0.010	0.25

Hot engine specifications

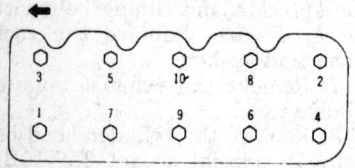

1468cc and 1997cc cylinder head bolt loosening sequence

tor, coolant temperature connectors, motor position sensor connector, idle speed control connector, TPS connector, injector connectors, EGR temperature sensor connector and control harness.

15. Connect the fuel hoses.

16. Connect the brake booster hose, EGR vacuum hoses and spark plug cables.

17. Connect the accelerator cable, breather hose, air intake hose and radiator hoses.

1468cc and 1997cc cylinder head bolt torque sequence

18. Connect the negative battery cable and refill the engine coolant. Adjust the timing and idle if needed.

1595cc DOHC Engine

1. Disconnect the negative battery cable.

2. Drain the engine and radiator coolant.

3. Remove the radiator assembly.

4. Disconnect the accelerator cable. Disconnect the air flow sensor wiring connector.

5. Disconnect all of the breather and vacuum hoses to the air intake. Remove the air cleaner assembly.

6. Remove the PCV hose. Disconnect the water bypass hose, the heater hose and vacuum lines from the water inlet connector.

7. Disconnect the vacuum hose to the power brake booster.

8. Release the fuel system pressure and disconnect the high pressure and fuel return lines. Remove the mounting O-rings.

9. Disconnect the oxygen sensor, engine coolant sensor, temperature gauge connection and the air conditioner coolant temperature switch.

10. Disconnect the fuel injector wiring harness, the ignition coil, power transistor, ISC motor and the EGR sensor connector.

11. Disconnect the detonation sensor, throttle position sensor and crankshaft angle sensor wiring connectors.

12. Remove the center cover and the spark plug wires. Disconnect the control wire harness connector.

13. Remove the timing belt.

14. Remove the rocker cover and rear half moon seal.

15. Remove the heat shield, turbocharger water and oil lines.

16. Disconnect the exhaust pipe from the turbocharger.

17. Remove the turbocharger, exhaust manifold and intake manifold assemblies.

18. Remove the head mounting bolts. Start at the outer ends of the head and loosen, in a criss-cross manner, toward the center of the head. Make 2-3 passes to loosen the bolts, a little at a time, in sequence.

19. Remove the cylinder head. Clean all gasket mounting surfaces. Make sure no gasket material gets into the cylinders, coolant passages or oil passages.

To install:

20. Position the cylinder head, with a new gasket, on the engine. Install and tighten the head mounting bolts.

21. Tighten the head bolts from the center outwards. Tighten in, 3 steps, to 65-72 ft. lbs. (88-98 Nm).

22. Install the turbocharger, exhaust manifold and intake manifold assemblies.

23. Connect the exhaust pipe to the turbocharger.

24. Install the heat shield, turbocharger water and oil lines.

25. Install the rocker cover and rear half moon seal.

26. Install the timing belt.

27. Install the center cover and the spark plug wires. Connect the control wire harness connector.

28. Connect the detonation sensor, throttle position sensor and crankshaft angle sensor wiring connectors.

29. Connect the fuel injector wiring harness, the ignition coil, power transistor, ISC motor and the EGR sensor connector.

30. Connect the oxygen sensor, engine coolant sensor, temperature gauge connection and the air conditioner coolant temperature switch.

31. Connect the high pressure and fuel return lines. Install the new O-rings.

32. Connect the vacuum hose to the power brake booster.

33. Install the PCV hose. Connect the water bypass hose, the heater hose and vacuum lines from the water inlet connector.

34. Connect all of the breather and vacuum hoses to the air intake. Install the air cleaner assembly.

35. Connect the accelerator cable. Connect the air flow sensor wiring connector.

36. Install the radiator assembly.

37. Replenish the engine and radiator coolant.

38. Connect the negative battery cable.

1755 cc and 1997cc Engines

1. Disconnect the negative battery cable. Remove the air cleaner assembly and the attached hoses.

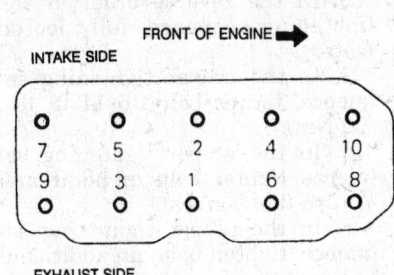

FRONT OF ENGINE →

INTAKE SIDE

```
7   5   2   4   10
9   3   1   6   8
```

EXHAUST SIDE

1595cc DOHC cylinder head bolt torque sequence

2. Drain the coolant, remove the upper radiator hose and the heater hoses.

3. On fuel injected vehicles, release the fuel system pressure. Remove the fuel line, disconnect the accelerator linkage, distributor vacuum lines, purge valve and water temperature gauge wire.

4. Remove the spark plug wires. Remove the distributor, where necessary.

5. Disconnect the exhaust pipe from the exhaust manifold flange.

6. Remove the exhaust manifold assembly.

7. Remove the intake manifold.

8. Turn the crankshaft to No. 1 piston at TDC on the compression stroke.

NOTE: During the following procedure, do not turn the crankshaft after locating TDC.

9. Align the timing mark on the upper under cover of the timing belt with that of the camshaft sprocket. Matchmark the timing belt and the timing mark on the camshaft sprocket with a felt tip pen. Remove the sprocket and insert a 2 in. (51mm) piece of timing belt or other material between the bottom of the camshaft sprocket and the sprocket holder, on the timing belt lower front cover, to hold the sprocket and belt so the valve timing will not be changed. Remove the timing belt upper under cover and rocker arm cover.

10. Loosen and remove the cylinder head bolts in 2-3 stages to avoid cylinder head warpage.

11. Remove the cylinder head from the engine block.

To install:

12. Clean the cylinder head and block mating surfaces and install a new cylinder head gasket.

13. Position the cylinder head on the engine block, engage the dowel pins front and rear and install the cylinder head bolts.

14. Tighten the head bolts in 3 stages and then torque to:
   1755cc engine — 50-54 ft. lbs. (68-73 Nm).
   1997cc engine — 65-72 ft. lbs. (88-97 Nm).

15. Install the timing belt upper under cover.

16. Locate the camshaft in original position. Pull the camshaft sprocket and belt or chain upward and install on the camshaft.

NOTE: If the dowel pin and the dowel pin hole does not align between the sprocket and the spacer or camshaft, move the camshaft by bumping either of the 2 projections provided at the rear of the No. 2 cylinder exhaust cam of the camshaft, with a light hammer or other tool, until the hole and pin align. Be certain the crankshaft does not turn.

17. Install the camshaft sprocket bolt and the distributor gear and tighten.

18. Install the timing belt upper front cover and spark plug cable support.

19. Apply sealant to the intake manifold gasket on both sides. Position the gasket and install the intake manifold. Torque the nuts to 11-14 ft. lbs. (15-20 Nm).

20. Install the exhaust manifold gaskets and the manifold assembly. Tighten the nuts to 11-14 ft. lbs. (15-20 Nm).

21. Connect the exhaust pipe to the exhaust manifold. Install the purge valve.

22. Install the water temperature gauge wire, heater hoses and the upper radiator hose.

23. Connect the fuel lines, accelerator linkage, vacuum hoses and the spark plug wires.

24. Fill the cooling system and connect the battery ground cable. Install the distributor.

25. Temporarily adjust the valve clearance to the cold engine specifications.

26. Install the gasket on the rocker arm cover and temporarily install the cover on the engine.

27. Start the engine and bring it to normal operating temperature. Stop the engine and remove the rocker arm cover.

28. Adjust the valves to hot engine specifications.

29. Install the rocker arm cover and tighten securely.

30. Install the air cleaner, hoses, purge valve hose and any other removed unit.

1834cc Engine

1. Relieve fuel system pressure. Disconnect the negative battery cable.

2. Drain the cooling system. Disconnect the brake booster vacuum hose and PVC valve connection.

3. Remove the upper radiator hose, overflow tube and the water hose from the thermostat to the throttle body.

4. Disconnect the air flow sensor connector. Remove the air cleaner case cover and the air intake hose.

5. Wrap the connection with a shop towel and disconnect the high pressure fuel line at the fuel rail.

6. Disconnect the fuel return hose and remove the O-ring.

7. Disconnect the accelerator cable connection from the throttle body and position aside.

8. Disconnect the electrical harnesses at the oil pressure switch, oxygen sensor, water temperature sensor connector, distributor, condenser, ISC, TPS, detonation sensor and the fuel injectors.

9. Disconnect the spark plug cables from each spark plug.

10. Unbolt the control harness assembly and position aside.

11. Remove the thermostat housing, thermostat and the thermostat case with O-ring from the engine.

12. Remove the rocker cover.

13. Remove the timing belt upper cover.

14. Rotate the crankshaft in the forward (right) direction to align the camshaft timing marks. Matchmark the camshaft sprocket and the timing belt. Tie the camshaft sprocket and the timing belt together so the sprocket will not move with respect to the timing belt.

15. While holding the camshaft sprocket in position using the appropriate wrench, remove the camshaft sprocket and with the belt attached. Wire the sprocket and belt aside making sure constant tension is maintained on the belt. Do not allow the belt to slacken or engine timing may be altered.

NOTE: When removing the camshaft sprocket, do not allow the crankshaft to rotate. If crankshaft rotation did occur, the engine timing may have been changed. Confirm proper engine timing during installation.

16. Loosen the cylinder head bolts in 2 or 3 steps in the appropriate order and remove from the cylinder head.

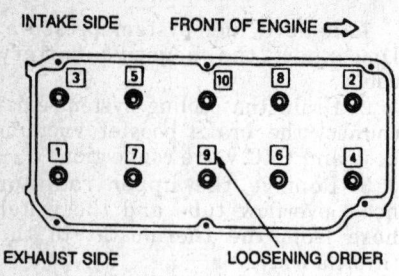

INTAKE SIDE   FRONT OF ENGINE ⟹

EXHAUST SIDE   LOOSENING ORDER

Cylinder head bolt loosening sequence — 1834cc engine

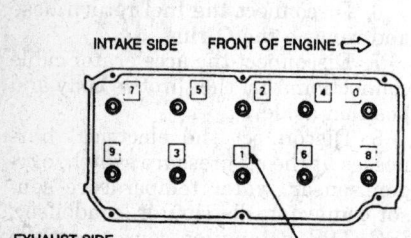

INTAKE SIDE   FRONT OF ENGINE ⟹

EXHAUST SIDE   TIGHTENING ORDER

Cylinder head bolt torquing sequence — 1834cc engine

17. Remove the cylinder head from the engine.

—— **CAUTION** ——
When placing the removed cylinder head upside down, take care not to bend or damage the plug guide. The plug guide can not be replaced.

18. Remove the cylinder head gasket from the block.
To install:
19. Thoroughly clean and dry the mating surfaces of the head and block. Check the cylinder head for

INSTALL SO THAT THE SAGGING SIDE MADE BY TAPPING OUT THE WASHER IS FACING UPWARD

WASHER

CYLINDER HEAD

Cylinder head bolt washer installation — 1834cc engine

cracks, damage or engine coolant leakage. Remove scale, sealing compound and carbon. Clean oil passages thoroughly. Check the head for flatness. End to end, the head should be within 0.002 in. (0.05mm) normally with 0.008 in. (0.200mm) the maximum allowed out of true. The total thickness allowed to be removed from the head and block is 0.008 in. (0.200mm) maximum.
20. Place a new head gasket on the cylinder block with the identification marks facing upward. Make sure the gasket has the proper identification mark for the engine. Do not use sealer on the gasket.
21. Carefully install the cylinder head on the block. Inspect the cylinder head bolt prior to installation, the length below the head of the bolts should be below the limit of 3.795 in. (96.4mm). Apply a small amount of engine oil to the thread section and the washer of the cylinder head bolt and install so the sagging side made by tapping out the washer is facing upward. (chamfer edge faces up).
22. Tighten the cylinder head bolts in the proper order as follows:
  a. In the proper tightening sequence, torque bolts to 54 ft. lbs. (75 Nm).

  b. In the reverse order of the tightening sequence, fully loosen bolts.
  c. In the proper tightening sequence, torque bolts to 14 ft. lbs. (20 Nm).
  d. In the proper tightening sequence, tighten bolts an additional ¼ turn (90 degrees).
  e. In the proper tightening sequence, tighten bolts an additional ¼ turn (90 degrees).
23. Install the camshaft sprocket and tighten bolt to 65 ft. lbs. (90 Nm), while holding the sprocket in place using the appropriate wrench. Confirm proper timing mark alignment.
24. Install the upper timing belt cover and rocker cover.
25. Loosen the water pipe mounting bolt.
26. Apply a thin bead of sealant MD970389 or equivalent, to the water tube connection on the thermostat case.
27. Apply a small amount of water to the O-ring of the water inlet pipe and press the thermostat case assembly onto the water inlet pipe. Install the thermostat case assembly mounting bolt tightening to 16 ft. lbs. (22 Nm).
28. Tighten the water pipe mounting bolt.
29. Install the thermostat into the housing so the jiggle valve is located at the top. Tighten the housing bolts to 10 ft. lbs. (14 Nm).
30. Connect the upper radiator hose to the thermostat housing.
31. Connect or install all previously disconnected hoses, cables and electrical connections. Adjust the throttle cable(s).
32. Replace the O-rings and reconnect the fuel lines.
33. Install the air intake hose. Connect the breather hose, air cleaner case cover and air flow sensor connector.
34. Change the engine oil and oil filter. Reconnect the brake booster and the PCV vacuum hoses.
35. Fill the system with coolant.
36. Connect the negative battery cable, run the vehicle until the thermostat opens, fill the radiator completely.
37. Check and adjust the idle speed and ignition timing.
38. Check all systems for leaks. Allow the engine to cool and recheck the coolant level.

2350cc Engine

1. Relieve fuel system pressure. Disconnect the negative battery cable.

INTAKE SIDE

IDENTIFICATION MARK (G9S)   ⟹ FRONT OF ENGINE

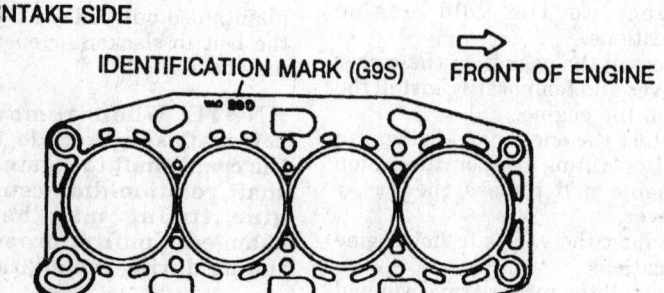

EXHAUST SIDE

Cylinder head gasket identification marks — 1834cc engine

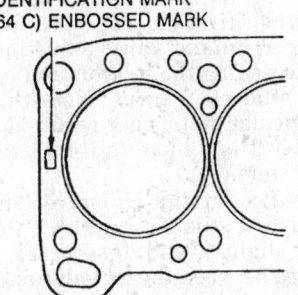

Cylinder head bolt loosening sequence — 2350cc engine

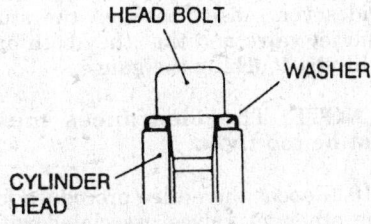

Cylinder head gasket identification marks — 2350cc engine

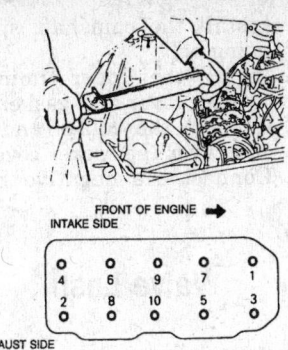

Cylinder head bolt torquing sequence — 2350cc engine

Cylinder head bolt washer installation — 2350cc engine

2. Drain the cooling system.

3. Disconnect the accelerator cable.

4. Remove the radiator.

5. Disconnect the air flow sensor connector and the air intake hose. Remove the air cleaner cover.

6. Disconnect the PCV hose.

7. Disconnect the water hose connection at the throttle body to water inlet pipe.

8. Disconnect the water hose connection at the throttle body to thermostat hose.

9. Wrap the connection with a shop towel and disconnect the high pressure fuel line at the fuel rail.

10. Disconnect the fuel return hose and remove the O-ring.

11. Disconnect the accelerator cables connection at the throttle body.

12. Disconnect the spark plug cables from the spark plugs.

13. Disconnect the electrical connectors from the oxygen sensor, water temperature gauge unit, engine coolant temperature sensor, TPS, power transistor connector, fuel injectors, ignition coil, distributor, and air conditioner compressor. Label prior to disconnecting to assure correct relocation on assembly.

14. Remove the bolt retaining the power steering hose and air conditioner hose clamp.

15. Remove the coolant reservoir. Remove the bolt holding the ground wire to the manifold.

16. Place a jack and wood block under the oil pan and carefully lift just enough to take the weight off the engine mounting bracket. Then remove the engine mounting bracket taking note of the position of the mount stopper.

17. Remove the valve cover, gasket and half-round seal.

18. Remove the timing belt front upper cover.

19. If possible, rotate the crankshaft clockwise until the timing marks on the cam sprocket and belt align. Matchmark the timing sprocket to the belt. Remove the sprocket bolt and remove the sprocket with the timing belt attached. Attach a flexible cord to the hood and suspend the sprocket so it cannot turn and there is no slack in the belt. Remove the timing belt rear upper cover.

20. Loosen the head bolts in the correct sequence in 2 or 3 steps. Remove the cylinder head bolts and head assembly from the block.

To install:

21. Thoroughly clean and dry the mating surfaces of the head and block. Check the cylinder head for cracks, damage or engine coolant leakage. Remove scale, sealing compound and carbon. Clean oil passages thoroughly. Check the head for flatness. End to end, the head should be within 0.002 in. (0.051mm) normally with 0.008 in. (0.200mm) the maximum allowed out of true. The total thickness allowed to be removed from the head and block is 0.008 in. (0.200mm) maximum.

22. Place a new head gasket on the cylinder block with the identification marks at the top (upward) position. Make sure the gasket has the proper identification mark for the engine. Do not use sealer on the gasket. Replace the turbo gasket and ring, if equipped.

23. Carefully install the cylinder head on the block. Install the cylinder head bolts and washer torquing in 3 even progressions to 76-83 ft. lbs. (105-115 Nm). This torque applies to a cold engine.

NOTE: Install the head bolt washer so the sagging side made by tapping out the washer is facing upward.

24. Install the camshaft sprocket and tighten bolt to 65 ft. lbs. (90 Nm), while holding the sprocket in place using the appropriate wrench. Confirm proper timing mark alignment.

25. Apply sealer to the perimeter of the half-round seal and to the lower edges of the half-round portions of the belt-side of the new gasket. Install the valve cover.

26. Install the engine mount positioning the stopper in the same direction as it was prior to removal.

27. Install the power steering and air conditioning compressor hose clamp in position and secure with the retainer bolt. Tighten the bolt to 9 ft. lbs. (12 Nm).

28. Install the coolant reservoir tank.

29. Reconnect all electrical harness connectors disconnect during disassembly. Connect the ground wire to the manifold.

30. Connect the accelerator cables and the spark plug cables.

31. Replace the O-rings and reconnect the fuel lines.

32. Reconnect the water hoses to throttle body, thermostat and the heater assembly.

33. Install the air intake case cover, air flow sensor connector and the radiator.

34. Fill the system with coolant. Adjust the accelerator cable.

35. Firmly set the parking brake. Start the engine and allow to idle until the thermostat opens, add coolant as required to fill system to the appropriate level.

36. Check all systems for leaks. Allow the engine to cool and recheck the coolant level.

Automatic Valve Lash Adjusters

REMOVAL AND INSTALLATION

1997cc, 2350cc Engines

1. Disconnect the negative battery cable.

2. Disconnect the cables and hoses that route over the rocker cover.

3. Remove the upper timing belt cover, rocker cover and gasket.

4. Remove the camshaft sprocket and timing belt. Secure with a piece of wire.

5. Before removing the rocker arm shaft assembly, use the special lash adjuster retaining tool MD998443 or equivalent, so the adjuster does not fall out. Remove the rocker arm shafts by loosening the bolts gradually from the center and moving outward.

6. Remove the lash adjuster. Mark each adjuster to ensure proper installation.

To install:

7. Insert the adjuster and retaining tool MD998443 or equivalent.

8. Install the rocker arm shaft and torque the large bolts to 14-15 ft. lbs. (19-21 Nm) and the small bolts to 15-19 ft. lbs. (20-27 Nm).

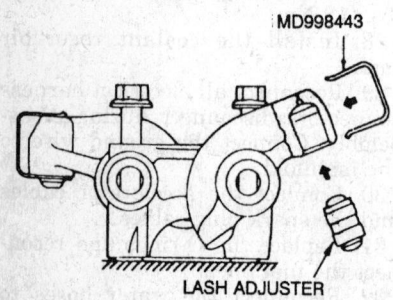

Automatic valve lash adjuster — 1997cc, 2350cc engines

9. Install the camshaft sprocket and timing belt.

10. Install the upper timing belt cover, rocker cover and gasket.

11. Connect the cables and hoses that route over the rocker cover.

12. Connect the negative battery cable.

Valve Lash

ADJUSTMENT

Except 2350cc Engine

Valve lash must be adjusted on all engines not equipped with automatic lash adjusters. Some engines have a third valve of very small size called a jet valve. The jet valve must be adjusted, whether the engine uses automatic lash adjusters for the normal intake and exhaust valves or not. Thus, on some engines, there are 3 valves per cylinder that must be adjusted.

1. Run the engine until operating temperature is reached.

2. Turn OFF the engine and block the wheels.

3. Remove all necessary components in order to gain access to the rocker cover.

4. Remove the spark plugs from the cylinder head for easy operations.

   a. On some engines it may be necessary to remove the air intake pipe.

   b. On some engines it may be necessary to disconnect the oxygen sensor connecting joint. Remove the engine bracket mounting, be sure to place a block of wood on the oil pan and jack it up into to place for the duration of the operation. Remove the upper front timing belt cover, remove the air cleaner assembly on the 1997cc engine or the air intake pipe on the 1755cc engine and remove the rocker cover.

   c. On all other vehicles, remove the air cleaner or air intake pipe assembly and remove the rocker cover.

5. Turn each cylinder head bolt, in sequence, back just until it is loose. Torque the cylinder head bolts in the proper sequence to specification.

6. Position the engine crankshaft at TDC with No. 1 cylinder at the firing position. Turn the engine by using a wrench on the bolt in the front of the crankshaft until the **0** degree timing mark on the timing cover lines up with the notch in the front pulley. On some engines, it may be

necessary to turn the crankshaft clockwise until the notch on the pulley is lined up with the **T** mark on the timing belt lower cover.

7. Observe the valve rockers for No. 1 cylinder. If both are in identical positions with the valves up, the engine is in the right position. If not, rotate the engine exactly 360 degrees until the **0** degree timing mark is again aligned. Each jet valve is associated with an intake valve that is on the same rocker lever. In this position, adjust all the valves marked **A**, including associated jet valves which are located on the rockers, on the intake side only.

8. To adjust the appropriate jet valves, first loosen the regular (larger) intake valve adjusting stud by loosening the locknut and backing the stud off 2 turns. Note that this particular step is not required on engines that have automatic lash adjusters.

9. Loosen the jet valve (smaller) adjusting stud locknut, back the stud out slightly and insert the feeler gauge between the jet valve and stud. Make sure the gauge lies flat on the top of the jet valve. Be careful not to twist the gauge or otherwise depress the jet valve spring, rotate the jet valve adjusting stud back in until it just touches the gauge. Tighten the locknut. Make sure the gauge still slides very easily between the stud and jet valve and that they both are still just touching the gauge.

NOTE: The clearances must not be too tight.

10. Repeat the entire procedure for the other jet valves associated with rockers labeled **A** (Dark Arrow).

11. On engines without automatic lash adjusters, repeat the procedure for the intake valves labeled **A** (Dark Arrow).

12. Repeat the basic adjustment procedure for exhaust valves labeled **A** on engines without automatic lash adjusters.

13. Turn the engine exactly 360 degrees, until the timing marks are again aligned at **0** degrees BTDC.

14. On engines with automatic lash adjusters, after the jet valves and rockers on the intake side and labeled **B** (Light Arrow) are adjusted, the valve adjustment procedure is completed. On engines without automatic lash adjusters, adjust the regular intake and exhaust valves labeled **B** (Light Arrow).

15. Reinstall the cam cover. Run the engine to check for oil leaks.

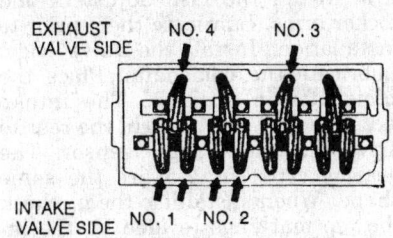

"A" and "B" valve adjusting sequence

Valve lash adjustment — 1468cc 12 valve engine

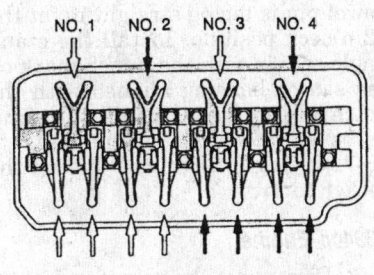

Valve clearance adjustment — all engines

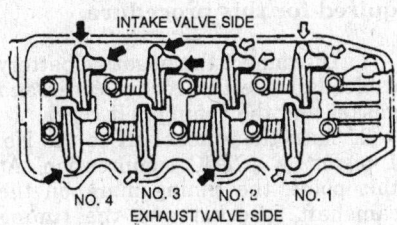

Valve lash adjustment — 2350cc engine

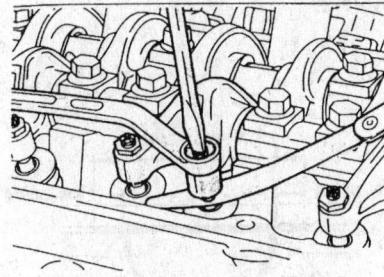

○: When No. 1 piston is at TDC on compression stroke

●: When No. 4 piston is at TDC on compression stroke

Jet valve adjusting

2393cc Engine

NOTE: Incorrect valve clearances will cause unsteady engine operation, excessive noise and reduced engine output. Check the valve clearances and adjust as required while the engine is hot.

1. Adjust the valves with the engine cold. Disconnect the negative battery cable.

2. Remove all spark plugs so engine can be easily turned by hand.

3. Remove the valve cover.

4. Turn the crankshaft clockwise until the notch on the pulley is aligned with the **T** mark on the timing belt lower cover. This brings both No. 1 and No. 4 cylinder pistons to Top Dead Center (TDC).

5. Wiggle the rocker arms on No. 1 and No. 4 cylinders up and down to determine which cylinder is at TDC on the compression stroke. Both rocker arms should move if the piston in that cylinder is at TDC on the compression stroke.

6. Measure the valve clearance with a feeler gauge. When the No. 1 piston is at TDC on the compression

stroke, check No. 1 intake and exhaust, No. 2 intake and No. 3 exhaust. Then turn the crankshaft clockwise 1 turn to bring No. 4 to TDC on its compression stroke. With No. 4 on TDC, compression stroke, check No. 2 exhaust, No. 3 intake and No. 4 intake and exhaust.

7. Valve lash specifications for 2350cc engine: Intake-0.0035 in. (0.09mm) cold: Exhaust-0.0079 in. (0.20mm) cold.

8. If the valve clearances are out of specification, loosen the rocker arm locknut and adjust the clearance using a feeler gauge while turning the adjusting screw. Be sure to hold the screw to prevent it from turning when tightening the locknut.

9. After adjusting the valves, install the valve cover and spark plugs, and connect the negative battery cable.

Rocker Arms/Shafts

REMOVAL AND INSTALLATION

1468cc and 1755cc Engines

1. Disconnect the negative battery cable. Remove the rocker cover. Matchmark the camshaft/rocker arm bearing caps to their cylinder head location, except 1468cc engine.

2. Loosen the bearing cap bolts or the rocker shaft bolts on 1468cc engine, from the cylinder head but do not remove them from the caps or shafts. Lift the rocker assembly from the cylinder head as a unit.

3. The rocker arm assembly can be disassembled by the removal of the mounting bolts and dowel pins on some vehicles, from the bearing caps and/or shafts.

NOTE: Keep the rocker arms and springs in the same order as disassembly. The left and right springs have different tension ratings and free length. Observe the location of the rocker arms as they are removed. Exhaust and intake, right and left, are different.

1595cc DOHC Engine

1. Remove the rocker cover, timing cover and cylinder head from the vehicle. Remove the crank angle sensor.

2. Remove both camshaft drive sprockets.

3. Remove both rear (opposite end of the drive sprockets) camshaft bearing caps.

4. Remove both front bearing caps and front oil seals.

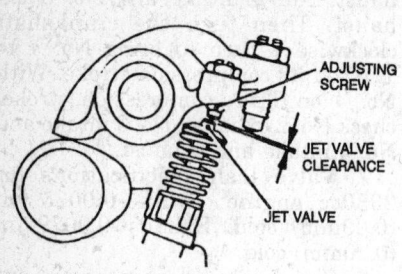

Valve adjustment sequence — typical

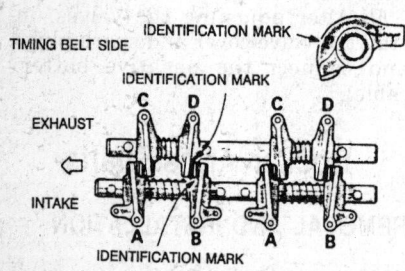

Rocker arm shaft assembly — 1468cc engine

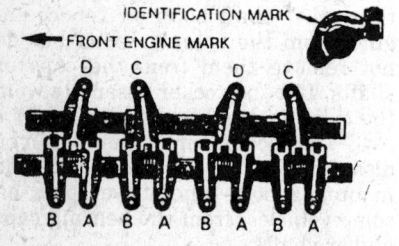

Rocker arm assembly — 1468cc 12 valve engine

5. Remove the remaining camshaft bearing caps alternating from the rear of the head to the front.

6. Remove the camshafts.

7. Remove the rocker arms and the lash adjusters. Remove the valve body assembly from the rear of the cylinder head.

8. Clean and inspect all parts. Check the rollers on the end of the rocker arms. If the rollers are worn or do not rotate smoothly, replace, as necessary.

To install:

9. Install the lash adjusters and rocker arms. Lubricate them prior to installation. Install the valve body. Lubricate the camshafts. Place the camshafts in position. The intake side camshaft has a slit in the rear to drive the crank angle sensor. The bearing caps No. 2-5 are the same shape. When installing them, check the top markings to identify the intake or exhaust side. **L** or **R** is marked on the front caps, **L** for the intake side; **R** for the exhaust side.

10. Tighten the bearing caps, in 2-3 steps, to 14-15 ft. lbs. (20-22 Nm).

11. Make sure the rocker arm is properly mounted on the lash adjuster and valve stem tip.

12. Install the front oil seals. Turn the intake camshaft until the front dowel pin is facing straight up at the 12 o'clock position. Install the crank angle sensor with the punch mark on the sensor housing aligned with the notch in the plate. Install the drive sprocket and tighten the bolts to 58-72 ft. lbs. (79-98 Nm). Install the rocker cover.

1834cc Engine

1. Disconnect the negative battery cable.

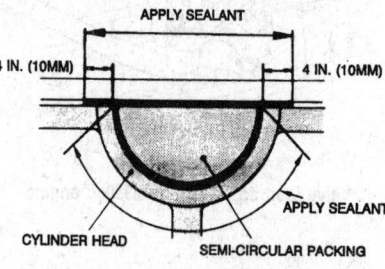

Half moon seal installation

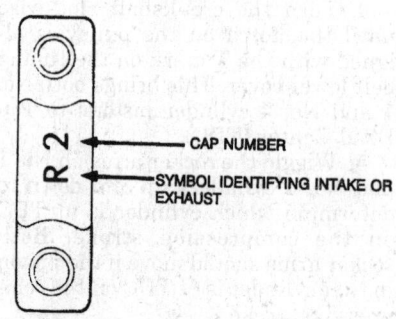

1595cc DOHC camshaft bearing cap identification

2. Remove the valve cover and discard the gasket.

3. Remove the rocker shaft holddown bolts gradually and evenly and remove the rocker shaft/arm assemblies.

4. If disassembly is required, keep all parts in the exact order of removal. Inspect the roller surfaces of the rockers. Replace if there are any signs of damage or if the roller does not turn smoothly. Check the inside bore of the rockers and the adjuster tip for wear.

To install:

5. Lubricate the rocker shaft with clean engine oil and install the rockers and springs in their proper places.

6. Install the rocker shaft assemblies on the engine and tighten the bolts gradually and evenly. Torque the rocker shaft bolts to 23 ft. lbs. (32 Nm).

7. Install the valve cover with a new gasket.

8. Connect the negative battery cable.

1997cc, 2350cc Engines with Automatic Lash Adjusters

NOTE: A special tool, MD998443 or equivalent, is required for this procedure.

1. Disconnect the negative battery cable. Remove the rocker cover and gasket and the timing belt cover.

2. Turn the crankshaft so the No. 1 piston is a TDC compression. At this point, the timing mark on the camshaft sprocket and the timing mark on the head to the left of the sprocket will be aligned.

3. Remove the camshaft bearing cap bolts.

4. Install the automatic lash adjuster retainer tool MD998443 or equivalent, to keep the adjuster from falling out of the rocker arms.

5. Lift off the bearing caps and rocker arm assemblies.

6. The rocker arms may now be removed from the shaft.

NOTE: Keep all parts in the order in which they were removed. None of the parts are interchangeable. The lash adjusters are filled with diesel fuel, which will spill out if they are inverted. If any diesel fuel is spilled, the adjusters must be bled.

7. Check all parts for wear or damage. Replace any damaged or excessively worn parts.

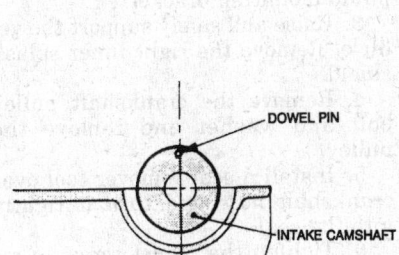

1595cc DOHC camshaft bearing cap installation torque sequence

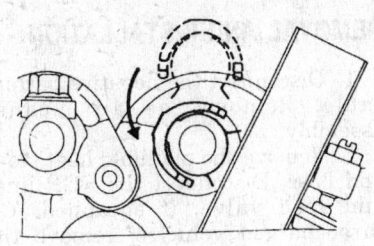

Rocker shaft spring location — 1834cc engine

move the arm up and down. Looseness should be felt. Full plunger stroke should be 0.0866 in. (2.2mm). If not, remove, clean and bleed the lash adjuster.

Intake Manifold

REMOVAL AND INSTALLATION

1. Disconnect the negative battery cable. Drain the cooling system. Disconnect the air intake hose, accelerator cable and the throttle body stay.

2. Disconnect the water bypass hose and the vacuum hose to the power brake booster.

3. Relieve the fuel system pressure.

4. Disconnect the fuel high pressure and return lines and their mounting O-rings.

5. Disconnect interfering vacuum hose, plug wires and wiring harness connections.

6. Disconnect the oxygen sensor, idle speed control, injector connector, ignition coil and power transistor connectors.

7. Disconnect the crank angle sensor, if equipped, the throttle position sensor and the control harness connectors.

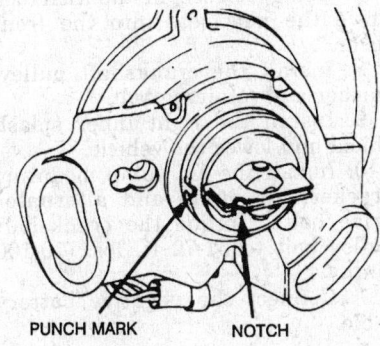

1595cc DOHC intake camshaft dowel pin position

special holding tool. If any of the diesel fuel is spilled, the adjuster must be bled.

14. Tighten the bearing cap bolts, working from the center towards the ends to 15 ft. lbs. (20 Nm).

15. Check the operation of each lash adjuster by positioning the camshaft so the rocker arm bears on the low or round portion of the cam pointed part of the can faces straight down. Insert a thin steel wire, or tool MD998442 or equivalent, in the hole in the top of the rocker arm, over the lash adjuster and depress the check ball at the top of the adjuster. While holding the check ball depressed,

1595cc DOHC crank angle sensor installation alignment

To install:

8. Assemble all parts in reverse order of the removal procedures. Note the following:

9. The rocker shafts are installed with the notches in the ends facing up.

10. The left rocker shaft is longer than the right.

11. The wave washers are installed on the left shaft.

12. Coat all parts with clean engine oil prior to assembly.

13. Insert the lash adjuster from under the rocker arm and install the

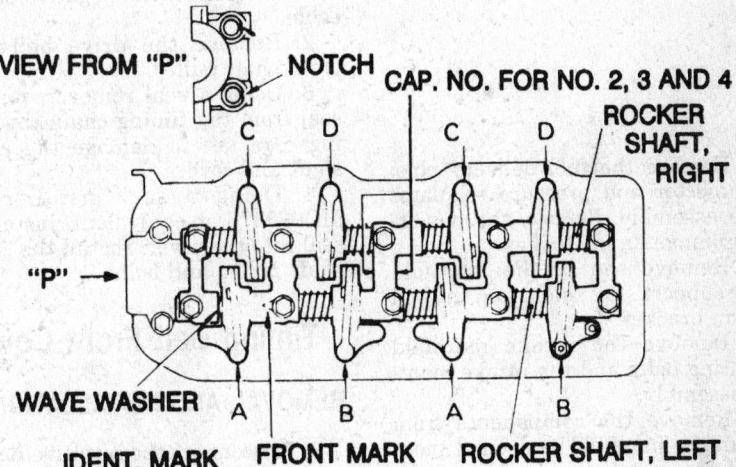

Rocker arm application

	Ident. mark	In.	Ex.
No. 1 & 3 cyl.	1–3	A	C
No. 2 & 4 cyl.	2–4	B	D

1997cc and 2350cc engines rocker arm shaft assembly

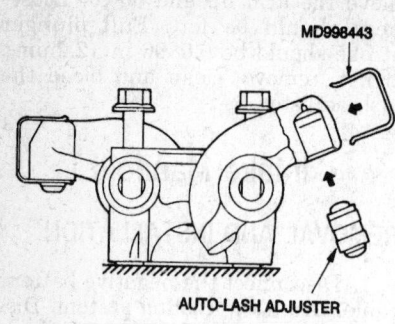

Automatic lash adjuster installation

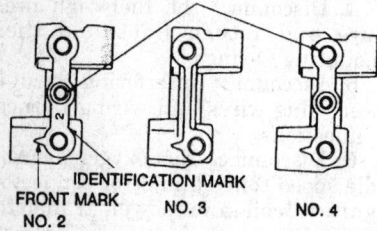

Camshaft bearing cap — 2350cc engine

8. Remove the fuel delivery pipe, fuel injector and pressure regulator as an assembly. Remove the mounting grommets and O-rings.

9. Remove the intake manifold lower support stay shield and the end tension bracket.

10. Remove the intake manifold mounting bolts and the intake manifold assembly.

11. Remove the components from the intake manifold and on 2 piece manifolds, separate the upper and lower halves.

To install:

12. Clean all gasket mounting surfaces.

13. Install all components and the intake manifold in reverse order of removal. Torque values follow: manifold to head bolts 11-14 ft. lbs. (15-20 Nm); upper to lower manifold 11-14 ft. lbs. (15-20 Nm); fuel delivery manifold 7-9 ft. lbs. (10-12 Nm); throttle body 11-16 ft. lbs. (14-21 Nm) on DOHC, 1997cc and 2393cc; 7-9 ft. lbs. (10-12 Nm) on 1468cc.

Exhaust Manifold

REMOVAL AND INSTALLATION

1. Disconnect the negative battery cable. Remove the air cleaner assembly.

2. Remove the manifold heat stove and hose. Disconnect the EGR lines and reed valve, if equipped. On turbocharged vehicles, remove the turbocharger.

3. Disconnect the exhaust pipe bracket from the engine block.

4. Remove the exhaust pipe flange bolts, 1 bolt and nut may have to be removed from under the vehicle.

5. Remove the manifold flange stud nuts and remove the manifold from the cylinder head.

To install:

6. Clean the gasket mating surfaces. Port liner gaskets may be used along with the exhaust manifold gaskets on some engine models. Torque the manifold to 11-14 ft. lbs. (15-20 Nm). Torque the pipe-to-manifold nuts to 15-20 ft. lbs. (20-27 Nm).

Front Cover Oil Seal

REMOVAL AND INSTALLATION

1. Disconnect the negative battery cable.

2. Remove the drive belts and crankshaft pulley.

3. Using a seal remover, pull the seal from the timing chain cover using care not to damage the crankshaft and cover.

4. Using a seal installer tool MD998376 or equivalent, install the seal into the cover. Install the crankshaft pulley and belts.

Timing Belt Front Cover

REMOVAL AND INSTALLATION

1. Disconnect the negative battery cable. Remove the all accessory drive belts.

2. Unbolt and remove the water pump drive pulley. Remove the bolt from the crankshaft pulley. Using a suitable puller, remove the crankshaft pulley.

3. Place a jack and piece of wood under the oil pan to support the engine. Remove the upper engine mount and bracket.

4. Remove the bolts from the upper and lower covers and remove them. Remove the upper cover first. In some cases, the timing belt side of

the engine may have to be raised to gain access to the timing covers.

5. Installation is the reverse order the removal procedures. If gaskets are damaged, replace with new. Torque the alternator bolts to 10-15 ft. lbs. (14-20 Nm) and the timing cover bolts to 7-9 ft. lbs. (10-12 Nm).

OIL SEAL REPLACEMENT

1. Disconnect the negative battery cable.

2. Remove the air pump and alternator drive belts. Remove the air pump mounting bracket.

3. Raise and safely support the vehicle. Remove the right inner splash shield.

4. Remove the crankshaft pulley bolt and washer and remove the pulley.

5. Install a seal remover tool over crankshaft nose and turn it tightly into the seal.

6. Tighten the thrust screw to remove the seal.

NOTE: If the front cover is removed from the engine, tap the side of the thrust screw to remove the seal.

To install:

7. Using a oil seal installation tool, drive the new seal into the front cover.

8. Install the crankshaft pulley, washer and retaining bolt.

9. Install the right inner splash shield and lower the vehicle.

10. Install the air pump mounting bracket, air pump and alternator drive belts. Torque the crankshaft pulley bolt to 51-72 ft. lbs. (70-100 Nm).

11. Connect the negative battery cable.

Timing Belt and Tensioner

ADJUSTMENT

1468cc Engine

1. Bring the engine to No. 1 piston at TDC timing marks aligned. Disconnect the negative battery cable.

2. Remove the drive belts, water pump pulley, spacer and timing belt cover.

3. Loosen the tensioner from it's temporary position so the spring pressure will allow it to contact the timing belt.

4. Rotate the crankshaft 2 complete turns in the normal rotation direction to remove any belt slack. Turn the crankshaft until the timing

marks are lined up. If the timing has slipped, remove the belt and repeat the procedure.

5. Tighten the tensioner mounting bolts, slotted side (right) first, then the spring side.

6. Once again rotate the engine 2 complete revolutions until the timing marks align. Recheck the belt tension.

NOTE: When the tension side of the timing belt and the tensioner are pushed in horizontally with a moderate force, about 11 lbs. (15 N). and the cogged side of the belt covers about ¼ in. (6.35mm) of the tensioner right side mounting bolt head, the across flats, the tension is correct.

7. Reinstall the timing belt cover, the water pump pulley, spacer, fan blades and drive belt.

8. Connect the negative battery cable.

1595cc DOHC Engine

1. Bring the engine to No. 1 piston at TDC timing marks aligned. Disconnect the negative battery cable.

2. Raise the vehicle and support it safely. Remove the under engine splash shield.

3. Place a piece of wood on a suitable floor jack and support the engine. Remove the engine mount bracket.

4. Remove the alternator and power steering drive belts. Remove the air conditioner drive belt and tensioner assembly.

5. Remove the water pump pulley and the crankshaft pulley.

6. Remove the upper and lower timing belt covers.

7. Lift up the tensioner pulley against the belt and tighten the center bolt to hold it in position.

8. Make sure the timing marks are aligned. Remove the binder clips. Rotate the crankshaft a ¼ turn counterclockwise. Then turn the crankshaft clockwise until the timing marks are aligned.

9. Place special tool MD998752 or equivalent, on a torque wrench. Insert the tool into the place provided on the tension pulley. Loosen the center pulley bolt and apply 2.2 ft. lbs. (3.1 Nm) of pressure against the timing belt with the tension pulley. While holding the required torque, tighten the center bolt. Screw in special tool MD998738 or equivalent, through the left engine support bracket until it contacts the tensioner arm bracket. Turn the tool a little

more to secure the tensioner and remove the locking wire placed into the automatic adjuster when it was reset.

10. Remove the special tool. Rotate the crankshaft 2 complete turns clockwise and allow it to set, for about 15 minutes. Then measure the protrusion of the automatic adjuster. It should be 0.015-0.018 in. (0.380-0.457mm). If the proper amount of protrusion is not present, repeat the tensioning process.

11. Install the upper and lower timing belt covers.

12. Install the crankshaft pulley and water pump pulley.

13. Install the alternator and power steering drive belts. Install the air conditioner drive belt and tensioner assembly.

14. Install the engine mount bracket and lower the engine.

15. Install the under engine splash shield.

16. Connect the negative battery cable.

1755cc Engine

1. Bring the engine to No. 1 piston at TDC, aligned. Disconnect the negative battery cable.

2. Remove the drive belts, water pump pulley, spacer and timing belt cover.

3. Ensure that the sprocket timing marks are aligned, before making the adjustment.

4. Loosen the tensioner mounting bolt and nut and allow the spring tension to move the tensioner against the belt.

NOTE: Make sure the belt comes in complete mesh with the sprocket by lightly pushing the tensioner up by hand toward the mounting nut.

5. Tighten the tensioner mounting nut and bolt.

NOTE: Be sure to tighten the nut before tightening the bolt. Too much tension could result from tightening the bolt first.

6. Recheck all sprocket alignments.

7. Turn the crankshaft through a complete rotation in the normal direction. Do not turn in a reverse direction or shake or push the belt.

8. Loosen the tensioner bolt and nut. Retighten the nut and then the bolt.

9. Reinstall the timing belt covers, the water pump pulley, spacer and drive belts. Connect the negative battery cable.

1834cc and 2350cc Engines

1. Disconnect negative battery cable.

2. Remove the timing belt covers.

3. On 2350cc engine, adjust the silent shaft (inner) belt tension first as follows:

    a. Loosen the idler pulley center bolt so the pulley can be moved.

    b. Move the pulley by hand so the long side of the belt deflects about ¼ in. (6.35mm).

    c. Hold the pulley tightly so the pulley cannot rotate when the bolt is tightened. Tighten the bolt to 15 ft. lbs. (20 Nm) and recheck the deflection amount.

4. To adjust the timing (outer) belt, first loosen the pivot side tensioner bolt and then the slot side bolt. Allow the spring to take up the slack.

5. Check to make sure the timing marks on each sprocket are aligned. Turn the crankshaft in normal direction (clockwise), by 2 teeth of the crankshaft sprocket.

NOTE: The purpose of Step 5 is to apply the proper amount of tension to the tension side of the timing belt, be sure not to turn the crankshaft in the opposite direction (counterclockwise).

6. Tighten the slot side tensioner bolt and then the pivot side bolt. If the pivot side bolt is tightened first, the tensioner could turn with bolt, causing over tension.

7. Lightly clamp the center of the span between the camshaft sprocket and the water pump sprocket on the belt tension side with a thumb and forefinger. Check to be sure the clearance between the reverse surface of the belt and the inside of the undercover seal line is at the standard value.

    a. 1834cc engine — 1.18 in. (30mm).

    b. 2350cc engine — 0.55 in. (14mm).

8. Install the timing belt covers and all related items.

9. Connect the negative battery cable.

1997cc Engine

1. Disconnect the negative battery cable. Remove the water pump drive belt and pulley.

2. Remove the crank adapter and crankshaft pulley.

3. Remove the upper and lower timing belt covers.

4. Check the tensioners for a smooth rate of movement.

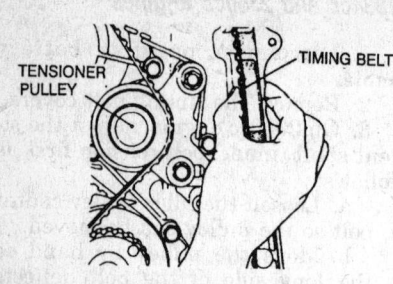

TENSIONER PULLEY

TIMING BELT

Checking the timing belt clearance between the belt and cover. The outside of the belt should be within 0.55 in. (14mm) of the cover

5. Replace any tensioner that shows grease leakage through the seal.

6. Install the silent shaft belt and adjust the tension, by moving the tensioner into contact with the belt, tighten enough to remove all slack. Tighten the tensioner bolt to 21 ft. lbs. (28 Nm).

7. Tighten the silent shaft sprocket bolt to 28 ft. lbs. (38 Nm)

8. Install the upper and lower timing belt covers.

9. Install the crank adapter and crankshaft pulley.

10. Install the water pump drive belt and pulley. Connect the negative battery cable.

REMOVAL AND INSTALLATION

NOTE: The timing chain case is cast aluminum, so exercise caution when handling this part.

1468cc Engine

1. Turn the engine until the No. 1 piston is on TDC with the timing marks aligned.

2. Disconnect the negative battery cable.

1. Condenser tank
2. Clamp section of air conditioner and power steering hose
3. Drive belt (power steering and air conditioner)
4. Drive belt (alternator)
5. Crankshaft bolt
6. Crankshaft pulley

7. Timing belt upper cover
8. Timing belt lower cover
9. Flange
10. Timing belt
11. Timing belt tensioner
12. Tensioner spacer
13. Tensioner spring

10 Nm
7 ft.lbs.

45 Nm
33 ft.lbs.

24 Nm
18 ft.lbs.

185 Nm
134 ft.lbs.

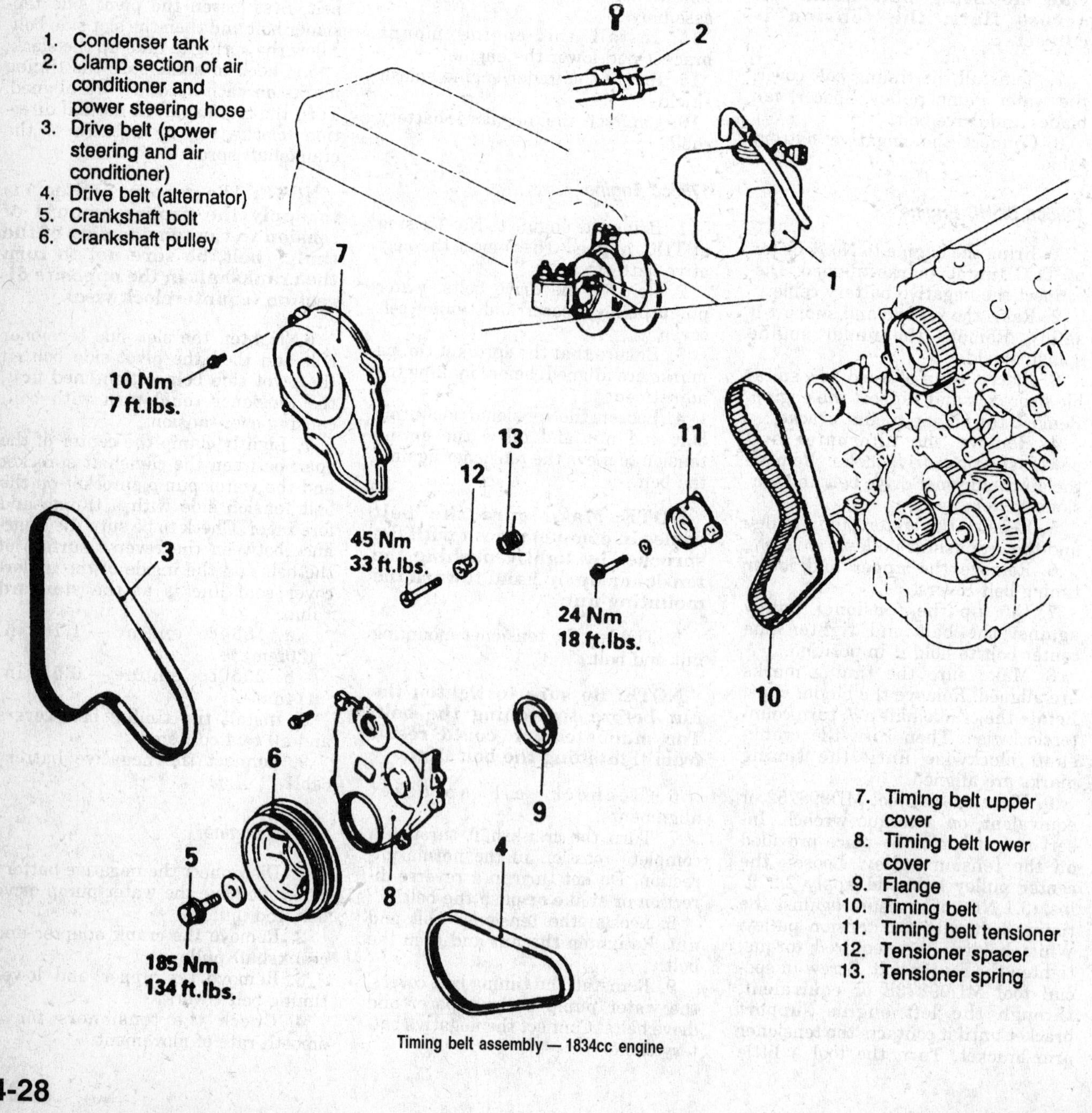

Timing belt assembly — 1834cc engine

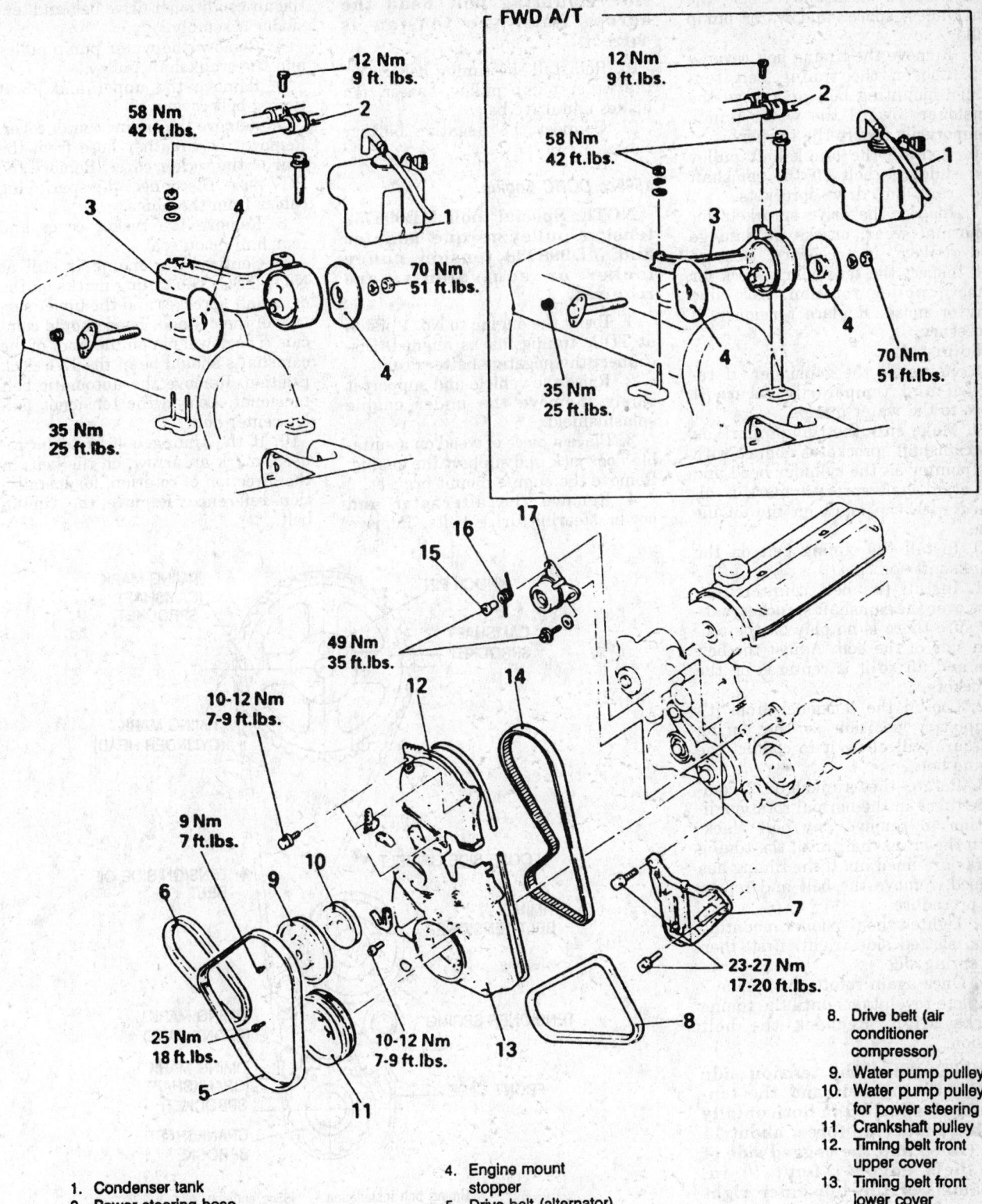

FWD A/T

12 Nm
9 ft. lbs.

58 Nm
42 ft. lbs.

70 Nm
51 ft. lbs.

35 Nm
25 ft. lbs.

12 Nm
9 ft.lbs.

58 Nm
42 ft.lbs.

70 Nm
51 ft.lbs.

35 Nm
25 ft.lbs.

49 Nm
35 ft.lbs.

10-12 Nm
7-9 ft.lbs.

9 Nm
7 ft.lbs.

25 Nm
18 ft.lbs.

10-12 Nm
7-9 ft.lbs.

23-27 Nm
17-20 ft.lbs.

1. Condenser tank
2. Power steering hose and air conditioner hose clamp bolt
3. Engine mount bracket
4. Engine mount stopper
5. Drive belt (alternator)
6. Drive belt (power steering oil pump)
7. Tensioner pulley bracket
8. Drive belt (air conditioner compressor)
9. Water pump pulley
10. Water pump pulley for power steering
11. Crankshaft pulley
12. Timing belt front upper cover
13. Timing belt front lower cover
14. Timing belt
15. Tension spacer
16. Tensioner spring
17. Timing belt tensioner

Timing belt assembly — 2350cc engine

3. Remove the fan drive belt, the fan blades, spacer and water pump pulley.

4. Remove the timing belt cover.

5. Loosen the timing belt tensioner mounting bolt and move the tensioner toward the water pump. Temporarily secure the tensioner.

6. Remove the crankshaft pulley and slide the belt off the camshaft and crankshaft drive sprockets.

7. Inspect the drive sprockets for abnormal wear, cracks or damage and replace, if necessary. Remove and inspect the tensioner. Check for smooth pulley rotation, excessive play or noise. Replace tensioner, if necessary.

To install:

8. Reinstall the tensioner, if removed and temporarily secure it close to the water pump.

9. Make sure the timing mark on the camshaft sprocket is aligned with the pointer on the cylinder head and the crankshaft sprocket mark is aligned with the mark on the engine case.

10. Install the timing belt on the crankshaft sprocket.

11. Install the belt counterclockwise over the camshaft sprocket making sure there is no play on the tension side of the belt. Adjust the belt fore and aft so it is centered on the sprockets.

12. Loosen the tensioner from it's temporary position so the spring pressure will allow it to contact the timing belt.

13. Rotate the crankshaft 2 complete turns in the normal rotation direction to remove ny belt slack. Turn the crankshaft until the timing marks are lined up. If the timing has slipped, remove the belt and repeat the procedure.

14. Tighten the tensioner mounting bolts, slotted side (right) first, then the spring side.

15. Once again rotate the engine 2 complete revolutions until the timing marks align. Recheck the belt tension.

NOTE: When the tension side of the timing belt and the tensioner are pushed in horizontally with a moderate force, about 11 lbs. (15 N) and the cogged side of the belt covers about ¼ in. (6.35mm) of the tensioner right

side mounting bolt head the across flats, the tension is correct.

16. Reinstall the timing belt cover, the water pump pulley, spacer, fan blades and drive belt.

17. Connect the negative battery cable.

1595cc DOHC Engine

NOTE: Special tools MD998752 tension pulley torque adapter and MD998738 tension pulley locker or equivalents, are required.

1. Bring the engine to No. 1 piston at TDC timing marks aligned. Disconnect the negative battery cable.

2. Raise the vehicle and support it safely. Remove the under engine splash shield.

3. Place a piece of wood on a suitable floor jack and support the engine. Remove the engine mount bracket.

4. Remove the alternator and power steering drive belts. Remove

the air conditioner drive belt and tensioner assembly.

5. Remove the water pump pulley and the crankshaft pulley.

6. Remove the upper and lower timing belt covers.

7. Remove the engine center cover. Remove the breather hose from the rear of the rocker cover. Remove the PCV hose. Disconnect the spark plug cables from the plugs.

8. Remove the rocker cover and rear half-moon seal.

9. Confirm the engine is still at No. 1 TDC. The timing marks on the camshaft sprocket and the upper surface of the cylinder head should coincide. The dowel pin on the front of the camshafts should be in the 12 o'clock position. Remove the automatic belt tensioner. Loosen the tensioner pulley center bolt.

10. If the timing belt is to be reused, mark an arrow, on the belt, in the direction of rotation, for installation reference. Remove the timing belt.

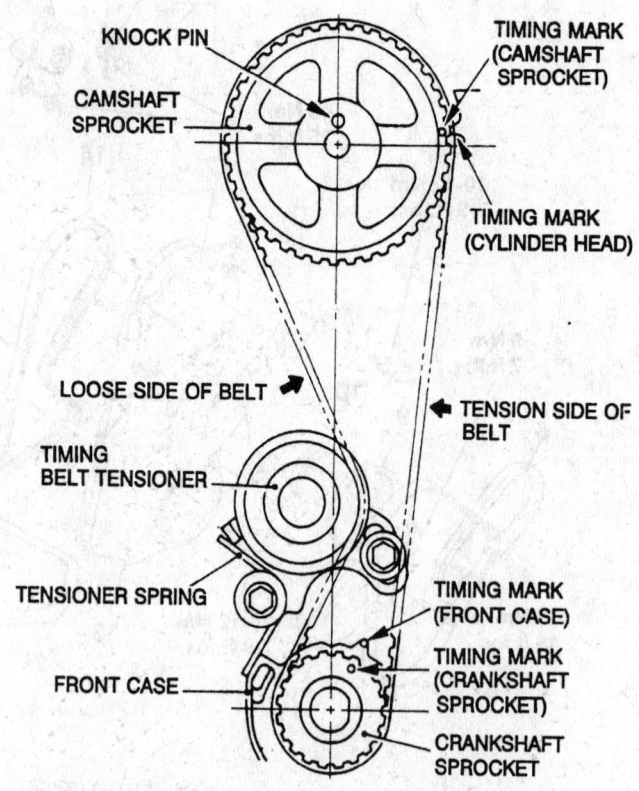

Timing belt installation — 1468cc engines

To install:

11. Install the automatic tensioner, after reset.

NOTE: To reset the tensioner: **Keep the adjuster level and clamp it in a soft jawed vise. Clamp with the extended adjuster on one side and the end mounting a plug on the other side. If the plug extends out of the adjuster body, place a suitable hole sized washer over the plug so the vise jaw pushes on the washer, not the plug. Close the vise slowly, forcing the adjuster back into the body. When the hole in the adjuster boss aligns with the adjuster rod, insert a snug fitting pin or wire into the holes to keep the rod in the compressed position. With the locking pin or wire in place, install the tensioner.**

12. Align the timing marks on the camshaft sprockets. Align the crankshaft timing marks. Align the oil pump timing marks. Place the timing belt around the intake camshaft and secure it to the sprocket with a stationary binder spring clip. Install the timing belt around the exhaust camshaft sprocket, check sprocket marks for alignment and secure the belt with a second binder clip on the exhaust sprocket.

13. Install the timing belt around the idler pulley, oil pump sprocket, crankshaft sprocket and the tensioner pulley.

14. Lift up the tensioner pulley against the belt and tighten the center bolt to hold it in position.

15. Check to see that all of the timing marks are aligned. Remove the binder clips. Rotate the crankshaft ¼ turn counterclockwise. Then turn the crankshaft clockwise until the timing marks are aligned.

16. Place special tool MD998752 or equivalent, on a torque wrench. Insert the tool into the place provided on the tension pulley. Loosen the center pulley bolt and apply 2.2 ft. lbs. (3.0 Nm) of pressure against the timing belt with the tension pulley. While holding the required torque, tighten the center bolt. Screw in special tool MD998738 or equivalent, through the left engine support bracket until it contacts the tensioner arm bracket. Turn the tool a little more to secure the tensioner and remove the locking wire place into the automatic adjuster when it was reset.

17. Remove the special tool. Rotate the crankshaft 2 complete turns clockwise and allow it to sit for about 15 minutes. Then measure the pro-

trusion of the automatic adjuster. It should be 0.015-0.018 in. (0.381-0.457mm). If the proper amount of protrusion is not present, repeat the tensioning process.

1755cc Engine

1. Drain the coolant and remove the radiator on rear wheel drive vehicles only. Disconnect the negative battery cable.

2. Remove the alternator and accessory belts. Remove the belt cover.

3. Rotate the crankshaft to bring No. 1 piston to TDC on the compression stroke. Align the notch on the

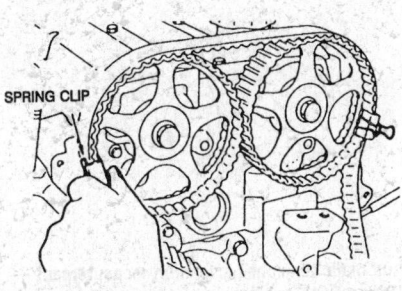

SPRING CLIP

Using binder clips to secure the timing belt

crankshaft pulley with the **T** mark on the timing indicator scale and the timing mark on the upper under cover of the timing belt with the mark on the camshaft sprocket. Mark and remove the distributor.

4. Remove the crankshaft pulley and bolt.

5. Remove the lower splash shield, if necessary.

6. Remove the timing belt covers, upper front and lower front.

7. Remove the crankshaft sprocket bolt.

8. Loosen the tensioner mounting nut and bolt. Move the tensioner away from the belt and retighten the nut to keep the tensioner in the off position. Remove the belt.

9. Remove the camshaft sprocket, crankshaft sprocket, flange and tensioner.

10. The water pump or cylinder head may be removed at this point, depending upon the type of repairs needed.

11. Raise the vehicle and support it safely. Remove any interfering splash pans.

12. Drain the oil pan and remove the pan from the block.

13. Remove the oil pump sprocket and cover.

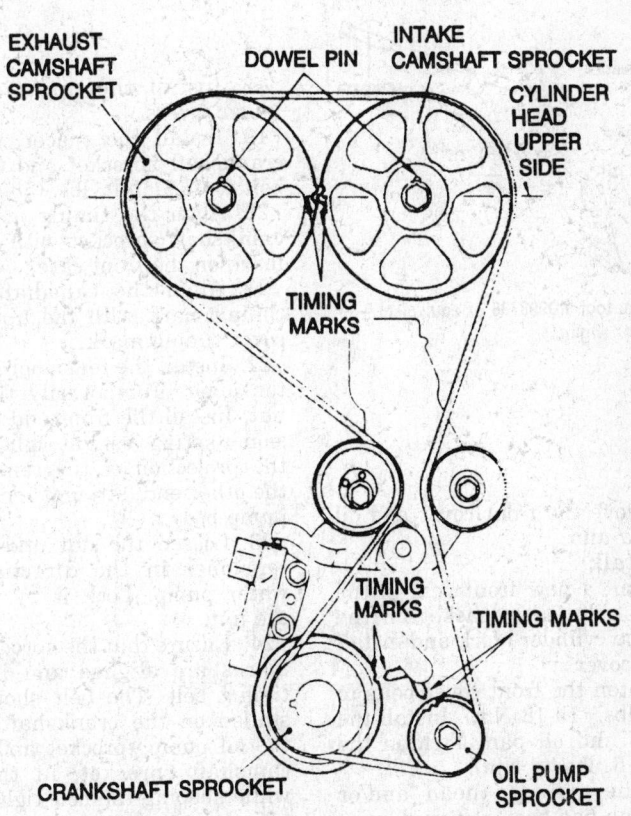

1595cc DOHC timing mark alignment for timing belt installation

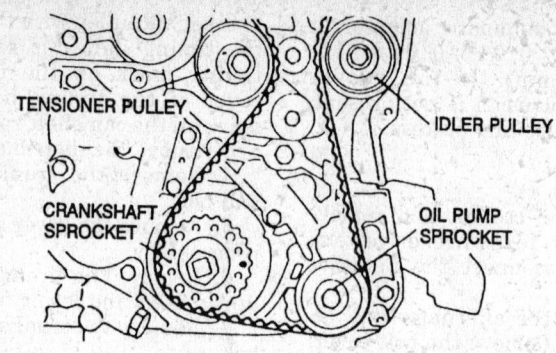

Installing the timing belt around the idler pulley, oil pump sprocket, crankshaft sprocket and tensioner

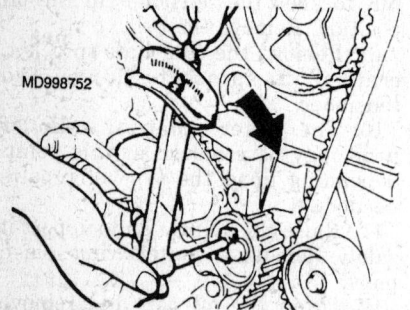

Using special tool MD998752 or equivalent — 1595cc DOHC engine

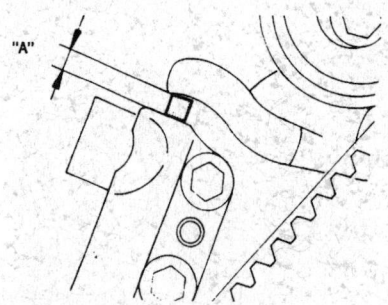

Automatic tensioner extension measurement — 1595cc DOHC engine

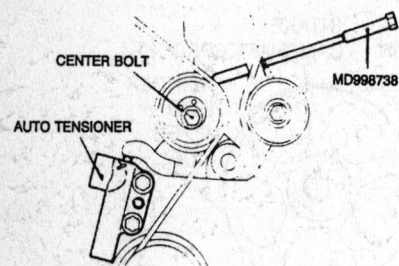

Using special tool MD998738 or equivalent — 1595cc DOHC engine

14. Remove the front cover and oil pump as a unit.

To install:

15. Install a new front seal in the cover. Install a new gasket on the front of the cylinder block and install the front cover.

16. Tighten the front cover bolts to 11-13 ft. lbs. (15-18 Nm). Install the oil screen and oil pan. Tighten the bolts to 5 ft. lbs. (7 Nm).

17. If the cylinder head and/or water pump had been removed, reinstall them, using new gaskets.

18. Install the upper and lower under covers.

19. Install the spacer, flange and crankshaft sprocket and tighten the bolt to 43.5-50 ft. lbs. (58-68 Nm).

20. Align the timing mark on the crankshaft sprocket with the timing mark on the front case.

21. Align the camshaft sprocket timing mark with the upper undercover timing mark.

22. Install the tensioner spring and tensioner. Temporarily tighten the nut. Install the front end of the tensioner spring (bent at right angles) on the projection of the tensioner and the other end (straight) on the water pump body.

23. Loosen the nut and move the tensioner in the direction of the water pump. Lock it by tightening the nut.

24. Ensure that the sprocket timing marks are aligned and install the timing belt. The belt should be installed on the crankshaft sprocket, the oil pump sprocket and then the camshaft sprocket, in that order, while keeping the belt tight.

25. Loosen the tensioner mounting bolt and nut and allow the spring tension to move the tensioner against the belt.

NOTE: Make sure the belt comes in complete mesh with the sprocket by lightly pushing the tensioner up by hand toward the mounting nut.

26. Tighten the tensioner mounting nut and bolt.

NOTE: Be sure to tighten the nut before tightening the bolt. Too much tension could result from tightening the bolt first.

27. Recheck all sprocket alignments.

28. Turn the crankshaft through a complete rotation in the normal direction. Do not turn in a reverse direction or shake or push the belt.

29. Loosen the tensioner bolt and nut. Retighten the nut and then the bolt.

30. Install the lower and upper front outer covers.

31. Install the crankshaft pulley and tighten the bolts to 7.5-8.5 ft. lbs. (10-11 Nm).

32. Install the alternator and belt and adjust. Install the distributor.

33. Install the radiator, fill the cooling system and inspect for leaks.

1834cc Engine

1. Disconnect the negative battery cable. Remove the engine under cover.

2. Raise and safely support the weight of the engine using the appropriate equipment. Remove the front engine mount bracket and accessory drive belts.

3. Remove the coolant reservoir tank.

4. Remove timing belt upper and lower covers.

5. Make a mark on the back of the timing belt indicating the direction of rotation so it may be reassembled in the same direction if it is to be reused. Loosen the timing belt tensioner and remove the timing belt.

NOTE: If coolant or engine oil comes in contact with the timing belt, they will drastically shorten its life. Also, do not allow engine oil or coolant to contact the timing belt sprockets or tensioner assembly.

6. Remove the tensioner spacer, tensioner spring and tensioner assembly.

7. Inspect the timing belt for cracks on back surface, sides, bottom and check for separated canvas.

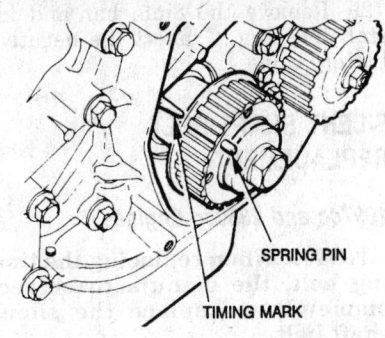

Crankshaft sprocket timing mark alignment — 1755cc engines

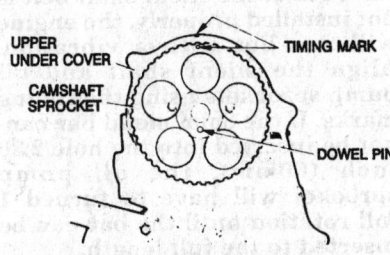

Camshaft sprocket installation alignment — 1755cc engines

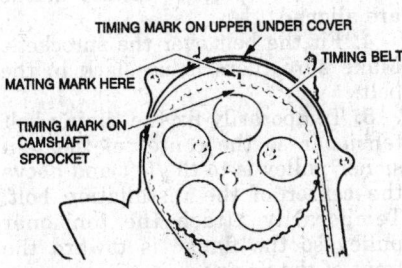

Camshaft timing mark alignment — 1755cc engines

Check the tensioner pulley for smooth rotation.

To install:

8. Position the tensioner, tensioner spring and tensioner spacer on engine block.

9. Align the timing marks on the camshaft sprocket and crankshaft sprocket. This will position No. 1 piston on TDC on the compression stroke.

10. Position the timing belt on the crankshaft sprocket and keeping the tension side of the belt tight, set it on the camshaft sprocket.

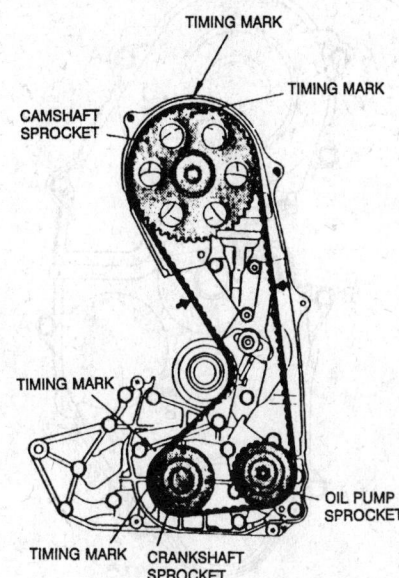

Timing belt installation — 1755cc engine

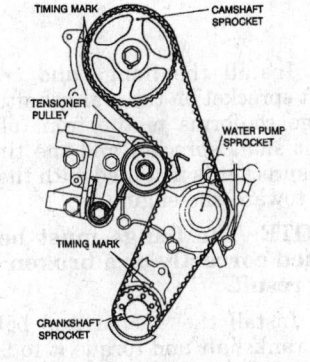

Timing belt alignment marks — 1834cc engine

11. Apply counterclockwise force to the camshaft sprocket to give tension to the belt and make sure all timing marks are aligned.

12. Loosen the pivot side tensioner bolt and the slot side bolt. Allow the spring to take up the slack.

13. Tighten the slot side tensioner bolt and then the pivot side bolt. If the pivot side bolt is tightened first, the tensioner could turn with bolt, causing over tension.

14. Turn the crankshaft clockwise. Loosen the pivot side tensioner bolt and then the slot side bolt to allow the spring to take up any remaining

slack. Tighten the adjuster bolt to 18 ft. lbs. (24 Nm).

15. Check the belt tension by holding the tensioner and timing belt together by hand and give the belt a slight thumb pressure at a point level with tensioner center. Make sure the belt cog crest comes as deep as about ¼ of the width of the slot side tensioner bolt head. Do not manually overtighten the belt or it will howl.

16. Install the timing belt covers and all related items.

17. Connect the negative battery cable.

1997cc and 2350cc Engines

NOTE: An 8mm diameter metal bar is needed for this procedure.

1. Disconnect the negative battery cable. Remove the water pump drive belt and pulley.

2. Remove the crank adapter and crankshaft pulley.

3. Remove the upper and lower timing belt covers.

4. Move the tensioner fully in the direction of the water pump and temporarily secure it there.

5. If the timing belt is to be reused, make a paint mark on the belt to indicate the direction of rotation. Slip the belt from the sprockets.

6. Remove the camshaft sprocket bolt and pull the sprocket from the camshaft.

7. Remove the crankshaft sprocket bolt and pull the crankshaft sprocket and flange from the crankshaft.

8. Remove the plug on the left side of the block and insert an 8mm diameter metal bar in the opening to keep the silent shaft in position.

9. Remove the oil pump sprocket retaining nut and remove the oil pump sprocket.

10. Loosen the right silent shaft sprocket mounting bolt until it can be turned by hand.

11. Remove the belt tensioner and remove the timing belt.

NOTE: Do not attempt to turn the silent shaft sprocket or loosen its bolt while the belt is off.

12. Remove the silent shaft belt sprocket from the crankshaft.

13. Check the belt for wear, damage or glossing. Replace it if any cracks, damage, brittleness or excessive wear are found.

14. Check the tensioners for a smooth rate of movement.

15. Replace any tensioner that shows grease leakage through the seal.

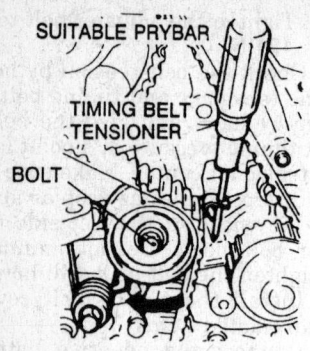

Set a prybar into the tensioner, press and lock in the direction of arrow — 1834cc engine

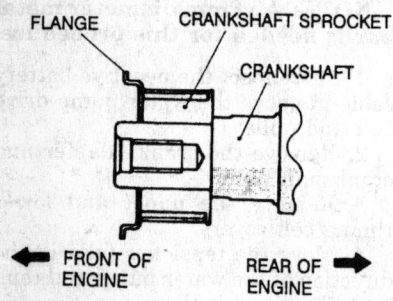

Crankshaft flange installation — 1834cc engine

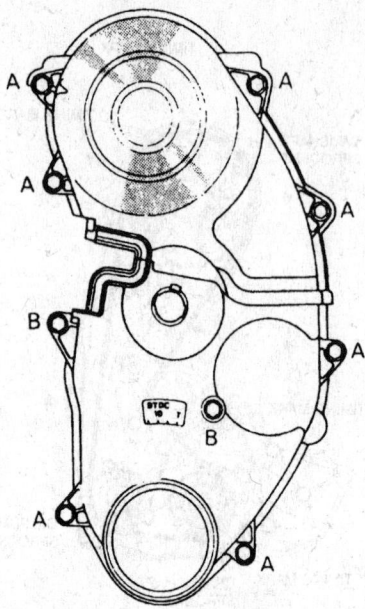

Timing belt cover bolts. Do not interchange — 1834cc engine

To install:

16. Install the silent shaft belt sprocket on the crankshaft, with the flat face toward the engine.

17. Apply light engine oil on the outer face of the spacer and install the spacer on the right silent shaft. The side with the rounded shoulder faces the engine.

18. Install the sprocket on the right silent shaft and install the bolt but do not tighten completely at this time.

NOTE: Align the silent shaft and oil pump sprockets using the timing marks. If the 8mm metal bar cannot be inserted into the hole 2.36 in. (60mm), the oil pump sprocket will have to be turned 1 full rotation until the bar can be inserted to the full length. If this procedure is not followed, the engine will run but vibrate at high engine rpm.

19. Install the silent shaft belt and adjust the tension, by moving the tensioner into contact with the belt, tight enough to remove all slack. Tighten the tensioner bolt to 21 ft. lbs. (28 Nm).

20. Tighten the silent shaft sprocket bolt to 28 ft. lbs. (38 Nm).

21. Install the flange and crankshaft sprocket on the crankshaft. The flange conforms to the front of the silent shaft sprocket and the timing belt sprocket is installed with the flat face toward the engine.

NOTE: The flange must be installed correctly or a broken belt will result.

22. Install the washer and bolt in the crankshaft and torque it to 94 ft. lbs. (127 Nm).

23. Install the camshaft sprocket and bolt and torque the bolt to 72 ft. lbs. (98 Nm).

24. Install the timing belt tensioner, spacer and spring.

25. Align the timing mark on each sprocket with the corresponding mark on the front case.

26. Install the timing belt on the sprockets and move the tensioner against the belt with sufficient force to allow a deflection of 5-7mm along its longest straight run.

27. Tighten the tensioner bolt to 21 ft. lbs. (28 Nm).

28. Install the upper and lower covers, the crankshaft pulley and the crank adapter. Tighten the bolts to 21 ft. lbs. (28 Nm).

29. Remove the 8mm bar and install the plug. Connect the negative battery cable.

SILENT SHAFT BELT REPLACEMENT

1997cc and 2350cc Engines

NOTE: When replacing the timing belt, the manufacturer recommends to replace the silent shaft belt.

1. After removing the timing belt, mark arrows on the belt to indicate direction of rotation (clockwise).

NOTE: If the silent shaft belt is not installed properly, the engine will run but with a vibration. Align the silent shaft and oil pump sprockets using the timing marks. If the 8mm metal bar cannot be inserted into the hole 2.36 inch (60mm), the oil pump sprocket will have to turned 1 full rotation until the bar can be inserted to the full length.

2. Align the timing marks before removal. Loosen the belt tensioner and remove the belt.

To install:

3. Make sure the crankshaft and silent shaft sprocket timing marks are aligned.

4. Fit the belt over the sprockets. Make sure there is no slack in the belt.

5. Temporarily fix the timing belt tensioner so the center of the tensioner pulley is to the left and above the center of the installation bolt. Temporarily attach the tensioner pulley so the flange is toward the front of the engine.

6. Adjust the belt so the slack between the 2 sprockets is within 0.20-0.28 inch (5-7mm).

Camshaft

REMOVAL AND INSTALLATION

1468cc Engine

1. Disconnect the negative battery cable.

2. Remove the cylinder head. Remove the cylinder head rear cover.

3. Remove the camshaft thrust case tightening bolt, located on top of the rear mounting boss.

4. Carefully slide the camshaft and thrust case, attached to the rear of the cam, out the rear of the cylinder head.

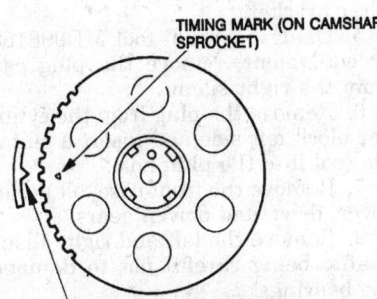

Timing mark alignment — 1997cc and 2350cc engines

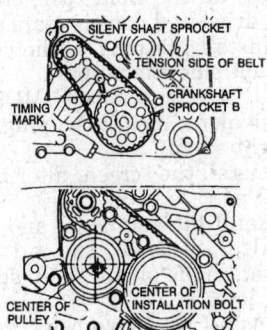

Camshaft timing mark alignment for No. 1 TDC — 1997cc and 2350cc engines

Silent shaft and belt — 1997cc and 2350cc engines

To install:

5. Carefully slide the camshaft and thrust case into the cylinder head from the front.

6. Install a new cylinder head gasket and install the cylinder head and bolts. Torque the cylinder head bolts to 50-54 ft. lbs. (68-73 Nm).

7. Install the cylinder head rear cover.

8. Reinstall the timing belt cover, the water pump pulley, spacer, fan blades and drive belt.

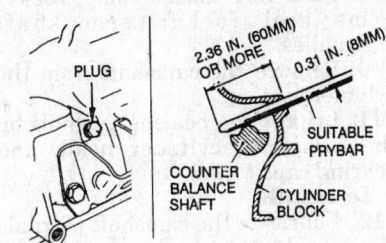

Silent shaft alignment — 1997cc and 2350cc engines

9. Connect the negative battery cable. Start the engine and test engine performance and check for leaks.

1595cc DOHC Engine

1. Disconnect the negative battery cable. Remove the cylinder head.

2. Remove the crank angle sensor. Remove both camshaft drive sprockets.

3. Remove both rear (opposite end of the drive sprockets) camshaft bearing caps.

4. Remove both front bearing caps and front oil seals.

5. Remove the remaining camshaft bearing caps alternating from the rear of the head to the front.

6. Remove the camshafts.

7. Clean and inspect all parts. Check the rollers on the end of the rocker arms. If the rollers are warn on do not rotate smoothly, replace as necessary.

To install:

8. Lubricate the camshafts. Place the camshafts in position. The intake side camshaft has a slit in the rear to drive the crank angle sensor. The bearing caps No. 2-5 are the same shape. When installing them, check the top markings to identify the intake or exhaust side. Left or Right is marked on the front caps, **L** for the intake side; **R** for the exhaust side.

9. Tighten the bearing caps, in 2 or 3 steps, to 14-15 ft. lbs. (20-22 Nm).

10. Make sure the rocker arm is properly mounted on the lash adjuster and valve stem tip.

11. Install the front oil seals. Turn the intake camshaft until the front dowel pin is facing straight up at the 12 o'clock position. Install the crank angle sensor with the punch mark on the sensor housing aligned with the notch in the plate. Install the drive sprocket and tighten the bolts to 58-72 ft. lbs. (79-98 Nm).

1755cc, 1997cc Engines

1. Disconnect the negative battery cable.

2. Remove the rocker cover. Matchmark the rocker arm bearing caps to the cylinder head.

3. Remove the bearing cap bolts from the cylinder head, but do not remove them from the bearing caps and shafts. Lift the rocker arm assembly from the cylinder head.

4. Make sure the timing marks on the camshaft sprocket and head are properly aligned, so No. 1 piston is at TDC of the compression stroke. If the camshaft sprocket is to be removed, do so before removing the camshaft from the head. If not, it will be difficult to remove the sprocket bolt. Prior to removing the bearing caps or belt, remove the camshaft sprocket bolt and lift off the sprocket and belt. Discard the camshaft oil seal.

5. Remove the camshaft from the bearing saddles.

NOTE: On some engines, a distributor drive gear and spacer are used on the front of the camshaft.

6. The valves, valve springs and valve guide seals can now be removed from the cylinder head.

7. Installation is the reverse of removal. Coat all parts with clean engine oil prior to installation. Use a seal driver to install the new oil seal after the camshaft is in place.

NOTE: If the dowel pin hole of the camshaft sprocket will not align with the dowel pin on the camshaft, the shaft can be easily turned by striking the projections on the shaft, just behind No. 2 exhaust valve cam, with a punch. Make sure the crankshaft does not turn. On the 1997cc engine, turn the camshaft until the dowel pin on the shaft end is in the 12 o'clock position. This will ensure correct camshaft sprocket installation.

8. Tighten the sprocket bolt to 50-60 ft. lbs. (68-81 Nm) on the 1997cc engines; 44-55 ft. lbs. (60-75 Nm) on the 1755cc engine. Tighten the rocker cover bolts to 5 ft. lbs. (7 Nm).

1834cc and 2350cc Engines

1. Disconnect the negative battery cable.

2. On 1834cc engine, remove the battery and battery cover. Disconnect the air flow sensor connector and remove the air cleaner case cover.

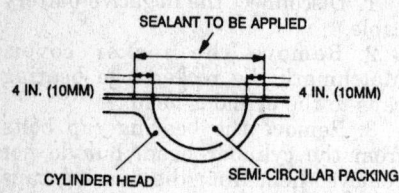

Sealant application on the rocker cover rear seal projection used for turning the shaft in hard-to-turn installations

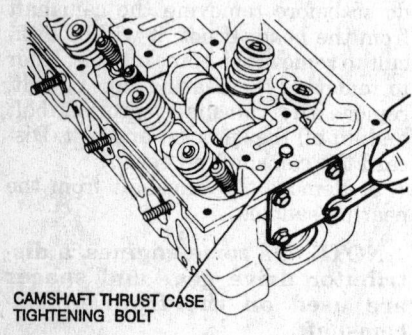

Removing the rear camshaft cover — 1468cc engine

3. Remove the breather hose. Disconnect the PCV hose.

4. Label and disconnect the spark plug cables.

5. On 1834cc engine, remove the distributor assembly.

6. Remove the rocker cover and the timing belt.

7. Remove the camshaft sprocket retainer bolt while holding shaft stationary with appropriate spanner wrench. Remove the sprocket from the shaft.

8. Remove the camshaft oil seal.

9. Install lash adjuster retainers on 2350cc engine. Remove both rocker arm shaft assemblies from the head. Do not disassembly rocker arms and rocker arm shaft assemblies.

10. Remove the camshaft from the cylinder.

11. Inspect the bearing journals on the camshaft, cylinder head, and bearing caps.

To install:

12. Lubricate the camshaft journals and camshaft with clean engine oil and install the camshaft in the cylinder head.

13. Install the rocker arm and shaft assemblies. On 1834cc engine, tighten the rocker arm shaft retainer bolts to 21-25 ft. lbs. (29-35 Nm). On 2350cc engine, tighten the rocker arm, bearing caps and shaft assembly to 14 ft. lbs. (20 Nm).

14. Remove the lash adjuster retainers. Install new camshaft oil seal.

15. Install camshaft sprocket and retainer bolt torqueing to 65 ft. lbs. (90 Nm).

16. Install the timing belt.

17. On 1834cc engine, install the distributor.

18. On 1834cc engine, check the valve lash adjustment using specifications for a cold engine. Install the rocker cover.

19. Connect the spark plug cables.

20. Install the breather hose and connect the PCV hose.

21. Connect the air flow sensor connector and install the air cleaner case cover.

22. On 1834cc engine, install the battery and battery cover.

23. Connect the negative battery cable. Run the engine at idle until normal operating temperature is reached. Check idle speed and ignition timing and adjust as required.

Silent Shafts

REMOVAL AND INSTALLATION

1997cc and 2350cc Engines

1. Disconnect the negative battery cable. Remove the engine from the vehicle.

2. Remove the drive belts, accessories, crankshaft pulley and timing belts.

3. Drain the engine oil and remove the filter. Remove the oil pump sprocket, right silent shaft sprocket and spacer.

4. Remove the oil pan, screen and filter bracket.

5. Using a special tool MD998162 or equivalent, remove the plug cap from the right silent.

6. Remove the plug from the cylinder block left side and insert a suitable tool into the plug hole.

7. Remove the front case, oil pump cover, drive and driven gears.

8. Remove the left and right silent shafts, being careful not to damage the bearings.

To install:

9. Install the left and right silent shafts, being careful not to damage the bearings.

10. Install the front case, oil pump cover, drive and driven gears.

11. Install the plug to the cylinder block left side silent shaft.

12. Using a special tool MD998162 or equivalent, install the plug cap to the right silent.

13. Install the screen, filter bracket and oil pan.

14. Refill the engine oil and install the filter. Install the oil pump sprocket, right silent shaft sprocket and spacer.

15. Install the drive belts, accessories, crankshaft pulley and timing belts.

16. Install the engine into the vehicle. Connect the negative battery cable.

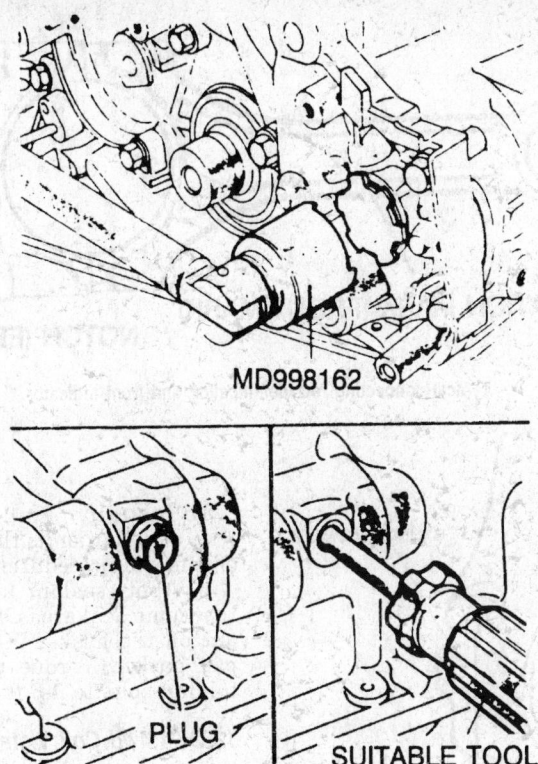

MD998162

PLUG   SUITABLE TOOL

Silent shaft removal — 1997cc engine

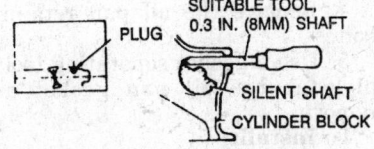

PLUG

SUITABLE TOOL,
0.3 IN. (8MM) SHAFT

SILENT SHAFT

CYLINDER BLOCK

Keeping the left silent shaft in position. The
tool must go into the hole at least 2.36 in.
(60mm). If not, the silent shaft will be out of
time and the engine will vibrate. Rotate the oil
pump sprocket 1 full revolution and insert
tool — 1997cc engine

Piston and Connecting Rod

POSITIONING

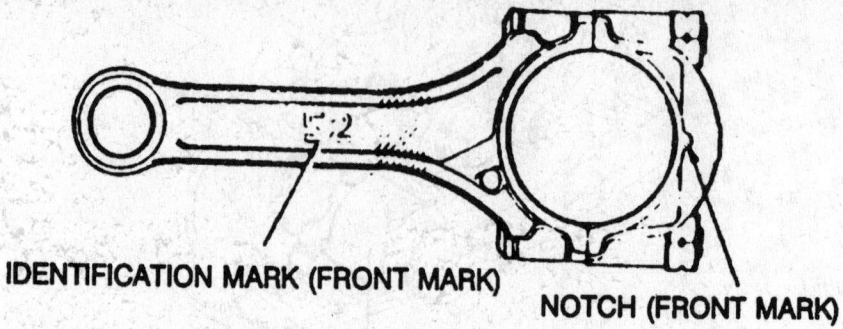

IDENTIFICATION MARK (FRONT MARK)   **NOTCH (FRONT MARK)**

Typical connecting rod identification and front indicator

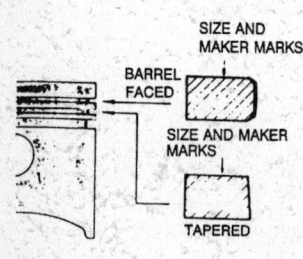

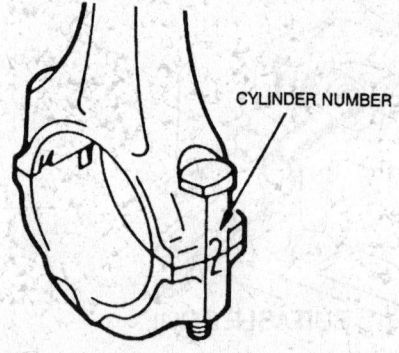

CYLINDER NUMBER

Location of cylinder number on connecting rod

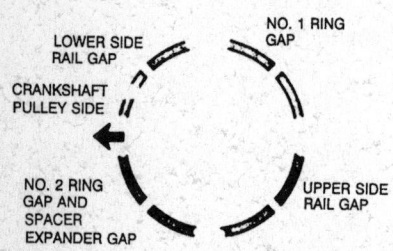

Using special tools to remove the hub from the knuckle

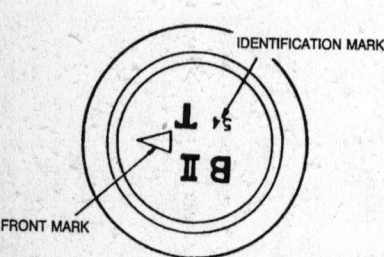

IDENTIFICATION MARK

FRONT MARK

Typical piston identification and direction indicator

ENGINE LUBRICATION

Oil Pan

REMOVAL AND INSTALLATION

The engine may have to be raised off its mount for the pan to clear the suspension crossmember. However, on most front wheel drive vehicles, there is usually enough clearance without raising the engine.

Except 1992-94 4wd Colt Vista

1. Raise the vehicle and support it safely. Remove the underbody splash shield.
2. Unbolt the left and right engine mounts, except on front wheel drive vehicles.
3. On rear wheel drive vehicles, place a jack under the bellhousing and raise the engine.
4. Remove the oil pan retaining bolts and remove the oil pan.

To install:

5. Installation is the reverse order of removal procedure.
6. Apply sealant to the front and rear main seal areas. Do not use sealant on the gasket itself. Use a new pan gasket. Torque the oil pan retaining bolts to 4-6 ft. lbs. (6-8 Nm).

1992-94 4wd Colt Vista

1. Disconnect the negative battery cable. Raise the vehicle and support safely. Drain the engine oil.
2. Remove the transfer case assembly and left halfshaft.
3. Remove the bellhousing cover.
4. Remove the oil pan retaining bolt.
5. Use a gasket separating tool to dislodge the oil pan gasket and remove.

To install:

6. Clean all gasket mating surfaces. Apply RTV gasket sealer to the oil pan and install within 5 minutes.
7. Torque the oil pan bolts to 5 ft. lbs. (7 Nm).
8. Install the bellhousing cover.
9. Install the transfer case and left halfshaft.
10. Refill the engine with oil, connect the battery cable, start the engine and check for leaks.

Oil Pump

REMOVAL AND INSTALLATION

1468cc Engine

1. Disconnect the negative battery cable and drain the oil. Remove the timing belt.
2. Remove the oil pan.
3. Remove the oil screen.
4. Unbolt and remove the front case assembly.
5. Remove the oil pump cover.

6. Remove the inner and outer gears from the front case.

NOTE: The outer gear has no identifying marks to indicate direction of rotation. Clean the gear and mark it with an indelible marker.

7. Remove the plug, relief valve spring and relief valve from the case.

To install:

8. Check the front case for damage or cracks. Replace the front seal. Replace the oil screen O-ring. Clean all parts thoroughly with a safe solvent.

9. Check the pump gears for wear or damage. Clean the gears thoroughly and place them in position in the case to check the clearances. There is a crescent shaped piece between the 2 gears. This piece is the reference point for 2 measurements. Use the following clearances for determining gear wear:

Outer gear face-to-case — 0.0039-0.0079 in. (0.0990-0.2000mm)

Outer gear teeth-to-crescent — 0.0087-0.0134 in. (0.2201-0.3404mm)

Outer gear endplay — 0.0016-0.0039 in. (0.0406-0.0990mm)

Inner gear teeth-to-crescent — 0.0083-0.0126 in. (0.2108-0.3200mm)

Inner gear endplay — 0.0016-0.0039 in. (0.0406-0.0990mm)

10. Check that the relief valve can slide freely in the case.

11. Check the relief valve spring for damage. The relief valve free length should be 1.850 in. (47.000mm) load length should be 9.5 lbs. (13.0 N) at 1.575 in. (40.000mm).

12. Thoroughly coat both oil pump gears with clean engine oil and install them in the correct direction of rotation.

13. Install the pump cover and torque the bolts to 7 ft. lbs. (10 Nm).

14. Coat the relief valve and spring with clean engine oil, install them and tighten the plug to 30-36 ft. lbs. (41-48 Nm).

15. Position a new front case gasket, coated with sealer, on the engine and install the front case. Torque the bolts to 10 ft. lbs. (14 Nm). Note that the bolts have different shank lengths.

16. Coat the lips of a new seal with clean engine oil and slide it along the crankshaft until it touches the front case. Drive it into place with a seal driver.

17. Install the sprocket, timing belt and pulley.

18. Install the oil screen.

19. Thoroughly clean both the oil pan and engine mating surfaces. Apply a 4mm wide bead of RTV sealer in the groove of the oil pan mating surface.

NOTE: The sealer will set in approximately 15 minutes.

20. Tighten the oil pan bolts to 5-6 ft. lbs. (7-8 Nm). Connect the battery cable and fill the crankcase with oil.

1595cc DOHC and 1755cc Engines

1. Remove the timing belt.
2. Drain the oil.
3. Remove the oil filter, on 1595cc DOHC engines. Remove the oil pan and screen.
4. Remove the oil filter bracket, on 1595cc DOHC engines. Unbolt and remove the front case assembly.

NOTE: On the 1755cc engine, if the front case assembly is difficult to remove from the block, there is a groove around the case into which a prybar may be inserted, to aid in removal. Pry slowly and evenly. Don't hammer.

5. On 1755cc engine, remove the oil pressure relief plug, spring and plunger.

6. On 1755cc engine, remove the oil pump cover.

7. On 1755cc engine, remove the pump rotor.

To install:

8. Check the case for cracks and damage.

9. Check the oil screen for damage.

10. Replace the oil screen O-ring.

11. Thoroughly clean all parts in a safe solvent.

12. Place the rotor back in the case to check clearances.

Side clearance — 0.0024-0.0047 in. (0.0601-0.1194mm)

Tip clearance — 0.0016-0.0047 in. (0.0406-0.1194mm)

Body clearance — 0.0039-0.0063 in. (0.0990-0.1600mm)

Shaft-to-cover clearance — 0.0008-0.0020 in. (0.0203-0.0508mm)

13. On 1755cc engines, check that the relief valve plunger slides smoothly in its bore.

14. On 1755cc engines: Check the relief valve spring. The free length should be 1.850 in. (47.000mm); the load length should be 9.5 lbs. (13.0 N) at 1.575 in. (40.000mm).

15. On 1755cc engines, install a new oil seal, coated with clean engine oil, into the oil pump cover. Drive it into place using a hammer and flat block.

16. On 1755cc, install a new cover gasket in the groove in the case.

17. On 1755cc, coat the rotor with clean engine oil and install it in the cover.

18. On 1755cc, install the cover and tighten the bolts.

19. On 1755cc, install the sprocket and tighten the nut to 28 ft. lbs. (38 Nm).

20. On 1755cc, coat the oil relief valve plunger with clean engine oil and install it, along with the spring and plug.

21. Install a new case gasket, coated with sealer, on the block and install the case. Torque the case bolts, on 1595cc DOHC engines, 20-25 ft. lbs. (28-34 Nm).

NOTE: There are 2 lengths of case bolts.

22. Install the screen. Tighten the bolts, on 1755cc engines, 18 ft. lbs. (25 Nm). On 1595cc DOHC engines, 11-16 ft. lbs. (14-22 Nm).

23. Install the oil pan.

1834cc Engine

1. Disconnect the negative battery cable and drain the engine oil.

2. Remove the oil filter and oil pan.

3. Remove the oil pump screen and gasket.

4. Remove the oil pump case (front cover). Matchmark the inner and outer rotors for installation.

5. Remove the oil pump cover, inner and outer rotor.

6. Check the tip clearance between the inner and outer rotor with a feeler gauge. The clearance should be 0.0024-0.0071 in. (0.06-0.18mm).

7. Check the side clearance with a straight-edge and feeler gauge across the 2 rotors. The clearance should be 0.0016-0.0039 in. (0.04-0.10mm).

8. Check the outer rotor-to-cover clearance with a feeler gauge. The clearance should to be 0.0039-0.0071 in. (0.10-0.18mm).

To install:

9. Clean all gasket mating surfaces.

10. Install the inner and outer rotors so the alignment marks are together. Install the oil pump cover and torque the screws to 7 ft. lbs. (10 Nm).

11. Install a new front oil seal with tool MD998717 or equivalent.

12. Apply RTV gasket sealer to the front cover and install. Torque the bolts to 11 ft. lbs. (14 Nm).

13. Install the oil screen and oil pan.

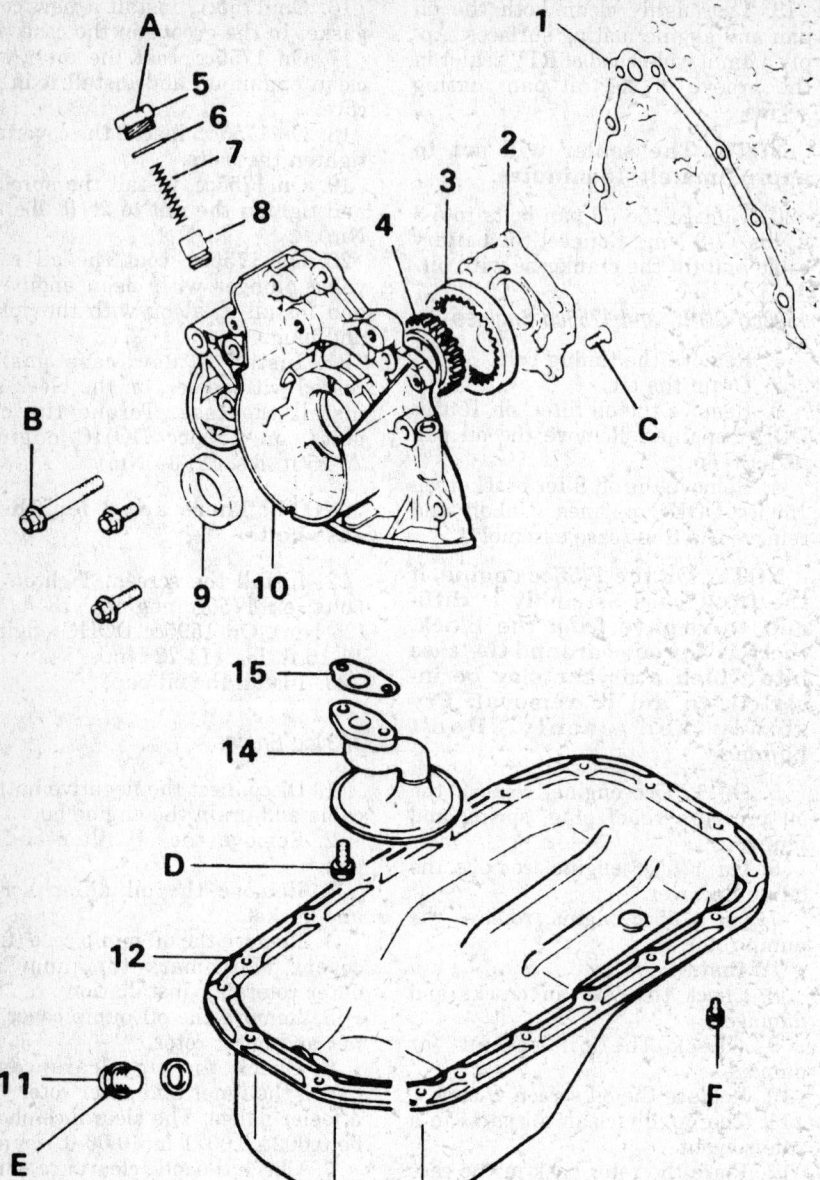

A. 30–36 ft. lbs. (40–49 Nm)
B. 8–11 ft. lbs. (12–14 Nm)
C. 6–8 ft. lbs. (8–9 Nm)
D. 13–18 ft. lbs. (18–24 Nm)
E. 26–32 ft. lbs. (35–44 Nm)
F. 4–5 ft. lbs. (6–7 Nm)

1. Front case gasket
2. Oil pump cover
3. Oil pump outer gear
4. Oil pump inner gear
5. Plug
6. Gasket
7. Relief spring
8. Relief plunger
9. Front oil seal
10. Front case
11. Drain plug
12. Oil pan
13. Oil screen
14. Oil screen gasket

Exploded view of oil pump, front cover and oil pan — 1468cc engine

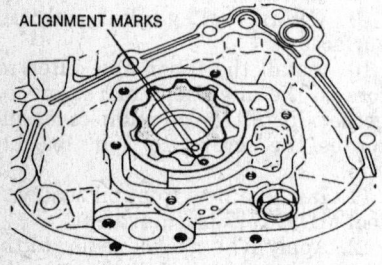

ALIGNMENT MARKS

Oil pump alignment marks — 1834cc engine

14. Install the remaining components.
15. Refill the engine with oil, connect the battery cable, start the engine and check for leaks.

1997cc and 2350cc Engines

1. Disconnect the negative battery cable and drain the engine oil.
2. Remove the oil pan and screen.
3. Remove the drive belts and crankshaft vibration damper. Remove the plug cap with the removing tool MD998162. Refer to the silent shaft section.
4. Remove the plug on the side of the engine block. Insert a phillips

screwdriver into the hole to block the silent shaft during removal.
5. Remove the oil pump driven gear bolt that secures the oil pump driven gear to the silent shaft.
6. Remove oil pump cover (front cover).
7. Check the side clearance with a straight edge and feeler gauge across the 2 rotors. The clearance should be no more than 0.0098 in. (0.25mm).
8. Check the outer rotor-to-cover clearance with a feeler gauge. The clearance should no more than 0.0098 in. (0.25mm).

To install:

9. Clean all gasket mating surfaces and lubricate all moving parts with clean engine oil.

10. Install the driven and drive gears with the alignment marks together.

11. Install a new front seal using tool C3095A, or equivalent.

12. Install an oil seal guide tool MD998285, or equivalent to the crankshaft to align the front cover during installation.

13. Install the oil pump cover and torque the bolts to 12 ft. lbs. (17 Nm). Apply RTV gasket sealer to the front cover.

14. Install the front cover and torque the bolts to 17 ft. lbs. (23 Nm).

15. Insert a phillips screwdriver into the silent shaft hole in the left side of the engine block to lock the silent shaft. Refer to silent shafts.

16. Secure the oil pump driven gear onto the left silent shaft by turning the driven gear bolt to 27 ft. lbs. (38 Nm).

17. Install the plug cap with a new O-ring. Use the special tool MD998162 and torque to 17 ft. lbs. (24 Nm).

18. Install the oil pan and screen.

19. Install the remaining components.

20. Refill the engine with oil, connect the battery cable, start the engine and check for leaks.

Rear Main Bearing Oil Seal

REMOVAL AND INSTALLATION

The rear main oil seal is located in a housing on the rear of the block.

1. Raise the vehicle and support it safely.

2. Remove the transmission/transaxle and flywheel.

3. Remove the oil seal housing from the block.

4. Remove the separator from the housing.

5. Pry out the oil seal.

To install:

6. Lightly oil the replacement seal. The oil seal should be installed so the seal plate fits into the inner contact surface of the seal case. Use seal installer tool MD998011 or equivalent to drive the seal into the case.

7. Install the separator with the oil holes facing down and install the oil housing.

8. Install the transmission/transaxle. Torque the flywheel

bolts to 94-101 ft. lbs. (130-140 Nm) and the transaxle bolts to 20-25 ft. lbs. (27-34 Nm).

9. Lower the vehicle. Refill the the engine with oil.

10. Connect the negative battery cable. Start the engine and check for leaks.

ENGINE COOLING

Radiator

REMOVAL AND INSTALLATION

1. Remove the splash panel from the bottom of the vehicle. Drain the radiator by opening the petcock. Remove the shroud, if equipped.

2. Disconnect the radiator hoses at the engine. On automatic transmission equipped vehicles, disconnect and plug the transmission lines to the bottom of the radiator.

3. Remove the 2 retaining bolts from either side of the radiator. Lift out the radiator. On front wheel drive vehicles, disconnect the electric fan wiring harness. Do not remove the fan motor, blades or bracket — remove as a unit with the radiator.

4. Remove the cooling and condenser fans, temperature switches and insulators from the radiator.

To install:

5. Install the cooling fans, temperature switches, insulator and remaining hardware to the radiator before installation.

6. Install the radiator and retaining bolts. Tighten the retaining bolts gradually in a criss-cross pattern.

NOTE: Work around the electric cooling fan when the engine is cold or disconnect the negative battery cable. On some vehicles, the fan will run to cool the engine even when the ignition is OFF.

7. Connect all hoses and tighten the clamps. Reconnect all electrical harnesses.

8. Install the remaining components. Refill the 50/50 percent engine coolant, start the engine and check for leaks and overheating.

Heater Core

REMOVAL AND INSTALLATION

Colt Wagon

1. Disconnect the negative battery cable and drain the engine coolant.

2. Disconnect the heater hoses.

3. Remove the steering wheel and lap air outlet. Use a steering wheel puller after removing the horn pad.

4. Remove the steering column upper and lower cover, shift knob and floor console assembly.

5. Remove the glove box by opening and quickly pulling up on the right corner of the box and remove the right hinge pin from the half hinge.

6. Remove the defroster duct and side joint from the heater unit.

7. Remove the instrument cluster hood attaching screws and clips. The clips are on the top.

8. Remove the instrument cluster screw and pull the cluster forwards. Disconnect the speedometer cable and electrical connections.

9. Remove the steering column-to-instrument panel bracket bolts.

10. Remove the heater control panel by pushing on the right side from behind the panel cover. Remove the heater control assembly-to-instrument panel retaining screws. Do not remove the control assembly.

11. Using a trim removal tool or equivalent, remove the upper instrument panel retaining screw covers. Be careful not to damage the assembly.

12. Remove the panel mounting bolts and remove the panel.

13. Disconnect the side and top ventilator ducts.

14. Remove the heater housing.

15. Remove the case half retaining clips and screws. Separate the 2 halves and remove the heater core.

To install:

16. Install the heater core, case half retaining clips and screws. Make sure the seals are not damaged.

17. Install the heater housing.

18. Connect the side and top ventilator ducts.

19. Install the instrument panel and mounting bolts.

20. Install the upper instrument panel retaining bolts and covers. Be careful not to damage the assembly.

21. Install the heater control panel.

22. Install the steering column-to-instrument panel bracket bolts.

23. Install the instrument cluster and hood.

24. Install the defroster duct and side joint to the heater unit.

25. Install the glove box.

26. Install the steering column upper and lower cover, shift knob and floor console assembly.

27. Install the steering wheel and lap air outlet.

28. Connect the heater hoses.

29. Connect the negative battery cable and refill the engine coolant.

Colt

1. Disconnect the negative battery cable.

2. Drain the cooling system and disconnect the heater hoses.

3. Remove the front seats by removing the covers over the anchor bolts, the underseat tray, the seat belt guide ring, the seat mounting nuts and bolts and disconnect the seat belt switch wiring harness from under the seat. Then lift out the seats.

4. Remove the floor console by first taking out the coin holder and the console box tray. Remove the remote control mirror switch or cover. All of these items require only a plastic trim tool to carefully pry them out.

5. Remove the rear half of the console.

6. Remove the shift lever knob on manual transmission vehicles.

7. Remove the front console box assembly.

8. A number of the instrument panel pieces may be retained by pin type fasteners. They may be removed using the following procedure:

a. This type of clip is removed by pressing down on the center pin with a suitable blunt pointed tool. Press down a little more than $\frac{1}{16}$ in. (2mm); this releases the clip. Pull the clip outward to remove it.

b. Do not push the pin inward more than necessary because it may damage the grommet or the pin may fall in if pushed in too far. Once the clips are removed, use a plastic trim stick to pry the piece loose.

9. Remove both lower cowl trim panels (kick panels).

10. Remove the ashtray.

11. Remove the center panel around the radio.

12. Remove the sunglass pocket at the upper left side of panel and the side panel into which it mounts.

13. Remove the driver's side knee protector and the hood release handle.

14. Remove the steering column top and bottom covers.

15. Remove the radio.

16. Remove the glove box striker and box assembly.

17. Remove the instrument panel lower cover, 2 small pieces in the center, by pulling forward.

18. Remove the heater control assembly screw.

19. Remove the instrument cluster bezel and pull out the gauge assembly.

20. Remove the speedometer adapter by disconnecting the speedometer cable at the transaxle pulling the cable sightly towards the vehicle interior and giving a slight twist on the adapter to release it.

21. Insert a small flat-tipped tool to open the tab on the gauge cluster connector. Remove the harness connectors.

22. Remove, by prying with a plastic trim tool, the right side speaker cover and the speaker, the upper side defroster grilles and the clock or plug to gain access to some of the instrument panel mounting bolts.

23. Lower the steering column by removing the bolt and nut.

24. Remove the instrument panel bolts and the instrument panel.

25. Disconnect the air selection, temperature and mode selection con-

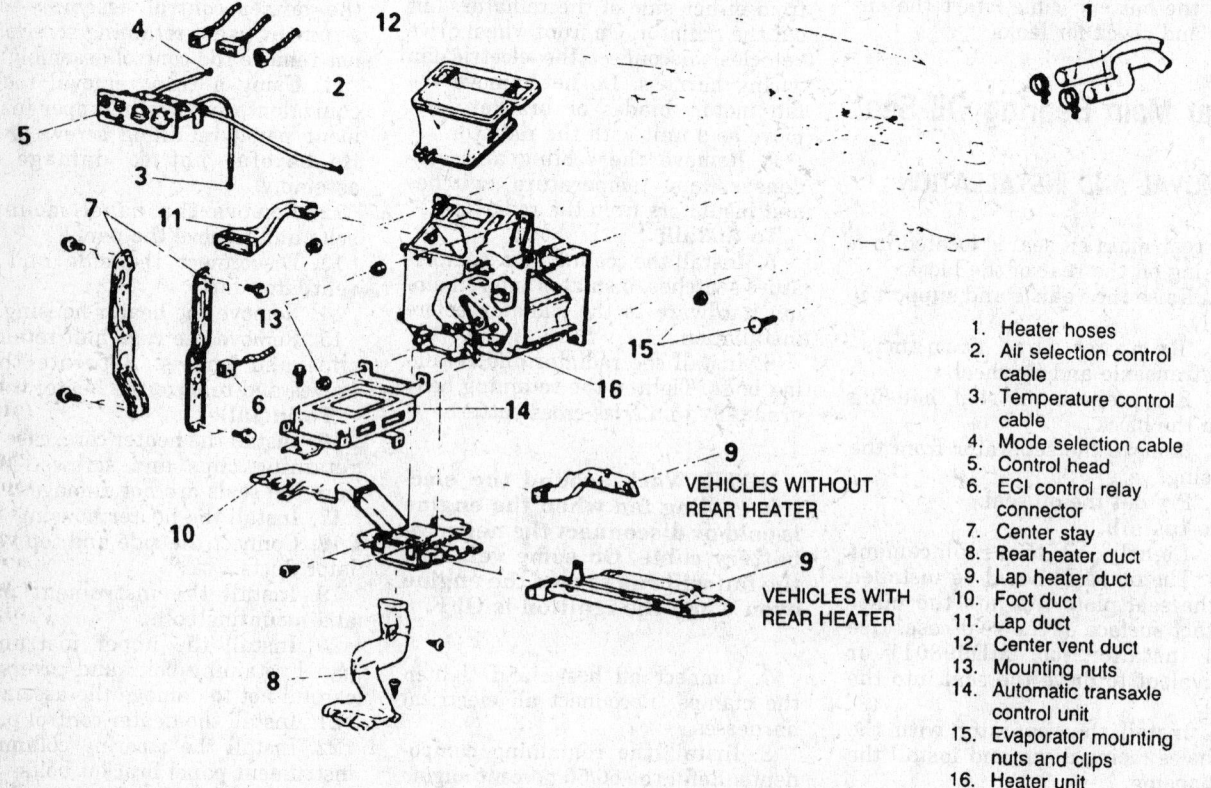

VEHICLES WITHOUT REAR HEATER

VEHICLES WITH REAR HEATER

1. Heater hoses
2. Air selection control cable
3. Temperature control cable
4. Mode selection cable
5. Control head
6. ECI control relay connector
7. Center stay
8. Rear heater duct
9. Lap heater duct
10. Foot duct
11. Lap duct
12. Center vent duct
13. Mounting nuts
14. Automatic transaxle control unit
15. Evaporator mounting nuts and clips
16. Heater unit

Heater case and related components — Colt

trol cables from the heater box and remove the heater control assembly.

26. Remove the connector for the ECI control relay.

27. Remove both stamped steel instrument panel supports.

28. Remove the heater ductwork.

29. Remove the heater box mounting nuts.

30. Remove the automatic transmission ELC control box.

31. Remove the evaporator mounting nuts and clips.

32. With the evaporator pulled toward the vehicle interior, remove the heater unit. Be careful not to damage the heater tubes or to spill coolant.

33. Remove the cover plate around the heater tubes and the core fastener clips. Pull the heater core from the heater box, being careful not to damage the fins or tank ends.

To install:

34. Thoroughly clean and dry the inside of the case. Install the heater core to the heater box. Install the clips and cover.

35. Install the evaporator and the automatic transmission ELC box.

36. Install the heater box and connect the duct work.

37. Connect all wires and control cables.

38. Install the instrument panel assembly and the console by reversing their removal procedures.

39. Install the seats.

40. Refill the cooling system.

41. Evacuate and recharge the air conditioning system. Add 2 oz. of refrigerant oil during the recharge if the evaporator was replaced.

42. Connect the negative battery cable and check the entire climate control system for proper operation. Check the system for leaks.

Colt Vista 1990-91

1. Disconnect the negative battery cable, drain the engine coolant and disconnect the heater hoses from the core tubes.

2. Remove the steering column under covers, steering column. This can be accomplished by removing the pinch bolt at the U-joint below the instrument panel, disconnecting the connectors and pulling the column from the U-joint yoke.

3. Remove the glove box assemblies, lap heater duct, ashtray and hood lock release cable from the instrument panel.

4. Remove the instrument cluster hood covers and hood. Pull the cluster out and disconnect the speedometer cable and electrical connectors.

5. Disconnect the control cables from the heater unit, remove the upper air ducts and disconnect the blower motor harness.

6. Remove the trim panels along the top of the instrument panel, disconnect the antenna feeder wire, remove the instrument panel retaining hardware and remove the assembly.

7. Remove the instrument panel absorber, duct from the right of the heater unit and unit mounting nuts. Remove the unit from the vehicle.

8. Disassemble the heater unit by removing the case clips and screws. Separate the 2 halves and remove the heater core.

To install:

9. Thoroughly clean and dry the inside of the case. Assemble the 2 halves being careful not to damage the seals.

10. Install the heater unit and mounting nuts.

11. Install the right side duct, instrument panel absorber bracket, and instrument panel.

12. Install the hood release cable, ashtray, lap heater duct and glove boxes.

13. Install the steering column and under covers.

14. Connect the heater hoses and refill the cooling system.

1. Heater hose
2. Instrument panel
3. Air intake
4. Duct
5. Temperature control cable
6. Mode selection control cable
7. Heater unit

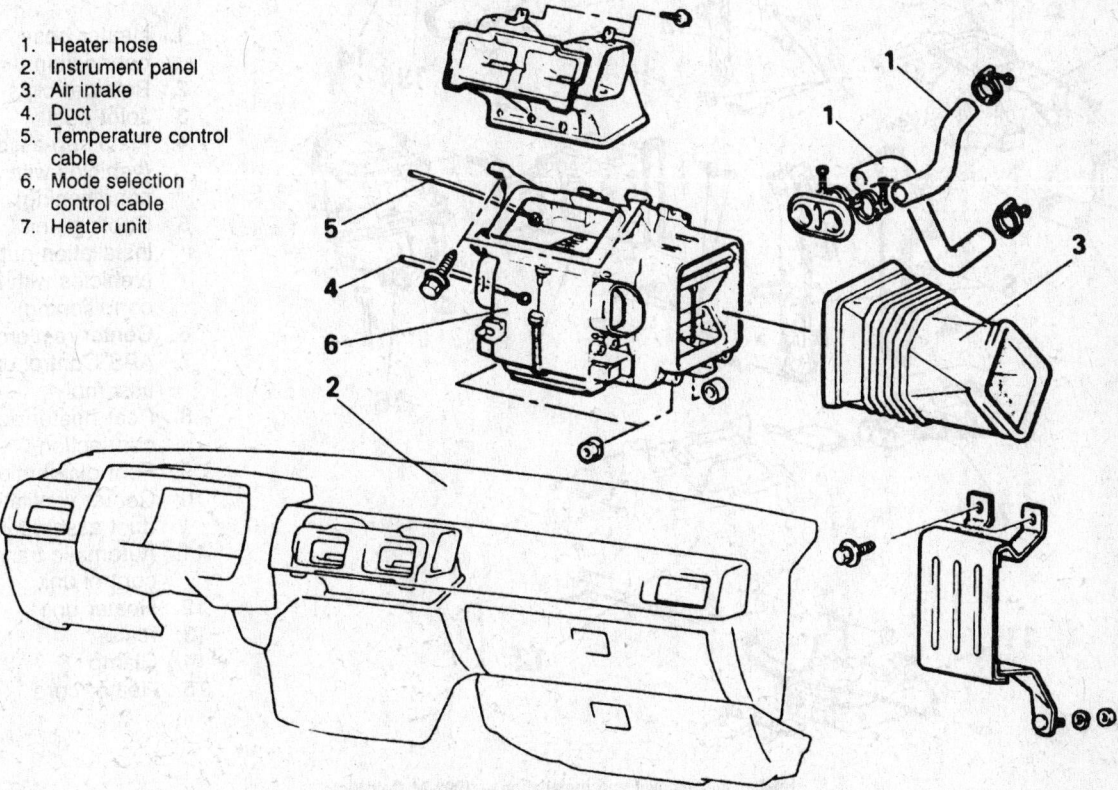

Heater core removal and installation — 1990-91 Colt Vista

15. Connect the negative battery cable and check the system for leaks and proper operation.

Colt Vista 1992-94

1. Disconnect negative battery cable.

2. Drain the engine coolant.

3. Remove the hood lock release handle, instrument panel under cover, lower frame, foot duct, lap duct and the lap heater duct.

4. Remove the glove box, speaker harness and the glove box frame.

5. Remove the meter hood and combination meter from the instrument panel. Remove the adapter lock and pull the speedometer cable into the passenger compartment slightly. Remove the rear of the adapter from the cable. Next, turn the adapter so the notched section is aligned with the tab on the cable section and slide adapter outward to remove.

6. Remove the ashtray from the center panel. Remove the mounting screws, radio and the center panel from the vehicle.

7. Remove the center air outlet from instrument panel by removing the clip on the lower section of the outlet. Next insert a flat tipped tool in between the fins and remove the clip on the top section while pulling the lock spring toward the inside. Remove the center air outlet assembly.

8. Disconnect the air selection, temperature and mode selection control cables from the heater box and remove the heater control assembly.

9. Remove the clock or plug from the upper instrument panel. Remove the instrument panel retaining bolt under the plug.

10. Lower the steering column by removing the bolt and nut under the column.

11. Remove the floor console side covers. If equipped with manual transaxle, remove the shifter knob.

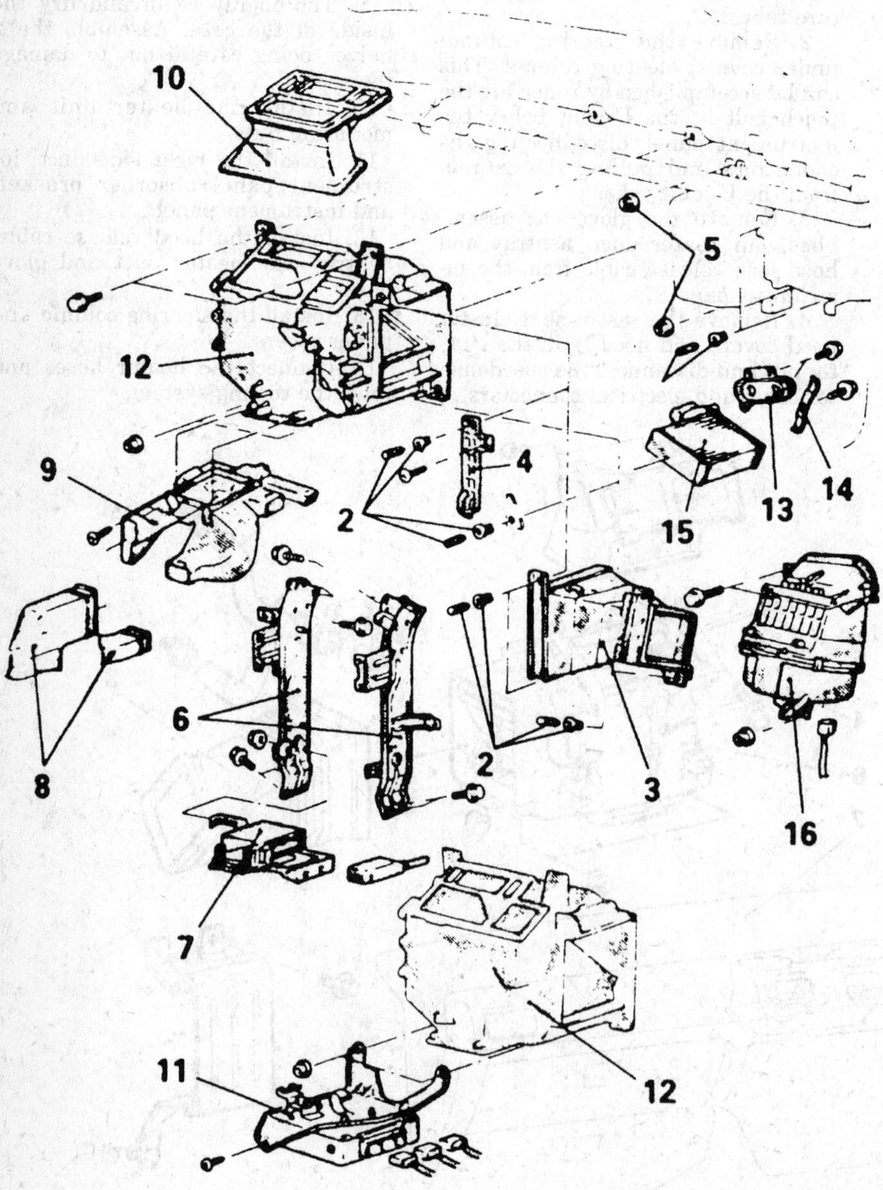

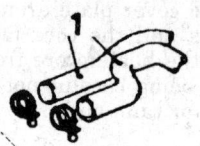

1. Heater hose connection
2. Retainer clips
3. Joint duct
4. Plate sub-assembly (vehicles with air conditioning)
5. Cooling unit installation nut (vehicles with air conditioning)
6. Center reinforcement
7. ABS Control unit assembly
8. Rear heater duct connection
9. Foot distribution duct
10. Center ventilation duct assembly
11. Automatic transaxle control unit
12. Heater unit
13. Plate
14. Clamp
15. Heater core

Heater unit removal and installation — 1992-94 Colt Vista

12. Remove the floor console switch panel, mounting bolts and the floor console from the vehicle.

13. Remove the instrument panel retainer bolts and the instrument panel.

14. Disconnect the heater hoses at the heater box.

15. Remove the heater joint duct by first removing the pin type retainer clips on the duct using the following procedure:

    a. This type of clip is removed by pressing down on the center pin with a blunt pointed tool. Press down a little more than 1/16 in. (2mm); this releases the clip. Pull the clip outward to remove it.

    b. Do not push the pin inward more than necessary because it may damage the grommet or the pin may fall in if pushed in too far. Once the clips are removed, use a plastic trim stick to pry the piece loose.

16. Remove the center reinforcement. Remove the cooling unit mounting nut if equipped with air conditioning.

17. Disconnect and remove the ABS control unit and the automatic transmission ELC control unit.

18. Remove the foot distribution duct and disconnect the rear heater duct connection.

19. Remove both stamped steel instrument panel supports.

20. Remove the mounting bolts and the heater unit from the vehicle. Be careful not to damage the heater tubes or to spill coolant inside the vehicle.

21. Remove the cover plate around the heater tubes and the core fastener clips. Pull the heater core from the heater box, being careful not to damage the fins or tank ends.

To install:

22. Thoroughly clean and dry the inside of the case. Install the heater core to the heater box. Install the clips and cover.

23. Install the heater unit into position on the vehicle and install the evaporator and heater unit mounting nuts and clips.

24. Install the automatic transaxle ELC box and the ABS control unit.

25. Connect the air selection, temperature and mode selection control cables from the heater box and install the heater control assembly.

26. Install both stamped steel instrument panel supports. Connect the connector for the ECI control relay.

27. Install the remaining instrument panel components reversing the removal procedure.

28. Install the center console as follows:

    a. Install the front console box assembly.

    b. Install the shift lever knob on manual transaxle vehicles.

    c. Install the rear console box assembly.

    d. Install the floor console switch panel

    e. Install the coin holder and the console box tray.

29. Refill the cooling system.

30. Evacuate and recharge the air conditioning system. Add 2 oz. of refrigerant oil during the recharge if the evaporator was replaced.

31. Connect the negative battery cable and check the entire climate control system for proper operation. Check the system for leaks.

Water Pump

REMOVAL AND INSTALLATION

Colt and 1990-91 Colt Vista

1. Drain the cooling system.

2. Remove the drive belt and water pump pulley.

3. Remove the timing belt covers and timing belt tensioner.

4. Remove the water pump bolts and alternator bracket.

5. Remove the water pump retaining bolts, it is important to observe the location of each bolt, they are different lengths.

6. Remove the water pump.

NOTE: The pump is not rebuildable. Check for driveshaft side to side play, if excessive replace the pump. If there are signs of damage or leakage from the seals or vent hole, the unit must be replaced.

To install:

7. Discard the O-ring in the front end of the water pipe. Install a new O-ring coated with water.

8. Using a new gasket, mount the water pump and alternator bracket on the engine. Torque the bolts with a head marked 4 to 9-11 ft. lbs. (12-15 Nm); the bolts with a head marked 7 to 14-20 ft. lbs. (20-27 Nm).

9. Complete the remainder of installation in the reverse order of removal procedure. Fill the system with coolant and check for leaks.

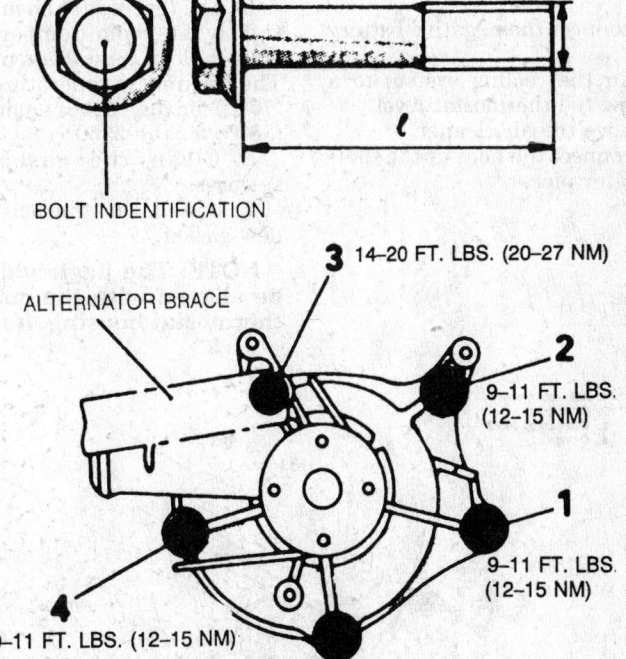

BOLT INDENTIFICATION

ALTERNATOR BRACE

3 14-20 FT. LBS. (20-27 NM)

2 9-11 FT. LBS. (12-15 NM)

1 9-11 FT. LBS. (12-15 NM)

4 9-11 FT. LBS. (12-15 NM)

2 9-11 FT. LBS. (12-15 NM)

Water pump bolt torque identification

1992-94 Colt Vista

1. Disconnect the negative battery cable and drain the engine coolant.
2. Remove the drive belts and move the accessories out of the way, if necessary. Remove the alternator bracket.
3. Align the crankshaft timing mark to TDC of No. 1 cylinder. Remove the timing belt cover and timing belt.
4. Remove the water pump.

To install:

5. Clean the gasket mating surfaces.
6. Install the water pump with a new gasket. The water pump bolts are different sizes. Make sure they are properly installed before tightening. Torque the bolts to 18 ft. lbs. (24 Nm). Install a new O-ring for the 2350cc engine.
7. Install the timing belt and cover.
8. Install the accessories and belts.
9. Install the remaining components.
10. Fill the engine with coolant, start the engine and check for leaks.

Thermostat

REMOVAL AND INSTALLATION

Colt and 1990-91 Colt Vista

1. Disconnect the negative battery cable.
2. Drain the cooling system to a point below the thermostat level.
3. Remove the air cleaner.
4. Disconnect the hose at the thermostat water pipe.

5. Remove the water pipe support bracket nut.

NOTE: This nut is also an intake manifold nut. It is very difficult to get to. A deep offset 12mm box wrench is used to remove or replace it.

6. Unbolt and remove the thermostat housing and pipe.
7. Lift out the thermostat. Discard the gasket.

To install:

8. Clean the mating surfaces of the housing and manifold thoroughly.
9. Install the thermostat with the spring facing downward and position a new gasket. The jiggle valve in the thermostat should be on the manifold side.
10. Install the housing and pipe assembly. Torque the housing bolts to 11 ft. lbs. (14 Nm); the intake manifold nut to 14 ft. lbs. (19 Nm).
11. Refill the system with coolant. Connect the negative battery cable.
12. Start the engine and check for leaks.

1992-94 Colt Vista

1. Drain the engine coolant to a level below the thermostat.
2. Remove the connection for the radiator upper hose.
3. Remove the water outlet fitting.
4. Remove the thermostat.

To install:

5. The thermostat should be closed tightly at room temperature and open 0.31 in. (8mm) when fully open. The opening temperature is 170°F (77°C) for the 1834cc engine or 190°F (88°C) for the 2350cc engine.
6. Clean the gasket mating surfaces.
7. Install the thermostat with a new gasket.

NOTE: The jiggle valve should be aligned with the mark on the thermostat housing. If there is no

mark, position the valve facing up. The main body of the thermostat should face the engine.

8. Install the remaining components. Torque the housing bolts to 14 ft. lbs. (19 Nm).
9. Refill the engine with coolant, start the engine and check for leaks.

Cooling System Bleeding

After working on the cooling system, even to replace the thermostat, the system must be bled. Air trapped in the system will prevent proper filling and leave the radiator coolant level low, causing a risk of overheating.

1. To bleed the system, start the system cool, the radiator cap off and the radiator filled to about an inch below the filler neck.

NOTE: The 1834cc engine has an air bleed screw at the throttle body assembly. Fill the engine until coolant spills from the hole. Torque the screw to 7 ft. lbs. (10 Nm).

2. Start the engine and run it at slightly above normal idle speed. This will insure adequate circulation. If air bubbles appear and the coolant level drops, fill the system with a mixture of anti-freeze and water to bring the level back to the proper level.
3. Run the engine this way until the thermostat opens. When this happens, the coolant will move abruptly across the top of the radiator and the temperature of the radiator will suddenly rise.
4. At this point, air is often expelled and the level may drop quite a bit. Keep refilling the system until the level is near the top of the radiator and remains constant.
5. If the vehicle has an overflow tank, fill the radiator up to the top of the filler neck.

ENGINE ELECTRICAL

NOTE: Disconnecting the negative battery cable on some vehicles may interfere with the functions of the on-board computer systems and may require the computer to undergo a relearning process, once the negative battery cable is reconnected.

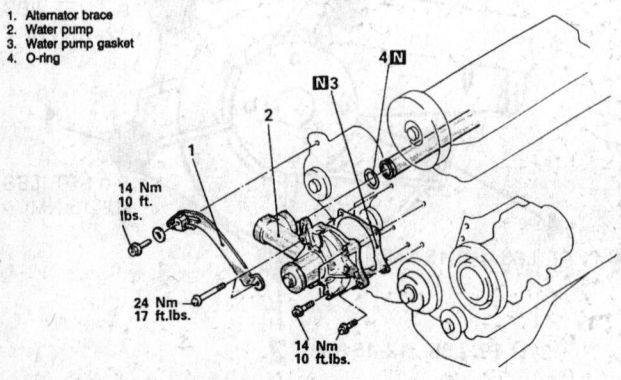

1. Alternator brace
2. Water pump
3. Water pump gasket
4. O-ring

14 Nm
10 ft. lbs.

24 Nm
17 ft.lbs.

14 Nm
10 ft.lbs.

Water pump assembly — 2350cc shown, 1834cc engine similar

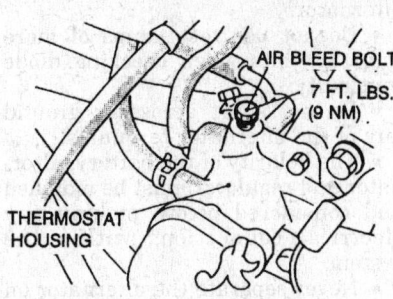

Cooling system bleeder screw — 1834cc engine

Distributor

REMOVAL

Before removing the distributor, position No. 1 cylinder at TDC on the compression stroke and align the timing marks.

1. Disconnect the negative battery cable.
2. Disconnect the spark plug wires from the distributor cap.
3. Disconnect the ignition coil high tension wire from the distributor cap.
4. Remove the vacuum hose from the advance unit, if equipped.
5. Remove the cap from the distributor.
6. Verify the rotor points to the No. 1 cylinder position and the timing marks on the crankshaft pulley and the timing tab are aligned at TDC.
7. Mark the distributor body to the exact place the rotor points. Matchmark both the distributor mounting flange and the cylinder head.
8. Loosen and remove the retaining nut from the mounting stud. Lift the distributor from the cylinder head. The rotor may turn slightly from the mark on the distributor body. Make note of how far. When the distributor is reinstalled, this is the point to position the rotor.

INSTALLATION

Timing Not Disturbed

1. Position the distributor into the engine while aligning the matchmarks made during removal.
2. Verify the rotor points to the No. 1 cylinder position and the timing marks on the crankshaft pulley and the timing tab are aligned at TDC.

3. Install the distributor retaining nut on the mounting stud and tighten.
4. Install the cap on the distributor.
5. Connect the spark plug wires to the distributor cap.
6. Connect the ignition coil high tension wire to the distributor cap.
7. Connect the negative battery cable to the battery.
8. Start the engine and check the ignition timing whenever the distributor has been removed.

Timing Disturbed

1. With the distributor removed from the engine, turn the crankshaft so the No. 1 piston is on the TDC of the compression stroke and the timing marks are aligned.
2. Turn the distributor shaft so the rotor points approximately 15 degrees before the rotor position that was marked on the distributor.
3. Insert the distributor, if resistance is met, slight wiggling of the rotor shaft will help seat the distributor.
4. When the distributor seats against the head, align the matchmarks and install the retaining nut. Do not tighten the retaining nut all the way, as the timing must be checked.
5. Reinstall the rotor, cap, plug wires, coil lead, primary lead or harness and connect the vacuum hoses.
6. Connect the negative battery cable. Start the engine, allow it to reach operating temperature and check the ignition timing.

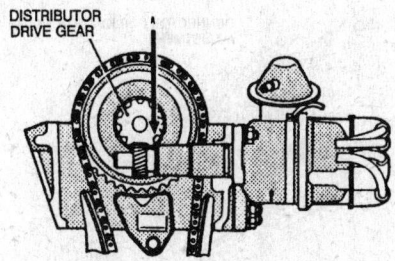

Distributor installation for cylinder head mounted distributors

Ignition Timing

ADJUSTMENT

Except 1595cc DOHC, 1834cc and 2350cc

1. Attach the timing light according to the manufacturer's instructions.
2. Locate the timing tab line on the front of the engine and the notch on the crankshaft pulley. Mark them so they are easily recognizable with the timing light. Connect a tachometer by inserting a paper clip into the connector at the distributor and connect the tachometer lead to the paper clip.
3. Start the engine and allow it to reach operating temperature.
4. Point the timing light at the crankshaft pulley marks. The marked line should align with the pulley notch.
5. If the marks do not align, loosen the distributor mounting nut and rotate the distributor slowly, in either direction, to align the timing marks.
6. Tighten the mounting nut when the ignition timing is correct. Stop the engine and remove the timing light.
7. Adjust engine idle if needed.

Except 1595cc DOHC, 1834cc and 2350cc

1. Run the engine until the normal operating temperature is reached. Shut OFF the engine. Make sure all lights and electrical accessories are OFF. Make sure the electric cooling fan is not operating when timing. Disconnect the fan harness, if necessary, but take care not to allow the engine to overheat.
2. Connect a timing light, following the light manufacturer's instructions.
3. Insert a paper clip along the terminal surface, of the terminal parallel to the fastener side of the ignition connector harness, in the engine compartment.
4. Locate the wire connector on the ignition coil connector. Insert a paper clip behind the TACH terminal connector to act as a tachometer adapter. Connect a tachometer to the paper clip. If not at specification, set the idle speed at the correct level.
5. Turn the engine OFF. Remove the water-proof cover from the ignition timing adjusting connector. This connector is located near the center of the firewall. Connect a jumper wire from this terminal to a good ground.

Aligning mating marks for installation of cylinder head mounted distributors

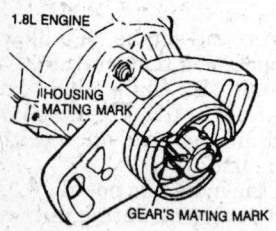

Distributor alignment marks — 1834cc and 2350cc engines

6. Start the engine and point the timing light at the pulley and timing cover marks. The base timing is 5 degrees before TDC.

7. If timing adjustment is necessary, loosen the crank angle sensor or distributor pivot bolt and turn the assembly. Turning the distributor or sensor to the right advances the timing, to the left retards it. Tighten the sensor pivot bolt when correct timing is reached. Do not allow the engine to overheat.

8. Stop the engine and disconnect the ground wire. Start the engine and check the curb idle speed. Check the

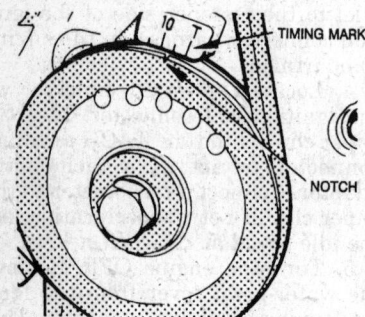

Timing marks positions — 1468cc, 1595cc, 1997cc, 1834cc and 2350cc engines

ignition timing, it should now be about 8 degrees before TDC.

9. Timing may vary depending upon the engine control module. If the timing is not about 8 degrees, check the base timing again. If the base timing is still 5 degrees, the ignition timing is functioning normally.

Alternator

PRECAUTIONS

Several precautions must be observed with alternator equipped vehicles to avoid damage to the unit.

• If the battery is removed for any reason, make sure it is reconnected with the correct polarity. Reversing the battery connections may result in damage to the one-way rectifiers.

• When utilizing a booster battery as a starting aid, always connect the positive to positive terminals and the negative terminal from the booster battery to a good engine ground on the vehicle being started.

• Never use a fast charger as a booster to start vehicles.

• Disconnect the battery cables when charging the battery with a fast charger.

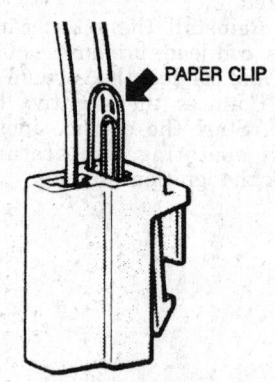

Paper clip installation

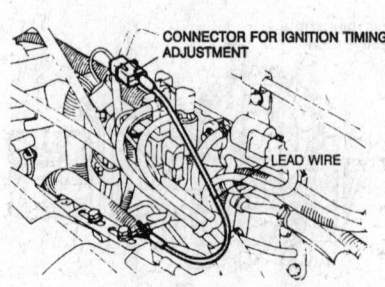

Lead wire connection

• Never attempt to polarize the alternator.

• Do not use test lamps of more than 12 volts when checking diode continuity.

• Do not short across or ground any of the alternator terminals.

• The polarity of the battery, alternator and regulator must be matched and considered before making any electrical connections within the system.

• Never separate the alternator on an open circuit. Make sure all connections within the circuit are clean and tight.

• Disconnect the battery ground terminal when performing any service on electrical components.

• Disconnect the battery if arc welding is to be done on the vehicle.

BELT TENSION ADJUSTMENT

1. Check the drive belts for cracking, fraying and any other deterioration. Replace if necessary.

2. To replace the belt, loosen the stationary mounting bolt and and pivot bolt. If equipped with an adjustment bolt, loosen it to provide the necessary slack for belt removal. Pivot the driven component in its bracket. Remove the old belt and slip the replacement belt over the pulleys.

3. Move the driven component or tighten the adjustment bolt, until the belt can be deflected $\frac{1}{4}$-$\frac{3}{8}$ in. (6.35-12.70mm) at its midpoint.

4. Tighten the mounting and pivot bolts.

REMOVAL AND INSTALLATION

Colt and Colt Wagon

1. Disconnect the negative battery cable.

2. Remove the condenser fan motor.

3. Remove the power steering pump from the bracket and support it on the oil reservoir using wire.

4. Remove the power steering pump bracket.

5. Disconnect the wiring connectors from the alternator.

6. Remove the lock bolt and the support bolt.

7. Remove the alternator and the adjusting bolt.

To install:

8. Installation is the reverse order of the removal procedure. Torque alternator brace bolts to to 9-11 ft. lbs. (12-15 Nm) and the pivot bolt to 15-18 ft. lbs. (20-25 Nm).

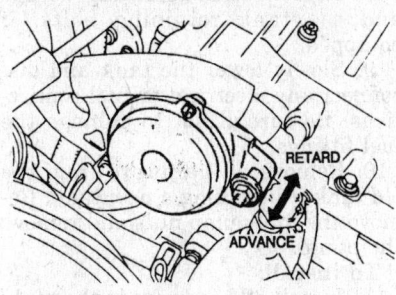

Timing adjustment with crank angle sensor — 1595cc DOHC engine

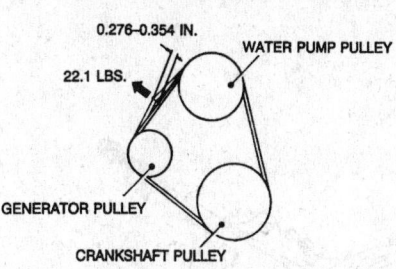

Belt tension adjustment

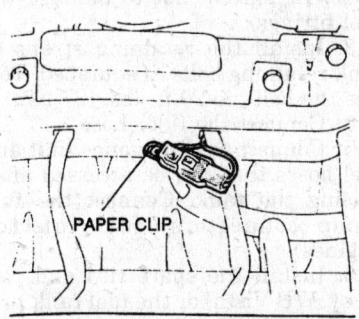

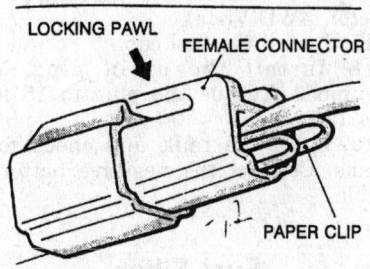

Tachometer hookup location — 1834cc and 2350cc engines

9. Adjust the belt to proper tension. Connect the negative battery cable.

Colt Vista

1. Disconnect the negative battery cable. Remove the left side cover panel if needed.
2. Remove the drive belts.
3. Remove both water pump pulleys.
4. Remove the alternator upper bracket/brace.
5. Disconnect the alternator electrical connectors and remove alternator.

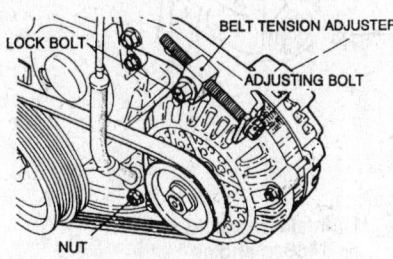

Alternator belt adjustment

To install:
6. Position the alternator on the lower mounting fixture and install the lower mounting bolt and nut. Tighten nut just enough to allow for movement of the alternator.
7. Install the alternator upper bracket/brace and connect the alternator electrical harness.
8. Install the water pump pulleys.
9. Install the drive belts and adjust to the proper tension.
10. Install the left side cover panel under the vehicle as required.
11. Connect the negative battery cable and check for proper operation.

Starter

REMOVAL AND INSTALLATION

NOTE: Always disconnect the negative battery cable when servicing the starter motor. A short circuit may cause vehicle damage and personal injury.

1. Disconnect the battery negative battery cable and the starter motor wiring. Remove the air cleaner assembly.
2. Raise and support the vehicle safely.

3. Remove the intake manifold-to-engine support bracket (Colt and Colt Wagon).
4. Remove the 2 starter attaching bolts and remove the starter motor.

To install:
5. Clean both surfaces of the starter motor flange and the rear plate.
6. Position the starter in the housing opening.
7. Install the manifold-to-engine support bracket (Colt and Colt Wagon).
8. Install the attaching bolts. Torque to 25 ft. lbs. (34 Nm) evenly to avoid binding.
9. Install the starter wiring and lower the vehicle.
10. Connect the negative battery cable and check operation.

EMISSION CONTROLS

FUEL SYSTEM

Fuel System Service Precautions

Safety is the most important factor when performing not only fuel system maintenance but any type of maintenance. Failure to conduct maintenance and repairs in a safe manner may result in serious personal injury or death. Maintenance and testing of the vehicle's fuel system components can be accomplished safely and effectively by adhering to the following rules and guidelines.

• To avoid the possibility of fire and personal injury, always disconnect the negative battery cable unless the repair or test procedure requires that battery voltage be applied.

• Always relieve the fuel system pressure prior to disconnecting any fuel system component (injector, fuel rail, pressure regulator, etc.), fitting or fuel line connection. Exercise extreme caution whenever relieving fuel system pressure to avoid exposing skin, face and eyes to fuel spray. Please be advised that fuel under

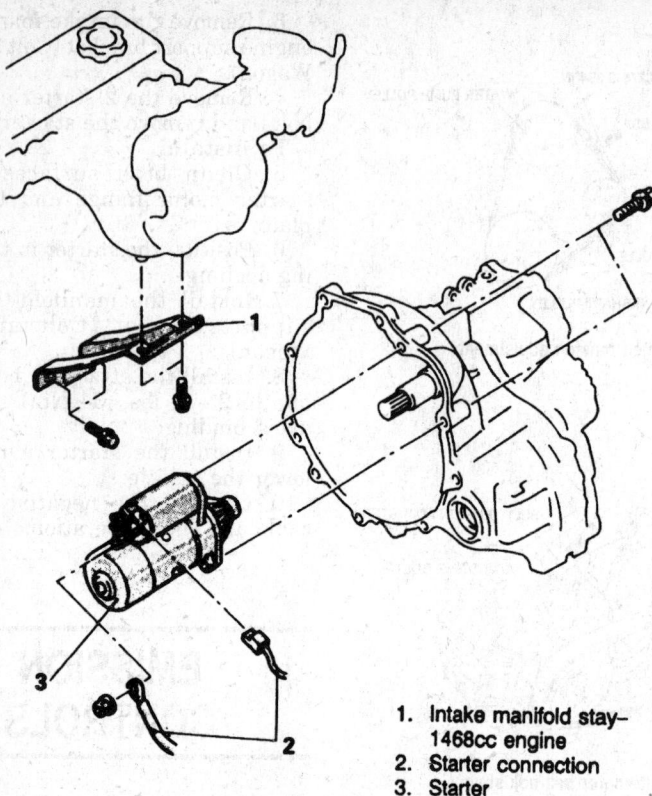

1. Intake manifold stay–
   1468cc engine
2. Starter connection
3. Starter

Starter motor removal and installation

pressure may penetrate the skin or any part of the body that it contacts.

• Always place a shop towel or cloth around the fitting or connection prior to loosening to absorb any excess fuel due to spillage. Ensure that all fuel spillage (should it occur) is quickly removed from engine surfaces. Ensure that all fuel soaked cloths or towels are deposited into a suitable waste container.

• Always keep a dry chemical (Class B) fire extinguisher near the work area.

• Do not allow fuel spray or fuel vapors to come into contact with a spark or open flame.

• Always use a backup wrench when loosening and tightening fuel line connection fittings. This will prevent unnecessary stress and torsion to fuel line piping. Always follow the proper torque specifications.

• Always replace worn fuel fitting O-rings with new. Do not substitute fuel hose or equivalent where fuel pipe is installed.

RELIEVING FUEL SYSTEM PRESSURE

1. Disconnect the fuel pump harness connector at the fuel tank side.

2. Start the engine and allow it to continue running until it stalls.

3. Set the ignition to the **OFF** position.

4. Reconnect the fuel pump harness connector.

Fuel Tank

REMOVAL AND INSTALLATION

Colt, Colt Wagon and Colt Vista

1. Disconnect the negative battery cable.

2. Drain the fuel tank using an approved tank pump and container. Remove and drain the remaining fuel using the drain plug, if equipped.

3. Remove the fuel cap.

4. Remove the spare tire and carrier (2WD Vista) or the fuel tank protector (4WD Vista).

5. Disconnect the fuel gauge unit and fuel hoses that can be accessed before lowering the tank. Disconnect the fuel pump connectors (fuel injected engines).

6. Disconnect the filler hose.

7. Place a floor jack and a piece of wood under the tank before removing the straps or retaining bolts.

8. Remove the retaining straps and the tank retaining bolts, if equipped.

9. Slowly lower the tank and disconnect any electrical or fuel connections. Be careful not to damage the fuel fittings.

10. Remove all hardware from the old tank if installing a new tank. Remove the fuel pump nuts and remove the pump.

To install:

11. Install all hardware to the tank, if installing a new tank. Always use new gaskets around the fuel pump and gauge unit. Install the pump and gauge unit. Torque the nuts or bolts to 1.4-2.2 ft. lbs. (2-3 Nm).

12. Slowly raise the tank and connect any electrical or fuel connections. Be careful not to damage the fuel fittings.

13. Install the retaining straps or tank retaining bolts, if equipped. Torque the bolts to 20 ft. lbs. (27 Nm).

14. Connect the filler hose.

15. Connect the fuel gauge unit and fuel hoses that can be accessed after raising the tank. Connect the fuel pump connectors (fuel injected engines).

16. Install the spare tire and carrier (2WD Vista) or the fuel tank protector (4WD Vista).

17. Install the fuel cap.

18. Install the drain plug, if equipped. Torque the plug to 15 ft. lbs. (20 Nm).

19. Refill the tank and check for leaks. Connect the negative battery cable.

Fuel Filter

REMOVAL AND INSTALLATION

1. Relieve the fuel system pressure.

2. Disconnect the negative battery cable. Remove the air cleaner.

3. Using a backup wrench, remove the fuel line fittings from the fuel filter.

NOTE: Some pressure may still remain in the system, cover the filter connections with a rag to prevent splashing.

4. Remove the fuel filter mounting bolts and the filter from the vehicle.

To install:

5. Installation is the reverse order of the removal procedures. Use a new fuel filter and O-rings. Torque the fuel line-to-filter connectors to 25 ft. lbs. (35 Nm).

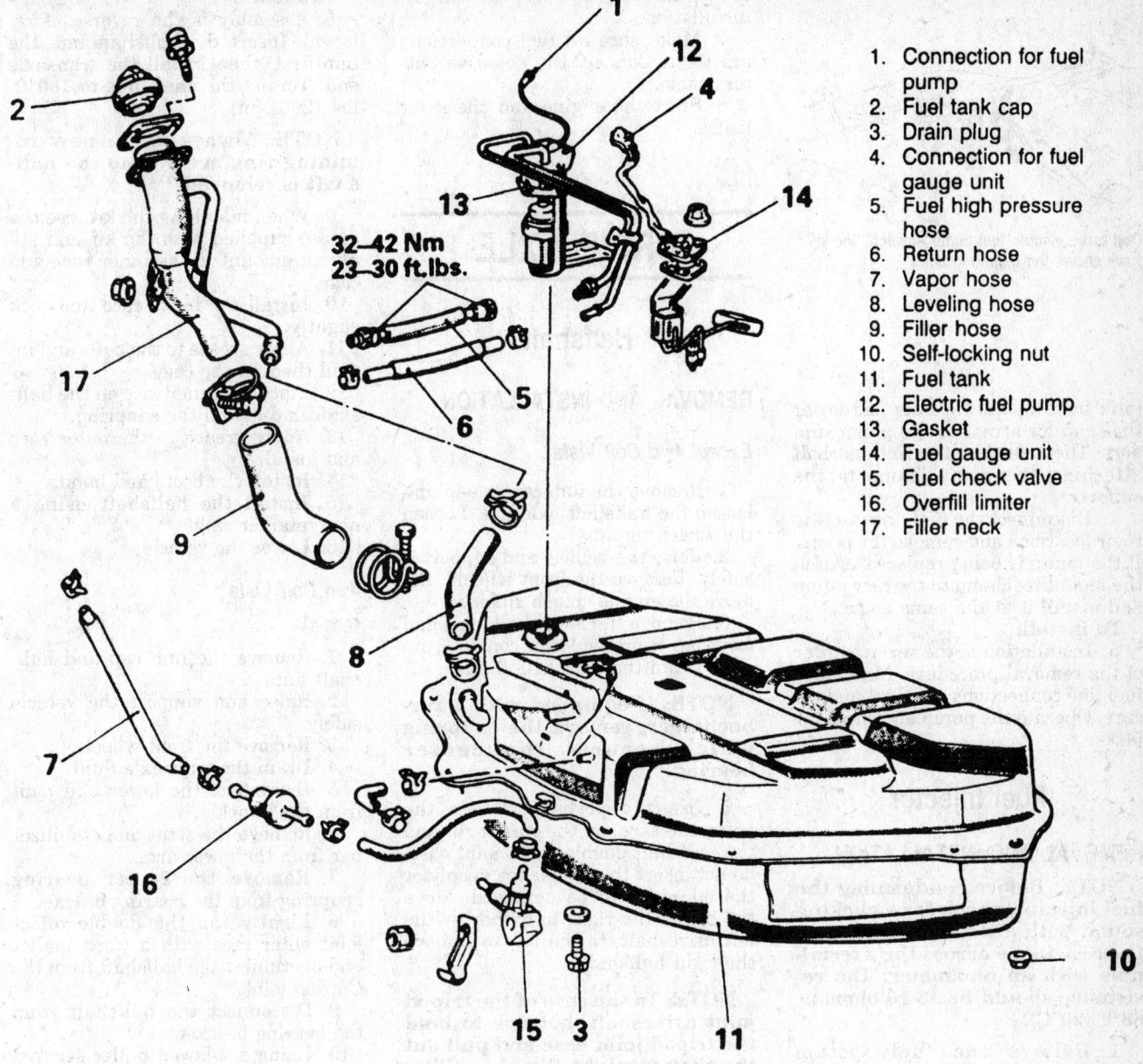

32–42 Nm
23–30 ft.lbs.

1. Connection for fuel pump
2. Fuel tank cap
3. Drain plug
4. Connection for fuel gauge unit
5. Fuel high pressure hose
6. Return hose
7. Vapor hose
8. Leveling hose
9. Filler hose
10. Self-locking nut
11. Fuel tank
12. Electric fuel pump
13. Gasket
14. Fuel gauge unit
15. Fuel check valve
16. Overfill limiter
17. Filler neck

Fuel tank removal

Electric Fuel Pump

PRESSURE TESTING

Colt and Colt Vista with Multi-Port Injection

1. Install a suitable fuel pressure gauge to the fuel delivery pipe, be sure to tighten the bolt at 18-25 ft. lbs. (25-34 Nm).

2. Apply voltage to the terminal for the fuel pump drive and activate the fuel pump; then, with fuel pressure applied, check that there is no fuel leakage from the pressure gauge or the special tool connection pipe.

3. Disconnect and plug the vacuum hose at the pressure regulator. Measure the fuel pressure during idling. The standard value is 47-50 psi (330-350 kPa).

4. Mea sure the fuel pressure when the vacuum hose is connected to the pressure regulator. The standard value is 38 psi (270 kPa).

5. If the fuel pressure readings are not within specifications, determine the probable cause and make the necessary repairs.

6. Remove all test equipment, use a new gasket and tighten the bolt on the delivery pipe to 18-25 ft. lbs.

(25-34). Start the engine and check for fuel leaks.

REMOVAL AND INSTALLATION

The fuel pump is mounted inside of the fuel tank.

1. Relieve the pressure from the fuel system. Disconnect the negative battery cable.

2. If equipped with a drain plug remove it and drain the fuel into a suitable container. Raise and support the vehicle safely. Remove the left rear wheel.

3. Support the fuel tank with a suitable floor jack. Loosen the fuel

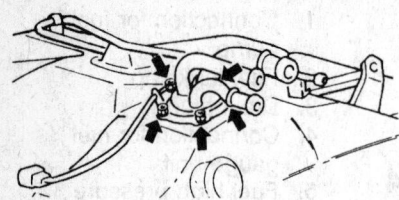

Colt turbo electric fuel pump location. The arrows shows the mounting bolts

tank band mounting nuts and lower the tank for access to the pump support. Then, remove the nut and bolt attaching the pump clamp to the support.

4. Disconnect the fuel lines, noting their locations and remove the pump. If the pump is being replaced, switch the mounting clamp to the new pump and install it at the same angle.

To install:

5. Installation is the reverse order of the removal procedure. Make sure fuel line connections are tight and secure. Operate the pump and check for leaks.

Fuel Injector

REMOVAL AND INSTALLATION

NOTE: Before condemning the fuel injector, check for a clicking sound with a stethoscope. Check the resistance across the 2 terminals with an ohmmeter. The resistance should be 13-16 ohms at 68°F (20°C).

1. Relieve the fuel system pressure.

2. Disconnect the negative battery cable.

3. Disconnect the fuel rail assembly, so the fuel injectors are easily accessible.

4. Remove the injector clip from the fuel rail and injector. Pull the injector straight out of the fuel rail receiver cup.

5. Check the injector O-ring for damage. If the O-ring is damaged, replace it. If the injector is being reused, install a protective cap on the injector tip to prevent damage.

To install:

6. Installation is the reverse order of the removal procedures. Before installing the injector, the rubber O-ring must be lubricated with a drop

of clean engine oil to aid in installation.

7. Make sure all fuel connections are tight. Connect the negative battery cable.

8. Start the engine and check for leaks.

DRIVE AXLE

Halfshaft

REMOVAL AND INSTALLATION

Except 4wd Colt Vista

1. Remove the hub center cap and loosen the halfshaft axle nut. Loosen the wheel lug nuts.

2. Raise the vehicle and support it safely. Remove the front wheels. Remove the engine splash shield.

3. Remove the lower ball joint and strut bar from the lower control arm.

4. Drain the transaxle fluid.

NOTE: If equipped with a turbocharger, remove the snapring which secures the center bearing.

5. Insert a prybar between the transaxle case, on the raised rib and the halfshaft double offset joint case; do not insert the prybar too deeply or the oil seal will be damaged. Move the bar to the right to withdraw the left driveshaft; to the left to remove the right halfshaft.

NOTE: In the case of the tripod joint driveshaft, be sure to hold the tripod joint case and pull out the shaft straight. Simply pulling the shaft out of position could cause damage to the tripod joint boot or the spider assembly slipping from the case.

6. Plug the transaxle case with a clean rag to prevent dirt from entering the case.

7. Use a special puller driver tool mounted on the wheel studs to push the halfshaft from the front hub. Take care to prevent the spacer from falling out of place.

NOTE: If equipped with a center bearing, after forcing out the halfshaft, remove it by lightly tapping the double offset joint outer race, with a plastic hammer.

To install:

8. Assembly is the reverse of removal. Insert the halfshaft into the hub first, then install the transaxle end. Torque the shaft nut to 180 ft. lbs. (260 Nm).

NOTE: Always use a new retaining ring every time the halfshaft is removed.

9. When installing the kit, use the grease supplied with the kit and apply an amount to the inner race and cage.

10. Install the inner race and cock slightly.

11. Apply grease to the balls and install them in the cage.

12. Place the inner race on the halfshaft and install the snapring.

13. Apply grease to the outer race and install.

14. Install the boots and bands.

15. Install the halfshaft using a new retainer ring.

16. Lower the vehicle.

4wd Colt Vista

1990-91

1. Remove the hub cap and halfshaft nut.

2. Raise and support the vehicle safely.

3. Remove the front wheels.

4. Drain the transaxle fluid.

5. Disconnect the lower ball joint from the knuckle.

6. Remove the strut and stabilizer bar from the lower arm.

7. Remove the center bearing snapring from the bearing bracket.

8. Lightly tap the double offset joint outer race with a wood mallet and disconnect the halfshaft from the Cardan joint.

9. Disconnect the halfshaft from the bearing bracket.

10. Using a 2-jawed puller secured to the hub lugs, press the halfshaft from the hub.

11. Unbolt and remove the bearing bracket.

12. Using a wood mallet, lightly tap the Cardan joint yoke and remove it from the transaxle. Never pry the Cardan joint from the transaxle. Prying will damage the Cardan joint dust cover.

To install:

13. Install the Cardan joint.

14. Apply a coating of chassis lube on the center bearing.

15. Attach a new O-ring to the oil seal retainer.

16. Install the bearing bracket. Torque the bolts to 40 ft. lbs. (54 Nm).

17. Insert the center bearing in the bearing bracket, making sure it is

fully seated, then secure it with the snapring.

18. Coat the halfshaft splines with chassis lube and slide it into the Cardan joint.

19. Slide the halfshaft into the hub and install the nut. Torque the nut to 188 ft. lbs. (255 Nm).

1992-94

1. Disconnect the negative battery cable, raise the vehicle and support safely. Remove the front wheel and place a drain pan under the transaxle.

2. Remove the cotter pin and halfshaft nut with a removing tool MB990767, or equivalent.

3. Remove the stabilizer bar from the control arm.

4. Remove the lower ball joint and tie rod end from the knuckle with a separator tool MB991113, or equivalent.

5. Use a special tool MB990241 to push the outer joint from the hub.

6. If the inner shaft and transaxle are tight, tap the center bearing bracket lightly with a plastic hammer to remove the halfshaft from the inner shaft.

7. Remove the inner shaft by prying the projecting part of the halfshaft inner joint from the transaxle.

To install:

8. Replace all circlips with new. Install the inner shaft into the transaxle until the circlip engages.

9. Install the halfshaft into the inner shaft and hub. Lubricate the splines to ease installation.

10. Install the lower ball joint and tie rod end to the knuckle. Torque the nut to 17-25 ft. lbs. (24-34 Nm) and install a new cotter pin.

11. Install the stabilizer bar to the control arm.

12. Install the washer and halfshaft nut. Use the holding tool MB990767 and torque the nut to 188 ft. lbs. (260 Nm). Install a new cotter pin.

13. Connect the negative battery cable, lower the vehicle and align the front end. Refill the transaxle with fluid.

CV-Boot

REMOVAL AND INSTALLATION

Inner Boot

1. Raise the vehicle and support it safely. Remove the wheel assembly.

2. Remove the halfshaft assembly from the vehicle.

3. Place the assembly in vise. Care must be taken not to crush the tubular shafts.

4. If inner joint needs replacement, cut the small rubber clamp, large metal clamp and remove the rubber boot. These items must be discarded.

5. Inspect for internal wear and/or damage.

6. Clean the grease by hand from inside the joint housing and around the ball trunnion assembly to inspect it.

7. Mark the tripod and housing for proper reassembly, if it is to be reinstalled.

8. To replace the boot, CV-joint or both, remove the snapring from the groove and tap the trunnion lightly with a brass drift pin. Leave the tripod bearings on the trunnion. Care must be taken to support the bearings as they may fall off.

To install:

9. Installation is the reverse order of the removal procedures.

10. When installing the tripod on the shaft place the chamfer face towards the retainer groove.

NOTE: The grease provided with the repair kit must be used. It cannot be substituted with any other type grease.

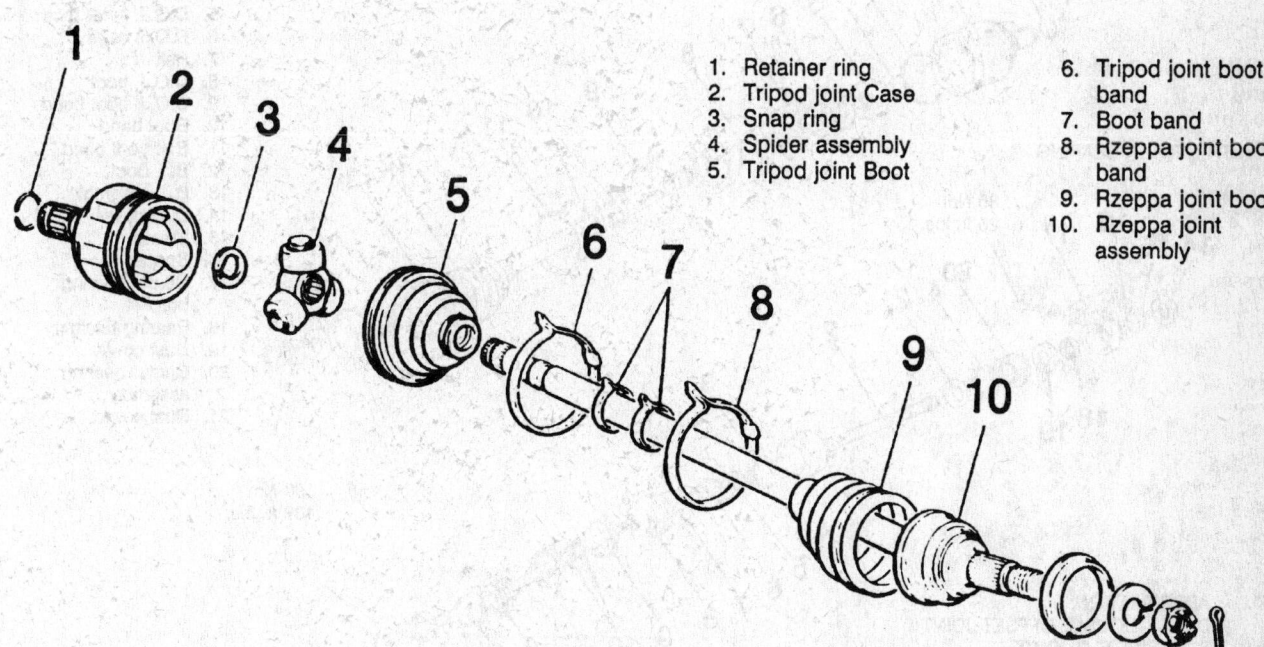

1. Retainer ring
2. Tripod joint Case
3. Snap ring
4. Spider assembly
5. Tripod joint Boot
6. Tripod joint boot band
7. Boot band
8. Rzeppa joint boot band
9. Rzeppa joint boot
10. Rzeppa joint assembly

Exploded view of the front driveshaft — Type T.J. and R.J.

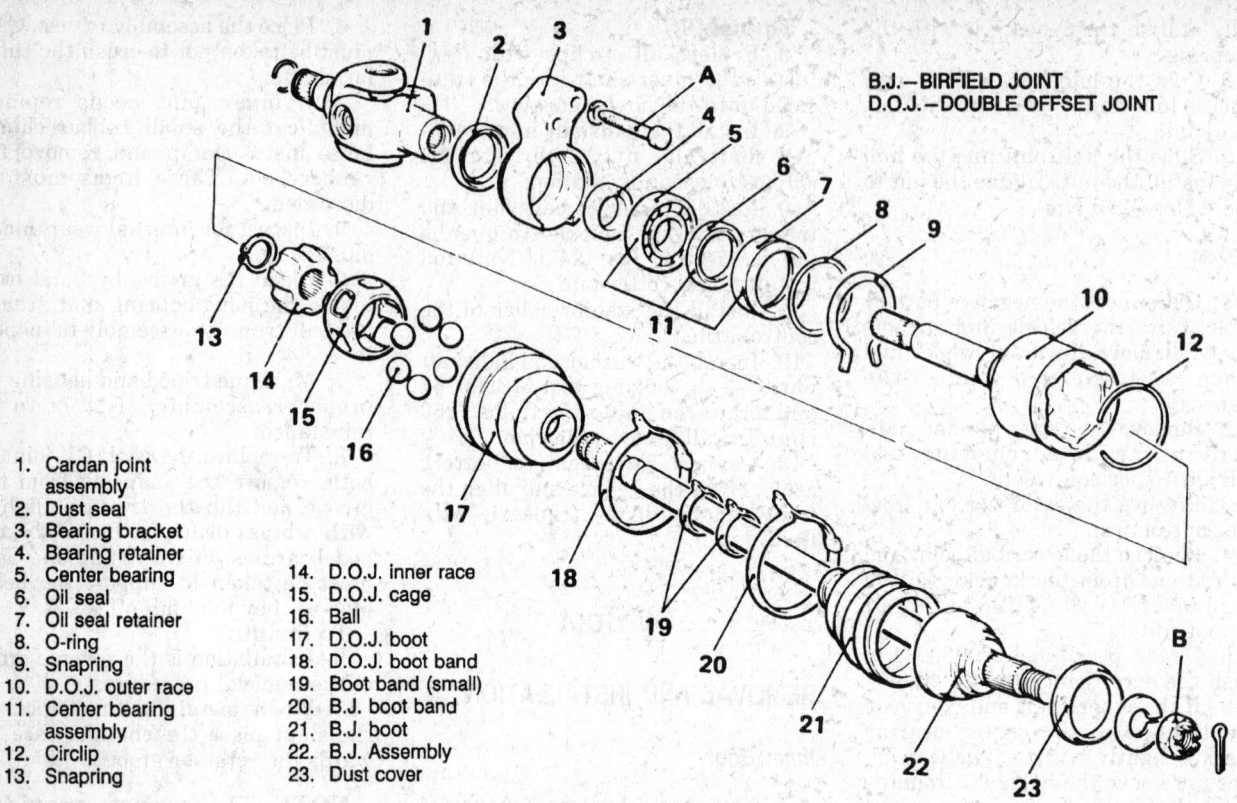

B.J.—BIRFIELD JOINT
D.O.J.—DOUBLE OFFSET JOINT

1. Cardan joint assembly
2. Dust seal
3. Bearing bracket
4. Bearing retainer
5. Center bearing
6. Oil seal
7. Oil seal retainer
8. O-ring
9. Snapring
10. D.O.J. outer race
11. Center bearing assembly
12. Circlip
13. Snapring
14. D.O.J. inner race
15. D.O.J. cage
16. Ball
17. D.O.J. boot
18. D.O.J. boot band
19. Boot band (small)
20. B.J. boot band
21. B.J. boot
22. B.J. Assembly
23. Dust cover

1990-91 4WD Colt Vista driveshaft

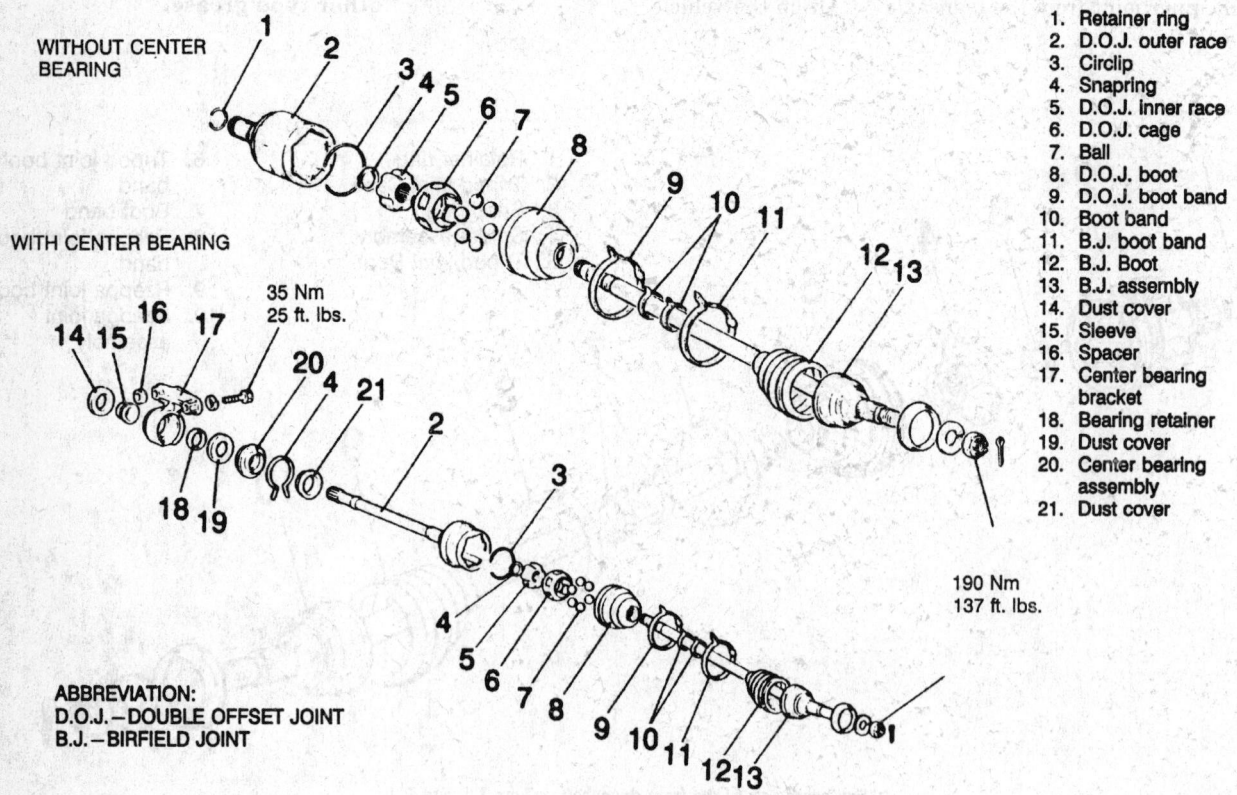

WITHOUT CENTER BEARING

WITH CENTER BEARING

35 Nm
25 ft. lbs.

190 Nm
137 ft. lbs.

1. Retainer ring
2. D.O.J. outer race
3. Circlip
4. Snapring
5. D.O.J. inner race
6. D.O.J. cage
7. Ball
8. D.O.J. boot
9. D.O.J. boot band
10. Boot band
11. B.J. boot band
12. B.J. Boot
13. B.J. assembly
14. Dust cover
15. Sleeve
16. Spacer
17. Center bearing bracket
18. Bearing retainer
19. Dust cover
20. Center bearing assembly
21. Dust cover

ABBREVIATION:
D.O.J.—DOUBLE OFFSET JOINT
B.J.—BIRFIELD JOINT

Exploded view of front driveshaft — Type D.O.J and B.J.

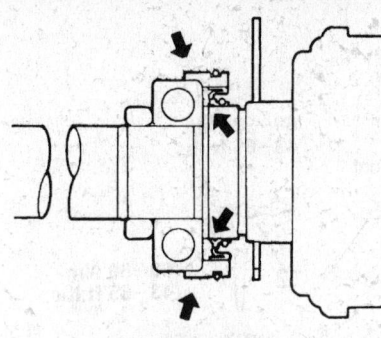

Lubricant application points

Driveshaft and U-Joints

REMOVAL AND INSTALLATION

Colt Wagon and 4WD Colt Vista

1. Raise the vehicle and support safely.
2. Mark the companion flanges for reassembly. Place a drain pan under the transaxle.
3. Remove the center exhaust pipe bracket.
4. Remove the center bearing nuts.
5. Remove the differential-to-driveshaft bolts.
6. Remove the driveshafts being careful not to damage the transfer case seal.
7. To disassemble the driveshaft: remove the U-joint snaprings and press the bearing caps from the yoke with tool MB990840, or equivalent.
8. Remove the lobro joint bolts, nut and companion flange with a gear puller.
9. Remove the lobro joint as follows.
    a. Matchmark the outer race and cage.
    b. Remove the outer cage and balls. If the outer cage can not be removed without excessive force, remove the entire assembly with a gear puller.
    c. Remove the inner race with cage from the center shaft with a gear puller.
    d. Remove the joint boot.
10. Assembly the lobro joint and pack with special grease for Constant Velocity (CV) joints. Torque the joint bolts to 25 ft. lbs. (35 Nm) and the shaft nut to 137 ft. lbs. (190 Nm).
11. Install the U-joint bearing cap into the yoke with a press.
12. Install the joint and other bearing caps with the press. Do not over-press the bearing caps.
13. Measure the space between the snapring and groove wall of the yoke. It should be 0.0008-0.0024 in. (0.02-0.06mm). If the measurement is excessive the bearing caps will bind against the U-joint. Different thickness snaprings are available.
    To install:
14. Install the driveshaft and torque the differential bolts to 25 ft. lbs. (35 Nm) and center bearing nuts to 30 ft. lbs. (41 Nm).
15. Drive the vehicle at about 40 mph. Check for excessive vibration.

Outer Boot

1. Raise the vehicle and support it safely. Remove the wheel assembly.
2. Remove the halfshaft assembly from the vehicle.
3. Place the assembly in vise. Care must be taken not to crush the tubular shafts.
4. At the inner joint, cut the small rubber clamp, large metal clamp and remove the rubber boot. These items must be discarded.
5. Inspect for internal wear and/or damage.
6. Clean the grease by hand from inside the joint housing and around the ball trunnion assembly to inspect it.
7. Mark the tripod and housing for proper reassembly, if it is to be reinstalled.
8. To replace the boot, CV-joint or both, remove the snapring from the groove and tap the trunnion lightly with a brass drift pin. Leave the tripod bearings on the trunnion. Care must be taken to support the bearings as they may fall off.
9. If equipped with a dynamic damper, remove the band and slide the damper from the shaft.
10. Cut both bands from the outer boot and slide the boot from the shaft.
    To install:
11. Installation is the reverse order of the removal procedures.
12. When installing the tripod on the shaft place the chamfer face towards the retainer groove.

NOTE: The grease provided with the repair kit must be used. It cannot be substituted with any other type grease.

Some vibration may be caused by unbalanced tires.

Rear Axle Shaft, Bearing and Seal

REMOVAL AND INSTALLATION

4WD Colt Vista

1990-91

1. Raise and support the vehicle safely.
2. Remove the rear wheels.
3. Remove the brake drums.
4. Remove the 3 bolts securing the halfshaft flange to the intermediate shaft flange.
5. Using a special tool, remove the halfshaft flange nut.
6. Using a slide hammer connected to a 2-jawed adapter secured under 2 lug nuts, pull the halfshaft from the housing.
7. Remove the lower arm.
8. Using a special tool, remove the dust cover and the outer wheel bearing and seal from the halfshaft at the same time. Discard the seal.
9. Using special driver tool and adapter, drive the inner bearing and seal from the housing. The new bearing should be thoroughly packed with chassis lube and driven into place with the same tools.
    To install:
10. Install a new inner bearing seal with a seal driver.
11. Using a special driver tool, tape a new dust cover into place. Tap evenly around the tool to seat the cover.
12. Coat the lip of a new seal with chassis lube and pack the new outer bearing thoroughly with chassis lube.
13. Using a press, install the bearing and seal.
14. Mount the inner arm in a vise and using a press, install the halfshaft.
15. Install the halfshaft and inner arm assembly.
16. Torque the halfshaft nut to 160 ft. lbs. (217 Nm).
17. Connect the halfshaft and intermediate shaft flanges and torque the bolts to 43 ft. lbs. (58 Nm).

1992-94

1. Disconnect the negative battery cable. Raise the vehicle and support safely.
2. Remove the bolts that attach the rear halfshaft to the rear carrier.

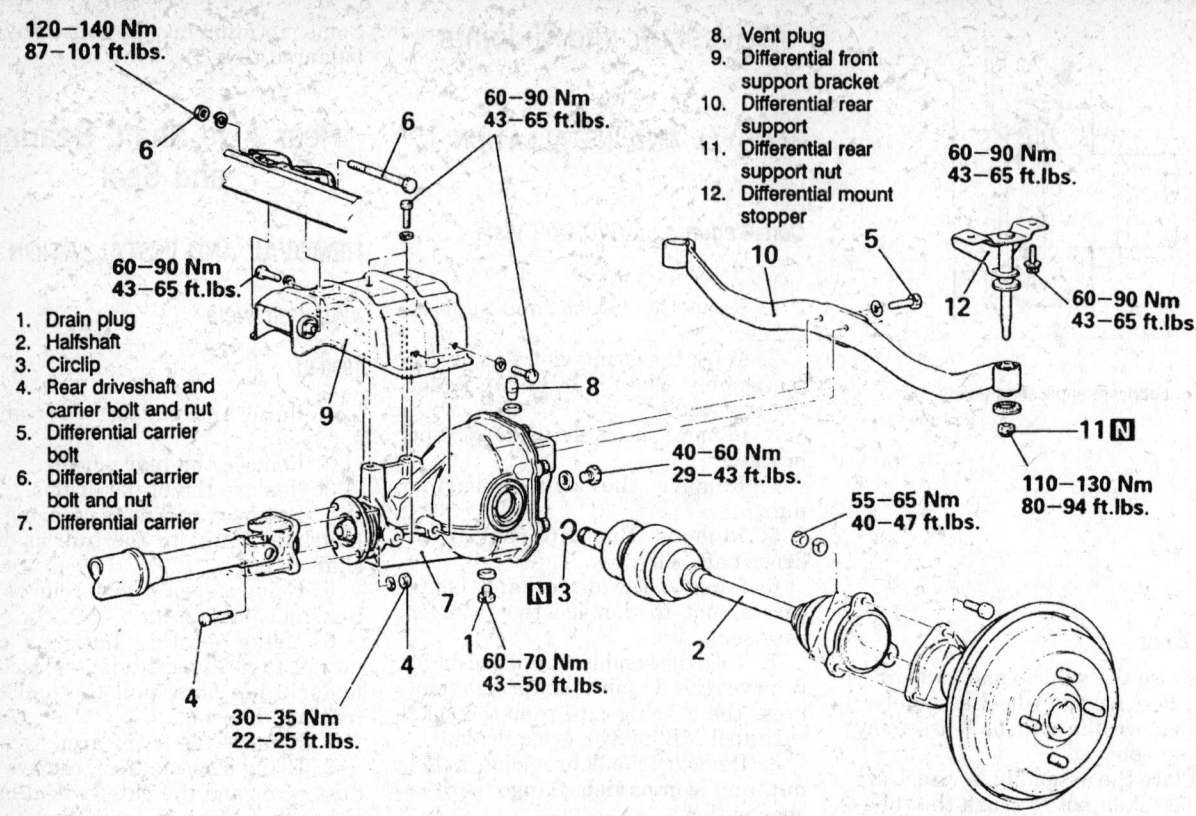

120—140 Nm
87—101 ft.lbs.

60—90 Nm
43—65 ft.lbs.

60—90 Nm
43—65 ft.lbs.

8. Vent plug
9. Differential front
   support bracket
10. Differential rear
    support
11. Differential rear
    support nut
12. Differential mount
    stopper

60—90 Nm
43—65 ft.lbs.

1. Drain plug
2. Halfshaft
3. Circlip
4. Rear driveshaft and
   carrier bolt and nut
5. Differential carrier
   bolt
6. Differential carrier
   bolt and nut
7. Differential carrier

40—60 Nm
29—43 ft.lbs.

55—65 Nm
40—47 ft.lbs.

110—130 Nm
80—94 ft.lbs.

60—70 Nm
43—50 ft.lbs.

30—35 Nm
22—25 ft.lbs.

Rear axle shaft bearing and seal — 1990-91 Colt Vista 4WD

3. Remove the cotter pin, driveshaft nut cover and nut from the rear driveshaft.

NOTE: Do not apply the vehicle weight to the wheel bearing while loosening the driveshaft nut or bearing damage may occur.

4. Separate the shaft from the hub using a puller MB990241, or equivalent. Remove the shaft from the flange and lift from the vehicle.
5. Remove the lower control arm and hub assembly. Remove the wheel hub using a slide hammer and puller tool MB990241.
6. Remove the wheel bearing inner race with a press.
7. Remove the wheel bearings from the lower control arm using tool MB990934 and a press. Remove the bearing seal.
To install:
8. Press the new bearing onto the lower control arm. Press the hub onto the bearing.
9. Install a wheel bearing preload tool MB990998 to the hub and bearing. Torque the tool nut to 145-188 ft. lbs. (200-240 Nm). Measure the rotating torque of the bearings with an inch lbs. torque wrench. The torque should be 9 inch lbs. (1.1 Nm) or less.

10. Install the remaining components. Torque the retainers on the rear carrier to 40-47 ft. lbs. (55-65 Nm) and the shaft end nut to 145-188 ft. lbs. (200-260 Nm).

Front Wheel Hub, Knuckle and Bearings

REMOVAL AND INSTALLATION

Colt and 1990-91 2WD Colt Vista

NOTE: The following procedure requires the use of several special tools.

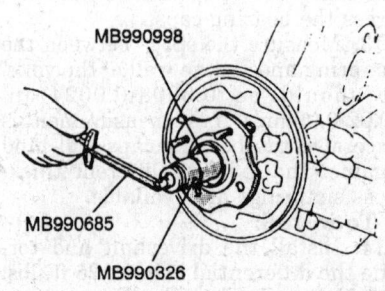

MB990998

MB990685

MB990326

Checking the wheel bearing turning torque

1. Remove the halfshaft nut.
2. Raise and support the the vehicle safely. Allow the front suspension to hang freely.
3. Remove the wheels.
4. Remove the caliper and suspend it out of the way, without disconnecting the brake hose.
5. Disconnect the lower ball joint from the knuckle.
6. Disconnect the tie rod end from the knuckle.
7. Using a 2-jawed puller, press the halfshaft from the hub.
8. Unbolt the strut from the knuckle. Remove the hub and knuckle assembly from the vehicle.
9. Install first the arm, then the body of special tool MB991056 (Colt) or MB991001 (Colt Vista) or their equivalent on the knuckle and tighten the nut.
10. Using special tool MB990998 or MB990781 or their equivalent, separate the hub from the knuckle.

NOTE: Prying or hammering will damage the bearing. Use these special tools or their equivalents, to separate the hub and knuckle.

11. Place the knuckle in a vise and separate the rotor from the hub.

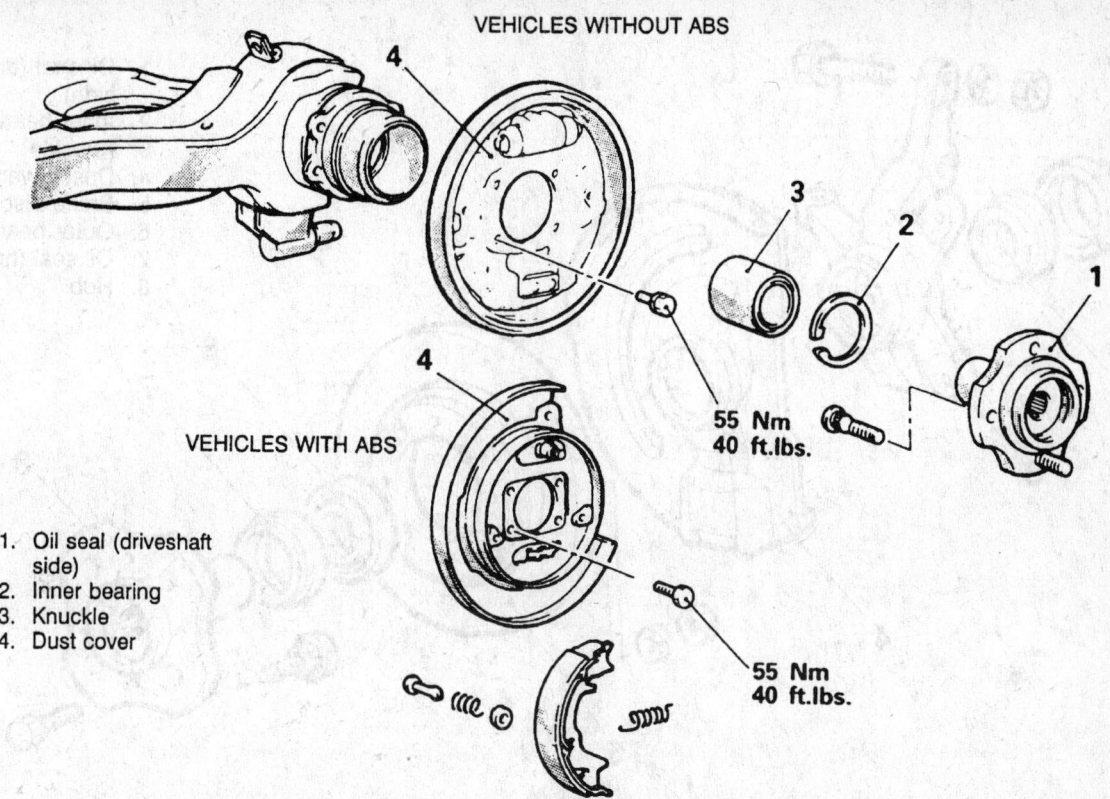

VEHICLES WITHOUT ABS

VEHICLES WITH ABS

1. Oil seal (driveshaft side)
2. Inner bearing
3. Knuckle
4. Dust cover

55 Nm
40 ft.lbs.

55 Nm
40 ft.lbs.

Removing the axle hub from the bearings — 1992-94 Colt Vista 4WD

12. Using special tools C-293-PA, SP-3183 and MB990781 or their equivalent, remove the outer bearing inner race.

13. Drive the oil seal and inner bearing inner race from the knuckle with a brass drift.

14. Drive out both outer races in a similar fashion.

NOTE: Always replace bearings and races as a set. Never replace just an inner or outer bearing. If either is in need of replacement, both sets must be replaced.

15. Thoroughly clean and inspect all parts. Any suspect part should be replaced.

To install:

16. Pack the wheel bearings with lithium based wheel bearing grease. Coat the inside of the knuckle with similar grease and pack the cavities in the knuckle. Apply a thin coating of grease to the outer surface of the races before installation.

17. Using special tools C-3893 and MB990776 or equivalent, install the outer races.

18. Install the rotor on the hub and torque the bolts to 36-43 ft. lbs. (48-58 Nm).

19. Drive the outer bearing inner race into position.

20. Coat the outer rim and lip of the oil seal and drive the hub side oil seal into place, using a seal driver.

21. Place the inner bearing in the knuckle.

22. Mount the knuckle in a vise. Position the hub and knuckle together. Install tool MB99098 or equivalent and tighten the tool to 147-192 ft. lbs. (190-265 Nm). Rotate the hub to seat the bearing.

23. With the knuckle still in the vise measure the hub starting torque with an inch lb. torque wrench and tool MB990998 or equivalent. Starting torque should be 11.5 inch lbs. (1.3 Nm) or less. If the starting torque is 0, measure the hub bearing axial play with a dial indicator. If axial play exceeds 0.0078 in. (0.1981mm), while the nut is tightened to 145-192 ft. lbs. (190-265 Nm), the assembly has not been done correctly. Disassemble the knuckle and hub, and start again.

24. Remove the special tool.

25. Place the outer bearing in the hub and drive the seal into place.

26. The remainder of installation is the reverse of removal.

1990-91 4WD Colt Vista

NOTE: The following procedure requires the use of several special tools.

1. Remove the hub cap and half-shaft nut.

2. Raise the vehicle and support it safely.

3. Remove the front wheels.

4. Drain the transaxle fluid.

5. Disconnect the lower ball joint from the knuckle.

6. Remove the strut and stabilizer bar from the lower arm.

7. Remove the center bearing snapring from the bearing bracket.

8. Lightly tap the double off-set joint outer race with a wood mallet and disconnect the halfshaft from the Cardan joint.

9. Disconnect the halfshaft from the bearing jacket.

10. Using a 2-jawed puller secured to the hub lugs, press the halfshaft from the hub.

11. Unbolt the strut from the hub. Remove the hub and knuckle assembly from the vehicle.

12. Install first the arm, then the body of special tool MB991001 or equivalent on the knuckle and tighten the nut.

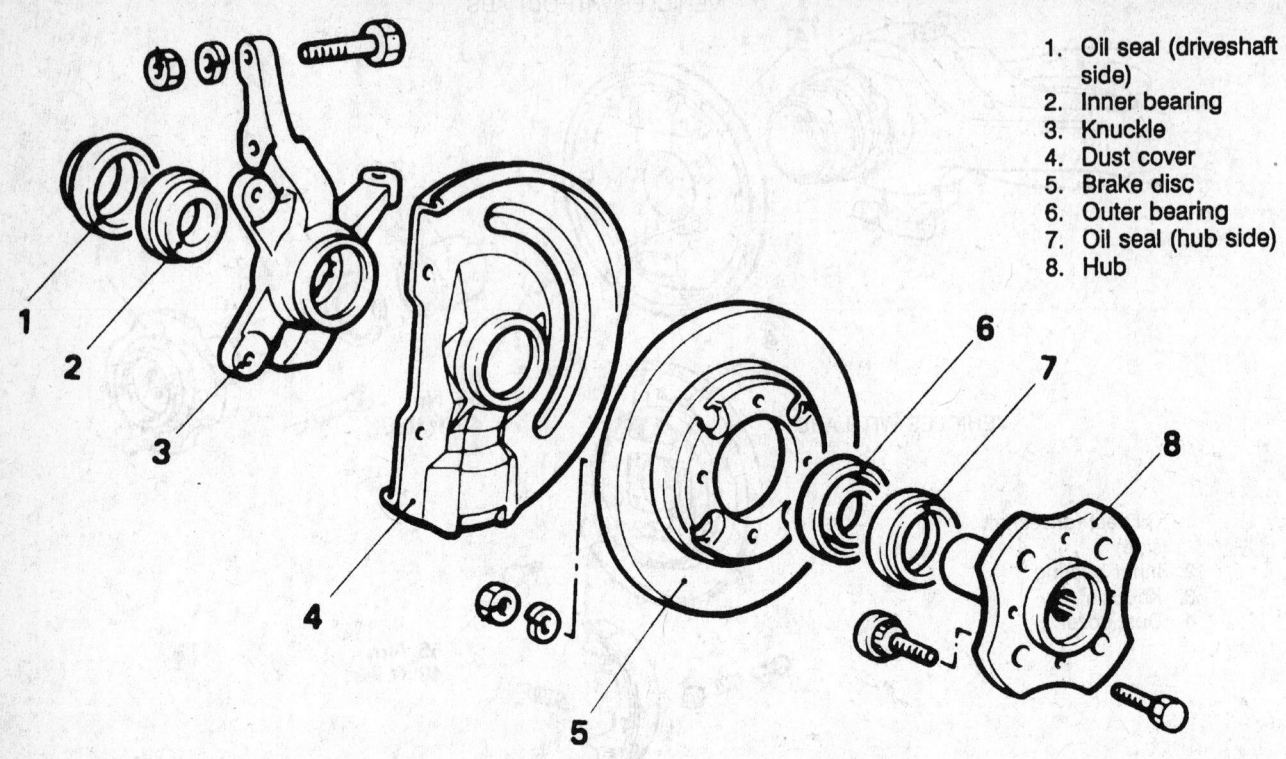

1. Oil seal (driveshaft side)
2. Inner bearing
3. Knuckle
4. Dust cover
5. Brake disc
6. Outer bearing
7. Oil seal (hub side)
8. Hub

Exploded view of the hub and knuckle — Colt, Colt Vista similar

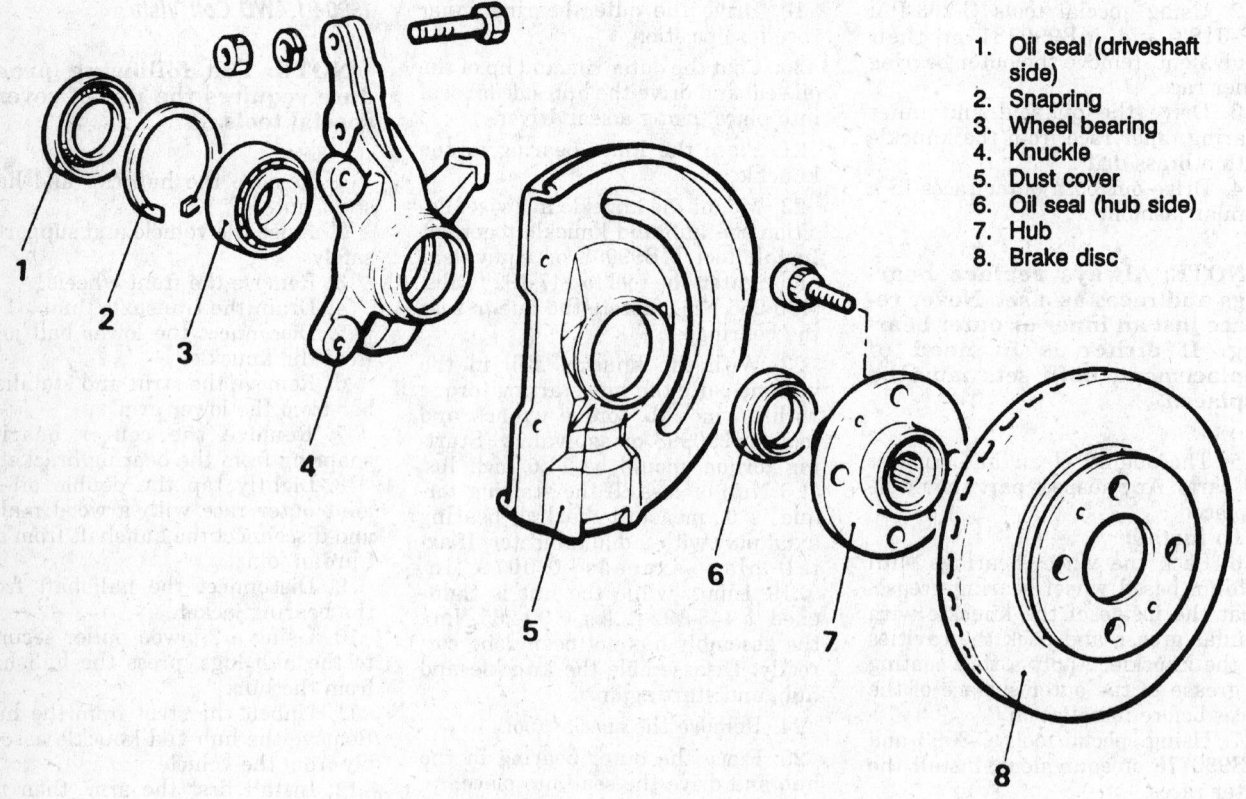

1. Oil seal (driveshaft side)
2. Snapring
3. Wheel bearing
4. Knuckle
5. Dust cover
6. Oil seal (hub side)
7. Hub
8. Brake disc

4WD Colt Vista front hub, knuckle and bearing

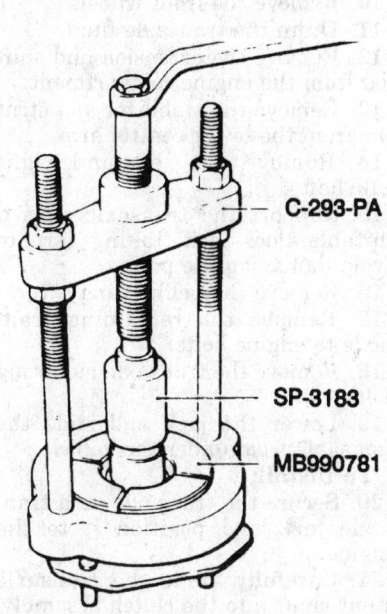

Removing the outer bearing inner race from the hub, using the special tools described

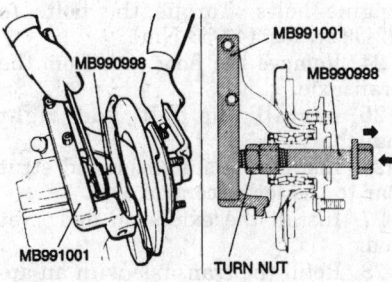

Using special tools to remove the hub from the knuckle

13. Using special tool MB9900998 or equivalent, separate the hub from the knuckle and tighten the nut.

NOTE: Prying or hammering will damage the bearing. Use these special tools or equivalent, to separate the hub and knuckle.

14. Matchmark the hub and rotor. The rotor should slide from the hub. If not, insert M8 x 1.25 bolts in the holes between the lugs and tighten

them alternately to press the hub from the rotor. Never hammer the rotor to remove it.

15. Using a 2-jawed puller, remove the outer bearing inner race.
16. Remove and discard the outer oil seal.
17. Remove and discard the inner oil seal.
18. Remove the bearing snapring from the knuckle.
19. Using special tools C-4628 and MB991056 or MB991001 or their equivalent, remove the bearing from the knuckle. Using a driver, drive the bearing from the knuckle.

NOTE: Always replace bearings and races as a set. Never replace just an inner or outer bearing. If either is in need of replacement, both sets must be replaced.

20. Thoroughly clean and inspect all parts. Any suspect part should be replaced.
21. Pack the wheel bearings with lithium based wheel bearing grease. Coat the inside of the knuckle with similar grease and pack the cavities in the knuckle. Apply a thin coating of grease to the outer surface of the races before installation.
To install:
22. Using special tools C-4171 and MB990985 or their equivalent, press the bearing into place in the knuckle. Install the snapring.
23. Coat the lips of a new hub side seal with lithium grease. Using a seal driver, install the seal. Make sure it is flush.
24. Install the rotor on the hub.
25. Using special tool MB990998 or equivalent, join the hub and knuckle. Torque the special tool nut to 188 ft. lbs. (260 Nm).
26. Rotate the hub several times to seat the bearing.
27. Mount the knuckle in a vise. Using MB990998 or equivalent and an inch lbs. torque wrench, measure the turning torque. Turning torque should be 15.6 inch lbs. (2.5 Nm) or less. Next, measure the axial play using a dial indicator. Axial play should be 0.008 in. (0.203mm). If either the axial play or the turning torque are not within the specified values, the hub and knuckle have not been properly assembled. Repeat the procedure. If everything checks out okay, go on to the next step.
28. Remove all the special tools.

29. Using a seal driver, drive a new seal coated with lithium grease, into place on the halfshaft side, until it contacts the snapring.
30. The remainder of installation is the reverse order of removal procedures.

1992-94 Colt Vista

1. Raise the vehicle and support safely. Remove the front wheel.
2. Disconnect the ABS speed sensor, if equipped.
3. Remove the brake disc caliper and hang with a wire.
4. Remove the brake disc.
5. Remove the halfshaft nut using tool MB9900767, or equivalent.
6. Disconnect the lower ball joint and tie rod end using tool MB991113, or equivalent.
7. Press the halfshaft from the hub using tool MB990241.
8. Remove the MacPherson strut bolts and knuckle/hub assembly.
9. Remove the hub from the knuckle using a press tool MB990998 and MB991056, or equivalent. If the tool is not available, have the local machine shop replace the bearings.
10. Crush the oil seal in opposite places so the tabs of tool MB990810 or equivalent, can remove the bearing inner race and seal.
11. Press the outer race from the knuckle.
To install:
12. Press the bearing into the knuckle and install the outer grease seal. Pack all bearings with chassis grease before reassembly.
13. Install a wheel bearing preload tool MB990998 or equivalent, to the hub and bearing. Torque the tool nut to 145-188 ft. lbs. (200-240 Nm). Measure the rotating torque of the bearings with an inch lbs. torque wrench. The torque should be 16 inch lbs. (1.8 Nm) or less.
14. Install the knuckle/hub assembly. Torque shaft end nut to 145-188 ft. lbs. (200-260 Nm), ball joint nut to 49 ft. lbs. (68 Nm), tie rod nut to 25 ft. lbs. (34 Nm) and strut bolts to 78 ft. lbs. (108 Nm).
15. Install the ABS speed sensor and measure the clearance between the rotor and sensor. The clearance should be 0.012-0.035 in. (0.3-0.9mm). If the clearance is not within specifications, the brake rotor is probably installed incorrectly.
16. Align the front end.

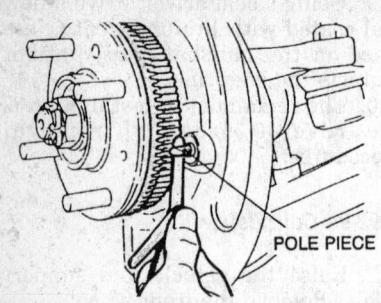

POLE PIECE

Measuring the clearance between the rotor and speed sensor — Anti-lock Brake System (ABS)

MANUAL TRANSAXLE

Transaxle Assembly

REMOVAL AND INSTALLATION

Colt

1. Disconnect the negative battery cable.

2. Disconnect from the transaxle: the clutch cable, speedometer cable, backup light harness, starter motor and the 4 upper bolts connecting the engine to the transaxle.

3. If with a turbocharger, remove the air cleaner case, the actuator mounting bolts, the pin coupling, the actuator and shaft and remove the actuator. Discard the collar used with the pin and replace it with a new collar. If equipped with a 5 speed transaxle, disconnect the selector control valve.

4. Raise and support the vehicle safely.

5. Remove the front wheels. Remove the splash shield. Drain the transaxle fluid.

6. Remove the shift rod and extension. It may be necessary to remove any heat shields that interfere.

7. If equipped, remove the stabilizer bar from the lower arm and disconnect the lower arm from the body side.

8. Remove the right and left halfshafts from the transaxle case.

9. Disconnect the range selector cable, if equipped. Remove the engine rear cover.

10. Support the weight of the engine from above. Support the transaxle and remove the remaining lower mounting bolts.

11. Remove the transaxle mount insulator bolt.

12. Remove the engine and transaxle by lowering the transaxle and raising the assembly on an angle.

To install:

13. Secure the transaxle on a transaxle jack and position it to the engine.

14. Carefully guide the transaxle input shaft into the clutch assembly. Make sure the transaxle is seated properly and is flush to the engine flange. Install 2 transaxle-to-engine bolts.

15. Install the transaxle mount insulator bolt. Torque the bolt to 29-36 ft. lbs. (40-50 Nm).

16. With the engine weight supported from above. Install the remaining lower transaxle mounting bolts.

17. Connect the range selector cable, if equipped. Install the engine rear cover.

18. Install the right and left halfshafts to the transaxle case.

19. If equipped, install the stabilizer bar to the lower arm.

20. Install the shift rod and extension. Install the heat shields, if removed.

21. Install the splash shield. Install the front wheels. Refill the transaxle fluid.

22. Lower the vehicle.

23. If equipped with a turbocharger, install the air cleaner case, the actuator mounting bolts, the pin coupling, the actuator shaft and actuator. Install new collar and pin. If equipped with a 5 speed transaxle, connect the selector control valve.

24. Connect to the transaxle: the clutch cable, speedometer cable, backup light harness, starter motor and the 4 upper bolts connecting the engine to the transaxle.

25. Connect the negative battery cable.

2WD Colt Vista

1. Disconnect the battery cables, negative cable first. Remove the battery and tray.

2. Remove the coolant reservoir.

3. Remove the air cleaner.

4. Disconnect the clutch cable, speedometer cable and backup light wiring from the transaxle.

5. Remove the upper engine-to-transaxle bolts.

6. Disconnect the select control lever and switch harness.

7. Remove the starter.

8. Disconnect and tag all wiring from the transaxle.

9. Raise and support the vehicle safely.

10. Remove the front wheels.

11. Drain the transaxle fluid.

12. Remove the extension and shift rod from the engine compartment.

13. Remove the stabilizer and strut bar from the lower control arm.

14. Remove the left and right halfshafts.

15. Support the transaxle with a suitable floor jack, taking care to avoid damaging the pan.

16. Remove the bellhousing cover.

17. Remove the remaining transaxle-to-engine bolts.

18. Remove the transaxle mounting bolt.

19. Lower the jack and slide the transaxle from under the vehicle.

To install:

20. Secure the transaxle on a transaxle jack and position it to the engine.

21. Carefully guide the transaxle input shaft into the clutch assembly. Make sure the transaxle is seated properly and is flush to the engine flange. Install 2 transaxle-to-engine bolts.

22. Install the transaxle mounting bolt. Torque the bolt to 29-36 ft. lbs. (40-50 Nm).

23. Install the lower transaxle-to-engine bolts. Torque the bolts to 32-39 ft. lbs. (43-53 Nm).

24. Remove the floor jack from the transaxle.

25. Install the left and right halfshafts.

26. Install the stabilizer and strut bar to the lower control arm.

27. Install the extension and shift rod.

28. Refill the transaxle with an approved gear oil.

29. Install the front wheels and lower the vehicle.

30. Connect all wiring to the transaxle.

31. Install the starter and mounting bolts. Torque the mounting bolts to 20-24 ft. lbs. (27-34 Nm).

32. Connect the select control lever and switch harness.

33. Install the upper engine-to-transaxle bolts. Torque the bolts to 32-39 ft. lbs. (43-53 Nm).

34. Connect the clutch cable, speedometer cable and backup light wiring to the transaxle.

35. Install the air cleaner.

36. Install the coolant reservoir and refill with coolant.

37. Install the battery tray and battery. Connect the battery cables, positive cable first.

4WD Colt Wagon

1. Disconnect the negative battery cable, drain the transaxle fluid and remove the under cover.

2. Remove the air cleaner, battery and battery tray.

3. Remove the split pin and disconnect the shift and select cables.

4. Disconnect the clutch cylinder line, backup light switch and speedometer cable.

5. Disconnect the stabilizer bar, tie rod ends, lower ball joint and driveshaft from the control arm and strut.

6. Remove the starter motor.

7. Place a jack under the transaxle and support the engine from above.

8. Remove the center crossmember with roll stopper bracket.

9. Remove the rear driveshaft and transfer case.

10. Remove the transaxle mount bracket and bellhousing bolts.

11. Using the jack, lower the transaxle and check for interference.

To install:

12. Using the jack, raise the transaxle and check for interference.

13. Install the transaxle mount bracket and bellhousing bolts. Torque the bolts to 35 ft. lbs. (47 Nm).

14. Install the rear driveshaft and transfer case. Torque the transfer bolts to 30 ft. lbs. (41 Nm).

15. Install the center crossmember with roll stopper bracket.

16. Remove the jack and engine support.

17. Install the starter motor and torque the bolts to 35 ft. lbs. (41 Nm).

18. Connect the stabilizer bar, tie rod ends, lower ball joint and driveshaft to the control arm and strut.

19. Connect the clutch cylinder line, backup light switch and speedometer cable.

20. Install the split pin and connect the shift and select cables.

21. Install the air cleaner, battery and battery tray.

22. Connect the negative battery cable, refill the transaxle fluid and install the under cover.

4WD Colt Vista

1. Disconnect the battery cables, negative cable first. Remove the battery.

2. Remove the coolant reserve tank.

3. Disconnect the speedometer cable, shift control cable and backup light harness at the transaxle.

4. Remove the range select control valves and connectors.

5. Tag and disconnect all other wiring attached to the transaxle.

6. Remove the clutch slave cylinder.

7. Remove the vacuum reservoir tank.

8. Disconnect the starter wiring and remove.

9. Remove the upper engine-to-transaxle bolts.

10. Raise and support the vehicle safely.

11. Remove the front wheels, lower engine cover and skid plate.

12. Drain the transaxle and transfer case.

13. Remove the driveshaft.

14. Remove the transfer case extension housing.

15. Remove the left and right halfshafts.

16. Disconnect the right strut from the lower arm.

17. Remove the right fender liner.

18. Take up the weight of the transaxle with a suitable floor jack.

19. Remove the bellhousing cover bolts and remove the cover.

20. Remove the remaining engine-to-transaxle bolts.

21. Remove the transaxle mount insulator bolt.

22. Remove the transaxle mounting bracket attaching bolts.

23. Move the transaxle/transfer case assembly to the right. Tilt the right side of the transaxle down, until the transfer case is about level with the upper part of the steering rack tube, then turn it to the left and lower the assembly.

To install:

24. Secure the transaxle/transfer case assembly to a transaxle jack.

25. Raise the assembly in position to the engine. It may be necessary to tilt or angle the assembly in and around the steering rack tube.

26. Once the transaxle/transfer assembly is positioned to the engine, carefully guide the input shaft into the clutch assembly.

27. Install the transaxle mounting bracket attaching bolts. Torque the bolts to 40-43 ft. lbs. (55-60 Nm).

28. Install the transaxle mount insulator bolt. Torque to 40-43 ft. lbs. (55-60 Nm).

29. Install the lower engine-to-transaxle bolts. Torque to 31-40 ft. lbs. (43-55 Nm).

30. Install the bellhousing cover bolts and install the cover.

31. Remove the the floor jack from the transaxle.

32. Install the right fender liner.

33. Connect the right strut to the lower arm.

34. Install the left and right halfshafts.

35. Install the transfer case extension housing and the driveshaft.

36. Refill the transaxle and transfer case with an approved gear oil.

37. Install the front wheels, lower engine cover and skid plate.

38. Lower the vehicle.

39. Install the upper engine-to-transaxle bolts. Torque the bolts to 40-43 ft. lbs. (55-60 Nm).

40. Install the starter motor and mounting bolts. Torque the bolts to 22-25 ft. lbs. (30-35 Nm). Connect the starter wiring.

41. Install the vacuum reservoir tank.

42. Install the clutch slave cylinder.

43. Connect all other wiring to the transaxle, as tagged.

44. Install the range select control valves and connectors.

45. Connect the speedometer cable, shift control cable and backup light harness at the transaxle.

46. Remove the coolant reserve tank.

47. Install the battery. Connect the battery cables, positive cable first.

LINKAGE ADJUSTMENT

1. Disconnect the negative battery cable.

2. Remove the console assembly from the vehicle.

3. At the shift selector assembly, remove the shift cable-to-shift selector cotter pins and disconnect the shift cables from the shift selector assembly.

4. Move the transaxle shift selector and shift selector into the **N** positions.

5. If necessary, turn the shift cable adjuster to adjust the cables length to align with shift lever in the **N** position. Connect the shift cable, flange side of the resin bushing should face cotter pin side of the shift lever, with lever Band install a new cotter pin.

6. At the shift selector, make sure dimensions A and B are equal; if they are not, turn the cable adjuster to make the necessary adjustment.

7. Adjust the other cable in the same fashion.

8. Move the shift selector into each position to make sure it is shifting smoothly.

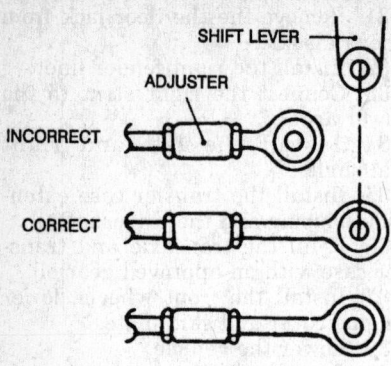

Shift cable position in neutral

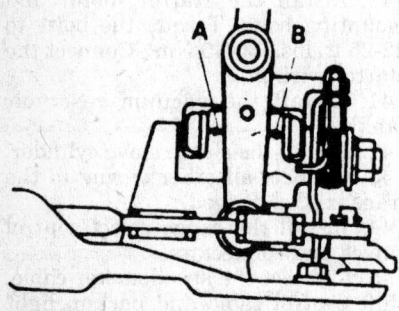

Adjusting the shift cable to make the shift selector's dimension A and B equal

CLUTCH

Clutch Assembly

REMOVAL AND INSTALLATION

1. Disconnect the negative battery cable.
2. Raise and support the vehicle safely. On the 4WD Colt Vista, remove the slave cylinder.
3. Remove the transmission or transaxle from the vehicle.
4. Insert a pilot shaft or an old input shaft into the center of the clutch disc, pressure plate and the pilot bearing in the crankshaft.
5. With the pilot tool supporting the clutch disc, loosen the pressure plate bolts gradually and in a criss-cross pattern.
6. Remove the pressure plate and clutch disc.
7. Clean the transmission or transaxle and clutch housing. Clean the

flywheel surface with a non-oil based solvent.

NOTE: Before assembly, slide the clutch disc up and down on the input shaft to check for any binding. Remove any rough spots with crocus cloth and then lightly coat the shaft with Lubriplate® or equivalent.

8. To remove the throwout bearing assembly:
   a. Remove the return clip and take out the throwout bearing carrier and the bearing.
   b. To replace the throwout arm use a 1/16 in. punch, knock out the throwout shaft spring pin and remove the shaft, springs and the center lever.
   c. Do not immerse the throwout bearing in solvent; it is permanently lubricated. Blow and wipe it clean. Check the bearing for wear, deterioration, or burning. Replace the bearing if there is any question about its condition.
   d. Check the shafts, lever and springs for wear and defects. Replace them if necessary.
9. Examine the clutch disc for the following before reusing it: loose rivets, burned facing, oil or grease on the facing, less than 0.012 in.

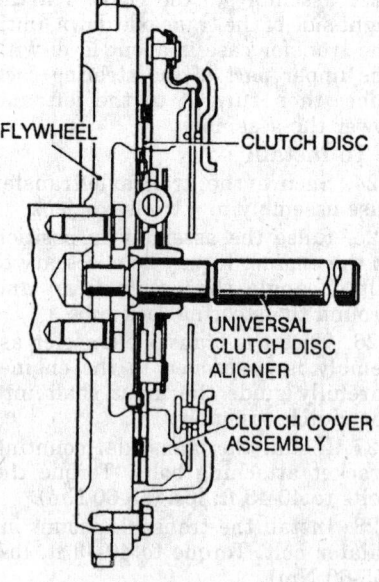

Clutch assembly with alignment tool

(0.305mm) left between the rivet head and the top of the facing.
10. Check the pressure plate and replace it if any of the following conditions exist: scored or excessive wear, bent or distorted diaphragm, loose rivets.

NOTE: Check the flywheel for excessive warpage, cracks and/or scoring. Clutch chatter indicates a warped flywheel surface. Matching a new clutch with a worn flywheel will cause premature clutch wear and/or failure.

To install:

11. Insert the control lever into the clutch housing. Install the 2 return springs and the throwout shaft.
12. Lock the shift lever to the shaft with the spring pin.
13. Fill the shaft oil seal with multi-purpose grease.
14. Install the throwout bearing carrier and the bearing. Install the return clip.
15. Grease the carrier groove and inner surface.
16. Lightly grease the clutch disc splines.

NOTE: The clutch is installed with the larger boss facing the transmission or transaxle.

17. Support the clutch disc and pressure plate with the pilot tool.
18. Turn the pressure plate so its balance mark aligns with the notch in the flywheel.
19. Install the pressure plate-to-flywheel bolts hand tight. Using a torque wrench and working in a criss-cross pattern, tighten the bolts to 11-15 ft. lbs. (15-20 Nm).
20. Install the transmission or transaxle.
21. Adjust the clutch free-play.
22. Lower the vehicle and connect the negative battery cable.

PEDAL HEIGHT/FREE-PLAY ADJUSTMENT

1. Measure the distance between the floor and the top of the clutch pedal.
2. The measurement should be as follows:
   Colt, Colt Wagon and 1990-1991 2WD Colt Vista — 6.20-6.40 in. (157.48-164.56mm)
   1990-91 4WD Colt Vista — 7.10-7.30 in. (180.34-185.42mm)
   1992-94 Colt Vista 7.68-7.87 in. (195.00-200.00mm)
3. If the measurement is not correct, loosen the clutch switch locknut

and move the switch in or out as necessary to obtain proper height.

4. Check to see if the clutch pedal free-play is within specifications. Measure the distance from the top of the pedal to the distance the pedal moves before resistance is felt. The distance should be as follows:

Colt, Colt Wagon and Colt Vista — 0.24-0.51 in. (6.10-12.95mm)

5. Adjust the Colt with cable type by turning the outer cable adjusting nut at the bulkhead in the engine compartment. The hydraulic systems are self-adjusting. If the clutch pedal free height is not within specifications, there is probably air in the hydraulic system or a malfunction in the clutch itself. Bleed the air out of the system or disassemble the clutch assembly.

Clutch Cable

ADJUSTMENT

1. Slightly pull the cable out from the firewall.
2. Turn the adjusting wheel on the cable until the play between the wheel and the cable is within the correct dimension.
3. Check the clutch free-play.
   a. Raise and and support the vehicle safely.
   b. Remove the rubber cover from the clutch housing.
   c. Using a 0.030 in. (0.760mm) feeler gauge, check the clearance between the pressure plate diaphragm spring and the throwout bearing.
4. If the free travel is not correct, make further adjustments at the cable adjusting wheel.

NOTE: Each turn of the adjusting wheel equals 0.060 in. (1.524mm) of adjustment to the wheel and retainer clearance.

5. Lower the vehicle and check the clutch operation.

REMOVAL AND INSTALLATION

1. Loosen the cable adjusting wheel inside the engine compartment.
2. Loosen the clutch pedal adjusting bolt locknut and loosen the adjusting bolt.
3. Remove the cable end from the clutch throwout lever.
4. Remove the cable end from the clutch pedal.

5. Installation is the reverse order of removal procedures.

NOTE: Lubricate the cable with engine oil and after installation, install pads isolating the cable from the intake manifold and from the rear side of the engine mount insulator.

Clutch Master Cylinder

REMOVAL AND INSTALLATION

1. Remove the air cleaner assembly.
2. Loosen the bleeder screw on the slave cylinder and drain the system.
3. Disconnect the pushrod from the clutch pedal.
4. Disconnect the clutch pedal from the pedal bracket.
5. Disconnect the fluid line and reservoir tube from the master cylinder.
6. Remove the reservoir and bracket on models with externally mounted fluid reservoirs. Unbolt and remove the master cylinder and remove.
7. Installation is the reverse order of removal procedures. Torque the cylinder retaining nuts to 9 ft. lbs. (13 Nm), the fluid pipe to 11 ft. lbs. (15 Nm) and the reservoir bracket bolts to 5 ft. lbs. (7 Nm).
8. Install the master cylinder and bleed the system.

NOTE: On the 4WD Colt Vista, the lower master cylinder mounting nut is accessed from inside the vehicle.

Clutch Slave Cylinder

REMOVAL AND INSTALLATION

1. Raise and support the vehicle safely.
2. Disconnect the clutch hose from the slave cylinder.
3. Unbolt and remove the cylinder from the clutch housing.
4. Installation is the reverse order of removal procedures. Bleed the system.

Hydraulic Clutch System Bleeding

NOTE: An assistant is needed for the bleeding operation.

1. Raise and support the vehicle safely.

2. Loosen the bleeder screw at the slave cylinder.
3. Make sure the master cylinder is full.
4. Attach a length of rubber hose to the bleeder screw nipple and place the other end in a glass jar half full of clean brake fluid.
5. Have the assistant push the clutch pedal down slowly to the floor. If air is in the system, bubbles will appear in the jar as the pedal is being depressed.
6. When the pedal is at the floor, tighten the bleeder screw.
7. Repeat Steps 5 and 6 until no bubbles are found. Check the master cylinder level frequently to make sure of fluid level.

AUTOMATIC TRANSAXLE

Transaxle Assembly

REMOVAL AND INSTALLATION

NOTE: The transaxle and converter must be removed and installed as an assembly.

Except 1992-94 Colt Vista

1. Disconnect the battery cables, negative first. Remove the battery and tray. Remove the air cleaner case.
2. Disconnect the throttle control cable at the carburetor. If equipped with fuel injection, disconnect the cable at the throttle body. Disconnect the manual control cable at the transaxle.
3. Disconnect from the transaxle: the inhibitor switch (neutral safety) connector, fluid cooler hoses and the 4 upper bolts connecting the engine to the transaxle.

NOTE: Cap oil cooler hoses to prevent fluid loss.

4. Raise and support the vehicle safely.
5. Remove the front wheels. Remove the engine splash shield.
6. Drain the transaxle fluid.
7. Disconnect the stabilizer bar at the lower arms and disconnect the control arms from the body. Remove the right and left halfshafts from the transaxle case.
8. Disconnect the speedometer cable. Remove the starter motor.

9. Remove the lower cover from the converter housing. Remove the bolts connecting the converter to the engine driveplate.

NOTE: Never support the full weight of the transaxle on the engine driveplate.

10. Turn and force the converter back and away from the engine driveplate.

11. Support the weight of the engine from above. Support the transaxle and remove the remaining mounting bolts.

12. Remove the transaxle mount insulator bolt.

13. Remove and the transaxle and converter as an assembly.

To install:

14. Secure the transaxle to a transmission jack.

15. Install the torque converter onto the transaxle input shaft. Make sure the converter is fully seated in to the front pump before bolting the transaxle to the engine.

16. Raise the transaxle and position it to the engine. Install the lower transmission-to-engine bolts. Torque the bolts to 31-39 ft. lbs. (43-54 Nm).

17. Install the transaxle mount insulator bolt. Torque the bolts to 31-40 ft. lbs. (43-54 Nm).

18. Install the remaining transaxle-to-engine bolts. Torque the bolts to 31-39 ft. lbs. (43-54 Nm).

19. From the converter housing, install the 3 bolts connecting the converter to the engine driveplate. Torque the bolts to 34-38 ft. lbs. (46-54 Nm).

20. Connect the speedometer cable.

21. Install the starter motor and connect the wiring to it.

22. Connect the stabilizer bar to the lower arms and connect the control arms to the body. Install the right and left halfshafts to the transaxle case.

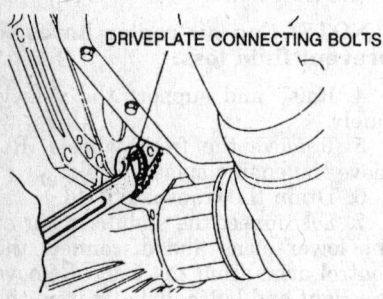

DRIVEPLATE CONNECTING BOLTS

Driveplate-to-torque converter bolts

23. Refill the transaxle fluid.

24. Install the engine splash shield. Install the front wheels.

25. Lower the vehicle.

26. Connect to the transaxle: the inhibitor switch (neutral safety) connector and the fluid cooler hoses.

27. Connect the throttle control cable to the transaxle.

28. Install the battery and tray. Connect the battery cables, positive first. If equipped with a turbocharger, install the air cleaner case.

1992-94 Colt Vista

1. Disconnect negative battery cable.

2. Remove the air cleaner assembly.

3. Disconnect the transaxle control lever. Disconnect and plug the oil cooler lines.

4. Disconnect the pulse generator connector, oil temperature connector, kickdown servo switch connector, inhibitor switch connector and solenoid valve connection.

5. Disconnect the speedometer cable connection. Remove the oil level dipstick and tube.

6. Install holding fixture to the top of the engine to support engine weight.

7. Remove the top transaxle upper coupling bolts.

8. Raise and safely support the vehicle.

9. Remove the starter motor leaving wire harness attached.

10. Remove the right side under cover. Drain the transaxle fluid.

11. Disconnect the tie rod ends, stabilizer bar and lower ball joints.

12. If equipped with 4WD, it will be necessary to remove the right driveshaft from the vehicle.

13. Except 4WD, remove the driveshafts from the transfer case, insert a prybar between the driveshaft and the transaxle case and pry the shaft from the transaxle housing. Swing the shafts out of the way keeping the joints straight, and suspend using wire. Turn the right shaft 90 degrees toward the front of the vehicle so it will not be a hindrance.

NOTE: Do not pull on the shaft during removal from the transaxle; doing so will damage the inboard joint. Do not insert the prybar so deep as to damage the oil seal.

14. Remove the lower bellhousing cover. Scribe a mark on the

driveplate and transaxle converter face using chalk. Remove the driveplate connecting bolts while turning the crankshaft.

15. Support the transaxle using a transmission jack. Remove the center support.

16. Remove the transaxle mount bolt and bracket.

17. If equipped with 4WD, disconnect the front exhaust pipe and remove the transfer assembly.

18. Remove the lower transaxle case coupling bolts, press the torque converter towards the transfer case to prevent separation during removal and lower the transfer case from the vehicle.

To install:

19. Install the transaxle into the vehicle and secure using the lower case coupling bolts.

20. Install the transaxle mount bolt and bracket, torque through bolt nut to 51 ft. lbs. (70 Nm).

21. Align the scribe marks on the converter and the driveplate. Install the driveplate connecting bolts torquing to 33-38 ft. lbs. (46-53 Nm).

22. Install the transfer assembly and the center crossmember. Remove the transmission jack.

23. Install the center exhaust pipe.

24. Install the drive axles into the transfer case taking care not to damage the oil seal lip part of the transaxle with the serrated part of the driveshaft.

25. Connect the tie rod ends, stabilizer bar and lower ball joints.

26. Install the right side under cover.

27. Lower the vehicle. Install the upper transaxle coupling bolts.

28. Connect the speedometer cable, and the electrical harness connectors disconnected during the removal procedure.

29. Install the starter motor torquing the retainer bolts to 35 ft. lbs. (49 Nm).

30. Connect the transaxle cooler hoses and the connections for the manual controls.

31. Install the air cleaner assembly and the oil level dipstick and tube.

32. Refill with Dexron II, Mopar ATF Plus type 7176, or equivalent automatic transaxle fluid.

33. Start the engine and allow to idle for 2 minutes. Apply parking brake and move selector through each gear position, ending in **N**. Recheck fluid level and add if necessary. Fluid level should be between the marks in the **HOT** range. Check operation of all gauges and meters.

SHIFT LINKAGE ADJUSTMENT

NOTE: When it is necessary to disconnect the linkage cable from the lever, which uses plastic grommets as retainers, the grommets should be replaced.

1. Set the parking brake.
2. Move the shift lever into **P**.
3. Loosen the clamp bolt on the gear shift cable bracket.
4. Make sure the preload adjustment spring engages the fork on the transaxle bracket.
5. Pull the shift lever all the way to the front detent position **P** and torque the lock screw to 100 inch lbs. (11 Nm).
6. Check the following conditions:
   a. The detent positions for **N** and **D** should be within limits of hand lever gate stops.
   b. Key start must occur only when the shift lever is in **P** or **N** positions.

THROTTLE LINKAGE ADJUSTMENT

Except 4-speed

1. Run the engine to normal operating temperature. Shut it off and

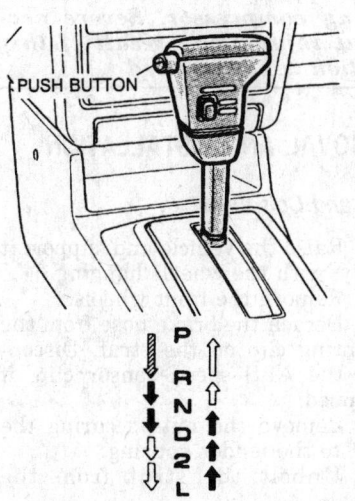

OPERATE WITH THE BUTTON PUSHED IN AND BRAKE PEDAL DEPRESSED
BUTTON NOT PRESSED
BUTTON PRESSED

Shift linkage adjustment

make sure the throttle plate is closed (curb idle position).
2. Raise the small cone shaped cover on the throttle cable to expose the nipple.
3. Loosen the lower cable bracket bolt.
4. Move the lower cable bracket until the distance between the nipple and the lower cover directly under it is 0.02-0.06 in. (0.51-1.52mm).
5. Tighten the bracket bolt to 9-11 ft. lbs. (12-15 Nm).

INHIBITOR SWITCH ADJUSTMENT

1. Place the manual valve in the neutral position.
2. Loosen the retaining bolts.
3. Turn the inhibitor switch body until the 0.472 inch (12.0mm) wide end of the manual control lever overlaps the switch body flange.
4. Torque the retaining bolts to 4-5 ft. lbs. (5-7 Nm).

LINE PRESSURE ADJUSTMENT

1. Attach a tachometer to the engine.
2. Install a pressure gauge into the line pressure take-off at the transaxle case.
3. Warm up the engine and raise the drive wheels and support safely.
4. For the 3-speed transaxle: pull the throttle control cable on the transaxle side to the wide open position. Pull the cable by hand in the engine compartment without racing the engine.
5. For the 3-speed transaxle: with the transaxle in **D** and the engine at 2500 rpm, the line pressure should be 98-100 psi (677-696 kPa).
6. For the 4-speed transaxle: with the transaxle in **D** and the engine at 2500 rpm, the line pressure should be 124-127 psi (870-890 kPa).
7. If not within specifications, drain the transaxle fluid and remove the oil pan.
8. Disconnect the throttle control cable (3-speed) from the cam or solenoid connector (4-speed) from the case.
9. Remove the valve body from the transaxle.
10. Turn the adjusting screw at the regulator valve to adjust the pressure.
11. For the 3-speed: turn the screw counterclockwise 1 turn will increase the line pressure by 3.7 psi (25 kPa). Turning clockwise will decrease the line pressure.
12. For the 4-speed: turn the screw counterclockwise 1 turn will increase

the line pressure by 5.4 psi (38 kPa). Turning clockwise will decrease the line pressure.
13. Install the valve body with a new gasket, accumulator spring and O-ring. Torque the bolts to 7.5-8.5 ft. lbs. (10-11 Nm).
14. Install the oil filter and connect the throttle cable.
15. Install the oil pan and torque to 8-9 ft. lbs. (10-11 Nm).
16. Refill the transaxle with approved fluid.
17. Start the engine and check for leaks and proper operation.

REDUCING PRESSURE ADJUSTMENT

4-Speed

1. Attach a tachometer to the engine.
2. Install a pressure gauge into the oil pressure take-off at the transaxle case.
3. The reducing pressure should be 60 psi (425 kPa).
4. If not within specifications, drain the fluid, remove the oil pan and filter.
5. The valve body does not have to be removed.
6. If the pressure is not within specifications, turn the adjusting screw on the lower valve body to the right to lower the pressure. Turn the screw to the left to increase. 1 turn of the screw will change the pressure by 6.4 psi (45 kPa).
7. Install the oil filter.
8. Install the oil pan and torque to 8-9 ft. lbs. (10-11 Nm).
9. Refill the transaxle with approved fluid.
10. Start the engine and check for leaks and proper operation.

KICKDOWN SERVO ADJUSTMENT

4-SPEED

1. Install a pressure gauge to the kickdown servo take-off port and test the pressure. Refer to the oil pressure table illustration.
2. Remove the kickdown switch snapring and switch.
3. To prevent rotation of the servo piston, install special tool MD998915 and MD998918. Do not press on the piston with the tool.
4. Loosen the locknut of the adjusting rod and tighten the tool inner portion until it contacts the locknut.
5. Engage the tool outer portion on the locknut. Rotate the outer cylinder counterclockwise and the inner por-

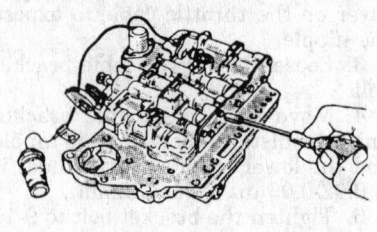

Throttle cable adjustment — except 4-speed automatic

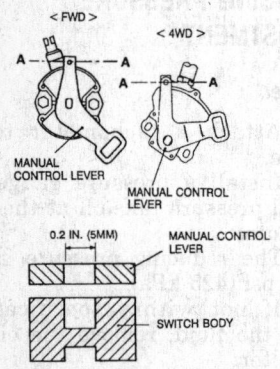

Inhibitor switch adjustment

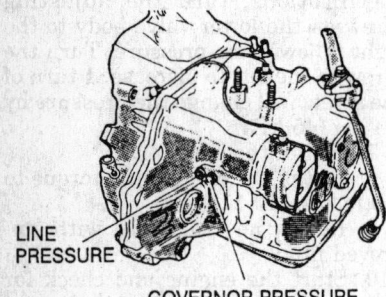

Line pressure fitting — 3-speed

Line pressure adjusting screw — 3-speed

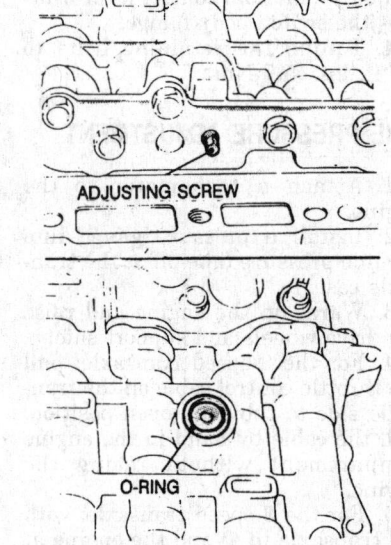

Line pressure adjuster and O-ring installation — 4-speed

tion clockwise. Lock the locknut with the special tool.

6. Attach a torque wrench to the special tool inner portion and repeat tightening and loosening at the torque of 7.2 ft. lbs. (10 Nm) 2 times.

7. Then, torque to 3.6 ft. lbs. (5 Nm).

8. Back off the special tool inner portion 2-2.5 turns for Colt, 2-2.25 turns for 4WD Colt Vista or 2.5-2.75 turns for 2WD Colt Vista.

9. Engage the special tool outer portion on the locknut. Rotate the outer cylinder clockwise and the inner cylinder counterclockwise to unlock the locknut. Always apply equal force to both tools.

10. Tighten the locknut by hand until it contacts the piston. Then, torque the locknut to 21 ft. lbs. (29 Nm).

11. Remove the special tools and install the servo switch.

12. Start the engine and check operation.

TRANSFER CASE

Transfer Case Assembly

REMOVAL AND INSTALLATION

4WD Colt vista

1. Raise the vehicle and support it safely. Remove the transaxle.

2. Unbolt the transfer case from the transaxle and using a small prybar, separate the two.

To install:

3. Installation is the reverse order of the removal procedure. Torque the attaching bolts to 40-43 ft. lbs. (54-58 Nm).

FRONT SUSPENSION

MacPherson Strut

— CAUTION —
The MacPherson strut spring is under extreme pressure. Do not remove the center strut shaft nut without having the strut assembly in an approved MacPherson strut spring compressor. Severe personal injury may result if this caution is not followed.

REMOVAL AND INSTALLATION

Colt and Colt Vista

1. Raise the vehicle and support it safely, with the wheels hanging.

2. Remove the front wheels.

3. Detach the brake hose from the mounting clip on the strut. Disconnect the ABS speed sensor clip, if equipped.

4. Remove the nuts securing the strut to the fender housing.

5. Unbolt the strut from the knuckle.

6. Remove the strut from the vehicle.

7. Remove the dust cover.

8. Install a MacPherson strut spring compressor and compress the spring. Compress the spring so the maximum length will be obtained.

9. Remove the shaft nut, strut insulator, upper spring seat and spring with the compressor installed.

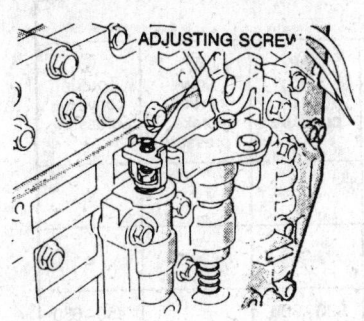

Reducing pressure adjustment — 4-speed

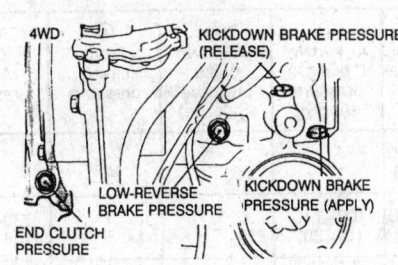

Transaxle pressure check locations — 4-speed

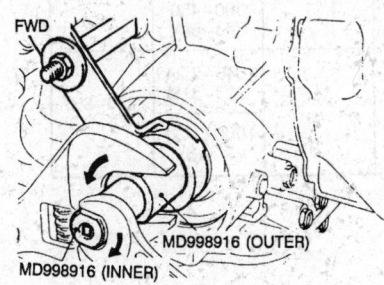

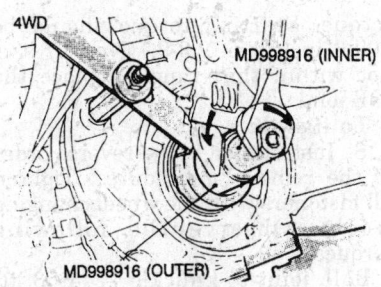

Kickdown servo adjustment — 4-speed

To install:

10. Install the spring (with compressor), upper spring seat, insulator and shaft nut. Align the spring end with the holes in the spring seats. Torque the shaft nut to 43-51 ft. lbs. (60-70 Nm). Remove the spring compressor.

11. Install the strut assembly into the vehicle in the reverse order of the removal procedures. Torque the strut-to-knuckle bolts to 80-94 ft. lbs. (110-130 Nm) on Colt. Torque the strut-to-fender housing nuts to 25-33 ft. lbs. (35-45) on Colt and 18-25 ft. lbs. (24-34 Nm) on Colt Vista.

Lower Ball Joints

INSPECTION

1. Raise and safely support the vehicle.
2. With the ball joint installed to the steering knuckle, Grasp the top and bottom of the wheel, then, move the wheel using an in and out shaking motion.
3. Observe any movement between the steering knuckle and the control arm. If movement exists, replace the ball joint.

REMOVAL AND INSTALLATION

Colt

The ball joint is not replaceable. The ball joint and lower control arm must be replaced as an assembly.

Colt Vista

1. Raise the vehicle and support it safely.
2. Remove the ball joint retaining bolt. Using a special tool, separate the ball joint from the steering knuckle. Remove the control arm from the vehicle.
3. Remove the ball joint dust cover.
4. Using snaping pliers, remove the snapring from the ball joint.
5. Using an adapter plate and driver, press the ball joint from the arm.

To install:

6. Installation is the reverse order of removal procedures. Invert the tool in the press for installation. Coat the lip and interior of the dust cover with lithium based chassis lube. Torque the ball joint nut to 43-52 ft. lbs. (60-72 Nm) and install a new cotter pin, if equipped.

Lower Control Arms

REMOVAL AND INSTALLATION

Colt

1. Raise the vehicle and support it safely. Remove the wheels. Remove the splash shield. If equipped, remove the center crossmember.
2. Disconnect the stabilizer bar from the lower arm.
3. Using a ball joint separator, disconnect the ball joint from the knuckle.
4. Unbolt the lower arm from the body and remove it from the vehicle.

NOTE: The ball joint cannot be separated from the control arm, but must be replaced as an assembly.

5. If the stabilizer bar is to be removed, disconnect the tie rod from the knuckle and unbolt and remove the stabilizer.
6. Check all parts for wear and damage and replace any suspect part.
7. Using an inch lb. torque wrench, check the ball joint starting torque. Nominal starting effort should be 22-87 inch lbs. (2.5-9.8 Nm). Replace if otherwise.

To install:

8. Installation is the reverse order of the removal procedures. Use a new dust cover, the lip and inside of which is coated with lithium based chassis lube. The dust cover should be hammered into place with a driver tool.
9. Install the stabilizer bar so the serrations on the horizontal part protrude 0.24 in. (6.00mm) to the inside of the clamp and 0.90 in. (23.00mm) of threaded stud appear below the nut at the control arm.
10. The washer on the lower arm shaft should be installed. The left side lower arm shaft has left handed threads. The lower arm shaft nut must be torqued with the wheels hanging freely. Observe the following torques:

Knuckle-to-strut — 54-65 ft. lbs. (73-88 Nm).

Lower arm shaft-to-body — 69-87 ft. lbs. (93-118 Nm).

Stabilizer bar-to-body — 12-20 ft. lbs. (16-27 Nm).

Ball joint-to-knuckle — 44-53 ft. lbs. (60-72 Nm).

Lower arm-to-shaft — 70-88 ft. lbs. (95-120 Nm).

Rear shaft bushing bracket-to-body — 43-58 ft. lbs. (59-79 Nm).

No.	Select lever position	Engine speed rpm	Shift position	① Reducing pressure	② Kickdown brake pressure (Apply)	③ Kickdown brake pressure (Release)	④ Front clutch pressure	⑤ Rear clutch pressure	⑥ End clutch pressure	⑦ Low-reverse brake pressure	⑧ Torque-converter pressure
						Standard oil pressure kPa (psi)					
1	N	Idling	Neutral	360–480 (51–68)	–	–	–	–	–	–	☆
2	D	Idling	2nd gear	360–480 (51–68)	100–210 (14–30)	–	–	730–830 (104–118)	–	–	☆
3	D (SW-ON)	Approx. 2,500	4th gear	360–480 (51–68)	830–900 (118–128)	–	–	–	830–900 (118–128)	–	450–650 (64–92)
4	D (SW-OFF)	Approx. 2,500	3rd gear	360–480 (51–68)	830–900 (118–128)	830–900 (118–128)	830–900 (118–128)	830–900 (118–128)	830–900 (118–128)	–	450–650 (64–92)
5	2	Approx. 2,500	2nd gear	360–480 (51–68)	830–900 (118–128)	–	–	830–900 (118–128)	–	–	450–650 (64–92)
6	L	Approx. 1,000	1st gear	360–480 (51–68)	–	–	–	830–900 (118–128)	–	300–450 (43–64)	☆
7	R	Approx. 2,500	Reverse	360–480 (51–68)	1,640–2,240 (223–319)	1,640–2,240 (223–319)	–	–	–	1,640–2,240 (223–319)	450–650 (64–92)
		Approx. 1,000	Reverse		1000 (142) or more	1000 (142) or more	–	–	–	1000 (142) or more	

NOTE
– must be 10 kPa (1.4 psi) or less.
SW-ON: Switch ON the overdrive control switch
SW-OFF: Switch OFF the overdrive control switch
☆: Hydraulic pressure is generated, but not the standard value.

Oil pressure tables — 4-speed

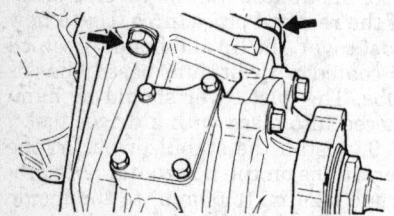

Transfer case attaching bolts

1990-91 Colt Vista

1. Raise the vehicle and support it safely.
2. Remove the wheels.
3. Disconnect the stabilizer bar and strut bar from the lower arm.
4. Remove the nut and disconnect the ball joint from the knuckle with a separator.
5. Unbolt the lower arm from the crossmember.
6. Check all parts for wear or damage and replace any suspect part.
7. Using an inch lb. torque wrench, check the ball joint starting

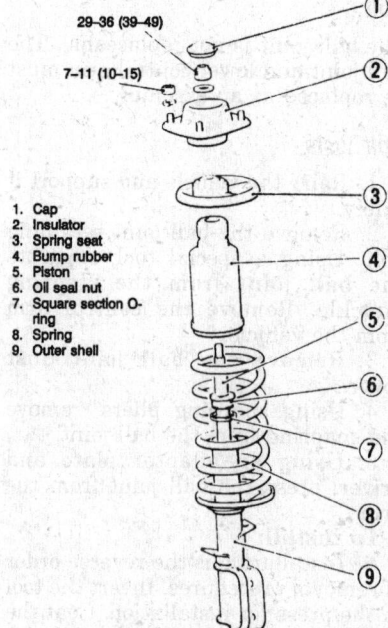

29–36 (39–49)
7–11 (10–15)

1. Cap
2. Insulator
3. Spring seat
4. Bump rubber
5. Piston
6. Oil seal nut
7. Square section O-ring
8. Spring
9. Outer shell

Front strut assembly — FWD Colt

torque. Starting torque should be 20-86 inch lbs. (2.3-9.7 Nm). If it is not within that range, replace the ball joint.

To install:

8. Installation is the reverse order of the removal procedures. Tighten all fasteners with the wheels hanging freely. Observe the following torques:

Ball joint-to-knuckle — 44-53 ft. lbs. (60-72 Nm).

Arm-to-crossmember-2WD to 90-111 ft. lbs.; 4WD to 58-68 ft. lbs. (78-92 Nm).

Stabilizer bar hanger brackets — 7-9 ft. lbs. (9.5-12.2 Nm).

9. When installing the stabilizer bar, the nut on the bar-to-crossmember bolts and the bar-to-lower arm bolts, are not torqued, but turned on until a certain length of thread is exposed above the nut:

2WD stabilizer bar-to-crossmember — 0.31-0.39 in. (7.87-9.91mm)

2WD stabilizer bar-to-lower control arm — 0.31-0.39 in. (7.87-9.91mm)

4WD stabilizer bar-to-crossmember — 0.31-0.39 in. (7.87-9.91mm)

4WD stabilizer bar-to-lower arm — 0.51-0.59 in. (12.95-15.00mm).

1992-94 Colt Vista

1. Disconnect the negative battery cable.
2. Raise the vehicle and support safely.
3. Remove sway bar links from lower control arm.
4. Disconnect the ball joint stud from the steering knuckle.
5. Remove the inner mounting frame-through bolt and nut.
6. Remove the rear mount bolts. Remove the clamp if equipped.
7. Remove the rear rod bushing if servicing.

To install:

8. Assemble the control arm and bushing.
9. Install the control arm to the vehicle and install the through bolt. Replace the nut and snug temporarily.
10. Install the rear mount clamp, bolts and replacement nuts. Torque the bolts to 51 ft. lbs. (70 Nm).
11. Connect the ball joint stud to the knuckle. Install a new nut and torque to 43-52 ft. lbs. (60-72 Nm).
12. Install the sway bar and links.
13. Lower the vehicle to the floor for the final torquing of the frame mount through bolt.
14. Once the full weight of the vehicle is on the floor, torque the frame mount through bolt nuts to 75-90 ft. lbs. (102-122 Nm).
15. Connect the negative battery cable and align the front end.

Stabilizer (Sway) Bar

REMOVAL AND INSTALLATION

Except 1992-94 Colt Vista

1. Raise and safely support the vehicle; allow the suspension to hang free. Remove the left front wheel assembly.
2. Disconnect the stabilizer link bolts and nuts from the control arms. Disconnect the stabilizer shaft from the support assemblies.
3. Loosen the front bolts and remove the bolts from the rear and center of the support assemblies, allowing the supports to be lowered enough to remove the stabilizer bar assembly. Remove the assembly from the vehicle.

To install:

4. Installation is the reverse order of the removal procedures. Loosely assemble all components while insuring that the stabilizer bar is centered, side-to-side. Torque the stabilizer bar

support assemblies to 9 ft. lbs. (13 Nm).
5. Lower the vehicle.

1992-94 Colt Vista

1834cc and 2350cc (4WD)

1. Raise the vehicle and support safely. Remove the front wheels.
2. Remove the driveshaft (4WD). Disconnect the exhaust pipe from the manifold.
3. Remove the stabilizer outer links nuts.
4. Remove the frame bolts, bracket and bushings.
5. Remove the stabilizer bar and bushings.

To install:

6. Install the stabilizer bar and hardware. Align the left edge of the marking on the stabilizer bar with the edge of the stabilizer bushing. Torque the frame bolts to 16 ft. lbs. (22 Nm), link nuts to 29 ft. lbs. (40 Nm) and the exhaust pipe nuts to 33 ft. lbs. (44 Nm).
7. Install the driveshaft (4WD).

2350CC (FWD)

1. Raise the vehicle and support safely. Remove the front wheels.
2. Remove the nut and disconnect the tie rod ends with separator tool MB991113, or equivalent.
3. Hold the link bolt still and remove the bushing nut.
4. Support the engine with a jack. Remove the center crossmember bolts and lower to gain enough run to remove the stabilizer bar.
5. Remove the frame, bolts, brackets and bushings.
6. Remove the stabilizer bar from the vehicle.

To install:

7. Install the stabilizer bar. Position the bar so the projecting lengths of the marking from the fixture are at the measurement of 0.27 in. (7mm). Torque the bracket bolts to 16 ft. lbs. (22 Nm).
8. Install the bushings, washer and nut. Torque the self-locking nut so 0.3-0.4 in. (8-10mm) is between the washer and top of the link bolt.
9. Install the remaining components. Torque the tie rod end nut to 17-25 ft. lbs. (24-34 Nm) and the crossmember bolts to 51 ft. lbs. (70 Nm).
10. Align the front end.

REAR SUSPENSION

Shock Absorbers

REMOVAL AND INSTALLATION

Except 4WD Colt Vista

1. Raise the vehicle and support it safely.
2. Remove the wheel. Remove the upper mounting bolt and nut.
3. While holding the bottom stud mount nut with one wrench, remove the locknut with another wrench.
4. Remove the shock absorber.
5. Check the shock for:
   a. Excessive oil leakage; some minor weeping is permissible.
   b. Bent center rod, damaged outer case, or other defects.
   c. Pump the shock absorber several times, if it offers even resistance on full strokes it may be considered serviceable.

To install:

6. Install the upper shock mounting nut and bolt. Hand tighten the nut.
7. Install the bottom eye of the shock over the spring stud. Tighten the lower nut to 12-15 ft. lbs. (15-19 Nm) on rear wheel drive vehicles; 47-58 ft. lbs. (64-79 Nm) on front wheel drive vehicles.
8. Finally, tighten the upper nut to 47-58 ft. lbs. (64-79 Nm) on all models except station wagons, which are tightened to 12-15 ft. lbs. (15-19 Nm).

1990-91 4WD Colt Vista

1. Raise the vehicle and support it safely.
2. Remove the rear wheels.
3. Using a suitable floor jack, raise the inner control arm slightly.
4. Unbolt the top, then the bottom of the shock absorber. Remove it from the vehicle.
5. Installation is the reverse order of the removal procedures. Torque the top nut to 55-58 ft. lbs. (75-79 Nm); the bottom bolt to 75-80 ft. lbs. (102-108 Nm).

1992-94 Colt Vista

1. Raise the vehicle and support safely.
2. Remove the access cover from inside the vehicle.
3. Remove the upper mount nuts.
4. Remove the lower mount nuts and washers.

5. Remove the shock from the vehicle and place in a vise.

6. Remove the nut, washer, collar, bushing, bracket, bushing, cup, bump stopper and dust cover from the shock.

To install:

7. Install the dust cover, bump stopper, cup, bushing, bracket, bushing, collar, washer and nut onto the shock.

8. Torque the nut to 33 ft. lbs. (45 Nm).

9. Install the shock assembly and torque the lower nut to 72 ft. lbs. (100 Nm) and upper nuts to 33 ft. lbs. (45 Nm).

MacPherson Strut

—— CAUTION ——

The MacPherson strut spring is under extreme pressure. Do not remove the center strut shaft nut without having the strut assembly in an approved MacPherson strut spring compressor. Severe personal injury may result if this caution is not followed.

REMOVAL AND INSTALLATION

Colt

1. Raise the vehicle and support it safely. Allow the lower arms and suspension to hang. Remove the wheels.

2. Raise the axle slightly to relax the strut and to support the axle when the strut is removed. Position an additional support under the axle.

3. Take care in jacking that no contact is made on the lateral rod.

4. On hatchback, remove the trunk side trim.

5. Remove the upper dust cover cap.

6. Remove the upper mounting nuts. Remove the lower mounting bolt and nut.

7. Remove the strut from the vehicle.

8. Remove the dust cover.

9. Install a MacPherson strut spring compressor and compress the spring. Compress the spring so the maximum length will be obtained.

10. Remove the shaft nut, strut insulator, upper spring seat and spring with the compressor installed.

To install:

11. Install the spring (with compressor), upper spring seat, insulator and shaft nut. Align the spring end with the holes in the spring seats. Torque the shaft nut to 43-51 ft. lbs. (60-70 Nm). Remove the spring compressor.

12. Installation is the reverse order of the removal procedures. Torque the lower mounting bolt and nut to 58-72 ft. lbs. (79-98 Nm); the upper mounting nuts to 18-25 ft. lbs. (24-34 Nm).

Coil Springs

REMOVAL AND INSTALLATION

1990-91 2WD Colt Vista

1. Raise the vehicle and support it safely. Allow the rear wheels to hang.

2. Place a suitable jack under the rear axle and remove the bottom bolts or nuts of the shock absorbers.

3. Lower the rear axle and remove the left and right coil springs.

4. Installation is the reverse order of the removal procedure.

NOTE: When installing the spring, pay attention to the difference in shape between the upper and lower spring seats.

1992-94 Colt Vista

1. Remove the rear stabilizer bar.

2. Using a jack, support the lower arm. Remove the rear shock absorber.

3. If equipped with 4WD, remove the rear driveshaft mounting bolts at the carrier flange and hang the driveshaft from the vehicle body using wire.

4. If equipped with ABS, remove the speed sensor clamp bolt and relocate out of the way. Do not apply tension to the wire harness of the connector.

5. Scribe mating marks on the lower arm shaft assembly and the crossmember. To remove the coil spring, loosen the shaft assembly nut and slowly lower the rear end of the lower arm. It is not necessary to remove the nut, only to loosen it.

To install:

6. Install the coil spring into the seats making sure both ends of the spring are correctly aligned with the spring seat groove.

7. Slowly raise the rear the rear end of the lower arm and align the scribe marks made during disassembly. Tighten shaft assembly nut to 69 ft. lbs. (95 Nm).

8. Install the speed sensor clamp to its' original location and secure the wire harness making.

9. Install the rear driveshaft to the flange and secure tightening mounting bolts to 40-47 ft. lbs. (55-65 Nm).

10. Reconnect the lower portion of the shock and tighten the retaining bolt to 72 ft. lbs. (100 Nm).

11. Lower the arm and remove the jack. Align all 4 wheels.

Torsion Bar and Control Arms

Instead of springs, the 1990-91 4WD Colt Vista uses transversely mounted torsion bars housed inside the rear crossmember, attached to which are inner and outer control arms. The conventional style shock absorbers are mounted on the inner arms.

REMOVAL AND INSTALLATION

1990-91 4WD Colt Vista

1. Raise the vehicle and support it safely.

2. Remove the differential.

3. Remove the intermediate shafts and halfshafts.

4. Remove the rear brake assemblies.

5. Disconnect the brake lines and parking brake cables from the inner arms.

6. Remove the main muffler.

7. Raise the inner arms slightly with a suitable floor jack and disconnect the shock absorbers.

8. Matchmark, precisely, the upper ends of the outer arms, the torsion bar ends and the top of the crossmember bracket and remove the inner and outer arm attaching bolts.

9. Remove the extension rods fixture attaching bolts.

10. Remove the crossmember attaching bolts and remove the rear suspension assembly from the vehicle.

11. Unbolt and remove the shock from the crossmember.

12. Remove the front and rear insulators from both ends of the crossmember.

13. Loosen but do not remove, the lock bolts securing the outer arm bushings at both ends of the crossmember.

14. Pull the outer arm from the crossmember. The torsion bar will slide out of the crossmember with the outer arm.

15. Remove the torsion bar from either the crossmember or outer arm.

16. Inspect all parts for wear or damage. Inspect the crossmember for bending or deformation.

17. Inner arm bushings may be replaced at this time using a press. The

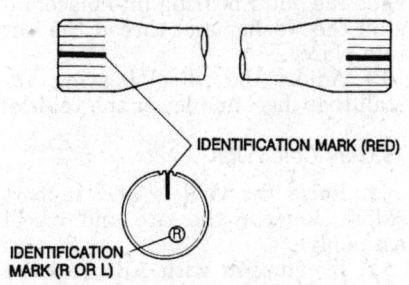

IDENTIFICATION MARK (RED)

IDENTIFICATION MARK (R OR L)

Torsion bar suspension identifying marks

thicker end of the bushing goes on the inner side.

To install:

18. Prior to installation note that the torsion bars are marked with an **L** or **R** on the outer end and are not interchangeable.

19. If the original torsion bars are being installed, align the identification marks on the torsion bar end, crossmember and outer arm, install the torsion bar and arm and tighten the lock bolts. Skip Step 20. If new torsion bars are being installed, proceed to Step 20.

20. A special alignment jig must be fabricated. The jig is bolted to the rear insulator hole on the crossmember bracket. Insert the torsion bar into the outer arm, aligning the red identification mark on the torsion bar end with the matchmark made on the outer arm top side. Install the torsion bar and arm so the center of the flanged bolt hole on the arm is 1.25 in. (32.00mm) below the lower marking line on the jig. Then, pull the outer arm off the torsion bar, leaving the bar undisturbed in the crossmember. Reposition the arm on the torsion bar, 1 serration counterclockwise from its former position. This will make the previously measured dimension, 1.30 in. (33.00mm) above the lower line. When the outer arm and torsion bar are properly positioned, the marking lines on the jig will run diagonally across the center of the toe-in adjustment hole. When the adjustment is complete, tighten the lock bolts. The clearance between the outer arm and the crossmember bracket, at the torsion bar, should be 0.20-0.27 in. (5.00-7.00mm).

21. The remainder of installation is the reverse order of the removal pro-

cedure. Observe the following torques:

Extension rod fixture bolts — 45-50 ft. lbs. (61-68 Nm).

Extension rod-to-fixture nut — 95-100 ft. lbs. (129-136 Nm).

Shock absorber lower bolt — 75-80 ft. lbs. (102-108 Nm).

Outer arm attaching bolts — 65-70 ft. lbs. (88-95 Nm).

Toe-in bolt — 95-100 ft. lbs. (129-136 Nm).

Lock bolts — 20-22 ft. lbs. (25-29 Nm).

Crossmember attaching bolts — 80-85 ft. lbs. (108-115 Nm).

Front insulator nuts — 7-10 ft. lbs. (9-13 Nm).

Inner arm-to-crossmember bolts — 60-65 ft. lbs. (81-88 Nm).

Damper-to-crossmember nuts — 15-20 ft. lbs. (20-27 Nm).

22. Lower the vehicle to the ground and check the ride height. The ride height is checked on both sides and is determined by measuring the distance between the center line of the toe-in bolt hole on the outer arm and the lower edge of the rebound bumper. The distance on each side should be 4.00-4.11 in. (101.60-104.39mm). If not or if there is a significant difference between sides, the torsion bars positioning is wrong.

Rear Control Arms

REMOVAL AND INSTALLATION

1992-94 Colt Vista

1. Disconnect negative battery cable.

2. Remove the rear stabilizer bar.

3. If equipped with 4WD, remove the rear axle shaft.

4. Remove the rear brake drum.

5. If equipped with ABS, remove the rear caliper assembly and brake disc.

6. Remove the rear hub assembly. If equipped with ABS, take care not to damage the rotor teeth during hub removal.

7. Disconnect the parking brake cable from the rear brake shoe.

8. If equipped with ABS, disconnect and remove the rear wheel sensor.

NOTE: The speed sensor has a pole piece projecting from it. This exposed tip must be pro-

tected from impact or scratches. **Do not allow the pole piece to contact the toothed wheel during removal or installation.**

9. Remove the rear shock and coil spring.

10. Remove the brake line and parking brake mounting bolts from the lower control arm.

11. Matchmark and remove the inboard lower arm pivot bolt. Remove the flange bolt and the arm from the vehicle.

To install:

12. Install the arm on the vehicle and secure with the flange bolt, temporarily tighten the nut. Install the arm pivot bolt and temporarily tighten the nut.

13. Install the rear shock and coil spring.

14. Install the brake line and parking brake mounting bolts to the lower control arm.

15. Connect the parking brake cable to the rear brake shoe.

16. Install the rear hub assembly.

17. Install the rear brake drum or if equipped with ABS, install the rear caliper assembly and brake disc.

18. Install the rear axle shaft.

19. Install and connect the rear wheel speed sensor. Use a brass or other non-magnetic feeler gauge to check the air gap between the tip of the pole piece and the toothed wheel. Correct gap is 0.012-0.035 in. (0.3-0.9mm). Tighten the 2 sensor bracket bolts to 10 ft. lbs. (14 Nm) with the sensor located so the gap is the same at several points on the toothed wheel. If the gap is incorrect, it is likely that the toothed wheel is worn or improperly installed.

20. Lower the vehicle and tighten the lower arm flange bolt nut and the arm pivot bolt to 69 ft. lbs. (95 Nm).

21. Install the rear stabilizer bar and reconnect the negative battery cable.

22. Bleed the brake system if any lines where opened. Adjust the parking brake and perform a rear wheel alignment.

Rear Wheel Bearings

NOTE: For the RWD and 4WD vehicles, please refer to the ""Drive Axle" section.

REMOVAL AND INSTALLATION

Colt

NOTE: The Colt and 1992-94 Colt Vista may be equipped with the removable tapered bearings and seal or a non-removable bearing/hub assembly. If the axle shaft is not tapered, the bearing/hub is serviced as an assembly.

1. Loosen the lug nuts. Raise the vehicle and support it safely.
2. Remove the wheel and tire assemblies.
3. Remove the grease cap.
4. Remove the nut.
5. Pull the drum off.
6. Colt equipped with removable bearings:
   a. The outer bearing will fall out while the drum is coming off. Do not drop it. If equipped with disc brakes; Remove the caliper assembly. Remove the disc rotor. Remove the hub assembly.
   b. Pry out the oil seal. Discard it.
   c. Remove the inner bearing.
   d. Check the bearing races. If any scoring, heat checking or damage is noted, they should be replaced.

NOTE: When bearing or races need replacement, replace them as a set.

   e. Inspect the bearings. If wear or looseness or heat checking is found, replace them.
   f. If the bearings and races are to be replaced, drive out the race with a brass drift.

To install:

7. Colt equipped with removable bearings:
   a. Before installing new races, coat them with lithium based wheel bearing grease. Drive into place with a brass drift. Make sure they are fully seated.
   b. Thoroughly pack the bearings with lithium based wheel bearing grease. Pack the hub with grease.
   c. Install the inner bearing and coat the lip and rim of the grease seal with grease. Drive the seal into place with a seal driver.
   d. If equipped with drum brakes, place the drum on the hub and install the outer bearing. Do not install the nut at this time.
8. Colt equipped with non-removable hub bearings. To determine if the self-locking nut is reusable:
   a. Screw in the self-locking nut until about 1/10 in. of the spindle is showing.

   b. Measure the torque required to turn the self-locking nut counterclockwise.
   c. The lowest allowable torque is 48 inch lbs. (5.5 Nm). If the measured torque is less than the specification, replace the nut.
   d. Install the drum and/or hub to the vehicle.
   e. Lubricate and install the outer wheel bearing to the spindle.
   f. Torque the self-locking nut to 108-145 ft. lbs. (150-200 Nm).
9. If equipped with drum brakes, use a pull scale attached to one of the lugs to measure the starting force necessary to get the drum to turn. Starting force should be 5 lbs. (6.8 N). If the starting torque is greater than specific, replace the bearings.
10. If equipped with drum brakes, install the nut on the halfshaft. Thread the nut on, to a point at which the back face of the nut is 0.079-0.118 in. (2.00-3.00mm) from the shoulder of the shaft, where the threads end.
11. Adjust the wheel bearing. Install the wheel and lower the vehicle.

1990-91 2WD Colt Vista

1. Loosen the lug nuts. Raise the vehicle and support it safely. Remove the wheel.
2. Remove the grease cap, cotter pin, nut and washer.
3. Remove the brake drum. While pulling the drum, the outer bearing will fall out. Do not drop it.
4. Pry out the grease seal and discard it.
5. Remove the inner bearing.
6. Check the bearing races. If any scoring, heat checking or damage is noted, they should be replaced.

NOTE: When bearing or races need replacement, replace them as a set.

7. Inspect the bearings. If wear or looseness or heat checking is found replace them.
8. If the bearings and races are to be replaced, drive out the races with a brass drift.

To install:

9. Before installing new races, coat them with lithium based wheel bearing grease. Drive into place with a brass drift. Make sure they are fully seated.
10. Thoroughly pack the bearings with lithium based wheel bearing grease. Pack the hub with grease.
11. Install the inner bearing and coat the lip and rim of the grease seal with grease. Drive the seal into place with a seal driver.

12. Mount the drum onto the hub, slide the outer bearing into place, install the washer and thread the nut into place.
13. Adjust the wheel bearing, install the wheel and lower the vehicle.

1992-94 Colt Vista

1. Raise the vehicle and support safely. Remove the tire and wheel assembly.
2. If equipped with ABS, remove the caliper assembly, brake disc and rear wheel speed sensor from the adapter. If not equipped with ABS, remove the brake drum.

NOTE: The speed sensor has a pole piece projecting from it. This exposed tip must be protected from impact or scratches. Do not allow the pole piece to contact the toothed wheel during removal or installation.

3. Remove the dust cap, nut and washer. Do not use an air gun to remove the nut.
4. Remove the rear hub assembly taking care not to scrape or damage the teeth of the speed rotor, if equipped.
5. Inspect the hub unit bearing for wear or damage. If replacement of the bearing is required, the hub assembly and bearing is to be replaced as a unit. The rear hub unit bearing assembly should should not be dismantled.
   To install:
6. Installation is the reverse of the removal procedure. Install the drum and/or hub to the vehicle. Lubricate and install the outer wheel bearing to the spindle. Torque the self-locking nut to 166 ft. lbs. (230 Nm). Stake the nut.
7. If equipped with ABS: insert a feeler gauge into the space between the speed sensor's pole piece and the toothed surface. Tighten the speed sensor at the position where the clearance at all places is 0.008-0.028 in. (0.2-0.7mm).

ADJUSTMENT

Colt

REMOVABLE BEARINGS

1. Raise the vehicle and support it safely. Remove the rear wheel and wheel bearing cap.
2. Using an inch lb. torque wrench, turn the nut counterclockwise 2-3 turns, noting the average force needed during the turning procedure. Turning torque for the nut should be about 48 inch lbs. (5.4 Nm).

If turning torque is not within 5 inch lbs. (0.5 Nm), either way, replace the nut.

3. Tighten the nut to 108-145 ft. lbs. (150-200 Nm).

4. Using a stand mounted gauge, check the axial play of the wheel bearings. Play should be less than 0.0079 in. (0.2007mm). If play cannot be brought within that figure, the unit is assembled incorrectly.

5. Pack the grease cap with wheel bearing grease and install it.

NON-REMOVABLE BEARINGS

Install the drum and/or hub to the vehicle. Lubricate and install the outer wheel bearing to the spindle. Torque the self-locking nut to 108-145 ft. lbs. (150-200 Nm). Stake the nut. Fill the cap with wheel bearings grease and install.

2WD Colt Vista

1990-91

1. Raise the vehicle and support it safely. Remove the rear wheel, wheel bearing cap and cotter pin.

2. Install a torque wrench on the nut. While turning the drum by hand, tighten the nut to 15 ft. lbs. (20 Nm). Back off the nut until it is loose, then tighten it to 7 ft. lbs. (9 Nm).

3. Install the lock cap and insert a new cotter pin. If the lock cap and hole don't align and repositioning the cap can't accomplish alignment, back off the nut no more than 15 degrees. If that won't align the holes either, try the adjustment procedure over again.

1992-94

Install the drum and/or hub to the vehicle. Lubricate and install the outer wheel bearing to the spindle. Torque the self-locking nut to 166 ft. lbs. (230 Nm). Stake the nut. Fill the cap with wheel bearing grease and install.

Rear Axle Assembly

NOTE: Please refer to the "Drive Axle" Section for RWD and 4WD vehicles.

REMOVAL AND INSTALLATION

Colt

1. Raise and safely support the vehicle. Remove the wheel and tire assemblies.

2. Remove brake fittings and retaining clips holding flexible brake line.

3. Remove parking brake cable adjusting connection nut.

4. Release both parking brake cables from brackets by slipping ball end of cables through brake connectors. Pull parking brake cable through bracket.

5. Pry off grease cap.

6. Remove cotter pin and castle lock.

7. Remove adjusting nut and brake drum.

8. Remove brake assembly and spindle bolts.

9. Set spindle aside and using a piece of wire, hang brake assembly aside.

10. Place supports under rear crossmember to support the rear suspension.

11. Remove shock absorber brackets.

12. Remove trailing arm-to-hanger bracket and control arm bolts.

13. Lower jack and remove axle assembly.

To Install:

14. Using a suitable jack, position the rear axle assembly under vehicle.

15. Install trailing arm-to-hanger mounting bracket and control arms, finger tighten bolts only.

16. Install shock absorber bolts loosely.

17. Place spindle and brake assembly in position; install bolts, do not tighten at this time.

18. Torque the bolts to 45 ft. lbs. (60 Nm).

19. Install brake drum or disc. Install washer and nut. Adjust wheel bearing. Install the dust cap.

20. Put parking brake cable through the bracket.

21. Slip ball end of parking brake cables through brake connectors on parking brake bracket.

22. Install both retaining clips.

23. Install parking brake cable adjusting connection nut. Tighten until all slack is removed from cables.

24. Install retaining clips and brake tube fittings. Torque fitting to 9 ft. lbs. (12 Nm).

25. Bleed rear brake system and readjust brakes.

26. Install wheel and tire assembly.

27. With vehicle on ground, torque trailing arm-to-hanger bracket mounting bolts to 58-72 ft. lbs. (80-100 Nm). Torque the control arm bolts to 94-108 ft. lbs. (130-150 Nm).

28. Torque shock absorber mounting bolts to 58-72 ft. lbs. (80-100 Nm).

Colt Vista

1990-91

1. Raise and safely support the vehicle. Remove the wheel assemblies.

2. Separate the parking brake cable at the connector and cable housing at the floor pan bracket.

3. Separate the brake line at backing plate.

4. Remove the muffler-to-middle exhaust pipe retaining bolts, remove the O-ring hangers and remove the exhaust system.

5. Remove the lower shock absorber through bolts and disconnect the shock at the axle end.

6. Lower the axle until the spring and isolator assemblies can be removed.

7. Remove the axle assembly from the vehicle.

To Install:

8. Using a suitable jack, position the rear axle assembly under vehicle.

9. Install the springs and isolators and carefully raise the axle assembly.

10. Install the shock absorber and through bolts; do not tighten.

11. Position brake support to the axle while routing the parking brake cable through the support. Lock it into place.

12. Connect the brake line fitting to the backing wheel cylinder. Torque to 9-12 ft. lbs. (13-17 Nm).

13. Install the hub and drum, if removed.

14. Route the parking brake cable through the fingers in the bracket and lock housing end into the floor pan bracket. Install the cable end into the intermediate connector.

15. Install the exhaust system and hangers. Torque the muffler-to-middle exhaust pipe retaining bolts to 22-29 ft. lbs. (30-40 Nm).

16. Install wheel assemblies and lower vehicle to floor. Torque the lower shock absorber bolts to 58-80 ft. lbs. (80-110 Nm). Torque the axle assembly-to-body mounting bolts to 87-108 ft. lbs. (120-150 Nm).

1992-94

This procedure is to remove and install the lower control arms and suspension crossmember.

1. Raise the vehicle and support safely. Remove the wheels.

2. Disconnect the center exhaust pipe, brake hose and ABS speed sensors (if equipped).

3. Remove the brake calipers and hang out of the way with wire.

4. Disconnect the parking brake cables from the backing plates and lower arms.

5. Position a floor jack under the lower arm and disconnect the shock absorbers.

6. Loosen the lower arm mounting bolts and remove the coil springs.

7. Remove the crossmember bracket, lower stopper and crossmember with the control arms attached.

To install:

8. Install the crossmember bracket, lower stopper and crossmember with the control arms attached. Torque the large bolts to 72 ft. lbs. (100 Nm), the small bolts to 33 ft. lbs. (45 Nm) and the nuts to 69 ft. lbs. (95 Nm). Do not torque the control arm bolts at this time.

9. Install the coil springs to their original position.

10. Connect the shock absorbers.

11. Connect the parking brake cables to the backing plates and lower arms.

12. Install the brake calipers.

13. Connect the center exhaust pipe, brake hose and ABS speed sensors (if equipped).

14. Install the wheels and lower the vehicle.

15. Torque the lower control arm bolts to 69 ft. lbs. (95 Nm) with vehicle's weight resting on the suspension. Align the rear end.

STEERING

Steering Wheel

REMOVAL AND INSTALLATION

1. Pull the lower end of the steering wheel center foam pad (horn button). Push up and out for the 1992-94 Colt Vista.

2. Remove the steering wheel retaining nut.

3. Mark the wheel and shaft for proper installation. Using a steering wheel puller, remove the wheel. Do not attempt this procedure without a steering wheel puller.

4. Make sure the front wheels are in a straight-ahead position. Each spline on the shaft equals about 10 degrees.

5. Installation is the reverse order of removal procedure. Tighten the nut to 30 ft. lbs. (41 Nm).

Manual Rack and Pinion

REMOVAL AND INSTALLATION

Colt

1. Loosen the lug nuts.
2. Raise and support the vehicle safely.
3. Remove the wheels.
4. Remove the steering shaft-to-pinion coupling bolt.
5. Disconnect the tie rod ends with a separator.
6. Remove the clamps or clamp and bolts securing the rack to the crossmember and remove the unit from the vehicle.

To install:

7. Install the rubber mount for the gear box with the slit on the downside.

8. The remainder of installation is the reverse order of the removal procedures. Torque as follows:

Rack-to-crossmember — 45-60 ft. lbs. (61-81 Nm).

Coupling bolt — 22-25 ft. lbs. (27-34 Nm).

Tie-rod nuts — 11-25 ft. lbs. (15-34 Nm).

9. Road test the vehicle.

1990-91 2WD Colt Vista

1. Loosen the lug nuts.
2. Raise and support the vehicle safely.
3. Remove the wheels.
4. Remove the steering shaft-to-pinion coupling bolt.
5. Disconnect the tie rod ends with a separator.
6. Remove the crossmember support bracket from the crossmember on the right side of the vehicle.
7. Remove the rear roll stopper-to-center member bolt and move the rear roll stopper forward.
8. Unbolt the rack from the crossmember.

NOTE: The rack is most easily removed using a ratchet and long extension, working from the engine compartment side.

9. Pull the rack out the right side of the vehicle. Pull it slowly to avoid damage.

To install:

10. Installation is the reverse order of the removal procedures. Torque the rack clamp bolts to 43-58 ft. lbs. (58-79 Nm), the tie rod nuts to 17-25 ft. lbs. (25-34 Nm and the coupling bolt to 22-25 ft. lbs. (27-34 Nm). Fill the system and road test the vehicle.

1990-91 4WD Colt Vista

1. Remove the steering column.
2. Raise and support the vehicle safely.
3. Remove the front wheels.
4. Using a separator, disconnect the tie rod from the knuckle.
5. Disconnect the steering shaft joint at the rack.
6. Remove the air cleaner.
7. Remove the rack attaching bolts from the rear of the No. 2 crossmember. The bolts are most easily accessed using a long extension and working from the top of the engine compartment.
8. Remove the rear roll stopper-to-center member bolt and move the rear roll stopper forward.
9. From under the vehicle, remove the gear box mounting bolts from the front of the No. 2 crossmember and pull out and to the left on the rack.
10. Lower the rack until the left edge of the left feed tube contacts the lower part of the left fender shield. At this point, remove the left and right feed tubes.
11. Remove the rack from the vehicle.

To install:

12. Position the rack to the No. 2 crossmember and connect the left and right feed tubes.

13. Install the rack, mounting brackets, bushing and retaining bolts. Torque the bolts to 43-58 ft. lbs. (60-80 Nm).

14. Connect the tie rods to the steering knuckle and install the retaining nuts. Torque the tie rod end retaining nuts to 17-25 ft. lbs. (24-34 Nm).

15. Install the wheel assemblies.

16. Install the steering column and connect the steering shaft joint to the rack shaft. Torque the steering shaft-to-rack bolts to 22-25 ft. lbs. (30-35 Nm).

17. Lower the vehicle. Install the air cleaner.

18. Replenish the powering fluid. Start the engine and check for leaks.

Power Steering Gear

REMOVAL AND INSTALLATION

1. Matchmark and disconnect the steering shaft from the gearbox main shaft.

2. Disconnect the tie rod end and pitman arm from the relay rod.

3. Remove the air cleaner and disconnect the pressure and return lines from the steering gear assembly.

4. Raise the vehicle and support it safely. Remove any interfering splash pans from under the vehicle.

5. If necessary, remove the kickdown linkage splash pan shield and bolts. Move the fuel line aside to avoid damage during removal.

6. Remove the frame bolts from the gearbox and lower the unit from the vehicle.

To install:

7. Make sure all matchmarks align. After tightening the pitman arm nut make sure the distance between the centerline of the lowest steering gear mounting bolt and the top of the pitman arm is 0.77 in. (19.50mm).

8. Observe the following torques:

Pitman arm nut — 94-109 ft. lbs. (127-148 Nm).

Steering gear mounting bolts — 40-47 ft. lbs. (54-64 Nm).

Tie rod socket and relay rod — 25-33 ft. lbs. (34-45 Nm).

High pressure hose — 22-29 ft. lbs. (29-39 Nm).

Return hose — 29-36 ft. lbs. (39-49 Nm).

Power Rack and Pinion

ADJUSTMENT

1. Disconnect the negative battery cable.

2. Raise the vehicle and support safely.

3. Remove the steering rack assembly from the vehicle.

4. Secure the steering rack assembly in a vise. Do not clamp the vise jaws on the steering housing tubes. Clamp the vise jaws only on the housing cast metal.

5. Remove the steering gear housing end plug from the steering gear shaft bore using tool 6103 or equivalent.

6. Remove the preload adjustment cap locknut from the steering gear housing bore using tool 6097 or equivalent.

7. With rack at center position, check torque on the rack support cover to 11 ft. lbs. (15 Nm).

8. With rack at center position, rotate the shaft clockwise 1 turn in 4-6 seconds. Return the rack support cover 30-60 degrees and adjust the total pinion torque to 5-11 inch lbs. (0.56-1.24 Nm). Set the standard value at its highest value when adjusting. Assure no ratcheting or catching when operating the rack towards the shaft direction.

9. Secure the preload adjustment cap with a new locknut using tool 6097 or equivalent. Do not allow the adjustment cap to rotate when tightening the locknut.

10. Install the end plug using tool 6103 or equivalent.

REMOVAL AND INSTALLATION

Colt

1. Loosen the lug nuts.

2. Raise the vehicle and support it safely.

3. Remove the wheels.

4. Remove the steering shaft-to-pinion coupling bolt.

5. Disconnect the tie rod ends with a separator.

6. Drain the fluid.

7. Disconnect the hoses from the rack.

8. Remove the band from the steering joint cover.

9. Unbolt and remove the stabilizer bar.

10. Remove the rack unit mounting clamp bolts and take the unit out the left side of the vehicle.

To install:

11. Make sure the rubber isolators have their nubs aligned with the holes in the clamps.

12. Apply rubber cement to the slits in the gear mounting grommet.

13. Torque the clamp bolt to 43-58 ft. lbs. (58-79 Nm), the tie rod nuts to 11-25 ft. lbs. (15-34 Nm) and the coupling bolt to 22-25 ft. lbs. (29-34 Nm).

14. Fill the system and road test the vehicle.

1990-91 2WD Colt Vista

1. Loosen the lug nuts.

2. Raise and support the vehicle safely.

3. Remove the wheels.

4. Remove the steering shaft-to-pinion coupling bolt.

5. Disconnect the tie rod ends with a separator.

6. Disconnect the hoses at the rack.

7. Remove the crossmember support bracket from the crossmember on the right side of the vehicle.

8. Unbolt the rack from the crossmember.

NOTE: The rack is most easily removed using a ratchet and long extension, working from the engine compartment side.

9. Pull the rack out the right side of the vehicle. Pull it slowly to avoid damage.

To install:

10. Installation is the reverse order of the removal procedures. Torque the rack clamp bolts to 43-58 ft. lbs. (58-79 Nm), the tie rod nuts to 17-25 ft. lbs. (23-34 Nm) and the coupling bolt to 22-25 ft. lbs. (29-34 Nm). Fill the system and road test the vehicle.

1990-91 4WD Colt Vista

1. Remove the steering column.

2. Raise and support the vehicle safely.

3. Remove the front wheels.

4. Using a separator, disconnect the tie rod from the knuckle.

5. Disconnect the steering shaft joint at the rack.

6. Disconnect the fluid lines at the gear box.

7. Remove the air cleaner.

8. Remove the rack attaching bolts from the rear of the No. 2 crossmember. The bolts are most easily accessed using a long extension and working from the top of the engine compartment.

9. From under the vehicle, remove the rack mounting bolts from the front of the No. 2 crossmember and pull out and to the left on the rack.

10. Lower the gear box until the left edge of the left feed tube contacts the lower part of the left fender shield. At this point, remove the left and right feed tubes.

11. Remove the rack from the vehicle.

To install:

12. Installation is the reverse order of the removal procedures. When installing the clamps, make sure the rubber projections are aligned with the holes in the clamps. Install the tie rods so 7.52-7.60 in. (191.00-193.00mm) shows between the tie rod end locknut and the beginning of the boot. Torque the gear box mounting bolts to 55-60 ft. lbs. (75-81 Nm); the tie rod-to-knuckle nut to 20-25 ft. lbs (27-34 Nm).

1992-94 Colt Vista

1. Disconnect the battery negative cable. Raise the vehicle and support safely.

2. Remove the pinch bolt holding the lower steering column joint to the rack and pinion input shaft.

3. Remove the cotter pins and disconnect the tie rod ends from the steering knuckle.

4. If equipped with 4WD, remove the transfer case rear bracket.

5. If equipped with 2350cc engine and FWD, disconnect the stabilizer bar and remove as required.

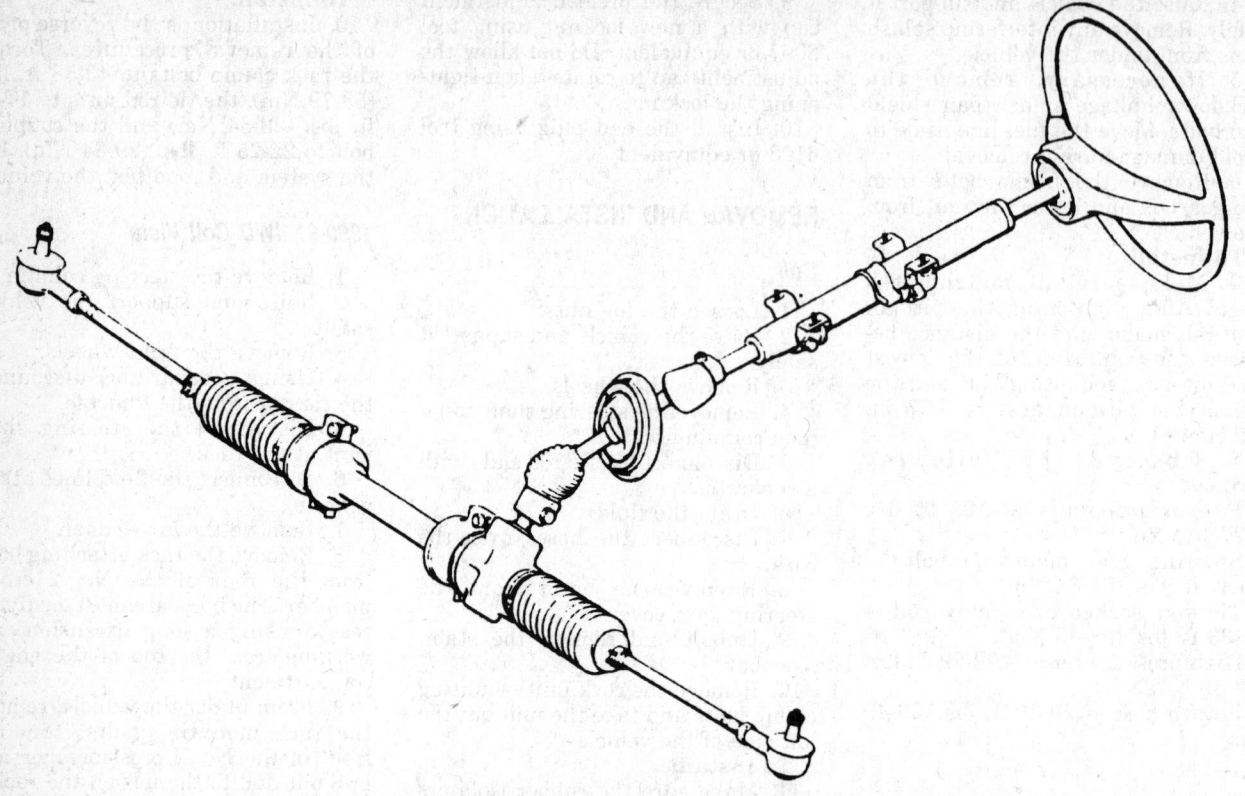

View of the steering system — Colt and Colt Vista

6. Disconnect the power steering fluid pressure pipe and return hose from the rack fittings.

7. Remove the rack and pinion steering assembly and its rubber mounts.

To install:

8. Install the steering gear into the vehicle and secure using the retainer clamps and bolts.

9. Connect the power steering fluid lines to the rack fittings.

10. Install the stabilizer bar and rear transaxle bracket.

11. Connect the tie rod ends to the steering knuckles.

12. Connect the negative battery cable. Refill the reservoir and bleed the system.

13. Perform a front end alignment.

Power Steering Pump

REMOVAL AND INSTALLATION

1. Remove the drive belt. If the pulley is to be removed, do so now.

2. Disconnect the pressure and return lines. Catch any leaking fluid. Remove the bango fitting nut on later model vehicles.

3. Remove the heat protector for the 1992-94 Colt Vista equipped with the 2350cc engine.

4. Remove the pump attaching bolts and lift the pump from the brackets.

To install:

5. Make sure the bracket-to-engine bolts are tight and install the pump to the brackets. Tighten the retaining bolts after installing the drive belt to the correct tension.

6. If the pulley has been removed, install it and tighten the nut securely. Bend the lock tab over the nut. Later model pulleys have to pressed on and off. Install the heat protector, if equipped.

7. Install the drive belt and adjust to a tension of 22 lbs. (30 N) at a deflection of 0.28-0.39 in. (7.11-9.91mm) at the top center of the belt. Torque the pump bolts to 21 ft. lbs. (30 Nm) and hold the belt tension.

8. Connect the pressure line and torque the banjo fitting nut to 13 ft. lbs. (18 Nm). Connect the return lines and fill the reservoir with Dexron® II automatic transmission fluid.

9. Bleed the system.

BELT ADJUSTMENT

1. Press the V-belt by applying pressure of 22 lbs. (30 N) at the center of the belt.

2. Measure the deflection to confirm that it is within the standard range.

a. Colt, standard value — 0.2-0.4 in. (6-9mm).

b. 1990-91 Colt Vista, standard value — 0.3-0.4 in. (7-10mm).

c. 1992-94 Colt Vista, standard value — 0.4-0.5 in. (9-12mm).

3. To adjust the tension of the belt, loosen the power steering pump mounting bolts, move the power steering pump and then retighten the bolts.

SYSTEM BLEEDING

1. The reservoir should be full of Dexron® II automatic transmission fluid.

2. Raise the vehicle and support it safely.

3. Turn the steering wheel fully to the right and left until no air bubbles appear in the fluid. Maintain the reservoir level.

4. Lower the vehicle and with the engine idling, turn the wheels fully to the right and left. Stop the engine.

5. Install a tube from the bleeder screw on the steering gear box or rack, to the reservoir.

6. Start the engine, turn the steering wheel fully to the left and loosen the bleeder screw.

7. Repeat the procedure until no air bubbles pass through the tube.

8. Tighten the bleeder screw and remove the tube. Refill the reservoir as needed and check that no further bubbles are present in the fluid. An abrupt rise in the fluid level after stopping the engine is a sign of incomplete bleeding. This will cause noise from the pump or control valve.

Tie Rod Ends

REMOVAL AND INSTALLATION

Outer

1. Raise the vehicle and support it safely.

2. Remove the cotter pin and loosen the nut from the tie rod.

3. Loosen the shaft jam nut before removing the joint. Remove the tie rod ends from the knuckle with a separator tool MB990635 or MB991113. The outer end is left hand threaded and the inner is right hand threaded. Keep the tie rod from turning while removing the tie rod end.

To install:

4. Grease the tie rod threads and install the ends. Turn each end in an equal amount.

5. Install the tie rod end assembly on the steering knuckle and tie rod. Torque the castellated nuts to 29-36 ft. lbs. (39-49 Nm) and the jam nut to 38 ft. lbs. (53 Nm). Use new cotter pins.

6. Adjust the toe-in.

Inner

Removal of the rack and pinion assembly may be needed to gain access to the inner tie rods. The inner tie rod is located inside the steering bellows. A large wrench is needed to turn the tie rod from the rack.

1. Raise the vehicle and support safely. Remove the front wheels.

2. Remove the rack and pinion assembly, if necessary.

3. Loosen the tie rod-to-tie rod end jam nut.

4. Remove the clamps and slide the bellows from the tie rod.

5. Using a punch, remove the stacked tab washer from the tie rod nut.

6. Use a large wrench to turn the tie rod from the rack.

To install:

7. Always use a new tab washer. Install the tab washer and tie rod. Torque the tie rod to 58-72 ft. lbs. (80-100 Nm). Stack over the tab washer.

8. Install the bellows and new clamps.

9. Install the remaining components.

10. Align the front end.

BRAKES

NOTE: For all brake system repair and service procedures not detailed below, please refer to "Brakes" in the Unit Repair section.

Master Cylinder

REMOVAL AND INSTALLATION

Colt and Colt Vista

1. Disconnect the fluid level sensor.

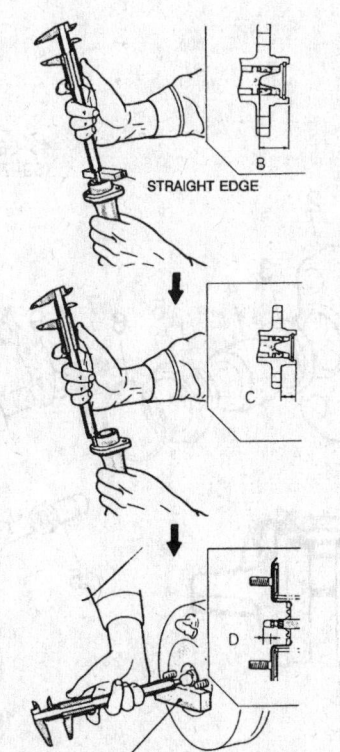

STRAIGHT EDGE

Brake booster pushrod-to-master cylinder clearance check

2. Disconnect the brake tubes from the master cylinder and cap them immediately. Always use a flare nut wrench.

3. If equipped with a turbocharger, remove the reservoir from the reservoir holder.

4. Unbolt and remove the master cylinder from the booster.

To install:

5. Measure the clearance between the brake booster pushrod and primary piston. Measure the distance from the bottom of the primary piston to the top of the round portion of the housing (measurement B), the distance from the mounting flange to the top of the round portion of the housing (measurement C) and the distance between the master cylinder mounting surface to the tip of the booster pushrod. The clearance should be as follows:

7 inch booster — 0.20-0.28 in. (0.5-0.7mm)

8 inch booster — 0.24-0.31 in. (0.6-0.8mm)

9 inch booster — 0.31-0.39 in. (0.8-1.0mm)

6. Mount the master cylinder to the power brake booster.

7. Connect all brake lines and wiring harnesses and fill the master cylinder reservoirs with clean fluid. Torque the brake lines and mounting nuts to 9-12 ft. lbs. (13-17 Nm).

8. Bleed the brake system.

Proportioning Valve

REMOVAL AND INSTALLATION

1. Disconnect the brake lines at the valve.

NOTE: Always use a flare nut wrench to avoid damage to the flare nuts and brake lines.

2. Remove the mounting bolts and the valve.

3. Install in the reverse order of the removal procedures. Torque the brake lines and mounting bolts to 9-12 ft. lbs. (13-17 Nm). Refill the master cylinder and bleed the brake system.

Power Brake Booster

REMOVAL AND INSTALLATION

1. Remove the master cylinder.

2. Disconnect the vacuum line from the booster.

3. Remove the pin connecting the power brake operating rod and the brake lever.

4. Unbolt and remove the booster.

5. Replace the packing on both sides of the booster-to-firewall spacer with new packing.

6. If the check valve was removed, make sure the direction of installation marking on the valve is followed.

To install:

7. Installation is the reverse order of the removal procedures. Torque the booster-to-firewall nuts to 6-9 ft. lbs. (9-13 Nm). Torque the master cylinder-to-booster nuts to 6-9 ft. lbs. (9-13 Nm). Torque the hydraulic lines to 9-12 ft. lbs. (13-17 Nm) with a flare nut wrench.

8. Adjust the brake pedal and master cylinder pushrod as explained earlier.

Brake Caliper

REMOVAL AND INSTALLATION

FRONT

1. Raise and support the vehicle safely and remove the wheel assembly.

NOTE: On late model vehicles equipped with the PFS15 type front disc brakes, the caliper and pads are retained to the adapter by 2 sleeve pin bolts. Remove the pin bolts and service the assembly as required. Sleeve bolt torque is 16-23 ft. lbs. (22-31 Nm).

2. Disconnect the brake hose from the caliper and plug.

3. Remove the upper and lower pin bolts and remove the caliper and brake pads as an assembly.

4. Remove the inner shim, the anti-squeal shim and the pads from the caliper support assembly.

To install:

5. Installation is the reverse order of the removal procedures. When installing the spacers, apply a coating of an approved grease on the spacers.

6. Torque the caliper retaining bolts to 16-23 ft. lbs. (22-32 Nm). Torque the brake hose fitting with a flare

nut wrench to 9-12 ft. lbs. (13-17 Nm).

Disc Brake Pads

REMOVAL AND INSTALLATION

FRONT

COLT

1. Raise the vehicle and support it safely. Remove the wheels.

NOTE: On late vehicles equipped with the PFS15 type front disc brakes; the caliper and pads are retained to the adapter by 2 sleeve pin bolts. Remove the pin bolts and service the assembly as required. Sleeve pin torque is 16-23 ft. lbs. (22-31 Nm).

2. Remove the lower sleeve bolt from the caliper and rotate the caliper upward.

NOTE: There is a grease coating on the bolt. Make sure it is not removed or contaminated.

3. Support the caliper by suspending it with wire or string from a nearby suspension member.

4. Remove the inner, then outer shims from the caliper.

1. Bleeder screw
2. Caliper, inner
3. Piston seal
4. Piston
5. Dust seal
6. Retaining ring
7. Cap plug
8. Torque plate pin cap
9. Oil seal retainer
10. Wiper seal
11. Torque plate
12. Pad assembly
13. Anti-squeak shim
14. Pad retaining pin
15. Torque plate pin bushing
16. K-spring
17. Pad protector
18. M-clip
19. Caliper, outer
20. Dust cover
21. Brake disc

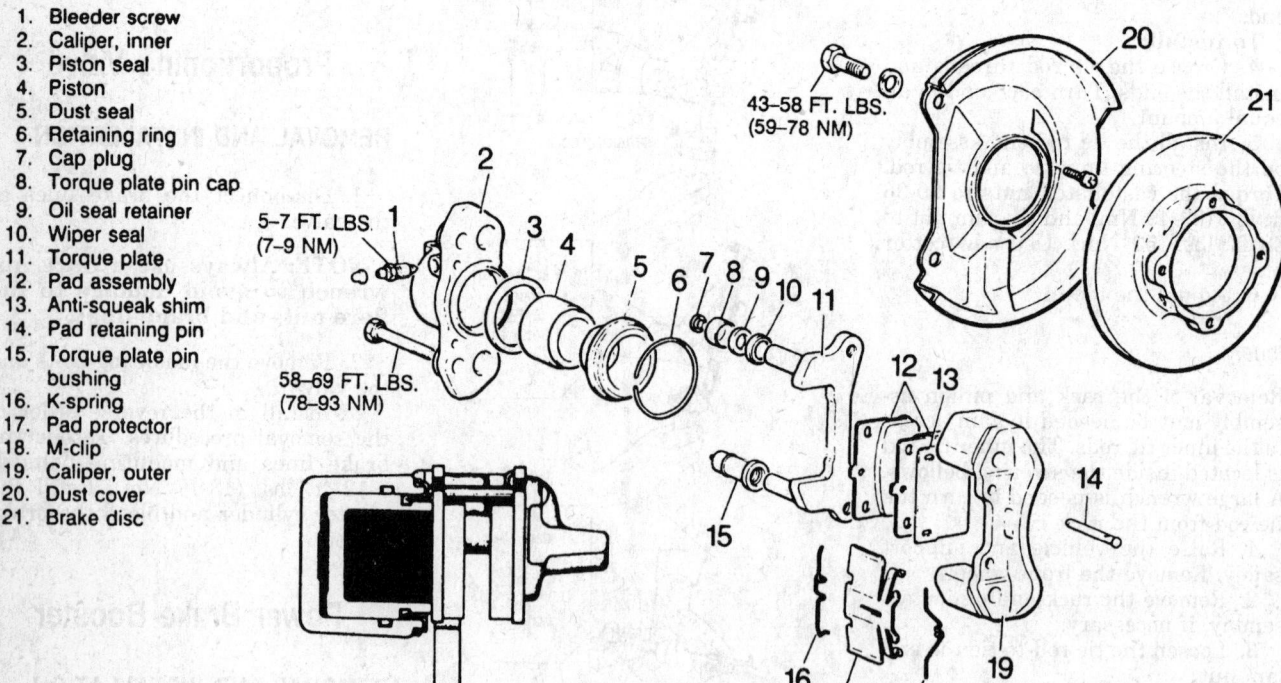

Typical pin type caliper

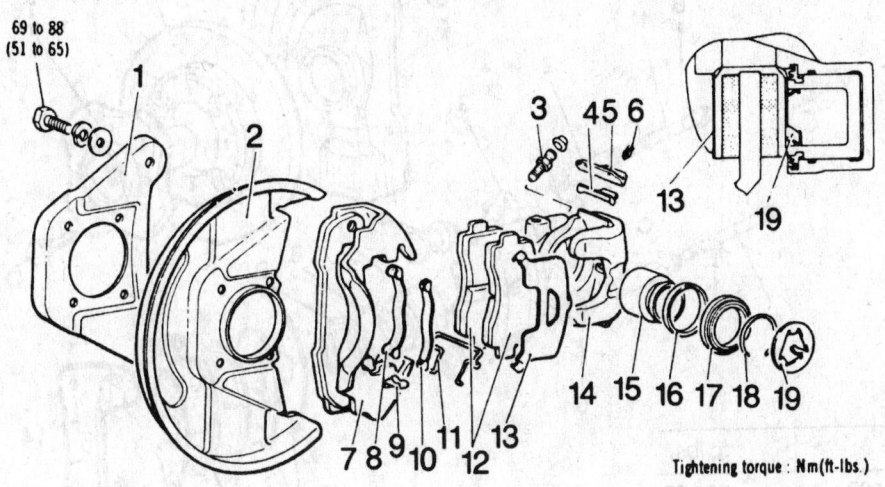

69 to 88
(51 to 65)

Tightening torque : Nm(ft-lbs.)

1. Disc brake adapter
2. Dust cover
3. Bleeder screw
4. Pad support plate
5. Stopper plug
6. Spigot pin
7. Caliper support
8. Pad clip (inner)
9. Pad clip B
10. Pad clip (outer)
11. Anti-rattle spring
12. Brake pad
13. Anti-squeak shim (outer)
14. Caliper body
15. Piston
16. Piston seal
17. Dust boot
18. Boot ring
19. Anti-squeak shim (inner)

Exploded view of a typical sliding type caliper

5. Lift out the brake pads.

6. Remove the pad liners.

To install:

7. Clean all parts in solvent made for brake parts.

8. Inspect the dust boot on the caliper piston. If it is torn or brittle, replace it. and consider rebuilding the caliper.

9. Inspect the shims and liners and replace them if damaged.

10. Remove the cap from the master cylinder reservoir and siphon off about ¼ in. (6.35mm) of fluid.

11. Using a C-clamp, force the piston back into the caliper as far as it will go. Remove the clamp.

12. Install the liners, pads and inner, then outer shims.

NOTE: Never replace just one set of pads, pads should be replaced on both front wheels at the same time.

13. Lower the caliper and install the lower sleeve bolt. Torque the bolt to 16-23 ft. lbs. (22-31 Nm).

14. Start the engine and depress the brake pedal several times. Hold it depressed for about 5 seconds. Turn the engine OFF.

15. Rotate the brake rotor a few times. Using a spring scale hooked to 1 of the lugs, measure the brake

drag. Remove the pads and perform the spring scale test again. The difference between the drag test with and without the pads should not exceed 15 lbs. (20 N). If the difference does exceed 15 lbs. (20 N), the caliper will have to be rebuilt or replaced. When servicing is complete, pump the brakes several times. Do not move the vehicle until a firm brake pedal is present.

COLT VISTA

1. Raise the vehicle and support it safely. Remove the front wheels.

NOTE: On late models equipped with the PFS15 type front disc brakes, the caliper and pads are retained to the adapter by 2 sleeve pin bolts. Remove the pin bolts and service the assembly as required. Sleeve bolt torque is 16-23 ft. lbs. (22-31 Nm).

2. Remove the lower pin bolt and rotate the caliper upwards. Support the caliper with wire or string from a nearby suspension member.

3. Remove the inner shim, the anti-squeal shim and the pads from the caliper support assembly.

4. Remove the clips from the pads.

To install:

5. Clean all parts in solvent made for brake parts.

6. Inspect the dust boot on the caliper piston. If it is torn or brittle, replace it and consider rebuilding the caliper.

7. Inspect the shims and liners and replace them if damaged.

8. Remove the cap from the master cylinder reservoir and siphon off about ¼ in. (6.35mm) of fluid.

9. Using a special tool, force the piston back into the caliper as far as it will go. Remove the clamp.

10. Install the pads with clips attached and the proper shims, in position, on the support.

NOTE: Never replace just one set of pads. Pads should be replaced on both front wheels at the same time.

11. Lower the caliper and install the lower pin bolt. Torque the bolt to 16-23 ft. lbs. (22-31 Nm).

12. Start the engine and depress the brake pedal. Hold it depressed for about 5 seconds. Turn the engine OFF.

13. Rotate the brake rotor a few times. Using a spring scale hooked to 1 of the lugs, measure the brake drag. Remove the pads and perform the spring scale test again. The difference between the drag test with and without the pads should not ex-

1. Sleeve bolt B
2. Sleeve
3. Caliper
4. Bushing
5. Sleeve bolt B
6. Pin boot
7. Piston
8. Piston seal
9. Dust boot
10. Inner shim
11. Pad assembly
12. Pad liner
13. Outer shim
14. Torque member
15. Brake disc
16. Hub

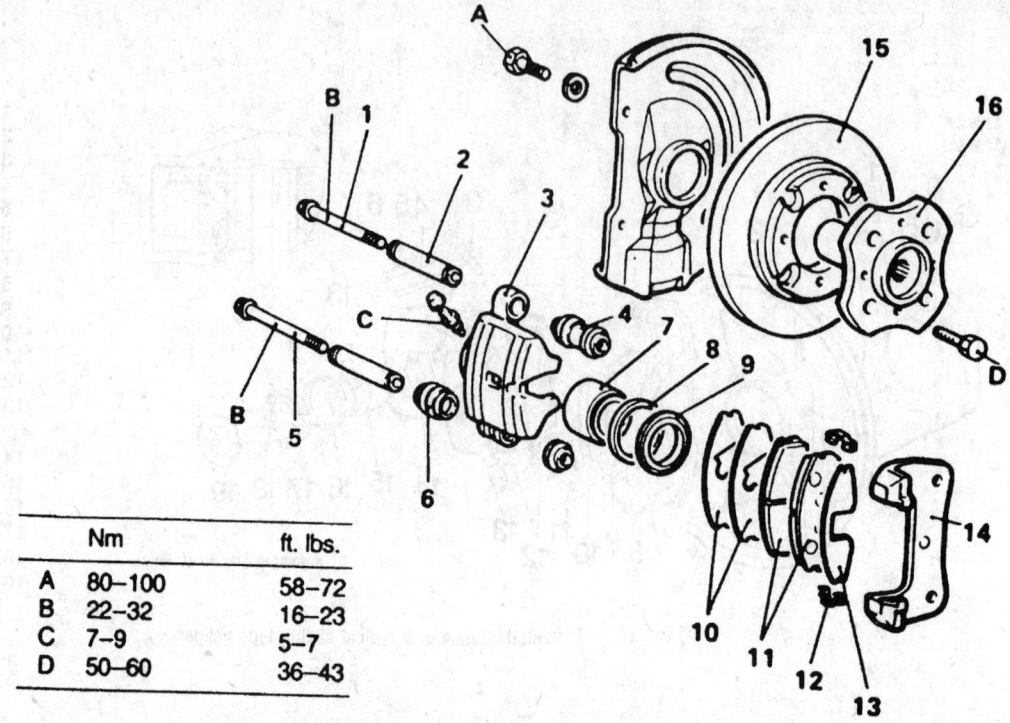

	Nm	ft. lbs.
A	80–100	58–72
B	22–32	16–23
C	7–9	5–7
D	50–60	36–43

Exploded view of the brake caliper assembly — Colt

ceed 15 lbs. (20 N). If the difference does exceed 15 lbs. (20 N), the caliper will have to be rebuilt or replaced.

14. When servicing is complete, pump the brakes several times, do not operate the vehicle until a firm brake pedal is present. Bleed the brakes if necessary.

REAR

1. Raise the vehicle and support it safely. Remove the rear wheel and the caliper dust cover.
2. Disconnect the parking brake cable, except 1992-94 Colt Vista.
3. Remove the spring pin and stopper plug.
4. Move the caliper back and forth to loosen, then remove the caliper from the support.

NOTE: The brake hose need not be disconnected; however, do not suspend the weight of the caliper from the hose.

5. Take time to examine the location of the various clips and springs. Remove the pads from the support. Do not mix up the inner and outer clips, they must be installed in the same location.
6. Seat the caliper piston by pushing in while turning clockwise. When fully seated, 1 of the grooves on the piston must be located vertically at 12 o'clock to accommodate a projection of the brake pad. Install new pads into the support and install the caliper.

Brake Rotor

REMOVAL AND INSTALLATION

FRONT

EXCEPT 1992-94 COLT VISTA

1. Raise the vehicle and support it safely.
2. Remove the wheel assembly. Remove the cotter pin and axle nut.
3. Support the caliper by suspending it with wire from a nearby suspension member.
4. Using halfshaft separator tool, separate the halfshaft from the hub assembly.
5. Matchmark the steering knuckle-to-strut bolts and remove the retaining bolts.
6. Remove the lower ball joint retaining nut. Using a ball joint separator tool, separate the ball joint from the knuckle assembly.

7. Remove the knuckle assembly from the vehicle.
8. Secure the knuckle and rotor assembly in a vise. Remove the rotor-to-hub retaining bolts and separate the rotor from the hub.

To install:

9. Installation is the reverse order of the removal procedures. Torque the rotor-hub-bolts to 56-72 ft. lbs. (80-100 Nm). Torque the steering knuckle-to-strut bolts to 54-65 ft. lbs. (75-90 Nm). Torque lower ball joint retaining nut to 43-52 ft. lbs. (60-72 Nm).

1992-94 COLT VISTA

1. Raise the vehicle and support it safely.
2. Remove the wheel assembly and remove the caliper assembly.
3. Support the caliper by suspending it with wire from a nearby suspension member. Remove the caliper support bracket from the knuckle.
4. Remove the brake rotor from the hub.
5. Installation is the reserve of removal. Install the support bracket and torque the bolts to 65 ft. lbs. (95 Nm).

	Nm	ft. lbs.
A	7–9	5–7
B	22–32	16–23
C	80–100	58–72
D	50–60	36–43

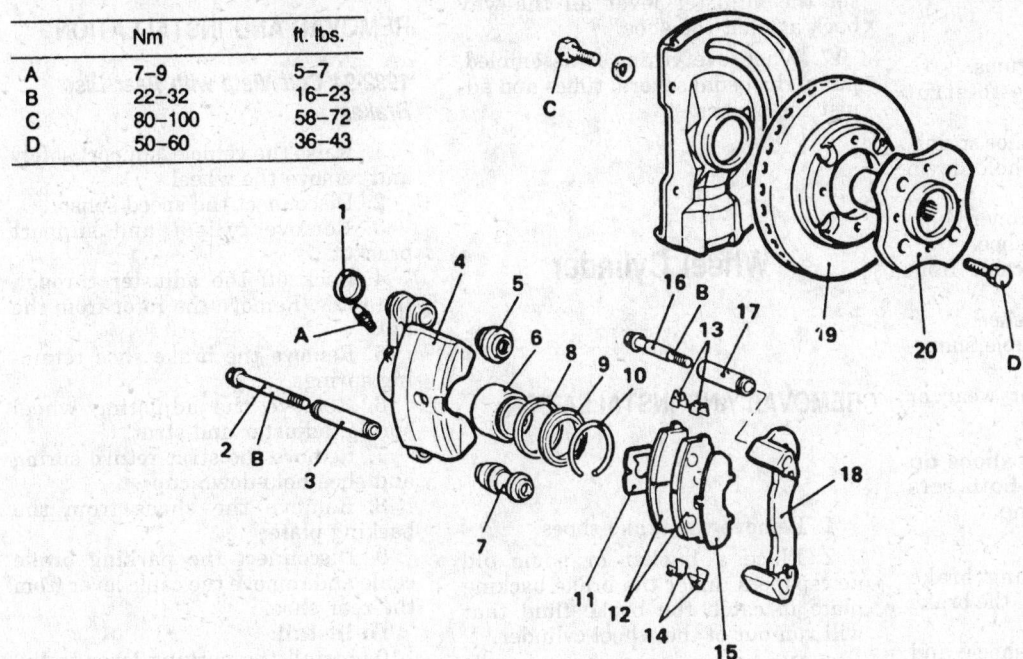

1. Lid
2. Lock pin
3. Sleeve
4. Caliper body
5. Guide pin boot
6. Piston
7. Lock pin boot
8. Piston seal
9. Piston boot
10. Boot ring
11. Inner shim
12. Pad assembly
13. Pad clip B
14. Pad clip C
15. Anti-squeak shim
16. Guide pin
17. Sleeve
18. Support mounting
19. Brake disc
20. Hub

Exploded view of the typical caliper used on the Colt Vista

REAR

ALL VEHICLES

1. Raise the vehicle and support it safely. Remove the wheel assembly.

2. Remove the caliper. Support the caliper by suspending it with wire from a nearby suspension member.

3. Remove the caliper support retaining bolts and remove the support.

4. Back off the parking brake shoe adjuster through the holes in the rotor for the 1992-94 Colt Vista.

5. Remove the rotor-to-hub retaining screws and slide the rotor from the hub. If equipped with retaining rings, remove the rings from the wheel lugs.

To install:

6. Slide the rotor on the hub and install the rotor-to-hub retaining screws. If equipped with retaining rings, install new rings on the wheel lugs.

7. Adjust the parking brake shoes so a slight drag is felt during rotation for the 1992-94 Colt Vista.

8. Install the caliper support and retaining bolts. Torque the bolts to 29-36 ft. lbs. (40-50 Nm), except 1992-94 Colt Vista. Torque the bolts to 40 ft. lbs. (55 Nm) for the 1992-94 Colt Vista.

9. Install the caliper, brake pads and caliper retaining bolts. Torque the bolts to 16-23 ft. lbs. (22-32 Nm).

10. Install the wheel assembly and lower the vehicle.

11. When servicing is complete, pump the brakes several times, do not operate the vehicle until a firm brake pedal is present. Bleed the brakes if necessary.

Brake Shoes

REMOVAL AND INSTALLATION

Colt

1. Raise the vehicle and support it safely. Remove rear wheel and brake drum.

2. Remove the lower pressed metal spring clip, the shoe return spring (the large one piece spring between the 2 shoes) and the 2 shoe hold-down springs.

3. Remove the shoes and adjuster as an assembly. Disconnect the parking brake cable from the lever, remove the spring between the shoes and the lever from the rear (trailing) shoe. Disconnect the adjuster retaining spring and remove the adjuster,

turn the star wheel in to the adjuster body after cleaning and lubricating the threads.

4. The wheel cylinder may be removed for service or replacement, if necessary.

To install:

5. Clean the backing plate. Install the wheel cylinder if it was removed. Lubricate all contact points on the backing plate, anchor plate, wheel cylinder to shoe contact and parking brake strut joints and contacts. Install the brake shoes after attaching the parking brake, lever and adjuster assemblies. Install the hold-down and return springs.

6. Pre-adjustment of the brake shoe can be made by turning the adjuster star wheel out until the drum will just slide on over the brake shoes. Before installing the drum make sure the parking brake is not adjusted too tightly, if it is, loosen or the adjustment of the rear brakes will not be correct.

7. If the wheel cylinders were serviced, bleed the brake system. The brake shoes are then adjusted by pumping the brake pedal and applying and releasing the parking brake, Adjust the parking brake stroke. Road test the vehicle.

Colt Vista

1. Raise the vehicle and support it safely.
2. Remove the wheels.
3. Remove the brake drums.
4. Remove the shoe-to-strut spring.
5. Remove the shoe-to-shoe spring.
6. Remove the shoe hold-down spring.
7. Remove the shoe retainer clip.
8. Remove the leading shoe.
9. Remove the brake cable from the lever.
10. Remove the trailing shoe.
11. Remove the brake cable snapring and remove the cable.
12. Inspect all parts for wear or damage.

NOTE: Never replace shoes on one side only. Replace both sets of shoes at the same time.

To install:

13. Assemble the parking brake and adjuster assemblies on the brake shoes.
14. Install the brake shoes and hold-downs. Connect the return springs.
15. Apply a small amount of lithium based grease to the contact pads of the backing plate before installing the shoes.

16. When installing the shoe-to-shoe spring and shoe-to-strut spring, set the adjuster lever all the way back against the shoe.
17. When everything is assembled, pump the pedal several times and adjust the brakes.

Wheel Cylinder

REMOVAL AND INSTALLATION

1. Remove the brake shoes.
2. Place a bucket or some old newspapers under the brake backing plate to catch the brake fluid that will run out of the wheel cylinder.
3. Disconnect the brake line and remove the cylinder mounting bolts.
4. Remove the cylinder from the backing plate.
5. Install the cylinder in the reverse order. Bleed the brake system.

Parking Brake Shoes

REMOVAL AND INSTALLATION

1992-94 Colt Vista with Rear Disc Brakes

1. Raise the vehicle, support safely and remove the wheel.
2. Disconnect the speed sensor.
3. Remove caliper and support bracket.
4. Back off the adjuster through the rotor. Remove the rotor from the hub.
5. Remove the brake shoe retaining springs.
6. Remove the adjusting wheel spring, adjuster and strut.
7. Remove the strut return spring and shoe hold-down cups.
8. Remove the shoes from the backing plate.
9. Disconnect the parking brake cable and remove the cable lever from the rear shoe.

To install:

10. Install the parking lever to the rear shoe with a new circlip. Bend the circlip around the rod.
11. Lubricate the shoe guide pads and adjuster with white lithium grease. Install the shoes to the backing plate.

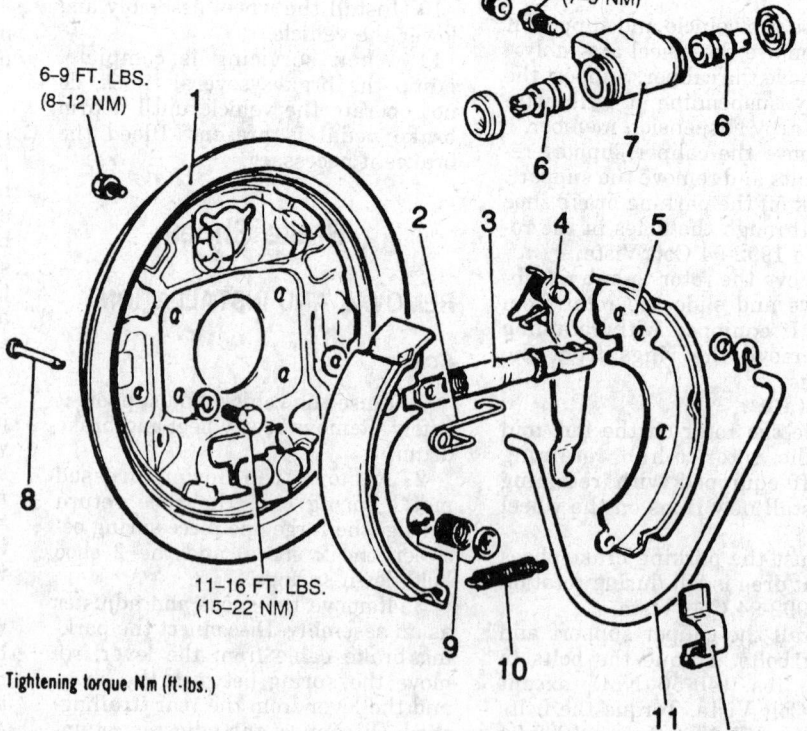

1. Backing plate
2. Spring
3. Adjuster
4. Parking lever
5. Shoe and lining assembly
6. Piston
7. Wheel cylinder body
8. Shoe hold spring pin
9. Shoe hold-down spring
10. Shoe to shore spring
11. Shoe return spring
12. Clip spring

6–9 FT. LBS. (8–12 NM)

5–7 FT. LBS. (7–9 NM)

11–16 FT. LBS. (15–22 NM)

Tightening torque Nm (ft-lbs.)

Typical rear drum brake system used on the front wheel drive — Except Colt Vista

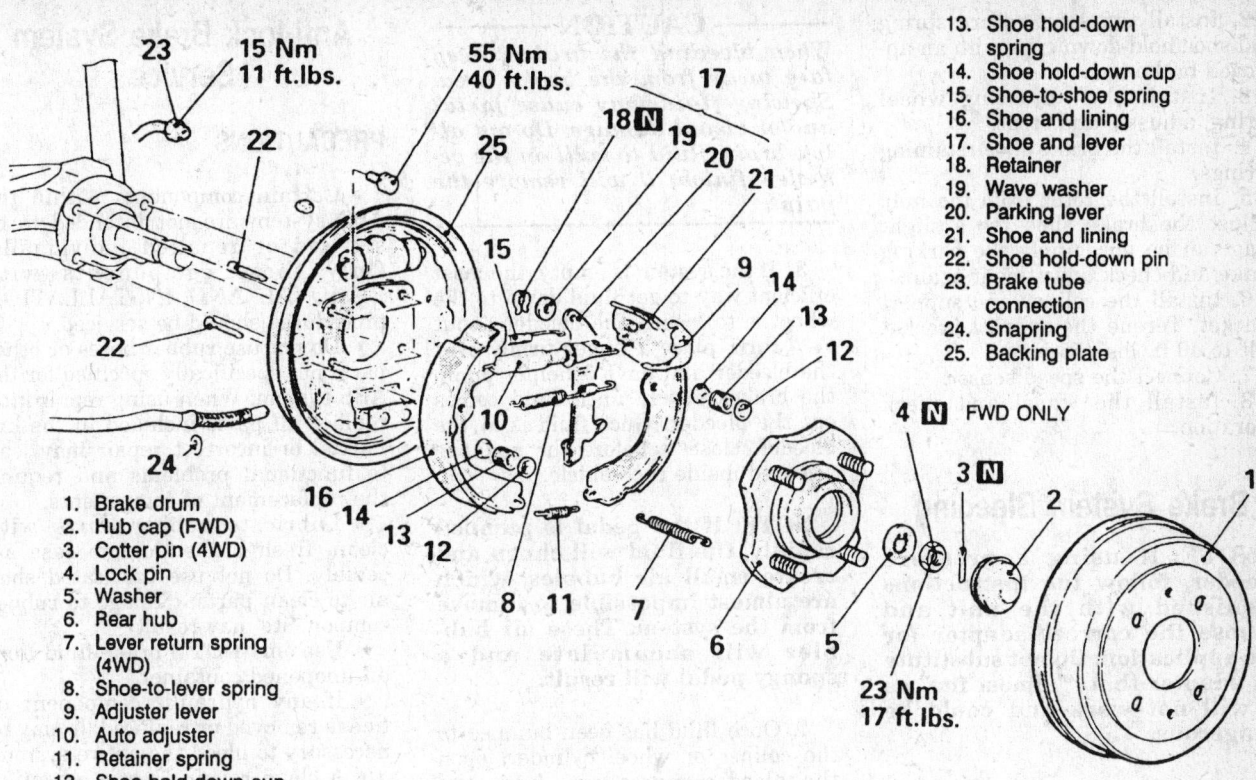

13. Shoe hold-down
    spring
14. Shoe hold-down cup
15. Shoe-to-shoe spring
16. Shoe and lining
17. Shoe and lever
18. Retainer
19. Wave washer
20. Parking lever
21. Shoe and lining
22. Shoe hold-down pin
23. Brake tube
    connection
24. Snapring
25. Backing plate

1. Brake drum
2. Hub cap (FWD)
3. Cotter pin (4WD)
4. Lock pin
5. Washer
6. Rear hub
7. Lever return spring
   (4WD)
8. Shoe-to-lever spring
9. Adjuster lever
10. Auto adjuster
11. Retainer spring
12. Shoe hold-down cup

Rear brake assembly — 1992-94 Colt Vista

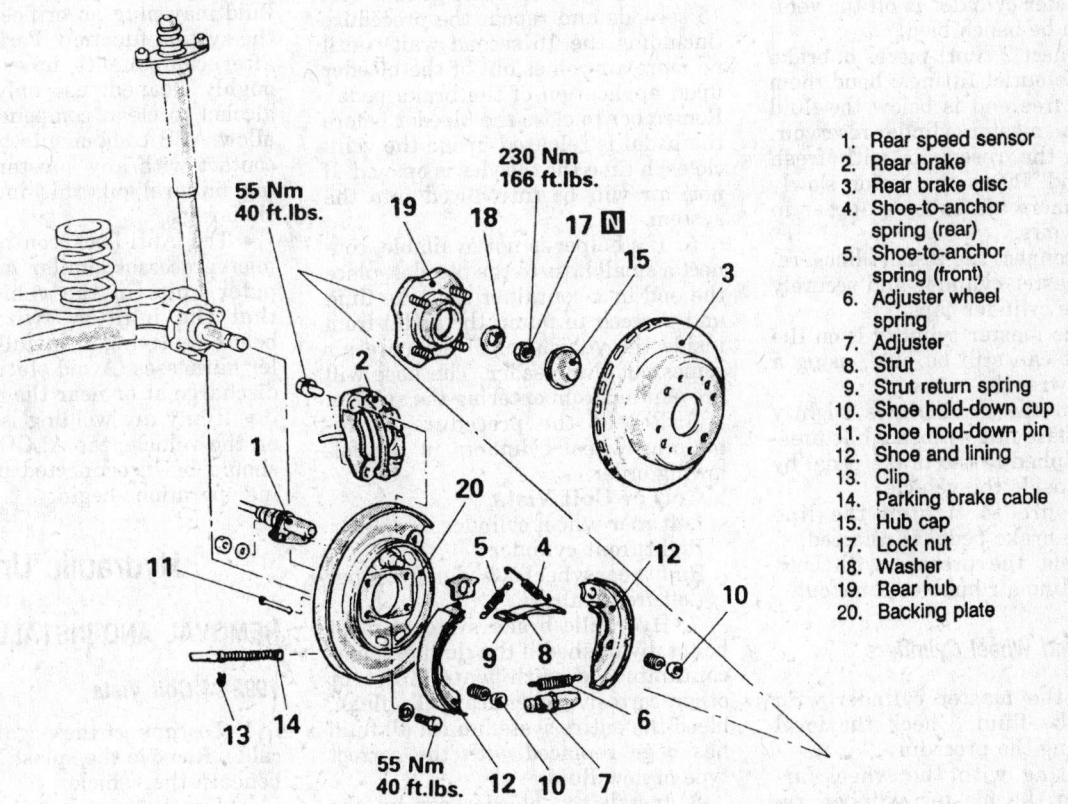

1. Rear speed sensor
2. Rear brake
3. Rear brake disc
4. Shoe-to-anchor
   spring (rear)
5. Shoe-to-anchor
   spring (front)
6. Adjuster wheel
   spring
7. Adjuster
8. Strut
9. Strut return spring
10. Shoe hold-down cup
11. Shoe hold-down pin
12. Shoe and lining
13. Clip
14. Parking brake cable
15. Hub cap
17. Lock nut
18. Washer
19. Rear hub
20. Backing plate

Parking brake assembly — 1992-94 Colt Vista with rear disc brakes

12. Install the strut return spring and shoe hold-down cups with an approved brake tool.

13. Install the adjusting wheel spring, adjuster and strut.

14. Install the brake shoe retaining springs.

15. Install the rotor from the hub. Adjust the brake shoes so a slight drag can be felt. Apply the parking brake and check adjustment again.

16. Install the caliper and support bracket. Torque the support bracket bolt to 40 ft. lbs. (55 Nm).

17. Connect the speed sensor.

18. Install the wheel and check operation.

Brake System Bleeding

NOTE: If using a pressure bleeder, follow the instructions furnished with the unit and choose the correct adaptor for the application. Do not substitute an adapter that ""almost fits" as it will not work and could be dangerous.

Master Cylinder

If the master cylinder is off the vehicle, it can be bench bled.

1. Connect 2 short pieces of brake line to the outlet fittings, bend them until the free end is below the fluid level in the master cylinder reservoir.

2. Fill the reservoir with fresh brake fluid. Pump the piston slowly until no more air bubbles appear in the reservoirs.

3. Disconnect the 2 short lines, refill the master cylinder and securely install the cylinder caps.

4. If the master cylinder is on the vehicle, it can still be bled, using a flare nut wrench.

5. Open the brake lines slightly with the flare nut wrench while pressure is applied to the brake pedal by a helper inside the vehicle.

6. Be sure to tighten the line before the brake pedal is released.

7. Repeat the process with both lines until no air bubbles come out.

Calipers and Wheel Cylinders

1. Fill the master cylinder with fresh brake fluid. Check the level often during the procedure.

2. Starting with the wheel farthest from the master cylinder, remove the protective cap from the bleeder and place where it will not be lost. Clean the bleeder screw.

---CAUTION---

When bleeding the brakes, keep face away from the brake area. Spewing fluid may cause facial and/or visual damage. Do not allow brake fluid to spill on the vehicle's finish; it will remove the paint.

3. If the system is empty, the most efficient way to get fluid down to the wheel is to loosen the bleeder about $\frac{1}{2}$-$\frac{3}{4}$ turn, place a finger firmly over the bleeder and have a helper pump the brakes slowly until fluid comes out the bleeder. Once fluid is at the bleeder, close it before the pedal is released inside the vehicle.

NOTE: If the pedal is pumped rapidly, the fluid will churn and create small air bubbles, which are almost impossible to remove from the system. These air bubbles will accumulate and a spongy pedal will result.

4. Once fluid has been pumped to the caliper or wheel cylinder, open the bleed screw again, have the helper press the brake pedal to the floor, lock the bleeder and have the helper slowly release the pedal. Wait 15 seconds and repeat the procedure (including the 15 second wait) until no more air comes out of the bleeder upon application of the brake pedal. Remember to close the bleeder before the pedal is released inside the vehicle each time the bleeder is opened. If not, air will be introduced into the system.

5. If a helper is not available, connect a small hose to the bleeder, place the end in a container of brake fluid and proceed to pump the pedal from inside the vehicle until no more air comes out the bleeder. The hose will prevent air from entering the system.

6. Repeat the procedure on remaining wheel cylinders in the following order:

Colt or Colt Vista
Left rear wheel cylinder or caliper
Right front cylinder
Right rear wheel cylinder or caliper
Left front caliper

7. Hydraulic brake systems must be totally flushed if the fluid becomes contaminated with water, dirt or other corrosive chemicals. To flush, bleed the entire system until all fluid has been replaced with the correct type of new fluid.

8. Install the bleeder cap on the bleeder to keep dirt out. Always road test the vehicle after brake work of any kind is done.

Anti-lock Brake System Service

PRECAUTIONS

• Certain components within the ABS system are not intended to be serviced or repaired individually. Only those components with REMOVAL AND INSTALLATION procedures should be serviced.

• Do not use rubber hoses or other parts not specifically specified for the ABS system. When using repair kits, replace all parts included in the kit. Partial or incorrect repair may lead to functional problems and require the replacement of components.

• Lubricate rubber parts with clean, fresh brake fluid to ease assembly. Do not use lubricated shop air to clean parts; damage to rubber components may result.

• Use only DOT 3 brake fluid from an unopened container.

• If any hydraulic component or line is removed or replaced, it may be necessary to bleed the entire system.

• A clean repair area is essential. Always clean the reservoir and cap thoroughly before removing the cap. The slightest amount of dirt in the fluid may plug an orifice and impair the system function. Perform repairs after components have been thoroughly cleaned; use only denatured alcohol to clean components. Do not allow ABS components to come into contact with any substance containing mineral oil; this includes used shop rags.

• The Anti-Lock control unit is a microprocessor similar to other computer units in the vehicle. Ensure that the ignition switch is **OFF** before removing or installing controller harnesses. Avoid static electricity discharge at or near the controller.

• If any arc welding is to be done on the vehicle, the ALCU connectors should be disconnected before welding operations begin.

Hydraulic Unit

REMOVAL AND INSTALLATION

1992-94 Colt Vista

1. Disconnect the negative battery cable. Remove the splash shield from beneath the vehicle.

2. Use a syringe or similar device to remove as much fluid as possible from the reservoir. Some fluid will be spilled from lines during removal of

the hydraulic unit; protect adjacent painted surfaces.

3. Remove the dust cover and the oil reservoir.

4. Disconnect the brake lines from the hydraulic unit. Correct reassembly is critical. Label or identify the lines before removal. Plug each line immediately after removal.

5. Disconnect the hydraulic unit electrical harness connectors.

6. Disconnect the hydraulic unit ground strap from the chassis.

7. Remove the 3 nuts holding the hydraulic unit. Remove the unit upwards.

NOTE: The hydraulic unit is heavy; use care when removing it. The unit must remain in the upright position at all times and be protected from impact and shock.

8. Set the unit upright supported by blocks on the workbench. The hydraulic unit must not be tilted or turned upside down. No component of the hydraulic unit should be loosened or disassembled.

9. The bracket assemblies and relays may be removed if desired.

To install:

10. Install the relays and brackets if removed.

11. Install the hydraulic unit into the vehicle, keeping it upright at all times.

12. Install the retaining nuts and tighten.

13. Connect the ground strap to the chassis bracket. Connect the hydraulic unit wiring harness.

14. Connect the hydraulic unit electrical harness connectors.

15. Install the dust cover and the oil reservoir.

16. Connect each brake line loosely to the correct port and double check the placement. Tighten each line to 10 ft. lbs. (13.5 Nm).

17. Fill the reservoir to the MAX line with brake fluid.

18. Bleed the master cylinder, then bleed the brake lines. Refill the master cylinder and check for proper operation.

Anti-Lock Control Unit

REMOVAL AND INSTALLATION

1. Ensure that the ignition switch is **OFF** throughout the procedure.

2. Remove the cup holder in front of the center console.

3. Remove the console side covers.

4. Disconnect the electrical harness from the control unit.

5. Remove the fasteners and the control unit from the vehicle.

6. Installation is the reverse of the removal procedure.

G-Sensor

The G-Sensor is found only on Four Wheel Drive (4WD) vehicles.

REMOVAL AND INSTALLATION

1. Disconnect negative battery cable.

2. Remove the floor console.

3. Disconnect the wiring harness connector from the sensor.

4. Remove the retaining screw and G-sensor from the mounting bracket.

5. Installation is the reverse of the removal procedure.

Wheel Speed Sensors

CAUTION

Vehicles equipped with air bag systems will have wiring and system components in the fender or wheel well area. The ABS components must be correctly identified before beginning repairs. Improper work procedures may cause impaired function of the ABS and/or SRS systems

REMOVAL AND INSTALLATION

1. Disconnect the negative battery cable. Raise and safely support the vehicle.

2. Remove the wheel and tire.

3. Remove the inner fender or splash shield.

4. Beginning at the sensor end, carefully disconnect or release each clip and retainer along the sensor wire. Take careful note of the exact position of each clip; they must be reinstalled in the identical position. Rear wheel sensor harnesses will be held by plastic wire ties; these may be cut away but must be replaced at reassembly.

5. Disconnect the sensor connector at the end of the harness.

6. Remove the 2 bolts holding the speed sensor bracket to the knuckle and remove the assembly from the vehicle.

NOTE: The speed sensor has a pole piece projecting from it. This exposed tip must be protected from impact or scratches.

Do not allow the pole piece to contact the toothed wheel during removal or installation.

7. Remove the sensor from the bracket.

To install:

8. Assemble the sensor onto the bracket and tighten the bolt to 10 ft. lbs. (14 Nm). Note that the brackets are different for the left and right front wheels. Each bracket has identifying letters stamped on it.

9. Temporarily install the speed sensor to the knuckle; tighten the bolts only finger-tight.

10. Route the cable correctly and loosely install the clips and retainers. All clips must be in their original position and the sensor cable must not be twisted. Improper installation may cause cable damage and system failure.

NOTE: The wiring in the harness is easily damaged by twisting and flexing. Use the white stripe on the outer insulation to keep the sensor harness properly placed.

11. Use a brass or other non-magnetic feeler gauge to check the air gap between the tip of the pole piece and the toothed wheel. Correct gap is 0.012-0.035 in. (0.3-0.9mm). Tighten the 2 sensor bracket bolts to 10 ft. lbs. (14 Nm) with the sensor located so the gap is the same at several points on the toothed wheel. If the gap is incorrect, it is likely that the toothed wheel is worn or improperly installed.

12. Tighten the screws and bolts for the cable retaining clips.

13. Install the inner fender or splash shield.

14. Install the wheel and tire. Lower the vehicle to the ground.

Front Toothed Wheel Rings

REMOVAL AND INSTALLATION

1. Disconnect the negative battery cable. Raise and safely support the vehicle.

2. Remove the wheel and tire.

3. Remove the wheel speed sensor and disconnect sufficient harness clips to allow the sensor and wiring to be moved out of the work area.

NOTE: The speed sensor has a pole piece projecting from it. This exposed tip must be protected from impact or scratches. Do not allow the pole piece to contact the toothed wheel during removal or installation.

4. Remove the front hub and knuckle assembly.

5. Remove the hub from the knuckle.

6. Support the hub in a vise with protected jaws. Remove the retaining bolts from the toothed wheel and remove the toothed wheel.

To install:

7. Fit the new toothed wheel onto the hub and tighten the retaining bolts to 7 ft. lbs. (10 Nm).

8. Assemble the hub to the knuckle

9. Install the hub and knuckle assembly to the vehicle.

10. Install the wheel speed sensor.

11. Install the wheel and tire.

12. Lower the vehicle to the ground.

Rear Toothed Wheel Rings

REMOVAL AND INSTALLATION

Front Wheel Drive

1. Disconnect the negative battery cable. Raise and safely support the vehicle.

2. Remove the wheel and tire.

3. Remove the wheel speed sensor and disconnect sufficient harness clips to allow the sensor and wiring to be moved out of the work area.

NOTE: The speed sensor has a pole piece projecting from it. This exposed tip must be protected from impact or scratches. Do not allow the pole piece to contact the toothed wheel during removal or installation.

4. Remove the hub assembly.

5. Support the hub in a vise with protected jaws. Remove the retaining bolts from the toothed wheel and remove the toothed wheel.

To install:

6. Fit the new toothed wheel onto the hub and tighten the retaining bolts to 7 ft. lbs. (10 Nm).

7. Install the hub assembly to the vehicle.

8. Install the tonged washer and hub nut. Torque the nut to 166 ft. lbs. (230 Nm). Crimp at the indentation and install the grease cap.

9. Install the wheel speed sensor.

10. Install the wheel and tire.

11. Lower the vehicle to the ground.

Four Wheel Drive (4WD)

1. Disconnect negative battery cable.

2. Raise and safely support the vehicle. Remove the tire and wheel assembly.

3. Remove the cotter pin, cover and driveshaft nut.

4. Remove the speed sensor and its O-ring. Disconnect sufficient clamps and wire ties to allow the sensor to be moved well out of the work area.

NOTE: The speed sensor has a pole piece projecting from it. This exposed tip must be protected from impact or scratches. Do not allow the pole piece to contact the toothed wheel during removal or installation.

5. Remove the rear driveshaft from the vehicle.

6. Fit the shaft assembly in a press with the toothed wheel completely supported by a bearing plate such as special tool MB990560 or equivalent.

7. Press the toothed wheel off the axle shaft.

To install:

8. Press the new toothed wheel onto the shaft with the groove facing the axle shaft flange.

9. Install the axle on vehicle. Tighten the inner flange retainers to 40-47 ft. lbs. (55 — 65 Nm).

10. Install the driveshaft nut and torque to 145-188 ft. lbs. (200-260 Nm). Secure using new cotter pin.

11. Install the speed sensor and secure the wiring harness in its' original location. Always use a new O-ring.

12. Install the tire and wheel assembly.

CHASSIS ELECTRICAL

Heater Blower Motor

REMOVAL AND INSTALLATION

Colt

1. Disconnect the negative battery cable.

2. Remove the glove box and parcel tray.

3. Disconnect the change over control wire and duct.

4. Disconnect the harness connector at the ECU unit and remove the ECU unit.

5. Remove the blower case assembly from the dash.

6. Unbolt and remove the blower motor from the case.

7. The fan is removable from the motor shaft.

To install:

8. Installation is the reverse of removal.

9. Connect the negative battery cable and test the blower motor operation.

Colt Vista

1. Disconnect the negative battery cable.

2. Remove the upper and lower glove boxes.

3. Disconnect the wiring from the blower assembly.

4. Remove the blower motor mounting bolts and lift out the motor. If the entire blower case is to be removed, the instrument panel will have to be removed first.

To install:

5. Installation is the reverse order of the removal procedures.

6. Connect the negative battery cable and test the blower motor operation.

Windshield Wiper Motor

REMOVAL AND INSTALLATION

Colt and Colt Vista

1. Disconnect the negative battery cable.

2. Remove the wiper arms.

3. Remove the front cowl trim plate.

4. Remove the pivot shaft mounting nuts and push the pivot shaft toward the inside.

5. Disconnect the linkage from the motor and lift out the linkage.

6. Disconnect the harness connector at the wiper motor.

7. Unbolt and remove the motor.

To install:

8. Installation is the reverse order the of removal procedures.

9. Connect the negative battery cable and test the wiper motor operation.

10. When installing the arms, the at-rest position of the blade tips-to-windshield molding should be as follows:

a. Colt passenger's side-0.79 in. (20.00mm); driver's side: 0.59 in. (15.00mm).

b. Colt Vista passenger's side-1.18 in. (30.00mm); driver's side: 0.98 in. (25.00mm).

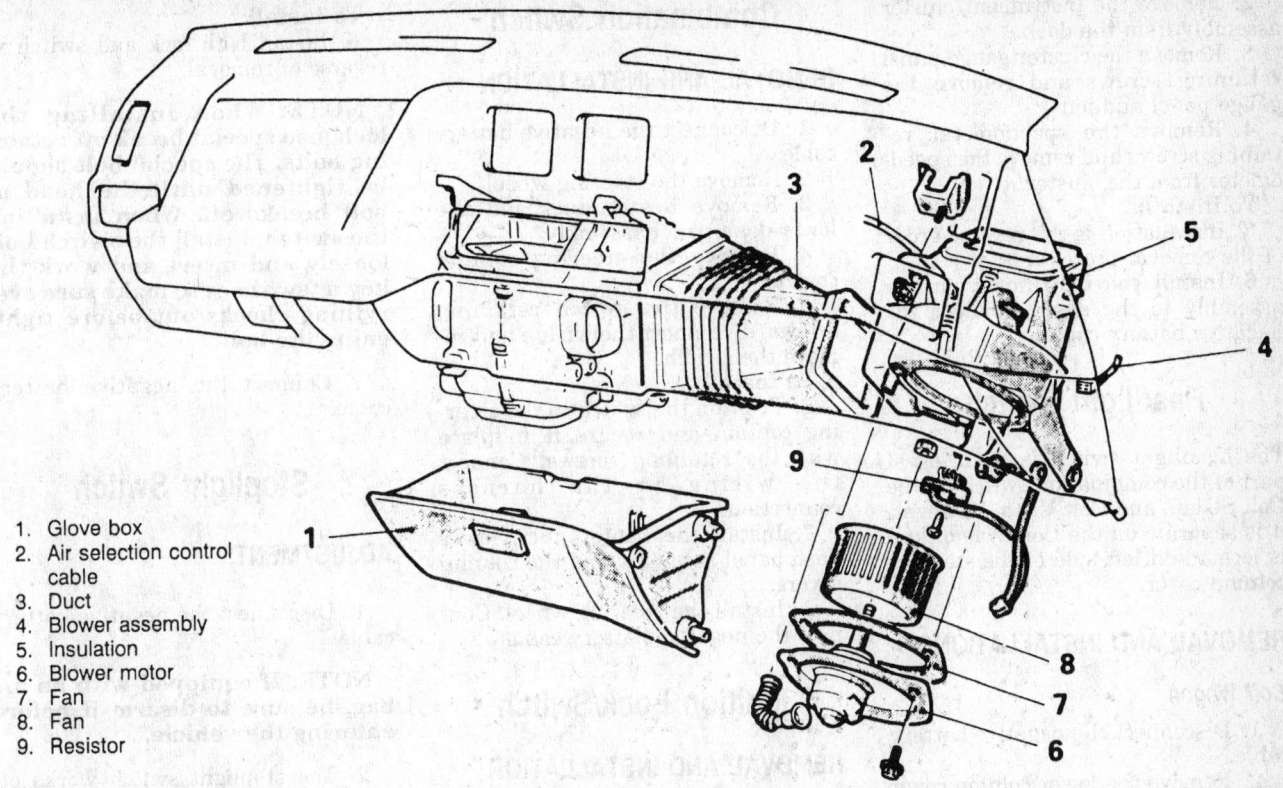

1. Glove box
2. Air selection control cable
3. Duct
4. Blower assembly
5. Insulation
6. Blower motor
7. Fan
8. Fan
9. Resistor

Blower motor removal and installation

Windshield Wiper Switch

REMOVAL AND INSTALLATION

NOTE: The wiper switch is integral with the turn signal switch.

1. Remove the steering wheel.
2. Remove the steering column cover.
3. Pull out and remove the switch knob.
4. Remove the 2 mounting screws and pull the switch out.
5. Installation is the reverse of removal.

Instrument Cluster

REMOVAL AND INSTALLATION

Colt

1. Disconnect the negative battery cable.
2. Remove the heater control cover.
3. Remove the knee protector or lower panel assembly.
4. Remove the cluster bezel and disconnect the electrical connectors.
5. Disconnect the speedometer cable. Remove the cluster retaining screws and pull the cluster out enough to disconnect the speedometer cable and electrical connectors. Release the cable by turning the adapter to the left or right and then remove.

To install:

6. Install the cluster and connect the speedometer and electrical cables.
7. Install the cluster bezel.
8. Install the knee protector or lower panel assembly.
9. Install the heater control cover.
10. Connect the negative battery cable.

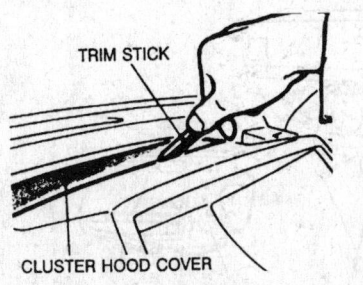

TRIM STICK

CLUSTER HOOD COVER

Cluster screw trim panel removal — Colt Vista

Colt Vista

1. Disconnect the negative battery cable.
2. Remove the steering wheel.
3. Remove the ashtray. Remove the cluster screw cover using a wood or plastic trim stick.
4. Remove the cluster trim panel retaining screws.
5. Pull the trim panel slightly toward the front and release the connectors. Lift the trim panel off.
6. Remove the 4 cluster mounting screws, pull the cluster slightly toward the front and disconnect the speedometer cable and electrical connectors.
7. Lift out the cluster.

To install:

8. Installation is the reverse order of the removal procedures.
9. Connect all electrical connectors. Connect the speedometer cable to the speedometer.
10. Connect the negative battery cable.

Speedometer

REMOVAL AND INSTALLATION

1. Disconnect the negative battery cable.

2. Remove the instrument cluster assembly from the dash.

3. Remove the cluster gauge panel retaining screws and remove the gauge panel and lens.

4. Remove the speedometer retaining screws and remove the speedometer from the cluster.

To install:

5. Installation is the reverse order of the removal procedures.

6. Install the instrument cluster assembly to the dash. Connect the negative battery cable.

Headlight Switch

The headlight switch is an integral part of the combination switch on the Colt Sedan, and Colt Vista. However, it is separate on the Colt Wagon and is located on left side of the steering column cover.

REMOVAL AND INSTALLATION

Colt Wagon

1. Disconnect the negative battery cable.

2. Remove the lower column cover and harness band.

3. Disconnect the electrical connections from the switch.

4. Remove the switch knob retainer screw and knob.

5. Pull the switch out, from behind the upper column cover panel.

To install:

6. Install the switch under and through the upper column cover opening, on the left side of column.

7. Install the knob and retaining screw, securing the switch in place.

8. Connect the electrical connections to the switch. Secure the harness in place with the band.

9. Install the lower column cover and retaining screws. Connect the negative battery cable and test the switch operation.

Combination Switch

REMOVAL AND INSTALLATION

1. Disconnect the negative battery cable.

2. Remove the steering wheel.

3. Remove heater duct and the lower dash panel assembly.

4. Remove the steering column covers.

5. Remove the switch retaining screws, disconnect the wiring and remove the switch.

To install:

6. Position the switch to the steering column and secure it in place with the retaining screws. Connect the wiring to the harness connections.

7. Install the heater duct, lower dash panel assembly and the column covers.

8. Install the steering wheel. Connect the negative battery cable.

Ignition Lock/Switch

REMOVAL AND INSTALLATION

NOTE: When replacing the ignition switch or key reminder switch only, remove the column cover, remove the screw holding the switch and pull out the switch.

1. Disconnect the negative battery cable.

2. Remove the turn signal switch.

3. Cut a notch in the lock bracket bolt head with a hacksaw. If removing the lock cylinder bracket, use a hacksaw to cut the special bolts from the steering lock bracket side.

4. Remove the bolt and lock.

5. Remove the column cover and unbolt and remove the ignition switch.

To install:

6. Install both lock and switch in reverse of removal.

NOTE: When installing the lock, use special break off retaining bolts. The special bolt should be tightened until the head of bolt breaks off. When installing the switch, install the switch bolt loosely and insert and work the key a few times to make sure everything checks out before tightening the bolt.

7. Connect the negative battery cable.

Stoplight Switch

ADJUSTMENT

1. Disconnect the negative battery cable.

NOTE: If equipped with an air bag, be sure to disarm it before entering the vehicle.

2. The stoplight switch works off the brake pedal lever. To adjust, disconnect the electrical connection and loosen the switch locknut.

3. Screw the switch inward until it contacts the stop on the brake pedal arm. Back out the switch $\frac{1}{2}$-1 full turn. The distance between the end of the switch plunger bore and the brake lever stop should be 0.020-0.040 in. (0.5-1.0mm).

4. Tighten the locknut and connect the wires.

5. Connect the negative battery cable.

6. Make sure the stoplights come ON when the brake pedal is depressed and go out when the pedal is released. Also, make sure the cruise control system operates properly.

REMOVAL AND INSTALLATION

1. Disconnect the negative battery cable.

2. Remove the lower dash trim panel.

3. Disconnect the electrical connections from the switch assembly.

4. Remove the adjustment nut from the switch and pull the switch from the support.

To install:

5. Installation is the reverse order of the removal procedure. Adjust the switch.

6. Connect the negative battery cable and test switch operation.

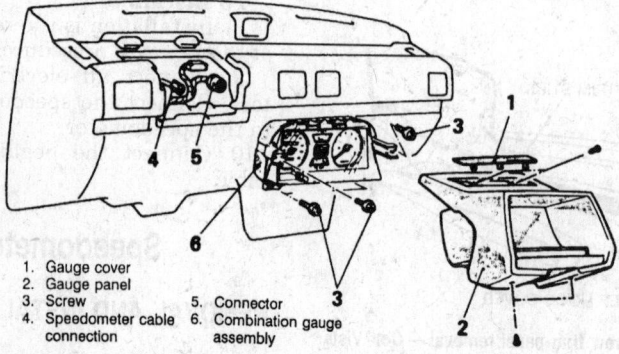

1. Gauge cover
2. Gauge panel
3. Screw
4. Speedometer cable connection
5. Connector
6. Combination gauge assembly

Speedometer removal and installation

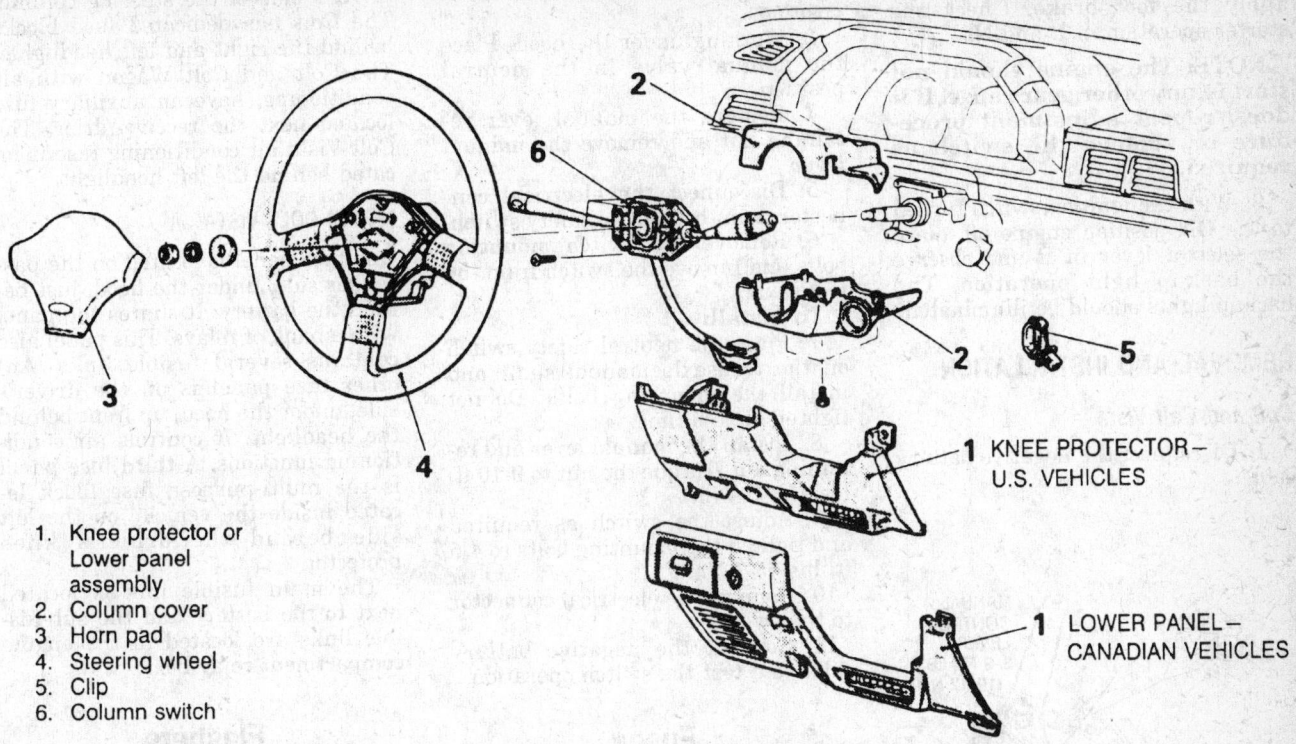

1. Knee protector or Lower panel assembly
2. Column cover
3. Horn pad
4. Steering wheel
5. Clip
6. Column switch

Combination switch removal and installation

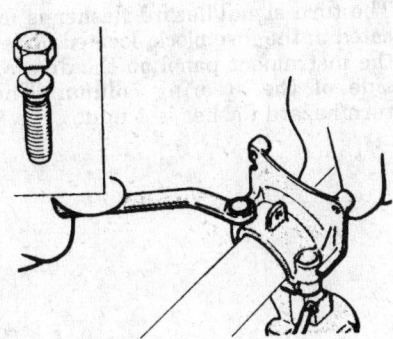

Ignition lock/switch installation

2. Measure the gap between the switch plunger and the arm stop. The gap should be 0.140 in. (3.5mm).

3. If adjustment is necessary, loosen the locknut and rotate the switch until the desired clearance is obtained. Tighten locknut to lock switch in place.

4. After completing the adjustment, check that the pedal free-play, measured at the face of the pedal pad is 0.240-0.510 in. (6-13mm). The distance between the pedal pad and the firewall when the clutch is disengaged (applied) should be 2.20 in. (55.88mm) or more for Colt, 1.77 in. (44.96mm) or more on Colt Vista. If these dimensions are not right, the hydraulic clutch system may need further servicing.

Clutch Switch

ADJUSTMENT

The clutch interlock switch is located at the top of the clutch pedal arm. Note that there may be 2 switches; 1 will be a cruise control cut-out switch.

1. Clutch interlock switch adjustment is made with the pedal fully depressed.

REMOVAL AND INSTALLATION

1. Disconnect the negative battery cable.
2. Remove the lower dash trim panel.
3. Disconnect the electrical connections from the switch assembly.
4. Remove the adjustment nut from the switch and pull the switch from the support.

To install:

5. Installation is the reverse order of the removal procedure. Adjust the switch.
6. Connect the negative battery cable and test switch operation.

Neutral Safety Switch

ADJUSTMENT

Colt and Colt Vista

1. Disconnect the negative battery cable.
2. Place the selector lever in the **N** position.
3. Working under the hood. Place the manual valve in the neutral position.
4. Loosen the switch mounting bolts.
5. Turn the switch until the small end of the the manual lever aligns with the alignment flange on the switch.
6. Tighten the mounting bolts, being careful not to allow the switch to move out of position. Torque the mounting bolts to 7-8 ft. lbs. (10-11 Nm).
7. Connect the negative battery cable.

8. Place the selector lever in **P** and apply the foot brake. Check the starter operation in **P** and **N**.

NOTE: The engine should not start in any other gear range. If it does, repeat adjustment procedure or replace the switch as required.

9. With the ignition switch turned to the **ON** position engine off, place the selector lever in **R** and observe the backup light operation. The backup lights should be illuminated.

REMOVAL AND INSTALLATION

Colt and Colt Vista

1. Disconnect the negative battery cable.

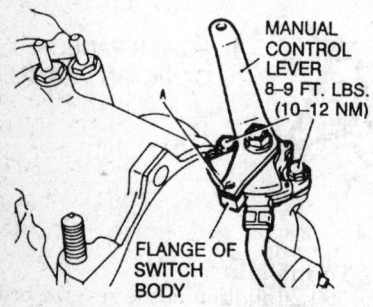

MANUAL CONTROL LEVER 8-9 FT. LBS. (10-12 NM)

FLANGE OF SWITCH BODY

Neutral start switch adjustment

2. Place the selector lever in the **N** position.

3. Working under the hood. Place the manual valve in the neutral position.

4. Remove the manual lever retaining nut and remove the manual lever.

5. Disconnect the electrical connector from the neutral safety switch.

6. Remove the switch mounting bolts and remove the switch from the transaxle.

To install:

7. Place the neutral safety switch on the transaxle manual shaft and install the mounting bolts. Do not tighten at this time.

8. Install the manual lever and retaining nut. Torque the nut to 9-10 ft. lbs. (12-14 Nm).

9. Adjust the switch as required and tighten the mounting bolts to 4-5 ft. lbs. (5-7 Nm).

10. Connect the electrical connector to the switch.

11. Connect the negative battery cable and test the switch operation.

Fuses

LOCATION

Fuse Block

EXCEPT 1992-94 COLT VISTA

The main fuse block is located up under the instrument panel on the driver's side of the steering column. The Colt has dedicated fuse blocks behind the right and left headlights. The Colt and Colt Wagon with air conditioning, have an auxiliary fuse located next the receiver/drier. The Colt Vista air conditioning fuse is located behind the left headlight.

1992-94 COLT VISTA

One fuse panel is located on the passenger side, under the hood, just behind the battery. It shares the panel with a bank of relays. This panel also contains several fusible links. Another fuse panel is on the driver's side, under the hood, up front behind the headlight. It controls air conditioning functions. A third fuse panel is the multi-purpose fuse block located inside the vehicle, on the left side behind the driver's knee protector.

The main fusible link is located next to the battery and the sub-fusible links are located in the engine compartment relay box.

Flashers

LOCATION

The turn signal/hazard flasher is located in the fuse block, located under the instrument panel on the driver's side of the steering column. The turn/hazard flasher is 1 unit.

SERIAL NUMBER IDENTIFICATION

Vehicle Identification Plate

The code plate is attached to the bulkhead on the firewall, in the en- gine compartment. The plate shows model code, engine family, transaxle code and body color.

Vehicle Identification Number

The VIN plate is attached to the in- strument panel on the driver's side, near the windshield. The VIN num- ber is a 17 digit number, the 8th digit denotes engine family and the 10th digit denotes vehicle model year.

VEHICLE IDENTIFICATION CHART

It is important for servicing and ordering parts to be certain of the vehicle and engine identification. The VIN (vehicle identification number) is a 17 digit number visible through the windshield on the driver's side of the dash and contains the vehicle and engine identification codes. The tenth digit indicates model year and the eighth digit indicates engine code. It can be interpreted as follows:

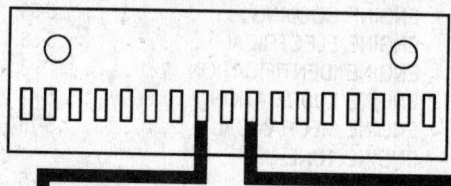

| | | Engine Code | | | | | Model Year | |
Code	Liters	Cu. In. (cc)	Cyl.	Fuel Sys.	Eng. Mfg.	Code		Year
5③	1.0	61 (993)	3	EFI	Suzuki	L		1990
6③	1.0	61 (993)	3	EFI	Suzuki	M		1991
5②④⑤	1.6	97 (1590)	4	MFI	Isuzu	N		1992
6②	1.6	97 (1590)	4	MFI	Isuzu	P		1993
5①④⑤	1.6	97 (1590)	4	MFI	Toyota	Q		1994
6④⑤	1.6	97 (1590)	4	MFI	Toyota			
8②④⑤	1.8	110 (1803)	4	MFI	Isuzu			
8①④⑤	1.8	110 (1803)	4	MFI	Toyota			

EFI—Electronic Fuel Injection
MFI—Multi-Port Fuel Injection
① Prizm
② Storm
③ Metro
④ Twin Cam
⑤ GSi model

ENGINE IDENTIFICATION

Year	Model	Engine Displacement Liters (cc)	Engine Series (ID/VIN)	Fuel System	No. of Cylinders	Engine Type
1990	Metro	1.0 (993)	5	EFI	3	SOHC
	Prizm ①	1.6 (1590)	5	MFI	4	DOHC
	Prizm	1.6 (1590)	6	MFI	4	DOHC
	Storm ①	1.6 (1590)	5	MFI	4	DOHC
	Storm	1.6 (1590)	6	MFI	4	SOHC
1991	Metro	1.0 (993)	6	EFI	3	SOHC
	Prizm ①	1.6 (1590)	5	MFI	4	DOHC
	Prizm	1.6 (1590)	6	MFI	4	DOHC
	Storm ①	1.6 (1590)	5	MFI	4	DOHC
	Storm	1.6 (1590)	6	MFI	4	SOHC
1992	Metro	1.0 (993)	6	EFI	3	SOHC
	Prizm ①	1.6 (1590)	5	MFI	4	DOHC
	Prizm	1.6 (1590)	6	MFI	4	DOHC
	Storm	1.6 (1590)	6	MFI	4	SOHC
	Storm ①	1.8 (1803)	8	MFI	4	DOHC
1993	Metro	1.0 (993)	6	EFI	3	SOHC
	Prizm	1.6 (1590)	6	MFI	4	DOHC
	Prizm ①	1.8 (1803)	8	MFI	4	DOHC
	Storm	1.6 (1590)	6	MFI	4	SOHC
	Storm ①	1.8 (1803)	8	MFI	4	DOHC
1994	Metro	1.0 (993)	6	EFI	3	SOHC
	Prizm	1.6 (1590)	6	MFI	4	DOHC
	Prizm ①	1.8 (1803)	8	MFI	4	DOHC
	Storm	1.6 (1590)	6	MFI	4	SOHC
	Storm ①	1.8 (1803)	8	MFI	4	DOHC

EFI—Electronic Fuel Injection
MFI—Multi-Point Fuel Injection
SOHC—Single Overhead Camshaft
DOHC—Double Overhead Camshaft
① GSi Model

GENERAL ENGINE SPECIFICATIONS

Year	Engine ID/VIN	Engine Displacement Liters (cc)	Fuel System Type	Net Horsepower @ rpm	Net Torque @ rpm (ft. lbs.)	Bore × Stroke (in.)	Com-pression Ratio	Oil Pressure @ rpm
1990	5	1.0 (993)	EFI	49 @ 4700	58 @ 3300	2.91 × 3.03	9.5:1	50 @ 3000
	5②	1.6 (1590)	MFI	130 @ 6800	105 @ 6000	3.20 × 3.00	10.3:1	56 @ 3000
	6①	1.6 (1590)	MFI	102 @ 5800	101 @ 4800	3.20 × 3.00	9.5:1	56 @ 3000
	5④	1.6 (1590)	MFI	130 @ 7000	102 @ 5800	3.15 × 3.11	9.8:1	29 @ 3000
	6③	1.6 (1590)	MFI	95 @ 5800	97 @ 4800	3.15 × 3.11	9.1:1	29 @ 3000
1991	6	1.0 (993)	EFI	55 @ 5700	58 @ 3300	2.91 × 3.03	9.5:1	50 @ 3000
	5②	1.6 (1590)	MFI	130 @ 6800	105 @ 6000	3.20 × 3.00	10.3:1	56 @ 3000
	6①	1.6 (1590)	MFI	102 @ 5800	101 @ 4800	3.20 × 3.00	9.5:1	56 @ 3000
	5④	1.6 (1590)	MFI	130 @ 7000	102 @ 5800	3.15 × 3.11	9.8:1	66 @ 3000
	6③	1.6 (1590)	MFI	95 @ 5800	97 @ 4800	3.15 × 3.11	9.1:1	58 @ 3000
1992	6	1.0 (993)	EFI	52 @ 5700	58 @ 3300	2.91 × 3.03	9.5:1	50 @ 3000
	5②	1.6 (1590)	MFI	130 @ 6800	105 @ 6000	3.20 × 3.00	10.3:1	54 @ 3000
	6①	1.6 (1590)	MFI	102 @ 5800	101 @ 4800	3.20 × 3.00	9.5:1	54 @ 3000
	6③	1.6 (1590)	MFI	95 @ 5800	97 @ 4800	3.15 × 3.11	9.1:1	58 @ 3000
	8④	1.8 (1803)	MFI	140 @ 6400	120 @ 4600	3.15 × 3.54	9.7:1	71 @ 3000
1993	6	1.0 (993)	EFI	55 @ 5700	58 @ 3300	2.91 × 3.03	9.5:1	50 @ 3000
	6①	1.6 (1590)	MFI	108 @ 6000	105 @ 4800	3.20 × 3.03	9.5:1	54 @ 3000
	8②	1.8 (1803)	MFI	115 @ 5600	115 @ 4800	3.18 × 3.37	9.5:1	54 @ 3000
	6③	1.6 (1590)	MFI	95 @ 5800	97 @ 4800	3.15 × 3.11	9.1:1	58 @ 3000
	8④	1.8 (1803)	MFI	140 @ 6400	120 @ 4600	3.15 × 3.54	9.7:1	71 @ 3000
1994	6	1.0 (993)	EFI	55 @ 5700	58 @ 3300	2.91 × 3.03	9.5:1	50 @ 3000
	6①	1.6 (1590)	MFI	108 @ 6000	105 @ 4800	3.20 × 3.03	9.5:1	54 @ 3000
	8②	1.8 (1803)	MFI	115 @ 5600	115 @ 4800	3.18 × 3.37	9.5:1	54 @ 3000
	6③	1.6 (1590)	MFI	95 @ 5800	97 @ 4800	3.15 × 3.11	9.1:1	58 @ 3000
	8④	1.8 (1803)	MFI	140 @ 6400	120 @ 4600	3.15 × 3.54	9.7:1	71 @ 3000

EFI—Electronic Fuel Injection
MPI—Multi-Point Fuel Injection
① Prizm Models
② Prizm GSi Model
③ Storm Models
④ Storm GSi Model

GASOLINE ENGINE TUNE-UP SPECIFICATIONS

Year	Engine ID/VIN	Engine Displacement Liters (cc)	Spark Plugs Gap (in.)	Ignition Timing (deg.)		Com-pression Pressure (psi)	Fuel Pump (psi)	Idle Speed (rpm)		Valve Clearance	
				MT	AT			MT	AT	In.	Ex.
1990	5	1.0 (993)	0.039–0.043	6B④	6B④	199	23–30	750	850	Hyd.	Hyd.
	5①③	1.6 (1590)	0.031	10B	10B	190	38–44	700	700	0.006–0.010	0.008–0.012
	6①	1.6 (1590)	0.031	10B	10B	190	38–44	700	700	0.006–0.010	0.008–0.012
	5②③	1.6 (1590)	0.041	10B	10B	142–191	40–47	700	700	0.004–0.008	0.008–0.012
	6②	1.6 (1590)	0.041	10B	10B	142–191	40–47	700	700	0.006	0.010
1991	6	1.0 (993)	0.039–0.043	6B④	6B④	199	23–30	750	850	Hyd.	Hyd.
	5①③	1.6 (1590)	0.031	10B	10B	190	38–44	700	700	0.006–0.010	0.008–0.012
	6①	1.6 (1590)	0.031	10B	10B	190	38–44	700	700	0.006–0.010	0.008–0.012
	5②③	1.6 (1590)	0.041	10B	10B	142–191	40–47	700	700	0.004–0.008	0.008–0.012
	6②	1.6 (1590)	0.041	10B	10B	142–191	40–47	700	700	0.006	0.010
1992	6	1.0 (993)	0.039–0.043	5B④	5B④	199	23–30	800	850	Hyd.	Hyd.
	5①③	1.6 (1590)	0.031	10B	10B	142–191	38–44	700	700	0.006–0.010	0.008–0.012
	6①	1.6 (1590)	0.031	10B	10B	142–191	38–44	700	700	0.006–0.010	0.008–0.012
	6②	1.6 (1590)	0.041	10B	10B	159	41–47	700	700	0.006	0.010
	8②③	1.8 (1803)	0.041	10B	10B	170	41–47	700	700	Hyd.	Hyd.
1993	6	1.0 (993)	0.039–0.043	5B④	5B④	199	23–30	800	850	Hyd.	Hyd.
	6①	1.6 (1590)	0.031	10B	10B	142–191	38–44	700	700	0.006–0.010	0.008–0.012
	8①③	1.8 (1803)	0.031	10B	10B	142–191	38–44	700	700	0.006–0.010	0.008–0.012
	6②	1.6 (1590)	0.041	10B	10B	159	41–47	700	700	0.006	0.010
	8②③	1.8 (1803)	0.041	10B	10B	170	41–47	700	700	Hyd.	Hyd.
1994	6	1.0 (993)	0.039–0.043	5B④	5B④	199	23–30	800	850	Hyd.	Hyd.
	6①	1.6 (1590)	0.031	10B	10B	142–191	38–44	700	700	0.006–0.010	0.008–0.012
	8①③	1.8 (1803)	0.031	10B	10B	142–191	38–44	700	700	0.006–0.010	0.008–0.012
	6②	1.6 (1590)	0.041	10B	10B	159	41–47	700	700	0.006	0.010
	8②③	1.8 (1803)	0.041	10B	10B	170	41–47	700	700	Hyd.	Hyd.

NOTE: The lowest cylinder pressure should be within 75% of the highest cylinder pressure reading. For example, if the highest cylinder is 134 psi, the lowest should be 101. Engine should be at normal operating temperature with throttle valve in the wide open position.
The underhood specifications sticker often reflects tune-up specification changes in production. Sticker figures must be used if they disagree with those in this chart.
B—Before Top Dead Center
Hyd.—Hydraulic valves
① Prizm
② Storm
③ GSi Model
④ Vacuum Advance Disconnected

FIRING ORDERS

NOTE: To avoid confusion, always replace spark plug wires one at a time.

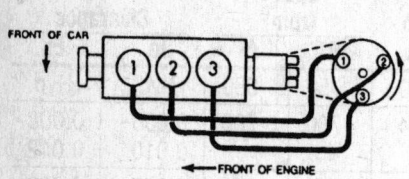

1.0L (Suzuki) Engine
Engine Firing Order: 1-3-2
Distributor Rotation: Counterclockwise

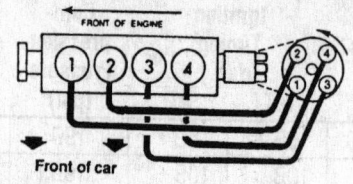

1.5L Engine
1.6L (Toyota) Engine Code 6
1.8L (Toyota) Engine Code 8
1.6L Isuzu Engine (Code 6)
1.6L Isuzu Engine (Code 5)
1.8L Isuzu Engine (Code 8)
Engine Firing Order: 1-3-4-2
Distributor Rotation: Counterclockwise

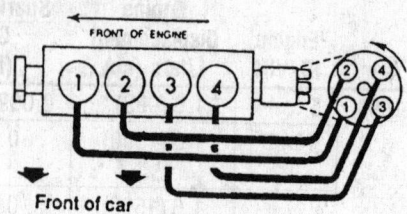

1.6L (Toyota) Engine Code 5
Engine Firing Order: 1-3-4-2
Distributor Rotation: Counterclockwise

CAPACITIES

Year	Model	Engine ID/VIN	Engine Displacement Liters (cc)	Engine Crankcase with Filter	Transmission (pts.)			Transfer Case (pts.)	Drive Axle		Fuel Tank (gal.)	Cooling System (qts.)
					4-Spd	5-Spd	Auto.		Front (pts.)	Rear (pts.)		
1990	Metro	5	1.0 (993)	3.7	—	4.1	10.1	—	—	—	10.0	4.5
	Prizm	6	1.6 (1590)	3.4	—	4.1	10.8③	—	—	—	13.0	6.3
	Prizm①	5	1.6 (1590)	3.9	—	5.4	⑥	—	—	3.0⑦	13.2	⑧
	Storm	6	1.6 (1590)	3.2	—	4.0	14.0③	—	—	—	12.4	④
	Storm①	5	1.6 (1590)	4.0	—	4.0	14.0③	—	—	—	12.4	④
1991	Metro	6	1.0 (993)	3.7	—	4.1	10.1	—	—	—	10.0	4.2②
	Prizm	6	1.6 (1590)	3.4	—	5.4	⑥	—	—	3.0⑦	13.2	⑧
	Prizm①	5	1.6 (1590)	3.9	—	5.4	⑥	—	—	3.0⑦	13.2	⑧
	Storm	6	1.6 (1590)	3.2	—	4.0	14.0③	—	—	—	12.4	④
	Storm①	5	1.6 (1590)	4.0	—	4.0	14.0③	—	—	—	12.4	⑤
1992	Metro	6	1.0 (993)	3.7	—	4.1	10.1	—	—	—	10.0	4.2②
	Prizm	6	1.6 (1590)	3.4	—	5.4	⑥	—	—	3.0⑦	13.2	⑧
	Prizm①	5	1.6 (1590)	3.9	—	5.4	⑥	—	—	3.0⑦	13.2	⑧
	Storm	6	1.6 (1590)	3.2	—	4.0	14.0③	—	—	—	12.4	④
	Storm①	8	1.8 (1803)	4.0	—	4.0	14.0③	—	—	—	12.4	⑤
1993	Metro	6	1.0 (993)	3.7	—	4.1	10.1	—	—	—	10.0	4.2②
	Prizm	6	1.6 (1590)	3.5	—	5.5	⑩	—	—	3.0⑦	13.2	⑧
	Prizm①	8	1.8 (1803)	4.3	—	5.5	⑩	—	—	3.0⑦	13.2	⑨
	Storm	6	1.6 (1590)	3.2	—	4.0	14.0③	—	—	—	12.4	④
	Storm①	8	1.8 (1803)	4.0	—	4.0	14.0③	—	—	—	12.4	⑤
1994	Metro	6	1.0 (993)	3.7	—	4.1	10.1	—	—	—	10.0	4.2②
	Prizm	6	1.6 (1590)	3.5	—	5.5	⑩	—	—	3.0⑦	13.2	⑧
	Prizm①	8	1.8 (1803)	4.3	—	5.5	⑩	—	—	3.0⑦	13.2	⑨
	Storm	6	1.6 (1590)	3.2	—	4.0	14.0③	—	—	—	12.4	④
	Storm①	8	1.8 (1803)	4.0	—	4.0	14.0③	—	—	—	12.4	⑤

① GSi model
② Manual transaxle: 4.1 qts.
③ After complete overhaul, less for drain and refill
④ Manual transaxle: 7.2 qts.
  Automatic transaxle: 7.7 qts.
⑤ Manual transaxle: 7.3 qts.
  Automatic transaxle: 7.8 qts.

⑥ 3 speed automatic: 11.6 pts.
  4 speed automatic: 15.2 pts.
⑦ 3 speed automatic only
⑧ Manual transaxle: 6.0 qts.
  3 speed automatic transaxle: 5.8 qts.
  4 speed automatic transaxle: 6.1 qts.

⑨ 1.6L w/Manual—6.3 qts.
  w/Automatic—6.2 qts.
  1.8L w/Manual—6.6 qts.
  w/Automatic—6.4 qts.
⑩ 3 speed automatic: 5.3 pts.
  4 speed automatic: 7.0 pts.
  (Incl. differential)

CAMSHAFT SPECIFICATIONS

All measurements given in inches.

Year	Engine ID/VIN	Engine Displacement Liters (cc)	Journal Diameter					Elevation		Bearing Clearance	Camshaft End Play
			1	2	3	4	5	In.	Ex.		
1990	5	1.0 (993)	1.0220–1.0228	1.1795–1.1803	1.1795–1.1803	—	—	1.5601–1.5664	1.5601–1.5664	0.0008–0.0024	—
	6①	1.6 (1590)	0.9822	0.9035	0.9035	0.0935	—	1.3700	1.3590	0.0014–0.0028	0.0043
	5①	1.6 (1590)	0.9822	0.9035	0.9035	0.0935	—	1.3700	1.3590	0.0014–0.0028	0.0043
	6②	1.6 (1590)	1.0157	1.0157	1.0157	1.0157	—	1.4260	1.4260	0.0059	0.0080
	5②	1.6 (1590)	1.0157	1.0157	1.0157	1.0157	—	1.5030	1.5030	0.0059	0.0080
	6①	1.6 (1590)	1.0610–1.0616	1.0610–1.0616	1.0610–1.0616	1.0610–1.0616	—	1.3941–1.3980	1.3941–1.3980	0.0014–0.0028	0.0031–0.0075
	5①	1.6 (1590)	0.9822	0.9035	0.9035	0.0935	—	1.3700	1.3590	0.0014–0.0028	0.0043
	6②	1.6 (1590)	1.0157	1.0157	1.0157	1.0157	—	1.4260	1.4260	0.0059	0.0080
	5②	1.6 (1590)	1.0157	1.0157	1.0157	1.0157	—	1.5030	1.5030	0.0059	0.0080
1991	6	1.0 (993)	1.0220–1.0228	1.1795–1.1803	1.1795–1.1803	—	—	1.5601–1.5664	1.5601–1.5664	0.0008–0.0024	—
	6①	1.6 (1590)	1.0610–1.0616	1.0610–1.0616	1.0610–1.0616	1.0610–1.0616	—	1.3941–1.3980	1.3941–1.3980	0.0014–0.0028	0.0031–0.0075
	5①	1.6 (1590)	0.9822	0.9035	0.9035	0.0935	—	1.3700	1.3590	0.0014–0.0028	0.0043
	6②	1.6 (1590)	1.0157	1.0157	1.0157	1.0157	—	1.4260	1.4260	0.0059	0.0080
	5②	1.6 (1590)	1.0157	1.0157	1.0157	1.0157	—	1.5030	1.5030	0.0059	0.0080
1992	6	1.0 (993)	1.0220–1.0228	1.1795–1.1803	1.1795–1.1803	—	—	1.5601–1.5664	1.5601–1.5664	0.0008–0.0024	—
	6①	1.6 (1590)	0.9822	0.9035	0.9035	0.0935	—	1.3700	1.3590	0.0014–0.0028	0.0043
	5①	1.6 (1590)	1.0610–1.0616	1.0610–1.0616	1.0610–1.0616	1.0610–1.0616	—	1.3941–1.3980	1.3941–1.3980	0.0014–0.0028	0.0031–0.0075
	6②	1.6 (1590)	1.0157	1.0157	1.0157	1.0157	—	1.4260	1.4260	0.0059	0.0080
	8②	1.8 (1803)	1.0157	1.0157	1.0157	1.0157	—	1.5030	1.5030	0.0059	0.0080
1993	6	1.0 (993)	1.0220–1.0228	1.1795–1.1803	1.1795–1.1803	—	—	1.5601–1.5664	1.5601–1.5664	0.0008–0.0024	—
	6①	1.6 (1590)	0.9035–0.9041	0.9035–0.9041	0.9035–0.9041	0.9035–0.9041	0.9035–0.9041	1.6500–1.6539	1.6520–1.6560	0.0014–0.0028	0.0012–③0.0033
	8①	1.8 (1803)	0.9035–0.9041	0.9035–0.9041	0.9035–0.9041	0.9035–0.9041	0.9035–0.9041	1.6500–1.6539	1.6520–1.6560	0.0014–0.0028	0.0012–③0.0033
	6②	1.6 (1590)	1.0157	1.0157	1.0157	1.0157	—	1.4260	1.4260	0.0059	0.0080
	8②	1.8 (1803)	1.0157	1.0157	1.0157	1.0157	—	1.5030	1.5030	0.0059	0.0080
1994	6	1.0 (993)	1.0220–1.0228	1.1795–1.1803	1.1795–1.1803	—	—	1.5601–1.5664	1.5601–1.5664	0.0008–0.0024	—
	6①	1.6 (1590)	0.9035–0.9041	0.9035–0.9041	0.9035–0.9041	0.9035–0.9041	0.9035–0.9041	1.6500–1.6539	1.6520–1.6560	0.0014–0.0028	0.0012–③0.0033
	8①	1.8 (1803)	0.9035–0.9041	0.9035–0.9041	0.9035–0.9041	0.9035–0.9041	0.9035–0.9041	1.6500–1.6539	1.6520–1.6560	0.0014–0.0028	0.0012–③0.0033
	6②	1.6 (1590)	1.0157	1.0157	1.0157	1.0157	—	1.4260	1.4260	0.0059	0.0080
	8②	1.8 (1803)	1.0157	1.0157	1.0157	1.0157	—	1.5030	1.5030	0.0059	0.0080

① Prizm
② Storm
③ Intake shown
　 Exhaust = 0.0014–0.0035

CRANKSHAFT AND CONNECTING ROD SPECIFICATIONS

All measurements are given in inches.

Year	Engine ID/VIN	Engine Displacement Liters (cc)	Crankshaft Main Brg. Journal Dia.	Crankshaft Main Brg. Oil Clearance	Crankshaft Shaft End-play	Crankshaft Thrust on No.	Connecting Rod Journal Diameter	Connecting Rod Oil Clearance	Connecting Rod Side Clearance
1990	5	1.0 (993)	③	0.0012	0.0044–0.0122	3	1.6529–1.6535	0.0012–0.0019	0.0039–0.0078
	6①	1.6 (1590)	1.8891–1.8898	0.0006–0.0013	0.0008–0.0073	3	1.6529–1.6535	0.0008–0.0020	0.0059–0.0098
	5①	1.6 (1590)	1.8891–1.8898	0.0006–0.0013	0.0008–0.0087	3	1.6529–1.6535	0.0008–0.0020	0.0059–0.0098
	6②	1.6 (1590)	2.0440–2.0448	0.0007–0.0019	0.0024–0.0095	2	1.5722–1.5728	0.0007–0.0018	0.0079–0.0138
	5②	1.6 (1590)	2.0440–2.0448	0.0007–0.0019	0.0024–0.0095	2	1.5722–1.5728	0.0009–0.0022	0.0079–0.0138
1991	6	1.0 (993)	③	0.0012	0.0044–0.0122	3	1.6529–1.6535	0.0012–0.0019	0.0039–0.0078
	6①	1.6 (1590)	1.8891–1.8898	0.0006–0.0013	0.0008–0.0087	3	1.6529–1.6535	0.0008–0.0020	0.0059–0.0098
	5①	1.6 (1590)	1.8891–1.8898	0.0006–0.0013	0.0008–0.0087	3	1.6529–1.6535	0.0008–0.0020	0.0059–0.0098
	6②	1.6 (1590)	2.0440–2.0448	0.0007–0.0019	0.0024–0.0095	2	1.5722–1.5728	0.0007–0.0018	0.0079–0.0138
	5②	1.6 (1590)	2.0440–2.0448	0.0007–0.0019	0.0024–0.0095	2	1.5722–1.5728	0.0009–0.0022	0.0079–0.0138
1992	6	1.0 (993)	③	0.0012	0.0044–0.0122	3	1.6529–1.6535	0.0012–0.0019	0.0039–0.0078
	6①	1.6 (1590)	1.8891–1.8898	0.0006–0.0013	0.0008–0.0073	3	1.6529–1.6535	0.0008–0.0020	0.0059–0.0098
	5①	1.6 (1590)	1.8891–1.8898	0.0006–0.0013	0.0008–0.0087	3	1.6529–1.6535	0.0008–0.0020	0.0059–0.0098
	6②	1.6 (1590)	2.0440–2.0448	0.0007–0.0019	0.0024–0.0095	2	1.5722–1.5728	0.0009–0.0022	0.0079–0.0138
	8②	1.8 (1803)	2.0440–2.0448	0.0007–0.0019	0.0024–0.0095	2	1.5722–1.5728	0.0009–0.0022	0.0079–0.0138
1993	6	1.0 (993)	③	0.0012	0.0044–0.0122	3	1.6529–1.6535	0.0012–0.0019	0.0039–0.0078
	6①	1.6 (1590)	1.8891–1.8898	0.0006–0.0013	0.0008–0.0073	3	1.5742–1.5748	0.0008–0.0020	0.0059–0.0098
	8①	1.8 (1803)	1.8891–1.8898	0.0006–0.0013	0.0008–0.0087	3	1.8891–1.8898	0.0008–0.0020	0.0059–0.0098
	6②	1.6 (1590)	2.0440–2.0448	0.0007–0.0019	0.0024–0.0095	2	1.5722–1.5728	0.0009–0.0022	0.0079–0.0138
	8②	1.8 (1803)	2.0440–2.0448	0.0007–0.0019	0.0024–0.0095	2	1.5722–1.5728	0.0007–0.0018	0.0079–0.0138

CRANKSHAFT AND CONNECTING ROD SPECIFICATIONS

All measurements are given in inches.

Year	Engine ID/VIN	Engine Displacement Liters (cc)	Crankshaft				Connecting Rod		
			Main Brg. Journal Dia.	Main Brg. Oil Clearance	Shaft End-play	Thrust on No.	Journal Diameter	Oil Clearance	Side Clearance
1994	6	1.0 (993)	③	0.0012	0.0044–0.0122	3	1.6529–1.6535	0.0012–0.0019	0.0039–0.0078
	6 ①	1.6 (1590)	1.8891–1.8898	0.0006–0.0013	0.0008–0.0073	3	1.5742–1.5748	0.0008–0.0020	0.0059–0.0098
	8 ①	1.8 (1803)	1.8891–1.8898	0.0006–0.0013	0.0008–0.0087	3	1.8891–1.8898	0.0008–0.0020	0.0059–0.0098
	6 ②	1.6 (1590)	2.0440–2.0448	0.0007–0.0019	0.0024–0.0095	2	1.5722–1.5728	0.0009–0.0022	0.0079–0.0138
	8 ②	1.8 (1803)	2.0440–2.0448	0.0007–0.0019	0.0024–0.0095	2	1.5722–1.5728	0.0007–0.0018	0.0079–0.0138

① Prizm
② Storm
③ Bearing Cap Stamped:
  No. 1—1.7710–1.7712
  No. 2—1.7712–1.7714
  No. 3—1.7714–1.7716
  No. 4—1.7710–1.7712

VALVE SPECIFICATIONS

Year	Engine ID/VIN	Engine Displacement Liters (cc)	Seat Angle (deg.)	Face Angle (deg.)	Spring Test Pressure (lbs. @ in.)	Spring Installed Height (in.)	Stem-to-Guide Clearance (in.)		Stem Diameter (in.)	
							Intake	Exhaust	Intake	Exhaust
1990	5	1.0 (993)	45	45	41–47.2 @ 1.28	1.28	0.0008– 0.0021	0.0014– 0.0024	0.2148– 0.2157	0.2146– 0.2151
	6①	1.6 (1590)	45	45.5	32.2	1.36	0.0031	0.0039	0.2350– 0.2356	0.2348– 0.2354
	5②	1.6 (1590)	45	45.5	32.2	1.36	0.0031	0.0039	0.2350– 0.2356	0.2348– 0.2354
1991	6	1.0 (993)	45	45	41–47.2 @ 1.28	1.28	0.0008– 0.0021	0.0014– 0.0024	0.2148– 0.2157	0.2146– 0.2151
	6①	1.6 (1590)	45	45.5	—	—	0.0010 0.0024	0.0012 0.0026	0.2350– 0.2356	0.2348– 0.2354
	5①	1.6 (1590)	45	45.5	32.2	1.36	0.0031	0.0039	0.2350– 0.2356	0.2348– 0.2354
	6②	1.6 (1590)	45	45.5	—	—	0.0090	0.0018	0.2335	0.2335
	5②	1.6 (1590)	45	45.5	—	—	0.0090	0.0018	0.2335	0.2335
1992	6	1.0 (993)	45	45	41–47.2 @ 1.28	1.28	0.0008– 0.0021	0.0014– 0.0024	0.2148– 0.2157	0.2146– 0.2151
	6①	1.6 (1590)	45	45.5	32.2	—	0.0031	0.0039	0.2350– 0.2356	0.2348– 0.2354
	5②	1.6 (1590)	45	45.5	32.2	1.36	0.0031	0.0039	0.2350– 0.2356	0.2348– 0.2354
	6②	1.6 (1590)	45	45.5	—	—	0.0090	0.0018	0.2335	0.2335
	8②	1.8 (1803)	45	45.5	—	—	0.0009– 0.0080	0.0012– 0.0080	0.2320	0.2320
1993	6	1.0 (993)	45	45	41–47.2 @ 1.28	1.28	0.0008– 0.0021	0.0014– 0.0024	0.2148– 0.2157	0.2146– 0.2151
	6①	1.6 (1590)	45	45.5	37.3	1.25	0.0010 0.0024	0.0012 0.0026	0.2350– 0.2356	0.2348– 0.2354
	8①	1.8 (1803)	45	45.5	37.3	1.25	0.0010 0.0024	0.0012 0.0026	0.2350– 0.2356	0.2348– 0.2354
	6②	1.6 (1590)	45	45.5	—	—	0.0090	0.0018	0.2335	0.2335
	8②	1.8 (1803)	45	45.5	—	—	0.0009– 0.0080	0.0012– 0.0080	0.2320	0.2320
1994	6	1.0 (993)	45	45	41–47.2 @ 1.28	1.28	0.0008– 0.0021	0.0014– 0.0024	0.2148– 0.2157	0.2146– 0.2151
	6①	1.6 (1590)	45	45.5	37.3	1.25	0.0010 0.0024	0.0012 0.0026	0.2350– 0.2356	0.2348– 0.2354
	8①	1.8 (1803)	45	45.5	37.3	1.25	0.0010 0.0024	0.0012 0.0026	0.2350– 0.2356	0.2348– 0.2354
	6②	1.6 (1590)	45	45.5	—	—	0.0090	0.0018	0.2335	0.2335
	8②	1.8 (1803)	45	45.5	—	—	0.0009– 0.0080	0.0012– 0.0080	0.2320	0.2320

① Prizm
② Storm

PISTON AND RING SPECIFICATIONS

All measurements are given in inches.

Year	Engine ID/VIN	Engine Displacement Liters (cc)	Piston Clearance	Ring Gap			Ring Side Clearance		
				Top Compression	Bottom Compression	Oil Control	Top Compression	Bottom Compression	Oil Control
1990	5	1.0 (993)	0.0008–0.0015	0.0079–0.0129	0.0079–0.0137	0.0079–0.0275	0.0012–0.0027	0.0008–0.0023	—
	6①	1.6 (1590)	0.0035–0.0043	0.0098–0.0138	0.0059–0.0118	0.0039–0.0236	0.0016–0.0031	0.0012–0.0028	—
	6②	1.6 (1590)	0.0011–0.0019	0.0110–0.0157	0.0177–0.0236	0.0039–0.0236	0.0011–0.0031	0.0007–0.0023	—
	5②	1.6 (1590)	0.0019–0.0027	0.0110–0.0157	0.0177–0.0236	0.0039–0.0236	0.0011–0.0031	0.0007–0.0023	—
1991	5	1.0 (993)	0.0008–0.0015	0.0079–0.0129	0.0079–0.0137	0.0079–0.0275	0.0012–0.0027	0.0008–0.0023	—
	6①	1.6 (1590)	0.0039–0.0047	0.0098–0.0185	0.0079–0.0165	0.0059–0.0205	0.0012–0.0028	0.0012–0.0028	0.0039–0.0236
	5①	1.6 (1590)	0.0035–0.0043	0.0098–0.0138	0.0059–0.0118	0.0039–0.0236	0.0016–0.0031	0.0012–0.0028	—
	6②	1.6 (1590)	0.0011–0.0019	0.0110–0.0157	0.0177–0.0236	0.0039–0.0236	0.0011–0.0031	0.0007–0.0023	—
	5②	1.6 (1590)	0.0019–0.0027	0.0110–0.0157	0.0177–0.0236	0.0039–0.0236	0.0011–0.0031	0.0007–0.0023	—
1992	6	1.0 (993)	0.0008–0.0015	0.0079–0.0129	0.0079–0.0137	0.0079–0.0275	0.0012–0.0027	0.0008–0.0023	—
	6①	1.6 (1590)	0.0024–0.0031	0.0098–0.0138	0.0059–0.0118	0.0039–0.0236	0.0016–0.0031	0.0012–0.0028	—
	5①	1.6 (1590)	0.0039–0.0047	0.0098–0.0185	0.0079–0.0165	0.0059–0.0205	0.0012–0.0028	0.0012–0.0028	0.0039–0.0236
	6②	1.6 (1590)	0.0011–0.0019	0.0110–0.0157	0.0177–0.0236	0.0039–0.0236	0.0011–0.0031	0.0007–0.0023	—
	8②	1.8 (1803)	0.0019–0.0027	0.0110–0.0157	0.0177–0.0236	0.0039–0.0236	0.0011–0.0031	0.0007–0.0023	—
1993	6	1.0 (993)	0.0008–0.0015	0.0079–0.0129	0.0079–0.0137	0.0079–0.0275	0.0012–0.0027	0.0008–0.0023	—
	6①	1.6 (1590)	0.0033–0.0041	0.0098–0.0138	0.0138–0.0234	0.0039–0.0177	0.0018–0.0035	0.0012–0.0028	—
	8①	1.8 (1803)	0.0033–0.0041	0.0098–0.0138	0.0138–0.0234	0.0039–0.0177	0.0018–0.0035	0.0012–0.0028	—
	6②	1.6 (1590)	0.0011–0.0019	0.0110–0.0157	0.0177–0.0236	0.0039–0.0236	0.0011–0.0031	0.0007–0.0023	—
	8②	1.8 (1803)	0.0019–0.0027	0.0110–0.0157	0.0177–0.0236	0.0039–0.0236	0.0011–0.0031	0.0007–0.0023	—
1994	6	1.0 (993)	0.0008–0.0015	0.0079–0.0129	0.0079–0.0137	0.0079–0.0275	0.0012–0.0027	0.0008–0.0023	—
	6①	1.6 (1590)	0.0033–0.0041	0.0098–0.0138	0.0138–0.0234	0.0039–0.0177	0.0018–0.0035	0.0012–0.0028	—
	8①	1.8 (1803)	0.0033–0.0041	0.0098–0.0138	0.0138–0.0234	0.0039–0.0177	0.0018–0.0035	0.0012–0.0028	—
	6②	1.6 (1590)	0.0011–0.0019	0.0110–0.0157	0.0177–0.0236	0.0039–0.0236	0.0011–0.0031	0.0007–0.0023	—
	8②	1.8 (1803)	0.0019–0.0027	0.0110–0.0157	0.0177–0.0236	0.0039–0.0236	0.0011–0.0031	0.0007–0.0023	—

① Prizm　② Storm

TORQUE SPECIFICATIONS
All readings in ft. lbs.

Year	Engine ID/VIN	Engine Displacement Liters (cc)	Cylinder Head Bolts	Main Bearing Bolts	Rod Bearing Bolts	Crankshaft Damper Bolts	Flywheel Bolts	Manifold		Spark Plugs	Lug Nut
								Intake	Exhaust		
1990	5	1.0 (993)	54	40	26	8	45	17	17	18	44
	6①	1.6 (1590)	44	44	36	87	58④	14	18	13	76
	5①	1.6 (1590)	44	44	36	87	58④	14	18	13	76
	6②	1.6 (1590)	58	44	11⑤	87	22⑤	17	30	18	87
	5②	1.6 (1590)	58	44	11⑤	87	22⑤	17	30	18	87
1991	6	1.0 (993)	54	40	26	8	45	17	17	18	44
	6①	1.6 (1590)	44	44	36	87	58④	14	18	13	76
	5①	1.6 (1590)	44	44	36	87	58④	14	18	13	76
	6②	1.6 (1590)	58	44	11⑤	87	22⑤	17	30	18	87
	5②	1.6 (1590)	58	44	11⑤	87	22⑤	17	30	18	87
1992	6	1.0 (993)	54	40	26	8	45	17	17	18	44
	6①	1.6 (1590)	44	44	36	87	58④	14	18	13	76
	5①	1.6 (1590)	44	44	36	87	58④	14	18	13	76
	6②	1.6 (1590)	58	44	11⑤	87	22⑤	17	30	21	87
	8②	1.8 (1803)	③	65⑥	18⑦	108	22	17	30	21	87
1993	6	1.0 (993)	54	40	26	8	45	17	17	18	44
	6①	1.6 (1590)	22⑧	44	22⑨	87	58④	14	25	13	76
	8①	1.8 (1803)	22⑧	44	22⑨	87	58④	14	25	13	76
	6②	1.6 (1590)	58	44	11⑤	87	22⑤	17	30	21	87
	8②	1.8 (1803)	③	65⑥	18⑦	108	22	17	30	21	87
1994	6	1.0 (993)	54	40	26	8	45	17	17	18	44
	6①	1.6 (1590)	22⑧	44	22⑨	87	58④	14	25	13	76
	8①	1.8 (1803)	22⑧	44	22⑨	87	58④	14	25	13	76
	6②	1.6 (1590)	58	44	11⑤	87	22⑤	17	30	21	87
	8②	1.8 (1803)	③	65⑥	18⑦	108	22	17	30	21	87

① Prizm
② Storm
③ 1st Step: 29 ft. lbs.
   2nd Step: 58 ft. lbs.

④ 47 ft. lbs. with automatic transaxle
⑤ Plus an additional 45 to 60 degrees
⑥ Do not tighten in 1 step, make 3 passes to reach the torque

⑦ Tighten an additional 100 degrees
⑧ Plus 2 additional steps of 90 degrees
⑨ Plus an additional 90 degrees

BRAKE SPECIFICATIONS

All measurements in inches unless noted.

Year	Model	Master Cylinder Bore	Original Thickness	Brake Disc Minimum Thickness	Maximum Runout	Brake Drum Diameter Original Inside Diameter	Max. Wear Limit	Maximum Machine Diameter	Minimum Lining Thickness Front	Rear
1990	Metro	0.825	0.394	0.315	0.004	7.09	7.16	7.16	0.31 ①	0.11 ①
	Prizm	NA	0.709	0.669	0.003	7.87	7.91	7.91	0.030	0.039
	Prizm ③	NA	0.354	0.315	0.003	—	—	—	—	0.039
	Storm	0.810	0.866	0.811	0.005	7.87	7.93	7.93	0.039	0.039
1991	Metro	0.825	0.394	0.315	0.004	7.09	7.16	7.16	0.31 ①	0.11 ①
	Prizm	NA	0.709	0.669	0.003	7.87	7.91	7.91	0.030	0.039
	Prizm ③	NA	0.354	0.315	0.003	—	—	—	—	0.039
	Storm	0.810 ②	0.866	0.811	0.005	7.87	7.93	7.93	0.039	0.039
1992	Metro	0.825	0.394	0.315	0.004	7.09	7.16	7.16	0.31 ①	0.11 ①
	Prizm	NA	0.709	0.669	0.003	7.87	7.91	7.91	0.030	0.039
	Prizm ③	NA	0.354	0.315	0.003	—	—	—	—	0.039
	Storm	0.810 ②	0.866	0.811	0.005	7.87	7.93	7.93	0.039	0.039
1993	Metro	0.825	0.394	0.315	0.004	7.09	7.16	7.16	0.31 ①	0.11 ①
	Prizm	NA	0.886	0.787	0.0035	7.87	7.91	7.91	0.039	0.039
	Storm	0.810 ②	0.866	0.811	0.005	7.87	7.93	7.93	0.039	0.039
1994	Metro	0.825	0.394	0.315	0.004	7.09	7.16	7.16	0.31 ①	0.11 ①
	Prizm	NA	0.886	0.787	0.0035	7.87	7.91	7.91	0.039	0.039
	Storm	0.810 ②	0.866	0.811	0.005	7.87	7.93	7.93	0.039	0.039

NA—Not available
① Lining plus shoe rim
② GSi models: 0.875 in.
③ GSi model with rear disk brakes, front brake specifications are the same as the Base and LSi models

WHEEL ALIGNMENT

Year	Model	Caster Range (deg.)	Caster Preferred Setting (deg.)	Camber Range (deg.)	Camber Preferred Setting (deg.)	Toe-in (in.)	Steering Axis Inclination (deg.)
1990	Metro	1P–5P	3P	1N–1P	0	0	$25^{11}/_{16}$
	Prizm	$^{11}/_{16}$P–$2^3/_{16}$P ①	$1^7/_{16}$P	$^9/_{16}$N–$1^5/_{16}$P	$^3/_{16}$P	$^3/_{64}$	NA
	Prizm	$^9/_{16}$P–$2^1/_8$P ②	$1^5/_{16}$P	$^1/_2$N–P	$^1/_4$P	$^3/_{64}$	NA
	Storm	2P–4P	3P	1N–$^1/_4$P	$^3/_8$N	0	$10^3/_{16}$
1991	Metro	1P–5P	3P	1N–1P	0	0	$25^{11}/_{16}$
	Prizm	$^{11}/_{16}$P–$2^3/_{16}$P ①	$1^7/_{16}$P	$^9/_{16}$N–$1^5/_{16}$P	$^3/_{16}$P	$^3/_{64}$	NA
	Prizm	$^9/_{16}$P–$2^1/_8$P ②	$1^5/_{16}$P	$^1/_2$N–P	$^1/_4$P	$^3/_{64}$	NA
	Storm	2P–4P	3P	1N–$^1/_4$P	$^3/_8$N	0	$10^3/_{16}$
1992	Metro	1P–5P	3P	1N–1P	0	0	$25^{11}/_{16}$
	Prizm	$^{11}/_{16}$P–$2^3/_{16}$P ①	$1^7/_{16}$P	$^9/_{16}$N–$1^5/_{16}$P	$^3/_{16}$P	$^3/_{64}$	NA
	Prizm	$^9/_{16}$P–$2^1/_8$P ②	$1^5/_{16}$P	$^1/_2$N–P	$^1/_4$P	$^3/_{64}$	NA
	Storm	2P–4P	3P	1N–$^1/_4$P	$^3/_8$N	0	$10^3/_{16}$
1993	Metro	1P–5P	3P	1N–1P	0	0	$25^{11}/_{16}$
	Prizm	$^9/_{16}$P–$2^1/_{16}$P	$1^5/_{16}$P	$^{15}/_{16}$N–$^9/_{16}$P	$^3/_{16}$N	$^3/_{64}$	NA
	Prizm ③	—	—	$1^{11}/_{16}$P–$^3/_{16}$N	$^{15}/_{16}$N	$^5/_{64}$	NA
	Storm	2P–4P	3P	1N–$^1/_4$P	$^3/_8$N	0	$10^3/_{16}$
1994	Metro	1P–5P	3P	1N–1P	0	0	$25^{11}/_{16}$
	Prizm	$^9/_{16}$P–$2^1/_{16}$P	$1^5/_{16}$P	$^{15}/_{16}$N–$^9/_{16}$P	$^3/_{16}$N	$^3/_{64}$	NA
	Prizm ③	—	—	$1^{11}/_{16}$P–$^3/_{16}$N	$^{15}/_{16}$N	$^5/_{64}$	NA
	Storm	2P–4P	3P	1N–$^1/_4$P	$^3/_8$N	0	$10^3/_{16}$

N—Negative
P—Positive
① Manual transaxle
② Automatic transaxle

ENGINE MECHANICAL

NOTE: Disconnecting the negative battery cable on some vehicles may interfere with the functions of the on-board computer systems and may require the computer to undergo a relearning process, once the negative battery cable is reconnected.

Engine Assembly

REMOVAL AND INSTALLATION

Metro

1. Relieve the fuel pressure from the fuel system.
2. Using a scratch awl, scribe the hood hinge-to-hood outline, then, using an assistant, remove the hood.
3. Disconnect the negative battery cable. Drain the cooling system.
4. Remove the air cleaner assembly. Remove the radiator assembly along with the cooling fan.
5. Disconnect and tag all the necessary electrical connections.
6. Disconnect and tag all the necessary vacuum lines.
7. Disconnect the fuel return hose and fuel feed hose from the throttle body.
8. Disconnect the heater inlet and outlet hoses.
9. Disconnect the following cables:
   a. The accelerator cable from the throttle body.
   b. The clutch cable from the transaxle (for manual transaxle models).
   c. The gear select cable and the oil pressure control cable from the transaxle (for automatic transaxle models).
   d. The speedometer cable from the transaxle.
10. Raise and safely support the vehicle.
11. Disconnect the exhaust pipe from the exhaust manifold.
12. Disconnect the gear shift control shaft and the extension to the transaxle for manual transaxle models.
13. Drain the engine oil and transaxle oil.
14. Remove the drive axles from the differential side gears of the transaxle. For the engine/transaxle removal, it is not necessary to remove

the drive axle from the steering knuckle.
15. Remove the engine rear torque rod bracket from the transaxle for automatic transaxle models.
16. Lower the vehicle.
17. Install a suitable chain hoist to the lifting device on the engine.
18. Remove the right side engine mounting from its bracket.
19. If equipped with an automatic transaxle, remove the transaxle rear mounting nut.
20. If equipped with a manual transaxle, remove the transaxle rear mounting from the body.
21. Remove the transaxle left side mounting bracket.
22. Lift the engine and transaxle assembly out from the vehicle. Separate the transaxle from the engine.

To install:
23. Install the transaxle to the engine, then a suitable hoist onto the engine lifting brackets.
24. Install engine and transaxle into vehicle and leave the hoist connected to the lifting device.
25. If equipped with an automatic transaxle, install the transaxle rear mounting nut.
26. If equipped with a manual transaxle, install the transaxle rear mounting from the body.
27. Install the transaxle left side mounting bracket.
28. Install the transaxle right side engine mounting to its bracket.
29. Tighten all the bolts and nuts.
30. Remove the lifting device.
31. To complete the installation procedure, reverse the removal procedure.
32. Adjust the clutch pedal free-play.
33. Adjust the gear select cable and oil pressure control cable.
34. Adjust the accelerator cable play.
35. Refill the transaxle with the recommended fluid. Do the same for the engine oil and engine coolant.
36. Reconnect the negative battery cable. Start the engine and check for leakage of any kind. Make all necessary repairs and adjustments.
37. Torque the transaxle-to-engine bolts and nuts to 37 ft. lbs. (50 Nm).
38. Torque the engine mounting nuts to 37 ft. lbs. (50 Nm).
39. Torque the engine mounting left hand bracket bolts to 37 ft. lbs. (50 Nm).
40. Torque the exhaust pipe to manifold bolts to 37 ft. lbs. (50 Nm).
41. Torque the flywheel retaining bolts to 47 ft. lbs. (64 Nm).

Prizm

1990

1. Remove the hood, with the aid of a helper.
2. Disconnect the negative battery cable, then the positive battery cable and remove the battery.
3. Raise the vehicle and safely support it.
4. Remove the left and right splash shields.
5. Drain the engine oil and the transmission oil.
6. Drain the engine coolant and save it in closed containers for reuse.
7. Remove the air cleaner hose and the air cleaner assembly.
8. Remove the coolant reservoir. Remove the radiator and fan assembly.
9. Disconnect the accelerator cable and if equipped with automatic transaxle, the throttle cable.
10. Disconnect and remove the cruise control actuator.
11. Label and disconnect the main engine wiring harness from its related sensors and switches.
12. Remove the ground strap connector and its bolt. Disconnect the wiring to the vacuum sensor, the oxygen sensor and the air conditioning compressor.
13. Label and disconnect the brake booster vacuum hose, the power steering vacuum hose, the charcoal canister vacuum hose and the vacuum switch vacuum hose.
14. Carefully disconnect the fuel inlet and return lines.

— CAUTION —
The fuel system is under pressure. Release pressure slowly and contain spillage. Observe no smoking/no open flame precautions. Have a Class B-C (dry powder) fire extinguisher within arm's reach at all times.

15. Disconnect the heater hoses.
16. Loosen the power steering pump mounting bolt and through bolt. Remove the drive belt.
17. Remove the 4 bolts holding the air conditioner compressor and remove the compressor. Do not loosen or remove any lines or hoses. Move the compressor out of the way and hang it from a piece of stiff wire.
18. Disconnect the speedometer cable from the transaxle.
19. On vehicles with manual transaxles, unbolt the clutch slave cylinder from the bell housing and move the cylinder out of the way. Don't disconnect any lines or hoses. Disconnect the shift control cables by re-

moving the 2 clips, the washers and retainers.

20. On vehicles with automatic transaxles, remove the clip and retainer and separate the control cable from the shift lever.

21. Raise the vehicle and support it safely.

22. Remove the 2 bolts from the exhaust pipe flange and separate the pipe from the exhaust manifold.

23. Remove the nuts and bolts and separate the halfshafts from the transaxle.

24. Remove the through bolt from the rear transaxle mount.

25. Remove the nuts from the center transaxle mount and the rear mount.

26. Lower the vehicle to the ground and attach the lifting equipment to the brackets on the engine. Take tension on the hoist line or chain just enough to support the motor but no more. Hang the engine wires and hoses on the chain or cable.

27. Remove the 3 exhaust hanger bracket nuts and the hanger. Remove the 2 center crossmember-to-main crossmember bolts. Remove the 3 center crossmember-to-radiator support bolts.

---------- **CAUTION** ----------

Support the crossmembers with a jack when loosening the bolts. The pieces are heavy and could fall.

---

28. Remove the 8 crossmember-to-body bolts, then remove the 2 bolts holding the control arm brackets to the underbody. Remove the 2 center mount-to-transaxle bolts and remove the mount. Carefully lower the center mount and crossmember and remove from under the vehicle.

29. At the left engine mount, remove the 3 bolts and the bracket, then remove the bolt, 2 nuts, through bolt and mounting. Remove the 3 bolts and the air cleaner bracket.

30. Loosen and remove the 5 bolts and disconnect the mounting bracket from the transaxle bracket. Remove the through bolt and mounting.

31. Carefully and slowly raise the engine and transaxle assembly out of the vehicle. Tilt the transaxle down to clear the right engine mount. Be careful not to hit the steering gear housing. Make sure the engine is clear of all wiring, lines and hoses.

32. Support the engine assembly on a suitable stand; do not allow it to remain on the hoist for any length of time.

33. With the engine properly supported, disconnect the reverse light

switch and the neutral safety switch (automatic transaxle).

34. Remove the rear end cover plate.

35. For automatic transaxles, remove the 6 torque converter mounting bolts.

36. Remove the starter.

37. Support the transaxle, remove the retaining bolts in the case and remove the transaxle from the engine. Pull the unit straight off the engine; do not allow it to hang partially removed on the shaft. Keep the automatic transaxle level; if it tilts forward the converter may fall off.

To install:

38. Before reinstalling the engine in the car, several components must be reattached or connected. Install the transaxle to the engine; tighten the 12mm bolts to 47 ft. lbs. (64 Nm) and the 10mm bolts to 34 ft. lbs. (46 Nm).

39. Install the starter, its cable and connector. Tighten the mounting bolts to 29 ft. lbs. (39 Nm).

40. Install the 6 torque converter-to-flexplate bolts on automatic transaxles. Tighten the bolts to 20 ft. lbs. (27 Nm).

41. Install the rear cover plate and connect the wiring to the reverse light switch and the neutral safety switch (automatic transaxle).

42. Attach the chain hoist or lift apparatus to the engine and lower it into the engine compartment. Before it is completely in position, attach the power steering pump and its through bolt to the motor.

NOTE: Tilt the transaxle downward and lower the engine to clear the left motor mount. As before, be careful not to hit the power steering housing (rack) or the throttle position sensor. Be sure the engine is clear of all wiring, hoses and cables.

43. Level the engine and align each mount with its bracket.

44. Install the right mounting insulator (bushing) to the engine bracket with the 2 nuts and bolt. Tighten the bolt temporarily.

45. Align the right insulator with the body bracket and install the through bolt and nut. Temporarily tighten the nut and bolt.

46. Align the left mounting insulator with the transaxle case bracket. Temporarily install the 3 bracket bolts.

47. With the engine held in place by these mounts, repeat steps 44, 45 and 46. Tightening the bolts to the following tightness:

a. Step 44 to 38 ft. lbs. (52 Nm)

b. Step 45 to 64 ft. lbs. (87 Nm)

c. Step 46 to 35 ft. lbs. (47 Nm)

48. Install the left side mounting support with its 2 bolts; tighten them to 15 ft. lbs. (20 Nm).

49. With the engine securely mounted in the vehicle, the lifting equipment may be removed. Elevate the vehicle and support it safely.

50. Install the center mount to the transaxle with its 2 bolts and tighten them to 45 ft. lbs. (61 Nm).

51. Position the center mount over the front and rear studs and start 2 nuts on the center mount only. Loosely install the 3 center support-to-radiator support bolts.

52. Loosely install the 2 front mount bolts. Raise the main crossmember into place over the rear studs and align all the underbody bolts.

53. Install the 2 rear mount nuts; leave them loose.

54. Loosely install the 8 underbody bolts, the lower control arm bracket bolts, the 2 center support-to-crossmember bolts and the exhaust hanger bracket and nuts.

55. With everything loose but in place, make a second pass over all the nuts and bolts tightening them to the following specifications:

Crossmember-to-underbody bolts to 152 ft. lbs. (206 Nm).

Lower control arm bracket-to-underbody bolts to 94 ft. lbs. (127 Nm).

Center support-to-radiator support bolts to 45 ft. lbs. (61 Nm).

Center support-to-crossmember bolts to 45 ft. lbs. (61 Nm).

Front, center and rear mount bolts to 45 ft. lbs. (61 Nm).

Exhaust hanger bracket nuts to 9 ft. lbs. (12 Nm).

56. Install the rear transaxle mount and tighten the bolt to 64 ft. lbs. (87 Nm).

57. Install the nuts on the center transaxle mount and tighten to 45 ft. lbs. (61 Nm).

58. Reconnect the halfshafts to the transaxle.

59. Using a new gasket, connect the exhaust pipe to the manifold and install the exhaust pipe bolts, tightening them to 18 ft. lbs. (24 Nm).

60. Lower the vehicle to the ground.

61. Either connect the control cables to the shift outer lever and selector lever and attach the control cables to manual transaxles or reconnect the control cable to the shift lever and install the clip and retainer on automatic transaxles. If equipped with manual transaxle, reattach the clutch slave cylinder to its mount.

62. Attach the speedometer cable to the transaxle.

63. Install the air conditioning compressor and drive belt, if equipped.

64. Install the power steering pump, pivot bolt and drive belt, if equipped. Adjust the belts to the correct tension.

65. Install the fuel inlet and outlet lines.

66. Connect the heater hoses. Make sure they are in the correct positions and that the clamps are in sound condition.

67. Connect the vacuum hoses to the vacuum switch, the charcoal canister, the vacuum sensor, the power steering and the brake booster.

68. Connect the wiring to the air conditioning, the oxygen sensor and the vacuum sensor.

69. Observing the labels made at the time of disassembly, reconnect the main engine harness to its sensors and switches. Work carefully and make sure each connector is properly matched and firmly seated.

70. Install the ground strap connector and its bolt; connect the wiring at the No. 2 junction block in the engine compartment.

71. Install the cruise control actuator, if equipped.

72. Connect the accelerator cable and throttle cable (automatic transaxle) to their brackets.

73. Install the radiator and cooling fan assembly. Install the overflow reservoir.

74. Install the air cleaner assembly and the air intake hose.

75. Install the battery. Connect the positive cable to the starter terminal, then to the battery. Do not connect the negative battery cable at this time.

76. Fill the transaxle with the correct amount of fresh fluid.

77. Refill the engine coolant.

78. Fill the engine with the correct amount of fresh oil.

79. Double check all installation items, paying particular attention to loose hoses or hanging wires, loosened nuts, poor routing of hoses and wires (too tight or rubbing) and tools left in the engine area.

80. Connect the negative battery cable. Start the engine and allow it to idle. As the engine warms up, shift the automatic transaxle into each gear range allowing it to engage momentarily. After each gear has been selected, put the shifter in **P** and check the transaxle fluid level.

81. Shut the engine OFF and check the engine area carefully for leaks, particularly around any line or hose which was disconnected during removal.

82. Raise and support the vehicle. Replace the left and right splash shields and lower the vehicle.

83. With the help of an assistant, reinstall the hood. Adjust the hood for proper fit and latching.

1991-94

1. Disconnect the negative terminal from the battery.

2. Using a scratch awl, scribe the hood hinge-to-hood outline. Disconnect the windshield washer fluid lines from the hood. Remove the 4 hood hinge bolts (2 on each side) disengaging the hood from the hinge. Using an assistant, remove the hood.

3. Properly relieve the fuel system pressure.

4. Raise and safely support the vehicle.

5. Remove the left and right stone shields.

6. Drain the engine oil and the cooling system.

7. Drain the transaxle fluid. Lower the vehicle.

8. Remove the air cleaner hose and air cleaner assembly. Remove the radiator, cooling fan and cooling overflow reservoir.

9. Disconnect the accelerator cable and throttle cable from the bracket.

10. Remove the cruise control actuator.

11. Disconnect and tag all electrical component connectors.

12. Disconnect and tag all the necessary vacuum lines.

13. Remove the fuel inlet and outlet lines.

14. Remove the heater hoses from the engine.

15. Remove the power steering pump and bracket from the engine and set it off to the side. Leave the power steering hydraulic lines hook up to the pump.

16. Remove the air conditioning compressor and bracket bolts from the engine and set it off to the side. Leave the freon lines hooked up to the compressor.

17. Remove the speedometer cable from the transaxle.

18. Disconnect the clutch release cylinder without disconnecting the line and hose (manual transaxles only).

19. On the manual transaxle models, disconnect the transaxle control cables by removing the 2 clips, washers and retainers. Disconnect the control cables from the shift outer lever and select outer lever.

20. Disconnect the control cable from the shift lever (automatic transaxle only).

21. Raise and safely support the vehicle.

22. Disconnect the front exhaust pipe from the exhaust manifold.

23. Remove the transaxle mounts. Lower the vehicle.

24. Remove the engine mounts.

25. Attach a suitable chain hoist to the lifting device on the engine. Slowly lift the engine/transaxle assembly out of the vehicle and place it in a suitable engine stand.

To install:

26. Attach a suitable chain hoist to the lifting device on the engine. Slowly lift the engine/transaxle assembly into the vehicle.

27. Tilt the transaxle downward to clear the left mount.

28. Raise and safely support the vehicle. Install the engine and transaxle mounts.

29. Install the drive axles.

30. Install the exhaust pipe to the exhaust manifold.

31. Install the right and left stone shields. Lower the vehicle.

32. Install the control cable to the shift lever (automatic transaxle).

33. If equipped with manual transaxles, install the control cables to the shift outer lever and select outer lever. Install the clutch release cylinder.

34. Install the air conditioner compressor bracket, compressor and bolts.

35. Install the power steering pump and bracket to the engine.

36. Install the heater hoses to the engine.

37. Install the fuel inlet and outlet lines.

38. Reconnect the disconnected vacuum lines.

39. Reconnect the disconnected electrical connectors.

40. Install the cruise control actuator.

41. Install the accelerator and throttle cable to the bracket.

42. Install the radiator, cooling fan and overflow reservoir. Refill the cooling system.

43. Install the air cleaner hose and air cleaner assembly.

44. Refill the transaxle.

45. Refill the engine with the recommended oil.

46. Reconnect the battery.

47. Install the hood assembly.

48. Start the engine and check for leakage of any kind. Make all necessary repairs and adjustments.

49. Torque the center transaxle mount-to-center crossmember nuts to 45 ft. lbs. (61 Nm)

50. Torque the rear transaxle mount-to-main crossmember nuts to 45 ft. lbs. (61 Nm).

51. Torque the right engine mount through bolt to 64 ft. lbs. (87 Nm).

52. Torque the right engine mount support bolts to 35 ft. lbs. (47 Nm).

53. Torque the right engine mount support bolts to 35 ft. lbs. (47 Nm).

54. Torque the engine mount-to-engine bracket nuts to 45 ft. lbs. (61 Nm).

55. Torque the engine mount-to-bracket bolt to 45 ft. lbs. (61 Nm).

56. If equipped with an automatic transaxle, torque the flywheel retaining bolts to 47 ft. lbs. (64 Nm).

57. If equipped with a manual transaxle, torque the flywheel retaining bolts to 58 ft. lbs. (78 Nm).

Storm

1. Relieve fuel system pressure.
2. Drain engine and transaxle oil.
3. Disconnect the battery cables, then remove battery and battery tray from vehicle.
4. Scribe matchmarks on the hood hinge-to-hood, then remove the hood.
5. Discharge air conditioning system.
6. Drain cooling system, then disconnect the accelerator cable from the throttle valve.
7. Disconnect the breather hose from the intake air duct, then remove the intake air duct from the throttle valve.
8. Remove the air cleaner cover, filter and the body from the vehicle.
9. Remove the MAP sensor hose from the MAP sensor, then the brake booster vacuum hose.
10. Disconnect the 2 canister hoses from the pipes on the intake manifold (common chamber). If equipped with DOHC engine, remove the canister pipe support bracket.
11. Disconnect the 2 cable harness connectors, located near the left shock tower.
12. Disconnect the ignition coil ground cable from the terminal on the thermostat housing flange.
13. Disconnect the ignition coil-to-distributor wire, the 2 primary wires from the ignition coil, then remove the ignition coil and bracket from the vehicle.
14. Disconnect the engine harness ground cable from the left inner fender.
15. Disconnect the harness terminal from the relay and fuse box.

16. Disconnect the cooling fan electrical connector and the 2 battery cable connectors.
17. Disconnect the oxygen sensor electrical connector, then the ground cable terminals from the left front side of the common chamber and the rear of the cylinder head cover.
18. If equipped with automatic transaxle, disconnect the electrical connectors from transaxle.
19. If equipped with manual transaxle, loosen the tow adjusting nuts and disconnect the clutch cable. Disconnect the 2 transaxle shaft cables by removing the cotter pin and clip from the shaft cable bracket.
20. If equipped with automatic transaxle, disconnect the shift cable by removing the cotter pin from the shaft cable lever.
21. On all vehicles, remove the 2 heater hoses from the engine.
22. Disconnect the speedometer from the transaxle, then the upper radiator hose from the radiator.
23. Disconnect the fuel feed line and fuel return hose, near the filter, then the coolant recovery tank with bracket.
24. Remove the power steering belt, power steering pump and bracket from the vehicle.
25. Remove the cooling fan and shroud, then raise and support the vehicle safely.
26. Remove the right and left undercovers and the lower radiator hose from the engine.
27. If equipped with automatic transaxle, disconnect the oil cooler lines from the transaxle.
28. Remove the air conditioning compressor bracket bolts and position compressor aside.
29. Remove the front tire and wheel assemblies, then the halfshafts.
30. Remove the front exhaust pipe from the exhaust manifold.
31. Lower the vehicle and install a suitable engine hoist onto the lifting brackets on the engine.
32. Remove the engine mounts and transaxle mounts, then lift the engine and transaxle assembly out from the vehicle. Separate the transaxle from the engine.

To install:

33. Install the transaxle to the engine, then a suitable hoist onto the engine lifting brackets.
34. Install engine and transaxle into vehicle, then the transaxle mounts and engine mounts.
35. Remove the engine hoist from the vehicle, then raise and support vehicle safely.

36. Install the front exhaust pipe to the exhaust manifold, then the halfshafts.
37. Install the tire and wheel assemblies, then the 2 air conditioning bracket mounting bolts.
38. If equipped with automatic transaxle, connect the 2 cooler lines to the transaxle.
39. Install the lower radiator hose, then the right and left undercovers. Lower the vehicle.
40. Install the cooling fan and shroud, then the power steering pump and belt onto the engine.
41. Install the coolant recovery tank with bracket, then connect the fuel feed line and fuel return hose.
42. Install the upper radiator hose, then connect the speedometer cable to the transaxle.
43. Connect the 2 heater hoses to the engine, then the transaxle shift cables, if equipped.
44. If equipped with manual transaxle, connect the clutch cable and adjust.
45. If equipped with automatic transaxle, connect the electrical connectors to the transaxle.
46. Connect the ground cable terminal to the rear of the cylinder head cover.
47. Connect the 2 ground terminals to the right side of the intake manifold (common chamber). If equipped with DOHC engine, install the canister pipe support bracket.
48. Connect the oxygen sensor electrical connector and the 2 battery cable harness connectors.
49. Connect the cooling fan harness connector, then the chassis harness terminal connector to the relay and fuse box.
50. Connect the engine ground cable to the left inner fender, then install the ignition coil and bracket.
51. Connect the 2 primary wires to the ignition coil and the ignition coil-to-distributor wire.
52. Connect the ignition coil ground wire to the terminal at the thermostat housing.
53. Connect the 2 cable harness connectors, located near the left shock tower.
54. Connect the 2 canister hoses to the intake manifold (common chamber).
55. Connect the brake booster vacuum hose, then the MAP sensor hose to the MAP sensor.
56. Install the air cleaner body, air cleaner filter and the cover.
57. Connect the air intake duct to the throttle body and the breather hose to the air intake duct.

58. Connect the accelerator cable to the throttle valve.

59. Fill the cooling system, engine oil and transaxle with suitable fluids. Install the battery tray and battery.

60. Align matchmarks on the hood hinge during removal and install the hood. Connect the battery negative cable. Start the engine and check for leaks.

Spectrum

1. Remove the hood, relieve the fuel system pressure and disconnect the negative battery cable.

2. Drain the cooling system.

3. If equipped with carburetor, remove the air cleaner and the throttle cable at the carburetor.

4. Disconnect the heater hoses at the intake manifold, the coolant hose at the thermostat housing and the thermostat housing at the cylinder head.

5. Remove the distributor from the cylinder head.

6. Disconnect the oxygen sensor electrical connector.

7. Support the engine using a vertical lift and remove the right motor mount.

8. Disconnect the necessary electrical connectors and vacuum hoses.

9. Disconnect the flex hose at the exhaust manifold and the lower radiator hose at the block.

10. Remove the upper air conditioning compressor bolt and remove the belt.

11. Disconnect the power steering bracket at the block and remove the belt.

12. Disconnect the fuel lines from the fuel pump and the electrical connectors from under the carburetor, if equipped.

13. Remove the upper starter bolt. Raise and support the vehicle safely.

14. Drain the oil from the crankcase and remove the oil filter.

15. Disconnect the oil temperature switch connector.

16. Disconnect the exhaust pipe bracket at the block and the exhaust pipe at the manifold.

17. Remove the air conditioning compressor and move to one side. Do not disconnect the air conditioning refrigerant lines. Remove the alternator wires.

18. Remove the flywheel cover and the converter bolts, then install a flywheel holding tool J-35271 or equivalent.

19. Disconnect the starter wires and remove the starter.

20. Remove the front right wheel and inner splash shield.

21. Lower the engine by lowering the crossmember enough to gain access to the crankshaft pulley bolts, then remove the pulley.

22. Raise the engine and crossmember. Remove the engine support.

23. Lower the vehicle and support the transaxle.

24. Remove the transaxle to engine bolts. Remove the engine.

To install:

25. Install engine, transaxle and engine bolts.

26. Remove transaxle support, then raise and support the vehicle.

27. Support the engine, then lower the engine by lowering the crossmember enough to install the crankshaft pulley and torque the crankshaft pulley bolt to 108 ft. lbs. (146 Nm).

28. Raise the engine and crossmember. Install the right front wheel and inner splash shield.

29. Install the starter and connect the starter wires.

30. Install torque converter bolts and flywheel cover.

31. Install the air conditioning compressor and connect the alternator wires.

32. Install the exhaust pipe to the exhaust manifold and exhaust pipe bracket to the block.

33. Install a new oil filter and the oil drain plug, if not already installed.

34. Connect fuel lines to the fuel pump and electrical connectors under the carburetor, if equipped.

35. Install the power steering bracket to the block and install the power steering and air conditioning belts.

36. Connect the lower radiator hose at the block and the flex hose at the exhaust manifold.

37. Connect the remaining vacuum hoses and electrical connectors.

38. Support the engine and install the right engine mount.

39. Connect the oxygen sensor wire and install the distributor.

40. Install the thermostat housing and torque the bolts to 17 ft. lbs. (23 Nm).

41. Connect the coolant hose to the thermostat housing and the heater hoses to the intake manifold.

42. Connect the throttle cable and install the air cleaner.

43. Adjust the drive belts and refill the fluids.

44. Check the connections at all electrical connectors and vacuum lines.

45. Connect the battery negative cable. Start engine and check for leaks.

Cylinder Head

REMOVAL AND INSTALLATION

Metro

1. Disconnect the negative battery cable and relieve the fuel system pressure.

2. Drain the cooling system.

3. Remove the air cleaner and the cylinder head cover.

4. Remove the distributor cap, then mark the position of the rotor and the distributor housing with the cylinder head. Remove the distributor and the case from the cylinder head.

5. Disconnect and tag all the necessary electrical connectors. Disconnect and tag all necessary vacuum lines.

6. Disconnect the throttle switch or throttle position solenoid.

7. Remove the fuel injectors.

8. Remove the vacuum switching valve for the EGR valve.

9. Disconnect the idle speed control solenoid valve.

10. Remove the ground wires from the intake manifold.

11. Disconnect the oxygen sensor and release the wire harness above from the clamps.

12. Disconnect the heater and coolant hoses.

13. Disconnect the fuel return hose and fuel feed hose from the throttle body.

14. Disconnect the accelerator cable from the throttle body.

15. Raise and safely support the vehicle.

16. Disconnect the No. 1 exhaust pipe from the exhaust manifold.

17. Remove the cylinder head cover.

18. Remove the cylinder head bolts. Remove the cylinder head with throttle body, intake manifold and exhaust manifold. With the camshaft still mounted to the cylinder, 1 of the 6 valves is out toward combustion chamber (it is open). Be sure not to place the cylinder head on any flat surface with its mating surface with the cylinder block facing down. It will cause damage to the open valve.

To install:

19. Install the new cylinder head gasket with the TOP mark provided on the gasket on the top side, toward the cylinder head and on the crankshaft pulley side.

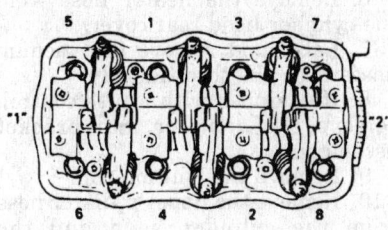

Cylinder head bolt torque sequence — Metro

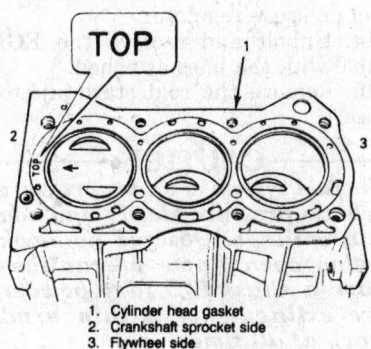

1. Cylinder head gasket
2. Crankshaft sprocket side
3. Flywheel side

Cylinder head gasket positioning — Metro

20. Install the cylinder head. Apply clean engine oil to the threads of the cylinder head bolts. Install the bolts and gradually tighten them with a torque wrench to 54 ft. lbs. (73 Nm).
21. Install the rubber seal between the water pump and the cylinder head.
22. Install the timing belt.
23. Install the distributor assembly.
24. To complete the installation procedure, reverse the removal procedure.
25. Adjust the water pump belt.
26. Adjust the accelerator cable play.

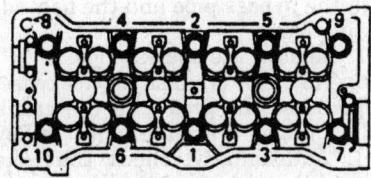

Cylinder head bolt torque sequence — Prizm (engine code 6 and 8)

27. Refill the cooling system. Reconnect the negative battery cable.
28. Start the vehicle and check for leaks of any kind. Make all repairs and adjustments as necessary.

Prizm

1990

1. Disconnect the negative battery cable. Relieve the fuel system pressure. Drain the coolant.
2. Raise and support the vehicle safely. Remove the right lower stone shield.
3. Remove the 2 mount nut and stud protectors. Remove the 2 rear transaxle mount to main crossmember mount nuts.
4. Remove the 2 center mount to center crossmember nuts. Lower the vehicle.
5. Remove the air cleaner assembly, disconnect the throttle cable and the cruise control actuator cable.
6. Disconnect the transaxle kickdown cable. Disconnect all necessary electrical connections and vacuum lines.
7. Disconnect the fuel inlet line. Disconnect the cold start injector pipe. Remove the fuel rail. Disconnect the coolant and heater hoses.
8. Remove the water outlet and inlet housings. Disconnect the spark plug wires and remove the PCV valve.
9. Remove the cylinder head cover. Loosen the air conditioning compressor, power steering pump and generator brackets as applicable.
10. Remove the accessory drive belts. Remove the air conditioning idler pulley. Disconnect the electrical connections at cruise control actuator and remove the cruise control actuator and bracket.
11. Remove windshield washer reservoir. Support the engine with a J-28467-A support fixture or its equivalent.
12. Remove the right engine mount through bolt. Raise the engine and properly support it.
13. Remove the water pump pulley. Lower the engine. Disconnect the engine wiring harness from upper timing belt cover.
14. Raise and suitably support the vehicle. Remove the cylinder head-to-cylinder block bracket.
15. Remove the exhaust manifold support bracket. Disconnect the exhaust pipe from exhaust manifold.
16. Remove the upper and center timing belt cover. Remove the right engine mount bracket.
17. Set the No. 1 cylinder at TDC on its compression stroke. Turn the crankshaft pulley and align its groove with the **0** mark of the timing belt cover. Remove the distributor.
18. Check that the camshaft gear hole is aligned with the exhaust camshaft cap mark. Remove the plug from the lower timing belt cover.
19. Place alignment marks on the camshaft timing gear and belt.
20. Loosen the idler pulley mount bolt and push the idler pulley toward the left as far as it will go, then tighten temporarily.
21. Remove the timing belt from the camshaft timing gear after marking its position in relation to the camshaft timing gear.
22. Hold the timing belt with a cloth.

NOTE: Support the belt so the meshing of the crankshaft timing gear and timing belt does not shift. Be careful not to drop anything inside the timing belt cover. Do not allow the belt to come in contact with oil, water or dust.

23. Remove the cylinder head bolts, in sequence, using a 10mm, 12 point deep well socket.

NOTE: Head warping or cracking could result from incorrect removal.

24. Remove the cylinder head with intake and exhaust manifolds. If the head is difficult to lift off, carefully pry with a bar between the cylinder head and a cylinder block projection.

NOTE: Be careful not to damage the cylinder head and block mating surface. Lift the cylinder head from the dowels on the cylinder block and place it on wooden blocks on a bench.

25. Remove the intake and exhaust manifolds.
26. Remove as necessary the camshafts, the valve lifters and shims, the spark plug tubes, the valves using a J-8062 spring compressor and a J-37979-A adapter, the valve stem oil seals and the half circle plug.
To install:
27. Install the half circle plug to the cylinder head. Apply GM No. 1052751 sealant or equivalent, to the plug.
28. Install the valves. Install the new oil seals on the valves using a J-38232 seal installer.

NOTE: The intake valve oil seal is brown and the exhaust valve oil seal is black.

29. Install the spring seat, spring and spring retainer on the cylinder

head. Using a J-8062 spring compressor and a J-37979-A adapter, compress the valve springs and place the 2 keepers around valve stem. Remove the J-8062 spring compressor and the J-37979-A adapter.

30. Apply GM No. 1052751 sealant to the spark plug tube hole of the cylinder head and using a press, install a new spark plug tube to a protrusion height of 1.835 — 1.866 in. (46.6 — 47.4mm).

31. Install the engine hangers to the cylinder head. Install the valve lifters and shims. Install the camshafts. Install the intake manifold.

32. Carefully install the cylinder head in position on the cylinder head gasket.

NOTE: Apply a light coating of engine oil on the bolt threads and under the bolt head before installation.

33. Install the 10 cylinder head bolts, in several passes and in sequence. Tighten the cylinder head bolts to 44 ft. lbs. (60 Nm).

34. Install the timing belt. Install the distributor. Install the engine mount bracket. Install the air conditioning idler pulley.

35. Install the center and upper timing belt covers. Raise and suitably support the vehicle. Install the exhaust manifold to exhaust pipe with a new gasket.

36. Install the 2 new exhaust pipe bolts. Tighten the exhaust pipe bolts to 18 ft. lbs. (25 Nm). Install the exhaust manifold support bracket.

37. Install the cylinder head-to-cylinder block bracket. Lower the vehicle.

38. Connect the engine harness to upper timing belt cover. Raise and properly support the engine.

39. Install the water pump pulley. Lower engine. Install the right engine mount through bolt. Tighten to 64 ft. lbs. (87 Nm).

40. Remove the J-28467-A support fixture. Install the windshield washer reservoir.

41. Install the cruise control actuator and bracket and connect the electrical connector.

42. Install the accessory drive belts and adjust to the proper tensions, as applicable.

43. Install the cylinder head cover. Install the PCV valve and spark plug wires. Install the water inlet and outlet housings.

44. Install the heater hoses and all coolant hoses. Install the fuel rail. Install the cold-start injector pipe.

45. Install the fuel inlet line. Connect all necessary electrical connections and vacuum lines.

46. Install the transaxle kickdown cable, connect the cruise control actuator cable and the throttle cable. Install the air cleaner assembly.

47. Raise and safely support the vehicle. Install the 2 rear mount-to-main crossmember nuts. Install the 2 center transaxle mount-to-center crossmember nuts.

48. Tighten the rear transaxle mount-to-main crossmember nuts to 45 ft. lbs. (61 Nm). Tighten the center transaxle mount-to-center crossmember nuts to 45 ft. lbs. (61 Nm).

49. Install both mount nut and stud protectors. Install the right lower stone shield.

50. Lower the vehicle. Refill coolant and install the battery negative cable.

1991-94

1. Disconnect the negative battery cable

2. Open the drain cocks on the engine and radiator. Collect the coolant in clean containers.

3. Remove the air cleaner assembly.

4. Disconnect the cruise control cable, if equipped.

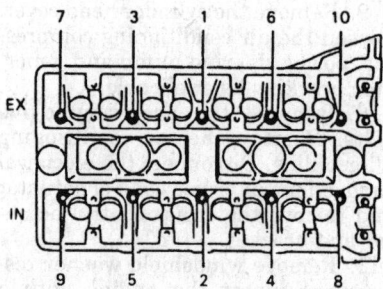

Cylinder head bolt torque sequence — Prizm (engine code 5)

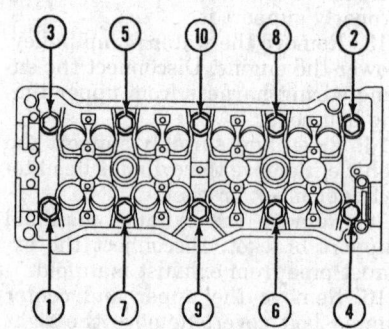

Cylinder head bolt removal sequence — Prizm (engine code 6 and 8)

5. Disconnect the throttle cable from the throttle linkage.

6. Remove the heater hose from the cylinder head rear cover.

7. Label and remove the vacuum hoses from the throttle body.

8. If equipped with cruise control, remove the actuator and bracket assembly.

9. Remove the ignition coil.

10. Remove the upper radiator hose from the cylinder head and the radiator.

11. Remove the brake booster vacuum hose.

12. Remove the PCV hose.

13. Unbolt and remove as a unit the fuel pressure regulator.

14. Unbolt and remove the EGR valve with the lines attached.

15. Remove the cold start injector hose.

—————— CAUTION ——————

The fuel system is under pressure. Release pressure slowly and contain spillage. Observe no smoking/no open flame precautions. Have a Class B-C (dry powder) fire extinguisher within arm's reach at all times.

16. Remove the No. 1 fuel line.

17. Remove the first and second water bypass hoses from the auxiliary air valve.

18. Remove the vacuum pipe and the cylinder head rear cover.

19. Remove, disconnect or reposition the wiring harness(es) around the head as necessary.

20. Remove the distributor.

21. Remove the exhaust manifold and its gaskets.

22. Remove the fuel delivery pipe and the injectors. Do not drop the injectors.

23. Remove the intake manifold support bracket; remove the intake manifold and the intake air control valve.

24. Remove the power steering drive belt.

25. Remove the upper timing belt cover and the valve covers.

26. Remove the water outlet fitting with the bypass pipe and the belt adjusting bar.

27. Remove the spark plugs.

28. Turn the crankshaft clockwise, stopping so the groove in the crank pulley aligns with the idler pulley bolt. Additionally, check that the valve lifters on No. 1 cylinder are loose (the camshaft lobes are not depressing the lifters). If the valves are under tension, rotate the crank one full revolution and check again. The engine is now on TDC/compression.

29. Remove the right motor mount.
30. Remove the water pump pulley.
31. Remove the lower and middle (Nos. 2 and 3) timing belt covers.

NOTE: The bolts are different lengths. Label or diagram the correct location of each bolt as it is removed. Improper placement during reassembly can cause engine damage.

32. Place matchmarks on the timing belt and the belt pulleys. Make sure to mark each pulley and the belt clearly. Additionally, mark an arrow on the belt showing the direction of rotation.
33. Carefully slide the timing belt off the camshaft pulleys. Do not pry on the belt with tools. Keep the belt under light upward tension so the bottom (crankshaft) end doesn't shift position on its pulley.
34. Remove the camshaft pulleys. Use an adjustable wrench to counter hold the camshaft during removal. Look for the flats on the camshaft and fit the wrench to them.
35. With the pulleys removed, the end-plate (otherwise called No. 4 timing cover) may be removed.
36. Mark the intake and exhaust camshaft gear positions in relation to each other.
37. Remove the camshafts, intake then exhaust.
38. Remove the front camshaft bearing caps.
39. Secure the intake camshaft sub-gear to the main gear with a 16-20mm long **x** 6mm **x** 1.0mm thread bolt.
40. When removing the exhaust camshaft, set the camshaft so the knock pin is properly located.

———— WARNING ————
The camshaft being removed must be held level during removal. If it is not, the area of the cylinder head receiving the shaft thrust might crack or be damaged. This could cause the camshaft to seize or break. Positioning the exhaust camshaft in the prescribed manner, will cause the No. 1 and No. 3 cylinder camshaft lobes to press on those valve lifters evenly.

41. Loosen and remove camshaft caps in several steps and in sequence.
42. If the camshaft cannot be lifted out straight and level, retighten no. 3 bearing cap and alternately loosen the bolts slowly while lifting up on the camshaft gear.
43. Remove the camshafts from the head.

44. Loosen the head bolts in the proper sequence. Make 3 complete passes, loosening them slowly, evenly and in order.
45. Remove the cylinder head. If it is difficult to remove, it may be pried up gently with a suitable tool. Be very careful not to scratch or gouge the mating surfaces when prying the head up.
46. Keeping the head upright, place it on wooden blocks on the workbench. If the head is to receive further work, the various components will need to be removed. If the head is not to be worked on, the mating surface must be cleaned of all gasket and sealant material before reinstallation.
47. Clean the engine block mating surface of all gasket and sealant material. Use plastic or wooden scrapers so as not gouge the metal. Remove all traces of liquids from the surface and clean out the bolt holes.

To install:
48. Install the new head gasket on the block. Make sure it is properly placed and that all the holes and passages in the block line up with the holes in the gasket.
49. Place the head in position and make sure it is properly seated and aligned.
50. Apply a light coat of oil to the threads of the cylinder head bolts.
51. Install the 10 cylinder head bolts.

NOTE: The bolts for the exhaust side are 108mm long; the bolts for the intake side are 90mm long.

52. Tighten the cylinder head bolts in 3 passes and in sequence. The first pass should tighten them to 8-10 ft. lbs. (11-14 Nm), the second pass to 16 ft. lbs. (22 Nm) and the third pass to 44 ft. lbs. (60 Nm).
53. On 1993-94 vehicles, torque the cylinder head bolts to 22 ft. lbs. (29 Nm), then tighten the bolts in 2 more steps of 90 degree turns each.
54. Apply RTV sealer or similar to the cylinder head. Install new camshaft end seals and coat them lightly with multi-purpose grease.
55. Install the exhaust camshaft as follows:
   a. Install the exhaust camshaft so the knock pin is in it's proper position.
   b. Apply a light coat of oil to the threads of the bearing cap bolts.
   c. Install camshaft bearing caps in several steps and torque the bolts to 115 inch lbs. (13 Nm).
56. Apply lithium grease to the new oil seal lip and install the seal. Make

certain the lip faces the camshaft, the seal in completely in the cylinder head and the seal is not slanted.
57. Install the intake camshaft as follows:
   a. Position the exhaust camshaft so the knock pin is slightly above the top of the cylinder head.
   b. Apply lithium grease to the thrust area of the intake camshaft.
   c. Engage the intake camshaft gear with the exhaust camshaft gear using the marks made during removal.

NOTE: There are TDC marks on each camshaft gear. Do not use them!

   d. Roll the intake camshaft onto the journals while engaging the camshaft gears. This allows the No. 1 and No. 3 cylinder camshaft lobes to press evenly on their lifters.
   e. Apply a light coat of oil to the threads of the bearing cap bolts.
   f. Install camshaft bearing caps in several steps and torque the bolts to 115 inch lbs. (13 Nm).
58. Install the end-plate or No. 4 timing cover.
59. Install the right side engine mount bracket and tighten its bolts to 64 ft. lbs. (87 Nm).
60. Install the camshaft pulleys. Be sure to align the camshaft knock pin and the camshaft pulley. Tighten the pulley bolts to 34 ft. lbs. (47 Nm).
61. Install the lower and middle (No. 2 and 3) timing belt covers. Remember that the bolts are different lengths; make certain the correct bolt is in the correct location.
62. Install the water pump pulley.
63. Install the right engine mount. Tighten the through bolt to 64 ft. lbs. (87 Nm).
64. Install the spark plugs. Correct tightness is 13 ft. lbs. (18 Nm).
65. Reinstall the water outlet with the bypass pipe and the belt adjusting bar.
66. Install the valve covers.
67. Install the alternator and power steering drive belts. Adjust the belts to the correct tension.
68. Install the intake manifold and intake air control valve. Tighten the bolts to 20 ft. lbs. (27 Nm).
69. Install the bracket and support for the intake manifold.
70. Install the fuel delivery pipe and the injectors. Make sure the insulators and spacers have been placed properly. Make sure the injectors rotate smoothly in their seats.
71. Tighten the delivery pipe retaining bolts to 13 ft. lbs. (18 Nm).

72. Install the exhaust manifold tighten its nuts and bolts to 18 ft. lbs. (25 Nm).

73. Reinstall the distributor.

74. Attach, reposition or connect the wiring harness(es) around the head. Make sure all retaining clips are used and are secure. Double check the wiring to eliminate any contact with moving parts.

75. Install the vacuum pipe and the cylinder head rear cover with a new gasket.

76. Connect the first and second by-pass hoses to the auxiliary air valve.

77. Connect the No. 1 fuel line.

78. Use new gaskets and connect the cold-start injector line. Tighten the bolts to 13 ft. lbs. (18 Nm).

79. Replace the EGR valve and use a new gasket.

80. Use a new O-ring and attach the fuel pressure regulator. Tighten the regulator bolts to 6.8 ft. lbs (9.2 Nm).

81. Install the PCV hose and the brake vacuum hose.

82. Install the radiator hose at the radiator and the cylinder head.

83. Install the ignition coil.

84. Install the cruise control actuator and bracket assembly, if equipped.

85. Observing the labels made earlier, connect the vacuum hose to the throttle body.

86. Attach the heater hose to the cylinder head rear cover.

87. Connect the throttle valve and accelerator cables.

88. Connect the cruise control cable, if equipped.

89. Install the air cleaner assembly.

90. Confirm that the drain cocks on the radiator and engine block are closed. Fill the cooling system with coolant.

91. Double check all installation items, paying particular attention to loose hoses or hanging wires, loosened nuts, poor routing of hoses and wires (too tight or rubbing) and tools left in the engine area.

92. Connect the negative battery cable.

93. Start the engine. During the warm up period, check for any sign of leakage or overheating. Check engine timing and adjust the idle speed if necessary.

94. After the engine is shut OFF, check the drive belts and adjust the tension if necessary.

Storm

1. Disconnect the battery negative cable.

2. Drain cooling system.

3. Disconnect the accelerator cable from the throttle valve, then the breather hose from the intake air duct.

4. Disconnect the intake air duct from the throttle valve, then the MAP sensor hose from the MAP sensor.

5. Disconnect the brake booster hose, then the 2 canister hoses from the pipes on the intake manifold (common chamber).

6. Disconnect the EGR vacuum hoses, then the oxygen sensor harness electrical connector.

7. Disconnect the ignition coil ground cable from the thermostat housing flange.

8. Disconnect the coolant temperature sensor and thermo unit harness connector from the thermostat housing.

9. Remove the cable harness clip from the coolant outlet pipe bracket.

10. Disconnect the 2 cable harness electrical connectors, located near the left strut tower.

11. Disconnect the engine heater hoses, then the upper radiator hose from the radiator.

12. Disconnect the fuel feed and return hoses, then raise and support vehicle safely.

13. Remove the right undercover, then the front exhaust pipe from the exhaust manifold. Lower the vehicle.

14. Remove the right engine mount, then the alternator drive belt.

15. Remove the power steering belt.

16. Remove the engine mounting bracket from the timing case cover, then remove the timing belt.

17. Remove the cylinder head center cover, cylinder head bolts, then the cylinder head.

To install:

18. Clean the cylinder head gasket mounting surfaces, then install the cylinder head with a new gasket.

19. First torque cylinder head bolts in sequence to 29 ft. lbs. (40 Nm), then a final torque in sequence of 58 ft. lbs. (79 Nm).

20. Install the timing belt and the cylinder head cover, then the engine mounting bracket onto the timing case cover.

21. Raise and safely support the vehicle, then install the right engine mount.

22. Install the front exhaust pipe to the exhaust manifold, then right side undercover. Lower the vehicle.

23. Connect the fuel feed line and fuel return hose.

24. Connect the coolant bypass pipe bracket to the cylinder head.

25. Install the upper radiator hose, then the 2 heater hoses onto the engine.

26. Connect the 2 cable harness connectors, located near the left strut tower.

27. Connect the 2 ground cable terminals, located to the right side of the intake manifold (common chamber).

28. Connect the coolant temperature sensor and thermo unit electrical connectors on the thermostat housing.

29. Connect the ignition coil ground cable to the terminal on the thermostat housing flange.

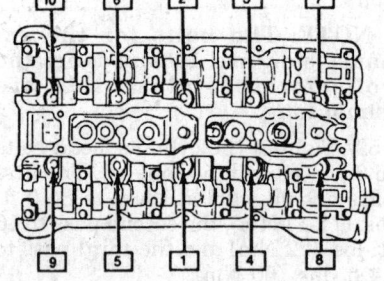

Cylinder head bolt torque sequence — Storm DOHC engine

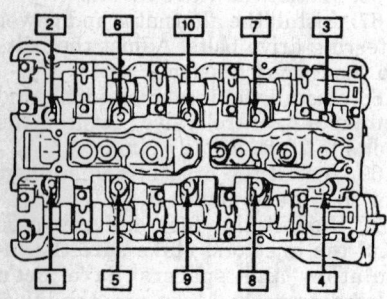

Cylinder head bolt removal sequence — Storm DOHC engine

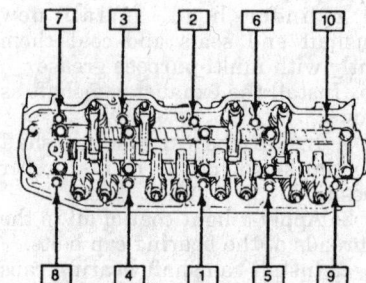

Cylinder head bolt installation sequence — Storm SOHC engine

30. Connect the oxygen sensor electrical connector.

31. Connect the canister hoses to the canister pipes on the intake manifold (common chamber).

32. Connect the brake booster vacuum hose and the MAP sensor vacuum hose.

33. Install the intake air duct to the throttle valve, then the PCV hose to the intake air duct.

34. Connect the accelerator cable to the throttle valve.

35. Connect the battery negative cable and fill cooling system. Start engine and check for leaks.

Spectrum

1. Relieve the fuel system pressure. Disconnect the negative battery terminal from the battery.

2. Drain the cooling system.

3. Remove the air cleaner. Remove the suction pipe and clips for the air induction system.

4. Disconnect the flex hose and oxygen sensor at the exhaust manifold.

5. Disconnect the exhaust pipe bracket at the block and the exhaust pipe at the manifold.

6. Disconnect the spark plug wires.

7. Remove the thermostat housing, the distributor, the vacuum advance hoses and the ground cable at the cylinder head.

8. Disconnect the fuel hoses at the fuel pump.

9. From the carburetor, if equipped. Remove the necessary hoses and the throttle cable.

10. Remove engine harness assembly from fuel injectors.

11. Disconnect the vacuum switching valve electrical connector and the heater hoses.

12. Remove the alternator, power steering and air conditioning adjusting bolts, brackets and drive belts.

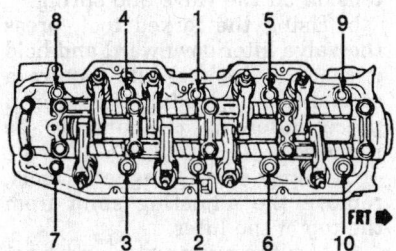

Cylinder head bolt torque sequence — Spectrum

13. Support the engine using a vertical hoist. Remove the right hand motor mount and the bracket at the front cover.

14. Rotate the engine to align the timing marks, then remove the timing gear cover.

15. Loosen the tension pulley and remove the timing belt from the camshaft timing pulley.

16. Disconnect the carburetor fuel line at the fuel pump and remove the fuel pump.

17. Disconnect the intake manifold coolant hoses.

18. Remove the cylinder head bolts (remove the bolts from both ends at the same time, working toward the middle) and the cylinder head.

To install:

19. Clean all of the mounting surfaces and carefully place a new head gasket onto the cylinder block.

20. Carefully install the cylinder head onto the cylinder block dowel pins. Apply oil to the bolt threads and torque the head bolts.

NOTE: When tightening the cylinder head bolts, work from the middle toward both ends, alternating from one side to the other. First, torque the bolts to 29 ft. lbs. (40 Nm) and then final torque them to 58 ft. lbs. (79 Nm).

21. Connect the coolant hoses at the intake manifold.

22. Install the fuel pump and connect the fuel lines.

23. Check the alignment of the timing marks before installing the timing belt.

24. Adjust the timing belt and install the timing gear cover.

25. Install the right hand motor mount and the bracket at the front cover.

26. Install the air conditioning, power steering and alternator brackets, adjusting bolts.

27. Install and adjust drive belts.

28. Connect the heater hoses and vacuum switching valve connector.

29. Connect the throttle cable, vacuum hoses and fuel lines to the carburetor.

30. Install the distributor and vacuum advance hoses.

31. Connect the ground cable at the cylinder head and spark plug wires.

32. Install the thermostat housing and torque the bolts to 17 ft. lbs. (23 Nm).

33. Connect the exhaust pipe to the exhaust manifold and exhaust pipe bracket to the block.

34. Install the air induction system suction pipe and clips.

35. Install the air cleaner assembly and fill the cooling system.

36. Connect the negative battery terminal.

37. Check and adjust engine timing if necessary and check for coolant leaks.

Valve Lifters

REMOVAL AND INSTALLATION

NOTE: The Metro 1.0L and the Storm 1.6L DOHC engines are the only engines using hydraulic valve adjusters. All the other engines that are being used in these vehicles are of the single or dual overhead camshaft design without valve adjusters.

Valve Adjuster

REMOVAL AND INSTALLATION

Metro

1. Disconnect the negative battery cable.

2. Remove the air cleaner assembly.

3. Remove the cylinder head cover assembly.

4. Set the engine up on top dead center of the compression stroke on the No. 1 cylinder. Make an alignment mark on the distributor cap and engine block and remove the distributor assembly.

5. Remove the crankshaft pulley, timing belt outside cover and the timing belt.

NOTE: After removing the timing belt, set the key on the crankshaft in position by turning the crankshaft. This is to prevent interference between the valves and the piston when reinstalling the camshaft.

6. Remove the camshaft timing belt gear. Lock the camshaft with a proper size rod inserted into the hole 0.39 in. (10mm) in it. Loosen the camshaft timing belt gear bolt.

NOTE: The mating surface of the cylinder head and cover must not be damaged. So, put a clean shop cloth between the rod and mating surfaces and use care not to bump the rod against the mating surfaces when loosening.

7. Remove the camshaft housing from the cylinder head.

8. Remove the camshaft from the cylinder head.

9. Remove the valve lash adjuster from the cylinder head.

NOTE: **Never disassemble the hydraulic valve lash adjuster. Do not apply force to the body of the valve adjuster. Immerse the removed adjuster in clean engine oil until it is reinstalled. If the adjuster is left in the air, place it with its valve lash adjuster body facing down. Do not place it on its side or with the valve lash adjuster body facing up.**

10. Check the adjuster for pitting, scratches or damage. If any of these conditions are found.

To install:

11. Before installing the valve lash adjuster to the cylinder head, fill the oil passage of the cylinder head with the engine oil. Pour the engine oil through the camshaft journal oil holes and check that the oil comes out from the oil holes in the sliding part of the valve lash adjuster.

12. Apply the engine oil around the valve lash adjuster and then install it to the cylinder head.

13. Install the camshaft to cylinder head. After applying engine oil to the camshaft journal and all around the camshaft, then position the camshaft into the cylinder head so the camshaft timing belt gear pin hole in camshaft is at the lower position.

14. Install the camshaft housing to the camshaft and the cylinder head.

15. Apply the engine oil to the sliding surface of each housing against the camshaft journal.

16. Apply the sealant to the mating surface of the No. 1 and No. 3 housing which will mate with the cylinder head.

17. There are marks provided on each camshaft housing indicating position and direction for installation. Install the housing as indicated by these marks.

18. As the camshaft housing No. 1 retains the camshaft in the proper position as to the thrust direction, make sure to first fit the No. 1 housing to the No. 1 journal of the camshaft securely.

19. After applying the engine oil to the housing bolts, tighten them temporarily. Then tighten in the proper sequence. Tighten the bolts a little at a time and evenly among bolts, repeat the tightening sequence 3 to 4 times before they are tightened to the proper torque of 8 ft. lbs. (11 Nm).

20. Install the camshaft oil seal. After applying engine oil to the oil seal lip, press-fit the camshaft oil seal until the oil seal surface becomes flush with the housing surfaces.

21. Install the camshaft timing belt gear to the camshaft after installing the dwell pin to the camshaft. While locking the camshaft, install the camshaft pulley and retaining bolt and torque the bolt to 44 ft. lbs. (60 Nm).

22. Install the cylinder head cover to the cylinder head.

23. Install the timing belt, timing belt outside cover, crankshaft pulley, coolant pump pulley and coolant pump belt.

24. Install the distributor assembly into the engine.

25. Install the air cleaner assembly and reinstall the negative battery cable.

26. Adjust the ignition timing.

NOTE: **Do not turn the camshaft or start the engine for about a half an hour after reinstalling the hydraulic valve lash adjusters and camshaft. As it takes time for valves to settle in place, operating engine within a half an hour after their installation may cause interference to occur between the valves and piston.**

27. If air is trapped in the valve lash adjuster, the valve may make tapping sound when engine is operated after valve lash adjuster is installed. In such a case, run the engine for about a half hour at approximately 2000 rpm and then the air will be purged and the tapping sound should cease. Should the tapping sound not cease, it is possible that the valve lash adjuster is defective. Among the 6 of them, if a defective adjuster can not be located, check as follows:

a. Stop the engine and remove the cylinder head cover.

b. Push the adjuster downward by hand (with less than 33 lbs. of force) when the camshaft lobe is not on the adjuster to be checked and check if the clearance exists between the camshaft and the adjuster. If it does, the adjuster is defective and needs to be replaced.

Storm

1. Disconnect the negative battery cable.

2. Remove the camshaft assemblies.

3. Remove the selective shims and valve lash (tappets) adjusters.

NOTE: **When removing selective shims and tappets, be sure to arrange them in order of removal to ensure proper installation. Measure the valve lash (tappet)** adjuster outside diameter using a micrometer. If the diameter is less than 1.218 in. (31mm), replace the tappet.

4. Install the selective shims and valve lash (tappets) adjusters.

5. Install the camshaft assemblies. Adjust the valve lash.

6. Reconnect the negative battery cables.

Valve Lash

ADJUSTMENT

Prizm

NOTE: **The use of the correct special tools or their equivalent is required for this procedure. The valve adjustment requires removal of the adjusting shims (Tool kit J-37141 or equivalent) and accurate measurement of the shims with a micrometer. A selection of replacement shims is also required.**

1. Remove the valve cover.

2. Turn the crankshaft to align the groove in the crankshaft pulley with the **0** mark on the timing belt cover. Removing the spark plugs makes this easier but is not required.

3. Check that the lifters on No. 1 cylinder are loose and those on No. 4 are tight. If not, turn the crankshaft pulley one full revolution (360 degrees).

4. Using the feeler gauge, measure the clearance on the 4 valves. Make a written record of any measurements which are not within specification.

5. Rotate the crankshaft pulley one full turn (360 degrees) and check the clearance on the other 4 valves. Any measurements not within specification should be recorded.

6. For any given valve needing adjustment:

a. Turn the crankshaft pulley until the camshaft lobe points upward over the valve. This takes the tension off the valve and spring.

b. Using the forked tool, press the valve lifter downward and hold it there. Some tool kits require a second tool for holding the lifter in place, allowing the first to be removed.

c. Using small magnetic tools, remove the adjusting shim from the top of the lifter.

d. Use the micrometer and measure the thickness of the shim removed. Determine the thickness of the new shim using the formula below. For the purposes of the follow-

Installed Shim Thickness (mm)

Column headers (Installed Shim Thickness, mm): 2.500, 2.525, 2.550, 2.575, 2.600, 2.620, 2.625, 2.640, 2.650, 2.660, 2.675, 2.680, 2.700, 2.720, 2.725, 2.740, 2.750, 2.760, 2.775, 2.800, 2.820, 2.825, 2.840, 2.850, 2.860, 2.875, 2.880, 2.900, 2.920, 2.925, 2.940, 2.950, 2.960, 2.975, 2.980, 3.000, 3.020, 3.025, 3.040, 3.050, 3.060, 3.075, 3.080, 3.100, 3.120, 3.125, 3.140, 3.150, 3.160, 3.175, 3.180, 3.200, 3.225, 3.250, 3.275, 3.300

Measured Clearance (mm) ranges (row labels):

Measured Clearance (mm)
0.000 – 0.009
0.010 – 0.025
0.026 – 0.040
0.041 – 0.050
0.051 – 0.070
0.071 – 0.090
0.091 – 0.100
0.101 – 0.120
0.121 – 0.140
0.141 – 0.150
0.151 – 0.170
0.171 – 0.190
0.191 – 0.199
0.200 – 0.300
0.301 – 0.320
0.321 – 0.325
0.326 – 0.340
0.341 – 0.350
0.351 – 0.370
0.371 – 0.375
0.376 – 0.390
0.391 – 0.400
0.401 – 0.420
0.421 – 0.425
0.426 – 0.440
0.441 – 0.450
0.451 – 0.470
0.471 – 0.475
0.476 – 0.490
0.491 – 0.500
0.501 – 0.520
0.521 – 0.525
0.526 – 0.540
0.541 – 0.550
0.551 – 0.570
0.571 – 0.575
0.576 – 0.590
0.591 – 0.600
0.601 – 0.620
0.621 – 0.625
0.626 – 0.640
0.641 – 0.650
0.651 – 0.670
0.671 – 0.675
0.676 – 0.690
0.691 – 0.700
0.701 – 0.720
0.721 – 0.725
0.726 – 0.740
0.741 – 0.750
0.751 – 0.770
0.771 – 0.775
0.776 – 0.790
0.791 – 0.800
0.801 – 0.820
0.821 – 0.825
0.826 – 0.840
0.841 – 0.850
0.851 – 0.870
0.871 – 0.875
0.876 – 0.890
0.891 – 0.900
0.901 – 0.925
0.926 – 0.950
0.951 – 0.975
0.976 – 1.000
1.001 – 1.025
1.026 – 1.050
1.051 – 1.075

AVAILABLE SHIMS mm (in.)

Shim No.	Thickness	Shim No.	Thickness
02	2.500 (0.0984)	20	2.950 (0.1161)
04	2.550 (0.1004)	22	3.000 (0.1181)
06	2.600 (0.1024)	24	3.050 (0.1201)
08	2.650 (0.1043)	26	3.100 (0.1220)
10	2.700 (0.1063)	28	3.150 (0.1240)
12	2.750 (0.1083)	30	3.200 (0.1260)
14	2.800 (0.1102)	32	3.250 (0.1280)
16	2.850 (0.1122)	34	3.300 (0.1299)
18	2.900 (0.1142)		

Exhaust valve clearance (cold):
0.20 – 0.30 mm (0.008 – 0.012 in.)

Example: A 2.800 mm shim is installed and the measured clearance is 0.450 mm. Replace the 2.800 mm shim with shim No. 22 (3.000 mm).

Exhaust valve shim size selection chart — Prizm

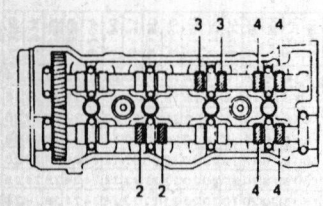

First pass when checking the valve clearance — Prizm DOHC engine

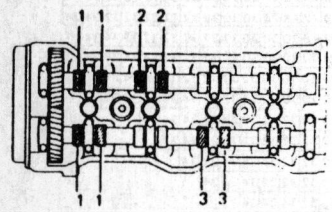

Second pass when checking the valve clearance — Prizm DOHC engine, the camshaft needs to be rotated 360 degrees

ing formula, T = Thickness of the old shim; A = Valve clearance measured; N = Thickness of the new shim.

For the intake side (camshaft nearest to the intake manifold): N = T + (A − 0.008 in. or 0.20mm)

For the exhaust side (camshaft nearest to the exhaust manifold): N = T + (A − 0.10 in. or 0.25mm)

e. Select a shim closest to the calculated thickness. Use the lifter depressor tool to press down the lifter and install the shim. Shims are available in 17 sizes from 0.0984-0.1299 in. (2.50-3.30mm).

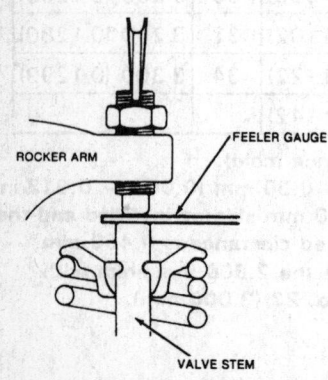

ROCKER ARM

FEELER GAUGE

VALVE STEM

Valve lash adjustment — Spectrum

The standard increment is 0.002 in. (0.05mm).

f. Repeat Steps **a-e** for each valve needing adjustment.

7. Reinstall the valve cover.

8. Check and adjust the timing and idle speed.

Spectrum and Storm

Except DOHC Engine

1. Remove the cylinder head cover.

2. Rotate the engine until the notched line on the crankshaft pulley aligns with the **0** degree mark on the timing gear case. The position of the No. 1 piston should be at TDC of the compression stroke.

NOTE: The notch on the crankshaft pulley should align with the 0 degree mark on the timing gear case. Make sure the rocker arms on the No. 1 cylinder are loose and the rockers on the No. 4 cylinder are tight. If not, turn the crankshaft one complete revolution and align the marks again.

3. The valve lash between the rocker arm the valve stem on the intake and exhaust valves on the No. 1 cylinder, the intake valves on the No. 2 cylinder and the exhaust valves on the No. 3 cylinder. If the valve lash on the intake valves is not 0.006 in. (0.15mm), adjust the valve lash. If the valve lash on the exhaust valve is not 0.010 in. (0.25mm), adjust the valve lash.

4. Adjust the valve lash by loosening the adjusting screw locknut and turning the adjusting screw until the proper specification is obtained. Tighten the adjusting screw locknut.

5. Set the intake valve to 0.006 in. (1.5mm) (cold) for No. 1 and 2 cylinders; exhaust valves to 0.010 in. (0.25mm) (cold) for No. 1 and 3 cylinders.

6. With the engine cold and the piston in No. 4 cylinder is at TDC on compression stroke, set the intake valves to 0.006 in. (1.5mm) for No. 3 and 4 cylinders; exhaust valves to 0.010 in. (0.25mm) for No. 2 and 4 cylinders.

7. After the adjustment has been completed, replace the head cover.

Storm

DOHC ENGINE

1. Disconnect the negative battery cable.

2. Remove the cylinder head cover.

3. Position the No. 1 cylinder at TDC on its compression stroke.

NOTE: The notch on the crankshaft pulley should align with the 0 degree mark on the timing gear case. Make sure the rocker arms on the No. 1 cylinder are loose and the rockers on the No. 4 cylinder are tight. If not, turn the crankshaft one complete revolution and align the marks again.

4. Using a feeler gauge, measure the clearance between the camshaft lobe and the selective shim on the intake and exhaust valves on the No. 1 cylinder, then the intake valves on the No. 2 cylinder and the exhaust valves on the No. 3 cylinder. Note readings.

5. Rotate the crankshaft 360 degrees. Using a feeler gauge, measure the clearance between the camshaft lobe and the selective shim on the intake and exhaust valves on the No. 4 cylinder, then the intake valves on the No. 3 cylinder and the exhaust valves on the No. 2 cylinder. Note readings.

6. The valve clearance obtained on the exhaust valves should be between 0.008-0.012 in. (0.20-0.30mm). If not, replace the selective shim by turning the camshaft lobe downward and installing tool J-38413-2 or J-38413-3 between the camshaft journal and the camshaft lobe next to the selective shim. Turn camshaft lobe upward and remove the selective shim. Install new shim using the selective shim chart.

7. The valve clearance obtained on the intake valves should be between 0.004-0.008 in. (0.10-0.20mm). If not, replace the selective shim by turning the camshaft lobe downward and installing tool J-38413-2 or J-38413-3 between the camshaft journal and the camshaft lobe next to the selective shim. Turn camshaft lobe upward and remove the selective shim. Install new shim using the selective shim chart.

8. Install the cylinder head covers and connect the battery negative cable. Start the engine and check for leaks.

Rocker Arms/Shafts

REMOVAL AND INSTALLATION

Prizm

The DOHC engines (one camshaft for the intake valves and one for the exhaust valves) use direct-acting camshafts; that is, the lobes of the

Intake valve shim size selection chart

Measured clearance (mm)	Measured clearance (inch)	2.52	2.54	2.56	2.58	2.60	2.62	2.64	2.66	2.68	2.70	2.72	2.74	2.76	2.78	2.80	2.82	2.84	2.86	2.88	2.90	2.92	2.94	2.96	2.98	3.00	3.02	3.04	3.06	3.08	3.10	3.12	3.14	3.16	3.18	3.20	3.22	3.24	3.26	3.28	3.30	3.32	3.34	3.36	3.38	3.40	3.42	3.44	3.46	3.48
0.000–0.025	0.000–0.001									1	1	2	2	2	3	3	4	4	4	5	5	6	6	6	7	7	8	8	8	9	9	10	10	10	11	11	12	12	12	13	13	14	14	14	15	15	16	16	16	17
0.026–0.050	0.001–0.002							1	1	1	2	2	3	3	3	4	4	5	5	5	6	6	7	7	7	8	8	9	9	9	10	10	11	11	11	12	12	13	13	13	14	14	15	15	15	16	16	17	17	17
0.051–0.075	0.002–0.003						1	1	1	2	2	3	3	3	4	4	5	5	5	6	6	7	7	7	8	8	9	9	9	10	10	11	11	11	12	12	13	13	13	14	14	15	15	15	16	16	17	17	17	18
0.076–0.100	0.003–0.004					1	1	2	2	2	3	3	4	4	4	5	5	6	6	6	7	7	8	8	8	9	9	10	10	10	11	11	12	12	12	13	13	14	14	14	15	15	16	16	16	17	17	18	18	18
0.101–0.200	0.004–0.008	Replacement not to be required																																																
0.201–0.225	0.008–0.009	2	2	2	3	3	4	4	4	5	5	6	6	6	7	7	8	8	8	9	9	10	10	10	11	11	12	12	12	13	13	14	14	14	15	15	16	16	16	17	17	18	18	18	19	19				
0.226–0.250	0.009–0.010	2	3	3	3	4	4	5	5	5	6	6	7	7	7	8	8	9	9	9	10	10	11	11	11	12	12	13	13	13	14	14	15	15	15	16	16	17	17	17	18	18	19	19	19					
0.251–0.275	0.010–0.011	3	3	3	4	4	5	5	5	6	6	7	7	7	8	8	9	9	9	10	10	11	11	11	12	12	13	13	13	14	14	15	15	15	16	16	17	17	17	18	18	19	19	19						
0.276–0.300	0.011–0.012	3	4	4	4	5	5	6	6	6	7	7	8	8	8	9	9	10	10	10	11	11	12	12	12	13	13	14	14	14	15	15	16	16	16	17	17	18	18	18	19	19								
0.301–0.325	0.012–0.013	4	4	4	5	5	6	6	6	7	7	8	8	8	9	9	10	10	10	11	11	12	12	12	13	13	14	14	14	15	15	16	16	16	17	17	18	18	18	19	19									
0.326–0.350	0.013–0.014	4	5	5	5	6	6	7	7	7	8	8	9	9	9	10	10	11	11	11	12	12	13	13	13	14	14	15	15	15	16	16	17	17	17	18	18	19	19	19										
0.351–0.375	0.014–0.015	5	5	5	6	6	7	7	7	8	8	9	9	9	10	10	11	11	11	12	12	13	13	13	14	14	15	15	15	16	16	17	17	17	18	18	19	19	19											
0.376–0.400	0.015–0.016	5	6	6	6	7	7	8	8	8	9	9	10	10	10	11	11	12	12	12	13	13	14	14	14	15	15	16	16	16	17	17	18	18	18	19	19													
0.401–0.425	0.016–0.017	6	6	6	7	7	8	8	8	9	9	10	10	10	11	11	12	12	12	13	13	14	14	14	15	15	16	16	16	17	17	18	18	18	19	19														
0.426–0.450	0.017–0.018	6	7	7	7	8	8	9	9	9	10	10	11	11	11	12	12	13	13	13	14	14	15	15	15	16	16	17	17	17	18	18	19	19	19															
0.451–0.475	0.018–0.019	7	7	7	8	8	9	9	9	10	10	11	11	11	12	12	13	13	13	14	14	15	15	15	16	16	17	17	17	18	18	19	19	19																
0.476–0.500	0.019–0.020	7	8	8	8	9	9	10	10	10	11	11	12	12	12	13	13	14	14	14	15	15	16	16	16	17	17	18	18	18	19	19																		
0.501–0.525	0.020–0.021	8	8	8	9	9	10	10	10	11	11	12	12	12	13	13	14	14	14	15	15	16	16	16	17	17	18	18	18	19	19																			
0.526–0.550	0.021–0.022	8	9	9	9	10	10	11	11	11	12	12	13	13	13	14	14	15	15	15	16	16	17	17	17	18	18	19	19	19																				
0.551–0.575	0.022–0.023	9	9	9	10	10	11	11	11	12	12	13	13	13	14	14	15	15	15	16	16	17	17	17	18	18	19	19	19																					
0.576–0.600	0.023–0.024	9	10	10	10	11	11	12	12	12	13	13	14	14	14	15	15	16	16	16	17	17	18	18	18	19	19																								
0.601–0.625	0.024–0.025	10	10	10	11	11	12	12	12	13	13	14	14	14	15	15	16	16	16	17	17	18	18	18	19	19																									
0.626–0.650	0.025–0.026	10	11	11	11	12	12	13	13	13	14	14	15	15	15	16	16	17	17	17	18	18	19	19	19																										
0.651–0.675	0.026–0.027	11	11	11	12	12	13	13	13	14	14	15	15	15	16	16	17	17	17	18	18	19	19	19																											
0.676–0.700	0.027–0.028	11	12	12	12	13	13	14	14	14	15	15	16	16	16	17	17	18	18	18	19	19																													
0.701–0.725	0.028–0.029	12	12	12	13	13	14	14	14	15	15	16	16	16	17	17	18	18	18	19	19																														
0.726–0.750	0.029–0.030	12	13	13	13	14	14	15	15	15	16	16	17	17	17	18	18	19	19	19																															
0.751–0.775	0.030–0.031	13	13	13	14	14	15	15	15	16	16	17	17	17	18	18	19	19	19																																
0.776–0.800	0.031–0.032	13	14	14	14	15	15	16	16	16	17	17	18	18	18	19	19																																		
0.801–0.825	0.032–0.033	14	14	14	15	15	16	16	16	17	17	18	18	18	19	19																																			
0.826–0.850	0.033–0.034	14	15	15	15	16	16	17	17	17	18	18	19	19	19																																				
0.851–0.875	0.034–0.035	15	15	15	16	16	17	17	17	18	18	19	19	19																																					
0.876–0.900	0.035–0.036	15	16	16	16	17	17	18	18	18	19	19																																							
0.901–0.925	0.036–0.037	16	16	16	17	17	18	18	18	19	19																																								
0.925–0.950	0.0365–0.0374	16	17	17	17	18	18	19	19	19																																									
0.951–0.975	0.037–0.038	17	17	17	18	18	19	19	19																																										
0.976–1.000	0.038–0.039	17	18	18	18	19	19																																												
1.001–1.025	0.039–0.040	18	18	18	19	19																																													
1.026–1.050	0.040–0.041	18	19	19	19																																														
1.051–1.075	0.041–0.042	19	19	19																																															
1.076–1.100	0.042–0.043	19																																																

Original Adjuster (Shim) Thickness (mm)

Thickness of available adjuster (Shim)

NO in Chart	Thickness (mm)	NO in Chart	Thickness (mm)
1	2.55	11	3.05
2	2.60	12	3.10
3	2.65	13	3.15
4	2.70	14	3.20
5	2.75	15	3.25
6	2.80	16	3.30
7	2.85	17	3.35
8	2.90	18	3.40
9	2.95	19	3.45
10	3.00		

How to use the chart

[Example]
Measured clearance; 0.550mm
Original adjuster thickness; 2.96mm
(Thickness mark (2.96) is printed
on the adjuster surface)

1. Draw straight lines as shown
   in the chart.
2. Select No.17 available adjuster
   to be replaced by finding
   cross point of straight lines.
3. Replace the 2.96mm adjuster
   with No.17 (3.35mm) adjuster.

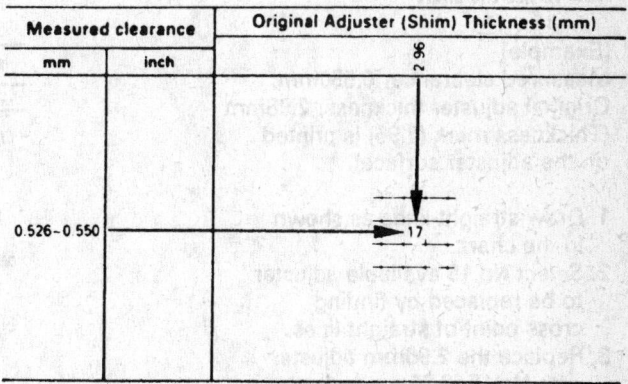

Measured clearance		Original Adjuster (Shim) Thickness (mm)
mm	inch	2.96
0.526–0.550		17

Intake valve shim size selection chart — Storm DOHC engine

Exhaust valve shim size selection chart — Storm DOHC engine

Measured clearance mm	inch	2.52	2.54	2.56	2.58	2.60	2.62	2.64	2.66	2.68	2.70	2.72	2.74	2.76	2.78	2.80	2.82	2.84	2.86	2.88	2.90	2.92	2.94	2.96	2.98	3.00	3.02	3.04	3.06	3.08	3.10	3.12	3.14	3.16	3.18	3.20	3.22	3.24	3.26	3.28	3.30	3.32	3.34	3.36	3.38	3.40	3.42	3.44	3.46	3.48
0.000–0.025	0.000–0.001														1	1	2	2	2	3	3	4	4	4	5	5	6	6	6	7	7	8	8	8	9	9	10	10	10	11	11	12	12	12	13	13	14	14	14	15
0.026–0.050	0.001–0.002												1	1	1	2	2	3	3	3	4	4	5	5	5	6	6	7	7	7	8	8	9	9	9	10	10	11	11	11	12	12	13	13	13	14	14	15	15	15
0.051–0.075	0.002–0.003											1	1	1	2	2	3	3	3	4	4	5	5	5	6	6	7	7	7	8	8	9	9	9	10	10	11	11	11	12	12	13	13	13	14	14	15	15	15	16
0.076–0.100	0.003–0.004										1	1	2	2	2	3	3	4	4	4	5	5	6	6	6	7	7	8	8	8	9	9	10	10	10	11	11	12	12	12	13	13	14	14	14	15	15	16	16	16
0.101–0.125	0.004–0.005									1	1	2	2	2	3	3	4	4	4	5	5	6	6	6	7	7	8	8	8	9	9	10	10	10	11	11	12	12	12	13	13	14	14	14	15	15	16	16	16	17
0.126–0.150	0.005–0.006							1	1	1	2	2	3	3	3	4	4	5	5	5	6	6	7	7	7	8	8	9	9	9	10	10	11	11	11	12	12	13	13	13	14	14	15	15	15	16	16	17	17	17
0.151–0.175	0.006–0.007						1	1	1	2	2	3	3	3	4	4	5	5	5	6	6	7	7	7	8	8	9	9	9	10	10	11	11	11	12	12	13	13	13	14	14	15	15	15	16	16	17	17	17	18
0.176–0.200	0.007–0.008					1	1	2	2	2	3	3	4	4	4	5	5	6	6	6	7	7	8	8	8	9	9	10	10	10	11	11	12	12	12	13	13	14	14	14	15	15	16	16	16	17	17	18	18	18
0.201–0.300	0.008–0.012																				Replacement not to be required																													
0.301–0.325	0.012–0.013	2	2	2	3	3	4	4	4	5	5	6	6	6	7	7	8	8	8	9	9	10	10	10	11	11	12	12	12	13	13	14	14	14	15	15	16	16	16	17	17	18	18	18	19	19				
0.326–0.350	0.013–0.014	2	3	3	3	4	4	5	5	5	6	6	7	7	7	8	8	9	9	9	10	10	11	11	11	12	12	13	13	13	14	14	15	15	15	16	16	17	17	17	18	18	19	19	19					
0.351–0.375	0.014–0.015	3	3	3	4	4	5	5	5	6	6	7	7	7	8	8	9	9	9	10	10	11	11	11	12	12	13	13	13	14	14	15	15	15	16	16	17	17	17	18	18	19	19	19						
0.376–0.400	0.015–0.016	3	4	4	4	5	5	6	6	6	7	7	8	8	8	9	9	10	10	10	11	11	12	12	12	13	13	14	14	14	15	15	16	16	16	17	17	18	18	18	19	19								
0.401–0.425	0.016–0.017	4	4	4	5	5	6	6	6	7	7	8	8	8	9	9	10	10	10	11	11	12	12	12	13	13	14	14	14	15	15	16	16	16	17	17	18	18	18	19	19									
0.426–0.450	0.017–0.018	4	5	5	5	6	6	7	7	7	8	8	9	9	9	10	10	11	11	11	12	12	13	13	13	14	14	15	15	15	16	16	17	17	17	18	18	19	19	19										
0.451–0.475	0.018–0.019	5	5	5	6	6	7	7	7	8	8	9	9	9	10	10	11	11	11	12	12	13	13	13	14	14	15	15	15	16	16	17	17	17	18	18	19	19	19											
0.476–0.500	0.019–0.020	5	6	6	6	7	7	8	8	8	9	9	10	10	10	11	11	12	12	12	13	13	14	14	14	15	15	16	16	16	17	17	18	18	18	19	19													
0.501–0.525	0.020–0.021	6	6	6	7	7	8	8	8	9	9	10	10	10	11	11	12	12	12	13	13	14	14	14	15	15	16	16	16	17	17	18	18	18	19	19														
0.526–0.550	0.021–0.022	6	7	7	7	8	8	9	9	9	10	10	11	11	11	12	12	13	13	13	14	14	15	15	15	16	16	17	17	17	18	18	19	19	19															
0.551–0.575	0.022–0.023	7	7	7	8	8	9	9	9	10	10	11	11	11	12	12	13	13	13	14	14	15	15	15	16	16	17	17	17	18	18	19	19	19																
0.576–0.600	0.023–0.024	7	8	8	8	9	9	10	10	10	11	11	12	12	12	13	13	14	14	14	15	15	16	16	16	17	17	18	18	18	19	19																		
0.601–0.625	0.024–0.025	8	8	8	9	9	10	10	10	11	11	12	12	12	13	13	14	14	14	15	15	16	16	16	17	17	18	18	18	19	19																			
0.626–0.650	0.025–0.026	8	9	9	9	10	10	11	11	11	12	12	13	13	13	14	14	15	15	15	16	16	17	17	17	18	18	19	19	19																				
0.651–0.675	0.026–0.027	9	9	9	10	10	11	11	11	12	12	13	13	13	14	14	15	15	15	16	16	17	17	17	18	18	19	19	19																					
0.676–0.700	0.027–0.028	9	10	10	10	11	11	12	12	12	13	13	14	14	14	15	15	16	16	16	17	17	18	18	18	19	19																							
0.701–0.725	0.028–0.029	10	10	10	11	11	12	12	12	13	13	14	14	14	15	15	16	16	16	17	17	18	18	18	19	19																								
0.726–0.750	0.029–0.030	10	11	11	11	12	12	13	13	13	14	14	15	15	15	16	16	17	17	17	18	18	19	19	19																									
0.751–0.775	0.030–0.031	11	11	11	12	12	13	13	13	14	14	15	15	15	16	16	17	17	17	18	18	19	19	19																										
0.776–0.800	0.031–0.032	11	12	12	12	13	13	14	14	14	15	15	16	16	16	17	17	18	18	18	19	19																												
0.801–0.825	0.032–0.033	12	12	12	13	13	14	14	14	15	15	16	16	16	17	17	18	18	18	19	19																													
0.826–0.850	0.033–0.034	12	13	13	13	14	14	15	15	15	16	16	17	17	17	18	18	19	19	19																														
0.851–0.875	0.034–0.035	13	13	13	14	14	15	15	15	16	16	17	17	17	18	18	19	19	19																															
0.876–0.900	0.035–0.036	13	14	14	14	15	15	16	16	16	17	17	18	18	18	19	19																																	
0.901–0.925	0.036–0.037	14	14	14	15	15	16	16	16	17	17	18	18	18	19	19																																		
0.926–0.950	0.0365–0.0374	14	15	15	15	16	16	17	17	17	18	18	19	19	19																																			
0.951–0.975	0.037–0.038	15	15	15	16	16	17	17	17	18	18	19	19	19																																				
0.976–1.000	0.038–0.039	15	16	16	16	17	17	18	18	18	19	19																																						
1.001–1.025	0.039–0.040	16	16	16	17	17	18	18	18	19	19																																							
1.026–1.050	0.040–0.041	16	17	17	17	18	18	19	19	19																																								
1.051–1.075	0.041–0.042	17	17	17	18	18	19	19	19																																									
1.076–1.100	0.042–0.043	17	18	18	18	19	19																																											
1.101–1.125	0.043–0.044	18	18	18	19	19																																												
1.126–1.150	0.044–0.045	18	19	19	19																																													
1.151–1.175	0.045–0.046	19	19	19																																														
1.176–1.200	0.046–0.047	19																																																

Thickness of available adjuster (Shim)

NO in Chart	Thickness (mm)	NO in Chart	Thickness (mm)
1	2.55	11	3.05
2	2.60	12	3.10
3	2.65	13	3.15
4	2.70	14	3.20
5	2.75	15	3.25
6	2.80	16	3.30
7	2.85	17	3.35
8	2.90	18	3.40
9	2.95	19	3.45
10	3.00		

Note; Thickness mark is printed on the surface to be contacted with tappet.

How to use the chart

[Example]
Measured clearance; 0.550mm
Original adjuster thickness; 2.96mm
(Thickness mark (2.96) is printed on the adjuster surface)

1. Draw straight lines as shown in the chart.
2. Select No.15 available adjuster to be replaced by finding cross point of straight lines.
3. Replace the 2.96mm adjuster with No.15 (3.25mm) adjuster.

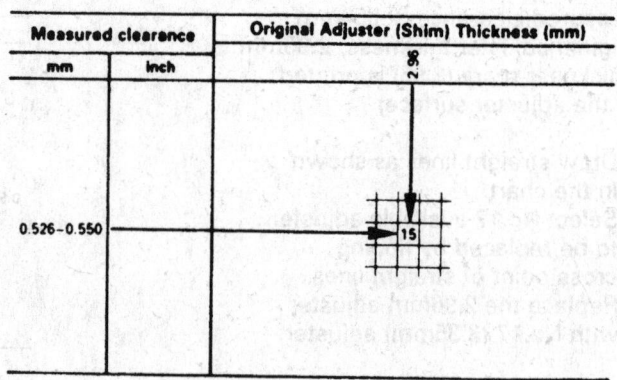

Measured clearance mm	inch	Original Adjuster (Shim) Thickness (mm) 2.96
0.526–0.550		15

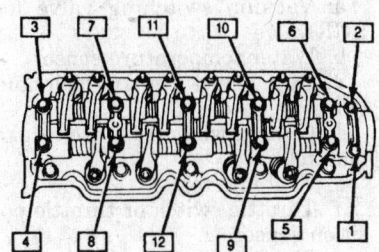

Rocker arm shaft bolt removal sequence — Storm SOHC engine

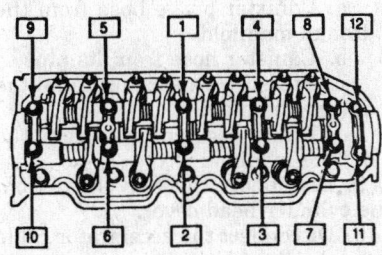

Rocker arm shaft bolt torque sequence — Storm SOHC engine

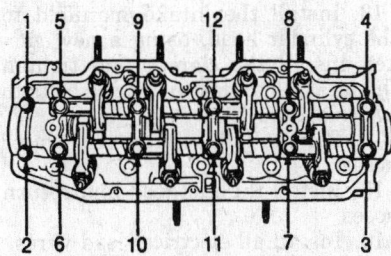

Rocker arm shaft bolt torque sequence — Spectrum

camshaft act directly on the valve mechanism. These engines do not have rocker arms.

Storm

1. Disconnect the battery negative cable.
2. Remove the cylinder head valve cover.
3. Remove the rocker arm bracket bolts in the proper order.
4. Remove the rocker shaft/arm assembly from the vehicle.
5. Remove the rocker arms from the rocker shaft.

To install:

6. Apply a light coat of engine oil to the rocker arm brackets.
7. Install the rocker arms on the rocker arm shafts.
8. Install the rocker arm shafts on the engine with the ID marks toward the front of the engine.
9. Apply a suitable silicone sealant to the No. 1 and No. 5 rocker brackets.
10. Install the rocker arm brackets. Torque the rocker arm bracket bolts in sequence to 16 ft. lbs. (22 Nm).
11. Adjust the valves and install the cylinder head cover. Reconnect the battery negative cable.

Spectrum

1. Disconnect the negative battery terminal from the battery. Remove the PCV hoses.
2. Remove the spark plug wires from the mounting clip.
3. Remove the ground wire from the right rear side of the head cover.
4. Support the engine and remove the right side engine mounting rubber, bolts and plate.
5. Remove the mounting bracket on the timing cover.
6. Remove the 4 bolts holding the timing cover and the 2 bolts holding the cylinder head cover.

7. Loosen the timing cover and remove the cylinder head cover.

NOTE: If the cylinder head cover sticks, strike the end of the cover with a rubber mallet.

8. Remove the rocker arm bracket bolts in sequence, work from both ends equally, toward the middle.
9. Remove the rocker arm shafts and then the rocker arms from the shafts.
10. Using the proper tool, clean the sealing surfaces of the cover and the cylinder head.

To install:

11. To install, apply sealer to the sealing surfaces and reverse the removal procedures.

NOTE: The rocker arm shafts are different from each other, make sure they are installed in the same position that they were removed. Install the rocker arms with the identification marks toward the front of the engine. Apply sealant to the bracket and cylinder head mating surfaces of the front and rear rocker brackets.

12. To complete the installation, mount the rocker assemblies securely to the dowel pins on the cylinder head. Torque the rocker arm bolts to

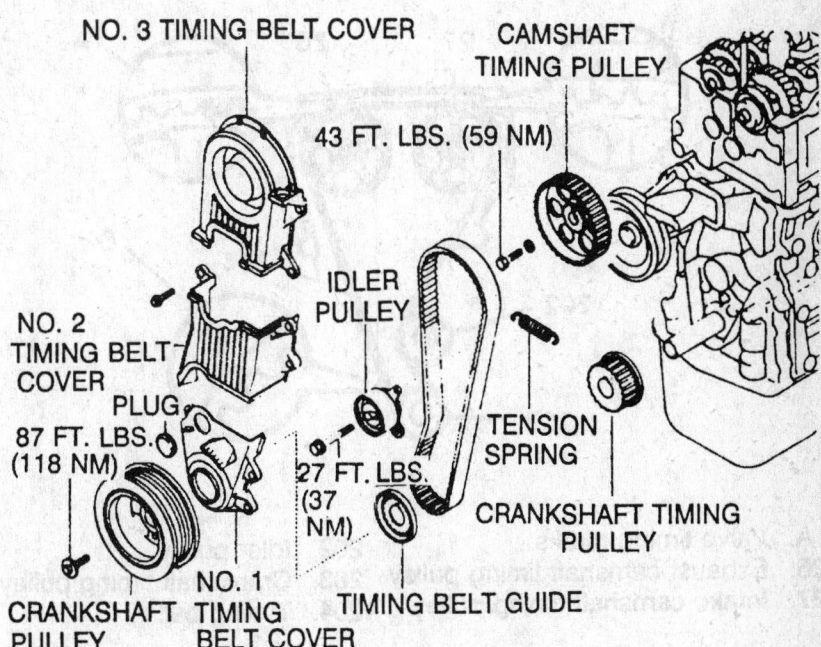

Exploded view of the timing belt assembly — Prizm

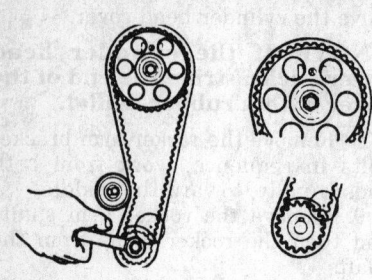

Mark the timing belt and camshaft timing gear — Prizm (engine code 6)

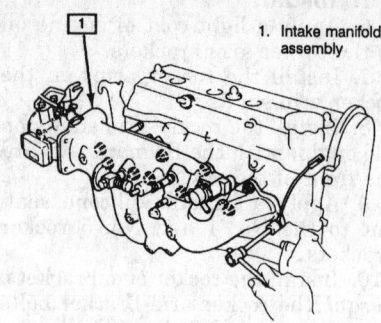

1. Intake manifold assembly

Intake manifold assembly — 1990-92 Prizm

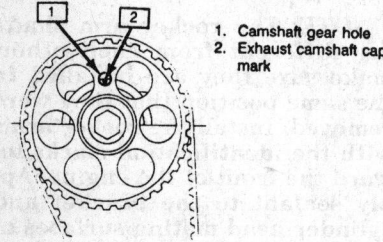

1. Camshaft gear hole
2. Exhaust camshaft cap mark

Aligning the camshaft gear hole and exhaust camshaft cap mark — Prizm (engine code 6)

16 ft. lbs. (22 Nm). Start the engine and check for leaks.

Intake Manifold

REMOVAL AND INSTALLATION

Metro

1. Relieve the fuel system pressure.
2. Disconnect the negative battery cable.
3. Drain the cooling system.
4. Remove the air cleaner assembly.

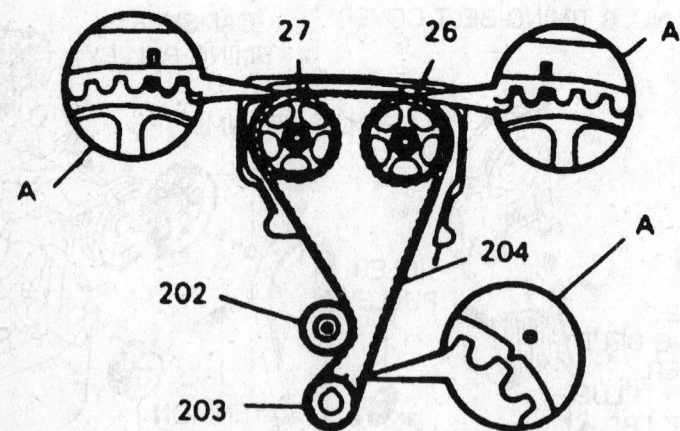

A. Valve timing marks
26. Exhaust camshaft timing pulley
27. Intake camshaft timing pulley
202. Idler pulley
203. Crankshaft timing pulley
204. Timing belt

Aligning the valve timing marks — 1990-92 Prizm (engine code 5)

5. Disconnect the following wires:
   a. Vacuum switching valve for EGR valve
   b. Water temperature sensor
   c. Idle speed control solenoid valve
   d. Ground wires from the intake manifold
   e. Fuel injector
   f. Throttle switch or throttle position sensor
   g. Water temperature gauge
6. Disconnect the fuel return and feed hoses from the throttle body.
7. Disconnect the water hoses from the throttle body and the intake manifold.
8. Disconnect the following hoses:
   a. Canister purge hose from the intake manifold
   b. Canister hose from its pipe
   c. Pressure sensor hose from the intake manifold
   d. Brake booster hose from the intake manifold
9. Disconnect the PCV hose from the cylinder head cover.
10. Disconnect the accelerator cable from the throttle body.
11. Disconnect any other lines and cables, as necessary.
12. Remove the intake manifold with the throttle body from the cylinder head.

To install:

13. Install the intake manifold to the cylinder head, using a new gasket, install the clamps and tighten the intake manifold retaining bolts to 17 ft. lbs. (23 Nm).
14. Reinstall all vacuum and water hoses.
15. Install the fuel feed and return hoses.
16. Install all electrical lead wires.
17. Install the accelerator cable to the throttle body.
18. Install the air cleaner assembly.
19. Fill the cooling system and reconnect the negative battery cable.

Prizm

1990

1. Disconnect the negative battery cable.
2. Drain the cooling system.
3. Remove the air cleaner assembly.
4. Label and disconnect the vacuum hoses at the manifold.
5. Label and disconnect the wiring to the throttle position sensor, the cold start injector, the injector connectors, the air control valve and the vacuum sensor.
6. Disconnect the cold start injector pipe.

―――――― **CAUTION** ――――――

The fuel system is under pressure. Release pressure slowly and contain spillage. Observe no smoking/no open flame precautions. Have a Class B-C (dry powder) fire extinguisher within arm's reach at all times.

7. Disconnect the water hose from the air valve.

8. Raise and safely support the vehicle.

9. Remove the intake manifold support bracket. Lower the vehicle to the ground.

10. Remove the 7 bolts, 2 nuts and the ground cable. Remove the intake manifold and its gaskets.

To install:

11. Measure the intake manifold mating surface with a precision straightedge and a feeler gauge. If the warpage exceeds 0.008 in. (0.2mm), the manifold must be replaced.

12. To reassemble, install the manifold with new gaskets in position. Attach the 7 bolts, 2 nuts and the ground cable connector.

13. Raise and safely support the car; install the manifold support bracket and its bolts. Lower the vehicle to the ground.

14. Tighten the manifold mounting nuts and bolts evenly to 14 ft. lbs. (19 Nm).

15. Connect the water hose to the air valve.

16. Connect the fuel line to the cold-start injector.

17. Connect the wiring to the throttle position sensor, the cold start injector, the injector connectors, the air control valve and the vacuum sensor.

18. Observing the labels made earlier, install the vacuum lines. Be careful of the routing and make sure each line fits snugly on its port. Double check each line for crimps or twists.

19. Connect the accelerator and throttle valve (automatic transaxle) cables to their brackets.

20. Refill the coolant.

21. Install the air cleaner assembly and connect the negative battery cable.

1991-92

1. Disconnect the negative battery cable.

2. Drain the cooling system.

3. Remove the air cleaner assembly.

4. Remove the upper radiator hose at the engine.

5. Disconnect the accelerator cable and, on automatic transaxles, the throttle valve cable.

6. Label and disconnect vacuum hoses at the manifolds.

7. Disconnect and remove the fuel delivery pipe (fuel rail) and remove the injectors. During removal, be careful not to drop the injectors.

―――――― **CAUTION** ――――――

The fuel system is under pressure. Release pressure slowly and contain spillage. Observe no smoking/no open flame precautions. Have a Class B-C (dry powder) fire extinguisher within arm's reach at all times.

8. Disconnect the vacuum hose to the brake booster and remove the heat shield(s) from the manifold(s).

9. Raise the vehicle and support it safely.

10. Disconnect the wire for the water temperature sensor and remove the water outlet housing (thermostat housing) and the bypass pipe.

11. Remove the exhaust bracket and disconnect the exhaust pipe at the manifold. Remove the support bracket for the intake manifold.

12. Lower the vehicle to the ground.

13. Remove the intake manifold with the air control valve and gaskets and/or remove the exhaust manifold with its gaskets.

14. Using a precision straightedge and a feeler gauge, check the mating surfaces of the manifolds for warpage. If the warpage is greater than the maximum allowable specification, replace the manifold. **Maximum allowable warpage:**

Intake Manifold: 0.002 in. (0.05mm)

Exhaust Manifold: 0.012 in. (0.30mm)

Air Control Valve: 0.002 in. (0.05mm)

To install:

15. When reinstalling, always use new gaskets and make sure they are properly positioned. Place the manifold(s) in position and loosely install the nuts and bolts until all are just snug. Double check the placement of the manifold(s) and in 2 passes, tighten the retaining nuts and bolts. The exhaust manifold retaining bolts should be tightened to 18 ft. lbs. (25 Nm) and the intake manifold bolts should be tightened to 20 ft. lbs. (27 Nm). The bolts for the intake support bracket should also be tightened to 20 ft. lbs. (27 Nm).

16. With the manifold(s) in place, elevate and support the vehicle; install the support bracket for the intake manifold and connect the exhaust pipe to the exhaust manifold. Attach the exhaust bracket.

17. Install the bypass pipe, the water outlet housing and connect the wiring to the water temperature sensor.

18. Lower the vehicle to the ground and install the heat shield(s) on the manifolds.

19. Connect the vacuum hose for the brake vacuum booster.

20. Install the fuel delivery pipe and the injectors. Tighten the mounting bolts to 13 ft. lbs. (18 Nm).

21. Observing the labels made earlier, install the vacuum lines. Be careful of the routing and make sure each line fits snugly on its port.

22. Double check each line for crimps or twists.

23. Connect the accelerator cable and throttle valve cable (automatic transaxle)

24. Reconnect the upper radiator hose.

25. Install the air cleaner assembly.

26. Refill the coolant.

27. Connect the negative battery cable.

1993-94

1. Relieve fuel system pressure.

2. Disconnect accelerator cable and cruise control cable, if equipped.

3. Disconnect the intake air temperature sensor.

4. Disconnect the air cleaner hose from the throttle body.

5. Remove the air cleaner lid with the hose attached.

6. If equipped with an automatic transaxle, disconnect the transaxle throttle cable.

7. Disconnect 1 evaporative emissions hose, throttle position sensor connector, idle air control valve connector, 2 bolts, 2 nuts and throttle body from the intake manifold.

8. Remove the throttle body gasket and air pipe.

9. On vehicles with California emissions, remove EGR valve, pipe modulator, bracket and hoses.

10. Remove the vacuum hose from the fuel pressure regulator and the PCV hose.

11. Remove 2 nuts, 3 Allen® head screws, plenum chamber cover and gasket.

12. Disconnect fuel injector connectors.

13. Place a shop towel or a container under the fuel feed hose-to-fuel rail connection.

14. Remove 1 bolt and fuel feed hose from the fuel rail.

15. Place a shop towel or a container under the fuel return hose-to-fuel rail connection and disconnect the fuel return hose.

16. Remove 2 bolts and fuel rail with fuel injectors attached.

17. Remove and discard the 4 insulators and 2 spacers from intake manifold.

18. Remove 7 bolts, ground strap, 2 nuts, intake manifold and gasket.

19. If necessary, clean mating surfaces of gasket and sealant materials.

To install:

20. Install the intake manifold with new gasket, 2 nuts, 7 bolts, ground strap and torque to 14 ft. lbs. (19 Nm).

21. Install 4 new insulators and 2 new spacers to intake manifold.

22. Install the fuel rail with injectors to the intake manifold and hand tighten the bolts. Make certain each injector can be smoothly rotated. If they do not rotate smoothly, the O-ring is not in its correct position.

23. Torque the fuel rail bolts to 11 ft. lbs. (15 Nm).

24. Connect the fuel return hose and fuel injector connectors.

25. Install the plenum chamber cover with new gasket and torque 2 nuts and 3 Allen® screws to 14 ft. lbs. (19 Nm).

26. Install the vacuum hose to the fuel pressure regulator and the PCV hose.

27. On vehicles with California emissions, install EGR valve, pipe modulator, bracket and hoses.

28. Install fuel feed hose to fuel rail, using new gaskets and torque the bolt to 21 ft. lbs. (28 Nm).

29. Install a new throttle body gasket and throttle body. Torque nuts and bolts to 16 ft. lbs. (22 Nm).

30. Connect idle air control valve, throttle position sensor, evaporative emissions hose and automatic transaxle throttle cable, if equipped.

31. Install air cleaner lid and hose.

32. Install accelerator cable and cruise control cable, if equipped.

33. Install the negative battery cable.

34. Turn the ignition switch to the **ON** position and back to the **LOCK** position to pressurize the fuel system and check for leaks.

Storm

EXCEPT DOHC ENGINE

1. Disconnect the battery negative cable and the ignition coil wire.

2. Properly relieve the fuel system pressure. Disconnect the accelerator cable from the throttle valve and the intake manifold (common chamber).

3. Disconnect the 2 cable harness connectors, located near the left shock tower.

4. Disconnect the cable harness from the MAT sensor, then the TPS sensor and the intake air control valve.

5. Remove the intake air duct from the throttle valve, then the PCV hose from the cylinder head cover.

6. Disconnect the EGR valve and canister vacuum hoses from the throttle valve.

7. Disconnect the EGR pipe from the EGR valve and the exhaust manifold.

8. Remove the intake manifold (common chamber) bracket bolt, then the throttle valve assembly bolts and the throttle valve.

9. Remove the coolant bypass pipe clip bolt, then disconnect the MAP sensor from the intake manifold (common chamber).

10. Disconnect the brake booster vacuum hose, then the canister vacuum hose from the intake manifold (common chamber) and the throttle valve.

11. Disconnect the pressure regulator vacuum hose from the common chamber, then the EGR vacuum hose.

12. Remove the engine hanger bolt, then the intake manifold (common chamber) attaching nuts and bolts. Remove the intake manifold (common chamber) from the vehicle.

To install:

13. Install the intake manifold (common chamber) and a new gasket onto the induction port. Torque nuts and bolts to 17 ft. lbs. (23 Nm).

14. Install the coolant bypass pipe clip bolts.

15. Install the throttle valve with a new gasket. Torque throttle valve bolts to 17 ft. lbs. (23 Nm).

16. Connect the EGR pipe flange to the exhaust manifold. Torque flange bolts to 17 ft. lbs. (23 Nm).

17. Connect the EGR vacuum hose, then the pressure regulator vacuum hose to the intake manifold (common chamber).

18. Connect the canister vacuum hose to the common chamber and the throttle valve, then the breather hose to the intake air duct.

19. Connect the cable harness to the MAT sensor, TPS and the intake air control valve.

20. Connect the 2 cable harness connectors, located near the left shock tower.

21. Connect the accelerator cable to the throttle valve and to the intake manifold (common chamber).

22. Connect the ignition coil wire. Connect the battery negative cable and fill cooling system. Start engine and check for leaks.

1990-91 DOHC ENGINE

1. Disconnect the battery negative cable.

2. Disconnect the accelerator cable clip and the PCV hose from the intake air duct.

3. Disconnect the accelerator cable from the throttle valve.

4. Disconnect the MAP sensor hose from the MAP sensor if equipped, then the vacuum hose form the brake vacuum booster.

5. Disconnect the 2 canister hoses from intake manifold (common chamber).

6. Remove the canister pipe bracket from the intake manifold (common chamber).

7. Disconnect the vacuum hose from the fuel pressure regulator, then the vacuum hose from the induction port.

8. Remove the throttle valve from the intake manifold (common chamber).

9. Remove the alternator harness clip, then the 3 fuel injector harness cable clips.

10. Loosen the EGR pipe bracket on the exhaust manifold and the EGR clip on the thermostat housing.

11. Remove the 2 intake manifold (common chamber) bracket attaching bolts, located on the left side of the engine and the engine hanger bolt, located on the right side of the intake manifold (common chamber).

12. Remove the intake manifold (common chamber) attaching nuts and bolts, then remove the intake manifold (common chamber) from the induction port assembly.

To install:

13. Install the intake manifold (common chamber) with a new gasket onto the induction port assembly. Torque nuts and bolts to 17 ft. lbs. (23 Nm).

14. Install the intake manifold (common chamber) bracket bolts, located on the left side of the engine and the hanger bolt, located on the right side of the engine.

15. Install the EGR pipe bracket bolts on the exhaust manifold and the EGR clip on the thermostat housing. Torque EGR bracket bolts to 32 ft. lbs. (44 Nm).

16. Install the alternator harness cable clip, then the 3 fuel injector harness cable clips.

17. Install the throttle valve onto the intake manifold (common cham-

Exhaust Manifold

1. Exhaust manifold
2. Gasket
3. No. 1 pipe
4. Pipe Seal
5. Oxygen sensor
6. Cover

| 5 | OXYGEN SENSOR |
| 6 | COVER |

Intake manifold assembly — Storm 1.8L engine

REMOVAL AND INSTALLATION

Metro

1. Disconnect the negative battery cable.
2. Remove the exhaust pipe from the exhaust manifold.
3. Remove the manifold retaining bolts and remove the exhaust manifold and gaskets.
4. Reverse procedure to install. Install a new manifold gasket and torque the bolts to 17 ft. lbs. (23 Nm). Reconnect the oxygen sensor coupler and the battery negative cable.

Prizm

1. Disconnect the negative battery cable.
2. Remove the 5 bolts and remove the upper heat shield (insulator) from the manifold.
3. Raise and safely support the vehicle.
4. Disconnect the exhaust pipe from the exhaust manifold and remove the manifold support and its 2 bolts.
5. Lower the vehicle to the ground. Disconnect the oxygen sensor wire.
6. Remove the 2 nuts and 3 bolts holding the manifold to the engine. Remove the manifold and its gaskets. When the manifold is clear of the vehicle, remove the lower heat shield.
7. Measure the exhaust manifold mating surface with a precision straightedge and a feeler gauge. If the warpage exceeds 0.010 in. (0.28mm), the manifold must be replaced.
   To install:
8. Before reinstalling, attach the lower heat shield to the manifold with the 3 bolts. Tighten the bolts to 18 ft. lbs. (25 Nm).
9. Install the manifold with new gaskets and tighten its bolts and nuts to 18 ft. lbs. (25 Nm).
10. Raise the vehicle and safely support. Install the manifold support and tighten the bolts to 18 ft. lbs. (25 Nm).
11. Connect the exhaust pipe to the manifold with new gaskets and tighten the bolts to 18 ft. lbs. (25 Nm).
12. Lower the vehicle to the ground. Install the upper heat shield on the manifold and tighten its 5 bolts to 18 ft. lbs. (25 Nm).
13. Connect the wiring to the oxygen sensors.
14. Connect the negative battery cable.

ber), then connect the induction control valve vacuum hose.
18. Connect the fuel pressure regulator vacuum hose to the intake manifold (common chamber).
19. Connect the canister pipe bracket onto the intake manifold (common chamber).
20. Connect the brake booster vacuum hose, then the MAP sensor hose to the MAP sensor.
21. Connect the accelerator cable clip to the intake air duct.
22. Connect the battery negative cable and fill cooling system. Start engine and check for leaks.

Spectrum

1. Disconnect the negative battery terminal from the battery. Drain the cooling system.
2. Remove the bolt securing the alternator adjusting plate to the engine.
3. Disconnect and label all of the hoses attached to the air cleaner and remove the air cleaner.
4. Disconnect the air inlet temperature switch wiring connector.
5. Disconnect and label the hoses, electrical connectors and control cable attached to the carburetor.
6. If equipped with air conditioning, disconnect the FIDC vacuum

hose, the pressure tank control valve hose, the distributor 3-way connector hose and the VSV wiring connector.
7. Remove the carburetor attaching bolts, located beneath the intake manifold, then remove the carburetor and the EFE heater.
8. At the intake manifold, remove the PCV hose, the water bypass hose, the heater hoses, the EGR valve/canister hose, the distributor vacuum advance hose and the ground wires.
9. Disconnect the thermometer unit switch wiring connector.
10. Remove the intake manifold attaching nuts/bolts and the intake manifold.
11. Clean the sealing surfaces of the intake manifold and cylinder head.
   To install:
12. Use new gaskets and install the manifold.
13. Torque the intake manifold to 17 ft. lbs. (23 Nm); then adjust the engine control cable and the alternator belt tension. Refill the engine with coolant and check for leaks.
14. Installation is the reverse of removal.

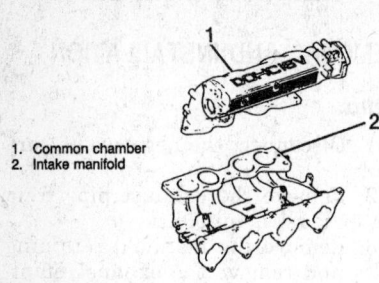

1. Common chamber
2. Intake manifold

Exhaust manifold components — Metro

Storm

1. Disconnect the battery negative cable.

2. Remove the heat protector, then disconnect the oxygen sensor electrical connector.

3. If equipped with DOHC engine, disconnect the EGR pipe clip from the thermostat housing.

4. Disconnect the EGR pipe from the exhaust manifold and the EGR valve.

5. Remove the front exhaust pipe from the exhaust manifold.

6. Remove the exhaust manifold attaching nuts and bolts, then remove the exhaust manifold from the engine.

To install:

7. Reverse procedure to install. Using the proper tool, clean the gasket mounting surfaces. Inspect the exhaust manifold for damage and/or warpage; maximum warpage is 0.0157 in. (0.4mm), if the warpage is greater, replace the exhaust manifold.

8. Torque exhaust manifold attaching nuts and bolts to 30 ft. lbs. (41 Nm) and the EGR pipe bolts to 32 ft. lbs. (44 Nm).

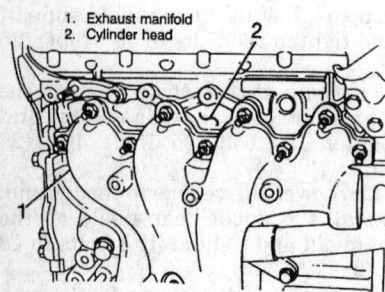

1. Exhaust manifold
2. Cylinder head

Exhaust manifold assembly — Storm 1.8L engine

Spectrum

1. Disconnect the negative battery terminal from the battery and the oxygen sensor wiring connector.

2. Disconnect the Thermostatic Air Cleaner (TAC) flex hose.

3. Remove the hot air cover and raise the vehicle.

4. Disconnect the exhaust pipe from the exhaust manifold and lower the vehicle.

5. Remove the nuts and bolts securing the exhaust manifold to the cylinder head. Clean the gasket mounting surfaces.

6. To install, use new gaskets and reverse the removal procedures. Torque the exhaust manifold to 17 ft. lbs. (23 Nm). Start the engine and check for leaks.

Timing Belt Front Cover

REMOVAL AND INSTALLATION

Metro

1. Disconnect the negative battery cable.

2. Raise and support the vehicle safely.

3. Remove the fender apron extension on the right side. Remove the clip after pushing the center pin.

4. Remove the water pump belt and its pulley. Loosen the generator pivot bolts and remove the water bolt.

5. Remove the crankshaft pulley by removing the pulley bolts. It is not necessary to loosen the crankshaft timing belt pulley bolt at the center.

6. Remove the timing belt outside cover.

7. To install, reverse the removal procedures.

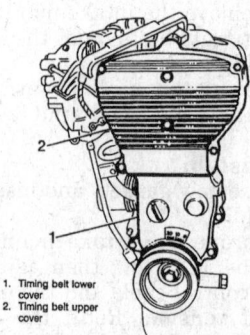

1. Timing belt lower cover
2. Timing belt upper cover

View of the timing belt covers — Storm 1.8L engine

Prizm

1990

1. Disconnect the negative battery cable.

2. Elevate the vehicle and safely support it.

3. Remove the right splash shield under the vehicle.

4. Lower the vehicle. Remove the wiring harness from the upper timing belt cover.

5. Depending on equipment, loosen the air conditioner compressor, the power steering pump and the alternator on their adjusting bolts. Remove the drive belts.

6. Remove the crankshaft pulley. The use of a counter holding tool such as J-8614-01 or similar is highly recommended.

7. Remove the valve cover.

8. Remove the windshield washer reservoir.

9. Elevate and safely support the vehicle.

10. Support the engine either from above (Tool 28467-A or chain hoist) or below (floor jack and wood block) and remove the through bolt at the right engine mount.

11. Remove the protectors on the mount nuts and studs for the center and rear transaxle mounts.

12. Remove the 2 rear transaxle mount-to-main crossmember nuts. Remove the 2 center transaxle mount-to-center crossmember nuts.

13. Carefully elevate the engine enough to gain access to the water pump pulley.

14. Remove the water pump pulley. Lower the engine to its normal position.

15. Remove the 4 bolts and the lower timing cover. Remove the center timing cover and its bolt, then the upper cover with its 4 bolts.

16. If further work is to be done, the vehicle may be lowered to the ground but the engine must remain supported until the mount(s) are reinstalled.

To install:

17. When reinstalling, make certain that the gaskets and their mating surfaces are clean and free from dirt and oil. The gasket itself must be free of cuts and deformations and must fit securely in the grooves of the covers.

18. Install the covers and the bolts; tighten the bolts to 3.6 ft. lbs. (5 Nm).

19. Elevate the engine and install the water pump pulley.

20. Lower the engine to its normal position. Install the through bolt in the right engine mount and tighten it

to 64 ft. lbs. (87 Nm) with the bolt secure, the engine lifting apparatus may be removed.

21. Install the valve cover.

22. Install the crankshaft pulley and tighten its bolt to 87 ft. lbs. (118 Nm).

23. Reinstall the air conditioning compressor, the power steering pump and the alternator. Install their belts and adjust them to the correct tension.

24. Reconnect the wiring harness to the upper timing belt cover.

25. Raise the vehicle and safely support it.

26. Install the 2 nuts on the center transaxle mount and the rear transaxle mount. Tighten all the nuts to 45 ft. lbs. (61 Nm).

27. Install the protectors on the nuts and studs.

28. Install the splash shield under the vehicle.

29. Lower the vehicle to the ground.

30. Install the windshield washer reservoir and connect the negative battery cable.

1991-94

1. Disconnect the negative battery cable.

2. Elevate the vehicle and safely support it on jackstands.

3. Remove the right front wheel.

4. Remove the splash shield from under the vehicle.

5. Drain the coolant into clean containers. Close the drain cocks when the system is empty.

6. Lower the vehicle to the ground. Disconnect the accelerator cable and, if equipped, the cruise control cable.

7. Remove the cruise control actuator, if equipped.

8. Carefully remove the ignition coil.

9. Disconnect the radiator hose at the water outlet.

10. Remove the power steering drive belt and the alternator drive belt.

11. Remove the spark plugs.

12. Rotate the crankshaft clockwise and set the engine to TDC compression on No. 1 cylinder. Align the crankshaft marks at 0; look through the oil filler hole and make sure the small hole in the end of the camshaft can be seen.

13. Raise and safely support the vehicle. Disconnect the center engine mount.

14. Lower the vehicle to the ground.

15. Support the engine either from above or below. Disconnect the right engine mount from the engine.

16. Raise the engine and remove the mount.

17. Remove the water pump pulley.

18. Remove the crankshaft pulley. The use of a counter holding tool such as J-8614-01 or similar is highly recommended.

19. Remove the 10 bolts and remove the timing belt covers with their gaskets.

NOTE: The bolts are different lengths; they must be returned to their correct location at reassembly. Label or diagram the bolts during removal.

20. When reinstalling, make certain that the gaskets and their mating surfaces are clean and free from dirt and oil. The gasket itself must be free of cuts and deformations and must fit securely in the grooves of the covers.

To install:

21. Reinstall the covers and their gaskets and the 10 bolts in their proper positions.

22. Install the crankshaft pulley, again using the counter holding tool. Tighten the bolt to 87 ft. lbs. (118 Nm).

23. Install the water pump pulley.

24. Install the right engine mount. Tighten the through bolt to 64 ft. lbs. (87 Nm).

25. Reinstall the spark plugs and their wires.

26. Install the alternator drive belt and the power steering drive belt. Adjust the belts to the correct tension.

27. Connect the radiator hose to the water outlet port.

28. Install the ignition coil.

29. Install the cruise control actuator and the cruise control cable, if equipped.

30. Connect the accelerator cable.

31. Refill the cooling system with the correct amount of anti-freeze and water.

32. Connect the negative battery cable.

33. Start the engine and check for leaks. Allow the engine to warm up and check the work areas carefully for seepage.

34. Install the splash shield under the vehicle.

35. Install the right front wheel.

Storm

EXCEPT DOHC ENGINE

1. Disconnect the battery negative cable.

2. Remove the alternator belt, then the power steering belt.

3. Using tool J-28467-A or equivalent, support the engine.

4. Remove the right engine mount.

5. Remove the timing belt cover attaching screws, then the timing belt cover from the vehicle.

6. Reverse procedure to install. Connect the battery negative cable.

DOHC ENGINE

1. Disconnect the battery negative cable.

2. Using tool J-28467-A or equivalent, support the engine.

3. Remove the right engine mount.

4. Remove the alternator and power steering belts.

5. Remove the upper timing belt cover attaching screws, then the upper timing belt cover from the vehicle.

6. Raise and support the vehicle safely.

7. Remove the crankshaft pulley bolt, then the crankshaft pulley.

8. Lower the vehicle, then remove the lower timing belt cover.

9. Reverse procedure to install. Connect the battery negative cable.

Spectrum

1. Disconnect negative battery cable.

2. Support the engine.

3. Remove the front mount bracket attached to the front cover.

4. Remove front cover.

5. To install, reverse the removal procedures.

Front Cover Oil Seal

REMOVAL AND INSTALLATION

The front cover oil seal replacement can and should be done when the front timing belt cover has been removed.

1. With the timing cover containing the oil seal removed, use a suitable seal removal tool and remove the front oil seal from the cover.

2. To install, apply a light coat of oil to the crankshaft and the lip of the new oil seal.

3. Using a suitable seal driver tool, drive in the new oil seal into the cover until the end of the seal sits squarely with the cover.

4. Reinstall the cover on the vehicle.

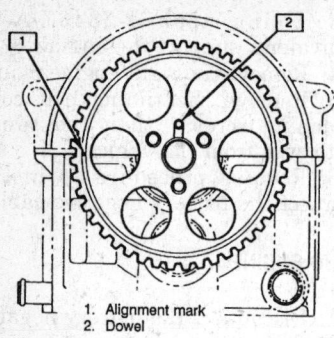

1. Alignment mark
2. Dowel

Camshaft pulley alignment — Storm SOHC engine

Timing Belt and Tensioner

ADJUSTMENT

Metro

1. Disconnect the battery negative cable.
2. Remove the front cover.
3. Take up the slack of the timing belt by turning the crankshaft 2 rotations clockwise after installing it. After making sure the belt is free from slack, tighten the tensioner stud first to 8 ft. lbs. (11 Nm) and the tensioner bolt to 20 ft. lbs. (27 Nm). Then confirm again that the 2 sets of marks are aligned respectively.
4. Install the timing belt outside cover. Before installing, make sure the seal is between the water pump and oil pump case. Tighten the timing belt cover bolts to 8 ft. lbs. (11 Nm).

Prizm

1. Remove the front cover assembly.
2. Using finger pressure on the longest span between pulleys (except 1990-92 GSi VIN 5) or between the camshaft pulleys (1990-92 GSi VIN 5), measure the timing belt deflection; 4.4 lbs. at 0.24-0.28 inch (except 1990-92 GSi VIN 5) or 0.16 inch (1990-92 GSi VIN 5).
3. If adjustment is not correct, loosen the idler pulley bolt and correct the belt tension.
4. To install, the front covers, reverse the removal procedures.

Spectrum and Storm

1. Remove the front cover.
2. Loosen the timing belt tension pulley bolt.

NOTE: If the belt has been removed or replaced with a new one, perform the following procedures to stretch the belt.

3. Using an Allen wrench, insert it into the hexagonal hole of the tension pulley. Hold the pulley stationary and temporarily tighten the tension pulley-to-engine bolt.
4. Rotate the crankshaft 2 complete revolutions and align the crankshaft timing pulley groove with the mark on the oil pump.
5. Loosen the tension pulley-to-engine bolt.
6. Using the Allen wrench and a timing belt tension gauge, apply 38 lbs. (52 N) of tension to the timing belt for the Spectrum or 31 lbs. (42 N) of tension on the timing belt for the Storm. Hold the pulley stationary and torque the tension pulley-to-engine bolt to 37 ft. lbs. (50 Nm) for the Spectrum or 31 ft. lbs. (42 Nm) for the Storm.
7. To complete the adjustment, install the front cover.

REMOVAL AND INSTALLATION

NOTE: Timing belts must always be handled carefully and kept completely free of dirt, grease, fluids and lubricants. This includes any accidental contact from spillage, fingerprints, rags, etc. These same precautions apply to the pulleys and contact surfaces on which the belt rides. The belt must never be crimped, twisted or bent. Never use tools to pry or wedge the belt into place. Such actions will damage the structure of the belt and possibly cause breakage.

Prizm

1990

1. Remove the timing belt covers.
2. If not done as part of the cover removal, rotate the crankshaft clockwise to the TDC compression position for No. 1 cylinder.
3. Loosen the timing belt idler pulley to relieve the tension on the belt, move the pulley away from the belt and temporarily tighten the bolt to hold it in the loose position.
4. Make matchmarks on the belt and both pulleys showing the exact placement of the belt. Mark an arrow on the belt showing its direction of rotation.
5. Carefully slip the timing belt off the pulleys.

NOTE: Do not disturb the position of the camshafts or the crankshaft during removal.

6. Remove the idler pulley bolt, pulley and return spring.

7. Use an adjustable wrench mounted on the flats of the camshaft to hold the camshaft from moving. Loosen the center bolt in the camshaft timing pulley and remove the pulley.
8. Check the timing belt carefully for any signs of cracking or deterioration. Pay particular attention to the area where each tooth or cog attaches to the backing of the belt. If the belt shows signs of damage, check the contact faces of the pulleys for possible burrs or scratches.
9. Check the idler pulley by holding it and spinning it. It should rotate freely and quietly. Any sign of grinding or abnormal noise indicates replacement of the pulley.
10. Check the free length of the tension spring. Correct length is 1.5 in. (38.5mm) measured at the inside faces of the hooks. A spring which has stretched during use will not apply the correct tension to the pulley; replace the spring.

To install:
11. Test the tension of the spring, look for 8.4 lbs. of tension at 2.0 in. (50mm) of length. If in doubt, replace the spring.
12. Reinstall the camshaft timing belt pulley, making sure the pulley fits properly on the shaft and that the timing marks align correctly. Tighten the center bolt to 43 ft. lbs. (58 Nm).
13. Before reinstalling the belt, double check that the crank and camshafts are exactly in their correct positions. The alignment mark on the end of the camshaft bearing cap should show through the small hole in the camshaft pulley and the small mark on the crankshaft timing belt pulley should align with the mark on the oil pump.
14. Reinstall the timing belt idler pulley and the tension spring. Pry the pulley to the left as far as it will go and temporarily tighten the retaining bolt. This will hold the pulley in its loosest position.
15. Install the timing belt, observing the matchmarks made earlier. Make sure the belt is fully and squarely seated on the upper and lower pulleys.
16. Loosen the retaining bolt for the timing belt idler pulley and allow it to tension the belt.
17. Temporarily install the crankshaft pulley bolt and turn the crank clockwise 2 full revolutions from TDC to TDC. Insure that each timing mark realigns exactly.
18. Tighten the timing belt idler pulley retaining bolt to 27 ft. lbs. (37 Nm).

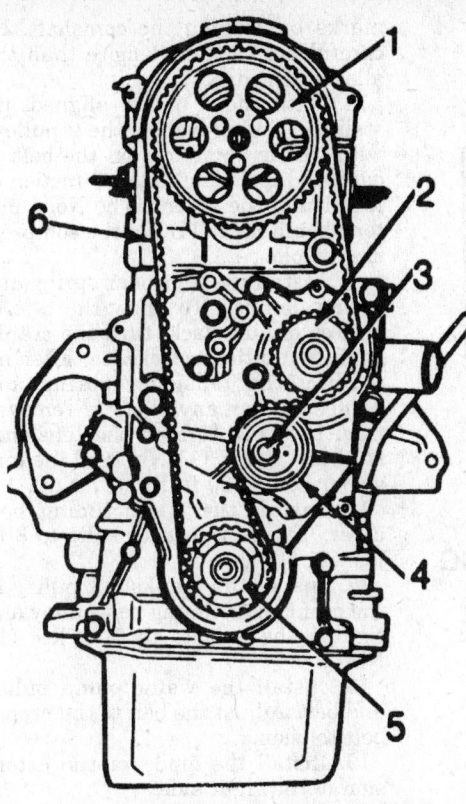

1. Camshaft timing pulley
2. Water pump timing pulley
3. Bolt
4. Tension pulley
5. Crankshaft timing pulley
6. Timing belt

View of the timing belt assembly — Spectrum and Storm

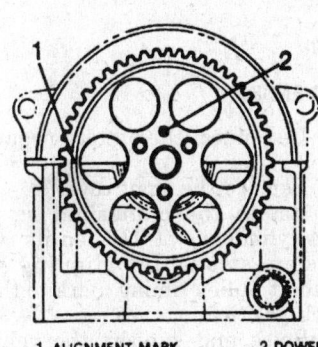

1 ALIGNMENT MARK   2 DOWEL

Aligning the camshaft pulley — Spectrum

19. Measure the timing belt deflection tool No. 23600-B or similar, looking for 0.20-0.24 in. (5-6mm) of deflection at 4.4 pounds of pressure. If the deflection is not correct, readjust the idler pulley by repeating Steps 15 through 18.

20. Remove the bolt from the end of the crankshaft.

21. Install the timing belt guide onto the crankshaft and install the lower timing belt cover.

22. Continue reassembly of the timing belt covers.

1991-94

1. Remove the timing belt covers.

2. Remove the timing belt guide from the crankshaft pulley.

3. Loosen the timing belt idler pulley, move it to the left (to take tension off the belt) and tighten its bolt.

4. Make matchmarks on the belt and all pulleys showing the exact placement of the belt. Mark an arrow on the belt showing its direction of rotation.

5. Carefully slip the timing belt off the pulleys.

NOTE: Do not disturb the position of the camshafts or the crankshaft during removal.

6. Remove the idler pulley bolt, pulley and return spring.

7. Remove the PCV hose and the valve covers.

8. Use an adjustable wrench to counter hold the camshaft. Be careful not to damage the cylinder head. Loosen the center bolt in each camshaft pulley and remove the pulley. Label the pulleys and keep them clean.

9. Check the timing belt carefully for any signs of cracking or deterioration. Pay particular attention to the area where each tooth or cog attaches to the backing of the belt. If the belt shows signs of damage, check the contact faces of the pulleys for possible burrs or scratches.

10. Check the idler pulley by holding and spinning it. It should rotate freely and quietly. Any sign of grinding or abnormal noise indicates replacement of the pulley.

11. Check the free length of the tension spring. Correct length is 1.7 in. (43.5mm) measured at the inside faces of the hooks. A spring which has stretched during use will not apply the correct tension to the pulley; replace the spring.

12. Test the tension of the spring, look for 22 lbs. of tension at 2.0 in. (50mm) of length. If in doubt, replace the spring.

To install:

13. Align the camshaft knock pin and the pulley. Reinstall the camshaft timing belt pulleys, making sure the pulley fits properly on the shaft and that the timing marks align correctly. Tighten the center bolt on each pulley to 34 ft. lbs. (46 Nm). Be careful not to damage the cylinder head during installation.

14. Before reinstalling the belt, double check that the crank and camshafts are exactly in their correct positions. The alignment marks on the pulleys should align with the cast marks on the head and oil pump.

15. Reinstall the valve covers and the PCV hose.

16. Install the timing belt idler pulley and its tensioning spring. Move the idler to the left and temporarily tighten its bolt.

17. Carefully observing the matchmarks made earlier, install the timing belt onto the pulleys.

18. Slowly release tension on the idler pulley bolt and allow the idler to take up tension on the timing belt. Do not allow the idler to slam into the belt; the belt may become damaged.

19. Temporarily install the crankshaft pulley bolt. Turn the engine clockwise through 2 complete revolutions, stopping at TDC. Check that each pulley aligns with its marks.

20. Using tool J 23600-B or similar, check the tension of the timing belt at a point halfway between the 2 camshaft sprockets. The correct deflection is 0.15 in.(4mm) at 4.4 lbs. pressure. If the belt tension is incorrect, readjust it by repeating Steps 19 and 20. If the tension is correct, tighten the idler pulley bolt to 27 ft. lbs. (37 Nm).

21. Remove the crankshaft pulley bolt.

22. Install the timing belt guide onto the crankshaft timing pulley.

23. Reinstall the timing belt covers, following procedures outlined previously in this chapter.

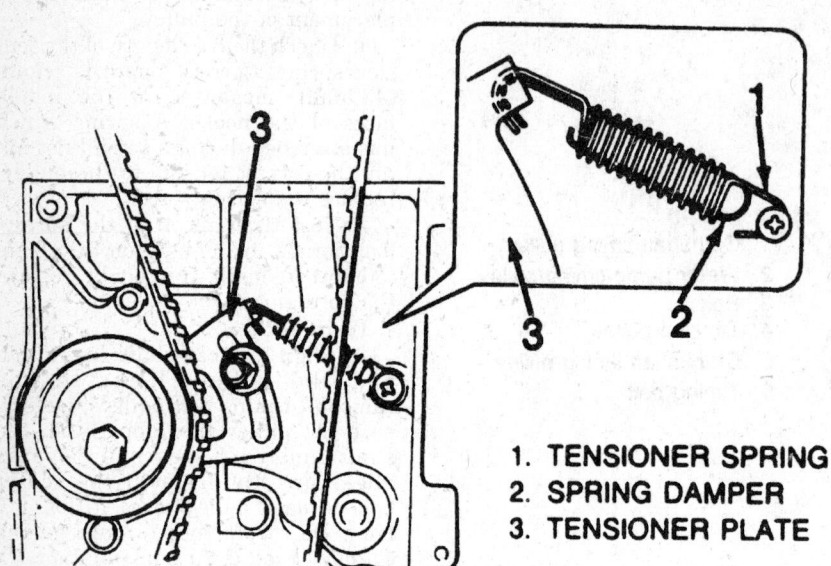

1. **TENSIONER SPRING**
2. **SPRING DAMPER**
3. **TENSIONER PLATE**

Installing the tensioner spring and damper — Metro

Metro

1. Disconnect the negative battery cable.

2. Raise and safely support the vehicle.

3. Remove the fender apron extension on the right side. Remove the clip after pushing the center pin.

4. Loosen the alternator pivot bolts and its adjusting bolt and remove the water pump belt and pulley.

5. Remove the 4 crankshaft pulley bolts and remove the crankshaft pulley. It is not necessary to loosen the crankshaft timing belt pulley bolt at the center.

6. Remove the timing belt cover. Before removing the timing belt, align the 4 timing marks by turning the crankshaft.

7. Remove the timing belt tensioner, tensioner plate, tensioner spring, spring damper and timing belt.

NOTE: After the timing belt is removed, never turn the camshaft or crankshaft independently. If turned, interference may occur among the pistons and valves and parts related to the pistons and valves may be damaged.

8. Inspect the timing belt for wear or cracks and replace as necessary. Check the tensioner for smooth rotation.

To install:

9. Install the tensioner plate to the tensioner.

10. Insert the lug of the tensioner plate into the hole of the tensioner.

11. Install the tensioner, tensioner plate and spring. Do not tighten the tensioner bolt and stud, make the bolt hand-tight only.

NOTE: Be sure plate movement is installed in the proper direction that causes the same directional movement of the tensioner inner race. If no movement between the plate and inner race occurs, remove the tensioner and plate again and reinsert the plate lug into the tensioner hole.

12. Check that the timing mark on the camshaft timing pulley is aligned with the V-mark on the cylinder head cover. If not, align the 2 marks by turning the camshaft. Be careful not to turn it more than the allowable range.

13. Check that the punchmark on the crankshaft timing belt pulley is aligned with the arrow mark on the oil pump case. If not align the 2 marks by turning the camshaft. Be careful not to turn it more than the allowable range.

14. With the 4 marks aligned, install the timing belt on the 2 pulleys with the arrow marks on the belt, if equipped, pointing in the direction of rotation of the engine. The No. 1 piston should be at TDC of the compression stroke.

15. Install the tensioner spring and spring damper. To allow the belt to be free of any slack, turn the crankshaft 2 rotations clockwise, after installing the tensioner spring and damper. After any slack is removed from the belt, tighten the tensioner stud to 8 ft. lbs. (11 Nm) and the tensioner bolt to 20 ft. lbs. (27 Nm).

16. Install the outer timing belt cover. Torque the cover bolts to 8 ft. lbs. (11 Nm).

17. Install the crankshaft pulley to the crankshaft timing belt pulley and tighten the 4 bolts to 8 ft. lbs. (11 Nm).

18. Install the water pump pulley and belt. Adjust the belt to the proper belt tension.

19. Install the fender apron extension of the right side.

20. Lower the vehicle and connect the negative battery cable.

Storm

SOHC ENGINE

1. Disconnect the battery negative cable.

2. Remove the front cover(s).

3. Rotate the crankshaft so the No. 4 cylinder is at TDC on its compression stroke by aligning the camshaft pulley timing mark to the 9 o'clock position.

4. Raise and support the vehicle safely.

5. Remove the crankshaft pulley bolt, the 4 crankshaft pulley side bolts and the crankshaft pulley from the vehicle.

6. Lower the vehicle. Loosen the belt tension pulley bolt, then the timing belt tensioner and timing belt from the vehicle.

To install:

7. Install the timing belt around the crankshaft timing pulley, tensioner pulley, water pump pulley and the camshaft timing pulley.

8. Tighten the belt tensioner retaining bolt. Make sure the belt is tight and aligned evenly around all the pulleys.

9. Check that the camshaft is still aligned to the 9 o'clock position.

10. Install the timing belt cover, secure it with the 2 lower mounting

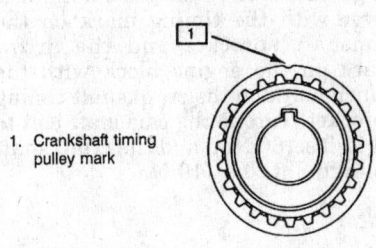

1. Crankshaft timing pulley mark

Crankshaft pulley alignment mark — Storm SOHC engine

bolts and torque the bolts to 89 inch lbs. (10 Nm).

11. Install the crankshaft pulley to the crankshaft dampener, secure the center bolt and the 4 side bolts. Torque the center bolt to 87 ft. lbs. (118 Nm) and the 4 side bolts to 17 ft. lbs. (23 Nm).

12. Install the right side undercover. Lower the vehicle. Install the 4 upper timing belt cover retaining bolts.

13. Install the right engine mount.

14. Install the power steering pump drive belt, alternator drive belt and any other drive belts that have been

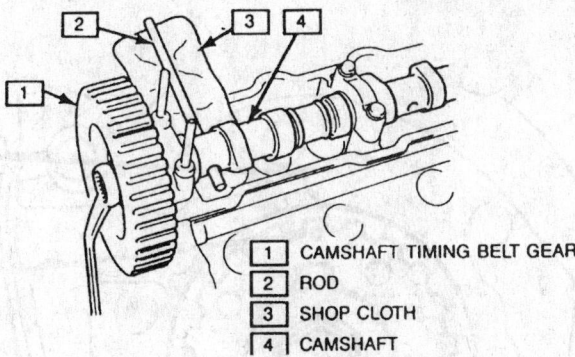

1	CAMSHAFT TIMING BELT GEAR
2	ROD
3	SHOP CLOTH
4	CAMSHAFT

Loosening the camshaft sprocket bolt — Metro

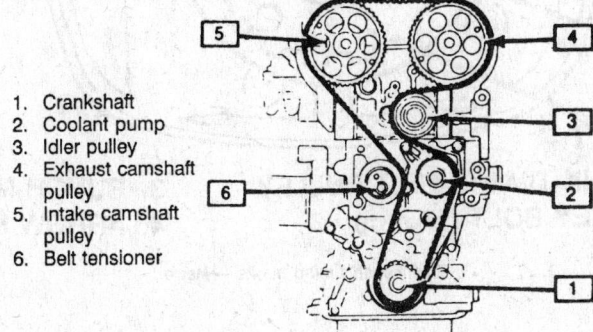

1. Crankshaft
2. Coolant pump
3. Idler pulley
4. Exhaust camshaft pulley
5. Intake camshaft pulley
6. Belt tensioner

Timing belt installation sequence — Storm DOHC engine

removed. Adjust them to the proper belt tension.

15. Remove engine support fixture tool J-28467-A or equivalent from the engine and reconnect the negative battery cable.

DOHC ENGINE

1. Disconnect the negative battery cable.

2. Install engine support fixture tool J-28467-A or equivalent.

3. Remove the right engine mount.

4. Remove the power steering belt and alternator belt.

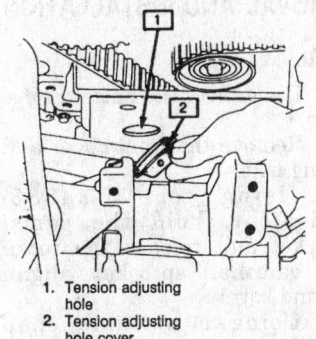

1. Tension adjusting hole
2. Tension adjusting hole cover

Timing Belt Hole Cover — Prizm

5. Remove the upper timing belt cover.

6. Raise and safely support the vehicle.

7. Remove the crankshaft pulley.

8. Lower the vehicle.

9. Remove the lower timing belt cover.

10. Align the crankshaft pulley to the TDC mark.

11. Loosen the tensioner pulley retaining bolt, turn and remove the timing belt.

To install:

12. Align the camshaft pulleys timing mark.

13. Raise and safely support the engine.

14. Install the crankshaft pulley. Torque the crankshaft pulley bolt to 87 ft. lbs. (118 Nm).

15. Lower the vehicle.

16. Install the timing belt over the crankshaft pulley, the coolant pump pulley, the idler pulley, the exhaust camshaft pulley, the intake camshaft pulley and then the tensioner pulley.

17. Install the timing belt tensioner and torque the retaining bolt to 31 ft. lbs. (42 Nm).

18. Rotate the crankshaft 2 turns to ensure that the crankshaft timing pulleys marks and the camshaft timing pulleys mark are correctly aligned.

19. Install the lower timing belt cover.

20. Raise and safely support the vehicle.

21. Install the crankshaft pulley bolt and torque the crankshaft pulley bolt to 87 ft. lbs. (118 Nm).

22. Lower the vehicle and install the upper timing cover.

23. Install the alternator and power steering belt. Adjust the belts to the proper belt tension.

24. Install the right engine mount.

25. Remove the engine support fixture tool. Reconnect the negative battery cable.

Spectrum

1. Remove the engine and mount the engine to an engine stand.

2. Remove the accessory drive belts.

3. Remove the engine mounting bracket from the timing cover.

4. Rotate the crankshaft until the notch on the crankshaft pulley aligns with the **0** degree mark on the timing cover and the No. 4 cylinder is on TDC of the compression stroke.

5. Remove the starter and install the flywheel holding tool J-35271 or equivalent.

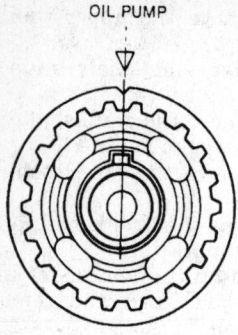

OIL PUMP

Crankshaft pulley timing mark alignment —
Spectrum

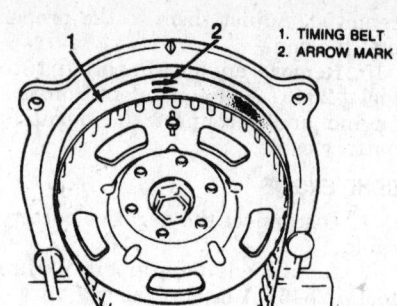

1. TIMING BELT
2. ARROW MARK

Arrow marks on the timing belt show the direction of rotation — Metro

Timing Sprockets

REMOVAL AND INSTALLATION

Metro

1. Disconnect the battery negative cable.
2. Remove the front cover and the timing belt.
3. Using tool J-34836 or equivalent, hold the camshaft sprocket and remove the retaining bolt, camshaft sprocket, alignment pin and cover.
4. Using a suitable spanner wrench, remove the crankshaft pulley bolt and the crankshaft pulley.

5. Reverse procedure to install. Align the **V**-mark on the timing belt cover with the timing mark on the camshaft sprocket and the arrow mark on the engine block with the punch mark on the crankshaft timing sprocket. Torque the camshaft bolt to 44 ft. lbs. (60 Nm) and the crankshaft bolts to 8 ft. lbs. (10 Nm).

Prizm

EXCEPT 1990-92 GSi

1. Disconnect the negative battery cable.
2. Remove the timing belt.
3. To remove the crankshaft timing belt pulley, simply pull it and the key from the crankshaft.
4. To remove the camshaft pulley, perform the following procedures:
   a. Remove the valve cover.
   b. Using an open end wrench, place it on the camshaft flats to secure it.
   c. Using a socket wrench on the camshaft pulley bolt, remove the camshaft pulley bolt and the camshaft pulley.
To install:
5. Torque the camshaft pulley-to-camshaft bolt to 34 ft. lbs. (46 Nm).
6. After installing the crankshaft pulley bolt, rotate the crankshaft 2 complete revolutions and recheck the

6. Remove the crankshaft bolt, boss and pulley.
7. Remove the timing cover bolts and the timing cover.
8. Loosen the tension pulley bolt.
9. Insert an Allen wrench into the tension pulley hexagonal hole and loosen the timing belt by turning the tension pulley clockwise.
10. Remove the timing belt.
11. Remove the head cover.

NOTE: Inspect the timing belt for signs of cracking, abnormal wear and hardening. Never expose the belt to oil, sunlight or heat. Avoid excessive bending, twisting or stretching.

To install:
12. Position the Woodruff key on the crankshaft followed by the crankshaft timing gear. Align the groove on the timing gear with the mark on the oil pump.
13. Align the camshaft timing gear mark with the upper surface of the cylinder head and the dowel pin in its uppermost position.
14. Place the timing belt arrow in the direction of the engine rotation and install the timing belt. Tighten the tension pulley bolt.
15. Turn the crankshaft 2 complete revolutions and realign the crankshaft timing gear groove with the mark on the oil pump.
16. Loosen the tension pulley bolt and apply tension to the belt with an Allen wrench. Torque the pulley bolt to 37 ft. lbs. (50 Nm) while holding the pulley stationary.
17. Adjust the valve clearances.
18. To complete the installation, reverse the removal procedures. Torque the crankshaft pulley-to-crankshaft bolt to 109 ft. lbs. (148 Nm).

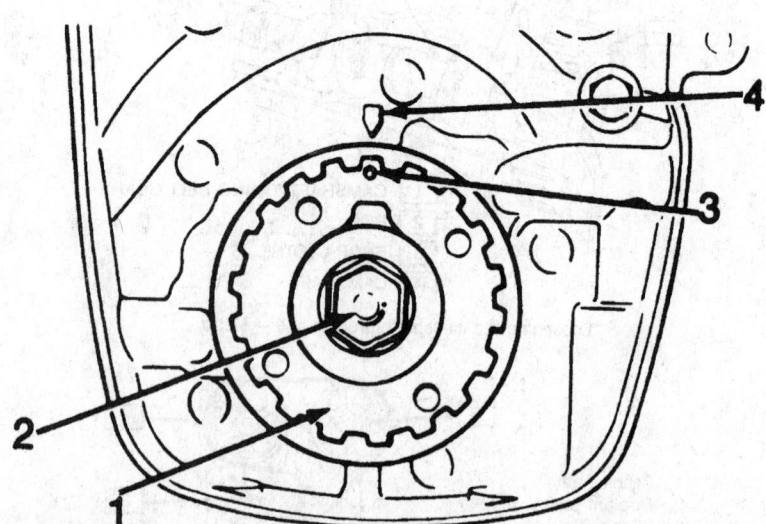

1. **CRANK TIMING BELT PULLEY**
2. **PULLEY BOLT (17 mm)**
3. **PUNCH MARK**
4. **ARROW MARK**

Crankshaft timing marks — Metro

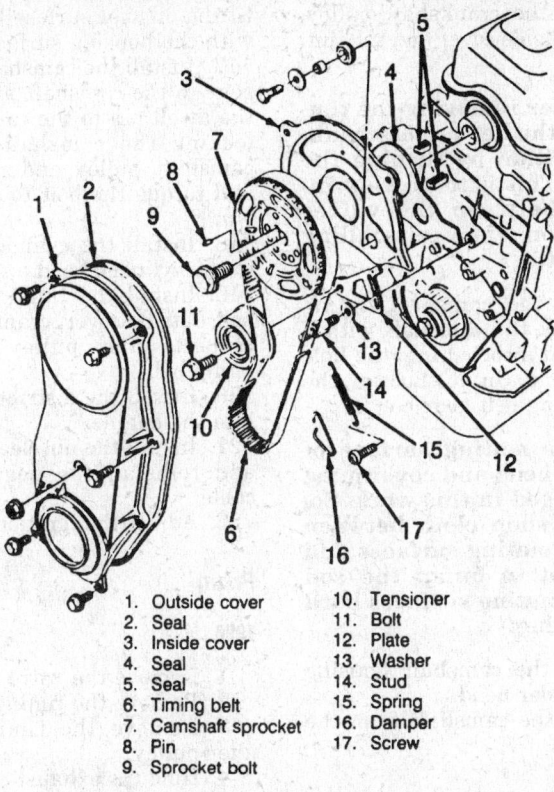

1. Outside cover
2. Seal
3. Inside cover
4. Seal
5. Seal
6. Timing belt
7. Camshaft sprocket
8. Pin
9. Sprocket bolt
10. Tensioner
11. Bolt
12. Plate
13. Washer
14. Stud
15. Spring
16. Damper
17. Screw

Exploded view of the timing belt assembly — Metro

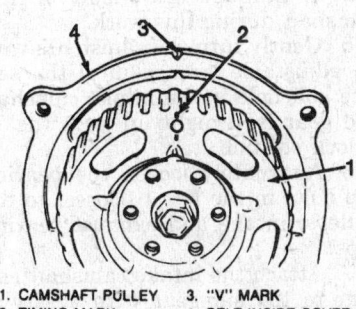

1. CAMSHAFT PULLEY
2. TIMING MARK
3. "V" MARK
4. BELT INSIDE COVER

Camshaft timing marks — Metro

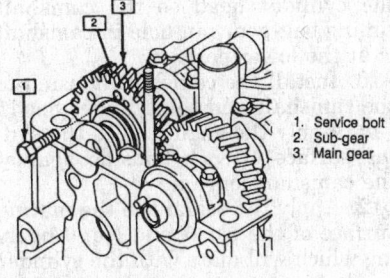

1. Service bolt
2. Sub-gear
3. Main gear

Always install a service bolt to lock the intake camshaft — Prizm (engine code 6 and 8)

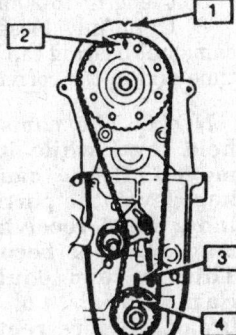

1. V mark on cylinder head cover
2. Timing mark on camshaft timing belt gear
3. Arrow mark on oil pump case
4. Punch mark on crankshaft timing belt gear

Aligning the timing marks — Metro

alignment. Check and/or adjust the timing belt tension. Torque the idler pulley mounting bolt to 27 ft. lbs. (37 Nm).

7. To complete the installation, reverse the removal procedures.

1990-92 GSi

1. Disconnect the negative battery cable.

2. Remove the timing belt.

3. To remove the crankshaft timing belt pulley, simply pull it and the key from the crankshaft.

4. To remove the camshaft pulleys, perform the following procedures:

  a. Remove both valve covers.

  b. Secure each camshaft, then, using a socket wrench on the camshaft pulley bolt, remove the camshaft pulley bolt.

  c. Using the pulley remover tool J-1859-03 or equivalent, press each camshaft pulley from the camshafts.

To install:

5. To install the camshaft pulleys, align each with the knock pin and reverse the removal procedures. Torque the camshaft pulley-to-camshaft bolt to 34 ft. lbs. (47 Nm).

6. To install the crankshaft timing pulley, simply align it with the keyway and slide it onto the crankshaft.

7. Align the timing belt marks with the pulley marks and install the timing belt.

8. After installing the crankshaft pulley bolt, rotate the crankshaft 2 complete revolutions and recheck the alignment. Check and/or adjust the timing belt tension. Torque the idler pulley mounting bolt to 27 ft. lbs. (37 Nm).

9. To complete the installation, reverse the removal procedures.

Spectrum and Storm

EXCEPT DOHC ENGINE

1. Disconnect the negative battery terminal from the battery.

2. On Spectrum, rotate the crankshaft to place the No. 4 cylinder on the TDC of compression stroke.

3. On Storm, rotate the crankshaft to place the No. 1 cylinder on TDC of the compression stroke.

4. Remove the front cover-to-mount bracket bolt and the bracket from the vehicle.

5. Remove the front cover-to-engine bolts and the front cover from the engine.

NOTE: Make sure the camshaft dowel pin is positioned at the top and the mark on the camshaft sprocket is aligned with the upper cylinder head surface.

6. Loosen the timing belt tension pulley-to-engine bolt, then remove the timing belt.

7. Remove the camshaft sprocket-to-camshaft bolts, the camshaft sprocket and allow the timing belt to hang.

8. If the engine has not been disturbed, reverse the removal procedures. On Spectrum, torque the camshaft sprocket-to-camshaft bolt to 7 ft. lbs. (10 Nm) or 9 ft. lbs. (12 Nm) on Storm. Adjust the timing belt.

9. To complete the installation, reverse the removal procedures.

DOHC ENGINE

1. Disconnect the battery negative cable.

2. Remove the cylinder head cover.

3. Rotate the crankshaft to bring the No. 1 cylinder to TDC of the compression stroke. The camshaft pulley's timing marks should align.

4. Loosen the timing belt tension pulley and remove the timing belt from the camshaft pulleys.

5. Remove the camshaft attaching bolts and the camshafts from the vehicle.

6. Reverse procedure to install. Torque the camshaft attaching bolts to 43 ft. lbs. (59 Nm).

Camshaft

REMOVAL AND INSTALLATION

Metro

1. Disconnect the negative battery cable.

2. Remove the air cleaner assembly.

3. Remove the cylinder head cover assembly.

4. Set the engine up on top dead center of the compression stroke on the No. 1 cylinder. Make an alignment mark on the distributor cap and engine block and remove the distributor assembly.

5. Remove the crankshaft pulley, timing belt outside cover and the timing belt.

NOTE: After removing the timing belt, set the key on the crankshaft in position by turning the crankshaft. This is to prevent interference between the valves and the piston when reinstalling the camshaft.

6. Remove the camshaft timing belt gear. Lock the camshaft with a proper size rod inserted into the hole 0.39 in. (10mm) in it. Loosen the camshaft timing belt gear bolt.

NOTE: The mating surface of the cylinder head and cover must not be damaged in this work. So, put a clean shop cloth between the rod and mating surfaces and use care not to bump the rod against the mating surfaces hard when loosening.

7. Remove the camshaft housing from the cylinder head.

8. Remove the camshaft from the cylinder head.

To install:

9. Install the camshaft to cylinder head. After applying engine oil to the camshaft journal and all around the cam, the position the camshaft into the cylinder head so the camshaft timing belt gear pin hole in camshaft is at the lower position.

10. Install the camshaft housing to the camshaft and the cylinder head.

11. Apply the engine oil to the sliding surface of each housing against the camshaft journal.

12. Apply the sealant to the mating surface of the No. 1 and No. 3 housing which will mate with the cylinder head.

13. There are marks provided on each camshaft housing indicating position and direction for installation. Install the housing as indicated by these marks.

14. As the camshaft housing No. 1 retains the camshaft in the proper position as to the thrust direction, make sure to first fit the No. 1 housing to the No. 1 journal of the camshaft securely.

15. After applying the engine oil to the housing bolts, tighten them temporarily. Then tighten in the proper sequence. Tighten the bolts a little at a time and evenly among bolts, repeat the tightening sequence 3 to 4 times before they are tighten to the proper torque of 8 ft. lbs. (11 Nm).

16. Install the camshaft oil seal. After applying engine oil to the oil seal lip, press-fit the camshaft oil seal un-

til the oil seal surface becomes flush with the housing surfaces.

17. Install the camshaft timing belt gear to the camshaft after installing the dwell pin to the camshaft. While locking the camshaft, install the camshaft pulley and retaining bolt and torque the bolt to 44 ft. lbs. (60 Nm).

18. Install the cylinder head cover to the cylinder head.

19. Install the timing belt, timing belt outside cover, crankshaft pulley, coolant pump pulley and coolant pump belt.

20. Install the distributor assembly into the engine.

21. Install the air cleaner assembly and reinstall the negative battery cable.

22. Adjust the ignition timing.

Prizm

1990

1. Remove the valve cover.

2. Remove the timing belt covers.

3. Remove the timing belt and idler pulley.

4. Hold the exhaust camshaft with an adjustable wrench and remove the camshaft timing belt gear. Be careful not to damage the head or the camshaft during this work.

5. Gently turn the camshafts with an adjustable wrench until the service bolt hole in the intake camshaft end gear is straight up or in the 12 o'clock position.

6. Alternately loosen the bearing cap bolts in the No. 1 (closest to the pulleys) intake and exhaust bearing caps.

7. Attach the intake camshaft end gear to the sub-gear with a service bolt. The service bolt should match the following specifications:
   Thread diameter: 6.0mm
   Thread pitch: 1.0mm
   Bolt length: 16-20mm

8. Uniformly loosen each intake camshaft bearing cap bolt a little at a time and in the correct sequence.

NOTE: The camshaft must be held level while it is being removed. If the camshaft is not kept level, the portion of the cylinder head receiving the thrust may crack or become damaged. This in turn could cause the camshaft to bind or break. Before removing the intake camshaft, make sure the rotational force has been removed from the sub-gear; that is, the gear should be in a neutral or "unloaded" state.

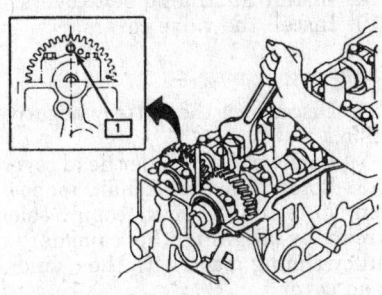

The correct position of the service bolt before removing the intake camshaft — Prizm (engine code 6 and 8)

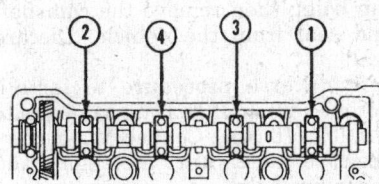

Remove the camshaft bearing caps in the order shown. The intake camshaft is shown, however the exhaust camshaft is removed the same way — Prizm (engine code 6 and 8)

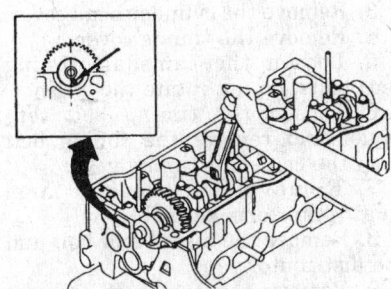

Setting the exhaust camshaft guide pin to just past the 5 o'clock position — Prizm (engine code 6 and 8)

9. Remove the bearing caps and remove the intake camshaft.

NOTE: If the camshaft cannot be removed straight and level, re-tighten the No. 3 bearing cap. Alternately loosen the bolts on the bearing cap a little at a time while pulling upwards on the camshaft gear. Do not attempt to pry or force the camshaft loose with tools.

10. With the intake camshaft removed, turn the exhaust camshaft approximately 105 degrees, so the guide pin in the end is just past the 5

o'clock position. This puts equal loadings on the camshaft, allowing easier and safer removal.

11. Loosen the exhaust camshaft bearing cap bolts a little at a time and in the correct sequence.

12. Remove the bearing caps and remove the exhaust camshaft.

NOTE: If the camshaft cannot be removed straight and level, re-tighten the No. 3 bearing cap. Alternately loosen the bolts on the bearing cap a little at a time while pulling upwards on the camshaft gear. Do not attempt to pry or force the camshaft loose with tools.

13. When reinstalling, remember that the camshafts must be handled carefully and kept straight and level to avoid damage.

To install:

14. Place the exhaust camshaft on the cylinder head so the camshaft lobes press evenly on the lifters for cylinders No. 1 and 3. This will put the guide pin just past the 5 o'clock position.

15. Place the bearing caps in position according to the number cast into the cap. The arrow should point towards the pulley end of the motor.

16. Tighten the bearing cap bolts gradually and in the proper sequence to 9.5 ft. lbs. (13 Nm).

17. Apply multi-purpose grease, such as GM 1051344 or similar, to a new exhaust camshaft oil seal.

18. Install the exhaust camshaft oil seal using tool J-35403 or equivalent. Be very careful not to install the seal on a slant or allow it to tilt during installation.

19. Turn the exhaust camshaft until the camshaft lobes of No. 4 cylinder press down on their lifters.

20. Hold the intake camshaft next to the exhaust camshaft and engage the gears by matching the alignment marks on each gear.

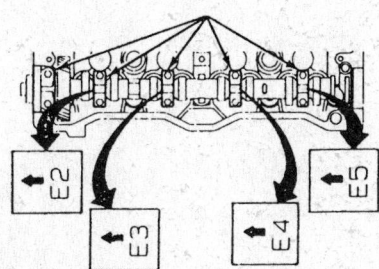

Examples of the bearing cap marking — Prizm (engine code 6 and 8)

21. Keeping the gears engaged, roll the intake camshaft down and into its bearing journals.

22. Place the bearing caps for No. 2, 3, 4 and 5 in position. Observe the numbers on each cap and make certain the arrows point to the pulley end of the motor.

23. Gradually tighten each bearing cap bolt in the same order as the exhaust camshaft bolts. Tighten each bolt to 9.5 ft. lbs. (13 Nm)

24. Remove any retaining pins or bolts in the intake camshaft gears.

25. Install the No. 1 bearing cap for the intake camshaft.

NOTE: If the No. 1 bearing cap does not fit properly, gently push the camshaft gear towards the rear of the engine by levering between the gear and the head.

26. Turn the exhaust camshaft one full revolution from TDC/compression on No. 1 cylinder to the same position. Check that the mark on the exhaust camshaft gear matches exactly with the mark on the intake camshaft gear.

27. Counter hold the exhaust camshaft and install the timing belt pulley. Tighten the bolt to 43 ft. lbs. (59 Nm).

28. Double check both the crankshaft and camshaft positions, insuring that they are both set to TDC/compression for No. 1 cylinder.

29. Install the timing belt.

30. Install the timing belt covers and the valve cover.

1991-94

1. Remove the valve covers and the timing belt cover.

2. Make certain the engine is set to TDC/compression on No. 1 cylinder. Remove the timing belt.

3. Remove the crankshaft pulley, if desired.

4. Remove the camshaft timing belt pulleys.

5. Loosen and remove the camshaft bearing caps in the proper sequence. It is recommended that the bolts be loosened in 2 or 3 passes.

6. With the bearing caps removed, the camshaft(s) may be lifted clear of the head. If both camshafts are to be removed, label them clearly — they are not interchangeable.

To install:

7. When reinstalling, place the camshaft(s) in position on the head. The exhaust camshaft has the distributor drive gear on it. Observe the markings on the bearing caps and place them according to their numbered positions. The arrow should point to the front of the engine.

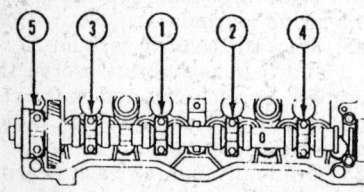

Torque the camshaft bearing caps in the order shown. The exhaust camshaft is shown, however the intake camshaft is installed the same way — Prizm (engine code 6 and 8)

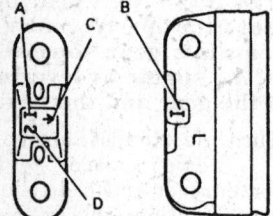

A. I = intake; E = exhaust
B. I = intake; E = exhaust
C. Front mark
D. I.D. for bearing No. 2 thru No.5

Example of the bearing cap markings. Note that the bearing on the right is used for position 1 only — 1990-92 Prizm (engine code 5)

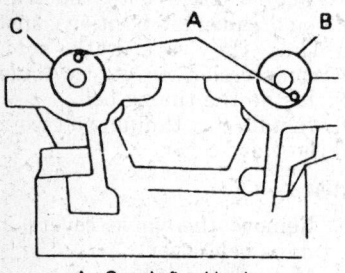

A. Camshaft guide pins
B. Exhaust camshaft
C. Intake camshaft

Correct position of guide pins on the camshaft — 1990-92 Prizm (engine code 5)

8. Tighten the bearing cap bolts in the correct sequence and in 3 passes

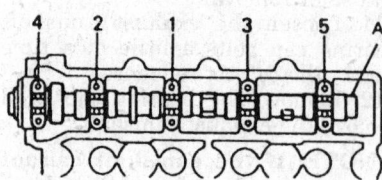

Install the camshaft bearing caps in the order shown — 1990-92 (engine code 5)

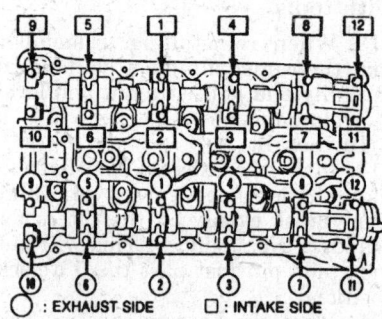

○ : EXHAUST SIDE   □ : INTAKE SIDE

Camshaft bearing cap torque sequence — Storm DOHC engine

to a final tightness of 9 ft. lbs. (12 Nm).

9. Position the camshafts so the guide pins (knock pins) are in the proper position. This step is critical to the correct valve timing of the engine.

10. Install the camshaft timing pulleys and tighten the bolts to 34 ft. lbs. (47 Nm).

11. Double check the positioning of the camshaft pulleys and the guide pin.

12. Install the crankshaft pulley if it was removed. Tighten its bolt to 87 ft. lbs. (118 Nm) and double check its position to be on TDC.

13. Install the timing belt and tensioner. Adjust the belt to the proper tension.

14. Install the timing belt covers.
15. Install the valve covers.

Storm

1. Disconnect the battery negative cable.
2. Remove the cylinder head cover.
3. Rotate the crankshaft to position No. 1 at TDC on its compression stroke by aligning the camshaft(s) pulley timing mark with the cylinder head cover.
4. Loosen the timing belt tensioner.
5. Remove the timing belt pulley(s) from the camshaft(s).
6. Remove the distributor.
7. Remove the camshaft(s) bearing cap bolts, then remove the camshaft and seal from the vehicle. Discard seal.
8. Reverse procedure to install. Torque camshaft bearing cap bolts to 8 ft. lbs. (10 Nm). Connect the battery negative cable. Start the engine and check for leaks.

Spectrum

1. Disconnect the negative battery terminal from the battery.
2. Align the crankshaft pulley notch with the **0** degree mark on the timing cover.
3. Remove the cylinder head cover.
4. Remove the timing cover.
5. Loosen the camshaft timing gear bolts; do not rotate the engine.
6. Loosen the timing belt tensioner and remove the timing belt from the camshaft timing gear.
7. Remove the rocker arm shaft/rocker arm assembly.
8. Remove the distributor bolt and the distributor.
9. Remove the camshaft and the camshaft seal.
10. To install, drive a new camshaft seal on the camshaft using the seal installation tool J-35268 or equivalent, reverse the removal procedures, adjust the valves and the timing belt.

Piston and Connecting Rod

POSITIONING

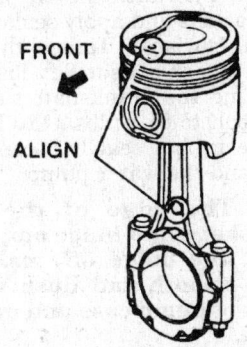

Piston alignment marks — Storm and Prizm

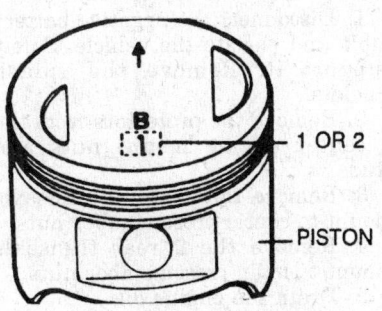

Piston alignment marks — Metro

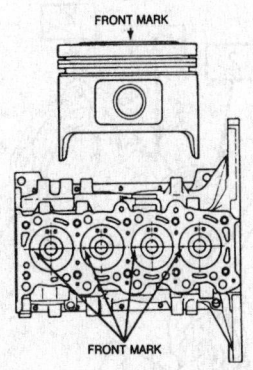

Piston alignment marks — Spectrum

ENGINE LUBRICATION

Oil Pan

REMOVAL AND INSTALLATION

Metro

1. Remove the negative battery cable.
2. Raise and support the vehicle safely.
3. Drain the engine oil.
4. Remove the flywheel dust cover.
5. Remove the exhaust pipe at the exhaust manifold.
6. Remove the oil pan bolts, the pan and the oil pump strainer.
7. Clean the gasket mating surfaces.
8. To install, use new gaskets and reverse the removal procedures. Torque the oil pan bolts to 9 ft. lbs. (11 Nm). Refill the engine oil.

Prizm

EXCEPT 1993-94 GSi

1. Disconnect the negative battery cable.
2. Safely raise and support the vehicle on jackstands.
3. Drain the engine oil and replace the drain plug when the pan is empty.
4. Remove the right splash shield.
5. Remove the front exhaust pipe. Disconnect it at the manifold and the catalytic converter.
6. Remove the exhaust bracket.
7. Remove the oil pan bolts. Remove the oil pan. If the pan is difficult to remove, tap it gently with a rubber or plastic mallet. Do not use a prybar to release it.

NOTE: Do not bend or deform the edge (flange) of the oil pan during removal.

8. Clean the pan thoroughly and remove all sludge and solid matter. Clean the mating surfaces of the pan and the engine, removing all traces of old gasket material and sealer. During the cleaning, remove the drain bolt and clean the threads.
To install:
9. Install a new gasket on the bolt and install the bolt in the pan. Apply a new gasket and/or sealant to the pan and install the pan to the engine.
10. Install and tighten the pan bolts to 4 ft. lbs. (5.4 Nm).

11. Install the front exhaust pipe and its bracket.
12. Install the right splash shield.
13. Lower the vehicle to the ground.
14. Refill the engine oil and connect the negative battery cable.
15. Start the engine and check for leaks.

1993-94 GSi

1. Disconnect the negative battery cable and oxygen sensor.
2. Raise and safely support the vehicle.
3. Drain the oil from the engine.
4. Remove the lower engine splash shields.
5. Remove the front exhaust pipe.
6. Remove 2 bolts and lower the front end of the center support.
7. Remove 13 bolts, 2 nuts and oil pan from the bottom of the block.

NOTE: Use caution when removing the oil pan. The front of the engine or the edge of the pan may be damaged during removal.

8. Remove 2 nuts, 2 bolts and oil baffle plate.
9. Remove 3 bolts, oil pickup and gasket.
10. Remove 3 transaxle mounting bolts from thew rear engine plate.
11. Remove 14 bolts from the lower cylinder block reinforcement brace.
12. Remove 6 Torx® bolts and the lower cylinder block reinforcement brace from the block using a suitable prybar to pry between the block and brace.

NOTE: Use caution when prying the brace from the block. Do not damage the brace-to-block mating surfaces, oil pump body or rear main oil seal housing.

13. Clean the pan thoroughly and remove all sludge and solid matter. Clean the mating surfaces of the pan and the engine, removing all traces of old gasket material and sealer. During the cleaning, remove the drain bolt and clean the threads.
To install:
14. Apply a new gasket and/or sealant to the lower cylinder block reinforcement brace and install the lower cylinder block reinforcement brace to the engine.
15. Torque 6 Torx® bolts to 11 ft. lbs. (15 Nm) and 14 bolts to 71 inch lbs. (8 Nm).
16. Install 3 transaxle mounting bolts and torque to 17 ft. lbs. (23 Nm).
17. Install a new gasket and oil pickup with 3 bolts and torque to 62 inch lbs. (7 Nm).

18. Install the oil baffle plate with 2 nuts and 2 bolts and torque to 62 inch lbs. (7 Nm).

19. Install a new gasket on the bolt and install the bolt in the pan. Apply a new gasket and/or sealant to the pan and install the pan to the engine.

20. Install and tighten the 2 nuts and 13 pan bolts to 44 inch lbs. (5 Nm).

21. Install the front exhaust pipe and new gaskets.

22. Torque the front pipe-to-converter bolts to 32 ft. lbs. (43 Nm), the front pipe-to-manifold nuts to 46 ft. lbs. (62 Nm) and front pipe hanger bolts to 14 ft. lbs. (19 Nm).

23. Install lower engine splash shields.

24. Raise and install the front end of the center support and torque the bolts to 45 ft. lbs. (61 Nm).

25. Lower the vehicle and fill crankcase with new oil.

26. Connect the negative battery cable and oxygen sensor.

27. Start the engine and check for leaks.

Storm

1. Disconnect the battery negative cable.

2. Raise and support the vehicle safely, then drain engine oil.

3. Remove the right undercover.

4. Remove the front exhaust pipe from the exhaust manifold, then remove the torque rod.

5. Remove the flywheel dust cover. Remove the stiffener from the cylinder head, if equipped.

6. Remove the oil pan attaching bolts, then remove the oil pan.

7. Reverse procedure to install. Apply suitable sealant to the oil pan gasket. Torque bolts to 89 inch lbs. (10 Nm). Connect battery negative cable. Start engine and check for leaks.

Spectrum

1. Disconnect the negative battery terminal from the battery.

2. Raise and support the vehicle safely, then drain the crankcase.

3. Disconnect the exhaust pipe bracket from the block and the exhaust pipe at the manifold.

4. Disconnect the right hand tension rod located under the front bumper.

5. Remove the oil pan bolts and oil pan, then clean the sealing surfaces.

6. To install, reverse the removal procedures. Use a new gasket, apply sealant to the oil pump housing and the rear retainer housing. Torque the oil pan bolts to 7 ft. lbs. (10 Nm). Tor-

que the exhaust pipe-to-manifold nuts to 42 ft. lbs. (57 Nm). Torque the exhaust pipe-to-converter bolts to 20 ft. lbs. (28 Nm).

Oil Pump

REMOVAL AND INSTALLATION

Metro

1. Remove the negative battery cable.

2. Raise and support the vehicle safely.

3. Drain the engine oil.

4. Remove the water pump belt, pulley, alternator, alternator bracket and air conditioning mounting bracket, if equipped.

5. Remove the crankshaft pulley, timing belt outside cover, timing belt and tensioner.

6. Disconnect the engine oil level gauge.

7. Remove the crankshaft timing belt gear and timing belt guide. With the crankshaft locked, remove the crankshaft timing belt pulley bolt.

8. Remove the oil pan bolts, oil pan, oil strainer fixing bolt and the oil strainer assembly.

9. Remove the oil pump bolts and the oil pump assembly.

10. Remove the sealing material from the oil pump and engine block sealing surfaces.

11. To install, reverse the removal procedures. Lubricate the oil pump, use new gaskets and apply sealant to the sealing surfaces. Torque the oil pump and oil pan bolts to 8 ft. lbs. (11 Nm). Torque the crankshaft timing belt gear bolt to 81 ft. lbs. (110 Nm). Install the rubber seal between the oil pump and the water pump.

NOTE: The edge of the oil pump gasket could bulge out; if it does, cut the bulge off, making the edge smooth and flush with end faces of pump case and cylinder block.

Prizm

EXCEPT GSi

1. Disconnect the negative battery cable and elevate the vehicle. Safely support it. Remove the splash shield(s).

2. Remove the protectors from the 2 center engine mount nuts and studs.

3. Remove the 2 center transaxle mount-to-center crossmember nuts.

4. Remove the 2 rear transaxle mount-to-main crossmember nuts.

5. Drain the engine oil.

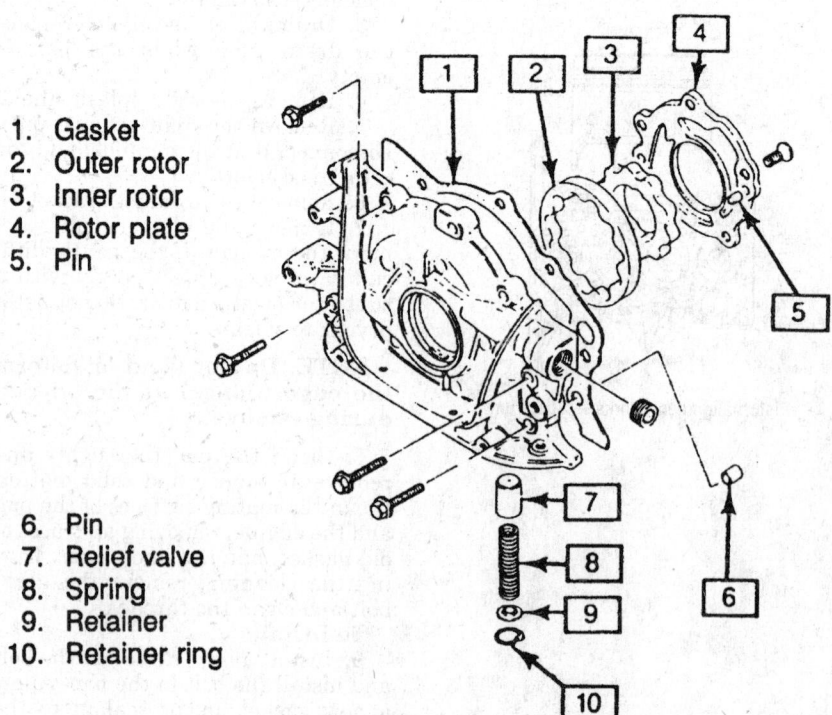

1. Gasket
2. Outer rotor
3. Inner rotor
4. Rotor plate
5. Pin

6. Pin
7. Relief valve
8. Spring
9. Retainer
10. Retainer ring

Exploded view of the oil pump — Metro

6. Remove the oil pan. Remove the oil pickup and strainer assembly.

7. Lower the vehicle to the ground.

8. Depending on equipment, loosen the air conditioning compressor bracket, the power steering pump bracket and the alternator bracket as applicable. Remove the drive belts.

9. Remove the alternator from its mounts and place it out of the way. The wiring may be left attached.

10. Lift out the windshield washer fluid reservoir.

11. Support the engine. This may be done from above with tool J-28467-A or a chain hoist or from below with a floor jack. Be very careful of the jack placement (the oil pan is removed); use a piece of wood to distribute the load and protect the engine.

12. Remove the through bolt in the right engine mount.

13. Remove the water pump pulley.

14. Lower the engine to its normal position.

15. Remove the crankshaft pulley.

16. Remove the timing belt covers.

17. Remove the timing belt guide from the crank pulley.

18. Loosen the idler pulley bolt, push it all the way to the left and tighten the bolt. This removes tension from the belt.

19. Matchmark the belt and all the pulleys so the belt may be reinstalled exactly as it was before. Mark an arrow on the belt showing direction of rotation.

20. Remove the timing belt from the lower pulley (crankshaft timing pulley). If careful, the belt may remain undisturbed on the camshaft pulleys.

21. Remove the idler pulley and spring.

22. Remove the dipstick and dipstick tube.

23. Remove the crankshaft timing pulley.

24. Raise the vehicle and safely support it.

25. Remove the 7 bolts holding the oil pump.

26. Remove the 7 bolts in the oil pump and carefully remove the pump. If it is difficult to remove, tap it lightly with a plastic or rubber mallet. Do not pry it off or strike it with a metal hammer.

To install:

27. When reinstalling, place a new gasket on the block. Install the oil pump to the crankshaft with the spline teeth to the drive gear engaged with the large teeth of the crankshaft.

28. Install the 7 retaining bolts and tighten them to 16 ft. lbs. (22 Nm).

29. Lower the vehicle to the ground.

30. Install the timing belt idler pulley.

31. Install the dipstick tube and dipstick.

32. Install the timing belt.

33. Install the timing belt guide. It should install with the cupped side facing outward.

34. Make sure the gaskets are properly seated in the timing belt covers and reinstall the covers. Make sure each bolt is in the correct hole.

35. Install the crankshaft pulley. Tighten the bolt to 87 ft. lbs. (118 Nm).

36. Raise the engine to gain access to the water pump.

37. Install the water pump pulley.

38. Install the right engine mount through bolt. Tighten the through bolt to 64 ft. lbs. (87 Nm). When the bolt is secure, the engine lifting apparatus may be removed.

39. Position and install the alternator.

40. Reinstall the drive belts for the alternator, power steering and air conditioning as applicable. Adjust the belts to the correct tension.

41. Raise the vehicle and safely support it.

42. Install the oil pickup and strainer assembly.

43. Apply a continuous bead of sealer (GM 1050026 or similar) to both sides of the new pan gasket.

44. Place the gasket on the pan and install the pan to the block. Tighten the bolts and nuts to 4 ft. lbs. (5.4 Nm).

45. Install the 2 rear transaxle mount-to-main crossmember nuts and tighten them to 45 ft. lbs. (61 Nm). Install the 2 center transaxle mount-to-center crossmember nuts and tighten them to 45 ft. lbs. (61 Nm).

46. Install the protectors over the nuts and studs for the mounts.

47. Lower the vehicle to the ground.

48. Install the windshield washer fluid reservoir.

49. Refill the engine with the correct amount of fresh oil.

50. Connect the negative battery cable.

51. Start the engine and check for leaks. Allow the engine to warm up to normal operating temperature and check the work area carefully for signs of seepage.

52. With the engine shut off, check the tension of the drive belts and adjust if necessary. Reinstall the splash guard(s) under the vehicle.

1991-92 GSi

1. Disconnect the negative battery cable.

2. Remove the oil pan.

3. Remove the oil pickup and strainer.

4. Remove the oil pan baffle plate.

5. Drain the cooling system.

6. Disconnect the accelerator cable or linkage.

7. Remove the cruise control actuator, if equipped.

8. Remove the washer tank.

9. Remove the upper radiator hose at the engine block.

10. Remove the power steering and/or the air conditioning drive belt(s).

11. Loosen the bolts to the water pump pulley and then remove the alternator drive belt.

12. Remove the spark plugs.

13. Rotate the crankshaft and position the engine at TDC/compression. Align the crankshaft marks at **0** and view the camshaft through the oil filler cap. The camshaft should have a small cavity pointing upward.

14. Use a floor jack and a piece of wood to slightly elevate the engine. Remove the right engine mount; then remove the 3 bolts and remove the right reinforcing plate for the engine mount.

15. Remove the water pump pulley.

16. Remove the crankshaft pulley. Counter hold the crankshaft or block the flywheel to prevent the crankshaft from turning.

17. Remove the timing belt covers.

NOTE: The timing belt cover bolts are different lengths and must be returned to the proper hole at reassembly. During removal, diagram or label each bolt and its correct position.

18. Remove the timing belt guide.

19. Loosen the idler pulley bolt, push it all the way to the left and tighten the bolt. This removes tension from the belt.

20. Matchmark the belt and all the pulleys so the belt may be reinstalled exactly as it was before. Mark an arrow on the belt showing direction of rotation.

21. Remove the timing belt from the lower pulley (crankshaft timing pulley). If careful, the belt may remain undisturbed on the camshaft pulleys.

22. Remove the idler pulley and spring.

23. Remove the crankshaft timing pulley.

24. Remove the PCV hose.

25. Remove the dipstick and tube.

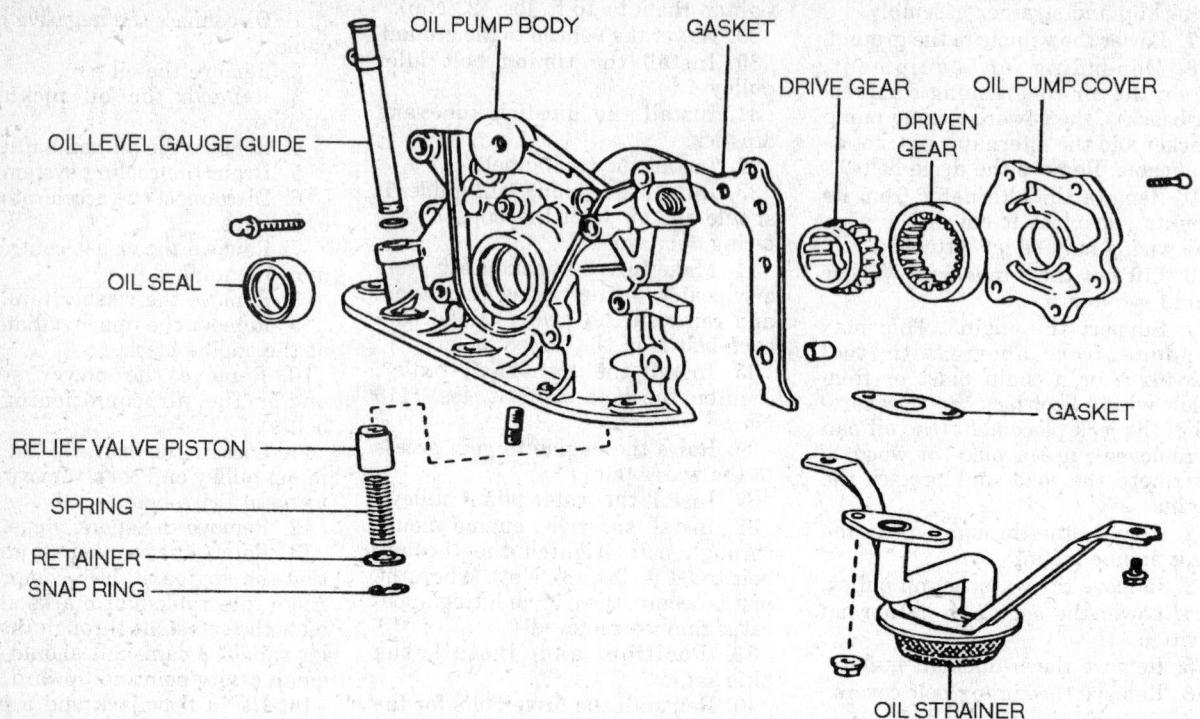

Exploded view of the oil pump — Prizm

OIL PUMP BODY
GASKET
DRIVE GEAR
OIL PUMP COVER
DRIVEN GEAR
OIL LEVEL GAUGE GUIDE
OIL SEAL
RELIEF VALVE PISTON
SPRING
RETAINER
SNAP RING
GASKET
OIL STRAINER

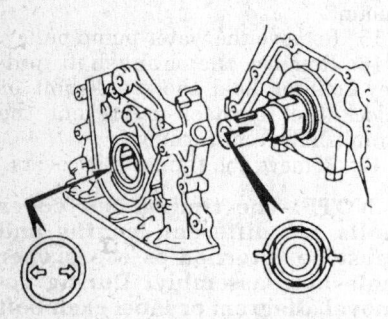

Correct position for installation of the oil pump — Prizm

26. Remove the 7 bolts in the oil pump and carefully remove the pump. If it is difficult to remove, tap it lightly with a plastic or rubber mallet. Do not pry it off or strike it with a metal hammer.

To install:
27. Place a new gasket on the block. Install the oil pump to the crankshaft with the spline teeth to the drive gear engaged with the large teeth of the crankshaft.
28. Install the 7 retaining bolts and tighten them to 7 ft. lbs. (10 Nm).
29. Install the dipstick tube and dipstick.

30. Install the crankshaft timing pulley.
31. Install the timing belt idler pulley.
32. Install the timing belt.
33. Install the timing belt guide. It should install with the cupped side facing outward.
34. Make sure the gaskets are properly seated in the timing belt covers and reinstall the covers. Make sure each bolt is in the correct hole.
35. Install the crankshaft pulley. Again using a counter holding device, tighten the bolt to 87 ft. lbs. (118 Nm).
36. Install the water pump pulley and tighten the bolts finger-tight. Install the valve covers.
37. Install the right side engine mount. Tighten the through bolt to 64 ft. lbs. (87 Nm).
38. Install the reinforcement for the right motor mount and tighten the bolts to 31 ft. lbs. (43 Nm).
39. Install the spark plugs.
40. Install the alternator drive belt and tighten the water pump pulley bolts.
41. Install and adjust the power steering and/or the air conditioner drive belts.
42. Connect the upper radiator hose.

43. Install the windshield washer reservoir.
44. If equipped with cruise control, reinstall the cruise control actuator.
45. Connect the accelerator cable or linkage.
46. Install the oil pan baffle plate. Clean the contact surfaces thoroughly, apply a bead of sealer to the baffle plate and press the baffle plate into position. Be very careful not to get any sealant into the oil passages.
47. Install the oil pickup and strainer assembly. Install the PCV hose.
48. Install the oil pan.
49. Using new gaskets, reconnect the exhaust pipe. Tighten the bolts to the exhaust manifold 46 ft. lbs. (62 Nm).
50. Install the flywheel cover.
51. Install the stiffener plate and the center engine mount.
52. Refill the engine with oil.
53. Refill the coolant system.
54. Start the engine and check for leaks. Allow the engine to warm up to normal operating temperature and check the work area carefully for signs of seepage.
55. With the engine shut off, check the tension of the drive belts and adjust if necessary. Reinstall the splash guards under the vehicle.

1993-94 GSi

1. Disconnect the negative battery cable and elevate the vehicle. Safely support it. Remove the splash shield(s).

2. Remove the protectors from the 2 center engine mount nuts and studs.

3. Remove the 2 center transaxle mount-to-center crossmember nuts.

4. Remove the 2 rear transaxle mount-to-main crossmember nuts.

5. Drain the engine oil and remove the oil pan.

6. Remove the lower engine reinforcement brace, the oil pickup and strainer assembly.

7. Lower the vehicle to the ground.

8. Depending on equipment, loosen the air conditioning compressor bracket, the power steering pump bracket and the alternator bracket as applicable. Remove the drive belts.

9. Remove the alternator from its mounts and place it out of the way. The wiring may be left attached.

10. Lift out the windshield washer fluid reservoir.

11. Support the engine. This may be done from above with tool J-28467-A or a chain hoist or from below with a floor jack. Be very careful of the jack placement (the oil pan is removed); use a piece of wood to distribute the load and protect the engine.

12. Remove the through bolt in the right engine mount.

13. Remove the water pump pulley.

14. Lower the engine to its normal position.

15. Remove the crankshaft pulley.

16. Remove the timing belt covers.

17. Remove the timing belt guide from the crank pulley.

18. Loosen the idler pulley bolt, push it all the way to the left and tighten the bolt. This removes tension from the belt.

19. Matchmark the belt and all the pulleys so the belt may be reinstalled exactly as it was before. Mark an arrow on the belt showing direction of rotation.

20. Remove the timing belt from the lower pulley (crankshaft timing pulley). If careful, the belt may remain undisturbed on the camshaft pulleys.

21. Remove the idler pulley and spring.

22. Remove the dipstick and dipstick tube.

23. Remove the crankshaft timing pulley.

24. Raise the vehicle and safely support it.

25. Remove the 7 bolts holding the oil pump.

26. Remove the 7 bolts in the oil pump and carefully remove the pump. If it is difficult to remove, tap it lightly with a plastic or rubber mallet. Do not pry it off or strike it with a metal hammer.

To install:

27. Place a new gasket on the block. Install the oil pump to the crankshaft with the spline teeth to the drive gear engaged with the large teeth of the crankshaft.

28. Install the 7 retaining bolts and tighten them to 16 ft. lbs. (22 Nm).

29. Lower the vehicle to the ground.

30. Install the timing belt idler pulley.

31. Install the dipstick tube and dipstick.

32. Install the timing belt.

33. Install the timing belt guide. It should install with the cupped side facing outward.

34. Make sure the gaskets are properly seated in the timing belt covers and reinstall the covers. Make sure each bolt is in the correct hole.

35. Install the crankshaft pulley. Tighten the bolt to 87 ft. lbs. (118 Nm).

36. Elevate the motor to gain access to the water pump.

37. Install the water pump pulley.

38. Install the right engine mount through bolt. Tighten the through bolt to 64 ft. lbs. (87 Nm). When the bolt is secure, the engine lifting apparatus may be removed.

39. Position and install the alternator.

40. Reinstall the drive belts for the alternator, power steering and air conditioning as applicable. Adjust the belts to the correct tension.

41. Raise the vehicle and safely support it.

42. Install lower engine reinforcement brace.

43. Install the oil pickup and strainer assembly.

44. Apply a continuous bead of sealer GM 1050026 or similar, to both sides of the new pan gasket.

45. Place the gasket on the pan and install the pan to the block. Tighten the bolts and nuts to 4 ft. lbs. (5.4 Nm).

46. Install the 2 rear transaxle mount-to-main crossmember nuts and tighten them to 45 ft. lbs. (61 Nm). Install the 2 center transaxle mount-to-center crossmember nuts and tighten them to 45 ft. lbs. (61 Nm).

47. Install the protectors over the nuts and studs for the mounts.

48. Lower the vehicle to the ground.

49. Install the windshield washer fluid reservoir.

50. Refill the engine with the correct amount of fresh oil.

51. Connect the negative battery cable.

52. Start the engine and check for leaks. Allow the engine to warm up to normal operating temperature and check the work area carefully for signs of seepage.

53. With the engine shut OFF, check the tension of the drive belts and adjust if necessary. Reinstall the splash guard(s) under the vehicle.

Storm

1. Disconnect the battery negative cable.

2. Remove the power steering and alternator belts.

3. Remove the timing belt.

4. Raise and support the vehicle safely.

5. Remove the crankshaft pulley.

6. Remove the oil pump attaching bolts, then the oil pump from the vehicle.

7. Reverse procedure to install. Apply suitable sealant to the oil pump gasket. Install bolts and torque to 89 inch lbs. (10 Nm). Connect the battery negative cable. Start engine and check for leaks.

Spectrum

1. Remove the engine from the vehicle. Drain the engine oil from the crankcase.

2. Remove the alternator belt. Remove the starter assembly.

3. Install the flywheel holding tool J-35271 or equivalent, to secure the flywheel.

4. Remove the crankshaft pulley and boss.

5. Remove the timing cover bolts and the timing cover.

6. Loosen the tension pulley and remove the timing belt.

7. Remove the crankshaft timing gear and the tension pulley.

8. Remove the oil pan bolts, oil pan, oil strainer fixing bolt and the oil strainer assembly.

9. Remove the oil pump bolts and the oil pump assembly.

10. Remove the sealing material from the oil pump and engine block sealing surfaces.

11. To install, lubricate the oil pump, use new gaskets, apply seal-

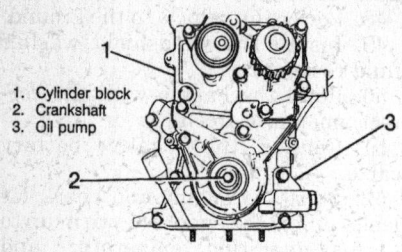

1. Cylinder block
2. Crankshaft
3. Oil pump

Oil pump mounting — Storm 1.8L engine

ant to the sealing surfaces and reverse the removal procedures.

NOTE: Before installing the oil pump, it would be a good idea to check the oil pressure relief valve and spring incorporated into the oil pump assembly. Remove the relief valve retaining plug along with the spring. Clean or replace the valve and spring assembly as necessary and reinstall it. Torque the retaining plug to 27 ft. lbs. (37 Nm). Torque the oil pump mounting bolts to 7 ft. lbs. (10 Nm). Be careful not to accidentally force the garter spring out of position during the oil pump assembly.

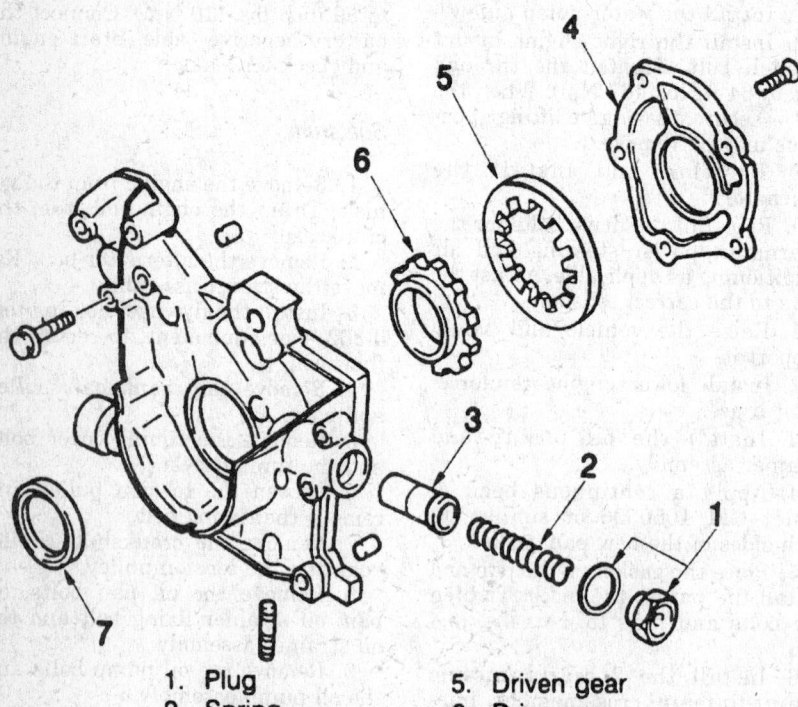

1. Plug
2. Spring
3. Relief valve
4. Oil pump cover
5. Driven gear
6. Drive gear
7. Oil seal

Exploded view of the oil pump — Spectrum

Rear Main Bearing Oil Seal

REMOVAL AND INSTALLATION

Metro

1. Remove the transaxle.
2. Raise and support the vehicle safely. Drain the oil and remove the oil pan.
3. Remove the pressure plate, the clutch plate and the flywheel.
4. Remove the mounting bolts and the rear seal housing.
5. Pry the oil seal from the oil seal housing.
6. To install, use new gaskets/seals and reverse the removal procedures. Torque the oil seal housing to 7-9 ft. lbs. (10-12 Nm) and the flywheel to the proper specification.

NOTE: After installing the oil seal housing, trim the gasket flush with the bottom of the case.

Prizm

1. Remove the transaxle from the vehicle.
2. If equipped with a manual transaxle, perform the following procedures:
   a. Matchmark the pressure plate-to-flywheel.

b. Remove the pressure plate-to-flywheel bolts and the clutch assembly from the vehicle.
   c. Remove the flywheel-to-crankshaft bolts and the flywheel.
3. If equipped with an automatic transaxle, perform the following procedures:
   a. Matchmark the flywheel-to-crankshaft.
   b. Remove the torque converter driveplate-to-crankshaft bolts and the torque converter driveplate.
4. Remove the rear end-plate-to-engine bolts and the rear end plate.
5. If removing the rear oil seal retainer, perform the following procedures:
   a. Remove the rear oil seal retainer-to-engine bolts, rear oil seal retainer to oil pan bolts and the rear oil seal retainer.
   b. Using a small prybar, pry the rear oil seal retainer from the mating surfaces.
   c. Using a drive punch, drive the oil seal from the rear bearing retainer.
   d. Using the proper tool, clean the gasket mounting surfaces.
6. To remove the rear oil seal, with the rear oil seal retainer installed, use a small prybar and pry the seal from the rear oil seal retainer.

NOTE: When removing the rear oil seal, be careful not to damage the seal mounting surface.

To install:
7. Clean the oil seal mounting surface.
8. Using multi-purpose grease, lubricate the new seal lips.
9. Using an rear oil seal installation tool J-35388 or equivalent, tap the seal straight into the bore of the retainer.
10. If the rear oil seal retainer was removed from the vehicle, use a new gasket and sealant, if necessary and reverse the removal procedures; be careful when installing the oil seal over the crankshaft.
11. To complete the installation, reverse the removal procedures. Torque the flywheel-to-crankshaft bolts to 58 ft. lbs. (78 Nm) if equipped with automatic transaxles or to 47 ft. lbs. (64 Nm) if equipped with manual transaxles.
12. Torque the converter drive plate-to-crankshaft bolts to 61 ft. lbs. (83 Nm).

Spectrum and Storm

1. Remove the transaxle.

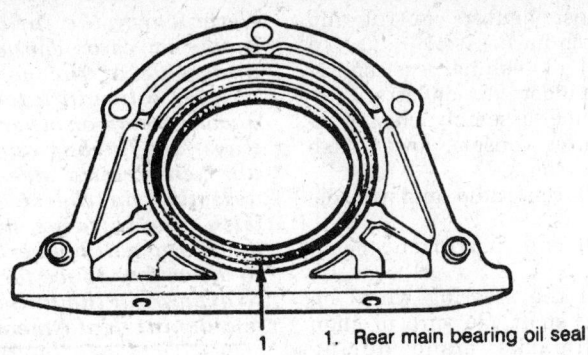

1. Rear main bearing oil seal

Rear main oil seal installed in housing — Metro

2. Remove the oil pan. On Storm, remove the right and left undercovers.

3. Remove the pressure plate and clutch on manual transaxle or the torque converter on automatic transaxle, the flywheel bolts and the flywheel from the crankshaft.

4. Remove the rear oil seal retainer and remove the oil seal from the retainer. Clean the sealing surfaces.

5. Using a new oil seal, install the new seal in the oil seal retainer.

6. To install, use new gaskets, apply sealer to the mounting surfaces, apply oil to the seal lips, align the dowel pins of the retainer with the engine block and reverse the removal procedures.

ENGINE COOLING

Radiator

REMOVAL AND INSTALLATION

Metro

1. Disconnect the battery negative cable.

2. Drain the cooling system.

3. Disconnect the cooling fan motor electrical connector and the air inlet hose.

4. Remove the inlet, outlet and the reservoir tank hoses from the radiator.

5. If equipped with automatic transaxle, disconnect the oil cooler lines from the radiator.

6. Remove the mounting bolts, cooling fan motor, shroud and the radiator from the vehicle.

7. Reverse procedure to install. Connect the battery negative cable and refill system.

Prizm

1. Disconnect the negative battery cable.

2. Drain the coolant by opening the engine block and radiator drain cocks.

3. Remove the coolant overflow reservoir.

4. Disconnect the upper radiator hose from the radiator and the lower radiator hose from the thermostat housing.

5. If equipped with automatic transmission, disconnect the oil cooler lines running to the radiator.

6. Remove the upper radiator brackets.

7. Disconnect the wiring running to the fan(s).

8. Remove the radiator and fan assembly from the vehicle. If the radiator is to be worked on or replaced, the fan and shroud assembly, the lower hose and the lower rubber mounts must be removed. Don't forget to install them on the new unit before installing it.

To install:

9. With the necessary parts mounted on the radiator, install the radiator in the vehicle. Install the upper mounting brackets. Tighten to 7.5 ft. lbs. (10 Nm).

10. Install the oil cooler hoses to the radiator, if equipped with automatic transaxle.

11. Connect the electrical lead(s) to the fan(s).

12. Replace the coolant overflow reservoir and connect the hose.

13. Install and secure the upper and lower radiator hoses. Use new clamps.

14. Connect the negative battery cable.

15. Confirm that the drain cocks on the engine and radiator are closed.

Refill the cooling system with the proper amount of engine coolant.

16. Add automatic transaxle fluid in an amount equal to that lost from the oil cooler during removal.

17. Start the engine and check hose and line connections for leaks. Allow the engine to warm up to normal operating temperature. Check carefully for leaks under both cold and hot conditions.

18. Check the automatic transmission fluid and add if necessary.

Spectrum

1. Disconnect the battery negative cable.

2. Drain the cooling system.

3. Remove the air intake duct.

4. Remove the fan motor cable from the fan motor socket and disconnect the thermo-switch cable.

5. Remove the fan motor assembly.

6. Remove the radiator hoses at the radiator, the coolant recovery hose at the filler neck and the oil cooler lines, if equipped with automatic transaxle.

7. Remove the radiator attaching bolts and the radiator.

8. Reverse procedure to install. Connect the battery negative cable.

Storm

1. Disconnect the battery negative cable.

2. Drain cooling system.

3. If equipped with automatic transaxle, disconnect the oil cooler lines from the radiator.

4. Remove the upper and lower radiator hoses.

5. Disconnect the fan motor cable from the rear of the fan motor socket.

6. Remove the coolant recovery hose from the radiator filler neck.

7. Remove the radiator attaching bolts and the radiator with fan and motor assembly from the vehicle.

8. Reverse procedure to install. Connect the battery negative cable and refill system. Start engine and check for leaks.

Heater Core

REMOVAL AND INSTALLATION

Metro

1. Disconnect the negative battery cable. Drain the cooling system.

2. Remove the clamps and heater core hoses from the heater core.

3. Remove the instrument panel carrier assembly.

4. Remove the heater control assembly from the instrument support member.

5. Remove the temperature and mode control cables from the heater case.

6. Remove the 2 mounting bolts and 2 mounting nuts from the heater case. Remove the heater case from the vehicle.

7. Remove all the heater case retaining clips and 2 attaching screws from the heater case.

8. Separate the heater case halves.

9. Carefully pull the heater core from the heater case.

10. To install, reverse the removal procedures. Refill the cooling system. Start the engine, bring it to normal operating temperature and check for leaks.

Prizm

1990-92

1. Disconnect the negative battery cable.

2. Remove the steering wheel nut and mark the position of the steering wheel relative to the steering shaft.

3. Remove the trim bezel from the instrument panel.

4. Remove the cup holder from the console.

5. Remove the radio.

6. Remove the instrument panel assembly, cluster assembly, center console and all console trim, lower dash trim, side window air deflectors and all instrument panel wiring harnesses.

7. Drain the coolant from the cooling system.

8. Disconnect all cables and ducts from the heater case.

9. Disconnect the blower switch harness and the heater control assembly.

10. Disconnect the 2 center console support braces.

11. Remove all mounting bolts, nuts and clips from the heater and air distribution cases.

12. Remove the heater and air distribution cases.

13. Remove the screws and clips from the case, separate the case halves and remove the core from the case.

To install:

14. Install the heater core into the case halves and secure with clips.

15. Install the heater and air distribution cases and attaching bolts, nuts and clips.

16. Install the 2 center console support braces.

17. Connect heater control and blower switch harnesses.

18. Install all dash harness connectors, side window air deflectors, instrument panel assembly, cluster assembly, center console, lower dash and console trim.

19. Install the radio and console cup holder.

20. Install the instrument panel trim bezel.

21. Install the steering wheel on the steering shaft. Be sure to align the matchmarks made during removal.

22. Connect the negative battery cable and fill the cooling system.

23. Start the vehicle and check for leaks.

1993-94

The heater case and core are located directly behind the center console. The access the case and core, the entire console must be removed as well as most of the instrument panel assembly.

1. If equipped, with an air bag system, disable the air bag system as follows:

 a. Position the vehicles front wheels to point straight-ahead.

 b. Turn the ignition switch to the **LOCK** position.

 c. Remove the IGN and CIG & RADIO fuses from the fuse block.

 d. Remove the Connector Position Assurance (CPA).

 e. Disconnect the lower steering column connector.

2. Disconnect the negative battery cable.

3. Remove the 2 side covers from the steering column.

4. Remove the upper and lower column covers.

5. Remove and set aside the left front carpet retainer. Remove 2 screws and disconnect the hood release lever from the knee bolster.

6. Remove 2 trim caps, unbolt and remove the knee bolster from the instrument panel.

7. With the air bag system disabled, remove the air bag inflator module as follows:

 a. Remove the 2 Torx® head screws.

 b. Remove the Connector Position Assurance (CPA) and disconnect the upper steering column connector.

 c. Remove the inflator module from the steering wheel.

——— CAUTION ———
When carrying a live inflator module, keep the air bag and trim cover pointed away from you.

Never carry the inflator module by the wires or connector on the underside of the module. When placing a live inflator module on a work bench or other surface, always face the bag and trim cover up. Never rest a steering column assembly on the steering wheel with the inflator module face down and column vertical. This is to allow free space for the air bag to expand in the unlikely event of accidental deployment.

8. With the inflator module removed, remove the horn connector.

9. Remove the steering wheel nut and mark the position of the steering wheel relative to the steering shaft.

10. Remove the trim bezel from the instrument panel.

11. Remove the cup holder from the console.

12. Remove the radio.

13. Remove the instrument panel assembly, cluster assembly, center console and all console trim, lower dash trim, side window air deflectors and all instrument panel wiring harnesses.

14. Drain the coolant from the cooling system.

15. Disconnect all cables and ducts from the heater case.

16. Disconnect the blower switch harness and the heater control assembly.

17. Disconnect the 2 center console support braces.

18. Remove all mounting bolts, nuts and clips from the heater and air distribution cases.

19. Remove the heater and air distribution cases.

20. Remove the screws and clips from the case, separate the case halves and remove the core from the case.

To install:

21. Install the core into the case.

22. Connect the case halves and install the screws and clips to the case.

23. Install the heater and air distribution cases and all mounting bolts, nuts and clips.

24. Connect the 2 center console support braces, the blower switch harness and the heater control assembly.

25. Connect all cables and ducts to the heater case.

26. Install all instrument panel wiring harnesses, side window air deflectors, lower dash trim, center console and all console trim, cluster assembly and the instrument panel assembly.

27. Install the radio and cup holder.

28. Install the instrument trim bezel.

29. Install the steering wheel, aligning the matchmarks made during removal.

30. Install the steering wheel nut and torque to 25 ft. lbs. (34 Nm).

31. Connect the horn connector.

32. Install the air bag inflator module.

33. Connect the upper steering column connector and secure with CPA.

34. Install the 2 Torx® head screws. Torque to 78 inch lbs. (8.8 Nm).

35. Install the upper and lower column covers with 2 screws.

36. Install the 2 steering column sidecovers.

37. Install the knee bolster with 4 bolts.

38. Install the left front carpet and retainer.

39. Reactivate the air bag system as follows:

    a. Turn the ignition switch to the **LOCK** position.

    b. Connect the lower steering column connector.

    c. Secure the lower steering column connector with Connector Position Assurance (CPA).

    d. Install the IGN and CIG & RADIO fuses.

    e. Turn the ignition switch to the **ACC** or **ON** position.

    f. Observe the **INFLATABLE RESTRAINT** indicator lamp. If the lamp does not illuminate for approximately 60 seconds and turn OFF, there is a problem in the air bag system and further diagnostic testing of the system is needed.

40. Fill the cooling system and check for leaks.

Spectrum

1. Disconnect the negative battery cable. Disconnect the heater hoses in the engine compartment.

2. At the lower part of the heater unit case, remove the 6 retaining clips.

3. Using a small prybar, pry open the lower part of the case and remove it.

4. Remove the core assembly insulator and the core assembly.

5. To install, reverse the removal procedures.

Storm

1. Disconnect the battery negative cable.

2. Disconnect heater hoses from inside the engine compartment.

3. Remove the instrument panel assembly.

4. If equipped with air conditioning, remove the evaporator assembly.

5. Remove the duct between the blower motor and the heater unit.

6. Remove the center ventilation duct.

7. Remove the 4 nuts attaching the heater unit and remove the heater unit from the vehicle.

8. Remove the 5 screws attaching the mode control case to the heater core case, then the mode control case. Do not remove the link assembly as this time.

9. Remove 5 screws to separate the 2 halves of the heater core case and remove the heater core from the case.

10. Reverse procedure to install. Connect the battery negative cable.

Water Pump

REMOVAL AND INSTALLATION

Metro

1990-91

1. Disconnect the negative battery cable.

2. Drain the cooling system.

3. Remove the water pump belt and pulley.

4. Remove the crankshaft pulley, the timing belt outside cover, the timing belt and the tensioner.

5. Remove the mounting bolts and the water pump.

6. Clean the gasket mating surfaces.

7. To install, use a new gasket/sealer and reverse the removal procedures. Torque the water pump bolts to 7.5-9.0 ft. lbs. (10-13 Nm). Adjust the water pump belt deflection to 1/4-3/8 inch between the water pump and the crankshaft pulleys.

1992-94

1. Disconnect the negative battery cable.

2. Drain the cooling system.

3. Remove the air cleaner, if needed.

4. Remove the A/C pipe bracket, if equipped.

5. Raise and safely support the vehicle. Then remove the right lower splash shield, if needed.

6. Remove the A/C drive belt from the compressor and crank shaft, if equipped.

7. Remove the lower alternator cover plate, loosen the alternator and remove the alternator/water pump drive belt.

8. Remove the crankshaft pulley, the timing belt outside cover, the timing belt and the tensioner.

9. Remove the water pump pulley.

10. Remove the mounting bolts and the water pump.

11. Clean the gasket mating surfaces.

12. To install, use a new gasket/sealer and reverse the removal procedures. Torque the water pump bolts to 7.5-9.0 ft. lbs. (10-13 Nm). Adjust the water pump belt deflection to 1/4-3/8 inch between the water pump and the crankshaft pulleys.

Prizm

1990

1. Remove the radiator cap. Drain the engine coolant by opening the radiator and engine block drain cocks.

2. Raise and safely support the vehicle on jackstands.

3. Remove the 2 nuts for the rear motor mount.

4. Lower the vehicle to the ground.

5. Remove the windshield washer fluid container.

6. If equipped, remove the cruise control bracket with the control module.

7. Remove the through bolt for the right motor mount.

8. Place a jack under the engine. Use a piece of wood between the engine and the jack.

9. Raise the engine slowly and carefully. Keep a close watch on lines and cables. The engine need only be raised enough to gain access to various nuts and bolts.

10. Loosen the water pump pulley bolts but leave them in place.

11. Loosen the alternator lock bolt and pivot nut; swing the alternator towards the engine and remove the drive belt.

12. Loosen the pivot bolts and the lock bolt for the power steering pump and move it towards the engine; remove the power steering belt.

13. With the belts removed, the water pump pulley may be removed from the pump.

14. Lower the jack, allowing the engine to return to place.

15. Remove the water inlet and water bypass hoses from the water inlet pipe.

16. Remove the clamp holding the water inlet pipe to the engine. Loosen and remove the 2 nuts holding the inlet pipe to the water pump. Remove the pipe and its O-ring.

17. Remove the mounting bolt for the dipstick tube; remove the tube and dipstick. Immediately plug the

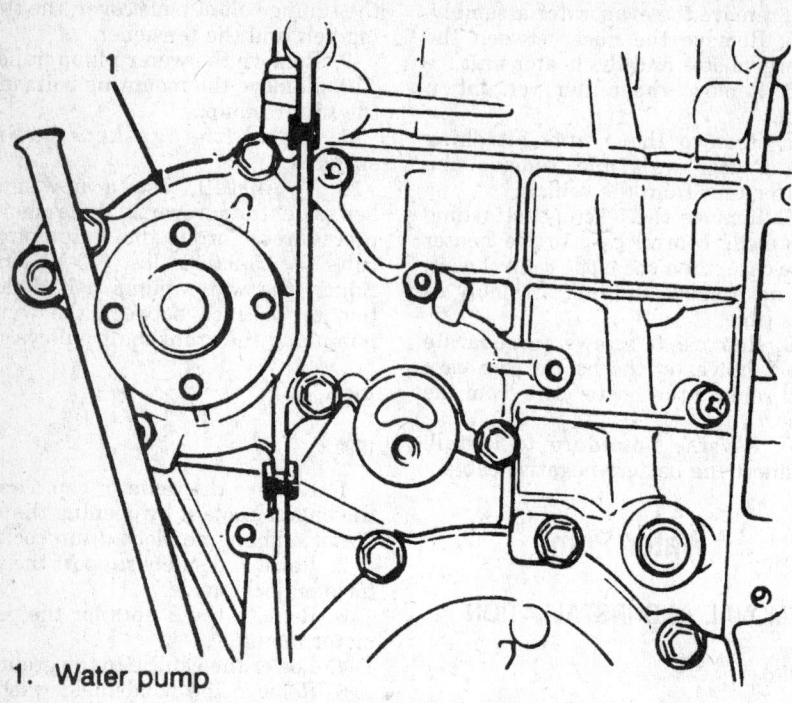

1. Water pump

Water pump mounting — Metro

hole in block to prevent fluid from polluting the oil.

NOTE: During the following steps, if coolant should get by the plug in the dipstick hole and run into the motor, the engine oil must be changed before starting the motor. Failure to do so can damage the engine bearings.

18. Remove the upper timing belt cover.

NOTE: The timing belt is exposed with the cover(s) removed. Do not allow oil or coolant to contact the belt. This includes any fluid which may be accidentally transferred through rags, fingerprints, etc.

19. Remove the 3 water pump bolts and remove the water pump.

To install:

20. When reinstalling, position a new O-ring on the engine and fit the water pump. Tighten the 3 bolts to 11 ft. lbs. (15 Nm).

21. Install the upper timing belt cover.

22. Install a new O-ring on the dipstick tube.

23. Remove the plug in the engine and install the tube. Tighten the mounting bolt.

24. Using a new O-ring, install the water inlet pipe at the back of the water pump. Tighten the 2 nuts to 14 ft. lbs. (19 Nm).

25. Connect the water inlet and water bypass hoses to the water inlet pipe.

26. Following the same jacking procedure as before, elevate the motor with the floor jack.

27. Install the water pump pulley and tighten the bolts finger-tight. It will be easier to do the final tightening when the belts are installed.

28. Install the power steering belt and adjust its tension.

29. Install the alternator drive belt and adjust its tension.

30. Tighten the water pump pulley bolts to 17 ft. lbs. (23 Nm).

31. Lower the jack, allowing the engine to return to its normal place.

32. Install the through bolt for the right motor mount. Tighten it to 64 ft. lbs. (86 Nm).

33. Reinstall the cruise control module and the bracket, if equipped.

34. Raise and safely support the vehicle.

35. Install the 2 nuts for the rear mount and tighten them to 38 ft. lbs. (52 Nm).

36. Lower the vehicle to the ground.

37. Replace the washer fluid container.

38. Confirm that the drain cocks on the radiator and engine block are closed. Refill the cooling system with coolant.

39. Start the engine and check for leaks. Pay particular attention to any hose or fitting which was disassembled during the repair.

40. After the engine is shut OFF, double check the drive belts for proper tension and adjust as necessary.

1991-94

1. Disconnect the negative battery cable.

2. Drain the cooling system.

3. Support the engine using a J-28467-A or equivalent, universal support fixture.

4. Remove right engine mount.

5. Remove upper and middle timing belt covers.

6. If the vehicle is equipped with power steering, proceed as follows:

   a. Raise and safely support the vehicle.

   b. Remove the front transaxle mount.

   c. Remove the radiator fan and shroud.

7. Remove the engine harness retainer.

8. Remove the dipstick, 1 bolt, dipstick tube and plug the dip stick tube hole.

9. Disconnect the engine coolant temperature sender.

10. Remove the coolant hose from pump-to-inlet pipe.

11. Remove 2 nuts and engine coolant inlet pipe.

12. Remove 3 bolts and water pump from the vehicle.

To install:

13. When reinstalling, position a new O-ring on the engine and fit the water pump. Tighten the 3 bolts to 11 ft. lbs. (15 Nm).

14. Using a new O-ring, install the water inlet pipe at the back of the water pump. Tighten the 2 nuts to 11 ft. lbs. (15 Nm).

15. Connect the coolant hose to the pump-to-inlet pipe.

16. Connect the engine coolant temperature sensor.

17. Using a new O-ring, install the dipstick tube and dipstick.

18. Connect the engine harness retainer.

19. If equipped with power steering, proceed as follows:

   a. Install the radiator fan and shroud.

   b. Install the front transaxle mount and through bolt. Torque the mounting bolts to 45 ft. lbs. (61

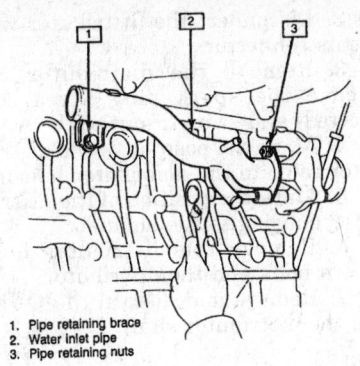

1. Pipe retaining brace
2. Water inlet pipe
3. Pipe retaining nuts

Removing the water pump inlet pipe — Prizm

Nm) and the through bolt to 69 ft. lbs. (87 Nm).

c. Lower the vehicle.

20. Install upper and middle timing covers.

21. Install right engine mount. Torque the through bolt to 64 ft. lbs. (87 Nm).

22. Torque 1 engine mount-to-engine bracket bolt and 2 engine mount-to-engine bracket nuts to 45 ft. lbs. (65 Nm).

23. Remove the engine support fixture.

24. Fill the cooling system and connect the battery negative cable. Start engine and check for leaks.

Storm

EXCEPT DOHC ENGINE

1. Disconnect the battery negative cable and drain cooling system.

2. Remove the power steering pump belt and the timing belt.

3. Remove the belt tension pulley.

4. Remove the water pump-to-block attaching bolts and the water pump from the vehicle.

5. Reverse procedure to install. Clean mating surfaces of all gasket material. Torque water pump bolts to 17 ft. lbs. (23 Nm). Connect battery negative cable and refill cooling system.

DOHC ENGINE

1. Disconnect the battery negative cable and drain cooling system.

2. Support the engine using a suitable floor jack and remove the right front engine mount.

3. Remove the engine mount bridge and the upper timing belt cover.

4. Remove the power steering belt and the lower timing belt cover.

5. Loosen the timing belt tension pulley and remove the timing belt.

6. Remove the power steering pump and bracket.

7. Remove the water pump attaching bolts, then the water pump from the vehicle.

8. Reverse procedure to install. Connect the battery negative cable and refill cooling system. Start engine and check for leaks.

Spectrum

1. Disconnect the negative battery cable and drain the cooling system.

2. Loosen the power steering pump adjustment bolts and remove the belt.

3. Remove the timing belt.

4. Remove the tension pulley and spring.

5. Remove the water pump mounting bolts, the water pump and gasket. Clean the mounting surfaces of all gasket material.

6. To install, reverse the removal procedures. Torque the water pump to 17 ft. lbs. (23 Nm) and the tension pulley to 30 ft. lbs. (41 Nm).

Thermostat

REMOVAL AND INSTALLATION

Metro

1. Disconnect the battery negative cable.

2. Drain cooling system to a level below the thermostat.

3. Remove the air cleaner.

4. Disconnect the electrical connectors at the thermostat cap.

5. Remove the inlet hose, cap mounting bolts and the thermostat from the thermostat housing.

6. Clean the gasket mounting surfaces. Ensure that the thermostat air bleed hose is clear.

7. Reverse procedure to install. Install thermostat into housing with the spring side down. Fill cooling system and connect the battery negative cable. Start engine and check for leaks.

Prizm

1990-92

NOTE: A thermostat with an internal bypass should never be removed as a countermeasure to overheating. Removing the thermostat actually makes the problem worse because more coolant bypasses the radiator, thereby reducing cooling even more.

1. Drain the cooling system.

2. Remove the water inlet housing and remove the thermostat. Carefully observe the positioning of the thermostat within the housing.

To install:

3. Install the new thermostat in the housing, making sure it is in correctly. It is possible to install it backwards.

4. Additionally, make certain that the air bleed valve aligns with the protrusion on the water inlet housing. Failure to observe this placement can result in poor air bleeding and possible overheating.

5. Install the 2 hold-down bolts and tighten them to 20 ft. lbs. (27 Nm). Do not overtighten these bolts.

6. Refill the cooling system with coolant.

7. Start the engine. During the warm up period, observe the temperature gauge for normal behavior. Also during this period, check the water inlet housing area for any sign of leakage. Remember to check for leaks under both cold and hot conditions.

1993-94

NOTE: A thermostat with an internal bypass should never be removed as a countermeasure to overheating. Removing the thermostat actually makes the problem worse because more coolant bypasses the radiator, thereby reducing cooling even more.

1. Drain the cooling system.

2. Disconnect the engine coolant temperature sensor.

3. Loosen the lower radiator hose clamp and remove the lower hose from the housing.

4. Remove 2 nuts and thermostat housing.

5. Remove the thermostat and discard the old O-ring type gasket.

To install:

6. Install a new O-ring type gasket on the thermostat.

7. Install the thermostat.

8. Make certain that the air bleed valve is positioned within 10 degrees on either side of the top thermostat housing stud.

9. Install the thermostat housing, 2 nuts and torque the nuts to 84 inch lbs. (9.5 Nm).

10. Install the lower radiator hose and connect the coolant temperature sensor.

11. Refill the cooling system with coolant.

12. Start the engine. During the warm up period, observe the temperature gauge for normal behavior. Also during this period, check the water inlet housing area for any sign of leakage. Remember to check for

leaks under both cold and hot conditions.

Spectrum and Storm

1. Disconnect the battery negative cable. Drain cooling system.
2. Remove the top radiator hose from the outlet pipe.
3. Remove the outlet pipe bolts, outlet pipe, gasket and thermostat from the thermostat housing.
4. Reverse procedure to install. Refill cooling system. Connect battery negative cable. Start engine and check for leaks.

Cooling System Bleeding

After performing any repairs on the cooling system, it must be bled. Air trapped in the system will prevent proper filling and leave the radiator coolant level low, causing a risk of overheating.

1. To bleed the system, start with the system cool, radiator cap off and the radiator filled to about an inch below the filler neck.
2. Start the engine and run it at slightly above normal idle speed. This will ensure adequate circulation. If air bubbles appear and the

coolant level drops, fill the cooling system to bring the level back to the proper level.

3. Run the engine until the thermostat opens. When this happens, coolant will move abruptly across the top of the radiator and the temperature of the radiator will suddenly rise.
4. At this point, air is often expelled and the level may drop quite a bit. Keep refilling the system until the level is near the top of the radiator and remains constant.
5. If the vehicle has an overflow tank, fill the radiator right up to the filler neck. Replace the radiator filler cap.

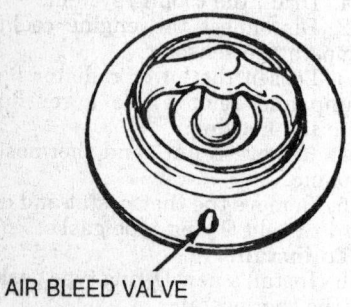

AIR BLEED VALVE

Air bleed valve type thermostat

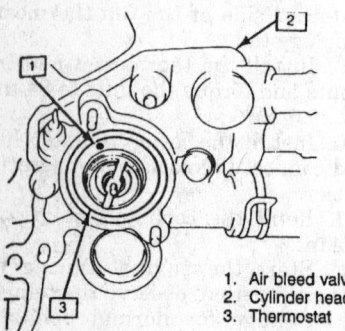

1. Air bleed valve
2. Cylinder head
3. Thermostat

The correct position for the air bleed valve during thermostat replacement — Prizm

---

ENGINE ELECTRICAL

NOTE: Disconnecting the negative battery cable on some vehicles may interfere with the functions of the on-board computer systems and may require the computer to undergo a relearning process, once the negative battery cable is reconnected.

Distributor

REMOVAL

Metro

1. Disconnect the negative battery cable.
2. Disconnect the wiring harnesses and/or vacuum lines at the distributor.
3. Remove the distributor cap.

NOTE: Mark the distributor body in reference to where the rotor is pointing. Mark the distributor hold-down bracket and cylinder head for a reinstallation location point.

4. Remove the hold-down bolt and the distributor from the cylinder head. Do not rotate the engine after the distributor has been removed.
5. Remove and discard the old O-ring from the distributor shaft.

1990-92 Prizm

EXCEPT GSi

1. Disconnect the negative battery cable.

2. Disconnect the distributor wire at its connector.
3. Remove the distributor cap (leave the spark plug wires connected) and swing it out of the way.
4. Mark the position of the distributor rotor to the distributor housing.
5. Mark the position of the distributor housing to the engine.
6. Remove the distributor hold-down bolts and the distributor.
7. Remove and discard the O-ring on the distributor shaft.

GSi

1. Disconnect the negative battery cable.
2. Label and disconnect the coil and spark plug wiring at the distributor cap.
3. Disconnect the distributor wire at its connector.
4. Mark the position of the distributor relative to the engine. Use a marker or tape so the mark doesn't rub off during the handling of the case.
5. Remove the distributor hold-down bolts.
6. Carefully pull the distributor out until it stops turning counterclockwise.
7. Mark the position of the rotor relative to the distributor. Use a marker or tape so the mark doesn't rub off during the handling of the case.
8. Remove the distributor from the engine.
9. Remove the O-ring from the distributor shaft.

1993-94 Prizm

1. Disconnect the negative battery cable.
2. Disconnect the distributor wires at their connectors.
3. Remove the spark plug wire lock retainers on the distributor cap.
4. Mark and remove the spark plug wires.
5. Remove the 3 bolts and the distributor cap.
6. Mark the position of the distributor rotor relative to the distributor.
7. Mark the position of the distributor relative to the engine.
8. Remove the hold-down bolts and the distributor.
9. Remove and discard the O-ring on the distributor shaft.

Storm

1. Disconnect the negative battery cable.
2. Disconnect all electrical connections at the distributor, including the plug wires.

Aligning the distributor driveshaft with the housing — Prizm (engine code 5)

3. Remove the distributor cap.

4. Mark the position of the distributor case relative to the engine. Use a marker or tape so the mark doesn't rub off during the handling of the case. Also mark the position of the distributor rotor relative to the case.

5. Remove the distributor mounting bolts.

6. Remove the distributor from the engine and remove the O-ring from the distributor shaft.

Spectrum

1. Disconnect the negative battery terminal from the battery.

2. Remove the distributor cap.

3. Mark and remove all electrical leads and vacuum lines connected to the distributor assembly.

4. Mark the relationship of the rotor to the distributor housing and the distributor housing to the engine.

5. Remove the hold-down bolt, clamp and distributor.

INSTALLATION

Timing Not Disturbed

METRO

1. Install a new O-ring on the distributor shaft.

2. Align the reference marks on the distributor housing to the distributor hold-down bracket.

3. Install the distributor into the offset slot in the camshaft, then the hold-down bolt.

4. Connect vacuum hoses and/or electrical connectors to the distributor.

5. Install the distributor cap, then connect the battery negative cable. Check and/or adjust the ignition timing.

1990-92 PRIZM EXCEPT GSi

1. Install a new O-ring on the distributor shaft.

2. Install the distributor into the engine. Make sure all the markings on the engine, distributor and rotor line up properly.

3. Install the distributor cap.

4. Install distributor wires and negative battery cable.

5. Check and adjust the timing as necessary.

1990-92 PRIZM GSi

1. Install a new O-ring and lubricate it with clean engine oil.

2. Align the rotor with it's mark made during removal. Then install the distributor, aligning the marks made on the distributor and engine during removal.

3. Install the distributor hold-down bolts.

4. Install the distributor cap and connect the negative battery cable.

5. Check and adjust the timing as necessary.

1993-94 PRIZM

1. Install a new O-ring and lubricate it with clean engine oil.

2. Install the distributor, matching the alignment marks made during removal.

3. Install the distributor hold-down bolts.

4. Connect the distributor wires at their connectors.

5. Install the distributor cap and bolts.

6. Connect the spark plug wires to the distributor cap.

7. Install the spark plug wire lock retainers on the distributor cap.

8. Connect the negative battery cable.

9. Check and adjust the timing as necessary.

STORM — EXCEPT DOHC ENGINE

1. Use a new O-ring on the distributor housing, lubricate the drive gear teeth with engine oil, align the protrusion at the bottom of the distributor housing with the pin on the side of the distributor drive gear, mesh the gears and install the distributor.

NOTE: Ensure that alignment marks on the distributor housing-to-engine and the rotor-to-distributor housing align before installing distributor.

2. Install the distributor cap.

3. Connect all vacuum hoses and electrical connectors.

4. Connect the battery negative cable.

5. Check and/or adjust the ignition timing.

STORM — DOHC ENGINE

1. Turn the distributor to align the halfshaft drilled mark with housing cavity.

2. Align the center of the distributor flange with the center of the cylinder head bolt hole, then, install the distributor.

3. Install the hold-down bolt and torque it to 14 ft. lbs. (19 Nm).

4. Connect the spark plug wires and ignition coil wire.

5. Connect the distributor electrical connector.

6. Connect the battery negative cable. Check and/or adjust the ignition timing.

SPECTRUM

1. Align the marks on the distributor housing and the distributor housing-to-the engine, then install the distributor.

2. Connect all vacuum hoses and electrical connectors.

3. Install the distributor cap and spark plug wires.

4. Connect the battery negative cable. Check and/or adjust ignition timing.

Timing Disturbed

METRO

Place the engine on TDC of the compression stroke to obtain the proper ignition timing.

1. Remove the No. 1 spark plug.

2. Place thumb over the spark plug hole. Crank the engine slowly until compression is felt. It will be easier to have someone rotate the engine by hand, using a wrench on the crankshaft pulley.

3. Align the timing mark on the crankshaft pulley with the **0** degree mark on the timing scale attached to the front of the engine. This places the engine at TDC of the compression stroke.

4. Align the marks on the distributor drive coupling and distributor shaft.

5. Install the distributor into the engine. Be sure to align the distributor-to-engine block mark made earlier.

6. Install the No. 1 spark plug. Connect all vacuum hoses and/or electrical connectors to the distributor.

7. Install distributor cap, then connect the battery negative cable.

8. Check and/or adjust ignition timing.

1990-92 PRIZM EXCEPT GSi

1. Remove the No. 1 spark plug.

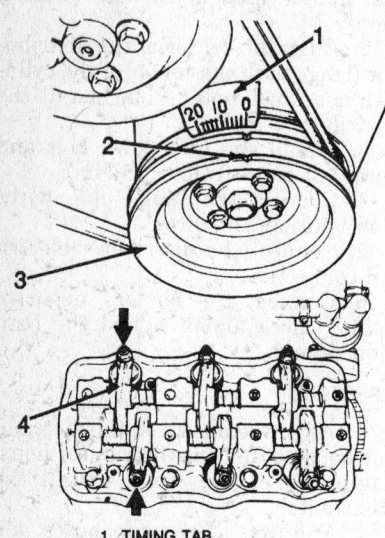

1. TIMING TAB
2. TIMING NOTCH
3. CRANKSHAFT PULLEY
4. NO. 1 CYLINDER

Timing mark and zero mark — Metro

2. Place finger over the spark plug hole. Crank the engine slowly until compression is felt. It would be easier to have someone rotate the engine by hand, using a wrench on the crankshaft pulley.

3. Align the timing mark on the crankshaft pulley with the **0** degree mark on the timing scale attached to the front of the engine. This places the engine at TDC of the compression stroke.

4. Turn the rotor until the groove in the distributor drive is aligned with the protrusion on the distributor housing.

5. Check the position of the exhaust camshaft to verify the TDC position of No. 1 cylinder.

6. Install the distributor.

7. Check and adjust the timing as necessary.

1990-92 PRIZM GSi

1. Remove the No. 1 spark plug.

2. Place finger over the spark plug hole. Crank the engine slowly until compression is felt. It would be easier to have someone rotate the engine by hand, using a wrench on the crankshaft pulley.

3. Align the timing mark on the crankshaft pulley with the **0** degree

mark on the timing scale attached to the front of the engine. This places the engine at TDC of the compression stroke.

4. To verify the TDC position of No. 1 cylinder, remove the oil cap to see that the groove on the camshaft is visible.

5. Align the drilled mark on the distributor gear with the groove in the distributor housing.

6. Install the distributor while centering the bolt holes on the cylinder head in the distributor mounting flange holes.

7. Install distributor hold-down bolts.

8. Check and adjust the timing as necessary.

1993-94 PRIZM

1. Remove the No. 1 spark plug.

2. Place finger over the spark plug hole. Crank the engine slowly until compression is felt. It would be easier to have someone rotate the engine by hand, using a wrench on the crankshaft pulley.

3. Align the timing mark on the crankshaft pulley with the **0** degree mark on the timing scale attached to the front of the engine. This places the engine at TDC of the compression stroke.

4. Turn the rotor until the groove in the distributor drive is aligned with the protrusion on the distributor housing.

5. Check the position of the exhaust camshaft to verify the TDC position of No. 1 cylinder.

6. Install the distributor.

7. Check and adjust the timing as necessary.

STORM — EXCEPT DOHC ENGINE

Place the engine on TDC of the compression stroke to obtain the proper ignition timing.

1. Remove the No. 1 spark plug.

2. Place finger over the spark plug hole. Crank the engine slowly until compression is felt. It would be easier to have someone rotate the engine by hand, using a wrench on the crankshaft pulley.

3. Align the timing mark on the crankshaft pulley with the **0** degrees mark on the timing scale attached to the front of the engine. This places the engine at TDC of the compression stroke.

4. Turn the distributor shaft until the rotor points to the No. 1 spark plug tower on the cap.

5. Install the distributor into the engine. Be sure to align the distribu-

tor-to-engine block mark made earlier.

6. To complete the installation, reverse the removal procedures and check the timing.

STORM — DOHC ENGINE

Place the engine on TDC of the compression stroke to obtain the proper ignition timing.

1. Remove the No. 1 spark plug.

2. Place thumb over the spark plug hole. Crank the engine slowly until compression is felt. It will be easier to have someone rotate the engine by hand, using a wrench on the crankshaft pulley.

3. Align the timing mark on the crankshaft pulley with the **0** degree mark on the timing scale attached to the front of the engine. This places the engine at TDC of the compression stroke.

4. Turn the distributor shaft until the rotor points to the No. 1 spark plug tower on the cap.

5. Install the distributor into the engine. Be sure to align the distributor-to-engine block mark made earlier.

6. Install spark plug and wire.

7. Connect battery negative cable. Check and/or adjust ignition timing.

SPECTRUM

If the engine was cranked while the distributor was removed, place the engine on TDC of the compression stroke to obtain the proper ignition timing.

1. Remove the No. 1 spark plug.

2. Place thumb over the spark plug hole. Crank the engine slowly until compression is felt. It will be easier to have someone rotate the engine by hand, using a wrench on the crankshaft pulley.

3. Align the timing mark on the crankshaft pulley with the **0** degree mark on the timing scale attached to the front of the engine. This places the engine at TDC of the compression stroke.

4. Turn the distributor shaft until the rotor points to the No. 1 spark plug tower on the cap.

5. Install the distributor into the engine. Be sure to align the distributor-to-engine block mark made earlier.

6. Install the No. 1 spark plug and connect all vacuum hoses and electrical connectors.

7. Install distributor cap, then connect the battery negative cable.

8. Check and/or adjust the ignition timing.

Ignition Timing

ADJUSTMENT

NOTE: When connecting the tachometer in the following procedures, be sure not to ground the tachometer terminal. Grounding the tachometer could result in damage to the igniter or ignition coil. Be sure the tachometer being used is compatible with the ignition system before installation. Incompatible equipment installation could cause damage to the ignition system.

Metro

Before setting timing , make sure the headlights, heater fan, engine cooling fan and any other electrical equipment are turned off. If any current drawing systems are operating, the idle up system will operate and cause the idle speed to be higher than normal.

1. Connect a tachometer to the negative terminal of the ignition coil. Connect a timing light to the No. 1 spark plug wire. Refer to the underhood sticker.

NOTE: On the Metro vehicles equipped with the Electronic Spark Control Distributor (Base and Xfi models), remove the diagnostic check connector cap (this connector is located next to the ignition coil). Insert a fused jumper wire between terminals C and D of the diagnostic connector.

2. Start and run the engine until it reaches normal operating temperature.

3. Check and/or adjust the idle speed. Correct speed should be 750 rpm for engines with manual transaxle or 850 rpm on engines with automatic transaxles.

NOTE: To adjust the idle speed, turn the throttle adjustment screw on the carburetor.

4. With the engine at the proper idle speed, aim the timing light at the crankshaft pulley and timing marks.

5. To adjust the ignition timing, loosen the distributor hold-down bolt and rotate the distributor until the correct timing marks are aligned. Tighten the distributor hold-down bolt and recheck the timing.

6. With the timing adjusted, stop the engine and remove the testing equipment.

1990 Prizm

EXCEPT GSi

1. Firmly apply the parking brake and place the transaxle in the **N** detent.

2. Connect a tachometer to the battery and the diagnostic connector. Do not ground the tachometer terminal.

3. Run the engine until normal operating temperatures are reached, then stop the engine.

4. Remove the diagnostic check connector cap (located on the left in-

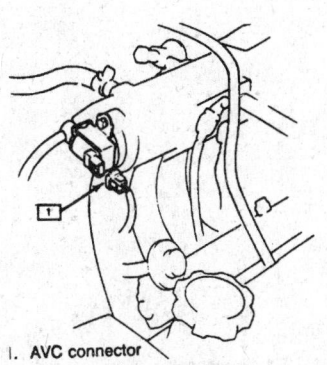

I. AVC connector

Removing the AVC connector — Prizm

ner fender) and insert a jumper wire between terminals **E1** and **T** of the diagnostic check connector. This will disconnect the ECM's control of the ignition timing, leaving the vehicle to operate on base timing.

5. Using a timing light, connect it to the No. 1 spark plug wire. Loosen the distributor hold-down bolt until it is finger-tight.

6. Start the engine, then, check and/or adjust the idle speed; it should be 700 rpm.

7. Aim the timing light at the timing cover plate near the crankshaft pulley; the notch on the crankshaft pulley should align with the specified timing mark on the timing plate.

8. To adjust the engine timing, turn the distributor slightly to align the marks, then, tighten the hold-down bolt and recheck the timing.

9. When the adjustment is correct, remove the jumper wire from diagnostic connector and install the cap.

10. Disconnect the ACV connector.

11. Recheck the timing marks. The timing should now be 10 degrees BTDC.

12. Reconnect the ACV connector.

13. Disconnect the timing light.

1991-94 Prizm

EXCEPT 1991-92 GSi

1. Firmly apply the parking brake and place the transaxle in the **N** detent.

2. Connect a tachometer to the battery and the diagnostic connector. Do not ground the tachometer terminal.

3. Run the engine until normal operating temperatures are reached, then stop the engine.

4. Remove the diagnostic check connector cap (located on the left inner fender) and insert a jumper wire between terminals **E1** and **TE1** of the diagnostic check connector. This will disconnect the ECM's control of the ignition timing, leaving the vehicle to operate on base timing.

5. Using a timing light, connect it to the No. 1 spark plug wire. Loosen the distributor hold-down bolt until it is finger-tight.

6. Start the engine, then, check and/or adjust the idle speed; it should be 700 rpm.

7. Aim the timing light at the timing cover plate near the crankshaft pulley; the notch on the crankshaft pulley should align with the specified timing mark on the timing plate.

8. To adjust the engine timing, turn the distributor slightly to align the marks, then, tighten the hold-down bolt and recheck the timing.

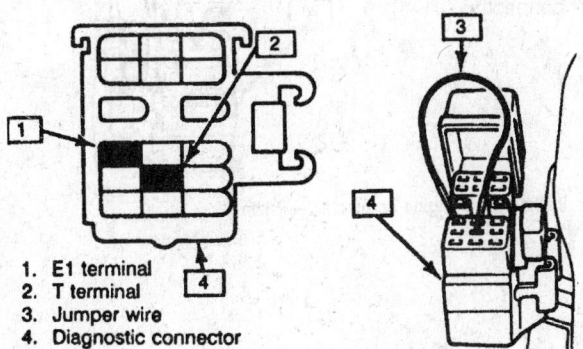

1. E1 terminal
2. T terminal
3. Jumper wire
4. Diagnostic connector

Diagnostic connector with jumper wire — 1990 Prizm

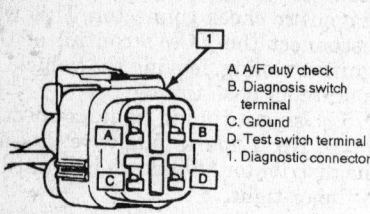

A. A/F duty check
B. Diagnosis switch terminal
C. Ground
D. Test switch terminal
1. Diagnostic connector

Exploded view of the check engine connector terminal — Metro

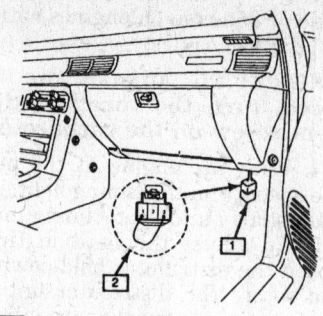

1. ALDL CONNECTOR C-52
2. JUMPER WIRE

ALDL connector Location — Storm

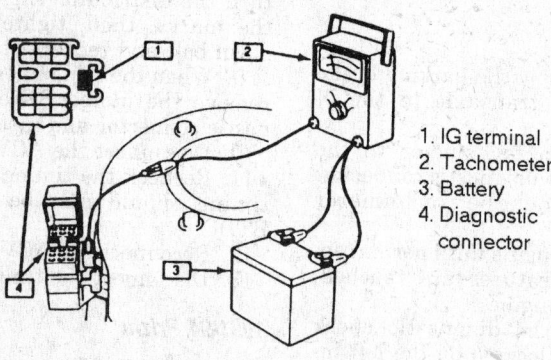

1. IG terminal
2. Tachometer
3. Battery
4. Diagnostic connector

Tachometer connections — Prizm

9. When the adjustment is correct, remove the jumper wire from diagnostic connector and install the cap.

10. Recheck ignition timing. Ignition timing should vary from 0-20 degrees BTDC.

11. Disconnect the timing light.

1991-92 GSi

1. Firmly apply the parking brake and place the transaxle in the **N** detent.

2. Connect a tachometer to the battery and the diagnostic connector. Do not ground the tachometer terminal.

3. Run the engine until normal operating temperatures are reached, then stop the engine.

4. Remove the diagnostic check connector cap (located on the left inner fender) and insert a jumper wire between terminals **E1** and **T** of the diagnostic check connector. This will disconnect the ECM's control of the ignition timing, leaving the vehicle to operate on base timing.

NOTE: On the 1992 Prizm GSi model, insert the jumper wire between terminal E1 and TE1 of the diagnostic connector.

5. Using a timing light, connect it to the No. 1 spark plug wire. Loosen

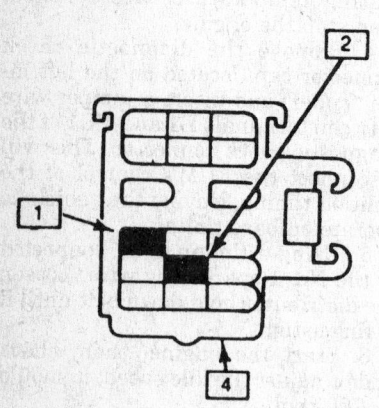

1. E1 trerminal
2. TE1 terminal
3. Service wire
4. Check connector

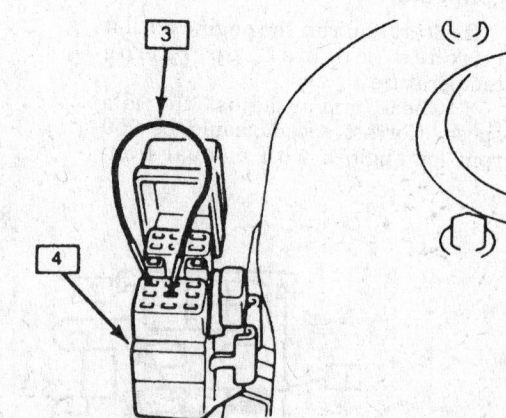

Installing the jumper wire in the check engine connector — Prizm

the distributor hold-down bolt until it is finger-tight.

6. Start the engine, then, check and/or adjust the idle speed; it should be 700 rpm.

7. Aim the timing light at the timing cover plate near the crankshaft pulley; the notch on the crankshaft pulley should align with the specified timing mark on the timing plate.

8. To adjust the engine timing, turn the distributor slightly to align the marks, then, tighten the hold-down bolt and recheck the timing.

9. When the adjustment is correct, remove the jumper wire from diagnostic connector and install the cap.

10. Recheck the timing marks. The timing should now be 10 degrees BTDC.

11. Disconnect the timing light.

Storm

1. Apply the parking brake and place the transaxle in the **N** detent.

2. Connect a tachometer to the battery and the diagnostic connector. Do not ground the tachometer terminal.

3. Run the engine until normal operating temperatures are reached, then stop the engine.

4. Connect a fused jumper wire between terminals **1** and **3** on the ALDL connector (located under the right hand instrument panel).

5. Using a timing light, connect it to the No. 1 spark plug wire. Loosen the distributor hold-down bolt until it is finger-tight.

6. Start the engine, then, check and/or adjust the idle speed; it should be 700 rpm.

7. Aim the timing light at the timing cover plate near the crankshaft pulley; the notch on the crankshaft pulley should align with the specified timing mark on the timing plate.

8. To adjust the engine timing, turn the distributor slightly to align the marks, then, tighten the hold-down bolt and recheck the timing.

9. When the adjustment is correct, remove the jumper wire from the ALDL connector.

10. Disconnect the timing light.

Spectrum

1. Set the parking brake and block the wheels.

2. Place the manual transaxle in neutral or the automatic transaxle in the **P** detent.

3. Allow the engine to reach normal operating temperature. Make sure the choke valve is open. Turn OFF all of the accessories.

4. If equipped with power steering, place the front wheels in a straight line.

5. Disconnect and plug the distributor vacuum line, the canister purge line, the EGR vacuum line and the ITC valve vacuum line at the intake manifold.

6. Connect a timing light to the No. 1 spark plug wire and a tachometer to the tachometer filter connector on the coil, tachometer filter is mounted near distributor hold-down bolt.

NOTE: Check the idle speed and adjust as needed.

7. Loosen the distributor flange bolt.

8. Using the timing light, align the notch on the crankshaft pulley with the mark on the timing cover by turning the distributor.

NOTE: Adjust the timing to 15 degrees BTDC at 750 rpm for manual transaxle or 10 degrees BTDC at 1000 rpm for automatic transaxle.

9. After the timing marks have been aligned, tighten the distributor flange bolt, then reinstall all vacuum lines.

Alternator

PRECAUTIONS

Several precautions must be observed to avoid damage to the unit.

• If the battery is removed for any reason, make sure it is reconnected with the correct polarity. Reversing the battery connections may result in damage to the 1-way rectifiers.

• When utilizing a booster battery as a starting aid, always connect the positive to positive terminals and the negative terminal from the booster battery to a good engine ground on the vehicle being started.

• Never use a fast charger as a booster to start vehicles.

• Disconnect the battery cables when charging the battery with a fast charger.

• Never attempt to polarize the alternator.

• Do not use test lamps of more than 12 volts when checking diode continuity.

• Do not short across or ground any of the alternator terminals.

• The polarity of the battery, alternator and regulator must be matched and considered before making any electrical connections within the system.

• Never separate the alternator on an open circuit. Make sure all connections within the circuit are clean and tight.

• Disconnect the battery ground terminal when performing any service on electrical components.

• Disconnect the battery if arc welding is to be done on the vehicle.

BELT TENSION ADJUSTMENT

Metro

1. Disconnect the negative battery cable.

2. Place a suitable belt tension gauge on the belt.

3. Adjust the drive belt to have 1/4-3/8in. play on the longest run of the drive belt.

Prizm and Storm

1. Disconnect the battery negative cable.

2. Place a suitable belt tension gauge on the belt.

3. Belt tension should be 110-150 lbs. (220-330 Kg) on a old belt and 140-180 lbs. (308-396 Kg) on a new belt.

4. If specifications are not as indicated, loosen the upper and lower alternator bolts and adjust as necessary.

5. Connect the battery negative cable.

Spectrum

NOTE: The following procedure requires the use of GM belt tension gauge tool BT-33-95-ACBN for regular V-belts or BT-33-97M for poly V-belts.

1. If the belt is cold, operate the engine, at idle speed, for 15 minutes; the belt will seat itself in the pulleys allowing the belt fibers to relax or stretch. If the belt is hot, allow it to cool, until it is warm to touch.

NOTE: A used belt is one that has been rotated at least 1 complete revolution on the pulleys. This begins the belt seating process and it must never be tensioned to the new belt specifications.

2. Loosen the component-to-mounting bracket bolts.

3. Using a belt tension gauge, place the gauge at the center of the belt between the longest span.

4. Applying belt tension pressure on the component, adjust the drive belt tension to the correct specifica-

tion. Belt tension should deflect about ¼ in. over a 7-10 inch span or ½ inch over a 13-16 inch span.

5. While holding the correct tension on the component, tighten the component-to-mounting bracket bolt.

6. When the belt tension is correct, 70-110 lbs. (154-242 Kg), remove the tension gauge.

REMOVAL AND INSTALLATION

Metro

1. Disconnect the negative battery cable.

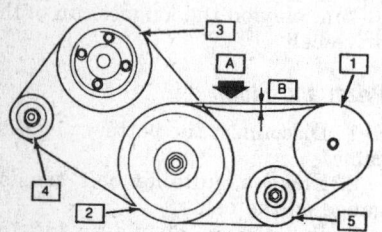

A. Thumb pressure (22 lbs.)
B. Deflection (5.0–6.5mm)
1. Magnetic clutch pulley
2. Crankshaft pulley
3. Water pump pulley
4. Alternator pulley
5. Idler pulley

Belt tension checking — Metro

2. Disconnect the wiring connectors from the back of the alternator.

3. Remove the adjusting arm mounting bolt, the lower pivot bolt and the drive belt.

4. Remove the alternator.

5. To install, reverse the removal procedures. Adjust the drive belt to have ¼-⅜inch play on the longest run of the drive belt.

Prizm

1990

1. Disconnect the negative battery cable.

2. Disconnect the large connector from the alternator.

3. Remove the nut and the single wire from the alternator.

4. Loosen the adjusting lock (lower) bolt and pivot (upper) bolt. Remove the drive belt.

NOTE: It may be necessary to remove other belts for access.

5. Remove the lower bolt first, support the alternator and remove the upper pivot bolt. Remove the alternator from the vehicle.

6. Installation is reverse of the above procedure. When reinstalling, remember to leave the bolts finger-tight so the belt may be adjusted.

7. Make sure the plugs and connectors are properly seated and secure in their mounts.

NOTE: The drive belt serrations run along the length of the belt. Make sure the serrations align with indentations on the pulleys; all serrations must ride inside the pulley surface.

1990-92

1. Disconnect the negative battery terminal.

NOTE: Failure to disconnect the negative cable may result in injury from the positive battery lead at the alternator and may short the alternator and regulator during the removal process.

2. Remove the rubber protector, nut and wire from the battery **B** terminal on the alternator.

3. Remove the 3-wire alternator connector.

4. On the 1991-92 Prizm Base and LSi models, use the following steps:

   a. Remove the upper and lower alternator bolts and nuts.

   b. Remove alternator.

5. On the 1990-92 Prizm GSi models use the following steps:

   a. Raise and support the vehicle safely.

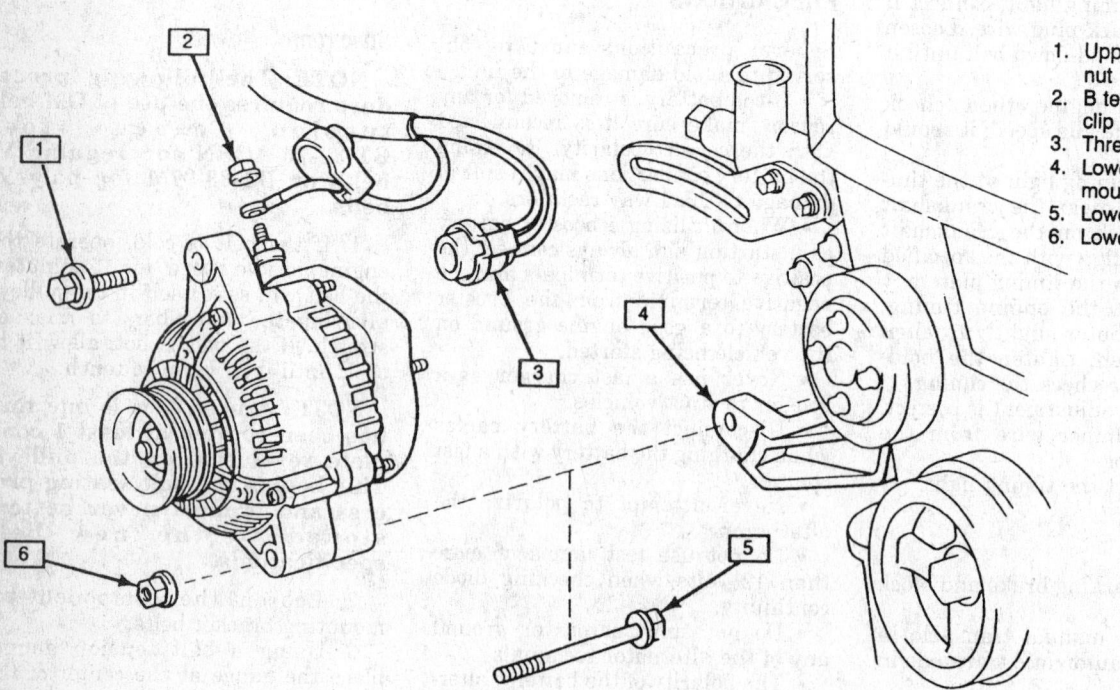

1. Upper adjustment nut
2. B terminal retaining clip
3. Three wire connector
4. Lower alternator mounting bracket
5. Lower mounting bolt
6. Lower mounting nut

Alternator mounting — Prizm GSi models

b. Remove the power steering and air conditioning drive belts.

c. Remove the lower mounting bolt and nut from the alternator bracket.

d. Remove the alternator drive belt from the pulley.

e. Remove the lower alternator mounting bracket (1 nut and 2 bolts).

NOTE: Removal of the alternator mounting bracket is necessary because of the nature of the engine compartment design. There is no way of getting the alternator out of the vehicle with the mounting bracket in place.

f. Remove the alternator from the vehicle through the space between the right splash shield and the oil pan.

6. Installation is reverse of the removal procedure. When reinstalling, remember to leave the bolts finger-tight so the belt may be adjusted.

7. Make sure the plugs and connectors are properly seated and secure in their mounts.

1993-94

1. Disconnect the negative battery cable.

NOTE: Failure to disconnect the negative cable may result in injury from the positive battery lead at the alternator and may short the alternator and regulator during the removal process.

2. Loosen the pivot and adjusting lock bolts.

3. Remove the drive belt.

4. Remove the rubber protector, nut and wire from the battery **B** terminal on the alternator.

5. Remove the 2 clips and wire harness.

6. Remove the 2 bolts, 1 nut and alternator from it's mounting bracket.

7. Installation is reverse of the removal procedure. When reinstalling, remember to leave the bolts finger-tight so the belt may be adjusted.

8. Make sure the plugs and connectors are properly seated and secure in their mounts.

Spectrum

1. Disconnect the negative battery terminal from the battery.

NOTE: Failure to disconnect the negative cable may result in injury from the positive battery lead at the alternator and may short the alternator and regulator during the removal process.

2. Disconnect and label the 2 terminal plug and the battery leads from the rear of the alternator.

3. Loosen the mounting bolts. Push the alternator inwards and slip the drive belt off the pulley.

4. Remove the mounting bolts and remove the alternator.

To install:

5. Place the alternator in its brackets and install the mounting bolts. Do not tighten.

6. Slip the belt back over the pulley. Pull outwards on the unit and adjust the belt tension. Tighten the mounting and adjusting bolts.

7. Install the electrical leads and the negative battery cable.

Storm

1. Disconnect the battery negative cable and remove the belt adjusting bolt from the alternator.

2. Raise and support vehicle and remove the right undercover.

3. Loosen the lower retaining bolt. Remove the alternator belt, then tag and disconnect electrical leads from the alternator.

4. Remove alternator mounting bracket-to-engine block attaching bolts, then remove the alternator and bracket from the vehicle.

5. Installation is reverse of the above procedure. When reinstalling, remember to leave the bolts finger-tight so the belt may be adjusted.

6. Make sure the plugs and connectors are properly seated and secure in their mounts.

Starter

REMOVAL AND INSTALLATION

Metro

1. Disconnect the negative battery cable.

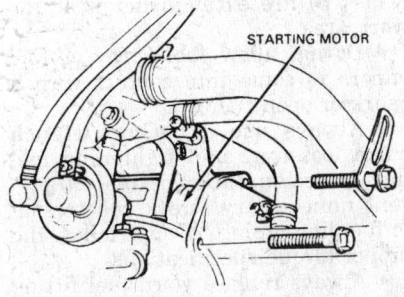

Starter motor mounting — Metro

2. Disconnect the ignition switch wire and the battery cable from the starter.

3. Remove the 2 engine-to-starter mounting bolts and remove the starter.

4. To install, reverse the removal procedures.

Prizm

1990-91, EXCEPT GSi

1. Disconnect the negative battery cable.

2. Disconnect the positive battery cable from the starter solenoid by removing the nut from terminal **30** stud.

3. Disconnect the ignition switch lead from terminal **50**.

4. Remove the 2 starter assembly retaining bolts and remove the starter assembly.

5. To install, reverse the removal procedures. Torque the starter-to-engine bolts to 26 ft. lbs. (35 Nm).

1992, EXCEPT GSi

1. Remove the negative battery cable.

2. Remove the wire harness retaining bracket.

3. Remove the upper starter mounting bolt.

4. Safely raise and support the vehicle.

5. Disconnect the positive battery cable from the starter solenoid by removing the nut from terminal **30** stud.

6. Disconnect the ignition switch lead from terminal **50**.

7. Remove the lower mounting bolt and starter from the vehicle.

8. To install, reverse the removal procedures. Torque the starter-to-engine bolts to 29 ft. lbs. (39 Nm).

GSi

1. Disconnect the negative battery cable.

2. Remove the rear cooling fan assembly.

3. Raise and safely support the vehicle safely.

4. Remove the right and left splash shields.

5. Disconnect the oxygen sensor connector from the front exhaust pipe.

6. Disconnect the front exhaust pipe.

7. Remove the starter assembly mounting bolts.

8. Disconnect the positive battery cable from the starter solenoid by removing the nut from terminal **30** stud.

9. Disconnect the ignition switch lead from terminal **50**. Remove the starter assembly from the vehicle.

10. To install, reverse the removal procedures. Torque the starter-to-engine bolts to 29 ft. lbs. (39 Nm).

1993-94

1. Disconnect the negative battery cable.

2. Remove the intake air temperature sensor from the air cleaner.

3. Loosen the air cleaner hose clamp.

4. Remove the 4 air cleaner lid clips, hose and air cleaner lid from the lower air cleaner housing and throttle body.

5. Remove the wire clamp from the starter.

6. Remove the ignition lead from the starter terminal.

7. Remove the positive battery cable and nut from the starter terminal.

8. To install, reverse the removal procedures. Torque the starter-to-engine bolts to 29 ft. lbs. (39 Nm).

1990-92 Storm

1. Disconnect the negative terminal from the battery.

2. Disconnect the electrical connectors from the starter terminals.

3. Remove the transaxle cable and bracket from the transaxle.

4. Remove the starter-to-engine bolts and the starter from the vehicle.

5. To install, reverse the removal procedures. Torque the starter-to-engine bolts to 29 ft. lbs. (39 Nm).

1993-94 Storm

1. Disconnect the negative terminal from the battery.

2. Raise and safely support the vehicle.

3. Remove 1 bolt, 1 nut and frame support bracket.

4. Disconnect the electrical connectors from the starter terminals.

5. Remove 1 bolt, 1 nut and starter from engine.

6. To install, reverse the removal procedures. Torque the starter-to-engine bolt and nut to 29 ft. lbs. (39 Nm).

Spectrum

1. Disconnect the negative battery terminal from the battery.

2. Disconnect the ignition switch lead wire and the battery cable from the starter motor terminal.

3. Remove the 2 mounting bolts from the starter and remove the starter.

4. To install, reverse the removal procedures.

FUEL SYSTEM

Fuel System Service Precautions

Safety is the most important factor when performing not only fuel system maintenance but any type of maintenance. Failure to conduct maintenance and repairs in a safe manner may result in serious personal injury or death. Maintenance and testing of the vehicle's fuel system components can be accomplished safely and effectively by adhering to the following rules and guidelines.

• To avoid the possibility of fire and personal injury, always disconnect the negative battery cable unless the repair or test procedure requires that battery voltage be applied.

• Always relieve the fuel system pressure prior to disconnecting any fuel system component (injector, fuel rail, pressure regulator, etc.), fitting or fuel line connection. Exercise extreme caution whenever relieving fuel system pressure to avoid exposing skin, face and eyes to fuel spray. Please be advised that fuel under pressure may penetrate the skin or any part of the body that it contacts.

• Always place a shop towel or cloth around the fitting or connection prior to loosening to absorb any excess fuel due to spillage. Ensure that all fuel spillage (should it occur) is quickly removed from engine surfaces. Ensure that all fuel soaked cloths or towels are deposited into a suitable waste container.

• Always keep a dry chemical (Class B) fire extinguisher near the work area.

• Do not allow fuel spray or fuel vapors to come into contact with a spark or open flame.

• Always use a backup wrench when loosening and tightening fuel line connection fittings. This will prevent unnecessary stress and torsion to fuel line piping. Always follow the proper torque specifications.

• Always replace worn fuel fitting O-rings with new. Do not substitute fuel hose or equivalent where fuel pipe is installed.

RELIEVING FUEL SYSTEM PRESSURE

Metro

1. Loosen the fuel filler cap on the gas tank to relieve fuel tank vapor pressure.

2. Place the transaxle gear shift lever in the **N** or **P** position. Set the parking brake and block the drive wheels.

3. Remove the main fuse block cover and engine coolant reservoir from its bracket.

4. Remove the screws holding the main fuse block.

5. Remove the coupler holding the fuel pump relay and disconnect it from the fuel pump relay.

6. Start the engine and let it run until it stalls. Crank the engine for 3 seconds to insure there is no fuel left in the lines.

7. After completing the repairs. Reverse Steps 2-4.

Prizm

NOTE: Make sure the engine is cold before disconnecting any portion of the fuel system.

1. Disconnect the negative battery cable.

2. Disconnect the circuit opening relay located under the dash panel, near the ECM.

3. Crank the engine and allow it to run for until it stalls, crank the engine for an additional 30 seconds. Then disconnect the negative battery.

4. Loosen the fuel filler cap to relieve tank vapor pressure.

5. Using a shop rag, wrap it around the fuel line fitting.

6. Slowly loosen and remove the cold start injector valve fuel line at the fuel rail.

7. Place a shop towel on the end of the fuel line to absorb any excess fuel remaining in the line.

8. When replacing the be sure to install a new O-ring.

Spectrum and Storm

1. Remove the fuel cap from the fuel tank.

2. Remove the fuel pump relay from the underhood relay center.

3. Start the engine and allow it to stall. Crank the engine for an additional 3 seconds.

4. Disconnect the negative battery cable.

5. Install the fuel pump relay and tighten the fuel cap.

Fuel Tank

REMOVAL AND INSTALLATION

NOTE: Before removing fuel system parts, clean them with a spray-type engine cleaner. Follow the instructions on the cleaner. Do not soak fuel system parts in liquid cleaning solvent.

— CAUTION —

The fuel injection system is under pressure. Release pressure slowly and contain spillage. Observe no smoking/no open flame precautions. Have a Class B-C (dry powder) fire extinguisher within arm's reach at all times.

Metro

1. Relieve the fuel system pressure and disconnect the negative battery cable.
2. Remove the fuel filler cap from the fuel tank.
3. Have a Class B fire extinguisher near the work area. Use a hand operated pump device to drain as much fuel through the fuel filler neck as possible.
4. Use a siphon to remove the remainder of the fuel in the tank by connecting the siphon to the fuel pump outlet fitting.

— CAUTION —

Never drain or store fuel in an open container because there is the possibility of a fire or an explosion.

5. Reinstall the fuel filler cap.
6. Remove the rear seat cushion from vehicle, if equipped.
7. Disconnect the fuel pump motor connector and sending unit electrical connectors.
8. Disconnect the wire harness grommet and harness through the vehicle floorpan.
9. Raise and safely support the vehicle.
10. Remove the fuel filler hose clamp from the filler neck assembly.
11. Remove the fuel breather hose clamp from the filler neck assembly.
12. Remove the fuel filter inlet hose clamp and hose from the filter.

NOTE: A small amount of fuel may be released after the fuel hose is disconnected. In order to reduce the chance of personal injury, cover the fitting to be disconnected with a shop towel.

13. Remove the fuel vapor clamp and hose and fuel return hose clamps and hose from the respective fuel lines.
14. Using a suitable transaxle jack, support the fuel tank.
15. Remove the fuel tank retaining bolts and lower the tank.
    To install:
16. Place the fuel tank in its proper space using the transaxle jack and install the fuel tank retaining bolts.
17. Remove the transaxle jack.
18. Reconnect all fuel hoses, lines and the fuel breather hose to the fuel tank.
19. Install the fuel breather hose and hose clamp to the filler neck assembly.
20. Install the fuel vapor hose and hose clamps. Install the fuel return hose and hose clamp to the respective fuel lines.
21. Install the fuel filter inlet hose and hose clamp to the filter.
22. Lower the vehicle. Install the wire harness and grommet through the vehicle floor pan.
23. Connect the fuel pump motor and the sending unit connectors.
24. Install the rear seat cushion. Reconnect the negative battery cable.

Prizm

1. Remove the filler cap.
2. Using a siphon or pump, drain the fuel from the tank and store it in a proper metal container with a tight cap.
3. Remove the rear seat cushion to gain access to the electrical wiring.
4. Disconnect the fuel pump and sending unit wiring at the connector.
5. Raise the vehicle and safely support it on jackstands.
6. Loosen the clamp and remove the filler neck and overflow pipe from the tank.
7. Remove the supply hose from the tank. Wrap a rag around the fitting to collect escaping fuel. Disconnect the breather hose from the tank, again using a rag to control spillage.
8. Cover or plug the end of each disconnected line to keep dirt out and fuel in.
9. Support the fuel tank with a floor jack or transaxle jack. Use a broad piece of wood to distribute the load. Be careful not to deform the bottom of the tank.
10. Remove the fuel tank support strap bolts.
11. Swing the straps away from the tank and lower the jack.
12. Remove the fuel filler pipe extension, the breather pipe assembly and the sending unit assembly. Keep these items in a clean, protected area away from the vehicle.

13. While the tank is out and disassembled, inspect it for any signs of rust, leakage or metal damage. If any problem is found, replace the tank. Clean the inside of the tank with water and a light detergent and rinse the tank thoroughly several times.
14. Inspect all of the lines, hoses and fittings for any sign of corrosion, wear or damage to the surfaces. Check the pump outlet hose and the filter for restrictions.
15. When reassembling, always replace the sealing gaskets with new ones. Also replace any rubber parts showing any sign of deterioration.
    To install:
16. Connect the breather pipe assembly and the filler pipe extension.

NOTE: Tighten the breather pipe screw to 17 inch lbs. (23 Nm) and all other attaching screws to 30 inch lbs. (41 Nm).

17. Place the fuel tank on the jack and elevate it into place within the vehicle. Attach the straps and install the strap bolts, tightening them to 29 ft. lbs. (40 Nm).
18. Connect the breather hose to the tank pipe, the return hose to the tank pipe and the supply hose to its tank pipe. Tighten the supply hose fitting to 21 ft. lbs. (28 Nm).
19. Connect the filler neck and overflow pipe to the tank. Make sure the clamps are properly seated and secure.
20. Lower the vehicle to the ground.
21. Connect the pump and sending unit electrical connectors to the harness.
22. Install the rear seat cushion.
23. Using a funnel, pour the fuel that was drained from its container into the fuel filler.
24. Install the fuel filler cap.
25. Start the engine and check carefully for any sign of leakage around the tank and lines.

Storm

1990-92

1. Relieve the fuel system pressure and disconnect the negative battery cable.
2. Remove the fuel filler cap from the fuel tank.
3. Have a Class B fire extinguisher near the work area. Use a hand operated pump device to drain as much fuel through the fuel filler neck as possible.
4. Use a siphon to remove the remainder of the fuel in the tank by connecting the siphon to the fuel pump outlet fitting.

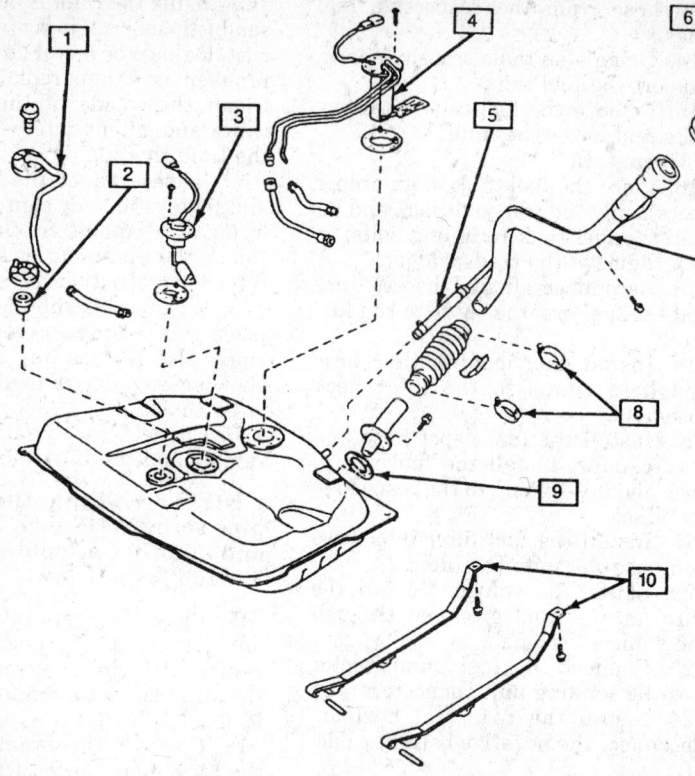

1. Fuel tank breather pipe
2. Fuel cut-off valve
3. Fuel tank sending unit
4. Fuel pump
5. Overflow pipe
6. Fuel filler neck bezel
7. Fuel filler neck
8. Clamps
9. Gasket
10. Fuel tank mounting straps

Fuel tank and components — Prizm

— CAUTION —

Never drain or store fuel in an open container because there is the possibility of a fire or an explosion.

5. Reinstall the fuel pump outlet hose to its fitting, install the fuel filler cap.

6. Raise and safely support the vehicle.

7. Remove the exhaust pipe from the catalytic converter.

8. Loosen the clamp on the fuel filler neck hose from the fuel tank.

9. Loosen the clamp for the fuel overflow pipe hose from the fuel tank.

10. Disconnect the fuel gauge sending unit and fuel pump electrical connector.

11. Spread the clamp for the fuel vapor hose on the fuel tank.

12. Remove the fuel pump supply hose from the fuel pipe.

13. Remove the fuel pump return hose.

14. Using a suitable transaxle jack, support the fuel tank.

15. Remove the 6 fuel tank retaining bolts and lower the tank.

To install:

16. Place the fuel tank in its proper space using the transaxle jack. Install the 6 fuel tank retaining bolts and torque them to 14 ft. lbs. (19 Nm).

17. Remove the transaxle jack. Install the fuel return hose.

18. Install the fuel pump supply hose, vapor hose and fuel gauge and fuel pump electrical connector. Torque the fuel pump supply hose fitting nut to 25 ft. lbs. (34 Nm).

19. Install the fuel overflow pipe hose.

20. Install the exhaust pipe to the catalytic converter. Install the fuel filler neck hose.

21. Lower the vehicle. Refill the fuel tank and install the fuel filler cap. Install the negative battery cable.

1993-94

1. Relieve the fuel system pressure and disconnect the negative battery cable.

2. Remove the fuel filler cap from the fuel tank.

3. Have a Class B fire extinguisher near the work area. Use a hand operated pump device to drain as much fuel through the fuel filler neck as possible.

4. Use a siphon to remove the remainder of the fuel in the tank by connecting the siphon to the fuel pump outlet fitting.

— CAUTION —

Never drain or store fuel in an open container because there is the possibility of a fire or an explosion.

5. Reinstall the fuel pump outlet hose to its fitting, install the fuel filler cap.

6. Raise and safely support the vehicle.

7. Remove the exhaust pipe from the catalytic converter.

8. Loosen the clamp on the fuel filler neck hose from the fuel tank.

9. Loosen the clamp for the fuel overflow pipe hose from the fuel tank.

10. Disconnect the fuel gauge sending unit and fuel pump electrical connector.

11. Spread the clamp for and remove the fuel vapor hose from the fuel tank.

12. Remove the fuel pump supply hose from the fuel pipe.

13. Remove the fuel pump return hose.

14. Remove 2 bolts and parking brake cables.

15. Remove the 4 fuel tank retaining bolts and lower the tank.

16. Using a suitable transaxle jack, support the fuel tank.

To install:

17. Place the fuel tank in its proper space using the transaxle jack, Install the 6 fuel tank retaining bolts and torque them to 14 ft. lbs. (19 Nm).

18. Remove the transaxle jack. Install the fuel return hose.

19. Install the fuel pump supply hose, vapor hose and fuel gauge and fuel pump electrical connector. Torque the fuel pump supply hose fitting nut to 25 ft. lbs. (34 Nm).

20. Install the fuel overflow pipe hose.

21. Install the exhaust pipe to the catalytic converter. Install the fuel filler neck hose.

22. Lower the vehicle. Refill the fuel tank and install the fuel filler cap. Connect the negative battery cable.

Spectrum

1. Relieve the fuel system pressure and disconnect the negative battery cable.

2. Remove the fuel filler cap from the fuel tank.

3. Have a Class B fire extinguisher near the work area. Use a hand operated pump device to drain as much fuel through the fuel filler neck as possible.

4. Use a siphon to remove the remainder of the fuel in the tank by connecting the siphon to the fuel pump outlet fitting.

—— CAUTION ——

Never drain or store fuel in an open container because there is the possibility of a fire or an explosion.

5. Reinstall the fuel filler cap.

6. Disconnect the sending unit wire from the fuel tank terminal.

7. Unfasten the clips and disconnect the 3 rubber hoses on the rear side of the fuel tank.

8. Unfasten the clips and disconnect the fuel delivery and fuel return hose from the side of the fuel tank.

9. Remove the fuel filler pipe bracket bolts.

10. Using a suitable transaxle jack, support the fuel tank.

11. Remove the fuel tank retaining bolts and lower the tank.

To install:

12. Place the fuel tank in its proper space using the transaxle jack, Install the fuel tank retaining bolts.

13. Install the fuel filler pipe bracket bolts.

14. Install the clips and reconnect the fuel delivery and fuel return hose to the side of the fuel tank.

15. Install the clips and reconnect the 3 rubber hoses on the rear side of the fuel tank.

Fuel Filter

REMOVAL AND INSTALLATION

Metro

1. Relieve the pressure in the fuel system.

2. Disconnect the negative battery cable.

3. Remove and replace the fuel tank cap. This releases the fuel pressure within the fuel system.

4. Raise and support the vehicle safely.

5. Place a drain pan under the fuel filter. Disconnect the fuel filter inlet hose clamp and the hose from the filter. Disconnect the fuel filter outlet hose clamp and the hose from the fuel feed line.

—— CAUTION ——

A small amount of fuel may be released after the fuel hose is disconnected. In order to reduce the chance of personal injury, cover the fittings to be disconnected with a shop towel.

6. Remove the fuel filter, mounting bracket and outlet hose as an assembly from the vehicle.

7. Disconnect the fuel filter outlet hose clamp and hose from the filter. Remove the mounting bracket from the filter.

8. Reverse procedure to install. Start engine and check for leaks.

Prizm

The fuel filter is located on the firewall. The element inside the filter reduces the flow speed of the fuel

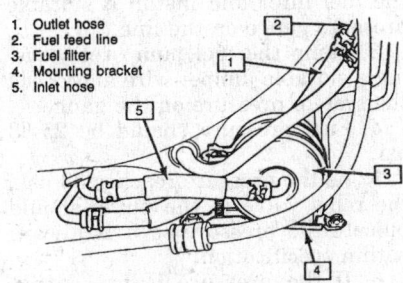

1. Outlet hose
2. Fuel feed line
3. Fuel filter
4. Mounting bracket
5. Inlet hose

Fuel filter mounting — Metro

causing dirt particles that are heavier than gasoline to settle to the bottom. The lighter particles are filtered by the element.

—— CAUTION ——

The fuel system is under pressure. Release pressure slowly and contain spillage. Observe no smoking/no open flame precautions. Have a Class B-C (dry powder) fire extinguisher within arm's reach at all times. Perform this procedure only on a cold engine.

NOTE: There is also a sock type fuel filter attached to the fuel pump which is located in the fuel tank. This filter does not require routine maintenance but when ever the fuel pump is replaced it would be wise to change the sock type fuel filter.

1. Disconnect the negative battery cable.

2. Relieve the pressure in the fuel line as follows:

   a. Fit a wrench of the exact size onto the upper line connection and fit a second wrench on the flats of the filter. This counterholding arrangement will prevent the filter and lines from turning during removal.

   b. Wrap the upper filter area in layers of rags to absorb spray and spillage.

   c. Slowly loosen the bolt holding the line to the filter. When the pressure is equalized, remove the bolt and the line. Plug the line immediately.

3. Again using 2 wrenches, disconnect the lower line to the filter. Be prepared to deal with fuel spillage. Be very careful not to crimp or bend the fuel line. Plug the line immediately.

4. Remove the filter from its holder and install a new one.

To install:

5. Apply a thin coat of oil to the threads and connect the bottom fuel line to the filter. Always begin the threads by hand, then tighten to 22 ft. lbs. (30 Nm).

6. Install the upper line with new gaskets. Make sure the line is held within the forked bracket on the filter and begin the bolt by hand to insure proper threading.

7. Tighten the bolt to 22 ft. lbs. (30 Nm). Reconnect the negative battery cable.

8. Start the engine and check for leaks. The engine may require a longer period of cranking until it starts due to loss of fuel pressure.

Spectrum

1. Relieve the pressure in the fuel system. Remove the fuel filler cap.
2. Note the routing of inlet and outlet lines and the direction of flow as marked by the arrow on the filter. With a pair of pliers, shift the clips on the inlet and outlet hoses back and well away from the connections on the filter.

NOTE: The fuel filter is located under the power brake booster.

3. Disconnect the fuel lines, using a twisting motion to break them loose. Pull the filter out of its retaining clip. Plug the lines immediately to prevent spillage.
To install:
4. Install the filter in the holder. When reconnecting the fuel lines, make sure the hoses are connected to the correct ports on the filter. The arrow on the filter indicates direction of flow and points towards the carburetor.
5. Install the hose clips to the inside of the bulged sections of the fuel filter connections and not right at the ends of the fuel lines. Start the engine and check for leaks.
6. Install the fuel filler cap.

Storm

1. Relieve the pressure in the fuel system.
2. Disconnect the negative battery cable.
3. Remove the air intake duct.
4. Disconnect the fuel filter outlet pipe from the fuel filter upper fitting.
5. Raise and support the vehicle safely. Be sure to cap the ends of the fuel pipe fittings to prevent both the entry of dirt and the spillage of fuel.
6. Loosen the fuel filter bracket clamp bolt.
7. Remove the fuel filter from the bracket as follows.
   a. Fit a wrench of the exact size onto the upper line connection and fit a second wrench on the flats of the filter. This counterholding arrangement will prevent the filter and lines from turning during removal.
   b. Wrap the upper filter area in layers of rags to absorb spray and spillage.
   c. Slowly loosen the bolt holding the line to the filter. When the pressure is equalized, remove the bolt and the line. Plug the line immediately.
   d. Again using 2 wrenches, disconnect the lower line to the filter. Be prepared to deal with fuel spill-

age. Be very careful not to crimp or bend the fuel line. Plug the line immediately.
8. Remove the filter from its holder and install a new one.
9. Installation is the reverse order of the removal procedure. Torque the fuel fitting nuts to 25 ft. lbs. (34 Nm).

Mechanical Fuel Pump

PRESSURE TESTING

Spectrum

1. Disconnect the fuel line from the carburetor. Install a rubber hose about 10 inches long. Attach a low reading pressure gauge.
2. Hold the gauge at least 16 inches above the fuel pump. If equipped, pinch the fuel return line.
3. Start the engine and run it at slow idle, using the fuel that is left in the carburetor.
4. Fuel pump pressure should be 3.8-4.7 psi. If specification obtained is not as indicated, replace the fuel pump or filter.

REMOVAL AND INSTALLATION

Spectrum

1. Disconnect the fuel and return hoses from the fuel pump.
2. Remove the bolts, fuel pump and heat insulator assembly.
3. After removing the fuel pump, cover the mounting face of the cylinder head to prevent oil discharge.
4. Reverse procedure to install. Replace the heat insulator assembly.

Electric Fuel Pump

PRESSURE TESTING

Metro

1. Relieve fuel system pressure.
2. Disconnect the fuel inlet line at the fuel filter and install a suitable pressure gauge on the line.
3. Jump the fuel pump relay, using a suitable jumper wire and check the system pressure on the gauge.
4. Fuel pressure should be 25-33 psi.
5. As the pressure reaches 33 psi., the relief valve in the pump should pulsate the pressure so it is always within specification.
6. If the pressure is not within specification, check for restrictions in the fuel lines or replace the in-tank fuel pump.

7. Before removing the pressure gauge, relieve the fuel pressure again.
8. Reconnect the fuel line. Start the engine and check for leaks.

Prizm

1. Disconnect the battery negative cable.
2. Using a shop cloth, wrap it around the cold start injector pipe and slowly loosen the union bolt and remove. Discard the gaskets.
3. Remove the delivery pipe to cold start injector banjo fitting bolt and the 2 gaskets. Discard the gaskets.
4. Install pressure gauge tools J-34370-1 and J-38347 onto the fuel delivery pipe. Close the gauge valve.
5. Reconnect the battery negative cable.
6. Open the gauge valve and turn the ignition switch to the **RUN** position.
7. Install a jumper wire between the **+B** and **FP** terminals of the fuel pump check connector. The fuel pump connector is located near the wiper motor.
8. Open the gauge air bleed valve and purge the air from the gauge. Use a suitable container to catch the fuel from the gauge air bleed valve.
9. The gauge reading should be 38-44 psi. If the pressure is too high, replace the pressure regulator or a restricted fuel return line. If the pressure is low, check the fuel pump, fuel filter, pressure regulator, the hoses and connections.
10. Pinch the fuel pressure regulator return hose. The pressure should be 57 psi.
11. Remove the fuel pump jumper wire and observe the pressure gauge. A very slow drop in pressure is normal.
12. The fuel pressure at idle should be 30-33 psi.
13. Remove the fuel pressure regulator sensing hose and plug the hose end. The fuel pressure gauge should read 38-44 psi.
14. Connect the vacuum sensing hose and quickly open and close the throttle valve for the air induction system. The fuel pressure gauge should show quick increases in pressure as the throttle is snapped open and decreases as it returns to idle.
15. Stop the engine. If improper pressure readings are shown, check the fuel pump, pressure regulator and/or the injectors, restricted fuel lines or filter and for improper injector control, thermal timer/ECM.
16. Connect the battery negative cable.

17. Use the fuel pressure gauge air bleed valve to relieve the system pressure.

18. Remove the fuel pressure gauge and adapter.

19. Using new gaskets, reconnect the cold start injector fitting bolt and torque to 13 ft. lbs. (18 Nm). Check for leaks using the fuel jumper wire.

Storm

1. Relieve fuel system pressure.

2. Disconnect the fuel pressure line from the fuel filter. Wrap a shop towel around the line catch any fuel leakage.

3. Install fuel gauge adapter J-35957-10 between the fuel pressure line and the fuel filter, located on the fuel rail.

4. Install fuel gauge J-34730-1 to the adapter.

5. Disconnect the vacuum hose from the pressure regulator.

6. Turn the ignition switch to the ON position. Fuel pressure should be 30-46 psi for the 1.6L engine or 41-47 psi for the 1.8L engine.

7. If pressure is within specification but not holding, proceed as follows:

a. Turn the ignition switch to the OFF position.

b. Using battery voltage, connect a jumper wire between the BLK/RED wire and the RED/WHT wire on the fuel pump relay connector, located in the engine compartment.

c. Pinch the pressure line and remove the jumper wire from the test connector. If pressure held, check for a leaking coupling hose or a faulty in-tank pump. If pressure did not hold, repeat Step 7b by pinching the fuel return line.

d. If pressure holds, replace the pressure regulator assembly. If pressure does not hold, check for leaking injector and spark plugs.

8. If pressure obtained is below specification, proceed as follows:

a. Check for a restricted inline fuel filter; replace, if necessary.

b. Turn the ignition switch to the OFF position.

c. Apply battery voltage to the fuel pump relay connector with the fuel pump removed.

d. Pinch the fuel return line and note pressure. Pressure should be above 65 psi.

e. If not, check for a faulty in-tank pump. If pressure is above 65 psi, replace the pressure regulator.

9. If pressure obtained is above specification, proceed as follows:

a. Disconnect the vacuum line to the pressure regulator and the fuel return line hose.

b. Install a hose to the pressure regulator side of the return line and insert the other end into a suitable container.

c. Turn the ignition switch to the ON position and check the fuel pressure. Fuel pressure should be 30-46 psi for the 1.6L engine or 41-47 psi for the 1.8L engine. If not, replace the pressure regulator.

d. If fuel pressure is 30-46 psi for the 1.6L engine or 41-47 psi for the 1.8L engine, check for a restriction in the fuel return line.

10. If no pressure was obtained on the pressure gauge, proceed as follows:

a. Remove the gas cap and turn the ignition switch to the ON position. Fuel pump should operate for approximately 2 seconds.

b. If fuel pump operates, check for faulty wiring and connectors.

c. If fuel pump does not operate, remove the fuel pump relay from the relay center. Using a suitable test light, check RED/WHT wire on the fuel pump relay connector for power.

d. If test light does not light, check for an open circuit in the RED/WHT wire. If test light illuminates, install a jumper wire between the RED/WHT and BLK/RED wire on the fuel pump relay connector. Fuel pump should operate.

e. If fuel pump does not operate, check the fuel pump connector at the fuel tank using the test light. Test light should illuminate. If not, check the BLK/RED wire for an open circuit. If test light illuminates, check for an open circuit in the fuel ground and/or a faulty fuel pump.

f. If the fuel pump operates, turn the ignition switch OFF for approximately 10 seconds. Connect a test light between the BLK wire and the PNK/WHT wire on the fuel pump relay connector. Turn the ignition switch ON, test light should light for approximately 2 seconds.

g. If test light illuminates, check for a faults fuel pump relay. If test light does not illuminate, turn the ignition switch OFF for approximately 10 seconds. Using the test light check the A1 terminal of the ECM. Turn the ignition switch ON. Test light should light for approximately 2 seconds. If not, replace the ECM. If test light illuminates, check for an open circuit in the PNK/WHT wire and/or the BLK wire.

Spectrum

1. Relieve the fuel system pressure.

2. Disconnect the fuel hoses between the pressure regulator and the fuel distributor pipe.

3. Connect fuel pressure gauge J-33945 between the pressure regulator and the fuel distributor pipe.

4. Start the engine and check the fuel pressure under the 2 different conditions:

a. With the vacuum hose for the pressure regulator disconnected, intake manifold side end of hose must be plugged. The pressure should read 35.6 psi.

b. With the vacuum hose for the pressure regulator connected, at engine speed of 900 rpm. The pressure should read 28.4 psi.

5. After on-vehicle inspection is made, remove the fuel pressure gauge, reconnect fuel line and check for leaks.

REMOVAL AND INSTALLATION

— CAUTION —

The fuel injection system is under pressure. Release pressure slowly and contain spillage. Observe no smoking/no open flame precautions. Have a Class B-C (dry powder) fire extinguisher within arm's reach at all times.

Metro

1. Relieve the fuel system pressure.

2. Disconnect the negative battery cable.

3. Raise and support the vehicle safely.

4. Drain the fuel tank by pumping or siphoning the fuel out through the fuel feed line (tank to fuel filter line).

5. Remove the tank from the vehicle.

6. Fuel feed and return clamps and hoses from the fuel pump assembly.

7. Remove the 12 attaching screws from the fuel pump assembly and remove the assembly with the gasket from the fuel tank.

8. Remove the 1 mounting screw from the fuel pump motor assembly. Remove the 2 fuel pump motor connectors and remove the fuel pump motor from the fuel pump assembly.

9. Installation is the reverse order of the removal procedure.

Prizm

1. Remove the filler cap.

2. Using a siphon or pump, drain the fuel from the tank and store it in a proper metal container with a tight cap.

3. Remove the rear seat cushion to gain access to the electrical wiring.

4. Disconnect the fuel pump and sending unit wiring at the connector.

5. Raise the vehicle and safely support it.

6. Loosen the clamp and remove the filler neck and overflow pipe from the tank.

7. Remove the supply hose from the tank. Wrap a rag around the fitting to collect escaping fuel. Disconnect the breather hose from the tank, again using a rag to control spillage.

8. Cover or plug the end of each disconnected line to keep dirt out and fuel in.

9. Support the fuel tank with a floor jack or transaxle jack. Use a broad piece of wood to distribute the load. Be careful not to deform the bottom of the tank.

10. Remove the fuel tank support strap bolts.

11. Swing the straps away from the tank and lower the jack. Balance the tank with a hand or have a helper assist. The tank is bulky and may have some fuel left in it. If its balance changes suddenly, the tank may fall.

12. Remove the fuel filler pipe extension, the breather pipe assembly and the sending unit assembly. Keep these items in a clean, protected area away from the vehicle.

13. To remove the electric fuel pump:

   a. Disconnect the 2 pump-to-harness wires.

   b. Loosen the pump outlet hose clamp at the bracket pipe.

   c. Remove the pump from the bracket and the outlet hose from the bracket pipe.

   d. Separate the outlet hose and the filter from the pump.

14. While the tank is out and disassembled, inspect it for any signs of rust, leakage or metal damage. If any problem is found, replace the tank. Clean the inside of the tank with water and a light detergent and rinse the tank thoroughly several times.

15. Inspect all of the lines, hoses and fittings for any sign of corrosion, wear or damage to the surfaces. Check the pump outlet hose and the filter for restrictions.

To install:

16. When reassembling, always replace the sealing gaskets with new ones. Also replace any rubber parts showing any sign of deterioration.

17. Assemble the outlet hose and filter onto the pump; then attach the pump to the bracket.

18. Connect the outlet hose clamp to the bracket pipe and connect the pump wiring to the harness wire.

19. Install the fuel pump and bracket assembly onto the tank.

20. Install the sending unit assembly.

21. Connect the breather pipe assembly and the filler pipe extension.

NOTE: Tighten the breather pipe screw to 17 inch lbs. (2.0 Nm) and all other attaching screws to 30 inch lbs. (3.3 Nm).

22. Place the fuel tank on the jack and elevate it into place within the vehicle. Attach the straps and install the strap bolts, tightening them to 29 ft. lbs. (39 Nm).

23. Connect the breather hose to the tank pipe, the return hose to the tank pipe and the supply hose to its tank pipe. Tighten the supply hose fitting to 21 ft. lbs. (28 Nm).

24. Connect the filler neck and overflow pipe to the tank. Make sure the clamps are properly seated and secure.

25. Lower the vehicle to the ground.

26. Connect the pump and sending unit electrical connectors to the harness.

27. Install the rear seat cushion.

28. Using a funnel, pour the fuel that was drained from its container into the fuel filler.

29. Install the fuel filler cap.

30. Start the engine and check carefully for any sign of leakage around the tank and lines.

Storm

1. Relieve the fuel system pressure, then disconnect the battery negative cable.

2. Drain the fuel from the fuel tank, then remove the fuel tank assembly.

3. Remove 8 fuel pump attaching screws, then the fuel pump/bracket from the fuel tank.

4. Remove the fuel pump supply hose extension from the bracket.

5. Remove the gasket from the fuel pump bracket and/or tank.

6. Remove the filter from the pump pickup tube.

7. Disconnect the electrical connectors from the fuel pump, outlet hose from pump and remove the pump from the bracket.

8. Reverse procedure to install. Connect battery negative cable. Start engine and check for leaks.

Spectrum

1. Relieve fuel pressure then disconnect negative battery cable.

2. Raise and support the vehicle safely. Drain fuel tank.

3. Remove all fuel line hose connections and fuel pump ground wire.

4. Remove filler neck hose and clamp.

5. Remove breather hose and clamp.

6. Disconnect fuel tank hose to evaporator pipe.

7. Remove fuel tank mounting bolts and lower tank from vehicle. At this point remove hose from pump to fuel filter.

8. Remove fuel pump bracket plate and fuel pump as an assembly.

9. Remove pump bracket, rubber cushion and fuel pump filter.

10. To install, reverse the removal procedures. Be careful, to push the lower side of the fuel pump, together with the rubber cushion, into the fuel pump bracket.

Carburetor

REMOVAL AND INSTALLATION

Spectrum

1. Disconnect the negative battery terminal from the battery.

2. Remove the air cleaner.

3. Disconnect the harness connector and hoses.

4. Remove the accelerator cable from the carburetor.

5. Remove the bolts securing the carburetor to the intake manifold. Remove the carburetor and place a cover over the intake manifold.

6. To install, reverse the removal procedures and torque carburetor fixing bolts to 7.2 ft. lbs. (9 Nm), then start the engine and check for leaks.

Fuel Injector

REMOVAL AND INSTALLATION

---------- **CAUTION** ----------

The fuel system is under pressure. Release pressure slowly and contain spillage. Observe no smoking/no open flame precautions. Have a Class B-C (dry powder) fire extinguisher within arm's reach at all times.

Metro

1. Relieve the fuel system pressure.
2. Disconnect the negative battery cable.
3. Remove the air cleaner assembly.
4. Remove the injector cover and upper insulator.
5. Disconnect the electrical connector and remove the injector.

To install:

6. Apply a thin coat of transaxle fluid or gasoline to the new upper and lower O-rings and install them on the injectors.
7. Install a new lower injector insulator into the injector cavity.
8. Push the injector straight into the fuel injection cavity. Do not twist.
9. Install a new upper insulator and the injection cover.
10. Install the injector cover screws to 31 inch lbs. (3.5 Nm).
11. Connect the electrical connector to the injector, facing it lug side upward on clamp sub-wire securely.
12. Connect the negative battery cable.

Prizm

1990

1. Disconnect the negative battery cable.
2. Disconnect the PCV hoses from the valve cover and the vacuum sensing hose from the fuel pressure regulator.
3. Disconnect the fuel return hose from the fuel pressure regulator.
4. Remove the wiring connectors from the injectors.
5. Remove the pressure regulator by loosening the 2 bolts and pulling the regulator from the delivery pipe.
6. Label and remove the 4 vacuum hoses running to the EGR vacuum modulator. Remove the nut and bracket with the modulator.
7. Disconnect the fuel union bolt at the inlet pipe. Remove the pipe and the 2 gaskets.

8. Remove the 2 bolts holding the delivery pipe and then remove the delivery pipe and the injectors. Don't drop the injectors.
9. Remove the 2 spacers and the 4 insulators from the cylinder head.
10. Pull the injectors free of the delivery pipe.

To install:

11. Before installing the injectors back into the fuel rail, install a new O-ring on each injector.
12. Coat each O-ring with a light coat of gasoline (never use oil of any sort) and install the injectors into the delivery pipe. Make certain each injector can be smoothly rotated. If they do not rotate smoothly, the O-ring is not in its correct position.
13. Install the 4 insulators and 2 spacers in place.
14. Place the delivery pipe and injectors on the cylinder head and again check that the injectors rotate smoothly. Install the 2 bolts and tighten them to 11 ft. lbs. (15 Nm).
15. Install 2 new gaskets and attach the inlet pipe and fuel union bolt. Tighten the bolt to 22 ft. lbs. (30 Nm).
16. Install the EGR vacuum modulator with its bracket and nut. Connect the 4 vacuum hoses to their proper ports.
17. Install new gaskets and connect the cold start injector pipe to the delivery pipe and cold start injector. Install the fuel line union bolts and tighten them to 13 ft. lbs. (18 Nm).
18. Install a new O-ring on the pressure regulator. Push the regulator into the delivery pipe and install the 2 bolts. Tighten the bolts to 5.5 ft. lbs. (7.5 Nm)
19. Connect the injector wiring connectors.
20. Connect the fuel return hose and the vacuum sensing hose to the pressure regulator. Attach the PCV hoses to the valve cover.

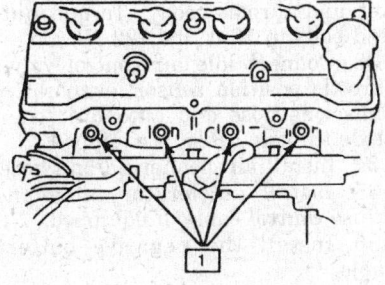

1. Insulators

Injector seal locations — Prizm

21. Connect the battery cable to the negative battery terminal. Start the engine and check for leaks.

---------- **CAUTION** ----------

If there is a leak at any fitting, the line will be under pressure and the fuel may spray in a fine mist. This mist is extremely explosive. Shut the engine OFF immediately if any leakage is detected. Use rags to wrap the leaking fitting until the pressure diminishes and wipe up any fuel from the engine area.

1991-92

1. Disconnect the negative battery cable.
2. Disconnect the PCV hose from the valve cover.
3. Remove the vacuum sensing hose from the pressure regulator.
4. Disconnect the fuel return hose from the pressure regulator.
5. Place a towel or container under the cold start injector pipe. Loosen the 2 union bolts at the fuel line and remove the pipe with its gaskets.
6. Remove the fuel inlet pipe mounting bolt and disconnect the fuel inlet hose by removing the fuel union bolt, the 2 gaskets and the hose.
7. Disconnect the injector electrical connections.
8. At the fuel delivery pipe (rail), remove the 3 bolts. Lift the delivery pipe and the injectors free of the engine. Don't drop the injectors.
9. Remove the 4 insulators and 3 collars from the cylinder head.
10. Pull the injectors free of the delivery pipe.

To install:

11. Before installing the injectors back into the fuel rail, install a new O-ring on each injector.
12. Coat each O-ring with a light coat of gasoline (never use oil of any sort) and install the injectors into the delivery pipe. Make certain each injector can be smoothly rotated. If they do not rotate smoothly, the O-ring is not in its correct position.
13. Install the insulators into each injector hole. Place the 3 spacers on the delivery pipe mounting holes in the cylinder head.
14. Place the delivery pipe and injectors on the cylinder head and again check that the injectors rotate smoothly. Install the 3 bolts and tighten them to 13 ft. lbs. (18 Nm).
15. Connect the electrical connectors to each injector.
16. Install 2 new gaskets and attach the inlet pipe and fuel union

bolt. Tighten the bolt to 22 ft. lbs. (30 Nm). Install the mounting bolt.

17. Install new gaskets and connect the cold start injector pipe to the delivery pipe and cold start injector. Install the fuel line union bolts and tighten them to 13 ft. lbs. (18 Nm).

18. Connect the fuel return hose and the vacuum sensing hose to the pressure regulator. Attach the PCV hose to the valve cover.

19. Connect the battery cable to the negative battery terminal. Start the engine and check for leaks.

——— CAUTION ———

If there is a leak at any fitting, the line will be under pressure and the fuel may spray in a fine mist. This mist is extremely explosive. Shut the engine OFF immediately if any leakage is detected. Use rags to wrap the leaking fitting until the pressure diminishes and wipe up any fuel from the engine area.

1993-94

1. Relieve fuel system pressure.
2. Disconnect accelerator cable and cruise control cable if equipped.
3. Disconnect the intake air temperature sensor.
4. Disconnect the air cleaner hose from the throttle body.
5. Remove the air cleaner lid with the hose attached.
6. If equipped with an automatic transaxle, disconnect the transaxle throttle cable.
7. Disconnect 1 evaporative emissions hose, throttle position sensor connector, idle air control valve connector, 2 bolts, 2 nuts and throttle body from the intake manifold.
8. Remove the throttle body gasket and air pipe.
9. On vehicles with California emissions, remove EGR valve, pipe modulator, bracket and hoses.
10. Remove the vacuum hose from the fuel pressure regulator and the PCV hose.
11. Remove 2 nuts, 3 Allen® head screws, plenum chamber cover and gasket.
12. Disconnect fuel injector connectors.
13. Place a shop towel or a container under the fuel feed hose-to-fuel rail connection.
14. Remove 1 bolt and fuel feed hose from the fuel rail.

15. Place a shop towel or a container under the fuel return hose-to-fuel rail connection and disconnect the fuel return hose.

16. Remove 2 bolts and fuel rail with fuel injectors attached.

17. Remove and discard the 4 insulators and 2 spacers from intake manifold.

18. Remove the 4 injectors from the fuel rail.

19. Remove and discard the old O-rings and grommets from the injectors.

20. Remove 2 bolts and fuel pressure regulator.

To install:

21. Install the fuel pressure regulator and torque the bolts to 82 inch lbs. (9.3 Nm).

22. Before installing the injectors back into the fuel rail, install a new O-ring on each injector.

23. Coat each O-ring with a light coat of gasoline (never use oil of any sort) and install the injectors into the fuel rail.

24. Install 4 new insulators and 2 new spacers to intake manifold.

25. Install the fuel rail with injectors to the intake manifold and hand tighten the bolts. Make certain each injector can be smoothly rotated. If they do not rotate smoothly, the O-ring is not in its correct position.

26. Torque the fuel rail bolts to 11 ft. lbs. (15 Nm).

27. Connect the fuel return hose and fuel injector connectors.

28. Install the plenum chamber cover with new gasket and torque 2 nuts and 3 Allen® screws to 14 ft. lbs. (19 Nm).

29. Install the vacuum hose to the fuel pressure regulator and the PCV hose.

30. On vehicles with California emissions, install EGR valve, pipe modulator, bracket and hoses.

31. Install fuel feed hose to fuel rail, using new gaskets and torque the bolt to 21 ft. lbs. (28 Nm).

32. Install a new throttle body gasket and throttle body. Torque nuts and bolts to 16 ft. lbs. (22 Nm).

33. Connect idle air control valve, throttle position sensor, evaporative emissions hose and automatic transaxle throttle cable, if equipped.

34. Install air cleaner lid and hose.

35. Install accelerator cable and cruise control cable, if equipped.

36. Install the negative battery cable.

37. Turn the ignition switch to the **ON** position and back to the **LOCK** position to pressurize the fuel system. Check for leaks.

Storm

1. Relieve fuel system pressure.
2. Disconnect the negative battery cable and cruise control cable, if equipped.
3. Remove the air duct assembly.
4. Disconnect the throttle cable at the throttle body, the throttle cable from the bracket and the TPS electrical connector.
5. Disconnect the idle air control valve and the intake air temperature sensor electrical connectors.
6. Disconnect the 2 vacuum hose and the 2 coolant hoses at the throttle body.
7. Remove the 4 retaining bolts at the throttle body assembly.
8. Remove the throttle body.
9. Remove the 4 vacuum hoses at the plenum.
10. Disconnect the PCV valve at the plenum. Disconnect the ECM ground wires.
11. Remove the engine lift hook brackets.
12. Remove the plenum support brackets.
13. Remove the 9 plenum retaining nuts and bolts. Remove the plenum assembly. Remove the 2 fuel rail retaining bolts.
14. Remove the 4 injector electrical connectors.
15. Slide the injector retaining clip along the fuel rail ledge away from the injector to disengage, then spread the clip open while pulling downward. Discard the clip after it has been removed.
16. Remove the injector assembly.
17. Remove the O-ring from the top and bottom of the injectors and discard them.

To install:

NOTE: Different injectors are calibrated for different flow rates. When ordering new fuel injectors, be sure to order the identical part number that is inscribed on the old injector.

18. Install new O-rings to the top and bottom of the injectors and lubricate them with clean engine oil.

19. Install the fuel injectors into the fuel rail. Install the new injector retaining clip. Be sure the clip is par-

allel to the injector electrical connector.

NOTE: Be sure to install the injector assembly into the fuel rail injector socket, with the electrical connector and retaining clip facing outward. Line up the injector with the injector socket, push upward slowly to engage the retaining clip on the fuel rail ledge then push the injector all the way in to firmly seat it in the socket.

20. Install the 4 injector electrical connectors.
21. Install the 2 fuel rail retaining bolts and torque them to 28 ft. lbs. (38 Nm).
22. Install the plenum assembly. Install the 9 plenum retaining nuts and bolts.
23. Install the plenum support brackets.
24. Install the engine lift hook brackets.
25. Reconnect the PCV valve at the plenum and the ECM ground wires.
26. Install the 4 vacuum hoses at the plenum.
27. Install the throttle body.
28. Install the 4 retaining bolts at the throttle body assembly. Torque the bolts 16 ft. lbs. (22 Nm).
29. Reconnect the 2 vacuum hose and the 2 coolant hoses at the throttle body.
30. Reconnect the idle air control valve and the intake air temperature sensor electrical connectors.
31. Reconnect the throttle cable at the throttle body, the throttle cable from the bracket and the TPS electrical connector.
32. Install the air duct assembly.
33. Reconnect the negative battery cable.

DRIVE AXLE

Halfshaft

REMOVAL AND INSTALLATION

Metro

1. Remove the grease cap, the cotter pin and the halfshaft nut from both front wheels.
2. Loosen the wheel nuts.
3. Raise and support the vehicle safely.
4. Remove the front wheels.

5. Drain the transaxle fluid.
6. Using a prybar, pry on the inboard joints of the right and left hand halfshafts to detach the halfshafts from the snaprings of the differential side gears.
7. Remove the stabilizer bar mounting bolts and the ball joint stud bolt. Pull down on the stabilizer bar and remove the ball joint stud from the steering knuckle.
8. Pull the halfshafts out of the transaxle's side gear, first and then from the steering knuckles.

NOTE: To prevent the halfshaft boots from becoming damaged, be careful not to bring them into contact with any parts. If any malfunction is found in the either of the joints, replace the joints as an assembly.

To install:
9. To install, snap the halfshaft into the transaxle first and then into the steering knuckle.
10. To complete the installation, reverse the removal procedures. Torque the stabilizer bar mounting bolts to 32 ft. lbs. (43 Nm); the ball joint stud bolt to 44 ft. lbs. (60 Nm) and the halfshaft nut to 129 ft. lbs. (175 Nm).

Prizm

1. Remove the wheel cover.
2. Remove the cotter pin, hub nut cap, hub nut and washer.
3. Loosen the wheel nuts.
4. Elevate and safely support the vehicle.
5. Remove the front wheel.
6. Remove the lower control arm to ball joint attaching nuts and bolts.
7. Use a ball joint separator such as GM J-24319-01 or equivalent, to remove the tie rod ball joint from the knuckle.
8. Remove the bolts holding the brake caliper bracket to the steering knuckle. Use stiff wire to suspend the caliper out of the way; do not let the caliper hang by its hose. Remove the brake disc.
9. Push the axle from the hub using a brass or plastic hammer.

NOTE: If the axle cannot be separated from the hub using a brass or plastic hammer. Use a puller such as GM J-25287 or equivalent, to push the axle from the hub.

10. Use a slide hammer and appropriate end fitting (GM J-2619-01 and J-35762 or equivalents) to pull the halfshaft from the transaxle. Remove the shaft from the vehicle.

To install:
11. When reinstalling, install shaft into transaxle. If necessary, use a long brass drift and a hammer to drive the housing ribs onto the inner joint.
12. Install the shaft into the wheel hub.
13. Install the lower control arm to the lower ball joint. Tighten the nuts and bolts to 105 ft. lbs. (142 Nm).
14. Install the tie rod end to the steering knuckle and tighten the nut to 36 ft. lbs. (49 Nm).
15. Install the brake disc; install the brake caliper and tighten the bolts to 65 ft. lbs. (88 Nm).
16. Install the wheel.
17. Install the hub nut and washer.
18. Lower the vehicle to the ground.
19. Tighten the wheel lugs to 76 ft. lbs. (103 Nm). Tighten the hub nut to 137 ft. lbs. (186 Nm).
20. Install the nut, cap, cotter pin and washer. Install the wheel cover.

Spectrum

1. Raise and support the vehicle safely, allowing the wheels to hang.
2. Remove the front wheel assemblies, the hub grease caps, the hub nuts and the cotter pins.
3. Install the halfshaft boot seal protector tool J-28712 or equivalent, on the outer CV-joints and the halfshaft boot seal protector tool J-34754 or equivalent, on the inner Tri-pot joints.

NOTE: Clean the halfshaft threads and lubricate them with a thread lubricant.

4. Have an assistant depress the brake pedal, then remove the hub nut and washer.
5. Remove the caliper-to-steering knuckle bolts and support the caliper, on a wire, out of the way.
6. Remove the rotor. Remove the drain plug and drain the oil from the transaxle.
7. Using a slide hammer puller and the puller attachment tool J-34866 or equivalent, pull the hub from the halfshaft.
8. Remove the tie rod-to-steering knuckle cotter pin and the nut. Using the ball joint separator tool J-21687-02 or equivalent, press the tie rod ball joint from the steering knuckle.
9. Remove the lower ball joint-to-control arm nuts/bolts.
10. Swing the steering knuckle assembly outward and slide the halfshaft from the steering knuckle.
11. Place a large prybar between the differential case and the inboard

constant velocity joint. Pry the halfshaft from the differential case.

12. Remove the halfshaft assembly.

NOTE: When installing the halfshaft, press it into the differential case until it locks with snapring.

To install:

13. Use new cotter pins and reverse the removal procedures.

14. Torque the ball joint-to-control arm nuts/bolts to 80 ft. lbs. (108 Nm), the caliper-to-steering knuckle bolts to 41 ft. lbs. (55 Nm) and the halfshaft-to-hub nut to 137 ft. lbs. (186 Nm).

15. Check and/or adjust the front alignment.

Storm

1. Remove the wheel cover.
2. Loosen the wheel nuts.
3. Elevate and safely support the vehicle.
4. Remove the front wheel.
5. Install the halfshaft boot seal protector tool J-28712 or equivalent, on the outer CV-joints and the halfshaft boot seal protector tool J-34754 or equivalent, on the inner Tri-pot joints.
6. Unstake the hub nut. Have an assistant depress the brake pedal, then remove the hub nut and washer.
7. Remove the lower control arm to ball joint attaching nuts and bolts.
8. Use a ball joint separator such as GM J-24319-01 or equivalent, to remove the tie rod ball joint from the knuckle.
9. Remove the bolts holding the brake caliper bracket to the steering knuckle. Use stiff wire to suspend the caliper out of the way; do not let the caliper hang by its hose. Remove the brake disc.
10. Push the axle from the hub using a brass or plastic hammer.

NOTE: If the axle can not be separated from the hub using a brass or plastic hammer. Use a puller such as GM J-25287 or equivalent, to push the axle from the hub.

11. Use a slide hammer and appropriate end fitting GM J-2619-01 and J-35762 or equivalents, to pull the driveshaft from the transaxle. Remove the shaft from the vehicle.

To install:

12. When reinstalling, install shaft into transaxle. If necessary, use a long brass drift and a hammer to drive the housing ribs onto the inner joint.

13. Install the shaft into the wheel hub.

14. Install the lower control arm to the lower ball joint. Tighten the nuts and bolts to 115 ft. lbs. (156 Nm).

15. Install the tie rod end to the steering knuckle and tighten the nut to 40 ft. lbs. (54 Nm).

16. Install the brake disc; install the brake caliper and tighten the bolts to 65 ft. lbs. (88 Nm).

17. Install the wheel.

18. Install the hub nut and washer.

19. Lower the vehicle to the ground.

20. Tighten the wheel lugs to 76 ft. lbs. (103 Nm). Tighten the hub nut to 137 ft. lbs. (186 Nm).

21. Install the nut, cap, cotter pin and washer. Install the wheel cover.

CV-Boot

REMOVAL AND INSTALLATION

Metro

NOTE: Do not disassemble the wheel side joint (outboard). Replace if found to be defective. Do not disassemble the spider of the differential side joint. If the spider is found to be defective, replace the differential side joint assembly.

1. With the axleshaft removed from the vehicle, remove the boot band from the differential side joint.
2. Remove the housing from the differential side joint.
3. Remove the snapring and spider from the shaft.
4. Remove the inside and outside boots from the shaft.

To install:

5. Liberally apply the joint grease to the wheel side joint. Use the black joint grease in the tube included in the wheel side boot set or wheel side joint assembly.
6. Fit the wheel side boot on the shaft. Fill the inside of the boot with the joint grease, approximately 80 grams and fix the boot bands.
7. Fit the differential side boot on the shaft.
8. Liberally apply the joint grease to the differential side joint on the shaft. Use the yellow grease in the tube included in the differential side boot set or differential side joint assembly.
9. Install the spider of the differential side joint on the shaft, facing its chamfered side to the wheel side joint.

10. After installing the spider, fit the snapring in the groove on the shaft.

11. Fill the inside of the differential side boot with the joint grease, approximately 130 gram and install the housing. Fix the boot to the housing with a boot band.

12. Correct any distortions or bends in the boots.

13. Install the halfshaft in the vehicle.

Prizm

1. Raise and safely support the vehicle and remove the tire and wheel assembly.
2. Remove the halfshaft assembly.
3. Remove the boot retaining clamps.
4. Remove the inboard joint tulip.
5. Remove the tripod joint snapring and the tripod joint from the halfshaft.
6. Remove the inboard and outboard joint boots.
7. To install, reverse the removal procedures; the inboard joint and clamp is larger than the outboard clamp. Face the beveled side of the tripod axial spline towards the outboard joint.

Storm

OUTER

1. Raise and safely support the vehicle and remove the tire and wheel assembly.
2. Remove the halfshaft.
3. Place halfshaft into a suitable vise.
4. Using a suitable prybar, remove the circlip.
5. Remove the case housing from the shaft.
6. Remove the 6 balls from the ball guide, then move ball guide towards center of shaft.
7. Remove the snapring from the shaft, then the ball guide and ball retainer from the shaft.
8. Remove boot from shaft.
9. Installation is the reverse of removal. Pack new boot with suitable grease.

INNER

1. Raise and safely support the vehicle and remove the tire and wheel assembly.
2. Remove halfshaft.
3. Place halfshaft into a suitable vise and remove the large boot clamp.
4. Remove the Tri-pot housing from the drive halfshaft.

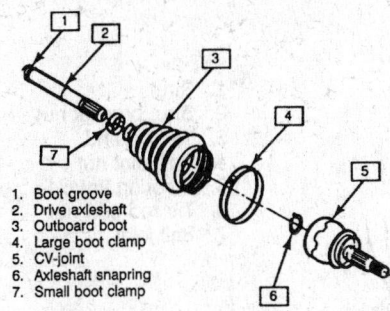

1. Boot groove
2. Drive axleshaft
3. Outboard boot
4. Large boot clamp
5. CV-joint
6. Axleshaft snapring
7. Small boot clamp

Exploded view of the CV-joint — Prizm

5. Using a suitable brass drift and hammer, remove the spider assembly from the halfshaft.

6. Remove the small boot clamp, then the boot from the shaft. Note the alignment marks on the spider assembly and the halfshaft and on the drive halfshaft and the Tri-pot housing. If no marks are present, make alignment marks for easy installation.

7. Installation is the reverse of removal. Pack new boot with a suitable grease.

Spectrum

INNER

1. Disconnect the negative battery terminal from the battery.

2. Raise and support the vehicle safely, the remove the front wheels.

3. Remove the outer boot assembly.

4. Remove the boot retaining clamps and the spacer ring.

5. Slide the axle and the spider bearing assembly out of the Tri-pot housing. Install the spider retainer onto the spider bearing assembly.

6. Remove the spider assembly and the boot from the axle.

7. Installation is the reverse of removal. Pack new boot with a suitable grease.

OUTER

1. Disconnect the negative battery terminal from the battery.

2. Raise and support the vehicle safely, then remove the front wheels.

3. Remove the brake caliper and support on a wire, then remove the rotor.

4. Slide the outer CV-joint assembly off the halfshaft.

5. Remove the bearing retaining ring, the boot retainer, the clamp and the outer boot.

6. Installation is the reverse of removal. Pack new boot with a suitable grease.

Front Wheel Hub, Knuckle and Bearings

REMOVAL AND INSTALLATION

Metro

1. Raise and support the vehicle safely. Remove the front wheel assembly. Remove the hub from the steering knuckle.

2. Remove the tie rod end cotter pin and nut.

3. Using the ball joint removal tool J-21687-02, remove the ball joint from the steering knuckle.

4. Remove the ball stud bolt from the steering knuckle.

5. Remove the strut-to-steering knuckle bolts.

6. Remove the steering knuckle and support the axleshaft.

7. Using a brass drift, drive the inner and outer wheel bearings from the steering knuckle.

8. Remove the spacer and clean the steering knuckle cavity.

To install:

9. Lubricate the new bearings and the steering knuckle cavity.

10. Using the installation tool J-34856, drive the new bearings, with the internal seals facing outward, into the steering knuckle.

11. Using the seal installation tool J-34881, drive the new seal into the steering knuckle, grease the seal lip.

12. To complete the installation, reverse the removal procedures.

13. Torque the strut-to-steering knuckle bolts to 59 ft. lbs. (80 Nm). Torque the ball joints-to-steering knuckle nuts to 44 ft. lbs. (60 Nm).

14. Torque the axleshaft castle nut to 129 ft. lbs. (175 Nm).

Prizm

1. Loosen the wheel nuts and the center axle nut.

2. Raise the vehicle and safely support it.

3. Remove the wheel.

4. Remove the center axle nut.

5. Remove the brake caliper and hang it out of the way on a piece of stiff wire. Do not disconnect the brake line; do not allow the caliper to hang by the hose.

6. Remove the brake disc.

7. Remove the cotter pin and nut from the tie rod end.

8. Remove the tie rod end from the knuckle using a joint separator GM tool J-6627-A or equivalent.

9. Remove the bolt and 2 nuts holding the bottom of the ball joint to the control arm and remove the arm from the knuckle.

10. Remove the 2 nuts from the steering knuckle. Place a protective cover or shield over the CV-boot on the halfshaft.

11. Using a plastic mallet, tap the halfshaft free of the hub assembly.

12. Remove the 2 bolts and remove the axle hub assembly.

13. Clamp the knuckle in a vise with protected jaws.

14. Remove the dust deflector. Loosen the nut holding the ball joint to the knuckle. Use a ball joint separator GM tool J-35413 or equivalent, to loosen and remove the joint

15. Use a slide hammer/extractor GM tool J-26941 or equivalent, to remove the outer oil seal.

16. Remove the snapring.

17. Using a hub puller and pilot GM tools J-25287 and J-35378 or equivalents, pull the axle hub from the knuckle.

18. Remove the brake splash shield (3 bolts).

19. Use a split plate bearing remover, puller pilot and a shop press, remove the inner bearing race from the hub.

20. Remove the inner oil seal with the same tools used to remove the outer seal.

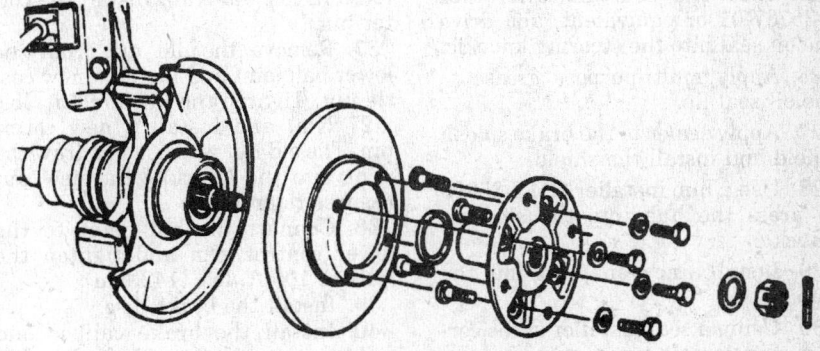

Front wheel hub and bearing assembly — Metro

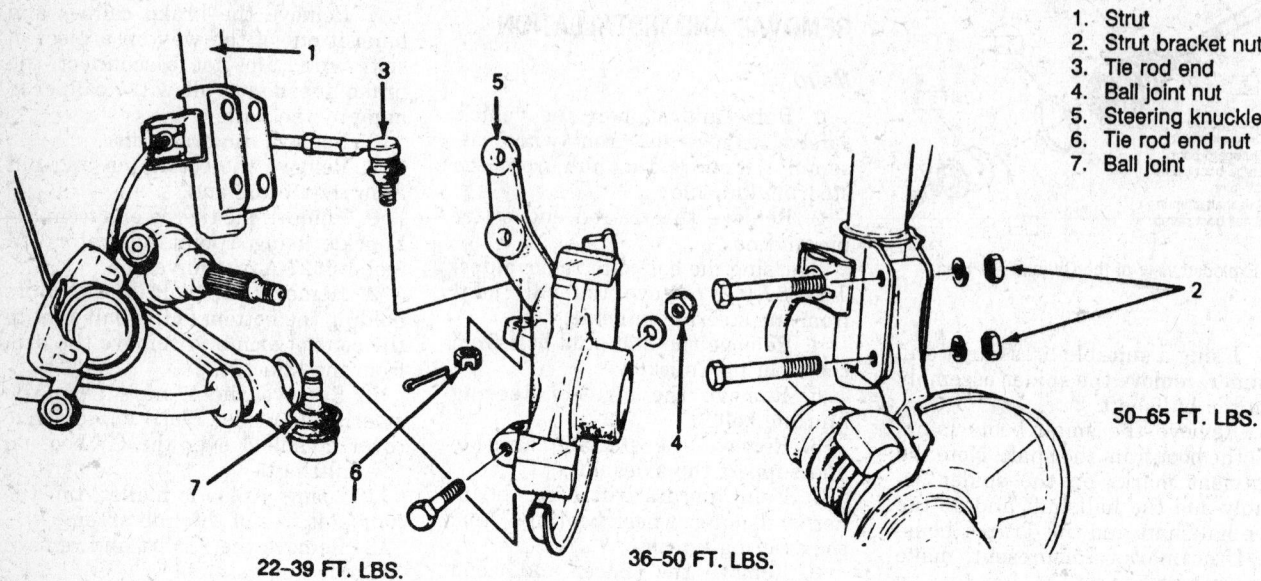

1. Strut
2. Strut bracket nut
3. Tie rod end
4. Ball joint nut
5. Steering knuckle
6. Tie rod end nut
7. Ball joint

50–65 FT. LBS.

22–39 FT. LBS.

36–50 FT. LBS.

Steering knuckle assembly — Metro

21. Place the inner race in the bearing. Support the knuckle and use an axle hub remover GM tool J-35399 with a plastic mallet to drive out the bearing.

22. Clean and inspect all parts but do not wash or clean the wheel bearing; it cannot be repacked. If the bearing is damaged or noisy, it must be replaced.

To install:

23. Press a new bearing race into the steering knuckle using a bearing driver of the correct size GM J-8092 and J-37777 or equivalent.

24. Place a new bearing inner race on the hub bearing.

25. Insert the side lip of a new oil seal into the seal installer GM J-35737-01 or equivalent, and drive the oil seal into the steering knuckle.

26. Apply multi-purpose grease to the oil seal lip.

27. Apply sealer to the brake splash shield and install the shield.

28. Use a hub installer GM J-35399 to press the hub into the steering knuckle.

29. Install a new snapring into the hub.

30. Using a seal installer of the correct size, install a new outer oil seal into the steering knuckle.

31. Apply multi-purpose grease to the seal surfaces which will contact the halfshaft.

32. Support the knuckle and drive in a new dust deflector.

33. Install the ball joint into the knuckle and tighten the nut to 94 ft. lbs. (127 Nm).

34. Temporarily install the hub assembly to the lower control arm and fit the halfshaft into the hub.

35. Install the knuckle to strut bolts, then install the tie rod end to the knuckle.

36. Tighten the steering knuckle to strut assembly nuts to 194 ft. lbs. (263 Nm) and the strut assembly bracket to body nuts to 29 ft. lbs. (39 Nm) and tighten the tie rod end nut to 36 ft. lbs. (49 Nm). Install the cotter pin.

37. Remove the old nut from the lower ball joint and install a new castle nut. Tighten the nut to 94 ft. lbs. (127 Nm) and install a new cotter pin. The old nut was used to draw the joint into the knuckle; the new nut assures retention.

38. Connect the ball joint to the lower control arm and tighten the nuts to 105 ft. lbs. (142 Nm).

39. Install the brake disc.

40. Install the brake caliper and tighten the bolts to 65 ft. lbs. (88 Nm).

41. Install the center nut and washer on the halfshaft.

42. Install the wheel.

43. Lower the vehicle to the ground.

44. Tighten the wheel nuts to 76 ft. lbs. (103 Nm) and the axle bolt to 137 ft. lbs. (186 Nm). Install the cap and cotter pin.

45. Remove the protective cover from the CV boot.

Spectrum and Storm

1. Raise and support the vehicle safely, allowing the wheels to hang.

2. Remove the front wheel assemblies, the hub grease caps and the cotter pins.

3. Install the halfshaft boot seal protector tool J-28712 or equivalent, on the outer CV-joints and the halfshaft boot seal protector tool J-34754 or equivalent, on the inner Tri-pot joints.

NOTE: Clean the halfshaft threads and lubricate them with a thread lubricant.

4. Remove the hub nut and washer.

5. Remove the caliper-to-steering knuckle bolts and support the caliper, on a wire, out of the way.

6. Remove the rotor.

7. Using a slide hammer puller and the puller attachment tool

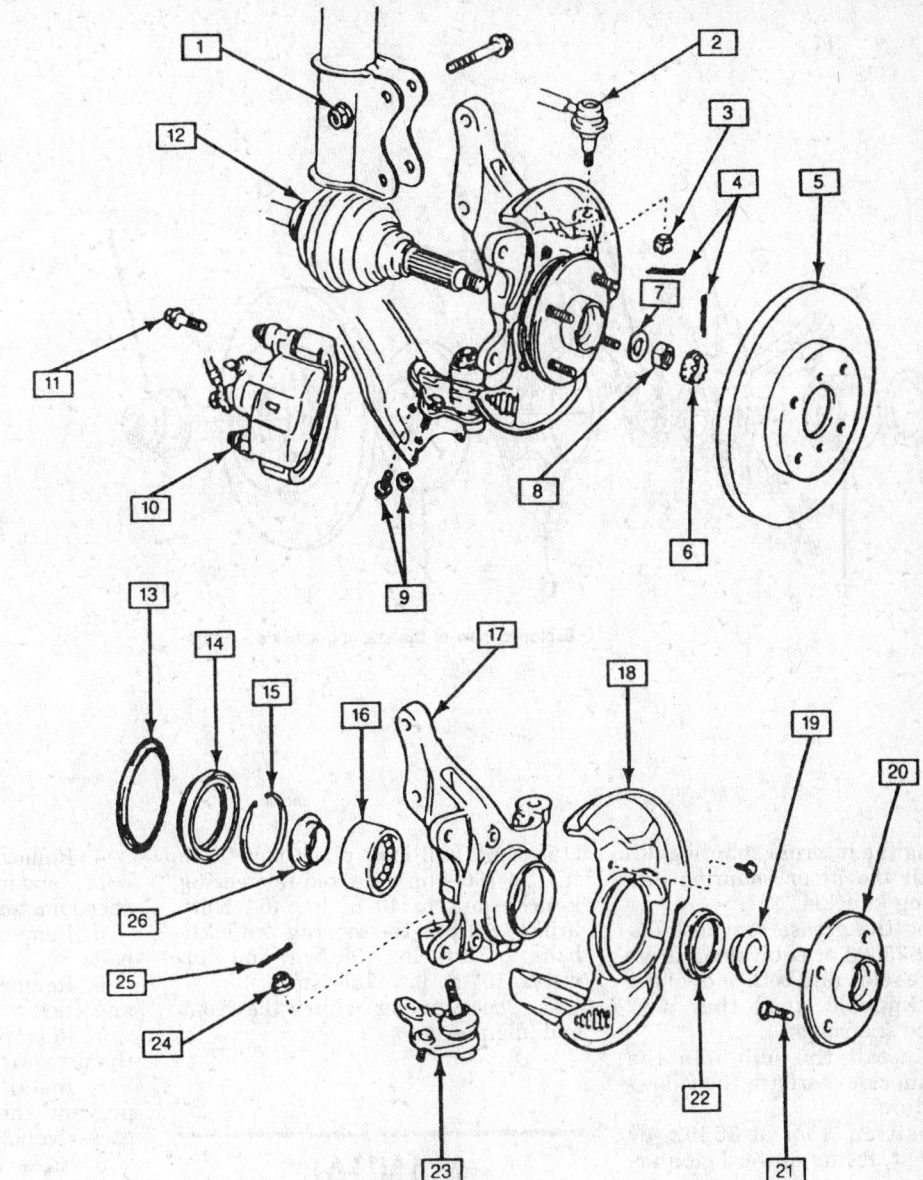

1. Strut mounting nut
2. Tie rod end
3. Tie rod bolt
4. Cotter pin
5. Rotor disc
6. Locknut cap
7. Washer
8. Bearing locknut
9. Ball joint mounting nut and bolt
10. Disc brake caliper
11. Caliper mounting bolt
12. Driveshaft
13. Dust deflector
14. Inner oil seal
15. Snapring
16. Hub bearing
17. Steering knuckle
18. Dust cover
19. Bearing inner race (outside)
20. Axle hub
21. Wheel stud
22. Outer oil seal
23. Ball joint
24. Ball joint castle nut
25. Cotter pin
26. Bearing inner race

Exploded view of the steering knuckle — Prizm

J-34866 or equivalent, pull the hub from the halfshaft.

8. Remove the tie rod-to-steering knuckle cotter pin and the nut. Using the ball joint separator tool J-21687-02 or equivalent, press the tie rod ball joint from the steering knuckle.

9. To remove the steering knuckle from the vehicle, perform the following procedures:

a. Remove the lower ball joint-to-control arm nuts/bolts.

NOTE: Before separating the steering knuckle from the strut, be sure to scribe matchmarks on each component.

b. Remove the steering knuckle-to-strut nuts/bolts and the steering knuckle from the vehicle.

10. Using a medium prybar, pry the grease seals from the steering knuckle. Using a pair of internal snapring pliers, remove the internal snaprings from the steering knuckle.

11. Support the steering knuckle (face down) on an arbor press (on 2 press blocks). Position tool J-35301 or equivalent, on the rear-side of the hub bearing, then, press the bearing from the steering knuckle.

12. Using an arbor press, the wheel puller tool J-35893 or equivalent and a piece of bar stock, press the bearing inner race from the wheel hub.

13. Clean the parts in solvent and blow dry with compressed air.

To install:

14. Using wheel bearing grease, lubricate the inside of the steering knuckle.

15. Using the internal snapring pliers, install the outer snapring into the steering knuckle.

16. Position the steering knuckle on a arbor press (outer face down), a new wheel bearing and the bearing installation tool J-35301 or equivalent, then press the bearing inward until it stops against the snapring.

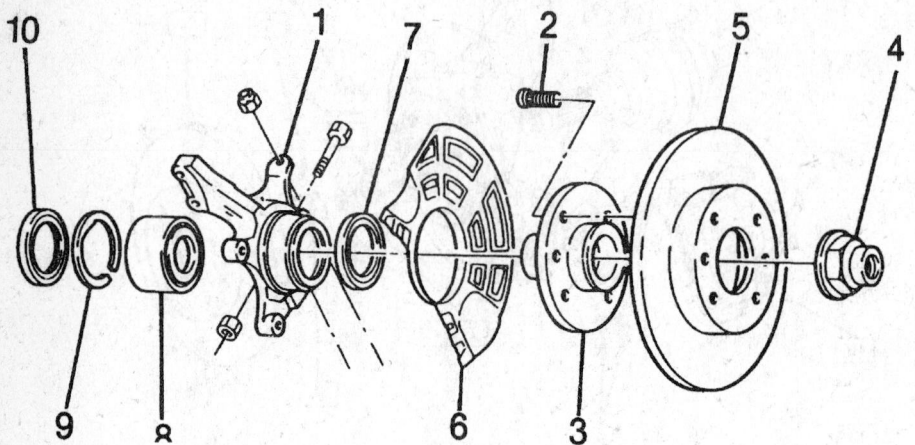

1. Steering knuckle
2. Wheel stud
3. Hub
4. Hub axle nut
5. Brake rotor
6. Dust cover
7. Outer oil seal
8. Bearing assembly
9. Inner snapring
10. Inner oil seal

Exploded view of the steering knuckle — Storm

17. Using the internal snapring pliers, install the inner snapring into the steering knuckle.

18. Using the grease seal installation tool J-35303 or equivalent, drive new grease seals into both ends of the steering knuckle until they seat against the snaprings.

19. To install the hub into the steering knuckle, perform the following procedure:

   a. Position tool J-35302 or equivalent, facing upward on a arbor press.

   b. Position the steering knuckle (facing upward) on the tool J-35302, the wheel hub and a piece of bar stock (on top).

   c. Press the assembly together until the hub bottoms out on the wheel bearing.

20. To install steering knuckle, use new cotter pins and reverse the removal procedures. Lubricate the new bearing seal with wheel bearing grease.

21. For Spectrum, torque the steering knuckle-to-strut bolts to 87 ft. lbs. (118 Nm), the ball joint-to-control arm nuts/bolts to 80 ft. lbs. (108 Nm), caliper-to-steering knuckle bolts to 41 ft. lbs. (55 Nm) and the halfshaft-to-hub nut to 137 ft. lbs. (186 Nm).

22. For Storm, torque steering knuckle nuts and bolts to 115 ft. lbs.

(156 Nm), ball joint pinch bolt to 48 ft. lbs. (66 Nm), tie rod-to-steering knuckle nut to 40 ft. lbs. (54 Nm), brake caliper-to-steering knuckle bolts to 72 ft. lbs. (98 Nm) and hub nut to 137 ft. lbs. (186 Nm).

23. Check and/or adjust the front end alignment.

MANUAL TRANSAXLE

Transaxle Assembly

REMOVAL AND INSTALLATION

Metro

1. Disconnect the negative battery cable and the ground strap at the transaxle.

2. Remove the clutch cable adjusting nuts, retaining clip from the cable and cable from the bracket.

3. Disconnect and tag all the wiring harness clamps and connectors involved with the transaxle removal.

4. Remove the speedometer cable boot, speedometer case clip and speedometer cable from the case.

5. Remove the transaxle retaining bolts.

6. Remove the starter assembly and starter motor plate.

7. Remove the vacuum hose from the pressure sensor.

8. Install the engine support to prevent the engine from lowering excessively.

9. Raise and support the vehicle safely. Drain the transaxle oil.

10. Remove the gear shaft control shaft bolt and nut and detach the control shaft from the gear shift shaft.

11. Extension rod nut and remove the rod with washers.

12. Remove the exhaust pipe front and rear flange bolts.

13. Remove the clutch housing lower plate.

14. Remove the left front wheel.

15. Remove the left tie rod end.

16. Remove the left ball joint by removing the joint stud bolt.

17. Remove both halfshafts at the transaxle.

18. Support the transaxle with a suitable jack and remove the transaxle retaining bolts and nuts.

19. Remove the 2 rear engine mounting bolts.

20. Remove the 3 bolts and 2 nuts from the transaxle mounting left hand bracket, remove the left hand bracket.

21. Lower the transaxle with the engine attached in order to detach it from the stud bolt at the engine rear mounting portion. Pull the transaxle straight out toward the left side to disconnect the input shaft from the clutch cover, lower and remove the transaxle assembly.

To install:

22. While the transaxle is being raised into its correct position, install the right hand halfshaft into the differential.

23. Install the transaxle along with the transaxle to engine nuts and bolts. Install the left hand bracket with its 3 bolts and 2 nuts. Torque them to 37 ft. lbs. (50 Nm).

24. Install the 2 rear engine mounting nuts and torque them to 37 ft. lbs. (50 Nm).

25. Lower the transaxle supporting jack. Torque the transaxle-to-engine bolt and nut to 37 ft. lbs. (50 Nm).

26. Install the left hand halfshaft to the transaxle. Be sure to push each driveaxle in fully to engage the snaprings with the differential gear.

27. Install the left ball joint and ball joint stud bolt. Torque the ball joint bolt and nut to 44 ft. lbs. (60 Nm).

28. Install the left tie rod end, castle nut and cotter pin. Torque the castle nut to 32 ft. lbs. (43 Nm).

29. Install the left front wheel.

30. Install the clutch housing lower plate.

31. Install the exhaust pipe front and rear flange nuts.

32. Install the extension rod nut and washers. Torque the rod nut to 24 ft. lbs. (33 Nm).

33. Install the control shaft to gear shift and install the gear shift control shaft bolt and nut. Torque the gear shift control shaft bolt and nut to 13 ft. lbs. (18 Nm).

34. Refill the transaxle with the recommended lubricant.

35. Lower the vehicle.

36. Remove the engine support fixture.

37. Install the vacuum hose to the pressure sensor.

38. Install the starter, starter motor plate and 2 bolts.

39. Install the transaxle retaining bolts. Torque the retaining bolts to 37 ft. lbs. (50 Nm).

40. Install the speedometer cable to case, speedometer case clip and speedometer cable boot.

41. Install the clutch cable bracket, retaining clip to cable and clutch cable adjusting nut. Adjust the clutch free-play as necessary.

42. Install the negative battery cable and the ground strap to the transaxle.

Prizm

1. Install an engine support and tension it to support the engine without raising it.

2. Remove the battery hold-down, the battery and tray.

3. Disconnect the electrical connector to the reverse lights and disconnect the ground strap running to the transaxle.

4. Remove the 2 actuator mounting bolts and the actuator line bracket.

5. Remove the shift cable retainers and end-clips.

6. Remove the shift cables from their brackets and place the cables out of the way.

7. Remove the cover and brace from the left transaxle mount.

8. Remove the through bolt from the mount.

9. Remove the 2 upper transaxle to engine bolts.

10. Remove the upper starter bolt and remove the speedometer cable.

11. Raise the vehicle and safely support it.

—————— **CAUTION** ——————

The engine hoist is in place and under tension. Use care when repositioning the vehicle and make necessary adjustments to the engine support.

12. Remove the splash shields. Drain the transaxle oil.

13. Disconnect the electrical connections at the starter.

14. Remove the bottom starter bolt and the starter.

15. Remove the drive axles.

16. Remove the 3 bolts holding the center crossmember to the radiator support.

17. Remove the covers from the front and center mount bolts.

18. Remove the 2 front mount bolts, then the center mount bolts and then the 2 rear mount bolts.

19. Remove the 2 bolts holding the center crossmember to the main crossmember.

20. Remove the 3 exhaust hanger bracket nuts and the exhaust hanger.

21. Use a floor jack and a wide piece of wood to support the main crossmember.

22. Remove the 8 bolts holding the main crossmember to the body.

23. Remove the 2 bolts holding the lower control arm brackets to the body.

—————— **CAUTION** ——————

The crossmembers are loose and free to fall. Make sure they are properly supported.

24. Slowly lower the main crossmember while holding onto the center crossmember.

25. At the front transaxle mount, remove the through bolt and mount.

26. Remove the front mounting bracket from the transaxle.

27. Remove the center mount from the transaxle with its 2 bolts.

28. Remove the inspection cover bolt.

29. Remove the 2 lower transaxle bracket to transaxle mount bolts.

30. Lower the vehicle to the ground.

—————— **CAUTION** ——————

The engine hoist is in place and under tension. Use care when repositioning the vehicle and make necessary adjustments to the engine support.

31. Remove the remaining transaxle mount to transaxle bracket bolt.

32. Slowly lower the engine support device to gain clearance for the removal of the transaxle.

33. Remove the transaxle mount.

34. Safely elevate and support the vehicle.

—————— **CAUTION** ——————

The engine hoist is in place and under tension. Use care when repositioning the vehicle and make necessary adjustments to the engine support.

35. Support the transaxle with a floor jack, making sure it is properly placed and balanced.

36. Remove the lower front and rear bolts holding the transaxle to the engine.

37. Remove the transaxle assembly from the engine and lower it slowly on the floor jack.

To install:

38. Elevate the transaxle into position, making sure the input shaft aligns with the clutch splines.

39. Install the lower front and rear bolts holding the transaxle to the engine.

40. Remove the floor jack from under the transaxle.

41. Attach the electrical wiring to the starter.

42. Install the lower starter bolt snugly.

43. Lower the vehicle to the ground

─── CAUTION ───

The engine hoist is in place and under tension. Use care when repositioning the vehicle and make necessary adjustments to the engine support.

44. Install the left transaxle mount upper bolt and 2 lower bolts snugly.

45. Take tension on the engine support device and raise the transaxle. Install the through bolt loosely in the mount.

46. Tighten the through bolt to 69 ft. lbs. (87 Nm). Tighten the upper transaxle mount bolt to 45 ft. lbs. (61 Nm).

47. Install the mount cover and bracket. Tighten the cover bolts to 45 ft. lbs. (61 Nm).

48. Install the 2 upper transaxle to engine bolts and tighten them to 34 ft. lbs. (46 Nm).

49. Install the upper starter bolt and tighten it to 29 ft. lbs. (39 Nm).

50. Connect the speedometer cable.

51. Position the shift cables into the brackets and connect the cable retainers and end clips.

52. Install the 2 actuator mounting bolts snugly, then install the actuator line bracket and bolt. Tighten the actuator line and mounting bolts to 15 ft. lbs. (20 Nm).

53. Connect the ground strap and the electrical connector for the reverse lights.

54. Install the air cleaner assembly.

55. Elevate and safely support the vehicle.

─── CAUTION ───

The engine hoist is in place and under tension. Use care when repositioning the vehicle and make necessary adjustments to the engine support.

56. Tighten the 2 remaining lower transaxle mount bolts to 45 ft. lbs. (61 Nm). (These are the bolts installed in Step 39).

57. Tighten the lower starter bolt to 29 ft. lbs. (39 Nm).

58. Install the center mount and its 2 bolts and tighten them to 45 ft. lbs. (61 Nm). Install the inspection cover bolt and tighten it to 45 ft. lbs. (61 Nm).

59. Install the front mount bracket on the transaxle.

60. Install the front mount and through bolt loosely.

NOTE: When installing the front mount, the weight on the mount must go toward the transaxle for proper mount alignment.

61. Position the center crossmember over the center and rear transaxle mount studs; start 2 nuts on the center mount.

62. Loosely install the 3 bolts holding the center crossmember to the radiator support.

63. Loosely install the 2 front mount bolts.

64. Raise the main crossmember into position over the rear mount studs and align all underbody bolts. Install the 2 rear mount nuts loosely.

65. Install the 8 main crossmember-to-underbody bolts loosely.

66. Install the 2 lower control arm bracket bolts loosely.

67. Loosely install the 2 bolts holding the center crossmember to the main crossmember.

68. Install the exhaust hanger bracket and its 3 nuts. The crossmembers, mounts, through bolts and brackets should now all be in place and held loosely by their nuts and bolts. If any repositioning is necessary, do so now.

69. Tighten the components below in the order listed to the correct torque specification:

    a. Main crossmember-to-underbody bolts: 152 ft. lbs. (206 Nm).

    b. Lower control arm bolts: 94 ft. lbs. (127 Nm).

    c. Center crossmember-to-radiator support bolts: 45 ft. lbs. (61 Nm).

    d. Front, center and rear mount bolts: 45 ft. lbs. (61 Nm).

    e. Exhaust hanger bracket nuts: 9.5 ft. lbs. (12.5 Nm)

    f. Front mount through bolt: 69 ft. lbs. (87 Nm).

70. Install the covers on the front and center mount bolts.

71. Reinstall the halfshafts.

72. Fill the transaxle with the correct amount of oil.

73. Install the splash shields.

74. Lower the vehicle to the ground. Remove the engine support apparatus.

75. Install the battery tray, battery and hold-down clamp.

Storm

1. Disconnect the battery cables, then remove the battery and tray from the vehicle.

2. Drain the transaxle fluid.

3. Remove the air cleaner assembly.

4. Disconnect the electrical connectors from the transaxle.

5. Disconnect the ground cable and engine wiring harness clamp from the transaxle.

6. Disconnect the ignition coil ground cable from the engine, then the ground cable at the ignition coil.

7. Disconnect the speedometer cable, clutch cable and shifter cables.

8. Support the engine using engine support tool J-28467-A or equivalent.

9. Raise and support the vehicle safely, then remove the tire and wheel assemblies.

10. Remove the front undercovers, then the ball joints from the steering knuckles.

11. Remove the left and right halfshaft, then the front exhaust pipe.

12. Remove the torque rod and bracket, then the left transaxle mount.

13. Remove the front transaxle through bolt, then the center beam with the rear transaxle mount.

14. Remove the engine stiffener attaching bolts, then the engine stiffener from the vehicle.

15. Remove the flywheel dust cover from the clutch housing. Support the transaxle using a suitable jack.

16. Remove the transaxle-to-engine attaching bolts, then the transaxle from the vehicle.

To install:

17. Install the transaxle, then the transaxle-to-engine attaching bolts. Torque bolts to 55 ft. lbs. (75 Nm).

18. Remove the engine support tool J-28467-A or its equivalent.

19. Install the flywheel dust cover, engine stiffener and center beam with the rear transaxle mount.

20. Install the left transaxle mount, then the front transaxle mount through bolt.

21. Torque the center crossmember bolts to 45 ft. lbs. (61 Nm). Torque the left transaxle mount bolts to 29 ft. lbs. (39 Nm) and the front transaxle through bolt to 64 ft. lbs. (87 Nm).

22. Install the torque rod and bracket, then the front exhaust pipe.

23. Install the right and left halfshafts, then the ball joints onto the steering knuckles.

24. Install the front undercovers, then the front tire and wheel assemblies.

25. Lower the vehicle and remove the engine support tool.

26. Connect the shift cable, clutch cable and speedometer cable.

27. Install the battery bracket and the ignition coil assembly.

28. Install the ignition coil ground cable onto the engine.

29. Install the engine harness wiring clamp, then the ground cable.

30. Connect all electrical connectors to the transaxle. Install the battery and battery tray.

31. Connect the battery cables. Adjust the shift cables, if necessary. Start engine and check for leaks.

Spectrum

1. Disconnect the negative battery terminal from the battery and the transaxle.

2. Disconnect the wiring connectors, speedometer cable, clutch cable and shift cables from the transaxle.

3. Remove the air cleaner heat tube.

4. Remove the upper transaxle-to-engine bolts.

5. Raise and support the vehicle safely. Drain the oil from the transaxle.

6. Remove the left front wheel assembly and splash shield.

7. Disconnect the left tie rod at the steering knuckle and the left tension rod.

8. Disconnect the halfshafts and remove the shafts by pulling them straight out from the transaxle, avoid damaging the oil seals.

9. Remove the dust cover at the clutch housing.

10. Using a floor jack, support the transaxle, then remove the transaxle-to-engine retaining bolts.

11. While sliding the transaxle away from the engine, carefully lower the jack, guiding the right halfshaft out of the transaxle.

NOTE: The right halfshaft must be installed into the transaxle when the transaxle is being mated to the engine.

To install:

12. When installing the transaxle, guide the right halfshaft into the shaft bore as the transaxle is being raised.

13. Install the transaxle-to-engine mounting bolts. Torque bolts to 55 ft. lbs. (75 Nm).

14. Install the left halfshaft into its bore on the transaxle.

15. Install the left tension rod and torque bolts to 80 ft. lbs. (108 Nm).

16. Install the tie rod to the steering knuckle.

17. Install the clutch housing dust cover bolts and the splash shield.

18. Install the tire and wheel assembly and lower the vehicle.

19. Install the remaining transaxle-to-engine attaching bolts. Torque bolts to 55 ft. lbs. (75 Nm).

20. Connect the ground cable at transaxle, clutch cable, speedometer cable and the battery negative cable.

21. Start engine and check for leaks.

LINKAGE ADJUSTMENT

Spectrum and Storm

1. Loosen the adjusting nuts.

2. Place the transaxle and the shift lever in the **N** position.

3. Turn the adjusting nuts until the shift lever is in the vertical position.

4. Tighten the adjusting nuts.

Metro

1. At the console, loosen the gear shift control housing nuts and the guide plate bolts.

2. Adjust the guide plate by displacing it toward the front and rear so the gear shift control lever is brought in the middle of the guide plate at the right angle.

3. Once the guide plate is positioned properly, tighten the guide plate bolts to 7 ft. lbs. (9 Nm) and then the housing nuts to 4 ft. lbs. (5 Nm).

CLUTCH

Clutch Assembly

REMOVAL AND INSTALLATION

Metro

1. Remove the transaxle.

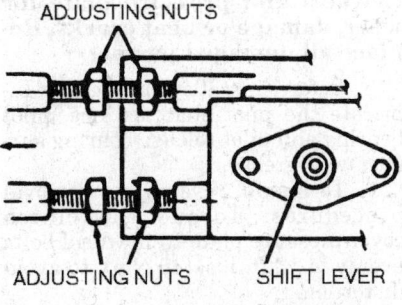

Adjusting the shift linkage — Spectrum

2. Install tool J-34860 (J-37761 on the Metro) into the pilot bearing to support the clutch assembly.

3. Loosen the clutch cover-to-flywheel bolts, one turn at a time (evenly) until the spring pressure is released.

4. Remove the clutch cover and clutch disc.

5. Inspect the parts for wear, if necessary, replace the parts.

6. To install, reverse the removal procedures. Torque the clutch cover bolts to 18 ft. lbs. (23 Nm).

Prizm

NOTE: Do not allow grease or oil to contaminate any of the disc, pressure plate or flywheel friction surfaces.

1. Remove the transaxle from the vehicle.

2. Remove the clutch cover and disc from the bell housing.

3. Unfasten the release fork bearing clips. Withdraw the release bearing hub, complete with the release bearing.

4. Remove the tension spring from the clutch linkage.

5. Remove the release fork and support.

6. Punch matchmarks on the clutch cover (pressure plate) and flywheel so the pressure plate can be returned to its original position during installation.

7. Slowly unfasten the screws which attach the retracting springs. Loosen each screw 1 turn at a time until the tension is released.

— **CAUTION** —

If the screws are released too quickly, the clutch assembly will fly apart, causing possible injury.

8. Separate the pressure plate from the clutch cover/spring assembly.

9. Inspect the parts for wear or deterioration. It is strongly recommended that all 3 components of the clutch system-disc, pressure plate and bearing be replaced as a unit, if any part is worn.

10. Inspect the flywheel for any signs of cracking, bluing in the steel (a sign of extreme heat) or scoring. Any bluing or cracks which are found require replacement of the flywheel. While the flywheel will not be perfectly smooth, it should be free of all but the slightest ridges and valleys or scores. A scored flywheel will immediately attack a new clutch disc, causing slippage and vibration.

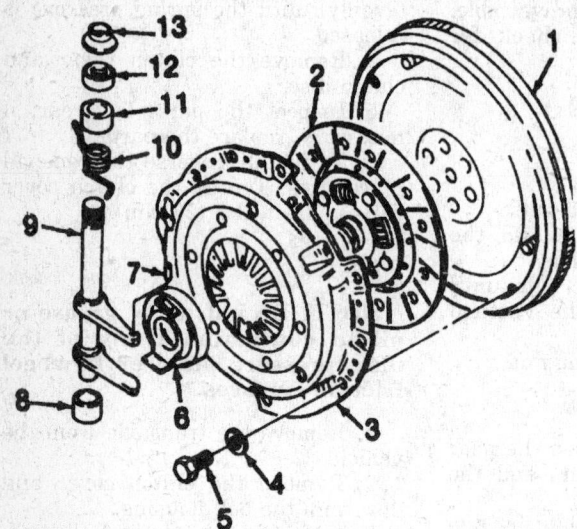

1. Flywheel
2. Disc
3. Clutch Cover
4. Lock Washer
5. Bolt
6. Release Bearing
7. Release Fork Pin
8. No. 2 Bushing
9. Release Shaft
10. Return Spring
11. No. 1 Bushing
12. Shaft Seal
13. Shaft Cover

Exploded view of the clutch assembly — Metro

To install:

11. When reassembling, apply a thin coating of multipurpose grease to the release bearing hub and release fork contact points. Also, pack the groove inside the clutch hub with multipurpose grease and lubricate the pivot points of the release fork.

12. Align the matchmarks on the clutch cover and flywheel which were made during disassembly. Install the clutch and pressure plate assembly and tighten the retaining bolts just finger-tight.

13. Center the clutch disc by using a clutch pilot tool or an old input shaft. Insert the pilot into the end of the input shaft front bearing, wiggle it gently to align the clutch disc and pressure plate and tighten the retaining bolts. The bolts should be tightened in 2 or 3 steps, gradually and evenly. Final bolt torque is 14 ft. lbs. (19 Nm).

14. Install the release bearing, fork and boot.

15. Reinstall the transaxle.

Spectrum and Storm

1. Remove the transaxle.

2. Install the pilot shaft tool J-35282 or equivalent, into the pilot bearing to support the clutch assembly during the removal procedures.

NOTE: Observe the alignment marks on the clutch and the clutch cover and pressure plate assembly. If the markings are not present, be sure to add them.

3. Loosen the clutch cover and pressure plate assembly retaining bolts evenly, one at a time, until the spring pressure is released.

4. Remove the clutch cover and pressure plate assembly and clutch plate.

NOTE: Check the clutch disc, flywheel and pressure plate for wear, damage or heat cracks. Replace all damaged parts.

5. Before installation, lightly lubricate the pilot shaft splines, pilot bearing and pilot release bearing surface with grease.

6. To install, reverse the removal procedures. Torque the clutch cover/pressure plate-to-flywheel bolts evenly to 13 ft. lbs. (18 Nm), to avoid distortion.

PEDAL HEIGHT/FREE-PLAY ADJUSTMENT

Metro

1. At the transaxle, move the clutch release arm to check the free-play, it should be 0.08-0.16 in. (15-30mm).

2. If necessary, turn the clutch cable joint nut to adjust the cable length.

NOTE: The clutch pedal height should be adjusted so the clutch pedal is within 0.3 in. (8mm) of the brake pedal height. The pedal is adjusted at the stop bolt on the upper end of the pedal pivot.

Prizm

1. Check pedal height as measured from the insulating sheet on the floor to the front-center of the pedal; it should be 5.71-6.10 in. (145-155mm). If the height is not correct, perform the following procedures:

   a. Remove the lower instrument finish panel and air duct.

   b. Loosen the locknut on the pedal stopper bolt, located at the top of the pedal.

   c. Turn the stopper bolt inward (to decrease) or outward (to increase) until it is within specifications.

   d. Tighten the locknut, recheck and readjust, if necessary.

2. To check and/or adjust the clutch pedal free-play, perform the following procedures:

   a. Measure the clutch pedal height.

   b. Push the pedal until increased resistance is felt as the clutch pressure plate springs begin to be compressed. Measure the pedal at this point, then, subtract the smaller figure from the larger one; this is the free-play dimension.

NOTE: The free-play dimension should be 0.20-0.59 in. (5-15mm).

   c. If necessary to adjust the free-play, loosen the pushrod locknut, located between the pedal and the clutch master cylinder. Turn the pushrod, clockwise to decrease or counter-clockwise to increase, until the dimension is within specifications.

   d. Tighten the locknut, recheck and readjust, if necessary.

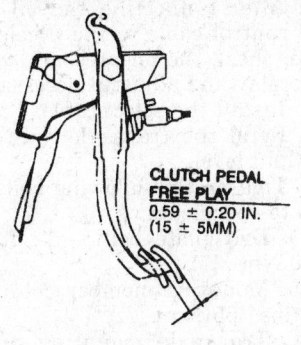

Clutch pedal free-play adjustment — Spectrum and Storm

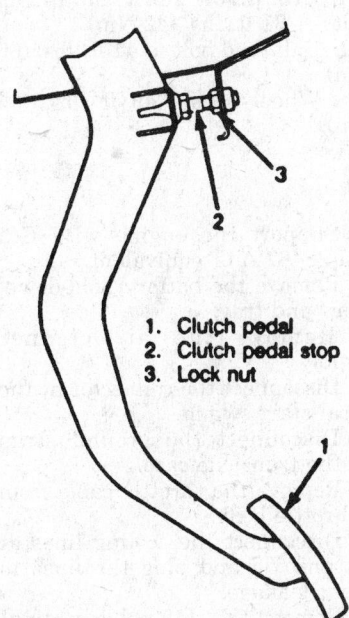

1. Clutch pedal
2. Clutch pedal stop
3. Lock nut

Clutch pedal height adjustment — Metro

Spectrum and Storm

1. Disconnect the negative battery terminal from the battery.
2. Loosen the adjusting nut and pull the cable to the rear until it turns freely.
3. Adjust the cable length by turning the adjusting nut.
4. When the clutch pedal free-play travel reaches 0.39-0.79 in. (10-20mm) on the Spectrum or 0.20-0.59 in. (5-15mm) on the Storm release the cable.
5. When the adjustment has been completed, tighten the locknut.

Clutch Cable

REMOVAL AND INSTALLATION

Metro

1. Disconnect the negative battery cable.
2. Remove the clutch cable joint nut and disconnect the cable from the release arm.
3. Remove the clutch cable bracket mounting nuts and remove the bracket from the cable.
4. Remove the cable retaining bolts at the clutch pedal.
5. Remove the cable from the vehicle.
To install:
6. Before installation, apply grease to the hook and pin end of the cable.
7. Connect the cable to the clutch pedal and install the retaining bolts.
8. Install the clutch cable bracket on the cable.
9. Position the bracket on the transaxle and install the mounting bolts.
10. Connect the cable to the release lever and install the joint nut on the cable.
11. Adjust the pedal free-play. Connect the negative battery cable.

Spectrum and Storm

1. Disconnect the negative battery terminal.
2. Loosen the clutch cable adjusting nuts. Disconnect the cable from the release arm and cable bracket.
3. At the clutch pedal, remove the cable retaining bolt.
4. Disconnect the cable from the front of the dash.
5. Remove the clutch cable from the vehicle.
6. To install, grease the clutch cable pin and reverse the removal procedures.
7. Adjust the pedal free-play.

Clutch Master Cylinder

REMOVAL AND INSTALLATION

Prizm

1. Drain or siphon the fluid from the master cylinder.
2. Disconnect the hydraulic line to the clutch from the master cylinder.

NOTE: Do not spill brake fluid on the painted surfaced of the vehicle.

3. Inside the vehicle, remove the underdash panel and the air duct.
4. Remove the pedal return spring.
5. Remove the spring clip and clevis pin.
6. Unfasten the bolts which secure the master cylinder to the firewall. Withdraw the assembly from the firewall side.
To install:
7. Install the master cylinder with its retaining nuts to the firewall.
8. Connect the line from the clutch to the master cylinder.
9. Connect the clevis and install the clevis pin and spring clip.
10. Install the pedal return spring.
11. Fill the reservoir with clean, fresh brake fluid and bleed the system.
12. Check the cylinder and the hose connection for leaks.
13. Adjust the clutch pedal.
14. Reinstall the air duct and underdash cover panel.

Clutch Slave Cylinder

REMOVAL AND INSTALLATION

Prizm

NOTE: Do not spill brake fluid on the painted surface of the vehicle.

1. Raise the front of the vehicle and support it safely.
2. If necessary, remove the rear splash shield to gain access to the release cylinder.
3. Remove the clutch fork return spring.
4. Unfasten the hydraulic line from the release cylinder by removing its retaining nut.
5. Remove the release cylinder retaining nuts and remove the cylinder.
To install:
6. Reinstall the cylinder to the clutch housing and tighten the bolts to 9 ft. lbs. (12 Nm).
7. Connect the hydraulic line and tighten it to 11 ft. lbs. (15 Nm).
8. Install the clutch release spring.
9. Bleed the system and remember to top up the fluid in the master cylinder when finished.
10. Install the splash shield if it was removed.
11. Lower the vehicle to the ground.

Hydraulic Clutch System Bleeding

Prizm

1. Fill the clutch master cylinder reservoir with brake fluid.

NOTE: Do not spill brake fluid on the painted surface of the vehicle.

2. Fit a vinyl bleeder tube over the bleeder screw at the front of the slave cylinder and place the other end in a clean jar half filled with brake fluid.

3. Have an assistant depress the clutch pedal several times. Loosen the bleeder screw and allow the fluid to flow into the jar.

4. Tighten the screw and have the assistant release the clutch pedal.

5. Repeat bleeding procedure until no air bubbles are present in the fluid.

6. Refill the master cylinder to the specified level, check the system for leaks, then, adjust the clutch pedal height and free-play.

AUTOMATIC TRANSAXLE

Transaxle Assembly

REMOVAL AND INSTALLATION

Metro

1. Disconnect the air suction guide from the air cleaner.

2. Disconnect the negative and the positive battery cables.

3. Remove the battery and the battery bracket tray.

4. Remove the negative cable from the transaxle.

5. Disconnect the solenoid wire coupler and the shift lever switch wire couplers.

6. Remove the wiring harness from the transaxle.

7. Remove the speedometer cable from the transaxle.

8. Disconnect the oil pressure control cable from the accelerator cable and the accelerator cable from the transaxle.

9. Remove the select cable from the transaxle.

10. Remove the starter motor.

11. Drain the transaxle fluid.

12. Disconnect the oil outlet and inlet hoses from the oil pipes. After disconnecting, plug the 2 oil hoses to prevent fluid in the hoses and oil cooler from draining.

13. Raise the vehicle and support it safely.

14. Remove the exhaust No. 1 pipe.

15. Remove the clutch housing lower plate.

16. Remove the 6 driveplate bolts. To lock the driveplate, engage a prybar with the driveplate gear through the notch provided at the under side of the transaxle case.

17. Remove the left hand front halfshaft.

18. Detach the inboard joint of the right hand halfshaft from the differential.

19. Disconnect the transaxle mounting member.

20. Securely support the transaxle with a suitable jack for removal.

21. Remove the transaxle left mounting.

22. Remove the bolts fastening the engine and the transaxle.

23. Disconnect the transaxle from the engine by sliding towards the left side and carefully lower the jack.

NOTE: When removing the transaxle assembly from the engine, move it in parallel with the crankshaft and use care so as not to apply excessive force to the driveplate and torque converter. After removing the transaxle assembly, be sure to keep it so the oil pan is at the bottom. If the transaxle is tilted, fluid in it may flow out.

To install:

24. Reverse the removal procedure noting the following important steps.

25. Before installing the transaxle assembly apply grease around the cup at the center of the torque converter. Then measure the distance between the torque converter flange nut and the transaxle case housing. The distance should be more than 0.85 in. (21.4mm). If the distance is less than 0.85 in. (21.4mm), the torque converter has been installed incorrectly and must be removed and reinstalled correctly.

26. When installing the transaxle, guide the right halfshaft into the differential side gear as the transaxle is being raised.

27. After inserting the inboard joints of the right hand and left hand halfshafts into the differential side gears, push the inboard joints into the side gears until the snaprings on the halfshafts engage the side gears.

28. After connecting the oil pressure control cable to the accelerator cable, check the oil pressure control cable play and adjust if necessary.

29. Install the select cable.

30. Refill the transaxle and check the fluid level.

31. Tighten the following bolts and nuts to specifications.

    a. Driveplate bolts — 14 ft. lbs. (19 Nm).

    b. Mounting member bolts — 40 ft. lbs. (55 Nm).

    c. Transaxle mounting nuts — 33 ft. lbs. (45 Nm).

    d. Transaxle mounting bolts (8mm) — 40 ft. lbs. (55 Nm).

    e. Transaxle mounting nuts (8mm) — 40 ft. lbs. (55 Nm).

    f. Stabilizer shaft mounting bolts — 31 ft. lbs. (42 Nm).

    g. Ball stud bolt — 44 ft. lbs. (60 Nm).

    h. Wheel nuts — 40 ft. lbs. (55 Nm).

Prizm

1. Support the engine with GM tool J-28467-A or equivalent.

2. Remove the battery hold-down, battery and tray.

3. Remove the air cleaner assembly

4. Disconnect the connector at the neutral start switch.

5. Disconnect the ground strap from the transaxle case.

6. Remove the throttle cable from the throttle body.

7. Disconnect the cooling lines at the transaxle and plug the lines to prevent leakage.

8. Remove the shift cable retainer and end clip.

9. Remove the shift cable from its brackets and place the cable out of the way.

10. Remove the upper shift cable bracket from the transaxle housing.

11. Remove the left transaxle mount brace.

12. Remove the through bolt in the mount.

13. Remove the 2 upper transaxle-to-engine bolts.

14. Remove the upper starter bolts.

15. Disconnect the speedometer cable.

16. Raise the vehicle and safely support it.

17. Remove the splash shields from below the vehicle.

18. Drain the transaxle oil.

19. Disconnect the electrical connections to the starter. Remove the bottom starter bolt and remove the starter.

20. Remove the halfshafts from the transaxle.

21. Remove the 3 bolts holding the center crossmember to the radiator support.

22. Remove the covers from the front and center mount bolts; remove the 2 front mount bolts, then the 2 center mount bolts.

23. Remove the 2 nuts from the rear mount.

24. Remove the 2 bolts holding the center crossmember to the main crossmember.

25. Remove the 3 nuts holding the exhaust hanger bracket and remove the bracket.

26. Use a floor jack to support the main crossmember. Check its placement carefully so the crossmember will be balanced during removal.

27. Remove the 8 bolts holding the main crossmember to the underbody.

28. On the left and right sides, remove the 2 bolts holding the control arm bracket to the underbody.

--- CAUTION ---

Lower the main crossmember slowly while holding onto the center crossmember. The center crossmember is free to fall at this point and could cause serious injury or damage.

29. At the front mount, remove the through bolt and the mount.

30. Remove the front mount bracket from the transaxle.

31. Remove the center mount from the transaxle with its 2 bolts.

32. Remove the torque converter bolt shield and remove the bolts holding the torque converter to the flywheel.

33. Remove the 2 bolts holding the lower transaxle mount to the bracket.

34. Lower the vehicle to the ground.

35. Remove the remaining transaxle mount-to-bracket bolt.

36. Adjust the engine support apparatus to lower the transaxle and gain clearance for removal.

37. Disconnect the transaxle mount.

38. Raise and safely support the vehicle.

39. Use a floor jack to support the transaxle. Make sure it is properly positioned.

40. Remove the front and rear lower bolts holding the transaxle to the engine.

41. Carefully remove the transaxle, keeping it as level as possible. Remove the torque converter.

To install:

42. Before installing the transaxle, make sure the torque converter is all the way into the pump and bushing. Use a straightedge across the front of the transaxle case and measure the inset to the converter. Clearance must be at least 0.79 in. (20mm).

43. Lightly coat the converter to flywheel contact point with multi-purpose grease.

44. Support the transaxle on the floor jack and move it into place. Install the transaxle and hold it in place with the front and rear lower transaxle-to-engine bolts. Tighten the bolts snugly; they will be final tightened later.

45. Remove the jack from under the transaxle.

46. Install the starter and its lower bolt snugly. Connect the starter wiring.

47. Lower the vehicle to the ground.

NOTE: The engine support apparatus has been repositioned and the crossmembers are removed. Be very careful when moving the vehicle.

48. Install the left transaxle mount.

49. Install the bolt for the upper mount bracket and the 2 bolts for the lower bracket snugly.

50. Adjust the engine support apparatus to raise the transaxle into position.

51. Install the through bolt for the transaxle mount and tighten it to 64 ft. lbs. (87 Nm). Tighten the upper transaxle mounting bracket bolt to 45 ft. lbs. (61 Nm).

52. Install the brace at the mount and tighten the bolts to 13 ft. lbs. (18 Nm).

53. Install the 2 upper transaxle-to-engine bolts snugly.

54. Install the upper starter bolt snugly.

55. Tighten all the transaxle-to-engine bolts to 34 ft. lbs. (46 Nm).

56. Tighten the upper starter bolt to 29 ft. lbs. (40 Nm).

57. Install the speedometer cable.

58. Install the upper shift cable bracket, position the shift cable into the bracket and install the cable retainer and end-clips.

59. Install the oil cooling lines.

60. Connect the throttle cable at the throttle body.

61. Install the ground strap to the transaxle case.

62. Install the connector to the neutral start switch.

63. Install the air cleaner assembly.

64. Raise and safely support the vehicle.

65. Tighten the 2 lower transaxle mount bolts to 45 ft. lbs. (61 Nm).

66. Tighten the lower starter bolt to 29 ft. lbs. (40 Nm).

67. Install the torque converter-to-flywheel bolts and tighten them to 31 ft. lbs. (42 Nm).

68. Install the converter bolt shield.

69. Install the center mount with 2 bolts to the transaxle; tighten the bolts to 45 ft. lbs. (61 Nm).

70. Install the front mount bracket on the transaxle and tighten the bolts to 13 ft. lbs. (18 Nm).

71. Install the front mount. Loosely install the through bolt.

NOTE: As the front mount is installed, the weight on the mount must go towards the transaxle; this allows the mount to align properly.

72. Position the center crossmember over the center and rear transaxle mount studs. Start 2 nuts on the center mount.

73. Loosely install the 3 bolts which hold the center crossmember to the radiator support.

74. Loosely install the 2 front mount bolts.

75. Raise the main crossmember into position over the rear mounting studs.

76. Align all the underbody bolts and bolt holes.

77. Install the 2 rear mount nuts loosely.

78. Loosely install the 8 bolts to hold the main crossmember to the underbody.

79. On each side, loosely install the 2 bolts holding the control arm brackets to the underbody.

80. Loosely install the 2 bolts holding the center crossmember to the main crossmember.

81. Install the exhaust hanger bracket and its 3 nuts. The crossmembers, mounts, through bolts and brackets should now all be in place and held loosely by their nuts and bolts. If any repositioning is necessary, do so now.

82. Tighten the components below in the order listed to the correct torque specification:

   a. Main crossmember-to-underbody bolts: 152 ft. lbs. (206 Nm).

   b. Lower control arm bolts: 94 ft. lbs. (127 Nm).

   c. Center crossmember-to-radiator support bolts: 45 ft. lbs. (61 Nm).

   d. Front, center and rear mount bolts: 45 ft. lbs. (61 Nm).

   e. Exhaust hanger bracket nuts: 9.5 ft. lbs. (13 Nm).

   f. Front mount through bolt: 64 ft. lbs. (87 Nm).

83. Install the covers on the front and center mount bolts.

84. Reinstall the drive axles.

85. Fill the transaxle with the correct amount of Dexron® II ATF. If the transaxle has been disassembled and drained, install 5.8 US qts. If the transaxle was not disassembled and still contains fluid, add 2.4 US qts.

86. Double check all installation items, paying particular attention to loose hoses or hanging wires, loosened nuts, poor routing of hoses and wires (too tight or rubbing) and tools left in the engine area.

87. Install the splash shields below the engine. Install the left front wheel and lower the vehicle to the ground.

88. Remove the engine support apparatus.

89. Install the battery tray, battery and hold-down.

90. Start the engine and allow it to idle. With the wheels blocked front and rear and the brake depressed, engage each gear and check that the transaxle engages properly. Check that the vehicle will not roll in **P**.

91. Allow the engine to idle with the transaxle in **P**; check the fluid level on the dipstick. Check all assembly points for any sign of leakage.

Storm

1. Disconnect the battery cables, then remove the battery and tray from the vehicle.

2. Remove the intake air duct and breather tube from the air cleaner assembly.

3. Disconnect the electrical connectors, shift cable, shift cable bracket, breather hose and speedometer cable from the transaxle.

4. Disconnect the vacuum diaphragm hose from the vacuum diaphragm, if equipped.

5. Install engine support tool J-28467-A or equivalent, then remove the left transaxle through bolt.

6. Remove 4 transaxle-to-engine attaching bolts, then raise and support the vehicle safely.

7. Remove the right and left undercovers, then the front wheel and tire assemblies.

8. Disconnect the left control arm from the steering knuckle, then drain the transaxle fluid.

9. Remove the halfshafts and suspend on a wire.

10. Remove the front transaxle mount through bolt, then the dampener from the rear mount through bolt.

11. Remove the rear transaxle mount through bolt, then the 2 front center crossmember mounting bolts.

12. Remove the front exhaust pipe-to-exhaust manifold attaching nuts,

then 2 rear front pipe bolts. Disconnect the front pipe from the exhaust manifold.

13. Remove the 2 rear center crossmember mounting bolts, then the crossmember from the vehicle. Lower the vehicle.

14. Lower the engine using engine support tool J-28467 or equivalent.

15. Raise and safely support the vehicle, then position a suitable jack under the transaxle.

16. Remove the rear mount to transaxle case bolt, then the front mount attaching bolt.

17. Remove the front mounting bracket attaching bolts, then the front mounting bracket from the engine.

18. Remove the flywheel cover, then the flywheel-to-torque converter attaching bolts.

19. Disconnect the oil cooler lines from the transaxle, then remove the 2 rear transaxle mount bolts. Lower the transaxle from the vehicle.

To install:

20. Raise the transaxle into position, then install the 2 rear transaxle mounting bolts. Remove transaxle jack.

21. Lower the vehicle, then install the 4 transaxle-to-engine mounting bolts.

22. Using engine support tool J-28467-A or equivalent, raise the engine slightly.

23. Install the through bolt on the left transaxle mount. Torque through bolt to 64 ft. lbs. (87 Nm).

24. Raise and safely support the vehicle, then install the flywheel-to-torque converter attaching bolts. Torque converter bolts to 31 ft. lbs. (42 Nm).

25. Install the flywheel cover, then connect the oil cooler lines to the transaxle. Torque oil cooler line trunnion bolts to 10 ft. lbs. (15 Nm).

26. Install the front transaxle mount nut and bolt. Torque bolt to 45 ft. lbs. (61 Nm).

27. Install the rear mount through bolt. Torque rear transaxle mount attaching bolts to 29 ft. lbs. (39 Nm) and the rear mount through bolt to 64 ft. lbs. (87 Nm).

28. Install the center crossmember. Torque crossmember bolts to 45 ft. lbs. (61 Nm).

29. Install the front mount through bolt. Torque bolt to 64 ft. lbs. (87 Nm).

30. Install the dampener on the rear mount through bolt.

31. Install the front pipe to the exhaust manifold, the 2 rear front pipe attaching bolts.

32. Install the halfshafts.

33. Install the left control arm onto the steering knuckle, then the right and left undercovers.

34. Install the tire and wheel assemblies, then lower the vehicle. Torque the engine-to-transaxle attaching bolts to 31 ft. lbs. (42 Nm).

35. Remove the engine support tool, then install the speedometer to the transaxle.

36. Install the breather hose, shaft cable bracket and shift cable to the transaxle.

37. Install the vacuum hose to the vacuum diaphragm, if equipped.

38. Connect the electrical connectors to the transaxle.

39. Install the air breather tube and the air intake duct onto the air cleaner assembly.

40. Install the battery and battery tray. Connect the battery cables and check transaxle fluid. Start engine and check for leaks.

Spectrum

1. Disconnect the negative battery terminal from the battery.

2. Remove the air duct tube from the air cleaner.

3. From the transaxle, disconnect the shift cable, speedometer cable, vacuum diaphragm hose, engine wiring harness clamp and the ground cable.

4. At the left fender, disconnect the inhibitor switch and the kickdown solenoid wiring connectors.

5. Disconnect the oil cooler lines from the transaxle.

6. Remove the 3 upper transaxle-to-engine mounting bolts. Raise and support the vehicle safely.

7. Remove both front wheels and the left front fender splash shield.

8. Disconnect both tie rod ends at the steering knuckles.

9. Remove both front tension rod brackets and disconnect the rods from the control arms.

10. Disengage the halfshafts from the transaxle.

11. Remove the flywheel dust cover and the converter-to-flywheel attaching bolts.

12. Remove the transaxle rear mount through bolt.

13. Disconnect the starter wiring and the starter. Support the transaxle.

14. Remove the lower transaxle-to-engine mounting bolts and remove the transaxle.

To install:

15. Install transaxle onto engine and converter to the flywheel. Torque the converter-to-flywheel at 30 ft. lbs.

(41 Nm), the transaxle-to-engine at 56 ft. lbs. (76 Nm).

16. Install the flywheel dust cover.

17. Install both halfshafts into the transaxle.

18. Install the tension rod brackets and both tie rod ends to the steering knuckle.

19. Install the splash shield to the left front fender and the tire and wheel assemblies.

20. Connect the transaxle cooler lines.

21. Connect all electrical connectors and hoses that were disconnected during the removal.

22. Connect the speedometer cable and shift cable to the transaxle.

23. Connect the battery negative cable, adjust the shift linkage and fill the transaxle with Dexron® II automatic transaxle fluid. Start engine and check for leaks.

SHIFT LINKAGE ADJUSTMENT

Metro

1. Place the shift lever in the **N** position.

2. Turn the adjusting nut in until it contacts the manual select cable joint.

3. Tighten the locknut.

4. To adjust the interlock cable (back drive cable), use the following procedure.

   a. Shift the selector to the **P** position.

   b. Loosen the adjusting and locknut on the interlock cable.

   c. Pull the outer wire (interlock cable) forward so there is no deflection on the inner wire, tighten the adjusting nut hand-tight only and then tighten the locknut.

NOTE: After tightening the nuts, make sure with the shifter lever shifted to the P position, the ignition key can be turned from the ACC to the LOCK position and the key can be removed from the ignition switch. With the selector lever shifted to any range other than the P position, the ignition key cannot be turned from the ACC to LOCK position.

5. On the Metro, adjust the shift lock solenoid so it will operate as follows:

   a. When the ignition switch is turned **OFF**, the solenoid is not operated.

   b. When the ignition switch is turned **ON** and the brake pedal is depressed, the solenoid is operated and the lockplate is positioned properly.

   c. There is no clearance between the lockplate and the guide plate.

   d. If the manual release knob is pulled when the ignition switch is turned **OFF**, the selector lever can be shifted from the **P** range to any other range.

NOTE: After tightening the solenoid retaining nuts, make sure with the shifter lever shifted to the P position, the ignition key can be turned from the ACC to the LOCK position and the key can be removed from the ignition switch.

Prizm

1. Loosen the swivel nut on the lever.

2. Push the manual lever fully towards the right side of the vehicle.

3. Return the lever 2 notches to the **N** position.

4. Set the shift lever in the **N** position.

5. While holding the lever lightly towards the **R** position, tighten the swivel nut.

6. On the 1991-92 Prizm, use the following procedure;

   a. Loosen the cap nut on the manual lever.

   b. Position the manual lever in the **N** position.

   c. Position the shift selector lever in the **N** position.

   d. Tighten the cap nut to 89 inch lbs. (10 Nm).

Spectrum

1. Loosen the 2 adjusting nuts at the control rod link and connect the shift cable to the link on the transaxle.

2. Shift the transaxle into the **N** detent.

3. Place the shifter lever into the **N** position.

4. Rotate the link assembly clockwise to remove slack in the cable.

5. Tighten the rear adjusting nut until it makes contact with the link. Tighten the front adjusting nut until it makes contact with the link and tighten the adjusting nuts.

Storm

1. Place the ignition switch in the **LOCK** position.

2. Set the selector lever in the **P** position.

3. Loosen the adjuster nuts at the transaxle.

4. Be sure the shift lever at the transaxle is in the **P** position.

5. Pull the cable forward and tighten the forward adjuster nut until it contacts the shift lever.

6. Tighten the rear nut until it comes in contact with the shift lever.

7. Tighten both adjuster nuts.

8. To adjust the brake drive cable, use the following procedure:

   a. Place the shift lever to the **P** position.

   b. Place the ignition switch to the **LOCK** position.

   c. Pull the cable forward at the shift lever bracket and tighten the forward adjuster nut until it makes contact with the bracket.

   d. Tighten the rear nut until it makes contact with the shift lever bracket and then tighten both the adjuster nuts.

THROTTLE LINKAGE ADJUSTMENT

Prizm

1. With the ignition **OFF**, depress the accelerator pedal all the way.

2. Peel the rubber dust boot back from the throttle valve cable.

3. Loosen the adjustment nuts on the throttle cable bracket (rocker cover) just enough to allow cable housing movement.

4. Have an assistant depress the accelerator pedal fully.

5. Adjust the cable housing so the distance between its end and the cable stop collar is 0-0.4 in. (0-1.0mm).

6. Tighten the adjustment nuts. Make sure the adjustment hasn't changed. Install the dust boot.

Storm

1. Position the ignition switch/key in the **LOCK** position.

2. Place the selector lever in the **P** position.

3. Loosen the adjuster nuts on the transaxle. Ensure that the shift lever on the transaxle is in the **P** position.

4. Pull the cable forward, then tighten the forward adjuster nut until it contacts the shift lever. Tighten the rear nut until it contacts the shift lever.

5. Tighten both adjuster nuts.

FRONT SUSPENSION

MacPherson Strut

REMOVAL AND INSTALLATION

Metro

1. Raise and support the vehicle safely.
2. Remove the tire and wheel assembly.
3. Remove the brake hose clip, then the hose from the strut.
4. Remove the upper strut support nuts from the engine compartment.
5. Remove the strut-to-steering knuckle bolts, then the strut assembly from the vehicle.
6. Reverse procedure to install. Torque upper mounting nuts to 20 ft. lbs. (27 Nm) and the strut-to-steering knuckle bolts to 59 ft. lbs. (80 Nm).

Prizm

1. Under the hood, remove the 3 or 4 small nuts holding the top of the strut to the shock tower. Do not loosen the larger center nut.
2. Loosen the wheel lug nuts at the appropriate wheel.
3. Raise the vehicle and safely support it. It need not be any higher than the distance necessary to separate the tire from the ground. Do not place the jackstands under the control arms.
4. Remove the wheel. Install a cover over the halfshaft boot to protect it from fluid and impact damage.
5. Disconnect the brake hose from the brake caliper and drain the fluid into a small pan. Remove the clip from the brake hose and remove the hose from the bracket.
6. Use a sharp instrument or scribing tool to make matchmarks in all 3 dimensions on the steering knuckle. The strut must be reinstalled in its exact previous position.
7. Remove the 2 bolts which attach the shock absorber to the steering knuckle. The steering knuckle bolt holes have collars that extend about 0.20 in. (5.0mm). Be careful to clear them when separating the steering knuckle from the strut assembly.

NOTE: Press down on the lower suspension arm in order to remove the strut assembly. This must be done to clear the collars on the steering knuckle bolt holes when removing the strut assembly.

8. Remove the strut assembly. Remember that the spring is still under tension. It will stay in place as long as the top nut on the shock piston shaft is not loosened. Handle the strut carefully and do not allow the coating on the spring to become damaged.

To install:

9. Loosely assemble all components onto the strut assembly. Make sure the mark on the upper spring seat is facing the outside of the vehicle.

NOTE: Never reuse a self-locking nut. Always replace self-locking nuts with new hardware.

10. Compress the spring, carefully aligning the shaft guide rod with the hole in the upper mount. Align the lower spring seat. Do not over-compress the spring; compress it just enough to allow installation of the shaft nut.
11. Install the shaft nut and tighten it until the strut shaft begins to rotate.
12. Double check that the spring is correctly seated in the upper and lower mounts and reposition it as needed. Slowly release the tension on the spring compressor and remove it from the strut assembly.
13. Tighten the shaft nut to 34 ft. lbs. (46 Nm).
14. Place the strut assembly in position and install the strut to knuckle attaching bolts. Tighten the bolts to 194 ft. lbs. (263 Nm).
15. Using a floor jack and a piece of wood, gently elevate the control arm to the point that the upper mount can be aligned with the holes in the shock tower. Insert the bolts into the upper holes and install the nuts and torque to 29 ft. lbs. (39 Nm).
16. Pack the shaft nut area with grease and install the dust cover.
17. Install the brake hose in the bracket and install the clip. Connect the hose to the caliper and tighten the fitting to 22 ft. lbs. (30 Nm).
18. Install the wheel and install the lug nuts snugly.
19. Lower the vehicle to the ground. Tighten the wheel lug nuts to 76 ft. lbs. (103 Nm).
20. Bleed the brake system and top up the brake fluid level.

Spectrum and Storm

1. From in the engine compartment, remove the nuts attaching the strut to the body.
2. Loosen the wheel nuts. Raise and support the vehicle safely. Lower the vehicle slightly so the weight of the vehicle rests on the support and not the control arms.
3. Remove the wheel and tire assembly.
4. Remove the brake hose clip at the strut bracket.
5. Disconnect the brake hose at the brake caliper. Cap all openings.
6. Pull the brake hose through the opening in the strut bracket.
7. Remove the nuts attaching the strut to the steering knuckle, then the strut assembly from the vehicle.
8. Reverse procedure to install.
9. On the Spectrum, torque the strut-to-body nuts to 80 ft. lbs. (108 Nm) and the upper strut retaining nuts to 41 ft. lbs. (55 Nm).
10. On the Storm, torque the upper strut retaining nuts to 58 ft. lbs. (78 Nm). Torque the steering knuckle to strut assembly nuts to 116 ft. lbs. (157 Nm).

Tension Rods

REMOVAL AND INSTALLATION

Spectrum

1. Raise and support the vehicle safely.
2. If equipped with a stabilizer bar, remove the nuts, bolts and insulators attaching it to the tension rod.
3. Remove the nut and washer attaching the tension rod to the body.
4. Remove the nuts and bolts attaching the tension rod to the control arm, then the tension rod from the vehicle.
5. Reverse procedure to install. Torque tension rod-to-body nuts to 72 ft. lbs. (98 Nm) and the tension rod-to-control arm nuts to 80 ft. lbs. (108 Nm).

Lower Ball Joints

INSPECTION

Metro

The lower joint is part of the lower control arm. Therefore, if ball joint replacement is necessary, it must be replace as an assembly.

Prizm

1. Turn the front wheels so they are in a straight-ahead position, then chock the rear wheels.

2. Raise and support the front of the vehicle, then place a wooden block approximately 7-8 inches under it. Lower the vehicle onto the block until the spring is compressed to only about half its compression when the vehicle is resting on it.

3. Attempt to move the lower arm up and down. There should be no noticeable play.

4. If the ball joint is removed from the vehicle, check the required rotating torque with an inch lb. torque wrench. Flip the ball joint back and forth several times. Install the nut and turn the stud with a torque wrench at a rate of about 1 turn in 3 seconds. At the fifth turn, measure the required torque; it should be 9-30 inch lbs. (1.0-3.4 Nm). If specifications are not as indicated, replace the ball joint.

Spectrum and Storm

Raise the front of the vehicle and safely support it on stands. Do not place stands under the control arms; the arms must hang free. Grasp the tire at the top and bottom and move the top of the tire through an in-and-out motion. Look for any horizontal motion in the steering knuckle relative to the control arm. Such motion is an indication of looseness within the ball joint. If the joint is checked while disconnected from the knuckle, it should have minimal or no free-play and should not twist in its socket under finger pressure. Replace any joint showing looseness or free-play.

REMOVAL AND INSTALLATION

Prizm

1. Elevate and safely support the front of the vehicle. Do not place the support under the control arms; they must hang free.

NOTE: Do not allow the driveshaft joints to over-extend. The CV-joints can become disconnected under extreme extension.

2. Install a protective cover over the CV-boot.

3. Remove the wheel.

4. Remove the cotter pin from the ball joint nut.

5. Loosen the castle nut but do not remove it. Unscrew it just to the top of the threads and install the ball joint separator GM tool 34754 or equivalent. Use the nut to bear on the tool; this protects the threaded shaft from damage during removal.

6. Use the separator to loosen the ball joint from the steering knuckle.

7. Remove the nuts and bolt holding the ball joint to the control arm.

8. Remove the ball joint from the control arm and steering knuckle.

To install:

9. When reinstalling, attach the ball joint to the control arm and tighten the 2 bolts to 105 ft. lbs. (142 Nm).

10. Carefully install the ball joint to the steering knuckle. Use a new castle nut and tighten it to 94 ft. lbs. (127 Nm).

11. Install the cotter pin through the castle nut and stud.

12. Remove the protector from the CV-boot.

13. Install the wheel.

14. Lower the vehicle to the ground.

Spectrum and Storm

1. Loosen the wheel nuts.

2. Loosen the wheel nuts. Raise and support the vehicle safely. Lower the vehicle slightly so the weight of the vehicle rests on the supports and not the control arms.

3. Remove the tire and wheel assembly.

NOTE: Care must be exercised to prevent the CV-joints from being over extended. When either end of the halfshaft is disconnected, over extension of the joint will result in separation of the internal components and possible joint failure. Drive axle joint seal protectors should be used any time service is performed on or near the drive axles. Failure to observe this could result in interior joint or seal damage and possible joint failure.

4. Install a inner drive joint seal protector J-34754 or equivalent, to the drive axle boot.

5. Remove the 2 nuts attaching the ball joint to the tension rod and the control arm assembly.

6. Remove the pinch bolt attaching the ball joint to the steering knuckle, then the ball joint from the vehicle.

7. Installation is the reverse order of the removal procedure. On Spectrum, torque the knuckle-to-ball joint nut to 51 ft. lbs. (69 Nm) and the tension rod-to-control arm nuts to 72 ft. lbs. (98 Nm). On Storm, torque the ball joint-to-control arm bolts to 115 ft. lbs. (156 Nm) and the pinch bolt to 49 ft. lbs. (66 Nm).

Lower Control Arms

REMOVAL AND INSTALLATION

Metro

1. Raise and support the vehicle safely.

2. Remove the wheel assemblies.

3. Remove the ball stud bolts.

4. Remove the suspension arm bracket nut.

5. Remove the suspension arm bracket bolts.

6. Remove the rear bracket and suspension arm.

7. Installation is the reverse order of the removal procedure. Torque the ball stud nut to 44 ft. lbs. (60 Nm). Torque the suspension arm rear bracket bolts to 32 ft. lbs. (43 Nm).

Prizm

NOTE: Both lower control arms and the suspension crossmember must be removed as a unit even if only 1 arm is damaged.

1. Raise and safely support the vehicle. Do not place the stands under the control arms or the suspension crossmember.

2. Remove the nuts and bolts holding the ball joints to the lower control arms.

3. Remove the nut and bolt holding the control arm rear brackets to the crossmember.

4. Place a floor jack under the suspension crossmember. Use a broad piece of wood between the jack and crossmember to evenly distribute the loading.

5. Remove the 6 bolts and 2 nuts holding the suspension crossmember. Carefully lower the crossmember (with the control arms attached) and remove from the vehicle.

6. Remove the mounting bolt holding the control arm to the crossmember and remove the arm. Inspect the arm and bushing for damage, deformation or corrosion damage.

To install:

7. Install the control arm(s) to the crossmember and partially tighten the bolts. They should be tight enough to hold firmly, yet still be able to pivot when moderate force is applied.

8. Install the suspension crossmember and control arms to the body of the vehicle and tighten the 8 nuts.

9. Install the bolts holding the rear control arm brackets and partially tighten them.

10. Connect the ball joints to each arm and tighten the bolts to 105 ft. lbs. (142 Nm).

11. Lower the vehicle to the ground. Bounce the front end up and down several times to stabilize the suspension. The partially tightened joints will flex and seek a normal position.

12. With the vehicle on the ground (don't raise it or the suspension position will be lost), tighten the bolt holding the arm to the crossmember to 152 ft. lbs. (206 Nm). Tighten the nut and bolt holding the rear bracket to the crossmember to 14 ft. lbs. (19 Nm) and the rear bracket bolts to 94 ft. lbs. (127 Nm). On the 1991-92 Prizm, torque the lower control arm nut to 152 ft. lbs. (206 Nm).

13. Check the alignment.

Storm

1. Raise and support the vehicle safely.

2. Remove the tire and wheel assembly.

3. Remove the stabilizer bar from the control arm.

4. Remove the ball stud from the steering knuckle.

5. Remove the front bushing-to-body attaching bolt, then the rear bushing-to-crossmember attaching bolts.

6. Remove the control arm from the vehicle.

7. Reverse procedure to install. Torque the rear bushing-to-crossmember bolt to 51 ft. lbs. (69 Nm); front bushing-to-body attaching bolt to 95 ft. lbs. (129 Nm) and the ball stud-to-knuckle pinch bolt to 46 ft. lbs. (62.5 Nm).

Spectrum

1. Raise and safely support the vehicle.

2. Remove the tire and wheel assembly.

3. Remove the control arm-to-tension arm attaching nuts and bolts.

4. Remove the nut and bolt attaching the control arm to the body, then the control arm from the vehicle.

5. Reverse procedure to install.

NOTE: Raise the control arm to a distance of 15 inches from the top of the wheelwell to the center of the hub. Retorque the control arm-to-body bolts to 41 ft. lbs. (55 Nm) and the control arm-to-tension rod bolts to 80 ft. lbs. (108 Nm). This procedure aligns the bushing arm to the body.

Stabilizer Bar

REMOVAL AND INSTALLATION

Prizm

GSi MODELS

1. Raise and safely support the vehicle.

2. Remove the left stabilizer link from the stabilizer bar.

3. Remove the right stabilizer link from the stabilizer bar.

4. Remove the catalytic converter from the front exhaust pipe.

5. Remove the right stabilizer bracket from the floor pan.

6. Remove the left stabilizer bracket from the floor pan.

7. Remove the stabilizer bar from the vehicle. Remove the bushing brackets and retainers from the stabilizer bar.

To install:

8. Use the following torque specifications:

 a. Torque the bushing bracket retaining bolts to 29 ft. lbs. (39 Nm).

 b. Torque the left and right stabilizer link nuts to 26 ft. lbs. (35 Nm).

 c. Torque the left and right stabilizer bracket bolts to 94 ft. lbs. (127 Nm).

 d. Torque the left and right stabilizer bracket nut and bolt to 14 ft. lbs. (19 Nm).

9. To remove the stabilizer link, use the following procedure.

 a. With the vehicle still raise and safely supported, remove the stabilizer link from the stabilizer bar.

 b. Remove the stabilizer link from the control arm.

 c. Remove the stabilizer link from the vehicle.

10. Torque the stabilizer link nuts to 26 ft. lbs. (35 Nm).

Storm

1. Install engine support tool J-28467-A onto the engine.

2. Raise the vehicle, then position suitable support under the suspension supports. Lower the vehicle onto the support, not the control arms.

3. Remove the tire and wheel assemblies.

4. Disconnect the front exhaust pipe from the exhaust manifold.

5. Disconnect the power steering lines from the rack and pinion gear.

6. From inside the vehicle, remove the boot from the steering shaft, then the steering shaft.

7. Remove the ball joints and tie rods from the steering knuckles.

8. Remove the engine torque rod from the center beam.

9. Remove the engine rear mount.

10. Remove the 2 bolts from the center beam and the 4 bolts from the crossmember, then the center beam and crossmember assembly with the rack and pinion gear and stabilizer bar.

11. Remove the rack and pinion assembly from the crossmember, then the stabilizer bar from the crossmember.

To install:

12. Install the stabilizer bar and rack and pinion assembly to the crossmember.

13. Install the center beam and crossmember assembly with the rack and pinion gear and stabilizer bar.

14. Install the 2 bolts at the center beam and the 4 bolts at the crossmember.

15. Install the rear engine mount.

16. Install the engine torque rod at the center beam, then the tie rods to the steering knuckle.

17. From inside the vehicle, install the steering shaft and boot.

18. Install the front exhaust pipe, then the tire and wheels.

19. Torque ball joint bolt to 48 ft. lbs. (66 Nm); tie rod-to-knuckle bolt 40 ft. lbs. (54 Nm); rack and pinion-to-crossmember nuts 65 ft. lbs. (73 Nm); stabilizer bar-to-control arm bolts 19 ft. lbs. (26 Nm); stabilizer bar-to-crossmember bolts to 12 ft. lbs. (16 Nm) and the crossmember-to-body bolts to 137 ft. lbs. (186 Nm).

20. Lower the vehicle and remove the engine support tool.

REAR SUSPENSION

Shock Absorbers

REMOVAL AND INSTALLATION

Spectrum

1. Open the trunk and lift off the trim cover for hatchback vehicles only. Remove the upper shock absorber nut and raise and safely support the vehicle.

2. Remove the shock absorber lower attaching bolt.

3. Remove the shock absorber from the vehicle.

4. Reverse procedure to install.

NOTE: When replacing the shock absorber, never reuse the old lower bolt, always use a new one.

Metro

1. Raise and safely support the vehicle. Remove the wheels.
2. Place a support under the suspension arm.
3. Remove the shock (strut) support nuts and push the shock down.
4. Remove the lower shock mount bolt.
5. Remove the shock from the knuckle by pulling the upper side of the knuckle. Compress the shock as short as possible for removal. If the shock is hard to remove, open the slit of the knuckle by inserting a wedge.

NOTE: Do not open the knuckle slit wider than necessary. Do not lower the jack more than necessary during the strut removal to prevent the coil spring from coming off or a brake flexible hose from stretching.

6. Installation is the reverse order of the removal procedure. Torque the shock lower mounting bolt to 44 ft. lbs. (60 Nm). Torque the upper shock to vehicle bolts to 24 ft. lbs. (30 Nm).

MacPherson Strut

REMOVAL AND INSTALLATION

Prizm

1. On Sedans, remove the seatback side cushion. On Hatchbacks, remove the rear sill side panel.
2. Raise and safely support the vehicle, then place a suitable support under the suspension support.
3. Lower the vehicle slightly so the weight rest on the jackstands and not the suspension arms.
4. Remove the tire and wheel assembly.
5. Disconnect the brake line hose and backing plate, then the brake hose from the brake hose bracket.
6. Disconnect the stabilizer bar link from the strut assembly, then the strut assembly mounting nuts and bolts.
7. Remove the strut assembly mounting nuts holding the top of the strut support, then the strut assembly from the vehicle.

8. Reverse procedure to install. Torque the strut to body nuts to 29 ft. lbs. (39 Nm); strut assembly to knuckle mounting bolts to 105 ft. lbs. (142 Nm) and the stabilizer bar link to the strut assembly to 26 ft. lbs. (35 Nm). Bleed the brake system.

Storm

1. Raise and safely support the rear of the vehicle, then place a support under the suspension support. Remove the tire and wheel assembly.
2. Lower the vehicle slightly so the weight rest on the support and not the suspension arms.
3. Remove the flexible bake hose clip at the strut and the brake hose from the brake pipe.
4. Disconnect the stabilizer bar link from the strut assembly, then the strut assembly mounting nuts and bolts.
5. Open the rear hatch, then remove the trim cover panel from the strut tower.
6. Remove the strut assembly mounting nuts holding the top of the strut support, then the strut assembly from the vehicle.
7. Reverse procedure to install. Torque strut tower nuts to 50 ft. lbs. (68 Nm) and the strut to knuckle bolts to 116 ft. lbs. (157 Nm).

Coil Springs

REMOVAL AND INSTALLATION

Spectrum

1. Raise and safely support the vehicle.
2. Remove the tire and wheel assembly.
3. At the center of the rear axle , remove the brake line, retaining clip and flexible hose.
4. Remove the parking brake tension spring, located on the rear axle.
5. Disconnect the parking brake cable from the turnbuckle and the cable joint.
6. Support the axle with a jack, then remove the lower shock absorber bolt and the shock absorber from the vehicle.
7. Reverse procedure to install.

NOTE: Raise the axle assembly to a distance of 15.2 in. (386mm) from the top of the wheel to the center of the axle hub, then torque the fasteners. Always replace the lower shock absorber bolt with a new one.

Metro

1. Raise and support the vehicle safely.

NOTE: To facilitate the toe adjustment after reinstallation, confirm which one of the lines stamped on the washer is in the closest alignment with the stamped line on the control rod. If not marked, add the alignment marks.

2. Remove the control rod inside bolt (body center side).
3. Remove the outside (wheel side) of the control rod from the rear knuckle stud bolt.
4. Loosen the rear mount not on the suspension arm, but do not remove the bolt.
5. Loosen the front nut of the suspension arm.
6. Loosen the lower mount nut of the knuckle, then place a jack under the suspension arm to prevent it from lowering and remove the lower mount nut of the knuckle.
7. Raise the jack placed under the suspension arm enough to allow the removal of the lower mount bolt of the knuckle.
8. Move the brake drum/backing plate toward the outside of the vehicle body so as to separate the lower mount of the knuckle from the suspension arm. Then lower the jack gradually and remove the coil spring.
9. Remove the suspension arm.
   To install:
10. Install the 4 mounting bracket bolts. Torque the mounting bracket bolts to 33 ft. lbs. (45 Nm).
11. Install the rear and front mounting nuts but do not torque them at this time.

NOTE: Make sure the front mounting washer is installed in the proper direction.

12. Place the jack under the suspension arm.
13. Install the coil spring on the spring seat of the suspension arm then raise the suspension arm. When seating the coil spring, mate the spring end with the stepped part of the suspension arm spring.
14. Install the lower knuckle mount bolt. Torque the bolt to 37 ft. lbs. (50 Nm).
15. Remove the jack from under the suspension arm.
16. Install the inside and outside control rod bolts, but do not tighten them at this time.
17. Install the wheel assemblies and lower the vehicle.

18. Install the control rod inside and outside nut and torque them to 59 ft. lbs. (80 Nm).

NOTE: When tightening the nuts, it is most desirable to have the vehicle off the hoist and in a non-loaded state. Also when tightening the inside nut, align the line stamped on the body with the line on the washer as confirmed before removal or align the matchmarks.

19. Install the suspension arm front and rear nuts. Torque the front nuts to 44 ft. lbs. (60 Nm) and the rear nuts to 37 ft. lbs. (50 Nm). After tightening the suspension arm outer nut, make sure the washer is not tilted.

20. Check the rear wheel alignment.

Rear Control Arms

REMOVAL AND INSTALLATION

Metro

1. Raise and support the vehicle safely.

NOTE: To facilitate the toe adjustment after reinstallation, confirm which one of the lines stamped on the washer is in the closest alignment with the stamped line on the control rod. If not marked, add the alignment marks.

2. Remove the brake hose from the control rod buy pulling off the E-ring.

3. Remove the outside (wheel side) of the control rod from the rear knuckle stud bolt.

4. Remove the control rod inside bolt (body center side). Hold the inside bolt with another wrench to prevent it from turning as the nut is turned.

5. Remove the control rod inside bolt and the control rod.

6. Installation is the reverse order of the removal procedure. To determine the installing direction of the control rod, note the angle of the brake flexible hose mounting brackets welded to the control rod. Torque the control rod outside and inside nut to 59 ft. lbs. (80 Nm).

Prizm

1. Raise and safely support the vehicle.

2. Remove the rear suspension arm to body attaching nut, then suspension knuckle bolt.

3. Remove the rear suspension arm to rear knuckle mounting bolts.

4. Remove the rear suspension arm from the vehicle.

To install:

5. When installing the rear suspension arm, align the matchmarks on the camshaft and body. Lower the vehicle and bounce the vehicle up and down to stabilize the suspension. Torque suspension arm mounting bolts to 87 ft. lbs. (118 Nm).

6. Check the rear wheel alignment.

7. To remove the strut rod, use the following procedure.

a. Raise and safely support the vehicle.

b. Remove the strut rod to body mounting bolt and nut.

c. Remove the strut rod to rear suspension knuckle mounting bolt and nut.

d. Remove the strut rod.

8. Installation is the reverse order of the removal procedure. Torque the strut rod-to-rear suspension knuckle bolt to 87 ft. lbs. (118 Nm). Torque the strut rod-to-body bolt and nut to 87 ft. lbs. (118 Nm).

Storm

1. Raise and safely support the vehicle.

2. Remove the tire and wheel assembly.

3. Remove trailing control arm nuts, then the trailing control arm from the vehicle.

4. Remove the right and left lateral control arms as follows:

a. Remove the right lateral control arm attaching bolts from the rear crossmember and the rear suspension knuckle, then the right lateral control arm from the vehicle.

b. Remove the left lateral control arms by loosening the 2 rear crossmember-to-body attaching bolts/nuts, then push crossmember down as far as possible and support with a jack. Remove the bolt from the rear crossmember and rear suspension knuckle, then the left lateral control arms from the vehicle.

5. When removing the stabilizer bar use the following procedure:

a. With the vehicle still in the raised and supported position and the wheel assemblies removed.

b. Remove the bolts on the shackle at both strut sides.

c. Remove the mounting bolts and brackets from stabilizer bar on the crossmember.

d. Remove the stabilizer bar.

6. Torque the link retaining bolts to 19 ft. lbs. (26 Nm) and torque the stabilizer mounting bracket bolts to 71 ft. lbs. (96 Nm).

7. Reverse procedure to install. Torque all nuts and bolts to 94 ft. lbs. (128 Nm).

Rear Axleshaft, Bearing and Seal

REMOVAL AND INSTALLATION

Metro

1. Raise and safely support the vehicle.

2. Remove the tire and wheel assemblies, then the brake line, retaining clip and flexible hose from the center of the rear axle.

3. Remove the tension spring from the rear axle, disconnect the parking brake cable from the turnbuckle and the cable joint.

4. Remove the brake backing plate from the knuckle after removing the 4 plate retaining bolts.

5. Using a suitable jack, support the under suspension are to prevent it from lowering.

NOTE: As a preparatory step for this removal, check the stamped line on the washer to use for a guide in the reinstallation.

6. Remove the lower strut mounting bolt.

7. Remove the lower knuckle mounting bolt.

8. Remove the knuckle (spindle) from the suspension arm and knuckle from the strut.

NOTE: If it is hard to remove the knuckle from the strut, open the slit in the knuckle by inserting a wedge. Do not open the slit wider than necessary.

To install:

9. Install the knuckle to the strut. Align the projection on the strut against the slit of the knuckle and push the strut into the knuckle until it is properly positioned.

10. Install the lower mount strut bolt. Torque it to 44 ft. lbs. (60 Nm).

11. Install the lower mount end of the knuckle to suspension arm. Torque the nut to 44 ft. lbs. (60 Nm).

12. Remove the jack from under suspension arm.

13. Torque the knuckle lower mount nut to 37 ft. lbs. (50 Nm).

14. Install the backing plate. Torque the retaining bolts to 17 ft. lbs. (23 Nm).

15. Install the brake hose bracket to the knuckle. Install the brake line to the wheel cylinder and tighten the line to 12 ft. lbs. (16 Nm).

16. Install the breather plug cap to the breather plug. Install the brake drum assembly.

17. Install the control rod and control rod nuts. Torque the nuts to 59 ft. lbs. (80 Nm).

18. Bleed the brake system and adjust the brakes as necessary.

19. If removing the wheel bearing use the following procedure:

a. Raise and support the vehicle safely.

b. Remove the wheel assembly.

c. Remove the dust cap, the cotter pin, the castle nut and the washer.

d. Loosen the adjusting nuts of the parking brake cable.

e. Remove the plug from the rear of the backing plate. Insert a suitable tool through the hole, making contact with the shoe hold-down spring, then push the spring to release the parking brake shoe lever.

f. Using a slide hammer tool and a brake drum remover tool, pull the brake drum from the halfshaft.

g. Using a brass drift and a hammer, drive the rear wheel bearings from the brake drum.

NOTE: When installing the wheel bearings, face the sealed sides (numbered sides) outward. Fill the wheel bearing cavity with bearing grease.

h. Drive the new bearings into the brake drum with the bearing installation tool.

i. To install, use a new seal and reverse the removal procedures. Torque the hub castle nut to 41 ft. lbs. (55 Nm). Bleed the brake system. Operate the brakes 3-5 times to obtain the proper drum-to-shoe clearance. Adjust the parking brake cable.

Prizm

1. Raise and safely support the vehicle.

2. Remove the wheel.

3. Remove the brake drum or brake caliper and brake disc. If the caliper is removed, suspend it out of the way with a piece of stiff wire; do not let it hang by the hose.

4. Remove the 4 bolts holding the axle hub/bearing assembly to the axle carrier and remove the hub and bearing assembly.

5. Remove the O-ring from the backing plate.

6. Mount the hub/bearing assembly in a vise with protected jaws.

7. Use a hammer and chisel to unstake the wheel bearing lock nut.

8. Remove the locknut.

9. Using a split plate bearing remover, a race puller pilot and an halfshaft puller GM tools J-22912, J-38278 and J-8433 respectively, separate the halfshaft from the hub.

10. Using the same tools, remove the inner bearing race.

11. Use a slide hammer and seal puller to remove the oil seal from the halfshaft.

12. Press the inner race off with a bearing race remover such as GM tool J-35400 or equivalent.

13. Clean all components thoroughly and examine for any signs of cracking, abrasion or corrosion. Whenever the wheel bearings are removed or disassembled, they must be replaced with new bearings. Reuse of the old bearings is not recommended.

To install:

14. To reassemble, apply multi-purpose grease around the outer race of a new bearing and install the bearing into the inner race.

15. Using a seal installer and slide hammer, install a new oil seal onto the halfshaft.

16. Using the proper size installation tool, press the bearing and bearing outer race into the axle hub.

17. Press the bearing inner race into the axle hub.

18. Press the outer race onto the halfshaft.

19. Install a new wheel bearing lock nut and tighten it to 90 ft. lbs. (123 Nm). Use a hammer and chisel to stake the nut in place.

20. Install a new O-ring onto the knuckle.

21. Place the axle hub/bearing assembly in position, install the bolts and tighten them to 59 ft. lbs. (80 Nm).

22. Reinstall the brake drum.

23. Install the wheel and lower the vehicle to the ground.

24. Although this repair should not have affected the rear alignment, it is recommended that the alignment be checked and adjusted if necessary.

Spectrum

1. Raise and safely support the vehicle.

2. Remove the tire and wheel assemblies, then the brake line, retaining clip and flexible hose from the center of the rear axle.

3. Remove the tension spring from the rear axle, disconnect the parking brake cable from the turnbuckle and the cable joint.

4. Using a suitable jack, support the lower side of the rear axle and remove the lower shock absorber bolt, then the shock absorber from the vehicle.

5. Carefully lower the jack and remove the coil spring.

6. Remove the bolts attaching the rear axle to the body, then the rear axle assembly from the vehicle.

7. If removing the wheel bearing use the following procedure:

a. Raise and support the vehicle safely.

b. Remove the rear wheel assemblies.

c. Remove the hub cap, cotter pin, hub nut, washer and outer bearing.

d. Remove the hub.

e. Using a slide hammer puller and attachment, pull the oil seal from the hub. Remove the inner bearing.

f. Using a brass drift and a hammer, drive both bearing races from the hub.

g. Clean, inspect and/or replace all parts.

h. To install, pack the bearings with grease, coat the oil seal lips with grease and reverse the removal procedures. Torque hub nut to 22 ft. lbs. (29 Nm).

NOTE: If the cotter pin holes are out of alignment upon reassembly, use a wrench to tighten the nut until the hole in the shaft and a slot of the nut align.

8. Reverse procedure to install. Set rear trim height.

Storm

1. Raise and safely support the vehicle.

2. Remove the tire and wheel assemblies, then the brake line, retaining clip and flexible hose from the center of the rear axle.

3. Remove the tension spring from the rear axle, disconnect the parking brake cable from the turnbuckle and the cable joint.

4. Using a suitable jack, support the under suspension are to prevent it from lowering.

5. Before removing the hub assembly, check the end-play as follows:

a. Using a suitable dial indicator tool J-8001 or equivalent, along with the magnetic base J-26900-1 or equivalent, measure the hub assembly end-play.

b. If the end-play exceeds 0.020 in. (0.05mm), replace the axle hub bearing.

c. Press the axle hub bearing out of the hub assembly or if possible use a brass drift and a hammer and drive the rear wheel bearings from the axle hub.

d. Drive the new bearings into the axle hub assembly with a bearing installation tool.

6. Remove the 4 retaining bolts holding the hub assembly to the knuckle.

7. Remove the hub assembly from the knuckle.

8. Remove the brake backing plate from the knuckle after removing the 4 plate retaining bolts.

9. Remove the through bolt from the trailing link at the axle side.

10. Remove the through bolt from the lateral link at the axle side.

11. Remove the knuckle (spindle) assembly from the strut.

To install:

12. Install the knuckle (spindle) assembly to the strut.

13. Install the through bolt to the lateral link at the axle side. Torque the bolt to 94 ft. lbs. (128 Nm).

14. Install the through bolt from the trailing link at the axle side. Torque the bolt to 94 ft. lbs. (128 Nm).

15. Install the brake backing plate to the knuckle along with the 4 plate retaining bolts. Torque the bolts to 12 ft. lbs. (16 Nm).

16. Install the rear suspension knuckle mounting bolts and nuts to the strut assembly.

17. Install the lateral link mounting bolt to the rear suspension and partially tighten.

18. Install the trailing link mounting bolt to the rear suspension and partially tighten.

19. Install the hub assembly to the knuckle. Install the retaining bolts and torque them to 49 ft. lbs. (66 Nm).

20. Torque the following:

a. Lateral link bolt-to-knuckle to 94 ft. lbs. (128 Nm).

b. Trailing link bolt-to-knuckle to 94 ft. lbs. (128 Nm).

c. Strut-to-knuckle nuts and bolts to 116 ft. lbs. (157 Nm).

21. Check the rear wheel alignment.

22. Install the tire and wheel assemblies.

23. Raise the vehicle and remove the jack. Lower the vehicle and bounce the vehicle up and down to stabilize the suspension.

STEERING

Steering Wheel

---CAUTION---

If equipped with an air bag, the air bag system must be disarmed before working around the steering wheel or instrument panel. Failure to do so may result in deployment of the air bag and possible personal injury.

REMOVAL AND INSTALLATION

Metro

1. If equipped, with an air bag system, disable the air bag system as follows:

a. Turn the ignition switch to the **OFF** position.

b. Remove the **SIR IG** fuse in the supplemental inflatable restraint fuse block.

c. Remove the rear plastic access cover to the air bag module.

d. Disconnect the yellow 2-way connector and Connector Position Assurance (CPA) inside the inflator module housing.

2. Disconnect the negative battery cable.

3. Remove the air bag module attaching screws, then the air bag assembly from the vehicle.

---CAUTION---

When carrying a live air bag module, make sure the bag and trim cover are pointed away from you. Never carry the air bag module by the wires or the connector on the underside of the air bag module. In case of an accidental deployment, the bag will then deploy with minimal chance of injury. When placing a live air bag module on a bench or other surface, always face the bag and trim cover in the up position, away from the surface. Never rest a steering column assembly on the steering wheel with the air bag module face down and the column vertical. This is necessary so a free space is provided to allow the air bag to expand in the unlikely event of accidental deployment. Otherwise, personal injury could result.

NOTE: The air bag system coil assembly is easily damaged if the correct steering wheel puller tools are not used.

4. Remove the steering wheel attaching nut, then using a suitable puller, remove the steering wheel.

5. Disconnect the electrical connectors from the steering wheel, then the rear steering wheel cover.

To install:

6. Reverse procedure to install. Torque steering nut to 25 ft. lbs. (34 Nm) and the air bag module attaching screws to 44 inch lbs. (5 Nm).

7. Reactivate the air bag system as follows:

a. Turn the ignition switch to the **OFF** position.

b. Connect the yellow 2-way connector and Connector Position Assurance (CPA) inside the inflator module housing.

c. Install the **SIR IG** fuse in the supplemental inflatable restraint fuse block.

d. Install the rear plastic access cover to the air bag module.

e. Turn the ignition switch to the **RUN** position. Observe the **INFLATABLE RESTRAINT** indicator lamp. If the lamp does not flash 7-9 times and then remain OFF, there is a problem in the air bag system and further diagnostic testing of the system is needed.

Prizm

1990-92

1. Disconnect the negative terminal from the battery.

2. Remove the screws from the bottom of the steering wheel pad and pull the pad upward and off the steering wheel.

3. Remove the steering wheel-to-steering column nut. Matchmark the steering wheel-to-steering column relationship.

4. Using a steering wheel puller tool, screw the bolts into both sides of the steering column, turn the puller center bolt to press the steering wheel from the steering shaft.

NOTE: When working on the steering column, be careful not to strike the column in any way, for it is constructed of a collapsible design and will not withstand major shock.

5. To install, align the matchmarks and reverse the removal procedures. Torque the steering wheel-to-steering column nut to 25 ft. lbs. (34 Nm).

1993-94

1. If vehicle is equipped with an air bag system, disable the air bag system as follows:

a. Position the vehicles front wheels to point straight-ahead.

b. Turn the ignition switch to the **LOCK** position.

c. Remove the IGN and CIG & RADIO fuses from the fuse block.

d. Remove the Connector Position Assurance (CPA).

e. Disconnect the lower steering column connector.

2. Disconnect the negative battery cable.

3. With the air bag system disabled, remove the air bag inflator module as follows:

a. Remove the 2 side covers from the steering column.

b. Remove the 2 Torx® head screws.

c. Remove the Connector Position Assurance (CPA) and disconnect the upper steering column connector.

d. Remove the inflator module from the steering wheel.

CAUTION

When carrying a live inflator module, keep the air bag and trim cover pointed away from you. Never carry the inflator module by the wires or connector on the underside of the module. When placing a live inflator module on a work bench or other surface, always face the bag and trim cover up. Never rest a steering column assembly on the steering wheel with the inflator module face down and column vertical. This is to allow free space for the air bag to expand in the unlikely event of accidental deployment.

4. With the inflator module removed, remove the horn connector.

5. Remove the steering wheel nut and mark the position of the steering wheel relative to the steering shaft.

6. Remove the steering wheel.

To install:

7. Install the steering wheel, aligning the matchmarks made during removal.

8. Install the steering wheel nut and torque to 25 ft. lbs. (34 Nm).

9. Connect the horn connector.

10. Install the air bag inflator module.

11. Connect the upper steering column connector and secure with CPA.

12. Install the 2 Torx® head screws.

13. Install the 2 steering column side covers.

14. Reactivate the air bag system as follows:

a. Turn the ignition switch to the **LOCK** position.

b. Connect the lower steering column connector.

c. Secure the lower steering column connector with Connector Position Assurance (CPA).

d. Install the IGN and CIG & RADIO fuses.

e. Turn the ignition switch to the **ACC** or **ON** position.

f. Observe the **INFLATABLE RESTRAINT** indicator lamp. If the lamp does not illuminate for approximately 60 seconds and turn OFF, there is a problem in the air bag system and further diagnostic testing of the system is needed.

Storm

1. If equipped with an air bag system, disable the air bag system as follows:

a. Turn the ignition switch to the **OFF** position.

b. Disconnect the battery negative cable.

c. Remove fuses C-22 and C-23 from the fuse box.

d. Disconnect the orange 3-way connector at the base of the steering column.

2. Remove the air bag module attaching screws, then the air bag assembly from the vehicle.

CAUTION

When carrying a live air bag module, make sure the bag and trim cover are pointed away from you. Never carry the air bag module by the wires or the connector on the underside of the air bag module. In case of an accidental deployment, the bag will then deploy with minimal chance of injury. When placing a live air bag module on a bench or other surface, always face the bag and trim cover in the up position, away from the surface. Never rest a steering column assembly on the steering wheel with the air bag module face down and the column vertical. This is necessary so a free space is provided to allow the air bag to expand in the unlikely event of accidental deployment. Otherwise, personal injury could result.

3. Remove the steering wheel attaching nut, then using a suitable puller, remove the steering wheel.

4. Disconnect the electrical connectors from the steering wheel, then the rear steering wheel cover.

To install:

5. Reverse procedure to install. Torque steering nut to 25 ft. lbs. (34 Nm) and the air bag module attaching screws to 44 inch lbs. (5 Nm).

6. Reactivate the air bag system as follows:

a. Turn the ignition switch to the **OFF** position.

b. Connect the orange 3-way connector at the base of the steering column.

c. Install fuses C-22 and C-23 to the fuse box.

d. Connect the battery negative cable.

Spectrum

1. Disconnect the negative battery terminal from the battery.

2. Using a suitable tool, remove the shroud screws from the rear-side of the steering wheel (Type 1) or pry the shroud from the steering wheel (Type 2).

3. Disconnect the horn connector and remove the shroud.

4. Remove the nut/washer retaining the steering wheel to the steering shaft.

5. Using a steering wheel puller, remove the steering wheel.

NOTE: The steering shaft and the steering column are designed to absorb impact from collision. Be careful not to severely jar the steering column and shaft during the removal and installation.

6. To install, reverse the removal procedures.

Manual Rack and Pinion

REMOVAL AND INSTALLATION

Metro

1. Slide the driver's seat back as far as possible.

2. Pull off the front part of the floor mat on the driver's side and remove the steering shaft joint cover.

3. Loosen the steering shaft upper joint bolt but do not remove.

4. Remove the steering shaft lower joint bolt and disconnect the lower joint from the pinion.

5. Raise and support the vehicle safely.

6. Remove the tie rod ends from the steering knuckles. Mark the left and right tie rods accordingly.

7. From under the dash, remove the steering joint cover.

8. Remove the lower steering shaft-to-steering gear clinch bolt and separate the steering shaft from the steering gear.

9. Remove the steering gear mounting bolts, the brackets and the steering gear case from the vehicle.

10. Installation is the reverse order of the removal procedure.

11. Torque the steering gear case bolts to 18 ft. lbs. (25 Nm); the steering gear-to-steering shaft bolt to 18 ft. lbs. (25 Nm) and the tie rod end-to-steering knuckle nut to 32 ft. lbs. (43 Nm).

Prizm

1. Remove the cover from the intermediate shaft.

2. Loosen the upper pinch bolt. Remove the lower pinch bolt at the pinion shaft.

3. Loosen the wheel lug nuts.

4. Elevate and safely support the vehicle.

5. Remove both front wheels.

6. Install an engine support and tension it to support the engine without raising it.

CAUTION

The engine hoist is in place and under tension. Use care when repositioning the vehicle and make necessary adjustments to the engine support.

7. Remove the 3 bolts holding the center crossmember to the radiator support.

8. Remove the covers from the front and center mount bolts.

9. Remove the 2 front mount bolts, then the center mount bolts.

10. Support the crossmember and remove the 2 rear mount bolts.

11. Remove the 2 bolts holding the center crossmember to the main crossmember.

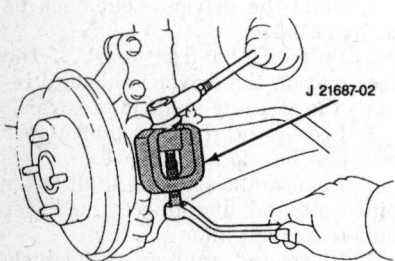

J 21687-02

Removing the tie rod ends — Prizm

12. Use a floor jack and a wide piece of wood to support the main crossmember.

13. Remove the 8 bolts holding the main crossmember to the body.

14. Remove the 2 bolts holding the lower control arm brackets to the body.

NOTE: The crossmembers are loose and free to fall. Make sure they are properly supported.

15. Slowly lower the main crossmember while holding onto the center crossmember.

16. Remove the cotter pins from both ball joints and remove the nuts.

17. Using a tie rod separator, remove both tie rod joints from the knuckles.

18. Remove the nuts and bolts attaching the steering rack to the body.

19. Remove the rack through the right side wheel well.

To install:

20. To reinstall the rack, place it in position through the right wheel well and tighten the bracket bolts to 45 ft. lbs. (59 Nm).

21. Attach the tie rods to the knuckles. Tighten the nuts to 36 ft. lbs. (49 Nm) and install new cotter pins.

22. Position the center crossmember over the center and rear transaxle mount studs; start 2 nuts on the center mount.

23. Loosely install the 3 bolts holding the center crossmember to the radiator support.

24. Loosely install the 2 front mount bolts.

25. Raise the main crossmember into position over the rear mount studs and align all underbody bolts. Install the 2 rear mount nuts loosely.

26. Install the 8 main crossmember to underbody bolts loosely.

27. Install the 2 lower control arm bracket bolts loosely.

28. Loosely install the 2 bolts holding the center crossmember to the main crossmember.

29. The crossmembers, bolts and brackets should now all be in place and held loosely by their nuts and bolts. If any repositioning is necessary, do so now.

30. Tighten the components below in the order listed to the correct torque specification:

   a. Main crossmember-to-underbody bolts: 152 ft. lbs. (206 Nm).

   b. Lower control arm bolts: 94 ft. lbs. (127 Nm).

   c. Center crossmember-to-radiator support bolts: 45 ft. lbs. (59 Nm).

   d. Front, center and rear mount bolts: 45 ft. lbs. (59 Nm).

31. Install the covers on the front and center mount bolts.

32. Install the front wheels.

33. Lower the vehicle to the ground.

34. Connect the yoke to the pinion and tighten both the upper and lower bolts to 26 ft. lbs. (35 Nm).

35. Install the yoke cover.

Spectrum

1. Remove the intermediate shaft cover.

2. Loosen the upper pinch bolt. Remove the lower pinch bolt at the pinion shaft.

3. Raise and safely support the vehicle. Remove the wheel assemblies.

4. Remove both tie rod ends from the steering knuckles and the left inner tie rod from the rack.

5. Remove the steering gear-to-body attaching nuts and the rack and pinion assembly from the vehicle.

6. Installation is the reverse order of the removal procedure.

Power Rack and Pinion

REMOVAL AND INSTALLATION

Prizm

1. Place a drain pan under the steering rack.

2. Remove the cover from the intermediate shaft.

3. Loosen the upper pinch bolt. Remove the lower pinch bolt at the pinion shaft.

4. Loosen the wheel lug nuts.

5. Elevate and safely support the vehicle.

6. Remove both front wheels.

7. Install an engine support and tension it to support the engine without raising it.

NOTE: The engine hoist is now in place and under tension. Use care when repositioning the vehicle and make necessary adjustments to the engine support.

8. Remove the 3 bolts holding the center crossmember to the radiator support.

9. Remove the covers from the front and center mount bolts.

10. Remove the 2 front mount bolts, then the center mount bolts and then the 2 rear mount bolts.

11. Remove the 2 bolts holding the center crossmember to the main crossmember.

12. Use a floor jack and a wide piece of wood to support the main crossmember.

13. Remove the 8 bolts holding the main crossmember to the body.

14. Remove the 2 bolts holding the lower control arm brackets to the body.

—————— CAUTION ——————

The crossmembers are loose and free to fall. Make sure they are properly supported.

15. Slowly lower the main crossmember while holding onto the center crossmember.

16. Remove the cotter pins from both tie rod ball joints and remove the nuts.

17. Using a tie rod separator, remove both tie rod joints from the knuckles.

18. Label and disconnect the fluid pressure and return lines from the rack.

19. Remove the nuts and bolts attaching the steering rack to the body.

20. Remove the rack through the right side wheel well.

To install:

21. To reinstall the rack, place it in position through the right wheel well and tighten the bracket bolts to 43 ft. lbs. (58 Nm).

22. Connect the fluid lines to the rack and tighten the fittings to 33 ft. lbs. (44 Nm). Make certain the fittings are correctly threaded before tightening them.

23. Attach the tie rods to the knuckles. Tighten the nuts to 36 ft. lbs. (49 Nm) and install new cotter pins.

24. Position the center crossmember over the center and rear transaxle mount studs; start 2 nuts on the center mount.

25. Loosely install the 3 bolts holding the center crossmember to the radiator support.

26. Loosely install the 2 front mount bolts.

27. Raise the main crossmember into position over the rear mount studs and align all underbody bolts. Install the 2 rear mount nuts loosely.

28. Install the 8 main crossmember to underbody bolts loosely.

29. Install the 2 lower control arm bracket bolts loosely.

30. Loosely install the 2 bolts holding the center crossmember to the main crossmember.

31. The crossmembers, bolts and brackets should now all be in place and held loosely by their nuts and bolts. If any repositioning is necessary, do so now.

32. Tighten the components below in the order listed to the correct torque specification:

   a. Main crossmember-to-underbody bolts: 152 ft. lbs. (206 Nm).

   b. Lower control arm bolts: 94 ft. lbs. (127 Nm).

   c. Center crossmember-to-radiator support bolts: 45 ft. lbs. (61 Nm).

   d. Front, center and rear mount bolts: 45 ft. lbs. (61 Nm).

33. Install the covers on the front and center mount bolts.

34. Install the front wheels.

35. Lower the vehicle to the ground.

36. Connect the yoke to the pinion and tighten both the upper and lower bolts to 26 ft. lbs. (35 Nm).

37. Install the yoke cover.

38. Add power steering fluid to the reservoir and bleed the system.

Spectrum

1. Raise and support the vehicle safely.

2. Remove both tie rod ends from the steering knuckles and the right inner tie rod from the rack.

3. Place a drain pan under the rack assembly and clean around the pressure lines at the rack valve.

4. Cut the plastic retaining straps at the power steering lines and hose.

5. Remove the power steering pump lines, the rack valve and drain the fluid into the pan.

6. Remove the rack and pinion.

7. To install, reverse the removal procedures, add fluid, bleed the system and check the toe-in.

Storm

1. Remove the steering shaft cover and 3 retaining nuts on the dust boot retaining ring.

2. Raise and safely support the vehicle. Remove the tires and wheels.

3. Remove the dust boot from the bulkhead. Place a drain pan beneath the vehicle.

4. Remove the pinch bolt from the intermediate steering shaft. Disconnect the tie rod ends from the steering knuckles.

5. Remove the hold-down bracket from the steering lines.

6. Remove the high pressure line from the steering rack and pinion. Remove the rack to crossmember bolts.

7. Remove the retaining brackets from the rack mounts. Position the rack away from the mounts.

8. Remove the return line from the rack. Remove the intermediate steering shaft knuckle.

9. Remove the rack and pinion from the right side of the vehicle.

10. Installation is the reverse order of the removal procedure.

   a. Torque the rack-to-crossmember bolts to 41 ft. lbs. (59 Nm).

   b. Torque the high pressure and return lines to 20 ft. lbs. (27 Nm).

   c. Torque the tie rod end nuts to 40 ft. lbs. (54 Nm).

Power Steering Pump

REMOVAL AND INSTALLATION

1990 Prizm

1. Place a drain pan below the pump.

2. Elevate and safely support the vehicle.

3. Remove the right front wheel.

4. Place a floor jack under the engine block and support it. Use a broad piece of wood to spread the load evenly and prevent damage.

5. Remove the bolt from the right side engine mount and lower the engine about 2.0 in. (50mm) to gain access to the lower power steering pump through bolt.

6. Working through the right wheel well, remove the lower pump through bolt.

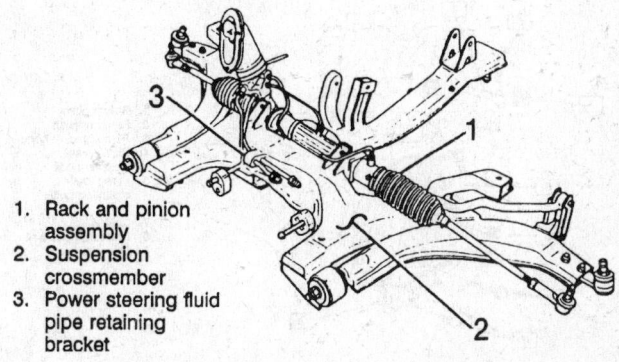

1. Rack and pinion assembly
2. Suspension crossmember
3. Power steering fluid pipe retaining bracket

Steering rack and pinion mounting — Storm

7. Disconnect the fluid lines from the pump and plug them immediately.

8. Remove the upper mounting bolt from the pump and remove the pump.

To install:

9. When reinstalling, place the pump in position and install the mounting bolts. Tighten them to 29 ft. lbs. (39 Nm).

10. Raise the engine to its normal position and install the engine mount bolt, tightening it to 69 ft. lbs. (93 Nm).

11. Connect the fluid lines to the pump and tighten the pressure hose fitting to 34 ft. lbs. (46 Nm).

12. Install the belt and adjust it to the proper tension.

13. Install the right front wheel.

14. Remove the jack and drain pan from under the engine.

15. Lower the vehicle to the ground.

16. Fill the reservoir to the proper level with power steering fluid and bleed the system.

17. After the vehicle has been driven for about an hour, double check the belt adjustment.

NOTE: If replacing the pump, switch the pulley and the mounting nut to the new pump.

1991-94 Prizm

BASE AND LSI MODELS

1. Disconnect the negative battery cable. Remove the air cleaner.

2. Remove the power steering pump drive belt.

3. Loosen the power steering hose retaining clip and remove the return hose from the power steering pump.

4. Remove the pressure hose from the pump using a injection line wrench J-29698 or equivalent.

5. Remove the upper mounting bolt from the pump.

6. Remove the vacuum hoses from the power steering switch. Remove the 3 bolts retaining the pump bracket mount and the 2 from the engine block and the one from the engine mount.

7. Remove the lower mounting bolt and the power steering pump from the vehicle.

8. Installation is the reverse order of the removal procedure. Torque the power steering pump mounting brackets to 29 ft. lbs. (39 Nm). Connect the pressure hose to the power steering pump union bolt and torque it to 32 ft. lbs. (44 Nm). Adjust the belt tension and bleed the system.

GSi MODEL

1. Disconnect the negative battery cable. Place a drain pan under the vehicle.

2. Remove the windshield washer reservoir retaining bolt; position the reservoir out of the way.

3. Loosen the drive pulley retaining nut. Use a J-35416 or equivalent adjusting screw wrench to keep the pulley from turning while loosening the retaining nut.

4. Raise and support the vehicle safely. Loosen the jam nut on the idler pulley. Lower the vehicle and remove the power steering pump drive belt.

5. Remove the drive pulley retaining nut from the shaft and remove the pulley from the pump.

6. Remove the power steering pressure lines from the pump.

7. Remove the 2 power steering pump retaining bolts and remove the pump from the bracket.

8. Installation is the reverse order of the removal procedure. Torque the power steering pump mounting brackets to 29 ft. lbs. (39 Nm). Connect the pressure hose to the power steering pump union bolt and torque it to 32 ft. lbs. (44 Nm). Adjust the belt tension and bleed the system.

Spectrum and Storm

1. Disconnect the negative battery cable.

2. Place a drain pan below the pump.

3. Remove the pressure hose clamp, pressure hose and return hose. Drain the fluid from the pump and reservoir.

4. Remove the adjusting bolt, pivot bolt and drive belt.

5. Remove the pump assembly.

6. To install, reverse the removal procedures, tighten the pressure hose to 20 ft. lbs. (27 Nm) and the pivot bolt to 15 ft. lbs. (20 Nm), adjust the drive belt, fill the reservoir and bleed the system.

BELT ADJUSTMENT

Prizm

1990

1. Install a J-23600B or equivalent, belt tension gauge on the pump belt. Loosen the 2 pump attaching bolts and nuts.

2. Using a suitable belt tension adjusting tool (between the pump and the engine block), push the pump away from the engine until the belt tension is set to specifications.

　a. If a new belt is being used, tighten the belt tensioner to 100-150 lbs.

　b. If a used belt is being installed, tighten the belt tensioner to 60-100 lbs.

3. Torque the upper bolt and then the lower through bolt to 29 ft. lbs. (39 Nm).

1991-94

1. Disconnect the negative battery cable. Loosen the upper and lower alternator mounting bolts.

2. Remove the alternator drive belt.

3. Loosen the upper and lower power steering mounting bolts.

4. Make sure the power steering drive belt is properly aligned in the grooves on the pulleys. Install a J-23600-B or equivalent, belt tension gauge on the pump belt.

5. Using a suitable belt tension adjusting tool (between the pump and the engine block), push the pump away from the engine until the belt tension is set to specifications.

　a. If a new belt is being used, tighten the belt tensioner to 30-46 lbs.

　b. If a used belt is being installed, tighten the belt tensioner to 18-30 lbs.

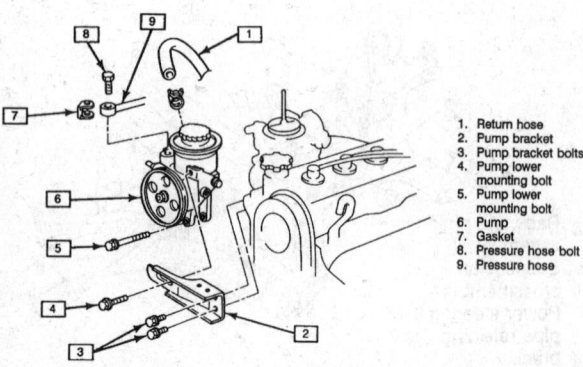

1. Return hose
2. Pump bracket
3. Pump bracket bolts
4. Pump lower mounting bolt
5. Pump lower mounting bolt
6. Pump
7. Gasket
8. Pressure hose bolt
9. Pressure hose

Power steering pump mounting — Prizm

6. Torque the upper bolt and then the lower through bolt to 29 ft. lbs. (39 Nm).

7. Make sure the alternator drive belt is properly aligned in the grooves on the pulleys. Install a J-23600-B or equivalent, belt tension gauge on the pump belt.

8. Using a suitable belt tension adjusting tool apply tension on the alternator until the belt tension is set to specifications.

a. If a new belt is being used, tighten the belt tensioner to 141-182 lbs.

b. If a used belt is being installed, tighten the belt tensioner to 111-152 lbs.

9. Torque the upper bolt to 17 ft. lbs. (23 Nm) and then the lower through bolt and nut to 26 ft. lbs. (35 Nm).

Storm

ENGINE CODE 6

1. Install belt tension gauge J-23600-B or equivalent, onto the pump drive belt.

2. Loosen the pump attaching nuts and bolts.

3. Using a ½ in. drive ratchet or breaker bar, move pump until the correct belt tension is obtained.

4. Belt tension should be 90 lbs. If equipped with air conditioning, belt tension should be 145 lbs.

5. Adjust the pivot and adjusting bolts to 15 ft. lbs. (20 Nm).

ENGINE CODE 8

The 1.8L engine uses a serpentine drive belt that has an automatic tensioner. Regular adjustment of the belt is not needed.

Spectrum

NOTE: The following procedures require the use of GM belt tension gauge BT-33-95-ACBN for regular V-belts or BT-33-97M for poly V-belts.

1. If the belt is cold, operate the engine, at idle speed, for 15 minutes; the belt will seat itself in the pulleys allowing the belt fibers to relax or stretch. If the belt is hot, allow it to cool, until it is warm to the touch.

NOTE: A used belt is one that has been rotated at least 1 complete evolution on the pulleys. This begins the belt seating process and it must never be tensioned to the new belt specifications.

2. Loosen the component-to-mounting bracket bolts.

3. Using a GM belt tension gauge BT-33-95-ACBN for standard V-belts or BT-33-97M for poly V-belts, place the tension gauge at the center of the belt between the longest span.

4. Applying belt tension pressure on the component, adjust the drive belt tension to the correct specifications. The belt tension should deflect about ½ inch over a 7-10 inch span or ½ inch over a 13-16 inch span.

5. While holding the correct tension on the component, tighten the component-to-mounting bracket bolt.

6. When the belt tension is 70-110 lbs., remove the tension gauge.

SYSTEM BLEEDING

Prizm

1. With the engine running, turn the wheel all the way to the left and shut off the engine.

2. Add power steering fluid to the COLD or MIN mark on the indicator.

3. Start the engine and run at fast idle for about 15 seconds. Stop the engine and recheck the fluid level. Add to the COLD mark as needed.

4. Start the engine and bleed the system by turning the wheels from left to right 3 or 4 times.

5. Stop the engine and check the fluid level and condition. Fluid with air in it is a light tan color. This air must be eliminated from the system before normal operation can be obtained. Repeat Steps 3 and 4 until the correct fluid color and fluid level is obtained.

Spectrum and Storm

1. Turn the wheels to the extreme left.

2. With the engine stopped, add power steering fluid to the MIN mark on the fluid indicator.

3. Start the engine and run it for 15 seconds at fast idle.

4. Stop the engine, recheck fluid level and refill to the MIN mark.

5. Start the engine and turn the wheels from side to side, 3 times.

6. Stop the engine check the fluid level.

NOTE: If air bubbles are still present in the fluid, the procedures must be repeated.

Tie Rod Ends

REMOVAL AND INSTALLATION

Metro

1. Raise and safely support the front of the vehicle. Remove the front wheel assembly.

2. Remove the cotter pin and the castle nut from the tie rod end.

3. Using the ball joint removal tool J-21687-02, remove the tie rod end ball joint from the steering knuckle.

4. Loosen the locknut on the tie rod end.

5. Unscrew the tie rod end from the tie rod, count the number of revolutions necessary to remove the tie rod end, for installation purposes.

6. At the steering gear, remove the boot clamps and pull the boot back over the tie rod.

7. Using a pair of pliers, bend the lockwasher back from the tie rod joint.

8. Using 2 wrenches, hold the steering rack and unscrew the tie rod end. Remove the tie rod and slide the boot from the tie rod.

To install:

9. Installation is the reverse order of the removal procedure, reverse the removal procedure.

10. Torque the tie rod end locknut to 33 ft. lbs. (45 Nm) and the tie rod end to steering knuckle nut to 32 ft. lbs. (43 Nm).

11. With the tie rod secured to the steering gear, bend the lockwasher over the flat spot on the tie rod ball end.

Prizm

1. Raise the front of the vehicle and support it safely. Remove the wheel.

2. Remove the cotter pin and nut holding the tie rod to the steering knuckle.

3. Using a tie rod separator, press the tie rod out of the knuckle.

NOTE: Use only the correct tool to separate the tie rod joint. Replace the joint if the rubber boot is cracked or ripped.

4. Matchmark the inner end of the tie rod to the end of the steering rack.

5. Loosen the locknut and remove the tie rod from the steering rack.

To install:

6. Install the tie rod ends onto the rack ends and align the matchmarks made earlier.

7. Tighten the locknuts to 35 ft. lbs. (47 Nm).

8. Connect the tie rod joint to the knuckle. Tighten the nut to 36 ft. lbs.(49 Nm) and install a new cotter pin.

9. Install the wheel and lower the vehicle to the ground.

Spectrum and Storm

1. Raise and safely support the vehicle. Remove the tire and wheel assemblies.

2. Remove the castle nut from the ball joint. Using a ball joint removal tool, separate the tie rod from the steering knuckle.

3. Disconnect the retaining wire from the inner boot and pull back the boot.

4. Using a chisel, straighten the staked part of the locking washer between the tie rod and the rack.

5. Remove the tie rod from the rack.

6. Reverse procedure to install.

BRAKES

Master Cylinder

REMOVAL AND INSTALLATION

NOTE: Be careful not to spill brake fluid on the painted surfaces of the vehicle; it will damage the finish.

Metro

1. Disconnect the negative battery cable. Clean around the reservoir cap and take some of the fluid out with a syringe.

2. Disconnect and plug the brake tubes from the master cylinder.

3. Remove the mounting nuts and washers.

4. Remove the master cylinder.

5. To install, reverse the removal procedures. Torque the mounting bolts to 8-12 ft. lbs. (11-16 Nm). Bleed the brake system.

Prizm

1. Disconnect the negative battery cable.

2. Clean the area at the reservoir and brake lines to prevent entry of dirt into the system.

3. Disconnect the wiring to the brake fluid level switch. Release the wiring from any clips.

4. Remove the air intake duct.

5. Use a syringe to remove the fluid from the reservoir. Store the fluid in a clean glass jar with a lid.

6. Disconnect the brake lines from the master cylinder. Plug or tape the lines immediately to keep dirt and moisture out of the system.

7. Remove the retaining nuts holding the master cylinder to the brake booster.

8. Remove the 3-way union from the booster stud.

9. Remove the master cylinder from the studs.

10. Remove the seal or gasket from the booster.

To install:

11. When reinstalling, always use a new gasket or seal and install the master cylinder to the booster.

12. Install the 3-way union bracket over the stud and install the retaining nuts finger-tight.

13. Connect the brake lines to the master cylinder. Make certain each fitting is correctly threaded and tighten each fitting 1-2 turns. The job is made easier by having a small amount of movement available at the master cylinder mounting studs.

14. Tighten the master cylinder retaining nuts to 9.5 ft. lbs. (13 Nm).

15. Tighten the brake line fittings to 11 ft. lbs. (15 Nm). Do not overtighten these fittings.

16. Install the air intake duct.

17. Connect the wiring to the brake fluid sensing switch and attach any wiring clips.

18. Fill the master cylinder reservoir.

19. Bleed the brake system.

20. Connect the negative battery cable

Spectrum and Storm

1. Disconnect the negative battery cable. Remove some brake fluid from the master cylinder with a syringe.

2. On Storm, remove the top of the air cleaner and the air duct.

3. Disconnect and cap or tape the openings of the brake tube.

4. Disconnect the brake fluid level warning switch connector.

5. Remove the 2 nuts securing the master cylinder to the power brake booster.

6. Remove the master cylinder from the power brake booster.

7. To install, reverse the removal procedures, add fluid to the reservoir and bleed the brake system.

NOTE: It may be necessary to adjust the brake booster pushrod length. Adjuster the pushrod length until the pushrod lightly touches the pin head.

Proportioning Valve

REMOVAL AND INSTALLATION

Prizm

The proportioning valve, if equipped is located on the center of the firewall under the hood. Except for leakage or impact damage, it rarely needs replacement. If it must be removed, all 5 brake lines must be labeled and removed and the valve removed from its mount. Clean the fittings before removal to prevent dirt from entering the ports.

1. Disconnect and plug the brake lines from the proportioning valve unions.

2. Remove the proportioning valve-to-bulkhead bolts, then the valves.

NOTE: If the proportioning valve is defective, it must be replaced as an assembly; it cannot be rebuilt.

3. To install, reverse the removal procedure. Bleed the brake system and check for leaks.

Spectrum

1. Clean the area around the reservoir and the brake pipe connections.

2. Remove the brake fluid from the master cylinder reservoir using a syringe.

3. Disconnect the brake pipes from the proportioning valve. Cap all openings.

4. While holding the master cylinder, use a box wrench and remove the proportioning valves from the master cylinder.

NOTE: It may be necessary to remove the master cylinder and place it into a suitable vise to sufficiently hold it while removing the proportioning valves.

5. To install, reverse the removal procedure. Fill the reservoir and bleed the system.

Power Brake Booster

REMOVAL AND INSTALLATION

Metro

1. Disconnect the negative battery cable.

2. Remove the master cylinder.

3. Disconnect the pushrod clevis pin from the brake pedal arm.

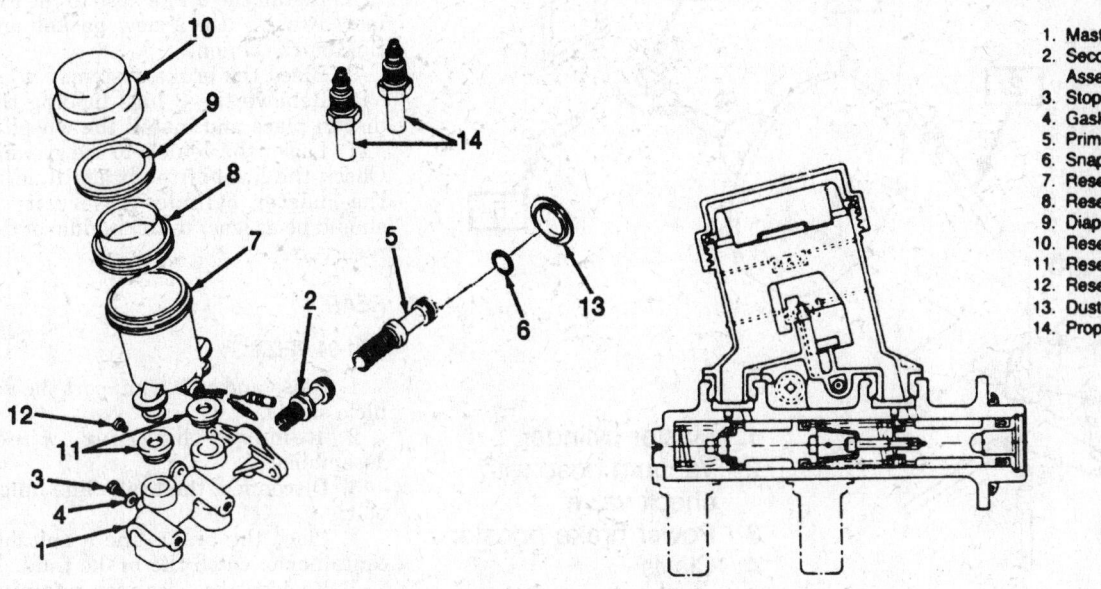

1. Master Cylinder Body
2. Secondary Piston Assembly
3. Stopper Bolt
4. Gasket
5. Primary Piston Assembly
6. Snap Ring
7. Reservoir
8. Reservoir Diaphragm
9. Diaphragm Retainer
10. Reservoir Cap
11. Reservoir Grommets
12. Reservoir Screw
13. Dust Seal
14. Proportioning Valves

Exploded view of the master cylinder assembly — Spectrum

4. Disconnect the vacuum hose from the brake booster.

5. Remove the mounting nuts from under the dash and the booster.

6. To install, reverse the removal procedures. Torque the booster-to-cowl nuts to 14-20 ft. lbs. (19-27 Nm). Bleed the brake system, if necessary.

Prizm

NOTE: To perform this procedure, use a booster pushrod gauge GM tool J-34873-A or equivalent, to set the booster pushrod length.

1. Disconnect the negative battery cable.

2. Remove the top of the air cleaner and the intake duct. Remove the charcoal canister mounting nuts.

3. Remove the brake master cylinder from the booster.

4. Remove the vacuum hose from the booster.

5. Inside the vehicle, disconnect the pedal return spring. Disconnect the clip and the clevis pin.

6. Remove the brake booster retaining nuts. It will be helpful to have a helper support the booster while the nuts are loosened.

7. Remove the booster from the engine compartment.

8. To adjust the power brake booster pushrod, perform the following procedures:

a. Using the pushrod gauge tool J-34873-A or equivalent, set the short side on the booster.

NOTE: The head of the pin sits near the end of the booster pushrod.

b. Check the gap between the head of the tool's pin and the pushrod; it should be 0. If necessary, adjust the pushrod by turning it until the pushrod just touches the pin.

To install:

9. When reinstalling, have a helper hold the booster in position while installing the retaining nuts. Tighten the nuts to 9.5 ft. lbs. (13 Nm).

10. Install the clevis pin and clip, then install the pedal return spring.

11. Connect the vacuum hose to the booster.

12. Install the master cylinder onto the booster and tighten the nuts to 9.5 ft. lbs. (13 Nm).

13. Install the charcoal canister mounting bolts and install the air cleaner top and intake duct.

14. Connect the negative battery cable.

15. Bleed the brake system.

Spectrum and Storm

1. Disconnect the negative battery cable.

2. On Storm, remove the top of the air cleaner and the air cleaner duct.

3. Remove the master cylinder.

4. Remove the vacuum hose from the vacuum servo.

5. Remove the clevis pin from the brake pedal.

6. Remove the 4 nuts from the brake assembly under the dash and remove the power booster from the engine compartment.

7. To install, reverse the removal procedures.

Brake Caliper

REMOVAL AND INSTALLATION

FRONT

1. Raise and safely support the front of the vehicle. Set the parking brake and block the rear wheels.

2. Siphon a sufficient quantity of brake fluid from the master cylinder reservoir to prevent the brake fluid from overflowing the master cylinder when removing or installing the calipers. This is necessary as the piston must be forced into the cylinder bore

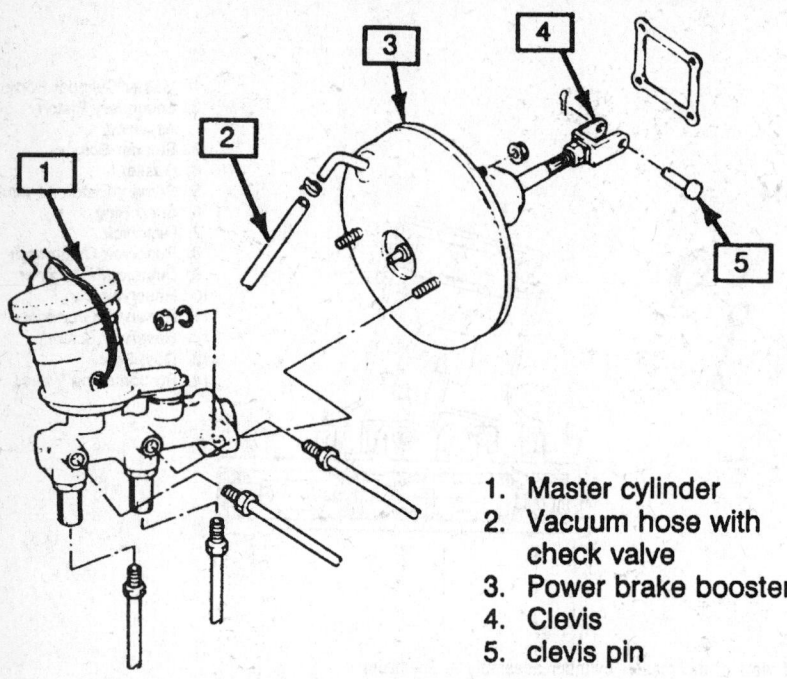

1. Master cylinder
2. Vacuum hose with check valve
3. Power brake booster
4. Clevis
5. clevis pin

Power brake booster mounting — Storm

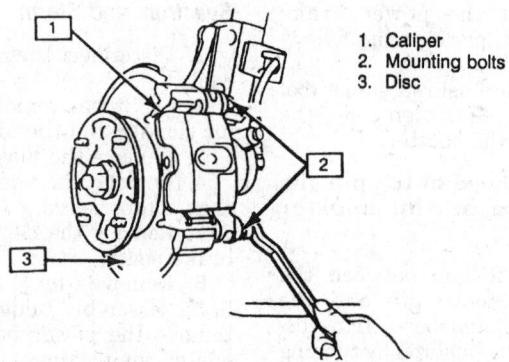

1. Caliper
2. Mounting bolts
3. Disc

Removing the front brake caliper bolts — Metro

not hold up under the extreme temperatures generated by the brakes. Tighten the bolts.

8. Install the brake hose to the caliper. Always use a new gasket and tighten the union.

9. Bleed the brake system.

10. Remove the 2 lugs holding the disc in place and install the wheel.

11. Lower the vehicle to the ground. Check the level of the brake fluid in the master cylinder reservoir; it should be at least to the middle of the reservoir.

REAR

1991-94 PRIZM

1. Raise and safely support the vehicle safely.

2. Remove the rear wheel assemblies.

3. Disconnect the brake line union bolt.

4. Place the brake line a suitable container to catch the brake fluid.

5. Remove the 2 caliper retaining bolts.

6. Remove the brake caliper from the vehicle.

7. Installation is the reverse order of the removal procedure. Install the caliper retaining bolts and torque them to 14 ft. lbs. (20 Nm). Torque the brake line union bolt to 22 ft. lbs. (30 Nm).

Disc Brake Pads

REMOVAL AND INSTALLATION

1. Raise and safely support the front of the vehicle. Set the parking brake and block the rear wheels.

2. Siphon a sufficient quantity of brake fluid from the master cylinder reservoir to prevent the brake fluid from overflowing the master cylinder when removing or installing the brake pads. This is necessary as the piston must be forced into the cylinder bore to provide sufficient clearance to install the pads.

3. Remove the wheel, then reinstall 2 lug nuts finger-tight to hold the disc in place.

NOTE: Disassemble brakes one wheel at a time. This will prevent parts confusion and also prevent the opposite caliper piston from popping out during pad installation.

4. Remove the 2 caliper mounting bolts and then remove the caliper from the mounting bracket. Position the caliper out of the way and sup-

to provide sufficient clearance to install the caliper.

3. Remove the wheel, then reinstall 2 lug nuts finger-tight to hold the disc in place.

NOTE: Disassemble brakes one wheel at a time. This will prevent parts confusion and also prevent the opposite caliper piston from popping out during installation. On Prizm, mark the relationship between the wheel and the axle hub before removing the tire and wheel assembly.

4. Disconnect the hose union at the caliper. Use a pan to catch any

spilled fluid and immediately plug the disconnected hose.

5. Remove the 2 caliper mounting bolts and then remove the caliper from the mounting bracket.

To install:

6. Use a caliper compressor, a C-clamp or large pair of pliers to slowly press the caliper piston back into the caliper.

7. Install the caliper assembly to the mounting plate. Before installing the retaining bolts, apply a thin, even coating of anti-seize compound to the threads and slide surfaces. Don't use grease or spray lubricants; they will

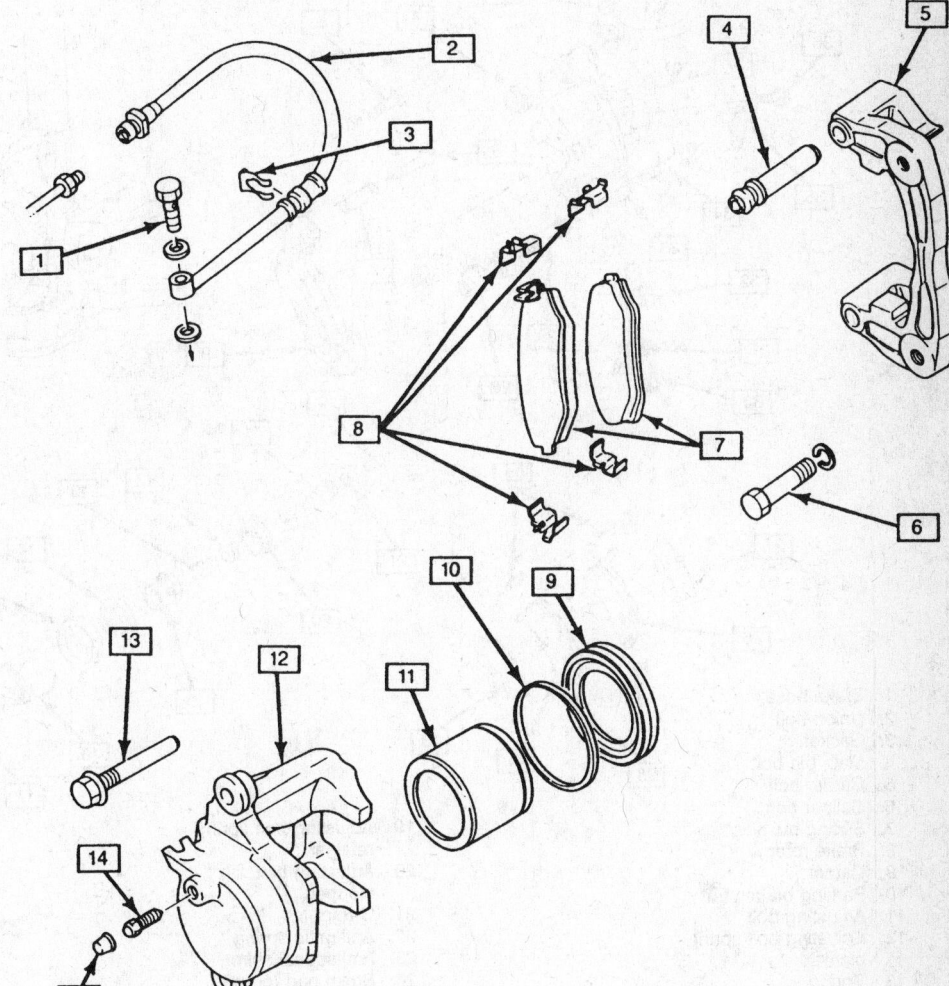

1. Brake hose union bolt
2. Brake hose
3. Brake hose retaining clip
4. Slide pin bushing
5. Bracket
6. Lower slide pin
7. Brake pads
8. Pad retainers
9. Piston boot
10. Piston seal
11. Piston
12. Caliper body
13. Upper slide pin bolt
14. Bleeder screw
15. Cap

Exploded view of the front brake caliper — Storm

port it with wire so it doesn't hang by the brake line.

NOTE: It may be necessary to rock the caliper back and forth a bit in order to reposition the piston so it will clear the brake pads.

5. Remove the brake pads, the wear indicators, the anti-squeal shims, the support plates and the anti-squeal springs, if equipped. Disassemble slowly and take note of how the parts fit together. This will save much time during reassembly.

6. Inspect the brake disc (both sides) for scoring or gouging. Measure the disc for both thickness and run-out. Complete inspection procedures are given later in this section.

7. Inspect the pads for remaining thickness and condition. Any sign of uneven wear, cracking, heat checking or spotting is cause for replacement. Compare the wear of the inner pad to the outer pad. While they will not wear at exactly the same rate, the remaining thickness should be about the same on both pads. If one is heavily worn and the other is not, suspect either a binding caliper piston or dirty slides in the caliper mount.

8. Examine the 2 caliper retaining bolts and the slide bushings in which they run. Everything should be clean and dry. If cleaning is needed, use spray solvents and a clean cloth. Do not wire brush or sand the bolts-this will cause grooves in the metal which will trap more dirt. Check the condition of the rubber dust boots and replace them if damaged.

To install:

9. Install the pad support plates onto the mounting bracket.

10. Install new pad wear indicators onto each pad, making sure the arrow on the tab points in the direction of disc rotation.

11. Install new anti-squeal pads to the back of the pads.

12. Install the pads into the mounting bracket and install the anti-squeal springs.

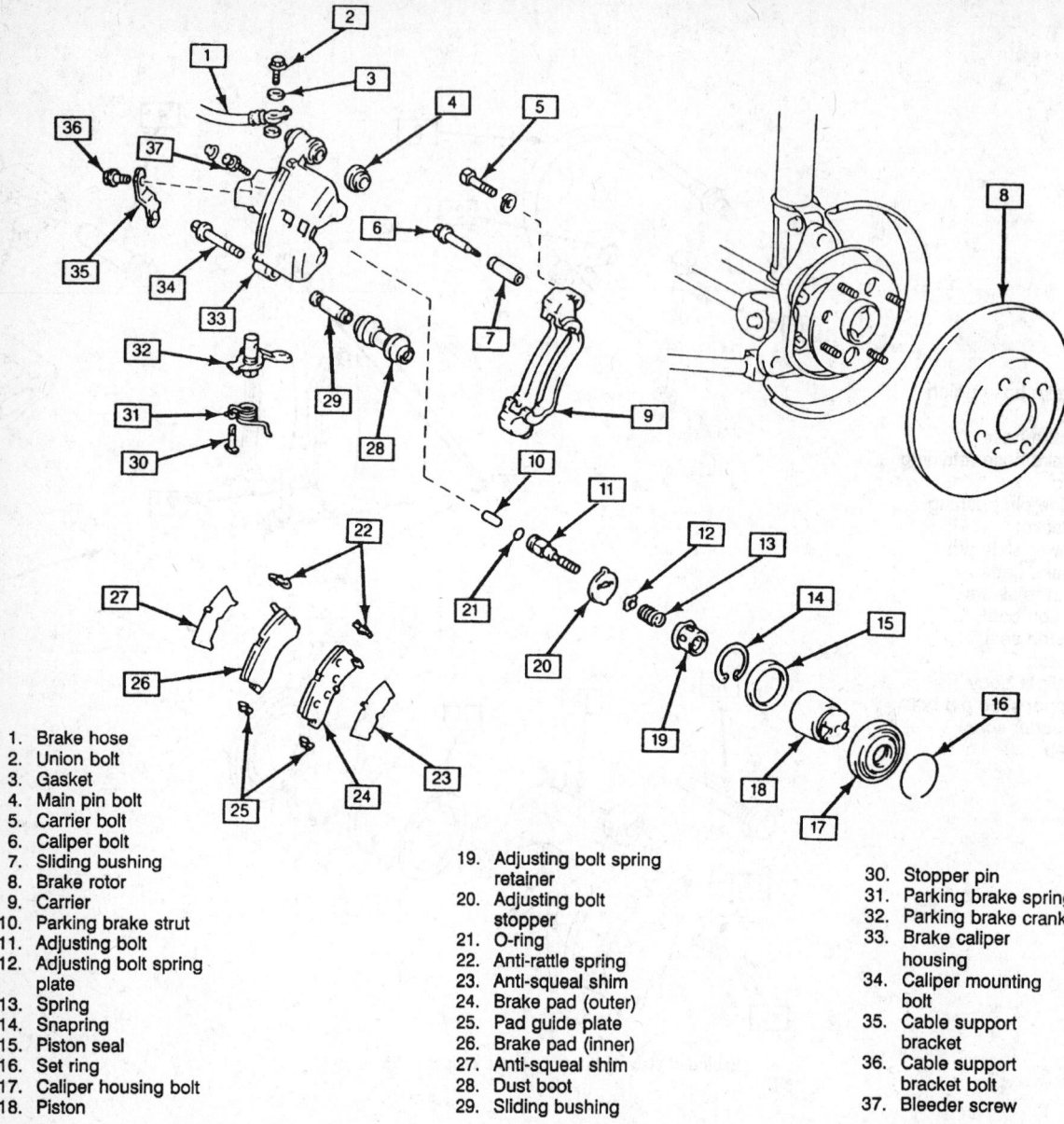

1. Brake hose
2. Union bolt
3. Gasket
4. Main pin bolt
5. Carrier bolt
6. Caliper bolt
7. Sliding bushing
8. Brake rotor
9. Carrier
10. Parking brake strut
11. Adjusting bolt
12. Adjusting bolt spring plate
13. Spring
14. Snapring
15. Piston seal
16. Set ring
17. Caliper housing bolt
18. Piston
19. Adjusting bolt spring retainer
20. Adjusting bolt stopper
21. O-ring
22. Anti-rattle spring
23. Anti-squeal shim
24. Brake pad (outer)
25. Pad guide plate
26. Brake pad (inner)
27. Anti-squeal shim
28. Dust boot
29. Sliding bushing
30. Stopper pin
31. Parking brake spring
32. Parking brake crank
33. Brake caliper housing
34. Caliper mounting bolt
35. Cable support bracket
36. Cable support bracket bolt
37. Bleeder screw

Exploded view of the rear disc brake components — Prizm

13. Use a caliper compressor or a C-clamp to slowly press the caliper piston back into the caliper. If the piston is frozen or if the caliper is leaking hydraulic fluid, the caliper must be overhauled or replaced.

14. Install the caliper assembly to the mounting plate. Before installing the retaining bolts, apply a thin, even coating of anti-seize compound to the threads and slide surfaces. Don't use grease or spray lubricants; they will not hold up under the extreme temperatures generated by the brakes. Tighten the bolts to specification.

15. Remove the 2 lugs holding the disc in place and install the wheel.

16. Lower the vehicle to the ground. Check the level of the brake fluid in the master cylinder reservoir; it should be at least to the middle of the reservoir.

17. Depress the brake pedal several times and make sure the movement feels normal. The first brake pedal application may result in a very "long" pedal due to the pistons being retracted. Always make several brake applications before starting the vehicle. Bleeding is not usually necessary after pad replacement.

18. Recheck the fluid level and add to the MAX line, if necessary.

NOTE: Braking should be moderate for the first 5 miles or so until the new pads seat correctly. The new pads will seat best if put through several moderate heating and cooling cycles. Avoid hard braking until the brakes have experienced several long, slow stops with time to cool in between. Taking the time to properly seat the brakes will yield quieter operation, more efficient stopping and contribute to extended brake life.

Brake Rotor

REMOVAL AND INSTALLATION

FRONT

1. Elevate and safely support the vehicle. If only the front end is supported, set the parking brake and block the rear wheels.
2. Remove the wheel.
3. Remove the brake caliper from its mount and suspend it out of the way. Don't disconnect the hose and don't let the caliper hang by the hose. Remove the brake pads with all the clips, shims, etc.
4. Install all the lug nuts to hold the rotor in place. If the nuts are open at both ends, it is helpful to install them backwards (tapered end out) to secure the disc. Tighten the nuts a bit tighter than finger-tight but make sure all are at approximately the same tightness.
5. Check the run-out and thickness measurements of the rotor.
6. Remove the 2 bolts holding the caliper mounting bracket to the steering knuckle. These bolts will be tight. Remove the 4 lug nuts holding the rotor.
7. Remove the bracket from the knuckle. Before removing the rotor, make a mark on the rotor indexing one wheel stud to one hole in the rotor. This assures the rotor will be reinstalled in its original position, serving to eliminate minor vibrations in the brake system.
   To install:
8. When reinstalling, make certain the rotor is clean and free of any particles of rust or metal from resurfacing. Observe the index mark made earlier and fit the rotor over the wheel lugs. Install 2 lug nuts to hold it in place.
9. Install the caliper mounting bracket in position and tighten the bolts.
10. Install the brake pads and the hardware.
11. Install the caliper. Tighten the mounting bolts.
12. Install the wheel and lower the vehicle to the ground.

REAR

1991-94 PRIZM

1. Raise and safely support the vehicle safely.
2. Remove the rear wheel assemblies.

3. Remove the 2 caliper retaining bolts.
4. Remove the brake caliper from the vehicle. Position the caliper out of the way and support it with wire so it doesn't hang by the brake line.
5. Remove the 2 brake pads, 2 anti-squeal shims and 4 pad guide plates.
6. Remove the rotor assembly.
7. Installation is the reverse order of the removal procedure. Torque the caliper retaining bolts to 14 ft. lbs. (20 Nm).

Brake Drums

REMOVAL AND INSTALLATION

Metro

1. Raise and support the vehicle safely.
2. Remove the tire and wheel assembly.
3. Remove the spindle cap without damaging the sealing portion of the cap.
4. Unfasten the staked portion of the nut using a suitable chisel.
5. Remove the castle nut and washer.
6. Slacken the parking brake cable by loosening its adjusting nuts.
7. Remove the backing plate plug, located on the back side of the backing plate.
8. Insert a suitable tool into the plug until the tip contacts the shoe hold-down and push the spring in the direction of the leading shoe. The allows a greater clearance between the shoes and the drum.
9. Using slide hammer J-2619-01 and drum remover J-34866 or equivalent, remove the drum.
10. Reverse procedure to install.

Prizm and Storm

1. Raise and support the vehicle safely.
2. Remove the tire and wheel assembly.
3. Insert a suitable tool through the hole in the backing plate and hold the automatic adjusting lever away from the adjusting bolt.
4. Using another suitable tool, turn the adjusting bolt to reduce the brake shoe adjustment.
5. Remove the brake drum.
6. Reverse procedure to install. Adjust brakes.

Spectrum

1. Raise and support the vehicle safely.
2. Remove the tire and wheel assembly.
3. Remove the cotter pin, nut and washer, then the hub and drum.
4. Reverse procedure to install.

Brake Shoes

REMOVAL AND INSTALLATION

Prizm and Storm

1. Disconnect the battery negative cable.
2. Raise and support the vehicle safely.
3. Remove the brake drums.
4. Remove the return spring, retainers, hold-down springs and pins.
5. Remove the anchor spring, then disconnect the parking brake cable from the parking brake lever.
6. Remove the adjuster spring, then the shoes and adjuster.
7. Reverse procedure to install. Adjust brakes.

Spectrum

1. Raise and support the vehicle safely.
2. Remove the brake drums.
3. Remove the return spring and the automatic adjuster spring.
4. Remove the leading shoe holding pin, then the shoe and adjuster.
5. Remove the trailing shoe holding pin, then disconnect the parking brake cable from the lever and remove the trailing shoe. Remove the lever from the shoe.
6. Reverse procedure to install. Adjust brakes.

Metro

1. Disconnect the battery negative cable.
2. Raise and support the vehicle safely.
3. Remove the brake drum.
4. Remove the brake shoe hold-down spring, then disconnect the parking brake shoe lever and remove the parking brake shoes.
5. Disconnect the bottom return spring, then remove the strut and upper return spring from the shoe.
6. Remove the parking brake shoe lever from the shoe.
7. Reverse procedure to install. Adjust brakes.

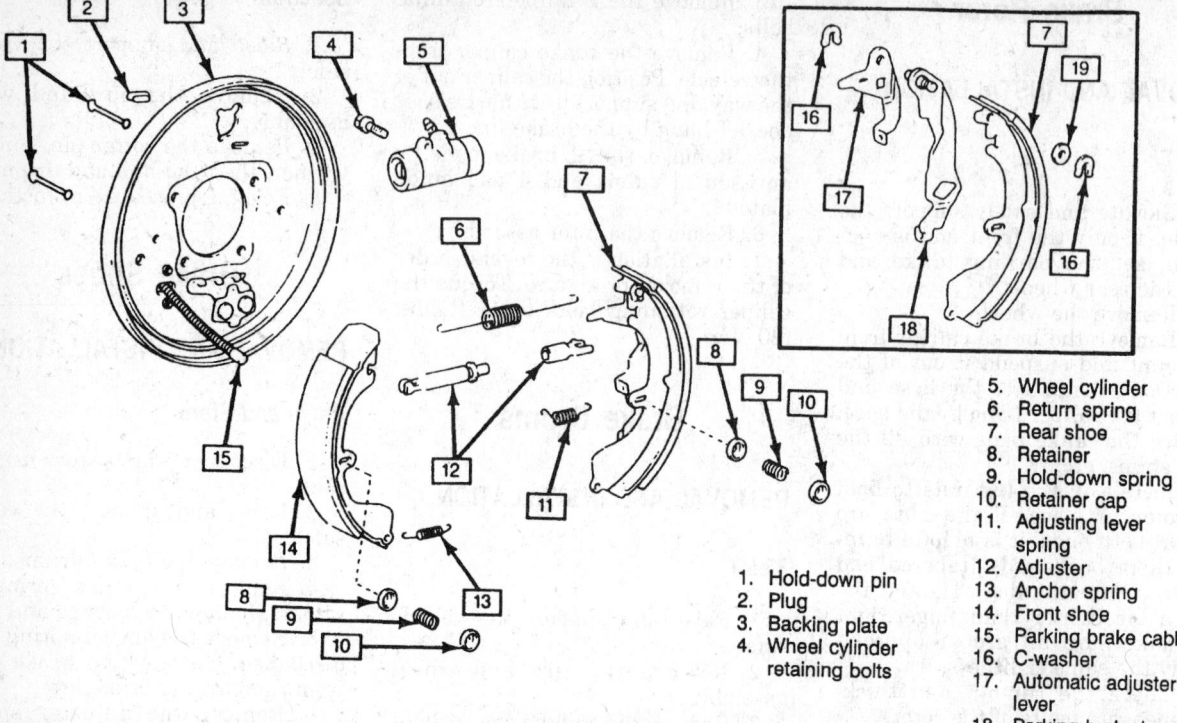

1. Hold-down pin
2. Plug
3. Backing plate
4. Wheel cylinder retaining bolts

5. Wheel cylinder
6. Return spring
7. Rear shoe
8. Retainer
9. Hold-down spring
10. Retainer cap
11. Adjusting lever spring
12. Adjuster
13. Anchor spring
14. Front shoe
15. Parking brake cable
16. C-washer
17. Automatic adjuster lever
18. Parking brake lever
19. Shim

Exploded view of the rear drum brake components — Prizm and Storm

Wheel Cylinder

REMOVAL AND INSTALLATION

Metro

1. Disconnect the battery negative cable.
2. Raise and support the vehicle safely, then remove the tire and wheel assembly.
3. Remove the brake drum and shoes.
4. Remove the bleeder screw from the wheel cylinder.
5. Loosen the brake pipe flarenut, then remove the wheel cylinder attaching bolts. Disconnect the brake pipe from the wheel cylinder. Cap all openings.
6. Reverse procedure to install. Fill the master cylinder with brake fluid and bleed the system.

Prizm and Storm

1. Raise and safely support the rear of the vehicle.
2. Remove the rear tire and wheel assembly.
3. Disconnect and plug the brake line at the wheel cylinder to prevent hydraulic fluid from leaking.
4. Remove the brake drums and shoes.

5. Remove the wheel cylinder-to-backing plate attaching bolts, then the wheel cylinder from the vehicle.
6. Reverse procedure to install. Torque the wheel cylinder-to-backing plate bolts to 7 ft. lbs. (10 Nm). Bleed system and adjust brakes.

Spectrum

1. Disconnect the battery negative cable.
2. Raise and support the vehicle safely.
3. Remove the brake drums and shoes.
4. Clean the area around the brake pipe, then disconnect the brake pipe from the wheel cylinder. Cap all openings.
5. Remove the 2 wheel cylinder attaching bolts, then the wheel cylinder from the vehicle.
6. Reverse procedure to install. Torque the wheel cylinder attaching bolts to 7 ft. lbs. (10 Nm). Bleed system and adjust brakes.

Brake System Bleeding

1. Clean the bleeder screw at each wheel.
2. Start with the wheel farthest from the master cylinder (right rear).

3. Attach a rubber hose to the bleeder screw and place the end in a clear container of brake fluid.
4. Fill the master cylinder with brake fluid. Have an assistant slowly pump up the brake pedal and hold the pressure.
5. Open the bleed screw about ¼ turn, press the brake pedal to the floor, close the bleed screw and slowly release the pedal. Continue until no more air bubbles are forced from the cylinder on application of the brake pedal.
6. Repeat procedure on remaining wheel cylinders and calipers, still working from the cylinder/caliper farthest from the master cylinder.

NOTE: Master cylinders equipped with bleed screws may be bled independently. When bleeding the master cylinder, it is necessary to cap 1 reservoir section while bleeding the other to prevent pressure loss through the cap vent hole.

1993-94 Prizm

The use of pressure bleeding equipment is preferred, although the system may be bled manually if necessary. Before bleeding is begun, the front and rear displacement cylinder pistons must be returned to the top-most position. This should be done with the use of the Tech-1 scan tool or equivalent.

When using the Tech-1, enter the manual control function and apply the front and rear motors. Make certain the enable relay is ON. These operations will move the pistons to the top of their travel.

If the scan tools are not available, the pistons may still be reset. Bleed the front brakes. Start the engine and allow it to run for at least 10 seconds; do not touch the brake pedal during this time. The ABS warning lamp must go OFF after about 3 seconds; if the lamp stays lit, the cause of the problem must be identified and repaired before continuing. The ABS system will initialize itself, returning the pistons to the top position. Switch the engine **OFF** and re-bleed the entire system. If the entire system is to be bled, the calipers must be bled in this order:

1. Right rear
2. Left rear
3. Right front
4. Left front

Pressure Bleeding

The pressure bleeding equipment must be of the diaphragm type, preventing the entry of air, moisture or other contaminants into the brake fluid.

1. Clean the brake fluid reservoir cap before removing it. Fill the reservoir to the correct level with fresh brake fluid.
2. Make certain the pistons have been set to the UP or HOME position. Install the adapter cap J-35589 or equivalent, to the fluid reservoir.
3. Connect the pressure bleeding equipment to the adapter. Charge the pressure bleeder to 30-35 psi.
4. Bleed the modulator assembly first. Connect a transparent tube over the rear bleeder valve on the modulator; submerge the other end in a clean container of brake fluid. Slowly open the bleeder valve about ¾ turn. Allow the fluid to flow until no air is seen in the bleeder hose. Close the bleeder valve and tighten it to 65 inch lbs. (7 Nm).
5. Repeat the bleeding procedure at the front bleeder valve on the modulator.
6. Use the same bleeding procedure at each brake caliper in the proper order. To aid in releasing trapped air, tap lightly on each caliper with a small rubber mallet. Tighten each caliper bleed valve to 8 ft. lbs. (11 Nm).

7. After circuits are bled, remove the pressure bleeding equipment. Refill the reservoir to the correct level and install the cap.
8. Turn the ignition **ON** but do not start the engine. Apply the brake pedal with moderate force and hold. The pedal should feel firm and without excessive travel; if so, start the engine and confirm pedal feel and travel. If still satisfactory, the vehicle may be road tested.
9. If the pedal feel is not correct, use the scan tool to apply and release the pistons 2 or 3 times, leaving them in the UP or HOME position when finished. Rebleed the system and recheck. If still not satisfactory, suspect leaks or mechanical failure in the system.
10. When road testing the vehicle, make several normal stops from moderate speeds.
11. Make 1-2 ABS stops from approximately 50 mph.
12. After testing, it is recommended to bleed the system again and recheck pedal feel and travel. If satisfactory, the vehicle need not be road tested a second time.

Manual Bleeding

1. Clean the brake fluid reservoir cap before removing it. Fill the reservoir to the correct level with fresh brake fluid. The reservoir must be kept at least half-full during the entire bleeding procedure. Reinstall the cap to prevent spillage.
2. Make certain the pistons have been set to the UP or HOME position.
3. Prime the modulator assembly first. Connect a transparent tube over the rear bleeder valve on the modulator; submerge the other end in a clean container of brake fluid. Slowly open the bleeder valve about ¾ turn. Depress the brake pedal and hold until fluid begins to flow. Close the bleeder valve, tighten it to 65 inch lbs. (7 Nm), then release the brake pedal.
4. Repeat the bleeding procedure at the front bleeder valve on the modulator.

NOTE: Once fluid flows from both modulator bleed valves, the master cylinder and modulator are sufficiently full of fluid but may still contain air. At this point, bleed the wheel circuits at the brakes. Return to the modulator and rebleed it after the wheel circuits are bled.

5. Inspect the fluid level in the reservoir, filling as necessary.

6. Use the same bleeding procedure at each brake caliper in the proper order. To aid in releasing trapped air, tap lightly on each caliper with a small rubber mallet. During bleeding, wait at least 5 seconds after the brake pedal is released before reapplying the pedal. Tighten each caliper bleed valve to 8 ft. lbs. (11 Nm).

NOTE: If no fluid flows when bleeding the rear brakes, it may mean that the displacement pistons are not at the UP or HOME position.

7. After circuits are bled, refill the reservoir to the correct level and install the cap.
8. Rebleed the modulator and master brake cylinder.
9. Turn the ignition **ON** but do not start the engine. Apply the brake pedal with moderate force and hold. The pedal should feel firm and without excessive travel; if so, start the engine and confirm pedal feel and travel. If still satisfactory, the vehicle may be road tested.
10. If the pedal feel is not correct, use the scan tool to apply and release the pistons 2-3 times, leaving them in the UP or HOME position when finished. Rebleed the system and recheck. If still not satisfactory, suspect leaks or mechanical failure in the system.
11. When road testing the vehicle, make several normal stops from moderate speeds.
12. Make 1-2 ABS stops from approximately 50 mph.
13. After testing, it is recommended to bleed the entire system again and recheck pedal feel and travel. If satisfactory, the vehicle need not be road tested a second time.

Anti-Lock Brake System Service

SERVICE PRECAUTIONS

1993-94 Prizm

• If equipped with an air bag (SIR) system, always properly disable this system before working on or around its components. Failure to disarm the system may result in unintentional deployment of the air bag, personal injury, property damage and/or additional repairs.
• Certain components within the ABS system are not intended to be serviced or repaired individually. Only those components with removal

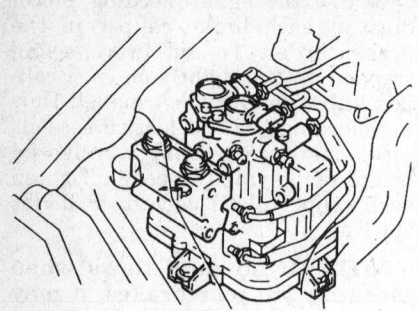

ABS Hydraulic Modulator

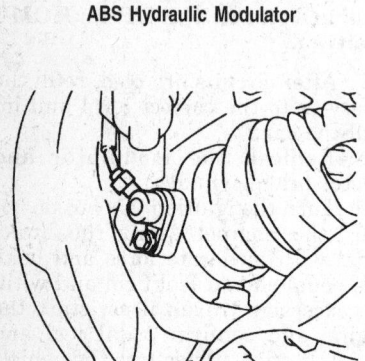

ABS Front Wheel Speed Sensor

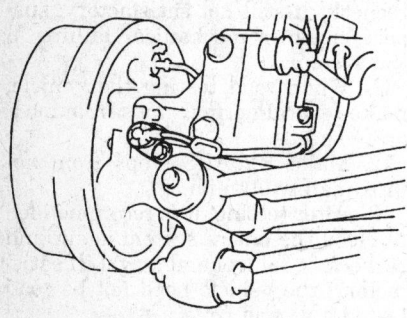

ABS Rear Wheel Speed Sensor

and installation procedures should be serviced.

• Do not use rubber hoses or other parts not specifically specified for the ABS system. When using repair kits, replace all parts included in the kit. Partial or incorrect repair may lead to functional problems and require the replacement of the additional components.

• Lubricate rubber parts with clean, fresh brake fluid to ease assembly. Do not use lubricated shop

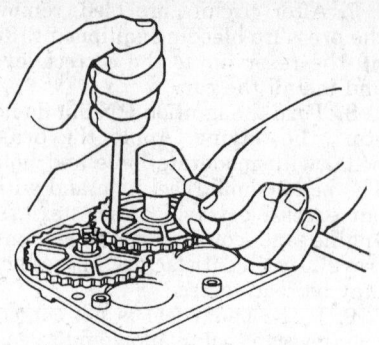

ABS Hydraulic Modulator Gears

air to clean parts; damage to rubber components may result.

• Use only DOT 3 brake fluid from an unopened container. Use of DOT 5 silicone brake fluid is specifically prohibited.

• If any hydraulic component or line is removed or replaced, it may be necessary to bleed the entire system.

• A clean repair area is essential. Perform repairs after components have been thoroughly cleaned; use only denatured alcohol to clean components. Do not allow ABS components to come into contact with any substance containing mineral oil; this includes used shop rags.

• Remove the lock pin before disconnecting CPA connectors.

• The Anti-lock brake controller is a microprocessor similar to other computer units in the vehicle. Insure that the ignition switch is **OFF** before removing or installing controller harnesses. Avoid static electricity discharge at or near the controller.

• Fault codes stored within the system can only be read with a bi-directional scanner such as the GM Tech-1 scanner or equivalent. Some scanners may require an additional cartridge to read the system.

• The brake controller is equipped with on-board diagnostic programs beyond the setting of codes. Not all scanners are capable of using these other features. Consult the scanner manufacturer's manual for directions and capabilities.

RELIEVING ANTI-LOCK BRAKE SYSTEM PRESSURE

The Deco 6 ABS system on the 1993-94 Prizm, is a low pressure system and should require no special depressurization procedures.

System Components

HYDRAULIC MODULATOR ASSEMBLY

―――――― CAUTION ――――――
The ABS modulator pistons are normally in the HOME or TOP position. In this position the modulator drive gears are under spring tension and will turn suddenly during disassembly if not unloaded. The sudden rotation of gears and release of tension may cause injury or damage. If the unit is being removed with intent to disassemble it, the gear tension must be relieved using the Tech-1 or equivalent, to perform the GEAR TENSION RELIEF SEQUENCE. This will run the modulator pistons down and release spring tension.

REMOVAL AND INSTALLATION

1. Remove 6 Torx® screws and gear cover from the hydraulic modulator.
2. Remove 4 Torx® screws and motor pack from the hydraulic modulator.

NOTE: Use caution to ensure that the motor pack connector is not damaged when handling the motor pack. Damage to the connector could cause accidental leaking of brake fluid into the motor pack causing permanent motor pack failure. If the motor pack is dropped or damaged while handling, the motor pack must be replaced.

3. Remove 2 banjo fittings and the proportioning valve from the hydraulic modulator.
4. Remove 2 transfer tubes and O-rings from the proportioning valve or hydraulic modulator.
5. Remove 2 banjo bolts and O-rings from the proportioning valve or hydraulic modulator.

To install:

NOTE: The hydraulic modulator is not serviceable and is replaced as a unit. If the hydraulic modulator is replaced, install the 3 gears in the same location on the replacement modulator. Use new transfer tubes when assembling the proportioning valve to the hydraulic modulator. Be certain 2 new O-rings are properly installed on each transfer tube.

6. Lubricate the new transfer tube O-rings with clean brake fluid.

7. Install the transfer tubes into the ports of the hydraulic modulator, seating the tubes by hand.

8. Lubricate the new banjo bolt O-rings with clean brake fluid and install the banjo bolts into the hydraulic modulator and proportioning valve.

9. Connect the proportioning valve to the hydraulic modulator by:

a. Gently rock the hydraulic modulator into position on the proportioning valve, inserting the transfer tubes into the proportioning valve ports.

b. Secure the proportioning valve to the hydraulic modulator with 2 banjo bolts.

c. Torque the banjo bolts to 17 ft. lbs. (24 Nm).

10. Hold the hydraulic modulator upside down or gears facing up and rotate each gear counterclockwise until each gear stops. This positions the pistons near the top of their bores, making bleeding easier.

11. Align the 3 motor pack gears with the 3 modulator gears while installing the motor pack into the hydraulic modulator.

12. Install the 4 Torx® screws and tighten to 40 inch lbs. (4.5 Nm).

13. Install the gear cover to the hydraulic modulator with the 6 Torx® screws and tighten to 35 inch lbs. (4 Nm).

Gear

REMOVAL AND INSTALLATION

1. Remove 6 Torx® screws and gear cover from the hydraulic modulator.

2. Remove 4 Torx® screws and motor pack from the hydraulic modulator.

NOTE: Use caution when removing and installing the gears. Place the modulator pistons in the center of their travel. Keep the pistons in position by placing a suitable prybar through the holes in the gears and into the recessed hole in the modulator base.

3. Remove 3 bolts and gears from the hydraulic modulator.

To install:

4. Install the 3 gears and bolts to the hydraulic modulator and torque the nuts to 76 inch lbs. (8.5 Nm).

5. Align the 3 motor pack gears with the 3 modulator gears while in-

stalling the motor pack into the hydraulic modulator.

6. Install the 4 Torx® screws and tighten to 40 inch lbs. (4.5 Nm).

7. Install the gear cover to the hydraulic modulator with the 6 Torx® screws and tighten to 35 inch lbs. (4 Nm).

Electronic Brake Control Module (EBCM)

REMOVAL AND INSTALLATION

1. Disconnect the negative battery cable.

2. Loosen the carpet from under the right side of the dash. Pull the carpet back to expose the EBCM cover panel.

3. Remove 4 nuts and the EBCM panel from the floor.

4. Disconnect the EBCM connectors and remove the EBCM from the vehicle.

To install:

5. Install the EBCM into vehicle and connect the connectors.

6. Install the EBCM cover panel with 4 nuts.

7. Replace the floor carpet.

8. Connect the negative battery cable.

Front Wheel Speed Sensor

The front wheel speed sensor is not a serviceable component and is replaced as a unit.

REMOVAL AND INSTALLATION

1. Disconnect the negative battery cable.

2. Raise and safely support the vehicle.

3. Remove the wheelhouse from the front wheelwell.

4. Disconnect the front wheel speed sensor connector.

5. Remove the 3 bolts attaching the front wheel speed sensor harness to the body and front strut assembly.

6. Remove 1 bolt and front wheel speed sensor from front steering knuckle.

To install:

7. Install the front wheel sensor to the front steering knuckle and torque the bolt to 69 inch lbs. (7.8 Nm).

8. Secure the front wheel speed sensor harness to the body and front strut assembly and torque the 3 bolts to 48 inch lbs. (5.4 Nm).

9. Connect the front wheel speed sensor.

10. Install the wheelhouse to the wheelwell.

11. Lower the vehicle and connect the negative battery cable.

Rear Wheel Speed Sensors

The rear wheel speed sensor is not a serviceable component and is replaced as a unit.

REMOVAL AND INSTALLATION

1. Disconnect the negative battery cable.

2. Remove the rear seat cushion and inner side trim panel.

3. Disconnect the rear speed sensor harness.

4. Raise and safely support the vehicle.

5. Pull the rear wheel speed sensor harness and grommet out through the body.

6. Remove the 3 bolts attaching the rear wheel speed sensor harness to the body and rear strut assembly.

7. Remove 1 bolt and rear wheel speed sensor from rear suspension knuckle.

To install:

8. Install the rear wheel sensor to the rear suspension knuckle and torque the bolt to 69 inch lbs. (7.8 Nm).

9. Secure the rear wheel speed sensor harness to the body and rear strut assembly and torque the 3 bolts to 48 inch lbs. (5.4 Nm).

10. Pull the rear wheel speed sensor harness and grommet back in through the body

11. Lower the vehicle and connect the rear wheel speed sensor harness.

12. Install the rear inner side panel and connect the negative battery cable.

ABS Lamp Driver Module

The lamp driver module is located on the instrument panel harness attached to the back of the instrument panel.

REMOVAL AND INSTALLATION

1. Remove the negative battery cable.

2. Remove the instrument panel.

3. Disconnect the lamp driver connector and remove the lamp driver module from the instrument panel harness.

4. To install, reverse the removal procedures.

Enable Relay

The enable relay is located under the hood on the right side wheel apron.

REMOVAL AND INSTALLATION

1. Disconnect the negative battery cable.
2. Remove 1 bolt and enable relay from the wheel apron.
3. Disconnect and remove the enable relay from the vehicle.
4. To install, reverse the removal procedures.

CHASSIS ELECTRICAL

Air Bag

DISARMING

Metro

1. If equipped, with an air bag system, disable the air bag system as follows:
    a. Position the vehicles front wheels to point straight ahead.
    b. Turn the ignition switch to the **OFF** position.
    c. Remove the **SIR IG** fuse in the supplemental inflatable restraint fuse block.
    d. Remove the rear plastic access cover to the air bag module.
    e. Disconnect the yellow 2-way connector and Connector Position Assurance (CPA) inside the inflator module housing.
2. Disconnect the negative battery cable.
3. Reactivate the air bag system as follows:
    a. Turn the ignition switch to the **OFF** position.
    b. Connect the yellow 2-way connector and Connector Position Assurance (CPA) inside the inflator module housing.
    c. Install the **SIR IG** fuse in the supplemental inflatable restraint fuse block.
    d. Install the rear plastic access cover to the air bag module.
    e. Turn the ignition switch to the **RUN** position. Observe the **INFLATABLE RESTRAINT** indicator lamp. If the lamp does not

flash 7-9 times and then remain OFF, there is a problem in the air bag system and further diagnostic testing of the system is needed.

1993ndash;94 Prizm

1. If equipped, with an air bag system, disable the air bag system as follows:
    a. Position the vehicles front wheels to point straight ahead.
    b. Turn the ignition switch to the **LOCK** position.
    c. Remove the IGN and CIG & RADIO fuses from the fuse block.
    d. Remove the Connector Position Assurance (CPA).
    e. Disconnect the lower steering column connector.
2. Disconnect the negative battery cable.
3. Reactivate the air bag system as follows:
    a. Turn the ignition switch to the **LOCK** position.
    b. Connect the lower steering column connector.
    c. Secure the lower steering column connector with Connector Position Assurance (CPA).
    d. Install the IGN and CIG & RADIO fuses.
    e. Turn the ignition switch to the **ACC** or **ON** position.
    f. Observe the **INFLATABLE RESTRAINT** indicator lamp. If the lamp does not illuminate for approximately 60 seconds and turn OFF, there is a problem in the air bag system and further diagnostic testing of the system is needed.

Storm

1. Disable the air bag system as follows:
    a. Turn the ignition switch to the **OFF** position.
    b. Disconnect the battery negative cable.
    c. Remove fuses C-22 and C-23 from the fuse box.
    d. Disconnect the orange 3-way connector at the base of the steering column.
2. Reactivate the air bag system as follows:
    a. Turn the ignition switch to the **OFF** position.
    b. Connect the orange 3-way connector at the base of the steering column.
    c. Install fuses C-22 and C-23 to the fuse box.
    d. Connect the battery negative cable.

Heater Blower Motor

REMOVAL AND INSTALLATION

Metro

1. Disconnect the negative battery cable.
2. Remove the 2 attaching screws from the glove box striker and remove the striker.
3. Remove the 1 attaching screw from the rear of the glove box upper panel and remove the panel.
4. Remove the blower motor and blower resistor electrical connections.
5. Remove the fresh/recirculate control cable from the blower case assembly.
6. Remove the 3 blower case mounting bolts and case from the vehicle.
7. Remove the air hose from the blower case. Remove the 3 blower motor mounting screws and remove the blower motor from the case.
8. Installation is the reverse order of the removal procedure.

Prizm

1. Disconnect the negative battery cable.
2. Remove the rubber duct running between the heater case and the blower.
3. Disconnect the wiring from the motor.
4. Remove the 3 screws holding the motor and remove the blower motor.
5. With the blower removed, check the case for any debris or signs of fan contact. Inspect the fan for wear spots, cracked blades or hub, loose retaining nut or poor alignment.
6. To reinstall, place the blower in position, making sure it is properly aligned within the case. Install the 3 screws and tighten them.
7. Connect the wiring to the motor.
8. Install the rubber air duct and connect the negative battery cable.

Storm

The blower motor is located under the instrument panel at the far right side of the vehicle. It is accessible from below the instrument panel.
1. Disconnect the negative battery cable.
2. Disconnect the rubber air duct between the motor and the heater assembly.
3. Disconnect the electrical connector from the motor.

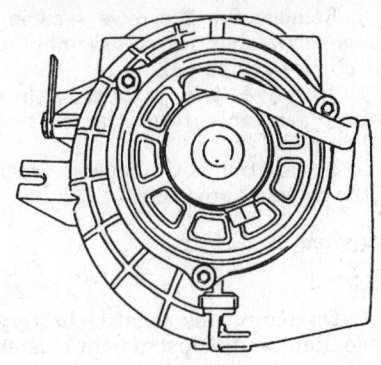

Blower motor mounting — Metro

4. Remove the 4 screws retaining the motor and remove the motor.

5. Installation is the reverse of removal.

Spectrum

1. Disconnect the negative battery cable. Disconnect the blower motor electrical connector at the motor case.

2. If equipped with air conditioning, remove the rubber hose from the blower case.

3. Rotate the blower motor case counterclockwise and remove the blower motor assembly.

4. To install, reverse the removal procedures.

Windshield Wiper Motor

REMOVAL AND INSTALLATION

Metro

FRONT

1. Disconnect the negative battery cable.

2. Remove the wiper motor retaining bolts.

NOTE: On 1992-94 vehicles, the front and rear wiper motor crank arms are not serviced separately and should not be disconnected from the wiper motor. At this point, gently pry the wiper linkage from the wiper motor crank arm. For other vehicles, proceed with the next steps.

3. Disconnect the crank arm from the wiper motor.

4. Remove the wiper motor from the vehicle.

5. To install, reverse the removal procedures.

REAR

1. Disconnect the negative battery cable.

2. Remove the right and left speakers from the hatchback door inner trim panel, if equipped.

3. Remove the retaining clips and hatchback door inner trim panel from the vehicle.

4. Remove the wiper motor electrical connector and wiper motor ground screw.

5. Remove the wiper cranking arm retaining nut from the wiper motor shaft.

6. Remove the 3 wiper motor mounting screws and the wiper motor assembly from the vehicle.

7. Installation is the reverse order of the removal procedure.

Prizm

FRONT

1. Disconnect the negative battery terminal.

2. Disconnect the electrical connector from the wiper motor.

3. Remove the mounting bolts and remove the motor from the firewall.

4. Remove the wiper linkage from the wiper motor assembly.

5. Installation is the reverse of removal.

REAR

The rear wiper motor is located in the rear hatch.

1. Disconnect the negative terminal from the battery.

A. Blower case upper insulator
B. Blower case (upper half)
C. Air mix door
D. Blower case (lower half)
E. Sub-lever
F. Door lever
1. Blower motor case
2. Blower motor fan and blower motor

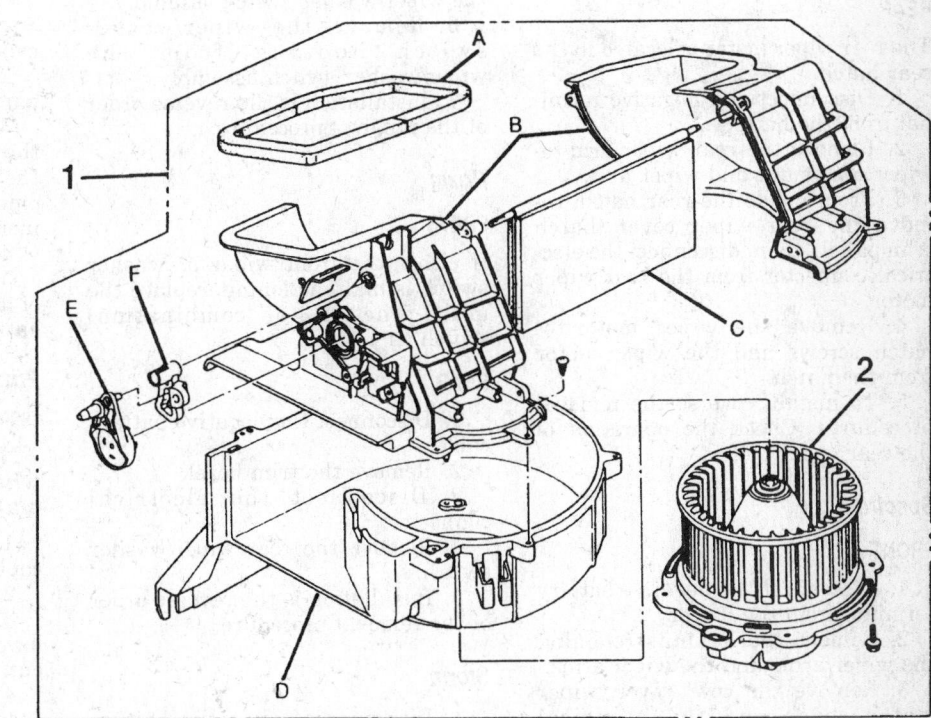

Blower motor assembly — Storm

2. Remove the rear wiper arm-to-wiper motor nut and wiper arm.

3. From inside the rear hatch, remove the rear wiper cover, then, disconnect the electrical connector from the rear wiper motor.

4. Remove the wiper motor-to-hatch screws and the wiper motor from the hatch.

5. To install, reverse the removal procedures. Check the operation of the rear wiper motor.

Storm

FRONT

1. Disconnect the negative terminal from the battery.

2. Remove the cowl vent grille. From the engine compartment, disconnect the electrical connector from the windshield wiper motor.

3. Disconnect the wiper motor from the windshield wiper crank arm; be careful not to bend the linkage.

4. Remove the 2 retaining bolts from the charcoal canister mounting bracket, allowing the canister to slip down and provide access to the wiper motor mounting bolts.

5. Remove the wiper motor-to-chassis screws.

6. To install, reverse the removal procedures. Check the operation of the front windshield wiper motor.

REAR

The rear wiper motor is located in the rear hatch.

1. Disconnect the negative terminal from the battery.

2. Remove the rear wiper arm-to-wiper motor nut and wiper arm.

3. From inside the rear hatch, remove the rear wiper cover (hatch trim panel), then, disconnect the electrical connector from the rear wiper motor.

4. Remove the wiper motor-to-hatch screws and the wiper motor from the hatch.

5. To install, reverse the removal procedures. Check the operation of the rear wiper motor.

Spectrum

FRONT

1. Disconnect the negative battery terminal from the battery.

2. Remove the locknuts retaining the wiper arms and the wiper arms.

3. Remove the cowl cover, wiper motor cover and the electrical connector.

4. Disconnect the drive arm from the wiper link.

5. Remove the mounting bolts and the wiper motor.

6. To install, reverse the removal procedures.

REAR

1. Disconnect the negative battery terminal from the battery.

2. Remove the trim pad and the wiper arm assemblies.

3. Remove the mounting bolts and the motor assembly.

4. Disconnect the electrical connector.

5. To install, reverse the removal procedures.

Windshield Wiper Switch

REMOVAL AND INSTALLATION

Metro

1. Disconnect the negative battery cable.

2. Remove the cluster switch panel.

3. Remove the 2 screws securing the wiper/washer switch assembly to the cluster switch panel.

4. Remove the wiper/washer switch assembly from the cluster switch panel.

5. Remove the 2 screws securing the wiper/washer switch housing to the wiper/washer switch assembly.

6. Remove the wiper/washer switch housing from the wiper/washer switch assembly.

7. Installation is the reverse order of the removal procedure.

Prizm

FRONT

If either the front wiper or washer switch is malfunctioning, replace the multi-function (or combination) switch as a unit.

REAR

1. Disconnect the negative battery cable.

2. Remove the trim bezel.

3. Disconnect the electrical connector.

4. Remove the rear wiper/washer switch.

5. Installation is the reverse order of the removal procedure.

Storm

1. Disconnect the negative battery cable.

2. Remove the cluster switch panel.

3. Remove the 2 screws securing the wiper/washer switch assembly to the cluster switch panel.

4. Remove the wiper/washer switch assembly from the cluster switch panel.

5. Installation is the reverse order of the removal procedure.

Spectrum

FRONT

1. Disconnect the negative battery cable. Remove the instrument cluster bezel.

2. Remove the wiper switch electrical connector, attaching nuts and bracket.

3. Remove the wiper switch.

4. To install, reverse the removal procedures.

REAR

1. Disconnect the negative battery cable. Using a small tool, pry the switch panel from the dash.

2. Pull the switch out and disconnect the electrical connector.

3. To install, reverse the removal procedures.

Instrument Cluster

REMOVAL AND INSTALLATION

Metro

1. Disconnect battery negative cable.

2. Remove the cluster switch panel.

3. Remove the 4 screws securing the instrument cluster. Disconnect the electrical connectors and speedometer from the back of the instrument cluster.

4. Remove the cluster assembly.

5. Installation is the reverse order of the removal procedure. Connect battery negative cable.

Prizm

1990-92

NOTE: Removing the steering wheel is not required but may make the job easier.

1. Disconnect the negative battery cable.

2. Remove the hood release lever.

3. Remove the 4 screws from the lower left dash trim and pull the trim out.

4. Disconnect the wiring from the radio speaker.

5. If equipped with air conditioning, remove the duct work from the lower air outlet.

6. Remove the trim panel from the vehicle.

7. Remove the upper and lower steering column covers.

8. Remove the 2 screws from the trim panel (bezel).

9. Pull the panel out, releasing the spring clips behind the dash. With the panel loose, disconnect the wiring to the dash switches.

10. Remove the switches from the panel.

11. Remove the 2 electrical connectors and the cigarette lighter from the trim bezel and remove the bezel from the vehicle.

12. Remove the 4 screws holding the instrument cluster trim.

13. Disconnect the wiring from the hazard (4-way) flasher and dimmer switches.

14. Remove the cluster trim panel.

15. Remove the 4 attaching screws holding the cluster, move it away from the dash and disconnect the wiring harnesses and the speedometer cable.

16. Remove the instrument cluster from the vehicle.

To install:

17. When reinstalling, connect the speedometer and electrical cables to the cluster. Install the cluster and the 4 retaining screws.

18. Attach the wiring connectors for the hazard flasher and the dimmer switches.

19. Install the cluster trim bezel.

20. Place the dash switches in place on the lower trim bezel and connect the wiring to the switches.

21. Install the lower trim bezel, making sure all the clips engage.

22. Install the steering column upper and lower covers.

23. Connect the air conditioning duct work to the lower air outlet, if equipped.

24. Attach the wiring to the radio speaker.

25. Install the lower left dashboard trim panel and its 4 screws.

26. Install the hood release lever.

27. Connect the negative battery cable.

1993-94

1. Disconnect the negative battery cable.

2. Remove 2 screws and instrument cluster trim panel, while disengaging the 2 lower clips.

3. Remove 4 screws and the instrument cluster assembly.

4. Disconnect the 3 electrical connectors.

5. Remove 2 screws and 7 clips which secure the instrument cluster bezel with lens to the instrument cluster housing.

6. Remove the instrument cluster bezel with lens.

7. Remove 4 screws and speedometer.

─────── **WARNING** ───────
Removal of the speedometer needle is not recommended. The speedometer shaft has no flats or detents for correct replacement of the speedometer needle.
───────────────────────

To install:

8. Install the speedometer and 4 screws into the instrument cluster.

9. Pressing firmly, install the instrument cluster bezel with lens. When all 7 clips are engaged, install 2 screws.

10. Connect 3 electrical connectors.

11. Install the instrument cluster assembly into the instrument panel and install 4 screws,

12. While engaging the 2 lower clips, install the instrument cluster trim panel and 2 screws. Connect the negative battery terminal.

Storm

1. Disconnect battery negative cable.

2. Remove the cluster switch panel.

3. Remove the 4 screws securing the instrument cluster. Disconnect the electrical connectors and speedometer from the back of the instrument cluster.

4. Remove the cluster assembly.

5. Installation is the reverse order of the removal procedure. Connect battery negative cable.

Spectrum

1. Disconnect the negative battery terminal.

2. Remove the instrument cluster bezel retaining screws and bezel.

3. Disconnect the windshield wiper and lighting switch connectors.

4. Remove the instrument cluster retaining screws and pull out the assembly.

5. Remove the trip reset knob and the assembly glass.

6. Remove the buzzer, sockets and bulbs.

7. Remove the speedometer assembly, fuel and temperature gauge.

8. Remove the tachometer, if equipped.

9. To install, reverse the removal procedures.

Speedometer

REMOVAL AND INSTALLATION

1. Disconnect the negative battery cable.

2. Remove the instrument cluster from the instrument panel.

3. Remove the cluster lens and retainer from the cluster.

4. Remove the speedometer retaining screws from the rear of the cluster.

5. Remove the speedometer/odometer from the cluster.

6. Installation is the reverse order of the removal procedure. Connect battery negative cable.

Concealed Headlights

MANUAL OPERATION

1990-91 Storm

The headlight door actuator motor is located behind the center of the grille. If the actuator motor should fail with the head lights closed, the covers can be manually opened using a knob on the bottom of the actuator motor.

Headlight Switch

REMOVAL AND INSTALLATION

1990-91 Metro

1. Disconnect the negative battery cable.

2. Remove the instrument cluster switch panel.

3. Remove the 2 screws securing the light switch assembly to the cluster switch panel.

4. Remove the light switch assembly from the cluster switch panel.

5. Remove the 2 screws securing the light switch housing to the light switch assembly.

6. Remove the light switch housing from the light switch assembly.

7. To install, reverse the removal procedures.

Storm

The headlight control switch is located at the left hand side of the instrument panel on the meter hood.

1. Disconnect the battery negative cable.

2. Remove the meter hood.

3. Remove the instrument cluster from the meter hood.

4. Remove the 2 clips attaching headlight control harness.

5. Remove the 4 screws attaching the headlight switch to the meter hood.

6. Disconnect electrical connectors from the switch and remove the switch.

7. Reverse procedure to install. Connect battery negative cable.

Spectrum

The headlight control switch is a 3 position, push type switch which is located at the left side of the instrument panel.

1. Disconnect the negative battery cable. Remove the instrument cluster bezel retaining screw and the bezel.

2. Disconnect the electrical connectors.

3. Place the bezel on a bench and remove the 2 nuts securing the headlight control switch.

4. Remove the headlight control switch.

5. To install, reverse the removal procedures.

Combination Switch

REMOVAL AND INSTALLATION

Metro

1. Place the ignition switch in the **LOCK** position. If equipped, with an air bag system, disable the air bag system as follows:

a. Turn the ignition switch to the **OFF** position.

b. Remove the **SIR IG** fuse in the supplemental inflatable restraint fuse block.

c. Remove the rear plastic access cover to the air bag module.

d. Disconnect the yellow 2-way connector and Connector Position Assurance (CPA) inside the inflator module housing.

2. Disconnect the negative battery cable.

3. Remove the 6 screws retaining upper and lower column covers.

4. Remove the steering column covers from the steering cover.

5. Remove the 4 electrical connectors, 2 from the fuse block, 1 from the air bag wire harness and 1 from the main wire harness.

6. Remove the 4 screws retaining the air bag coil and turn signal/dimmer switch assembly.

7. Remove the switch assembly from the steering column.

NOTE: The coil assembly will become uncentered if the steering column is separated from the steering gear and it is allowed to rotate.

To install:

8. Installation is the reverse order of the removal procedure.

9. Reactivate the air bag system as follows:

a. Turn the ignition switch to the **OFF** position.

b. Connect the yellow 2-way connector and Connector Position Assurance (CPA) inside the inflator module housing.

c. Install the **SIR IG** fuse in the supplemental inflatable restraint fuse block.

d. Install the rear plastic access cover to the air bag module.

e. Turn the ignition switch to the **RUN** position. Observe the **INFLATABLE RESTRAINT** indicator lamp. If the lamp does not flash 7-9 times and then remain OFF, there is a problem in the air bag system and further diagnostic testing of the system is needed.

Prizm

1990-92

1. Disconnect the negative battery cable. Remove the steering wheel.

2. Remove the lower left side instrument finish panel.

3. Remove the upper and lower steering column covers.

4. Disconnect the combination switch connector.

5. Disconnect the 4 bolts holding the combination switch and remove the switch from the vehicle.

6. To install, reverse the removal procedures.

1993-94

1. If equipped, with an air bag system, disable the air bag system as follows:

a. Position the vehicles front wheels to point straight ahead.

b. Turn the ignition switch to the **LOCK** position.

c. Remove the IGN and CIG & RADIO fuses from the fuse block.

d. Remove the Connector Position Assurance (CPA).

e. Disconnect the lower steering column connector.

2. Disconnect the negative battery cable.

3. With the air bag system disabled, remove the air bag inflator module as follows:

a. Remove the 2 side covers from the steering column.

b. Remove the 2 Torx® head screws.

c. Remove the Connector Position Assurance (CPA) and disconnect the upper steering column connector.

d. Remove the inflator module from the steering wheel.

--- CAUTION ---

When carrying a live inflator module, keep the air bag and trim cover pointed away from you. Never carry the inflator module by the wires or connector on the underside of the module. When placing a live inflator module on a work bench or other surface, always face the bag and trim cover up. Never rest a steering column assembly on the steering wheel with the inflator module face down and column vertical. This is to allow free space for the air bag to expand in the unlikely event of accidental deployment.

4. With the inflator module removed, remove the horn connector.

5. Remove the steering wheel nut and mark the position of the steering wheel relative to the steering shaft.

6. Remove the steering wheel.

7. Remove the upper and lower column covers.

8. Remove and set aside the left front carpet retainer.

9. Remove 2 screws and disconnect the hood release lever from the knee bolster.

10. Remove 2 trim caps, unbolt and remove the knee bolster from the instrument panel.

11. Untape the SRS coil harness from the combination switch harness and disconnect the SRS coil harness from the SRS coil.

12. Remove 4 screws and the SRS coil assembly from the combination switch.

13. Disconnect the combination switch connector.

14. Remove 4 screws and combination switch from the steering column.

To install:

15. Install combination switch to the steering column with 4 mounting screws.

16. Connect the combination switch connector.

17. Center the SRS coil assembly as follows:

    a. Make sure the front wheels of the vehicle are positioned straight-ahead.

    b. Turn the SRS coil counter-clockwise by hand until it becomes harder to turn the cable.

    c. Turn the SRS coil clockwise approximately 3 turns to align the red mark.

18. Install the SRS coil to the combination switch with 4 mounting screws.

19. Connect the SRS coil harness to the SRS coil and tape the SRS coil harness to the combination switch harness.

20. Install the knee bolster with 4 bolts.

21. Install the left front carpet and retainer.

22. Install the upper and lower column covers with 2 screws.

23. Install the steering wheel, aligning the matchmarks made during removal.

24. Install the steering wheel nut and torque to 25 ft. lbs. (34 Nm).

25. Connect the horn connector.

26. Install the air bag inflator module.

27. Connect the upper steering column connector and secure with CPA.

28. Install the 2 Torx® head screws.

29. Install the 2 steering column side covers.

30. Reactivate the air bag system as follows:

    a. Turn the ignition switch to the **LOCK** position.

    b. Connect the lower steering column connector.

    c. Secure the lower steering column connector with Connector Position Assurance (CPA).

    d. Install the IGN and CIG & RADIO fuses.

    e. Turn the ignition switch to the **ACC** or **ON** position.

    f. Observe the **INFLATABLE RESTRAINT** indicator lamp. If the lamp does not illuminate for approximately 60 seconds and turn OFF, there is a problem in the air bag system and further diagnostic testing of the system is needed.

Spectrum

1. Disconnect the negative battery terminal from the battery.

2. Remove the horn shroud, steering wheel nut/washer and steering wheel assembly.

3. Remove the steering cowl attaching screw and steering cowl.

4. Disconnect the combination/starter switch connector.

5. Remove the turnsignal/dimmer switch attaching screw and switch.

6. To install, reverse the removal procedures.

Storm

1. Disable the air bag system as follows:

    a. Set the front wheels to a straight-ahead position and turn the ignition switch to the **OFF** position.

    b. Disconnect the battery negative cable.

    c. Remove fuses C-22 and C-23 from the fuse box.

    d. Disconnect the orange 3-way connector at the base of the steering column.

2. Remove the 4 bolts attaching the inflator module to the steering wheel. Disconnect the inflator module electrical connector.

3. Disconnect the electrical connector from the horn.

4. Remove the steering wheel nut and the steering wheel.

5. Remove the steering wheel cowl assembly and harness.

6. Remove the combination switch attaching screws, disconnect electrical connectors and the combination switch from the vehicle.

7. Reverse procedure to install. Reactivate the air bag system as follows:

    a. Turn the ignition switch to the **OFF** position.

    b. Connect the orange 3-way connector at the base of the steering column.

    c. Install fuses C-22 and C-23 to the fuse box.

    d. Connect the battery negative cable.

Ignition Lock/Switch

REMOVAL AND INSTALLATION

Metro

1. Place the ignition switch in the **LOCK** position. If equipped, with an air bag system, disable the air bag system as follows:

    a. Turn the ignition switch to the **OFF** position.

    b. Remove the **SIR IG** fuse in the supplemental inflatable restraint fuse block.

    c. Remove the rear plastic access cover to the air bag module.

    d. Disconnect the yellow 2-way connector and Connector Position Assurance (CPA) inside the inflator module housing.

2. Disconnect the negative battery cable.

3. Remove the 6 screws retaining upper and lower column covers.

4. Remove the steering column covers from the steering cover.

5. Remove the 4 electrical connectors, 2 from the fuse block, 1 from the air bag wire harness and 1 from the main wire harness.

6. Remove the 4 screws retaining the air bag coil and turn-signal/dimmer switch assembly.

NOTE: The coil assembly will become uncentered if the steering column is separated from the steering gear and it is allowed to rotate.

7. Remove the 1 screw and ignition switch assembly from the steering column. Remove the 2 screws and ignition key warning switch from the steering column.

8. Pull the ignition switch harness free from the instrument panel and remove it from the vehicle.

9. Installation is the reverse order of the removal procedure.

10. Reactivate the air bag system as follows:

    a. Turn the ignition switch to the **OFF** position.

    b. Connect the yellow 2-way connector and Connector Position Assurance (CPA) inside the inflator module housing.

    c. Install the **SIR IG** fuse in the supplemental inflatable restraint fuse block.

    d. Install the rear plastic access cover to the air bag module.

    e. Turn the ignition switch to the **RUN** position. Observe the **INFLATABLE RESTRAINT** indicator lamp. If the lamp does not flash 7-9 times and then remain OFF, there is a problem in the air bag system and further diagnostic testing of the system is needed.

Prizm

1990-92

1. Disconnect the negative battery cable. Remove the combination switch.

2. If equipped with a tilt steering column, perform the following procedures:

    a. Remove the tension springs and grommets, the tilt lever screw (left hand thread), the adjusting nut/washer and tilt lever.

    b. Pull out the lock bolt, then, remove the upper and lower column supports.

3. From the lower steering column, disconnect the ignition switch electrical connector.

4. Remove the retainer-to-upper bracket screws and the retainer from the upper bracket.

5. Using snapring pliers, remove the snapring from the upper bracket.

6. Insert the key into the ignition switch and release the steering lock.

7. Using a hammer and a pin punch, drive the tapered bolt from the upper bracket.

8. Remove the upper bracket-to-steering column tube bolts and the upper bracket.

To install:

9. Release the steering lock and install the upper bracket-to steering column bolts, tighten the bolts finger-tight. Torque the upper bracket-to-steering column bolts to 14 ft. lbs. (19 Nm).

10. If installing the tilt steering mechanism, perform the following procedures:

a. Apply grease to the bushings and the O-rings, then, install the lower support-to-tube.

b. Using multi-purpose grease, apply it to the tilt bracket-to-steering column mating surfaces, then, install the upper support and lock bolt.

NOTE: If there is any play in the adjusting support, snug-up the adjusting nut.

c. Install the tilt lever. Move the lever to loosen the bracket-to-column bolt, adjust the column height and move the lever to lock the column position; if the lever is out of position, reposition the adjusting nut.

d. Install the tilt lever retaining screw (left hand thread) and torque it. Install the tension springs and grommets.

11. To complete the installation, reverse the removal procedures.

1993-94

1. If equipped, with an air bag system, disable the air bag system as follows:

a. Position the vehicles front wheels to point straight ahead.

b. Turn the ignition switch to the **LOCK** position.

c. Remove the IGN and CIG & RADIO fuses from the fuse block.

d. Remove the Connector Position Assurance (CPA).

e. Disconnect the lower steering column connector.

2. Disconnect the negative battery cable.

3. Remove the 2 side covers from the steering column.

4. Remove the upper and lower column covers.

5. Remove and set aside the left front carpet retainer. Remove 2 screws and disconnect the hood release lever from the knee bolster.

6. Remove 2 trim caps, unbolt and remove the knee bolster from the instrument panel.

7. With the air bag system disabled, remove the air bag inflator module as follows:

a. Remove the 2 Torx® head screws.

b. Remove the Connector Position Assurance (CPA) and disconnect the upper steering column connector.

c. Remove the inflator module from the steering wheel.

CAUTION

When carrying a live inflator module, keep the air bag and trim cover pointed away from you. Never carry the inflator module by the wires or connector on the underside of the module. When placing a live inflator module on a work bench or other surface, always face the bag and trim cover up. Never rest a steering column assembly on the steering wheel with the inflator module face down and column vertical. This is to allow free space for the air bag to expand in the unlikely event of accidental deployment.

8. With the inflator module removed, remove the horn connector.

9. Remove the steering wheel nut and mark the position of the steering wheel relative to the steering shaft.

10. Untape the SRS coil harness from the combination switch harness and disconnect the SRS coil harness from the SRS coil.

11. Remove 4 screws and the SRS coil assembly from the combination switch.

12. Disconnect the combination switch connector.

13. Remove 4 screws and combination switch from the steering column.

14. If equipped with a tilt steering column, perform the following procedures:

a. Remove the tension springs and grommets, the tilt lever (the bolt has left hand threads), the adjusting nut/washer.

b. Pull out the lock bolt, then, remove the upper and lower column supports.

15. From the lower steering column, disconnect the ignition switch electrical connector.

16. Remove the retainer-to-upper bracket screws and the retainer from the upper bracket.

17. Using snapring pliers, remove the snapring from the upper bracket.

18. Insert the key into the ignition switch and release the steering lock.

19. Using a hammer and a pin punch, drive the tapered bolt from the upper bracket.

20. Remove the upper bracket-to-steering column tube bolts and the upper bracket.

To install:

21. Release the steering lock and install the upper bracket-to steering column bolts, tighten the bolts finger-tight. Torque the upper bracket-to-steering column bolts to 14 ft. lbs. (19 Nm).

22. If installing the tilt steering mechanism, perform the following procedures:

a. Apply grease to the bushings and the O-rings, then, install the lower support-to-tube.

b. Using multi-purpose grease, apply it to the tilt bracket-to-steering column mating surfaces, then, install the upper support and lock bolt.

NOTE: If there is any play in the adjusting support, snug-up the adjusting nut.

c. Install the tilt lever. Move the lever to loosen the bracket-to-column bolt, adjust the column height and move the lever to lock the column position; if the lever is out of position, reposition the adjusting nut.

d. Install the tilt lever retaining screw (left hand thread) and torque it.

e. Install the tension springs and grommets.

23. Install combination switch to the steering column with 4 mounting screws.

24. Connect the combination switch connector.

25. Center the SRS coil assembly as follows:

a. Make sure the front wheels of the vehicle are positioned straight-ahead.

b. Turn the SRS coil counter-clockwise by hand until it becomes harder to turn the cable.

c. Turn the SRS coil clockwise approximately 3 turns to align the red mark.

26. Install the SRS coil to the combination switch with 4 mounting screws.

27. Connect the SRS coil harness to the SRS coil and tape the SRS coil harness to the combination switch harness.

28. Install the steering wheel, aligning the matchmarks made during removal.

29. Install the steering wheel nut and torque to 25 ft. lbs. (34 Nm).

30. Connect the horn connector.

31. Install the air bag inflator module.

32. Connect the upper steering column connector and secure with CPA.

33. Install the 2 Torx® head screws. Torque to 78 inch lbs. (8.8 Nm).

34. Install the upper and lower column covers with 2 screws.

35. Install the 2 steering column side covers.

36. Install the knee bolster with 4 bolts.

37. Install the left front carpet and retainer.

38. Reactivate the air bag system as follows:

a. Turn the ignition switch to the **LOCK** position.

b. Connect the lower steering column connector.

c. Secure the lower steering column connector with Connector Position Assurance (CPA).

d. Install the IGN and CIG & RADIO fuses.

e. Turn the ignition switch to the **ACC** or **ON** position.

f. Observe the **INFLATABLE RESTRAINT** indicator lamp. If the lamp does not illuminate for approximately 60 seconds and turn OFF, there is a problem in the air bag system and further diagnostic testing of the system is needed.

Spectrum

1. Disconnect the negative battery cable. Remove the combination switch.

2. Insert the key into the ignition and place the key in the **ON** position, the lock bar must be pulled all the way in.

3. Remove the snapring and rubber cushion from the steering shaft.

4. Disconnect the switch wires at the connectors.

5. Remove the 2 screws retaining the ignition/starter switch and remove the switch.

6. To install, reverse the removal procedures.

Storm

1. Disable the air bag system as follows:

a. Set the front wheels to a straight-ahead position and turn the ignition switch to the **OFF** position.

b. Disconnect the battery negative cable.

c. Remove fuses C-22 and C-23 from the fuse box.

d. Disconnect the orange 3-way connector at the base of the steering column.

2. Remove the 4 bolts attaching the inflator module to the steering wheel. Disconnect the inflator module electrical connector.

3. Disconnect the electrical connector from the horn.

4. Remove the steering wheel nut and the steering wheel.

5. Remove the steering wheel cowl assembly and harness.

6. With the key in the **OFF** position, depress the retaining pin and remove the ignition lock cylinder from the ignition switch. Disconnect the electrical connector from the switch.

7. Remove the ignition switch snapring, rubber seal and spacer collar from the steering shaft.

8. Remove the back drive cable from the ignition switch. Remove the ignition switch retaining screws and remove the switch from the steering column.

9. Installation is the reverse order of the removal procedure.

10. Reactivate the air bag system as follows:

a. Turn the ignition switch to the **OFF** position.

b. Connect the orange 3-way connector at the base of the steering column.

c. Install fuses C-22 and C-23 to the fuse box.

d. Connect the battery negative cable.

Stoplight Switch

ADJUSTMENT

Metro, Spectrum and Storm

1. Pull the brake pedal as far rearward as it will go.

2. Adjust the switch so there is 0.02-0.04 in. (0.51-1.02mm) clearance between the contact plate and the end of the threads on the switch.

3. Adjust the switch so there is 0.02-0.04 in. clearance between the contact plate and the end of the threads on the switch.

4. Tighten the locknut and check the clearance again.

Prizm

1. Adjust the stoplight switch by turning the switch until the end of the plunger measures 0.02-0.09 in. (0.51-2.23mm) from the threaded part of the switch.

2. Tighten the stoplight switch locknut and check the clearance again.

REMOVAL AND INSTALLATION

Metro

1. Disconnect the negative battery cable. Disconnect the stoplight switch wiring at the brake pedal.

2. Remove the switch from the plate and install the new one.

3. Adjust the stoplight switch.

4. Connect the battery cable and check that the stoplights are not on with the pedal in the resting position.

Prizm

1. Disconnect the negative battery cable.

2. Remove the hood release cable from it's holder and the hood release lever from the knee bolster.

3. Remove the knee bolster cover plates, 2 screws, 4 bolts and knee bolster from instrument panel.

4. Remove the ventilation duct from the left side outlet.

5. Remove the old stoplight switch.

To install:

6. Install the new stoplight switch but do not tighten the locknut.

7. Adjust the stoplight switch.

8. Tighten the stoplight switch locknut. The remaining installation is the reverse of removal.

Spectrum

1. Disconnect the negative battery cable. Remove stoplight switch locknut.

2. Remove switch by pulling straight out of pedal assembly.

To install:

3. Push switch straight in, push the brake pedal by turning the stoplight switch, so free-play in the brake pedal is eliminated, then tighten the stoplight switch locknut.

Storm

1. Disconnect the negative battery cable. Disconnect the stoplight switch wiring at the brake pedal.

2. Remove the switch from the plate and install the new one.

3. Adjust the stoplight switch.

4. Connect the battery cable and check that the stoplights are not on with the pedal in the resting position.

Clutch Switch

ADJUSTMENT

The clutch start switch clearance is adjusted by loosening the front locknut and depressing the clutch pedal fully. Adjust the clutch start switch and tighten the locknut.

REMOVAL AND INSTALLATION

Metro and Storm

1. Disconnect the negative battery terminal from the battery.

2. Disconnect the electrical connector from the switch.

3. Loosen the locknut then unscrew the clutch start switch from the clutch pedal.

4. To install, reverse the removal procedures

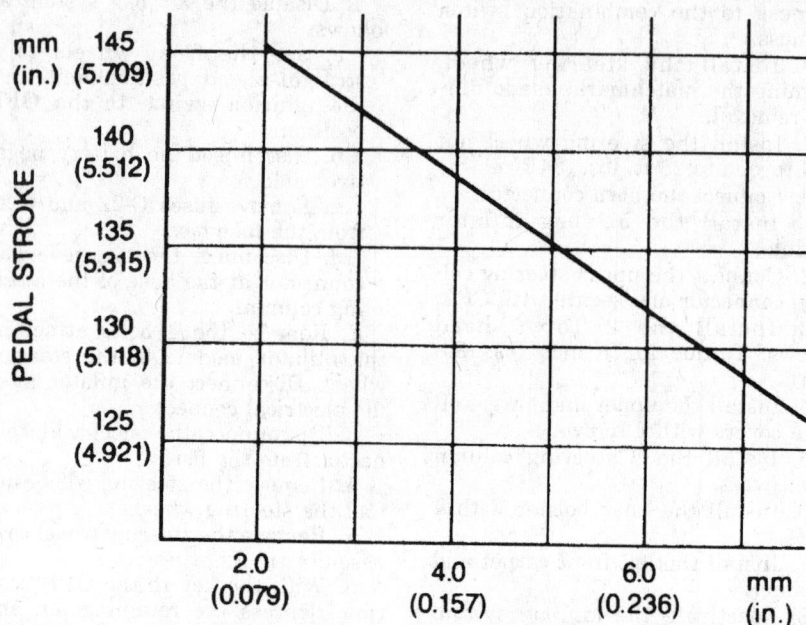

Clutch start switch clearance chart

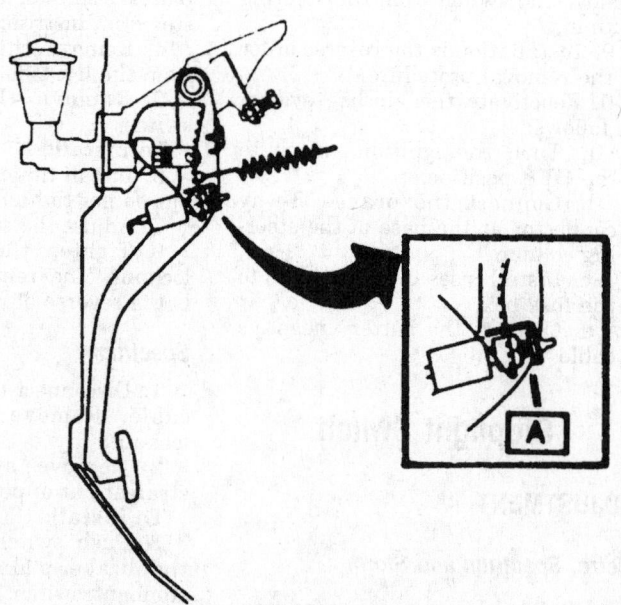

A CLUTCH START SWITCH CLEARANCE

Clutch start switch clearance check

Prizm

1. Disconnect the negative terminal from the battery.

2. Remove the necessary trim panels in order to gain access to the clutch switch retaining screws.

3. Remove the clutch switch retaining screws and front locknut.

4. Pull the switch down from its retainer and disconnect the electrical connections.

5. To install, reverse the removal procedures.

Spectrum

1. Disconnect the negative battery terminal from the battery.

2. Disconnect the electrical connector from the switch.

3. Remove the clutch start switch-to-brake pedal stop bracket screw and the switch from the clutch pedal.

4. To install, reverse the removal procedures

Neutral Safety Switch

ADJUSTMENT

Metro

1. Place selector lever in the **N** position.

2. Using a suitable tool, turn the neutral safety switch joint clockwise or counterclockwise to position the slot at the 11 o'clock position. Check that a click is heard from the switch in this position.

3. Now turn the switch by hand and stop at the position where a click is heard from the joint.

4. Torque the neutral safety switch retaining bolts to 17 ft. lbs. (23 Nm).

Prizm and Spectrum

1990-91

1. Loosen the neutral start switch bolts and set the shift lever in the **N** position.

2. Disconnect the neutral start switch electrical connector.

3. Connect an ohmmeter between the terminals on the switch.

4. Adjust the switch to the point where there is continuity between the terminals.

5. Connect the neutral switch electrical connector. Torque switch bolts to 48 inch lbs. (5.4 Nm). Check switch operation.

1992-94

1. Loosen the neutral start switch bolts and set the shift lever in the **N** position.

2. Disconnect the neutral start switch electrical connector.

3. Align the line scribed on the switch with the groove in the top of the manual shift shaft.

4. Connect the neutral switch electrical connector. Torque switch bolts to 71 inch lbs. (8 Nm). Check switch operation.

Storm

1. Remove the intake air duct and air breather tube from the air cleaner assembly.

2. Loosen the neutral safety switch attaching screws.

3. Place selector lever in the **N** position.

4. Install a pin into the adjustment holes in both the neutral safety switch and the switch lever.

5. Torque the retaining screws to 26 inch lbs. (3 Nm).

6. Install the air breather tube and intake air duct onto the air cleaner assembly.

NOTE: ON 1992-94 Storm with 3-speed automatic transaxle the neutral safety switch is not adjustable.

REMOVAL AND INSTALLATION

Metro

1. Disconnect the negative battery cable.

2. Raise and support the vehicle safely.

3. Disconnect the neutral safety switch couplers.

4. Remove the neutral safety switch retaining screws. Remove the switch from the transaxle.

5. Installation is the reverse order of the removal procedure. Adjust the switch as necessary.

Prizm

1. Disconnect the negative battery cable.

2. Place gear selector in **N** position.

3. Raise the vehicle and support it safely.

4. Remove 6 bolts and left under side splash shield.

5. Disconnect the electrical connector at the switch.

6. Remove the shift cable select lever.

7. Remove manual shaft lock plate and retaining nut.

8. Remove the switch retaining bolts and remove the switch.

9. Installation is the reverse of removal. Adjust the switch before completely tightening the switch mounting bolts.

10. Check and make sure the engine starts in only the **P** and **N** detents.

Storm

1. Disconnect the negative battery cable.

2. Remove the intake air duct and breather tube from the air cleaner assembly.

3. Disconnect the shift control cable from the selector cable.

4. Remove the neutral safety switch attaching screws and disconnect electrical connectors.

5. Remove the neutral safety switch. Reverse procedure to install. Adjust neutral safety switch, if necessary.

6. Disconnect the electrical connector at the switch.

7. Raise the vehicle and support it safely.

8. Remove the switch retaining bolts and remove the switch.

9. Installation is the reverse of removal. Align the groove and neutral basic line. Hold the switch in position and tighten the bolts to 48 inch lbs. (5.4 Nm)

10. Check and make sure the engine starts in only the **P** and **N** detents.

Spectrum

1. Disconnect the negative battery cable.

2. Disconnect the electrical connector for the switch at the left fender.

3. Raise the vehicle and support it safely.

4. Remove the switch retaining bolts and remove the switch.

5. Installation is the reverse of removal. Add transaxle fluid as necessary.

6. Check and make sure the engine starts in only the **P** and **N** detents.

Fuses, Circuit Breakers and Relays

LOCATION

Fusible Links

Fusible links are located in the engine harness at the starter solenoid and the left hand front of the dash at the battery junction block. On the Prizm, there is a fusible link box located on the positive battery cable.

Circuit Breakers

The circuit breakers can be found incorporated in the switch it represents or they can be found on the fuse and relay boards, mounted to the boards with blades similar to the fuses. Before removing a breaker, always disconnect the negative battery cable to prevent potentially damaging electrical "spikes" within the system. Simply remove the breaker by pulling straight out from the relay board. Do not twist the relay or damage may occur to the connectors inside the housing.

NOTE: Some circuit breakers on the Prizm do not reset automatically. Once tripped, they must be reset by hand. Use a small prybar or similar tool; insert it in the hole in the back of the breaker and push gently. Once the breaker is reset, either check it for continuity with an ohmmeter or reinstall it and check the circuit for function.

Reinstall the circuit breaker by pressing it straight in to its mount. Make certain the blades line up correctly and that the circuit breaker is fully seated. Reconnect the negative battery cable and check the circuit for function.

Fuse Panels

METRO

The main fuse/relay box is located on the left hand side of the engine compartment near the battery. The fuse junction block is located under the left side of the instrument panel.

PRIZM

The main fuse panel is attached to the number 1 junction block on the lower left hand shroud. There is also a ECM-IG fuse attached to the number 1 junction block.

STORM

The main fuse panel is attached to the junction block behind the left hand kick panel inside the vehicle. There is also a fuse/relay box located

on the left hand side of the engine compartment near the battery. There is also a relay box located on the right hand side of the engine compartment near the strut tower.

SPECTRUM

The fuse panel is located at the lower left hand side of the instrument panel, concealed by a cover.

Flashers

LOCATION

Metro

The flasher is located near the junction/fuse block, under the left hand side of the instrument panel.

Prizm

The turn signal flasher is located on the driver's side kick panel. In order

to gain access to the unit, it will be necessary to first remove certain under dash padding.

Storm

The turn signal and hazard flasher are located above the fuse box, under the left hand dash panel.

Spectrum

The turn signal flasher is located behind the instrument panel, on the left hand side of the steering column. Replacement is accomplished by unplugging the old flasher and inserting a new one.

The hazard flasher is located behind the instrument panel, on the left hand side of the steering column. Replacement is accomplished by unplugging the old flasher and inserting a new one.

ENGINE IDENTIFICATION

Year	Model	Engine Displacement Liters (cc)	Engine Series (ID/VIN)	Fuel System	No. of Cylinders	Engine Type
1990	Civic	1.5 (1493)	D15B1	DP-FI	4	SOHC 16-valve
	Civic/CRX	1.5 (1493)	D15B2	DP-FI	4	SOHC 16-valve
	Civic/CRX, HF	1.5 (1493)	D15B6	MPFI	4	SOHC 8-valve
	Civic/CRX, Si	1.6 (1590)	D16A6	MPFI	4	SOHC 16-valve
	Accord, DX/LX	2.2 (2156)	F22A1 ①	MPFI	4	SOHC 16-valve
	Accord EX	2.2 (2156)	F22A4 ②	MPFI	4	SOHC 16-valve
	Prelude S	2.0 (1955)	B20A3	Carb	4	SOHC 12-valve
	Prelude Si	2.0 (1955)	B20A5	MPFI	4	DOHC 16-valve
	Prelude Si	2.1 (2056)	B21A1	MPFI	4	DOHC 16-valve
1991	Civic	1.5 (1493)	D15B1	DP-FI	4	SOHC 16-valve
	Civic/CRX	1.5 (1493)	D15B2	DP-FI	4	SOHC 16-valve
	Civic/CRX, HF	1.5 (1493)	D15B6	MPFI	4	SOHC 8-valve
	Civic/CRX, Si	1.6 (1590)	D16A6	MPFI	4	SOHC 16-valve
	Accord, DX/LX	2.2 (2156)	F22A1 ①	MPFI	4	SOHC 16-valve
	Accord EX	2.2 (2156)	F22A4 ②	MPFI	4	SOHC 16-valve
	Accord SE	2.2 (2156)	F22A6 ③	MPFI	4	SOHC 16-valve
	Prelude Si	2.0 (1955)	B20A5	MPFI	4	DOHC 16-valve
	Prelude Si	2.1 (2056)	B21A1	MPFI	4	DOHC 16-valve
1992	Civic	1.5 (1493)	D15B7	MPFI	4	SOHC 16-valve
	Civic	1.5 (1493)	D15B8	MPFI	4	SOHC 8-valve
	Civic	1.5 (1493)	D15Z1 ④	MPFI	4	SOHC 16-valve
	Civic	1.6 (1590)	D16Z6 ④	MPFI	4	SOHC 16-valve
	Accord, DX/LX	2.2 (2156)	F22A1 ①	MPFI	4	SOHC 16-valve
	Accord EX	2.2 (2156)	F22A4 ②	MPFI	4	SOHC 16-valve
	Accord EX-R	2.2 (2156)	F22A6 ③	MPFI	4	SOHC 16-valve
	Prelude S	2.2 (2156)	F22A1	MPFI	4	SOHC
	Prelude Si	2.3 (2259)	H23A1	MPFI	4	DOHC
1993	Civic	1.5 (1493)	D15B7	MPFI	4	SOHC 16-valve
	Civic	1.5 (1493)	D15B8	MPFI	4	SOHC 8-valve
	Civic	1.5 (1493)	D15Z1 ④	MPFI	4	SOHC 16-valve
	Civic	1.6 (1590)	D16Z6 ④	MPFI	4	SOHC 16-valve
	del Sol	1.5 (1493)	D15B7	MPFI	4	SOHC 16-valve
	del Sol	1.6 (1590)	D16Z6 ④	MPFI	4	SOHC 16-valve
	Accord, DX/LX	2.2 (2156)	F22A1 ①	MPFI	4	SOHC 16-valve
	Accord EX	2.2 (2156)	F22A4 ②	MPFI	4	SOHC 16-valve
	Accord EX-R	2.2 (2156)	F22A6 ③	MPFI	4	SOHC 16-valve
	Prelude S	2.2 (2156)	F22A1	MPFI	4	SOHC 16-valve
	Prelude Si	2.2 (2156)	H22A1 ④	MPFI	4	DOHC 16-valve
	Prelude Si	2.3 (2259)	H23A1	MPFI	4	DOHC 16-valve

ENGINE IDENTIFICATION

Year	Model	Engine Displacement Liters (cc)	Engine Series (ID/VIN)	Fuel System	No. of Cylinders	Engine Type
1994	Civic	1.5 (1493)	D15B7	MPFI	4	SOHC 16-valve
	Civic	1.5 (1493)	D15B8	MPFI	4	SOHC 8-valve
	Civic	1.5 (1493)	D15Z1 ④	MPFI	4	SOHC 16-valve
	Civic	1.6 (1590)	D16Z6 ④	MPFI	4	SOHC 16-valve
	del Sol	1.5 (1493)	D15B7	MPFI	4	SOHC 16-valve
	del Sol	1.6 (1590)	D16Z6 ④	MPFI	4	SOHC 16-valve
	Accord, DX/LX	2.2 (2156)	F22A1 ①	MPFI	4	SOHC 16-valve
	Accord EX	2.2 (2156)	F22A4 ②	MPFI	4	SOHC 16-valve
	Accord EX-R	2.2 (2156)	F22A6 ③	MPFI	4	SOHC 16-valve
	Prelude S	2.2 (2156)	F22A1	MPFI	4	SOHC 16-valve
	Prelude Si	2.2 (2156)	H22A1 ④	MPFI	4	DOHC 16-valve
	Prelude Si	2.3 (2259)	H23A1	MPFI	4	DOHC 16-valve

DP-FI—Dual Point Fuel Injected
MP-FI—Multi Point Fuel Injected
MP-PFI—Multi Point Port Fuel Injected
VTEC—Variable Valve Timing and Lift Electronic
Control System
① Single exhaust manifold
② Dual exhaust manifold
③ Dual intake manifold
④ VTEC-E

GENERAL ENGINE SPECIFICATIONS

Year	Engine ID/VIN	Engine Displacement Liters (cc)	Fuel System Type	Net Horsepower @ rpm	Net Torque @ rpm (ft. lbs.)	Bore × Stroke (in.)	Compression Ratio	Oil Pressure @ rpm
1990	D15B1	1.5 (1493)	DP-FI	70 @ 5500	83 @ 3000	2.95 × 3.33	9.2:1	50 @ 3000
	D15B2	1.5 (1493)	DP-FI	92 @ 6000	89 @ 4500	2.95 × 3.33	9.2:1	50 @ 3000
	D15B6	1.5 (1493)	MP-FI	62 @ 4500	90 @ 2000	2.95 × 3.33	9.2:1	50 @ 3000
	D16A6	1.6 (1590)	MP-FI	108 @ 6000	100 @ 5000	2.95 × 3.54	9.1:1	50 @ 3000
	F22A1	2.2 (2156)	MP-FI	125 @ 5200	137 @ 4000	3.35 × 3.74	8.8:1	50 @ 3000
	F22A4	2.2 (2156)	MP-FI	130 @ 5200	142 @ 4000	3.35 × 3.74	8.8:1	50 @ 3000
	B20A3	2.0 (1955)	Dual Sidedraft	①	111 @ 4000	3.19 × 3.74	9.1:1	50 @ 3000
	B20A5	2.0 (1955)	MP-FI	135 @ 6200	127 @ 4000	3.19 × 3.74	9.0:1	50 @ 3000
	B21A1	2.1 (2056)	MP-FI	140 @ 5800	135 @ 5000	3.27 × 3.74	9.4:1	50 @ 3000
1991	D15B1	1.5 (1493)	DP-FI	70 @ 5500	83 @ 3000	2.95 × 3.33	9.2:1	50 @ 3000
	D15B2	1.5 (1493)	DP-FI	92 @ 6000	89 @ 4500	2.95 × 3.33	9.2:1	50 @ 3000
	D15B6	1.5 (1493)	MP-FI	62 @ 4500	90 @ 2000	2.95 × 3.33	9.6:1	50 @ 3000
	D16A6	1.6 (1590)	MP-FI	108 @ 6000	100 @ 5000	2.95 × 3.54	9.1:1	50 @ 3000
	F22A1	2.2 (2156)	MP-FI	125 @ 5200	137 @ 4000	3.35 × 3.74	8.8:1	50 @ 3000
	F22A4	2.2 (2156)	MP-FI	130 @ 5200	142 @ 4000	3.35 × 3.74	8.8:1	50 @ 3000
	F22A6	2.2 (2156)	MP-FI	140 @ 5600	142 @ 4500	3.35 × 3.74	8.8:1	50 @ 3000
	F20A5	2.0 (1958)	MP-FI	135 @ 6200	127 @ 4000	3.19 × 3.74	9.0:1	50 @ 3000
	B21A1	2.1 (2056)	MP-FI	140 @ 5800	135 @ 5000	3.27 × 3.74	9.4:1	50 @ 3000
1992	D15B7	1.5 (1493)	MP-FI	102 @ 5900	98 @ 5000	2.95 × 3.33	9.2:1	50 @ 3000
	D15B8	1.5 (1493)	MP-FI	70 @ 5000	91 @ 2000	2.95 × 3.33	9.1:1	50 @ 3000
	D15Z1	1.5 (1493)	MP-FI	92 @ 5500	97 @ 4500	2.95 × 3.33	9.3:1	50 @ 3000
	D16Z6	1.6 (1590)	MP-FI	125 @ 6600	106 @ 5200	2.95 × 3.54	9.2:1	50 @ 3000
	F22A1	2.2 (2156)	MP-FI	135 @ 5200	137 @ 4000	3.35 × 3.74	8.8:1	50 @ 3000
	F22A4	2.2 (2156)	MP-FI	125 @ 5200	137 @ 4000	3.35 × 3.74	8.8:1	50 @ 3000
	F22A6	2.2 (2156)	MP-FI	140 @ 5600	142 @ 4000	3.35 × 3.74	8.8:1	50 @ 3000
	H23A1	2.3 (2259)	MP-FI	160 @ 5800	156 @ 4500	3.43 × 3.74	9.8:1	50 @ 3000
1993	D15B7	1.5 (1493)	MP-FI	102 @ 5900	98 @ 5000	2.95 × 3.33	9.2:1	50 @ 3000
	D15B8	1.5 (1493)	MP-FI	70 @ 5000	91 @ 2000	2.95 × 3.33	9.1:1	50 @ 3000
	D15Z1	1.5 (1493)	MP-FI	92 @ 5500	97 @ 4500	2.95 × 3.33	9.3:1	50 @ 3000
	D16Z6	1.6 (1590)	MP-FI	125 @ 6600	106 @ 5200	2.95 × 3.54	9.2:1	50 @ 3000
	F22A1	2.2 (2156)	MP-FI	135 @ 5200	137 @ 4000	3.35 × 3.74	8.8:1	50 @ 3000
	F22A4	2.2 (2156)	MP-FI	125 @ 5200	137 @ 4000	3.35 × 3.74	8.8:1	50 @ 3000
	F22A6	2.2 (2156)	MP-FI	140 @ 5600	142 @ 4000	3.35 × 3.74	8.8:1	50 @ 3000
	H22A1	2.2 (2156)	MP-FI	190 @ 6800	158 @ 5300	3.43 × 3.57	10.0:1	50 @ 3000
	H23A1	2.3 (2259)	MP-FI	160 @ 5800	156 @ 4500	3.43 × 3.74	9.8:1	50 @ 3000

GENERAL ENGINE SPECIFICATIONS

Year	Engine ID/VIN	Engine Displacement Liters (cc)	Fuel System Type	Net Horsepower @ rpm	Net Torque @ rpm (ft. lbs.)	Bore × Stroke (in.)	Compression Ratio	Oil Pressure @ rpm
1994	D15B7	1.5 (1493)	MP-FI	102 @ 5900	98 @ 5000	2.95 × 3.33	9.2:1	50 @ 3000
	D15B8	1.5 (1493)	MP-FI	70 @ 5000	91 @ 2000	2.95 × 3.33	9.1:1	50 @ 3000
	D15Z1	1.5 (1493)	MP-FI	92 @ 5500	97 @ 4500	2.95 × 3.33	9.3:1	50 @ 3000
	D16Z6	1.6 (1590)	MP-FI	125 @ 6600	106 @ 5200	2.95 × 3.54	9.2:1	50 @ 3000
	F22A1	2.2 (2156)	MP-FI	135 @ 5200	137 @ 4000	3.35 × 3.74	8.8:1	50 @ 3000
	F22A4	2.2 (2156)	MP-FI	125 @ 5200	137 @ 4000	3.35 × 3.74	8.8:1	50 @ 3000
	F22A6	2.2 (2156)	MP-FI	140 @ 5600	142 @ 4000	3.35 × 3.74	8.8:1	50 @ 3000
	H22A1	2.2 (2156)	MP-FI	190 @ 6800	158 @ 5300	3.43 × 3.57	10.0:1	50 @ 3000
	H23A1	2.3 (2259)	MP-FI	160 @ 5800	156 @ 4500	3.43 × 3.74	9.8:1	50 @ 3000

NOTE: Horsepower and torque are SAE net figures. They are measured at the rear of the transmission with all accessories installed and operating. Since the figures vary when a given engine is installed in different models, some are representative rather than exact.
DP-FI—Dual Point Fuel Injected
MP-FI—Multi Point Fuel Injected
MP-PFI—Multi Point Port Fuel Injected
① Manual transaxle—104 @ 5800
   Automatic transaxle—105 @ 5800

GASOLINE ENGINE TUNE-UP SPECIFICATIONS

Year	Engine ID/VIN	Engine Displacement Liters (cc)	Spark Plugs Gap (in.)	Ignition Timing (deg.) MT	AT	Fuel Pump (psi)	Idle Speed (rpm) MT	AT	Valve Clearance In.	Ex.
1990	D15B1	1.5 (1493)	0.042	18B	18B	36	700–800	700–800	0.007–0.009	0.009–0.011
	D15B2	1.5 (1493)	0.042	18B	18B	36	700–800	700–800	0.007–0.009	0.009–0.011
	D15B6	1.5 (1493)	0.042	14B	14B	36	600–700 ①	700–800	0.005–0.007	0.007–0.009
	D16A6	1.5 (1590)	0.042	18B	18B	36	700–800	700–800	0.007–0.009	0.009–0.011
	F221A	2.2 (2156)	0.042	15B	15B	36	650–750	650–750	0.0094–0.011	0.011–0.012
	F22A4	2.2 (2156)	0.042	15B	15B	36	650–750	650–750	0.0094–0.011	0.0110–0.0126
	B20A3	2.0 (1955)	0.042	20B ②	15B ④	1.3–2.1	750–850	700–800	0.005–0.007	0.010–0.012
	B20A5	2.0 (1955)	0.042	15B	15B	36	700–800	700–800	0.003–0.005	0.006–0.008
	B21A1	2.1 (2056)	0.042	15B	15B	36	700–800	700–800	0.003–0.005	0.006–0.008
1991	D15B1	1.5 (1493)	0.042	18B	18B	36	700–800	700–800	0.007–0.009	0.009–0.011
	D15B2	1.5 (1493)	0.042	18B	18B	36	700–800	700–800	0.007–0.009	0.009–0.011
	D15B6	1.5 (1493)	0.042	14B	14B	36	550–650	550–650	0.005–0.007	0.007–0.009
	D1646	1.6 (1590)	0.042	18B	18B	36	700–800	700–800	0.007–0.009	0.009–0.011
	F22A1	2.2 (2156)	0.042	15B	15B	36	700–800	700–800	0.0094–0.011	0.011–0.012
	F22A4	2.2 (2156)	0.042	15B	15B	36	700–800	700–800	0.094–0.011	0.011–0.012
	F22A6	2.2 (2156)	0.042	15B	15B	36	700–800	700–800	0.094–0.011	0.011–0.012
	F20A5	2.0 (1958)	0.042	15B	15B	36	700–800	700–800	0.003–0.005	0.006–0.008
	B21A1	2.1 (2056)	0.042	15B	15B	36	700–800	700–800	0.003–0.005	0.006–0.008
1992	D15B7	1.5 (1493)	0.039–0.043	16B	16B	40	370–470	370–470	0.007–0.009	0.009–0.011
	D15B8	1.5 (1493)	0.039–0.043	12B	12B	40	370–470	370–470	0.007–0.009	0.009–0.011
	D15Z1	1.5 (1493)	0.039–0.043	16B	16B	40	370–470	370–740	0.007–0.009	0.009–0.011
	D16Z6	1.6 (1590)	0.039–0.043	16B	16B	40	370–470	370–470	0.007–0.009	0.009–0.001
	F22A1	2.2 (2156)	0.039–0.043	15B	15B	36	650–750	650–750	0.009–0.011	0.011–0.013
	F22A4	2.2 (2156)	0.039–0.043	15B	15B	40	650–750	650–750	0.009–0.011	0.011–0.012

GASOLINE ENGINE TUNE-UP SPECIFICATIONS

Year	Engine ID/VIN	Engine Displacement Liters (cc)	Spark Plugs Gap (in.)	Ignition Timing (deg.) MT	Ignition Timing (deg.) AT	Fuel Pump (psi)	Idle Speed (rpm) MT	Idle Speed (rpm) AT	Valve Clearance In.	Valve Clearance Ex.
1992	F22A6	2.2 (2156)	0.039–0.043	15B	15B	40	650–750	650–750	0.009–0.011	0.011–0.012
	H23A1	2.3 (2259)	0.039–0.043	15B	15B	36	650–750	650–750	0.003–0.004	0.006–0.007
1993	D15B7	1.5 (1493)	0.039–0.043	16B	16B	40	370–470	370–470	0.007–0.009	0.009–0.011
	D15B8	1.5 (1493)	0.039–0.043	12B	12B	40	370–470	370–470	0.007–0.009	0.009–0.011
	D15Z1	1.5 (1493)	0.039–0.043	16B	16B	40	370–470	370–740	0.007–0.009	0.009–0.011
	D16Z6	1.6 (1590)	0.039–0.043	16B	16B	40	370–470	370–470	0.007–0.009	0.009–0.001
	F22A1	2.2 (2156)	0.039–0.043	15B	15B	36	650–750	650–750	0.009–0.011	0.011–0.013
	F22A4	2.2 (2156)	0.039–0.043	15B	15B	40	650–750	650–750	0.009–0.011	0.011–0.012
	F22A6	2.2 (2156)	0.039–0.043	15B	15B	40	650–750	650–750	0.009–0.011	0.011–0.012
	H22A1	2.2 (2156)	0.039–0.043	15B	15B	36	650–750	650–750	0.006–0.007	0.007–0.008
	H23A1	2.3 (2259)	0.039–0.043	15B	15B	36	650–750	650–750	0.003–0.004	0.006–0.007
1994	D15B7	1.5 (1493)	0.039–0.043	16B	16B	40	370–470	370–470	0.007–0.009	0.009–0.011
	D15B8	1.5 (1493)	0.039–0.043	12B	12B	40	370–470	370–470	0.007–0.009	0.009–0.011
	D15Z1	1.5 (1493)	0.039–0.043	16B	16B	40	370–470	370–740	0.007–0.009	0.009–0.011
	D16Z6	1.6 (1590)	0.039–0.043	16B	16B	40	370–470	370–470	0.007–0.009	0.009–0.001
	F22A1	2.2 (2156)	0.039–0.043	15B	15B	36	650–750	650–750	0.009–0.011	0.011–0.013
	F22A4	2.2 (2156)	0.039–0.043	15B	15B	40	650–750	650–750	0.009–0.011	0.011–0.012
	F22A6	2.2 (2156)	0.039–0.043	15B	15B	40	650–750	650–750	0.009–0.011	0.011–0.012
	H22A1	2.2 (2156)	0.039–0.043	15B	15B	36	650–750	650–750	0.006–0.007	0.007–0.008
	H23A1	2.3 (2259)	0.039–0.043	15B	15B	36	650–750	650–750	0.003–0.004	0.006–0.007

NOTE: The underhood specifications sticker often reflects tune-up specification changes in production. Sticker figures must be used if they disagree with those in this chart.

B   Before top dead center

① Aim timing light at red mark on flywheel or torque converter drive plate with the distributor vacuum hose connected at the specified idle speed.

② California—20B

③ California—15B

FIRING ORDERS

NOTE: To avoid confusion, always replace spark plug wires one at a time.

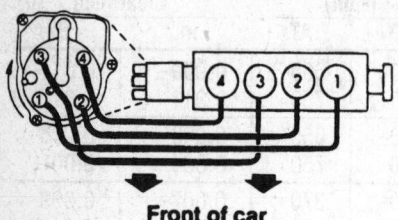

Front of car

1990-91 1.5L and 1.6L Engines
Engine Firing Order: 1-3-4-2
Distributor Rotation: Clockwise

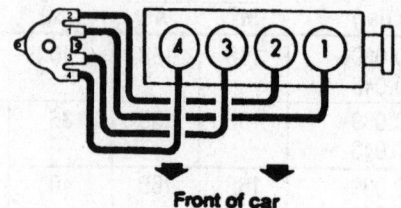

Front of car

2.0L (DOHC) and 2.1L Engines
Engine Firing Order: 1-3-4-2
Distributor Rotation: Clockwise

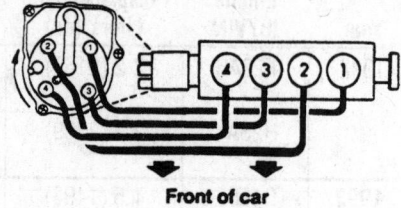

Front of car

1992-94 1.5L and 1.6L Engines 2.2L and 2.3L
Engines
Engine Firing Order: 1-3-4-2
Distributor Rotation: Clockwise

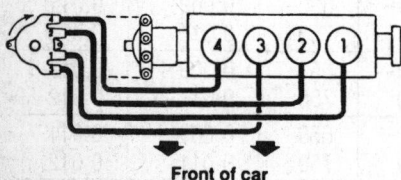

Front of car

2.0L (SOHC) Engine
Engine Firing Order: 1-3-4-2
Distributor Rotation: Clockwise

CAPACITIES

Year	Model	Engine ID/VIN	Engine Displacement Liters (cc)	Engine Crankcase with Filter (qts.)	Transmission (pts.)			Transfer case (pts.)	Drive Axle		Fuel Tank (gal.)	Cooling System (qts.)
					4-Spd	5-Spd	Auto.		Front (pts.)	Rear (pts.)		
1990	Civic	D15B1	1.5 (1493)	3.7	—	4.0[1]	5.0[2]	—	—	1.4[9]	11.9[3]	[4]
	Civic/CRX	D15B2	1.5 (1493)	3.7	—	4.0[1]	5.0[2]	—	—	—	11.9[3]	[4]
	Civic/CRX, HF	D15B6	1.5 (1493)	3.7	—	4.0[1]	5.0[2]	—	—	—	11.9[3]	[4]
	Civic/CRX, Si	D16A6	1.6 (1590)	3.7	—	4.0[1]	5.0[2]	—	—	1.4[9]	11.9[3]	[4]
	Accord, DX/LX	F22A1	2.2 (2156)	4.0	—	4.0	5.0	—	—	—	17.0	[7]
	Accord EX	F22A4	2.2 (2156)	4.0	—	4.0	5.0	—	—	—	17.0	[7]
	Prelude S	B20A3	2.0 (1955)	4.0	—	4.4	6.0	—	—	—	15.9	[8]
	Prelude Si	B20A5	2.0 (1955)	4.0	—	4.4	6.0	—	—	—	15.9	[8]
	Prelude Si	B21A1	2.1 (2056)	4.0	—	4.4	6.0	—	—	—	15.9	8.2
1991	Civic	D15B1	1.5 (1493)	3.7	—	4.0	5.0	—	—	1.4[9]	11.9[3]	[4]
	Civic/CRX	D15B2	1.5 (1493)	3.7	—	4.0	5.0	—	—	—	11.9[3]	[4]
	Civic/CRX, HF	D15B6	1.5 (1493)	3.7	—	4.0	5.0	—	—	—	11.9[3]	[4]
	Civic/CRX, Si	D16A6	1.6 (1590)	3.7	—	4.0[1]	5.0	—	—	1.4[9]	11.9[3]	[4]
	Accord, DX/LX	F22A1	2.2 (2156)	4.0	—	4.0	5.0	—	—	—	17.0	[7]
	Accord EX	F22A4	2.2 (2156)	4.0	—	4.0	5.0	—	—	—	17.0	[7]
	Accord SE	F22A6	2.2 (2156)	4.0	—	4.0	5.0	—	—	—	17.0	[7]
	Prelude Si	B20A5	2.0 (1955)	4.0	—	4.4	6.0	—	—	—	15.9	[8]
	Prelude Si	B21A1	2.1 (2056)	4.0	—	4.4	6.0	—	—	—	15.9	8.2
1992	Civic	B15B7	1.5 (1493)	3.5	—	4.0	5.6	—	—	—	11.9	[11]
	Civic	B15B8	1.5 (1493)	3.5	—	4.0	5.6	—	—	—	11.9	[11]
	Civic	B15Z1	1.5 (1493)	3.5	—	4.0	5.6	—	—	—	11.9	[11]
	Civic	B16Z6	1.6 (1590)	3.5	—	4.0	5.6	—	—	—	11.9	[12]
	Accord, DX/LX	F22A1	2.2 (2156)	4.0	—	4.0	5.0	—	—	—	17.0	[10]
	Accord EX	F22A4	2.2 (2156)	4.0	—	4.0	5.0	—	—	—	17.0	[10]
	Accord EX-R	F22A6	2.2 (2156)	4.0	—	4.0	5.0	—	—	—	17.0	[10]
	Prelude S	F22A1	2.2 (2156)	4.0	—	4.0	5.6	—	—	—	15.9	[13]
	Prelude Si	H23A1	2.3 (2259)	4.5	—	4.0	5.6	—	—	—	15.9	[14]
1993	Civic	B15B7	1.5 (1493)	3.5	—	4.0	5.6	—	—	—	11.9	[11]
	Civic	B15B8	1.5 (1493)	3.5	—	4.0	5.6	—	—	—	11.9	[11]
	Civic	B15Z1	1.5 (1493)	3.5	—	4.0	5.6	—	—	—	11.9	[11]
	Civic	B16Z6	1.6 (1590)	3.5	—	4.0	5.6	—	—	—	11.9	[12]
	del Sol	D15B7	1.5 (1493)	3.5	—	4.0	5.6	—	—	—	11.9	[11]
	del Sol	D15B7	1.6 (1590)	3.5	—	4.0	5.6	—	—	—	11.9	[12]
	Accord, DX/LX	F22A1	2.2 (2156)	4.0	—	4.0	5.0	—	—	—	17.0	[10]
	Accord EX	F22A4	2.2 (2156)	4.0	—	4.0	5.0	—	—	—	17.0	[10]
	Accord EX-R	F22A6	2.2 (2156)	4.0	—	4.0	5.0	—	—	—	17.0	[10]
	Prelude S	F22A1	2.2 (2156)	4.0	—	4.0	5.6	—	—	—	15.9	[13]
	Prelude Si	H22A1	2.2 (2156)	5.0	—	4.0	5.6	—	—	—	15.9	[14]
	Prelude Si	H23A1	2.3 (2259)	4.5	—	4.0	5.6	—	—	—	15.9	[14]

CAPACITIES

Year	Model	Engine ID/VIN	Engine Displacement Liters (cc)	Engine Crankcase with Filter (qts.)	Transmission (pts.)			Transfer case (pts.)	Drive Axle		Fuel Tank (gal.)	Cooling System (qts.)
					4-Spd	5-Spd	Auto.		Front (pts.)	Rear (pts.)		
1990	Civic	D15B1	1.5 (1493)	3.7	—	4.0①	5.0②	—	—	1.4⑨	11.9③	④
	Civic/CRX	D15B2	1.5 (1493)	3.7	—	4.0①	5.0②	—	—	—	11.9③	④
	Civic/CRX, HF	D15B6	1.5 (1493)	3.7	—	4.0①	5.0②	—	—	—	11.9③	④
	Civic/CRX, Si	D16A6	1.6 (1590)	3.7	—	4.0①	5.0②	—	—	1.4⑨	11.9③	④
	Accord, DX/LX	F22A1	2.2 (2156)	4.0	—	4.0	5.0	—	—	—	17.0	⑦
	Accord EX	F22A4	2.2 (2156)	4.0	—	4.0	5.0	—	—	—	17.0	⑦
	Prelude S	B20A3	2.0 (1955)	4.0	—	4.4	6.0	—	—	—	15.9	⑧
	Prelude Si	B20A5	2.0 (1955)	4.0	—	4.4	6.0	—	—	—	15.9	⑧
	Prelude Si	B21A1	2.1 (2056)	4.0	—	4.4	6.0	—	—	—	15.9	8.2
1991	Civic	D15B1	1.5 (1493)	3.7	—	4.0	5.0	—	—	1.4⑨	11.9③	④
	Civic/CRX	D15B2	1.5 (1493)	3.7	—	4.0	5.0	—	—	—	11.9③	④
	Civic/CRX, HF	D15B6	1.5 (1493)	3.7	—	4.0	5.0	—	—	—	11.9③	④
	Civic/CRX, Si	D16A6	1.6 (1590)	3.7	—	4.0①	5.0	—	—	1.4⑨	11.9③	④
	Accord, DX/LX	F22A1	2.2 (2156)	4.0	—	4.0	5.0	—	—	—	17.0	⑦
	Accord EX	F22A4	2.2 (2156)	4.0	—	4.0	5.0	—	—	—	17.0	⑦
	Accord SE	F22A6	2.2 (2156)	4.0	—	4.0	5.0	—	—	—	17.0	⑦
	Prelude Si	B20A5	2.0 (1955)	4.0	—	4.4	6.0	—	—	—	15.9	⑧
	Prelude Si	B21A1	2.1 (2056)	4.0	—	4.4	6.0	—	—	—	15.9	8.2
1992	Civic	B15B7	1.5 (1493)	3.5	—	4.0	5.6	—	—	—	11.9	⑪
	Civic	B15B8	1.5 (1493)	3.5	—	4.0	5.6	—	—	—	11.9	⑪
	Civic	B15Z1	1.5 (1493)	3.5	—	4.0	5.6	—	—	—	11.9	⑪
	Civic	B16Z6	1.6 (1590)	3.5	—	4.0	5.6	—	—	—	11.9	⑫
	Accord, DX/LX	F22A1	2.2 (2156)	4.0	—	4.0	5.0	—	—	—	17.0	⑩
	Accord EX	F22A4	2.2 (2156)	4.0	—	4.0	5.0	—	—	—	17.0	⑩
	Accord EX-R	F22A6	2.2 (2156)	4.0	—	4.0	5.0	—	—	—	17.0	⑩
	Prelude S	F22A1	2.2 (2156)	4.0	—	4.0	5.6	—	—	—	15.9	⑬
	Prelude Si	H23A1	2.3 (2259)	4.5	—	4.0	5.6	—	—	—	15.9	⑭
1993	Civic	B15B7	1.5 (1493)	3.5	—	4.0	5.6	—	—	—	11.9	⑪
	Civic	B15B8	1.5 (1493)	3.5	—	4.0	5.6	—	—	—	11.9	⑪
	Civic	B15Z1	1.5 (1493)	3.5	—	4.0	5.6	—	—	—	11.9	⑪
	Civic	B16Z6	1.6 (1590)	3.5	—	4.0	5.6	—	—	—	11.9	⑫
	del Sol	D15B7	1.5 (1493)	3.5	—	4.0	5.6	—	—	—	11.9	⑪
	del Sol	D15B7	1.6 (1590)	3.5	—	4.0	5.6	—	—	—	11.9	⑫
	Accord, DX/LX	F22A1	2.2 (2156)	4.0	—	4.0	5.0	—	—	—	17.0	⑩
	Accord EX	F22A4	2.2 (2156)	4.0	—	4.0	5.0	—	—	—	17.0	⑩
	Accord EX-R	F22A6	2.2 (2156)	4.0	—	4.0	5.0	—	—	—	17.0	⑩
	Prelude S	F22A1	2.2 (2156)	4.0	—	4.0	5.6	—	—	—	15.9	⑬
	Prelude Si	H22A1	2.2 (2156)	5.0	—	4.0	5.6	—	—	—	15.9	⑭
	Prelude Si	H23A1	2.3 (2259)	4.5	—	4.0	5.6	—	—	—	15.9	⑭

CRANKSHAFT AND CONNECTING ROD SPECIFICATIONS

All measurements are given in inches.

Year	Engine ID/VIN	Engine Displacement Liters (cc)	Crankshaft				Connecting Rod		
			Main Brg. Journal Dia.	Main Brg. Oil Clearance	Shaft End-play	Thrust on No.	Journal Diameter	Oil Clearance	Side Clearance
1990	D15B1	1.5 (1493)	1.7707–1.7718	②	0.004–0.014	4	1.6526–1.6535	0.0008–0.0015	0.006–0.012
	D16A6	1.6 (1590)	2.1644–2.1654	③	0.004–0.014	4	1.7707–1.7717	0.0008–0.0015	0.006–0.012
	F22A1	2.2 (2156)	④	⑤	0.004–0.014	4	1.7710–1.7717	0.0008–0.0017	0.006–0.012
	B20A3	2.0 (1955)	2.1644–2.1654⑦	③	0.004–0.014	3	1.7707–1.7717	⑥	0.006–0.012
	B21A1	2.1 (2056)	2.1644–2.1654	③	0.004–0.014	3	1.8888–1.8900	0.0010–0.0017	0.006–0.012
1991	D15B1	1.5 (1493)	1.7707–1.7718	②	0.004–0.014	4	1.6526–1.6535	0.0008–0.0015	0.006–0.012
	D16A6	1.6 (1590)	2.1644–2.1654	③	0.004–0.014	4	1.7707–1.7717	0.0008–0.0015	0.006–0.012
	F22A1	2.2 (2156)	④	⑤	0.004–0.014	4	1.7710–1.7717	0.0008–0.0017	0.006–0.012
	B20A5	2.0 (1955)	2.1644–2.1654⑦	③	0.004–0.014	3	1.7707–1.7717	⑥	0.006–0.012
	B21A1	2.1 (2056)	2.1644–2.1654	③	0.004–0.014	3	1.8888–1.8900	0.0010–0.0017	0.006–0.012
1992	D15B7	1.5 (1493)	1.7707–1.7718	②	0.004–0.014	4	1.7707–1.7717	0.0010–0.0017	0.008–0.014
	D16Z6	1.6 (1590)	2.1644–2.1654	③	0.004–0.014	4	1.7707–1.7717	0.0010–0.0017	0.008–0.014
	F22A1	2.2 (2156)	①	⑧	0.004–0.014	4	1.7710–1.7717	0.0008–0.0019	0.008–0.014
	H23A1	2.3 (2259)	①	⑧	0.004–0.014	4	1.7710–1.7717	0.0011–0.0022	0.008–0.014
1993	D15B7	1.5 (1493)	1.7707–1.7718	②	0.004–0.014	4	1.7707–1.7717	0.0010–0.0017	0.008–0.014
	D16Z6	1.6 (1590)	2.1644–2.1654	③	0.004–0.014	4	1.7707–1.7717	0.0010–0.0017	0.008–0.014
	F22A1	2.2 (2156)	①	⑧	0.004–0.014	4	1.7710–1.7717	0.0008–0.0019	0.008–0.014
	H22A1	2.2 (2156)	①	⑧	0.004–0.014	4	1.8888–1.8898	0.0011–0.0022	0.006–0.012
	H23A1	2.3 (2259)	①	⑧	0.004–0.014	4	1.7710–1.7717	0.0011–0.0022	0.008–0.014

CRANKSHAFT AND CONNECTING ROD SPECIFICATIONS

All measurements are given in inches.

| Year | Engine ID/VIN | Engine Displacement Liters (cc) | Crankshaft | | | | Connecting Rod | | |
			Main Brg. Journal Dia.	Main Brg. Oil Clearance	Shaft End-play	Thrust on No.	Journal Diameter	Oil Clearance	Side Clearance
1994	D15B7	1.5 (1493)	1.7707–1.7718	②	0.004–0.014	4	1.7707–1.7717	0.0010–0.0017	0.008–0.014
	D16Z6	1.6 (1590)	2.1644–2.1654	③	0.004–0.014	4	1.7707–1.7717	0.0010–0.0017	0.008–0.014
	F22A1	2.2 (2156)	①	⑧	0.004–0.014	4	1.7710–1.7717	0.0008–0.0019	0.008–0.014
	H22A1	2.2 (2156)	①	⑧	0.004–0.014	4	1.8888–1.8898	0.0011–0.0022	0.006–0.012
	H23A1	2.3 (2259)	①	⑧	0.004–0.014	4	1.7710–1.7717	0.0011–0.0022	0.008–0.014

① No. 1, 2—1.9676–1.9685
No. 3—1.9674–1.9683
No. 4—1.9665–1.9688
No. 5—1.9680–1.9690

② No. 2, 3, 4—0.0010–0.0017
No. 1, 5—0.0007–0.0014

③ No. 1, 5—0.0007–0.0014
No. 2, 4—0.0010–0.0017
No. 3—0.0012–0.0019

④ No. 1, 2—1.9676–1.9685
No. 3—1.9674–1.9683
No. 4, 5—1.9655–1.9688

⑤ No. 1, 2—0.0009–0.0018
No. 3—0.0014–0.0017
No. 4, 5—0.0005–0.0015

⑥ Prelude 2.0S—0.0008–0.0015
Prelude 2.0Si—0.0010–0.0017

⑦ No. 3—2.1642–2.1651

⑧ No. 1, 2—0.0008–0.0018
No. 3—0.0010–0.0019
No. 4—0.0005–0.0015
No. 5—0.0004–0.0013

VALVE SPECIFICATIONS

Year	Engine ID/VIN	Engine Displacement Liters (cc)	Seat Angle (deg.)	Face Angle (deg.)	Spring Test Pressure (lbs. @ in.)	Spring Installed Height (in.)	Stem-to-Guide Clearance (in.)		Stem Diameter (in.)	
							Intake	Exhaust	Intake	Exhaust
1990	D15B1	1.5 (1493)	45	45	NA	NA	0.001–0.002	0.002–0.003	0.2157–0.2161	0.2147–0.2150
	D16A6	1.6 (1590)	45	45	NA	NA	0.001–0.002	0.002–0.003	0.2157–0.2161	0.2147–0.2150
	F22A1	2.2 (2156)	45	45	NA	NA	0.0009–0.0019	0.002–0.003	0.2157–0.2161	0.2146–0.2150
	B20A3	2.0 (1955)	45	45	NA	NA	0.001–0.002	①	0.2591–0.2594	②
	B21A1	2.1 (2056)	45	45	NA	NA	0.001–0.002	0.002–0.003	0.2591–0.2594	0.2579–0.2583
1991	D15B1	1.5 (1493)	45	45	NA	NA	0.001–0.002	0.002–0.003	0.2157–0.2161	0.2147–0.2150
	D16A6	1.6 (1590)	45	45	NA	NA	0.001–0.002	0.002–0.003	0.2157–0.2161	0.2147–0.2150
	F22A1	2.2 (2156)	45	45	NA	NA	0.0009–0.0019	0.002–0.003	0.2157–0.2161	0.2146–0.2150
	B20A5	2.0 (1955)	45	45	NA	NA	0.001–0.002	①	0.2591–0.2594	②
	B21A1	2.1 (2056)	45	45	NA	NA	0.001–0.002	0.002–0.003	0.2591–0.2594	0.2579–0.2583
1992	D15B7	1.5 (1493)	45	45	NA	NA	0.001–0.002	0.002–0.003	0.2157–0.2161	0.2146–0.2150
	D16Z6	1.6 (1590)	45	45	NA	NA	0.001–0.002	0.002–0.003	0.2157–0.2161	0.2146–0.2150
	F22A1	2.2 (2156)	45	45	NA	NA	0.0008–0.0020	0.0021–0.0031	0.2159–0.2163	0.2145–0.2149
	H23A1	2.3 (2259)	45	45	NA	NA	0.001–0.002	0.002–0.003	0.2591–0.2594	0.2579–0.2583
1993	D15B7	1.5 (1493)	45	45	NA	NA	0.001–0.002	0.002–0.003	0.2157–0.2161	0.2146–0.2150
	D16Z6	1.6 (1590)	45	45	NA	NA	0.001–0.002	0.002–0.003	0.2157–0.2161	0.2146–0.2150
	F22A1	2.2 (2156)	45	45	NA	NA	0.0008–0.0020	0.0021–0.0031	0.2159–0.2163	0.2145–0.2149
	H22A1	2.2 (2156)	45	45	NA	NA	0.0010–0.0022	0.0020–0.0031	0.2156–0.2159	0.2156–0.2159
	H23A1	2.3 (2259)	45	45	NA	NA	0.001–0.002	0.002–0.003	0.2591–0.2594	0.2579–0.2583
1994	D15B7	1.5 (1493)	45	45	NA	NA	0.001–0.002	0.002–0.003	0.2157–0.2161	0.2146–0.2150
	D16Z6	1.6 (1590)	45	45	NA	NA	0.001–0.002	0.002–0.003	0.2157–0.2161	0.2146–0.2150
	F22A1	2.2 (2156)	45	45	NA	NA	0.0008–0.0020	0.0021–0.0031	0.2159–0.2163	0.2145–0.2149
	H22A1	2.2 (2156)	45	45	NA	NA	0.0010–0.0022	0.0020–0.0031	0.2156–0.2159	0.2156–0.2159
	H23A1	2.3 (2259)	45	45	NA	NA	0.001–0.002	0.002–0.003	0.2591–0.2594	0.2579–0.2583

NA—Not available
① Prelude 2.0S—0.002–0.004
   Prelude 2.0Si—0.002–0.003
② Prelude 2.0S—0.2732–0.2736
   Prelude 2.0Si—0.2579–0.2583

PISTON AND RING SPECIFICATIONS
All measurements are given in inches.

| Year | Engine ID/VIN | Engine Displacement Liters (cc) | Piston Clearance | Ring Gap | | | Ring Side Clearance | | |
				Top Compression	Bottom Compression	Oil Control	Top Compression	Bottom Compression	Oil Control
1990	D15B1	1.5 (1493)	0.0004–0.0016	0.006–0.012	0.012–0.018	0.008–0.031	0.0012–0.0024	0.0012–0.0022	Snug
	D16A6	1.6 (1590)	0.0004–0.0016	0.006–0.012	0.012–0.018	0.008–0.031	0.0012–0.0024	0.0012–0.0022	Snug
	F22A1	2.2 (2156)	0.0008–0.0016	0.008–0.014	0.016–0.022	0.007–0.027	0.0014–0.0024	0.0011–0.0022	Snug
	B20A3	2.0 (1955)	0.0008–0.0016	0.008–0.014	0.016–0.022	0.008–0.020	0.0012–0.0022	0.0012–0.0022	Snug
	B21A1	2.1 (2056)	0.0004–0.0013	0.010–0.014	0.018–0.022	0.008–0.020	0.0014–0.0026	0.0012–0.0024	Snug
1991	D15B1	1.5 (1493)	0.0004–0.0016	0.006–0.012	0.012–0.018	0.008–0.031	0.0012–0.0024	0.0012–0.0022	Snug
	D16A6	1.6 (1590)	0.0004–0.0016	0.006–0.012	0.012–0.018	0.008–0.031	0.0012–0.0024	0.0012–0.0022	Snug
	F22A1	2.2 (2156)	0.0008–0.0016	0.008–0.014	0.016–0.022	0.007–0.027	0.0014–0.0024	0.0011–0.0022	Snug
	B20A5	2.0 (1955)	0.0008–0.0016	0.008–0.014	0.016–0.022	0.008–0.020	0.0012–0.0022	0.0012–0.0022	Snug
	B21A1	2.1 (2056)	0.0004–0.0013	0.010–0.014	0.018–0.022	0.008–0.020	0.0014–0.0026	0.0012–0.0024	Snug
1992	D15B1	1.5 (1493)	0.0004–0.0016	0.006–0.012	0.012–0.018	0.008–0.028	0.0012–0.0024	0.0012–0.0022	Snug
	D16Z6	1.6 (1590)	0.0004–0.0016	0.006–0.012	0.012–0.018	0.008–0.024	0.0012–0.0024	0.0012–0.0022	Snug
	F22A1	2.2 (2156)	0.0008–0.0016	0.008–0.014	0.016–0.022	0.008–0.028	0.0014–0.0024	0.0011–0.0022	Snug
	H23A1	2.3 (2259)	0.0003–0.0012	0.010–0.014	0.016–0.022	0.008–0.028	0.0014–0.0024	0.0012–0.0022	Snug
1993	D15B1	1.5 (1493)	0.0004–0.0016	0.006–0.012	0.012–0.018	0.008–0.028	0.0012–0.0024	0.0012–0.0022	Snug
	D16Z6	1.6 (1590)	0.0004–0.0016	0.006–0.012	0.012–0.018	0.008–0.024	0.0012–0.0024	0.0012–0.0022	Snug
	F22A1	2.2 (2156)	0.0008–0.0016	0.008–0.014	0.016–0.022	0.008–0.028	0.0014–0.0024	0.0011–0.0022	Snug
	H22A1	2.2 (2156)	0.0003–0.0012	0.010–0.014	0.024–0.030	①	0.0014–0.0024	0.0012–0.0022	Snug
	H23A1	2.3 (2259)	0.0003–0.0012	0.010–0.014	0.016–0.030	①	0.0014–0.0024	0.0012–0.0022	Snug
1994	D15B1	1.5 (1493)	0.0004–0.0016	0.006–0.012	0.012–0.018	0.008–0.028	0.0012–0.0024	0.0012–0.0022	Snug
	D16Z6	1.6 (1590)	0.0004–0.0016	0.006–0.012	0.012–0.018	0.008–0.024	0.0012–0.0024	0.0012–0.0022	Snug
	F22A1	2.2 (2156)	0.0008–0.0016	0.008–0.014	0.016–0.022	0.008–0.028	0.0014–0.0024	0.0011–0.0022	Snug
	H22A1	2.2 (2156)	0.0003–0.0012	0.010–0.014	0.024–0.030	①	0.0014–0.0024	0.0012–0.0022	Snug
	H23A1	2.3 (2259)	0.0003–0.0012	0.010–0.014	0.016–0.030	①	0.0014–0.0024	0.0012–0.0022	Snug

① Teikoku piston ring: 0.008–0.020
Riken piston ring: 0.008–0.028

TORQUE SPECIFICATIONS

All readings in ft. lbs.

Year	Engine ID/VIN	Engine Displacement Liters (cc)	Cylinder Head Bolts	Main Bearing Bolts	Rod Bearing Bolts	Crankshaft Pulley Bolts	Flywheel Bolts	Manifold		Spark Plugs	Lug Nuts
								Intake	Exhaust		
1990	D15B1	1.5 (1493)	47	33②	23	119②	87①	16	23	13	80
	D16A6	1.6 (1590)	47	47②	23	119②	87①	16	23	13	80
	F22A1	2.2 (2156)	78	52②	34	159②	76①	16	23	13	80
	B20A3	2.0 (1955)	49②	49②	23⑥	108②	76①	16	22	13	80
	B21A1	2.1 (2056)	49②	49②	34	108②	76①	16	22	13	80
1991	D15B1	1.5 (1493)	47	33②	23	119②	87①	16	23	13	80
	D16A6	1.6 (1590)	47	47②	23	119②	87①	16	23	13	80
	F22A1	2.2 (2156)	78	52②	34	159②	76①	16	23	13	80
	B20A5	2.0 (1955)	49②	49②	23③	108②	76①	16	22	13	80
	B21A1	2.1 (2056)	49②	49②	34	108②	76①	16	22	13	80
1992	D15B7	1.5 (1493)	47	33②	23	119②	87①	16	23	13	80
	D16Z6	1.6 (1590)	47	38②	23	119②	87①	16	23	13	80
	F22A1	2.2 (2156)	78	54②	34	159②	76①	16	23	13	80
	H23A1	2.3 (2259)	72	54②	34	159②	76①	16	23	13	80
1993	D15B7	1.5 (1493)	47	33②	23	119②	87①	16	23	13	80
	D16Z6	1.6 (1590)	47	38②	23	119②	87①	16	23	13	80
	F22A1	2.2 (2156)	78	54②	34	159②	76①	16	23	13	80
	H22A1	2.2 (2156)	72	54②	34	159②	76①	16	23	13	80
	H23A1	2.3 (2259)	72	54②	34	159②	76①	16	23	13	80
1994	D15B7	1.5 (1493)	47	33②	23	119②	87①	16	23	13	80
	D16Z6	1.6 (1590)	47	38②	23	119②	87①	16	23	13	80
	F22A1	2.2 (2156)	78	54②	34	159②	76①	16	23	13	80
	H22A1	2.2 (2156)	72	54②	34	159②	76①	16	23	13	80
	H23A1	2.3 (2259)	72	54②	34	159②	76①	16	23	13	80

① Auto transaxle: 54 ft. lbs.
② Dip bolts in clean engine oil
③ Fuel injected engine—34 ft. lbs.

BRAKE SPECIFICATIONS

All measurements in inches unless noted.

Year	Model	Master Cylinder Bore	Brake Disc Original Thickness	Brake Disc Minimum Thickness	Maximum Runout	Brake Drum Diameter Original Inside Diameter	Brake Drum Diameter Max. Wear Limit	Brake Drum Diameter Maximum Machine Diameter	Minimum Lining Thickness Front	Minimum Lining Thickness Rear
1990	Civic	NA	0.83	0.75	0.004	7.09	7.13	7.13	0.120	0.079
	Civic SW	NA	0.75	0.67 ⑨	0.004	7.90	7.95	7.95	0.120	0.080
	CRX	NA	⑤ ⑫	0.67 ⑪	0.004	7.09	7.13	7.13	0.120	0.080
	Accord	NA	0.91 F 0.39 R	0.83 F 0.32 R	0.004	8.661	8.701	8.701	0.063	0.080
	Prelude	NA	0.83 F 0.39 R	0.75 F 0.31 R	⑥	—	—	—	0.120	0.080
1991	Civic	NA	0.75 ⑦	0.67 ⑧	0.004	7.09	7.13	7.13	0.120	0.079
	Civic Wagon	NA	0.83 ④	0.75 ⑩	0.004	7.90	7.95	7.95	0.120	0.080
	CRX	NA	⑤	0.67 ⑨	0.004	7.09	7.13	7.13	0.120	0.080
	Accord	NA	0.91 F 0.39 R	0.83 F 0.32 R	0.004	8.661	8.701	8.701	0.120	0.080
	Prelude	NA	0.83 F 0.39 R	0.75 F 0.31 R	0.004	—	—	—	0.080	0.080
1992	Civic	NA	0.827 F 0.350 R	0.748 F 0.320 R	0.004	7.09 ①	7.15 ②	7.13 ③	0.080	0.080
	Accord	NA	0.906 F 0.390 R	0.827 F 0.315 R	0.004	8.661	8.701	8.701	0.120	0.080
	Prelude	NA	0.906 F 0.390 R	0.827 F 0.320 R	0.004	—	—	—	0.080	0.080
1993	Civic	NA	0.827 F 0.350 R	0.748 F 0.320 R	0.004	7.09 ①	7.15 ②	7.13 ③	0.080	0.080
	del Sol	NA	0.830 F 0.350 R	0.750 F 0.310 R	0.004	7.09	7.13	7.11	0.060	0.080
	Accord	NA	0.906 F 0.390 R	0.827 F 0.315 R	0.004	8.661	8.701	8.701	0.120	0.080
	Prelude	NA	0.906 F 0.390 R	0.827 F 0.320 R	0.004	—	—	—	0.080	0.080
1994	Civic	NA	0.827 F 0.350 R	0.748 F 0.320 R	0.004	7.09 ①	7.15 ②	7.13 ③	0.080	0.080
	del Sol	NA	0.830 F 0.350 R	0.750 F 0.310 R	0.004	7.09	7.13	7.11	0.060	0.080
	Accord	NA	0.906 F 0.390 R	0.827 F 0.315 R	0.004	8.661	8.701	8.701	0.120	0.080
	Prelude	NA	0.906 F 0.390 R	0.827 F 0.320 R	0.004	—	—	—	0.080	0.080

NA—Not available
F—Front
R—Rear
① Except 1.5L 4-door with A/T and 1.6L—7.87
② Except 1.5L 4-door with A/T and 1.6L—7.95
③ Except 1.5L 4-door with A/T and 1.6L—7.91
④ 4WD—0.75
⑤ CRX Std.—0.83
  CRX HF—0.67
  CRX Si—0.75

⑥ Front—0.004
  Rear—0.006
⑦ Civic EX—0.83
⑧ Civic EX—0.750
⑨ CRX Std.—0.750
  CRX HF—0.590
⑩ 4WD—0.67
⑪ Rear—0.31
⑫ Rear—0.39

WHEEL ALIGNMENT

Year	Model	Caster Range (deg.)	Caster Preferred Setting (deg.)	Camber Range (deg.)	Camber Preferred Setting (deg.)	Toe-in (in.)	Steering Axis Inclination (deg.)
1990	Civic	2P–4P	3P	1N–1P	0	0	—
	Civic SW	$1\frac{15}{16}$P–$3\frac{15}{16}$P	$2\frac{15}{16}$P	$\frac{11}{16}$N–$\frac{15}{16}$P	$\frac{5}{16}$P	0	—
	Civic 4WD	$1\frac{15}{16}$P–$3\frac{15}{16}$P	$2\frac{15}{16}$P	$\frac{7}{16}$N–$1\frac{9}{16}$P	$\frac{9}{16}$P	0	—
	Accord	2P–4P	3P	1N–1P	0	0	—
	Prelude	$1\frac{13}{16}$P–$2\frac{13}{16}$P	$2\frac{3}{8}$P	1N–1P	0	0	—
1991	Civic	2P–4P	3P	1N–1P	0	0	—
	Civic SW	$1\frac{15}{16}$P–$3\frac{15}{16}$P	$2\frac{15}{16}$P	$\frac{11}{16}$N–$\frac{15}{16}$P	$\frac{5}{16}$P	0	—
	Civic 4WD	$1\frac{15}{16}$P–$3\frac{15}{16}$P	$2\frac{15}{16}$P	$\frac{7}{16}$N–$1\frac{9}{16}$P	$\frac{9}{16}$P	0	—
	Accord	2P–4P	3P	1N–1P	0	0	—
	Prelude	$1\frac{13}{16}$P–$2\frac{13}{16}$P	$2\frac{3}{8}$P	1N–1P	0	0	—
1992	Civic	$\frac{1}{10}$P–$2\frac{1}{10}$P	$1\frac{1}{10}$P	1N–1P	0	0	—
	Accord	2P–4P	3P	1N–1P	$\frac{9}{16}$P	0	—
	Prelude	$1\frac{13}{16}$P–$2\frac{13}{16}$P	$2\frac{3}{8}$P	1N–1P	0	0	—
1993	Civic	$\frac{1}{10}$P–$2\frac{1}{10}$P	$1\frac{1}{10}$P	1N–1P	0	0	—
	del Sol	$\frac{1}{10}$P–$2\frac{1}{10}$P	$1\frac{1}{10}$P	①	②	0	—
	Accord	2P–4P	3P	1N–1P	$\frac{9}{16}$P	0	—
	Prelude	$1\frac{13}{16}$P–$2\frac{13}{16}$P	$2\frac{3}{8}$P	1N–1P	0	0	—
1994	Civic	$\frac{1}{10}$P–$2\frac{1}{10}$P	$1\frac{1}{10}$P	1N–1P	0	0	—
	del Sol	$\frac{1}{10}$P–$2\frac{1}{10}$P	$1\frac{1}{10}$P	①	②	0	—
	Accord	2P–4P	3P	1N–1P	$\frac{9}{16}$P	0	—
	Prelude	$1\frac{13}{16}$P–$2\frac{13}{16}$P	$2\frac{3}{8}$P	1N–1P	0	0	—

N—Negative
P—Positive
① Front: $1\frac{1}{16}$N–$\frac{15}{16}$P
　Rear: $1\frac{1}{3}$N–$\frac{2}{3}$P
② Front: $\frac{1}{16}$N
　Rear: $\frac{1}{3}$N

ENGINE MECHANICAL

Engine Assembly

REMOVAL AND INSTALLATION

1990-91 Civic and CRX

1. Disconnect the negative battery cable. Remove the battery and the battery tray.

2. Apply the parking brake and place blocks behind the rear wheels. Raise and safely support the vehicle.

3. Scribe a line where the hood brackets meet the inside of the hood.

4. Disconnect the windshield washer fluid tubes. Unbolt and remove the hood.

5. Remove the engine and wheel-well splash shields.

6. Drain the oil from the engine, the coolant from the radiator and the transaxle oil from the transaxle.

7. Remove the air intake duct and the front air intake duct.

8. Relieve the fuel pressure from the fuel system, by slowly loosening the banjo bolt on the fuel filler approximately 1 turn.

NOTE: Keep any and all open flames away from the work area. Before disconnecting any fuel lines, the fuel pressure should be relieved. Place a suitable shop towel over the fuel filler to prevent the pressurized fuel from spraying over the engine.

9. Disconnect and tag the engine compartment harness connectors, battery wires and transaxle ground cable.

10. Remove the throttle cable by loosening the locknut and the throt-

tle cable adjust nut, then slip the throttle cable end out of the throttle bracket and accelerator linkage. Be sure not to bend the cable when removing it. Do not use pliers to remove the cable from the linkage. Always replace a kinked cable with a new one.

11. Disconnect and tag the engine wire connectors and spark plug wires. Bring the engine up to TDC on the No. 1 cylinder. Mark the position of the distributor rotor in relation to the distributor housing and the distributor in relation to the engine block. Remove the distributor assembly from the cylinder head.

12. Disconnect the radiator hoses and heater hoses. Disconnect the transaxle fluid cooler lines. Remove the speedometer cable.

NOTE: Do not remove the speedometer cable holder, because the speedometer gear may fall into the transaxle housing.

13. If equipped with power steering, remove the mounting bolts and power steering belt, then without disconnecting the hoses, pull the pump away from it's mounting bracket and lay aside.

14. Disconnect and tag the alternator wiring, remove the alternator adjusting bolts, mounting bolts and belt. Remove the alternator from the vehicle.

15. Loosen the air conditioning belt adjust bolt and the idler puller nut. Remove the compressor mounting bolts. Disconnect the air conditioning suction and discharge lines, only if it is necessary. Lift the compressor out of the bracket with the air conditioning hoses attached and wire the compressor to the front beam of the vehicle.

NOTE: If it is necessary to remove the air conditioning suction and discharge lines, properly discharge the refrigerant from the air conditioning system.

———— CAUTION ————
An approved R-12 recovery/recycling machine that meets SAE standard J-1991 should be employed when discharging the air conditioning system. Follow the operating instructions provided with the approved equipment exactly to properly discharge the system.

16. If equipped with an automatic transaxle, proceed as follows:
   a. Remove the header pipe, header pipe bracket, torque con-

verter cover and shift control cable holder.
   b. Remove the shift control cable by removing the cotter pin, control pin and control lever roller from the control lever.

17. If equipped with manual transaxles, remove the shift lever torque rod, shift rod and clutch cable. On reassembly, slide the retainer back into place after driving in the spring pin.

18. Remove the wheelwell splash shields and engine splash shields. Remove the right and left halfshafts from the transaxle and cover the shafts with a plastic bag so as to prevent the oil from spilling over the work area. Be sure to coat all precision finished surfaces with clean engine oil or grease.

19. On 4WD vehicles equipped with automatic transaxles, remove the cable clip and the control pin. Loosen the shift control cable nut and then remove the control cable.

20. On 4WD vehicles equipped with manual transaxles, remove the cotter pins and the 3 cable bracket mounting bolts. Remove the cable bracket from the rear of the transaxle mount bracket.

21. Attach a suitable chain hoist to the engine block hoist brackets and raise the hoist just enough to remove the slack from the chain. To attach the rear engine chain, remove the plastic radiator hose bracket and hook the chain to the top of the clutch cable bracket.

22. Remove the rear transaxle mount bracket. Remove the bolts from the front transaxle bolt mount. Remove the bolts from the engine side mount. Remove the bolts from the engine side transaxle mounts.

23. Check that the engine/transaxle assembly are completely free of vacuum, fuel, coolant hoses and electrical wires.

24. Slowly raise the engine approximately 6 inches and stop. Check again that the engine/transaxle assembly are completely free of vacuum, fuel, coolant hoses and electrical wires.

25. Raise the engine/transaxle assembly all the way up and out of the vehicle, once it is clear from the vehicle, lower the assembly into a suitable engine stand.

To install:
26. Installation is the reverse order of the removal procedure. Use the following steps to aid in the installation procedure.

27. Torque the engine mount bolts in the following sequence; be sure to

replace the rear transaxle bolt and the front transaxle bolt with new bolts:
   Side transaxle mount — 40 ft. lbs. (54 Nm).
   Rear transaxle mount bracket — 43 ft. lbs. (58 Nm).
   Front transaxle mount — 43 ft. lbs. (58 Nm).
   Engine side mount — 40 ft. lbs. (54 Nm).

NOTE: Failure to tighten the bolts in the proper sequence can cause excessive noise and vibration and reduce bushing life. Be sure to check that the bushings are not twisted or offset.

28. Check that the spring clip on the end of each driveshaft clicks into place. Be sure to use new spring clips on installation.

29. After assembling the fuel line parts, turn the ignition switch (do not operate the starter) to the **ON** position so the fuel pump is operated for approximately 2 seconds so as to pressurize the fuel system. Repeat this procedure 2-3 times and check for a possible fuel leak.

30. Bleed the air from the cooling system at the bleed bolt with the heater valve open.

31. Adjust the throttle cable tension, install the air conditioning compressor and belt and adjust all belt tensions. Adjust the clutch cable freeplay and check that the transaxle shifts into gear smoothly.

32. Check the ignition timing.

33. Install the speedometer cable, be sure to align the tab on the cable end with the slot holder. Install the clip so the bent leg is on the groove side. After installing, pull the speedometer cable to make sure it is secure.

1992-94 Civic and Civic Del Sol

1. Disconnect the negative battery cable.

2. Apply the parking brake and place blocks behind the rear wheels. Raise the vehicle and support it safely.

3. Remove the radiator cap.

4. Remove the front tires and wheels and remove the engine splash shield.

5. Drain the coolant, transaxle oil and engine oil.

6. Lower the vehicle, open the hood and secure it as far open as possible.

7. Remove the underhood ABS fuse/relay box.

8. Remove the air intake hose, resonator and air cleaner assembly.

9. Relieve the system fuel pressure by turning the fuel filter service bolt one turn.

10. Remove the fuel feed hose and charcoal canister hose from the intake manifold.

11. Remove the throttle cable by loosening the locknut and slipping the cable end out of the accelerator linkage.

12. Disconnect the engine wire harness connectors at the left side of the engine compartment.

13. Remove the fuel return hose and brake booster vacuum hose.

14. Remove the engine wire harness connectors, terminal and clamps on the right side of the engine compartment.

15. Remove the battery/starter cable from the underhood fuse/relay box. Remove the ABS power cable from the battery terminal.

16. Remove the engine ground cable from the cylinder head.

17. Remove the power steering pump and belt, but do not disconnect the power steering hoses.

18. Remove the air conditioning belt and compressor and disconnect the electrical connector, but do not disconnect the air conditioning hoses.

19. Remove the transaxle ground cable and remove the ATF cooler lines, if equipped with automatic transaxle.

20. Remove the upper and lower radiator hoses and remove the heater hoses.

21. Remove the exhaust pipe and stay.

22. On automatic transaxle, disconnect the shift cable.

23. On manual transaxle, remove the clutch slave cylinder and pipe/hose assembly. Disconnect the shift rod and extension rod from the transaxle.

24. Remove the damper fork and disconnect the suspension lower arm ball joint, using the special tool.

25. Remove the driveshafts.

26. Attach an engine lifting device to the engine and remove the left and right engine stopper rubbers and brackets.

27. Remove the rear engine mounting bracket. Remove the engine support nuts.

28. Loosen the mount bolt and pivot the engine side mount out of the way.

29. Remove the transaxle mount nuts and pivot the mount out of the way.

30. Raise the engine lifting device so it is tight.

31. Check that all electrical, vacuum, coolant and fuel lines are clear and disconnected.

32. Remove engine from the vehicle.

To install:

33. Torque the engine mount bolts in the following sequence:

Side transaxle mount — 40 ft. lbs. (55 Nm).

Rear engine mount bracket — 40 ft. lbs. (55 Nm).

Right front transaxle mount — 28 ft. lbs. (39 Nm).

Engine side mount nut — 65 ft. lbs. (40 Nm).

Engine side mount bolt — 28 ft. lbs. (38 Nm)

NOTE: Failure to tighten the bolts in the proper sequence can cause excessive noise and vibration and reduce bushing life. Be sure to check that the bushings are not twisted or offset.

34. Check that the spring clip on the end of each driveshaft clicks into place. Be sure to use new spring clips on installation.

35. After assembling the fuel line parts, turn the ignition switch (do not operate the starter) to the **ON** position so the fuel pump is operated for approximately 2 seconds so as to pressurize the fuel system. Repeat this procedure 2-3 times and check for a possible fuel leak.

36. Bleed the air from the cooling system at the bleed bolt with the heater valve open.

37. Adjust the throttle cable tension, install the air conditioning compressor and belt and adjust all belt tensions. Adjust the clutch cable freeplay and check that the transaxle shifts into gear smoothly.

38. Check the ignition timing.

39. Install the speedometer cable, be sure to align the tab on the cable end with the slot holder. Install the clip so the bent leg is on the groove side. After installing, pull the speedometer cable to make sure it is secure.

1990-91 Prelude

1. Raise the vehicle and support it safely.

2. Disconnect both battery cables from the battery. Remove the battery, and then remove the battery tray from the engine compartment.

3. Remove the knob caps covering the headlights' manual retracting knobs, then turn the knobs to bring the headlights to the ON position.

4. Remove the 5 screws retaining the grille and remove the grille.

5. Remove the splash guard from under the engine. Unbolt and remove the hood.

6. Remove the oil filler cap and drain the engine oil.

7. Remove the radiator cap, then open the radiator drain petcock and drain the coolant from the radiator.

8. Remove the transaxle filler plug, then remove the drain plug and drain the transaxle.

9. On carbureted vehicles:

a. Label and then remove the wires at the coil and the engine secondary ground cable located on the valve cover.

b. Remove the air cleaner cover and filter.

c. Remove the air intake ducts. Remove the 2 nuts and 2 bolts from the air cleaner, remove the air control valve. Remove the air cleaner as required.

d. Loosen the locknut on the throttle cable and loosen the cable adjusting nut, then slip the cable end out of the carburetor linkage.

NOTE: Be careful not to bend or kink the throttle cable. Always replace a damaged cable.

e. Disconnect the No. 1 control box connector. Remove the control box from its bracket and let it hang next to the engine.

f. Disconnect the fuel line at the fuel filter and remove the solenoid vacuum hose at the charcoal canister.

g. On California and high altitude vehicles, remove the air jet controller.

10. On fuel injected vehicles:

a. Remove the air intake duct. Disconnect the cruise control vacuum tube from the air intake duct and remove the resonator tube.

b. Remove the secondary ground cable from the top of the engine.

c. Disconnect the air box connecting tube. Unscrew the tube clamp bolt and disconnect the emission tubes.

d. Remove the air cleaner case mounting nuts and remove the air cleaner case assembly.

e. Loosen the locknut on the throttle cable and loosen the cable adjusting nut, then slip the cable end out of the bracket and linkage.

NOTE: Be careful not to bend or kink the throttle cable. Always replace a damaged cable.

f. Disconnect the following wires, the ground cable at the fuse box. The engine compartment subharness connector and clamp. The high tension wire and ignition primary leads at the coil. The radio condenser connector at the coil.

g. Using the following procedures relieve the fuel system pressure by placing a shop rag over the fuel filter to absorb any gasoline which may be sprayed on the engine while relieving the pressure. Slowly loosen the service bolt approximately 1 full turn. This will relieve any pressure in the system. Using a new sealing washer, tighten the service bolt.

h. Disconnect the fuel return hose from the pressure regulator. Remove the banjo nut and then remove the fuel hose.

i. Disconnect the vacuum hose from the brake booster.

11. Disconnect the radiator and heater hoses at the engine. Label the heater hoses so they can be installed correctly.

12. On automatic transaxle equipped vehicles, disconnect the transaxle oil cooler hoses at the transaxle, let the fluid drain from the hoses, then hang the hoses up near the radiator.

13. On manual transaxle equipped vehicles, loosen the clutch cable adjusting nut and remove the clutch cable from the release arm.

14. Disconnect the battery cable at the transaxle and the starter cable at the starter motor terminal.

15. Disconnect both engine harness connectors.

16. Remove the speedometer cable clip, then pull the cable out of the holder.

NOTE: Do not remove the holder as the speedometer gear may drop into the transaxle.

17. If equipped with power steering:

a. Remove the speed sensor complete with hoses.

b. Remove the adjusting bolt and the drive belt.

c. Without disconnecting the hoses, pull the pump away from its mounting bracket and position it out of the way.

d. Remove the power steering hose bracket from the cylinder head.

18. Remove the center beam beneath the engine.

19. If equipped with air conditioning:

a. Remove the compressor clutch lead wire.

b. Loosen the belt adjusting bolt.

NOTE: Do not remove the air conditioner hoses. The air conditioner compressor can be moved without discharging the air conditioner system.

c. Remove the compressor mounting bolts, then lift the compressor out of the bracket with the hoses attached, and hang it on the front bulkhead with a piece of wire.

20. If equipped with manual transaxle, remove the shift rod yoke attaching bolt and disconnect the shift lever torque rod from the clutch housing.

21. If equipped with automatic transaxle:

a. Remove the center console.

b. Place the shift lever in reverse, then remove the lock pin from the end of the shift cable.

c. Unscrew the cable mounting bolts and remove the shift cable holder.

d. Remove the throttle cable from the throttle lever. Loosen the lower locknut, then remove the cable from the bracket.

NOTE: Do not loosen the upper locknut as it will change the transaxle shift points.

22. Disconnect the right and left lower ball joints and the tie rod ends.

23. Remove the halfshafts as follows:

a. Lower the vehicle. Loosen the 32mm spindle nuts with a socket. Raise and support the vehicle safely.

b. Remove the front wheel the spindle nut.

c. Remove the damper fork and the damper pinch bolts.

d. Remove the ball joint bolt and separate the ball joint from the lower arm control (Prelude).

e. Disconnect the tie rods from the steering knuckles.

f. Pull the front hub outward and off the halfshafts.

g. Using a small prybar, pry out the inboard CV-joint approximately 1/2 in. (13mm) in order to release the spring clip from the differential, then pull the halfshaft out of the transaxle case.

NOTE: When installing the halfshaft, insert the shaft until the spring clip clicks into the groove. Always use a new spring clip when installing driveshafts.

24. On fuel injected vehicles, disconnect the sub-engine harness connectors and clamp.

25. Remove the exhaust header pipe.

26. Attach a chain hoist to the engine and raise it just enough to remove the slack.

27. Disconnect the No. 2 control box connector, lift the control box off its bracket, and let it hang next to the engine.

28. If equipped with air conditioning, remove the idle control solenoid valve.

29. Remove the air chamber, if equipped.

30. Remove the 3 engine mount bolts located under the air chamber, then push the engine mount into the engine mount tower.

31. Remove the front engine mount nut, then remove the rear engine mount nut.

32. Loosen and remove the alternator belt. Disconnect the alternator wire harness and remove the alternator.

33. Remove the bolt from the rear torque rod at the engine, then loosen the bolt in the frame mount and swing the rod up and out of the way.

34. Raise the engine carefully from the vehicle, checking that all wires and hoses have been removed from the engine/transaxle. Raise the engine all the way up and remove it from the vehicle.

To install:

35. Installation is the reverse of the removal procedure. Use the following steps to aid in the installation procedure.

36. Tighten the engine mount bolts in the following sequence:

a. Replace the 3 rear engine mount bolts with new ones and tighten to 40 ft. lbs. (55 Nm).

b. Replace the rear engine mount-to-frame bolt with a new one and tighten temporarily.

c. Replace the front engine mount-to-frame bolt with a new one and tighten temporarily.

d. Tighten the transaxle mount bolts to 28 ft. lbs. (39 Nm) for the vertical bolt and 40 ft. lbs. (55 Nm) for the horizontal bolt. Tighten the transaxle mount-to-frame bolt to 54 ft. lbs. (75 Nm).

e. Tighten the side engine mount bolts to 28 ft. lbs. (39 Nm) and the side engine mount through bolt to 54 ft. lbs. (75 Nm).

f. Tighten the rear engine mount-to-frame bolt to 51 ft. lbs. (70 Nm).

g. Tighten the front engine mount-to-frame bolt to 51 ft. lbs. (70 Nm).

NOTE: Failure to tighten the bolts in the proper sequence can cause excessive noise and vibration and reduce bushing life. Check that the bushings are not twisted or offset.

37. Check that the spring clip on the end of each halfshaft clicks into the differential. Use new clips on installation.

38. After assembling the fuel line parts, turn the ignition switch (do not operate the starter) to the **ON** position, so the fuel pump is operated for approximately 2 seconds so as to pressurize the fuel system. Repeat this procedure 2-3 times and check for a possible fuel leak.

39. Bleed the air from the cooling system at the bleed bolt, with the heater valve open.

40. Adjust the throttle cable tension, install the air conditioning compressor and belt and adjust all belt tensions. Adjust the clutch cable free-play and check that the transaxle shifts into gear smoothly.

41. Check the ignition timing.

Accord

1. Disconnect the battery cables and remove the battery and battery case.

2. Raise and safely support the vehicle.

3. Place the hood in a vertical position and safely support it in place. Do not remove the hood.

4. Remove the engine splash shield. Drain the engine oil, coolant and transaxle fluid.

5. Remove the air intake duct and the air cleaner case.

6. Relieve the fuel system pressure by slowly loosening the service bolt on the fuel pipe about 1 turn.

7. Remove the fuel feed hose from the fuel pipe and the return hose from the pressure control valve.

8. Disconnect the 2 connectors and remove the control box from the firewall.

NOTE: Do not disconnect the vacuum hoses.

9. Disconnect the vacuum hose from the charcoal canister and the charcoal canister hose from the throttle body.

10. Remove the ground cable from the transaxle.

11. Remove the throttle cable by loosening the locknut, then slip the cable end out of the throttle bracket and accelerator linkage.

NOTE: Be careful not to bend the cable when removing. Do not use pliers to remove the cable from the linkage. Always replace a kinked cable with a new one.

12. Disconnect the connector and the vacuum hose, then remove the cruise control actuator.

13. Remove the brake booster vacuum hose and mount vacuum hose from the intake manifold.

14. Disconnect the 3 engine wire harness connectors from the main wire harness at the right side of the engine compartment and remove the engine wire harness terminal and the starter cable terminal from the underhood relay box and clamps. Then remove the transaxle ground terminal.

15. Disconnect the 2 engine wire harness connectors from the main harness and the resistor at the left side of the engine compartment.

16. Remove the engine ground wire from the cylinder head cover and power steering pump bracket.

17. Remove the mounting bolts and the power steering belt from the power steering pump, then without disconnecting the hoses, pull the pump away from it's mounting bracket. Support the pump out of the way.

18. Remove the mounting bolts and belt from the air conditioning compressor, then without disconnecting the hoses, pull the compressor away from it's mounting bracket. Support the compressor out of the way.

19. Disconnect the heater hoses. Disconnect the radiator hoses, automatic transaxle cooler hoses and the cooling fan motor connectors. Remove the radiator/cooling fan assembly.

20. Remove the speed sensor without disconnecting the hoses or connector.

21. Remove the center beam.

22. Remove the exhaust pipe nuts and bracket mounting bolts.

23. Remove the halfshafts as follows:

   a. Remove the wheel and tire assemblies.

   b. Raise the locking tab on the spindle nut and remove it.

   c. Remove the damper fork nut and damper pinch bolt and remove the damper fork.

   d. Remove the cotter pin and castle nut from the lower ball joint.

   e. Using a suitable puller, separate the lower control arm from the knuckle.

   f. Pull the knuckle outward and remove the halfshaft outboard CV-joint from the knuckle using a suitable plastic hammer.

   g. Using a suitable prybar, pry the halfshaft out to force the set ring at the end of the halfshaft past the groove.

   h. Pull the inboard CV-joint and remove the halfshaft and CV-joint out of the differential case or intermediate shaft as an assembly.

NOTE: Do not pull on the halfshaft, as the CV-joint may come apart. Tie plastic bags over the halfshaft ends to protect them.

24. On manual transaxle equipped vehicles, remove the clutch release hose from the clutch damper on the transaxle housing. Remove the shift cable and the select cable with the cable bracket from the transaxle.

NOTE: Be careful not to bend the cable when removing. Do not use pliers to remove the cable. Always replace a kinked cable with a new one.

25. On automatic transaxle equipped vehicles, remove the engine stiffener, then remove the torque converter cover. Remove the cable holder, then remove the shift control lever bolt and shift control cable.

NOTE: Be careful not to bend the cable when removing. Do not use pliers to remove the cable. Always replace a kinked cable with a new one.

26. Attach a suitable lifting device to the engine. Raise the engine to unload the engine mounts.

27. Remove the front and rear engine mounting bolts.

28. Remove the engine side mount and mounting bolt and the side transaxle mount and mounting bolt.

29. Make sure the engine/transaxle assembly is completely free of vacuum hoses, fuel and coolant hoses and electrical wires.

30. Slowly raise the engine approximately 6 in. (152mm). Check again that all hoses and wires have been disconnected from the engine/transaxle assembly.

31. Raise the engine/transaxle assembly all the way and remove it from the vehicle.

   To install:

32. Installation is the reverse of the removal procedure. Attention to the following steps will aid installation.

33. Tighten the engine mounting bolts in the following sequence:

   a. Tighten the rear engine mount-to-frame bolts snug only.

b. Replace the rear engine mount through bolt with a new one and tighten snug only.

c. Replace the front engine mount through bolt with a new one and tighten snug only.

d. Tighten the side transaxle mount through bolt snug only.

e. Tighten the engine side mount through bolt snug only.

f. Tighten the side transaxle mount-to-block nuts to 28 ft. lbs. (39 Nm).

g. Tighten the engine side mount-to-block bolt and nut to 40 ft. lbs. (55 Nm).

h. Tighten the rear engine mount through bolt to 47 ft. lbs. (65 Nm).

i. Tighten the rear engine mount-to-frame bolts to 40 ft. lbs. (55 Nm).

j. Tighten the front engine mount through bolt to 47 ft. lbs. (65 Nm).

k. Tighten the side transaxle mount through bolt to 40 ft. lbs. (55 Nm).

l. Tighten the engine side mount through bolt to 40 ft. lbs. (55 Nm).

NOTE: Failure to tighten the bolts in the proper sequence can cause excessive noise and vibration and reduce bushing life. Check that the bushings are not twisted or offset.

34. Make sure the spring clip on the end of each halfshaft clicks into place. Use new clips when installing.

35. Bleed the air from the cooling system at the bleed bolt with the heater valve open.

36. Adjust the throttle cable tension and check the clutch pedal freeplay.

37. Check that the transaxle shifts into gear smoothly.

38. Adjust the tension of the accessory drive belts.

39. After assembling the fuel line parts, turn the ignition switch **ON**, but do not operate the starter, so the fuel pump is operated for approximately 2 seconds and the fuel is pressurized. Repeat 2-3 times and check for fuel leakage.

40. Check the ignition timing.

1992-94 Prelude

1. Disconnect the battery cables and remove the battery and battery case.

2. Raise and safely support the vehicle.

3. Place the hood in a vertical position and safely support it in place. Remove the radiator cap.

4. Remove the front wheels and remove the engine splash shield. Drain the engine oil, coolant and transaxle fluid.

5. Remove the air intake duct and the air cleaner case.

6. Relieve the fuel system pressure by slowly loosening the service bolt on the fuel pipe about 1 turn.

7. Remove the fuel feed hose from the fuel pipe.

8. Disconnect the resistor connector from the resistor on the left side of the engine compartment.

9. Disconnect the throttle cable by loosening the locknut and slipping the cable end out of the accelerator linkage.

NOTE: Be careful not to bend or kink the cable when removing it. If cable is kinked it must be replaced.

10. Remove the engine wire harness connectors, terminal and clamps from the right side of the engine.

11. Disconnect the power cable from the under hood fuse/relay box.

12. Disconnect the brake booster vacuum hose and emission control vacuum tubes from the intake manifold.

13. Disconnect the vacuum tube and electrical connector from the cruise control actuator and remove the actuator.

14. Remove the engine ground cable from the cylinder head.

15. Remove the power steering belt and pump. Do not disconnect the power steering hoses.

16. Remove the air conditioning condenser fan and shroud and place a shield in front of the radiator.

17. Remove the air conditioning compressor drive belt and compressor. Do not remove the air conditioning lines. Position the compressor aside.

18. Remove the upper and lower radiator hoses and the heater hoses.

19. On automatic transaxle, remove the shift cable, transaxle ground cable and the cooler lines.

20. On manual transaxle, remove the shift cable and select cable. Remove the clutch slave cylinder and pipe/hose assembly.

21. Remove the clutch damper assembly and the speed sensor assembly.

22. Remove the exhaust pipe and stay.

23. Remove the damper fork and using the special tool, disconnect the suspension lower arm ball joint.

24. Remove the driveshaft and swing it out of the way, under the fender.

25. Attach an engine lifting device to the engine.

26. Remove the rear mounting bracket. Remove the front mounting bracket.

27. Remove the left side engine mount and remove the transaxle mount and mounting bracket.

28. Raise the engine and check that all necessary disconnections were made.

29. Remove the engine from the vehicle.

To install:

30. Installation is the reverse of the removal procedure. Attention to the following steps will aid installation.

31. Tighten the engine mounting bolts in the following sequence:

a. Tighten the rear engine mount-to-frame bolts snug only.

b. Replace the rear engine mount through bolt with a new one and tighten snug only.

c. Replace the rear engine mount through bolt with a new one and tighten snug only.

d. Tighten the side transaxle mount through bolt snug only.

e. Tighten the engine side mount through bolt snug only.

f. Tighten the side transaxle mount-to-block nuts to 28 ft. lbs. (39 Nm).

g. Tighten the engine side mount-to-block bolt and nut to 40 ft. lbs. (55 Nm).

h. Tighten the rear engine mount through bolt to 47 ft. lbs. (65 Nm).

i. Tighten the rear engine mount-to-frame bolts to 40 ft. lbs. (55 Nm).

j. Tighten the front engine mount through bolt to 47 ft. lbs. (65 Nm).

k. Tighten the side transaxle mount through bolt to 40 ft. lbs. (55 Nm).

l. Tighten the engine side mount through bolt to 40 ft. lbs. (55 Nm).

NOTE: Failure to tighten the bolts in the proper sequence can cause excessive noise and vibration and reduce bushing life. Check that the bushings are not twisted or offset.

32. Make sure the spring clip on the end of each halfshaft clicks into place. Use new clips when installing.

33. Bleed the air from the cooling system at the bleed bolt with the heater valve open.

34. Adjust the throttle cable tension and check the clutch pedal freeplay.

35. Check that the transaxle shifts into gear smoothly.

36. Adjust the tension of the accessory drive belts.

37. After installing all fuel system components, pressurize the fuel system by cycling the ignition switch **ON** and then **OFF**. Do not operate the starter. Repeat 2-3 times and check for fuel leakage.

38. Check the ignition timing.

Cylinder Head

REMOVAL AND INSTALLATION

———— **WARNING** ————
To avoid damaging the cylinder head, wait until the engine coolant temperature drops below 100°F (38°C) before loosening the cylinder head bolts. Also, inspect the timing belt before removing the cylinder head.

1.5L and 1.6L Engines

1. Disconnect the negative battery cable.
2. Remove the radiator cap and drain the cooling system.
3. Relieve the fuel system pressure.
4. Remove the brake booster vacuum hose from the brake master cylinder power booster. Remove the engine secondary ground cable from the valve cover.
5. Remove the air intake hose and the air chamber. Relieve the fuel pressure. Disconnect the fuel hoses and fuel return hose.
6. Remove the air intake hose and resonator hose. Disconnect the throttle cable at the throttle body. If equipped with automatic transaxles, disconnect the throttle control cable at the throttle body.
7. Disconnect the charcoal canister hose at the throttle valve.
8. Disconnect the following engine wire connectors from the cylinder head and the intake manifold:
   a. 14 prong connector from the main wiring harness
   b. EACV connector
   c. Intake air temperature sensor connector
   d. Throttle angle sensor connector
   e. Injector connectors
   f. Ignition coil from the distributor
   g. Top dead center/crank sensor connector from the distributor.

h. Coolant temperature gauge sender connector.
   i. Coolant temperature sensor connector.
   j. Oxygen sensor.

9. Disconnect the vacuum hoses and the water bypass hoses from the intake manifold and throttle body.

10. Remove the upper radiator hose and the heater hoses from the cylinder head.

11. Remove the PCV hose, charcoal canister hose and vacuum hose from the intake manifold. Remove the vacuum hose from the brake master cylinder power booster.

12. Loosen the air conditioning idler pulley and remove the air conditioning belt. Remove the alternator belt. If equipped with power steering, remove the power steering belt and pump bracket.

13. Remove the intake manifold bracket. Remove the exhaust manifold bracket, then remove the header pipe.

14. Remove the exhaust manifold shroud, then remove the exhaust manifold.

15. Mark the position of the distributor in relation to the engine block, remove and tag the spark plug wires and remove the distributor assembly.

16. Remove the valve cover. Remove the timing belt cover.

17. Mark the direction of rotation on the timing belt. Loosen the timing belt adjuster bolt, then remove the timing belt from the camshaft pulley.

NOTE: Do not crimp or bend the timing belt more than 90 degrees or smaller than 1 in. (25mm) in diameter.

18. Remove the cylinder head bolts. Once the bolts are all removed, remove the cylinder head along with the intake manifold from the engine. Remove the intake manifold from the cylinder head.

To install:
19. Install the cylinder head in the reverse order of the removal procedure.
20. Always use a new head gasket.
21. Be sure the cylinder head and the engine block surfaces are clean, level and straight.
22. Be sure the **UP** mark on the timing belt pulley is at the top.
23. Install the intake manifold and tighten the nuts in a crisscross pattern in 2-3 steps to 17 ft. lbs. (23 Nm) starting with the inner nuts.
24. Be sure the cylinder head dowel pins and control jet are aligned.
25. Install the bolts that secure the intake manifold to its bracket but do not tighten them at this point.

26. Position the camshaft correctly and install the cylinder head bolts.

27. Tighten the cylinder head bolts in 2 steps. On the first step, tighten all the bolts, in sequence, to 22 ft. lbs. (30 Nm). On the final step, using the same sequence, tighten the bolts to 47 ft. lbs. (65 Nm).

28. On 16-valve engines, install the exhaust manifold and tighten the nuts in a crisscross pattern in 2 or 3 steps to 25 ft. lbs. (34 Nm) starting with the inner nuts.

29. On 8-valve engines, install the catalytic converter to the exhaust manifold, then install the exhaust manifold assembly and tighten the bolts to 30 ft. lbs. (34 Nm).

30. Install the header pipe onto the exhaust manifold. tighten the bolts to the intake manifold bracket. Install the header pipe on to its bracket.

31. After the installation procedure is complete, check that all tubes, hoses and connectors are installed correctly. Adjust the valve timing.

2.0L (SOHC) Engine

ACCORD

1. Be sure the engine is cold. Disconnect the battery ground cable.
2. Raise and safely support the vehicle. Drain the cooling system.
3. Remove the vacuum hose from the brake booster.
4. Remove the air intake ducts from the air cleaner case.
5. On fuel injected vehicles, relieve the fuel pressure using the following procedure:
   a. Slowly loosen the service bolt on the top of the fuel filter about 1 turn.

NOTE: Place a rag under the filter during this procedure to prevent fuel from spilling onto the engine.

   b. Disconnect the fuel return hose from the pressure regulator. Remove the special nut and then remove the fuel hose.
6. Remove the secondary ground cable from the valve cover.
7. Remove the air cleaner, tagging all hoses for installation.
8. Disconnect the wires from the automatic choke and the fuel cut-off solenoid valve.
9. Disconnect the throttle cable and the fuel lines.
10. Disconnect the connector and hoses from the distributor.
11. On fuel injected vehicles, disconnect the engine sub-harness connectors and the following couplers

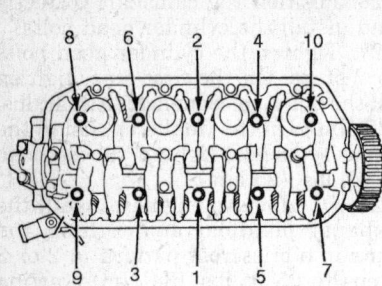

Cylinder head torque sequence — 1990-91 1.5L (16-valve) and 1.6L engines

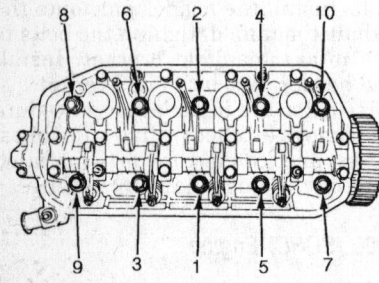

Cylinder head torque sequence — 1990-91 1.5L (8-valve) engine

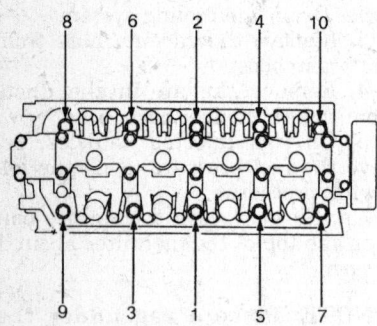

Cylinder head torque sequence — 1992-94 1.6L (SOHC VTEC) engine

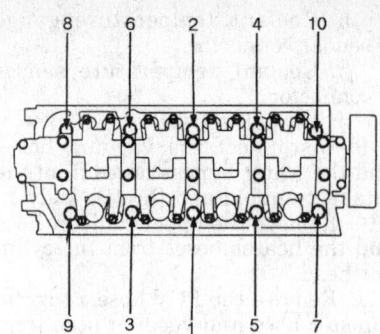

Cylinder head torque sequence — 1992-94 1.5L (SOHC VTEC-E, 16-valve) engine

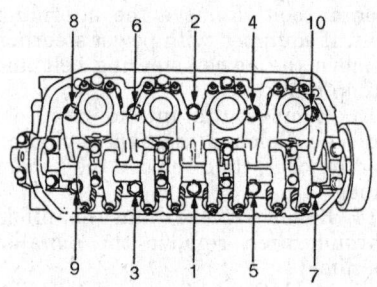

Cylinder head torque sequence — 1992-94 1.5L (SOHC, 16-valve) engine

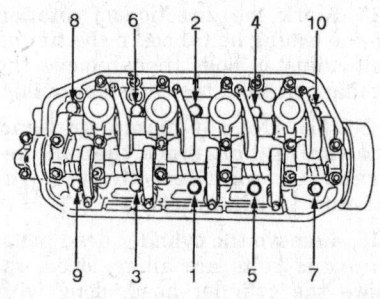

Cylinder head torque sequence — 1992-94 1.5L (SOHC, 8-Valve) engine

from the head and the intake manifold:

   a. The 4 injector couplers
   b. The TA sensor connector
   c. The ground connector
   d. The TW sensor connector
   e. The throttle sensor connector
   f. The crankshaft angle sensor coupler
   g. EGR valve connector
   h. Four wire harness connectors and clamps

12. Disconnect the No. 1 control box hoses from the tubing manifold.

13. On California and high altitude vehicles, disconnect the air jet controller hoses.

14. Disconnect the oxygen sensor coupler.

15. Disconnect the cooling system hoses at the cylinder head.

16. Remove the power steering pump, if equipped. Do not disconnect the pump hoses. Also, remove the hose clamp bolt on the cylinder head.

17. Remove the power steering pump bracket.

18. Remove the cruise control actuator, if equipped.

19. If equipped with air conditioning, disconnect the idle boost solenoid hoses.

20. Remove the engine splash guard from under the vehicle, if equipped.

21. Remove the exhaust header pipe and pull it clear of the exhaust manifold.

22. Remove the air cleaner base mount bolts and disconnect the hose from the intake manifold to the breather chamber.

23. Remove the valve cover, upper timing belt cover and then loosen the belt tensioner to remove the belt.

24. Remove the cylinder head bolts and remove the head.

NOTE: Loosen the cylinder head bolts in the reverse order of the torque sequence, 1/3 turn at a time to prevent warpage to the cylinder head.

To install:

25. Installation is the reverse of the removal procedure.

26. Make sure the cylinder head gasket surfaces are clean.

27. Make sure the **UP** mark on the timing belt pulley is at the top.

28. Install the intake and exhaust manifolds and tighten the nuts in a crisscross pattern in 2-3 steps, beginning with the inner nuts.

29. Make sure the head dowel pins and oil control jet are aligned.

30. Install the bolts that secure the intake manifold to it's bracket, but do not tighten them yet.

31. Position the camshaft correctly.

32. Tighten the cylinder head bolts in 2 steps. Tighten all bolts in sequence to 22 ft. lbs. (30 Nm) and then to 49 ft. lbs. (68 Nm) in the same sequence.

33. Install the exhaust pipe on the exhaust manifold. Tighten the bolts for the intake manifold bracket.

34. Install the exhaust pipe on it's bracket.

35. After installation, check that the tubes, hoses and connectors are installed correctly.

36. Adjust the valve timing.

PRELUDE

1. Disconnect the negative battery cable.

2. Bring the No. 1 cylinder to TDC.

3. Drain the cooling system.

4. Remove the brake booster vacuum hose from the tubing manifold.

5. Remove the engine secondary ground cable from the valve cover.

6. Disconnect the radio condenser connector, ignition coil wire and ignition primary connector.

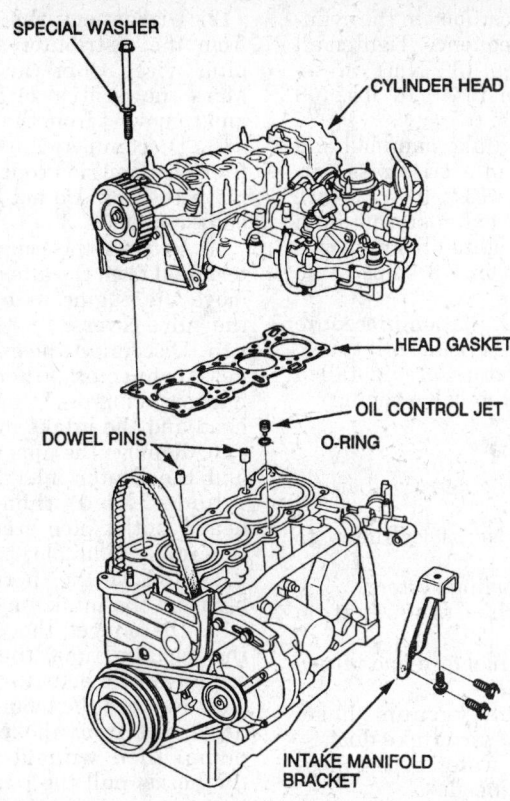

SPECIAL WASHER

CYLINDER HEAD

HEAD GASKET

OIL CONTROL JET

DOWEL PINS

O-RING

INTAKE MANIFOLD BRACKET

Cylinder head installation — 1990-91 1.5L (16-valve) and 1.6L engines

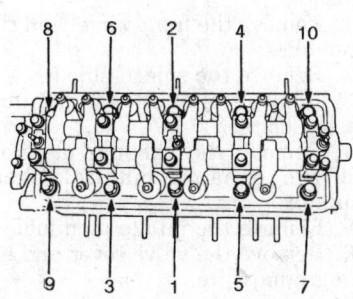

Cylinder head torque sequence — 2.0L (12-Valve) SOHC engine

7. Remove the air cleaner cover.

8. Remove the fuel tube from the fuel filter.

9. Disconnect the throttle cable from the carburetor.

10. Disconnect the engine wire harness connectors from the cylinder head.

11. Remove the emission control box and vacuum tank, then disconnect the 2 connectors. Do not remove the emission hoses.

12. Disconnect the charcoal canister vacuum hoses and the upper radiator, heater and bypass hoses.

13. If equipped with cruise control, remove the actuator.

14. Remove the power steering and alternator belts.

15. Disconnect the inlet hose of the power steering pump, then remove the pump from the cylinder head.

NOTE: When the hose is disconnected, fluid will run out. Protect the alternator by covering it with a shop towel. Plug the inlet hose.

16. Remove the alternator.

17. Remove the intake manifold bracket.

18. Remove the exhaust manifold bracket and the exhaust pipe.

19. Remove the valve cover and the timing belt upper cover.

20. Remove the crankshaft pulley, then remove the timing belt lower cover.

21. Loosen the timing belt adjust bolt, then remove the timing belt.

22. Remove the cylinder head bolts and remove the cylinder head.

23. Remove the EGR pipe, if equipped. Remove the air suction pipe from the intake and exhaust manifolds.

24. Remove the exhaust manifold shroud, oxygen sensor and exhaust manifold from the cylinder head.

25. Remove the intake manifold from the cylinder head.

To install:

26. Install the cylinder head in the reverse order of removal. Always use a new head gasket and make sure the cylinder head and block surfaces are clean. Check the cylinder head surface for warpage. If warpage is less than 0.002 in. (0.05mm), resurfacing is not required. The maximum resurface limit is 0.008 in. (0.2mm) based on a cylinder head height of 3.54 in. (90.0mm).

27. The **UP** mark on the timing belt pulley should be at the top.

28. Install the intake and exhaust manifolds and tighten the nuts in a crisscross pattern in 2-3 steps, beginning with the inner nuts.

29. Make sure the head dowel pins and oil control jet are aligned.

30. Install the bolts that secure the intake manifold to it's bracket, but do not tighten.

31. Position the camshaft correctly.

32. Tighten the cylinder head bolts in 2 steps. Tighten all bolts in sequence to 22 ft. lbs. (30 Nm) and then to 49 ft. lbs. (68 Nm) in the same sequence.

33. Install the exhaust pipe on the exhaust manifold. Tighten the bolts for the intake manifold bracket.

34. Install the exhaust pipe on it's bracket.

35. After installation, check that the tubes, hoses and connectors are installed correctly.

36. Adjust the valve timing.

2.0L and 2.1L (DOHC) Engines

1. Be sure the engine is cold. Disconnect the negative battery cable.

2. Drain the cooling system.

3. Remove the brake booster vacuum hose from the intake manifold.

4. Remove the engine secondary ground cable from the valve cover. Disconnect the radio condenser connector and the ignition coil wire.

5. Remove the air cleaner assembly. Relieve the fuel system pressure.

6. Disconnect the fuel lines. Remove the air intake hose and the resonator hose. Disconnect the throttle cable at the throttle body.

7. Disconnect the throttle control cable at the throttle body, if equipped with automatic transaxle. Disconnect the charcoal canister hose at the throttle valve.

8. Disconnect and tag all the necessary wire harness connectors from the cylinder head. Remove the emission control box and vacuum tank, then disconnect the 2 connectors. Do not remove the emission hoses.

9. Remove the upper radiator hose. Remove the heater hoses from the cylinder head. Remove the water bypass hoses from the water pump inlet pipe.

10. If equipped with cruise control, remove the actuator.

11. Remove the power steering pump belt and the alternator belt. Also remove the air conditioning belt, if equipped.

12. Disconnect the inlet hose from the power steering pump and remove the power steering pump from the cylinder head. Remove the alternator assembly as well.

13. Remove the intake manifold bracket. Remove the exhaust manifold bracket and then the header pipe.

14. Mark the position of the distributor rotor in relation to the distributor housing and the distributor housing in relation to the cylinder head. Remove and tag the ignition wires and then remove the distributor assembly.

15. Remove the cylinder sensor. Remove the valve cover. Remove the timing belt middle cover.

16. Remove the crankshaft pulley and then remove the lower timing belt cover. Loosen the timing belt adjusting bolt and then remove the timing belt. Be sure to mark the rotation of the timing belt, if the belt is to be used again.

NOTE: Do not crimp or bend the timing belt more than 90 degrees or smaller than 1 in. (25mm) in diameter.

17. Remove the camshaft holders, camshafts and rocker arms. Remove the cylinder head bolts taking notice of the bolt holes that the 2 longer bolts come out of and remove the cylinder head.

18. Remove the exhaust manifold shroud and EGR pipe, then remove the exhaust manifold from the cylinder head. Remove the intake manifold from the cylinder head.

To install:

19. Installation is the reverse of the removal procedure. Attention to the following steps will aid installation.

20. Thoroughly clean the mating surfaces of the head and block.

21. Always use a new gasket.

22. Make sure the head dowel pins and oil control jet are aligned. Make sure the **UP** marks or cut-out on the timing belt pulleys are at the top. Tighten the cylinder head bolts in 2 equal steps. Apply engine oil to all the cylinder head bolts and the washers. Place the 2 longer bolts in the

No. 1 and No. 2 positions in the cylinder head torque sequence. Tighten all bolts to 22 ft. lbs. (30 Nm), in sequence, and then to 49 ft. lbs. (68 Nm) in sequence.

23. Install the intake manifold and tighten the nuts in a crisscross pattern in 2-3 steps to 16 ft. lbs. (21 Nm).

24. Install the exhaust manifold and bracket and tighten the nuts in a crisscross pattern in 2-3 steps to 26 ft. lbs. (35 Nm).

25. After the installation procedure is complete, check that all tubes, hoses and connectors are installed correctly. Adjust the valve timing.

2.2L (SOHC) Engine

1. Disconnect the negative battery cable.

2. Bring the No. 1 cylinder to TDC.

3. Drain the cooling system.

4. Relieve the fuel system pressure.

5. Remove the fuel feed and return hose.

6. Remove the vacuum hose, breather hose and air intake duct.

7. Remove the water bypass hose from the cylinder head.

8. Remove the charcoal canister hose from the throttle body.

9. Remove the brake booster vacuum hose from the intake manifold. On automatic transaxle equipped vehicles, remove the vacuum hose mount.

10. Remove the cruise control vacuum hose.

11. Remove the throttle cable from the throttle body. On automatic transaxle equipped vehicles, remove the throttle control cable at the throttle body.

NOTE: Be careful not to bend the cable when removing. Do not use pliers to remove the cable from the linkage. Always replace a kinked cable with a new one.

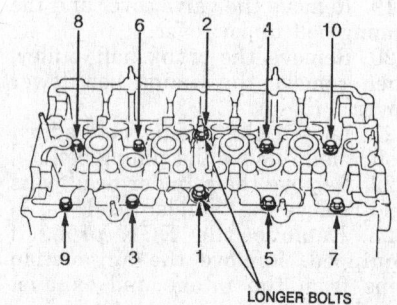

Cylinder head torque sequence — 2.0L and 2.1L (16-valve) DOHC engines

12. Disconnect the 2 connectors from the distributor and the spark plug wires from the spark plugs. Mark the position of the distributor and remove it from the cylinder head.

13. Disconnect the 2 connectors from the emission control box and remove the box. Do not disconnect the emission hoses.

14. Remove the connector and the terminal from the alternator, then remove the engine wire harness from the valve cover.

15. Disconnect the engine wire harness connectors, then remove the harness clamps from the cylinder head and the intake manifold.

16. Remove the upper radiator hose and the heater inlet hose from the cylinder head, then remove the heater outlet pipe bracket bolt from the intake manifold.

17. Remove the thermostat assembly from the intake manifold.

18. Disconnect the connector and the vacuum tube, then remove the cruise control actuator.

19. Remove the mounting bolts and drive belt from the power steering pump, then without disconnecting the hoses, pull the pump away from the mounting bracket. Support the pump out of the way.

20. Raise and safely support the vehicle.

21. Remove the front wheel and tire assemblies.

22. Remove the splash shield.

23. Remove the intake manifold bracket bolts.

24. Remove the exhaust manifold and the exhaust manifold heat insulator.

25. Remove the intake manifold.

26. Remove the valve cover and engine ground wire.

27. Remove the side engine mount bracket stay, then remove the timing belt upper cover.

28. Mark the rotation of the timing belt if it is to be used again. Loosen the timing belt adjusting bolt and then release the timing belt.

NOTE: Push the tensioner to release tension from the belt, then tighten the adjusting bolt.

29. Remove the timing belt from the driven pulley.

30. Remove the cylinder head bolts, then remove the cylinder head.

NOTE: To prevent warpage, unscrew the bolts in sequence ⅓ turn at a time. Repeat the sequence until all bolts are loosened.

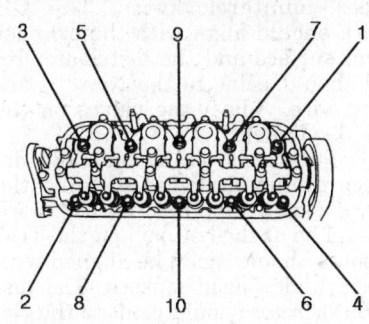

Cylinder head bolts loosening sequence — 2.2L (SOHC) engine

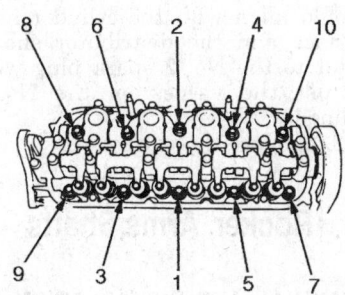

Cylinder head torque sequence — 2.2L (SOHC) engine

To install:

31. Installation is the reverse of the removal procedure. Attention to the following steps will aid installation.

32. Make sure all cylinder head and block gasket surfaces are clean. Check the cylinder head for warpage. If warpage is less than 0.002 in. (0.05mm), cylinder head resurfacing is not required. Maximum resurface limit is 0.008 in. (0.2mm) based on a cylinder head height of 3.935 in. (99.95mm).

33. Always use a new head gasket.

34. The **UP** mark on the camshaft pulley should be at the top.

35. Make sure the No. 1 cylinder is at TDC.

36. The cylinder head dowel pins and oil control jet must be aligned.

37. Install the bolts that secure the intake manifold to it's bracket but do not tighten them.

38. Position the camshaft correctly.

39. Tighten the cylinder head bolts sequentially in 3 steps:
   Step 1 — 29 ft. lbs. (40 Nm).
   Step 2 — 51 ft. lbs. (70 Nm).
   Step 3 — 78 ft. lbs. (108 Nm).

40. Install the intake manifold and tighten the nuts in a crisscross pattern, in 2-3 steps, beginning with the

inner nuts. Final torque should be 16 ft. lbs. (22 Nm). Always use a new intake manifold gasket.

41. Install the heat insulator to the cylinder head and the block.

42. Install the exhaust manifold and tighten the nuts in a crisscross pattern in 2-3 steps, beginning with the inner nut. Final torque should be 23 ft. lbs. (32 Nm). Always use a new exhaust manifold gasket.

43. Install the exhaust manifold bracket, then install the exhaust pipe, the bracket and upper shroud.

44. Check the ignition timing.

2.2L and 2.3L (DOHC) Engines

1. Disconnect the negative battery cable. Drain the cooling system and properly relieve the fuel pressure.

2. Remove the air flow tube. Remove the fuel feed hose and charcoal canister hose from the intake manifold.

3. If equipped with automatic transaxle, remove the throttle control cable from the throttle body.

4. Remove the fuel feed hose, fuel return hose and brake booster vacuum hose.

5. Disconnect the 4 injector connectors, the TA sensor connector, the EACV connector, throttle sensor connector and the EGR valve lift sensor connector from the cylinder head and the intake manifold.

6. Disconnect the ground terminal, cooling fan thermoswitch connector, oxygen sensor connector, TW sensor connector and temperature sensor connector.

7. Disconnect the ignition coil connector, crankshaft (TDC sensor) sensor connector and the speed sensor connector.

8. Remove the engine ground cable from the cylinder head cover. Remove the power steering belt and pump. Do not disconnect the power steering hoses.

9. Remove the engine wire harness from the cylinder head cover and remove the ignition coil.

10. Remove the ignition coil and remove the emission vacuum hoses and water bypass hoses from the intake manifold assembly.

11. Remove the radiator, heater and water bypass hoses. Remove the thermostat housing.

12. Remove the intake manifold bracket and brace and remove the intake manifold.

13. Remove the nuts and disconnect the exhaust pipe from the exhaust manifold.

14. Remove the heatshield and bracket and remove the exhaust manifold.

15. Remove the cylinder head cover and remove the timing belt middle cover.

16. Loosen the timing belt adjusting bolt 180 degrees. Push on the tensioner to release tension from timing belt and then tighten the adjusting bolt.

17. Remove the belt form the camshaft pulleys and remove the pulleys.

18. Loosen the rocker arm adjusting screws and remove the camshaft holders and the camshafts.

19. Remove the side engine mount bracket stay B and the back timing belt cover.

20. Remove the cylinder head bolts and remove the cylinder head.

NOTE: Unscrew the cylinder head bolts in sequence $\frac{1}{3}$ turn at a time to prevent head warpage.

To install:

21. Align the cylinder head dowel pins and oil control jet. Install the cylinder head with a new gasket to the engine block.

22. Tighten the cylinder head bolts in the proper sequence in 3 steps:
   Step 1 — 29 ft. lbs. (40 Nm)
   Step 2 — 51 ft. lbs. (70 Nm)
   Step 3 — 72 ft. lbs. (100 Nm)

23. Install the intake manifold, exhaust manifold and bracket.

24. Install the camshafts and camshaft pulleys.

25. Install the timing belt and adjust to proper tension.

26. Install the timing belt covers and cylinder head cover.

27. Connect the coolant hoses, the thermostat housing and install the ignition coil.

28. Connect the electrical connectors to the cylinder head cover.

29. Install the power steering pump and belt.

30. Connect all previously disconnected electrical connectors to the cylinder head and intake manifold.

31. Connect the fuel feed hose, fuel return hose and brake booster vacuum hose.

32. Connect the throttle cable to the throttle body, if equipped with automatic transaxle.

33. Install the charcoal canister hose and the air flow tube. Refill the coolant to the proper level.

34. Connect the negative battery cable, start the vehicle and allow to idle. Inspect for any coolant or exhaust leaks.

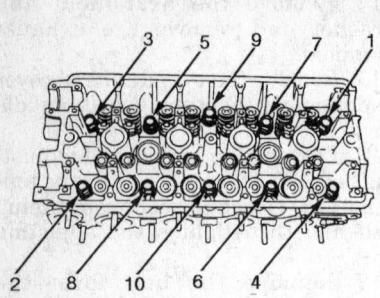

Cylinder head bolts loosening sequence — 2.3L (DOHC) engine

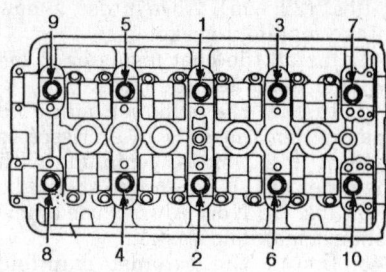

Cylinder head torque sequence — 2.2L (DOHC VTEC) engine

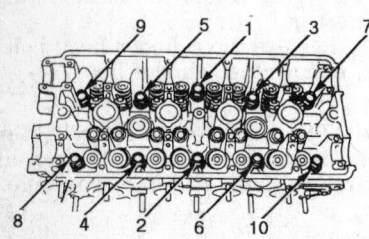

Cylinder head torque sequence — 2.3L (DOHC) engine

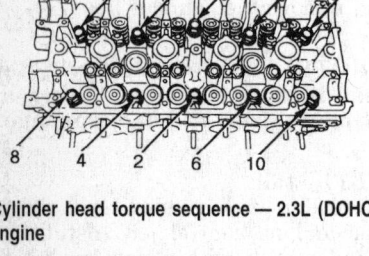

Cylinder head bolts loosening sequence — 2.2L (DOHC VTEC) engine

Valve Lash

ADJUSTMENT

NOTE: The valves should be adjusted cold. Cylinder head temperature must be less than 100°F (38°C). Adjustment is the same for intake and exhaust valves.

1. Disconnect the negative battery cable and remove the valve cover.
2. Bring the No. 1 piston to TDC. The **UP** mark on the pulley(s) should be at the top and the TDC grooves on the back side of the pulley(s) should align with the cylinder head surface. The distributor rotor must be pointing towards the No. 1 spark plug wire.
3. Adjust the valves on the No. 1 cylinder. Valve clearance is as follows:
1.5L (16 valve) and 1.6L engines:
Intake and auxiliary, if equipped — 0.007-0.009 in. (0.17-0.22mm)
Exhaust — 0.009-0.011 in. (0.22-0.27mm)
1.5L (8 valve) engine:
Intake — 0.005-0.007 in. (0.12-0.17mm)
Exhaust — 0.007-0.009 in. (0.17-0.22mm)
2.0L (SOHC) engine:
Intake — 0.005-0.007 in. (0.12-0.17mm)
Exhaust — 0.010-0.012 in. (0.25-0.30mm)
2.2L (SOHC) engine:
Intake — 0.009-0.011 in. (0.24-0.28mm)
Exhaust — 0.011-0.013 in. (0.28-0.32mm)
2.0L and 2.1L (DOHC) engines:
Intake — 0.003-0.005 in. (0.08-0.12mm)
Exhaust — 0.006-0.008 in. (0.16-0.20mm)
2.2L and 2.3L (DOHC) engines:
Intake — 0.004-0.005 in. (0.09-0.13)
Exhaust — 0.006-0.007 in. (0.15-0.19mm)
4. Loosen the locknut and turn the adjusting screw until the feeler gauge slides back and forth with a slight amount of drag.
5. Tighten the locknut and check the clearance again. Repeat adjustment if necessary.
6. Rotate the crankshaft 180 degrees counterclockwise. The camshaft pulley(s) will turn 90 degrees counterclockwise. The **UP** mark should align with the cylinder head surface and the distributor rotor should point to the No. 3 spark plug wire. Adjust the valves on the No. 3 cylinder.
7. Rotate the crankshaft 180 degrees counterclockwise to bring the No. 4 piston to TDC. The **UP** mark should be at the bottom and the TDC grooves should again be aligned with the cylinder head surface. The distributor rotor should point to the No. 4 spark plug wire. Adjust the valves on the No. 4 cylinder.
8. Rotate the crankshaft 180 degrees counterclockwise to bring the No. 2 piston to TDC. The **UP** mark should align with the cylinder head surface and the distributor should point to the No. 2 spark plug wire. Adjust the valves on the No. 2 cylinder.
9. Replace the valve cover.

Rocker Arms/Shafts

REMOVAL AND INSTALLATION

Except DOHC Engine

1. Disconnect the negative battery cable.
2. Remove the valve cover and bring the No. 1 cylinder to TDC.
3. Remove the rocker arm bolts. Unscrew the bolts 2 turns at a time, in a crisscross pattern, to prevent damaging the valves or rocker assembly.
4. Remove the rocker arm/shaft assemblies. Leave the rocker arm bolts in place as the shafts are removed to keep the bearing caps, springs and rocker arms in place on the shafts.
5. If the rocker arms or shafts are to be replaced, identify the parts as they are removed from the shafts to ensure reinstallation in the original location.
To install:
6. Lubricate the camshaft journals and lobes.
7. Set the rocker arm assembly in place and loosely install the bolts. Tighten each bolt 2 turns at a time in the proper sequence to ensure that the rockers do not bind on the valves. Tighten the rocker arm bolts to 16 ft. lbs. (22 Nm) except on 1990-92 Accord. On 1990-92 Accord tighten the 6mm bolts to 9 ft. lbs. (12 Nm) and the 8mm bolts to 16 ft. lbs. (22 Nm).
8. Replace the valve cover and connect the negative battery cable.

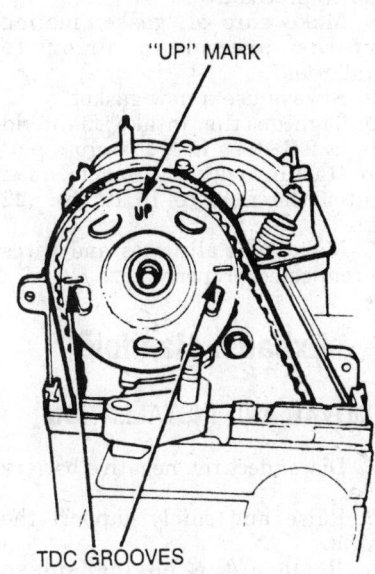

Position of the sprocket marks for No. 1 TDC on Civic, Civic del Sol and CRX with single camshaft engine

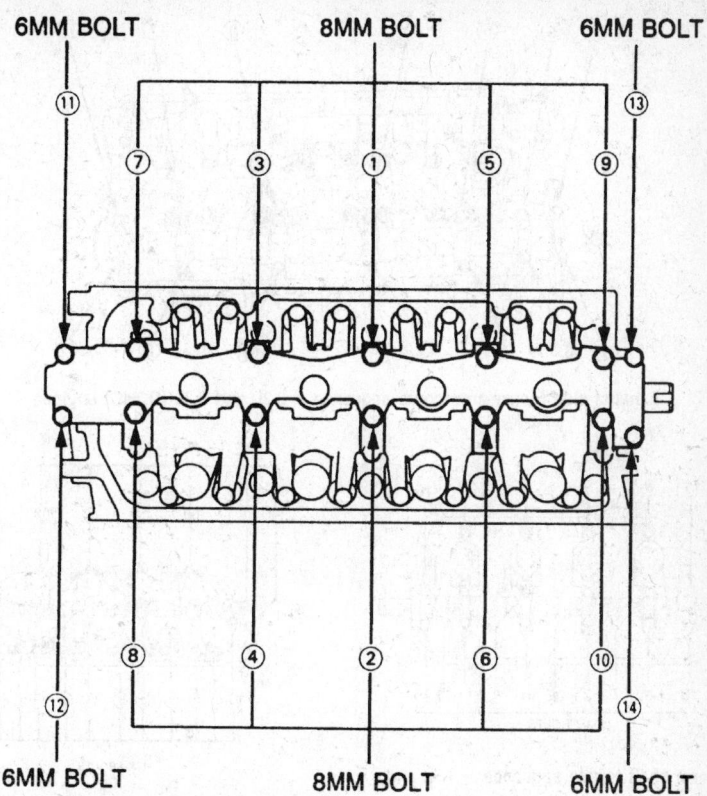

Rocker arm torque sequence — 1.5L (VTEC-E) and 1.6L (VTEC) engines

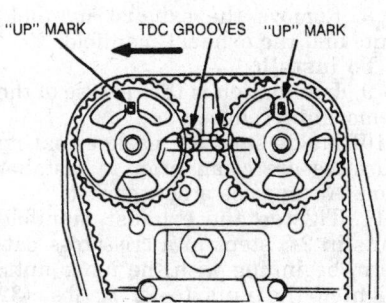

Position of the sprocket marks for No. 1 TDC on dual camshaft engines

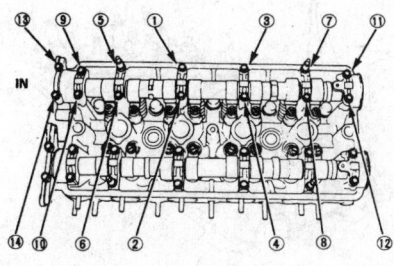

Intake side rocker arm torque sequence — 2.2L and 2.3L (DOHC) engines

Intake Manifold

REMOVAL AND INSTALLATION

Carbureted Engine

1. Disconnect the negative battery cable. Drain the coolant from the radiator.
2. Remove the air cleaner and case from the carburetor(s).
3. Remove the air valve, EGR valve, air suction valve and air chamber, if equipped.
4. Label and remove all wires and vacuum hoses running to the intake manifold.
5. Remove the intake manifold attaching nut in a crisscross pattern, beginning from the center. Then remove the manifold.

To install:
6. Installation is the reverse of the removal procedure.
7. Clean all the old gasket material from the manifold and the cylinder head.
8. Always use a new gasket.
9. Tighten the nuts in a crisscross pattern in 2-3 steps, starting with the inner nuts. Tighten the nuts to 16 ft. lbs. (22 Nm).
10. Be sure all hoses and wires are connected properly.

DOHC Engine

1. Disconnect the negative battery cable.
2. Remove the valve cover and bring the No. 1 cylinder to TDC.
3. Remove the timing belt cover and the timing belt.
4. Remove the camshaft bearing caps and remove the camshafts.
5. Remove the rocker arms.

To install:
6. Lubricate the camshaft journals and lobes.
7. Set the rocker arm assembly in place and loosely install the bolts.

8. Apply liquid gasket to the No. 1 and No. 6 camshaft bearing caps and install them with the rest of the caps. Make sure the caps are installed in their proper positions as indicated by their markings.
9. Tighten each camshaft bearing cap bolt gradually, to prevent binding. Tighten the bolts to 9 ft. lbs. (12 Nm). On the 1992-94 Civic and del Sol, tighten the 8mm bolts to 16 ft. lbs. (22 Nm) and the 6 mm bolts to 9 ft. lbs. (12 Nm).

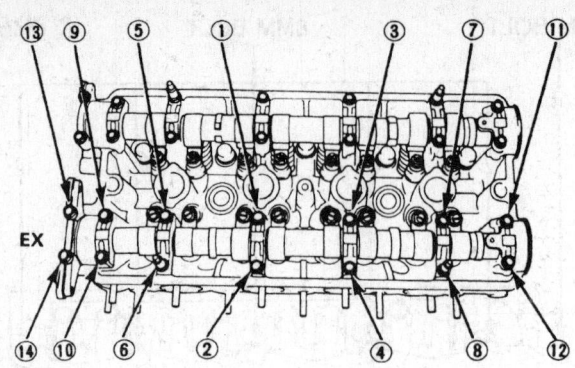

Exhaust side rocker arm torque sequence — 2.2L and 2.3L (DOHC) engines

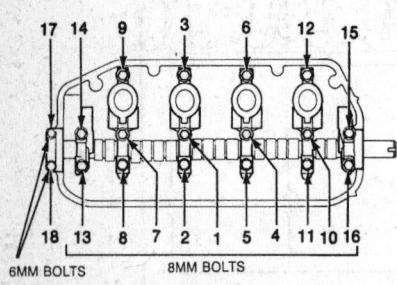

Rocker arm shaft torque sequence — 1.5L and 1.6L engines

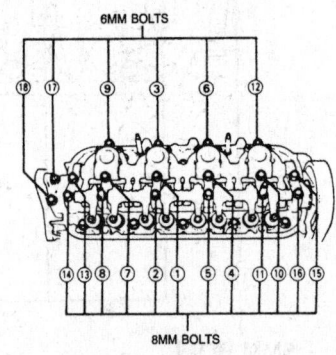

Rocker arm shaft torque sequence — 2.0L, 2.1L, 2.2L and 2.3L (DOHC) engines

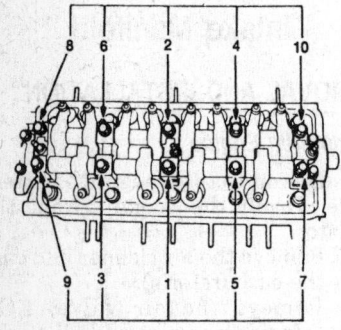

Rocker arm shaft torque sequence — 2.0L and 2.2L (SOHC) engines

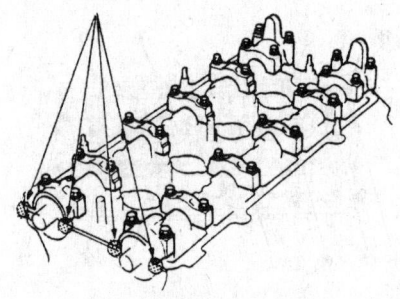

Use non-hardening sealant when installing the valve cover on dual camshaft engines

Fuel Injected Engine

1. Disconnect the negative battery cable. Drain the cooling system.
2. Label and disconnect all required electrical connectors and vacuum lines.
3. Properly relieve the fuel system pressure.
4. Remove the throttle body assembly on 1.5L engines with dual-point fuel injection. On all other engines, remove the fuel injector manifold and fuel injectors.

5. As required, remove the fast idle control valve, the air bleed valve, the EGR valve and all related brackets.
6. Remove the intake manifold retaining bolts. Remove the intake manifold assembly from the vehicle. Discard the gaskets.

NOTE: Some Accord and Prelude engines have an upper and lower manifold chamber. Separate the upper chamber from the lower manifold before removing the assembly from the vehicle.

To install:
7. Installation is the reverse of the removal procedure.
8. Make sure all gasket mating surfaces are clean prior to installation.
9. Always use a new gasket.
10. Tighten the intake manifold nuts in 2-3 steps in a crisscross pattern starting with the inside nuts. Tighten the nuts to 16 ft. lbs. (22 Nm).
11. Make sure all hoses and wires are connected properly.

Exhaust Manifold

REMOVAL AND INSTALLATION

1. Disconnect the negative battery cable.
2. Raise and safely support the vehicle.
3. Remove the engine splash shield, as necessary.
4. Disconnect the exhaust pipe or catalytic converter, as required.
5. Lower the vehicle.
6. Remove the exhaust manifold heatshield.
7. Disconnect the exhaust manifold brackets, EGR tube and oxygen sensor, as required.
8. Remove the exhaust manifold nuts and the exhaust manifold.

To install:
9. Installation is the reverse of the removal procedure.
10. Make sure all gasket mating surfaces are clean prior to installation. Always use a new gasket.
11. Tighten the exhaust manifold nuts in 2-3 steps in a crisscross pattern, beginning with the inner nuts. Tighten the nuts to 22 ft. lbs. (32 Nm).

Timing Belt Front Cover

REMOVAL AND INSTALLATION

1.5L and 1.6L Engines

1. Disconnect the negative battery cable.
2. Raise and safely support the vehicle.
3. Remove the left front wheel and tire assembly.
4. Remove the left front wheelwell splash shield.
5. If equipped, remove the power steering belt and pump.
6. If equipped with air conditioning, remove the adjust pulley with bracket and the belt.

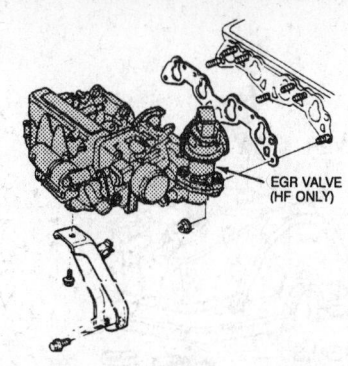

Intake manifold installation — 1.5L (MPFI) and 1.6L engines

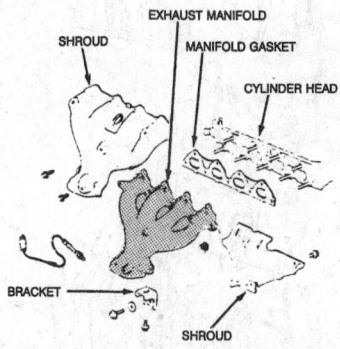

Exhaust manifold installation — 1.5L (16-valve) and 1.6L engines shown, others similar

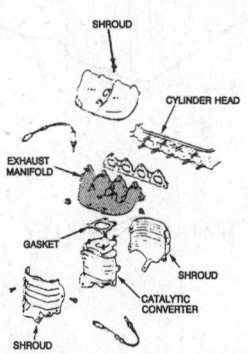

Exhaust system on CRX HF has the catalytic converter close coupled to the manifold

7. Remove the power steering bracket, loosen the alternator adjust bolt and through bolt and remove the alternator belt.

8. Use a suitable device to support the engine. Remove the engine side support bolts and nut and then remove the side mount rubber.

9. Remove the valve cover, the crankshaft pulley bolt and the crankshaft pulley.

10. Remove the timing belt upper and lower cover.

11. Installation is the reverse of the removal procedure. Apply engine oil

to the crankshaft pulley. On 1990-91 models, torque the pulley bolt to 119 ft. lbs. (165 Nm). On 1992-94 models, torque the pulley bolt to 134 ft. lbs. (185 Nm).

2.0L (SOHC) Engine

1. Disconnect the negative battery cable.

2. Bring the piston of the No. 1 cylinder to TDC.

3. Remove all accessory drive belts.

4. Remove the water pump pulley.

5. Remove the crankshaft pulley bolt and using a suitable puller, remove the crankshaft pulley.

6. Remove the timing belt cover bolts and the upper and lower covers.

7. Installation is the reverse of the removal procedure. Tighten the crankshaft pulley bolt to 108 ft. lbs. (150 Nm).

2.2L (SOHC) Engine

1. Disconnect the negative battery cable.

2. Raise and safely support the vehicle.

3. Remove the engine splash shield.

4. Disconnect the connector, then remove the cruise control actuator. Do not disconnect the control cable.

5. Remove the mounting bolt, nut and drive belt from the power steering pump, then without disconnecting the hoses, pull the pump away from the mounting bracket.

6. Disconnect the alternator terminal and the connector, then remove the engine wire harness from the valve cover.

7. Loosen the alternator mounting bolt, nut and adjusting nut, then remove the alternator belt or if equipped, the air conditioning belt.

8. Remove the valve cover. Remove the side engine mount bracket stay, if equipped.

9. Remove the upper timing belt cover.

10. Use a suitable device to support the engine, then remove the side engine bolt.

11. Remove the dipstick and pipe and remove the timing belt tensioner adjusting nut.

12. Remove the crankshaft pulley bolt and the crankshaft pulley. Remove the 2 rear bolts from the center beam, to allow the engine to drop down and give clearance to remove the lower timing belt cover. Remove the lower cover.

To install:

13. Installation is the reverse of the removal procedure.

14. Apply oil to the threads of the crankshaft pulley bolt and tighten it to 159 ft. lbs. (220 Nm).

15. After installing the lower cover, the timing belt and balancer belt tension must be adjusted as follows:

a. Make sure the No. 1 cylinder is at TDC.

b. Loosely install the adjusting nut.

c. Rotate the crankshaft counterclockwise 3 teeth on the camshaft pulley to create tension on the timing belt.

d. Tighten the adjusting nut.

e. If the crankshaft pulley loosens while turning the crankshaft, tighten it to 159 ft. lbs. (220 Nm).

2.0L, 2.1L, 2.2L and 2.3L (DOHC) Engines

1. Disconnect the negative battery cable.

2. Raise and safely support the vehicle.

3. Remove the engine splash shield.

4. Use a suitable device to support the engine. Remove the engine support bolts and nuts, then remove the side mount rubber and side mount bracket. Remove the actuator, if equipped with cruise control.

5. Remove the power steering pump adjusting pulley nut and the adjusting bolt, then remove the adjusting pulley, power steering pump and belt.

6. Remove the alternator through bolt, mount bolt and adjust nut, then remove the alternator and belt.

7. If equipped with air conditioning, remove the air conditioning compressor mount bolts, then remove the air conditioning compressor and the belt.

8. Remove the ignition wire and the engine wire harness protector from the valve cover, if necessary.

9. Remove the valve cover.

10. Remove the crankshaft pulley bolt and the crankshaft pulley.

11. Remove the timing belt covers.

12. Installation is the reverse of the removal procedure. Apply engine oil to the threads of the crankshaft pulley bolt and tighten it to 108 ft. lbs. (150 Nm) on 1990-91 Prelude or to 159 ft. lbs. (220 Nm) on 1992-94 Prelude.

OIL SEAL REPLACEMENT

1. Disconnect the negative battery cable.

2. Remove the timing belt cover and the timing belt.

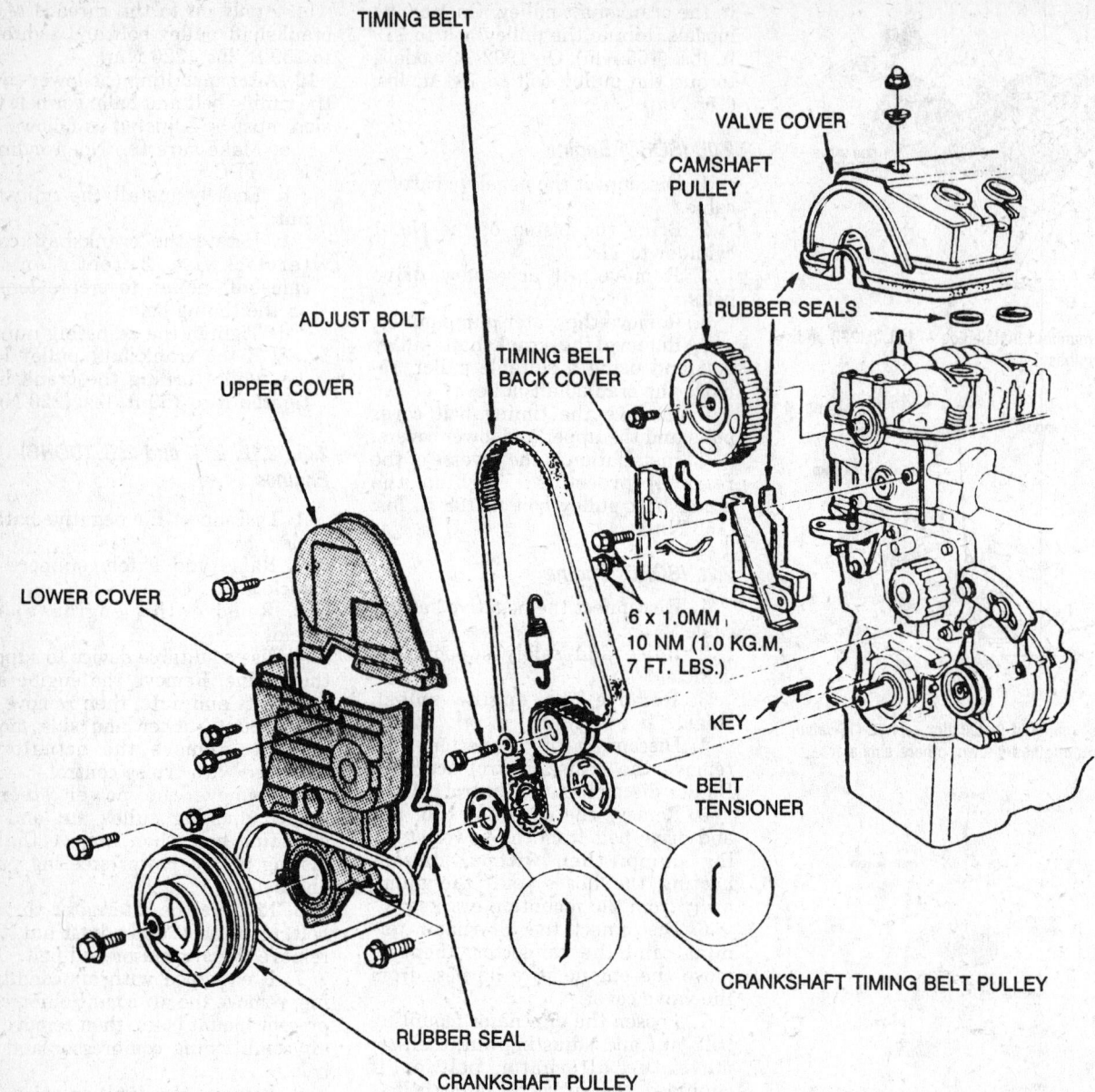

TIMING BELT

VALVE COVER

CAMSHAFT PULLEY

RUBBER SEALS

ADJUST BOLT

TIMING BELT BACK COVER

UPPER COVER

LOWER COVER

6 x 1.0MM
10 NM (1.0 KG.M, 7 FT. LBS.)

KEY

BELT TENSIONER

CRANKSHAFT TIMING BELT PULLEY

RUBBER SEAL

CRANKSHAFT PULLEY

Timing belt and cover installation — 1.5L and 1.6L engines

3. Remove the crankshaft timing sprocket.

4. Using a suitable seal removal tool, remove the seal from the front of the engine.

5. Installation is the reverse of the removal procedure. Place a thin coat of oil on the seal lip prior to installation. Use a suitable seal driver to install the seal. Be sure to install the seal with the open (spring) side facing the inside of the engine.

Timing Belt and Tensioner

ADJUSTMENT

NOTE: The timing belt tensioner is spring loaded, to apply proper tension to the belt automatically, after making the following adjustment.

1. Disconnect the negative battery cable.

2. Remove the valve cover or upper timing belt cover.

3. Set the piston in No. 1 cylinder at TDC.

4. Loosen the adjusting bolt/nut ⅔-1 turn.

5. Rotate the crankshaft counterclockwise 3 teeth on the camshaft pulley to create tension on the timing belt.

6. Tighten the adjusting bolt/nut.

7. If the crankshaft pulley broke loose while turning the crankshaft, tighten it to specification.

8. Reinstall or connect the remaining components after adjustment is completed.

REMOVAL AND INSTALLATION

1. Disconnect the negative battery cable.

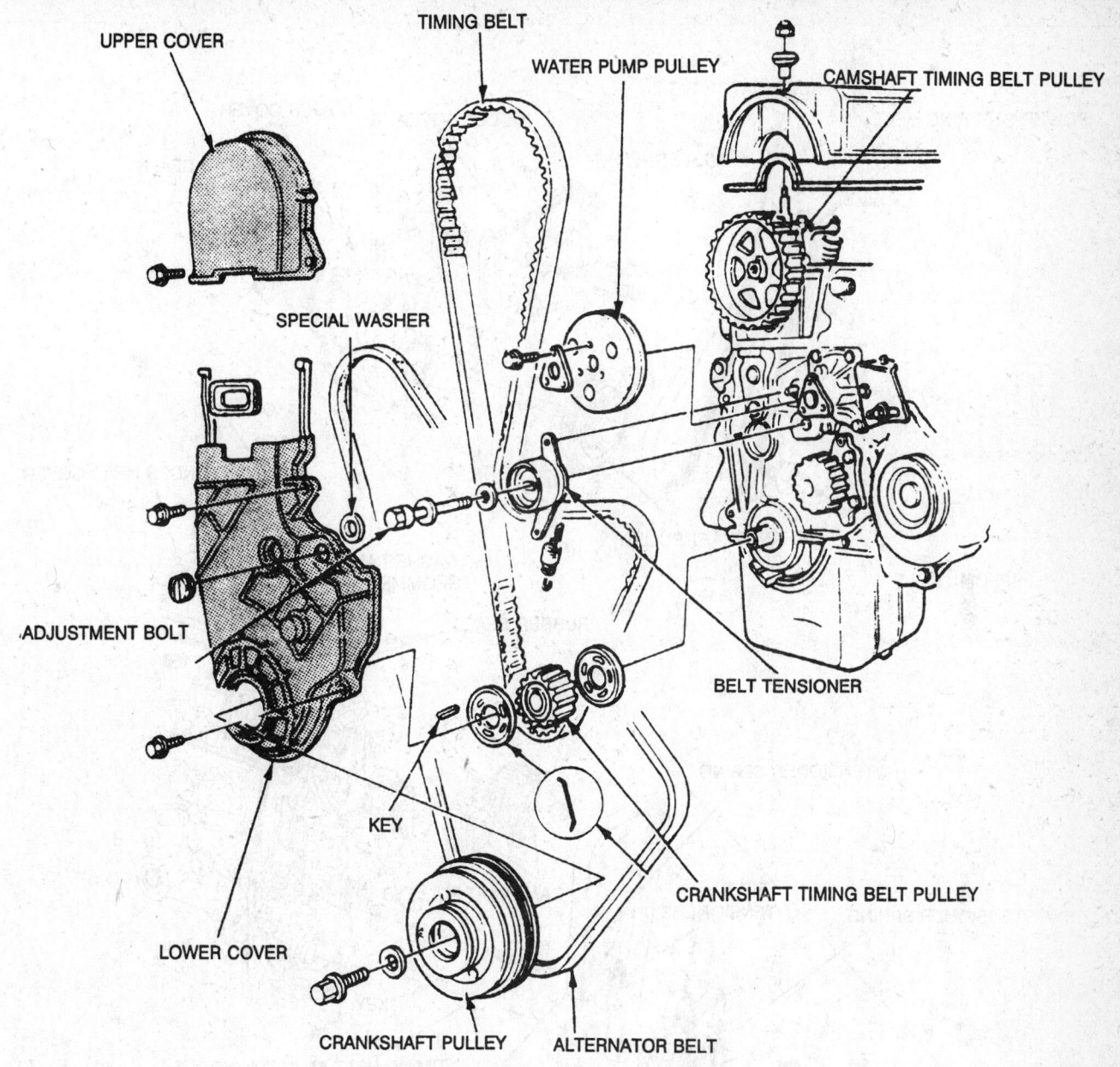

UPPER COVER

TIMING BELT

WATER PUMP PULLEY

CAMSHAFT TIMING BELT PULLEY

SPECIAL WASHER

ADJUSTMENT BOLT

BELT TENSIONER

KEY

CRANKSHAFT TIMING BELT PULLEY

LOWER COVER

CRANKSHAFT PULLEY

ALTERNATOR BELT

Timing belt and cover installation — 2.0L (SOHC) engine

2. Bring the piston in No. 1 cylinder to TDC on the compression stroke.

3. Remove the valve cover and timing belt front covers.

4. Mark the direction of timing belt rotation. On 1990-92 Accord and 1992-94 Prelude, mark the direction of timing balancer belt rotation.

5. On all except Accord and 1992-94 Prelude, loosen the adjusting bolt and remove the timing belt. On Accord and 1992-94 Prelude, push the timing balancer belt tensioner and the timing belt tensioner to remove tension on the belts, then reinstall and tighten the adjusting nut. Remove the timing balancer belt and the timing belt.

To install:

6. Align the camshaft sprocket(s) and crankshaft sprocket as follows:

  a. Make sure the **UP** mark on the camshaft sprocket(s) is at the top most position. The sprocket timing marks should be aligned with the cylinder head upper surface.

  b. On Accord and Prelude, remove the timing inspection hole cover at the rear of the engine block. Make sure the TDC mark on the flywheel, indicated by a white painted mark, is aligned with the pointer in the inspection hole.

  c. On Civic, Civic del Sol and CRX, temporarily reinstall the lower timing belt cover and crankshaft pulley. Make sure the TDC mark on the crankshaft pulley, indicated by a white painted mark, is aligned with the pointer on the timing cover. Remove the lower timing belt cover and crankshaft pulley.

7. Install the timing belt. If the old timing belt is reused, install the belt in the same rotational direction, as indicated by the mark that was made during removal.

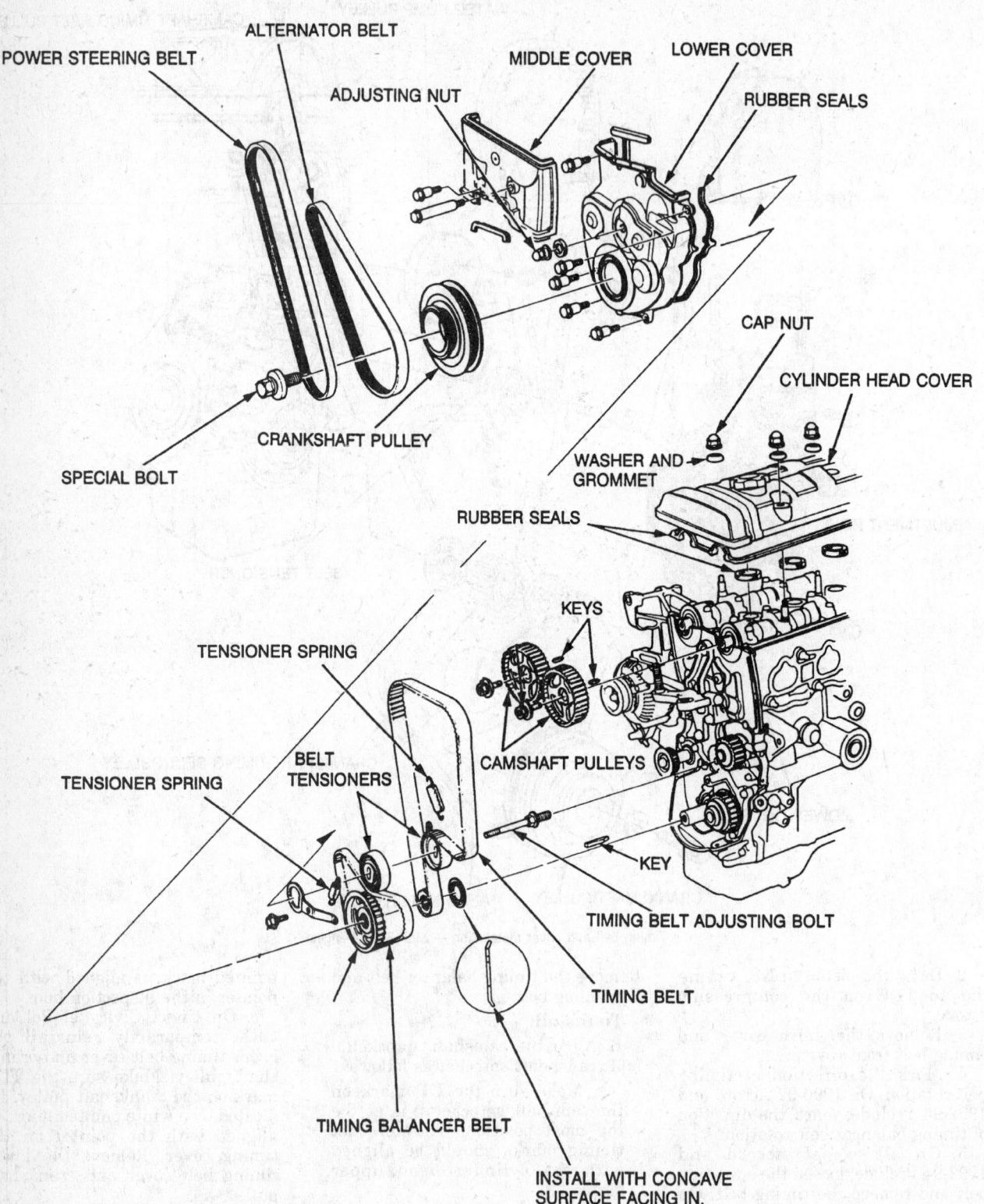

Timing belt and timing balancer belt installation — 2.2L and 2.3L (DOHC) engines

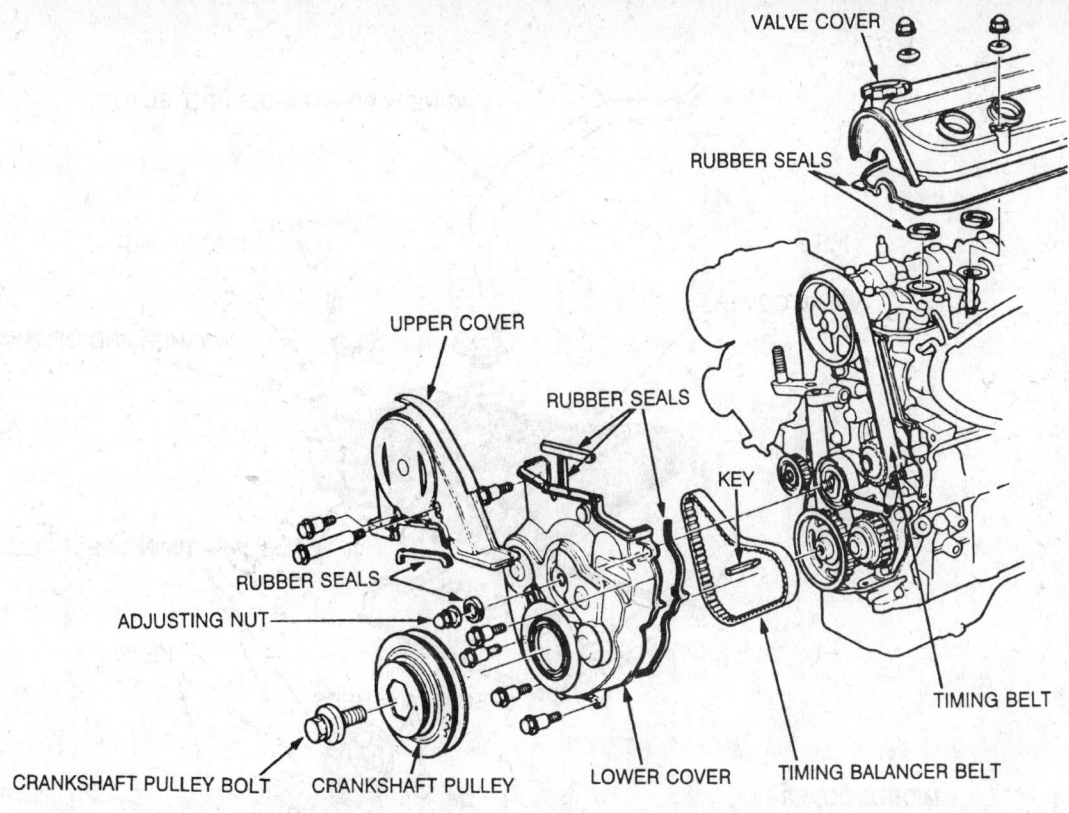

Timing belt and cover installation — 2.2L (SOHC) engine

8. On 1990-92 Accord and 1992-94 Prelude, align the timing belt balancer pulleys and install the balancer belt as follows:

a. The timing belt balancer drive pulley should already be at TDC, if the timing belt is installed correctly.

b. Align the groove on the front timing balancer belt driven pulley with the pointer on the oil pump body.

c. Remove the bolt from the maintenance hole on the cylinder block, next to the rear balancer shaft. Align the rear timing balancer belt driven pulley using a 6 **x**100mm bolt, or equivalent. Mark a line at 3 in. (74mm) length of the bolt. Align the pulley by inserting the bolt through the maintenance hole. The bolt must be inserted to a depth where the line is flush with the maintenance hole surface.

d. Install the timing balancer belt. If the old balancer belt is reused, install the belt in the same rotational direction, as indicated by the mark that was made during removal. After the balancer belt is installed, remove the rear balancer belt driven pulley alignment bolt and reinstall the original bolt in

the maintenance hole. Tighten the bolt to 22 ft. lbs. (30 Nm).

9. Installation of the remaining components is the reverse of the removal procedure. Be sure to properly adjust the timing belt tension. On 1990-92 Accord, the balancer belt tension is automatically adjusted when the timing belt tension is adjusted.

10. Torque the crankshaft pulley bolt as follows:

1990-91 Prelude and 1989 Accord — 108 ft. lbs. (150 Nm)

1990-92 Civic and CRX — 119 ft. lbs. (165 Nm)

1990-92 Accord and 1992-94 Prelude — 159 ft. lbs. (220 Nm)

Timing Sprockets

REMOVAL AND INSTALLATION

1. Disconnect the negative battery cable.

2. Remove the valve cover, timing belt covers and the timing belt.

3. Remove the crankshaft and camshaft timing sprockets.

4. Installation is the reverse of the removal procedure. Tighten the camshaft sprocket retaining bolts to 27 ft. lbs. (38 Nm).

Camshaft

REMOVAL AND INSTALLATION

Except DOHC Engine

1. Disconnect the negative battery cable.

2. Bring the piston in No. 1 cylinder to TDC on the compression stroke.

3. Remove the valve cover, timing belt front covers and the timing belt.

4. Remove the camshaft sprocket.

5. Remove the rocker arm/shaft assembly.

6. Remove the camshaft and camshaft seal.

To install:

7. Installation is the reverse of the removal procedure. Lubricate the lobes and journals of the camshaft prior to installation. Install the camshaft with the keyway facing up.

8. Install the rocker arm/shaft assembly as follows:

a. Loosen the rocker arm locknuts and back off the adjust screws.

b. Set the rocker arm/shaft assembly in place and loosely install the bolts.

c. Tighten each bolt 2 turns at a time in the proper sequence to en-

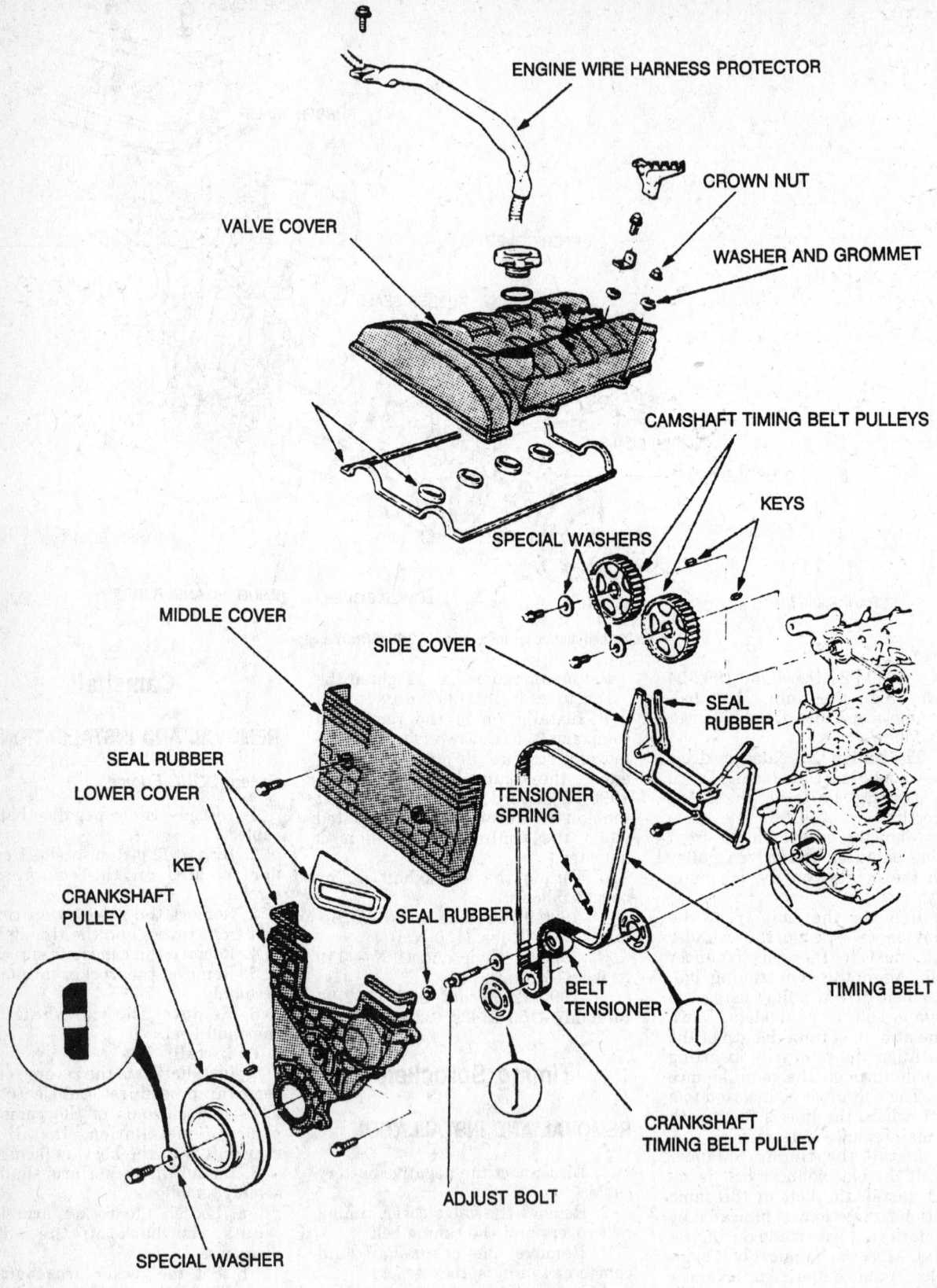

ENGINE WIRE HARNESS PROTECTOR

CROWN NUT

WASHER AND GROMMET

VALVE COVER

CAMSHAFT TIMING BELT PULLEYS

KEYS

SPECIAL WASHERS

MIDDLE COVER

SIDE COVER

SEAL RUBBER

SEAL RUBBER

LOWER COVER

TENSIONER SPRING

KEY

CRANKSHAFT PULLEY

SEAL RUBBER

TIMING BELT

BELT TENSIONER

CRANKSHAFT TIMING BELT PULLEY

ADJUST BOLT

SPECIAL WASHER

Timing belt and cover installation — 2.0L, 2.1L, 2.2L and 2.3L (DOHC) engines

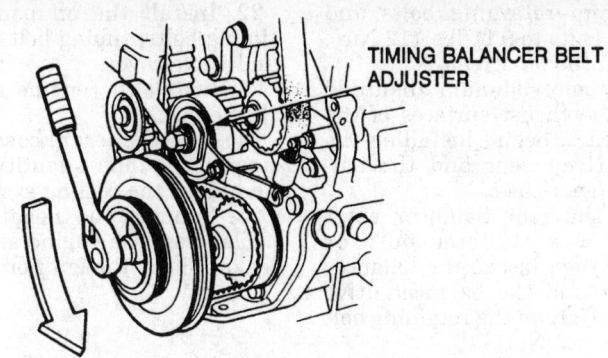

Timing balancer belt adjustment — 1992-94 Prelude

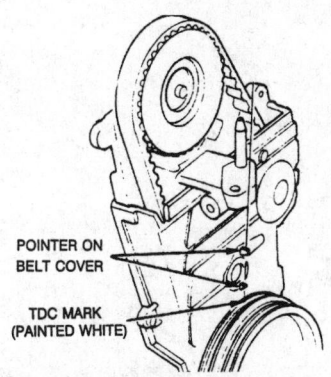

TDC locating marks — SOHC engines

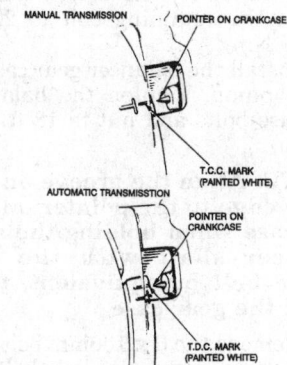

TDC locating marks — 2.0L (SOHC) engine

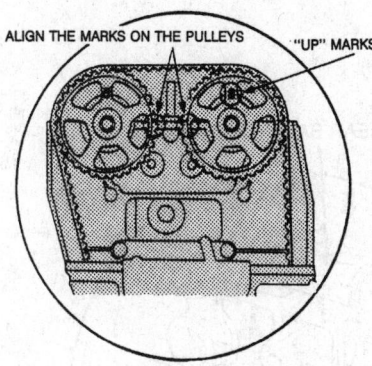

Aligning the timing marks — DOHC engines

sure that the rockers do not bind on the valves.

d. Tighten the rocker arm bolts to 16 ft. lbs. (22 Nm) except on Accord. On Accord tighten the 6mm bolts to 9 ft. lbs. (12 Nm) and the 8mm bolts to 16 ft. lbs. (22 Nm).

9. Lubricate a new camshaft seal and install using a suitable tool.

10. Properly set the tension of the timing belt after installation. Tighten the crankshaft pulley bolt to specification. Adjust the valve lash.

DOHC Engine

1. Disconnect the negative battery cable.

2. Bring the piston in the No. 1 cylinder to TDC on the compression stroke.

3. Remove the valve cover, timing belt front covers and the timing belt.

4. Remove the camshaft sprockets.

5. Remove the camshaft bearing caps and the camshafts and camshaft seals.

To install:

6. Installation is the reverse of the removal procedure. Inspect the rocker arms for wear or damage and replace as necessary prior to installation of the camshafts. The rocker arm locknuts and adjust screws should be backed off before installation of the camshafts. Lubricate the lobes and journals of the camshafts before installing. Install the camshafts with keyways facing UP.

7. Apply liquid gasket to the No. 1 and No. 6 camshaft bearing caps and install them with the rest of the caps. Make sure the caps are installed in their proper positions as indicated by their markings.

8. Tighten each camshaft bearing cap bolt gradually, to prevent bind-

ing. Tighten the bolts to 9 ft. lbs. (12 Nm).

9. Lubricate new camshaft seals and install using a suitable tool.

10. Properly tension the timing belt after installation. Tighten the crankshaft pulley to specification. Adjust the valve lash.

Balancer Shafts

REMOVAL AND INSTALLATION

2.2L (SOHC) Engine

1. Disconnect the negative battery cable.

2. Remove the engine/transaxle assembly from the vehicle.

3. Separate the engine from the transaxle.

4. Remove the valve cover, timing belt front covers and the timing belt.

5. Remove the oil pan.

6. Remove the balancer drive gear case.

7. Insert a suitable tool into the maintenance hole in the front balancer shaft, in order to hold the shaft in place and remove the front balancer driven pulley.

8. Remove the maintenance hole bolt from the cylinder block, next to the rear balancer shaft. Insert a 6 **x** 100mm bolt or equivalent to a depth of 3 in. (74mm) through the maintenance hole and into the rear balancer shaft. Remove the balancer shaft driven gear.

9. Remove the oil screen and pump.

10. Turn the crankshaft so the No. 2 and No. 3 crankpins are at the bottom.

11. Remove the bolts and the thrust plate, then remove the front and rear balancer shaft.

To install:

12. Clean all gasket mating surfaces of old gasket material.

13. Lubricate the balancer shaft bearings.

14. Insert the balancer shafts into the block, then install the thrust plate to the front balancer shaft and the block. Tighten the thrust plate bolts to 9 ft. lbs. (12 Nm).

15. Apply liquid gasket to the block mating surfaces of the oil pump, then install it on the engine block. Apply grease to the lips of the oil pump seal and the balancer seal. Then, install the oil pump onto the inner rotor to the crankshaft. When the pump is in place, clean any excess grease off the crankshaft and the balancer shaft, then check that the oil seal lips are not distorted. Apply liquid gasket to

Adjusting the timing belt tensioner — 2.0L and 2.1L (DOHC) engines

the oil pump retaining bolts and tighten the bolts to 9 ft. lbs. (12 Nm).

16. Install the oil screen.

17. Apply molybdenum disulfide grease to the thrust surfaces of the balancer gears, before installing the balancer driven gear and the balancer drive gear case.

18. Hold the rear balancer shaft with the 6 x 100mm bolt or equivalent, then install the balancer driven gear and the balancer drive belt pulley. Tighten the retaining bolt to 18 ft. lbs. (25 Nm).

19. Hold the front balancer shaft with a suitable tool, then install the timing balancer belt driven pulley. Tighten the retaining bolt to 22 ft. lbs. (30 Nm).

20. Install the balancer gear case to the oil pump. Tighten the balancer gear case bolts and nut to 18 ft. lbs. (25 Nm).

NOTE: Align the groove on the pulley edge to the pointer on the gear case when holding the rear balancer shaft with the 6 x 100mm bolt or equivalent, then install the gear case.

21. Remove the 6 x 100mm bolt and install the maintenance hole bolt.

22. Install the oil pan, balancer, timing belts, timing belt front covers and valve cover.

23. Install the engine assembly in the vehicle.

24. Fill the crankcase with the proper type and quantity of oil. Fill and bleed the cooling system.

25. Connect the negative battery cable, start the engine and check for leaks. Check the ignition timing.

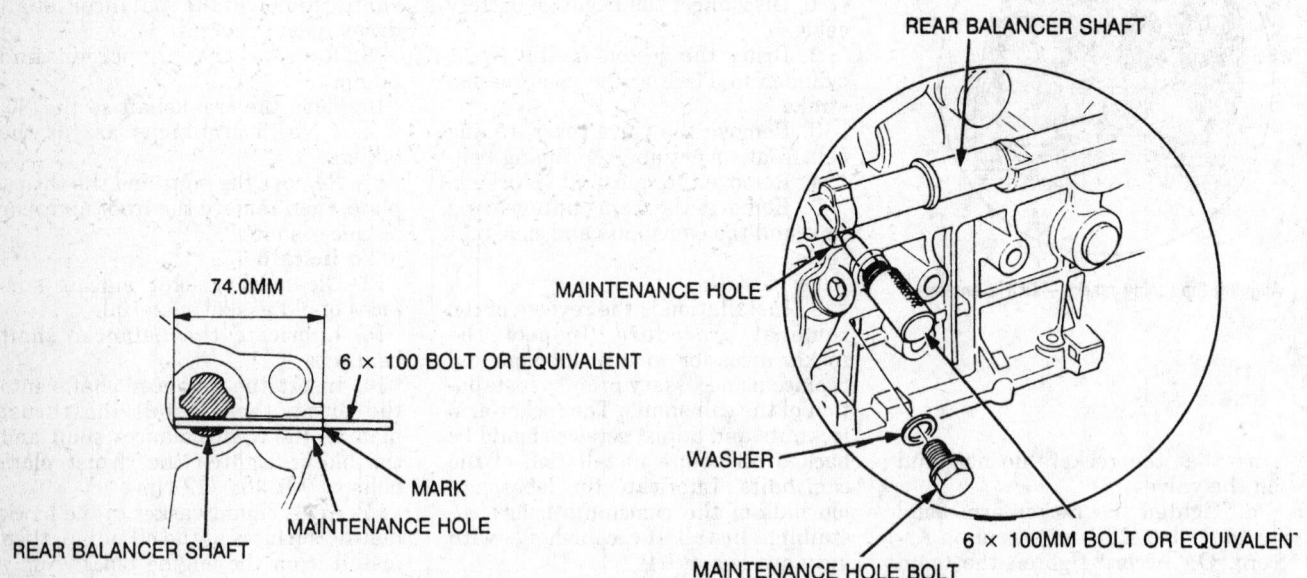

Aligning the belt driven rear timing balancer — 2.2L (SOHC) engine

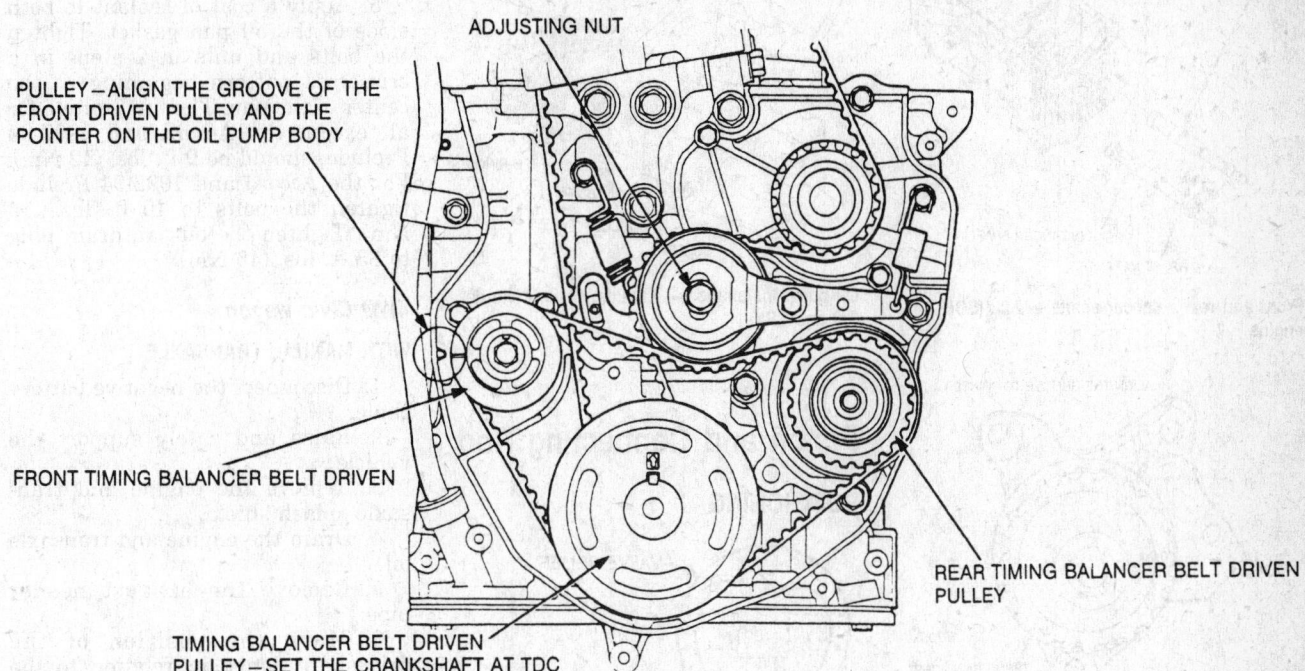

ADJUSTING NUT

PULLEY—ALIGN THE GROOVE OF THE
FRONT DRIVEN PULLEY AND THE
POINTER ON THE OIL PUMP BODY

FRONT TIMING BALANCER BELT DRIVEN

TIMING BALANCER BELT DRIVEN
PULLEY—SET THE CRANKSHAFT AT TDC

REAR TIMING BALANCER BELT DRIVEN
PULLEY

Timing balancer belt installation — 2.2L (SOHC) engine

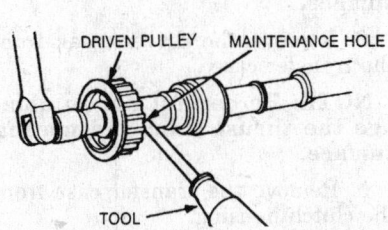

DRIVEN PULLEY   MAINTENANCE HOLE

TOOL

Front balancer shaft driven gear installation —
2.2L (SOHC) engine

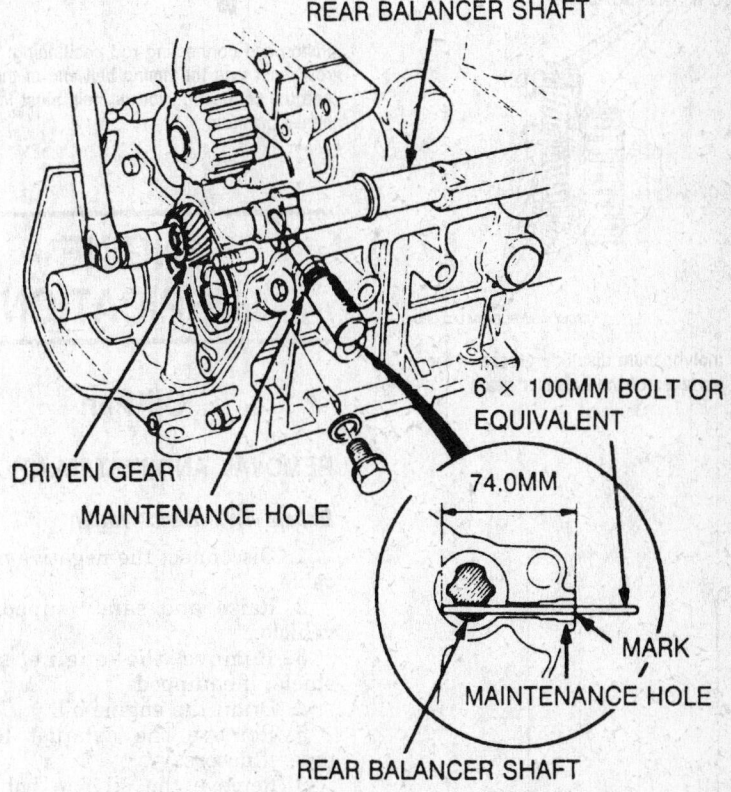

REAR BALANCER SHAFT

6 × 100MM BOLT OR
EQUIVALENT

74.0MM

DRIVEN GEAR

MAINTENANCE HOLE

MARK

MAINTENANCE HOLE

REAR BALANCER SHAFT

Rear balancer shaft driven gear installation — 2.2L (SOHC) engine

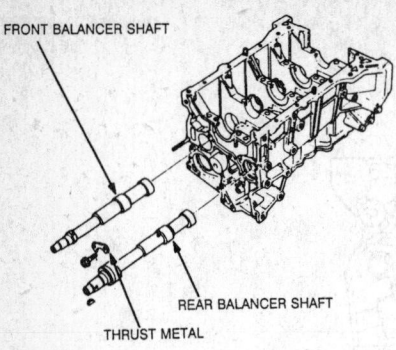

Front and rear balancer shafts — 2.2L (SOHC) engine

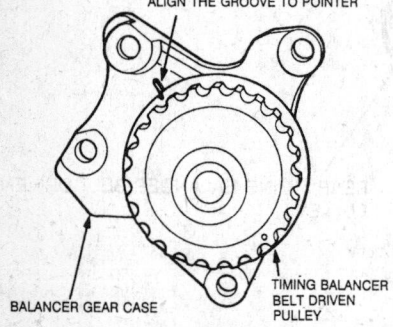

Timing balancer belt driven pulley — 2.2L (SOHC) engine

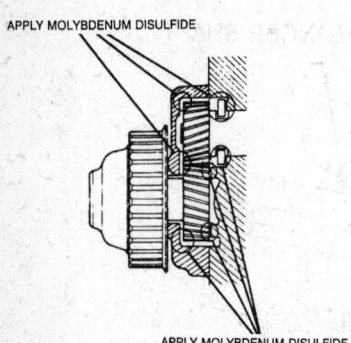

Apply molybdenum disulfide grease to the thrust surfaces of the balancer gears

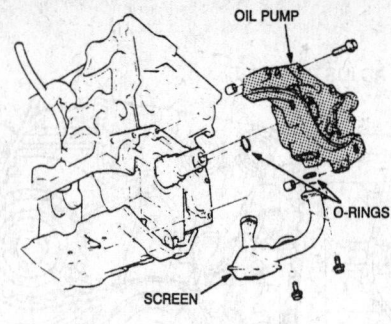

Oil pump installation — Prelude, Civic, Civic del Sol and CRX

Piston and Connecting Rod

POSITIONING

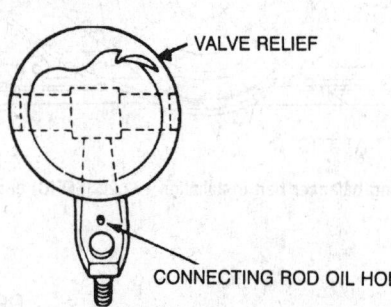

Piston and connecting rod positioning: The arrow must face the timing belt end of the engine and the connecting rod oil hole must face the intake manifold

ENGINE LUBRICATION

Oil Pan

REMOVAL AND INSTALLATION

Except 4WD Civic Wagon

1. Disconnect the negative battery cable.
2. Raise and safely support the vehicle.
3. Remove the engine splash shield, if equipped.
4. Drain the engine oil.
5. Remove the exhaust header pipe, if necessary.
6. Remove the oil pan bolts and nuts and the oil pan.
7. Installation is the reverse of the removal procedure. Make sure all gasket mating surfaces are clean prior to installation.
8. Apply a coat of sealant to both sides of the oil pan gasket. Tighten the bolts and nuts in 2 steps in a crisscross pattern beginning at the center of the pan. The final torque for all except the Accord and 1992-94 Prelude, should be 9 ft. lbs. (12 Nm). For the Accord and 1992-94 Prelude tighten the bolts to 10 ft. lbs. (14 Nm). Tighten the oil pan drain plug to 33 ft. lbs. (45 Nm).

4WD Civic wagon

WITH MANUAL TRANSAXLE

1. Disconnect the negative battery cable.
2. Raise and safely support the vehicle.
3. Remove the engine and transaxle splash shield.
4. Drain the engine and transaxle oil.
5. Remove the exhaust header pipe.
6. Mark the position of the driveshaft flange in relation to the companion flange and remove the driveshaft.
7. Remove the left side cover from the transfer case.

NOTE: Be careful not to damage the thrust shim and mating surface.

8. Remove the driven gear from the transfer case.

NOTE: Be careful not to damage the thrust shim and mating surface.

9. Remove the transfer case from the clutch housing.
10. Remove the clutch case cover.
11. Remove the oil pan by removing the bolts and nuts.
   To install:
12. Clean all gasket mating surfaces.
13. Apply sealant to both sides of a new oil pan gasket and install the gasket and the oil pan. Tighten the bolts and nuts in 2 steps in a crisscross pattern starting at the center of the pan. The final torque should be 9 ft. lbs. (12 Nm).
14. Install and tighten the oil drain plug to 33 ft. lbs. (45 Nm).
15. Apply liquid gasket to the clutch housing mating surface of the transfer case. Install the transfer case on the clutch housing. Tighten the transfer case bolts to 33 ft. lbs. (45 Nm).
16. Install the drive gear thrust shim on the transfer shaft. Lubricate the drive gear and install it on the

transfer shaft. Install the transfer thrust shim and left side cover on the transfer case. Apply liquid gasket to the side cover bolts and tighten them to 33 ft. lbs. (45 Nm).

17. Apply a thin film of sealant at the top and bottom of the transfer case opening and install the driven gear thrust shim and the driven gear. Tighten the mounting bolts to 19 ft. lbs. (26 Nm).

18. Install the driveshaft, aligning the marks that were made during the removal procedure. Tighten the bolts to 24 ft. lbs. (33 Nm).

19. Install the exhaust header pipe and the engine and transaxle splash shields. Install and tighten the transaxle drain plug to 30 ft. lbs. (40 Nm).

20. Fill the transaxle with the proper type of oil, to the required level.

21. Lower the vehicle and fill the crankcase with the proper type of oil, to the required level.

22. Connect the negative battery cable, start the engine and check for leaks.

WITH AUTOMATIC TRANSAXLE

1. Disconnect the negative battery cable.

2. Raise and safely support the vehicle.

3. Remove the engine and transaxle splash shield.

4. Drain the engine and transaxle oil.

5. Remove the exhaust header pipe.

6. Mark the position of the driveshaft flange in relation to the companion flange and remove the driveshaft.

7. Remove the driven gear assembly from the transfer case.

8. Remove the left side cover and then the drive gear from the transfer case. Rotate the cover using the bolt closest to the front of the vehicle as the axis. This bolt is not removed from the cover.

NOTE: Be careful not to damage the thrust shim and mating surface.

9. Remove the transfer case from the clutch housing.

10. Remove the clutch case cover.

11. Remove the oil pan by removing the bolts and nuts.

To install:

12. Clean all gasket mating surfaces.

13. Apply sealant to both sides of a new oil pan gasket and install the gasket and the oil pan. Tighten the bolts and nuts in 2 steps in a crisscross pattern starting at the center of the pan. The final torque should be 9 ft. lbs. (12 Nm).

14. Install and tighten the oil drain plug to 33 ft. lbs. (45 Nm).

15. Apply liquid gasket to the clutch housing mating surface of the transfer case. Attach a new O-ring to the groove in the transfer left side cover.

16. Install the transfer case on the clutch housing. Install the bolt that remained in the left side cover, in the transfer case before installing the case on the clutch housing. Tighten the transfer case bolts to 33 ft. lbs. (45 Nm).

17. Install the drive gear thrust shim on the transfer shaft. Lubricate the drive gear and install it on the transfer shaft. Install the transfer thrust shim and left side cover on the transfer case. Apply liquid gasket to the side cover bolts and tighten them to 33 ft. lbs. (45 Nm).

18. Apply a thin film of sealant at the top and bottom of the transfer case opening and install the driven gear thrust shim and the driven gear. Tighten the mounting bolts to 19 ft. lbs. (26 Nm).

19. Install the driveshaft, aligning the marks that were made during the removal procedure. Tighten the bolts to 24 ft. lbs. (33 Nm).

20. Install the exhaust header pipe and the engine and transaxle splash shields. Install and tighten the transaxle drain plug to 29 ft. lbs. (40 Nm).

21. Lower the vehicle and fill the crankcase with the proper type of oil, to the required level. Fill the transaxle with the proper type and quantity of oil.

22. Connect the negative battery cable, start the engine and check for leaks.

Oil Pump

REMOVAL AND INSTALLATION

All Models

1. Disconnect the negative battery cable.

2. Raise and safely support the vehicle.

3. Drain the engine oil.

4. Bring the No. 1 cylinder to TDC. On Civic, Civic del Sol and CRX, the mark on the crankshaft pulley should align with the index mark on the timing cover. On Accord and Prelude, the mark on the flywheel should align with the pointer in the inspection hole.

5. Remove the necessary accessory drive belts and the crankshaft pulley.

6. Remove the valve cover and the timing belt covers.

7. On Accord and 1992-94 Prelude, remove the following:

   a. Timing balancer belt
   b. Timing belt
   c. Timing belt tensioner
   d. Timing balancer belt tensioner
   e. Timing belt drive pulley
   f. Timing balancer belt driven pulley. Insert a suitable tool into the maintenance hole in the front balancer shaft in order to hold the shaft in place and remove the front balancer driven pulley.
   g. Balancer drive gear case
   h. Balancer driven gear. Remove the maintenance hole bolt from the cylinder block next to the rear balancer shaft. Insert a 6 **x** 100mm bolt or equivalent, to a depth of 3 in. (74mm) through the maintenance hole and into the rear balancer shaft. Remove the balancer shaft driven gear.

8. On all other vehicles, remove the following:

   a. Timing belt tensioner
   b. Timing belt
   c. Timing belt drive pulley

9. Remove the oil pan and oil screen.

10. Remove the oil pump mount bolts and the oil pump assembly.

To install:

11. Installation is the reverse of the removal procedure. Make sure all gasket mating surfaces are clean prior to installation.

12. Inspect the crankshaft oil seal and replace as necessary prior to installing the oil pump.

13. Apply liquid gasket to the cylinder block mating surface of the block. Apply a light coat of oil to the crankshaft seal lip. Install a new O-ring on the cylinder block and install the oil pump. Apply liquid gasket to the threads of the oil pump mounting bolts and tighten them to 9 ft. lbs. (12 Nm).

14. Install the oil screen.

15. On Accord and 1992-94 Prelude, perform the following procedure:

   a. Apply molybdenum disulfide grease to the thrust surfaces of the balancer gears, before installing the balancer driven gear and the balancer drive gear case.

   b. Hold the rear balancer shaft with the 6 **x** 100mm bolt or equivalent, then install the balancer driven gear and the balancer drive belt pulley. Tighten the retaining bolt to 18 ft. lbs. (25 Nm).

   c. Hold the front balancer shaft with a suitable tool, then install the timing balancer belt driven pulley. Tighten the retaining bolt to 22 ft. lbs. (30 Nm).

d. Install the balancer gear case to the oil pump. Align the groove on the pulley edge to the pointer on the gear case when holding the rear balancer shaft with the 6 **x** 100mm bolt or equivalent, then install the gear case. Tighten the balancer gear case bolts to 18 ft. lbs. (25 Nm).

e. Remove the 6 **x** 100mm bolt and install the maintenance hole bolt.

16. Install the oil pan and the remainder of the components. Be sure to properly tension the timing belt after installation. Tighten the crankshaft pulley bolt to specification.

Rear Main Bearing Oil Seal

REMOVAL AND INSTALLATION

The rear main seal is housed in a separate cover which is mounted on the engine block with 4 bolts.

1. Disconnect the negative battery cable.
2. Raise and safely support the vehicle.
3. Remove the transaxle assembly.

4. On Civic Wagon with 4WD, remove the transfer case.
5. Remove the flywheel.
6. Remove the oil pan.
7. Remove the 4 bolts and the seal housing. Remove the rear main seal.

To install:

8. Installation is the reverse of the removal procedure. Lubricate the lip of the seal prior to installation. Pack the inner spring pocket of the seal with grease to prevent the spring from dislodging during installation.

9. Install the rear main seal in the seal housing using a suitable installation tool. Install the seal with the

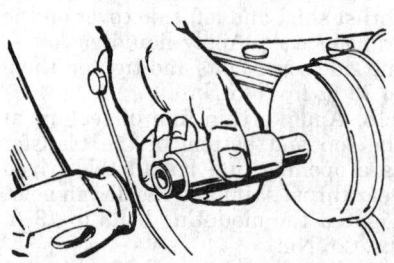

Installing the rear main seal — 2.0L (SOHC) engine

part number side towards the installation tool. Apply liquid gasket to the block mating surface and the seal housing retainer bolts. Install the seal housing on the block. Tighten the bolts to 9 ft. lbs. (12 Nm).

10. Install the remainder of the components.

ENGINE COOLING

Radiator

REMOVAL AND INSTALLATION

1. Disconnect the negative battery cable. Drain the radiator.
2. Disconnect the thermo-switch wire and the fan motor wire.
3. Disconnect the upper coolant hose at the upper radiator tank and the lower hose at the water pump connecting pipe. Disconnect and plug the automatic transaxle cooling lines at the bottom of the radiator, if equipped.
4. Remove the hoses to the coolant reservoir, if equipped.

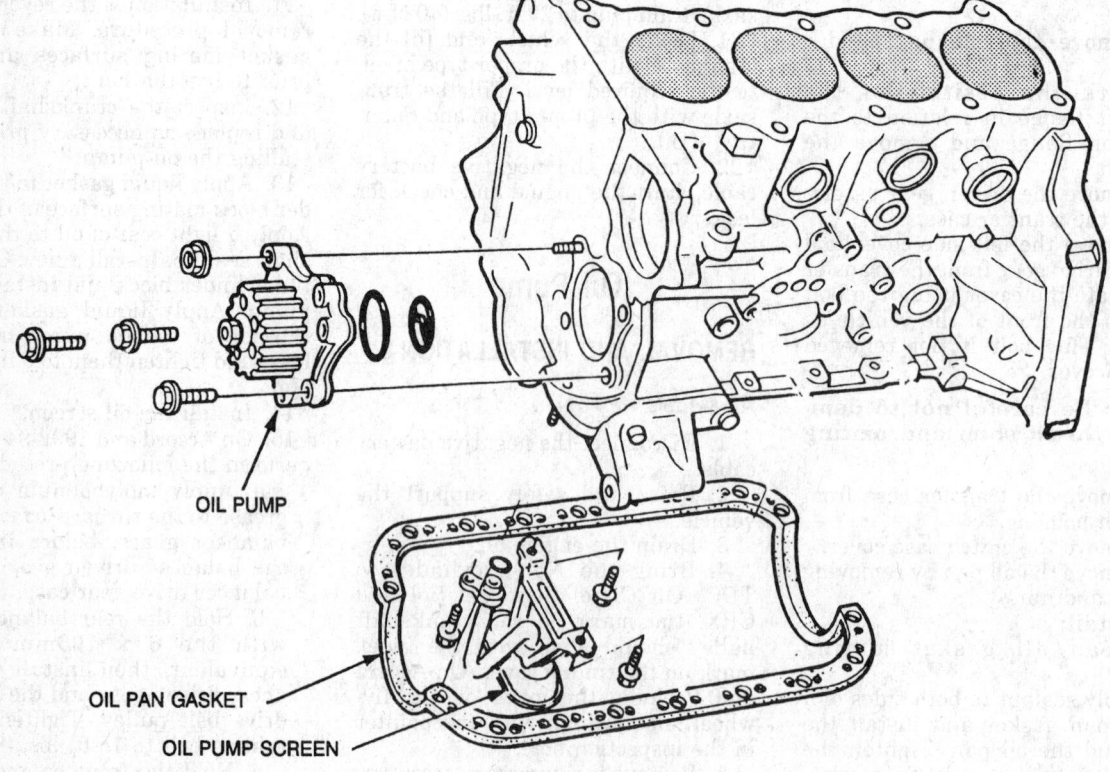

OIL PUMP

OIL PAN GASKET

OIL PUMP SCREEN

Oil pump installation — 2.0L engine

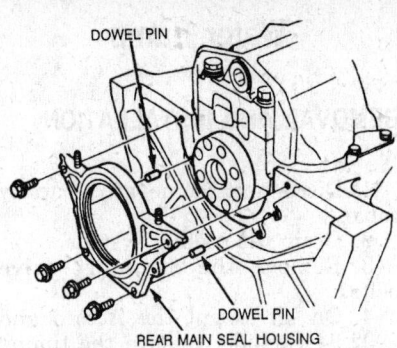

Installing the rear main seal housing — except 2.0L (SOHC) engine

5. Detach the radiator mounting bolts and remove the radiator with the fan attached.

6. Remove the cooling fan and shroud assembly from the radiator.

7. To install, reverse the removal procedure. Refill and bleed the cooling system.

Heater Core

REMOVAL AND INSTALLATION

CIVIC AND CIVIC DEL SOL

1. Disconnect the negative battery cable.

2. Disable the Supplemental Restraint System (SRS) on the 1992-94 Civic and del Sol models.

3. Drain the cooling system.

4. Disconnect the heater hoses from the heater at the firewall.

5. Disconnect the water valve cable from the water valve and remove the heater unit attaching nut from the firewall.

6. Remove the dashboard by performing the following procedure:

a. Slide the seats back fully and remove the center console.

b. Remove the fuse lid.

c. Remove the knee bolster.

d. Disconnect the wire harnesses from the connector holder and disconnect the sunroof switch connector, if equipped. Remove the fuse box mounting nuts and lower the fuse box, if necessary.

e. Disconnect the ground cable at the right of the steering column and the power door mirror switch connector.

f. Remove the knob, then remove the side air vent face plate.

g. Remove the 2 screws attaching the side air vent control lever.

h. Remove the center panel and radio, then remove the 3 screws attaching the heater control panel to the dashboard.

i. Remove the gauge upper panel or instrument panel, as necessary.

j. Disconnect the speedometer cable.

k. Remove the center upper lid from the top of the dashboard.

l. Remove the side defroster garnishes from both ends of the dashboard.

m. Lower the steering column.

n. Remove the dashboard mounting bolts, lift and remove the dashboard.

7. Remove the heater duct.

8. Remove the heater lower mounting nut.

9. Remove the steering column bracket and duct assembly.

10. Remove the 2 heater mounting bolts and the clip, then remove the heater assembly.

11. Remove the tapping screws and heater core cover.

12. Remove the tapping screw and clamp and remove the heater core.

To install:

13. Install the heater core into the housing and make sure the cover is properly sealed.

14. Install the heater assembly and connect the ducting.

15. Fit the dashboard into place and secure the steering column.

16. Install the instruments and connect the wiring.

17. Install the center console and connect the wiring and heater controls.

18. Install the fuse box and connect the wiring.

19. Connect the heater hoses and fill and bleed the cooling system. Adjust the controls as required.

20. Connect the negative battery cable and enable the SRS system.

21. Start the engine and check for leaks.

CRX

1. Disconnect the negative battery cable.

2. Drain the cooling system.

3. Disconnect the heater hoses at the firewall.

4. Disconnect the water valve cable from the water valve.

5. Remove the dashboard by performing the following procedure:

a. Slide the seats back fully and remove the front console.

b. Remove the fuse lid. Disconnect the wire harnesses from the connector holder and disconnect the sunroof switch connector, if equipped. Remove the fuse box mounting nuts and lower the fuse box, if necessary.

c. Disconnect the ground cable at the right of the steering column.

d. Remove the coin box.

e. Remove the knob, then remove the side air vent face plate.

f. Remove the 2 screws attaching the side air vent control lever.

g. Remove the 3 screws attaching the heater control panel to the dashboard.

h. Remove the instrument panel.

i. Disconnect the speedometer cable.

j. Remove the center upper lid from the top of the dashboard.

k. Remove the side defroster garnishes from both ends of the dashboard.

l. Lower the steering column.

m. Remove the dashboard mounting bolts, lift and remove the dashboard.

6. Remove the heater duct.

7. Remove the heater lower mounting nut.

8. Remove the steering column bracket and duct assembly.

9. Remove the 2 heater mounting bolts, disconnect the wire harness connector from the function control motor and then remove the heater assembly.

10. Remove the tapping screws and heater core cover.

11. Remove the tapping screw and clamp. Remove the heater core.

To install:

12. Install the heater core into the housing and make sure the cover is properly sealed.

13. Install the heater assembly and connect the ducts and wiring.

14. Fit the dashboard into place and secure the steering column.

15. Install the instruments and connect the wiring.

16. Install the center console and connect the wiring and heater controls.

17. Install the fuse box and connect the wiring.

18. Connect the heater hoses and negative battery cable.

19. Fill and bleed the cooling system.

20. Start the engine and check for leaks. Adjust the controls as required.

Accord

1. Disconnect the negative battery cable. Disable the SRS system (air bag), if equipped.

2. Drain the cooling system.

3. Disconnect the heater hoses at the heater.

4. Disconnect the heater valve cable from the heater valve.

5. Remove the dashboard by performing the following procedure:

a. Slide the seats back fully and remove the console.

b. Remove the knee bolster, lower panel and steering column.

c. Disconnect the dashboard wire harness from the connectors and fuse box.

d. Remove the carpet clips and disconnect the antenna lead.

e. Disconnect the heater control cable and function control cable.

f. Remove the caps from both sides of the dash and the clock.

g. Remove the 7 dashboard mounting bolts, lift and remove the dashboard.

6. Remove the heater duct.

7. Remove the instrument sub-pipe.

8. Remove the 4 heater mounting nuts and the heater assembly.

9. Remove the air mix rod from the clip, the self-tapping screws and heater core cover and the self-tapping screw and clamp. Remove the heater core from the heater housing.

To install:

10. Install the heater core into the housing and make sure the cover is properly sealed. Install the air mix door rod.

11. Install the heater assembly and connect the ducts.

12. Install the instrument sub-pipe.

13. Carefully fit the dashboard into place and install the bolts.

14. Connect the heater controls and wiring.

15. Install the console and knee bolster and secure the steering column in place.

16. Connect the heater hoses and negative battery cable.

17. Fill and bleed the cooling system.

18. Start the engine and check for leaks. Adjust the controls as required.

PRELUDE

1. Disconnect the negative battery cable. If equipped with SRS, disable the system.

2. Drain the cooling system.

3. Disconnect the heater hoses at the heater.

4. Disconnect the heater valve cable from the heater.

5. Remove the dashboard by performing the following procedure:

a. Slide the seats back fully and remove the dashboard lower panel and the front and rear consoles.

b. Disconnect the wire harnesses from the connector holder and fuse box.

c. Remove the 6 screws and radio panel, then disconnect the wire connectors and antenna cable.

d. Remove the radio assembly.

e. Disconnect the heater control cable and the connector and wire harnesses from the heater control unit.

f. Remove the clock from the top of the dashboard.

g. Lower the steering column.

h. Remove the dashboard mounting bolts. Lift the dashboard as it is removed, so it will slide up and off the guide pin in the middle. Hold the dashboard from underneath so it will not fall when it comes off the pin.

6. Remove the heater duct.

7. Remove the heater lower mounting nuts.

8. Remove the steering column bracket.

9. Remove the 2 heater mounting bolts, disconnect the wire harness connector from the function control motor and then remove the heater assembly.

10. Remove the integrated control unit and bracket from the heater assembly.

11. Remove the 2 tapping screws, bracket, set-plate and heater core cover.

12. Remove the 2 tapping screws, heater core set-plate and clamp.

13. Pull the heater core from the heater housing.

To install:

14. Install the heater core into the housing and make sure the cover is properly sealed. Complete the heater assembly.

15. Install the heater assembly and connect the ducts and wiring.

16. Install the instrument sub-pipe.

17. Carefully fit the dashboard into place and install the bolts.

18. Connect the heater controls and wiring.

19. Install the radio and connect the wiring.

20. Connect the wiring to the fuse box.

21. Connect the heater hoses and negative battery cable.

22. Fill and bleed the cooling system.

23. Enable the SRS system, if equipped.

24. Start the engine and check for leaks. Adjust the controls as required.

Water Pump

REMOVAL AND INSTALLATION

1. Disconnect the negative battery cable.

2. Drain the cooling system.

3. Remove the accessory drive belts.

4. On all except the Accord and 1992-94 Prelude, remove the timing belt cover and belt. On the Accord and the 1992-94 Prelude, remove the timing balancer belt assembly and then remove the timing belt.

5. Remove the water pump mounting bolts and the water pump.

To install:

6. Install the water pump into position, using new O-ring seal. Install the mounting bolts. Tighten the water pump mounting bolts to 9 ft. lbs. (12 Nm).

7. On all except the Accord and 1992-94 Prelude, install the timing belt and cover. On the Accord and the 1992-94 Prelude, install the timing belt and balancer assembly.

8. Install the accessory drive belts.

9. Connect the negative battery cable. Fill and bleed the cooling system.

10. Start the engine and check for leaks.

Thermostat

The thermostat housing is located on the cylinder head, with the exception of Civic, CRX, del Sol and Accord. The Civic, CRX, del Sol and Accord thermostat is located at the end of the water pump inlet tube.

REMOVAL AND INSTALLATION

1. Disconnect the negative battery cable.

2. Drain the cooling system.

3. Disconnect the radiator hose from the thermostat housing outlet.

4. Remove the thermostat housing outlet and remove the thermostat.

5. Installation is the reverse of the removal procedure. Use new gaskets and O-rings. Install the thermostat with the pin towards the thermostat housing outlet. Tighten the thermostat housing outlet bolts to 9 ft. lbs. (12 Nm).

6. Fill and bleed the cooling system.

Cooling System Bleeding

1. Loosen the air bleed bolt in the water outlet and fill the radiator to the bottom of the filler neck with antifreeze/coolant. Tighten the bleed bolt as soon as the coolant starts to run out in a steady stream without any air bubbles in it.

2. With the radiator cap off, start the engine and allow it to warm up (the cooling fan should go on at least twice). Recheck the coolant level. If necessary, add more antifreeze/coolant to bring the level back up to the bottom of the filler neck.

3. Put the radiator cap on, restart the engine and check for any leaks.

ENGINE ELECTRICAL

NOTE: Disconnecting the negative battery cable on some vehicles may interfere with the functions of the on-board computer systems and may require the computer to undergo a relearning process, once the negative battery cable is reconnected.

Distributor

REMOVAL

1. Disconnect the negative battery cable.

2. Disconnect the spark plug wires and tag for reassembly in the same positions.

3. Disconnect the coil wire and primary lead wire, if equipped.

4. Disconnect the vacuum advance hoses, if equipped.

5. Disconnect the necessary electrical connectors.

6. Remove the distributor cap.

7. Using a suitable marking tool, mark the position of the distributor rotor in relation to the distributor housing and mark the position of the distributor housing in relation to the cylinder head.

8. Remove the distributor hold-down bolts and remove the distributor. Remove and discard the distributor O-ring.

INSTALLATION

Timing Not Disturbed

1. Coat a new distributor O-ring with engine oil and install on the distributor. Install the distributor, aligning the distributor housing and distributor rotor with the marks that were made during the removal procedure.

NOTE: The distributor is equipped with locating lugs which mesh with corresponding grooves in the end of the camshaft. The lugs and grooves are both offset to prevent installing the distributor 180 degrees out of time.

2. Install the distributor hold-down bolts and tighten temporarily.

3. Install the distributor cap.

4. Connect the electrical connectors.

5. Connect the vacuum hoses, if equipped.

6. Connect the coil wire and the primary lead wire, if equipped.

7. Connect the spark plug wires in their original positions.

8. Check the ignition timing and tighten the distributor hold-down bolts to 16 ft. lbs. (22 Nm). Recheck the ignition timing.

Timing Disturbed

1. Disconnect the spark plug wire from the No. 1 cylinder spark plug and remove the spark plug.

2. Place a finger over the spark plug hole and turn the engine over slowly, by hand until compression is felt.

3. On Civic and del Sol vehicles, align the **RED** timing mark on the crankshaft pulley with the pointer on the timing belt cover. On Accord and Prelude vehicles, remove the rubber cap from the inspection window at the rear of the cylinder block. Align the **RED** timing mark on the driveplate (automatic transaxle) or flywheel (manual transaxle) with the pointer on the cylinder block.

4. Coat a new distributor O-ring with engine oil and install on the distributor. Install the distributor with the distributor rotor pointing to the No. 1 spark plug tower on the distributor cap.

NOTE: The distributor is equipped with locating lugs which mesh with corresponding grooves in the end of the camshaft. The lugs and grooves are both offset to prevent installing the distributor 180 degrees out of time.

5. Install the distributor hold-down bolts and tighten temporarily.

6. Install the distributor cap.

7. Connect the electrical connectors.

8. Connect the vacuum hoses, if equipped.

9. Connect the coil wire and the primary lead wire, if equipped.

10. Install the No. 1 spark plug and tighten to 13 ft. lbs. (18 Nm). Connect the No. 1 spark plug wire to the spark plug.

11. Connect the spark plug wires to the distributor cap in their original positions.

12. Set the ignition timing and tighten the distributor hold-down bolts to 16 ft. lbs. (22 Nm). Recheck the ignition timing.

Ignition Timing

ADJUSTMENT

Carburetor equipped Prelude

1. Remove the rubber cap from the inspection window of the cylinder block.

2. Start the engine and allow it to warm up. The cooling fan must come ON at least once.

3. Disconnect the vacuum hoses from the vacuum advance diaphragm and plug them.

4. Connect the pickup lead from a suitable timing light to the No. 1 spark plug wire. Make the remaining timing light connections according to the manufacturers instructions.

5. With the engine idling, aim the timing light at the pointer on the engine block and the driveplate (automatic transaxle) or flywheel (manual transaxle).

6. Adjust the ignition timing according to the specification listed on the underhood emission label. Adjust as necessary by loosening the distributor adjusting bolts and turning the distributor housing counterclockwise to advance the timing, or clockwise to retard the timing.

7. Tighten the adjusting bolts to 16 ft. lbs. (22 Nm) and recheck the timing.

8. Connect the vacuum advance hoses and replace the rubber cap to the inspection window.

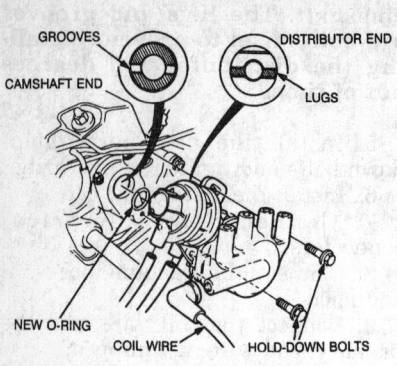

Distributor installation

Civic, CRX, Civic Del Sol, Accord and Prelude with Fuel Injection

1. On Accord and Prelude vehicles, remove the rubber cap from the inspection window of the cylinder block.

2. Start the engine and allow it to warm up. The engine cooling fan must come ON at least once.

3. On Civic, CRX and Civic del Sol, pull out the blue ignition timing adjusting connector located under the right side of the dash and connect the brown and green/white connector.

4. On Accord, connect the orange/red and green/white terminals of the blue service check connector with a jumper wire. The service check connector is located in the far right corner under the dashboard.

5. On 1990-91 Prelude, remove the yellow cap from the ignition timing adjusting connector located behind the ignition coil and connect the brown and green/white terminals with a jumper wire. On 1992-94 Prelude, pull out the service check connector from under the center of the dash and connect the blue/white terminal to the brown/white terminal.

6. Connect the pickup lead of a suitable timing light to the No. 1 spark plug wire. Make the other timing light connections according to the manufacturers instructions.

7. With the engine idling, aim the timing light at the pointer on the timing belt cover and the crankshaft pulley on Civic, CRX and del Sol. On Accord and Prelude, aim the timing light at the pointer on the cylinder block and the driveplate (automatic transaxle) or flywheel (manual transaxle).

8. Adjust the ignition timing to the specification listed on the underhood vehicle emission label. Adjust as necessary by loosening the distributor adjusting bolts and turn-

ing the distributor housing counterclockwise to advance the timing, or clockwise to retard the timing.

9. Tighten the adjusting bolts to 16 ft. lbs. (22 Nm) and recheck the timing.

10. Remove the jumper wire from the ignition timing adjusting connector on Civic, CRX, del Sol and Prelude, and install the yellow rubber cap, if equipped. On Accord, remove the jumper wire from the blue service check connector and install the rubber cap to the inspection window.

Alternator

PRECAUTIONS

Several precautions must be observed with alternator equipped vehicles to avoid damage to the unit:

• If the battery is removed for any reason, make sure it is reconnected with the correct polarity. Reversing the battery connections may result in damage to the 1-way rectifiers.

• When utilizing a booster battery as a starting aid, always connect the positive to positive terminals and the

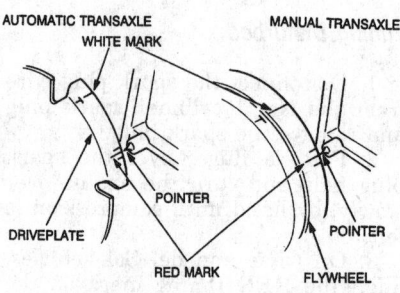

Location of ignition timing marks — Prelude

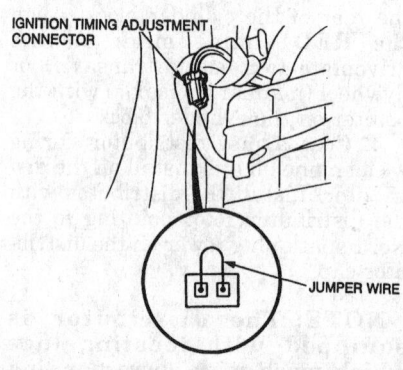

Underdash ignition timing adjustment connector

negative terminal from the booster battery to a good engine ground on the vehicle being started.

• Never use a fast charger as a booster to start vehicles.

• Disconnect the battery cables when charging the battery with a fast charger.

• Never attempt to polarize the alternator.

• Do not use test lamps of more than 12 volts when checking diode continuity.

• Do not short across or ground any of the alternator terminals.

• The polarity of the battery, alternator and regulator must be matched and considered before making any electrical connections within the system.

• Never separate the alternator on an open circuit. Make sure all connections within the circuit are clean and tight.

• Disconnect the battery ground terminal when performing any service on electrical components.

• Disconnect the battery if arc welding is to be done on the vehicle.

BELT TENSION ADJUSTMENT

1. Apply a force of 22 lbs. and measure the deflection of the alternator belt between the alternator and the crankshaft pulley.

2. On a belt in service, the deflection should be as follows:
1990 Civic and CRX — 0.35-0.43 in. (9-11mm)
1992-94 Civic and del Sol — 0.28-0.41 in. (7-11mm)
Accord — 0.39-0.47 in. (10-12mm)
Prelude — 0.39-0.47 in. (10-12mm)

3. If the belt deflection is not as specified, loosen the alternator pivot bolt. On Civic, CRX and del Sol, loosen the alternator adjusting bolt and move the alternator using a suitable prybar positioned against the front of the alternator housing. Tighten the adjusting bolt when the proper tension is obtained. On Accord and Prelude, loosen the alternator nut or bolt and turn the adjusting nut or bolt until the proper tension is obtained. Tighten the alternator nut or bolt and the pivot bolt. Recheck the belt deflection.

4. If a new belt is installed, the deflection should be as follows when first measured:
1990 Civic and CRX — 0.25-0.35 in. (7-9mm)
1991-94 Civic and del Sol — 0.22-0.31 in. (5.5-8mm)
Accord

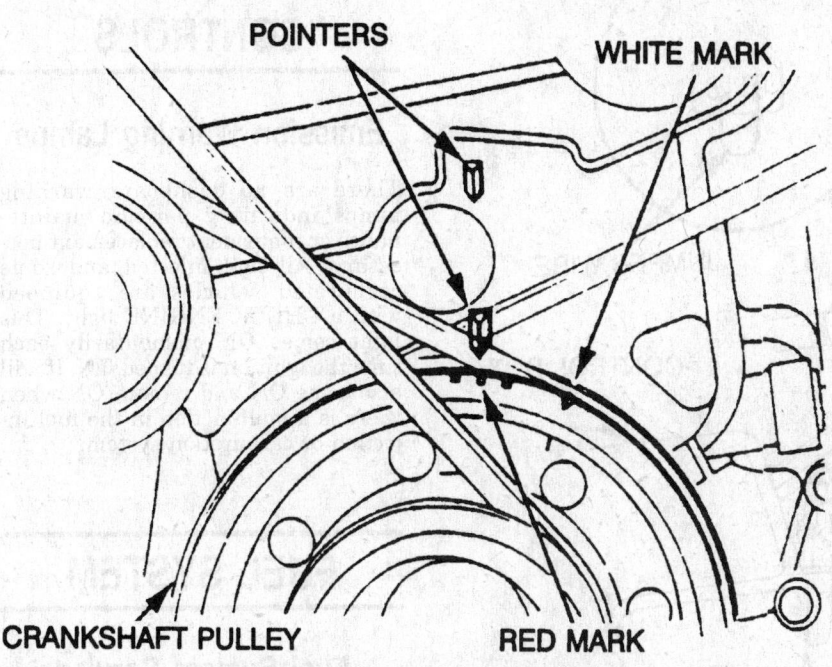

Location of ignition timing marks — Civic and CRX

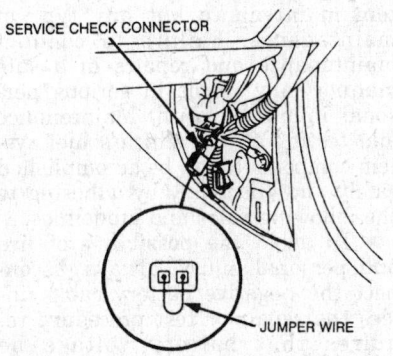

Location of service check connector — Accord

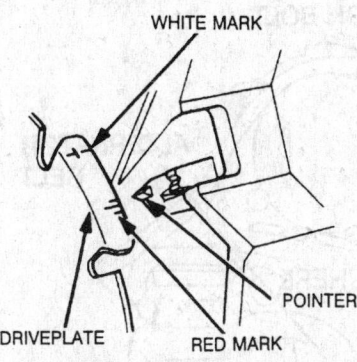

Timing pointer and timing marks — Accord

nut to 33 ft. lbs. (45 Nm). Tighten the alternator adjusting bolt on Civic, del Sol and CRX and the alternator bolt on 1990-91 Prelude and Accord to 17 ft. lbs. (24 Nm).

Accord and 1992-94 Prelude

1. Disconnect the negative battery cable.
2. Remove the power steering pump and the cruise control actuator. Do not disconnect the actuator cable.
3. Disconnect the electrical connectors from the alternator.
4. Loosen the adjusting bolt, then remove the alternator nut. Remove the alternator belt from the alternator pulley.
5. Remove the adjusting bolt, the lower through bolt and the stay.
6. Remove the upper through bolt and the alternator. If necessary, remove the 4 mount bracket bolts, the mount bracket and the heat insulator.
7. Installation is the reverse of the removal procedure. Tighten the upper through bolt to 33 ft. lbs. (45 Nm) and the alternator nut to 18 ft. lbs. (26 Nm). If the mount bracket was removed, apply liquid gasket to the mount bracket bolt threads and tighten to 36 ft. lbs. (50 Nm).

Voltage Regulator

The voltage regulator on all vehicles is an internal part of the alternator. It can still usually be replaced separately but the alternator must be removed and partially disassembled.

Starter

REMOVAL AND INSTALLATION

1. Disconnect the negative battery cable.
2. Disconnect the starter cable from the starter motor.
3. Remove the engine compartment wire harness from the harness clip on the starter motor, if equipped.
4. Disconnect the wire from the starter solenoid.
5. Remove the 2 bolts retaining the starter motor and remove the starter motor.
6. Installation is the reverse of the removal procedure. Tighten the starter motor retaining bolts to 32 ft. lbs. (45 Nm).

Without air conditioning — 0.33-0.43 in. (8.5-11mm)
With air conditioning — 0.18-0.28 in. (4.5-7mm)
Prelude — 0.31-0.39 in. (8-10mm)

REMOVAL AND INSTALLATION

Except Accord and 1992-94 Prelude

1. Disconnect the negative battery cable.
2. Remove the air cleaner assembly, if necessary.

3. Disconnect the electrical connectors from the alternator.
4. Loosen the alternator adjusting bolt or nut and through bolt and remove the alternator belt.
5. Remove the alternator adjusting bolt or nut and through bolt and remove the alternator. If necessary, remove the mount bracket bolts and the upper and lower mount brackets.
6. Installation is the reverse of the removal procedure. Tighten the alternator through bolt or through bolt

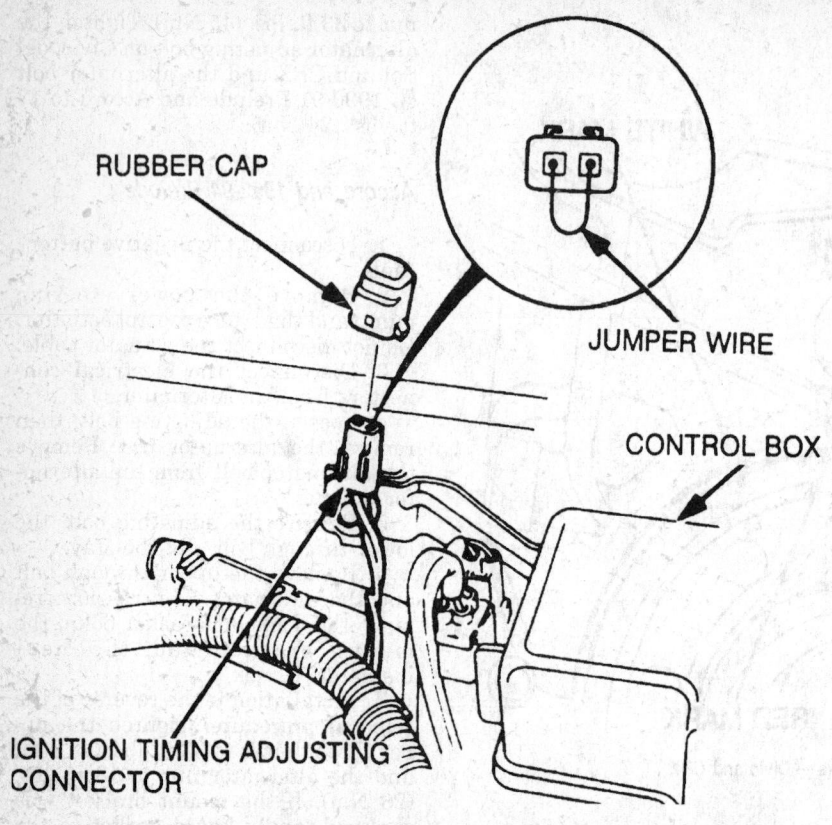

RUBBER CAP

JUMPER WIRE

CONTROL BOX

IGNITION TIMING ADJUSTING CONNECTOR

Location of ignition timing adjusting connector — 1990-91 Prelude with fuel injection

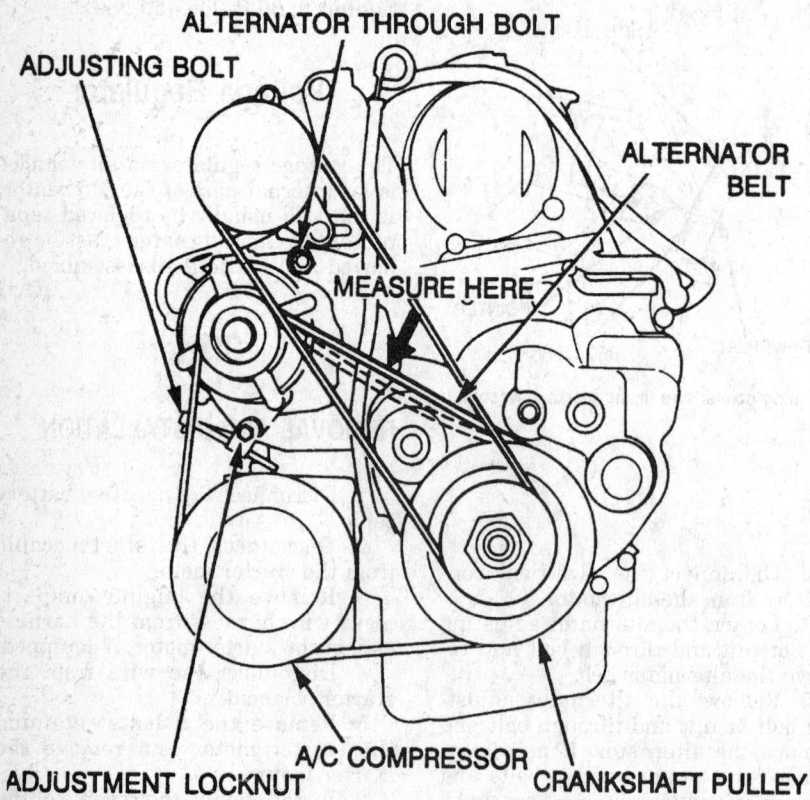

ALTERNATOR THROUGH BOLT

ADJUSTING BOLT

ALTERNATOR BELT

MEASURE HERE

ADJUSTMENT LOCKNUT

A/C COMPRESSOR

CRANKSHAFT PULLEY

Alternator belt adjustment — Accord and 1992-94 Prelude with air conditioning

EMISSION CONTROLS

Emission Warning Lamps

There are no dashboard warning lamps indicating periodic maintenance or component replacement necessary. All fuel injected and some carbureted vehicles are equipped with a CHECK ENGINE light. This light comes ON momentarily each time the ignition is turned **ON**. It will also come ON and remain ON when there is a malfunction in the fuel injection or carburetion system.

FUEL SYSTEM

Fuel System Service Precautions

Safety is the most important factor when performing not only fuel system maintenance but any type of maintenance. Failure to conduct maintenance and repairs in a safe manner may result in serious personal injury or death. Maintenance and testing of the vehicle's fuel system components can be accomplished safely and effectively by adhering to the following rules and guidelines.

• To avoid the possibility of fire and personal injury, always disconnect the negative battery cable unless the repair or test procedure requires that battery voltage be applied.

• Always relieve the fuel system pressure prior to disconnecting any fuel system component (injector, fuel rail, pressure regulator, etc.), fitting or fuel line connection. Exercise extreme caution whenever relieving fuel system pressure to avoid exposing skin, face and eyes to fuel spray. Please be advised that fuel under pressure may penetrate the skin or any part of the body that it contacts.

• Always place a shop towel or cloth around the fitting or connection prior to loosening to absorb any excess fuel due to spillage. Ensure that all fuel spillage (should it occur) is quickly removed from engine surfaces. Ensure that all fuel soaked

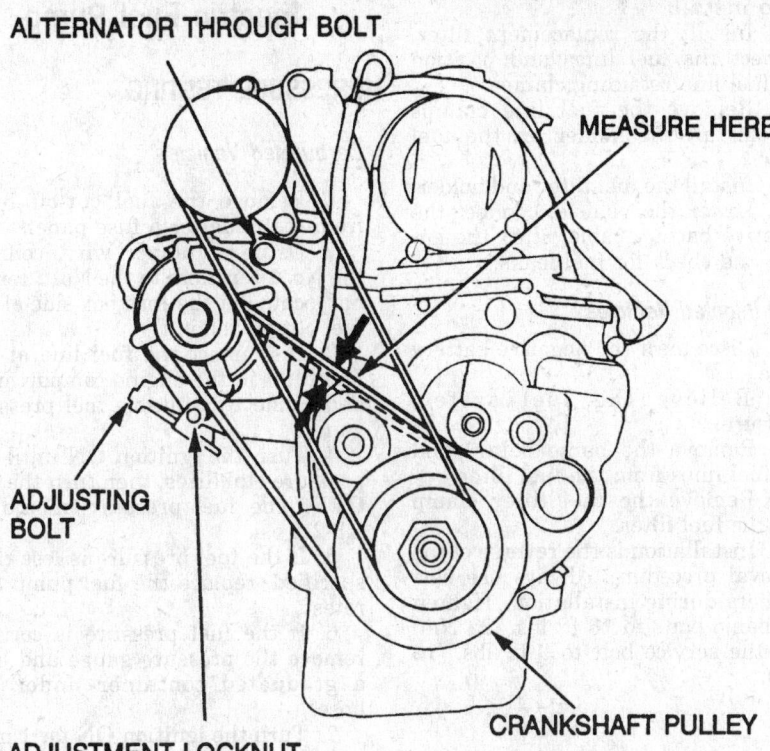

ALTERNATOR THROUGH BOLT

MEASURE HERE

ADJUSTING BOLT

ADJUSTMENT LOCKNUT

CRANKSHAFT PULLEY

Alternator belt adjustment — Accord and 1992-94 Prelude without air conditioning

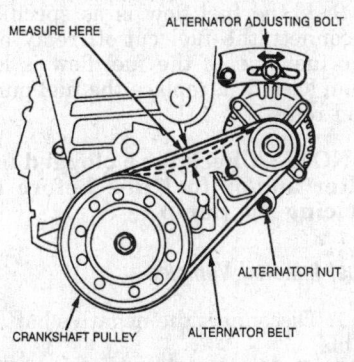

MEASURE HERE

ALTERNATOR ADJUSTING BOLT

ALTERNATOR NUT

CRANKSHAFT PULLEY

ALTERNATOR BELT

Alternator belt adjustment — Civic, Civic del Sol and CRX

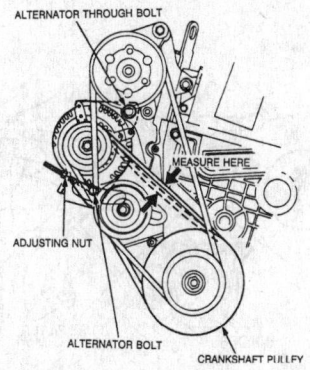

ALTERNATOR THROUGH BOLT

MEASURE HERE

ADJUSTING NUT

ALTERNATOR BOLT

CRANKSHAFT PULLEY

Alternator belt adjustment — Prelude

cloths or towels are deposited into a suitable waste container.

• Always keep a dry chemical (Class B) fire extinguisher near the work area.

• Do not allow fuel spray or fuel vapors to come into contact with a spark or open flame.

• Always use a backup wrench when loosening and tightening fuel line connection fittings. This will prevent unnecessary stress and torsion to fuel line piping. Always follow the proper torque specifications.

• Always replace worn fuel fitting O-rings with new. Do not substitute fuel hose or equivalent where fuel pipe is installed.

RELIEVING FUEL SYSTEM PRESSURE

1. Make sure the engine is cold.
2. Disconnect the negative battery cable.
3. Remove the fuel filler cap.
4. Use a suitable box end wrench on the 6mm service bolt at the top of the fuel filter (fuel pipe on Accord

and 1992-94 Prelude), while holding the special banjo bolt with another wrench.

5. Place a rag or shop towel over the 6mm service bolt.

6. Slowly loosen the 6mm service bolt 1 complete turn.

Fuel Tank

REMOVAL AND INSTALLATION

1. Disconnect the negative battery cable.

2. Raise and safely support the vehicle and remove the rear wheels.

3. Remove the drain bolt and drain the fuel from the tank. Be sure to take the appropriate fire safety precautions.

4. In the luggage area on the Accord and Prelude, remove the access covers and disconnect the fuel pump and gauge unit wiring. On Civic and del Sol vehicles, the access cover is under the rear seat.

5. To disconnect the hoses, loosen the clamps and slide them back. Carefully twist the hose while pulling it off the fitting to avoid damage to the hose or the flared fittings.

6. On 4WD vehicles, remove the exhaust pipe and muffler and the rear propeller shaft.

7. Place a jack under the tank and remove the nuts/bolts to allow the tank straps to fall free. The tank may stick to the vehicle's undercoating but it can be pried out of the mounts. Be careful not to damage the fittings.

To install:

8. Position the tank under the vehicle and install the straps, washers and nuts onto the hooks.

9. Wiggle the tank while tightening the nuts a few turns at a time to make sure the tank seats properly into the mount. Torque the strap nuts on all, except Accord and 1992-94 Prelude, to 16 ft. lbs. (22 Nm). Torque the strap bolts on the Accord and 1992-94 Prelude to 27 ft. lbs. (38 Nm).

10. Make sure the drain plug in installed with a new gasket and torque to 36 ft. lbs. (50 Nm).

11. Connect the hoses and wiring.

12. On 4WD vehicles, install the drive shaft and torque the bolts to 24 ft. lbs. (33 Nm). Use new self-locking nuts when attaching the exhaust pipe to the catalytic converter and torque to 25 ft. lbs. (34 Nm).

13. Install the tire and wheel assemblies.

14. Lower the vehicle. Connect the negative battery cable.

15. Refill the fuel tank.

Fuel Filter

REMOVAL AND INSTALLATION

Carburetor Equipped Vehicles

FRONT FILTER

1. Disconnect the negative battery cable.
2. Use suitable fuel line clamps to pinch off the fuel lines and prevent fuel from leaking.
3. Slide the fuel line retaining clamps back. Remove the fuel lines from the filter by using a twisting motion as the line is pulled off.
4. Remove the fuel filter.

To install:
5. Install the replacement filter, connect the fuel lines and position the fuel line retaining clamps.
6. Remove the fuel line clamps and connect the negative battery cable.
7. Start the engine and check for fuel leaks.

REAR FILTER

1. Disconnect the negative battery cable.
2. Raise and safely support the vehicle.
3. Remove the fuel filter and holder.
4. Push in the tab of the fuel filter to release the holder, then remove the filter from the holder.
5. Attach suitable fuel line clamps to pinch off the fuel lines and prevent fuel from leaking.
6. Slide the fuel line retaining clamps back. Remove the fuel lines from the filter by using a twisting motion as the line is pulled off.
7. Remove the fuel filter.

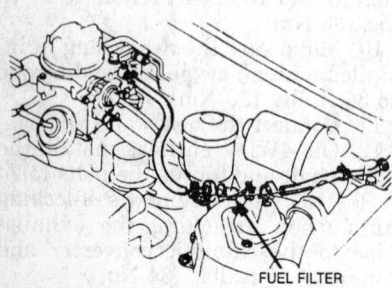

Front fuel filter location — Accord equipped with carburetor

To install:
8. Install the replacement filter, connect the fuel lines and position the fuel line retaining clamps.
9. Remove the fuel line clamps and install the holder on the fuel filter.
10. Install the fuel filter and holder.
11. Lower the vehicle, connect the negative battery cable, start the engine and check for fuel leaks.

Fuel Injected Vehicles

1. Disconnect the negative battery cable.
2. Relieve the fuel system pressure.
3. Remove the banjo bolt(s) and the fuel lines from the fuel filter.
4. Remove the fuel filter clamp and the fuel filter.
5. Installation is the reverse of the removal procedure. Always use new washers during installation. Tighten the banjo bolts to 16 ft. lbs. (22 Nm) and the service bolt to 9 ft. lbs. (12 Nm).

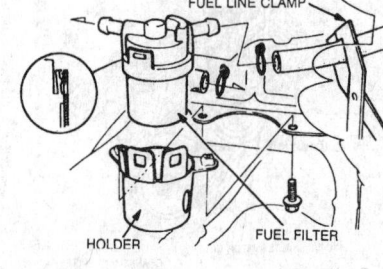

Rear fuel filter location — vehicles with carburetor

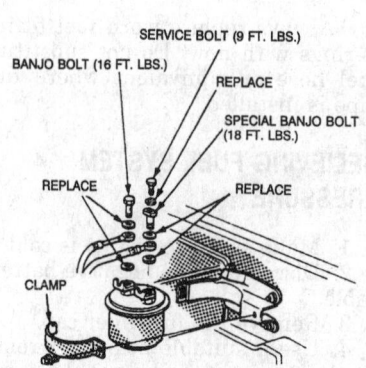

Fuel filter installation — fuel injected vehicles

Electric Fuel Pump

PRESSURE TESTING

Carbureted Vehicles

1. Remove the fuel cut-off relay from the underdash fuse panel.
2. Using a jumper wire, connect the No. 1 terminal to the No. 2 terminal located at the fuse box side of the fuel cut-off relay.
3. Disconnect the fuel line at the fuel filter in the engine compartment and connect a suitable fuel pressure gauge.
4. Turn the ignition **ON** until the pressure stabilizes, then turn the key **OFF**. The fuel pressure should be 1.3-2.1 psi.
5. If the fuel pressure is less than specified, replace the fuel pump and retest.
6. If the fuel pressure is correct, remove the pressure gauge and hold a graduated container under the hose.
7. Turn the ignition **ON** for 1 minute, then turn the ignition **OFF** and measure the amount of fuel flow.
8. The fuel flow should be 20 oz. (600cc) or more.
9. If the fuel flow is as specified, reconnect the fuel cut-off relay and the fuel line. If the fuel flow is less than specified, replace the fuel pump and retest.

NOTE: Check for a clogged fuel filter and/or fuel line before replacing the pump.

Fuel Injected Vehicles

1. Disconnect the negative battery cable.
2. Relieve the fuel system pressure.
3. Attach a suitable fuel pressure gauge to service port of the fuel filter (fuel pipe on Accord and 1992-94 Prelude).
4. Connect the negative battery cable and disconnect the vacuum hose at the pressure regulator.
5. Start the engine and allow it to idle. The fuel pressure should be as follows:

Civic, CRX and del Sol: 40-50 psi
Accord: 40-47 psi
Prelude: 37-44 psi

6. If the fuel pressure is not as specified, check for battery voltage at the fuel pump. If battery voltage is available, replace the fuel pump. If there is no voltage, check the main relay and wire harness.

7. If the fuel pump is okay, check the following:

a. If the fuel pressure is higher than specified, inspect for a pinched or clogged fuel return hose or pipe or a faulty pressure regulator.

b. If the fuel pressure is lower than specified, inspect for a clogged fuel filter, pressure regulator failure or leakage in the fuel line.

REMOVAL AND INSTALLATION

Prelude

The fuel pump is located in the fuel tank.

1. Disconnect the negative battery cable.

2. Relieve the fuel system pressure on fuel injected vehicles.

3. Remove the maintenance access cover in the trunk.

4. Disconnect the fuel lines.

5. Remove the fuel pump mounting bolts and remove the fuel pump from the fuel tank. If the pump is hard to remove, slightly lower the fuel tank by loosening the fuel tank mounting nuts.

6. Installation is the reverse of the removal procedure. Use a new O-ring when installing the pump. Before installing the maintenance access cover, turn the ignition switch **ON** and check for fuel leaks.

NOTE: When installing the maintenance access cover, make sure the seal is attached to the cover.

Civic, CRX, Civic Del Sol and Accord

The fuel pump is located in the fuel tank.

1. Disconnect the negative battery cable.

2. Relieve the fuel system pressure.

3. Raise and safely support the vehicle.

4. Remove the fuel tank drain bolt and drain the fuel into a suitable container.

5. On Civic, del Sol and Accord, disconnect the fuel pump electrical connector in the trunk. On CRX, remove the storage compartment and disconnect the fuel pump electrical connector. On Civic Wagon, remove the rear seat and disconnect the fuel pump electrical connector.

6. On Civic Wagon with 4WD, remove the driveshaft from the rear differential and the exhaust pipe and muffler.

7. Remove the 2-way valve cover and fuel hose protector.

8. Disconnect the fuel lines.

9. Place a suitable support under the fuel tank.

10. Remove the fuel tank strap nuts and let the straps hang.

11. Remove the fuel tank.

12. Remove the fuel pump mounting nuts and the fuel pump.

To install:

13. Install the pump assembly into the tank and make sure the unit is properly sealed.

14. Install the tank into the vehicle and tighten the strap nuts. Connect the hoses and wiring.

15. On 4WD vehicles, connect the driveshaft and the exhaust system.

16. Lower the vehicle and connect the negative battery cable.

17. Fill the tank with approximately 3 gallons of fuel and test the system.

Carburetor

REMOVAL AND INSTALLATION

1990 Prelude

1. Disconnect the negative battery cable.

2. Disconnect the fresh air intake duct and hot air intake hose from the air cleaner cover.

3. Disconnect the vacuum hose from the hot air intake control diaphragm and remove the air cleaner cover and element.

4. Disconnect the breather hose from the valve cover. Disconnect the vacuum lines from the air cleaner base and mark their positions for proper reassembly.

5. Disconnect the electrical connectors from the air cleaner base and remove the bolts from the air cleaner base.

6. Remove the retaining nuts, air screens, flanges and the air cleaner base.

7. Disconnect all vacuum hoses and electrical connectors and mark their position for proper reassembly.

8. Disconnect the throttle cable and the fuel line.

9. Loosen the insulator bands and remove the carburetor.

To install:

10. Place the carburetor into position and tighten the insulator bands.

11. Connect the fuel line, throttle cable, vacuum hoses and electrical connectors.

12. Install the retaining nuts, air screens, flanges and the air cleaner base.

13. Install the air cleaner assembly.

14. Connect the negative battery cable. Start the engine and check for leaks.

IDLE SPEED ADJUSTMENT

NOTE: The carburetors must be properly synchronized before making idle speed adjustments.

1. Start the engine and allow it to reach normal operating temperature. The cooling fan must come ON at least once.

2. Disconnect the vacuum hose from the intake air control diaphragm and clamp the hose end.

3. Connect a tachometer according to the manufacturers instructions.

4. Make sure the fast idle lever is not seated against the fast idle cam. If it is, replace the left carburetor.

5. Check the idle speed with the headlights, heater blower, rear window defroster, cooling fan and air conditioner OFF. Check the underhood emission label for idle speed specification.

6. Adjust the idle speed, if necessary, by turning the throttle stop screw.

7. If the engine speed is excessively high, check the throttle control as follows:

a. Disconnect the vacuum hose from the throttle controller and check the engine speed. The engine speed should be 1700-2700 rpm on manual transaxle equipped vehicles or 1400-2400 rpm on automatic transaxle equipped vehicles.

b. If the engine speed is excessively high, adjust the engine speed by bending the tab.

c. If the engine speed does not change, connect a suitable vacuum pump to the throttle control vacuum hose and check the vacuum. There should be vacuum.

d. If there is no vacuum, check the vacuum hose for proper connection, cracks or a bad check valve and replace as necessary. If there is vacuum, replace the throttle controller and retest.

e. Reconnect the vacuum hose to the throttle controller and check the idle speed.

Fuel Injector

REMOVAL AND INSTALLATION

Except 1.5L Engine with Dual Point Fuel Injection

1. Disconnect the negative battery cable.

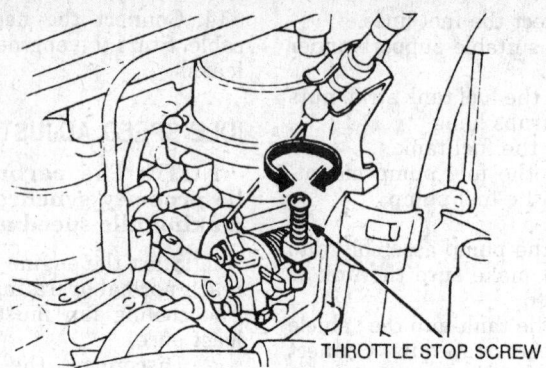

Throttle stop screw location — Prelude

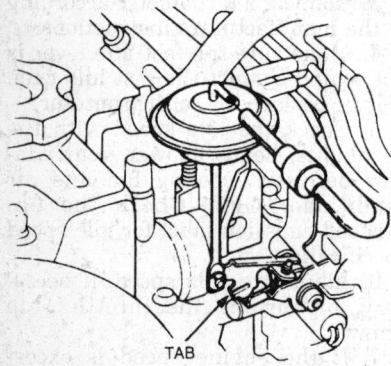

Throttle controller adjusting tab — Prelude

2. Relieve the fuel pressure.

3. Disconnect the electrical connectors from the fuel injectors.

4. Disconnect the vacuum hose and fuel return hose from the fuel pressure regulator.

NOTE: Place a rag or shop towel over the hose and tube before disconnecting them.

5. Disconnect the fuel line from the fuel pipe.

6. On 1990-91 Prelude, disconnect the EACV from the intake manifold.

7. Remove the fuel pipe retainer nuts and the fuel pipe.

8. Remove the injectors from the intake manifold.

To install:

9. Slide new cushion rings onto the injectors.

10. Coat new O-rings with clean engine oil and install them on the injectors.

11. Insert the injectors into the fuel pipe first.

12. Coat new seal rings with clean engine oil and press them into the intake manifold.

13. Install the injectors and fuel pipe assembly in the intake manifold.

NOTE: To prevent damage to the O-rings, install the injectors in the fuel pipe first, then install them in the intake manifold.

14. Align the centerline marking on the fuel injector with the mark on the fuel pipe.

15. Install and tighten the fuel pipe retainer nuts.

16. Connect the fuel line to the fuel pipe and the vacuum hose and fuel return line to the pressure regulator.

17. Connect the electrical connectors to the injectors.

18. Connect the negative battery cable and turn the ignition switch **ON** for 2 seconds, but do not operate the starter. Repeat 2-3 times and check for fuel leaks.

1.5L Engine with Dual Point Fuel Injection

1. Disconnect the negative battery cable.

2. Relieve the fuel pressure.

3. Remove the air intake chamber.

4. Disconnect the electrical connector from the fuel injector.

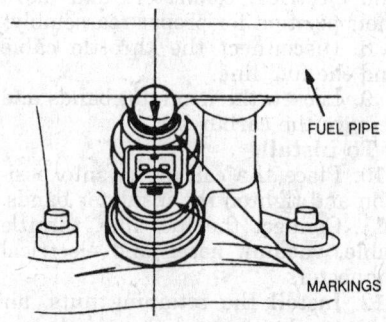

Aligning the fuel injector and fuel pipe marks

5. Loosen the screws and remove the injector from the throttle body. Place a rag or shop towel over the throttle body after removal.

To install:

6. Install the injector into the throttle body, using new O-rings. Lubricate the O-rings with engine oil prior to installation. After the injector is inserted, make sure it turns smoothly approximately 30 degrees. Secure the electrical connector.

7. Before installing the air intake chamber, connect the negative battery cable and turn the ignition switch **ON** for approximately 2 seconds. Repeat 2-3 times and check for fuel leaks. Correct leak, if necessary.

8. Install the air intake chamber.

DRIVE AXLE

Halfshaft

REMOVAL AND INSTALLATION

Front

NOTE: Do not tighten or loosen a spindle nut unless the vehicle is sitting on all 4 wheels. The torque is high enough to cause the vehicle to fall even when properly supported.

1. Loosen the front spindle nut.

2. Raise and safely support the vehicle.

3. Remove the front wheel and tire assemblies and the spindle nut.

4. Drain the transaxle fluid and replace the drain plug.

5. Remove the damper fork nut and damper pinch bolt.

6. Remove the damper fork.

7. Remove the knuckle-to-lower arm cotter pin and castle nut.

8. Using a suitable puller, separate the lower arm from the knuckle.

9. Pull the knuckle outward and remove the halfshaft outboard joint, from the knuckle, using a plastic hammer.

10. Using a suitable tool, pry on the inner CV-joint in order to force the set ring at the end of the halfshaft assembly out of the groove.

11. Pull on the inboard CV-joint and remove the halfshaft and joint

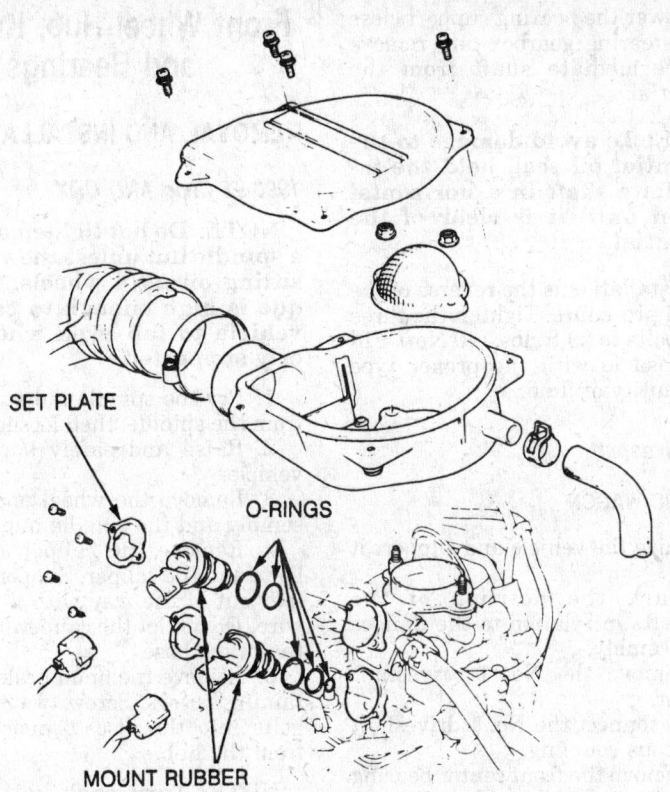

SET PLATE

O-RINGS

MOUNT RUBBER

Fuel injector installation — 1.5L engine with dual-point fuel injection

from the differential case or intermediate shaft.

NOTE: Do not pull on the halfshaft as the CV-joint may come apart. Use care when prying out the assembly and pull it straight to avoid damaging the differential oil seal or intermediate shaft dust seal.

To install:

12. Installation is the reverse of the removal procedure. Always install new set rings on the ends of the halfshafts.

13. Make sure the set ring locks in the differential side gear groove and the halfshaft bottoms in the differential or intermediate shaft.

14. Install the spindle nut but do not torque it yet.

15. Assemble the suspension in the reverse order. Torque the upper damper pinch bolt to 32 ft. lbs. (44 Nm) and the fork nut to 47 ft. lbs. (65 Nm). Install the halfshaft.

16. Torque the ball joint nut to 40 ft. lbs. (55 Nm), then tighten as required to install a new cotter pin.

17. With the vehicle resting on all 4 wheels, torque the spindle nut to the

proper specification and stake the nut in place.

1990-91 Civic and CRX — 134 ft. lbs. (185 Nm)

1992-94 Civic and del Sol — 181 ft. lbs. (250 Nm)

Accord and Prelude — 180 ft. lbs. (245 Nm)

18. Fill the transaxle with the proper type and quantity of fluid.

Rear

4WD CIVIC WAGON

NOTE: Do not tighten or loosen a spindle nut unless the vehicle is sitting on all 4 wheels. The tor-

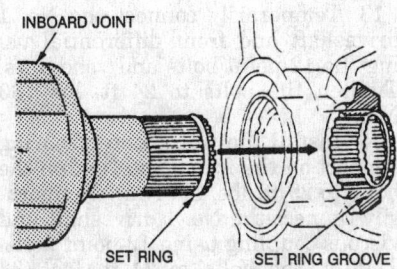

INBOARD JOINT

SET RING   SET RING GROOVE

Installing the inboard CV-joint into the differential assembly

que is high enough to cause the vehicle to fall even when properly supported.

1. Pry the spindle nut stake away from the spindle. Loosen the nut. Loosen the wheel nuts.

2. Raise and support the vehicle safely. Remove the tire and wheel assemblies.

3. Disconnect the brake hose from the brake pipe.

4. Using a floor jack, raise the rear suspension until the weight of the lower arm is relieved.

5. Remove the trailing arm bushing bolts. Disconnect the upper arm and the lower arm from the trailing arm.

6. Pull the trailing arm outward. Remove the rear halfshaft outboard joint from the trailing arm, using the proper tool.

7. Using a suitable tool, pry the halfshaft assembly to force the set ring at the halfshaft end past the groove.

8. Pull the inboard joint and remove the halfshaft and the CV-joint from the differential case as an assembly.

To install:

9. Always install a new set ring on the end of the halfshaft. Make sure the set ring locks in the differential side gear groove and the CV-joint sub-axle bottoms in the differential.

10. Reassemble the suspension and torque the upper and lower arm bushing bolts to 40 ft. lbs. (55 Nm) and the trailing arm bushing bolts to 47 ft. lbs. (65 Nm).

11. When the vehicle is resting on all 4 wheels, torque the spindle nut to 134 ft. lbs. (185 Nm).

CV-Boot

REMOVAL AND INSTALLATION

1. Raise and safely support the vehicle.

2. Remove the halfshaft.

3. If replacing the inboard CV-joint boot, perform the following procedure:

   a. Place the halfshaft in a suitable holding fixture where it will remain in position during disassembly.

   b. Remove the boot bands. If the boot bands are the welded type, they must be cut to be removed. After removing the bands, push the CV-joint boot away from the end of the halfshaft to gain access to the CV-joint.

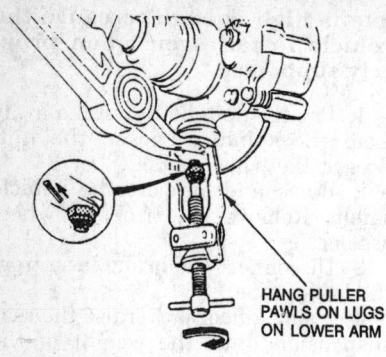

HANG PULLER
PAWLS ON LUGS
ON LOWER ARM

Separating the steering knuckle from the lower arm assembly

c. Remove the inboard CV-joint. Mark the components during disassembly to ensure proper positioning during reassembly.

d. Remove the CV-joint boot.

e. Installation is the reverse of the removal procedure. Check the CV-joint components for wear prior to installation and replace as necessary.

f. Thoroughly pack the inboard CV-joint and boot with molybdenum disulfide grease. Always install new boot bands.

4. If replacing the outboard CV-joint boot, perform the following procedure:

a. Place the halfshaft in a suitable holding fixture where it will remain in position during disassembly.

b. Remove the inboard CV-joint and boot. Do not try to remove or disassemble the outboard CV-joint.

c. Remove the boot bands and the outboard CV-joint boot.

d. Installation is the reverse of the removal procedure. Thoroughly pack the outboard CV-joint boot with molybdenum disulfide grease. Always install new boot bands.

5. Install the halfshaft in the reverse order of the removal procedure.

Driveshaft and U-Joints

REMOVAL AND INSTALLATION

Intermediate shaft

4WD CIVIC WAGON, PRELUDE AND ACCORD

1. Raise the vehicle and support it safely.

2. Drain the transaxle fluid and replace the drain plug.

3. Remove the driver's side halfshaft.

4. Remove the flange and hex bolts.

5. Lower the bearing support close to the steering gearbox and remove the intermediate shaft from the differential.

NOTE: To avoid damage to the differential oil seal, hold the intermediate shaft in a horizontal position until it is clear of the differential.

6. Installation is the reverse of the removal procedure. Tighten the three 10mm bolts to 29 ft. lbs. (40 Nm). Fill the transaxle with the proper type and quantity of fluid.

Rear Driveshaft

4WD CIVIC WAGON

1. Raise the vehicle and support it safely.

2. Mark the position of the driveshafts in relation to the flanges for reassembly.

3. Remove the No. 1 driveshaft protector.

4. Disconnect the No. 1 driveshaft and viscous coupling.

5. Remove the front center bearing support from the body.

6. Remove the No. 1 driveshaft by disconnecting the U-joint.

7. Remove the No. 3 driveshaft protector.

8. Disconnect the No. 3 driveshaft and rear differential.

9. Remove the rear center bearing support from the body, then remove the viscous coupling and No. 3 driveshaft.

To install:

10. Install the rear center bearing support on the frame and tighten the bolts to 29 ft. lbs. (40 Nm).

11. Temporarily connect the No. 3 driveshaft and rear differential using the 12-point bolts and yoke nuts. Tighten the bolts to 24 ft. lbs. (33 Nm).

12. Install the No. 3 driveshaft protector and tighten the bolts to 29 ft. lbs. (40 Nm).

13. Temporarily connect the No. 1 driveshaft and front differential using the 12-point bolts and yoke nuts. Tighten the bolts to 24 ft. lbs. (33 Nm).

14. Install the front center bearing support on the frame and tighten the bolts to 29 ft. lbs. (40 Nm). Temporarily connect the No. 1 driveshaft and viscous coupling using 12-point bolts. Tighten the bolts to 24 ft. lbs. (33 Nm).

15. Install the No. 1 driveshaft protector and tighten the bolts to 29 ft. lbs. (40 Nm).

Front Wheel Hub, Knuckle and Bearings

REMOVAL AND INSTALLATION

1990-91 Civic AND CRX

NOTE: Do not tighten or loosen a spindle nut unless the vehicle is sitting on all 4 wheels. The torque is high enough to cause the vehicle to fall even when properly supported.

1. Pry the spindle nut stake away from the spindle, then loosen the nut.

2. Raise and safely support the vehicle.

3. Remove the wheel and tire assembly and the spindle nut.

4. Remove the caliper mounting bolts and the caliper. Support the caliper out of the way with a length of wire. Do not let the caliper hang from the brake hose.

5. Remove the 6mm brake disc retaining screws. Screw two 8 x 12mm bolts into the disc to push it away from the hub.

NOTE: Turn each bolt 2 turns at a time to prevent cocking the brake disc.

6. Remove the cotter pin from the tie rod castle nut, then remove the nut. Break the tie rod ball joint using a suitable ball joint remover, then lift the tie rod out of the knuckle.

7. Remove the cotter pin and loosen the lower arm ball joint nut half the length of the joint threads.

8. Separate the ball joint and lower arm using a suitable puller with the pawls applied to the lower arm.

NOTE: Avoid damaging the ball joint boot. If necessary, apply penetrating type lubricant to loosen the ball joint.

9. Remove the knuckle protector.

10. Remove the cotter pin and remove the upper ball pin nut.

11. Separate the upper ball joint and knuckle using a suitable tool.

12. Remove the knuckle and hub by sliding them off the halfshaft.

13. Remove the splash guard screws from the knuckle.

14. Position the knuckle/hub assembly on a hydraulic press. Press the hub from the knuckle using a suitable driver while supporting the knuckle with a suitable base.

NOTE: The bearing must be replaced with a new one after removal.

15. Remove the 76mm snapring and knuckle ring from the knuckle.

16. Press the wheel bearing out of the knuckle using a suitable driver while supporting the knuckle with a suitable base.

17. Remove the outboard bearing inner race from the hub using a suitable bearing puller.

To install:

18. Clean the knuckle and hub thoroughly before reassembly.

19. Press a new wheel bearing into the hub using a suitable driver while supporting the knuckle with a suitable base.

20. Install the 76mm snapring securely in the knuckle groove.

21. Install the splash guard and tighten the screws to 7 ft. lbs. (10 Nm).

22. Place the knuckle into position on the hydraulic press and press onto the hub using a suitable driver. The maximum press load should be 2 tons.

23. Install the front knuckle ring on the knuckle.

24. Install the knuckle/hub assembly onto the vehicle in the reverse order of the removal procedure. Tighten the upper ball pin nut and tie rod nut to 32 ft. lbs. (44 Nm) and the lower ball joint castle nut to 40 ft. lbs. (55 Nm).

25. With all 4 wheels resting on the ground, torque the spindle nut to 134 ft. lbs. (185 Nm).

1992-94 Civic and Del Sol

1. Raise and safely support the vehicle.

2. Remove the wheel and tire assembly.

3. Raise the locking tab on the spindle nut and remove the nut.

4. Remove the brake hose mounting bracket and remove the caliper mounting bolts and the caliper. Support the caliper out of the way with a length of wire. Do not let the caliper hang from the brake hose.

5. Remove the 6mm brake disc retaining screws. Screw two 8 **x** 12mm bolts into the disc to push it away from the hub.

NOTE: Turn each bolt 2 turns at a time to prevent cocking the brake disc.

6. Remove the speed sensor wire bracket and remove the speed sensor from the knuckle. Do not disconnect the speed sensor.

7. Remove the cotter pin from the steering arm castle nut, then remove the nut. Break the tie rod ball joint using a suitable ball joint remover,

then lift the tie rod out of the knuckle.

8. Remove the cotter pin and loosen the lower arm ball joint nut half the length of the joint threads.

9. Separate the ball joint and lower arm using a suitable puller with the pawls applied to the lower arm.

NOTE: Avoid damaging the ball joint boot. If necessary, apply penetrating type lubricant to loosen the ball joint.

10. Remove the knuckle protector.

11. Remove the cotter pin and remove the upper ball pin nut.

12. Separate the upper ball joint and knuckle using a suitable tool.

13. Remove the knuckle and hub by sliding them off the halfshaft.

14. Remove the splash guard screws from the knuckle.

15. Position the knuckle/hub assembly on a hydraulic press. Press the hub from the knuckle using a suitable driver while supporting the knuckle with a suitable base.

NOTE: The bearing must be replaced with a new one after removal.

16. Remove the 76mm snapring and knuckle ring from the knuckle.

17. Press the wheel bearing out of the knuckle using a suitable driver while supporting the knuckle with a suitable base.

18. Remove the outboard bearing inner race from the hub using a suitable bearing puller.

To install:

19. Clean the knuckle and hub thoroughly before reassembly.

20. Press a new wheel bearing into the hub using a suitable driver while supporting the knuckle with a suitable base.

21. Install the 76mm snapring securely in the knuckle groove.

22. Install the splash guard and tighten the screws to 7 ft. lbs. (10 Nm).

23. Place the knuckle into position on the hydraulic press and press onto the hub using a suitable driver. The maximum press load should be 2 tons.

24. Install the front knuckle ring on the knuckle.

25. Install the knuckle/hub assembly onto the vehicle in the reverse order of the removal procedure. Tighten the upper ball pin nut and tie rod nut to 32 ft. lbs. (44 Nm) and the lower ball joint castle nut to 40 ft. lbs. (55 Nm).

26. Install the spindle nut and torque to 134 ft. lbs. (185 Nm).

27. Install the wheel and lower the vehicle.

1990-91 Prelude

NOTE: Do not tighten or loosen a spindle nut unless the vehicle is sitting on all 4 wheels. The torque is high enough to cause the vehicle to fall even when properly supported.

1. Pry the spindle nut stake away from the spindle and loosen the nut.

2. Raise and safely support the vehicle.

3. Remove the wheel and tire assembly and the spindle nut.

4. Remove the caliper mounting bolts and the caliper. Support the caliper out of the way with a length of wire. Do not let the caliper hang from the brake hose.

5. Remove the 6mm brake disc retaining screws. Screw two 8 **x** 1.25 **x** 12mm bolts into the disc to push it away from the hub.

NOTE: Turn each bolt 2 turns at a time to prevent cocking the brake disc.

6. Remove the cotter pin from the tie rod castle nut, then remove the nut. Break the tie rod ball joint using a suitable ball joint remover, then lift the tie rod out of the knuckle.

7. Remove the cotter pin and loosen the lower arm ball joint nut half the length of the joint threads.

8. Separate the ball joint and lower arm using a suitable puller with the pawls applied to the lower arm.

NOTE: Avoid damaging the ball joint boot. If necessary, apply penetrating type lubricant to loosen the ball joint.

9. Remove the upper ball joint shield, if equipped.

10. Pry off the cotter pin and remove the upper ball joint nut.

11. Separate the upper ball joint and knuckle using a suitable tool.

12. Remove the knuckle and hub by sliding them off the halfshaft.

13. Remove the splash guard screws from the knuckle.

14. Position the knuckle/hub assembly in a hydraulic press. Press the hub from the knuckle using a suitable driver while supporting the knuckle.

NOTE: The bearing must be replaced with a new one after removal.

15. Remove the splash guard and snapring from the knuckle.

16. Press the wheel bearing out of the knuckle using a suitable driver while supporting the knuckle.

17. Remove the outboard bearing inner race from the hub using a suitable bearing puller.

To install:

18. Clean the knuckle and hub thoroughly.

19. Press a new wheel bearing into the knuckle using a suitable driver while supporting the knuckle.

20. Install the snapring.

21. Install the splash shield and tighten the screws to 4 ft. lbs. (5 Nm).

22. Press the knuckle onto the hub using a suitable fixture.

23. Install the front knuckle ring on the knuckle.

24. Install the knuckle/hub assembly on the vehicle in the reverse of the removal procedure. Tighten the upper ball joint nut and tie rod end nut to 32 ft. lbs. (44 Nm). Install new cotter pins. Tighten the lower ball joint nut to 40 ft. lbs. (55 Nm) and install a new cotter pin.

25. With all 4 wheels resting on the ground, torque the spindle nut to 180 ft. lbs. (250 Nm).

Accord

NOTE: Do not tighten or loosen a spindle nut unless the vehicle is sitting on all 4 wheels. The torque is high enough to cause the vehicle to fall even when properly supported.

1. Pry the spindle nut stake away from the spindle, then loosen the nut.

2. Raise and safely support the vehicle.

3. Remove the wheel and tire assembly and the spindle nut.

4. Remove the caliper mounting bolts and the caliper. Support the caliper out of the way with a length of wire. Do not let the caliper hang from the brake hose.

5. Remove the cotter pin from the tie rod castle nut, then remove the nut. Break loose the tie rod ball joint using a suitable ball joint remover, then lift the tie rod out of the knuckle.

6. Remove the cotter pin and loosen the lower arm ball joint nut half the length of the joint threads.

7. Separate the ball joint and lower arm using a suitable puller with the pawls applied to the lower arm.

NOTE: Avoid damaging the ball joint boot. If necessary, apply penetrating type lubricant to loosen the ball joint.

8. Pull the knuckle outward and remove the halfshaft outboard joint from the knuckle using a suitable tool.

9. Remove the cotter pin and the upper ball joint nut. Break loose the upper ball joint using a suitable tool.

NOTE: Avoid damaging the ball joint boot. If necessary, apply penetrating type lubricant to loosen the ball joint.

10. Remove the 4 bolts and remove the knuckle from the hub unit.

11. Remove the splash guard screws and the splash guard from the knuckle.

12. Remove the 4 bolts, then separate the hub unit from the brake disc.

13. Position the hub in a suitable hydraulic press. Press the wheel bearing from the hub while adequately supporting the hub.

14. Remove the outboard bearing inner race from the hub using a suitable bearing puller.

NOTE: The wheel bearing must be replaced with a new one after removal.

To install:

15. Clean the knuckle and hub thoroughly.

16. Position the hub in a suitable hydraulic press. Press a new wheel bearing into the hub using a suitable driver.

17. Install the hub on the brake disc and tighten the bolts to 40 ft. lbs. (55 Nm).

18. Install the splash guard and tighten the screws to 7 ft. lbs. (10 Nm).

19. Install the knuckle on the hub and tighten the bolts to 33 ft. lbs. (45 Nm).

20. Installation of the knuckle/hub assembly on the vehicle is the reverse of the removal procedure. Tighten the upper ball joint nut and the tie rod nut to 32 ft. lbs. (44 Nm) and install new cotter pins. Tighten the lower ball joint nut to 40 ft. lbs. (55 Nm) and install a new cotter pin.

21. With all 4 wheels resting on the ground, install a new spindle nut and torque to 180 ft. lbs. (245 Nm). After tightening, use a suitable drift to stake the spindle nut shoulder against the spindle.

1992-94 Prelude

NOTE: Do not tighten or loosen a spindle nut unless the vehicle is sitting on all 4 wheels. The torque is high enough to cause the vehicle to fall even when properly supported.

1. Pry the spindle nut stake away from the spindle and loosen the nut.

2. Raise and safely support the vehicle.

3. Remove the wheel and tire assembly and the spindle nut.

4. Remove the mounting bolts for the brake hose bracket. Remove the caliper mounting bolts and the caliper. Support the caliper out of the way with a length of wire. Do not let the caliper hang from the brake hose.

5. Remove the 6mm brake disc retaining screws. Screw two 8 x 12mm bolts into the disc to push it away from the hub and remove the disc from the hub.

NOTE: Turn each bolt 2 turns at a time to prevent cocking the brake disc.

6. Remove the speed sensor wire bracket and remove the speed sensor from the knuckle. Do not disconnect the speed sensor wire.

7. Remove the cotter pin from the tie rod castle nut, then remove the nut. Break the tie rod ball joint using a suitable ball joint remover, then lift the tie rod out of the knuckle.

8. Remove the cotter pin and loosen the lower arm ball joint nut half the length of the joint threads.

9. Separate the ball joint and lower arm using a suitable puller with the pawls applied to the lower arm.

NOTE: Avoid damaging the ball joint boot. If necessary, apply penetrating type lubricant to loosen the ball joint.

10. Remove the upper ball joint shield, if equipped.

11. Pry off the cotter pin and remove the upper ball joint nut.

12. Separate the upper ball joint and knuckle using a suitable tool.

13. Remove the knuckle and hub by sliding them off the halfshaft.

14. Remove the splash guard screws from the knuckle.

15. Position the knuckle/hub assembly in a hydraulic press. Press the hub from the knuckle using a suitable driver while supporting the knuckle.

NOTE: The bearing must be replaced with a new one after removal.

16. Remove the splash guard and snapring from the knuckle.

17. Press the wheel bearing out of the knuckle using a suitable driver while supporting the knuckle.

18. Remove the outboard bearing inner race from the hub using a suitable bearing puller.

To install:

19. Clean the knuckle and hub thoroughly.

20. Press a new wheel bearing into the knuckle using a suitable driver while supporting the knuckle.

21. Install the snapring.

22. Install the splash shield and tighten the screws to 4 ft. lbs. (5 Nm).

23. Press the knuckle onto the hub using a suitable fixture.

24. Install the front knuckle ring on the knuckle.

25. Install the knuckle/hub assembly on the vehicle in the reverse of the removal procedure. Tighten the upper ball joint nut and tie rod end nut to 32 ft. lbs. (44 Nm). Install new cotter pins. Tighten the lower ball joint nut to 40 ft. lbs. (55 Nm) and install a new cotter pin.

26. With all 4 wheels resting on the ground, torque the spindle nut to 180 ft. lbs. (250 Nm).

Pinion Seal

REMOVAL AND INSTALLATION

4WD Civic Wagon

1. Raise and safely support the vehicle.

2. Remove the rear wheel and tire assemblies.

3. Keep the rear halfshafts in their normal horizontal position by raising the lower arms to their normal road level position.

4. Mark the position of the driveshaft in relation to the pinion flange, then disconnect the driveshaft from the pinion flange.

5. Using a suitable inch lb. torque wrench, turn the pinion flange by the pinion nut and record the reading. This is the total bearing preload.

6. Hold the pinion flange using a suitable holding tool and remove the pinion nut.

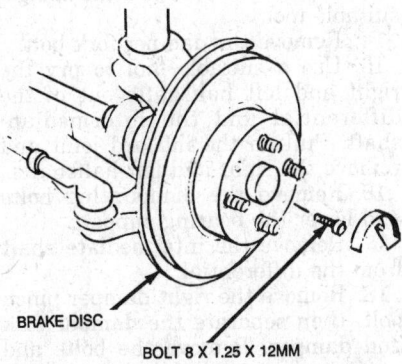

BRAKE DISC

BOLT 8 X 1.25 X 12MM

Disc brake rotor removal — except Accord

7. Remove the pinion flange and use a suitable removal tool to remove the pinion seal.

To install:

8. Lubricate the lip of a new pinion seal.

9. Use a suitable installation tool to install the pinion seal.

10. Install the pinion flange and pinion nut. Tighten the pinion nut until the reading on an inch lb. torque wrench is the same as that recorded prior to removal.

11. Connect the driveshaft to the pinion flange, aligning the marks that were made during the removal procedure. Tighten the bolts to 24 ft. lbs. (33 Nm).

12. Install the wheel and tire assemblies.

13. Lower the vehicle.

Differential Carrier

REMOVAL AND INSTALLATION

4WD Civic Wagon

1. Raise and safely support the vehicle.

2. Drain the oil from the differential and replace the drain bolt.

3. Remove the driveshaft and the right and left rear halfshafts.

4. Remove the differential mounting bolts from the lower differential mounting bracket.

5. Remove the 2 bolts from the upper differential bracket and remove the differential and bracket as an assembly.

6. Remove the upper differential bracket from the differential and remove the differential carrier from the differential housing.

To install:

7. Clean the mating surfaces of the differential carrier and differential housing.

8. Apply sealant to the mating surfaces and install the carrier to the housing, aligning the dowel pin. Apply sealant to the bolt threads and tighten them to 16 ft. lbs. (22 Nm).

9. Install the differential bracket on the differential and tighten the bolts to 40 ft. lbs. (55 Nm).

10. Install the differential and upper bracket and tighten the upper bracket bolts to 43 ft. lbs. (59 Nm).

11. Install and tighten the lower differential bracket bolts to 40 ft. lbs. (55 Nm).

12. Installation of the remainder of the components is the reverse of the removal procedure.

MANUAL TRANSAXLE

Transaxle Assembly

REMOVAL AND INSTALLATION

1990-91 Civic and CRX

1. Disconnect the battery cables from the battery.

2. Remove the 3 mount bolts and loosen the 1 bolt located at the side of the battery base. Remove the intake hose band at the throttle body.

3. Remove the air cleaner case complete with the intake hose. Disconnect the starter and transaxle ground cables.

4. Disconnect the speedometer, but be sure not to disassemble the speedometer gear holder.

5. Disconnect the backup light switch connector and the clutch cable release arm.

6. Drain the transaxle fluid into a suitable drain pan. Disconnect the connectors and remove the mount bolts.

7. Remove the distributor assembly, as required.

8. Remove the starter mounting bolts and remove the starter assembly. Remove the engine splash shield and the right wheelwell splash shield.

9. Remove the header pipe. Remove the cotter pin and the lower arm ball joint nut. Separate the ball joint and lower arm.

10. Remove the bolts and nut, then remove the right radius rod. Remove the right and left halfshafts. Remove the header pipe bracket. Remove the shift lever torque rod and shift rod from the clutch housing.

11. On 4WD vehicles, remove the driveshaft and the intermediate shaft. Remove the cable bracket and the side transaxle mount from the transaxle housing and body.

12. Install a bolt at the cylinder head and attach a suitable chain hoist to the bolt and the other end to the engine hanger plate. Lift the engine slightly to unload the mounts.

13. Place a suitable transaxle jack under the transaxle and raise it just enough to take the weights off the mounts.

14. Remove the front transaxle mounting bolts. Remove the rear transaxle mounting bolts. Remove the side transaxle mount, remove the

5 remaining transaxle mounting bolts and pull the transaxle assembly far enough away from the engine to clear the 14mm dowel pins.

15. Separate the mainshaft from the clutch pressure plate and remove the transaxle by lowering the jack.

To install:

16. Make sure the two 14mm dowel pins are installed in the clutch housing.

17. Raise the transaxle into position with the transaxle jack. Loosely install the transaxle mount bolts and then tighten to 43 ft. lbs. (60 Nm).

18. Install the engine side mount bolt and tighten to 50 ft. lbs. (68 Nm).

19. Install the transaxle-to-rear transaxle mount bracket. Tighten the bolts to 40 ft. lbs. (55 Nm).

20. Install the transaxle-to-front transaxle mount and tighten the bolts to 29 ft. lbs. (40 Nm).

21. Install the transaxle-to-side transaxle mount and tighten the bolts to 43 ft. lbs. (60 Nm).

22. Install the starter and tighten the starter bolts to 33 ft. lbs. (45 Nm).

23. Remove the transaxle jack and the chain hoist and bolts.

24. Install the shift lever torque rod and shift rod. After reassembly, slide the retainer back into place after driving in the spring pin.

25. Install the header pipe bracket and tighten the bolts to 16 ft. lbs. (22 Nm).

26. On 4WD vehicles, install the cable bracket to the rear transaxle mount bracket. Install the select and shift cables. Install the intermediate shaft and the driveshaft.

27. Install a new set ring on the end of each halfshaft. Install the right and left halfshafts. Turn the right steering knuckle fully outward and slide the axle into the differential, until the spring clip is felt to engage the differential side gear.

28. Install the damper fork and radius rod. Tighten the radius rod nut to 39 ft. lbs. (44 Nm).

29. Install the ball joints to the lower arm. Tighten the stud nuts to 40 ft. lbs. (55 Nm) and install a new cotter pin.

30. Install the splash shields and exhaust header pipe.

31. Install the distributor.

32. Connect the speedometer cable and connect the clutch cable to the release arm.

33. Connect the backup light switch connector.

34. Install the 3 bolts located at the side of the battery base and retighten the intake hose band of the throttle body.

35. Fill the transaxle with the proper type and quantity of oil.

36. Connect the starter and transaxle ground cable.

37. Install the air cleaner case and intake hose.

38. Connect the battery cables, start the engine and check the ignition timing.

1992-94 Civic and Civic Del Sol

1. Disconnect the battery cable from the battery. Drain the transaxle oil.

2. Remove the resonator, the air cleaner case and the air intake hose.

3. Disconnect the starter cables, the transaxle ground cable and remove the engine wire harness clip.

4. Disconnect the speed sensor connectors and the backup light switch.

5. Remove the clutch pipe bracket and slave cylinder.

6. Remove the transaxle housing bolts.

7. Raise and safely support the vehicle. Remove the driveshafts.

8. Disconnect and remove the front exhaust pipe.

9. Disconnect the shift rod and extension rod. Remove the splash guard and front stopper bracket.

10. Attach a lifting device to the engine and lift slightly to ease the tension on the mounts.

11. Place a jack under the transaxle and remove the transaxle side mount.

12. Remove the clutch cover and remove the transaxle rear mount bolts and transaxle housing bolts.

13. Pull the transaxle away from the engine until it clears the mainshaft. Remove the transaxle from the vehicle.

To install:

14. Place the transaxle on a transaxle jack and raise it to engine level.

15. Align the transaxle and engine. Install the transaxle mounting bolts and rear mount bolts.

16. Raise transaxle and install the side mount. Tighten the mount bolts to 47 ft. lbs. (65 Nm).

17. Remove the engine lifting device and install the clutch cover.

18. Install the front stopper bracket and splash guard.

19. Connect the shift rod, spring pin and clip. Connect the torque rod.

20. Install the front exhaust pipe and install the driveshafts.

21. Connect the lower arm ball joint and damper fork.

22. Install the transaxle-to-engine attaching bolts and tighten to 43 ft. lbs. (60 Nm).

23. Install the slave cylinder and clutch pipe stay.

24. Connect the speed sensor and backup light switch connectors.

25. Install the wire harness clamp. Install the resonator, air cleaner case and air intake hose.

26. Refill the transaxle with oil and connect the battery cables.

27. Check the clutch and transaxle operation.

Accord

1. Disconnect the battery cables and remove the battery.

2. Raise and safely support the vehicle.

3. Remove the air intake hose and battery base.

4. Disconnect the starter wires and remove the starter.

5. Disconnect the transaxle ground cable and the backup light switch wire.

6. Remove the cable stay and then disconnect the cables from the top housing of the transaxle. Remove both cables and the stay together.

7. Disconnect the connector and remove the speed sensor, but leave the speed sensor hoses connected.

8. Remove the front wheel and tire assemblies.

9. Remove the engine splash shield and drain the transaxle fluid.

10. Remove the mounting bolts and clutch slave cylinder with the clutch pipe and pushrod.

11. Remove the mounting bolt and clutch hose joint with the clutch pipe and clutch hose.

NOTE: Do not operate the clutch pedal once the slave cylinder has been removed. Be careful not to bend the pipe.

12. Remove the center beam and the header pipe.

13. Remove the cotter pins and lower arm ball joint nuts. Separate the ball joints and lower arms using a suitable tool.

14. Remove the damper fork bolt.

15. Use a suitable tool to pry the right and left halfshafts out of the differential and the intermediate shaft. Pull on the inboard joint and remove the right and left halfshafts.

16. Remove the 3 mounting bolts and lower the bearing support.

17. Remove the intermediate shaft from the differential.

18. Remove the right damper pinch bolt, then separate the damper fork and damper. Remove the bolts and nut, then remove the right radius rod.

19. Remove the engine stiffener and the clutch cover.

20. Remove the intake manifold bracket.

21. Remove the rear engine mount bracket stay and remove the 3 rear engine mount bracket mounting bolts.

22. Remove the transaxle housing mounting bolt on the engine side. Swing the right halfshaft to the inner fender.

23. Place a suitable jack under the transaxle and raise the transaxle just enough to take the weight off the mounts.

24. Remove the transaxle mount bolt and loosen the mount bracket nuts.

25. Remove the 3 transaxle housing mounting bolts.

26. Remove the transaxle from the vehicle.

To install:

27. Make sure the 4 dowel pins are installed.

28. Raise the transaxle into position.

29. Install the 3 transaxle mounting bolts and tighten to 47 ft. lbs. (65 Nm).

30. Install the transaxle mount and mount bracket. Install the through bolt and tighten temporarily. Make sure the engine is level and tighten the 3 mount bracket nuts to 40 ft. lbs. (55 Nm). Tighten the through bolt to 47 ft. lbs. (65 Nm).

31. Install the transaxle housing mounting bolts on the engine side and tighten to 47 ft. lbs. (65 Nm).

32. Install the 3 rear engine bracket mounting bolts and tighten to 40 ft. lbs. (55 Nm).

33. Install the rear engine mount bracket stay. Tighten the mounting bolt to 28 ft. lbs. (39 Nm) and then tighten the mounting nut to 15 ft. lbs. (21 Nm).

34. Install the intake manifold bracket and tighten the bolts to 16 ft. lbs. (22 Nm).

35. Install the clutch cover and tighten the bolts to 9 ft. lbs. (12 Nm).

36. Install the engine stiffener and loosely install the mounting bolts. Tighten the stiffener-to-transaxle case mounting bolt to 28 ft. lbs. (39 Nm), then tighten the 2 stiffener-to-cylinder block mounting bolts to 28 ft. lbs. (39 Nm) beginning with the bolt closest to the transaxle.

37. Install the radius rod. Tighten the radius rod mounting bolts to 76 ft. lbs. (105 Nm) and the radius rod nut to 32 ft. lbs. (44 Nm).

38. Install the damper fork. Tighten the damper pinch bolt to 32 ft. lbs. (44 Nm).

39. Install the intermediate shaft.

40. Install a new set ring on the end of each halfshaft. Install the right and left halfshafts. Turn the right and left steering knuckle fully outward and slide the axle into the differential, until the spring clip is felt engaging the differential side gear.

41. Install the damper fork bolt and ball joint nut to the lower arms. Tighten the nut while holding the damper fork bolt to 40 ft. lbs. (55 Nm). Tighten the ball joint nut to 40 ft. lbs. (55 Nm). Install a new cotter pin.

42. Install the header pipe and center beam. Tighten the center beam bolts to 28 ft. lbs. (39 Nm).

43. Install the clutch hose joint and clutch slave cylinder to the transaxle housing. Tighten the slave cylinder mounting bolts to 16 ft. lbs. (22 Nm).

44. Install the speed sensor. Tighten the mounting bolt to 13 ft. lbs. (18 Nm).

45. Install the shift cable and select cable to the shift arm lever and to the select lever respectively. Tighten the cable bracket mounting bolts to 16 ft. lbs. (22 Nm). Install new cotter pins.

46. Connect the backup light switch coupler.

47. Install the starter. Tighten the 10 x 1.25mm bolt to 32 ft. lbs. (45 Nm) and the 12 x 1.25mm bolt to 54 ft. lbs. (75 Nm). Connect the starter wires.

48. Install the transaxle ground cable.

49. Install the front wheel and tire assemblies.

50. Fill the transaxle with the proper type and quantity of oil.

51. Lower the vehicle.

52. Install the battery and connect the battery cables.

53. Check the clutch pedal freeplay.

54. Start the vehicle and check the transaxle for smooth operation.

1990-91 Prelude

1. Disconnect the negative battery cable at the battery and the transaxle. Raise and safely support the vehicle.

2. Disconnect the wiring for the starter and the backup light switch.

3. On fuel injected vehicles, remove the air cleaner case.

4. Remove the power steering speed sensor from the transaxle, without removing the power steering hoses.

5. Remove the shift cable and the select cable from the top cover of the transaxle. Remove the mounting bolt from the cable stay. Remove the cables and the stay together.

6. Remove the upper transaxle mounting bracket.

7. Remove the 4 transaxle-to-block attachment bolts, that must be removed from the engine compartment.

8. Raise and safely support the vehicle.

9. Remove the front wheel and tire assemblies.

10. Remove the engine splash shield.

11. Drain the transaxle oil.

12. Remove the clutch slave cylinder and the center beam.

13. Remove the right radius rod. Remove the right and left halfshafts.

14. Remove the intermediate shaft.

15. Remove the engine stiffener and the clutch cover.

16. Support the transaxle with a suitable jack.

17. Remove the 3 lower bolts from the rear engine mounting bracket. Loosen but do not remove the top bolt. This bolt will support the weight of the engine.

18. Remove the 2 remaining engine-to-transaxle mounting bolts.

19. Pull the transaxle away from the engine and disengage the input shaft from the clutch disc. Lower the transaxle and remove it from the vehicle.

To install:

20. Make sure the 14mm dowel pin is installed in the transaxle.

21. Raise the transaxle into position.

22. Install the engine side transaxle mount bolts and tighten to 47 ft. lbs. (65 Nm). Install the transaxle side transaxle mount bolts and tighten to 47 ft. lbs. (65 Nm).

23. Attach the transaxle mounting bracket. Tighten the transaxle mount bolts to 28 ft. lbs. (39 Nm) and the mount through bolt to 54 ft. lbs. (75 Nm).

24. Install and tighten the rear engine mounting bracket bolts to 54 ft. lbs. (75 Nm).

25. Attach the clutch cover and tighten the bolts to 9 ft. lbs. (12 Nm).

26. Attach the engine stiffener and tighten the mounting bolts to 28 ft. lbs. (39 Nm). Tighten the bolts using the following sequence:

   a. Tighten the upper most stiffener-to-transaxle case bolt.

   b. Tighten the remaining stiffener-to-transaxle bolts.

c. Tighten the stiffener-to-cylinder block bolt, closest to the transaxle.

d. Tighten the remaining stiffener-to-cylinder block bolts.

27. Install the intermediate shaft and the left and right halfshaft.

28. Install the center beam and tighten the bolts to 37 ft. lbs. (51 Nm).

29. Install the clutch slave cylinder with the clutch hose and pushrod. Tighten the slave cylinder bolts to 16 ft. lbs. (22 Nm).

30. Attach the transaxle side shift cable and select cable to the shift arm lever and to the select lever respectively. Tighten the bracket mounting bolts to 16 ft. lbs. (22 Nm).

31. Connect the backup light switch coupler.

32. Attach the right and left front damper forks.

33. Install the speed sensor assembly and the air cleaner case.

34. Connect the starter cable and connect the ground cable to the transaxle.

35. Install the wheel and tire assemblies.

36. Fill the transaxle with the proper type and quantity of oil.

37. Lower the vehicle and connect the negative battery cable. Check the clutch pedal free-play.

1992-94 Prelude

1. Disconnect the battery cables and remove the battery.

2. Raise and safely support the vehicle. Drain the transmission fluid.

3. Remove the air flow tube and air cleaner case. Remove the battery base.

4. Remove the vacuum tank and bracket. Do not disconnect the hoses.

5. Disconnect the starter wires and remove the starter.

6. Disconnect the transaxle ground cable and the backup light switch wire.

7. Remove the harness wire clamp and shift the transaxle to **R**. Remove both cables and the stay together.

8. Remove the cable bracket and disconnect the cables from the top housing of the transaxle. Remove both cables and the bracket together.

9. Disconnect the connector and remove the speed sensor, but leave the speed sensor hoses connected.

10. Remove the front wheel and tire assemblies.

11. Remove the mounting bolts and clutch slave cylinder with the clutch pipe and pushrod.

NOTE: Do not operate the clutch pedal once the slave cylinder has been removed. Be careful not to bend the pipe.

12. Remove the clutch damper mounting bolts and raise the clutch damper.

13. Remove the rear engine mount bracket stay.

14. Remove the cotter pins and lower arm ball joint nuts. Separate the ball joints and lower arms using a suitable tool.

15. Remove the damper fork bolt and remove the right radius rod.

16. Use a suitable tool to pry the right and left halfshafts out of the differential and the intermediate shaft. Pull on the inboard joint and remove the right and left halfshafts.

17. Remove the intermediate shaft from the differential.

18. Remove the center beam and remove the clutch cover.

19. Remove the rear beam stiffener and the intake manifold stay.

20. Remove the 3 rear engine mount bracket bolts.

21. Place a suitable jack under the transaxle and raise the transaxle just enough to take the weight off the mounts.

22. Remove the transaxle mount and mount bracket.

23. Remove the 2 upper transaxle housing mounting bolts and the 3 lower transaxle housing bolts.

24. Remove the transaxle from the vehicle.

To install:

25. Make sure the 4 dowel pins are installed.

26. Raise the transaxle into position.

27. Install the 3 lower and 2 upper transaxle mounting bolts and tighten to 47 ft. lbs. (65 Nm).

28. Install the transaxle mount and mount bracket. Install the through bolt and tighten temporarily. Make sure the engine is level and tighten the 3 mount bracket nuts and 2 bolts to 28 ft. lbs. (39 Nm). Tighten the through bolt to 47 ft. lbs. (65 Nm).

29. Install the transaxle housing mounting bolts on the engine side and tighten to 47 ft. lbs. (65 Nm).

30. Install the rear beam stiffener and tighten the bolts to 28 ft. lbs. (39 Nm).

31. Install the intake manifold stay and tighten the bolts to 16 ft. lbs. (22 Nm).

32. Install the clutch cover and tighten the bolts to 9 ft. lbs. (12 Nm).

33. Install the center beam and tighten the bolts to 43 ft. lbs. (60 Nm).

34. Install the intermediate shaft and driveshafts.

35. Install the radius rod. Tighten the radius rod mounting bolts to 76 ft. lbs. (105 Nm) and the radius rod nut to 32 ft. lbs. (44 Nm).

36. Install the ball joint to the lower arm.

37. Install the damper fork. Tighten the damper pinch bolt to 32 ft. lbs. (44 Nm).

38. Install the rear engine mount bracket stay. Tighten the nut to 15 ft. lbs. (21 Nm) and the bolt to 28 ft. lbs. (39 Nm).

39. Install the clutch damper and tighten the bolts to 16 ft. lbs. (22 Nm).

40. Install the clutch hose pipe and clutch slave cylinder to the transaxle housing. Tighten the slave cylinder mounting bolts to 16 ft. lbs. (22 Nm).

41. Install the speed sensor. Tighten the mounting bolt to 14 ft. lbs. (19 Nm).

42. Install the shift cable and select cable to the shift arm lever and to the select lever respectively. Tighten the cable bracket mounting bolts to 16 ft. lbs. (22 Nm). Install new cotter pins.

43. Connect the backup light switch coupler and the transmission ground cable. Install the harness clamp.

44. Install the starter. Tighten the 10 x 1.25mm bolt to 32 ft. lbs. (45 Nm) and the 12 x 1.25mm bolt to 54 ft. lbs. (75 Nm). Connect the starter wires.

45. Install the front wheel and tire assemblies.

46. Lower the vehicle.

47. Install the bracket and vacuum tank. Install the air cleaner case and air flow tube.

48. Fill the transaxle with the proper type and quantity of oil.

49. Install the battery base stay and the battery base. Install the battery and connect the battery cables.

50. Check the clutch pedal free-play.

51. Start the vehicle and check the transaxle for smooth operation.

LINKAGE ADJUSTMENT

The 1990-91 Prelude, Accord and Civic Wagon with 4WD, feature cable operated gear shift mechanisms that are adjustable. All other vehicles have non-adjustable, rod operated, gear shift linkage.

Select Cable

1990-91 PRELUDE AND 4WD CIVIC WAGON

1. Disconnect the negative battery cable.
2. Remove the console.
3. With the transaxle in neutral, check that the groove in the lever bracket is aligned with the index mark on the selector cable.
4. If the index mark is not aligned with the groove in the cable, loosen the locknuts and turn the adjuster as necessary.

NOTE: After adjustment, check the operation of the gear shift lever. Make sure the threads of the cables do not extend out of the cable adjuster by more than 0.4 in. (10mm).

5. Replace the console and connect the negative battery cable.

ACCORD

1. Disconnect the negative battery cable.
2. Remove the console.
3. Place the shift lever in the neutral position.
4. Measure the clearance between (A) and (B). It should be 8.37-8.40 in. (212.5-213.5mm).
5. If the clearance is incorrect, disconnect the select cable from the linkage, loosen the locknut and turn the adjuster, as necessary.
6. Tighten the locknut and connect the select cable to the linkage. Install a new cotter pin.

NOTE: Make sure the new cotter pin is seated firmly. After adjustment, check the operation of the shift lever.

7. Install the console and connect the negative battery cable.

(A)   (212.5-213.5MM)   (B)
                8.37-8.40 IN.

Select cable clearance measurement — Accord

Shift Cable

1990-91 PRELUDE AND 4WD CIVIC WAGON

1. Disconnect the negative battery cable.
2. Remove the console.
3. Place the transaxle in 4th gear.
4. Measure the clearance between the gear shift lever bracket and stopper, while pushing the lever forward. The clearance should be 0.24-28 in. (6.0-7.0mm).
5. If the clearance is outside specification, loosen the locknuts and turn the adjuster in or out until the correct clearance is obtained.

NOTE: After adjustment, check the operation of the gear shift lever. Make sure the threads of the cables do not extend out of the cable adjuster by more than 0.4 in. (10mm).

6. Replace the console and connect the negative battery cable.

ACCORD

1. Disconnect the negative battery cable.
2. Remove the console.
3. Place the shift lever in the neutral position.
4. Measure the clearance between (A) and (B). The clearance should be 6.86-6.90 in. (174.3-175.3mm).
5. If the clearance is incorrect, disconnect the shift cable from the change lever, loosen the locknut and turn the adjuster, as necessary.
6. Tighten the locknut and connect the shift cable to the change lever. Install a new cotter pin.

NOTE: Make sure the new cotter pin is seated firmly. After adjustment, check the operation of the gear shift lever.

7. Install the console and connect the negative battery cable.

CLUTCH

Clutch Assembly

REMOVAL AND INSTALLATION

1. Disconnect the negative battery cable. Raise and safely support the vehicle. Remove the transaxle from the vehicle. Matchmark the flywheel and clutch for reassembly.
2. Hold the flywheel ring gear with a tool made for this purpose, remove the retaining bolts and remove the pressure plate and clutch disc. Remove the bolts 2 turns at a time working in a crisscross pattern, to prevent warping the pressure plate.
3. At this time, inspect the flywheel for wear, cracks or scoring and resurface or replace, as necessary.
4. If the clutch release bearing is to be replaced, perform the following procedure on all except Prelude, 1992-94 Civic, Civic del Sol and Accord:

   a. Remove the 8mm special bolt.

   b. Remove the release shaft and the release bearing assembly.

   c. Separate the release fork from the bearing by removing the release fork spring from the holes in the release bearing.

5. To remove the release bearing on Prelude, 1992-94 Civic, Civic del Sol and Accord, perform the following procedure:

   a. Remove the boot from the clutch housing.

   b. Remove the release fork from the clutch housing by squeezing the release fork set spring with a suitable tool.

   c. Remove the release bearing from the release fork.

6. Check the release bearing for excessive play by spinning it by hand. Replace if there is excessive play.

To install:

7. If the flywheel was removed, make sure the flywheel and crankshaft mating surfaces are clean. Align the hole in the flywheel with the crankshaft dowel pin and install the flywheel bolts finger-tight. Install the ring gear holder and tighten the flywheel bolts in a crisscross pattern. Tighten the flywheel bolts to 76 ft. lbs. (105 Nm) on Prelude and Accord or 87 ft. lbs. (120 Nm) on Civic, Civic del Sol and CRX.
8. Install the clutch disc and pressure plate by aligning the dowels on the flywheel with the dowel holes in the pressure plate. If the same pressure plate is being installed that was removed, align the marks that were made during the removal procedure. Install the pressure plate bolts finger-tight.
9. Insert a suitable clutch disc alignment tool into the splined hole in the clutch disc. Tighten the pressure plate bolts in a crisscross pattern 2 turns at a time to prevent warping the pressure plate. The final torque should be 19 ft. lbs. (26 Nm).
10. Remove the alignment tool and ring gear holder.

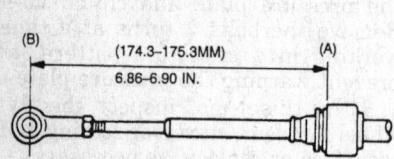

Shift cable clearance measurement — Accord

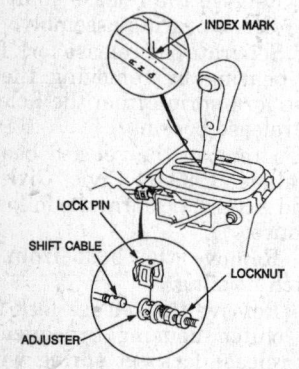

Shift cable adjustment — 1992-94 Prelude

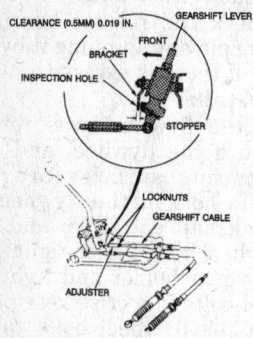

Gear shift cable adjustment — 4WD Civic Wagon and 1990-91 Prelude

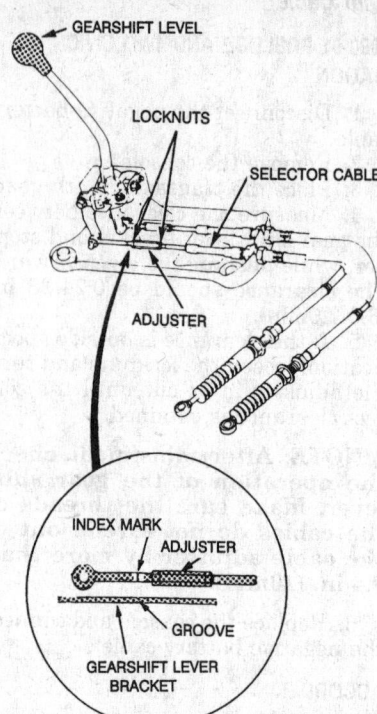

Selector cable adjustment — 4WD Civic Wagon and 1990-91 Prelude

PEDAL HEIGHT/FREE-PLAY ADJUSTMENT

1990-91 Civic, CRX

1. Measure the clutch pedal disengagement height.
2. Measure the clutch pedal free-play.
3. Adjust the clutch pedal free-play by turning the clutch cable adjusting nut, found at the end of the clutch cable housing near the release shaft.
4. Turn the adjusting nut until the clutch pedal free-play is 0.6-0.8 in. (15-20mm).
5. After adjustment, make sure the free-play at the tip of the release arm is 0.12-0.16 in. (3.0-4.0mm).

1992-94 Civic, Civic Del Sol, Prelude and Accord

NOTE: The clutch is self-adjusting to compensate for wear. The total clutch pedal free-play is 0.35-0.59 in. (9-15mm) for Prelude and Accord. For 1992-94 Civic and del Sol total clutch pedal free-play should be 0.47-0.83 in. (12-21mm). If there is no clearance between the master cylinder piston and pushrod, the release bearing is held against the

diaphragm spring of the pressure plate, which can result in clutch slippage or other clutch malfunction.

1. Loosen the locknut on clutch pedal switch A and back off the pedal switch until it no longer touches the clutch pedal. Clutch pedal switch A is the switch that contacts the clutch pedal below the clutch pedal pivot.
2. Loosen the locknut on the clutch master cylinder pushrod and turn the pushrod in or out to get the specified stroke and height at the clutch pedal.
3. The pedal stroke should be 5.3-5.7 in. (135-145mm) on Prelude, 1992-94 Civic and del Sol or 5.6 in. (142mm) on Accord.
4. The pedal height should be as follows:
   1992-94 Civic and del Sol — 6.46 in. (164mm)
   Prelude — 8.1 in. (207mm)
   Accord
   1990-91 — 8.27 in. (210mm)
   1992-94 — 7.24 in. (184mm)
5. Tighten the pushrod locknut.
6. Thread in clutch pedal switch A until it contacts the clutch pedal, then turn it in 1/4-1/2 turn further.
7. Tighten the locknut on clutch pedal switch A.

Clutch Cable

REMOVAL AND INSTALLATION

1. Disconnect the negative battery cable.
2. Disconnect the cable end from the brake pedal.
3. Remove the adjuster nut assembly from its mounting.
4. Raise and support the vehicle safely.
5. Disconnect the cable end from the release arm. Remove the cable from the vehicle.
6. Installation is the reverse of the removal procedure. Adjust the cable to specification.

Clutch Master Cylinder

REMOVAL AND INSTALLATION

Except 1992-94 Prelude

1. Disconnect the negative battery cable. Pry out the cotter pin and pull the pedal pin out of the yoke.
2. Remove the nuts and bolts retaining the clutch master cylinder and remove the cylinder from the engine compartment.

11. If the release bearing was removed, replace it in the reverse order of the removal procedure. Place a light coat of molybdenum disulfide grease on the inside diameter of the bearing prior to installation.
12. Install the transaxle, making sure the mainshaft is properly aligned with the clutch disc splines and the transaxle case is properly aligned with the cylinder block, before tightening the transaxle case bolts.
13. Adjust the clutch pedal free-play and connect the negative battery cable.

3. Disconnect and plug the hydraulic lines from the master cylinder.

4. Installation is the reverse order of the removal procedure. Bleed the clutch hydraulic system.

1992-94 Prelude

1. Disconnect the negative battery cable. Remove the reservoir hose from the master cylinder and drain the brake fluid into a suitable container.

2. Remove the reservoir from the engine compartment bulkhead.

3. Disconnect the clutch pipe from the clutch master cylinder.

4. Pry out the cotter pin and pull the pedal pin out of the yoke.

5. Remove the attaching nuts and remove the clutch master cylinder from the vehicle.

6. Installation is the reverse order of the removal procedure. Bleed the clutch hydraulic system.

Clutch Slave Cylinder

REMOVAL AND INSTALLATION

1. Disconnect the negative battery cable.

2. Disconnect and plug the clutch hose from the slave cylinder.

3. Remove the 2 retaining bolts and remove the slave cylinder.

4. Installation is the reverse of the removal procedure. Bleed the clutch hydraulic system.

Hydraulic Clutch System Bleeding

The hydraulic system must be bled whenever the system has been leaking or dismantled. The bleed screw is located on the slave cylinder.

1. Remove the bleed screw dust cap.

2. Attach a clear hose to the bleed screw. Immerse the other end of the hose in a clear jar, half filled with brake fluid.

3. Fill the clutch master cylinder with fresh brake fluid.

4. Open the bleed screw slightly and have an assistant slowly depress the clutch pedal. Close the bleed screw when the pedal reaches the end of its travel. Allow the clutch pedal to return slowly.

5. Repeat Steps 3-4 until all air bubbles are expelled from the system.

6. Discard the brake fluid in the jar. Replace the dust cap. Refill the master cylinder.

AUTOMATIC TRANSAXLE

Transaxle Assembly

REMOVAL AND INSTALLATION

1990-91 Civic and CRX

1. Disconnect the battery cables and remove the battery.

2. Raise and safely support the vehicle.

3. Remove the 3 mount bolts and loosen the 1 bolt located at the side of the battery base and intake hose band of the throttle body.

4. Remove the air cleaner case, complete with the intake hose.

5. Remove the starter and the transaxle ground cable.

6. Disconnect the lock-up control solenoid valve wire connector. On 4WD Civic Wagon, disconnect the lock-up control solenoid valve and shift control solenoid valve wire connectors and disconnect the automatic transaxle speed pulser connector.

7. Disconnect the control cable at the control lever.

8. Drain the transaxle fluid. Remove the filler plug to speed draining. After draining reinstall the drain plug with a new washer.

9. Disconnect and plug the cooler hoses at the joint pipes.

10. Mark the position of the distributor housing in relation to the cylinder head. Disconnect the connectors and remove the mount bolts, then remove the distributor from the cylinder head.

11. Remove the shift cable by removing the cotter pin, control pin, control lever roller and loosening the locknut.

12. Disconnect the speedometer cable. Do not disassemble the speedometer gear holder.

13. On 4WD Civic Wagon, remove the driveshaft.

14. Remove the torque converter cover and the plug. Remove the driveplate bolts.

15. Remove the engine splash shield and the right wheelwell splash shield.

16. Remove the header pipe.

17. Remove the cotter pins and lower arm ball joint nuts and then separate the ball joints using a suitable tool.

18. Remove the bolts and nut, then remove the right radius rod.

19. Remove the right and left halfshafts. On 4WD Civic Wagon, remove the intermediate shaft.

20. On 4WD Civic Wagon, remove the 9 mounting bolts, then remove the transaxle cover.

21. Install bolts in each end of the cylinder head and attach a suitable hoist to the bolts. Lift the engine slightly to unload the mounts.

22. Place a suitable jack under the transaxle and raise the transaxle just enough to take weight off the mounts.

23. On 4WD Civic Wagon, remove the transaxle mounting bolt on the engine side.

24. Remove the bolts from the front transaxle mount.

25. Remove the rear transaxle mount bracket by removing the 4 mounting bolts.

26. Remove the 4 mounting bolts. Remove the side transaxle mount.

27. Remove the transaxle-to-cylinder block mounting bolts.

28. On 4WD Civic Wagon, loosen the side engine mounting bolt and tilt the engine.

29. Pull the transaxle away from the engine until it clears the 14mm dowel pins, then lower the transaxle jack.

To install:

30. Make sure the two 14mm dowel pins are installed in the torque converter housing.

31. Raise the transaxle into position and loosely install the transaxle-to-cylinder block bolts. Tighten them to 43 ft. lbs. (60 Nm).

32. Install the engine side mounting bolt (12 x 1.25 x 70mm) and tighten to 50 ft. lbs. (68 Nm).

33. Install the transaxle to rear transaxle mount bracket and tighten the bolts to 40 ft. lbs. (55 Nm).

34. Install the transaxle to the front and side transaxle mounts. Tighten the mount retaining bolts to 29 ft. lbs. (40 Nm) and the mount through bolts to 40 ft. lbs. (55 Nm).

35. Remove the transaxle jack. On 4WD Civic Wagon, tighten the side engine mount bolt to 40 ft. lbs. (55 Nm).

36. Remove the hoist chain and bolts from the cylinder head.

37. Attach the torque converter to the driveplate with the eight 12mm bolts. Tighten the bolts in 2 steps, first to 4.5 ft. lbs. (6 Nm) in a criss-

cross pattern and finally to 9 ft. lbs. (12 Nm) in the same pattern.

38. Install the shift cable and cable holder.

39. Install the torque converter cover and header pipe bracket.

40. On 4WD Civic Wagon, install the transaxle cover and the intermediate shaft.

41. Install a new set ring on the end of each halfshaft.

42. Turn the right steering knuckle fully outward and slide the axle into the differential, until the spring clip can be felt engaging the differential side gear. Repeat the procedure on the left side.

43. Install the damper fork bolt and radius rod.

44. Install the ball joints to the lower arms and tighten the nuts to 40 ft. lbs. (55 Nm). Install new cotter pins.

45. On 4WD Civic Wagon, install the driveshaft.

46. Install the splash shields and header pipe.

47. Install the distributor.

48. Connect the lock-up control solenoid valve wire connector. On 4WD Civic Wagon, connect the lock-up control solenoid valve and shift control solenoid valve wire connectors and connect the automatic transaxle speed pulser connector.

49. Connect the transaxle cooler hoses to the joint pipes and the control cable to the control lever.

50. Connect the speedometer cable.

51. Install the starter and tighten the bolts to 33 ft. lbs. (45 Nm).

52. Connect the positive battery cable to the starter and connect the ground cable at the transaxle.

53. Install the air intake case and hose.

54. Install the 3 bolts located at the side of the battery base and retighten the intake hose band of the throttle body.

55. Lower the vehicle, install the battery and connect the battery cables.

56. Fill the transaxle with the proper type and quantity of fluid.

57. Start the engine, set the parking brake and shift through all gears 3 times. Check for proper control cable adjustment. Check the ignition timing.

58. Let the engine reach operating temperature with the transaxle in **N** or **P**, then turn the engine OFF and check the fluid level.

1992-94 Civic and Civic Del Sol

1. Disconnect both cables from the battery.

2. Remove the resonator, air intake hose and air cleaner case.

3. Disconnect the starter motor cable from the starter motor and remove the cable holder.

4. Remove the transaxle ground cable from the transaxle.

5. Disconnect the lock-up control solenoid valve connector.

6. Disconnect the speedometer sensor connector from the transaxle.

7. Remove the transaxle housing mounting bolts and the rear engine mounting bolt. Raise and safely support the vehicle.

8. Remove the transaxle drain plug and drain the ATF. Install the drain plug with a new washer.

9. Remove the cotter pins and castle nuts and separate the ball joints from the lower arm.

10. Remove the damper fork bolts and separate the damper fork and the damper.

11. Pry the right and left driveshafts out from the differential.

12. Pull on the inboard joint and remove the right and left driveshafts.

13. For protection purposes, tie plastic bags over the driveshaft ends.

14. Remove the splash shield and the exhaust pipe A.

15. Remove the shift cable cover, remove the control lever and remove the shift cable. Do not bend the shift control cable during removal.

16. Remove the stopper mount and remove the end of the throttle control cable from the throttle control lever.

17. Disconnect the ATF cooler hoses at the joint pipes. Turn the cooler hoses upward to prevent loss of fluid. Plug the joint pipes.

18. Remove the engine stiffeners and the torque converter cover.

19. Remove the driveplate bolts.

20. Attach an engine support fixture to the engine. Use the distributor mounting bolt.

21. Place a transmission jack below the transaxle and raise enough to take weight off the mounts. Remove the transaxle side mount.

22. Remove the transaxle housing mounting bolts and remove the rear engine mounting bolts.

23. Pull the transaxle away from the engine until it is clear of the 14mm dowel pins. Lower the transaxle out of the vehicle.

To install:

24. Make sure the two 14mm dowel pins are installed in the torque converter housing.

25. Raise the transaxle into position and install the 2 transaxle housing mounting bolts and the 2 rear engine mounting bolts. Tighten the transaxle housing bolts to 43 ft. lbs. (60 Nm) and the engine mounting bolts to 61 ft. lbs. (85 Nm).

26. Install the transaxle side mount and tighten the nuts and bolt to 40 ft. lbs. (55 Nm).

27. Install the upper rear engine mounting bolt and 3 transmission housing mounting bolts. Tighten the engine mounting bolt to 61 ft. lbs. (85 Nm) and the transaxle housing bolts to 43 ft. lbs. (60 Nm).

28. Remove the transaxle jack and engine support device.

29. Attach the torque converter to the driveplate with 8 bolts. Tighten the bolts in 2 steps, first to 4.5 ft. lbs. (6 Nm) in a crisscross pattern and finally to 9 ft. lbs. (12 Nm) in the same pattern. Check for free rotation after tightening the last bolt.

30. Install the torque converter cover and tighten the bolts to 9 ft. lbs. (12 Nm). Install the engine stiffener(s) and tighten the bolts to 33 ft. lbs. (45 Nm).

31. Connect the ATF cooler hoses to the joint pipes.

32. Connect the throttle control cable and install the stopper mount. Tighten the 10mm bolts to 28 ft. lbs. (39 Nm) and the 12mm bolts to 47 ft. lbs. (65 Nm)

33. Install the control lever with a new lock washer in place to the control shaft. Install the shift cable cover.

34. Install exhaust pipe A. Tighten the pipe to manifold nuts to 40 ft. lbs. (55 Nm). Tighten the pipe A to pipe B nuts to 16 ft. lbs. (22 Nm).

35. Install the splash shield.

36. Install a new set ring on the end of each driveshaft and install the driveshafts.

37. Turn the right steering knuckle fully outward and slide the axle into the differential until the spring clip is felt engaging the differential side gear. Repeat the procedure on the left side.

38. Install the damper fork bolts and ball joint nuts to the lower arms. Tighten the nut to 40 ft. lbs. (55 Nm) while holding the damper fork bolt. Tighten the ball joint nut to 40 ft. lbs. (55 Nm) and install a new cotter pin.

39. Connect the speedometer sensor connector and connect the lock-up control solenoid connector.

40. Connect the transaxle ground cable and the starter motor cable. Install the starter cable holder.

41. Install the air cleaner case, air intake hose and resonator.

42. Lower the vehicle and connect the battery cables at the battery.

43. Fill the transaxle with the proper type and quantity of fluid.

44. Start the engine, set the parking brake and shift the transaxle through all gears 3 times. Check for proper control cable adjustment.

45. Let the engine reach operating temperature with the transaxle in **N** or **P**, then turn the engine OFF and check the fluid level.

Accord

1. Disconnect the battery cable and remove the battery.

2. Raise and safely support the vehicle.

3. Remove the air intake hose, air cleaner case and battery base.

4. Disconnect the throttle cable from the throttle control lever.

5. Disconnect the transaxle ground cable and the speed sensor connectors.

6. Disconnect the starter cables and remove the starter.

7. Remove the rear mount bracket stay nut first. Remove the bolt, then remove the rear mount bracket stay.

8. Remove the speed sensor, but leave hoses connected.

9. Disconnect the lock-up control solenoid valve and shift control solenoid valve connectors.

10. Drain the transaxle fluid and reinstall the drain plug with a new washer.

11. Disconnect the transaxle cooler hoses from the joint pipes. Plug the hoses.

12. Remove the center beam.

13. Disconnect the oxygen sensor connector.

14. Remove the exhaust header pipe and the splash shield.

15. Remove the cotter pins and lower arm ball joint nuts, then separate the ball joints from the lower arms using a suitable tool.

16. Using a suitable tool, pry the right and left halfshafts out of the differential. Pull on the inboard CV-joints and remove the right and left halfshafts.

17. Remove the right damper pinch bolt, then separate the damper fork and damper.

18. Remove the bolts and nut, then remove the right radius rod.

19. Tie plastic bags over the halfshaft ends.

20. Remove the torque converter cover and control cable holder.

21. Remove the shift control cable by removing the cotter pin, control pin and control lever roller from the control lever.

22. Remove the plug, then remove the driveplate bolts.

23. Remove the rear, engine side transaxle housing mounting bolts.

24. Remove the mounting bolts from the rear engine mount bracket.

25. Attach a suitable hoist to the transaxle hoisting brackets, then lift the engine slightly.

26. Place a suitable jack under the transaxle and raise the jack just enough to take weight off the mounts.

27. Remove the 4 transaxle housing mounting bolts and 3 mount bracket nuts.

28. Pull the transaxle away from the engine until it clears the 14mm dowel pins, then lower it on the transaxle jack.

To install:

29. Make sure the two 14mm dowel pins are installed in the torque converter housing.

30. Raise the transaxle into position and install the 4 transaxle housing mounting bolts. Tighten the bolts to 47 ft. lbs. (65 Nm).

31. Install the transaxle to transaxle mount bracket and tighten the nuts to 28 ft. lbs. (39 Nm).

32. Remove the transaxle jack.

33. Install the 2 engine side transaxle housing mounting bolts and tighten to 47 ft. lbs. (65 Nm). Install the rear engine mount bracket bolts and tighten to 40 ft. lbs. (55 Nm).

34. Attach the torque converter to the driveplate with 8 bolts. Tighten the bolts in 2 steps, first to 4.5 ft. lbs. (6 Nm) in a crisscross pattern and finally to 9 ft. lbs. (12 Nm) in the same pattern. Check for free rotation after tightening the last bolt.

35. Install the shift control cable and control cable holder. Tighten the control cable holder bolts to 13 ft. lbs. (18 Nm).

36. Install the torque converter cover and tighten the bolts to 9 ft. lbs. (12 Nm).

37. Remove the hoist.

38. Install the radius rod. Tighten the mounting bolts to 76 ft. lbs. (105 Nm) and the nut to 32 ft. lbs. (44 Nm).

39. Install the damper fork. Tighten the damper pinch bolt to 32 ft. lbs. (44 Nm).

40. Install a new set ring on the end of each halfshaft.

41. Turn the right steering knuckle fully outward and slide the axle into the differential until the spring clip is felt engaging the differential side gear. Repeat the procedure on the left side.

42. Install the damper fork bolts and ball joint nuts to the lower arms. Tighten the nut to 40 ft. lbs. (55 Nm) while holding the damper fork bolt.

Tighten the ball joint nut to 40 ft. lbs. (55 Nm) and install a new cotter pin.

43. Install the splash shield, the center beam and the exhaust header pipe. Tighten the center beam bolts to 28 ft. lbs. (39 Nm).

44. Connect the oxygen sensor connector.

45. Install the speed sensor and tighten the bolt to 13 ft. lbs. (18 Nm).

46. Install the rear mount bracket stay. Tighten the mounting bolt first, to 28 ft. lbs. (39 Nm) and then tighten the nut to 15 ft. lbs. (21 Nm).

47. Install the starter and tighten the bolts to 33 ft. lbs. (45 Nm). Connect the cables to the starter.

48. Connect the lock-up control solenoid valve and shift control solenoid valve connectors.

49. Connect the speed sensor connectors and the transaxle ground cable.

50. Connect the transaxle cooler hoses to the joint pipes.

51. Install the battery base, air cleaner case and air intake hose. Install the battery.

52. Lower the vehicle and connect the battery cables at the battery.

53. Fill the transaxle with the proper type and quantity of fluid.

54. Start the engine, set the parking brake and shift the transaxle through all gears 3 times. Check for proper control cable adjustment.

55. Let the engine reach operating temperature with the transaxle in **N** or **P**, then turn the engine OFF and check the fluid level.

PRELUDE

1990-91

1. Disconnect the negative battery cable at the battery and the transaxle.

2. Drain the transaxle fluid and replace the drain plug.

3. Disconnect the wiring for the starter, lock-up control solenoids, shift control solenoids and speed pulser.

4. On fuel injected vehicles, remove the air inlet hose and the air cleaner case.

5. Remove the speed sensor from the transaxle without removing the hoses.

6. Disconnect the throttle control cable at the transaxle bracket.

7. Disconnect the transaxle cooler hoses at the joint pipes and cap the joint pipes.

8. Remove the upper transaxle mounting bracket.

9. Remove the transaxle-to-cylinder block attachment bolts that must

be removed from the engine compartment.

10. Raise and safely support the vehicle.

11. Remove the front wheel and tire assemblies.

12. Remove the splash shield and the center beam.

13. Remove the right radius rod completely.

14. Remove the right and left half-shafts and the intermediate shaft.

15. Remove the engine stiffener and the torque converter cover.

16. Remove the shift cable from the transaxle.

17. Remove the bolts from the driveplate.

18. Support the transaxle with a suitable jack.

19. Remove the lower bolt from the rear engine mounting bracket. Loosen, but do not remove the top bolt. This bolt will support the weight of the engine.

20. Remove the remaining engine-to-transaxle mounting bolts.

21. Separate the transaxle from the engine block. Disengage the two 14mm dowel pins and lower the transaxle.

To install:

22. Raise the transaxle into position and install the mounting bolts. Tighten the bolts to 47 ft. lbs. (65 Nm).

23. Attach the torque converter to the driveplate with the mounting bolts. Tighten the bolts in 2 steps, first to 4.5 ft. lbs. (6 Nm) in a criss-cross pattern and finally to 9 ft. lbs. (12 Nm) in the same pattern. Check for free rotation after tightening the last bolt.

24. Install the transaxle to the rear engine mount bracket with the mounting bolts. Tighten the bolts to 54 ft. lbs. (75 Nm).

25. Install the shift cable with the control pin and a new cotter pin.

26. Install the torque converter cover and the cable holder.

27. Install the engine stiffener. The engine stiffener bolts must be tightened to 28 ft. lbs. (39 Nm) in their proper order. First tighten the uppermost stiffener-to-transaxle housing bolt followed by the remaining stiffener-to-transaxle housing bolt. Next tighten the stiffener-to-cylinder block bolt closest to the transaxle followed by the remaining stiffener-to-cylinder block bolt.

28. Install the intermediate shaft and the halfshafts.

29. Install the center beam and the right and left front damper fork.

30. Install the radius rod on the transaxle side.

31. Install the transaxle mounting bracket and tighten the bolts to 28 ft. lbs. (39 Nm).

32. Connect the lock-up control solenoid valve connector, the shift control solenoid valve coupler and the connector of the speed pulser.

33. Connect the throttle control cable to the throttle control lever.

34. Install the speed sensor assembly and the air cleaner case.

35. Connect the oil cooler hoses and connect the starter and ground cables.

36. Connect the battery cables to the battery.

37. Start the engine, set the parking brake and shift the transaxle through all gears 3 times. Check for proper control cable adjustment.

38. Let the engine reach operating temperature with the transaxle in **N** or **P**, then turn the engine OFF and check the fluid level.

1992-94

1. Disconnect both cables from the battery.

2. Remove the battery hold-down and remove the battery.

3. Drain the ATF fluid and reinstall the drain plug complete with a new washer.

4. Remove the air intake hose, air cleaner case and resonator.

5. Disconnect the connector from the vacuum tank and remove the vacuum tank and tank bracket. Do not remove the vacuum tube from the vacuum tank.

6. Disconnect the ground cable from the transaxle and the body.

7. Remove the battery base with the ground cable and remove the battery base stay.

8. Disconnect the lock-up control solenoid valve and shift control solenoid valve connectors.

9. Disconnect the throttle control cable from the throttle control lever.

10. Disconnect the countershaft speed sensor connector.

11. Disconnect the ATF cooler hoses at the joint pipes. Turn the ends of the cooler hoses upward to prevent loss of ATF. Plug the joint pipes.

12. Remove the starter motor. Disconnect the vehicle speed sensor connector.

13. Remove the rear stiffener, then remove the vehicle speed sensor and power steering speed sensor.

NOTE: Do not disconnect the power steering pressure hoses from the vehicle speed sensor and power steering speed sensor.

14. Remove the upper transaxle housing mounting bolts.

15. Loosen the front engine mount bracket bolts and remove the transmission mount.

16. Remove the splash shield and remove the center beam and rear beam stiffener.

17. Remove the cotter pins and castle nuts and separate the ball joints from the lower arm.

18. Remove the damper fork bolts and separate the damper fork and the damper.

19. Pry the right and left driveshafts out from the differential.

20. Pull on the inboard joint and remove the right and left driveshafts.

21. For protection purposes, tie plastic bags over the driveshaft ends.

22. Remove the right damper pinch bolt and separate the damper fork and damper.

23. Remove the radius rod bolts and nut and remove the radius rod.

24. Remove the torque converter cover and control cable cover.

25. Remove the control lever lock bolt and remove the control cable with the lever. Do not bend the shift control cable during removal.

26. Remove the driveplate bolts.

27. Place a transaxle jack below the transaxle and raise it enough to take the weight off the mount.

28. Remove the intake manifold stay.

29. Remove the lower transaxle housing mounting bolts and lower rear engine mounting bolts.

30. Pull the transaxle away from the engine until it clears the dowel pins. Lower the transaxle out of the vehicle.

To install:

31. Place the transaxle on a transaxle jack and raise to the engine level.

32. Align the transaxle to the engine and install the transmission housing mounting bolts and lower rear engine mounting bolts. Tighten the engine mounting bolts to 40 ft. lbs. (55 Nm) and the transaxle mounting bolts to 47 ft. lbs. (65 Nm).

33. Tighten the front engine mount bracket bolts to 28 ft. lbs. (39 Nm).

34. Install the transaxle mount. Tighten the bolt to 47 ft. lbs. (65 Nm) and the nuts to 28 ft. lbs. (39 Nm).

35. Remove the transaxle jack.

36. Attach the torque converter to the driveplate with the mounting bolts. Tighten the bolts in 2 steps, first to 4.5 ft. lbs. (6 Nm) in a criss-cross pattern and finally to 9 ft. lbs. (12 Nm) in the same pattern. Check for free rotation after tightening the last bolt.

37. Install the shift control lever with the cable on the control shaft.

38. Install the torque converter cover and the shift cable cover.

39. Install the radius rod. Tighten the bolts to 76 ft. lbs. (105 Nm) and the nut to 40 ft. lbs. (55 Nm).

40. Install a new set ring on the end of each driveshaft.

41. Turn the right steering knuckle fully outward and slide the axle into the differential until the spring clip is felt engaging the differential side gear. Repeat the procedure on the left side.

42. Install the damper fork bolts and ball joint nuts to the lower arms. Tighten the damper pinch bolt to 32 ft. lbs. (44 Nm). Tighten the nut to 47 ft. lbs. (65 Nm) while holding the damper fork bolt. Tighten the ball joint nut to 47 ft. lbs. (65 Nm) and install a new cotter pin.

43. Install the rear beam stiffener and the center beam. Tighten the stiffener bolts to 28 ft. lbs. (39 Nm). Tighten the center beam bolts to 43 ft. lbs. (60 Nm).

44. Install the speedometer sensor and rear stiffener. Tighten the sensor bolt to 9 ft. lbs. (12 Nm), the stiffener bolt to 28 ft. lbs. (39 Nm) and the stiffener nut to 15 ft. lbs. (21 Nm).

45. Connect the ATF cooler hoses to the joint pipes.

46. Connect the lock-up control solenoid and shift control solenoid valve connectors.

47. Connect the vehicle speed sensor and power steering speed sensor connectors.

48. Connect the starter motor cables and install the battery base and base stay.

49. Connect the ground cables on the body and on the transaxle.

50. Install the vacuum tank, tank bracket and connect the connector.

51. Install the air cleaner case and air intake hose.

52. Lower the vehicle and connect the battery cables at the battery.

53. Fill the transaxle with the proper type and quantity of fluid.

54. Start the engine, set the parking brake and shift the transaxle through all gears 3 times. Check for proper control cable adjustment.

55. Let the engine reach operating temperature with the transaxle in **N**

or **P**, then turn the engine OFF and check the fluid level.

56. After road testing the vehicle, loosen the front engine mount brackets and torque them again to 28 ft. lbs. (39 Nm).

SHIFT CABLE ADJUSTMENT

1. Start the engine. Shift the transaxle to **R**, to see if the reverse gear engages.

2. Shut the engine OFF and disconnect the negative battery cable.

3. Remove the console.

4. On 1990-92 Civic and CRX, place the selector lever in **N** or **R**. On Accord, Prelude and 1992-94 Civic and del Sol, place the selector lever in **N**. Remove the lock pin from the cable adjuster.

5. Check that the hole in the adjuster is perfectly aligned with the hole in the shift cable.

NOTE: There are 2 holes in the end of the shift cable. They are positioned 90 degrees apart to allow cable adjustments in ¼ turn increments.

6. If not perfectly aligned, loosen the locknut on the shift cable and adjust as required.

7. Tighten the locknut and install the lock pin on the adjuster.

NOTE: If the lock pin feels like it is binding when being installed, the cable is still out of adjustment and must be adjusted again.

8. Connect the negative battery cable, start the engine and check the shift lever in all gears. Install the console.

THROTTLE LINKAGE ADJUSTMENT

Carbureted Engine

THROTTLE CONTROL CABLE BRACKET

1. Disconnect the negative battery cable.

2. Disconnect the throttle control cable from the throttle control lever.

3. Bend down the lock tabs of the lock-plate and remove the two 6mm bolts to free the bracket.

4. Loosely install a new lock-plate.

5. Adjust the position of the bracket by measuring the distance between the cable housing side of the bracket and the bracket side edge of the throttle control lever. Measure between the same points that the cable would pass through the bracket and lever.

6. Tighten the two 6mm bolts when the measurement is 6.18 in. (157.0mm). The bolts should be tightened to 9 ft. lbs. (12 Nm).

NOTE: Make sure the control lever does not get pulled toward the bracket side as the bolts are tightened.

7. Bend up the lock-plate tabs against the bolt heads, connect the throttle control cable and connect the negative battery cable.

THROTTLE CONTROL CABLE

1. Start the engine and bring it to normal operating temperature. The cooling fan must come ON at least once.

2. Make sure the throttle cable free-play and idle speed are correct.

3. Check the distance between the throttle control lever and throttle control bracket and adjust, as necessary.

4. On 1990-92 Prelude, disconnect the vacuum hose from the throttle controller and connect a vacuum pump to the controller and apply vacuum.

5. Apply light thumb pressure to the throttle control lever. Have an assistant depress the accelerator. The lever should move just as the engine speed increases above idle. If not, proceed to Step 6.

6. Loosen the nuts on the control cable at the transaxle end and synchronize the control lever to the throttle.

NOTE: The shift/lock-up characteristics can be tailored to the driver's expectations by adjusting the control cable up to 3mm shorter than the synchronized point.

Fuel Injected Engine

THROTTLE CONTROL CABLE

1. Start the engine and bring it up to operating temperature. The cooling fan must come ON at least once.

2. Make sure the throttle cable free-play and idle speed are correct.

3. On dash pot equipped vehicles, disconnect the vacuum hose from the dash pot, connect a vacuum pump and apply vacuum. This simulates a normal operating amount of pull by the dash pot as if the engine were running.

4. Remove any throttle cable free-play.

5. Apply light thumb pressure to the throttle control lever, then work the throttle linkage. The lever should move just as the engine speed in-

creases above idle. If not, proceed to Step 6.

6. Loosen the nuts on the control cable at the transaxle end and synchronize the control lever to the throttle.

NOTE: The shift/lock-up characteristics can be tailored to the driver's expectations by adjusting the control cable up to 3mm shorter than the synchronized point.

7. Remove the vacuum pump and connect the vacuum hose to the dash pot.

TRANSFER CASE

Transfer Case Assembly

REMOVAL AND INSTALLATION

Manual Transaxle

1. Disconnect the negative battery cable.
2. Raise and safely support the vehicle.
3. Drain the transaxle fluid and replace the drain plug.
4. Remove the exhaust header pipe.
5. Disconnect the driveshaft from the transfer case.
6. Remove the transaxle splash shield.
7. Remove the left side cover from the transfer case.
8. Remove the driven gear from the transfer case.

NOTE: Be careful not to damage the thrust shim and mating surface.

9. Remove the transfer case from the clutch housing.
10. Remove the clutch case cover.
   To install:
11. Make sure all mating surfaces are clean prior to installation.
12. Apply liquid gasket to the clutch housing mating surface of the transfer case and install the transfer case on the clutch housing. Tighten the bolts to 33 ft. lbs. (45 Nm).
13. Lubricate the drive gear with oil and install the drive gear thrust shim and the drive gear on the transfer shaft. Install the transfer thrust shim and left side cover on the transfer case. Apply liquid gasket to the

threads and tighten the bolts to 33 ft. lbs. (45 Nm).

14. Apply liquid gasket to the mating surface on the top and bottom of the transfer case opening, install a new O-ring and install the driven gear thrust shim and driven gear in the transfer case. Tighten the bolts to 19 ft. lbs. (26 Nm).
15. Installation of the remaining components is the reverse of the removal procedure. Lower the vehicle and fill the transaxle with the proper type and quantity of fluid.
16. Connect the negative battery cable, start the vehicle and check for leaks.

Automatic Transaxle

1. Disconnect the negative battery cable.
2. Raise and safely support the vehicle.
3. Drain the transaxle fluid and replace the drain plug.
4. Remove the exhaust header pipe.
5. Disconnect the driveshaft from the transfer case.
6. Remove the transaxle splash shield.
7. Remove the driven gear assembly from the transfer case.
8. Remove the drive gear from the transfer case. In this procedure, remove all of the left side cover bolts except the 1 closest to the front of the vehicle. Loosen this bolt and use it as the axis, about which the cover can be rotated to gain access to the drive gear. Leave this bolt in the cover and transfer case.

NOTE: Be careful not to damage the thrust shim and mating surface.

9. Remove the transfer case from the clutch housing.
10. Remove the clutch case cover.
   To install:
11. Make sure all mating surfaces are clean prior to installation.
12. Apply liquid gasket to the clutch housing mating surface of the transfer case. Attach a new O-ring to the groove on the left side cover.
13. Install the transfer case with the 1 bolt and left side cover still attached. Tighten the transfer case bolts to 33 ft. lbs. (45 Nm).
14. Lubricate the drive gear with oil and install the drive gear thrust shim and the drive gear on the transfer shaft. Install the transfer thrust shim and left side cover on the transfer case. Apply liquid gasket to the threads and tighten the bolts to 33 ft. lbs. (45 Nm).

15. Apply liquid gasket to the mating surface on the top and bottom of the transfer case opening. Install a new O-ring and install the driven gear thrust shim and driven gear in the transfer case. Tighten the bolts to 19 ft. lbs. (26 Nm).
16. Installation of the remaining components is the reverse of the removal procedure. Lower the vehicle and fill the transaxle with the proper type and quantity of fluid.
17. Connect the negative battery cable, start the vehicle and check for leaks.

FRONT SUSPENSION

MacPherson Strut

REMOVAL AND INSTALLATION

1. Raise and safely support the vehicle.
2. Remove the front tire and wheel assembly.
3. Remove the brake hose clamp bolts from the damper, if equipped.
4. Remove the damper fork bolts and remove the damper fork.
5. Remove the flange nuts and remove the strut assembly.
6. Installation is the reverse of the removal procedure. Tighten the damper fork nut to 47 ft. lbs. (65 Nm) while holding the damper fork bolt. Tighten the damper fork pinch bolt to 32 ft. lbs. (44 Nm).
7. The flange nuts should not be tightened until the strut is under vehicle load. Tighten the flange nuts to 28 ft. lbs. (39 Nm), except for 1992-94 Civic and del Sol. Tighten 1992-94 Civic and del Sol nuts to 36 ft. lbs. (50 Nm).

Upper Ball Joints

INSPECTION

1. Raise and safely support the vehicle.
2. Remove the front wheel and tire assembly.
3. Grasp the steering knuckle and move it back and forth.
4. If any play is detected, replace the upper control arm (except 1990-91 Prelude). On 1990-91 Prelude, replace the upper ball joint.

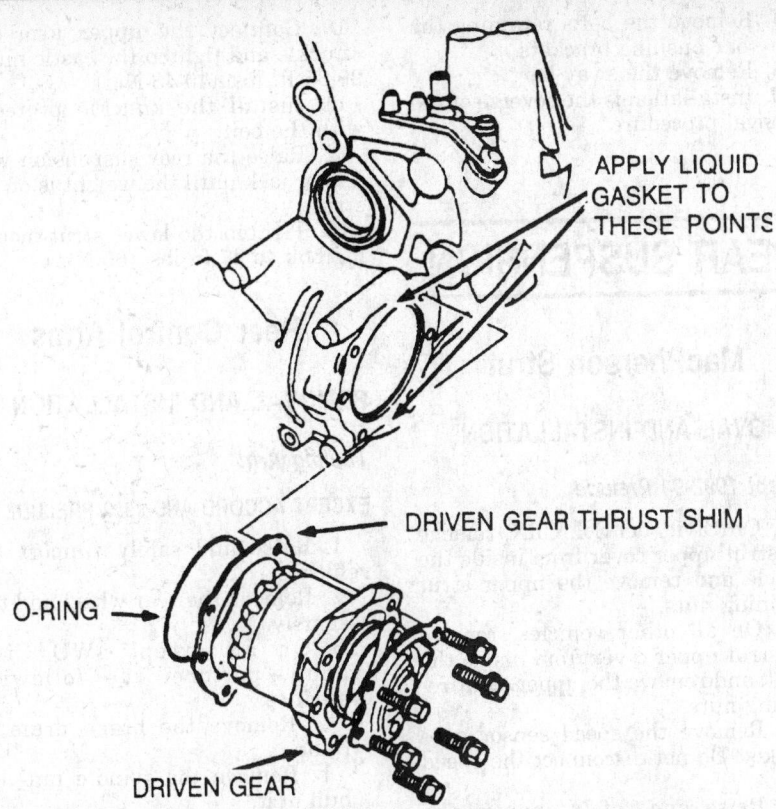

APPLY LIQUID GASKET TO THESE POINTS

DRIVEN GEAR THRUST SHIM

O-RING

DRIVEN GEAR

Transfer case driven gear installation — 4WD Civic Wagon with automatic transaxle

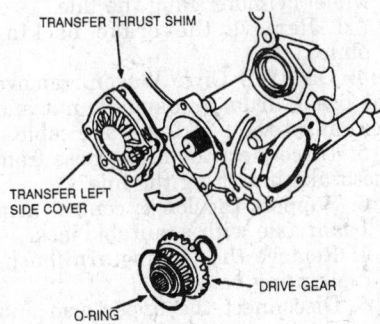

TRANSFER THRUST SHIM

TRANSFER LEFT SIDE COVER

DRIVE GEAR

O-RING

Transfer case drive gear and left side cover installation — 4WD Civic Wagon with automatic transaxle

REMOVAL AND INSTALLATION

Except 1990-91 Prelude

The upper ball joint is an integral component of the upper control arm. If the ball joint is defective, the entire upper control arm must be replaced.

1990-91 Prelude

1. Raise and safely support the vehicle.
2. Remove the front wheel and tire assembly.
3. Remove the cotter pin and castle nut from the upper ball joint.

4. Using a suitable tool, separate the upper ball joint from the steering knuckle.
5. Remove the 2 retaining nuts and the ball joint.
6. Installation is the reverse of the removal procedure. Tighten the ball joint-to-control arm retaining nuts to 40 ft. lbs. (55 Nm). Tighten the ball joint castle nut to 32 ft. lbs. (44 Nm) and install a new cotter pin.
7. Check the camber adjustment.

Lower Ball Joints

INSPECTION

1. Raise and safely support the vehicle.
2. Remove the wheel and tire assembly.
3. Grasp the steering knuckle close to the lower ball joint and move it back and forth. Replace the ball joint, if any movement is detected.

REMOVAL AND INSTALLATION

1. Raise and safely support the vehicle.
2. Remove the wheel and tire assembly.

3. Remove the steering knuckle.
4. Pry off the snapring and remove the boot.
5. Remove the circlip.
6. Install a suitable ball joint remover/installer 07965-SB00100 or equivalent, on the ball joint and tighten the ball joint nut.
7. Position ball joint remover base 07JAF-SH20200 or equivalent, over the ball joint and then set the assembly in a suitable vise. Press the ball joint out of the knuckle.
To install:
8. Place the ball joint in position by hand.
9. Install a suitable ball joint remover/installer 07965-SB00100 or equivalent, and ball joint installer base 07965-SB00200 or equivalent, over the ball joint and position in a suitable vise. Press the ball joint in.
10. Installation of the remaining components is the reverse of the removal procedure.

Upper Control Arms

REMOVAL AND INSTALLATION

Civic, Civic Del Sol, CRX and Accord

1. Raise and support the vehicle safely.
2. Remove the front wheels. Properly support the lower control arm assemblies.
3. Remove the self-locking nuts, upper control arm bolts and upper control anchor bolts. Separate the upper ball joint using a suitable ball joint separator tool.
4. Place the upper control arm assembly into a suitable holding fixture and drive out the upper arm bushing.
To install:
5. Drive the new upper arm bushing into the upper arm anchor bolts. On Civic, del Sol and CRX, center the bushing so 0.3543 in. (9mm) protrudes from each side of the anchor bolt. On Accord, drive in the bushing so the leading edges are flush with the anchor bolt.
6. Install the upper control arm assembly and install the upper arm bolts, then tighten the self-locking nuts. Be sure to align the upper arm anchor bolt with the mark on the upper arm.
7. Installation of the remaining components is the reverse of the removal procedure.

Prelude

1. Raise and support the vehicle safely.

2. Remove the front wheels. Properly support the lower control arm assemblies.

3. Remove the self-locking nuts, upper control arm bolts and upper control anchor bolts. Separate the upper ball joint using a suitable ball joint separator tool.

4. Place the upper control arm assembly into a suitable holding fixture and remove the self-locking nut, upper arm bolt, upper arm anchor bolts and housing seals.

5. Remove the upper arm collar. Drive out the upper arm bushing, using a suitable drift.

To install:

6. Replace the upper control arm bushings, bushing seals and upper control arm collar with new ones. Be sure to coat the ends and the insides of the upper control arm bushings, and the sealing lips of the upper control arm bushing with grease.

7. After Step 6 is completed, apply sealant to the threads and underside of the upper arm bolt heads and self-locking nut. Install the upper arm bolt and tighten the self-locking nut.

8. Installation of the remaining components is the reverse of the removal procedure.

Lower Control Arms

REMOVAL AND INSTALLATION

1. Raise the vehicle and support it safely. Remove the front wheels.

2. Properly support the lower control arm assembly. Disconnect the lower arm ball joint. Be careful not to damage the seal.

3. Remove the stabilizer bar retaining brackets, starting with the center brackets.

4. Remove the lower arm pivot bolt.

5. Disconnect the radius rod and remove the lower arm.

6. Installation is the reverse of the removal procedure. Tighten the lower control arm-to-chassis bolt to 40 ft. lbs. (55 Nm).

Sway Bar

REMOVAL AND INSTALLATION

1. Raise and safely support the vehicle.

2. Remove the front wheel and tire assemblies.

3. Disconnect the sway bar ends from both lower control arms.

4. Remove the bolts retaining the sway bar bushing brackets.

5. Remove the sway bar.

6. Installation is the reverse of the removal procedure.

REAR SUSPENSION

MacPherson Strut

REMOVAL AND INSTALLATION

Except 1992-94 Prelude

1. On Civic, del Sol, CRX, remove the strut upper cover from inside the vehicle and remove the upper strut retaining nuts.

2. On all other vehicles, remove the strut upper cover from inside the trunk and remove the upper strut retaining nuts.

3. Remove the speed sensor wire bracket. Do not disconnect the speed sensor.

4. Raise and safely support the vehicle.

5. Remove the rear wheel and tire assembly.

6. Remove the strut mounting bolt, lower the suspension and remove the strut.

7. Installation is the reverse of the removal procedure. Tighten the upper mounting nuts to 28 ft. lbs. (39 Nm). Tighten the strut lower mounting bolt to 40 ft. lbs. (55 Nm) with the strut under vehicle load.

1992-94 Prelude

1. Raise and safely support the vehicle.

2. Remove the trunk side trim and remove the 2 top strut nuts.

3. Remove the knuckle protector.

4. Remove the cotter pin and upper ball joint nut.

5. Fit a 10mm nut on the ball joint and separate the ball joint and the knuckle by using a ball joint removal tool.

6. Remove the lower strut mounting bolt and lower the suspension.

7. Remove the strut from the vehicle.

To install:

8. Install the strut to the vehicle and loosely install the lower mounting bolt. Do not tighten.

9. Install the upper strut mounting bolts. Tighten the bolts to 28 ft. lbs. (39 Nm).

10. Connect the upper arm and knuckle and tighten the castle nut to 29-35 ft. lbs. (40-48 Nm).

11. Install the knuckle protector with the bolt.

12. Raise the rear suspension with a floor jack until the weight is on the strut.

13. Tighten the lower strut mounting bolt to 47 ft. lbs. (65 Nm).

Rear Control Arms

REMOVAL AND INSTALLATION

Trailing Arm

EXCEPT ACCORD AND 1992 PRELUDE

1. Raise and safely support the vehicle.

2. Remove the rear wheel and tire assembly.

3. On all except 4WD Civic Wagon, perform the following procedure:

   a. Remove the brake drum or rotor.

   b. Remove the spindle nut and hub unit.

   c. Disconnect the parking brake cable and the brake line from the wheel cylinder. Plug the line.

   d. Remove the brake backing plate.

4. On 4WD Civic Wagon, remove the brake drum and spindle nut and disconnect the parking brake cable.

5. Disconnect the brake hose from the brake line. Plug the line.

6. Support the lower control arm or beam axle with a suitable jack.

7. Remove the trailing arm bushing mounting bolts.

8. Disconnect the upper arm and compensator arm from the trailing arm, if equipped.

9. On 4WD Civic Wagon, remove the rear halfshaft outboard CV-joint from the trailing arm using a suitable puller.

10. Remove the trailing arm from the vehicle.

11. Installation is the reverse of the removal procedure. Tighten all bolts and nuts with the vehicle on the ground. Bleed the brake system.

ACCORD AND 1992 PRELUDE

1. Raise and safely support the vehicle.

2. Remove the rear wheel and tire assembly.

3. Support the lower control arm using a suitable jack.

4. Remove the bolt from the trailing arm bushing.

5. Remove the mounting nuts from the knuckle and remove the trailing arm.

6. Installation is the reverse of the removal procedure.

Upper Control Arm

1. Raise and safely support the vehicle.

2. Remove the rear wheel and tire assembly.

3. Support the lower control arm or rear axle, as necessary.

4. On Accord and Prelude, remove the cotter pin and castle nut from the upper ball joint and use a suitable tool to separate the ball joint from the knuckle.

5. Remove the upper control arm mounting bolts and the upper control arm.

6. Installation is the reverse of the removal procedure.

Lower Control Arm

1. Raise and safely support the vehicle.

2. Remove the rear wheel and tire assembly.

3. Remove the strut and/or radius rod mounting bolts from the lower control arm, if necessary.

4. On Prelude, remove the cotter pin and castle nut from the ball joint and separate the ball joint from the knuckle using a suitable tool.

5. Remove the lower arm mounting bolts and remove the lower control arm.

6. Installation is the reverse of the removal procedure.

Rear Wheel Bearings

REMOVAL AND INSTALLATION

Accord and Civic

EXCEPT 4WD WAGON

NOTE: Do not tighten or loosen a spindle nut unless the vehicle is sitting on all 4 wheels. The torque is high enough to cause the vehicle to fall even when properly supported.

1. Loosen the rear lug nuts and the spindle nut. Raise the vehicle and support it safely.

2. Release the parking brake. Remove the rear wheel and the brake drum.

3. Remove the rear bearing hub cap and nut.

4. Pull the hub unit off the spindle.

5. Installation is the reverse order of removal. With the vehicle on the ground, torque the new spindle nut to 134 ft. lbs. (185 Nm), then stake the nut.

4WD WAGON

1. Raise and safely support the vehicle.

2. Remove the trailing arm from the vehicle.

3. Position the trailing arm in suitable hydraulic press. Press the hub from the trailing arm using a suitable driver while supporting the trailing arm.

NOTE: Be careful not to distort the brake backing plate. Hold onto the rear hub and trailing arm to keep it from falling when pressed clear.

4. Remove the outboard bearing inner race from the hub using a suitable bearing puller.

5. Remove the 64mm snapring.

6. Remove the bolts and the backing plate.

7. Remove the O-ring from the groove of the bearing holder plate.

8. Press the wheel bearing out of the trailing arm, using a suitable driver, while supporting the trailing arm.

To install:

9. Clean the trailing arm and hub thoroughly.

10. Press a new wheel bearing into the trailing arm, using a suitable driver, while supporting the trailing arm.

11. Install the O-ring on the groove of the bearing holder plate.

12. Install the backing plate and the snapring.

13. Press the trailing arm onto the hub, using a suitable guide and driver, while supporting the hub.

14. Installation of the remaining components is the reverse of the removal procedure.

1990-91 Prelude

1. Slightly loosen the rear lug nuts. Raise the vehicle and support it safely.

2. Release the parking brake. Remove the rear wheel and tire assemblies.

3. Remove the bolts retaining the brake caliper and remove the caliper from the knuckle. Do not let the caliper hang by the brake hose, support it with a length of wire.

4. Remove the two 6mm screws from the brake disc. Tighten the 8 x 12mm bolts into the holes of the brake disc, then remove the brake disc from the rear hub.

5. Remove the cotter pin of the lower arm B on 2 wheel steering vehicles or the tie rod on 4 wheel steering vehicles and remove the castle nut.

6. Separate the tie rod ball joint using a suitable ball joint removal tool.

7. Remove the cotter pin and loosen the lower arm ball joint nut half the length of the joint threads.

8. Separate the ball joint and lower arm using a suitable puller.

9. Remove the cotter pin and castle nut and separate the upper ball joint, using a ball joint removal tool. Remove the knuckle assembly from the vehicle.

10. Remove the rear hub spindle nut from the rear hub. Remove the splash guard mounting bolts. Using a hydraulic press, separate the hub from the knuckle.

NOTE: Set the rear hub at the hub/disc assembly base firmly, so the knuckle will not tilt the assembly in the press. Take care not to distort the splash guard. Hold onto the hub to keep it from falling after it is pressed out.

11. Remove the splash guard and 68mm circlip from the knuckle.

12. Using a hydraulic press and suitable press tools, press the wheel bearing out of the knuckle.

13. Remove the bearing inner race using a suitable bearing remover.

To install:

14. Place the rear wheel bearing in the tool fixture, then set the knuckle into position and apply downward pressure with a hydraulic press. Fit the 68mm circlip into the groove of the knuckle.

15. Install the splash guard. Place the hub in the tool fixture, then set the knuckle into position and apply downward pressure with a hydraulic press. Install the rear hub nut and torque the spindle nut to 180 ft. lbs. (250 Nm).

16. Install the knuckle assembly onto the vehicle and install all nuts and bolts loosely. Torque the lower ball joint nut to 40 ft. lbs. (55 Nm), then tighten as required to install a new cotter pin.

17. On vehicles with 4 wheel steering, torque the tie rod end joint to 32 ft. lbs. (44 Nm), then tighten as required to install a new cotter pin.

18. When everything is assembled, lower the vehicle and tighten the rubber bushing nuts and bolts with the weight of the vehicle on the wheels. Torque the upper bushing nut to 32

ft. lbs. (44 Nm) and the lower bushing bolt to 40 ft. lbs. (55 Nm).

19. Remove the exhaust header pipe.

20. Disconnect the hydraulic lines at the steering control unit. On 4 wheel steering vehicles, disconnect the driven drain hose.

21. Remove the mounting bolts and lower the front sway bar.

22. Move the tie rods aside.

23. Remove the gearbox mounting bolts.

24. Slide the gearbox right so the left tie rod clears the bottom of the rear beam. Remove the gearbox.

To install:

25. Position the gear box in the vehicle and torque the clamp bolts to 29 ft. lbs. (40 Nm).

26. Install the sway bar.

27. Connect the hydraulic lines and the exhaust pipe.

28. Connect the shift linkage.

29. Connect the tie rod ends to the steering knuckles. Torque the nuts to 32 ft. lbs. (44 Nm) and tighten as required to install a new cotter pin.

30. Connect the steering shaft coupling and torque to 22 ft. lbs. (30 Nm).

31. Fill the system with fluid and bleed the air from the system.

Power Steering Pump

REMOVAL AND INSTALLATION

1. Drain the fluid from the system as follows:

a. Disconnect the cooler return hose from the reservoir and place the end in a large container.

b. Start the engine and allow it to run at fast idle. Turn the steering wheel from lock-to-lock several times, until fluid stops running from the hose. Shut off the engine and discard the fluid.

c. Reattach the hose on all vehicles with a separate reservoir.

2. Disconnect the inlet and outlet hoses at the pump and plug them. Remove the drive belt.

3. Remove the bolts and remove the pump.

4. Installation is the reverse of the removal procedure. Adjust the belt tension, fill the reservoir and bleed the air from the system.

BELT ADJUSTMENT

1. Push on the belt mid way between the pulleys with a force of about 22 lbs. (98 N) The belt deflection should be as follows:

Civic and del Sol — 0.35-0.47 in. (9-12mm)

Accord — 0.50 — 0.62 in. (12.5-16mm)

Prelude

1990-91 — 0.43-0.51 in. (11-13mm)

1992-94 — 0.53-0.65 in. (13.5-16.5mm)

2. If belt deflection is not as specified, adjust as follows:

a. Accord — loosen the pivot bolt and mounting nut. Turn the adjusting bolt to get the proper tension. Tighten the pivot bolt to 33 ft. lbs. (45 Nm) and the mounting nut to 16 ft. lbs. (22 Nm).

b. Prelude and 1992-94 Civic and del Sol — loosen the adjusting pulley bolt and turn the adjusting bolt to get the proper tension. Tighten the pulley bolt to 35 ft. lbs. (49 Nm).

c. All others — loosen the pump pivot bolt and the adjusting nut or bolt. Pry the pump away from the engine to get the proper tension. Tighten the pivot bolt to 28 ft. lbs. (39 Nm). Tighten the adjusting nut or bolt to 28 ft. lbs. (39 Nm).

SYSTEM BLEEDING

1. Make sure the reservoir is filled to the full mark.

2. Start the engine and allow it to idle.

3. Turn the steering wheel from side-to-side several times, lightly contacting the stops.

4. Turn the engine OFF.

5. Check the fluid level in the reservoir and add if necessary.

Tie Rod Ends

REMOVAL AND INSTALLATION

1. Raise the vehicle and support it safely. Remove the front wheels.

2. Remove the cotter pins and castle nuts from the tie rod ends. Use a ball joint remover to remove the tie rod from the knuckle.

3. Disconnect the air tube at the dust seal joint. Remove the tie rod dust seal bellows clamps and move the rubber bellows on the tie rod rack joints.

4. Straighten the tie rod lock washer tabs at the tie rod-to-rack joint and remove the tie rod by turning it with a wrench.

5. To install, reverse the removal procedure. Always use a new tie rod

lock washer during reassembly. Install the locating lugs into the slots on the rack and bend the outer edge of the washer over the flat part of the rod, after the tie rod nut has been properly tightened.

6. Check the toe setting of the front end alignment.

STEERING

— CAUTION —

The 1991 Accord Wagon and all 1992-94 models are equipped with a driver's side air bag. Some 1992-94 Preludes are equipped with a passenger side air bag. To avoid accidental deployment and serious personal injury, the system must be disarmed before beginning any repair procedure.

Steering Wheel

REMOVAL AND INSTALLATION

All Except 1992-94 Civic, Civic Del Sol and Prelude

1. Disconnect the negative battery cable. Disarm the air bag, if equipped, and remove the air bag unit and/or the steering wheel pad. Disconnect the necessary electrical connections under the steering wheel pad.

2. Remove the steering wheel retaining nut. Remove the steering wheel by rocking it from side to side, as it is pulled up steadily by hand.

3. Installation is the reverse of the removal procedure. Be sure to tighten the steering wheel nut to 36 ft. lbs. (50 Nm).

1992-94 Civic, Civic Del Sol and Prelude

1. Disconnect the battery cables from the battery.

2. Remove the access panel from the lower half of the steering wheel rear cover.

3. Disconnect the connector between the air bag and the cable reel.

4. Connect the short connector to the electrical connector located on the air bag side.

5. Remove the lid and cruise control switch cover assembly.

6. Remove the Torx® bolt and the screw and remove the air bag.

7. Disconnect the horn and cruise control electrical connectors.

8. Remove the steering wheel nut and remove the steering wheel.

To install:

9. Center the cable reel by rotating the clockwise until it stops. Then rotate counterclockwise until the yellow gear tooth lines up with the mark on the cover and the arrow on the cable reel points straight up.

10. Install the steering wheel and tighten the bolt to 36 ft. lbs. (50 Nm).

11. The remaining steps are a reversal of the removal procedure.

Manual Rack and Pinion

REMOVAL AND INSTALLATION

1. Raise the vehicle and support it safely.

2. Remove the cover panel and steering joint cover. Unbolt and separate the steering shaft at the coupling.

3. Remove the front wheels.

4. Remove the cotter pins and unscrew the castle nuts on the tie rod ends. Using a ball joint tool disconnect the tie rod ends. Lift the tie rod ends out of the steering knuckles.

5. If equipped with manual transaxle, disconnect the shift lever torque rod from the clutch housing. Slide the pin retainer out of the way, drive out the spring pin and disconnect the shift rod.

6. If equipped with automatic transaxles, remove the shift cable guide from the floor and pull the shift cable down by hand.

7. Remove the 2 nut connecting the exhaust header pipe to the exhaust pipe and move the exhaust pipe out of the way.

8. Push the rack all the way to the right and remove the brackets or mounting bolts. Slide the tie rod ends all the way to the right.

9. Drop the rack far enough to permit the end of the pinion shaft to come out of the hole in the frame channel, then rotate it forward until the shaft is pointing rearward.

10. Slide the rack to the right until the left tie rod clears the exhaust pipe, then drop it down and out of the vehicle to the left.

To install:

11. Position the rack into the vehicle and torque the mounting bolts to 29 ft. lbs. (39 Nm).

12. Connect the exhaust pipe using a new gasket.

13. Reconnect the shift linkage and adjust as required.

14. Install the tie rod ends into the steering knuckle. Torque the nuts to 32 ft. lbs. (44 Nm), then tighten as required to install a new cotter pin.

15. Connect the steering shaft coupling and torque the bolt to 22 ft. lbs. (30 Nm).

Rear Wheel Steering Gear

Some Prelude are equipped with Four Wheel Steering (4WS).

REMOVAL AND INSTALLATION

1. Raise and safely support the vehicle.

2. Remove the rear wheel and tire assemblies.

3. Use a suitable tool to separate the tie-rods from the steering knuckles.

4. Slide the rear steering joint guard toward the front.

5. Remove the steering yoke bolt.

6. Remove the cap bolt and install rear steering center lock pin 07HAJ-1020A or equivalent, then remove the 4 rear steering gearbox bolts.

7. Remove the rear steering gearbox assembly.

8. Installation is the reverse of the removal procedure. Tighten the 4 gearbox mounting bolts to 29 ft. lbs. (40 Nm). Tighten the steering yoke bolt to 22 ft. lbs. (30 Nm). Tighten the tie-rod nuts to 32 ft. lbs. (44 Nm) and install new cotter pins.

Power Steering Rack and Pinion

REMOVAL AND INSTALLATION

Civic and Civic Del Sol

1. Disconnect the negative battery cable. Raise the vehicle and support it safely.

2. Remove the cover panel and steering joint cover. Unbolt and separate the steering shaft at the coupling.

3. Drain the power steering fluid by disconnecting the return hose at the box and running the engine while turning the steering wheel lock-to-lock until fluid stops draining. Remove the gearbox shield, if equipped. Remove the front wheels.

4. Remove the cotter pins and unscrew the castle nuts on the tie rod ends. Using a ball joint tool, disconnect the tie rod ends. Lift the tie rod ends out of the steering knuckles.

5. If equipped with manual transaxle, disconnect the shift lever torque rod from the clutch housing. Slide the pin retainer out of the way, drive out the spring pin and disconnect the shift rod.

6. If equipped with automatic transaxle, remove the shift cable guide from the floor and pull the shift cable down by hand.

7. On 1990-91 vehicles, remove the 2 nuts connecting the exhaust header pipe to the exhaust pipe and remove the exhaust header pipe. On the 1992-94 Civic and del Sol, remove the catalytic converter. Disconnect the 3 hydraulic lines from the control unit.

8. Slide the tie rod ends all the way to the right and remove the steering rack mounting bolts.

9. Drop the gearbox far enough to permit the end of the pinion shaft to come out of the hole in the frame channel, then rotate it forward until the shaft is pointing rearward.

10. Slide the gearbox to the right until the left tie rod clears the beam, then drop it down and out of the vehicle to the left.

11. Installation is the reverse of removal. Torque the mounting bracket bolts to 29 ft. lbs. (40 Nm). If equipped with a manual transaxle, reinstall the pin retainer after driving in the pin and be sure the projection on the pin retainer is in the hole.

12. Fill the system with fluid and bleed the air from the system.

Accord and Prelude

1. Disconnect the negative battery cable. Raise the vehicle and support it safely.

2. Remove the steering shaft joint cover and disconnect the steering shaft at the coupling.

3. Drain the power steering fluid by disconnecting the return hose at the box and running the engine, while turning the steering wheel lock-to-lock until fluid stops draining.

4. Remove the gearbox shield.

5. Remove the front wheels.

6. Using a ball joint tool, disconnect the tie rods from the knuckles.

7. If equipped with manual transaxle, remove the shift extension from the transaxle case. Disconnect the gear shift rod from the transaxle case by removing the 8mm bolt.

8. If equipped with automatic transaxle, remove the control cable clamp.

9. On Prelude, remove the center beam.

10. On the 4 wheel steering vehicles, separate the joint guard cap and

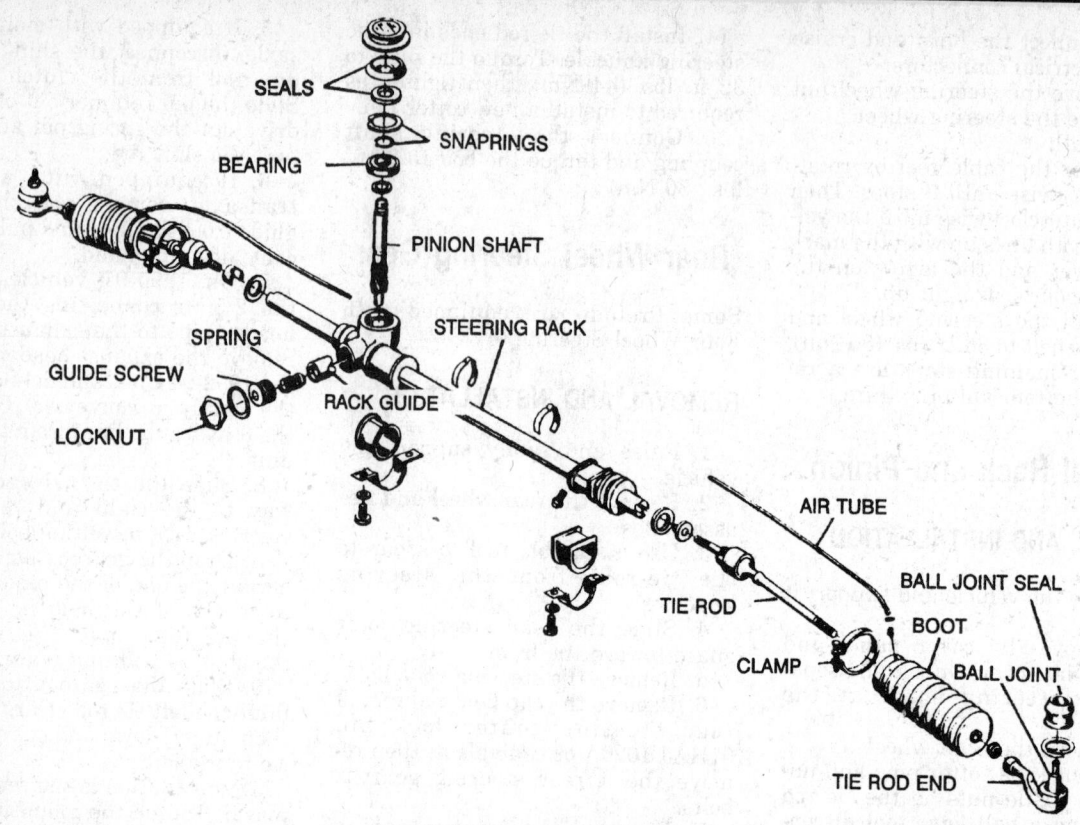

SEALS

SNAPRINGS

BEARING

PINION SHAFT

SPRING

GUIDE SCREW

STEERING RACK

LOCKNUT

RACK GUIDE

AIR TUBE

BALL JOINT SEAL

BOOT

TIE ROD

CLAMP

BALL JOINT

TIE ROD END

Manual steering box and linkage

the joint guard. Remove the joint bolt from the driven pinion side. Remove the joint bolt from the center steering shaft side, then slide the joint back to disconnect it from the driven pinion.

11. Remove the exhaust header pipe.

12. Disconnect the hydraulic lines at the steering control unit. On 4 wheel steering vehicles, disconnect the driven drain hose.

13. On Prelude, remove the mounting bolts and lower the front sway bar.

14. Move the tie rods aside.

15. Remove the gearbox mounting bolts.

16. Slide the gearbox right so the left tie rod clears the bottom of the rear beam. Remove the gearbox.

To install:

17. Position the gear box in the vehicle and torque the clamp bolts to 29 ft. lbs. (40 Nm).

18. On Prelude, install the sway bar.

19. Connect the hydraulic lines and the exhaust pipe.

20. Connect the shift linkage.

21. Connect the tie rod ends to the steering knuckles. Torque the nuts to 32 ft. lbs. (44 Nm) and tighten as required to install a new cotter pin.

22. Connect the steering shaft coupling and torque to 22 ft. lbs. (30 Nm).

23. Fill the system with fluid and bleed the air from the system.

Power Steering Pump

REMOVAL AND INSTALLATION

1. Drain the fluid from the system as follows:

   a. Disconnect the cooler return hose from the reservoir and place the end in a large container.

   b. Start the engine and allow it to run at fast idle. Turn the steering wheel from lock-to-lock several times, until fluid stops running from the hose. Shut off the engine and discard the fluid.

   c. Reattach the hose on all vehicles with a separate reservoir.

2. Disconnect the inlet and outlet hoses at the pump and plug them. Remove the drive belt.

3. Remove the bolts and remove the pump.

4. Installation is the reverse of the removal procedure. Adjust the belt tension, fill the reservoir and bleed the air from the system.

BELT ADJUSTMENT

1. Push on the belt mid way between the pulleys with a force of about 22 lbs. (98 N) The belt deflection should be as follows:

Civic and del Sol — 0.35-0.47 in. (9-12mm)

Accord — 0.50 — 0.62 in. (12.5-16mm)

Prelude

1990-91 — 0.43-0.51 in. (11-13mm)

1992-94 — 0.53-0.65 in. (13.5-16.5mm)

2. If belt deflection is not as specified, adjust as follows:

   a. Accord — loosen the pivot bolt and mounting nut. Turn the adjusting bolt to get the proper tension. Tighten the pivot bolt to 33 ft. lbs. (45 Nm) and the mounting nut to 16 ft. lbs. (22 Nm).

   b. Prelude and 1992-94 Civic and del Sol — loosen the adjusting pulley bolt and turn the adjusting bolt to get the proper tension. Tighten the pulley bolt to 35 ft. lbs. (49 Nm).

   c. All others — loosen the pump pivot bolt and the adjusting nut or bolt. Pry the pump away from the engine to get the proper tension. Tighten the pivot bolt to 28 ft. lbs.

(39 Nm). Tighten the adjusting nut or bolt to 28 ft. lbs. (39 Nm).

SYSTEM BLEEDING

1. Make sure the reservoir is filled to the full mark.
2. Start the engine and allow it to idle.
3. Turn the steering wheel from side-to-side several times, lightly contacting the stops.
4. Turn the engine OFF.
5. Check the fluid level in the reservoir and add if necessary.

Tie Rod Ends

REMOVAL AND INSTALLATION

1. Raise the vehicle and support it safely. Remove the front wheels.
2. Remove the cotter pins and castle nuts from the tie rod ends. Use a ball joint remover to remove the tie rod from the knuckle.
3. Disconnect the air tube at the dust seal joint. Remove the tie rod dust seal bellows clamps and move the rubber bellows on the tie rod rack joints.
4. Straighten the tie rod lock washer tabs at the tie rod-to-rack joint and remove the tie rod by turning it with a wrench.
5. To install, reverse the removal procedure. Always use a new tie rod lock washer during reassembly. Install the locating lugs into the slots on the rack and bend the outer edge of the washer over the flat part of the rod, after the tie rod nut has been properly tightened.
6. Check the toe setting of the front end alignment.

BRAKES

Master Cylinder

REMOVAL AND INSTALLATION

1. Disconnect the negative battery cable. Disconnect and plug the brake lines at the master cylinder.
2. Remove the master cylinder-to-vacuum booster attaching bolts and remove the master cylinder from the vehicle.
3. To install, reverse the removal procedure. Before operating the vehicle, bleed the brake system.

Proportioning Valve

REMOVAL AND INSTALLATION

1. Disconnect the negative battery cable.
2. Disconnect and plug the brake lines at the valve.
3. Remove the valve mounting bolts and the valve.
4. Installation is the reverse of the removal procedure. Bleed the brake system.

Power Brake Booster

REMOVAL AND INSTALLATION

1. Disconnect the negative battery cable. Disconnect the vacuum hose at the booster and remove the bracket.
2. It may be possible to remove the master cylinder to brake booster retaining nuts and then position the master cylinder assembly to the side on some vehicles. If not, the master cylinder will have to be removed from the vehicle.
3. It may be necessary to remove the throttle/cruise control cable bracket and the grommet from the bulkhead.
4. Remove the brake pedal-to-booster link pin and the 4 nuts retaining the booster. The pushrod and nuts are located inside the vehicle under the instrument panel.
5. Remove the booster assembly from the vehicle.
6. To install, reverse the removal procedure. If the master cylinder was removed, bleed the brake system.
7. Check and adjust the brake pedal height as necessary.

Brake Caliper

REMOVAL AND INSTALLATION

Front

1. Raise and safely support the vehicle.
2. Remove the front wheel and tire assembly.
3. Remove the banjo bolt and disconnect the brake hose from the caliper. Plug the hose.
4. Remove the mounting bolt(s) and the caliper.
To install:
5. Clean the caliper thoroughly. Place the caliper into position and install the mounting bolts. Use new gaskets on the banjo bolt and torque to 25 ft. lbs. (35 Nm).

6. On vehicles that have long pins below the threads of the caliper bolt, torque the bolt to 54 ft. lbs. (75 Nm).
7. On all vehicles except 1992-94 Civic and del Sol, that have short bolts with no pin beyond the threads, torque the bolt to 36 ft. lbs. (50 Nm). On 1992-94 Civic and del Sol, tighten the bolts to 20 ft. lbs. (27 Nm).
8. Bleed the brakes.

Rear

1. Raise and safely support the vehicle.
2. Remove the rear wheel and tire assembly.
3. Remove the caliper shield.
4. Disconnect the parking brake cable from the lever on the caliper by removing the lock pin.
5. Remove the banjo bolt and disconnect the brake hose from the caliper. Plug the hose.
6. Remove the 2 caliper mounting bolts and the caliper from the bracket.
7. Installation is the reverse of the removal procedure. Use new gaskets on the banjo bolt and torque to 25 ft. lbs. (35 Nm).
8. Torque the caliper bracket bolts to 20 ft. lbs. (25 Nm).
9. Bleed the brakes.

Disc Brake Pads

REMOVAL AND INSTALLATION

Front

1. Remove the master cylinder cover and remove half the quantity of brake fluid in the master cylinder.
2. Raise and support the vehicle safely. Remove the tire and wheel assemblies.
3. If required, separate the brake hose clamp from the knuckle by removing the retaining bolts.
4. Remove the lower caliper retaining bolt and pivot the caliper out of the way.
5. Remove the pad shim and pad retainers. Remove the disc brake pads from the caliper.
To install:
6. Clean the caliper thoroughly. Check the brake rotor for grooves or cracks and machine or replace, as necessary.
7. Install the pad retainers. Apply a suitable disc brake pad lubricant to both surfaces of the shims and the back of the disc brake pads. Do not get any lubricant on the braking surface of the pad.
8. Install the pads and shims.

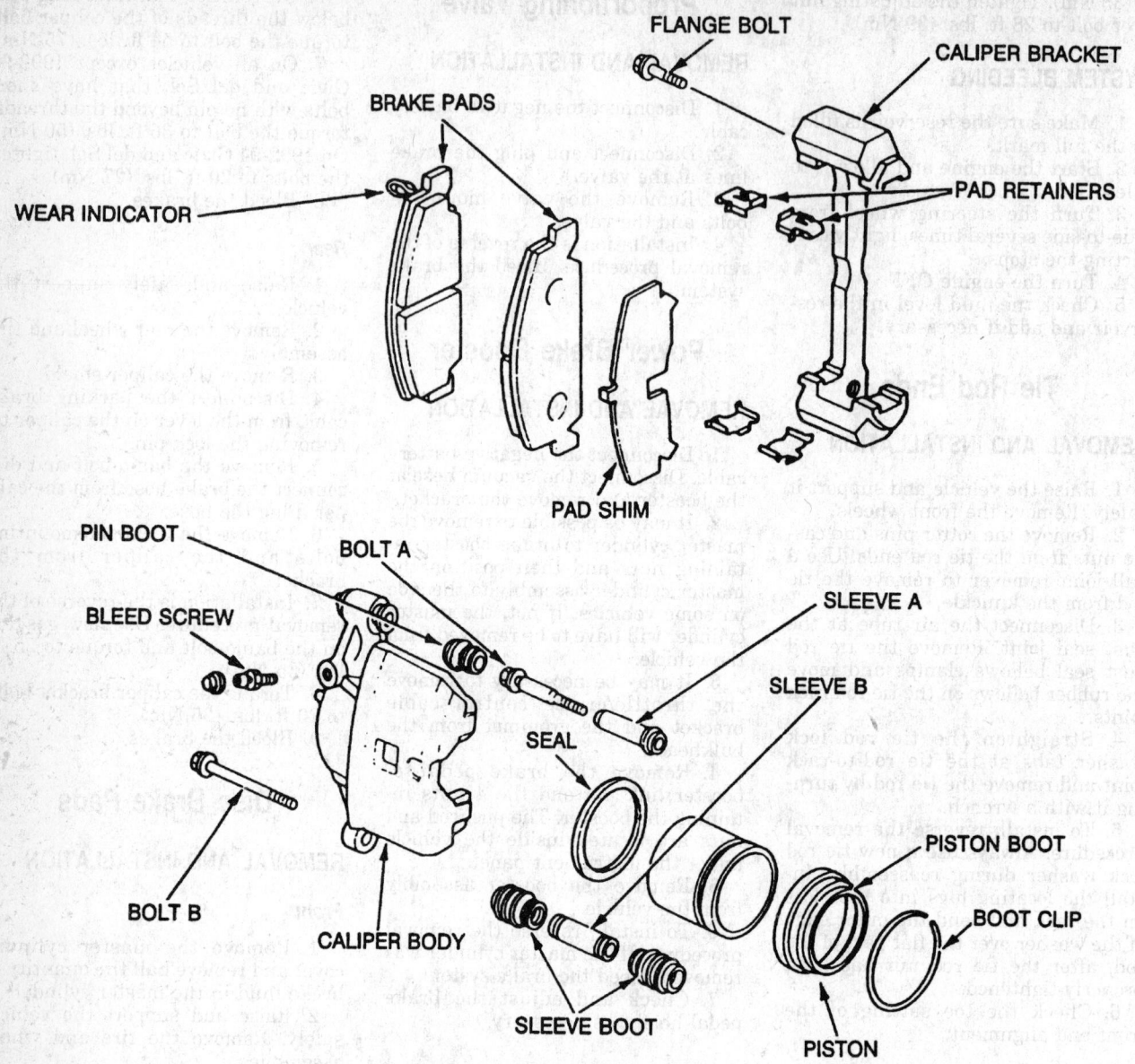

FLANGE BOLT

CALIPER BRACKET

BRAKE PADS

PAD RETAINERS

WEAR INDICATOR

PAD SHIM

PIN BOOT

BOLT A

SLEEVE A

BLEED SCREW

SLEEVE B

SEAL

PISTON BOOT

BOOT CLIP

BOLT B

CALIPER BODY

SLEEVE BOOT

PISTON

Front disc brake assembly — Civic shown, others similar

9. Use a suitable tool to push in the caliper piston so the caliper will fit over the pads.

10. Pivot the caliper down into position and tighten the mounting bolts.

11. Connect the brake hose to the knuckle, if removed. Install the wheel and tire assembly and lower the vehicle.

12. Check the master cylinder and add fluid as required, then replace the master cylinder cover. Depress the brake pedal several times to seat the pads.

Rear

1. Remove the master cylinder cover and remove half the quantity of brake fluid.

2. Raise and safely support the vehicle. Remove the rear wheel and tire assemblies.

3. Remove the caliper shield, if equipped.

4. Remove the 2 caliper mounting bolts and the caliper from the bracket.

5. Remove the pads, shims and pad retainers.

To install:

6. Clean the caliper thoroughly. Check the brake rotor for grooves or

cracks and machine or replace, as necessary.

7. Install the pad retainers. Apply a suitable disc brake pad lubricant to both surfaces of the shims and the back of the disc brake pads. Do not get any lubricant on the braking surface of the pad.

8. Install the pads and shims.

9. Use a suitable tool to rotate the caliper piston clockwise into the caliper bore, enough to fit over the brake pads. Lubricate the piston boot with silicone grease to avoid twisting the piston boot.

10. Install the brake caliper, aligning the cutout in the piston with the

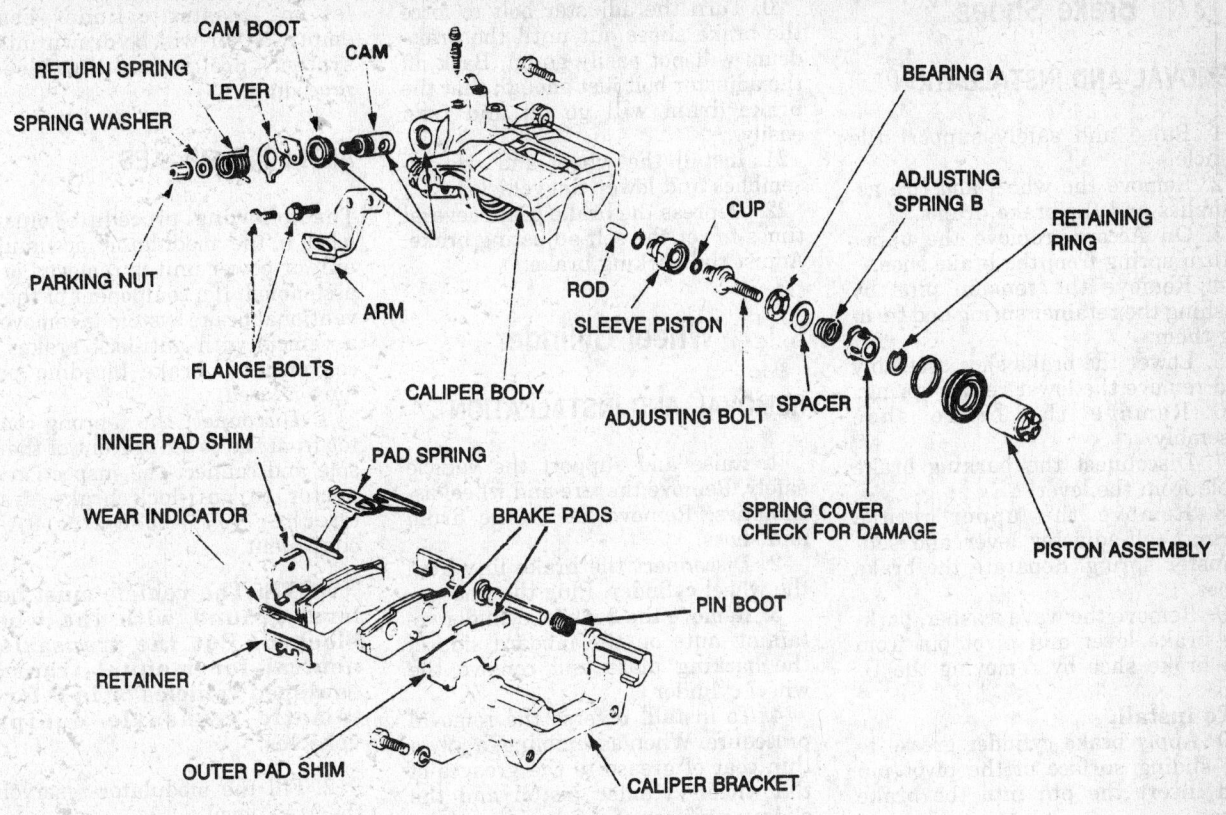

RETURN SPRING · CAM BOOT · CAM · LEVER · SPRING WASHER · PARKING NUT · FLANGE BOLTS · ARM · CALIPER BODY · ROD · SLEEVE PISTON · ADJUSTING BOLT · CUP · SPACER · SPRING COVER CHECK FOR DAMAGE · ADJUSTING SPRING B · BEARING A · RETAINING RING · PISTON ASSEMBLY · INNER PAD SHIM · WEAR INDICATOR · RETAINER · OUTER PAD SHIM · PAD SPRING · BRAKE PADS · PIN BOOT · CALIPER BRACKET

Rear disc brake assembly

tab on the inner pad. Tighten the mounting bolts.

11. Install the wheel and tire assemblies and lower the vehicle.

12. Check the fluid in the master cylinder and add, as required, then replace the master cylinder cover. Depress the brake pedal several times to seat the pads.

Brake Rotor

REMOVAL AND INSTALLATION

Except Accord

1. Raise and safely support the vehicle.

2. Remove the wheel and tire assembly.

3. Disconnect the caliper from the caliper bracket. Support the caliper out of the way with a length of wire. Do not allow the caliper to hang from the brake hose.

4. Remove the caliper bracket.

5. Remove the 6mm screws and the brake disc. If the brake disc is difficult to remove, install two 8mm bolts into the threaded holes and tighten them evenly to prevent cocking the rotor.

6. Installation is the reverse of the removal procedure.

Accord

1. Pry the spindle nut stake away from the spindle, then loosen the nut.

2. Raise and safely support the vehicle.

3. Remove the wheel and tire assembly and the spindle nut.

4. Remove the caliper and support it out of the way with a length of wire. Do not allow the caliper to hang from the brake hose. Remove the caliper bracket.

5. Remove the cotter pin and tie rod ball joint nut. Separate the tie rod from the steering knuckle using a suitable tool.

6. Remove the cotter pin and loosen the lower arm ball joint nut half the length of the joint threads. Separate the ball joint and lower arm using a suitable puller. Remove the lower ball joint nut.

7. Pull the steering knuckle outward and remove the halfshaft outboard CV-joint from the knuckle, using a suitable plastic hammer.

8. Remove the 4 bolts retaining the hub unit to the steering knuckle and remove the hub unit.

9. Remove the 4 bolts, then separate the hub unit from the brake rotor.

To install:

10. Assemble the disc to the hub unit and torque the bolts to 40 ft. lbs. (55 Nm).

11. When installing the hub to the knuckle, use new self-locking bolts and torque to 33 ft. lbs. (45 Nm).

12. When installing the steering knuckle, torque the upper nut to 32 ft. lbs. (44 Nm) and the lower ball joint nut to 40 ft. lbs. (55 Nm), then tighten as required to install a new cotter pin.

Brake Drums

REMOVAL AND INSTALLATION

1. Raise and safely support the vehicle.

2. Remove the rear wheel and tire assembly.

3. Remove the brake drum.

4. Installation is the reverse of the removal procedure. Adjust the brakes if necessary.

Brake Shoes

REMOVAL AND INSTALLATION

1. Raise and safely support the vehicle.
2. Remove the wheel and tire assemblies and the brake drums.
3. On Accord, remove the upper return spring from the brake shoe.
4. Remove the tension pins by pushing the retainer spring and turning them.
5. Lower the brake shoe assembly and remove the lower return spring.
6. Remove the brake shoe assembly.
7. Disconnect the parking brake cable from the lever.
8. Remove the upper return spring, self-adjuster lever and self-adjuster spring. Separate the brake shoes.
9. Remove the wave washer, parking brake lever and pivot pin from the brake shoe by removing the U-clip.

To install:

10. Apply brake cylinder grease to the sliding surface of the pivot pin and insert the pin into the brake shoe.
11. Install the parking brake lever and wave washer on the pivot pin and secure with the U-clip.

NOTE: Pinch the U-clip securely to prevent the pivot pin from coming out of the brake shoe.

12. Connect the parking brake cable to the parking brake lever.
13. Apply grease on each sliding surface of the brake backing plate.

NOTE: Do not allow grease to come in contact with the brake linings. Grease will contaminate the linings and reduce stopping power.

14. Clean the threaded portions of the adjuster bolt. Coat the threads with grease. Turn the adjuster bolt to shorten the clevises.
15. Hook the adjuster spring to the adjuster lever first, then to the brake shoe.
16. Install the adjuster bolt/clevis assembly and the upper return spring.
17. Install the brake shoes to the backing plate.
18. Install the lower return spring, the tension pins and retaining springs.
19. On Accord, connect the upper return spring.

20. Turn the adjuster bolt to force the brake shoes out until the brake drum will not easily go on. Back off the adjuster bolt just enough that the brake drum will go on and turn easily.
21. Install the wheel and tire assemblies and lower the vehicle.
22. Depress the brake pedal several times to set the self-adjusting brake. Adjust the parking brake.

Wheel Cylinder

REMOVAL AND INSTALLATION

1. Raise and support the vehicle safely. Remove the tire and wheel assemblies. Remove the brake drum and shoes.
2. Disconnect the brake line from the wheel cylinder. Plug the line.
3. Remove the 2 wheel cylinder retaining nuts on the inboard side of the backing plate and remove the wheel cylinder.
4. To install, reverse the removal procedure. When assembling, apply a thin coat of grease to the grooves of the wheel cylinder piston and the sliding surfaces of the backing plate. Bleed the brakes.

Brake System Bleeding

CONVENTIONAL BRAKES

1. Make sure the master cylinder reservoir is full.
2. Raise and safely support the vehicle.
3. Connect a suitable piece of clear tubing to the bleeder screw and submerge the other end in a clear container half filled with clean brake fluid.
4. Have an assistant slowly pump the brake pedal several times, then apply steady pressure.
5. Loosen the bleeder screw to allow air to escape from the system, then tighten the bleeder screw. Repeat Steps 4 and 5 until air bubbles no longer appear in the fluid.
6. This procedure should be repeated at each wheel. The brake system should be bled in the following sequence:

   Left front
   Right rear
   Right front
   Left rear

7. Periodically check the fluid level in the master cylinder during the brake bleeding procedure. Do not

let the master cylinder become empty, as air will be drawn into the system, prolonging the bleeding procedure.

ANTI-LOCK BRAKES

The following procedure must be used if the modulator, accumulator unit or power unit is removed or disassembled. If a component of the conventional brake system is removed on a vehicle with anti-lock brakes, the conventional brake bleeding procedure is used.

1. Disconnect the 6-prong connector from the cover in front of the console and connect the inspection connector to anti-lock brake system checker 07HAJ-SG0010A or equivalent.

NOTE: The vehicle must be on level ground with the wheels blocked. Put the transaxle in neutral for manual transaxle equipped vehicles or in P for automatic transaxle equipped vehicles.

2. Fill the modulator reservoir to the MAX level.

NOTE: Do not reuse aerated brake fluid that has been bled from the power unit.

3. Remove the red cap from the maintenance bleeder. Use bleeder T-wrench 07HAA-SG00101 or equivalent, to bleed high pressure fluid from the maintenance bleeder.
4. Start the engine and release the parking brake.
5. Turn the mode selector to 6 on the anti-lock brake checker, depress the brake pedal firmly and press the Start Test button. There should be at least 2 strong kickbacks. If not, repeat Steps 2-5, as necessary.
6. Fill the modulator reservoir up to the MAX level.
7. Install the reservoir cap.
8. Check the anti-lock brake function in all modes by using the anti-lock brake checker.

Anti-Lock Brake System Service

PRECAUTIONS

Before disassembling or removing the modulator, accumulator unit or power unit, the accumulator line pressure must be relieved.

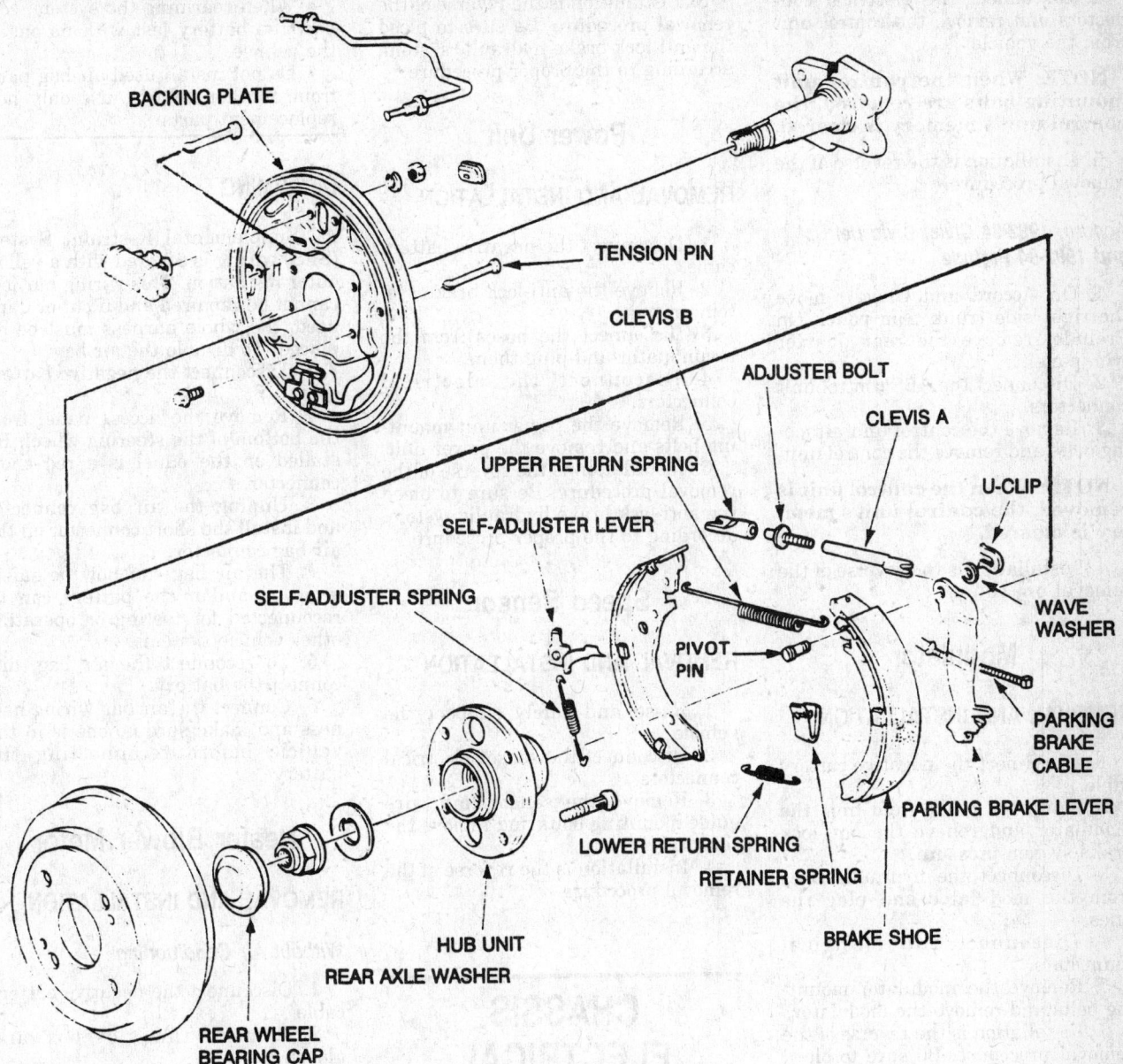

BACKING PLATE

TENSION PIN

CLEVIS B

ADJUSTER BOLT

CLEVIS A

U-CLIP

UPPER RETURN SPRING

SELF-ADJUSTER LEVER

WAVE WASHER

SELF-ADJUSTER SPRING

PIVOT PIN

PARKING BRAKE CABLE

PARKING BRAKE LEVER

LOWER RETURN SPRING

RETAINER SPRING

BRAKE SHOE

HUB UNIT

REAR AXLE WASHER

REAR WHEEL BEARING CAP

Rear drum brake assembly

RELIEVING ANTI-LOCK BRAKE SYSTEM PRESSURE

1. Drain the brake fluid from the master cylinder and modulator reservoir thoroughly. The master cylinder can be drained by loosening the bleed screw and pumping the brake pedal to drain the brake fluid. The brake fluid can be sucked out through the top of the modulator tank with a syringe.
2. Remove the red cap from the bleeder on the top of the power unit.

3. Install bleeder T-wrench 07HAA-SG00101 or equivalent, on the bleeder screw and turn it out slowly 90 degrees to collect high pressure fluid into the reservoir. Turn the T-wrench out 1 complete turn to drain the brake fluid thoroughly.
4. Retighten the bleeder screw and discard the fluid. Reinstall the red cap.

Anti-Lock Brake System Control Unit

REMOVAL AND INSTALLATION

1990-91 Prelude

1. Disconnect the negative battery cable.
2. Remove the cover that is mounted in front of the center console.
3. Remove the control unit mounting bolts, then remove the control unit.

4. Disconnect the electrical connectors and remove the control unit from the vehicle.

NOTE: When the control unit mounting bolts are removed, the control unit's memory is cleared.

5. Installation is the reverse of the removal procedure.

Accord, 1992-94 Civic, Civic Del Sol and 1992-94 Prelude

1. On Accord and Civic, remove the right side trunk trim panel. On Prelude, remove the rear quarter trim panel.
2. Disconnect the ABS control unit connectors.
3. Remove the control unit attaching bolts and remove the control unit.

NOTE: When the control unit is removed, the control unit's memory is cleared.

4. Installation is the reverse of the removal procedure.

Modulator

REMOVAL AND INSTALLATION

1. Disconnect the negative battery cable.
2. Drain the brake fluid from the modulator and relieve the anti-lock brake system pressure.
3. Disconnect the hydraulic lines from the modulator and plug the lines.
4. Disconnect the electrical connectors.
5. Remove the modulator mounting bolts and remove the modulator.
6. Installation is the reverse of the removal procedure. Be sure to bleed the anti-lock brake hydraulic system, according to the proper procedure.

Accumulator

REMOVAL AND INSTALLATION

1. Disconnect the negative battery cable.
2. Relieve the anti-lock brake system pressure.
3. Disconnect the hydraulic lines from the accumulator and plug the lines.
4. Disconnect the electrical connectors.
5. Remove the accumulator mounting bolts and remove the accumulator.

6. Installation is the reverse of the removal procedure. Be sure to bleed the anti-lock brake hydraulic system, according to the proper procedure.

Power Unit

REMOVAL AND INSTALLATION

1. Disconnect the negative battery cable.
2. Relieve the anti-lock brake system pressure.
3. Disconnect the hoses from the accumulator and plug them.
4. Disconnect the electrical connectors.
5. Remove the power unit mounting bolts and remove the power unit.
6. Installation is the reverse of the removal procedure. Be sure to bleed the anti-lock brake hydraulic system, according to the proper procedure.

Speed Sensor

REMOVAL AND INSTALLATION

1. Raise and safely support the vehicle.
2. Disconnect the sensor electrical connectors.
3. Remove the sensor and wire guide mounting bolts and remove the sensor.
4. Installation is the reverse of the removal procedure.

CHASSIS ELECTRICAL

Air Bag

——— CAUTION ———
To avoid accidental deployment and serious personal injury, the air bag system must be disarmed before beginning any repair procedure. Read the following safety precautions.

• Do not disassemble or tamper with the air bag assembly.
• Be sure to store a removed air bag assembly with the pad surface up. If the air bag is improperly stored face down, accidental deployment could propel the unit with enough force to cause serious injury.

• When rearming the system, connect the battery last with no one in the vehicle.
• Do not install used air bag parts from another vehicle, use only new replacement parts.

DISARMING

All Supplemental Restraint System (SRS) wiring is covered with a yellow outer insulation. This wiring harness cannot be repaired and if cut or damaged, the whole harness must be replaced. To disable the air bag:
1. Disconnect the negative battery cable.
2. Remove the access panel from the bottom of the steering wheel. Installed on the panel is a red short connector.
3. Unplug the air bag connector and install the short connector on the air bag connector.
4. The air bag can now be safely removed and/or the battery can be reconnected for testing or operating other vehicle systems.
5. To reconnect the air bag, disconnect the battery.
6. Connect the air bag wiring harness and make sure no one is in the vehicle before reconnecting the battery.

Heater Blower Motor

REMOVAL AND INSTALLATION

Without Air Conditioning

1. Disconnect the negative battery cable.
2. Remove the glovebox and glovebox frame.
3. Remove the heater duct.
4. Disconnect the electrical connectors from the blower motor.
5. Remove the blower motor mounting bolts and the blower motor.
6. Installation is the reverse of the removal procedure.

With Air Conditioning

EXCEPT ACCORD

1. Disconnect the negative battery cable.

NOTE: The air bag must be disabled before removing the blower motor on the 1992-94 Prelude.

2. Properly discharge the air conditioning system.

3. Disconnect the receiver line and suction hose from the evaporator.

NOTE: Cap the open fittings immediately to keep moisture out of the system.

4. Remove the glovebox and glovebox frame.

5. Disconnect the drain hose from the evaporator lower housing, if equipped.

6. Loosen the sealing band if equipped, and slide it to the right.

7. Disconnect the thermostat switch wire connector and pull the wire from the clamps.

8. Remove the evaporator and blower retaining bands, as necessary.

9. Remove the evaporator mounting bolts and remove the evaporator.

10. Disconnect the blower motor electrical connectors.

11. Remove the blower motor mounting bolts and remove the blower motor.

To install:

12. Install the blower motor and connect the wiring.

13. Install the evaporator and connect the switch wiring. Connect the drain hose to the housing.

14. Connect the air conditioning hoses. Evacuate and charge the system.

15. After the system is working properly, finish installing the glove compartment and other dashboard parts.

ACCORD

1. Disconnect the negative battery cable.

2. Remove the glovebox and the glovebox frame.

3. Turn over the carpet and remove the side cover. Remove the control unit bracket mounting nuts. Disconnect the connectors and remove the control unit bracket.

4. Remove the retaining band and remove the blower undercover.

NOTE: Be careful not to break the tabs while removing the blower undercover.

5. Remove the blower mounting nuts, disconnect the electrical connectors and remove the blower.

6. Installation is the reverse of the removal procedure. When installing the glovebox frame, the face which covers the dashboard is installed with double-sided adhesive tape.

Windshield Wiper Motor

REMOVAL AND INSTALLATION

1. Disconnect the negative battery cable.

2. Remove the wiper arm retaining nuts and remove the wiper arms.

3. Remove the front air scoop, if equipped, and hood seal located over the wiper linkage at the bottom of the windshield.

4. Disconnect the linkage from the wiper motor.

5. Remove the wiper motor water seal cover clamp and remove the cover, if equipped.

6. Disconnect the wiper motor electrical connector, remove the motor mounting bolts and remove the motor.

To install:

7. Place the motor into position and install the mounting bolts. Connect the motor electrical connector.

8. Coat the linkage joints with grease and install. Make sure the linkage moves smoothly.

9. Install the front air scoop, if equipped, and hood seal located over the wiper linkage at the bottom of the windshield.

10. Install the wiper arms.

11. Connect the negative battery cable. Check the wipers operation.

Windshield Wiper Switch

REMOVAL AND INSTALLATION

1. Disconnect the negative battery cable.

2. Remove the dashboard lower cover and knee bolster panel.

3. Remove the upper and lower steering column covers.

4. Disconnect the switch electrical connector and remove the retaining screws. Remove the switch from the vehicle.

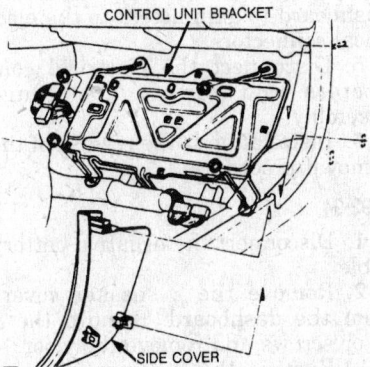

Control unit location — Accord

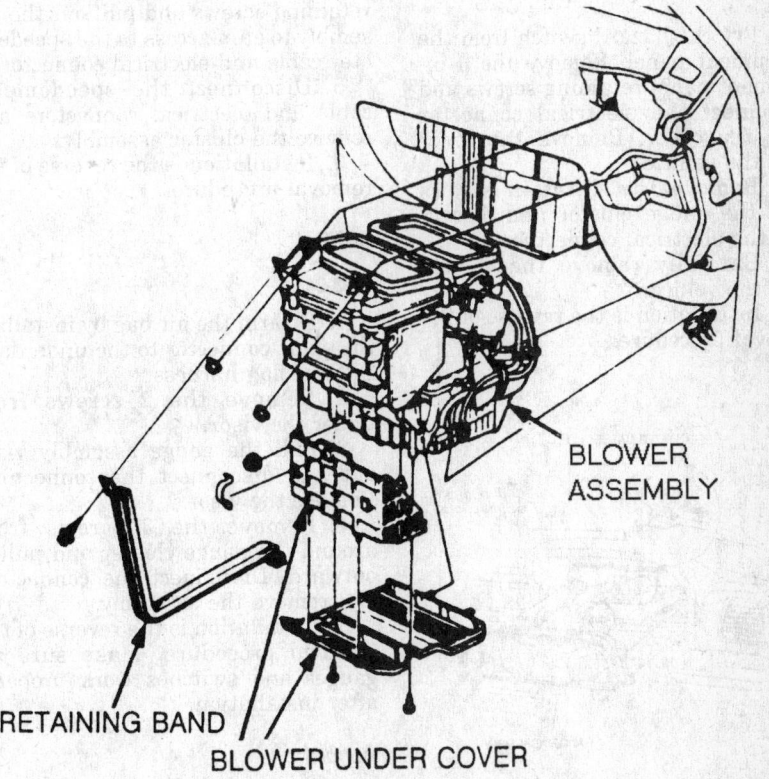

Blower installation — Accord

5. Installation is the reverse of the removal procedure.

Instrument Cluster

REMOVAL AND INSTALLATION

Civic

1990-91

1. Disconnect the negative battery cable.
2. Remove the caps positioned over the 2 gauge visor retaining screws. Remove the gauge visor retaining screws and remove the gauge visor.
3. Remove the 4 screws retaining the instrument panel to the dashboard, disconnect the switch connectors and remove the instrument panel.
4. Remove the 4 screws retaining the gauge assembly and pull out the assembly to gain access to the speedometer cable and the electrical connectors.
5. Disconnect the speedometer cable and electrical connectors and remove the cluster assembly.
6. Installation is the reverse of the removal procedure.

1992-94

1. Disconnect the negative battery cable.
2. Pry the hazard switch from the instrument panel. Remove the 3 instrument panel retaining screws and disconnect the electrical connector from the cover. Remove the cover from the vehicle.
3. Remove the 4 retain screws from the gauge cluster and disconnect the electrical connectors.
4. Carefully remove the cluster from the vehicle.
5. Installation is the reverse of the removal procedure.

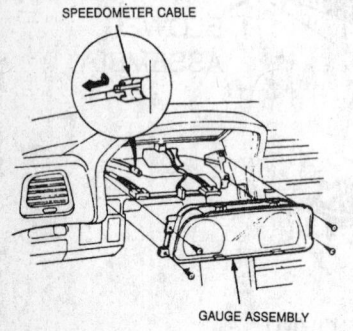

SPEEDOMETER CABLE

GAUGE ASSEMBLY

Instrument cluster installation — 1990-91 Civic (1992-94 similar)

Civic Wagon

1. Disconnect the negative battery cable.
2. Remove the caps positioned over the upper instrument panel retaining screws. Remove the upper and lower instrument panel retaining screws.
3. Disconnect the switch connectors and remove the instrument panel.
4. Remove the 4 gauge assembly retaining screws and pull out the assembly to gain access to the speedometer cable and electrical connectors.
5. Disconnect the speedometer cable and electrical connectors and remove the gauge assembly.
6. Installation is the reverse of the removal procedure.

CRX

1990-91

1. Disconnect the negative battery cable.
2. Remove the caps positioned over the upper instrument panel retaining screws. Remove the upper and lower instrument panel retaining screws.
3. Disconnect the switch connectors and remove the instrument panel.
4. Remove the 4 gauge assembly retaining screws and pull out the assembly to gain access to the speedometer cable and electrical connectors.
5. Disconnect the speedometer cable and electrical connectors and remove the cluster assembly.
6. Installation is the reverse of the removal procedure.

Del Sol

1993-94

1. Disarm the air bag by installing the short connector to the underdash SRS/air bag harness.
2. Remove the 2 screws from under the visor.
3. Pull the gauge assembly visor out and disconnect the connectors. Remove the visor.
4. Remove the 3 screws from around the gauge cluster and pull it outward. Disconnect the connectors and remove the assembly.
5. Installation is the reverse of the removal procedure. Make sure all gauges and switches work properly after installation.

Accord

1. Disconnect the negative battery cable.

2. Remove the front console mounting screws. On manual transaxle equipped vehicles, remove the shift lever knob.
3. Remove the front console.
4. Remove the ashtray and ashtray holder.
5. Loosen the 2 screws retaining the radio and disconnect the wire harness connector and the antenna lead. Remove the radio.
6. Remove the coin box, cruise control master switch, sunroof switch and panel brightness controller.
7. Remove the side and center air vents.
8. Remove the 12 mounting screws and disconnect the electrical connectors.
9. Remove the instrument panel.
10. Remove the 4 cluster assembly screws and the cluster assembly. Disconnect the electrical connectors from the cluster assembly.

To install:

11. Place the cluster assembly into position and install retaining screws.
12. Install the side and center air vents.
13. Install the coin box, cruise control master switch, sunroof switch and panel brightness controller.
14. Install the radio, ashtray and ashtray holder.
15. On manual transaxle, install the shift lever knob.
16. Connect the negative battery cable.

PRELUDE

1990-91

1. Disconnect the negative battery cable.
2. Remove the dash light brightness controller and retractor/fog light switch from the instrument panel and disconnect the connectors.
3. Remove the 5 retaining screws and the instrument panel from the gauge visor.
4. Remove the 4 screws and pull out the gauge assembly from the dashboard to gain access to the electrical connectors.
5. Disconnect the electrical connectors and remove the gauge assembly.
6. Installation is the reverse of the removal procedure.

1992-94

1. Disconnect the negative battery cable.
2. Remove the 2 speaker covers from the dashboard. Remove the 8 visor screws and remove the visor.
3. Remove the 3 screws and remove the black face panel. Discon-

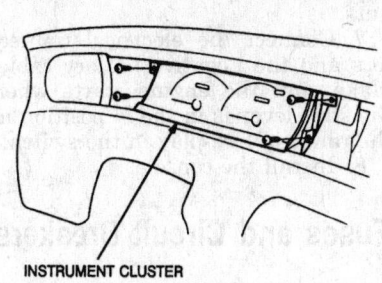

INSTRUMENT CLUSTER

Instrument cluster installation — 1992-94 Prelude

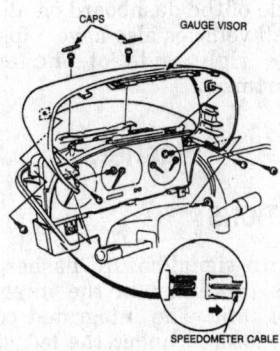

CAPS   GAUGE VISOR

SPEEDOMETER CABLE

Instrument cluster installation — 1990-91 Prelude

nect the electrical connector from the clock switch.

4. Remove the 4 screws from the gauge cluster and pull cluster out. Disconnect the electrical connectors and remove the cluster.

5. Installation is the reverse of the removal procedure.

Concealed Headlights

MANUAL OPERATION

1. Remove the cover from the engine compartment fuse box and remove the fuse for the headlight motor that does not work.

NOTE: Always remove the fuse before manually operating a headlight motor, otherwise the motor may suddenly activate.

2. Remove the cap from the top of the headlight motor, then turn the knob in the direction of the arrow (clockwise) until the headlight is as far up or down as it will go.

3. Replace the cap and reinstall the fuse.

Combination Switch

REMOVAL AND INSTALLATION

Accord, Civic, Del Sol and Prelude

1. Disconnect the negative battery cable.

2. Remove the lower dashboard cover and knee bolster.

3. Remove the upper and lower steering column covers.

4. Remove the combination switch retaining screws, disconnect the connector and remove the switch assembly.

5. Installation is the reverse of the removal procedure.

Ignition Switch

REMOVAL AND INSTALLATION

1. Disconnect the negative battery cable and disarm the SRS air bag.

2. Remove the steering wheel and steering column covers as necessary, to gain access to the switch.

3. Disconnect the electrical connector.

4. Insert the ignition key and turn it to the **O** position.

5. Remove the switch cover and remove the 2 screws and the switch.

6. Installation is the reverse of the removal procedure.

Ignition Lock

REMOVAL AND INSTALLATION

1. Disconnect the negative battery cable and disarm the SRS air bag.

2. Remove the steering wheel and the steering column covers.

3. Disconnect the ignition switch connector.

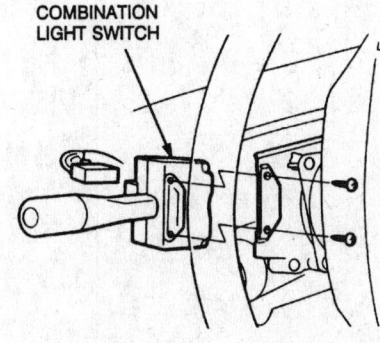

COMBINATION LIGHT SWITCH

Combination switch installation

4. Center punch each of the 2 shear bolts and drill their heads off with a suitable drill bit.

NOTE: Do not damage the switch body when removing the shear bolt heads.

5. Remove the shear bolts from the switch body and remove the switch.

To install:

6. Install the new ignition switch without the key inserted.

7. Loosely tighten the new shear bolts.

NOTE: Make sure the projection on the ignition switch is aligned with the hole in the steering column.

8. Insert the ignition key and check for proper operation of the steering wheel lock and that the ignition key turns freely.

9. Tighten the shear bolts until the hex heads twist off.

Stoplight Switch

ADJUSTMENT

1. Loosen the stoplight switch locknut and back off the stoplight switch until it is no longer touching the brake pedal.

2. Loosen the brake pushrod locknut and screw the pushrod in or out until the pedal height from the floor is as follows:

1990-91 Civic and CRX — 6.02 in. (153mm).

1992-94 Civic and del Sol
  With manual transaxle — 6.30 in. (160mm).
  With automatic transaxle — 6.50 in. (165mm).

1990-91 Accord
  With manual transaxle — 7.48 in. (190mm).
  With automatic transaxle — 7.68 in. (195mm).

1992-94 Accord
  With manual transaxle — 6.50 in. (165mm).
  With automatic transaxle — 6.69 in. (170mm).

1990-91 Prelude
  With manual transaxle — 7.0 in. (176mm).
  With automatic transaxle — 7.2 in. (183mm).

1992-94 Prelude
  With manual transaxle — 6.50 in. (165mm).
  With automatic transaxle — 7.32 in. (186mm).

3. After adjustment, tighten the brake pushrod locknut.

4. Screw in the stoplight switch until it's plunger is fully depressed, threaded end touching the pad on the pedal arm, then back off the switch ½ turn and tighten the locknut.

NOTE: Make sure the brake lights go OFF when the pedal is released.

REMOVAL AND INSTALLATION

1. Disconnect the negative battery cable.
2. Disconnect the electrical connector.
3. Loosen the locknut and unscrew the switch from it's mounting.
4. Installation is the reverse of removal procedure. The switch must be adjusted after installation.

Clutch Switch

ADJUSTMENT

1. Loosen the locknut on the clutch interlock switch.
2. Depress the clutch pedal fully and then release 0.59-0.79 in. (15-20mm) from the fully depressed position and hold. Adjust the position of the clutch switch so the engine will start with the clutch pedal in this position.

3. Thread the clutch switch in further ¼-½ turn and tighten the locknut.

REMOVAL AND INSTALLATION

1. Disconnect the negative battery cable.
2. Disconnect the electrical connector from the switch.
3. Loosen the locknut on the clutch switch and unscrew the switch from it's mounting.
4. Installation is the reverse of the removal procedure. Adjust the switch after installation.

Neutral Safety Switch

REMOVAL AND INSTALLATION

1. Disconnect the negative battery cable.
2. Remove the console and disconnect the electrical connectors from the neutral safety switch.
3. Remove the 2 neutral safety switch mounting nuts and remove the neutral safety switch.
   To install:
4. Position the switch slider to the **N** position.
5. Shift the selector lever to **N**, then slip the neutral safety switch into position.

6. Attach the switch with the 2 nuts.
7. Connect the electrical connectors and the negative battery cable. Make sure the engine starts when the shift lever is in the **N** position in the range of free-play in the switch.
8. Install the console.

Fuses and Circuit Breakers

Location

Fuses

The fuse panel is located under the left side of the dashboard on all vehicles. All vehicles also have a fuse box in the right side of the engine compartment.

Flashers

LOCATIONS

The turn signal/hazard flasher function is contained in the integrated control unit. The integrated control unit is located under the left side of the dashboard on Civic, CRX and del Sol, under the dash on the left kick panel on Accord, under the center of the dash on 1990-91 Prelude and in the underdash fuse panel on the 1992-94 Prelude.

ENGINE IDENTIFICATION

Year	Model	Engine Displacement Liters (cc)	Engine Series (ID/VIN) ③	Fuel System	No. of Cylinders	Engine Type
1990	Excel	1.5 (1468)	M	2bbl	4	OHC
	Excel	1.5 (1468)	J	MPI	4	OHC
	Sonata	2.4 (2351)	S	MPI	4	OHC
	Sonata	3.0 (2972)	T	MPI	6	OHC
1991	Excel	1.5 (1468)	M	2bbl	4	OHC
	Excel	1.5 (1468)	J	MPI	4	OHC
	Sonata	2.4 (2351)	S	MPI	4	OHC
	Sonata	3.0 (2972)	T	MPI	6	OHC
	Scoupe	1.5 (1468)	J	MPI	4	OHC
1992	Excel	1.5 (1468)	M	2bbl	4	OHC
	Excel	1.5 (1468)	J	MPI	4	OHC
	Sonata	2.0 (1997)	F	MPI	4	DOHC
	Sonata	3.0 (2972)	T	MPI	6	OHC
	Scoupe	1.5 (1468)	J	MPI	4	OHC
	Elantra	1.6 (1596)	R	MPI	4	DOHC
1993	Excel ②	1.5 (1468)	M	2bbl	4	OHC
	Excel	1.5 (1468)	J	MPI	4	OHC
	Sonata	2.0 (1997)	F	MPI	4	DOHC
	Sonata	3.0 (2972)	T	MPI	6	OHC
	Scoupe	1.5 (1495)	N	MPI	4	OHC
	Scoupe ①	1.5 (1495)	N	MPI	4	OHC
	Elantra	1.6 (1596)	R	MPI	4	DOHC
	Elantra	1.8 (1836)	M	MPI	4	DOHC
1994	Excel ②	1.5 (1468)	M	2bbl	4	OHC
	Excel	1.5 (1468)	J	MPI	4	OHC
	Sonata	2.0 (1997)	F	MPI	4	DOHC
	Sonata	3.0 (2972)	T	MPI	6	OHC
	Scoupe	1.5 (1495)	N	MPI	4	OHC
	Scoupe ①	1.5 (1495)	N	MPI	4	OHC
	Elantra	1.6 (1596)	R	MPI	4	DOHC
	Elantra	1.8 (1836)	M	MPI	4	DOHC

MPI—Multi-Point Fuel Injection
OHC—Overhead Camshaft
DOHC—Double Overhead Camshaft
2 bbl—2 Barrel carburetor
① Scoupe Turbo
② Canada only
③ Engine identification is sixth position (not sixth digit) of VIN

GENERAL ENGINE SPECIFICATIONS

Year	Engine ID/VIN	Engine Displacement Liters (cc)	Fuel System Type	Net Horsepower @ rpm	Net Torque @ rpm (ft. lbs.)	Bore × Stroke (in.)	Compression Ratio	Oil Pressure @ rpm
1990	M	1.5 (1468)	2bbl	77 @ 5300	84 @ 3000	2.97 × 3.23	9.4:1	45 @ 2000
	J	1.5 (1468)	MPI	81 @ 5500	91 @ 3000	2.97 × 3.23	9.4:1	45 @ 2000
	S	2.4 (2351)	MPI	126 @ 5100	180 @ 2600	3.41 × 3.94	8.5:1	45 @ 2000
	T	3.0 (2972)	MPI	142 @ 5000	168 @ 2500	3.59 × 2.99	8.9:1	30–80 @ 3000
1991	M	1.5 (1468)	2bbl	77 @ 5300	84 @ 3000	2.97 × 3.23	9.4:1	45 @ 2000
	J	1.5 (1468)	MPI	81 @ 5500	91 @ 3000	2.97 × 3.23	9.4:1	12 @ 750
	S	2.4 (2351)	MPI	126 @ 5100	180 @ 2600	3.41 × 3.94	8.5:1	45 @ 2000
	T	3.0 (2972)	MPI	142 @ 5000	168 @ 2500	3.59 × 2.99	8.9:1	30–80 @ 3000
1992	M	1.5 (1468)	2bbl	77 @ 5300	84 @ 3000	2.97 × 3.23	9.4:1	45 @ 2000
	J	1.5 (1468)	MPI	81 @ 5500	91 @ 3000	2.97 × 3.23	9.4:1	12 @ 750
	R	1.6 (1596)	MPI	113 @ 6000	102 @ 5000	3.24 × 2.95	9.2:1	12 @ 750
	F	2.0 (1997)	MPI	128 @ 6000	121 @ 5000	3.35 × 3.46	9.0:1	12 @ 750
	T	3.0 (2972)	MPI	142 @ 5000	168 @ 2500	3.59 × 2.99	8.9:1	30–80 @ 3000
1993	M ②	1.5 (1468)	2bbl	77 @ 5300	84 @ 3000	2.97 × 3.23	9.4:1	45 @ 2000
	J	1.5 (1468)	MPI	81 @ 5500	91 @ 3000	2.97 × 3.23	9.4:1	12 @ 750
	N	1.5 (1495)	MPI	92 @ 5500	97 @ 4500	2.97 × 3.29	10.0:1	21 @ 800
	N ①	1.5 (1495)	MPI	115 @ 5500	123 @ 4500	2.97 × 3.29	7.5:1	21 @ 800
	M	1.8 (1836)	MPI	124 @ 6000	116 @ 5000	3.17 × 3.46	9.2:1	12 @ 750
	R	1.6 (1596)	MPI	113 @ 6000	102 @ 5000	3.24 × 2.95	9.2:1	12 @ 750
	F	2.0 (1997)	MPI	128 @ 6000	121 @ 5000	3.35 × 3.46	9.0:1	12 @ 750
	T	3.0 (2972)	MPI	142 @ 5000	168 @ 2500	3.59 × 2.99	8.9:1	30–80 @ 3000
1994	M ②	1.5 (1468)	2bbl	77 @ 5300	84 @ 3000	2.97 × 3.23	9.4:1	45 @ 2000
	J	1.5 (1468)	MPI	81 @ 5500	91 @ 3000	2.97 × 3.23	9.4:1	12 @ 750
	N	1.5 (1495)	MPI	92 @ 5500	97 @ 4500	2.97 × 3.29	10.0:1	21 @ 800
	N ①	1.5 (1495)	MPI	115 @ 5500	123 @ 4500	2.97 × 3.29	7.5:1	21 @ 800
	M	1.8 (1836)	MPI	124 @ 6000	116 @ 5000	3.17 × 3.46	9.2:1	12 @ 750
	R	1.6 (1596)	MPI	113 @ 6000	102 @ 5000	3.24 × 2.95	9.2:1	12 @ 750
	F	2.0 (1997)	MPI	128 @ 6000	121 @ 5000	3.35 × 3.46	9.0:1	12 @ 750
	T	3.0 (2972)	MPI	142 @ 5000	168 @ 2500	3.59 × 2.99	8.9:1	30–80 @ 3000

MPI—Multi-Point Fuel Injection
2 bbl—2 Barrel carburetor
① Scoupe Turbo
② Canada only

ENGINE TUNE-UP SPECIFICATIONS

Year	Engine ID/VIN	Engine Displacement Liters (cc)	Spark Plugs Gap (in.)	Ignition Timing (deg.)		Fuel Pump (psi)	Idle Speed (rpm)		Valve Clearance	
				MT	AT		MT	AT	In.	Ex.
1990	M	1.5 (1468)	0.039–0.043	5B	5B	2.8–3.6	700	700	0.006	0.010
	J	1.5 (1468)	0.039–0.043	5B	5B	48	700	700	0.006	0.010
	S	2.4 (2351)	0.039–0.043	5B	5B	48	750	750	Hyd.	Hyd.
	T	3.0 (2972)	0.039–0.043	5B	5B	48	750	750	Hyd.	Hyd.
1991	M	1.5 (1468)	0.039–0.043	5B	5B	2.8–3.6	700	700	0.006	0.010
	J	1.5 (1468)	0.039–0.043	5B	5B	48	700	700	0.006	0.010
	S	2.4 (2351)	0.039–0.043	5B	5B	48	750	750	Hyd.	Hyd.
	T	3.0 (2972)	0.039–0.043	12B	12B	48	750	750	Hyd.	Hyd.
1992	M	1.5 (1468)	0.039–0.043	5B	5B	2.8–3.6	700	700	0.006	0.010
	J	1.5 (1468)	0.039–0.043	5B	5B	48	700	700	0.006	0.010
	R	1.6 (1596)	0.039–0.043	5B	5B	48	750	750	Hyd.	Hyd.
	F	2.0 (1997)	0.039–0.043	5B	5B	48	750	750	Hyd.	Hyd.
	T	3.0 (2972)	0.039–0.043	12B	12B	48	750	750	Hyd.	Hyd.
1993	M②	1.5 (1468)	0.039–0.043	5B	5B	2.8–3.6	700	700	0.006	0.010
	J	1.5 (1468)	0.039–0.043	5B	5B	48	700	700	0.006	0.010
	N	1.5 (1495)	0.039–0.043	9B	9B	43	800	800	0.007	0.009
	N①	1.5 (1495)	0.039–0.043	9B	9B	43	800	800	0.007	0.009
	R	1.6 (1596)	0.039–0.043	5B	5B	48	750	750	Hyd.	Hyd.
	M	1.8 (1836)	0.039–0.043	5B	5B	48	750	750	Hyd.	Hyd.
	F	2.0 (1997)	0.039–0.043	5B	5B	48	750	750	Hyd.	Hyd.
	T	3.0 (2972)	0.039–0.043	12B	12B	48	750	750	Hyd.	Hyd.
1994	M②	1.5 (1468)	0.039–0.043	5B	5B	2.8–3.6	700	700	0.006	0.010
	J	1.5 (1468)	0.039–0.043	5B	5B	48	700	700	0.006	0.010
	N	1.5 (1495)	0.039–0.043	9B	9B	43	800	800	0.007	0.009
	N①	1.5 (1495)	0.039–0.043	9B	9B	43	800	800	0.007	0.009
	R	1.6 (1596)	0.039–0.043	5B	5B	48	750	750	Hyd.	Hyd.
	M	1.8 (1836)	0.039–0.043	5B	5B	48	750	750	Hyd.	Hyd.
	F	2.0 (1997)	0.039–0.043	5B	5B	48	750	750	Hyd.	Hyd.
	T	3.0 (2972)	0.039–0.043	12B	12B	48	750	750	Hyd.	Hyd.

NOTE: The lowest cylinder pressure should be within 75% of the highest cylinder pressure reading. For example, if the highest cylinder is 134 psi, the lowest should be 101. Engine should be at normal operating temperature with throttle valve in the wide open position.
The underhood specifications sticker often reflects tune-up specification changes in production. Sticker figures must be used if they disagree with those in this chart.
Hyd.—Hydraulic
① Scoupe Turbo
② Canada only

FIRING ORDERS

NOTE: To avoid confusion, always replace spark plug wires one at a time.

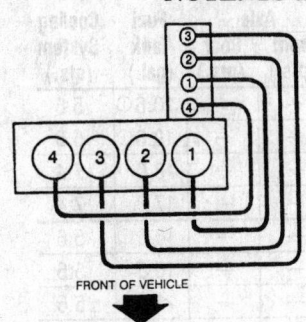

FRONT OF VEHICLE

1495cc, 1596cc, 1796cc and 1997cc Engines
Engine Firing Order: 1-3-4-2
Distributorless Ignition System

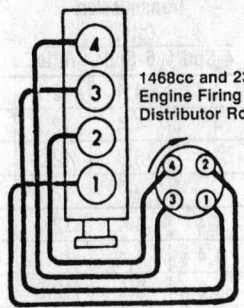

1468cc and 2351cc Engines
Engine Firing Order: 1-3-4-2
Distributor Rotation: Clockwise

1468cc and 2351cc Engines
Engine Firing Order: 1-3-4-2
Distributor Rotation: Clockwise

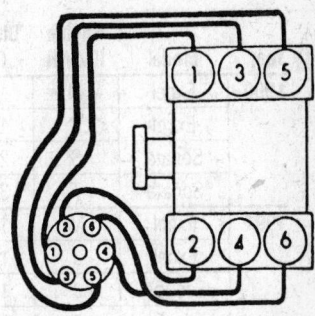

2972cc Engine
Engine Firing Order: 1-2-3-4-5-6
Distributor Rotation: Counterclockwise

CAPACITIES

Year	Model	Engine ID/VIN	Engine Displacement Liters (cc)	Engine Crankcase with Filter (qts.)	Transmission (pts.) 4-Spd	5-Spd	Auto.	Transfer Case (pts.)	Drive Axle Front (pts.)	Rear (pts.)	Fuel Tank (gal.)	Cooling System (qts.)
1990	Excel	M	1.5 (1468)	3.6	4.4	4.4	12.2	—	—	—	10.6①	5.6
	Excel	J	1.5 (1468)	3.6	4.4	4.4	12.2	—	—	—	10.6①	5.6
	Sonata	S	2.4 (2351)	4.0	—	5.3	12.3	—	—	—	16.0	7.4
	Sonata	T	3.0 (2972)	4.0	—	—	12.3	—	—	—	17.0	7.4
1991	Excel	M	1.5 (1468)	3.6	4.4	4.4	12.2	—	—	—	10.6①	5.6
	Excel	J	1.5 (1468)	3.6	4.4	4.4	12.2	—	—	—	10.6①	5.6
	Scoupe	J	1.5 (1468)	3.6	3.8	3.8	12.8	—	—	—	11.9①	5.6
	Sonata	S	2.4 (2351)	4.0	—	5.3	12.3	—	—	—	16.0	7.4
	Sonata	T	3.0 (2972)	4.0	—	—	12.3	—	—	—	17.0	7.4
1992	Excel	M	1.5 (1468)	3.6	4.4	4.4	12.2	—	—	—	10.6①	5.6
	Excel	J	1.5 (1468)	3.6	4.4	4.4	12.2	—	—	—	10.6①	5.6
	Scoupe	J	1.5 (1468)	3.6	3.8	3.8	12.8	—	—	—	11.9①	5.6
	Elantra	R	1.6 (1596)	3.6	—	3.8	12.8	—	—	—	13.8	5.4
	Sonata	F	2.0 (1997)	4.0	—	4.0	12.8	—	—	—	17.2	7.7
	Sonata	T	3.0 (2972)	4.0	—	—	12.3	—	—	—	17.0	7.4
1993	Excel③	M	1.5 (1468)	3.6	4.4	4.4	12.2	—	—	—	10.6①	5.6
	Excel	J	1.5 (1468)	3.6	4.4	4.4	12.2	—	—	—	10.6①	5.6
	Scoupe	N	1.5 (1495)	3.4	—	4.4	12.8	—	—	—	11.9	5.6
	Scoupe②	N	1.5 (1495)	3.4	—	4.4	12.8	—	—	—	11.9	5.6
	Elantra	R	1.6 (1596)	4.6	—	3.8	12.8	—	—	—	13.8	5.4
	Elantra	M	1.8 (1836)	4.6	—	3.8	12.8	—	—	—	13.8	5.4
	Sonata	F	2.0 (1997)	4.0	—	4.0	12.8	—	—	—	17.2	7.7
	Sonata	T	3.0 (2972)	4.0	—	—	12.3	—	—	—	17.0	7.4
1994	Excel③	M	1.5 (1468)	3.6	4.4	4.4	12.2	—	—	—	10.6①	5.6
	Excel	J	1.5 (1468)	3.6	4.4	4.4	12.2	—	—	—	10.6①	5.6
	Scoupe	N	1.5 (1495)	3.4	—	4.4	12.8	—	—	—	11.9	5.6
	Scoupe②	N	1.5 (1495)	3.4	—	4.4	12.8	—	—	—	11.9	5.6
	Elantra	R	1.6 (1596)	4.6	—	3.8	12.8	—	—	—	13.8	5.4
	Elantra	M	1.8 (1836)	4.6	—	3.8	12.8	—	—	—	13.8	5.4
	Sonata	F	2.0 (1997)	4.0	—	4.0	12.8	—	—	—	17.2	7.7
	Sonata	T	3.0 (2972)	4.0	—	—	12.3	—	—	—	17.0	7.4

① Optional 13.2 gallon tank
② Scoupe Turbo
③ Canada only

CAMSHAFT SPECIFICATIONS

All measurements given in inches.

Year	Engine ID/VIN	Engine Displacement Liters (cc)	Journal Diameter (in.)					Elevation		Bearing Clearance	Camshaft End Play
			1	2	3	4	5	In.	Ex.		
1990	M	1.5 (1468)	1.338	1.338	1.338	1.338	—	1.532	1.522	0.0020–0.0035	0.004–0.008
	J	1.5 (1468)	1.338	1.338	1.338	1.338	—	1.532	1.534	0.0020–0.0035	0.004–0.008
	S	2.4 (2351)	1.336–1.337	1.336–1.337	1.336–1.337	1.336–1.337	1.336–1.337	1.753	1.753	0.0020–0.0035	0.004–0.008
	T	3.0 (2972)	1.336–1.337	1.336–1.337	1.336–1.337	1.336–1.337	—	1.620–1.628	1.620–1.628	0.0020–0.0035	0.004–0.008
1991	M	1.5 (1468)	1.338	1.338	1.338	1.338	—	1.532	1.522	0.0020–0.0035	0.004–0.008
	J	1.5 (1468)	1.338	1.338	1.338	1.338	—	1.532	1.534	0.0020–0.0035	0.004–0.008
	S	2.4 (2351)	1.336–1.337	1.336–1.337	1.336–1.337	1.336–1.337	1.336–1.337	1.753	1.753	0.0020–0.0035	0.004–0.008
	T	3.0 (2972)	1.336–1.337	1.336–1.337	1.336–1.337	1.336–1.337	—	1.620–1.628	1.620–1.628	0.0020–0.0035	0.004–0.008
1992	M	1.5 (1468)	1.338	1.338	1.338	1.338	—	1.532	1.522	0.0020–0.0035	0.004–0.008
	J	1.5 (1468)	1.338	1.338	1.338	1.338	—	1.532	1.534	0.0020–0.0035	0.004–0.008
	R	1.6 (1596)	1.020	1.020	1.020	1.020	1.020	1.386	1.374	0.0020–0.0035	0.004–0.008
	F	2.0 (1997)	1.020	1.020	1.020	1.020	1.020	1.753	1.753	0.0020–0.0035	0.004–0.008
	T	3.0 (2972)	1.336–1.337	1.336–1.337	1.336–1.337	1.336–1.337	—	1.620–1.628	1.620–1.628	0.0020–0.0035	0.004–0.008
1993	M②	1.5 (1468)	1.338	1.338	1.338	1.338	—	1.532	1.522	0.0020–0.0035	0.004–0.008
	J	1.5 (1468)	1.338	1.338	1.338	1.338	—	1.532	1.534	0.0020–0.0035	0.004–0.008
	N	1.5 (1495)	1.338	1.338	1.338	1.338	—	①	1.625	0.0020–0.0035	0.004–0.008
	R	1.6 (1596)	1.020	1.020	1.020	1.020	1.020	1.386	1.374	0.0020–0.0035	0.004–0.008
	M	1.8 (1836)	1.020	1.020	1.020	1.020	1.020	1.386	1.374	0.0020–0.0035	0.004–0.008
	F	2.0 (1997)	1.020	1.020	1.020	1.020	1.020	1.753	1.753	0.0020–0.0035	0.004–0.008
	T	3.0 (2972)	1.336–1.337	1.336–1.337	1.336–1.337	1.336–1.337	—	1.620–1.628	1.620–1.628	0.0020–0.0035	0.004–0.008

CAMSHAFT SPECIFICATIONS

All measurements given in inches.

Year	Engine ID/VIN	Engine Displacement Liters (cc)	Journal Diameter (in.)					Elevation		Bearing Clearance	Camshaft End Play
			1	2	3	4	5	In.	Ex.		
1994	M②	1.5 (1468)	1.338	1.338	1.338	1.338	—	1.532	1.522	0.0020–0.0035	0.004–0.008
	J	1.5 (1468)	1.338	1.338	1.338	1.338	—	1.532	1.534	0.0020–0.0035	0.004–0.008
	N	1.5 (1495)	1.338	1.338	1.338	1.338	—	①	1.625	0.0020–0.0035	0.004–0.008
	R	1.6 (1596)	1.020	1.020	1.020	1.020	1.020	1.386	1.374	0.0020–0.0035	0.004–0.008
	M	1.8 (1836)	1.020	1.020	1.020	1.020	1.020	1.386	1.374	0.0020–0.0035	0.004–0.008
	F	2.0 (1997)	1.020	1.020	1.020	1.020	1.020	1.753	1.753	0.0020–0.0035	0.004–0.008
	T	3.0 (2972)	1.336–1.337	1.336–1.337	1.336–1.337	1.336–1.337	—	1.620–1.628	1.620–1.628	0.0020–0.0035	0.004–0.008

① 1.617 on Non-Turbo Models
  1.625 on Turbocharged Models
② Canada only

CRANKSHAFT AND CONNECTING ROD SPECIFICATIONS

All measurements are given in inches.

Year	Engine ID/VIN	Engine Displacement Liters (cc)	Crankshaft Main Brg. Journal Dia.	Crankshaft Main Brg. Oil Clearance	Crankshaft Shaft End-Play	Crankshaft Thrust on No.	Connecting Rod Journal Diameter	Connecting Rod Oil Clearance	Connecting Rod Side Clearance
1990	M	1.5 (1468)	1.8898	0.0008–0.0020	0.002–0.007	3	1.6535	0.0006–0.0017	0.004–0.010
	J	1.5 (1468)	1.8898	0.0008–0.0020	0.002–0.007	3	1.6535	0.0006–0.0017	0.004–0.010
	S	2.4 (2351)	2.2436	0.0008–0.0020	0.002–0.007	3	1.7709–1.7715	0.0008–0.0020	0.004–0.010
	T	3.0 (2972)	2.3622	0.0008–0.0020	0.002–0.007	3	1.9685	0.0006–0.0017	0.004–0.010
1991	M	1.5 (1468)	1.8898	0.0008–0.0020	0.002–0.007	3	1.6535	0.0006–0.0017	0.004–0.010
	J	1.5 (1468)	1.8898	0.0008–0.0020	0.002–0.007	3	1.6535	0.0006–0.0017	0.004–0.010
	S	2.4 (2351)	2.2436	0.0008–0.0020	0.002–0.007	3	1.7709–1.7715	0.0008–0.0020	0.004–0.010
	T	3.0 (2972)	2.3622	0.0008–0.0020	0.002–0.007	3	1.9685	0.0006–0.0017	0.004–0.010
1992	M	1.5 (1468)	1.8898	0.0008–0.0020	0.002–0.007	3	1.6535	0.0006–0.0017	0.004–0.010
	J	1.5 (1468)	1.8898	0.0008–0.0020	0.002–0.007	3	1.6535	0.0006–0.0017	0.004–0.010
	R	1.6 (1596)	2.2400	0.0008–0.0020	0.002–0.007	3	1.7700	0.0008–0.0020	0.004–0.010
	F	2.0 (1997)	2.2433–2.2439	0.0008–0.0020	0.002–0.007	3	1.7709–1.7715	0.0008–0.0020	0.004–0.010
	T	3.0 (2972)	2.3622	0.0008–0.0020	0.002–0.007	3	1.9685	0.0006–0.0017	0.004–0.010
1993	M①	1.5 (1468)	1.8898	0.0008–0.0020	0.002–0.007	3	1.6535	0.0006–0.0017	0.004–0.010
	J	1.5 (1468)	1.8898	0.0008–0.0020	0.002–0.007	3	1.6535	0.0006–0.0017	0.004–0.010
	N	1.5 (1495)	1.9685	0.0013–0.0020	0.002–0.007	3	1.6535	0.0013–0.0022	0.004–0.010
	R	1.6 (1596)	2.2400	0.0008–0.0020	0.002–0.007	3	1.7700	0.0008–0.0020	0.004–0.010
	M	1.8 (1836)	2.2400	0.0008–0.0020	0.002–0.007	3	1.7700	0.0008–0.0020	0.004–0.010
	F	2.0 (1997)	2.2433–2.2439	0.0008–0.0020	0.002–0.007	3	1.7709–1.7715	0.0008–0.0020	0.004–0.010
	T	3.0 (2972)	2.3622	0.0008–0.0020	0.002–0.007	3	1.9685	0.0006–0.0017	0.004–0.010

CRANKSHAFT AND CONNECTING ROD SPECIFICATIONS

All measurements are given in inches.

Year	Engine ID/VIN	Engine Displacement Liters (cc)	Crankshaft				Connecting Rod		
			Main Brg. Journal Dia.	Main Brg. Oil Clearance	Shaft End-Play	Thrust on No.	Journal Diameter	Oil Clearance	Side Clearance
1994	M ①	1.5 (1468)	1.8898	0.0008–0.0020	0.002–0.007	3	1.6535	0.0006–0.0017	0.004–0.010
	J	1.5 (1468)	1.8898	0.0008–0.0020	0.002–0.007	3	1.6535	0.0006–0.0017	0.004–0.010
	N	1.5 (1495)	1.9685	0.0013–0.0020	0.002–0.007	3	1.6535	0.0013–0.0022	0.004–0.010
	R	1.6 (1596)	2.2400	0.0008–0.0020	0.002–0.007	3	1.7700	0.0008–0.0020	0.004–0.010
	M	1.8 (1836)	2.2400	0.0008–0.0020	0.002–0.007	3	1.7700	0.0008–0.0020	0.004–0.010
	F	2.0 (1997)	2.2433–2.2439	0.0008–0.0020	0.002–0.007	3	1.7709–1.7715	0.0008–0.0020	0.004–0.010
	T	3.0 (2972)	2.3622	0.0008–0.0020	0.002–0.007	3	1.9685	0.0006–0.0017	0.004–0.010

① Canada only

VALVE SPECIFICATIONS

Year	Engine ID/VIN	Engine Displacement Liters (cc)	Seat Angle (deg.)	Face Angle (deg.)	Spring Test Pressure (lbs. @ in.)	Spring Installed Height (in.)	Stem-to-Guide Clearance (in.)		Stem Diameter (in.)	
							Intake	Exhaust	Intake	Exhaust
1990	M	1.5 (1468)	45	45	53 @ 1.07 ①	1.42 ②	0.0012–0.0024	0.0020–0.0035	0.2598	0.2598
	J	1.5 (1468)	45	45	53 @ 1.07	1.42 ②	0.0012–0.0024	0.0020–0.0035	0.2598	0.2598
	S	2.4 (2351)	45	45	73 @ 1.591 ①	1.59 ②	0.0012–0.0024	0.0020–0.0035	0.3150	0.3150
	T	3.0 (2972)	44–44.5	45	74 @ 1.591 ①	1.59	0.0012–0.0024	0.0020–0.0035	0.3150	0.3134
1991	M	1.5 (1468)	45	45	53 @ 1.07 ①	1.42 ②	0.0012–0.0024	0.0020–0.0035	0.2598	0.2598
	J	1.5 (1468)	45	45	53 @ 1.07	1.42 ②	0.0012–0.0024	0.0020–0.0035	0.2598	0.2598
	S	2.4 (2351)	45	45	73 @ 1.591 ①	1.59 ②	0.0012–0.0024	0.0020–0.0035	0.3150	0.3150
	T	3.0 (2972)	44–44.5	45	74 @ 1.591 ①	1.59	0.0012–0.0024	0.0020–0.0035	0.3150	0.3134
1992	M	1.5 (1468)	45	45	53 @ 1.07 ①	1.42 ②	0.0012–0.0024	0.0020–0.0035	0.2598	0.2598
	J	1.5 (1468)	45	45	53 @ 1.07	1.42 ②	0.0012–0.0024	0.0020–0.0035	0.2598	0.2598
	R	1.6 (1596)	44–44.5	45–45.5	66 @ 1.575	③	0.0008–0.0019	0.0020–0.0033	0.2585	0.2591
	F	2.0 (1997)	44–44.5	45–45.5	66 @ 1.575	③	0.0008–0.0019	0.0020–0.0033	0.2585	0.2591
	T	3.0 (2972)	44–44.5	45–45.5	74 @ 1.591 ①	1.59	0.0012–0.0024	0.0020–0.0035	0.3150	0.3134
1993	M ④	1.5 (1468)	45	45	53 @ 1.07 ①	1.42 ②	0.0012–0.0024	0.0020–0.0035	0.2598	0.2598
	J	1.5 (1468)	45	45	53 @ 1.07	1.42 ②	0.0012–0.0024	0.0020–0.0035	0.2598	0.2598
	N	1.5 (1495)	45	45	53 @ 1.07	1.42	0.0012–0.0024	0.0020–0.0031	0.2598	0.2598
	R	1.6 (1596)	44–44.5	45–45.5	66 @ 1.575	③	0.0008–0.0019	0.0020–0.0033	0.2585	0.2591
	M	1.8 (1836)	45–45.5	45–45.5	66 @ 1.575	③	0.0008–0.0019	0.0020–0.0033	0.2591	0.2579
	F	2.0 (1997)	44–44.5	45–45.5	66 @ 1.575	③	0.0008–0.0019	0.0020–0.0033	0.2585	0.2591
	T	3.0 (2972)	44–44.5	45–45.5	74 @ 1.591 ①	1.59	0.0012–0.0024	0.0020–0.0035	0.3150	0.3134

VALVE SPECIFICATIONS

Year	Engine ID/VIN	Engine Displacement Liters (cc)	Seat Angle (deg.)	Face Angle (deg.)	Spring Test Pressure (lbs. @ in.)	Spring Installed Height (in.)	Stem-to-Guide Clearance (in.)		Stem Diameter (in.)	
							Intake	Exhaust	Intake	Exhaust
1994	M ④	1.5 (1468)	45	45	53 @ 1.07 ①	1.42 ②	0.0012–0.0024	0.0020–0.0035	0.2598	0.2598
	J	1.5 (1468)	45	45	53 @ 1.07	1.42 ②	0.0012–0.0024	0.0020–0.0035	0.2598	0.2598
	N	1.5 (1495)	45	45	53 @ 1.07	1.42	0.0012–0.0024	0.0020–0.0031	0.2598	0.2598
	R	1.6 (1596)	44–44.5	45–45.5	66 @ 1.575	③	0.0008–0.0019	0.0020–0.0033	0.2585	0.2591
	M	1.8 (1836)	45–45.5	45–45.5	66 @ 1.575	③	0.0008–0.0019	0.0020–0.0033	0.2591	0.2579
	F	2.0 (1997)	44–44.5	45–45.5	66 @ 1.575	③	0.0008–0.0019	0.0020–0.0033	0.2585	0.2591
	T	3.0 (2972)	44–44.5	45–45.5	74 @ 1.591 ①	1.59	0.0012–0.0024	0.0020–0.0035	0.3150	0.3134

① Jet valve—7.7 @ 0.846
② Jet valve—0.846
③ Free length—1.902
④ Canada only

PISTON AND RING SPECIFICATIONS

All measurements are given in inches.

Year	Engine ID/VIN	Engine Displacement Liters (cc)	Piston Clearance	Ring Gap			Ring Side Clearance		
				Top Compression	Bottom Compression	Oil Control	Top Compression	Bottom Compression	Oil Control
1990	M	1.5 (1468)	0.0008–0.0016	0.008–0.014	0.008–0.014	0.008–0.028	0.0012–0.0028	0.0008–0.0024	NA
	J	1.5 (1468)	0.0008–0.0016	0.008–0.014	0.008–0.014	0.008–0.028	0.0012–0.0028	0.0008–0.0024	NA
	S	2.4 (2351)	0.0004–0.0012	0.010–0.016	0.008–0.014	0.008–0.028	0.0012–0.0028	0.0008–0.0024	NA
	T	3.0 (2972)	0.0008–0.0016	0.012–0.018	0.010–0.016	0.008–0.028	0.0012–0.0035	0.0008–0.0024	NA
1991	M	1.5 (1468)	0.0008–0.0016	0.008–0.014	0.008–0.014	0.008–0.028	0.0012–0.0028	0.0008–0.0024	NA
	J	1.5 (1468)	0.0008–0.0016	0.008–0.014	0.008–0.014	0.008–0.028	0.0012–0.0028	0.0008–0.0024	NA
	S	2.4 (2351)	0.0004–0.0012	0.010–0.016	0.008–0.014	0.008–0.028	0.0012–0.0028	0.0008–0.0024	NA
	T	3.0 (2972)	0.0008–0.0016	0.012–0.018	0.010–0.016	0.008–0.028	0.0012–0.0035	0.0008–0.0024	NA
1992	M	1.5 (1468)	0.0008–0.0016	0.008–0.014	0.008–0.014	0.008–0.028	0.0012–0.0028	0.0008–0.0024	NA
	J	1.5 (1468)	0.0008–0.0016	0.008–0.014	0.008–0.014	0.008–0.028	0.0012–0.0028	0.0008–0.0024	NA
	R	1.6 (1596)	0.0008–0.0016	0.010–0.016	0.014–0.020	0.008–0.028	0.0012–0.0028	0.0012–0.0028	NA
	F	2.0 (1997)	0.0004–0.0012	0.010–0.018	0.014–0.020	0.008–0.028	0.0012–0.0028	0.0012–0.0028	NA
	T	3.0 (2972)	0.0008–0.0016	0.012–0.018	0.010–0.016	0.008–0.028	0.0012–0.0035	0.0008–0.0024	NA
1993	M ①	1.5 (1468)	0.0008–0.0016	0.008–0.014	0.008–0.014	0.008–0.028	0.0012–0.0028	0.0008–0.0024	NA
	J	1.5 (1468)	0.0008–0.0016	0.008–0.014	0.008–0.014	0.008–0.028	0.0012–0.0028	0.0008–0.0024	NA
	Y	1.5 (1495)	0.0008–0.0016	0.012–0.020	0.012–0.020	0.010–0.030	0.0016–0.0031	0.0016–0.0031	NA
	R	1.6 (1596)	0.0008–0.0016	0.010–0.016	0.014–0.020	0.008–0.028	0.0012–0.0028	0.0012–0.0028	NA
	M	1.8 (1836)	0.0008–0.0016	0.010–0.016	0.018–0.024	0.008–0.028	0.0012–0.0028	0.0012–0.0028	NA
	F	2.0 (1997)	0.0004–0.0012	0.010–0.018	0.014–0.020	0.008–0.028	0.0012–0.0028	0.0012–0.0028	NA
	T	3.0 (2972)	0.0008–0.0016	0.012–0.018	0.010–0.016	0.008–0.028	0.0012–0.0035	0.0008–0.0024	NA

PISTON AND RING SPECIFICATIONS

All measurements are given in inches.

Year	Engine ID/VIN	Engine Displacement Liters (cc)	Piston Clearance	Ring Gap			Ring Side Clearance		
				Top Compression	Bottom Compression	Oil Control	Top Compression	Bottom Compression	Oil Control
1994	M ①	1.5 (1468)	0.0008–0.0016	0.008–0.014	0.008–0.014	0.008–0.028	0.0012–0.0028	0.0008–0.0024	NA
	J	1.5 (1468)	0.0008–0.0016	0.008–0.014	0.008–0.014	0.008–0.028	0.0012–0.0028	0.0008–0.0024	NA
	Y	1.5 (1495)	0.0008–0.0016	0.012–0.020	0.012–0.020	0.010–0.030	0.0016–0.0031	0.0016–0.0031	NA
	R	1.6 (1596)	0.0008–0.0016	0.010–0.016	0.014–0.020	0.008–0.028	0.0012–0.0028	0.0012–0.0028	NA
	M	1.8 (1836)	0.0008–0.0016	0.010–0.016	0.018–0.024	0.008–0.028	0.0012–0.0028	0.0012–0.0028	NA
	F	2.0 (1997)	0.0004–0.0012	0.010–0.018	0.014–0.020	0.008–0.028	0.0012–0.0028	0.0012–0.0028	NA
	T	3.0 (2972)	0.0008–0.0016	0.012–0.018	0.010–0.016	0.008–0.028	0.0012–0.0035	0.0008–0.0024	NA

NA—Not available
① Canada only

TORQUE SPECIFICATIONS
All readings in ft. lbs.

Year	Engine ID/VIN	Engine Displacement Liters (cc)	Cylinder Head Bolts	Main Bearing Bolts	Rod Bearing Bolts	Crankshaft Damper Bolts	Flywheel Bolts	Manifold Intake	Manifold Exhaust	Spark Plugs	Lug Nut
1990	M	1.5 (1468)	①	36–39	23–25	72	94–101	12–14	12–14	18	80
	J	1.5 (1468)	①	36–39	23–25	72	94–101	12–14	12–14	18	80
	S	2.4 (2351)	②	36–40	38	94	94–101	11–14	12–14	18	80
	T	3.0 (2972)	②	55–61	36–38	109–115	65–70	11–14	11–16	18	80
1991	M	1.5 (1468)	①	36–39	23–25	72	94–101	12–14	12–14	18	80
	J	1.5 (1468)	①	36–39	23–25	72	94–101	12–14	12–14	18	80
	S	2.4 (2351)	②	36–40	38	94	94–101	11–14	12–14	18	80
	T	3.0 (2972)	②	55–61	36–38	109–115	65–70	11–14	11–16	18	80
1992	M	1.5 (1468)	①	36–39	23–25	72	94–101	12–14	12–14	18	80
	J	1.5 (1468)	①	36–39	23–25	72	94–101	12–14	12–14	18	80
	R	1.6 (1596)	②	47–51	36–38	80–94	94–101	③	18–22	15–21	80
	F	2.0 (1997)	76–83	47–51	38	80–94	94–101	22	18–22	14–22	80
	T	3.0 (2972)	②	55–61	36–38	109–115	65–70	11–14	11–16	18	80
1993	M⑤	1.5 (1468)	①	36–39	23–25	72	94–101	12–14	12–14	18	80
	J	1.5 (1468)	①	36–39	23–25	72	94–101	12–14	12–14	18	80
	N	1.5 (1495)	①	39–43	25–27	137–145	94–101	12–14	12–14	18	80
	R	1.6 (1596)	②	47–51	36–38	80–94	94–101	③	18–22	15–21	80
	M	1.8 (1836)	76–83④	47–51	36–38	80–94	94–101	③	18–22	15–21	80
	F	2.0 (1997)	76–83	47–51	38	80–94	94–101	22	18–22	14–22	80
	T	3.0 (2972)	②	55–61	36–38	109–115	65–70	11–14	11–16	18	80
1994	M⑤	1.5 (1468)	①	36–39	23–25	72	94–101	12–14	12–14	18	80
	J	1.5 (1468)	①	36–39	23–25	72	94–101	12–14	12–14	18	80
	N	1.5 (1495)	①	39–43	25–27	137–145	94–101	12–14	12–14	18	80
	R	1.6 (1596)	②	47–51	36–38	80–94	94–101	③	18–22	15–21	80
	M	1.8 (1836)	76–83④	47–51	36–38	80–94	94–101	③	18–22	15–21	80
	F	2.0 (1997)	76–83	47–51	38	80–94	94–101	22	18–22	14–22	80
	T	3.0 (2972)	②	55–61	36–38	109–115	65–70	11–14	11–16	18	80

① Cold: 51–54 ft. lbs.; Warm: 58–61 ft. lbs.
② Cold: 65–72 ft. lbs.; Warm: 72–80 ft. lbs.
③ M8 bolt: 11–14 ft. lbs.
  Except M8 bolt: 22–30 ft. lbs.
④ Cold Engine
⑤ Canada only

BRAKE SPECIFICATIONS

All measurements in inches unless noted.

Year	Model		Master Cylinder Bore	Brake Disc Original Thickness	Brake Disc Minimum Thickness	Maximum Runout	Brake Drum Diameter Original Inside Diameter	Brake Drum Diameter Max. Wear Limit	Brake Drum Diameter Maximum Machine Diameter	Minimum Lining Thickness Front	Minimum Lining Thickness Rear
1990	Excel		0.812	0.750	0.670	0.006	7.100	—	7.200	0.040	0.413
	Sonata	Front disc		0.886	0.787	0.004	—	—	—	0.079	—
		Bendix system w/rear disc	1.024	0.472	0.413	0.005	—	—	—	0.079	0.413
		Mando system w/rear drum	1.000	—	—	—	9.000	—	9.079	0.079	0.059
1991	Excel		0.875	0.750	0.669	0.006	7.100	—	7.165	0.039	0.039
	Sonata	Front disc	1.024	0.866	0.787	0.004	—	—	—	0.079	—
		Rear disc	—	0.472	0.413	0.005	—	—	—	—	0.031
		Rear drum	—	—	—	—	8.858	—	8.936	—	0.031
	Scoupe		0.875	0.750	0.669	0.006	7.100	—	7.165	0.039	0.039
1992	Excel		0.875	0.750	0.669	0.006	7.100	—	7.165	0.039	0.039
	Sonata	Front disc	1.024	0.866	0.787	0.004	—	—	—	0.079	—
		Rear disc	—	0.472	0.413	0.005	—	—	—	—	0.031
		Rear drum	—	—	—	—	8.858	—	8.936	—	0.031
	Scoupe		0.875	0.750	0.669	0.006	7.100	—	7.165	0.039	0.039
	Elantra		0.875	0.866	0.787	0.006	8.000	—	8.079	0.079	0.059
1993	Excel		0.875	0.750	0.669	0.006	7.100	—	7.165	0.039	0.039
	Sonata	Front disc	1.024	0.866	0.787	0.004	—	—	—	0.079	—
		Rear disc	—	0.472	0.413	0.005	—	—	—	—	0.031
		Rear drum	—	—	—	—	8.858	—	8.936	—	0.031
	Scoupe		0.875	0.750	0.669	0.006	7.100	—	7.165	0.039	0.039
	Elantra		0.875	0.866	0.787	0.006	8.000	—	8.079	0.079	0.059
1994	Excel		0.875	0.750	0.669	0.006	7.100	—	7.165	0.039	0.039
	Sonata	Front disc	1.024	0.866	0.787	0.004	—	—	—	0.079	—
		Rear disc	—	0.472	0.413	0.005	—	—	—	—	0.031
		Rear drum	—	—	—	—	8.858	—	8.936	—	0.031
	Scoupe		0.875	0.750	0.669	0.006	7.100	—	7.165	0.039	0.039
	Elantra		0.875	0.866	0.787	0.006	8.000	—	8.079	0.079	0.059

WHEEL ALIGNMENT

Year	Model	Caster Range (deg.)	Caster Preferred Setting (deg.)	Camber Range (deg.)	Camber Preferred Setting (deg.)	Toe-in (in.)	Steering Axis Inclination (deg.)
1990	Excel	$1/2$P–$1\,1/6$P	$5/6$P	0–1P	$1/2$P	$1/16$in–$5/64$out	①
	Sonata	$1\,1/2$P–$2\,1/2$P	2P	0–1P	$1/2$P	$1/16$in–$5/64$out	③
1991	Excel	$1/2$P–$1\,1/6$P	$5/6$P	0–1P	$1/2$P	$1/16$in–$5/64$out	①
	Sonata	$1\,1/2$P–$2\,1/2$P	2P	0–1P	$1/2$P	$1/16$in–$5/64$out	③
	Scoupe	$1/2$P–$1\,1/2$P	②	$2/3$N–$1/3$P	$1/6$N	0.157in–0.079out	④
1992	Excel	$1/2$P–$1\,1/6$P	$5/6$P	0–1P	$1/2$P	$1/16$in–$5/64$out	①
	Sonata	$1\,1/2$P–$2\,1/2$P	2P	0–1P	$1/2$P	$1/16$in–$5/64$out	③
	Scoupe	$1/2$P–$1\,1/2$P	②	$2/3$N–$1/3$P	$1/6$N	0.157in–0.079out	④
	Elantra	—	$2\,1/3$P	$1/2$N–$1/2$P	0	0.120in–0.120out	⑤
1993	Excel	$1/2$P–$1\,1/6$P	$5/6$P	0–1P	$1/2$P	$1/16$in–$5/64$out	①
	Sonata	$1\,1/2$P–$2\,1/2$P	2P	0–1P	$1/2$P	$1/16$in–$5/64$out	③
	Scoupe	$1/2$P–$1\,1/2$P	②	$2/3$N–$1/3$P	$1/6$N	0.157in–0.079out	④
	Elantra	—	$2\,1/3$P	$1/2$N–$1/2$P	0	0.120in–0.120out	⑤
1994	Excel	$1/2$P–$1\,1/6$P	$5/6$P	0–1P	$1/2$P	$1/16$in–$5/64$out	①
	Sonata	$1\,1/2$P–$2\,1/2$P	2P	0–1P	$1/2$P	$1/16$in–$5/64$out	③
	Scoupe	$1/2$P–$1\,1/2$P	②	$2/3$N–$1/3$P	$1/6$N	0.157in–0.079out	④
	Elantra	—	$2\,1/3$P	$1/2$N–$1/2$P	0	0.120in–0.120out	⑤

P—Positive
N—Negative
① Inside wheel—$35\,2/3$: outside wheel—$29\,9/32$
② Manual steering $1\,1/2$P
  Power steering 1P
③ King pin angle $13\,2/5$
④ King pin angle $13\,1/4$
⑤ King pin angle $12\,1/2$

SERIAL NUMBER IDENTIFICATION

Vehicle Identification Plate

The Vehicle Identification Number (VIN) is located on a plate attached to the left front of the dash panel, so it can be seen through the windshield when standing beside the vehicle.

Use care when decoding a vehicle's VIN number. Hyundai uses 3 letters/numbers to identify the country of origin, yet it is considered only the first place of the VIN. The letters and numbers in the VIN digits can be interpreted according to their positions in the sequence as follows:
1. World manufacturer's identifier code (country)
  a. KMH-Hyundai Motor Co., Korea
  b. 2HM-Bromont Assembly Plant, Canada
2. Drive-line type
  a. V-LHD
  b. U-RHD
3. Body type
4. Body style and version
  a. 1-Standard
  b. 2-Deluxe (GL)
  c. 3-Super Delux (GLS)
5. Restraint type
  a. 1-Active system
  b. 2-Passive system
6. Engine size
7. Check digit (manufacture's use only)
8. Model year
  a. L-1990
  b. M-1991
  c. N-1992
  d. P-1993
  e. Q-1994
9. Plant build code
10. Serial number

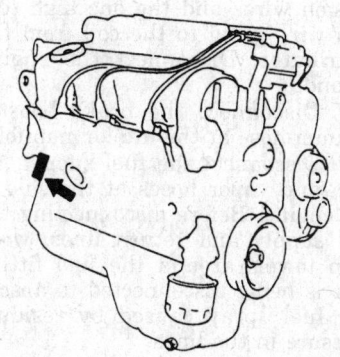

Engine number location — 6 cylinder engine

Engine Number

The engine model and serial numbers in all cases are stamped on the top edge of the block near the front of the engine. In most cases, they are located on the right side of the engine.

Vehicle Identification Number

The Vehicle Identification Label (VIN) is located on the top center of the firewall in the engine compartment.

ENGINE MECHANICAL

NOTE: Disconnecting the negative battery cable on some vehicles may interfere with the functions of the on-board computer systems and may require the computer to undergo a relearning process, once the negative battery cable is reconnected.

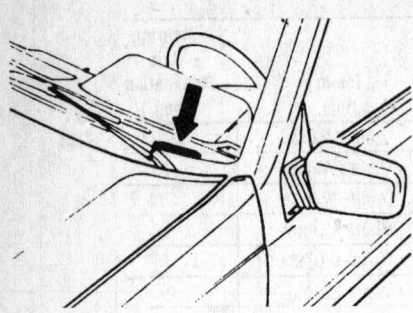

Serial number location

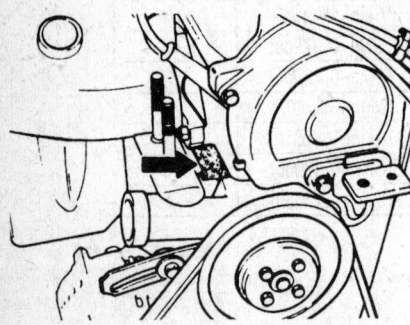

Engine number location — 4 cylinder

Engine model number

Engine Assembly

REMOVAL AND INSTALLATION

4-Cylinder Engine

NOTE: The factory recommends that the engine and transaxle be removed as a unit. Slight variations in this procedure may occur due to extra connections, etc., but the basic procedure should cover all 4-cylinder engines.

1. If equipped with fuel injection, relieve fuel system pressure as follows:

   a. Turn the ignition to the **OFF** position.

   b. Loosen the fuel filler cap to release fuel tank pressure.

   c. Disconnect the fuel pump harness connector located under the rear seat cushion on Elantra or in the area of the fuel tank on the remaining models.

   d. Start the vehicle and allow it to run until it stalls from lack of fuel. Turn the key to the **OFF** position.

   e. Disconnect the negative battery cable, then reconnect the fuel pump connector.

2. Matchmark the hood and hinges and remove the hood assembly. Remove the air cleaner assembly and all adjoining air intake duct work.

3. Remove the undercover if equipped.

4. Disconnect the purge control vacuum hose from the purge valve. Remove the purge control valve mounting bracket. Remove the windshield washer reservoir, radiator tank and carbon canister.

5. Drain the coolant from the radiator. Disconnect the upper and lower radiator hoses and then remove the radiator assembly with the electric cooling fan attached. Be sure to disconnect the fan wiring harness prior to removal.

6. Disconnect the electrical connectors for the backup lights and engine harness, located near the battery tray. If equipped with a 5 speed transaxle, disconnect the select control valve connector. Disconnect the alternator harness connectors and the oil pressure sending unit.

7. Label and disconnect the automatic transaxle oil cooler hoses. Avoid spilling oil and cap the openings.

8. Label and disconnect all low tension wires and the one high tension wire going to the coil from the distributor. Disconnect the engine ground.

9. Disconnect the brake booster vacuum hose at the intake manifold.

10. Disconnect the fuel supply, return and vapor hoses at the side of the engine. Before disconnecting the fuel supply and return lines, wrap shop towels around the fuel fitting that is being disconnected to absorb any fuel spray caused by residual pressure in the lines.

11. Disconnect the heater hoses from the side of the engine. Disconnect the accelerator cable at the engine side.

12. Disconnect the clutch control cable for manual transaxle. Disconnect the shifter control cable for automatic transaxle.

13. Unscrew and disconnect the speedometer cable at the transaxle.

14. Remove the air conditioner drive belt and the air conditioning compressor. Leave the hoses attached. Do not discharge the system. Wire the compressor aside.

15. Raise and safely support the vehicle. Remove the splash shield. Remove the drain plug and drain the transaxle fluid. Disconnect the exhaust pipe at the manifold and suspend the pipe securely with wire.

16. If equipped with a manual transaxle, remove the shift control rod and extension rod.

17. Disconnect the stabilizer bar at both lower control arms. Remove the bolts that attach the lower control arms to the body on either side. Support the arms from the body.

18. Remove the front halfshafts. Then, seal off the openings in the transaxle to prevent damage caused by the introduction of foreign substances into the transaxle. Be sure to replace the circlips holding the halfshafts in the transaxle during assembly.

19. Attach an engine lift, via chains or cables, to both the engine lifting hooks. Put just a little tension on the cables. Then, remove the nut and bolt from the front roll stopper; unbolt the brace from the top of the engine damper.

20. Separate the rear roll stopper from the No. 2 crossmember. Remove the attaching nut from the left mount insulator bolt, but do not remove the bolt.

21. Raise the engine just enough that the lifting device is supporting its weight. Check that everything is disconnected from the engine.

22. Remove the blind cover from the inside of the right fender inner shield. Remove the transaxle mounting bracket bolts.

23. Remove the left mount insulator bolt. Then, press downward on the transaxle while lifting the engine/transaxle assembly to guide it up and out of the vehicle.

NOTE: Make sure the transaxle does not hit the battery bracket during engine and transaxle removal.

To install:

24. Using a lifting device, lower the engine and transaxle carefully into position and loosely install the

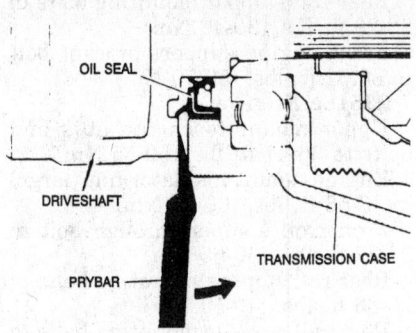

Removing the driveshafts

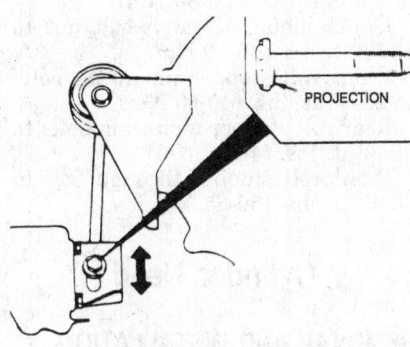

Installing the lower bolt on the roll stopper

Remove the front roll stop nut and the bolt; or, remove the attaching bolts from the engine damper

mounting bolts. Temporarily tighten the front and rear roll control rods mounting bolts. Lower the full weight of the engine and transaxle onto the mounts and tighten the nuts and bolts. Loosen and retighten the roll control rods.

25. Install the transaxle mounting bracket bolts. Install the blind cover to the inside of the right fender inner shield.

26. Assemble the rear roll stopper to the No. 2 crossmember. Install retaining nut and bolt.

27. Install new circlips on the half-shafts and install in position.

28. Attach the lower control arms to the body on either side. Connect the stabilizer bar to both lower control arms.

29. If equipped with a manual transaxle, install the shift control rod and extension rod.

30. Raise the vehicle and support it safely. Connect the exhaust pipe at the manifold. Install the splash shield.

31. Connect the speedometer cable at the transaxle. Connect the air conditioning compressor to the mounting bracket.

32. Install the clutch control cable, for manual transaxle, or shifter control cable, for automatic transaxle, to the transaxle.

33. Lower the vehicle. Connect the heater hoses to the engine. Connect the accelerator cable at the engine side.

34. Connect the fuel supply, return and vapor hoses with new O-rings installed.

35. Connect the brake booster vacuum hose at the intake manifold.

36. Connect all low tension wires and the high tension wire going to the coil from the distributor. Connect the engine ground and the fuel injectors.

37. Connect the automatic transaxle oil cooler hoses.

38. Connect the electrical connectors for the backup lights and engine harness, located near the battery tray. If equipped with 5 speed, connect the select control valve connector. Connect the alternator harness connectors and the oil pressure sending unit.

39. Install the radiator and electric cooling fan assembly. Connect the upper and lower radiator hoses.

40. Fill all fluids to the proper levels. Adjust the transaxle control cables, accessory drive belts and accelerator linkages as required. Reconnect the negative battery cable.

41. Start the engine and check for leaks as well as proper gauge operation. Allow the vehicle to reach normal operating temperature and recheck all fluid levels.

42. Replace the hood making sure to align the matchmarks made during removal. Allow the engine to cool and recheck the coolant level.

6-Cylinder Engine

NOTE: The factory recommends that the engine and transaxle be removed as a unit.

1. If equipped with fuel injection, relieve fuel system pressure as follows:

   a. Turn the ignition to the **OFF** position.

   b. Loosen the fuel filler cap to release fuel tank pressure.

   c. Disconnect the fuel pump harness connector normally located under the vehicle towards the rear of the fuel tank.

   d. Start the vehicle and allow it to run until it stalls from lack of fuel. Turn the key to the **OFF** position.

   e. Disconnect the negative battery cable, then reconnect the fuel pump connector.

2. Remove the undercover, if equipped.

3. Matchmark the hood and hinges and remove the hood assembly. Remove the air cleaner assembly and all adjoining air intake duct work.

4. Disconnect the fuel supply line, return line and vent hoses. Prior to disconnecting the fuel supply or return lines, wrap shop towels around the fitting that is being disconnected to absorb any fuel spray caused by residual pressure in the lines.

5. Disconnect the backup light, engine, alternator and oil pressure harnesses.

6. Drain the engine coolant.

7. Label and disconnect the transaxle oil cooler lines, radiator hoses and remove the radiator assembly.

8. Disconnect the brake booster, fuel, evaporative canister and heater hoses.

9. Disconnect the accelerator, transaxle, cruise control and speedometer cables.

10. Detach the air conditioning compressor from the mounting bracket and hang out of the way with a piece of wire. Do not disconnect the refrigerant lines.

11. Remove the power steering pump and wire aside.

12. Raise the vehicle and support safely.

13. Remove the oil pan shield and drain the transaxle.

14. Disconnect the front exhaust pipe.

15. Remove the lower arm ball joint and stabilizer bar at the point where it is mounted to the lower arms.

16. Remove the halfshaft from the housing by prying against the transaxle housing with a prybar.

17. Suspend the lower arm and driveshafts aside using wire attached to the vehicle underbody.

18. Attach an engine lifting device to the engine. Raise the engine just enough to take the tension off the engine mounts.

19. Remove the front roll stopper, engine damper and rear roll stopper.

20. Remove the engine mount bolts.

21. Remove the blind plugs from the inside of the right fender shield and remove the transaxle mounting bracket bolts.

22. Remove the left mount insulator bolt.

23. Raise the engine and transaxle slightly and inspect to make sure all cables, hoses and harness connectors are disconnected.

24. While directing the transaxle side downward, lift the engine and transaxle assembly up and out of the vehicle.

To install:

25. While directing the transaxle side downward, direct the engine and transaxle assembly into the vehicle. Install all mounting hardware and control bracket retainers.

26. Tighten the center crossmember-to-body bolts to 43-58 ft. lbs. (58-77 Nm).

27. Once the engine is securely in place, remove the engine lifting device.

28. Connect the lower arm and the remaining suspension components disassembled during engine removal.

29. Install the halfshafts to the transaxle housing. Make sure the new C-clips are fully engaged into the differential assembly.

30. Connect the front exhaust pipe. Refill the transaxle with fluid.

31. Install the oil pan shield and lower the vehicle.

32. Install the power steering pump.

33. Reconnect the fuel lines using new O-rings where required.

34. Install the air conditioning compressor to the mounting bracket.

35. Connect the accelerator, transaxle, cruise control and speedometer cables.

36. Connect the brake booster, fuel, evaporative canister and heater hoses.

37. Install the radiator. Connect the transaxle oil cooler lines and radiator hoses.

38. Refill the engine coolant.

39. Connect the backup light, engine, alternator and oil pressure harnesses.

40. Connect the negative battery cable. Install the air cleaner assembly.

41. Start the engine and check for leaks. Allow the engine to run until normal operating temperature is reached and recheck all fluid levels.

42. Replace the hood making sure to align the matchmarks made during removal. Allow the engine to cool and recheck the coolant level.

Engine Mounts

REMOVAL AND INSTALLATION

1. Disconnect the negative battery cable.

2. Remove the air cleaner and all necessary air duct work.

3. Using the proper equipment, raise and safely support the engine so it is not resting on the engine mount.

4. Note the position of the stopper plates on the upper engine mount and mark their orientation for installation. Remove the engine mount insulator bolts and remove the insulators brackets from the engine.

To install:

5. Make sure to install the stopper plates in the same direction prior to removal. If reference marks were not made on plate prior to stopper plate removal and alignment arrows are present, make sure the arrows face towards the center of the engine.

6. Torque the engine mounting hardware as follows:

1468cc and 1495cc Engines
Upper mount to engine nuts and bolts to 36-47 ft. lbs. (50-65 Nm)
Upper mount through bolt nut to 65-80 ft. lbs. (90-110 Nm)
Front roll stopper mounting bolts to 22-29 ft. lbs. (30-40 Nm)
Rear roll stopper mounting bolts to 33-43 ft. lbs. (45-60 Nm)
Front roll stopper through bolt to 36-47 ft. lbs. (50-65 Nm)

1596cc and 1796cc Engines
Upper mount to engine nuts and bolts to 36-47 ft. lbs. (50-65 Nm)
Upper mount through bolt nut to 65-80 ft. lbs. (90-110 Nm)
Front roll stopper mounting bolts to 22-29 ft. lbs. (30-40 Nm).
Rear roll stopper mounting bolts to 33-43 ft. lbs. (45-60 Nm)
Front roll stopper through bolt to 33-43 ft. lbs. (44-59 Nm)
Rear roll stopper through bolt to 33-43 ft. lbs. (44-59 Nm)

1997cc Engine
Upper mount to engine nuts and bolts to 36-47 ft. lbs. (50-65 Nm)
Engine mount insulator nut (large) to 43-58 ft. lbs. (60-80 Nm)
Front roll stopper through bolt to 36-47 ft. lbs. (50-65 Nm)
Rear roll stopper mounting bolts to 29-36 ft. lbs. (40-50 Nm)

Rear roll stopper mounting bolts to 22-29 ft. lbs. (30-40 Nm)
Front engine support bracket bolt to 36-51 ft. lbs. (50-70 Nm)

2351cc Engine
Upper mount to engine nuts and bolts to 36-47 ft. lbs. (50-65 Nm)
Engine mount insulator nut (large) to 43-58 ft. lbs. (60-80 Nm)
Front roll stopper through bolt to 36-47 ft. lbs. (50-65 Nm)
Rear roll stopper mounting bolts to 29-36 ft. lbs. (40-50 Nm)
Rear roll stopper mounting bolts to 22-29 ft. lbs. (30-40 Nm)

2972cc Engine
Upper engine mount bracket nuts to 43-58 ft. lbs. (60-80 Nm)
Upper mount through bolt nut to 43-58 ft. lbs. (60-80 Nm)
Front roll stopper mounting bolts to 29-36 ft. lbs. (40-50 Nm)
Rear roll stopper mounting bolts to 29-36 ft. lbs. (40-50 Nm)
Front roll stopper through bolt to 36-47 ft. lbs. (50-65 Nm)

Cylinder Head

REMOVAL AND INSTALLATION

NOTE: Do not remove the cylinder head unless the engine is cold. A hot cylinder head will warp.

1468CC Engine

1. Release the fuel system pressure and disconnect the negative battery cable.

2. Drain the cooling system and then disconnect the upper radiator hose. Remove the PCV hose that runs between the air cleaner and the rocker cover.

3. Remove the air cleaner. Label and disconnect any vacuum lines running to the cylinder head, manifold or carburetor from other parts of the engine compartment. Disconnect the heater hoses going to the head.

4. Disconnect the fuel supply line, return line and vent hoses. Prior to disconnecting the fuel supply or return lines, wrap shop towels around the fitting that is being disconnected to absorb any fuel spray caused by residual pressure in the lines.

5. Label and disconnect the spark plug wires, injectors and any other electronic components that will be removed with the cylinder head. Remove the rocker cover.

6. Turn the crankshaft until the TDC timing marks align and both No. 1 cylinder valves are closed, both rockers are off the cams. The engine

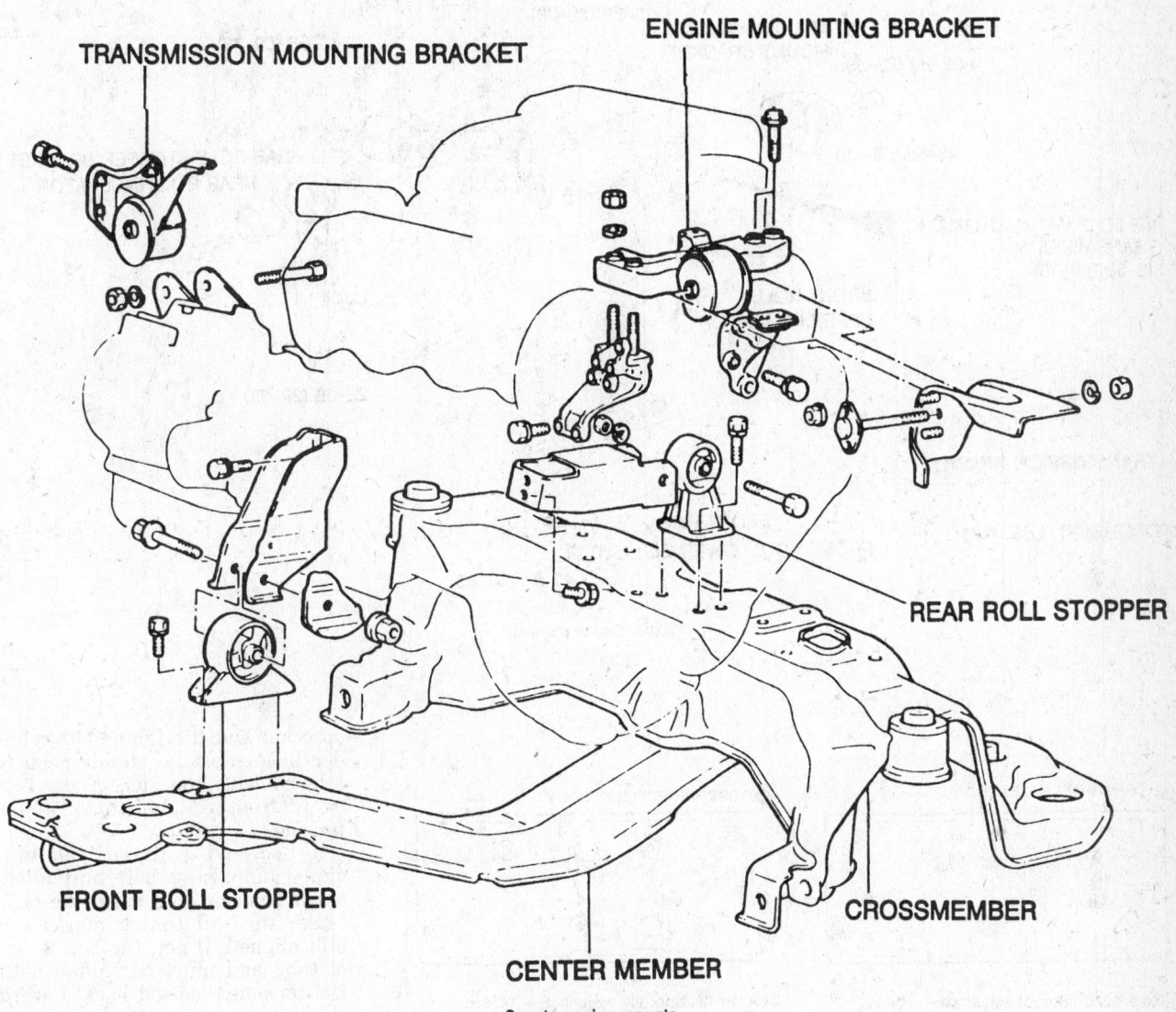

TRANSMISSION MOUNTING BRACKET

ENGINE MOUNTING BRACKET

REAR ROLL STOPPER

FRONT ROLL STOPPER

CROSSMEMBER

CENTER MEMBER

Sonata engine mounts

will now be at top dead center with No. 1 piston on its' compression stroke.

7. Remove the distributor cap and matchmark the rotor tip to the distributor housing and the housing to the engine. Now, remove the distributor.

NOTE: with the distributor removed, do not crank the engine. If rotated with the distributor removed, the engine will have to be positioned with No. 1 cylinder at top dead center of its' compression stroke prior to installing the distributor.

8. Remove the carburetor, if equipped. Remove the intake and the exhaust manifolds.

9. Remove the timing belt cover. Note the location of the camshaft sprocket timing mark. Loosen both timing belt tensioner mounting bolts and move tensioner toward the water pump as far as it will go. Retighten the adjusting bolt to hold the tensioner in this position. Pull the timing belt off the camshaft sprocket but leave it engaged with the other sprockets.

10. Using a hex type wrench, loosen the head bolts in the proper sequence. When all have been loosened,

remove them. Then, pull the head off the engine block, rocking it slightly to break it loose.

11. Inspect the head with a straight-edge and a flat feeler gauge of 0.002 in. (0.05mm) thickness. The tolerance for warping of a used head is 0.002 in. (0.05mm). The block deck must be flat within the same tolerance. The height of the head should be 3.5 in. (89mm) with a maximum machining limit of 0.012 in. (0.3mm).

To install:

12. Clean the combustion chambers of carbon with a scraper that is not excessively sharp, being careful not to damage the aluminum surface.

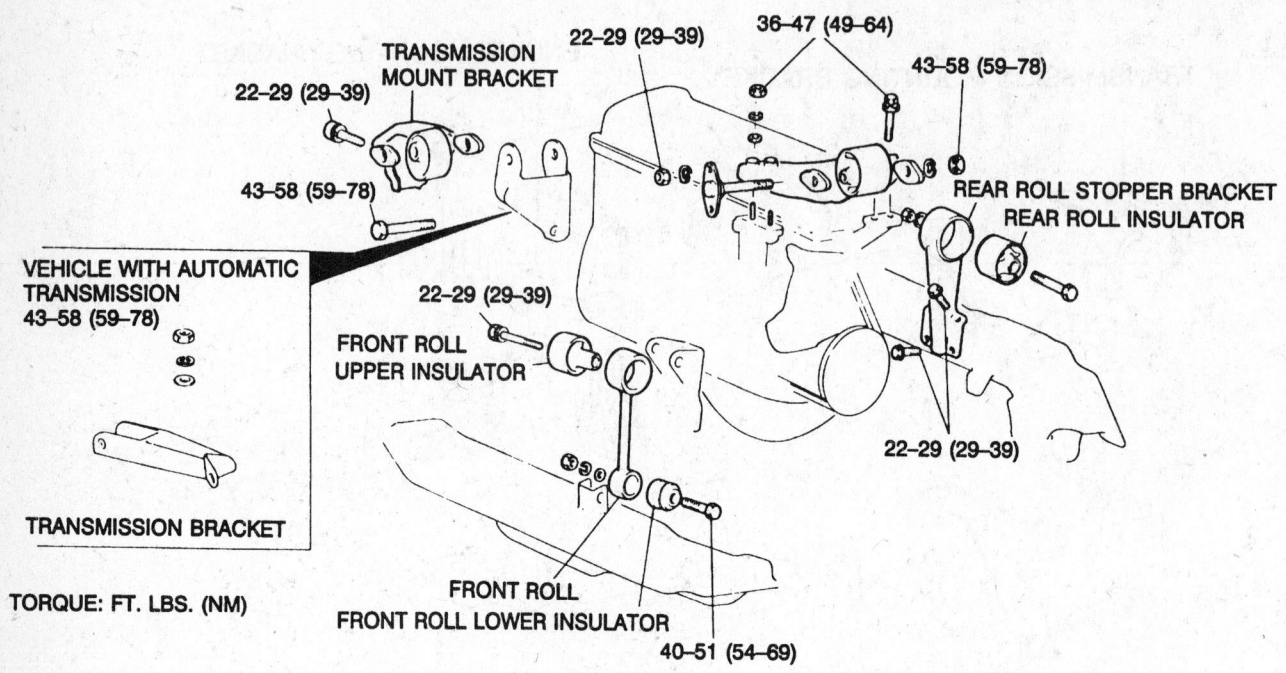

Excel engine mounts

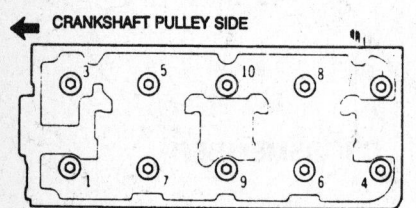

Cylinder head removal sequence — 1468cc engine

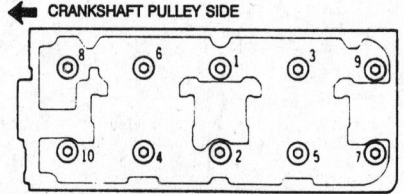

Cylinder head torque sequence — 1468cc engine

Sharp edges in the combustion chambers can cause detonation. Clean the gasket mating surfaces with a scraper and solvent.

13. The oil and water passages should be cleaned thoroughly. Also, blow compressed air through all the small oil passages to ensure that they are clear. Check that the EGR and air pump passages are also clear. Both gasket surfaces must be completely free of dirt.

14. Install a new head gasket, without sealant, and position the head on the cylinder block. Install all the bolts finger-tight. Torque the bolts in sequence. First step to 15 ft. lbs. (20 Nm), 2nd step to 25 ft. lbs. (35 Nm). Then, torque again, in sequence, to 51-54 ft. lbs. (69-74 Nm).

15. Align the matchmarks and install the distributor to the engine.

16. Install the timing belt on the camshaft tensioner and rotate the camshaft sprocket backward so the belt is tight on what is normally the tension side.

a. Make sure all the timing marks are now aligned. That is, timing marks on the crankshaft sprocket and front case must align; and the marks on the camshaft sprocket and the tab on the cylinder head must be simultaneously aligned with the side of the belt away from the tensioner under tension.

b. Loosen the timing belt tensioner adjusting bolt and allow spring tension to tension the belt. Make sure all timing marks are still aligned. If not, the belt is out of time and must be shifted with the tensioner moved back, toward the water pump and locked there.

c. Torque the adjusting bolt on the right side, working through a slot, to 15-18 ft. lbs. (20-25 Nm). After the tensioner adjusting bolt is torqued, torque the hinged mounting bolt located on the opposite side. Don't torque the mounting bolt first or the tension on the belt will be too great.

17. Turn the crankshaft 1 full turn in the normal direction of rotation. Loosen first the tensioner pivot bolt and then the adjusting bolt. Now torque them exactly as before, adjusting bolt, working in the slot. This extra step is necessary to ensure the timing belt is properly seated before final tension is adjusted.

18. Install the cylinder head cover and tighten the bolts to 13-16 inch lbs. (1.5-2.0 Nm).

19. Install the timing belt cover.

20. Install the intake manifold using a new gasket and tighten the bolts and nut to 12-14 ft. lbs. (16-19 Nm).

21. Install the exhaust manifold using a new gasket and tighten the nuts to 12-14 ft. lbs. (16-19 Nm).

22. Install the carburetor or throttle body assembly.

23. Install the distributor. Connect all hoses, lines and the air cleaner.

24. Refill the cooling system. Operate the engine and check for leaks. After the engine has reached normal operating temperature, turn it OFF and remove the air cleaner and rocker cover. Retighten the cylinder head bolts to 58-61 ft. lbs. (78-83 Nm), in the sequence.

25. Reinstall the rocker cover and the air cleaner.

1495cc Engine

The following applies to the 12 valve head on the VIN (N) engine introduced on the 1993-94 Scoupe. It is available normally aspirated or turbocharged.

1. Drain the coolant and disconnect the upper radiator hose. Disconnect the negative battery cable.

2. It is generally a good idea to set the engine to TDC on No.1 cylinder, making sure all the timing marks line up. This will save much time at reassembly.

3. Remove the breather hose between the air cleaner and the rocker cover. Remove the air intake pipe on turbocharged engines and the air intake hose.

4. Remove the vacuum hose, fuel hose and water hose.

5. Remove the cables from the spark plugs.

6. Remove the distributor.

7. Remove the surge tank.

8. Remove the intake manifold.

9. Remove the heat protector and exhaust manifold assembly.

10. Remove the water pump pulley and the crankshaft pulley.

11. Remove the timing belt cover.

12. Move the timing belt tensioner pulley toward the water pump and temporarily secure it.

13. Remove the timing belt. If the timing belt is to be reused, make arrow marks indicating the turning direction or front of engine to make sure the timing belt is reinstalled in the same direction as before.

14. Remove the rocker cover.

15. Remove the cylinder head bolts using the proper wrench and sequence.

16. Remove the head gasket and clean the block deck and cylinder bores.

17. Check the head for cracks and flatness. Out-of-true dimension limit is 0.004 in. (0.0054mm) in any direction.

18. Make sure oil and coolant passages as well as all holes for the head bolts are clean. The proper size metric tap can be used to make sure the head bolt holes in the engine block are free of corrosion and debris. This is important to obtain an accurate torque reading when the head is installed.

To install:

19. Always use a new head gasket. Do not apply sealant to the gasket. Make sure the gasket surface on the bottom of the head is absolutely clean and install the head. Use care when setting the head onto the block to avoid gasket damage.

20. Install the cylinder head bolts. New bolts are recommended. Starting at top center, tighten all cylinder head bolts in the proper sequence. Torque the head bolts in several steps to 51-54 ft. lbs. (70-74 Nm).

21. Move the timing belt tensioner pulley toward the water pump and temporarily secure it.

22. Install the timing belt on the camshaft sprocket. Make sure the tension side of the belt is tight. If the engine was set to TDC on No. 1 at disassembly, the timing marks should line-up. Adjust the timing belt as required.

23. Install the rocker cover. Do not overtighten the fasteners. Torque to only 1.1-1.4 ft. lbs. (1.5-2.0 Nm).

24. Install the timing belt cover.

25. Install a new intake gasket and install the intake manifold. Torque fasteners to 11-14 ft. lbs. (15-19 Nm).

26. Install a new exhaust gasket and install the exhaust manifold. Torque fasteners to 11-14 ft. lbs. (15-19 Nm).

27. Install the surge tank, distributor and remaining vacuum, coolant and fuel hoses.

28. Refill with coolant. Test run, check for leaks.

2351cc Engine

1. Disconnect the negative battery cable. Drain the engine coolant.

2. Remove the intake and exhaust manifolds.

3. Remove the air cleaner. Detach and tag all vacuum hoses, heater hoses and gauge connectors which connect with the cylinder head or would obstruct its removal.

4. Remove the throttle air valve.

5. Remove the timing belt cover.

6. Remove the rocker cover.

7. Rotate the crankshaft until the timing marks are at TDC with No. 1 cylinder at the firing position, front valves closed fully. If the rockers are not all the way off the cams, turn the engine another 360 degrees.

8. Label and disconnect all spark plug wires at the plugs.

9. Remove the distributor.

10. Remove the timing belt.

11. Using an 8mm hex socket loosen the head bolts, in order, in 3 stages, alternating from bolt to bolt. Rock the head to break it loose and then remove the head and the gasket from the block.

12. Inspect the head with a straight-edge and a flat feeler gauge of 0.004 in. (0.10mm) thickness. Run the gauge in every direction. The tolerance for warping of a used head is 0.002 in. (0.05mm) across the entire length. The block deck must be flat within the same tolerance. The refacing limit is 0.008 in. (0.20mm). The overall head height should be 3.539-3.547 in. (89.9-90.1mm).

To install:

13. Clean the combustion chambers of carbon with a scraper that is not excessively sharp and use it carefully to avoid damaging the relatively soft aluminum surface. Clean the gasket mating surfaces with a scraper and solvent.

14. The oil and water passages should be cleaned thoroughly, Blow compressed air through all the small oil passages to ensure that they are clear. Check that the EGR and air pump passages are also clear. Both gasket surfaces must be completely free of dirt.

15. Apply sealant around the 4 oil drain holes on the cylinder head gasket. Install the head gasket on the block deck, with the identification mark facing upward toward the cylinder head.

16. Put the head into position and install the head bolts. The bolts must be torqued to a cold specification, which is 65-72 ft. lbs. (88-98 Nm), in 3 stages. Using the proper sequence, torque the bolts, in order, to 25 ft. lbs. (34 Nm) and then to 33-36 ft. lbs. (45-48 Nm). Then, repeat the operation, tightening them to the full torque of 72 ft. lbs. (98 Nm).

17. Perform the remaining steps in reverse of the removal procedure.

18. Connect the negative battery cable.

19. Start the engine, check for leaks and run the engine to normal operating temperature. Stop the engine. Re-

move the valve cover and torque the head bolts, warm, in sequence, to 72-80 ft. lbs. (96-108 Nm). Replace the valve cover.

1596cc, 1796cc and 1997cc Engines

1. Release the fuel system pressure. Disconnect the negative battery cable and drain the cooling system.

2. Disconnect the accelerator cable, PCV hoses, breather hoses, spark plug cables and the remove the valve cover.

3. Rotate the crankshaft clockwise and align the timing marks so No. 1 piston will be at TDC of the compres-

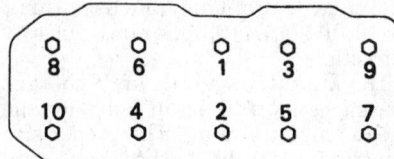

⟵ FRONT OF ENGINE

Cylinder head tightening sequence — 2351cc engine

⟵ FRONT OF ENGINE

Cylinder head loosening sequence — 2351cc engine

sion stroke. At this time the timing marks on the camshaft sprocket and the upper surface of the cylinder head should coincide, and the dowel pin of the camshaft sprocket should be at the upper side.

NOTE: Always rotate the crankshaft in a clockwise direction. Make a mark on the back of the timing belt indicating the direction of rotation so it may be reassembled in the same direction if it is to be reused.

4. Remove the timing belt upper and lower covers.

5. Remove the timing belt.

6. Remove the crank angle sensor.

7. Loosen the cylinder head mounting bolts in 3 steps, starting from the outside and working inward. Lift off the cylinder head assembly and remove the head gasket.

To install:

8. Thoroughly clean and dry the mating surfaces of the head and block. Check the cylinder head for cracks, damage or engine coolant leakage. Remove scale, sealing compound and carbon. Clean oil passages thoroughly. Check the head for flatness. End to end, the head should be within 0.002 in. (0.05mm) normally with 0.008 in. (0.20mm) the maximum allowed out-of-true. The total thickness allowed to be removed from the head and block is 0.008 in. (0.20mm) maximum.

9. Place a new head gasket on the cylinder block with the identification marks at the front top (upward) position. Make sure the gasket has the proper identification mark for the engine. Do not use sealer on the gasket.

10. Carefully install the cylinder head on the block. Using 3 even steps, torque the head bolts in sequence to 76-83 ft. lbs. (105-115 Nm) on 1997cc engine. On 1596cc and 1796cc engines, torque the head bolts in sequence to 65-72 ft. lbs. (90-100 Nm) using 3 even steps. These torques apply to a cold engine.

11. Install the timing belt and all related items.

12. Align the punch mark on the crank angle sensor housing with the notch on the plate. Install the crank angle sensor into the cylinder head.

NOTE: The crank angle sensor can be installed even when the punch mark is positioned opposite the notch; however, the position results in incorrect fuel injection and ignition timing.

13. Apply sealer to the perimeter of the half-round seal and to the lower edges of the half-round portions of the belt-side of the new gasket. Install the valve cover.

14. Connect or install all previously disconnected hoses, cables and electrical connections. Adjust the throttle cable(s).

15. Install the spark plug cable center cover.

16. Replace the O-rings and connect the fuel lines.

17. Install the air cleaner and intake hose. Connect the breather hose.

18. Change the engine oil and oil filter.

19. Fill the system with coolant. Connect the negative battery cable. Run the vehicle until the thermostat

8a. Camshaft bearing cap
8b. No. 2, 3 and 4 caps
8c. Camshaft bearing cap (rear)
10. Cylinder head
11a. Intake valve seat ring
11b. Exhaust valve seat ring
12. Cylinder head bolt
13a. Exhaust valve guide
13b. Intake valve guide
14. Cylinder head gasket

Exploded view of the cylinder head — 2351cc engine

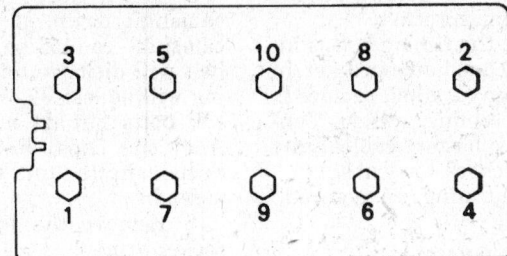

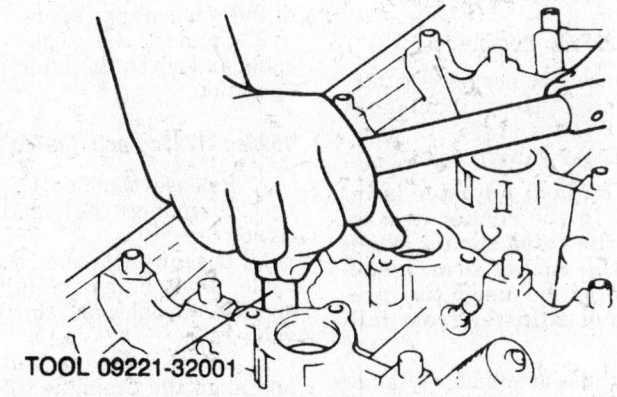

TOOL 09221-32001

Cylinder head bolt removal sequence — 1596cc, 1796cc and 1997cc DOHC engines

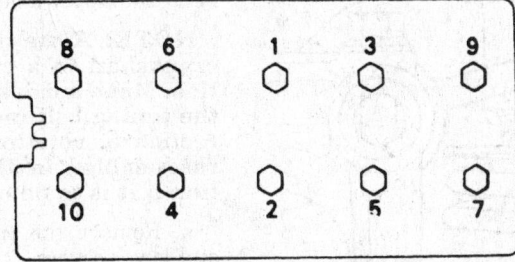

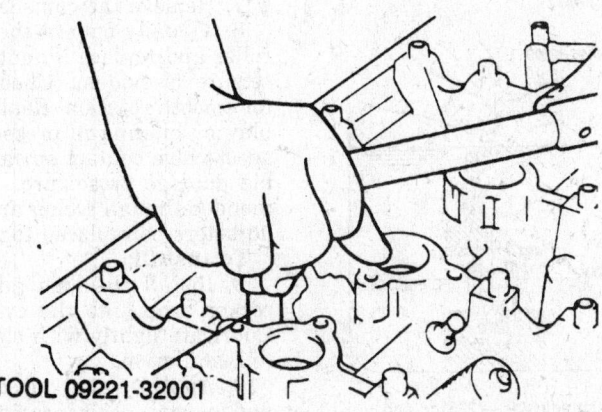

TOOL 09221-32001

Cylinder head bolt tightening sequence — 1596cc, 1796cc and 1997cc DOHC engines

opens and fill the radiator completely.

20. Check and adjust the idle speed and ignition timing.

21. Once the vehicle has cooled, recheck the coolant level.

2972cc Engine

1. Relieve the fuel pressure. Disconnect the negative battery cable. Drain the cooling system.

2. Remove the compressor drive belt and the air conditioning compressor from its mount and support it aside. Using a ½ in. drive breaker bar, insert it into the square hole of the serpentine drive belt tensioner, rotate it counterclockwise to reduce the belt tension and remove the belt. Remove the alternator and power steering pump from the brackets and move them aside.

3. Raise the vehicle and support safely. Remove the right front wheel and the inner splash shield.

4. Remove the crankshaft pulleys and the torsional damper.

5. Lower the vehicle. Using a floor jack and a block of wood positioned under the oil pan, raise the engine slightly. Remove the engine mount bracket from the timing cover end of the engine and the timing belt covers.

6. To remove the timing belt, perform the following procedures:

   a. Rotate the crankshaft to position the No. 1 cylinder on the TDC of its compression stroke; the crankshaft sprocket timing mark should align with the oil pan timing indicator and the camshaft sprockets timing marks (triangles) should align with the rear timing belt covers timing marks.

   b. Mark the timing belt in the direction of rotation for reinstallation purposes.

   c. Loosen the timing belt tensioner and remove the timing belt.

NOTE: When removing the timing belt from the camshaft sprocket, make sure the belt does not slip off the other camshaft sprocket. Support the belt so it can not slip off the crankshaft sprocket and opposite side camshaft sprocket.

7. Remove the air cleaner assembly. Label and disconnect the spark plug wires and the vacuum hoses.

8. Remove the valve cover.

9. Install auto lash adjuster retainer tools MD998443 or equivalent, on the rocker arms.

10. If removing the front cylinder head, matchmark the distributor rotor to the distributor housing and the

housing to distributor extension locations. Remove the distributor and the distributor extension.

11. Remove the camshaft bearing assembly to cylinder head bolts but do not remove the bolts from the assembly. Remove the rocker arms, rocker shafts and bearing caps as an assembly, as required. Remove the camshafts from the cylinder head and inspect them for damage.

12. Remove the intake manifold assembly.

13. Remove the exhaust manifold.

14. Remove the cylinder head bolts, starting from the outside and working inward. Remove the cylinder head from the engine.

15. Clean the gasket mounting surfaces and check the heads for warpage; maximum warpage is 0.008 in. (0.20mm).

To install:

16. Install the new cylinder head gasket over the dowels on the engine block.

17. Install the cylinder head(s) on the engine and torque the cylinder head bolts, in sequence, using 3 even steps, to 70 ft. lbs. (95 Nm).

18. Install or connect all items that were removed or disconnected during the removal procedure.

19. When installing the timing belt on the camshaft sprocket, use care not to allow the belt to slip off the opposite camshaft sprocket.

20. Make sure the timing belt is installed on the camshaft sprocket in the same position as when removed.

21. Refill the cooling system. Connect the negative battery cable. Start the engine and check for leaks.

22. Adjust the timing, as required.

Valve Lifters

REMOVAL AND INSTALLATION

2351cc and 2972cc Engines

1. Disconnect the negative battery cable. Remove the air cleaner assembly.

2. Remove the valve cover.

NOTE: The lash adjuster is incorporated in the rocker arm on the side of the valve spring. When removing the rocker arm, a special tool must be used the prevent the lash adjuster from falling out.

3. Using the lash adjuster retainer tools MD998443 or equivalent, install them on the rocker arms.

4. On the right side cylinder head, remove the distributor extension.

5. Hold the rear end of the camshaft down. If the rear of the camshaft cannot be held down, the belt will dislodge and the valve timing will be lost. Loosen the camshaft cap bolts but do not remove them from the caps. Remove the caps, arms, shafts and bolts all as an assembly.

6. Remove the lifter(s) from the rocker arm(s).

7. Lubricate the lifter(s) and their bore(s) with clean engine oil.

8. The installation is the reverse of the removal procedure.

9. Connect the negative battery cable and check the lifters for proper operation.

1596cc, 1796cc and 1997cc Engines

1. Release the fuel system pressure. Disconnect the negative battery cable.

2. Disconnect the accelerator cable, PCV hoses, breather hoses, spark plug cables and the remove the valve cover.

3. Rotate the crankshaft clockwise and align the timing marks so No. 1 piston will be at TDC of the compression stroke. At this time the timing marks on the camshaft sprocket and the upper surface of the cylinder head should coincide, and the dowel pin of the camshaft sprocket should be at the upper side.

NOTE: Always rotate the crankshaft in a clockwise direction. Make a mark on the back of the timing belt indicating the direction of rotation so it may be reassembled in the same direction if it is to be reused.

4. Remove the timing belt upper and lower covers.

5. Remove the timing belt.

6. Remove the crank angle sensor.

7. Remove the camshafts.

8. Visually inspect the rocker arm roller and replace if dent, damage or seizure is evident. Check the roller for smooth rotation. Replace if excess play or binding is present. Also, inspect valve contact surface for possible damage or seizure. It is recommended that all rocker arms and lash adjusters be replaced together.

To install:

9. Install the lash adjusters and rocker arms into the cylinder head. Lubricate lightly with clean oil prior to installation.

10. Apply engine oil to the lobes and journals of each camshaft. Install the camshafts into the cylinder head

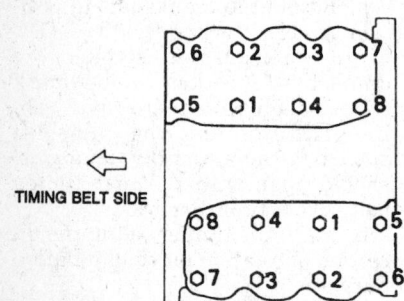

Cylinder head bolt torque sequence — 2972cc engine

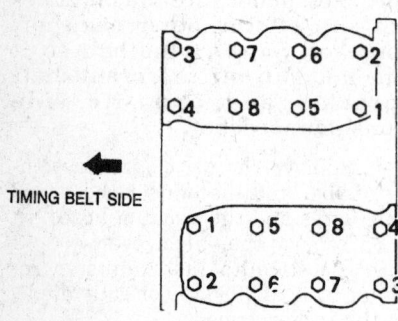

Cylinder head bolt loosening sequence — 2972cc engine

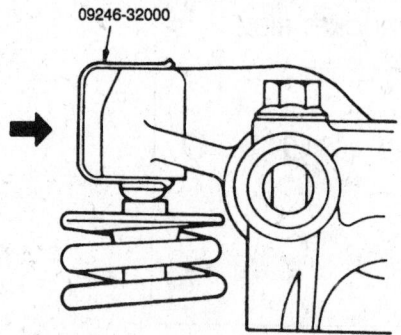

Lash adjuster holding tool installed — 2351cc and 2972cc engines

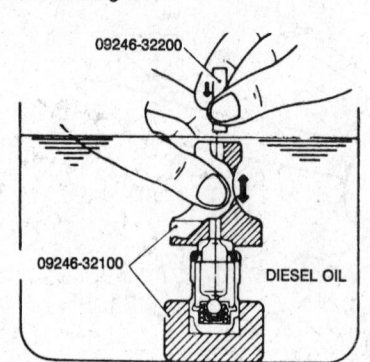

Bleeding the lash adjuster — 2351cc and 2972cc engines

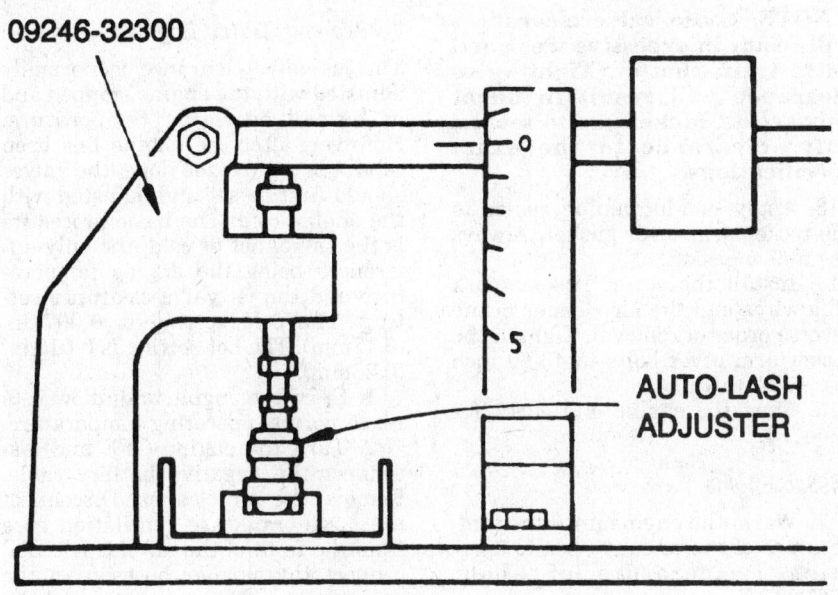

09246-32300

AUTO-LASH ADJUSTER

Lash adjuster leak down — 2351cc and 2972cc engines

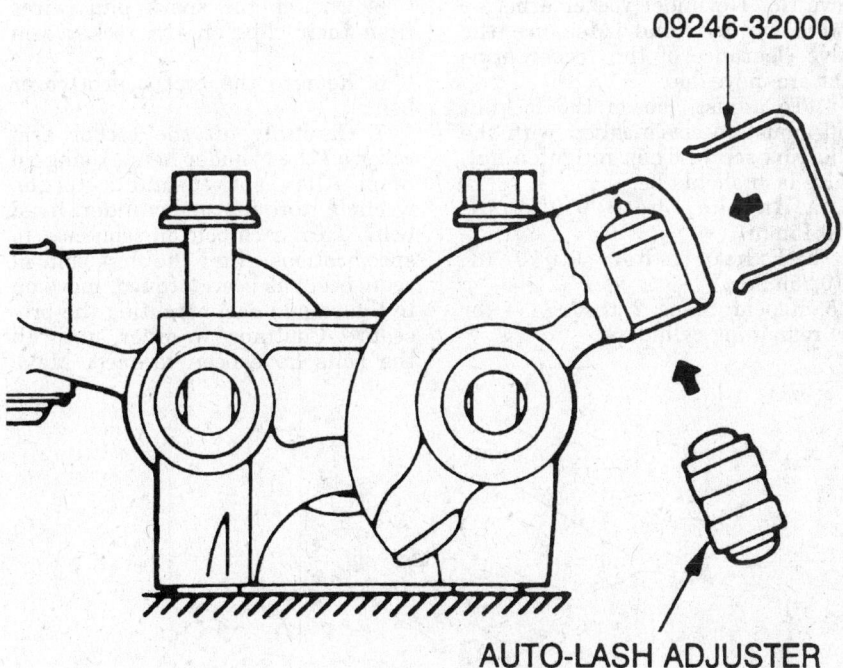

09246-32000

AUTO-LASH ADJUSTER

Lash adjuster installation

taking care not to confuse the intake and the exhaust camshaft; the intake camshaft has a slit on its rear end for driving the crank angle sensor. Align shafts so dowel pins on camshaft sprocket end are located on the top.

11. Install and tighten the camshaft bearing caps in the proper sequence tightening to 14-15 ft. lbs. (19-21 Nm), in 3 even progressions.

12. Replace the camshaft oil seals and install the sprockets.

13. Locate the dowel pin on the sprocket end of the intake camshaft at the top position, if not already done.

14. Align the punch mark on the crank angle sensor housing with the notch on the sensor plate. Install the crank angle sensor into the cylinder head.

15. Install the timing belt, covers and related components.

16. Install the valve cover using new gasket. Reconnect all related components.

17. Reconnect the negative battery cable.

BLEEDING THE LASH ADJUSTERS

If the lash adjuster is removed and the diesel fuel contained inside is spilled, submerge the adjuster in clean diesel fuel and compress it several times to expel the air. If air is still trapped after assembly and installation and a clattering noise is heard when the engine is started, the air can be bled by increasing engine speed from idle to 3000 rpm and back to idle over a minute period. Do this several times, or until the clattering stops. If this does not stop the clattering, remove and submerge the lifter in clean diesel fuel, compressing it several times. If clattering continues, replace the lash adjuster.

Valve Lash

ADJUSTMENT

1468cc Engine

Valve clearance is adjusted with the engine OFF.

1. Run the engine until it reaches normal operating temperature and then turn it OFF.

2. Remove the air cleaner. Pull the large crankcase ventilation hose off the front of the air cleaner. Disconnect the 2 smaller hoses, one goes to the rear of the rocker arm cover and the other to the intake manifold.

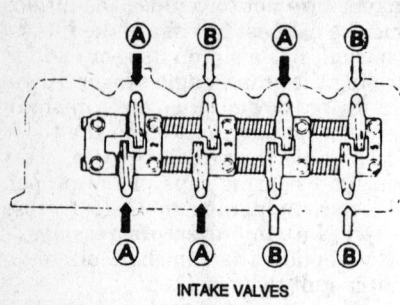

INTAKE VALVES

"A" and "B" valve adjusting positions — 2351cc engine

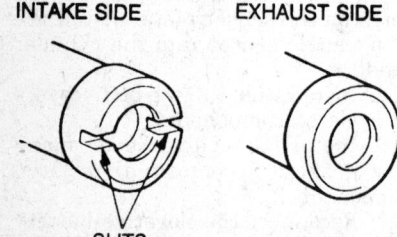

Camshaft identification marks. The intake camshaft has a slit on its rear end which is used for driving the crank angle sensor — 1596cc, 1796cc and 1997cc DOHC engines

3. Loosen and remove the nuts and bracket which attach the air cleaner to the rocker arm cover.

4. On carburetor equipped vehicles, lift the bottom housing of the air cleaner off the carburetor and the hose coming up from the exhaust manifold heat stove.

5. Remove the spark plug wires from their clips on the rocker arm cover.

6. Using a deep socket or box wrench, remove the rocker arm cover bolts.

7. Carefully lift the rocker arm cover off the cylinder head. Using a 5/16 in. (8mm) Allen socket and a torque wrench, make sure the cylinder head bolts are all tightened to specification.

8. Hot valve clearance is 0.006 in. (0.15mm) for the intake valves and 0.010 in. (0.25mm) for the exhaust.

9. Turn the crankshaft pulley to bring the piston to TDC of the compression stroke on the cylinder being adjusted.

10. Loosen the rocker arm adjusting screw locknuts.

11. Using the correct thickness feeler gauge, turn the adjusting screw until the gauge just snaps through the valve stem and the rocker arm.

12. Repeat the procedure to adjust the valves of each cylinder.

NOTE: Loose valve clearances will result in excessive wear and valve train chatter. Tight valve clearance will result in burnt valve seats. Make sure to set the valve clearance to the exact specifications.

13. Apply non-hardening sealer to the rocker arm cover gasket. Always use a new gasket.

14. Install the cover, hoses, spark plug wires and the air cleaner in the reverse order of removal. Tighten the rocker arm cover bolts to 48-60 inch lbs. (5.5-7.0 Nm).

15. Start the engine and check for leaks.

1495cc Engine

1. Warm the engine until the temperature of the coolant rises to operating temperature of about 176°-205°F.

2. Shut OFF the engine. Turn the crankshaft clockwise until the notch on the pulley is lined up with the **T** mark on the timing belt lower cover. This should place the piston of No. 1 cylinder at TDC of the compression stroke.

3. Remove the rocker cover and move No. 1 cylinder rocker arms up and down by hand. Measure the valve clearance of the rocker arms that are moveable.

4. To adjust, loosen the locknut and adjust to specification with the adjusting screw. Then retighten nut. Valve lash should be:

    a. Intake, hot: 0.006 in. (0.15mm)

    b. Exhaust, hot: 0.010 in. (0.25mm)

5. Repeat Steps 2 through 4 for the remaining cylinders.

Jet Valve

Adjustment

1468cc and 2351cc Engines

The jet valve clearance is normally adjusted with the engine stopped and at normal operating temperature. However, after the engine has been rebuilt or a valve job done, the valves should first be set and adjusted with the engine cold. The basic procedure is the same, hot or cold, the only differences being the engine temperature and the jet valve clearance setting. The cold setting is 0.007 in. (0.17mm). The hot setting is 0.010 in. (0.25mm).

1. Start the engine and allow it to reach normal operating temperature.

2. Turn the engine OFF and disconnect the negative battery cable. Remove the air cleaner. Disconnect the large crankcase ventilation hose from the front of the air cleaner. Disconnect the smaller hoses from the rear of the rocker arm cover and the intake manifold.

3. Loosen and remove the nuts and bracket which secure the air cleaner to the rocker arm cover.

4. Lift the bottom housing of the air cleaner off the intake, with the hose from the exhaust manifold heat stove attached.

5. Unsnap the spark plug wires from their clips on the rocker arm cover.

6. Remove the rocker arm cover bolts.

7. Carefully lift the rocker arm cover off the cylinder head. Using an 8mm Allen socket and a torque wrench, torque the cylinder head bolts. Turn each bolt, in sequence, to specifications. After the first bolt, in sequence, has been torqued, move on to the second one, repeating the procedure. Continue, in order, until all the bolts have been torqued. Make

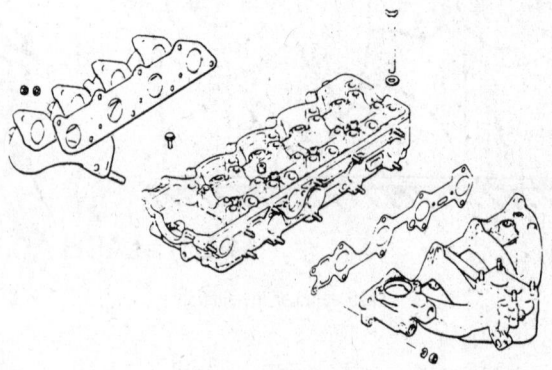

1468cc engine intake and exhaust manifolds — carburetor shown, fuel injected similar

sure the cylinder head bolts are all tightened, in sequence, to specification.

8. Remove the spark plugs.
9. Remove the distributor cap.

NOTE: A crankshaft pulley access hole is located on the left side frame member. Remove the covering plug and use a ratchet extension to turn the crankshaft when adjusting the valves.

10. Rotate the crankshaft until the No. 1 cylinder is at TDC of the compression stroke. Turn the engine by using a wrench on the bolt in the front of the crankshaft until the **TDC** or **0** timing mark on the timing cover lines up with the notch in the front pulley. Observe the valve rockers for No. 1 cylinder. If both are in identical positions with the valves up, the engine is in the right position. If not, rotate the engine exactly 360 degrees until the **TDC** or **0** degree timing mark is again aligned. Each jet valve is associated with an intake valve that is on the same rocker lever. In this position, adjust No. 1 and No. 2 jet valves, which are located on the rockers on the intake side only.

11. To adjust the appropriate jet valves:

   a. Loosen the regular (larger) intake valve adjusting stud by loosening the locknut and backing the stud off 2 turns (1468cc engine only).

   b. Loosen the jet valve (smaller) adjusting stud locknut, back the stud out slightly and insert an 0.010 in. (0.25mm) feeler gauge between the jet valve and stud. Make sure the gauge lies flat on the top of the jet valve. Being careful not to twist the gauge or otherwise depress the jet valve spring, rotate the jet valve adjusting stud back in until it just touches the gauge. Tighten the locknut.

   c. Make sure the gauge still slides very easily between the stud and jet valve and they both are still just touching the gauge. Readjust, if necessary. Note that, especially with the jet valve, the clearance must not be too tight.

   d. Repeat entire the procedure for the other jet valves associated with rockers labeled No. 1 and 2.

12. Turn the engine exactly 360 degrees, until the timing marks are again aligned at **TDC** or **0**. First, perform the adjustment procedure for all

the jet valves on rockers labeled No. 3 and 4, intake side only.

NOTE: Loose valve clearances will result in excessive wear and valve train chatter; tight valve clearance will result in burnt valve seats.

13. Apply non-hardening sealer to the rocker arm cover gasket. Always use a new gasket.
14. Install the cover, hoses, spark plug wires and the air cleaner in the reverse order of removal. Tighten the rocker arm cover bolts to 48-60 inch lbs. (5.5-7.0 Nm).
15. Start the engine and check for leaks. It's best to install new gaskets and seals wherever they are used and to observe torque specifications for the camshaft cover bolts.

Rocker Arms/Shafts

REMOVAL AND INSTALLATION

1468cc Engine

1. Disconnect the negative battery cable. Remove the PCV hose running from the rocker cover and the air cleaner. Remove the air cleaner.
2. Remove the upper timing belt cover. Remove the rocker cover.
3. Loosen the bearing cap bolts or the rocker shaft mounting bolts but do not remove them and remove each rocker shaft, rocker arms and springs as an assembly. Disassemble the whole assembly by progressively removing each bolt and then the associated springs and rockers, keeping all parts in the exact order of disassembly. The left and right springs have different tension ratings and free length. Observe the location of the rocker arm as they are removed. Exhaust and intake, right and left are different. Do not mix them up.
4. Check the rocker arm face contacting the camshaft lobe and the adjusting screw that contacts the valve stem for excess wear. Inspect the fit of the rockers on the shaft. Replace adjusting screws, rockers, and/or shafts that show excessive wear. Pay special attention to the contact pad ends of the rocker arms and the ball surface of the adjusting studs. Check the diameter of the shaft at the rocker mounting points and subtract that number from the measured inside diameter of the corresponding rocker arm. Clearance should be 0.0005-0.0017 in. (0.013-0.043mm). The service limit is 0.004 in. (0.1mm). Check the rocker shaft bend. Total

rocker shaft bend should be 0.002 in. (0.05mm). Check the spring free length. Maximum free length should be 2.1 in. (53.3mm) for the exhaust side springs; 2.6 in. (66mm) for intake side springs.

To install:
5. Assemble all the parts, noting the differences between intake and exhaust parts. The intake rocker shaft is much longer; the intake rocker shaft springs are over 3 in. long, while those for the exhaust side are less than 2 in. long; intake rockers have the extra adjusting screw for the jet valve; rockers are labeled 1-3 and 2-4 for the cylinder with which they are associated. Torque the rocker shaft mounting bolts to 15-19 ft. lbs. (20-26 Nm).
6. Adjust the valve clearances. This step may be omitted only if all parts are being reused.
7. Install the rocker cover with a new gasket, torquing the bolts to 12-18 inch lbs. (1.5-2.0 Nm).
8. Install the air cleaner and PCV valve. Connect the battery cable.
9. Run the engine at idle speed until it is hot. Then, unless valves did not require adjustment, remove the valve cover again and adjust the valve clearances with the engine hot.
10. Replace the rocker cover and timing belt cover, air cleaner and PCV valve.

1495cc Engine

1. Remove the air intake pipe, if turbocharged.
2. Remove the breather hose and secondary hose.
3. Remove the timing belt cover.
4. Remove the rocker cover.
5. Loosen the flanged bolts that hold down the rocker arm shafts and remove the shaft, rocker arms and springs as an assembly.
6. Remove the bolts, rocker arms and shaft springs from the shaft. Use care to keep the parts in proper order if to be reused.

To install:
7. Installation is the reverse of the removal procedure. Clean an inspect all parts well. Check the rocker faces where the rocker contacts the camshaft lobes for wear. Replace as required. Check the valve cap face that contacts the valve stem. This cap should be replaced if worn. Inspect the shafts for wear.
8. Install the rocker arms and rocker arm shaft springs to the shafts. Note the difference between the **A** and **B** type rocker arms. The exhaust side uses only the **A** type. Install the assembly to the cylinder

head. Torque the mounting bolts to 14-20 ft. lbs. (19-27 Nm).

9. Adjust the valve lash.

10. Install the rocker cover. The hold-down bolts should be just snug, not over-tightened. Torque to only 1.1-1.4 ft. lbs. (1.5-2.0 Nm).

NOTE: Sealant must be applied to the top surface of the cylinder head and camshaft cap. Don't use too much or excess sealant will be squeezed out into the engine.

11. Install the timing cover, air cleaner and breather hose.

2351cc Engine

NOTE: A special tool 09246-32000 (MD998443) or equivalent, is required to retain the automatic lash adjusters in this procedure.

1. Disconnect the negative battery cable. Remove the rocker cover and gasket and the timing belt cover.

2. Turn the crankshaft so the No. 1 piston is at TDC compression. At this point, the timing mark on the camshaft sprocket and the timing mark on the head to the left of the sprocket will be aligned.

3. Remove the camshaft bearing cap bolts.

4. Install the automatic lash adjuster retainer tool 09246-32000 (MD998443) or equivalent, to keep the adjuster from falling out of the rocker arms.

5. Lift off the bearing caps and rocker arm assemblies.

6. The rocker arms may now be removed from the shafts.

NOTE: Keep all parts in the order in which they were removed. None of the parts are interchangeable. The lash adjusters are filled with diesel fuel, which will spill out if they are inverted. If any diesel fuel is spilled, the adjusters must be bled.

To install:

7. Check all parts for wear or damage. Replace any damaged or excessively worn part.

8. Service as required, assemble all parts. Note the following:

a. The rocker shafts are installed with the notches in the ends facing up.

b. The left rocker shaft is longer than the right.

c. The wave washers are installed on the left shaft.

d. Coat all parts with clean engine oil prior to assembly.

e. Insert the lash adjuster from under the rocker arm and install

the special holding tool. If any of the diesel fuel is spilled, the adjuster must be bled.

f. Tighten the bearing cap bolts, working from the center towards the ends, to 15 ft. lbs. (20 Nm).

g. Check the operation of each lash adjuster by positioning the camshaft so the rocker arm bears on the low or round portion of the cam. Insert a thin steel wire, tool MD998442 or equivalent, in the hole in the top of the rocker arm, over the lash adjuster and depress the check ball at the top of the adjuster. While holding the check ball depressed, move the arm up and down. Looseness should be felt. Full plunger stroke should be 2.2mm. If not, remove, clean and bleed the lash adjuster.

Intake Manifold

REMOVAL AND INSTALLATION

1468cc Engine

1. Disconnect the negative battery cable. Remove the air cleaner assembly.

2. Disconnect the fuel line and the EGR lines, if equipped with EGR. Tag and disconnect all vacuum hoses.

3. Disconnect the throttle positioner and fuel cut-off solenoid wires.

4. Disconnect the throttle linkage.

5. If equipped with an automatic transaxle, disconnect the shift cable linkage.

6. Disconnect the power brake booster vacuum line.

7. Drain the cooling system.

8. Disconnect the choke water hose at the manifold.

9. Remove the heater and water outlet hoses, disconnect the water temperature sending unit.

10. Remove the mounting nuts that hold the manifold to the cylinder head. Remove the intake manifold.

To install:

11. Clean all mounting surfaces. Before installing the manifold, coat both sides of a new gasket with a gasket sealer.

NOTE: If equipped with jet air system, take care not to get any sealer into the jet air intake passage.

12. Install the intake manifold assembly to the engine block.

13. Reconnect the heater and water outlet hoses. Connect the water temperature sending unit.

14. Connect the brake booster vacuum line. Connect the choke hose at the manifold.

15. Connect the throttle and shift cable linkages, the fuel lines and all vacuum hoses. Install the air cleaner.

16. Refill the engine with coolant. Connect the negative battery cable.

1495cc Engine

These engines use a 2-piece intake manifold.

1. Disconnect the negative battery cable. Remove the idle speed actuator.

2. Remove the air intake hose connected to the throttle body on non-turbocharged engines. On turbocharged engines, remove the intake pipe connected to the turbocharger.

3. Remove the accelerator cable.

4. Remove the water hose and throttle body.

5. Remove the PCV hose and brake booster vacuum hose.

6. Disconnect the vacuum hose connections. Tag as necessary.

7. Relieve the fuel system pressure. Disconnect the high pressure fuel line.

8. Remove the intake manifold brace.

9. Remove the upper intake manifold assembly and gasket.

10. Disconnect the fuel injector harness connector.

11. Remove the fuel rail, fuel injectors and pressure regulator as an assembly. Use care not to allow the injectors to drop out of the fuel rail. They are not retained by any fasteners.

12. Remove the insulator from the lower intake manifold and disconnect the heater hose.

13. Remove the lower intake manifold and gasket.

To install:

14. Installation is the reverse of the removal procedure. Check the manifolds for cracks or damage. Clean all parts well. Use care not to damage the gasketing surfaces.

15. Install the fuel rail and injector assembly. Make sure the injectors are correctly seated.

16. Use new gaskets when installing the manifolds. Torque all manifold-to-head nuts to 11-14 ft. lbs. (15-19 Nm).

2351cc Engine

1. Disconnect the negative battery cable. Remove the air cleaner assembly.

2. Release fuel system pressure. Disconnect the fuel line and the EGR

lines. Tag and disconnect all vacuum hoses.

3. Disconnect the throttle positioner and fuel cut-off solenoid wires.

4. Disconnect the throttle linkage. If equipped with automatic transaxle, disconnect the shift cable linkage.

5. Remove the heater and water outlet hoses, disconnect the water temperature sending unit. Disconnect the oxygen sensor connector, power transistor connector, ISC connector, ignition coil connector, etc. and the distributor.

6. Remove the mounting nuts that hold the manifold to the cylinder head. Remove the intake manifold lower and upper sections with injector assembly as a unit.

7. Clean all mounting surfaces. Before installing the manifold, coat both sides with a gasket sealer.

To install:

8. Clean all mounting surfaces. Before installing the manifold, coat both sides of a new gasket with a gasket sealer.

NOTE: If equipped with jet air system, take care not to get any sealer into the jet air intake passage.

9. Install the intake manifold lower and upper sections with injector assembly as a unit. Install the mounting nuts that hold the manifold to the cylinder head.

10. Install the heater and water outlet hoses, disconnect the water temperature sending unit. Connect the oxygen sensor connector, power transistor connector, ISC connector, ignition coil connector, etc. and the distributor.

11. Connect the throttle linkage. If equipped with automatic transaxle, connect the shift cable linkage.

12. Connect the throttle positioner and fuel cut-off solenoid wires.

13. Connect the fuel line the EGR lines. Connect all vacuum hoses.

14. Refill the engine with coolant. Connect the negative battery cable.

1596cc, 1796cc and 1997cc Engines

1. Relieve the fuel system pressure.

2. Disconnect battery negative cable and drain the cooling system.

3. Disconnect the accelerator cable, breather hose and air intake hose.

4. Disconnect the upper radiator hose, heater hose and water bypass hose.

5. Remove all vacuum hoses and pipes as necessary, including the brake booster vacuum line.

6. Disconnect the high pressure fuel line, fuel return hose and remove throttle control cable brackets.

7. Tag and disconnect the electrical connectors from the oxygen sensor, coolant temperature sensor, thermo switch, idle speed control connection, spark plug wires, etc. that may interfere with the manifold removal procedure.

8. Remove the fuel delivery pipe, fuel injectors, pressure regulator and insulators from the engine. Be careful not to drop the injectors when removing the assembly from the engine.

9. Disconnect the water hose connections at the throttle body, water inlet and heater assembly.

10. If the thermostat housing is preventing removal of the intake manifold, remove it.

11. Disconnect the vacuum connection at the power brake booster and the PCV valve if still connected.

12. Remove the intake manifold mounting bolts and remove the intake manifold assembly.

To install:

13. Clean all gasket material from the cylinder head intake mounting surface and intake manifold assembly. Check both surfaces for cracks or other damage. Check the intake manifold water passages for clogging and clean if necessary.

14. Install a new intake manifold gasket to the head and install the manifold. Torque the manifold in a crisscross pattern, starting from the inside and working outwards to 11-14 ft. lbs. (15-19 Nm).

15. Install the fuel delivery pipe, injectors and pressure regulator from the engine. Torque the retaining bolts to 7-9 ft. lbs. (10-13 Nm).

16. Install the thermostat housing, intake manifold brace bracket, distributor and throttle body stay bracket.

17. Connect or install all hoses, cables and electrical connectors that were removed or disconnected during the removal procedure.

18. Fill the system with coolant.

19. Connect the negative battery cable, run the vehicle until the thermostat opens, fill the radiator completely.

20. Adjust the accelerator cable. Check and adjust the idle speed as required.

21. Once the vehicle has cooled, recheck the coolant level.

2972cc Engine

1. Disconnect the negative battery cable. Relieve the fuel system pressure.

2. Drain the cooling system.

3. Remove the throttle body to air cleaner hose.

4. Remove the throttle body and transaxle kickdown linkage.

5. Remove the AIS motor and TPS wiring connectors from the throttle body.

6. Remove and label the vacuum hose harness from the throttle body.

7. From the air intake plenum, remove the PCV and brake booster hoses and the EGR tube flange.

8. Disconnect and label the charge air temperature sensor wiring at the intake manifold.

9. Remove the vacuum connections from the air intake plenum vacuum connector.

10. Remove the fuel hoses from the fuel rail.

11. Remove the air intake plenum mounting bolts and the plenum.

12. Remove the vacuum hoses from the fuel rail and pressure regulator.

13. Disconnect the fuel injector wiring harness from the engine wiring harness.

14. Remove the fuel pressure regulator mounting bolts and the regulator from the fuel rail.

15. Remove the fuel rail mounting bolts and the fuel rail from the intake manifold.

16. Separate the radiator hose from the thermostat housing and heater hoses from the heater pipe.

17. Remove the intake manifold mounting bolts and the manifold from the engine.

18. Clean the gasket mounting surfaces on the engine and intake manifold.

To install:

19. Using new gaskets, position the intake manifold on the engine and install the mounting nuts and washers.

20. Torque the mounting nuts gradually and evenly, in sequence, to 15 ft. lbs. (20 Nm).

21. Make sure the injector holes are clean. Lubricate the injector O-rings with a drop of clean engine oil and install the injector assembly onto the engine.

22. Install and torque the fuel rail mounting bolts to 10 ft. lbs. (14 Nm).

23. Install the fuel pressure regulator onto the fuel rail.

24. Install the fuel supply and return tube and the vacuum crossover hold-down bolt.

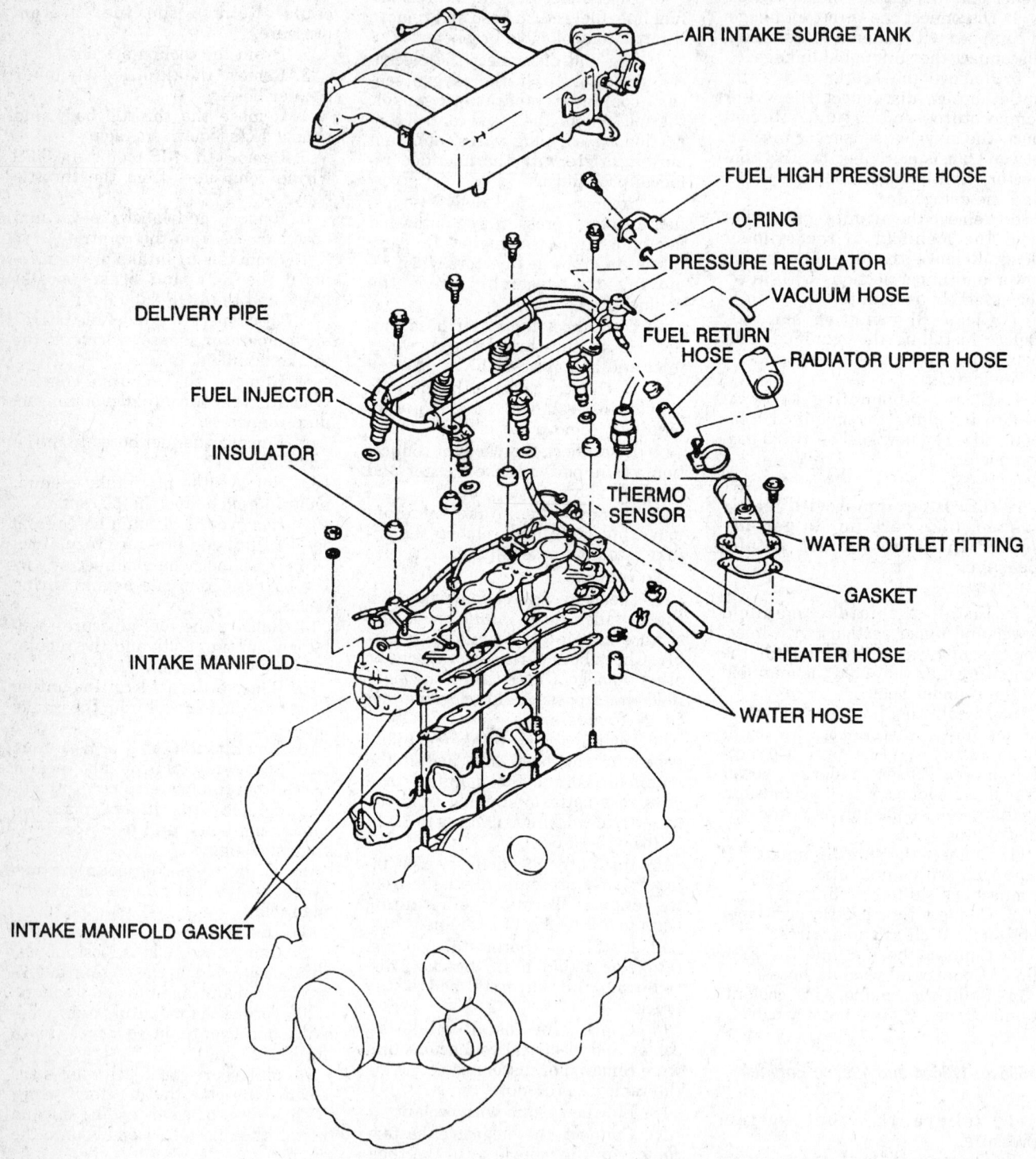

AIR INTAKE SURGE TANK

FUEL HIGH PRESSURE HOSE

O-RING

PRESSURE REGULATOR

VACUUM HOSE

DELIVERY PIPE

FUEL RETURN HOSE

RADIATOR UPPER HOSE

FUEL INJECTOR

INSULATOR

THERMO SENSOR

WATER OUTLET FITTING

GASKET

INTAKE MANIFOLD

HEATER HOSE

WATER HOSE

INTAKE MANIFOLD GASKET

Engine intake manifold and related components — 2972cc engine

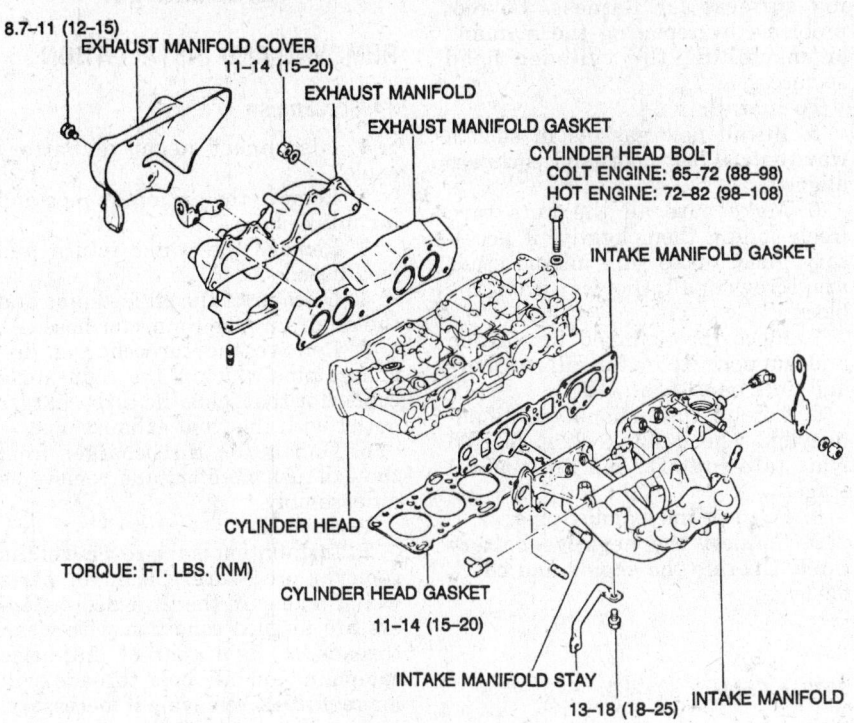

8.7–11 (12–15)
EXHAUST MANIFOLD COVER
11–14 (15–20)
EXHAUST MANIFOLD
EXHAUST MANIFOLD GASKET
CYLINDER HEAD BOLT
COLT ENGINE: 65–72 (88–98)
HOT ENGINE: 72–82 (98–108)
INTAKE MANIFOLD GASKET
CYLINDER HEAD
TORQUE: FT. LBS. (NM)
CYLINDER HEAD GASKET
11–14 (15–20)
INTAKE MANIFOLD STAY
13–18 (18–25)   INTAKE MANIFOLD

2351cc engine intake and exhaust manifolds

25. Connect the fuel injection wiring harness to the engine wiring harness.

26. Connect the vacuum harness to the fuel pressure regulator and fuel rail assembly.

27. Remove the cover from the lower intake manifold and clean the mating surface.

28. Place the intake plenum gasket with the beaded sealant side up, on the intake manifold. Install the air intake plenum and torque the mounting bolts gradually and evenly, in sequence, to 10 ft. lbs. (14 Nm).

29. Connect or install all remaining items that were disconnected or removed during the removal procedure.

30. Refill the cooling system. Connect the negative battery cable and check for leaks.

Exhaust Manifold

REMOVAL AND INSTALLATION

1468cc Engine

1. Disconnect the negative battery cable. Remove the air cleaner. Remove the heat stove and/or heat shield on the exhaust manifold, if equipped. with the manifold cool,

soak all manifold nuts and studs with a liquid penetrant.

2. Disconnect the exhaust pipe at the exhaust manifold. Disconnect and remove the oxygen sensor. If there is a secondary air line connected to the exhaust manifold, disconnect it. First remove the exhaust pipe, then the secondary air supply pipe.

3. Support the manifold and remove all attaching nuts and washers. Slide the manifold from the cylinder head. Remove the converter mounting bolts. When the converter is disconnected, remove the exhaust manifold, if necessary, rock it to break it loose.

4. Thoroughly clean the sealing surfaces on the cylinder head and manifold. Replace any nuts, washers or studs that are excessively rusted or may have been damaged during removal. Use a straight-edge to check the manifold and cylinder head sealing surfaces for flatness. Correct problems by replacing the manifold or machining the cylinder head surface.

To install:

5. Install new gaskets in such a way that all bolt holes and ports are aligned.

6. Make sure all the nuts turn freely, oiling them lightly, if neces-

sary. Also, make sure all the studs are screwed all the way into the block.

7. Place the manifold in position and support it, install all washers and nuts hand-tight.

8. Torque the exhaust manifold-to-cylinder head nuts to 14 ft. lbs. (20 Nm), alternately and in several stages.

9. Install piping, heat stoves and shields. Connect the exhaust pipe or primary catalytic converter.

10. Connect the negative battery cable. Operate the engine and check for leaks.

1495cc Engine

1. Disconnect the negative battery cable. Remove the air cleaner. Remove the heat stove and/or heat shield on the exhaust manifold, if equipped. with the manifold cool, soak all manifold nuts and studs with a liquid penetrant.

2. Disconnect the exhaust pipe at the exhaust manifold. On turbocharged engines, this pipe is at the bottom of the 90 degree adapter which is bolted to the turbocharger outlet.

3. Disconnect and remove the oxygen sensor.

4. Support the manifold and remove all attaching nuts and washers. Remove the manifold from the cylinder head. Use care not to damage the turbocharger, if equipped. Tape over the turbocharger opening to keep out dirt and debris.

5. Thoroughly clean the sealing surfaces on the cylinder head and manifold. Replace any nuts, washers or studs that are excessively rusted or may have been damaged during removal. Use a straight-edge to check the manifold and cylinder head sealing surfaces for flatness. Correct problems by replacing the manifold or machining the cylinder head surface.

To install:

6. Installation is the reverse of the removal procedure. Use new gaskets and make sure the openings are aligned.

7. Make sure all the nuts turn freely, oiling them lightly, if necessary. Apply anti-seize compound on the threads to make future removal easier. Make sure all the studs are screwed all the way into the block.

8. Place the manifold in position and support it, install all washers and nuts hand-tight.

9. Torque the exhaust manifold-to-cylinder head nuts to 14 ft. lbs. (20

Nm) alternately and in several stages.

10. Install piping, heat stoves and shields as necessary. Connect the exhaust pipe.

11. Connect the negative battery cable. Operate the engine and check for leaks.

2351cc Engine

1. Disconnect the negative battery cable. Remove the air cleaner assembly.

2. Disconnect any EGR or heat lines. Disconnect the reed valve, if equipped.

3. Remove the exhaust pipe support bracket from the engine block, if equipped.

4. Remove the exhaust pipe from exhaust manifold by removing the exhaust pipe flange nuts. It may be necessary to remove 1 nut or bolt from underneath the vehicle.

5. If equipped with a catalytic converter mounted between the exhaust manifold and exhaust pipe, remove the exhaust pipe and the secondary air supply pipe.

6. Remove the nuts mounting the exhaust manifold to the cylinder head. Slide the manifold from the cylinder head, to provide enough room to remove the converter mounting bolts. When the converter is disconnected, remove the exhaust manifold.

To install:

7. Installation is the reverse order of the removal procedure. Install the exhaust manifold with new gaskets. New gaskets should be used and on some engines, port liner gaskets are used.

8. Torque the exhaust manifold-to-cylinder head bolts to 14 ft. lbs. (20 Nm).

1596cc, 1796cc and 1997cc Engines

1. Disconnect the negative battery cable. Remove the air cleaner. Remove the heat shield on the exhaust manifold. with the manifold cool, soak all manifold nuts and studs with a liquid penetrant.

2. Disconnect the exhaust pipe at the exhaust manifold. Disconnect and remove the oxygen sensor.

3. Support the manifold and remove all attaching nuts and washers. Slide the manifold from the cylinder head.

4. Thoroughly clean the sealing surfaces on the cylinder head and manifold. Replace any nuts, washers or studs that are excessively rusted or may have been damaged during removal. Use a straight-edge to check

the manifold and cylinder head sealing surfaces for flatness. Correct problems by replacing the manifold or machining the cylinder head surface.

To install:

5. Install new gaskets in such a way that all bolt holes and ports are aligned.

6. Make sure all the nuts turn freely, oiling them lightly, if necessary. Also, make sure all the studs are screwed all the way into the block.

7. Place the manifold in position and support it, install all washers and nuts hand-tight.

8. Torque the exhaust manifold-to-cylinder head nuts to 22 ft. lbs. (30 Nm), alternately and in several stages.

9. Connect the exhaust pipe.

10. Connect the negative battery cable. Operate the engine and check for leaks.

2972cc Engine

1. Disconnect the negative battery cable. Raise the vehicle and support safely.

2. Disconnect the exhaust pipe from the rear exhaust manifold at the articulated joint.

3. Disconnect the EGR tube from the rear manifold and unplug the oxygen sensor wire.

4. Remove the crossover pipe to manifold bolts.

5. Remove the rear manifold to cylinder head nuts and the manifold.

6. Lower the vehicle and remove the heat shield from the manifold.

7. Remove the front manifold-to-cylinder head nuts and the manifold.

8. Clean the gasket mounting surfaces. Inspect the manifolds for cracks, flatness and/or damage.

To install:

9. When installing, the numbers 1-3-5 on the gaskets are used with the rear cylinders and 2-4-6 are on the gasket for the front cylinders. Torque the manifold-to-cylinder head nuts to 14 ft. lbs. (20 Nm).

10. Install the crossover pipe to the manifold.

11. Connect the EGR tube and oxygen sensor wire.

12. Connect the exhaust pipe to the rear exhaust manifold, at the articulated joint.

13. Connect the negative battery cable and check the manifolds for leaks.

Turbocharger

REMOVAL AND INSTALLATION

1495cc Engine

1. Disconnect negative battery cable.

2. Remove the air intake pipe and air intake hose.

3. Remove the water return and feed hose.

4. Disconnect the oil feed pipe and the oil drain pipe connector hose.

5. Remove the turbocharger discharge pipe which is the right angle connector that joins the turbocharger outlet with the front exhaust pipe.

6. Unbolt the turbocharger from the exhaust manifold and remove as an assembly.

To install:

7. Installation is the reverse of the removal procedure. Clean all parts well. Make sure the threaded fasteners are in good condition with clean threads. A light coat of anti-seize compound on all bolt threads will make future removal, if necessary, easier. Use new gaskets.

8. Before attaching oil feed line, pour clean engine oil into the turbocharger so it will be lubricated at startup.

9. Install all hoses, start vehicle and check for exhaust, water and oil leaks.

Timing Belt Front Cover

REMOVAL AND INSTALLATION

Except 2972cc Engine

1. Disconnect the negative battery cable.

2. Remove the engine undercover.

3. Using the proper equipment, slightly raise the engine to take the weight off the side engine mount. Remove the engine mount bracket.

4. Remove the accessory drive belts, tension pulley brackets, water pump pulley and crankshaft pulley.

5. Remove all attaching screws and remove the upper and lower timing belt covers.

6. The installation is the reverse of the removal procedure. Make sure all pieces of packing are positioned in the inner grooves of the covers when installing.

2972cc Engine

1. Disconnect the negative battery cable.

2. Remove the engine undercover.

3. Remove the accessory drive belts.

4. Remove the air conditioner compressor tension pulley assembly.

5. Remove the tension pulley bracket.

6. Using the proper equipment, slightly raise the engine to take the weight off the side engine mount.

7. Disconnect the power steering pump pressure switch connector. Remove the power steering pump and wire aside.

8. Remove the engine support bracket.

9. Remove the crankshaft pulley.

10. Remove the timing belt cover cap.

11. Remove the timing belt upper and lower covers.

To install:

12. Install the timing covers. Make sure all pieces of packing are positioned in the inner grooves of the covers when installing.

13. Install the crankshaft pulley. Torque the bolt to 108-116 ft. lbs. (150-160 Nm).

14. Install the engine support bracket.

15. Install the power steering pump and reconnect wire harness at the power steering pump pressure switch.

16. Install the engine mounting bracket and remove the engine support fixture.

17. Install the tension pulleys and drive belts.

18. Install the cruise control actuator.

19. Install the engine undercover.

20. Connect the negative battery cable.

Timing Belt and Tensioner

Adjustment

1468cc Engine

1. Rotate the crankshaft clockwise and align the timing marks so No. 1 piston will be at TDC of the compression stroke. Disconnect the negative battery cable.

2. Remove the timing belt covers.

3. Loosen the tensioner lower mounting bolt first, then the uppermost bolt.

4. Check to insure that the timing marks are in correct alignment and secure tightening the uppermost bolt first.

5. Rotate the crankshaft 1 revolution in operating direction (clockwise), and realign the timing marks.

Loosen the tensioner lower mounting bolt first, then the uppermost bolt.

6. Retighten the attaching bolts, uppermost first, to 14-20 ft. lbs. (20-27 Nm).

7. Apply a moderate pressure to the tension side of the timing belt and measure the belt deflection. The inner (cog) side of the belt should be depressed to the center of the tensioner mounting bolt head. If the deflection point is correct, the tension adjustment of the timing belt is correct.

8. If a tension gauge is used, measure the tension in the middle of the tension side span. The desired reading is 32-47 lbs.

9. Install the timing belt covers and all related components.

10. Reconnect the negative battery cable.

1495cc Engine

The timing belt has an automatic tension adjusting mechanism. Adjustment can be made by the following procedure:

1. Turn the steering wheel fully counterclockwise.

2. Place a suitable block of wood under the engine oil pan and carefully raise the engine. Raise just enough to permit removing the right engine mount and bracket.

3. Remove the water pump pulley and crankshaft pulley.

4. Remove the timing belt upper cover.

5. Check the entire belt for cracking, peeling or other damage.

6. Rotate the crankshaft so the No. 1 piston is at TDC of the compression stroke. The timing mark on the camshaft sprocket should align with the mark on the cylinder head at approximately the 3 o'clock position. Use care to only turn the crankshaft clockwise. Never turn backwards or the tension will be wrong.

7. Remove the timing belt lower cover.

8. Loosen the tensioner mounting bolts, the lower first, then the upper to give the timing belt tension. Recheck that the belt is not out of position.

9. Tighten the tensioner bolts, the top first, then the bottom. Be sure to tighten the bolts in this order because if the lower bolt is tightened first, the tensioner will move with the bolt and the belt will be overtightened.

10. Give the crankshaft 1 turn in the operating direction (clockwise) and realign the crankshaft sprocket timing mark with the TDC position.

Again, do not turn the crankshaft backwards.

11. Loosen the tensioner mounting bolts, the lower first, then the upper. Then retighten the tensioner bolts, the top first, then the bottom. Torque the bolts to 14-20 ft. lbs. (20-27 Nm).

12. Recheck the belt tension. When the tensioner and the tension side of the timing belt are squeezed moderately, the timing belt cog should cover approximately half the bolt head.

13. If a specialized belt tension gauge is available (Borroughs BT-33-73F or equivalent) rotate the crankshaft to 90 degrees BTDC. Measure the tension at the belt midpoint. The gauge should read 21-36 lbs.

2351cc Engine

1. Disconnect the negative battery cable.

2. Remove the upper and lower timing belt covers.

3. Check the tensioners for a smooth rate of movement and leaking seal. Replace any tensioner that binds or shows grease leakage through the seal.

4. Rotate the crankshaft clockwise and align the timing marks so No. 1 piston will be at TDC of the compression stroke. Do not rotate the crankshaft in a counterclockwise direction as this can cause improper timing belt ension.

5. Loosen the timing belt tensioner bolt and nut, using a 0.55 in. (14mm) socket wrench.

6. Rotate the crankshaft and camshaft sprocket clockwise 2 teeth. Do not turn the engine counterclockwise. Momentarily apply slight pressure behind the tensioner to assure tensioner is not sticking and then release pressure. After tension has equalized, tighten the tensioner mounting bolt (lower side) first, and then tighten the upper mounting nut. Be sure to tighten the mounting hardware in that order. If the nut it tightened first, the tensioner will rotate with the nut and the belt will be loose.

7. Check to ensure proper tension by measuring belt deflection. The standard value is 0.200-0.276 in. (5-7mm) with moderate pressure applied to the center of the timing belt.

8. Install the upper and lower timing belt covers.

9. Install the crankshaft pulley.

10. Install the water pump drive belt and pulley. Connect the negative battery cable.

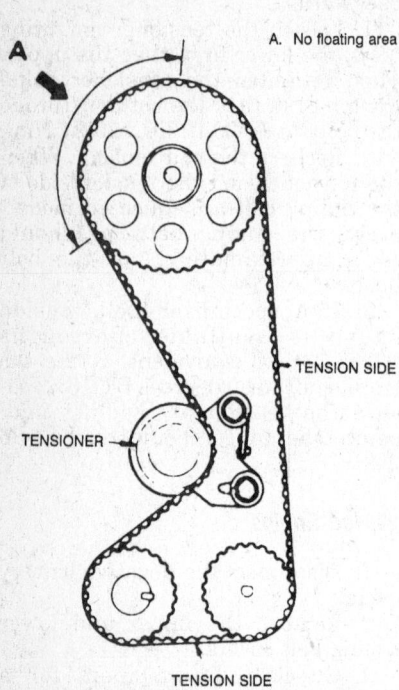

A. No floating area

TENSION SIDE

TENSIONER

TENSION SIDE

Timing belt and tensioner — 2351cc engine

1596cc, 1796cc and 1997cc Engines

1. Disconnect the negative battery cable.

2. Remove the timing belt covers.

3. Adjust the silent shaft (inner) belt tension first. Loosen the idler pulley center bolt so the pulley can be moved.

4. Move the pulley by hand so the long side of the belt deflects about ¼ in. (6mm).

5. Hold the pulley tightly so the pulley cannot rotate when the bolt is tightened. Tighten the bolt to 15 ft. lbs. (20 Nm) and recheck the amount of deflection.

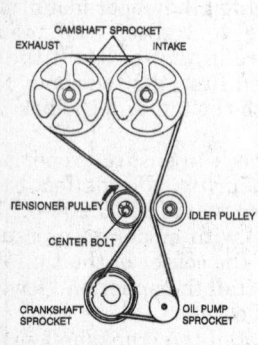

CAMSHAFT SPROCKET
EXHAUST   INTAKE

TENSIONER PULLEY   IDLER PULLEY

CENTER BOLT

CRANKSHAFT SPROCKET   OIL PUMP SPROCKET

Temporarily tightening the timing belt tension — 1596cc, 1796cc and 1997cc DOHC engines

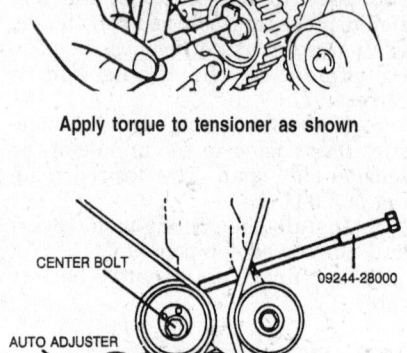

09244-28100

Apply torque to tensioner as shown

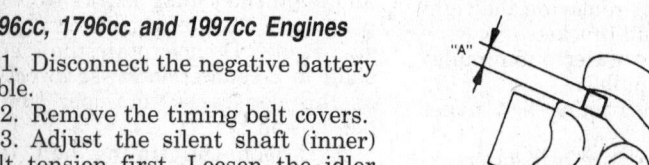

CENTER BOLT

09244-28000

AUTO ADJUSTER

Adjusting tensioner using alternate method and special tool — 1596cc, 1796cc and 1997cc DOHC engines

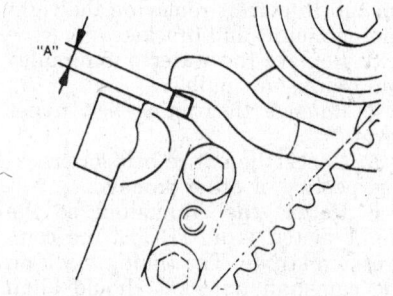

"A"

Measure the auto tensioner protrusion at "A", the distance between the tensioner arm and the auto tensioner body — 1596cc, 1796cc and 1997cc DOHC engines

6. To adjust the timing (outer) belt, turn the crankshaft ¼ turn counterclockwise, then turn it clockwise to move No. 1 cylinder to TDC.

7. Loosen the center bolt. Using tool MD998752 or equivalent and a torque wrench, apply a torque of 1.88-2.03 ft. lbs. (2.6-2.8 Nm). If the body of the vehicle interferes with the special tool and the torque wrench, use a jack and slightly raise the engine assembly. Holding the tensioner pulley, tighten the center bolt.

8. Screw special tool MD998738 or exact equivalent into the engine left support bracket until its end makes contact with the tensioner arm. At this point, screw the special tool in some more and remove the set wire attached to the auto tensioner, if wire was not previously removed. Then remove the special tool.

9. Rotate the crankshaft 2 complete turns clockwise and let it sit for approximately 15 minutes. Then, measure the auto tensioner protrusion (the distance between the tensioner arm and auto tensioner body) to ensure that it is within 0.15-0.18 in. (3.8-4.5mm). If out of specification, repeat Step 1-4 until the specified value is obtained.

10. If the timing belt tension adjustment is being performed with the engine mounted in the vehicle, and clearance between the tensioner arm and the auto tensioner body cannot be measured, the following alternative method can be used:

a. Screw in special tool MD998738 or equivalent, until its end makes contact with the tensioner arm.

b. After the special tool makes contact with the arm, screw it in some more to retract the auto tensioner pushrod while counting the number of turns the tool makes until the tensioner arm is brought into contact with the auto tensioner body. Make sure the number of turns the special tool makes conforms with the standard value of 2½-3 turns.

c. Install the rubber plug to the timing belt rear cover.

11. Install the timing belt covers and all related items.

12. Connect the negative battery cable.

2972cc Engine

1. Disconnect the negative battery cable.

2. If equipped with air conditioning, remove the compressor drive belt.

3. Remove the access cover located in the lower timing belt cover.

4. Loosen the timing belt tensioner mounting bolt 1-2 turns.

5. Rotate the engine clockwise 2 revolutions.

6. Tighten the timing belt tensioner mounting bolt.

7. Install the access cover and the air compressor drive belt.

8. Reconnect the negative battery cable.

REMOVAL AND INSTALLATION

1468cc Engine

1. Disconnect the negative battery cable. Remove the timing belt cover.

2. Rotate the crankshaft clockwise and align the timing marks so No. 1 piston will be at TDC of the compression stroke. Loosen the tensioning bolt, it runs in the slotted portion of the tensioner, and the pivot bolt on the timing belt tensioner. Move the tensioner as far as it will go toward the water pump. Tighten the adjusting bolt. Mark the timing belt with an arrow showing direction of rotation if the belt is to be reused.

3. Remove the timing belt.

4. Remove the camshaft sprocket as required.

5. Remove the crankshaft sprocket bolts and remove the crankshaft sprocket and flange, noting the direction of installation for each. Remove the timing belt tensioner.

6. Inspect the belt thoroughly. The back surface must be pliable and rough. If it is hard and glossy, the belt should be replaced. Any cracks in the belt backing or teeth or missing teeth mean the belt must be replaced. The canvas cover should be intact on all the teeth. If rubber is exposed anywhere, the belt should be replaced.

7. Inspect the tensioner for grease leaking from the grease seal and any roughness in rotation. Replace a tensioner for either defect.

8. The sprockets should be inspected and replaced, if there is any sign of damaged teeth or cracking. Do not immerse sprockets in solvent, as solvent that has soaked into the metal may cause deterioration of the timing belt later. Do not clean the tensioner in solvent either, as this may wash the grease out of the bearing.

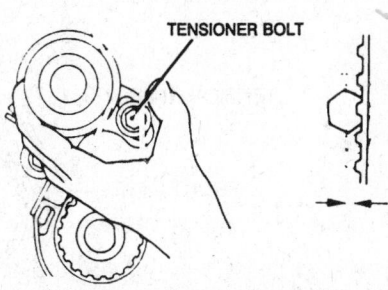

Checking belt tension on the 1468cc engine

To install:

9. Install the flange and crankshaft sprocket. The flange must go on first with the chamfered area outward. The sprocket is installed with the boss forward and the studs for the fan belt pulley outward. Install and torque the crankshaft sprocket bolt to 51-72 ft. lbs. (69-98 Nm). Install the camshaft sprocket and bolt, torquing it to 47-54 ft. lbs. (64-74 Nm).

10. Align the timing marks of the camshaft sprocket. Check that the crankshaft timing marks are still in alignment (the locating pin on the front of the crankshaft sprocket is aligned with a mark on the front case).

11. Mount the tensioner, spring and spacer with the bottom end of the spring free. Then, install the bolts and tighten the adjusting bolt slightly with the tensioner moved as far as possible away from the water pump. Install the free end of the spring into the locating tang on the front case. Position the belt over the crankshaft sprocket and then over the camshaft sprocket. Slip the back of the belt over the tensioner wheel. Turn the camshaft sprocket in the opposite of its normal direction of rotation until the straight side of the belt is tight and make sure the timing

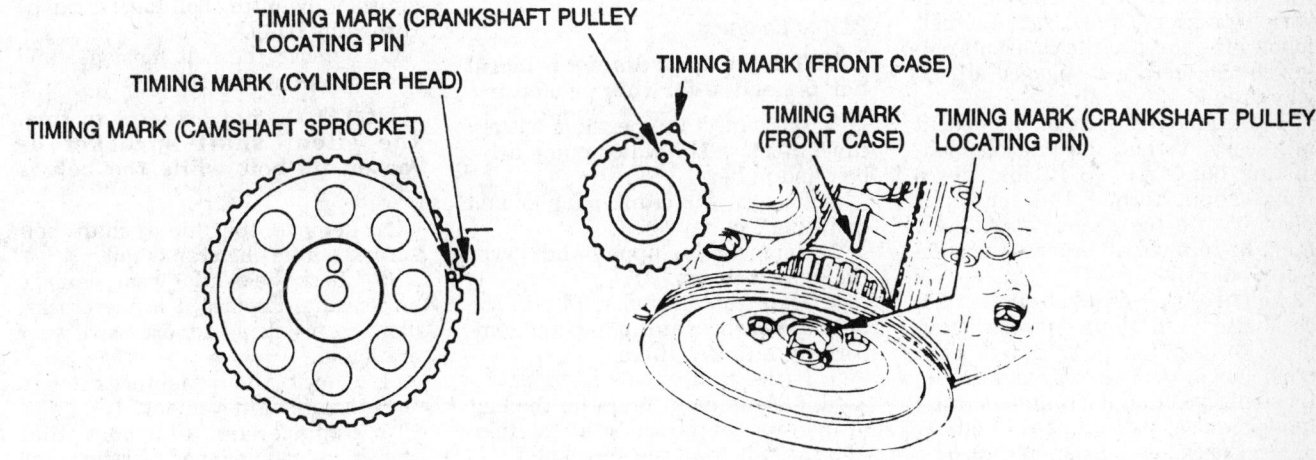

Installing the crankshaft and camshaft sprockets on the 1468cc engine

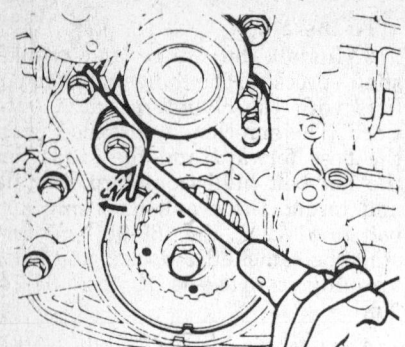

Installing the belt tensioner spring on the 1468cc engine

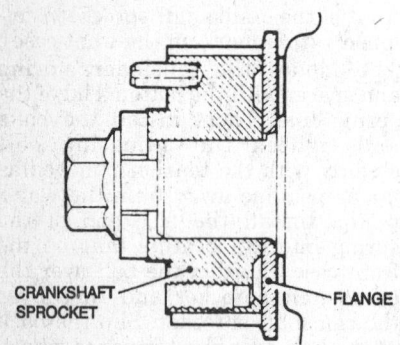

Installing the crankshaft sprocket on the 1468cc engine

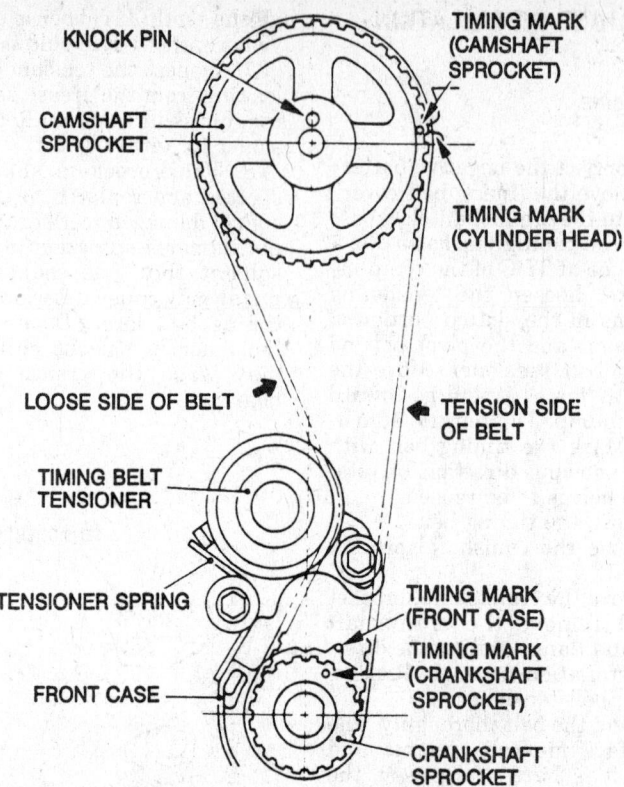

1468cc engine timing belt installation and timing mark alignment

marks align. If not, shift the belt 1 tooth at a time in the appropriate direction until this occurs.

12. Loosen the tensioner mounting bolts so the tensioner works, without the interference of any friction, under spring pressure. Make sure the belt follows the curve of the camshaft pulley so the teeth are engaged all the way around.

13. Correct the path of the belt, if necessary. Torque the tensioner adjusting bolt to 15-18 ft. lbs. (20-26 Nm). Then, torque the tensioner pivot bolt to the same figure. Bolts must be torqued, in order, or tension won't be correct.

14. Turn the crankshaft 1 turn clockwise until timing marks again align to seat the belt. Loosen both tensioner attaching bolts and let the tensioner position itself under spring tension as before. Torque the bolts in order. Check belt tension by putting a finger on the water pump side of the tensioner wheel and pull the belt toward it. The belt should move toward the pump until the teeth are about ¼ of the way across the head of the tensioner adjusting bolt. Retension the belt, if necessary.

15. Install the timing belt covers.

16. Install the crankshaft pulley, making sure the pin on the crankshaft sprocket fits through the hole in the rear surface of the pulley. Install the bolts and torque to 7.5-8.5 ft. lbs. (9-12 Nm). Connect the negative battery cable.

2351cc Engine

NOTE: An 8mm diameter metal bar is needed for this procedure.

1. Disconnect the negative battery cable. Remove the water pump drive belt and pulley.

2. Remove the crank adapter and crankshaft pulley.

3. Remove the upper and lower timing belt covers.

4. Move the tensioner fully in the direction of the water pump and temporarily secure it there.

5. If the timing belt is to be reused, make a paint mark on the belt to indicate the direction of rotation. Slip the belt from the sprockets.

6. Remove the camshaft sprocket bolt and pull the sprocket from the camshaft.

7. Remove the crankshaft sprocket bolt and pull the crankshaft sprocket and flange from the crankshaft.

8. Remove the plug on the left side of the block and insert an 8mm diam-

eter metal bar in the opening to keep the silent shaft in position.

9. Remove the oil pump sprocket retaining nut and remove the oil pump sprocket.

10. Loosen the right silent shaft sprocket mounting bolt until it can be turned by hand.

11. Remove the belt tensioner and remove the timing belt.

NOTE: Do not attempt to turn the silent shaft sprocket or loosen its bolt while the belt is off.

12. Remove the silent shaft belt sprocket from the crankshaft.

13. Check the belt for wear, damage or glossing. Replace it if any cracks, damage, brittleness or excessive wear are found.

14. Check the tensioners for a smooth rate of movement.

15. Replace any tensioner that shows grease leakage through the seal.

To install:

16. Install the silent shaft belt sprocket on the crankshaft, with the flat face toward the engine.

17. Apply light engine oil on the outer face of the spacer and install the spacer on the right silent shaft.

The side with the rounded shoulder faces the engine.

18. Install the sprocket on the right silent shaft and install the bolt but do not tighten completely at this time.

NOTE: Align the silent shaft and oil pump sprockets using the timing marks. If the 8mm metal bar cannot be inserted into the hole 2.36 inch (60mm), the oil pump sprocket will have to turned 1 full rotation until the bar can be inserted to the full length. The above step assures that the oil pump sprocket and silent shafts are in correct orientation. This step must not be skipped or a vibration may develop during engine operation.

19. Install the silent shaft belt and adjust the tension, by moving the tensioner into contact with the belt, tight enough to remove all slack. Tighten the tensioner bolt to 21 ft. lbs. (28 Nm).
20. Tighten the silent shaft sprocket bolt to 28 ft. lbs. (36 Nm).
21. Install the flange and crankshaft sprocket on the crankshaft. The flange conforms to the front of the silent shaft sprocket and the timing belt sprocket is installed with the flat face toward the engine.

NOTE: The flange must be installed correctly or a broken belt will result.

22. Install the washer and bolt in the crankshaft and torque it to 94 ft. lbs. (130 Nm).
23. Install the camshaft sprocket and bolt and torque the bolt to 72 ft. lbs. (96 Nm).
24. Install the timing belt tensioner, spacer and spring.
25. Align the timing mark on each sprocket with the corresponding mark on the front case.
26. Install the timing belt on the sprockets and move the tensioner against the belt with sufficient force to allow a deflection of 0.197-0.275 in. (5-7mm) along its longest straight run.
27. Tighten the tensioner bolt to 21 ft. lbs. (28 Nm).
28. Install the upper and lower covers, the crankshaft pulley and the crank adapter. Tighten the bolts to 21 ft. lbs. (28 Nm).
29. Remove the 8mm bar and install the plug. Connect the negative battery cable.

1495CC, 1596CC, 1796CC AND 1997CC ENGINES

NOTE: The 1495cc and 1596cc engines are not equipped with silent shafts. Disregard all instructions pertaining to silent shafts if working one of these engines.

1. Disconnect the negative battery cable.
2. Remove the timing belt upper and lower covers.
3. Rotate the crankshaft clockwise and align the timing marks so No. 1 piston will be at TDC of the compression stroke. At this time the timing marks on the camshaft sprocket and the upper surface of the cylinder head should coincide, and the dowel pin of the camshaft sprocket should be at the upper side.

NOTE: Always rotate the crankshaft in a clockwise direction. Make a mark on the back of the timing belt indicating the direction of rotation so it may be reassembled in the same direction if it is to be reused.

4. Remove the auto tensioner and remove the outermost timing belt.
5. Remove the timing belt tensioner pulley, tensioner arm, idler pulley, oil pump sprocket, special washer, flange and spacer.
6. Remove the silent shaft (inner) belt tensioner and remove the inner belt.

To install:
7. Align the timing marks on the crankshaft sprocket and the silent shaft sprocket. Fit the inner timing belt over the crankshaft and silent shaft sprocket. Ensure that there is no slack in the belt.
8. While holding the inner timing belt tensioner with your fingers, adjust the timing belt tension by applying a force towards the center of the belt, until the tension side of the belt is taut. Tighten the tensioner bolt.

NOTE: When tightening the bolt of the tensioner, ensure that the tensioner pulley shaft does not rotate with the bolt. Allowing it to rotate with the bolt can cause excessive tension on the belt.

9. Check belt for proper tension by depressing the belt on its long side with your finger and noting the belt deflection. The desired reading is 0.20-0.28 in. (5-7mm). If tension is not correct, readjust and check belt deflection.
10. Install the flange, crankshaft and washer to the crankshaft. The flange on the crankshaft sprocket must be installed towards the inner timing belt sprocket. Tighten bolt to 80-94 ft. lbs. (110-130 Nm).
11. To install the oil pump sprocket, insert a Phillips screwdriver with a shaft 0.31 in. (8mm) in diameter into the plug hole in the left side of the cylinder block to hold the left silent shaft. Tighten the nut to 36-43 ft. lbs. (50-60 Nm).
12. Using a wrench, hold the camshaft hexagon found between journal No. 2 and 3 and tighten bolt to 58-72 ft. lbs. (80-100 Nm). If no hexagon is present between journal No. 2 and 3, hold the sprocket stationary with a spanner wrench while tightening the retainer bolt.
13. Carefully push the auto tensioner rod in until the set hole in the rod aligned up with the hole in the cylinder. Place a wire into the hole to retain the rod.
14. Install the tensioner pulley onto the tensioner arm. Locate the pinhole in the tensioner pulley shaft to the left of the center bolt. Then, tighten the center bolt finger-tight.
15. When installing the timing belt, turn the 2 camshaft sprockets so their dowel pins are located on top. Align the timing marks facing each other with the top surface of the cylinder head. When you let go of the exhaust camshaft sprocket, it will rotate 1 tooth in the counter-clockwise direction. This should be taken into account when installing the timing belts on the sprocket.

NOTE: Both camshaft sprockets are used for the intake and exhaust camshafts and are provided with 2 timing marks. When the sprocket is mounted on the exhaust camshaft, use the timing mark on the right with the dowel pin hole on top. For the intake camshaft sprocket, use the 1 on the left with the dowel pin hole on top.

16. Align the crankshaft sprocket and oil pump sprocket timing marks.
17. After alignment of the oil pump sprocket timing marks, remove the plug on the cylinder block and insert a Phillips screw driver with a shaft diameter of 0.31 in. (8mm) through the hole. If the shaft can be inserted 2.4 in. (70mm) deep, the silent shaft is in the correct position. If the shaft of the tool can only be inserted 0.8 — 1.0 in. (20-25mm) deep, turn the oil pump sprocket 1 turn and realign the marks. Reinsert the tool making sure it is inserted 2.4 in. (70mm) deep.

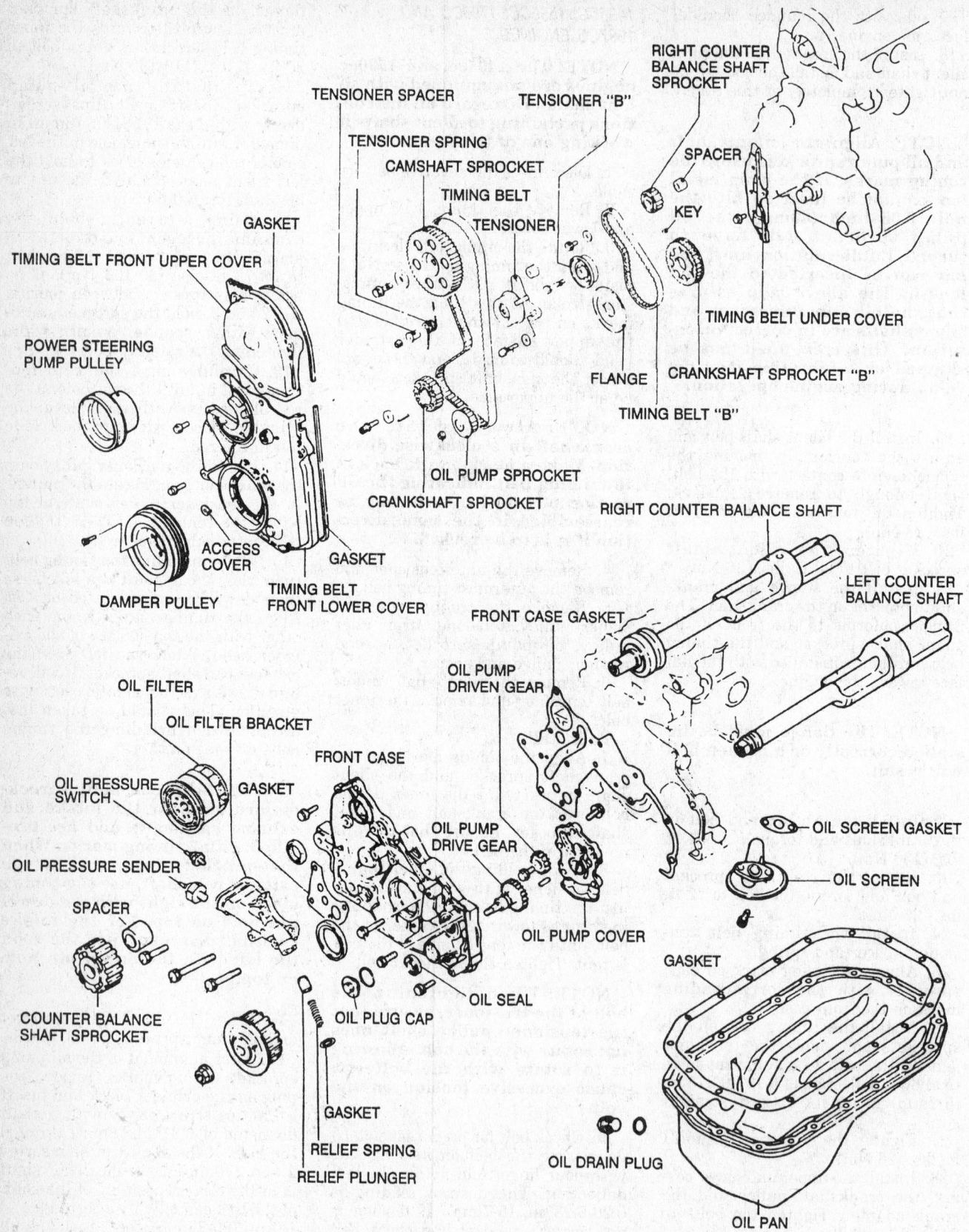

TIMING BELT FRONT UPPER COVER

GASKET

TENSIONER SPACER

TENSIONER SPRING

CAMSHAFT SPROCKET

TIMING BELT

TENSIONER "B"

TENSIONER

RIGHT COUNTER BALANCE SHAFT SPROCKET

SPACER

KEY

TIMING BELT UNDER COVER

CRANKSHAFT SPROCKET "B"

TIMING BELT "B"

FLANGE

POWER STEERING PUMP PULLEY

DAMPER PULLEY

ACCESS COVER

GASKET

TIMING BELT FRONT LOWER COVER

OIL PUMP SPROCKET

CRANKSHAFT SPROCKET

RIGHT COUNTER BALANCE SHAFT

LEFT COUNTER BALANCE SHAFT

FRONT CASE GASKET

OIL PUMP DRIVEN GEAR

OIL FILTER

OIL FILTER BRACKET

OIL PRESSURE SWITCH

OIL PRESSURE SENDER

SPACER

COUNTER BALANCE SHAFT SPROCKET

FRONT CASE

GASKET

OIL PUMP DRIVE GEAR

OIL PUMP COVER

OIL SCREEN GASKET

OIL SCREEN

GASKET

OIL SEAL

OIL PLUG CAP

GASKET

RELIEF SPRING

RELIEF PLUNGER

OIL DRAIN PLUG

OIL PAN

Counterbalance shafts and related drive components — 2351cc engine

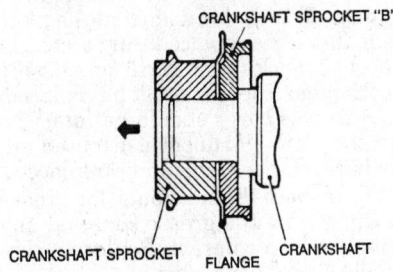

Crankshaft sprocket installation on the 2351cc

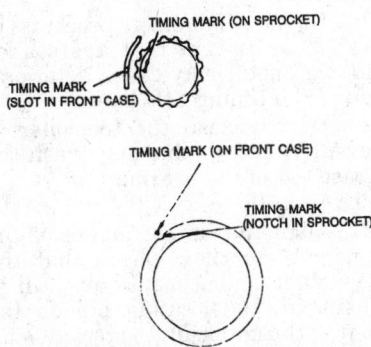

2351cc right counterbalance shaft timing mark alignment

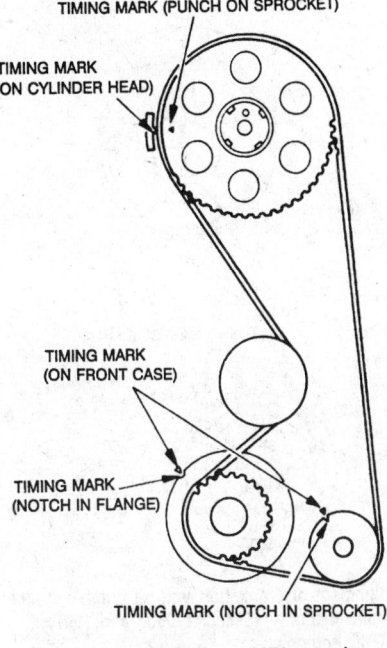

Timing belt installation — 2351cc engine

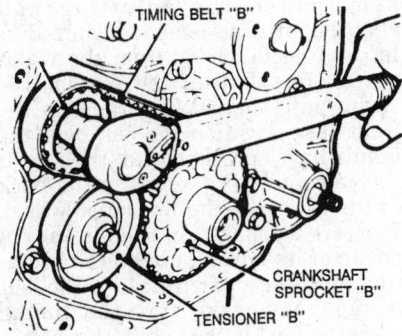

Removing tensioner "B" — 2351cc engine

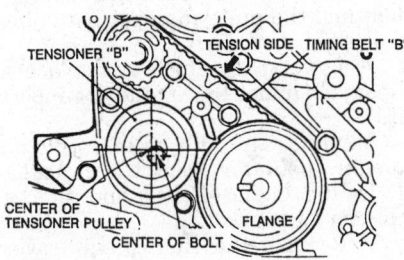

Checking timing belt tension on the 2351cc engine

Keep the tool inserted in hole for the remainder of this procedure.

NOTE: The above step assures that the oil pump socket is in correct orientation to the silent shafts. This step must not be skipped or a vibration may develop during engine operation.

18. Install the timing belt as follows:

a. Install the timing belt around the intake camshaft sprocket and retain it with 2 spring clips or binder clips.

b. Install the timing belt around the exhaust sprocket, aligning the timing marks with the cylinder head top surface using 2 wrenches. Retain the belt with 2 spring clips.

c. Install the timing belt around the idler pulley, oil pump sprocket, crankshaft sprocket and the tensioner pulley. Remove the 2 spring clips.

d. Lift upward on the tensioner pulley in a clockwise direction and tighten the center bolt. Make sure all timing marks are aligned.

e. Rotate the crankshaft ¼ turn counterclockwise. Then, turn in

clockwise until the timing marks are aligned again.

19. To adjust the timing (outer) belt, turn the crankshaft ¼ turn counterclockwise, then turn it clockwise to move No. 1 cylinder to TDC.

20. Loosen the center bolt. Using tool MD998738 or equivalent and a torque wrench, apply a torque of 1.88-2.03 ft. lbs. (2.6-2.8 Nm). Tighten the center bolt.

21. Screw the special tool into the engine left support bracket until its end makes contact with the tensioner arm. At this point, screw the special tool in some more and remove the set wire attached to the auto tensioner, if the wire was not previously removed. Then remove the special tool.

22. Rotate the crankshaft 2 complete turns clockwise and let it sit for approximately 15 minutes. Then, measure the auto tensioner protrusion (the distance between the tensioner arm and auto tensioner body) to ensure that it is within 0.15-0.18 in. (3.8-4.5mm). If out of specification, repeat Step 1-4 until the specified value is obtained.

23. If the timing belt tension adjustment is being performed with the engine mounted in the vehicle, and clearance between the tensioner arm and the auto tensioner body cannot be measured, the following alternative method can be used:

a. Screw in special tool MD998738 or equivalent, until its end makes contact with the tensioner arm.

b. After the special tool makes contact with the arm, screw it in some more to retract the auto tensioner pushrod while counting the number of turns the tool makes until the tensioner arm is brought into contact with the auto tensioner body. Make sure the number of turns the special tool makes conforms with the standard value of 2½-3 turns.

c. Install the rubber plug to the timing belt rear cover.

24. Install the timing belt covers and all related items.

25. Connect the negative battery cable.

2972cc Engine

1. Disconnect the negative battery cable.

2. To remove the air conditioning compressor belt, loosen the adjustment pulley locknut, turn the screw counterclockwise to reduce the drive belt tension and remove the belt.

3. To remove the serpentine drive belt, insert a ½ in. breaker bar in to

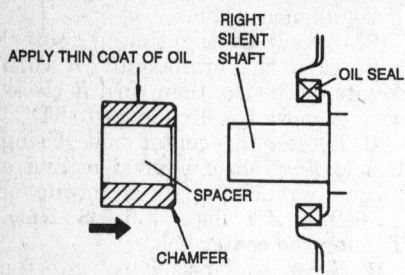

Right counterbalance shaft seal installation — 2351cc engine

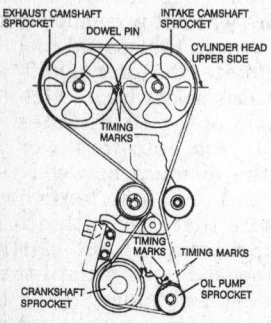

Correct alignment of engine timing marks and belt installation — 1596cc, 1796cc and 1997cc DOHC engines

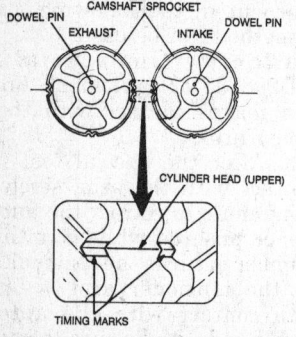

Alignment of camshaft sprocket timing marks — 1596cc, 1796cc and 1997cc DOHC engines

the square hole of the tensioner pulley, rotate it counterclockwise to reduce the drive belt tension and remove the belt.

4. Remove the air conditioning compressor and the air compressor bracket, power steering pump and alternator from the mounts and support them to the side. Remove power steering pump/alternator automatic belt tensioner bolt and the tensioner.

5. Raise the vehicle and support safely. Remove the right inner fender splash shield.

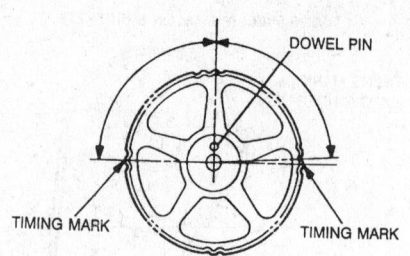

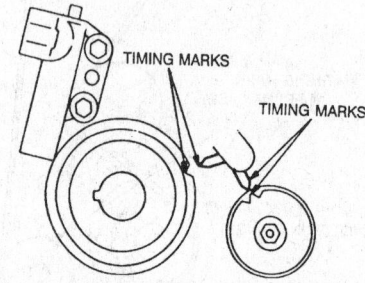

Alignment of crankshaft and oil pump sprocket timing marks — 1596cc, 1796cc and 1997cc DOHC engines

6. Remove the crankshaft pulley bolt and the pulley/damper assembly from the crankshaft.

7. Lower the vehicle and place a floor jack under the engine to support it.

8. Separate the front engine mount insulator from the bracket. Raise the engine slightly and remove the mount bracket.

9. Remove the timing belt cover bolts and the upper and lower covers from the engine.

10. Turn the crankshaft until the timing marks on the camshaft sprocket and cylinder head are aligned.

11. Loosen the tensioning bolt, it runs in the slotted portion of the tensioner, and the pivot bolt on the timing belt tensioner.

12. Move the tensioner counterclockwise as far as it will go. Tighten the adjusting bolt.

13. Mark the timing belt with an arrow showing direction of rotation.

14. Remove the timing belt from the camshaft sprocket.

15. Remove the crankshaft pulley. Then, remove the timing belt. Remove the timing belt tensioner. Remove the retainer bolts from the timing sprockets and remove as required.

16. Inspect the belt thoroughly. The back surface must be pliable and rough. If it is hard and glossy, the belt should be replaced. Any cracks in the belt backing or teeth or missing teeth mean the belt must be replaced. The canvas cover should be intact on all the teeth. If rubber is exposed anywhere, the belt should be replaced.

17. Inspect the tensioner for grease leaking from the grease seal and any roughness in rotation. Replace a tensioner for either defect.

18. The sprockets should be inspected and replaced if there is any sign of damaged teeth or cracking anywhere.

19. Do not immerse sprockets in solvent, as solvent that has soaked into the metal may cause deterioration of the timing belt later.

20. Do not clean the tensioner in solvent either, as this may wash the grease out of the bearing.

To install:

21. Align the timing marks of the camshaft sprocket. Check that the crankshaft timing marks are still in alignment, the locating pin on the front of the crankshaft sprocket is aligned with a mark on the front case.

22. Mount the tensioner, spring and spacer with the bottom end of the spring free. Then, install the bolts and tighten the adjusting bolt slightly with the tensioner moved as far as possible away from the water pump. Install the free end of the spring into the locating tang on the front case. Position the belt over the crankshaft sprocket and then over the camshaft sprocket. Slip the back of the belt over the tensioner wheel. Turn the camshaft sprocket in the opposite of its normal direction of rotation until the straight side of the belt is tight and make sure the timing marks align. If not, shift the belt 1 tooth at a time in the appropriate direction until this occurs.

23. Loosen the tensioner mounting bolts so the tensioner works, without the interference of any friction, under spring pressure. Make sure the belt follows the curve of the camshaft pulley so the teeth are engaged all the way around.

24. Correct the path of the belt, if necessary. Torque the tensioner adjusting bolt to 16-21 ft. lbs. (22-29 Nm). Then, torque the tensioner pivot bolt to the same figure. Bolts must be torqued in that order, or tension won't be correct.

25. Turn the crankshaft 1 turn clockwise until timing marks again align to seat the belt. Then loosen both tensioner attaching bolts and let

the tensioner position itself under spring tension as before. Finally, torque the bolts in the proper order exactly as before. Check belt tension by putting a finger on the water pump side of the tensioner wheel and pull the belt toward it. The belt should move toward the pump until the teeth are about ¼ of the way across the head of the tensioner adjusting bolt. Retension the belt, if necessary.

26. Install the timing belt covers.

27. Install the crankshaft pulley, making sure the pin on the crankshaft sprocket fits through the hole in the rear surface of the pulley. Install the retaining bolt and torque to 108-116 ft. lbs. (147-157 Nm).

28. Install the engine mount bracket and secure with the mounting hardware.

29. Install the pulley damper assembly to the crankshaft. Torque the bolt to 110 ft. lbs. (149 Nm). Install the splash shield.

30. Install the power steering pump/alternator automatic belt tensioner.

31. Install the air conditioning compressor bracket, compressor, power steering pump and alternator.

32. Install the accessory drive belt.

33. Connect the negative battery cable and check all disturbed components for proper operation.

Timing Sprockets and Oil Seals

REMOVAL AND INSTALLATION

1. Disconnect the negative battery cable.

2. Remove the valve cover(s) and timing belt(s).

3. Remove the crankshaft pulley retainer bolts and remove the pulley.

4. Remove the crankshaft sprocket retainer bolt and washer from the sprocket, if used, and remove sprocket. If sprocket is difficult to remove or there are no bolts on the puller, the appropriate puller should be used to facilitate remove.

5. Hold the camshaft stationary using the hexagon cast between journals No. 2 and 3 and remove the retainer bolt. Remove the sprocket from the camshaft. If the camshaft does not have a hexagon cast between journals No. 2 and 3, use an appropriate spanner wrench to hold the shaft in position while removing the bolt.

6. Pry the seals from the bores and replace using the proper installation tools.

7. The sprockets should be inspected and replaced if there is any sign of damaged teeth or cracking. Do not immerse sprockets in solvent, as solvent that has soaked into the metal may cause deterioration of the timing belt later.

To install:

8. Install the sprockets to their shafts. Install the retainer bolts and torque the camshaft sprocket as follows:

 1468cc engine to 54 ft. lbs. (75 Nm)

 1495, 1596cc and 1796 engines to 58-72 ft. lbs. (80-100 Nm)

 1997cc engine to 58-72 ft. lbs. (80-100 Nm)

 2351cc engine to 72 ft. lbs. (98 Nm)

 2972cc engine to 72 ft. lbs. (98 Nm)

9. Install the flange and crankshaft sprocket. The flange must go on first with the chamfered area outward. The sprocket is installed with the boss forward and the studs for the fan belt pulley outward. Torque the crankshaft sprocket retaining bolt as follows:

 1468cc engine to 72 ft. lbs. (98 Nm)

 1495cc engine to 137-145 ft. lbs. (190-200 Nm)

 1596cc and 1996 engines to 80-94 ft. lbs. (110-130 Nm)

 1997cc engine to 80-94 ft. lbs. (110-130 Nm)

 2351cc engine to 94 ft. lbs. (127 Nm)

 2972cc engine to 116 ft. lbs. (157 Nm)

10. Install the timing belt(s) and valve cover(s).

11. Connect the negative battery cable and check for leaks.

Camshaft

REMOVAL AND INSTALLATION

1468cc Engine

1. Remove the rocker cover. Remove the timing belt cover. Remove the distributor.

2. Loosen the 2 bolts and move the timing belt tensioner toward the water pump as far as it will go, then retighten the timing belt tensioner adjusting bolt. Disengage the timing belt from the camshaft sprocket and unbolt and remove the sprocket. The timing belt may be left engaged with

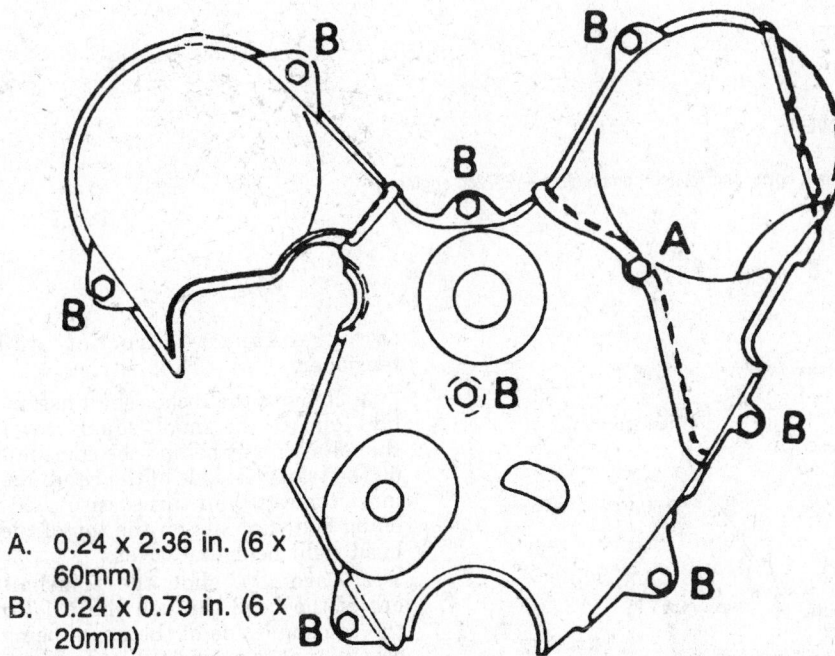

A. 0.24 x 2.36 in. (6 x 60mm)
B. 0.24 x 0.79 in. (6 x 20mm)

Timing belt cover bolt locations — 2972cc engine

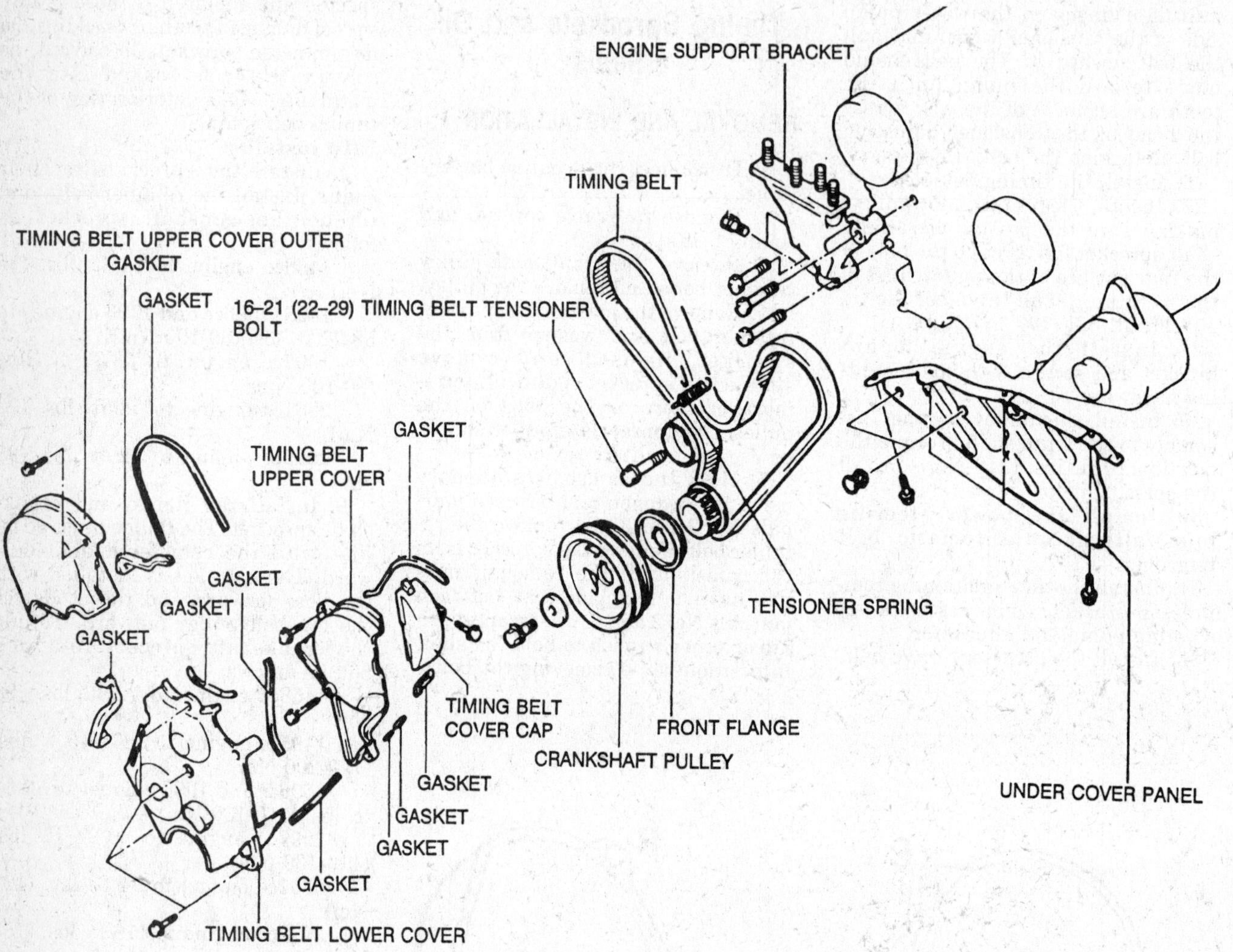

ENGINE SUPPORT BRACKET

TIMING BELT

TIMING BELT UPPER COVER OUTER
GASKET

GASKET

16–21 (22–29) TIMING BELT TENSIONER
BOLT

GASKET

TIMING BELT
UPPER COVER

GASKET

GASKET

GASKET

TENSIONER SPRING

TIMING BELT
COVER CAP

FRONT FLANGE

CRANKSHAFT PULLEY

UNDER COVER PANEL

GASKET

GASKET

GASKET

GASKET

TIMING BELT LOWER COVER

Timing belt cover and related components — 2972cc engine

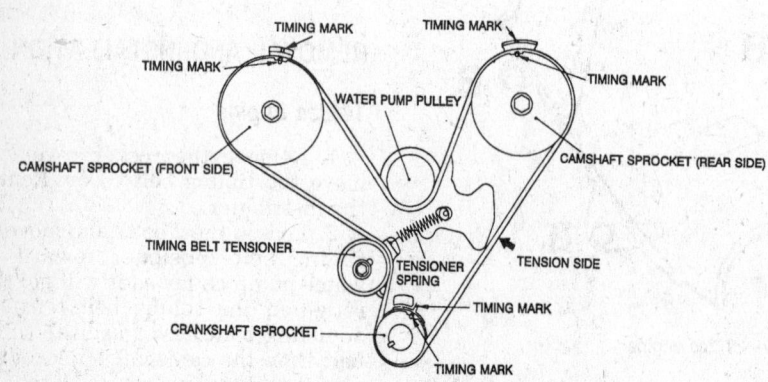

TIMING MARK

TIMING MARK

TIMING MARK

TIMING MARK

WATER PUMP PULLEY

CAMSHAFT SPROCKET (FRONT SIDE)

CAMSHAFT SPROCKET (REAR SIDE)

TIMING BELT TENSIONER

TENSIONER
SPRING

TENSION SIDE

TIMING MARK

CRANKSHAFT SPROCKET

TIMING MARK

Alignment of timing marks with belt installed — 2972cc engine

the crankshaft sprocket and tensioner.

3. Remove the rocker shaft assembly. Remove the small, square cover that sits directly behind the camshaft on the transaxle side of the head. Remove the camshaft thrust case tightening bolt that sits on the top of the head right near that cover.

4. Carefully, slide the camshaft out of the head through the hole in the camshaft side of the head, being careful that the camshaft lobes do not strike the bearing bores in the head.

To install:

5. Lubricate all journal and thrust surfaces with clean engine oil.

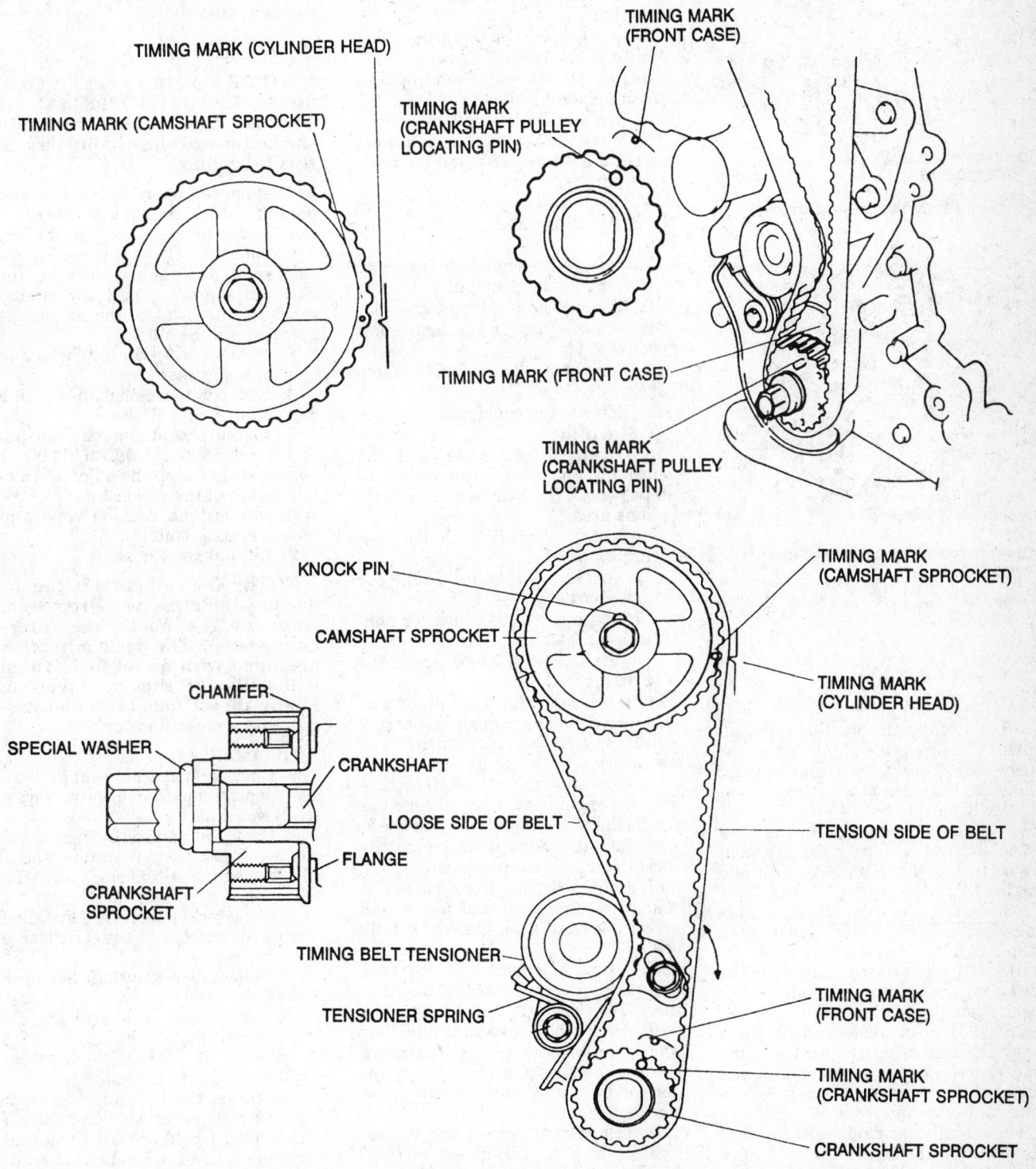

TIMING MARK (CYLINDER HEAD)

TIMING MARK (CAMSHAFT SPROCKET)

TIMING MARK (FRONT CASE)

TIMING MARK (CRANKSHAFT PULLEY LOCATING PIN)

TIMING MARK (FRONT CASE)

TIMING MARK (CRANKSHAFT PULLEY LOCATING PIN)

KNOCK PIN

CAMSHAFT SPROCKET

TIMING MARK (CAMSHAFT SPROCKET)

TIMING MARK (CYLINDER HEAD)

CHAMFER

SPECIAL WASHER

CRANKSHAFT

LOOSE SIDE OF BELT

TENSION SIDE OF BELT

FLANGE

CRANKSHAFT SPROCKET

TIMING BELT TENSIONER

TENSIONER SPRING

TIMING MARK (FRONT CASE)

TIMING MARK (CRANKSHAFT SPROCKET)

CRANKSHAFT SPROCKET

Timing belt sprockets, components and timing mark relationship — 1495cc 12 valve engine — 1993-94 Scoupe

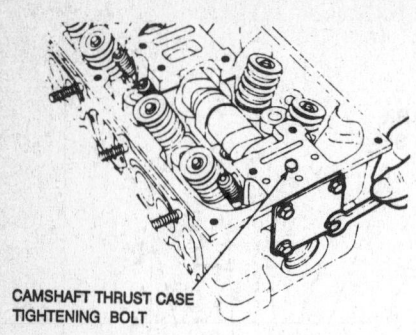

CAMSHAFT THRUST CASE
TIGHTENING BOLT

Rear camshaft cover — 1468cc engine

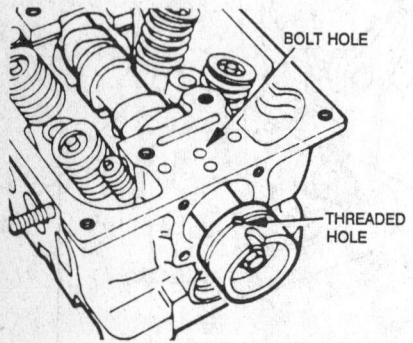

BOLT HOLE

THREADED
HOLE

Camshaft positioning during installation —
1468cc engine

6. Carefully, insert the camshaft into the engine. Make sure the camshaft goes in with the threaded hole in the top of the thrust case straight upward.

7. Align the bolt hole in the trust case and the cylinder head surface.

8. Install the thrust case bolt and tighten firmly.

9. Install the rear cover with a new gasket and install and tighten the bolts.

10. Coat the external surface of the front oil seal with engine oil.

11. Using special installer tool MD 998306-01 or equivalent, drive the a new front camshaft oil seal into the clearance between the camshaft and head at the forward end, making sure the seal seats fully.

12. Install the camshaft sprocket and torque the bolt to 47-54 ft. lbs. (64-74 Nm).

13. Reconnect the timing belt, check the timing and adjust the belt tension.

14. Reinstall the rocker shaft assembly. Adjust the valves and install the rocker and timing belt covers.

1495cc Engine

1. Disconnect the negative battery cable. Remove the air intake pipe, if turbocharged.

2. Disconnect the breather hose and the secondary air hose.

3. Remove the water pump pulley and crankshaft pulley.

4. Remove the timing belt cover.

5. Move the timing belt tensioner toward the water pump and temporarily secure it.

6. Remove the timing belt from the camshaft sprocket and the timing belt.

7. Remove the camshaft sprocket.

8. Remove the distributor.

9. Remove the rocker cover.

10. Remove the rocker arm shaft assembly.

11. Remove the camshaft bearing caps.

12. Remove the camshaft.

To install:

13. Clean all parts well. If the camshaft is be reused, use a micrometer to check the lobe height. Specifications are:

    a. Intake: 1.5318 inch for non-turbocharged

    b. Intake: 1.4990 inch for turbocharged

    c. Exhaust: 1.5344 inch for non-turbocharged

    d. Exhaust: 1.5020 inch for turbocharged

14. If the camshaft lobes, front seal wear area or the camshaft bearing saddles are worn, replace as necessary.

15. Lubricate the camshaft with a suitable engine assembly lubricant or fresh engine oil. Install the camshaft.

16. Install the distributor then the rocker arm and shaft assembly.

17. Lubricate the front camshaft seal with engine oil and use a seal driver to install until the seal is fully seated.

18. Install the camshaft sprocket and torque the center bolt to 58-72 ft. lbs. (77-98 Nm).

19. Align the camshaft sprocket and crankshaft sprocket timing marks. The piston in the No. 1 cylinder will be at TDC of the compression stroke.

20. Temporarily adjust the valves. Cold setting is: Intake — 0.007 in. (0.18mm); Exhaust — 0.009 in. (0.23mm).

21. Install a new gasket in the rocker cover groove and temporarily install the rocker cover.

22. Install the timing belt cover, water pump and crankshaft pulley.

23. Start the engine, allow to idle and warm to operating temperature. Adjust valves if required.

24. Install air intake pipe, if turbocharged.

2351cc Engine

NOTE: A special tool 09246-32000 (MD998443) or equivalent, is required to retain the automatic lash adjusters in this procedure.

1. Remove the rocker cover and gasket and the timing belt cover.

2. Turn the crankshaft so the No. 1 piston is at TDC compression. At this point, the timing mark on the camshaft sprocket and the timing mark on the head to the left of the sprocket will be aligned.

3. Remove the timing belt and camshaft sprocket.

4. Remove the camshaft bearing cap bolts.

5. Install the automatic lash adjuster retainer tool 09246-32000 or equivalent, to keep the adjuster from falling out of the rocker arms.

6. Lift off the bearing caps and rocker arm assemblies.

7. Lift out the camshaft.

NOTE: Keep all parts in the order in which they were removed. None of the parts are interchangeable. The lash adjusters are filled with diesel fuel, which will spill out if they are inverted. If any diesel fuel is spilled, the adjusters must be bled.

To install:

8. Check all parts for wear or damage. Replace any damaged or excessively worn part.

9. Coat the camshaft with clean engine oil and place it on the head.

10. Assemble all parts. Note the following:

    a. The rocker shafts are installed with the notches in the ends facing up.

    b. The left rocker shaft is longer than the right.

    c. The wave washers are installed on the left shaft.

    d. Coat all parts with clean engine oil prior to assembly.

    e. Insert the lash adjuster from under the rocker arm and install the special holding tool. If any of the diesel fuel is spilled, the adjuster must be bled.

    f. Tighten the bearing cap bolts, working from the center towards the ends, to 15 ft. lbs. (20 Nm), in 3 steps.

    g. Check the operation of each lash adjuster by positioning the camshaft so the rocker arm bears on the low or round portion of the cam. The pointed part of the cam faces straight down. Insert a thin steel wire, or tool MD998442 or equivalent, in the hole in the top of the rocker arm, over the lash adjuster and depress the check ball at the top of the adjuster. While holding the check ball depressed, move the arm up and down. Looseness should be felt. Full plunger stroke should be 0.087 in. (2.2mm). If not, remove, clean and bleed the lash adjusters.

1596cc, 1796cc and 1997cc Engines

1. Relieve the fuel system pressure.
2. Disconnect battery negative cable.
3. Disconnect the accelerator cable.
4. Remove the timing belt cover and timing belt.
5. Remove the center cover, breather and PCV hoses and spark plug cables.
6. Remove the rocker cover, semi-circular packing, throttle body stay, crankshaft angle sensor, both camshaft sprockets and oil seals.
7. Loosen the bearing cap bolts in 2-3 steps. Label and remove all camshaft bearing caps.

NOTE: If the bearing caps are difficult to remove, use a plastic hammer to gently tap the rear part of the camshaft.

8. Remove the intake and exhaust camshafts.
9. Check the camshaft journals for wear or damage. Check the camshaft lobes for damage. Also, check the cylinder head oil holes for clogging.

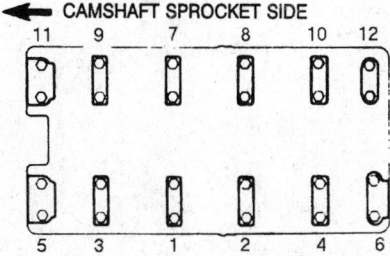

← CAMSHAFT SPROCKET SIDE

Tighten camshaft bearing caps to the specified torque in 2 or 3 steps using the above sequence

To install:

10. Lubricate the camshafts with heavy engine oil and position the camshafts on the cylinder head.

NOTE: Do not confuse the intake camshaft with the exhaust camshaft. The intake camshaft has a split on its rear end for driving the crank angle sensor.

11. Make sure the dowel pin on both camshaft sprocket ends are located on the top.
12. Install the bearing caps. Tighten the caps in sequence and in 2 or 3 steps. No. 2 and 5 caps are of the same shape. Check the markings on the caps to identify the cap number and intake/exhaust symbol. Only **L** (intake) or **R** (exhaust) is stamped on No. 1 bearing cap. Also, make sure the rocker arm is correctly mounted on the lash adjuster and the valve stem end. Torque the retaining bolts to 15 ft. lbs. (20 Nm).
13. Apply a coating of engine oil to the oil seal. Using tool MD998307 or equivalent, press-fit the seal into the cylinder head.
14. Align the punch mark on the crank angle sensor housing with the notch in the plate. with the dowel pin on the sprocket side of the intake camshaft at top, install the crank angle sensor on the cylinder head.

NOTE: Do not position the crank angle sensor with the punch mark positioned opposite the notch; this position will result in incorrect fuel injection and ignition timing.

15. Install the timing belt, valve cover and all related parts.
16. Connect the negative battery cable and check for leaks.

2972cc Engine

1. Disconnect the negative battery cable. Remove the air cleaner assembly and valve covers.
2. Install auto lash adjuster retainer tools MD998443 or equivalent on the rocker arms.
3. If removing the right side (front) camshaft, remove the distributor extension.
4. Remove the camshaft bearing caps but do not remove the bolts from the caps.
5. Remove the rocker arms, rocker shafts and bearing caps, as an assembly.
6. Remove the camshaft from the cylinder head.
7. Inspect the bearing journals on the camshaft, cylinder head and bearing caps.

To install:

8. Lubricate the camshaft journals and camshaft with clean engine oil and install the camshaft in the cylinder head.
9. Align the camshaft bearing caps with the arrow mark depending on cylinder numbers and install in numerical order.
10. Apply sealer at the ends of the bearing caps and install the assembly.
11. Torque the rocker arm and shaft assembly bolts to 15 ft. lbs. (21 Nm).
12. Install the distributor extension, if removed.
13. Install the valve cover and all related parts. Torque the valve cover retaining bolts to 7 ft. lbs. (10 Nm).
14. Connect the negative battery cable and road test the vehicle.

Counterbalance Shafts

REMOVAL AND INSTALLATION

1997cc and 2351cc Engines

1. Disconnect the negative battery cable.
2. Remove the oil filter, oil pressure switch, oil gauge sending unit, oil filter mounting bracket and gasket.
3. Raise and safely support the vehicle. Drain engine oil. Remove engine oil pan.
4. Lower the vehicle. Remove the timing belts.
5. Remove the crankshaft sprocket (inner) and counterbalance shaft sprocket.
6. Remove the front engine cover which is also the oil pump cover. Different length bolts are used. Take note of their locations. Discard the shaft seal and gasket.
7. Remove the oil pump driven gear flange bolt. When loosening this bolt, first remove the plug at the bottom of the left side of the cylinder block and insert a tool approximately ³/₈ in. in diameter into the hole. The tool will hold the silent shaft in position. The tool must be inserted at least 2.4 in. into the hole. If depth of insertion is not correct, rotate the oil pump sprocket 1 revolution, and align the timing marks. Insert the tool shaft again, and watch the amount of insertion, which should be at least 2.4 in.
8. Remove the oil pump gears and remove the front case assembly. Remove the threaded plug, the oil pressure relief spring and plunger.

9. Remove the shaft alignment tool, front cover and oil pump as a unit, with the left counter shaft attached.

10. Remove the oil pump gear and left counterbalance shaft.

NOTE: To aid in removal of the front cover, a driver groove is provided on the cover, above the oil pump housing. Avoid prying on the thinner parts of the housing flange or hammering on it to remove the case.

11. Remove the right counterbalance shaft from the engine block.

To install:

12. Install a new front seal in the cover. Install the oil pump drive and driven gears in the front case, aligning the timing marks on the pump gears.

13. Install the left counterbalance shaft in the driven gear and temporarily tighten the bolt.

14. Install the right counterbalance shaft into the cylinder block.

15. Install an oil seal guide on the end of the crankshaft and install a new gasket on the front of the engine block for the front cover.

16. Install a new front case packing.

17. Insert the left counterbalance shaft into the engine block and at the

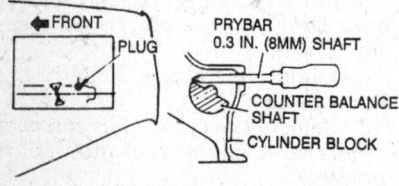

Holding the counter balance shaft in position during oil pump sprocket retainer nut removal. This procedure is also used to assure correct orientation of the oil pump sprocket and counter balance shaft.

same time, guide the front cover into place on the front of the engine block.

18. Install an O-ring on the oil pump cover and install it on the front cover.

19. Tighten the oil pump cover bolts and the front cover bolts to 11-13 ft. lbs. (15-18 Nm).

20. Install the upper and lower undercovers.

21. Install the spacer on the end of the right counterbalance shaft, with the chambered edge toward the rear of the engine.

22. Install the counterbalance shaft sprocket and temporarily tighten the bolt.

23. Install the inner crankshaft sprocket and align the timing marks on the sprockets with those on the front case.

24. Install the inner tensioner (B) with the center of the pulley on the left side of the mounting bolt and with the pulley flange toward the front of the engine.

25. Lift the tensioner by hand, clockwise, to apply tension to the belt. Tighten the bolt to secure the tensioner.

26. Check that all alignment marks are in their proper places and the belt deflection is approximately ¼-½ in. on the tension side.

NOTE: When the tensioner bolt is tightened, make sure the shaft of the tensioner does not turn with the bolt. If the belt is too tight there will be noise and if the belt is too loose, the belt and sprocket may come out of mesh.

27. Tighten the counterbalance shaft sprocket bolt to 22-28.5 ft. lbs. (29-40 Nm).

28. Install the flange and crankshaft sprocket. Tighten the bolt to 43-50 ft. lbs. (58-67 Nm).

29. Install the camshaft spacer and sprocket. Tighten the bolt to 44-57 ft. lbs. (61-75 Nm).

30. Align the camshaft sprocket timing mark with the timing mark on the upper inner cover.

31. Install the oil pump sprocket, tightening the nut to 25-28 ft. lbs. (34-39 Nm). Align the timing mark on the sprocket with the mark on the case.

NOTE: To be assured that the phasing of the oil pump sprocket and the left counterbalance shaft is correct, a metal rod should be inserted in the plugged hole on the left side of the cylinder block. If it can be inserted more than 2.4 in., the phasing is correct. If the tool can only be inserted approximately 1.0 in., turn the oil pump sprocket through 1 turn and realign the timing marks. Keep the metal rod inserted until the installation of the timing belt is completed. Remove the tool from the hole and install the plug, before starting the engine.

32. Install the tensioner spring and tensioner. Temporarily tighten the nut. Install the front end of the tensioner spring (bent at right angles) on the projection of the tensioner and the other end (straight) on the water pump body.

33. If the timing belt is correctly tensioned, there should be about 12mm clearance between the outside of the belt and the edge of the belt cover. This is measured about half-way down the side of the belt opposite the tensioner.

34. Complete the assembly by installing the oil screen, gasket and oil pan.

35. Install the crankshaft pulley, alternator and accessory belts and adjust to specifications.

36. Install the radiator, fill the cooling system with antifreeze and the crankcase with clean engine oil. Connect the negative battery cable and start the engine.

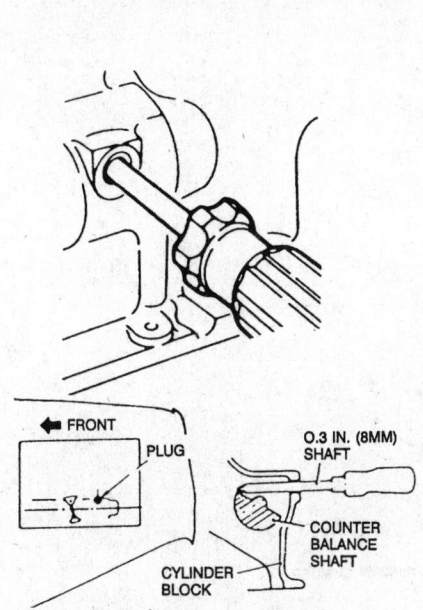

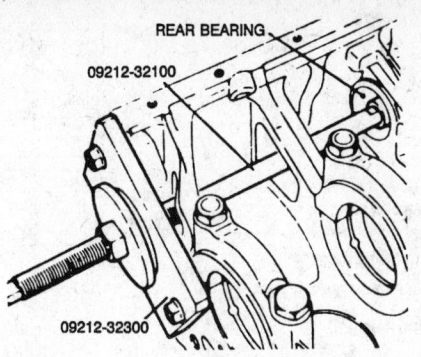

Removing the left counterbalance shaft — 2351cc engine

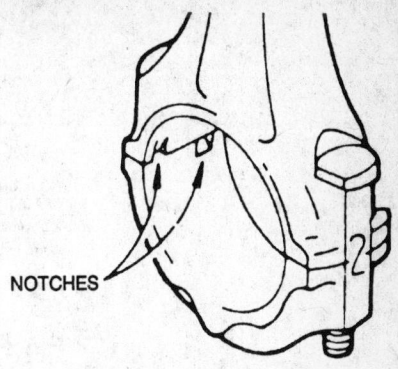

NOTCHES

Connecting rod cap installation

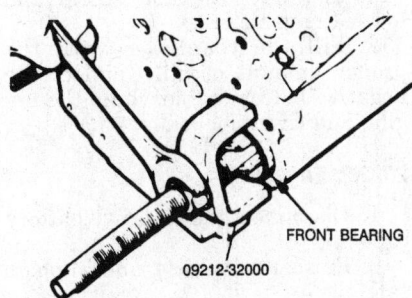

FRONT

PLUG

0.3 IN. (8MM) SHAFT

COUNTER BALANCE SHAFT

CYLINDER BLOCK

Checking orientation of counterbalance shaft by removing plug and inserting 8mm shaft into hole

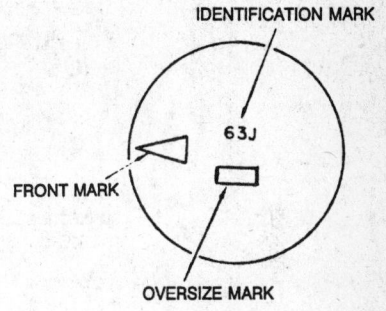

IDENTIFICATION MARK

6 3 J

FRONT MARK

OVERSIZE MARK

Piston installation

Piston and Connecting Rod

POSITIONING

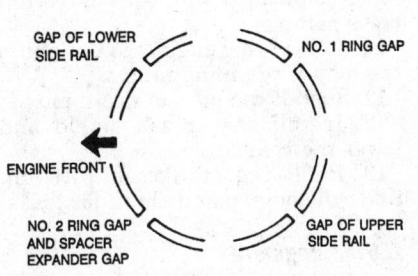

GAP OF LOWER SIDE RAIL

NO. 1 RING GAP

ENGINE FRONT

NO. 2 RING GAP AND SPACER EXPANDER GAP

GAP OF UPPER SIDE RAIL

Piston ring positioning

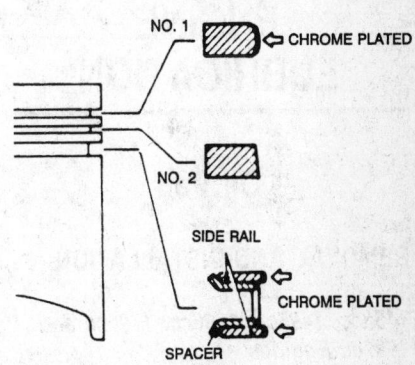

NO. 1   CHROME PLATED

NO. 2

SIDE RAIL

CHROME PLATED

SPACER

Piston ring installation

Removing the right counterbalance shaft — 2351cc engine

FRONT BEARING

09212-32000

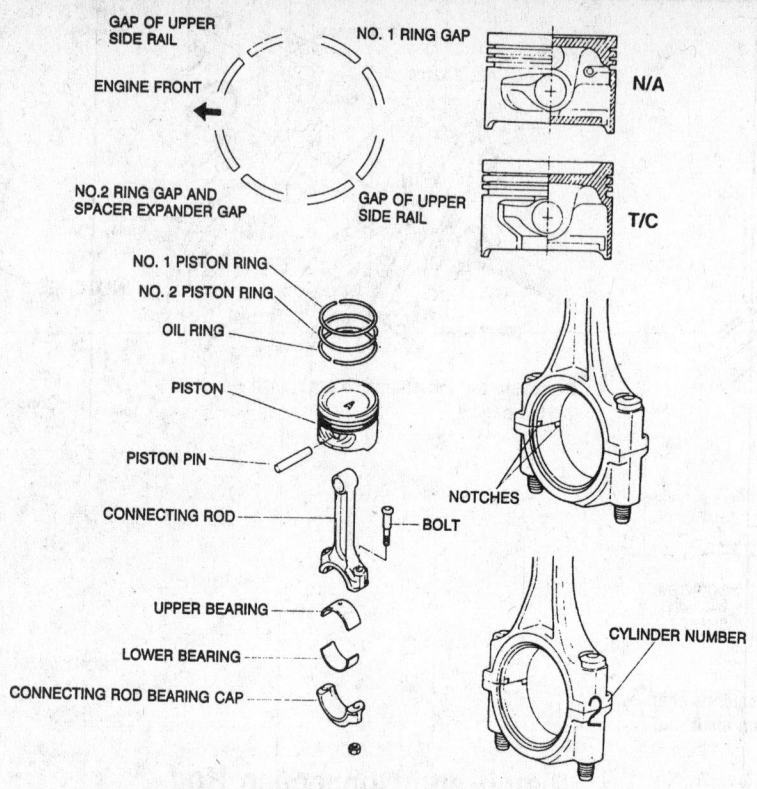

GAP OF UPPER SIDE RAIL

ENGINE FRONT

NO. 1 RING GAP

N/A

T/C

NO.2 RING GAP AND SPACER EXPANDER GAP

GAP OF UPPER SIDE RAIL

NO. 1 PISTON RING
NO. 2 PISTON RING
OIL RING
PISTON
PISTON PIN
CONNECTING ROD
BOLT
NOTCHES
UPPER BEARING
LOWER BEARING
CONNECTING ROD BEARING CAP
CYLINDER NUMBER

Piston and connecting rod identification — 1495cc 12 valve engine — 1993-94 Scoupe

ENGINE LUBRICATION

Oil Pan

REMOVAL AND INSTALLATION

1468cc, 1495cc, 1596cc, 1796cc and 1997cc Engines

1. Disconnect the negative battery cable. Raise the vehicle and support it safely.
2. Drain the oil.
3. Remove the underbody splash shield.
4. Remove the oil pan bolts, drop the pan and slide it out from under the vehicle.
5. Clean the mating surfaces of the oil pan and the engine block.
6. Apply a ⅛ in. (3mm) bead of RTV sealer along the groove in the oil pan.
To install:
7. Using non-hardening sealer, glue a new gasket to the oil pan.
8. Install the oil pan. Hand-tighten the retaining bolts.

9. Starting at one end of the pan, gradually tighten the retaining bolts to 48-72 inch lbs. (6-8 Nm) in a criss-cross pattern.
10. Lower the engine and tighten the mount retaining nuts.
11. Install the oil pan drain plug.
12. Install the splash shield and lower the vehicle.
13. Refill the crankcase with oil. Start the engine and check for leaks.

2351cc Engine

1. Disconnect the negative battery cable. Raise the vehicle and support it safely.
2. Drain the oil.
3. Remove the underbody splash shield.
4. Remove the oil pan bolts, drop the pan and slide it out from under the vehicle.
5. Clean the mating surfaces of the oil pan and the engine block.
To install:
6. Apply sealer to the engine block at the block-to-chain case and block-to-rear oil seal case joint faces.
7. Use a non-hardening sealer and secure a new gasket to the oil pan.
8. Install the oil pan. Hand-tighten the retaining bolts.
9. Starting at one end of the pan, tighten the pan bolts to 48-72 inch lbs. (6-8 Nm) in a crisscross pattern.

10. Install the oil pan drain plug.
11. Install the splash shield and lower the vehicle.
12. Fill the crankcase with the proper amount of oil. Connect the negative battery cable. Start the engine and check for leaks.

2972cc Engine

1. Disconnect the negative battery cable.
2. Raise the vehicle and support safely.
3. Remove the torque converter bolt access cover.
4. Drain the engine oil.
5. Remove the oil pan retaining screws and remove the oil pan and gasket.
To install:
6. Thoroughly clean and dry all sealing surfaces, bolts and bolt holes.
7. Apply silicone sealer to the chain cover to block mating seam and the rear main seal retainer to block seam, if equipped.
8. Install a new pan gasket or apply silicone sealer to the sealing surface of the pan and install to the engine.
9. Install the retaining screws and torque to 50 inch lbs. (6 Nm).
10. Install the torque converter bolt access cover, if equipped. Lower the vehicle.

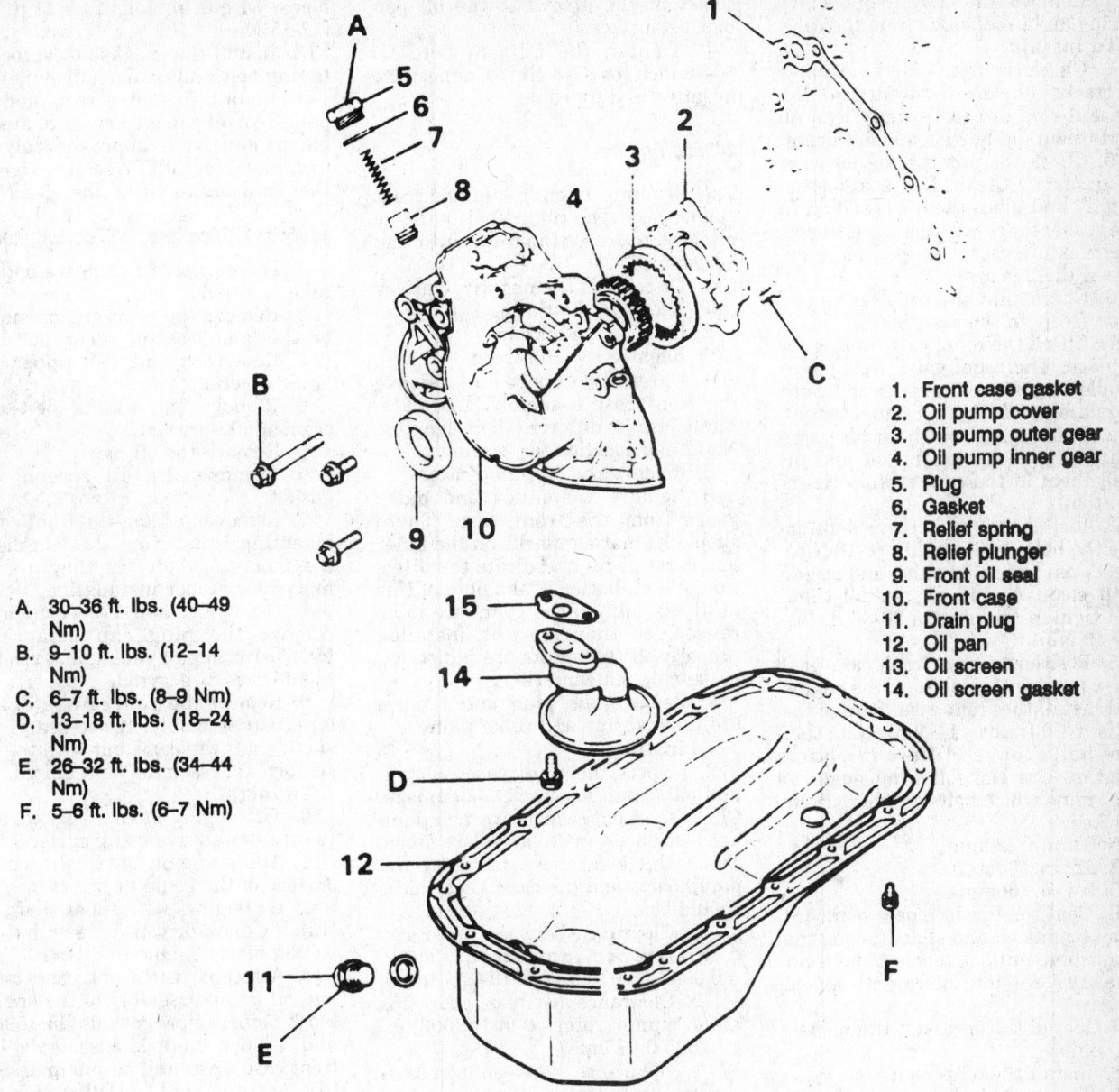

A. 30–36 ft. lbs. (40–49 Nm)
B. 9–10 ft. lbs. (12–14 Nm)
C. 6–7 ft. lbs. (8–9 Nm)
D. 13–18 ft. lbs. (18–24 Nm)
E. 26–32 ft. lbs. (34–44 Nm)
F. 5–6 ft. lbs. (6–7 Nm)

1. Front case gasket
2. Oil pump cover
3. Oil pump outer gear
4. Oil pump inner gear
5. Plug
6. Gasket
7. Relief spring
8. Relief plunger
9. Front oil seal
10. Front case
11. Drain plug
12. Oil pan
13. Oil screen
14. Oil screen gasket

Oil pan and related components — 1468cc engine

Application guide for the formed-in-place gasket on the oil pan — 2351cc engine shown

11. Install the dipstick. Fill the engine with the proper amount of oil.
12. Connect the negative battery cable and check for leaks.

Oil Pump

REMOVAL AND INSTALLATION

NOTE: Whenever the oil pump is disassembled or the cover removed, the gear cavity must be filled with petroleum jelly for priming purposes. Do not use grease.

1468cc Engine

1. Disconnect the negative battery cable. Remove the timing belt.
2. Remove the oil pan.
3. Remove the oil screen.
4. Unbolt and remove the front case assembly.
5. Remove the oil pump cover.
6. Remove the inner and outer gears from the front case.

NOTE: The outer gear has no identifying marks to indicate direction of rotation. Clean the gear and mark it with an indelible marker.

7. Remove the plug, relief valve spring and relief valve from the case.

To install:

8. Check the front case for damage or cracks. Replace the front seal. Replace the oil screen O-ring. Clean all parts thoroughly with a safe solvent.

9. Check the pump gears for wear or damage. Clean the gears thoroughly and place them in position in the case to check the clearances. There is a crescent-shaped piece between the 2 gears.

10. Check that the relief valve can slide freely in the case.

11. Check the relief valve spring for damage. The relief valve free length should be 1.8 in. (47mm). Load length should be 13.4 lbs. at 1.6 in. (40mm).

12. Thoroughly coat both oil pump gears with clean engine oil and install them in the correct direction of rotation.

13. Install the pump cover and torque the bolts to 6-7 ft. lbs. (8-10 Nm).

14. Coat the relief valve and spring with clean engine oil, install them and tighten the plug to 30-36 ft. lbs. (39-49 Nm).

15. Position a new front case gasket, coated with sealer, on the engine and install the front case. Torque the bolts to 10 ft. lbs. (14 Nm). Note that the bolts have different shank lengths. Use the following guide to determine which bolts go where. Bolts marked:
   A: 0.08 in. (20mm)
   B: 1.2 in. (30mm)
   C: 2.4 in. (60mm)

16. Coat the lips of a new seal with clean engine oil and slide it along the crankshaft until it touches the front case. Drive it into place with a seal driver.

17. Install the sprocket, timing belt and pulley.

18. Install the oil screen.

19. Thoroughly clean both the oil pan and engine mating surfaces. Apply a 1/8 in. (3mm) wide bead of RTV

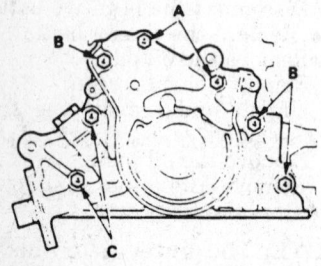

Installing the bolts for the 1468cc engine's oil pump. Bolts of 0.79 in. (20mm) length are at location A; of 1.18 in. (30mm) length are at location B; and those of 2.36 in. (60mm) length are at C.

sealer in the groove of the oil pan mating surface.

20. Tighten the oil pan bolts to 60-72 inch lbs. (7-8 Nm). Connect the negative battery cable.

1495cc Engine

The oil pump is built into the front engine case. The timing belt must be removed to access the front cover and oil pump.

1. Disconnect the negative battery cable. Remove the timing belt.

2. Remove the oil pan.

3. Remove the oil screen.

4. Carefully unbolt and remove the front case assembly. Use care. There are 4 different bolt lengths. Note their location for assembly.

5. Remove the oil pump cover.

6. Remove the inner and outer gears from the front case. There should be mating marks on the inner and outer gears to indicate the direction of installation. Take note of this at disassembly if the gears are to be reused, so they may be installed properly. If the marks are indistinct, make new matchmarks.

7. Remove the plug and remove the relief spring and relief plunger.

To install:

8. Inspect the front case, oil pan and oil screen for cracks or damage. Check the front case for worn or damaged surfaces. with a feeler gauge, check the clearances between the pump parts and the case. Clearances should be:
   a. Clearance between outer circumference and front case: 0.0047-0.0070 in. (0.119-0.178mm).
   b. Clearance between gear tips and pump rotor: 0.001-0.003 in. (0.025-0.076mm).
   c. Clearance between straight-edge and top of pump rotor: 0.0016-0.0034 in. (0.040-0.086mm).

9. Check relief spring and valve. Spring free height should be 1.835 in. (46.60mm). The valve should not be varnished or scored.

10. Clean all parts well. Coat all parts with clean engine oil. Install the pump gears into the case. Make sure the inner and outer gears are installed in the proper direction. Install the pump cover and tighten the bolts to 6-9 ft. lbs. (8-12 Nm).

11. Coat with oil, then install the relief valve and spring. Tighten the plug to 29-36 ft. lbs. (40-50 Nm). Install a new front seal with a seal driver.

12. Install the front case assembly with a new gasket. Make sure the proper length bolts are in the correct

holes. Torque all bolts to 9-11 ft. lbs. (12-15 Nm).

13. Install the crankshaft sprocket, timing belt and crankshaft pulley.

14. Install the oil screen and oil pan. If an oil pan gasket is not available, run a bead approximately 3/16 inch diameter of RTV sealer. Tighten the pan bolts to 4-6 ft. lbs. (5-8 Nm).

1596cc, 1796cc and 1997cc Engines

1. Disconnect the negative battery cable.

2. Remove the front engine mount bracket and accessory drive belts.

3. Remove timing belt upper and lower covers.

4. Remove the timing belt and crankshaft sprocket.

5. Remove the oil pan.

6. Remove the oil screen and gasket.

7. Remove and tag the front cover mounting bolts. Note the lengths of the mounting bolts as they are removed for proper installation.

8. On 1596cc and 1796cc engines, remove the plug cap using tool MD998162 or equivalent, and remove the oil pressure switch.

9. Remove the front case cover and oil pump assembly. If necessary, the silent shaft can come out with the assembly. Disassemble as required.

To install:

10. Thoroughly clean all gasket material from all mounting surfaces.

11. Apply engine oil to the entire surface of the gears or rotors.

12. On engines with silent shaft, install the drive/driven gears with the 2 timing marks aligned.

13. Assemble the front case cover and oil pump assembly to the engine block using a new gasket. On 1596cc and 1796cc engines, assemble the front case cover and oil pump assembly using tool MD998285 or equivalent, on the front end of the crankshaft.

14. Install the oil screen with new gasket.

15. Install the oil pan and timing belts.

16. Connect the negative battery cable and check for adequate oil pressure.

2351cc Engine

1. Disconnect the negative battery cable. Remove the timing belt.

2. Remove the oil pump cover and gears.

3. Remove the relief valve plug, spring and plunger.

4. Thoroughly clean all parts in a safe solvent and check for wear and damage.

5. Clean all orifices and passages.

6. Place the gear back in the pump body and check clearances.

Tip clearance, drive gear — 0.0063-0.0083 in. (0.16-0.21mm)

Limit — 0.0098 in. (0.25mm)

Tip clearance, driven gear — 0.0051-0.0071 in. (0.13-0.18mm)

Limit — 0.0098 in. (0.25mm)

Side clearance, drive gear — 0.0031-0.0055 in. (0.08-0.14mm)

Limit — 0.0098 in. (0.25mm)

Side clearance, driven gear — 0.0024-0.0047 in. ((0.06-0.12mm)

Limit — 0.0098 in. (0.25mm)

NOTE: If gear replacement is necessary, the entire pump body must be replaced.

7. Check the relief valve spring for wear or damage. Free length should be 1.835 in. (47mm).

To install:

8. Assembly the pump components. Make sure the gears are installed with the mating marks aligned.

9. Install the timing belt. Connect the negative battery cable.

2972cc Engine

1. Disconnect the negative battery cable. Remove the dipstick.

2. Raise the vehicle and support safely. Remove the timing belt, drain the engine oil and remove the oil pan from the engine. Remove the oil pickup.

3. Remove the oil pump mounting bolts and remove the pump from the front of the engine. Note the different length bolts and their position in the pump for installation.

To install:

4. Clean the gasket mounting surfaces of the pump and engine block.

5. Prime the pump by pouring fresh oil into the pump and turning the rotors. Using a new gasket, install the oil pump on the engine and torque all bolts to 11 ft. lbs. (15 Nm).

6. Install the balancer and crankshaft sprocket to the end of the crankshaft.

7. Clean out the oil pickup or replace, if necessary. Replace the oil pickup gasket ring and install the pickup to the pump.

8. Install the timing belt, oil pan and all related parts.

9. Install the dipstick. Fill the engine with the proper amount of oil.

10. Connect the negative battery cable and check the oil pressure.

Rear Main Bearing Oil Seal

REMOVAL AND INSTALLATION

NOTE: The rear main seal is located in a housing on the rear of the block. To replace the seal, it is necessary to remove the transaxle and perform the work from underneath the vehicle or remove the engine and perform the work on an engine stand.

1. Raise the vehicle and support it safely. Remove the transaxle from the vehicle.

2. Unscrew the retaining bolts and remove the housing from the cylinder block. Remove the separator from the housing.

3. Using a small prybar, pry out the old seal.

4. Clean the housing and the separator.

To install:

5. Lightly oil the replacement seal. Tap the seal into the housing. The oil seal should be installed so the seal plate fits into the inner contact surface of the seal case.

6. Install the separator into the housing so the oil hole faces down.

7. Oil the lips of the seal and install the housing on the rear of the engine block.

8. Install the transaxle in the vehicle.

9. Lower the vehicle. Start the engine and check for leaks.

Piston Oil Cooling Jet

REMOVAL AND INSTALLATION

1495cc Turbocharged Engine

1. Remove oil pan.

2. Locate jets attached to oil gallery in lower side of block.

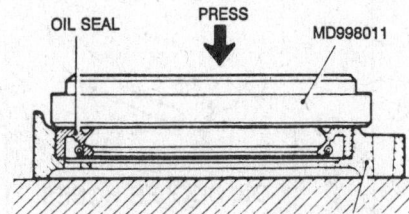

Pressing a new rear main seal into place

3. Remove the jets by unscrewing the hex-shape check valve which acts like a retaining bolt.

4. Check the cooling jet body for damage, cracks and wear. Replace as necessary.

5. Check the oil hole. If the hole is clogged, clean with solvent and blow dry with compressed air. Examine the check valve. The free spring height is 0.787 in. (20mm).

6. Installation is the reverse of the removal procedure. Tighten the cooling jet bolt to 2-3 ft. lbs. (2.7-4.0 Nm).

7. Install oil pan.

ENGINE COOLING

Radiator

REMOVAL AND INSTALLATION

1. Disconnect the negative battery cable.

2. On Scoupe and Elantra, set the warm water flow control knob of the heater control to the HOT position.

3. Drain the radiator. Raise the vehicle and support it safely. Remove the splash shield from under the vehicle.

4. Remove the fan shroud and disconnect the fan motor wiring harness.

5. Disconnect the radiator hoses and, if equipped, the automatic transaxle cooler hoses. Plug the end of the oil cooler hoses to prevent the transaxle fluid from spilling out and foreign material from getting in.

6. Disconnect the expansion tank hose.

7. Remove the radiator mounting bolts and lift out the radiator and fan assembly. The fan and motor may be left attached to the radiator and removed with the radiator as one unit.

To install:

8. Install the radiator. Tighten the retaining bolts gradually in a crisscross pattern.

9. Connect the expansion tank hose, the radiator hoses and the automatic transaxle oil cooler lines.

10. Install the fan shroud and connect the fan wiring.

11. Install the splash shield and refill the engine with coolant.

12. Connect the negative battery cable, run the vehicle until the thermostat opens, fill the radiator completely and check the automatic transaxle fluid level, if equipped.

13. Once the vehicle has cooled, recheck the coolant level.

Heater Core

REMOVAL AND INSTALLATION

Elantra

1. Disconnect the negative battery cable.

2. Position the heater control to **HOT** and drain the cooling system.

3. Disconnect the heater hoses from the heater core tubes at the firewall.

4. Remove the evaporator drain hose.

5. Using the proper equipment, drain the air conditioning system.

6. Disconnect the suction and liquid line connections at the firewall and cap to prevent contamination of the system.

7. Remove the floor console assembly as follows:

   a. Remove the center console plate and then loosen 1 screw.

   b. Disconnect the outside mirror control switch connector and remove the switch.

   c. Remove the transaxle shift control lever knob.

   d. Remove the 4 screws securing the front console to the front and the center mounting brackets.

   e. Remove the remaining rear console mounting screws and remove the console assembly.

8. Remove the glove box assembly.

9. Remove the hood release handle and the side lower crash pads.

10. Remove the lower crash pad center facia panel and disconnect the electrical harness connectors. Remove the radio making sure to disconnect all connectors.

11. Remove the mounting screws from the lower main crash pad and remove from the vehicle. Remove the

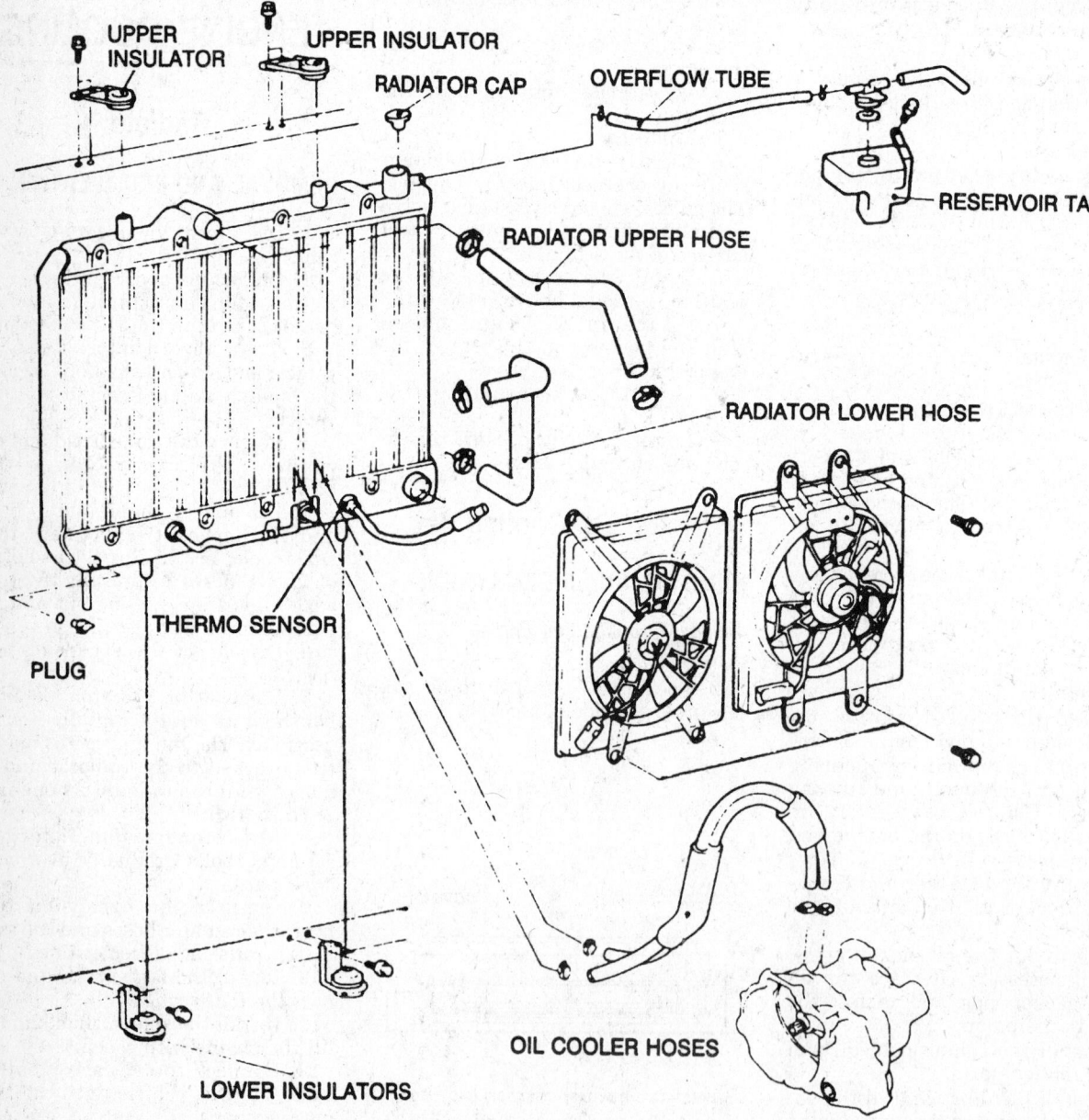

Radiator and cooling fan installation as seen on Scoupe — other models similar

lower crash pad support bracket assembly.

12. Disconnect and remove the air conditioning/heater control assembly. Disconnect the electrical harness at the blower motor.

13. Remove the evaporator mounting screws and the evaporator unit assembly.

14. Remove the rear heating joint duct assembly.

15. Remove the heater unit from the vehicle.

16. Separate the case halves and remove the heater core.

To install:

17. Install the heater unit into the vehicle.

18. Install the rear heating joint duct assembly.

19. Install the evaporator unit assembly and secure with the mounting screws.

20. Install the air conditioning/heater control assembly. Connect the electrical harness at the blower motor.

21. Install the lower crash pad support bracket assembly and lower crash pad on vehicle.

22. Install the radio connecting all harness connectors.

23. Connect the electrical harness connectors while installing the lower crash pad center facia panel.

24. Install the lower side crash pads and the hood release handle.

25. Install the glove box assembly.

26. Install the floor console assembly.

27. Connect the suction and the liquid line connections at the firewall making sure to use new gaskets at all unions.

28. Connect the heater hoses to the heater core tubes at the firewall.

29. Refill the cooling system to the proper level.

30. Install the drain hose to the evaporator drain, evacuate and recharge the air conditioning system, if equipped.

31. Reconnect the negative battery cable.

32. Start the vehicle and run until normal operating temperature is reached. Check the operation of the air conditioning and heating systems and inspect for leaks.

33. Shut the engine OFF and allow to cool. Carefully remove the radiator cap. Add coolant as required to fill the system to the appropriate level.

Excel

1. Disconnect the negative battery cable.

2. Set the heater control to **HOT** and drain the cooling system.

3. Disconnect the coolant hoses at the heater core tubes, in the engine compartment.

4. Remove the lower instrument panel section.

5. Remove the center console and on-board computer.

6. Loosen the heater duct mounting screw.

7. While pushing downward and gently pulling, remove the heater ducts.

8. Disconnect the heater control cable.

9. Disconnect the wiring at the motor.

10. Remove the heater case mounting bolts and remove the heater case from under the dash.

11. Separate the case halves and remove the blower motor and the heater core assembly.

To install:

12. Install the heater core into the case and assemble the case halves. Install the blower.

13. Install the heater case into the vehicle and secure using the mounting bolts.

14. Connect the electrical harness at the motor.

15. Connect the heater control cable.

16. Install the heater ducts.

17. Tighten the heater duct mounting screw.

18. Install the center console and on-board computer.

19. Install the lower instrument panel section.

20. Connect the coolant hoses at the heater core tubes, in the engine compartment.

21. Set the heater control to **HOT** and refill the cooling system.

22. Connect the negative battery cable.

23. Start the vehicle and run until normal operating temperature is reached. Check the operation of the air conditioning and heating systems and inspect for leaks.

24. Shut the engine OFF and allow to cool. Carefully remove the radiator cap. Add coolant as required to fill the system to the appropriate level.

Sonata

1. Disconnect the negative battery cable.

2. Place the control in the **HOT** position.

3. Drain the cooling system.

4. Remove the heater hoses from the core tubes.

5. Discharge the air conditioning system.

6. Disconnect the suction and liquid refrigerant lines at the firewall connectors. Always use backup wrenches. Cap all openings at once.

7. Remove the front and rear center consoles.

8. Remove the heater side covers.

9. Remove the glove box, center crash pad cover, center crash pad and the radio.

10. Remove the lower crash pad.

11. Remove the console mounting bracket and center support.

12. Remove the left and right rear heat duct assemblies and the rear heating joint duct.

13. Remove the control unit.

14. Disconnect the blower speed actuator connector and, on Canadian vehicles, disconnect the blend door actuator connector.

15. Remove the heater/air conditioning unit.

16. Remove the blower motor from the case.

17. Separate the case halves and lift out the core.

To install:

18. Assemble the case halves.

19. Install the blower motor to the case.

20. Install the heater/air conditioning unit.

21. Connect the blower speed actuator connector and, on Canadian vehicles, connect the blend door actuator connector.

22. Install the control unit.

23. Install the left and right rear heat duct assemblies and the rear heating joint duct.

24. Install the console mounting bracket and center support.

25. Install the lower crash pad.

26. Install the glove box, center crash pad cover, center crash pad and the radio.

27. Install the heater side covers.

28. Install the front and rear center consoles.

29. Connect the suction and liquid refrigerant lines at the firewall connectors. Always use backup wrenches.

30. Recharge the air conditioning system.

31. Install the heater hoses to the core tubes.

32. Refill the cooling system.

33. Connect the negative battery cable.

34. Start the vehicle and run until normal operating temperature is reached. Check the operation of the air conditioning and heating systems and inspect for leaks.

35. Shut the engine OFF and allow to cool. Carefully remove the radiator cap. Add coolant as required to fill the system to the appropriate level.

Scoupe

1. Disconnect the negative battery cable.
2. Set the heater control to **HOT** and drain the cooling system.
3. Disconnect the coolant hoses at the heater core tubes, in the engine compartment.
4. Remove the console assembly, cluster facia panel and lower crash pad center skin.
5. Loosen the heater duct mounting screw.
6. Remove the heater ducts.
7. Disconnect the heater control cable.
8. Disconnect the wiring at the motor.
9. Remove the heater case mounting bolts and remove the heater case from under the dash.
10. Separate the case halves and remove the blower.

To install:

11. Assemble the case halves.
12. Install the heater case and mounting bolts.
13. Connect the wiring at the motor.
14. Connect the heater control cable.
15. Install the heater ducts.
16. Tighten the heater duct mounting screw.
17. Install the console assembly, cluster facia panel and lower crash pad center skin.
18. Connect the coolant hoses at the heater core tubes, in the engine compartment.
19. Refill the cooling system.
20. Connect the negative battery cable.
21. Start the vehicle and run until normal operating temperature is reached. Check the operation of the air conditioning and heating systems and inspect for leaks.
22. Shut the engine OFF and allow to cool. Carefully remove the radiator cap. Add coolant as required to fill the system to the appropriate level.

Water Pump

REMOVAL AND INSTALLATION

1468cc Engine

1. Disconnect the negative battery cable.

2. Loosen the 4 bolts attaching the water pump pulley to the pulley flange. Loosen the alternator mounting bolts, slide the alternator toward the engine and remove the belt. Remove the radiator cap, open the drain cock at the bottom of the radiator and drain the coolant from the radiator into a clean container.
3. Remove the timing belt covers, timing belt and tensioner.
4. Remove the water pump mounting bolts, noting the 3 different lengths and locations. Remove the pump and gasket, disconnecting the outlet at the water pipe (don't lose the O-ring).

To install:

5. Clean gasket surfaces and coat a new gasket with sealer. Then, position the gasket on the front of the block with all bolt holes aligned. Replace the O-ring for the outlet water pipe.
6. Install the pump connecting the outlet water pipe. Install the bolts with the shortest at the bottom; 2 just slightly longer at the 1 and 4 o'clock positions on the right side of the pump; next-to-longest bolt at the 8 o'clock position, just under the outlet; and the longest bolt at the 11 o'clock position and also attaching the alternator brace. Torque the bolts with a head mark, 4, to 9-11 ft. lbs. (12-15 Nm); those with a head mark 7, to 14-20 ft. lbs. (20-26 Nm).
7. Install the remaining parts in reverse order. Final tightening of the water pump pulley bolts is done after the V-belt has been installed and tensioned. Recheck tension after the pulley bolts are tightened. Close the radiator drain and refill the system. Run the engine until the thermostat opens and then add coolant until the level stabilizes before replacing the radiator cap. Check for leaks. Connect the negative battery cable.

1495cc Engine

1. Disconnect the negative battery cable. Drain the cooling system.
2. Disconnect the radiator outlet hose from the water pump. Remove the drive belt and water pump pulley.
3. Remove the timing belt covers and the timing belt tensioner.
4. Remove the water pump mounting bolts. Take note of the positions of the bolts since the lengths vary. Remove the alternator brace.
5. Remove the water pump assembly from the cylinder block.
6. Check the pump for cracks, corrosion damage or for leaks. If coolant had previously been dripping from the vent opening it likely means the

water pump internal seal is worn out and the pump should be replaced.

To install:

7. Clean the gasket surfaces well. Install a new O-ring onto the groove on the front end of the water pipe, then wet the O-ring with water. Do not use oil or grease.
8. Install a new gasket to the water pump. Install the pump and tighten the mounting bolts to 9-11 ft. lbs. (12-15 Nm).
9. Install the timing belt tensioner and timing belt and adjust the timing belt tension.
10. Install the timing belt covers, the water pump pulley and drive belt.
11. Refill the cooling system with clean coolant, run the engine and check for leaks.

1596cc, 1796cc and 1997cc Engines

1. Disconnect the negative battery cable. Drain the cooling system.
2. Remove all drive belts and water pump pulley.
3. Rotate the crankshaft clockwise and align the timing marks so No. 1 piston will be at TDC of the compression stroke. Remove the timing belt covers and the timing belt tensioner.
4. Remove the water pump mounting bolts and the alternator mounting brace.
5. Remove the water pump assembly from the engine block.
6. Thoroughly clean all gasket mounting surfaces to prevent leaks after reassembly.

To install:

7. Install new O-rings on the front end of the water pipe, then wet the O-ring with water to aid in installation. Do not apply oil or grease to the O-ring.
8. Install the water pump onto the block with new gasket in place. Position the alternator brace on pump and install the mounting screws. Tighten mounting bolts as follows:

   a. Head mark 4 bolt to 9-11 ft. lbs. (12-15 Nm)
   b. Head mark 7 bolt to 14-20 ft. lbs. (20-27 Nm)

9. Install the timing belt tensioner and the timing belt. Install the timing belt front covers.
10. Install the water pump pulley and drive belts. Adjust the drive belt tension.
11. Refill the cooling system and reconnect the negative battery cable.
12. Start the vehicle and run until normal operating temperature is reached. Check the operation of the heating system and inspect for leaks.
13. Shut the engine OFF and allow to cool. Carefully remove the radiator

cap. Add coolant as required to fill the system to the appropriate level.

2351cc Engine

1. Disconnect the negative battery cable. Drain the cooling system.
2. Remove all drive belts and the water pump pulley.
3. Remove the timing belt covers, timing belt tensioner and timing belt.
4. Remove the water pump mounting bolts.
5. Remove the water pump from the engine block.

NOTE: The pump is not rebuildable. If there are signs of damage or leakage from the seals or vent hole, the unit must be replaced.

To install:

6. Discard the O-ring in the front end of the water pipe. Install a new O-ring coated with water.
7. Using a new gasket, mount the water pump. Torque the bolts with a head marked 4, to 10 ft. lbs. (14 Nm) or the bolts with a head marked 7, to 20 ft. lbs. (27 Nm).
8. Install the timing belt tensioner, timing belt and belt covers.
9. Install the water pump pulley and accessory drive belts.
10. Connect the negative battery cable and fill the cooling system to the proper level.
11. Start the vehicle and run until normal operating temperature is reached. Check the operation of the heating system and inspect for leaks.
12. Shut the engine OFF and allow to cool. Carefully remove the radiator cap. Add coolant as required to fill the system to the appropriate level.

2972cc Engine

1. Disconnect the negative battery cable.
2. Drain the cooling system.
3. Remove the timing cover. If the same timing belt will be reused, mark the direction of the timing belt's rotation, for installation in the same direction. Make sure the engine is positioned so the No. 1 cylinder is at the TDC of its compression stroke and the sprockets timing marks are aligned with the engine's timing mark indicators.
4. Loosen the timing belt tensioner bolt and remove the belt. Position the tensioner as far away from the center of the engine as possible and tighten the bolt. Remove the water pump mounting bolts, separate the pump from the water inlet pipe and remove the pump from the engine.

To install:

5. Install the pump with a new gasket to the engine. Torque the water pump mounting bolts to 20 ft. lbs. (27 Nm).
6. If not already done, position both camshafts so the marks align with those on the alternator bracket (rear bank) and inner timing cover (front bank). Rotate the crankshaft so the timing mark aligns with the mark on the oil pump.
7. Install the timing belt on the crankshaft sprocket and while keeping the belt tight on the tension side (right side), install the belt on the front camshaft sprocket.
8. Install the belt on the water pump pulley, then the rear camshaft sprocket and the tensioner.
9. Rotate the front camshaft counterclockwise to tension the belt between the front camshaft and the crankshaft. If the timing marks became misaligned, repeat the procedure.
10. Install the crankshaft sprocket flange.
11. Loosen the tensioner bolt and allow the spring to tension the belt.
12. Turn the crankshaft 2 full turns in the clockwise direction only until the timing marks align again. Now that the belt is properly tensioned, torque the tensioner lock bolt to 21 ft. lbs. (29 Nm).
13. Refill the cooling system. Connect the negative battery cable and road test the vehicle.

Thermostat

REMOVAL AND INSTALLATION

1468cc Engine

1. Disconnect the negative battery cable. Remove the air cleaner.
2. Drain the cooling system to a point below the level of the tubes in the top tank of the radiator.
3. Disconnect the hose at the thermostat water pipe.
4. Remove the water pipe support bracket nut.
5. Unbolt and remove the thermostat housing and pipe.
6. Lift out the thermostat. Discard the gasket.

To install:

7. Clean the mating surfaces of the housing and manifold thoroughly.
8. Install the thermostat with the spring facing downward and position a new gasket. The jiggle valve in the thermostat should be on the manifold side.

9. Install the housing and pipe assembly. Torque the housing bolts to 10 ft. lbs. (14 Nm); the intake manifold nut to 14 ft. lbs. (19 Nm).
10. Refill the cooling system. Connect the negative battery cable.

1495cc, 1596cc, 1796cc and 1997cc Engines

1. Disconnect the negative battery cable.
2. Drain the cooling system.
3. Disconnect the upper radiator hose from the thermostat housing.
4. Remove the thermostat housing and gasket.
5. Remove the thermostat taking note of its original positioning in the housing.

To install:

6. Install the thermostat so its flange seats tightly in the machined groove in the thermostat case. Refer to its location prior to removal.
7. Use a new gasket and reinstall the thermostat housing. Torque the housing mounting bolts to 12-14 ft. lbs. (17-20 Nm).
8. Fill the system with coolant.
9. Connect the negative battery cable, run the vehicle until the thermostat opens and fill the radiator completely.
10. Once the vehicle has cooled, recheck the coolant level.

2351cc Engine

1. Connect the negative battery cable. Remove the air cleaner.
2. Drain the cooling system down well below the level of the tubes in the top tank of the radiator.
3. Disconnect the hose at the thermostat water pipe.
4. Unbolt and remove the thermostat housing.
5. Lift out the thermostat. Discard the gasket.
6. Clean the mating surfaces of the housing and manifold thoroughly.

To install:

7. Install the thermostat with the spring facing downward and position a new gasket.
8. Install the housing. Torque the housing bolts to 14 ft. lbs. (19 Nm).
9. Refill the cooling system. Connect the negative battery cable.

2972cc Engine

1. Connect the negative battery cable. Remove the air cleaner.
2. Drain the cooling system down well below the level of the tubes in the top tank of the radiator.
3. Disconnect the hose at the thermostat water pipe.

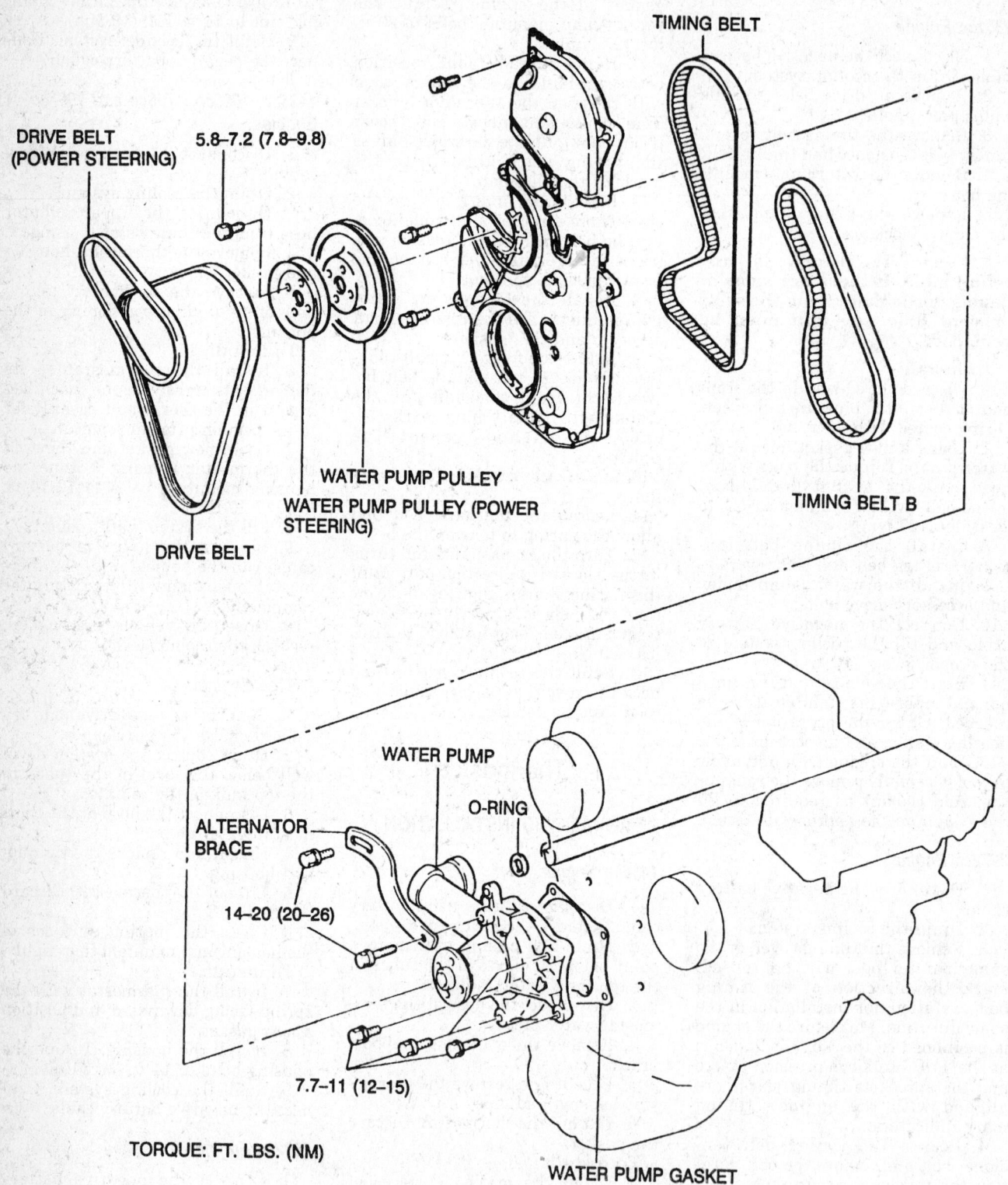

TIMING BELT

DRIVE BELT (POWER STEERING)

5.8–7.2 (7.8–9.8)

WATER PUMP PULLEY

WATER PUMP PULLEY (POWER STEERING)

DRIVE BELT

TIMING BELT B

WATER PUMP

O-RING

ALTERNATOR BRACE

14–20 (20–26)

7.7–11 (12–15)

TORQUE: FT. LBS. (NM)

WATER PUMP GASKET

Water pump and related components — 2351cc engine

4. Unbolt and remove the thermostat housing.

5. Lift out the thermostat. Discard the gasket.

6. Clean the mating surfaces of the housing and manifold thoroughly.

To install:

7. Install the thermostat with the spring facing downward and position a new gasket.

8. Install the housing. Torque the housing bolts to 14 ft. lbs. (19 Nm).

9. Refill the cooling system. Connect the negative battery cable.

Cooling System Bleeding

After working on the cooling system, even to replace the thermostat, the system must bled. Air trapped in the system will prevent complete filling leaving the radiator coolant level low, causing a risk of overheating.

1. To bleed the system, start with the system cool, the radiator cap off and the radiator filled to about 1 in. below the filler neck.

2. Start the engine and run it at slightly above normal idle speed. This will insure adequate circulation. If air bubbles appear and the coolant level drops, fill the system with a mixture of anti-freeze and water to bring the solution back to the proper level.

3. Run the engine this way until the thermostat opens. When this happens, the coolant will move abruptly across the top of the radiator and the temperature of the radiator will rise.

4. At this point, air is often expelled and the fluid level may drop quite a bit. Keep refilling the system until the level is near the top of the radiator and remains constant.

5. If the vehicle has an overflow tank, fill the radiator to the top of the filler neck.

ENGINE ELECTRICAL

NOTE: Disconnecting the negative battery cable on some vehicles may interfere with the functions of the on-board computer systems and may require the computer to undergo a relearning process, once the negative battery cable is reconnected.

Distributor

REMOVAL

1. Disconnect the negative battery cable. Remove the ignition wire cover, if equipped.

2. Disconnect the distributor harness electrical connectors.

3. Unscrew the distributor cap hold-down screws or release the clips, and lift off the distributor cap with all ignition wires still connected. Remove the coil wire, if necessary.

4. Matchmark the rotor to the distributor housing and the distributor housing to the engine.

NOTE: Do not crank the engine during this procedure. If the engine is cranked, the matchmarks must be disregarded.

5. Remove the hold-down nut.

6. Carefully remove the distributor from the engine.

INSTALLATION

NOTE: Some engines may be sensitive to the routing of the distributor sensor wires. If routed near the high-voltage coil wire or the spark plug wires, the electromagnetic field surrounding the high voltage wires could generate an occasional disruption of the ignition system operation.

Timing Not Disturbed

1. Install a new distributor housing O-ring and lubricate with clean oil.

2. Install the distributor in the engine so the rotor is aligned with the matchmark on the housing and the housing is aligned with the matchmark on the engine. Make sure the distributor is fully seated and the distributor shaft is fully engaged.

3. Install the hold-down nut.

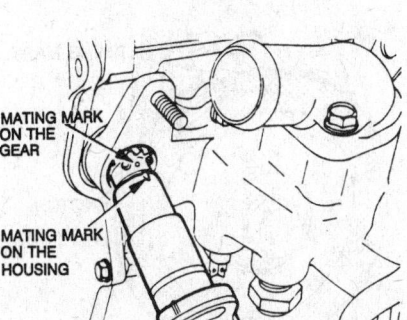

Aligning mating marks for installation of cylinder head mounted distributors

4. Connect the distributor harness connectors.

5. Make sure the sealing O-ring is in place, install the distributor cap and tighten the screws or secure the clips.

6. Connect the negative battery cable.

7. Adjust the ignition timing and tighten the hold-down nut.

Timing Disturbed

1. Install a new distributor housing O-ring and lubricate with clean oil.

2. Position the engine so the No. 1 piston is at TDC of its compression stroke and the mark on the vibration damper is aligned with **0** or **T** on the timing indicator.

3. Align the distributor housing and gear mating marks. Install the distributor in engine so the slot or groove of the distributor's installation flange aligns with the distributor installation stud in the engine block. Make sure the distributor is fully seated. Inspect alignment of the distributor rotor making sure the rotor is aligned with the position of the No. 1 ignition wire in the distributor cap.

NOTE: Make sure the rotor is pointing to where the No. 1 runner originates inside the cap, if equipped, and not where the No. 1 ignition wire plugs into the cap.

4. Install the hold-down nut.

5. Connect the distributor harness connectors.

6. Make sure the sealing O-ring is in place, install the distributor cap and tighten the screws or secure the clips.

7. Connect the negative battery cable.

8. Adjust the ignition timing and tighten the hold-down bolt.

Distributorless Ignition

REMOVAL AND INSTALLATION

Crank Angle Sensor

1. Rotate the crankshaft clockwise and align the timing marks so No. 1 piston is at TDC of the compression stroke and the mark on the vibration damper is aligned with **0** or **T** on the timing indicator.

2. Disconnect the negative battery cable.

3. Disconnect the crank angle sensor harness connector.

4. Remove the hold-down nut.

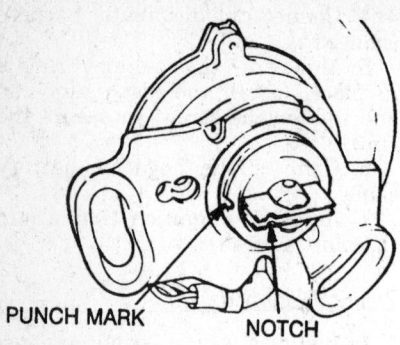

PUNCH MARK NOTCH

Aligning the mating marks on the crank angle sensor — 1596cc, 1796cc and 1997cc engines

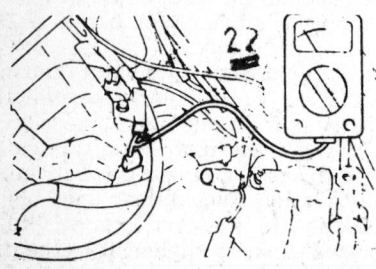

Installation of a tachometer during ignition timing adjustment procedure

5. Carefully remove the crank angle sensor assembly from the engine.
To install:
6. Install a new housing O-ring and lubricate with clean oil.
7. Install the sensor in the engine so the factory matchmark on the coupling (notch) is aligned with the matchmark on the housing (punch mark) and the housing is aligned with the matchmark on the engine. Make sure the sensor assembly is fully seated and the shaft is fully engaged.
8. Install the hold-down nut.
9. Connect the harness connector.
10. Connect the negative battery cable.
11. Adjust the ignition timing and tighten the hold-down nut.

Ignition Coil

1. Disconnect the negative battery cable.
2. Tag and remove the spark plug wires from the ignition coil by gripping the boot and not the cable.
3. Remove the mounting screws and coil from engine.
4. Installation is the reverse of the removal procedure.

Power Transistor

1. Disconnect the negative battery cable.
2. Tag and disconnect the wires from the power transistor.
3. Remove the retaining screw and lift the power transistor from the engine.
4. Installation is the reverse of the removal procedure.

Ignition Timing

ADJUSTMENT

1468cc Engine with Feedback Carburetor

1. Locate the timing tab line on the front of the engine and the notch on the crankshaft pulley. Mark them with chalk.
2. Run the engine until it is at normal operating temperature.
3. Leave the engine idling, apply the parking brake and put the transaxle in neutral if equipped with manual transaxle or **P** if equipped

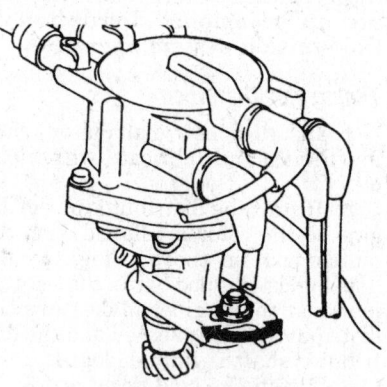

Adjusting ignition timing — 2972cc engine

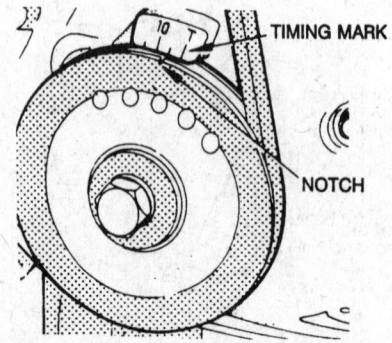

TIMING MARK

NOTCH

Timing marks on crankshaft and front engine case

with automatic transaxle. Turn all accessories OFF.

NOTE: On high altitude engines equipped with vacuum advance, the distributor vacuum hoses must be disconnected and plugged.

4. Install a tachometer, according to the manufacturer's instructions.
5. Check the engine idle speed and adjust to specifications as required.
6. Connect a timing light according to the manufacturer's instructions.
7. Direct the timing light at the crankshaft pulley marks. Check the basic ignition timing and adjust as required. The desired reading is 5 degrees BTDC. After adjustment, securely tighten the distributor mounting nut.
8. Turn the engine OFF and disconnect the timing light and tachometer. Reconnect the vacuum hose at the distributor as required.

1468cc Engine without Feedback Carburetor

1. Set the parking brake, start and run the engine until normal operating temperature is obtained. Keep all lights and accessories OFF and the front wheels straight-ahead. Place the transaxle in **P** for automatic transaxle or neutral for manual transaxle.
2. Locate the wire connector on the ignition coil connector. Insert a paper clip behind the TACH terminal connector to act as a tachometer adapter. Connect a tachometer to the paper clip. If not at specification, set the idle speed at the correct level.
3. Turn the engine OFF. Remove the water-proof cover from the ignition timing adjusting connector, located in the engine compartment. Connect a jumper wire from this terminal to a good ground.
4. Connect a conventional power timing light to the No. 1 cylinder spark plug wire. Start the engine and run at idle.
5. Aim the timing light at the timing scale located near the crankshaft pulley.
6. Loosen the distributor or crank angle sensor hold-down nut just enough so the housing can be rotated.
7. Turn the housing in the proper direction until the specified timing is reached. Tighten the hold-down nut and recheck the timing. Turn the engine OFF.
8. Remove the jumper wire from the ignition timing adjusting terminal and install the water-proof cover.

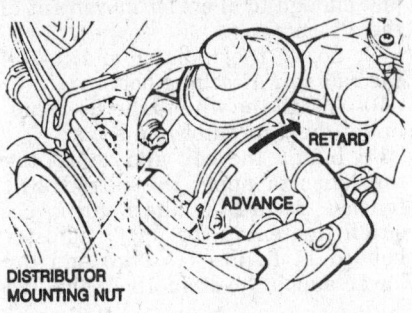

**DISTRIBUTOR
MOUNTING NUT**

Adjusting ignition timing as seen on 1468cc engine

9. Start the engine and check the actual timing (the timing without the terminal grounded). This reading should be approximately 3 degrees more than the basic timing. Actual timing may increase according to altitude. Also, actual timing may fluctuate because of slight variation accomplished by the ECU. As long as the basic timing is correct, the engine is timed correctly.

10. Turn the engine OFF. Disconnect the timing apparatus and tachometer.

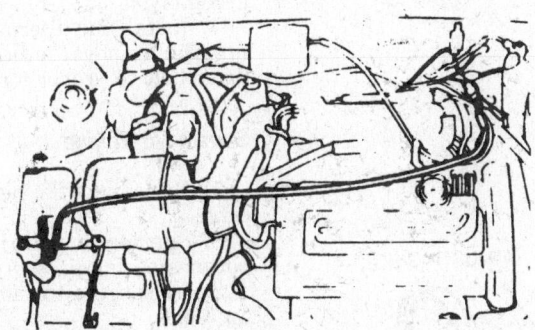

Grounding the ignition timing adjustment terminal located in the engine compartment — 1596cc and 1796cc engines

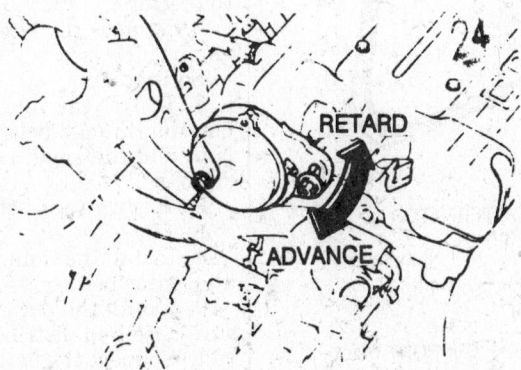

RETARD

ADVANCE

Adjustment of the ignition timing — 1596cc and 1796cc engines

Alternator

PRECAUTIONS

Several precautions must be observed with alternator equipped vehicles to avoid damage to the unit.

• If the battery is removed for any reason, make sure it is reconnected with the correct polarity. Reversing the battery connections may result in damage to the 1-way rectifiers.

• When utilizing a booster battery as a starting aid, always connect the positive to positive terminals and the negative terminal from the booster battery to a good engine ground on the vehicle being started.

• Never use a fast charger as a booster to start vehicles.

• Disconnect the battery cables when charging the battery with a fast charger.

• Never attempt to polarize the alternator.

• Do not use test lamps of more than 12 volts when checking diode continuity.

• Do not short across or ground any of the alternator terminals.

• The polarity of the battery, alternator and regulator must be matched

and considered before making any electrical connections within the system.

• Never separate the alternator on an open circuit. Make sure all connections within the circuit are clean and tight.

• Disconnect the battery ground terminal when performing any service on electrical components.

• Disconnect the battery if arc welding is to be done on the vehicle.

BELT TENSION ADJUSTMENT

The alternator drive belt is correctly tensioned when the longest span of belt between pulleys can be depressed 1/8-1/2 in. by moderate thumb pressure (about 22 lbs). To adjust, loosen the adjusting bolt or fixing bolt locknut on the alternator, alternator bracket or tension pulley. Then move the alternator or turn the adjusting bolt to adjust belt tension. Secure the bolt or locknut when finished.

Loosen the adjusting bolt or fixing bolt locknut on the alternator, alternator bracket or tension pulley. Then move the alternator or turn the adjusting bolt to adjust belt tension. Secure the bolt or locknut when finished.

V-belts under 39 in. (100cm) in length should deflect about 1/8 in. (3mm). Belts over 40 in. (101cm) long should deflect about 1/2 in. (13mm).

NOTE: Be careful not to overtighten the belt, as this may damage the alternator bearings.

REMOVAL AND INSTALLATION

Elantra, Excel and Sonata with 4-cylinder Engine

EXCEPT 1596CC, 1796CC AND 1997CC ENGINES

1. Turn OFF the ignition switch and disconnect both battery cables.

2. Loosen the support bolt and adjusting bolt and then shift the alternator toward the engine so belt tension is relieved. Remove the belt.

3. Note the locations of all connectors. Make a drawing, if necessary. Unplug the plug type connectors and unscrew the fastening nuts for terminal type connectors. Clean any dirty connections.

4. Remove the adjusting bolt. Remove the nut from the rear of the mounting bolt.

5. Remove the alternator.

To install:

6. To install the alternator, first position it so the mounting bolt can be inserted. Install the mounting bolt loosely.

NOTE: If equipped with Delco alternators, spacers are required between the front leg of the alternator mounting bracket and the front case. Spacers are available in thicknesses of 0.2mm. Enough should be installed so they do not fall out when removed.

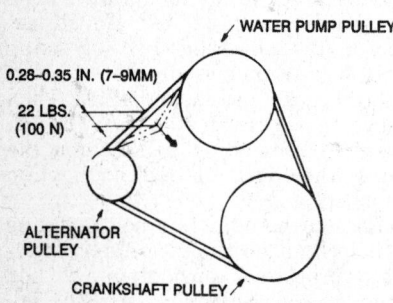

Adjusting the tension on the drive belts

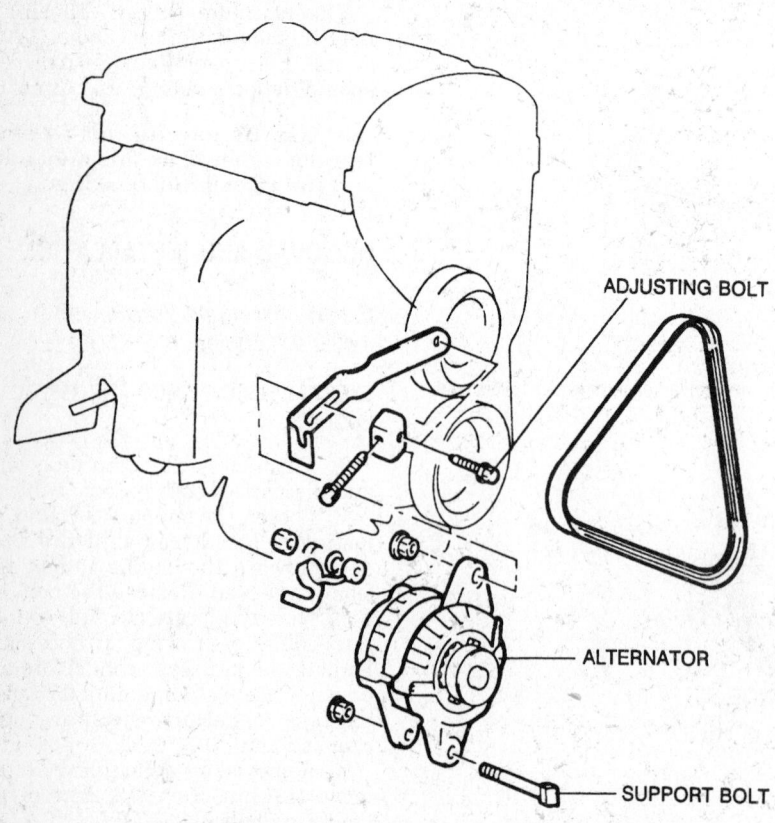

Alternator assembly — 1992 Elantra equipped with 1596cc engine

7. Install the adjusting bolt loosely. Install the belt and turn the alternator to put tension on the belt. Tighten the adjusting bolt 10 ft. lbs. (14 Nm) and the mounting bolt/nut to 15-18 ft. lbs. (20-25 Nm).

1596CC, 1796CC AND 1997CC ENGINES

1. Disconnect the negative battery cable.
2. Raise and safely support the vehicle. Remove the left side mud guard and engine cover panel from under the vehicle.
3. Lower the vehicle. Remove the radiator attaching bolts.
4. Disconnect the coolant reserve hose, oil pressure switch and the fan motor connectors.
5. Loosen the belt tensioner and remove the accessory drive belt.
6. Remove the terminal nut and the wire from the **B+** terminal of the alternator.
7. While lifting up on the radiator, remove the alternator from the vehicle.

To install:

8. While lifting the radiator, position the alternator on the engine mounting fixture. Install the lower mounting bolt and nut. Tighten nut just enough to allow for movement of the alternator.
9. Lower the radiator and install the radiator attaching bolts.
10. Install the wire to the **B+** terminal of the alternator and secure.
11. Install the belt and adjust the tensioner to apply the correct belt tension. Secure the alternator in position tightening the upper adjuster bolt to 11 ft. lbs. (15 Nm) and the lower support bolt to 18 ft. lbs. (25 Nm).
12. Connect the coolant reserve hose, oil pressure switch and the fan motor connectors.
13. Install the left side cover and panel under the vehicle.
14. Connect the negative battery cable and check the charging system for proper operation.

Scoupe

1. Disconnect the negative battery cable.
2. Loosen the belt tension and remove the belt.
3. Raise and safely support the vehicle.
4. Remove the left hand mud guard.
5. Disconnect the alternator **B+** terminal wire.
6. Remove the alternator assembly.
7. Install the alternator by reversing the removal procedure. Adjust drive belt to proper tension.

Sonata V6 Engine

1. Disconnect the negative battery cable.
2. Remove the distributor cap and power steering pressure hose nut.
3. Loosen the tension and remove the belt.
4. Remove the timing belt cover cap and timing belt upper cover.
5. Disconnect the electrical connectors.
6. Remove the alternator from the engine.

To install:

7. Install the alternator and torque the through bolt to 18 ft. lbs. (25 Nm) and the small bolt to 11 ft. lbs. (15 Nm).
8. Reconnect the electrical connectors.
9. Install the timing belt cover and alternator belt.
10. Install the power steering pressure hose and distributor cap.
11. Connect the battery cable, start the engine and check the power steering fluid.

Starter

REMOVAL AND INSTALLATION

Except Scoupe

1. Disconnect the negative battery cable. On some models, it may be helpful to remove the battery and the battery tray from the engine compartment during this procedure.
2. Raise and support the vehicle safely.
3. Remove the engine undercover. Disconnect the electrical harness from the starter solenoid, noting position of wires for correct installation.
4. Remove the starter mounting bolts and the starter from the vehicle.
5. Clean the surfaces of the starter motor flange and the flywheel housing where the starter attaches.
   To install:
6. Install the starter motor and secure with the retainer bolts. Tighten the bolts to 23 ft. lbs. (30 Nm) for 4 cylinder engines or 20-25 ft. lbs. (27-34 Nm) for the V6 engine.
7. Connect the electrical harness to the starter solenoid. Install the battery and tray, if removed.
8. Reconnect the negative battery cable.

Scoupe

1. Disconnect the negative battery cable.
2. Remove the EGR valve assembly and coil wire for access, if necessary.
3. Remove the speedometer cable and the heater valve, if necessary.
4. Disconnect the starter motor connector and terminal.
5. Remove the starter motor retainer bolts and the starter assembly from the vehicle.
   To install:
6. Install the starter assembly to the engine and secure using the re-

tainer bolts tightening to 20-25 ft. lbs. (26-33 Nm).
7. Connect the starter motor electrical connector and terminal.
8. Install the speedometer cable and the heater valve as required.
9. Install the EGR valve assembly and torque the retaining bolts to 7-11 ft. lbs. (10-15 Nm).
10. Connect the negative battery cable and check the starting system for proper operation.

FUEL SYSTEM

Fuel System Service Precautions

Safety is the most important factor when performing not only fuel system maintenance but any type of maintenance. Failure to conduct maintenance and repairs in a safe manner may result in serious personal injury or death. Maintenance and testing of the vehicle's fuel system components can be accomplished safely and effectively by adhering to the following rules and guidelines.

• To avoid the possibility of fire and personal injury, always disconnect the negative battery cable unless the repair or test procedure requires that battery voltage be applied.

• Always relieve the fuel system pressure prior to disconnecting any fuel system component (injector, fuel rail, pressure regulator, etc.), fitting or fuel line connection. Exercise extreme caution whenever relieving fuel system pressure to avoid exposing skin, face and eyes to fuel spray. Please be advised that fuel under pressure may penetrate the skin or any part of the body that it contacts.

• Always place a shop towel or cloth around the fitting or connection prior to loosening to absorb any excess fuel due to spillage. Ensure that all fuel spillage (should it occur) is quickly removed from engine surfaces. Ensure that all fuel soaked cloths or towels are deposited into a suitable waste container.

• Always keep a dry chemical (Class B) fire extinguisher near the work area.

• Do not allow fuel spray or fuel vapors to come into contact with a spark or open flame.

• Always use a backup wrench when loosening and tightening fuel

line connection fittings. This will prevent unnecessary stress and torsion to fuel line piping. Always follow the proper torque specifications.

• Always replace worn fuel fitting O-rings with new. Do not substitute fuel hose or equivalent where fuel pipe is installed.

RELIEVING FUEL SYSTEM PRESSURE

1. Turn the ignition to the **OFF** position.
2. Loosen the fuel filler cap to release fuel tank pressure.
3. Disconnect the fuel pump harness connector which is located under the rear seat cushion on Elantra or in the area of the fuel tank on the remaining models.
4. Start the vehicle and allow it to run until engine stalls from lack of fuel. Turn the key to the **OFF** position.
5. Disconnect the negative battery cable, then reconnect the fuel pump connector.
6. Service the fuel system as required.

Fuel Tank

REMOVAL AND INSTALLATION

Fuel Injected Engine

1. Have an approved fire extinguisher close to the vehicle. Relieve the fuel pressure and disconnect the negative battery cable.
2. Raise and support the vehicle safely.
3. Drain the fuel from the fuel tank into an approved container.
4. Disconnect the high pressure lines, return and vapor hoses and all connectors connected to the pump/sending unit.

— **CAUTION** —
Cover all fuel hose connections with a shop towel, prior to disconnecting, to prevent splash of fuel that could be caused by residual pressure remaining in the fuel line.

5. Check to make sure all hoses and electrical harness connectors are disconnect and positioned out of the way as not to interfere with the removal of the fuel tank.
6. Place a jack under the fuel tank and remove locking nuts and the tank support bands. Lower the tank

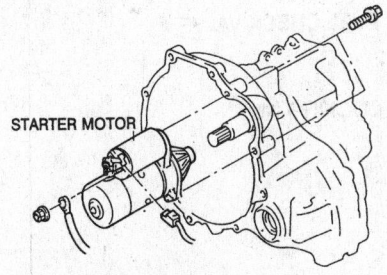

STARTER MOTOR

Starter motor assembly — 1992 Elantra equipped with 1596cc engine

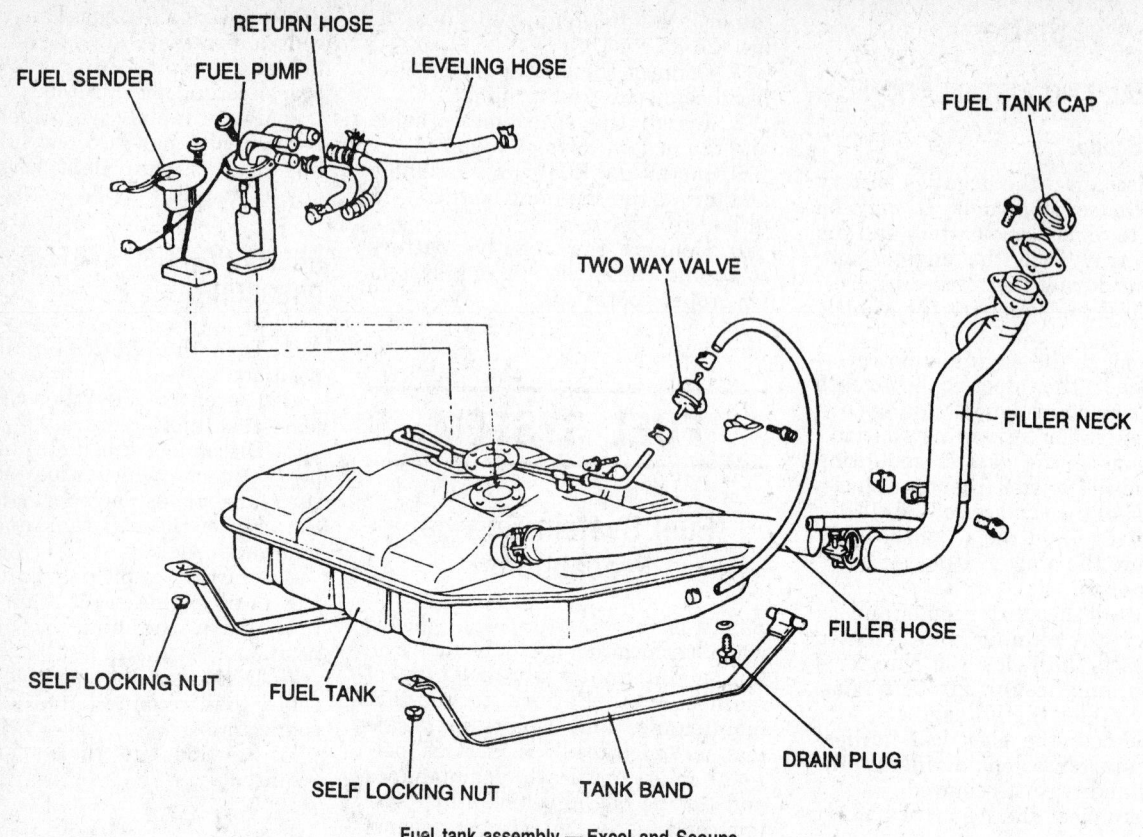

Fuel tank assembly — Excel and Scoupe

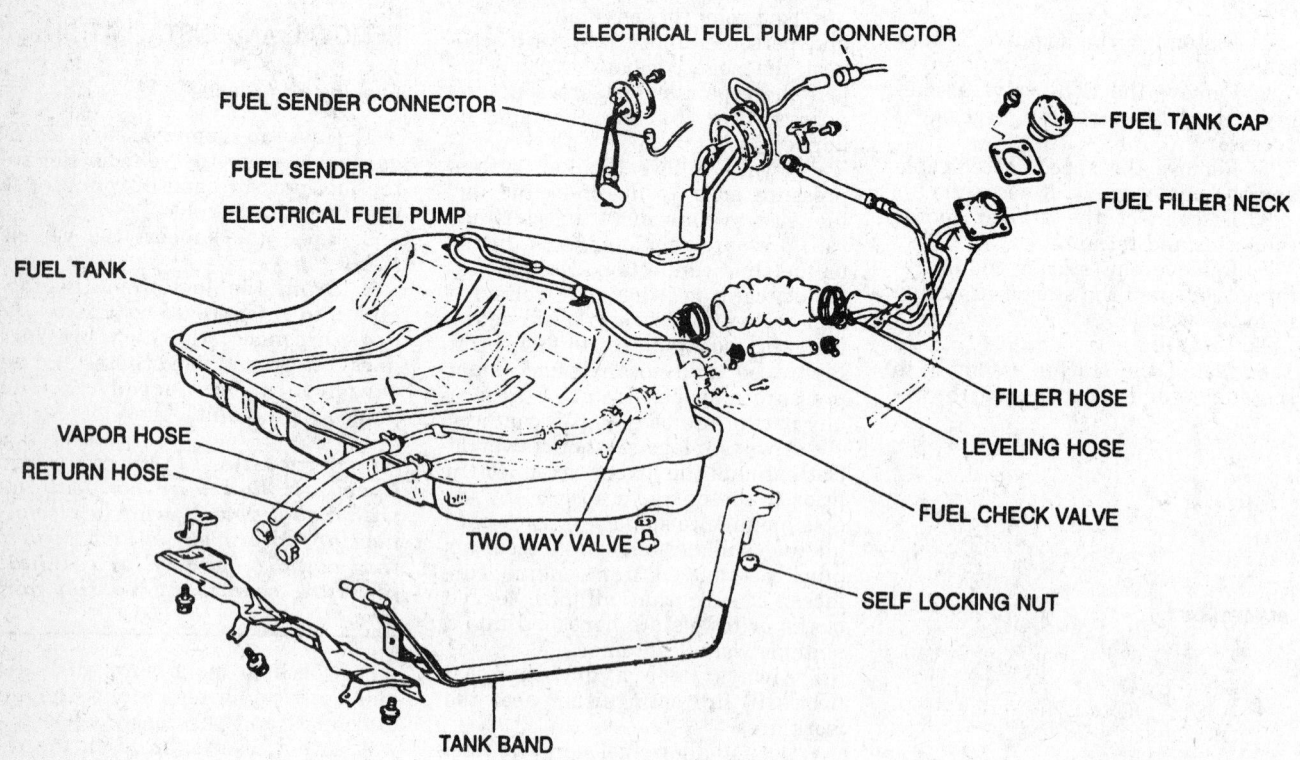

Fuel tank assembly — Sonata

enough to disconnect any remaining fuel hoses or electrical connections.

7. Remove the fuel tank from the vehicle. Check the tank for deformation, corrosion or cracking. Inspect the in-tank fuel filter for restriction or damage.

To install:

8. Confirm that the insulation pads are fully bonded to the tank.

9. Raise the tank far enough to connect the hoses and connectors that cannot be accessed after the tank is in place.

10. Install the tank straps and tighten the nuts until the rear end of the tank contacts the body.

11. Connect all electrical connectors and fuel hoses.

12. Connect the fuel filler hose.

13. Refill the tank and check for leaks before connecting the battery cable.

14. Connect the negative battery cable. Check for proper operation of the fuel pump and for leaks in the fuel system.

Carbureted Engine

1. Have an approved fire extinguisher close to the vehicle. Relieve the fuel pressure and disconnect the negative battery cable.

2. Raise and support the vehicle safely.

3. Drain the fuel from the fuel tank into an approved container.

4. Loosen the fuel hose clamps from the supply and return hoses and disconnect.

5. Disconnect the filler hose and breather hose from the filler neck.

6. After removing the tank protector, if equipped, support the weight of the tank using a jack.

7. Remove the locking nut and the tank retainer bands. Lower the tank using the jack slightly and disconnect the fuel gauge unit harness.

8. Remove the fuel tank from the vehicle. Inspect the fuel tank for rust formation, cracks, corrosion or any other damage. A badly corroded or damaged tank should be replaced.

To install:

9. Confirm that the pad is fully bonded to the tank.

10. Raise the tank and connect the fuel gauge unit harness connectors. Position the tank in place and secure by tightening the locknuts.

11. Connect all remaining hoses to the fuel and tubes.

12. Fill the fuel tank and check for leaks. Install the tank protector, if equipped.

Fuel Filter

REMOVAL AND INSTALLATION

Carbureted Engine

The fuel filter is of the inline type. The filter is located at low center of the firewall.

NOTE: Remove the fuel tank cap to release pressure in the fuel lines.

1. Turn OFF the engine and allow it to cool. Loosen the screws in the fuel line clamps (at the filter) and then, using a pair of pliers, force open the clamps on the fuel lines and back them away from the connections.

2. Work the fuel lines off the filter connections. If they are difficult to remove, pull them off with a twisting motion. Remove the filter from its mounting clip.

To install:

3. Inspect the fuel lines for cracks or breaks and replace, if necessary.

4. Install the new filter in the same position the old one was in the clamp. Connect the inlet fuel line to the inlet fitting on the bottom of the filter. Connect the outlet to the outlet fitting on top. Make sure the hoses are fully installed over the bulged-out portions of the fittings. Then, with pliers, move the clamps over the filter fittings so they are beyond the bulged-out sections of the fittings but a small distance away from the ends of the hoses and secure.

5. Start the vehicle and check for fuel leakage.

Fuel Injected Engine

Prior to opening the fuel system of a vehicle equipped with fuel injection, the fuel system pressure must be released.

────── **CAUTION** ──────
Do not use conventional fuel filters, hoses or clamps when servicing fuel injection systems. They are not compatible with the injection system and could fail, causing personal injury or damage to the vehicle. Use only hoses and clamps specifically designed for fuel injection.

1. Relieve the fuel system pressure.

2. Disconnect the negative battery cable.

3. The filter is located in the engine compartment, mounted either on the firewall or inner fender panel.

4. Hold the fuel filter nut securely with a backup or spanner wrench. Cover the hoses with shop towels and remove the eye bolt. Discard the old gaskets.

5. The high pressure hose connection is accomplished with another eye bolt connection; hold the fuel filter nut securely with a backup or spanner wrench. Cover the hoses with shop towels and remove the eye bolt. Discard the old gaskets.

6. Remove the mounting bolts if equipped, and remove the fuel filter from the vehicle.

To install:

7. Install the filter into the mounting bracket.

8. Install new gaskets and connect the high pressure hose and eye bolt, then the main pipe and eye bolt. While holding the fuel filter nut, tighten the eye bolts to 22 ft. lbs. (30 Nm).

9. Connect the negative battery cable, install the fuel filler cap, turn the key to the **ON** position to pressurize the fuel system and check for leaks. Release the fuel pressure and repair leaks as required.

Mechanical Fuel Pump

PRESSURE TESTING

1. Disconnect the inlet line coming from the filter, at the pump.

2. Connect a vacuum gauge to the pump nipple.

3. Remove the high tension cable at the coil. Crank the engine and observe the gauge reading.

4. A vacuum of 2.7-3.7 psi should be produced. If there is a blow-back of pressure, the inlet valve on the pump is leaking and the unit must be replaced.

5. Disconnect the hose at the carburetor and connect a fuel pressure gauge.

6. Disconnect the return hose at the pump and plug the fitting at the pump.

7. Check the pressure while the engine is idling. The pressure should be 2.76-3.63 psi.

8. Check the pump volume by disconnecting the carburetor fuel hose and insert the end into a graduated container. Start the engine and measure the amount of fuel pumped within 1 minute. The volume should be 0.85 pint (0.60 liters).

9. Reconnect all disconnected hoses and check for leaks.

REMOVAL AND INSTALLATION

The mechanical fuel pump operates directly off a camshaft eccentric. A fuel return valve is located in the upper body of the pump. If the fuel temperature rises above 122°F (50°C), the valve opens and routes fuel back to the tank, preventing percolation.

1. Disconnect the negative battery cable. Remove the 2 screws and remove the plastic heat shield.
2. Disconnect the 3 fuel pump lines.
3. Unscrew the retaining nuts and remove the fuel pump and pushrod.
4. Remove the gaskets and the insulator.
5. Clean the fuel pump and pump mounting surfaces.

To install:

6. Apply non-hardening sealer to both sides of the gaskets. Position a gasket, the insulator and the other gasket on the head studs.
7. Set the No. 1 piston at TDC of the compression stroke and insert the pushrod into the head. Install the pump and torque the nuts to 25 ft. lbs. (34 Nm).
8. Connect the negative battery cable.

Electric Fuel Pump

All fuel injected vehicles are equipped with an electric fuel pump. The fuel pump is in the gas tank.

OPERATION TEST

If the fuel pump does not work:
1. Check the fuse.
2. Check all wiring connections.
3. Check the control relay which is located in the engine compartment, next to the ignition coil. If the engine starts when the ignition switch is turned to **START**, but stops when it is turned to **ON**, the relay is defective. Jumper terminals **1** and **2** of the test connector, the fuel pump should operate. If the pump fails to operate when the the jumper is connected, the pump is probably defective.

PRESSURE TESTING

1. Relieve fuel system pressure. Disconnect the battery negative cable.
2. Hold the upper fuel filter nut securely with a backup or spanner wrench. Cover the hoses with shop towels and remove the upper eye bolt. Discard the gaskets.
3. Using a fuel pressure gauge with the appropriate adapters, install the pressure gauge to the fuel filter.
4. Connect the negative battery terminal. Apply battery voltage to the fuel pump test connector located in the engine compartment, which will energize the fuel pump. With pressure applied, check for fuel leakage at the gauge. If no leaks are present, continue with the test procedure.
5. Start the engine and run at curb idle speed.
6. Measure the fuel pressure and compare to specifications.
7. Locate and disconnect the vacuum hose running to the fuel pressure regulator. Plug the end of the hose and record the fuel pressure again. The fuel pressure should have increased approximately 10 psi.
8. If the pressure readings were not at the desired specifications, perform the following diagnostic procedure:
   a. If fuel pressure is too low, check for a clogged fuel filter, a defective fuel pressure regulator or a defective fuel pump, any of which will require replacement.
   b. If fuel pressure is too high, the fuel pressure regulator is defective and will have to be replaced or the fuel return is bent or clogged. If the fuel pressure reading does not change when the vacuum hose is disconnected, the hose is clogged or the valve is stuck in the fuel pressure regulator and it will have to be replaced.
   c. Stop the engine and check for changes in the fuel pressure gauge. It should not drop. If the gauge reading does drop, watch the rate of drop. If fuel pressure drops slowly, the likely cause is a leaking injector which will require replacement. If the fuel pressure drops immediately after the engine is stopped, the check valve in the fuel pump isn't closing and the fuel pump will have to be replaced.
9. Relieve fuel system pressure.
10. Remove the fuel pressure gauge.
11. Install a new O-ring and the pressure hose to the filter. After installation, apply battery voltage to the terminal for fuel pump activation to run the fuel pump. Check for leaks.

REMOVAL AND INSTALLATION

1. Reduce pressure in the fuel lines as follows:
   a. Turn the ignition to the **OFF** position.
   b. Loosen the fuel filler cap to release fuel tank pressure.
   c. Disconnect the fuel pump harness connector located under the rear seat cushion on Elantra or in the area of the fuel tank on the remaining models.
   d. Start the vehicle and allow it to run until it stalls from lack of fuel. Turn the key to the **OFF** position.
   e. Disconnect the negative battery cable, then reconnect the fuel pump connector.
2. Raise the vehicle and support it safely.
3. Remove the fuel tank from the vehicle.
4. Disconnect the hoses at the pump.
5. Unbolt and remove the pump from the tank.

To install:

6. Install the new pump with new gasket in place into the fuel tank and secure.
7. Install the fuel tank into the vehicle.
8. Connect the fuel lines and the electrical connectors to the fuel pump and sending unit.
9. Connect the negative battery cable, pressurize the fuel system and check for leaks.

Carburetor

REMOVAL AND INSTALLATION

USA Vehicles

1. Disconnect the negative battery cable. Drain the coolant down to below the level of the intake manifold.
2. Remove the air cleaner. Disconnect the throttle cable at the carburetor.
3. Disconnect and label all vacuum hoses.

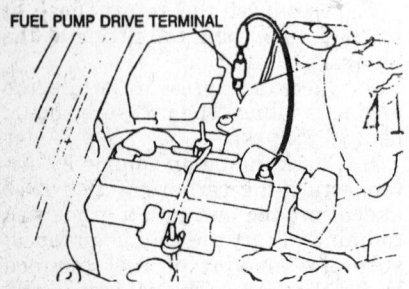

FUEL PUMP DRIVE TERMINAL

Fuel pump drive terminal location — fuel injected vehicle

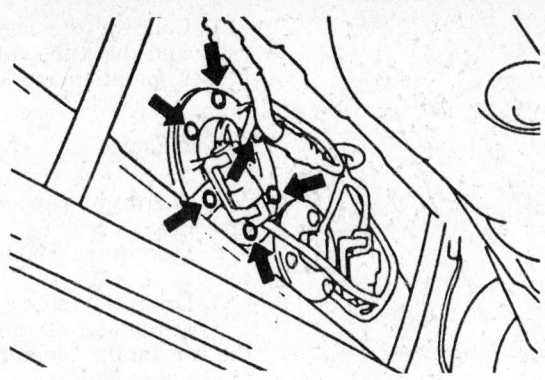

Electric fuel pump attaching screws

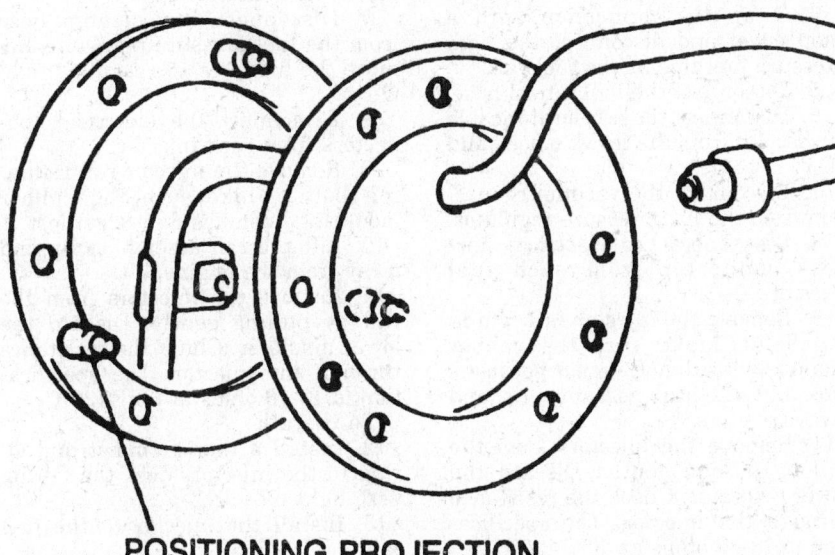

POSITIONING PROJECTION

During electric fuel pump installation, make sure positioning studs on the packing collar are properly positioned

4. Disconnect the connectors for the solenoid valves and the Throttle Position Sensor (TPS).

5. Place a pan under the fuel connections and then disconnect them. Remove the container, avoiding the spilling of fuel.

6. Remove the mounting bolts, lift the carburetor off the engine and remove it to a workbench, keeping it level to avoid the spilling of fuel from the float bowl.

To install:

7. Inspect the mating surfaces of the carburetor and manifold. They should be clean and free of nicks or burrs. Clean and, if necessary, remove any slight imperfections with crocus cloth. Put a new carburetor gasket on the surface of the manifold.

8. Position the carburetor on top of the gasket with all holes aligned. Install the carburetor bolts and tighten them alternately and evenly.

9. Connect the throttle linkage. Depress the accelerator pedal and make sure the throttle blade opens all the way. Adjust, if necessary.

10. Connect the vacuum hoses. Make sure all are soft and free of cracks to make a good seal. Replace hoses that are hard and cracked. Reconnect the fuel hoses.

11. Install the remaining parts in reverse order. Connect the negative battery cable. To start the engine, set the choke and operate the starter. Do not attempt to prime the engine by pouring gas into the carburetor inlet. Check for leaks with the engine running.

Canadian Vehicles

1. Disconnect the negative battery cable.

2. Drain the coolant to a level just below the intake manifold.

3. Remove the air cleaner.

4. Disconnect the wiring from the fuel cutoff solenoid.

5. Disconnect the accelerator rod and, if equipped with automatic transaxle, the shift rod.

6. Tag and disconnect the vacuum hoses from the carburetor.

7. Place a container under the fuel inlet and return hoses to catch any leaking fuel and disconnect the hoses.

8. Disconnect the water hose which runs between the carburetor and the cylinder head.

9. Unscrew the 4 retaining nuts and remove the carburetor. Hold the carburetor level to avoid a fuel spill.

To install:

10. Mount the carburetor on the intake manifold and install nuts. Attach the choke water hose to the carburetor.

11. Reconnect the fuel lines and vacuum hoses to the carburetor.

12. Connect the accelerator or shift rod.

13. Reconnect the fuel cut-off solenoid and replace the air cleaner.

14. Refill the system with coolant. Connect the negative battery cable.

Fuel Injector

REMOVAL AND INSTALLATION

1596cc, 1796cc and 1997cc Engines

1. Relieve the fuel system pressure.

2. Disconnect the negative battery cable.

3. Wrap the connection with a shop towel and disconnect the high pressure fuel line at the fuel rail.

4. Disconnect the fuel return hose.

5. Disconnect the vacuum hose from the fuel pressure regulator. Remove the fuel pressure regulator and O-ring.

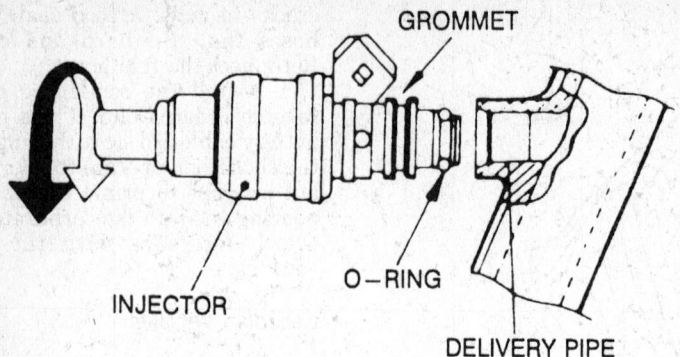

GROMMET

INJECTOR

O—RING

DELIVERY PIPE

Fuel injector installation

6. Disconnect and remove the PCV hose.

7. Label and disconnect the electrical connectors from each injector.

8. Remove the injector rail retaining bolts. Make sure the rubber mounting bushings do not get lost.

9. Lift the rail assembly up and away from the engine.

10. Remove the injectors from the rail by pulling gently. Discard the lower insulator. Check the resistance through the injector. The specification is 13-16 ohms at 70°F (20°C). If resistance is out of desired reading, replace the injector.

To install:

11. Install a new grommet and O-ring to the injector. Coat the O-ring with light oil.

12. Install the injector to the fuel rail turning to the left and right during installation.

13. Install the fuel rail and injectors to the manifold. Make sure the rubber bushings are in place before tightening the mounting bolts.

14. Tighten the retaining bolts to 72 inch lbs. (11 Nm).

15. Connect the electrical harness connectors to the injectors. Install and connect the PCV hose.

16. Replace the O-ring, lightly lubricate it and connect the fuel pressure regulator.

17. Connect the fuel return hose.

18. Replace the O-ring, lightly lubricate it and connect the high pressure fuel line.

19. Connect the negative battery cable and check the entire system for proper operation and leaks.

1468cc and 2351cc Engines

1. Relieve the fuel system pressure.

2. Disconnect the negative battery cable.

3. Disconnect and remove the air intake hoses as required.

4. Wrap the connection with a shop towel and disconnect the high pressure fuel line at the fuel rail.

5. Disconnect the fuel return hose.

6. Disconnect the accelerator cable connection from the throttle body and position aside.

7. Disconnect the vacuum connection from the fuel pressure regulator.

8. Disconnect the electrical harness connector from each fuel injector.

9. Remove the injector rail retaining bolts. Make sure the rubber mounting insulators do not get lost.

10. Lift the rail assembly up and away from engine.

11. Remove the injectors from the rail by pulling gently. Discard the lower insulator. Check the resistance through the injector. The specification is 13-16 ohms at 70°F (20°C).

To install:

12. Install a new grommet and O-ring to the injector. Coat the O-ring with light weight oil.

13. Install the injector to the fuel rail.

14. Install the fuel rail and injectors to the manifold. Make sure the rubber bushings are in place before tightening the mounting bolts.

15. Tighten the retaining bolts to 9 ft. lbs. (12 Nm).

16. Connect the electrical connectors to the injectors.

17. Replace the O-ring on the fuel pressure regulator, lightly lubricate and install on the delivery pipe. Connect the vacuum hose to the fuel pressure regulator.

18. Connect the fuel return hose.

19. Replace the O-ring on high pressure fuel line, lightly lubricate it and connect to delivery pipe.

20. Reconnect the accelerator cable to the throttle body and adjust to specifications.

21. Connect the negative battery cable and check the entire system for proper operation and leaks.

2972cc Engine

1. Relieve the fuel system pressure.

2. Disconnect the negative battery cable.

3. Drain the cooling system.

4. Disconnect all components from the air intake plenum and remove the plenum from the intake manifold. Discard the gaskets.

5. Wrap the connection with a shop towel and disconnect the high pressure fuel line at the fuel rail.

6. Disconnect the fuel return hose and remove the O-ring.

7. Disconnect the vacuum hose from the fuel pressure regulator. Remove the fuel pressure regulator and O-ring.

8. Disconnect the electrical connectors from each injector.

9. Remove the injector rail retaining bolts. Make sure the rubber mounting bushings do not get lost.

10. Lift the rail assemblies up and away from the engine.

11. Remove the injectors from the rail by pulling gently. Discard the lower insulator. Check the resistance through the injector. The specification is 13-16 ohms at 68°F (20°C).

To install:

12. Install a new grommet and O-ring to the injector. Coat the O-ring with light oil.

13. Install the injector to the fuel rail.

14. Replace the seats in the intake manifold, if equipped. Install the fuel rails and injectors to the manifold. Make sure the rubber bushings are in place before tightening the mounting bolts.

15. Tighten the retaining bolts to 72 inch lbs. (11 Nm). Install the fuel pipe with new gasket.

16. Connect the electrical connectors to the injectors.

17. Replace the O-ring, lightly lubricate it and connect the fuel pressure regulator.

18. Connect the fuel return hose.

19. Replace the O-ring, lightly lubricate it and connect the high pressure fuel line.

20. Using new gaskets, install the intake plenum and all related items. Torque the plenum mounting bolts to 13 ft. lbs. (18 Nm).

21. Fill the cooling system.

22. Connect the negative battery cable and check the entire system for proper operation and leaks.

DRIVE AXLE

Halfshaft

REMOVAL AND INSTALLATION

NOTE: If the vehicle is going to be rolled while the halfshafts are out of the vehicle, obtain 2 outer CV-joints or proper equivalent tools and install to the hubs. If the vehicle is rolled without the proper torque applied to the front wheel bearings, the bearings will no longer be usable.

1. Disconnect the negative battery cable.
2. Remove the cotter pin, halfshaft nut and washer.
3. Raise the vehicle and support safely. Remove the lower ball joint and the tie rod end from the steering knuckle.
4. On vehicles with an inner shaft, remove the center support bearing bracket bolts and washers.
5. On vehicles with an inner shaft, remove the halfshaft by setting up a puller on the outside wheel hub and pushing the halfshaft from the front hub. Then tap the shaft union at the joint case with a plastic hammer to remove the halfshaft shaft and inner shaft from the transaxle.
6. On vehicles without an inner shaft, remove the halfshaft by setting up a puller on the outside wheel hub and pushing the halfshaft from the front hub. After pressing the outer shaft, insert a prybar between the transaxle case and the halfshaft and pry the shaft from the transaxle. Do not pull on the shaft; doing so damages the inboard joint. Do not insert the prybar too far or the oil seal in the case may be damaged.

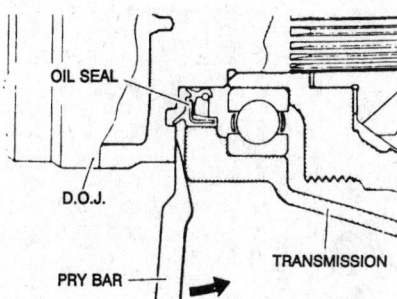

OIL SEAL

D.O.J.

PRY BAR

TRANSMISSION

Removing halfshaft from the transaxle case extension housing

To install:

7. Inspect the halfshaft boot for damage or deterioration. Check the ball joints and splines for wear.
8. Replace the circlips on the ends of the halfshafts.
9. Insert the halfshaft into the transaxle. Make sure it is fully seated.
10. Pull the strut assembly out and install the other end to the hub.
11. Install the center bearing bracket bolts and tighten to 33 ft. lbs. (45 Nm).
12. Install the washer so the chamfered edge faces outward. Install the nut and tighten temporarily.
13. Install the tie rod end, stabilizer bar and ball joint.
14. Install the wheel and lower the vehicle to the floor. Tighten the axle nut with the brakes applied. Tighten the nut to a maximum torque of 188 ft. lbs. (260 Nm). Install the cotter pin and bend to secure.

CV-Boot

The vehicles use several different types of joints. Engine size, transaxle type, whether the joint is an inboard or outboard joint, even which side of the vehicle is being serviced could make a difference in joint type. Be sure to properly identify the joint before attempting joint or boot replacement. Look for identification numbers at the large end of the boots and/or on the end of the metal retainer bands.

The 3 types of joints used are the Birfield Joint, (B.J.), the Tripod Joint (T.J.) and the Double Offset Joint (D.O.J.). Take note that the Birfield Joint, (B.J.) assembly, which is normally the inner joint, is not to be disassembled. In addition, some left side shafts will have a round dynamic damper installed on the shaft. Special grease is generally used with these joints and is often supplied with the replacement joint and/or boot. Do not use regular chassis grease.

The distance between the large and small boot bands is important and should be checked prior to and after boot service. This is so the boot will not be installed either too loose or too tight, which could cause early wear and cracking, allowing the grease to get out and water and dirt in, leading to early joint failure.

REMOVAL AND INSTALLATION

Double Offset Joint

The Double Offset Joint (D.O.J.) is bigger than other joints and in these applications, is normally used as an inboard joint.

1. Remove the halfshaft from the vehicle.
2. Side cutter pliers can be used to cut the metal retaining bands. Remove the boot from the joint outer race.
3. Locate and remove the large circlip at the base of the joint. Remove the outer race (the body of the joint).
4. Remove the small snapring and take off the inner race, cage and balls as an assembly. Clean the inner race, cage and balls without disassembling.
5. If the boot is to be reused, wipe the grease from the splines and wrap the splines in vinyl tape before sliding the boot from the shaft.
6. Remove the inner (D.O.J.) boot from the shaft. If the outer (B.J.) boot is to be replaced, remove the boot retainer rings and slide the boot down and off the shaft at this time.

To install:

7. Be sure to tape the shaft splines before installing the boots. Fill the inside of the boot with the specified grease. Often the grease supplied in the replacement parts kit is meant to be divided in half, with half being used to lubricate the joint and half being used inside the boot.
8. Install the cage onto the halfshaft so the small diameter side of the cage is installed first. With a brass drift pin, tap lightly and evenly around the inner race to install the race until it comes into contact with the rib of the shaft. Apply the specified grease to the inner race and cage and fit them together. Insert the balls into the cage.
9. Install the outer race (the body of the joint) after filling with the specified grease. The outer race should be filled with this grease.
10. Tighten the boot bands securely. Make sure the distance between the boot bands is correct.
11. Install the halfshaft to the vehicle.

Except Double Offset Joint

1. Disconnect the negative battery cable. Remove the halfshaft.
2. Use side cutter pliers to remove the metal retaining bands from the boot(s) that will be removed. Slide the boot from the T.J. case.

3. Remove the snapring and the tripod joint spider assembly from the halfshaft. Do not disassemble the spider and use care in handling.

4. If the boot is be reused, wrap vinyl tape around the spline part of the shaft so the boot(s) will not be damaged when removed. Remove the dynamic damper, if used, and the boots from the shaft.

To install:

5. Double check that the correct replacement parts are being installed. Wrap vinyl tape around the splines to protect the boot and install the boots and damper, if used, in the correct order.

6. Install the joint spider assembly to the shaft and install the snapring.

7. Fill the inside of the boot with the specified grease. Often the grease supplied in the replacement parts kit is meant to be divided in half, with half being used to lubricate the joint and half being used inside the boot. Keep grease off the rubber part of the dynamic damper (if used).

8. Secure the boot bands with the halfshaft in a horizontal position. Make sure distance between boot bands is correct.

9. Install the halfshaft to the vehicle and reconnect the negative battery cable.

Front Wheel Hub, Knuckle and Bearings

REMOVAL AND INSTALLATION

NOTE: The following procedure requires the use of a number of special tools. Always replace bearings and races as a set. Never replace just an inner or outer bearing. If either is in need of replacement, both sets must be replaced.

1. Remove the center hub cap and halfshaft nut. Raise the vehicle and support it safely, positioned so the wheels hang freely. Remove the front wheel and tire assembly.

2. Remove the brake caliper and suspend it out of the way with a piece of wire. It is not necessary to disconnect the hydraulic line from the caliper.

3. Disconnect the tie rod end and the lower arm ball joint at the steering knuckle using puller 09568-31000 or equivalent.

4. Press the halfshaft out of the hub with a 2 jawed puller 09526-11001 or equivalent, and remove the halfshaft from the transaxle.

5. Unbolt the hub and knuckle assembly from the bottom of the strut and remove hub assembly from the vehicle.

6. Several special tools are required to press the hub and disc from the steering knuckle and to remount them. Use 09517-21600 or equivalent. Do not attempt to hammer the parts apart, or damage to the bearing may result. Install the arm of the special tool then the body onto the knuckle and tighten the nut manually. Using special tool

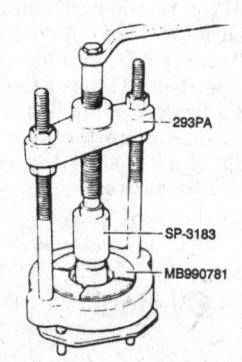

Removing the outer bearing inner race from the hub

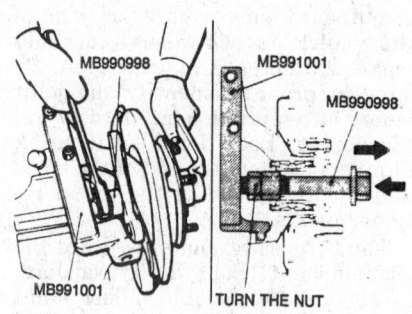

Removing the hub from the knuckle

09517-21500, separate the hub from the knuckle.

7. Secure the knuckle in a vise. Remove the outer bearing inner race from the hub using puller and adapter 09532-11000, 09532-11301 and 09517-21100 or exact equivalents. Remove the inner bearing race and oil seal from the knuckle.

8. Drive out the bearing outer race from the knuckle using the appropriate driver. If one of the bearing races requires replacement, they both must be replaced as a set.

To install:

9. Apply a multi-purpose grease SAE J310, NLGI No. 2 or equivalent, to the outside surface of the bearing race. Install the bearing race into the steering knuckle using the appropriate driver.

10. Install the disc to the hub and torque the retainers to 36-43 ft. lbs. (50-60 Nm).

11. Apply a multi-purpose grease SAE J310, NLGI No. 2 or equivalent, to the bearing and the inside surface of the hub. Place the outside bearing inner race into the knuckle. Drive the oil seal into the knuckle using the correct size driver. Apply multi-purpose grease SAE J310, NLGI No. 2 or equivalent, to the surfaces of the oil seal that contacts the hub.

12. Place the inner bearing into the knuckle. Tighten the hub and knuckle to 167 ft. lbs. (235 Nm) using tool 09517-21500 or exact equivalent. Rotate the hub on the tool to seat the bearing.

13. Measure the hub bearing starting torque and compare to the desired reading of 11 inch lbs. (1.3 Nm), or less. If starting torque is 0 inch lbs. (0 Nm), measure the bearing end-play.

14. If the hub axial end-play exceeds the limit of 0.0043 in. (0.11mm), the bearing and hub assembly is improperly installed. Re-

1. Oil seal (driveshaft side)
2. Inner bearing
3. Knuckle
4. Dust cover
5. Brake disc
6. Outer bearing
7. Oil seal (hub side)
8. Hub

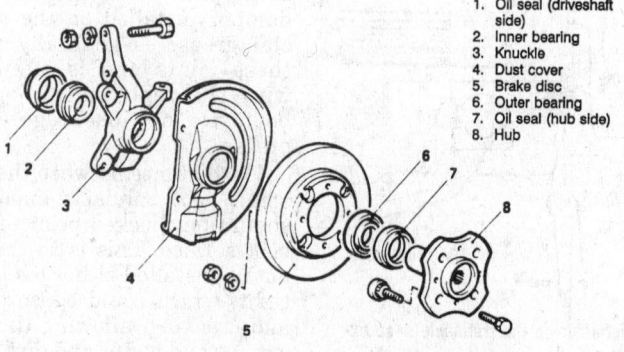

Front hub, knuckle and related components — Excel

peat the hub disassembly and assembly procedure again.

15. Remove the special mounting tool and drive the seal into the knuckle until it contacts the bearing outer race.

16. Install the steering knuckle onto the lower ball joint and loosely install the retaining nut.

17. Install the axle shaft into the transaxle, with new locking ring in place. Guide the stub shaft through the steering knuckle and loosely install the washer and the axle nut.

18. Install the lower strut mounting bolts and secure. The final torque will be reached after the front end of the vehicle has been aligned.

19. Connect the tie rod stud to the steering knuckle and torque to 25 ft. lbs. (34 Nm). Install new cotter pin, if equipped.

20. Torque the lower ball joint retainer nut to 52 ft. lbs. (72 Nm) and install new cotter pin, if equipped.

21. Install the caliper assembly to the adapter.

22. Tighten the axle nut, while applying the brakes, to 188 ft. lbs. (260 Nm) and install new cotter pin.

23. Install the tire and wheel assembly. Align the front suspension tightening the lower strut-to knuckle mounting bolts to 65 ft. lbs. (88 Nm).

MANUAL TRANSAXLE

Transaxle Assembly

NOTE: If the vehicle is going to be rolled while the halfshafts are out of the vehicle, obtain 2 outer CV-joints or proper equivalent tools and install to the hubs. If the vehicle is rolled without the proper torque applied to the front wheel bearings, the bearings will no longer be usable.

REMOVAL AND INSTALLATION

Except 1993-94 Scoupe with 1495cc Engine

1. Disconnect the negative battery cable. Remove the air cleaner assembly, battery and battery tray as required.

2. On 5 speed transaxle, disconnect the electrical connector for the selector control valve.

NOTE: The actuator-to-shaft coupling pin collar is not reusable; replace it.

3. Disconnect and remove the speedometer cable.

4. If equipped with a cable operated clutch, disconnect the clutch cable from the transaxle assembly.

5. If equipped with a hydraulically operated clutch, remove the clevis pin connecting the slave cylinder to the release fork shaft and remove the slave cylinder mounting bolts. Remove the bolts attaching the hydraulic line support bracket to the transaxle. Remove and support the slave cylinder assembly out of the way with a length of mechanics wire.

6. Disconnect the backup lamp electrical connector. Remove the starter motor electrical harness.

7. Remove the transaxle mounting bolts accessible from the top side of the transaxle.

8. Unbolt and remove the starter motor.

9. Raise the vehicle and support it safely. Then, remove the splash shield from under the engine. Drain the transaxle fluid.

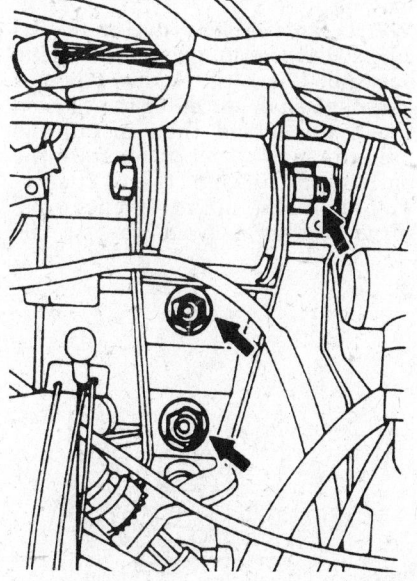

Transaxle mount insulator bolt locations

10. Disconnect the extension rod and the shift rod at the transaxle end and lower them.

11. Disconnect the stabilizer bar at the lower control arm.

12. Remove the halfshafts from the transaxle assembly.

13. Support the transaxle from below with a floor jack. Make sure the support is spread wide enough that the transaxle pan will not be damaged. Then, remove the attaching bolts and the bell housing cover.

14. Remove the lower bolts attaching the transaxle to the engine.

15. Remove the transaxle insulator mount bolt. Remove the cover from inside the right fender shield and remove the transaxle support bracket.

16. Remove the transaxle mount bracket.

17. Pull the assembly away from the engine and lower it from the vehicle.

To install:

18. Install the transaxle to the engine and install the mounting bolts. Tighten the mounting bolts as follows:

M10-7T engine-to-transaxle bolts to 35 ft. lbs. (48 Nm)

M8-10T engine-to-transaxle bolts to 25 ft. lbs. (34 Nm)

19. When installing the halfshafts, use new circlips on the axle ends. Take care to get the inboard joint parts straight, not bent relative to the axle. Care must be taken to ensure that the oil seal lip of the transaxle is not damaged by the serrated part of the driveshaft.

20. Install the undercover.

21. Install the mounting brackets and torque the mounting bracket bolt to 40 ft. lbs. (54 Nm).

22. Install the starter making sure to fasten the ground wire with the upper fastener and the harness fastener with the lower fastener.

23. Connect the backup light switch connector and speedometer cable.

24. Install the clutch and shifter actuation components. If the hydraulic system was opened, it should be bled after installation.

25. Install the air cleaner and battery.

26. Make sure the vehicle is level when refilling the transaxle. Use Hypoid gear oil or equivalent, GL-4 or higher.

27. Connect the negative battery cable and check the transaxle for proper operation. Make sure the reverse lights come ON when in reverse.

1993-94 Scoupe with 1495cc Engine

1. Disconnect the negative battery cable.
2. Remove the clutch cylinder.
3. Remove the air cleaner assembly.
4. Remove the select and shift cable.
5. Disconnect the backup light switch connector.
6. Remove the speedometer cable.
7. Disconnect the clutch cable or clutch tube.
8. Remove the starter motor mounting bolts. Remove the transaxle assembly upper connecting bolts and transaxle mounting bracket bolt.
9. Remove the splash shield.
10. Remove the intermediate shaft by removing the 2 bolts (turbocharged only).
11. Disconnect the tie rod end, lower the arm ball joint and driveshaft.
12. Remove the bell housing cover.
13. Remove the transaxle assembly lower mounting bolts with the transaxle supported on a suitable jack. Use care to spread the weight. Lifting force from the jack concentrated on a small area could damage the transaxle case.
14. Remove the transaxle.

To install:

15. Installation is the reverse of the removal procedure. Use care not force the assembly. Make sure the input shaft correctly aligns with the clutch disc.
16. Transaxle total oil capacity is 2.3 quarts. Use SAE 75/85W API-GL4 HP gear oil.

CLUTCH

Clutch Assembly

REMOVAL AND INSTALLATION

Cable Operated System

1. Remove the transaxle. Insert the forward end of an old transaxle input shaft or a clutch disc guide tool into the splined center of the clutch disc, pressure plate and the pilot bearing in the crankshaft. This will keep the disc from dropping when the pressure plate is removed from the flywheel.
2. Loosen the clutch mounting bolts alternately and diagonally in very small increments, no more than 2 turns at a time, so as to avoid warping the cover flange.
3. Remove the pressure plate and disc.
4. Remove the return clip and the clutch release bearing.
5. Insert tool 09414-24000 in the spring pin and attach the round nut to the end of the tool. While holding the shaft of the special tool, rotate the sleeve with a wrench to force the spring pin out.
6. Remove the clutch release shaft, packings, return spring and the release fork.

To install:

7. Apply a light coating of multi-purpose grease to the release fork shaft and the throw out bearing contact surfaces.
8. Align the lock pin holes of the release fork and shaft and drive 2 new spring pins into the holes. Make sure the spring pin slot is at right angles to the centerline of the control shaft.
9. Apply grease into the groove in the release bearing and install bearing into the front bearing retainer in the transaxle. Install the return clip to the release bearing and fork.
10. Make sure the surfaces of the pressure plate and flywheel are wiped clean of grease and lightly sand them with crocus cloth. Lightly grease the clutch disc and transaxle input shaft splines making sure not to allow any grease to contact the clutch disc material or clutch slip may result.
11. Locate the clutch disc on the flywheel with the stamped mark facing outward. Use a clutch disc guide or old input shaft to center the disc on the flywheel and then install the pressure plate over it. Install the bolts and tighten them evenly. Tighten them in increments of 2 turns or less to avoid warping the pressure plate. Torque to 11-15 ft. lbs. (15-21 Nm).
12. Remove the clutch disc centering tool. Install the transaxle. Adjust the clutch free-play.

Hydraulic System

ELANTRA

1. Disconnect the negative battery cable. Raise and safely support the vehicle.
2. Remove the transaxle assembly from the vehicle.
3. Remove the pressure plate attaching bolts. If the pressure plate is to be reused, loosen the bolts in succession, 1 or 2 turns at a time to prevent warping the the cover flange.
4. Remove the pressure plate release bearing assembly and the clutch disc. Do not use solvent to clean the bearing.
5. Inspect the condition of the clutch components and replace any worn parts.

To install:

6. Inspect the flywheel for heat damage or cracks. Resurface or replace the flywheel as required, using new bolts.
7. Using the proper alignment tool, install the clutch disc to the flywheel. Install the pressure plate assembly and tighten the pressure plate bolts evenly to 14 ft. lbs. (22 Nm). Remove the alignment tool.
8. Apply a very light coat of high temperature grease to the clutch fork at the ball pivot and where the fork contacts the bearing. Also a little bit of grease can be applied to end of the release cylinder's pushrod and to the pushrod hole on the fork. Apply a light coat of grease on the transaxle input shaft splines.
9. Install a new clutch release bearing. Pack its inner surface with grease.
10. Install the transaxle assembly and check for proper clutch operation.

Except Elantra

1. Disconnect the negative battery cable. Raise and safely support the vehicle.
2. Remove the transaxle assembly from the vehicle.
3. Remove the pressure plate attaching bolts. If the pressure plate is to be reused, loosen the bolts in succession, 1 or 2 turns at a time to prevent warping the the cover flange.
4. Remove the pressure plate and disc.
5. Remove the return clip and the clutch release bearing.

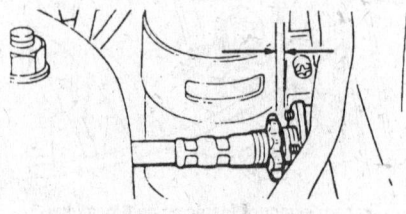

Clutch cable adjustment

6. Insert tool 09414-24000 in the spring pin and attach the round nut to the end of the tool. While holding the shaft of the special tool, rotate the sleeve with a wrench to force the spring pin out.

7. Remove the clutch release shaft, packings, return spring and the release fork.

To install:

8. Apply a light coating of multipurpose grease to the release fork shaft and the throw out bearing contact surfaces.

9. Align the lock pin holes of the release fork and shaft and drive 2 new spring pins into the holes. Make sure the spring pin slot is at right angles to the centerline of the control shaft.

10. Apply grease into the groove in the release bearing and install bearing into the front bearing retainer in the transaxle. Install the return clip to the release bearing and fork.

11. Make sure the surfaces of the pressure plate and flywheel are wiped clean of grease and lightly sand them with crocus cloth. Lightly grease the clutch disc and transaxle input shaft splines making sure not to allow any grease to contact the clutch disc material or clutch slip may result.

12. Locate the clutch disc on the flywheel with the stamped mark facing outward. Use a clutch disc guide or old input shaft to center the disc on the flywheel and then install the pressure plate over it. Install the bolts and tighten them evenly. Tighten them in increments of 2 turns or less to avoid warping the pressure plate. Torque to 11-15 ft. lbs. (15-21 Nm).

13. Remove the clutch disc centering tool. Install the transaxle. Adjust the clutch free-play.

CLUTCH PEDAL HEIGHT ADJUSTMENT

Elantra

Measure the pedal height from the top of the pedal pad to the closest point on the floor. The distance should be 7.0 in. (182mm). If incorrect and the vehicle is not equipped with cruise control, adjust the height by loosening the locknut on the pedal stop bolt and adjusting the bolt to the proper length. Secure the adjustment by tightening the locknut. If the vehicle is equipped with cruise control, adjust as follows:

1. Disconnect the clutch switch wiring.

2. Loosen the locknut and turn the switch, as required.

3. Tighten the locknut.

Excel

Measure the pedal height from the top of the pedal pad to the closest point on the floor. The distance should be 7.3-7.6 in. (185-192mm). Loosen the clutch switch locknut and move the pedal stop bolt. Then, tighten the locknut.

Sonata

Measure the pedal height from the face of the pedal to the floorboard. Pedal height should be 6.97-7.17 in. (177-182mm). If incorrect and the vehicle is not equipped with cruise control, adjust the height by loosening the locknut on the pedal stop bolt and adjusting the bolt to the proper length. Secure the adjustment by tightening the locknut. If the vehicle is equipped with cruise control, adjust as follows:

1. Disconnect the clutch switch wiring.

2. Loosen the locknut and turn the switch, as required.

3. Tighten the locknut.

Scoupe

Measure the pedal height from the top of the pedal pad to the closest point on the floor. The distance should be 7 in. (178mm). Loosen the clutch switch locknut and move the pedal stop bolt. Then, tighten the locknut.

CLEVIS PIN PLAY ADJUSTMENT

Clevis pin play is measure at the pedal while observe the pin. Play should be 0.04-0.12 in. (1-3mm). If not, loosen the locknut and turn the pushrod, as required. Tighten the locknut.

FREE-PLAY ADJUSTMENT

Clutch pedal free-play cannot be adjusted on hydraulic clutch systems. If the free-play deviates from the desired reading of 0.2-0.5 in. (6-13mm), it is probably due to air in the hydraulic system or a defective clutch master cylinder or clutch disc.

Excel

Slightly pull the cable away from the firewall. Turn the adjusting wheel on the cable until the play between the wheel and the cable retainer is 0.20-0.25 in. (5-6mm). Release the cable and make sure the end of the tension spring engages the adjusting wheel, so the wheel won't turn. Check the clutch pedal free-play. Free-play should be 0.8-1.2 in. (20-30mm). If it is outside specification, adjust it by means of the adjusting wheel on the cable.

Clutch Cable

REMOVAL AND INSTALLATION

1. Back-off the cable adjusting wheel in the engine compartment.

2. Raise and support the vehicle safely.

3. Pull out the split pin from the end of the clutch control lever and disconnect the cable from the lever.

4. Disconnect the cable at the clutch pedal and remove the clutch cable from the vehicle.

5. Installation is the reverse of removal. Adjust the clutch.

Clutch Master Cylinder

REMOVAL AND INSTALLATION

1. Loosen the bleeder screw on the slave cylinder and drain the fluid from the system.

2. Disconnect the pushrod from the clutch pedal.

3. Disconnect the clutch pedal from the pedal bracket.

4. Disconnect the fluid line from the master cylinder.

5. Unbolt and remove the clutch master cylinder.

6. Install the master cylinder and bleed the system. Torque the mounting nuts to 7-10 ft. lbs. (9-14 Nm) and the hydraulic fitting to 7-10 ft. lbs. (9-14 Nm).

Clutch Slave Cylinder

REMOVAL AND INSTALLATION

1. Disconnect the clutch hose from the slave cylinder.

2. Unbolt the cylinder from the clutch housing and remove.

3. Inspect the cylinder for leakage or torn boots and repair or replace as required.

To install:

4. Apply a thin coating of grease to the contact points of the release fork and the cylinder and install the slave cylinder to the clutch housing. Tighten the cylinder retainer bolts to 11-16 ft. lbs. (15-22 Nm).

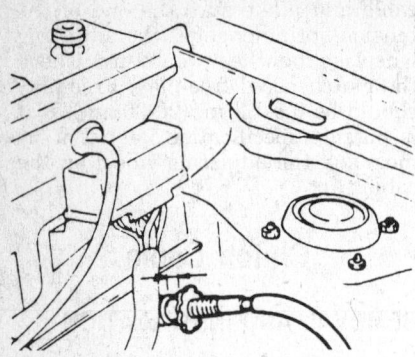

Clutch pedal height adjustment

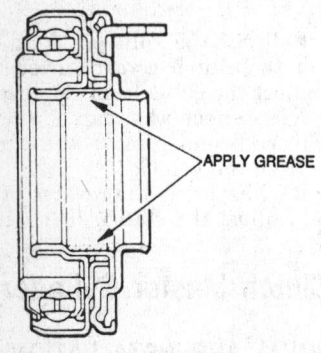

APPLY GREASE

Grease the groove in the throwout bearing as shown

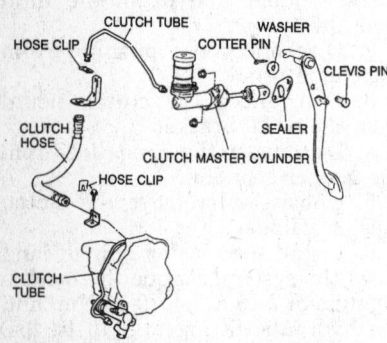

CLUTCH TUBE
WASHER
HOSE CLIP
COTTER PIN
CLEVIS PIN
CLUTCH HOSE
SEALER
CLUTCH MASTER CYLINDER
HOSE CLIP
CLUTCH TUBE

Hydraulic clutch system components — 1992 Sonata

5. Connect the fluid line to the cylinder and tighten the fitting to 7-10 ft. lbs. (9-14 Nm).

6. Add clean DOT3 brake fluid to the system and bleed.

Hydraulic Clutch System Bleeding

Whenever the clutch tubes, hoses or the clutch master cylinder have been removed, bleeding of the clutch system is required. If the clutch pedal feels spongy, it is possibly due to air in the system and the clutch system should be bleed. Use DOT3 brake fluid in the clutch system.

1. Raise the vehicle and support it safely.

2. Loosen the bleeder screw at the slave cylinder.

3. Make sure the master cylinder is full.

4. Attach a length of rubber hose to the bleeder screw nipple and place the other end in a glass jar half full of clean brake fluid.

5. Have an assistant push the clutch pedal slowly to the floor. If air is in the system, bubbles will appear in the jar as the pedal is depressed.

6. When the pedal is at the floor, have an assistant hold it there. Tighten the bleeder screw.

7. Repeat this bleeding procedure until no bubbles exit the tube. Check the master cylinder level frequently to make sure the reservoir doesn't run low on fluid.

AUTOMATIC TRANSAXLE

Transaxle Assembly

REMOVAL AND INSTALLATION

Except 1993-94 Scoupe with 1495cc Engine

NOTE: The transaxle and torque converter must be removed and installed as an assembly.

1. Disconnect the negative battery cable. Remove the battery and battery tray, as required.

2. Disconnect and remove the air cleaner and housing.

3. Disconnect the throttle control cable and the manual control cable. Loosen the locknut which uses a star washer and locates the cable housing on the bracket. Also, remove the locknut at the very end of the cable, where it connects with the neutral safety switch.

4. Disconnect the inhibitor switch connector, pulse generator connector, oil cooler hoses, solenoid valve connector and speedometer cable from the transaxle. Immediately install clean caps in the open ends of the hoses. Keep the hoses pointed up so fluid will not escape until the caps are installed.

5. Remove the speedometer cable from the transaxle.

6. Remove the bolts attaching the transaxle to the engine that are accessible from above.

7. Support the weight of the engine from above. Raise the vehicle and support it safely. Remove the engine undercover, if equipped.

8. Label and disconnect the electrical connector from the starter motor and the transaxle assembly. Remove the mounting bolts and the starter assembly from the transaxle.

9. Remove both front tire and wheel assemblies.

10. Drain the transaxle fluid by removing the drain plug.

11. Remove the transaxle mounting bolts and bracket.

12. Remove the under guard pan.

13. Disconnect the steering tie rod end and the ball joint from the steering arm.

14. Remove both halfshafts.

15. Remove the bell housing cover.

16. Rotate the engine by hand to expose the driveplate bolts and remove from the converter. Make sure to push the converter as far as it will go toward the transaxle after the bolts have been removed.

17. Properly support the transaxle assembly using the appropriate jack. Remove the transaxle mount insulator bolts and the remaining transaxle retaining bolts. Do not forget to remove the lower connecting bolt located just over the left halfshaft housing.

18. Move the transaxle away from the engine slightly and press the converter towards the transaxle as far as it will go. Lower the assembly from the vehicle.

To install:

19. Install the transaxle into the vehicle, guiding the dowels into the transaxle case. Install the lower mounting bolts and torque to 26-35 ft. lbs. (35-48 Nm).

20. Install the transaxle mount insulator bolts. Remove the transaxle jack once the transaxle is securely in place.

21. Install the torque converter-to-flexplate bolts to 34-39 ft. lbs. (46-53 Nm).

22. Install the bell housing cover.

23. Install both halfshafts making sure to replace both inner retainer clips prior to installation.

24. Connect the steering tie rod end and the ball joint to the steering arm making sure to replace cotter pins.

25. Install the transaxle mounting bolts and bracket.

26. Install the under guard pan.

27. Lower the vehicle. Reconnect the electrical connectors disconnected during the removal procedure.

28. Connect the oil cooler hoses and the speedometer cable to the transaxle assembly.

29. Connect the throttle control cable and the manual control cable.

30. Install the battery and battery tray, as required.

31. Adjust the throttle control cable and neutral safety switch. Test the neutral safety switch.

32. Refill the transaxle to the proper level. Make sure the neutral safety switch wiring does not rub against the insulator mount bracket.

33. Start the engine and allow to come to normal operating temperature. Check fluid level in the transaxle.

1993-94 Scoupe with 1495cc Engine

1. Disconnect the battery negative cable. Remove the drain plug and drain out the transaxle fluid.

2. Disconnect and remove the air cleaner assembly.

Disconnecting the shift control cable at the transaxle

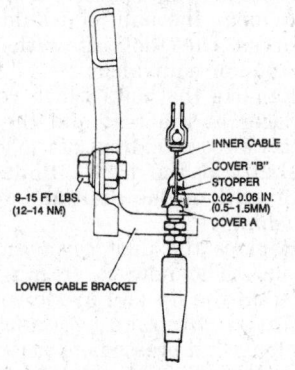

Excel throttle cable adjustment

3. Loosen the mounting clamps and disconnect the fluid return and supply hose. Plug end to keep out dirt.

4. Remove the control cable.

5. Remove the speedometer cable.

6. Separate the electrical connectors for the pulse generator, inhibitor switch, kickdown servo switch, solenoid valve and oil temperature switch. Tag connectors, if necessary.

7. Remove the transaxle-to-engine bolts from the upper portion of the transaxle.

8. Remove the transaxle mounting bracket.

9. While supporting the lower part of the transaxle with a suitable jack, remove the center member mounting bolts. Support the transaxle over a wide area. Lifting force concentrated in a small area could cause damage to the oil pan.

10. Remove the bell housing cover.

11. Remove the 6 special bolts connecting the converter to the flywheel. Turn the crankshaft with a box wrench to access the bolts for removal.

12. After removing the converter bolts, reinstall the center member assembly.

13. Remove the lower arm ball joint.

14. Remove the remaining engine connecting bolts while at the same time supporting the transaxle with the jack. Lower and remove transaxle from vehicle.

To install:

15. Install the torque converter to the transaxle. Do not try to install the torque converter to the flywheel first or the front seal will be damaged.

16. Lift the transaxle up into place and mount the transaxle assembly onto the engine.

17. Connect the lower ball joint and tighten the nut to 43-52 ft. lbs. (60-72 Nm). Install the crossmember.

18. Install the torque converter-to-drive plate bolts. Torque to 7-10 ft. lbs. (9-14 Nm).

19. Connect all brackets and wiring take off during the removal process.

20. Install the control cable and speedometer cable.

21. Connect the oil cooler lines.

22. Adjust the transaxle control cable.

23. Fill with 6 quarts MOPAR ATF Plus Type 7176 automatic transmission fluid.

SHIFT LINKAGE ADJUSTMENT

1. Move the shift lever and the inhibitor switch to the **N** position and install the control cable.

2. When connecting the control cable to the transaxle mounting bracket, install the clip until it contacts the control cable.

3. Remove any free-play in the control cable by adjusting nut and then checking to see that the selector lever moves smoothly.

4. Check to see that the cable has been adjusted correctly.

THROTTLE CONTROL CABLE ADJUSTMENT

Excel

1. Make sure the engine is at normal operating temperature, with the throttle in normal idling position.

2. Loosen the lower cable bracket mounting bolt. Pull the small rubber cover located near the transaxle back toward the housing to expose the nipple. Now, move the cable bracket until the distance between the nipple and the outer end of the cover next to the bracket is 0.02-0.06 in. (0.5-1.5mm). Then, torque the bracket mounting bolt to 9-11 ft. lbs. (12-15 Nm).

3. With the engine **OFF**, open the throttle all the way and hold it there. Then, pull the cable further upward to make sure it still has freedom of movement; that it has not bottomed out. If necessary, repeat the adjustment.

INHIBITOR SWITCH ADJUSTMENT

1. Disconnect the negative battery cable.

2. Place the selector lever in the **N** position. Loosen the manual control lever flange nut to free up the cable and the lever.

3. Place the manual control lever in the **N** position.

4. Turn the inhibitor switch body until the 0.47 in. (12mm) wide end of the manual control lever aligns with the switch body flange. Tighten the mounting bolts to 7-9 ft. lbs. (10-12 Nm) torque.

NOTE: .When setting up the switch body, be careful not to drop the O-ring from the switch body. Tighten the switch body carefully.

FRONT SUSPENSION

MacPherson Strut

REMOVAL AND INSTALLATION

1. Raise the vehicle and support it safely. Remove the front wheels. Detach the brake hose bracket at the strut.
2. Remove the nuts securing the strut to the fender well.
3. Unbolt the strut lower end from the knuckle.
4. Remove the strut from the vehicle.

To install:

5. Reposition the strut and tighten the bolts. Install the brake assembly. Observe the following torques:

Strut-to-knuckle bolts to 80-94 ft. lbs. (110-130 Nm) for Elantra.

Strut-to-knuckle bolts to 55-65 ft. lbs. (75-88 Nm) for Excel.

Strut-to-knuckle bolts to 65-76 ft. lbs. (88-103 Nm) for Sonata.

Strut-to-knuckle bolts to 54-64 ft. lbs. (74-87 Nm) for Scoupe.

Strut-to-fenderwell nuts to 25-33 ft. lbs. (35-45 Nm) for Elantra.

Strut-to-fenderwell nuts to 7-11 ft. lbs. (10-15 Nm) for Excel.

Strut-to-fenderwell nuts to 18-25 ft. lbs. (25-34 Nm) for Sonata.

Strut-to-fenderwell nuts to 11-14 ft. lbs. (15-19 Nm) for Scoupe.

Lower Ball Joints

INSPECTION

Raise the vehicle and support it safely. Disconnect the ball joint at the lower end of the strut. Install the nut back onto the ball stud. Then, with an inch lbs. torque wrench, measure the torque required to start the ball joint rotating. The figures are 1.4-7.0 ft. lbs. (2.0-9.5 Nm). If the figures are within specification, the ball joint is satisfactory. If the figure is too high, the joint should be replaced. If the figure is too low, reuse the joint, provided its rotation is smooth and even. If there is roughness or play, it must be replaced. Inspect the dust cover for cracks and check all bolts for straightness and replace any damaged components.

REMOVAL AND INSTALLATION

Elantra

1. Raise the vehicle and support it safely.
2. Unbolt the ball joint from the control arm and using the special tool 09568-31000 or equivalent, disconnect the lower arm ball joint from the control arm.
3. Remove the stabilizer bar link self-locking nut and detach the stabilizer bar from the lower control arm.
4. Remove the ball joint mounting bolts and remove the joint from the arm.
5. Remove the dust cover from the ball joint.

To install:

6. Park the specified grease in the new dust cover and press the cover to the ball joint using cup driver tool 09545-21100 or equivalent.
7. Install the joint to the lower arm. Tighten the ball joint mounting bolts.
8. Connect the ball joint to the steering knuckle and tighten the nut to 52 ft. lbs. (72 Nm).
9. Connect the stabilizer bar to the lower control arm and tighten the bar link self-locking nut to 40 ft. lbs. (55 Nm).
10. Install the tire and wheel assembly to the vehicle.

Excel and Scoupe

1. Raise the vehicle and support it safely.
2. Unbolt the ball joint from the control arm.
3. Remove the stud retaining nut.
4. Use a ball joint removing tool and separate the ball joint from the steering knuckle.
5. Replace the ball joint and tighten the ball joint to control arm nut to 69-87 ft. lbs. (99-118 Nm). Torque the ball joint stud nut 43-52 ft. lbs. (59-71 Nm).

Sonata

1. Raise the vehicle and support it safely. Remove the tire and wheel assemblies.
2. Remove the lower control arm from the vehicle.
3. Remove the ball joint dust cover. Using a special tool, press the ball joint from the control arm.

To install:

4. Apply grease to the lip of the control arm and to the ball joint contact surfaces.
5. Place the ball joint in the control arm. Using a special tool, press the ball joint into the control arm. The ball joint must be pressed evenly into the control arm.
6. Install a new dust cover on the ball joint. Install the control arm assembly into the vehicle. Torque the ball joint-to-steering knuckle retaining nut to 52 ft. lbs. (71 Nm).
7. Install the wheel and tire assembly. Lower the vehicle.

Lower Control Arms

REMOVAL AND INSTALLATION

Elantra and 1991-94 Excel

1. Raise the vehicle and support it safely. Remove the front tire and wheel assembly.
2. Unbolt the ball joint from the control arm and using the special tool 09568-31000 or equivalent, disconnect the lower arm ball joint from the control arm.
3. Remove the stabilizer bar link self-locking nut and detach the stabilizer bar from the lower control arm.
4. Remove the lower arm mounting bolts and nuts and remove the arm from the vehicle.
5. Installation is the reverse of the removal procedure. Torque the lower arm retainer clamp mounting bolts on both models, to 43-58 ft. lbs. (60-80 Nm) and the inner through bolt and nut on Elantra to 69-87 ft. lbs. (95-120 Nm). On Excel, tighten the lower arm mounting shaft bolts to 116-137 ft. lbs. (160-190 Nm).

1990 Excel

1. Raise the vehicle and support it safely. Remove the front wheel and tire assembly.
2. Remove the undercover.
3. Disconnect the stabilizer bar from the lower arm. Remove the nut from under the control arm and take off the washer and spacer.
4. Remove the ball joint stud nut and press the tool off with tool MB991113 or equivalent.
5. Remove the bolts which retain the spacer at the rear and the nut and washers on the front of the lower arm shaft (at the front). Slide the arm forward, off the shaft and out of the bushing.
6. Replace the dust cover on the ball joint. The new cover must be greased on the lip and inside with 2 EP multi-purpose grease or equivalent, and pressed on, with special tool MB990800 or equivalent, until it is fully seated.

To install:

7. When installing the control arm, the nut on the stabilizer bar bolt must be torqued until the link shows 0.8-0.9 in. (21-23mm) of threads below the bottom of the nut.

8. The washer for the lower arm must be installed as shown. The left side arm shaft has a left hand thread.

9. Torque the all fasteners with the vehicle on the ground. Observe the following torques:

Knuckle-to-strut bolts to 54-65 ft. lbs. (75-88 Nm)

Lower arm shaft-to-body bolts to 69-87 ft. lbs. (94-120 Nm)

Stabilizer bar-to-body bolts to 22-29 ft. lbs. (29-38 Nm)

Stabilizer bar-to-strut bar bolts to 48-60 inch lbs. (5-7 Nm)

Ball joint-to-knuckle bolts to 44-53 ft. lbs. (60-73 Nm)

Lower arm-to-strut bar bolts to 70-88 ft. lbs. (95-120 Nm)

Strut bar-to-body bolts to 55-60 ft. lbs. (75-81 Nm)

Strut bar inner locknut to 55-60 ft. lbs. (75-81 Nm)

Scoupe

1. Disconnect the negative battery cable. Raise the vehicle and safely support.

2. Using a ball joint separator, disconnect the lower ball joint from the knuckle.

3. Remove the stabilizer bar mounting bolt, nut and bar.

4. Remove the lower arm bracket and remove the lower arm.

5. Inspect the arm for cracks, bushings for deterioration and boot damage.

6. There should be no vertical play in the ball joint.

To install:

7. Install the control arm. Loosely attach all hardware to the control arm.

8. Do not tighten the control bushing nuts before the suspension is loaded. Torque the ball joint to 43-52 ft. lbs. (59-71 Nm), lower arm mounting shaft to 116-137 ft. lbs. (157-187 Nm) and the stabilizer shaft nut to 43-58 ft. lbs. (59-78 Nm).

9. Load the suspension and torque the lower bushing nuts to 69-87 ft. lbs. (93-117 Nm).

Sonata

1. Raise the vehicle and support it safely.

2. Loosen the ball joint nut and, using special tool 09568-3100 or equivalent. Disconnect the joint from the knuckle. Be sure to secure the tool's cord to a nearby part.

3. Once the ball joint is free, remove the nut.

4. Remove the stabilizer bar.

5. Remove the control arm-to-crossmember bolt.

To install:

6. Installation is the reverse of removal. Torque the control arm-to-crossmember bolt to 70-87 ft. lbs. (95-110 Nm). Install the stabilizer bar link nut until 5-7mm of threads show beneath the nut. Torque the ball joint stud nut to 50 ft. lbs. (68 Nm).

Scoupe

1. Raise and safely support the vehicle.

2. Remove the tire and wheel assembly.

3. Using special tool 09545-21000 or equivalent, disconnect the lower arm ball joint from the knuckle.

4. Remove the stabilizer bar mounting bolt and nut and detach the stabilizer bar from the lower arm.

5. Detach the lower arm bracket. Remove the lower arm mounting shaft bolts and separate.

6. Remove the lower arm.

7. Install the lower control arm by reversing the removal procedure observing the following torque values:

Lower arm shaft-to-body bolts to 69-87 ft. lbs. (95-115 Nm)

Lower arm rear bushing bracket-to-body bolts to 43-58 ft. lbs. (60-79 Nm)

Stabilizer bar-to-body bolts to 12-19 ft. lbs. (16-26 Nm)

Ball joint-to-knuckle bolts to 43-52 ft. lbs. (60-70 Nm)

Ball joint-to-lower arm nut to 69-87 ft. lbs. (94-115 Nm)

Stabilizer Bar

REMOVAL AND INSTALLATION

Elantra

1. Raise the vehicle and support it safely.

2. Disconnect and separate the tie rod end and the ball joint from the lower control arm and the steering knuckle.

3. Remove the stabilizer link self locking nut using a 14mm spanner wrench.

4. Remove the stabilizer bar through the access opening. Detach the upper and the lower fixtures; then remove the bushings.

To install:

5. Install the bushings onto the bar. Align the upper and the lower

fixtures with the bushings making sure the projections are securely in the space between the fixtures.

NOTE: Distinguish the side the fixtures are to be installed by locating the identification marks stamped on each; R will denote the right side and L will denote the left side fixture. They are not the same and should be installed as labeled.

6. Using the access opening, install the rod to the vehicle. Temporarily tighten the bushing fixtures.

7. Tighten the stabilizer bar link with a spanner wrench and install the self-locking nut tighten to 51 ft. lbs. (70 Nm).

8. Connect the tie rod end and the ball joint to the steering knuckle and control arm tightening the ball joint stud nut to 52 ft. lbs. (72 Nm).

9. Install the tire and wheel assembly and lower the vehicle.

Excel

1. Raise the vehicle and support it safely.

2. Unbolt the stabilizer clamps from the crossmember.

3. Unbolt the stabilizer bar from the strut bar.

4. Examine the bushings for cracks and wear, if one is worn or cracked all the bushings must be replaced.

5. Installation is the reverse order of the removal procedures. Reposition the stabilizer bar and tighten the chassis clamp bolts to 29 ft. lbs. (39 Nm); the strut bar clamps to 50 inch lbs. (6 Nm).

Sonata

1. Raise the vehicle and support it safely.

2. Remove the stabilizer bar brackets from the crossmember.

3. Lower the rear of the center member and lower the stabilizer bar.

4. Disconnect the end links and remove the stabilizer.

5. Installation is the reverse order of the removal procedures. Torque the end link nuts to 45 ft. lbs. (61 Nm); the bracket bolts to 30 ft. lbs. (41 Nm).

Scoupe

1. Raise and safely support the vehicle.

2. Remove the tire and wheel assembly.

3. Disconnect the tie rod end ball joint from the knuckle using special tool 09568-31000 or equivalent.

4. Remove the rear roll stopper mounting bolt and rear roll bracket assembly mounting bolt.

5. Pull the rear roll bracket assembly forward.

6. Loosen the stabilizer link bolt and nut, then separate the stabilizer bar from the lower arm.

7. Loosen the stabilizer bar mounting bolts through the steering gear box access opening provided on the vehicle body.

8. Remove the stabilizer through the access opening.

9. Detach the upper and lower bracket, then remove the bushing.

10. Install the stabilizer bar by reversing the removal procedure, observing the following torque values:

Stabilizer bar bracket bolts to 12-19 ft. lbs. (15-26 Nm).

Ball joint-to-knuckle to 43-52 ft. lbs. (58-70 Nm).

Strut Bar

REMOVAL AND INSTALLATION

Excel

1. Raise the vehicle and support it safely.

2. Unbolt the stabilizer bar from the strut bar.

3. Remove the bolts securing the strut bar to the control arm.

4. Remove the strut bar-to-frame bracket outer nut and pull the bar from the bracket.

5. Inspect all parts and replace any cracked, dry or deformed parts. The strut bar bend must not exceed 0.19 in. (3mm) over its entire length.

To install:

NOTE: The left side bar is identified with a dab of white paint.

6. When installing the strut bar at the strut bar bracket, the distance between the inner locknut and the end of the strut bar must be 80.5mm.

7. Torque the stabilizer bar-to-strut bar clamp bolts to 50 inch lbs. (5.5 Nm); the strut bar-to-control arm bolts to 87 ft. lbs. (120 Nm); the strut bar-to-bracket nut to 60 ft. lbs. (81 Nm).

REAR SUSPENSION

Shock Absorbers

REMOVAL AND INSTALLATION

Elantra

1. Raise the vehicle and support it safely. Remove the wheel.

2. Remove the trim cover inside the rear compartment for access to the top mounting nuts.

3. Support the lower arm with a jack and compress the coil spring. Remove the lower mounting nut.

4. Remove the cap from the upper end of the shock.

5. Remove the upper mounting nut and the shock from the vehicle.

To install:

6. Install the shock absorber to the lower arm, install the lower nut and tighten to 72 ft. lbs. (100 Nm).

7. Install the upper nut and torque to 33 ft. lbs. (45 Nm).

8. Install the cap and cover.

9. Lower the arm and remove the jack.

Excel and Scoupe

1. Remove the wheel cover. Loosen the lug nuts.

2. Raise the vehicle and support it safely. Remove the wheel.

3. Remove the upper mounting bolt or nut.

4. While holding the bottom stud mount nut with one wrench, remove the locknut with another wrench, or on some vehicles, remove the nut and bolt from the mounting bracket.

5. Remove the shock absorber.

6. Check the shock for:

a. Excessive oil leakage, some minor weeping is permissible

b. Bent center rod, damaged outer case, or other defects

c. Pump the shock absorber several times. If it offers even resistance on full strokes it may be considered serviceable.

To install:

7. Install the upper shock mounting nut and bolt. Hand-tighten the nut.

8. Install the bottom eye of the shock over the spring stud or into the mounting bracket and insert the bolt and nut. Tighten the nut to 47-58 ft. lbs. (64-78 Nm).

9. Tighten the upper fasteners to 47-58 ft. lbs. (64-78 Nm).

Sonata

1. Raise the vehicle and support it safely. Allow the lower arms and suspension to hang. Remove the wheels.

2. Place a block of wood on a floor jack and position the jack under the axle beam. Raise the axle slightly to relax the strut and to support the axle when the strut is removed. Position an additional support under the axle.

3. Take care in jacking that no contact is made on the lateral rod.

4. Remove the upper dust cover cap from the strut assembly.

5. Remove the upper mounting nuts. Remove the lower mounting bolt and nut.

6. Remove the strut.

7. Installation is the reverse order of the removal procedures. Torque the lower mounting bolt and nut to 58-72 ft. lbs. (79-96 Nm); the upper mounting nuts to 18-25 ft. lbs. (25-34 Nm).

Coil Springs

REMOVAL AND INSTALLATION

Elantra

1. Raise the vehicle and support it safely. Remove the wheel.

2. Remove the trim cover inside the rear compartment for access to the top mounting nuts.

3. Support the lower arm with a jack and compress the coil spring. Remove the lower mounting nut.

4. Remove the cap from the upper end of the shock.

5. Remove the upper mounting nut and the shock from the vehicle.

6. Compress the spring on the shock using spring compressor 09546-11000 or equivalent. Remove the piston rod tightening nut at the top of the strut while holding the piston rod with a wrench.

7. Disassemble the upped dust cover, bushing, pad, bracket and cup assembly taking note of positioning to assure correct installation. Remove the spring from the shock absorber.

To install:

8. Install the compressed spring to the shock absorber assembly and install the bump rubber, cup assembly, upper bushing, upper spring pad, collar, bracket assembly, upper bushing, washer and self-locking nut to the shock absorber in that order. Make sure the components are in the same orientation as was prior to removal.

9. Tighten the upper rod nut to 14-22 ft. lbs. (20-30 Nm).

10. Remove the spring compressor tool.

11. Install the shock absorber to the lower arm, install the lower mounting nut and tighten to 72 ft. lbs. (100 Nm).

12. Install the upper nut and torque to 33 ft. lbs. (45 Nm).

13. Install the cap and cover.

14. Lower the arm and remove the jack.

Excel and Scoupe

1. Raise the vehicle and support it safely. Remove the rear wheels.

2. Support the rear suspension arm with a floor jack. Then, remove the lower shock absorber attaching bolt, nut and lock washer.

3. Slowly, lower the jack just to the point where the spring can be removed and remove the spring. If the spring is being replaced, transfer the spring seat to the new spring.
To install:

4. When installing the coil spring, make sure the smaller diameter is upward. Make sure the spring identification and load markings match up.

5. Torque the lower shock mounting nut/bolt to 47-58 ft. lbs. (64-78 Nm).

Rear Suspension Arms

REMOVAL AND INSTALLATION

Excel and Scoupe

1. Raise the vehicle and support it safely.

2. Remove the rear wheels.

3. Remove the brake drums and brake shoes.

4. Remove the muffler assembly.

5. Raise the suspension arm assembly slightly and keep in this position.

6. Disconnect the parking brake cable from the arm.

7. Remove the shock absorber.

8. Disconnect the brake hoses from their clips on the suspension members.

9. Lower the suspension slightly and carefully remove the coil spring.

10. Remove the rear suspension from the vehicle as an assembly.

11. Before removing any fixtures from the suspension arm matchmark all parts for assembly reference; this is extremely important! If equipped with stabilizer bars, make a mark on the bar in line with the punch mark on the bracket.

12. Remove the dust cover clamp.

13. Remove the nuts securing the control arms and pull them apart. Leave the dust cover attached to the right arm.

14. Remove the rubber stopper from the right arm.

15. Using a flat blade chisel, drive bushing from the right arm.

16. Using a brass drift, drive bushing out from the left arm.

17. Coat the inside of the left arm and the outside of the bushing with chassis lube and drive it into place with driver tools 09555-21100 and 09555-21000 or equivalent. Drive the bushing in until the notch on 09555-21000 or equivalent, reaches the end of the arm.

18. Coat the inside of the arm and the outside of the bushing with chassis lube and drive it into the arm until it is fully seated.

19. Install the dust cover to the center position of the right arm, about 400mm.

20. Apply chassis lube to the surface of the right arm and install the rubber stopper.

21. Align all matchmarks, including the stabilizer bar and slowly push the suspension halves together.

22. Install all remaining bushing, washers and attaching parts.

NOTE: The toothed sides of the washers face the bushings.

23. Install the end nuts and torque them loosely at this time.
To install:

24. Raise the assembly into position and torque the suspension-to-body bolts to 50 ft. lbs. (68 Nm).

25. Install the coil springs and loosely install the shock absorbers.

26. Install the rear brake assembly and related components.

27. Attach the parking brake cable and brake hoses to their clips on the suspension arm.

28. Install the tire and wheel assemblies.

29. Lower the vehicle and tighten the suspension arm end nuts to 65-80 ft. lbs. (88-108 Nm) for Scoupe, 65-80 ft. lbs. (88-108 Nm) for 1990-91 Excel or 94-108 ft. lbs. for 1992-94 Excel. Tighten the shock mounting bolts to 47-58 ft. lbs. (63-79 Nm).

30. Adjust the rear brake shoe clearance.

Elantra

1. Raise the vehicle and support it safely.

2. Support the rear torsion axle.

3. Remove the lateral rod assembly from the inner body mount and tie the rod to the axle beam using wire.

4. Remove the brake drums and brake shoes. Disconnect the brake line from the wheel cylinder and cap closed. Disconnect the parking brake cables and remove the brake backing plate from the rear hub.

5. Using a floor jack, support the slightly raise the rear torsion axle and arm assembly.

6. Remove the shock absorber lower mounting bolt. Using the floor jack, lower the arm enough to separate the shock from the trailing arm.

7. Remove the trailing arm mounting bolts and the arm from the vehicle.
To install:

8. Install the trailing arm to the vehicle and secure in place with mounting bolts. Tightened to 94-108 ft. lbs. (100-120 Nm) once weight of the vehicle is applied to the rear suspension. Install the shock absorber.

9. Attach the lateral rod to the inner mount and tighten bolt to 58-72 ft. lbs. (80-100 Nm).

10. Install the backing plate, brake lines and related components. Torque the rear wheel bearing nut to and check the end-play of the bearing. Install the hub nut cap after filling with multi-purpose grease.

11. Install the tire and wheel assembly, adjust the rear brake shoes and bleed the brake system.

Sonata

1. Raise and safely support the vehicle.

2. Support the rear torsion axle assembly using floor jack or equivalent.

3. Disconnect the lateral rod at the axle and support aside. Remove the lower shock attaching bolts.

4. Remove the tire and wheel assemblies.

5. If equipped with drum brakes, remove the brake drums, brake shoes and hubs. Disconnect the brake fluid lines to the wheel cylinders and cap closed.

6. If equipped with rear disc brakes, remove the caliper assemblies and brake pads. Support the calipers out of the way using wire. Take care not to twist the brake hoses or lines.

7. Disconnect the parking brake cables.

8. Remove the trailing arm mounting bolts and lower the assembly from the vehicle.
To install:

9. Install the trailing arm assembly to the vehicle and secure using

the mounting hardware. Once weight of the vehicle is on the rear suspension, torque the trailing arm-to-frame mounting bolts to 72-87 ft. lbs. (96-120 Nm), and the trailing arm-to-torsion axle to 72-87 ft. lbs. (100-120 Nm).

10. Connect the parking brake cables.

11. If equipped with rear disc brakes, install the caliper assemblies and brake pads. Take care not to twist the brake hoses or lines during installation.

12. If equipped with drum brakes, install the brake drums, brake shoes and hubs. Connect the brake fluid lines to the wheel cylinders.

13. Install the tire and wheel assemblies.

14. Connect the lateral rod to the axle and tighten fasteners to 58-72 ft. lbs. (80-100 Nm).

15. Install the lower shock attaching bolts and tighten to 58-72 ft. lbs. (80-100 Nm).

16. Bleed the brake system if any brake fluid lines were opened. Adjust the rear brake shoes, if equipped with drum brakes.

Lateral Rod

REMOVAL AND INSTALLATION

Elantra and Sonata

1. Raise the vehicle and support it safely.

2. Disconnect the rod at each end and remove it from the vehicle.

3. Install the bar to the vehicle with the same orientation as prior to removal.

4. Install the bar retainer bolts and nuts at each end to hold bar in place. Do not apply final torque to the fasteners at this time.

5. Lower the vehicle so the weight of the car is resting on the suspension and torque the nuts to 58-72 ft. lbs. (78-97 Nm).

Rear Wheel Bearings

REMOVAL AND INSTALLATION

NOTE: Sodium-based grease is not compatible with lithium-based grease. If there is any doubt as to the type of grease used, completely clean the old grease from the bearing and hub before replacing.

Elantra

1. Safely raise and support the rear of the vehicle. Remove the tire and wheel assembly.

2. Remove the grease cap, axle shaft nut and washer.

3. Pull outward on the brake drum slightly to remove the outer wheel bearing.

4. Slide the drum down the spindle and remove from the vehicle.

5. Pry the inner grease seal from the rear hub of the drum and discard.

6. Remove the inner wheel bearing. If the bearings are being replaced, drive the bearing races from the hub taking care not to damage the inner surface of the drum.

To install:

7. Coat the new races with EP lithium wheel bearing grease and drive them into the hub, making sure they are fully and squarely seated.

8. Pack the hub cavity with new EP lithium wheel bearing grease.

9. Install the inner bearing and drive a new grease seal into place. Make sure to pack the bearings completely with grease prior to installing into the drum.

10. Before installing the rear drum assembly, inspect the rear bearing nut as follows:

   a. Thread the wheel nut onto the spindle until it gap between the shoulder of the spindle and the nut is 0.07-0.11 in. (2.0-3.0mm).

   b. Measure the torque required to rotate the rear wheel bearing nut while turning counterclockwise. The limit is 48 inch lbs. (5.5 Nm). If torque is less than the limit, replace the nut.

11. Install the brake drum and bearing assembly onto the spindle and install the outer bearing and shaft nut. Tighten the nut to 108-145 ft. lbs. (150-200 Nm).

12. Check for correct bearing endplay by placing a dial indicator on the hub surface and moving the hub outward. Note the movement of the gauge and compare to the desired reading of 0.008 in. or less (0.2mm or less). If end-play exceeds the desired reading, retighten the rear hub bearing nut and recheck end-play. If reading is still excessive, replace the hub unit.

13. If end-play is correct, check the starting torque by attaching a spring balance to the hub lug bolts and pulling at a 90 degree angle while noting the required force to turn the hub. If the torque required is above the desired reading of 4.9 lbs. (2.2 Kg) or less, loosen the nut and again tighten to the desired torque. Recheck the

starting torque. If torque is still above the desired reading, replace the rear bearings.

14. Install the tire and wheel assembly and lower the vehicle. Prior to moving the vehicle, pump the brakes until a firm pedal is obtained.

Excel

1. Safely raise and support the rear of the vehicle. Remove the tire and wheel assembly.

2. Remove the grease cap, cotter pin, serrated nut cap, axle shaft nut and washer from the spindle as equipped.

3. Pull outward on the brake drum slightly to remove the outer wheel bearing.

4. Slide the drum down the spindle and remove assembly from the vehicle.

5. Pry the inner grease seal from the rear hub of the drum and discard.

6. Remove the inner wheel bearing. If the bearings are being replaced, drive the bearing races from the hub taking care not to damage the inner surface of the drum.

To install:

7. Coat the new races with EP lithium wheel bearing grease and drive them into the hub, making sure they are fully and squarely seated.

8. Pack the hub cavity with new EP lithium wheel bearing grease.

9. Install the inner bearing and drive a new grease seal into place. Make sure to pack the bearings completely with grease prior to installing into the drum.

10. Install the brake drum onto the spindle. Install the outer bearing, washer and shaft nut onto spindle.

11. On 1990 vehicles equipped with castellated nut and cotter pin, torque the bearing nut to 15 ft. lbs. (20 Nm) while turning the drum. Back off the nut until it is loose, then torque it to 48 inch lbs. (5.4 Nm). Install the serrated nut cap and a new cotter pin. If the cotter pin holes have to be re-aligned, back off the nut no more than 15 degrees; if not, repeat the adjustment procedure.

12. On 1991-94 vehicles equipped with bearing locknut, install and tighten bearing locknut as follows:

   a. Prior to installation, inspect the rear bearing nut by threading the nut onto the spindle until the distance between the shoulder of the spindle and the inner flat on the nut is 0.07-0.11 in. (2.0-3.0mm).

   b. Measure the torque required to rotate the rear wheel bearing locknut while turning counterclockwise. The limit is 48 ft. lbs. (5.5 Nm). If required torque is less than the limit, replace the nut.

c. Install the brake drum and outer bearing onto the spindle. Install and torque the nut to 108-145 ft. lbs. (147-196 Nm).

d. Check for correct bearing end-play by placing a dial indicator on the hub surface and moving the drum outward. Note the movement of the gauge and compare to the desired reading of 0.0043 in. (0.11mm) or less. If end-play exceeds the desired reading, retighten the rear hub bearing nut and recheck end-play. If reading is still excessive, replace the hub unit.

e. If end-play is correct, check the starting torque by attaching a spring balance to the hub lug bolts and pulling at a 90 degree angle while noting the required force to turn the hub. If the torque required is above the desired reading of 4.9 lbs. (2.2 Kg) or less, loosen the nut and again tighten to the desired torque. Recheck the starting torque. If torque is still above the desired reading, replace the rear bearings.

f. After final tightening the wheel bearing nut, align with the spindle's indentation and crimp the edge of the nut to swedge in position.

13. Install the tire and wheel assembly and lower the vehicle. Prior to moving the vehicle, pump the brakes until a firm pedal is obtained.

Scoupe

1. Safely raise and support the rear of the vehicle. Remove the tire and wheel assembly.

2. Remove the grease cap, axle shaft nut and washer.

3. Pull outward on the brake drum slightly to remove the outer wheel bearing.

4. Slide the drum down the spindle and remove from the vehicle.

5. Pry the inner grease seal from the rear hub of the drum and discard.

6. Remove the inner wheel bearing. If the bearings are being replaced, drive the bearing races from the hub taking care not to damage the inner surface of the drum.

To install:

7. Coat the new races with EP lithium wheel bearing grease and drive them into the hub, making sure they are fully and squarely seated.

8. Pack the hub cavity with new EP lithium wheel bearing grease.

9. Install the inner bearing and drive a new grease seal into place. Make sure to pack the bearings completely with grease prior to installing into the drum.

10. Before installing the rear drum assembly, inspect the rear bearing nut as follows:

a. Thread the wheel nut onto the spindle until it gap between the shoulder of the spindle and the nut is 0.07-0.11 in. (2.0-3.0mm).

b. Measure the torque required to rotate the rear wheel bearing nut while turning counterclockwise. The limit is 48 ft. lbs. (5.5 Nm). If torque is less than the limit, replace the nut.

11. Install the brake drum and bearing assembly onto the spindle and install the outer bearing and shaft nut. Tighten the nut to 108-145 ft. lbs. (150-200 Nm).

12. Check for correct bearing end-play by placing a dial indicator on the hub surface and moving the hub outward. Note the movement of the gauge and compare to the desired reading of 0.0043 in. (0.11mm) or less. If end-play exceeds the desired reading, retighten the rear bearing nut and recheck end-play. If reading is still excessive, replace the rear bearings.

13. Once end-play is correct, check the hub and drum starting force by attaching a spring balance to the lug bolts and pulling at a 90 degree angle while noting the required force to turn the drum assembly. If the torque required is above the desired reading of 4.8 lbs. (2 Kg) or less, loosen the nut and again tighten to the desired torque. Recheck the starting torque. If torque is still above the desired reading, replace the rear bearings.

14. After final tightening the wheel bearing nut, align with the spindle's indentation and crimp the edge of the nut to swedge in position.

15. Install the tire and wheel assembly and lower the vehicle. Prior to moving the vehicle, pump the brakes until a firm pedal is obtained.

Sonata

1990-91

NOTE: The rear hub bearing unit cannot be disassembled. If the hub shows signs of wear or damage, replacement of the unit is required.

1. Safely raise and support the rear of the vehicle. Remove the tire and wheel assembly.

2. If equipped with rear disc brakes, remove the brake caliper and support out of the way using wire. Do not disconnect the brake hose from the caliper. Remove the brake rotor. If equipped with drum brakes, remove the brake drum from the hub assembly.

3. Remove the grease cap, cotter pin, serrated nut cap, axle shaft nut and washer from the spindle as equipped.

4. Pull outward on the rear hub assembly slightly to remove the outer wheel bearing.

5. Slide the hub down the spindle and remove assembly from the vehicle.

6. Pry the inner grease seal from the hub and discard.

7. Remove the inner wheel bearing. If the bearings are being replaced, drive the bearing races from the hub taking care not to damage the inner surface of the hub.

To install:

8. Coat the new races with EP lithium wheel bearing grease and drive them into the hub, making sure they are fully and squarely seated.

9. Pack the hub cavity with new EP lithium wheel bearing grease.

10. Install the inner bearing and drive a new grease seal into place. Make sure to pack both bearings completely with grease prior to installing into the hub.

11. Install the hub assembly onto the spindle. Install the outer bearing, washer and shaft nut onto spindle.

12. Torque the bearing nut to 14 ft. lbs. (20 Nm) while turning the hub or drum. Back off the nut until it is loose, then torque it to 7 ft. lbs. (10 Nm). Install the serrated nut cap and a new cotter pin. If the cotter pin holes have to be re-aligned, back off the nut no more than 15 degrees; if not, repeat the adjustment procedure.

13. If equipped with drum brakes, install the brake drum to the hub assembly and adjust the brake shoes as required. If equipped with disc brakes, install the rotor and caliper.

14. Install the tire and wheel assembly and lower the vehicle. Pump the brake pedal to seat the brake pads against the rotors prior to moving the vehicle.

1992-94

NOTE: The rear hub bearing unit cannot be disassembled. If the hub shows signs of wear or damage, replacement of the unit is required.

1. Safely raise and support the rear of the vehicle. Remove the tire and wheel assembly.

2. If equipped with rear disc brakes, remove the brake caliper and support out of the way using wire. Do not disconnect the brake hose from the caliper. Remove the brake rotor. If equipped with drum brakes, remove the brake drum from the hub assembly.

3. Remove the grease cap, wheel bearing nut and washer from the center of the hub bearing unit. Remove the rear hub unit from the vehicle.

To install:

4. Install the rear bearing unit onto the spindle. Install the outer bearing and the tonged washer into the rear hub unit.

NOTE: Press the inner race further until the inner race contacts with the spindle end.

5. Install and tighten the rear wheel bearing nut to 174-217 ft. lbs. (240-300 Nm).

6. Check for correct bearing end play by placing a dial indicator on the hub surface and moving the hub outward. Note the movement of the gauge and compare to the desired reading of 0.004 in. or less (0.01mm or less). If end-play exceeds the desired reading, retighten the rear hub bearing nut and recheck end-play. If reading is still excessive, replace the hub unit.

7. If end-play is correct, check the starting torque by attaching a spring balance to the hub lug bolts and pulling at a 90 degree angle while noting the required force to turn the hub. If the torque required is above the desired reading of 7 lbs. or less (31 N or less), loosen the nut and again tighten to the desired torque. Recheck the starting torque. If torque is still above the desired reading, replace the rear hub bearing unit.

8. After final tightening the wheel bearing nut, align with the spindle's indentation and crimp the edge of the nut to swedge in position.

9. If equipped with rear disc brakes, install the brake disc and caliper to the vehicle. If equipped with drum brakes, install drum to hub assembly.

10. Install the tire and wheel assembly and lower the vehicle. Pump the brake pedal to assure correct brake operation, prior to moving the vehicle.

ADJUSTMENT

Excel

1. Raise the vehicle and support it safely. Remove the rear wheel assembly.

2. Remove dust cover from the hub.

3. On 1990 vehicles equipped with castellated nut and cotter pin, remove the cotter pin and nut cap. Torque the bearing nut to 15 ft. lbs. (20 Nm) while turning the drum. Back off the nut until it is loose, then torque it to 48 inch lbs. Install the serrated nut cap and a new cotter pin. If the cotter pin holes have to be re-aligned, back off the nut no more than 15 degrees; if not, repeat the adjustment procedure.

4. On 1991-94 vehicles equipped with bearing locknut, adjust bearing locknut as follows:

a. Loosen the nut and then torque nut to 108-145 ft. lbs. (147-196 Nm).

b. Check for correct bearing end-play by placing a dial indicator on the hub surface and moving the drum outward. Note the movement of the gauge and compare to the desired reading of 0.0043 in. or less (0.11mm or less). If end-play exceeds the desired reading, retighten the rear hub bearing nut and recheck end-play. If reading is still excessive, replace the hub unit.

c. If end-play is correct, check the starting torque by attaching a spring balance to the hub lug bolts and pulling at a 90 degree angle while noting the required force to turn the hub. If the torque required is above the desired reading of 4.9 lbs. or less (22 N or less), loosen the nut and again tighten to the desired torque. Recheck the starting torque. If torque is still above the desired reading, replace the rear bearings.

d. After final tightening the wheel bearing nut, align with the spindle's indentation and crimp the edge of the nut to swedge in position.

5. Fill the dust cap with grease and install.

6. Install the tire and wheel assembly.

Sonata

1990-91

1. Safely raise and support the rear of the vehicle. Remove the tire and wheel assembly.

2. Remove the grease cap, cotter pin and serrated nut cap.

3. Torque the bearing nut to 14 ft. lbs. (20 Nm) while turning the hub or drum. Back off the nut until it is loose, then torque it to 7 ft. lbs. (10 Nm). Install the serrated nut cap and a new cotter pin. If the cotter pin holes have to be re-aligned, back off the nut no more than 15 degrees; if not, repeat the adjustment procedure.

4. Install the nut lock and a new cotter pin.

5. Install the tire and wheel assembly and lower the vehicle. Pump the brake pedal to seat the brake pads against the rotors prior to moving the vehicle.

1992-94

1. Safely raise and support the rear of the vehicle. Remove the tire and wheel assembly.

2. If equipped with rear disc brakes, remove the brake caliper and support out of the way using wire. Do not disconnect the brake hose from the caliper. Remove the brake rotor. If equipped with drum brakes, remove the brake drum from the hub assembly.

3. Remove the grease cap and loosen the wheel bearing nut.

4. Tighten the rear wheel bearing nut to 174-217 ft. lbs. (240-300 Nm).

5. Check for correct bearing end-play by placing a dial indicator on the hub surface and moving the hub outward. Note the movement of the gauge and compare to the desired reading of 0.004 in. (0.01mm) or less. If end-play exceeds the desired reading, retighten the rear hub bearing nut and recheck end-play. If reading is still excessive, replace the hub unit.

6. If end-play is correct, check the starting torque by attaching a spring balance to the hub lug bolts and pulling at a 90 degree angle while noting the required force to turn the hub. If the torque required is above the desired reading of 7 lbs. (3 Kg), loosen the nut and again tighten to the desired torque. Recheck the starting torque. If torque is still above the desired reading, replace the rear hub bearing unit.

7. After final tightening the wheel bearing nut, align with the spindle's indentation and crimp the edge of the nut to swedge in position.

8. If equipped with rear disc brakes, install the brake disc and caliper to the vehicle. If equipped with drum brakes, install drum to hub assembly.

9. Install the tire and wheel assembly and lower the vehicle. Pump the brake pedal to assure correct brake operation, prior to moving the vehicle.

Elantra

1. Safely raise and support the rear of the vehicle. Remove the tire and wheel assembly.

2. Remove the grease cap and loosen the axle shaft nut.

3. Tighten the nut to 108-145 ft. lbs. (150-200 Nm).

4. Check for correct bearing end-play by placing a dial indicator on the hub surface and moving the hub outward. Note the movement of the gauge and compare to the desired reading of 0.008 in. (0.20mm). If end-play exceeds the desired reading, re-tighten the rear hub bearing nut and recheck end-play. If reading is still excessive, replace the hub unit.

5. If end-play is correct, check the starting torque by attaching a spring balance to the hub lug bolts and pulling at a 90 degree angle while noting the required force to turn the hub. If the torque required is above the desired reading of 4.9 lbs. (2.2 Kg) or less, loosen the nut and again tighten to the desired torque. Recheck the starting torque. If torque is still above the desired reading, replace the rear bearings.

6. Install the tire and wheel assembly and lower the vehicle. Prior to moving the vehicle, pump the brakes until a firm pedal is obtained.

Scoupe

1. Safely raise and support the rear of the vehicle. Remove the tire and wheel assembly.

2. Remove the grease cap and loosen the axle shaft nut.

3. Tighten the nut to 108-145 ft. lbs. (150-200 Nm).

4. Check for correct bearing end-play by placing a dial indicator on the hub surface and moving the hub outward. Note the movement of the gauge and compare to the desired reading of 0.0043 in. (0.11mm) or less. If end-play exceeds the desired reading, retighten the rear bearing nut and recheck end-play. If reading is still excessive, replace the rear bearings.

5. Once end-play is correct, check the hub and drum starting force by attaching a spring balance to the lug bolts and pulling at a 90 degree angle while noting the required force to turn the drum assembly. If the torque required is above the desired

reading of 4.8 lbs. (2.2 Kg) or less, loosen the nut and again tighten to the desired torque. Recheck the starting torque. If torque is still above the desired reading, replace the rear bearings.

6. After final tightening the wheel bearing nut, align with the spindle's indentation and crimp the edge of the nut to swedge in position.

7. Install the tire and wheel assembly and lower the vehicle. Prior to moving the vehicle, pump the brakes until a firm pedal is obtained.

Rear Axle Assembly

REMOVAL AND INSTALLATION

1. Raise and safely support the vehicle. Remove the wheel assemblies.

2. Separate the parking brake cable at the connector and cable housing at the floor pan bracket.

3. Separate the brake line at backing plate.

4. Remove the muffler-to-middle exhaust pipe retaining bolts, remove the O-ring hangers and remove the exhaust system.

5. Remove the lower shock absorber through bolts and disconnect the shock at the axle end.

6. Lower the axle until the spring and isolator assemblies can be removed.

7. Remove the axle assembly from the vehicle.

To install:

8. Using floor jacks, position the rear axle assembly under vehicle.

9. Install the springs and isolators and carefully raise the axle assembly.

10. Install the shock absorber and through bolts, do not tighten.

11. Position brake support to the axle while routing the parking brake cable through the support. Lock it into place.

12. Connect the brake line fitting to the backing wheel cylinder. Torque to 9-12 ft. lbs. (13-17 Nm).

13. Install the hub and drum, if removed.

14. Route the parking brake cable through the fingers in the bracket and lock housing end into the floor pan bracket. Install the cable end into the intermediate connector.

15. Install the exhaust system and hangers. Torque the muffler-to-middle exhaust pipe retaining bolts to 22-29 ft. lbs. (30-40 Nm).

STEERING

Steering Wheel

REMOVAL AND INSTALLATION

Excel and Scoupe

1. Disconnect the negative battery cable. Pull off the horn cover at the center of the wheel by grasping the upper edge for Excel and prying off at the lower edge for Scoupe. Then, disconnect the horn wire connector.

2. Remove the steering wheel retaining nut. Matchmark the relationship between the wheel and shaft.

3. Remove the steering wheel dynamic dampener.

4. Screw the 2 bolts of a steering wheel puller into the wheel. Then, turn the bolt at the center of the puller to force the wheel off the steering shaft. Do not pound on the wheel to remove it or the collapsible steering shaft may be damaged.

To install:

5. The steering wheel can be pushed onto the shaft splines by hand far enough to start the retaining nut. Install the retaining nut and torque it to 26-32 ft. lbs. (34-44 Nm).

Elantra and Sonata

1. Disconnect the negative battery cable.

2. Remove the screws from the back of the horn pad and lift it off.

3. Disconnect the horn wire connector.

4. Pull the dynamic damper forward and off.

5. Remove the steering wheel retaining nut. Matchmark the relationship between the wheel and shaft.

6. Screw the 2 bolts of a steering wheel puller into the wheel. Then, turn the bolt at the center of the puller to force the wheel off the steering shaft. Do not pound on the wheel to remove it or the collapsible steering shaft may be damaged.

To install:

7. Install the steering wheel to the shaft aligning the matchmarks made during removal.

8. Install and tighten the retainer nut to 29-36 ft. lbs. (39-49 Nm).

9. Install the dynamic damper and horn pad to the steering shaft. Make sure to connect the horn wire to the pad prior to installation.

10. Fasten the horn pad to the wheel and reconnect the negative battery cable.

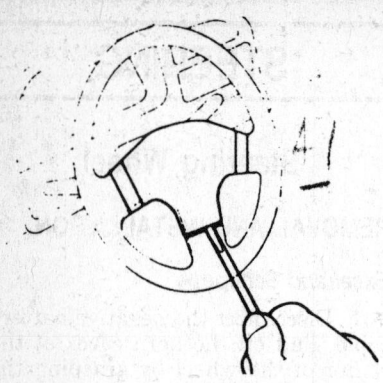

Removing the horn pad — Scoupe

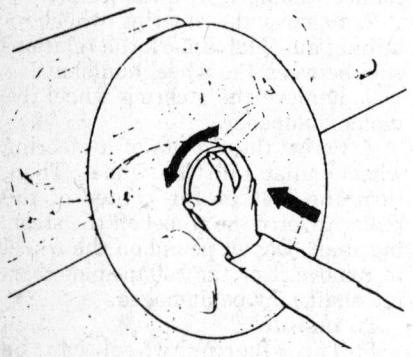

Removing the horn pad — Excel

Manual Rack and Pinion

REMOVAL AND INSTALLATION

Excel and Scoupe

1. Loosen the lug nuts.
2. Raise the vehicle and support it safely.
3. Remove the wheels.
4. Remove the steering shaft-to-pinion coupling bolt.
5. Disconnect the tie rod ends with a separator.

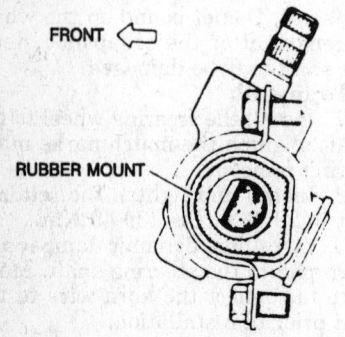

FRONT ⟵

RUBBER MOUNT

Install the rubber rack and pinion mount as shown — Excel

6. Removing the clamps securing the rack to the crossmember and remove the unit from the vehicle. The tie rod ends can now be removed. Use a tie rod puller to pop the tie rod studs from the steering knuckle.
   a. If the tie rod ends are going to be placed, prior to removal, count the exact number of exposed threads on the tie rod ends, then loosen the locknut and unscrew the tie rod end.
   b. When installing new tie rod ends, oil the threads and screw them into place so the previously noted number of threads is visible with the locknut tight.
   c. As a further reference, the distance between the end of the tie rod boot and the centerline of the tie rod ball stud should be 9.6 in. (243.5mm). Torque the locknut to 38 ft. lbs. (52 Nm).

To install:

7. Install the rubber mount for the gear box with the slit on the downside.
8. Observe the following torques:
Rack-to-crossmember bolts to 43-58 ft. lbs. (58-78 Nm).
Coupling bolt to 11-14 ft. lbs. (15-19 Nm)
Tie rod end slotted nuts to 11-25 ft. lbs. (15-34 Nm)

Power Rack and Pinion

ADJUSTMENT

Excel and Scoupe

1. Mount the rack in a soft jawed vise, clamping the vise on the rack mounting areas, only.
2. Using a spline adapter on an inch-pound torque wrench, rotate the pinion shaft several times, lock-to-lock and note the total pinion preload. Preload should be 5-11 inch lbs. (0.6-1.2 Nm).
3. If the preload is note within specifications, adjust the position of the rack support cover and recheck the preload. If it does not work, the rack support cover components are defective.

NOTE: Complete gear replacement with a new or reconditioned unit may be more cost and/or time efficient than repairing the original unit and may reduce the risk of damage or injury due to a part failure. Assessment of the situation may prove to be beneficial.

REMOVAL AND INSTALLATION

Excel and Scoupe

1. Loosen the lug nuts.
2. Raise the vehicle and support it safely.
3. Remove the wheels.
4. Remove the steering shaft-to-pinion coupling bolt.
5. Disconnect the tie rod ends with a separator.
6. Drain the fluid.
7. Disconnect the hoses from the steering gear.
8. Remove the band from the steering joint cover.
9. Unbolt and remove the stabilizer bar.
10. Remove the rear roll stopper-to-center member bolt and move the rear roll stopper forward, as required.
11. Remove the rack unit mounting clamp bolts and take the unit out the left side of the vehicle. The tie rod ends can now be removed. Prior to removal, count the exact number of exposed threads on the tie rod ends, then loosen the locknut and unscrew the tie rod end.

To install:

12. When installing new tie rod ends, oil the threads and screw them into place so the previously noted number of threads is visible with the locknut tight. As a further reference, the distance between the end of the tie rod boot and the point at which the locknut touches the tie rod ball socket body should be 6.1-6.2 in. (155.5-157.5mm) except Scoupe; 6.9-7.0 in. (174.3-176.3mm) for Scoupe. Torque the locknut to 38 ft. lbs. (52 Nm).
13. When installing the power steering rack, make sure the rubber isolators have their nubs aligned with the holes in the clamps.
14. Apply rubber cement to the slits in the gear mounting grommet.
15. Tighten the clamp bolt to 43-58 ft. lbs. (58-78 Nm), the tie rod end slotted nuts to 11-25 ft. lbs. (14-34 Nm) and the coupling bolt to 11-14 ft. lbs. (14-19 Nm).
16. Fill the system with Dexron®II ATF.

Elantra and Sonata

1. Raise the vehicle and support it safely.
2. Remove the wheels.
3. Drain the fluid from the power steering system.
4. Remove the steering shaft-to-pinion coupling bolt.

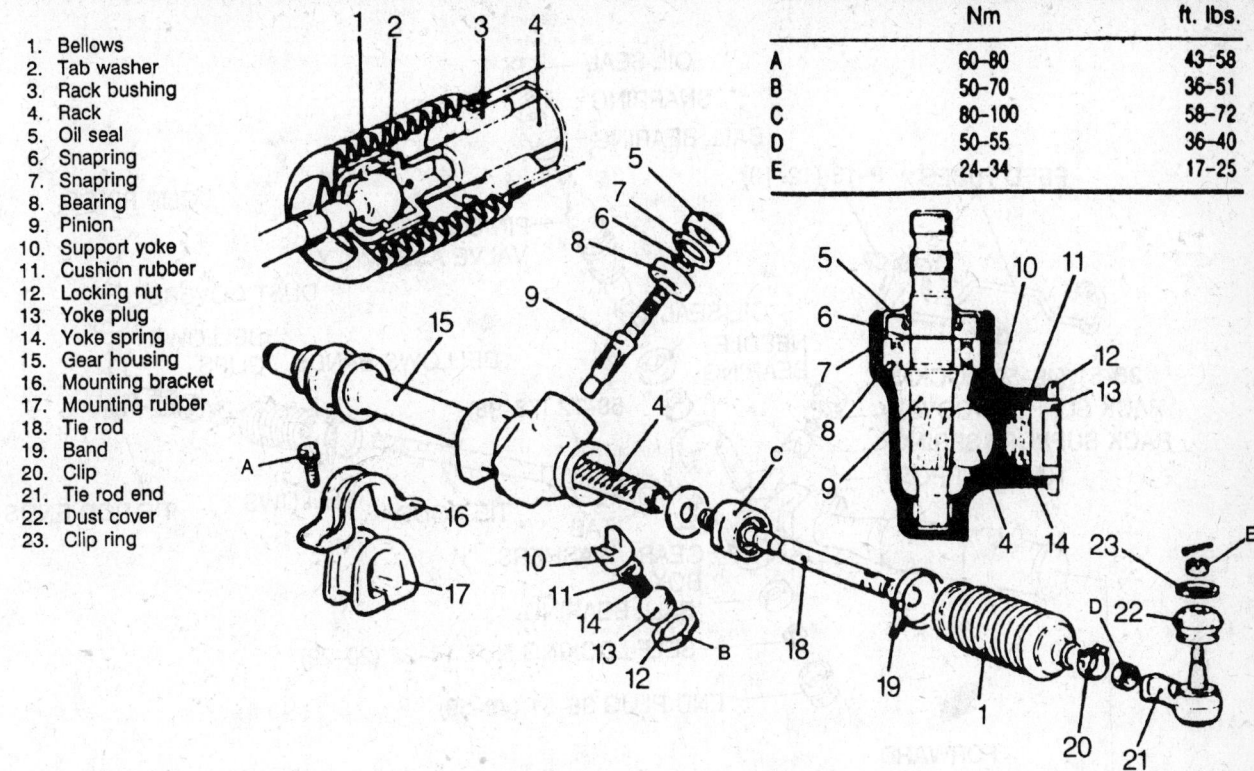

1. Bellows
2. Tab washer
3. Rack bushing
4. Rack
5. Oil seal
6. Snapring
7. Snapring
8. Bearing
9. Pinion
10. Support yoke
11. Cushion rubber
12. Locking nut
13. Yoke plug
14. Yoke spring
15. Gear housing
16. Mounting bracket
17. Mounting rubber
18. Tie rod
19. Band
20. Clip
21. Tie rod end
22. Dust cover
23. Clip ring

	Nm	ft. lbs.
A	60–80	43–58
B	50–70	36–51
C	80–100	58–72
D	50–55	36–40
E	24–34	17–25

Manual rack and pinion steering assembly

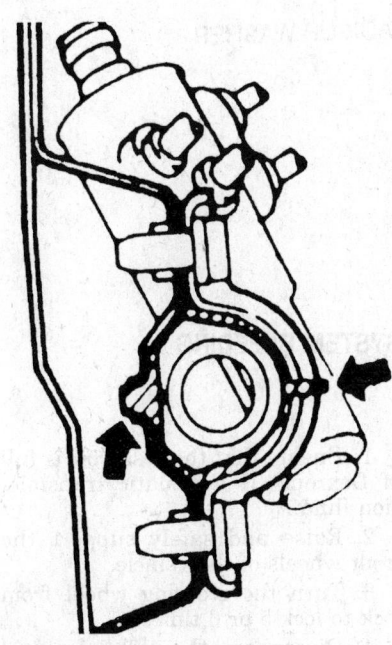

Rubber isolator alignment on the power steering rack — Excel

5. Remove the retainer nut and disconnect both tie rod ends using an appropriate puller.

6. Disconnect the left lower arm from the steering knuckle. This will increase clearance as the gear assembly will be removed from the left side of the vehicle.

7. Disconnect the fluid hoses from the gear box.

8. Remove the center member and temporarily retighten the front muffler.

9. Unbolt and remove the stabilizer bar.

10. Remove the rack unit mounting clamp bolts and move the rack towards the right and then take the unit out on the left side of the vehicle. The tie rod ends can now be removed. Prior to removal, count the exact number of exposed threads on the tie rod ends, then loosen the locknut and unscrew the tie rod end.

To install:

11. When installing new tie rod ends, oil the threads and screw them into place so the previously noted number of threads is visible with the locknut tight. As a further reference, the distance between the end of the tie rod boot and the point at which the locknut touches the tie rod ball socket body should be 7.38 in.

(187.4mm). Torque the locknut to 38 ft. lbs. (52 Nm).

12. When installing the power steering rack, make sure the rubber isolators have their nubs aligned with the holes in the clamps.

13. Apply rubber cement to the slits in the gear mounting grommet. Tighten the clamp bolt to 43-58 ft. lbs. (58-78 Nm), the tie rod nuts to 11-25 ft. lbs. (14-34 Nm) and the coupling bolt to 22-25 ft. lbs. (29-34 Nm).

14. Fill the system with Dexron®II ATF.

Power Steering Pump

REMOVAL AND INSTALLATION

1. Place a drain pan under the pump.

NOTE: In order to prevent alternator contamination due to spilled power steering fluid from the pump, cover the alternator prior to removing any hoses at the pump.

2. Disconnect the pressure hose from the pump.

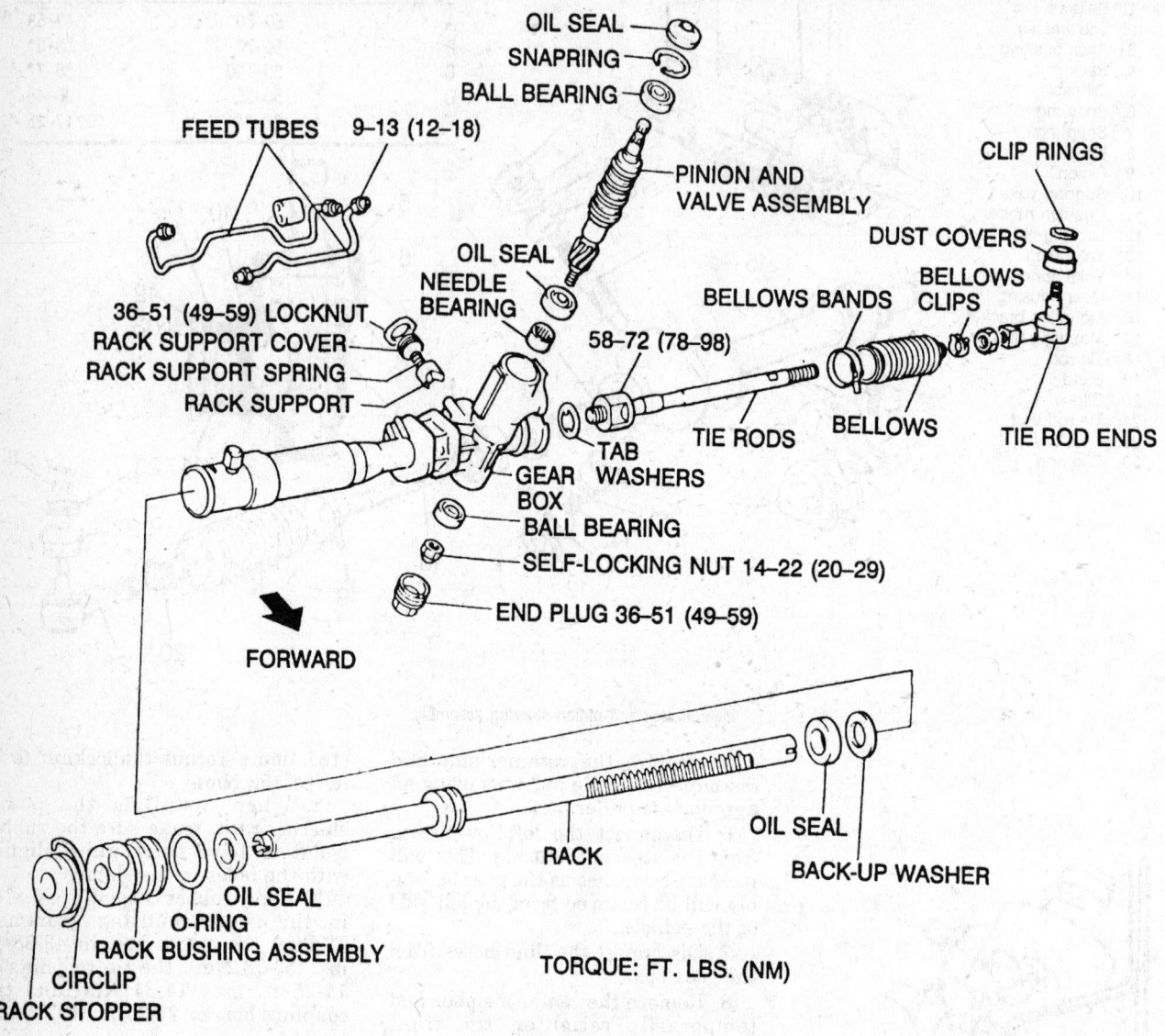

OIL SEAL
SNAPRING
BALL BEARING

FEED TUBES — 9–13 (12–18)

PINION AND VALVE ASSEMBLY

CLIP RINGS
DUST COVERS

OIL SEAL
NEEDLE BEARING

BELLOWS BANDS
BELLOWS CLIPS

36–51 (49–59) LOCKNUT
RACK SUPPORT COVER
RACK SUPPORT SPRING
RACK SUPPORT

58–72 (78–98)

TIE RODS

BELLOWS

TIE ROD ENDS

TAB WASHERS

GEAR BOX
BALL BEARING
SELF-LOCKING NUT 14–22 (20–29)
END PLUG 36–51 (49–59)

FORWARD

OIL SEAL
O-RING
RACK BUSHING ASSEMBLY
CIRCLIP
RACK STOPPER

OIL SEAL

RACK

BACK-UP WASHER

TORQUE: FT. LBS. (NM)

Sonata steering components

3. Disconnect the return hose and the oil pressure switch from the pump.

4. Loosen the pump mounting bolts and remove the drive belt.

5. Remove the pump-to-mounting bracket bolts and lift out the pump.

To install:

6. Install the power steering pump. When installing the return line, push it at least 1.2 in. (30mm) onto the return tube. Fill the system with Dexron®II ATF, start the engine and turn the steering lock-to-lock several times to bleed any trapped air.

BELT ADJUSTMENT

1. Press the V-belt by applying pressure of 22 lbs. (98 N) at the center of the belt.

2. Deflection of the belt should be 0.28-0.39 in. (7-10mm).

3. To adjust the tension of the belt except V6 engine, loosen the oil pump mounting bolts, move the oil pump and then retighten the bolts. On V6 engine, loosen the adjuster mounting bolts, move tensioner to adjust tension and tighten bolts.

SYSTEM BLEEDING

1. Ensure that the reservoir is full of Dexron® II automatic transmission fluid.

2. Raise and safely support the front wheels of the vehicle.

3. Turn the steering wheel from lock to lock 5 or 6 times.

4. Disconnect the coil wire and connect to a solid ground. Operate the starter motor intermittently for 15 to 20 seconds and turn the steer-

ing wheel from lock to lock 5 or 6 times.

NOTE: Ensure that the reservoir is full during air bleeding to prevent the fluid level from falling below the lower position of the filter.

5. Connect the coil wire and start the engine.
6. Turn the steering wheel from lock to lock until no more air bubbles are visible in the reservoir.
7. Confirm that the oil is not milky and that the fluid level is correct.
8. Confirm that there is little change in the fluid level when the steering wheel is turned to the left and right.

NOTE: An abrupt rise in the fluid level after stopping the engine is a sign of incomplete bleeding. If this occurs, repeat the bleeding procedure.

Tie Rod Ends

REMOVAL AND INSTALLATION

1. Raise the vehicle and support it safely. Remove the front wheels.
2. Remove the cotter pin and then remove the ball stud retaining nut. Use a vise-like tool MB991113 or equivalent, to press the ball stud down and out of the steering knuckle.
3. Using a backup wrench on the flats at the inner end of the tie rod end, loosen the nut that retains the end to the tie rod coming out of the steering box. Unscrew the tie rod end, counting the turns required to remove it.
To install:
4. Install the new tie rod end in reverse order. Torque the castellated nut retaining the ball stud to 11-25 ft. lbs. (15-33 Nm). Then, turn it just far enough to align the castellations with the hole in the stud and install a new cotter pin. Torque the inner nut to 36-40 ft. lbs. (49-54 Nm).

BRAKES

Master Cylinder

REMOVAL AND INSTALLATION

1. Disconnect the negative battery cable. Disconnect the fluid level sensor.

2. Disconnect the brake tubes from the master cylinder and cap them immediately.
3. Unbolt and remove the master cylinder from the booster.
To install:
4. Position the master cylinder to the booster and install the mounting bolts. Torque the mounting bolts to 10-16 ft. lbs. (14-22 Nm) for Scoupe or 9 ft. lbs. (12 Nm) for remaining models.
5. Connect the brake tubes to the master cylinder. Torque the tubes to 9-12 ft. lbs. (13-17 Nm).
6. Bleed the brake system. Connect the negative battery cable. Road test the vehicle.

Proportioning Valve

On Excel and Sonata, the proportioning valve is located under the master cylinder on a mounting bracket. On Scoupe and Sonata V6 the proportioning valves are threaded into the master cylinder where the hydraulic fittings connect. It does not require routine check or adjustment.

REMOVAL AND INSTALLATION

1. Disconnect the negative battery cable. Disconnect the brake lines at the valve.

NOTE: Use a flare nut wrench to avoid damage to the lines and fittings.

2. Remove the mounting bolts and remove the valve.

NOTE: If the proportioning valve is found to be defective, it must be replaced.

3. Install the proportioning valve and tighten the mounting bolts to 15 ft. lbs. (20 Nm).
4. Refill the system with fluid and bleed the brakes. Connect the negative battery cable.

Power Brake Booster

REMOVAL AND INSTALLATION

1. Disconnect the negative battery cable. Slide back the clip and disconnect the vacuum supply line at the brake booster. Pull gently in order to avoid damaging the check valve.
2. Remove the master cylinder.
3. Disconnect the pushrod at the brake pedal. This requires pulling the lockpin out of the pedal clevis pin

and then pulling the latter out of the pedal lever and clevis rod.
4. Remove the mounting bolts and nuts from the firewall and remove the booster.
To install:
5. Installation is the reverse of the removal procedures. Install the brake booster on the firewall and tighten the mounting nuts to 10-12 ft. lbs. (13-17 Nm) for Scoupe or 8 ft. lbs. (12 Nm) for the remaining models. Bleed the brake system.

Front Brake Caliper

REMOVAL AND INSTALLATION

1. Raise the vehicle and support safely.
2. Remove the tire and wheel assembly.
3. Remove the caliper mounting pin(s).
4. Lift the caliper off the rotor. Remove the outer pad from the caliper.
5. Remove the brake hose retaining bolt from the caliper.
To install:
6. Install the brake hose to the caliper using new copper washers.
7. Position the caliper over the rotor so the caliper engages the adapter correctly. Install the mounting pin(s). Install the hold-down spring, if equipped.
8. Fill the master cylinder and bleed the brakes.
9. Install the wheel and tire assembly.
10. Lower the vehicle.

Rear Brake Caliper

REMOVAL AND INSTALLATION

SONATA

1. Raise the vehicle and support it safely.
2. Remove the tire and wheel assemblies.
3. Remove the screw which holds the trailing shoe key onto the anchor plate. Bias the caliper assembly against the thin key and slide the trailing shoe outward.
4. Remove both caliper support pins which holds the caliper to the anchor plate. While pressing the caliper assembly against the leading shoe key, swing the front end of the caliper up and past the anchor plate rail. The caliper should be free for removal. Disconnect the brake hose from the caliper, remove the brake

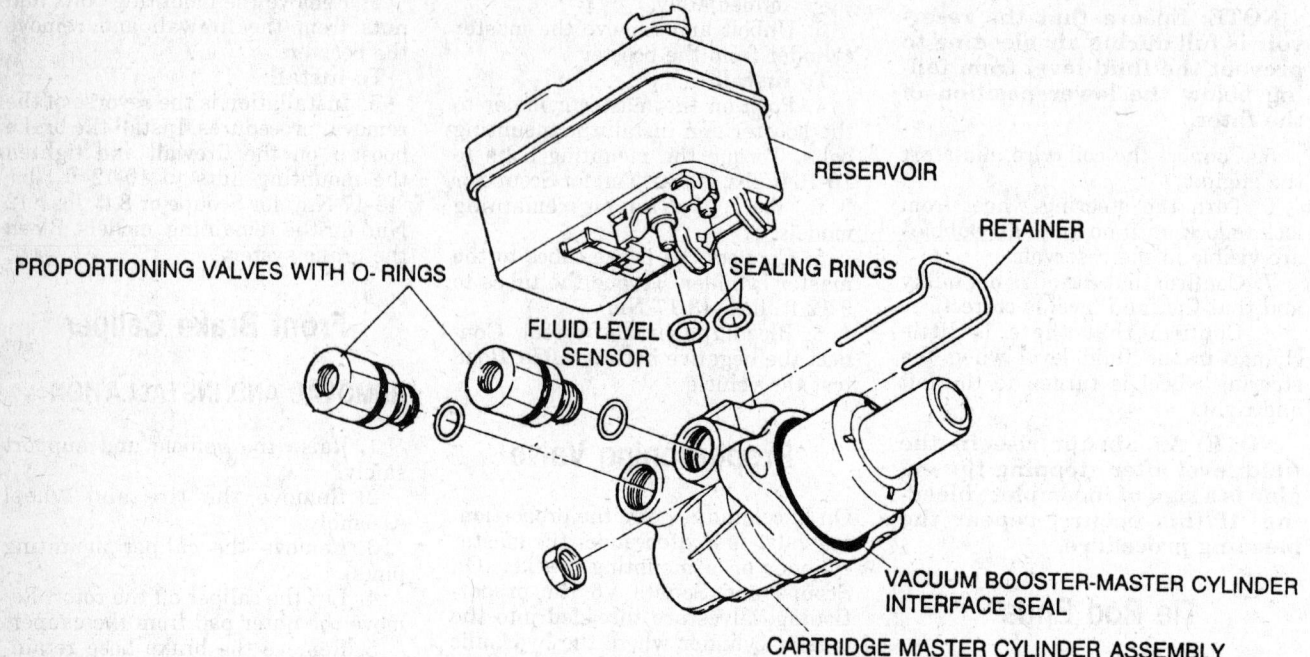

PROPORTIONING VALVES WITH O- RINGS

RESERVOIR

RETAINER

SEALING RINGS

FLUID LEVEL SENSOR

VACUUM BOOSTER-MASTER CYLINDER INTERFACE SEAL

CARTRIDGE MASTER CYLINDER ASSEMBLY

Master cylinder and related components — 1992 Sonata

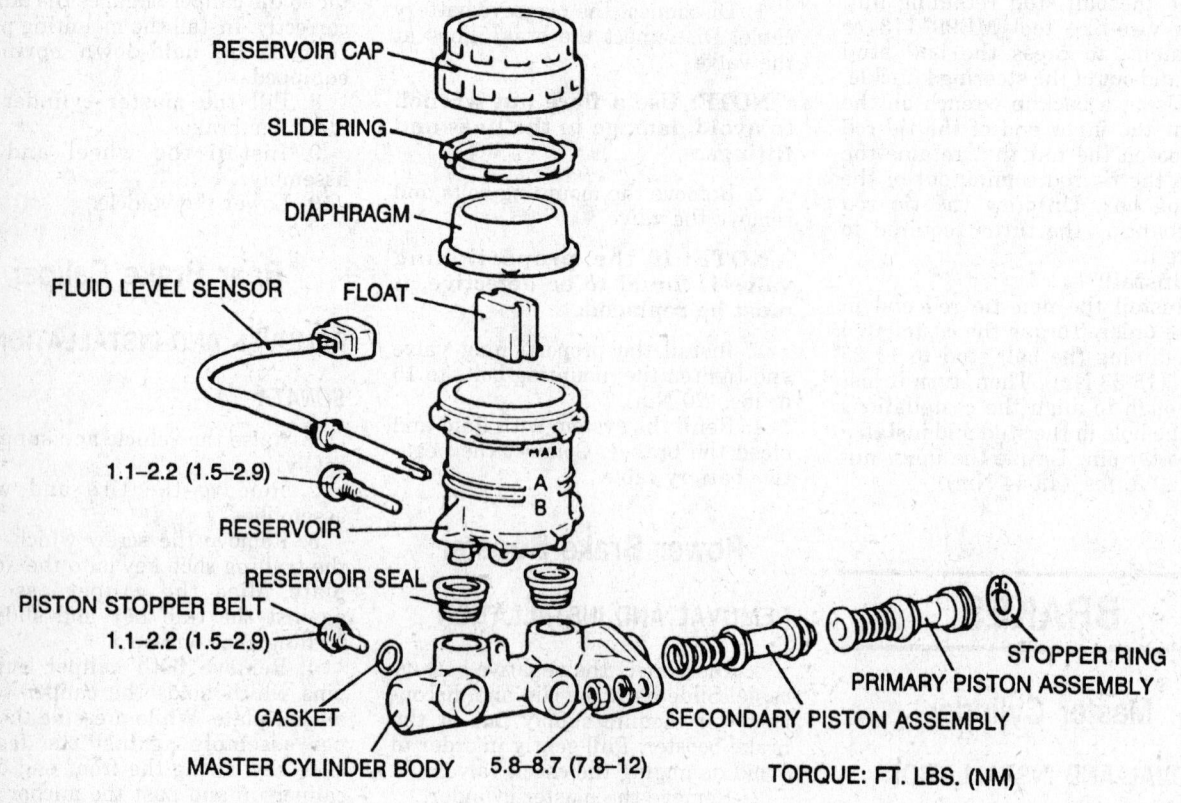

RESERVOIR CAP

SLIDE RING

DIAPHRAGM

FLUID LEVEL SENSOR

FLOAT

1.1–2.2 (1.5–2.9)

RESERVOIR

RESERVOIR SEAL

PISTON STOPPER BELT

1.1–2.2 (1.5–2.9)

GASKET

MASTER CYLINDER BODY

5.8–8.7 (7.8–12)

SECONDARY PISTON ASSEMBLY

PRIMARY PISTON ASSEMBLY

STOPPER RING

TORQUE: FT. LBS. (NM)

Excel master cylinder

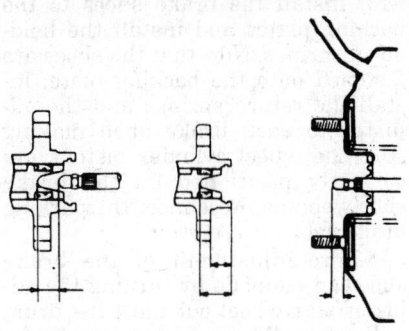

Determining brake booster pushrod clearance

shoes and the caliper from the vehicle.

To install:

5. Install the brake hose to the caliper using new copper gaskets. Position the brake pads into the caliper and install the caliper onto vehicle.

6. Install the bolts and torque to 25 ft. lbs. (34 Nm).

7. Refill the master cylinder, bleed the brake system, install the tire and wheel assemblies and pump the brake pedal until firm.

Front Disc Brake Pads

REMOVAL AND INSTALLATION

Excel and Scoupe

1. Raise the vehicle and support it safely.

2. Remove the front wheels.

3. Pry off the dust shield from the caliper.

4. Depress the center of the outboard spring clip and remove the clip by slipping the ends from the pins.

5. Remove the inboard spring clip with pliers.

6. Using pliers, pull the retaining pins from the caliper.

7. Lift the pads and anti-squeal shims from the caliper.

8. Clean all caliper parts, especially the torque plate shafts, with a solvent made for brake parts.

NOTE: Replace all brake pads at the same time. Never replace the pads on 1 wheel only.

9. If the dust protector or spring clips are weak, damaged or deformed, replace them.

10. Remove the cap from the master cylinder reservoir and, using a clean suction gun, remove about ⅓ of the fluid.

To install:

11. Using a C-clamp, force the caliper piston back into the caliper as far as it will go.

12. Install the inboard pad and anti-squeal shim.

13. Install the outboard pad and anti-squeal shim.

14. Install the pins.

15. Install the spring clips.

16. Install the dust shield.

17. Install the wheels and lower the vehicle.

18. Replenish the brake fluid supply. Depress the brake pedal a few times. The first couple of strokes on the pedal will feel overly long. However, the pads will set themselves and the stroke will return to normal.

19. Check brake fluid level.

Elantra and Sonata

1. Raise the vehicle and support it safely.

2. Remove the front wheel and tire assemblies.

3. Remove the 2 bolts from the torque plate and lift off the caliper. Suspend the caliper safely with wire. Don't stretch the brake hose.

4. Remove the pads and anti-rattle clips from the caliper.

5. Remove the cap from the master cylinder reservoir and siphon off about ⅓ of the fluid.

To install:

6. Using a large C-clamp, press the piston all the way back into the caliper.

7. Install the new pads and clips. Position the pad with the wear sensor on the piston side and upwards.

8. Position the caliper and install the bolts. Torque the bolts to 23 ft. lbs. (32 Nm).

Rear Disc Brake Pads

REMOVAL AND INSTALLATION

Sonata

1. Raise the vehicle and support it safely.

2. Remove the tire and wheel assemblies.

3. Remove the screw which holds the trailing shoe key onto the anchor plate. Push the caliper assembly against the thin key and slide the trailing shoe outward.

4. Remove both caliper support pins which holds the caliper to the anchor plate. While pushing the caliper assembly against the leading shoe key, swing the front end of the caliper up and past the anchor plate

rail. The caliper should be free. Support the caliper using wire making sure not to twist the brake fluid hose during removal.

5. To remove the outer shoe, push the outer shoe inward off the caliper legs. The locator buttons must clear the slots in the housing before the shoe can be removed. Remove the inner shoe by pulling the shoe outward until the shoe clears the piston.

To install:

6. Remove the cap from the master cylinder reservoir and, using a clean suction gun, remove about ⅓ of the fluid. Using a large C-clamp, press the piston all the way back into the caliper.

7. Install the new pads and clips. Position the pad with the wear sensor on the piston side and upwards.

8. Position the caliper and install the bolts. Torque the bolts to 25 ft. lbs. (34 Nm).

9. Refill the master cylinder, install the tire and wheel assemblies and pump the brake pedal until firm.

Brake Rotor

REMOVAL AND INSTALLATION

All Models

1. Remove the center hub cap and halfshaft nut. Then raise the vehicle and support it safely. Allow the wheels to hang freely. Then remove the front wheel.

2. Remove the brake caliper without disconnecting the hydraulic line and suspend it out of the way with a piece of wire.

3. Disconnect the stabilizer bar and strut bar from the lower control arm.

4. Remove the halfshaft from the transaxle and press the halfshaft out of the hub using tool 09526-11001 or equivalent.

5. Unbolt and remove the hub and knuckle from the bottom of the strut and remove the hub and knuckle assembly from the vehicle.

6. Several special tools are required to press the hub and disc from the steering knuckle and to remount them. Use 09517-21600 or equivalent. Do not attempt to hammer the parts apart, or the bearing will be damaged. Install the arm of the special tool then the body onto the knuckle and tighten the nut manually. Using special tool 09517-21500, separate the hub from the knuckle. Pull the bearings out, noting their positions and direction of

installation (smaller diameter inward).

7. Matchmark the relationship between the brake disc and hub. Then place the knuckle in a vise and separate the rotor from the hub by removing the attaching bolts.

To install:

8. Install the hub to the rotor and attaching bolts.

9. Install the hub and knuckle to the bottom of the strut.

10. Install the halfshaft to the transaxle.

11. Connect the stabilizer bar and strut bar to the lower control arm, if disconnected.

12. Install the brake caliper.

13. Install the halfshaft nut and center hub cap and halfshaft nut.

14. Install the front wheel and lower the vehicle.

15. Torque the hub nut to 188 ft. lbs. (255 Nm).

Brake Drum

REMOVAL AND INSTALLATION

1. Raise the vehicle and support safely.

2. Remove the wheel and tire assembly.

3. On some vehicles, the drum will simply pull off the brake assembly after removing small retainer screws from the face of the drum. If the drum is difficult to remove, remove the plug from the rear of the backing plate and push the self adjuster lever away from the star wheel. Rotate the star wheel to retract the shoes.

4. Other vehicles must have the hub nut removed. On these vehicles, remove the dust cap, cotter pin, nut lock, wheel bearing nut and washer from the spindle. Remove the outer wheel bearing. Remove the drum with the inner wheel bearing from the spindle. If the drum is difficult to remove, remove the plug from the rear of the backing plate and push the self adjuster lever away from the star wheel. Rotate the star wheel to retract the shoes. Remove the grease seal.

To install:

5. Lubricate and install the inner wheel bearing, if the brake drum includes the hub. Install a new grease seal. Install the drum to the spindle. Lubricate and install the outer wheel bearing, washer and nut. Adjust the bearing preload following the procedure outlined in the "Rear Wheel Bearing" of this section. When the bearing preload is properly set, install the nut lock and a new cotter pin. Install the grease cap.

NOTE: Late model vehicles may not have a cotter (split) pin retainer. The nut now used to retain the rear axle hub is a self-locking type that must be replaced with by a new one every time it is removed. This nut is to be torqued to 108-145 ft. lbs. (145-200 Nm).

6. On vehicles where the drum is separate from the hub, simply install the brake drum to the hub assembly and install the retaining screws.

7. Install the wheel and tire assembly. Adjust the rear brakes as required.

8. Apply the brakes until a firm pedal is obtained, prior to moving the vehicle.

Drum Brake Shoes

REMOVAL AND INSTALLATION

Excel and Scoupe

1. Raise the vehicle and support it safely.

2. Remove the rear wheels.

3. Remove the brake drum from the vehicle.

4. Thoroughly clean the spindle.

5. Remove the lower pressed metal spring clip, the shoe return spring, the large 1 piece spring between the 2 shoes, and the shoe hold-down springs.

6. Remove the shoes and adjuster as an assembly.

7. Disconnect the parking brake cable from the lever.

8. Remove the spring between the shoes and the lever from the rear (trailing) shoe.

9. Disconnect the adjuster retaining spring and remove the adjuster, turn the star wheel into the adjuster body after cleaning and lubricating the threads.

To install:

10. Clean both backing plates and all brake components using the appropriate equipment.

11. Lubricate all contact points on the backing plate, anchor plate, wheel cylinder to shoe contact and parking brake strut joints and contacts with lithium based grease.

12. Install the parking brake lever to the new rear (trailing) shoe.

13. Install the brake shoes to the backing plates and install the hold-down springs. Now that the shoes are fastened onto the backing plate, install the return springs and the adjuster to each brake shoe making sure the wheel cylinder pistons are correctly positioned on the brake shoe webbing. Reconnect the parking brake cable, if removed.

14. Pre-adjustment of the brake shoe can be made by turning the adjuster star wheel out until the drum will just slide on over the brake shoes. Before installing the drum make sure the parking brake is not adjusted too tightly, if it is, loosen it, or the adjustment of the rear brakes will not be correct.

15. Install the hub and drum assembly onto each spindle and set bearing preload, if equipped.

16. Install the tire and wheel assemblies. Check the fluid in the master cylinder reservoirs.

17. The brakes shoes are adjusted by pumping the brake pedal and applying and releasing the parking brake. Adjust the parking brake stroke. Road test the vehicle.

Elantra and Sonata

1. Raise the vehicle and support it safely.

2. Remove both tire and wheel assemblies.

3. Remove the hub nut, outer wheel bearing and brake drum.

4. Thoroughly clean the spindle.

5. Clean the brake shoes and backing plate using the appropriate equipment.

6. Remove the lower spring return springs.

7. Remove the upper spring return springs.

8. Remove the hold-down springs.

9. Remove the shoes and adjuster as an assembly.

10. Disconnect the parking brake cable from the adjuster arm.

To install:

11. Apply a thin coating of lithium based grease to the backing plate pads.

12. Connect the parking brake cable to the adjuster.

13. Position the shoes on the backing plate and install the hold-down springs and pins.

14. Install the upper spring, then the lower spring and lastly the adjuster spring.

15. Install the drum and adjust the wheel bearing.

Wheel Cylinder

REMOVAL AND INSTALLATION

1. Raise the vehicle and support it safely. Remove the tire and wheel assembly.
2. Remove the brake drums and shoes.
3. Disconnect the brake line from the wheel cylinder. Plug the open end of the brake line to prevent any damage to painted surfaces due to contact with brake fluid.
4. Remove the bolts that fasten the wheel cylinder to the backing plate and remove the wheel cylinder.

To install:

5. Install the wheel cylinder to the backing plate and tighten the mounting bolts to 8 ft. lbs. (11 Nm) for Excel or 13 ft. lbs. (18 Nm) for the remaining models. Reconnect the fluid line to the cylinder.
6. Install the brake shoes, drum and wheel assembly onto the vehicle.
7. Lower the vehicle and check the fluid in the master cylinder reservoir, add as required to correct the level.
8. Adjust the rear brake shoes and the parking brake, if necessary. Bleed the brake system.

Brake System Bleeding

NOTE: If using a pressure bleeder, follow the instructions furnished with the unit and choose the correct adapter for the application. Do not substitute an adapter that "almost fits" as it will not work and could be dangerous.

1. Fill the master cylinder with fresh brake fluid. Check the level often during the procedure.
2. Starting with the right rear wheel, remove the protective cap from the bleeder, if equipped, and place where it will not be lost. Clean the bleed screw.

———— **CAUTION** ————

When bleeding the brakes, keep face away from the brake area. Spewing fluid may cause facial and/or visual injury. Do not allow brake fluid to spill on the vehicle's finish; it will remove the paint.

3. If the system is empty, the most efficient way to get fluid down to the wheel is to loosen the bleeder about $1/2$-$3/4$ turn, place a finger firmly over the bleeder and have a helper pump the brakes slowly until fluid comes out the bleeder. Once fluid is at the bleeder, close it before the pedal is released inside the vehicle.

NOTE: If the pedal is pumped rapidly, the fluid will churn and create small air bubbles, which are almost impossible to remove from the system. These air bubbles will eventually congregate and a spongy pedal will result.

4. Once fluid has been pumped to the caliper or wheel cylinder, open the bleed screw again, have an assistant press the brake pedal to the floor, lock the bleeder and have an assistant slowly release the pedal. Wait 15 seconds and repeat the procedure, including the 15 second wait, until no more air comes out of the bleeder upon application of the brake pedal. Remember to close the bleeder before the pedal is released inside the vehicle each time the bleeder is opened. If not, air will be induced into the system.
5. If a helper is not available, connect a small hose to the bleeder, place the end in a container of brake fluid and proceed to pump the pedal from inside the vehicle until no more air comes out the bleeder. The hose will prevent air from entering the system.
6. Repeat the procedure on remaining wheel cylinders in order:
   a. Left front caliper
   b. Left rear wheel cylinder or caliper
   c. Right front caliper
7. Hydraulic brake systems must be totally flushed, if the fluid becomes contaminated with water, dirt or other corrosive chemicals. To flush, bleed the entire system until all fluid has been replaced with the correct type of new fluid.
8. Install the bleeder cap(s) on the bleeder to keep dirt out. Always road test the vehicle.

Anti-lock Brake System Service

PRECAUTIONS

- Certain components within the ABS system are not intended to be serviced or repaired individually. Only those components with removal and installation procedures should be serviced.
- Do not use rubber hoses or other parts not specifically specified for the ABS system. When using repair kits, replace all parts included in the kit. Partial or incorrect repair may lead to functional problems and require the replacement of components.
- Lubricate rubber parts with clean, fresh brake fluid to ease assembly. Do not use lubricated shop air to clean parts; damage to rubber components may result.
- Use only DOT 3 brake fluid from an unopened container.
- If any hydraulic component or line is removed or replaced, it may be necessary to bleed the entire system.
- A clean repair area is essential. Always clean the reservoir and cap thoroughly before removing the cap. The slightest amount of dirt in the fluid may plug an orifice and impair the system function. Perform repairs after components have been thoroughly cleaned; use only denatured alcohol to clean components. Do not allow ABS components to come into contact with any substance containing mineral oil; this includes used shop rags.
- The Anti-Lock Control Unit (ALCU) is a microprocessor similar to other computer units in the vehicle. Ensure that the ignition switch is **OFF** before removing or installing controller harnesses. Avoid static electricity discharge at or near the controller.
- If any arc welding is to be done on the vehicle, the ALCU connectors should be disconnected before welding operations begin.

Proportioning Valves

REMOVAL AND INSTALLATION

1. Disconnect the negative battery cable.
2. Remove the right rear and the left rear tubes from the modulator.
3. Remove the right rear and the left rear proportioning valves from the modulator.
4. Inspect the O-ring of each proportioning valve and replace as required.

To install:

5. Install the proportioning valves in the modulator.
6. Tighten each valve to 13 ft. lbs. (18 Nm).
7. Install the right and left rear tubes to the modulator.

Front Wheel Sensors

REMOVAL AND INSTALLATION

1. Disconnect the negative battery cable.

2. Disconnect the sensor electrical connector.

3. Remove the sensor cable mounting bolts and the sensor head mounting bolt.

4. Remove the sensor from the mount.

5. Installation is the reverse of the removal procedure. Torque the sensor mounting bolt to 9 ft. lbs. (12 Nm).

Rear Wheel Sensors

REMOVAL AND INSTALLATION

1. Disconnect the negative battery cable.

2. Remove the tire and wheel assembly.

3. Disconnect the sensor electrical connector at the body wire harness.

4. Remove the sensor cable mounting bolts and the sensor mounting bolt and remove the sensor.

To install:

5. Install the sensor cable mounting bolts.

NOTE: When you install the sensor cables, you must tighten the mounting clamps so they will attach firmly to the grommets. Make sure the harness is not twisted during installation.

6. Install the sensor mounting bolt to the backing plate and tighten the bolt to 9 ft. lbs. (12 Nm). Connect the electrical connector.

7. Install the tire and wheel assembly and lower the vehicle. Reconnect the negative battery cable.

Modulator

REMOVAL AND INSTALLATION

1. Disconnect the negative battery cable.

2. Drain the master cylinder reservoir by following the procedure under "ABS System Bleeding".

NOTE: Do not allow any brake fluid to remain on a painted surface, wash off immediately or damage to the finish will result.

3. Disconnect the 6 brake tubes from the modulator assembly and label for aid during installation.

4. Remove the 4 mounting bolts and washers at the modulator and lift the modulator from the vehicle. Remove the 3 mounting brackets from the modulator.

To install:

5. Install the 3 mounting bracket to the modulator assembly and tighten the fasteners to 20 ft. lbs. (26 Nm).

6. Install the modulator to the vehicle and install the 4 mounting bolts with washers. Torque the mounting bolts to 12 ft. lbs. (16 Nm).

7. Install the brake tubes to the modulator and tighten to as follows:

   a. Left front tube nut to 17 ft. lbs. (23 Nm)

   b. Left rear tube nut to 17 ft. lbs. (23 Nm)

   c. Right front tube nut to 17 ft. lbs. (23 Nm)

   d. Right rear tube nut to 17 ft. lbs. (23 Nm)

   e. Primary bolt to 23 ft. lbs. (31 Nm)

   f. Secondary bolt to 23 ft. lbs. (31 Nm)

8. Connect the body harness electrical connector to the modulator connector.

9. Refill the cylinder reservoir as outlined in the ABS bleeding procedure. Connect the negative battery cable. Operate the brakes to assure a firm pedal and correct brake operation prior to moving the vehicle.

ANTI-LOCK BRAKE SYSTEM BLEEDING

This procedure should be used to insure correct and adequate bleeding and filling of the ABS unit, brake lines, master cylinder and calipers. A Multi-Use Tester (MUT), will be required for this procedure.

1. After work has been completed, check all brake lines for correct attachment and no leaks. Bleed the normal brake circuit using the procedure listed for conventional braking systems.

2. Connect the Multi-Use Tester (MUT) to the terminal located under the dash near the fuse box.

3. Turn the key to the **ON** position, but do not start the engine.

4. Follow each of the steps listed for each bleed screw in the order shown:

   a. Install clear bleeder tube on the screw to be bled.

   b. Apply light pressure to the brake pedal.

   c. Using the MUT, actuate the appropriate valve and bleed the system.

5. Loosen the bleed screw and observe the fluid flow, the flow will be cycled OFF and on with the MUT.

NOTE: Fluid can flow at high pressure. Never open bleed screw without attaching flexible hose.

6. Close the bleed screw and release the pressure on the brake pedal. Re-apply the brake pedal and open the bleeder as required to rid the system of air. Stop the valve activation when bleeding is complete.

CHASSIS ELECTRICAL

Heater Blower Motor

REMOVAL AND INSTALLATION

NOTE: On Excel and Sonata, in order to remove either the blower or core, the heater case must be removed.

Sonata

— CAUTION —

It has been determined that the discharge of R-12 refrigerant into the atmosphere depletes the earth's protective ozone layer. It is recommended that R-12 be recovered and recycled when possible.

1. Disconnect the negative battery cable.

2. Place the control in the HOT position.

3. Drain the cooling system.

4. Remove the heater hoses from the core tubes.

5. Discharge the air conditioning system.

6. Disconnect the suction and liquid refrigerant lines at the firewall connectors. Always use backup wrenches. Cap all openings at once.

7. Remove the front and rear center consoles.

8. Remove the heater side covers.

9. Remove the glove box, center crash pad cover, center crash pad and the radio.

10. Remove the lower crash pad.

11. Remove the console mounting bracket and center support.

12. Remove the left and right rear heat duct assemblies and the rear heating joint duct.

13. Remove the control unit.

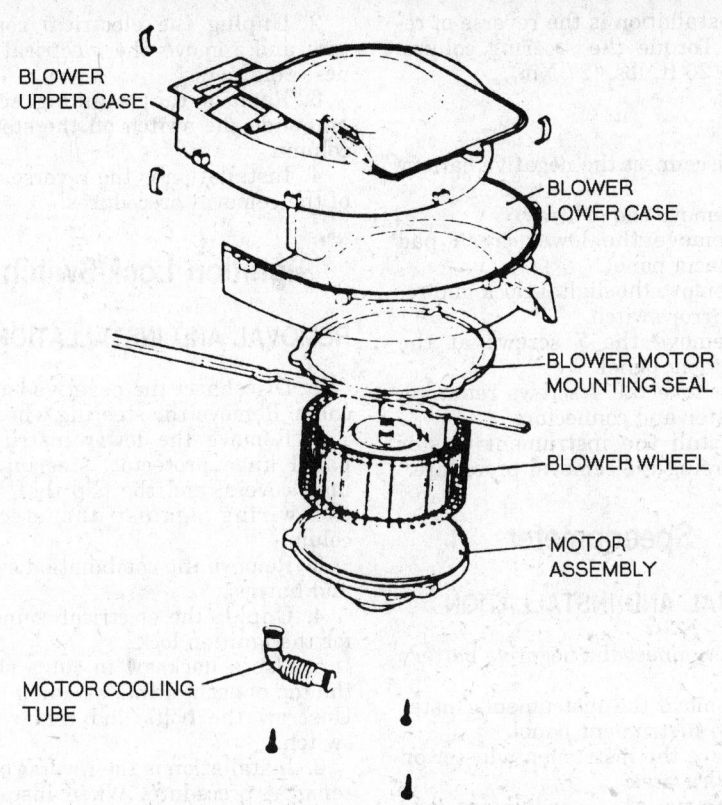

BLOWER
UPPER CASE

BLOWER
LOWER CASE

BLOWER MOTOR
MOUNTING SEAL

BLOWER WHEEL

MOTOR
ASSEMBLY

MOTOR COOLING
TUBE

Blower motor assembly — Excel, Elantra and Scoupe

14. Disconnect the blower speed actuator connector and, in Canada, disconnect the blend door actuator connector.

15. Remove the heater/air conditioning unit.

16. Remove the blower motor from the case.

   To install:

17. Install the blower motor to the case.

18. Install the heater/air conditioning unit.

19. Connect the blower speed actuator connector and, in Canada, connect the blend door actuator connector.

20. Install the control unit.

21. Install the left and right rear heat duct assemblies and the rear heating joint duct.

22. Install the console mounting bracket and center support.

23. Install the lower crash pad.

24. Install the glove box, center crash pad cover, center crash pad and the radio.

25. Install the heater side covers.

26. Install the front and rear center consoles.

27. Connect the suction and liquid refrigerant lines at the firewall con-

nectors. Always use backup wrenches.

28. Evacuate, recharge and leak test the air conditioning system.

29. Install the heater hoses to the core tubes.

30. Refill the cooling system.

31. Connect the negative battery cable, start the engine and check for leaks.

Scoupe, Elantra and Excel

1. Disconnect the negative battery cable.

2. Remove the glove box housing cover assembly.

3. Disconnect the resistor and blower motor connector.

4. Pull out the blower unit and disconnect the fresh/recirc vacuum connector.

5. Install the blower motor by reversing the removal procedure.

Windshield Wiper Motor

REMOVAL AND INSTALLATION

Front

1. Disconnect the negative battery cable. Remove the wiper arm and

blade assemblies. Remove the air inlet and cowl front center trim panels. Remove the 3 pivot shaft mounting nuts and push the pivot shafts into the area under the cowl.

2. Remove the motor mounting bolts. Pull the motor into the best possible position for access and remove the linkage off the motor crank arm. Remove the motor and then the linkage as required.

3. If the motor is being replaced, matchmark the position of the crank arm of the motor shaft of the new motor and then remove the nut and crank arm, transferring both to the new motor.

   To install:

4. Torque the pivot shaft nuts to 4.3-5.8 ft. lbs. (5-8 Nm).

5. Position the wiper arms so, on the Excel and Elantra, the blades are about 15mm above the lower windshield molding, on the driver's side and 20mm above it, on the passenger's side.

6. On the Sonata, each blade tip should be about 30mm above the molding. On Scoupe, the driver's side blade tip should be about 50mm above the lower windshield molding and the passenger side blade tip should be about 30mm above the lower windshield molding. Torque the wiper arm mounting nuts to 7-12 ft. lbs. (10-15 Nm).

7. Make sure the wiper motor is securely grounded. Connect the negative battery cable.

Rear

1. Remove the wiper blade and arm by lifting the wiper blade locknut cover and removing the locknut. Then, pull the arm from the shaft.

2. Remove the lift gate trim panel and disconnect the wiring harness connector.

3. Matchmark the relationship of the crank arm to the motor and remove the crank arm.

4. Remove the inside and outside motor mounting nuts and remove the motor.

5. Installation is the reverse of the removal procedures.

   NOTE: When installing the wiper arm, the distance between the tip of the blade and the lower window molding should be 40mm.

Windshield Wiper Switch

REMOVAL AND INSTALLATION

Rear

1. Pry the switch bezel from the instrument panel.
2. Reach behind the panel and disconnect the wiring from the switch.
3. Depress the 2 retainers and pull the switch from the panel.
4. Installation is the reverse order of the removal procedures.

Instrument Cluster

REMOVAL AND INSTALLATION

Elantra

1. Disconnect the negative battery cable.
2. Remove the coin box, ashtray and lower crash pad center facial panel.
3. Separate the connectors from the clock, hazard switch, air conditioning switch, rear heater switch and the cruise control switch.
4. Remove the 3 screws at the cluster facia panel. If the speedometer is to be removed, do so now.
5. Remove the 4 screws retaining the cluster and connectors to the instrument panel. Remove the cluster assembly from the vehicle.
6. Installation is the reverse of the removal procedure.

Excel

1. Disconnect the negative battery cable. Remove the meter hood attaching screws, located at the bottom and tilt the lower meter hood outward. Pull the hood downward to release the locking tangs at the top and remove it.
2. Remove the meter assembly mounting screws and pull the unit outward. Disconnect the speedometer cable and all connectors. Remove the unit.
3. Installation is the reverse order of the removal procedures.

Sonata

1. Disconnect the negative battery cable. Remove the steering column support bolts and carefully lower the column on the front seat.
2. Remove the cluster trim panel.
3. Remove the cluster mounting screws and slowly pull the cluster outward. Disconnect the wires.

4. Installation is the reverse of removal. Torque the steering column bolts to 20 ft. lbs. (27 Nm).

Scoupe

1. Disconnect the negative battery cable.
2. Remove the ashtray.
3. Remove the lower crash pad center facia panel.
4. Remove the digital clock and remote mirror switch.
5. Remove the 7 screws at the cluster facia panel.
6. Remove the 4 screws retaining the cluster and connectors
7. Install the instrument cluster by reversing the removal procedure.

Speedometer

REMOVAL AND INSTALLATION

1. Disconnect the negative battery cable.
2. Remove the instrument cluster from the instrument panel.
3. Place the instrument cluster on clean work area.
4. Remove the speedometer lens retaining screws from the side of the cluster and remove the lens.
5. From the rear side of the cluster, remove the speedometer retaining screws and carefully remove the speedometer from the cluster assembly.
   To install:
6. Install the speedometer into the cluster and install the retaining screws.
7. Position the cluster assembly to the dash, while inserting the speedometer cable into the speedometer, push in securely.
8. Install the instrument cluster face plate and lens to the panel.
9. Connect the negative battery cable.

Combination Switch

NOTE: The headlights, turn signals, dimmer switch, horn switch, windshield wiper/washer, intermittent wiper switch and the cruise control function are all built into 1 multi-function combination switch that is mounted on the steering column.

REMOVAL AND INSTALLATION

1. Disconnect the negative battery cable. Remove the steering wheel. Remove the steering column covers.

2. Unplug the electrical connectors and remove the electrical harness retainers.
3. Remove the retaining screws and slide the switch off the steering column.
4. Installation is the reverse order of the removal procedures.

Ignition Lock/Switch

REMOVAL AND INSTALLATION

1. Disconnect the negative battery cable. Remove the steering wheel.
2. Remove the lower instrument panel knee protector, steering column covers, and the clip that holds the wiring against the steering column.
3. Remove the combination switch and harness.
4. Unplug the electrical connector for the ignition lock.
5. Use a hacksaw to cut a slit in the top of each of the fastening bolts. Unscrew the bolts and remove the switch.
6. Installation is the reverse of the removal procedure. When installing the new switch, align the halves of the assembly around the steering column, align the assembly with the column boss and then install the special new installation bolts loosely. Verify that the ignition switch works and tighten the bolts until their heads break off.

Stoplight Switch

The switch is located on a bracket above the brake pedal arm.

ADJUSTMENT

1. Disconnect the negative battery cable.
2. The stoplight switch works off the brake pedal lever. To adjust, disconnect the electrical connection and loosen the switch locknut.
3. Screw the switch inward until it contacts the stop on the brake pedal arm. Back out the switch ½-1 full turn. The distance between the end of the switch plunger bore and the brake lever stop should be 0.020-0.040 in. (0.5-1.0mm).
4. Tighten the locknut and connect the wires.
5. Connect the negative battery cable.
6. Make sure the stoplights come ON when the brake pedal is depressed and go out when the pedal is

Combination switch removal

released. Also, make sure the cruise control system operates properly.

REMOVAL AND INSTALLATION

1. Disconnect the negative battery cable.
2. Locate the stoplight switch above the brake pedal lever.
3. Disconnect the wiring connectors from the switch and unscrew the switch.

To install:

4. Thread the stoplight switch into the switch holding bracket. Adjust the switch to achieve correct operation.
5. Connect the stoplight wires.
6. Connect the negative battery cable.
7. Make sure the stoplights come on when the brake pedal is depressed and go out when the pedal is released. Also, make sure the cruise control system operates properly.

Clutch Ignition Lock Switch

ADJUSTMENT

The clutch ignition lock switch is located at the top of the clutch pedal arm. Note that there may be 2 switches; 1 will be a clutch cruise control cut-out switch.

1. Clutch ignition lock switch adjustment is made with the pedal fully depressed. Remove the lower instrument trim panel and locate the switch.
2. Measure the gap between the switch plunger and the arm stop. The gap should be 0.140 in. (3.5mm).
3. If adjustment is necessary, loosen the locknut and rotate the switch until the desired clearance is obtained. Tighten locknut to lock switch in place.

REMOVAL AND INSTALLATION

1. Disconnect the negative battery cable.
2. Locate the interlock switch above the clutch pedal lever.
3. Disconnect the wiring connectors from the switch and unscrew the switch.

To install:

4. Thread the switch into the mounting bracket and adjust to 0.140 in. (3.5mm) clearance.
5. Reconnect the interlock wires.
6. Make sure the engine will not start unless the clutch pedal is depressed. Also, make sure the cruise control system operates properly.

Clutch Cruise Control Cut-out Switch

ADJUSTMENT

1. Disconnect the negative battery cable.
2. Remove the lower, left cover on the clutch pedal support.
3. Disconnect the electrical connector from the switch and remove the switch, by twisting it out of the tubular retaining clip.
4. Pull back on the clutch pedal and push the switch through the retaining clip noting the clicks: repeat this procedure until no more clicks can be heard.
5. Connect the electrical connector to the switch.
6. Connect the negative battery cable and check the switch operation.

REMOVAL AND INSTALLATION

1. Disconnect the negative battery cable.
2. Remove the lower, left trim panel. Locate the switch on the clutch pedal support.

3. Disconnect the electrical connector from the switch and remove the switch, by twisting it out of the tubular retaining clip.

To install:

4. Using a new retaining clip, install the switch and connect the electrical connector.
5. To adjust the switch, pull back on the clutch pedal, push the switch through the retaining clip, noting the clicks; repeat this procedure until no more clicks can be heard.
6. Connect the negative battery cable and check the switch operation.

Neutral Safety Switch

ADJUSTMENT

Excel and Scoupe

1. Apply the parking brake. Place the gearshift lever in **N** position.
2. Loosen the mounting screws of the neutral switch so it can be rotated. Now, rotate it so the end of the operating lever (A) is directly over the flange on the switch body and the holes in that flange and the outer end of the lever are aligned.
3. Hold the switch securely in place while torquing the mounting screws to 7 ft. lbs. (10 Nm).
4. Recheck the function of the switch by attempting to start the engine in all selector positions. It should start only in **P** and **N**.

Sonata

1. Place the shifter in the **N** position.
2. Loosen the control cable coupler and free the cable.
3. Place the control lever in the neutral position.
4. Turn the switch body until the wide (12mm) end of the control lever aligns with the switch body's widest part or turn the switch body until; the 5mm hole in the control lever aligns with the 5mm hole in the switch body. Tighten the nuts to 9 ft. lbs. (12 Nm).

Elantra

1. Place the shifter in the **N** position.
2. Loosen the manual control lever flange nut to free up the cable and lever.
3. Place the manual control lever in the **N** position.
4. Turn the switch body until the 0.47 in. (12mm) wide end of the manual control lever aligns with the

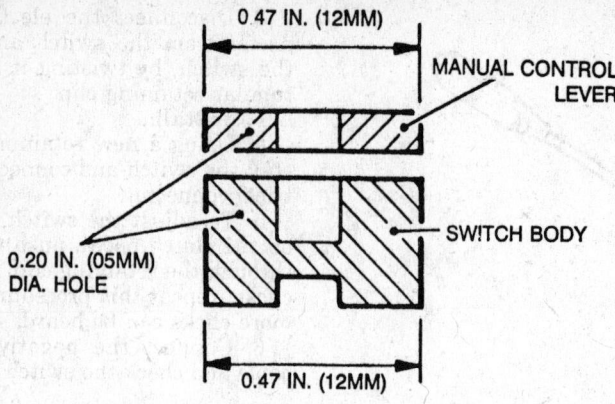

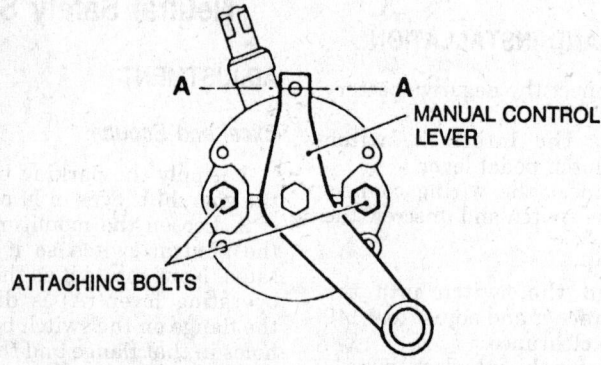

Neutral start switch adjustments — Sonata

switch body flange 0.472 in. (12mm) wide portion.

5. Tighten the attaching bolts to 9 ft. lbs. (12 Nm).

NOTE: When setting the switch body, be careful not to drop the O-ring from the switch body. Tighten the attaching bolts carefully.

6. Make sure the selector lever is in the **N** position. Adjust the flange nut so there is no slack in the control

cable and make sure the selector lever operates smoothly.

7. Run the vehicle and confirm that the transaxle is set in each range when the selector lever is shifted to each position.

REMOVAL AND INSTALLATION

1. Disconnect the negative battery cable.

2. Raise the vehicle and support it safely. Disconnect the shift linkage from the transaxle.

3. Disconnect the electrical connector from the switch.

4. Remove the switch to transaxle bolts and the switch from the vehicle.

To install:

5. Position the shifter shaft in the **N** position.

6. Align the shifter shaft flats with the switch and assemble the mounting bolts loosely.

7. Adjust the switch. Connect the negative battery cable and test operation.

Circuit Protection

Location

Fuse Block

The fuse block is located up under the instrument panel on the driver's side of the steering column.

Fusible Link

On all except Elantra, the main fusible link is located under the hood, inline of the positive battery cable. On Elantra, the main fusible link is mounted at the positive battery terminal. There is also a sub-fuse link located in the engine compartment, mounted on the right fender.

Flashers

LOCATION

The turn signal and hazard flashers are located in the fuse block, located under the instrument panel on the driver's side of the steering column.

Infiniti 8

G20, J30, M30, Q45

SERIAL NUMBER IDENTIFICATION

Vehicle Identification Number

The vehicle identification number plate is located at the upper left corner of the dash panel, as viewed through the windshield.

Engine Number

The engine number is located at the rear of the engine block. It is centrally positioned on Q45, slightly right of center on M30 and J30. It is at the left side of the engine on the G20.

Chassis Number

The chassis number plate is located in the engine compartment, at the upper right portion of the firewall.

Transaxle Number

The G20 manual transaxle identification number is located at the top of the case near the bellhousing. The G20 automatic transaxle identification number is located at the top of the case on the governor cap.

Transmission Number

The automatic transmission identification number for the J30, M30 and Q45 is located at the right rear of the case on the tailshaft.

ENGINE IDENTIFICATION

Year	Model	Engine Displacement Liters (cc)	Engine Series ID (VIN)	Fuel System	No. of Cylinders	Engine Type
1990	Q45	4.5 (4494)	VH45DE (N)	MPFI	8	DOHC
	M30	3.0 (2960)	VG30 (H)	MPFI	6	SOHC
1991	Q45	4.5 (4494)	VH45DE (N)	MPFI	8	DOHC
	M30	3.0 (2960)	VG30 (H)	MPFI	6	SOHC
	G20	2.0 (1998)	SR20DE (C)	MPFI	4	DOHC
1992	Q45	4.5 (4494)	VH45DE (N)	MPFI	8	DOHC
	M30	3.0 (2960)	VG30 (H)	MPFI	6	SOHC
	G20	2.0 (1998)	SR20DE (C)	MPFI	4	DOHC
1993	Q45	4.5 (4494)	VH45DE (N)	MPFI	8	DOHC
	G20	2.0 (1998)	SR20DE (C)	MPFI	4	DOHC
	J30	3.0 (2960)	VG30DE (A)	MPFI	6	DOHC
1994	Q45	4.5 (4494)	VH45DE (N)	MPFI	8	DOHC
	G20	2.0 (1998)	SR20DE (C)	MPFI	4	DOHC
	J30	3.0 (2960)	VG30DE (A)	MPFI	6	DOHC

MPFI—Multi-Point Fuel Injection
SOHC—Single Overhead Camshaft
DOHC—Dual Overhead Camshaft

GENERAL ENGINE SPECIFICATIONS

Year	Engine ID/VIN	Engine Displacement Liters (cc)	Fuel System Type	Net Horsepower @ rpm	Net Torque @ rpm (ft. lbs.)	Bore × Stroke (in.)	Compression Ratio	Oil Pressure @ rpm
1990	N	4.5 (4494)	MPFI	278 @ 6000	280 @ 4000	3.66 × 3.26	10.2:1	67–81 @ 3000
	H	3.0 (2960)	MPFI	162 @ 5200	180 @ 3600	3.43 × 3.27	9.0:1	53–65 @ 3200
1991	N	4.5 (4494)	MPFI	278 @ 6000	280 @ 4000	3.66 × 3.26	10.2:1	67–81 @ 3000
	H	3.0 (2960)	MPFI	162 @ 5200	180 @ 3600	3.43 × 3.27	9.0:1	53–65 @ 3200
	C	2.0 (1998)	MPFI	140 @ 6400	132 @ 4800	3.39 × 3.39	9.5:1	46–57 @ 3200
1992	N	4.5 (4494)	MPFI	278 @ 6000	292 @ 4000	3.66 × 3.26	10.2:1	67–81 @ 3000
	H	3.0 (2960)	MPFI	162 @ 5200	180 @ 3600	3.43 × 3.27	9.0:1	53–65 @ 3200
	C	2.0 (1998)	MPFI	140 @ 6400	132 @ 4800	3.39 × 3.39	9.5:1	46–57 @ 3200
1993	N	4.5 (4494)	MPFI	278 @ 6000	292 @ 4000	3.66 × 3.26	10.2:1	67–81 @ 3000
	C	2.0 (1998)	MPFI	140 @ 6400	132 @ 4800	3.39 × 3.39	9.5:1	46–57 @ 3200
	A	3.0 (2960)	MPFI	210 @ 6400	193 @ 4800	3.43 × 3.27	10.5:1	51–65 @ 3000
1994	N	4.5 (4494)	MPFI	278 @ 6000	292 @ 4000	3.66 × 3.26	10.2:1	67–81 @ 3000
	C	2.0 (1998)	MPFI	140 @ 6400	132 @ 4800	3.39 × 3.39	9.5:1	46–57 @ 3200
	A	3.0 (2960)	MPFI	210 @ 6400	193 @ 4800	3.43 × 3.27	10.5:1	51–65 @ 3000

MPFI—Sequential Multi-Point Fuel Injection

GASOLINE ENGINE TUNE-UP SPECIFICATIONS

Year	Engine ID/VIN	Engine Displacement Liters (cc)	Spark Plugs Gap (in.)	Ignition Timing (deg.) MT	AT	Fuel Pump (psi)	Idle Speed (rpm) MT	AT	Valve Clearance In.	Ex.
1990	N	4.5 (4494)	0.039–0.043	—	15B	①	—	750	Hyd.	Hyd.
	H	3.0 (2960)	0.039–0.043	—	15B	①	—	800	Hyd.	Hyd.
1991	N	4.5 (4494)	0.039–0.043	—	15B	①	—	650	Hyd.	Hyd.
	H	3.0 (2960)	0.039–0.043	—	15B	①	—	800	Hyd.	Hyd.
	C	2.0 (1998)	0.039–0.043	15B	15B	①	800	800	Hyd.	Hyd.
1992	N	4.5 (4494)	0.039–0.043	—	15B	①	—	650	Hyd.	Hyd.
	H	3.0 (2960)	0.039–0.043	—	15B	①	—	800	Hyd.	Hyd.
	C	2.0 (1998)	0.039–0.043	15B	15B	①	800	800	Hyd.	Hyd.
1993	N	4.5 (4494)	0.039–0.043	—	15B	①	—	650	Hyd.	Hyd.
	C	2.0 (1998)	0.039–0.043	15B	15B	①	800	800	Hyd.	Hyd.
	A	3.0 (2960)	0.039–0.043	—	15B	①	—	720	Hyd.	Hyd.
1994	N	4.5 (4494)	0.039–0.043	—	15B	①	—	650	Hyd.	Hyd.
	C	2.0 (1998)	0.039–0.043	15B	15B	①	800	800	Hyd.	Hyd.
	A	3.0 (2960)	0.039–0.043	—	15B	①	—	720	Hyd.	Hyd.

NOTE: The lowest cylinder pressure should be within 75% of the highest cylinder pressure reading. For example, if the highest cylinder is 134 psi, the lowest should be 101. Engine should be at normal operating temperature with throttle valve in the wide open position.
The underhood specifications sticker often reflects tune-up specification changes in production. Sticker figures must be used if they disagree with those in this chart.
B—Before Top Dead Center
Hyd.—Hydraulic
① 34 psi with regulator vacuum hose connected
43 psi with regulator vacuum hose disconnected

FIRING ORDERS

NOTE: To avoid confusion, always replace spark plug wires one at a time.

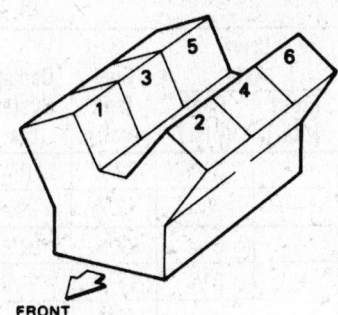

3.0L (VG30DE) Engine
Engine Firing Order: 1-2-3-4-5-6
Distributorless Ignition System

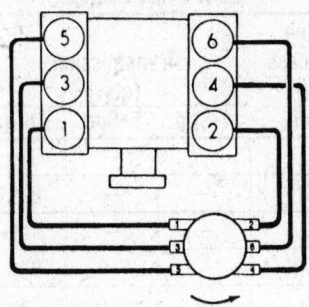

3.0L (VG30) Engine
Engine Firing Order: 1-2-3-4-5-6
Distributor Rotation: Counterclockwise

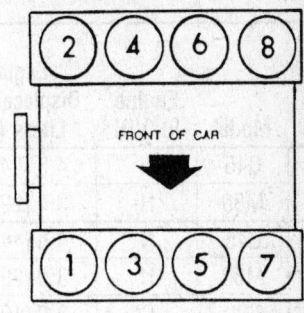

4.5L Engine
Engine Firing Order: 1-8-7-3-6-5-4-2
Distributorless Ignition System

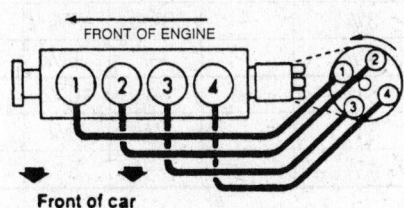

2.0L Engine
Engine Firing Order 1-3-4-2
Distributor Rotation: Clockwise

CAPACITIES

Year	Model	Engine ID/VIN	Engine Displacement Liters (cc)	Engine Crankcase with Filter	Transmission (qts.)			Transfer case (pts.)	Drive Axle		Fuel Tank (gal.)	Cooling System (qts.)
					4-Spd	5-Spd	Auto.		Front (pts.)	Rear (pts.)		
1990	Q45	N	4.5 (4494)	6³⁄₈	—	—	9¹⁄₈	—	—	3¹⁄₈	22¹⁄₂	10⁷⁄₈
	M30	H	3.0 (2960)	4⁵⁄₈	—	—	8³⁄₄	—	—	2³⁄₄	17¹⁄₈	9⁵⁄₈
1991	Q45	N	4.5 (4494)	6³⁄₈	—	—	10³⁄₄	—	—	3¹⁄₈	22¹⁄₂	10⁷⁄₈
	M30	H	3.0 (2960)	4⁵⁄₈	—	—	8³⁄₄	—	—	2³⁄₄	17¹⁄₈	9⁵⁄₈
	G20	C	2.0 (1998)	3⁵⁄₈	—	3⁷⁄₈	7³⁄₈	—	—	—	15⁷⁄₈	①
1992	Q45	N	4.5 (4494)	6³⁄₈	—	—	10³⁄₄	—	—	3¹⁄₈	22¹⁄₂	10⁷⁄₈
	M30	H	3.0 (2960)	4⁵⁄₈	—	—	8³⁄₄	—	—	2³⁄₄	17¹⁄₈	9⁵⁄₈
	G20	C	2.0 (1998)	3⁵⁄₈	—	3⁷⁄₈	7³⁄₈	—	—	—	15⁷⁄₈	①
1993	Q45	N	4.5 (4494)	6³⁄₈	—	—	10³⁄₄	—	—	3¹⁄₈	22¹⁄₂	10⁷⁄₈
	G20	C	2.0 (1998)	3⁵⁄₈	—	3⁷⁄₈	7³⁄₈	—	—	—	15⁷⁄₈	①
	J30	A	3.0 (2960)	4¹⁄₂	—	—	8³⁄₄	—	—	3¹⁄₈	19	10⁷⁄₈
1994	Q45	N	4.5 (4494)	6³⁄₈	—	—	10³⁄₄	—	—	3¹⁄₈	22¹⁄₂	10⁷⁄₈
	G20	C	2.0 (1998)	3⁵⁄₈	—	3⁷⁄₈	7³⁄₈	—	—	—	15⁷⁄₈	①
	J30	A	3.0 (2960)	4¹⁄₂	—	—	8³⁄₄	—	—	3¹⁄₈	19	10⁷⁄₈

① 6¹⁄₂ qts. M/T, 6⁷⁄₈ qts. A/T

CAMSHAFT SPECIFICATIONS

All measurements given in inches.

Year	Engine ID/VIN	Engine Displacement Liters (cc)	Journal Diameter					Elevation		Bearing Clearance	Camshaft End Play
			1	2	3	4	5	In.	Ex.		
1990	N	4.5 (4494)	1.0211–1.0218	1.0211–1.0218	1.0211–1.0218	1.0211–1.0218	—	1.4929–1.5004	1.3889–1.3964	0.0018–0.0034	0.0028–0.0058
	H	3.0 (2960)	1.8866–1.8874	1.8472–1.8480	1.8472–1.8480	1.8472–1.8480	1.6701–1.6709	1.5566–1.5641	1.5566–1.5641	0.0024–0.0041	0.0012–0.0024
1991	N	4.5 (4494)	1.0211–1.0218	1.0211–1.0218	1.0211–1.0218	1.0211–1.0218	—	1.4929–1.5004	1.3889–1.3964	0.0018–0.0034	0.0028–0.0058
	H	3.0 (2960)	1.8866–1.8874	1.8472–1.8480	1.8472–1.8480	1.8472–1.8480	1.6701–1.6709	1.5566–1.5641	1.5566–1.5641	0.0024–0.0041	0.0012–0.0024
	C	2.0 (1998)	1.0998–1.1006	1.0998–1.1006	1.0998–1.1006	1.0998–1.1006	1.0998–1.1006	1.5121–1.5196	1.4929–1.5004	0.0018–0.0034	0.0022–0.0055
1992	N	4.5 (4494)	1.0211–1.0218	1.0211–1.0218	1.0211–1.0218	1.0211–1.0218	—	1.4929–1.5004	1.3889–1.3964	0.0018–0.0034	0.0028–0.0058
	H	3.0 (2960)	1.8866–1.8874	1.8472–1.8480	1.8472–1.8480	1.8472–1.8480	1.6701–1.6709	1.5566–1.5641	1.5566–1.5641	0.0018–0.0035	0.0012–0.0024
	C	2.0 (1998)	1.0998–1.1006	1.0998–1.1006	1.0998–1.1006	1.0998–1.1006	1.0998–1.1006	1.5121–1.5196	1.4929–1.5004	0.0018–0.0034	0.0022–0.0055
1993	N	4.5 (4494)	1.0211–1.0218	1.0211–1.0218	1.0211–1.0218	1.0211–1.0218	—	1.4929–1.5004	1.3889–1.3964	0.0018–0.0034	0.0028–0.0058
	C	2.0 (1998)	1.0998–1.1006	1.0998–1.1006	1.0998–1.1006	1.0998–1.1006	1.0998–1.1006	1.5121–1.5196	1.4929–1.5004	0.0018–0.0034	0.0022–0.0055
	A	3.0 (2960)	1.0998–1.1006	1.0998–1.1006	1.0998–1.1006	1.0998–1.1006	1.0998–1.1006	1.5907–1.5982	1.5907–1.5982	0.0018–0.0034	0.0012–0.0031
1994	N	4.5 (4494)	1.0211–1.0218	1.0211–1.0218	1.0211–1.0218	1.0211–1.0218	—	1.4929–1.5004	1.3889–1.3964	0.0018–0.0034	0.0028–0.0058
	C	2.0 (1998)	1.0998–1.1006	1.0998–1.1006	1.0998–1.1006	1.0998–1.1006	1.0998–1.1006	1.5121–1.5196	1.4929–1.5004	0.0018–0.0034	0.0022–0.0055
	A	3.0 (2960)	1.0998–1.1006	1.0998–1.1006	1.0998–1.1006	1.0998–1.1006	1.0998–1.1006	1.5907–1.5982	1.5907–1.5982	0.0018–0.0034	0.0012–0.0031

CRANKSHAFT AND CONNECTING ROD SPECIFICATIONS

All measurements are given in inches.

| Year | Engine ID/VIN | Engine Displacement Liters (cc) | Crankshaft | | | | Connecting Rod | | |
			Main Brg. Journal Dia.	Main Brg. Oil Clearance	Shaft End-play	Thrust on No.	Journal Diameter	Oil Clearance	Side Clearance
1990	N	4.5 (4494)	①	0.0005–0.0012	0.0039–0.0102	3	②	0.0008–0.0018	0.0079–0.0138
	H	3.0 (2960)	③	0.0011–0.0022	0.0020–0.0067	4	1.9667–1.9675	0.0006–0.0021	0.0079–0.0138
1991	N	4.5 (4494)	①	0.0005–0.0012	0.0039–0.0102	3	②	0.0008–0.0018	0.0079–0.0138
	H	3.0 (2960)	③	0.0011–0.0022	0.0020–0.0067	4	1.9667–1.9675	0.0006–0.0021	0.0079–0.0138
	C	2.0 (1998)	④	0.0002–0.0009	0.0039–0.0102	3	⑤	0.0008–0.0018	0.0079–0.0138
1992	N	4.5 (4494)	①	0.0005–0.0012	0.0039–0.0102	3	②	0.0008–0.0018	0.0079–0.0138
	H	3.0 (2960)	③	0.0011–0.0022	0.0020–0.0067	4	1.9667–1.9675	0.0006–0.0021	0.0079–0.0138
	C	2.0 (1998)	④	0.0002–0.0009	0.0039–0.0102	3	⑤	0.0008–0.0018	0.0079–0.0138
1993	N	4.5 (4494)	①	0.0005–0.0012	0.0039–0.0102	3	②	0.0008–0.0018	0.0079–0.0138
	C	2.0 (1998)	④	0.0002–0.0009	0.0039–0.0102	3	⑤	0.0008–0.0018	0.0079–0.0138
	A	3.0 (2960)	③	0.0011–0.0022	0.0020–0.0071	4	⑥	0.0011–0.0019	0.0079–0.0138
1994	N	4.5 (4494)	①	0.0005–0.0012	0.0039–0.0102	3	②	0.0008–0.0018	0.0079–0.0138
	C	2.0 (1998)	④	0.0002–0.0009	0.0039–0.0102	3	⑤	0.0008–0.0018	0.0079–0.0138
	A	3.0 (2960)	③	0.0011–0.0022	0.0020–0.0071	4	⑥	0.0011–0.0019	0.0079–0.0138

① Grade No. 0—2.5180–2.5183
  Grade No. 1—2.5178–2.5180
  Grade No. 2—2.5176–2.5178
  Grade No. 3—2.5173–2.5176
② Grade No. 0—2.0460–2.0462
  Grade No. 1—2.0457–2.0460
  Grade No. 2—2.0455–2.0457
③ Grade No. 0—2.4790–2.4793
  Grade No. 1—2.4787–2.4790
  Grade No. 2—2.4784–2.4787
④ Grade No. 0—2.1643–2.1646
  Grade No. 1—2.1641–2.1643
  Grade No. 2—2.1639–2.1641
  Grade No. 3—2.1636–2.1639
⑤ Grade No. 0—1.8885–1.8887
  Grade No. 1—1.8883–1.8885
  Grade No. 2—1.8880–1.8883
⑥ Grade No. 0—1.9672–1.9675
  Grade No. 1—1.9670–1.9672
  Grade No. 2—1.9667–1.9670

VALVE SPECIFICATIONS

Year	Engine ID/VIN	Engine Displacement Liters (cc)	Seat Angle (deg.)	Face Angle (deg.)	Spring Test Pressure (lbs. @ in.)	Spring Installed Height (in.)	Stem-to-Guide Clearance (in.)		Stem Diameter (in.)	
							Intake	Exhaust	Intake	Exhaust
1990	N	4.5 (4494)	45°15′ 45°45′	44°53′ 45°07′	120.4 @ 1.055	1.862 ①	0.0008– 0.0014	0.0012– 0.0016	0.2746– 0.2752	0.3136– 0.3140
	H	3.0 (2960)	45°15′ 45°45′	45°	②	① ③	0.0008– 0.0021	0.0012– 0.0021	0.2742– 0.2748	0.3136– 0.3138
1991	N	4.5 (4494)	45°15′ 45°45′	44°53′ 45°07′	120.4 @ 1.055	1.862 ①	0.0011– 0.0020	0.0014– 0.0020	0.2743– 0.2744	0.3134– 0.3136
	H	3.0 (2960)	45°15′ 45°45′	45°	②	① ③	0.0008– 0.0021	0.0016– 0.0029	0.2742– 0.2748	0.3136– 0.3138
	C	2.0 (1998)	45°15′ 45°45′	44°53′ 45°07′	127–144 @ 1.181	1.943 ①	0.0008– 0.0021	0.0016– 0.0029	0.2348– 0.2354	0.2341– 0.2346
1992	N	4.5 (4494)	45°15′ 45°45′	44°53′ 45°07′	120.4 @ 1.055	1.862 ①	0.0011– 0.0020	0.0014– 0.0020	0.2743– 0.2744	0.3134– 0.3136
	H	3.0 (2960)	45°15′ 45°45′	45°	②	① ③	0.0008– 0.0021	0.0016– 0.0029	0.2742– 0.2748	0.3136– 0.3138
	C	2.0 (1998)	45°15′ 45°45′	44°53′ 45°07′	②	1.943 ①	0.0008– 0.0021	0.0016– 0.0029	0.2348– 0.2354	0.2341– 0.2346
1993	N	4.5 (4494)	45°15′ 45°45′	44°53′ 45°07′	120.4 @ 1.055	1.862 ①	0.0011– 0.0020	0.0014– 0.0020	0.2743– 0.2744	0.3134– 0.3136
	C	2.0 (1998)	45°15′ 45°45′	44°53′ 45°07′	②	1.943 ①	0.0008– 0.0021	0.0016– 0.0029	0.2348– 0.2354	0.2341– 0.2346
	A	3.0 (2960)	45°15′ 45°45′	45°	120.6 @ 1.043	1.697 ①	0.0008– 0.0021	0.0016– 0.0029	0.2348– 0.2354	0.2341– 0.2346
1994	N	4.5 (4494)	45°15′ 45°45′	44°53′ 45°07′	120.4 @ 1.055	1.862 ①	0.0011– 0.0020	0.0014– 0.0020	0.2743– 0.2744	0.3134– 0.3136
	C	2.0 (1998)	45°15′ 45°45′	44°53′ 45°07′	②	1.943 ①	0.0008– 0.0021	0.0016– 0.0029	0.2348– 0.2354	0.2341– 0.2346
	A	3.0 (2960)	45°15′ 45°45′	45°	120.6 @ 1.043	1.697 ①	0.0008– 0.0021	0.0016– 0.0029	0.2348– 0.2354	0.2341– 0.2346

① Free height
② Inner—57.3 @ 0.984
 Outer—117.7 @ 1.181
③ Inner—1.736
 Outer—2.016

PISTON AND RING SPECIFICATIONS

All measurements are given in inches.

Year	Engine ID/VIN	Engine Displacement Liters (cc)	Piston Clearance	Ring Gap Top Compression	Ring Gap Bottom Compression	Ring Gap Oil Control	Ring Side Clearance Top Compression	Ring Side Clearance Bottom Compression	Ring Side Clearance Oil Control
1990	N	4.5 (4494)	0.0004–0.0012	0.0106–0.0181	0.0154–0.0248	0.0079–0.0272	0.0016–0.0031	0.0012–0.0028	—
	H	3.0 (2960)	0.0010–0.0018	0.0083–0.0173	0.0071–0.0173	0.0079–0.0299	0.0016–0.0029	0.0012–0.0025	—
1991	N	4.5 (4494)	0.0004–0.0012	0.0106–0.0181	0.0154–0.0248	0.0079–0.0272	0.0016–0.0031	0.0012–0.0028	—
	H	3.0 (2960)	0.0006–0.0014	0.0083–0.0173	0.0071–0.0173	0.0079–0.0299	0.0016–0.0029	0.0012–0.0025	—
	C	2.0 (1998)	0.0004–0.0012	0.0079–0.0118	0.0138–0.0197	0.0079–0.0236	0.0018–0.0031	0.0012–0.0026	—
1992	N	4.5 (4494)	0.0004–0.0012	0.0106–0.0181	0.0154–0.0248	0.0079–0.0272	0.0016–0.0031	0.0012–0.0028	—
	H	3.0 (2960)	0.0006–0.0014	0.0083–0.0173	0.0071–0.0173	0.0079–0.0299	0.0016–0.0029	0.0012–0.0025	—
	C	2.0 (1998)	0.0004–0.0012	0.0079–0.0118	0.0138–0.0197	0.0079–0.0236	0.0018–0.0031	0.0012–0.0026	—
1993	N	4.5 (4494)	0.0004–0.0012	0.0106–0.0181	0.0154–0.0248	0.0079–0.0272	0.0016–0.0031	0.0012–0.0028	—
	C	2.0 (1998)	0.0004–0.0012	0.0079–0.0118	0.0138–0.0197	0.0079–0.0236	0.0018–0.0031	0.0012–0.0026	—
	A	3.0 (2960)	0.0006–0.0014	0.0083–0.0157	0.0197–0.0299	0.0079–0.0299	0.0016–0.0029	0.0012–0.0025	0.0006–0.0073
1994	N	4.5 (4494)	0.0004–0.0012	0.0106–0.0181	0.0154–0.0248	0.0079–0.0272	0.0016–0.0031	0.0012–0.0028	—
	C	2.0 (1998)	0.0004–0.0012	0.0079–0.0118	0.0138–0.0197	0.0079–0.0236	0.0018–0.0031	0.0012–0.0026	—
	A	3.0 (2960)	0.0006–0.0014	0.0083–0.0157	0.0197–0.0299	0.0079–0.0299	0.0016–0.0029	0.0012–0.0025	0.0006–0.0073

TORQUE SPECIFICATIONS

All readings in ft. lbs.

Year	Engine ID/VIN	Engine Displacement Liters (cc)	Cylinder Head Bolts	Main Bearing Bolts	Rod Bearing Bolts	Crankshaft Damper Bolts	Flywheel Bolts	Manifold		Spark Plugs	Lug Nut
								Intake	Exhaust		
1990	N	4.5 (4494)	①	②	③	260–275	61–69	12–15	20–23	14–22	72–87
	H	3.0 (2960)	④	67–74	③	90–98	61–69	12–14	13–16	14–22	76–90
1991	N	4.5 (4494)	①	②	③	260–275	61–69	12–15	20–23	14–22	72–87
	H	3.0 (2960)	④	67–74	③	90–98	61–69	12–14	13–16	14–22	76–90
	C	2.0 (1998)	⑤	⑥	③	105–112	61–69	13–15	27–35	14–22	72–87
1992	N	4.5 (4494)	①	②	③	260–275	61–69	12–15	20–23	14–22	72–87
	H	3.0 (2960)	④	67–74	③	90–98	61–69	12–14	13–16	14–22	76–90
	C	2.0 (1998)	⑤	⑥	③	105–112	61–69	13–15	27–35	14–22	72–87
1993	N	4.5 (4494)	①	②	③	260–275	61–69	12–15	20–23	14–22	72–87
	C	2.0 (1998)	⑤	⑥	③	105–112	61–69	13–15	27–35	14–22	72–87
	A	3.0 (2960)	⑧	67–74	⑦	159–174	61–69	12–15	17–20	14–22	72–87
1994	N	4.5 (4494)	①	②	③	260–275	61–69	12–15	20–23	14–22	72–87
	C	2.0 (1998)	⑤	⑥	③	105–112	61–69	13–15	27–35	14–22	72–87
	A	3.0 (2960)	⑧	67–74	⑦	159–174	61–69	12–15	17–20	14–22	72–87

NOTE: Always tighten bolts in specified sequence
① Step 1: Tighten all bolts to 22 ft. lbs.
  Step 2: Tighten all bolts to 69 ft. lbs.
  Step 3: Loosen all bolts completely
  Step 4: Tighten all bolts to 18–25 ft. lbs.
  Step 5: Tighten all bolts an additional
      90–95 degrees or tighten all bolts
      to 69–72 ft.lbs.

② See text
③ Step 1: Tigthen all bolts to 10–12 ft. lbs.
  Step 2: Tighten all bolts an additional
      60–65 degrees or tighten all bolts
      to 28–33 ft.lbs.
④ Step 1: Tighten all bolts to 22 ft. lbs.
  Step 2: Tighten all bolts to 43 ft. lbs.
  Step 3: Loosen all bolts completely
  Step 4: Tighten all bolts to 22 ft. lbs.
  Step 5: Tighten all bolts an additional
      60–65 degrees or tighten all bolts
      to 40–47 ft.lbs.
⑤ Step 1: Tighten all bolts to 29 ft. lbs.
  Step 2: Tighten all bolts to 58 ft. lbs.
  Step 3: Loosen all bolts completely
  Step 4: Tighten all bolts to 25–33 ft. lbs.
  Step 5: Tighten all bolts 90–100 degrees
  Step 6: Tighten all bolts an additional 90–100
      degrees
  Note: Do not turn any bolt 180–200 degrees all
      at once
⑥ Step 1: Tighten all bolts to 24–28 ft. lbs.
  Step 2: Tighten all bolts 45–50 degrees or
      tighten to 54–61 ft. lbs.
⑦ Step 1: Tighten all bolts to 10–12 ft. lbs.
  Step 2: Tighten all bolts to 43–48 ft. lbs. or
      tighten an additional 60–65 degrees
⑧ Step 1: Tighten all bolts to 29 ft. lbs.
  Step 2: Tighten all bolts to 90 ft. lbs.
  Step 3: Loosen all bolts completely
  Step 4: Tighten all bolts to 25–33 ft. lbs.
  Step 5: Tighten all bolts to 90 ft. lbs. or tighten
      an additional 70–75 degrees

BRAKE SPECIFICATIONS

All measurements in inches unless noted.

| Year | Model | Master Cylinder Bore | Brake Disc | | Minimum Lining Thickness | |
			Minimum Thickness	Maximum Runout	Front	Rear
1990	Q45	1.625	Front: 1.024 Rear: 0.315	0.0028	0.079	0.079
	M30	1.000	Front: 0.787 Rear: 0.354	0.0028	0.079	0.079
1991	Q45	1.625	Front: 1.024 Rear: 0.315	0.0028	0.079	0.079
	M30	1.000	Front: 0.787 Rear: 0.354	0.0028	0.079	0.079
	G20	0.937	Front: 0.787 Rear: 0.310	0.0028	0.079	0.079
1992	Q45	1.000	Front: 1.024 Rear: 0.315	0.0028	0.079	0.079
	M30	1.000	Front: 0.787 Rear: 0.354	0.0028	0.079	0.079
	G20	0.937	Front: 0.787 Rear: 0.310	0.0028	0.079	0.079
1993	Q45	1.000	Front: 1.024 Rear: 0.315	0.0028	0.079	0.079
	G20	0.937	Front: 0.787 Rear: 0.310	0.0028	0.079	0.079
	J30	1.000	Front: 1.024 Rear: 0.551	0.0028	0.079	0.079
1994	Q45	1.000	Front: 1.024 Rear: 0.315	0.0028	0.079	0.079
	G20	0.937	Front: 0.787 Rear: 0.310	0.0028	0.079	0.079
	J30	1.000	Front: 1.024 Rear: 0.551	0.0028	0.079	0.079

WHEEL ALIGNMENT

| Year | Model | Front/Rear | Caster | | Camber | | Toe-in (in.) | Steering Axis Inclination (deg.) |
			Range (deg.)	Preferred Setting (deg.)	Range (deg.)	Preferred Setting (deg.)		
1990	Q45	Front:	$5\frac{3}{4}$P–$7\frac{1}{4}$P	NA	$1\frac{19}{32}$N–$\frac{3}{32}$N	NA	0–$\frac{3}{32}$N	$12\frac{3}{4}$
		Rear:	—	—	$1\frac{19}{32}$N–$\frac{19}{32}$N	NA	0–$\frac{3}{16}$N	—
	Q45 ①	Front:	$6\frac{3}{16}$P–$7\frac{11}{16}$P	NA	$1\frac{11}{16}$N–$\frac{3}{16}$N	NA	$\frac{1}{16}$P–$\frac{1}{16}$N	$12\frac{15}{16}$
		Rear:	—	—	2N–1N	NA	0–$\frac{3}{8}$N	—
	M30	Front:	$3\frac{15}{16}$P–$5\frac{7}{16}$P	NA	$\frac{19}{32}$N–$\frac{15}{16}$P	NA	$\frac{1}{32}$P–$\frac{1}{32}$N	$12\frac{11}{16}$
		Rear:	—	—	$1\frac{3}{32}$N–$\frac{13}{32}$P	NA	$\frac{1}{32}$P–$\frac{5}{16}$N	—
1991	Q45	Front:	$5\frac{3}{4}$P–$7\frac{1}{4}$P	NA	$1\frac{19}{32}$N–$\frac{3}{32}$N	NA	0–$\frac{3}{32}$N	$12\frac{3}{4}$
		Rear:	—	—	$1\frac{19}{32}$N–$\frac{19}{32}$N	NA	0–$\frac{3}{16}$N	—
	Q45 ①	Front:	$6\frac{3}{16}$P–$7\frac{11}{16}$P	NA	$1\frac{11}{16}$N–$\frac{3}{16}$N	NA	$\frac{1}{16}$P–$\frac{1}{16}$N	$12\frac{15}{16}$
		Rear:	—	—	2N–1N	NA	0–$\frac{3}{8}$N	—
	M30	Front:	$3\frac{15}{16}$P–$5\frac{7}{16}$P	NA	$\frac{19}{32}$N–$\frac{15}{16}$P	NA	$\frac{1}{32}$P–$\frac{1}{32}$N	$12\frac{11}{16}$
		Rear:	—	—	$1\frac{3}{32}$N–$\frac{13}{32}$P	NA	$\frac{1}{32}$P–$\frac{5}{16}$N	—
	G20	Front:	$1\frac{3}{32}$P–$2\frac{19}{32}$P	NA	$\frac{3}{4}$N–$\frac{3}{4}$P	NA	0–$\frac{3}{16}$N	$14\frac{1}{2}$
		Rear:	—	—	$1\frac{3}{4}$N–$\frac{1}{4}$N	NA	$\frac{3}{16}$P–$\frac{3}{16}$N	—
1992	Q45	Front:	$5\frac{3}{4}$P–$7\frac{1}{4}$P	NA	$1\frac{19}{32}$N–$\frac{3}{32}$N	NA	0–$\frac{3}{32}$N	$12\frac{3}{4}$
		Rear:	—	—	$1\frac{19}{32}$N–$\frac{19}{32}$N	NA	0–$\frac{3}{16}$N	—
	Q45 ①	Front:	$6\frac{3}{16}$P–$7\frac{11}{16}$P	NA	$1\frac{11}{16}$N–$\frac{3}{16}$N	NA	$\frac{1}{16}$P–$\frac{1}{16}$N	$12\frac{15}{16}$
		Rear:	—	—	2N–1N	NA	0–$\frac{3}{8}$N	—
	M30	Front:	$3\frac{15}{16}$P–$5\frac{7}{16}$P	NA	$\frac{19}{32}$N–$\frac{15}{16}$P	NA	$\frac{1}{32}$P–$\frac{1}{32}$N	$12\frac{11}{16}$
		Rear:	—	—	$1\frac{3}{32}$N–$\frac{13}{32}$P	NA	$\frac{1}{32}$P–$\frac{5}{16}$N	—
	G20	Front:	$1\frac{3}{32}$P–$2\frac{19}{32}$P	NA	$\frac{3}{4}$N–$\frac{3}{4}$P	NA	0–$\frac{3}{16}$N	$14\frac{1}{2}$
		Rear:	—	—	$1\frac{3}{4}$N–$\frac{1}{4}$N	NA	$\frac{3}{16}$P–$\frac{3}{16}$N	—
1993	Q45	Front:	$5\frac{3}{4}$P–$7\frac{1}{4}$P	NA	$1\frac{19}{32}$N–$\frac{3}{32}$N	NA	0–$\frac{3}{32}$N	$12\frac{3}{4}$
		Rear:	—	—	$1\frac{19}{32}$N–$\frac{19}{32}$N	NA	0–$\frac{3}{16}$N	—
	Q45 ①	Front:	$6\frac{3}{16}$P–$7\frac{11}{16}$P	NA	$1\frac{11}{16}$N–$\frac{3}{16}$N	NA	$\frac{1}{16}$P–$\frac{1}{16}$N	$12\frac{15}{16}$
		Rear:	—	—	2N–1N	NA	0–$\frac{3}{8}$N	—
	G20	Front:	$1\frac{3}{32}$P–$2\frac{19}{32}$P	NA	$\frac{3}{4}$N–$\frac{3}{4}$P	NA	0–$\frac{3}{16}$N	$14\frac{1}{2}$
		Rear:	—	—	$1\frac{3}{4}$N–$\frac{1}{4}$N	NA	$\frac{3}{16}$P–$\frac{3}{16}$N	—
	J30	Front:	$5\frac{7}{8}$P–$7\frac{3}{8}$P	NA	$1\frac{1}{2}$N–0	NA	0–$\frac{5}{64}$N	—
		Rear:	—	—	$1\frac{1}{2}$N–$\frac{1}{2}$N	NA	0–$\frac{11}{64}$N	—
1994	Q45	Front:	$5\frac{3}{4}$P–$7\frac{1}{4}$P	NA	$1\frac{19}{32}$N–$\frac{3}{32}$N	NA	0–$\frac{3}{32}$N	$12\frac{3}{4}$
		Rear:	—	—	$1\frac{19}{32}$N–$\frac{19}{32}$N	NA	0–$\frac{3}{16}$N	—
	Q45 ①	Front:	$6\frac{3}{16}$P–$7\frac{11}{16}$P	NA	$1\frac{11}{16}$N–$\frac{3}{16}$N	NA	$\frac{1}{16}$P–$\frac{1}{16}$N	$12\frac{15}{16}$
		Rear:	—	—	2N–1N	NA	0–$\frac{3}{8}$N	—
	G20	Front:	$1\frac{3}{32}$P–$2\frac{19}{32}$P	NA	$\frac{3}{4}$N–$\frac{3}{4}$P	NA	0–$\frac{3}{16}$N	$14\frac{1}{2}$
		Rear:	—	—	$1\frac{3}{4}$N–$\frac{1}{4}$N	NA	$\frac{3}{16}$P–$\frac{3}{16}$N	—
	J30	Front:	$5\frac{7}{8}$P–$7\frac{3}{8}$P	NA	$1\frac{1}{2}$N–0	NA	0–$\frac{5}{64}$N	—
		Rear:	—	—	$1\frac{1}{2}$N–$\frac{1}{2}$N	NA	0–$\frac{11}{64}$N	—

① With active suspension

ENGINE MECHANICAL

NOTE: **Disconnecting the negative battery cable on some vehicles may interfere with the functions of the on-board computer systems and may require the computer to undergo a relearning process, once the negative battery cable is reconnected.**

Engine Assembly

REMOVAL AND INSTALLATION

G20

1. Disconnect the negative battery cable. Raise and support the vehicle safely. Remove the engine undercover. Matchmark the hood with the hood hinges and remove.
2. Drain the coolant from both the cylinder block and radiator.
3. Drain the engine oil.
4. Release fuel system pressure and remove fuel line.
5. Label and remove all vacuum lines and wiring harness connectors.
6. Remove exhaust tubes, ball joints and drive shafts.
7. Remove the radiator and fans.
8. Remove the drive belts.
9. Remove the alternator, compressor and power steering pump from the engine and lay them aside. Do not disconnect the compressor or power steering pump lines.
10. Support the engine with a hoist and the transmission with a suitable jack. Raise the engine and transaxle slightly and remove the center member.
11. Remove the bolts from the rear engine mount and slowly lower the hoist and transaxle jack.
12. Remove the engine and transaxle from beneath the vehicle.
   To install:
13. Install the center member bracket (manual transmission) on the engine, if removed. Ensure that all insulators are correctly positioned on the brackets. Tighten insulator through bolts to 32-41 ft. lbs. (43-55 Nm).
14. If equipped with manual transaxle, ensure that the distance between the center of the insulator through bolt and the center member is 2.28-2.36 in. (58-60mm). Tighten through bolt to 46-58 ft. lbs. (62-78 Nm).

15. Carefully install the engine and tighten the center member-to-frame bolts to 57-72 ft. lbs. (77-98 Nm).
16. Install the alternator, compressor and power steering pump.
17. Connect all vacuum hoses and wiring harness connectors. Connect the fuel line.
18. Install the exhaust tubes, ball joints, driveshafts, the radiator and fans and drive belts.
19. Fill the coolant system and the crankcase with oil.
20. Install the engine undercover and hood. Road test the vehicle for proper operation.

J30

1. Disconnect the negative battery cable.
2. Raise and support the vehicle safely.
3. Remove the engine undercover. Remove the hood after matchmarking it to the hinges.
4. Drain the cooling system. Use the cylinder block drain plugs to drain the engine.
5. Label and disconnect all vacuum hoses, fuel tubes, wires, harnesses and connectors from the engine.
6. Remove the propeller shaft.
7. Remove the radiator.
8. Remove the drive belts, cooling fan and coupling.
9. Remove the power steering pump, alternator, air conditioner pump and starter motor from the engine.
10. Remove the exhaust tube front nuts. Remove the front tubes after removing the exhaust tube bracket.
11. Remove the fluid charging pipe front the transmission.
12. Remove the cooler pipes from the transmission.
13. Remove the control linkage from the selector lever.
14. Disconnect the inhibitor switch and solenoid harness connectors.
15. Remove the gusset securing the transmission to the engine.
16. Remove the bolts securing torque converter to driveplate.
17. Support the engine and separate engine from transmission.
18. Lift the engine slightly and remove the engine mounting bolts from both sides.
19. Carefully remove the engine from the top side of the vehicle.
   To install:
20. Lower the engine into the vehicle and tighten the engine mounting bolts to 32-41 ft. lbs. (43-55 Nm).
21. Install the transmission into the vehicle. Tighten the converter

bolts to 33-43 ft. lbs. (44-59 Nm). Tighten the engine-to-transmission bolts as follows:
   a. Tighten the upper 6 bolts to 29-36 ft. lbs. (39-49 Nm).
   b. Tighten the lower 4 bolts to 22-29 ft. lbs. (29-39 Nm).
22. Connect the inhibitor switch and solenoid harness connectors.
23. Install the control linkage on the selector lever.
24. Install the cooler pipes on the transmission.
25. Install the fluid charging pipe on the transmission.
26. Install the front exhaust tubes and exhaust tube bracket. Tighten the nuts to 33-44 ft. lbs. (45-60 Nm).
27. Install the power steering pump, alternator, air conditioner pump and starter motor.
28. Install the drive belts, cooling fan and coupling. Tension the accessory drive belts.
29. Install the radiator. Install the driveshaft.
30. Connect all vacuum hoses, fuel tubes, wires, harnesses and connectors to the engine.
31. Check and fill the cooling system, engine oil, transmission fluid and power steering fluid.
32. Install the engine hood and undercover.
33. Connect the negative battery cable.
34. Start the engine and allow it to reach operating temperature. Make any necessary adjustments and check for leaks. Road test the vehicle for proper operation.

M30

1. Mark the hood hinge relationship and remove the hood and engine undercover.
2. Release the fuel system pressure and disconnect the negative battery cable. Raise and support the vehicle safely.
3. Remove the vacuum hoses, fuel tubes, wires, harnesses and connectors.
4. Remove the radiator with shroud and cooling fan.
5. Remove the drive belts, power steering oil pump and air conditioner compressor.
6. Remove the front exhaust tubes. Install engine slingers.
7. Remove or disconnect the transmission assembly.
8. Hoist engine and remove engine mounting bolts from both sides.
9. Remove the engine from the top side of the vehicle.

To install:

10. Lower the engine in vehicle. Connect the transmission to the engine.

11. Install all remaining components in reverse order.

12. Install or connect all hoses, belts, harnesses, connectors and components that were necessary to remove the engine.

13. Fill all fluids to the proper levels.

14. Install the hood and connect the negative battery cable.

15. Make all the necessary adjustments. Road test the vehicle for proper operation.

Q45

1. Disconnect the negative battery cable.

2. Relieve the pressure from the fuel system.

3. Mark the relation of the hood to the hinge brackets and remove the hood.

4. Raise and safely support the vehicle.

5. Remove the engine splash shield.

6. Drain the coolant and the engine oil.

7. Disconnect the transmission cooler lines from the radiator.

8. Remove the radiator hoses and remove the radiator and shroud.

9. Tag and disconnect all vacuum hoses, fuel lines and electrical connectors.

10. Disconnect the exhaust pipes from the exhaust manifolds.

11. Mark the position of the driveshaft on the flanges and remove the driveshaft.

12. Remove the accessory drive belts.

13. Remove the alternator, air conditioning compressor and power steering pump.

14. Remove the lower steering joint.

15. Remove the sway bar, transverse link and tension rod with bracket.

16. Place a suitable jack under the transmission and disconnect the transmission rear mount.

17. Remove the suspension member attaching bolts.

18. Remove the engine mounting bolts.

19. Attach a suitable hoist to the engine. Lower the transmission jack and the hoist and lower the engine and transmission from under the vehicle.

To install:

20. Install the engine and transmission into position. Check the clearance between the frame and transaxle and make sure the engine mount bolts are seated in the groove of the mounting bracket.

21. Tighten the engine mounts to the following torque specifications:

    a. Front engine mount bracket-to-engine bolts to 32-41 ft. lbs. (43-55 Nm).

    b. Front engine mount-to-frame bolts to 41-49 ft. lbs. (55-67 Nm).

    c. Rear engine mount-to-crossmember bolts to 16-21 ft. lbs. (22-28 Nm).

    d. Rear crossmember-to-frame bolts to 32-41 ft. lbs. (43-55 Nm).

22. Install the suspension member bolts.

23. Remove the hoist and the transmission jack.

24. Install the sway bar, transverse link and the tension rod with bracket.

25. Install the lower steering joint.

26. Install the alternator, air conditioning compressor and power steering pump.

27. Install and adjust the accessory drive belts.

28. Install the radiator and shroud. Install the radiator hoses.

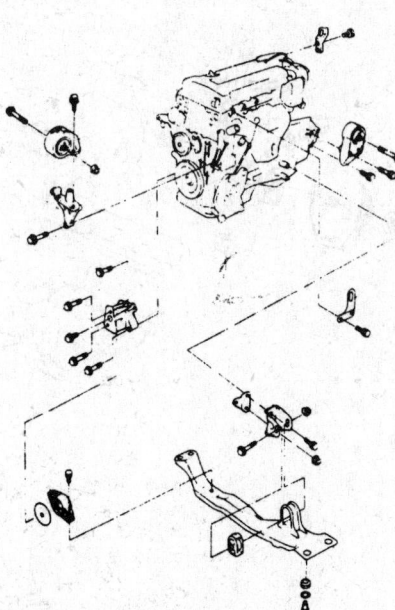

Engine mounts — G20

29. Install the driveshaft, aligning the marks that were made during the removal procedure.

30. Connect the exhaust pipes to the exhaust manifolds.

31. Connect all electrical connectors, fuel lines and vacuum hoses.

32. Fill the crankcase with the proper type of engine oil to the required level. Fill the cooling system with the proper type and quantity of coolant.

33. Install the hood, aligning the marks that were made during the removal procedure.

34. Connect the negative battery cable, start the engine and check for leaks. Road test the vehicle for proper operation.

Engine Mount

REMOVAL AND INSTALLATION

G20

1. Disconnect the negative battery cable.

2. Matchmark the engine mount to its frame mounting location.

3. Raise the vehicle and support safely, if necessary. Using the proper equipment, support the weight of the engine.

4. Inspect all mounts to determine which is defective. A defective mount will have the rubber portion of the mount separated from the metal backing or stud.

5. Remove all bolts and nuts that attach the mount to the engine, transaxle or frame and remove the mount assembly from the vehicle.

6. Remove the through bolt and separate the insulator from the bracket, as required.

7. Installation is the reverse of removal.

8. If equipped with manual transaxle, ensure that the distance between the center of the front mounting bracket through bolt and the center member is 2.28-2.36 in. (58-60mm). Tighten through bolt to 46-58 ft. lbs. (62-78 Nm).

9. Tighten center member bolts to 57-72 ft. lbs. (77-98 Nm); front and rear engine mount to 32-41 ft. lbs. (43-55 Nm).

J30

1. Raise and support the vehicle safely.

2. Attach a hoist to the engine and lift until the slack in the chain is taken up.

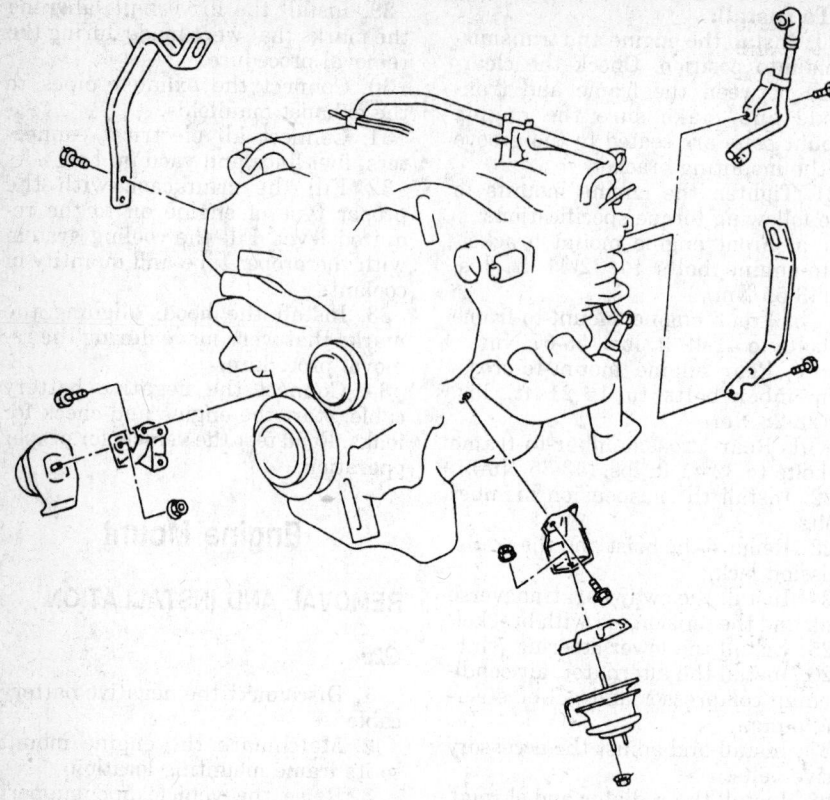

Engine mounts — J30

3. Remove the nuts from the engine mounts.

NOTE: Inspect the engine compartment for components that may bind when the engine is raised. Disconnect these components.

4. Lift the engine the exact amount needed to remove the engine mount. Do not lift any higher.

5. Remove the engine mounts.

To install:

6. Install the engine mounts.

7. Lower the engine and tighten the engine mount-to-engine nuts to 32-41 ft. lbs. (43-55 Nm). Tighten the engine mount-to-frame nuts to 41-49 ft. lbs. (55-67 Nm).

8. Remove the engine hoist and lower the vehicle.

M30

1. Disconnect the negative battery cable.

2. Matchmark the engine mount to its frame mounting location.

3. Raise the vehicle and support safely, if necessary. Using the proper equipment, support the weight of the engine.

4. Inspect all mounts to determine which is defective. A defective mount will have the rubber portion of the

mount separated from the metal backing or stud.

5. Remove all bolts and nuts that attach the mount to the engine, transmission or frame and remove the mount assembly from the vehicle.

6. Remove the through bolt and separate the insulator from the bracket, as required.

7. Installation is the reverse of removal.

8. Tighten bolts as follows: engine mount-to-frame bolt to 29-36 ft. lbs. (39-49 Nm); engine mount-to-bracket bolt to 29-36 ft. lbs. (39-49 Nm); transmission mount-to-crossmember bolt to 16-21 ft. lbs. (22-28 Nm); crossmember-to-frame bolt to 32-41 ft. lbs. (43-55 Nm).

Q45

1. Disconnect the negative battery cable.

2. Matchmark the engine mount to its frame mounting location.

3. Raise the vehicle and support safely, if necessary. Using the proper equipment, support the weight of the engine.

4. Inspect all mounts to determine which is defective. A defective mount will have the rubber portion of the mount separated from the metal backing or stud.

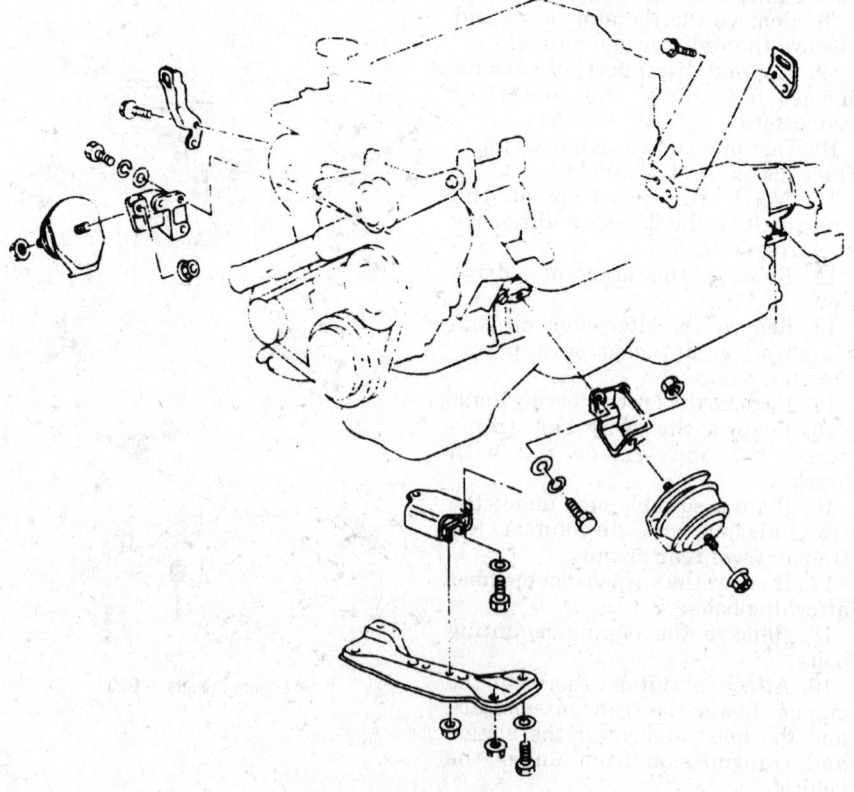

Engine mounts — M30, Q45 similar

5. Remove all bolts and nuts that attach the mount to the engine, transmission or frame and remove the mount assembly from the vehicle.

6. Remove the through bolt and separate the insulator from the bracket, as required.

7. Installation is the reverse of removal.

8. Tighten bolts as follows:
Engine mount-to-frame bolt to 41-49 ft. lbs. (55-67 Nm)
Engine mount-to-engine bolt to 32-41 ft. lbs. (43-55 Nm)
Transmission mount-to-crossmember bolt to 16-21 ft. lbs. (22-28 Nm)
Crossmember-to-frame bolt to 32-41 ft. lbs. (43-55 Nm).

Cylinder Head

REMOVAL AND INSTALLATION

G20

1. Relieve the fuel system pressure and disconnect the negative battery cable.

2. Drain the coolant from the radiator and engine block. Remove the radiator.

3. Remove the right front wheel and engine side cover.

4. Remove the air duct to the intake manifold.

5. Remove the drive belts, water pump pulley, alternator and power steering pump.

6. Label and remove the vacuum hoses, fuel hoses and wire harness connectors.

7. Remove all the spark plugs, the AIV valve and resonator.

8. Remove the rocker cover and oil separator. Loosen rocker cover bolts, using 2-3 steps, in the opposite sequence of tightening

9. Remove the intake manifold supports.

10. Remove the oil filter bracket and power steering oil pump bracket.

11. Set No. 1 piston at TDC on the compression stroke by rotating the crankshaft. Rotate the crankshaft until the mating marks on the camshaft sprockets are at the 11 o'clock and 1 o'clock positions.

12. Remove the chain tensioner.

13. Remove the distributor. Do not turn the rotor with the distributor removed.

14. Remove the timing chain guide, camshaft sprockets, camshafts, brackets, oil tubes and baffle plate. The camshaft bracket bolts must be loosened in sequence to prevent damage to the camshafts or the head.

15. Remove the cylinder block water hose and heater hoses.

16. Remove the starter motor and water pipe bolt.

17. Remove the outside cylinder head bolts, then the inside cylinder head bolts by loosening in 2-3 steps, in the reverse order of the tightening sequence.

18. Remove the cylinder head with the intake and exhaust manifolds attached.

To install:

19. Apply a continuous bead of liquid gasket to the mating surface of the cylinder block before installing the head gasket.

20. Install the the gasket and cylinder head on the block.

NOTE: Cylinder head bolts may be reused providing the dimension from the bottom of the head to the end of the bolt does not exceed 6.228 in. (158.2mm). If the dimension exceeds the specification, install replacement cylinder head bolts.

21. Tighten cylinder head bolts as follows:
   a. Tighten all bolts to 29 ft. lbs. (39 Nm) using the proper sequence.
   b. Tighten all bolts to 58 ft. lbs. (78 Nm) using the proper sequence.
   c. Loosen all bolts completely.
   d. Tighten all bolts to 25-33 ft. lbs. (34-44 Nm) using the proper sequence.
   e. Tighten all bolts 90-100 degrees.
   f. Tighten all bolts an additional 90-100 degrees.

22. Install the cylinder head outside bolts.

23. Install the water pipe bolt, starter motor and water hoses.

24. Clean the left hand camshaft end bracket and coat with liquid gasket. Install the camshafts, camshaft brackets, oil tubes and baffle plate. Ensure the left camshaft key is at 12 o'clock and the right camshaft key is at 10 o'clock.

25. The procedure for tightening camshaft bolts must be followed exactly to prevent camshaft damage. Tighten bolts as follows:
   a. Tighten right camshaft bolts 9 and 10 (in that order) to 1.5 ft. lbs. (2 Nm), then tighten bolts 1 through 8 (in that order) to the same specification.
   b. Tighten left camshaft bolts 11 and 12 (in that order) to 1.5 ft. lbs. (2 Nm), then tighten bolts 1 through 10 (in that order) to the same specification.
   c. Tighten all bolts in sequence to 4.5 ft. lbs. (6 Nm).

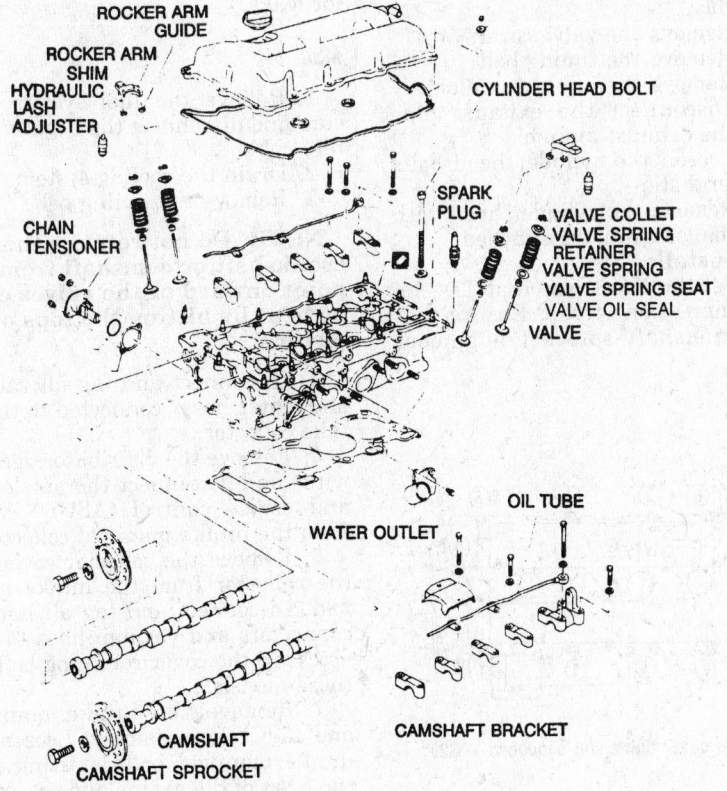

ROCKER ARM GUIDE
ROCKER ARM SHIM
HYDRAULIC LASH ADJUSTER
CYLINDER HEAD BOLT
CHAIN TENSIONER
SPARK PLUG
VALVE COLLET
VALVE SPRING RETAINER
VALVE SPRING
VALVE SPRING SEAT
VALVE OIL SEAL
VALVE
OIL TUBE
WATER OUTLET
CAMSHAFT BRACKET
CAMSHAFT
CAMSHAFT SPROCKET

Cylinder head components — G20

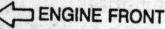

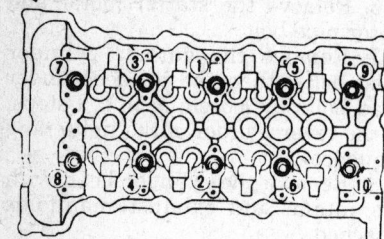

Cylinder head inside bolt torque sequence — G20

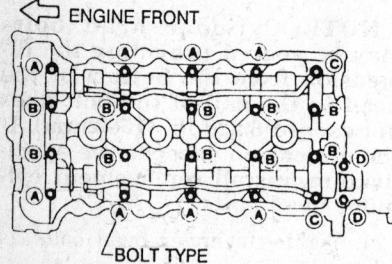

Camshaft bracket bolt type — G20

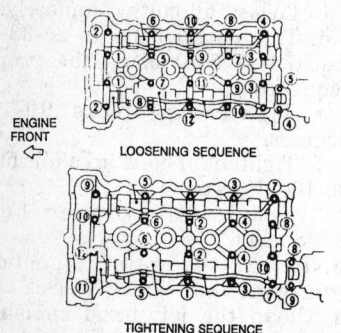

Camshaft bracket loosening and tightening sequence — G20

d. Tighten all bolts in sequence to 6.5-8.5 ft. lbs. (9-12 Nm) for type A, B and C bolts and 13-19 ft. lbs. (18-25 Nm) for type D bolts.

26. Line up the mating marks on the timing chain and camshaft sprockets and install the sprockets. Tighten sprocket bolts to 101-116 ft. lbs. (137-157 Nm).

27. Install the timing chain guide, distributor (ensure that rotor head is at 5 o'clock position), chain tensioner, oil filter bracket and power steering oil pump bracket.

28. Install intake manifold supports. Clean the rocker cover and mating surfaces and apply a continuous bead of liquid gasket to the mating surface.

29. Install the rocker cover and oil separator. Tighten the rocker cover bolts as follows:

    a. Tighten nuts 1, 10, 11 and 8, in that order to 3 ft. lbs. (4 Nm).

    b. Tighten nuts 1 through 13 as indicated in the figure to 6-7 ft. lbs. (8-10 Nm).

30. Install the AIV and resonator, spark plugs, power steering pump, alternator water pump pulley and drive belts, air duct to the intake manifold and the radiator.

31. Install all vacuum and fuel hoses and reconnect all electrical connections.

32. Install the engine side cover, right front wheel and engine undercover.

33. Refill the cooling system.

J30

1. Relieve the fuel system pressure. Drain the cooling system.

2. Label and disconnect all electrical connectors and vacuum hoses.

3. Disconnect the intake air ducts from the throttle body.

4. Remove the intake manifold collector.

5. Remove the injector pipe assembly.

6. Remove the valve covers.

7. Remove the timing belt.

8. Remove the intake manifold.

9. Disconnect the exhaust pipe from the exhaust manifold.

10. Loosen the cylinder head bolts in several steps.

11. Remove the cylinder head with the exhaust manifold attached.

To install:

12. Set the No. 1 piston at TDC on its compression stroke. Ensure that the crankshaft sprocket alignment

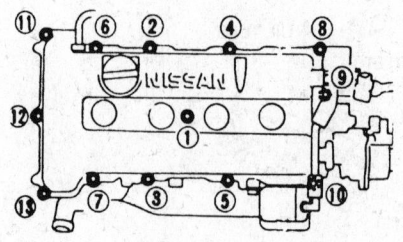

Rocker cover tightening sequence — G20

mark is aligned with the one on the oil pump body and the camshaft sprocket alignment mark is aligned with the one on the timing belt rear cover.

13. Install the cylinder head using a new gasket. Install the cylinder head bolts with washers.

14. Tighten the cylinder head bolts as follows:

    a. Tighten all bolts to 29 ft. lbs. (39 Nm).

    b. Tighten all bolts to 90 ft. lbs. (123 Nm).

    c. Loosen all bolts completely.

    d. Tighten all bolts to 25-33 ft. lbs. (34-44 Nm).

    e. Tighten all bolts to 90 ft. lbs. (123 Nm).

15. Tighten the bolts on the outer corners of each head (bolts marked M6) to 7-9 ft. lbs. (10-12 Nm).

16. Install the valve covers, timing belt and intake manifold.

17. Install the exhaust pipe on the exhaust manifold.

18. Install the injector pipe assembly and intake manifold collector.

19. Connect the intake air ducts to the throttle body.

20. Connect all electrical connectors and vacuum hoses.

21. Make any necessary adjustments.

22. Start the engine and allow it to reach operating temperature. Check for leaks.

M30

1. Relieve the fuel system pressure and disconnect the negative battery cable.

2. Drain the cooling system.

3. Remove the timing belt.

NOTE: Do not rotate either the crankshaft or camshaft from this point onward or the valves could be bent by hitting the tops of the pistons.

4. Disconnect and tag all vacuum and water hoses connected to the intake collector.

5. Remove the distributor, ignition wires and disconnect the accelerator and cruise control (ASCD) cables from the intake manifold collector.

6. Remove the collector cover and the collector from the intake manifold. Disconnect and tag all harness connectors and vacuum lines to gain access to the cover retaining bolts on these models.

7. Remove the intake manifold and fuel tube assembly. Loosen the intake manifold bolts starting from the front of the engine and proceed in crisscross pattern towards the center.

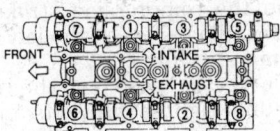

LEFT CYLINDER HEAD

RIGHT CYLINDER HEAD

Cylinder head torquing sequence — J30

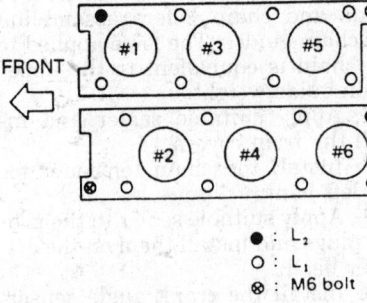

FRONT

● : L₂
○ : L₁
⊗ : M6 bolt

Tighten the outer cylinder head bolts to 7-9 ft. lbs. (10-12 Nm) — J30

8. Remove the exhaust collector bracket.

9. Remove the exhaust manifold covers.

10. Disconnect the exhaust manifold from the exhaust pipe.

11. Remove the camshaft pulleys and the rear timing cover securing bolts. Remove the distributor and ignition wires. Remove the rocker arm covers.

12. Separate the air conditioning compressor and alternator from the their mounting brackets. Remove the mounting brackets. Do not disconnect

the refrigerant lines from the compressor or serious injury will result.

13. Remove the cylinder head bolts in the correct sequence. Lift the cylinder head off the engine block with the exhaust manifolds attached. It may be necessary to tap the head lightly with a rubber mallet to loosen it.

To install:

14. Make sure the No. 1 cylinder is set at TDC on its compression stroke as follows:

a. Align the crankshaft timing mark with the mark on the oil pump housing.

b. The knock pin in the front end of the camshaft should be facing upward.

NOTE: Do not rotate crankshaft and camshaft separately because valves will hit piston head.

15. Install the cylinder head with a new gasket. Apply clean engine oil to the threads and seats of the bolts and install the bolts with washers in the correct position. Note that bolts 4, 5, 12 and 13 are 4.95 in. (127mm) long. The other bolts are 4.13 in. (106mm) long.

16. Torque the bolts in the proper sequence as follows:

a. Torque all bolts, in sequence, to 22 ft. lbs. (29 Nm).

b. Torque all bolts, in sequence, to 43 ft. lbs. (58 Nm).

c. Loosen all bolts completely.

d. Torque all bolts, in sequence, to 22 ft. lbs. (29 Nm).

e. Using an angle torque wrench, torque all bolts in sequence an additional 60-65 degrees. If an angle torque wrench is not available, tighten all bolts in sequence to 40-47 ft. lbs. (54-64 Nm).

17. Install the rocker covers. Install the alternator and air conditioner compressor mounting brackets. Mount the compressor and alternator.

18. Install the rear timing cover bolts. Install the camshaft pulleys. Make sure the pulley marked **R3** goes on the right and that marked **L3** goes on the left. Align the timing marks if necessary and install the timing belt and adjust the belt tension.

19. Connect the exhaust manifold to the exhaust pipe.

20. Install the exhaust manifold covers.

21. Install the exhaust collector bracket.

22. Install the intake manifold and fuel tube assembly.

23. Install the distributor and ignition wires. Install the intake manifold collector cover.

24. Connect the accelerator and cruise control cables to the intake manifold and install the distributor and ignition wires.

25. Connect the vacuum and water hoses to the intake collector.

26. Install and tension the timing belt.

27. Fill the cooling system and connect the negative battery cable.

28. Make all the necessary engine adjustments.

NOTE: If valve clatter is noticed when engine is started, the hydraulic lifters must be bled. Run the engine at 1000 rpm for 10 minutes to bleed lifters.

Q45

1. Disconnect the negative battery cable.

2. Remove the engine and transmission assembly from the vehicle.

3. Remove the suspension member and engine mounts from the engine.

4. Remove the air compressor bracket and the exhaust manifolds.

5. Remove the cooling fan with coupling and the engine gusset.

6. Separate the engine from the transmission and mount the engine on a suitable workstand.

7. Remove the oil pan. Remove the intake collector.

8. Disconnect the injector harness connector and remove the injector tube assembly with injector. Loosen bolts in opposite sequence of torquing..

NOTE: Be careful not to let the rubber washer fall into the intake manifold.

9. Remove the intake manifold.

10. Remove the ornamental rocker cover and remove the ignition coils and spark plugs.

11. Bring the No. 1 piston to TDC on the compression stroke.

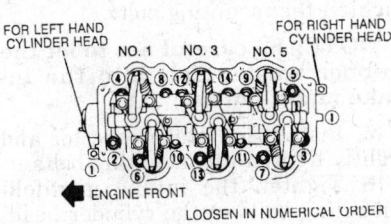

FOR LEFT HAND CYLINDER HEAD   FOR RIGHT HAND CYLINDER HEAD

NO. 1   NO. 3   NO. 5

ENGINE FRONT

LOOSEN IN NUMERICAL ORDER

Cylinder head bolt removal sequence — M30

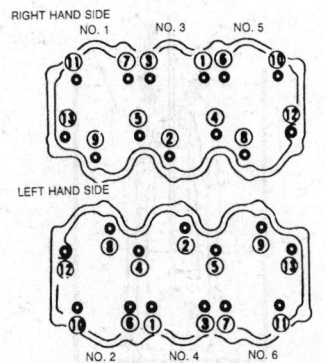

RIGHT HAND SIDE

NO. 1   NO. 3   NO. 5

LEFT HAND SIDE

NO. 2   NO. 4   NO. 6

Cylinder head bolt tightening sequence — M30

12. Use a suitable puller to remove the crankshaft pulley.

13. Remove the rocker cover.

14. Remove the crank angle sensor and the Valve Timing Control (VTC) solenoid.

15. Remove the chain tensioners and the upper front covers.

16. Remove the front timing chain cover.

NOTE: The timing chain will not be disengaged or dislocated from the crankshaft sprocket unless the front cover is removed. The cast portion of the front cover is located on the lower side of the crankshaft sprocket so the timing chain is not disengaged from the sprocket.

17. Remove the VTC assembly and the camshaft sprocket.

18. Remove the oil pump chain and the timing chains.

NOTE: Do not attempt to disassemble the VTC assembly since they are difficult to reassemble accurately in the field. If it should be disassembled, the VTC assembly must be replaced with a new one.

19. Remove the camshaft brackets in the reverse order of torquing sequence. Use 2-3 steps. Remove the camshafts. Mark the parts so they can be reinstalled in their original positions.

20. Remove the rocker arm and hydraulic lash adjuster. Be sure to identify each adjuster so it can be reinstalled in it's original position.

21. Remove the cylinder head and gasket. Loosen the head bolts in 2-3 steps working from the outside bolts in towards the center bolts.

To install:

22. Make sure all mating surfaces are clean before installation.

23. Check the cylinder head surface for warpage using a feeler gauge and a suitable straightedge. If the cylinder head is warped more than 0.004 in. (0.1mm), it must be resurfaced or replaced. The total amount machined from the head or head and block combined, cannot total more than 0.008 in. (0.2mm).

24. Make sure the No. 1 piston is still at TDC of the compression stroke, then turn the crankshaft until the No. 1 piston is at approximately 45 degrees before TDC on the compression stroke. At this point, the No. 3 piston will be at the same height as the No. 1 piston to prevent interference of the valves and pistons.

25. Install the cylinder heads with new gaskets. Temporarily tighten the

cylinder head bolts to avoid damaging the cylinder head gaskets. Be sure to install washers between the bolts and the cylinder heads. Do not rotate the crankshaft or camshaft separately or the valves will hit the pistons.

26. Install the hydraulic lash adjusters and check them as follows:

    a. When the rocker arm can be moved at least 0.04 in. (1.0mm) by pushing at the hydraulic lash adjuster location, it indicates that there is air in the high pressure chamber. Noise will be emitted from the hydraulic lash adjuster if the engine is started without bleeding the air.

    b. Remove the hydraulic lash adjuster and dip in a container filled with engine oil. While pushing the top of the plunger down, insert a suitable thin rod through the hole in the top of the plunger and lightly push the check ball. Air is completely bled when the plunger no longer moves.

NOTE: Air cannot be bled from the lash adjusters by running the engine.

27. Install the rocker arms, camshafts and camshaft brackets on the right bank and tighten in the proper sequence to 9-10 ft. lbs (12-14 Nm).

28. Install the VTC assembly and the exhaust camshaft sprocket on the right bank.

29. After making sure the camshafts are still correctly positioned, turn the crankshaft clockwise to bring the No. 1 piston to TDC on the compression stroke.

30. Install the timing chain on the right bank, aligning the mating marks on the chain with those on the crankshaft and camshaft sprockets.

31. Install the chain tensioner on the right bank.

32. Turn the crankshaft approximately 120 degrees clockwise from

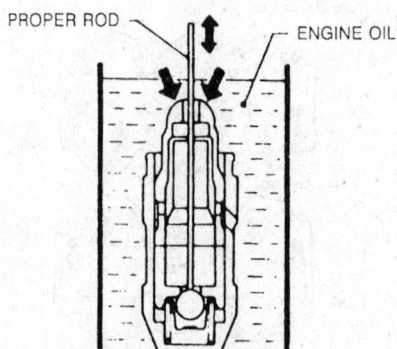

Hydraulic lash adjuster bleeding — Q45

the point where the No. 1 piston is at TDC on the compression stroke. At this point, the valves on the left bank still remain unlifted.

33. Correctly position the camshafts and tighten brackets in the proper sequence to 9-10 ft. lbs. (12-14 Nm). Install the VTC assembly and the exhaust cam sprocket.

34. Install the timing chain on the left bank, aligning the mating marks on the chain with those on the crankshaft and camshaft sprockets.

35. Install the oil pump chain and sprockets.

36. Install the oil pump chain guides. Place a 0.04 in. (1.0mm) feeler gauge between the upper chain guide and chain before assembling the chain guides. The force applied to the chain is equivalent to the upper chain guide weight.

37. Apply suitable sealer and install the front covers.

38. Install the chain tensioner for the left bank.

39. Apply suitable sealer to the rubber plugs and install them on the cylinder head.

40. Install the crank angle sensor, VTC solenoid, rocker cover and crank pulley.

41. Bring the piston in No. 1 cylinder to TDC on the compression stroke.

42. Tighten the cylinder head bolts in the proper torque sequence as follows:

    a. Tighten the bolts in sequence to 22 ft. lbs. (29 Nm).

    b. Tighten the bolts in sequence to 69 ft. lbs. (93 Nm).

    c. Loosen the bolts completely.

    d. Tighten the bolts in sequence to 18-25 ft. lbs. (25-34 Nm).

    e. Turn the bolts in sequence 90-95 degrees or 69-72 ft. lbs. (93-98 Nm).

43. Install the intake manifold bolts in their proper positions on the cylinder head and lightly tighten the mounting bolts.

44. Connect the injector tube assemblies, including the fuel injectors, to the intake manifolds and lightly tighten the mounting bolts.

NOTE: Be careful not to let the rubber washer fall into the intake manifold.

45. Install the intake collector and lightly tighten the mounting bolts.

46. Tighten the intake manifold mounting bolts at the cylinder head, remove the intake collectors and tighten the intake manifolds to 12-15 ft. lbs. (16-21 Nm).

47. Tighten the sub-fuel tubes, in sequence, first to 3.1-4.3 ft. lbs.

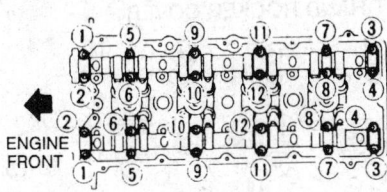

Camshaft bracket bolt torque sequence — Q45

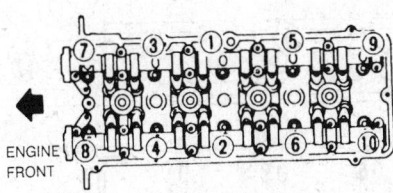

Cylinder head torque sequence — Q45

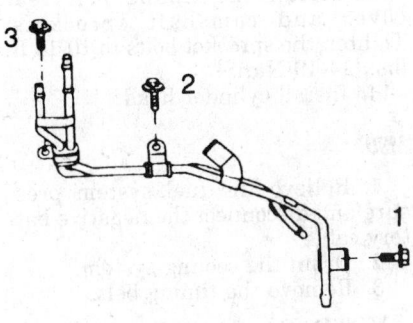

Sub-fuel tubes torque sequence

(4.2-5.9 Nm) and then to 6.2-8.0 ft. lbs. (8.4-10.8 Nm).

48. Tighten the injector tube assemblies, in sequence, first to 6.9-8.0 ft. lbs. (9.3-10.8 Nm) and then to 15-20 ft. lbs. (21-26 Nm).

49. Install the intake collectors and tighten to 9-11 ft. lbs. (12-15 Nm).

50. Install the exhaust manifolds.

51. Install the rocker covers and tighten in the proper sequence to 5-7 ft. lbs. (7-10 Nm).

52. Install all other remaining components. Join the engine and trans-

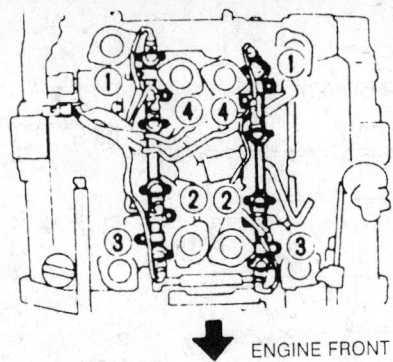

ENGINE FRONT

Injector tube torque sequence

mission and install the assembly in the vehicle.

Hydraulic Lash Adjusters

REMOVAL AND INSTALLATION

G20

1. Relieve the fuel system pressure and Disconnect the negative battery cable.

2. Drain the coolant from the radiator and engine block. Remove the radiator.

3. Raise and support the vehicle safely. Remove the right front wheel and engine side cover.

4. Remove the air duct to the intake manifold.

5. Remove the drive belts, water pump pulley, alternator and power steering pump.

6. Label and remove the vacuum hoses, fuel hoses and wire harness connectors.

7. Remove all the spark plugs, the AIV valve and resonator.

8. Remove the rocker cover and oil separator. Loosen rocker cover bolts, using 2-3 steps, in the opposite sequence of tightening

9. Remove the intake manifold supports.

10. Remove the oil filter bracket and power steering oil pump bracket.

11. Set No. 1 piston at TDC on the compression stroke by rotating the crankshaft.

12. Remove the chain tensioner.

13. Remove the distributor. Do not turn the rotor with the distributor removed.

14. Remove the timing chain guide, camshaft sprockets, camshafts, brackets, oil tubes and baffle plate. The camshaft bracket bolts must be loosened in sequence to prevent damage to the camshafts or the head.

15. Remove the hydraulic lash adjuster and rocker arm assembly.

To install:

16. Install the hydraulic lash adjusters and check them as follows:

a. When the rocker arm can be moved at least 0.04 in. (1.0mm) by pushing at the hydraulic lash adjuster location, it indicates that there is air in the high pressure chamber. Noise will be emitted from the hydraulic lash adjuster if the engine is started without bleeding the air.

b. Remove the hydraulic lash adjuster and dip in a container filled with engine oil. While pushing the top of the plunger down, insert a suitable thin rod through the hole in the top of the plunger and lightly push the check ball. Air is completely bled when the plunger no longer moves.

NOTE: Air cannot be bled from the lash adjusters by running the engine.

17. Clean the camshaft end bracket and coat with liquid gasket. Install the camshafts, camshaft brackets, oil tubes and baffle plate. Ensure the left camshaft key is at 12 o'clock and the right camshaft key is at 10 o'clock.

18. The procedure for tightening camshaft bracket bolts must be followed exactly to prevent camshaft damage. Tighten bolts as follows:

a. Tighten right camshaft bolts 9 and 10 (in that order) to 1.5 ft. lbs. (2 Nm) then tighten bolts 1 through 8 (in that order) to the same specification.

b. Tighten left camshaft bolts 11 and 12 (in that order) to 1.5 ft. lbs. (2 Nm) then tighten bolts 1 through 10 (in that order) to the same specification.

c. Tighten all bolts in sequence to 4.5 ft. lbs. (6 Nm).

d. Tighten all bolts in sequence to 6.5-8.5 ft. lbs. (9-12 Nm) for type A, B and C bolts and 13-19 ft. lbs. (18-25 Nm) for type D bolts.

19. Line up the mating marks on the timing chain and camshaft sprockets and install the sprockets. Tighten sprocket bolts to 101-116 ft. lbs. (137-157 Nm).

20. Install the timing chain guide, distributor (ensure that rotor head is at 5 o'clock position) and chain tensioner.

21. Install intake manifold supports. Clean the rocker cover and mating surfaces and apply a continuous bead of liquid gasket to the mating surface.

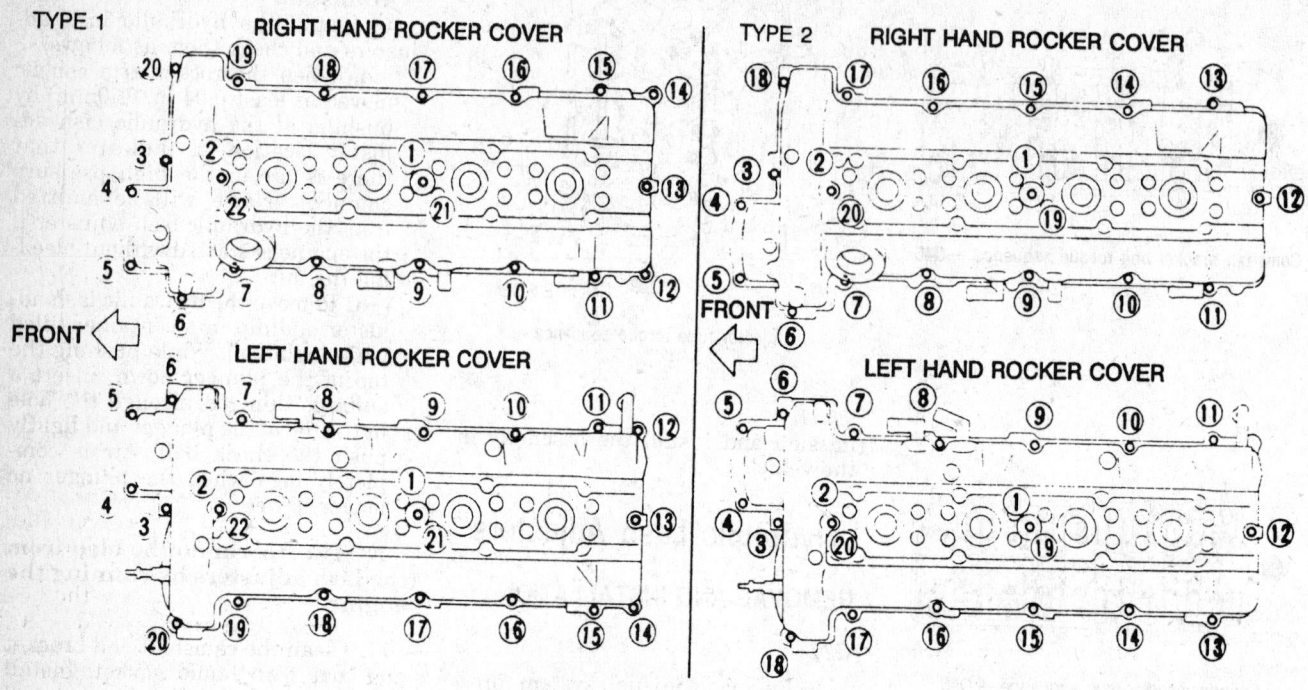

Rocker cover bolt torque sequence — Q45

22. Install the rocker cover and oil separator. Tighten the rocker cover bolts as follows:

  a. Tighten nuts 1, 10, 11 and 8, in that order to 3 ft. lbs. (4 Nm).

  b. Tighten nuts 1 through 13 in the proper sequence to 6-7 ft. lbs. (8-10 Nm).

23. Installation of the remaining components is the reverse of removal procedures.

J30

1. Disconnect the negative battery cable.

2. Remove the cylinder head.

3. Remove the exhaust manifold from the cylinder head.

4. Remove the camshaft sprockets and timing belt rear cover.

5. Remove the VTC solenoid valve.

6. Measure the camshaft end-play for installation reference.

7. Loosen the camshaft bracket bolts in several steps. Remove the camshaft brackets.

8. Remove the oil seals, camshafts and hydraulic valve lifters.

To install:

9. Install the hydraulic valve lifters and camshafts. Align the camshaft knock pins at 90 degrees to the top surface of the cylinder head.

NOTE: The left side exhaust camshaft has a spline for the crankshaft position sensor.

10. Coat the VTC solenoid valve surfaces with liquid gasket and install.

11. Apply liquid gasket to the front sealing surfaces of the front camshaft brackets.

12. Install the camshaft brackets and tighten from the center outward in several steps to 7-9 ft. lbs. (9-12 Nm).

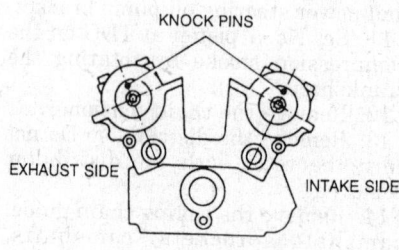

KNOCK PINS

EXHAUST SIDE

INTAKE SIDE

Aligning the camshafts — J30

13. Install the timing belt rear cover and camshaft sprockets. Tighten the sprocket bolts to 10-14 ft. lbs. (14-19 Nm).

14. Install cylinder head.

M30

1. Relieve the fuel system pressure and disconnect the negative battery cable.

2. Drain the cooling system.

3. Remove the timing belt.

NOTE: Do not rotate either the crankshaft or camshaft from this point onward or the valves could be bent by hitting the tops of the pistons.

4. Disconnect and tag all vacuum and water hoses connected to the intake collector.

5. Remove the distributor, ignition wires and disconnect the accelerator and cruise control (ASCD) cables from the intake manifold collector.

6. Remove the collector cover and the collector from the intake manifold. Disconnect and tag all harness connectors and vacuum lines to gain access to the cover retaining bolts on these models.

7. Remove the intake manifold and fuel tube assembly. Loosen the intake manifold bolts starting from

the front of the engine and proceed in crisscross pattern towards the center.

8. Remove the exhaust bracket.

9. Remove the exhaust manifold covers.

10. Disconnect the exhaust manifold from the exhaust pipe.

11. Remove the camshaft pulleys and the rear timing cover securing bolts. Remove the rocker arm covers.

12. Separate the air conditioning compressor and alternator from the their mounting brackets. Remove the mounting brackets.

13. Remove the rocker shafts with the rocker arms. The bolts should be loosened in 2-3 steps.

14. Remove the hydraulic valve lifters and the lifter guide. Hold the valve lifter with wire so they do not fall from the lifter guide.

To install:

15. Install the valve lifters into the valve lifter guide.

16. Assemble the lifters to their original position and hold all the lifters with wire to prevent the lifters from falling out. After installing them, remove the wire.

17. Install the rocker shafts with the rocker arms. Tighten the bolts gradually in 2-3 stages. Before tightening, be sure to set camshaft lobe at the position where lobe is not lifted. Set each cylinder 1 at a time or follow the procedure below. The cylinder head, intake manifold, collector and timing belt must be installed:

a. Set No. 1 piston at TDC of compression stroke and tighten rocker shaft bolts for No. 2, 4 and 6 cylinders.

b. Set No. 4 piston at TDC of compression stroke and tighten rocker shaft bolts for No. 1, 3 and 5 cylinders.

c. Torque specification for the rocker shaft retaining bolts is 13-16 ft. lbs. (18-22 Nm).

18. Install the alternator and air conditioner compressor mounting brackets. Mount the compressor and alternator.

19. Install the rear timing cover bolts. Install the camshaft pulleys. Make sure the pulley marked **R3** goes on the right and that marked **L3** goes on the left. Align the timing marks if necessary, install the timing belt and adjust the belt tension.

20. Connect the exhaust manifold to the exhaust pipe.

21. Install the exhaust manifold covers.

22. Install the exhaust collector bracket.

23. Install the intake manifold and fuel tube assembly.

24. Install the intake manifold collector cover.

25. Connect the accelerator and cruise control cables to the intake manifold and install the distributor and ignition wires.

26. Connect the vacuum and water hoses to the intake collector.

27. Install and tension the timing belt.

28. Fill the cooling system and connect the negative battery cable.

29. Make all the necessary engine adjustments.

Q45

1. Disconnect the negative battery cable.

2. Remove the engine and transmission assembly from the vehicle.

3. Remove the suspension member and engine mounts from the engine.

4. Remove the air compressor bracket.

5. Remove the cooling fan with coupling and the engine gusset.

6. Separate the engine from the transmission and mount the engine on a suitable workstand.

7. Remove the oil pan.

8. Remove the ornamental rocker cover and remove the ignition coils and spark plugs.

9. Bring the No. 1 piston to TDC on the compression stroke.

10. Use a suitable puller to remove the crankshaft pulley.

11. Remove the rocker cover.

12. Remove the crank angle sensor and the Valve Timing Control (VTC) solenoid.

13. Remove the chain tensioners and the upper front covers.

14. Remove the front timing chain cover.

NOTE: The timing chain will not be disengaged or dislocated from the crankshaft sprocket unless the front cover is removed. The cast portion of the front cover is located on the lower side of the crankshaft sprocket so the timing chain is not disengaged from the sprocket.

15. Remove the VTC assembly and the camshaft sprocket.

16. Remove the oil pump chain and the timing chains.

NOTE: Do not attempt to disassemble the VTC assembly since they are difficult to reassemble accurately in the field. If it should be disassembled, the VTC assembly must be replaced with a new one.

17. Remove the camshaft brackets and the camshafts. Mark the parts so they can be reinstalled in their original positions.

18. Remove the rocker arm and hydraulic lash adjuster. Be sure to identify each adjuster so it can be reinstalled in it's original position.

To install:

19. Make sure all mating surfaces are clean before installation.

20. Install the hydraulic lash adjusters and check them as follows:

a. When the rocker arm can be moved at least 0.04 in. (1.0mm) by pushing at the hydraulic lash adjuster location, it indicates that there is air in the high pressure chamber. Noise will be emitted from the hydraulic lash adjuster if the engine is started without bleeding the air.

b. Remove the hydraulic lash adjuster and dip in a container filled with engine oil. While pushing the top of the plunger down, insert a suitable thin rod through the hole in the top of the plunger and lightly push the check ball. Air is completely bled when the plunger no longer moves.

NOTE: Air cannot be bled from the lash adjusters by running the engine.

21. Install the rocker arms, camshafts and camshaft brackets on the right bank.

22. Install the VTC assembly and the exhaust cam sprocket on the right bank.

23. Make sure the camshafts are still correctly positioned and the piston in the No. 1 cylinder is still at TDC.

24. Install the timing chain on the right bank, aligning the mating marks on the chain with those on the crankshaft and camshaft sprockets.

25. Install the chain tensioner on the right bank.

26. Turn the crankshaft approximately 120 degrees clockwise from the point where the No. 1 piston is at TDC on the compression stroke. At this point, the valves on the left bank still remain unlifted.

27. Correctly position the camshafts for the left cylinder head. Install the VTC assembly and the exhaust cam sprocket.

28. Install the timing chain on the left bank, aligning the mating marks on the chain with those on the crankshaft and camshaft sprockets.

29. Install the oil pump chain and sprockets.

30. Install the oil pump chain guides. Place a 0.04 in. (1.0mm)

feeler gauge between the upper chain guide and chain before assembling the chain guides. The force applied to the chain is equivalent to the upper chain guide weight.

31. Apply suitable sealer and install the front covers.

32. Install the chain tensioner for the left bank.

33. Apply suitable sealer to the rubber plugs and install them on the cylinder head.

34. Install the crank angle sensor, VTC solenoid, rocker cover and crank pulley.

35. Installation of the remaining components is the reverse of the removal procedure.

Rocker Arms/Shafts

REMOVAL AND INSTALLATION

G20

1. Relieve the fuel system pressure and Disconnect the negative battery cable.

2. Drain the coolant from the radiator and engine block. Remove the radiator.

3. Raise and support the vehicle safely. Remove the right front wheel and engine side cover.

4. Remove the air duct to the intake manifold.

5. Remove the drive belts, water pump pulley, alternator and power steering pump.

6. Label and remove the vacuum hoses, fuel hoses and wire harness connectors.

7. Remove all the spark plugs, the AIV valve and resonator.

8. Remove the rocker cover and oil separator. Loosen rocker cover bolts, using 2-3 steps, in the opposite sequence of tightening

9. Remove the intake manifold supports.

10. Remove the oil filter bracket and power steering oil pump bracket.

11. Set No. 1 piston at TDC on the compression stroke by rotating the crankshaft.

12. Remove the chain tensioner.

13. Remove the distributor. Do not turn the rotor with the distributor removed.

14. Remove the timing chain guide, camshaft sprockets, camshafts, brackets, oil tubes and baffle plate. The camshaft bracket bolts must be loosened in sequence to prevent damage to the camshafts or the head.

15. Remove rocker arm assembly.

To install:

16. Check the hydraulic lash adjusters to ensure they did not bleed down during disassembly. If bleed down has occured, remove the lash adjuster and reprime.

NOTE: Air cannot be bled from the lash adjusters by running the engine.

17. Clean the camshaft end bracket and coat with liquid gasket. Install the camshafts, camshaft brackets, oil tubes and baffle plate. Ensure the left camshaft key is at 12 o'clock and the right camshaft key is at 10 o'clock.

18. The procedure for tightening camshaft bracket bolts must be followed exactly to prevent camshaft damage. Tighten bolts as follows:

    a. Tighten right camshaft bolts 9 and 10 (in that order) to 1.5 ft. lbs. (2 Nm) then tighten bolts 1-8 (in that order) to the same specification.

    b. Tighten left camshaft bolts 11 and 12 (in that order) to 1.5 ft. lbs. (2 Nm) then tighten bolts 1-10 (in that order) to the same specification.

    c. Tighten all bolts in sequence to 4.5 ft. lbs. (6 Nm).

    d. Tighten all bolts in sequence to 6.5-8.5 ft. lbs. (9-12 Nm) for type A, B and C bolts and 13-19 ft. lbs. (18-25 Nm) for type D bolts.

19. Line up the mating marks on the timing chain and camshaft sprockets and install the sprockets. Tighten sprocket bolts to 101-116 ft. lbs. (137-157 Nm).

20. Install the timing chain guide, distributor (ensure that rotor head is at 5 o'clock position) and chain tensioner.

21. Install intake manifold supports. Clean the rocker cover and mating surfaces and apply a continuous bead of liquid gasket to the mating surface.

22. Install the rocker cover and oil separator. Tighten the rocker cover bolts as follows:

    a. Tighten nuts 1, 10, 11 and 8, in that order to 3 ft. lbs. (4 Nm).

    b. Tighten nuts 1-13 in the proper sequence to 6-7 ft. lbs. (8-10 Nm).

23. Installation of the remaining components is the reverse of removal procedures.

M30

1. Relieve the fuel system pressure and disconnect the negative battery cable.

2. Drain the cooling system.

3. Remove the timing belt.

NOTE: Do not rotate either the crankshaft or camshaft from this point onward or the valves could be bent by hitting the tops of the pistons.

4. Disconnect and tag all vacuum and water hoses connected to the intake collector.

5. Remove the distributor, ignition wires and disconnect the accelerator and cruise control (ASCD) cables from the intake manifold collector.

6. Remove the collector cover and the collector from the intake manifold. Disconnect and tag all harness connectors and vacuum lines to gain access to the cover retaining bolts on these models.

7. Remove the intake manifold and fuel tube assembly. Loosen the intake manifold bolts starting from the front of the engine and proceed in crisscross pattern towards the center.

8. Remove the exhaust bracket.

9. Remove the exhaust manifold covers.

10. Disconnect the exhaust manifold from the exhaust pipe.

11. Remove the camshaft pulleys and the rear timing cover securing bolts. Remove the rocker arm covers.

12. Separate the air conditioning compressor and alternator from their mounting brackets. Remove the mounting brackets.

13. Remove the rocker shafts with the rocker arms. The bolts should be loosened in 2-3 steps.

To install:

14. Install the rocker shafts with the rocker arms. Tighten the bolts gradually in 2-3 stages. Before tightening, be sure to set camshaft lobe at the position where lobe is not lifted or the valve closed. Set each cylinder 1 at a time or follow the procedure below. The cylinder head, intake manifold, collector and timing belt must be installed:

    a. Set No. 1 piston at TDC of the compression stroke and tighten rocker shaft bolts for No. 2, 4 and 6 cylinders.

    b. Set No. 4 piston at TDC of the compression stroke and tighten rocker shaft bolts for No. 1, 3 and 5 cylinders.

    c. Torque specification for the rocker shaft retaining bolts is 13-16 ft. lbs. (18-22 Nm).

15. Install the alternator and air conditioner compressor mounting brackets. Mount the compressor and alternator.

16. Install the rear timing cover bolts. Install the camshaft pulleys. Make sure the pulley marked **R3**

goes on the right and that marked **L3** goes on the left. Align the timing marks, if necessary, and then install the timing belt and adjust the belt tension.

17. Connect the exhaust manifold to the exhaust pipe.
18. Install the exhaust manifold covers.
19. Install the exhaust bracket.
20. Install the intake manifold and fuel tube assembly.
21. Install the intake manifold collector cover.
22. Connect the accelerator and cruise control cables to the intake manifold and install the distributor and ignition wires.
23. Connect the vacuum and water hoses to the intake collector.
24. Install and tension the timing belt.
25. Fill the cooling system and connect the negative battery cable.
26. Make all the necessary engine adjustments.

Q45

1. Disconnect the negative battery cable.
2. Remove the engine and transmission assembly from the vehicle.
3. Remove the suspension member and engine mounts from the engine.
4. Remove the air compressor bracket.
5. Remove the cooling fan with coupling and the engine gusset.
6. Separate the engine from the transmission and mount the engine on a suitable workstand.
7. Remove the oil pan.
8. Remove the ornamental rocker cover and remove the ignition coils and spark plugs.
9. Bring the No. 1 piston to TDC on the compression stroke.
10. Use a suitable puller to remove the crankshaft pulley.
11. Remove the rocker cover.
12. Remove the crank angle sensor and the Valve Timing Control (VTC) solenoid.
13. Remove the chain tensioners and the upper front covers.
14. Remove the front timing chain cover.

NOTE: The timing chain will not be disengaged or dislocated from the crankshaft sprocket unless the front cover is removed. The cast portion of the front cover is located on the lower side of the crankshaft sprocket so the timing chain is not disengaged from the sprocket.

15. Remove the VTC assembly and the camshaft sprocket.
16. Remove the oil pump chain and the timing chains.

NOTE: Do not attempt to disassemble the VTC assembly since they are difficult to reassemble accurately in the field. If it should be disassembled, the VTC assembly must be replaced with a new one.

17. Remove the camshaft brackets and the camshafts. Mark the parts so they can be reinstalled in their original positions.
18. Remove the rocker arms. Be sure to identify each rocker arm so it can be reinstalled in it's original position.
   To install:
19. Make sure all mating surfaces are clean before installation.
20. Install the rocker arms, camshafts and camshaft brackets on the right bank. Properly lubricate the rocker arms and camshafts prior to installation.
21. Install the VTC assembly and the exhaust cam sprocket on the right bank.
22. Make sure the camshafts are still correctly positioned and the piston in the No. 1 cylinder is still at TDC.
23. Install the timing chain on the right bank, aligning the mating marks on the chain with those on the crankshaft and camshaft sprockets.
24. Install the chain tensioner on the right bank.
25. Turn the crankshaft approximately 120 degrees clockwise from the point where the No. 1 piston is at TDC on the compression stroke. At this point, the valves on the left bank still remain closed.
26. Correctly position the camshafts and rocker arms for the left cylinder head. Properly lubricate the rocker arms and camshafts prior to installation. Install the VTC assembly and the exhaust cam sprocket.
27. Install the timing chain on the left bank, aligning the mating marks on the chain with those on the crankshaft and camshaft sprockets.
28. Install the oil pump chain and sprockets.
29. Install the oil pump chain guides. Place a 0.04 in. (1.0mm) feeler gauge between the upper chain guide and chain before assembling the chain guides. The force applied to the chain is equivalent to the upper chain guide weight.
30. Apply suitable sealer and install the front covers.

31. Install the chain tensioner for the left bank.
32. Apply suitable sealer to the rubber plugs and install them on the cylinder head.
33. Install the crank angle sensor, VTC solenoid, rocker cover and crank pulley.
34. Installation of the remaining components is the reverse of the removal procedure.

Intake Manifold

REMOVAL AND INSTALLATION

G20

1. Disconnect the negative battery cable.
2. Properly relieve the fuel system pressure.
3. Drain the cooling system.
4. Tag and disconnect the fuel lines, vacuum hoses and electrical connectors. Disconnect the throttle linkage.
5. Remove the intake manifold collector. Loosen the retaining bolts from the ends, working toward the center position.
6. Remove the injector tube assembly and remove the intake manifold. Loosen bolts in the reverse order of the torquing sequence.
   To install:
7. Make sure all mating surfaces are clean prior to installation.
8. Install the intake manifold bolts, in their proper positions, on the cylinder head and lightly tighten the mounting bolts.
9. Connect the injector tube assembly, including the fuel injectors, to the intake manifold and lightly tighten the mounting bolts.
10. Install the intake collector and lightly tighten the mounting bolts.
11. To tighten the intake manifold mounting bolts at the cylinder head, remove the intake collector bolts and tighten the intake manifold in sequence to 13-15 ft. lbs. (18-21 Nm).
12. Tighten the injector tube assembly, first to 6.9-8.0 ft. lbs. (9.3-10.8 Nm) and then to 15-20 ft. lbs. (21-26 Nm).
13. Install the intake collector and tighten the bolts to 12-15 ft. lbs. (16-21 Nm).
14. Reconnect the fuel lines, vacuum hoses and electrical connectors. Disconnect the throttle linkage.
15. Refill the cooling system, connect the negative battery cable, start engine and test for leaks.

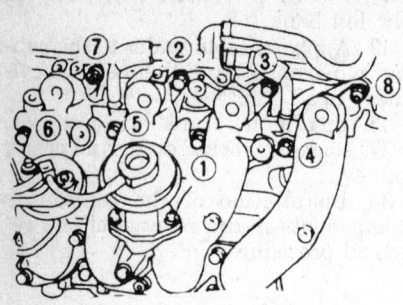

Intake manifold bolt torque sequence — G20

J30

1. Disconnect the negative battery cable.
2. Remove the air ducts. Drain the cooling system.
3. Label and disconnect all electrical harnesses and vacuum hoses.
4. Disconnect the accelerator linkage and all other accessories attached to the intake manifold collector.
5. Remove the intake manifold collector.
6. Relieve the fuel system pressure. Disconnect the fuel feed and return pipe.
7. Remove the injector pipe assembly.
8. Remove the timing belt, idler pulley and stud bolt.
9. Remove the intake manifold.
To install:
10. Install the intake manifold using new gaskets and sealant where necessary.
11. Tighten the intake manifold bolts hand-tight, then torque to 12-14 ft. lbs. (16-20 Nm).
12. Tighten the intake manifold nuts hand-tight, then torque to 17-20 ft. lbs. (24-27 Nm).
13. Install the stud bolt, idler pulley and timing belt.
14. Install the injector pipe assembly.
15. Connect the fuel feed and return pipes.
16. Install the intake manifold collector and tighten the attaching bolts to 12-15 ft. lbs. (16-21 Nm).
17. Connect the accelerator linkage and all other accessories attached to the intake manifold collector.
18. Connect all electrical harnesses and vacuum hoses.
19. Connect the air ducts.
20. Fill the cooling system.
21. Make any necessary adjustments. Start the engine and allow it to reach operating temperature. Check for leaks.

M30

1. Relieve the fuel system pressure, disconnect the negative battery cable and drain the cooling system.
2. Remove the distributor and the ignition wires.
3. Disconnect the ASCD and accelerator wires from the intake manifold collector.
4. Disconnect the harness connectors for the AAC valve, throttle sensor and idle switch.
5. Disconnect the air cut out valve water hose.
6. Disconnect the PCV valve hoses.
7. Disconnect the vacuum hoses from the vacuum gallery, swirl control valve, master brake cylinder, EGR control valve and EGR flare tube.
8. Loosen the upper collector cover bolts and remove the upper intake manifold collector from the engine. Remove the collector gasket.
9. Disconnect the engine ground harness.
10. Loosen the lower collector bolts and remove the lower intake manifold collector from the engine.
11. Disconnect the harness connectors for all injectors, engine temperature switch and sensor, power valve control solenoid valve, EGR control solenoid valve, EGR. temperature sensor (California only).
12. Disconnect the vacuum gallery hoses.
13. Disconnect the pressure regulator valve vacuum hose, heater hose, fuel feed and return hose.
14. Remove the intake manifold and fuel tube assembly. Loosen intake manifold bolts in numerical order.
To install:
15. Install the intake manifold and fuel tube assembly with a new gasket. Tighten the manifold bolts and nuts, in sequence to 12-14 ft. lbs. (16-20 Nm).
16. Connect the hoses and electrical wires to the intake manifold and fuel tube.
17. Install the upper and lower collector and collector cover with new gaskets. Tighten collector to intake manifold bolts, in 2-3 stages, working from the center to the end position.
18. Connect the vacuum lines, hoses, cables and brackets to the collector cover and collector assembly.
19. Install the distributor and ignition wires.
20. Fill the cooling system to the proper level and connect the negative battery cable.

21. Make all the necessary engine adjustments.

Q45

1. Disconnect the negative battery cable.
2. Properly relieve the fuel system pressure.
3. Drain the cooling system.
4. Tag and disconnect the fuel lines, vacuum hoses and electrical connectors. Disconnect the throttle linkage.
5. Remove the intake manifold collector.
6. Remove the injector tube assembly and remove the intake manifolds.
To install:
7. Make sure all mating surfaces are clean prior to installation.
8. Install the intake manifolds, gaskets and bolts in their proper positions, on the cylinder head and lightly tighten the mounting bolts.
9. Connect the injector tube assemblies, including the fuel injectors, to the intake manifolds and lightly tighten the mounting bolts.

NOTE: Be careful not to let the rubber washer fall into the intake manifold.

10. Install the intake collector and lightly tighten the mounting bolts.
11. Tighten the intake manifolds mounting bolts at the cylinder head. Remove the intake collectors and tighten the intake manifolds to 12-15 ft. lbs. (16-21 Nm).
12. Tighten the sub-fuel tubes, in sequence, first to 3.1-4.3 ft. lbs. (4.2-5.9 Nm) and then to 6.2-8.0 ft. lbs. (8.4-10.8 Nm).
13. Tighten the injector tube assemblies, in sequence, first to 6.9-8.0 ft. lbs. (9.3-10.8 Nm) and then to 15-20 ft. lbs. (21-26 Nm).
14. Install the intake collector and tighten to 9-11 ft. lbs. (12-15 Nm).
15. Install the remaining components in the reverse order of their removal.

Exhaust Manifold

REMOVAL AND INSTALLATION

G20

1. Disconnect the negative battery cable. Raise and support the vehicle safely.
2. Remove the undercover and dust covers, if equipped. Disconnect the exhaust pipe at the manifold flange.

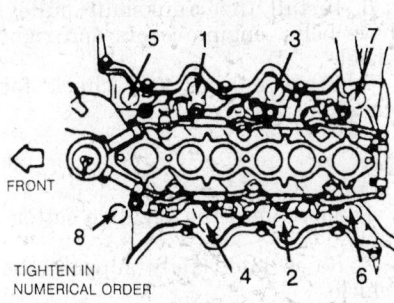

Intake manifold installation torque sequence — M30

3. Remove the AIV, AIV tube and attaching bracket.

4. Disconnect the exhaust gas sensor electrical connection and remove the sensor.

5. Remove the exhaust manifold cover.

6. Remove the exhaust manifold nuts in reverse order of torquing sequence.

7. Remove the exhaust manifold and gasket.

To install:

8. Clean the gasket mating surface and intall a new exhaust manifold gasket.

9. Install the exhaust manifold and tighten the manifold nuts, in steps and sequence, to 27-35 ft. lbs. (37-48 Nm).

10. Install the exhaust manifold cover and exhaust gas sensor. Reconnect the sensor electrical connection.

11. Install the AIV, AIV tube and attaching bracket.

12. Install the exhaust pipe to the manifold flange and tighten the nuts to 30- 35 ft. lbs. (41-48 Nm).

13. Lower the vehicle, start the engine and check for leaks.

J30 AND M30

1. Disconnect the negative battery cable.

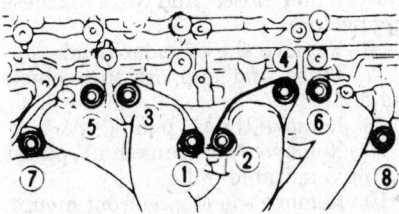

Exhaust manifold tightening sequence — G20

2. Raise and support the vehicle safely.

3. Remove the air cleaner or collector assembly, if necessary for access.

4. Remove the heatshield(s), if equipped.

5. Disconnect the exhaust pipe from the exhaust manifold.

6. Remove or disconnect the temperature sensors, oxygen sensors, air induction pipes, bracketry and other attachments from the manifold.

7. Loosen and remove the exhaust manifold attaching nuts and remove the manifold(s) from the block. Discard the exhaust manifold gaskets and replace with new.

8. Clean the gasket surfaces and check the manifold for cracks and warpage.

To install:

9. Install the exhaust manifold with a new gasket. Torque the manifold fasteners from the center outward in several stages.

10. Install or connect the temperature sensors, oxygen sensors, air induction pipes, brackets and other attachments to the manifold.

11. Connect the exhaust pipe to the manifold using a new gasket.

12. Install the heatshields.

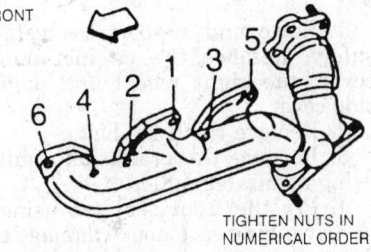

Left hand exhaust manifold installation torque sequence — M30

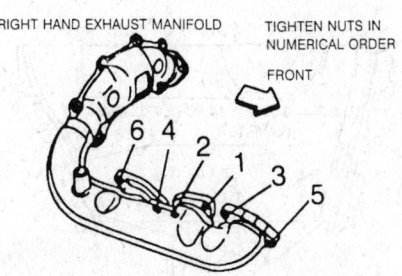

Right hand exhaust manifold installation torque sequence — M30

13. Install the air cleaner or collector assembly.

14. Install the undercovers and dust covers.

15. Connect the negative battery cable.

Q45

1. Disconnect the negative battery cable. Raise and support the vehicle safely.

2. Remove the undercover and dust covers, if equipped. Disconnect the exhaust pipe at the manifold flange.

3. Disconnect the exhaust gas sensor electrical connection and if necessary, remove the sensor.

4. Remove the exhaust manifold nuts in reverse order of torquing sequence.

5. Remove the exhaust manifold and gasket.

To install:

6. Clean the gasket mating surface and install a new exhaust manifold gasket.

7. Install the exhaust manifold and tighten the manifold nuts, in sequence, to 20-23 ft. lbs. (27-31 Nm).

8. Install exhaust gas sensor and tighten to 30-37 ft. lbs. (40-50 Nm). Reconnect the sensor electrical connection.

9. Install the exhaust pipe to the manifold flange and tighten the nuts to 33-44 ft. lbs. (45-60 Nm).

10. Lower the vehicle, start the engine and check for leaks.

Timing Chain Front Cover

REMOVAL AND INSTALLATION

G20

1. Disconnect the negative battery cable.

2. Drain the engine oil and coolant.

3. Remove the cylinder head.

4. Raise and support the vehicle safely. Remove the oil pan, oil strainer and baffle plate.

5. Remove the crankshaft pulley using a suitable puller. Removal of the radiator may be necessary to gain clearance.

6. Place a suitable jack under the main bearing beam. Remove the front engine mount.

7. Loosen the front cover bolts in 2-3 steps and remove the front cover.

To install:

8. Clean all mating surfaces of liquid gasket material.

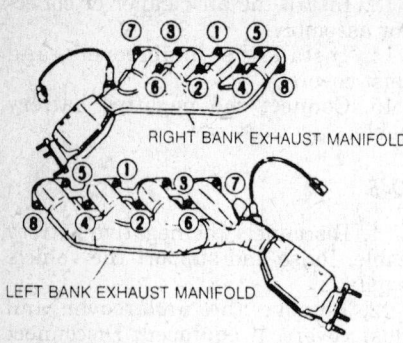

Exhaust manifold torque sequence — Q45

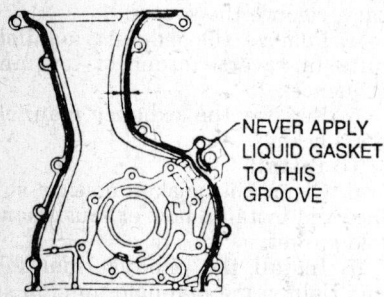

NEVER APPLY LIQUID GASKET TO THIS GROOVE

Front timing cover gasket sealing surface — G20

9. Apply a continuous bead of liquid gasket to the mating surface of the timing cover. Install the oil pump drive spacer and front cover. Tighten front cover bolts to 5-6 ft. lbs. (6-8 Nm). Wipe excess liquid gasket material.

10. Install front engine mount.

11. Install crankshaft pulley and tighten bolt to 105-112 ft. lbs. (142-152 Nm). Set No. 1 piston at TDC on the compression stroke.

12. Install the oil strainer and baffle. Install the oil pan.

13. Before installing the cylinder head, place a bead of liquid gasket at the parting line between the front cover and the engine block.

14. Install the cylinder head.

15. Lower the vehicle, connect the negative battery cable, start the engine and check for leaks.

Q45

1. Disconnect the negative battery cable.

2. Remove the engine and transmission assembly from the vehicle.

3. Remove the suspension member and engine mounts from the engine.

4. Remove the air compressor bracket.

5. Remove the cooling fan with coupling and the engine gusset.

6. Separate the engine from the transmission and mount the engine on a suitable workstand.

7. Remove the oil pan.

8. Remove the ornamental rocker cover and remove the ignition coils and spark plugs.

9. Bring the No. 1 piston to TDC on the compression stroke.

10. Use a suitable puller to remove the crankshaft pulley.

11. Remove the rocker cover.

12. Remove the crank angle sensor and the Valve Timing Control (VTC) solenoid.

13. Remove the chain tensioners and the upper front covers.

14. Remove the front timing chain cover.

15. Installation is the reverse of the removal procedure. Make sure all mating surfaces are clean prior to installation. Apply a suitable sealant to the proper locations on the timing chain covers.

16. Tighten the cover bolts to 4.6-6.1 ft. lbs. (6.3-8.3 Nm) and the crankshaft pulley bolt to 260-275 ft. lbs. (353-373 Nm).

Front Cover Oil Seal

REPLACEMENT

G20

1. Raise and support the vehicle safely. Remove the engine undercover, the right wheel and engine side cover.

2. Remove the drive belts.

3. Remove the crankshaft pulley using a suitable puller.

4. Pry the front seal out using a prybar taking care not to damage the front cover.

To install:

5. Install a new seal lubricated with engine oil using a seal driver.

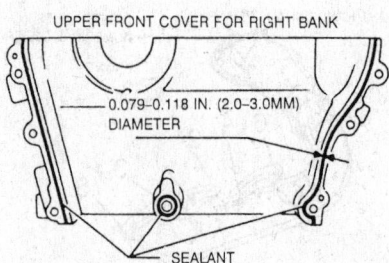

UPPER FRONT COVER FOR RIGHT BANK

0.079-0.118 IN. (2.0-3.0MM) DIAMETER

SEALANT

Upper front right cover sealant application areas — Q45

6. Install the crankshaft pulley, drive belts, engine covers and right wheel.

7. Start engine and check for leaks.

Q45

1. Disconnect the negative battery cable.

2. Raise and safely support the vehicle.

3. Remove the engine splash shield.

4. Remove the cooling fan and the engine gusset.

5. Remove the necessary accessory drive belts.

6. Remove the lower rear plate in order to remove the crankshaft pulley bolt.

7. Remove the crankshaft pulley bolt and the crankshaft pulley.

8. Use a suitable tool to remove the front cover oil seal.

9. Installation is the reverse of the removal procedure. Lubricate the seal lip prior to installation. Tighten the crank pulley bolt to 260-275 ft. lbs. (353-373 Nm).

Timing Chain and Sprockets

REMOVAL AND INSTALLATION

G20

1. Relieve the fuel system pressure and Disconnect the negative battery cable.

2. Drain the coolant from the radiator and engine block. Remove the radiator.

3. Raise and support the vehicle safely. Remove the right front wheel and engine side cover and lower the vehicle.

4. Remove the drive belts, water pump pulley, alternator and power steering pump.

5. Label and remove the vacuum hoses, fuel hoses and wire harness connectors.

6. Remove the cylinder head.

7. Raise and support the vehicle safely.

8. Remove the oil pan.

9. Remove the crankshaft pulley using a suitable puller.

10. Remove the engine front mount.

11. Remove the front cover.

12. Remove the timing chain guides and timing chain. Check the timing chain for excessive wear at the roller links. Replace the chain, if necessary.

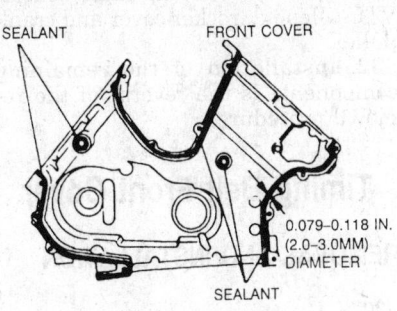

SEALANT FRONT COVER

0.079–0.118 IN.
(2.0–3.0MM)
DIAMETER

SEALANT

Front cover sealant application areas — Q45

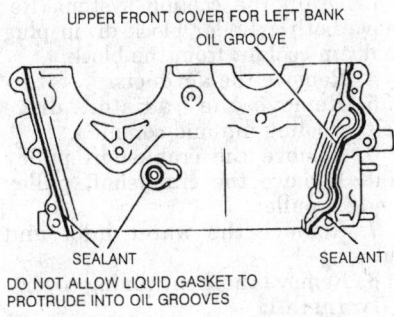

UPPER FRONT COVER FOR LEFT BANK
OIL GROOVE

SEALANT SEALANT

DO NOT ALLOW LIQUID GASKET TO
PROTRUDE INTO OIL GROOVES

Upper front left cover sealant application areas — Q45

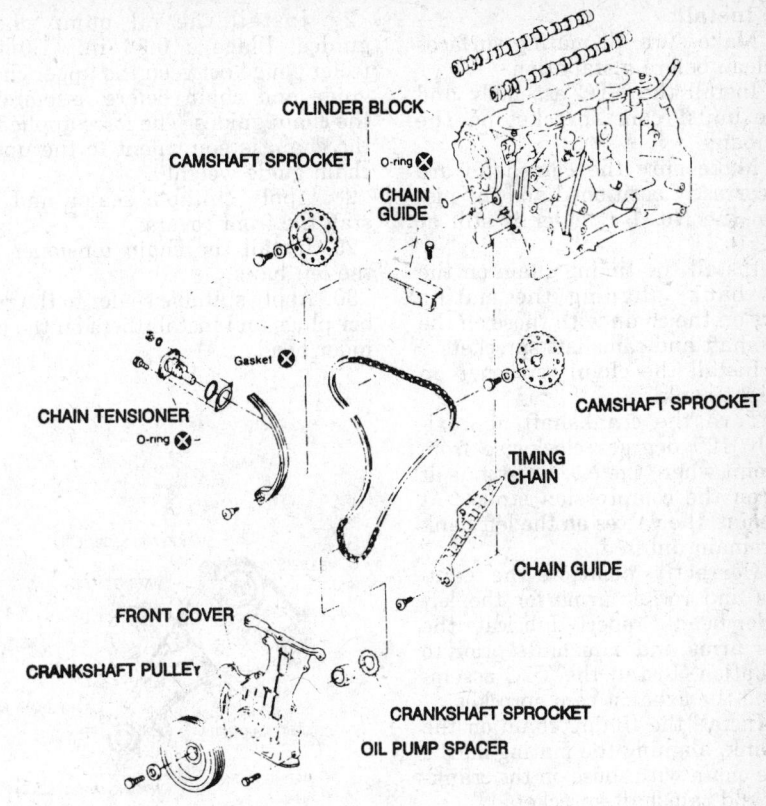

CYLINDER BLOCK

CAMSHAFT SPROCKET O-ring CHAIN GUIDE

CHAIN TENSIONER

O-ring Gasket

CAMSHAFT SPROCKET

TIMING CHAIN

CHAIN GUIDE

FRONT COVER

CRANKSHAFT PULLEY

CRANKSHAFT SPROCKET

OIL PUMP SPACER

Timing chain assembly — G20

To install:

13. Install the crankshaft sprocket. Position the crankshaft so No. 1 piston is set at TDC (keyway at 12 o'clock, mating mark at 4 o'clock). Fit the timing chain to crankshaft sprocket so mating mark is inline with mating mark on crankshaft sprocket. The mating marks on the camshaft sprockets should be silver. The mating mark on the crankshaft sprocket should be gold.

14. Install the timing chain and timing chain guides.

15. Install front engine mount.

16. Install the crankshaft pulley and set No. 1 piston at TDC on the compression stroke.

17. Install the oil strainer, baffle plate and oil pan.

18. Install the cylinder head, camshafts, oil tubes and baffles. Position the left camshaft key at 12 o'clock and the right camshaft key at 10 o'clock.

19. Install the camshaft sprockets by lining up the mating marks on the timing chain with the mating marks on the camshaft sprockets. Tighten the camshaft bolts to 101-116 ft. lbs. (137-157 Nm).

20. Install the timing chain guide and distributor. Ensure rotor is at 5 o'clock position.

21. Install the chain tensioner. Press the camshaft stopper down and the press-in sleeve until the hook can be engaged on the pin. When tensioner is bolted in position the hook will release automatically. Ensure the arrow on the outside faces the front of the engine.

22. Install all other components in reverse order of removal.

Q45

1. Disconnect the negative battery cable.

2. Remove the engine and transmission assembly from the vehicle.

3. Remove the suspension member and engine mounts from the engine.

4. Remove the air compressor bracket.

5. Remove the cooling fan with coupling and the engine gusset.

6. Separate the engine from the transmission and mount the engine on a suitable workstand.

7. Remove the oil pan.

8. Remove the ornamental rocker cover and remove the ignition coils and spark plugs.

9. Bring the No. 1 piston to TDC on the compression stroke.

10. Use a suitable puller to remove the crankshaft pulley.

11. Remove the rocker cover.

12. Remove the crank angle sensor and the Valve Timing Control (VTC) solenoid.

13. Remove the chain tensioners and the upper front covers.

14. Remove the front timing chain cover.

NOTE: The timing chain will not be disengaged or dislocated from the crankshaft sprocket unless the front cover is removed. The cast portion of the front cover is located on the lower side of the crankshaft sprocket so the timing chain is not disengaged from the sprocket.

15. Remove the VTC assembly and the camshaft sprocket.

16. Remove the oil pump chain and the timing chains.

NOTE: Do not attempt to disassemble the VTC assembly since they are difficult to reassemble accurately in the field. If it should be disassembled, the VTC assembly must be replaced with a new one.

17. Use a suitable tool to remove the crankshaft sprocket.

To install:

18. Make sure all mating surfaces are clean before installation.

19. Install the VTC assembly and the exhaust cam sprocket on the right bank.

20. Make sure the camshafts are still correctly positioned and the piston in the No. 1 cylinder is still at TDC.

21. Install the timing chain on the right bank, aligning the mating marks on the chain with those on the crankshaft and camshaft sprockets.

22. Install the chain tensioner on the right bank.

23. Turn the crankshaft approximately 120 degrees clockwise from the point where the No. 1 piston is at TDC on the compression stroke. At this point, the valves on the left bank still remain unlifted.

24. Correctly position the camshafts and rocker arms for the left cylinder head. Properly lubricate the rocker arms and camshafts prior to installation. Install the VTC assembly and the exhaust cam sprocket.

25. Install the timing chain on the left bank, aligning the mating marks on the chain with those on the crankshaft and camshaft sprockets.

26. Install the oil pump chain and sprockets.

27. Install the oil pump chain guides. Place a 0.04 in. (1.0mm) feeler gauge between the upper chain guide and chain before assembling the chain guides. The force applied to the chain is equivalent to the upper chain guide weight.

28. Apply suitable sealer and install the front covers.

29. Install the chain tensioner for the left bank.

30. Apply suitable sealer to the rubber plugs and install them on the cylinder head.

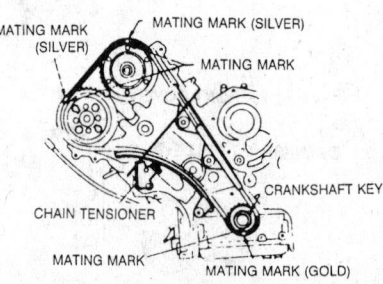

Right bank timing chain alignment — Q45

31. Install the crank angle sensor, VTC solenoid, rocker cover and crank pulley.

32. Installation of the remaining components is the reverse of the removal procedure.

Timing Belt Front Cover

REMOVAL AND INSTALLATION

J30

1. Disconnect the negative battery cable.

2. Remove the engine undercover.

3. Drain the cooling system. Remove both cylinder block drain plug to drain coolant from the block.

4. Remove the air ducts.

5. Remove the radiator, drive belts, cooling fan and coupling.

6. Remove the crankshaft pulley bolt. Remove the crankshaft pulley using a puller.

7. Remove the water inlet and outlet.

8. Remove the front timing covers.

To install:

9. Install the front timing covers and tighten bolts to 24-38 inch lbs. (3-5 Nm).

10. Install the water inlet and outlet.

11. Install the crankshaft pulley and bolt. Tighten the crankshaft pulley bolt to 159-174 ft. lbs. (216-235 Nm).

12. Install the cooling fan and fan coupling, drive belts and radiator.

13. Install the air ducts.

14. Fill the cooling system and install the engine undercover.

M30

1. Disconnect the negative battery cable.

2. Raise and support the front of the vehicle safely.

3. Remove the engine undercovers.

4. Drain the cooling system.

5. Remove the right front wheel.

6. Remove the engine side cover.

7. Remove the alternator, power steering and air conditioning compressor drive belts from the engine. When removing the power steering drive belt, loosen the idler pulley from the right side wheel housing.

8. Remove the upper radiator and water inlet hoses. Remove the water pump pulley.

9. Remove the idler bracket of the compressor drive belt.

10. Remove the crankshaft pulley with a suitable puller.

MATING MARK (SILVER

MATING MARK (GOLD)

MATING MARK

MATING MARK

Left bank timing chain alignment — Q45

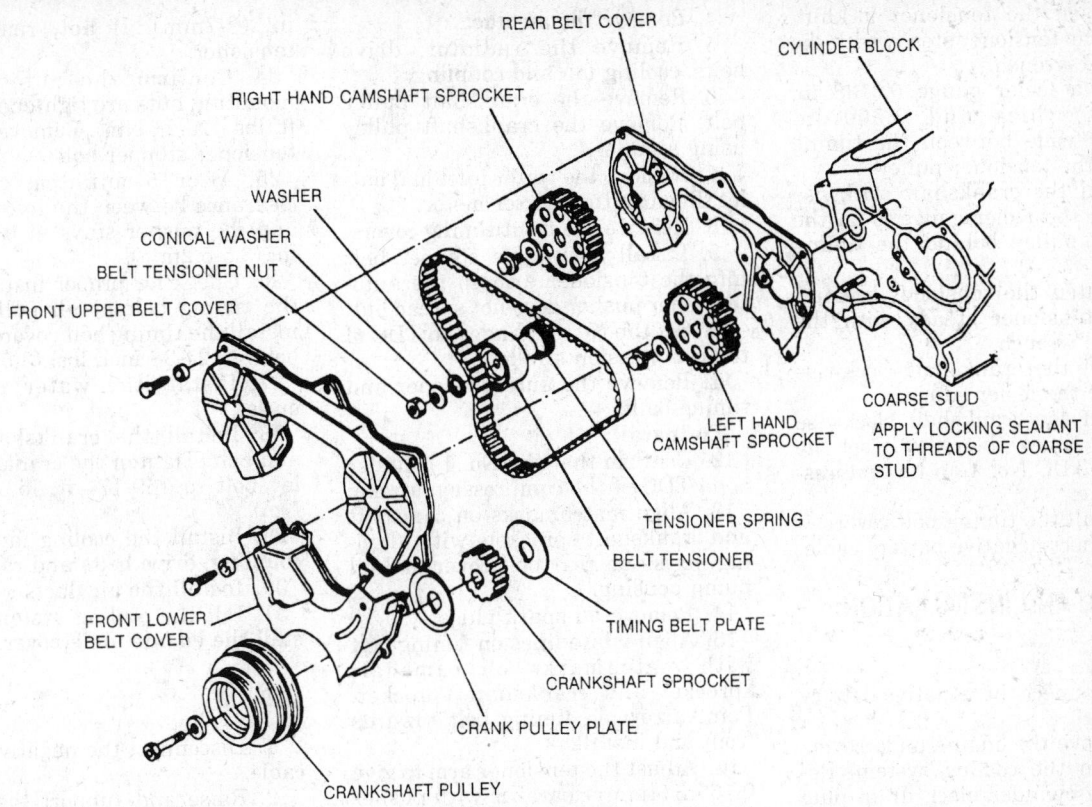

Timing belt installation — M30

11. Remove the upper and lower
timing belt covers and gaskets.

To install:

12. Install the upper and lower timing belt covers with new gaskets.

13. Install the crankshaft pulley. Torque the pulley bolt to 90-98 ft. lbs. (123-132 Nm).

14. Install the compressor drive belt idler bracket.

15. Install the water pump pulley and torque the nuts to 12-15 ft. lbs. (16-21 Nm); install the upper radiator and water inlet hoses.

16. Install the drive belts.

17. Install the engine side cover.

18. Mount the front right wheel.

19. Install the engine undercovers.

20. Lower the vehicle.

21. Fill the cooling system and connect the negative battery cable.

OIL SEAL REPLACEMENT

J30

1. Disconnect the negative battery cable.

2. Remove the timing belt and crankshaft sprocket.

3. Remove the oil pan and oil pump assembly.

4. Remove the front oil seal from the oil pump body.

5. Installation is the reverse of the removal procedure.

M30

1. Disconnect the negative battery cable.

2. Remove the timing belt.

3. Remove the crankshaft sprocket.

4. Remove the oil pan and oil pump.

5. Using a suitable tool, pry the oil seal from the front cover.

NOTE: When removing the oil seal, be careful not the gouge or scratch the seal bore or crankshaft surface.

To install:

6. Wipe the seal bore with a clean rag.

7. Lubricate the lip of the new seal with clean engine oil.

8. Install the seal into the front cover with a suitable seal installer.

9. Install the oil pump and oil pan.

10. Install the crankshaft sprocket.

11. Install the timing belt.

12. Connect the negative battery cable.

Timing Belt and Tensioner

ADJUSTMENT

J30

The timing belt on the J30 is automatically tensioned by an auto-tensioner device. No adjustment is necessary.

M30

1. Disconnect the negative battery cable.

2. Remove timing belt front covers.

3. Set engine to TDC No. 1 cylinder on its compression stroke.

4. Loosen the tensioner locknut, keeping the tension steady with the hexagonal wrench.

5. Turn tensioner 70-80 degrees clockwise with the hexagonal wrench. Temporarily tighten locknut.

6. Turn crankshaft clockwise at least 2 times, then slowly set the engine to TDC No. 1 cylinder on its compression stroke.

7. Push the middle of the timing belt between the right hand camshaft sprocket and tensioner pulley with a force of 22 lbs. (98 N).

8. Loosen the tensioner locknut, keeping the tensioner steady with the hexagonal wrench.

9. Set a feeler gauge 0.0138 in. (0.35mm) thick and 0.500 in. (12.7mm) wide between the timing belt and the tensioner pulley.

10. Turn the crankshaft clockwise and until the feeler gauge is on the tensioner pulley behind the timing belt.

11. Tighten the tensioner locknut, keeping tensioner steady with the hexagonal wrench.

12. Turn the crankshaft clockwise to remove the feeler gauge.

13. Turn the crankshaft clockwise at least 2 times, then slowly set the engine to TDC No. 1 on its compression stroke.

14. Install the timing belt covers.

15. Connect negative battery cable.

REMOVAL AND INSTALLATION

J30

1. Disconnect the negative battery cable.

2. Remove the engine undercover.

3. Drain the cooling system. Remove both cylinder block drain plug to drain coolant from the block.

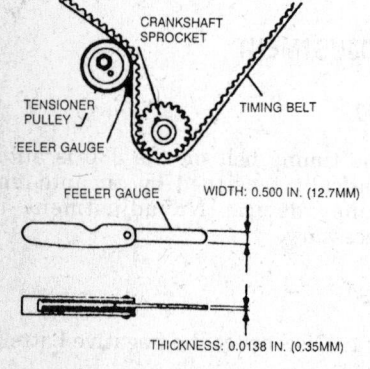

CRANKSHAFT SPROCKET

TENSIONER PULLEY

TIMING BELT

FEELER GAUGE

FEELER GAUGE   WIDTH: 0.500 IN. (12.7MM)

THICKNESS: 0.0138 IN. (0.35MM)

Setting timing belt tension — M30

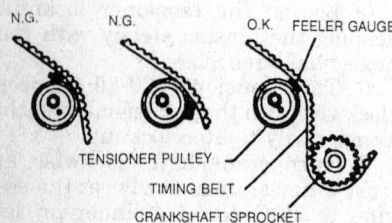

N.G.   N.G.   O.K.   FEELER GAUGE

TENSIONER PULLEY

TIMING BELT

CRANKSHAFT SPROCKET

Proper feeler gauge position for setting timing belt tension — M30

4. Remove the air ducts.

5. Remove the radiator, drive belts, cooling fan and coupling.

6. Remove the crankshaft pulley bolt. Remove the crankshaft pulley using a puller.

7. Remove the water inlet and outlet. Remove the starter motor.

8. Remove the front timing covers.

9. Install a suitable stopper bolt into the tensioner arm so the auto-tensioner pusher does not spread out.

10. Set the No. 1 cylinder on TDC of the compression stroke.

11. Remove the auto-tensioner and timing belt.

   To install:

12. Confirm that the No. 1 cylinder is on TDC of the compression stroke.

13. Align matchmarks on camshaft and crankshaft sprockets with aligning marks on rear belt cover and oil pump housing.

14. Remove all spark plugs.

15. Align white lines on timing belt with matchmarks on camshaft sprocket and crankshaft sprocket. Point arrow on timing belt towards front and install.

16. Adjust the tensioner arm to give 0.16 in. (4mm) clearance with pusher of auto-tensioner using a suitable vise, and then insert stopper bolt into tensioner arm so clearance does not change.

17. Install the auto-tensioner and tighten lower bolts hand tight. Push auto-tensioner toward belt until contact is made. Then push slightly more. Turn the crankshaft 10 degrees clockwise and tighten the tensioner nuts to 12-15 ft. lbs. 16-21 Nm).

18. Turn the crankshaft 120 degrees counterclockwise.

19. Loosen tensioner bolts ½ turn and move tensioner away from timing belt as far as it will move.

20. Turn the crankshaft clockwise and set No. 1 cylinder to TDC on its compression stroke.

21. Push the end of a pusher tool J-38387 with 13 lbs. of force and tighten the auto-tensioner bolts to 12-15 ft. lbs. (16-21 Nm).

22. Turn the crankshaft 120 degrees clockwise, then turn crankshaft 120 degrees counterclockwise. and set No. 1 cylinder to TDC on the compression stroke.

23. Prepare a steel plate measuring 0.12 x 0.39 in. (3 x 10mm). Set the plate on the timing belt and push it using a Pusher tool (J-38387) with 11 lbs. of force at a point midway between the camshaft sprockets. Also use the tool between the camshaft sprockets and the idler/tensioner pulleys. Deflection should be 0.24-0.28

in. (6-7mm). If not, readjust the tensioner.

24. Confirm the auto-tensioner mounting nuts are tightened to 12-15 ft. lbs. (16-21 Nm). Remove the auto-tensioner stopper bolt.

25. After 5 minutes, check the clearance between the tensioner arm and the pusher stays at 0.138-0.205 in. (3.5-5.2mm).

26. Check for proper installation of the timing belt at all pulleys, then install the timing belt covers. Tighten bolts to 24-38 inch lbs. (3-5 Nm).

27. Install the water inlet and outlet.

28. Install the crankshaft pulley and bolt. Tighten the crankshaft pulley bolt to 159-174 ft. lbs. (216-235 Nm).

29. Install the cooling fan and fan coupling, drive belts and radiator.

30. Install the air ducts.

31. Fill the cooling system and install the engine undercover.

M30

1. Disconnect the negative battery cable.

2. Raise and support the front of the vehicle safely.

3. Remove the engine undercovers.

4. Drain the cooling system.

5. Remove the front right side wheel.

6. Remove the engine side cover.

7. Remove the alternator, power steering and air conditioning compressor drive belts from the engine. When removing the power steering drive belt, loosen the idler pulley from the right side wheel housing.

8. Remove the upper radiator and water inlet hoses; remove the water pump pulley.

9. Remove the idler bracket of the compressor drive belt.

10. Remove the crankshaft pulley with a suitable puller.

11. Remove the upper and lower timing belt covers and gaskets.

12. Rotate the engine with a socket wrench on the crankshaft pulley bolt to align the punch mark on the left hand camshaft pulley with the mark on the upper rear timing belt cover. Align the punchmark on the crankshaft with the notch on the oil pump housing and temporarily install the crankshaft pulley bolt to allow for crankshaft rotation.

13. Use a hex wrench to turn the belt tensioner clockwise and tighten the tensioner locknut just enough to hold the tensioner in position. Then, remove the timing belt.

To install:

14. Before installing the timing belt, confirm that No. 1 cylinder is at TDC of the compression stroke. Install tensioner and tensioner spring. If stud is removed, apply locking sealant to threads before installing.

15. Swing tensioner fully clockwise with hexagon wrench and temporarily tighten locknut.

16. Point the arrow on the timing belt toward the front belt cover. Align the white lines on the timing belt with the punch marks on all 3 pulleys.

NOTE: There are 133 total timing belt teeth. If timing belt is installed correctly there will be 40 teeth between left hand and right hand camshaft sprocket timing marks. There will be 43 teeth between left hand camshaft sprocket and crankshaft sprocket timing marks.

17. Loosen tensioner locknut, keeping tensioner steady with a hexagon wrench.

18. Swing tensioner 70-80 degrees clockwise with hexagon wrench and temporarily tighten locknut.

19. Turn crankshaft clockwise 2-3 times, then slowly set No. 1 cylinder at TDC of the compression stroke.

20. Push middle of timing belt between right hand camshaft sprocket and tensioner pulley with a force of 22 lbs.

21. Loosen tensioner locknut, keeping tensioner steady with a hexagon wrench.

22. Insert a 0.138 in. (0.35mm) thick and 0.5 in. (12.7mm) wide feeler gauge between the bottom of tensioner pulley and timing belt. Turn crankshaft clockwise and position gauge completely between tensioner pulley and timing belt. The timing belt will move about 2.5 teeth.

23. Tighten tensioner locknut, keeping tensioner steady with a hexagon wrench.

24. Turn crankshaft clockwise or counterclockwise and remove the gauge.

25. Rotate the engine 3 times, then set No. 1, to TDC, on its compression stroke.

26. Install the upper and lower timing belt covers with new gaskets.

27. Install the crankshaft pulley. Torque the pulley bolt to 90-98 ft. lbs. (123-132 Nm).

28. Install the compressor drive belt idler bracket.

29. Install the water pump pulley and torque the nuts to 12-15 ft. lbs.

(16-21 Nm). Install the upper radiator and water inlet hoses.

30. Install the drive belts.

31. Install the engine side cover.

32. Mount the front right wheel.

33. Install the engine undercovers.

34. Lower the vehicle.

35. Fill the cooling system and connect the negative battery cable.

Timing Sprockets

REMOVAL AND INSTALLATION

J30 AND M30

1. Disconnect the negative battery cable.

2. Set the No. 1 piston to TDC of the compression stroke.

3. Remove the timing belt covers.

4. Remove the timing belt.

5. Using a suitable spanner wrench and a socket wrench, remove the camshaft pulley bolt and washer. Remove the front plate, O-ring and spring from the intake camshaft to gain access to the sprocket bolt. The left camshaft sprocket is held in place by plate and 4 bolts.

6. Using a suitable puller, remove the crankshaft gear and timing belt plates from the crankshaft. Be careful not to gouge or scratch the surface of the crankshaft when removing the gear.

7. Inspect the timing gear teeth for wear and replace, as necessary.

To install:

8. Install the crankshaft gear with new Woodruff keys.

9. Install the camshaft sprockets. Torque the sprocket bolts to 90-98 ft. lbs. (123-132 Nm) for intake and 10-14 ft. lbs. (14-19 Nm) for exhaust.

NOTE: The right hand and left hand camshaft pulleys are different. Install them in their correct positions. The right hand pulley has an R3 identification mark and the left hand pulley has an L3.

10. Install the timing belt.

11. Install the timing belt covers.

12. Connect the negative battery cable.

Camshaft

REMOVAL AND INSTALLATION

G20

1. Disconnect the negative battery cable. Remove the rocker cover and oil separator.

2. Rotate the crankshaft until the No. 1 piston is at TDC on the compression stroke. Then rotate the crankshaft until the mating marks on the camshaft sprockets line up with the mating marks on the timing chain.

3. Remove the timing chain tensioner.

4. Remove the distributor.

5. Remove the timing chain guide.

6. Remove the camshaft sprockets. Use a wrench to hold the camshaft while loosening the sprocket bolt.

7. Loosen the camshaft bracket bolts in the opposite order of the torquing sequence.

8. Remove the camshaft.

To install:

9. Clean the left hand camshaft end bracket and coat the mating surface with liquid gasket. Install the camshafts, camshaft brackets, oil tubes and baffle plate. Ensure the left camshaft key is at 12 o'clock and the right camshaft key is at 10 o'clock.

10. The procedure for tightening camshaft bolts must be followed exactly to prevent camshaft damage. Tighten bolts as follows:

a. Tighten right camshaft bolts 9 and 10 (in that order) to 1.5 ft. lbs. (2 Nm) then tighten bolts 1-8 (in that order) to the same specification.

b. Tighten left camshaft bolts 11 and 12 (in that order) to 1.5 ft. lbs. (2 Nm) then tighten bolts 1-10 (in that order) to the same specification.

c. Tighten all bolts in sequence to 4.5 ft. lbs. (6 Nm).

d. Tighten all bolts in sequence to 6.5-8.5 ft. lbs. (9-12 Nm) for type A, B and C bolts or 13-19 ft. lbs. (18-25 Nm) for type D bolts.

11. Line up the mating marks on the timing chain and camshaft sprockets and install the sprockets. Tighten sprocket bolts to 101-116 ft. lbs. (137-157 Nm).

12. Install the timing chain guide, distributor (ensure that rotor head is at 5 o'clock position) and chain tensioner.

13. Clean the rocker cover and mating surfaces and apply a continuous bead of liquid gasket to the mating surface.

14. Install the rocker cover and oil separator. Tighten the rocker cover bolts as follows:

a. Tighten nuts 1, 10, 11 and 8, in that order to 3 ft. lbs. (4 Nm).

b. Tighten nuts 1-13 as indicated in the figure to 6-7 ft. lbs. (8-10 Nm).

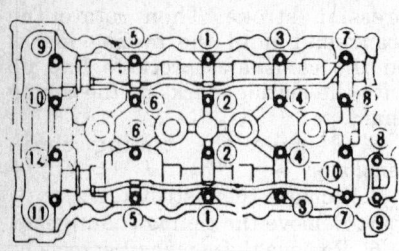

Camshaft bracket bolt torque sequence — G20

J30

1. Disconnect the negative battery cable.
2. Remove the cylinder head.
3. Remove the exhaust manifold from the cylinder head.
4. Remove the camshaft sprockets and timing belt rear cover.
5. Remove the VTC solenoid valve.
6. Measure the camshaft end-play for installation reference.
7. Loosen the camshaft bracket bolts in several steps. Remove the camshaft brackets.
8. Remove the oil seals, camshafts and hydraulic valve lifters.

To install:

9. Install the hydraulic valve lifters and camshafts. Align the camshaft knock pins at 90 degrees to the top surface of the cylinder head.

NOTE: The left side exhaust camshaft has a spline for the crankshaft position sensor.

10. Coat the VTC solenoid valve surfaces with liquid gasket and install.
11. Apply liquid gasket to the front sealing surfaces of the front camshaft brackets.
12. Install the camshaft brackets and tighten from the center outward in several steps to 7-9 ft. lbs. (9-12 Nm).
13. Install the timing belt rear cover and camshaft sprockets.
14. Install cylinder head.

M30

1. Disconnect the negative battery cable.
2. Drain the cooling system.
3. Remove the timing belt.
4. Remove the collector assembly.
5. Remove the intake manifold.
6. Remove the cylinder head.
7. Remove the rocker shafts with rocker arms. Bolts should be loosened in several steps in the proper sequence.

8. Remove hydraulic valve lifters and lifter guide. Hold hydraulic valve lifters with wire so they will not drop from lifter guide.
9. Using a dial gauge, measure the camshaft end-play. If the camshaft end-play exceeds the limit 0.0012-0.0024 in. (0.03-0.06mm), select the thickness of a cam locate plate so the end-play is within specification. For example: if camshaft end-play measures 0.0031 in. (0.08mm) with shim 2 used, then change shim 2 to shim 3 so the camshaft end-play is 0.0020 in. (0.05mm).
10. Remove the camshaft front oil seal and slide camshaft out the front of the cylinder head assembly.

To install:

11. Install camshaft, locater plates, cylinder head rear cover and front oil seal. Set camshaft knock pin at 12 o'clock position. Install cylinder head with new gasket to engine.
12. Install valve lifter guide assembly. Assemble valve lifters in their original position. After installing them in the correct location remove the wire holding them in lifter guide.
13. Install rocker shafts in correct position with rocker arms. Tighten bolts, in 2-3 stages, to 13-16 ft. lbs. (18-22 Nm). Before tightening, be sure to set camshaft lobe at th position where lobe is not lifted or the valve closed. Set each cylinder 1 at a time or follow the procedure below. The cylinder head, intake manifold, collector and timing belt must be installed:

  a. Set No. 1 piston at TDC of compression stroke and tighten rocker shaft bolts for Nos. 2, 4 and 6 cylinders.

  b. Set No. 4 piston at TDC of compression stroke and tighten rocker shaft bolts for Nos. 1, 3 and 5 cylinders.

  c. Torque specification for the rocker shaft retaining bolts is 13-16 ft. lbs. (18-22 Nm).

14. Fill the cooling system to the proper level.
15. Connect the negative battery cable.

Q45

1. Disconnect the negative battery cable.
2. Remove the engine and transmission assembly from the vehicle.
3. Remove the suspension member and engine mounts from the engine.
4. Remove the air compressor bracket.
5. Remove the cooling fan with coupling and the engine gusset.

6. Separate the engine from the transmission and mount the engine on a suitable workstand.
7. Remove the oil pan.
8. Remove the ornamental rocker cover and remove the ignition coils and spark plugs.
9. Bring the No. 1 piston to TDC on the compression stroke.
10. Use a suitable puller to remove the crankshaft pulley.
11. Remove the rocker cover.
12. Remove the crank angle sensor and the Valve Timing Control (VTC) solenoid.
13. Remove the chain tensioners and the upper front covers.
14. Remove the front timing chain cover.

NOTE: The timing chain will not be disengaged or dislocated from the crankshaft sprocket unless the front cover is removed. The cast portion of the front cover is located on the lower side of the crankshaft sprocket so the timing chain is not disengaged from the sprocket.

15. Remove the VTC assembly and the camshaft sprocket.
16. Remove the oil pump chain and the timing chains.

NOTE: Do not attempt to disassemble the VTC assembly since they are difficult to reassemble accurately in the field. If it should be disassembled, the VTC assembly must be replaced with a new one.

17. Remove the camshaft brackets and the camshafts. Mark the parts so they can be reinstalled in their original positions.
18. Remove the rocker arms. Be sure to identify each rocker arm so it can be reinstalled in it's original position.

To install:

19. Make sure all mating surfaces are clean before installation.
20. Install the rocker arms, camshafts and camshaft brackets on the right bank. Properly lubricate the rocker arms and camshafts prior to installation. Tighten the camshaft bracket bolts to 9-10 ft. lbs. (12-14 Nm) in the proper sequence.
21. Install the VTC assembly and the exhaust cam sprocket on the right bank.
22. Make sure the camshafts are still correctly positioned and the piston in the No. 1 cylinder is still at TDC.
23. Install the timing chain on the right bank, aligning the mating

marks on the chain with those on the crankshaft and camshaft sprockets.

24. Install the chain tensioner on the right bank.

25. Turn the crankshaft approximately 120 degrees clockwise from the point where the No. 1 piston is at TDC on the compression stroke. At this point, the valves on the left bank still remain unlifted.

26. Correctly position the camshafts and rocker arms for the left cylinder head. Properly lubricate the rocker arms and camshafts prior to installation. Tighten the camshaft bracket bolts to 9-10 ft. lbs. (12-14 Nm) in the proper sequence. Install the VTC assembly and the exhaust cam sprocket.

27. Install the timing chain on the left bank, aligning the mating marks on the chain with those on the crankshaft and camshaft sprockets.

28. Install the oil pump chain and sprockets.

29. Install the oil pump chain guides. Place a 0.04 in. (1.0mm) feeler gauge between the upper chain guide and chain before assembling the chain guides. The force applied to the chain is equivalent to the upper chain guide weight.

30. Apply suitable sealer and install the front covers.

31. Install the chain tensioner for the left bank.

32. Apply suitable sealer to the rubber plugs and install them on the cylinder head.

33. Install the crank angle sensor, VTC solenoid, rocker cover and crank pulley.

34. Installation of the remaining components is the reverse of the removal procedure.

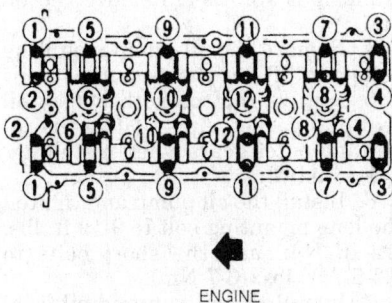

ENGINE FRONT

Camshaft bracket torque sequence — Q45

Piston and Connecting Rod

POSITIONING

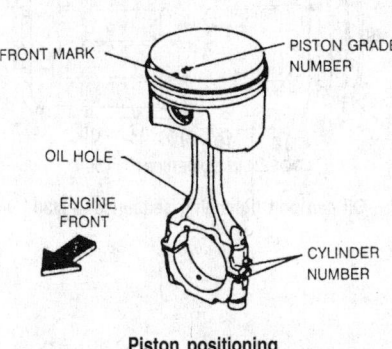

Piston positioning

ENGINE LUBRICATION

Oil Pan

REMOVAL AND INSTALLATION

G20

1. Raise and support the vehicle safely. Remove the engine undercover and drain the oil.

2. Remove the steel oil pan bolts in the proper sequence. Remove the steel oil pan. Insert tool KV10111100 between steel oil pan and aluminum oil pan to pry apart.

3. Remove the oil baffle bolts and oil baffle. Remove the front exhaust tube.

4. Set a suitable jack under the transaxle and raise the engine with and engine hoist.

5. If equipped with an automatic transaxle, remove the transaxle shift control cable.

6. Remove the compressor gussets, the rear cover plate and all aluminum oil pan bolts. Loosen aluminum oil pan bolts in the proper sequence.

7. Remove the 2 engine to transaxle bolts and refit the them into vacant vacant holes at the bottom of the oil pan. Remove the aluminum oil pan. Use tool KV10111100 to pry oil pan from block. Remove the engine to transaxle bolts.

To install:

8. Clean the oil pan rail of all liquid gasket and apply a new bead of ⅛ inch thickness to the oil pan rail.

9. Install the aluminum oil pan and torque bolts 1-16 to 12-14 ft. lbs. (16-19 Nm) and bolts 17-18 to 5-6 ft. lbs. (6-8 Nm) in the opposite order of removal.

10. Install the 2 engine to transaxle bolts, rear cover plate, compressor gussets, automatic transmission shift control cable (if equipped), center member, front exhaust tube and baffle plate.

11. Clean the oil pan rail of all liquid gasket and apply a new bead of ⅛ inch thickness to the oil pan rail.

12. Install the steel oil pan and install bolts until snug. Tighten bolts in the reverse order of removal sequence and wait 30 minutes before refilling crankcase with oil.

J30 AND M30

1. Disconnect the negative battery cable. Raise and support the vehicle safely.

2. Remove the engine undercover and drain the engine oil.

3. Remove the air ducts.

4. Remove the upper and lower radiator shrouds and radiator, if needed. Disconnect the oil cooler lines on vehicles with automatic transmissions.

5. Remove the fan coupling.

6. Remove the stabilizer bar, as required.

7. Place a suitable support under the transmission.

8. Remove the engine mounting insulator lower attaching nuts from both sides of the engine. Hoist the engine so enough clearance is provided for oil pan removal.

9. Remove the oil pan bolts. Insert oil pan removal tool J-37228 or equivalent, between the cylinder block and oil pan. Slide tool around oil pan to break the gasket seal.

10. Remove the oil strainer and lay it in the oil pan. Remove the oil pan.

To install:

11. Clean all gasket mating surfaces thoroughly.

12. Apply sealant to oil pump gasket and rear oil seal retainer gasket.

13. Apply a continuous bead of liquid gasket to the oil pan mating surface. Be sure the bead is ⅛ inch wide.

14. Place oil pan under engine and install oil strainer.

15. Install oil pan and tighten bolts in the proper sequence to 5-6 ft. lbs. (7-8 Nm).

16. Lower the engine an install the engine mount insulator bolts.

17. Install the stabilizer bar.

18. Install the radiator, if removed, the radiator hoses, shroud and transmission oil cooler lines.

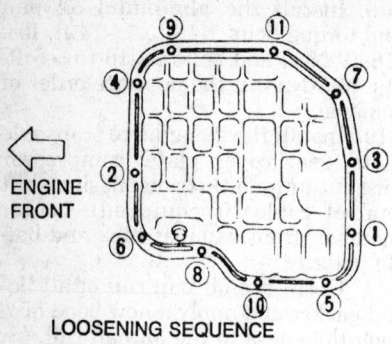

Steel oil pan bolt removal sequence — G20

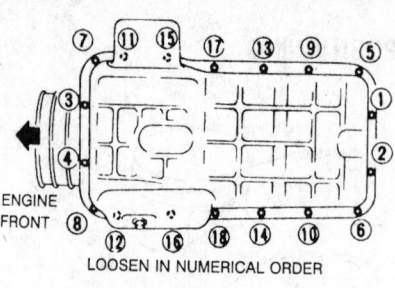

Oil pan bolt tightening sequence — M30

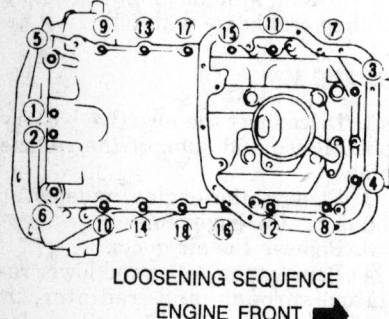

Aluminum oil pan bolt removal sequence — G20

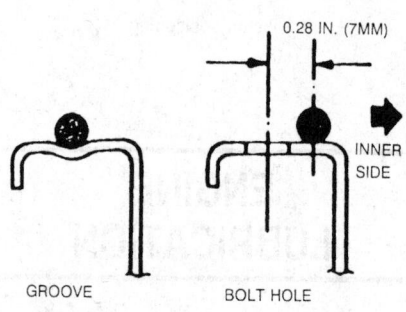

Oil pan liquid sealant bead — all engines

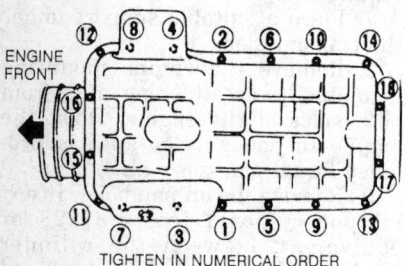

Oil pan bolt loosening sequence — M30

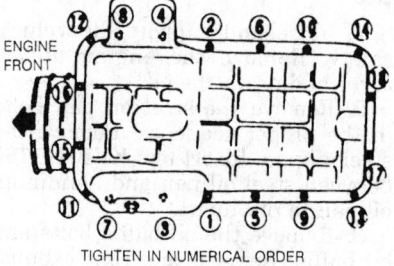

Oil pan installation torque sequence — Q45

equivalent, between the cylinder block and oil pan. Slide tool around oil pan to break the gasket seal.

9. Remove the oil pan.

To install:

10. Clean all gasket mating surfaces thoroughly.

11. Apply a continuous bead of liquid gasket to the oil pan mating surface. Be sure the bead is 1/8 inch wide.

12. Install oil pan and tighten bolts in the proper sequence to 5-6 ft. lbs. (7-8 Nm).

13. Install all remaining components in the reverse order of removal.

14. Fill the engine with oil. Start the engine and allow it to reach normal operating temperature. Check for leaks.

Oil Pump

REMOVAL AND INSTALLATION

G20

1. Remove the drive belts.
2. Remove the cylinder head and oil pans.
3. Remove the oil strainer and baffle plate.
4. Remove the front cover assembly.

To install:

5. Clean the mating surfaces of liquid gasket and apply a fresh bead of 1/8 inch sealer to the surface.

6. Coat the oil pump gears with oil. Using a new oil seal and O-ring, install the front cover assembly.

7. Install the oil strainer, baffle plate, oil pans, cylinder head and drive belts.

J30 and M30

1. Raise and safely support the vehicle.
2. Drain the engine oil. Remove the oil level gauge.
3. Remove the timing belt and crankshaft sprocket. Remove the oil pan.
4. Remove the oil pump mounting bolts and lift out the oil pump.
5. Always replace with a new oil seal and gasket. Apply oil to the inner and outer gears when installing.

To install:

6. Install the oil pump and tighten the long mounting bolt to 9-12 ft. lbs. (12-16 Nm) and the short bolts to 4.3-5.1 ft. lbs. (6-7 Nm).

7. Install the oil pan and oil level gauge.

8. Fill the engine with oil. Start the engine and check for leaks.

19. Install the fan coupling.
20. Install the air ducts and engine undercover.
21. Fill the engine with oil. Start the engine and allow it to reach normal operating temperature. Check for leaks.

Q45

1. Disconnect the negative battery cable. Raise and support the vehicle safely.
2. Remove the engine undercover and drain the engine oil.

3. Remove the fan coupling with the fan.
4. Remove the drive belts, alternator, air conditioning compressor and engine gusset.
5. Matchmark and remove the steering lower joint.
6. Place a suitable support under the transmission. Hoist the engine with engine slinger.
7. Remove the suspension member assembly.
8. Remove the oil pan bolts. Insert oil pan removal tool J-37228 or

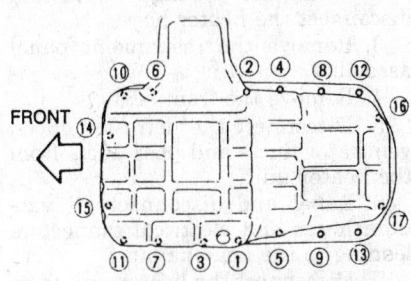

FRONT

TIGHTEN IN NUMERICAL ORDER

Oil pan bolt torquing sequence — J30

Q45

1. Disconnect the negative battery cable.

2. Remove the engine and transmission assembly from the vehicle.

3. Remove the suspension member and engine mounts from the engine.

4. Remove the air compressor bracket.

5. Remove the cooling fan with coupling and the engine gusset.

6. Separate the engine from the transmission and mount the engine on a suitable workstand.

7. Remove the oil pan.

8. Remove the ornamental rocker cover and remove the ignition coils and spark plugs.

9. Bring the No. 1 piston to TDC on the compression stroke.

10. Use a suitable puller to remove the crankshaft pulley.

11. Remove the rocker cover.

12. Remove the crank angle sensor and the Valve Timing Control (VTC) solenoid.

13. Remove the chain tensioners and the upper front covers.

14. Remove the front timing chain cover.

NOTE: The timing chain will not be disengaged or dislocated from the crankshaft sprocket unless the front cover is removed. The cast portion of the front cover is located on the lower side of the crankshaft sprocket so the timing chain is not disengaged from the sprocket.

15. Remove the VTC assembly and the camshaft sprocket.

16. Remove the oil pump chain and the timing chains.

17. Remove the mounting bolts and lift out the oil pump.

To install:

18. Thoroughly clean the mounting surfaces. Apply engine oil to the gears.

19. Install the oil pump with a new seal and gasket. Tighten the long bolts to 12-15 ft. lbs. (16-20 Nm) and the short bolts to 3.3-4.3 ft. lbs. (4-6 Nm).

20. Make sure all mating surfaces are clean before installation.

21. Install the VTC assembly and the exhaust cam sprocket on the right bank.

22. Make sure the camshafts are still correctly positioned and the piston in the No. 1 cylinder is still at TDC.

23. Install the timing chain on the right bank, aligning the mating marks on the chain with those on the crankshaft and camshaft sprockets.

24. Install the chain tensioner on the right bank.

25. Turn the crankshaft approximately 120 degrees clockwise from the point where the No. 1 piston is at TDC on the compression stroke. At this point, the valves on the left bank still remain unlifted.

26. Correctly position the camshafts and rocker arms for the left cylinder head. Properly lubricate the rocker arms and camshafts prior to installation. Install the VTC assembly and the exhaust cam sprocket.

27. Install the timing chain on the left bank, aligning the mating marks on the chain with those on the crankshaft and camshaft sprockets.

28. Install the oil pump chain and sprockets.

29. Install the oil pump chain guides. Place a 0.04 in. (1.0mm) feeler gauge between the upper chain guide and chain before assembling the chain guides. The force applied to the chain is equivalent to the upper chain guide weight.

30. Apply suitable sealer and install the front covers.

31. Install the chain tensioner for the left bank.

32. Apply suitable sealer to the rubber plugs and install them on the cylinder head.

33. Install the crank angle sensor, VTC solenoid, rocker cover and crank pulley.

34. Installation of the remaining components is the reverse of the removal procedure.

Rear Main Bearing Oil Seal

The rear main oil seal is a solid type seal located in the rear oil seal retainer at the rear of the engine.

REMOVAL AND INSTALLATION

1. Raise and safely support the vehicle. Remove the transaxle or transmission.

2. Remove the flywheel or driveplate.

3. Remove the rear oil seal retainer from the block.

4. Using a suitable prying tool, remove the oil seal from the retainer.

To install:

5. Thoroughly scrape the surface of the retainer to remove any traces of the existing sealant or gasket material.

6. Wipe the seal bore with a clean rag.

7. Apply clean engine oil to the new oil seal and carefully install it into the retainer using the proper seal installation tool.

8. Install the rear oil seal retainer into the engine, along with a new gasket.

9. Install the flywheel or driveplate. Install the transaxle or transmission. Lower the vehicle.

ENGINE COOLING

Radiator

REMOVAL AND INSTALLATION

G20

1. Disconnect the negative battery cable. Drain the coolant system, remove the upper radiator hose and reservoir tank.

2. Remove the lower radiator hose and transmission cooler lines.

3. Unplug the radiator fan motor connector and remove the radiator fan.

4. Remove all radiator attaching bolts and remove the radiator.

To install:

5. Lower the radiator into position. Take care not to damage the radiator fins as this will effect cooling efficiency.

6. Install all attaching bolts and tighten securely.

7. Install the radiator fan and reconnect the radiator fan motor connector.

8. Install the radiator upper and lower hoses, and the reservoir tank.

9. Fill the cooling system, start the engine and allow it to reach normal operating temperature. Bleed

the cooling system and check for leaks.

J30

1. Drain the coolant.
2. Remove the engine undercover.
3. Disconnect the radiator upper and lower hoses. Disconnect the overflow tank hose.
4. Disconnect and plug the automatic transmission oil cooler hoses.
5. Remove the radiator lower shroud.
6. Remove the radiator.

To Install:

7. Install the radiator and tighten the mounting brackets to 5-6 ft. lbs. (6-8 Nm).
8. Connect the automatic transmission oil cooler hoses.
9. Connect the radiator upper and lower hoses. Connect the overflow tank hose.
10. Fill the system with coolant.
11. Install the engine undercover. Start the engine and allow it to reach operating temperature. Check for leaks.

M30 and Q45

1. Disconnect the negative battery cable.
2. Remove the engine undercover. Drain the coolant.
3. Remove the upper hose and coolant reserve tank hose from the radiator.
4. Unbolt the shroud and move it backward in order to remove the fan and coupling. Remove the fan to water pump bolts and remove the fan, coupling, water pump pulley and shroud.
5. Raise the vehicle and support safely. Remove the lower hose from the radiator.
6. Disconnect and plug the automatic transmission cooler hoses. Disconnect the coolant thermo switch. Lower the vehicle.
7. Remove the mounting brackets or unbolt the radiator from the support and carefully lift out of the engine compartment.
8. Remove the cooling fans from the radiator.

To install:

9. Lower the radiator into position.
10. Install the mounting brackets or bolts.
11. Raise the vehicle and support safely. Connect the automatic transmission cooler lines and the thermo switch connector.
12. Connect the lower hose. Lower the vehicle.

13. Install the shroud, pulley, coupling and fan. Torque the water pump pulley nuts to 7 ft. lbs. (10 Nm). Adjust the belt.
14. Connect the upper hose and coolant reserve tank hose.
15. On the M30, open the air release plug. Fill the cooling system and check for leaks.
16. Connect the negative battery cable, run the vehicle until the thermostat opens, fill the radiator completely and check the automatic transmission fluid level. Recheck for coolant leaks.
17. Once the vehicle has cooled, recheck the coolant level.

Heater Core

REMOVAL AND INSTALLATION

G20

1. Disconnect the negative battery cable.
2. With the temperature control lever set to the HOT position, drain the cooling system.
3. Disconnect the heater hoses a the driver's side of the heater unit.
4. Remove the glove compartment and the front panel from the center console.
5. Remove the radio and heater/air conditioner controls to remove the lower portion of the center console.
6. Disconnect the output vent ducts and remove the heater unit.
7. Disassemble the housing to remove the heater core.

To install:

8. Install the heater core and assemble the heater unit housing. Use new gaskets and seals as required, and check for smooth movement of the doors and linkage.
9. Install the heater unit and attach the ducts. Take care not to damage the gasket between the heater and cooling units.
10. Install the lower center console, the radio and the heater controls. Before completing the assemble, connect the battery and adjust the door motor linkage, if necessary.
11. Install the glove compartment and console panel.
12. Connect the heater hoses and refill the cooling system with the temperature control set at the HOT position. Bleed the cooling system.

J30

1. Disconnect the negative battery cable.

2. Drain the cooling system and disconnect the heater hoses.
3. Remove the instrument panel assembly.
4. Remove the front seats.
5. Disconnect the defroster ducts, ventilator ducts and floor ducts from the heater unit.
6. Label and disconnect all vacuum hoses and electrical connectors leading to the heater unit.
7. Disconnect the heater unit from the cooling unit. Take care not to damage the air conditioning pipe.
8. Remove the heater unit attaching bolts. Remove the heater unit from the passenger compartment.
9. Disassemble the heater unit and remove the heater core.

To install:

10. Install the heater core and assemble the heater unit.
11. Install the heater unit in the passenger compartment and tighten the attaching bolts securely.
12. Connect the cooling unit to the heater unit.
13. Connect all previously disconnected vacuum hoses and electrical connectors.
14. Connect the defroster ducts, ventilator ducts and floor ducts to the heater unit.
15. Install the front seats.
16. Install the instrument panel assembly.
17. Connect the heater hoses and fill the cooling system.
18. Connect the negative battey cable, start the engine and check for leaks. Check system for proper operation.

M30

1. Disconnect the negative battery cable.
2. Drain the coolant.
3. Disconnect the heater hoses from the heater core tubes and plug them.
4. Remove the steering column covers.
5. Remove the front pillar garnish and lower instrument covers.
6. Remove the cluster lid and instrument cluster.
7. Remove the radio bezel, radio and climate control switch assembly.
8. Remove the glovebox.
9. Remove the instrument reinforcement and the shift lever cover.
10. Remove the console assembly.
11. Remove the defroster grille and sensors.
12. Remove the hood lock cable bracket and rear heater ducts.

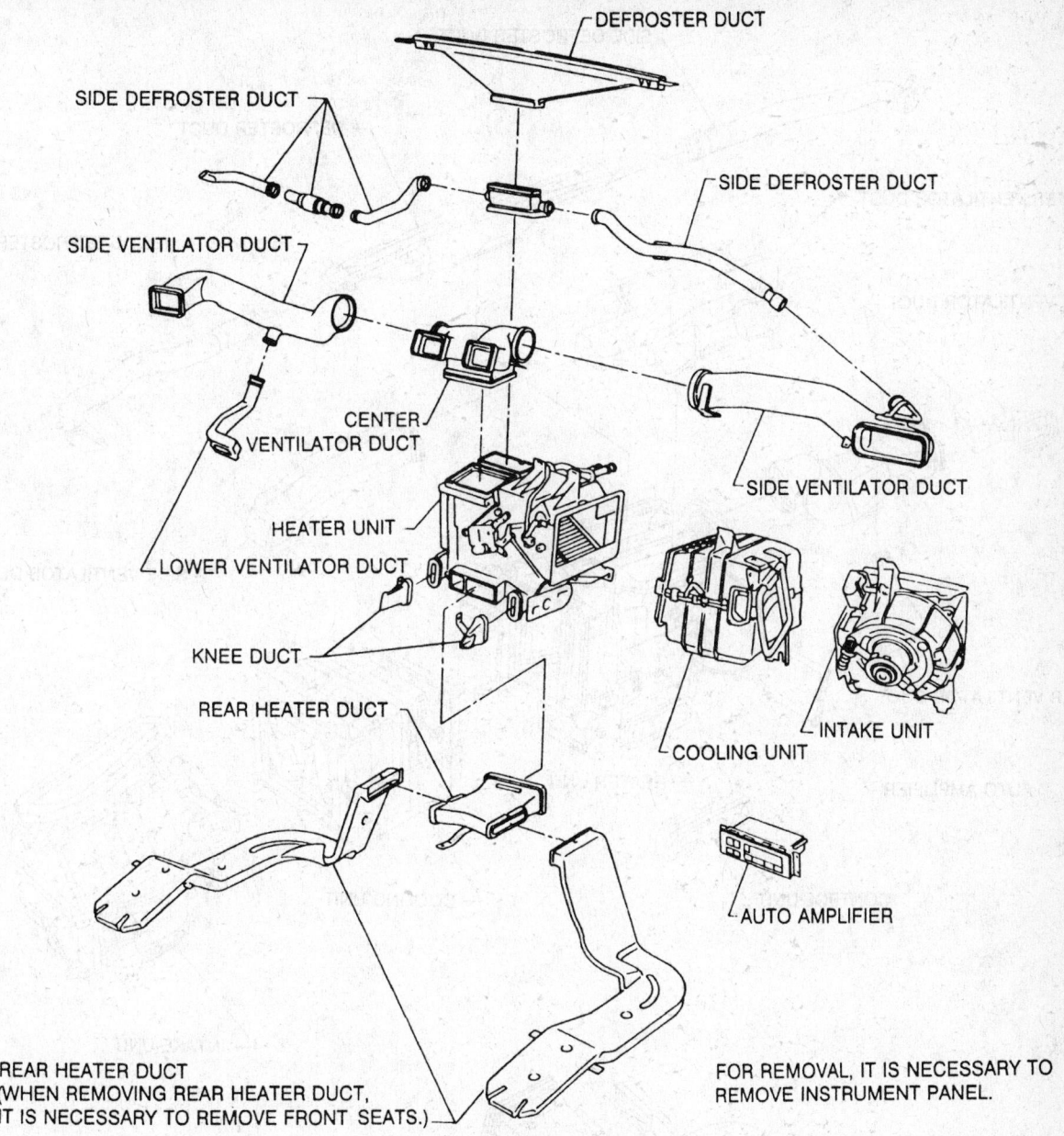

DEFROSTER DUCT

SIDE DEFROSTER DUCT

SIDE DEFROSTER DUCT

SIDE VENTILATOR DUCT

CENTER VENTILATOR DUCT

SIDE VENTILATOR DUCT

HEATER UNIT

LOWER VENTILATOR DUCT

KNEE DUCT

COOLING UNIT

INTAKE UNIT

REAR HEATER DUCT

AUTO AMPLIFIER

REAR HEATER DUCT
(WHEN REMOVING REAR HEATER DUCT,
IT IS NECESSARY TO REMOVE FRONT SEATS.)

FOR REMOVAL, IT IS NECESSARY TO
REMOVE INSTRUMENT PANEL.

Heater and air conditioner assembly — G20

13. Remove the fuse block and disconnect the Super Multiple Junction (SMJ).

14. Remove the steering column mounting bolts and lower the column.

15. Remove the caps that cover the instrument panel securing screws, remove the screws and remove the instrument panel assembly.

16. Remove the air distribution ducts from the heater unit.

17. Disconnect all wires and cables that connect to the unit.

18. Remove the mounting bolts and nuts and remove the heater unit from the vehicle.

19. Disassemble and remove the heater core from the unit.

To install:

20. Clean the inside of the unit out, install the heater core and assemble the unit.

21. Install the unit to the vehicle and connect all wires and cables. Install the air distribution ducts.

22. Install the instrument panel assembly and snap the screw caps in place.

23. Raise and secure the steering column.

24. Connect the SMJ and install the fuse block.

25. Install the rear heater ducts and hood lock cable bracket.

26. Install the defroster grille and sensors.

27. Install the console assembly and shift lever cover.

28. Install the instrument reinforcement and glove box.

29. Install the climate control switch assembly, radio and bezel.

30. Install the instrument cluster and lid.

31. Install the lower instrument panel covers and pillar garnish.

32. Install the steering column covers.

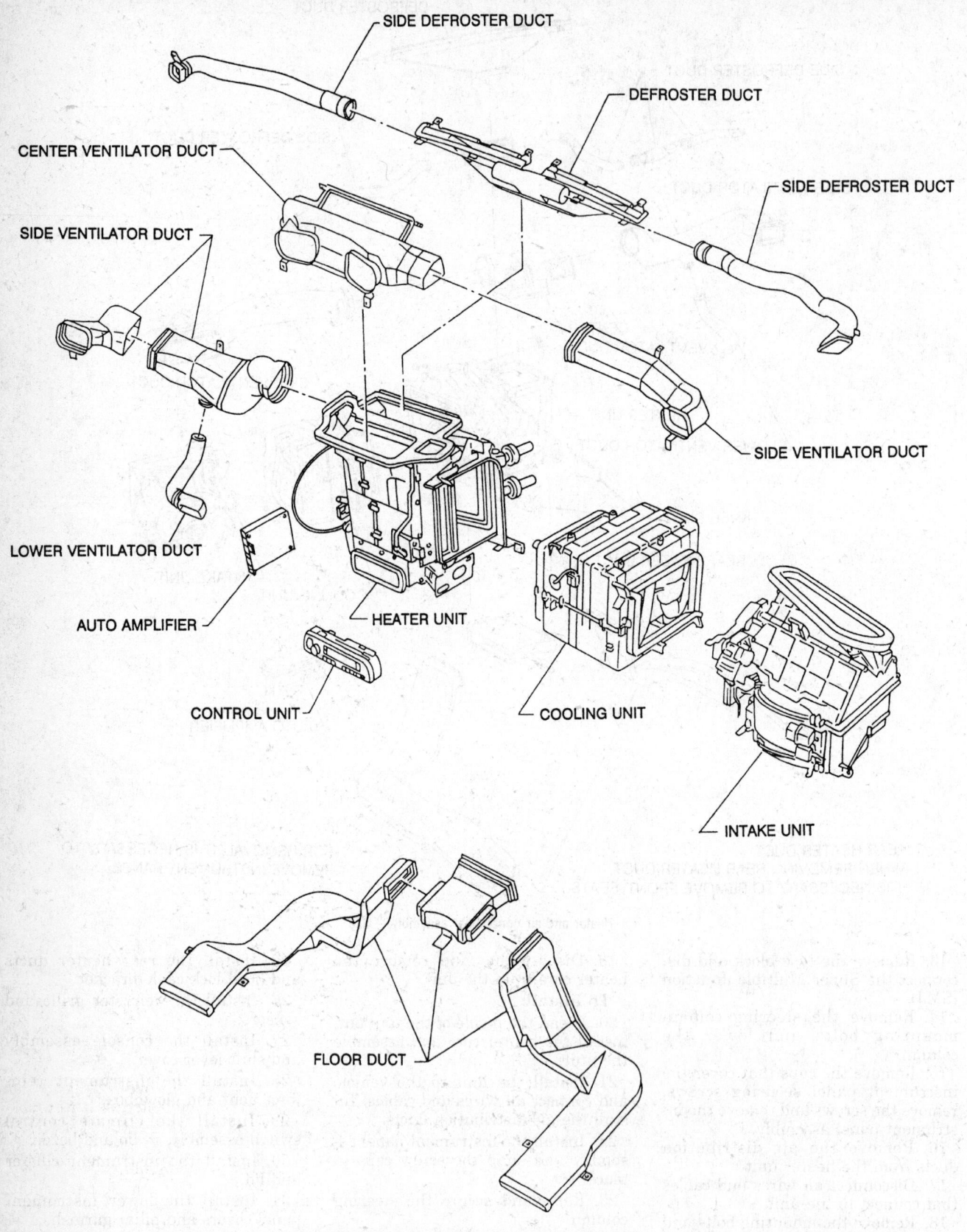

SIDE DEFROSTER DUCT

DEFROSTER DUCT

CENTER VENTILATOR DUCT

SIDE DEFROSTER DUCT

SIDE VENTILATOR DUCT

SIDE VENTILATOR DUCT

LOWER VENTILATOR DUCT

AUTO AMPLIFIER

HEATER UNIT

CONTROL UNIT

COOLING UNIT

INTAKE UNIT

FLOOR DUCT

Heating and cooling system component layout — J30

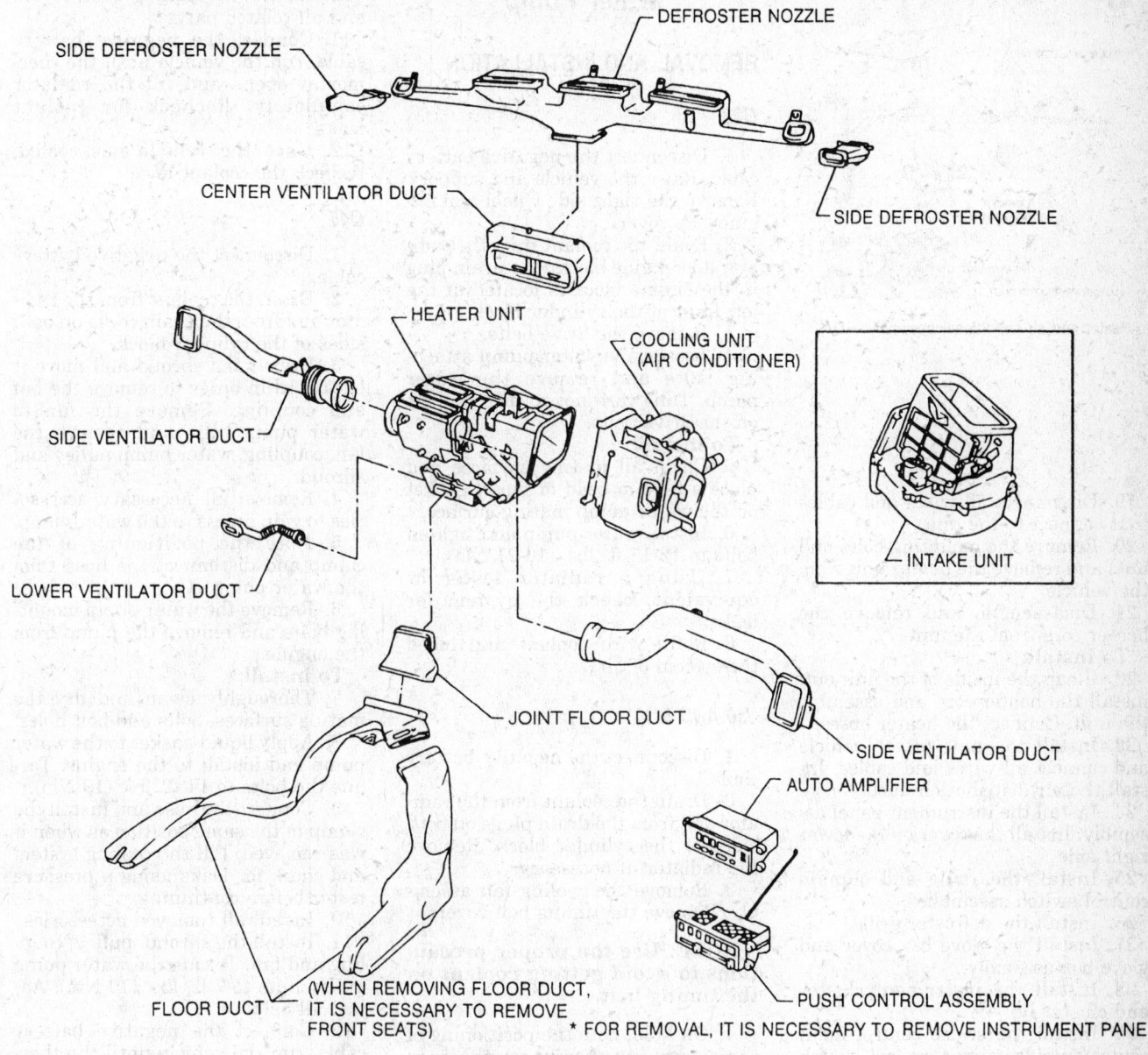

SIDE DEFROSTER NOZZLE

DEFROSTER NOZZLE

CENTER VENTILATOR DUCT

SIDE DEFROSTER NOZZLE

HEATER UNIT

COOLING UNIT
(AIR CONDITIONER)

SIDE VENTILATOR DUCT

LOWER VENTILATOR DUCT

INTAKE UNIT

JOINT FLOOR DUCT

SIDE VENTILATOR DUCT

AUTO AMPLIFIER

FLOOR DUCT

(WHEN REMOVING FLOOR DUCT,
IT IS NECESSARY TO REMOVE
FRONT SEATS)

PUSH CONTROL ASSEMBLY

* FOR REMOVAL, IT IS NECESSARY TO REMOVE INSTRUMENT PANE

Heater and air conditioner assembly — M30

33. Connect the heater core tubes to the heater core tubes.

34. Open the air release plug. Fill the cooling system and check for leaks.

35. Connect the negative battery cable, run the vehicle until the thermostat opens, fill the radiator completely and check the automatic transmission fluid level. Recheck for coolant leaks.

36. Once the vehicle has cooled, recheck the coolant level.

Q45

1. Disconnect the negative battery cable.

2. Drain the coolant.

3. Disconnect the heater hoses from the heater core tubes and plug them.

4. Remove the steering wheel and column covers.

5. Remove the shifter lever bezel.

6. Remove the ashtray assembly.

7. Remove the radio assembly.

8. Remove the climate control switch bezel.

9. Remove the lower instrument panel covers.

10. Remove the front and rear floor console assemblies.

11. Remove the cruise control main switch/outside mirror control switch assembly.

12. Remove the cluster lid and instrument cluster.

13. Remove the glove box and glove box cover.

14. Remove the cover on the lower right side of the instrument panel.

15. Remove the defroster grille.

16. Remove the radio and climate control switch assemblies.

17. Remove the remaining mounting screws remove the instrument panel assembly.

18. Remove the air distribution ducts from the heater unit.

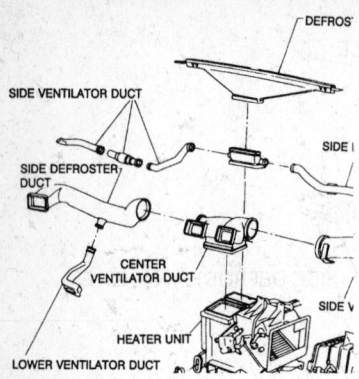

DEFROS'

SIDE VENTILATOR DUCT

SIDE DEFROSTER DUCT

SIDE

CENTER VENTILATOR DUCT

SIDE V

HEATER UNIT

LOWER VENTILATOR DUCT

Heater and air conditioner assembly — Q45

19. Disconnect all wires and cables that connect to the unit.

20. Remove the mounting bolts and nuts and remove the heater unit from the vehicle.

21. Disassemble and remove the heater core from the unit.

To install:

22. Clean the inside of the unit out, install the heater core and assemble the unit. Connect the heater hoses.

23. Install the unit to the vehicle and connect all wires and cables. Install the air distribution ducts.

24. Install the instrument panel assembly. Install the cover on the lower right side.

25. Install the radio and climate control switch assemblies.

26. Install the defroster grille.

27. Install the glove box cover and glove box assembly.

28. Install the instrument cluster and cluster lid.

29. Install the cruise control main switch/outside mirror control switch assembly.

30. Install the console assemblies.

31. Install the lower instrument panel covers.

32. Install the radio and climate control switch bezel.

33. Install the ashtray assembly.

34. Install the shifter lever bezel.

35. Install the steering wheel and column covers.

36. Fill the cooling system and check for leaks.

37. Connect the negative battery cable, run the vehicle until the thermostat opens, fill the radiator completely and check the automatic transmission fluid level. Recheck for coolant leaks.

38. Once the vehicle has cooled, recheck the coolant level.

Water Pump

REMOVAL AND INSTALLATION

G20

1. Disconnect the negative battery cable. Raise the vehicle and support. Remove the right side wheel and engine side cover.

2. Drain the coolant from the radiator and engine block. The drain plug in the engine block is located at the left front of the cylinder block.

3. Remove the drive belts.

4. Loosen the water pump attaching bolts and remove the water pump. Take care not to drip coolant on the drive belts.

To install:

5. Clean all mating surfaces and place a 2-3mm bead of liquid gasket on the water pump mating surface.

6. Install water pump and tighten bolts to 12-15 ft. lbs. (16-21 Nm).

7. Using a radiator tester or equivalent, check the system for leaks.

8. Refill with coolant and bleed the system of air.

J30 AND M30

1. Disconnect the negative battery cable.

2. Drain the coolant from the radiator and from the drain plugs on both sides of the cylinder block. Remove the radiator, if necessary.

3. Remove the cooling fan assembly. Remove the timing belt covers.

NOTE: Use the proper precautions to avoid getting coolant on the timing belt.

4. On M30, note the positioning of the clamp and disconnect the hose from the water pump.

5. Remove the water pump mounting bolts and remove the pump from the engine.

To install:

6. Thoroughly clean and dry the mating surfaces, bolts and bolt holes.

7. Apply liquid gasket to the water pump and install to the engine. Torque the bolts to 12-15 ft. lbs. (16-21 Nm).

8. On M30, connect the hose and install the clamp in the same position as when it was removed to provide adequate clearance between it and the timing belt cover.

9. Open the air release plug, as required. Fill the cooling system and check for leaks using a pressure tester before continuing.

10. Install the timing belt covers and all related parts.

11. Connect the negative battery cable, run the vehicle until the thermostat opens and fill the radiator completely. Recheck for coolant leaks.

12. Once the vehicle has cooled, recheck the coolant level.

Q45

1. Disconnect the negative battery cable.

2. Drain the coolant from the radiator and from the drain cocks on both sides of the cylinder block.

3. Unbolt the shroud and move it backward in order to remove the fan and coupling. Remove the fan to water pump bolts and remove the fan, coupling, water pump pulley and shroud.

4. Remove all necessary accessories to gain access to the water pump.

5. Note the positioning of the clamp and disconnect the hose from the water pump.

6. Remove the water pump mounting bolts and remove the pump from the engine.

To install:

7. Thoroughly clean and dry the mating surfaces, bolts and bolt holes.

8. Apply liquid gasket to the water pump and install to the engine. Torque the bolts to 14 ft. lbs. (19 Nm).

9. Connect the hose and install the clamp in the same position as when it was removed. Fill the cooling system and check for leaks using a pressure tester before continuing.

10. Install all removed accessories.

11. Install the shroud, pulley, coupling and fan. Torque the water pump pulley nuts to 7 ft. lbs. (10 Nm). Adjust all belts.

12. Connect the negative battery cable, run the vehicle until the thermostat opens and fill the radiator completely. Recheck for coolant leaks.

13. Once the vehicle has cooled, recheck the coolant level.

Thermostat

REMOVAL AND INSTALLATION

G20

1. Drain the engine coolant.

2. Remove the lower radiator hose.

3. Remove the water inlet, then remove the thermostat.

4. Install the new thermostat with the air bleeder or jiggle valve facing upward.

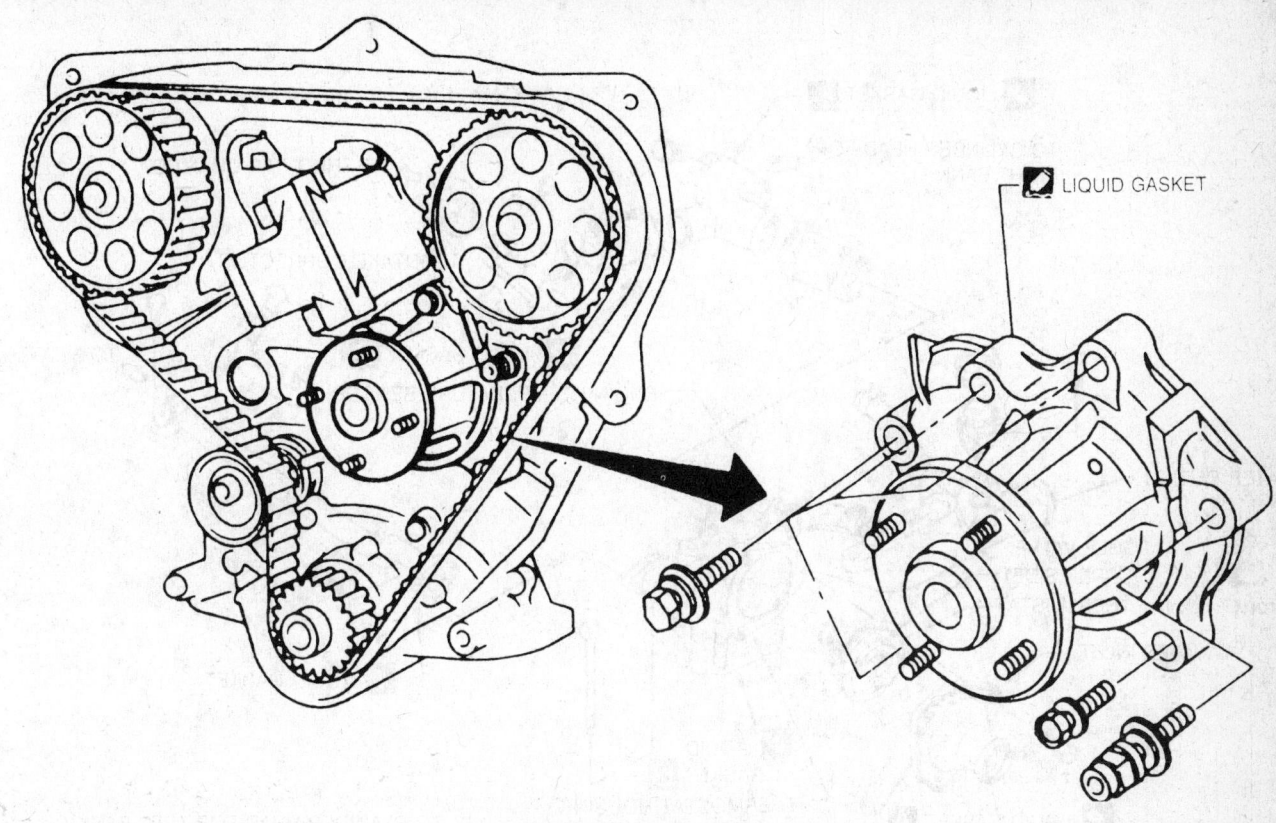

LIQUID GASKET

Water pump location — M30

5. Clean all mating surfaces and apply a 2-3mm bead of liquid gasket to the water inlet.

6. Install the water pump inlet and tighten bolts to 5-6 ft. lbs. (6-8 Nm).

7. Install the lower radiator hose, refill and bleed the coolant system and check for leaks.

J30 AND M30

1. Disconnect the negative battery cable. Drain the cooling system.

2. Disconnect the upper radiator hose from the thermostat housing.

3. Remove the thermostat housing (remove cooling fan assemble if necessary) and thermostat.

To install:

4. Thoroughly clean and dry the mating surfaces, bolts and bolt holes.

5. Install the thermostat with the **UPR** mark and arrow at the top or with the jiggle valve at the top.

6. Apply liquid gasket to the thermostat housing. Install the housing and torque the bolts to 12-15 ft. lbs. (16-21 Nm). Install cooling fan assemble, if necessary.

7. Open the air release plug, as required. Fill the cooling system.

8. Connect the negative battery cable, run the vehicle until the ther-mostat opens and fill the radiator completely. Recheck for coolant leaks.

9. Once the vehicle has cooled, recheck the coolant level.

Q45

1. Disconnect the negative battery cable. Drain the cooling system.

2. Remove the front ornament cover.

3. Disconnect the upper hose from the coolant inlet.

4. Remove the inlet and thermostat.

To install:

5. Thoroughly clean and dry the mating surfaces, bolts and bolt holes.

6. Install the thermostat with the jiggle valve at the top.

7. Apply liquid gasket to the inlet. Install and torque the bolts to 14 ft. lbs. (19 Nm).

8. Fill the cooling system.

9. Connect the negative battery cable, run the vehicle until the ther-mostat opens and fill the radiator completely. Recheck for coolant leaks.

10. Once the vehicle has cooled, recheck the coolant level.

COOLING SYSTEM BLEEDING

G20

1. Set the heater temperature con-trol lever to MAX hot position. Re-move the radiator cap, air relief plug (located at the thermostat housing) and the air bleeder cap (located near the heater core).

2. Refill the reservoir bottle to the MAX line. Reinstall the the air relief plug when coolant spills from the hole. Reinstall the air bleeder cap.

3. Install a steel wire between the negative pressure valve and the seat of the radiator cap. Install the cap and warm the engine to normal oper-ating temperature.

4. Run the engine at 2500 rpm for 10 seconds and return to idle. Repeat this 2-3 times. Turn the engine off and allow car to cool.

5. Remove the radiator cap and check the coolant level. If necessary refill the radiator with coolant up to the filler neck.

6. Remove the radiator cap and re-move the steel wire. Install the cap and warm the engine and check for

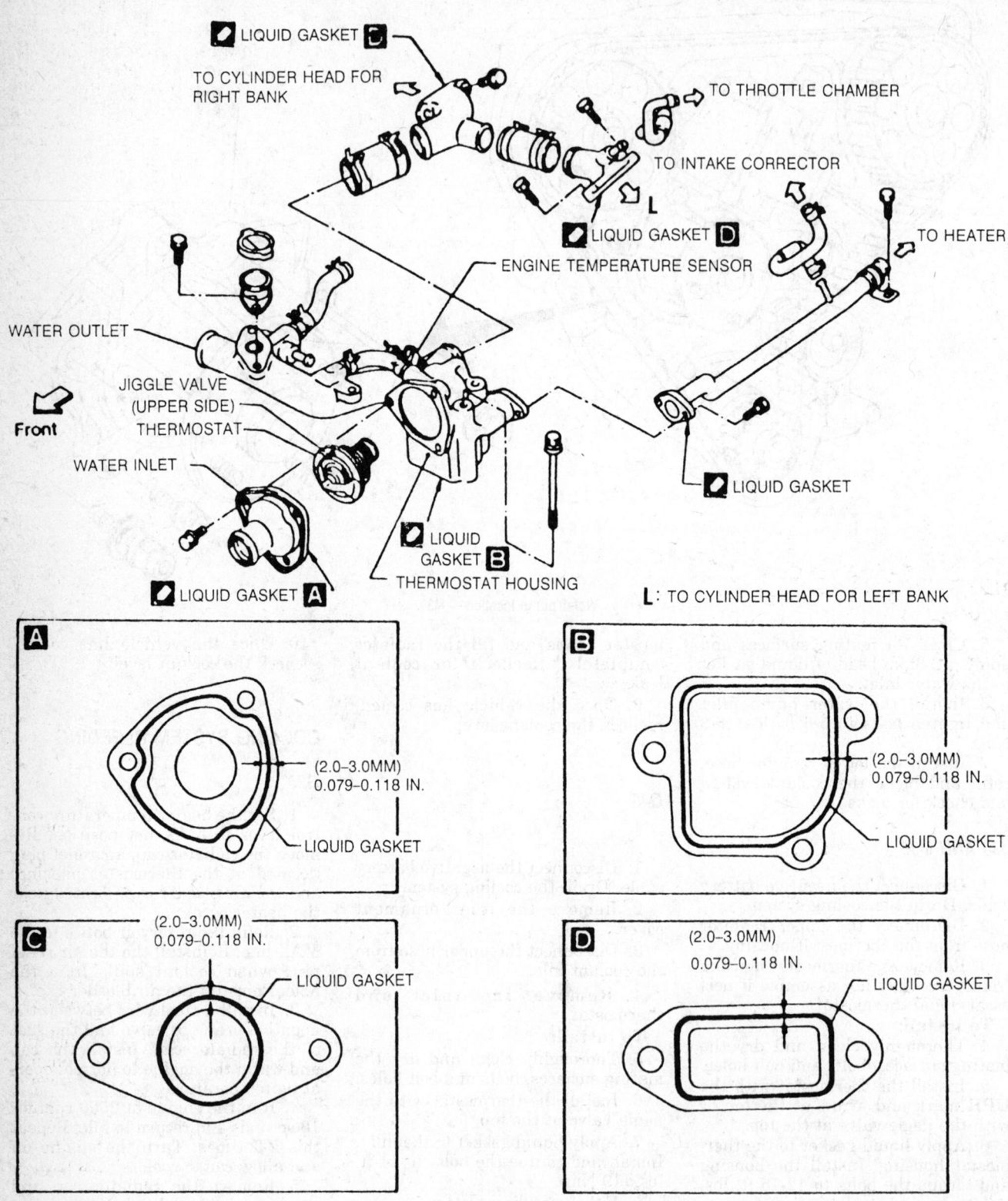

Thermostat location — Q45

the sound of coolant flow with engine running from idle to 4000 rpm. If a sound is heard, bleed air from the cooling system as follows:

a. Cool engine and remove the air bleeder cap on the heater inlet hose.

b. Attach a suitable transparent hose at the air bleeder pipe and put the opposite end of the hose into the coolant reservoir.

c. Install the radiator cap with the steel wire inserted and check for proper connection of all coolant related hoses.

d. Start the engine and check for bubbles in the reservoir tank.

e. Set the heater control lever to MAX cool and run the engine up to 2300 rpm until the bubbles disappear in the hose.

f. After bubbles disappear, set the heater control lever to MAX hot and listen for coolant system sound. If sound is heard, perform Steps a-e again.

g. After all air has been bled from the system, remove the steel wire from the radiator cap, remove the transparent hose, install the air bleeder cap and check the coolant reservoir to ensure it is full.

M30

The M30 is equipped with a air release plug inline with a coolant hose on the right side of the ornamental collector cover. When filling the coolant system open the plug to bleed air from the system.

Q45 AND J30

The Q45 and J30 use a thermostat which is equipped with a jiggle valve. This valve bleeds air as the system is being filled, thus the cooling system requires no further bleeding.

NOTE: Pour coolant through coolant filler neck slowly to allow air in system to escape.

ENGINE ELECTRICAL

NOTE: Disconnecting the negative battery cable on some vehicles may interfere with the functions of the on-board computer systems and may require the computer to undergo a relearning process, once the negative battery cable is reconnected.

Distributor

Removal

G20 AND M30

1. Disconnect the negative battery cable.
2. Remove the splash shield, if equipped. Disconnect the distributor connectors.
3. Unscrew the distributor cap hold-down screws and lift off the distributor cap with all ignition wires still connected.
4. Matchmark the rotor to the distributor housing and the distributor housing to the engine.

NOTE: Do not crank the engine during this procedure. If the engine is cranked, the matchmark must be disregarded.

5. Remove the hold-down bolt.
6. Remove the distributor from the engine.

INSTALLATION

Timing Not Disturbed

1. Install a new distributor housing O-ring.
2. Install the distributor in the engine so the rotor is aligned with the matchmark on the housing and the housing is aligned with the matchmark on the engine. Make sure the distributor is fully seated and the distributor gear is fully engaged.
3. Install and snug the hold-down bolt.
4. Connect the distributor pickup lead wires.
5. Install the distributor cap and tighten the screws. Install the splash shield.
6. Connect the negative battery cable.
7. Adjust the ignition timing and tighten the hold-down bolt.

Timing Disturbed

1. Install a new distributor housing O-ring.
2. Position the engine so the No. 1 piston is at TDC of its compression stroke and the mark on the vibration damper is aligned with **0** on the timing indicator.
3. Install the distributor in the engine so the rotor is aligned with the position of the No. 1 ignition wire on the distributor cap (4-5 o'clock position on the G20). Make sure the dis-

tributor is fully seated and that the distributor shaft is fully engaged.

NOTE: There are distributor cap runners inside the cap on 3.0L engine. Make sure the rotor is pointing to where the No. 1 runner originates inside the cap.

4. Install and snug the hold-down bolt.
5. Connect the distributor pickup lead wires.
6. Install the distributor cap and tighten the screws. Install the splash shield, if equipped.
7. Connect the negative battery cable.
8. Adjust the ignition timing and tighten the hold-down bolt.

Distributorless Ignition

REMOVAL AND INSTALLATION

Power Transistor Unit

J30 AND Q45

1. Disconnect the negative battery cable.
2. Remove the air intake duct, if necessary.
3. Disconnect the connector.
4. Remove the bolts that attach the unit to the ornamental rocker cover.
5. Remove the unit from the engine.
6. The installation is the reverse of the removal procedure.

Ignition Coil

1. Disconnect the negative battery cable.
2. Remove the air intake duct, if necessary.
3. Disconnect the power transistor unit connector.
4. Remove the ornamental rocker cover.
5. Remove the ignition coil bracket mounting bolts and pull out the bracket with the ignition coils.
6. Separate the coil from the bracket and remove from the engine.
7. The installation is the reverse of the removal procedure.

Crank Angle Sensor

1. Disconnect the negative battery cable.
2. Remove the air intake duct.
3. Matchmark the position of the crankshaft sensor assembly to the head.
4. Disconnect the connector, remove the mounting bolts and remove

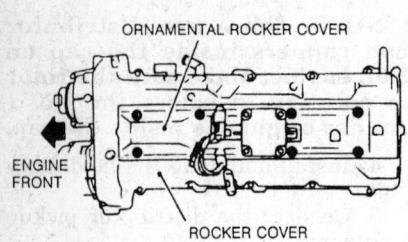

Ornamental rocker cover — 4.5L engine

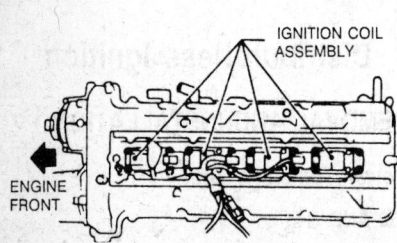

Ignition coil assembly — 4.5L engine

the crank angle sensor from the engine.

5. The installation is the reverse of the removal procedure.

6. Check the ignition timing and adjust, if necessary.

Ignition Timing

ADJUSTMENT

Except J30

1. Start the engine, set the parking brake and run the engine until at normal operating temperature. Keep all lights and accessories OFF.

2. Connect a timing light to the No. 1 cylinder spark plug wire.

3. Use the Nissan Consult System Checking tool in the Data Monitor mode to check engine rpm. Adjust, if necessary.

4. Aim the timing light at the timing scale.

5. On the G20, run the engine at 2000 rpm for 2 minutes and race engine 2-3 times under no load. Return engine to idle. Turn engine OFF and disconnect the throttle sensor harness connector. Start engine and race at 2000-3000 rpm 2-3 times. Check

ignition timing with a timing light. Specification is 13-17 degrees BTDC (manual transmission) or 13-17 degrees BTDC in **N** (automatic transmission). Adjust timing as necessary by loosening distributor hold-down clamp and rotating distributor.

6. On the M30 and Q45, run the engine at 2000 rpm for 2 minutes and race engine 2-3 times under no load. Return engine to idle. Check ignition timing with a timing light. Specification is 13-17 degrees BTDC. Adjust timing as necessary by loosening the hold-down clamp and rotating distributor (crankshaft position sensor).

J30

1. Remove the No. 1 or No. 6 ignition coil and spark plug from the cylinder head.

2. Using a suitable high tension wire, connect the wire in series with the coil and spark plug. Modify the wire end.

3. Attach the timing light inductive pickup to the high tension wire and check the ignition timing.

4. Run the engine at 2000 rpm for 2 minutes and race engine 2-3 times under no load. Return engine to idle.

5. Check ignition timing with a timing light. Specification is 13-17

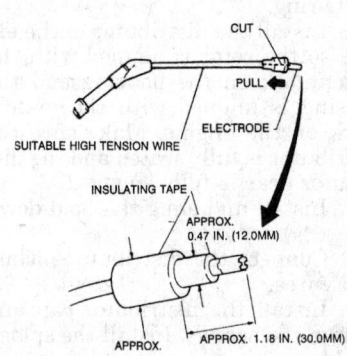

Modifying a high tension wire to check ignition timing — J30

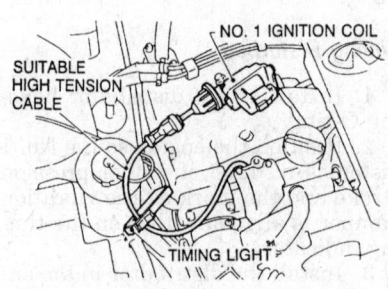

Installing the high tension wire to check ignition timing — J30

degrees BTDC. Adjust timing as necessary by loosening the hold-down clamp and rotating crankshaft position sensor.

Alternator

PRECAUTIONS

Several precautions must be observed with alternator equipped vehicles to avoid damage to the unit.

• If the battery is removed for any reason, make sure it is reconnected with the correct polarity. Reversing the battery connections may result in damage to the 1-way rectifiers.

• When utilizing a booster battery as a starting aid, always connect the positive to positive terminals and the negative terminal from the booster battery to a good engine ground on the vehicle being started.

• Never use a fast charger as a booster to start vehicles.

• Disconnect the battery cables when charging the battery with a fast charger.

• Never attempt to polarize the alternator.

• Do not use test lamps of more than 12 volts when checking diode continuity.

• Do not short across or ground any of the alternator terminals.

• The polarity of the battery, alternator and regulator must be matched and considered before making any electrical connections within the system.

• Never separate the alternator on an open circuit. Make sure all connections within the circuit are clean and tight.

• Disconnect the battery ground terminal when performing any service on electrical components.

• Disconnect the battery if arc welding is to be done on the vehicle.

BELT TENSION ADJUSTMENT

G20

1. Disconnect the negative battery cable.

2. Loosen the nut that secures the T-bolt to the slotted adjustment bracket.

3. Turn the adjustment bolt until the belt deflects approximately 0.28-0.31 in. (7-8mm) (alternator) and 0.16-0.20 in. (4-5mm) (power steering) at its longest expanse.

4. Tighten the T-bolt nut to 12-16 ft. lbs. (16-22 Nm).

5. Connect the negative battery cable.

J30 and M30

1. Disconnect the negative battery cable.
2. Loosen the nut that secures the T-bolt to the slotted adjustment bracket.
3. Turn the adjustment bolt until the belt deflects approximately 0.3 in. (8mm) at its longest expanse.
4. Tighten the T-bolt nut to 11 ft. lbs. (15 Nm).
5. Connect the negative battery cable.

Q45

1. Disconnect the negative battery cable.
2. Loosen the nut that secures the T-bolt to the alternator belt idler pulley.
3. Turn the adjustment bolt until the belt deflects approximately 0.3 in. (8mm) at its longest expanse.
4. Tighten the T-bolt nut to 24 ft. lbs. (32 Nm).
5. Connect the negative battery cable.

REMOVAL AND INSTALLATION

Except Q45

1. Disconnect the negative battery cable.
2. Loosen the alternator belt and remove from the pulley.
3. Disconnect the harness connector and cable from the rear of the alternator.
4. Remove the adjusting bracket.

NOTE: On some models, the front mounting bolt cannot be removed separately because of insufficient clearance between the alternator and engine coolant inlet tube.

5. Remove the rear mounting bolt loosen the front mounting bolt.
6. Remove the alternator with the front mounting bolt.
   To install:
7. The installation is the reverse of the removal procedure. Torque the mounting bolts to 15 ft. lbs. (20 Nm).
8. Adjust the belt so it deflects approximately 0.3 in. (8mm) at its longest expanse.
9. Connect the negative battery cable and check the alternator for proper operation.

Q45

1. Disconnect the negative battery cable.
2. Remove the radiator shroud and cooling fan.
3. Drain a sufficient amount of coolant and remove the upper radiator hose.
4. Remove the upper alternator bracket and the air conditioner pipe mounting bracket.
5. Remove the idler pulley and belt.
6. Remove the 2 power steering cooler pipe mounting screws.
7. Remove the mounting through bolt.
8. Pull the alternator toward the radiator and remove the harness heatshield.
9. Disconnect the wires from the rear of the alternator and remove from the vehicle.
   To install:
10. Position the alternator and connect the wires. Install the heatshield.
11. Install the mounting through bolt loosely.
12. Install the 2 power steering cooler pipe mounting screws.
13. Install the idler pulley and belt.
14. Install the air conditioner pipe mounting bracket and upper alternator bracket. Tighten the through bolt.
15. Adjust the belt so it deflects approximately 0.3 in. (8mm) at its widest expanse.
16. Install the upper radiator hose and refill the cooling system.
17. Install the cooling fan and radiator shroud.
18. Connect the negative battery cable and check the alternator for proper operation.

Starter

REMOVAL AND INSTALLATION

1. Disconnect the negative battery cable.
2. Raise the vehicle and support safely.
3. Remove the engine undercover.
4. Remove exhaust components, as required, in order to gain access to the starter.
5. Remove the starter mounting bolts and remove the starter.
6. The installation is the reverse of the removal procedure. Torque the mounting bolts to 25 ft. lbs. (34 Nm).
7. Connect the negative battery cable and check the starter for proper operation.

EMISSION CONTROLS

Due to the complex nature of modern electronic engine contol systems, comprehensive diagnosis and testing procedures fall outside the confines of this repair manual. For complete information on diagnosis, testin and repair procedures concerning all modern engine and emission control systems, please refer to "Chilton's Guide to Fuel Injecton and Electronic Engine Controls".

FUEL SYSTEM

Fuel System Service Precautions

Safety is the most important factor when performing not only fuel system maintenance but any type of maintenance. Failure to conduct maintenance and repairs in a safe manner may result in serious personal injury or death. Maintenance and testing of the vehicle's fuel system components can be accomplished safely and effectively by adhering to the following rules and guidelines.

• To avoid the possibility of fire and personal injury, always disconnect the negative battery cable unless the repair or test procedure requires that battery voltage be applied.

• Always relieve the fuel system pressure prior to disconnecting any fuel system component (injector, fuel rail, pressure regulator, etc.), fitting or fuel line connection. Exercise extreme caution whenever relieving fuel system pressure to avoid exposing skin, face and eyes to fuel spray. Please be advised that fuel under pressure may penetrate the skin or any part of the body that it contacts.

• Always place a shop towel or cloth around the fitting or connection prior to loosening to absorb any excess fuel due to spillage. Ensure that all fuel spillage (should it occur) is quickly removed from engine surfaces. Ensure that all fuel soaked cloths or towels are deposited into a suitable waste container.

• Always keep a dry chemical (Class B) fire extinguisher near the work area.

• Do not allow fuel spray or fuel vapors to come into contact with a spark or open flame.

• Always use a backup wrench when loosening and tightening fuel line connection fittings. This will prevent unnecessary stress and torsion to fuel line piping. Always follow the proper torque specifications.

• Always replace worn fuel fitting O-rings with new. Do not substitute fuel hose or equivalent where fuel pipe is installed.

RELIEVING FUEL SYSTEM PRESSURE

1. Disable the fuel system either by pulling the fuel pump fuse, located in the interior fuse box or by disconnecting the fuel pump relay or module located in the trunk.
2. Start the engine and run until it stalls.
3. Crank the engine 2-3 more times to ensure that all pressure is relieved.
4. Disconnect the negative battery cable. Install or reconnect the fuse, relay or module.
5. Erase the created code using a Nissan Consult Tester or equivalent, when servicing is finished.

Fuel Tank

REMOVAL AND INSTALLATION

1. Relieve the fuel system pressure.
2. Disconnect the negative battery cable. Raise and support the rear of the vehicle safely.
3. Using the proper equipment, drain the fuel tank.
4. Remove the fuel tank and filler neck protective plates. Remove the filler neck to quarter panel attaching bolts. Disconnect the ventilation pipes and remove the fuel filler assembly.
5. Disconnect the wiring harness connector for the fuel pump/sending unit assembly.
6. Place a suitable jack under the center of the tank and apply slight pressure. Remove the tank retaining bolts.
7. Lower the tank and disconnect the fuel hoses from the pump/sending unit assembly and plug them. Some vehicles are equipped with an inspection cover under the rear seat. Remove this cover to gain access to the

fuel hoses prior to lowering the fuel tank.
8. Remove the fuel tank from the vehicle.

To install:
9. If the pump/sending unit was removed from the fuel tank, use a new O-ring and install the assembly on the fuel tank.
10. Install the fuel tank. Torque the retaining bolts to 24 ft. lbs. (33 Nm).
11. Connect all fuel lines and harness connections. Connect the filler neck and overflow tube.
12. Install the protective plates.
13. Lower the vehicle. Install the bolts that attach the filer neck to the quarter panel.
14. Connect the negative battery cable, start the engine and check for leaks.

Fuel Filter

REMOVAL AND INSTALLATION

———— CAUTION ————
Do not use conventional fuel filters, hoses or clamps when servicing this fuel system. They are not compatible with the high pressures of the injection system and could fail, causing personal injury. Use only components specifically designed for fuel injection.

1. Relieve the fuel system pressure.
2. Disconnect the negative battery cable.
3. Disconnect the fuel hoses from the fuel filter, located in the right side of the engine compartment.
4. Remove the filter mounting screws and remove from the vehicle.
5. Inspect all hoses and clamps for damage of any type. Replace parts, as required.
6. Installation is the reverse of the removal procedure.

Fuel Pump

The fuel pump on all models is located inside the fuel tank assembly.

PRESSURE TESTING

1. Relieve the fuel system pressure.
2. Disconnect the fuel hose between the fuel filter and the fuel tube leading to the engine.
3. Install an appropriate fuel pressure gauge between the filter and tube.

4. Start the engine and check for fuel leaks.
5. Observe the fuel pressure. The specification is 34-36 psi at idle or 43 psi when the fuel pressure regulator vacuum hose is pinched off.
6. Stop the engine, disconnect the vacuum hose to the pressure regulator and plug it.
7. Connect a hand-held vacuum pump to the regulator.
8. Start the engine and observe the fuel pressure as the vacuum is varied. The fuel pressure should decrease as the vacuum is increased.

REMOVAL AND INSTALLATION

G20

1. Release the fuel system pressure.
2. Remove the inspection hole cover located beneath the rear seat.
3. Disconnect the connectors and fuel tubes.
4. Remove the fuel gauge locking ring using tool SST-X38879 or equivalent.
5. Remove the fuel gauge assembly and disconnect the tubes and connector.
6. Remove the fuel pump by sliding it out on an angle.

To install:
7. Use a new O-ring on the fuel gauge assembly locking ring.
8. Install the new fuel pump and attach all fuel lines and connectors.
9. Using tool SST-X38879 or equivalent, tighten the locking ring to 22-26 ft. lbs. (30-35 Nm).
10. Install the inspection cover and test fuel system pressure at the injectors.

Except G20

1. Relieve the fuel system pressure.
2. Disconnect the negative battery cable.
3. Remove the fuel tank.
4. Disconnect the wiring harness. Remove the fuel tank sender unit attaching bolts. Remove the fuel tank sender and discard the O-ring.
5. Remove the fuel pump from the sender unit.

To install:
6. Install the new fuel pump on the sender unit assembly.
7. Using a new O-ring, install the sender unit in the fuel tank. Tighten the bolts to 2 ft. lbs. (3 Nm).
8. Connect the wiring harness and install the fuel tank. Tighten the fuel tank attaching strap bolts to 20-27 ft. lbs. (26-36 Nm).

9. Connect the negative battery cable, start the engine and check for leaks.

Fuel Injector

REMOVAL AND INSTALLATION

G20

1. Disconnect the negative battery cable. Relieve fuel system pressure.
2. Disconnect injector harness connectors.
3. Disconnect vacuum hose from pressure regulator.
4. Disconnect fuel hoses from fuel tube assembly.
5. Remove injectors with fuel tube assembly. Loosen bolts in reverse order of torquing sequence.
6. To remove injector, push out of the fuel tube assembly.

NOTE: Do not remove injector by pinching connector.

To install:
7. Replace or clean injector as necessary.
8. Install injector on fuel tube assembly using a new O-ring and insulator. Lubricate O-rings with silicone oil.
9. Install injectors with fuel tube assembly onto intake manifold. Tighten fuel tube assembly bolts in sequence to 7-8 ft. lbs. (9-10 Nm), and then retighten to 15-20 ft. lbs. (21-26 Nm).
10. Install fuel hoses, lubricating them with silicone oil.
11. Connect the injector harness connector, start the engine and check for leaks.

J30

1. Relieve the fuel system pressure. Disconnect the negative battery cable.

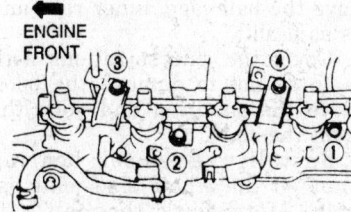

ENGINE FRONT

Fuel tube torquing sequence — G20

2. Disconnect the accelerator cable and as required the cruise control cable.
3. Disconnect the air ducts. Label and disconnect all electrical connectors, vacuum lines and hoses.
4. Remove the intake manifold collector.
5. Remove the fuel injector electrical connector, attaching screws and cover.
6. Remove the fuel injector. Discard the O-ring.

To install:
7. Install the fuel injector with a new O-ring. Install the cover, attaching screws and electrical connector.
8. Install the intake manifold collector.
9. Connect all electrical connectors, vacuum lines and hoses.
10. Connect the accelerator cable and as required the cruise control cable.
11. Connect the negative battery cable. Start the engine and check for leaks.

M30

1. Relieve the fuel system pressure. Disconnect the negative battery cable.
2. Disconnect the cruise control and throttle cables from the throttle body.
3. Remove the intake manifold collector.
4. Disconnect the vacuum hose from the fuel pressure regulator.
5. Disconnect and plug the fuel hoses.
6. Disconnect all injector harness connectors.
7. Disconnect the fuel temperature sensor connector.
8. Remove the injector fuel fuel tube assembly retaining bolts and remove the assembly from the engine.
9. Remove the injector(s) and short fuel hose(s) from the fuel tube. Do not reuse the rubber hose(s).

To install:
10. Wet the inside of the new rubber hose(s) with fuel.
11. Push the end of the rubber hose with hose sockets into the injector tail piece and fuel tube end as far as they will go. Clamps are not used at these connections.
12. Install the injector fuel tube assembly.
13. Connect the fuel temperature sensor connector.
14. Connect all injector harness connectors.
15. Connect the fuel hoses and the regulator vacuum hose.

16. Install the intake manifold collector.
17. Connect the cruise control and throttle cables to the throttle body.
18. Connect the negative battery cable and check for leaks.

Q45

1. Relieve the fuel system pressure. Disconnect the negative battery cable.
2. Drain the coolant.
3. Remove the EGR control valve.
4. Remove the intake manifold collector.
5. Disconnect the harness connector(s) from the fuel injector(s).
6. Remove the injector(s) from the injector tube assembly. Do not reuse the O-ring(s).

To install:
7. Using new O-ring(s), install the injector(s) to the injector tube.
8. Connect the harness connector(s).
9. Install the intake manifold collector.
10. Install the EGR control valve.
11. Fill the cooling system.
12. Connect the negative battery cable and check for leaks.

DRIVE AXLE

NOTE: Final tightening of any suspension component must be performed with the suspension unladen with the tires on the ground.

Halfshaft

REMOVAL AND INSTALLATION

G20

1. Raise and support the vehicle safely. Remove the wheel bearing locknut.
2. Remove the brake caliper assembly and rotor. Using a piece of wire, position the caliper so it is not supported by the brake line.
3. Separate the tie-rod from the ball joint.
4. Separate the kingpin from the knuckle.
5. Remove the halfshaft from the wheel hub/knuckle by lightly tapping it with a wood drift. Take care not to damage the CV-boots.
6. Remove the halfshaft from the transaxle by prying outward with a suitable tool at the transaxle case.

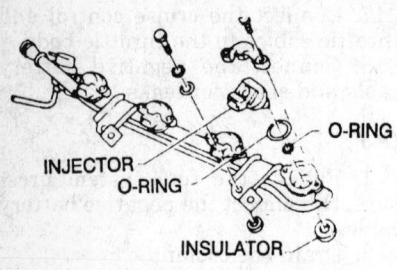

Fuel tube components — G20

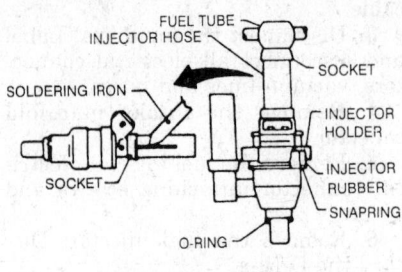

Injector assembly — M30

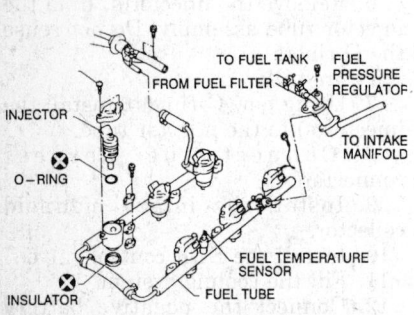

Fuel rail and injectors — J30

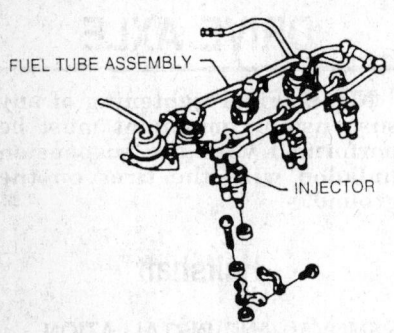

Fuel tube assembly — M30

7. On automatic transaxle models, remove the left halfshaft by tapping it out with a drift from the right side of the transaxle case. Take care not to damage the pinion mate shaft and side gear.

To install:

8. Drive a new oil seal into the transaxle. Set tool KV38106800 or equivalent, along the inner circumference of the oil seal.

9. Insert the halfshaft into the transaxle. Ensure that the serrations are aligned. Remove the tool.

Fuel tube assembly — Q45

10. Push the halfshaft inward and install the circular clip in the groove of the side gear. After inserting the clip, pull outward on the flange of the slide joint to ensure the clip is properly meshed with the side gear. If if pulls out, the clip was not installed properly.

11. Install the halfshaft into the wheel hub/knuckle. Tighten the upper knuckle nut to 72-87 ft. lbs. (98-118 Nm) and wheel bearing locknut to 174-231 ft. lbs. (235-314 Nm).

12. Using a dial indicator, check wheel bearing axial end-play. Specification calls for 0.0020 in. (0.05mm) or less.

M30

1. Raise the vehicle and support safely.

2. Remove the 6 bolts and nuts attaching the outer CV-joint to the companion flange.

3. Remove the inner CV-joint from the differential carrier by prying with a suitable tool.

To install:

4. Install the inner CV-joint into the differential carrier.

---

5. Connect the outer CV-joint to the companion flange with the 6 bolts and nuts. Tighten to 20-27 ft. lbs. (27-37 Nm).

6. Lower the vehicle.

J30 and Q45

1. Raise the vehicle and support safely.

2. Remove the rear wheel.

3. Remove the differential side flange bolts and nuts and separate shaft.

4. Remove the cotter pin, adjusting cap, insulator, wheel bearing locknut and washer from halfshaft.

5. Remove the halfshaft by lightly tapping it with a copper hammer.

6. Remove the halfshaft assembly from the vehicle.

To install:

7. Insert halfshaft into wheel hub and install washer and wheel bearing locknut. Temporarily tighten the locknut.

8. Connect the halfshaft with the differential side flange. Install the nuts and bolts.

9. Tighten the wheel bearing locknut to 152-203 ft. lbs. (206-275 Nm). Install the insulator, adjusting cap and a new cotter pin.

10. Install the rear wheel.

11. Lower the vehicle.

CV-Boot

REMOVAL AND INSTALLATION

G20

1. Raise and support the vehicle safely.

2. Remove halfshaft assembly from vehicle and place in a suitable working fixture.

3. Remove the boot bands. Matchmark the transaxle side slide joint housing and the inner race before separating the joint assembly.

4. Remove the snapring and disassemble the slide joint housing.

5. Matchmark the inner race and halfshaft. Remove the snapring, then remove the ball cage, inner race and balls as a unit.

6. Cover the axle serrations with tape so as not to damage the boot. Remove the snapring and slide the boot off the shaft.

7. Install the wheel bearing locknut on the wheel side joint assembly. Matchmark the halfshaft and joint assembly. Using a suitable puller, separate the joint assembly.

NOTE: The wheel side joint assembly cannot be disassembled.

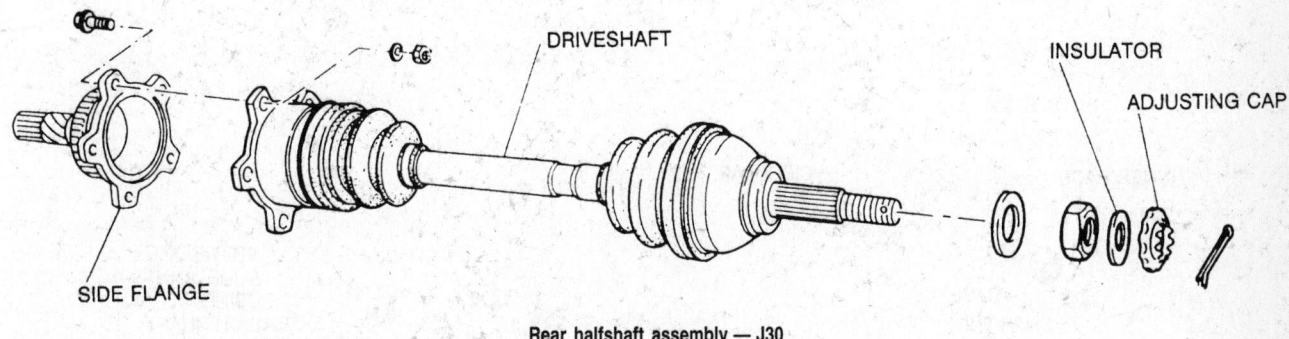

DRIVESHAFT

INSULATOR

ADJUSTING CAP

SIDE FLANGE

Rear halfshaft assembly — J30

8. Cover the axle serrations with tape so as not to damage the boot. Remove the snapring and slide the boot off the shaft.

To install:

9. Install the transaxle side boot and joint assembly. Ensure that all snaprings are secure. If a snapring is loose or damaged, replace it. Ensure that the matchmarks made during assembly are mated.

10. Install the wheel side boot and joint by setting the joint assembly on the halfshaft. Lightly tap the joint to seat it on the shaft. Ensure that the matchmarks made during disassembly are mated.

11. Pack the joint assemblies with 3.6-4.2 oz. (105-125ml) of grease. Install the boots so the length is 3.86 in. (98.5mm) for the wheel side and 3.96 in. (100.5mm) for the transaxle side. Lock the boot bands securely in place.

12. Install the halfshaft assembly and lower the vehicle.

M30

1. Raise the vehicle and support safely.

2. Remove the halfshaft from the vehicle and place in a vise.

3. Remove the plug seal from the slide joint housing by lightly tapping around the slide joint housing.

4. Remove the boot bands.

5. Put matchmarks on the slide joint housing, halfshaft and spider assembly before separating the joint assembly.

6. Remove the snapring on the halfshaft and remove spider assembly.

7. Remove the CV-joint housing.

8. Remove the boot from the shaft.

NOTE: Cover the shaft splines with tape to protect the boot.

To install:

9. Install boot onto shaft.

10. Install CV-joint housing onto shaft.

11. Install spider assembly onto shaft observing matchmarks made on disassembly. Ensure that the spider assembly chamfer faces the shaft.

12. Install snapring onto shaft.

13. With the CV-joint housing held vertically in the vise, install the coil spring, spring cap and new plug seal.

NOTE: The CV-joint housing is held vertically to prevent the coil spring from tilting or falling over.

14. Pack the halfshaft with the 6.52-6.88 oz. (185-195g) of grease.

15. Set the boot so it does not swell or deform when installed.

16. Install a new large boot band and lock in place.

17. Install a new small boot band and lock in place.

18. Install halfshaft assembly in vehicle.

19. Lower vehicle.

J30 and Q45

1. Raise the vehicle and support safely.

2. Remove the halfshaft assembly from the vehicle and place in a vise.

3. Remove the boot bands on both inner and outer joints.

4. Put matchmarks on the slide joint housing and inner race before separating the joint assembly.

5. Remove large snapring retaining slide joint and remove slide joint from halfshaft.

6. Put matchmarks on the inner race and the halfshaft.

7. Remove small snapring and remove the ball cage, inner race and balls as a unit.

8. Remove the boot.

9. Before separating the joint assembly on the wheel side, put matchmarks on the halfshaft and joint assembly.

NOTE: The joint on the wheel side cannot be disassembled.

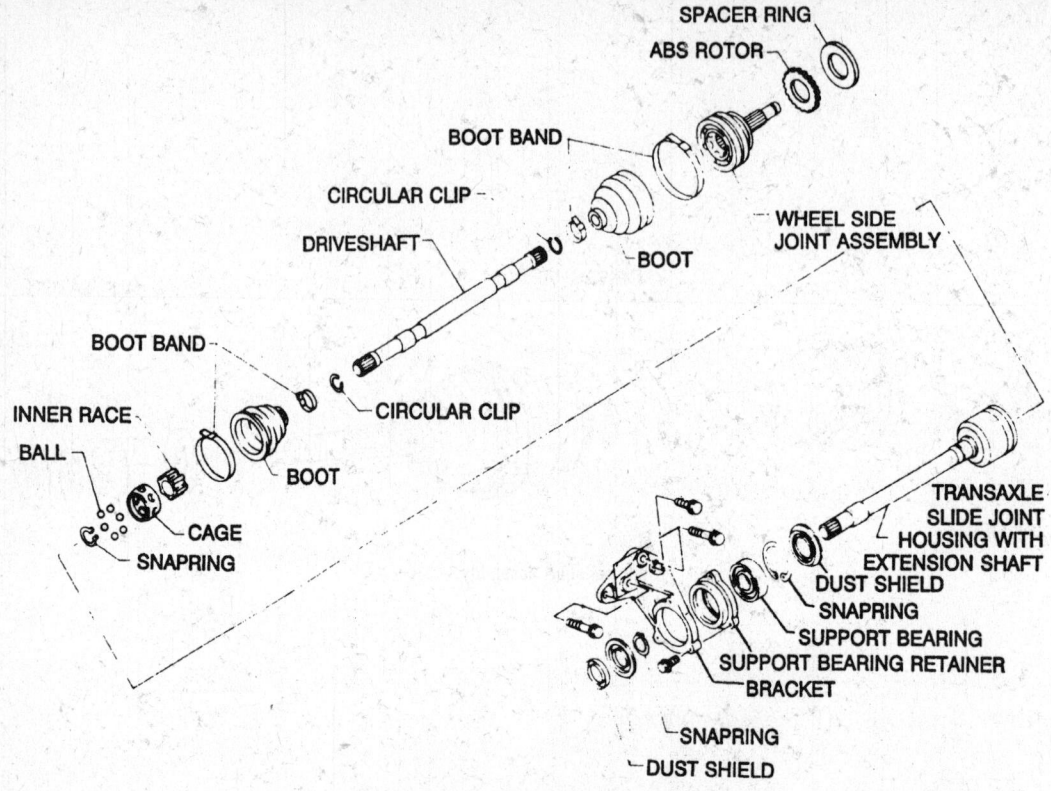

SPACER RING
ABS ROTOR
BOOT BAND
CIRCULAR CLIP
DRIVESHAFT
BOOT
WHEEL SIDE JOINT ASSEMBLY
BOOT BAND
INNER RACE
BALL
BOOT
CIRCULAR CLIP
CAGE
SNAPRING
TRANSAXLE SLIDE JOINT HOUSING WITH EXTENSION SHAFT
DUST SHIELD
SNAPRING
SUPPORT BEARING
SUPPORT BEARING RETAINER
BRACKET
SNAPRING
DUST SHIELD

Halfshaft assembly exploded view — G20

10. Separate the joint assembly from the halfshaft using a slide hammer or equivalent.

11. Remove the boot.

To install:

12. Apply tape to the halfshaft splines to prevent damage to the boots.

13. Install a new small boot band and a new boot on the wheel side of the halfshaft.

14. Set the joint assembly onto the halfshaft and seat the joint by lightly tapping it. Ensure that the matchmarks are aligned when assembling.

15. Pack the halfshaft with 6.00-6.70 oz. (170-190g).

16. Set boot so it does not swell or deform when installed in the vehicle.

17. Lock new larger and smaller boot band securely with a suitable tool.

18. Install a new small boot band and a new boot on the differential side of the halfshaft.

19. Install the ball cage, inner race and balls as a unit. Ensure that the matchmarks are aligned when assembling.

20. Install a new large snapring.

21. Pack the halfshaft with 6.35-7.05 oz. (180-200g) of grease.

22. Install slide joint housing and install a new small snapring.

23. Set the boot so it does not swell or deform when installed in the vehicle.

24. Lock the new larger and smaller boot bands securely with a suitable tool.

25. Install the halfshaft assembly in the vehicle.

26. Install the rear wheel.

27. Lower the vehicle.

Driveshaft and U-Joints

REMOVAL AND INSTALLATION

J30, M30 and Q45

1. Raise the vehicle and support safely.

2. Matchmark the final drive flange, driveshaft flanges, center bearing flanges, transmission yoke and transmission.

3. Remove the attaching bolts and separate driveshaft from the differential carrier.

4. Remove the bolts attaching the driveshaft to the center bearing flange and remove the rear driveshaft.

5. Remove the nuts attaching the center bearing. Slide the front driveshaft rearward to remove it from the transmission. Plug the rear opening of the transmission extension housing to prevent oil spills.

6. Inspect the rear driveshaft runout. Runout should not exceed 0.024 in. (0.6mm).

To install:

7. Remove the plug front the transmission. Align and install the front driveshaft. Tighten the center bearing attaching nuts to 18-22 ft. lbs. (25-29 Nm).

8. Align and install the rear driveshaft. Tighten the differential carrier-to-driveshaft bolts to 41-48 ft. lbs. (55-65 Nm) on J30 and M30 models or 65-72 ft. lbs. (88-98 Nm) on the Q45 model. Torque the center bearing flange-to-driveshaft bolts to 29-33 ft. lbs. (39-44 Nm) on J30 and M30 models or 40-47 ft. lbs. (54-65 Nm) on all others.

9. Lower the vehicle.

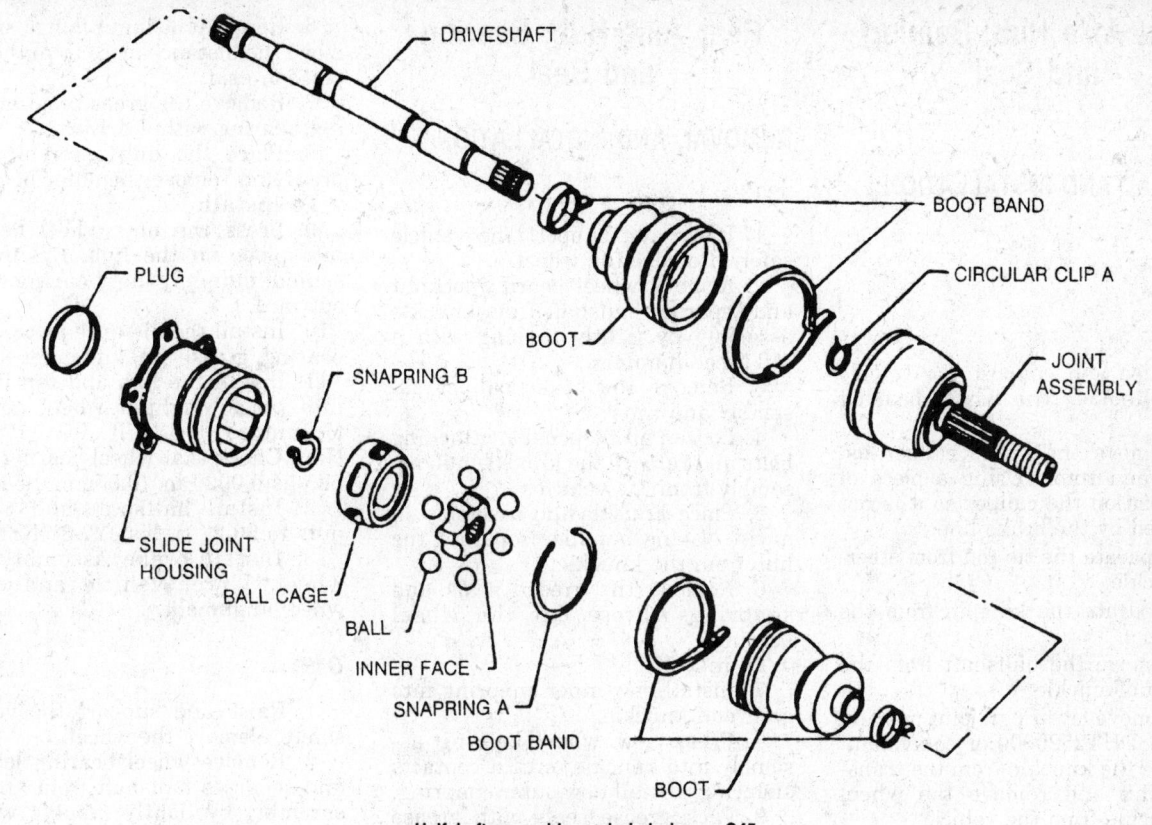

Halfshaft assembly exploded view — Q45

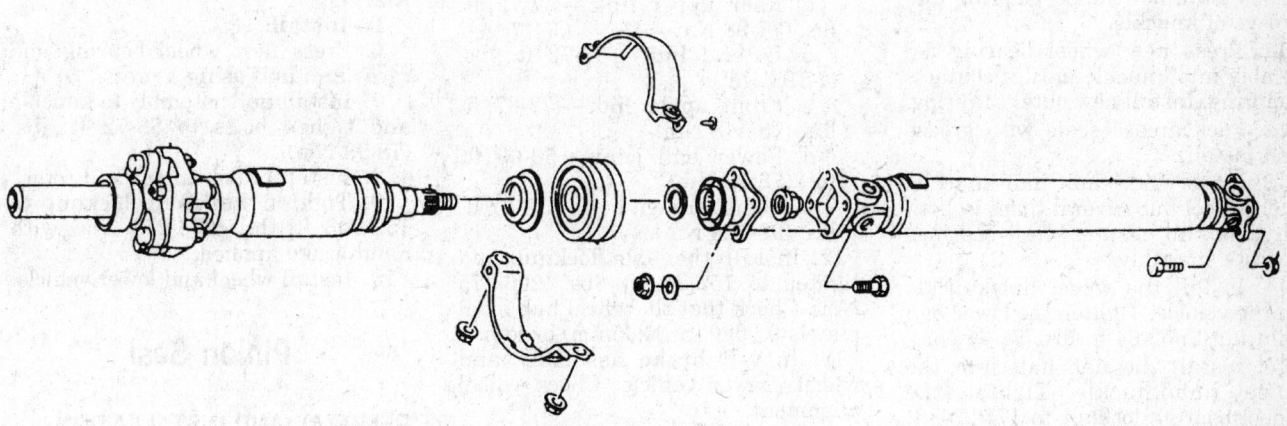

Driveshaft assembly — J30, M30 and Q45

Front Axle Hub, Bearing and Seal

REMOVAL AND INSTALLATION

G20

1. Raise and support the vehicle safely. Remove the wheel bearing locknut.
2. Remove the brake caliper assembly and rotor. Using a piece of wire, position the caliper so it is not supported by the brake line.
3. Separate the tie-rod from steering knuckle.
4. Separate the kingpin from the knuckle.
5. Remove the halfshaft from the wheel hub/knuckle.
6. Remove lower ball joint nut and using tool HT2520000 or equivalent. Separate the knuckle from the transverse link and remove the wheel hub/knuckle from the vehicle.
7. Place the wheel hub/knuckle assembly in a vise and drive out the hub from the rear side of the knuckle.
8. Remove the inner grease seal, inner and outer snaprings.
9. Press out the wheel bearing.

To install:
10. Install new inner snapring into groove of knuckle.
11. Press new wheel bearing assembly into knuckle until it contacts snapring. Install new outer snapring.
12. Pack grease seals with grease and install.
13. Press wheel hub into knuckle. Spin wheel hub several times in both directions to ensure wheel bearings operate smoothly.
14. Install the wheel hub/knuckle on the vehicle. Tighten the lower ball joint nut to 52-64 ft. lbs. (71-86 Nm).
15. Install the halfshaft into the wheel hub/knuckle. Tighten the wheel bearing locknut to 174-231 ft. lbs. (235-314 Nm) and the kingpin nut to 72-87 ft. lbs. (98-118 Nm).
16. Install the tie-rod on the steering knuckle and tighten to 22-29 ft. lbs. (29-39 Nm). Install new cotter pin.
17. Check that the wheel hub axial play is 0.0020 in. (0.05mm) or less.
18. Install the brake assembly and wheel. Lower the vehicle. Check wheel alignment.

Rear Axle Hub, Bearing and Seal

REMOVAL AND INSTALLATION

J30

1. Raise and support the vehicle safely. Remove the wheel.
2. Remove wheel bearing locknut and separate halfshaft from knuckle assembly by lightly tapping with a soft faced hammer.
3. Remove the brake caliper assembly and rotor.
4. Loosen all suspension attaching bolts and remove the knuckle/hub assembly from the vehicle.
5. Place knuckle/hub assembly in a vise. Using a puller separate the hub from the knuckle.
6. Remove the grease seals and snaprings. Press out the wheel bearing.

To install:
7. Install new inner snapring into groove of knuckle.
8. Press new wheel bearing assembly into knuckle until it contacts snapring. Install new outer snapring.
9. Pack grease seals with grease and install.
10. Press wheel hub into knuckle. Spin wheel hub several times in both directions to ensure wheel bearings operate smoothly.
11. Install knuckle/hub assembly on vehicle and tighten suspension arm through bolts as follows:
   a. Rear upper link — 57-72 ft. lbs. (77-98 Nm).
   b. Lateral link — 57-72 ft. lbs. (77-98 Nm).
   c. Front upper link — 72-87 ft. lbs. (98-118 Nm).
   d. Lower ball joint — 58-69 ft. lbs. (78-93 Nm).
   e. Strut through bolt — 72-87 ft. lbs. (98-118 Nm).
12. Install the axle locknut and tighten to 152-203 ft. lbs. (206-275 Nm). Check that the wheel hub axial play is 0.0020 in. (0.05mm) or less.
13. Install brake assembly and wheel. Lower vehicle. Check wheel alignment.

M30

1. Raise and support the vehicle safely. Remove the wheel.
2. Disconnect the halfshaft.
3. Remove the wheel bearing locknut.
4. Remove the brake caliper and rotor.
5. Draw out the rear axle using puller.
6. Remove the inner flange and remove the distance piece from the suspension arm.
7. Remove the grease seal and inner bearing with a driver.
8. Place the hub assembly in a press and remove the outer bearing.

To install:
9. Press the new wheel bearing into place on the hub. Ensure the sealed side of the bearing faces outward.
10. Install the distance piece, inner bearing, grease seal and inner flange.
11. Install the hub and tap lightly into place. Tighten wheel bearing locknut to 94-130 ft. lbs. (127-177 Nm). Check that wheel bearing axial play is 0.0020 in. (0.05mm) or less.
12. Install halfshaft and tighen nuts to 20-27 ft. lbs. (27-37 Nm).
13. Install brake assembly and wheel. Lower vehicle and check wheel alignment.

Q45

1. Raise and support the vehicle safely. Remove the wheel.
2. Remove wheel bearing locknut and separate halfshaft from knuckle assembly by lightly tapping with a soft faced hammer.
3. Remove the brake caliper assembly and rotor.
4. Loosen the wheel bearing flange nuts from the rear of the knuckle assembly and remove the wheel bearing flange with the hub attached.
5. Use a press to remove the wheel bearing.

To install:
6. Press new wheel bearing and races into hub using a press.
7. Install hub assembly to knuckle and tighen bolts to 58-72 ft. lbs. (78-98 Nm).
8. Install brake caliper and rotor.
9. Tighten halfshaft locknut to 152-203 ft. lbs. (206-275 Nm) with hand brake applied.
10. Install wheel and lower vehicle.

Pinion Seal

REMOVAL AND INSTALLATION

J30, M30 and Q45

1. Raise the vehicle and support safely.
2. Remove the driveshaft.
3. Loosen the drive pinion nut (note torque specification before removal).
4. Remove the companion flange using a suitable puller.

5. Remove the pinion seal using a suitable seal puller.

To install:

6. Apply a multi-purpose grease to the sealing lips of the new pinion seal. Install the new seal into the carrier using a suitable seal installer.

7. Install the companion flange and drive pinion nut. Tighten to 137-217 ft. lbs. (186-294 Nm).

8. Install the driveshaft.

9. Lower the vehicle.

Differential Carrier

REMOVAL AND INSTALLATION

J30, M30 and Q45

1. Raise the vehicle and support safely.

2. Remove the driveshaft. On the Q45, remove the exhaust pipes.

NOTE: Plug rear opening in transmission extension housing.

3. Remove the halfshafts.

4. Support the weight of the differential carrier.

5. Remove the nuts and bolts securing the differential carrier to the suspension member.

6. Remove the bolts and nuts securing the differential mounting insulator to the body.

7. On M30, move the differential carrier toward the rear of the vehicle with the jack. On J30 and Q45, move the differential carrier forward together with the jack, then remove the rear cover stud bolts from the suspension member.

8. Lower the differential carrier using the jack.

To install:

9. Position the differential carrier in the vehicle.

10. On M30, install bolts and nuts securing the differential mounting insulator to the body. Tighten bolts to 22-29 ft. lbs. (29-39 Nm). Tighten the nuts to 43-58 ft. lbs. (59-78 Nm). Install the differential carrier to the suspension member. Tighten the nuts to 43-65 ft. lbs. (59-88 Nm).

11. On J30 and Q45, install the nuts securing the differential carrier rear cover to the suspension member. Tighten to 72-87 ft. lbs. (98-118 Nm). Install the differential carrier mounting member to the front of the differential carrier. Tighten to 72-87 ft. lbs. (98-118 Nm).

12. Remove the jack.

13. Install the halfshafts.

14. Install the driveshaft.

15. Install the exhaust tube.

16. Lower the vehicle.

MANUAL TRANSAXLE

Transaxle Assembly

REMOVAL AND INSTALLATION

G20

1. Disconnect the negative battery cable and disconnect the air duct.

2. Disconnect the clutch control cable and speedometer cable from the transaxle.

3. Disconnect the backup light switch, neutral switch and ground harness connectors.

4. Remove the starter, shift control rod and support rod from the transaxle.

5. Drain the gear oil from the transaxle and remove the exhaust front tube.

6. Remove the halfshafts.

7. Support the engine with a suitable jack under the oil pan.

8. Remove the rear and left engine mounts

9. Raise the jack and remove the lower transaxle housing bolts. Lower

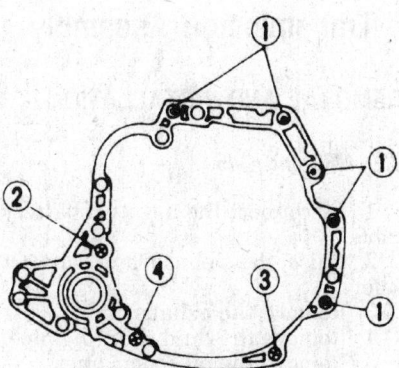

1. 51–59 ft. lbs. (70–79 Nm) – 2.17 in. (55mm) length
2. 51–59 ft. lbs. (70–79 Nm) – 2.56 in. (65mm) length
3. 22–30 ft. lbs. (30–40 Nm) – 1.38 in. (35mm) length
4. 22–30 ft. lbs. (30–40 Nm) – 1.77 in. (45mm) length

Transaxle mounting bolt torque specifications

jack and remove the upper housing bolts. Keep the bolts in order as they are different lengths and must be returned to the same position.

10. Lower the transaxle.

To install:

11. Raise the transaxle into place and install the attaching bolts. Tighten bolts to the torque specified.

12. Install the rear and left engine mounts.

13. Install the driveshafts.

14. Install the shift control rods, support rod and starter on the transaxle.

15. Connect the backup light switch, neutral switch and ground harness connectors.

16. Connect the clutch control cable and speedometer cable from the transaxle.

17. Connect the air duct and install the negative battery cable. Road test the vehicle.

CLUTCH

Clutch Assembly

REMOVAL AND INSTALLATION

G20

1. Disconnect the negative battery cable.

2. Raise and support the vehicle safely.

3. Remove the transaxle.

4. Insert tool KV30101000 or equivalent, into the clutch disc hub and loosen pressure plate bolts in 2-3 steps in sequence.

5. Remove the pressure plate and clutch disc as an assembly.

6. Remove the release bearing by pulling the bearing retainers outward from the transaxle case.

7. Inspect the clutch disc for surface wear. Measure from the friction surface to the top of the rivets. Wear limit is 0.012 in. (0.3mm). Replace clutch disc as necessary.

8. Inspect the contact surface of the flywheel for burns or discoloration. Check flywheel runout. Maximum runout is 0.0059 in. (0.15mm).

9. Using tools ST20050100 and ST20050010 or equivalent, check pressure plate diaphragm springs. Measure from the pressure plate/flywheel mating surface to the top of the diaphragm spring. Height should be 1.201-1.280 in.

(30.5-32.5mm). Replace pressure plate as necessary.

10. Inspect the release bearing for damage. Spin the bearing to see that it rolls freely.

To install:

11. Lightly lubricate the transaxle input shaft, input shaft collar, clutch lever assembly and the clutch release bearing with a lithium based grease.

NOTE: Keep clutch disc and all clutch components clean during installation. Do not allow grease to contact the clutch disc.

12. Insert tool KV30101000 or equivalent, into the clutch disc hub. Install the clutch disc and pressure plate on the tool and tighten the pressure plate bolts to 16-22 ft. lbs. (22-29 Nm) in 2-3 steps using a crisscross pattern. Remove the tool.

13. Install release bearing in the transaxle. Ensure that the bearing retainer clips are fully engaged.

14. Install the transaxle.

15. Adjust clutch pedal height and free-play.

16. Lower vehicle, connect negative battery cable and road test vehicle.

PEDAL HEIGHT/FREE-PLAY ADJUSTMENT

1. Adjust pedal height with pedal stopper or Automatic Speed Control Device (ASCD) cancel switch. Pedal height specification is 6.28-6.67 in. (159.5-169.5mm) from the top of the pedal to the floor well (when measured at a 90 degree angle to the top of the pedal).

2. Adjust the withdrawl lever play on the top of the transaxle, by pushing the withdrawl lever until resistance is felt and then adjusting the nut. Turn the adjusting nut 2.5-3.5 turns back and then tighten the locknut. Withdrawal lever play should be 0.098-0.138 in. (2.5-3.5mm). Tighten the locknut to 2-3 ft. lbs. (3-4 Nm).

3. As a final check, measure pedal free travel at the center of the pedal pad. Pedal free travel should be 0.425-0.594 in. (10.8-15.1mm).

4. On U.S. models only, adjust the clearance between the stopper rubber and the threaded end of the clutch interlock switch while depressing the clutch pedal fully. Adjust the clearance to 0.039-0.004 in. (0.1-1.0mm).

Clutch Cable

REMOVAL AND INSTALLATION

G20

1. Raise and support the vehicle safely.

2. Loosen the locknut and adjusting nut on the clutch cable at the withdrawl lever and disconnect the cable.

3. Disconnect the cable from the clutch pedal under the dash.

4. Remove any clips or ties holding the cable to the chassis and remove the cable.

To install:

5. Install the cable using the original routing.

6. Connect the cable at the clutch pedal and withdraw lever.

7. Adjust the pedal height and free-play.

8. Lower the vehicle and road test.

AUTOMATIC TRANSMISSION

Transmission Assembly

REMOVAL AND INSTALLATION

J30, M30 and Q45

1. Disconnect the negative battery cable.

2. Raise the vehicle and support safely.

3. Remove the exhaust tube.

4. Remove the fluid charging pipe.

5. Remove the oil cooler lines.

6. Plug fluid charging and oil cooler fittings after removing lines.

7. Remove the control linkage from the selector lever.

8. Disconnect the neutral safety switch and solenoid harness connectors.

9. Disconnect the speedometer cable or speed sensor connection.

10. Remove the driveshaft. Insert plug into rear seal opening to prevent loss of fluid.

11. Remove the starter motor.

12. Support the transmission safely.

13. Remove the gusset securing the transmission to the engine. Remove

the bolts attaching the transmission to the engine.

NOTE: The bolts securing the transmission to the engine are of different lengths. Note the length of the bolts as they are removed.

14. Remove the bolts securing the torque converter to the flexplate.

15. Support the engine safely. Avoid jacking directly under the oil pan drain plug.

16. Remove the transmission from the vehicle.

To install:

17. Position the transmission in the vehicle and install the torque converter-to-flexplate bolts. Tighten to 33-43 ft. lbs. (44-59 Nm).

18. Secure the transmission to the engine. Torque the:

- 60mm bolts to 29-36 ft. lbs. (39-49 Nm)
- 50mm bolts to 29-36 ft. lbs. (39-49 Nm)
- 45mm bolts to 29-36 ft. lbs. (39-49 Nm)
- 25mm bolts to 22-29 ft. lbs. (29-39 Nm)
- 20mm gusset bolts to 22-29 ft. lbs. (29-39 Nm)

19. Install the starter motor.

20. Install the driveshaft.

21. Connect the speedometer cable or speed sensor connection.

22. Connect the neutral safety switch and solenoid harness connectors.

23. Install the control linkage to the selector lever.

24. Install the fluid charging and oil cooler lines.

25. Connect the exhaust tube.

26. Lower the vehicle.

27. Connect negative battery cable.

SHIFT LINKAGE ADJUSTMENTS

1. Place the selector lever in **P** range.

2. Loosen the locknuts.

3. Without pushing the button, pull selector lever toward **R** and tighten locknut X until it touches trunnion.

4. Back off locknut X one turn and tighten locknut Y to 8-11 ft. lbs. (11-15 Nm).

THROTTLE LINKAGE ADJUSTMENT

Adjust throttle wire end-play to 0.04-0.12 in. (1-3mm). Tighten locknut to 6-7 ft. lbs. (8-10 Nm).

7. Support the engine with a suitable stand and use a suitable jack to support the transaxle.

8. Remove the transaxle mounting bolts and the transaxle-to-engine bolts. Lower the transaxle.

To install:

9. Place a straightedge across the bell housing of the transaxle and measure the distance to the mounting bosses on the torque converter. The distance should be 0.626 in. (15.9mm). If not, the torque converter is not installed correctly.

10. Check the driveplate runout with a dial indicator. Maximum allowable runout is 0.008 in. (0.2mm).

11. Raise the transaxle into position and install the torque converter bolts. Tighten bolts to 33-43 ft. lbs. (44-59 Nm). Rotate the crankshaft to gain access to the bolts.

12. Install the halfshafts, exhaust front tube and starter.

13. Connect the control cable and transaxle coolant lines.

14. Connect the transaxle solenoid harness and inhibitor switch harness connector. Disconnect the throttle wire at the engine side.

15. Fill the transaxle with lubricant, install the negative battery cable and road test the vehicle.

CONTROL CABLE ADJUSTMENT

The control cable is adjusted by loosening the locknut on the manual shaft (located at the top of the transaxle) and sliding the cable. After adjustment, move the selector lever from **P** to **L** range and make sure the selector lever moves smoothly without making a sliding noise.

THROTTLE WIRE ADJUSTMENT

1. Turn ignition switch **OFF**.

2. Move adjusting tube toward the transaxle side while pressing the lockplate. Then return the lockplate to lock the adjusting tube.

3. Put a mark on the throttle wire to use as a reference while measuring.

4. Move the throttle drum from the idling position to the full throttle position quickly. The adjusting tube should move in the direction of the engine side depressing the lockplate.

5. Ensure that the throttle wire stroke is 1.54-1.69 in. (39-43mm). If the throttle drum is too far toward the transaxle, kickdown range will greatly increase. If the throttle drum is too far toward the engine, kickdown will not occur.

6. After properly adjusting the throttle wire, ensure the parting line is as straight as possible.

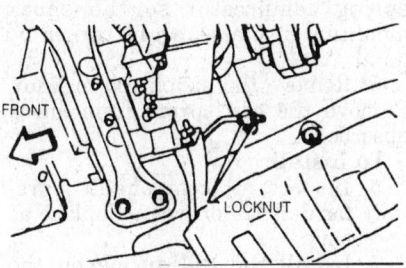

Manual control linkage locknut

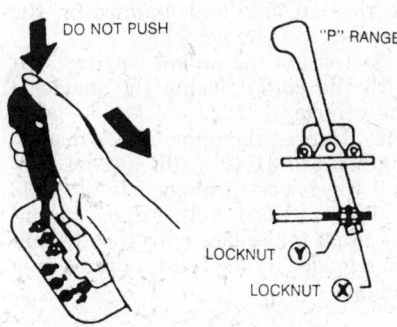

Manual control linkage adjustment

AUTOMATIC TRANSAXLE

Transaxle Assembly

REMOVAL AND INSTALLATION

G20

1. Disconnect the negative battery cable and the air duct.

2. Raise and support the vehicle safely. Disconnect the transaxle solenoid harness and inhibitor switch harness connector. Disconnect the throttle wire at the engine side.

3. Drain the transaxle fluid.

4. Disconnect the control cable and transaxle coolant lines.

5. Remove the halfshafts, exhaust front exhaust tube and starter.

6. Remove the rear plate cover and the bolts securing the torque converter to the driveplate. Rotate the crankshaft to gain access to the bolts.

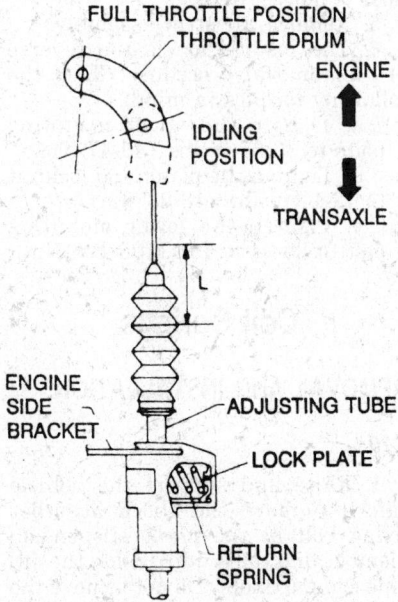

Throttle wire adjustment — G20

FRONT SUSPENSION

Shock Absorbers

Removal and Installation

G20

1. Raise and support the vehicle safely. Remove the shock absorber fixing bolt at the lower suspension member and the 3 nuts inside the engine compartment. Do not remove the piston rod locknut.

2. Remove the shock absorber assembly and place in a suitable holding device.

3. Using a prybar to hold the spring, loosen the piston rod locknut.

4. Compress the spring with a spring compressor so the shock mounting insulator can be turned by hand.

5. Remove the piston rod locknut. Remove the shock absorber.

To install:

6. Inspect all components carefully for damage or wear. Replace as necessary.

7. Install shock absorber and tighten rod locknut to 13-17 ft. lbs. (18-24 Nm).

8. Install the shock absorber assembly in the vehicle. Ensure the bend in the lower shock bracket faces rearward on the left side and forward on the right side of the vehicle.

9. Install the upper spring seat with the cutout facing the inside of the vehicle.

10. Tighten the upper shock mounting bolts to 31-40 ft. lbs. (42-54 Nm) and the lower through bolt to 82-93 ft. lbs. (112-126 Nm). Final tightening must take place with the suspension loaded (vehicle at normal ride height).

Q45

1. Remove the upper shock absorber mounting insulator bolts.

2. Raise and safely support the vehicle.

3. Remove the lower shock mounting bolt and lift out the shock assembly.

4. Lower the vehicle.

5. The installation is the reverse of the removal procedure. Keep the following torques in mind:

   a. Tighten the upper mounting bolts to 30-35 ft. lbs. (40-47 Nm).

   b. Tighten the piston rod locknut to 13-17 ft. lbs. (18-23 Nm).

   c. Tighten the lower mounting bolt to 80-94 ft. lbs. (108-128 Nm).

MacPherson Strut

REMOVAL AND INSTALLATION

J30

1. Raise and support the vehicle safely.

2. Remove the front wheel.

3. Remove the brake caliper and rotor. Hang the brake caliper out of the way using a piece of wire.

4. Remove the tie rod ball joint and lower ball joint using a ball joint tool.

5. Remove the stabilizer connecting rod upper nut, separate the strut assembly and stabilizer connecting rod.

6. Matchmark the strut assembly to the body and remove the strut assembly upper nuts.

7. Remove the strut assembly.

To install:

8. Install the strut assembly and loosely install the upper assembly nuts.

9. Install the stabilizer connecting rod and loosely install the connecting rod upper nut.

10. Connect the tie rod and ball joint to the strut assembly. Loosely install the attaching nuts.

11. Align all components to their proper positions then tighten the strut assembly upper nuts to 43-54 ft. lbs. (59-74 Nm).

12. Tighten the tie rod ball joint to 22-29 ft. lbs. (29-39 Nm) and the lower ball joint to 71-88 ft. lbs. (98-118 Nm).

13. Tighten the stabilizer connecting rod nut to 54-67 ft. lbs. (74-90 Nm).

14. Install the brake caliper and rotor. Install the wheel.

15. Align the front suspension as necessary. Lower the vehicle.

M30

1. Disconnect the negative battery cable.

2. Disconnect the sub-harness connector strut actuator mounting bolt.

3. Remove the strut assembly mounting nut. Do not remove the piston rod locknut on the vehicle.

4. Raise and safely support the vehicle. Remove the tension rod nuts and the strut-to-steering knuckle mounting bolts. Make sure the brake hose is not twisted.

5. Remove the strut assembly.

6. The installation is the reverse of the removal procedure. Keep the following torques in mind:

   a. Tighten the upper mounting bolts to 30-35 ft. lbs. (40-47 Nm).

   b. Tighten the piston rod locknut to 13-17 ft. lbs. (18-23 Nm).

   c. Tighten the lower mounting bolt to 80-94 ft. lbs. (108-128 Nm)

Coil Springs

REMOVAL AND INSTALLATION

G20

1. Raise and support the vehicle safely. Remove the shock absorber fixing bolt at the lower suspension member and the 3 nuts inside the engine compartment. Do not remove the piston rod locknut.

2. Remove the shock absorber assembly and place in a suitable holding device.

3. Using a prybar to hold the spring, loosen the piston rod locknut.

4. Compress the spring with a spring compressor so the shock mounting insulator can be turned by hand.

5. Remove the piston rod locknut. Remove the coil spring from shock absorber.

To install:

6. Inspect all components carefully for damage or wear. Replace as necessary.

7. Install the coil spring on the shock absorber and tighten rod locknut to 13-17 ft. lbs. (18-24 Nm).

8. Install the coil spring assembly in the vehicle. Ensure the bend in the lower shock bracket faces rearward on the left side and forward on the right side of the vehicle.

9. Install the upper spring seat with the cutout facing the inside of the vehicle.

10. Tighten the upper shock mounting bolts to 31-40 ft. lbs. (42-54 Nm) and the lower through bolt to 82-93 ft. lbs. (112-126 Nm). Final tightening must take place with the suspension loaded (vehicle at normal ride height).

J30

1. Raise and support the vehicle safely.

2. Remove the front wheel.

3. Remove the disc brake and rotor.

4. Remove the strut assembly.

5. Place the strut assembly in a vise using special tool ST-35652000 or equivalent.

6. Loosen, but do not remove the piston rod locknut.

7. Compress the spring with a spring compressor so the strut mounting insulator can be turned by hand.

8. Remove the piston rod locknut and coil spring.

To install:

9. Install coil spring with flat end on top. Install upper spring seat with its cutout facing the outer side of the vehicle.

10. After spring is in position, tighten locknut to 43-54 ft. lbs. (59-74 Nm).

11. Install the strut assembly, rotor and disc brake assembly.

12. Install the wheel and lower the vehicle.

M30

1. Disconnect the negative battery cable.

2. Disconnect the sub-harness connector strut actuator mounting bolt.

3. Remove the strut assembly mounting nut. Do not remove the piston rod locknut on the vehicle.

4. Raise and safely support the vehicle. Remove the tension rod nuts and the steering knuckle mounting bolts. Make sure the brake hose is not twisted.

5. Secure the strut assembly in suitable holding fixture and loosen the piston rod locknut. Do not remove it.

6. Compress the spring with the proper tool so the shock absorber mounting insulator can be turned by hand.

7. Remove the piston rod locknut and the coil spring assembly.

8. Remove the gland packing with the proper tool. Retract the piston, by pushing it down until it bottoms.

9. Slowly, remove the piston rod from the cylinder together with the piston guide.

To install:

10. Inspect the rubber parts for deterioration.

11. Lubricate the sealing lip of the gland packing.

12. Install the gland packing while covering the piston rod with tape so not to damage the oil sealing lip.

13. Tighten the gland packing to 51-94 ft. lbs. (69-128 Nm) without the special tool.

14. The flat portion of the spring goes in the top position.

15. Install the spring seat with it's cutout facing the outer side of the vehicle. Tighten the following:

  a. The upper cover mounting bolts to 22-29 ft. lbs. (29-39 Nm).

  b. The upper piston rod locknut to 43-58 ft. lbs. (58-79 Nm).

  c. The lower strut-to-knuckle arm mounting bolts to 53-72 ft. lbs. (72-97 Nm).

Q45

1. Remove the upper shock absorber mounting insulator bolts.

2. Raise and safely support the vehicle.

3. Remove the lower shock mounting bolt and lift out the shock assembly.

4. Secure the shock absorber in a suitable holding fixture.

5. Loosen the piston rod locknut. Do not remove the locknut.

6. Compress the spring with the proper tool so the shock absorber mounting insulator can be turned by hand.

7. Remove the piston rod locknut. Remove the spring assembly, dust cover and rubber seat.

8. Remove the shock absorber. Inspect the rubber parts for deterioration.

9. The installation is the reverse of the removal procedure. Keep the following torques in mind:

  a. Tighten the upper mounting bolts to 30-35 ft. lbs. (40-47 Nm).

  b. Tighten the piston rod locknut to 13-17 ft. lbs. (17-23 Nm).

  c. Tighten the lower mounting bolt to 80-94 ft. lbs. (108-128 Nm).

NOTE: When installing the coil spring, be careful not to reverse the top and bottom direction. The top end is flat.

Upper Kingpin

On some model applications, the upper kingpin assembly is an integral part of the front knuckle and replaced as an assembly.

REMOVAL AND INSTALLATION

Q45

1. Raise and support the vehicle safely. Remove the wheel.

2. Remove the brake caliper and rotor.

3. Disconnect the shock absorber at the lower mount.

4. Remove the upper nut cap. Remove the upper and lower kingpin nuts.

5. Remove the kingpin.

To install:

6. Install the kingpin and tighten the upper nut to 72-87 ft. lbs. (98-118 Nm) and the lower nut to 108-137 ft. lbs. (147-186 Nm). Install the upper nut cap.

NOTE: Final tightening must be done with vehicle at normal ride height with tires on ground and suspension loaded.

7. Connect the shock absorber and tighten the lower nut to 76-94 ft. lbs. (103-127 Nm).

8. Install the brake caliper and rotor.

9. Install the wheel and lower the vehicle.

Lower Ball Joint

The lower ball joints are an integral part of the the lower control arm and replaced as an assembly.

INSPECTION

1. Turn the ball joint at least 10 revolutions before checking.

2. Measure the swing force using the proper tool. The G20 and Q45 should be 1.8-11.9 ft. lbs. (2.4-16 Nm), the J30 should be 2.0-13.5 ft. lbs. (2.7-18 Nm) or the M30 should read 5.5-18.1 ft. lbs. (7.5-25 Nm).

3. The turning torque should read 4.3-30.4 inch lbs. (0.5-3.4 Nm) on the G20 and Q45; 4.3-30.4 inch lbs. (0.5-3.4 Nm) on the J30 or 13-43 inch lbs. (1.3-4.7 Nm) on the M30.

4. The vertical end-play should be 0 in. (0mm) on the all vehicles except the M30 or 0.004-0.051 in. (0.1-1.3mm) on the M30.

5. After inspecting, if the play exceeds these specifications replace the transverse arm.

Upper Control Arm

The upper control arm assembly consists of the upper link and third link.

REMOVAL AND INSTALLATION

G20

1. Raise and support the vehicle safely.

2. Remove the cap and kingpin nut.

3. Remove the shock absorber attaching nuts and upper link attaching bolts.

4. Remove the stabilizer connecting rod, third link and upper link.

To install:

5. Pack kingpin housing with 0.14 oz. (4g) of multi-purpose grease. Pack the cap with 0.35 oz. (10g) of multi-purpose grease.

NOTE: Final tightening must be done with vehicle at normal ride height with tires on ground and suspension loaded.

6. Install the third link and cap. Tighten kingpin bolt to 72-87 ft. lbs. (98-118 Nm) and stabilizer connecting rod bolt to 12-16 ft. lbs. (16-22 Nm).

7. Install the upper link. Tighten upper link-to-third link through bolt to 82-93 ft. lbs. (112-126 Nm) and upper link-to-bracket bolt to 65-90 ft. lbs. (88-123 Nm).

Q45

1. Raise and safely support the vehicle. Support the wheel assembly with a suitable jacking device.

2. Remove the cap and the upper kingpin mounting nut. Do not remove the lower nut.

3. Remove the shock absorber mounting nut and the upper link mounting bolts.

4. Remove the third link and the upper link.

5. Installation is the reverse of removal. Upper link bushings cannot be disassembled.

6. Always install the upper link with the (A) facing the axle and the side without a character facing the vehicle body.

7. Tighten the upper kingpin mounting nut to 72-87 ft. lbs. (98-118 Nm) and the lower kingpin mounting nut to 108-137 ft. lbs. (147-186 Nm).

Lower Control Arm

REMOVAL AND INSTALLATION

G20

1. Raise and support the vehicle safely.

2. Remove the stabilizer bar.

3. Support the steering knuckle with a suitable jack and remove the lower ball joint nut.

4. Remove the bolts attaching the lower control arm to the chassis. Remove the lower control arm.

To install:

5. Check the lower ball joint for damage or wear. If present, replace the lower control arm assembly. The ball joint is not serviceable separately.

6. Installation is the reverse of removal.

NOTE: Final tightening must be done with the vehicle at normal ride height, tires on the ground and the chassis loaded.

7. Tighten lower control arm bolts to 87-108 ft. lbs. (118-147 Nm) and gusset nut to 69-87 ft. lbs. (93-118 Nm). Tighten ball joint nut to 52-64 ft. lbs. (71-86 Nm). Install new cotter pin.

J30 and M30

1. Raise and safely support the vehicle.

2. Remove the bolts and disconnect the stabilizer bar.

3. Remove the bolt and disconnect the transverse arm from the knuckle arm, using the proper tool.

4. Remove the transverse arm and joint assembly.

To install:

5. Install the stabilizer bar with the ball joint socket in a straight position, not cocked.

NOTE: Final tightening must be done with the vehicle at normal ride height, tires on the ground and the chassis loaded.

6. The installation is the reverse of the removal procedure. Tighten the following to:

   a. The stabilizer bar mounting bolt to 14-22 ft. lbs. (19-29 Nm).

   b. The tension rod mounting bolts to 35-43 ft. lbs. (47-58 Nm).

   c. The ball joint-to-steering knuckle mounting nut to 71-88 ft. lbs. (96-119 Nm). Install new cotter pin.

Q45

1. Raise and safely support the vehicle. Support the wheel assembly with a suitable jacking device.

2. Remove the mounting bolts and disconnect the tension rod and stabilizer bar.

3. Remove the bolt and disconnect the transverse arm from the knuckle arm, using the proper tool.

4. Remove the transverse arm and joint assembly.

5. The installation is the reverse of the removal procedure. The final tightening must be at curb weight with the tires on the ground.

NOTE: Final tightening must be done with the vehicle at normal ride height, tires on the ground and the chassis loaded.

6. Tighten the following to:

   a. The stabilizer bar mounting bolt to 14-22 ft. lbs. (19-29 Nm).

   b. The tension rod mounting bolts to 72-87 ft. lbs. (97-118 Nm).

   c. The ball joint-to-steering knuckle mounting nut to 65-80 ft. lbs. (88-108 Nm). Install new cotter pin.

Stabilizer Bar

REMOVAL AND INSTALLATION

1. Raise and support the vehicle safely.

2. Using a backup wrench to support the connecting rod, remove the stabilizer to connecting rod bolt.

3. Remove the stabilizer bracket bolts. Remove the stabilizer.

To install:

4. Install the stabilizer with the paint mark to the right of the bracket when viewed from the front of the vehicle. Install the bracket with the elongated hole toward the rear of the vehicle. Tighten the bracket bolts to 29-36 ft. lbs. (39-49 Nm). On the M30 tighten bolts to 40-47 ft. lbs. (54-64 Nm).

NOTE: Final tightening must be done with the vehicle at normal ride height, tires on the ground and the chassis loaded.

5. Ensure that the ball socket on the connecting rod is straight, then attach the connecting rod and tighten the bolt to 30-38 ft. lbs. (41-51 Nm). Use a backup wrench to keep the connecting rod straight.

Front Wheel Bearings

PRELOAD ADJUSTMENT

J30

1. Thoroughly clean all parts to prevent dirt entry.

2. Apply the recommended multipurpose grease to the following components:

   a. The rubbing surface of the spindle.

   b. The contact surface between the lock washer and the outer wheel bearing.

   c. The inside of the dust cap.

   d. The grease seal lip.

3. Install the wheel hub and tighten wheel bearing locknut to 152-210 ft. lbs. (206-284 Nm).

4. Turn the wheel hub several times in both directions to seat the wheel bearing correctly.

5. Attach a spring balance to wheel hub bolt and pull it at a speed of 10 rpm to measure rotation torque. Torque should be 2-18 inch lbs. (0.25-2.11 Nm).

6. If bearing preload does not meet specification, replace the wheel bearing.

7. Clinch locknut and install the cap.

M30

1. Thoroughly clean all parts to prevent dirt entry.

2. Apply the recommended multipurpose grease to the following components:

   a. The rubbing surface of the spindle.

   b. The contact surface between the lock washer and the outer wheel bearing.

   c. The inside of the dust cap.

   d. The grease seal lip.

3. Tighten the wheel bearing lock to 25-29 ft. lbs. (34-39 Nm). Turn the wheel hub several times in both directions to seat the wheel bearing correctly.

4. Again, tighten the wheel bearing to the specified torque. Turn back the wheel bearing locknut 90 degrees.

5. Install the adjusting cap and the locknut. Do not turn the nut back for cotter pin insertion. Align the cotter pin by re-tightening the nut within 15 degrees. Spread cotter pin.

6. Measure the wheel bearing preload and the axle end-play limit with the proper tool. The wheel bearing preload, measure at the wheel hub bolt should be 3.1 lbs. (13.7 N) or less. The axle end-play limit is 0.0020 in. (0.05mm).

7. Repeat procedure until the correct bearing preload is obtained.

Q45

1. Thoroughly clean all parts to prevent dirt entry.

2. After installing wheel bearing and hub, tighten wheel bearing locknut to 152-210 ft. lbs. (206-284 Nm).

3. Check that wheel bearing operates smoothly, then stake wheel bearing locknut.

REMOVAL AND INSTALLATION

J30

1. Raise and safely support the vehicle. Remove the brake caliper assembly and the brake rotor. The brake line need not be disconnected.

2. Remove the wheel hub from the spindle.

3. Remove the grease seal and snapring.

4. Press out the bearing and race as a set.

To install:

5. Press a new wheel bearing assembly into the wheel hub. Do not press the inner race of the wheel bearing assembly.

6. Install the snapring.

7. Pack grease seal lip with multipurpose grease.

8. Install the grease seal

9. Install the wheel hub and tighten the wheel bearing to 152-210 ft. lbs. (206-284 Nm).

10. Adjust wheel bearing preload.

M30

1. Raise and safely support the vehicle. Remove the brake caliper assembly and the brake rotor. The brake line need not be disconnected.

2. Remove the wheel hub and the wheel bearing from the spindle.

3. Secure the hub in a suitable holding fixture. Drive out the outer race with the proper tool.

4. Inspect all the components for damage or excessive wear.

To install:

5. Install the bearing outer race with the proper tool until it seat in the hub.

6. Coat the bearing with the recommended multi-purpose grease and install. Pack the grease seal lip with the recommended grease.

7. Install the seal with the proper tool until it seats in the hub. Pack the hub and dust cap with the recommended grease.

8. Adjust the wheel bearing preload.

9. The remainder of the installation is the reverse of the removal procedure.

Q45

1. Raise and safely support the vehicle. Remove the brake caliper assembly and the brake rotor. The brake line need not be disconnected.

2. Disconnect the tie rod and transverse arm from the steering knuckle assembly with the proper tool.

NOTE: The steering knuckle is made from aluminum alloy, Be careful not to hit the knuckle.

3. Remove the kingpin lower nut and the steering knuckle assembly. Secure the steering knuckle in a suitable holding fixture.

4. Remove the dust cap and the wheel bearing locknut. Remove the wheel hub with the proper tool.

5. Remove the circular clip and press out the bearing assembly from the steering knuckle with the proper tools.

6. Drive out the wheel bearing inner race from the wheel hub and remove the grease seal with the suitable tools.

To install:

7. Press a new wheel bearing assembly into the steering knuckle from outside the of the steering knuckle. The maximum press load is 3.9 tons. Do not press the inner race of the wheel bearing assembly.

8. Install the circular clip into the groove of the steering knuckle. Apply a multi-purpose grease to the sealing and install the grease seal and splash guard.

9. Press the wheel hub onto the steering knuckle with the proper tool. The maximum press load is 3.3 tons.

10. Tighten the wheel bearing locknut to 152-210 ft. lbs. (206-284 Nm).

11. Stake the wheel bearing locknut and install the dust cap.

12. The remainder of the installation is the reverse of the removal procedure.

REAR SUSPENSION

Shock Absorbers

REMOVAL AND INSTALLATION

J30

1. Raise and support the vehicle safely.

2. Remove the rear parcel shelf as required to gain access to shock upper mounting nuts.

NOTE: Do not remove piston rod locknut on vehicle.

3. Remove shock upper and lower mounting nuts. Remove shock absorber.

To install:

4. Install shock absorber.

5. Tighten upper shock mounting nuts to 12-14 ft. lbs. (16-19 Nm). Tighten lower shock mounting nut to 72-87 ft. lbs. (98-118 Nm).

6. Install parcel shelf and lower vehicle.

M30

1. Disconnect the negative battery cable.

2. Remove the rear parcel shelf. Disconnect the sub-harness connector.

3. Remove the strut mounting cap.

4. Remove the shock absorber actuator mounting bolts and the upper end mounting nuts.

5. Raise and safely support the vehicle. Disconnect the hydraulic brake line and the parking brake cable.

6. Disconnect the propeller shaft. Remove the lower mounting bolt.

7. Remove the shock absorber and spring assembly.

To install:

8. Place the shock absorber and spring assembly into position. Install propeller shaft.

9. Tighten the lower mounting bolt to 43-58 ft. lbs. (58-78 Nm) and the upper mounting insulator bolts to 23-31 ft. lbs. (31-42 Nm).

10. Install the brake line and parking brake cable. Lower the vehicle.

11. Connect the sub-harness connector and install the rear parcel shelf. Connect the negative battery cable and test drive the vehicle.

Q45

1. Raise and safely support the vehicle. Remove the exhaust tube.

2. Disconnect the propeller shaft at the rear of the vehicle.

3. Disconnect the parking brake cable from the front of the vehicle.

4. If equipped, with High Capacity Actively Controlled Steering (HICAS). Remove the ball joints by removing the snapring and pressing out the ball joint from the axle housing with proper tools.

5. Remove the tire and wheel assembly. Remove the brake caliper assembly. It is not necessary to disconnect the brake line.

6. Remove the upper shock absorber end nuts. Do not remove the piston rod nut.

7. Remove the rear suspension mounting nuts. Draw out the rear axle and rear suspension assembly.

8. Remove the shock absorber upper and lower mounting nuts. Do not remove the piston rod nut.

9. Remove the shock absorber and spring assembly.

To install:

10. Install the shock absorber and spring assembly. It may be necessary to install the rear axle and suspension assembly prior to installing the shock assembly.

11. Tighten the lower shock mounting bolt to 57-72 ft. lbs. (77-98 Nm) and the upper spring seat mounting bolts to 12-14 ft. lbs. (16-19 Nm).

12. Install the brake caliper, wheel and tire, parking brake cable, propeller shaft and exhaust tube.

13. Lower the vehicle and test drive.

MacPherson Strut

REMOVAL AND INSTALLATION

G20

1. Raise and support the vehicle safely.

2. Remove the rear seat and finisher to gain access to the top shock absorber bolts. Remove the 3 top shock mount bolts.

3. Remove the rear stabilizer connecting rod where it attaches the knuckle assembly.

4. Remove the shock absorber through bolts at the knuckle assembly and remove the shock absorber assembly.

5. Set the shock absorber assembly in a vise using attachment ST25652000 or equivalent. Loosen the piston rod locknut, but do not remove.

6. Compress the spring with a suitable tool so the strut mounting insulator can be turned by hand.

7. Remove the piston rod locknut and spring with compressor attached.

To install:

8. Replace the bound rubber bumpers. Install the coil spring on the shock absorber and tighten the piston rod locknut to 43-58 ft. lbs. (59-78 Nm). Gradually release the spring compressor. When the coil spring is located correctly, there should be 2 identification color codes on the lower side.

9. Installation is the reverse of removal.

10. Tighten the shock assembly upper attaching bolts to 31-40 ft. lbs. (42-54 Nm); lower attaching bolts to 72-87 ft. lbs. (98-118 Nm) and the stabilizer bar connecting rod bolts to 30-35 ft. lbs. (41-47 Nm)

Coil Springs

REMOVAL AND INSTALLATION

G20

1. Raise and support the vehicle safely.

2. Remove the shock absorber assembly.

3. Set the shock absorber assembly in a vise using attachment ST25652000 or equivalent. Loosen the piston rod locknut, but do not remove.

4. Compress the spring with a suitable tool so the strut mounting insulator can be turned by hand.

5. Remove the piston rod locknut and spring with compressor attached.

To install:

6. Replace the bound rubber bumpers. Install the coil spring on the shock absorber and tighten the piston rod locknut to 43-58 ft. lbs. (59-78 Nm). Gradually release the spring compressor. When the coil spring is located correctly, there should be 2 identification color codes on the lower side.

7. Install the shock absorber assembly. Lower the vehicle.

8. Final tightening of all rubber parts should take place with the tires on the ground and the chassis at normal ride height.

J30

1. Raise and support the vehicle safely.

2. Remove rear shock absorber assembly.

3. Matchmark coil spring and shock absorber assembly.

4. Set shock absorber on a vise with holding attachment HT-71780000 or equivalent and loosen rod locknut. Do not remove rod locknut.

5. Compress spring with a spring compressor so the strut upper spring seat can be turned by hand.

6. Remove piston rod locknut and disassemble.

To install:

7. Install the coil spring. Install upper spring seat with its cutout facing the outer side of the vehicle.

8. Ensure that the coil spring ends are held firmly in the spring seat pockets.

9. Compress spring and install rod locknut. Tighten to 43-54 ft. lbs. (59-74 Nm).

10. Install rear shock assembly and lower vehicle.

M30

1. Raise and support the vehicle safely.

2. Remove the rear parcel shelf and disconnect the shock absorber actuator wiring connector.

3. Remove the strut mounting cap, spacer and insulator bolts.

4. Remove the lower mounting bolt. Remove the shock absorber assembly.

5. Place the shock absorber assembly in an appropriate holding fixture and loosen the piston locknut.

6. Compress the coil spring with a spring compressor, then remove the locknut. Remove the coil spring with the compressor still attached.

To install:

7. Install the new coil spring with the spring compressor attached.

8. Assemble the shock absorber components and tighten the piston rod locknut.

9. Installation is the reverse of removal.

10. Tighten the lower shock mount bolt to 43-58 ft. lbs. (59-78 Nm) and shock insulator bolts to 23-31 ft. lbs. (31-42 Nm).

11. Final tightening of all rubber parts should take place with the tires on the ground and the chassis at normal ride height.

Q45

1. Raise and support the vehicle safely.

2. Remove the upper shock assembly attaching nuts. It may be necessary to remove the rear parcel shelf to gain access to the nuts.

3. Remove the lower shock assembly mounting bolt at the axle assembly.

4. Place the shock absorber assembly in a suitable holding fixture and loosen the piston rod locknut.

5. Using a spring compressor, compress the coil spring, then remove the piston rod locknut. Remove the coil spring with the compressor attached.

To install:

6. Install the spring compressor, if removed, and assemble the shock absorber assembly. Remove the spring compressor.

7. Installation is the reverse of removal.

8. Tighten the piston rod locknut to 13-17 ft. lbs. (18-24 Nm), upper shock mount nuts to 12-14 ft. lbs. (16-19 Nm) and lower shock mount bolts to 57-72 ft. lbs. (77-98 Nm).

9. Final tightening of all rubber parts should take place with the tires on the ground and the chassis at normal ride height.

Rear Control Arm

REMOVAL AND INSTALLATION

G20

1. Raise and support the vehicle safely.

2. Remove the brake caliper assembly and rotor.

3. Support the suspension under the knuckle assembly with a floor jack.

4. Remove the parallel link attaching bolts. Remove the parallel link.

5. Installation is the reverse of removal.

6. Tighten all parallel link bolts to 80-94 ft. lbs. (108-127 Nm).

J30 and M30

1. Raise and support the vehicle. Remove the axleshaft assembly, as required.

2. Remove the stabilizer bar bolt and disconnect the parking brake cable.

3. Disconnect the lower shock absorber bolt. Using a splitter, separate the ball joint from the spindle, if equipped.

4. Matchmark the suspension arm to the body side bolt and remove the body side bolt.

5. Remove the lower suspension arm.

To install:

6. Install the lower suspension arm and tighten the body side bolts to 57-72 ft. lbs. (77-98 Nm) on the J30 or 72-87 ft. lbs. (97-118 Nm) on the M30.

NOTE: Tighten all suspension bolts to specification when vehicle is unladen with the wheels on the ground.

7. Tighten the ball joint nut to 58-69 ft. lbs. (78-93 Nm), if equipped. Install new cotter pin.

8. Connect the lower shock absorber bolt and tighten to 72-87 ft. lbs. (98-118 Nm).

9. Install the stabilizer bar bolt and connect the parking brake cable.

10. Check the rear wheel alignment.

Q45

1. Raise and safely support the vehicle. Remove the exhaust tube.

2. Disconnect the propeller shaft at the rear of the vehicle.

3. Disconnect the parking brake cable from the front of the vehicle.

4. If equipped with high capacity actively controlled steering (HICAS), remove the ball joints by removing the snapring and pressing out the ball joint from the axle housing with proper tools.

5. Remove the tire and wheel assembly. Remove the brake caliper assembly. It is not necessary to disconnect the brake line.

6. Remove the upper shock absorber end nuts. Do not remove the piston rod nut.

7. Remove the rear suspension mounting nuts. Draw out the rear axle and rear suspension assembly.

8. The installation is the reverse of the removal procedure. Tighten the lower arm adjusting pin bolts to 57-72 ft. lbs. (77-97 Nm).

9. Tighten the ball joint nut to 58-69 ft. lbs. (78-93 Nm). Install new cotter pin.

10. Check rear wheel alignment.

Rear Wheel Bearings

REMOVAL AND INSTALLATION

G20

1. Raise and support the vehicle safely.

2. Remove the rear wheel and tire assembly.

3. Remove the rear wheel hub cap, cotter pin, locknut, washer and wheel hub bearing.

NOTE: The wheel bearing is integral with the hub and cannot be serviced separately.

4. Installation is the reverse of removal. Tighten the wheel bearing locknut to 137-188 ft. lbs. (186-255 Nm).

STEERING

Steering Wheel

─────── **CAUTION** ───────
On vehicles equipped with an air bag, disconnect the negative battery cable and allow 10 minutes to elapse before working on the system. Failure to do so may result in deployment of the air bag and possible personal injury.

REMOVAL AND INSTALLATION

Without Air Bag

1. Disconnect the negative battery cable.

2. Ensure that the steering wheel and front tires are positioned in the straight-ahead position.

3. Using an appropriate tool, pry the horn pad off the steering wheel.

4. Remove the steering wheel locknut.

5. Using an appropriate puller, remove the steering wheel.

To install:

6. Apply multi-purpose grease to the entire surface of the turn signal cancel pin and the horn contact clipring.

7. Install the steering wheel and tighten the locknut to 22-29 ft. lbs. (29-39 Nm).

8. Install the horn pad. Reconnect the negative battery cable.

With Air Bag

1. Make sure the wheels are pointing straight-ahead. Disconnect the negative battery cable and allow 10 minutes to elapse.

2. Remove the lower lid from the steering column and disconnect the air bag module connector.

NOTE: The air bag module is a fragile component. Always place it with the pad side facing upward. Do not allow oil, grease or water to come in contact with the module. Do not drop the module; if it is damaged in any way, do not reinstall it to the steering wheel.

3. Remove the side access lids, remove the left and right T50H Torx® bolts and discard them. These bolts are specially coated and should not be reused.

4. Carefully remove the air bag module and place in a safe location with the pad side facing upward.

5. Disengage the spiral cable and disconnect the horn connector. Remove the steering wheel hold-down nut.

6. Using an appropriate puller, remove the steering wheel.

7. Attach the spiral cable to the stopper.

8. Remove the steering column covers.

9. Disconnect the connector, remove the 4 mounting screws and remove the spiral cable.

To install:

10. Connect the spiral cable connectors and install to the column. Disengage the stopper by pulling the 2 pin guides on the spiral cable unit.

11. Pull the spiral cable through the steering wheel opening and install the steering wheel, setting the pin guides.

12. Connect the horn connector and engage the spiral cable with the pawls in the steering wheel.

13. Install the hold-down nut and torque to 22-29 ft. lbs. (29-39 Nm).

14. Carefully position the air bag module. Install new Torx® bolts and torque to 15 ft. lbs. (20 Nm). Connect the air bag module connector.

15. Install the 3 access lids and the column covers.

16. Connect the negative battery cable.

17. Using the Nissan Consult System Checking tool, conduct self-diagnosis to ensure the system is operating properly.

18. If the Consult tool is not available, perform the following:

a. From the passenger seat, turn the ignition switch to the **ON** position.

b. Observe the **AIR BAG** warning light on the instrument cluster.

c. The warning light should illuminate for about 7 seconds, then go out.

d. If the warning light illuminates in any sequence except the above, perform the proper diagnostics before continuing.

Power Rack and Pinion

REMOVAL AND INSTALLATION

1. Disconnect the negative battery cable.

2. Raise the vehicle and support safely.

3. Remove the front wheels.

4. Disconnect the outer tie rods from the steering knuckle.

5. Remove the setscrew from the lower steering column universal joint. Disconnect the shaft from the joint.

6. Remove the power steering fluid lines from the rack assembly.

7. Remove the bolts attaching the power steering rack assembly to the body.

8. Remove the rack assembly from the vehicle.

9. Complete the installation of the power steering rack assembly by reversing the removal procedure. Pay close attention to the following:

a. Tighten the rack mounting bolts to 62-80 ft. lbs. (84-108 Nm).

b. Initially, tighten the tie rod-to-steering knuckle nuts bolts to 22-29 ft. lbs. (29-39 Nm). Tighten the nut further to expose first pin hole and install a new cotter pin.

c. Tighten the pinion shaft-to-universal joint setscrew to 17-22 ft. lbs. (24-29 Nm).

d. On all models except Q45, tighten low pressure power steering lines to 20-29 ft. lbs. (27-39 Nm). Tighten high pressure lines to 11-18 ft. lbs. (15-25 Nm).

e. On Q45 models, tighten low pressure power steering lines to 27-30 ft. lbs. (36-40 Nm). Tighten high pressure lines to 22-26 ft. lbs. (30-35 Nm).

Power Steering Pump

REMOVAL AND INSTALLATION

1. Disconnect the negative battery cable.

2. Remove the power steering belt pump drive belt.

3. Disconnect the power steering fluid lines.

4. Remove the power steering pump mounting bolts and remove the pump.

5. Complete the installation of the power steering pump by reversing the removal procedure.

BELT ADJUSTMENT

1. Loosen the power steering pump tension locknut.

2. On the all models except the Q45, using a suitable belt tension gauge, adjust the belt tension to 0.55-0.63 in. (14-16mm) with a force of 22 lbs. (98 N) applied at the midpoint of the belt run between the crankshaft and power steering pump pulleys.

3. On the Q45, using a suitable belt tension gauge, adjust the belt tension to 0.35-0.39 in. (9-10mm) with a force of 22 lbs. (98 N) applied at the mid-point of the belt run between the crankshaft and power steering pump pulleys for vehicles without Super HICAS or full-active suspension. Vehicles with Super HICAS or full-active suspension, adjust the tension to 0.28-0.31 in. (7-8mm) with a force of 22 lbs. (98 N) applied at the mid-point of the belt run between the crankshaft and power steering pump pulleys.

4. Tighten the power steering pump tension locknut.

SYSTEM BLEEDING

1. Raise and support the vehicle safely.

2. Ensure that the reservoir is full.

3. Quickly turn the wheels from side to side lightly touching the steering stops.

4. Repeat steps 2 and 3 until the fluid level no longer decreases in the reservoir.

5. Start the engine.

6. Air in the system may cause one or all of the following:

a. Air bubbles to appear in the reservoir.

b. Generation of a clicking noise in the oil pump.

c. Excessive buzzing in the oil pump.

Tie Rod Ends

REMOVAL AND INSTALLATION

1. Raise the vehicle and support safely.

2. Remove the front wheel.

3. Matchmark the position of tie rod end locknut on the threaded section of the tie rod.

4. Loosen the tie rod end locknut.

5. Remove the cotter pin and tie rod end nut.

6. Separate the tie rod end from the steering knuckle using a suitable tool.

7. Remove the tie rod end from the tie rod.

To install:

8. Install the new tie rod end on the tie rod.

9. Install the tie rod end on the steering knuckle. Initially, tighten the tie rod-to-steering knuckle nuts bolts to 22-29 ft. lbs. (29-39 Nm). Tighten the nut further to expose first pin hole and install a new cotter pin.

10. Adjust the toe-in to the matchmark made on the threaded section of the tie rod. Tighten the locknut.

11. Install the front wheel.

12. Lower the vehicle.

13. Check alignment to verify proper toe-in setting.

BRAKES

Master Cylinder

REMOVAL AND INSTALLATION

NOTE: Prevent brake fluid from coming in contact with painted surfaces. Clean up any spills immediately.

1. Loosen the brake line flarenuts and remove brake lines from master cylinder fittings.

2. Remove the master cylinder mounting nuts.

3. Remove the master cylinder.

To install:

4. Bench bleed the master cylinder.

5. Install the master cylinder in the vehicle. Tighten bolts to 6-8 ft. lbs. (8-11 Nm).

6. Connect the brake lines to the master cylinder and finger-tighten the flarenuts.

7. Bleed the air from the brake lines. Tighten the flarenuts.

Proportioning Valve

On most models (except G20) the proportioning valve is integral to the master cylinder and cannot be serviced or removed separately.

On vehicles that do not use a proportioning valve that is integral to the master cylinder, remove all pressure fittings and mounting bolts, remove the valve from the vehicle.

Power Brake Booster

REMOVAL AND INSTALLATION

1. Remove the master cylinder.

2. Remove the clevis pin connecting the brake pedal to the booster input rod.

3. Remove the brake pedal bracket to booster mounting nuts.

4. Remove the brake booster.

5. Complete the installation of the brake booster by reversing the removal procedure. Tighten the brake booster nuts to 9-12 ft. lbs. (13-16 Nm).

Brake Caliper

REMOVAL AND INSTALLATION

NOTE: Prevent brake fluid from coming in contact with painted surfaces. Clean up any spills immediately.

1. Raise the vehicle and support safely.

2. Remove the wheel.

3. Loosen the brake hose connecting bolt.

4. Remove the bolts connecting the caliper to the torque member.

5. Slide the caliper out from the rotor and remove the pad, shim and shim cover.

6. Remove the brake hose connecting bolt from the caliper.

7. Remove the caliper from the vehicle.

8. Complete the installation of the brake caliper by reversing the removal procedure. Tighten the caliper bolts to 16-23 ft. lbs. (22-31 Nm). Bleed the air from the system.

Disc Brake Pads

REMOVAL AND INSTALLATION

1. Remove the cap from the master cylinder reservoir and extract a small amount of brake fluid from the reservoir.

2. Raise the vehicle and support safely.

3. Remove the wheel.

4. On Q45 models, if servicing the right front brake, disconnect the sensor harness by pushing the connector pin and pulling the connector. Remove the bracket from the cylinder body. If servicing the right rear brake, remove the sensor harness by pushing it toward the pad, turning it counterclockwise and removing it.

5. Remove the lower pin bolt.

6. Pivot the caliper body upward and remove pad retainers, inner and outer shims and pads.

To install:

7. Place the old pad in place over the caliper cylinders. Use a C-clamp to compress the cylinder pistons to allow for the added thickness of the new pads.

8. Install the new pads and install caliper on rotor. Install pin bolts.

9. Install connector harness, if removed. Pump brakes to seat pads and then refill master cylinder.

Brake Rotor

REMOVAL AND INSTALLATION

1. Raise the vehicle and support safely.

2. Remove the wheel.

3. Remove the caliper from the torque member and support using a length of mechanics wire.

4. Remove the bolts attaching the torque member and remove.

5. Remove the rotor from the hub assembly.

6. Complete the installation of the brake rotor by reversing the removal procedure.

Brake System Bleeding

1. Fill the brake master cylinder reservoir with brake fluid.

2. Raise and safely support the vehicle.

3. Connect a length of vinyl hose to the bleeder plug.

4. Submerge one end of the vinyl hose in a container filled with brake fluid. Connect the other end of the vinyl hose to the wheel cylinder bleeder plug.

5. Have an assistant slowly depress the brake pedal and hold it.

6. Open the bleeder plug of the right rear wheel cylinder 1/3-1/2 turn until the bubbles stop coming out of the tube. Close the bleeder plug.

7. Have the assistant release the brake pedal.

NOTE: The assistant must keep the brake pedal depressed until the bleeder plug is closed.

8. Continue the above procedure until air bubbles are no longer observed in the brake fluid.
9. Remove the vinyl tube and replace the bleeder plug cap.
10. Bleed the system without antilock brakes in the following order:
    a. Left rear
    b. Right rear
    c. Left front
    d. Right front
11. Bleed the system with anti-lock brakes as follows:
    a. For G20 vehicles, bleed the system in this order: left rear, right front, right rear and left front.
    b. On all other vehicles, the system should be bled in this order: left rear, right rear, left front, right front, front side bleeder on ABS actuator and rear side bleeder on the ABS actuator.
12. Check the brake fluid level in the master cylinder reservoir frequently during the bleeding operation.

Anti-Lock Brake System Service

PRECAUTIONS

- Carefully monitor the brake fluid level in the master cylinder at all times during the bleeding procedure. Keep the reservoir full at all times.
- Only use brake fluid that meets or exceeds DOT 3 specifications.
- Place a suitable container under the master cylinder to avoid spillage of brake fluid.
- Do not allow brake fluid to come in contact with any painted surface.
- Make sure to use the proper bleeding sequence.

RELIEVING ANTI-LOCK BRAKE SYSTEM PRESSURE

To relieve the pressure from the ABS system, turn the ignition switch to the **OFF** position. Disconnect the connectors from the ABS actuator. Wait a few minutes to allow for the system to bleed down, then disconnect the negative battery cable.

Wheel Speed Sensor

REMOVAL AND INSTALLATION

Front

1. Raise and safely support the front of the vehicle.
2. Remove the tire and wheel.
3. On some models, it may be necessary to remove the inner fender liner.
4. With the ignition switch **OFF**, disconnect the wheel speed sensor lead from the ABS harness. Remove any retaining bolts or clips holding the harness in place.

NOTE: Clips and retainers must be reinstalled in their exact original location. Take careful note of the position of each retainer and of the correct harness routing during removal.

5. Remove the single bolt holding the speed sensor.
6. Carefully remove the sensor straight out of its mount. Do not subject the sensor to shock or vibration; protect the tip of the sensor at all times.
   To install:
7. Fit the sensor into position. Make certain the sensor sits flush against the mounting surface; it must not be crooked.
8. Install the retaining bolt. Correct bolt tightness for all vehicles is 9 ft. lbs. (12 Nm).
9. Route the sensor cable correctly and install the harness clips and retainers. The cable must be in its original position and completely clear of moving components.
10. Connect the sensor cable to the ABS harness.
11. Install the inner fender liner if it was removed.
12. Install the wheel and tire.
13. Lower the vehicle to the ground.

Rear

1. Raise and safely support the rear of the vehicle.
2. Remove the tire and wheel.
3. Disconnect the wheel speed sensor lead from the ABS harness. Remove any retaining bolts or clips holding the harness in place.

NOTE: Clips and retainers must be reinstalled in their exact original location. Take careful note of the position of each retainer and of the correct harness routing during removal.

4. Remove the single bolt holding the speed sensor.

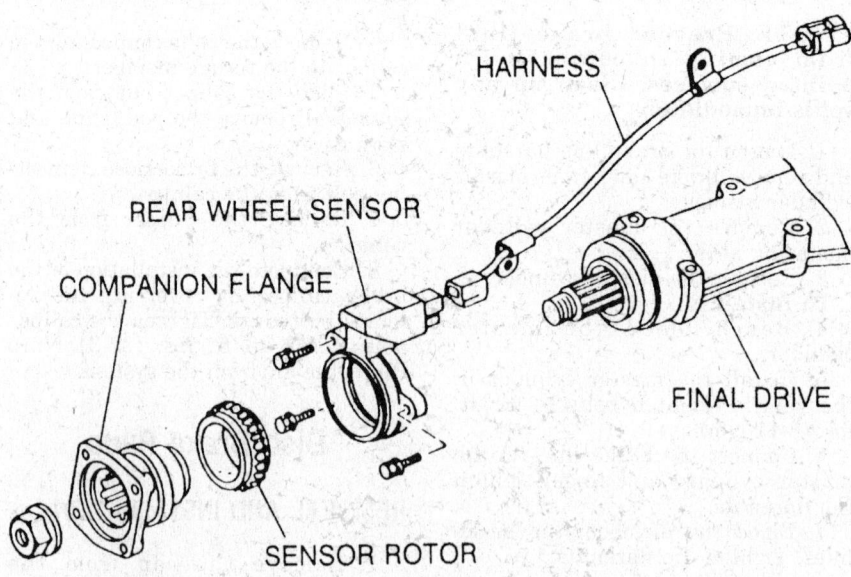

Rear wheel sensor assembly — M30

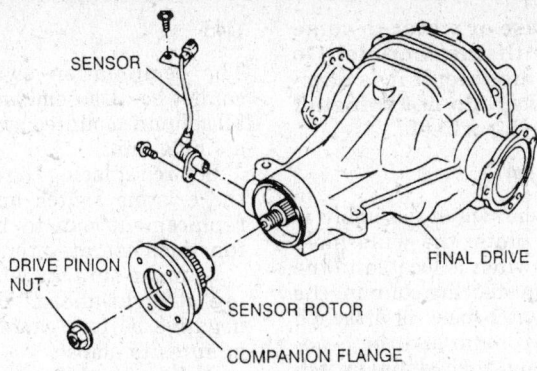

SENSOR

DRIVE PINION NUT

SENSOR ROTOR

COMPANION FLANGE

FINAL DRIVE

Rear wheel sensor assembly — Q45

5. Carefully remove the sensor straight out of its mount. Do not subject the sensor to shock or vibration; protect the tip of the sensor at all times.

To install:

6. Fit the sensor into position. Make certain the sensor sits flush against the mounting surface; it must not be crooked.

7. Install the retaining bolt. Tighten the bolt to 9 ft. lbs. (12 Nm).

8. Route the sensor cable correctly and install the harness clips and retainers. The cable must be in its original position and completely clear of moving components.

9. Connect the sensor cable to the ABS harness.

10. Install the wheel and tire.

11. Lower the vehicle to the ground.

Hydraulic Actuator

REMOVAL AND INSTALLATION

1. Disconnect the negative battery cable.

2. Drain the brake fluid from the system. Use a syringe or similar tool to empty the master cylinder reservoir. Connect a plastic tube to each brake bleeder. Proceed as if bleeding the brakes; pump each line clear of fluid by operating the brake pedal.

3. Disconnect the wiring connectors at the actuator.

4. Apply dots of colored paint to identify each actuator brake line and its correct port. Using tool GG 94310000 or equivalent, carefully disconnect each brake line from the actuator.

5. Remove the retaining nuts holding the actuator. Make certain the brake lines are out of the way, then remove the actuator from the engine compartment.

To install:

6. Install the actuator into the engine compartment.

7. Connect the brake lines to the actuator temporarily, finger-tight only. Make certain each is in the correct location.

8. Tighten the actuator mounting bolts to 12 ft. lbs. (16 Nm.)

9. Tighten the actuator brake line fittings to 11 ft. lbs. (15 Nm).

10. Connect the wiring connectors to the actuator.

11. Refill the system with DOT 3 brake fluid from unopened containers. Since the system was drained, a substantial amount may be required.

12. Bleed the system at all 4 wheels and at the ABS actuator, if required. Each line may require repeated bleeding to eliminate all air within.

13. Connect the negative battery cable.

CHASSIS ELECTRICAL

— CAUTION —

It is possible for the air bag to inflate for 10 minutes after the battery has been disconnected. Therefore, disconnect the negative battery cable and wait 10 minutes before working on the system. Failure to do so may result in deployment of the air bag and possible personal injury.

Air Bag

DISARMING

Before servicing any component, turn the ignition switch **OFF**, disconnect the negative battery cable and wait for at least 10 minutes. This will disarm the air bag.

Heater Blower Motor

REMOVAL AND INSTALLATION

1. Disconnect the negative battery cable. Remove the lower right side instrument panel cover.

2. Remove the screws that attach the blower housing to the intake unit.

3. Remove the housing and remove the blower motor from the housing.

4. The installation is the reverse of the removal procedure.

5. Connect the negative battery cable and check the climate control system for proper operation.

Windshield Wiper Motor

REMOVAL AND INSTALLATION

1. Disconnect the negative battery cable.

2. Disconnect the leads at the motor.

3. Remove the motor mounting bolts.

4. Pull the motor out and remove the wiper motor linkage attaching nut.

5. Remove the motor from the firewall.

6. The installation is the reverse of the removal procedure.

7. Connect the negative battery cable and check all windshield wiper and washer functions for proper operation.

Instrument Cluster

REMOVAL AND INSTALLATION

Except Q45

1. Disconnect the negative battery cable.

2. Remove the steering column covers.

3. Remove the screws that fasten the cluster lid to the instrument panel and remove the lid.

4. Remove the screws that fasten the instrument cluster to the instrument panel, pull the cluster out, disconnect all connectors and remove the cluster.

5. Disassemble the cluster, as required.

6. The installation is the reverse of the removal procedure.

7. Connect the negative battery cable and check all gauges for proper operation.

Q45

1. Disconnect the negative battery cable.
2. Remove the steering column covers.
3. Remove the gear shifter bezel from the console.
4. Remove the ashtray assembly.
5. Remove the screws that fasten the radio and climate control switch bezel to the instrument panel. Pull the bezel down and out, disconnect the rear window defogger switch and remove the bezel.
6. Remove the cruise control main switch/outside mirror control switch assembly.
7. Remove the screws that fasten the cluster lid to the instrument panel and remove the lid.
8. Remove the screws that attach the instrument cluster to the instrument panel, pull the cluster out, disconnect all connectors and remove the cluster.
9. Disassemble the cluster, as required.

To install:

10. Assemble the cluster, connect all connectors and install to the instrument panel.
11. Connect the negative battery cable and check all gauges for proper operation. If everything is operating properly, disconnect the negative battery cable and proceed.
12. Install the cluster lid and cruise control main switch/outside mirror control switch assembly.
13. Install the radio and climate control switch bezel to the instrument panel.
14. Install the ashtray and gear shifter bezel.
15. Install the steering column covers.
16. Connect the negative battery cable and check all gauges for proper operation.

Combination Switch

REMOVAL AND INSTALLATION

NOTE: On vehicles equipped with an air bag, it is imperative that the exact steering wheel REMOVAL AND INSTALLATION procedure is followed. The air bag module is a fragile component. Always place it with the pad side facing upward. Do not allow oil, grease or water to come in contact with the module. Do not drop the module; if it is damaged in any way, do not reinstall it to the steering wheel.

G20, M30 and J30

The combination switch assembly is made up of 3 units; the windshield wiper/washer switch is located to the right side of the steering column, the combination switch base is attached to the steering column and the headlight, dimmer and turn signal switch is located to the left of the steering column. The 2 switches can be removed without removing the switch base.

1. Disconnect the negative battery cable.
2. Remove the steering column covers. Disconnect the connector.
3. Remove the combination switch mounting screws and remove the switch(s) from the switch base.
4. The installation is the reverse of the removal procedure.
5. Connect the negative battery cable and check all functions of the combination switch for proper operation.

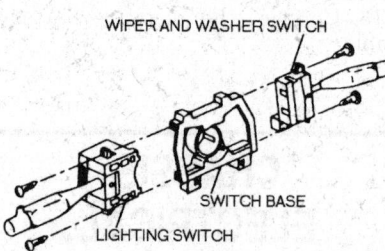

Combination switch assembly — G20 and M30

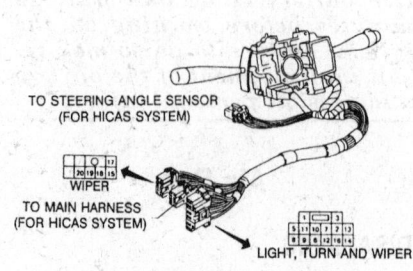

Combination switch assembly — Q45

Q45

The combination switch assembly cannot be disassembled and refers to all column-mounted stalk switches as a single unit.

Before replacing the switch, unplug the existing switch and plug in the replacement one to make sure all functions operate properly.

1. Make sure the wheels are pointing straight-ahead. Disconnect the negative battery cable and allow 10 minutes to elapse.
2. Remove the steering wheel.
3. Disconnect all combination switch connectors from underneath the steering column.
4. Remove the screws that fasten the combination switch to the steering column and remove from the vehicle.
5. The installation is the reverse of the removal procedure.
6. Connect the negative battery cable and check all functions of the combination switch for proper operation.

Combination Switch Base

REMOVAL AND INSTALLATION

NOTE: On vehicles equipped with air bags, it is imperative that the exact steering wheel REMOVAL AND INSTALLATION procedure is followed. The air bag module is a fragile component. Always place it with the pad side facing upward. Do not allow oil, grease or water to come in contact with the module. Do not drop the module; if it is damaged in any way, do not reinstall it to the steering wheel.

J30

1. Make sure the wheels are pointing straight-ahead. Disconnect the negative battery cable and allow 10 minutes to elapse.
2. Remove the steering wheel.
3. Disconnect all combination and windshield wiper switch connectors and remove the switches from the switch base.
4. Insert a suitable tool between the combination switch base and the steering column. Lift the base and pull outward to remove.
5. The installation is the reverse of the removal procedure.
6. Connect the negative battery cable and check all functions of the combination and windshield wiper switches for proper operation.

M30 and G20

1. Make sure the wheels are pointing straight-ahead. Disconnect the negative battery cable and allow 10 minutes to elapse.

2. Remove the steering wheel.

3. Disconnect all combination and windshield wiper switch connectors and remove the switches from the switch base.

4. To remove the combination switch base, remove the base attaching screw and turn after pushing it.

5. The installation is the reverse of the removal procedure.

6. Connect the negative battery cable and check all functions of the combination and windshield wiper switches for proper operation.

Ignition Lock/Switch

REMOVAL AND INSTALLATION

NOTE: On vehicles equipped with air bags, it is imperative that the exact steering wheel REMOVAL AND INSTALLATION procedure is followed. The air bag module is a fragile component. Always place it with the pad side facing upward. Do not allow oil, grease or water to come in contact with the module. Do not drop the module; if it is damaged in any way, do not reinstall it to the steering wheel.

1. Make sure the wheels are pointing straight-ahead. Disconnect the negative battery cable and allow 10 minutes to elapse.

2. Remove the steering wheel and combination switch or switch base.

3. Disconnect the ignition switch wiring.

4. Lower the steering column.

5. Using a hacksaw blade, cut a groove into the heads of the special

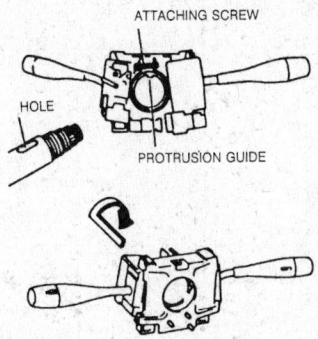

Combination switch base removal — M30 and G20

self-shearing screws and remove the screws.

6. Remove the assembly from the column.

To install:

7. With the key inserted in the switch, install the assembly onto the column with new self-shearing screws. Tighten the screws gradually, testing the key for binding often. Tighten the screws until the heads shear off.

8. Raise and secure the steering column.

9. Install the combination switch or switch base and steering wheel.

10. Connect the negative battery cable and check the ignition switch for proper operation in all positions.

Stoplight Switch

ADJUSTMENT

1. Measure the free height of the brake pedal at its bottom edge. The specification is 6.0 in. (152mm) for the manual transmission or 6.0-7.0 in. (152-177mm) for the automatic transaxle on the G20; 7.2-7.6 in. (184-194mm) for the J30; 8.0 in. (205mm) for M30 or 7.4 in. (190mm) for Q45. Adjust by loosening the booster input rod locknut and turning the input rod.

2. The stoplight switch is to the right of the cruise control cancel switch on the bracket above the brake pedal. Adjust both switches during this procedure.

3. Measure the clearance between the threaded end of the switches and the pedal stopper. The specification is 0.025 in. (0.06mm) for both.

4. Adjust be loosening the locknut and turning each switch.

5. Check the pedal free-play. The specification is 0.04-0.12 in. (1-3mm) for the G20 or 0.039-0.118 in. (1.0-1.3mm) for all other vehicles.

6. Make sure the brake lights illuminate when the pedal is depressed and they go out when the pedal is released.

7. Also, make sure the cruise control cancels when the brake pedal is depressed.

REMOVAL AND INSTALLATION

1. Disconnect the negative battery cable.

2. Remove the locknut.

3. Remove the switch from the bracket above the brake pedal.

4. The installation is the reverse of the removal procedure.

5. Adjust the switch.

6. Connect the negative battery cable and check the switch for proper operation.

Neutral Safety Switch

ADJUSTMENT

1. Disconnect the negative battery cable.

2. Raise the vehicle and support safely.

3. Disconnect the manual control linkage from the manual shift shaft.

4. Set the manual shift shaft in the **N** detent.

5. Loosen the neutral safety switch mounting bolts.

6. Align the switch with the shift shaft by inserting a suitable pin in the alignment holes.

7. Tighten the switch mounting bolts and connect the control linkage.

8. Make sure the vehicle does not start in any gear except **P** or **N** and does start in both **P** and **N**.

REMOVAL AND INSTALLATION

1. Disconnect the negative battery cable.

2. Raise the vehicle and support safely.

3. Disconnect the wires to the switch.

4. Remove the switch mounting screws.

5. Remove the switch from the transmission/transaxle.

6. The installation is the reverse of the removal procedure.

7. Adjust the switch.

8. Make sure the vehicle does not start in any gear except **P** or **N** and does start in both **P** and **N**.

Clutch Switch

ADJUSTMENT

1. Ensure that the clutch pedal height and free travel adjustments are within specification.

2. With the clutch pedal fully depressed, measure the clearance between the rubber stopper and the threaded end of the clutch switch. Clearance should be 0.004-0.039 in. (0.1-1.0mm).

3. If the clearance is not within specification, adjust the switch by loosening the locknut and adjusting the switch.

REMOVAL AND INSTALLATION

1. Disconnect the negative battery cable.
2. Disconnect the wiring harness from the clutch switch.
3. Loosen the locknut and remove the clutch switch.
4. Installation is the reverse of removal.
5. Adjust the switch.

Fuses and Circuit Breakers

LOCATION

A fuse, fusible link and relay box is located in the engine compartment, near the battery. Release the latch and remove the protective covering to access the desired component. The radio has its own fuse behind it. Other various relays are located throughout the vehicle.

There is a second fuse box located behind an access door to the left of the steering column on the instrument panel. The circuit breaker for the power door locks and seats is located near this fuse box. The circuit breaker for the power windows and the sunroof is located behind the left side kick panel.

Flasher

LOCATION

The combination flasher unit is located under the instrument panel to the right of the steering column on the G20, J30 and M30 or near the interior fuse box on the Q45.

SPECIFICATIONS

ENGINE IDENTIFICATION

Year	Model	Engine Displacement Liters (cc)	Engine Series (ID/VIN)	Fuel System	No. of Cylinders	Engine Type

ENGINE IDENTIFICATION

Year	Model	Engine Displacement Liters (cc)	Engine Series (ID/VIN)	Fuel System	No. of Cylinders	Engine Type
1990	Impulse	1.6 (1588)	4XE1-W	EFI	4	DOHC
1991	Impulse XS	1.6 (1588)	4XE1-W	EFI	4	DOHC
	Impulse RS (Turbo)	1.6 (1588)	4XE1-WT	EFI	4	DOHC
	Stylus XS	1.6 (1588)	4XE1-W	EFI	4	DOHC
	Stylus S	1.6 (1588)	4XE1-V	EFI	4	SOHC
1992	Impulse RS (Turbo)	1.6 (1588)	4XE1-WT	EFI	4	DOHC
	Impulse XS	1.8 (1809)	4XF1-W	EFI	4	DOHC
	Stylus S	1.6 (1588)	4XE1-V	EFI	4	SOHC
	Stylus RS	1.8 (1809)	4XF1-W	EFI	4	DOHC
1993	Stylus S	1.6 (1588)	4XE1-V	EFI	4	SOHC

EFI—Electronic Fuel Injection
DOHC—Double Overhead Camshaft
SOHC—Single Overhead Camshaft

GENERAL ENGINE SPECIFICATIONS

Year	Engine ID/VIN	Engine Displacement Liters (cc)	Fuel System Type	Net Horsepower @ rpm	Net Torque @ rpm (ft. lbs.)	Bore × Stroke (in.)	Compression Ratio	Oil Pressure @ rpm
1990	4XE1-W	1.6 (1588)	EFI	125 @ 6800	138 @ 5400	3.15 × 3.11	9.8:1	49 @ 5200
1991	4XE1-W	1.6 (1588)	EFI	130 @ 6600	102 @ 4600	3.15 × 3.11	9.8:1	49 @ 5200
	4XE1-WT	1.6 (1588)	EFI	160 @ 6600	150 @ 4800	3.15 × 3.11	8.5:1	49 @ 5200
	4XE1-V	1.6 (1588)	EFI	95 @ 5800	97 @ 4800	3.15 × 3.11	9.1:1	49 @ 5200
1992	4XE1-WT	1.6 (1588)	EFI	160 @ 6600	150 @ 4800	3.15 × 3.11	8.5:1	51–80 @ 3000
	4XF1-W	1.8 (1809)	EFI	140 @ 6400	120 @ 4600	3.15 × 3.54	9.7:1	51–80 @ 3000
	4XE1-V	1.6 (1588)	EFI	96 @ 5800	97 @ 3400	3.15 × 3.11	9.1:1	51–80 @ 3000
1993	4XE1-V	1.6 (1588)	EFI	96 @ 5800	97 @ 3400	3.15 × 3.11	9.1:1	51–80 @ 3000

EFI—Electronic Fuel Injection

GASOLINE ENGINE TUNE-UP SPECIFICATIONS

Year	Engine ID/VIN	Engine Displacement Liters (cc)	Spark Plugs Gap (in.)	Ignition Timing (deg.) MT	Ignition Timing (deg.) AT	Fuel Pump (psi)	Idle Speed (rpm) MT	Idle Speed (rpm) AT	Valve Clearance In.	Valve Clearance Ex.
1990	4XE1-W	1.6 (1588)	0.041	10B	10B	35–38	850	850	0.006	0.010
1991	4XE1-W	1.6 (1588)	0.041	10B	10B	35–38	850	850	0.006	0.010
	4XE1-WT	1.6 (1588)	0.030	10B	10B	35–38	900	900	0.006	0.010
	4XE1-V	1.6 (1588)	0.041	10B	10B	35–38	850	940	0.006	0.010
1992	4XE1-WT	1.6 (1588)	0.030	10B	10B	35–42	900	900	0.006	0.010
	4XF1-W	1.8 (1809)	0.040	10B	10B	35–42	850	850	Hyd.	Hyd.
	4XE1-V	1.6 (1588)	0.041	10B	10B	35–42	850	940	0.006	0.010
1993	4XE1-V	1.6 (1588)	0.041	10B	10B	35–42	850	940	0.006	0.010

NOTE: The lowest cylinder pressure should be within 75% of the highest cylinder pressure reading. For example, if the highest cylinder is 134 psi, the lowest should be 101. Engine should be at normal operating temperature with throttle valve in the wide open position.
The underhood specifications sticker often reflects tune-up specification changes in production. Sticker figures must be used if they disagree with those in this chart.
B—Before Top Dead Center
Hyd.—Hydraulic
① At 900 rpm with vacuum hose of the pressure regulator disconnected.
② ±50 rpm

FIRING ORDERS

NOTE: To avoid confusion, always replace spark plug wires one at a time.

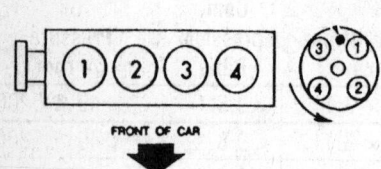

1.6L and 1.8L Non-Turbocharged Engines
Engine Firing Order: 1-3-4-2
Distributor Rotation: Counterclockwise

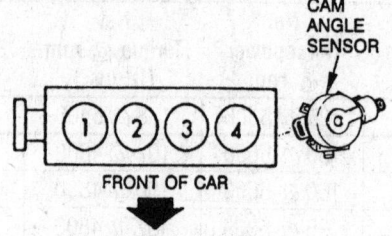

1.6L DOHC Turbocharged Engine
Engine Firing Order: 1-3-4-2
Distributorless Ignition System

CAPACITIES

Year	Model	Engine ID/VIN	Engine Displacement Liters (cc)	Engine Crankcase with Filter (qts.)	Transmission (pts.)			Drive Axle (pts.)	Fuel Tank (gal.)	Cooling System (qts.)
					4-Spd	5-Spd	Auto.			
1990	Impulse	4XE1-W	1.6 (1588)	4.2	—	4.0	14.0	NA	12.4	①
1991	Impulse XS	4XE1-W	1.6 (1588)	4.2	—	8.0	14.0	NA	12.4	①
	Impulse RS (Turbo)	4XE1-WT	1.6 (1588)	4.6	—	8.0	14.0	③	12.4	7.9
	Stylus XS	4XE1-W	1.6 (1588)	4.2	—	8.0	14.0	NA	12.4	①
	Stylus S	4XE1-V	1.6 (1588)	4.2	—	8.0	14.0	NA	12.4	①
1992	Impulse RS	4XE1-WT	1.6 (1588)	4.6	—	8.0	14.0	③	12.4	7.9
	Impulse XS	4XF1-W	1.8 (1809)	4.2	—	8.0	14.0	NA	12.4	②
	Stylus S	4XE1-V	1.6 (1588)	4.2	—	8.0	14.0	NA	12.4	②
	Stylus RS	4XF1-W	1.8 (1809)	4.2	—	8.0	14.0	NA	12.4	②
1993	Stylus S	4XE1-V	1.6 (1588)	4.2	—	8.0	14.0	NA	12.4	②

NA—Not available
① Manual transaxle: 7.3 qts.
  Automatic transaxle: 7.8 qts.
② Manual transaxle: 7.5 qts.
  Automatic transaxle: 8.0 qts.
③ Rear axle (4WD): 1.5 pts.

CAMSHAFT SPECIFICATIONS

All measurements given in inches.

Year	Engine ID/VIN	Engine Displacement Liters (cc)	Journal Diameter					Elevation		Bearing Clearance	Camshaft End Play
			1	2	3	4	5	In.	Ex.		
1990	4XE1-W	1.6 (1588)	1.021–1.022	1.021–1.022	1.021–1.022	1.021–1.022	1.021–1.022	1.503	1.503	0.0011–0.0031	0.0020–0.0060
1991	4XE1-V	1.6 (1588) SOHC	1.021–1.022	1.021–1.022	1.021–1.022	1.021–1.022	1.021–1.022	1.426	1.426	0.0024–0.0044	0.0020–0.0060
	4XE1-W	1.6 (1588) DOHC	1.021–1.022	1.021–1.022	1.021–1.022	1.021–1.022	1.021–1.022	1.503	1.503	0.0011–0.0031	0.0020–0.0060
	4XE1-WT	1.6 (1588) Turbo	1.021–1.022	1.021–1.022	1.021–1.022	1.021–1.022	1.021–1.022	1.525	1.525	0.0011–0.0031	0.0020–0.0060
1992	4XE1-WT	1.6 (1588)	1.050–1.051	1.050–1.051	1.050–1.051	1.050–1.051	1.050–1.051	1.525	1.525	0.0011–0.0031	0.0020–0.0060
	4XF1-W	1.8 (1809)	1.050–1.051	1.050–1.051	1.050–1.051	1.050–1.051	1.050–1.051	1.503	1.503	0.0011–0.0031	0.0020–0.0060
	4XE1-V	1.6 (1588)	1.050–1.051	1.050–1.051	1.050–1.051	1.050–1.051	1.050–1.051	1.503	1.503	0.0011–0.0031	0.0020–0.0060
1993	4XE1-V	1.6 (1588)	1.050–1.051	1.050–1.051	1.050–1.051	1.050–1.051	1.050–1.051	1.503	1.503	0.0011–0.0031	0.0020–0.0060

DOHC—Double Overhead Camshaft
SOHC—Single Overhead Camshaft

CRANKSHAFT AND CONNECTING ROD SPECIFICATIONS

All measurements are given in inches.

Year	Engine ID/VIN	Engine Displacement Liters (cc)	Crankshaft				Connecting Rod		
			Main Brg. Journal Dia.	Main Brg. Oil Clearance	Shaft End-play	Thrust on No.	Journal Diameter	Oil Clearance	Side Clearance
1990	4XE1-W	1.6 (1588)	2.0439–2.0448	0.0008–0.0020	0.0024–0.0095	2	1.5724–1.5728	0.0010–0.0023	0.0079–0.0138
1991	4XE1-V	1.6 (1588) SOHC	2.0243	0.0008–0.0020	0.0024–0.0095	2	1.5526	0.0010–0.0023	0.0079–0.0138
	4XE1-W, 4XE1-WT	1.6 (1588) DOHC & Turbo	2.0439–2.0448	0.0008–0.0020	0.0024–0.0095	2	1.5724–1.5728	0.0010–0.0023	0.0079–0.0138
1992	4XE1-WT	1.6 (1588)	2.0439–2.0448	0.0008–0.0020	0.0024–0.0095	2	1.5724–1.5728	0.0010–0.0023	0.0079–0.0138
	4XF1-W	1.8 (1809)	2.0439–2.0448	0.0008–0.0020	0.0024–0.0095	2	1.8083–1.8088	0.0011–0.0023	0.0079–0.0138
	4XE1-V	1.6 (1588)	2.0439–2.0448	0.0008–0.0020	0.0024–0.0095	2	1.5724–1.5728	0.0010–0.0023	0.0079–0.0138
1993	4XE1-V	1.6 (1588)	2.0439–2.0448	0.0008–0.0020	0.0024–0.0095	2	1.5724–1.5728	0.0010–0.0023	0.0079–0.0138

DOHC—Double Overhead Camshaft
SOHC—Single Overhead Camshaft

VALVE SPECIFICATIONS

Year	Engine ID/VIN	Engine Displacement Liters (cc)	Seat Angle (deg.)	Face Angle (deg.)	Spring Test Pressure (lbs. @ in.)	Spring Installed Height (in.)	Stem-to-Guide Clearance (in.)		Stem Diameter (in.)	
							Intake	Exhaust	Intake	Exhaust
1990	4XE1-W	1.6 (1588)	45	45	44.1 @ 1.504	1.504	0.0009–0.0022	0.0012–0.0025	0.2348–0.2356	0.2346–0.2352
1991	4XE1-V	1.6 (1588) SOHC	45	45	①	1.504	0.0009–0.0022	0.0012–0.0025	0.2348–0.2356	0.2346–0.2352
	4XE1-W	1.6 (1588) DOHC	45	45	44.1 @ 1.504	1.504	0.0009–0.0022	0.0012–0.0025	0.2348–0.2356	0.2346–0.2352
	4XE1-WT	1.6 (1588) Turbo	45	45	44.1 @ 1.504	1.504	0.0009–0.0022	0.0012–0.0025	0.2348–0.2356	0.2346–0.2352
1992	4XE1-WT	1.6 (1588)	45	45	44.1 @ 1.504	1.504	0.0009–0.0022	0.0012–0.0025	0.2348–0.2356	0.2346–0.2352
	4XF1-W	1.8 (1809)	45	45	44.1 @ 1.504	1.504	0.0009–0.0022	0.0012–0.0025	0.2348–0.2356	0.2346–0.2352
	4XE1-V	1.6 (1588)	45	45	①	1.504	0.0009–0.0022	0.0012–0.0025	0.2348–0.2356	0.2346–0.2352
1993	4XE1-V	1.6 (1588)	45	45	①	1.504	0.0009–0.0022	0.0012–0.0025	0.2348–0.2356	0.2346–0.2352

DOHC—Double Overhead Camshaft
SOHC—Single Overhead Camshaft
① 44 @ 1.504 in.—Intake
   55 @ 1.504 in.—Exhaust

PISTON AND RING SPECIFICATIONS

All measurements are given in inches.

Year	Engine ID/VIN	Engine Displacement Liters (cc)	Piston Clearance	Ring Gap			Ring Side Clearance		
				Top Compression	Bottom Compression	Oil Control	Top Compression	Bottom Compression	Oil Control
1990	4XE1-W	1.6 (1588)	0.0019–0.0027	0.0110–0.0157	0.0177–0.0236	0.0039–0.0236	0.0018–0.0032	0.0008–0.0024	NA
1991	4XE1-V	1.6 (1588) SOHC	0.0011–0.0019	0.0110–0.0157	0.0177–0.0236	0.0039–0.0236	0.0018–0.0032	0.0008–0.0024	NA
	4XE1-W, 4XE1-WT	1.6 (1588) DOHC & Turbo	0.0019–0.0027	0.0110–0.0157	0.0177–0.0236	0.0039–0.0236	0.0018–0.0032	0.0008–0.0024	NA
1992	4XE1-WT	1.6 (1588)	0.0019–0.0027	0.0110–0.0157	0.0177–0.0236	0.0039–0.0236	0.0018–0.0032	0.0008–0.0024	NA
	4XF1-W	1.8 (1809)	0.0019–0.0027	0.0110–0.0157	0.0177–0.0236	0.0039–0.0236	0.0018–0.0032	0.0008–0.0024	NA
	4XE1-V	1.6 (1588)	0.0011–0.0019	0.0110–0.0157	0.0177–0.0236	0.0039–0.0236	0.0018–0.0032	0.0008–0.0024	NA
1993	4XE1-V	1.6 (1588)	0.0011–0.0019	0.0110–0.0157	0.0177–0.0236	0.0039–0.0236	0.0018–0.0032	0.0008–0.0024	NA

NA—Not available
DOHC—Double Overhead Camshaft
SOHC—Single Overhead Camshaft

TORQUE SPECIFICATIONS

All readings in ft. lbs.

Year	Engine ID/VIN	Engine Displacement Liters (cc)	Cylinder Head Bolts	Main Bearing Bolts	Rod Bearing Bolts	Crankshaft Damper Bolts	Flywheel Bolts	Manifold		Spark Plugs	Lug Nut
								Intake	Exhaust		
1990	4XE1-W	1.6 (1588)	②	65①	③	109	④	17	30	11–14	87
1991	4XE1-V	1.6 (1588) SOHC	②	65①	③	109	④	17	30	11–14	87
	4XE1-W, 4XE1-WT	1.6 (1588) DOHC & Turbo	②	65①	③	109	④	17	30	11–14	87
1992	4XE1-WT	1.6 (1588)	②	65①	③	109	④	17	30	14	87
	4XF1-W	1.8 (1809)	②	65①	③	109	④	17	30	14	87
	4XE1-V	1.6 (1588)	②	65①	③	109	④	17	30	14	87
1993	4XE1-V	1.6 (1588)	②	65①	③	109	④	17	30	14	87

DOHC—Double Overhead Camshaft
SOHC—Single Overhead Camshaft
① See text for proper sequence
② 1st step—29 ft. lbs.
  2nd step—58 ft. lbs.
③ 1st step—11 ft. lbs.
  2nd step—turn an additional 45–60 degrees
④ 1st step—22 ft. lbs.
  2nd step—turn an additional 45–60 degrees

BRAKE SPECIFICATIONS

All measurements in inches unless noted

Year	Model	Master Cylinder Bore	Brake Disc			Brake Drum Diameter			Minimum Lining Thickness	
			Original Thickness	Minimum Thickness	Maximum Runout	Original Inside Diameter	Max. Wear Limit	Maximum Machine Diameter	Front	Rear
1990	Impulse	0.875	②	①	0.0059	NA	NA	NA	0.039	0.039
1991	Impulse	0.875	②	①	0.0059	NA	NA	NA	0.039	0.039
	Stylus	0.875	②	①	0.0059	7.87	NA	7.526	0.039	0.039
1992	Impulse	0.875	②	①	0.0059	NA	NA	NA	0.039	0.039
	Stylus	0.875	②	①	0.0059	7.87	NA	7.526	0.039	0.039
1993	Stylus	0.875	②	①	0.0059	7.87	NA	7.526	0.039	0.039

NA—Not available
DOHC—Double Overhead Camshaft
① Front—0.810
  Rear—0.299
② Front—0.866
  Rear—0.350

WHEEL ALIGNMENT

Year	Model	Caster Range (deg.)	Caster Preferred Setting (deg.)	Camber Range (deg.)	Camber Preferred Setting (deg.)	Toe-in (in.)	Steering Axis Inclination (deg.)
1990	Impulse	2P–4P	3P	1¼N–¼P	½N	0	NA
1991	Impulse	2P–4P	3P	1¼N–¼P	½N	1/32–3/32	NA
	Stylus	2P–4P	3P	1¼N–¼P	½N	1/32–3/32	NA
1992	Impulse	2P–4P	3P	1¼N–¼P	½N	0	NA
	Stylus	2P–4P	3P	1¼N–¼P	½N	0	NA
1993	Stylus S	2P–4P	3P	1¼N–¼P	½N	0	NA

NOTE: Caster angle is pre-set and cannot be serviced
NA—Not available
DOHC—Double Overhead Camshaft
N—Negative
P—Positive

ENGINE MECHANICAL

NOTE: Disconnecting the negative battery cable on some vehicles may interfere with the functions of the on-board computer systems and may require the computer to undergo a relearning process, once the negative battery cable is reconnected.

Engine Assembly

REMOVAL AND INSTALLATION

1. Relieve the fuel system pressure. Disconnect and remove the battery and tray from the vehicle.
2. Mark the position of the hood on the hood hinges and remove the hood.
3. Raise and safely support the vehicle.
4. Drain the coolant from the radiator and the oil from the transaxle. Remove the left and right undercovers.
5. Disconnect the accelerator cable from the throttle valve and the common chamber.
6. Disconnect the breather hose from the intake air duct side and remove the intake air duct from the throttle valve.
7. On turbocharged engine, remove the intercooler and breather hose.
8. Remove the air cleaner cover and element and the air cleaner body.
9. Disconnect the MAP sensor hose from the MAP sensor side, the vacuum hose from the vacuum booster side and the 2 canister vacuum hoses from the common chamber and throttle valve.
10. Remove the bracket which supports the 2 canister pipes and the MAP sensor pipe from the common chamber.
11. Disconnect the following electrical connectors and tag them for reassembly:
    a. Two cable harness connectors near the left front strut tower.
    b. Ignition wire from the ignition coil side.
    c. Bonding cable connector from the terminal at the thermostat housing flange.
    d. Both primary connections from the ignition coil.
    e. Ground cable from the driver's side inner fender.
    f. Positive cable terminal in fuse box.
    g. Cooling fan harness connector.
    h. Both harness connectors at the front of the battery.
    i. Oxygen sensor harness connector.
    j. Ground cable terminals from the right side of the common chamber.
    k. Bonding cable terminal from the right side of the induction control assembly.
    l. If equipped with an automatic transaxle, the 4 connectors of the automatic transaxle control system on the automatic transaxle assembly.
    m. Disconnect the oil cooler pipes, turbocharged engine.
12. Remove the ignition coil with the battery bracket.
13. If equipped with a manual transaxle, loosen both adjusting nuts and remove the clutch cable and disconnect the cotter pin and clip from the shift cable bracket.
14. If equipped with an automatic transaxle, disconnect the cotter pin and joint from the shift cable lever.
15. Disconnect the heater hoses, radiator hoses, fuel lines and speedometer cable.

16. Remove the coolant reservoir tank.

17. Remove the power steering pump and air conditioning compressors. Position them aside without disconnecting their lines.

18. If equipped with an automatic transaxle, disconnect the oil cooler lines from the radiator.

19. Remove the cooling fan and the shroud.

20. Remove the front wheel and tire assemblies.

21. Loosen but do not remove, the strut tower nuts.

22. Disconnect the lower ball joints and tie rod ends and remove the halfshafts.

23. Remove the engine splash shield. Disconnect the exhaust pipe.

24. Attach an engine hoist to the engine/transaxle assembly and lift the engine slightly to take weight off of the mounts.

25. Disconnect the torque rod from the center beam.

26. Remove the center bolt of the rear side engine mounting after removing the damper weight.

27. Remove the left side engine mount.

28. Remove the cruise control pump and VSV assembly. Remove the right side engine mount.

29. If equipped with a manual transaxle, disconnect the axle shaft center bearing support bracket from the cylinder bracket.

30. Remove the engine/transaxle assembly.

31. Separate the engine from the transaxle.

To install:

32. Connect the transaxle to the engine and position the assembly in the vehicle.

33. Connect the halfshaft center bearing support bracket to the cylinder bracket.

34. Install the right side engine mount. Tighten the mount attaching bolt to 89 ft. lbs. (121 Nm), the mount attaching nut to 37 ft. lbs. (50 Nm) and the through bolt to 51 ft. lbs. (69 Nm).

35. Install the left side engine mount and tighten the through bolt to 51 ft. lbs. (69 Nm).

36. Install the rear side engine mount. Tighten the through bolt to 76 ft. lbs. (103 Nm) and the damper weight to 37 ft. lbs. (50 Nm).

37. Install the torque rod. Tighten the center beam side bolt to 51 ft. lbs. (69 Nm) and the engine side bolt to 95 ft. lbs. (128 Nm).

38. Connect the exhaust pipe and install the engine splash shield.

39. Install the halfshafts and connect the tie rods and lower ball joints. Tighten the lower ball joint nuts to 48 ft. lbs. (66 Nm) and the tie rod nuts to 29 ft. lbs. (39 Nm).

40. Tighten the strut tower nuts to 51 ft. lbs. (69 Nm) and install the front wheel and tire assemblies.

41. Install the cooling fan and shroud. On automatic transaxle vehicles, connect the transaxle cooling lines.

42. Install the power steering pump and air conditioning compressor. Install and adjust the drive belts.

43. Install the coolant reservoir tank.

44. Connect the radiator and heater hoses, fuel lines and speedometer cable. Install the intercooler and hoses. On turbocharged engine, connect the oil cooler lines.

45. Connect the transaxle shift cable. On manual transaxle vehicles, connect the clutch cable.

46. Install the ignition coil with the battery bracket.

47. Connect all electrical connectors.

48. Install the bracket that supports the 2 canister pipes and the MAP sensor pipe to the common chamber.

49. Connect all vacuum hoses.

50. Install the air cleaner assembly.

51. Install the intake air duct and connect the breather hose to the intake air side.

52. Connect the accelerator cable and install the hood. Aligning the marks that were made during the removal procedure.

53. Install the battery tray and the battery.

54. Fill the cooling system and engine crankcase with the proper type and quantity of fluids.

55. Install the battery and battery tray. Connect the battery cables, start the engine and check for leaks. Adjust the clutch cable.

Cylinder Head

REMOVAL AND INSTALLATION

1.6L DOHC and 1.8L Engines

1. Relieve the fuel system pressure. Disconnect the negative battery cable.

2. Mark the position of the hood on the hinge brackets and remove the hood.

3. Drain the cooling system.

4. Remove the accelerator cable from the throttle valve and common chamber.

5. Disconnect the breather hose from the intake air duct side.

6. Disconnect the MAP sensor hose from the MAP sensor side, the vacuum booster hose from the vacuum booster and the 2 canister hoses from the pipes on the common chamber.

7. Remove the bracket that supports the 2 canister pipes and MAP sensor pipe from the common chamber.

8. Disconnect the following electrical connectors and tag them for reassembly:

  a. Oxygen sensor.

  b. Ignition wire from the coil side.

  c. Bonding cable connector from the terminal at the thermostat housing flange.

  d. Temperature sensor and thermometer unit connector at the thermostat housing.

  e. Ground cable terminals from the right side of the common chamber.

  f. Bonding cable terminal from the right side of the induction control assembly.

  g. The 2 cable harness connectors near the left front strut tower.

  h. Fuel injector connectors.

9. Disconnect the heater hose, upper radiator hose, throttle valve heating hose and the fuel lines.

10. Remove the coolant bypass stay pipe from the cylinder head.

11. Raise and safely support the vehicle.

12. Remove the engine splash shield and disconnect the exhaust pipe.

13. Use a hoist to support the engine and remove the right side engine mount.

14. Remove the coolant recovery tank with the bracket.

15. Remove the accessory drive belts.

16. Remove the 2 bolts from the power steering pump bracket, without disconnecting the feed lines and position the pump and bracket aside.

17. Remove the engine mounting bridge bracket and the cylinder head center cover.

18. Disconnect the spark plug wires, ignition coil and clips and the PCV hose from the valve cover.

19. Remove the upper timing belt cover, the power steering pump bracket and valve cover.

20. Remove the tension adjusting hole cover and align the camshaft pulley timing marks even with the top edge of the cylinder head.

21. Loosen the tension pulley lock bolt and turn the tension pulley clockwise to loosen the timing belt. Remove the timing belt from the camshaft pulleys.

22. Remove the cylinder head bolts, starting at each end of the cylinder head and working toward the center.

23. Raise the cylinder head and remove the coolant hose from the oil cooler.

24. Remove the cylinder head assembly.

To install:

25. Take note of the following points.

26. Make sure all mating surfaces are clean prior to installation.

27. Check the cylinder head for flatness before installing. If the head is warped more than 0.008 in. (0.2mm), it must be resurfaced. If the head is warped more than 0.016 in. (0.4mm), it must be replaced.

28. Use a new gasket and align the cylinder head on the block dowel pins. Apply engine oil to the threads and seating faces of the cylinder head bolts.

29. Tighten the bolts, in 2 steps, following the proper sequence. First, tighten the bolts to 29 ft. lbs. (40 Nm), in sequence, and finally to 59 ft. lbs. (79 Nm), in sequence.

30. Apply a 0.08-0.12 in. (2-3mm) width bead of sealant to the arched area of the No. 1 and No. 5 camshaft bearing caps. Tighten the cylinder head cover bolts to 27 inch lbs. (3 Nm) in the proper sequence.

31. Properly adjust the timing belt after installation.

32. Be sure to torque the following components to specification:

Upper timing cover — 7 ft. lbs. (10 Nm).

Engine mounting bridge bracket — 30 ft. lbs. (40 Nm).

Right side engine mount through bolt — 51 ft. lbs. (69 Nm).

Right side engine mount nut — 37 ft. lbs. (50 Nm).

Right side engine mount bolt — 89 ft. lbs. (121 Nm).

Exhaust pipe nuts — 42 ft. lbs. (57 Nm).

1.6L SOHC

1. Relieve the fuel system pressure. Disconnect the negative battery cable and drain the cooling system.

2. Rotate the engine until the engine is at TDC on the compression stroke of the No. 1 cylinder. Remove the distributor cap. Matchmark the distributor rotor to housing position and housing to cylinder head position. Remove the distributor holddown bolt and remove the distributor.

3. Disconnect the radiator inlet and outlet hoses and remove the radiator.

4. Remove the alternator and the air conditioner drive belts. Remove the engine cooling fan.

5. Remove the crankshaft pulley center bolt and remove the pulley and hub assembly.

6. Remove the air pump belt and position the air pump aside. If equipped, remove the air condition-

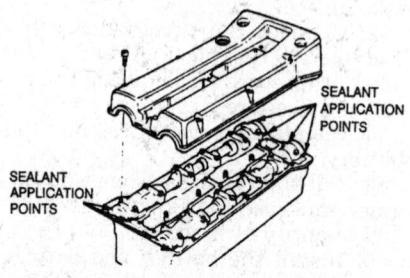

Installing the cylinder head cover — 1.6L DOHC engine

ing compressor and position it aside. Remove the compressor mounting bracket.

7. Remove the water pump pulley. Remove the top section of the front cover and the water pump.

8. Remove the lower section of the front cover.

9. Remove the tension spring. Loosen the top bolt of the tension pulley and draw the tension pulley fully to the water pump side.

10. Remove the timing belt.

11. Remove camshaft cover.

12. Loosen and remove the rocker arm shaft retaining nuts, starting from the outermost. Remove the rocker arm shaft with the bracket as an assembly.

13. Raise and safely support the vehicle. Disconnect the exhaust pipe at the exhaust manifold. On turbocharged vehicles, disconnect the exhaust pipe from the wastegate manifold and remove the control cable for the turbocharger.

14. Lower the vehicle and disconnect all necessary lines, hoses and electrical connectors. Tag them for reassembly.

15. Disconnect the accelerator linkage. On turbocharged vehicles, remove the engine wiring harness assembly from the fuel injectors and fuel line from fuel injector pipe.

16. Remove the cylinder head bolts, beginning with the outer bolts and working in towards the center on both sides.

17. Remove the cylinder head.

To install:

18. Make sure all mating surfaces are clean prior to installation.

19. Check the cylinder head surface for flatness before installing. If the head is warped more than 0.008 in. (0.2mm), it must be resurfaced. If the head is warped more than 0.016 in. (0.4mm), it must be replaced.

20. Install a new cylinder head gasket and the cylinder head, aligning them on the dowels on the cylinder block.

21. Apply a thin coat of engine oil to the cylinder head bolt threads and install the bolts. Tighten them, in 2 steps, in sequence. First tighten to 58 ft. lbs. (80 Nm), in sequence and then to 72 ft. lbs. (100 Nm), in sequence.

22. Properly adjust the timing belt tension.

23. Adjust the drive belts. Refill and bleed the cooling system. Fill the engine crankcase, transaxle and power steering reservoir with the proper fluids.

24. After the installation is completed, road test the vehicle. Recheck

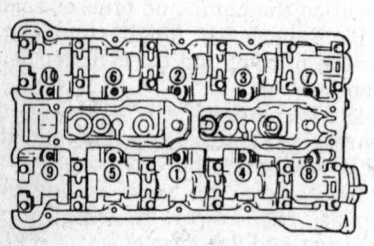

Cylinder head bolt torque sequence — 1.6L and 1.8L DOHC engines

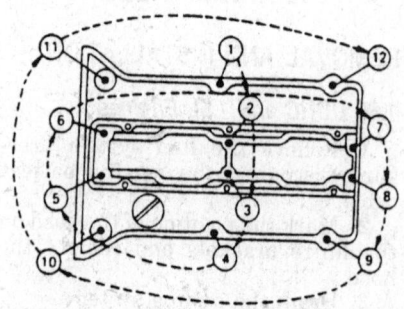

Cylinder head cover bolt torque sequence — 1.6L DOHC engine

the fluid levels and check for any leaks.

Valve Lifters

Only the 1.6L and 1.8L DOHC engines use hydraulic valve lifters. In all other engines, the camshaft acts directly on the rocker arm to activate the valve.

REMOVAL AND INSTALLATION

1.6L and 1.8L DOHC Engines

1. Disconnect the negative battery cable.
2. Disconnect the PCV hoses and the center cover.
3. Disconnect the spark plug wires and remove the upper timing cover.
4. Remove the valve cover.
5. Bring the No. 1 cylinder to TDC of the compression stroke. The timing marks on the camshafts should be even with the top edge of the cylinder head.
6. Loosen the camshaft pulley bolts and loosen the timing belt tension pulley bolt ½ turn. Loosen the timing belt by rotating the tension pulley and remove the belt from the camshaft pulleys.

NOTE: Be careful not to rotate the engine.

7. Remove the camshaft pulleys.
8. Remove the distributor cap. Mark the position of the distributor rotor in relation to the distributor housing and the distributor housing in relation to the cylinder head. Remove the distributor.
9. Remove the camshaft bearing cap bolts, beginning with the end caps and working gradually toward the center of the cylinder head.
10. Remove the camshafts and the camshaft oil seals.

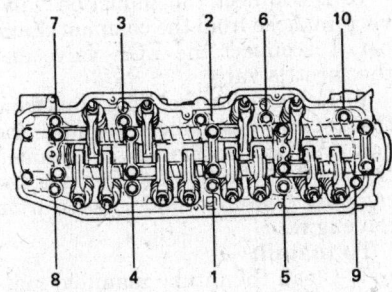

Cylinder head bolt torque sequence — 1.6L SOHC engines

11. Remove the lifters and arrange them in order so they can be reinstalled in the same position.

NOTE: Remove the lifters with the adjusting shims. Submerge the lifters in engine oil when removed. This will prevent air from mixing with the oil in the lifter and causing noise when reinstalled.

To install:

12. Be sure to coat the lifters and camshaft lobes and journals with engine oil before installing.
13. Apply sealant to the contact surfaces of No. 1 and No. 5 bearing caps. Install the caps and tighten to 89 inch lbs. (10 Nm), in sequence.

NOTE: Do not allow sealant to contact the bearing surfaces of the bearing cap.

14. Adjust the valve clearance.
15. Lubricate the sealing lip of new camshaft seals and install using with a seal installer.
16. Tighten the camshaft pulleys to 43 ft. lbs. (59 Nm), install the timing belt and properly adjust the tension.
17. Tighten the cylinder head cover bolts to 27 inch lbs. (3 Nm), in sequence.

Valve Lash

ADJUSTMENT

Valve lash adjustments must be made when the engine is cold.

Except 1.6L DOHC Engine

1. Disconnect the negative battery cable.
2. Remove the valve cover.
3. Before proceeding further, check the rocker shaft bolts for looseness and tighten to 16 ft. lbs. (22 Nm), as necessary.
4. Remove the distributor cap. Turn the crankshaft 1 full turn in the normal direction of rotation. Align the distributor rotor with the No. 1 cylinder spark plug wire on the distributor cap and align the notched line on the crank pulley with the 0 mark on the timing gear case cover.
5. The following valves can be adjusted: Intake — No. 1 and No. 2. Exhaust — No. 1 and No. 3.
6. Measure the clearance between the rocker arm and the valve stem using a feeler gauge. Adjust by loosening the locknut and turning the adjustment stud until a slight drag is felt on the feeler gauge.

7. Adjust the valve clearance to the following specifications:
Intake — 0.006 in. (0.15mm)
Exhaust — 0.010 in. (0.25mm)
8. After adjustment is completed, rotate the engine 1 revolution until the notched line on the crank pulley is aligned with the 0 mark on the timing gear case cover and the distributor rotor is aligned with the No. 4 spark plug wire on the distributor cap.
9. The remaining valves can now be adjusted.
10. After all valves have been adjusted, install the remaining components in the reverse of their removal procedure.

1.6L DOHC Engine

NOTE: The 1.6L SOHC engine uses hydraulic lifters which require no adjustment.

1. Disconnect the negative battery cable.
2. Remove the valve cover and remove the spark plugs.
3. Check the torque of the camshaft bearing cap bolts. Tighten to 89 inch lbs. (10 Nm), as necessary.
4. Rotate the engine and align the notched line on the crank pulley with the 0 mark on the timing cover. The lifters on the No. 1 cylinder should have play and the lifters on the No. 4 cylinder should not. If not, rotate the engine 1 more revolution and align the marks again. The No. 1 cylinder is on TDC of the compression stroke.
5. The following valves can be measured for valve clearance: Intake — No. 1 and No. 2. Exhaust — No. 1 and No. 3.
6. Measure the clearance, using feeler gauge. Record the measurements of those that are out of adjustment.
7. Rotate the engine 1 revolution, until the No. 4 cylinder is at TDC. Measure the clearance of the remaining valves. Record the measurements of those that are out of adjustment.
8. Adjust the valve clearance by replacing the adjuster shim, as follows:
   a. Turn the camshaft and use the cam lift to press down the lifter.
   b. Place spacer J-38413-2, J-38413-3 or equivalent, on the upper circumference of the lifter from outside the cylinder head.
   c. Release the cam lift by turning the camshaft and hold the lifter down with the spacer. Remove the

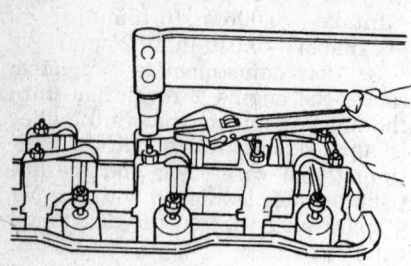

Checking rocker shaft for tightness

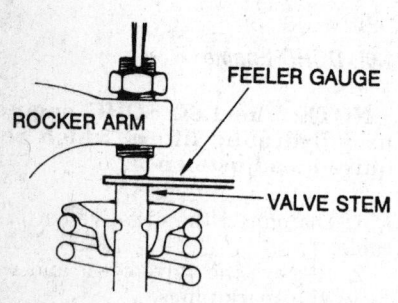

Adjusting the valve clearance

adjuster shim to the spark plug side, using a tool.

NOTE: Before pressing down the lifter, turn the cutaway of the lifter toward the position at which the adjuster shim is easily removed.

d. Measure the thickness of the adjuster shim, using a suitable micrometer. Calculate the needed thickness of the replacement shim by adding the thickness of the original shim to the required clearance. Select the available adjuster shim

with a thickness as close as possible to the calculated values.

NOTE: Adjuster shims are available in 19 sizes in thickness increments of 0.05mm, ranging from 2.55-3.45mm.

e. Place the selected adjuster shim on the lifter and press down the lifter by turning the camshaft and removing the spacer.

9. After valve adjustment is completed, install the remaining components in the reverse order of their removal.

Rocker Arms/Shafts

REMOVAL AND INSTALLATION

1. Disconnect the negative battery cable.
2. Remove the valve cover and the timing belt cover.
3. Bring the No. 1 cylinder to TDC on the compression stroke.
4. On Impulse, remove the tension spring and loosen the bolt. Draw the timing cover tension pulley fully to the water pump side to loosen the timing belt.
5. Loosen and remove the rocker arm shaft tightening bolts starting with the outermost one and working toward the center of the cylinder head.
6. Remove the rocker arm shafts.
7. Inspect the rocker arms and shafts for wear and replace, as necessary. When disassembling, label the components and keep them in order so they may be reinstalled in their original positions. Apply engine oil to the rocker arms and shafts when reassembling.
   To install:
8. Installation is the reverse of the removal procedure.
9. On Impulse, remove any oil from the contact surface of the No. 1

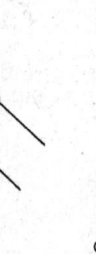
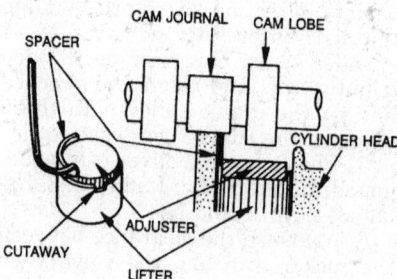

Valve adjuster shim removal — 1.6L DOHC engine

Installing valve adjustment spacer tool — 1.6L DOHC engine

rocker arm bracket and apply sealant to the contact surface before installation.
10. On Impulse, tighten the rocker arm shaft bolts to 16 ft. lbs. (22 Nm) with the exception of the 2 small bolts at the front of the No. 1 bearing cap which are tightened to 5 ft. lbs. (8 Nm).
11. Properly adjust the timing belt tension.

Intake Manifold

REMOVAL AND INSTALLATION

1.6L Engine

SOHC ENGINE

1. Disconnect negative battery cable. Drain cooling system. Remove the air cleaner duct hose from the common or intake chamber.
2. Disconnect and tag the following vacuum lines and wiring harness:
   a. Fast idle vacuum hose from the air duct hose.
   b. The MAP sensor vacuum hose from the common chamber.
   c. Disconnect the TPC valve vacuum hose from the common chamber.
   d. Disconnect the canister vacuum hose from the common chamber.
   e. Electronic control gas injection harness, disconnect the 2 ECM ground connectors from the bracket located on top of the common chamber. Disconnect the 2 green and black multi-pin connectors on the top of the common chamber.
   f. Remove the MAT sensor connector.
3. Disconnect the accelerator cable from the throttle body and at the common chamber. Disconnect the PCV valve hose from the valve cover.
4. Disconnect the master vacuum hose from the master vacuum tube at the common chamber side.
5. Disconnect the induction valve vacuum hose from the common chamber. Disconnect the EGR valve and the throttle valve.
6. Remove the fuel hose clips from the common chamber. Remove the bolt and nuts retaining the common chamber to the engine. Remove the common chamber and gasket from the engine.
   To install:
7. Clean the intake manifold mating surfaces.
8. Install the intake manifold using a new gaskets. Torque the intake manifold to 17 ft. lbs. (24 Nm).

Measured clearance mm	inch	2.52	2.54	2.56	2.58	2.60	2.62	2.64	2.66	2.68	2.70	2.72	2.74	2.76	2.78	2.80	2.82	2.84	2.86	2.88	2.90	2.92	2.94	2.96	2.98	3.00	3.02	3.04	3.06	3.08	3.10	3.12	3.14	3.16	3.18	3.20	3.22	3.24	3.26	3.28	3.30	3.32	3.34	3.36	3.38	3.40	3.42	3.44	3.46	3.48
0.000-0.025	0.000-0.001									1	1	2	2	2	3	3	4	4	4	5	5	6	6	6	7	7	8	8	8	9	9	10	10	10	11	11	12	12	12	13	13	14	14	14	15	15	16	16	16	17
0.026-0.050	0.001-0.002							1	1	1	2	2	3	3	3	4	4	5	5	5	6	6	7	7	7	8	8	9	9	9	10	10	11	11	11	12	12	13	13	13	14	14	15	15	15	16	16	17	17	17
0.051-0.075	0.002-0.003						1	1	1	2	2	3	3	3	4	4	5	5	5	6	6	7	7	7	8	8	9	9	9	10	10	11	11	11	12	12	13	13	13	14	14	15	15	15	16	16	17	17	17	18
0.076-0.100	0.003-0.004					1	1	2	2	2	3	3	4	4	4	5	5	6	6	6	7	7	8	8	8	9	9	10	10	10	11	11	12	12	12	13	13	14	14	14	15	15	16	16	16	17	17	18	18	18
0.101-0.200	0.004-0.008	Replacement not to be required																																																
0.201-0.225	0.008-0.009	2	2	2	3	3	4	4	4	5	5	6	6	6	7	7	8	8	8	9	9	10	10	10	11	11	12	12	12	13	13	14	14	14	15	15	16	16	16	17	17	18	18	18	19	19				
0.226-0.250	0.009-0.010	2	3	3	3	4	4	5	5	5	6	6	7	7	7	8	8	9	9	9	10	10	11	11	11	12	12	13	13	13	14	14	15	15	15	16	16	17	17	17	18	18	19	19	19					
0.251-0.275	0.010-0.011	3	3	3	4	4	5	5	5	6	6	7	7	7	8	8	9	9	9	10	10	11	11	11	12	12	13	13	13	14	14	15	15	15	16	16	17	17	17	18	18	19	19	19						
0.276-0.300	0.011-0.012	3	4	4	4	5	5	6	6	6	7	7	8	8	8	9	9	10	10	10	11	11	12	12	12	13	13	14	14	14	15	15	16	16	16	17	17	18	18	18	19	19								
0.301-0.325	0.012-0.013	4	4	4	5	5	6	6	6	7	7	8	8	8	9	9	10	10	10	11	11	12	12	12	13	13	14	14	14	15	15	16	16	16	17	17	18	18	18	19	19									
0.326-0.350	0.013-0.014	4	5	5	5	6	6	7	7	7	8	8	9	9	9	10	10	11	11	11	12	12	13	13	13	14	14	15	15	15	16	16	17	17	17	18	18	19	19	19										
0.351-0.375	0.014-0.015	5	5	5	6	6	7	7	7	8	8	9	9	9	10	10	11	11	11	12	12	13	13	13	14	14	15	15	15	16	16	17	17	17	18	18	19	19	19											
0.376-0.400	0.015-0.016	5	6	6	6	7	7	8	8	8	9	9	10	10	10	11	11	12	12	12	13	13	14	14	14	15	15	16	16	16	17	17	18	18	18	19	19													
0.401-0.425	0.016-0.017	6	6	6	7	7	8	8	8	9	9	10	10	10	11	11	12	12	12	13	13	14	14	14	15	15	16	16	16	17	17	18	18	18	19	19														
0.426-0.450	0.017-0.018	6	7	7	7	8	8	9	9	9	10	10	11	11	11	12	12	13	13	13	14	14	15	15	15	16	16	17	17	17	18	18	19	19	19															
0.451-0.475	0.018-0.019	7	7	7	8	8	9	9	9	10	10	11	11	11	12	12	13	13	13	14	14	15	15	15	16	16	17	17	17	18	18	19	19	19																
0.476-0.500	0.019-0.020	7	8	8	8	9	9	10	10	10	11	11	12	12	12	13	13	14	14	14	15	15	16	16	16	17	17	18	18	18	19	19																		
0.501-0.525	0.020-0.021	8	8	8	9	9	10	10	10	11	11	12	12	12	13	13	14	14	14	15	15	16	16	16	17	17	18	18	18	19	19																			
0.526-0.550	0.021-0.022	8	9	9	9	10	10	11	11	11	12	12	13	13	13	14	14	15	15	15	16	16	17	17	17	18	18	19	19	19																				
0.551-0.575	0.022-0.023	9	9	9	10	10	11	11	11	12	12	13	13	13	14	14	15	15	15	16	16	17	17	17	18	18	19	19	19																					
0.576-0.600	0.023-0.024	9	10	10	10	11	11	12	12	12	13	13	14	14	14	15	15	16	16	16	17	17	18	18	18	19	19																							
0.601-0.625	0.024-0.025	10	10	10	11	11	12	12	12	13	13	14	14	14	15	15	16	16	16	17	17	18	18	18	19	19																								
0.626-0.650	0.025-0.026	10	11	11	11	12	12	13	13	13	14	14	15	15	15	16	16	17	17	17	18	18	19	19	19																									
0.651-0.675	0.026-0.027	11	11	11	12	12	13	13	13	14	14	15	15	15	16	16	17	17	17	18	18	19	19	19																										
0.676-0.700	0.027-0.028	11	12	12	12	13	13	14	14	14	15	15	16	16	16	17	17	18	18	18	19	19																												
0.701-0.725	0.028-0.029	12	12	12	13	13	14	14	14	15	15	16	16	16	17	17	18	18	18	19	19																													
0.726-0.750	0.029-0.030	12	13	13	13	14	14	15	15	15	16	16	17	17	17	18	18	19	19	19																														
0.751-0.775	0.030-0.031	13	13	13	14	14	15	15	15	16	16	17	17	17	18	18	19	19	19																															
0.776-0.800	0.031-0.032	13	14	14	14	15	15	16	16	16	17	17	18	18	18	19	19																																	
0.801-0.825	0.032-0.033	14	14	14	15	15	16	16	16	17	17	18	18	18	19	19																																		
0.826-0.850	0.033-0.034	14	15	15	15	16	16	17	17	17	18	18	19	19	19																																			
0.851-0.875	0.034-0.035	15	15	15	16	16	17	17	17	18	18	19	19	19																																				
0.876-0.900	0.035-0.036	15	16	16	16	17	17	18	18	18	19	19																																						
0.901-0.925	0.036-0.037	16	16	16	17	17	18	18	18	19	19																																							
0.926-0.950	0.0365-0.0374	16	17	17	17	18	18	19	19	19																																								
0.951-0.975	0.037-0.038	17	17	17	18	18	19	19	19																																									
0.976-1.000	0.038-0.039	17	18	18	18	19	19																																											
1.001-1.025	0.039-0.040	18	18	18	19	19																																												
1.026-1.050	0.040-0.041	18	19	19	19																																													
1.051-1.075	0.041-0.042	19	19	19																																														
1.076-1.100	0.042-0.043	19																																																

Thickness of available adjuster (Shim)

NO in Chart	Thickness (mm)	NO in Chart	Thickness (mm)
1	2.55	11	3.05
2	2.60	12	3.10
3	2.65	13	3.15
4	2.70	14	3.20
5	2.75	15	3.25
6	2.80	16	3.30
7	2.85	17	3.35
8	2.90	18	3.40
9	2.95	19	3.45
10	3.00		

Intake adjuster shim chart — 1.6L DOHC engine

9. Install the remaining components by reversing their removal procedures. Reconnect all wiring, hoses and cables to the original location.

10. Refill the cooling system.

11. Reconnect the negative battery cable. Start the engine and check for leaks.

DOHC ENGINE

1. Disconnect the negative battery cable.

2. Disconnect the ground cable terminals from the common chamber, the 2 cable harness connectors from the throttle valve assembly and the MAT sensor harness connector and accelerator cable from the throttle valve assembly and common chamber.

3. Disconnect the air intake duct.

4. On turbocharged engine, remove the intercooler and back pressure transducer.

5. Disconnect the PCV hose, MAP sensor hose, fuel pressure regulator vacuum hose, canister hoses and vacuum booster hose.

6. Remove the canister pipes and MAP sensor pipe with the bracket.

7. Disconnect the heating hoses and throttle valve assembly from the common chamber.

8. On turbocharged engine, remove the intercooler rear bracket and breather hoses.

9. Loosen the EGR pipe and valve retainers and clip.

10. Disconnect the induction control vacuum hose and the alternator harness clip.

11. Disconnect the common chamber bracket and the engine hanger from the common chamber. Remove the common chamber.

12. Disconnect the VSV cable harness connector and oil cooler pipe bracket from the bosses beneath the intake manifold.

Exhaust adjuster shim chart — 1.6L DOHC engine

Measured clearance mm	inch	2.52	2.54	2.56	2.58	2.60	2.62	2.64	2.66	2.68	2.70	2.72	2.74	2.76	2.78	2.80	2.82	2.84	2.86	2.88	2.90	2.92	2.94	2.96	2.98	3.00	3.02	3.04	3.06	3.08	3.10	3.12	3.14	3.16	3.18	3.20	3.22	3.24	3.26	3.28	3.30	3.32	3.34	3.36	3.38	3.40	3.42	3.44	3.46	3.48
0.000~0.025	0.000~0.001														1	1	2	2	2	3	3	4	4	4	5	5	6	6	6	7	7	8	8	8	9	9	10	10	10	11	11	12	12	12	13	13	14	14	14	15
0.026~0.050	0.001~0.002											1	1	1	2	2	3	3	3	4	4	5	5	5	6	6	7	7	7	8	8	9	9	9	10	10	11	11	11	12	12	13	13	13	14	14	15	15	15	
0.051~0.075	0.002~0.003										1	1	1	2	2	3	3	3	4	4	5	5	5	6	6	7	7	7	8	8	9	9	9	10	10	11	11	11	12	12	13	13	13	14	14	15	15	15	16	
0.076~0.100	0.003~0.004									1	1	2	2	2	3	3	4	4	4	5	5	6	6	6	7	7	8	8	8	9	9	10	10	10	11	11	12	12	12	13	13	14	14	14	15	15	16	16	16		
0.101~0.125	0.004~0.005								1	1	2	2	2	3	3	4	4	4	5	5	6	6	6	7	7	8	8	8	9	9	10	10	10	11	11	12	12	12	13	13	14	14	14	15	15	16	16	16	17		
0.126~0.150	0.005~0.006						1	1	1	2	2	3	3	3	4	4	5	5	5	6	6	7	7	7	8	8	9	9	9	10	10	11	11	11	12	12	13	13	13	14	14	15	15	15	16	16	17	17	17			
0.151~0.175	0.006~0.007					1	1	1	2	2	3	3	3	4	4	5	5	5	6	6	7	7	7	8	8	9	9	9	10	10	11	11	11	12	12	13	13	13	14	14	15	15	15	16	16	17	17	17	18			
0.176~0.200	0.007~0.008				1	1	2	2	2	3	3	4	4	4	5	5	6	6	6	7	7	8	8	8	9	9	10	10	10	11	11	12	12	12	13	13	14	14	14	15	15	16	16	16	17	17	18	18	18				
0.201~0.300	0.008~0.012	Replacement not to be required																																																
0.301~0.325	0.012~0.013	2	2	2	3	3	4	4	4	5	5	6	6	6	7	7	8	8	8	9	9	10	10	10	11	11	12	12	12	13	13	14	14	14	15	15	16	16	16	17	17	18	18	18	19	19				
0.326~0.350	0.013~0.014	2	3	3	3	4	4	5	5	5	6	6	7	7	7	8	8	9	9	9	10	10	11	11	11	12	12	13	13	13	14	14	15	15	15	16	16	17	17	17	18	18	19	19	19					
0.351~0.375	0.014~0.015	3	3	3	4	4	5	5	5	6	6	7	7	7	8	8	9	9	9	10	10	11	11	11	12	12	13	13	13	14	14	15	15	15	16	16	17	17	17	18	18	19	19	19						
0.376~0.400	0.015~0.016	3	4	4	4	5	5	6	6	6	7	7	8	8	8	9	9	10	10	10	11	11	12	12	12	13	13	14	14	14	15	15	16	16	16	17	17	18	18	18	19	19								
0.401~0.425	0.016~0.017	4	4	4	5	5	6	6	6	7	7	8	8	8	9	9	10	10	10	11	11	12	12	12	13	13	14	14	14	15	15	16	16	16	17	17	18	18	18	19	19									
0.426~0.450	0.017~0.018	4	5	5	5	6	6	7	7	7	8	8	9	9	9	10	10	11	11	11	12	12	13	13	13	14	14	15	15	15	16	16	17	17	17	18	18	19	19	19										
0.451~0.475	0.018~0.019	5	5	5	6	6	7	7	7	8	8	9	9	9	10	10	11	11	11	12	12	13	13	13	14	14	15	15	15	16	16	17	17	17	18	18	19	19	19											
0.476~0.500	0.019~0.020	5	6	6	6	7	7	8	8	8	9	9	10	10	10	11	11	12	12	12	13	13	14	14	14	15	15	16	16	16	17	17	18	18	18	19	19												
0.501~0.525	0.020~0.021	6	6	6	7	7	8	8	8	9	9	10	10	10	11	11	12	12	12	13	13	14	14	14	15	15	16	16	16	17	17	18	18	18	19	19													
0.526~0.550	0.021~0.022	6	7	7	7	8	8	9	9	9	10	10	11	11	11	12	12	13	13	13	14	14	15	15	15	16	16	17	17	17	18	18	19	19	19														
0.551~0.575	0.022~0.023	7	7	7	8	8	9	9	9	10	10	11	11	11	12	12	13	13	13	14	14	15	15	15	16	16	17	17	17	18	18	19	19	19															
0.576~0.600	0.023~0.024	7	8	8	8	9	9	10	10	10	11	11	12	12	12	13	13	14	14	14	15	15	16	16	16	17	17	18	18	18	19	19																	
0.601~0.625	0.024~0.025	8	8	8	9	9	10	10	10	11	11	12	12	12	13	13	14	14	14	15	15	16	16	16	17	17	18	18	18	19	19																		
0.626~0.650	0.025~0.026	8	9	9	9	10	10	11	11	11	12	12	13	13	13	14	14	15	15	15	16	16	17	17	17	18	18	19	19	19																			
0.651~0.675	0.026~0.027	9	9	9	10	10	11	11	11	12	12	13	13	13	14	14	15	15	15	16	16	17	17	17	18	18	19	19	19																				
0.676~0.700	0.027~0.028	9	10	10	10	11	11	12	12	12	13	13	14	14	14	15	15	16	16	16	17	17	18	18	18	19	19																						
0.701~0.725	0.028~0.029	10	10	10	11	11	12	12	12	13	13	14	14	14	15	15	16	16	16	17	17	18	18	18	19	19																							
0.726~0.750	0.029~0.030	10	11	11	11	12	12	13	13	13	14	14	15	15	15	16	16	17	17	17	18	18	19	19	19																								
0.751~0.775	0.030~0.031	11	11	11	12	12	13	13	13	14	14	15	15	15	16	16	17	17	17	18	18	19	19	19																									
0.776~0.800	0.031~0.032	11	12	12	12	13	13	14	14	14	15	15	16	16	16	17	17	18	18	18	19	19																											
0.801~0.825	0.032~0.033	12	12	12	13	13	14	14	14	15	15	16	16	16	17	17	18	18	18	19	19																												
0.826~0.850	0.033~0.034	12	13	13	13	14	14	15	15	15	16	16	17	17	17	18	18	19	19	19																													
0.851~0.875	0.034~0.035	13	13	13	14	14	15	15	15	16	16	17	17	17	18	18	19	19	19																														
0.876~0.900	0.035~0.036	13	14	14	14	15	15	16	16	16	17	17	18	18	18	19	19																																
0.901~0.925	0.036~0.037	14	14	14	15	15	16	16	16	17	17	18	18	18	19	19																																	
0.926~0.950	0.0365~0.0374	14	15	15	15	16	16	17	17	17	18	18	19	19	19																																		
0.951~0.975	0.037~0.038	15	15	15	16	16	17	17	17	18	18	19	19	19																																			
0.976~1.000	0.038~0.039	15	16	16	16	17	17	18	18	18	19	19																																					
1.001~1.025	0.039~0.040	16	16	16	17	17	18	18	18	19	19																																					
1.026~1.050	0.040~0.041	16	17	17	17	18	18	19	19	19																																						
1.051~1.075	0.041~0.042	17	17	17	18	18	19	19	19																																							
1.076~1.100	0.042~0.043	17	18	18	18	19	19																																									
1.101~1.125	0.043~0.044	18	18	18	19	19																																										
1.126~1.150	0.044~0.045	18	19	19	19																																											
1.151~1.175	0.045~0.046	19	19	19																																												
1.176~1.200	0.046~0.047	19																																														

Thickness of available adjuster (Shim)

NO in Chart	Thickness (mm)	NO in Chart	Thickness (mm)
1	2.55	11	3.05
2	2.60	12	3.10
3	2.65	13	3.15
4	2.70	14	3.20
5	2.75	15	3.25
6	2.80	16	3.30
7	2.85	17	3.35
8	2.90	18	3.40
9	2.95	19	3.45
10	3.00		

Note; Thickness mark is printed on the surface to be contacted with tappet.

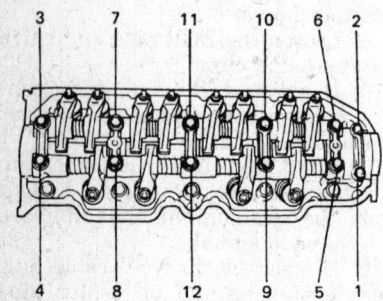

Rocker arm shaft bolt torque sequence — 1.6L SOHC engine

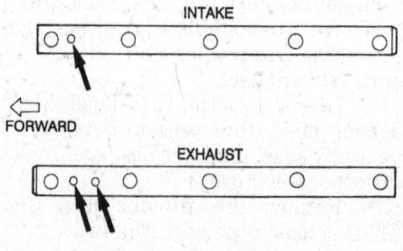

Rocker arm shaft positioning — 1.6L SOHC engines

13. Remove the EGR transducer and the VSV bracket.

14. Disconnect the fuel lines. Remove the fuel injector harness and the fuel rail with the fuel injectors.

15. Remove the intake manifold.

To install:

16. Clean the intake manifold mating surfaces.

17. Install the intake manifold using a new gaskets. Torque the manifold retaining bolts and nuts to 17 ft. lbs. (24 Nm).

18. Install the remaining components by reversing their removal procedures. Reconnect all wiring, hoses and cables to the original location.

19. Reconnect the negative battery cable. Start the engine and check for leaks.

1.8L DOHC Engine

1. Disconnect the negative battery cable.

2. Disconnect the ground cable terminals from the common chamber. Remove the 2 cable harness connectors, MAT sensor connector and accelerator cable from the throttle valve assembly.

3. Disconnect the air intake duct.

4. Disconnect the PCV hose, MAP sensor hose, fuel pressure regulator vacuum hose, the canister hoses and the vacuum booster hose.

5. Remove the canister pipes and the MAP sensor pipe with the bracket.

6. Disconnect the heating hoses and throttle valve assembly from the common chamber.

7. Remove the fuel pipe bracket retaining bolts at the intake manifold.

8. Remove the EGR valve retaining bolts from the exhaust manifold.

9. Remove the EGR pipe retaining bolts from the exhaust manifold.

10. Remove the EGR pipe bracket retaining bolt from the water inlet manifold with the ground cable. Remove the EGR valve.

11. Disconnect the ground cable from the manifold.

12. Disconnect the vacuum booster hose.

13. Disconnect the fuel return pipe bracket from the manifold.

14. Disconnect the oil cooler pipe bracket from under the intake manifold.

15. Remove the manifold retaining bolts from the front and rear side of the intake manifold.

16. Remove the 3 injector harness clips from the intake manifold.

17. Remove the 7 bolts and 2 nuts, then remove the intake manifold.

To install:

18. Clean the intake manifold mating surfaces.

19. Install the intake manifold using a new gaskets. Torque the manifold retaining bolts and nuts to 17 ft. lbs. (24 Nm).

20. Install the remaining components by reversing their removal procedures. Reconnect all wiring, hoses and cables to the original location.

21. Reconnect the negative battery cable. Start the engine and check for leaks.

Exhaust Manifold

REMOVAL AND INSTALLATION

———— **CAUTION** ————
Perform this operation only after components are cool. Exhaust components operate at very high temperatures and can cause serious burns.

Exc. Turbocharged Engines

1. Disconnect the negative battery cable.

2. Disconnect the oxygen sensor connector and the EGR pipe.

3. Remove the heat protector.

4. Raise and safely support the vehicle.

5. Disconnect the exhaust pipe from the exhaust manifold.

6. Lower the vehicle.

7. Remove the exhaust manifold nuts and the exhaust manifold.

To install:

8. Check the manifold for cracks or other damage. Check the manifold for flatness using a straight-edge and feeler gauge. The manifold must be replaced if the warpage exceeds 0.016 in. (0.4mm).

9. Installation is the reverse of the removal procedure. Make sure all

gasket mating surfaces are clean prior to installation.

10. Tighten the manifold mounting nuts to 30 ft. lbs. (39 Nm). 17 ft. lbs. (23 Nm) for the SOHC engine.

Turbocharged Engines

1. Disconnect the negative battery cable.

2. Drain the engine coolant.

3. Remove the intercooler, left and right undercovers, front exhaust pipe from the manifold and intake ducts from turbocharger. Remove the power steering pump and position aside. Do not disconnect the power steering pump lines.

4. Remove the bracket from the wastegate and heat protector from the turbocharger.

5. Disconnect the turbocharger coolant and oil lines.

6. Remove the bracket from the manifold converter.

7. Remove the EGR pipe and clip.

8. Remove the exhaust manifold with the turbocharger and manifold converter as an assembly.

9. Remove all components from the manifold.

To install:

10. Make sure all gasket mating surfaces are clean prior to installation.

11. Install the manifold and turbocharger and torque the bolts to 43 ft. lbs. (59 Nm).

12. Install the wastegate manifold and torque the bolts to 21 ft. lbs. (28 Nm).

13. Install the EGR pipe and torque to 21 ft. lbs. (28 Nm).

14. Install all wiring, hoses and cables.

15. Reconnect the negative battery cable. Start the engine and check for leaks.

Turbocharger

REMOVAL AND INSTALLATION

———— **CAUTION** ————
Perform this operation only after components are cool. Exhaust components operate at very high temperatures and can cause serious burns.

1.6L Engine

1. Disconnect the negative battery cable.

2. Remove the exhaust manifold.

3. Disconnect the coolant pipe and the oil pipe from the turbocharger.

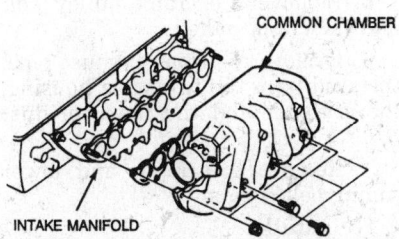

Intake manifold and common chamber — 1.6L DOHC engine

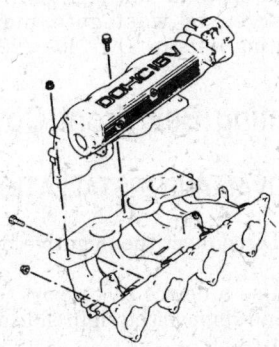

Common chamber and intake manifold — 1.8L DOHC engine

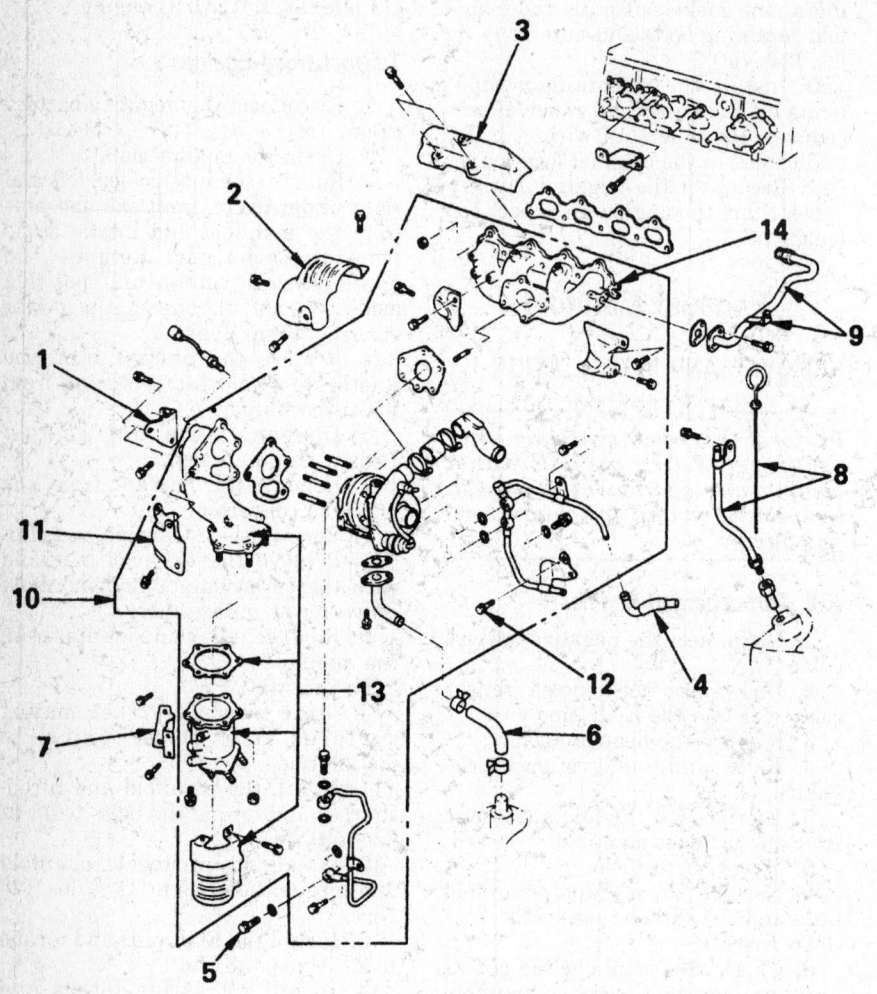

1. Bracket from wastegate manifold
2. Heat protector from turbocharger
3. Upper heat protector from exhaust manifold
4. Turbocharger coolant hose from coolant pipe
5. Turbocharger oil feed pipe joint bolt from cylinder block
6. Turbocharger oil return hose from turbocharger
7. Bracket from manifold convertor
8. Oil level gauge and guide tube from cylinder block
9. EGR pipe and clip
10. Exhaust manifold with turbocharger and manifold convertor
11. Heat protector from wastegate manifold
12. Coolant pipe bracket fixing bolts from exhaust manifold
13. Wastegate manifold with manifold convertor from turbocharger
14. Exhaust manifold

Exhaust manifold and turbocharger assembly — 1.6L turbocharged engine

4. Remove the turbocharger assembly.

To install:

5. Before reinstalling the turbocharger, connect a pressure gauge and make sure the pressure is 597-694mm Hg with the control rod moved 2mm.

6. Install the pressure gauge to the wastegate and apply approximately 560mm Hg to the wastegate. The rod should begin to move when this pressure is applied. Do not allow the pressure applied to the wastegate to exceed 720mm Hg.

7. Installation is the reverse of the removal procedure. Make sure all gasket mating surfaces are clean prior to installation. Tighten the turbocharger to wastegate manifold mounting nuts to 21 ft. lbs. (29 Nm).

Timing Belt Front Cover

REMOVAL AND INSTALLATION

1. Disconnect the negative battery cable.

2. Use a device to support the engine and remove the right side engine mount.

3. Remove the necessary accessory drive belts.

4. Remove the right side engine mounting bridge bracket and the torque rod.

5. Remove the crank pulley bolt and the crank pulley.

6. Remove the front exhaust pipe, the stud from the transaxle housing, the stiffener and the flywheel dust cover.

7. Remove the upper and lower timing belt covers.

To install:

8. Install the front cover and gaskets.

9. Tighten the timing belt cover bolts to 89 inch lbs. (10 Nm). Tighten

the crank pulley bolt to 109 ft. lbs. (147 Nm).

OIL SEAL REPLACEMENT

1. Disconnect the negative battery cable.
2. Remove the timing belt cover and the timing belt.
3. Use an extractor tool to remove the crankshaft timing sprocket.
4. Remove the oil seal using a removal tool.
5. Lubricate the lip of a new oil seal and install it using a suitable installation tool.
6. Install the remaining components in the reverse order of their removal.

Timing Belt and Tensioner

ADJUSTMENT

1.6L SOHC Engines

1. Disconnect the negative battery cable.
2. Remove the timing belt cover.
3. Loosen the tension pulley bolt.
4. Insert an Allen wrench into the tension pulley hexagonal hole. Hold the pulley stationary and temporarily tighten the bolt.
5. Turn the crankshaft 2 complete revolutions in the reverse direction of normal rotation (counterclockwise) and align the crankshaft timing sprocket groove with the mark on the oil pump.
6. Loosen the tension pulley bolt and apply tension to the belt.
7. Insert the Allen wrench into the tension pulley hexagonal hole. Hold the pulley stationary and tighten the bolt to 37 ft. lbs. (51 Nm).
8. Move the crankshaft back to about 50 degrees BTDC. Turn the crankshaft 2 complete revolutions in the reverse direction of normal rotation and align the crank timing sprocket groove with the mark on the oil pump.
9. Use a belt tension gauge to check the timing belt tension. The tension should be 39.6-48.4 lbs. (18-22 kg).

1.6L and 1.8L DOHC Engines

1. Disconnect the negative battery cable.
2. Remove the timing belt covers.
3. Loosen the tensioner bolt.

NOTE: On used belts, do not tension with other than the spring force applied. When a new belt is used, push the tension pulley in the direction of belt tension.

4. Tighten the tensioner bolt to 31 ft. lbs. (42 Nm).
5. Turn the crankshaft 2 complete revolutions and align the crankshaft and camshaft sprocket timing marks correctly.
6. Turn the crankshaft 60 degrees and measure the deflection of the belt. Deflection is measured with a down force of 22 lbs. (10 kg) applied to the timing belt at a point between the camshaft sprockets. The deflection should be 0.28-0.33 in. (7-8.5mm) for a new belt or 0.35-0.41 in. (9-10.5mm) for a used belt.

REMOVAL AND INSTALLATION

1.6L SOHC Engines

1. Disconnect the negative battery cable.
2. Remove the timing belt cover.
3. Bring the piston in No. 4 cylinder to TDC on the compression stroke. The crankshaft sprocket timing mark should be aligned with the triangular mark on the oil pump housing. The notch on the camshaft sprocket should be aligned with the left upper corner of the cylinder head, with the dowel pin in the up position.
4. Remove the crank pulley bolt and the crank pulley, being careful not to disturb the position of the crankshaft.
5. Loosen the bolts retaining the tension pulley. Using a suitable Allen wrench, turn the tension pulley clockwise and relieve the tension on the timing belt.
6. Mark the direction of rotation on the timing belt and remove the timing belt from the vehicle.
To install:
7. If a new belt is used, set the letters marked on the belt in the direction of engine rotation. If the old belt is used, install it in the same direction as before, as indicated by the mark that was made during the removal procedure.
8. Install the belt over the crankshaft sprocket, camshaft sprocket, water pump pulley and tension pulley, in that order.

NOTE: There must be no slack in the belt after it has been installed. The teeth of the belt and the teeth of the pulley must be in perfect alignment.

9. Properly tension the timing belt.
10. Install the crankshaft pulley hub with the taper face to the belt. Tighten the crank pulley bolt to 108 ft. lbs. (150 Nm).
11. Install the remainder of the components in the reverse order of their removal.

1.6L and 1.8L DOHC Engines

1. Disconnect the negative battery cable.
2. Remove the timing belt cover.
3. Rotate the crankshaft to align the timing marks. The mark on the crankshaft timing sprocket should be aligned with the triangular mark on the oil pump. The keyway should be at the top of the crankshaft, towards the cylinder head. The marks on the camshaft sprockets should be directly across from each other and aligned with the top edge of the cylinder head.
4. Loosen the tension pulley attaching bolt ½ turn. Insert a hex wrench into the tension pulley hexagonal hole and loosen the timing belt by rotating the tension pulley.
5. Mark the rotational direction of the timing belt and remove it from the vehicle.
To install:
6. Make sure the timing marks are still in alignment.

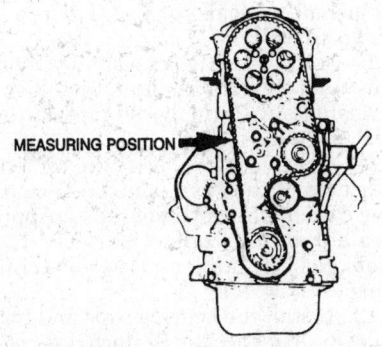

Timing belt tension measuring position — 1.6L SOHC Engines

MEASURING POSITION

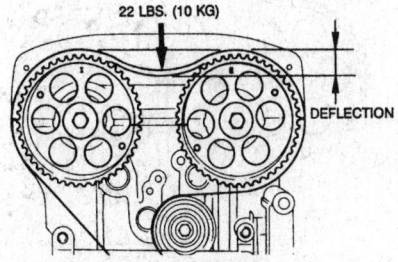

22 LBS. (10 KG)

DEFLECTION

Timing belt deflection measuring position — 1.6L and 1.8L DOHC engines

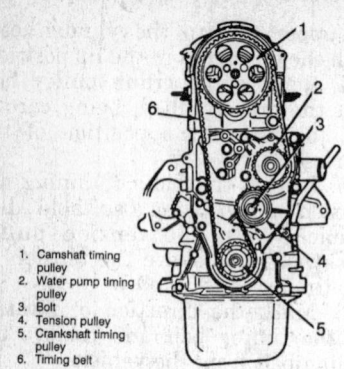

1. Camshaft timing pulley
2. Water pump timing pulley
3. Bolt
4. Tension pulley
5. Crankshaft timing pulley
6. Timing belt

Timing belt installed — 1.6L SOHC engines

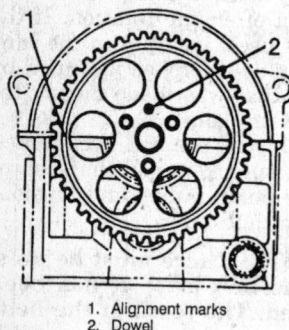

1. Alignment marks
2. Dowel

Camshaft sprocket alignment — 1.6L SOHC engines

CYLINDER HEAD SIDE

ENGINE ROTATION DIRECTION

ISUZU

TIMING BELT

New timing belt positioning — 1.6L SOHC engines

7. Lock the camshaft sprockets in position by inserting 6mm bolts through the camshaft sprockets and into the cylinder heads.

8. Install the timing belt. A new belt is installed correctly if the lettering can be read while viewing it from the passenger side fender. If the old belt is being used, it must be installed in the same direction as was marked during the removal procedure. The belt must be installed in the following order:

a. Crankshaft timing sprocket.
b. Water pump pulley.

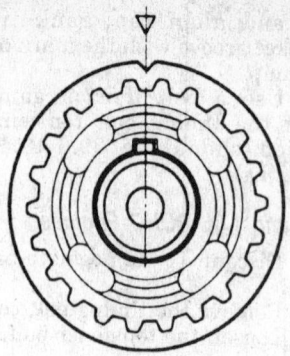

Crankshaft sprocket alignment

c. Idler pulley.
d. Exhaust camshaft sprocket.
e. Intake camshaft sprocket.
f. Tensioner pulley.

NOTE: There must be no slack in the belt after it has been installed. The teeth of the belt and the teeth of the sprocket must be in perfect alignment.

9. Properly tension the belt.
10. Install the remainder of the components in the reverse order of their removal.

Timing Sprockets

REMOVAL AND INSTALLATION

1. Disconnect the negative battery cable.
2. Remove the timing belt cover and the timing belt.
3. Use an extractor tool to remove the crankshaft sprocket.
4. Remove the camshaft sprocket retaining bolt(s) and the camshaft sprocket(s).
5. Installation is the reverse of the removal procedure. Tighten the camshaft sprocket retaining bolt(s) to 43 ft. lbs. (59 Nm).

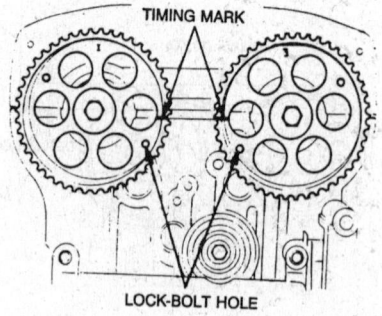

TIMING MARK

LOCK-BOLT HOLE

Aligning the camshaft sprocket timing marks — 1.6L and 1.8L DOHC engines

Camshaft

REMOVAL AND INSTALLATION

1.6L SOHC Engines

1. Disconnect the negative battery cable.
2. Remove the cylinder head cover.
3. Remove the timing belt cover.
4. Align the timing marks properly and remove the timing belt.
5. Mark the position of the distributor rotor in relation to the distributor housing. Mark the distributor housing in relation to the cylinder head. Remove the distributor.
6. Remove the camshaft sprocket.
7. Remove the rocker arm shafts and remove the camshaft and seal.

To install:

8. Lubricate the camshaft thoroughly. Install the camshaft with the dowel pin in the UP position.
9. Lubricate the lip of a new camshaft seal and install it.
10. Properly tension the timing belt, adjust the valve lash and check the ignition timing.

1.6L and 1.8L DOHC Engines

1. Disconnect the negative battery cable.
2. Remove the valve cover.
3. Bring the piston in the No. 1 cylinder to TDC on the compression stroke.
4. Remove the timing belt cover.
5. Loosen the camshaft sprocket bolts and loosen the timing belt tension.
6. Remove the camshaft sprockets.
7. Mark the position of the distributor rotor in relation to the distributor housing and the distributor housing in relation to the cylinder head. Remove the distributor.
8. Remove the camshaft bearing caps working from the outside caps toward the center of the cylinder head.
9. Remove the camshafts and camshaft oil seals.

To install:

10. Lubricate the camshafts thoroughly before installation. Install the camshafts with the dowel pins in the UP position.
11. Remove any oil from the contact surfaces of the No. 1 and No. 5 bearing caps and the cylinder head. Apply sealant to the contact surfaces. Do not get sealant on the bearing surface.
12. Install the bearing caps and torque in sequence to 89 inch lbs. (10 Nm). Adjust the valve clearance using the appropriate shims.

13. Lubricate the sealing lip of the new camshaft seals. Install the seals using a tool of the proper size.

14. Properly tension the timing belt and check the ignition timing.

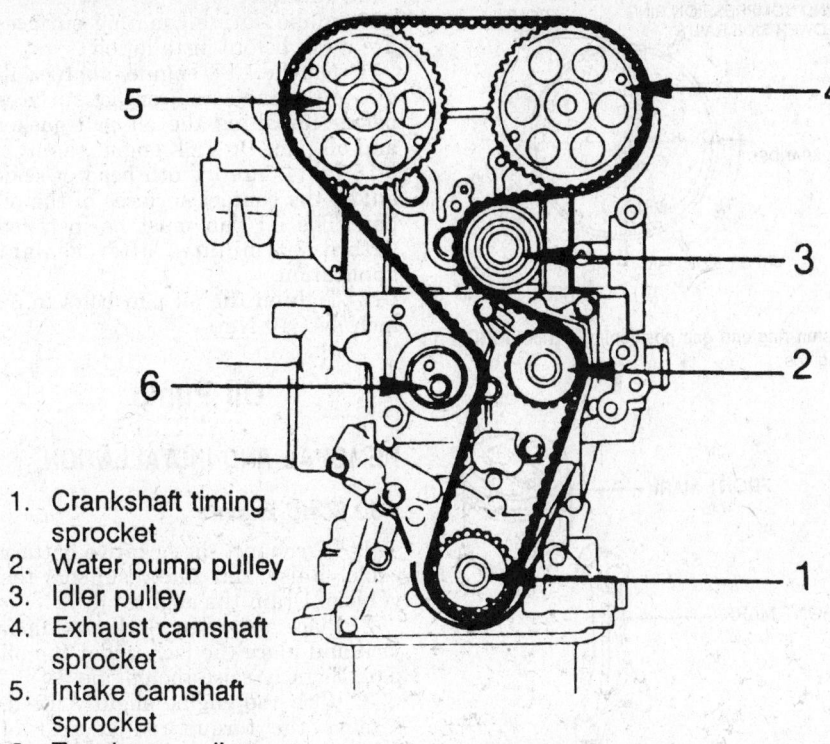

1. Crankshaft timing sprocket
2. Water pump pulley
3. Idler pulley
4. Exhaust camshaft sprocket
5. Intake camshaft sprocket
6. Tensioner pulley.

Timing belt installed — 1.6L and 1.8L DOHC engines

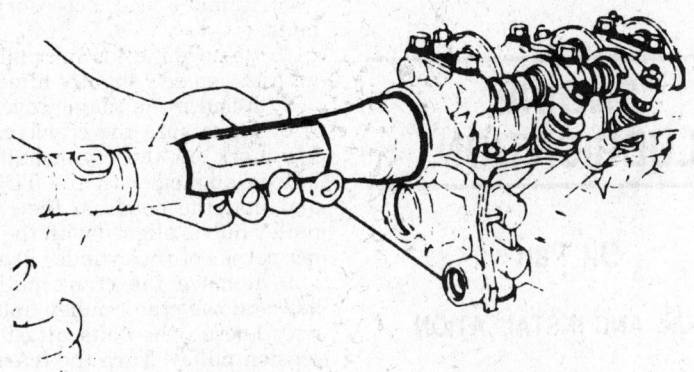

Installing the camshaft oil seal — 1.6L SOHC engines

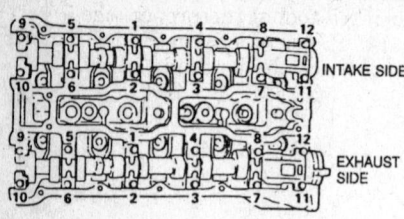

Camshaft bearing cap torque sequence — 1.6L DOHC engine

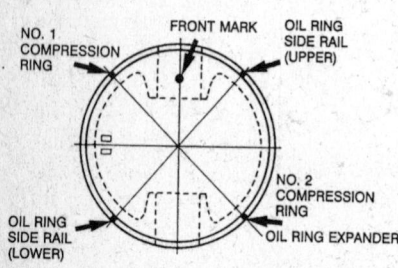

Sealant application points — 1.6L DOHC engine

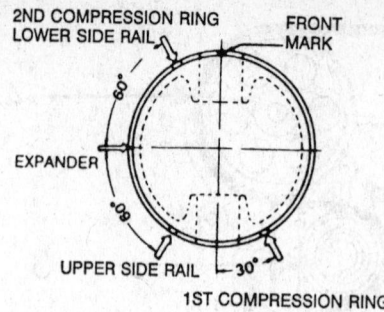

Piston ring end gap positioning — 1.6L SOHC engines

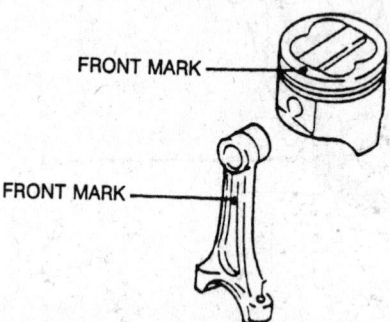

Piston and connecting rod alignment: marks toward front of engine

ENGINE LUBRICATION

Oil Pan

REMOVAL AND INSTALLATION

1. Disconnect the negative battery cable.
2. Raise and safely support the vehicle.
3. Drain the engine oil and replace the drain plug.
4. Remove the torque rod and stiffener.
5. Remove the engine splash shield.
6. Remove the exhaust header pipe, if necessary.
7. Remove the flywheel dust shield.
8. Remove the oil pan retaining bolts.
9. If required, raise the engine to provide sufficient room for the oil pan removal. Remove the pan from the vehicle.

To install:

10. Make sure all mating surfaces are clean before installation.
11. On the 1.8L engine, apply sealant to the indicated contact surfaces before installing the oil pan gasket and oil pan. On 1.6L engine, apply a 0.18 in. (4.5mm) width bead of sealant to the contact surfaces of the oil pan. The oil pan must be installed within 30 minutes after sealant application.
12. Tighten the oil pan bolts to 89 inch lbs. (10 Nm).

Oil Pump

REMOVAL AND INSTALLATION

1.6L SOHC Engines

1. Disconnect the negative battery cable. Raise and safely support the vehicle. Drain the engine oil.
2. Place a wooden block on a floor jack and place the jack under the oil pan. Slightly raise the engine.
3. With the engine slightly lifted, remove the torque rod at rear of engine.
4. Remove the right side engine mount, then remove the body side bracket and the engine side bracket.
5. Remove the accessory drive belts.
6. Remove the 4 crank pulley bolts with the engine slightly lifted.
7. Remove the timing cover.
8. Make sure the crankshaft timing mark on the crankshaft pulley hub is aligned with the TDC mark and that the notch on the camshaft pulley hub is aligned with the left upper corner of the cylinder head.
9. Remove the crank pulley hub bolt and the crank pulley hub.
10. Loosen the bolts attaching the tension pulley. Turn the tension pulley clockwise with an Allen wrench, then remove the timing belt.
11. Use an extractor tool to remove the crankshaft timing sprocket.
12. Temporarily reinstall the right side engine mount brackets and mount. Lower the engine. Remove the jack and remove the oil pan.
13. Remove the oil pump retaining bolts and remove the oil pump assembly.
14. Check the outside of the oil pump assembly for cracking or other damage. Disassemble the oil pump and check the gears and housing for wear and proper clearance. Replace as necessary.

To install:

15. Make sure all mating surfaces are clean before installation.

Piston and Connecting Rod

POSITIONING

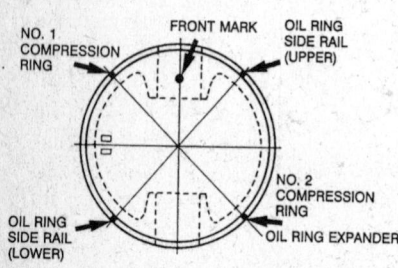

Piston ring end gap positioning — 1.6L and 1.8L DOHC engines

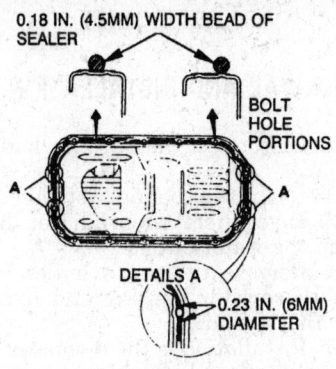

Oil pan sealer application — 1.6L engine

16. Apply oil to the sealing lip of the oil seal and apply sealant to the pump fitting face.

17. Install the pump and tighten the retaining bolts to 7.2 ft. lbs. (10 Nm).

18. Install the timing cover and torque the bolts to 15 ft. lbs. (20 Nm).

19. Install all wiring, hoses and cables.

20. Start the engine and check for leaks.

1.6L and 1.8L DOHC Engines

1. Disconnect the negative battery cable. Raise and safely support the vehicle. Drain the engine oil.

2. Remove the timing belt cover and the timing belt.

3. Remove the crankshaft timing sprocket using a tool.

4. Remove the oil pan.

5. Remove the oil pump bolts and the oil pump.

To install:

6. Check the outside of the oil pump assembly for cracking or other damage. Disassemble the oil pump and check the gears and housing for wear and proper clearance. Replace as necessary.

7. Installation is the reverse of the removal procedure. Make sure all mating surfaces are clean prior to installation.

8. Apply sealant to the oil pump fitting face, being careful not to get sealant on the oil ports. Apply engine oil to the oil seal lip and install the pump. Tighten the pump mounting bolts to 17 ft. lbs. (24 Nm).

Rear Main Bearing Oil Seal

REMOVAL AND INSTALLATION

1. Disconnect the negative battery cable.

2. Raise and safely support the vehicle.

3. Drain the engine oil and replace the drain plug.

4. Remove the transaxle assembly.

5. If equipped with manual transmission, remove the clutch assembly.

6. Remove the flywheel.

7. Remove the oil pan.

8. Remove the rear oil seal retainer bolts and remove the oil seal retainer.

9. Remove the seal from the retainer.

To install:

10. Make sure all mating surfaces are clean prior to installation.

11. Use an installation tool to install a new seal in the retainer.

12. Apply sealant to the seal retainer mounting surface and oil to the lip of the seal and install the retainer, aligning it with the dowel pins.

13. Install the remaining components by reversing their removal procedures.

14. Lower the vehicle. Reconnect the negative battery cable. Start the engine and check for leaks.

ENGINE COOLING

Radiator

REMOVAL AND INSTALLATION

1. Disconnect the negative battery cable.

2. Remove the radiator cap and loosen the drain plug to drain the radiator.

3. Disconnect the fan motor and thermo switch connectors.

4. Disconnect the radiator and surge tank hoses from the radiator.

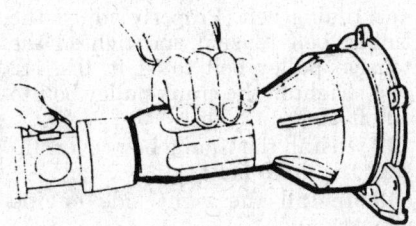

Installing rear main bearing oil seal

5. Disconnect the transaxle cooler hoses, if equipped.

6. Remove the radiator mounting bolts and the radiator and fan assembly.

7. Separate the cooling fan from the radiator.

8. Installation is the reverse of the removal procedure. Fill the radiator with enough water and anti-freeze to provide the required cooling, freezing and corrosion protection.

Heater Core

——— CAUTION ———
Always disarm the SIR system, when working on or around the steering column. Failure to disarm the SIR system, may result in deployment of the air bag and possible personal injury. To disarm the Supplemental Inflatable Restraint (SIR) system, disconnect and tape the negative battery cable.

REMOVAL AND INSTALLATION

Without Air conditioning

1. Disconnect the negative battery cable.

2. Drain the engine coolant into a container.

3. Disconnect the heater hoses. Be careful not to damage the core by pulling on the hose to remove. Cut the hoses if they will not come off easily.

4. Remove the instrument panel.

5. Disconnect the resistor assembly.

6. Remove the duct.

7. Remove the center vent duct and heater unit.

8. Disassemble the heater unit by removing the duct, mode control case, core assembly and heater core.

To install:

9. Install the heater core, making sure all the seals are in place.

10. Assemble the heater unit, making sure all the seals are in place.

11. Install the center vent duct and heater unit.

12. Install the duct.

13. Connect the resistor assembly.

14. Install the instrument panel.

15. Connect the heater hoses. Be careful not to damage the core by pulling on the hose to remove. Cut the hoses if they will not come off easily.

16. Refill the engine coolant.

17. Connect the negative battery cable and check for leaks.

With Air Conditioning

1. Disconnect the negative battery cable.

2. Drain the cooling system and properly discharge the air conditioning system.

3. Remove the instrument panel as follows:

   a. Pull the switch bezel out and disconnect the switch connectors.

   b. Pull the cigarette lighter bezel out and disconnect the electrical connectors, then remove the bezel.

   c. Disconnect the engine hood opener cable.

   d. Remove the knee pad assembly.

   e. Remove the 2 hinge pins from inside the glove box and remove the glove box.

   f. Remove the front console bracket.

   g. Remove the instrument cluster hood and the instrument cluster.

   h. Remove the front hole covers and the front cover.

   i. Remove the instrument panel assembly.

4. Disconnect and plug the heater hoses at the heater core.

5. Disconnect the resistor connector.

6. Disconnect and plug the air conditioning lines at the evaporator.

7. Disconnect the hose and the electrical connectors at the evaporator.

8. Remove the 3 mounting nuts and the evaporator.

9. Remove the center ventilator duct.

10. Remove the heater unit.

11. Disassemble the heater unit and remove the heater core.

To install:

12. Assemble the heater unit.

13. Install the heater unit into the vehicle.

14. Install the center ventilator duct.

15. Install the 3 mounting nuts and the evaporator.

16. Connect the hose and the electrical connectors at the evaporator.

17. Reconnect the air conditioning lines at the evaporator.

18. Connect the resistor connector.

19. Connect the heater hoses at the heater core.

20. Install the instrument panel as follows:

   a. Install the instrument panel assembly.

   b. Install the front hole covers and the front cover.

   c. Install the instrument cluster and hood.

   d. Install the front console bracket.

   e. Install the 2 hinge pins to the inside of the glove box.

   f. Install the knee pad assembly.

   g. Connect the engine hood opener cable.

   h. Install the cigarette lighter and bezel.

   i. Install the switch bezel.

21. Connect the negative battery cable.

22. Fill and bleed the cooling system. Evacuate and recharge the air conditioning system.

Water Pump

REMOVAL AND INSTALLATION

1. Disconnect the negative battery cable.

2. Drain the cooling system.

3. Place a wooden block on a floor jack and support the engine under the oil pan.

4. Remove the right side engine mount.

5. Remove the drive belts.

6. Remove the crank pulley and the timing cover.

7. Bring the No. 1 cylinder to TDC.

8. Loosen the tension pulley lock bolt, turn the tension pulley clockwise and remove the timing belt.

9. Remove the water pump.

To install:

10. Make sure all gasket mating surfaces are clean prior to installation. Install the water pump using a new gasket. Tighten the water pump mounting bolts to 17 ft. lbs. (24 Nm).

11. Install the tensioner assembly and timing belt. Properly adjust the timing belt tension and tighten the tension pulley bolt to 31 ft. lbs. (42 Nm). Tighten the crank pulley bolt to 109 ft. lbs. (147 Nm).

12. Install the timing belt cover. Install the drive belts.

13. Install the right side engine mount.

14. Reconnect the negative battery cable.

15. Fill and bleed the cooling system.

Thermostat

REMOVAL AND INSTALLATION

1. Disconnect the negative battery cable.

2. Drain the cooling system.

3. Disconnect the radiator hose from the water outlet.

4. Remove the water outlet from the thermostat housing and remove the thermostat.

5. Installation is the reverse of the removal procedure. Make sure all gasket mating surfaces are clean prior to installation. Install the thermostat with the jiggle valve toward the water outlet and the spring toward the thermostat housing.

COOLING SYSTEM BLEEDING

1. Make sure the engine and radiator are cold before proceeding.

2. Remove the radiator cap and the coolant reserve tank cap.

3. Check that the radiator is full to the base of the filler neck and the coolant reserve tank is filled to a level between the MAX and MIN lines. Add coolant, as necessary.

4. Block the drive wheels and apply the parking brake. Place the transmission in **P** (automatic transmissions) or neutral (manual transmission).

5. Run the engine, with the radiator cap removed, until the upper radiator hose is hot. With the engine idling, add coolant to the radiator until it is full. Install the radiator cap.

6. Allow the engine to cool down to outside air temperature and check the coolant level in the coolant reservoir. The coolant level should be at the MAX mark. Add coolant, as necessary.

ENGINE ELECTRICAL

NOTE: Disconnecting the negative battery cable on some vehicles may interfere with the functions of the on-board computer systems and may require the computer to undergo a relearning process, once the negative battery cable is reconnected.

Distributor

REMOVAL

NOTE: The 1.6L DOHC turbocharged engine does not have a distributor. The engine is equipped with a Direct Ignition System (DIS). The cam angle sensor is removed in the same manner as the conventional distributor.

1. Turn the engine over and bring the No. 1 piston up to TDC on the compression stroke.
2. Disconnect the negative battery cable.
3. Remove the distributor cap and disconnect the electrical connectors from the distributor.
4. Mark the position of the distributor rotor in relation to the distributor housing and the distributor housing in relation to the cylinder head or block.
5. Remove the distributor hold-down bolt and remove the distributor.

INSTALLATION

Timing Not Disturbed

1. Install the distributor, aligning the marks that were made during the removal procedure.
2. Install the distributor hold-down bolt and tighten temporarily.
3. Connect the distributor electrical connectors and install the distributor cap.
4. Connect the negative battery cable, start the engine, check the ignition timing and adjust as necessary. Tighten the distributor hold-down bolt.

Timing Disturbed

1. Disconnect the spark plug wire and remove the spark plug from the No. 1 cylinder.
2. Place a finger over the spark plug hole and rotate the crankshaft until compression is felt.
3. Align the notched line on the crankshaft pulley with the 0 mark on the timing scale of the timing cover.
4. Install the distributor so the distributor rotor points to the No. 1 spark plug wire tower of the distributor cap.
5. Install the distributor hold-down bolt and tighten temporarily.

6. Connect the distributor electrical connectors and install the distributor cap.
7. Install the No. 1 spark plug and connect the No. 1 spark plug wire.
8. Connect the negative battery cable, start the engine and adjust the ignition timing. Tighten the distributor hold-down bolt.

Cam Angle Sensor

REMOVAL

1. Rotate the engine and bring up the No. 1 cylinder to top dead center of its compression stroke.

NOTE: To bring the engine to TDC of the No. 1 compression stroke, remove the spark plug for the No. 1 cylinder. With the engine cool, turn the crankshaft over until compression is forced out of the spark plug hole. Watch the crankshaft damper while feeling for compression. When compression is felt, align the mark on the crankshaft damper with the 0 degree mark on the timing cover.

2. Disconnect the negative battery cable.
3. Remove the intercooler and disconnect the sensor electrical connector.
4. Mark the cylinder block and camshaft angle sensor before removing. Remove the mounting bolt and cam angle sensor.

INSTALLATION

1. Install the sensor to its original position and install the mounting bolt.

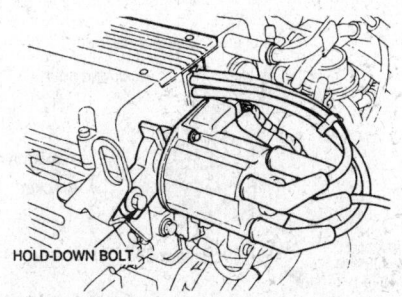

Distributor location — 1.6L Non-turbocharged engine

2. Connect the wiring connectors.
3. Install the intercooler and connect the battery cable.
4. Start the engine and adjust the timing.

Ignition Timing

ADJUSTMENT

NOTE: The timing marks are located at the front of the crankshaft pulley. They consist of a graduated scale attached to the timing cover and a notch in the crankshaft pulley.

NOTE: The 1.6L DOHC turbocharged engine is equipped with a Direct Ignition System. Timing can be adjusted by moving the cam angle sensor. The sensor is mounted in the same location as a conventional distributor for non-turbocharged engines.

1. Apply the parking brake and start the engine.
2. Place the transaxle in N.
3. Make sure the CHECK ENGINE light is not ON.
4. Locate the ALDL connector under the right hand side of the instrument panel. Connect the terminals 1 and 3 on both ends of the ALDL connector with a jumper wire.
5. Connect the timing light lead to the No. 1 spark plug wire.
6. Using the timing light, check that the center of fluctuation of a white notched line on the crankshaft pulley against the scale on the timing cover is between 9-11 degrees BTDC. If the fluctuation is too large, open the throttle valve a little to increase the engine speed to 1500-2000 rpm. The fluctuation will be reduced so the timing can be confirmed.
7. If the timing is incorrect, loosen the hold-down bolt on the distributor or cam angle sensor and turn the assembly clockwise or counterclockwise to adjust the timing. After adjustment, tighten the bolt to 17 ft. lbs. (24 Nm).

NOTE: When tightening the distributor or cam angle sensor hold-down bolt, make sure the assembly body does not rotate together with the mounting bolt.

8. Turn the ignition switch OFF and remove the jumper wire from the ALDL connector.

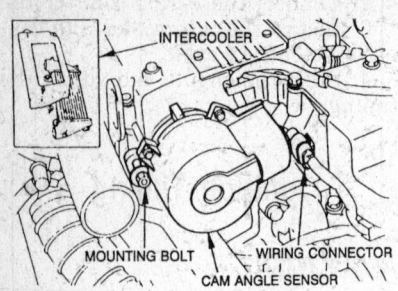

Camshaft angle sensor — 1.6L DOHC
Turbocharged engine

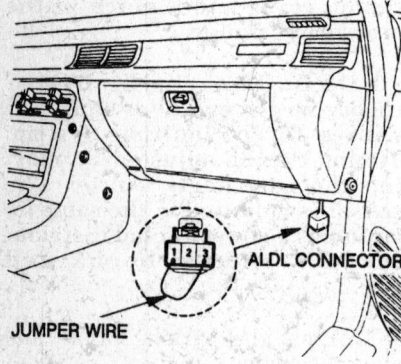

ALDL connector location

Alternator

PRECAUTIONS

Several precautions must be observed with alternator-equipped vehicles to avoid damage to the unit.

• If the battery is removed for any reason, make sure it is reconnected with the correct polarity. Reversing the battery connections may result in damage to the one-way rectifiers.

• When utilizing a booster battery as a starting aid, always connect the positive to positive terminals and the negative terminal from the booster battery to a good engine ground on the vehicle being started.

• Never use a fast charger as a booster to start vehicles.

• Disconnect the battery cables when charging the battery with a fast charger.

• Never attempt to polarize the alternator.

• Do not use test lamps of more than 12 volts when checking diode continuity.

• Do not short across or ground any of the alternator terminals.

• The polarity of the battery, alternator and regulator must be matched

and considered before making any electrical connections within the system.

• Never disconnect the battery with the engine operating.

• Disconnect the battery ground terminal when performing any service on electrical components.

• Disconnect the battery if arc welding is to be done on the vehicle.

BELT TENSION ADJUSTMENT

1. Check the belt tension between the pulleys using a belt tension gauge. The tension should be 70-110 lbs. (95-149 N).

2. If the tension is incorrect, loosen the alternator pivot and adjusting bolts. Pry on the alternator until the proper belt tension is obtained.

REMOVAL AND INSTALLATION

1. Disconnect the negative battery cable.

2. Remove the right tie rod end, lower ball joint and driveshaft (4WD only).

3. Remove the adjuster plate bolt.

4. Disconnect the electrical connector.

5. Remove the alternator bracket bolts, alternator and bracket.

To install:

6. Install the alternator bracket bolts, alternator and bracket.

7. Connect the electrical connector.

8. Install the adjuster plate bolt.

9. Install the right tie rod end, lower ball joint and driveshaft (4WD only).

10. Connect the negative battery cable.

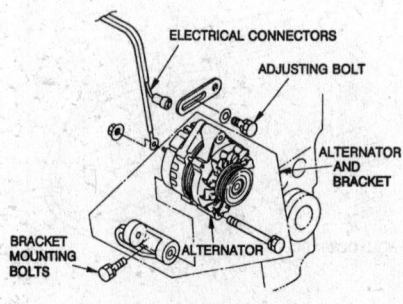

Alternator installation

Starter

REMOVAL AND INSTALLATION

1. Disconnect the negative battery cable.

2. Disconnect the electrical connectors at the starter.

3. Remove the starter mounting nuts or bolts and remove the starter.

4. Installation is the reverse of the removal procedure.

EMISSION CONTROLS

Emission Warning Lamps

Isuzu vehicles do not employ emission warning lamps that would indicate scheduled component replacement. A CHECK ENGINE lamp is used to indicate component malfunction. When the CHECK ENGINE lamp comes ON, the vehicle should be checked as soon as possible. Use the proper diagnostic procedures to locate the malfunction.

FUEL SYSTEM

Fuel System Service Precautions

Safety is the most important factor when performing not only fuel system maintenance but any type of maintenance. Failure to conduct maintenance and repairs in a safe manner may result in serious personal injury or death. Maintenance and testing of the vehicle's fuel system components can be accomplished safely and effectively by adhering to the following rules and guidelines.

• To avoid the possibility of fire and personal injury, always disconnect the negative battery cable unless the repair or test procedure requires that battery voltage be applied.

• Always relieve the fuel system pressure prior to disconnecting any fuel system component (injector, fuel rail, pressure regulator, etc.), fitting or fuel line connection. Exercise extreme caution whenever relieving fuel system pressure to avoid exposing skin, face and eyes to fuel spray. Please be advised that fuel under pressure may penetrate the skin or any part of the body that it contacts.

• Always place a shop towel or cloth around the fitting or connection prior to loosening to absorb any excess fuel due to spillage. Ensure that all fuel spillage is quickly removed from engine surfaces. Ensure that all fuel soaked cloths or towels are deposited into a waste container.

• Always keep a dry chemical (Class B) fire extinguisher near the work area.

• Do not allow fuel spray or fuel vapors to come into contact with a spark or open flame.

• Always use a backup wrench when loosening and tightening fuel line connection fittings. This will prevent unnecessary stress and torsion to fuel line piping. Always follow the proper torque specifications.

• Always replace worn fuel fitting O-rings with new. Do not substitute fuel hose or equivalent where fuel pipe is installed.

RELIEVING FUEL SYSTEM PRESSURE

1. Remove the fuel pump fuse from the fuse block or disconnect the fuel pump harness connector at the tank.

2. Start the engine. It should run and then stall when the fuel in the lines is exhausted. When the engine stops, crank the starter for about 3 seconds to make sure all pressure in the fuel lines is released.

3. Install the fuel pump fuse after repair is made.

Fuel Tank

REMOVAL AND INSTALLATION

1. Disconnect the negative battery cable. Relieve the fuel system pressure.

2. Drain the tank with an approved pump and container.

3. Remove the rear and center exhaust pipes.

4. Remove the 3rd driveshaft, fuel filler and air breather hose.

5. Disconnect the feed, return and evaporative hoses.

6. Disconnect the parking brake cable bracket and return spring.

7. Disconnect the tank harness connectors.

8. Place a floor jack under the tank and remove the tank retainers. Lower the tank and disconnect any wiring or hoses.
   To install:

9. Raise the tank into position and install the tank retainers. Torque the retainers to 15 ft. lbs. (20 Nm).

10. Connect the tank harnesses and hoses.

11. Connect the parking brake cable bracket and return spring.

12. Connect the feed, return and evaporative hoses.

13. Install the 3rd driveshaft, fuel filler and air breather hoses.

14. Install the rear and center exhaust pipes.

15. Refill the tank and check for leaks.

16. Connect the battery cable.

Fuel Filter

REMOVAL AND INSTALLATION

1. Disconnect the negative battery cable.

2. Relieve the fuel system pressure and remove the fuel filler cap.

3. Disconnect the engine harness connector and remove the air duct with the air cleaner cover.

4. Disconnect and plug the fuel lines at the fuel filter.

5. On Impulse, loosen the filter clamp bolt.

6. Remove the fuel filter.

7. Installation is the reverse of the removal procedure. Make sure the filter is installed in the proper direction of fuel flow.

8. Start the engine and check for leaks.

Electric Fuel Pump

PRESSURE TESTING

1. Relieve the fuel system pressure.

2. Install a fuel pressure gauge between the fuel filter and the fuel distributor pipe.

3. Disconnect the vacuum hose from the pressure regulator.

4. Make sure the ignition has been **OFF** for at least 10 seconds and the air conditioning is OFF.

5. Turn the ignition **ON**. The fuel pump should run for about 2 seconds. The fuel pressure reading should be 35-38 psi for the non-turbocharged engine or 39-47 psi for the turbocharged engine.

6. Turn the ignition **OFF** and disconnect the fuel pressure gauge.

REMOVAL AND INSTALLATION

The electric fuel pump is located in the fuel tank.

1. Relieve the fuel system pressure, then disconnect the negative battery cable.

2. Loosen the fuel filler cap and drain the fuel system.

3. Remove the fuel filler and air breather hoses and disconnect the fuel lines.

4. Remove the parking brake cable brackets and the parking brake return spring.

5. Disconnect the fuel gauge and fuel pump harness connectors.

6. Support the fuel tank and remove the mounting bolts. Lower the tank onto the exhaust pipe.

7. Peel off the harness fixing tape. Remove the fuel pump assembly attaching screws and pull the fuel pump assembly out of the tank.
   To install:

8. Install the fuel pump assembly into the tank and tighten the retaining screws.

9. Raise the tank and install the retaining bolts. Torque the bolts to 15 ft. lbs. (20 Nm).

10. Connect the fuel gauge and fuel pump harness connectors.

11. Install the parking brake cable brackets and the parking brake return spring.

12. Install the fuel filler and air breather hoses.

13. Refill the tank, check for leaks and install the fuel filler cap.

14. Connect the negative battery cable.

Fuel Injector

REMOVAL AND INSTALLATION

1. Disconnect the negative battery cable. Remove the air cleaner and duct.

2. Relieve the fuel system pressure.

3. Remove the intercooler assembly, if equipped.

4. Disconnect the throttle cable, hoses and electrical connectors from the throttle body. Remove the throttle body.

5. Disconnect the vacuum line at the pressure regulator and the electrical connectors at the fuel injectors.

6. Disconnect the fuel lines at the fuel rail.

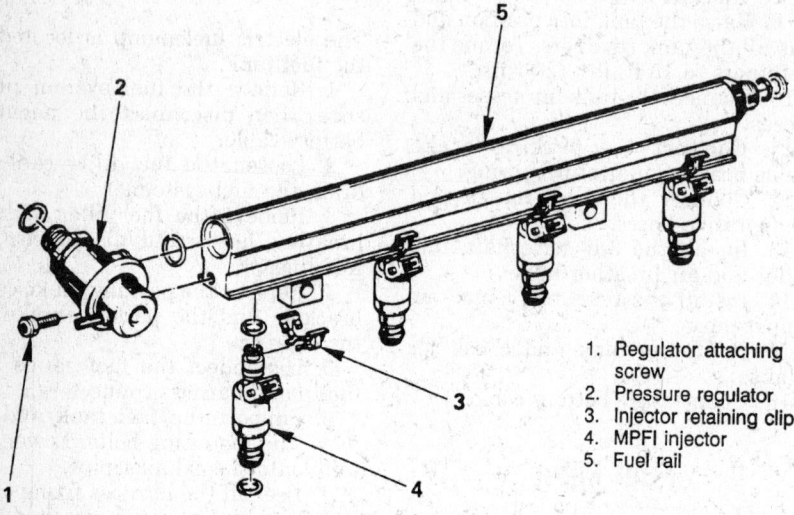

1. Regulator attaching screw
2. Pressure regulator
3. Injector retaining clip
4. MPFI injector
5. Fuel rail

Fuel rail and injector

DRIVE AXLE

Halfshaft

REMOVAL AND INSTALLATION

1. Raise and safely support the vehicle. Drain the oil from the transaxle and replace the drain plug.
2. Remove the front wheel and tire assembly.
3. Remove the hub nut.
4. Disconnect the tie rod end from the steering knuckle, using a removal tool.
5. Loosen the pinch bolt and disconnect the lower control arm from the knuckle.
6. Carefully pull the hub and knuckle assembly from the halfshaft. When pulling the hub assembly, pull just enough to push the shaft off. If necessary, strike the end of the halfshaft with a plastic mallet.
7. To detach the snapring, fitted on the spline of the inboard CV-joint, pry out the inboard joint using a tool.

NOTE: To prevent damaging the CV-joint, never pull out the halfshaft. To prevent damage to

7. Remove the fuel rail mounting bolts and remove the fuel rail and injectors.

To install:

8. Replace all O-rings. Lubricate O-rings with engine oil before installing.
9. Install the fuel rail and mounting bolts. Torque the bolts to 10 ft. lbs. (13 Nm).
10. Connect the fuel lines at the fuel rail.
11. Connect the vacuum line at the pressure regulator and the electrical connectors at the fuel injectors.
12. Connect the throttle cable, hoses and electrical connectors to the throttle body.
13. Install the intercooler assembly, if equipped.
14. Install the air cleaner. Connect the negative battery cable.

the CV-boots, be careful not to bring them into contact with other parts when removing the halfshaft assembly.

To install:

8. Installation is the reverse of the removal procedure. Tighten the ball joint pinch bolt to 48 ft. lbs. (65 Nm). Tighten the tie rod end nut to 29 ft. lbs. (39 Nm).
9. Replace the locking nub nut with a new one.
10. Apply grease to the hub nut fitting surfaces and the shaft threads. Tighten the nut to 137 ft. lbs. (186 Nm) and stake the nut.

CV-Boot

REMOVAL AND INSTALLATION

1. Raise and safely support the vehicle.
2. Remove the halfshaft assembly.
3. Mount the halfshaft in a vice.

NOTE: The outer CV-joint cannot be disassembled. The inboard CV-joint must be removed to replace either CV-joint boot. The right halfshaft uses a Tri-pot inboard CV-joint (automatic transaxle). All other inboard CV-joints are the double offset type. A different REMOVAL AND INSTALLATION procedure is used for each.

4. Remove the double offset CV-joint as follows:
   a. Mark the position of the case in relation to the shaft. Use paint or ink. Do not use a punch.
   b. Remove the big end band clip.
   c. Remove the circular clip and remove the outer case.
   d. Turn the ball guide on an angle and move it to the center shaft side. Remove the balls.
   e. Remove the snapring. Mark the position of the ball retainer in relation to the shaft and remove the ball retainer.
   f. Remove the ball guide and small end band clip. Remove the boot.
   g. If the outer boot is to be replaced, remove the band clips and remove the outer boot.

5. Remove the Tri-pot CV-joint as follows:
   a. Mark the position of the case in relation to the shaft. Use paint or ink. Do not use a punch.
   b. Remove the big end band clip.
   c. Remove the outer case.
   d. Remove the snapring and pull the Tri-pot from the shaft. It may

be necessary to use a brass drift to dislodge the Tri-pot from the splines.

e. Remove the small band clip and boot.

To install:

6. When assembling, apply special grease to ½ of the space within the double offset joint and Tri-pot joint. Make sure the band clips are securely tightened and the boot is not twisted.

7. Install the Tri-pot CV-joint, boots and clips.

8. Install the halfshaft and lower the vehicle. Torque the halfshaft nut to 137 ft. lbs. (186 Nm) and stake the nut or install a new cotter pin.

Driveshaft and U-Joints

REMOVAL AND INSTALLATION

1990-92 Impulse with AWD

1. Raise and safely support the vehicle.

2. Apply alignment marks on the flange at the center bearing.

3. Remove the bolts at the rear axle side and center bearing.

4. Remove the shaft from the vehicle.

5. Installation is the reverse of the removal procedure. Align the marks and install the bolts. Torque the center bearing bolts to 14 ft. lbs. (19 Nm) and the rear bolts to 26 ft. lbs. (35 Nm).

Rear Axle Shaft, Bearing and Seal

REMOVAL AND INSTALLATION

1. Raise and safely support the vehicle.

2. Remove the rear wheel and tire assembly.

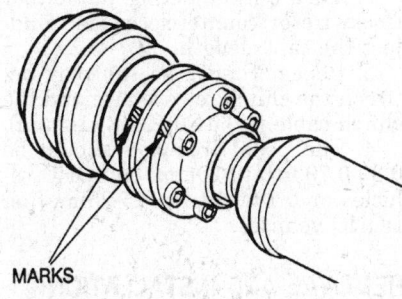

MARKS

Halfshaft alignment marks — Impulse with All Wheel Drive

3. Remove the caliper from the rotor. Support the caliper with a length of wire, do not let it hang from the brake hose.

4. Remove the disc brake rotor.

5. Working through the access hole, remove the plate-to-axle housing bolts.

6. Attach a slide hammer to the axle flange and remove the axle from the axle housing.

7. Remove the oil seal from the axle housing.

8. Press the axle bearing from the shaft.

To install:

9. Use an installation tool to set the oil seal in the axle housing. Apply approximately 1.4 ozs. of wheel bearing grease to the inner face of the rear axle case.

10. Install the O-ring on the outer circumference of the outer race. Install the bearing with the O-ring turned to the splined end of the axle shaft. Install the sleeve with the flanged side facing towards the ball bearing. Press the bearing onto the axle using a hydraulic press.

11. Insert the axle into the axle housing and install the plate-to-axle housing bolts. Tighten the bolts to 27 ft. lbs. (38 Nm).

12. Install the rotor and the brake caliper. Tighten the caliper bolts to 36 ft. lbs. (50 Nm).

13. Install the wheel and tire assembly and lower the vehicle.

Front Wheel Hub, Knuckle and Bearings

REMOVAL AND INSTALLATION

NOTE: Do not remove the hub from the knuckle unless it is absolutely necessary.

1. Raise and safely support the vehicle.

2. Remove the front wheel and tire assembly.

3. Remove the brake caliper and support it with a length of wire. Do not let the caliper hang from the brake hose.

4. Remove the disc brake rotor.

5. Pry the hub nut open and remove it from the end of the halfshaft.

6. Attach a slide hammer to the hub and remove the hub from the vehicle.

7. Remove the dust shield.

8. Disconnect the tie rod end from the knuckle, using a suitable removal tool.

9. Remove the pinch bolt and separate the ball joint from the knuckle.

10. Remove the bolts from the strut and remove the knuckle assembly.

11. Remove the inner and outer seals. Remove the 1 inner snapring.

12. Mount the knuckle in a hydraulic press and press out the bearing, using a fixture.

To install:

13. Mount the knuckle in a hydraulic press. Using a fixture, press in a new bearing.

14. Install the inner snapring and the inner and outer seals. Install the dust cover.

15. Mount the knuckle in a hydraulic press and press the hub onto the knuckle, using a fixture.

16. Install the hub and knuckle assembly onto the halfshaft and tighten the hub nut temporarily.

17. Install the strut bolts and tighten to 115 ft. lbs. (156 Nm).

18. Connect the ball joint to the knuckle and tighten the pinch bolt to 48 ft. lbs. (65 Nm).

19. Connect the tie rod end to the knuckle and tighten the nut to 29 ft. lbs. (39 Nm).

20. Remove the hub nut and apply grease to the halfshaft's thread. Install the hub nut and tighten it to 137 ft. lbs. (186 Nm). Stake the nut after installation.

21. Install the brake rotor and the caliper.

22. Install the wheel and tire assembly and lower the vehicle.

Pinion Seal

REMOVAL AND INSTALLATION

1. Raise and safely support the vehicle.

2. Remove the driveshaft and the differential flange.

3. Carefully pry out the pinion seal.

4. Installation is the reverse of the removal procedure. Lubricate the lip of the seal.

5. Tighten the flange nut to 130-202 ft. lbs. (180-280 Nm).

Axle Housing

REMOVAL AND INSTALLATION

Except 1990-92 Impulse with AWD

1. Raise and safely support the vehicle.

2. Remove the rear wheel and tire assemblies.

3. Remove the driveshaft.

4. Remove the calipers and support them with a length of wire. Do

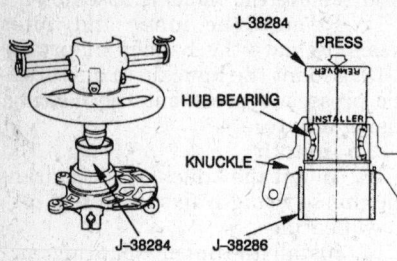

Removing front hub bearings

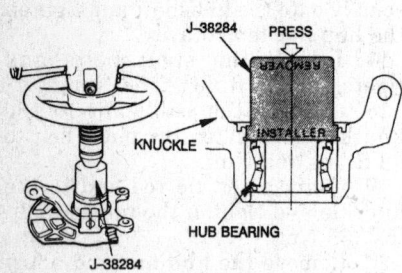

Installing front hub bearings

not let the calipers hang by the brake hoses. Disconnect the parking brake cables.

5. Remove the exhaust pipe and muffler, if necessary.

6. Disconnect the sway bar from the axle housing.

7. Support the axle housing with a jack.

8. Remove the Panhard rod.

9. Disconnect the shock absorbers from the axle housing.

10. Lower the axle housing slowly, enough to remove the coil springs.

11. Disconnect the control arms from the axle housing and lower the axle housing from the vehicle.

To install:

12. Connect the control arms to the axle housing.

13. Raise the axle housing slowly enough to install the coil springs.

14. Connect the shock absorbers to the axle housing.

15. Install the panhard rod.

16. Connect the sway bar to the axle housing and torque to 58 ft. lbs. (78 Nm).

17. Install the exhaust pipe and muffler, if removed.

18. Install the calipers. Connect the parking brake cables.

19. Install the driveshaft. Torque the nut to 137 ft. lbs. (186 Nm).

20. Install the rear wheel and tire assemblies. Torque the lug nuts to 100 ft. lbs. (136 Nm).

21. Lower the vehicle.

1990-92 Impulse with AWD

1. Drain the rear differential fluid.

2. Disconnect the ball joint for both side of the stabilizer bar.

3. Disconnect the lateral links at the wheel side.

NOTE: Never pull out the driveshaft. Damage to the boots and joints may result.

4. Pry the inboard joint against the differential housing to dislodge the snapring inside the differential assembly. Use a prybar to remove the rear axle shafts from the vehicle.

5. Remove the rear driveshaft.

6. Support the differential assembly using a jack. Remove the 2 bolts in the rear mounting and disconnect the breather hose.

7. Remove the bolt from the front mounting and remove the assembly from the vehicle.

To install:

8. Install the assembly into the vehicle and install the bolt to the front mounting.

9. Install the 2 bolts in the rear mounting and connect the breather hose.

10. Install the rear driveshaft.

11. Install the rear axle shafts to the vehicle.

12. Connect the lateral links at the wheel side.

13. Connect the ball joint for both side of the stabilizer bar.

14. Refill the rear differential with fluid.

CLUTCH

Clutch Assembly

REMOVAL AND INSTALLATION

1. Disconnect the negative battery cable.

2. Raise and safely support the vehicle.

3. Remove the transmission/transaxle assembly.

4. Mark the position of the pressure plate on the flywheel. Remove the pressure plate and the clutch disc.

5. Remove the release bearing from the clutch fork.

6. Inspect the flywheel for scoring or heat cracks. Resurface or replace, as necessary.

7. Inspect the pressure plate and clutch disc for wear or scoring. Replace as necessary.

8. Inspect the release bearing for wear or binding. Replace as necessary.

To install:

9. Install the flywheel if it was removed. Make sure the crankshaft flange and the mating surface of the flywheel are clean. Tighten the flywheel bolts in a crisscross pattern.

10. Tighten the bolts on 1.6L engines in 2 steps, first to 22 ft. lbs. (29 Nm) and then repeat the pattern turning the bolts another 45 degrees each.

11. Lubricate the pilot bearing with a grease. Install a clutch alignment tool.

12. Install the clutch disc and the pressure plate on the flywheel. If the old pressure plate is used, make sure it is installed in the position that was marked during the removal procedure. Tighten the pressure plate bolts in a crisscross pattern in 2-3 steps to avoid warping the pressure plate. The final bolt torque should be 13 ft. lbs. (18 Nm).

13. Remove the clutch alignment tool.

14. Apply grease to the sliding surface of the release bearing and the contact surface of the clutch fork. Install the release bearing.

15. Install the remaining components in the reverse order of their removal. Adjust the clutch cable or pedal height, as required.

Clutch Cable

ADJUSTMENT

1. Pull the clutch cable to the rear until the adjusting nut turns freely.

2. Turn the adjusting nut either clockwise or counterclockwise to adjust the cable length.

3. Repeat Step 2 so the play between the clutch release arm and the clutch cable is 0.04-0.12 in. (1-3mm).

4. The pedal free-play should be 0.39-0.79 in. (10-20mm) on SOHC vehicles or 0.19-0.59 in. (15-25mm) on DOHC vehicles.

REMOVAL AND INSTALLATION

1. Disconnect the negative battery cable.

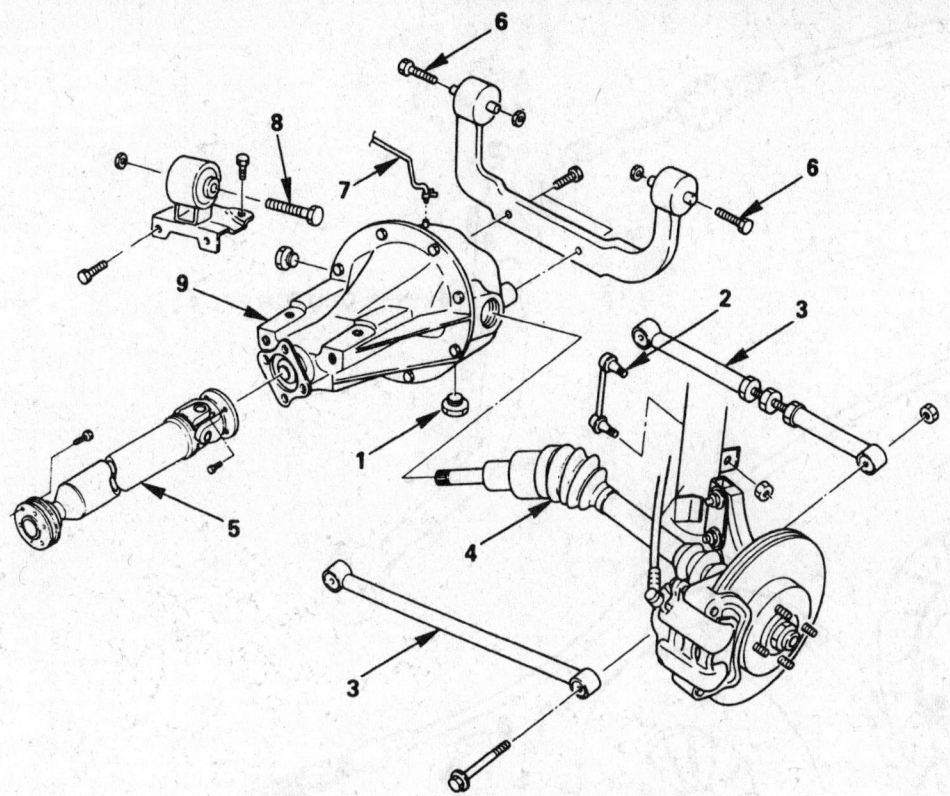

1. Drain plug
2. Ball joint
3. Lateral links
4. Drive axle shaft
5. Rear driveshaft
6. Bolt from rear
7. Breather hose
8. Bolt from front
9. Rear differential assembly

Rear differential assembly — Impulse with All Wheel Drive

2. Raise and support safely the front of the vehicle.

3. Disconnect the clutch cable from the clutch housing and transaxle. Remove all necessary snaprings and locknuts to free the clutch cable.

4. Remove the clutch cable from the clutch pedal and pull the cable out from the engine compartment.

5. Installation is the reverse of the removal procedure. Adjust the clutch cable.

Clutch Master Cylinder

REMOVAL AND INSTALLATION

1. Disconnect the negative battery cable.

2. Disconnect clutch pedal return spring and joint pin from clutch pedal.

3. Disconnect and plug the hydraulic line and the hose at the clutch master cylinder.

4. Remove 2 hold-down nuts from inside of passenger compartment.

5. Remove clutch master cylinder from engine compartment.

6. Installation is the reverse of removal procedure. Bleed the hydraulic system.

Clutch Slave Cylinder

REMOVAL AND INSTALLATION

1. Disconnect the negative battery cable.

2. Raise and safely support the vehicle.

3. Disconnect and plug the hydraulic line at the slave cylinder.

4. Remove the slave cylinder mounting bolts and disconnect the pushrod from the clutch fork. Remove the slave cylinder.

5. Installation is the reverse of the removal procedure. Bleed the hydraulic system.

Hydraulic Clutch System Bleeding

1. Fill the clutch fluid reservoir with brake fluid and keep it filled during the bleeding operation.

2. Remove the bleeder rubber cap and connect a clear plastic length of hose to the bleeder. Submerge the other end of the hose in a transparent container half-filled with brake fluid.

3. Pump the clutch pedal several times and hold the pedal depressed.

4. With the pedal depressed, loosen the bleeder ½ turn to release brake fluid with air and tighten it immediately.

5. Repeat Steps 3 and 4 until air bubbles disappear completely from the fluid being forced out.

6. After bleeding is completed, check for pedal free-play and clutch disengagement, then check the brake fluid level in the reservoir.

AUTOMATIC TRANSMISSION

Transmission Assembly

REMOVAL AND INSTALLATION

1. Disconnect the negative battery cable.

2. Raise and safely support the vehicle. Drain the transmission and replace the drain plug.

3. Disconnect the throttle cable at the engine side. Remove the transmission dipstick.

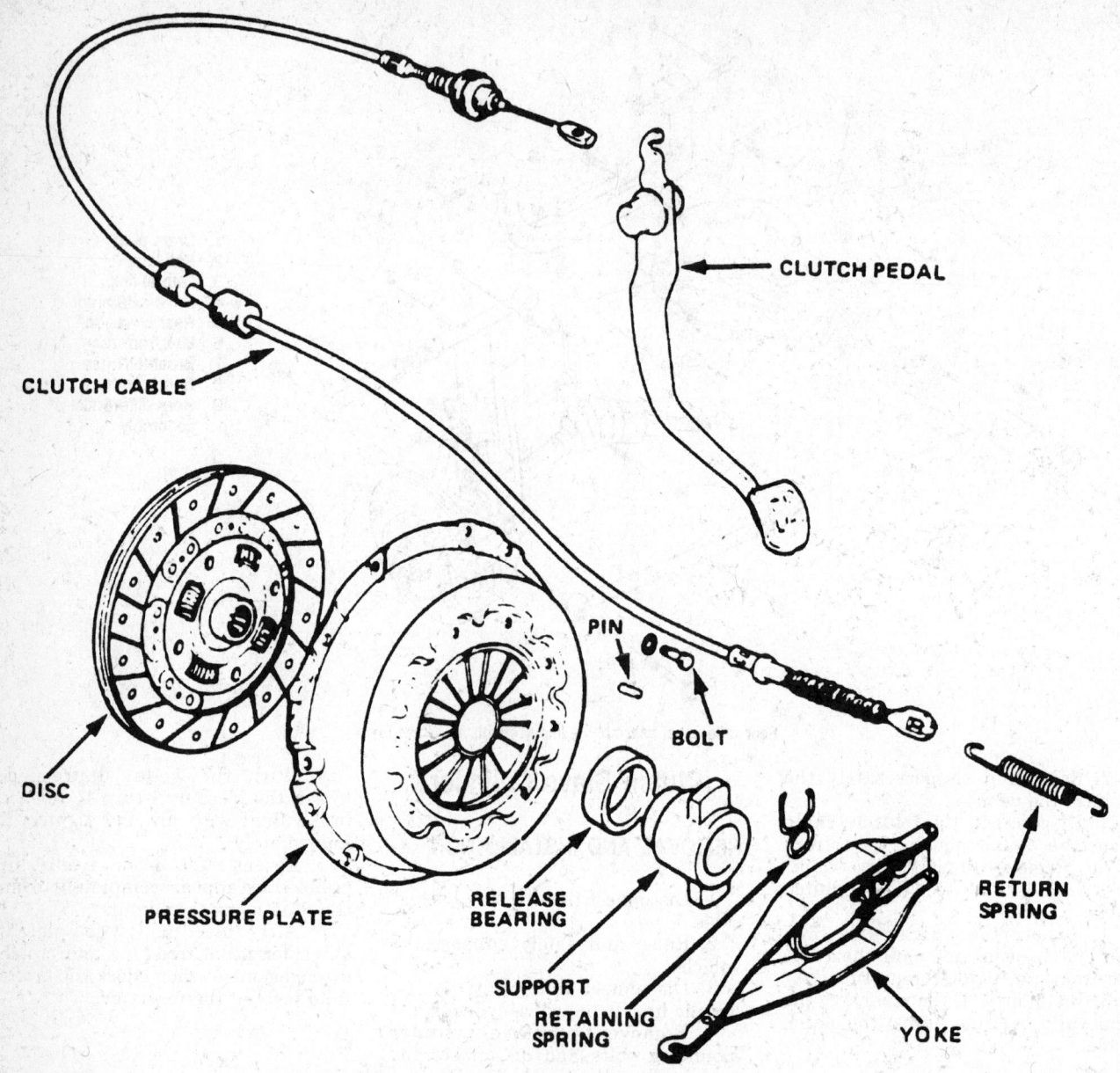

CLUTCH CABLE

CLUTCH PEDAL

PIN

BOLT

DISC

PRESSURE PLATE

RELEASE
BEARING

SUPPORT
RETAINING
SPRING

YOKE

RETURN
SPRING

Exploded view of clutch components

4. Disconnect the electrical connectors and remove the starter.

5. Matchmark the driveshaft to the differential flange and remove the driveshaft.

6. Disconnect the link rod at the shift lever side. Disconnect the speedometer cable.

7. Remove the exhaust header pipe.

8. Disconnect the transmission cooler lines from the transmission. Secure the lines close to the body to prevent damage during transmission removal.

9. Remove the flywheel dust cover and the engine splash shield.

10. Remove the 6 bolts attaching the converter to the flywheel. Rotate the engine at the crankshaft pulley to gain access to all of the bolts.

11. Support the transmission using a jack. Support the rear of the engine to hold it in position when the transmission is removed.

12. Remove the rear transmission mount and remove the transmission-to-engine mounting bolts.

13. Remove the transmission, being careful not to let the torque converter slip out of the transmission.

To install:

14. Install the transmission and torque the transmission-to-engine

mounting bolts to 47 ft. lbs. (65 Nm) and the converter attaching bolts to 13 ft. lbs. (19 Nm).

15. Install the driveshaft, aligning the marks that were made during the removal procedure. Tighten the bolts to 26 ft. lbs. (36 Nm).

16. Tighten the drain plug to 15 ft. lbs. (21 Nm). Adjust the link rod and the throttle cable.

17. Lower the vehicle and fill the transmission with approximately 4.2 qts. of the proper fluid. Start the engine and add fluid, as necessary, to bring the fluid to the proper level. Avoid racing the engine.

SHIFT LINKAGE ADJUSTMENT

1. Remove the adjustment nut attaching the select lever link to the control lever.

2. Move the manual valve lever forward to stop, then return to the **N** position (3rd stop).

3. Depress the manual valve lever toward the **R** position lightly and tighten the adjust nut.

4. Check that the control lever moves smoothly and that the position indicator works correctly.

THROTTLE LINKAGE ADJUSTMENT

1. Check that the throttle valve is held closed completely.

2. Adjust the setting of the adjustment nut, as necessary, so the clearance A between the inner cable stopper and the end of the rubber boot on the outer cable is adjusted to 0.032-0.059 in. (0.8-1.5mm).

3. Open the throttle valve fully and check that the inner cable stroke B is within the range of 1.30-1.34 in. (33-34mm).

TRANSFER CASE

Transfer Case Assembly

REMOVAL AND INSTALLATION

Impulse

1. Disconnect the negative battery cable.

2. Drain the transaxle and transfer fluid.

3. Remove the steering shaft protector, intermediate shaft pinch bolt and steering shaft boot.

4. Raise the vehicle and support safely.

5. Remove the front wheels.

6. Remove the left halfshaft nut and both tie rod ends.

7. Disconnect the lower ball joints. Remove all under covers, front exhaust pipe and rear driveshaft.

8. Remove the steering hoses and place a drain pan into position to catch the fluid.

9. Support the engine with an engine hoist.

10. Remove the torque rod bolt at the center beam.

11. Remove the rear rubber mounting bolt, center beam and cross-

member with the steering unit and stabilizer.

12. Disconnect the FWD halfshafts.

13. Disconnect the speedometer cable and support the transfer case with a jack.

14. Remove the transfer-to-transaxle attaching bolts and remove the assembly.

To install:

15. Install the assembly and attaching bolts. Torque the bolts to 25 ft. lbs. (34 Nm).

16. Connect the speedometer cable and support the transfer case with a jack.

17. Connect the FWD halfshafts.

18. Install the rear rubber mounting bolt, center beam and crossmember with the steering unit and stabilizer.

19. Install the torque rod bolt at the center beam.

20. Install the steering hoses, all undercovers, front exhaust pipe and rear driveshaft.

21. Connect the lower ball joints. Install the left halfshaft nut. Torque the nut to 137 ft. lbs. (186 Nm). Reconnect the tie rod ends.

22. Install the front wheels and lower the vehicle.

23. Install the steering shaft protector, intermediate shaft pinch bolt and steering shaft boot.

24. Refill the transaxle and transfer case with fluid.

25. Connect the battery cable and align the front end.

FRONT SUSPENSION

Shock Absorbers

REMOVAL AND INSTALLATION

1. Raise and safely support the vehicle.

2. Remove the front wheel and tire assemblies.

3. Remove the shock absorber caps and remove the upper shock mounting nuts.

4. Remove the lower shock mounting bolts and remove the shock absorbers.

5. Installation is the reverse of the removal procedure. Tighten the lower shock mounting bolts to 40 ft. lbs. (56 Nm).

MacPherson Strut

REMOVAL AND INSTALLATION

1. Raise and safely support the vehicle.

2. Remove the front wheel and tire assemblies.

3. Remove the brake hose clip at the strut bracket.

4. Disconnect and plug the brake hose at the caliper. Pull the brake hose back through the opening in the strut bracket.

5. Remove the strut-to-knuckle bolts.

6. Remove the strut mounting nuts and remove the strut.

To install:

7. Install the strut assembly and torque the strut mounting nuts to 50 ft. lbs. (68 Nm).

8. Torque the strut-to-knuckle bolts to 115 ft. lbs. (156 Nm).

9. Bleed the brake system. Install the wheel and tire assembly.

Coil Springs

REMOVAL AND INSTALLATION

1. Raise and safely support the vehicle.

2. Remove the front wheel and tire assembly.

3. Remove the disc brake caliper assembly. Support the caliper with a length of wire. Do not let the caliper hang from the brake hose.

4. Mark the position of the nuts on the front of the strut bar for reassembly. These nuts control the caster setting. Remove the strut bar.

5. Remove the sway bar brackets on both sides of the vehicle. Remove the bolt, tube and grommets holding the sway bar to the lower control arm. Move the sway bar aside.

6. Use a separator to disconnect the tie rod end from the steering knuckle. Turn the steering wheel to move the tie rod end aside.

7. Place a hydraulic floor jack under the lower control arm and apply slight upward pressure.

NOTE: Install a safety chain through 1 coil at the top of the spring and attach it to the upper control arm to prevent the spring from coming out unexpectedly.

8. Install a spring compressor tool J-36567 or equivalent, and slightly compress the spring.

9. Remove the upper and lower ball joint nuts. Using a suitable removal tool, disconnect the upper and

lower ball joints from the steering knuckle. Remove the steering knuckle from the vehicle.

10. Slowly lower the lower control arm until the spring is free of the lower control arm. Slowly and evenly release the spring compressor until the spring is fully extended. Remove the safety chain and the coil spring.

To install:

11. Make sure the lower end of the coil spring is aligned with the notch in the lower control arm.

12. Install new self-locking nuts on the upper and lower ball joint studs and tighten the upper ball joint nut to 39 ft. lbs. (54 Nm) and the lower ball joint nut to 58 ft. lbs. (80 Nm).

13. Install a new self-locking nut on the sway bar end link and tighten to 19 ft. lbs. (26 Nm). Tighten the sway bar bracket bolt to 14 ft. lbs. (19 Nm).

14. Install the strut bar to the chassis and tighten the locknuts. Install the strut bar-to-lower arm bolts, aligning the marks that were made during the removal procedure. Tighten the small bolt to 47 ft. lbs. (65 Nm) and the large bolt to 114 ft. lbs. (158 Nm).

15. Install the remaining components by reversing their removal procedures.

16. Tighten the tie rod end nut to 60 ft. lbs. (84 Nm). Check the front end alignment.

Upper Ball Joints

INSPECTION

1. Raise and safely support the vehicle.

2. Place a jack under the lower control arm. Raise the jack enough to slightly compress the coil spring.

3. Have an assistant grasp the front wheel and attempt to move the top of the wheel in and out toward the inside of the wheel well. If any play is observed in the ball joint during this procedure, the ball joint must be replaced.

REMOVAL AND INSTALLATION

1. Raise and safely support the vehicle.

2. Remove the front wheel and tire assembly.

3. Remove the disc brake caliper assembly. Support the caliper with a length of wire. Do not let the caliper hang from the brake hose.

4. Place a hydraulic floor jack under the lower control arm and apply slight upward pressure.

NOTE: Install a safety chain through 1 coil at the bottom of the spring and attach it to the lower control arm to prevent the spring from coming out unexpectedly.

5. Install a spring compressor, tool J-36567 or equivalent, and slightly compress the spring.

6. Remove the upper ball joint nut and use a separator to disconnect the upper ball joint from the steering knuckle.

7. Remove the upper ball joint from the upper control arm.

8. Installation is the reverse of the removal procedure. Install the ball joint with the cutaway portion turned outward. Tighten the ball joint mounting nuts to 40 ft. lbs. (56 Nm). Install a new self-locking nut on the upper ball joint stud and tighten to 39 ft. lbs. (54 Nm).

Lower Ball Joints

INSPECTION

1. Raise and safely support the vehicle.

2. Have an assistant grasp the front wheel and attempt to move the bottom of the wheel in and out toward the inside of the wheel well. If any play is observed in the ball joint during this procedure, the ball joint must be replaced.

REMOVAL AND INSTALLATION

1. Raise and safely support the vehicle.

2. Remove the front wheel and tire assembly.

3. Remove the pinch bolt and nut from the steering knuckle.

4. Remove the nuts and bolts retaining the lower ball joint to the lower control arm and remove the lower ball joint.

5. Installation is the reverse of the removal procedure. Tighten the bolts retaining the lower ball joint to the lower control arm to 115 ft. lbs. (156 Nm). Tighten the pinch bolt to 48 ft. lbs. (65 Nm).

Upper Control Arms

REMOVAL AND INSTALLATION

1. Raise and safely support the vehicle.

2. Remove the front wheel and tire assembly.

3. Remove the disc brake caliper assembly. Support the caliper with a length of wire. Do not let the caliper hang from the brake hose.

4. Place a hydraulic floor jack under the lower control arm and apply slight upward pressure.

NOTE: Install a safety chain through 1 coil at the bottom of the spring and attach it to the lower control arm to prevent the spring from coming out unexpectedly.

5. Install a spring compressor, tool J-36567 or equivalent, and slightly compress the spring.

6. Remove the upper ball joint nut and use a separator to disconnect the upper ball joint from the steering knuckle. Remove the upper control arm bolts and remove the upper control arm.

7. Installation is the reverse of the removal procedure. Install the upper control arm bolts but do not tighten.

8. After installing all other components, including wheel and tire assemblies, lower the vehicle. If possible, have 2 assistants sit in the front seats to simulate actual vehicle load; tighten the upper control arm bolts to 47 ft. lbs. (65 Nm).

9. Check front end alignment.

Lower Control Arms

REMOVAL AND INSTALLATION

1. Raise and safely support the vehicle.

2. Remove the front wheel and tire assembly.

3. Remove the pinch bolt from the steering knuckle and separate the ball joint from the knuckle.

4. Disconnect the sway bar from the lower control arm.

5. Remove the lower control arm bolt(s) and remove the lower control arm.

To install:

6. Before tightening the lower control arm bolt(s), the trim height must be set.

7. Raise the lower control arm with a jack and set the trim height to 3 in. (77mm) from the center of the

front lower control arm bushing to the center of the wheel hub.

8. Tighten the lower control arm bolt to 50 ft. lbs. (68 Nm) on the rear bolt and 94 ft. lbs. (128 Nm) on the front bolt.

Sway Bar

REMOVAL AND INSTALLATION

1. Raise and safely support the vehicle.
2. Remove the exhaust header pipe.
3. Disconnect and plug the power steering lines at the steering rack.
4. Remove the steering shaft boot nuts from inside the vehicle. Remove the steering shaft bolt.
5. Remove the pinch bolts and disconnect the lower ball joints from the steering knuckles.
6. Using a tool, disconnect the tie rod ends from the steering knuckle.
7. Place a jack under the engine and raise it to support the engine.
8. Disconnect the engine torque rod at the center beam.
9. Disconnect the rear engine mount. Remove 2 bolts at the center beam and 4 bolts at the crossmember. Lower the crossmember assembly with the steering rack carefully.
10. Remove the steering rack, then remove the sway bar from the crossmember.

NOTE: The sway bar cannot be removed unless the crossmember assembly is removed; however, the sway bar bushings can be replaced without removing the crossmember.

11. Installation is the reverse of the removal procedure. Tighten the 4 crossmember bolts to 137 ft. lbs. (186 Nm) and the 2 center beam bolts to 37 ft. lbs. (50 Nm). Tighten the lower ball joint pinch bolts to 48 ft. lbs. (65 Nm) and the steering shaft bolt to 30 ft. lbs. (40 Nm). Tighten the tie rod nuts to 40 ft. lbs. (54 Nm).
12. Install the remaining components by reversing their removal procedures.
13. Lower the vehicle and check the front end alignment.

Front Wheel Bearings

ADJUSTMENT

1. Raise and safely support the vehicle. Remove the front wheel and tire assembly.
2. Remove the dust cap and the cotter pin. Make sure the wheel bearings are clean and adequately greased before proceeding further.
3. Tighten the hub nut to 22 ft. lbs. (30 Nm) and turn the hub 2-3 turns in fore and aft directions to set the bearings.
4. Loosen the hub nut just enough, so it can be turned by hand. Hand tighten the hub nut using a socket wrench and check that the hub has no play in it.
5. Attach a pull scale to one of the hub studs. Adjust the tightness of the hub nut, so the hub begins to rotate when the pull scale is pulled forward with a force of 1.1-3.3 lbs. (1.3-4.2 N).
6. Install the cotter pin. If the cotter pin holes are not aligned, tighten the nut just enough to align the cotter pin holes.
7. Replace the dust cap, front wheel and tire assembly and lower the vehicle.

REMOVAL AND INSTALLATION

1. Raise and safely support the vehicle.
2. Remove the front wheel and tire assembly.
3. Remove the disc brake caliper and the caliper mounting bracket. Support the caliper with a length of wire, do not let it hang from the brake hose.
4. Remove the dust cap and the cotter pin. Remove the castle nut, washer and outer wheel bearing assembly. Remove the rotor/hub assembly with the inner wheel bearing and seal.
5. Remove the wheel seal. Remove the inner wheel bearing assembly.
6. Clean the wheel bearings, washer, castle nut and the inside of the hub thoroughly with a cleaning solvent and allow to air dry.
7. Inspect the wheel bearing rollers, cages and races for pitting, cracking or other wear and replace, as necessary. Bearings and bearing races must always be replaced as a unit. If the bearings or bearing races are worn or damaged, drive the races out of the hub using removal tools.

To install:
8. If the bearing races were removed, drive the new races into the hub using installation tools. Make sure the inside of the hub is clean before installation.
9. Pack the wheel bearings using a high temperature wheel bearing grease. If a bearing packer is not available, the bearings may be packed by hand, but care must be taken that grease thoroughly penetrates behind the bearing rollers.
10. Place a quantity of wheel bearing grease inside the hub between the races and coat the races with grease. Install the inner wheel bearing.
11. Carefully install a new wheel seal.
12. Install the rotor/hub assembly onto the spindle and install the outer wheel bearing, washer and the castle nut. Adjust the wheel bearings, install a new cotter pin and install the dust cap.
13. Install the disc brake caliper mounting bracket and the disc brake caliper.
14. Install the front wheel and tire assembly and lower the vehicle.

REAR SUSPENSION

MacPherson Strut

REMOVAL AND INSTALLATION

1. Raise and safely support the vehicle.
2. Remove the rear wheel and tire assembly. Open the rear hatch and remove the strut tower cover. Loosen the strut mount.
3. Remove the brake line clip at the strut. Disconnect and plug the brake hose at the strut. Disconnect the speed sensor cable, if equipped with ABS brakes.
4. Disconnect the sway bar end. Remove the strut-to-knuckle bolts.
5. Open the rear hatch and remove the strut tower cover. Remove the strut mounting nuts and remove the strut.
6. Installation is the reverse of the removal procedure. Tighten the strut mounting nuts to 51 ft. lbs. (69 Nm) and the strut-to-knuckle bolts to 116 ft. lbs. (157 Nm).
7. Bleed the brakes.

Rear Control Arms

REMOVAL AND INSTALLATION

Trailing Arm

1. Raise and safely support the vehicle.
2. Remove the rear wheel and tire assembly.
3. Remove the trailing arm mounting bolts and remove the trailing arm.

To install:

4. Installation is the reverse of the removal procedure. Set the trim height before tightening the trailing arm mounting bolts. The trim height is set as follows:
   a. Raise the rear suspension assembly using a jack until the center of the hub is 1.3 in. (33mm) above the center line of the body side lateral arm bushing.
   b. Tighten the trailing arm mounting bolts to 94 ft. lbs. (127 Nm).

Lateral Arm

NOTE: Do not loosen the turn buckle of the trailing lateral arm unless it is absolutely necessary.

1. Raise and safely support the vehicle.
2. Remove the rear wheel and tire assembly.
3. Remove the lateral arm mounting bolts and remove the lateral arm.

NOTE: To remove the lateral arm on the left side, loosen the crossmember bolts and push the crossmember down as far as possible. This will prevent interference with the fuel tank and create space to pull the bolt free. Place a jack under the crossmember for safety when dropping down the crossmember.

To install:

4. Installation is the reverse of the removal procedure. Tighten the crossmember mounting bolts to 94 ft. lbs. (127 Nm). Set the trim height before tightening the lateral arm mounting bolts. The trim height is set as follows:
   a. Raise the rear suspension assembly using a jack until the center of the hub is 1.3 in. (33mm) above the center line of the body side lateral arm bushing.
   b. Tighten the lateral arm mounting bolts to 94 ft. lbs. (127 Nm).
5. Check the rear wheel alignment.

Rear Wheel Bearings

REMOVAL AND INSTALLATION

NOTE: The hub, hub bearing and the spindle are a single unit and cannot be disassembled. If the hub axial play is excessive or abnormal noise occurs, replace the entire hub unit assembly.

1. Raise and safely support the vehicle.
2. Remove the rear wheel and tire assembly.
3. Remove the disc brake caliper and caliper mounting bracket. Remove the disc brake rotor.
4. Remove the hub unit assembly mounting bolts and remove the hub assembly.
5. Installation is the reverse of the removal procedure. Tighten the hub unit assembly mounting bolts to 49 ft. lbs. (66 Nm).

Rear Knuckle

REMOVAL AND INSTALLATION

1. Raise and safely support the vehicle. Disconnect the negative battery cable.
2. If equipped with ABS, disconnect the ABS speed sensor.
3. Remove the brake caliper and rotor.
4. If equipped with All Wheel Drive, remove the hub nut.
5. Remove the hub assembly, retained by 4 bolts.
6. Remove the backing plate.
7. Disconnect the lateral link, trailing link and remove the knuckle from the vehicle.
8. Installation is the reverse of the removal procedure. Torque the knuckle-to-strut bolts to 116 ft. lbs. (157 Nm), trailing link-to-knuckle bolts to 94 ft. lbs. (127 Nm), lateral link-to-knuckle bolts to 116 ft. lbs. (157 Nm), hub-to-knuckle bolts to 49 ft. lbs. (66 Nm) and 4WD hub nut to 137 ft. lbs. (186 Nm).

STEERING

Steering Wheel

——————— **CAUTION** ———————
On vehicles equipped with an air bag, the negative battery cable must be disconnected and tape,
before working on the system. Failure to do so may result in deployment of the air bag and possible personal injury.

REMOVAL AND INSTALLATION

1. Disconnect the negative battery cable.
2. Remove the 4 bolts securing the Supplemental Inflatable Restraint (SIR) module to the steering wheel.
3. Disconnect the module connector and remove the SIR module.

——————— **CAUTION** ———————
The SIR module should always be carried with the urethane cover away from the body. It should always be laid on a flat surface with the urethane side up. This is necessary because a free space is provided to allow the air cushion to expand in the unlikely event of accidental deployment. Failure to follow this precaution may result is personal injury.

4. Disconnect the horn connector and remove the steering wheel nut.
5. Use a puller to remove the steering wheel.

To install:

6. Mount the steering wheel on the column and tighten the steering wheel nut to 25 ft. lbs. (35 Nm).

NOTE: Be careful not to damage the harness section of the coil when installing the steering wheel. At this time, the cancel cam for the turn signal switch must be closely inserted into a boss hole in the steering wheel.

7. Support the SIR module and carefully connect the module connector. Pass the lead wire through the tabs on the plastic cover (wire protector) of the inflator to prevent the lead wire from being pinched.
8. Install the module retaining bolts and tighten them to 3.6 ft. lbs. (5 Nm).
9. Connect the negative battery cable. Turn the ignition switch **ON** and observe the warning light. The light should flash 7-9 times and then go OFF. If the light does not operate correctly, there is a problem in the SIR system.

Manual Rack and Pinion

REMOVAL AND INSTALLATION

Stylus

1. Disconnect the negative battery cable.
2. Remove the steering column protector and spline shaft pinch bolt.
3. Remove the steering shaft boot nuts.
4. Mark the position of the hood in relation to the hinge brackets and remove the hood.
5. Raise the vehicle and support safely. Remove the front wheels.
6. Disconnect the exhaust pipe.
7. Using a tie rod remover tool J-21687-02 or equivalent, remove the tie rod ends from the knuckle.
8. Using a ball joint remover tool, disconnect the ball joints from the knuckles.
9. Remove the crossmember assembly and manual steering assembly.

To install:
10. Install the steering assembly and torque the nuts to 51 ft. lbs. (69 Nm).
11. Install the crossmember and torque the bolts to 137 ft. lbs. (186 Nm).
12. Install the knuckle to the ball joints and torque the nuts to 37 ft. lbs. (50 Nm).
13. Install the tie rod ends and torque the nuts to 40 ft. lbs. (54 Nm).
14. Install the exhaust pipe.
15. With an assistant, install the engine hood.
16. Install the steering shaft boot and nuts and the spline shaft pinch bolt. Torque the bolt to 30 ft. lbs. (40 Nm).
17. Install the front wheels and lower the vehicle.
18. Connect the battery cable.
19. Check the front end alignment.

Power Rack and Pinion

REMOVAL AND INSTALLATION

1. Disconnect the negative battery cable. Mark the position of the hood on the hinge brackets and remove the hood.
2. Remove the column protector and remove the spline shaft pinch bolts. Remove the steering shaft boot nuts.
3. Raise and safely support the vehicle. Remove the front wheel and tire assemblies.

4. Attach a hoist to the engine and support it.
5. Remove the exhaust header pipe. Place a drain pan below the steering rack and disconnect the power steering lines.
6. Use a separator to disconnect the tie rod ends from the steering knuckle.
7. Disconnect the ball joints from the steering knuckle and remove the crossmember assembly. Separate the steering rack from the crossmember.

To install:
8. Install the steering rack to the crossmember. Install the crossmember and rack assembly.
9. Connect the ball joints and tie rod ends to the steering knuckle.
10. Install the exhaust header pipe. Connect the power steering lines.
11. Remove the engine hoist.
12. Install the column protector, spline shaft pinch bolts and steering shaft boot nuts.
13. Tighten the following components to specification:
   a. Steering rack-to-chassis bolts — 37 ft. lbs. (50 Nm).
   b. Crossmember assembly — 137 ft. lbs. (186 Nm).
   c. Front beam-to-chassis bolts — 37 ft. lbs. (50 Nm).
   d. Ball joint — 48 ft. lbs. (65 Nm).
   e. Tie rod ends — 40 ft. lbs. (54 Nm).
   f. Exhaust pipe — 49 ft. lbs. (67 Nm).
   g. Spline shaft pinch bolt — 30 ft. lbs. (40 Nm).
14. Install the front wheels and lower the vehicle.
15. Connect the negative battery cable. With an assistant, install the hood.
16. Fill the reservoir with the proper type of fluid and bleed the air from the system. Adjust the front end alignment.

Power Steering Pump

REMOVAL AND INSTALLATION

1. Disconnect the negative battery cable.
2. Remove the engine splash shield, if so equipped.
3. Disconnect the pressure and return lines from the pump.
4. Remove the drive belt from the pump pulley.
5. Installation is the reverse of removal procedure. Adjust the drive belt, fill the reservoir with the proper type of fluid and bleed the air from the system.

BELT ADJUSTMENT

1. Loosen the pump adjusting bolt and the pivot bolt. Use a tool to force the pump away from the engine until the correct belt tension is reached.
2. On all the 1.8L engine, exert a force of approximately 22 lbs. to the belt at a point midway between the pump pulley and the crank pulley. The belt tension is correct if the belt deflects 0.2-0.4 in. when this force is applied.
3. On 1.6L engine, use a belt tension gauge and set the belt tension to 120-150 lbs. for a used belt or 130-160 lbs. for a new belt.

SYSTEM BLEEDING

1. Turn the wheels to the extreme left.
2. With the engine stopped, add power steering fluid to the MIN mark on the fluid indicator.
3. Start the engine and run it for 15 seconds at fast idle.
4. Stop the engine, recheck the fluid level and refill to the MIN mark.
5. Start the engine and turn the wheels from side to side 3 times.
6. Stop the engine and check the fluid level.

NOTE: If air bubbles are still present in the fluid, the procedure must be repeated.

Tie Rod Ends

REMOVAL AND INSTALLATION

1. Raise and safely support the vehicle. Remove the front wheel and tire assembly.
2. Remove the nut from the tie rod end stud. Using a removal tool, separate the tie rod from the steering knuckle.
3. Disconnect the retaining wire from the inner boot and pull back the boot.
4. Using a tool, straighten the staked part of the locking washer between the tie rod and the rack.
5. Remove the tie rod from the rack.
6. Installation is the reverse of the removal procedure. Tighten the tie rod end nut to 40 ft. lbs. (54 Nm).
7. Adjust the toe setting.

BRAKES

Master Cylinder

REMOVAL AND INSTALLATION

1. Disconnect the negative battery cable.
2. Disconnect the electrical connector from the master cylinder.
3. Disconnect and plug the brake lines at the master cylinder.
4. Remove the master cylinder mounting nuts and remove the master cylinder.
5. Installation is the reverse of the removal procedure. Tighten the mounting nuts to 9 ft. lbs. (13 Nm). Bleed the master cylinder.

Proportioning Valve

REMOVAL AND INSTALLATION

There are 2 proportioning valves attached to the master cylinder.
1. Disconnect the negative battery cable.
2. Disconnect and plug the brake lines at the master cylinder.
3. Remove the proportioning valves from the master cylinder.
4. Installation is the reverse of the removal procedure. Tighten the proportioning valves to 30 ft. lbs. (40 Nm). Bleed the brake system.

Power Brake Booster

REMOVAL AND INSTALLATION

1. Disconnect the negative battery cable.
2. On Impulse, remove the air cleaner duct.
3. Remove the master cylinder assembly.
4. Disconnect the vacuum hose from the power brake booster.
5. Remove the clevis pin from the brake pedal.
6. Remove the booster attaching nuts and remove the booster.
To install:
7. Install the power brake booster and tighten the booster attaching nuts to 13 ft. lbs. (18 Nm).
8. If a different booster is installed than was removed, or if the booster has been rebuilt, the pushrod must be adjusted before the master cylinder is installed.

9. Measure the distance from the flange face of the booster to the end of the pushrod using a pushrod gauge J-34873-A. Turn the locknut at the end of the pushrod.

Brake Caliper

REMOVAL AND INSTALLATION

Front

1. Raise and safely support the vehicle.

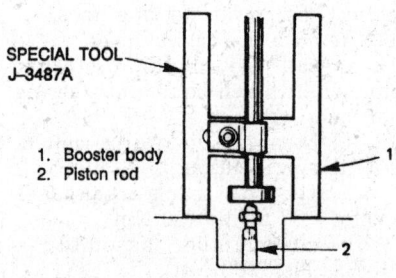

SPECIAL TOOL
J–3487A

1. Booster body
2. Piston rod

Adjusting pushrod length using special tool

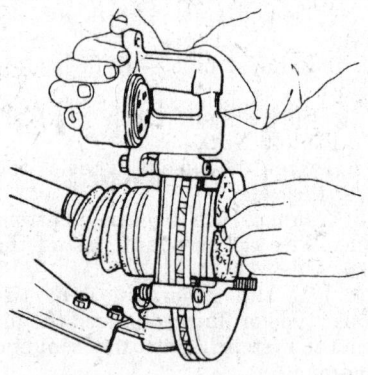

Front disc brake caliper, removal

2. Remove the front wheel and tire assemblies.
3. Disconnect and plug the brake hose at the caliper.
4. Remove the caliper slide pin(s) and remove the caliper.
5. Installation is the reverse of the removal procedure. Tighten the slide pin(s) to 36 ft. lbs. (50 Nm). Bleed the brake system.

Rear

1. Raise and safely support the vehicle.
2. Remove the rear wheel and tire assemblies.
3. Disconnect and plug the brake hose at the caliper.

NOTE: The banjo bolt retaining the brake hose on the right side has left-hand threads.

4. Disconnect the rear parking brake cable from the front cable, remove the brake cable from the cable support bracket and disconnect the brake cable from the brake lever.
5. Remove the lower slide pin and remove the caliper assembly.
6. Installation is the reverse of the removal procedure. Tighten to 32 ft. lbs. (43 Nm).
7. Bleed the brake system.
8. Adjust the parking brake.

Disc Brake Pads

REMOVAL AND INSTALLATION

1. Remove ½ brake fluid from the master cylinder.
2. Raise and safely support the vehicle.
3. Remove the wheel and tire assemblies.
4. Remove the brake caliper without disconnecting the brake line. Support the caliper with a length of wire. Do not let the caliper hang from the brake hose.

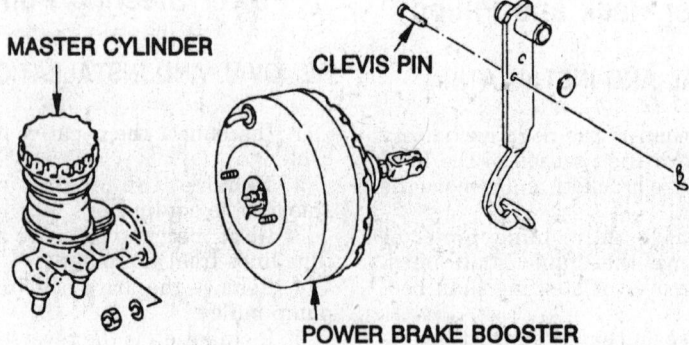

MASTER CYLINDER

CLEVIS PIN

POWER BRAKE BOOSTER

Master cylinder and power brake booster assembly

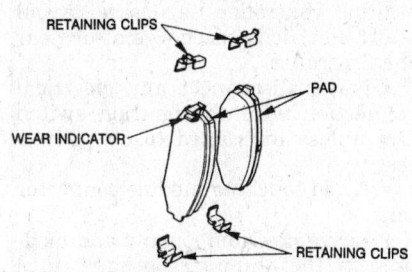

Front disc brake pads assembly

5. Remove the brake pads and shims. Inspect the brake rotor and machine or replace, as necessary. Check the minimum thickness specification when machining.

To install:

6. Push the caliper piston into its bore. Push the piston in by rotating it clockwise until it stops. Set the piston by aligning the uneven section on the piston surface with the caliper center.

7. Apply a thin coat of grease to the rear face of the brake pad and install the shim. Install the brake pads. The brake pad is provided with a pinion. The automatic adjuster becomes inoperative when the pinion is not placed correctly into the indentation of the piston.

8. Install the calipers. Install the wheel and tire assemblies and lower the vehicle.

9. Apply the brakes several times to seat the pads. Check the fluid in the master cylinder and add, as necessary.

Brake Rotor

REMOVAL AND INSTALLATION

1. Raise and safely support the vehicle.
2. Remove the wheel and tire assembly.
3. Remove the caliper and the caliper bracket.
4. Remove the brake rotor.
5. Installation is the reverse of the removal procedure.

Brake Drum

REMOVAL AND INSTALLATION

1. Raise and safely support the vehicle.

2. Remove the rear wheel and tire assembly.
3. Remove the dust cap and cotter pin. Remove the castle nut, washer and outer wheel bearing.
4. Remove the brake drum/hub assembly with the inner wheel bearing.
5. Installation is the reverse of the removal procedure. Properly adjust the wheel bearings and install a new cotter pin.

Brake Shoes

REMOVAL AND INSTALLATION

1. Raise and safely support the vehicle.
2. Remove the rear wheel and tire assemblies.
3. Remove the brake drums.
4. Remove the brake return springs.
5. Remove the leading shoe holding pin and spring and the leading shoe.
6. Remove the self adjuster and the adjuster lever.
7. Remove the trailing shoe holding pin and spring.
8. Disconnect the parking brake cable from the trailing shoe and remove the trailing shoe. Remove the parking brake lever from the trailing shoe.

To install:

9. Apply a thin coat of high temperature grease to the shoe contact pads on the brake backing plate prior to installation.
10. Check the brake drum for scoring or other wear and machine or replace, as necessary. Check the maximum brake drum diameter specification when machining. If the drum is machined, the wheel bearings must be removed and the hub .thoroughly cleaned before reinstalling.
11. Adjust the brake shoes.

Wheel Cylinder

REMOVAL AND INSTALLATION

1. Raise and safely support the vehicle.
2. Remove the rear wheel and tire assembly.
3. Remove the brake drum and the brake shoes.
4. Disconnect and plug the brake line at the wheel cylinder.
5. Remove the wheel cylinder attaching bolts and the wheel cylinder.

6. Installation is the reverse of the removal procedure. Bleed the brake system.

Brake System Bleeding

NOTE: The vacuum booster will be damaged if the bleeding operation is performed with the engine OFF.

1. Set the parking brake fully and block the drive wheels. Start the engine.
2. Remove the master cylinder reservoir cap and fill the reservoir with brake fluid. Keep the reservoir at least half full during the bleeding operation.
3. If the master cylinder is replaced or overhauled, first bleed the air from the master cylinder and then from each caliper or wheel cylinder.

NOTE: If equipped with Anti-Lock Brake System (ABS), the ABS main fuse (40A), located at the relay/fuse box assembly, must first be removed. This is necessary to properly remove all the air from the brake hydraulic system and to avoid damage to the hydraulic unit.

4. Bleed the master cylinder as follows:

a. Disconnect the left front wheel brake line from the master cylinder.

b. Have an assistant depress the brake pedal slowly once and hold it depressed.

c. Seal the delivery port of the master cylinder where the line was disconnected with a finger, then release the brake pedal slowly.

d. Release the finger from the delivery port when the brake pedal returns completely.

e. Repeat Steps c-e until the brake fluid comes out of the delivery port during Step c.

f. Reconnect the brake line to the master cylinder.

g. Have an assistant depress the brake pedal slowly once and hold it depressed.

h. Loosen the front wheel brake line at the master cylinder.

i. Retighten the brake line, then release the brake pedal slowly.

j. Repeat Steps g-i until no air comes out from the port when the brake line is loosened.

k. Bleed the air from the right front wheel brake line connection by repeating Steps a-j.

5. Bleed the air from each wheel in the following order: left front caliper, right rear caliper or wheel cylinder,

right front caliper, left rear caliper or wheel cylinder. Bleed the air as follows:

    a. Place the proper size box wrench over the bleeder screw.

    b. Cover the bleeder screw with a transparent tube and submerge the free end of the tube in a transparent container containing brake fluid.

    c. Have an assistant pump the brake pedal 3 times, then hold it depressed.

    d. Remove the air along with the brake fluid by loosening the bleeder screw.

    e. Retighten the bleeder screw, then release the brake pedal slowly.

    f. Repeat Steps c-e until the air is completely removed. It may be necessary to repeat the bleeding procedure 10 or more times for front wheels and 15 or more times for rear wheels.

    g. Go to the next wheel in sequence after each wheel is bled.

6. Depress the brake pedal to check if sponginess is felt after the air has been removed from all wheel cylinders and calipers. If the pedal feels spongy, the entire bleeding procedure must be repeated.

7. After the bleeding operation is completed on each individual wheel, check the level of brake fluid in the reservoir and replenish up to the MAX level, if necessary.

8. Install the master cylinder reservoir cap and stop the engine.

Anti-lock Brake System Service

Some diagnostic procedures require the installation of a pinout box, tool J-35592 or equivalent, in order to prevent damage to the 35-pin Electronic Brake Control Module (EBCM) connector. The pinout box should be installed prior to probing any circuit with a digital multi-meter.

PINOUT BOX INSTALLATION

1. Ensure that the ignition switch is in the **OFF** position when removing the 35-pin EBCM connector.

2. Disconnect the connector by depressing the locking plate and rotating the connector toward the front of the vehicle.

3. Inspect the 35-pin connector for damage. Install the pinout box tool J-35592 on the connector.

4. Proceed with self-diagnostic test.

SYSTEM SELF-DIAGNOSIS

The ABS is equipped with a self-diagnostic capability which is used to isolate ABS failures.

Electrical failures in the ABS are detected by the ECBM, located under the passenger seat, and result in the anti-lock warning light illuminating. The anti-lock warning light is intended to inform the driver that a condition exists which results in the ABS being disabled. The anti-lock warning light is connected to a Light Emitting Diode (LED) on the EBCM. The LED assists the individual servicing the system by flashing trouble codes which pinpoint the defective component or circuit.

NOTE: If more than one failure in the system is detected, the first failure to occur will be flashed in code on the LED. Once this failure has been corrected, the next failure code will be will be flashed.

The EBCM enters diagnostic mode any time a trouble code is set; the anti-lock light illuminates. To read the ABS trouble code, count the number of times the LED on the EBCM turns ON and OFF. Trouble codes are erased from the EBCM memory when the ignition key is turned OFF.

SERVICE PRECAUTIONS

• Do not use rubber hoses or other parts not specifically specified for the ABS system. When using repair kits, replace all parts included in the kit. Partial or incorrect repair may lead to functional problems.

• Lubricate rubber parts with clean, fresh brake fluid to ease assembly. Do not use lubricated shop air to clean parts; damage to rubber components may result.

• Use only brake fluid from an unopened container. Use of suspect or contaminated brake fluid can reduce system performance and/or durability.

• A clean repair area is essential. Perform repairs after components have been thoroughly cleaned; use only denatured alcohol to clean components. Do not allow components to come into contact with any substance containing mineral oil; this includes used shop rags.

• The ABS ECU is a microprocessor similar to other computer units in

the vehicle. Insure that the ignition switch is **OFF** before removing or installing controller harnesses. Avoid static electricity discharge at or near the controller.

• Never disconnect any electrical connection with the ignition switch **ON** unless instructed to do so in a test.

• Avoid touching module connector pins.

• Leave new components and modules in the shipping package until ready to install them.

• To avoid static discharge, always touch a vehicle ground after sliding across a vehicle seat or walking across carpeted or vinyl floors.

• Never allow welding cables to lie on, near or across any vehicle electrical wiring.

• Do not allow extension cords for power tools or droplights to lie on, near or across any vehicle electrical wiring.

• If welding is to be performed on the vehicle using an electric arc welder, the EBCM and valve block connectors should be disconnected.

• Hydraulic units of the anti-lock brake system are not separately serviceable and must be replaced as assemblies. Do not disassemble any component which is designated as non-serviceable.

Hydraulic Unit

REMOVAL AND INSTALLATION

1. Disconnect negative battery cable.

2. Raise and support vehicle safely.

3. Remove under cover to gain access to hydraulic unit.

4. Remove tire, if necessary. Remove inner fender liner.

5. Disconnect harness connectors from hydraulic unit.

6. Remove radiator reservoir tank.

7. Remove brake lines using a flare nut wrench. Cap or tape brake line ends to prevent entry of foreign matter.

8. Disconnect hydraulic motor ground cable.

9. Remove bracket attaching bolt, hydraulic unit attaching nut, bracket and hydraulic unit.

To install:

10. Installation is the reverse of the removal procedure. Torque the hydraulic unit attaching nut, bracket attaching bolt and ground cable bolt to 17 ft. lbs. (22 Nm). Torque brake line to 9 ft. lbs. (12 Nm).

11. Bleed the brake system.

NOTE: Replace all components included in repair kits used to service this system. Lubricate rubber parts with clean, fresh brake fluid to ease assembly. Do not use lubricated shop air to clean parts, as damage to rubber components may result. Always bleed the braking system after repairing or replacing hydraulic components.

12. Install the wheels, if removed. Lower the vehicle and connect the negative battery cable.
13. Road test the vehicle.

Electric Brake Control Unit (EBCM)

REMOVAL AND INSTALLATION

The EBCM is located under the passenger side seat on the Impulse.
1. Disconnect the negative battery cable.
2. It may be necessary to move the passenger seat out of the way to gain access to the EBCM. If so, remove the seat attaching bolts and move the seat.
3. Remove the EBCM attaching bolts.
4. Remove the EBCM wiring harness connector. Remove the EBCM.
5. Installation is the reverse of removal. Tighten EBCM attaching bolts to 62 inch lbs. (7.0 Nm).

G-Sensor

REMOVAL AND INSTALLATION

1. Disconnect negative battery cable.
2. Remove center console.
3. Remove G-Sensor wiring harness connector.
4. Remove G-Sensor attaching bolt. Remove the G-Sensor.
5. Place G-Sensor on a known level surface and check continuity between terminals. If no continuity, replace the G-Sensor.
6. Incline the G-Sensor to a 30 degree angle and retest for continuity. If continuity exists, replace the G-Sensor.

NOTE: Ensure that G-Sensor is installed in the direction indicated.

7. Installation is the reverse of removal. Torque attaching bolts to 53 inch lbs. (5.4 Nm).

Speed Sensor

REMOVAL AND INSTALLATION

1. Disconnect negative battery cable.
2. Raise and support vehicle safely.
3. Remove wheel assembly. Remove inner fender liner.
4. Disconnect speed sensor wire connector.
5. Remove sensor cable attaching bolts and screws.
6. Remove sensor attaching bolts. Remove sensor.
To install:
7. Inspect the speed sensor for damage.
   a. Check the speed sensor pole piece for dirt and gently clean it if needed.
   b. Check the pole piece for damage and replace, if necessary.
   c. Check for continuity while flexing the sensor cable. Replace sensor cable, if a short or open is found.
   d. Check the sensor rotor for damage including tooth chipping. If sensor rotor is damaged, replace the driveshaft assembly.
8. Install the speed sensor, taking care not to damage the pole piece. Tighten the attaching bolt to 62 inch lbs. (6.8 Nm).
9. Check the clearance between the speed sensor pole piece and the rotor. Clearance should be 0.0079-0.0315 in. (0.20-0.80mm).
10. Install the sensor cable fixing bolt and tighten to 13 ft. lbs. (17 Nm). Tighten screw to 9 ft. lbs. (12 Nm).
11. Ensure the white line marked on the cable is not twisted. If so, loosen connections and straighten cable.
12. Reconnect sensor wire connector. Install the inner liner and wheel and tire assemblies. Lower the vehicle and reconnect negative battery cable.
13. Road test the vehicle.

CHASSIS ELECTRICAL

Air Bag

DISARMING

——— CAUTION ———
To disarm the Supplemental Inflatable Restraint (SIR) system, disconnect and TAPE the negative battery cable. Failure to disarm the SIR system, when working on or around the steering column, may result in deployment of the air bag and possible personal injury.

REMOVAL AND INSTALLATION

1. Disconnect the negative battery cable.
2. Disconnect the wire connector from the blower motor.
3. Disconnect the rubber hose on vehicles equipped with air conditioning.
4. Remove the retaining clip and the blower motor.
5. Installation is the reverse of the removal procedure.

Windshield Wiper Motor

REMOVAL AND INSTALLATION

Front

1. Disconnect the negative battery cable.
2. Remove the wiper arm cap, nut and the wiper arm and blade.
3. Remove the cowl cover, if equipped.
4. Disconnect the wiper motor from the wiper linkage.
5. Disconnect the electrical connectors.
6. Remove the mounting bolts and the wiper motor.
7. Installation is the reverse of the removal procedure. Be sure to apply grease to the crank arm ball joint.

Rear

1. Disconnect the negative battery cable.
2. Remove the cover, nut and rear wiper arm and blade.
3. Remove the rear hatch trim panel, if equipped.

4. Disconnect the electrical connector at the wiper motor.

5. On Impulse, remove the nut, cap washer and seal. Remove the wiper motor mounting bolts and remove the wiper motor.

6. Installation is the reverse of the removal procedure.

Windshield Wiper Switch

REMOVAL AND INSTALLATION

1. Disconnect the negative battery cable.

2. Remove the instrument cluster hood attaching screws. Disconnect the electrical connectors so the hood can be removed.

3. Remove the instrument cluster, if necessary.

4. Remove the windshield wiper switch.

5. Installation is the reverse of the removal procedure.

Instrument Cluster

─────── CAUTION ───────

Always disarm the SIR system, when working on or around the steering column. Failure to disarm the SIR system, may result in deployment of the air bag and possible personal injury. To disarm the Supplemental Inflatable Restraint (SIR) system, disconnect and TAPE the negative battery cable.

─────────────────────

REMOVAL AND INSTALLATION

1. Disconnect the negative battery cable.

2. Remove the instrument cluster hood screw hole covers and remove the hood attaching screws.

3. Disconnect the lighting and windshield wiper switch connectors and remove the instrument cluster hood.

4. Disconnect the speedometer cable and electrical connectors from the instrument cluster.

5. Remove the instrument cluster.

6. Remove the trip meter and clock reset knob and the gauge screen.

7. Remove the instrument cluster bezel and remove the speedometer from the gauge case.

To install:

8. Install the instrument cluster bezel and speedometer to the gauge case.

9. Install the trip meter and clock reset knob and the gauge screen.

10. Install the instrument cluster.

11. Connect the speedometer cable and electrical connectors to the instrument cluster. Install the cluster hood.

12. Connect the lighting and windshield wiper switch connectors.

13. Install the instrument cluster hood screw hole covers.

14. Connect the negative battery cable.

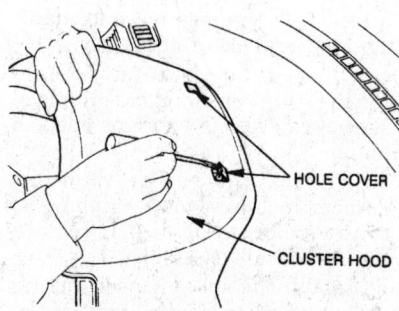

HOLE COVER

CLUSTER HOOD

Removing the cluster hood screw covers

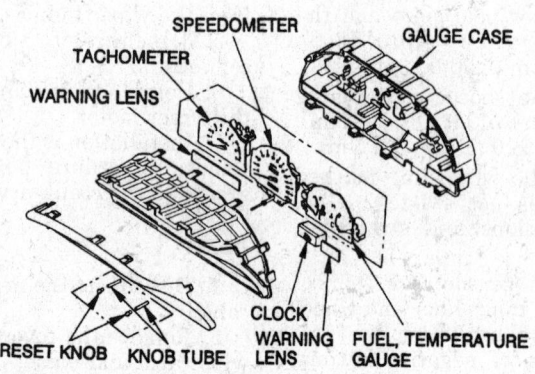

SPEEDOMETER

TACHOMETER

WARNING LENS

GAUGE CASE

RESET KNOB KNOB TUBE

CLOCK
WARNING LENS

FUEL, TEMPERATURE GAUGE

Instrument cluster assembly

Concealed Headlights

MANUAL OPERATION

1. Raise the hood and disconnect the electrical connector at the headlight cover motor.

2. Turn the manual operation knob located on the headlight cover motor to open or close the headlight covers.

Headlight Switch

REMOVAL AND INSTALLATION

1. Disconnect the negative battery cable.

2. Remove the instrument cluster hood attaching screws. Disconnect the electrical connectors so the hood can be removed.

3. Remove the instrument cluster, if necessary.

4. Remove the headlight switch.

5. Installation is the reverse of the removal procedure.

Dimmer Switch

REMOVAL AND INSTALLATION

1. Disconnect and tape the negative battery cable.

2. Place the front wheels in the straight-ahead position and the ignition key in the **LOCK** position.

3. Remove the 4 bolts from the lower side of the steering wheel. These bolts hold the Supplemental Inflatable Restraint (SIR) module to the steering wheel. Disconnect the module connector and remove the SIR module.

─────── CAUTION ───────

The SIR module should always be carried with the urethane cover away from the body and should always be laid on a flat surface with the urethane side up. This is necessary because a free space is provided to allow the air cushion to expand in the unlikely event of accidental deployment. Otherwise, personal injury may result.

─────────────────────

4. Disconnect the horn lead and remove the steering wheel nut. Use a steering wheel puller to remove the steering wheel.

5. Remove the knee pad and the steering column cover.

6. Disconnect the electrical connector from the coil/switch assembly.

Manual operation of the headlight cover — Impulse

7. Remove the retaining screws and the coil/switch assembly.

8. Separate the coil from the switch.

To install:

9. Install the switch, trim panels and connect the electrical connectors.

NOTE: Whenever the coil/switch assembly is be replaced, the vehicle's front wheels must be straight-ahead. Failure to do so will cause the coil assembly to be removed without being centered. Installing an uncentered coil assembly can cause damage to the coil assembly.

10. Install the steering wheel and torque the nut to 25 ft. lbs. (34 Nm).

11. Install and connect the horn pad or SIR module.

12. Connect the battery cable and check operation.

Turn Signal Switch

———— **CAUTION** ————

Always disarm the SIR system, when working on or around the steering column. Failure to disarm the SIR system, may result in deployment of the air bag and possible personal injury. To disarm the Supplemental Inflatable Restraint (SIR) system, disconnect and TAPE the negative battery cable.

REMOVAL AND INSTALLATION

1. Disconnect and tape the negative battery cable.

2. Place the front wheels in the straight-ahead position and the ignition key in the **LOCK** position.

3. Remove the 4 bolts which hold the Supplemental Inflatable Restraint (SIR) module from the lower

side of the steering wheel. Disconnect the module connector and remove the SIR module.

———— **CAUTION** ————

The SIR module should always be carried with the urethane cover away from the body and should always be laid on a flat surface with the urethane side up. This is necessary because a free space is provided to allow the air cushion to expand in the unlikely event of accidental deployment. Otherwise, personal injury may result.

4. Disconnect the horn lead and remove the steering wheel nut. Use a steering wheel puller to remove the steering wheel.

5. Remove the knee pad and the steering column cover.

6. Disconnect the electrical connector from the coil/switch assembly.

7. Remove the retaining screws and the coil/switch assembly.

8. Separate the coil from the switch.

To install:

9. Install the switch, trim panels and connect the electrical connectors.

NOTE: Whenever the coil/switch assembly is be replaced, the vehicle's front wheels must be straight-ahead. Failure to do so will cause the coil assembly to be removed without being centered. Installing an uncentered coil assembly can cause damage to the coil assembly.

10. Install the steering wheel and torque the nut to 25 ft. lbs. (34 Nm).

11. Install and connect the horn pad or SIR module.

12. Connect the battery cable and check operation.

Ignition Lock/Switch

———— **CAUTION** ————

Always disarm the SIR system, when working on or around the steering column. Failure to disarm the SIR system, may result in deployment of the air bag and possible personal injury. To disarm the Supplemental Inflatable Restraint (SIR) system, disconnect and tape the negative battery cable.

REMOVAL AND INSTALLATION

1. Disconnect and tape the negative battery cable.

2. If equipped with an air bag, perform the following procedure:

a. Place the front wheels in the straight-ahead position and the ignition key in the **LOCK** position.

b. Remove the 4 bolts which hold the Supplemental Inflatable Restraint (SIR) module from the lower side of the steering wheel. Disconnect the module connector and remove the SIR module.

———— **CAUTION** ————

The SIR module should always be carried with the urethane cover away from the body and should always be laid on a flat surface with the urethane side up. This is necessary because a free space is provided to allow the air cushion to expand in the unlikely event of accidental deployment. Otherwise, personal injury may result.

3. If not equipped with an air bag, remove the horn pad.

4. Disconnect the horn lead and remove the steering wheel nut. Use a steering wheel puller to remove the steering wheel.

5. Remove the knee pad.

6. Remove the steering column covers.

7. Remove the steering shaft retaining ring and washer.

8. Disconnect the ignition switch electrical connector, remove the steering lock retaining screws and remove the lock/switch assembly.

NOTE: Whenever the coil/switch assembly is be replaced, the vehicle's front wheels must be straight-ahead. Failure to do so will cause the coil assembly to be removed without being centered. Installing an uncentered coil assembly can cause damage to the coil assembly.

To install:

9. Install and connect the ignition switch electrical connector.

10. Install the steering shaft retaining ring and washer.

11. Install the steering column covers.

12. Install the knee pad.

13. Install the steering wheel and nut. Torque the nut to 25 ft. lbs. (34 Nm). Connect the horn lead.

14. If not equipped with an air bag, install the horn pad.

15. Install the 4 bolts holding the Supplemental Inflatable Restraint (SIR) module to the steering wheel.

16. Connect the negative battery cable.

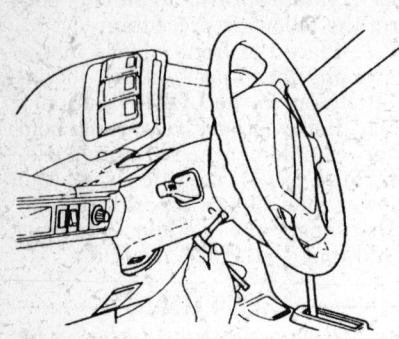

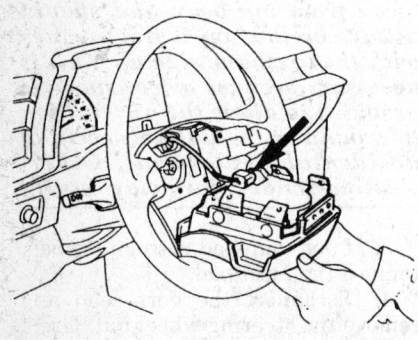

Supplemental Inflatable Restraint SIR module removal

Stoplight Switch

REMOVAL AND INSTALLATION

1. Loosen the locknut.
2. Place the tip of the switch so it rests gently against the rubber stopper on the pedal arm.

3. Rotate the stoplight switch until the switch housing contacts lightly with the pedal stopper.

NOTE: Do not attempt to force the brake pushrod into position during the stoplight switch adjustment procedure.

4. Tighten the locknut.

Clutch Switch

REMOVAL AND INSTALLATION

1. Disconnect the negative battery cable.
2. Disconnect the electrical connector at the switch.
3. Remove the switch retaining screws and the switch.
4. Installation is the reverse of the removal procedure.

Neutral Safety Switch

REMOVAL AND INSTALLATION

1. Raise and safely support the vehicle.
2. Disconnect the electrical connector to the switch.
3. Remove the switch from the transmission.
4. Installation is the reverse of the removal procedure.

NOTE: This adjustment is necessary only if the engine will start with the shift selector in other positions than N or P.

5. Loosen the neutral start switch bolt and set the shift selector into the **N** range.
6. Align the groove and the neutral basic line.
7. Hold it in position and torque the bolt to 9 ft. lbs. (12 Nm).

Fuses

LOCATION

Fuses are located in both the junction block located on the left kick panel and in the relay and fuse box located in the left side of the engine compartment.

Circuit Breakers

LOCATION

Stylus and Impulse have 2 circuit breaker locations on the junction box, with only 1 being used for the power windows and sunroof.

Flashers

LOCATION

Flashers are located under the left side of the dashboard.

SPECIFICATIONS

ENGINE IDENTIFICATION

Year	Model	Engine Displacement Liters (cc)	Engine Series (ID/VIN)	Fuel System	No. of Cylinders	Engine Type
1990	ES 250	2.5 (2508)	2VZ-FE	EFI	6	DOHC
	LS 400	4.0 (3969)	1UZ-FE	EFI	8	DOHC
1991	ES 250	2.5 (2508)	2VZ-FE	EFI	6	DOHC
	LS 400	4.0 (3969)	1UZ-FE	EFI	8	DOHC
1992	ES 300	3.0 (2959)	3VZ-FE	EFI	6	DOHC
	SC 300	3.0 (2997)	2JZ-GE	EFI	6	DOHC
	LS 400	4.0 (3969)	1UZ-FE	EFI	8	DOHC
	SC 400	4.0 (3969)	1UZ-FE	EFI	8	DOHC
1993	ES 300	3.0 (2959)	3VZ-FE	EFI	6	DOHC
	SC 300	3.0 (2997)	2JZ-GE	EFI	6	DOHC
	LS 400	4.0 (3969)	1UZ-FE	EFI	8	DOHC
	SC 400	4.0 (3969)	1UZ-FE	EFI	8	DOHC
1994	ES 300	3.0 (2959)	3VZ-FE	EFI	6	DOHC
	SC 300	3.0 (2997)	2JZ-GE	EFI	6	DOHC
	LS 400	4.0 (3969)	1UZ-FE	EFI	8	DOHC
	SC 400	4.0 (3969)	1UZ-FE	EFI	8	DOHC

EFI: Electronic Fuel Injection
DOHC: Double Overhead Camshaft

GENERAL ENGINE SPECIFICATIONS

Year	Engine ID/VIN	Engine Displacement Liters (cc)	Fuel System Type	Net Horsepower @ rpm	Net Torque @ rpm (ft. lbs.)	Bore x Stroke (in.)	Compression Ratio	Oil Pressure @ rpm
1990	2VZ-FE	2.5 (2508)	EFI	156 @ 5600	160 @ 4400	3.44 x 2.74	9.0:1	43–78 @ 3000
	1UZ-FE	4.0 (3969)	EFI	250 @ 5600	260 @ 4400	3.44 x 3.25	10.0:1	36–71 @ 3000
1991	2VZ-FE	2.5 (2508)	EFI	156 @ 5600	160 @ 4400	3.44 x 3.25	9.0:1	43–78 @ 3000
	1UZ-FE	4.0 (3969)	EFI	250 @ 5600	260 @ 4400	3.44 x 3.25	10.0:1	36–71 @ 3000
1992	3VZ-FE	3.0 (2959)	EFI	185 @ 5200	195 @ 4400	3.44 x 3.23	9.6:1	43–78 @ 3000
	2JZ-GE	3.0 (2997)	EFI	225 @ 6000	210 @ 4800	3.39 x 3.39	10.2:1	43–78 @ 3000
	1UZ-FE	4.0 (3969)	EFI	250 @ 5600	260 @ 4400	3.44 x 3.25	10.0:1	36–71 @ 3000
1993	3VZ-FE	3.0 (2959)	EFI	185 @ 5200	195 @ 4400	3.44 x 3.23	9.6:1	43–78 @ 3000
	2JZ-GE	3.0 (2997)	EFI	225 @ 6000	210 @ 4800	3.39 x 3.39	10.2:1	43–78 @ 3000
	1UZ-FE	4.0 (3969)	EFI	250 @ 5600	260 @ 4400	3.44 x 3.25	10.0:1	36–71 @ 3000
1994	3VZ-FE	3.0 (2959)	EFI	185 @ 5200	195 @ 4400	3.44 x 3.23	9.6:1	43–78 @ 3000
	2JZ-GE	3.0 (2997)	EFI	225 @ 6000	210 @ 4800	3.39 x 3.39	10.2:1	43–78 @ 3000
	1UZ-FE	4.0 (3969)	EFI	250 @ 5600	260 @ 4400	3.44 x 3.25	10.0:1	36–71 @ 3000

EFI—Electronic Fuel Injection

TUNE-UP SPECIFICATIONS

Year	Engine ID/VIN	Displacement Liters (cc)	Spark Plugs Gap (in.)	Ignition Timing ① (deg.)		Fuel Pump (psi)	Idle Speed (rpm)		Valve Clearance	
				MT	AT		MT	AT	In.	Ex.
1990	2VZ-FE	2.5 (2508)	0.043	10B	10B	38–44	600–700	650–750	0.005	0.015
	1UZ-FE	4.0 (3969)	0.043	—	8–12B	38–44	—	600–700	0.006–0.010	0.010–0.014
1991	2VZ-FE	2.5 (2508)	0.043	10B	10B	38–44	600–700	650–750	0.005	0.015
	1UZ-FE	4.0 (3969)	0.043	—	8–12B	38–44	—	600–700	0.006–0.010	0.010–0.014
1992	3VZ-FE	3.0 (2959)	0.043	10B	10B	38–44	600–700	650–750	0.005–0.009	0.011–0.015
	2JZ-GE	3.0 (2997)	0.043	10B	10B	38–44	650–750	600–700	0.006–0.010	0.010–0.014
	1UZ-FE	4.0 (3969)	0.043	—	8–12B	38–44	—	600–700	0.006–0.010	0.010–0.014
1993	3VZ-FE	3.0 (2959)	0.043	10B	10B	38–44	600–700	650–750	0.005–0.009	0.011–0.015
	2JZ-GE	3.0 (2997)	0.043	10B	10B	38–44	650–750	600–700	0.006–0.010	0.010–0.014
	1UZ-FE	4.0 (3969)	0.043	—	8–12B	38–44	—	600–700	0.006–0.010	0.010–0.014
1994	3VZ-FE	3.0 (2959)	0.043	10B	10B	38–44	600–700	650–750	0.005–0.009	0.011–0.015
	2JZ-GE	3.0 (2997)	0.043	10B	10B	38–44	650–750	600–700	0.006–0.010	0.010–0.014
	1UZ-FE	4.0 (3969)	0.043	—	8–12B	38–44	—	600–700	0.006–0.010	0.010–0.014

NOTE: The lowest cylinder pressure should be within 75% of the highest cylinder pressure reading. For example, if the highest cylinder is 134 psi, the lowest should be 101. Engine should be at normal operating temperature with throttle valve in the wide open position.

The underhood specifications sticker often reflects tune-up specification changes in production. Sticker figures must be used if they disagree with those in this chart.

B: Before Top Dead Center

① Terminals TE_1 and E_1 of the check connector must be connected.

FIRING ORDERS

NOTE: To avoid confusion, always replace spark plug wires one at a time.

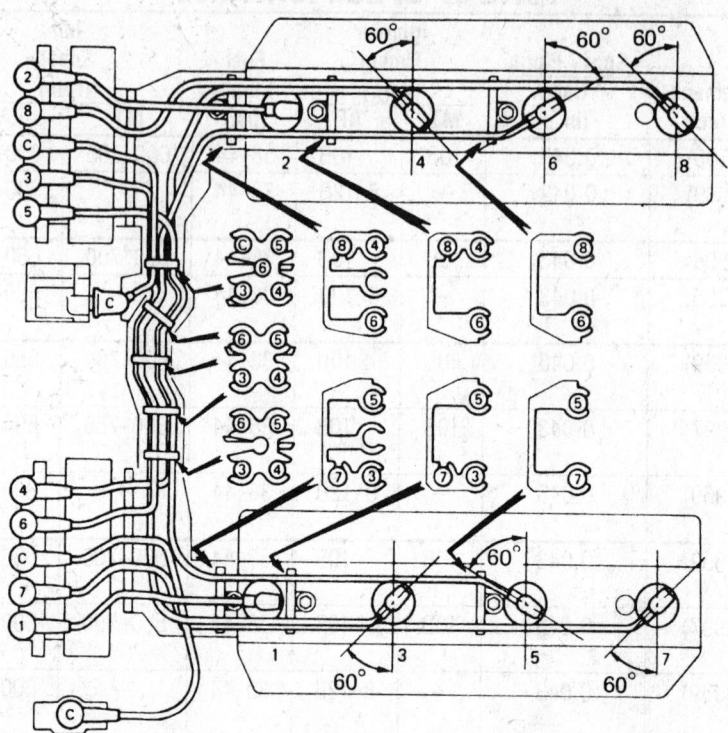

4.0L Engine (1UZ-FE)
Engine Firing Order: 1-8-4-3-6-5-7-2
Distributor Rotation: Clockwise

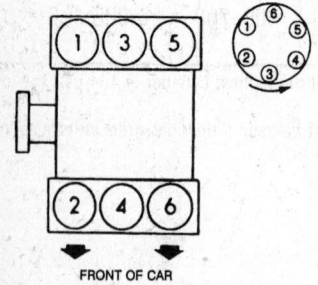

FRONT OF CAR

2.5L and 3.0L Engines (2VZ-FE, 3VZ-FE)
Engine Firing Order: 1-2-3-4-5-6
Distributor Rotation: Counterclockwise

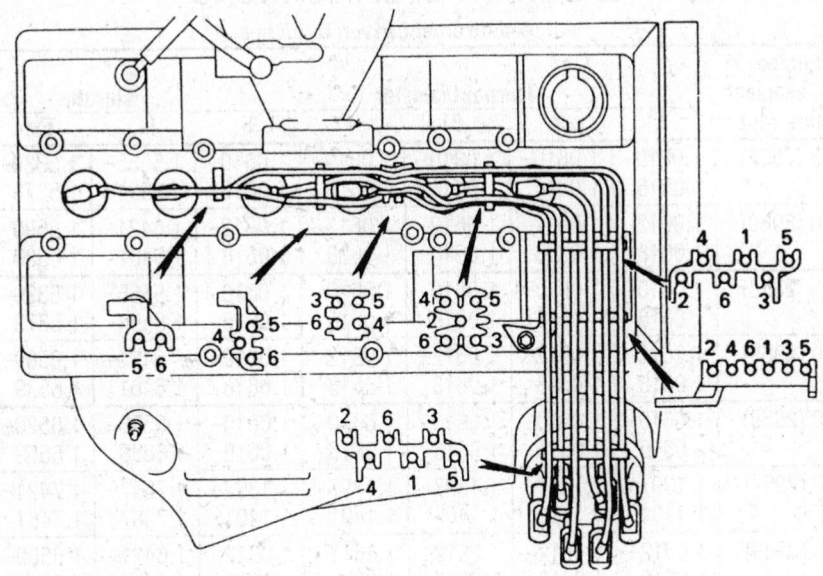

2JZ-GE Engine
Engine Firing Order: 1-5-3-6-2-4
Distributor Rotation: Clockwise

CAPACITIES

Year	Model	Engine ID/VIN	Engine Displacement Liters (cc)	Engine Crankcase with Filter (qts.)	Transmission (pts.) 4-Spd	5-Spd	Auto.	Transfer case (pts.)	Drive Axle Front (pts.)	Rear (pts.)	Fuel Tank (gal.)	Cooling System (qts.)
1990	ES250	2VZ-FE	2.5 (2508)	4.1	—	4.4	5.2	—	2.2	—	15.9	10.0
	LS400	1UZ-FE	4.0 (3969)	5.6	—	—	4.0	—	—	2.8	22.5	11.2
1991	ES250	2VZ-FE	2.5 (2508)	4.1	—	4.4	5.2	—	2.2	—	15.9	10.0
	LS400	1UZ-FE	4.0 (3969)	5.6	—	—	4.0	—	—	2.8	22.5	11.2
1992	ES300	3VZ-FE	3.0 (2959)	4.5	—	8.8	6.6	—	1.6	—	18.5	9.0
	SC300	2JZ-GE	3.0 (2997)	5.1	—	5.4	3.4	—	—	2.8	22.5	8.9
	LS400	1UZ-FE	4.0 (3969)	5.6	—	—	4.0	—	—	2.8	22.5	11.2
	SC400	1UZ-FE	4.0 (3969)	5.1	—	—	4.0	—	—	2.8	22.5	11.4
1993	ES300	3VZ-FE	3.0 (2959)	4.5	—	8.8	6.6	—	1.6	—	18.5	9.0
	SC300	2JZ-GE	3.0 (2997)	5.1	—	5.4	3.4	—	—	2.8	22.5	8.9
	LS400	1UZ-FE	4.0 (3969)	5.6	—	—	4.0	—	—	2.8	22.5	11.2
	SC400	1UZ-FE	4.0 (3969)	5.1	—	—	4.0	—	—	2.8	22.5	11.4
1994	ES300	3VZ-FE	3.0 (2959)	4.5	—	8.8	6.6	—	1.6	—	18.5	9.0
	SC300	2JZ-GE	3.0 (2997)	5.1	—	5.4	3.4	—	—	2.8	22.5	8.9
	LS400	1UZ-FE	4.0 (3969)	5.6	—	—	4.0	—	—	2.8	22.5	11.2
	SC400	1UZ-FE	4.0 (3969)	5.1	—	—	4.0	—	—	2.8	22.5	11.4

CAMSHAFT SPECIFICATIONS

All measurement given in inches

Year	Engine ID/VIN	Engine Displacement Liters (cc)	Journal Diameter					Elevation		Bearing Clearance	Camshaft End Play
			1	2	3	4	5	In.	Ex.		
1990	2VZ-FE	2.5 (2508)	1.0610–1.0616	1.0610–1.0616	1.0610–1.0616	1.0610–1.0616	1.0610–1.0616	1.5555–1.5594	1.5339–1.5378	0.0014–0.0028	0.0012–0.0031
	1UZ-FE ①	4.0 (3969)	1.0612–1.0618	1.0612–1.0618	1.0612–1.0618	1.0612–1.0618	1.0612–1.0618	1.6421–1.6461	1.6500–1.6539	0.0012–0.0026	0.0016–0.0035
1991	2VZ-FE	2.5 (2508)	1.0610–1.0616	1.0610–1.0616	1.0610–1.0616	1.0610–1.0616	1.0610–1.0616	1.5555–1.5594	1.5339–1.5378	0.0014–0.0028	0.0012–0.0031
	1UZ-FE ①	4.0 (3969)	1.0612–1.0618	1.0612–1.0618	1.0612–1.0618	1.0612–1.0618	1.0612–1.0618	1.6421–1.6461	1.6500–1.6539	0.0012–0.0026	0.0016–0.0035
1992	3VZ-FE	3.0 (2959)	1.0610–1.0616	1.0610–1.0616	1.0610–1.0616	1.0610–1.0616	1.0610–1.0616	1.6598–1.6638	1.6520–1.6559	0.0014–0.0028	0.0013–0.0031
	2JZ-GE	3.0 (2997)	1.1397–1.1401	1.1397–1.1401	1.1397–1.1401	1.1397–1.1401	1.1397–1.1401	1.7547–1.7587	1.7421–1.7461	0.0014–0.0028	0.0031–0.0075
	1UZ-FE ①	4.0 (3969)	1.0612–1.0618	1.0612–1.0618	1.0612–1.0618	1.0612–1.0618	1.0612–1.0618	1.6421–1.6461	1.6500–1.6539	0.0012–0.0026	0.0016–0.0035
1993	3VZ-FE	3.0 (2959)	1.0610–1.0616	1.0610–1.0616	1.0610–1.0616	1.0610–1.0616	1.0610–1.0616	1.6598–1.6638	1.6520–1.6559	0.0014–0.0028	0.0013–0.0031
	2JZ-GE	3.0 (2997)	1.1397–1.1401	1.1397–1.1401	1.1397–1.1401	1.1397–1.1401	1.1397–1.1401	1.7547–1.7587	1.7421–1.7461	0.0014–0.0028	0.0031–0.0075
	1UZ-FE ①	4.0 (3969)	1.0612–1.0618	1.0612–1.0618	1.0612–1.0618	1.0612–1.0618	1.0612–1.0618	1.6421–1.6461	1.6500–1.6539	0.0012–0.0026	0.0016–0.0035
1994	3VZ-FE	3.0 (2959)	1.0610–1.0616	1.0610–1.0616	1.0610–1.0616	1.0610–1.0616	1.0610–1.0616	1.6598–1.6638	1.6520–1.6559	0.0014–0.0028	0.0013–0.0031
	2JZ-GE	3.0 (2997)	1.1397–1.1401	1.1397–1.1401	1.1397–1.1401	1.1397–1.1401	1.1397–1.1401	1.7547–1.7587	1.7421–1.7461	0.0014–0.0028	0.0031–0.0075
	1UZ-FE ①	4.0 (3969)	1.0612–1.0618	1.0612–1.0618	1.0612–1.0618	1.0612–1.0618	1.0612–1.0618	1.6421–1.6461	1.6500–1.6539	0.0012–0.0026	0.0016–0.0035

① The exhaust camshaft thrust portion of journal
diameter is 0.9433–0.9439 in.; of bearing
clearance is 0.0010–0.0024 in.

CRANKSHAFT AND CONNECTING ROD SPECIFICATIONS

All measurements are given in inches.

Year	Engine ID/VIN	Engine Displacement Liters (cc)	Crankshaft				Connecting Rod		
			Main Brg. Journal Dia.	Main Brg. Oil Clearance	Shaft End-play	Thrust on No.	Journal Diameter	Oil Clearance	Side Clearance
1990	2VZ-FE	2.5 (2508)	2.5191–2.5197	0.0011–0.0022	0.0008–0.0087	3	1.8892–1.8898	0.0011–0.0026	0.0059–0.0130
	1UZ-FE	4.0 (3969)	2.6373–2.6378	0.0010–0.0018	0.0008–0.0087	3	2.0465–2.0472	0.0011–0.0021	0.0063–0.0114
1991	2VZ-FE	2.5 (2508)	2.5191–2.5197	0.0011–0.0022	0.0008–0.0087	3	1.8892–1.8898	0.0011–0.0026	0.0059–0.0130
	1UZ-FE	4.0 (3969)	2.6373–2.6378	0.0010–0.0018	0.0008–0.0087	3	2.0465–2.0472	0.0011–0.0021	0.0063–0.0114
1992	3VZ-FE	3.0 (2959)	2.5191–2.5197	0.0011–0.0022	0.0008–0.0087	3	2.1648–2.1654	0.0011–0.0026	0.0059–0.0130
	2JZ-GE	3.0 (2997)	①	0.0010–0.0016	0.0008–0.0087	3	②	0.0014–0.0021	0.0098–0.0158
	1UZ-FE	4.0 (3969)	2.6373–2.6378	0.0010–0.0018	0.0008–0.0087	3	2.0465–2.0472	0.0011–0.0021	0.0063–0.0114
1993	3VZ-FE	3.0 (2959)	2.5191–2.5197	0.0011–0.0022	0.0008–0.0087	3	2.1648–2.1654	0.0011–0.0026	0.0059–0.0130
	2JZ-GE	3.0 (2997)	①	0.0010–0.0016	0.0008–0.0087	3	②	0.0014–0.0021	0.0098–0.0158
	1UZ-FE	4.0 (3969)	2.6373–2.6378	0.0010–0.0018	0.0008–0.0087	3	2.0465–2.0472	0.0011–0.0021	0.0063–0.0114
1994	3VZ-FE	3.0 (2959)	2.5191–2.5197	0.0011–0.0022	0.0008–0.0087	3	2.1648–2.1654	0.0011–0.0026	0.0059–0.0130
	2JZ-GE	3.0 (2997)	①	0.0010–0.0016	0.0008–0.0087	3	②	0.0014–0.0021	0.0098–0.0158
	1UZ-FE	4.0 (3969)	2.6373–2.6378	0.0010–0.0018	0.0008–0.0087	3	2.0465–2.0472	0.0011–0.0021	0.0063–0.0114

① Mark 0: 2.44087–2.44095 in.
  Mark 1: 2.44079–2.44087 in.
  Mark 2: 2.44071–2.44079 in.
  Mark 3: 2.44063–2.44071 in.
  Mark 4: 2.44055–2.44063 in.
  Mark 5: 2.44047–2.44055 in.
  Mark 6: 2.44039–2.44047 in.
  Mark 7: 2.44031–2.44039 in.
② Mark 0: 2.0470–2.0472 in.
  Mark 1: 2.0468–2.0470 in.
  Mark 2: 2.0465–2.0468 in.

VALVE SPECIFICATIONS

Year	Engine ID/VIN	Engine Displacement Liters (cc)	Seat Angle (deg.)	Face Angle (deg.)	Spring Test Pressure (lbs.)	Spring Installed Height (in.)	Stem-to-Guide Clearance (in.)		Stem Diameter (in.)	
							Intake	Exhaust	Intake	Exhaust
1990	2VZ-FE	2.5 (2508)	NA	44.5	41.0–47.2	1.677	0.0010–0.0024	0.0012–0.0026	0.2350–0.2356	0.2348–0.2354
	1UZ-FE	4.0 (3969)	NA	44.5	41.9–46.3	1.717	0.0010–0.0024	0.0012–0.0026	0.2350–0.2356	0.2348–0.2354
1991	2VZ-FE	2.5 (2508)	NA	44.5	41.0–47.2	1.677	0.0010–0.0024	0.0012–0.0026	0.2350–0.2356	0.2348–0.2354
	1UZ-FE	4.0 (3969)	NA	44.5	41.9–46.3	1.717	0.0010–0.0024	0.0012–0.0026	0.2350–0.2356	0.2348–0.2354
1992	3VZ-FE	3.0 (2959)	NA	44.5	38.4–42.4	1.630	0.0010–0.0024	0.0012–0.0026	0.2350–0.2356	0.2348–0.2354
	2JZ-GE	3.0 (2997)	NA	44.5	41.9–46.3	①	0.0010–0.0024	0.0012–0.0026	0.2350–0.2356	0.2348–0.2354
	1UZ-FE	4.0 (3969)	NA	44.5	41.9–46.3	1.717	0.0010–0.0024	0.0012–0.0026	0.2350–0.2356	0.2348–0.2354
1993	3VZ-FE	3.0 (2959)	NA	44.5	38.4–42.4	1.630	0.0010–0.0024	0.0012–0.0026	0.2350–0.2356	0.2348–0.2354
	2JZ-GE	3.0 (2997)	NA	44.5	41.9–46.3	①	0.0010–0.0024	0.0012–0.0026	0.2350–0.2356	0.2348–0.2354
	1UZ-FE	4.0 (3969)	NA	44.5	41.9–46.3	1.717	0.0010–0.0024	0.0012–0.0026	0.2350–0.2356	0.2348–0.2354
1994	3VZ-FE	3.0 (2959)	NA	44.5	38.4–42.4	1.630	0.0010–0.0024	0.0012–0.0026	0.2350–0.2356	0.2348–0.2354
	2JZ-GE	3.0 (2997)	NA	44.5	41.9–46.3	①	0.0010–0.0024	0.0012–0.0026	0.2350–0.2356	0.2348–0.2354
	1UZ-FE	4.0 (3969)	NA	44.5	41.9–46.3	1.717	0.0010–0.0024	0.0012–0.0026	0.2350–0.2356	0.2348–0.2354

NA—Not available
① Pink mark: 1.6433 in.
  White mark: 1.6339 in.

PISTON AND RING SPECIFICATIONS

All measurements are given in inches

Year	Engine ID/VIN	Engine Displacement Liters (cc)	Piston Clearance	Ring Gap			Ring Side Clearance		
				Top Compression	Bottom Compression	Oil Control	Top Compression	Bottom Compression	Oil Control
1990	2VZ-FE	2.5 (2508)	0.0018–0.0026	0.0118–0.0213	0.0138–0.0244	0.0079–0.0224	0.0004–0.0031	0.0012–0.0028	—
	1UZ-FE	4.0 (3969)	0.0008–0.0016	0.0098–0.0177	0.0138–0.0236	0.0059–0.0197	0.0008–0.0024	0.0006–0.0022	—
1991	2VZ-FE	2.5 (2508)	0.0018–0.0026	0.0118–0.0213	0.0138–0.0244	0.0079–0.0224	0.0004–0.0031	0.0012–0.0028	—
	1UZ-FE	4.0 (3969)	0.0008–0.0016	0.0098–0.0177	0.0138–0.0236	0.0059–0.0197	0.0008–0.0024	0.0006–0.0022	—
1992	3VZ-FE	3.0 (2959)	0.0051–0.0059	0.0011–0.0197	0.0150–0.0236	0.0059–0.0224	0.0004–0.0031	0.0012–0.0028	—
	2JZ-GE	3.0 (2997)	0.0022–0.0031	0.0120–0.0188	0.0138–0.0208	0.0051–0.0180	0.0004–0.0028	0.0012–0.0028	—
	1UZ-FE	4.0 (3969)	0.0008–0.0016	0.0098–0.0177	0.0138–0.0236	0.0059–0.0197	0.0008–0.0024	0.0006–0.0022	—
1993	3VZ-FE	3.0 (2959)	0.0051–0.0059	0.0011–0.0197	0.0150–0.0236	0.0059–0.0224	0.0004–0.0031	0.0012–0.0028	—
	2JZ-GE	3.0 (2997)	0.0022–0.0031	0.0120–0.0188	0.0138–0.0208	0.0051–0.0180	0.0004–0.0028	0.0012–0.0028	—
	1UZ-FE	4.0 (3969)	0.0008–0.0016	0.0098–0.0177	0.0138–0.0236	0.0059–0.0197	0.0008–0.0024	0.0006–0.0022	—
1994	3VZ-FE	3.0 (2959)	0.0051–0.0059	0.0011–0.0197	0.0150–0.0236	0.0059–0.0224	0.0004–0.0031	0.0012–0.0028	—
	2JZ-GE	3.0 (2997)	0.0022–0.0031	0.0120–0.0188	0.0138–0.0208	0.0051–0.0180	0.0004–0.0028	0.0012–0.0028	—
	1UZ-FE	4.0 (3969)	0.0008–0.0016	0.0098–0.0177	0.0138–0.0236	0.0059–0.0197	0.0008–0.0024	0.0006–0.0022	—

TORQUE SPECIFICATIONS
All readings in ft. lbs.

Year	Engine ID/VIN	Engine Displacement Liters (cc)	Cylinder Head Bolts	Main Bearing Bolts	Rod Bearing Bolts	Crankshaft Damper Bolts	Flywheel Bolts	Manifold		Spark Plugs	Lug Nut
								Intake	Exhaust		
1990	2VZ-FE	2.5 (2508)	①	②	③	181	61	13	29	13	76
	1UZ-FE	4.0 (3969)	④	⑤	③	181	72	13	29	13	76
1991	2VZ-FE	2.5 (2508)	①	②	③	181	61	13	29	13	76
	1UZ-FE	4.0 (3969)	④	⑤	③	181	72	13	29	13	76
1992	3VZ-FE	3.0 (2959)	①	②	③	181	61	13	29	13	76
	2JZ-GE	3.0 (2997)	①	⑥	⑦	239	⑧	15	29	13	76
	1UZ-FE	4.0 (3969)	④	⑤	③	181	72	13	33	13	76
1993	3VZ-FE	3.0 (2959)	①	②	③	181	61	13	29	13	76
	2JZ-GE	3.0 (2997)	①	⑥	⑦	239	⑧	15	29	13	76
	1UZ-FE	4.0 (3969)	④	⑤	③	181	72	13	33	13	76
1994	3VZ-FE	3.0 (2959)	①	②	③	181	61	13	29	13	76
	2JZ-GE	3.0 (2997)	①	⑥	⑦	239	⑧	15	29	13	76
	1UZ-FE	4.0 (3969)	④	⑤	③	181	72	13	33	13	76

① Tighten in 3 steps:
  1—tighten to 25 ft. lbs.
  2—turn 90 degrees
  3—turn 90 degrees
  Recessed bolt on 3VZ-FE: 13 ft. lbs.
② Tighten in 2 steps:
  1—tighten to 45 ft. lbs.
  2—turn 90 degrees
③ Tighten in 2 steps:
  1—tighten to 18 ft. lbs.
  2—turn 90 degrees
④ Tighten in 2 steps:
  1—tighten to 29 ft. lbs.
  2—turn 90 degrees
⑤ Tighten in 2 steps:
  1—tighten to 20 ft. lbs.
  2—turn 90 degrees
⑥ Tighten in 2 steps:
  1—tighten to 33 ft. lbs.
  2—turn 90 degrees
⑦ Tighten in 2 steps:
  1—tighten to 22 ft. lbs.
  2—turn 90 degrees
⑧ Driveplate: 72 ft. lbs.
  Flywheel:
  1—tighten to 36 ft. lbs.
  2—turn 90 degrees

BRAKE SPECIFICATIONS
All measurements in inches unless noted.

Year	Model	Master Cylinder Bore	Brake Disc			Brake Drum Diameter			Minimum Lining Thickness	
			Original Thickness	Minimum Thickness	Maximum Runout	Original Inside Diameter	Max. Wear Limit	Maximum Machine Diameter	Front	Rear
1990	ES250	NA	0.984 ⑤	0.945 ①	0.0028 ②	NA	NA	NA	0.039	0.039
	LS400	NA	1.102 ④	0.906 ③	0.0020	NA	NA	NA	0.039	0.039
1991	ES250	NA	0.984 ⑤	0.945 ①	0.0028 ②	NA	NA	NA	0.039	0.039
	LS400	NA	1.102 ④	0.906 ③	0.0020	NA	NA	NA	0.039	0.039
1992	ES300	NA	1.102 ⑤	1.063 ①	0.0020 ②	NA	NA	NA	0.039	0.039
	SC300	NA	1.102 ④	1.024 ③	0.0020	NA	NA	NA	0.039	0.039
	LS400	NA	1.102 ④	1.024 ③	0.0020	NA	NA	NA	0.039	0.039
	SC400	NA	1.260 ④	1.181 ③	0.0020	NA	NA	NA	0.039	0.039
1993	ES300	NA	1.102 ⑤	1.063 ①	0.0020 ②	NA	NA	NA	0.039	0.039
	SC300	NA	1.102 ④	1.024 ③	0.0020	NA	NA	NA	0.039	0.039
	LS400	NA	1.102 ④	1.024 ③	0.0020	NA	NA	NA	0.039	0.039
	SC400	NA	1.260 ④	1.181 ③	0.0020	NA	NA	NA	0.039	0.039
1994	ES300	NA	1.102 ⑤	1.063 ①	0.0020 ②	NA	NA	NA	0.039	0.039
	SC300	NA	1.102 ④	1.024 ③	0.0020	NA	NA	NA	0.039	0.039
	LS400	NA	1.102 ④	1.024 ③	0.0020	NA	NA	NA	0.039	0.039
	SC400	NA	1.260 ④	1.181 ③	0.0020	NA	NA	NA	0.039	0.039

NA—Not applicable
① Rear: 0.354 in.
② Rear: 0.059 in.
③ Rear: 0.591 in.
④ Rear: 0.630 in.
⑤ Rear: 0.394 in.

WHEEL ALIGNMENT

Year	Model		Caster Range (deg.)	Caster Preferred Setting (deg.)	Camber Range (deg.)	Camber Preferred Setting (deg.)	Toe-in (in.)	Steering Axis Inclination (deg.)
1990	ES250	Front	50'P–2°20'P	1°35'P	20'N–1°10'P	25'P	0.04	12°55'
		Rear	—	—	1°25'N–5'P	40'N	0.16	
	LS400	Front	8°25'P–9°55'P①	9°10'P①	45'N–45'P②	0②	0.08③	8°45'④
		Rear	—	—	45'N–45'P⑤	0⑤	0.08⑥	—
1991	ES250	Front	50'P–2°20'P	1°35'P	20'N–1°10'P	25'P	0.04	12°55'
		Rear	—	—	1°25'N–5'P	40'N	0.16	
	LS400	Front	8°25'P–9°55'P①	9°10'P①	45'N–45'P②	0②	0.08③	8°45'④
		Rear	—	—	45'N–45'P⑤	0⑤	0.08⑥	—
1992	ES300	Front	30'P–2°P	1°15'P	1°25'N–5'P	40'N	0	13°05'
		Rear	—	—	1°15'N–15'P	30'N	0.16	—
	SC300	Front	2°11'P–3°41'P	2°56'P	44'N–46'P	1'P	0.04	8°58'
		Rear	—	—	1°38'N–8'N	53'N	0.177	—
	LS400	Front	8°25'P–9°55'P①	9°10'P①	45'N–45'P②	0②	0.08③	8°45'④
		Rear	—	—	45'N–45'P⑤	0⑤	0.08⑥	—
	SC400	Front	2°11'P–3°41'P	2°56'P	15'P–1°45'P	1°P	0.04	8°58'
		Rear	—	—	1°39'N–8'N	53'N	0.177	—
1993	ES300	Front	30'P–2°P	1°15'P	1°25'N–5'P	40'N	0	13°05'
		Rear	—	—	1°15'N–15'P	30'N	0.16	—
	SC300	Front	2°11'P–3°41'P	2°56'P	44'N–46'P	1'P	0.04	8°58'
		Rear	—	—	1°38'N–8'N	53'N	0.177	—
	LS400	Front	8°25'P–9°55'P①	9°10'P①	45'N–45'P②	0②	0.08③	8°45'④
		Rear	—	—	45'N–45'P⑤	0⑤	0.08⑥	—
	SC400	Front	2°11'P–3°41'P	2°56'P	15'P–1°45'P	1°P	0.04	8°58'
		Rear	—	—	1°39'N–8'N	53'N	0.177	—
1994	ES300	Front	30'P–2°P	1°15'P	1°25'N–5'P	40'N	0	13°05'
		Rear	—	—	1°15'N–15'P	30'N	0.16	—
	SC300	Front	2°11'P–3°41'P	2°56'P	44'N–46'P	1'P	0.04	8°58'
		Rear	—	—	1°38'N–8'N	53'N	0.177	—
	LS400	Front	8°25'P–9°55'P①	9°10'P①	45'N–45'P②	0②	0.08③	8°45'④
		Rear	—	—	45'N–45'P⑤	0⑤	0.08⑥	—
	SC400	Front	2°11'P–3°41'P	2°56'P	15'P–1°45'P	1°P	0.04	8°58'
		Rear	—	—	1°39'N–8'N	53'N	0.177	

① W/Air Suspension: 9°5'P–10°35'P, 9°50'P
② W/Air Suspension: 50'N–40'P, 5'N
③ W/Air Suspension: 0.04 in.
④ W/Air Suspension: 8°50'
⑤ W/Air Suspension: 1°30'N–0, 45'N
⑥ W/Air Suspension: 0.12 in.

ENGINE MECHANICAL

NOTE: Disconnecting the negative battery cable on some vehicles may interfere with the functions of the on-board computer systems and may require the computer to undergo a relearning process, once the negative battery cable is reconnected.

Engine Assembly

REMOVAL AND INSTALLATION

ES250

1. Disconnect the negative battery cable. Disconnect the positive battery cable.
2. Remove the hood assembly. Remove the battery from the vehicle and disconnect the ground cable.
3. Remove the engine undercovers and drain the cooling system.
4. Raise and safely support the vehicle. Drain the engine oil. Lower the vehicle.
5. Remove the suspension upper brace.
6. Disconnect the igniter connector, noise filter connector and the high tension electrical cord.
7. Remove the ignition coil, igniter and bracket assembly.
8. Remove the radiator, alternator, alternator belt and the adjusting bar.
9. Remove the radiator reservoir tank and disconnect the accelerator cable from the throttle body.
10. Disconnect the throttle cable from the throttle body, on vehicles equipped with automatic transaxle.
11. Remove the cruise control actuator.
12. Disconnect the air flow meter connector, ISC valve air hose and the vacuum pipe air hose.
13. Disconnect the air cleaner hose, air cleaner cap, hoses and the air flow meter. Remove the mounting bolts and the air cleaner assembly.
14. Disconnect the following:
    a. Check connector
    b. Ground straps from the left side fender apron
    c. Connectors from the relay box
    d. Engine compartment wire connector.
15. Disconnect the following hoses:
    a. Brake booster vacuum hose to the air intake chamber.

b. Air conditioning control valve vacuum hose.
    c. Charcoal canister vacuum hose.
16. Disconnect the ground strap from the transaxle.
17. Disconnect the heater hoses and the fuel line hoses. Use a suitable container to catch any excess fuel.
18. Remove the starter, if equipped with manual transaxle.
19. Remove the clutch release cylinder and tube clamp, do not disconnect the tube, if equipped with manual transaxle.
20. Disconnect the speedometer cable and the transaxle control cable(s).
21. Remove the engine undercover and glove compartment box.
22. Disconnect the following connectors:
    a. Three engine and ECT Electronic Control Unit (ECU) connectors.
    b. Circuit opening relay connector.
    c. Cowl wire connector.
    d. Instrument panel wire connector.
23. Remove the engine wire from the cowl panel.
24. Raise and safely support the vehicle. Remove the bolts and the suspension lower crossmember.
25. Disconnect the front exhaust pipe.
26. Disconnect the air conditioning wire connectors and remove the mounting bolts. Position and support the compressor aside.
27. Remove the halfshafts.
28. Remove the power steering pump and support. Do not disconnect the hoses.
29. Remove the mounting bolts and the engine crossmember. Support the engine with a lifting device.
30. Remove the front, center and rear engine mounting insulators and brackets.
31. Remove the power steering reservoir tank, without disconnecting the hoses. Remove the ground strap.
32. Remove the mounting brackets on both sides of the engine assembly. Lower the vehicle, keeping the engine supported.
33. Attach a suitable engine hoist to the engine hangers. Disconnect the clamps of the power steering oil cooler lines.
34. Remove the mounting insulators on both sides of the engine. Lift the engine and transaxle out of the vehicle.
35. Remove the starter, if equipped with automatic transaxle.

36. Separate the engine from the transaxle.

To install:

37. Assemble the engine to the transaxle. Install the starter, if equipped with an automatic transaxle. Tighten the mounting bolts to 29 ft. lbs. (40 Nm).
38. Lower the engine and the transaxle into the vehicle with a suitable engine hoist. Tilt the transaxle downward to clear the left side mounting bracket.
39. Align the right side and the left side mounting with the body bracket. Attach the right side mounting insulator to the mounting bracket and install the bolts.
40. Install the left side mounting bracket to the transaxle case and tighten the mounting bolts to 38 ft. lbs. (52 Nm).
41. Attach the left side mounting insulator to the mounting bracket. Tighten the mounting bolts to 38 ft. lbs. (52 Nm) and the through bolt to 64 ft. lbs. (87 Nm).
42. Tighten the nuts and bolts of the right side mounting insulator. Tighten the bolts to 47 ft. lbs. (64 Nm). Tighten the bracket nuts to 38 ft. lbs. (52 Nm) and the body nuts to 65 ft. lbs. (88 Nm).
43. Remove the engine hoist from the engine and connect the power steering cooler line clamp.
44. Connect the right side engine mounting brackets. Tighten the bolts to 38-48 ft. lbs. (52-65 Nm) and the nut 38 ft. lbs. (52 Nm).
45. Connect the left side engine mounting bracket. Tighten the bolt to 14 ft. lbs. (19 Nm) and the nuts to 38 ft. lbs. (52 Nm).
46. Install the automatic transaxle mounting bracket, if equipped. Tighten the 12mm nut to 15 ft. lbs. (20 Nm) and the 14mm nut to 38 ft. lbs. (52 Nm).
47. Install the power steering reservoir tank and connect the ground strap.
48. Install the front engine mounting bracket and insulator. Tighten the bolts to 57 ft. lbs. (77 Nm).
49. Install the center mounting bracket and insulator. Tighten the mounting bolts to 38 ft. lbs. (52 Nm).
50. Install the rear engine mounting bracket and insulator. Tighten the mounting bolts to 57 ft. lbs. (77 Nm).
51. Install the engine mounting crossmember and tighten the bolts to 29 ft. lbs. (40 Nm).
52. Install and tighten the bolts holding the insulators to the crossmember. Tighten the bolts to 54 ft.

lbs. (73 Nm). Tighten the mounting insulator through bolts to 64 ft. lbs. (87 Nm).

53. Install the power steering pump and the halfshafts.

54. Install the air conditioning compressor and tighten the mounting bolts. Connect the electrical connection.

55. Raise and safely support the vehicle. Install the front exhaust pipe . Tighten the manifold nuts to 46 ft. lbs. (62 Nm) and the converter nuts 32 ft. lbs. (43 Nm).

56. Install the suspension crossmember and tighten the bolts and nuts to 153 ft. lbs. (207 Nm). Lower the vehicle.

57. Push in the engine wire through the cowl panel.

58. Connect the following connectors:

  a. Three engine and ECT Electronic Control Unit (ECU) connectors

  b. Circuit opening relay connector

  c. Cowl wire connector

  d. Instrument panel wire connector

59. Install the glove compartment box and the engine undercover.

60. Connect the transaxle control cables and the speedometer cable.

61. Install the clutch release cylinder and tube clamp, if equipped with manual transaxle.

62. Install the starter, if equipped with manual transaxle.

63. Connect the heater hoses and fuel line hoses. Connect the ground strap to the transaxle case.

64. Connect the following hoses:

  a. Brake booster vacuum hose to the air intake chamber

  b. Air conditioning control valve vacuum hose

  c. Charcoal canister vacuum hose

65. Connect the following:

  a. Check connector

  b. Ground straps from the left side fender apron

  c. Connectors from the relay box

  d. Engine compartment wire connector

66. Install the air cleaner case and tighten the mounting bolt. Connect the air cleaner hose, air cleaner cap, hoses and the air flow meter.

67. Install the cruise control actuator.

68. Install the throttle control cable and adjust, if equipped with automatic transaxle.

69. Install the accelerator cable and adjust. Replace the radiator reservoir tank.

70. Install the alternator belt adjusting bar, the alternator and belt.

71. Install the radiator assembly.

72. Replace the ignition coil, igniter and bracket assembly. Connect the igniter connector, noise filter connector and the high tension electrical cord.

73. Install the suspension upper brace and tighten the mounting bolts to 47 ft. lbs. (64 Nm).

74. Install the battery and refill the cooling system. Fill the engine crankcase to the proper oil level.

75. Install the engine undercovers and the hood assembly.

76. Connect the battery cables. Start the engine and check for leaks. Check the ignition timing. Adjust, if necessary. Recheck the cooling system and the oil level.

ES300

1. Disconnect the negative battery cable.

2. Remove the battery and its tray.

3. Remove the hood.

4. Remove the engine undercover and then drain the engine coolant and oil.

5. Disconnect the accelerator cable from the throttle body. On models with automatic transaxle, its the throttle cable, not the accelerator.

6. Remove the air cleaner assembly, resonator and the air intake hose.

7. On models with cruise control, remove the actuator cover, unplug the connector, remove the 3 bolts and then disconnect the actuator with the bracket.

8. Disconnect the ground strap at the battery carrier.

9. Remove the radiator and then disconnect the coolant reservoir hose.

10. Remove the 3 washer tank mounting bolts, disconnect the connector and hose and then lift out the tank.

11. Tag and disconnect the:

  a. Three connectors to the engine relay box

  b. Two connectors from the left side fender apron

  c. Igniter connector

  d. Noise filter connector

  e. Connector at the fender apron

  f. Check connector

  g. Ground strap at the right fender apron

  h. Backup light switch and speed sensor models with manual transaxle

12. Disconnect the heater hoses and the fuel return hose and the fuel inlet

hose. All of these may leak coolant or fuel

13. On models with manual transaxle, remove the starter and then remove the clutch release cylinder. Don't disconnect the hydraulic line, simply hang the cylinder out of the way.

14. Disconnect the transaxle control cables at the transaxle.

15. Tag and disconnect all remaining vacuum hoses.

16. Remove the undercover beneath the glove box. Remove the lower instrument panel, the glove box door and the box itself. Tag and disconnect the 3 ECU connectors, the 5 cowl wire connectors and the cooling fan ECU connector. Remove the 2 nuts and then pull the engine harness into the engine compartment.

17. Without disconnecting the refrigerant lines, remove the A/C compressor and hang it carefully out of the way.

18. Loosen the 2 bolts and disconnect the front exhaust pipe bracket. Remove the 3 nuts attaching the front pipe to the manifold. Disconnect the pipe.

19. Remove the halfshafts.

20. Without disconnecting the hydraulic lines, remove the power steering pump and hang it aside. Disconnect the hydraulic cooling fan pressure hose.

21. Remove the 3 bolts on manual transaxle or 4 bolts on automatic transaxle and then disconnect the left engine mounting insulator. Pop out the plugs, remove the 4 nuts and then remove the rear engine mounting insulator. Remove the 4 bolts and remove the mount absorber. Remove the 3 bolts and disconnect the front engine mounting insulator.

22. Attach an engine lifting device to the lift hooks. Remove the 3 bolts and disconnect the control rod. Slowly and carefully, lift the engine/transaxle assembly out of the engine compartment.

To install:

23. Carefully lower the engine into the engine compartment. With the engine level and all the mounts aligned with their brackets, install the engine control rod. Tighten the 3 bolts, in the sequence shown, to 47 ft. lbs. (64 Nm). Install the right side mounting stays and tighten the small bolt to 23 ft. lbs. (31 Nm) and the larger bolts to 46 ft. lbs. (62 Nm).

24. Connect the front engine mount and tighten the bolts to 59 ft. lbs. (80 Nm). Connect the engine mount absorber and tighten the bolts to 35 ft. lbs. (48 Nm). Connect the rear mount

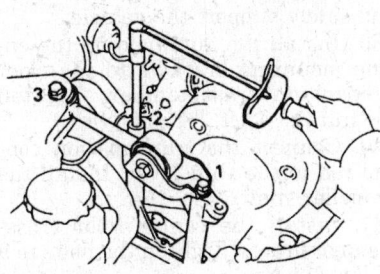

Tighten the engine control rod in this sequence — ES300

and tighten the nuts to 48 ft. lbs. (66 Nm). Don't forget the plugs.

25. Connect the left mount and tighten the bolts (3 or 4) to 47 ft. lbs. (64 Nm).

26. Install the power steering pump and tighten the bolts to 31 ft. lbs. (43 Nm).

27. Install the halfshafts. Connect the cooling fan pressure hose.

28. Connect the front pipe to the manifold and tighten the new nuts to 46 ft. lbs. (62 Nm), tighten the converter nuts to 32 ft. lbs. (43 Nm). Don't forget to install the bracket.

29. Install the A/C compressor and tighten the cylinder block bolts to 20 ft. lbs. (27 Nm); tighten the bracket bolts to 14 ft. lbs. (20 Nm).

30. Feed the engine harness through the cowl and reconnect it. Install the glove box.

31. Connect the vacuum hoses and the transaxle control cables.

32. Install the release cylinder and the starter.

33. Connect the fuel inlet hose and tighten it to 22 ft. lbs. (29 Nm). Connect the return hose and the 2 heater hoses.

34. Reconnect all wires disconnected previously.

35. Install the washer tank and connect the electrical lead and hose.

36. Install the coolant reservoir hose and the radiator.

37. Connect the ground strap to the battery carrier and then install the cruise control actuator. Install the air cleaner assembly.

38. Connect the throttle/accelerator cable and adjust it.

39. Fill the engine with oil and coolant. Connect the battery cable, start the engine and check for any leaks.

SC300

1. Disconnect the negative battery cable.

2. Remove the battery and its tray.

3. Remove the hood.

4. Remove the engine undercover and then drain the engine coolant and oil.

5. Disconnect the accelerator cable from the throttle body. On models with automatic transmission, its the throttle cable, not the accelerator.

6. On models with cruise control, remove the actuator cover, unplug the connector, remove the 3 bolts and then disconnect the actuator with the bracket.

7. Remove the air cleaner assembly, resonator and the air intake hose.

8. Remove the drive belt, fan (with fluid coupling attached) and the water pump pulley.

9. Remove the radiator and then disconnect the coolant reservoir hose.

10. Tag and disconnect the vacuum hoses and then remove the charcoal canister.

11. Without disconnecting the refrigerant or hydraulic lines, remove the power steering pump and A/C compressor and position them out of the way.

12. Tag and disconnect all wires electrical lead and vacuum hoses.

13. On models with manual transmission, remove the shift knob and center console. Remove the 8 mounting bolts and lift out the shift lever.

14. Remove the undercover beneath the glove box. Remove the lower instrument panel, the glove box door and the box itself. Tag and disconnect the 3 ECU connectors, the 5 cowl wire connectors and the cooling fan ECU connector. Remove the 2 nuts and then pull the engine harness into the engine compartment.

15. Remove the 2 clamp bolts and disconnect the power steering pipe from the engine block.

16. Remove the union bolt and 2 gaskets and disconnect the fuel inlet hose. Make sure you have a rag or container nearby to catch any dripping fuel.

17. Unbolt and remove the clutch master cylinder; move it aside without disconnecting the hydraulic lines.

18. Disconnect the front exhaust pipe and then remove the heat shield.

19. Disconnect the automatic transmission control rod at the shift lever.

20. Remove the intermediate shaft. Some vehicles are not equipped with adjusting washers.

21. Remove the 2 nuts holding the engine to the suspension crossmember. Remove the 4 bolts and 4 nuts and lift out the rear engine mount.

22. Attach an engine lifting device to the lift hooks. Slowly and carefully, lift the engine/transaxle assembly out of the engine compartment.

To install:

23. Carefully lower the engine into the engine compartment. With the engine level and all the mounts aligned with their brackets, install the rear mount. Tighten the 4 bolts to 10 ft. lbs. (13 Nm). Tighten the 4 nuts to 19 ft. lbs. (25 Nm).

24. Connect the intermediate shaft and tighten the bolts and nuts to 54 ft. lbs. (74 Nm). Tighten the bolts to 36 ft. lbs. (49 Nm).

25. Connect the transmission control rod to the shift lever (automatic transmission only).

26. Install the exhaust shield and then reconnect the front pipe. Tighten the new nuts to 46 ft. lbs. (62 Nm). Tighten the bolts and nuts on the No. 2 pipe to 32 ft. lbs. (43 Nm).

27. Install the clutch release cylinder and tighten the bolts to 9 ft. lbs. (12 Nm).

28. Reconnect the fuel inlet hose with 2 new gaskets and tighten the union bolt to 25 ft. lbs. (34 Nm).

29. Install the power steering pipe and then reconnect the engine harness.

30. Install the shift lever on models with manual transmission.

31. Reconnect all wires, electrical leads and vacuum hoses.

32. Install the A/C compressor and tighten the through bolt to 19 ft. lbs. (26 Nm). Tighten the other bolt and nut to 38 ft. lbs. (52 Nm).

33. Install the charcoal canister and connect the hoses.

34. Install the water pump pulley, the fan and the drive belt. Tighten the 4 pulley nuts to 12 ft. lbs. (16 Nm).

35. Install the air cleaner assembly.

36. Install the coolant reservoir hose and the radiator.

37. Connect the ground strap to the battery carrier and then install the cruise control actuator.

38. Connect the throttle/accelerator cable.

39. Install battery and reconnect the battery cables.

40. Install engine undercover. Install the hood.

41. Fill the engine with oil and coolant. Check all fluid levels. Start the engine and check for any leaks. Road test the vehicle for proper operation.

LS400 and SC400

1. Disconnect the negative battery cable and the positive battery cable. Remove the hood assembly.

2. Remove the dust covers and the air duct above the radiator assembly. Drain the cooling system.

3. Remove the battery from the vehicle. Raise and safely support the vehicle.

4. Remove the engine undercover and drain the engine oil. Lower the vehicle.

5. Disconnect the radiator upper hose from the water inlet. Loosen the nuts holding the fluid coupling to the fan bracket.

6. Loosen the drive belt tension by turning the belt tensioner counterclockwise. Remove the drive belt.

7. Remove the radiator assembly.

8. Disconnect the air flow meter connector, the mounting bolts and the the air cleaner hose. Remove the air cleaner, the air flow meter and hose assembly.

9. Remove the igniter cover and disconnect the igniter connectors.

10. Remove the bolts, nut and the throttle body cover. Disconnect the accelerator and cruise control actuator cables.

11. Disconnect the air hose from the ISC valve and the power steering air control valve.

12. Disconnect the air connector pipe from the throttle body and remove the air connector pipe. Remove the bolt and connector pipe bracket.

13. Disconnect the air hose from the air intake chamber. Remove the power steering pump mounting bolts and nut. Position the pump aside.

14. Disconnect the coolant level sensor connector and remove the radiator reservoir tank. Remove the mounting bolts and reservoir tank bracket.

15. Disconnect the following hoses:
   a. Heater and bypass hoses
   b. Fuel hoses (plug the open end and catch the fuel in a suitable container)
   c. Vacuum hose from the brake booster on the air intake chamber
   d. Air conditioning control valve vacuum hoses
   e. EVAP and BVSV vacuum hoses

16. Remove the relay box cover. Disconnect the connector and ground cables from the engine compartment relay box. Remove the ground straps from under the fender aprons.

17. Remove the cruise control actuator cover.

18. Remove the instrument panel undercover and the lower the trim panel the ECU for the engine and transmission.

19. Disconnect the glove box door, the glove box light and remove the glove box assembly.

20. Disconnect the ABS ECU and the heater air duct.

21. Disconnect the following connectors:
   a. The 3 engine and Electronic Controlled Transmission (ECT) ECU connectors
   b. Circuit opening relay connector
   c. Cowl wire connector
   d. Instrument panel wire connector

22. Remove the mounting bolts and pull out the engine wire from the cowl panel.

23. Raise and safely support the vehicle.

24. Remove the mounting bolts and disconnect the power steering oil cooler pipe from the oil pan.

25. Remove the mounting bolts and the steering damper.

26. Disconnect the grommet from the floor and the sub-oxygen sensor from the exhaust pipe. Disconnect the 2 sub-oxygen sensors.

27. Remove the sub-oxygen sensor covers and the exhaust pipe. Remove the exhaust pipe support brackets.

28. Remove the catalytic converters and the exhaust pipe heat insulator.

29. Remove the center floor cross-member braces. Remove the driveshaft.

30. Disconnect the shift control rod from the shift lever. Lower the vehicle.

31. Attach a suitable engine hoist to the engine hangers and support the engine.

32. Remove the nuts holding the engine mounting insulators to the front suspension crossmember.

33. Remove the rear engine mounting member. Disconnect the ground strap.

34. Lift out the engine with the transmission attached. Place the engine assembly on a suitable holding fixture. Separate the engine from the transmission.

To install:

35. Connect the engine to the transmission. Attach a suitable engine hoist to the engine hangers.

36. Lower the engine assembly into the vehicle. Insert the stud bolts of the front engine mounting brackets into the stud bolt holes of the front suspension crossmember.

37. Install the rear engine mounting member and tighten the bolts to 19 ft. lbs. (26 Nm) and the nuts to 10 ft. lbs. (14 Nm). Install the ground strap.

38. Remove the engine hoist. Raise and safely support the vehicle.

39. Install the nuts holding the engine mounting brackets to the front suspension crossmember. Tighten the nuts to 43 ft. lbs. (59 Nm).

40. Connect the transmission control rod to the shift lever. Install the propeller shaft.

41. Install the center floor cross-member braces. Tighten the bolts to 9 ft. lbs. (11 Nm).

42. Install the exhaust pipe heat insulator. Replace the catalytic converters and tighten the bolts to 46 ft. lbs. (62 Nm).

43. Install the front exhaust pipe and the sub-oxygen sensor covers. Tighten the bolts to 32 ft. lbs. (43 Nm). Install the sub-oxygen sensors to the exhaust pipe and tighten to 33 ft. lbs. (44 Nm).

44. Install the steering damper and tighten the mounting bolts to 20 ft. lbs. (26 Nm). Connect the engine wire to the wire bracket on the front suspension crossmember.

45. Install the power steering oil cooler pipe to the engine oil pan. Lower the vehicle.

46. Push in the engine wire through the cowl panel and install the wire retainer.

47. Connect the following connectors:
   a. Three engine and ECT ECU connectors
   b. Circuit opening relay connector
   c. Cowl wire connector
   d. Instrument panel wire connector

48. Install the heater duct and the glove compartment.

49. Install the right side lower instrument panel pad and the engine and ECT electronic control units. Replace the right side instrument panel undercover.

50. Install the cruise control actuator. Connect the connectors and ground cables to the relay box.

51. Install the upper cover to the relay box. Connect the 2 ground straps to the underside of the fender aprons.

52. Connect the following hose:
   a. The heater bypass water hoses
   b. Fuel hoses
   c. Vacuum hose to the brake booster on the air intake chamber
   d. Vacuum hose to the EVAP BVSV

53. Install the air conditioning compressor. Tighten the bolts to 36 ft. lbs. (49 Nm) and the nut to 22 ft. lbs.

(29 Nm). Connect the electrical connectors.

54. Install the radiator reservoir tank bracket, the reservoir and connect the coolant level sensor connector.

55. Install the power steering pump and tighten the mounting bolts to 29 ft. lbs. (39 Nm) and the nuts to 32 ft. lbs. (43 Nm). Connect the air hose to the air intake manifold.

56. Connect the air connector pipe to the throttle body. Connect the air hose to the ISC valve and the power steering control valve.

57. Connect the accelerator cable and the cruise control actuator cable to the throttle body. Install the throttle body cover.

58. Connect the igniter connectors and install the igniter cover.

59. Connect the air cleaner hose to the intake air connector pipe.

60. Install the air cleaner, the air flow meter and hose assembly. Connect the air flow meter connector.

61. Install the radiator.

62. Temporarily install the fan pulley, the fan and the fluid coupling assembly. Install the drive belt by turning the belt tensioner counterclockwise.

63. Tighten the bolts holding the fluid coupling to the fan bracket to 16 ft. lbs. (21 Nm).

64. Install the battery. Replace the air ducts and dust covers.

65. Refill the cooling system and the crankcase to the proper levels.

66. Install the engine undercover and hood assembly.

67. Connect the battery cables. Start the engine and check for leaks. Check the timing.

68. Recheck the fluid levels.

Engine Mounts

REMOVAL AND INSTALLATION

ES250

FRONT

1. Raise and safely support the vehicle.
2. Support the engine with a suitable jacking device.
3. Remove the nut and the through bolt.
4. Remove the insulator. Remove the mounting bolts and the bracket, if necessary.
5. The installation is the reverse of the removal procedure. Tighten the bolts to 57 ft. lbs. (77 Nm).

CENTER

1. Raise and safely support the vehicle.
2. Support the engine with a suitable jacking device.
3. Remove the nut and the through bolt.
4. Remove the insulator. Remove the mounting bolts and the bracket, if necessary.
5. The installation is the reverse of the removal procedure. Tighten the bolts to 38 ft. lbs. (52 Nm).

REAR

1. Raise and safely support the vehicle.
2. Support the engine with a suitable jacking device.
3. Remove the nut and the through bolt.
4. Remove the insulator. Remove the mounting bolts and the bracket, if necessary.
5. The installation is the reverse of the removal procedure. Tighten the bolts to 57 ft. lbs. (77 Nm). Remove the jacking device and lower the vehicle.

ES300

FRONT

1. Raise and safely support the vehicle.
2. Support the engine with a suitable jacking device.
3. Remove the 3 bolts.
4. Remove the insulator. Remove the mounting bolts and the bracket, if necessary.
5. The installation is the reverse of the removal procedure. Tighten the bolts to 57 ft. lbs. (77 Nm).

REAR

1. Raise and safely support the vehicle.
2. Support the engine with a suitable jacking device.
3. Remove the nut and the through bolt.
4. Remove the insulator. Remove the mounting bolts and the bracket, if necessary.
5. The installation is the reverse of the removal procedure. Tighten the bolts to 57 ft. lbs. (77 Nm). Remove the jacking device and lower the vehicle.

SC300, LS400 AND SC400

REAR

1. Raise and safely support the vehicle.
2. Support the engine with a suitable jacking device.

3. Remove the 4 bolts and 4 mounting nuts and the mounting insulator. Remove the mounting bracket, if necessary.
4. The installation is the reverse of the removal procedure. Tighten the bolts to 19 ft. lbs (25 Nm) and the nuts to 10 ft. lbs. (14 Nm). Remove the jacking device and lower the vehicle.

Cylinder Head

——— CAUTION ———
On models with an air bag, wait at least 90 seconds from the time that the ignition switch is turned to the LOCK position and the battery is disconnected before performing any further work.

REMOVAL AND INSTALLATION

ES250 and ES300

1. Disconnect the negative battery cable.
2. Drain the cooling system.
3. If equipped with automatic transmission, disconnect the throttle cable and bracket from the throttle body.
4. Disconnect the accelerator cable and bracket from the throttle body and intake chamber.
5. If equipped with cruise control, remove the actuator, vacuum pump and bracket (2VZ-FE engine).
6. Remove the air cleaner hose.
7. Remove the alternator.
8. Remove the oil pressure gauge, engine hangers and alternator upper bracket.
9. Loosen the lug nuts on the right wheel and raise and support the vehicle safely.
10. Remove the right tire and wheel assembly.
11. Remove the right undercover.
12. Remove the suspension lower crossmember (2VZ-FE engine).
13. Disconnect the exhaust pipe from the catalytic converter.
14. Separate the exhaust pipe from the catalytic converter.
15. Remove the distributor. Remove the V-bank cover on the 3VZ-FE engine.
16. Disconnect the water temperature sender gauge connector, water temperature sensor connector, cold start injector time switch connector, upper radiator hose, water hoses, and the emission control vacuum hoses. Unbolt and remove the water outlet and gaskets.
17. Remove the water bypass pipe with O-rings and gasket.

18. Remove the EGR valve and vacuum modulator. Remove the exhaust crossover pipe

19. Remove the throttle body.

20. Remove the cold start injector pipe for 2VZ-FE engine.

21. Disconnect the air chamber hose, throttle body air hose and power steering hoses, if equipped. Remove the air tube.

22. Remove the intake manifold stay and disconnect the vacuum sensing hose. Remove the intake manifold and gasket.

23. Remove the fuel delivery pipe and the injectors.

24. Remove the rear cylinder head plate. On the 3VZ-FE engine, remove the emission control valve set and the left side engine harness.

25. Remove the exhaust manifolds. Remove the spark plugs. On the 3VZ-FE, remove the oil dipstick.

26. Remove the timing belt, all camshaft timing pulleys and the No. 2 idler pulley.

27. Remove the No. 3 timing belt cover. Support the belt carefully so the belt and pulley mesh does not shift.

28. Remove the cylinder head covers. Remove the spark plug tube gaskets on the 2VZ-FE engine.

29. Remove the intake and exhaust camshafts from each cylinder head. On the 3VZ-FE engine, remove the power steering pump bracket and the left side engine hanger.

30. Remove the 2 (one on each head) 8mm hex bolts. Loosen and remove the 8 head bolts evenly, in 3 passes, in the order. Carefully lift the head from the engine and place it on wood blocks in a clean work area.

NOTE: If the cylinder head bolts are loosened out of sequence, warpage or cracking could result.

31. Remove the cylinder head gasket. With a gasket scraper, remove all the old gasket material from the cylinder head and engine block surfaces.

To install:

32. Place the new cylinder head gasket onto the cylinder block. Place the cylinder head onto the gasket.

33. Coat the threads of the 8 cylinder head bolts (12-sided) with clean engine oil and install the bolts into the cylinder head. Uniformly torque the bolts in 3 passes to an ultimate torque of 25 ft. lbs. (34 Nm), using the sequence. If any of the bolts does not meet the torque, replace it.

34. Mark the forward edge of each bolt with paint and then retighten

each bolt an additional 90 degrees, in the order. Now repeat the process once more, for an additional 90 degrees. Check that each painted mark is now at a 180 degrees angle to the front, facing the rear.

35. Coat the threads of the 2 remaining 8mm bolts with engine oil and install them. Tighten to 13 ft. lbs. (18 Nm).

36. Install the left engine hanger and tighten it to 27 ft. lbs. (37 Nm). Install the power steering pump bracket on the 3VZ-FE engine.

37. Install the camshafts. On the 2VZ-FE engine, install the spark plug tube gaskets.

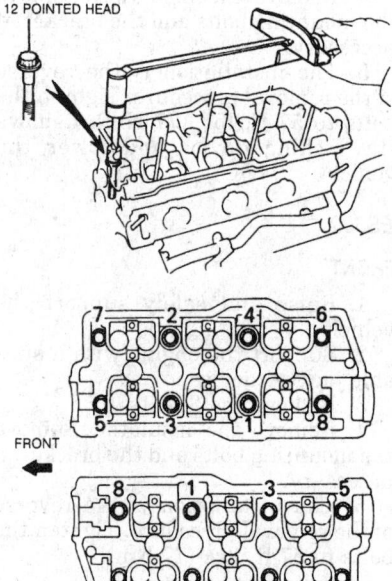

12 POINTED HEAD

FRONT

Cylinder head bolt tightening sequence — ES250, ES300

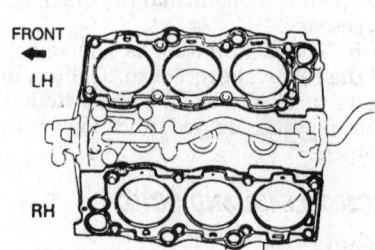

FRONT
LH
RH

Cylinder head gasket positioning — ES250 and ES300

38. Install the cylinder head covers and tighten the bolts to 52 inch lbs. (5.9 Nm).

39. Install the No. 3 timing belt cover and tighten the 6 bolts to 65 inch lbs. (7.4 Nm). Install the No. 2 idler pulley, the camshaft timing pulleys and the timing belt.

40. Install the spark plugs.

41. Install the right and left side exhaust manifolds and tighten them to 29 ft. lbs. (39 Nm).

42. Install the intake manifold and the No. 2 idler pulley bracket. Tighten all bolts to 13 ft. lbs. (18 Nm).

43. Install the cylinder head rear plate and the oil dipstick tube.

44. Install the water bypass outlet and tighten the bolts to 14 ft. lbs. (20 Nm) on the 2VZ-FE engine or 74 inch lbs. (8.3 Nm) on the 3VZ-FE engine. On the 2VZ-FE engine, install the water outlet.

45. Install the injectors and delivery pipe. Tighten the bolts to 9 ft. lbs. (13 Nm).

46. On the 3VZ-FE engine, install the air pipe, the engine harness and the No. 1 EGR cooler. Tighten the pipe to 73 inch lbs. (8.3 Nm) and the cooler to 13 ft. lbs. (18 Nm).

47. Install the air intake chamber. Tighten the mounting bolts to 32 ft. lbs. (43 Nm), the stays to 27 ft. lbs. (37 Nm) on the 2VZ-FE engine or 29 ft. lbs. (39 Nm) on the 3VZ-FE engine.

48. Install the cold start injector. Install the distributor and the EGR assembly. Tighten the EGR bolts to 13 ft. lbs. (18 Nm).

49. On the 2VZ-FE engine, install the crossover pipe and tighten the bolts to 25 ft. lbs. (34 Nm) and the nuts to 29 ft. lbs. (39 Nm). On the 3VZ-FE engine, install the emission control valve set and tighten it to 73 inch lbs. (8.3 Nm).

50. Install the EGR pipe and tighten the bolt to 13 ft. lbs. (18 Nm) and the union nut to 58 ft. lbs. (78 Nm).

51. Install the throttle body and the ISC valve. Tighten both sets of bolts to 9 ft. lbs. (13 Nm).

52. On the 3VZ-FE engine, install the V-bank cover.

53. Install the front exhaust pipe and tighten the manifold nuts to 46 ft. lbs. (62 Nm), tighten the torque converter nuts to 32 ft. lbs. (43 Nm). Install the engine undercover on the 2VZ-FE engine.

54. Install the alternator and adjust the drive belt tension.

55. Install the air cleaner hose.

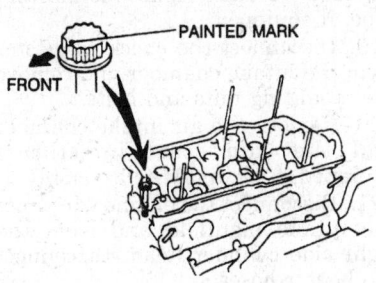

Mark the front of the bolt with paint — ES250, ES300 and SC300

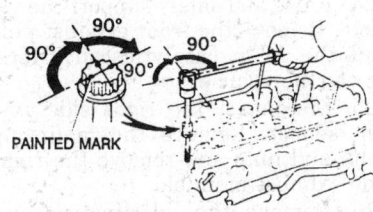

Check that the painted mark is 180 degrees to the front — ES250, ES300 and SC300

56. If equipped, install the cruise control actuator and bracket.

57. Install and adjust the accelerator cable.

58. If equipped with automatic transaxle, connect and adjust the throttle cable.

59. Fill the cooling system to the proper level with coolant.

60. Connect the negative battery cable. Start the engine and check for leaks.

61. Adjust the valves and the ignition timing.

62. Road test the vehicle and check for unusual noise, shock, slippage, correct shift points and smooth operation.

63. Recheck the coolant and engine oil levels.

SC300

1. Disconnect the negative battery cable.

—————— **CAUTION** ——————
On models with an air bag, wait at least 90 seconds from the time that the ignition switch is turned to the LOCK position and the battery is disconnected before performing any further work.

2. Drain the cooling system.

3. Tag and disconnect the spark plug wires at the spark plugs.

4. Remove the spark plugs. Remove the distributor with the spark plug leads attached.

5. Remove the radiator and then remove the water pump pulley.

6. Place matchmarks on the timing belt and sprockets, support the belt and then slide it off the timing sprockets.

7. Remove the No. 2 front exhaust pipe. Disconnect the two O_2 sensor leads, remove the 4 nuts and then remove the manifold heatshield. Remove the exhaust manifolds.

8. Loosen the 2 bolts and remove the water bypass outlet and the No. 1 bypass pipe. Remove the three O-rings from the outlet and the pipe.

9. Loosen the 2 bolts and nut and remove the water outlet. Loosen the clamp and remove the No. 1 bypass hose.

10. Remove the vacuum control valve set and the No. 2 vacuum pipe.

11. Disconnect the fuel return hose from the oil dipstick guide, remove the mounting bolt, and pull the guide and dipstick from the pan. Plug the hole.

12. Remove the air intake chamber. Remove the fuel delivery pipe and then pull out the injectors. Remove the No. 1 and 2 fuel pipes.

13. Disconnect the engine harness from the intake manifold.

14. Remove the intake manifold and then remove the cylinder head covers.

15. While holding the camshaft with a wrench, loosen the timing sprocket bolt and remove the sprocket. Repeat this procedure for the other camshaft.

16. Remove the No. 4 (inner) timing belt cover.

17. Loosen and remove the camshafts.

18. Using the correct tool (10mm bi-hexagon socket) loosen and remove

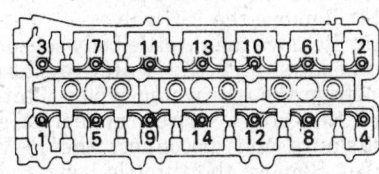

Cylinder head bolt loosening sequence — SC300

the 10 head bolts evenly, in 3 passes, in the order. Remove the 14 plate washers. Carefully lift the head from the engine and place it on wood blocks in a clean work area.

NOTE: If the cylinder head bolts are loosened out of sequence, warpage or cracking could result.

19. Remove the cylinder head gasket. With a gasket scraper, remove all the old gasket material from the cylinder head and engine block surfaces.

To install:

20. Place the new cylinder head gasket onto the cylinder block. Place the cylinder head onto the gasket and connect the heater water hose to the union.

21. Coat the threads of the cylinder head bolts with clean engine oil and install the bolts into the cylinder head. Don't forget the plate washers. Uniformly tighten the bolts in 3 passes to an ultimate torque of 25 ft. lbs. (34 Nm), using the sequence. If any of the bolts does not meet the torque, replace it.

22. Mark the forward edge of each bolt with paint and then retighten each bolt an additional 90 degrees, in the order. Now repeat the process once more, for an additional 90 degrees. Check that each painted mark is now at a 180 degrees angle to the front — facing the rear.

23. Install the camshafts and tighten them evenly to 14 ft. lbs. (20 Nm). Be sure to follow the proper procedures for setting the camshafts.

24. Check and adjust the valve clearance.

25. Install the No. 4 timing belt cover and tighten the bolts to 78 inch lbs. (8.8 Nm).

26. Align the knock pins and grooves and install the camshaft sprockets. Tighten the bolts to 59 ft. lbs. (79 Nm).

27. Install the cylinder head covers and tighten the bolts to 4 ft. lbs. (5.4 Nm).

28. Using a new gasket, install the intake manifold and tighten the bolts and nuts to 15 ft. lbs. (21 Nm). Install the mounting stay and tighten the bolts to 29 ft. lbs. (39 Nm). Connect the engine harness to the manifold.

29. Install the 2 fuel pipes and tighten the bolts to 78 inch lbs. (8.8 Nm). Install the delivery pipe and injectors. Tighten the pipe bolts to 15 ft. lbs. (21 Nm).

30. Install the air intake chamber and tighten it to 15 ft. lbs. (21 Nm). Install the 2 stays and tighten them to 13 ft. lbs. (18 Nm); The No. 1 stay

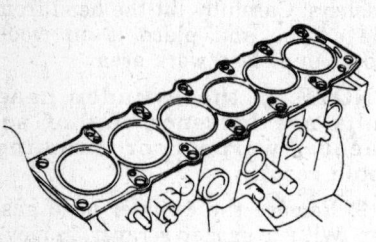

Cylinder head gasket positioning — SC300

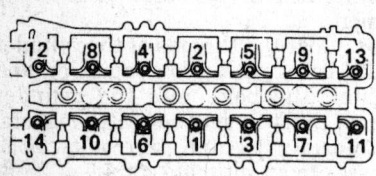

Cylinder head bolt tightening sequence — SC300

is marked with an **F** and the No. 2 stay is marked with an **R**.

31. Use a new O-ring and install the oil dipstick and guide.

32. Install the VCV set and the vacuum pipe. Tighten the set mounting bolts to 15 ft. lbs. (21 Nm).

33. Install the water bypass outlet and the pipe, tighten the bolts to 78 inch lbs. (8.8 Nm).

34. Using a new gasket, install the exhaust manifolds. Tighten the bolts to 29 ft. lbs. (39 Nm). Install the heat shield and tighten it to 13 ft. lbs. (18 Nm). Install the No. 2 front pipe.

35. Install the timing belt.

36. Install the radiator and water pump pulley.

37. Install the distributor and spark plugs. Connect the plug wires to the plugs.

38. Fill the cooling system to the proper level.

39. Connect the negative battery cable. Start the engine and check for leaks.

40. Adjust the valves and the ignition timing.

41. Road test the vehicle and check for unusual noise, shock, slippage, correct shift points and smooth operation.

42. Recheck the coolant and engine oil levels.

LS400 and SC400

1. Disconnect the negative battery cable. Drain the cooling system.

CAUTION

On models with an air bag, wait at least 90 seconds from the time that the ignition switch is turned to the LOCK position and the battery is disconnected before performing any further work.

2. Remove the camshaft timing pulleys. Remove the cooling fan hydraulic pump on the SC400.

3. Disconnect the accelerator cable, the throttle control cable, if equipped with automatic transmission and the cruise control actuator cable.

4. Remove the high tension cord cover and the right side ignition coil.

5. Remove the water inlet housing mounting bolts and disconnect the water bypass hose from the ISC valve.

6. Remove the water inlet and inlet housing assemblies. Remove the O-ring from the water inlet housing.

7. Remove the EGR pipe.

8. Disconnect the following:
   a. VSV connector
   b. Vacuum pipe hose
   c. EGR water bypass pipe
   d. Fuel pressure VSV

9. Disconnect the EGR vacuum hoses and remove the EGR VSV.

10. Disconnect the following hoses:
   a. Water bypass pipe hose from the ISC valve.
   b. Water bypass joint hose.
   c. Vacuum pipe hoses.

11. Disconnect the EGR gas temperature sensor (California only). Remove the EGR valve adapter.

12. Disconnect the following:
   a. Fuel pressure regulator vacuum hose.
   b. Air intake chamber vacuum hose.
   c. Vacuum hose from the EVAP BVSV.

13. Remove the mounting bolts, hoses and the vacuum pipe.

14. Remove the ISC valve.

15. Remove the throttle body sensor connectors and the water bypass pipefrom the rear water bypass joint.

16. Remove the mounting bolts/nuts and disconnect the PCV valve. Remove the throttle body and gasket.

17. Disconnect the accelerator cable bracket and the brake booster vacuum union and hose.

18. Disconnect the cold start injector connector and the cold start injec-

tor tube from the right side delivery pipe, if equipped.

19. Disconnect the check connector from the intake chamber and remove the mounting nuts and bolts.

20. Remove the air intake chamber and the cold start injector if equipped, tube and wire assembly.

21. Disconnect the engine wire from the intake manifold and from the right side cylinder head. Disconnect the heater hoses.

22. Remove the delivery pipes and the fuel injectors. Remove the mounting bolts and nuts. Lift up the intake manifold.

23. Remove the front and rear water bypass joint.

24. Raise and safely support the vehicle. Remove the front exhaust pipe and the main catalytic converters. Lower the vehicle.

25. Disconnect the right side oxygen sensor. Remove the mounting bolts and nuts and remove the right side exhaust manifold.

26. Remove the oil dipstick and guide. Disconnect the left side oxygen sensor.

27. Remove the mounting bolts and nuts and remove the left side exhaust manifold.

28. Remove the 2 engine hangers and the wire brackets from the right side cylinder head.

29. Remove the bolts, washers and the cylinder head cover. Remove the semi-circular plugs, if necessary.

30. Remove the intake and exhaust camshafts from each cylinder head assembly.

31. Disconnect the ground straps and clamp of the engine wire from the rear of the cylinder heads.

32. Uniformly, loosen the head bolts of 1 side of the cylinder head then on the other side. Remove the head bolts and washers.

33. Lift out the cylinder head from the dowels on the cylinder block and place on a suitable holding fixture. Remove the gasket and clean the mounting surface.

To install:

34. Place new cylinder gasket into position on the cylinder block. Install the cylinder head.

35. The cylinder head bolts are tightened in 2 steps:
   a. Apply a light coat of engine oil on the threads of the bolts. Temporarily, install the washers and bolts. Uniformly, tighten the head bolts on 1 side of the cylinder head in the proper sequence then the other side. Tighten the bolts to 29 ft. lbs. (39 Nm).

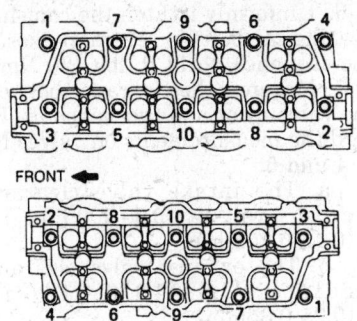

Cylinder head bolt loosening sequence —
LS400, SC400

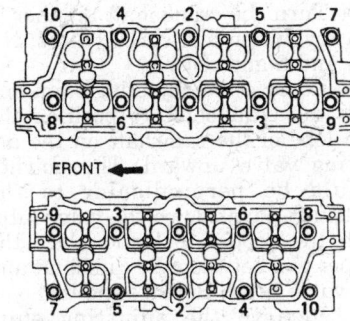

Cylinder head bolt tightening sequence —
LS400, SC400

b. Mark the front the cylinder head bolt with paint. Retighten the cylinder head bolts in the proper sequence 90 degrees. Check that the painted mark is at a 90 degree angle to the front.

36. Connect the engine wire to the cylinder head(s), tighten the clamps.

37. Install the circular plugs on the cylinder head with the cup side facing forward.

38. Remove any old packing and apply new seal packing to the bearing caps.

39. Install the bearing cap on the right side cylinder head, marked **I1**, in position with the arrow mark facing the rear. Install the bearing cap on the left side cylinder head, marked **I6**, in position with the arrow mark facing the front.

40. Apply a light coat of oil on the threads of the cap bolts. Install the bearing cap bolts with new washers and tighten to 12 ft. lbs. (16 Nm).

41. Install the intake and exhaust camshafts assemblies.

42. Install the camshaft oil seals with the proper tool. Install the semicircular plugs with the proper seal packing.

43. Install the cylinder head covers with the proper seal packing and gas-

ket. Tighten the mounting bolts to 52 inch lbs. (5.9 Nm).

44. Install the engine wire bracket and hangers. Tighten the hanger bolts to 27 ft. lbs. (37 Nm).

45. Install the right side exhaust manifold with a new gasket and tighten the mounting bolts to 29 ft. lbs. (40 Nm).

46. Connect the right side oxygen sensor connector.

47. Install the left side exhaust manifold with a new gasket and tighten the mounting bolts to 29 ft. lbs. (40 Nm). Connect the left side oxygen sensor connector.

48. Install the oil dipstick and guide. Raise and safely support the vehicle.

49. Install the catalytic converters and front exhaust pipe. Lower the vehicle.

50. Install the front and rear water bypass joints. Tighten the mounting bolts to 13 ft. lbs. (18 Nm).

51. Install the intake manifold, using new gaskets. Tighten the mounting nuts and bolts to 13 ft. lbs. (18 Nm).

52. Install the delivery pipes and fuel injectors. Install the fuel return pipe with new gaskets. Tighten the union bolt to 26 ft. lbs. (35 Nm).

53. Connect the fuel hoses and the injector connectors. Connect the engine wire to the delivery pipes.

54. Connect the connectors on the left side delivery pipe, the water temperature sensor connector, cold start injector time switch connector and the water temperature sender gauge connector.

55. Connect the heater hoses and engine wire bracket. Install the engine wire to the bracket.

56. Install the cold start injector, tube and wire assembly as necessary. Tighten the mounting bolts to 69 inch lbs. (8 Nm).

57. Install the air intake chamber with new gaskets and tighten the mounting bolts to 13 ft. lbs. (18 Nm).

58. Connect the cold start injector tube to the right side delivery pipe and tighten the union bolt to 11 ft. lbs. (15 Nm), if equipped.

59. Connect the cold start injector connector, as necessary. Install the accelerator cable bracket.

60. Install the brake booster union and connect the vacuum hose. Tighten the union bolt to 22 ft. lbs. (30 Nm).

61. Connect the water bypass hose to the throttle body and the PCV hose to the cylinder head cover.

62. Install the throttle body, using a new gasket. Tighten the mounting bolts to 13 ft. lbs. (18 Nm).

63. Install the water bypass pipe and connect the sensor connectors. Install the ISC valve and tighten the mounting bolts to 13 ft. lbs. (18 Nm). Connect the water bypass hose.

64. Install the vacuum pipe and the following hoses:
    a. Fuel pressure regulator vacuum hose.
    b. Vacuum hose to the upper port of the EVAP BVSV.
    c. Air intake chamber vacuum hose.
    d. Throttle body vacuum hoses.

65. Install the EGR valve adapter with a new gasket. Tighten the mounting bolts to 13 ft. lbs. (18 Nm).

66. Connect the EGR gas temperature sensor connector (California only).

67. Install the EGR valve and vacuum modulator. Connect the water bypass hoses and the vacuum hoses.

68. Install the EGR and fuel pressure VSV and connect the hoses and connectors. Replace the EGR pipe and tighten the mounting bolts to 13 ft. lbs. (18 Nm).

69. Install the timing belt rear plates and tighten the bolts to 69 inch lbs. (8 Nm). Install the water inlet and inlet hosing and tighten the bolts to 13 ft. lbs. (18 Nm).

70. Install the right side ignition coil and the high tension cord cover.

71. Connect and adjust the accelerator cable, the automatic transmission throttle cable and the cruise control actuator cable.

72. Install the cooling fan hydraulic pump on the SC400. Install the camshaft timing pulley.

73. Fill the cooling system and connect the negative battery cable. Start the engine and check for leaks.

74. Recheck all the fluid levels and check the ignition timing.

Valve Lifters

REMOVAL AND INSTALLATION

1. Disconnect the negative battery cable.

2. Remove the camshaft from the cylinder head assembly.

3. Remove the lifters and the adjusting shims, using the proper tool.

NOTE: Be sure to store the lifters and shims in the proper order.

4. Install the valve lifters and shims.

5. Check that the valve lifter rotates smoothly.

6. Install the camshaft in the cylinder head assembly.

7. Connect the negative battery cable.

Valve Lash

ADJUSTMENT

——— CAUTION ———

On models with an air bag, wait at least 90 seconds from the time that the ignition switch is turned to the LOCK position and the battery is disconnected before performing any further work.

ES250 AND ES300

NOTE: Adjust the valve clearance when the engine is cold.

1. Disconnect the negative battery cable.

2. Disconnect the accelerator/throttle cable from the throttle linkage.

3. Remove the air intake chamber.

4. On the 3VZ-FE engine, remove the V-bank cover with a 5mm allen wrench.

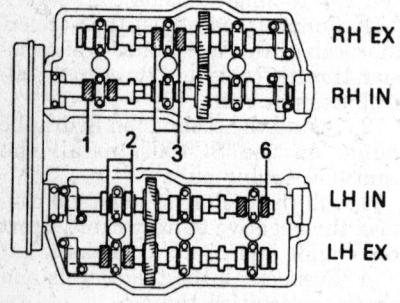

RH EX
RH IN
LH IN
LH EX

Adjust these valves FIRST — ES250 and ES300

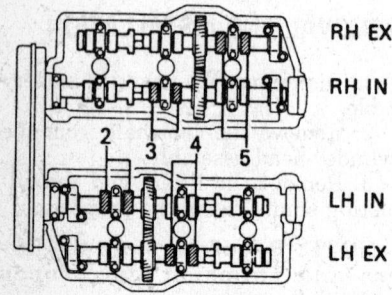

RH EX
RH IN
LH IN
LH EX

Adjust these valves SECOND — ES250 and ES300

5. Remove the cylinder head covers.

6. Turn the crankshaft pulley and align it's groove with the timing mark **0** of the No. 1 timing cover.

7. Check that the valve lifters on the No. 1 intake are loose and the exhaust are tight. If not, turn the crankshaft on complete revolution (360 degrees).

8. Measure the clearance between the valve lifter and the camshaft. Record the measurements on valves No. 1, 2, 3 and 6.

a. The intake valve clearance cold is 0.005-0.009 in. (0.13-0.23mm).

b. The exhaust valve clearance cold is 0.011-0.015 in. (0.27-0.37mm).

9. Turn the crankshaft ⅔ of a revolution (240 degrees) and check the clearance on valves No. 2, 3, 4 and 5 and record.

10. Turn the crankshaft another ⅔ of a revolution and check valves; No. 1, 4, 5 and 6 and record.

11. Remove the adjusting shim and turn the crankshaft to position the cam lobe of the camshaft on the adjusting valve upward. Press down the valve lifter with the proper tool and place the proper tool between the camshaft and the valve lifter. Remove the tool.

12. Remove the adjusting shim with the proper tool.

13. Use the accompanying charts to determine the correct size replacement shim. Install the specified valve shim on the valve lifter with the proper tool.

14. Recheck the valve clearance.

15. Install the cylinder head covers and intake chamber.

16. Connect the negative battery cable.

SC300

NOTE: Adjust the valve clearance when the engine is cold.

1. Disconnect the negative battery cable.

2. Disconnect the accelerator/throttle cable from the throttle linkage.

3. Remove the cylinder head covers.

4. Turn the crankshaft pulley and align it's groove with the timing mark **0** of the No. 1 timing cover.

5. Check that the timing marks on the camshaft sprockets are in alignment with the marks on the No. 4 timing cover. If not, turn the crankshaft 1 complete revolution (360 degrees).

6. Uniformly tighten the camshaft bearing cap bolts in several passes, in the sequence, to 14 ft. lbs. (20 Nm).

7. Measure the clearance between the valve lifter and the camshaft. Record the measurements on valves No. 1, 4 and 5.

a. The intake valve clearance cold is 0.006-0.010 in. (0.15-0.25mm).

b. The exhaust valve clearance cold is 0.010-0.014 in. (0.25-0.35mm).

8. Turn the crankshaft ⅔ of a revolution (240 degrees) and check the clearance on valves No. 3, 5 and 6 and record.

9. Turn the crankshaft another ⅔ of a revolution and check valves; No. 2, 4 and 6 and record.

10. Remove the adjusting shim and turn the crankshaft to position the cam lobe of the camshaft on the adjusting valve upward. The notches should be perpindicular to the camshaft. Press down the valve lifter with the proper tool and place the proper tool between the camshaft and the valve lifter. Remove the tool.

11. Remove the adjusting shim with the proper tool (a magnetic finger).

12. Use the accompanying charts to determine the correct size replacement shim. Install the specified valve shim on the valve lifter with the proper tool.

13. Recheck the valve clearance.

14. Install the cylinder head covers and intake chamber.

15. Connect the negative battery cable.

LS400 and SC400

1. Disconnect the negative battery cable.

2. Remove the No. 3 timing belt covers.

3. Disconnect the spark plug wires and remove the cylinder head covers.

4. Turn the crankshaft pulley and align it's groove with the timing mark **0** of the No. 1 timing cover. Check that the timing marks of the camshaft timing pulleys and timing belt rear plates are aligned. If not, turn the crankshaft 1 revolution (360 degrees) and align the mark.

5. Measure the clearance between the valve lifter and the camshaft on the valves in the first sequence and record.

a. The intake valve clearance cold is 0.006-0.010 in. (0.15-0.25mm).

b. The exhaust valve clearance cold is 0.010-0.014 in. (0.25-0.35mm).

Intake Manifold

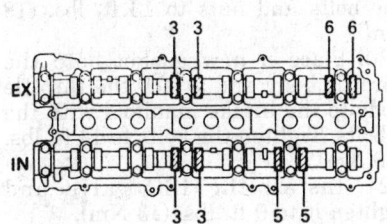

Adjust these valves SECOND — SC300

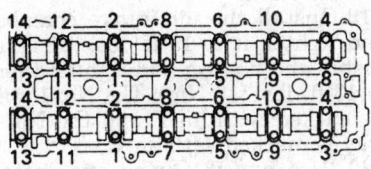

Camshaft bearing cap bolt tightening sequence — SC300

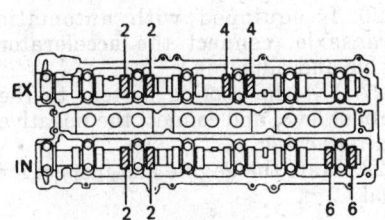

Adjust these valves THIRD — SC300

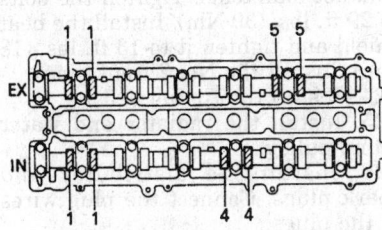

Adjust these valves FIRST — SC300

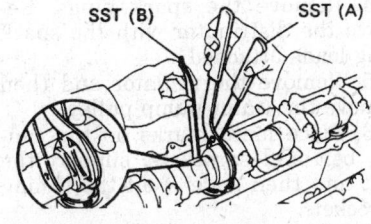

Press down the valve lifter with a special tool — SC300 shown — others similar

Adjust these valves THIRD — ES250 and ES300

CAUTION
On models with an air bag, wait at least 90 seconds from the time that the ignition switch is turned to the LOCK position and the battery is disconnected before performing any further work.

REMOVAL AND INSTALLATION

ES250 and ES300

1. Disconnect the negative battery cable. Drain the engine coolant.
2. Disconnect the throttle/accelerator cable from the throttle body.
3. Disconnect the air cleaner hose at the air intake chamber and remove it.
4. Remove the V-bank cover on the 3VZ-FE engine.
5. Tag and disconnect all lines and hoses and then remove both the ISC valve and the throttle body.
6. Remove the EGR valve and vacuum modulator. Remove the distributor.
7. On the 3VZ-FE engine, remove the emission control valve set and then disconnect the left side engine harness.
8. Remove the cylinder head rear plate.
9. Remove the intake chamber stays, any wires and then remove the air intake chamber.
10. Remove the fuel injection delivery pipe and the injectors.
11. Remove the water outlet and the bypass outlet.
12. Remove the 2 bolts and the No. 2 idler pulley bracket stay. Remove the 8 bolts and 4 nuts and then lift out the intake manifold.
   To install:
13. Thoroughly clean the intake manifold and cylinder head surfaces. Using a machinist's straight edge and a feeler gauge, check the surface of the intake manifold for warpage. If the warpage is greater than 0.0039 in. (0.10mm), replace the intake manifold.
14. Place new gaskets onto the intake manifold and position the intake manifold between the cylinder heads. Tighten the nuts and bolts to 13 ft. lbs. (18 Nm). Tighten the No. 2 pulley bracket bolts to 13 ft. lbs. (18 Nm).
15. Install the water bypass outlet and tighten the bolts to 14 ft. lbs. (20 Nm) on the 2VZ-FE engine or 74 inch lbs. (8.3 Nm) on the 3VZ-FE engine.

6. Turn the crankshaft 1 full revolution (360 degrees) and align the mark.
7. Measure the clearance between the valve lifter and the camshaft on the valves in the second sequence and record.
8. Remove the adjusting shim and turn the crankshaft to position the cam lobe of the camshaft on the adjusting valve upward. Position the hole in the shim toward the outside of the cylinder head. Press down the valve lifter with the proper tool and place the proper tool between the

camshaft and the valve lifter. Remove the tool.
9. Remove the adjusting shim with the proper tool.
10. Use the accompanying charts to determine the correct replacement shim. Install the specified valve shim on the valve lifter with the proper tool.
11. Recheck the valve clearance. Install the cylinder head covers.
12. Connect the spark plug wires and install the No. 3 timing belt covers.
13. Connect the negative battery cable.

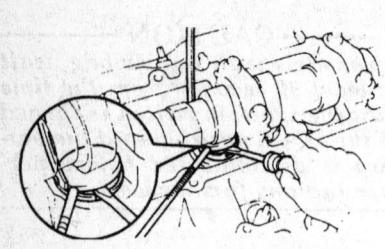

Removing the adjusting shim — SC300 shown — others similar

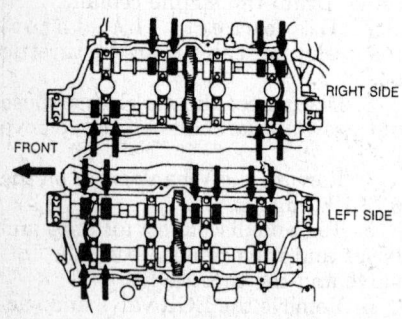

Adjust these valves FIRST — LS400 and SC400

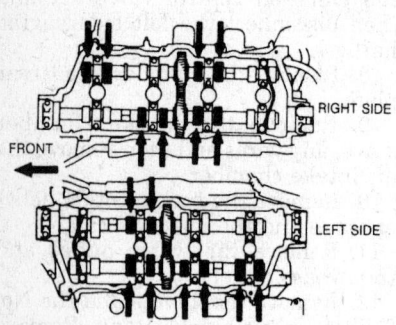

Adjust these valves SECOND — LS400 and SC300

Tighten the water outlet to 74 inch lbs. (8.3 Nm).

16. Install the injectors and delivery pipe.

17. Install the air intake chamber and tighten the 2 bolts and 2 nuts to 32 ft. lbs. (43 Nm); use an 8mm hex wrench. Install the chamber stays and tighten the mounting bolts to 27 ft. lbs. (37 Nm) on the 2VZ-FE engine or 29 ft. lbs. (39 Nm) on the 3VZ-FE engine.

18. Install the distributor. Install the emission control valve set on the 3VZ-FE engine and tighten the 2 bolts to 73 inch lbs. (8.3 Nm).

19. Install the EGR valve and modulator (with new gaskets). Tighten the bolts and nuts to 13 ft. lbs. (18 Nm).

20. Place a new gasket onto the throttle body and attach the throttle body to the intake manifold with the 4 bolts. Tighten the bolts to 14 ft. lbs. (19 Nm).

21. Install the ISC valve and tighten it to 9 ft. lbs. (13 Nm).

22. Unplug and connect all hoses.

23. Connect the throttle position sensor and ISC valve connectors.

24. Connect the air cleaner hose and tighten the hose clamp.

25. Connect the throttle cable with bracket onto the throttle body. Install the return spring.

26. If equipped with automatic transaxle, connect the accelerator cable and adjust it.

27. Fill the cooling system to the proper level and connect the negative battery cable.

28. Start the engine and inspect for leaks.

SC300

1. Disconnect the negative battery cable.

2. Drain the cooling system.

3. Tag and disconnect the spark plug wires at the spark plugs.

4. Remove the spark plugs. Remove the distributor with the spark plug leads attached.

5. Remove the radiator and then remove the water pump pulley.

6. Place matchmarks on the timing belt and sprockets, support the belt and then slide it off the timing sprockets.

7. Remove the No. 2 front exhaust pipe. Disconnect the 2 O_2 sensor leads, remove the 4 nuts and then remove the manifold heat shield. Remove the exhaust manifolds.

8. Loosen the 2 bolts and remove the water bypass outlet and the No. 1 bypass pipe. Remove the 3 O-rings from the outlet and the pipe.

9. Loosen the 2 bolts and nut and remove the water outlet. Loosen the clamp and remove the No. 1 bypass hose.

10. Remove the vacuum control valve set and the No. 2 vacuum pipe.

11. Disconnect the fuel return hose from the oil dipstick guide, remove the mounting bolt, and pull the guide and dipstick from the pan. Plug the hole.

12. Remove the air intake chamber. Remove the fuel delivery pipe and then pull out the injectors. Remove the No. 1 and 2 fuel pipes.

13. Disconnect the engine harness from the intake manifold.

14. Loosen the 2 bolts and remove the intake manifold stay. Loosen the 6 bolts and 2 nuts and then lift out the intake manifold.

To install:

15. Using a new gasket, install the intake manifold and tighten the bolts and nuts to 15 ft. lbs. (21 Nm).

16. Install the mounting stay and tighten the bolts to 29 ft. lbs. (39 Nm).

17. Connect the engine harness to the manifold.

18. Install the 2 fuel pipes and tighten the bolts to 78 inch lbs. (8.8 Nm). Install the delivery pipe and injectos. Tighten the pipe bolts to 15 ft. lbs. (21 Nm).

19. Install the air intake chamber and tighten it to 15 ft. lbs. (21 Nm). Install the 2 stays and tighten them to 13 ft. lbs. (18 Nm); The No. 1 stay is marked with an **F** and the No. 2 stay is marked with an **R**.

20. Use a new O-ring and install the oil dipstick and guide.

21. Install the VCV set and the vacuum pipe. Tighten the set mounting bolts to 15 ft. lbs. (21 Nm).

22. Install the water bypass outlet and the pipe, tighten the bolts to 78 inch lbs. (8.8 Nm).

23. Using a new gasket, install the exhaust manifolds. Tighten the bolts to 29 ft. lbs. (39 Nm). Install the heat shield and tighten it to 13 ft. lbs. (18 Nm). Install the No. 2 front pipe.

24. Install the timing belt.

25. Install the radiator and water pump pulley.

26. Install the distributor and spark plugs. Connect the plug wires to the plugs.

27. Fill the cooling system to the proper level with coolant.

28. Connect the negative battery cable. Start the engine and check for leaks.

29. Road test the vehicle and check for unusual noise, shock, slippage, correct shift points and smooth operation.

30. Recheck the coolant and engine oil levels.

LS400 and SC400

1. Disconnect the negative battery cable. Drain the cooling system.

2. Remove the camshaft timing pulleys. Remove the cooling fan hydraulic pump on the SC400.

3. Disconnect the accelerator cable, the throttle control cable, if equipped with automatic transmission and the cruise control actuator cable.

New shim thickness   mm (in.)

Shim No.	Thickness	Shim No.	Thickness
01	2.50 (0.0984)	38	2.95 (0.1161)
63	2.55 (0.1004)	43	3.00 (0.1181)
06	2.60 (0.1024)	48	3.05 (0.1201)
66	2.65 (0.1043)	51	3.10 (0.1220)
13	2.70 (0.1063)	77	3.15 (0.1240)
18	2.75 (0.1083)	56	3.20 (0.1260)
23	2.80 (0.1102)	80	3.25 (0.1280)
28	2.85 (0.1122)	61	3.30 (0.1299)
33	2.90 (0.1142)		

Exhaust valve shim selection chart — ES250, ES300 and SC300

New shim thickness — mm (in.)

Shim No.	Thickness	Shim No.	Thickness
01	2.50 (0.0984)	38	2.95 (0.1161)
63	2.55 (0.1004)	43	3.00 (0.1181)
06	2.60 (0.1024)	48	3.05 (0.1201)
66	2.65 (0.1043)	51	3.10 (0.1220)
13	2.70 (0.1063)	77	3.15 (0.1240)
18	2.75 (0.1083)	56	3.20 (0.1260)
23	2.80 (0.1102)	80	3.25 (0.1280)
28	2.85 (0.1122)	61	3.30 (0.1299)
33	2.90 (0.1142)		

Intake valve shim selection chart — ES250, ES300 and SC300

Installed shim thickness (mm)

Column headers (left → right): 2.500, 2.525, 2.550, 2.575, 2.600, 2.620, 2.640, 2.650, 2.660, 2.680, 2.700, 2.720, 2.740, 2.750, 2.760, 2.780, 2.800, 2.820, 2.840, 2.850, 2.860, 2.880, 2.900, 2.920, 2.940, 2.950, 2.960, 2.980, 3.000, 3.020, 3.040, 3.050, 3.060, 3.080, 3.100, 3.120, 3.140, 3.150, 3.160, 3.180, 3.200, 3.225, 3.250, 3.275, 3.300

Measured clearance (mm)	Shim numbers (read across installed-shim-thickness columns)
0.000 – 0.025	02 02 02 02 02 02 04 04 04 06 06 06 08 08 08 10 10 10 12 12 12 14 14 14 16 16 16 18 18 18 20 20 20 22 22 22 24 24 24 26 26 28
0.026 – 0.050	02 02 02 02 02 02 04 04 06 06 06 06 08 08 10 10 10 10 12 12 14 14 14 14 16 16 18 18 18 18 20 20 22 22 22 22 24 24 26 26 28 28
0.051 – 0.075	02 02 02 02 04 04 04 06 06 06 08 08 08 10 10 10 12 12 12 14 14 14 16 16 16 18 18 18 20 20 20 22 22 22 24 24 24 26 26 28 28 30
0.076 – 0.100	02 02 02 04 04 04 04 06 06 08 08 08 08 10 10 12 12 12 12 14 14 16 16 16 16 18 18 20 20 20 20 22 22 24 24 24 24 26 26 28 28 30 30
0.101 – 0.125	02 02 02 04 04 04 06 06 06 08 08 08 10 10 10 12 12 12 14 14 14 16 16 16 18 18 18 20 20 20 22 22 22 24 24 24 26 26 26 28 28 30 30 32
0.126 – 0.129	02 02 04 04 04 06 06 06 08 08 08 10 10 10 12 12 12 14 14 14 16 16 16 18 18 18 20 20 20 22 22 22 24 24 24 26 26 26 28 28 28 30 30 32
0.130 – 0.230	
0.231 – 0.250	04 06 06 08 08 10 10 10 10 12 12 14 14 14 14 16 16 18 18 18 18 20 20 22 22 22 22 24 24 26 26 26 26 28 28 30 30 30 30 32 32 34 34 34
0.251 – 0.275	06 06 08 08 10 10 10 12 12 12 14 14 14 16 16 16 18 18 20 20 20 22 22 22 24 24 24 26 26 26 28 28 28 30 30 30 32 32 32 34 34 34
0.276 – 0.300	06 08 08 10 10 12 12 12 12 14 14 16 16 16 16 18 18 20 20 20 22 22 24 24 24 26 26 28 28 28 28 30 30 32 32 32 32 34 34 34
0.301 – 0.325	08 08 10 10 12 12 12 14 14 14 16 16 16 18 18 18 20 20 20 22 22 22 24 24 24 26 26 26 28 28 30 30 30 32 32 32 34 34 34 34
0.326 – 0.350	08 10 10 12 12 14 14 14 14 16 16 18 18 18 18 20 20 22 22 22 22 24 24 26 26 26 26 28 28 30 30 30 30 32 32 34 34 34 34
0.351 – 0.375	10 10 12 12 14 14 14 16 16 16 18 18 18 20 20 20 22 22 22 24 24 24 26 26 26 28 28 28 30 30 30 32 32 32 34 34 34 34
0.376 – 0.400	10 12 12 14 14 16 16 16 16 18 18 20 20 20 20 22 22 24 24 24 24 26 26 28 28 28 28 30 30 32 32 32 32 34 34 34 34
0.401 – 0.425	12 12 14 14 16 16 16 18 18 18 20 20 20 22 22 22 24 24 24 26 26 26 28 28 28 30 30 30 32 32 32 34 34 34 34
0.426 – 0.450	12 14 14 16 16 18 18 18 18 20 20 22 22 22 22 24 24 26 26 26 26 28 28 30 30 30 30 32 32 34 34 34 34
0.451 – 0.475	14 14 16 16 18 18 18 20 20 20 22 22 22 24 24 24 26 26 26 28 28 28 30 30 30 32 32 32 34 34 34 34
0.476 – 0.500	14 16 16 18 18 20 20 20 20 22 22 24 24 24 24 26 26 28 28 28 28 30 30 32 32 32 32 34 34 34 34
0.501 – 0.525	16 16 18 18 20 20 20 22 22 22 24 24 24 26 26 26 28 28 28 30 30 30 32 32 32 34 34 34 34
0.526 – 0.550	16 18 18 20 20 22 22 22 22 24 24 26 26 26 26 28 28 30 30 30 30 32 32 34 34 34 34
0.551 – 0.575	18 18 20 20 22 22 22 24 24 24 26 26 26 28 28 28 30 30 30 32 32 32 34 34 34 34
0.576 – 0.600	18 20 20 22 22 24 24 24 24 26 26 28 28 28 28 30 30 32 32 32 32 34 34 34 34
0.601 – 0.625	20 20 22 22 24 24 26 26 26 28 28 28 30 30 30 32 32 32 34 34 34 34
0.626 – 0.650	20 22 22 24 24 26 26 26 28 28 30 30 30 30 32 32 34 34 34 34 34
0.651 – 0.675	22 22 24 24 26 26 28 28 28 30 30 30 32 32 32 34 34 34 34 34
0.676 – 0.700	22 24 24 26 26 28 28 28 28 30 30 32 32 32 32 34 34 34 34
0.701 – 0.725	24 24 26 26 28 28 30 30 30 32 32 32 34 34 34 34
0.726 – 0.750	24 26 26 28 28 30 30 30 30 32 32 34 34 34 34 34
0.751 – 0.775	26 26 28 28 30 30 30 32 32 32 34 34 34 34
0.776 – 0.800	26 28 28 30 30 32 32 32 32 34 34 34 34 34
0.801 – 0.825	28 28 30 30 32 32 32 34 34 34 34
0.826 – 0.850	28 30 30 32 32 32 34 34 34 34 34
0.851 – 0.875	30 30 32 32 34 34 34 34 34
0.876 – 0.900	30 32 32 34 34 34 34 34
0.901 – 0.925	32 32 34 34 34 34
0.926 – 0.950	32 34 34 34 34
0.951 – 0.975	34 34 34 34
0.976 – 1.000	34 34 34
1.001 – 1.025	34 34
1.026 – 1.030	34

New shim thicknesses   mm (in.)

Shim No.	Thickness	Shim No.	Thickness
02	2.500 (0.0984)	20	2.950 (0.1161)
04	2.550 (0.1004)	22	3.000 (0.1181)
06	2.600 (0.1024)	24	3.050 (0.1201)
08	2.650 (0.1043)	26	3.100 (0.1220)
10	2.700 (0.1063)	28	3.150 (0.1240)
12	2.750 (0.1083)	30	3.200 (0.1260)
14	2.800 (0.1102)	32	3.250 (0.1280)
16	2.850 (0.1122)	34	3.300 (0.1299)
18	2.900 (0.1142)		

Intake valve shim selection chart — LS400 and SC400

Installed Shim thickness (mm)

Measured clearance (mm)	2.500	2.525	2.550	2.575	2.600	2.620	2.640	2.650	2.660	2.680	2.700	2.720	2.740	2.750	2.760	2.780	2.800	2.820	2.840	2.850	2.860	2.880	2.900	2.920	2.940	2.950	2.960	2.980	3.000	3.020	3.040	3.050	3.060	3.080	3.100	3.120	3.140	3.150	3.160	3.180	3.200	3.225	3.250	3.275	3.300
0.000 – 0.025																	02	02	04	04	04	04	06	06	08	08	08	08	10	10	12	12	12	12	14	14	16	16	16	16	18	18	20	20	22
0.026 – 0.050															02	02	02	04	04	04	06	06	06	08	08	08	10	10	10	12	12	12	14	14	14	16	16	16	18	18	18	20	20	22	22
0.051 – 0.075													02	02	02	02	04	04	06	06	06	06	08	08	10	10	10	10	12	12	14	14	14	14	16	16	18	18	18	18	20	20	22	22	24
0.076 – 0.100												02	02	02	04	04	04	06	06	06	08	08	08	10	10	10	12	12	12	14	14	14	16	16	16	18	18	18	20	20	20	22	22	24	24
0.101 – 0.125											02	02	04	04	04	04	06	06	08	08	08	08	10	10	12	12	12	12	14	14	16	16	16	16	18	18	20	20	20	20	22	22	24	24	26
0.126 – 0.150									02	02	02	04	04	04	06	06	06	08	08	08	10	10	10	12	12	12	14	14	14	16	16	16	18	18	18	20	20	20	22	22	22	24	24	26	26
0.151 – 0.175							02	02	02	02	04	04	06	06	06	06	08	08	10	10	10	10	12	12	14	14	14	14	16	16	18	18	18	18	20	20	22	22	22	22	24	24	26	26	28
0.176 – 0.200						02	02	02	04	04	04	06	06	06	08	08	08	10	10	10	12	12	12	14	14	14	16	16	16	18	18	18	20	20	20	22	22	22	24	24	24	26	26	28	28
0.201 – 0.225					02	02	04	04	04	04	06	06	08	08	08	08	10	10	12	12	12	12	14	14	16	16	16	16	18	18	20	20	20	20	22	22	24	24	24	24	26	26	28	28	30
0.226 – 0.250				02	02	04	04	04	06	06	06	08	08	08	10	10	10	12	12	12	14	14	14	16	16	16	18	18	18	20	20	20	22	22	22	24	24	24	26	26	26	28	28	30	30
0.251 – 0.269			02	02	04	04	06	06	06	06	08	08	10	10	10	10	12	12	14	14	14	14	16	16	18	18	18	18	20	20	22	22	22	22	24	24	26	26	26	26	28	28	30	30	32
0.270 – 0.370																																													
0.371 – 0.375	04	06	06	08	08	08	10	10	10	12	12	12	14	14	14	16	16	16	18	18	18	20	20	20	22	22	22	24	24	24	26	26	26	28	28	28	30	30	30	32	32	34	34		
0.376 – 0.400	04	06	06	08	08	10	10	10	12	12	12	14	14	14	16	16	16	18	18	18	20	20	20	22	22	22	24	24	24	26	26	26	28	28	28	30	30	30	32	32	32	34	34		
0.401 – 0.425	06	06	08	08	10	10	12	12	12	12	14	14	16	16	16	16	18	18	20	20	20	20	22	22	24	24	24	24	26	26	28	28	28	28	30	30	32	32	32	32	34	34			
0.426 – 0.450	06	08	08	10	10	12	12	12	14	14	14	16	16	16	18	18	18	20	20	20	22	22	22	24	24	24	26	26	26	28	28	28	30	30	30	32	32	32	34	34	34				
0.451 – 0.475	08	08	10	10	12	12	14	14	14	14	16	16	18	18	18	18	20	20	22	22	22	22	24	24	26	26	26	26	28	28	30	30	30	30	32	32	34	34	34						
0.476 – 0.500	08	10	10	12	12	14	14	14	16	16	16	18	18	18	20	20	20	22	22	22	24	24	24	26	26	26	28	28	28	30	30	30	32	32	32	34	34	34							
0.501 – 0.525	10	10	12	12	14	14	16	16	16	16	18	18	20	20	20	20	22	22	24	24	24	24	26	26	28	28	28	28	30	30	32	32	32	32	34	34									
0.526 – 0.550	10	12	12	14	14	16	16	16	18	18	18	20	20	20	22	22	22	24	24	24	26	26	26	28	28	28	30	30	30	32	32	32	34	34	34										
0.551 – 0.575	12	12	14	14	16	16	18	18	18	18	20	20	22	22	22	22	24	24	26	26	26	26	28	28	30	30	30	30	32	32	34	34	34												
0.576 – 0.600	12	14	14	16	16	18	18	18	20	20	20	22	22	22	24	24	24	26	26	26	28	28	28	30	30	30	32	32	32	34	34	34													
0.601 – 0.625	14	14	16	16	18	18	20	20	20	20	22	22	24	24	24	24	26	26	28	28	28	28	30	30	32	32	32	32	34	34															
0.626 – 0.650	14	16	16	18	18	20	20	20	22	22	22	24	24	24	26	26	26	28	28	28	30	30	30	32	32	32	34	34	34																
0.651 – 0.675	16	16	18	18	20	20	22	22	22	22	24	24	26	26	26	26	28	28	30	30	30	30	32	32	34	34	34																		
0.676 – 0.700	16	18	18	20	20	22	22	22	24	24	24	26	26	26	28	28	28	30	30	30	32	32	32	34	34	34																			
0.701 – 0.725	18	18	20	20	22	22	24	24	24	24	26	26	28	28	28	28	30	30	32	32	32	32	34	34																					
0.726 – 0.750	18	20	20	22	22	24	24	24	26	26	26	28	28	28	30	30	30	32	32	32	34	34	34																						
0.751 – 0.775	20	20	22	22	24	24	26	26	26	26	28	28	30	30	30	30	32	32	34	34	34																								
0.776 – 0.800	20	22	22	24	24	26	26	26	28	28	28	30	30	30	32	32	32	34	34	34																									
0.801 – 0.825	22	22	24	24	26	26	28	28	28	28	30	30	32	32	32	32	34	34																											
0.826 – 0.850	22	24	24	26	26	28	28	28	30	30	30	32	32	32	34	34	34																												
0.851 – 0.875	24	24	26	26	28	28	30	30	30	30	32	32	34	34	34																														
0.876 – 0.900	24	26	26	28	28	30	30	30	32	32	32	34	34	34																															
0.901 – 0.925	26	26	28	28	30	30	32	32	32	32	34	34																																	
0.926 – 0.950	26	28	28	30	30	32	32	32	34	34	34																																		
0.951 – 0.975	28	28	30	30	32	32	34	34	34																																				
0.976 – 1.000	28	30	30	32	32	34	34	34																																					
1.001 – 1.025	30	30	32	32	34	34																																							
1.026 – 1.050	30	32	32	34	34																																								
1.051 – 1.075	32	32	34	34																																									
1.076 – 1.100	32	34	34																																										
1.101 – 1.125	34	34																																											
1.126 – 1.150	34																																												
1.151 – 1.170	34																																												

New shim thicknesses — mm (in.)

Shim No.	Thickness	Shim No.	Thickness
02	2.500 (0.0984)	20	2.950 (0.1161)
04	2.550 (0.1004)	22	3.000 (0.1181)
06	2.600 (0.1024)	24	3.050 (0.1201)
08	2.650 (0.1043)	26	3.100 (0.1220)
10	2.700 (0.1063)	28	3.150 (0.1240)
12	2.750 (0.1083)	30	3.200 (0.1260)
14	2.800 (0.1102)	32	3.250 (0.1280)
16	2.850 (0.1122)	34	3.300 (0.1299)
18	2.900 (0.1142)		

Exhaust valve shim selection chart — LS400 and SC400

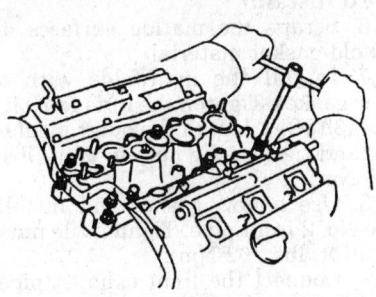

Removing the intake manifold — ES250 and ES300

4. Remove the high tension cord cover and the right side ignition coil.

5. Remove the water inlet housing mounting bolts and disconnect the water bypass hose from the ISC valve.

6. Remove the water inlet and inlet housing assemblies. Remove the O-ring from the water inlet housing.

7. Remove the EGR pipe.

8. Disconnect the following:
   a. VSV connector
   b. Vacuum pipe hose
   c. EGR water bypass pipe
   d. Fuel pressure VSV

9. Disconnect the EGR vacuum hoses and remove the EGR VSV.

10. Disconnect the following hoses:
   a. Water bypass pipe hose from the ISC valve.
   b. Water bypass joint hose.
   c. Vacuum pipe hoses.

11. Disconnect the EGR gas temperature sensor, California only. Remove the EGR valve adapter.

12. Disconnect the following:
   a. Fuel pressure regulator vacuum hose.
   b. Air intake chamber vacuum hose.
   c. Vacuum hose from the EVAP BVSV.

13. Remove the mounting bolts, hoses and the vacuum pipe.

14. Remove the ISC valve.

Removing the intake manifold — LS400 and SC400

15. Remove the throttle body sensor connectors and the water bypass pipe from the rear water bypass joint.

16. Disconnect the PCV valve hose. Remove the throttle body and gasket.

17. Disconnect the accelerator cable bracket and the brake booster vacuum union and hose.

18. Disconnect the cold start injector connector and the cold start injector tube from the right side delivery pipe, if equipped.

19. Disconnect the check connector from the intake chamber and remove the mounting nuts and bolts.

20. Remove the air intake chamber and the cold start injector, if equipped, tube and wire assembly.

21. Disconnect the engine wire from the intake manifold and from the right side cylinder head. Disconnect the heater hoses.

22. Remove the delivery pipes and the fuel injectors. Remove the mounting bolts and nuts. Lift up the intake manifold.

To install:

23. Install the intake manifold, using new gaskets. Tighten the mounting nuts and bolts to 13 ft. lbs. (18 Nm).

NOTE: Align the port holes of the gasket and cylinder head. Be careful of the installation direction.

24. Install the delivery pipes and fuel injectors. Install the fuel return pipe with new gaskets. Tighten the union bolt to 26 ft. lbs. (35 Nm).

25. Connect the fuel hoses and the injector connectors. Connect the engine wire to the delivery pipes.

26. Connect the connectors on the left side delivery pipe, the water temperature sensor connector, cold start injector time switch connector and the water temperature sender gauge connector.

27. Connect the heater hoses and engine wire bracket. Install the engine wire to the bracket.

28. Install the cold start injector, tube and wire assembly if equipped. Tighten the mounting bolts to 69 inch lbs. (7.8 Nm).

29. Install the air intake chamber with new gaskets and tighten the mounting bolts to 13 ft. lbs. (18 Nm).

30. Connect the cold start injector tube to the right side delivery pipe and tighten the union bolt to 11 ft. lbs. (15 Nm), if equipped.

31. Connect the cold start injector connector as necessary. Install the accelerator cable bracket.

32. Install the brake booster union and connect the vacuum hose.

Tighten the union bolt to 22 ft. lbs. (29 Nm).

33. Connect the water bypass hose to the throttle body and the PCV hose to the cylinder head cover.

34. Install the throttle body, using a new gasket. Tighten the mounting bolts to 13 ft. lbs. (18 Nm).

35. Install the water bypass pipe and connect the sensor connectors. Install the ISC valve and tighten the mounting bolts to 13 ft. lbs. (18 Nm). Connect the water bypass hose.

36. Install the vacuum pipe and the following hoses:
   a. Fuel pressure regulator vacuum hose.
   b. Vacuum hose to the upper port of the EVAP BVSV.
   c. Air intake chamber vacuum hose.
   d. Throttle body vacuum hoses.

37. Install the EGR valve adapter with a new gasket. Tighten the mounting bolts to 13 ft. lbs. (18 Nm).

38. Connect the EGR gas temperature sensor connector (California only).

39. Install the EGR valve and vacuum modulator. Connect the water bypass hoses and the vacuum hoses.

40. Install the EGR and fuel pressure VSV and connect the hoses and connectors. Replace the EGR pipe and tighten the mounting bolts to 13 ft. lbs. (18 Nm).

41. Install the timing belt rear plates and tighten the bolts to 69 inch lbs. (7.8 Nm). Install the water inlet and inlet hosing and tighten the bolts to 13 ft. lbs. (18 Nm).

42. Install the right side ignition coil and the high tension cord cover.

43. Connect and adjust the accelerator cable, the automatic transmission throttle cable and the cruise control actuator cable.

44. Install the cooling fan hydraulic pump on the SC400. Install the camshaft timing pulleys.

45. Fill the cooling system and connect the negative battery cable. Start the engine and check for leaks.

46. Recheck all the fluid levels. Roadtest the vehicle for proper operation.

Exhaust Manifold

— **CAUTION** —

On models with an air bag, wait at least 90 seconds from the time that the ignition switch is turned to the LOCK position and the battery is disconnected before performing any further work.

REMOVAL AND INSTALLATION

ES250

1. Disconnect the negative battery cable.

2. Raise the vehicle, support it on safety stands and then remove the engine undercovers.

3. Remove the lower suspension crossmember. Remove the 2 front exhaust pipe stay bolts. Disconnect the front pipe from the center pipe and remove the gasket. Loosen the 3 nuts and then remove the front pipe.

4. Remove the 6 nuts and 2 bolts and lift out the upper crossover pipe and its gaskets.

5. Disconnect the O_2 sensor at the right side manifold. Remove the 3 mounting nuts and lift off the outside heat insulator.

6. Remove the 6 nuts and lift off the right side manifold and gasket. Remove the bolt and pull off the inner insulator.

7. Loosen the 2 nuts and lift off the left side heat insulator. Remove the 6 nuts and lift off the left side manifold and gaskets.

To install:

8. Scrape the mating surfaces of all old gasket material.

9. Install the right inner heat insulator and then position the manifold with a new gasket. Tighten the nuts to 29 ft. lbs. (39 Nm). Install the outer insulator.

10. Use a new gasket and install the left manifold. Tighten the nuts to 29 ft. lbs. (39 Nm). Install the outer insulator.

11. Use new gaskets and install the crossover pipe. Tighten the 6 nuts to 29 ft. lbs. (39 Nm) and the 2 bolts to 25 ft. lbs. (34 Nm).

12. Install the front exhaust pipe and tighten the manifold-to-pipe nuts to 46 ft. lbs. (62 Nm). Tighten the pipe-to-converter nuts to 32 ft. lbs. (43 Nm).

13. Install the lower suspension crossmember and tighten all bolts and nuts to 153 ft. lbs. (207 Nm).

14. Connect the O_2 sensor and then lower the vehicle. Connect the battery cable.

ES300

1. Disconnect the negative battery cable.

2. Raise the vehicle, support it on safety stands and then remove the engine undercovers.

3. Remove the 2 front exhaust pipe stay bolts. Disconnect the front pipe from the center pipe and remove the gasket. Loosen the 3 nuts and then remove the front pipe.

4. Disconnect the O_2 sensor at the right side manifold. Remove the 3 mounting nuts and lift off the outside heat insulator.

5. Remove the 6 nuts and lift off the right side manifold and gasket.

6. Loosen the 2 nuts and bolt and lift off the left side heat insulator. Remove the 6 nuts and lift off the left side manifold and gaskets.

To install:

7. Scrape the mating surfaces of all old gasket material.

8. Install the right manifold with a new gasket. Tighten the nuts to 29 ft. lbs. (39 Nm). Install the outer insulator.

9. Use a new gasket and install the left manifold. Tighten the nuts to 29 ft. lbs. (39 Nm). Install the outer insulator.

10. Install the front exhaust pipe and tighten the manifold-to-pipe nuts to 46 ft. lbs. (62 Nm). Tighten the pipe-to-converter nuts to 32 ft. lbs. (43 Nm).

11. Connect the O_2 sensor, install the undercovers and then lower the vehicle. Connect the battery cable.

SC300

1. Disconnect the negative battery cable.

2. Raise the vehicle, support it on safety stands and then remove the engine undercovers.

3. Remove the No. 2 front exhaust pipe bolts and disconnect it from the front exhaust pipe. Loosen the 4 nuts and then remove the front pipe.

4. Disconnect the 2 O_2 sensors at the manifold. Remove the 4 mounting nuts and lift off the outside heat insulator.

5. Remove the 4 nuts and disconnect the manifolds from the pipe. Loosen the mounting bolts and remove the 2 manifolds and the gasket.

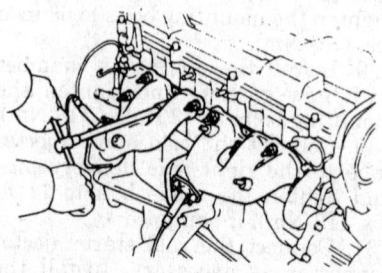

Removing the exhaust manifolds — SC300

To install:

6. Scrape the mating surfaces of all old gasket material.

7. Install the manifolds with a new gasket. Tighten the nuts to 29 ft. lbs. (39 Nm). Install the outer insulator and tighten the nuts to 13 ft. lbs. (18 Nm).

8. Use a new gasket and install the No. 2 front pipe. Tighten the nuts to 46 ft. lbs. (62 Nm).

9. Connect the front exhaust pipe and tighten the bolts and nuts to 32 ft. lbs. (43 Nm).

10. Connect the O_2 sensors, install the undercovers and then lower the vehicle. Connect the battery cable.

LS400 and SC400

1. Disconnect the negative battery cable. Drain the cooling system.

2. Remove the camshaft timing pulleys. Remove the cooling fan hydraulic pump on the SC400.

3. Disconnect the accelerator cable, the throttle control cable, if equipped with automatic transaxle and the cruise control actuator cable.

4. Remove the high tension cord cover and the right side ignition coil.

5. Remove the water inlet housing mounting bolts and disconnect the water bypass hose from the ISC valve.

6. Remove the water inlet and inlet housing assemblies. Remove the O-ring from the water inlet housing.

7. Remove the EGR pipe.

8. Disconnect the following:
   a. VSV connector
   b. Vacuum pipe hose
   c. EGR water bypass pipe
   d. Fuel pressure VSV

9. Disconnect the EGR vacuum hoses and remove the EGR VSV.

10. Disconnect the following hoses:
   a. Water bypass pipe hose from the ISC valve.
   b. Water bypass joint hose.
   c. Vacuum pipe hoses.

11. Disconnect the EGR gas temperature sensor, California only. Remove the EGR valve adapter.

12. Disconnect the following:
   a. Fuel pressure regulator vacuum hose.
   b. Air intake chamber vacuum hose.
   c. Vacuum hose from the EVAP BVSV.

13. Remove the mounting bolts, hoses and the vacuum pipe.

14. Remove the ISC valve.

15. Remove the throttle body sensor connectors and the water bypass pipe from the rear water bypass joint.

16. Disconnect the PCV valve hose. Remove the throttle body and gasket.

17. Disconnect the accelerator cable bracket and the brake booster vacuum union and hose.

18. Disconnect the cold start injector connector and the cold start injector tube from the right side delivery pipe, if equipped.

19. Disconnect the check connector from the intake chamber and remove the mounting nuts and bolts.

20. Remove the air intake chamber and the cold start injector, tube and wire assembly, if equipped.

21. Disconnect the engine wire from the intake manifold and from the right side cylinder head. Disconnect the heater hoses.

22. Remove the delivery pipes and the fuel injectors. Remove the mounting bolts and nuts. Lift up the intake manifold.

23. Remove the front and rear water bypass joint.

24. Raise and safely support the vehicle. Remove the front exhaust pipe and the main catalytic converters. Lower the vehicle.

25. Disconnect the right side oxygen sensor. Remove the mounting bolts and nuts and remove the right side exhaust manifold.

26. Remove the oil dipstick and guide. Disconnect the left side oxygen sensor.

27. Remove the mounting bolts and nuts and remove the left side exhaust manifold.

To install:

28. Install the right side exhaust manifold with a new gasket (the painted marks should face the manifold) and tighten the mounting bolts to 29 ft. lbs. (39 Nm). Connect the right side oxygen sensor connector.

29. Install the left side exhaust manifold with a new gasket (the painted marks should face the manifold) and tighten the mounting bolts to 29 ft. lbs. (39 Nm). Connect the left side oxygen sensor connector.

30. Install the oil dipstick and guide. Raise and safely support the vehicle.

31. Install the catalytic converters and front exhaust pipe. Lower the vehicle.

32. Install the front and rear water bypass joints. Tighten the mounting bolts to 13 ft. lbs. (18 Nm).

33. Install the intake manifold, using new gaskets. Tighten the mounting nuts and bolts to 13 ft. lbs. (18 Nm).

34. Install the delivery pipes and fuel injectors. Install the fuel return pipe with new gaskets. Tighten the union bolt to 26 ft. lbs. (35 Nm).

35. Connect the fuel hoses and the injector connectors. Connect the engine wire to the delivery pipes.

36. Connect the connectors on the left side delivery pipe, the water temperature sensor connector, cold start injector time switch connector and the water temperature sender gauge connector.

37. Connect the heater hoses and engine wire bracket. Install the engine wire to the bracket.

38. Install the cold start injector, tube and wire assembly. Tighten the mounting bolts to 69 inch lbs. (7.8 Nm), if equipped.

39. Install the air intake chamber with new gaskets and tighten the mounting bolts to 13 ft. lbs. (18 Nm).

40. Connect the cold start injector tube to the right side delivery pipe and tighten the union bolt to 11 ft. lbs. (15 Nm), if equipped.

41. Connect the cold start injector connector, if necessary. Install the accelerator cable bracket.

42. Install the brake booster union and connect the vacuum hose. Tighten the union bolt to 22 ft. lbs. (29 Nm).

43. Connect the water bypass hose to the throttle body and the PCV hose to the cylinder head cover.

44. Install the throttle body, using a new gasket. Tighten the mounting bolts to 13 ft. lbs. (18 Nm).

45. Install the water bypass pipe and connect the sensor connectors. Install the ISC valve and tighten the mounting bolts to 13 ft. lbs. (18 Nm). Connect the water bypass hose.

46. Install the vacuum pipe and the following hoses:

    a. Fuel pressure regulator vacuum hose.

    b. Vacuum hose to the upper port of the EVAP BVSV.

    c. Air intake chamber vacuum hose.

    d. Throttle body vacuum hoses.

47. Install the EGR valve adapter with a new gasket. Tighten the mounting bolts to 13 ft. lbs. (18 Nm).

48. Connect the EGR gas temperature sensor connector (California only).

49. Install the EGR valve and vacuum modulator. Connect the water bypass hoses and the vacuum hoses.

50. Install the EGR and fuel pressure VSV and connect the hoses and connectors. Replace the EGR pipe and tighten the mounting bolts to 13 ft. lbs. (18 Nm).

51. Install the timing belt rear plates and tighten the bolts to 69 inch lbs. (8 Nm). Install the water inlet and inlet hosing and tighten the bolts to 13 ft. lbs. (18 Nm).

52. Install the right side ignition coil and the high tension cord cover.

53. Connect and adjust the accelerator cable, the automatic transmission throttle cable and the cruise control actuator cable. Install the cooling fan hydraulic pump on the SC400. Install the camshaft timing pulleys.

54. Fill the cooling system and connect the negative battery cable. Start the engine and check for leaks.

55. Recheck all the fluid levels. Roadtest for proper operation.

Timing Belt Front Cover

— CAUTION —

On models with an air bag, wait at least 90 seconds from the time that the ignition switch is turned to the LOCK position and the battery is disconnected before performing any further work.

REMOVAL AND INSTALLATION

ES250 and ES300

1. Disconnect the cable from the negative battery terminal.

2. Remove the power steering pump reservoir and position it out of the way. Remove the right fender apron seal and then remove the alternator and power steering belts. On 2VZ-FE engine, remove the cruise control actuator and vacuum pump.

3. On the 3VZ-FE engine, remove the coolant reservoir hose, the washer tank and then the coolant overflow tank.

4. Remove the right side engine mount stays.

5. Position a piece of wood on a floor jack and then slide the jack under the oil pan. Raise the jack slightly until the pressure is off the engine mounts.

6. On the 2VZ-FE engine, remove the right side engine mount insulator. On the 3VZ-FE engine, remove the engine control rod.

7. Remove the spark plugs.

8. Remove the right side engine mounting bracket.

9. Remove the 8 bolts and lift off the upper (No. 2) cover.

10. Paint matchmarks on the timing belt at all points where it meshes with the pulleys and the lower timing cover.

11. Set the No. 1 cylinder to TDC of the compression stroke and check that the timing marks on the camshaft timing pulleys are aligned with those on the No. 3 timing cover.

If not, turn the engine 1 complete revolution (360 degrees) and check again.

12. Remove the timing belt tensioner and the dust boot.

13. Turn the right camshaft pulley clockwise slightly to release tension and then remove the timing belt from the pulleys.

14. Use a spanner wrench to hold the pulley, loosen the set bolt and then remove the camshaft timing pulleys along with the knock pin. Be sure to keep track of which is which.

15. Remove the No. 2 idler pulley.

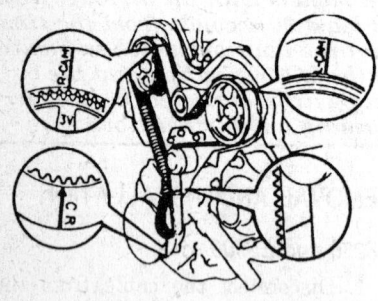

Before removing the timing belt, make sure all marks are there — ES250 and ES300

Check that the marks on the camshaft sprocket and the No. 3 cover are there

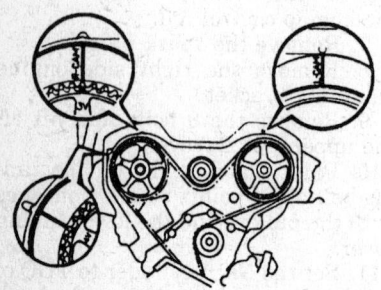

Before removing the timing belt, make sure all marks are there — ES250 and ES300

16. Remove the crankshaft pulley and then pull off the lower (No. 1) timing belt cover.

To install:

17. Install the lower (No. 1) timing cover and tighten the bolts.

18. Align the crankshaft pulley set key with the key groove on the pulley and slide the pulley on. Tighten the bolt to 181 ft. lbs. (245 Nm).

19. Install the No. 2 idler pulley and tighten the bolt to 29 ft. lbs. (39 Nm). Check that the pulley moves smoothly.

20. Install the left camshaft pulley with the flange side outward. Align the knock pin hole in the camshaft with the knock pin groove on the pulley and then install the pin. Tighten the bolt to 80 ft. lbs. (108 Nm).

21. Set the No. 1 cylinder to TDC again. Turn the right camshaft until the knock pin hole is aligned with the timing mark on the No. 3 belt cover. Turn the left pulley until the marks on the pulley are aligned with the mark on the No. 3 timing cover.

22. Check that the mark on the belt matches with the edge of the lower cover. If not, shift it on the crank pulley until it does. Turn the left pulley clockwise a bit and align the mark on the timing belt with the timing mark on the pulley. Slide the belt over the left pulley. Now move the pulley until the marks on it align with the 1 on the No. 3 cover. There should be tension on the belt between the crankshaft pulley and the left camshaft pulley.

23. Align the installation mark on the timing belt with the mark on the right side camshaft pulley. Hang the belt over the pulley with the flange facing inward. Align the timing marks on the right pulley with the 1 on the No. 3 cover and slide the pulley onto the end of the camshaft. Move the pulley until the camshaft knock pin hole is aligned with the groove in the pulley and then install the knock pin. Tighten the bolt to 55 ft. lbs. (75 Nm).

24. Position a plate washer between the timing belt tensioner and the a block and then press in the pushrod until the holes are aligned between it and the housing. Slide a 1.27mm (3VZ-FE engine — 1.5mm) allen wrench through the hole to keep the pushrod set. Install the dust boot and then install the tensioner. Tighten the bolts to 20 ft. lbs. (26 Nm). Don't forget to pull out the allen wrench.

25. Turn the crankshaft clockwise 2 complete revolutions and check that all marks are still in alignment. If

they aren't, remove the timing belt and start over again.

26. Install the right engine mount bracket and tighten it to 30 ft. lbs. (39 Nm).

27. Position a new gasket and then install the upper (No. 2) timing cover.

28. Install the spark plugs.

29. On the 2VZ-FE engine, install the right engine mount insulator. Tighten the bolt to 47 ft. lbs. (64 Nm), the bracket nut to 38 ft. lbs. (52 Nm) and the body nut to 65 ft. lbs. (88 Nm). Install the No. 1 stay and tighten it to 38 ft. lbs. (52 Nm). Install the No. 2 stay and tighten the bolt to 48 ft. lbs. (66 Nm) and the nut to 38 ft. lbs (52 Nm).

30. On the 3VZ-FE engine, install the control rod and tighten the bolts to 47 ft. lbs. (64 Nm). Install the right stay and tighten it to 23 ft. lbs. (31 Nm).

31. Install and adjust the drive belts.

32. Install the fender apron seal and the wheel.

33. On the 3VZ-FE engine, install the No. 2 stay and tighten the bolt to 55 ft. lbs. (75 Nm), the nut to 46 ft. lbs. (62 Nm). Install the No. 3 stay and tighten it to 54 ft. lbs. (73 Nm).

34. Install the coolant overflow tank and the washer tank.

35. Install the power steering reservoir tank and the cruise control actuator.

36. Connect the battery cable, start the vehicle and check for any leaks.

SC300

1. Disconnect the negative battery cable.

2. Drain the engine coolant. Remove the water pump pulley. Remove the radiator.

3. Remove the oil filler cap.

4. Using a 5mm Allen wrench, remove the 9 bolts and lift off the No. 2 and No. 3 timing covers, the top 2.

5. Rotate the crankshaft pulley clockwise so its groove is aligned with the **0** mark in the No. 1 (lower) timing cover. Check that the timing marks on the camshaft timing sprockets are aligned with the marks on the No. 4 (inner) cover, if not, rotate the crankshaft 1 complete revolution (360 degrees).

6. Alternately loosen the 2 tensioner mounting bolts and remove them, the tensioner and the dust boot. Slide the timing belt off of the 2 camshaft sprockets. Its a good idea to matchmark the belt to the pulleys.

7. Making sure the timing belt is securely supported, hold the crankshaft pulley with a spanner wrench

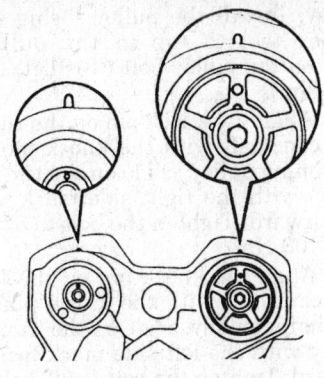

Camshaft sprocket alignment

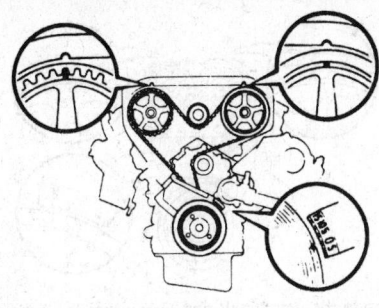

Check that the sprocket aligns with the timing marks — ES250 and ES300

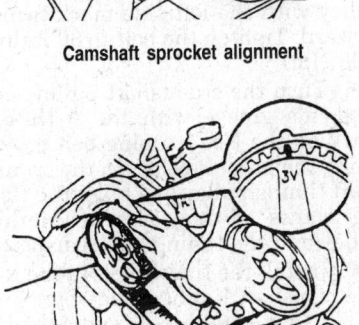

Align the marks on the right sprocket and the No. 3 cover and then slide the belt on

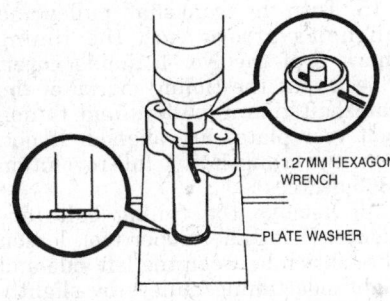

1.27MM HEXAGON WRENCH

PLATE WASHER

Align the holes on the pushrod and the housing and then insert an Allen wrench — ES250 and ES300

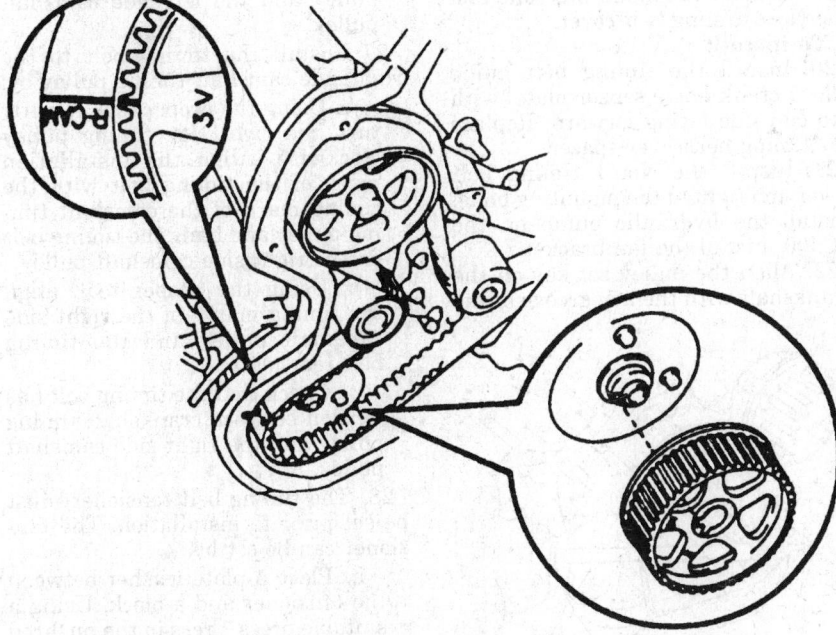

Align the installation mark on the belt with the mark on the right side sprocket

and loosen the mounting bolt. Remove the bolt and the pulley.

8. Remove the 5 bolts and then lift off the lower No. 1 timing cover.

To install:

9. Position 2 new gaskets on the lower cover and then install the cover.

10. Align the crankshaft pulley set key with the groove in the pulley and slide it onto the shaft. Secure the pulley with a spanner and tighten the bolt to 239 ft. lbs. (324 Nm).

11. Make sure the crankshaft timing marks and the camshaft sprocket marks are still in alignment and carefully slide the timing belt back over the sprockets. The marks you made previously on the belt and sprockets should still be in alignment.

12. Press the tensioner pushrod into the housing and slide an 1.5mm hex key through the holes to keep it retracted. Install the dust boot and tensioner and tighten the bolts to 20 ft. lbs. (26 Nm). Remove the hex key.

13. Rotate the crankshaft 2 complete revolutions and check that all timing marks are still in alignment. If they aren't, reinstall the belt and try it again.

14. Install the 2 upper covers.

15. Install the radiator and water pump pulley. Refill the engine with coolant. Connect the battery and road test the vehicle.

LS400 and SC400

1. Disconnect the negative battery cable and the positive battery cable. Remove the battery.

2. Remove the air duct and dust covers. Remove the engine undercover.

3. Drain the cooling system. Remove the drive belt, fan, fluid coupling and fan pulley.

4. Remove the radiator, air cleaner and throttle body cover. Remove the air intake connector pipe.

5. Remove the air conditioning compressor and power steering pump. Do not disconnect the hoses.

6. Remove the upper high tension cord cover and the right side engine wire cover.

7. Disconnect the PCV hose and remove the left side engine wire cover. Remove the right side No. 3 timing cover.

8. Disconnect and tag the vacuum hoses and remove the left side engine wire cover. Disconnect the spark plug wires.

9. Remove the bolt, cover plate and idler pulley.

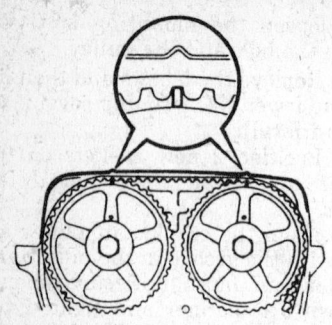

Check that the timing marks on the camshaft sprocket are aligned with the marks on the No. 4 cover — SC300

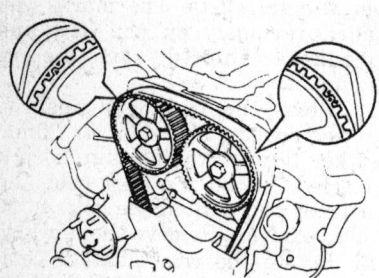

Place matchmarks on the belt and sprockets — SC300

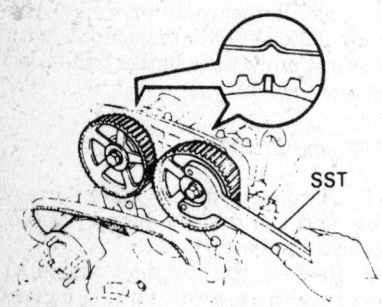

Rotate the camshaft until the timing marks on the sprockets and No. 4 timing cover are aligned — SC300

10. Disconnect the camshaft position sensor connector and remove the right side No. 2 timing belt cover.

11. Disconnect and remove the ignition coil. Disconnect the hoses and wires from the water bypass pipe. Remove the water bypass pipe.

12. Disconnect the camshaft position sensor connector and remove the left No. 2 timing belt cover.

13. Remove the distributor caps and rotors. Disconnect and remove both distributor housings.

14. Disconnect and remove the alternator. Remove the drive belt tensioner and the spark plugs.

Rotate the crankshaft and check that the timing marks are still in alignment — SC300

15. Turn the crankshaft pulley and align it's groove with the timing mark **0** of the No. 1 timing cover. Check that the timing marks of the camshaft timing pulleys and timing belt rear plates are aligned. If not, turn the crankshaft 1 full revolution (360 degrees).

16. Remove the timing belt tensioner. Using the proper tool, loosen the tension between the left side and right side timing pulleys by slightly turning the left side camshaft clockwise.

17. Disconnect the timing belt from the camshaft timing pulleys. Using the proper tool, remove the bolt and the timing pulleys.

18. Remove the bolt and the crankshaft pulley with the proper tool. Remove the fan bracket. Remove the hydraulic pump on the SC400.

19. Remove the mounting bolts and the No. 1 timing belt cover.

To install:

20. Install the timing belt guide (No. 1 crank angle sensor plate) with the cup side facing forward. Replace the timing belt cover spacer.

21. Install the No. 1 timing belt cover and tighten the mounting bolts. Install the hydraulic pump on the SC400. Install the fan bracket.

22. Align the pulley set key on the crankshaft with the key groove of the

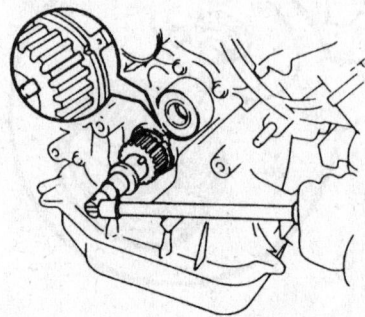

Aligning the timing mark of the crankshaft timing pulley and oil pump body — LS400

pulley. Install the pulley, using the proper tool to tap in the pulley. Tighten the pulley bolt to 181 ft. lbs. (245 Nm).

23. Align the knock pin on the right side camshaft with the knock pin of the timing pulley. Slide on the timing pulley with the right side mark facing forward. Tighten the bolt to 80 ft. lbs. (108 Nm).

24. Align the knock pin on the left side camshaft with the knock pin of the timing pulley. Slide on the timing pulley with the left side mark facing forward. Tighten the bolt to 80 ft. lbs. (108 Nm).

25. Turn the crankshaft pulley and align it's groove with the **0** timing mark on the No. 1 timing belt cover. Using the proper tool, turn the crankshaft timing pulley and align the timing marks of the camshaft timing pulley and the timing belt rear plate.

26. Install the timing belt to the left side camshaft timing pulley by:

    a. Using the proper tool, slightly turn the left side timing pulley clockwise. Align the installation mark of the timing belt with the timing mark of the camshaft timing pulley and hang the timing belt on the left side camshaft pulley.

    b. Using the proper tool, align the timing marks of the left side camshaft pulley and the timing belt rear plate.

    c. Check that the timing belt has tension between crankshaft timing pulley and the left side camshaft pulley.

27. Install the timing belt to the right side camshaft timing pulley by:

    a. Using the proper tool, slightly turn the right side timing pulley clockwise. Align the installation mark of the timing belt with the timing mark of the camshaft timing pulley and hang the timing belt on the right side camshaft pulley.

    b. Using the proper tool, align the timing marks of the right side camshaft pulley and the timing belt rear plate.

    c. Check that the timing belt has tension between crankshaft timing pulley and the right side camshaft pulley.

28. The timing belt tensioner must be set prior to installation. The tensioner can be set by:

    a. Place a plate washer between the tensioner and a block. Using a suitable press, press in the pushrod using 220-2205 lbs. of pressure.

    b. Align the holes of the pushrod and housing, pass the proper tool (an 1.27mm allen wrench) through

Aligning the timing mark of the camshaft timing pulley and timing belt rear cover — LS400

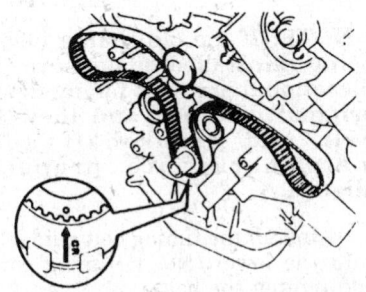

Aligning the installation mark on the timing belt with the drilled mark of the crankshaft timing pulley — LS400

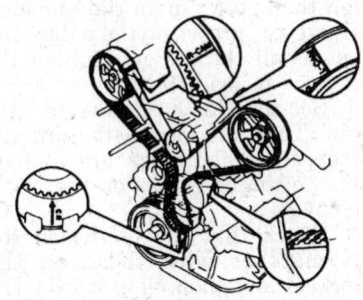

Checking the timing belt installation marks on a reinstalled used timing belt — LS400

the holes to keep the setting position of the pushrod.

c. Release the press and install the dust boot to the tensioner.

29. Install the tensioner and tighten the bolts to 20 ft. lbs. (26 Nm). Remove the tool from the tensioner.

30. Turn the crankshaft pulley 2 complete revolutions from TDC to TDC. Always turn the crankshaft clockwise. Check that each pulley aligns with the timing marks.

31. Install the spark plugs and tighten to 13 ft. lbs. (18 Nm). Install

the drive belt tensioner and tighten the bolt to 12 ft. lbs. (16 Nm).

32. Install the alternator and engine wire bracket. Tighten the nut and bolt to 26 ft. lbs. (35 Nm) on the LS400 or 27 ft. lbs. (37 Nm) on the SC400. Connect the electrical connections at the alternator.

33. Install both distributor housings and tighten the mounting bolts to 13 ft. lbs. (18 Nm). Replace the distributor rotors and caps.

34. Install the right side No. 2 timing belt cover and tighten the 10mm bolts to 69 inch lbs. (7.8 Nm) and the 12mm bolts to 12 ft. lbs. (16 Nm). Connect the camshaft position sensor connector.

35. Install the left side No. 2 timing belt cover and connect the camshaft position sensor connector.

36. Install the water bypass pipe and connect the hoses and connectors.

37. Replace the left side ignition coil and connect the coil connector. Install the idler pulley and cover plate. Tighten the bolt to 27 ft. lbs. (37 Nm).

38. Install and secure the ignition wires. Install the right side No. 3 timing belt cover.

39. Install the left side No. 3 timing belt cover and connect the vacuum hose and connectors. Install the right side engine wire cover.

40. Install the left side engine wire cover and connect the vacuum hoses.

41. Install the upper high tension cord covers. Fit the front side claw groove of the upper cover to claw of the lower cover.

42. Install the power steering pump and the air conditioning compressor.

43. Install the throttle body cover and the air cleaner.

44. Install the radiator, fan pulley, fan coupling, fan and drive belt.

45. Install the engine undercover and replace the battery.

46. Install the air ducts and dust covers. Connect the battery cables.

47. Refill the cooling system. Check the ignition timing.

Timing Belt and Tensioner

REMOVAL AND INSTALLATION

ES250 and ES300

1. Remove the upper and lower timing belt covers as previously detailed.

2. Remove the timing belt guide.

3. Remove the timing belt.

NOTE: If the timing belt is to be reused, draw a directional arrow on the timing belt in the direction of engine rotation (clockwise) and place matchmarks on the timing belt and crankshaft gear to match the drilled mark on the pulley.

4. With a 10mm hex wrench, remove the setbolt, plate washer and the No. 1 idler pulley.

To install:

5. Turn the crankshaft until the key groove in the crankshaft timing pulley is facing upward. Slide the timing pulley on so the flange side faces inward.

6. Apply bolt adhesive to the first few threads of the No. 1 idler pulley setbolt, install the plate washer and pulley and then tighten the bolt to 25 ft. lbs. (34 Nm).

7. Install the timing belt on the crankshaft timing, No. 1 idler and water pump pulleys.

NOTE: If the old timing belt is being reinstalled, make sure the directional arrow is facing in the original direction and that the belt and crankshaft gear matchmarks are properly aligned.

8. Install the lower (No. 1) timing cover and tighten the bolts.

9. Align the crankshaft pulley set key with the key groove on the pulley and slide the pulley on. Tighten the bolt to 181 ft. lbs. (245 Nm).

10. Install the No. 2 idler pulley and tighten the bolt to 29 ft. lbs. (39 Nm). Check that the pulley moves smoothly.

11. Install the left camshaft pulley with the flange side outward. Align the knock pin hole in the camshaft with the knock pin groove on the pulley and then install the pin. Tighten the bolt to 80 ft. lbs. (108 Nm).

12. Set the No. 1 cylinder to TDC again. Turn the right camshaft until the knock pin hole is aligned with the timing mark on the No. 3 belt cover. Turn the left pulley until the marks on the pulley are aligned with the mark on the No. 3 timing cover.

13. Check that the mark on the belt matches with the edge of the lower cover. If not, shift it on the crank pulley until it does. Turn the left pulley clockwise a bit and align the mark on the timing belt with the timing mark on the pulley. Slide the belt over the left pulley. Now move the pulley until the marks on it align with the 1 on the No. 3 cover. There should be tension on the belt between the crank-

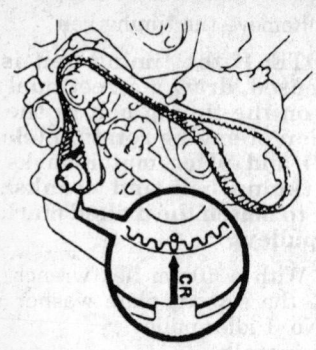

Matchmark the belt to the drilled mark on the crankshaft sprocket — ES250 and ES300

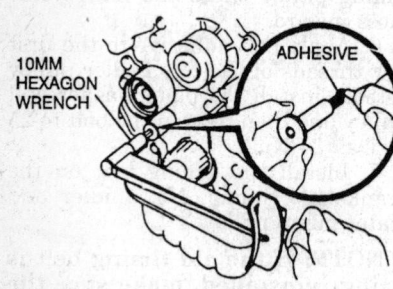

Coat the end of the idler pulley set bolt with adhesive — ES250 and ES300

shaft pulley and the left camshaft pulley.

14. Align the installation mark on the timing belt with the mark on the right side camshaft pulley. Hang the belt over the pulley with the flange facing inward. Align the timing marks on the right pulley with the 1 on the No. 3 cover and slide the pulley onto the end of the camshaft. Move the pulley until the camshaft knock pin hole is aligned with the groove in the pulley and then install the knock pin. Tighten the bolt to 55 ft. lbs. (75 Nm).

15. Position a plate washer between the timing belt tensioner and the a block and then press in the pushrod until the holes are aligned between it and the housing. Slide a 1.27mm, except 3VZ-FE engine or 1.5mm for 3VZ-FE Allen wrench through the hole to keep the pushrod set. Install the dust boot and then install the tensioner. Tighten the bolts to 20 ft. lbs. (26 Nm). Don't forget to pull out the allen wrench.

16. Turn the crankshaft clockwise 2 complete revolutions and check that all marks are still in alignment. If they aren't, remove the timing belt and start over again.

17. Install the right engine mount bracket and tighten it to 30 ft. lbs. (39 Nm).

18. Position a new gasket and then install the upper (No. 2) timing cover.

19. Install the spark plugs.

20. On the 2VZ-FE engine, install the right engine mount insulator. Tighten the bolt to 47 ft. lbs. (64 Nm), the bracket nut to 38 ft. lbs. (52 Nm) and the body nut to 65 ft. lbs. (88 Nm). Install the No. 1 stay and tighten it to 38 ft. lbs. (52 Nm). Install the No. 2 stay and tighten the bolt to 48 ft. lbs. (66 Nm) and the nut to 38 ft. lbs. (52 Nm).

21. On the 3VZ-FE engine, install the control rod and tighten the bolts to 47 ft. lbs. (64 Nm). Install the right stay and tighten it to 23 ft. lbs. (31 Nm).

22. Install and adjust the drive belts.

23. Install the fender apron seal and the wheel.

24. On the 3VZ-FE engine, install the No. 2 stay and tighten the bolt to 55 ft. lbs. (75 Nm), the nut to 46 ft. lbs. (62 Nm). Install the No. 3 stay and tighten it to 54 ft. lbs. (73 Nm).

25. Install the coolant overflow tank and the washer tank.

26. Install the power steering reservoir tank and the cruise control actuator.

27. Connect the battery cable, start the vehicle and check for any leaks.

SC300

1. Remove the 2 upper and lower timing belt covers.
2. Remove the timing belt guide.
3. Remove the timing belt.

NOTE: If the timing belt is to be reused, draw a directional arrow on the timing belt in the direction of engine rotation (clockwise) and place matchmarks on the timing belt and crankshaft gear to match the drilled mark on the pulley.

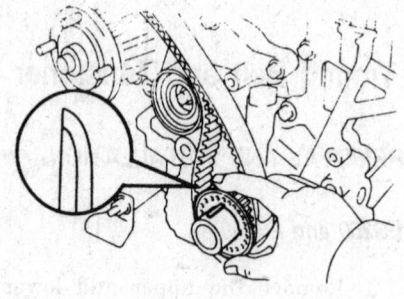

Install the timing belt guide with the cup side out — SC300

4. With a 10mm hex wrench, remove the pivot bolt, plate washer and the idler pulley.

To install:

5. Turn the crankshaft until the key groove in the crankshaft timing pulley is facing upward. Slide the timing pulley on so the flange side faces inward.

6. Apply bolt adhesive to the first few threads of the idler pulley pivot bolt, install the plate washer and pulley and then tighten the bolt to 25 ft. lbs. (34 Nm).

7. Install the timing belt on the crankshaft timing pulley and the idler pulleys.

NOTE: If the old timing belt is being reinstalled, make sure the directional arrow is facing in the original direction and that the belt and crankshaft gear matchmarks are properly aligned.

8. Install the timing belt guide. Install the lower (No. 1) timing cover and tighten the bolts.

9. Align the crankshaft pulley set key with the key groove on the pulley and slide the pulley on. Tighten the bolt to 239 ft. lbs. (324 Nm).

10. Install the camshaft pulleys. Align the knock pin on the camshaft with the key groove on the pulley and then install the pulley. Tighten the bolt to 59 ft. lbs. (79 Nm).

11. Set the No. 1 cylinder to TDC again. Turn the camshaft until the sprocket timing marks are aligned with the timing marks on the No. 4 belt cover.

12. Check that the marks on the belt matches with those on the sprockets and then slide it over the sprockets. If not, shift it on the crank pulley until it does.

13. Position a plate washer between the timing belt tensioner and the a block and then press in the pushrod until the holes are aligned between it and the housing. Slide a 1.5mm Allen wrench through the hole to keep the pushrod set. Install the dust boot and then install the tensioner. Tighten the bolts to 20 ft. lbs. (26 Nm). Don't forget to pull out the Allen wrench.

14. Turn the crankshaft clockwise 2 complete revolutions and check that all marks are still in alignment. If they aren't, remove the timing belt and start over again.

15. Position new gaskets and then install the upper (No. 2 and No. 3) timing covers.

16. Install and adjust the drive belts.

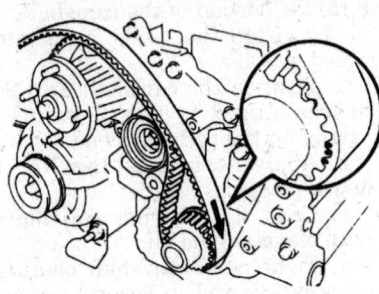

Draw a directional arrow on the belt

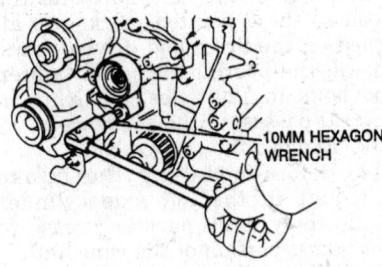

10MM HEXAGON WRENCH

Removing the idler pulley — SC300

17. Connect the battery cable, start the vehicle and check for any leaks.

LS400 and SC400

1. Remove the 2 upper and lower timing belt covers.
2. Remove the timing belt guide (No. 1 crank position sensor plate).
3. Remove the timing belt.

NOTE: If the timing belt is to be reused, draw a directional arrow on the timing belt in the direction of engine rotation (clockwise) and place matchmarks on the timing belt and crankshaft gear to match the drilled mark on the pulley.

To install:

4. Align the installation mark on the timing belt with the drilled mark of the crankshaft timing pulley. Install the timing belt on the crankshaft timing pulley, No. 1 idler pulley and the No. 2 idler pulley.

NOTE: If the old timing belt is being reinstalled, make sure the directional arrow is facing in the original direction and that the belt and crankshaft gear matchmarks are properly aligned.

5. Install the timing belt guide (No. 1 crank angle sensor plate) with the cup side facing forward. Replace the timing belt cover spacer.

6. Install the No. 1 timing belt cover and tighten the mounting bolts. Install the hydraulic pump on the SC400. Install the fan bracket.

7. Align the pulley set key on the crankshaft with the key groove of the pulley. Install the pulley, using the proper tool to tap in the pulley. Tighten the pulley bolt to 181 ft. lbs. (245 Nm).

8. Align the knock pin on the right side camshaft with the knock pin of the timing pulley. Slide on the timing pulley with the right side mark facing forward. Tighten the bolt to 80 ft. lbs. (108 Nm).

9. Align the knock pin on the left side camshaft with the knock pin of the timing pulley. Slide on the timing pulley with the left side mark facing forward. Tighten the bolt to 80 ft. lbs. (108 Nm).

10. Turn the crankshaft pulley and align it's groove with the **0** timing mark on the No. 1 timing belt cover. Using the proper tool, turn the crankshaft timing pulley and align the timing marks of the camshaft timing pulley and the timing belt rear plate.

11. Install the timing belt to the left side camshaft timing pulley by:

a. Using the proper tool, slightly turn the left side timing pulley clockwise. Align the installation mark of the timing belt with the timing mark of the camshaft timing pulley and hang the timing belt on the left side camshaft pulley.

b. Using the proper tool, align the timing marks of the left side camshaft pulley and the timing belt rear plate.

c. Check that the timing belt has tension between crankshaft timing pulley and the left side camshaft pulley.

12. Install the timing belt to the right side camshaft timing pulley by:

a. Using the proper tool, slightly turn the right side timing pulley clockwise. Align the installation mark of the timing belt with the timing mark of the camshaft timing pulley and hang the timing belt on the right side camshaft pulley.

b. Using the proper tool, align the timing marks of the right side camshaft pulley and the timing belt rear plate.

c. Check that the timing belt has tension between crankshaft timing pulley and the right side camshaft pulley.

13. The timing belt tensioner must be set prior to installation. The tensioner can be set by:

a. Place a plate washer between the tensioner and a block. Using a suitable press, press in the pushrod using 220-2205 lbs. of pressure.

b. Align the holes of the pushrod and housing, pass the proper tool (1.27mm allen wrench) through the holes to keep the setting position of the pushrod.

c. Release the press and install the dust boot to the tensioner.

14. Install the tensioner and tighten the bolts to 20 ft. lbs. (26 Nm). Remove the tool from the tensioner.

15. Turn the crankshaft pulley 2 complete revolutions from TDC to TDC. Always turn the crankshaft clockwise. Check that each pulley aligns with the timing marks.

16. Install the spark plugs and tighten to 13 ft. lbs. (18 Nm). Install the drive belt tensioner and tighten the bolt to 12 ft. lbs. (16 Nm).

17. Install the alternator and engine wire bracket. Tighten the nut and bolt to 26 ft. lbs. (35 Nm) on the LS400 or 27 ft. lbs. (37 Nm) on the SC400. Connect the electrical connections at the alternator.

18. Install both distributor housings and tighten the mounting bolts to 13 ft. lbs. (18 Nm). Replace the distributor rotors and caps.

19. Install the right side No. 2 timing belt cover and tighten the 10mm bolts to 69 inch lbs. (7.8 Nm) and the 12mm bolts to 12 ft. lbs. (16 Nm). Connect the camshaft position sensor connector.

20. Install the left side No. 2 timing belt cover and connect the cam position sensor connector.

21. Install the water bypass pipe and connect the hoses and connectors.

22. Replace the left side ignition coil and connect the coil connector. Install the idler pulley and cover plate. Tighten the bolt to 27 ft. lbs. (37 Nm).

23. Install and secure the ignition wires. Install the right side No. 3 timing belt cover.

24. Install the left side No. 3 timing belt cover and connect the vacuum hose and connectors. Install the right side engine wire cover.

25. Install the left side engine wire cover and connect the vacuum hoses.

26. Install the upper high tension cord covers. Fit the front side claw groove of the upper cover to claw of the lower cover.

27. Install the power steering pump and the air conditioning compressor.

28. Install the throttle body cover and the air cleaner.

29. Install the radiator, fan pulley, fan coupling, fan and drive belt.

30. Install the engine undercover and replace the battery.

31. Install the air ducts and dust covers. Connect the battery cables.

32. Refill the cooling system. Check the ignition timing.

Timing Sprockets

REMOVAL AND INSTALLATION

1. Remove the timing belt.

2. Using a spanner wrench to hold the camshaft pulley, remove the setbolt.

3. Install a 2-armed puller and remove the camshaft pulley. Be careful, the pulley may spring off so don't drop it.

To install:

4. Align the camshaft knockpin with the groove in the camshaft timing pulley and slide the pulley onto the shaft (flange side outward). Install the setbolt and plate washer and tighten it to 80 ft. lbs. (108 Nm) on the ES250, ES300, LS400 and SC400 or 59 ft. lbs. (79 Nm) on the SC300.

5. Install the timing belt and covers.

Camshaft

REMOVAL AND INSTALLATION

ES250 and ES300

1. Remove the cylinder head covers.

NOTE: Being that the thrust clearance on both the intake and exhaust camshafts is small, the camshafts must be kept level dur-

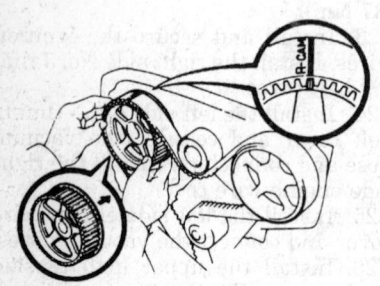

Installing the right camshaft sprocket — ES250 and ES300

ing removal. If the camshafts are removed without being kept level, the camshaft may be caught in the cylinder head causing the head to break or the camshaft to seize.

2. To remove the exhaust camshaft from the right side cylinder head, proceed as follows:

   a. Turn the camshaft with a wrench until the 2 pointed marks on the drive and driven gears are aligned.

   b. Secure the exhaust camshaft sub-gear to the main gear using a service bolt. The manufacturer recommends a bolt 0.63-0.79 in. (16-20mm) long with a thread diameter of 6mm and a 1mm thread pitch. When removing the exhaust camshaft be sure the torsional spring force of the sub-gear has been eliminated.

   c. Remove eight bearing cap bolts and remove the caps. Uniformly loosen and remove bearing cap bolts in several passes and in the proper sequence.

   d. Remove the exhaust camshaft from the engine.

3. Uniformly loosen and remove the 10 bearing cap bolts in several passes, in the sequence. Remove the bearing caps and oil seal and then lift out the intake camshaft.

4. To remove the exhaust camshaft from the left side cylinder head, proceed as follows:

   a. Turn the camshaft with a wrench until the pointed marks on the drive and driven gears are aligned.

   b. Secure the exhaust camshaft sub-gear to the main gear using a service bolt. The manufacturer recommends a bolt 0.63-0.79 in. (16-20mm) long with a thread diameter of 6mm and a 1mm thread pitch. When removing the exhaust camshaft be sure the torsional spring force of the sub-gear has been eliminated.

   c. Remove eight bearing cap bolts and remove the caps. Uniformly loosen and remove bearing cap bolts in several passes and in the proper sequence.

   d. Remove the exhaust camshaft from the engine.

5. Uniformly loosen and remove the 10 bearing cap bolts in several passes, in the sequence. Remove the bearing caps and oil seal and then lift out the intake camshaft.

To install:

6. Before installing the intake camshaft in the right side cylinder

head, apply multi-purpose grease to the thrust portion of the camshaft.

7. To install the intake camshaft, proceed as follows:

   a. Position the camshaft at a 90 degree angle to the 2 pointed marks on the cylinder head.

   b. Apply sealant to the No. 1 bearing cap.

   c. Coat the bearing cap bolts with clean engine oil.

   d. Tighten the camshaft bearing caps evenly and in several passes to 12 ft. lbs. (16 Nm) in the proper sequence.

8. Apply multi-purpose grease to the thrust portion of the exhaust camshaft (right side head).

9. Position the camshaft into the head so the 2 pointed marks are aligned on the drive and driven gears. Install the bearing caps and tighten the bolts to 12 ft. lbs. (16 Nm), in several passes, in the sequence.

10. Remove the service bolt.

11. Before installing the intake camshaft in the left side cylinder head, apply multi-purpose grease to the thrust portion of the camshaft.

12. To install the intake camshaft, proceed as follows:

   a. Position the camshaft at a 90 degree angle to the pointed mark on the cylinder head.

   b. Apply sealant to the No. 1 bearing cap.

   c. Coat the bearing cap bolts with clean engine oil.

   d. Tighten the camshaft bearing caps evenly and in several passes to 12 ft. lbs. (16 Nm) in the proper sequence.

13. Apply multi-purpose grease to the thrust portion of the exhaust camshaft (left side head).

14. Position the camshaft into the head so the pointed marks are aligned on the drive and driven gears. Install the bearing caps and tighten the bolts to 12 ft. lbs. (16 Nm), in several passes, in the sequence.

15. Remove the service bolt.

16. Install the head cover.

17. Start the engine and check for leaks.

18. Adjust the valves if necessary and check the ignition timing.

SC300

1. Remove the cylinder head covers.

2. While holding the camshaft with a wrench, loosen the camshaft sprocket bolt and remove the sprocket.

3. Remove the 4 bolts and lift out the No. 4 (inner) timing belt cover.

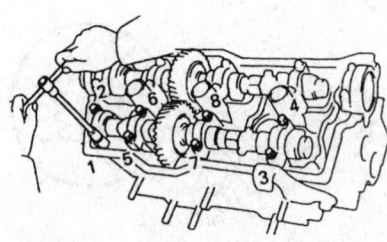

Secure the right side exhaust camshaft sub-gear with a service bolt — ES250 and ES300

Installing the right and left camshaft sprockets — LS400 and SC400

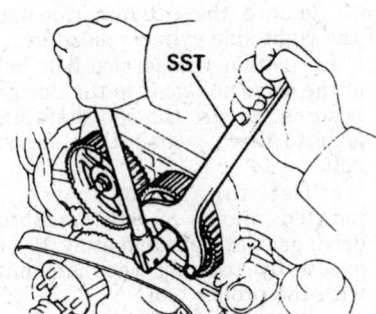

Removing the camshaft sprockets — SC300

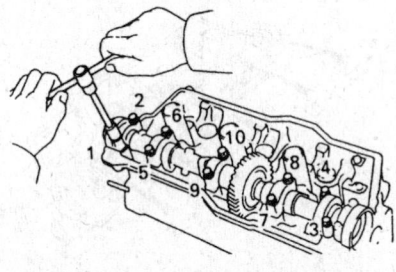

Right side exhaust camshaft bearing cap bolt loosening sequence — ES250 and ES300

Right side intake camshaft bearing cap bolt loosening sequence — ES250 and ES300

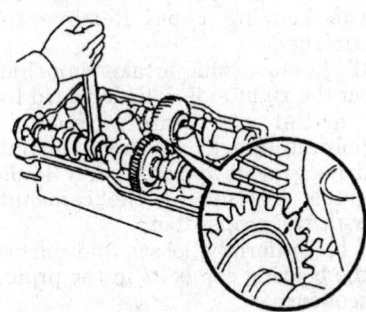

Align the 2 pointed marks on the gears — ES250 and ES300

4. Uniformly loosen and then remove the 4 No. 1 camshaft bearing cap bolts. These are the ones directly behind the sprockets. Remove the bearing caps.

5. Uniformly, and in the sequence, loosen and remove the remaining bearing cap bolts. Lift off all 12 bearing caps.

6. Lift out the exhaust and intake camshafts.

To install:

7. Coat the thrust portions of each camshaft with engine oil and then position them in the cylinder head with the cam lobes facing up and the knock pins.

8. Position the No. 3 and No. 7 bearing caps in place, coat the bolt threads with oil and then tighten them temporarily.

9. Coat new oil seals with multi-purpose grease and then slide them over the camshafts.

10. Clean the mating surfaces of the 2 No. 1 bearing caps and then squeeze on some sealant. Install the bolts.

11. Install all remaining bearing caps, coat the threads of each bolt with clean oil and then tighten them, in several passes, in the sequence, to 14 ft. lbs. (20 Nm).

12. Press the oil seal in as far as it will go and then rotate the camshaft until the forward straight pin is upward. Loosen the bearing cap bolts, until they can be turned by hand and then tighten them to 14 ft. lbs. (20 Nm).

13. Turn each camshaft ⅓ of a revolution (120 degrees), loosen the bearing cap bolts and then retighten them to 14 ft. lbs. (20 Nm).

14. Turn each camshaft an additional ⅓ of a revolution, loosen the bearing cap bolts and then retighten them to 14 ft. lbs. (20 Nm).

15. Check and adjust the valve clearance.

16. Install the cylinder head covers.

LS400 and SC400

1. Disconnect the negative battery cable. Drain the cooling system.

2. Remove the camshaft timing pulleys. Remove the cooling fan hydraulic pump on the SC400.

3. Disconnect the accelerator cable, the throttle control cable, if equipped with automatic transmission and the cruise control actuator cable.

4. Remove the high tension cord cover and the right side ignition coil.

5. Remove the water inlet housing mounting bolts and disconnect the water bypass hose from the ISC valve.

6. Remove the water inlet and inlet housing assemblies. Remove the O-ring from the water inlet housing.

7. Remove the EGR pipe.

8. Disconnect the following:
   a. VSV connector
   b. Vacuum pipe hose
   c. EGR water bypass pipe
   d. Fuel pressure VSV

9. Disconnect the EGR vacuum hoses and remove the EGR VSV.

10. Disconnect the following hoses:
   a. Water bypass pipe hose from the ISC valve.

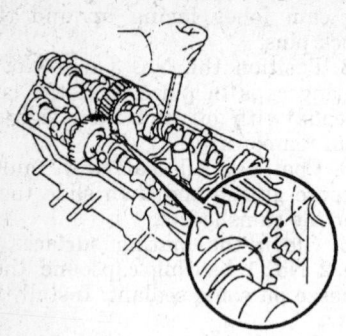

Align the pointed marks on the gears — ES250 and ES300

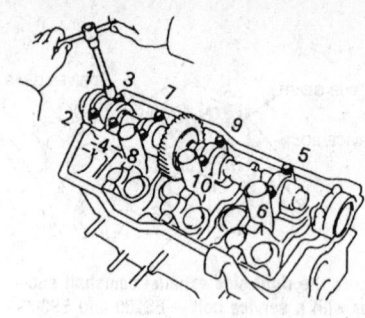

Left side intake camshaft bearing cap bolt loosening sequence — ES250 and ES300

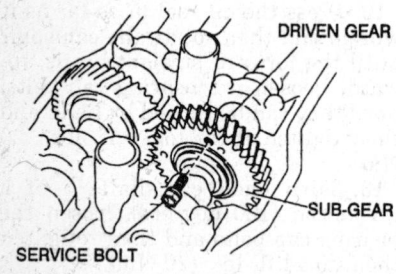

Secure the left side exhaust camshaft sub-gear with a service bolt — ES250 and ES300

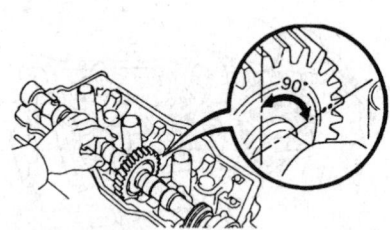

Install the right side intake camshaft like this — ES250 and ES300

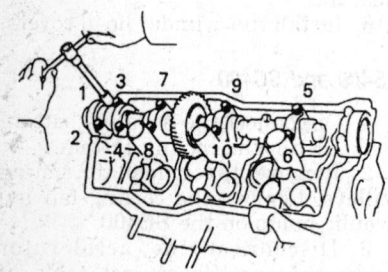

Left side exhaust camshaft bearing cap bolt loosening sequence — ES250 and ES300

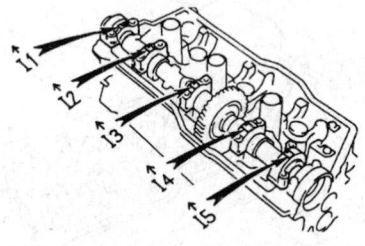

Install the right side intake camshaft bearing caps — ES250 and ES300

b. Water bypass joint hose.

c. Vacuum pipe hoses.

11. Disconnect the EGR gas temperature sensor, California only. Remove the EGR valve adapter.

12. Disconnect the following:

a. Fuel pressure regulator vacuum hose.

b. Air intake chamber vacuum hose.

c. Vacuum hose from the EVAP BVSV.

13. Remove the mounting bolts, hoses and the vacuum pipe.

14. Remove the ISC valve.

15. Remove the throttle body sensor connectors and the water bypass pipe from the rear water bypass joint.

16. Disconnect the PCV valve hose. Remove the throttle body and gasket.

17. Disconnect the accelerator cable bracket and the brake booster vacuum union and hose.

18. Disconnect the cold start injector connector and the cold start injector tube from the right side delivery pipe, if equipped.

19. Disconnect the check connector from the intake chamber and remove the mounting nuts and bolts.

20. Remove the air intake chamber and the cold start injector, tube and wire assembly, if equipped.

21. Disconnect the engine wire from the intake manifold and from the right side cylinder head. Disconnect the heater hoses.

22. Remove the delivery pipes and the fuel injectors. Remove the mounting bolts and nuts. Lift up the intake manifold.

23. Remove the front and rear water bypass joint.

24. Raise and safely support the vehicle. Remove the front exhaust pipe and the main catalytic converters. Lower the vehicle.

25. Disconnect the right side oxygen sensor. Remove the mounting bolts and nuts and remove the right side exhaust manifold.

26. Remove the oil dipstick and guide. Disconnect the left side oxygen sensor.

27. Remove the mounting bolts and nuts and remove the left side exhaust manifold.

28. Remove the 2 engine hangers and the wire brackets from the right side cylinder head.

29. Remove the bolts, washers and the cylinder head cover. Remove the semi-circular plugs, if necessary.

30. Remove the exhaust camshaft of the right side cylinder head by:

a. Position the service bolt hole of the drive sub-gear to the upright position. Secure the camshaft sub-gear to drive gear with a service bolt.

b. Set the timing mark, 1 pointed mark, of the camshaft drive gear at approximately 10 degrees, by turning the camshaft with the proper tool.

c. Alternately, loosen and remove the bearing cap bolts holding the intake camshaft side of the oil feed pipe to the cylinder head.

d. Uniformly, loosen and remove the bearing cap bolts, in sequence.

e. Remove the oil feed pipe and the bearing caps. Remove the camshaft.

31. Remove the intake camshaft from the right side cylinder head by:

a. Set the timing mark, 1 pointed mark, of the camshaft drive gear at approximately 45 degrees, by turning the camshaft with the proper tool.

b. Uniformly, loosen and remove the bearing cap bolts in the proper sequence.

c. Remove the bearing caps, oil seal and the intake camshaft.

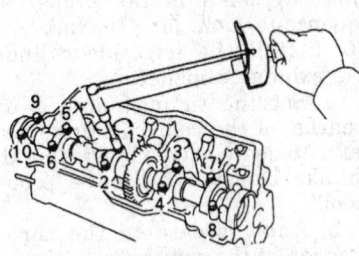

Right side intake camshaft bearing cap bolt tightening sequence — ES250 and ES300

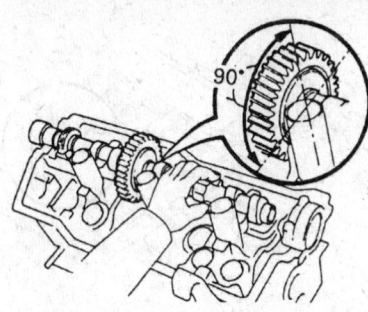

Installing the left side intake camshaft — ES250 and ES300

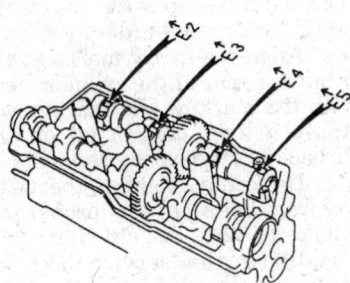

Install the right side exhaust camshaft bearing caps — ES250 and ES300

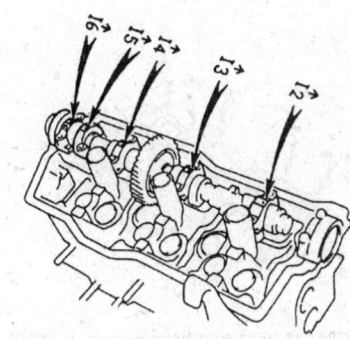

Install the left side intake camshaft bearing caps — ES250 and ES300

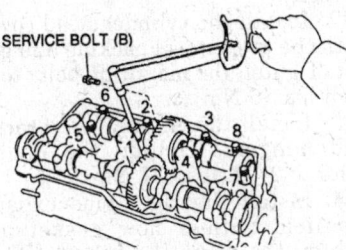

Right side exhaust camshaft bearing cap bolt tightening sequence — ES250 and ES300

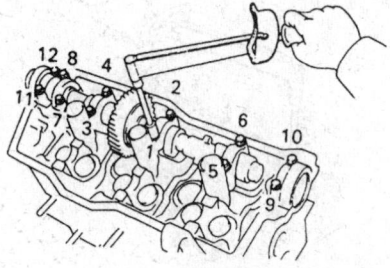

Left side intake camshaft bearing cap bolt tightening sequence — ES250 and ES300

32. Remove the exhaust camshaft of the left side cylinder head by:

a. Position the service bolt hole of the drive sub-gear to the upright position. Secure the camshaft sub-gear to drive gear with a service bolt.

NOTE: When removing the camshaft, make sure the torsional spring force of the sub-gear has been eliminated.

b. Set the timing mark, 2 pointed marks, of the camshaft drive gear at approximately 15 de-

grees, by turning the camshaft with the proper tool.

c. Alternately, loosen and remove the bearing cap bolts holding the intake camshaft side of the oil feed pipe to the cylinder head.

d. Uniformly, loosen and remove the bearing cap bolts in the proper sequence.

e. Remove the oil feed pipe and the bearing caps. Remove the camshaft.

33. Remove the intake camshaft from the left side cylinder head by:

a. Set the timing mark, 1 pointed mark, of the camshaft

drive gear at approximately 60 degrees, by turning the camshaft with the proper tool.

b. Uniformly, loosen and remove the bearing cap bolts, in sequence.

c. Remove the bearing caps, oil seal and the intake camshaft.

To install:

34. Remove any old packing and apply new seal packing to the bearing caps.

35. Install the bearing cap on the right side cylinder head, marked **I1**, in position with the arrow mark facing the rear. Install the bearing cap on the left side cylinder head, marked **I6**, in position with the arrow mark facing the front.

36. Apply a light coat of oil on the threads of the cap bolts. Install the nearing cap bolts with new washers and tighten to 12 ft. lbs. (16 Nm).

37. Install the right side cylinder head intake camshaft by:

a. Apply grease to the thrust portion of the camshaft.

b. Place the intake camshaft at a 45 degree angle of the timing mark (1 pointed mark) on the cylinder head.

c. Remove any old packing and apply new seal packing to the bearing cap marked **I6** and install the front bearing cap, marked **I6** with the arrow facing rearward.

d. Align the arrows at the front and rear of the cylinder head with the bearing cap.

e. Install the remaining bearing caps in the proper sequence with the arrow mark facing rearward. Install the oil feed pipe and the mounting bolts.

f. Uniformly, tighten the bearing cap bolts in the proper sequence to 12 ft. lbs. (16 Nm).

38. Install the right side cylinder head exhaust camshaft by:

a. Set the timing mark, 1 pointed mark, of the camshaft drive gear at a 10 degree angle by turning the intake camshaft with the proper tool.

b. Apply grease to the thrust portion of the camshaft.

c. Align the timing marks, 1 pointed mark, of the camshaft drive and driven gears.

d. Place the exhaust camshaft in the cylinder head. Install the rear bearing cap with the arrow mark facing rearward.

e. Align the arrow marks at the front and rear of the cylinder head with the mark on the bearing cap. Apply a light coat of oil on the threads of the bearing cap bolts.

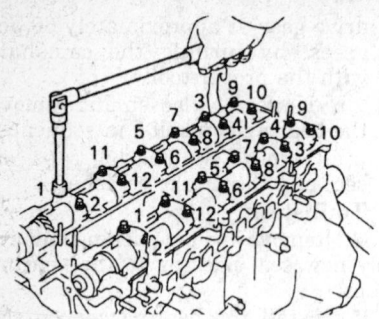

Camshaft bearing cap bolt loosening sequence (remember, both No. 1 caps have already been removed) — SC300

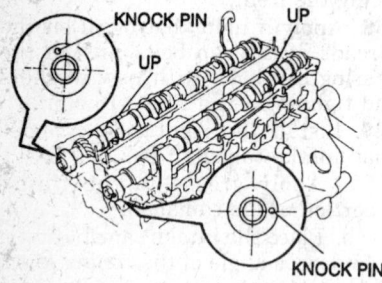

Camshaft positioning — SC300

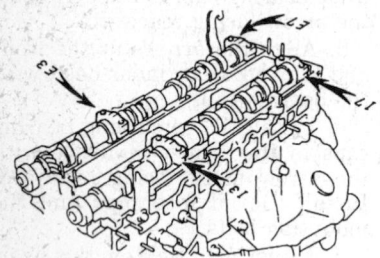

Install the No. 3 and No. 7 bearing caps — SC300

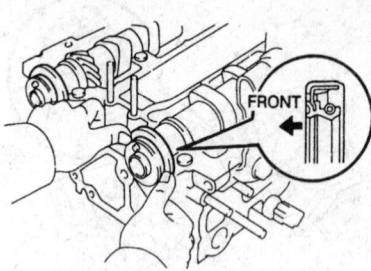

Oil seal installation — SC300

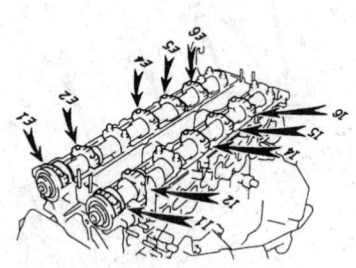

Install the remaining bearing caps — SC300

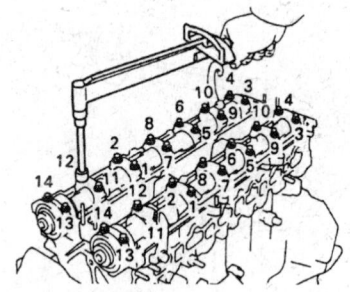

Camshaft bearing cap bolt tightening sequence — SC300

f. Uniformly, tighten the bearing cap bolts in the proper sequence to 12 ft. lbs. (16 Nm).

g. Bring the service bolt installed upward by turning the camshaft with the proper tool. Remove the service bolt.

39. Install the left side cylinder head intake camshaft by:

a. Apply grease to the thrust portion of the camshaft.

b. Place the intake camshaft at a 60 degree angle of the timing mark, 1 pointed mark, on the cylinder head.

c. Remove any old packing and apply new seal packing to the bearing cap marked I6 and install the front bearing cap, marked I1 with the arrow facing rearward.

d. Align the arrows at the front and rear of the cylinder head with the bearing cap. Apply a light coat of oil on the threads of the bearing cap bolts.

e. Install the remaining bearing caps in the proper sequence with the arrow mark facing rearward. Install the oil feed pipe and the mounting bolts.

f. Uniformly, tighten the bearing cap bolts in the proper sequence to 12 ft. lbs. (16 Nm).

40. Install the left side cylinder head exhaust camshaft by:

a. Set the timing mark, 2 dot marks, of the camshaft drive gear at a 15 degree angle by turning the intake camshaft with the proper tool.

b. Apply grease to the thrust portion of the camshaft.

c. Align the timing marks, 2 dot marks, of the camshaft drive and driven gears.

d. Place the exhaust camshaft ion the cylinder head. Install the rear bearing cap with the arrow mark facing rearward.

e. Align the arrow marks at the front and rear of the cylinder head with the mark on the bearing cap. Apply a light coat of oil on the threads of the bearing cap bolts.

f. Uniformly, tighten the bearing cap bolts in the proper sequence to 12 ft. lbs. (16 Nm).

g. Bring the service bolt installed upward by turning the camshaft with the proper tool. Remove the service bolt.

41. Install the camshaft oil seals with the proper tool. Install the semicircular plugs with the proper seal packing.

42. Install the cylinder head covers with the proper seal packing and gasket. Tighten the mounting bolts to 52 inch lbs. (6 Nm).

43. Install the engine wire bracket and hangers. Tighten the hanger bolts to 27 ft. lbs. (37 Nm).

44. Install the right side exhaust manifold with a new gasket and tighten the mounting bolts to 29 ft. lbs. (40 Nm). Connect the right side oxygen sensor connector.

45. Install the right side exhaust manifold with a new gasket and tighten the mounting bolts to 29 ft. lbs. (40 Nm). Connect the right side oxygen sensor connector.

46. Install the left side exhaust manifold with a new gasket and tighten the mounting bolts to 29 ft. lbs. (40 Nm). Connect the left side oxygen sensor connector.

47. Install the oil dipstick and guide. Raise and safely support the vehicle.

48. Install the catalytic converters and front exhaust pipe. Lower the vehicle.

49. Install the front and rear water bypass joints. Tighten the mounting bolts to 13 ft. lbs. (18 Nm).

50. Install the intake manifold, using new gaskets. Tighten the mount-

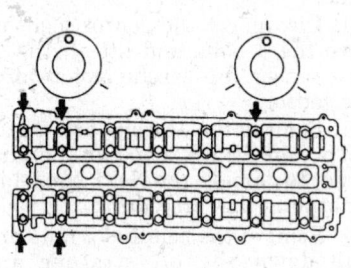

Loosen the bearing cap bolts as shown

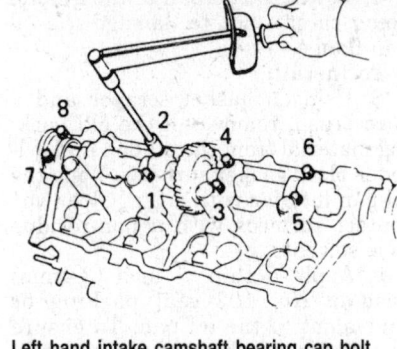

Left hand intake camshaft bearing cap bolt tightening sequence — LS400 and SC400

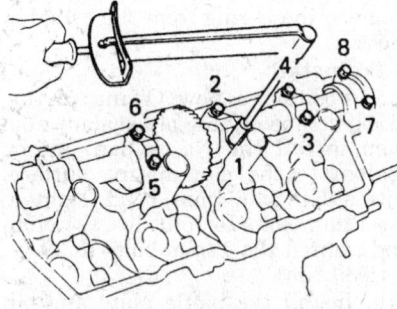

Right hand intake camshaft bearing cap bolt tightening sequence — LS400 and SC400

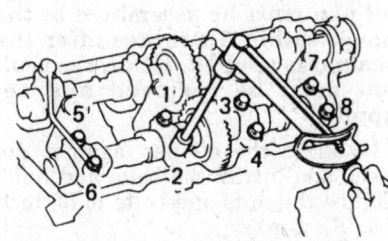

Left hand exhaust camshaft bearing cap bolt tightening sequence — LS400 and SC400

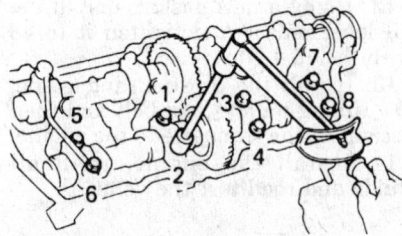

Right hand exhaust camshaft bearing cap bolt tightening sequence — LS400 and SC400

ing nuts and bolts to 13 ft. lbs. (18 Nm).

51. Install the delivery pipes and fuel injectors. Install the fuel return pipe with new gaskets. Tighten the union bolt to 26 ft. lbs. (36 Nm).

52. Connect the fuel hoses and the injector connectors. Connect the engine wire to the delivery pipes.

53. Connect the connectors on the left side delivery pipe, the water temperature sensor connector, cold start injector time switch connector and the water temperature sender gauge connector.

54. Connect the heater hoses and engine wire bracket. Install the engine wire to the bracket.

55. Install the cold start injector, tube and wire assembly. Tighten the mounting bolts to 69 inch lbs. (8 Nm), if equipped.

56. Install the air intake chamber with new gaskets and tighten the mounting bolts to 13 ft. lbs. (18 Nm).

57. Connect the cold start injector tube to the right side delivery pipe and tighten the union bolt to 11 ft. lbs. (15 Nm), if equipped.

58. Connect the cold start injector connector, if necessary. Install the accelerator cable bracket.

59. Install the brake booster union and connect the vacuum hose. Tighten the union bolt to 22 ft. lbs. (30 Nm).

60. Connect the water bypass hose to the throttle body and the PCV hose to the cylinder head cover.

61. Install the throttle body, using a new gasket. Tighten the mounting bolts to 13 ft. lbs. (18 Nm).

62. Install the water bypass pipe and connect the sensor connectors. Install the ISC valve and tighten the mounting bolts to 13 ft. lbs. (18 Nm). Connect the water bypass hose.

63. Install the vacuum pipe and the following hoses:
   a. Fuel pressure regulator vacuum hose.
   b. Vacuum hose to the upper port of the EVAP BVSV.
   c. Air intake chamber vacuum hose.
   d. Throttle body vacuum hoses.

64. Install the EGR valve adapter with a new gasket. Tighten the mounting bolts to 13 ft. lbs. (18 Nm).

65. Connect the EGR gas temperature sensor connector (California only).

66. Install the EGR valve and vacuum modulator. Connect the water bypass hoses and the vacuum hoses.

67. Install the EGR and fuel pressure VSV and connect the hoses and connectors. Replace the EGR pipe and tighten the mounting bolts to 13 ft. lbs. (18 Nm).

68. Install the timing belt rear plates and tighten the bolts to 69 inch lbs. Install the water inlet and inlet housing and tighten the bolts to 13 ft. lbs. (18 Nm).

69. Install the right side ignition coil and the high tension cord cover.

70. Connect and adjust the accelerator cable, the automatic transmission throttle cable and the cruise control actuator cable. Install the camshaft timing pulley.

71. Fill the cooling system and connect the negative battery cable. Start the engine and check for leaks.

72. Recheck all the fluid levels and check the ignition timing.

Piston and Connecting Rod

POSITIONING

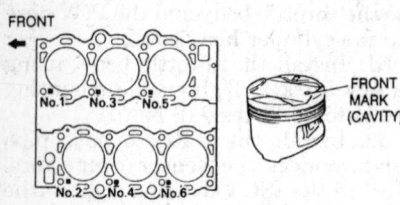

Piston installation location — ES250

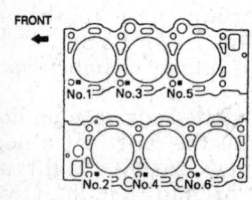

Piston installation location — ES300

ENGINE LUBRICATION

Oil Pan

REMOVAL AND INSTALLATION

ES250 and ES300

1. Raise the support the front end on jackstands.
2. Drain the oil and remove the dipstick.
3. Remove the right engine undercover.
4. Disconnect the exhaust pipe, remove the lower suspension cross-member, engine mounting center member and the stiffener plate.
5. Remove the 15 bolts and 4 nuts from the oil pan flange.
6. Using a prybar, separate the oil pan from the cylinder block.

7. Lower the oil pan to the ground being careful not to damage the oil pan flange.
   To install:
8. Using a gasket scraper and a wire brush, remove all the old packing material from the oil pan and cylinder block gasket surfaces. Wipe the oil pan interior with a rag. Clean the contact surfaces with a non-residue type solvent.
9. Apply a thin ⅛ inch (3-4mm) bead of No. 102 seal packing or equivalent to the oil pan. To ensure the proper size bead, cut the nozzle on the tube.

NOTE: Avoid applying too much sealant to the oil pan. The oil pan must be assembled to the block within 3 minutes after the sealant is applied. If not, the sealant must be removed and reapplied.

10. Place the oil pan against the block and install the bolts and nuts. Torque the nuts and bolts to 65 inch lbs. (5.4 Nm)
11. Install the stiffener plate and torque the mounting bolts to 27 ft. lbs. (37 Nm) for 14mm bolts or 13 ft. lbs. (18 Nm) for 12mm bolts. Install the engine mounting center member. Connect the exhaust pipe.
12. Install the right engine cover or covers.
13. Fill the engine with oil to the proper level.
14. Start the engine and check for leaks. Recheck the engine oil level.

SC300

1. Remove the engine/transmission assembly and then separate the transaxle from the engine.
2. With the engine on a stand, remove the timing belt, the idler pulley and the crankshaft timing pulley.

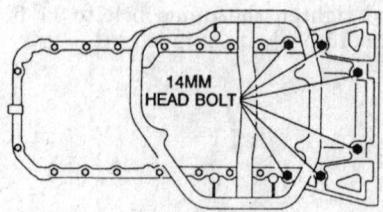

Install the 14mm bolts here — SC300

3. Remove the oil dipstick and guide.
4. Disconnect the sensor lead, remove the 4 bolts and lift off the oil level sensor. Be careful not to drop this sensor.
5. Remove the 14 bolts and 2 nuts and pry off the No. 2 oil pan. Be careful not to damage the No. 1 pan while performing this procedure.
6. Remove the bolt and 2 nuts and drop down the oil strainer and gasket.
7. Remove the 5 bolts and 2 nuts and drop down the baffle plate.
8. Remove the 22 bolts and the carefully pry off the No. 1 oil pan. Remove the O-ring from the cylinder block.
   To install:
9. Position a new O-ring in the block, scrape off any old sealant and then install the No. 1 pan. Apply sealant to the pan mating surface with a ⅛ inch (3-4mm) bead. Tighten the 12mm bolts to 15 ft. lbs. (21 Nm) and tighten the 14mm bolts to 29 ft. lbs. (39 Nm).
10. Install the baffle plate and oil strainer. Tighten them both to 78 inch lbs. (8.8 Nm).
11. Install the No. 2 pan as you did the No. 1 and tighten the bolts to 78 inch lbs. (8.8 Nm).
12. Using a new gasket, install the oil level sensor and tighten it to 48 inch lbs. (5.4 Nm).
13. Install the dipstick and guide, the timing pulleys and belt and then reconnect the transaxle to the engine.
14. Install the engine, refill all fluids and road test the vehicle.

LS400

1. Raise the support the front end on jackstands.
2. Drain the oil and remove the dipstick.
3. Remove the right engine undercover(s).
4. Remove the mounting bolts and drop down the oil pan. Remove any old packing or sealer from the mounting surfaces.
   To install:
5. Using a gasket scraper and a wire brush, remove all the old packing material from the oil pan and cylinder block gasket surfaces. Wipe the oil pan interior with a rag. Clean the contact surfaces with a non-residue type solvent.
6. Apply a thin ⅛ inch (3-4mm) bead of No. 102 seal packing or equivalent to the oil pan. To ensure

the proper size bead, cut the nozzle on the tube.

NOTE: Avoid applying too much sealant to the oil pan. The oil pan must be assembled to the block within 3 minutes after the sealant is applied. If not, the sealant must be removed and re-applied.

7. Place the oil pan against the block and install the bolts and nuts. Torque the nuts and bolts to 65 inch lbs. (5.4 Nm)

8. Install the engine cover or covers.

9. Fill the engine with oil to the proper level.

10. Start the engine and check for leaks. Recheck the engine oil level.

SC400

1. Remove the engine/transmission assembly and then separate the transmission from the engine.

2. With the engine on a stand, remove the timing belt, the idler pulleys and the crankshaft timing pulley.

3. Remove the oil dipstick and guide.

4. Remove the main O_2 sensor bracket. Disconnect the sensor lead,

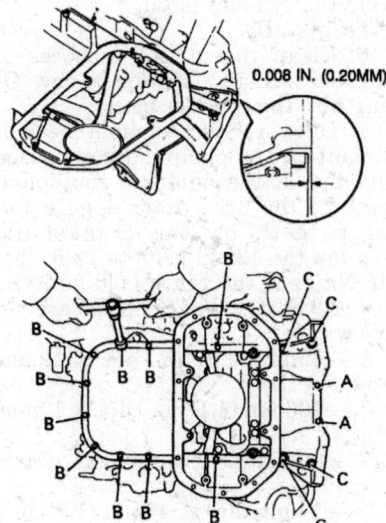

0.008 IN. (0.20MM)

No. 1 oil pan bolt positioning: (A) 20mm length, 10mm head; (B) 35mm length, 10mm head; (C) 55mm length, 12mm head — SC400

remove the 4 bolts and lift off the oil level sensor. Be careful not to drop this sensor.

5. Remove the 12 bolts and 2 nuts and pry off the No. 2 oil pan. Be careful not to damage the No. 1 pan while performing this procedure.

6. Remove the 6 bolts and 2 nuts and drop down the baffle plate.

7. Remove the 16 bolts and the carefully pry off the No. 1 oil pan. There are slots for inserting the prybar.

To install:

8. Scrape off any old sealant and then install the No. 1 pan. Apply sealant to the pan mating surface with a ⅛ inch (3-4mm) bead. Tighten the 12mm bolts to 13 ft. lbs. (18 Nm); tighten the 10mm bolts to 69 inch lbs. (7.8 Nm). Refer to the illustration for proper sizing and installation of each bolt.

9. Install the baffle plate and tighten it to 69 inch lbs. (7.8 Nm).

10. Install the No. 2 pan as you did the No. 1 and tighten the bolts to 69 inch lbs. (7.8 Nm). Make sure the bolts are 14mm in length.

11. Using a new gasket, install the oil level sensor and tighten it to 48 inch lbs. (5.4 Nm).

12. Install the dipstick and guide, the timing pulleys and belt and then reconnect the transaxle to the engine.

13. Install the engine, refill all fluids and road test the vehicle.

Oil Pump

REMOVAL AND INSTALLATION

ES250 and ES300

1. Remove the oil pan.
2. Remove the oil pan baffle plate.
3. Remove the oil strainer and O-ring.
4. Remove the timing belt. Remove the No. 1 idler and the crankshaft timing pulleys.

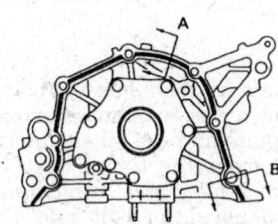

SEAL WIDTH 0.08–0.12 IN. (2.0–3.0MM)

Oil pump sealant location — ES250 and ES300

5. Remove the alternator and the A/C compressor. Also, remove the compressor bracket and the power steering pump adjusting bar.

6. Remove the 9 oil pump retaining bolts.

7. With a soft-faced hammer or rubber mallet, tap the oil pump loose from the block.

8. Remove the oil pump gasket and replace a new one.

To install:

9. Clean the cylinder block and oil pump gasket contact surfaces.

10. Draw a ⅛ inch (3-4mm) bead of seal packing.

11. Insert a new O-ring and then engage the spline teeth on the drive gear with the large teeth on the end of the crankshaft.

12. Tighten the oil pump mounting bolts to; 12mm bolts (C and D) to 14 ft. lbs. (20 Nm) and the 14mm bolts (A and B) to 30 ft. lbs. (41 Nm).

13. Install the power steering belt adjusting bar, the A/C compressor bracket and the alternator.

14. Install the timing belt. Don't forget the No. 1 idler and crankshaft pulleys.

15. Install the baffle plate.

16. Place a new O-ring on the strainer pipe outlet and install the strainer. Tighten the bolt and 2 nuts to 61 inch lbs. (7 Nm).

17. Install the oil pan and refill the engine oil.

18. Start the engine and inspect for leaks.

19. Recheck the engine oil level.

SC300

1. Remove the No. 1 and No. 2 oil pans.

2. Loosen the 9 mounting bolts and drive the pump off the cylinder block using a brass drift. Remove the 2 O-rings.

3. Position the 2 new O-rings in the cylinder block. Scrape any old sealant from the mating surfaces and install the pump. Draw a ⅛ inch (3-4mm) bead of sealant around the pump mating surface. Tighten the bolts to 15 ft. lbs. (21 Nm). Its a good idea to tighten the bolts (A) by hand first.

4. Install the oil pans.

LS400

1. Disconnect the negative battery cable. Raise and safely support the vehicle.

2. Remove the engine undercover.

3. Drain the oil, using a suitable container. Remove the oil dipstick.

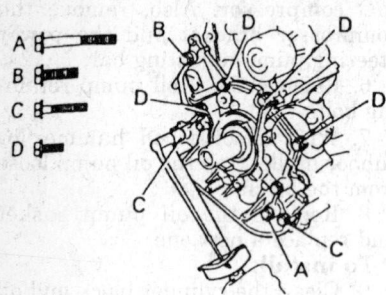

Oil pump bolt positioning — ES300

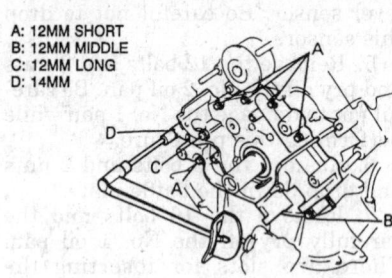

A: 12MM SHORT
B: 12MM MIDDLE
C: 12MM LONG
D: 14MM

Oil pump bolt positioning — LS400

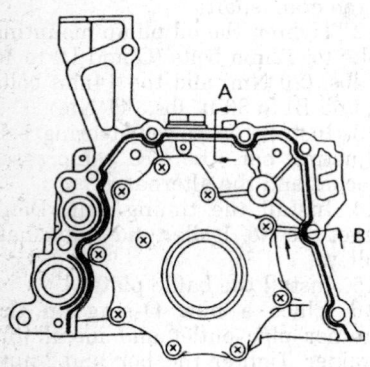

SEAL WIDTH 0.08–0.12 IN. (2.0–3.0MM)

Oil pump sealant location — SC300

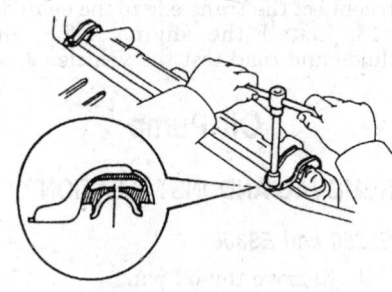

Oil pump bolt positioning — SC400

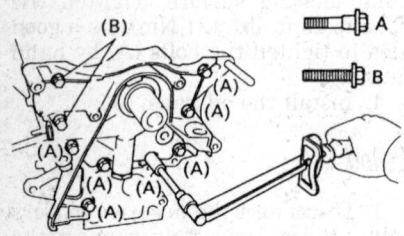

Oil pump bolt positioning — SC300

To install:

7. Install a new O-ring and align the oil drive rotor groove with the pump body mark.

8. Install the pump to the crankshaft with the spine teeth of the drive gear engaged with the large teeth of the crankshaft. Tighten the mounting bolts; 12mm bolts to 12 ft. lbs. (16 Nm) and 14mm bolts to 22 ft. lbs. (30 Nm).

9. Install the pickup sensor with the bolt and tighten to 56 inch lbs. (6.4 Nm). Replace the stud bolt.

10. Install the crankshaft timing pulley, No. 1 and No. 2 idler pulley and the timing belt. Install the oil strainer and tighten to 69 inch lbs. (7.8 Nm).

11. Install the baffle plate and the oil pan. Tighten the mounting bolts to 69 inch lbs. (7.8 Nm).

12. Install the engine undercover. Lower the vehicle.

13. Install the dipstick and refill the crankcase.

SC400

1. Remove the No. 1 and No. 2 oil pans.

2. Remove the 2 bolts and 2 nuts and lift off the oil strainer and gasket.

3. Remove the oil filter and mounting bracket.

4. Disconnect the lead and remove the engine speed sensor.

5. Remove the 8 bolts and pry off the oil pump. Remove the O-ring from the cylinder block.

To install:

6. Clean the mating surfaces of any old sealant. Position a new O-ring into the cylinder block.

7. Draw a ⅛ inch (3-4mm) bead of sealant on the pump mating surface and install the pump so the spline teeth of the drive rotor engage the large teeth on the crankshaft. Tighten the 12mm bolts to 12 ft. lbs. (16 Nm) and the 14mm bolts to 22 ft. lbs. (29 Nm). Bolt lengths are as follows:

A — 50mm (1.97 in.) dia. **x** 12mm long

B — 106mm (4.17 in.) dia. **x** 12mm long

C — 30mm (1.18 in.) dia. **x** 12mm long

D — 14mm dia. **x** 40mm (1.57 in.) long

8. Install the speed sensor and tighten it to 56 inch lbs. (6.4 Nm).

9. With 2 new O-rings, install the oil filter bracket assembly and tighten it to 13 ft. lbs. (18 Nm).

10. Install the oil strainer and tighten it to 69 inch lbs. (7.8 Nm).

Be sure the rubber support cushions are not pinched when installing the radiator

4. Remove the mounting bolts and pull down the oil pan. Remove the baffle plate and the oil strainer.

5. Remove the timing belt, No. 1 and No. 2 idler and crankshaft pulleys. Remove the bolt and pickup sensor.

6. Remove the stud bolts and mounting bolts. Remove the oil pump with the proper tool to pry away from the cylinder block. Clean and remove any packing from the mounting surfaces.

11. Install the oil pans.

Rear Main Bearing Oil Seal

REMOVAL AND INSTALLATION

1. Remove the transmission/transaxle.
2. On manual transmission/transaxle equipped vehicles, remove the clutch cover assembly and flywheel.
3. On automatic transmission/transaxle equipped vehicles, remove the driveplate.
4. Remove the rear end-plate.
5. Remove the 6 bolts and remove the oil seal retainer.
6. Use a small prybar to pry the oil seal from the retaining plate. Be careful not to damage the plate.

To install:

7. Clean the retainer contact surfaces thoroughly and lubricate the new oil seal with multi-purpose grease.
8. Using a block of wood, drive the oil seal into the retainer until its surface is flush with the edge of the retainer. Make sure the seal is installed evenly in the retainer to ensure proper sealing.
9. Apply a ⅛ inch (3-4mm) bead of sealant to the oil seal retainer. Bolt the retainer with the 6 bolts and install the dust seal. Tighten the bolts to 69 inch lbs. (7.8 Nm).
10. Install the rear endplate.
11. On automatic transmission/transaxle equipped vehicles, install the driveplate.
12. On manual transmission/transaxle equipped vehicles, install the clutch disc ans clutch cover.
13. Install the transmission/transaxle.

ENGINE COOLING

NOTE: On the LS400, a design change has been made to the cylinder head coolant core plug and gasket. The newly designed plug has eliminated the sealant on the flat surface of the plug. There was also some molybdenum disulfide coating added to the plug gasket. Torque the new coolant core plug to 58 ft. lbs. (79 Nm). Always replace the screw plugs and gaskets as a set and only with the new style parts.

Radiator

REMOVAL AND INSTALLATION

ES250

1. Position a suitable drain pan under the radiator and drain the cooling system by opening the radiator draincock.
2. Disconnect the coolant reservoir hose.
3. Remove the battery. Remove the ignition coil/igniter assembly.
4. Disconnect the engine and air conditioning cooling fan motor connectors.
5. Disconnect the upper and lower hoses from the radiator.
6. Unbolt and remove the engine electric cooling fan assembly (shroud and motor).
7. If equipped with air conditioning, remove the air conditioning electric cooling fan assembly (shroud and motor).
8. If equipped with automatic transaxle, disconnect the 2 cooler hoses from the cooler pipes at the bottom of the radiator.
9. Support the radiator by hand and remove the 2 bolts and radiator supports.
10. Remove the radiator from the vehicle.

To install:

11. Place the radiator in position and support it by hand. Install the 2 radiator supports with bolts. Tighten the bolts to 9 ft. lbs. (13 Nm). Make sure the rubber cushion of each support is not depressed or crimped.
12. If equipped with automatic transaxle, connect and tighten the 2 oil cooler hoses.
13. If equipped with air conditioning, install the air conditioning electric cooling fan assembly.
14. Install the engine electric cooling fan assembly.
15. Connect the cooling fan motor connectors.
16. Connect the upper and lower hoses to the radiator.
17. Connect the coolant reservoir hose.
18. Install the battery. Install the ignition coil/igniter assembly.
19. Fill the cooling system to the proper level with coolant.
20. Start the engine and inspect for leaks.
21. Remember to check the transmission fluid level on cars with automatic transaxles. Add fluid as required.

ES300

1. Disconnect the cable at the negative battery terminal.
2. Drain the engine coolant into a suitable container.
3. Remove the cruise control actuator cover.
4. Remove the union bolt and gasket and then disconnect the pressure line from the hydraulic fan motor. You may lose some hydraulic fluid here, so have a container ready.
5. Disconnect the upper radiator hose and the coolant reservoir hose. Disconnect the hydraulic motor return hose.
6. Remove the engine undercover.
7. Disconnect the lower radiator hose and the oil cooler lines.
8. Remove the 2 bolts and the upper supports and lift out the radiator/fan assembly. Remove the 6 bolts and separate the fan from the radiator.

To install:

9. Install the fan assembly to the radiator and then install the radiator. Tighten the 2 support bolts to 9 ft. lbs. (13 Nm). Be sure the rubber support cushions are not pinched.
10. Connect the oil cooler hoses and the lower radiator hose.
11. Install the engine undercover.
12. Connect the hydraulic motor return line.
13. Connect the reservoir and upper radiator hoses.
14. Connect the pressure line to the hydraulic motor with a new gasket. Tighten the union bolt to 47 ft. lbs. (64 Nm).
15. Install the actuator cover.
16. Fill the engine with coolant, connect the battery, start the car and check for leaks.

SC300

1. Disconnect the battery cables and remove the battery.
2. Remove the engine undercover and drain the coolant.
3. Disconnect the coolant reservoir hose and the upper radiator hose. Disonnect the lower radiator hose and the 2 oil cooler hoses.
4. Pinch out the 2 clips and remove the No. 2 radiator shroud.
5. Remove the 2 bolts and screw and remove the upper radiator support. Remove the 2 radiator supports.
6. Lift out the radiator.

To install:

7. Position the radiator, install the supports and tighten the bolts and screw to 9 ft. lbs. (12 Nm).
8. Install the No. 2 fan shroud.

9. Connect the upper and lower radiator hoses, the reservoir hose and the 2 oil cooler lines.

10. Fill the engine with coolant, install the undercover, start the engine and check for leaks.

LS400

1. Disconnect the negative battery cable. Drain the cooling system.

2. Remove the air intake duct and disconnect and plug the automatic transmission lines.

3. Disconnect the cooling fan motor connector.

4. Disconnect the water hose from the coolant reservoir and remove both radiator hoses.

5. Remove the radiator supports and the radiator.

6. Remove both fan shrouds.

7. The installation is the reverse of the removal procedure.

SC400

1. Disconnect the battery cables and remove the battery.

2. Remove the engine undercovers and drain the coolant.

3. Remove the coolant reservoir tank.

4. Loosen the clamps and remove the 2 radiator hoses and the 2 A/T oil cooler hoses.

5. Disconnect the pressure and return lines from the cooling fan hydraulic motor.

6. Remove the 2 bolts, the brackets and bushings and then disconnect the cooling fan inlet pipe from the shroud.

7. Disconnect the cooling fan hydraulic reservoir from the fan shroud.

8. Disconnect the water temperature sensor connector.

9. Remove the 2 bolts and screw and lift out the upper radiator support.

10. Lift the radiator slightly and disconnect the 2 oil cooler hoses (for

the cooling fan) from the clamp on the shroud. Remove the radiator.

To install:

11. Press the lower radiator supports onto the radiator and then slide into position. Lift it slightly and reconnect the 2 cooler hoses.

12. Install the upper supports and tighten them to 9 ft. lbs. (12 Nm).

13. Connect the temperature sensor. Install the reservoir tank and the inlet pipe to the fan shroud and tighten them both to 43 inch lbs. (4.9 Nm).

14. Connect the 2 hydraulic lines and tighten them to 47 ft. lbs. (64 Nm). Reconnect all remaining lines and hoses.

15. Install the coolant tank and the battery. Fill the engine with coolant, start the engine and check for leaks.

Heater Core

———— CAUTION ————
On models with an air bag, wait at least 90 seconds from the time that the ignition switch is turned to the LOCK position and the battery is disconnected before performing any further work.

REMOVAL AND INSTALLATION

ES250, ES300, SC300 AND SC400

1. Disconnect the negative battery cable. Drain the cooling system.

2. Remove the console, if equipped, by removing the shift knob (manual), wiring connector and console attaching screws.

3. Remove the carpeting from the tunnel.

4. If necessary, remove the cigarette lighter and ash tray.

5. Remove the package tray, if access to the heater core is difficult.

6. Remove the bottom cover/intake assembly screws and withdraw the A/C-heater assembly.

7. Remove the heater protector on the ES300. Remove the cover from the water valve.

8. Remove the water valve.

9. Remove the hose clamps and remove the hoses from the core.

10. Remove the heater core.

11. Installation is the reverse of the removal procedure. Fill the cooling system to the proper level. Operate the heater and check for leaks.

LS400

1. Disconnect the negative battery cable. Drain the cooling system.

2. Properly discharge the air conditioning system.

3. Disconnect the mounting nuts and hoses. Remove the heater valve.

4. Remove the cooling and blower unit.

5. Disconnect the inlet and outlet water hoses. Remove the mounting nuts and the insulator retainer.

6. Remove the instrument cluster and the radio assembly with the air conditioning control attached.

7. Remove the undercover.

8. Remove the glove box by performing the following:

a. Remove the glove box compartment panel and disconnect the left side check arm from the door.

b. Remove the retaining clips. Insert the proper tool between the upper side of the compartment and the safety pad, pry out the compartment to remove.

c. Disconnect the connector from the glove box compartment.

9. Disconnect the mounting bolts and remove the right side lower pad. Remove the connectors from the pad.

10. Remove the glove box door. Disconnect the connectors and remove the ABS Electronic Control Unit (ECU).

11. Remove the air ducts.

12. On the driver's side, loosen the lockbolt and disconnect the junction block. Disconnect the retaining clips at the floor. Remove the combination switch.

13. On the passenger side, disconnect the connectors and the bond cable. Disconnect the retaining clips at the floor carpet.

14. Remove the bolts and nut from the safety pad and lift out the pad.

15. Remove the heater ducts.

16. Remove the mounting screws and lift out the heater unit. Disconnect the connector and remove the servo motor.

17. Remove the mounting screws and remove the aspirator.

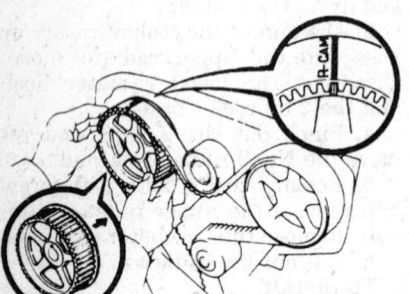

Lift the radiator slightly before disconnecting the oil cooler hoses — SC400

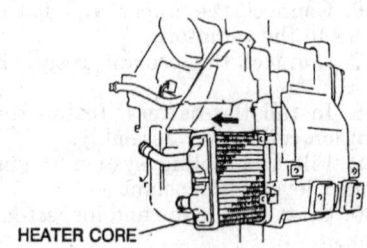

HEATER CORE

Removing the heater core — ES300

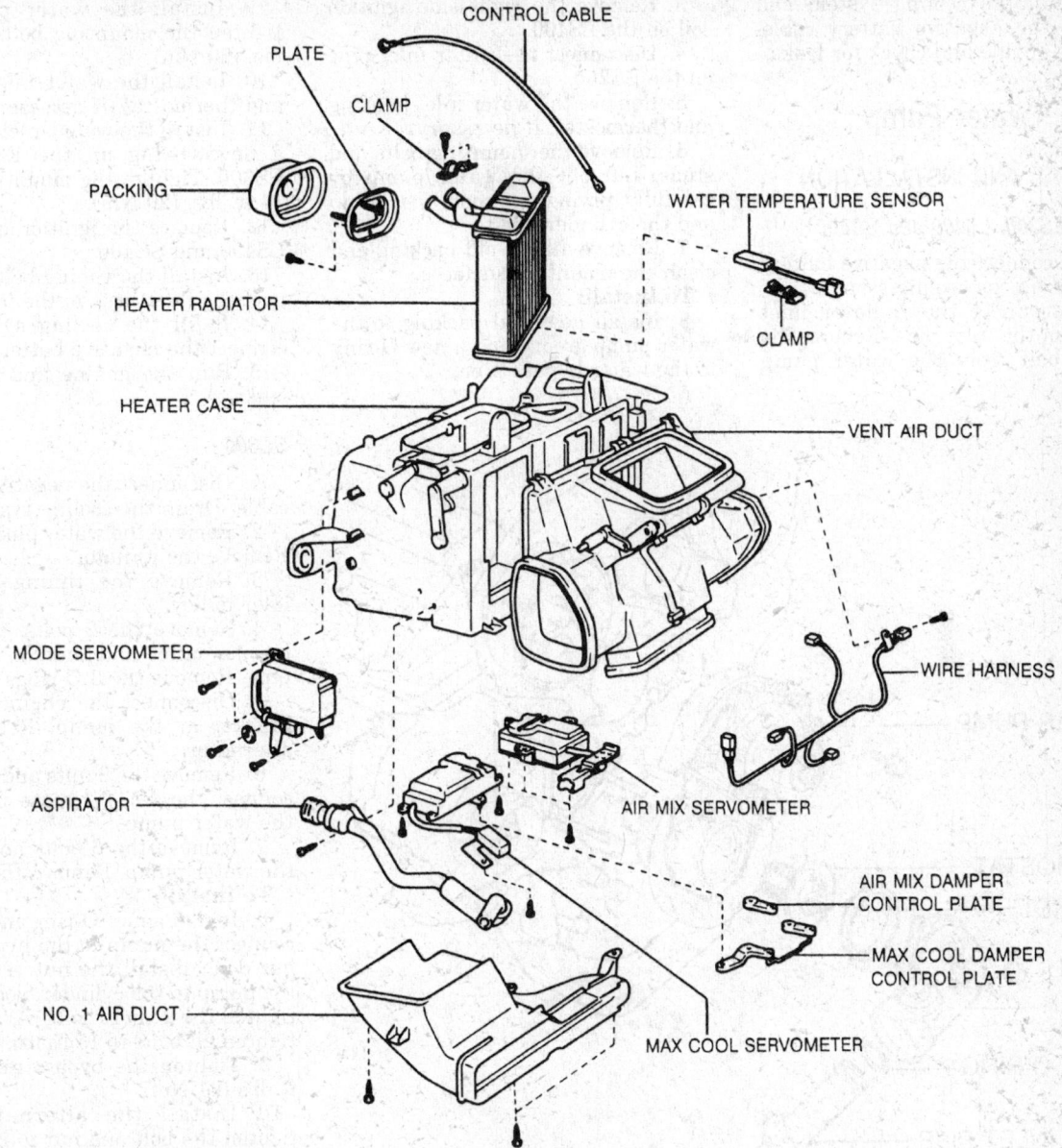

CONTROL CABLE

PLATE

CLAMP

PACKING

WATER TEMPERATURE SENSOR

HEATER RADIATOR

CLAMP

HEATER CASE

VENT AIR DUCT

MODE SERVOMETER

WIRE HARNESS

AIR MIX SERVOMETER

ASPIRATOR

AIR MIX DAMPER
CONTROL PLATE

MAX COOL DAMPER
CONTROL PLATE

NO. 1 AIR DUCT

MAX COOL SERVOMETER

Heater assembly — LS400

18. Remove the packing, screw, plate and the retaining screws. Pull out the heater core assembly.

To install:

19. Install the heater core. Replace the retaining screws, plate, screw and install the packing.

20. Install the aspirator and the servo motor. Connect the connector.

21. Install the heater unit and tighten the retaining screws. Replace the heater ducts.

22. Install the safety pad and tighten the mounting bolts and nut.

23. On the passenger side, connect the connectors and the bond cable. Connect the retaining clips at the floor carpet.

24. On the driver's side, connect the junction block and tighten the lock bolt. Connect the retaining clips at the floor. Replace the combination switch.

25. Replace the glove box door. Connect the connectors and replace the ABS Electronic Control Unit (ECU).

26. Install the air ducts.

27. Replace the right side lower pad and tighten the mounting bolts. Replace the connectors to the pad.

28. Replace the glove box by performing the following:

a. Connect the connector to the glove box compartment.

b. Install the glove box and replace the retaining clips.

c. Replace the glove box compartment panel and connect the left side check arm from the door.

29. Install the undercover.

30. Replace the instrument cluster and the radio assembly with the air conditioning control attached.

31. Connect the inlet and outlet water hoses. Replace the mounting nuts and the insulator retainer.

32. Replace the cooling and blower unit.

33. Install the heater valve. Connect the mounting nuts and hoses.

34. Properly, evacuate and recharge the air conditioning system.

35. Refill the cooling system and connect the negative battery cable. Run the engine and check for leaks.

Water Pump

REMOVAL AND INSTALLATION

ES250, ES300, LS400 and SC400

1. Disconnect the negative battery cable. Drain the cooling system.

2. Disconnect the radiator inlet hose from the inlet pipe. Remove the timing belt from the water pump pulley.

3. Remove the right side ignition coil on the LS400.

4. Disconnect the water inlet pipe on the ES250.

5. Remove the water inlet housing and thermostat, if necessary.

6. Remove the mounting bolts and studs. Lift out the water pump by carefully prying between the pump and the cylinder head.

7. Remove all the old packing and clean the mounting surfaces.

To install:

8. Install new seal packing to the water pump groove and a new O-ring to the water bypass pipe.

9. Install the water pump and tighten the mounting bolts to 14 ft. lbs. (20 Nm).

10. Install the water inlet housing and thermostat, if necessary.

11. Install the water inlet pipe with a new O-ring on the ES250 and ES300. Tighten the mounting bolt to 14 ft. lbs. (20 Nm).

12. Replace the ignition coil on the LS400 and SC400.

13. Install the timing belt and connect the inlet hose to the inlet pipe.

14. Refill the cooling system and connect the negative battery cable.

15. Run the engine and check for leaks.

SC300

1. Disconnect the negative battery cable. Drain the cooling system.

2. Remove the water pump pulley. Remove the radiator.

3. Remove the timing belt and idler pulley.

4. Remove the 2 bolts, the water bypass outlet and the No. 1 bypass pipe. Remove the 3 O-rings.

5. Disconnect the engine harness bracket at the pump. Remove the alternator.

6. Remove the 2 nuts and then disconnect the No. 2 bypass pipe from the water pump.

7. Remove the 6 bolts and pry off the water pump. Remove the O-ring.

To install:

8. Install a new O-ring and gasket. connect the pump to the bypass pipe but don't install the nut yet. Install the pump to the cylinder block, hand-tighten the 2 short bolts (A) and then tighten all bolts to 15 ft. lbs. (21 Nm).

9. Tighten the bypass nuts to 15 ft. lbs (21 Nm).

10. Install the alternator and tighten the bolt and nut to 29 ft. lbs. (39 Nm). Install the engine harness bracket.

11. Install the bypass outlet and the No. 1 pipe with new O-rings. Tighten the bolts to 78 inch lbs. (8.8 Nm).

12. Installation of the remaining components is in the reverse order of removal.

Thermostat

REMOVAL AND INSTALLATION

1. Position a suitable drain pan under the radiator drain cock and drain the cooling system.

2. Disconnect the water temperature switch connector from the water inlet housing.

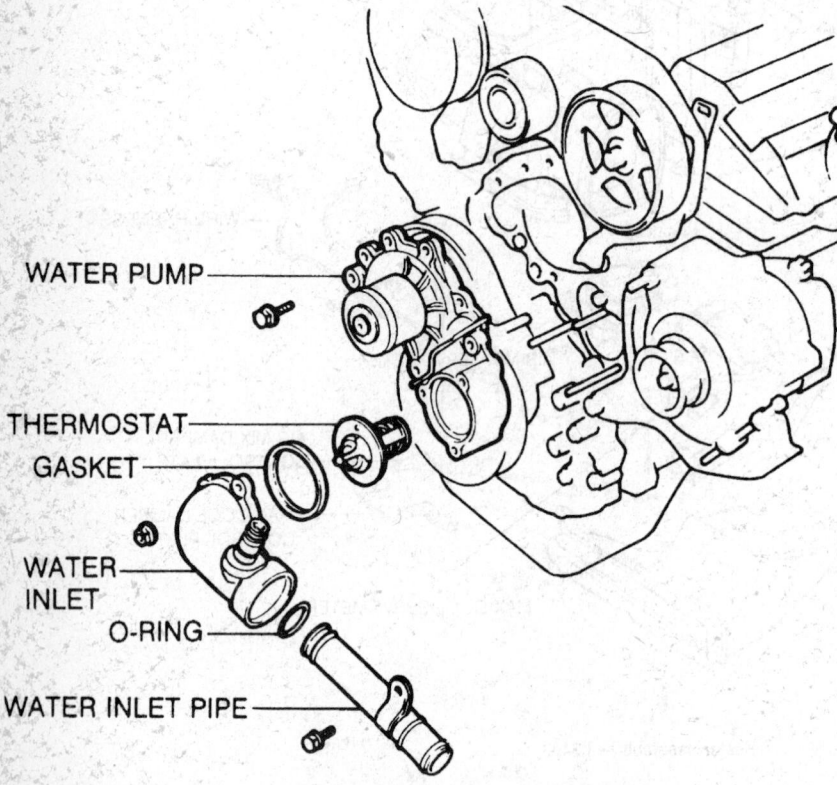

WATER PUMP

THERMOSTAT

GASKET

WATER INLET

O-RING

WATER INLET PIPE

Water pump assembly — ES250 and ES300

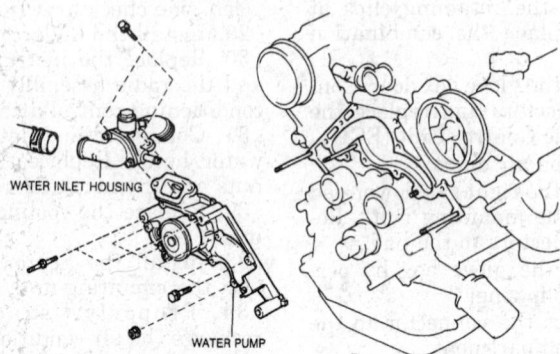

WATER INLET HOUSING

WATER PUMP

Water pump assembly — LS400 and SC400

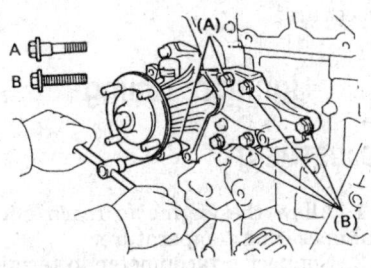

Water pump bolt installation — SC300

3. Loosen the hose clamp and disconnect the lower radiator hose from the water inlet housing.

4. Remove the 2 nuts from the water inlet housing and remove the housing from the water pump studs.

5. Remove the thermostat and rubber O-ring gasket from the water inlet housing.

To install:

6. Make sure all the gasket surfaces are clean. Clean the inside of the inlet housing and the radiator hose connection with a rag.

7. Install the new rubber O-ring gasket onto the thermostat. On the

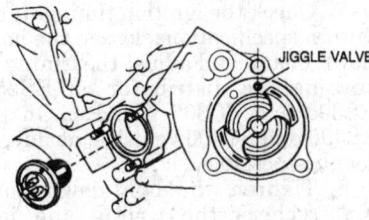

Thermostat installation — SC300

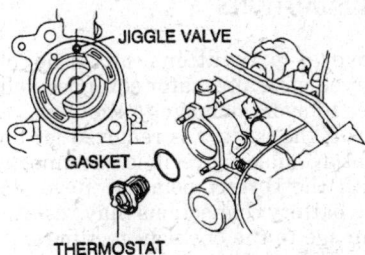

Thermostat installation — LS400

ES250 and ES300, align the jiggle valve with the stud bolt (A). On the SC300, align the jiggle valve with the protrusion on the mating surface — it may be within 10 degrees of either side. On the LS400 and SC400, position the jiggle valve so it is pointing straight upward; on the SC400, it can be within 30 degrees of either side. Insert the thermostat into the housing.

8. Position the water inlet housing with the thermostat over the studs on the water pump and install the 2 nuts. Torque the 2 nuts to 78 inch lbs. (8.8 Nm) on the SC300 or 13-14 ft. lbs. (18-20 Nm) on all others.

9. Connect the lower radiator hose to the inlet housing and install the hose clamp. On the ES300, tighten the bolt holding the water inlet hose to the alternator belt adjusting bar to 14 ft. lbs. (20 Nm).

10. Connect the water temperature switch connector.

11. Install the oil filter and check the oil level.

12. Fill the cooling system with a good brand of eythylene glycol based coolant.

13. Start the engine and inspect for leaks.

ENGINE ELECTRICAL

NOTE: Disconnecting the negative battery cable on some vehicles may interfere with the functions of the on-board computer systems and may require the computer to undergo a relearning process, once the negative battery cable is reconnected.

Distributor

REMOVAL

———— **CAUTION** ————
On models with an air bag, wait at least 90 seconds from the time that the ignition switch is turned to the LOCK position and the battery is disconnected before performing any further work.

ES250 and ES300

1. Disconnect the negative battery cable. Remove the upper brace if necessary.

2. Remove the air cleaner top. Disconnect the air flow meter and the air cleaner hose.

3. Remove the wires from the distributor cap and disconnect the distributor wire connector.

4. Remove the hold-down bolts and pull out the distributor. Remove the O-ring.

5. Remove the distributor.

SC300

1. Disconnect the negative battery cable.

2. Tag and disconnect the spark plug wires at the distributor. Disconnect the distributor connector.

3. Set No. 1 cylinder to TDC of the compression stroke. Remove the oil filler cap. Rotate the crankshaft clockwise until the camshaft nose can be seen through the hole. Turn the crankshaft counterclockwise approximately 120 degrees. Turn it an additional 10-40 degrees clockwise until the timing marks on the crankshaft pulley and timing cover are aligned.

4. Loosen the hold-down bolt and remove the distributor.

LS400 and SC400

RIGHT

1. Disconnect the negative battery cable. Remove the air duct assembly.

2. Disconnect the air flow meter connector and air hose.

3. Remove the air flow meter assembly and the throttle body cover.

4. Disconnect the ISC and power steering idle-up air hose. Remove the No. 1 air hose.

5. Remove the high tension cable upper cover and the right side engine wire cover.

6. Disconnect the mounting bolts and remove the No. 3 timing belt cover.

7. Disconnect the sensor connector. Remove the mounting bolts, the wire cover and take off the No. 2 timing belt cover.

8. Disconnect the electrical wires from the distributor cap.

9. Remove the distributor cap and the rotor.

10. Remove the mounting bolts and lift out the distributor housing.

LEFT

1. Disconnect the negative battery cable. Drain the cooling system and remove the engine wire cover.

2. Remove the No. 2 junction block cover and the No. 3 timing belt cover.

3. Disconnect the water inlet housing hose and the reservoir tank hose.

4. Remove the mounting bolts and the water pipe from the No. 2 timing belt cover.

5. Disconnect the sensor connector, the connector boot and remove the No. 2 timing belt cover.

6. Disconnect the electrical connections from the cap and the housing. Remove the distributor cap and the rotor.

7. Remove the mounting screws and lift out the distributor housing.

INSTALLATION

Timing Not Disturbed

ES250 AND ES300

1. Install a new O-ring in the housing. Lubricate the O-ring with engine oil.

2. Align the cutout marks of the coupling and the housing.

3. Insert the distributor, aligning the line of the distributor housing with the cutout of the distributor attachment bearing cap. Tighten the hold-down bolts.

4. Install the rotor and the distributor cap. Connect the cables to the distributor cap. Align the spline of the distributor cap with the spline groove of the holder.

5. Connect the electrical connections to the distributor. Replace the air cleaner cap, air flow meter and the air cleaner hose.

6. Install the upper brace if necessary and connect the negative battery cable.

7. Adjust the timing.

SC300

1. Lubricate a new O-ring with engine oil and install it.

2. Check that the No. 1 cylinder is still at TDC.

3. Align the groove on the distributor housing with the protrusion on the drive gear. Insert the distributor so the center of the flange is aligned with that of the bolt hole on the cylinder head.

4. Tighten the hold-down bolt.

5. Connect the distributor connector and the spark plug wires.

6. Connect the battery cable and check the ignition timing.

LS400 and SC400

RIGHT

1. Install the distributor housing. Replace the rotor. Match the protrusion on the rear of the rotor with the hollow on the camshaft timing pulley and install the rotor with the tip of

the rotor towards the matchmark on the distributor housing and the distributor cap.

2. Connect the ignition cables to the distributor cap.

3. Connect the sensor connector. Install the No. 2 timing belt cover and boots.

4. Install the No. 3 timing belt cover and engine wire cover. Tighten the mounting bolts.

5. Install the electrical connection upper cover and the upper throttle body cover.

6. Replace the No. 1 air hose, the PS idle-up air hose and the ISC air hose.

7. Install the air flow meter assembly and connect the air hose and the meter connector.

8. Connect the negative battery cable. Adjust the timing.

LEFT

1. Install the distributor housing and tighten the mounting bolts.

2. Install the rotor. Match the protrusion on the rear of the rotor with the hollow on the camshaft timing pulley and install the rotor with the tip of the rotor towards the matchmark on the distributor housing and replace the distributor cap.

3. Connect the ignition cables to the distributor cap.

4. Connect the sensor connector. Install the No. 2 timing belt cover and boots.

5. Connect the water inlet housing hose and the reservoir tank hose.

6. Replace the water pipe to the No. 2 timing belt cover.

7. Install the No. 3 timing belt cover and replace the No. 2 junction block cover.

8. Install the engine wire cover and tighten the mounting bolts.

9. Refill the cooling system and connect the negative battery cable. Adjust the timing.

Timing Disturbed

1. Turn the crankshaft pulley and align the groove on the pulley with the timing mark 0 of the No. 1 timing belt cover.

2. On the LS400 and SC400, check that the timing marks of the camshaft timing pulleys and the timing belt rear plates or covers are aligned. If not, turn the crankshaft 1 revolution (360 degrees).

3. On the ES250 and ES300, position the slit of the intake camshaft (right side cylinder head) in the proper position for distributor installation.

4. On all engines, install the distributor following the proper procedure.

Ignition Timing

ADJUSTMENT

1. Allow the engine to reach normal operating temperature.

2. Connect a tachometer to terminal IG (-) of the check connector. On the LS400 and SC400, set the tachometer to the 4 cylinder range.

NOTE: Never allow the tachometer test probe to touch ground as it could result in damage to the igniter and or ignition coil. As some tachometers are not compatible with this ignition system, it is recommended to confirm the compatibility of the unit before use.

3. Check the idle speed.

4. Connect the proper jumper wire to terminals TE_1 and E_1 of the check connector in the engine compartment.

5. Connect the timing light to spark plug wire for the No. 1 cylinder on the ES250, ES300 and SC300 or the No. 6 cylinder on the LS400 and SC400.

6. Start the engine and check the timing with the transmission in **N** position.

7. Check the ignition timing. If not within specifications, loosen the hold-down bolt(s) and adjust the timing by turning the distributor on ES250, ES300 and SC300 vehicles. On the LS400 and SC400 vehicles, no adjustment is possible.

8. Tighten the hold-down bolts and recheck the timing and idle speed, adjust as necessary. Remove the jumper wires and test equipment.

Alternator

PRECAUTIONS

Several precautions must be observed with alternator equipped vehicles to avoid damage to the unit.

• If the battery is removed for any reason, make sure it is reconnected with the correct polarity. Reversing the battery connections may result in damage to the one-way rectifiers.

• When utilizing a booster battery as a starting aid, always connect the positive to positive terminals and the negative terminal from the booster

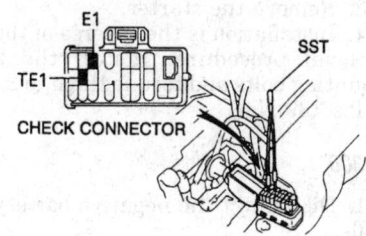
Short the check connector — ES300

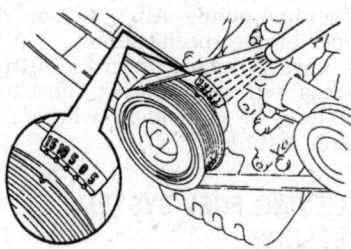
Timing mark location — ES300

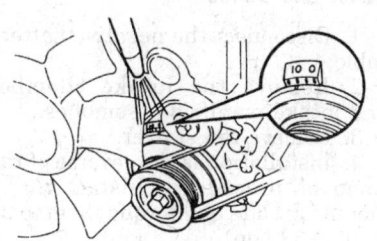
Timing mark location — SC300

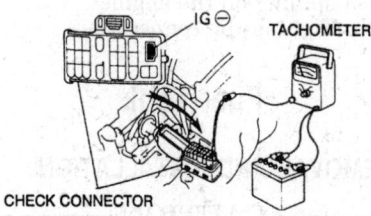
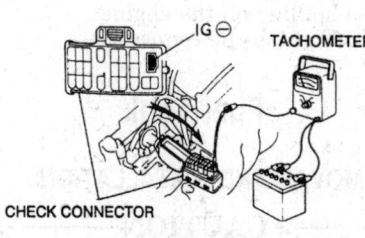
Tachometer connection — SC300

battery to a good engine ground on the vehicle being started.

• Never use a fast charger as a booster to start vehicles.

• Disconnect the battery cables when charging the battery with a fast charger.

• Never attempt to polarize the alternator.

• Do not use test lamps of more than 12 volts when checking diode continuity.

• Do not short across or ground any of the alternator terminals.

• The polarity of the battery, alternator and regulator must be matched and considered before making any electrical connections within the system.

• Never separate the alternator on an open circuit. Make sure all connections within the circuit are clean and tight.

• Disconnect the battery ground terminal when performing any service on electrical components.

• Disconnect the battery if arc welding is to be done on the vehicle.

BELT TENSION ADJUSTMENT

LS400, SC400 and SC300

An automatic belt tensioner is used to maintain the proper amount of pressure on the drive belt. The bolt on the SC300 tensioner is a left hand thread.

ES250 and ES300

1. Disconnect the negative battery cable.

2. Loosen the adjusting lock bolt and the pivot bolt.

3. Move the alternator to adjust the belt tension to 5 lbs. on a new belt or 20 lbs. on a used belt.

4. Tighten the adjusting and pivot bolts.

5. Connect the negative battery cable.

REMOVAL AND INSTALLATION

CAUTION

On models with an air bag, wait at least 90 seconds from the time that the ignition switch is turned to the LOCK position and the battery is disconnected before performing any further work.

ES250 and ES300

1. Disconnect the negative battery cable.

2. Remove the 2 bolts and the No. 3 right hand engine mounting stay on the ES300. Remove the bolt and nut and then remove the No. 2 right hand engine mounting stay.

3. Disconnect the electrical connector and wire (and nut) from the alternator.

4. Unfasten the bolts which attach the adjusting link to the alternator.

5. Remove the alternator drive belt from the pulley.

6. Unfasten the alternator attaching bolt and then withdraw the alternator from its bracket.

To install:

7. Mount the alternator on the alternator brackets with the pivot and adjusting bolts. Do not tighten the bolts at this time.

8. Install the No. 2 stay and tighten the bolts to 55 ft. lbs. (75 Nm), the nut to 46 ft. lbs. (62 Nm). Install the No. 3 stay and tighten the 2 bolts to 54 ft. lbs. (73 Nm).

9. Install the drive belt onto the pulley making sure the grooves on the belt and the grooves on the pulley are properly aligned.

10. Adjust the drive belt tension and properly tighten the pivot and adjusting bolts.

11. Connect the wire (nut) and connector to the alternator.

12. Connect the negative and starter battery cables.

13. Start the engine and allow it warm. Visually inspect the drive belt and listen for any abnormal vibration. Stop the engine and recheck the belt tension.

SC300

1. Disconnect the negative battery cable.

2. Remove the engine undercover.

3. Remove the drive belt.

4. Tag and disconnect the alternator electrical leads, remove the bolt and nut and remove the alternator.

To install:

5. Install the alternator and tighten the bolts to 27 ft. lbs. (37 Nm).

6. Install the drive belt and connect the battery.

LS400 and SC400

1. Disconnect the negative battery cable. Turn the ignition switch to the **LOCK** position.

2. Remove the drive belt and the engine undercover.

3. Disconnect the electrical connections at the alternator.

4. Remove the through bolt and nut. Remove the alternator.

5. The installation is the reverse of the removal procedure.

NOTE: On the LS400, there has been a problem on occasion with the alternator connector not being fully inserted into its socket. Should this condition exist, the vehicle may experience diminished alternator output which in turn will effect the battery charging system. When installing the connector to the alternator socket, be sure to reconnect the connector to the socket until a click is heard. Fasten the rubber boot and check to see that the rubber boot is fastened properly.

Starter

REMOVAL AND INSTALLATION

———— CAUTION ————
On models with an air bag, wait at least 90 seconds from the time that the ignition switch is turned to the LOCK position and the battery is disconnected before performing any further work.

ES250

1. Disconnect both battery cables, remove the battery and the battery tray.

2. Remove the igniter bracket and all necesary wiring.

3. Disconnect connector and wire from the starter.

4. Remove the starter.

5. Installation is the reverse of the removal procedure. Install the 2 mounting bolts and torque them to 29 ft. lbs. (39 Nm).

ES300

1. Disconnect both battery cables and remove the battery.

2. Remove the cruise control actuator cover and actuator.

3. Remove the starter.

4. Installation is the reverse of the removal procedure. Install the 2 mounting bolts and torque them to 29 ft. lbs. (39 Nm).

SC300

1. Disconnect the negative battery cable.

2. Remove the starter.

3. Installation is the reverse of the removal procedure. Install the 2 mounting bolts and torque them to 29 ft. lbs. (39 Nm)

LS400 and SC400

1. Disconnect the negative battery cable.

2. Remove the intake chamber and intake manifold assemblies.

3. Remove the starter.

4. Installation is the reverse of the removal procedure. Install the 2 mounting bolts and torque them to 29 ft. lbs. (39 Nm).

FUEL SYSTEM

Fuel System Service Precautions

Safety is the most important factor when performing not only fuel system maintenance but any type of maintenance. Failure to conduct maintenance and repairs in a safe manner may result in serious personal injury or death. Maintenance and testing of the vehicle's fuel system components can be accomplished safely and effectively by adhering to the following rules and guidelines.

• To avoid the possibility of fire and personal injury, always disconnect the negative battery cable unless the repair or test procedure requires that battery voltage be applied.

• Always relieve the fuel system pressure prior to disconnecting any fuel system component (injector, fuel rail, pressure regulator, etc.), fitting or fuel line connection. Exercise extreme caution whenever relieving fuel system pressure to avoid exposing skin, face and eyes to fuel spray. Please be advised that fuel under pressure may penetrate the skin or any part of the body that it contacts.

• Always place a shop towel or cloth around the fitting or connection prior to loosening to absorb any excess fuel due to spillage. Ensure that all fuel spillage (should it occur) is quickly removed from engine surfaces. Ensure that all fuel soaked cloths or towels are deposited into a suitable waste container.

• Always keep a dry chemical (Class B) fire extinguisher near the work area.

• Do not allow fuel spray or fuel vapors to come into contact with a spark or open flame.

• Always use a backup wrench when loosening and tightening fuel line connection fittings. This will prevent unnecessary stress and torsion to fuel line piping. Always follow the proper torque specifications.

• Always replace worn fuel fitting O-rings with new. Do not substitute fuel hose or equivalent where fuel pipe is installed.

RELIEVING FUEL SYSTEM PRESSURE

1. Be sure the engine is cold.

2. Relieve the fuel pressure by slowly loosening the connection at the pressure regulator.

3. Be sure to place a rag under the pressure regulator to prevent the fuel from spilling on the engine.

4. Tighten the connection.

Fuel Tank

REMOVAL AND INSTALLATION

———— CAUTION ————
The fuel injection system is under pressure. Release pressure slowly and contain spillage. Observe no smoking/no open flame precautions. Have a Class B-C (dry powder) fire extinguisher within arm's reach at all times.

ES250 and ES300

1. Relieve the fuel system pressure. Remove the filler cap.

2. Using a siphon or pump, drain the fuel from the tank and store it in a proper metal container with a tight cap.

3. Disconnect the fuel pump and sending unit wiring at the connector.

4. Raise the vehicle and safely support it.

5. Loosen the clamp and remove the filler neck and overflow pipe from the tank.

6. Remove the supply hose from the tank. Wrap a rag around the fitting to collect escaping fuel. Disconnect the breather hose from the tank, again using a rag to control spillage.

7. Cover or plug the end of each disconnected line to keep dirt out and fuel in.

8. Support the fuel tank with a floor jack or transmission jack. Use a broad piece of wood to distribute the load. Be careful not to deform the bottom of the tank.

9. Remove the fuel tank protectors.

10. Remove the fuel tank support strap bolts.

11. Swing the straps away from the tank and lower the jack. Balance the tank.

12. Remove the fuel filler pipe extension assembly, the breather pipe assembly, sending unit assembly and fuel pump assembly. Keep these items in a clean, protected area away from the vehicle.

13. While the tank is out and disassembled, inspect it for any signs of rust, leakage or metal damage. If any problem is found, replace the tank. Clean the inside of the tank and rinse the tank thoroughly several times.

14. Inspect all of the lines, hoses and fittings for any sign of corrosion, wear or damage to the surfaces. Check the pump outlet hose and the filter for restrictions.

15. When reassembling, always replace the sealing gaskets with new ones. Also, replace any rubber parts showing any sign of deterioration.

To install:

16. Install the fuel pump and or the sending unit assembly. Connect the breather pipe assembly and the filler pipe extension. Make sure all fuel tank cushions are in the proper location.

NOTE: Tighten all fuel tank attaching screws to 35 inch lbs. (3.9 Nm).

17. Place the fuel tank on the jack and elevate it into place within the vehicle. Attach the straps and install the strap bolts, tightening them evenly to 29 ft. lbs. (39 Nm).

18. Install the fuel tank protectors.

19. Connect the breather hose to the tank pipe, the return hose to the tank pipe and the supply hose to its tank pipe. Tighten the supply hose fitting to 21 ft. lbs. (28 Nm).

20. Connect the filler neck and overflow pipe to the tank. Make sure the clamps are properly seated and secure.

21. Lower the vehicle to the ground.

22. Connect the pump and sending unit electrical connectors to the harness.

23. Using a funnel, pour the fuel that was drained from its container into the fuel filler.

24. Install the fuel filler cap.

25. Start the engine and check carefully for any sign of leakage around the tank and lines.

SC300, LS400 and SC400

1. Relieve the fuel system pressure. Remove the filler cap.

2. Using a siphon or pump, drain the fuel from the tank and store it in a proper metal container with a tight cap.

3. Disconnect the fuel pump and sending unit wiring at the connectors.

4. Raise the vehicle and safely support it.

5. Loosen the clamp and remove the filler neck and overflow pipe from the tank.

6. Remove the supply hose from the tank. Wrap a rag around the fitting to collect escaping fuel. Disconnect the breather hose from the tank, again using a rag to control spillage.

7. Cover or plug the end of each disconnected line to keep dirt out and fuel in.

8. Support the fuel tank with a floor jack or transmission jack. Use a broad piece of wood to distribute the load. Be careful not to deform the bottom of the tank.

9. Remove the No. 1 and No. 2 fuel tank cover cases.

10. Remove the fuel tank retaining nuts and bolts.

11. Lower the jack and balance the tank with by hand. The tank is bulky and may have some fuel left in it. If its balance changes suddenly, the tank may fall.

12. Remove the fuel filler pipe extension, the breather pipe assembly, sending unit assembly and or fuel pump assembly. Keep these items in a clean, protected area away from the vehicle.

13. While the tank is out and disassembled, inspect it for any signs of rust, leakage or metal damage. If any problem is found, replace the tank. Clean the inside of the tank with water and a light detergent and rinse the tank thoroughly several times.

14. Inspect all of the lines, hoses and fittings for any sign of corrosion, wear or damage to the surfaces. Check the pump outlet hose and the filter for restrictions.

15. When reassembling, always replace the sealing gaskets and O-rings

with new ones. Also replace any rubber parts showing any sign of deterioration.

To install:

16. Install the fuel pump and or the sending unit assembly. Connect the breather pipe assembly and the filler pipe extension. Make sure all fuel tank cushions are in the proper location.

NOTE: Tighten all fuel tank attaching screws to 26 inch lbs. (2.9 Nm).

17. Place the fuel tank on the jack and elevate it into place within the vehicle. Attach the retaining nuts and bolts, tightening them to 18 ft. lbs. (25 Nm).

18. Install the No. 1 and No. 2 fuel tank cover cases.

19. Connect the breather hose to the tank pipe, the return hose to the tank pipe and the supply hose to its tank pipe. Torque the inlet tank pipe screws to 26 inch lbs. (2.9 Nm). Install the fuel main tank tube and torque the bolt to 22 ft. lbs. (29 Nm). Install the No. 2 fuel return tank tube and torque the bolt to 18 ft. lbs. (25 Nm).

20. Connect the filler neck and overflow pipe to the tank. Make sure the clamps are properly seated and secure.

21. Lower the vehicle to the ground.

22. Connect the pump and sending unit electrical connectors to the harness.

23. Using a funnel, pour the fuel that was drained from its container into the fuel filler.

24. Install the fuel filler cap.

25. Start the engine and check carefully for any sign of leakage around the tank and lines.

Fuel Filter

REMOVAL AND INSTALLATION

ES250 and ES300

The fuel filter is located under the hood, on the driver's side, by the fenderwell.

1. Disconnect the negative battery cable.

2. Disconnect and plug the fuel lines to the filter. Place a rag under the filter to catch any fuel that may spill.

3. Disconnect the mounting bolt(s) and remove the fuel filter.

4. Install a new filter and tighten the line connections to 22 ft. lbs. (29 Nm).

5. Connect the negative battery cable. Start the engine and check for leaks.

SC300

The fuel filter is located under the vehicle, on the driver's side, in front of the rear axle.

1. Disconnect the negative battery cable.
2. Disconnect and plug the fuel lines to the filter. Place a rag under the filter to catch any fuel that may spill.
3. Disconnect the mounting bolt(s) and remove the fuel filter.
4. Install a new filter and tighten the line connections to 22 ft. lbs. (29 Nm).
5. Connect the negative battery cable. Start the engine and check for leaks.

LS400 and SC400

The fuel filter is located under the vehicle on the driver's side before the rear axle.

1. Disconnect the negative battery cable. Raise and safely support the vehicle.
2. Disconnect and plug the fuel lines to the filter. Place a rag under the filter to catch any fuel that may spill.
3. Disconnect the mounting bolt(s) and remove the fuel filter.
4. Install a new filter and tighten the line connections to 22 ft. lbs. (29 Nm). Lower the vehicle.
5. Connect the negative battery cable. Start the engine and check for leaks.

Electric Fuel Pump

PRESSURE TESTING

ES250 and ES300

1. Check that the battery voltage is above 12 volts. Disconnect the negative battery cable.
2. Disconnect the cold start injector.
3. Place a suitable container or shop towel under the cold start injector.
4. Remove the union bolt and gaskets. Disconnect the cold start injector tube from the delivery pipe.
5. Install the proper pressure gauge to the delivery pipe and tighten the washers and bolt to 13 ft. lbs. (18 Nm) on the ES250 or 11 ft. lbs. (15 Nm) on the ES300.
6. Short terminals **+B** and **FP** of the check connector. Reconnect the

negative battery cable and turn the ignition switch to the **ON** position.
7. Measure the fuel pressure. The pressure should be 38-44 psi (262-303 kPa).
8. Remove the pressure gauge (disconnect the jumper wire on the ES300) and tighten the union bolt with the gaskets to 13 ft. lbs. (18 Nm) on the ES250 or 11 ft. lbs. (15 Nm) on the ES300.
9. Connect the cold start injector tube to the left side delivery pipe. Install the cold start injector.
10. Start the engine and check for leaks.

SC300

1. Check that the battery voltage is above 12 volts. Disconnect the negative battery cable.
2. Remove the union bolt and 2 gaskets. Disconnect the No. 1 fuel pipe from the delivery pipe.
3. Place a suitable container or shop towel under the delivery pipe.
4. Install the proper pressure gauge to the delivery pipe and tighten the washers and bolt to 30 ft. lbs. (42 Nm).
5. Short terminals **+B** and **FP** of the check connector. Reconnect the negative battery cable and turn the ignition switch to the **ON** position.
6. Measure the fuel pressure. The pressure should be 38-44 psi (262-303 kPa).
7. Remove the pressure gauge (disconnect the jumper wire) and tighten the union bolt with the gaskets to 30 ft. lbs. (42 Nm).
8. Connect the fuel pipe to the delivery pipe.
9. Start the engine and check for leaks.

LS400 and SC400

1. Check that the battery voltage is above 12 volts. Disconnect the negative battery cable.
2. Disconnect the VSV (or remove filter) for the EGR, if equipped.
3. Place a suitable container or shop towel under the rear end of the left side delivery pipe.
4. Slowly, loosen the bolt on the left side of the rear fuel pipe and remove the bolt and gaskets from the delivery pipe.
5. Drain the fuel in the left side delivery pipe.
6. Install the proper pressure gauge and connect with the gaskets and bolt. Tighten to 29 ft. lbs (39 Nm).
7. Reconnect the negative battery cable. Connect terminals **+B** and **FP**

of the check connector with the proper tool.
8. Turn the ignition switch to the **ON** position.
9. Measure the fuel pressure. The pressure should be 38-44 psi (262-303 kPa).
10. Remove the pressure gauge. Install the bolt AND gasket to the delivery pipe.
11. Connect the VSV for the EGR as necessary. Start the engine AND check for leaks.

REMOVAL AND INSTALLATION

———— **CAUTION** ————
On models with an air bag, wait at least 90 seconds from the time that the ignition switch is turned to the LOCK position and the battery is disconnected before performing any further work.

ES250

1. Disconnect the negative battery cable. Raise and safely support the vehicle.
2. Drain the fuel from the fuel tank. Disconnect and clamp the fuel lines.
3. Remove both fuel tank protector shields. Support the tank with a suitable jacking device.
4. Remove the mounting bolts and take down both tank band straps. Lower the tank and disconnect the electrical connections.
5. Remove the fuel tank.
6. Remove the fuel pump bracket. Disconnect the fuel line and electrical connector.
7. Remove the mounting nuts and the pump assembly.
   To install:
8. Install the fuel pump to the mounting bracket. Connect the mounting nuts, fuel line and electrical connectors.
9. Raise the fuel tank and connect the electrical connections.
10. Install the tank band straps and tighten the strap bolts to 29 ft. lbs. (39 Nm).
11. Install both fuel tank protector shields. Connect the fuel lines.
12. Remove the jacking device. Lower the vehicle.
13. Connect the negative battery cable. Fill the fuel tank.

ES300

1. Disconnect the negative battery cable.
2. Remove the rear seat cushion and take up the pump service cover.

3. Remove the fuel filler cap. Disconnect the fuel outlet pipe and the return hose from the pump bracket.

4. Remove the 8 screws and lift out the pump/bracket assembly with gasket.

To install:

5. Using a new gasket, install the pump and tighten the screws to 35 inch lbs. (3.9 Nm).

6. Connect the fuel pipe and return hose to the pump and tighten the bolts to 22 ft. lbs. (29 Nm).

7. Connect the wire, install the service cover and replace the rear seat.

8. Connect the battery, start the engine and check for leaks.

SC300

1. Disconnect the negative battery cable.

2. Remove the floor mat in the trunk. Remove the spare tire. Remove the trunk trim cover that separates the trunk and seats.

3. Disconnect the fuel pump connector.

4. Remove the rear seat cushion and back. Pry up the pump service cover.

5. Remove the 8 bolts and disconnect the fuel pump set plate from the tank.

6. Remove the 3 nuts and disconnect the pump bracket from the tank. Disconnect the fuel line and then remove the whole assembly.

To install:

7. Install a new gasket on the set plate, connect the fuel line to the pump bracket and then install the assembly into the tank. Tighten the 3 nuts to 48 inch lbs. (5.4 Nm). Install the set plate and tighten it to 35 inch lbs. (3.9 Nm).

8. Tape the cover plate into position and install the seat cushions.

9. Connect the pump connector and then put the trunk back together.

10. Connect the battery cable, start the engine and check for leaks.

LS400 and SC400

1. Disconnect the negative battery cable. Drain the fuel from the fuel tank.

2. Remove the front trim panel from inside the trunk.

3. Remove the seat back assembly by performing the following:

   a. Disconnect the hook and remove the clips, using the proper tool.

   b. Disconnect the wire harness clamp and connectors.

c. Disconnect the side hooks and remove the mounting bolts and seat back assembly.

4. Remove the partition panel plug. Disconnect the fuel pump connector.

5. Remove the mounting bolts and the fuel pump set plate. Move the clips aside and disconnect and plug the fuel hose.

6. Remove the mounting bolts and the fuel pump assembly.

7. The installation is the reverse of the removal procedure. Tighten the fuel pump mounting bolts to 48 inch lbs. (5.4 Nm) and the fuel pump set plate bolts to 35 inch lbs. (3.9 Nm).

8. Connect the negative battery cable.

Fuel Injector

REMOVAL AND INSTALLATION

———— **CAUTION** ————
On models with an air bag, wait at least 90 seconds from the time that the ignition switch is turned to the LOCK position and the battery is disconnected before performing any further work.

ES250

1. Disconnect the negative battery cable. Drain the cooling system.

2. Disconnect the throttle cable from the throttle body and bracket, if equipped with automatic transaxle.

3. Disconnect the accelerator and bracket from the throttle body and air intake chamber.

4. Remove the air cleaner cap, the air flow meter and the air cleaner hose.

5. Disconnect and tag the following hoses:

   a. PCV hoses
   b. Vacuum sensing hose
   c. Water bypass hose
   d. Fuel pressure VSV hose
   e. Emission control vacuum hoses
   f. ISC connector
   g. Throttle position sensor connector
   h. EGR gas temperature sensor for California only.

6. Remove the right side mounting bracket.

7. Disconnect the cold start injector and the cold start injector tube.

8. Disconnect and tag the following:

   a. Brake booster vacuum hose
   b. Power steering vacuum and air hoses

   c. Cruise control vacuum hose
   d. Ground strap connector
   e. Wire harness and clamp

9. Disconnect the EGR pipe. Disconnect the engine hanger and the air intake chamber stay from the air intake chamber.

10. Remove the air intake chamber. Disconnect and tag the cold start injector connector, water temperature sensor connector and the 6 injector connectors.

11. Disconnect the wire harness from the left side delivery pipe.

12. Disconnect the fuel inlet and return hoses. Remove the fuel line.

13. Remove the 2 bolts and the left side delivery pipe with the 3 injectors. Remove the 3 bolts and the right side delivery pipe with the fuel pipe and the injectors attached.

14. Pull out the 6 injectors from the delivery pipe. Remove the 6 insulators and the 4 spacers from the intake manifold.

To install:

15. Install a new grommet and O-ring to the injector. Apply a light coat of gasoline to the new O-ring.

16. Install the injectors to the delivery pipes, while turning to left and right.

17. Place the insulators and the spacers in the proper position on the intake manifold.

18. Install the 3 injectors together with the right side delivery pipe and the fuel pipe in the proper position on the intake manifold.

19. Install the 3 injectors together with the left side delivery pipe in the proper position on the intake manifold.

NOTE: Make sure the injectors rotate smoothly. If the injectors do not rotate smoothly, the probable cause is the incorrect installation of the O-rings. Replace the O-rings.

20. Position the injector connector upward and install the mounting bolts. Tighten to 9 ft. lbs. (12 Nm)

21. Install the No. 2 fuel pipe with new gaskets. Tighten the mounting bolts to 24 ft. lbs. (33 Nm).

22. Connect the fuel inlet and return hoses. Connect the wire harness clamps to the left side delivery pipe.

23. Connect the 6 injector connectors, the cold start injector connector and the water temperature connector.

24. Install the air intake chamber, using a new gasket. Tighten the mounting bolts to 32 ft. lbs. (44 Nm).

25. Connect the EGR pipe and tighten to 58 ft. lbs. (79 Nm). Connect the wire harness clamp.

26. Connect the air intake chamber stay and tighten the bolts to 27 ft. lbs. (37 Nm).

27. Install the engine hanger and tighten the mounting bolts to 27 ft. lbs. (37 Nm).

28. Connect the following:
   a. Brake booster vacuum hose
   b. Power steering vacuum and air hoses
   c. Cruise control vacuum hose
   d. Ground strap connector
   e. Wire harness and clamp

29. Connect the cold start injector and the cold start injector tube.

30. Replace the right side mounting stay and tighten the bolts to 38 ft. lbs. (52 Nm).

31. Connect the following hoses:
   a. PCV hoses
   b. Vacuum sensing hose
   c. Water bypass hose
   d. Fuel pressure VSV hose
   e. Emission control vacuum hoses
   f. ISC connector
   g. Throttle position sensor connector
   h. EGR gas temperature sensor for California only.

32. Replace the air cleaner cap, the air flow meter and the air cleaner hose.

33. Connect the accelerator and bracket to the throttle body and air intake chamber.

34. Connect the throttle cable and bracket, if equipped with automatic transaxle.

35. Refill the cooling system. Connect the negative battery cable.

ES300

1. With the ignition switch in the **LOCK** position, disconnect the negative battery terminal. If equipped with an air bag system, wait at least 90 seconds before performing any other work.

2. Drain the engine coolant.

3. Disconnect the accelerator cable from the throttle linkage.

4. If equipped with automatic transmission, disconnect the throttle cable from the throttle linkage.

5. Remove the air cleaner cap, air flow meter and the air cleaner hose as a unit.

6. Remove the two 5mm bolts holding the V-cover; remove the cover.

7. Disconnect the EGR temperature connector clamp from the set of emission control valves.

8. Label and remove the hoses from the fuel pressure control VSV. Disconnect the hoses from the IACV,

disconnect the VSV wiring connectors and remove the emission control valve set.

9. Label and disconnect the brake booster vacuum hose, PS air hose, PCV hose and IACV vacuum hose.

10. Disconnect the 2 ground straps.

11. Remove the wiring connector from the cold start injector. Disconnect the fuel line from the cold start injector.

12. Remove the No. 1 engine hanger and the air intake chamber support.

13. Remove the EGR pipe.

14. Remove the bolt and disconnect the hydraulic pressure pipe from the air intake chamber.

15. Disconnect the 3 hoses at the air intake plenum, disconnect the 2 coolant bypass hoses and disconnect the EGR temperature sensor connector, if equipped.

16. Disconnect the throttle position sensor connector. Detach the connector for the ISC valve and remove the air hoses from the ISC valve. Remove the PS air hose.

17. Remove the bolts and nuts holding the air plenum; remove the air plenum and gasket.

18. Disconnect the fuel return hoses from the No. 1 fuel pipe; then disconnect the fuel inlet hose from the filter.

19. Disconnect the wiring connectors from each injector.

20. Remove the No. 2 fuel pipe.

21. Remove the left delivery pipe or fuel rail; be careful not to drop the injectors during removal.

22. Remove the 3 injectors from the delivery pipe. Remove the rail spacers from the intake manifold.

23. Disconnect the 2 air hoses; remove the air pipe with the hoses attached.

24. Remove the right fuel rail and injectors. Take care not to drop an injector. Remove the injectors from the rail.

   To install:

25. Install new grommets on each injector.

26. Apply a light coat of clean gasoline to new O-rings and install 2 on each injector.

27. Install each injector into the fuel rail while turning the injector left and right. Once installed, the injector should turn freely in the rail. If not, remove the injector and inspect the O-ring for damage or dislocation.

28. Place the rail spacers on the manifold. Clean the injector ports and install the right rail and injector assembly. Again check that the injectors turn freely in place.

29. Position the injector wiring connector upward. Install the bolts holding the delivery pipe and tighten them to 9 ft. lbs. (13 Nm).

30. Install the air pipe and hoses; tighten the retaining bolts only to 74 inch lbs. (8.3 Nm).

31. Repeat Steps 28 and 29 to install the left side delivery pipe and injectors.

32. Install the No. 2 fuel pipe connecting the 2 fuel rails. Use new gaskets at each union bolt. Tighten the union bolts to 25 ft. lbs. (34 Nm).

33. Connect the IACV vacuum hose.

34. Attach the wiring connectors to their proper injectors.

35. Install the inlet hose to the fuel filter using new gaskets; tighten the bolt to 22 ft. lbs. (29 Nm). Connect the return hose to the No. 1 fuel pipe.

36. Using a new gasket, install the air intake chamber. Tighten the mounting nuts to 32 ft. lbs (43 Nm).

37. Connect the throttle position sensor harness, ISC valve wiring, ISC air hose and PS air hose.

38. Connect the EGR temperature sensor wiring.

39. Install the coolant bypass hose to the throttle body. Install the coolant bypass hose to the EGR cooler.

40. Connect the vacuum hoses to the BVSV.

41. Attach the hydraulic pressure pipe to the air intake chamber.

42. Install the EGR pipe with a new gasket and new sleeve ball. Tighten the bolts to 13 ft. lbs (18 Nm) and the union nut to 58 ft. lbs. (78 Nm).

43. Install the No. 1 engine hanger and the air intake chamber stay. Tighten the bolts to 29 ft. lbs. (39 Nm).

44. Connect the injector pipe with new gaskets to the cold start injector. Tighten the bolts to 11 ft. lbs. (15 Nm). Attach the cold start injector wiring connector.

45. Connect the 2 ground straps.

46. Connect the brake booster vacuum hose, PS air hose, PCV hose and the IACV vacuum hose.

47. Install the emission valve set and tighten the bolts. Connect the VSV connectors and attach the 2 vacuum hoses to the IACV VSV. Install the 2 hoses to the fuel pressure VSV. Connect the EGR temperature sensor connector clamp to the valve set.

48. Install the V-bank cover on the engine.

49. Install the air cleaner cover, air flow meter and air hose as a unit. Make certain the clips are correctly engaged.

50. Connect and adjust the throttle control cable if it was removed.

51. Connect the accelerator cable and adjust it as needed.

52. Refill the engine coolant.

53. Connect the negative battery cable.

SC300

1. Disconnect the negative battery cable.

2. Drain the engine coolant.

3. Remove the throttle body along with the intake air connector.

4. Remove the union bolt and 2 gaskets and then disconnect the No. 1 fuel pipe at the fuel delivery pipe.

5. Remove the union bolt and 2 gaskets and then disconnect the No. 2 fuel pipe at the fuel pressure regulator.

6. Remove the air intake chamber stays.

7. Tag and disconnect the vacuum sensing hose at the regulator and the injector connectors.

8. Remove the 2 bolts and turn the control valve actuator sideways to disconnect it. Wrap the actuator with tape and attach it to the intake chamber.

9. Remove the 3 bolts and then lift out the delivery pipe along with the injectors. Pull the injectors out of the pipe, remove the O-ring and grommet from each injector and then remove the 6 insulators and 3 spacers from the cylinder head.

To install:

10. Install the grommet to each injector. Coat new O-rings with gasoline and slide them onto each injector.

11. While swiveling the injector back and forth, press it onto the delivery pipe so the connector is facing outward.

12. Position the insulators and spacers on the head and press the delivery pipe with the injectors installed into place. Hand-tighten the 3 mounting bolts and then check that the injectors rotate smoothly. Position the injector connector so it is now pointing upward and then tighten the mounting bolts to 15 ft. lbs. (21 Nm).

NOTE: If the injectors do not rotate smoothly, remove them and install new O-rings.

13. Install the control valve actuator and tighten the 2 bolts to 61 inch lbs. (6.8 Nm).

14. Install the injector connectors. The No. 1, 3 and 5 connectors are gray, while the No. 2, 4 and 6 connectors are dark gray.

15. Connect the vacuum sensing hose. Install the air intake chamber stays and tighten to 13 ft. lbs. (18 Nm).

16. Connect the No. 2 fuel pipe to the regulator and tighten the union bolt to 20 ft. lbs. (27 Nm). Don't forget to use new gaskets.

17. Connect the No. 1 fuel pipe to the delivery pipe and tighten the union bolt to 30 ft. lbs. (42 Nm). Don't forget to use new gaskets.

18. Install the throttle body, fill the engine with coolant and connect the battery cable. Start the engine and check for leaks.

LS400 and SC400

RIGHT

1. Disconnect the negative battery cable. Remove the air cleaner with the air flow meter.

2. Remove the throttle body by performing the following:

    a. Disconnect the vacuum hoses from the throttle body and the pressure regulator.

    b. Remove the upper electrical wire cover and the bypass pipe from the ISC valve.

    c. Disconnect the throttle valve motor connector, the sub-throttle position sensor connector and the main throttle position sensor, if equipped.

    d. Remove the nuts and bolts. Separate the throttle body from the intake chamber.

    e. Remove the PCV hose from the cylinder head cover and the bypass pipe from the throttle body.

    f. Remove the throttle body.

3. Remove the left side and right side engine wire covers.

4. Remove the right side and left side No. 3 timing belt covers.

5. Remove the right side ignition coil and the lower electrical wire cover.

6. Disconnect the wire harness from the delivery pipe.

7. Disconnect the water temperature sensor connector, water temperature sender gauge connector, start injector time switch connector and 4 injector connectors.

8. Disconnect the fuel return pipe, cold start injector tube, if equipped and the front fuel pipe.

9. Disconnect the rear fuel pipe, leave on the vehicle.

10. Disconnect the vacuum hoses from the pressure regulator.

11. Remove the delivery pipe with the injectors attached. Remove the insulators from the intake manifold.

12. Remove the injectors from the delivery pipe.

To install:

13. Install a new grommet and O-ring to the injector. Apply a light coat of gasoline to the new O-ring.

14. Install the injectors to the delivery pipes, while turning to left and right. Make sure the injectors rotate smoothly.

15. Place the insulators and the spacers in the proper position on the intake manifold.

16. Install the injectors together with the delivery pipe in the proper position on the intake manifold.

NOTE: Make sure the injectors rotate smoothly. If the injectors do not rotate smoothly, the probable cause is the incorrect installation of the O-rings. Replace the O-rings.

17. Temporarily install the rear fuel pipe and the front fuel pipe. Tighten the delivery pipe first, then the front and rear fuel pipes. Tighten the delivery pipe to 13 ft. lbs. (18 Nm) and the front and rear fuel pipes to 22 ft. lbs. (30 Nm) on 1990-91 vehicles or 29 ft. lbs. (39 Nm) on 1992-94 vehicles.

18. Connect the cold start injector tube, if equipped, tighten to 11 ft. lbs. (15 Nm). Install the fuel return pipe and tighten the union bolt to 22 ft. lbs. (30 Nm) on 1990-91 vehicles or 26 ft. lbs. (35 Nm) on 1992-94 vehicles.

19. Connect the fuel injector connectors, the start injector time switch connector, the water temperature sensor connector and the water temperature sender gauge connector.

20. Install the wire harness to the delivery pipe and tighten the mounting bolts to 74 inch lbs. (8 Nm).

21. Install the lower electrical wire cover and the right side ignition coil.

22. Install the right side and left side No. 3 timing covers.

23. Install the throttle body by performing the following:

    a. Install the bypass hoses and the PCV hose. Install a new gasket to the air intake chamber.

    b. Connect the PCV hose to the cylinder head cover and the bypass hose to the throttle body.

    c. Install the throttle body to the air intake chamber. Tighten the nuts and bolts to 13 ft. lbs. (18 Nm).

    d. Connect the main throttle position sensor connector to the throttle body. Connect the sub-throttle position sensor and the throttle valve motor connector, if equipped.

    e. Install the bypass hose to the ISC valve and the upper electrical wire cover.

f. Connect the vacuum hoses to the throttle body and the pressure regulator.

24. Install the intake air connector pipe and tighten to 45 inch lbs. (4 Nm).

25. Install the air cleaner and the air flow meter. Refill the engine coolant.

26. Connect the negative battery cable. Run the engine and check for leaks.

LEFT

1. Disconnect the negative battery cable. Drain the cooling system.

2. Disconnect the PCV hose. Remove the upper electrical wire cover and the left side wire cover.

3. Disconnect the following hoses:
   a. Vacuum hoses from the air pipe
   b. Vacuum hose from the BVSV
   c. Vacuum hose from the VSV for the EGR
   d. EGR vacuum modulator hose

4. Remove the EGR vacuum modulator with the mounting bracket. Disconnect the check connector from the bracket.

5. Disconnect the connectors and remove the mounting bolts from the 2 VSV's. Remove the VSV's.

6. Remove the water bypass pipes.

7. Disconnect the engine wire from the delivery pipe.

8. Disconnect the following connectors:
   a. Distributor connector
   b. Engine speed sensor connector
   c. EGR gas temperature sensor connector, California only
   d. Injector connectors

9. Remove the bolt, pulsation damper and disconnect the fuel inlet hose from the delivery pipe.

10. Disconnect the front fuel pipe and disconnect the rear fuel pipe.

11. Remove the delivery pipe with the injectors attached. Remove the insulators from the intake manifold.

12. Remove the injectors from the delivery pipe.

To install:

13. Install a new grommet and O-ring to the injector. Apply a light coat of gasoline to the new O-ring.

14. Install the injectors to the delivery pipes, while turning to left and right. Make sure the injectors rotate smoothly.

15. Place the insulators and the spacers in the proper position on the intake manifold.

16. Install the injectors together with the delivery pipe in the proper position on the intake manifold.

NOTE: Make sure the injectors rotate smoothly. If the injectors do not rotate smoothly, the probable cause is the incorrect installation of the O-rings. Replace the O-rings.

17. Temporarily, install the rear fuel pipe and the front fuel pipe. Tighten the delivery pipe first, then the front and rear fuel pipes. Tighten the delivery pipe to 13 ft. lbs. (18 Nm) and the front and rear fuel pipes to 22 ft. lbs. (30 Nm) for 1990-91 or 29 ft. lbs. (39 Nm) for 1992-94.

18. Install the fuel return pipe and tighten the union bolt to 22 ft. lbs. (30 Nm) for 1990-91 or 29 ft. lbs. (39 Nm) for 1992-94.

19. Connect the fuel inlet hose to the delivery pipe and replace the pulsation damper and bolt. Tighten the damper to 22 ft. lbs. (30 Nm) for 1990-91 or 29 ft. lbs. (39 Nm) for 1992-94 and the bolt to 69 inch lbs. (7.8 Nm).

20. Connect the following connectors:
   a. Distributor connector
   b. Engine speed sensor connector
   c. EGR gas temperature sensor connector, California only
   d. Injector connectors

21. Connect the engine wire to the delivery pipe and tighten the mounting bolts to 74 inch lbs.

22. Install the water bypass pipes.

23. Install the VSV's and tighten the bolts to 13 ft. lbs. (18 Nm). Connect the connectors.

24. Connect the check connector to the bracket. Replace the EGR vacuum modulator with the mounting bracket.

25. Connect the following hoses:
   a. Vacuum hoses from the air pipe
   b. Vacuum hose from the BVSV
   c. Vacuum hose from the VSV for the EGR
   d. EGR vacuum modulator hose

26. Connect the PCV hose. Replace the upper electrical wire cover and the left side wire cover.

27. Refill the cooling system. Connect the negative battery cable.

28. Run the engine and check for leaks.

DRIVE AXLE

Halfshafts

REMOVAL AND INSTALLATION

ES250 and ES300

FRONT

NOTE: The hub bearing could be damaged if it is subjected to the vehicle weight, such as when moving the vehicle with halfshaft removed.

1. Raise and safely support the vehicle. Remove the front fender apron seal, front tire and wheel assembly. Remove the cotter pin and locknut cap. Loosen the bearing locknut.

2. Disconnect the steering knuckle from the lower ball joint with the proper tool.

3. Disconnect the tie rod end from the steering knuckle with the proper tool.

4. On the ES300, disconnect the stabilizer bar link from the lower control arm.

5. Place matchmarks on the halfshaft and center halfshaft. Using the proper tool, loosen the mounting bolts.

NOTE: Do not remove the bolts. Finger-tighten them so the halfshaft does not fall.

6. Disconnect the halfshaft from the axle hub. Remove the left side halfshaft and the joint cover gasket.

7. Remove the bearing lock bolt and the snapring with the proper tool. Pull out the left side halfshaft with the center halfshaft.

NOTE: If the halfshaft cannot be pulled out, tap out the driveshaft with the proper tool.

8. Push the side gear shaft to the differential, in order to replace. Measure and note the distance between the transaxle case and the side gear shaft. Remove the side gear shaft with the proper tool.

9. If necessary, replace the side gear gear shaft oil seal.

To install:

10. Install the left side gear shaft, using a suitable tool to tap in the driveshaft until it makes contact with the pinion shaft. Ensure a new snapring is positioned securely in the groove of the side gear shaft.

11. Check that the side gear will not come out by hand. Push the side gear shaft to the differential and

measure the distance between side gear shaft and the transaxle case. Make sure the distance is the same measurement taken before removing the side gear shaft.

12. Pack the side gear shaft with a suitable grease.

13. Align the matchmarks on the side gear shaft and the halfshaft. Install the left side halfshaft and finger-tighten the bolts.

14. Install the right side halfshaft with the center halfshaft to the transaxle through the bearing bracket. Install the snapring. On the ES300, install a new bearing lock-bolt and tighten it to 24 ft. lbs. (32 Nm).

15. Install the outboard joint side of the halfshaft to the axle hub. Temporarily, connect the steering knuckle to the lower ball joint.

16. Connect the tie rod end to the steering knuckle and tighten the bolt to 36 ft. lbs. (49 Nm). Tighten the lower ball joint mounting bolts to 83 ft. lbs. (113 Nm) on the ES250 or 94 ft. lbs. (127 Nm) on the ES300.

17. Connect the stabilizer bar link to the lower arm on the ES300 and tighten it to 47 ft. lbs. (64 Nm).

18. Tighten the hexagon bolts to 48 ft. lbs. (65 Nm).

19. Replace the front tire and wheel assembly. Lower the vehicle. Check front wheel alignment.

SC300, LS400 AND SC400
REAR

1. Raise and safely support the vehicle. Remove the rear tire and wheel assembly.

2. Remove the cotter pin, locknut cap and locknut.

3. Remove the tail pipe O-rings and suspend the tail pipe, using a piece of wire.

4. Disconnect the height control sensor, if equipped with air suspension (LS400).

5. Place matchmarks on the halfshaft and the side gear shaft. Remove the hexagon bolts and washers with the proper tool.

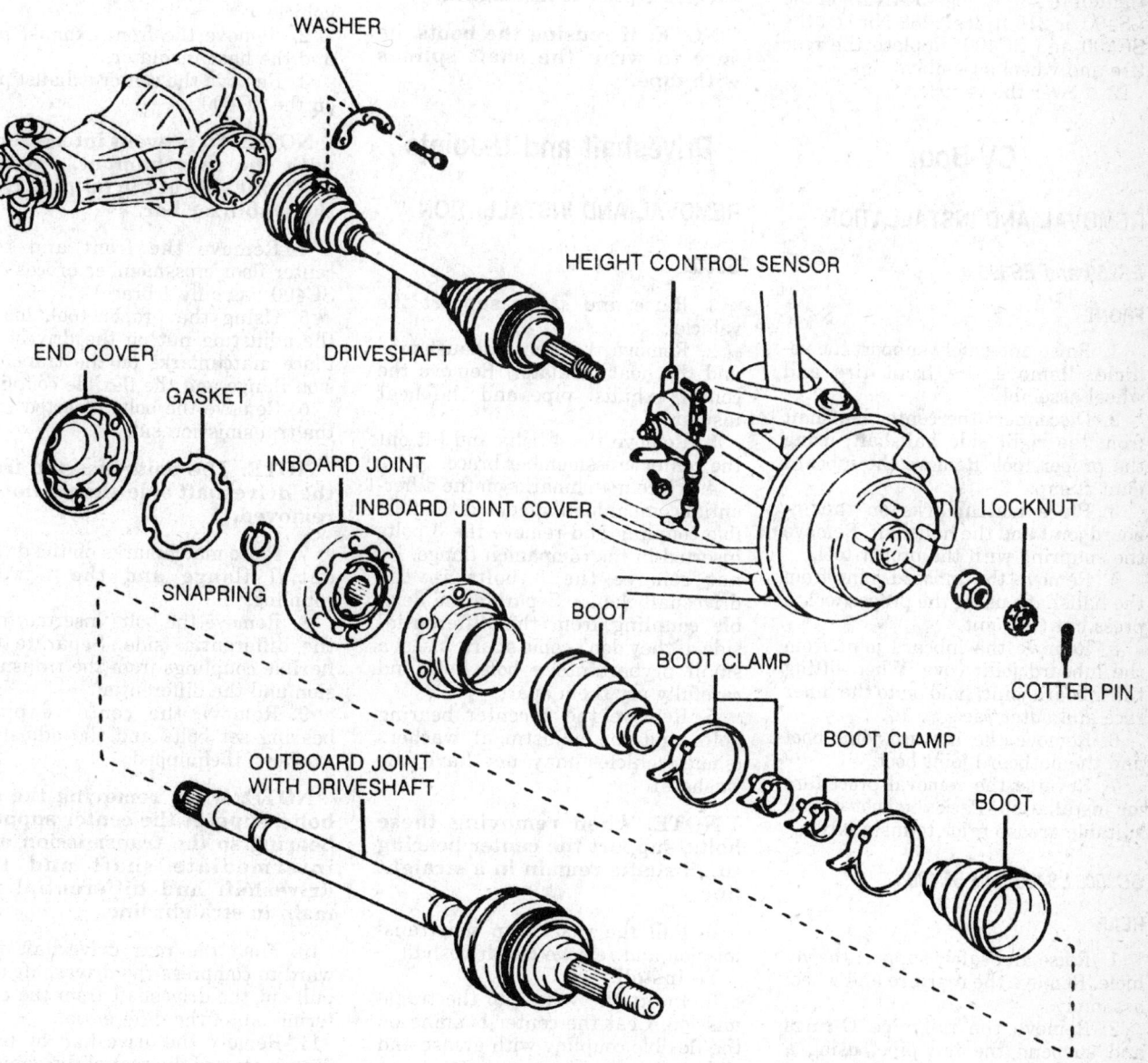

WASHER

HEIGHT CONTROL SENSOR

END COVER

DRIVESHAFT

GASKET

INBOARD JOINT

INBOARD JOINT COVER

SNAPRING

BOOT

BOOT CLAMP

LOCKNUT

COTTER PIN

BOOT CLAMP

BOOT

OUTBOARD JOINT WITH DRIVESHAFT

Exploded view of the rear halfshaft — SC300, LS400 and SC400

6. Hold the inboard joint side of the halfshaft so the outboard joint side does not bend too much. Tap the end of the halfshaft with a rubber mallet and disengage the axle hub.

7. Remove the halfshaft.

To install:

8. Insert the outboard joint side of the halfshaft and align the matchmarks on the side gear shaft and the halfshaft.

9. Coat the threads with clean oil and install the hexagon bolts and tighten to 61 ft. lbs. (83 Nm).

10. Connect the height control sensor, if equipped. Replace the O-rings supporting the tail pipe.

11. Install the bearing locknut and tighten to 253 ft. lbs. (344Nm) on the LS400 or 213 ft. lbs. (289 Nm) on the SC300 and SC400. Replace the rear tire and wheel assembly.

12. Lower the vehicle.

CV-Boot

REMOVAL AND INSTALLATION

ES250 and ES300

FRONT

1. Raise and safely support the vehicle. Remove the front tire and wheel assembly.

2. Disconnect the center halfshaft from the right side halfshaft, using the proper tool. Remove the inboard joint clamp.

3. Place matchmarks on the inboard joint and the halfshaft. Remove the snapring with the proper tool.

4. Remove the inboard joint from the halfshaft, using the proper tool to press out the joint.

5. Remove the inboard joint from the inboard joint cove. When lifting the inboard joint, hold on to the inner race and outer race.

6. Remove the inboard joint boot and the outboard joint boot.

7. Reverse the removal procedure for installation. Pack the boot with a suitable grease prior to installation.

SC300, LS400 and SC400

REAR

1. Raise and safely support the vehicle. Remove the rear tire and wheel assembly.

2. Remove the tail pipe O-rings and suspend the tail pipe, using a piece of wire.

3. Disconnect the height control sensor, if equipped.

4. Remove the halfshaft.

5. Secure the halfshaft in a suitable holding fixture. Tap out the end cover with the proper tools.

6. Remove the boot clamps from the inboard and outboard joint boots.

7. Place matchmarks on the inboard joint and halfshaft. Remove the snapring, using the proper pliers.

8. Press out the inboard joint from the halfshaft with the proper tools. Secure the inboard joint in a suitable holding fixture.

9. Tap out the inboard joint cover. Remove both the inboard and outboard joint boots.

10. The installation is the reverse of the removal procedure. Pack the boots and the end cover with a suitable grease prior to installation.

NOTE: If reusing the boots, be sure to wrap the shaft splines with tape.

Driveshaft and U-Joints

REMOVAL AND INSTALLATION

SC300

1. Raise and safely support the vehicle.

2. Remove the front exhaust pipe and the heat insulator. Remove the center exhaust pipe and the heat insulator.

3. Remove the 4 bolts and lift out the center crossmember brace.

4. Place matchmarks on the differential companion flange and the flexible coupling and remove the 3 bolts inserted in the companion flange. Do not remove the 3 bolts in the driveshaft flange. Separate the flexible coupling from the differential side, if they don't come apart, insert a small prybar into a bolt hole and carefully pry them apart.

5. Remove the 2 center bearing bolts and the adjustment washers (some vehicles may not have the washers).

NOTE: When removing these bolts, support the center bearing so all shafts remain in a straight line.

6. Pull the yoke from the transmission and remove the driveshaft.

To install:

7. Insert the yoke into the transmission. Coat the center bushing on the flexible coupling with grease and slide it into position.

8. Coat the threads of the coupling bolts with clean engine oil, align the matchmarks and insert the bolts

from the driveshaft side. Tighten them to 69 ft. lbs. (93 Nm).

9. Position the center bearing and tighten the bolts to 36 ft. lbs. (49 Nm).

10. Install the crossmember brace and tighten it to 9 ft. lbs. (13 Nm).

11. Install the center pipe with 4 new nuts and tighten them to 14 ft. lbs. (19 Nm).

12. Install the front pipe with 4 new nuts and tighten them to 32 ft. lbs. (43 Nm). Tighten the O_2 sensors to 33 ft. lbs. (44 Nm).

13. Lower the vehicle.

LS400 and SC400

1. Raise and safely support the vehicle.

2. Remove the front exhaust pipe and the heat insulator.

3. Remove the center exhaust pipe on the SC400.

NOTE: To prevent interference with the rear bumper, suspend the front side of the tailpipe from the stabilizer bar.

4. Remove the front and rear center floor crossmember braces (the SC400 has only 1 brace).

5. Using the proper tool, loosen the adjusting nut on the driveshaft. Place matchmarks on the transmission flange and the flexible coupling.

6. Remove the bolts inserted from the transmission side.

NOTE: The bolts inserted from the driveshaft side should not be removed.

7. Place matchmarks on the differential flange and the flexible coupling.

8. Remove the bolts inserted from the differential side. Separate the flexible couplings from the transmission and the differential.

9. Remove the center support bearing set bolts and the adjusting washers, if equipped.

NOTE: When removing the set bolts, support the center support bearing so the transmission and intermediate shaft and the driveshaft and differential remain in straight line.

10. Push the rear driveshaft forward to compress the driveshaft and pull out the driveshaft from the centering pin of the differential.

11. Remove the driveshaft by pulling out toward the rear of the vehicle.

To install:

12. Apply a suitable grease to the flexible coupling centering bushings.

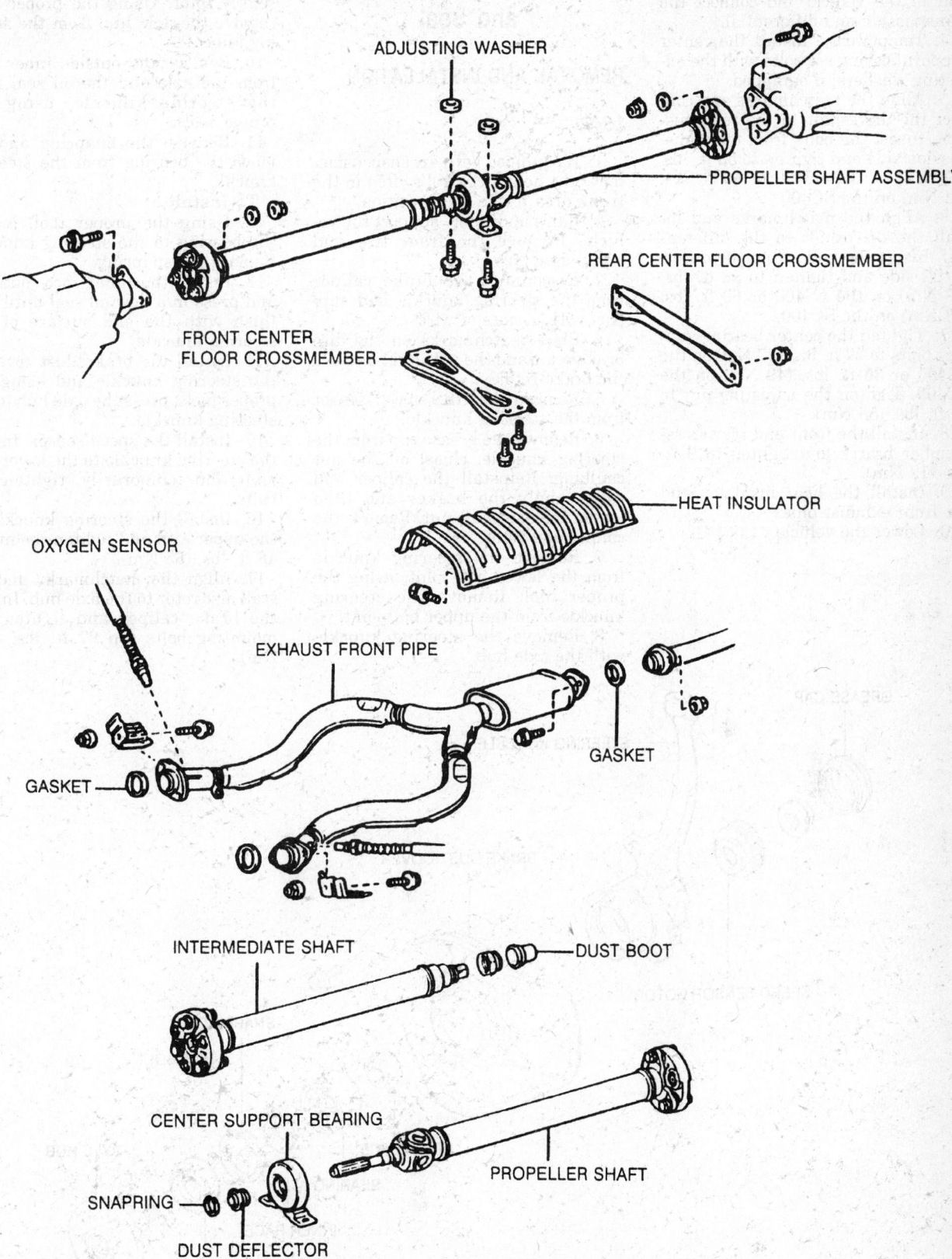

ADJUSTING WASHER

PROPELLER SHAFT ASSEMBLY

REAR CENTER FLOOR CROSSMEMBER

FRONT CENTER
FLOOR CROSSMEMBER

HEAT INSULATOR

OXYGEN SENSOR

EXHAUST FRONT PIPE

GASKET

GASKET

INTERMEDIATE SHAFT

DUST BOOT

CENTER SUPPORT BEARING

PROPELLER SHAFT

SNAPRING

DUST DEFLECTOR

Exploded view of the driveshaft — LS400 and SC400

13. Insert the driveshaft from the rear of the vehicle and connect the transmission and differential.

14. Temporarily, install the center support bearing set bolts with the adjusting washers, if equipped.

15. Align the matchmarks and connect the driveshaft to the transmission. Insert the bolts from the transmission side and tighten to 58 ft. lbs. (79 Nm) on the LS400 or 69 ft. lbs. (93 Nm) on the SC400.

16. Align the matchmarks and install the driveshaft to the differential. Insert the bolts from the differential side and tighten to 58 ft. lbs. (79 Nm) on the LS400 or 69 ft. lbs. (93 Nm) on the SC400.

17. Tighten the center bearing support bolts to 27 ft. lbs. (37 Nm) on the LS400 or 36 ft. lbs. (49 Nm) on the SC400. Tighten the adjusting nut to 39 ft. lbs. (53 Nm).

18. Install the front and rear crossmember braces and tighten to 9 ft. lbs. (12 Nm).

19. Install the heat insulator and the front exhaust pipe.

20. Lower the vehicle.

Front Axle Hub, Bearing and Seal

REMOVAL AND INSTALLATION

LS400

1. If equipped with air suspension, move the height control switch in the trunk area to the OFF position.

2. Raise and safely support the vehicle. Remove the front tire and wheel assembly.

3. Disconnect the brake caliper from the steering knuckle and support with a piece of wire.

4. Place matchmarks on the disc brake rotor and the axle hub. Remove the brake rotor.

5. Remove the ABS speed sensor from the steering knuckle.

6. Remove the grease cap from the steering knuckle, chisel off the nut caulking. Reinstall the caliper and rotor, apply the brakes and then loosen the axleshaft nut. Remove the caliper and rotor.

7. Remove the steering knuckle from the lower ball joint, using the proper tool. Remove the steering knuckle from the upper ball joint.

8. Remove the steering knuckle with the axle hub.

9. Remove the nut and the speed sensor rotor. Using the proper tool, remove the axle hub from the steering knuckle.

10. Remove the outside inner race from the axle and the oil seal from the steering knuckle, using the proper tools.

11. Remove the snapring and remove the bearing from the steering knuckle.

To install:

12. Using the proper tool, install the bearing to the steering knuckle. Replace the snapring.

13. Install the inner race (outside) and press in a new oil seal until it is flush with the end surface of the steering knuckle.

14. Install the brake dust cover to the steering knuckle and using the proper tools, press the axle hub to the steering knuckle.

15. Install the speed sensor. Install the steering knuckle to the lower ball joint and temporarily, tighten the bolts.

16. Install the steering knuckle to the upper arm and tighten the nut to 48 ft. lbs. (65 Nm).

17. Align the matchmarks and install disc rotor to the axle hub. Install the brake caliper and tighten the mounting bolts top 87 ft. lbs. (118 Nm).

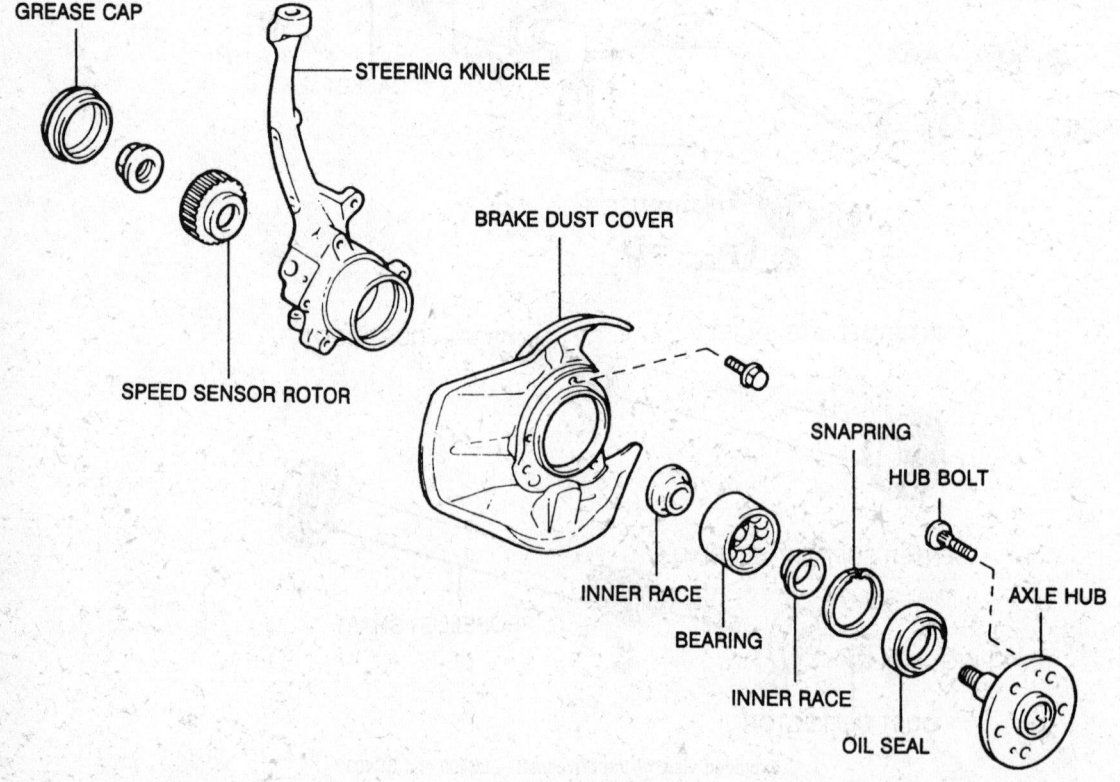

Exploded view of the front axle hub and bearing — LS400

18. Tighten the axle shaft nut to 147 ft. lbs. (199 Nm). Install the speed sensor to the steering knuckle.

19. Replace the front tire and wheel assembly. Lower the vehicle.

20. If equipped with air suspension, turn the height control switch to the ON position.

SC300 and SC400

1. Raise and safely support the vehicle. Remove the front tire and wheel assembly.

2. Remove the brake caliper and support, using a piece of wire. Place matchmarks on the rotor disc and the axle hub. Remove the rotor.

3. Disconnect the ABS speed sensor.

4. Remove the cotter pin and nut and disconnect the tie rod from the steering knuckle.

5. Remove the cotter pin and nut and disconnect the steering knuckle from the upper arm.

6. Remove the clip and nut and press the knuckle off the lower arm.

7. Pry the hub bearing cap from the steering knuckle. Using a hammer and chisel, loosen the staked part of the hub nut and remove it. Remove the ABS sensor rotor.

8. Remove the 4 bolts and shift the brake dust shield toward the hub (outside). Using a 2-armed puller, remove the axle shaft from the knuckle.

9. With a puller, remove the inner bearing race from the axle shaft. Pry out the oil seal.

10. Remove the bearing snapring and then position the inner race above the bearing on the inner side. Press the bearing out.

To install:

11. Press the bearing into the knuckle. If the inner race and balls come loose from the outer race, be sure to install them on the same side as before.

12. Install the snapring and inner race and then tap in a new oil seal until it is flush with the end surface of the knuckle.

13. Install the brake dust cover and tighten the bolts to 74 inch lbs. (8.3 Nm).

14. Press the hub into the knuckle and install the speed sensor.

15. Install a new locknut and tighten it to 147 ft. lbs. (199 Nm). Stake the nut with a chisel. Tap the bearing cap into place.

16. Connect the knuckle to the upper arm and tighten the nut to 76 ft. lbs (103 Nm). Install a new cotter pin. Connect the knuckle to the lower arm and tighten the nut to 92 ft. lbs. (125 Nm). Install a new clip.

17. Install the rotor and caliper. Tighten the caliper bolts to 87 ft. lbs. (118 Nm).

18. Connect the speed sensor to the knuckle and tighten the bolt to 69 inch lbs. (7.8 Nm).

19. Install the front wheel and tighten the lug nuts to 76 ft. lbs. (103 Nm). Lower the vehicle and check the front end alignment.

Rear Axle Hub, Bearing and Seal

REMOVAL AND INSTALLATION

ES250 and ES300

1. Raise and safely support the vehicle. Remove the rear tire and wheel assembly.

2. Remove the brake caliper and support, using a piece of wire. Place matchmarks on the rotor disc and the axle hub. Remove the rotor.

3. Remove the 4 bolts and pull off the rear axle hub. Remove the O-ring.

4. Coat a new O-ring with grease and install it.

5. Position the hub on the carrier and tighten the bolts to 59 ft. lbs. (80 Nm).

6. Install the rotor and caliper. Tighten the caliper mounting bolts to 34 ft. lbs. (47 Nm).

7. Install the wheel, tighten the lug nuts to 76 ft. lbs. (103 Nm) and lower the vehicle.

Rear Axle Shaft Bearing and Seal

REMOVAL AND INSTALLATION

LS400

1. If equipped with air suspension, move the height control switch in the trunk area to the **OFF** position.

2. Raise and safely support the vehicle. Remove the rear tire and wheel assembly.

3. Disconnect the brake caliper from the rear axle carrier and support with a piece of wire.

4. Place matchmarks on the disc brake rotor and the axle hub. Remove the brake rotor.

5. Remove the speed sensor. Remove the strut rod and lower suspension rods.

6. Remove the nut on the lower side of the shock absorber. Do not remove the bolt.

7. Remove the upper arm set bolts and the bolt on the lower side of the shock absorber. Remove the axle with the arm.

8. Remove the upper arm and the dust deflector, using the proper tools. Remove the inner oil seal.

9. Remove the axle hub and the backing plate. Remove the inner race (outside) from the axle hub.

10. Pry out the outer oil seal. Remove the snapring and the bearing, using the proper tools.

To install:

11. Install the bearing to the axle carrier.

NOTE: If the inner races come loose from the bearing outer race, be sure to install them on the same side as before.

12. Install the snapring. Replace the backing plate to the axle carrier and tighten the mounting bolts 43 ft. lbs. (58 Nm).

13. Install the inner race (outside) and a new oil seal.

14. Install the inner race (inside) and press in the axle hub with the proper tools.

15. Install the inner oil seal. Align the holes for the speed sensor in the dust deflector and axle carrier. Install the dust deflector.

16. Install the upper arm to the axle carrier. Tighten the nut and bolt to 80 ft. lbs. (108 Nm).

17. Replace the nut on the lower side of the shock absorber.

18. Install the speed sensor. Replace the strut rod and lower suspension rods.

19. Install the brake rotor. Connect the brake caliper to the rear axle carrier.

20. Replace the rear tire and wheel assembly. Lower the vehicle.

SC300 and SC400

1. Raise and safely support the vehicle. Remove the rear tire and wheel assembly.

2. Disconnect the brake caliper from the rear axle carrier and support with a piece of wire.

3. Place matchmarks on the disc brake rotor and the axle hub. Remove the brake rotor.

4. Remove the speed sensor.

5. Remove the rear halfshaft. Remove the parking brake shoes.

6. Remove the 2 bolts at the parking brake cable. Remove the 2 hub bolts and the hex bolt. Slide the backing plate to the outside and disconnect the parking brake cable.

7. Disconnect the strut rod at the carrier.

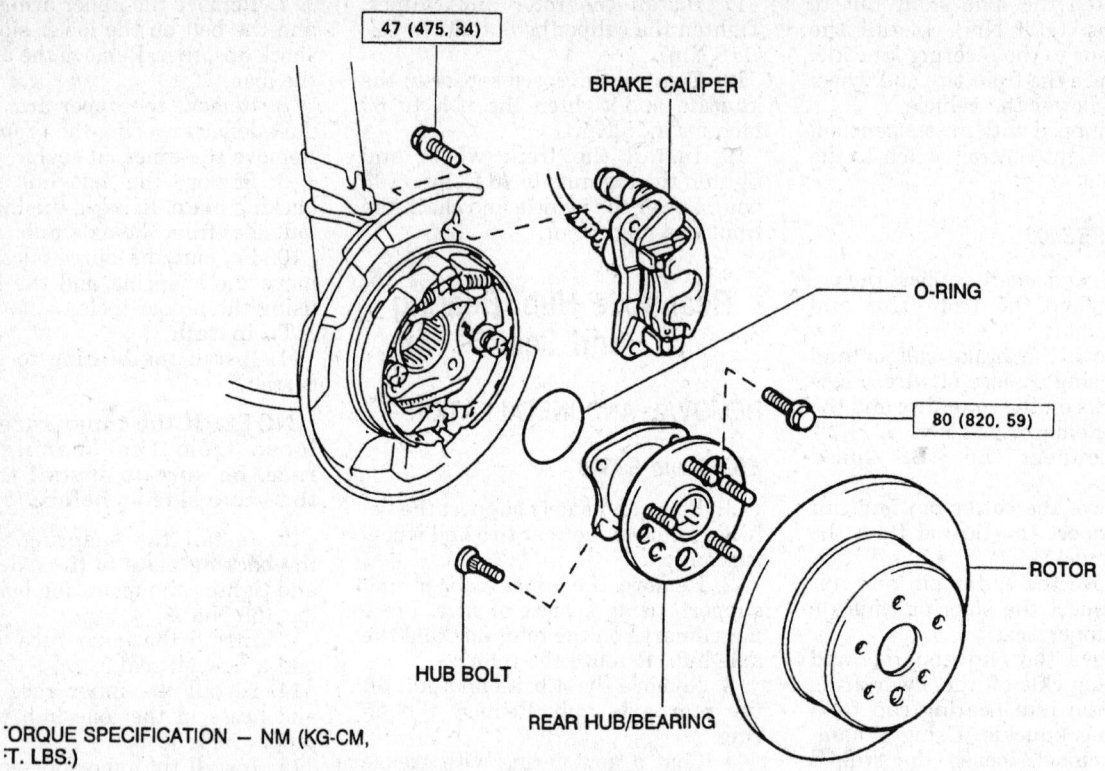

47 (475, 34)

BRAKE CALIPER

O-RING

80 (820, 59)

ROTOR

HUB BOLT

REAR HUB/BEARING

TORQUE SPECIFICATION — NM (KG-CM, T. LBS.)

Exploded view of the rear axle hub and bearing — ES250 and ES300

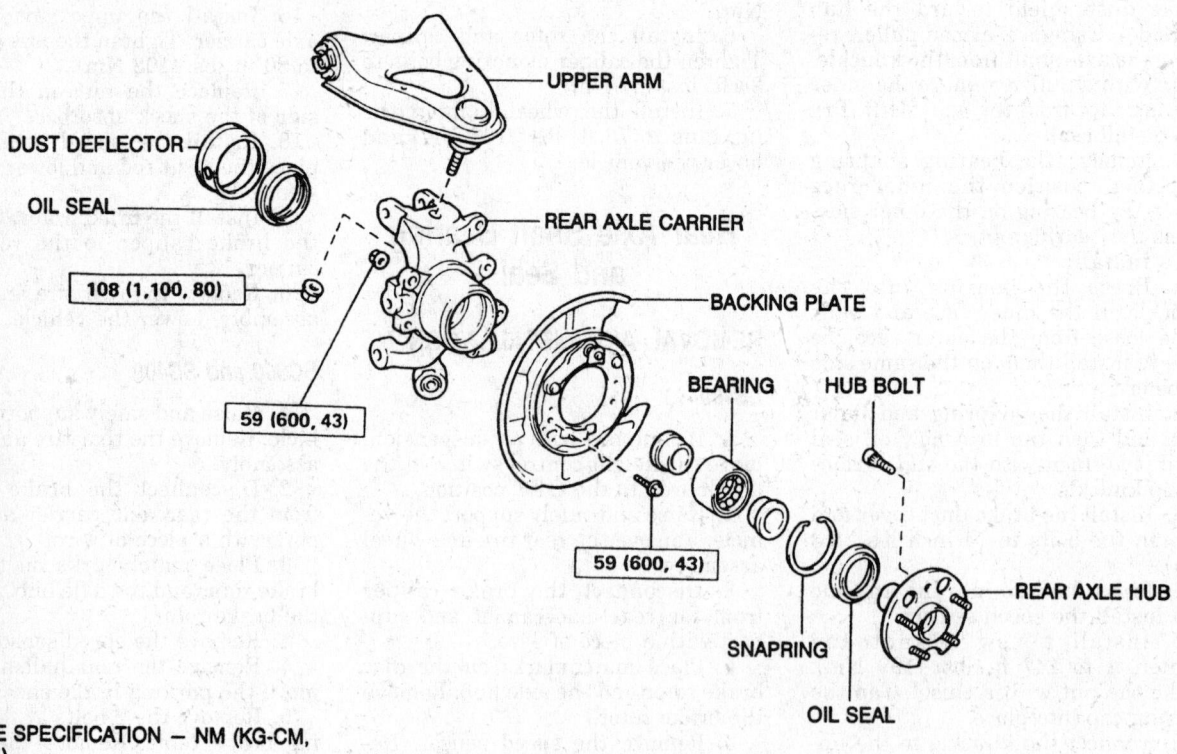

UPPER ARM

DUST DEFLECTOR

OIL SEAL

REAR AXLE CARRIER

108 (1,100, 80)

BACKING PLATE

BEARING   HUB BOLT

59 (600, 43)

59 (600, 43)

REAR AXLE HUB

SNAPRING

OIL SEAL

TORQUE SPECIFICATION — NM (KG-CM, T. LBS.)

Exploded view of the rear axle hub and bearing — LS400

8. Remove the nut and then press out the No. 1 lower suspension arm. Remove the nut and then press out the No. 2 lower suspension arm. Remove the nut and then press out the upper suspension arm. Remove the axle carrier.

9. Remove the dust deflector ans pull out the oil seal.

10. Using a 2-armed puller, remove the axle hub from the carrier. Remove the backing plate.

11. Pull out the inner race (outside) and then remove the oil seal. Remove the snapring.

12. Install the inner race over the bearing and tap out the bearing.

To install:

13. Install the bearing to the axle carrier.

NOTE: If the inner races come loose from the bearing outer race, be sure to install them on the same side as before.

14. Install the snapring. Install the inner race and a new oil seal.

15. Install the backing plate. Install the inner race (inside) and press in the axle hub with the proper tools.

16. Install the inner oil seal. Align the holes for the speed sensor in the dust deflector and axle carrier. Install the dust deflector.

17. Install the upper arm to the axle carrier. Tighten the nut and bolt to 80 ft. lbs. (109 Nm).

18. Connect the No. 2 lower arm to the carrier and tighten a new nut to 110 ft. lbs. (150 Nm). Connect the No. 1 lower arm to the carrier and tighten a new nut to 43 ft. lbs. (59 Nm).

19. Connect the strut rod to the carrier. Connect the parking brake cable and slide the backing plate to the inside. Install the hex bolt and tighten it to 132 ft. lbs. (180 Nm). Install the 2 hub bolts and tighten them to 19 ft. lbs. (26 Nm).

20. Install the 2 bolts at the cable and tighten them to 69 inch lbs. (7.8 Nm). Install the parking brake shoes and the ABS sensor.

21. Install the halfshafts. Tighten the locknut to 213 ft. lbs. (289 Nm).

22. Install the brake rotor. Connect the brake caliper to the rear axle carrier.

23. Replace the rear tire and wheel assembly. Lower the vehicle and bounce it a few times to stabilize the suspension. Raise the vehicle again, support the axle carrier and tighten the strut rod to 136 ft. lbs. (184 Nm).

Front Wheel Hub, Knuckle and Bearings

REMOVAL AND INSTALLATION

ES250

1. Raise and safely support the vehicle. Remove the front tire and wheel assembly.

2. Remove the brake caliper and support, using a piece of wire. Place matchmarks on the rotor disc and the axle hub. Remove the rotor.

3. Disconnect the ABS speed sensor.

4. Disconnect the lower ball joint from the steering knuckle with the proper tool. Disconnect the tie rod end from the steering knuckle.

5. Disconnect the steering knuckle from the shock absorber.

6. Remove the steering knuckle with the axle hub from the halfshaft.

7. Remove the dust protector and pry out the inner oil seal with the proper tool.

8. Remove the snapring from the steering knuckle and separate the dust cover from the steering knuckle.

9. Push out the axle hub and remove the inner race (inside) from the bearing, using the proper tool.

10. Remove the sensor control rotor from the axle hub. Remove the bearing inner race (outside) from the axle hub.

11. Pry out the oil seal with the proper tool and tap out the bearing.

To install:

12. Install the sensor control rotor to the axle hub and press in a new bearing into the steering knuckle.

13. Install the outer oil seal and the disc brake dust cover.

14. Apply a suitable multi-purpose grease between the oil seal lip, the oil seal and the bearing. Install the axle hub into the steering knuckle, using the proper tool.

15. Install the snapring into the steering knuckle.

16. Install the oil seal into the steering knuckle with a suitable seal installer tool. Apply a suitable multipurpose grease to the oil seal lip.

17. Tap the dust deflector into the steering knuckle

18. Install the steering knuckle with the axle hub to the halfshaft. Tighten the lower mounting nuts to 224 ft. lbs. (304 Nm).

19. Connect the tie rod end to the steering knuckle and tighten the bolts to 36 ft. lbs. (49 Nm).

20. Tighten the lower ball joint mounting bolts to 83 ft. lbs. (113 Nm). Connect the ABS speed sensor.

21. Align the matchmarks and install the brake rotor. Replace the brake caliper and tighten the mounting bolts to 79 ft. lbs. (107 Nm).

22. Tighten the bearing locknut to 137 ft. lbs. (186 Nm). Replace the tire and wheel assembly.

23. Lower the vehicle. Check front wheel alignment.

ES300

1. Raise the vehicle and support safely. Remove the front wheels and the fender apron seal.

2. While applying the front brakes, remove the driveshaft lock nut. Remove the ABS speed sensor.

3. Disconnect and separate the tie rod end from the steering knuckle.

4. Remove the left and right stabilizer end brackets from the lower arms.

5. Remove the 2 nuts and disconnect the lower arm from the ball joint.

6. Remove the driveshaft from the axle hub. Secure the shaft out of the way using wire. Be careful not to damage the shaft boot or ABS sensor rotor.

7. Remove the 2 brake cylinder mounting bolts and remove the cylinder. Support cylinder from the vehicle using wire. Remove the disc rotor.

8. If equipped with ABS, remove the sensor from the steering knuckle.

9. Remove the 2 nuts on the lower end of the shock and remove the steering knuckle.

10. Clamp the steering knuckle in a vise with soft jaws to protect the knuckle.

11. Carefully pry the dust deflector from the hub.

12. Drive out the bearing inner oil seal from the knuckle.

13. After the seal is removed, use snapring pliers to remove the hole snapring from the knuckle bore.

14. Unbolt and separate the dust deflector from the steering knuckle.

15. Using a 2-armed mechanical puller, pull the axle hub from the dust deflector.

16. Using the puller, remove the inner (inside) bearing race from the bearing.

17. Using Torx® wrench, remove the sensor control rotor from the axle hub.

18. Using the puller, remove the outer bearing race. Set the outer race aside.

19. Remove the outer bearing seal in the same manner as the inner seal.

20. Take the inner (outside) race and install it inside the bearing.

21. With a piece of brass stock, tap the bearing from the steering knuckle.

To install:

22. Clean all the oil seal and bearing seating surfaces with a clean, dry rag.

23. Install tool 09608-32010 into the bore of the steering knuckle and press the bearing into the bore. Leave the tool in place.

24. Turn and insert the side lip of the new outer oil seal into a tool and drive the seal into the steering knuckle.

25. Connect the brake disc cover to the steering knuckle with the bolts.

26. Apply multi-purpose grease between the oil seal lip, oil seal and bearing and press the hub into the knuckle.

27. Install a new snapring in the knuckle.

28. Press a new oil seal into the knuckle and coat the seal with multi-purpose grease.

29. Press the dust deflector into the knuckle.

30. Install the steering knuckle onto the vehicle and temporarily install the lower shock bolts.

31. Connect the lower ball joint to the lower arm and tighten the bolt and nuts to 94 ft. lbs. (127 Nm).

32. Connect the tie rod to the knuckle and tighten the nut to 36 ft. lbs. (49 Nm). Install new cotter pin.

33. Torque the nuts on the lower end of the shock to 156 ft. lbs. (211 Nm).

34. Install both side stabilizer end brackets to the lower arm and tighten to 43 ft. lbs. (58 Nm).

35. Install the front ABS sensor and torque to 69 inch lbs. (7.8 Nm).

36. Install the front brake rotor and cylinder. Tighten the cylinder mounting bolts to 79 ft. lbs. (107 Nm).

37. Install the driveshaft locknut, and while applying the brakes, torque to 217 ft. lbs. (294 Nm). Install lock cap and new cotter pin.

38. Install front fender apron seal and the front wheel. Torque the front wheel to 76 ft. lbs. (103 Nm).

Differential Carrier

REMOVAL AND INSTALLATION

SC300, LS400 and SC400

1. Raise and safely support the vehicle. Remove the front exhaust pipe.

2. Remove the driveshaft. Drain the differential oil in a suitable container.

3. Place matchmarks on the driveshafts and side gear shafts. Using the proper tool, disconnect the driveshafts from the differential.

4. Support the driveshafts, using a piece of wire.

5. Support the differential with a suitable jacking device. Remove the bolts and lower the differential.

6. Remove the mount upper stopper from the differential carrier.

NOTE: Some vehicles have the adjusting shim for adjusting the driveshaft joint angle installed on the mount upper stopper.

To install:

7. Install the mount upper stopper on the differential carrier. Install the adjusting shim, if equipped.

8. Support the differential with a proper jacking device and install the washer and bolt. Tighten to bolt to 87 ft. lbs. (118 Nm).

9. Tighten the upper mounting bolts to 90 ft. lbs. (122 Nm).

10. Align the matchmarks and connect the driveshafts to the differential. Tighten the bolts to 61 ft. lbs. (83 Nm).

11. Install the driveshaft and connect the front exhaust pipe. Refill the differential to the specified level.

12. Lower the vehicle.

MANUAL TRANSMISSION

CAUTION

On models with an air bag, wait at least 90 seconds from the time that the ignition switch is turned to the LOCK position and the battery is disconnected before performing any further work.

Transmission Assembly

REMOVAL AND INSTALLATION

SC300

1. Disconnect the negative battery cable.

2. Pry out the rear side of the cup holder and remove the cup holder.

Unscrew the shift lever knob. Pry up the upper rear console panel. Remove the 6 mounting screws and then pry out the upper console panel. Remove the eight bolts and lift out the shift lever.

3. Raise the vehicle and support it on safety stands. Remove the undercover and drain the transmission fluid.

4. Remove the front exhaust pipe and support bracket. Remove the center exhaust pipe.

5. Remove the heat insulator.

6. Remove the 4 bolts and the crossmember brace.

7. Remove the driveshaft. Remove the clutch release cylinder and disconnect the ground cable.

8. Tag and disconnect the starter leads and then remove the starter.

9. Remove the transmission mounting bolt. Disconnect the backup light switch connector and the speed sensor connector.

10. Raise the transmission slightly until its weight is off the rear support. Remove the 4 nuts and bolts and then remove the rear mounting member.

11. Remove the 5 mounting bolts, lower the rear of the engine and remove the transmission.

To install:

12. Align the input spline with the clutch disc and install the transmission to the engine. Tighten the mounting bolts to 53 ft. lbs. (72 Nm).

13. Install the rear engine mount and tighten the nuts to 10 ft. lbs. (13 Nm) and the bolts to 19 ft. lbs. (25 Nm).

14. Connect the speed sensor and backup light switch. Install the transmission mounting bolt and tighten it to 27 ft. lbs. (37 Nm).

15. Install the starter and tighten the bolts to 29 ft. lbs. (39 Nm). Connect the starter leads.

16. Install the release cylinder and tighten the 2 bolts to 9 ft. lbs. (12 Nm). Tighten the ground wire to 27 ft. lbs. (37 Nm).

17. Install the driveshaft.

18. Install the crossmember brace and tighten the bolts to 9 ft. lbs. (13 Nm).

19. Install the heat insulator and exhaust pipes. Tighten the center pipe to 14 ft. lbs. (19 Nm), the front pipe to 32 ft. lbs. (43 Nm) and the bracket to 27 ft. lbs. (37 Nm).

20. Fill the transmission with oil, install the undercover, lower the vehicle, install the shifter and connect the battery.

MANUAL TRANSAXLE

Transaxle Assembly

REMOVAL AND INSTALLATION

ES250 and ES300

1. Disconnect the negative battery cable. Remove the clutch release cylinder and tube clamp. Remove the clutch tube bracket.

—————— CAUTION ——————

On models with an air bag, wait at least 90 seconds from the time that the ignition switch is turned to the LOCK position and the battery is disconnected before performing any further work.

2. Disconnect the control cables. Disconnect the backup light switch electrical connector. Remove the ground strap.
3. Remove the starter assembly. Remove the transaxle upper mounting bolts.
4. Raise and support the vehicle safely. Remove the undercovers. Drain the transaxle fluid. Disconnect the speedometer cable.
5. Remove the suspension lower crossmember. Remove the engine mounting center member.
6. Disconnect both halfshafts. Disconnect the left steering knuckle from the lower control arm. Remove the stabilizer bar.
7. Properly support the engine and remove the left engine mount.
8. Properly support the transaxle assembly. Remove the engine-to-transaxle bolts, lower the left side of the engine and carefully ease the transaxle out of the engine compartment.
9. Installation is the reverse of the removal procedure. Please note the following:
   a. Tighten the 12mm mounting bolts to 47 ft. lbs. (64 Nm) and the 10mm bolts to 34 ft. lbs. (46 Nm).
   b. Tighten the left engine mount to 38 ft. lbs. (52 Nm).
   c. Tighten the 4 center engine mount bolts to 29 ft. lbs. (39 Nm).
   d. Tighten the front and rear engine mount bolts to 32 ft. lbs. (43 Nm).
   e. Tighten the lower crossmember bolts to 153 ft. lbs. (207

Nm) for 4 outer or to 29 ft. lbs. (39 Nm) for 2 inner bolts.

CLUTCH

Clutch Assembly

REMOVAL AND INSTALLATION

ES250, ES300 and SC300

1. Disconnect the negative battery cable. Remove the transmission/transaxle assembly from the vehicle.

—————— CAUTION ——————

On models with an air bag, wait at least 90 seconds from the time that the ignition switch is turned to the LOCK position and the battery is disconnected before performing any further work.

2. Place matchmarks on the flywheel and clutch cover. Remove the clutch pressure plate retaining bolts. Remove the pressure plate assembly.
3. Remove the clutch disc.
4. Installation is the reverse of the removal procedure.
5. Tighten the pressure plate mounting bolts to 14 ft. lbs. (19 Nm) in X-type pattern.

FREE-PLAY ADJUSTMENT

ES250, ES300 and SC300

1. Loosen the locknut and turn the clutch master cylinder pushrod until the freeplay is correct.
2. After adjusting the pedal freeplay, check pedal height. The correct specifications are for the ES250 pedal freeplay is 0.20-0.59 in. (5-15mm) and pedal height from the asphalt sheet 7.52-7.91 in. (191-201mm).
3. On the ES300 pedal freeplay is 0.197-0.591 in. (5-15mm) and pedal height from the asphalt sheet 6.48-6.88 in. (164.7-174.7mm).
4. On the SC300 pedal freeplay is 0.20-0.59 in. (5-15mm) and pedal height from the asphalt sheet 5.92-6.31 in. (150.4-160.4mm).

Clutch Master Cylinder

REMOVAL AND INSTALLATION

ES250, ES300 and SC300

1. Disconnect the negative battery cable.
2. Remove the ABS control relay, if equipped.
3. Remove the pushrod clevis pin and clip.

NOTE: On some vehicles it will be necessary to remove the under dash panel in order to gain access to the pushrod clevis pin.

4. Disconnect the fluid line. Remove the clutch master cylinder retaining bolts. Remove the component from the vehicle.
5. Install the master cylinder and tighten to 58 inch lbs. (7.8 Nm) on the ES250 and ES300 or 9 ft. lbs. (13 Nm) on the SC300.
6. Connect the hydraulic line and tighten the union bolt to 11 ft. lbs. (15 Nm).
7. Connect the pushrod and install the clevis pin.
8. Fill the master cylinder with fluid and bleed the system.

Clutch Slave Cylinder

REMOVAL AND INSTALLATION

ES250, ES300 and SC300

1. Disconnect the negative battery cable. Raise and support the vehicle safely.
2. Remove the gravel shield, if equipped. Disconnect the fluid line from the assembly.
3. Remove the slave cylinder retaining bolts. Remove the clutch slave cylinder from the vehicle.
4. Install the slave cylinder and tighten to 9 ft. lbs. (13 Nm).
5. Connect the hydraulic line and tighten the union bolt to 11 ft. lbs. (15 Nm).
6. Fill the master cylinder with fluid and bleed the system.

Hydraulic Clutch System Bleeding

1. Check and fill the clutch fluid reservoir to the specified level as necessary. During the bleeding process, continue to check and replenish the reservoir to prevent the fluid level from getting lower than ¾ the specified level.

2. Remove the dust cap from the bleeder screw on the clutch slave cylinder and connect a tube to the bleeder screw and insert the other end of the tube into a clean glass or metal container ½ filled with clean brake fluid.

NOTE: Take precautionary measures to prevent the brake fluid from getting on any painted surfaces.

3. Pump the clutch pedal several times, hold it down and loosen the bleeder screw slowly.

4. Tighten the bleeder screw and release the clutch pedal gradually. Repeat this operation until air bubbles disappear from the brake fluid being expelled out through the bleeder screw.

5. Repeat until all evidence of air bubbles completely disappears from the fluid being pumped out of the tube.

6. When the air is completely removed, tighten the bleeder screw and replace the dust cap.

7. Check and refill the master cylinder reservoir as necessary.

8. Depress the clutch pedal several times to check the operation of the clutch and check for leaks.

AUTOMATIC TRANSMISSION

Transmission Assembly

REMOVAL AND INSTALLATION

SC300, LS400 and SC400

1. Disconnect the negative battery cable. Remove the air cleaner assembly. Disconnect the transmission throttle cable.

2. Raise and support the vehicle safely. Drain the transmission fluid. Remove the driveshaft along with the center bearing.

3. Remove the exhaust pipe together with the catalytic converter. Disconnect the manual shift linkage. Remove the speedometer cable.

4. Disconnect the oil cooler lines. As necessary, remove the transmission oil filler tube. As required, remove the starter assembly. Remove the speedometer cable.

5. Remove both stiffener plates and the catalytic converter cover

from the transmission housing and cylinder block.

6. Support the engine and transmission using the proper jacking device. Remove the rear crossmember.

7. Remove the torque converter cover. Remove the torque converter-to-engine retaining bolts.

8. Remove the bolts retaining the transmission to the engine. Carefully remove the transmission from the vehicle.

9. Installation is the reverse of the removal procedure. Tighten the transmission housing bolts to 47 lbs. (64 Nm) on the LS400. On the SC300 and SC400, tighten the 14mm bolts to 27 ft. lbs. (37 Nm) and the 17mm bolts to 53 ft. lbs. (72 Nm). Tighten the torque converter bolts to 25 ft. lbs. (33 Nm) on all models.

SHIFT LINKAGE ADJUSTMENT

1. Loosen the nut on the shift linkage. Push the selector lever all the way to the rear of the vehicle.

2. Return the lever 2 notches to the **N** shift position.

3. While holding the selector lever slightly toward the **R** shift position, tighten the connecting rod nut.

THROTTLE CABLE ADJUSTMENT

1. Remove the air cleaner.

2. Confirm that the accelerator linkage opens the throttle fully. Adjust the linkage as necessary.

3. Peel the rubber dust boot back from the throttle cable.

4. Loosen the adjustment nuts on the throttle cable bracket (cylinder head cover) just enough to allow cable housing movement.

5. Have an assistant depress the accelerator pedal fully.

6. Adjust the cable housing so the distance between its end and the cable stop collar is 0.04 in. (1-2mm).

7. Tighten the adjustment nuts. Make sure the adjustment hasn't changed. Install the dust boot and the air cleaner.

NOTE: When reinstalling the transmission assembly after repair or replacement, it is critical that the correct torque converter mounting bolts are used.

AUTOMATIC TRANSAXLE

Transaxle Assembly

REMOVAL AND INSTALLATION

ES250

1. Disconnect the negative battery cable. Remove the air flow meter and the air cleaner assembly.

2. Disconnect the transaxle wire connector. Disconnect the neutral safety switch electrical connector.

3. Disconnect the transaxle ground strap. Disconnect the throttle cable from the throttle linkage.

4. Remove the transaxle case protector. Disconnect the speedometer cable. Disconnect the control cable.

5. Disconnect the oil cooler hoses. Remove the upper starter retaining bolts, as required remove the starter assembly. Remove the upper transaxle housing bolts. Remove the engine rear mount insulator bracket set bolt.

6. Raise and support the vehicle safely. Drain the transaxle fluid.

7. Remove the left front fender apron seal. Disconnect both halfshafts.

8. Remove the suspension lower crossmember assembly. Remove the center halfshaft.

9. Remove the engine mounting center crossmember. Remove the stabilizer bar. Remove the left steering knuckle from the lower control arm.

10. Remove the torque converter cover. Remove the torque converter retaining bolts.

11. Properly support the engine and transaxle assembly. Remove the rear engine mounting bolts. Remove the remaining transaxle-to-engine retaining bolts.

12. Carefully remove the transaxle assembly from the vehicle.

13. Installation is the reverse of the removal procedure. Tighten the 12mm transaxle housing bolts to 47 ft. lbs. (64 Nm); tighten the 10mm bolts to 34 ft. lbs. (46 Nm). Tighten the rear engine mount set bolts to 38 ft. lbs. (52 Nm). Tighten the torque converter mounting bolts to 20 ft. lbs. (27 Nm).

ES300

1. Disconnect the negative battery cable. Remove the air cleaner assembly.

2. Remove the starter.

3. Disconnect speed sensor connectors, park/neutral position switch, solenoid connector.

4. Disconnect shift control cable. Disconnect oil cooler hoses.

5. Remove the 2 front side transaxle and engine mounting bolts.

6. Remove the 3 upper transaxle to engine bolts.

7. Install a engine support fixture. Tie steering gear housing to engine support fixture.

8. Raise and safely support the vehicle. Drain fluid and remove the front wheel.

9. Remove the exhaust pipe.

10. Remove the engine side covers and undercovers.

11. Disconnect both halfshafts.

12. Remove the front side engine mounting nut. Remove the rear side engine mounting bolts (remove hole plugs).

13. Remove the left side transaxle mounting bolts. Remove the steering gear housing.

14. Remove the front frame assembly.

15. Properly support the engine and transaxle assembly. Remove the rear engine mounting bolts. Remove the remaining transaxle-to-engine retaining bolts.

16. Remove the torque converter cover. Remove the torque converter retaining bolts.

17. Carefully remove the transaxle assembly from the vehicle.

18. Installation is the reverse of the removal procedure. Torque the following bolts to:
    Transaxle housing bolts
        12mm bolts — 47 ft. lbs. (64 Nm)
        10mm bolts — 34 ft. lbs. (46 Nm)
    Rear engine mount set bolts — 38 ft. lbs. (52 Nm)
    Torque converter mounting bolts evenly with sealer — 20 ft. lbs. (27 Nm)
    Front frame assembly head bolts
        19mm bolts — 134 ft. lbs. (181 Nm)
        12mm head bolts — 24 ft. lbs (32 Nm)
    Steering gear housing bolts — 134 ft. lbs. (181 Nm)

SHIFT CABLE ADJUSTMENT

ES250 and ES300

1. Loosen the swivel nut on the selector lever.

2. Push the lever fully toward the right side of the vehicle.

3. Return the lever 2 notches to the **N** position.

4. Set the shift lever in the **N** position.

5. While holding the selector lever slightly toward the **R** shift position and tighten the swivel nut to 48 inch lbs. (5.4 Nm).

THROTTLE CABLE ADJUSTMENT

ES250 and ES300

1. Remove the air cleaner.

2. Confirm that the accelerator linkage opens the throttle fully. Adjust the linkage as necessary.

3. Peel the rubber dust boot back from the throttle cable.

4. Loosen the adjustment nuts on the throttle cable bracket (cylinder head cover) just enough to allow cable housing movement.

5. Depress the accelerator pedal fully.

6. Adjust the cable housing so the distance between its end and the cable stop collar is 0.04 in. (1mm)

7. Tighten the adjustment nuts. Make sure the adjustment hasn't changed. Install the dust boot and the air cleaner.

FRONT SUSPENSION

Pneumatic Cylinder

REMOVAL AND INSTALLATION

LS400 with Air Suspension

1. Move the height control switch, located in the trunk area to the **OFF** position.

2. Raise and safely support the vehicle. Remove the steering knuckle from the upper ball joint with the proper tool.

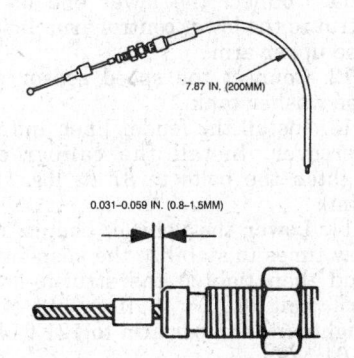

Throttle cable adjustment — ES250 and ES300

3. Support the steering knuckle using a piece of wire. Disconnect speed sensor wire connector.

4. Remove the height control sensor link from the shock absorber lower bracket.

5. Disconnect the shock absorber from the lower mounting bracket. Remove the grommet and disconnect the air tube from the shock absorber.

6. Remove the mounting bolts and the actuator cover. Remove the mounting bolts and the actuator.

7. Remove the 3 upper mounting nuts and remove the shock absorber from the vehicle.

8. The installation is the reverse of the removal procedure. Tighten the upper mounting nuts to 27 ft. lbs. (39 Nm), actuator cover mounting nuts to 27 ft. lbs. (39 Nm) and the lower shock mount nut to 106 ft. lbs. (144 Nm).

MacPherson Strut

REMOVAL AND INSTALLATION

ES250 and ES300

1. Raise and safely support the vehicle. Remove the tire and wheel assembly.

2. Disconnect the ABS speed sensor connector. Disconnect the brake hose from the brake caliper.

3. Disconnect the steering knuckle and the strut assembly from the lower mount.

4. Remove the upper mounting nuts from the top suspension mount and remove the strut assembly.

5. The installation is the reverse of the removal procedure. Tighten the upper strut mount nuts to 47 ft. lbs. (64 Nm) on the ES250 or 59 ft. lbs. (80 Nm) on the ES300. Torque the lower strut mount nuts to 224 ft. lbs. (304 Nm) on the ES250 or 156 ft. lbs. (211 Nm) for all others.

NOTE: On the ES250, the front strut bar cushion retainers have been changed to a new resin formed casting cover to improve the front suspension noise during suspension compression and rebound.

LS400

1. Raise and safely support the vehicle. Remove the tire and wheel assembly.

2. Remove the steering knuckle from the upper ball joint with the proper tool. Support the steering knuckle using a piece of wire.

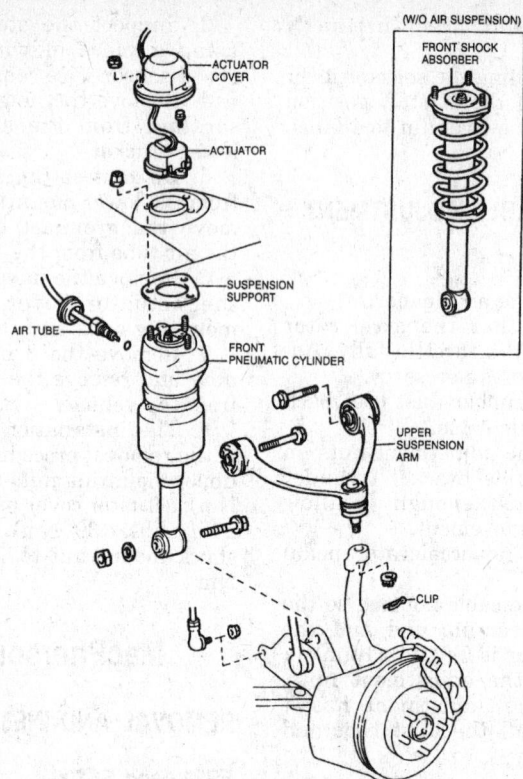

(W/O AIR SUSPENSION)

FRONT SHOCK ABSORBER

ACTUATOR COVER

ACTUATOR

SUSPENSION SUPPORT

AIR TUBE

FRONT PNEUMATIC CYLINDER

UPPER SUSPENSION ARM

CLIP

Front suspension assembly — LS400

3. Disconnect the strut assembly from the lower strut bracket. Remove the plug from the upper strut mount.

4. Loosen the nut on the middle of the strut mount support. Do not remove it.

5. Remove the other 3 mounting nuts and remove the strut assembly with the coil spring from the vehicle.

6. The installation is the reverse of the removal procedure. Tighten the upper strut mount nuts to 27 ft. lbs. (37 Nm) and the lower strut mount nut to 106 ft. lbs. (144 Nm).

SC300 and SC400

1. Raise and safely support the vehicle. Remove the tire and wheel assembly.

2. Remove the brake caliper and suspend it with a piece of wire.

3. Remove the fender liner, engine undercover and the front fender wheel opening moulding.

4. If removing the left side strut, disconnect the windshield washer tank.

5. Remove the bolt and disconnect the ABS speed sensor at the steering knuckle. Remove the 3 bolts and then disconnect the wire harness clamp in order to prevent the harness from be-

ing damaged when removing the through bolt.

6. Remove the plug from the upper strut mount. Loosen the nut on the middle of the strut mount support. Do not remove it.

7. Disconnect the upper control arm and position it out of the way.

8. Disconnect the strut at the lower control arm.

9. Remove the 3 upper mounting nuts and remove the strut assembly with the coil spring from the vehicle.

To install:

10. Install the strut and tighten the upper strut mount nuts to 26 ft. lbs. (35 Nm). Tighten the middle nut to 22 ft. lbs. (29 Nm) and install the plug.

11. Connect the lower end of the strut to the lower control arm. Install the upper arm.

12. Connect the speed sensor and the washer tank.

13. Install the fender liner and undercover. Install the caliper and tighten the bolts to 87 ft. lbs. (118 Nm).

14. Lower the vehicle, bounce it a few times to stabilize the suspension and then tighten the strut-to-lower arm bolt to 106 ft. lbs. (143 Nm). Tighten the upper arm to 121 ft. lbs. (164 Nm).

15. Check the front end alignment.

Strut Bar

REMOVAL AND INSTALLATION

LS400

1. Disconnect the negative battery cable. Raise and support the vehicle safely.

2. Remove the steering knuckle with the axle hub.

3. Remove the strut assembly or the pneumatic cylinder, depending on what the vehicle is equipped with.

4. Remove the strut assembly lower bracket.

5. Place matchmarks on the screw part and nut of the strut bar.

6. Remove the nut and washer from the front side of the strut bar.

7. Remove the 2 nuts and remove the strut bar from the lower arm.

8. Remove the 3 nuts and remove the strut bar cushion and strut bar.

9. Installation is the reverse order of the removal procedure. Be sure to align the matchmarks on the strut bar when installing it.

10. Use the following torque specifications during installation:

a. Torque the 2 strut bar bolts to 59 ft. lbs. (80 Nm).

b. Torque the 2 strut bar nuts to 121 ft. lbs. (164 Nm).

c. Torque the through bolt of the strut assembly bracket to 83 ft. lbs. (113 Nm) and the other bolt to 43 ft. lbs. (59 Nm).

d. Lower the vehicle and after stabilizing the suspension. Torque the front strut bar nut to 87 ft. lbs. (118 Nm).

Upper Ball Joints

INSPECTION

1. Raise and safely support the vehicle. Place a wooden block under the tire and wheel assembly.

2. Lower the lifting device until there is about 1/2 the load on the front spring.

3. Make sure the front wheels are in a straight forward position and block the wheel with wheel chocks.

4. Move the lower arm up and down and check that the ball joint has no excessive play. The ball joint vertical play limit is 0 in. (0mm) on the SC300 and SC400 or 0.012 in. (0.3mm) on the LS400.

REMOVAL AND INSTALLATION

SC300, LS400 and SC400

Upper ball joint replacement on these models is accomplished by replacing the upper arm. The upper ball joint is integral with the upper arm.

Lower Ball Joints

INSPECTION

1. Raise and safely support the vehicle. Place a wooden block under the tire and wheel assembly.
2. Lower the lifting device until there is about ½ the load on the front spring.
3. Make sure the front wheels are in a straight forward position and block the wheel with wheel chocks.
4. Move the lower arm up and down and check that the ball joint has no excessive play. The ball joint vertical play limit is 0 in. (0mm) on the ES250, ES300, SC300 and SC400 or 0.012 in. (0.3mm) on the LS400.

REMOVAL AND INSTALLATION

ES250

1. Raise and safely support the vehicle. Remove the tire and wheel assembly.
2. Loosen the nut holding the stabilizer bar to the lower suspension arm.
3. Loosen the nut holding the lower suspension arm to the lower suspension arm shaft.
4. Disconnect the lower ball joint from the lower suspension arm with the proper tool.
5. Remove the mounting bolts and using a suitable prybar, push down the lower suspension arm, the remove the ball joint.
6. The installation is the reverse of the removal procedure. Tighten the ball joint mounting bolts to 83 ft. lbs. (113 Nm), the castle nut to 90 ft. lbs. (12 Nm), the stabilizer bar lower suspension arm nuts to 156 ft. lbs. (212 Nm) and the lower arm shaft (lower suspension arm) nuts to 156 ft. lbs. (212 Nm).
7. Check the front wheel alignment.

ES300

1. Raise the front of the vehicle and support it safely. Remove the front wheels.
2. Remove side fender apron seal.
3. Remove the steering knuckle with the axle hub, from the vehicle.

4. Pry the dust deflector from the knuckle using a screw driver.
5. Remove the cotter pin and the nut from the ball joint stud.
6. Using puller, remove the lower ball joint from the steering knuckle.
To install:
7. Install the lower ball joint onto the steering knuckle and tighten nut to 90 ft. lbs. (123 Nm). Install new cotter pin.
8. Using the appropriate driver, install new dust deflector.
9. Install the steering knuckle onto the vehicle.
10. Install the fender apron seal and the front wheels.

LS400

1. If equipped with air suspension, move the height control switch, located in the trunk area to the **OFF** position.
2. Raise and safely support the vehicle. Remove the tire and wheel assembly.
3. Disconnect the brake caliper and support, using a piece of wire.
4. Loosen the lower mounting bolts. Do not remove.
5. Disconnect the tie rod end from the steering arm with the proper tool. Remove the bolts and disconnect the lower ball joint from the steering knuckle.
6. Remove the nut and disconnect the lower ball joint from the lower arm with the proper tool.
7. The installation is the reverse of the removal procedure. Tighten the ball joint castle nut to 112 ft. lbs. (152 Nm), the tie rod end nut to 43 ft. lbs. (58 Nm) and the lower ball joint bolts to 83 ft. lbs. (113 Nm).

SC300 AND SC400

The lower ball joint on these models is not replaceable. If out of specifications, replace the entire lower control arm.

Upper Control Arms

REMOVAL AND INSTALLATION

LS400

1. Raise and safely support the vehicle. Remove the tire and wheel assembly.
2. Remove the shock absorber or pneumatic cylinder, if equipped.
3. Remove the mounting bolts and the upper suspension arm.
4. Install the upper suspension arm and tighten the mounting bolts to 83 ft. lbs. (113 Nm).

5. Reverse the remainder of the procedures for installation.

SC300 and SC400

1. Raise the front of the vehicle and support it on safety stands. Remove the wheel.
2. Remove the front fender splash shield, fender liner and the wheel opening moulding.
3. If removing the left side arm, remove the washer tank.
4. Remove the bolt and disconnect the ABS speed sensor from the steering knuckle. Remove the 3 bolts and disconnect the wire harness clamp.
5. Remove the cotter pin and the nut and then press the upper ball joint from the knuckle.
6. Remove the bolt and nut and remove the upper control arm.
To install:
7. Install the upper arm. Connect the arm to the knuckle and tighten the nut to 76 ft. lbs. (103 Nm). Install a new cotter pin.
8. Connect the wire harness and the ABS speed sensor.
9. Install the washer tank, the fender liner, undercover and moulding.
10. Install the wheel, lower the vehicle and bounce the suspension several times to set the suspension. Support the lower arm and tighten the upper arm bolt and nut to 121 ft. lbs. (164 Nm). Check the front wheel alignment.

Lower Control Arms

REMOVAL AND INSTALLATION

ES250

1. Raise and safely support the vehicle.
2. Remove the nut holding the stabilizer to the lower suspension arm. Remove the nut holding the lower suspension arm to the lower suspension arm shaft.
3. Remove the mounting bolts and disconnect the lower ball joint from the steering knuckle with the proper tool.
4. Remove the suspension lower crossmember. Remove the mounting bolt and the lower arm with the shaft.
5. Remove the nut and disconnect the lower ball joint from the lower arm with the proper tool.
6. The installation is the reverse of the removal procedure. Tighten the lower arm shaft-to-body bolts to 153 ft. lbs. (207 Nm), ball joint-to-steer-

ing knuckle bolts to 83 ft. lbs. (113 Nm) and the lower suspension arm mounting nuts to 156 ft. lbs. (212 Nm).

ES300

1. Raise the vehicle and support safely. Remove the front wheels and the fender apron seal.

2. While applying the front brakes, remove the halfshaft locknut.

3. Disconnect and separate the tie rod end from the steering knuckle.

4. Remove the left and right stabilizer end brackets from the lower arms.

5. Remove the 2 nuts and disconnect the lower arm from the ball joint.

6. Remove the driveshaft from the axle hub. Secure the shaft out of the way using wire. Be careful not to damage the shaft boot or ABS sensor rotor.

7. Remove the bolts from the front side of the lower arm.

8. Remove the bolts and nuts from the rear side of the arm and remove arm from the vehicle.

To install:

9. Place the lower arm onto the vehicle and temporarily install the mounting nuts and bolts on the rear side of the arm.

10. Install the lower arm bushing stopper to the lower arm shaft. Install the bolts on the front side of the arm and tighten to 152 ft. lbs. (206 Nm).

11. Tighten the bolts on the rear side of the control arm to 152 ft. lbs. (206 Nm).

12. Install the driveshaft to the axle hub. Connect the lower arm to the lower ball joint and tighten the fasteners to 94 ft. lbs. (127 Nm).

13. Install both side stabilizer end brackets to the lower arm and tighten to 43 ft. lbs. (58 Nm).

14. Connect the tie rod end to the steering knuckle and tighten nut to 36 ft. lbs. (49 Nm). Install new cotter pin.

15. Install the driveshaft locknut and tighten to 217 ft. lbs. (294 Nm). Install new cotter pin.

16. Install front fender apron seal and the front wheel. Torque the front wheel to 76 ft. lbs. (103 Nm).

LS400

1. Raise and safely support the vehicle. Remove the tire and wheel assembly.

2. Remove the shock absorber or pneumatic cylinder, if equipped.

3. Disconnect the tie rod end from the steering knuckle with the proper tool. Remove the lower shock bracket.

4. Remove the nuts and disconnect the lower strut bar from the lower arm.

5. Place matchmarks on the camber adjusting cam. Remove the nut, the adjusting cam and the lower arm with the lower ball joint.

NOTE: To help remove the adjusting cam, fully pull the steering wheel toward the lower arm being removed.

To install:

6. Insert the camber adjusting cam from the rear side of the vehicle and temporarily tighten the nut. Put 2 strut bar bolts into the holes of the lower arm beforehand.

7. Connect the strut bar to the lower arm and tighten the bolts to 121 ft. lbs. (164 Nm). Install the lower shock bracket.

8. Connect the tie rod to the steering arm and tighten the nut to 43 ft. lbs. (58 Nm). Install a new clip.

9. Install the shock absorber or pneumatic cylinder, if equipped.

10. Install the steering knuckle with the axle hub. Replace the tire and wheel assembly.

11. Lower the vehicle and stabilize the suspension.

12. Support the lower arm with a lifting device and remove the tire and wheel assembly.

13. Align the matchmarks and tighten the nut to 185 ft. lbs. (250 Nm). Replace the tire and wheel assembly. Remove the lifting device.

14. Check the front end alignment.

SC300 and SC400

1. Raise the front of the vehicle and support it on safety stands. Remove the wheel and the engine undercover.

2. Remove the nut and disconnect the stabilizer bar from the lower control arm.

3. Remove the clip and nut and then press the lower ball joint out of the steering knuckle.

4. Disconnect the lower end of the strut. Matchmark the front and rear adjustment cams to the body and then remove the cams. Lift out the lower control arm.

To install:

5. Install the lower arm and tighten the ball joint nut to 92 ft. lbs. (125 Nm). Install a new clip.

6. Connect the strut to the arm and tighten the bolt to 106 ft. lbs. (143 Nm).

7. Connect the stabilizer bar link and tighten the nut to 47 ft. lbs. (64 Nm).

8. Install the wheel, lower the vehicle and bounce it several times to set the suspension. Support the lower arm, align the matchmarks on the adjusting cams and tighten the nuts to 166 ft. lbs. (226 Nm). Check the front wheel alignment.

Stabilizer Bar

REMOVAL AND INSTALLATION

ES250

1. Disconnect the negative battery cable. Raise and support the vehicle safely.

2. Remove the lower suspension crossmember.

3. Remove the nuts and retainers holding the stabilizer bar to the lower suspension arms.

4. Remove the stabilizer bar brackets.

5. Remove the the 2 engine undercovers. Remove the control cable clamp bolts from the engine center mounting member, if equipped. Remove the 10 bolts and engine center mounting member.

6. Pull off the stabilizer bar from the lower suspension arms. Remove the retainers and spacers from the stabilizer bar.

To install:

7. Install the stabilizer bar assembly to the lower suspension arm.

8. Install the stabilizer bar brackets.

9. Install the lower suspension crossmember.

10. Use the following torque specifications during installation:

    a. Torque the stabilizer bar bracket cushion bolts to 94 ft. lbs. (127 Nm).

    b. Torque the 2 bolts on the right hand end and the 2 bolts on the left hand end of the engine center mounting member to 29 ft. lbs. (39 Nm) and the other retaining bolts to 32 ft. lbs. (43 Nm).

    c. Torque the suspension lower crossmember bolts to 112 ft. lbs. (152 Nm).

    d. Torque the stabilizer bar mounting nuts 156 ft. lbs. (212 Nm).

ES300

1. Raise the front of the vehicle and support it safely. Remove the front wheels.

2. Remove both right and left side fender apron seals.

3. Remove the cotter pin and the nut from both side tie rod end studs. Using puller, disconnect right and left tie rod ends from the steering knuckle

4. Remove stabilizer bar links (bolts) from each control arm.

5. Remove the right and left bushing retainers and the bar bushings.

6. Remove the front exhaust pipe.

7. Remove the steering gear box mounting bolts and nuts.

8. Lift the steering gear box and remove the stabilizer bar from the vehicle.

To install:

9. Lift the steering gear box and install bar into position.

10. Install the steering gear box mounting bolts and nuts and torque to 134 ft. lbs. (181 Nm).

11. Install the front exhaust pipe.

12. Install the left and the right stabilizer bar bushings, bushing retainers and secure with the retaining bolts. Torque the retainer bolts to 14 ft. lbs. (19 Nm).

13. Install both side stabilizer bar links and torque to 47 ft. lbs. (64 Nm).

14. Connect both side tie rod ends to the steering knuckles and tighten the nut to 36 ft. lbs. (49 Nm).

15. Install the left and the right fender apron seals and the front wheels.

LS400

1. Disconnect the negative battery cable. Raise and support the vehicle safely.

2. Remove the steering knuckle with the axle hub.

3. Remove the strut assembly or the pneumatic cylinder.

4. Remove the strut assembly lower bracket.

5. Place matchmarks on the screw part and nut of the strut bar.

6. Remove the nut and washer from the front side of the strut bar.

7. Remove the 2 nuts and remove the strut bar from the lower arm.

8. Remove the 3 nuts and remove the strut bar cushion and strut bar.

9. Remove the right and left stabilizer bar bushings.

10. Remove the strut bar brackets with the stabilizer bar. Remove the stabilizer bar and inspect the stabilizer bar link as follows:

   a. Flip the ball joint stud back and forth 5 times.

   b. Using a torque gauge, turn the stud continuously 1 turn per

2-4 seconds and take the torque reading on the 5th turn.

   c. Turning torque should be 0.4-13 inch lbs. (0.05-1.0 Nm).

To install:

11. Install the strut bar bushings and brackets with the stabilizer bar to lower arm.

12. Install the strut assembly lower bracket.

13. Install the strut assembly or the pneumatic cylinder.

14. Install the steering knuckle with the axle hub.

15. Use the following torque specifications during installation:

   a. Torque the 2 strut bar bolts to 59 ft. lbs. (80 Nm).

   b. Torque the 2 strut bar nuts to 121 ft. lbs. (164 Nm).

   c. Torque the through bolt of the strut assembly bracket to 83 ft. lbs. (113 Nm) and the other bolt to 43 ft. lbs. (59 Nm).

   d. Lower the vehicle and after stabilizing the suspension. Torque the front strut bar nut to 87 ft. lbs. (118 Nm).

   e. Torque the stabilizer bar links to 70 ft. lbs. (95 Nm).

   f. Torque the stabilizer bar bushings to 21 ft. lbs. (28 Nm).

SC300 and SC400

1. Raise the front of the vehicle and support it on safety stands. Remove the wheel.

2. Remove the engine undercover.

3. Remove the nuts and the stabilizer bar links from the bar and the lower control arm.

4. Remove the 4 bracket mounting bolts and remove the bar and cushions.

To install:

5. Install the cushions so they touch the inside of the line painted on the stabilizer bar. Install the bar and tighten the bracket bolts to 13 ft. lbs. (18 Nm).

6. Install the links and tighten the nuts to 47 ft. lbs. (64 Nm).

7. Install the undercover and wheel, lower the vehicle and check the front wheel alignment.

Front Wheel Bearings

REMOVAL AND INSTALLATION

NOTE: For detailed procedures on all other models, please refer to the drive axle section.

LS400, SC400 and SC300

1. Raise and safely support the vehicle. Remove the tire and wheel assembly.

2. Remove the steering knuckle with the axle hub. Remove the nut and the speed sensor rotor.

3. Remove the 4 bolts and shift the brake dust cover towards the hub side (outside). Remove the axle shaft from the steering knuckle with the proper tool.

4. Using the proper tool, remove the inner race (outside) from the axle shaft. Pry out the oil seal from the steering knuckle with the proper tool.

5. Remove the snapring and press out the bearing from the steering knuckle with the proper tools.

To install:

6. Using the proper tool, press the new bearing into the steering knuckle. Install the snapring, using suitable snapring pliers.

7. Install the inner race (outside) and press in the new oil seal until it is flush with the end surface of the steering knuckle.

8. Install the brake dust cover to the steering knuckle. Press the axle hub to the steering knuckle with the proper tool.

9. Install the speed sensor rotor and the steering knuckle.

10. Replace the tire and wheel assembly. Lower the vehicle.

REAR SUSPENSION

Pneumatic Cylinder

REMOVAL AND INSTALLATION

LS400 With Air Suspension

1. Remove the rear seat cushion and seat back. Remove the rear scuff plates and the roof side inner trim panel and the speaker panel.

2. Remove the trunk trim panel. Move the height control switch, located in the trunk area to the off position.

3. Raise and safely support the vehicle. Remove the tire and wheel assembly.

4. Disconnect the stabilizer links from the stabilizer bar.

5. Disconnect and support the brake caliper, using a piece of wire. Do not disconnect the brake line.

6. Disconnect the height control sensor link from the suspension arm.

Remove the nut on the lower side of the shock absorber. Do not remove the bolt.

7. Support the rear axle assembly with a lifting device. Remove the grommet and disconnect the air tube from the shock absorber.

8. Remove the mounting bolts and the actuator cover. Remove the mounting bolts and the actuator.

9. Remove the upper mounting nuts and lower the rear axle assembly. Remove the bolt on the lower side of the shock absorber.

10. Remove the shock absorber.

To install:

11. Install the shock to the vehicle and tighten the upper mounting nuts to 43 ft. lbs. (58 Nm).

12. Install the actuator and replace the actuator cover. Tighten the mounting nuts to 13 ft. lbs. (18 Nm).

13. Install new O-rings and connect the air line to the shock absorber. Tighten the fitting to 13 ft. lbs. (18 Nm).

14. Install the shock to the rear axle carrier. Insert the bolt from the vehicle's rear and temporarily tighten the nut.

15. Connect the height control sensor link to suspension arm and tighten to 48 inch lbs. (5 Nm).

16. Install the rear brake caliper to the rear axle carrier and tighten the mounting bolts to 77 ft. lbs. (104 Nm).

17. Connect the stabilizer links and tighten to 26 ft. lbs. (35 Nm).

18. Stabilize the suspension by:

a. Install the tire and wheel assembly and lower the vehicle.

b. Move the height control switch to the on position. Start the engine an fill the pneumatic cylinder with air.

c. Bounce the vehicle up and down several times to stabilize the suspension.

19. Raise and safely support the vehicle. Remove the tire and wheel assembly.

20. Support the rear axle carrier with a lifting device. Tighten the lower shock bolt to 101 ft. lbs. (137 Nm).

21. Replace the tire and wheel assembly. Lower the vehicle.

22. Install the rear seat cushion and seat back. Replace the rear scuff plates, the roof side inner trim panel and the speaker panel.

23. Install the trunk trim panel. Check the rear wheel alignment.

MacPherson Strut

REMOVAL AND INSTALLATION

ES250 and ES300

1. Raise and safely support the vehicle. Remove the tire and wheel assembly.

2. Disconnect and plug the brake line from the strut assembly.

3. Disconnect the stabilizer link from the strut assembly.

4. Remove the rear seat back and package tray trim. Remove the dust cover from the upper suspension support. Loosen the nut but do not remove.

5. Remove the strut mounting bolts and disconnect the strut assembly. Remove the upper mounting bolts and remove the strut assembly.

6. The installation is the reverse of the removal procedure. Tighten the following to:

Upper mounting bolts — 29 ft. lbs. (39 Nm)

Lower strut-to-axle bolts
ES250 — 166 ft. lbs. (225 Nm)
ES300 — 188 ft. lbs. (255 Nm)
Upper center mounting nut — 36 ft. lbs. (49 Nm) — ES250 only
Stabilizer link top nut — 47 ft. lbs. (64 Nm)

LS400

1. Remove the rear seat cushion and seat back. Remove the rear scuff plates and the roof side inner trim panel and the speaker panel.

2. Raise and safely support the vehicle. Remove the tire and wheel assembly.

3. Remove the rear halfshaft and disconnect the stabilizer links.

4. Disconnect and support the brake caliper. Do not disconnect the brake line.

5. Remove the nut on the lower side of the strut. Do not remove the bolt.

6. Support the rear axle assembly with a lifting device. Remove the 3 nuts and the strut cap.

7. Loosen the nut in the middle of the suspension support. Do not remove it.

8. Remove the other 3 mounting bolts. Lower the rear axle assembly and remove the bolt on the lower side of the strut assembly.

9. Remove the strut assembly with the coil spring.

To install:

10. Install the strut assembly with the coil spring to the vehicle and tighten the nuts to 47 ft. lbs. (64 Nm). Tighten the nut in the middle of the

suspension support to 20 ft. lbs. (27 Nm).

11. Install the strut to the rear axle carrier. Install the bolt from the rear of the vehicle and temporarily tighten the nut.

12. Install the brake caliper and tighten the mounting bolts to 77 ft. lbs. (104 Nm). Connect the stabilizer links and tighten to 26 ft. lbs. (35 Nm).

13. Install the rear halfshaft. Replace the tire and wheel assembly. Lower the vehicle.

14. Bounce the vehicle up and down to stabilize the suspension.

15. Raise and safely support the vehicle. Remove the tire and wheel assembly.

16. Support the rear axle assembly with a lifting device. Tighten the bolt to 101 ft. lbs. (137 Nm).

17. Install the tire and wheel assembly. Lower the vehicle.

18. Replace the rear scuff plates and the roof side inner trim panel and the speaker panel.

19. Replace the rear seat cushion and seat back.

20. Check the rear wheel alignment.

SC300 and SC400

1. Raise the rear of the vehicle and support it with safety stands. Remove the wheel.

2. Remove the rear brake caliper and position it out of the way.

3. Remove the nut and bolt on the lower end of the strut.

4. Remove the cap and loosen (do not remove) the center nut on the upper end of the strut. Remove the 3 remaining upper nuts and lift out the strut.

To install:

5. Install the strut and tighten the 3 upper nuts and the center nut to 20 ft. lbs. (27 Nm). Install the cap.

6. Install the lower bolt and the caliper.

7. Install the wheel, lower the vehicle and bounce it several times to set the suspension. Support the lower arm and tighten the lower strut mounting bolt to 106 ft. lbs. (143 Nm).

Upper Control Arms

REMOVAL AND INSTALLATION

LS400

1. Raise and safely support the vehicle. Remove the tire and wheel assembly.

2. Remove the rear axle carrier with the upper arm assembly.

3. Install the axle carrier in a suitable holding fixture.

4. Disconnect the upper control arm from the axle carrier.

5. The installation is the reverse of the removal procedure. Tighten the upper arm-to-axle bolt to 80 ft. lbs. (108 Nm).

SC300 and SC400

1. Raise and safely support the vehicle. Remove the tire and wheel assembly.

2. Remove the rear halfshaft. Remove the 2 bolts and the ABS wire harness clamp.

3. Remove the nut and press the upper ball joint out of the axle carrier.

4. Remove the upper mounting bolts and nuts and lift out the control arm.

5. Position the arm and tighten the upper bolts and nuts to 121 ft. lbs. (164 Nm). Make sure the tip of the nut lock is facing down.

6. Use a new nut and tighten the ball joint to 80 ft. lbs. (109 Nm).

7. Install the halfshaft and the ABS clamp. Install the wheel and lower the vehicle.

Lower Suspension Arms and Strut Rod

REMOVAL AND INSTALLATION

ES250

1. Disconnect the negative battery cable. Raise and support the vehicle safely.

2. Disconnect the ABS speed sensor wire clamp from the No. 1 suspension arm.

3. Remove the bolt and nut holding the strut rod to the axle carrier and remove the strut rod from the carrier.

4. Place a matchmark on the adjusting cam and body of the No. 1 and No. 2 suspension arms. Remove the bolt and nut holding the No. 1 and No. 2 suspension arms to the axle carrier.

5. Remove the fuel tank protector by removing the 2 bolts and clips.

6. Remove the cam, cam bolt and No. 2 suspension arm from the body.

7. Remove the bolt, retainer, nut and No. 1 suspension arm.

To install:

NOTE: The right and left suspension arms have been stamped with an R and L respectively for identification. Install the suspension arm so the directional hole faces toward the outside of the rear of the vehicle. Temporarily install the No. 1 suspension arm to the body with the retaining bolt and nut. Install the No. 2 suspension arm, so the bushing with the slit side faces toward the rear. Then install the suspension arm with the small paint spot towards the outside of the vehicle. Place the No. 2 suspension arm, in position and temporarily install the cam bolt and cam to the body.

8. Torque the No. 1 suspension arm to the body mounting bolt with the vehicle weight on the suspension to 83 ft. lbs. (113 Nm).

9. Align the matchmarks on the adjusting cam and body, torque the No. 2 suspension arm to the body mounting bolt with the vehicle weight on the suspension to 83 ft. lbs. (113 Nm).

10. Torque the No. 1 and No. 2 suspension arms to the axle carrier mounting bolt and nut with the vehicle weight on the suspension to 134 ft. lbs. (181 Nm).

11. Torque the strut rod to the axle carrier mounting bolt with the vehicle weight on the suspension to 83 ft. lbs. (113 Nm).

12. Install the fuel tank protector and ABS speed sensor wire clamp.

13. Reconnect the negative battery cable and check the rear wheel alignment.

ES300

1. Raise the vehicle and support safely. Remove the rear wheels.

2. Remove the nut from the axle carrier. Remove the mounting bolts from the strut rod and disconnect from the carrier.

3. Disconnect Load Sensing Proportioning Valve (LSPV) spring from the lower arm, if equipped.

4. Disconnect No. 1 and No. 2 suspension arms from the axle carrier.

5. Remove the fasteners and pull the fuel tank protector down from the vehicle.

6. Place matchmarks on the toe adjust cam and suspension member.

7. Remove the service hole cover(s). Loosen the bolt and remove the toe adjust plate No. 2.

8. Remove the bolt with toe adjust cam, disconnect the No. 2 suspension arm and remove from the vehicle.

9. Remove the nut retainer from the body and remove the No. 1 suspension arm.

To install:

10. Install the stamped suspension arm No. 1 with the identification mark **L** for left and **R** for right on the proper side. Temporarily install the suspension arms with the bolt, washer and nut. Do not tighten at this time. Install with the bushing slit side towards the rear.

11. Face the paint mark on the No. 2 suspension arms toward the rear of the vehicle. Install the bushing with the slit side towards the rear of the vehicle.

12. Loosely install the bolt into the axle carrier. Connect the LSPV spring to the lower arm.

13. Connect the strut bar to the axle carrier and temporarily install the bolt and nut.

14. Install the fuel tank protector, rear wheels and lower the vehicle. Bounce the suspension up and down a few times.

15. Torque the strut rod bolts to 83 ft. lbs. (113 Nm) and the suspension arm nuts (inside and outside) to 134 ft. lbs. (181 Nm).

16. Have the rear wheel alignment checked.

LS400

1. Disconnect the negative battery cable. If equipped with air suspension. move the height control ON/OFF switch (located in the luggage compartment) to the OFF position.

2. Raise and support the vehicle safely and remove the rear wheel assembly.

3. Disconnect the strut rod from the rear axle carrier. Remove the strut rod.

4. Disconnect the height control sensor link, if equipped, from the No. 1 suspension arm.

5. Place matchmarks on the adjusting cam and body. Remove the adjusting cam. Remove the nut on the axle carrier side of the No. 1 lower suspension arm.

6. Using a tie rod removal tool, remove the No. 1 suspension arm.

7. Disconnect the stabilizer bar link from the No. 2 suspension arm.

8. Place matchmarks on the adjusting cam and body. Remove the adjusting cam. Remove the No. 2 lower suspension arm. Remove the arm cover.

9. Inspect the No. 1 lower suspension arm ball joint as follows.

   a. Flip the ball joint stud back and forth 5 times.

   b. Using a torque gauge, turn the stud continuously 1 turn per 2-4 seconds and take the torque reading on the 5th turn.

   c. Turning torque should be 7.4-30 inch lbs. (0.8-3.4 Nm).

   d. If not within specifications, replace the No. 1 suspension arm.

To install:

10. Temporarily install the No. 2 and No. 1 lower suspension arms. Install the bolt and nut into the No. 2 suspension arm, connected the No. 2 lower suspension arm to the axle carrier and torque the bolts to 121 ft. lbs. (164 Nm). Install a new nut to the No. 1 suspension arm ball joint and torque it to 43 ft. lbs. (59 Nm).

11. Connect the height control sensor link to the No. 1 lower suspension arm with a new nut. Torque it to 48 inch lbs. (5 Nm).

12. Temporarily install the strut rod.

13. Install the rear wheel assemblies and lower the vehicle.

14. Move the height control switch back to the ON position, if equipped. Bounce the vehicle up and down several times to stabilize the suspension.

15. Raise and safely support the vehicle. Remove the rear wheel assemblies.

16. Support the axle carrier. Torque the bolt and nut of the strut rod to 136 ft. lbs. (184 Nm). Torque the nut on the body side of the No. 1 lower suspension arm to 136 ft. lbs. (184 Nm). Torque the nut on the body side of the No. 2 lower suspension arm to 136 ft. lbs. (184 Nm).

17. Install the rear wheel assemblies, lower the vehicle and torque the rear wheel retaining nuts to 76 ft. lbs. (103 Nm).

18. Reconnect the negative battery cable. Check the rear wheel alignment.

SC300 and SC400

1. Raise the rear of the vehicle and support it on safety stands. Remove the wheel.

2. Remove the bolt and nut and disconnect the strut rod from the axle carrier. Remove the bolt and nut and lift out the strut rod.

3. Remove the nut and press the No. 1 arm out of the axle carrier. Place matchmarks on the adjusting cam, remove the cam and nut and lift out the No. 1 arm.

4. Disconnect the strut at the No. 2 lower arm. Disconnect the stabi-lizer bar link. Remove the nut and press the lower arm out of the axle carrier. Place matchmarks on the adjusting cam, remove the cam and nut and lift out the No. 2 arm.

To install:

5. Install the No. 2 arm to the carrier with a new nut and tighten it to 110 ft. lbs. (150 Nm).

6. Connect the No. 2 arm to the body and install the adjusting cam and nut, align the matchmarks. Connect the strut to the lower arm. Connect the stabilizer link and tighten the nut to 26 ft. lbs. (35 Nm).

7. Connect the No. 1 arm to the axle carrier and tighten the new nut to 43 ft. lbs. (59 Nm). Connect the No. 1 arm to the body and install the adjusting cam and nut, align the matchmarks.

8. Install the strut rod.

9. Install the wheel, lower the vehicle and bounce it several times to set the suspension. Support the axle carrier and tighten the strut rod to 136 ft. lbs. (184 Nm). Tighten the strut bolt to 106 ft. lbs. (143 Nm). Align the adjusting cam matchmarks and tighten the nuts to 136 ft. lbs. (184 Nm).

Strut Rod

REMOVAL AND INSTALLATION

ES250

1. Disconnect the negative battery cable. Raise and support the vehicle safely.

2. Disconnect the ABS speed sensor wire clamp from the No. 1 suspension arm.

3. Remove the bolt and nut holding the strut rod to the axle carrier and remove the strut rod from the carrier. If necessary, remove the rear floor heat upper insulator on the right hand side.

4. Installation is the reverse order of the removal procedure. Position the strut rod to the body and temporarily install the nut and bolt. Be sure the lip of the nut is resting on the flange of the bracket.

5. Torque the strut rod to the body mounting bolt with the vehicle weight on the suspension to 83 ft. lbs. (113 Nm).

6. Torque the strut rod to the axle carrier mounting bolt with the vehicle weight on the suspension to 83 ft. lbs. (113 Nm).

7. Reconnect the negative battery cable and Check the rear wheel alignment.

Stabilizer Bar

------ CAUTION ------

On models with an air bag, wait at least 90 seconds from the time that the ignition switch is turned to the LOCK position and the battery is disconnected before performing any further work.

REMOVAL AND INSTALLATION

ES250, ES300 and LS400

1. Disconnect the negative battery cable. Raise and support the vehicle safely.

2. Remove the tail pipe assembly.

3. Remove the stabilizer links. If the ball joint stud turns together with the nut, use a hexagon wrench to hold the stud.

4. Disconnect the ABS speed sensor wire clamp. Remove the 4 bolts, stabilizer brackets and cushions.

5. Using a lift and a block of wood, support the fuel tank. Remove the 2 fuel tank band installation bolts.

6. Lower the fuel tank approximately 1.57 in. (40mm) on the ES250, and then remove the stabilizer bar from the body.

7. Rotate the ball joint stud in all directions. If the movement is not smooth and free, replace the stabilizer link.

To install:

8. Install the fuel tank in its proper position, torque the tank strap retaining bolts to 29 ft. lbs. (39 Nm).

9. Install the stabilizer bar assembly. Torque the stabilizer bar cushions retaining bolts to 14 ft. lbs. (19 Nm) on the ES250 and ES300 or 13 ft. lbs. (18 Nm) on the LS400.

10. Torque the stabilizer link to 47 ft. lbs. (64 Nm) on the ES250 and ES300 or 26 ft. lbs. (35 Nm) on the LS400.

11. Reconnect the ABS speed sensor wire clamp.

12. Install the exhaust system. Torque the tail pipe clamp to 29 ft. lbs. (39 Nm).

SC300 and SC400

1. Disconnect the negative battery cable. Raise and support the vehicle safely.

2. Remove the tail pipe assembly.

3. Remove the stabilizer links. If the ball joint stud turns together with the nut, use a hexagon wrench to hold the stud.

4. Remove the 4 bolts, stabilizer brackets and cushions and lift out the bar.

5. Installation is the reverse order of the removal installation. Use the following torque specifications:

a. Torque the stabilizer bar cushions retaining bolts to 21 ft. lbs. (28 Nm).

b. Torque the stabilizer link to 26 ft. lbs. (35 Nm).

c. Torque the tail pipe clamp to 29 ft. lbs. (39 Nm).

Rear Wheel Bearings

REMOVAL AND INSTALLATION

NOTE: Rear wheel bearing removel and installation procedures for all RWD models are detailed in the Drive Axle section. On the ES300 the rear axle hub with bearing is replaced as a complete assembly.

ES250

1. Raise and safely support the vehicle. Remove the tire and wheel assembly.

2. Remove the rear brakes and rotor assembly.

3. Remove the axle hub mounting bolts and remove the axle hub with the parking brake assembly.

4. Using the proper tool, unstake the locknut and remove.

5. Push the rear axle shaft off the axle hub with the proper tool. Remove the bearing inner race (inside) with the proper tool.

6. Using the proper tool, pull off the bearing inner race (outside) from the axle shaft. Remove the oil seal.

7. Install the inner race (outside) of the bearing to be removed, using the proper tool, press out the bearing.

NOTE: Always replace the bearing as an assembly.

To install:

8. Apply a suitable multi-purpose grease to the outer race of a new bearing. Press the bearing into the axle hub with the proper tool.

9. Install a new bearing inner race (outside) and drive in a new oil seal with the proper tool. Apply a suitable multi-purpose grease to the seal lip.

10. Install a new bearing inner race (inside) and press the inner races onto the axle shaft, using the proper tool. Install and tighten the locknut to 90 ft. lbs. (122 Nm). Stake the nut.

11. Install the parking brake assembly and a new oil seal to the axle carrier.

12. Install the axle hub and tighten the bolts to 59 ft. lbs. (80 Nm).

13. Install the tire and wheel assembly. Lower the vehicle.

Rear Axle Carrier Assembly

REMOVAL AND INSTALLATION

NOTE: Rear axle carrier REMOVAL AND INSTALLATION procedures for all other models are detailed in the Drive Axle section.

ES250 and ES300

1. Raise and safely support the vehicle. Remove the tire and wheel assembly.

2. Remove the rear brakes and rotor assembly.

3. Remove the axle hub mounting bolts and remove the axle hub with the parking brake assembly. Remove the O-ring from the axle carrier.

NOTE: Be careful not to damage the sensor control rotor.

4. Remove the strut rod nut and bolt from the axle carrier. Remove the suspension arm mounting bolts from the axle carrier.

5. Supporting the axle carrier, remove the axle carrier mounting bolt and nut from the strut assembly. Remove the axle carrier assembly.

To install:

6. Place the axle carrier into position.

7. Install the axle carrier mounting bolt and nut to the strut assembly. Tighten to 166 ft. lbs. (225 Nm) on the ES250 or 188 ft. lbs. (255 Nm) on the ES300.

8. Temporarily, connect the suspension arms to axle carrier. Temporarily, connect the strut rod to the axle carrier.

9. Install the parking brake assembly and a new oil seal to the axle carrier.

10. Install the axle hub and tighten the mounting bolts to 59 ft. lbs. (80 Nm).

11. Install the rotor and disc brake assembly. Stabilize the suspension.

12. Tighten the axle carrier-to-strut rod mounting bolts to 83 ft. lbs. (113 Nm) and the suspension arm-to-axle carrier bolts to 134 ft. lbs. (181 Nm). Tighten with the vehicle weight on the suspension.

13. Check the rear wheel alignment.

LS400

1. Disconnect the negative battery cable. If the vehicle is equipped with air suspension. move the height control ON/OFF switch (located in the luggage compartment) to the off position.

2. Raise and support the vehicle safely and remove the rear wheel assembly.

3. Remove the brake caliper retaining bolts. Remove the caliper and support on the vehicle with a piece of safety wire.

4. Place matchmarks on the disc rotor and axle hub. Remove the 2 screws and remove the disc rotor retaining screws and remove the rotor.

5. Check the backlash in the bearing shaft, by placing a dial indicator near the center of the axle hub and check the backlash in the bearing shaft. Maximum backlash should be 0.0020 in. (0.05mm). If the backlash is greater than the maximum specification, replace the bearing.

6. Using a dial indicator, check the deviation at the surface of the axle hub outside the hub bolt. The maximum deviation should be 0.0028 in. (0.07mm) If the maximum deviation is greater than the specified amount, replace the axle hub.

7. Install the disc rotor and brake caliper. Remove the cotter pin and lock cap from the drive axle locknut.

8. While an assistant is applying the brakes, remove the drive axle locknut. Remove the brake caliper and rotor.

9. Remove the parking brake shoe and cable.

10. Remove the 3 speed sensor retaining brakes and remove the speed sensor.

11. Remove the strut rod and lower suspension arms.

12. Remove the nut on the lower side of the strut assembly.

13. Remove the 2 upper arm set bolts. Remove the bolt on the lower side of the strut assembly.

14. Remove the axle carrier with the upper arm. To remove the upper arm from the axle carrier, use the following procedure.

a. Install a bolt and 2 nuts to the axle carrier and secure it in a suitable vise.

b. Loosen the nut upper arm nut until it is just about off the bolt and tap on it with a soft face hammer.

c. Remove the upper arm.

15. Inspect the upper arm ball joint as follows:

a. Flip the ball joint stud back and forth 5 times.

b. Using a torque gauge, turn the stud continuously 1 turn per 2-4 seconds and take the torque reading on the 5th turn.

c. Turning torque should be 9-30 inch lbs. (1.0-3.4 Nm).

d. If not within specifications, replace the upper arm.

16. Install the upper arm to the axle carrier and install a new nut. Torque the nut to 80 ft. lbs. (108 Nm).

To install:

17. Install the rear axle carrier with upper arm. Temporarily install the driveshaft to the axle hub. Be careful not to damage the oil seal of the axle carrier and speed sensor rotor on the ddriveshaft. Install the upper arm with the 2 bolts and nuts and torque them to 121 ft. lbs. (164 Nm).

18. Install the strut assembly to the axle carrier and temporarily install the bolt and nut.

19. Install the speed sensor along with the 3 retaining bolts.

20. Temporarily install the No. 2 and No. 1 lower suspension arms.

21. Temporarily install the strut rod.

22. Align the matchmarks on the disc rotor and axle hub and install the disc rotor with the 2 screws.

23. Install the brake caliper and torque the retaining bolts to 77 ft. lbs. (104 Nm).

24. Install the driveshaft locknut and while an assistant applies the brake, torque the locknut to 253 ft. lbs. (343 Nm). Install the lock cap and new cotter pin.

25. Install the rear wheel assemblies and lower the vehicle.

26. Move the height control switch back to the on position, if equipped. Bounce the vehicle up and down several times to stabilize the suspension.

27. Raise and safely support the vehicle. Remove the rear wheel assemblies.

28. Support the axle carrier. Torque the bolt on the lower side of the strut assembly to 101 ft. lbs. (137 Nm).

29. Use the following torque specification:

a. Torque the No. 1 lower suspension arm-to-rear axle carrier bolt to 43 ft. lbs. (59 Nm).

b. Torque the No. 1 lower suspension arm-to-body bolt to 136 ft. lbs. (184 Nm).

c. Torque the No. 2 lower suspension arm-to-rear axle carrier bolt to 121 ft. lbs. (164 Nm).

d. Torque the No. 2 lower suspension arm-to-body bolt to 136 ft. lbs. (184 Nm).

e. Torque the strut rod-to-rear axle carrier bolt to 136 ft. lbs. (184 Nm).

f. Torque the strut rod-to-body bolt to 136 ft. lbs. (184 Nm).

30. Install the rear wheel and lower the vehicle. Torque the wheel retaining nuts to 76 ft. lbs. (103 Nm).

31. Reconnect the negative battery cable. Check the rear wheel alignment.

STEERING

Steering Wheel

CAUTION

If equipped with an air bag, the negative battery cable must be disconnected, before working on the system. Failure to do so may result in deployment of the air bag and possible personal injury. Work must be started after approximately 90 seconds or longer from the time the ignition switch is turned to the LOCK position and the negative battery cable is disconnected from the battery. If the wiring connector of the air bag system is disconnected with the ignition switch at ON or ACC, diagnostic coded will be recorded.

REMOVAL AND INSTALLATION

1. Disconnect the negative battery cable. Position the front wheels in a straight-ahead position.

AIR BAG WIRE HARNESS

Disconnect the air bag connector — ES300

2. Loosen the 3 Torx® screws until the groove along the screw circumference catches on the screw case.

3. Pull the wheel pad away from the steering wheel and disconnect the air bag connector.

NOTE: When removing the wheel pad, take care not to pull the air bag harness connector. When storing the wheel pad, keep the upper surface of the pad facing upward.

4. Disconnect the wire connector and remove the set nut. Place matchmarks on the steering wheel and mainshaft.

5. Remove the steering with a suitable puller.

To install:

6. Check that the front wheels are facing straight-ahead. Center the spiral cable. When centering the spiral cable be sure to use the following procedure:

a. Check that the front wheels are pointing straight-ahead.

b. Turn the spiral cable counterclockwise by hand until it becomes harder to turn the cable. The spiral cable will rotate approximately 2½ turns to either the left or right of the center (3 turns on the ES300, SC300 and SC400).

c. Then rotate the spiral cable clockwise approximately 2½ turns to align the red mark (3 turns on the ES300, SC300 and SC400).

7. Align the matchmarks and install the steering wheel. Tighten the set nut to 26 ft. lbs. (35 Nm).

8. Connect the connector.

9. Install the steering wheel pad after confirming that the circumference groove of the screws is caught on the screw case.

NOTE: Make sure the wheel pad is installed to the specified torque. If the wheel pad has been dropped, or there are cracks, dents or other defects in the case or connector, replace the wheel pad with a new one. When installing the wheel pad, be sure the wires and connectors do not interfere with other parts and are not pinched between other parts.

10. Tighten the screws to 65 inch lbs. (7.4 Nm) except ES300 or 78 inch lbs. (8.8 Nm) on the ES300. Connect the negative battery cable.

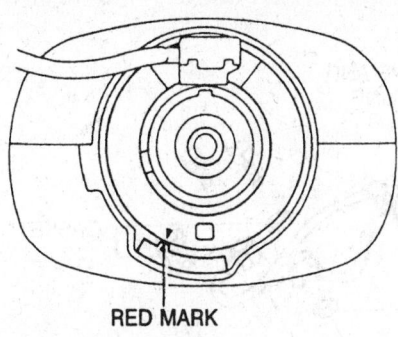

RED MARK

Rotate the spiral cable 3 turns to align the mark — ES300

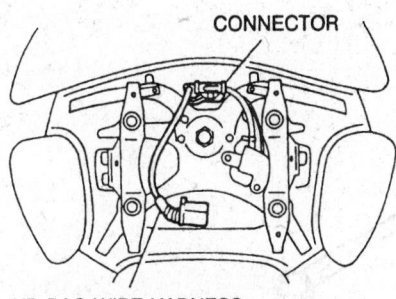

CONNECTOR

AIR BAG WIRE HARNESS

Installing the steering wheel — ES300

Power Steering Rack And Pinion

REMOVAL AND INSTALLATION

ES250 and ES300

1. Place the front wheels in a straight-ahead position, secure the steering wheel with a suitable device to prevent the wheel from turning.
2. Place matchmarks in the universal joint and control valve shaft. Disconnect the joint.
3. Disconnect and plug the hydraulic lines to rack assembly.
4. Raise and safely support the vehicle. On the ES250, disconnect the front exhaust pipe.
5. Remove the center support member and the crossmember on the ES250. On the ES300, disconnect and remove the stabilizer bar brackets.
6. Matchmark and disconnect the tie rod ends from the steering knuckle with the proper tool.
7. Remove the rear engine mount and mounting bracket. Raise the front of the engine with a lifting device.

NOTE: Do not over-tilt the engine.

8. Remove the mounting brackets and slide the gear housing to the right side to put the tie rod end in the body panel.
9. Pull the gear housing out through the opening in the left side lower side of the vehicle body.

NOTE: Do not damage the turn pressure tube and the transmission control cables.

10. Secure the gear housing in a suitable holding fixture. Remove the return and pressure tubes.

To install:

11. Connect the hydraulic tubes to the rack assembly and tighten to 38 ft. lbs. (51 Nm). Insert the rack assembly into position.
12. Replace the mounting brackets and tighten evenly to 43 ft. lbs. (58 Nm) on the ES250 vehicle and torque the housing-to-frame through mounting bolts to 134 ft. lbs. (182 Nm) on the ES300 vehicle.
13. Replace the rear engine mount and mounting bracket. Tighten the the through bolt to 64 ft. lbs. (85 Nm) (and the mounting bolts to 38 ft. lbs. (52 Nm). Lower the front of the engine with a lifting device. Remove the lifting device.
14. Connect the tie rod ends to the steering knuckle. Tighten to 36 ft. lbs. (49 Nm).
15. Replace the center support member and the crossmember on the ES250. Tighten the crossmember bolts to 153 ft. lbs. (207 Nm) and the center member support bolts to 29 ft. lbs. (39 Nm).
16. Install the front exhaust pipe on the ES250. Lower the vehicle.
17. Connect the hydraulic lines to the rack assembly.
18. Align the matchmarks on the universal joint and the control valve shaft and connect. Tighten the connecting bolt to 26 ft. lbs. (35 Nm).
19. Check the steering wheel center point and the toe-in. Refill the power steering reservoir.

SC300, LS400 and SC400

1. Disconnect the negative battery cable.
2. Place the front wheels in a straight-ahead position, secure the steering wheel with a suitable device to prevent the wheel from turning.
3. Place matchmarks in the universal joint and control valve shaft. Disconnect the joint.
4. Disconnect and plug the hydraulic lines to rack assembly.
5. Raise and safely support the vehicle. Disconnect the brake caliper and support with a piece of wire.

6. Disconnect the tie rod end from the steering knuckle with the proper tool.
7. Remove the steering damper and rack boot protector.
8. Disconnect the solenoid wiring and remove the mounting grommets and brackets. Remove the rack assembly.
9. The installation is the reverse of the removal procedure. Follow the following torque specifications:
   a. Joint connecting bolt — 26 ft. lbs. (35 Nm).
   b. Tie rod end nuts — 43 ft. lbs. (58 Nm) on the LS400 or 36 ft. lbs. (49 Nm) on the SC300 and SC400.
   c. Steering damper bolts — 20 ft. lbs. (27 Nm).
   d. Mounting bracket bolts — 56 ft. lbs. (76 Nm).

Power Steering Pump

REMOVAL AND INSTALLATION

ES250 and ES300

1. Disconnect the negative battery cable. Disconnect the hydraulic lines at the pump assembly.
2. Raise and safely support the vehicle. Disconnect the right side tie rod end with the proper tool.
3. Remove the lower crossmember and the front fender apron seal to gain access.
4. Loosen the adjusting and through bolt and push the power steering pump forward. Remove the drive belt.
5. Remove the adjusting bolt and through bolt, then remove the power steering pump.
6. Remove the pressure hose from the pump.
7. The installation is the reverse of the removal procedure. Follow the following torque specifications:
   a. Power steering pump mounting bolts — 29 ft. lbs. (39 Nm) on the ES250 or 43 ft. lbs. (58 Nm) on the ES300.
   b. Lower crossmember bolts — 153 ft. lbs. (207 Nm).
   c. Tie rod end nuts — 36 ft. lbs. (49 Nm).
   d. Pressure line fitting — 27-33 ft. lbs. (37-45 Nm) on the ES250 or 36 ft. lbs. (49 Nm) on the ES300.

SC300, LS400 and SC400

1. Disconnect the negative battery cable.
2. Remove the air cleaner cover, air duct and battery cover.

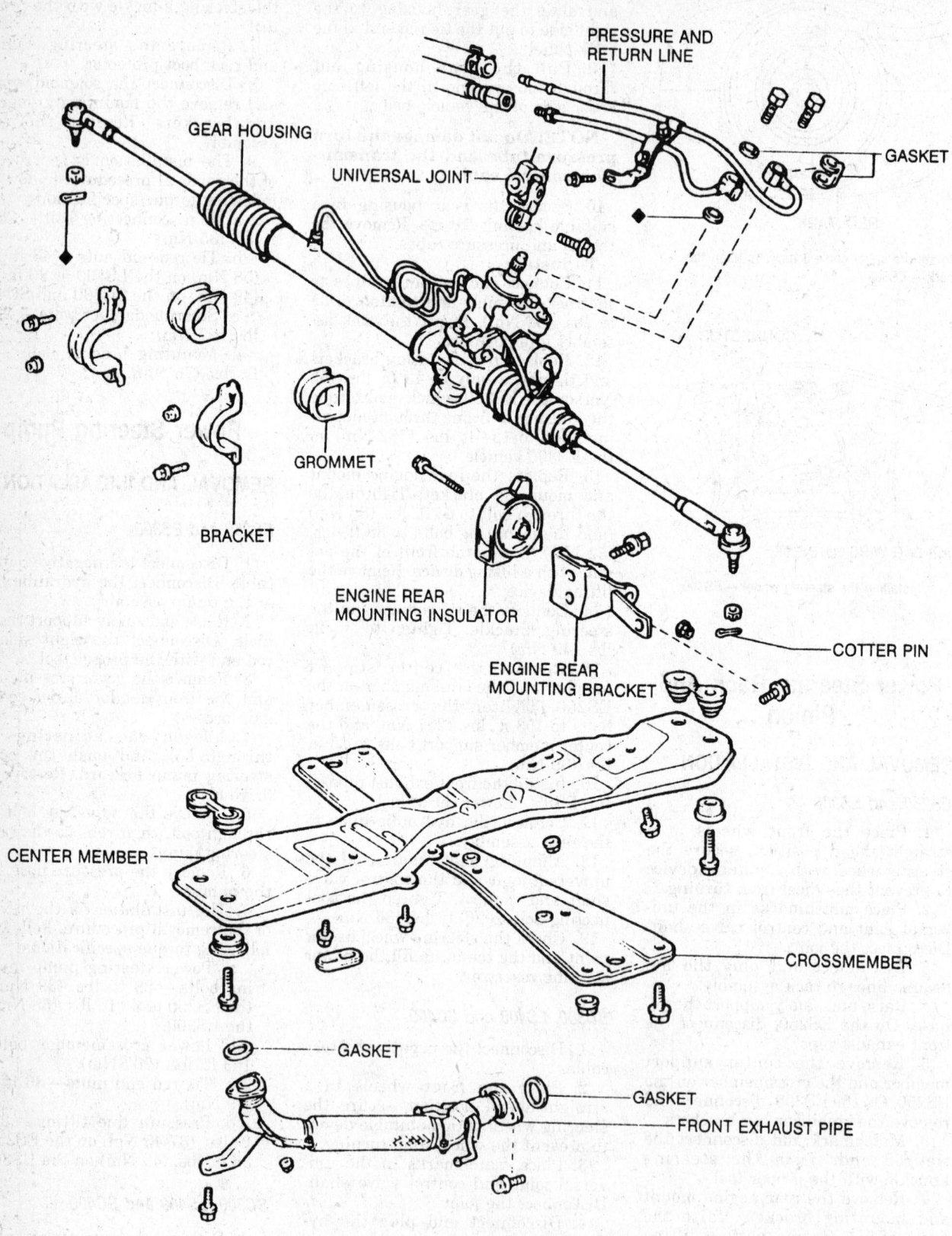

PRESSURE AND
RETURN LINE

GEAR HOUSING

UNIVERSAL JOINT

GASKET

GROMMET

BRACKET

ENGINE REAR
MOUNTING INSULATOR

ENGINE REAR
MOUNTING BRACKET

COTTER PIN

CENTER MEMBER

CROSSMEMBER

GASKET

GASKET

FRONT EXHAUST PIPE

Exploded view of the power steering rack — ES250 and ES300

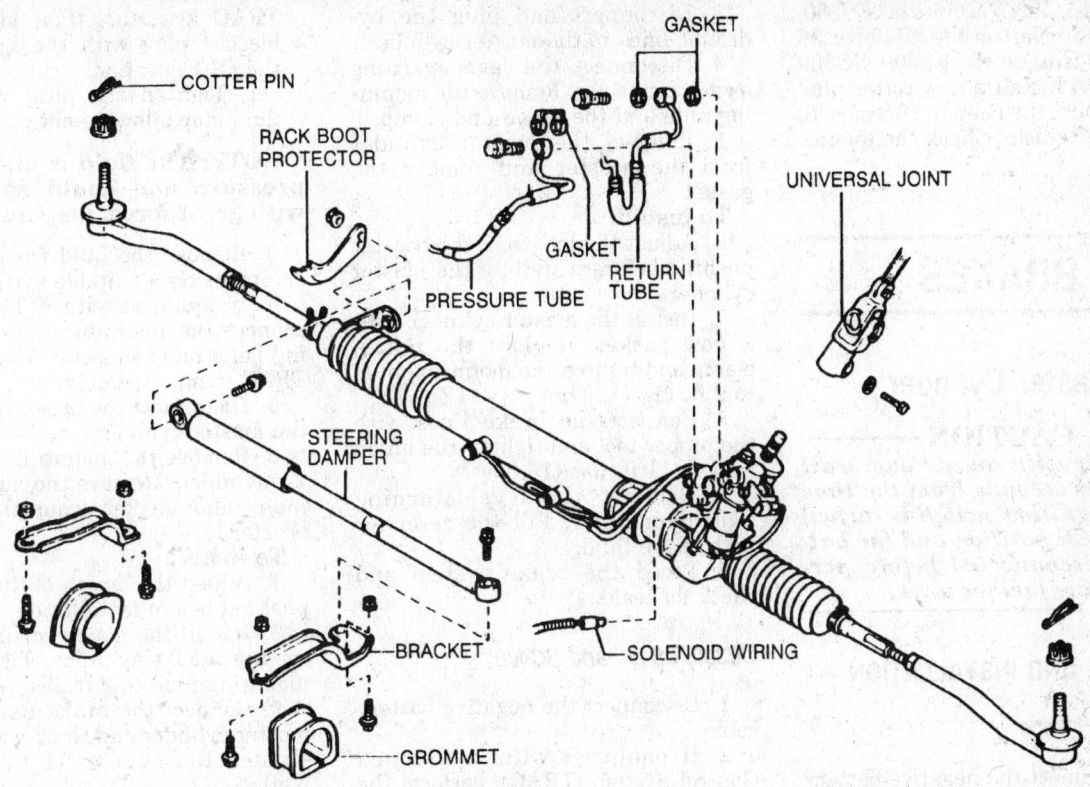

Exploded view of the power steering rack — SC300, LS400 and SC400

3. Turn the drive belt tensioner counterclockwise and remove the drive belt. Remove the pump pulley with the proper tool on the LS400 and SC300.

4. Raise and safely support the vehicle. Remove the engine undercover.

5. Disconnect the hydraulic and vacuum lines at the pump assembly.

6. Remove the pump mounting bolts and the pump assembly.

7. The installation is the reverse of the removal procedure. Follow the following torque specifications:

a. Pump mounting bolts — 29 ft. lbs. (40 Nm) on the LS400 or on the SC300 and SC400, tighten the bolts to 29 ft. lbs. (39 Nm) and the nut to 32 ft. lbs. (43 Nm).

b. Pump pulley bolt — 32 ft. lbs. (44 Nm).

c. Pressure line fitting — 36 ft. lbs. (49 Nm).

8. Bleed the power steering system.

NOTE: On the LS400, note the curvature of the No. 2 and No. 3 power steering return tubes and the rear left hand engine cover have been modified. The new curvature is a 50 degree bend. Previous and new parts are interchangeable as a set only.

BELT ADJUSTMENT

ES250 and ES300

1. Disconnect the negative battery cable.

2. Loosen the power steering pump adjusting bolt and the through bolt.

3. Using a proper tool, move the pump assembly to attain the proper belt tension.

4. Tighten the pump mounting bolts.

5. Connect the negative battery cable.

SC300, LS400 and SC400

On these models, a belt tensioner is used. There is no need for belt adjustment, tension adjustment is automatic.

SYSTEM BLEEDING

1. Check that the fluid level in the reservoir tank is at the maximum level.

2. Start the engine and turn the steering wheel from lock to lock and then keep it there for a few seconds until the air bubbles are removed from the fluid.

3. Stop the engine and measure the fluid level.

4. Make sure the rise of the fluid is not over 0.020 in. (5mm).

Tie Rod Ends

REMOVAL AND INSTALLATION

1. Raise and safely support the vehicle.

2. Place matchmarks on the threads of the tie rod end and the rack end.

3. On LS400, disconnect the brake caliper and suspend with a piece of wire. Do not disconnect the lines.

4. Remove the cotter pin and nut. Disconnect the tie rod end from the steering knuckle with a tie rod end puller.

5. Unscrew the tie rod end from the rack end.

To install:

6. Install the tie rod end to the rack end, counting the same number of threads as were removed until the marks align.

7. The measurement from the outer edge of the nut to the inner edge of the threads should be 1.06 in. (27mm) on the ES250 and ES300 or 1.26 in. (32mm) on the SC300, LS400 and SC400.

8. Connect the tie rod end to the steering knuckle. Tighten the nut to

41-43 ft. lbs. (59 Nm) on the ES250, 43 ft. lbs. (59 Nm) on the LS400 or 36 ft. lbs. (49 Nm) on the ES300, SC300 and SC400. Install a new cotter pin.

9. Connect the caliper, if removed. Lower the vehicle. Check the toe-in.

BRAKES

Master Cylinder

--- CAUTION ---
On models with an air bag, wait at least 90 seconds from the time that the ignition switch is turned to the LOCK position and the battery is disconnected before performing any further work.

REMOVAL AND INSTALLATION

ES250 and ES300

1. Disconnect the negative battery cable. On the ES250, remove the charcoal canister.

2. Remove the fluid from the reservoir, using a suitable syringe.

3. Disconnect and plug the hydraulic lines to the master cylinder.

4. Disconnect the level warning switch connector. Remove the mounting nuts and the union and clamp.

5. Remove the master cylinder from the booster and remove the gasket.

To install:

6. Adjust the length of the booster pushrod before installing the master cylinder.

7. Install the master cylinder with a new gasket. Replace the union, clamp and tighten the mounting nuts to 9 ft. lbs. (12 Nm).

8. Connect the brake lines with the proper tool and tighten the union nuts to 11 ft. lbs. (15 Nm).

9. Connect the level warning switch connector. Fill the reservoir with brake fluid.

10. Bleed the brake system and check for leaks.

SC300, LS400 and SC400

1. Disconnect the negative battery cable.

2. If equipped with a Traction Control System (TRAC), perform the following procedure:

a. Remove the air cleaner.

b. Connect a vinyl tube from a container to the bleeder plug of the TRAC actuator, then loosen the bleeder plug with the ignition in the **OFF** position.

c. Tighten the plug when the fluid stops flowing out.

NOTE: The fluid is under high pressure and could spray out with great force, use caution.

3. Remove the fluid from the reservoir, using a suitable syringe.

4. If equipped with a TRAC, disconnect the hydraulic lines, mounting bolts and connector. Remove the TRAC pump assembly.

5. Disconnect the brake lines from the master cylinder.

6. Remove the mounting nuts and 2-way union. Remove the master cylinder and gasket from the brake booster.

To install:

7. Adjust the length of the booster pushrod before installation.

8. Install the master cylinder and replace the 2-way union. Tighten the mounting nuts to 9 ft. lbs. (13 Nm).

9. Connect the brake lines to the master cylinder and the 2-way union. Tighten the nuts to 11 ft. lbs. (15 Nm).

10. Install the TRAC pump assembly, if equipped.

11. Bleed the brake system and the TRAC system, if equipped.

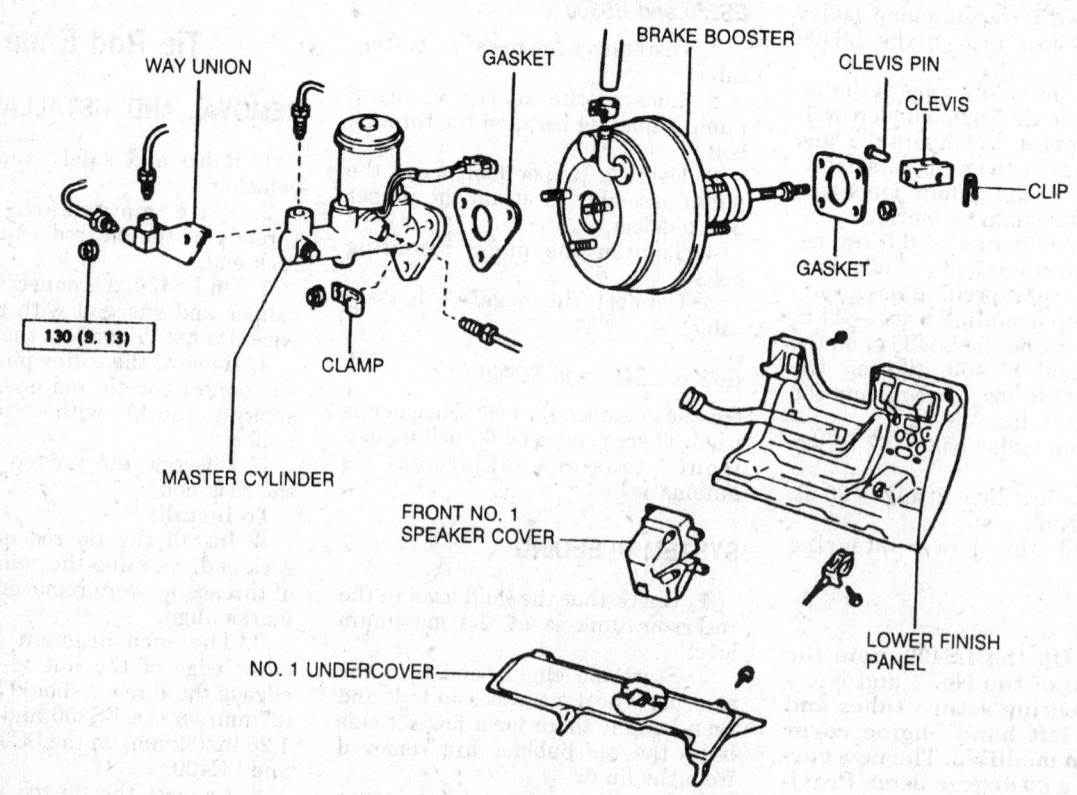

WAY UNION
GASKET
BRAKE BOOSTER
CLEVIS PIN
CLEVIS
CLIP
GASKET
130 (9, 13)
CLAMP
MASTER CYLINDER
FRONT NO. 1 SPEAKER COVER
LOWER FINISH PANEL
NO. 1 UNDERCOVER

Brake master cylinder and booster — ES250 and ES300

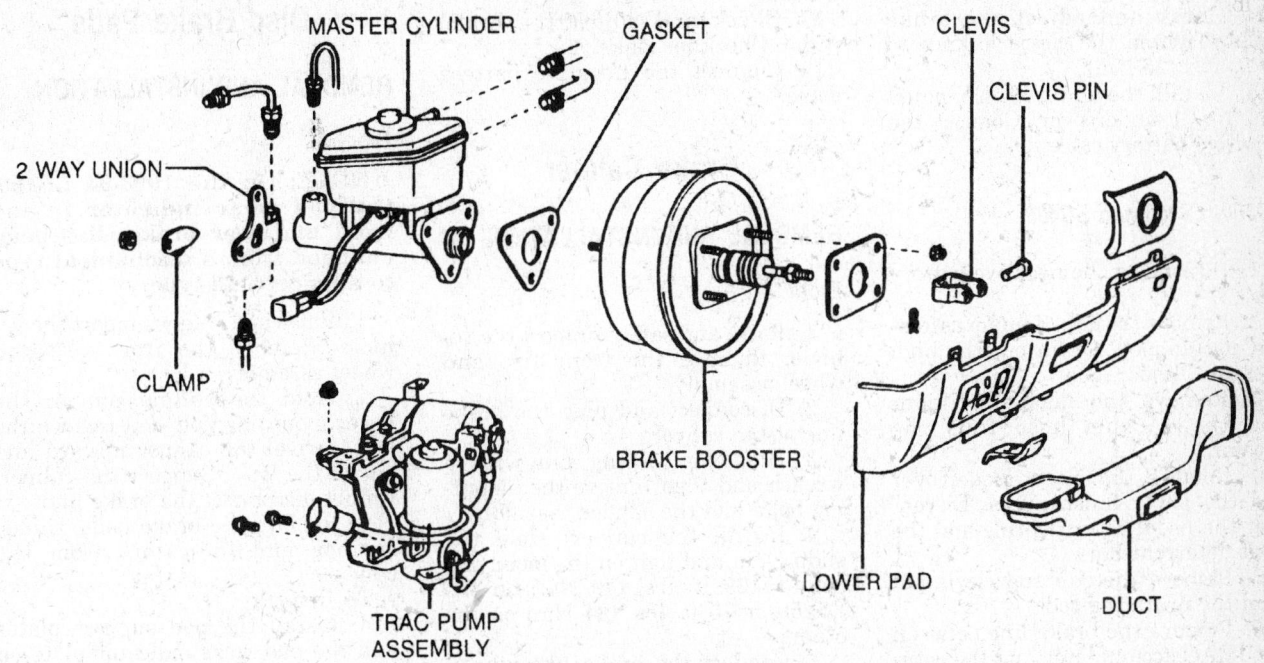

MASTER CYLINDER · GASKET · CLEVIS · CLEVIS PIN · 2 WAY UNION · CLAMP · BRAKE BOOSTER · TRAC PUMP ASSEMBLY · LOWER PAD · DUCT

Brake master cylinder and booster — SC300, LS400 and SC400

12. Check for leaks. Check and adjust the brake pedal, if needed.

Proportioning Valve

REMOVAL AND INSTALLATION

1. Disconnect the brake line from the valve union. Use caution if under pressure.
2. On the ES300, Remove the locknut on the adjusting bolt and then disconnect the bolt from the rear suspension arm.
3. Remove the valve mounting bolts and remove the valve assembly.
4. Install the valve and tighten the 2 bolts to 29 ft. lbs. (39 Nm).
5. On the ES300, install the adjusting bolt to the arm. Set the exposed shaft length to 1.08 in. (27.5mm).
6. Connect the hydraulic line and tighten the union bolt to 11 ft. lbs. (15 Nm).
7. Bleed the brake system. Check for leaks.

Power Brake Booster

— **CAUTION** —

On models with an air bag, wait at least 90 seconds from the time that the ignition switch is turned to the LOCK position and the battery is disconnected before performing any further work.

REMOVAL AND INSTALLATION

ES250 and ES300

1. Disconnect the negative battery cable. Remove the master cylinder and the vacuum hose.
2. Remove the charcoal canister. On the ES250, remove the No. 1 undercover and the lower finish panel. Disconnect the pedal return spring and the theft deterrent horn.
3. Remove the clip and clevis pin from the operating rod.
4. Remove the pedal bracket mounting bolt, the steering support nuts and the break-away bracket nuts. Lower the steering column.
5. Remove the mounting nuts and pull out the booster and gasket.

To install:
6. Adjust the length of the pushrod by:
   a. Install the gasket on the master cylinder. Place the proper tool on the gasket and lower the pin of the tool until it's tip slightly touches the pin.
   b. Turn the tool upside down and set it on the booster.
   c. Measure the distance pushrod, the clearance is 0 in. (0mm). Adjust the booster pushrod length until the pushrod slightly touches the pin head.
7. Install the booster and gasket. Replace the clevis pin to the operating rod.
8. Install and tighten the mounting nuts to 9 ft. lbs. (13 Nm).
9. Insert the clevis pin to the clevis and brake pedal. Install the clip to the clevis pin.
10. On the ES250, lift up the steering column and install the steering support nuts and break-away nuts. Tighten to 19 ft. lbs. (26 Nm).
11. Install the pedal bracket mounting bolt and tighten to 13 ft. lbs. (18 Nm). Replace the pedal return spring.
12. Install the master cylinder and connect the vacuum hose to the brake booster.

13. Fill the reservoir with brake fluid and bleed the brake system. Check for leaks.

14. Check and adjust the brake pedal. Tighten the clevis locknut to 19 ft. lbs. (26 Nm).

15. Install the lower finish panel and No. 1 undercover. Connect the negative battery cable.

SC300, LS400 and SC400

1. Disconnect the negative battery cable.

2. Remove the TRAC pump assembly, if equipped. Drain out the high pressure fluid.

3. Remove the master cylinder and the vacuum hose from the booster.

4. Remove the No. 1 undercover and the lower finish panel. Disconnect the pedal return spring and the theft deterrent horn.

5. Remove the clip and clevis pin from the operating rod.

6. Remove the brake line between the TRAC accumulator and the actuator from the clamp.

7. Remove the booster mounting nuts and lift out the booster.

To install:

8. Adjust the length of the pushrod by:

a. Install the gasket on the master cylinder. Place the proper tool on the gasket and lower the pin of the tool until it's tip slightly touches the pin.

b. Turn the tool upside down and set it on the booster.

c. Measure the distance pushrod, the clearance is 0 in. (0mm). Adjust the booster pushrod length until the pushrod slightly touches the pin head.

9. Install the brake booster and gasket. Replace the clevis on the operating rod.

10. Install and tighten the mounting nuts to 9 ft. lbs. (13 Nm) on the LS400 or 11 ft. lbs. (15 Nm) on the SC300 and SC400.

11. Insert the clevis pin into the clevis and brake pedal and install the clip on the clevis pin.

12. If equipped with a TRAC, install the brake tube between the TRAC accumulator and actuator to the No. 2 clamp.

13. Install the No. 1 undercover and lower finish panel.

14. Install the master cylinder and connect the vacuum hose to the booster.

15. Replace the TRAC pump, if equipped.

16. Fill the brake reservoir with brake fluid and bleed the brake system.

17. Check and adjust the brake pedal. Check for leaks.

18. Connect the negative battery cable.

Brake Caliper

REMOVAL AND INSTALLATION

Front

1. Raise and safely support the vehicle. Remove the front tire and wheel assembly.

2. Disconnect and plug the brake line at the caliper.

3. Hold the sliding pin with a wrench and then remove the mounting bolts and the caliper assembly.

4. Install the caliper. Hold the sliding pin and tighten the mounting bolts to 29 ft. lbs. (40 Nm) on the ES250 or 25 ft. lbs. (34 Nm) on the others.

5. Connect the brake line with 2 new gaskets and tighten the union to 21 ft. lbs. (27 Nm) on the ES250 and ES300 or 22 ft. lbs. (30 Nm) on the others.

NOTE: Insert the brake line securely into the lock hole in the caliper.

6. Bleed the brake system.

Rear

1. Raise and safely support the vehicle. Remove the rear tire and wheel assembly.

2. Disconnect and plug the brake line at the caliper.

3. Remove the mounting bolts and the caliper assembly. On the ES250 and ES300, remove the main pin.

4. Install the main pin and tighten it to 19 ft. lbs. (27 Nm).

5. Install the caliper. Hold the sliding pin and tighten the mounting bolts to 14 ft. lbs. (20 Nm) on the ES300 or 24 ft. lbs. (34 Nm) on the others.

6. Connect the brake line with 2 new gaskets and tighten the union to 14 ft. lbs. (29 Nm) on the ES250 and ES300, 22 ft. lbs. (30 Nm) on the SC300 and SC400 or 17 ft. lbs. (23 Nm) on the LS400. On the LS400, connect the brake line to the brake hose and tighten it to 11 ft. lbs. (15 Nm).

NOTE: Insert the brake line securely into the lock hole in the caliper.

7. Bleed the brake system.

Disc Brake Pads

REMOVAL AND INSTALLATION

Front

NOTE: On the 1993-94 LS400, the pad wear indicator in the front and rear brakes has been changed from a mechanical type to an electrical type.

1. Raise and safely support the vehicle. Remove the front tire and wheel assembly.

2. Hold the sliding pin on the lower mounting bolt and remove the bolt. Swivel the caliper upward and out of the way. Support the caliper. Do not disconnect the brake line.

3. Remove the brake pads, shims, springs and indicators from the caliper.

To install:

4. Install the pad support plates and the pad wear indicator plate on the inside pad.

5. Apply disc brake grease to both sides of the anti-squeal shims to each pad.

6. On the ES250, install the inside pad with the wear indicator facing upward. Install the outside pad. On all others, install both pads with the wear indicator plates facing upward on ES300 or downward on SC300, LS400 and SC400.

7. Install the anti-squeal springs. Press in the caliper piston(s) with large pliers or a C-clamp and install the caliper over the pads. Hold the sliding pin and tighten the mounting bolts to 29 ft. lbs. (40 Nm) on the ES250 or 25 ft. lbs. (34 Nm) on the others.

8. Install the front tire and wheel assembly. Lower the vehicle.

Rear

NOTE: On the 1993-94 LS400, the pad wear indicator in the front and rear brakes has been changed from a mechanical type to an electrical type.

1. Raise and safely support the vehicle. Remove the rear tire and wheel assembly.

2. Hold the sliding pin on the lower mounting bolt and remove the bolt. Swivel the caliper upward and out of the way. Support the caliper. Do not disconnect the brake line.

3. Remove the brake pads, shims, springs and indicators from the caliper.

To install:

4. Install the pad support plates and the pad wear indicator plate on the inside pad.

5. Apply disc brake grease to both sides of the anti-squeal shims to each pad.

6. On the ES250, install the inside pad with the wear indicator facing upward. Install the outside pad. On all others, install both pads with the wear indicator plates facing upward on the ES300 or downward on the SC300, LS400 and SC400.

7. Install the anti-squeal springs. Press in the caliper piston(s) with large pliers or a C-clamp and install the caliper over the pads. Hold the sliding pin and tighten the mounting bolts to 14 ft. lbs. (20 Nm) on the ES300 or 24 ft. lbs. (34 Nm) on all others.

8. Install the rear tire and wheel assembly. Lower the vehicle.

Brake Rotor

REMOVAL AND INSTALLATION

Front

1. Raise and safely support the vehicle. Remove the front tire and wheel assembly.

2. Remove the mounting bolts and lift off the caliper assembly. Support the caliper. Do not disconnect the brake line.

3. Remove the torque plate from the steering knuckle.

4. Remove the hub bolts and pull the brake rotor.

5. The installation is the reverse of the removal procedure. Tighten the torque plate bolts to 79 ft. lbs. (107 Nm) on the ES250 and ES300 or 87 ft. lbs. (118 Nm) on the others. Hold the sliding pin and tighten the caliper mounting bolts to 29 ft. lbs. (40 Nm) on the ES250 or 25 ft. lbs. (34 Nm) on the others.

Rear

1. Raise and safely support the vehicle. Remove the rear and wheel assembly.

2. Remove the 2 retaining bolts from the rear disc brake caliper. Suspend the caliper with a suitable piece of wire so as not to stretch the brake hose.

3. Place matchmarks on the rotor disc and the rear axle shaft. Remove the 2 rotor retaining screws from the rotor and remove the rotor.

NOTE: If the rotor disc cannot be removed easily, return the shoe adjuster until the wheel turns freely.

4. The installation is the reverse of the removal procedure. Tighten the torque plate bolts to 34 ft. lbs. (47 Nm) on the ES250 and ES300 or 77 ft. lbs. (104 Nm) on the others. Hold the sliding pin and tighten the caliper mounting bolts to 14 ft. lbs. (20 Nm) on the ES300 or 24 ft. lbs. (34 Nm) on the others.

Brake System Bleeding

1. Fill the reservoir to the maximum level with brake fluid.

2. To bleed the master cylinder:

   a. Disconnect the brake lines from the master cylinder.

   b. Depress the brake pedal and hold it.

   c. Block off the outer holes with fingers and release the brake pedal. Repeat 2-3 times.

3. To bleed the wheels:

   a. Start bleeding the brakes from the farthest point.

   b. Connect a vinyl tube to the brake cylinder bleeder plug and insert the other end of the tube in a ½ full container of brake fluid.

   c. Press on the brake pedal and loosen the bleeder plug until brake fluid comes out.

   d. Repeat until there is no more air bubbles in the fluid. Tighten the bleeder screw.

   e. Repeat the procedure for each wheel.

4. To bleed TRAC Control System:

   a. Remove the air cleaner, then temporarily reinstall it so the engine can be started.

   b. Connect a vinyl tube to the bleeder plug of the TRAC actuator, then loosen the bleeder plug.

   c. Start the engine, then operate the TRAC pump motor until all the air has been bled out of the fluid.

   d. Tighten the bleeder screw and stop the engine. Install the air cleaner.

Anti-Lock Brake System Service

The ABS system controls the hydraulic pressure of all 4 wheels during sudden braking and braking on slippery road surfaces, preventing the wheels from locking.

ABS Actuator

REMOVAL AND INSTALLATION

ES250 and ES300

1. Disconnect the negative battery cable. Remove brake fluid using a proper syringe.

2. Remove the actuator cover and disconnect the connectors from the actuator.

3. Remove the cover bracket and stud bolt.

4. Disconnect the brake tubes from the actuator, mounting nuts, wave washers and washers.

5. Remove the actuator from the actuator bracket.

To install:

6. Install the actuator to the actuator bracket. Replace the washers, wave washers and tighten the mounting nuts to 48 inch lbs. (5 Nm).

7. Connect the brake tubes to the actuator with the proper tool and tighten to 11 ft. lbs. (15 Nm).

8. Connect the connectors to the actuator. Install the stud and bracket.

9. Install the actuator cover.

10. Fill the brake reservoir to the proper level and bleed the brake system.

11. Connect the negative battery cable. Check for leaks.

SC300, LS400 and SC400

1. Disconnect the negative battery cable. Remove brake fluid using a proper syringe.

2. Disconnect the dust cover, air cleaner and the air duct.

3. Disconnect the brake line from the ABS, actuator with the proper tool. Disconnect the brake lines from the TRAC actuator, if equipped.

4. Remove the mounting bolts from the ABS actuator or TRAC actuator, if equipped.

5. Disconnect the connectors and remove the actuator.

To install:

6. Install the ABS actuator or TRAC actuator, if equipped. Tighten the mounting bolts to 9 ft. lbs. (12 Nm). Connect the actuator connectors.

7. Using the proper tool, connect the brake lines to the actuator and tighten to 11 ft. lbs. (15 Nm).

8. Connect the dust cover, air cleaner and the air duct.

9. Bleed the brake system and connect the negative battery cable.

10. Check for leaks.

Front Speed Sensor

REMOVAL AND INSTALLATION

ES250 and ES300

1. Disconnect the negative battery cable.
2. Raise and safely support the vehicle. Remove the tire and wheel assembly.
3. Disconnect the speed sensor connector.
4. Remove the front hub and steering knuckle assembly.
5. Remove the nut and the speed sensor rotor. Do not scratch the serrations of the speed sensor rotor.
6. The installation is the reverse of the removal procedure.

SC300, LS400 and SC400

1. Disconnect the negative battery cable.
2. Raise and safely support the vehicle. Remove the tire and wheel assembly.
3. Disconnect the speed sensor connector.
4. Remove the front axle hub from the steering knuckle. Remove the sensor control rotor from the axle hub with the proper tool.
5. The installation is the reverse of the removal procedure.

Rear Speed Sensor

REMOVAL AND INSTALLATION

ES250 and ES300

1. Disconnect the negative battery.
2. Remove the rear seat cushion and rear side seat back cushion.
3. Disconnect the sensor connector and pull out the sensor wire harness. Remove the 2 clamp bolts holding the sensor wire harness to the body and suspension arm.
4. Remove the axle carrier mounting bolt and nut of the upper side. Remove the 2 bolts and remove the disc brake caliper assembly. Be sure to suspend the disc brake caliper with a piece of safety wire.
5. Remove the rotor disc.
6. Remove the 4 axle hub mounting bolts. Remove the rear axle hub. Remove the backing plate with the parking brake assembly and O-ring.
7. Remove the speed sensor bolts and remove the speed sensor from the backing plate.

8. Installation is the reverse order of the removal procedure. Torque the following to:
   Speed sensor retaining bolts — 69 inch lbs. (7 Nm)
   Rear hub retaining bolts — 59 ft. lbs. (80 Nm)
   Brake caliper retaining bolts — 34 ft. lbs. (47 Nm)
   Upper axle carrier mounting bolt and nut — 166 ft. lbs. (226 Nm)

SC300, LS400 and SC400

1. Disconnect the negative battery cable.
2. Raise and safely support the vehicle. Remove the tire and wheel assembly.
3. Disconnect the speed sensor connector.
4. Remove the rear axle hub and backing plate.
5. Remove the mounting bolts and the speed sensor from the backing plate.
6. The installation is the reverse of the removal procedure.

CHASSIS ELECTRICAL

Air Bag

DISARMING

If equipped with an air bag, the negative battery cable must be disconnected, before working on the system. Failure to do so may result in deployment of the air bag and possible personal injury. Work must be started after approximately 90 seconds or longer from the time the ignition switch is turned to the **LOCK** position and the negative battery cable is disconnected from. If equipped with an air bag, the negative battery cable must be disconnected, before working on the system.

Heater Blower Motor

REMOVAL AND INSTALLATION

─────── CAUTION ───────
On models with an air bag, wait at least 90 seconds from the time that the ignition switch is turned

to the LOCK position and the battery is disconnected before performing any further work.

ES250

1. Disconnect the negative battery cable.
2. Disconnect the electrical connection at the blower motor.
3. Remove the mounting bolts and the blower motor.
4. The installation is the reverse of the removal procedure.

ES300

1. Disconnect the negative battery cable.
2. Remove the lower instrument panel and the No. 2 undercover.
3. Loosen the 2 screws and remove the connector bracket.
4. Disconnect the electrical lead, remove the 3 screws and let down the blower motor.
5. Install the motor and connect the electrical lead.
6. Install the connector bracket and replace the undercover. Install the lower instrument panel.

LS400

1. Disconnect the negative battery cable. Remove the right side instrument panel cover.
2. Remove the lower instrument panel and the No. 2 undercover.
3. Loosen the 2 screws and remove the connector bracket.
4. Remove the front passenger's door scuff plate. Pull back cowl side portion of the floor carpet.
5. Remove the blower lower case. Disconnect the electrical lead, remove the 3 screws and remove the blower motor.
6. Installation is the reverse of the removal procedure. Install the blower lower case control lever on the shaft by turning it counterclockwise.

SC300 and SC400

1. Disconnect the negative battery cable.
2. Remove the glove box.
3. Lift up the front edge of the carpet on the passenger side, remove the 2 screws and lift off the ECU cover.
4. Remove the connector bracket.
5. Disconnect the electrical connector at the blower motor, remove the 3 screws and lift out the motor.
6. Install the motor and reconnect the electrical lead.
7. Install the connector bracket, the ECU cover and the glove box.

Windshield Wiper Motor

REMOVAL AND INSTALLATION

—— CAUTION ——

On models with an air bag, wait at least 90 seconds from the time that the ignition switch is turned to the LOCK position and the battery is disconnected before performing any further work.

ES250

1. Disconnect the negative battery cable. Remove the wiper arm and blade assembly.
2. Disconnect the electrical connections at the wiper motor.
3. Remove the mounting bolts and disconnect the wiper arm.
4. Remove the wiper motor.
5. The installation is the reverse of the removal procedure.

ES300

1. Disconnect the negative battery cable.
2. Unscrew the nuts and remove the wiper blades and arms.
3. Using a clip remover tool, remove the eleven cowl louver retaining clips and the weather stripping. Remove the 2 remaining clips and pull the cowl out and forward.
4. Remove the 6 wiper link retaining bolts, disconnect the wiper motor electrical lead and then remove the 4 motor mounting bolts.
5. Connect the claw on the link to the panel, disconnect the motor from the link and remove it. Remove the link through the service hole.

To install:

6. Slide the link through the service hole and install the bolts.
7. Slide on the wire protector, hook the link claw on the panel and reconnect the motor. Install the bolts.

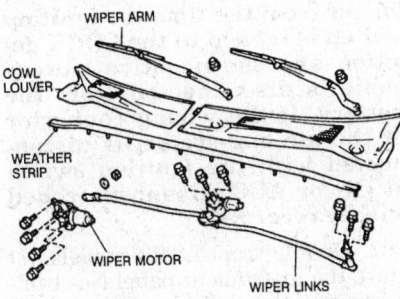

Wiper motor location — ES300

8. Position the cowl with the 2 clips, install the weatherstripping and install the remaining clips.
9. Install the wiper arm and blade assembly and tighten the retaining nuts to 18 ft. lbs. (25 Nm).

LS400

1. Disconnect the negative battery cable. Remove the wiper arm and blade assembly.
2. Remove the hood-to-cowl seal and remove the cowl louver.

NOTE: Raise the front side of the cowl louver up to remove the louver.

3. Remove the mounting bolts and disconnect the electrical connection.
4. Raise the front side of the wiper motor and link assembly up. Remove the wiper motor and link assembly.
5. Remove the wiper motor cover.
6. The installation is the reverse of the removal procedure. Tighten the mounting bolts to 48 inch lbs. (5.4 Nm).

NOTE: With the front side of the louver raised, install the protector on the glass, then push the louver down.

SC300 and SC400

1. Disconnect the negative battery cable.
2. Unscrew the nuts and remove the wiper blades and arms.
3. Remove the hood-to-cowl seal. Using a clip remover tool, remove the cowl louver retaining clips. Pull the cowl out and forward.
4. Remove the 5 wiper link retaining bolts and disconnect the wiper motor electrical lead.
5. Raise the front side of the link/motor assembly up and then remove the motor.

To install:

6. Slide the link/motor assembly into position and install the bolts. Tighten to 48 inch lbs. (5.4 Nm).
7. Position the cowl with the front side raised. Install the protector onto the glass and then push the cowl down into place.
8. Install the wiper arm and blade assembly and tighten the retaining nuts to 15 ft. lbs. (20 Nm).

Windshield Wiper Switch

—— CAUTION ——

On models with an air bag, wait at least 90 seconds from the time that the ignition switch is turned

to the LOCK position and the battery is disconnected before performing any further work.

REMOVAL AND INSTALLATION

1. Disconnect the negative battery cable.
2. Remove the combination switch assembly.
3. Remove the mounting screws and separate the wiper switch bracket from the combination switch body.
4. Remove the mounting screws and the switch from the switch body.
5. Remove the boot.
6. The installation is the reverse of the removal procedure.

Instrument Cluster

NOTE: Work must be started after approximately 90 seconds or longer from the time the ignition switch is turned to the LOCK position and the negative battery cable is disconnected.

REMOVAL AND INSTALLATION

ES250

1. Disconnect the negative battery cable.
2. Remove the steering wheel.
3. Pry out the clips and pull the front pillar molding upward and remove.
4. Remove the left lower dash panel. Disconnect the hood release lever and remove the panel cover.
5. Pry out the switch bases and the speaker panel with the proper tool. Remove the mounting screws and lower the lower column panel.
6. Remove the mounting screws and the cluster panel. Disconnect the electrical connections.
7. Remove the steering column cover.
8. Disconnect the mounting screws, the speedometer cable and the electrical connections. Remove the instrument cluster and the speedometer.
9. The installation is the reverse of the removal procedure.

ES300

1. Disconnect the negative battery cable.
2. Remove the steering wheel.
3. Remove the 2 mounting screws and pry out the cluster finish panel slightly. Disconnect any connectors and remove the panel.

4. Remove the 4 mounting screws, pull out the cluster slightly and disconnect any electrical leads. Remove the cluster.

To install:

5. Position the cluster in place and connect the electrical leads. Move the cluster all the way in and install the mounting screws.

6. Install the cluster finish panel. Install the steering wheel.

LS400

1. Disconnect the negative battery cable.

NOTE: Work must be started after approximately 90 seconds or longer from the time the ignition switch is turned to the LOCK position and the negative battery cable is disconnected.

2. Remove the steering wheel. Remove the left and right front pillar moldings.

3. Remove the steering column cover and the upper console panel, with the proper tool, to prevent damaging the cover.

4. Remove the front ash receptacle and disconnect the electrical connection.

5. Pry out the front side of the lower console cover and remove by sliding the cover forward.

6. Remove the mounting screws and pry out the lower console box. Remove the cup holder.

7. Pry out the rear end panel and disconnect the wire connector. Remove the console box.

8. Remove the left lower trim panel. Remove the hood release lever and disconnect the cable from the lever.

9. Remove the mounting bolts and the left trim pad. Disconnect the wire connections and hose from the pad.

10. Remove the key cylinder pad and disconnect the park brake lever. Remove the outer mirror switch assembly and disconnect the electrical connection.

11. Remove the mounting screws and carefully pry out the instrument cluster. Remove the speedometer from the cluster.

To install:

12. Install the instrument cluster and mounting screws.

13. Install the key cylinder pad and connect the park brake lever. Install the outer mirror switch assembly and connect the electrical connection.

14. Install the mounting bolts and the left trim pad.

15. Install the left lower trim panel and hood release lever.

16. Install the rear end panel and connect the wire connector. Install the console box.

17. Install the cup holder.

18. Install the front ash receptacle and connect the electrical connection.

19. Install the steering column cover and the upper console panel.

20. Install the steering wheel.

21. Connect the negative battery cable.

NOTE: A rattle or squeak noise from the glovebox door area may be apparent when the glovebox door is closes and/or the vehicle is driven over rough roads. This condition may be caused by the movement of the glovebox door check arm against the glovebox door and/or the check arm through hole in the dash.

SC300 and SC400

1. Disconnect the negative battery cable.

2. Lower the steering wheel to its lowest position and pull it out as far as it will go.

3. Remove the mounting screws and pry out the cluster finish panel slightly. Disconnect any connectors and remove the panel.

4. Remove the 4 mounting screws, pull out the cluster slightly and disconnect the 3 electrical leads. Remove the cluster.

To install:

5. Position the cluster in place and connect the electrical leads. Move the cluster all the way in and install the mounting screws.

6. Install the cluster finish panel.

Speedometer

The speedometer is an integral part of the instrument cluster on all models except the LS400 models. REMOVAL AND INSTALLATION as a separate unit is not possible.

REMOVAL AND INSTALLATION

LS400

1. Remove the combination meter from the vehicle and disassemble the meter.

2. Remove the retaining screws and remove the speedometer from the meter lens.

3. Keep the indicator needle horizontal.

4. Remove the indicator needle without it striking the lens.

5. To install, reverse the removal procedures.

Headlight Switch

REMOVAL AND INSTALLATION

1. Disconnect the negative battery cable.

2. Remove the combination switch assembly.

3. Remove the mounting screws and separate the headlight switch bracket from the combination switch body.

4. Remove the mounting screws and the switch from the switch body.

5. Remove the boot.

6. The installation is the reverse of the removal procedure.

Dimmer Switch

REMOVAL AND INSTALLATION

1. Disconnect the negative battery cable.

2. Remove the combination switch assembly.

3. Remove the mounting screws and separate the dimmer switch bracket from the combination switch body.

4. Remove the mounting screws and the switch from the switch body.

5. Remove the boot.

6. The installation is the reverse of the removal procedure.

Combination Switch

The combination switch incorporates the headlight switch, turn signal switch, dimmer switch and the windshield wiper switch.

REMOVAL AND INSTALLATION

1. Disconnect the negative battery cable.

NOTE: Position the front wheels in a straight-ahead position. Work must be started after approximately 90 seconds or longer from the time the ignition switch is turned to the LOCK position and the negative battery cable is disconnected from the battery. If the wiring connector of the air bag system is disconnected with the ignition switch at ON or ACC, diagnostic coded will be recorded.

2. On all except LS400 models, remove the instrument panel No. 1 undercover sub-assembly. Remove the instrument panel lower finish panel and cluster finish panel.

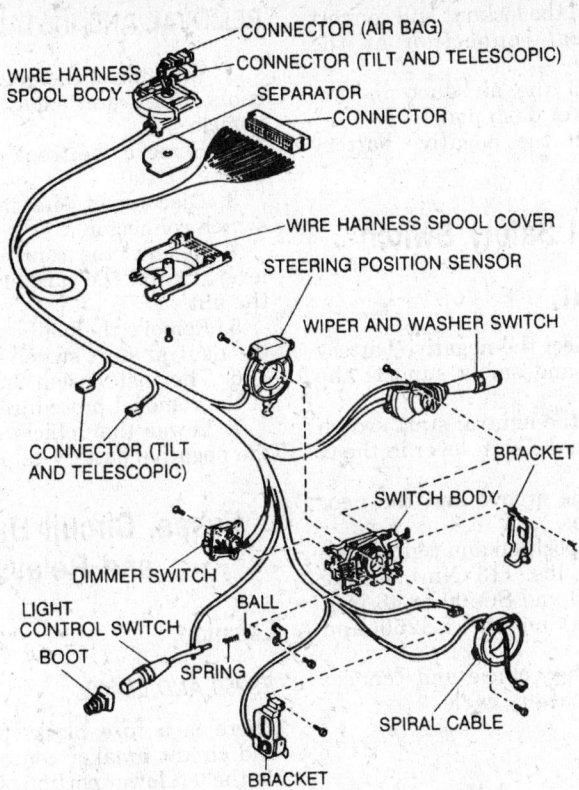

WIRE HARNESS SPOOL BODY — CONNECTOR (AIR BAG)
CONNECTOR (TILT AND TELESCOPIC)
SEPARATOR
CONNECTOR
WIRE HARNESS SPOOL COVER
STEERING POSITION SENSOR
WIPER AND WASHER SWITCH
CONNECTOR (TILT AND TELESCOPIC)
BRACKET
SWITCH BODY
DIMMER SWITCH
LIGHT CONTROL SWITCH
BALL
BOOT
SPRING
SPIRAL CABLE
BRACKET

Exploded view of the combination switch — LS400

3. On the LS400 models, remove the undercover, lower pad, key cylinder pad. The No. 3 finish panel mounting bracket. The No. 2 heater to register duct.

4. Remove the steering wheel center pad.

NOTE: When removing the wheel pad, take care not to pull the air bag harness connector. When storing the wheel pad, keep the upper surface of the pad facing upward. Since the air bag connector has a 2-stage lock, remove the 1st stage lock and disconnect the connector.

5. Remove the steering wheel assembly.

6. Remove the steering column cover. Remove the 4 combination switch retaining screws. Disconnect the connectors and remove the combination switch assembly from the steering column.

NOTE: Since the air bag connector has a 2 stage lock, remove the 1st stage lock and then disconnect the connector.

7. To remove the headlight switch:
   a. Remove the mounting screws and separate the bracket from the switch body.

b. Remove the screws and the ball set plate from the switch body.
   c. Remove the ball and slide out the switch from the switch body with the spring.
   d. Remove the boot.

8. Loosen the mounting screws and remove the dimmer switch and the turn signal switch from the switch body.

9. Separate the bracket from the wiper switch body. Remove the wiper switch from the switch body.

To install:
10. Install the wiper switch to the switch body and connect the mounting bracket.

11. Install the dimmer and turn signal switch to the switch body and tighten the mounting screws.

12. To install the headlight switch:
   a. Slide the switch and install the switch body.
   b. Set the lever in the HIGH position. Install the ball and plate.

13. Install the combination switch assembly to the steering column and tighten the mounting screws.

14. Connect the electrical connectors. Push in the terminals until they

are securely locked in the connector lug.

NOTE: The spiral cable matchmarks must be aligned for correct installation with the front wheels in the straight head position.

15. Replace both steering column covers. Install the steering wheel, using the proper tool.

16. Connect the air bag connector and replace the 1st stage lock.

17. Replace the cluster finish panel. Install the steering wheel center pad and connect the wire connector.

18. Replace the key cylinder trim pad assembly and heater duct register, if necessary.

19. Install the lower instrument trim panel and cover assembly.

20. Connect the negative battery cable.

Ignition Lock/Switch

REMOVAL AND INSTALLATION

1. Disconnect the negative battery cable.

2. Remove the lower trim panel and pad assembly, if necessary.

3. Remove the key cylinder trim panel and pad assembly. Disconnect the key cylinder lamp assembly, if equipped.

4. Remove the trim panel mounting bracket and the heater duct register, if necessary.

5. Remove the mounting screws and disconnect the electrical connections. Remove the ignition switch.

6. The installation is the reverse of the removal procedure.

Stoplight Switch

ADJUSTMENT

1. Disconnect the negative battery cable.

2. Remove the instrument panel undercover, the lower trim panel and air duct, if necessary.

3. Disconnect the connector from the stoplight switch.

4. Loosen the stoplight switch locknut, the switch and the pushrod locknut.

5. Adjust the pedal height by turning the pushrod. Return the stoplight switch until it contacts the pedal stopper and then retract it 1 complete turn.

6. Check that the clearance between the bottom of the switch

threads and the top of the pedal stop pad is 0.02-0.09 in. (0.5-2.4mm) all models except LS400. On the LS400, it should be 0.06-0.10 in. (1.5-2.6mm).

7. Tighten the stoplight switch locknut, the switch and the pushrod locknut. Connect the electrical connection at the switch.

8. Connect the negative battery cable.

9. Check that the stoplights come ON when the brake pedal is depressed and OFF when the pedal is released.

REMOVAL AND INSTALLATION

1. Disconnect the negative battery cable.

2. Remove the instrument panel undercover, the lower trim panel and air duct, if necessary.

3. Disconnect the connector from the stoplight switch. Loosen the pushrod locknut.

4. Remove the stoplight switch locknut and the stoplight switch.

To install:

5. Install the stoplight switch and replace the locknut, do not tighten.

6. Adjust the pedal height by turning the pushrod. Return the stoplight switch until it contacts the pedal stopper.

7. Tighten the stoplight switch locknut, the switch and the pushrod locknut. Connect the electrical connection at the switch.

8. Connect the negative battery cable.

9. Check that the stoplights come ON when the brake pedal is depressed and OFF when the pedal is released.

Clutch Switch

ADJUSTMENT

ES250, ES300 and SC300

1. Disconnect the negative battery cable.

2. Remove the lower dash trim panel and disconnect the air duct.

3. Loosen the locknut and disconnect the connection at the clutch switch. Turn the clutch switch until the pedal height is 7.52-7.91 in. (191-201mm) for the ES250, 6.48-6.88 in. (165-175mm) for the ES300 or 5.92-6.31 in. (150-160mm) for the SC300 from the asphalt sheet (under the carpet) to the top of the pedal pad.

4. Tighten the locknut and connect the electrical connection at the switch.

5. Connect the air duct and replace the lower dash panel.

6. Connect the negative battery cable.

Neutral Safety Switch

ADJUSTMENT

1. Disconnect the negative battery cable. Raise and safely support the vehicle.

2. Loosen the neutral start switch bolt and place the shift lever in the **N** position.

3. Align the groove and the neutral basic line.

4. Hold in position and tighten the bolt to 9 ft. lbs. (13 Nm) on the LS400, SC300 and SC400 or 48 inch lbs. (5.4 Nm) on the ES250 and ES300.

5. Lower the vehicle and connect the negative battery cable.

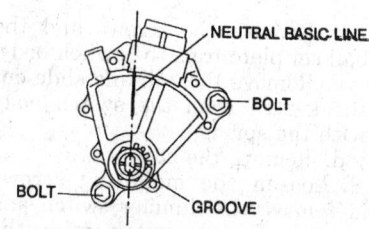

Neutral safety switch adjustment — ES250 and ES300

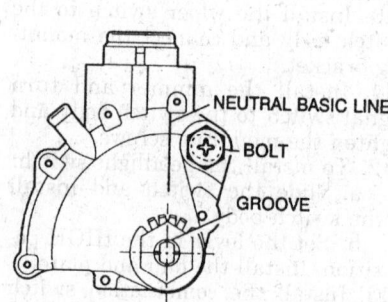

Neutral safety switch adjustment — SC300, SC400 and LS400

REMOVAL AND INSTALLATION

1. Disconnect the negative battery cable. Raise and safely support the vehicle.

2. Remove the front exhaust pipe on the LS400.

3. Disconnect the neutral start switch connector.

4. Remove the control shaft shift lever. Pry off the washer and remove the nut.

5. Remove the bolt(s) and pull out the neutral start switch.

6. The installation is the reverse of the removal procedure.

7. Lower the vehicle and connect the negative battery cable.

Fuses, Circuit Breakers and Relays

Location

ES250 AND LS400

There is a fuse block, relay center and circuit breaker center is located on the left lower portion of the instrument panel. There is a fuse block and relay center located in the engine compartment on the driver's side.

ES300

The main (No. 1) fuse/relay block is located under the lower left side of the instrument panel. There are relay blocks (Nos. 1 and 4) located on both the left and right kick panels, and there is a relay block (No. 6) found under and behind the glovebox.

In the engine compartment, there are 2 relay blocks (No. 5 and No. 7 for Canadian vehicles) and another fuse block; all found in the proximity of the battery.

SC300 AND SC400

The main fuse/relay block is located on the left side kick panel, under the instrument cluster. There are also 2 additional relay blocks in the engine compartment, along the left side.

Flashers

Location

The turn signal/hazard flasher is located on the left lower section of the instrument panel with the main fuse/relay block on all models, except on the ES300 which is located in a relay block behind the glovebox.

SERIAL NUMBER IDENTIFICATION

Vehicle Identification Plate

The Vehicle Identification Number (VIN) is stamped on a metal plate that is attached to the driver's side of the instrument panel and is visible through the lower left corner of the windshield.

Engine Number

The engine number is located on a plate attached to the engine or stamped into a machined pad on the engine block. The engine number consists of an identification number followed by a 6-digit production number.

On the 1.6L engine, the engine number is located on the right rear of the engine block, next to the cylinder head and just forward of the transmission. On the 1.8L 4-cylinder and 2.0L engines, the engine number is located on the left rear of the engine block, just forward of the transmission. On the 2.2L and 1990-91 3.0L engines, the engine number is located on the left side of the engine block, just forward of the exhaust manifold. The engine number on the 1992-94 3.0L engine is located on the top rear of the engine block, just forward of the transmission. On the 1.8L and 2.5L 6-cylinder engines, the engine number is located on the lower right side of the engine block, toward the front of the engine. The engine number on the 1.3L rotary engine is located on the left side, toward the front of the engine.

Vehicle Identification Label

The chassis number is located in the engine compartment on the right side of the firewall. Other important vehicle information and specifications can be found on the vehicle emission information label, located on the underside of the hood and on the motor vehicle safety certification label, located on the drivers door jamb.

Transmission/Transaxle Number

The transmission/transaxle model and serial number are either stamped on a plate that is bolted to the transmission case or stamped directly on the case. The location varies from vehicle-to-vehicle.

SPECIFICATIONS

ENGINE IDENTIFICATION

Year	Model	Engine Displacement Liters (cc)	Engine Series (ID/VIN)	Fuel System	No. of Cylinders	Engine Type
1990	323	1.6 (1597)	B6E	EFI	4	SOHC
	Protege	1.8 (1839)	BPE	EFI	4	SOHC
	Protege LX	1.8 (1839)	BPD	EFI	4	DOHC
	Miata	1.6 (1597)	B6ZE	EFI	4	DOHC
	626	2.2 (2184)	F2	EFI	4	SOHC
	626 GT	2.2 (2184)	F2	EFI	4	SOHC-Turbo
	MX6	2.2 (2184)	F2	EFI	4	SOHC
	MX6 GT	2.2 (2184)	F2	EFI	4	SOHC-Turbo
	RX7	1.3 (1308)	13B	EFI	—	Rotary
	RX7	1.3 (1308)	13B	EFI	—	Rotary-Turbo
	929	3.0 (2954)	JE	EFI	6	SOHC
	929S	3.0 (2954)	JE	EFI	6	DOHC
1991	323	1.6 (1597)	B6E	EFI	4	SOHC
	Protege	1.8 (1839)	BPE	EFI	4	SOHC
	Protege LX	1.8 (1839)	BPD	EFI	4	DOHC
	Miata	1.6 (1597)	B6ZE	EFI	4	DOHC
	626	2.2 (2184)	F2	EFI	4	SOHC
	626 GT	2.2 (2184)	F2	EFI	4	SOHC-Turbo
	MX6	2.2 (2184)	F2	EFI	4	SOHC
	MX6 GT	2.2 (2184)	F2	EFI	4	SOHC-Turbo
	RX7	1.3 (1308)	13B	EFI	—	Rotary
	RX7	1.3 (1308)	13B	EFI	—	Rotary-Turbo
	929	3.0 (2954)	JE	EFI	6	SOHC
	929S	3.0 (2954)	JE	EFI	6	DOHC
1992	323	1.6 (1597)	B6E	EFI	4	SOHC
	Protege	1.8 (1839)	BPE	EFI	4	SOHC
	Protege LX	1.8 (1839)	BPD	EFI	4	DOHC
	MX3	1.6 (1597)	B6E	EFI	4	SOHC
	MX3	1.8 (1844)	K8D	EFI	6	DOHC
	Miata	1.6 (1597)	B6ZE	EFI	4	DOHC
	626	2.2 (2184)	F2	EFI	4	SOHC
	626 GT	2.2 (2184)	F2	EFI	4	SOHC-Turbo
	MX6	2.2 (2184)	F2	EFI	4	SOHC
	MX6 GT	2.2 (2184)	F2	EFI	4	SOHC-Turbo
	929	3.0 (2954)	JE	EFI	6	DOHC

ENGINE IDENTIFICATION

Year	Model	Engine Displacement Liters (cc)	Engine Series (ID/VIN)	Fuel System	No. of Cylinders	Engine Type
1993	323	1.6 (1597)	B6E	EFI	4	SOHC
	Protege	1.8 (1839)	BPE	EFI	4	SOHC
	Protege LX	1.8 (1839)	BPD	EFI	4	DOHC
	MX3	1.6 (1597)	B6E	EFI	4	SOHC
	MX3	1.8 (1844)	K8D	EFI	6	DOHC
	Miata	1.6 (1597)	B6ZE	EFI	4	DOHC
	626	2.0 (1991)	FS	EFI	4	DOHC
	626 GT	2.5 (2496)	KL	EFI	4	DOHC
	MX6	2.0 (1991)	FS	EFI	4	DOHC
	MX6 LS	2.5 (2496)	KL	EFI	6	DOHC
	RX7	1.3 (1308)	13B	EFI	—	Rotary-Turbo
	929	3.0 (2954)	JE	EFI	6	DOHC
1994	323	1.6 (1597)	B6E	EFI	4	SOHC
	Protege	1.8 (1839)	BPE	EFI	4	SOHC
	Protege LX	1.8 (1839)	BPD	EFI	4	DOHC
	MX3	1.6 (1597)	B6E	EFI	4	SOHC
	MX3	1.8 (1844)	K8D	EFI	6	DOHC
	Miata	1.6 (1597)	B6ZE	EFI	4	DOHC
	626	2.0 (1991)	FS	EFI	4	DOHC
	626 GT	2.5 (2496)	KL	EFI	4	DOHC
	MX6	2.0 (1991)	FS	EFI	4	DOHC
	MX6 LS	2.5 (2496)	KL	EFI	6	DOHC
	RX7	1.3 (1308)	13B	EFI	—	Rotary-Turbo
	929	3.0 (2954)	JE	EFI	6	DOHC

EFI—Electronic Fuel Injection
DOHC—Double Overhead Cam
SOHC—Single Overhead Cam

GENERAL ENGINE SPECIFICATIONS

Year	Engine ID/VIN	Engine Displacement Liters (cc)	Fuel System Type	Net Horsepower @ rpm	Net Torque @ rpm (ft. lbs.)	Bore × Stroke (in.)	Compression Ratio	Oil Pressure @ rpm
1990	B6E	1.6 (1597)	EFI	82 @ 5000	92 @ 2500	3.07 × 3.29	9.3:1	43–57 @ 3000
	B6ZE	1.6 (1597)	EFI	116 @ 6500	100 @ 5500	3.07 × 3.29	9.4:1	43–57 @ 3000
	BPE	1.8 (1839)	EFI	103 @ 5500	111 @ 4000	3.27 × 3.35	8.9:1	43–57 @ 3000
	BPD	1.8 (1839)	EFI	125 @ 6500	114 @ 4500	3.27 × 3.35	9.0:1	43–57 @ 3000
	F2	2.2 (2184)	EFI	110 @ 4700	130 @ 3000	3.39 × 3.70	8.6:1	43–57 @ 3000
	F2	2.2 (2184)	EFI Turbo	145 @ 4300	190 @ 3500	3.39 × 3.70	7.8:1	43–57 @ 3000
	JE	3.0 (2954)	EFI	158 @ 5500	170 @ 4000	3.54 × 3.05	8.5:1	53–75 @ 3000
	JE	3.0 (2954)	EFI	190 @ 5600	191 @ 4500	3.54 × 3.05	8.9:1	46–71 @ 3000
1991	B6E	1.6 (1597)	EFI	82 @ 5000	92 @ 2500	3.07 × 3.29	9.3:1	43–57 @ 3000
	B6ZE	1.6 (1597)	EFI	①	②	3.07 × 3.29	③	43–57 @ 3000
	BPE	1.8 (1839)	EFI	103 @ 5500	111 @ 4000	3.27 × 3.35	8.9:1	43–57 @ 3000
	BPD	1.8 (1839)	EFI	125 @ 6500	114 @ 4500	3.27 × 3.35	9.0:1	43–57 @ 3000
	F2	2.2 (2184)	EFI	110 @ 4700	130 @ 3000	3.39 × 3.70	8.6:1	43–57 @ 3000
	F2	2.2 (2184)	EFI Turbo	145 @ 4300	190 @ 3500	3.39 × 3.70	7.8:1	43–57 @ 3000
	JE	3.0 (2954)	EFI	158 @ 5500	170 @ 4000	3.54 × 3.05	8.5:1	53–75 @ 3000
	JE	3.0 (2954)	EFI	190 @ 5600	191 @ 4500	3.54 × 3.05	8.9:1	46–71 @ 3000
1992	B6E	1.6 (1597)	EFI	④	⑤	3.07 × 3.29	⑥	43–57 @ 3000
	B6ZE	1.6 (1597)	EFI	①	②	3.07 × 3.29	③	43–57 @ 3000
	BPE	1.8 (1839)	EFI	103 @ 5500	111 @ 4000	3.27 × 3.35	8.9:1	43–57 @ 3000
	BPD	1.8 (1839)	EFI	125 @ 6500	114 @ 4500	3.27 × 3.35	9.0:1	43–57 @ 3000
	K8D	1.8 (1844)	EFI	130 @ 6500	115 @ 4500	2.95 × 2.74	9.2:1	48–71 @ 3000
	F2	2.2 (2184)	EFI	110 @ 4700	130 @ 3000	3.39 × 3.70	8.6:1	43–57 @ 3000
	F2	2.2 (2184)	EFI Turbo	145 @ 4300	190 @ 3500	3.39 × 3.70	7.8:1	46–71 @ 3000
	JE	3.0 (2954)	EFI	195 @ 5750	200 @ 3500	3.54 × 3.05	9.2:1	46–71 @ 3000
1993	B6E	1.6 (1597)	EFI	④	⑤	3.07 × 3.29	⑥	43–57 @ 3000
	B6ZE	1.6 (1597)	EFI	①	②	3.07 × 3.29	③	43–57 @ 3000
	BPE	1.8 (1839)	EFI	103 @ 5500	111 @ 4000	3.27 × 3.35	8.9:1	43–57 @ 3000
	BPD	1.8 (1839)	EFI	125 @ 6500	114 @ 4500	3.27 × 3.35	9.0:1	43–57 @ 3000
	K8D	1.8 (1844)	EFI	130 @ 6500	115 @ 4500	2.95 × 2.74	9.2:1	48–71 @ 3000
	FS	2.0 (1991)	EFI	118 @ 5500	127 @ 4500	3.27 × 3.62	9.0:1	57–71 @ 3000
	KL	2.5 (2496)	EFI	164 @ 5600	160 @ 4800	3.33 × 2.92	9.2:1	49–71 @ 3000
	JE	3.0 (2954)	EFI	195 @ 5750	200 @ 3500	3.54 × 3.05	9.2:1	46–71 @ 3000
1994	B6E	1.6 (1597)	EFI	④	⑤	3.07 × 3.29	⑥	43–57 @ 3000
	B6ZE	1.6 (1597)	EFI	①	②	3.07 × 3.29	③	43–57 @ 3000
	BPE	1.8 (1839)	EFI	103 @ 5500	111 @ 4000	3.27 × 3.35	8.9:1	43–57 @ 3000
	BPD	1.8 (1839)	EFI	125 @ 6500	114 @ 4500	3.27 × 3.35	9.0:1	43–57 @ 3000
	K8D	1.8 (1844)	EFI	130 @ 6500	115 @ 4500	2.95 × 2.74	9.2:1	48–71 @ 3000
	FS	2.0 (1991)	EFI	118 @ 5500	127 @ 4500	3.27 × 3.62	9.0:1	57–71 @ 3000
	KL	2.5 (2496)	EFI	164 @ 5600	160 @ 4800	3.33 × 2.92	9.2:1	49–71 @ 3000
	JE	3.0 (2954)	EFI	195 @ 5750	200 @ 3500	3.54 × 3.05	9.2:1	46–71 @ 3000

EFI—Electronic Fuel Injection
① Manual transmission—
  116 @ 6500 horsepower
  Automatic transmission—
  105 @ 6000 horsepower
② Manual transmission—100 @ 5500 ft. lbs.
  Automatic transmission—100 @ 4000 ft. lbs.
③ Manual transmission—9.4:1
④ 323—82 @ 5000 horsepower
  MX3—88 @ 5000 horsepower
⑤ 323—92 @ 2500 ft. lbs.
  MX3—98 @ 4000 ft. lbs.
⑥ 323—9.3:1
  MX3—9.0:1

GENERAL ENGINE SPECIFICATIONS—ROTARY ENGINE

Year	Engine ID/VIN	Engine Displacement Liters (cc)	Fuel System Type	Net Horsepower @ rpm	Net Torque @ rpm (ft. lbs.)	Rotor Displacement (cu. in.)	Compression Ratio	Oil Pressure @ rpm
1990	13B	1.3 (1308)	EFI	160 @ 7000	140 @ 4000	80	9.7:1	64–78 @ 3000
	13B	1.3 (1308)	EFI Turbo	200 @ 6500	196 @ 3500	80	9.0:1	64–78 @ 3000
1991	13B	1.3 (1308)	EFI	160 @ 7000	140 @ 4000	80	9.7:1	64–78 @ 3000
	13B	1.3 (1308)	EFI Turbo	200 @ 6500	196 @ 3500	80	9.0:1	64–78 @ 3000
1992	13B	1.3 (1308)	EFI	160 @ 7000	140 @ 4000	80	9.7:1	64–78 @ 3000
	13B	1.3 (1308)	EFI Turbo	200 @ 6500	196 @ 3500	80	9.0:1	64–78 @ 3000
1993	13B	1.3 (1308)	EFI Turbo	255 @ 6500	217 @ 5000	80	9.0:1	49–71 @ 3000
1994	13B	1.3 (1308)	EFI Turbo	255 @ 6500	217 @ 5000	80	9.0:1	49–71 @ 3000

EFI—Electronic Fuel Injection

GASOLINE ENGINE TUNE-UP SPECIFICATIONS

Year	Engine ID/VIN	Engine Displacement Liters (cc)	Spark Plugs Gap (in.)	Ignition Timing (deg.)		Fuel Pump (psi)	Idle Speed (rpm)		Valve Clearance	
				MT	AT		MT	AT	In.	Ex.
1990	B6	1.6 (1597)	0.041	7B	7B	64–85	750	①	Hyd.	Hyd.
	B6ZE	1.6 (1597)	0.041	10B	—	64–85	850	—	Hyd.	Hyd.
	BPE	1.8 (1839)	0.041	5B	5B	64–85	750	①	Hyd.	Hyd.
	BPD	1.8 (1839)	0.041	10B	10B	64–85	750	750	Hyd.	Hyd.
	F2	2.2 (2184)	0.041	6B	6B	64–85	750	750	Hyd.	Hyd.
	F2	2.2 (2184)	0.041	9B	9B	64–85	750	750	Hyd.	Hyd.
	JE	3.0 (2954)	0.041	—	15B	64–85	—	650	Hyd.	Hyd.
	JE	3.0 (2954)	0.041	—	8B	64–85	—	700	Hyd.	Hyd.
1991	B6E	1.6 (1597)	0.041	7B	7B	64–85	750	750	Hyd.	Hyd.
	B6ZE	1.6 (1597)	0.041	10B	8B	64–85	850	850	Hyd.	Hyd.
	BPE	1.8 (1839)	0.041	5B	5B	64–85	750	750	Hyd.	Hyd.
	BPD	1.8 (1839)	0.041	10B	10B	64–85	750	750	Hyd.	Hyd.
	F2	2.2 (2184)	0.041	6B	6B	64–85	750	750	Hyd.	Hyd.
	F2	2.2 (2184)	0.041	9B	9B	64–85	750	750	Hyd.	Hyd.
	JE	3.0 (2954)	0.041	—	15B	64–85	—	650	Hyd.	Hyd.
	JE	3.0 (2954)	0.041	—	8B	64–85	—	700	Hyd.	Hyd.
1992	B6E	1.6 (1597)	0.041	②	②	64–85	750	750	Hyd.	Hyd.
	B6ZE	1.6 (1597)	0.041	10B	8B	64–85	850	850	Hyd.	Hyd.
	BPE	1.8 (1839)	0.041	5B	5B	64–85	750	750	Hyd.	Hyd.
	BPD	1.8 (1839)	0.041	10B	10B	64–85	750	750	Hyd.	Hyd.
	K8D	1.8 (1844)	0.041	10B	10B	64–85	670	670	Hyd.	Hyd.
	F2	2.2 (2184)	0.041	6B	6B	64–85	750	750	Hyd.	Hyd.
	F2	2.2 (2184)	0.041	9B	9B	64–85	750	750	Hyd.	Hyd.
	JE	3.0 (2954)	0.041	—	12B	64–85	—	700	Hyd.	Hyd.
1993	B6E	1.6 (1597)	0.041	②	②	64–85	750	750	Hyd.	Hyd.
	B6ZE	1.6 (1597)	0.041	10B	8B	64–85	850	850	Hyd.	Hyd.
	BPE	1.8 (1839)	0.041	5B	5B	64–85	750	750	Hyd.	Hyd.
	BPD	1.8 (1839)	0.041	10B	10B	64–85	750	750	Hyd.	Hyd.
	K8D	1.8 (1844)	0.041	10B	10B	64–85	670	670	Hyd.	Hyd.
	F2	2.0 (1991)	0.041	12B	12B	64–92	700	700	Hyd.	Hyd.
	KL	2.5 (2497)	0.041	10B	10B	72–92	650	650	Hyd.	Hyd.
	JE	3.0 (2954)	0.041	—	12B	64–85	—	700	Hyd.	Hyd.
1994	B6E	1.6 (1597)	0.041	②	②	64–85	750	750	Hyd.	Hyd.
	B6ZE	1.6 (1597)	0.041	10B	8B	64–85	850	850	Hyd.	Hyd.
	BPE	1.8 (1839)	0.041	5B	5B	64–85	750	750	Hyd.	Hyd.
	BPD	1.8 (1839)	0.041	10B	10B	64–85	750	750	Hyd.	Hyd.
	K8D	1.8 (1844)	0.041	10B	10B	64–85	670	670	Hyd.	Hyd.
	F2	2.0 (1991)	0.041	12B	12B	64–92	700	700	Hyd.	Hyd.
	KL	2.5 (2497)	0.041	10B	10B	72–92	650	650	Hyd.	Hyd.
	JE	3.0 (2954)	0.041	—	12B	64–85	—	700	Hyd.	Hyd.

NOTE: The lowest cylinder pressure should be within 75% of the highest cylinder pressure reading. For example, if the highest cylinder is 134 psi, the lowest should be 101. Engine should be at normal operating temperature with throttle valve in the wide open position.

The underhood specifications sticker often reflects tune-up specification changes in production. Sticker figures must be used if they disagree with those in this chart.

B—Before Top Dead Center

Hyd.—Hydraulic

① Canadian vehicles—800 rpm

Except Canadian vehicles—750 rpm

② 323—7B

MX3—10B

TUNE-UP SPECIFICATIONS—ROTARY ENGINE

Year	Engine ID/VIN	Engine Displacement Liters (cc)	Spark Plugs Gap (in.)	Distributor	Ignition Timing (degrees)		Idle Speed (rpm)	
					Leading	Trailing	MT	AT
1990	13B	1.3 (1308)	0.056	Electronic	5A	20A	750	750
	13B	1.3 (1308)	0.056	Electronic	5A	20A	750	—
1991	13B	1.3 (1308)	0.056	Electronic	5A	20A	750	750
	13B	1.3 (1308)	0.056	Electronic	5A	20A	750	—
1992	13B	1.3 (1308)	0.056	Electronic	5A	20A	750	750
	13B	1.3 (1308)	0.056	Electronic	5A	20A	750	—
1993	13B	1.3 (1308)	0.056	DIS	5A	20A	725	725
1994	13B	1.3 (1308)	0.056	DIS	5A	20A	725	725

DIS—Distributorless Ignition System

FIRING ORDERS

NOTE: To avoid confusion, always replace spark plug wires one at a time.

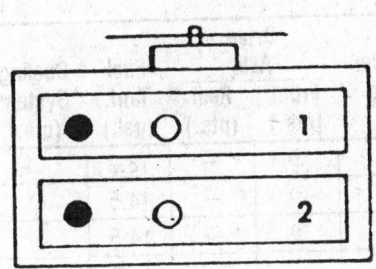

1.3L Rotary Engine
Distributorless Ignition System

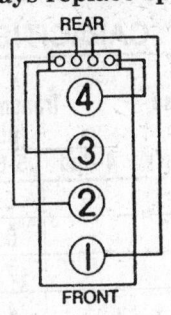

1.6L Engine (Miata) Engine
Firing Order: 1-3-4-2
Distributorless Ignition System

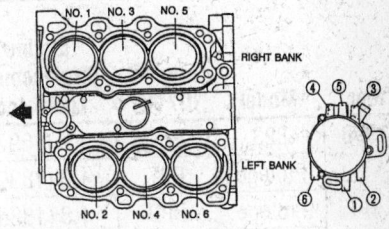

1.8L and 2.5L Engines
Engine Firing Order: 1-2-3-4-5-6
Distributor Rotation: Counterclockwise

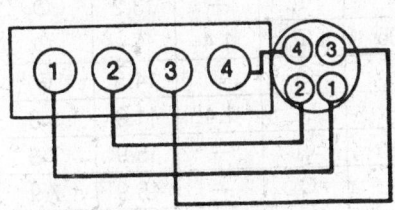

1.6L (except Miata), 1.8L and 2.2L Engines
Engine Firing Order: 1-3-4-2
Distributor Rotation: Counterclockwise

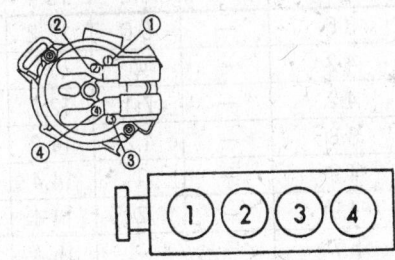

2.0L Engine
Engine Firing Order: 1-3-4-2
Distributor Rotation: Clockwise

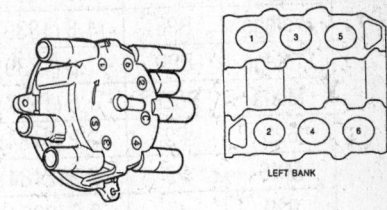

3.0L Engine
Engine Firing Order: 1-2-3-4-5-6
Distributor Rotation: Clockwise

CAPACITIES

Year	Model	Engine ID/VIN	Engine Displacement Liters (cc)	Engine Crankcase with Filter (qts.)	Transmission (pts.) 4-Spd	5-Spd	Auto.	Transfer Case (pts.)	Drive Axle Front (pts.)	Rear (pts.)	Fuel Tank (gal.)	Cooling System (qts.)
1990	323	B6E	1.6 (1597)	3.6	—	5.6	12.2	—	①	—	13.2	⑦
	Protege	BPE	1.8 (1839)	4.2	—	5.6	12.2	—	①	—	14.5	⑦
	Protege	BPD	1.8 (1839)	4.2	—	7.1	12.2	—	①	—	14.5	⑦
	Miata	B6ZE	1.6 (1597)	3.8	—	4.2	—	—	—	1.4	11.9	6.3
	626	F2	2.2 (2184)	4.9	—	②	14.4	—	①	—	③	④
	MX6	F2	2.2 (2184)	4.9	—	②	14.4	—	①	—	③	④
	929	JE	3.0 (2954)	5.7	—	—	15.4	—	—	2.8	18.5	9.9
	RX7	13B	1.3 (1308)	6.1	—	5.2	15.4	—	—	⑤	18.5	⑥
1991	323	B6E	1.6 (1597)	3.6	—	5.6	12.2	—	①	—	13.2	⑦
	Protege	BPE	1.8 (1839)	4.2	—	⑧	⑨	1.06	①	1.4	⑩	⑦
	Protege	BPD	1.8 (1839)	4.2	—	7.1	12.2	—	①	—	14.5	⑦
	Miata	B6ZE	1.6 (1597)	3.8	—	4.2	14.2	—	—	1.4	11.9	6.3
	626	F2	2.2 (2184)	4.9	—	②	14.4	—	①	—	15.9	7.9
	MX6	F2	2.2 (2184)	4.9	—	②	14.4	—	①	—	15.9	7.9
	929	JE	3.0 (2954)	5.7	—	—	15.4	—	—	2.8	18.5	9.9
	RX7	13B	1.3 (1308)	6.1	—	5.2	15.4	—	—	⑤	18.5	⑥
1992	323	B6E	1.6 (1597)	3.6	—	5.6	13.4	—	①	—	13.2	⑦
	Protege	BPE	1.8 (1839)	4.2	—	5.6	13.4	—	①	—	14.5	⑦
	Protege	BPD	1.8 (1839)	4.2	—	7.1	13.4	—	①	—	14.5	⑦
	Miata	B6ZE	1.6 (1597)	3.8	—	4.2	14.2	—	—	1.4	11.9	6.3
	MX3	B6E	1.6 (1597)	3.6	—	5.6	13.4	—	①	—	13.2	6.3
	MX3	K8D	1.8 (1844)	5.2	—	5.7	12.2	—	①	—	13.2	7.9
	626	F2	2.2 (2184)	4.9	—	②	14.4	—	①	—	15.9	7.9
	MX6	F2	2.2 (2184)	4.9	—	②	14.4	—	①	—	15.9	7.9
	929	JE	3.0 (2954)	5.7	—	—	18.2	—	—	2.8	18.5	⑪
1993	323	B6E	1.6 (1597)	3.6	—	5.6	13.4	—	①	—	13.2	⑦
	Protege	BPE	1.8 (1839)	4.2	—	5.6	13.4	—	①	—	14.5	⑦
	Protege	BPD	1.8 (1839)	4.2	—	7.1	13.4	—	①	—	14.5	⑦
	Miata	B6ZE	1.6 (1597)	3.8	—	4.2	14.2	—	—	1.4	11.9	6.3
	MX3	B6E	1.6 (1597)	3.6	—	5.6	13.4	—	①	—	13.2	6.3
	MX3	K8D	1.8 (1844)	5.2	—	5.7	12.2	—	①	—	13.2	7.9
	626	FS	2.0 (1991)	3.9	—	5.8	18.6	—	①	—	15.5	7.4
	626	KL	2.5 (2496)	5.2	—	5.8	18.6	—	①	—	15.5	7.9
	MX6	FS	2.0 (1991)	3.9	—	5.8	18.6	—	①	—	15.5	7.4
	MX6	KL	2.5 (2496)	5.2	—	5.8	18.6	—	①	—	15.5	7.9
	929	JE	3.0 (2954)	5.7	—	—	18.2	—	—	2.8	18.5	⑪
	RX7	13B	1.3 (1308)	⑫	—	5.2	18.2	—	—	2.8	20.1	9.3

CAPACITIES

Year	Model	Engine ID/VIN	Engine Displacement Liters (cc)	Engine Crankcase with Filter (qts.)	Transmission (pts.)			Transfer Case (pts.)	Drive Axle		Fuel Tank (gal.)	Cooling System (qts.)
					4-Spd	5-Spd	Auto.		Front (pts.)	Rear (pts.)		
1994	323	B6E	1.6 (1597)	3.6	—	5.6	13.4	—	①	—	13.2	⑦
	Protege	BPE	1.8 (1839)	4.2	—	5.6	13.4	—	①	—	14.5	⑦
	Protege	BPD	1.8 (1839)	4.2	—	7.1	13.4	—	①	—	14.5	⑦
	Miata	B6ZE	1.6 (1597)	3.8	—	4.2	14.2	—	—	1.4	11.9	6.3
	MX3	B6E	1.6 (1597)	3.6	—	5.6	13.4	—	①	—	13.2	6.3
	MX3	K8D	1.8 (1844)	5.2	—	5.7	12.2	—	①	—	13.2	7.9
	626	FS	2.0 (1991)	3.9	—	5.8	18.6	—	①	—	15.5	7.4
	626	KL	2.5 (2496)	5.2	—	5.8	18.6	—	①	—	15.5	7.9
	MX6	FS	2.0 (1991)	3.9	—	5.8	18.6	—	①	—	15.5	7.4
	MX6	KL	2.5 (2496)	5.2	—	5.8	18.6	—	①	—	15.5	7.9
	929	JE	3.0 (2954)	5.7	—	—	18.2	—	—	2.8	18.5	⑪
	RX7	13B	1.3 (1308)	⑫	—	5.2	18.2	—	—	2.8	20.1	9.3

① Included in transaxle
② Non-turbocharged engine—7 pts.
    Turbocharged engine—7.8 pts.
③ With 4-wheel steering—15 gal.
    Without 4-wheel steering—15.9 gal.
④ With heater—7.9 qts.
    Without heater—7.4 qts.
⑤ Except Turbo engine with limited slip—2.8 pts.
    Turbo engine with limited slip—3.0 pts.
⑥ Non-turbo engine—7.7 qts.
    Turbo engine—9.2 qts.
⑦ Manual trans.—5.3 qts.
    Automatic trans.—6.3 qts.
⑧ 2WD—5.6 pts.
    4WD—5.4 pts.
⑨ 2WD—12.2 pts.
    4WD—14.0 pts.
⑩ 2WD—14.5 gal.
    4WD—15.8 gal.
⑪ With heater—9.9 qts.
    Without heater—9.3 qts.
⑫ Except RI package—5.2 qts.
    RI package—5.7 qts.

CAMSHAFT SPECIFICATIONS
All measurements given in inches.

Year	Engine ID/VIN	Engine Displacement Liters (cc)	Journal Diameter 1	2	3	4	5	Elevation In.	Ex.	Bearing Clearance	Camshaft End Play
1990	B6E	1.6 (1597)	1.7102–1.7112	1.7091–1.7100	1.7102–1.7112	—	—	1.4272–1.4351	1.4272–1.4351	⑤	0.0020–0.0080
	B6ZE	1.6 (1597)	1.0213–1.0222	1.0213–1.0222	1.0213–1.0222	1.0213–1.0222	1.0213–1.0222	1.6019–1.6098	1.6019–1.6098	0.0014–0.0060	0.0028–0.0080
	BPE	1.8 (1839)	1.7102–1.7110	1.7096–1.7106	1.7091–1.7100	1.7096–1.7106	1.7102–1.7110	1.4092–1.4170	1.4202–1.4281	⑥	0.0024–0.0080
	BPD	1.8 (1839)	1.0213–1.0222	1.0213–1.0222	1.0213–1.0222	1.0213–1.0222	1.0213–1.0222	1.7281–1.7360	1.7480–1.7560	0.0014–0.0060	0.0028–0.0080
	F2	2.2 (2184)	1.2575–1.2585	1.2563–1.2573	1.2563–1.2573	1.2563–1.2573	1.2575–1.2585	1.6197–1.6295	1.6396–1.6495	③	0.0030–0.0080
	JE	3.0 (2954)	1.9268–1.9274	1.9258–1.9266	1.9258–1.9267	1.9268–1.9274	—	1.6084–1.6163	1.6178–1.6257	④	0.0020–0.0080
	JE①	3.0 (2954)	1.1787–1.1797	1.1776–1.1785	1.1776–1.1785	1.1787–1.1797	—	1.5898–1.5976	1.5856–1.5935	⑦	0.0012–0.0080
1991	B6E	1.6 (1597)	1.7102–1.7112	1.7091–1.7100	1.7102–1.7112	—	—	1.4272–1.4351	1.4272–1.4351	⑤	0.0020–0.0080
	B6ZE	1.6 (1597)	1.0213–1.0222	1.0213–1.0222	1.0213–1.0222	1.0213–1.0222	1.0213–1.0222	⑧	⑨	0.0014–0.0060	0.0028–0.0075
	BPE	1.8 (1839)	1.7102–1.7110	1.7096–1.7106	1.7091–1.7100	1.7096–1.7106	1.7102–1.7110	1.4092–1.4170	1.4202–1.4281	⑥	0.0024–0.0080
	BPD	1.8 (1839)	1.0213–1.0222	1.0213–1.0222	1.0213–1.0222	1.0213–1.0222	1.0213–1.0222	1.7281–1.7360	1.7480–1.7560	0.0014–0.0060	0.0028–0.0080
	F2	2.2 (2184)	1.2575–1.2585	1.2563–1.2573	1.2563–1.2573	1.2563–1.2573	1.2575–1.2585	1.6197–1.6295	1.6396–1.6495	③	0.0030–0.0080
	JE	3.0 (2954)	1.9268–1.9274	1.9258–1.9266	1.9258–1.9267	1.9268–1.9274	—	1.6084–1.6163	1.6178–1.6257	④	0.0020–0.0080
	JE①	3.0 (2954)	1.1787–1.1797	1.1776–1.1785	1.1776–1.1785	1.1787–1.1797	—	1.5898–1.5976	1.5856–1.5935	⑦	0.0012–0.0080
1992	B6E	1.6 (1597)	1.7102–1.7110	⑩	⑪	1.7096–1.7106⑫	1.7102–1.7110⑫	⑬	⑭	⑮	⑯
	B6ZE	1.6 (1597)	1.0213–1.0222	1.0213–1.0222	1.0213–1.0222	1.0213–1.0222	1.0213–1.0222	⑧	⑨	0.0014–0.0060	0.0028–0.0075
	BPE	1.8 (1839)	1.7102–1.7110	1.7096–1.7106	1.7091–1.7100	1.7096–1.7106	1.7102–1.7110	1.4092–1.4170	1.4202–1.4281	⑥	0.0024–0.0080
	BPD	1.8 (1839)	1.0213–1.0222	1.0213–1.0222	1.0213–1.0222	1.0213–1.0222	1.0213–1.0222	1.7281–1.7360	1.7480–1.7560	0.0014–0.0060	0.0028–0.0080
	K8D	1.8 (1844)	⑰	1.0201–1.0209	1.0201–1.0209	1.0201–1.0209	1.0213–1.0220	1.6718–1.6797	1.7054–1.7132	⑱	0.0020–0.0055
	F2	2.2 (2184)	1.2575–1.2585	1.2563–1.2573	1.2563–1.2573	1.2563–1.2573	1.2575–1.2585	1.6197–1.6295	1.6396–1.6495	③	0.0030–0.0080
	JE	3.0 (2954)	1.1787–1.1797	1.1776–1.1785	1.1776–1.1785	1.1787–1.1797	—	1.5800–1.5874	1.5794–1.5873	⑳	0.0012–0.0080

CAMSHAFT SPECIFICATIONS

All measurements given in inches.

Year	Engine ID/VIN	Engine Displacement Liters (cc)	Journal Diameter 1	2	3	4	5	Elevation In.	Ex.	Bearing Clearance	Camshaft End Play
1993	B6E	1.6 (1597)	1.7102–1.7110	⑩	⑪	1.7096–1.7106⑫	1.7102–1.7110⑫	⑬	⑭	⑮	⑯
	B6ZE	1.6 (1597)	1.0213–1.0222	1.0213–1.0222	1.0213–1.0222	1.0213–1.0222	1.0213–1.0222	⑧	⑨	0.0014–0.0060	0.0028–0.0075
	BPE	1.8 (1839)	1.7102–1.7110	1.7096–1.7106	1.7091–1.7100	1.7096–1.7106	1.7102–1.7110	1.4092–1.4170	1.4202–1.4281	⑥	0.0024–0.0080
	BPD	1.8 (1839)	1.0213–1.0222	1.0213–1.0222	1.0213–1.0222	1.0213–1.0222	1.0213–1.0222	1.7281–1.7360	1.7480–1.7560	0.0014–0.0060	0.0028–0.0080
	K8D	1.8 (1844)	⑰	1.0201–1.0209	1.0201–1.0209	1.0201–1.0209	1.0213–1.0220	1.6718–1.6797	1.7054–1.7132	⑱	0.0020–0.0055
	FS	2.0 (1991)	1.0213–1.0222	1.0213–1.0222	1.0213–1.0222	1.0213–1.0222	1.0213–1.0222	1.6859–1.6918	1.7003–1.7062	0.0014–0.0060	0.0032–0.0080
	KL	2.5 (2496)	⑰	1.0201–1.0209	1.0201–1.0209	1.0201–1.0209	1.0213–1.0220	1.7067–1.7145	1.7067–1.7145	⑲	0.0020–0.0056
	JE	3.0 (2954)	1.1787–1.1797	1.1776–1.1785	1.1776–1.1785	1.1787–1.1797	—	1.5800–1.5874	1.5794–1.5873	⑳	0.0012–0.0080
1994	B6E	1.6 (1597)	1.7102–1.7110	⑩	⑪	1.7096–1.7106⑫	1.7102–1.7110⑫	⑬	⑭	⑮	⑯
	B6ZE	1.6 (1597)	1.0213–1.0222	1.0213–1.0222	1.0213–1.0222	1.0213–1.0222	1.0213–1.0222	⑧	⑨	0.0014–0.0060	0.0028–0.0075
	BPE	1.8 (1839)	1.7102–1.7110	1.7096–1.7106	1.7091–1.7100	1.7096–1.7106	1.7102–1.7110	1.4092–1.4170	1.4202–1.4281	⑥	0.0024–0.0080
	BPD	1.8 (1839)	1.0213–1.0222	1.0213–1.0222	1.0213–1.0222	1.0213–1.0222	1.0213–1.0222	1.7281–1.7360	1.7480–1.7560	0.0014–0.0060	0.0028–0.0080
	K8D	1.8 (1844)	⑰	1.0201–1.0209	1.0201–1.0209	1.0201–1.0209	1.0213–1.0220	1.6718–1.6797	1.7054–1.7132	⑱	0.0020–0.0055
	FS	2.0 (1991)	1.0213–1.0222	1.0213–1.0222	1.0213–1.0222	1.0213–1.0222	1.0213–1.0222	1.6859–1.6918	1.7003–1.7062	0.0014–0.0060	0.0032–0.0080
	KL	2.5 (2496)	⑰	1.0201–1.0209	1.0201–1.0209	1.0201–1.0209	1.0213–1.0220	1.7067–1.7145	1.7067–1.7145	⑲	0.0020–0.0056
	JE	3.0 (2954)	1.1787–1.1797	1.1776–1.1785	1.1776–1.1785	1.1787–1.1797	—	1.5800–1.5874	1.5794–1.5873	⑳	0.0012–0.0080

① Double Overhead Cam
② No. 1 & No. 3—0.0010–0.0059
  No. 2—0.0030–0.0059
③ No. 1 & No. 5—0.0014–0.0059
  Nos. 2, 3 & 4—0.0026–0.0059
④ No. 1 & No. 4—0.0024–0.0059
  No. 2 & No. 3—0.0031–0.0059
⑤ No. 1 & No. 3—0.0014–0.0060
  No. 2—0.0020–0.0060
⑥ No. 1 & No. 5—0.0016–0.0060
  No. 2 & No. 4—0.0014–0.0060
  No. 3—0.0020–0.0060
⑦ No. 1 & No. 4—0.0014–0.0060
  No. 2 & No. 3—0.0026–0.0060
⑧ Manual trans.—1.6019–1.6098
  Automatic trans.—1.5662–1.5741
⑨ Manual trans.—1.6019–1.6098
  Automatic trans.—1.6018–1.6097
⑩ 323—1.7098–1.7108
  MX3—1.7096–1.7106

⑪ 323—1.7102–1.7110
  MX3—1.7091–1.7100
⑫ MX3 only
⑬ 323—1.4272–1.4351
  MX3—1.4027–1.4106
⑭ 323—1.4272–1.4351
  MX3—1.3960–1.4039
⑮ 323: No. 1 & No. 3—0.0021–0.0060
  No. 2—0.0023–0.0060
  MX3: No. 1 & No. 5—0.0016–0.0060
  No. 2 & No. 4—0.0014–0.0060
  No. 3—0.0020–0.0060
⑯ 323—0.0020–0.0080
  MX3—0.0023–0.0070
⑰ Right ex., left int.—1.0213–0.0220
  Right in., left ex.—1.1801–1.1811
⑱ No. 1 & No. 5—0.0016–0.0052
  No. 2, No. 3 & No. 4—0.0028–0.0063
⑲ No. 1 & No. 5—0.0016–0.0047
  No. 2, No. 3 & No. 4—0.0028–0.0059
⑳ No. 1 & No. 4—0.0016–0.0060
  No. 2 & No. 3—0.0028–0.0060

CRANKSHAFT AND CONNECTING ROD SPECIFICATIONS

All measurements are given in inches.

Year	Engine ID/VIN	Engine Displacement Liters (cc)	Crankshaft				Connecting Rod		
			Main Brg. Journal Dia.	Main Brg. Oil Clearance	Shaft End-play	Thrust on No.	Journal Diameter	Oil Clearance	Side Clearance
1990	B6E	1.6 (1597)	1.9647–1.9668	0.0007–0.0040	0.0031–0.0120	4	1.7680–1.7699	0.0011–0.0040	0.0043–0.0120
	B6ZE	1.6 (1597)	1.9647–1.9668	0.0007–0.0040	0.0031–0.0120	4	1.7680–1.7699	0.0011–0.0040	0.0043–0.0120
	BPE	1.8 (1839)	1.9647–1.9668	0.0007–0.0040	0.0031–0.0120	4	1.7680–1.7699	0.0011–0.0040	0.0043–0.0120
	BPD	1.8 (1839)	1.9647–1.9668	0.0007–0.0040	0.0031–0.0118	4	1.7680–1.7699	0.0011–0.0040	0.0043–0.0120
	F2	2.2 (2184)	2.3597–2.3604	①	0.0031–0.0118	3	2.0055–2.0061	0.0011–0.0039	0.0040–0.0120
	JE	3.0 (2954)	2.4385–2.4392	0.0010–0.0031	0.0031–0.0118	4	2.0842–2.0848	0.0009–0.0040	0.0070–0.0160
1991	B6E	1.6 (1597)	1.9647–1.9668	0.0007–0.0040	0.0031–0.0120	4	1.7680–1.7699	0.0011–0.0040	0.0043–0.0120
	B6ZE	1.6 (1597)	1.9647–1.9668	0.0007–0.0040	0.0031–0.0120	4	1.7680–1.7699	0.0011–0.0040	0.0043–0.0120
	BPE	1.8 (1839)	1.9647–1.9668	0.0007–0.0040	0.0031–0.0120	4	1.7680–1.7699	0.0011–0.0040	0.0043–0.0120
	BPD	1.8 (1839)	1.9647–1.9668	0.0007–0.0040	0.0031–0.0120	4	1.7680–1.7699	0.0011–0.0040	0.0043–0.0120
	F2	2.2 (2184)	2.3597–2.3604	①	0.0031–0.0120	3	2.0055–2.0061	0.0011–0.0039	0.0040–0.0120
	JE	3.0 (2954)	2.4385–2.4392	0.0010–0.0031	0.0031–0.0118	4	2.0842–2.0848	0.0009–0.0040	0.0070–0.0160
1992	B6E	1.6 (1597)	1.9647–1.9668	0.0007–0.0040	0.0031–0.0120	4	1.7680–1.7699	0.0011–0.0040	0.0043–0.0120
	B6ZE	1.6 (1597)	1.9647–1.9668	0.0007–0.0040	0.0031–0.0120	4	1.7680–1.7699	0.0011–0.0040	0.0043–0.0120
	BPE	1.8 (1839)	1.9647–1.9668	0.0007–0.0040	0.0031–0.0120	4	1.7680–1.7699	0.0011–0.0040	0.0043–0.0120
	BPD	1.8 (1839)	1.9647–1.9668	0.0007–0.0040	0.0031–0.0120	4	1.7680–1.7699	0.0011–0.0040	0.0043–0.0120
	K8D	1.8 (1844)	2.4382–2.4392	0.0015–0.0025	0.0031–0.0130	4	1.8872–1.8880	0.0009–0.0031	0.0070–0.0160
	F2	2.2 (2184)	2.3597–2.3604	①	0.0031–0.0120	3	2.0055–2.0061	0.0011–0.0039	0.0040–0.0120
	JE	3.0 (2954)	2.4385–2.4392	0.0010–0.0031	0.0031–0.0118	4	2.0842–2.0848	0.0009–0.0040	0.0070–0.0160
1993	B6E	1.6 (1597)	1.9647–1.9668	0.0007–0.0040	0.0031–0.0120	4	1.7680–1.7699	0.0011–0.0040	0.0043–0.0120
	B6ZE	1.6 (1597)	1.9647–1.9668	0.0007–0.0040	0.0031–0.0120	4	1.7680–1.7699	0.0011–0.0040	0.0043–0.0120
	BPE	1.8 (1839)	1.9647–1.9668	0.0007–0.0040	0.0031–0.0120	4	1.7680–1.7699	0.0011–0.0040	0.0043–0.0120
	BPD	1.8 (1839)	1.9647–1.9668	0.0007–0.0040	0.0031–0.0120	4	1.7680–1.7699	0.0011–0.0040	0.0043–0.0120
	K8D	1.8 (1844)	2.4382–2.4392	0.0015–0.0025	0.0031–0.0130	4	1.8872–1.8880	0.0009–0.0031	0.0070–0.0160

CRANKSHAFT AND CONNECTING ROD SPECIFICATIONS
All measurements are given in inches.

Year	Engine ID/VIN	Engine Displacement Liters (cc)	Crankshaft				Connecting Rod		
			Main Brg. Journal Dia.	Main Brg. Oil Clearance	Shaft End-play	Thrust on No.	Journal Diameter	Oil Clearance	Side Clearance
	FS	2.0 (1991)	2.2020–2.2029	②	0.0031–0.0118	4	1.8872–1.8880	0.0009–0.0026	0.0043–0.0120
	KL	2.5 (2496)	2.4382–2.4392	0.0015–0.0025	0.0032–0.0125	4	2.0841–2.0848	0.0009–0.0032	0.0070–0.0160
	JE	3.0 (2954)	2.4385–2.4392	0.0010–0.0031	0.0031–0.0118	4	2.0842–2.0848	0.0009–0.0040	0.0070–0.0160
1994	B6E	1.6 (1597)	1.9647–1.9668	0.0007–0.0040	0.0031–0.0120	4	1.7680–1.7699	0.0011–0.0040	0.0043–0.0120
	B6ZE	1.6 (1597)	1.9647–1.9668	0.0007–0.0040	0.0031–0.0120	4	1.7680–1.7699	0.0011–0.0040	0.0043–0.0120
	BPE	1.8 (1839)	1.9647–1.9668	0.0007–0.0040	0.0031–0.0120	4	1.7680–1.7699	0.0011–0.0040	0.0043–0.0120
	BPD	1.8 (1839)	1.9647–1.9668	0.0007–0.0040	0.0031–0.0120	4	1.7680–1.7699	0.0011–0.0040	0.0043–0.0120
	K8D	1.8 (1844)	2.4382–2.4392	0.0015–0.0025	0.0031–0.0130	4	1.8872–1.8880	0.0009–0.0031	0.0070–0.0160
	FS	2.0 (1991)	2.2020–2.2029	②	0.0031–0.0118	4	1.8872–1.8880	0.0009–0.0026	0.0043–0.0120
	KL	2.5 (2496)	2.4382–2.4392	0.0015–0.0025	0.0032–0.0125	4	2.0841–2.0848	0.0009–0.0032	0.0070–0.0160
	JE	3.0 (2954)	2.4385–2.4392	0.0010–0.0031	0.0031–0.0118	4	2.0842–2.0848	0.0009–0.0040	0.0070–0.0160

① No. 1, 2, 4 & 5—0.0010–0.0031
  No. 3—0.0012–0.0031
② No. 1, 2, 4 & 5—0.0009–0.0026
  No. 3—0.0012–0.0026

VALVE SPECIFICATIONS

Year	Engine ID/VIN	Engine Displacement Liters (cc)	Seat Angle (deg.)	Face Angle (deg.)	Maximum Out of Square	Spring Free Length	Stem-to-Guide Clearance (in.)		Stem Diameter (in.)	
							Intake	Exhaust	Intake	Exhaust
1990	B6E	1.6 (1597)	45	45	0.060	1.720	0.0010–0.0024	0.0011–0.0026	0.2744–0.2750	0.2742–0.2748
	B6ZE	1.6 (1597)	45	45	⑥	⑦	0.0010–0.0024	0.0012–0.0026	0.2350–0.2356	0.2348–0.2354
	BPE	1.8 (1839)	45	45	⑧	⑨	0.0010–0.0024	0.0011–0.0026	0.2350–0.2356	0.2348–0.2354
	BPD	1.8 (1839)	45	45	0.064	1.821	0.0010–0.0024	0.0012–0.0026	0.2350–0.2356	0.2348–0.2354
	F2	2.2 (2184)	45	45	0.067	③	0.0010–0.0024	0.0012–0.0026	0.2744–0.2750	0.2742–0.2748
	JE	3.0 (2954)	45	45	⑩	⑪	0.0010–0.0024	0.0012–0.0026	0.2744–0.2750	0.3159–0.3165
	JE①	3.0 (2954)	45	45	0.060	1.720	0.0010–0.0024	0.0012–0.0026	0.2750–0.2356	0.2348–0.2354
1991	B6E	1.6 (1597)	45	45	0.060	1.720	0.0010–0.0024	0.0011–0.0026	0.2744–0.2750	0.2742–0.2748
	B6ZE	1.6 (1597)	45	45	⑥	⑦	0.0010–0.0024	0.0012–0.0026	0.2350–0.2356	0.2348–0.2354
	BPE	1.8 (1839)	45	45	⑧	⑨	0.0010–0.0024	0.0011–0.0026	0.2350–0.2356	0.2348–0.2354
	BPD	1.8 (1839)	45	45	0.064	1.821	0.0010–0.0024	0.0012–0.0026	0.2350–0.2356	0.2348–0.2354
	F2	2.2 (2184)	45	45	0.067	③	0.0010–0.0024	0.0012–0.0026	0.2744–0.2750	0.2742–0.2748
	JE	3.0 (2954)	45	45	⑩	⑫	0.0010–0.0024	0.0012–0.0026	0.2744–0.2750	0.3159–0.3165
	JE①	3.0 (2954)	45	45	0.060	1.720	0.0010–0.0024	0.0012–0.0026	0.2750–0.2356	0.2348–0.2354
1992	B6E	1.6 (1597)	45	45	0.060	1.7188	0.0010–0.0024	0.0011–0.0026	0.2744–0.2750	0.2742–0.2748
	B6E②	1.6 (1597)	45	45	⑬	⑭	0.0010–0.0024	0.0012–0.0026	0.2350–0.2356	0.2348–0.2354
	B6ZE	1.6 (1597)	45	45	⑥	⑦	0.0010–0.0024	0.0012–0.0026	0.2350–0.2356	0.2348–0.2354
	BPE	1.8 (1839)	45	45	⑧	⑨	0.0010–0.0024	0.0011–0.0026	0.2350–0.2356	0.2348–0.2354
	BPD	1.8 (1839)	45	45	0.064	1.821	0.0010–0.0024	0.0012–0.0026	0.2350–0.2356	0.2348–0.2354
	K8D	1.8 (1844)	45	45	0.064	1.847	0.0010–0.0024	0.0012–0.0026	0.2350–0.2356	0.2348–0.2354
	F2	2.2 (2184)	45	45	0.067	③	0.0010–0.0024	0.0012–0.0026	0.2744–0.2750	0.2742–0.2748
	JE	3.0 (2954)	45	45	0.060	1.720	0.0010–0.0024	0.0012–0.0026	0.2750–0.2356	0.2348–0.2354

VALVE SPECIFICATIONS

Year	Engine ID/VIN	Engine Displacement Liters (cc)	Seat Angle (deg.)	Face Angle (deg.)	Maximum Out of Square	Spring Free Length	Stem-to-Guide Clearance (in.)		Stem Diameter (in.)	
							Intake	Exhaust	Intake	Exhaust
1993	B6E	1.6 (1597)	45	45	0.060	1.7188	0.0010– 0.0024	0.0011– 0.0026	0.2744– 0.2750	0.2742– 0.2748
	B6E ②	1.6 (1597)	45	45	⑬	⑭	0.0010– 0.0024	0.0012– 0.0026	0.2350– 0.2356	0.2348– 0.2354
	B6ZE	1.6 (1597)	45	45	⑥	⑦	0.0010– 0.0024	0.0012– 0.0026	0.2350– 0.2356	0.2348– 0.2354
	BPE	1.8 (1839)	45	45	⑧	⑨	0.0010– 0.0024	0.0011– 0.0026	0.2350– 0.2356	0.2348– 0.2354
	BPD	1.8 (1839)	45	45	0.064	1.821	0.0010– 0.0024	0.0012– 0.0026	0.2350– 0.2356	0.2348– 0.2354
	K8D	1.8 (1844)	45	45	0.064	1.847	0.0010– 0.0024	0.0012– 0.0026	0.2350– 0.2356	0.2348– 0.2354
	FS	2.0 (1991)	45	45	0.016	1.732	0.0010– 0.0024	0.0012– 0.0026	0.2351– 0.2356	0.2349– 0.2354
	KL	2.5 (2496)	45	45	0.0642	1.847	0.0010– 0.0023	0.0012– 0.0025	0.2351– 0.2356	0.2349– 0.2354
	JE	3.0 (2954)	45	45	0.060	1.720	0.0010– 0.0024	0.0012– 0.0026	0.2750– 0.2356	0.2348– 0.2354
1994	B6E	1.6 (1597)	45	45	0.060	1.7188	0.0010– 0.0024	0.0011– 0.0026	0.2744– 0.2750	0.2742– 0.2748
	B6E ②	1.6 (1597)	45	45	⑬	⑭	0.0010– 0.0024	0.0012– 0.0026	0.2350– 0.2356	0.2348– 0.2354
	B6ZE	1.6 (1597)	45	45	⑥	⑦	0.0010– 0.0024	0.0012– 0.0026	0.2350– 0.2356	0.2348– 0.2354
	BPE	1.8 (1839)	45	45	⑧	⑨	0.0010– 0.0024	0.0011– 0.0026	0.2350– 0.2356	0.2348– 0.2354
	BPD	1.8 (1839)	45	45	0.064	1.821	0.0010– 0.0024	0.0012– 0.0026	0.2350– 0.2356	0.2348– 0.2354
	K8D	1.8 (1844)	45	45	0.064	1.847	0.0010– 0.0024	0.0012– 0.0026	0.2350– 0.2356	0.2348– 0.2354
	FS	2.0 (1991)	45	45	0.016	1.732	0.0010– 0.0024	0.0012– 0.0026	0.2351– 0.2356	0.2349– 0.2354
	KL	2.5 (2496)	45	45	0.0642	1.847	0.0010– 0.0023	0.0012– 0.0025	0.2351– 0.2356	0.2349– 0.2354
	JE	3.0 (2954)	45	45	0.060	1.720	0.0010– 0.0024	0.0012– 0.0026	0.2750– 0.2356	0.2348– 0.2354

① Double Overhead Cam Engine
② MX3
③ Intake: 1.902–1.949
  Exhaust: 1.937–1.984
④ Intake:
  Outer: 0.070
  Inner: 0.064
  Exhaust:
  Outer: 0.083
  Inner: 0.074
⑤ Intake:
  Outer: 1.988–2.000
  Inner: 1.819–1.835
  Exhaust:
  Outer: 2.264–2.295
  Inner: 2.063–2.091

⑥ Intake: 0.0661
  Exhaust: 0.0665
⑦ Intake: 1.850–1.890
  Exhaust: 1.862–1.902
⑧ Intake: 0.063
  Exhaust: 0.060
⑨ Intake: 1.815
  Exhaust: 1.717
⑩ Intake:
  Outer: 0.071
  Inner: 0.063
  Exhaust:
  Outer: 0.080
  Inner: 0.073

⑪ Intake:
  Outer: 1.949–1.969
  Inner: 1.821–1.840
  Exhaust:
  Outer: 2.274–2.296
  Inner: 2.071–2.092
⑫ Intake:
  Outer: 1.984–2.003
  Inner: 1.821–1.840
  Exhaust:
  Outer: 2.274–2.296
  Inner: 2.071–2.092
⑬ Intake: 0.063
  Exhaust: 0.059
⑭ Intake: 1.816
  Exhaust: 1.687

PISTON AND RING SPECIFICATIONS

All measurements are given in inches.

Year	Engine ID/VIN	Engine Displacement Liters (cc)	Piston Clearance	Ring Gap			Ring Side Clearance		
				Top Compression	Bottom Compression	Oil Control	Top Compression	Bottom Compression	Oil Control
1990	B6E	1.6 (1597)	0.0015–0.0020	0.0060–0.0120	0.0060–0.0120	0.0080–0.0280	0.0012–0.0026	0.0012–0.0026	NA
	B6ZE	1.6 (1597)	0.0015–0.0020	0.0060–0.0120	0.0060–0.0120	0.0080–0.0280	0.0012–0.0028	0.0012–0.0028	NA
	BPE	1.8 (1839)	0.0015–0.0020	0.0060–0.0120	0.0060–0.0120	0.0080–0.0280	0.0012–0.0026	0.0012–0.0026	NA
	BPD	1.8 (1839)	0.0015–0.0020	0.0060–0.0120	0.0060–0.0120	0.0080–0.0280	0.0012–0.0026	0.0012–0.0028	NA
	F2	2.2 (2184)	0.0014–0.0030	0.0080–0.0138	0.0060–0.0120	0.0080–0.0276	0.0012–0.0028	0.0012–0.0028	NA
	JE	3.0 (2954)	0.0019–0.0026	0.0080–0.0140	0.0060–0.0120	0.0080–0.0280	①	①	NA
1991	B6E	1.6 (1597)	0.0015–0.0020	0.0060–0.0120	0.0060–0.0120	0.0080–0.0280	0.0012–0.0026	0.0012–0.0026	NA
	B6ZE	1.6 (1597)	0.0015–0.0020	0.0060–0.0120	0.0060–0.0180	0.0080–0.0280	0.0012–0.0028	0.0012–0.0028	NA
	BPE	1.8 (1839)	0.0015–0.0020	0.0060–0.0120	0.0060–0.0120	0.0080–0.0280	0.0012–0.0026	0.0012–0.0026	NA
	BPD	1.8 (1839)	0.0015–0.0020	0.0060–0.0120	0.0060–0.0120	0.0080–0.0280	0.0012–0.0026	0.0012–0.0028	NA
	F2	2.2 (2184)	0.0014–0.0030	0.0080–0.0140	0.0060–0.0120	0.0080–0.0280	0.0012–0.0028	0.0012–0.0028	NA
	JE	3.0 (2954)	0.0019–0.0026	0.0080–0.0140	0.0060–0.0120	0.0080–0.0280	①	①	NA
1992	B6E	1.6 (1597)	0.0015–0.0020	0.0060–0.0120	②	0.0080–0.0280	0.0012–0.0026	③	NA
	B6ZE	1.6 (1597)	0.0015–0.0020	0.0060–0.0120	0.0120–0.0180	0.0080–0.0280	0.0012–0.0028	0.0012–0.0028	NA
	BPE	1.8 (1839)	0.0015–0.0020	0.0060–0.0120	0.0060–0.0120	0.0080–0.0280	0.0012–0.0026	0.0012–0.0026	NA
	BPD	1.8 (1839)	0.0015–0.0020	0.0060–0.0120	0.0060–0.0120	0.0080–0.0280	0.0012–0.0026	0.0012–0.0028	NA
	K8D	1.8 (1844)	0.0011–0.0022	0.0060–0.0110	0.0100–0.0150	0.0080–0.0280	0.0080–0.0026	0.0012–0.0026	NA
	F2	2.2 (2184)	0.0014–0.0030	0.0080–0.0140	0.0060–0.0120	0.0080–0.0280	0.0012–0.0028	0.0012–0.0028	NA
	JE	3.0 (2954)	0.0009–0.0020	0.0080–0.0140	0.0060–0.0120	0.0080–0.0280	0.0012–0.0028	0.0012–0.0028	NA

PISTON AND RING SPECIFICATIONS

All measurements are given in inches.

| Year | Engine ID/VIN | Engine Displacement Liters (cc) | Piston Clearance | Ring Gap | | | Ring Side Clearance | | |
				Top Compression	Bottom Compression	Oil Control	Top Compression	Bottom Compression	Oil Control
1993	B6E	1.6 (1597)	0.0015–0.0020	0.0060–0.0120	②	0.0080–0.0280	0.0012–0.0026	③	NA
	B6ZE	1.6 (1597)	0.0015–0.0020	0.0060–0.0120	0.0120–0.0180	0.0080–0.0280	0.0012–0.0028	0.0012–0.0028	NA
	BPE	1.8 (1839)	0.0015–0.0020	0.0060–0.0120	0.0060–0.0120	0.0080–0.0280	0.0012–0.0026	0.0012–0.0026	NA
	BPD	1.8 (1839)	0.0015–0.0020	0.0060–0.0120	0.0060–0.0120	0.0080–0.0280	0.0012–0.0026	0.0012–0.0028	NA
	K8D	1.8 (1844)	0.0011–0.0022	0.0060–0.0110	0.0100–0.0150	0.0080–0.0280	0.0080–0.0026	0.0012–0.0026	NA
	FS	2.0 (1991)	0.0016–0.0020	0.0060–0.0110	0.0060–0.0110	0.0080–0.0270	0.0014–0.0025	0.0012–0.0025	NA
	KL	2.5 (2496)	0.0012–0.0022	0.0060–0.0118	0.0100–0.0150	0.0080–0.0270	0.0008–0.0026	0.0012–0.0026	NA
	JE	3.0 (2954)	0.0009–0.0020	0.0080–0.0140	0.0060–0.0120	0.0080–0.0280	0.0012–0.0028	0.0012–0.0028	NA
1994	B6E	1.6 (1597)	0.0015–0.0020	0.0060–0.0120	②	0.0080–0.0280	0.0012–0.0026	③	NA
	B6ZE	1.6 (1597)	0.0015–0.0020	0.0060–0.0120	0.0120–0.0180	0.0080–0.0280	0.0012–0.0028	0.0012–0.0028	NA
	BPE	1.8 (1839)	0.0015–0.0020	0.0060–0.0120	0.0060–0.0120	0.0080–0.0280	0.0012–0.0026	0.0012–0.0026	NA
	BPD	1.8 (1839)	0.0015–0.0020	0.0060–0.0120	0.0060–0.0120	0.0080–0.0280	0.0012–0.0026	0.0012–0.0028	NA
	K8D	1.8 (1844)	0.0011–0.0022	0.0060–0.0110	0.0100–0.0150	0.0080–0.0280	0.0080–0.0026	0.0012–0.0026	NA
	FS	2.0 (1991)	0.0016–0.0020	0.0060–0.0110	0.0060–0.0110	0.0080–0.0270	0.0014–0.0025	0.0012–0.0025	NA
	KL	2.5 (2496)	0.0012–0.0022	0.0060–0.0118	0.0100–0.0150	0.0080–0.0270	0.0008–0.0026	0.0012–0.0026	NA
	JE	3.0 (2954)	0.0009–0.0020	0.0080–0.0140	0.0060–0.0120	0.0080–0.0280	0.0012–0.0028	0.0012–0.0028	NA

NA—Not available
① SOHC engine—0.0010–0.0030
   DOHC engine—0.0012–0.0028
② 323—0.0060–0.0120
   MX3—0.0120–0.0180
③ 323—0.0012–0.0026
   MX3—0.0012–0.0028

TORQUE SPECIFICATIONS
All readings in ft. lbs.

Year	Engine ID/VIN	Engine Displacement Liters (cc)	Cylinder Head Bolts	Main Bearing Bolts	Rod Bearing Bolts	Crankshaft Sprocket Bolts	Flywheel Bolts	Manifold Intake	Manifold Exhaust	Spark Plugs	Lug Nut
1990	B6E	1.6 (1597)	56–60	40–43	35–38	80–87	71–76	14–19	12–17	11–17	65–87
	B6ZE	1.6 (1597)	56–60	40–43	37–40	80–87	71–76	14–19	28–34	11–17	65–87
	BPE	1.8 (1839)	56–60	40–43	36–38	80–87	71–76	14–19	12–17	11–17	65–87
	BPD	1.8 (1839)	56–60	40–43	37–40	80–87	71–76	14–19	28–34	11–17	65–87
	F2	2.2 (2184)	59–64	61–65	48–51	116–123	71–76	14–22	25–36	11–17	65–87
	JE	3.0 (2954)	①	②	③	116–123	76–81	14–19	16–21	④	65–87
1991	B6E	1.6 (1597)	56–60	40–43	35–38	80–87	71–76	14–19	12–17	11–17	65–87
	B6ZE	1.6 (1597)	56–60	40–43	37–40	80–87	71–76	14–19	28–34	11–17	65–87
	BPE	1.8 (1839)	56–60	40–43	36–38	80–87	71–76	14–19	12–17	11–17	65–87
	BPD	1.8 (1839)	56–60	40–43	35–37	80–87	71–76	14–19	28–34	11–17	65–87
	F2	2.2 (2184)	59–64	61–65	48–51	116–123	71–76	14–22	25–36	11–17	65–87
	JE	3.0 (2954)	①	②	③	116–123	76–81	14–19	16–21	④	65–87
1992	B6E	1.6 (1597)	56–60	40–43	⑤	116–123	71–76	14–19	12–17	11–17	65–87
	B6ZE	1.6 (1597)	56–60	40–43	37–40	116–123	71–76	14–19	28–34	11–17	65–87
	BPE	1.8 (1839)	56–60	40–43	36–38	116–123	71–76	14–19	12–17	11–17	65–87
	BPD	1.8 (1839)	56–60	40–43	35–37	116–123	71–76	14–19	28–34	11–17	65–87
	K8D	1.8 (1844)	⑧	⑥	⑦	116–123	45–50	14–19	14–19	11–17	65–87
	F2	2.2 (2184)	59–64	61–65	48–51	116–123	71–76	14–22	25–36	11–17	65–87
	JE	3.0 (2954)	①	②	③	116–123	76–81	14–19	16–21	10–13	65–87
1993	B6E	1.6 (1597)	56–60	40–43	⑤	116–123	71–76	14–19	12–17	11–17	65–87
	B6ZE	1.6 (1597)	56–60	40–43	37–40	116–123	71–76	14–19	28–34	11–17	65–87
	BPE	1.8 (1839)	56–60	40–43	36–38	116–123	71–76	14–19	12–17	11–17	65–87
	BPD	1.8 (1839)	56–60	40–43	35–37	116–123	71–76	14–19	28–34	11–17	65–87
	K8D	1.8 (1844)	⑧	⑥	⑦	116–123	45–50	14–19	14–19	11–17	65–87
	FS	2.0 (1991)	⑨	⑩	⑪	116–123	71–76	14–18	⑫	11–16	65–87
	KL	2.5 (2496)	⑧	⑥	⑪	116–123	45–49	14–18	14–18	11–16	65–87
	JE	3.0 (2954)	①	②	③	116–123	76–81		16–21	10–13	65–87
1994	B6E	1.6 (1597)	56–60	40–43	⑤	116–123	71–76	14–19	12–17	11–17	65–87
	B6ZE	1.6 (1597)	56–60	40–43	37–40	116–123	71–76	14–19	28–34	11–17	65–87
	BPE	1.8 (1839)	56–60	40–43	36–38	116–123	71–76	14–19	12–17	11–17	65–87
	BPD	1.8 (1839)	56–60	40–43	35–37	116–123	71–76	14–19	28–34	11–17	65–87
	K8D	1.8 (1844)	⑧	⑥	⑦	116–123	45–50	14–19	14–19	11–17	65–87
	FS	2.0 (1991)	⑨	⑩	⑪	116–123	71–76	14–18	⑫	11–16	65–87
	KL	2.5 (2496)	⑧	⑥	⑪	116–123	45–49	14–18	14–18	11–16	65–87
	JE	3.0 (2954)	①	②	③	116–123	76–81	14–19	16–21	10–13	65–87

① Tighten in 3 steps:
Step 1: 14 ft. lbs.
Step 2: Turn each bolt 90°, in sequence
Step 3: Turn each bolt 90°, in sequence

② Tighten in 3 steps:
Step 1: 14 ft. lbs.
Step 2: Turn each bolt 90°, in sequence
Step 3: Turn each bolt 45°, in sequence

③ Tighten in 2 steps:
Step 1: 22 ft. lbs.
Step 2: Turn each bolt 90°

④ SOHC engine—11–17 ft. lbs.
DOHC engine—10–13 ft. lbs.

⑤ 323—35–38 ft. lbs.
MX3—35–37 ft. lbs.

⑥ Tighten in sequence in 3 steps:
Step 1: Inner bolts—17–18 ft. lbs.
Outer bolts—13–15 ft. lbs.
Step 2: Inner bolts
Nos. 1, 2 & 3—Turn each bolt 70°
No. 4—Turn each bolt 80°
Outer bolts:
Turn each bolt 60°
Step 3: Repeat Step 2.

⑦ Tighten in 3 steps:
Step 1: 16–19 ft. lbs.
Step 2: Turn each bolt 90°
Step 3: Turn each bolt 90°

⑧ Tighten in 3 steps:
Step 1: 17–19 ft. lbs.
Step 2: Turn each bolt 90°, in sequence
Step 3: Turn each bolt 90°, in sequence

⑨ Tighten in 3 steps:
Step 1: 12.7–16.2 ft. lbs.
Step 2: Turn each bolt 90°, in sequence
Step 3: Turn each bolt 90°, in sequence

⑩ Tighten in 2 steps:
Step 1: 12.7–16.2 ft. lbs.
Step 2: Turn each bolt 90°, in sequence

⑪ Tighten in 2 steps:
Step 1: 16.3–19.8 ft. lbs.
Step 2: Turn each bolt 90°

⑫ Nut—15–20 ft. lbs.
Bolt—12–16 ft. lbs.

TORQUE SPECIFICATIONS—ROTARY ENGINE

All readings in ft. lbs.

Year	Engine ID/VIN	Engine Displacement Liters (cc)	Front Cover	Bearing Housing	Rear Stationary Gear	Eccentric Shaft Pulley Bolt	Flywheel-to-Eccentric Shaft Nut	Manifolds Intake	Manifolds Exhaust	Oil Pan	Tension Bolts
1990	13B	1.3 (1308)	12–17	12–17	12–17	80–98	289–362	14–19	23–34	6–8	23–29
1991	13B	1.3 (1308)	12–17	12–17	12–17	80–98	289–362	14–19	23–34	6–8	23–29
1993	13B	1.3 (1308)	12–17	12–16	12–16	80–98	290–360	12–16	48–57	7–8	24–28
1994	13B	1.3 (1308)	12–17	12–16	12–16	80–98	290–360	12–16	48–57	7–8	24–28

BRAKE SPECIFICATIONS
All measurements in inches unless noted.

Year	Model	Master Cylinder Bore	Brake Disc			Brake Drum Diameter			Minimum Lining Thickness	
			Original Thickness	Minimum Thickness	Maximum Runout	Original Inside Diameter	Max. Wear Limit	Maximum Machine Diameter	Front	Rear
1990	323	0.875	⑨	⑩	0.004	9.000	9.040	NA	0.080	0.040
	Protege	0.875	⑨	⑩	0.004	9.000	9.040	NA	0.080	0.040
	Miata	0.875	⑪	⑫	0.004	—	—	—	0.040	0.040
	626	0.875	①	②	0.004	9.000	9.060	NA	0.080	0.040
	MX6	0.875	①	②	0.004	9.000	9.060	NA	0.080	0.040
	929	0.875	⑬	⑭	0.004	6.690④	6.730④	NA	0.080	⑤
	RX7	⑥	⑦	⑧	0.004	—	—	—	0.080	0.040
1991	323	0.875	⑨	⑩	0.004	9.000	9.040	NA	0.080	0.040
	Protege	0.875	⑨	⑩	0.004	9.000	9.040	NA	0.080	0.040
	Miata	0.875	⑪	⑫	0.004	—	—	—	0.040	0.040
	626	0.875	①	②	0.004	9.000	9.060	NA	0.080	0.040
	MX6	0.875	①	②	0.004	9.000	9.060	NA	0.080	0.040
	929	0.875	⑬	⑭	0.004	6.690④	6.730④	NA	0.080	⑤
	RX7	⑥	⑦	⑧	0.004	—	—	—	0.080	0.040
1992	323	0.875	⑨	⑩	0.004	7.874	7.913	NA	0.080	0.040
	Protege	0.875	⑨	⑩	0.004	7.874	7.913	NA	0.080	0.040
	Miata	0.875	⑪	⑫	0.004	—	—	—	0.040	0.040
	MX3	⑮	⑨	③	0.004	7.874	7.913	NA	0.080	0.040
	626	0.875	①	②	0.004	9.000	9.060	NA	0.080	0.040
	MX6	0.875	①	②	0.004	9.000	9.060	NA	0.080	0.040
	929	NA	⑯	⑰	0.004	—	—	—	0.040	0.040
1993	323	0.875	⑨	⑩	0.004	7.874	7.913	NA	0.080	0.040
	Protege	0.875	⑨	⑩	0.004	7.874	7.913	NA	0.080	0.040
	Miata	0.875	⑪	⑫	0.004	—	—	—	0.040	0.040
	MX3	⑮	⑨	③	0.004	7.874	7.913	NA	0.080	0.040
	626	0.937	①	②	0.004	9.000	9.060	NA	0.040	0.040
	MX6	0.937	①	②	0.004	9.000	9.060	NA	0.040	0.040
	929	NA	⑯	⑰	0.004	—	—	—	0.040	0.040
	RX7	NA	⑦	⑧	0.004	—	—	—	0.040	0.040
1994	323	0.875	⑨	⑩	0.004	7.874	7.913	NA	0.080	0.040
	Protege	0.875	⑨	⑩	0.004	7.874	7.913	NA	0.080	0.040
	Miata	0.875	⑪	⑫	0.004	—	—	—	0.040	0.040
	MX3	⑮	⑨	③	0.004	7.874	7.913	NA	0.080	0.040
	626	0.937	①	②	0.004	9.000	9.060	NA	0.040	0.040
	MX6	0.937	①	②	0.004	9.000	9.060	NA	0.040	0.040
	929	NA	⑯	⑰	0.004	—	—	—	0.040	0.040
	RX7	NA	⑦	⑧	0.004	—	—	—	0.040	0.040

NA—Not available
① Front: 0.940
  Rear: 0.390
② Front: 0.870
  Rear: 0.310
③ Front: 0.790
  Rear: 0.310
④ Parking brake drum inside rear disc

⑤ Disc pad: 0.080
  Drum shoe: 0.040
⑥ Turbo: 0.937
  Non-turbo: 0.875

⑦ Front: 0.870
  Rear
    Ventilated disc: 0.790
    Solid disc: 0.390
⑧ Front: 0.790
  Rear
    Ventilated disc: 0.710
    Solid disc: 0.310

⑨ Front: 0.870
  Rear: 0.350
⑩ Front: 0.790
  Rear: 0.280
⑪ Front: 0.710
  Rear: 0.350

⑫ Front: 0.630
  Rear: 0.280
⑬ Front: 0.870
  Rear: 0.710
⑭ Front: 0.790
  Rear: 0.630

⑮ 1.6L engine: 0.875
  1.8L engine: 0.937
⑯ Front: 0.940
  Rear: 0.710
⑰ Front: 0.870
  Rear: 0.630

WHEEL ALIGNMENT

Year	Model		Caster Range (deg.)	Caster Preferred Setting (deg.)	Camber Range (deg.)	Camber Preferred Setting (deg.)	Toe-in (in.)	Steering Axis Inclination (deg.)
1990	323	Front	$1\frac{5}{16}$P–$2\frac{13}{16}$P	$2\frac{1}{16}$P	$\frac{13}{16}$N–$\frac{11}{16}$P	$\frac{1}{16}$N	$\frac{3}{32}$	$12\frac{7}{16}$
		Rear	—	—	$1\frac{1}{16}$N–$\frac{7}{16}$P	$\frac{5}{16}$N	$\frac{3}{32}$	—
	Protege	Front	$1\frac{5}{16}$P–$2\frac{13}{16}$P	$2\frac{1}{16}$P	$\frac{13}{16}$N–$\frac{11}{16}$P	$\frac{1}{16}$N	$\frac{3}{32}$	$12\frac{7}{16}$
		Rear	—	—	$1\frac{1}{16}$N–$\frac{7}{16}$P	$\frac{5}{16}$N	$\frac{3}{32}$	—
	Miata	Front	$3\frac{3}{4}$P–$5\frac{1}{4}$P	$4\frac{1}{2}$P	$\frac{3}{8}$N–$1\frac{1}{8}$P	$\frac{3}{8}$P	$\frac{1}{8}$	$11\frac{5}{16}$
		Rear	—	—	$1\frac{1}{4}$N–$\frac{1}{4}$N	$\frac{3}{4}$N	$\frac{1}{8}$	—
	626	Front	$\frac{7}{16}$P–$1\frac{15}{16}$P	$1\frac{3}{16}$P	$\frac{7}{16}$N–$1\frac{1}{16}$P	$\frac{5}{16}$P	0	$12\frac{13}{16}$
		Rear	—	—	①	②	$\frac{1}{8}$	—
	MX6	Front	$\frac{7}{16}$P–$1\frac{15}{16}$P	$1\frac{3}{16}$P	$\frac{7}{16}$N–$1\frac{1}{16}$P	$\frac{5}{16}$P	0	$12\frac{13}{16}$
		Rear	—	—	①	②	$\frac{1}{8}$	—
	929	Front	$3\frac{3}{4}$P–$5\frac{1}{4}$P	$4\frac{1}{2}$P	$\frac{1}{4}$P–$1\frac{3}{4}$P	1P	$\frac{5}{32}$	$12\frac{11}{16}$
		Rear	—	—	$\frac{3}{4}$N–$\frac{1}{4}$N	$\frac{1}{4}$N	$\frac{3}{32}$	—
	RX7	Front	$3\frac{15}{16}$P–$5\frac{7}{16}$P	$4\frac{11}{16}$P	$\frac{3}{16}$N–$\frac{13}{16}$P	$\frac{5}{16}$P	$\frac{1}{8}$	$13\frac{3}{4}$
		Rear	—	—	$1\frac{1}{4}$N–$\frac{1}{4}$N	$\frac{3}{4}$N	$\frac{1}{8}$	—
1991	323	Front	1P–$2\frac{7}{8}$P	$1\frac{15}{16}$P	$\frac{27}{32}$N–$\frac{21}{32}$P	$\frac{3}{32}$N	$\frac{3}{32}$	$12\frac{7}{16}$
		Rear	—	—	$1\frac{1}{16}$N–$\frac{7}{16}$P	$\frac{5}{16}$N	$\frac{3}{32}$	—
	Protege	Front	③	④	⑤	⑥	$\frac{3}{32}$	⑦
		Rear	—	—	$1\frac{1}{16}$N–$\frac{7}{16}$P	$\frac{5}{16}$N	$\frac{3}{32}$	—
	Miata	Front	$3\frac{11}{16}$P–$5\frac{3}{16}$P	$4\frac{7}{16}$P	$\frac{3}{8}$N–$1\frac{1}{8}$P	$\frac{3}{8}$P	$\frac{1}{8}$	$11\frac{5}{16}$
		Rear	—	—	$1\frac{1}{4}$N–$\frac{1}{4}$N	$\frac{3}{4}$N	$\frac{1}{8}$	—
	626	Front	$\frac{15}{16}$P–$2\frac{7}{16}$P	$1\frac{11}{16}$P	$\frac{7}{16}$N–$1\frac{1}{16}$P	$\frac{5}{16}$P	0	$12\frac{13}{16}$
		Rear	—	—	$1\frac{1}{4}$N–$\frac{1}{4}$N	$\frac{1}{2}$N	$\frac{1}{8}$	—
	MX6	Front	$\frac{15}{16}$P–$2\frac{7}{16}$P	$1\frac{11}{16}$P	$\frac{7}{16}$N–$1\frac{1}{16}$P	$\frac{5}{16}$P	0	$12\frac{13}{16}$
		Rear	—	—	$1\frac{1}{4}$N–$\frac{1}{4}$P	$\frac{1}{2}$N	$\frac{1}{8}$	—
	929	Front	$3\frac{3}{4}$P–$5\frac{1}{4}$P	$4\frac{1}{2}$P	$\frac{1}{4}$P–$1\frac{3}{4}$P	1P	$\frac{5}{32}$	$12\frac{11}{16}$
		Rear	—	—	$\frac{3}{4}$N–$\frac{1}{4}$N	$\frac{1}{4}$N	$\frac{3}{32}$	—
	RX7	Front	$3\frac{15}{16}$P–$5\frac{7}{16}$P	$4\frac{11}{16}$P	$\frac{3}{16}$N–$\frac{13}{16}$P	$\frac{5}{16}$P	$\frac{1}{8}$	$13\frac{3}{4}$
		Rear	—	—	$1\frac{1}{4}$N–$\frac{1}{4}$N	$\frac{3}{4}$N	$\frac{1}{8}$	—
1992	323	Front	1P–$2\frac{7}{8}$P	$1\frac{15}{16}$P	$\frac{27}{32}$N–$\frac{21}{32}$P	$\frac{3}{32}$N	$\frac{3}{32}$	$12\frac{7}{16}$
		Rear	—	—	$1\frac{1}{16}$N–$\frac{7}{16}$P	$\frac{5}{16}$N	$\frac{3}{32}$	—
	Protege	Front	1P–$2\frac{7}{8}$P	$1\frac{15}{16}$P	$\frac{27}{32}$N–$\frac{21}{32}$P	$\frac{3}{32}$N	$\frac{3}{32}$	$12\frac{7}{16}$
		Rear	—	—	$1\frac{1}{16}$N–$\frac{7}{16}$P	$\frac{5}{16}$N	$\frac{3}{32}$	—
	Miata	Front	$3\frac{11}{16}$P–$5\frac{3}{16}$P	$4\frac{7}{16}$P	$\frac{3}{8}$N–$1\frac{1}{8}$P	$\frac{3}{8}$P	$\frac{1}{8}$	$11\frac{5}{16}$
		Rear	—	—	$1\frac{1}{4}$N–$\frac{1}{4}$N	$\frac{3}{4}$N	$\frac{1}{8}$	—
	MX3	Front	$1\frac{7}{8}$P–$3\frac{3}{8}$P	$2\frac{5}{8}$P	$1\frac{9}{16}$N–$\frac{1}{16}$N	$\frac{13}{16}$N	$\frac{1}{8}$	$13\frac{3}{4}$
		Rear	—	—	$1\frac{11}{16}$N–$\frac{3}{16}$N	$\frac{15}{16}$N	$\frac{3}{32}$	—
	626	Front	$\frac{15}{16}$P–$2\frac{7}{16}$P	$1\frac{11}{16}$P	$\frac{7}{16}$N–$1\frac{1}{16}$P	$\frac{5}{16}$P	0	$12\frac{13}{16}$
		Rear	—	—	$1\frac{1}{4}$N–$\frac{1}{4}$P	$\frac{1}{2}$N	$\frac{1}{8}$	—
	MX6	Front	$\frac{15}{16}$P–$2\frac{7}{16}$P	$1\frac{11}{16}$P	$\frac{7}{16}$N–$1\frac{1}{16}$P	$\frac{5}{16}$P	0	$12\frac{13}{16}$
		Rear	—	—	$1\frac{1}{4}$N–$\frac{1}{4}$P	$\frac{1}{2}$N	$\frac{1}{8}$	—
	929	Front	$4\frac{11}{16}$P–$6\frac{3}{16}$P	$5\frac{7}{16}$P	$1\frac{1}{16}$N–$\frac{13}{16}$P	$\frac{1}{16}$P	$\frac{3}{32}$	$10\frac{9}{16}$
		Rear	—	—	$1\frac{1}{16}$N–$\frac{7}{16}$P	$\frac{5}{16}$N	$\frac{1}{8}$	—

WHEEL ALIGNMENT

Year	Model		Caster Range (deg.)	Caster Preferred Setting (deg.)	Camber Range (deg.)	Camber Preferred Setting (deg.)	Toe-in (in.)	Steering Axis Inclination (deg.)
1993	323	Front	1P–2$7/8$P	1$15/16$P	$27/32$N–$21/32$P	$3/32$N	$3/32$	12$7/16$
		Rear	—	—	1$1/16$N–$7/16$P	$5/16$N	$3/32$	—
	Protege	Front	1P–2$7/8$P	1$15/16$P	$27/32$N–$21/32$P	$3/32$N	$3/32$	12$7/16$
		Rear	—	—	1$1/16$N–$7/16$P	$5/16$N	$3/32$	—
	Miata	Front	3$11/16$P–5$3/16$P	4$7/16$P	$3/8$N–1$1/8$P	$3/8$P	$1/8$	11$5/16$
		Rear	—	—	1$1/4$N–$1/4$N	$3/4$N	$1/8$	—
	MX3	Front	1$7/8$P–3$3/8$P	2$5/8$P	1$9/16$N–$1/16$N	$13/16$N	$1/8$	13$3/4$
		Rear	—	—	1$11/16$N–$3/16$N	$15/16$N	$3/32$	—
	626	Front	1$7/8$P–3$3/8$P	2$5/8$P	1$3/8$N–$5/32$P	$19/32$N	$1/8$	15$1/16$
		Rear	—	—	$29/32$N–$19/32$P	$5/32$N	$1/8$	—
	MX6	Front	$15/16$P–2$7/16$P	3P	1$7/16$N–$1/16$P	$11/16$N	$1/8$	15$1/4$
		Rear	—	—	1$1/8$N–$3/8$P	$5/8$N	$1/8$	—
	929	Front	4$11/16$P–6$3/16$P	5$7/16$P	1$1/16$N–$13/16$P	$1/16$P	$3/32$	10$9/16$
		Rear	—	—	1$1/16$N–$7/16$P	$5/16$N	$1/8$	—
	RX7	Front	5$3/32$P–7$3/32$P	6$3/32$P	$21/32$N–$27/32$P	$3/32$P	$1/32$	13$15/16$
		Rear	—	—	1$31/32$N–$17/32$N	1$7/32$N	$3/32$	—
1994	323	Front	1P–2$7/8$P	1$15/16$P	$27/32$N–$21/32$P	$3/32$N	$3/32$	12$7/16$
		Rear	—	—	1$1/16$N–$7/16$P	$5/16$N	$3/32$	—
	Protege	Front	1P–2$7/8$P	1$15/16$P	$27/32$N–$21/32$P	$3/32$N	$3/32$	12$7/16$
		Rear	—	—	1$1/16$N–$7/16$P	$5/16$N	$3/32$	—
	Miata	Front	3$11/16$P–5$3/16$P	4$7/16$P	$3/8$N–1$1/8$P	$3/8$P	$1/8$	11$5/16$
		Rear	—	—	1$1/4$N–$1/4$N	$3/4$N	$1/8$	—
	MX3	Front	1$7/8$P–3$3/8$P	2$5/8$P	1$9/16$N–$1/16$N	$13/16$N	$1/8$	13$3/4$
		Rear	—	—	1$11/16$N–$3/16$N	$15/16$N	$3/32$	—
	626	Front	1$7/8$P–3$3/8$P	2$5/8$P	1$3/8$N–$5/32$P	$19/32$N	$1/8$	15$1/16$
		Rear	—	—	$29/32$N–$19/32$P	$5/32$N	$1/8$	—
	MX6	Front	$15/16$P–2$7/16$P	3P	1$7/16$N–$1/16$P	$11/16$N	$1/8$	15$1/4$
		Rear	—	—	1$1/8$N–$3/8$P	$5/8$N	$1/8$	—
	929	Front	4$11/16$P–6$3/16$P	5$7/16$P	1$1/16$N–$13/16$P	$1/16$P	$3/32$	10$9/16$
		Rear	—	—	1$1/16$N–$7/16$P	$5/16$N	$1/8$	—
	RX7	Front	5$3/32$P–7$3/32$P	6$3/32$P	$21/32$N–$27/32$P	$3/32$P	$1/32$	13$15/16$
		Rear	—	—	1$31/32$N–$17/32$N	1$7/32$N	$3/32$	—

N—Negative
P—Positive
① 2WD: 1$1/4$N–$1/4$P
  4WD: $3/4$N–$3/4$P
② 2WD: $1/2$N
  4WD: 0
③ 2WD: 1P–2$7/8$P
  4WD: 1$5/8$P–3$1/2$P

④ 2WD: 1$15/16$P
  4WD: 2$9/16$P
⑤ 2WD: $27/32$N–$21/32$P
  4WD: 1$1/2$N–0

⑥ 2WD: $3/32$N
  4WD: $3/4$N
⑦ 2WD: 12$7/16$
  4WD: 12$3/16$

ECCENTRIC SHAFT SPECIFICATIONS—ROTARY ENGINE

All measurements are given in inches.

Year	Engine ID/VIN	Engine Displacement Liters (cc)	Journal Diameter Main Bearing	Journal Diameter Rotor Bearing	Oil Clearance Main Bearing	Oil Clearance Rotor Bearing	Eccentric Shaft End-play Normal	Eccentric Shaft End-play Limit	Maximum Shaft Run-out
1990	13B	1.3 (1308)	1.6917–1.6923	2.9122–2.9128	0.0016–0.0039	0.0016–0.0039	0.0016–0.0028	0.0035	0.0047
1991	13B	1.3 (1308)	1.6917–1.6923	2.9122–2.9128	0.0016–0.0039	0.0016–0.0039	0.0016–0.0028	0.0035	0.0047
1993	13B	1.3 (1308)	1.6929	2.9130	①	0.0023–0.0039	0.0016–0.0028	0.0035	0.0027
1994	13B	1.3 (1308)	1.6929	2.9130	①	0.0023–0.0039	0.0016–0.0028	0.0035	0.0027

① Outside: 0.0031–0.0051
Inside: 0.0023–0.0043

ROTOR AND HOUSING SPECIFICATIONS—ROTARY ENGINE

All measurements are given in inches.

Year	Engine ID/VIN	Engine Displacement Liters (cc)	Rotor Side Clearance	Rotor Width	Housings Front and Rear Distortion Limit	Housings Front and Rear Wear Limit	Housings Rotor Width	Housings Rotor Distortion Limit	Housings Intermediate Distortion Limit	Housings Intermediate Wear Width
1990	13B	1.3 (1308)	0.0039–0.0083	3.1417–3.1437	0.0016	0.0039	3.1484–3.1500	0.0024	0.0016	0.0039
1991	13B	1.3 (1308)	0.0039–0.0083	3.1417–3.1437	0.0016	0.0039	3.1484–3.1500	0.0024	0.0016	0.0039
1993	13B	1.3 (1308)	0.0039–0.0083	3.1368	0.0020	0.0040	3.1496	0.0024	0.0020	0.0040
1994	13B	1.3 (1308)	0.0039–0.0083	3.1368	0.0020	0.0040	3.1496	0.0024	0.0020	0.0040

SEAL CLEARANCES—ROTARY ENGINE

All measurements are given in inches.

Year	Engine ID/VIN	Engine Displacement Liters (cc)	Apex Seals				Side Seal			
			To Side Housing		To Rotor Groove		To Rotor Groove		To Corner Seal	
			Normal	Limit	Normal	Limit	Normal	Limit	Normal	Limit
1990	13B	1.3 (1308)	—	—	①	0.0059	0.0011–0.0031	0.0039	0.0020–0.0059	0.016
1991	13B	1.3 (1308)	—	—	②	0.0059	0.0011–0.0031	0.0039	0.0020–0.0059	0.016
1993	13B	1.3 (1308)	—	—	0.002–0.004	0.0059	0.0011–0.0031	0.0039	0.0020–0.0059	0.016
1994	13B	1.3 (1308)	—	—	0.002–0.004	0.0059	0.0011–0.0031	0.0039	0.0020–0.0059	0.016

① Non-turbocharged engine: 0.0020–0.0036
   Turbochargd engine: 0.0016–0.0036
② Non-turbocharged engine: 0.0020–0.0040
   Turbochargd engine: 0.0024–0.0040

PISTON ENGINE MECHANICAL

NOTE: Disconnecting the negative battery cable on some vehicles may interfere with the functions of the on board computer systems and may require the computer to undergo a relearning process, once the negative battery cable is reconnected.

Engine Assembly

REMOVAL AND INSTALLATION

323 and Protege

1. Properly relieve the fuel system pressure. Raise and safely support the vehicle, as necessary.
2. Disconnect the battery cables and remove the battery and the battery tray. Raise and safely support the vehicle.
3. Remove the splash shield(s) from under the vehicle and drain the engine and transaxle oil and the coolant.
4. Remove the air cleaner assembly and resonance chamber, including the air flow meter and all of the ducting. Remove the oil dipstick.
5. Remove the radiator hoses. If equipped with automatic transaxle, disconnect and plug the oil cooler lines from the radiator. Disconnect the cooling fan and, if equipped, radiator switch electrical connectors and remove the radiator/cooling fan assembly. On 4WD vehicles, remove the crossmember from the underside of the vehicle.
6. Disconnect the throttle and the speedometer cable.
7. Label and disconnect the vacuum hoses and wiring.
8. Disconnect the fuel supply and return hoses and the heater hoses.
9. Disconnect the exhaust pipe from the manifold. On 4WD vehicles, remove the exhaust manifold. If equipped, remove the water inlet pipe and gasket.
10. Without disconnecting the hydraulic hoses, remove the power steering pump and hang it from the body with wire.
11. Without disconnecting the refrigerant lines, remove the air conditioning compressor and hang it from the body with wire.
12. If equipped with manual transaxle, disconnect the clutch cable and shift control rod. If equipped with hydraulic clutch, remove the slave cylinder from the transaxle without disconnecting the hydraulic line.
13. If equipped with automatic transaxle, disconnect the shift control cable.
14. Remove the nuts and disconnect the tie rod ends from the steering knuckles. Disconnect the stabilizer bar from the lower control arms.
15. Attach an engine lifting chain to the engine lifting eyes. Attach the chain to a suitable engine hoist and raise the hoist until there is tension on the chain.
16. Remove the engine mount nuts and the engine mount member bolts and nuts and remove the engine mount member. On 4WD vehicles, remove the front transaxle mount.

NOTE: Be careful so the engine does not fall when removing the engine mount member.

17. Remove the pinch bolts from the steering knuckle and pry the control arm down to slip lower ball joint out of the knuckle.
18. If equipped, remove the bolts from the right side intermediate shaft support and, using a suitable prybar, pry the intermediate shaft from the transaxle. Insert a suitable prybar between the inner CV-joint

and transaxle case and carefully pry the inner CV-joints out of the transaxle. Suspend the halfshafts with wire.

19. If equipped with 4WD, mark the position of the driveshaft on the transaxle and rear axle flanges. Remove the driveshaft, keeping all spacers, washers and bushings in order so they can be reinstalled in their original positions.

20. Remove the dynamic damper from the right side engine mount, if equipped. Remove the engine/transaxle mount nuts/bolts and right engine and, if equipped, left transaxle mounts. Carefully lift the engine/transaxle assembly from the vehicle.

21. Properly support the engine/transaxle assembly. Remove the intake manifold bracket, starter, torque converter nuts, stiffener, if equipped and No. 2 engine mount. Disconnect the throttle cable.

22. If equipped with 4WD, remove the center differential lock motor as follows:

a. Remove the set bolt and lock sensor switch.

b. Remove the plug from the end of the motor and use a small flat bladed tool to turn the shift rod ½ turn clockwise.

c. Remove the retaining bolts and the center differential lock motor.

23. Remove the transaxle mounting bolts and separate the transaxle from the engine.

To install:

24. Attach the transaxle to the engine and install the transaxle-to-engine bolts. If equipped with automatic transaxle, install the torque converter nuts and tighten to 25-36 ft. lbs. (34-49 Nm).

25. Connect the throttle cable. Install the No. 2 engine mount, stiffener, starter and intake manifold bracket. If equipped with 4WD, install the center differential lock motor as follows:

a. Install a new O-ring onto the motor. Make sure the flat edge of the shift rod is facing up.

b. Turn the shift rod ½ turn counterclockwise using a small flat bladed tool.

c. Install the lock motor and tighten the bolts to 14-22 ft. lbs. (20-29 Nm). Install the set bolt and lock sensor switch and tighten to 14-22 ft. lbs. (20-29 Nm).

26. On 2WD vehicles, proceed as follows:

a. Install the engine mount member and tighten the bolts/nuts to 47-66 ft. lbs. (64-89 Nm).

b. Carefully lower the engine/transaxle assembly into the engine compartment and align the engine mount bolts with the engine mount member mounting holes. Install the mount-to-mount member nuts and tighten to 27-38 ft. lbs. (37-52 Nm).

c. Install the right side engine mount. Tighten the mount-to-engine nut(s) to 54-76 ft. lbs. (74-103 Nm). Tighten the mount through bolt to 49-69 ft. lbs. (67-93 Nm).

d. Install the dynamic damper, to the right side mount and tighten to 41-59 ft. lbs. (55-80 Nm).

e. If equipped, install the left side transaxle mount. Loosely install the mount-to-transaxle nuts and align the mount bracket holes with the body holes. Install the mount-to-body bolts and tighten, in sequence, to 32-45 ft. lbs. (43-61 Nm). Tighten the mount-to-transaxle nuts to 49-69 ft. lbs. (67-93 Nm).

27. On 4WD vehicles, proceed as follows:

a. Carefully lower the engine/transaxle assembly into the vehicle.

b. Install the left and right side mounts and loosely tighten the bolts and nuts.

c. If equipped with manual transaxle, install the clutch hydraulic slave cylinder and pipe bracket assembly.

d. Install the front transaxle mount and tighten the mount-to-transaxle bolts to 27-38 ft. lbs. (37-52 Nm).

e. Align the engine mount member with the front and rear transaxle mount bolts and install the engine member-to-body bolts/nuts. Tighten the engine member-to-body bolts/nuts to 47-66 ft. lbs. (64-89 Nm) and the engine mount-to-member nuts to 27-38 ft. lbs. (37-52 Nm).

f. Tighten the left transaxle mount-to-body bolts, in sequence, to 32-43 ft. lbs. (43-61 Nm). Tighten the mount to transaxle nuts to 49-69 ft. lbs. (67-93 Nm).

g. Tighten the mount-to-engine nuts to 54-76 ft. lbs. (74-103 Nm) and the mount through bolt to 49-69 ft. lbs. (67-93 Nm). Install the dynamic damper and tighten the bolts/nuts to 41-59 ft. lbs. (55-80 Nm).

h. Install the driveshaft, aligning the marks that were made during removal. Tighten the shaft-to-flange bolts/nuts to 20-22 ft. lbs. (27-30 Nm) and the support bearing mounting nuts to 27-38 ft. lbs. (37-51 Nm).

28. Install new circlips on the inner CV-joint stub shafts and, if equipped, intermediate shaft. Grease the shaft splines and install the halfshaft/intermediate shaft into the transaxle.

29. If equipped, install the right intermediate shaft support bolts and tighten, in sequence, to 31-46 ft. lbs. (42-62 Nm).

30. Install the lower ball joint and torque the clamping bolt to 43 ft. lbs. (59 Nm). Install the tie rod ends and torque the nut to 42 ft. lbs. (57 Nm), then tighten as required to install a new cotter pin.

31. Attach the stabilizer bar and tighten the nuts so there is ¾ in. (19mm) of thread showing above the nut.

32. If equipped with manual transaxle, connect the extension bar and shift control rod. Connect the clutch cable or install the hydraulic slave cylinder, as necessary.

33. If equipped with automatic transaxle, connect the shift control cable.

34. Install a new gasket and connect the exhaust pipe to the manifold. Use new self-locking nuts and torque to 34 ft. lbs. (46 Nm).

35. Connect the wiring, heater, fuel and vacuum hoses.

36. Install the air conditioner compressor and power steering pump, if equipped. On 4WD vehicles, install the crossmember and tighten the bolts to 69-79 ft. lbs. (93-107 Nm).

37. Install the radiator/cooling fan assembly and connect the radiator hoses and the necessary electrical connectors.

38. Connect the accelerator and speedometer cables.

39. Install the battery tray assembly and battery. Install the air cleaner and air flow meter assembly and all the ducting. Connect the air flow sensor connector.

40. Install the splash shield(s).

41. Fill the engine and the transaxle with the proper types and quantities of oil. Fill the cooling system.

42. Connect the negative battery cable, start the engine and check for leaks. Check the ignition timing and the idle speed. Check all fluid levels.

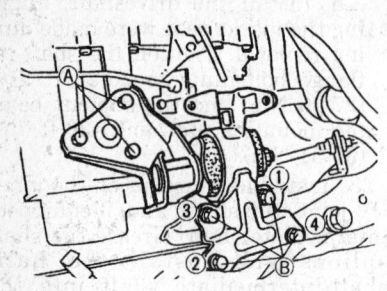

Left transaxle mount-to-body bolt torque sequence — 323, Protege and MX-3 with manual transaxle

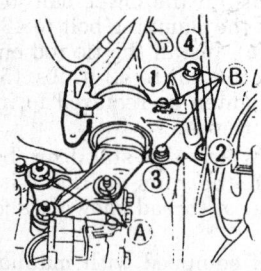

Left transaxle mount-to-body bolt torque sequence — 323, Protege and MX-3 with automatic transaxle

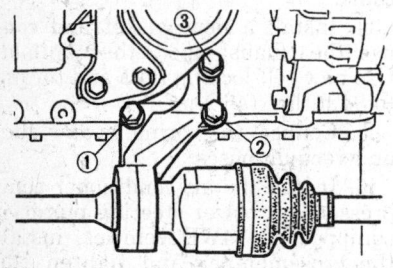

Intermediate shaft support bolt torque sequence — 323 and Protege

Miata

1. Mark the position of the hood on its hinges and remove the hood.

2. Properly relieve the fuel system pressure.

3. Raise the trunk lid and disconnect the negative battery cable. Remove the fresh air duct and the air cleaner/air flow meter assembly.

4. Disconnect the accelerator cable from the throttle body.

5. Raise and safely support the vehicle and remove the undercover.

Drain the engine and transmission oil and the coolant.

6. Disconnect the radiator hoses and the cooling fan electrical connector. Remove the radiator/cooling fans assembly.

7. Remove the accessory drive belts. Without disconnecting the hydraulic hoses, remove the power steering pump and secure it aside.

8. Without disconnecting the refrigerant, remove the air conditioner compressor and secure it aside.

9. Label and disconnect the wiring and all vacuum, fuel and coolant hoses.

10. Disconnect the exhaust pipe from the exhaust manifold.

11. Without disconnecting the hydraulic line, remove the clutch slave cylinder.

12. Remove the center console and the shifter assembly.

13. Disconnect the transmission electrical connectors and the speedometer cable.

14. Mark the position of the driveshaft on the differential flange and remove the bolts. Slide the driveshaft yoke from the transmission and remove the drive shaft.

15. The frame member between the transmission and differential must be removed. With the transmission properly supported, remove the bolts at both ends and remove the frame.

NOTE: Do not remove the upper frame-to-differential spacers from the frame. If they are removed, the entire frame must be replaced as a unit.

16. Install suitable lifting equipment onto the engine and make sure all hoses, wires and cables are disconnected.

17. Remove the engine mount nuts and lift the engine and transmission as an assembly from the vehicle.

18. Remove the starter.

19. If equipped with automatic transmission, remove the torque converter-to-flywheel bolts.

20. Remove the bolts to separate the transmission from the engine.

To install:

21. Assemble the engine to the transmission and torque the bolts to 66 ft. lbs. (89 Nm). If equipped with automatic transmission, install the torque converter-to-flywheel bolts and torque to 40 ft. lbs. (54 Nm).

22. Install the starter and torque the bolts to 38 ft. lbs. (52 Nm).

23. Carefully install the engine and transmission assembly into the vehicle. Start but do not tighten the mount nuts.

24. Install the transmission-to-differential frame and torque the bolts to 91 ft. lbs. (124 Nm). Torque the engine mount nuts to 58 ft. lbs. (78 Nm).

25. Connect the transmission wiring and speedometer cable and install the driveshaft. Torque the driveshaft bolts to 22 ft. lbs. (30 Nm).

26. Use a new gasket and attach the exhaust pipe to the manifold. Torque the nuts to 34 ft. lbs. (46 Nm).

27. Install the clutch slave cylinder and torque bolts to 19 ft. lbs. (25 Nm).

28. Connect and adjust the shift linkage as required.

29. Install the air conditioner compressor and power steering pump. Install and adjust the drive belts.

30. Install the radiator and fans and connect all cooling system hoses.

31. Connect all wiring and hoses.

32. Connect and adjust the accelerator cable as required.

33. Install the air cleaner and air flow meter assembly.

34. Check to make sure all wiring and hoses are properly connected. Fill and bleed the cooling system. Fill the engine and transmission with the proper type and quantity of oil.

35. Connect the negative battery cable, start the engine and bring to normal operating temperature. Check for leaks.

36. Check the ignition timing and idle speed. Check all fluid levels.

MX-3

1.6L ENGINE

1. Properly relieve the fuel system pressure.

2. Disconnect the battery cables and remove the battery and battery tray.

3. Mark the position of the hood on its hinges and remove the hood.

4. Raise and safely support the vehicle. Remove the front wheel and tire assemblies. Remove the splash shields.

5. Drain the cooling system and the engine and transaxle oil.

6. Disconnect the electrical connector from the air flow meter. Remove the air cleaner/air flow meter assembly and all air ducts.

7. Remove the radiator hoses and the accessory drive belts. If equipped with automatic transaxle, disconnect the oil cooler lines.

8. Remove the power steering pump and position aside, leaving the hoses connected.

9. Remove the A/C compressor and position aside, leaving the hoses connected.

10. Label and disconnect all necessary electrical connectors, vacuum hoses, fuel lines and heater hoses.

11. Disconnect the accelerator and speedometer cables.

12. If equipped with manual transaxle, remove the clutch slave cylinder and hydraulic line bracket and position aside, leaving the hydraulic line connected. Remove the shift control rod and extension bar.

13. If equipped with automatic transaxle, disconnect the shift control cable.

14. Disconnect the exhaust pipe from the exhaust manifold.

15. Disconnect the stabilizer bar and tie rod ends from the lower control arms.

16. Suspend the engine with suitable lifting equipment.

17. Remove the front and rear transaxle mount-to-engine mount member nuts. Remove the engine mount member-to-body bolts/nuts and remove the engine mount member.

NOTE: Be careful that the engine does not fall when removing the engine mount member.

18. Remove the ball joint pinch bolts/nuts from the steering knuckles. Use a suitable prybar to pull the lower control arm down and separate the ball joints from the steering knuckles. Use care so as not to damage the ball joint dust boots.

19. Insert a suitable prybar between the inner CV-joints and the transaxle case. Pry the halfshaft from the case, being careful not to damage the oil seal.

20. Remove the dynamic damper from the right side engine mount and remove the mount. Remove the left side transaxle mount and bracket.

21. Carefully lift the engine/transaxle assembly from the vehicle.

22. Safely support the engine/transaxle assembly and remove the starter and front transaxle mount.

23. If equipped with automatic transaxle, disconnect the throttle valve cable and remove the torque converter-to-flywheel nuts.

24. Remove the transaxle mounting bolts and separate the transaxle from the engine.

To install:

25. Assemble the transaxle to the engine and tighten the mounting bolts. Install the starter and front transaxle mount and tighten the bolts to 38 ft. lbs. (52 Nm).

26. If equipped with automatic transaxle, connect the throttle valve cable and install the torque con-

verter-to-flywheel nuts. Tighten the nuts to 36 ft. lbs. (49 Nm).

27. Install the engine mount member and tighten the bolts/nuts to 66 ft. lbs. (89 Nm).

28. Carefully lower the engine/transaxle assembly into the vehicle, aligning the front and rear transaxle mount bolts with the holes in the engine mount member. Install the nuts to the front and rear transaxle mounts and tighten to 38 ft. lbs. (52 Nm).

29. Install the right side engine mount and tighten the mount-to-engine nuts to 76 ft. lbs. (103 Nm). Install the mount through bolt and tighten the nut to 69 ft. lbs. (93 Nm). Install the dynamic damper and tighten the bolt/nut to 59 ft. lbs. (80 Nm).

30. Install the left transaxle mount/bracket assembly and loosely tighten the mount-to-transaxle nuts. Install the mount-to-body bolts and tighten, in sequence, to 45 ft. lbs. (61 Nm). Tighten the mount-to-engine nuts to 69 ft. lbs. (93 Nm).

31. Apply new circlips, with the gaps positioned upward, to the inner CV-joint stubs shafts and grease the splines. Install the halfshafts in the transaxle, being careful not to damage the oil seals. After installation, pull out on the hubs to make sure the circlips are seated in the differential side gears.

32. Insert the ball joints into the steering knuckles and install the pinch bolts. Tighten the pinch bolt nuts to 43 ft. lbs. (59 Nm).

33. Insert the tie rod ends into the knuckles and install the nuts. Tighten the nuts to at least 31 ft. lbs. (42 Nm), then continue tightening until the nut castellation is lined up with the ball stud hole. Install a new cotter pin.

34. Connect the stabilizer bar to the lower control arm.

35. If equipped with manual transaxle, connect the extension bar to the transaxle and tighten the nut to 34 ft. lbs. (46 Nm). Connect the shift control rod and tighten the nut to 17 ft. lbs. (23 Nm). Install the clutch slave cylinder and pipe bracket.

36. If equipped with automatic transaxle, connect the shift cable to the transaxle.

37. Connect the speedometer and accelerator cables.

38. Using a new gasket, connect the exhaust pipe to the exhaust manifold. Tighten the flange nuts to 34 ft. lbs. (46 Nm) and the bracket bolts to 38 ft. lbs. (52 Nm).

39. Connect the electrical connectors, vacuum hoses, heater hoses and fuel lines.

40. Install the A/C compressor and tighten the mounting bolts to 26 ft. lbs. (35 Nm). Install the power steering pump and bracket and tighten the bolts to 38 ft. lbs. (52 Nm). Install the accessory drive belts and adjust the belt tension.

41. Install the radiator hoses. If equipped with automatic transaxle, connect the oil cooler lines.

42. Install the battery tray and battery. Install the air flow meter/air cleaner assembly and related ducts. Connect the air flow sensor electrical connector.

43. Install the splash shields and the front wheel and tire assemblies. Lower the vehicle.

44. Install the hood, aligning the marks that were made during removal.

45. Connect the battery cables. Fill the engine and transaxle with the proper type and quantity of oil. Fill and bleed the cooling system.

46. Start the engine and bring to normal operating temperature. Check for leaks.

47. Check the ignition timing and idle speed. Check all fluid levels and road test the vehicle.

1.8L ENGINE

1. Properly relieve the fuel system pressure.

2. Disconnect the battery cables and remove the battery, battery tray and duct.

3. Mark the position of the hood on its hinges and remove the hood.

4. Raise and safely support the vehicle. Remove the front wheel and tire assemblies. Remove the splash shields.

5. Drain the cooling system and the engine and transaxle oil.

6. Remove the air cleaner assembly and all air ducts. Disconnect the accelerator cable and remove the coolant reservoir.

7. Remove the radiator hoses. Disconnect the cooling fan electrical connector and, if equipped with automatic transaxle, the oil cooler hoses. Remove the radiator, shroud and cooling fan assembly.

8. Remove the accessory drive belts.

9. Disconnect the power steering hose from the engine and disconnect the power steering pressure switch connector. Remove the power steering fluid reservoir and position aside. Remove the power steering pump pulley and mounting bolts and support the pump aside.

10. Remove the A/C compressor and position aside, leaving the hoses connected.

11. Label and disconnect all necessary electrical connectors, vacuum and heater hoses and fuel lines.

12. If equipped with manual transaxle, remove the clutch slave cylinder and line bracket and position the slave cylinder aside, leaving the hydraulic line connected. Disconnect the shift control rod and extension bar.

13. If equipped with automatic transaxle, disconnect the shift control cable.

14. Remove the transverse frame member from under the front of the vehicle. Disconnect the exhaust pipe from the exhaust manifolds.

15. Disconnect the stabilizer bar and tie rod ends from the lower control arms.

16. Suspend the engine with suitable lifting equipment.

17. Remove the front and rear transaxle mount-to-engine mount member nuts. Remove the engine mount member-to-body bolts/nuts and remove the engine mount member.

NOTE: Be careful that the engine does not fall when removing the engine mount member.

18. Remove the ball joint pinch bolts/nuts from the steering knuckles. Use a suitable prybar to pull the lower control arm down and separate the ball joints from the steering knuckles. Use care so as not to damage the ball joint dust boots.

19. Remove the right intermediate shaft support bolts and remove the intermediate shaft from the transaxle. Insert a suitable prybar between the left inner CV-joint and the transaxle case. Pry the halfshaft from the case, being careful not to damage the oil seal.

20. Remove the right engine mount and left transaxle mount. Carefully lift the engine/transaxle assembly from the vehicle.

21. Safely support the engine/transaxle assembly and remove the starter and front transaxle mount.

22. If equipped with automatic transaxle, disconnect the throttle valve cable and remove the torque converter-to-flywheel nuts.

23. Remove the transaxle mounting bolts and separate the transaxle from the engine.

To install:

24. Assemble the transaxle to the engine and tighten the mounting bolts to 73 ft. lbs. (99 Nm). Install the starter and front transaxle mount

and tighten the bolts to 38 ft. lbs. (52 Nm).

25. If equipped with automatic transaxle, connect the throttle valve cable and install the torque converter-to-flywheel nuts. Tighten the nuts to 36 ft. lbs. (49 Nm).

26. Install the engine mount member and tighten the bolts/nuts to 66 ft. lbs. (89 Nm).

27. Carefully lower the engine/transaxle assembly into the vehicle, aligning the front and rear transaxle mount bolts with the holes in the engine mount member. Install the nuts to the front and rear transaxle mounts and tighten to 38 ft. lbs. (52 Nm).

28. Install the right side engine mount. Tighten the mount-to-engine nuts to 76 ft. lbs. (103 Nm) and the mount through bolt to 69 ft. lbs. (93 Nm).

29. Install the left transaxle mount/bracket assembly and loosely tighten the mount-to-transaxle nuts. Install the mount-to-body bolts and tighten, in sequence, in 2-3 steps, to 45 ft. lbs. (61 Nm). Tighten the mount-to-transaxle nuts to 69 ft. lbs. (93 Nm).

30. Apply new circlips, with the gaps positioned upward, to the left inner CV-joint stub shaft and right intermediate shaft and grease the splines. Install the halfshaft and intermediate shaft in the transaxle, being careful not to damage the oil seals. Install the intermediate shaft support bolts and tighten, in sequence, to 46 ft. lbs. (62 Nm). After installation, pull out on the left hub to make sure the circlip on the left inner CV-joint stube shaft is seated in the differential side gear.

31. Insert the ball joints into the steering knuckles and install the pinch bolts. Tighten the pinch bolt nuts to 43 ft. lbs. (59 Nm).

32. Insert the tie rod ends into the knuckles and install the nuts. Tighten the nuts to at least 31 ft. lbs. (42 Nm), then continue tightening until the nut castellation is lined up with the ball stud hole. Install a new cotter pin.

33. Connect the stabilizer bar to the lower control arm.

34. If equipped with manual transaxle, connect the extension bar to the transaxle and tighten the nut to 34 ft. lbs. (46 Nm). Connect the shift control rod and tighten the nut to 17 ft. lbs. (23 Nm). Install the clutch slave cylinder and pipe bracket.

35. If equipped with automatic transaxle, connect the shift cable to the transaxle.

36. Using new gaskets, connect the exhaust pipe to the exhaust manifolds and tighten the nuts to 41 ft. lbs. (55 Nm).

37. Install the transverse member and tighten the mounting bolts to 93 ft. lbs. (127 Nm).

38. Connect the electrical connectors, vacuum hoses, heater hoses and fuel lines.

39. Install the A/C compressor and tighten the mounting bolts to 38 ft. lbs. (46 Nm).

40. Install the power steering pump. Tighten all mounting bolts to 34 ft. lbs. (46 Nm) except the bolt adjacent to the belt tensioning bolt. Tighten that bolt to 19 ft. lbs. (25 Nm). Connect the power steering hose bracket to the engine and connect the power steering pressure switch.

41. Install the power steering pump pulley and loosely tighten the nut. Insert a breaker bar and 12mm socket through 1 of the pulley holes and onto a pump bolt to keep the pulley from turning. Tighten the pulley nut to 69 ft. lbs. (93 Nm).

42. Install the power steering fluid reservoir and engine ground. Install the accessory drive belts and adjust the tension.

43. Install the battery duct and coolant reservoir.

44. Install the radiator/cooling fan assembly. Connect the hoses and the cooling fan electrical connector. If equipped with automatic transaxle, connect the oil cooler lines.

45. Connect the accelerator cable. Install the battery tray and battery.

46. Install the air cleaner assembly and ducts. Connect the air flow sensor connector.

47. Install the splash shields and the front wheel and tire assemblies. Lower the vehicle.

48. Install the hood, aligning the marks that were made during removal.

49. Connect the battery cables. Fill the engine and transaxle with the proper type and quantity of oil. Fill and bleed the cooling system.

50. Start the engine and bring to normal operating temperature. Check for leaks.

51. Check the ignition timing and idle speed. Check all fluid levels and road test the vehicle.

626 and MX-6

2.0L ENGINE

1. Properly relieve the fuel system pressure.

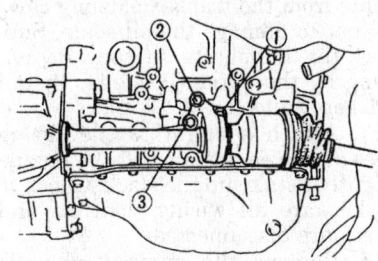

Intermediate shaft support bolt torque sequence — 1.8L and 2.5L 6-cylinder engine

2. Disconnect the battery cables and remove the battery, battery tray and duct.

3. Mark the position of the hood on its hinges and remove the hood.

4. Raise and safely support the vehicle. Remove the front wheel and tire assemblies. Remove the splash shields.

5. Drain the cooling system and the engine and transaxle oil.

6. Disconnect the electrical connectors and remove the air cleaner/air flow meter assembly and all air ducts. Disconnect the accelerator cable.

7. Remove the radiator hoses. Disconnect the cooling fan electrical connector and, if equipped with automatic transaxle, the oil cooler hoses. Remove the radiator, shroud and cooling fan assembly.

8. Remove the accessory drive belts.

9. Remove the power steering pump and position aside, leaving the hoses connected.

10. Remove the A/C compressor and position aside, leaving the hoses connected.

11. Label and disconnect all necessary electrical connectors, vacuum hoses, fuel lines and heater hoses. Remove the fuel filter.

12. If equipped with manual transaxle, remove the clutch slave cylinder and line bracket and position the slave cylinder aside, leaving the hydraulic line connected. Disconnect the shift control rod and extension bar.

13. If equipped with automatic transaxle, disconnect the shift control cable.

14. Remove the transverse frame member from under the front of the vehicle.

15. Suspend the engine with suitable lifting equipment.

16. Remove the mount-to-engine mount member nuts. Remove the engine mount member-to-body bolts/nuts and remove the engine mount member.

NOTE: Be careful that the engine does not fall when removing the engine mount member.

17. Remove the front exhaust pipe.

18. Disconnect the stabilizer bar and tie rod ends from the lower control arms.

19. Remove the ball joint pinch bolts/nuts from the steering knuckles. Use a suitable prybar to pull the lower control arm down and separate the ball joints from the steering knuckles. Use care so as not to damage the ball joint dust boots.

20. Remove the right intermediate shaft support bolts and remove the intermediate shaft from the transaxle. Insert a suitable prybar between the left inner CV-joint and the transaxle case. Pry the halfshaft from the case, being careful not to damage the oil seal.

21. Remove the (engine mounted) fuse box.

22. Remove the rear transaxle mount stay bracket and bolts. Remove the right engine mount and the left transaxle mount.

23. Carefully remove the engine/transaxle assembly from the vehicle.

24. Safely support the engine/transaxle assembly and remove the intake manifold bracket, starter and front transaxle mount. If equipped with automatic transaxle, remove the torque converter-to-flywheel nuts.

25. Remove the transaxle-to-engine bolts and separate the transaxle from the engine.

To install:

26. Assemble the transaxle to the engine and tighten the mounting bolts.

27. Install the front transaxle mount bracket and tighten the bolts to 44 ft. lbs. (60 Nm). Loosely tighten the mount through bolt.

28. Install the starter and intake manifold bracket and tighten the bolts to 38 ft. lbs. (51 Nm). If equipped with automatic transaxle, install the torque converter-to-flywheel nuts and tighten to 45 ft. lbs. (60 Nm).

29. Carefully lower the engine/transaxle assembly into the engine compartment.

30. Align the front engine mount bolts with the engine mount member mounting holes. Loosely tighten the mount-to-mount member nuts and tighten the mount member-to-body bolts/nuts to 68 ft. lbs. (93 Nm).

31. Install the rear transaxle mount-to-transaxle bolts and tighten to 68 ft. lbs. (93 Nm). Install the right engine mount and tighten the mount-to-engine nuts to 76 ft. lbs. (102 Nm) and the mount through bolt to 86 ft. lbs. (116 Nm).

32. Install the left transaxle mount bracket to the body. Loosely tighten the vertical bolts. Tighten the horizontal bolts to 59 ft. lbs. (80 Nm), then tighten the vertical bolts to the same specification.

33. Install the left transaxle mount. Tighten the mount-to-transaxle bolts/nuts to 68 ft. lbs. (93 Nm) and the mount through bolt to 86 ft. lbs. (116 Nm).

34. Remove the engine lifting equipment. Tighten the front transaxle mount-to-engine mount member nuts to 77 ft. lbs. (104 Nm) and the front engine mount through bolt to 86 ft. lbs. (116 Nm).

35. Install the center transaxle mount. Tighten the mount-to-transaxle bolts to 68 ft. lbs. (93 Nm) and the mount-to-mount member nuts to 44 ft. lbs. (60 Nm). Install the rear transaxle mount stay bracket and ground wire.

36. Apply new circlips, with the gaps positioned upward, to the left inner CV-joint stub shaft and right intermediate shaft and grease the splines. Install the halfshaft and intermediate shaft in the transaxle, being careful not to damage the oil seals. Install the intermediate shaft support bolts and tighten, in sequence, to 45 ft. lbs. (61 Nm). After installation, pull out on the left hub to make sure the circlip on the left inner CV-joint stub shaft is seated in the differential side gear.

37. Insert the ball joints into the steering knuckles and install the pinch bolts. Tighten the pinch bolt nuts to 41 ft. lbs. (56 Nm).

38. Insert the tie rod ends into the knuckles and install the nuts. Tighten the nuts to at least 32 ft. lbs. (44 Nm), then continue tightening until the nut castellation is lined up with the ball stud hole. Install a new cotter pin.

39. Connect the stabilizer bar to the lower control arm and tighten to 39 ft. lbs. (53 Nm).

40. If equipped with manual transaxle, connect the extension bar to the transaxle and tighten the nut to 38 ft. lbs. (51 Nm). Connect the shift control rod and tighten the nut to 16 ft. lbs. (22 Nm). Install the clutch slave cylinder and pipe bracket.

41. If equipped with automatic transaxle, connect the shift cable to the transaxle.

42. Using new gaskets, install the exhaust pipe and tighten the nuts and bracket bolts to 38 ft. lbs. (51 Nm).

43. Install the transverse member and tighten the bolts to 97 ft. lbs. (131 Nm).

44. Connect the electrical connectors, vacuum and heater hoses and fuel lines.

45. Install the A/C compressor and tighten the mounting bolts to 26 ft. lbs. (35 Nm).

46. Install the power steering pump adjuster and tighten the mounting bolts to 16 ft. lbs. (22 Nm). Install the pump and tighten the mounting bolts to 33 ft. lbs. (46 Nm). Connect the pump pressure switch electrical connector and install the power steering line brackets to the valve cover.

47. Install the accessory drive belts and adjust the tension.

48. Install the radiator/cooling fan assembly. Connect the radiator hoses and the cooling fan electrical connector.

49. Connect the accelerator cable.

50. Install the battery tray and battery. Install the air cleaner/air flow sensor assembly and the air ducts. Connect the air flow sensor and intake air thermosensor electrical connectors.

51. Install the splash shields and the front wheel and tire assemblies. Lower the vehicle.

52. Install the hood, aligning the marks that were made during removal.

53. Connect the battery cables. Fill the engine and transaxle with the proper type and quantity of oil. Fill and bleed the cooling system.

54. Start the engine and bring to normal operating temperature. Check for leaks.

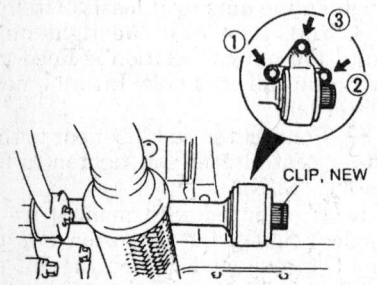

Intermediate shaft support bolt torque sequence — 2.0L engine

55. Check the ignition timing and idle speed. Check all fluid levels and road test the vehicle.

2.2L ENGINE

1. Properly relieve the fuel system pressure. Mark the position of the hood on the hinges and remove the hood.

2. Disconnect and remove the battery and the battery box. Raise and safely support the vehicle. Remove the wheel and tire assemblies.

3. Remove the splash shields at the front of the inner fenders and drain the engine and transaxle and the cooling system.

4. Remove the air cleaner assembly, including the air flow meter and all of the ducting. If equipped, remove the turbocharger pipe and hose and cover the turbocharger opening with a clean shop towel.

5. Remove the radiator hoses and disconnect the cooling fan electrical connector. If equipped with automatic transaxle, disconnect the oil cooler lines from the radiator. Remove the radiator/cooling fan assembly.

6. Disconnect the throttle and cruise control cables, if equipped, and the speedometer cable.

7. Label and disconnect the vacuum hoses and wiring.

8. Disconnect the fuel supply and return hoses and the heater hoses. Plug the fuel hoses to prevent leakage.

9. Disconnect the exhaust pipe from the manifold.

10. Without disconnecting the hydraulic hoses, remove the power steering pump and position it aside.

11. Without disconnecting the refrigerant lines, remove the air conditioning compressor and position it aside.

12. If equipped with manual transaxle, remove the clutch slave cylinder without disconnecting the hydraulic line. Disconnect the shift linkage.

13. If equipped with automatic transaxle, disconnect the shift cable.

14. Disconnect the stabilizer bar and the tie rod ends from the lower control arm.

15. Remove the pinch bolts from the steering knuckle and pry the control arm down to slip lower ball joint out of the knuckle.

NOTE: When the halfshafts are removed from the transaxle, the differential side gears must be held in place with service tool 49 G027 003 (manual) or 40 G030 455 (automatic), or equivalent.

16. Carefully pry the inner CV-joints from the transaxle, being careful not to damage the oil seals. Support the halfshafts so they do not hang by the outer CV-joints. Install the service tools.

17. Attach a chain to the lifting eyes on the engine and lift the engine slightly to take up the slack. Check to make sure all wiring, controls and hoses are disconnected.

18. Remove the engine/transaxle mount nuts/bolts and carefully lift the engine/transaxle assembly from the vehicle.

19. With the transaxle properly supported, remove the starter. If equipped with automatic transaxle, remove the flywheel-to-torque converter nuts.

20. Remove the transaxle mounting bolts and brackets and separate the transaxle from the engine.

To install:

21. Carefully fit the engine and transaxle together and torque the bolts to 86 ft. lbs. (117 Nm).

22. If equipped with automatic transaxle, install the flywheel-to-torque converter bolts and torque to 45 ft. lbs. (61 Nm).

23. On manual transaxle, when installing the clutch cover, seal the inner corners with silicone sealant.

24. Attach the stiffener brackets and torque the bolts to 38 ft. lbs. (52 Nm).

25. Attach the front transaxle mount to the engine and torque the bolts to 38 ft. lbs. (52 Nm) on non-turbocharged vehicles or to 68 ft. lbs. (92 Nm) on turbocharged vehicles.

26. Install the starter and torque the bolts to 38 ft. lbs. (52 Nm).

27. Carefully install the engine/transaxle with just the front and rear mounts attached. When the unit is in place, install the left and right mounts. Start all nuts and bolts first, then torque the following:

Left mount-to-transaxle nuts — 66 ft. lbs. (89 Nm).

Left mount-to-body bolts — 40 ft. lbs. (54 Nm).

Right mount-to-engine nuts — 76 ft. lbs. (103 Nm).

Right mount through bolt — 69 ft. lbs. (93 Nm).

Front mount-to-body nut — 69 ft. lbs. (93 Nm).

Rear mount through bolt — 86 ft. lbs. (117 Nm).

28. Use new gaskets and attach the exhaust pipe. Torque the pipe-to-manifold or turbocharger nuts to 36 ft. lbs. (49 Nm).

29. Connect the manual shift linkage and install the clutch slave

cylinder. Torque the shift rod bolt to 17 ft. lbs. (22 Nm) and the extension bar nut to 34 ft. lbs. (46 Nm).

30. Install new circlips on the inner CV-joint stub shafts with the gap facing upward. Grease the splines and push the halfshafts into the transaxle, being careful not to damage the oil seals. After installation, pull the hubs outward to make sure the circlips are seated in the differential side gears.

31. Install the lower ball joint and torque the pinch bolt to 40 ft. lbs. (54 Nm). Install the tie rod ends and torque the nut to 42 ft. lbs. (57 Nm), then tighten as required to install a new cotter pin.

32. Attach the stabilizer bar and tighten the nuts so there is 0.80 in. (20mm) of thread showing at the top of the long mounting bolt.

33. If equipped with automatic transaxle, connect and adjust the shift cable as required.

34. Connect the wiring and all water, fuel and vacuum hoses. Connect the accelerator cable.

35. Install the air conditioner compressor and power steering pump. Install the accessory drive belts and adjust the tension.

36. Install the radiator/cooling fan assembly and connect the hoses and cooling fan electrical connector.

37. Install the battery tray and the battery.

38. Install the air cleaner and air flow meter assembly and all the ducting. If equipped, install the turbocharger pipe and hoses.

39. Install the splash shields and the front wheel and tire assemblies. Lower the vehicle.

40. Install the hood, aligning the marks that were made during removal.

41. Connect the battery cables. Fill the engine and transaxle with the proper type and quantity of oil. Fill and bleed the cooling system.

42. Start the engine and bring to normal operating temperature. Check for leaks.

43. Check the ignition timing and idle speed. Check all fluid levels and road test the vehicle.

2.5L ENGINE

1. Properly relieve the fuel system pressure.

2. Disconnect the battery cables and remove the battery, battery tray and duct.

3. Mark the position of the hood on its hinges and remove the hood.

4. Raise and safely support the vehicle. Remove the front wheel and tire assemblies. Remove the splash shields.

5. Drain the cooling system and the engine and transaxle oil.

6. Remove the air cleaner assembly and all air ducts. Disconnect the accelerator cable.

7. Remove the radiator hoses. Disconnect the cooling fan electrical connector and, if equipped with automatic transaxle, the oil cooler hoses. Remove the radiator/cooling fan assembly.

8. Remove the accessory drive belts.

9. Remove the power steering fluid reservoir and position aside, leaving the hoses attached. Remove the power steering pump pulley and mounting bolts and support the pump aside, leaving the hoses attached.

10. Remove the A/C compressor and position aside, leaving the hoses connected.

11. Remove the fuel filter. Label and disconnect all necessary electrical connectors, vacuum and heater hoses, and fuel lines.

12. If equipped with manual transaxle, remove the clutch slave cylinder and line bracket and position the slave cylinder aside, leaving the hydraulic line connected. Disconnect the shift control rod and extension bar.

13. If equipped with automatic transaxle, disconnect the shift control cable.

14. Remove the transverse frame member from under the front of the vehicle. Remove the front exhaust pipe.

15. Disconnect the stabilizer bar and tie rod ends from the lower control arms.

16. Remove the ball joint pinch bolts/nuts from the steering knuckles. Use a suitable prybar to pull the lower control arm down and separate the ball joints from the steering knuckles. Use care so as not to damage the ball joint dust boots.

17. Remove the right intermediate shaft support bolts and remove the intermediate shaft from the transaxle. Insert a suitable prybar between the left inner CV-joint and the transaxle case. Pry the halfshaft from the case, being careful not to damage the oil seal.

18. Suspend the engine with suitable lifting equipment. Remove the right engine mount and left transaxle mount.

19. Remove the mount-to-engine mount member nuts. Remove the engine mount member-to-body

bolts/nuts and remove the engine mount member.

20. Carefully lift the engine/transaxle assembly from the vehicle.

21. Safely support the engine/transaxle assembly and remove the starter and front transaxle mount.

22. If equipped with automatic transaxle, remove the torque converter-to-flywheel nuts.

23. Remove the transaxle mounting bolts and separate the transaxle from the engine.

To install:

24. Assemble the transaxle to the engine and tighten the mounting bolts to 73 ft. lbs. (99 Nm). Install the starter and front transaxle mount bracket and tighten the bolts to 38 ft. lbs. (52 Nm). Install the front engine mount and loosely tighten the through bolt.

25. If equipped with automatic transaxle, install the torque converter-to-flywheel nuts. Tighten the nuts to 44 ft. lbs. (60 Nm).

26. Carefully lower the engine/transaxle assembly into the engine compartment.

27. Align the front engine mount bolts with the engine mount member mounting holes. Loosely tighten the mount-to-mount member nuts and tighten the mount member-to-body bolts/nuts to 68 ft. lbs. (93 Nm).

28. Install the rear transaxle mount-to-transaxle bolts and tighten to 68 ft. lbs. (93 Nm). Install the right engine mount and tighten the mount-to-engine nuts to 76 ft. lbs. (102 Nm) and the mount through bolt to 86 ft. lbs. (116 Nm).

29. Install the left transaxle mount bracket to the body. Loosely tighten the vertical bolts. Tighten the horizontal bolts to 59 ft. lbs. (80 Nm), then tighten the vertical bolts to the same specification.

30. Install the left transaxle mount. Tighten the mount-to-transaxle bolts/nuts to 68 ft. lbs. (93 Nm) and the mount through bolt to 86 ft. lbs. (116 Nm).

31. Remove the engine lifting equipment. Tighten the front engine mount through bolt to 86 ft. lbs. (116 Nm) and the front transaxle mount-to-engine mount member nuts to 77 ft. lbs. (104 Nm).

32. Install the center transaxle mount. Tighten the mount-to-transaxle bolts to 68 ft. lbs. (93 Nm) and the mount-to-mount member nuts to 44 ft. lbs. (60 Nm).

33. Apply new circlips, with the gaps positioned upward, to the left

inner CV-joint stub shaft and right intermediate shaft and grease the splines. Install the halfshaft and intermediate shaft in the transaxle, being careful not to damage the oil seals. Install the intermediate shaft support bolts and tighten, in sequence, to 45 ft. lbs. (61 Nm). After installation, pull out on the left hub to make sure the circlip on the left inner CV-joint stub shaft is seated in the differential side gear.

34. Insert the ball joints into the steering knuckles and install the pinch bolts. Tighten the pinch bolt nuts to 43 ft. lbs. (56 Nm).

35. Insert the tie rod ends into the knuckles and install the nuts. Tighten the nuts to at least 32 ft. lbs. (44 Nm), then continue tightening until the nut castellation is lined up with the ball stud hole. Install a new cotter pin.

36. Connect the stabilizer bar to the lower control arm and tighten to 39 ft. lbs. (53 Nm).

37. If equipped with manual transaxle, connect the extension bar to the transaxle and tighten the nut to 33 ft. lbs. (46 Nm). Connect the shift control rod and tighten the nut to 16 ft. lbs. (22 Nm). Install the clutch slave cylinder and pipe bracket.

38. If equipped with automatic transaxle, connect the shift cable to the transaxle.

39. Using new gaskets, install the front exhaust pipe. Tighten the pipe-to-exhaust system nuts to 65 ft. lbs. (89 Nm) and the pipe-to-manifold nuts to 40 ft. lbs. (54 Nm).

40. Install the transverse member and tighten the bolts to 93 ft. lbs. (126 Nm).

41. Install the fuel filter. Connect the electrical connectors, vacuum and heater hoses and fuel lines.

42. Install the A/C compressor and tighten the mounting bolts to 26 ft. lbs. (35 Nm).

43. Install the power steering pump. Tighten all mounting bolts to 34 ft. lbs. (46 Nm) except the bolt adjacent to the belt tensioning bolt. Tighten that bolt to 19 ft. lbs. (25 Nm). Connect the power steering pressure switch.

44. Install the power steering pump pulley and loosely tighten the nut. Insert a breaker bar and 12mm socket through 1 of the pulley holes and onto a pump bolt to keep the pulley from turning. Tighten the pulley nut to 69 ft. lbs. (93 Nm).

45. Install the power steering fluid reservoir and engine ground. Install the accessory drive belts and adjust the tension.

46. Install the radiator/cooling fan assembly. Connect the hoses and the cooling fan electrical connector. If equipped with automatic transaxle, connect the oil cooler lines.

47. Connect the accelerator cable. Install the battery tray and battery.

48. Install the air cleaner assembly and ducts. Connect the air flow sensor connector.

49. Install the splash shields and the front wheel and tire assemblies. Lower the vehicle.

50. Install the hood, aligning the marks that were made during removal.

51. Connect the battery cables. Fill the engine and transaxle with the proper type and quantity of oil. Fill and bleed the cooling system.

52. Start the engine and bring to normal operating temperature. Check for leaks.

53. Check the ignition timing and idle speed. Check all fluid levels and road test the vehicle.

929

1. Properly relieve the fuel system pressure. Disconnect the negative battery cable.

2. Mark the position of the hood on the hinges and remove the hood.

3. Remove the air cleaner assembly and the air ducts.

4. On 1992-94 vehicles, remove the battery and battery tray.

5. Raise and safely support the vehicle. Remove the splash shield.

6. Drain the cooling system and the engine and transmission oil.

7. Remove the cooling fan and fan shroud. Disconnect the radiator hoses and transmission cooler lines and remove the radiator.

8. Remove the accessory drive belts.

9. Remove the power steering pump pulley, using holder tool 49 W023 585A or equivalent, to hold the pulley while the nut is removed. Remove the power steering pump and position aside, leaving the hoses attached.

10. Remove the A/C compressor and position aside, leaving the refrigerant lines attached.

11. On DOHC engines, remove the upper intake manifold and throttle body assembly.

12. Label and disconnect all necessary wiring, vacuum hoses, heater hoses and fuel lines.

13. Remove the alternator.

14. Disconnect the accelerator cable.

15. Disconnect the exhaust pipes from the exhaust manifolds.

16. Remove the engine mount nuts.

17. Remove the starter and the transmission.

18. Attach suitable lifting equipment to the engine. Carefully remove the engine from the vehicle and position on a workstand.

To install:

19. Carefully lower the engine into the engine compartment. Loosely install the engine mount nuts.

20. Install the transmission. After the transmission and engine are bolted together, tighten the engine mount nuts to 36 ft. lbs. (49 Nm).

21. Install the starter.

22. Using new gaskets, connect the exhaust pipes to the exhaust manifolds. Tighten the nuts to 34 ft. lbs. (46 Nm).

23. Connect the electrical connectors, vacuum hoses, heater hoses and fuel lines.

24. On DOHC engines, use a new gasket and install the upper intake manifold and throttle body assembly. Tighten the bolts to 19 ft. lbs. (25 Nm).

25. Connect the accelerator cable and the electrical connectors and hoses to the upper intake manifold and throttle body assembly.

26. Install the power steering pump and tighten the mounting bolts to 34 ft. lbs. (46 Nm). Install the pump pulley and tighten the nut to 43 ft. lbs. (59 Nm).

27. Install the A/C compressor and tighten the mounting bolts to 29 ft. lbs. (39 Nm) on SOHC engine or 38 ft. lbs. (52 Nm) on DOHC engine.

28. Install the alternator and tighten the mounting bolts to 38 ft. lbs. (52 Nm).

29. Install the accessory drive belts and adjust the belt tension.

30. Install the radiator and tighten the mounting bolts to 19 ft. lbs. (26 Nm). Connect the radiator hoses and the transmission oil cooler lines.

31. Install the cooling fan and shroud.

32. Install the air cleaner assembly and ducts. Install the battery tray and battery, if removed.

33. Install the splash shield and lower the vehicle.

34. Install the hood, aligning the marks that were made during removal.

35. Connect the battery cables. Fill the engine and transaxle with the proper type and quantity of oil. Fill and bleed the cooling system.

36. Start the engine and bring to normal operating temperature. Check for leaks.

37. Check the ignition timing and idle speed. Check all fluid levels and road test the vehicle for proper operation.

Engine Mounts

REMOVAL AND INSTALLATION

1. Raise and support the vehicle safely.

2. Attach a hoist to the engine and lift until the slack in the chain is taken up.

3. Remove the nuts from the engine mounts.

NOTE: Inspect the engine compartment for components that may bind when the engine is raised. Disconnect these components.

4. Lift the engine the exact amount needed to remove the engine mount. Do not lift any higher.

5. Remove the engine mounts.

To Install:

6. Install the engine mounts.

7. Lower the engine and tighten the engine mount-to-engine nuts to 32-41 ft. lbs. (43-55 Nm). Tighten the engine mount-to-frame nuts to 41-49 ft. lbs. (55-67 Nm).

8. Remove the engine hoist and lower the vehicle.

Cylinder Head

REMOVAL AND INSTALLATION

323 and Protege

1. Properly relieve the fuel system pressure.

2. Disconnect the negative battery cable and remove the engine undercover.

3. Remove the air ducts from the air cleaner and throttle body. If equipped, remove the turbocharger air pipe and cover the turbocharger opening with a clean rag.

4. Tag and disconnect the spark plug wires from the spark plugs. Remove the spark plugs and the distributor cap and wires assembly. Remove the distributor.

5. Drain the cooling system and disconnect the radiator and heater hoses. On turbocharged engines, remove the radiator/cooling fan assembly.

6. Disconnect the exhaust pipe and remove the exhaust manifold. On turbocharged engines, disconnect the

turbocharger oil line and remove the manifold and the turbocharger as an assembly.

7. On DOHC engines, remove the coolant bypass pipe.

8. Disconnect the accelerator cable.

9. Label and disconnect all necessary electrical connections and vacuum hoses. Disconnect the fuel lines.

10. Remove the intake manifold bracket and the intake manifold.

11. Remove the cylinder head cover bolts and the cylinder head cover.

12. Remove the timing belt cover(s). Rotate the crankshaft, in the normal direction of rotation, until the No. 1 cylinder piston is at TDC on the compression stroke. Make sure the timing marks on the crankshaft and camshaft sprocket(s) are properly aligned and mark the direction of rotation of the belt.

13. Loosen the timing belt tensioner and remove the belt. Do not rotate the crankshaft until the timing belt is reinstalled.

14. When everything is disconnected, loosen the cylinder head bolts in the reverse of the tightening sequence in steps. Remove the bolts and lift the head off the engine.

To install:

15. Thoroughly, clean the cylinder head and the block contact surfaces. Examine the head gasket and check the cylinder head for cracks. Check the cylinder head for warpage using a feeler gauge and straightedge. The maximum allowable distortion is 0.006 in. (0.15mm) on 1.6L engine or 0.004 in. (0.10mm) on 1.8L engine.

16. Clean the cylinder head bolts and the threads in the block. Make sure the bolts turn freely in the block.

17. Install a new head gasket on the engine block. Make sure the camshaft sprocket timing marks are still aligned, as set during the removal procedure. Install the cylinder head.

18. Lubricate the bolt threads and seat surfaces with clean engine oil and install them. Torque the bolts in 2-3 steps to 56-60 ft. lbs. (75-81 Nm) in the proper sequence.

19. Make sure the crankshaft and camshaft sprocket timing marks are aligned, install the timing belt and set the tension. Carefully rotate the crankshaft 2 turns to make sure the timing marks still line up.

20. Apply a thin bead of sealant to the cylinder head cover and install the new gasket. Install the cover and torque the cover bolts to 78 inch lbs. (9 Nm).

21. Install the timing belt cover(s) and tighten the bolts to 95 inch lbs. (11 Nm).

22. Use new gaskets and install the manifolds. Torque the intake manifold bolts/nuts to 19 ft. lbs. (25 Nm) and install the intake manifold bracket. Torque the SOHC engine exhaust manifold bolts to 17 ft. lbs. (23 Nm). On DOHC engines, torque the exhaust manifold nuts to 34 ft. lbs. (46 Nm).

23. On turbocharged engines, connect the turbocharger oil line and install the turbocharger bracket.

24. Use a new gasket to connect the exhaust pipe and torque the nuts to 34 ft. lbs. (46 Nm).

25. If removed, install the radiator and connect all cooling system hoses. On DOHC engines, install the coolant bypass pipe.

26. Install the distributor, spark plugs, distributor cap and wires.

27. Connect all vacuum and fuel system hoses and connect all wiring.

28. Connect the accelerator cable and install the air ducts and engine undercover.

29. Connect the negative battery cable. Fill and bleed the cooling system. Change the engine oil.

30. Start the engine and bring to normal operating temperature. Check for leaks. Check the ignition timing and idle speed.

Miata

1. Properly relieve the fuel system pressure.

2. Disconnect the negative battery cable and drain the cooling system.

3. Remove the air cleaner and air flow meter assembly and the inlet air ducting. Disconnect the accelerator cable.

4. Disconnect the radiator and heater hoses.

5. Label and disconnect all necessary electrical connections and vacuum hoses. Disconnect the fuel lines.

6. Remove the ignition coil pack assembly with the spark plug wires.

7. Disconnect the exhaust pipe from the exhaust manifold and remove the exhaust manifold from the cylinder head.

8. Remove the cylinder head cover and the timing belt front covers.

9. Rotate the crankshaft, in the normal direction of rotation, until the No. 1 cylinder piston is at TDC on the compression stroke. Make sure the timing marks on the crankshaft and camshaft sprockets are properly aligned and mark the direction of rotation of the belt.

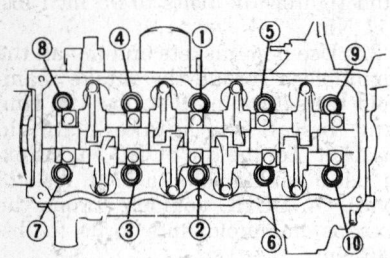

Cylinder head bolt torque sequence — 323, Protege and MX-3 with SOHC engine

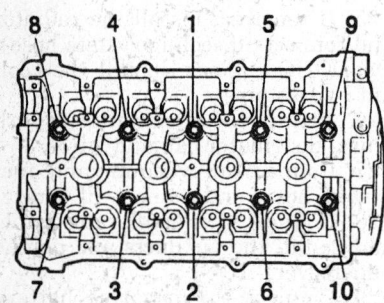

Cylinder head bolt torque sequence — 323, Protege and Miata with DOHC engine

10. Loosen the timing belt tensioner lock bolt. Pry the tensioner outward with a prybar and tighten the lock bolt with the tensioner spring fully extended. Remove the timing belt.

11. Remove the intake manifold-to-engine block bracket.

12. When everything is disconnected, loosen the cylinder head bolts in the reverse of the tightening sequence in steps. Remove the bolts and lift the head off the engine.

13. If necessary, remove the intake manifold from the cylinder head.

To install:

14. Thoroughly, clean the cylinder head and the block contact surfaces. Examine the head gasket and check the cylinder head for cracks. Check the cylinder head for warpage using a feeler gauge and straightedge. The maximum allowable distortion is 0.006 in. (0.15mm).

15. If removed, install the intake manifold using a new gasket. Tighten the intake manifold bolts to 19 ft. lbs. (25 Nm).

16. Clean the cylinder head bolts and the threads in the block. Make sure the bolts turn freely in the block.

17. Install a new head gasket on the engine block. Make sure the

camshaft sprocket timing marks are still aligned, as set during the removal procedure. Install the cylinder head.

18. Lubricate the bolt threads and seat surfaces with clean engine oil and install. Torque the bolts in 2-3 steps to 56-60 ft. lbs. (75-81 Nm) in the proper sequence.

19. Make sure the crankshaft and camshaft sprocket timing marks are aligned, install the timing belt and set the tension. Carefully rotate the crankshaft 2 turns to make sure the timing marks still line up. Install the timing belt covers.

20. Apply a thin bead of sealant to the cylinder head cover and install the new gasket. Install the cover and torque the cover bolts to 78 inch lbs. (9 Nm).

21. Using a new gasket, install the exhaust manifold and torque the nuts to 34 ft. lbs. (46 Nm). Install a new flange gasket and torque the nuts to 34 ft. lbs. (45 Nm).

22. Install the intake manifold-to-engine block bracket.

23. Install all cooling system hoses.

24. Install the ignition coil pack and spark plugs.

25. Connect all wiring and vacuum hoses. Connect the fuel lines.

26. Connect the accelerator cable. Install the air cleaner/air flow meter assembly and the air ducts.

27. Connect the negative battery cable. Fill and bleed the cooling system. Change the engine oil.

28. Start the engine and bring to normal operating temperature. Check for leaks. Check the ignition timing and idle speed.

MX-3

1.6L ENGINE

1. Properly relieve the fuel system pressure.

2. Disconnect the negative battery cable. Remove the engine undercover and drain the cooling system.

3. Remove the air ducts from the air cleaner and throttle body. Disconnect the accelerator and, if equipped, throttle valve cables.

4. Label and disconnect the necessary wiring, vacuum hoses and coolant hoses. Disconnect the fuel lines.

5. Remove the nut from the water bypass pipe bracket and remove the bracket from the stud.

6. Remove the accessory drive belts and the water pump pulley.

7. Remove the cylinder head and timing belt covers. Remove the crankshaft pulley.

8. Rotate the crankshaft, in the normal direction of rotation, until the

No. 1 cylinder piston is at TDC on the compression stroke. Make sure the timing marks on the crankshaft and camshaft sprockets are properly aligned and mark the direction of rotation of the belt.

9. Loosen the timing belt tensioner lock bolt. Pry the tensioner outward with a prybar and tighten the lock bolt with the tensioner spring fully extended. Remove the timing belt.

10. Disconnect the exhaust pipe from the exhaust manifold. Remove the intake manifold-to-cylinder head bracket.

11. Loosen the cylinder head bolts in the reverse order of the tightening sequence in steps. Remove the cylinder head.

12. If necessary, remove the intake and exhaust manifolds from the cylinder head.

13. Clean all gasket mating surfaces. Inspect the cylinder head for cracks or other damage. Check the cylinder head for warpage using a feeler gauge and straightedge. The maximum allowable distortion is 0.006 in. (0.15mm).

14. Clean the cylinder head bolts and the threads in the block. Make sure the bolts turn freely in the block.

To install:

15. If removed, install the intake and exhaust manifolds using new gaskets. Tighten the intake manifold bolts/nuts to 19 ft. lbs. (25 Nm) and the exhaust manifold bolts/nuts to 34 ft. lbs. (46 Nm).

16. Install a new head gasket on the engine block. Make sure the camshaft sprocket timing marks are still aligned, as set during the removal procedure. Install the cylinder head.

17. Lubricate the cylinder head bolt threads and seat surfaces with clean engine oil and install. Torque the bolts in 2-3 steps to 56-60 ft. lbs. (75-81 Nm) in the proper sequence.

18. Make sure the crankshaft and camshaft sprocket timing marks are aligned, install the timing belt and set the tension. Carefully rotate the crankshaft 2 turns to make sure the timing marks still line up. Install the timing belt covers.

19. Apply a thin bead of sealant to the cylinder head cover and install the new gasket. Install the cover and torque the cover bolts to 78 inch lbs. (9 Nm).

20. Install the crankshaft pulley and tighten the bolt to 123 ft. lbs. (167 Nm). Install the water pump pulley and accessory drive belts.

21. Install the water bypass pipe bracket over the stud and install the nut. Tighten to 17 ft. lbs. (23 Nm).

22. Connect the electrical connectors, vacuum and coolant hoses, and the fuel lines.

23. Connect the accelerator and, if equipped, throttle valve cables.

24. Install the air ducts and the engine undercover.

25. Connect the negative battery cable. Fill and bleed the cooling system. Change the engine oil.

26. Start the engine and bring to normal operating temperature. Check for leaks. Check the ignition timing and idle speed.

1.8L ENGINE

1. Properly relieve the fuel system pressure.

2. Disconnect the negative battery cable and drain the cooling system.

3. Remove the timing belt, then reinstall the right side engine mount to support the engine.

4. Remove the air cleaner assembly and air ducts. Remove the battery tray and battery.

5. Disconnect the accelerator and, if equipped, throttle valve cables.

6. Label and disconnect the spark plug wires, then remove the wires with the distributor cap. Disconnect the distributor electrical connector, remove the retaining bolts and remove the distributor.

7. Label and disconnect the necessary electrical connectors, vacuum hoses and coolant hoses. Disconnect and plug the fuel lines.

8. Remove the intake manifold stay. Remove the intake manifold bolts in 2-3 steps and remove the intake manifold.

9. If removing the left (front) cylinder head, disconnect the ventilation pipe from the cylinder head cover. Remove the cylinder head cover retaining bolts and remove the cylinder head cover.

10. Use a suitable wrench to hold the camshaft and remove the camshaft sprocket bolt. The wrench fits on a hexagon that is cast into the camshaft. Remove the camshaft sprocket.

11. Install engine support tool 49 G017 5A0 and support the engine. Remove the right side engine mount.

12. Remove the seal plate and water outlet from the front of the engine. Remove the engine lifting eyes.

13. Disconnect the exhaust pipe from the exhaust manifolds.

14. Turn the camshaft, using a wrench on the cast hexagon, until the camshaft knock pin aligns with the cylinder head marks.

NOTE: Do not remove the camshaft caps when the camshaft lobe is pressing the hydraulic lash adjuster, as this may damage the thrust journal support of the cylinder head.

15. Loosen the front camshaft cap bolts in 5-6 steps in the proper sequence. Bolt **A** is only on the right cylinder head.

16. Loosen the remaining camshaft cap bolts in 5-6 steps in the proper sequence. Mark the position of the camshaft caps so they can be reinstalled in their original positions. Remove the thrust cap last.

17. If removing the left (front) cylinder head, remove the alternator bracket.

18. Temporarily install the right side engine mount and remove the engine support tool.

19. Loosen the cylinder head bolts in 2-3 steps in the reverse order of the tightening sequence. Remove the cylinder head bolts and the cylinder head.

20. If necessary, remove the exhaust manifold.

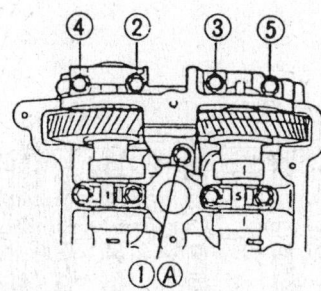

Front camshaft cap bolt loosening sequence — MX-3 1.8L engine and MX-6/626 2.5L engine

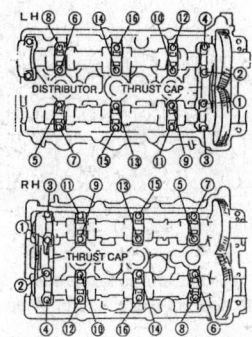

Camshaft cap bolt loosening sequence — MX-3 1.8L engine and MX-6/626 2.5L engine

21. Clean all gasket mating surfaces. Inspect the cylinder head for cracks or other damage. Check the cylinder head for warpage using a feeler gauge and straightedge. The maximum allowable distortion is 0.004 in. (0.10mm).

22. Measure the length of the cylinder head bolts; replace the bolt if it exceeds 5.31 in. (135mm) from just under the bolt head to the tip of the threads. Clean the cylinder head bolts and the threads in the block. Make sure the bolts turn freely in the block.

To install:

23. If removed, install the exhaust manifold using a new gasket and tighten the bolts/nuts to 19 ft. lbs. (25 Nm).

24. Measure the height of the oil control plug from the cylinder block deck; it should be 0.315-0.354 in. (8-9mm). If not within specification, remove the oil control plug and tap in a new one, to the specified height. Apply clean engine oil to a new O-ring and install on the plug.

25. Install a new cylinder head gasket. On the left bank, the **L** mark on the gasket should be facing up. On the right bank, the **R** mark should be facing up. Be careful not to damage the oil control plug O-ring.

26. Position the cylinder head on the block. Lubricate the cylinder head bolt threads and seat faces with clean engine oil and install them with the washers. Tighten the bolts as follows:

    a. Tighten the bolts in 2-3 steps to 19 ft. lbs. (26 Nm).

    b. Put a paint mark on each bolt head.

    c. Using the paint marks for reference, turn each bolt 90 degrees, in sequence.

    d. Using the paint marks for reference, turn each bolt an additional 90 degrees, in sequence.

27. Install the engine support tool and remove the right side engine mount.

28. Lubricate the camshaft lobes, journals and gears with clean engine oil. Align the camshaft gear timing marks and install the camshafts in the cylinder head.

NOTE: The thrust plate positions for the right and left cylinder head camshafts are different.

29. Make sure the camshaft cap and cylinder head surfaces are clean. Apply a small amount of sealant to the mating surface of the front camshaft cap on both cylinder heads and the rear exhaust camshaft cap on the left cylinder head. Do not get any

sealant on the camshaft rotating surfaces.

30. Install the front camshaft caps and thrust plate caps and tighten the bolts until the cap seats fully to the cylinder head. Install the remaining camshaft caps in their original locations and loosely tighten the bolts.

31. Tighten the camshaft cap bolts in 5-6 steps to 126 inch lbs. (14 Nm), in the proper sequence.

32. Apply clean engine oil to a new oil seal and the cylinder head. Install the seal, using a suitable installer. Apply sealant to a new blind cap and install, using a plastic hammer.

33. Install the engine lifting eyes and the alternator bracket. Install the seal plate and water outlet. Using new gaskets, connect the exhaust pipe to the exhaust manifolds and tighten the nuts to 41 ft. lbs. (55 Nm).

34. Temporarily install the right side engine mount and remove the engine support tool.

35. Install the camshaft sprockets. On the right cylinder head, install the sprocket so the **R** mark can be seen and the timing mark aligns with the camshaft knock pin. On the left cylinder head, install the sprocket so the **L** mark can be seen and the timing mark aligns with the camshaft knock pin.

36. Apply clean engine oil to the camshaft sprocket bolt threads and install. Hold the camshaft with a wrench on the cast hexagon and tighten the sprocket bolt to 103 ft. lbs. (140 Nm).

37. Coat a new gasket with sealant and install onto the cylinder head cover. Install the cover and tighten the bolts, in sequence, in 2-3 steps, to 78 inch lbs. (8.8 Nm). Install the ventilation pipe to the left cover.

38. Apply clean engine oil to a new O-ring and install on the distributor. Install the distributor with the blade fitting into the camshaft groove and loosely tighten the retaining bolt.

39. Install the intake manifold using a new gasket. Loosely install the bolts and nuts. Install the intake manifold stay and tighten the bolts to 19 ft. lbs. (25 Nm), then tighten the intake manifold bolts/nuts, in 2-3 steps, to 19 ft. lbs. (25 Nm).

40. Connect the wiring, vacuum and heater hoses, and the fuel lines.

41. Connect the accelerator and, if equipped, throttle valve cables.

42. Install the battery tray and the battery. Install the air cleaner assembly and the ducts.

43. Install the timing belt.

44. Connect the negative battery cable. Fill and bleed the cooling system. Change the engine oil.

45. Start the engine and bring to normal operating temperature. Check for leaks. Check the ignition timing and idle speed.

626 and MX-6

2.0L ENGINE

1. Properly relieve the fuel system pressure. Disconnect the negative battery cable.

2. Mark the position of the hood on the hinges and remove the hood.

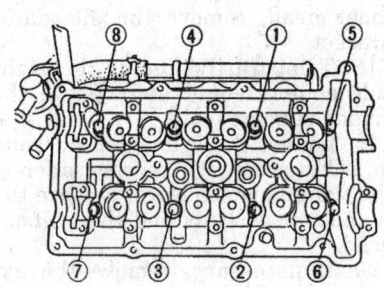

Cylinder head bolt torque sequence — MX-3 1.8L engine and MX-6/626 2.5L engine

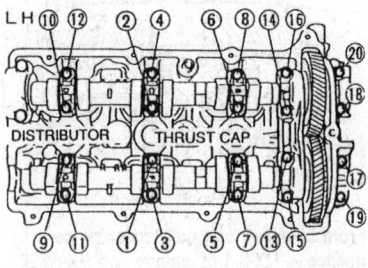

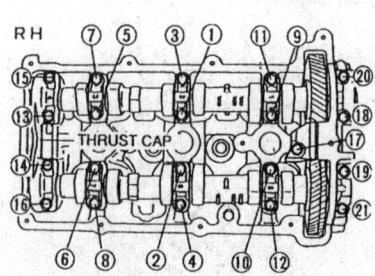

Camshaft cap bolt torque sequence — MX-3 1.8L engine and MX-6/626 2.5L engine

3. Remove the engine undercover and drain the cooling system.

4. Disconnect the air flow sensor and intake air temperature connectors. Remove the air cleaner assembly and air ducts.

5. Disconnect the accelerator cable. Label and disconnect the necessary wiring, vacuum and coolant hoses, and fuel lines.

6. Remove the accessory drive belts and the water pump pulley. Remove the power steering pump pulley shield.

7. Remove the power steering pump and position aside, leaving the hoses connected.

8. Hold the crankshaft pulley using a suitable tool and remove the bolt. Remove the crankshaft pulley.

9. Disconnect the spark plug wires and remove the spark plugs.

10. Loosen the cylinder head bolt cover bolts, in 2-3 steps, in the reverse order of the tightening sequence. Remove the cylinder head cover.

11. Remove the engine oil dipstick and dipstick tube.

12. Remove the timing belt covers.

13. Support the engine using engine support tool 49 G017 5A0. Remove the right side engine mount.

14. Turn the crankshaft, in the normal direction of rotation, until the crankshaft and camshaft sprocket timing marks are aligned. Mark the direction of rotation on the belt.

15. Turn the belt tensioner clockwise and disconnect the tensioner spring from the hook pin. Remove the timing belt.

16. Remove the distributor cap and spark plug wires assembly. Disconnect the electrical connector and remove the distributor.

17. Hold the camshaft using a wrench on the hexagon cast into the camshaft. Remove the camshaft sprocket bolts and the sprockets.

18. Loosen the camshaft cap bolts, in 2-3 steps, in the reverse order of the tightening sequence. Mark the position of the caps so they can be reinstalled in their original positions. Remove the caps and camshafts.

19. Remove the intake manifold-to-engine block bracket. Disconnect the exhaust pipe from the exhaust manifold.

20. Loosen the cylinder head bolts in the reverse order of the tightening sequence in steps. Remove the cylinder head bolts and cylinder head.

21. Remove the intake and exhaust manifolds, if necessary.

22. Clean all gasket mating surfaces. Inspect the cylinder head for

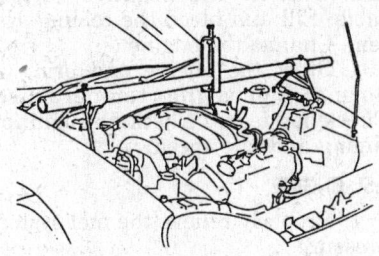

Supporting the engine with the engine support tool

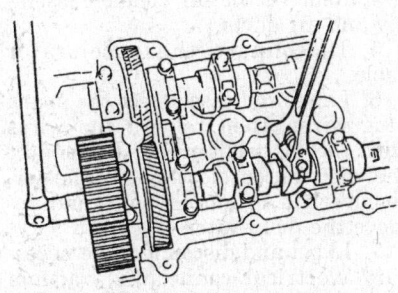

Hold the camshaft while removing/installing the sprocket — MX-3 1.8L engine and MX-6/626 2.5L engine

cracks or other damage. Check the cylinder head for warpage using a feeler gauge and straightedge. The maximum allowable distortion is 0.004 in. (0.10mm).

23. Measure the length of the cylinder head bolts; replace the bolt if it exceeds 4.154 in. (105.5mm) from just under the bolt head to the tip of the threads. Clean the cylinder head bolts and the threads in the block. Make sure the bolts turn freely in the block.

To install:

24. If removed, install the intake and exhaust manifolds using new gaskets. Tighten the intake manifold bolts/nuts to 18 ft. lbs. (25 Nm). Tighten the exhaust manifold nuts to 20 ft. lbs. (28 Nm) and the bolts to 16 ft. lbs. (22 Nm).

25. Position a new head gasket on the cylinder block and install the cylinder head. Lubricate the bolt threads and head seat with clean engine oil and install the bolts. Tighten the bolts as follows:

  a. Tighten the bolts, in sequence, to 16 ft. lbs. (22 Nm).

  b. Make paint marks on the bolt heads.

  c. Using the paint mark as a reference, tighten each bolt, in sequence, 90 degrees.

  d. Using the paint mark as a reference, tighten each bolt, in sequence, an additional 90 degrees.

26. Install the intake manifold bracket and tighten the bolts to 38 ft. lbs. (51 Nm). Connect the exhaust pipe to the exhaust manifold and tighten the nuts to 38 ft. lbs. (51 Nm).

27. Apply clean engine oil to the camshaft lobes and journals and install the camshafts in the cylinder head.

28. Apply silicone sealant to the cylinder head on the front camshaft caps mating surface. Do not get sealant on the camshaft journals.

29. Install the camshaft caps in their original positions. Install the cap bolts and tighten in 2-3 steps, in sequence, to 125 inch lbs. (14.2 Nm).

30. Apply clean engine oil to the lips of the new camshaft seals and install the seals with a suitable seal installer. The seals must be installed so they are flush with the edge of the camshaft caps.

31. Install the camshaft sprockets, positioning the dowels at 12 o'clock. Lubricate the sprocket bolt threads with clean engine oil and install in the camshafts. Tighten to 44 ft. lbs. (60 Nm) while holding the cast hexagon on the camshaft with a wrench.

32. Apply clean engine oil to a new O-ring and install on the distributor. Apply clean engine oil to the distributor drive gear and install the distributor in the cylinder head. Loosely tighten the mounting bolts.

33. Make sure the camshaft and crankshaft sprocket timing marks are aligned and install the timing belt. There should be no looseness at the idler side or between the camshaft sprockets.

34. Turn the crankshaft clockwise 2 turns and make sure the timing marks are aligned. Turn the tensioner clockwise and connect the tensioner spring to the hook pin. Make sure tension is applied to the timing belt.

35. Turn the crankshaft clockwise 2 turns and make sure the timing marks are aligned.

36. Install the right side engine mount. Tighten the mount-to-engine nuts to 86 ft. lbs. (116 Nm) and the mount through bolt to 76 ft. lbs. (102 Nm). Connect the ground harness and tighten the nut to 65 ft. lbs. (89 Nm).

37. Remove the engine support tool.

38. Install the timing belt covers, tightening the mounting bolts to 95 inch lbs. (10.7 Nm). Install the dipstick tube and dipstick.

39. Apply silicone sealer to the cylinder head cover and install a new gasket. Apply sealant to the cylinder head in the area adjacent to the front camshaft caps. Install the cylinder head cover and tighten the bolts in 2-3 steps, in sequence, to 69 inch lbs. (7.8 Nm).

40. Install the spark plugs and connect the spark plug wires.

41. Install the crankshaft pulley. Hold the pulley with a suitable tool and tighten the pulley bolt to 122 ft. lbs. (166 Nm).

42. Install the water pump pulley. Install the power steering pump and the pulley shield.

43. Install the accessory drive belts and adjust the belt tension.

44. Connect the electrical connectors, vacuum and coolant hoses and fuel lines. Connect the accelerator cable.

45. Install the air cleaner assembly with the ducts. Connect the electrical connectors for the air flow sensor and intake air temperature sensor.

46. Install the engine undercover. Install the hood, aligning the marks that were made during removal.

47. Connect the negative battery cable. Fill and bleed the cooling system. Change the engine oil.

48. Start the engine and bring to normal operating temperature. Check for leaks. Check the ignition timing and idle speed.

2.2L ENGINE

1. Properly relieve the fuel system pressure.

2. Disconnect the negative battery cable and drain the cooling system.

3. Disconnect the spark plug wires and remove the spark plugs and the distributor.

4. Disconnect the accelerator cable and if equipped, throttle valve cable.

5. Disconnect the air intake hose from the throttle body. Disconnect and plug the fuel lines.

6. Remove the upper radiator hose, water bypass hose, heater hose, oil cooler hose and brake vacuum hose. If equipped with turbocharger, disconnect the oil cooler hose.

7. Remove the 3-way solenoid and EGR solenoid valve assemblies.

8. Label and disconnect the wiring and vacuum hoses.

9. Remove the vacuum chamber and exhaust manifold shield.

10. Remove the EGR pipe, turbocharger oil pipe, if equipped, and exhaust pipe.

11. Remove the exhaust manifold. On turbocharged engines, remove the

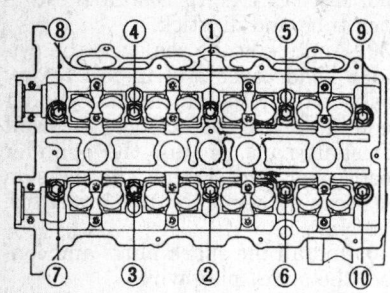

Cylinder head bolt torque sequence — 2.0L engine

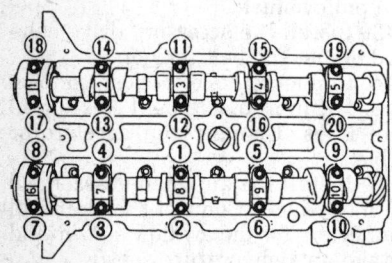

Camshaft cap bolt torque sequence — 2.0L engine

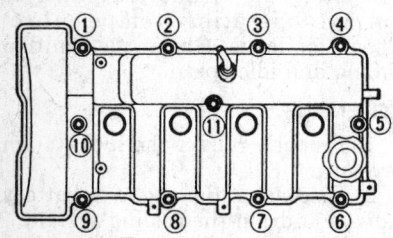

Cylinder head cover bolt torque sequence — 2.0L engine

manifold and turbocharger as an assembly.

12. Remove the intake manifold bracket and the intake manifold.

13. Remove the air conditioning compressor and bracket and position the compressor aside, without disconnecting the refrigerant lines.

14. Remove the upper timing belt cover.

15. To remove the timing belt, perform the following:

a. Rotate the crankshaft so the **1** on the camshaft sprocket is aligned with the timing mark on the front housing.

b. When timing marks are aligned, loosen the timing belt tensioner lock bolt. Pull the tensioner outward as far as possible and temporarily tighten the lock bolt.

c. Lift the timing belt from the camshaft pulley and position it aside.

16. Remove the cylinder head cover and gasket.

17. Loosen the cylinder head bolts in the reverse of the tightening sequence in steps, remove the cylinder head and head gasket.

18. Thoroughly clean all gasket mating surfaces. Check the cylinder head for cracks or other damage. Check the cylinder head for warpage using a feeler gauge and straightedge. The maximum allowable distortion is 0.006 in. (0.15mm).

19. Inspect the cylinder head bolts for damaged threads and make sure they turn freely in the threads in the block.

To install:

20. Position a new cylinder head gasket on the engine block and install the cylinder head.

21. Lubricate the bolt threads and seat surfaces with clean engine oil and install them. Torque the bolts in 2-3 steps to 59-64 ft. lbs. (80-86 Nm) and in the proper sequence.

22. Apply sealant to the 4 corners of the cylinder head and install the cover with a new gasket. Torque the cover bolts to 69 inch lbs. (8 Nm).

23. Make sure the camshaft sprocket and front housing timing marks are aligned and install the timing belt. Set the tension and carefully rotate the crankshaft 2 turns to make sure the timing marks still line up. Install the timing belt cover.

24. Use a new gasket and install the intake manifold. Torque the nuts/bolts to 22 ft. lbs. (30 Nm). Install the intake manifold bracket.

25. Use new gaskets and install the exhaust manifold. Torque the nuts to 36 ft. lbs. (49 Nm). On turbocharged engines, connect the turbocharger oil line.

26. Connect the exhaust pipe with a new gasket and torque the nuts to 34 ft. lbs. (46 Nm).

27. Install the EGR pipe, exhaust manifold shield and vacuum chamber. Install the EGR solenoid and 3-way solenoid.

28. Connect all the coolant, vacuum and fuel system hoses. Connect the air intake hose to the throttle body.

29. Install the distributor and spark plugs and connect all wiring

30. Connect the accelerator cable.

31. Connect the negative battery cable. Fill and bleed the cooling system. Change the engine oil.

32. Start the engine and bring to normal operating temperature. Check for leaks. Check the ignition timing and idle speed.

2.5L ENGINE

1. Properly relieve the fuel system pressure.

2. Disconnect the negative battery cable and drain the cooling system.

3. Remove the timing belt, then reinstall the right side engine mount to support the engine.

4. Remove the air cleaner assembly and air ducts.

5. Disconnect the accelerator cable.

6. Label and disconnect the spark plug wires, then remove the wires with the distributor cap. Disconnect the distributor electrical connector, remove the retaining bolts and remove the distributor.

7. Label and disconnect the necessary electrical connectors, vacuum hoses and coolant hoses. Disconnect and plug the fuel lines.

8. Remove the intake manifold stay, air cleaner housing bracket, fuel line and hose. Remove the intake manifold bolts/nuts in 2-3 steps and remove the intake manifold.

9. If removing the left (front) cylinder head, disconnect the ventilation pipe from the cylinder head cover. Remove the cylinder head cover retaining bolts and remove the cylinder head cover.

10. Use a suitable wrench to hold the camshaft and remove the camshaft sprocket bolt. The wrench fits on a hexagon that is cast into the camshaft. Remove the camshaft sprocket.

11. Install engine support tool 49 G017 5A0 and support the engine. Remove the right side engine mount.

12. Remove the seal plate and water outlet from the front of the engine. Remove the engine lifting eyes.

13. Disconnect the exhaust pipe from the exhaust manifolds.

14. Turn the camshaft, using a wrench on the cast hexagon, until the camshaft knock pin aligns with the cylinder head marks.

NOTE: Do not remove the camshaft caps when the camshaft lobe is pressing the hydraulic lash adjuster, as this may damage the thrust journal support of the cylinder head.

15. Loosen the front camshaft cap bolts in 5-6 steps in the proper se-

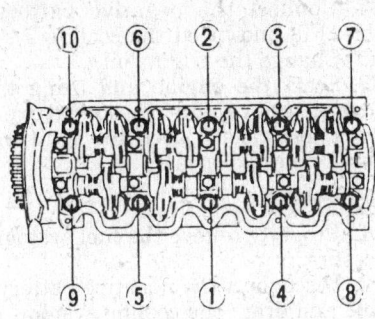

Cylinder head bolt torque sequence — 2.2L engine

quence. Bolt **A** is only on the right cylinder head.

16. Loosen the remaining camshaft cap bolts in 5-6 steps in the proper sequence. Mark the position of the camshaft caps so they can be reinstalled in their original positions. Remove the thrust cap last.

17. If removing the left (front) cylinder head, remove the alternator bracket.

18. Temporarily install the right side engine mount and remove the engine support tool.

19. Loosen the cylinder head bolts in 2-3 steps in the reverse order of the tightening sequence. Remove the cylinder head bolts and the cylinder head.

20. If necessary, remove the exhaust manifold.

21. Clean all gasket mating surfaces. Inspect the cylinder head for cracks or other damage. Check the cylinder head for warpage using a feeler gauge and straightedge. The maximum allowable distortion is 0.004 in. (0.10mm).

22. Measure the length of the cylinder head bolts; replace the bolt if it exceeds 5.31 in. (135mm) from just under the bolt head to the tip of the threads. Clean the cylinder head bolts and the threads in the block. Make sure the bolts turn freely in the block.

   To install:
23. If removed, install the exhaust manifold using a new gasket and tighten the bolts/nuts to 19 ft. lbs. (25 Nm).

24. Measure the height of the oil control plug from the cylinder block deck; it should be 0.512-0.551 in. (13-14mm). If not within specification, remove the oil control plug and tap in a new one to the specified height. Apply clean engine oil to a new O-ring and install on the plug.

25. Install a new cylinder head gasket. On the left bank, the **L** mark on

the gasket should be facing up. On the right bank, the **R** mark should be facing up. Be careful not to damage the oil control plug O-ring.

26. Position the cylinder head on the block. Lubricate the cylinder head bolt threads and seat faces with clean engine oil and install them with the washers. Tighten the bolts as follows:

   a. Tighten the bolts in 2-3 steps to 19 ft. lbs. (26 Nm).

   b. Put a paint mark on each bolt head.

   c. Using the paint marks for reference, turn each bolt 90 degrees, in sequence.

   d. Using the paint marks for reference, turn each bolt an additional 90 degrees, in sequence.

27. Install the engine support tool and remove the right side engine mount.

28. Lubricate the camshaft lobes, journals and gears with clean engine oil. Align the camshaft gear timing marks and install the camshafts in the cylinder head.

NOTE: The thrust plate positions for the right and left cylinder head camshafts are different.

29. Make sure the camshaft cap and cylinder head surfaces are clean. Apply a small amount of sealant to the mating surface of the front camshaft cap on both cylinder heads and the rear exhaust camshaft cap on the left cylinder head. Do not get any sealant on the camshaft rotating surfaces.

30. Install the front camshaft caps and thrust plate caps and tighten the bolts until the cap seats fully to the cylinder head. Install the remaining camshaft caps in their original locations and loosely tighten the bolts.

31. Tighten the camshaft cap bolts in 5-6 steps to 126 inch lbs. (14 Nm), in the proper sequence.

32. Apply clean engine oil to a new oil seal and the cylinder head. Install the seal, using a suitable installer. Apply sealant to a new blind cap and install, using a plastic hammer.

33. Install the engine lifting eyes and the alternator bracket. Install the seal plate and water outlet. Using new gaskets, connect the exhaust pipe to the exhaust manifolds and tighten the nuts to 41 ft. lbs. (55 Nm).

34. Temporarily install the right side engine mount and remove the engine support tool.

35. Install the camshaft sprockets. On the right cylinder head, install the sprocket so the **R** mark can be seen and the timing mark aligns with the camshaft knock pin. On the left

cylinder head, install the sprocket so the **L** mark can be seen and the timing mark aligns with the camshaft knock pin.

36. Apply clean engine oil to the camshaft sprocket bolt threads and install. Hold the camshaft with a wrench on the cast hexagon and tighten the sprocket bolt to 103 ft. lbs. (140 Nm).

37. Coat a new gasket with sealant and install onto the cylinder head cover. Install the cover and tighten the bolts, in sequence, in 2-3 steps, to 78 inch lbs. (8.8 Nm). Install the ventilation pipe to the left cover.

38. Apply clean engine oil to a new O-ring and install on the distributor. Install the distributor with the blade fitting into the camshaft groove and loosely tighten the retaining bolt.

39. Install the intake manifold using a new gasket. Loosely install the bolts and nuts. Install the intake manifold stay, bracket, fuel line and hoses, then tighten the intake manifold bolts/nuts, in 2-3 steps, to 19 ft. lbs. (25 Nm).

40. Connect the wiring, vacuum and heater hoses and the fuel lines.

41. Connect the accelerator cable.

42. Install the air cleaner assembly and the ducts.

43. Install the timing belt.

44. Connect the negative battery cable. Fill and bleed the cooling system. Change the engine oil.

45. Start the engine and bring to normal operating temperature. Check for leaks.

46. Check the ignition timing and idle speed.

929

SOHC ENGINE

1. Properly relieve the fuel system pressure.

2. Disconnect the negative battery cable and drain the cooling system.

3. Remove the air intake duct.

4. Disconnect and mark the spark plug wires and remove the spark plugs and the distributor.

5. Disconnect the accelerator cable.

6. Label and disconnect the wiring, fuel lines and vacuum hoses. Remove the upper radiator hose and disconnect the heater hoses as required.

7. Remove the fan shroud and the fan from the front of the engine.

8. Mark the intake runners so they can be returned to their original position. It may be easier to remove the throttle body before removing the runners and plenum chamber.

9. Remove the intake manifold. Loosen the bolts ½ turn at a time in the reverse order of the torque sequence.

10. Remove the cylinder head covers.

11. Disconnect the exhaust pipes and EGR tube and remove the exhaust manifolds. Remove the 3-way solenoid assembly.

12. Remove the accessory drive belts, timing belt cover and crankshaft pulley.

13. Rotate the crankshaft until the crankshaft and camshaft sprocket timing marks are aligned. Mark the direction of rotation of the belt, remove the belt tensioner and the timing belt.

14. Remove the seal plate at the front of the heads.

15. Loosen the cylinder head bolts in 2-3 steps in the reverse of the torque sequence.

16. Remove the bolts and lift the cylinder heads from the engine.

17. Thoroughly clean all gasket mating surfaces. Check the cylinder head for cracks or other damage. Check the cylinder head for warpage using a feeler gauge and straightedge. The maximum allowable distortion is 0.004 in. (0.10mm).

18. Measure the cylinder head bolt lengths and replace if they exceed the specified length. The intake side (short) bolts should not exceed 4.29 in. (109mm) measured from just under the bolt head to the tip of the threads. The exhaust side (long) bolts should not exceed 5.47 in. (139mm) measured from just under the bolt head to the tip of the threads. Make sure the bolt threads in the block are clean and that the bolts turn freely.

To install:

19. Check the oil control orifice plug projection at the cylinder block; it should be 0.209-0.224 in. (5.3-5.7mm). Apply clean engine oil to a new O-ring and install on the oil control plug.

20. Place the new cylinder head gasket on the left bank with the **L** mark facing up. Place the new cylinder head gasket on the right bank with the **R** mark facing up.

21. Carefully place the cylinder heads onto the block. Tighten the head bolts in the following manner:

a. Coat the threads and the seating faces of the head bolts with clean engine oil.

b. Torque the bolts, in sequence, to 14 ft. lbs. (20 Nm).

c. Place a paint mark on the head of each bolt.

d. Using the paint mark as a reference, tighten the bolts, in sequence, 90 degrees.

e. Using the paint mark as a reference, tighten the bolts, in sequence and an additional 90 degrees.

22. Install the seal plate.

23. Position the timing belt tensioner in a suitable press with a flat washer at the bottom of the tensioner to prevent damage to the body plug. Press in the tensioner rod slowly, not exceeding 2200 lbs. Install a pin to hold the tensioner rod in the tensioner body, then install the tensioner. Tighten the bolts to 19 ft. lbs. (25 Nm).

24. Make sure the camshaft and crankshaft timing marks are aligned.

25. With the upper idler pulley removed, install the timing belt in the original direction of rotation. Install the upper idler pulley and tighten to 38 ft. lbs. (52 Nm).

26. Turn the crankshaft twice in the normal direction of rotation and make sure the timing marks are aligned. Remove the pin from the automatic tensioner and rotate the crankshaft 2 more times. Make sure the timing marks are aligned.

27. Install the cylinder head covers with new gaskets and seal washers and torque the bolts to 39 inch lbs. (4.4 Nm).

28. Install the timing belt covers and crankshaft pulley. Install the accessory drive belts and adjust the tension.

29. Install the cooling fan and shroud.

30. Install the intake manifold with new gaskets. Torque the manifold bolts in the proper sequence in 2-3 steps to 19 ft. lbs. (25 Nm).

31. Install the intake runners with new O-rings and gaskets. Torque the nuts to 19 ft. lbs. (25 Nm).

32. Install the exhaust manifolds with new gaskets and torque the nuts to 21 ft. lbs. (28 Nm). Install the exhaust pipes with new gaskets and torque the nuts to 34 ft. lbs. (46 Nm).

33. Apply clean engine oil to a new O-ring and install on the distributor. Apply clean engine oil to the drive gear and install the distributor. Loosely tighten the distributor mounting bolt.

34. Install the EGR pipe and the 3-way solenoid assembly.

35. Connect all wiring, vacuum and coolant hoses and the fuel lines.

36. Connect the accelerator cable and install the air intake pipe.

37. Connect the negative battery cable. Fill and bleed the cooling system. Change the engine oil.

38. Start the engine and bring to normal operating temperature. Check for leaks. Check the ignition timing and idle speed.

DOHC ENGINE

1. Properly relieve the fuel system pressure.

2. Disconnect the negative battery cable and drain the cooling system.

3. Remove the air cleaner and air intake pipe.

4. Remove the cooling fan and fan shroud.

5. Disconnect and mark the spark plug wires and remove the spark plugs. Remove the idler pulleys and the accessory drive belts.

6. Remove the coolant bypass hose and the upper radiator hose. Disconnect the electrical connector and remove the distributor.

7. Hold the crankshaft pulley with a suitable tool and remove the bolt. Remove the crankshaft pulley. On 1992-94 vehicles, be careful not to damage the sensor rotor.

8. Remove the timing belt covers. Rotate the crankshaft until the camshaft and crankshaft sprocket timing marks are aligned.

9. Remove the upper idler pulley and the tensioner and pulley. Mark the direction of rotation on the timing belt and remove the timing belt.

10. Disconnect the accelerator cable. Disconnect and plug the fuel lines. Label and disconnect the necessary electrical connectors and vacuum hoses.

11. On 1990-91 vehicles, remove the upper intake manifold cover. Remove the upper intake manifold.

12. Loosen the lower intake manifold bolts in 2-3 steps, in the reverse order of the torque sequence. Remove the lower intake manifold.

13. Remove the bolts from the transmission dipstick tube bracket and the coolant bypass pipe.

14. Disconnect the exhaust pipe from the exhaust manifolds. Remove the exhaust manifold insulators and the manifolds.

15. Remove the cylinder head covers.

16. Hold the camshaft with a wrench on the hexagon cast into the camshaft and remove the camshaft sprocket bolt. Remove the camshaft sprockets.

17. Remove bolts **A** from the front camshaft cap on the left cylinder head. Loosen the remaining camshaft cap bolts in 2-3 steps in the proper sequence. Mark the position of the

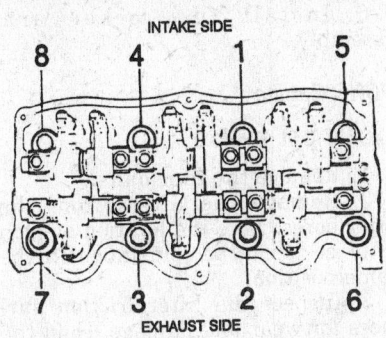

INTAKE SIDE

8   4   1   5

7   3   2   6

EXHAUST SIDE

Cylinder head bolt torque sequence — SOHC 3.0L engine

caps so they can be reinstalled in their original positions. Remove the caps and remove the camshafts. Label the camshafts so they can be reinstalled in their proper locations.

18. Remove the rocker arms.

19. Loosen the cylinder head bolts in 2-3 steps in the reverse of the tightening sequence. Remove the bolts and remove the cylinder heads.

20. Clean all gasket mating surfaces. Inspect the cylinder head for cracks or other damage. Check the cylinder head for warpage using a feeler gauge and a straightedge. The maximum allowable distortion is 0.004 in. (0.10mm).

21. Measure the length of the cylinder head bolts, from just under the bolt head to the tip of the threads. On 1990-91 vehicles, the bolt length should not exceed 4.29 in. (109mm). On 1992-94 vehicles, the intake bolts should not exceed 5.43 in. (138mm) and the exhaust bolts should not exceed 5.47 in. (139mm). Replace any bolts that exceed specification.

22. Clean the bolt threads and the threads in the cylinder block. Make sure the bolts turn freely in the cylinder block.

To install:

23. Measure the distance the oil control plug projects from the cylinder block deck; it should be 0.209-0.224 in. (5.3-5.7mm). Apply clean engine oil to new O-rings and install them on the oil control plugs.

24. Install new cylinder head gaskets. On the left bank the **L** mark on the gasket should face upward. On the right bank, the **R** mark should face up.

NOTE: Be careful not to damage the O-rings when installing the cylinder heads.

25. Carefully install the cylinder heads. Lubricate the cylinder bolt threads and head seat with clean en-

gine oil and install the bolts. Tighten the bolts as follows:

    a. Tighten the bolts, in sequence, to 14 ft. lbs. (20 Nm).

    b. Make a paint mark on each bolt head.

    c. Tighten each bolt, in sequence, 90 degrees.

    d. Turn each bolt, in sequence, an additional 90 degrees.

26. Lubricate the rocker arms with clean engine oil and install them over the valve stems and hydraulic lash adjusters.

27. Lubricate the camshaft lobes and journals with clean engine oil and install the camshafts on the cylinder heads. Apply clean engine oil to the lips of the new camshaft seals and install them on the camshafts.

28. Apply a small amount of silicone sealant to the cylinder head on the front camshaft cap mating surfaces. Do not allow sealant to get on the camshaft journal, oil seal face or camshaft thrust face.

29. Install the camshaft caps in their original locations. Gradually tighten the cap bolts, in sequence, to 24 ft. lbs. (32 Nm). Tighten the front cap bolts, **A**, on the left cylinder head to 95 inch lbs. (11 Nm).

30. Hold the camshafts using a wrench on the hexagon cast into the camshaft. Install the camshaft sprockets with the retaining bolts. Tighten the sprocket bolts on the right cylinder head to 59 ft. lbs. (80 Nm) and the sprocket bolts on the left cylinder head to 19 ft. lbs. (25 Nm).

31. Apply sealant to the cylinder head in the areas adjacent to the front camshaft caps. Install the cylinder head covers and tighten the nuts to 39 inch lbs. (4 Nm). On 1990-91 vehicles, apply sealant to the cylinder head cover and install the plug hole cover, tightening the bolts to 52 inch lbs. (5.9 Nm).

32. Using new gaskets, install the exhaust manifolds. Tighten the nuts to 21 ft. lbs. (28 Nm). Install the exhaust manifold insulators and tighten the bolts to 19 ft. lbs. (25 Nm).

33. Connect the exhaust pipes to the exhaust manifolds with new gaskets. Tighten the flange nuts to 38 ft. lbs. (52 Nm).

34. Install the bolts attaching the coolant bypass pipe and the transmission dipstick tube.

35. Install the lower intake manifold using new gaskets. Tighten the mounting nuts in 2-3 steps, in the proper sequence, to 19 ft. lbs. (25 Nm). Connect the fuel lines.

36. Install the upper intake manifold to the lower intake manifold, using a new gasket. Tighten the bolts to 19 ft. lbs. (25 Nm). On 1990-91 vehicles, install the upper intake manifold cover and tighten the bolts to 95 inch lbs. (11 Nm).

37. Connect the electrical connectors and vacuum hoses. Connect the accelerator cable.

38. Position the timing belt tensioner on a suitable press. Place a flat washer at the bottom of the tensioner body to prevent damage to the body plug. Slowly press in the tensioner rod, but do not exceed 2200 lbs. Insert a pin in the tensioner body to hold the rod in place, then install the tensioner and tighten the mounting bolts to 19 ft. lbs. (25 Nm).

39. Make sure the crankshaft and camshaft sprocket timing marks are properly aligned. Install the timing belt over the sprockets and pulleys in the following order: crankshaft sprocket, lower idler pulley, left cylinder head exhaust cam sprocket, left cylinder head intake cam sprocket, tensioner pulley, right cylinder head exhaust cam sprocket and right cylinder head intake cam sprocket.

40. Push the belt down and install the upper idler pulley. Tighten the upper idler pulley bolt to 38 ft. lbs. (52 Nm). Make sure the camshaft and crankshaft sprocket timing marks are still aligned after installing the upper idler pulley.

41. Turn the crankshaft 2 revolutions in the normal direction of rotation and realign the timing marks. Make sure all timing marks are correctly aligned.

42. Remove the pin from the automatic tensioner and again rotate the crankshaft 2 turns. Confirm that the timing marks are aligned.

43. Install the timing belt covers and tighten the bolts to 95 inch lbs. (11 Nm).

44. Install the crankshaft pulley. Hold the pulley with a suitable tool and tighten the pulley bolt to 123 ft. lbs. (167 Nm). On 1992-94 vehicles, be careful not to damage the sensor rotor.

45. Install the spark plugs and the distributor assembly. Connect the spark plug wires and the distributor electrical connector.

46. Install the upper radiator hose and water bypass hose. Install the idler pulleys and accessory drive belts. Adjust the belt tension.

47. Install the shroud and cooling fan. Install the air cleaner and ducts.

48. Connect the negative battery cable. Fill and bleed the cooling system. Change the engine oil.

49. Start the engine and bring to normal operating temperature. Check for leaks. Check the ignition timing and idle speed.

Valve Lifters

All double overhead camshaft engines except the 3.0L engine are equipped with conventional type hydraulic lifters, which are located over the valve stem and driven directly by

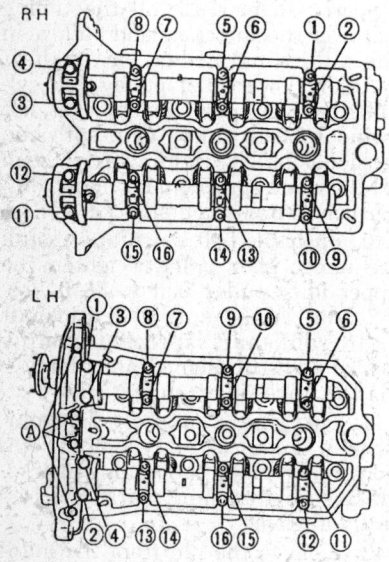

Camshaft cap bolt loosening sequence — DOHC 3.0L engine

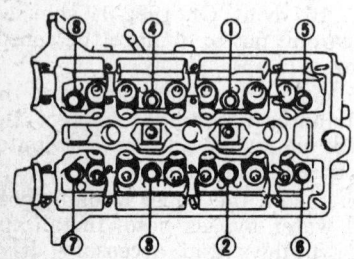

Cylinder head bolt torque sequence — DOHC 3.0L engine

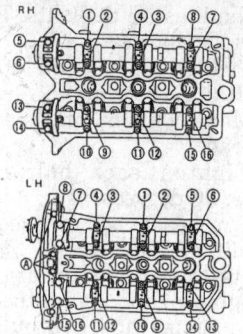

Camshaft cap bolt torque sequence — DOHC 3.0L engine

the camshaft. The 3.0L DOHC engine uses a hydraulic lash adjuster, mounted stationary in the cylinder head, to keep the rocker arm in contact with the camshaft.

All single overhead camshaft engines are equipped with hydraulic lash adjusters mounted in the rocker arms, located directly over the valve stem.

REMOVAL AND INSTALLATION

SOHC Engine

1. Remove the rocker arm assembly.

2. Inspect the hydraulic lash adjuster for obvious wear or damage.

3. If necessary, remove the hydraulic lash adjuster by hand. Use pliers, if the adjuster is difficult to remove.

NOTE: Do not remove the hydraulic lash adjuster from the rocker arm unless it is necessary, to avoid damaging the O-ring.

To install:

4. Pour clean engine oil into the rocker arm reservoir.

5. Apply clean engine oil to the new hydraulic lash adjuster and install into the rocker arm, being careful not to damage the O-ring.

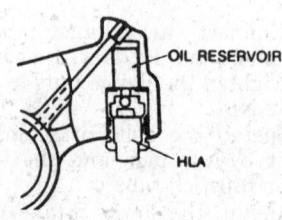

Hydraulic lash adjuster — SOHC engines

6. Install the rocker arm assembly.

DOHC Engine

EXCEPT 3.0L ENGINE

1. Remove the camshafts.

2. Remove the lifters from the lifter bores. Note the location of each lifter so it can be reinstalled in the same position.

3. Inspect the lifter friction surfaces for wear and damage. Hold the lifter body and try to press in the plunger by hand. If the plunger moves, or if the friction surfaces are worn or damaged, replace the lifter.

To install:

4. Lubricate the lifter and lifter bore with clean engine oil.

5. Install the lifters into the cylinder head. If the lifters are being reused, make sure they are installed in their original locations.

6. After installation, make sure all lifters move freely in the bores.

7. Install the camshafts.

3.0L ENGINE

1. Remove the camshafts and rocker arms.

2. Remove the hydraulic lash adjuster using pliers. Protect the lash adjuster by wrapping a rag around the jaws of the pliers. Note the position of each lash adjuster so it can be reinstalled in the same location.

NOTE: Do not remove the hydraulic lash adjuster unless it is necessary.

3. Check the hydraulic lash adjuster for wear or damage. Hold the lash adjuster between the thumb and forefinger and try to compress the plunger. If the plunger moves, or if there is obvious wear or damage, replace the hydraulic lash adjuster.

To install:

4. Place the hydraulic lash adjuster in a clean container filled with clean engine oil.

5. Bleed the air from the hydraulic lash adjuster by inserting a pin into the plunger hole and pressing the plunger until it no longer moves.

NOTE: Do not push the pin too hard, as it may damage the hydraulic lash adjuster.

6. Remove the excess engine oil from the hydraulic lash adjuster bore in the cylinder head.

7. Install a new O-ring on the hydraulic lash adjuster and install the lash adjuster in the cylinder head.

8. Install the rocker arms and camshafts.

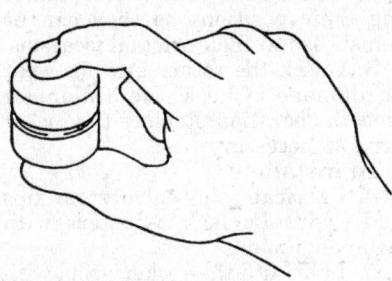

Checking the valve lifter plunger — except 3.0L DOHC engine

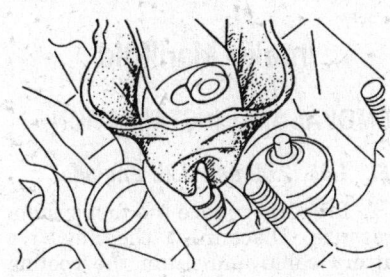

Removing the hydraulic lash adjuster — 3.0L DOHC engine

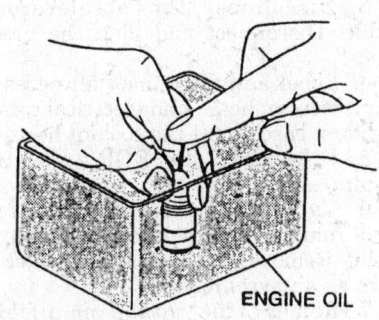

ENGINE OIL

Bleeding the air from the hydraulic lash adjuster — 3.0L DOHC engine

Rocker Arms/Shafts

REMOVAL AND INSTALLATION

1.6L and 1.8L SOHC Engines

1. Disconnect the negative battery cable.
2. Disconnect and mark the spark plug wires and the breather hoses and remove the cylinder head cover.
3. Loosen the rocker arm shaft bolts in 2-3 steps, in the reverse order of the torque sequence. Remove the rocker arms/shafts assembly with the bolts.
4. If necessary, disassemble the shaft assemblies. Note the position of the rocker arms and shafts so they can be reassembled in the same locations.
5. Inspect the rocker arms and shafts for wear or damage and replace parts, as necessary.

To install:

6. If disassembled, lubricate the rocker arms and shafts with clean engine oil and assemble with the springs and bolts. If reusing the original parts, make sure they are installed in the same locations.

NOTE: The installation bolt holes are different for the exhaust side and intake side shafts. On the 1.6L 8-valve engine, the shaft oil holes must face downward. On the 1.6L and 1.8L 16-valve engines, the identification marks at the end of the shafts must face upward.

7. Apply clean engine oil to the valve stems and camshaft lobes. Install the rocker arms/shafts assembly.
8. Tighten the rocker arm shaft bolts, in 2-3 steps, to 21 ft. lbs. (28 Nm) in the proper sequence.
9. Install the cylinder head cover. Tighten the cylinder head cover-to-cylinder head bolts to 78 inch lbs. (8.8 Nm) and the timing cover-to-cylinder head cover bolts to 95 inch lbs. (11 Nm).
10. Connect the breather hoses and spark plug wires. Connect the negative battery cable, start the engine and check for leaks.

2.2L Engines

1. Disconnect the negative battery cable.
2. Disconnect and mark the spark plug wires and the breather hoses

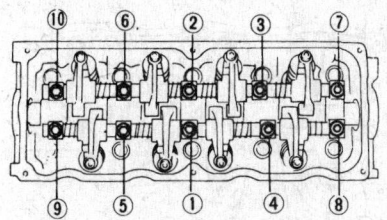

Rocker arm shaft bolt torque sequence — 1.6L, 1.8L and 2.2L SOHC engines

and remove the cylinder head cover. Remove the spark plugs.

3. Remove the timing belt cover. Turn the crankshaft until the 'arrow'1 mark on the camshaft sprocket aligns with the mark at the top of the front housing.
4. Loosen the timing belt tensioner lock bolt, move the tensioner as far outward as possible, then retighten the lock bolt.
5. Remove the timing belt from the camshaft sprocket and secure it aside.

NOTE: Do not rotate the crankshaft while the timing belt is removed.

6. Loosen the rocker arm shaft bolts in 2-3 steps in the reverse order of the torque sequence. Remove the rocker arm/shaft assemblies with the bolts.
7. If necessary, disassemble the shaft assemblies. Note the position of the rocker arms and shafts so they can be reassembled in the same locations.
8. Inspect the rocker arms and shafts for wear or damage and replace parts, as necessary.

To install:

9. If disassembled, lubricate the rocker arms and shafts with clean engine oil and assemble with the springs and bolts. If reusing the original parts, make sure they are installed in the same locations.

NOTE: The intake side shaft has twice as many oil holes as the exhaust side shaft. The stepped ends are the rear of the shafts.

10. Apply clean engine oil to the valve stems and camshaft lobes. Install the rocker arms/shafts assembly.
11. Tighten the rocker arm shaft bolts, in 2-3 steps, to 20 ft. lbs. (26 Nm) in the proper sequence.

NOTE: Make sure the rocker arms or spacers do not get caught between the shaft and camshaft cap.

12. Make sure the timing marks on the camshaft sprocket and front housing are aligned.
13. Install the timing belt over the camshaft sprocket. Make sure there is no looseness at the water pump pulley and idler pulley side.
14. Turn the crankshaft clockwise 2 revolutions and make sure the timing mark on the crankshaft sprocket aligns with the mark on the oil pump housing and the timing mark on the camshaft sprocket aligns with the mark on the front housing.

15. Loosen the tensioner lock bolt and apply tension to the belt. Tighten the lock bolt to 38 ft. lbs. (52 Nm).

16. Again rotate the crankshaft clockwise 2 turns and check the timing mark alignment. Install the timing belt cover.

17. Install a new gasket on the cylinder head cover, if necessary. Apply sealant to the cylinder head in the area adjacent to the front and rear camshaft caps and install the cylinder head cover. Tighten the bolts to 69 inch lbs. (8 Nm).

18. Install the spark plugs, connect the wires, breather hoses and negative battery cable.

19. Start the engine and check for leaks.

3.0L Engine

SOHC ENGINE

1. Properly relieve the fuel system pressure. Disconnect the negative battery cable.

2. If removing the rocker arm shafts from the left cylinder head, proceed as follows:

   a. Disconnect the accelerator cable and air intake hose from the throttle body.

   b. Label and disconnect the necessary vacuum hoses and electrical connectors.

   c. Remove the retaining nuts and remove the throttle body.

   d. Remove the distributor cap from the distributor, leaving the spark plug wires attached. Mark the position of the rotor in relation to the distributor housing and the position of the distributor housing on the cylinder head, and remove the distributor.

3. Disconnect and plug the fuel lines and remove the front engine lifting eye.

4. Remove the upper intake plenum-to-lower intake manifold runners.

5. Remove the spark plugs. Remove the distributor cap and wires assembly.

6. Disconnect the breather hoses and remove the cylinder head cover.

7. Loosen the rocker arm shaft bolts in 2-3 steps, in the reverse of the torque sequence. Remove the rocker arm/shaft assemblies.

8. If necessary, disassemble the shaft assemblies. Note the position of the rocker arms and shafts so they can be reassembled in the same locations.

9. Inspect the rocker arms and shafts for wear or damage and replace parts, as necessary.

To install:

10. If disassembled, lubricate the rocker arms and shafts with clean engine oil and assemble with the springs and bolts. If reusing the original parts, make sure they are installed in the same locations.

NOTE: The intake side shaft has twice as many oil holes as the exhaust side shaft.

11. Apply clean engine oil to the valve stems and camshaft lobes. Install the rocker arms/shafts assembly.

12. Tighten the rocker arm shaft bolts, in 2-3 steps, to 19 ft. lbs. (25 Nm) in the proper sequence.

NOTE: Make sure the rocker arm shaft spring does not get caught between the shaft and mounting boss.

13. Install a new gasket on the cylinder head cover and install the cover on the cylinder head. Install new seal washers and the bolts. Tighten the bolts to 39 inch lbs. (4.4 Nm).

14. Install the spark plugs.

15. Install the distributor, aligning the marks that were made during removal, and loosely tighten the mounting bolt. Install the distributor cap and connect the spark plug wires.

16. Install new O-rings and gaskets on the intake runners and install them on the manifolds. Tighten the nuts to 19 ft. lbs. (25 Nm).

17. Install the front engine lifting eye. Install the throttle body assembly.

18. Connect the fuel lines and the vacuum hoses and electrical connectors. Connect the accelerator cable and the air intake hose.

19. Connect the negative battery cable, start the engine and check for leaks. Check the idle speed and ignition timing.

DOHC ENGINE

1. Remove the camshafts.

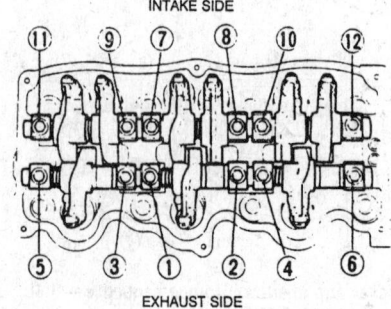

Rocker arm shaft bolt torque sequence — 3.0L SOHC engine

2. Remove the rocker arms, marking their positions so they can be reinstalled in their original locations.

3. Check the rocker arm for wear or damage. Check the roller for smooth operation. Replace the rocker arm, as necessary.

To install:

4. Lubricate the valve stem tips and hydraulic lash adjusters with clean engine oil.

5. Lubricate the rocker arms with clean engine oil and position over the valves and hydraulic lash adjusters. If reusing the original parts, make sure they are installed in their original locations.

6. Install the camshafts.

Intake Manifold

REMOVAL AND INSTALLATION

1.6L, 1.8L, 2.0L and 2.2L Engines

1. Properly relieve the fuel system pressure. Disconnect the negative battery cable and drain the cooling system.

2. Disconnect the air intake hose from the throttle body. Remove the hose and air cleaner assembly if necessary.

3. Disconnect the accelerator cable. Disconnect and plug the fuel lines.

4. Label and disconnect all necessary vacuum hoses and electrical connectors. Disconnect the coolant hoses.

5. Disconnect the EGR tube, if equipped.

6. On Miata, remove the air valve and remove the fuel rail attaching bolts. Remove the fuel rail and injectors as an assembly.

7. Remove the intake manifold support bracket. If necessary, remove the bolt retaining the dipstick tube bracket to the intake manifold.

8. Remove the intake manifold-to-cylinder bolts/nuts and remove the intake manifold assembly.

9. If necessary, remove the throttle body and separate the intake manifold upper and lower halves.

To install:

10. Clean all gasket mating surfaces.

11. If separated, connect the upper and lower intake manifolds using a new gasket. Tighten the nuts/bolts to 19 ft. lbs. (25 Nm). If removed, install the throttle body using a new gasket. Tighten the retaining nuts/bolts to 19 ft. lbs. (25 Nm).

12. Install the intake manifold assembly to the cylinder head using a new gasket. Tighten the nuts/bolts to

19 ft. lbs. (25 Nm) on all except 2.2L engine. On 2.2L engine, tighten to 22 ft. lbs. (30 Nm).

NOTE: On all except Miata 1.6L and MX-6/626 2.2L engines, torque the intake manifol-to-cylinder head bolts in the proper sequence. On Miata 1.6L and MX-6/626 2.2L engines, torque the bolts in the center of the manifold first and works outward toward the ends.

13. If equipped, install the bolt retaining the dipstick tube to the intake manifold. Install the intake manifold bracket. Tighten the attaching nuts/bolts to 38 ft. lbs. (52 Nm) on all except 323, Protege and MX-3. On 323, Protege and MX-3, tighten the attaching nuts/bolts to 19 ft. lbs. (25 Nm).

14. On Miata, install the fuel rail and injector assembly on the intake manifold using new insulators. Tighten the fuel rail mounting bolts to 19 ft. lbs. (25 Nm). Install the air valve and tighten the bolts to 57 inch lbs. (5.5 Nm).

15. Connect the EGR tube, if equipped. Connect the coolant and vacuum hoses, electrical connectors and fuel lines.

16. Connect the accelerator cable. Install the air cleaner assembly, if removed, and connect the air intake tube to the throttle body.

17. Connect the negative battery cable. Fill and bleed the cooling system.

18. Start the engine and bring to normal operating temperature. Check for leaks. Check the idle speed.

MX-3 1.8L and MX-6/626 2.5L Engines

1. Properly relieve the fuel system pressure.

2. Disconnect the negative battery cable and drain the cooling system.

3. On MX-3, remove the upper strut bar.

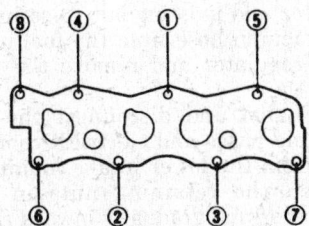

Intake manifold-to-cylinder head torque sequence — 323/Protege 1.6L engine

4. Remove the air cleaner assembly and ducts.

5. Disconnect the accelerator cable. Label and disconnect the necessary electrical connectors and vacuum hoses.

6. Disconnect and plug the fuel lines. Disconnect the coolant hose from the air bypass valve.

7. Remove the intake manifold support bracket. Remove the intake manifold-to-cylinder head bolts and remove the intake manifold.

8. If necessary, remove the throttle body and air intake pipe from the manifold.

9. Check the intake manifold for cracks or other damage. Check the surface of the cylinder heads and intake manifold for warpage using a straightedge. Replace the intake manifold, as necessary.

To install:

10. Clean all gasket mating surfaces.

11. If removed, install the throttle body using new gaskets. Tighten the nuts/bolts to 19 ft. lbs. (25 Nm).

12. If removed, apply clean engine oil to new O-rings and install the air intake pipe to the intake manifold. Tighten the bolts to 95 inch lbs. (10.8 Nm). On 1.8L engine, the bolts must be tightened in the proper sequence.

13. Position new gaskets and install the intake manifold to the cylinder head. Install the mounting bolts and tighten, in 2-3 steps, to 19 ft. lbs. (25 Nm), working from the center toward the ends of the manifold.

14. Install the intake manifold bracket and tighten the bolts to 19 ft. lbs. (25 Nm).

15. Connect the coolant hose to the air bypass valve. Connect the fuel lines.

16. Connect the vacuum hoses and electrical connectors. Connect the accelerator cable.

17. Install the air cleaner assembly and ducts. On MX-3, install the upper strut bar.

18. Connect the negative battery cable. Fill and bleed the cooling system.

19. Start the engine and bring to normal operating temperature. Check for leaks. Check the idle speed.

3.0L Engine

SOHC ENGINE

1. Properly relieve the fuel system pressure.

2. Disconnect the negative battery cable and drain the cooling system.

3. Disconnect the electrical connector from the air flow meter and

remove the air cleaner assembly and air ducts.

4. Disconnect the electrical connector from the air bypass valve. Label and disconnect the coolant hoses from the air bypass valve. Remove the air bypass valve.

5. Disconnect the throttle position sensor and accelerator cable from the throttle body. Remove the throttle body.

6. Label and disconnect the vacuum hoses, EGR pipe, EGR position sensor connector, coolant hose and ground wire from the air intake pipe. Remove the wiring bracket.

7. Remove the air intake pipe from the rear of the upper intake manifold.

8. Mark the position of the intake manifold runners connecting the upper and lower intake manifolds, so they can be reinstalled in their original locations. Remove the nuts and remove the intake manifold runners.

9. Label and disconnect the intake air thermosensor connector, vacuum hoses and ground wires from the upper intake manifold. Remove the upper intake manifold.

10. Label and disconnect the remaining necessary wiring connectors, vacuum and coolant hoses. Disconnect and plug the fuel lines.

11. Loosen the lower intake manifold nuts in 2-3 steps, working progressively from the ends of the manifold toward the center. Remove the lower intake manifold.

12. Inspect the upper and lower intake manifolds and the manifold runners for cracks or other damage. Replace as necessary.

To install:

13. Clean all gasket mating surfaces.

14. Position new gaskets to the cylinder heads and install the lower intake manifold. Install the intake manifold washers with the white paint mark facing upward.

15. Install the retaining nuts and tighten in 2-3 steps in the proper sequence.

16. Connect the fuel lines. Connect the coolant and vacuum hoses and the electrical connectors to the lower intake manifold.

17. Install a new drain hole O-ring on the lower intake manifold before installing the upper intake manifold. Install the upper intake manifold to the lower intake manifold and tighten the nuts to 19 ft. lbs. (25 Nm).

18. Connect the ground wires, vacuum hoses and intake air thermosensor connector to the upper intake manifold.

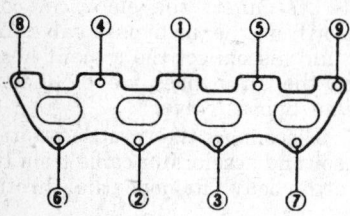

Intake manifold-to-cylinder head torque sequence — 323/Protege 1.8L engine

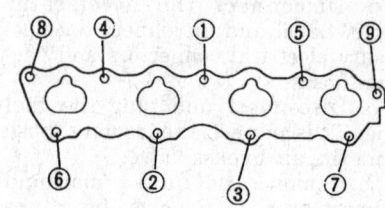

Intake manifold-to-cylinder head torque sequence — MX-3 1.6L engine

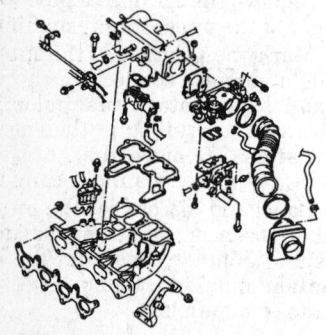

Intake manifold assembly and related components — 323/Protege 1.8L engine

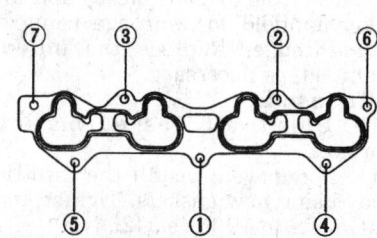

Intake manifold-to-cylinder head torque sequence — 2.0L engine

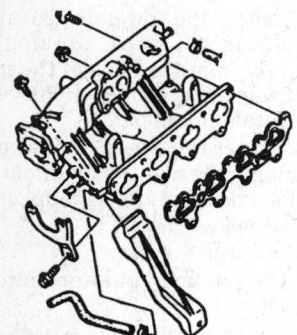

Intake manifold assembly and related components — Miata

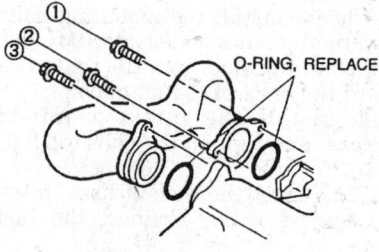

Air intake pipe-to-intake manifold torque sequence — MX-3 1.8L engine

26. Connect the negative battery cable. Fill and bleed the cooling system.

27. Start the engine and bring to normal operating temperature. Check for leaks. Check the idle speed.

DOHC ENGINE

1. Properly relieve the fuel system pressure.

2. Disconnect the negative battery cable and drain the cooling system.

3. Disconnect the air intake hose from the throttle body. If necessary, disconnect the air flow meter electrical connector and remove the air cleaner assembly and air ducts.

4. Disconnect the accelerator cable. Disconnect and plug the fuel lines.

5. On 1990-91 vehicles, remove the cover from the upper intake manifold.

6. Label and disconnect the necessary hoses and electrical connectors from the throttle body. On 1990-91 vehicles, remove the cold start injector from the throttle body, leaving the fuel line connected. Remove the throttle body.

7. On 1992-94 vehicles, disconnect the electrical connector, water hoses and air hose from the air bypass valve. Remove the retaining bolts/nuts and remove the air bypass valve. Remove the air intake pipe from the upper intake manifold.

8. Label and disconnect the necessary hoses and electrical connectors from the upper intake manifold. Remove the upper intake manifold retaining bolts and the upper intake manifold.

9. Label and disconnect the electrical connectors from the fuel injectors.

10. On 1990-91 vehicles, disconnect the vacuum hose from the fuel pressure regulator and remove the fuel rail retaining nuts. Remove the fuel rail with the injectors.

11. On 1992-94 vehicles, remove the retaining bolts and cap from the top of the injector. Remove the injector by grasping the plastic part of the injector and twisting out. Disconnect the vacuum hose from the fuel pressure regulator and remove the fuel rail.

12. Label and disconnect the remaining hoses and electrical connectors from the lower intake manifold. Loosen the retaining nuts in 2-3 steps working gradually inward from the ends of the manifold. Remove the lower intake manifold.

13. Clean all gasket mating surfaces. Inspect the manifolds for cracks or other damage.

19. Install new O-rings on the intake manifold runners. Using new gaskets, install the runners, in their original locations, on the upper and lower intake manifolds. Tighten the nuts to 19 ft. lbs. (25 Nm).

20. Using a new gasket, install the air intake pipe at the rear of the upper intake manifold. Tighten the nuts to 19 ft. lbs. (25 Nm). Install the wiring bracket.

21. Connect the EGR pipe, EGR position sensor, ground wires, vacuum and coolant hoses to the air intake pipe.

22. Install the throttle body, using a new gasket. Tighten the nuts to 19 ft. lbs. (25 Nm).

23. Connect the throttle position sensor electrical connector and accelerator cable to the throttle body.

24. Install the air bypass valve and tighten the retaining bolt to 22 ft. lbs. (30 Nm). Connect the electrical connector and coolant hoses.

25. Install the air cleaner assembly and air ducts. Connect the air flow meter electrical connector.

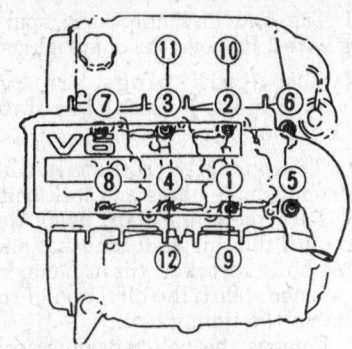

Lower intake manifold nut torque sequence — SOHC 3.0L engine

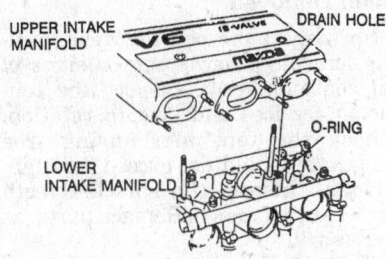

Install a new O-ring before installing the upper intake manifold — SOHC 3.0L engine

To install:

14. Position new gaskets and install the lower intake manifold. Install the retaining nut washers with the white paint mark facing upward. Tighten the retaining nuts in 2-3 steps to 19 ft. lbs. (25 Nm), in the proper sequence.

15. Connect the hoses and electrical connectors to the lower intake manifold.

16. On 1990-91 vehicles, apply clean engine oil to new injector O-rings and install on the injectors. Install the injectors on the intake manifold and retain with the fuel rail. Tighten the fuel rail nuts to 19 ft. lbs. (25 Nm).

17. On 1992-94 vehicles, install the fuel rail. Apply a small amount of clean engine oil to new injector O-rings and install on the injectors. Install the injectors in the fuel rail using a turning motion, to prevent damaging the O-rings. Install the injector retainer caps and tighten the screws to 30 inch lbs. (3.4 Nm).

18. Connect the injector electrical connectors and connect the vacuum hose to the fuel pressure regulator. Connect the fuel lines.

19. Using a new gasket, install the upper intake manifold on the lower intake manifold. Tighten the mounting bolts to 19 ft. lbs. (25 Nm).

20. Connect the electrical connectors and hoses to the upper intake manifold.

21. On 1992-94 vehicles, install the air intake pipe on the upper intake manifold using a new gasket, and tighten the mounting bolts to 17 ft. lbs. (23 Nm). Install the air bypass valve and tighten the nuts to 19 ft. lbs. (25 Nm). Connect the coolant hoses, air hose and electrical connector to the air bypass valve.

22. Install the throttle body, using a new gasket. Tighten the nuts to 19 ft. lbs. (25 Nm). On 1990-91 vehicles, install the cold start injector on the throttle body using a new gasket. Tighten to 8 ft. lbs. (11 Nm). Connect the hoses and electrical connectors to the throttle body.

23. On 1990-91 vehicles, install the cover on the upper intake manifold. Connect the accelerator cable.

24. If removed, install the air cleaner and air ducts. Connect the air intake to the throttle body.

25. Connect the negative battery cable. Fill and bleed the cooling system.

26. Start the engine and bring to normal operating temperature. Check for leaks. Check the idle speed.

Exhaust Manifold

REMOVAL AND INSTALLATION

1. Disconnect the negative battery cable.

2. Remove the retaining bolts and remove the exhaust manifold insulator.

3. Disconnect the oxygen sensor electrical connector. Remove the oxygen sensor, if necessary, if it is installed in the manifold.

4. Disconnect the EGR pipe, if equipped.

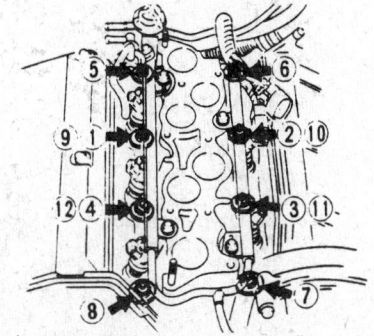

Lower intake manifold nut torque sequence — 1990-91 DOHC 3.0L engine

5. Raise and safely support the vehicle. Remove the nuts from the exhaust pipe flange and disconnect the exhaust pipe from the manifold or turbocharger, if equipped.

6. Lower the vehicle.

7. If equipped with turbocharger, proceed as follows:
   a. Drain the cooling system.
   b. Disconnect the air hose and coolant hoses from the turbocharger.
   c. Disconnect the oil feed and return lines.

8. On 3.0L SOHC engine, remove the retaining bolts and remove the center exhaust pipe from the exhaust manifolds.

9. Remove the mounting nuts/bolts and remove the exhaust manifold. On turbocharged vehicles, the manifold and turbocharger are removed as an assembly.

10. Installation is the reverse of the removal procedure. Make sure all gasket mating surfaces are clean prior to assembly.

11. Use new gaskets and tighten the exhaust manifold-to-cylinder head nuts/bolts to:
   17 ft. lbs. (23 Nm) for 1.6L and 1.8L SOHC engines
   34 ft. lbs. (46 Nm) for 1.6L, 1.8L DOHC and 2.2L 4-cylinder engines
   19 ft. lbs. (25 Nm) for 1.8L, 2.5L and 3.0L 6-cylinder engines.

12. On 2.0L engine, tighten the nuts to 20 ft. lbs. (26 Nm) and the bolts to 16 ft. lbs. (22 Nm).

13. Use a new gasket and tighten the exhaust pipe flange-to-exhaust manifold nuts to 34 ft. lbs. (46 Nm). On 3.0L SOHC engine, tighten the center exhaust pipe bolts to 22 ft. lbs. (30 Nm).

Turbocharger

REMOVAL AND INSTALLATION

1. Disconnect the negative battery cable.

2. Raise and safely support the vehicle. Remove the engine undercover and drain the cooling system.

3. Remove the inlet and outlet hoses from the turbocharger. Cover the turbocharger openings with clean rags to prevent the entry of dirt or foreign material.

4. Remove the retaining bolts and remove the insulator covers from the exhaust manifold and turbocharger.

5. Disconnect the coolant hoses.

6. Disconnect the oil feed and return lines. Cover the openings in the

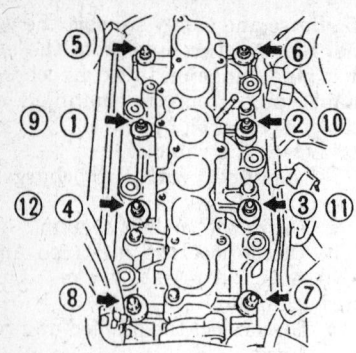

Lower intake manifold nut torque sequence — 1992-94 DOHC 3.0L engine

turbocharger to prevent the entry of dirt or foreign material.

7. Disconnect the oxygen sensor connector. On MX-6/626, disconnect the EGR pipe from the exhaust manifold.

8. Remove the nuts and disconnect the exhaust pipe from the turbocharger. On MX-6/626, remove the bolt from the turbocharger support bracket.

9. Remove the exhaust manifold-to-cylinder head nuts while supporting the manifold/turbocharger assembly.

10. Remove the exhaust manifold and turbocharger as an assembly.

11. Remove the nuts and separate the manifold from the turbocharger.

NOTE: Do not carry the turbocharger by the actuator rod. Be careful not to bend the actuator mounting or rod.

12. Clean all gasket mating surfaces of sealant and old gasket material.

To install:

13. Assemble the exhaust manifold to the turbocharger, using a new gasket. Tighten the nuts to 34 ft. lbs. (46 Nm).

14. Pour approximately 25cc of clean engine oil into the turbocharger oil inlet.

15. Install the turbocharger/exhaust manifold assembly to the cylinder head, using a new gasket. Tighten the nuts to 34 ft. lbs. (46 Nm).

16. On MX-6/626, connect the support bracket to the turbocharger. Tighten the bolt to 30 ft. lbs. (41 Nm).

17. Connect the exhaust pipe to the turbocharger, using a new gasket. Tighten the nuts to 34 ft. lbs. (46 Nm).

18. On MX-6/626, connect the EGR pipe to the exhaust manifold. Connect the oxygen sensor connector.

19. Connect the oil feed and return lines. Connect the coolant hoses.

20. Install the insulators on the exhaust manifold and turbocharger and secure with the bolts.

21. Install the turbocharger inlet and outlet hoses.

22. Check the engine oil level and add, as necessary. Change the oil and filter if the oil is dirty.

23. Install the engine undercover and lower the vehicle.

24. On 323, disconnect the connector from the ignition coil negative terminal. On MX-6/626, disconnect the connector from the igniter.

25. Connect the negative battery cable and crank the engine for at least 20 seconds.

26. Reconnect the electrical connector. Fill and bleed the cooling system.

27. Start the engine and run at idle for 30 seconds.

28. On MX-6/626, stop the engine and disconnect the negative battery cable. Depress the brake pedal for at least 5 seconds to cancel the malfunction code.

Timing Belt Cover, Belt and Tensioner

REMOVAL AND INSTALLATION

323 and Protege

SOHC ENGINE

1. Disconnect the negative battery cable. Remove the engine undercover.

2. Remove the accessory drive belts.

3. Remove the water pump pulley.

4. Remove the crankshaft pulley bolts and remove the crankshaft pulley and baffle plate. Using a suitable tool to hold the crankshaft pulley and remove the pulley lock bolt. Remove the crankshaft pulley boss.

5. Remove the upper and lower timing belt covers.

6. Tag and disconnect the spark plug wires. Remove the spark plugs.

NOTE: Spark plugs are removed to make it easier to rotate the engine.

7. Temporarily reinstall the crankshaft pulley boss and lock bolt.

8. Turn the crankshaft, using the bolt, until the camshaft sprocket and crankshaft sprocket timing marks are aligned. Mark the direction of rotation on the timing belt.

9. Remove the belt tensioner lock bolt, the tensioner wheel and the spring. Remove the timing belt.

NOTE: Do not rotate the engine after the timing belt has been removed.

10. Inspect the belt for wear, peeling, cracking, hardening or signs of oil contamination. Inspect the tensioner for free and smooth rotation. Check the tensioner spring free length; it should not exceed 2.520 in. (64mm). Inspect the sprocket teeth for wear or damage. Replace parts, as necessary.

To install:

11. Make sure the timing marks on the sprockets are properly aligned.

12. Install the timing belt tensioner and spring. Temporarily tighten the bolt with the spring fully extended.

13. Install the timing belt so there is no looseness on the tension side. If reusing the old timing belt, make sure it is reinstalled in the same direction of rotation.

14. Turn the crankshaft 2 turns clockwise and check the timing mark alignment. If the marks are not aligned, repeat Steps 11-14.

15. Loosen the tensioner lock bolt to set the tension, then torque the bolt to 19 ft. lbs. (25 Nm).

16. Turn the crankshaft 2 turns clockwise and check the alignment of the timing marks. If they are not aligned, repeat Steps 11-16.

1. Air bypass hose
2. Insulators
3. Oil pipe
4. Water hoses
5. EGR pipe
6. Oxygen sensor
7. Front pipe
8. Bolt

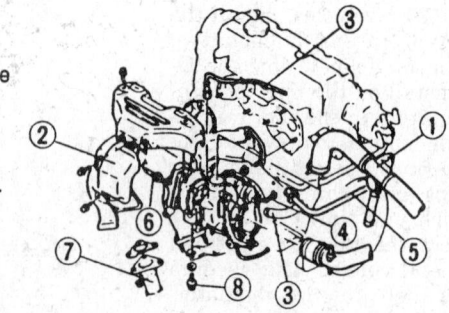

Turbocharger removal and Installation — MX-6/626

17. Apply approximately 22 lbs. pressure to the timing belt on the side opposite the tensioner, at a point midway between the sprockets. The belt should deflect 0.43-0.51 in. (11-13mm). If the tension is not as specified, repeat Steps 14-17 or, if necessary, replace the tensioner spring.

18. Install the spark plugs and connect the spark plug wires.

19. Install the upper and lower timing belt covers. Tighten the bolts to 95 inch lbs. (11 Nm).

20. Install the crankshaft pulley boss and tighten the lock bolt to 123 ft. lbs. (167 Nm), while holding the pulley boss with a suitable tool.

21. Install the crankshaft pulley and baffle plate.

22. Install the undercover or side cover. Connect the negative battery cable.

23. Start the engine and check for proper operation. Check the ignition timing.

DOHC ENGINE

1. Disconnect the negative battery cable. Remove the engine undercover.

2. Remove the accessory drive belts.

3. Remove the crankshaft pulley bolts and remove the crankshaft pulley.

4. Remove the outer timing belt guide plate. Remove the inner timing belt guide plate if so equipped.

5. Tag and disconnect the spark plug wires. Remove the spark plugs.

NOTE: Spark plugs are removed to make it easier to rotate the engine.

6. Remove the engine oil dipstick.

7. Remove the upper, middle and lower timing belt covers.

8. Turn the crankshaft until the timing marks on the crankshaft and camshaft sprockets are aligned. On 1992-94 vehicles, the pin on the pulley boss must face upward.

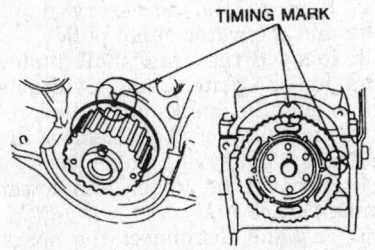

TIMING MARK

Crankshaft and camshaft sprocket timing mark alignment — 323/Protege with SOHC engine

9. On 1992-94 vehicles, hold the crankshaft pulley boss with a suitable tool and remove the pulley lock bolt, being careful not to rotate the crankshaft. Remove the crankshaft pulley boss.

10. Mark the direction of rotation on the timing belt. Loosen the tensioner lock bolt and pry the tensioner outward. Tighten the lock bolt with the tensioner spring fully extended. Remove the timing belt.

NOTE: Protect the tensioner with a shop towel before prying on it. Do not rotate the crankshaft after the timing belt has been removed.

11. Remove the tensioner and spring. If necessary, remove the idler pulley.

12. Inspect the belt for wear, peeling, cracking, hardening or signs of oil contamination. Inspect the tensioner for free and smooth rotation. Check the tensioner spring free length; it should not exceed 2.315 in. (58.8mm). Inspect the sprocket teeth for wear or damage. Replace parts, as necessary.

To install:

13. If removed, install the idler pulley and tighten the bolt to 38 ft. lbs. (52 Nm).

14. Install the tensioner and tensioner spring. Pry the tensioner outward and temporarily tighten the tensioner lock bolt with the tensioner spring fully extended.

15. Make sure the crankshaft sprocket timing mark is aligned with the mark on the oil pump housing and the camshaft sprocket timing marks are aligned with the marks on the seal plate.

16. Install the timing belt so there is no looseness at the idler pulley side or between the camshaft sprockets. If reusing the old belt, make sure it is installed in the same direction of rotation.

17. On 1992-94 vehicles, temporarily install the pulley boss and lock bolt.

18. Turn the crankshaft 2 turns clockwise and align the crankshaft sprocket timing mark. On 1992-94 vehicles, face the pin on the pulley boss upright. Make sure the camshaft sprocket timing marks are aligned. If they are not, repeat Steps 15-19.

19. Turn the crankshaft 1⅚ turns clockwise and align the crankshaft sprocket timing mark with the tension set mark for proper belt tension adjustment. On 1992-94 vehicles, remove the lock bolt and pulley boss.

20. Make sure the crankshaft sprocket timing mark is aligned with the tension set mark. Loosen the tensioner lock bolt and allow the spring to apply tension to the belt. Tighten the tensioner lock bolt to 38 ft. lbs. (52 Nm).

21. On 1992-94 vehicles, install the pulley boss and lock bolt.

22. Turn the crankshaft 2⅙ turns clockwise and make sure the timing marks are correctly aligned.

23. Apply approximately 22 lbs. pressure to the timing belt at a point midway between the camshaft sprockets. The belt should deflect 0.35-0.45 in. (9.0-11.5mm). If the deflection is not correct, repeat Steps 21-24.

24. On 1992-94 vehicles, hold the pulley boss with a suitable tool and tighten the lock bolt to 123 ft. lbs. (167 Nm).

25. Install the timing belt covers and tighten the bolts to 95 inch lbs. (11 Nm). Install the engine oil dipstick.

26. Install the spark plugs and connect the spark plug wires.

27. Install the timing belt inner guide plate, if equipped. Make sure the dished side of the plate faces away from the timing belt. Install the outer guide plate, if equipped.

28. Install the crankshaft pulley and tighten the bolts to 13 ft. lbs. (17 Nm).

29. Install the water pump pulley and the accessory drive belts. Adjust the belt tension.

30. Install the engine side or undercover, as necessary. Connect the negative battery cable.

31. Start the engine and check for proper operation. Check the ignition timing.

Miata

1. Disconnect the negative battery cable. Drain the cooling system.

2. Remove the air intake pipe.

3. Remove the upper radiator hose and disconnect the coolant hoses at the thermostat housing.

4. Remove the accessory drive belts and the water pump pulley.

5. Remove the crankshaft pulley bolts and the crankshaft pulley. On 1992-94 vehicles, hold the pulley boss with a suitable tool and remove the pulley lock bolt. Remove the pulley boss.

6. On 1990-91 vehicles, remove the outer and inner timing belt guide plates.

7. Tag and disconnect the spark plug wires from the spark plugs. Re-

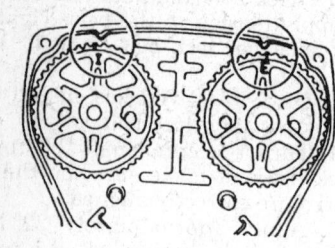

Crankshaft and camshaft sprocket timing mark alignment — 323/Protege with DOHC engine

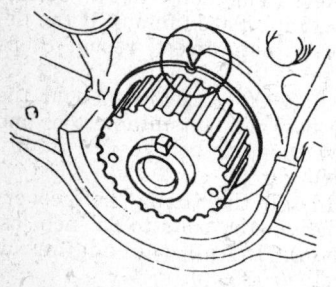

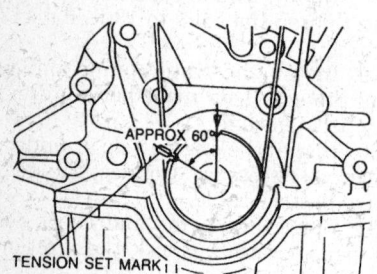

Timing belt tension set mark — 323/Protege and Miata with DOHC engine

move the ignition coil and plug wires assembly. Remove the spark plugs.

8. Remove the cylinder head cover. Remove the upper, middle and lower timing belt covers.

9. On 1992-94 vehicles, temporarily reinstall the pulley boss and lock bolt.

10. Turn the crankshaft until the crankshaft and camshaft sprocket timing marks are aligned. On 1992-94 vehicles, the pin on the pulley boss must face upward.

11. On 1992-94 vehicles, remove the pulley boss and lock bolt, being careful not to disturb the crankshaft.

12. Mark the direction of rotation on the timing belt. Loosen the tensioner lock bolt and pry the tensioner outward. Tighten the lock bolt with the tensioner spring fully extended. Remove the timing belt.

NOTE: Protect the tensioner with a shop towel before prying on it. Do not rotate the crankshaft after the timing belt has been removed.

13. Remove the tensioner and spring. If necessary, remove the idler pulley.

14. Inspect the belt for wear, peeling, cracking, hardening or signs of oil contamination. Inspect the tensioner for free and smooth rotation. Check the tensioner spring free length; it should not exceed 2.315 in. (58.8mm). Inspect the sprocket teeth for wear or damage. Replace parts, as necessary.

To install:

15. If removed, install the idler pulley and tighten the bolt to 38 ft. lbs. (52 Nm).

16. Install the tensioner and tensioner spring. Pry the tensioner outward and temporarily tighten the tensioner spring lock bolt with the tensioner spring fully extended.

17. Make sure the crankshaft sprocket timing mark is aligned with the mark on the oil pump housing and the camshaft sprocket timing marks are aligned with the marks on the seal plate.

18. Install the timing belt so there is no looseness at the idler pulley side or between the camshaft sprockets. If reusing the old belt, make sure it is installed in the same direction of rotation.

19. On 1992-94 vehicles, temporarily install the pulley boss and lock bolt.

20. Turn the crankshaft 2 turns clockwise and align the crankshaft sprocket timing mark. On 1992-94 vehicles, face the pin on the pulley boss upright. Make sure the camshaft sprocket timing marks are aligned. If they are not, repeat Steps 16-20.

21. Turn the crankshaft 1⁵/₆ turns clockwise and align the crankshaft sprocket timing mark with the tension set mark for proper belt tension adjustment. On 1992-94 vehicles, remove the lock bolt and pulley boss.

22. Make sure the crankshaft sprocket timing mark is aligned with the tension set mark. Loosen the tensioner lock bolt and allow the spring to apply tension to the belt. Tighten the tensioner lock bolt to 38 ft. lbs. (52 Nm).

23. On 1992-94 vehicles, install the pulley boss and lock bolt.

24. Turn the crankshaft 2¹/₆ turns clockwise and make sure the timing marks are correctly aligned.

25. Apply approximately 22 lbs. pressure to the timing belt at a point midway between the camshaft sprockets. The belt should deflect 0.35-0.45 in. (9.0-11.5mm). If the deflection is not correct, repeat Steps 22-25.

26. Install the timing belt covers and tighten the bolts to 95 inch lbs. (11 Nm).

27. Apply silicone sealer to the cylinder head in the area adjacent to the front and rear camshaft caps. Install the cylinder head cover and tighten the bolts to 78 inch lbs. (8.8 Nm).

28. Install the spark plugs. Install the ignition coil and tighten the bolts to 19 ft. lbs. (25 Nm). Connect the spark plug wires.

29. On 1990-91 vehicles, install the inner timing belt guide plate with the dished side facing away from the engine. Install the outer guide plate.

30. On 1992-94 vehicles, hold the pulley boss with a suitable tool and tighten the lock bolt to 123 ft. lbs. (167 Nm).

31. Install the crankshaft pulley. Tighten the bolts to 13 ft. lbs. (17 Nm).

32. Install the water pump pulley and the accessory drive belts. Adjust the belt tension.

33. Connect the coolant hoses to the thermostat housing and install the upper radiator hose.

34. Install the air intake pipe and connect the negative battery cable. Fill and bleed the cooling system.

35. Start the engine and bring to normal operating temperature. Check for leaks and proper operation. Check the ignition timing.

MX-3

1.6L ENGINE

1. Disconnect the negative battery cable. Remove the engine undercover.

2. Remove the accessory drive belts and the water pump pulley.

3. Remove the crankshaft pulley bolts and the plate. Using a suitable tool to hold the crankshaft pulley, remove the pulley lock bolt. Remove the crankshaft pulley and pulley boss.

4. Remove the upper and lower timing belt covers.

5. Tag and disconnect the spark plug wires. Remove the spark plugs.

NOTE: Spark plugs are removed to make it easier to rotate the engine.

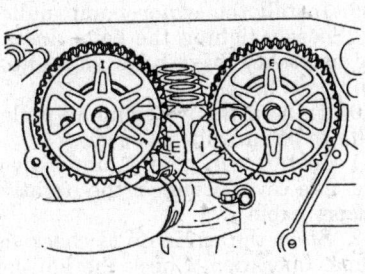

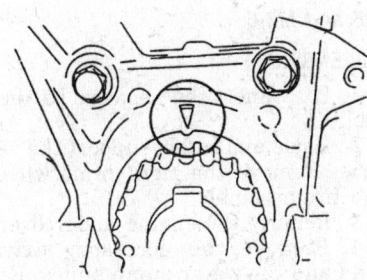

Crankshaft and camshaft sprocket timing mark alignment — Miata

6. Temporarily reinstall the pulley boss and lock bolt.

7. Turn the crankshaft, using the bolt, until the camshaft sprocket and crankshaft sprocket timing marks are aligned. The pin on the pulley boss faces up.

8. Mark the direction of rotation on the timing belt.

9. Remove the belt tensioner lock bolt, the tensioner wheel and the spring. Remove the timing belt.

NOTE: Do not rotate the engine after the timing belt has been removed.

10. Inspect the belt for wear, peeling, cracking, hardening or signs of oil contamination. Inspect the tensioner for free and smooth rotation. Check the tensioner spring free length; it should not exceed 2.520 in. (64mm). Inspect the sprocket teeth for wear or damage. Replace parts, as necessary.

To install:

11. Make sure the timing marks on the sprockets are properly aligned.

12. Install the timing belt tensioner and spring. Temporarily tighten the bolt with the spring fully extended.

13. Install the timing belt so there is no looseness on the tension side. If reusing the old timing belt, make

sure it is reinstalled in the same direction of rotation.

14. Turn the crankshaft 2 turns clockwise and check the timing mark alignment. If the marks are not aligned, repeat Steps 11-14.

15. Loosen the tensioner lock bolt to set the tension, then torque the bolt to 19 ft. lbs. (25 Nm).

16. Turn the crankshaft 2 turns clockwise and check the alignment of the timing marks. If they are not aligned, repeat Steps 11-16.

17. Apply approximately 22 lbs. (98 N) pressure to the timing belt on the side opposite the tensioner, at a point midway between the sprockets. The belt should deflect 0.43-0.51 in. (11-13mm). If the tension is not as specified, repeat Steps 14-17 or, if necessary, replace the tensioner spring.

18. Remove the pulley boss and lock bolt.

19. Install the spark plugs and connect the spark plug wires.

20. Install the upper and lower timing belt covers. Tighten the bolts to 95 inch lbs. (11 Nm).

21. Install the crankshaft pulley boss and crankshaft pulley. Tighten the lock bolt to 123 ft. lbs. (167 Nm), while holding the pulley boss with a suitable tool.

22. Install the crankshaft pulley plate and tighten the bolts to 13 ft. lbs. (17 Nm).

23. Install the water pump pulley and accessory drive belts. Adjust the belt tension.

24. Install the undercover. Connect the negative battery cable.

25. Start the engine and check for proper operation. Check the ignition timing.

1.8L ENGINE

1. Disconnect the negative battery cable. Remove the engine undercover and side cover.

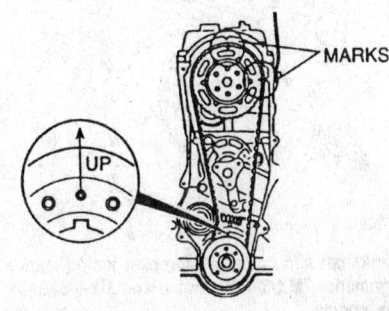

Crankshaft and camshaft sprocket timing mark alignment — MX-3 1.6L engine

2. Remove the accessory drive belts.

3. Remove the water pump pulley and the accessory drive belt idler pulley bracket.

4. Disconnect the power steering pump pressure switch connector and disconnect the power steering hose from the engine.

5. Remove the power steering pump reservoir bolts and secure the reservoir aside.

6. Keep the power steering pump pulley from turning, by installing a socket on the end of a breaker bar through one of the pulley holes and engaging a pump mounting bolt. Remove the pulley nut and the pulley.

7. Remove the power steering pump mounting bolts and remove the power steering pump. Secure the pump aside, leaving the hoses connected.

8. Hold the crankshaft pulley with a suitable tool and remove the pulley bolt. Remove the crankshaft pulley, being careful not to damage the crank angle sensor rotor on the rear of the pulley.

9. Disconnect the crank angle sensor connector and remove the clip from the engine oil dipstick tube. Remove the dipstick and tube. Plug the hole after removal to prevent the entry of dirt or foreign material.

10. Remove the knock sensor harness bracket and wiring harness from the timing belt cover.

11. Support the engine with engine support tool 49 G017 5A0 or equivalent.

12. Remove the right side engine mount.

13. Remove the right and left timing belt covers.

14. Install the crankshaft pulley bolt and turn the crankshaft until the No. 1 piston is at TDC on the compression stroke. Mark the direction of rotation on the timing belt.

15. Loosen the automatic tensioner bolts and remove the lower bolt. Hold the tensioner so the bolt threads are not damaged during removal.

16. Hold the upper idler pulley to reduce the belt resistance and remove the pulley bolts and pulley. Remove the timing belt. Remove the automatic tensioner and the remaining idler pulley.

NOTE: Do not rotate the engine after the timing belt has been removed.

17. Inspect the belt for wear, peeling, cracking, hardening or signs of oil contamination. Inspect the tensioner pulley for free and smooth rotation. Check the automatic ten-

sioner for oil leakage. Check the tensioner rod projection (free length); it should be 0.55-0.63 in. (14-16mm). Inspect the sprocket teeth for wear or damage. Replace parts, as necessary.

To install:

18. Position the automatic tensioner in a suitable press. Place a flat washer under the tensioner body to prevent damage to the body plug.

19. Slowly press in the tensioner rod, but do not exceed 2200 lbs. force. Insert a pin into the tensioner body to hold the rod in place.

20. Install the tensioner and loosely tighten the upper bolts so the tensioner can move.

NOTE: This is done to reduce the timing belt resistance when the upper idler pulley is installed.

21. If removed, install the lower idler pulley and tighten the bolt to 38 ft. lbs. (52 Nm).

22. Make sure the crankshaft and camshaft sprocket timing marks are aligned.

23. Install the timing belt over the crankshaft sprocket, lower idler pulley, left camshaft sprocket, tensioner pulley and right camshaft sprocket, in that order. Make sure the belt has no looseness at the tension side. If reusing the old timing belt, make sure it is installed in the same direction of rotation.

24. Install the upper idler pulley while applying pressure on the timing belt. Be careful not to damage the pulley bolt threads when installing. Tighten the upper idler pulley bolt to 34 ft. lbs. (46 Nm).

25. Push the bottom of the automatic tensioner away from the belt and tighten the mounting bolts to 19 ft. lbs. (25 Nm). Remove the pin from the tensioner, applying tension to the belt.

26. Turn the crankshaft twice in the normal direction of rotation and make sure the timing marks are aligned. If the timing marks are not aligned, repeat Steps 18-26.

27. Apply approximately 22 lbs. (98 N) pressure to the timing belt at a point midway between the automatic tensioner and the crankshaft sprocket. The belt should deflect 0.24-0.31 in. (6-8mm). If the deflection is not as specified, replace the automatic tensioner.

28. Install new gaskets and the right and left timing belt covers. Tighten the bolts to 95 inch lbs. (11 Nm).

29. Install the crank angle sensor and harness brackets and tighten the bolts to 95 inch lbs. (11 Nm).

30. Install the right side engine mount. Tighten the mount-to-engine nuts to 76 ft. lbs. (103 Nm) and the mount through bolt to 69 ft. lbs. (93 Nm).

31. Remove the engine support tool.

32. Apply clean engine oil to a new O-ring and install on the dipstick tube. Remove the plug and install the dipstick tube and dipstick. Tighten the tube bracket bolt to 95 inch lbs. (11 Nm).

33. Install the crank angle sensor harness and clip to the dipstick tube. Connect the electrical connector.

34. Remove the crankshaft pulley bolt and install the crankshaft pulley. Reinstall the bolt and hold the pulley with a suitable tool. Tighten the bolt to 123 ft. lbs. (167 Nm).

35. Install the power steering pump. Tighten the mounting bolts to 34 ft. lbs. (46 Nm) except the bolt to the right of the idler pulley. Tighten that bolt to 19 ft. lbs. (25 Nm).

36. Install the power steering pump pulley and loosely tighten the nut. Hold the pulley with the socket and breaker bar and tighten the nut to 69 ft. lbs. (93 Nm).

37. Connect the power steering hose to the engine and connect the pressure switch connector.

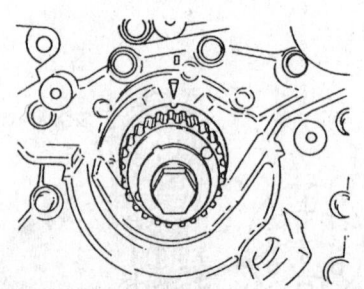

Crankshaft and camshaft sprocket timing mark alignment — MX-3 1.8L engine and MX-6/626 2.5L engine

38. Install the power steering fluid reservoir and engine ground. Tighten to 87 inch lbs. (9.8 Nm).

39. Install the water pump pulley and loosely tighten the bolts. Install the accessory drive belts and adjust the belt tension.

40. Tighten the water pump pulley bolts to 95 inch lbs. (11 Nm).

41. Install the engine undercover and side cover. Connect the negative battery cable.

42. Start the engine and check for proper operation. Check the ignition timing.

626 and MX-6

2.0L ENGINE

1. Disconnect the negative battery cable.

2. Raise and safely support the vehicle. Remove the right front wheel and tire assembly.

3. Remove the engine undercover.

4. Remove the accessory drive belts and the water pump pulley. Remove the power steering pump pulley shield.

5. Remove the power steering pump and position aside, leaving the hoses connected.

6. Hold the crankshaft pulley using a suitable tool and remove the bolt. Remove the crankshaft pulley and the guide plate.

7. Disconnect the spark plug wires and remove the spark plugs.

8. Loosen the cylinder head bolt cover bolts, in 2-3 steps, in the reverse order of the tightening sequence. Remove the cylinder head cover.

9. Remove the engine oil dipstick and dipstick tube.

10. Remove the upper and lower timing belt covers.

11. Support the engine using engine support tool 49 G017 5A0. Remove the right side engine mount.

12. Turn the crankshaft, in the normal direction of rotation, until the crankshaft and camshaft sprocket timing marks are aligned. Mark the direction of rotation on the belt.

13. Turn the belt tensioner clockwise and disconnect the tensioner spring from the hook pin. Remove the timing belt.

NOTE: Do not rotate the engine after the timing belt has been removed.

14. Inspect the belt for wear, peeling, cracking, hardening or signs of oil contamination. Inspect the tensioner pulley for free and smooth rotation and for oil leaks. Check the spring bracket and grommet for

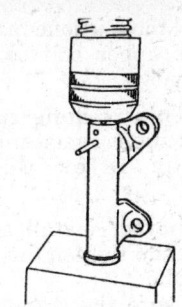

Insert a pin in the tensioner body after pressing in the tensioner rod — MX-3 1.8L engine and MX-6/626 2.5L engine

looseness or damage. Measure the tensioner spring free length; it should not exceed 1.441 in. (36.6mm). Check the sprockets for worn teeth or other damage.

To install:

15. Make sure the crankshaft and camshaft timing marks are aligned.

NOTE: It may be easier to check the camshaft sprocket alignment by looking behind the sprockets. The camshafts are properly aligned when the grooves on the rear of the sprockets are even with the cylinder head surface.

16. Install the timing belt so there is no looseness at the idler side or between the camshaft sprockets. If reusing the old timing belt, make sure it is installed in the same direction of rotation.

17. Turn the crankshaft clockwise 2 turns and make sure the timing marks are correctly aligned. If the marks are not aligned, repeat Steps 15-17.

18. Turn the tensioner clockwise and connect the tensioner spring to the hook pin. Make sure tension is applied to the timing belt.

19. Turn the crankshaft clockwise 2 turns and make sure the timing

marks are correctly aligned. If the marks are not aligned, repeat Steps 15-19.

20. Install the right side engine mount. Tighten the mount-to-engine nuts to 76 ft. lbs. (102 Nm) and the mount through bolt to 86 ft. lbs. (116 Nm). Install the ground harness and tighten the nut to 65 ft. lbs. (89 Nm).

21. Remove the engine support tool.

22. Install the timing belt covers and tighten the bolts to 95 inch lbs. (10.7 Nm). Install the dipstick tube and dipstick.

23. Apply silicone sealant to the contact surfaces of the cylinder head cover. Also apply sealant to the cylinder head surface in the area adjacent to the front camshaft caps.

24. Install the cylinder head cover and tighten the bolts in 2-3 steps to 69 inch lbs. (7.8 Nm), in the proper sequence.

25. Install the spark plugs and connect the spark plug wires.

26. Install the guide plate and the crankshaft pulley. Hold the pulley with a suitable tool and tighten the lock bolt to 122 ft. lbs. (166 Nm).

27. Install the power steering pump and tighten the bolts to 33 ft. lbs. (46 Nm).

28. Install the power steering pulley shield and the water pump pulley.

29. Install the accessory drive belts and adjust the belt tension.

30. Install the engine undercover and the right front wheel and tire assembly. Lower the vehicle.

31. Connect the negative battery cable. Start the engine and check for proper operation. Check the ignition timing.

2.2L ENGINE

1. Disconnect the negative battery cable. Tag and disconnect the spark plug wires and remove the spark plugs.

2. Remove the engine side cover from the fenderwell.

3. Remove the accessory drive belts.

4. Remove the retaining bolts and remove the crankshaft pulley.

5. Remove the upper and lower timing belt covers. Remove the baffle plate from in front of the crankshaft sprocket.

6. Turn the crankshaft clockwise until the 'arrow'**1** mark on the camshaft is aligned with the mark on top of the front housing. Unbolt and remove the tensioner and the tensioner spring.

7. Remove the timing belt. If the timing belt is to be reused, mark the direction of rotation.

NOTE: Do not rotate the engine after the timing belt has been removed.

8. Inspect the belt for wear, peeling, cracking, hardening or signs of oil contamination. Inspect the tensioner pulley for free and smooth rotation. Measure the tensioner spring free length; it should not exceed 2.480 in. (63mm). Check the sprockets for worn teeth or other damage.

To install:

9. Make sure the crankshaft and camshaft timing marks are aligned.

10. Install the timing belt tensioner and spring. Move the tensioner until the spring is fully extended and temporarily tighten the tensioner bolt to hold it in place.

11. Install the timing belt. Make sure there is no slack at the side of the water pump and idler pulleys. If reusing the old belt, it should be installed in the original direction of rotation.

12. Turn the crankshaft 2 turns clockwise and make sure the timing marks are aligned. If the marks are not aligned, repeat Steps 9-12.

13. Loosen the tensioner lock bolt to apply tension to the belt. Tighten the tensioner bolt to 38 ft. lbs. (52 Nm).

14. Turn the crankshaft 2 turns clockwise and make sure the timing marks are aligned. If the marks are not aligned, repeat Steps 9-14.

15. Apply approximately 22 lbs. (98 N) pressure to the timing belt at a point midway between the idler pulley and camshaft sprocket. A new belt should deflect 0.31-0.35 in. (8-9mm). A used belt should deflect 0.35-0.39 in. (9-10mm). If the deflection is not as specified, repeat Steps 12-15 or, if necessary, replace the tensioner spring.

16. Install the baffle plate with the dished side facing away from the engine.

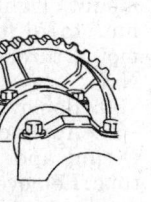

Camshaft sprocket alignment as seen from the rear of the sprockets — 2.0L engine

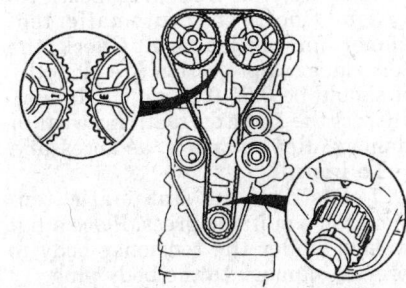

Crankshaft and camshaft sprocket timing mark alignment — 2.0L engine

17. Install the timing belt covers and tighten the bolts to 87 inch lbs. (10 Nm).

18. Install the crankshaft pulley and tighten the bolts to 13 ft. lbs. (17 Nm).

19. Install the accessory drive belts and adjust the belt tension.

20. Install the engine side cover in the fenderwell.

21. Install the spark plugs and connect the spark plug wires.

22. Connect the negative battery cable. Start the engine and check for proper operation. Check the ignition timing.

2.5L ENGINE

1. Disconnect the negative battery cable. Remove the engine undercover and side cover.

2. Remove the accessory drive belts.

3. Remove the water pump pulley and the accessory drive belt idler pulley bracket.

4. Remove the power steering pump reservoir bolts and secure the reservoir aside.

5. Keep the power steering pump pulley from turning, by installing a socket on the end of a breaker bar through one of the pulley holes and

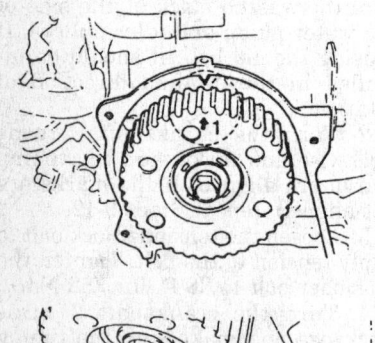

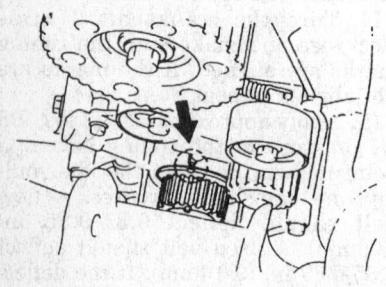

Crankshaft and camshaft sprocket timing mark alignment — 2.2L engine

engaging a pump mounting bolt. Remove the pulley nut and the pulley.

6. Remove the power steering pump mounting bolts and remove the power steering pump. Secure the pump aside, leaving the hoses connected.

7. Hold the crankshaft pulley with a suitable tool and remove the pulley bolt. Remove the crankshaft pulley, being careful not to damage the crank position sensor rotor on the rear of the pulley.

8. Disconnect the crank position sensor connector and remove the clip from the engine oil dipstick tube. Remove the dipstick and tube. Plug the hole after removal to prevent the entry of dirt or foreign material.

9. Remove the crank position sensor harness bracket and wiring harness bracket from the timing belt cover.

10. Support the engine with engine support tool 49 G017 5A0 or equivalent.

11. Remove the right side engine mount.

12. Remove the right and left timing belt covers.

13. Install the crankshaft pulley bolt and turn the crankshaft until the No. 1 piston is at TDC on the compression stroke. Mark the direction of rotation on the timing belt.

14. Loosen the automatic tensioner bolts and remove the lower bolt. Hold the tensioner so the bolt threads are not damaged during removal.

15. Hold the upper idler pulley to reduce the belt resistance and remove the pulley bolts and pulley. Remove the timing belt. Remove the automatic tensioner and the remaining idler pulley.

NOTE: Do not rotate the engine after the timing belt has been removed.

16. Inspect the belt for wear, peeling, cracking, hardening or signs of oil contamination. Inspect the tensioner pulley for free and smooth rotation. Check the automatic tensioner for oil leakage. Check the tensioner rod projection (free length); it should be 0.55-0.63 in. (14-16mm). Inspect the sprocket teeth for wear or damage. Replace parts, as necessary.

To install:

17. Position the automatic tensioner in a suitable press. Place a flat washer under the tensioner body to prevent damage to the body plug.

18. Slowly press in the tensioner rod, but do not exceed 2200 lbs. force. Insert a pin into the tensioner body to hold the rod in place.

19. Install the tensioner and loosely tighten the upper bolt so the tensioner can move.

NOTE: This is done to reduce the timing belt resistance when the upper idler pulley is installed.

20. If removed, install the lower idler pulley and tighten the bolt to 38 ft. lbs. (52 Nm).

21. Make sure the crankshaft and camshaft sprocket timing marks are aligned.

22. Install the timing belt over the crankshaft sprocket, lower idler pulley, left camshaft sprocket, tensioner pulley and right camshaft sprocket, in that order. Make sure the belt has no looseness at the tension side. If reusing the old timing belt, make sure it is installed in the same direction of rotation.

23. Install the upper idler pulley while applying pressure on the timing belt. Be careful not to damage the pulley bolt threads when installing. Tighten the upper idler pulley bolt to 34 ft. lbs. (46 Nm).

24. Push the bottom of the automatic tensioner away from the belt and tighten the mounting bolts to 19 ft. lbs. (25 Nm). Remove the pin from the tensioner, applying tension to the belt.

25. Turn the crankshaft twice in the normal direction of rotation and make sure the timing marks are aligned. If the timing marks are not aligned, repeat Steps 17-25.

26. Apply approximately 22 lbs. (98 N) pressure to the timing belt at a point midway between the automatic tensioner and the crankshaft sprocket. The belt should deflect 0.24-0.31 in. (6-8mm). If the deflection is not as specified, replace the automatic tensioner.

27. Install the right and left timing belt covers. Tighten the bolts to 95 inch lbs. (11 Nm).

28. Install the crank position sensor and harness brackets and tighten the bolts to 95 inch lbs. (11 Nm).

29. Install the right side engine mount. Tighten the mount-to-engine nuts to 76 ft. lbs. (103 Nm) and the mount through bolt to 86 ft. lbs. (116 Nm).

30. Remove the engine support tool.

31. Apply clean engine oil to a new O-ring and install on the dipstick tube. Remove the plug and install the dipstick tube and dipstick. Tighten the tube bracket bolt to 95 inch lbs. (11 Nm).

32. Install the crank angle sensor harness and clip to the dipstick tube. Connect the electrical connector.

33. Remove the crankshaft pulley bolt and install the crankshaft pulley. Reinstall the bolt and hold the pulley with a suitable tool. Tighten the bolt to 122 ft. lbs. (166 Nm).

34. Install the power steering pump. Tighten the mounting bolts to 34 ft. lbs. (46 Nm) except the bolt to the right of the idler pulley. Tighten that bolt to 19 ft. lbs. (25 Nm).

35. Install the power steering pump pulley and loosely tighten the nut. Hold the pulley with the socket and breaker bar and tighten the nut to 69 ft. lbs. (93 Nm).

36. Install the power steering fluid reservoir and engine ground. Tighten to 87 inch lbs. (9.8 Nm).

37. Install the water pump pulley and loosely tighten the bolts. Install the accessory drive belts and adjust the belt tension.

38. Tighten the water pump pulley bolts to 95 inch lbs. (11 Nm).

39. Install the engine undercover and side cover. Connect the negative battery cable.

40. Start the engine and check for proper operation. Check the ignition timing.

929

SOHC ENGINE

1. Disconnect the negative battery cable. Drain the cooling system.

2. Tag and disconnect the spark plug wires. Remove the spark plugs.

3. Remove the fresh air duct. Remove the cooling fan and the fan shroud.

4. Remove the accessory drive belts and the A/C compressor idler pulley.

5. Remove the crankshaft pulley and baffle plate.

6. Remove the coolant bypass hose and the upper radiator hose.

7. Remove the timing belt covers and gaskets.

8. Turn the crankshaft, in the normal direction of rotation, and align the crankshaft and camshaft sprocket timing marks. Mark the direction of rotation on the timing belt.

9. Remove the upper idler pulley and remove the timing belt. Remove the automatic tensioner.

NOTE: Do not rotate the engine after the timing belt has been removed.

10. Inspect the belt for wear, peeling, cracking, hardening or signs of oil contamination. Inspect the tensioner pulley for free and smooth rotation. Check the automatic tensioner for oil leakage. Check the tensioner rod projection (free length);

it should be 0.47-0.55 in. (12-14mm). Inspect the sprocket teeth for wear or damage. Replace parts, as necessary.

To install:

11. Position the automatic tensioner in a suitable press. Place a flat washer under the tensioner body to prevent damage to the body plug.

12. Slowly press in the tensioner rod, but do not exceed 2200 lbs. force. Insert a pin into the tensioner body to hold the rod in place.

13. Install the tensioner and tighten the bolts to 19 ft. lbs. (25 Nm).

14. Make sure the crankshaft and camshaft sprocket timing marks are aligned.

15. Install the timing belt over the crankshaft sprocket, lower idler pulley, left camshaft sprocket, right camshaft sprocket and tensioner pulley, in that order. If reusing the old timing belt, make sure it is installed in the same direction of rotation.

16. Install the upper idler pulley and tighten the bolt to 38 ft. lbs. (52 Nm).

17. Turn the crankshaft 2 turns, in the normal direction of rotation, and align the timing marks. If the timing marks are not aligned, repeat Steps 14-17.

18. Remove the pin from the automatic tensioner. Turn the crankshaft 2 turns, in the normal direction of rotation, and make sure the timing marks are aligned.

19. Apply approximately 22 lbs. (98 N) pressure to the timing belt at a point midway between the right camshaft sprocket and tensioner pulley. The belt should deflect 0.20-0.28 in. (5-7mm). If the deflection is not as specified, replace the timing belt or the automatic tensioner.

20. Install the timing belt covers with new gaskets. Tighten the bolts to 95 inch lbs. (11 Nm).

21. Install the upper radiator hose and coolant bypass hose.

22. Install the baffle plate and crankshaft pulley. Tighten the bolts to 130 inch lbs. (15 Nm).

23. Install the A/C compressor idler pulley and tighten the bolts to 19 ft. lbs. (25 Nm). Install the accessory drive belts and adjust the tension.

24. Install the fan shroud and cooling fan. Install the fresh air duct.

25. Install the spark plugs and connect the spark plug wires.

26. Connect the negative battery cable. Fill and bleed the cooling system.

27. Start the engine and bring to normal operating temperature.

Check for leaks and for proper operation. Check the ignition timing.

DOHC ENGINE

1. Disconnect the negative battery cable and drain the cooling system.

2. Remove the fresh air duct.

3. Remove the cooling fan and fan shroud.

4. Remove the air intake pipe from the throttle body and air cleaner.

5. Disconnect the spark plug wires and remove the spark plugs.

6. Remove the idler pulleys and the accessory drive belts.

7. Remove the coolant bypass hose and the upper radiator hose.

8. Disconnect the electrical connector and remove the distributor.

9. Hold the crankshaft pulley with a suitable tool and remove the bolt. Remove the crankshaft pulley. On 1992-94 vehicles, be careful not to damage the sensor rotor.

10. Remove the timing belt covers. Rotate the crankshaft until the camshaft and crankshaft sprocket timing marks are aligned.

11. Remove the upper idler pulley and the automatic tensioner and pulley. Mark the direction of rotation on the timing belt and remove the timing belt.

NOTE: Do not rotate the engine after the timing belt has been removed.

12. Inspect the belt for wear, peeling, cracking, hardening or signs of oil contamination. Inspect the tensioner pulley for free and smooth rotation. Check the automatic tensioner for oil leakage. Check the tensioner rod projection (free length); it should be 0.47-0.55 in. (12-14mm). Inspect the sprocket teeth for wear or damage. Replace parts, as necessary.

To install:

13. Position the automatic tensioner in a suitable press. Place a flat washer under the tensioner body to prevent damage to the body plug.

14. Slowly press in the tensioner rod, but do not exceed 2200 lbs. force. Insert a pin into the tensioner body to hold the rod in place.

15. Install the tensioner and tighten the bolts to 19 ft. lbs. (25 Nm).

16. Make sure the crankshaft and camshaft sprocket timing marks are aligned.

17. Install the timing belt over the crankshaft sprocket, lower idler pulley, left exhaust camshaft sprocket, left intake camshaft sprocket, tensioner pulley, right exhaust camshaft sprocket and right intake camshaft sprocket, in that order.

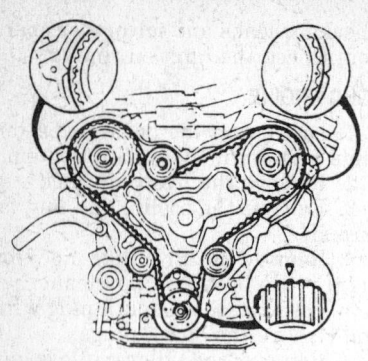

Crankshaft and camshaft sprocket timing mark alignment — SOHC 3.0L engine

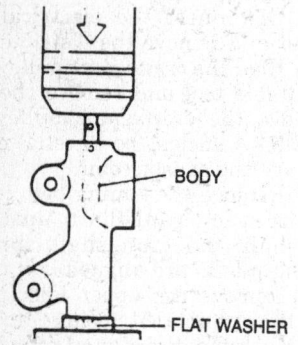

Pressing the rod into the automatic tensioner — SOHC 3.0L engine

18. Push the belt down and install the upper idler pulley. Tighten the bolt to 38 ft. lbs. (52 Nm). Make sure the timing marks are still aligned after installing the upper idler pulley.

19. Turn the crankshaft 2 revolutions in the direction of normal rotation and realign the timing marks. If the timing marks do not align, repeat Steps 16-20.

20. Remove the pin from the automatic tensioner. Again rotate the crankshaft 2 turns and make sure the timing marks are aligned.

21. Apply approximately 22 lbs. (98 N) pressure to the timing belt at a point midway between the right exhaust camshaft sprocket and the tensioner pulley. The belt should deflect 0.20-0.28 in. (5-7mm). If the deflection is not as specified, replace the automatic tensioner.

22. Install the timing belt cover and tighten the bolts to 95 inch lbs. (11 Nm).

23. Install the crankshaft pulley. Hold the pulley with a suitable tool and tighten the lock bolt to 123 ft. lbs. (167 Nm). On 1992-94 vehicles, be careful not to damage the sensor rotor.

24. Install the distributor and connect the electrical connector.

25. Install the upper radiator hose and coolant bypass hose.

26. Install the idler pulleys and the accessory drive belts. Adjust the belt tension.

27. Install the spark plugs and connect the spark plug wires.

28. Install the air intake pipe to the throttle body and air cleaner.

29. Install the cooling fan and radiator shroud. Install the fresh air duct.

30. Connect the negative battery cable. Fill and bleed the cooling system.

31. Start the engine and bring to normal operating temperature. Check for leaks and for proper operation. Check the ignition timing.

Front Oil Seal

REMOVAL AND INSTALLATION

Except 2.2L and SOHC 3.0L Engines

1. Remove the timing belt covers and the timing belt.

2. If not removed during the timing belt removal procedure, remove the crankshaft sprocket bolt.

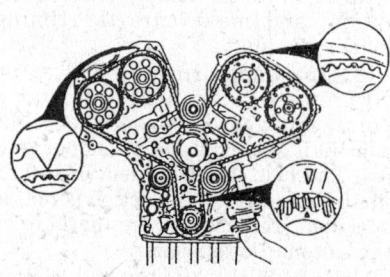

Crankshaft and camshaft sprocket timing mark alignment — DOHC 3.0L engine

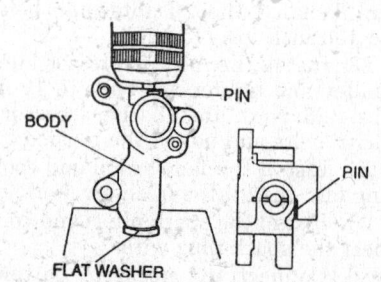

Pressing the rod into the automatic tensioner — 1992-94 DOHC 3.0L engine

3. Remove the crankshaft sprocket. It may be necessary to use a suitable puller.

4. Cut the seal lip with a razor knife. Protect the crankshaft with a shop towel and pry the seal from the engine.

To install:

5. Lubricate the seal lip with clean engine oil and push the seal slightly in by hand.

6. Tap the seal in evenly using a seal installer. Install the seal until it is flush with the oil pump body on all except 1.8L and 2.5L 6-cylinder engines. On the 1.8L engine, the seal must protrude from the pump body 0.020 in. (0.5mm). On the 2.5L engine, the seal must protrude from the pump body 0.030 in. (0.7mm).

7. Install the crankshaft sprocket. Install the sprocket key with the tapered side toward the oil pump body.

8. Install the remaining components in the reverse order of removal. Tighten the crankshaft bolt to 123 ft. lbs. (167 Nm) on all except 1990-91 1.6L and 1.8L engines, which should be torqued to 87 ft. lbs. (118 Nm).

2.2L and SOHC 3.0L Engines

Removal of the oil pump is required to replace the front oil seal on these engines.

Camshaft

REMOVAL AND INSTALLATION

1.6L, 1.8L and 3.0L SOHC Engines

NOTE: The camshaft is removed through the front of the cylinder head.

1. Remove the cylinder head from the vehicle and position in a suitable holding fixture.

NOTE: Do not lay the cylinder head flat on the head gasket surface as the valves may be damaged.

2. On 1.6L and 1.8L engines, hold the camshaft with a wrench on the hexagon cast into the front of the camshaft. Remove the sprocket bolt and the sprocket.

3. On 3.0L engine, use holder tool 49 H012 010 or equivalent, to hold the sprocket. Remove the bolt and the sprocket.

4. Loosen the rocker arm shaft bolts in 2-3 steps, in the reverse of the torque sequence. Remove the rocker arm and shaft assemblies.

5. Pry out the camshaft seal using a small prybar, being careful not to damage the camshaft or seal bore.

6. Remove the thrust plate at the rear of the cylinder head.

7. Carefully slide the camshaft from the cylinder head, being careful not to damage the cylinder head bearing surfaces.

To install:

8. Lubricate the camshaft lobes and journals and the cylinder head bearing surfaces with clean engine oil.

9. Carefully slide the camshaft into the cylinder head, being careful not to damage the bearing surfaces.

10. Install the camshaft thrust plate. On the 1.6L 8-valve engine and the 3.0L engine, tighten the thrust retaining bolt to 95 in. lbs. (11 Nm). On the 1.6L and 1.8L 16-valve engines, the thrust plate is held in place by the rocker arm and shaft assembly.

11. Lubricate the lip of a new camshaft seal with clean engine oil and install in the cylinder head, using a seal installer.

12. Lubricate the rocker arms and valve stem tips with clean engine oil. Install the rocker arm and shaft assemblies and tighten the bolts, in 2-3 steps, in the proper sequence. The final torque should be 21 ft. lbs. (28 Nm) on the 1.6L and 1.8L engines or 19 ft. lbs. (25 Nm) on the 3.0L engine.

13. Install the camshaft sprocket and retaining bolt. On 1.6L and 1.8L engines, hold the camshaft with the wrench on the hexagon and tighten the bolt to 45 ft. lbs. (61 Nm). On 3.0L engine, hold the sprocket with the holder tool and tighten the bolt to 59 ft. lbs. (80 Nm).

14. Install the cylinder head and the remaining components in the reverse order of removal.

1.6L, 1.8L and 2.0L DOHC Engines

1. Disconnect the negative battery cable. Drain the cooling system on Miata.

2. Label and disconnect the spark plug wires and remove the spark plugs.

3. Disconnect the hoses from the cylinder head cover, if equipped.

4. Remove the cylinder head cover bolts and remove the cylinder head cover. On 2.0L engine, loosen the bolts in 2-3 steps in the reverse of the torque sequence.

5. Remove the timing belt. Remove the distributor, or on Miata, remove the crank angle sensor.

6. Hold the camshaft with a wrench on the hexagon cast into the

camshaft. Remove the sprocket bolts and remove the sprockets.

7. Label the caps so they can be reinstalled in their original positions. Loosen the camshaft cap bolts in 2-3 steps in the reverse of the torque sequence, then remove the camshaft caps.

8. Remove the camshafts. Remove the camshaft oil seals from the camshafts.

To install:

9. Lubricate the camshaft journals and lobes with clean engine oil. Install the camshafts in the cylinder head.

10. Apply silicone sealant to the cylinder head on the front camshaft cap mating surfaces. Do not allow any sealant on the camshaft journals.

11. Install the camshaft caps in their original positions. Loosely install the cap bolts.

12. Tighten the camshaft cap bolts in 2-3 steps to 125 inch lbs. (14 Nm) in the proper sequence.

13. Apply clean engine oil to the lip of a new camshaft seal. Push the seal slightly in by hand. Tap the seal into position, using a seal installer, until it is flush with the edge of the camshaft cap.

14. Turn the camshafts until the dowel pins face straight up. Install the camshaft sprockets and the sprocket bolts.

15. Hold the camshaft with the wrench on the cast hexagon and tighten the sprocket bolts to 44 ft. lbs. (60 Nm).

16. Install the remaining components in the reverse order of removal.

2.2L Engine

1. Disconnect the negative battery cable.

2. Disconnect the spark plug wires and hoses from the cylinder head cover and remove the cylinder head cover.

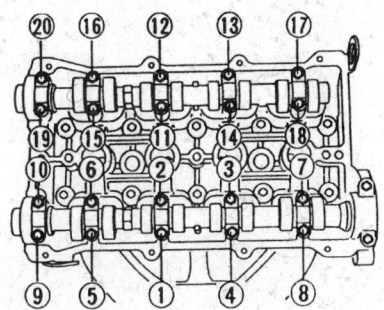

Camshaft cap bolt torque sequence — 323/Protege 1.6L and 1.8L DOHC engines

3. Remove the timing belt and the distributor.

4. Insert a suitable tool through one of the camshaft sprocket holes to keep the camshaft from turning. Remove the sprocket bolt and remove the sprocket.

5. Remove the front and rear housings from the cylinder head.

6. Loosen the rocker arm shaft bolts, in 2-3 steps, in the reverse of the torque sequence. Remove the rocker arm and shaft assemblies with the bolts.

7. Remove the camshaft caps. Label their position prior to removal so they can be reinstalled in their original locations.

8. Remove the camshaft.

To install:

9. Lubricate the camshaft journals and lobes with clean engine oil and position in the cylinder head with the dowel pin facing straight up.

10. Apply silicone sealant to cylinder head in the area adjacent to the front and rear camshaft journals. Do not allow sealant to get on the camshaft journals.

11. Install the camshaft caps in their original locations.

12. Apply clean engine oil to the valve stem tips and rocker arms.

13. Install the rocker arm and shaft assemblies. Tighten the bolts in 2-3 steps to 20 ft. lbs. (26 Nm) in the proper sequence.

NOTE: Make sure the rocker arms or spacers do not get caught between the shaft and camshaft cap.

14. Pry the old oil seal from the front housing. Apply engine oil to the front housing and a new oil seal and press the seal into the housing.

15. Install the front housing using a new gasket. Tighten the bolt and nut to 19 ft. lbs. (25 Nm).

16. Install the rear housing using a new gasket. Tighten the bolts/nuts to 19 ft. lbs. (25 Nm).

17. Apply silicone sealant at the front and rear corners of the cylinder head and install the cylinder head cover. Tighten the bolts to 69 inch lbs. (8 Nm). Connect the hoses and spark plug wires.

18. Install the camshaft sprocket on the camshaft with the sprocket bolt. Hold the camshaft sprocket using a suitable tool inserted through a sprocket hole and tighten the bolt to 48 ft. lbs. (65 Nm).

19. Install the timing belt and the remaining components in the reverse order of removal.

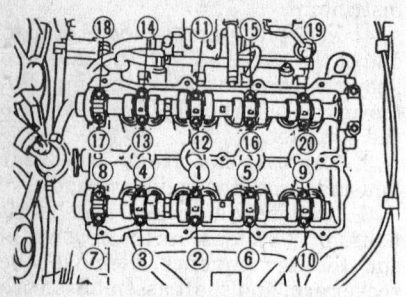

Camshaft cap bolt torque sequence — Miata

MX-3 1.8L and MX-6/626 2.5L Engines

1. Properly relieve the fuel system pressure. Disconnect the negative battery cable and drain the cooling system.

2. Remove the timing belt.

3. Disconnect the accelerator cable. On 1.8L engine, disconnect the throttle cable.

4. Label and disconnect the spark plug wires.

5. Label and disconnect the necessary wiring and hoses.

6. Remove the intake manifold and the cylinder head covers.

7. Remove the distributor.

8. Hold the camshaft with a wrench on the hexagon cast into the camshaft. Remove the sprocket bolt and remove the sprocket.

9. Turn the camshaft, using a wrench on the cast hexagon, until the camshaft knock pin is aligned with the cylinder head marks.

NOTE: Do not remove the camshaft caps when the camshaft lobe is pressing on a lifter, as the thrust journal support may become damaged.

10. Loosen the front camshaft cap bolts in 5-6 steps, in the proper sequence. Bolt **A** is only on the right cylinder head. Remove the front camshaft cap.

11. Mark the position of the camshaft caps so they can be reinstalled in their original locations. Loosen the remaining camshaft cap bolts in 5-6 steps, in the proper sequence, then remove the caps.

12. Remove the camshafts.

To install:

13. Lubricate the camshaft journals, lobes and gears with clean engine oil. Align the intake and exhaust camshaft timing marks and install the camshafts.

NOTE: The thrust plate positions for the right and left cylinder head camshafts are different.

14. Make sure the camshaft cap and cylinder head surfaces are clean. Apply a small amount of sealant to the mating surface of the front camshaft cap on both cylinder heads and the rear exhaust camshaft cap on the left cylinder head. Do not get any sealant on the camshaft rotating surfaces.

15. Install the front camshaft caps and thrust plate caps and tighten the bolts until the cap seats fully to the cylinder head. Install the remaining camshaft caps in their original locations and loosely tighten the bolts.

16. Tighten the camshaft cap bolts in 5-6 steps to 126 inch lbs. (14 Nm), in the proper sequence.

17. Apply clean engine oil to a new oil seal and the cylinder head. Install the seal, using a suitable installer. Apply sealant to a new blind cap and install, using a plastic hammer.

18. Install the camshaft sprockets. On the right cylinder head, install the sprocket so the **R** mark can be seen and the timing mark aligns with the camshaft knock pin. On the left cylinder head, install the sprocket so the **L** mark can be seen and the timing mark aligns with the camshaft knock pin.

19. Apply clean engine oil to the camshaft sprocket bolt threads and install. Hold the camshaft with a wrench on the cast hexagon and tighten the sprocket bolt to 103 ft. lbs. (140 Nm).

20. Coat a new gasket with sealant and install onto the cylinder head cover. Install the cover and tighten the bolts, in sequence, in 2-3 steps, to 78 inch lbs. (8.8 Nm). Install the ventilation pipe to the left cover.

21. Apply clean engine oil to a new O-ring and install on the distributor. Install the distributor with the blade fitting into the camshaft groove and loosely tighten the retaining bolt.

22. Install the intake manifold using a new gasket. Loosely install the

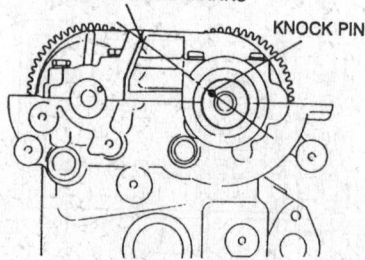

CYLINDER HEAD MARKS
KNOCK PIN

Align the camshaft knock pin with the cylinder head marks before removing the camshaft caps — MX-3 1.8L and MX-6/626 2.5L engines

bolts and nuts. Install the intake manifold stay and tighten the bolts to 19 ft. lbs. (25 Nm), then tighten the intake manifold bolts/nuts, in 2-3 steps, to 19 ft. lbs. (25 Nm).

23. Connect the wiring, hoses, and the fuel lines.

24. Connect the accelerator and, if equipped, throttle valve cables.

25. Install the timing belt.

26. Connect the negative battery cable. Fill and bleed the cooling system.

27. Start the engine and bring to normal operating temperature. Check for leaks. Check the ignition timing and idle speed.

3.0L DOHC Engine

1. Properly relieve the fuel system pressure.

2. Disconnect the negative battery cable and drain the cooling system.

3. Remove the fresh air duct and air intake pipe.

4. Remove the cooling fan and shroud.

5. Disconnect the spark plug wires and remove the spark plugs. Remove the idler pulleys and the accessory drive belts.

6. Remove the coolant bypass hose and the upper radiator hose. Disconnect the electrical connector and remove the distributor.

7. Hold the crankshaft pulley with a suitable tool and remove the bolt. Remove the crankshaft pulley. On 1992-94 vehicles, be careful not to damage the sensor rotor.

8. Remove the timing belt covers. Rotate the crankshaft until the camshaft and crankshaft sprocket timing marks are aligned.

9. Remove the upper idler pulley and the tensioner and pulley. Mark the direction of rotation on the timing belt and remove the timing belt.

10. Disconnect the accelerator cable. Disconnect and plug the fuel lines. Label and disconnect the necessary electrical connectors and vacuum hoses.

11. On 1990-91 vehicles, remove the upper intake manifold cover. Remove the upper intake manifold.

12. Loosen the lower intake manifold bolts in 2-3 steps, in the reverse order of the torque sequence. Remove the lower intake manifold.

13. Remove the cylinder head covers.

14. Hold the camshaft with a wrench on the hexagon cast into the camshaft and remove the camshaft sprocket bolt. Remove the camshaft sprockets.

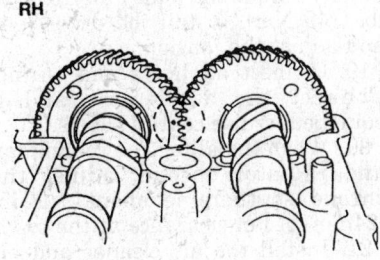

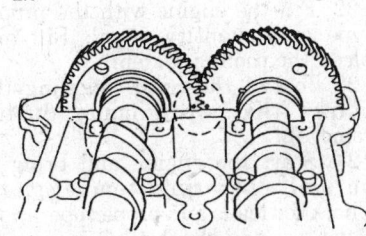

Intake and exhaust camshaft gear alignment —
MX-3 1.8L and MX-6/626 2.5L engines

15. Remove bolts **A** from the front camshaft cap on the left cylinder head. Loosen the remaining camshaft cap bolts in 2-3 steps in the proper sequence. Mark the position of the caps so they can be reinstalled in their original positions.

16. Remove the camshaft caps and remove the camshafts. Label the camshafts so they can be reinstalled in their proper locations.

To install:

17. Lubricate the camshaft lobes and journals with clean engine oil and install the camshafts on the cylinder heads. Apply clean engine oil to the lips of the new camshaft seals and install them on the camshafts.

18. Apply a small amount of silicone sealant to the cylinder head on the front camshaft cap mating surfaces. Do not allow sealant to get on the camshaft journal, oil seal face or camshaft thrust face.

19. Install the camshaft caps in their original locations. Gradually tighten the cap bolts, in sequence, to 24 ft. lbs. (32 Nm). Tighten the front cap bolts, **A**, on the left cylinder head to 95 inch lbs. (11 Nm).

20. Hold the camshafts using a wrench on the hexagon cast into the camshaft. Install the camshaft sprockets with the retaining bolts. Tighten the sprocket bolts on the right cylinder head to 59 ft. lbs. (80 Nm) and the sprocket bolts on the left cylinder head to 19 ft. lbs. (25 Nm).

21. Apply sealant to the cylinder head in the areas adjacent to the front camshaft caps. Install the cylinder head covers and tighten the nuts to 39 inch lbs. (4 Nm). On 1990-91 vehicles, apply sealant to the cylinder head cover and install the plug hole cover, tightening the bolts to 52 inch lbs. (5.9 Nm).

22. Install the lower intake manifold using new gaskets. Tighten the mounting nuts in 2-3 steps, in the proper sequence, to 19 ft. lbs. (25 Nm). Connect the fuel lines.

23. Install the upper intake manifold to the lower intake manifold, using a new gasket. Tighten the bolts to 19 ft. lbs. (25 Nm). On 1990-91 vehicles, install the upper intake manifold cover and tighten the bolts to 95 inch lbs. (11 Nm).

24. Connect the electrical connectors and vacuum hoses. Connect the accelerator cable.

25. Position the timing belt tensioner on a suitable press. Place a flat washer at the bottom of the tensioner body to prevent damage to the body plug. Slowly press in the tensioner rod, but do not exceed 2200 lbs. Insert a pin in the tensioner body to hold the rod in place, then install the tensioner and tighten the mounting bolts to 19 ft. lbs. (25 Nm).

26. Make sure the crankshaft and camshaft sprocket timing marks are properly aligned. Install the timing belt over the sprockets and pulleys in the following order: crankshaft sprocket, lower idler pulley, left cylinder head exhaust cam sprocket, left cylinder head intake cam sprocket, tensioner pulley, right cylinder head exhaust cam sprocket and right cylinder head intake cam sprocket.

27. Push the belt down and install the upper idler pulley. Tighten the upper idler pulley bolt to 38 ft. lbs. (52 Nm). Make sure the camshaft and crankshaft sprocket timing marks are still aligned after installing the upper idler pulley.

28. Turn the crankshaft 2 revolutions in the normal direction of rotation and realign the timing marks. Make sure all timing marks are correctly aligned.

29. Remove the pin from the automatic tensioner and again rotate the crankshaft 2 turns. Confirm that the timing marks are aligned.

30. Install the timing belt covers and tighten the bolts to 95 inch lbs. (11 Nm).

31. Install the crankshaft pulley. Hold the pulley with a suitable tool and tighten the pulley bolt to 123 ft. lbs. (167 Nm). On 1992-94 vehicles, be careful not to damage the sensor rotor.

32. Install the spark plugs and the distributor assembly. Connect the spark plug wires and the distributor electrical connector.

33. Install the upper radiator hose and water bypass hose. Install the idler pulleys and accessory drive belts. Adjust the belt tension.

34. Install the shroud and cooling fan. Install the air intake pipe and fresh air duct.

35. Connect the negative battery cable. Fill and bleed the cooling system.

36. Start the engine and bring to normal operating temperature. Check for leaks. Check the ignition timing and idle speed.

Piston and Connecting Rod

POSITIONING

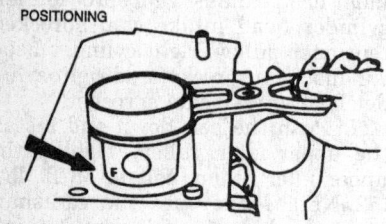

POSITIONING

On all 4-cylinder engines, the piston and connecting rod assembly is installed with the "F" mark facing the front of the engine

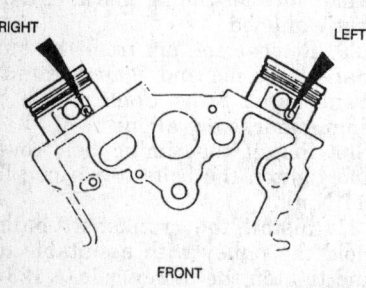

RIGHT   LEFT

FRONT

On all 6-cylinder engines, the piston and connecting rod assembly is installed with the "R", for right bank or "L", for left bank, facing the front of the engine

ROTARY ENGINE MECHANICAL

Engine Assembly

REMOVAL AND INSTALLATION

RX-7

1990-91

1. Mark the position of the hood on its hinges and remove the hood.
2. Properly relieve the fuel system pressure and disconnect the negative battery cable.
3. Remove the engine undercover and drain the engine oil and coolant. Remove the battery and battery box.
4. Remove the inlet air ducting and the air cleaner/air flow meter assembly. On turbocharged engines, remove the intercooler and turbocharger outlet duct.

5. Remove the cooling fan and upper and lower radiator hoses. Disconnect the heater return hose and pipe. If equipped with automatic transaxle, disconnect the transmission oil cooler lines. Remove the radiator and shroud.
6. Label and disconnect all fuel, vacuum and heater hoses and wiring connectors. Plug the fuel hoses. Disconnect the accelerator and, if equipped, cruise control cables.
7. Remove the accessory drive belts. Hold the power steering pump pulley with a suitable tool and remove the nut. Remove the power steering pump pulley.
8. Without disconnecting the hoses, remove the power steering pump and air conditioner compressor and secure them out of the way.
9. Without disconnecting the hydraulic line, remove the clutch slave cylinder and secure it out of the way.
10. Disconnect the oil cooler pipes at the engine and cover the fittings to protect the cooler.
11. Remove the exhaust system heat shields and the front exhaust pipe. On turbocharged vehicles, disconnect the air pipe and remove the catalytic converter.
12. Remove the starter. If equipped with automatic transmission, remove the cover and remove the torque converter-to-flywheel bolts.
13. Make sure all wiring and hoses are disconnected. Attach suitable lifting equipment to the engine. Remove the engine-to-transmission bolts and the engine mount nuts. Carefully remove the engine from the vehicle and position on a workstand.

To install:

14. Carefully lower the engine into the vehicle and connect it to the transmission. Torque the engine-to-transmission bolts and the engine mount nuts to 34 ft. lbs. (46 Nm).
15. If equipped with automatic transmission, install the torque converter-to-flywheel bolts and torque to 35 ft. lbs. (47 Nm). Install the cover.
16. Install the starter and torque the bolts to 34 ft. lbs. (46 Nm). Connect the wiring. Use new gaskets to install the exhaust pipe and, if removed, catalytic converter. Torque the nuts to 59 ft. lbs. (80 Nm) except the exhaust pipe-to-turbocharger nuts which are torqued to 40 ft. lbs. (54 Nm). Install the shields.
17. Use new sealing washers to connect the rear oil cooler pipe and torque the banjo bolt to 50 ft. lbs. (68 Nm). Torque the front oil cooler fitting to 40 ft. lbs. (54 Nm). If

equipped, install the clutch slave cylinder.
18. Install the air conditioner compressor and power steering pump and pulley. Torque the pulley nut to 36 ft. lbs. (49 Nm). Install the drive belts and adjust the tension.
19. Connect all hoses and wiring. Connect the accelerator and if equipped, cruise control cables.
20. When installing the cooling fan and radiator shroud, adjust the shroud so there is about $^{15}/_{16}$ in. (24mm) of fan clearance at the top.
21. Install the air cleaner and air ducts. Install the battery tray and battery and connect the cables.
22. Fill the engine with the proper type and quantity of oil. Fill and bleed the cooling system.
23. Install the hood, aligning the marks that were made during removal.
24. Start the engine and bring to normal operating temperature. Check for leaks and proper operation. Road test and check all fluid levels.

1993-94

1. Mark the position of the hood on its hinges and remove the hood.
2. Properly relieve the fuel system pressure and disconnect the negative battery cable.
3. Remove the engine undercover and drain the engine oil and cooling system.
4. Remove the transmission.
5. Disconnect the Engine Control Unit (ECU) as follows:
   a. Open the passenger side door and remove the sill plate.
   b. Remove the passenger side kick panel.
   c. Disconnect the electrical connectors from the ECU.
6. Remove the fresh air duct, air cleaner intake hose and air cleaner.
7. Remove the battery and the battery box.
8. Remove the strut bar and temporarily tighten the locknut to the stud bolt.
9. Disconnect the accelerator cable and remove the throttle body air intake hose.
10. Remove the upper and lower radiator hoses and disconnect the heater hose.
11. Remove the (engine mounted) fuse box and position aside, leaving the wiring harness connected.
12. Remove the accessory drive belts.
13. Hold the power steering pump pulley using a suitable tool and remove the pulley nut. Remove the pulley. Remove the power steering pump

and position aside, leaving the hoses connected.

14. Remove the A/C compressor and position aside, leaving the hoses connected.

15. Label and disconnect all necessary hoses and electrical connectors. Disconnect and plug the fuel lines.

16. Position a drain pan under the engine oil cooler lines. Remove the clips and disconnect the hoses from the engine oil cooler.

17. Remove the insulators from the exhaust pipe and turbocharger. Do not let oil get on the insulators.

18. Disconnect the oxygen sensor connector and remove the front exhaust pipe. Remove the split air pipe.

19. If equipped with automatic transmission, disconnect the oil cooler lines at the radiator. Remove the bolt and nut from the line support brackets and remove the lines.

20. Attach suitable lifting equipment to the engine and remove the engine mount nuts. Carefully remove the engine from the vehicle and position on a workstand.

To install:

21. Carefully lower the engine into the vehicle, aligning the engine mounts with the crossmember mounting holes.

22. Install the engine mount nuts and tighten to 49 ft. lbs. (67 Nm). Remove the engine lifting equipment.

23. If equipped with automatic transmission, install and connect the transmission oil cooler lines. Tighten the support bracket nut and bolt to 95 inch lbs. (10.7 Nm).

24. Install the front exhaust pipe, using new gaskets. Tighten the exhaust pipe-to-turbocharger nuts to 38 ft. lbs. (51 Nm) and the exhaust pipe-to-main converter nuts to 65 ft. lbs. (89 Nm). Connect the split air pipe.

25. Install the front exhaust pipe insulator, turbocharger insulator and center insulator, in that order. Tighten the bolts, after all 3 insulators have been installed, to 95 inch lbs. (10.7 Nm).

26. Install the engine mount insulator and tighten the bolts to 95 inch lbs. (10.7 Nm).

27. Connect the engine oil cooler hoses to the engine oil cooler and install the clips. Make sure the clips are securely locked.

28. Connect the fuel lines, hoses and electrical connectors.

29. Install the A/C compressor and tighten the bolts to 18 ft. lbs. (25 Nm).

30. Install the power steering pump and tighten the bolts to 33 ft. lbs. (46 Nm). Connect the electrical connector to the pump.

31. Install the power steering pump pulley and loosely tighten the nut. Hold the pulley with a suitable tool and tighten the nut to 43 ft. lbs. (58 Nm).

32. Install the accessory drive belts and adjust the belt tension.

33. Install the (engine mounted) fuse box and tighten the nut to 95 inch lbs. (10.7 Nm).

34. Install the radiator and heater hoses.

35. Install the throttle body air intake hose using a new gasket. Tighten the nuts to 95 inch lbs. (10.7 Nm). Connect the accelerator cable.

36. Remove the upper nuts and install the strut bar. Tighten the nuts to 26 ft. lbs. (36 Nm).

37. Install the air cleaner assembly and ducts. Tighten the bolts to 95 inch lbs. (10.7 Nm).

38. Install the battery box and tighten the bolts to 95 inch lbs. (10.7 Nm). install the battery.

39. Install the transmission.

40. Install the engine undercover.

41. Connect the ECU and install the kick panel and sill plate.

42. Fill the engine with the proper type and quantity of oil. Fill and bleed the cooling system.

43. Install the hood, aligning the marks that were made during removal.

44. Connect the battery cables, start the engine and bring to normal operating temperature. Check for leaks.

45. Check the ignition timing and idle speed. Check all fluid levels and road test.

DISASSEMBLY

NOTE: Because of the design of the rotary engine, it is not practical to attempt component removal and Installation. Procedures described here are for complete engine disassembly and assembly.

1. Remove the engine mounts, A/C compressor and power steering pump brackets and mount the engine on a workstand.

2. Label the vacuum and wiring connections and remove the harness as an assembly.

3. Remove the intake and exhaust systems. If equipped, cap the turbocharger inlets and outlets to protect the turbine wheels.

4. Remove the fuel and oil injectors and cap the nozzles and inlet tubes to keep them clean.

5. Remove the water pump.

6. Remove the oil metering pump and cover the openings to protect the internal parts.

7. When all accessories have been removed, invert the engine to remove the oil pan, oil strainer and gasket.

8. Identify the front and rear rotor housings with paint or a felt tip pen. These are common parts and must be identified to be assembled in their respective locations.

9. Turn the engine right side up and remove the eccentric shaft pulley and the pulley boss bolt. The bypass valve and spring will come out, then remove the pulley boss.

10. Turn the engine so the front end of the engine is up and remove the front cover. The oil pressure control valve is next to the oil pan gasket surface.

11. Remove the oil slinger and distributor drive gear from the shaft. Unbolt and remove the chain adjuster.

12. Remove the locknut and washer from the oil pump driven sprocket. Slide the oil pump drive sprocket and driven sprocket, together with the drive chain off the eccentric shaft and oil pump simultaneously.

13. Remove the keys from the eccentric and oil pump shafts and remove the oil pump.

14. Slide the balance weight, thrust washer, thrust bearing and spacer from the shaft.

15. On engines with a manual transmission, install a ring gear locking tool and remove the large flywheel-to-eccentric shaft nut. Use a puller to remove the flywheel

16. On engines with an automatic transmission, remove the 6 bolts and remove the driveplate. Use tool No. 49 0820 035, or equivalent, to hold the counter weight and remove the large nut. Use a puller to remove the counter weight.

NOTE: On engines equipped with an automatic transmission driveplate, do not hold the driveplate to hold the eccentric shaft when removing or installing the large nut. The torque on the nut is over 300 ft. lbs. (400 Nm) and the driveplate is not designed to withstand that much torque.

17. Working at the rear of the engine, loosen the long tension bolts 1 turn at a time in the reverse order of the assembly torque sequence. Since they are not all the same, mark tension bolts to replace them in their original holes during reassembly.

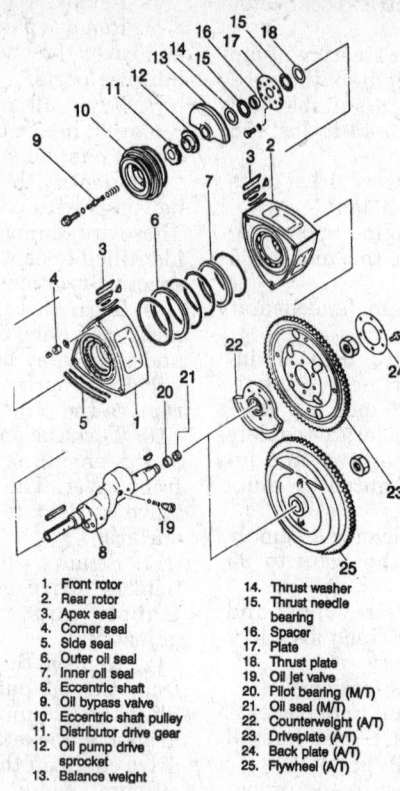

1. Front rotor
2. Rear rotor
3. Apex seal
4. Corner seal
5. Side seal
6. Outer oil seal
7. Inner oil seal
8. Eccentric shaft
9. Oil bypass valve
10. Eccentric shaft pulley
11. Distributor drive gear
12. Oil pump drive sprocket
13. Balance weight
14. Thrust washer
15. Thrust needle bearing
16. Spacer
17. Plate
18. Thrust plate
19. Oil jet valve
20. Pilot bearing (M/T)
21. Oil seal (M/T)
22. Counterweight (A/T)
23. Driveplate (A/T)
24. Back plate (A/T)
25. Flywheel (A/T)

Rotary engine internal components

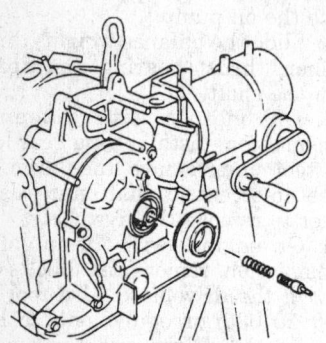

Eccentric shaft bypass valve, pulley boss and spring — rotary engine

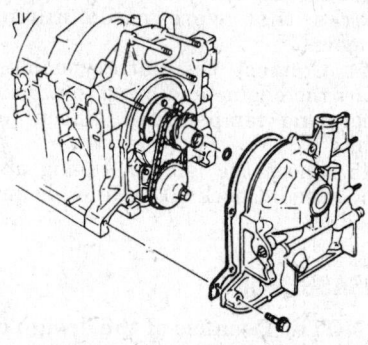

Front cover removal — rotary engine

18. Lift the rear housing off the shaft. Remove any seals that are stuck to the rotor sliding surface of the rear housing and reinstall them in their original locations.

19. Remove all the corner seal assemblies and the side seal assemblies from the rear side of the rotor. The seals are distinguished by the numbers near each groove on the rotor face. Store the seals in a way that their original locations can be easily identified.

20. Remove the tubular dowels from the rear rotor housing using the appropriate puller.

21. Lift the rear rotor housing away from the rear rotor, being careful not to drop the apex seals on the rear rotor. Remove the O-ring from the upper dowel hole.

22. Remove each apex seal, side piece and spring from the rear rotor and segregate them.

23. Remove the rear rotor from the eccentric shaft and place it upside down on a clean shop towel. The coated surfaces on the rotor must be protected from damage, do not place the rotor on a hard surface.

24. Remove each seal and spring from the other side of the rotor and

segregate them. If some of the seals fall off the rotor, be careful not to change the original position of each seal. Identify the bottom of each apex seal with a felt tip pen.

25. When removing the oil seals from the rotors, do not exert heavy pressure at only one place on the seal or it could be deformed. Replace the O-rings in the oil seal when the engine is overhauled.

26. Hold the intermediate housing down and remove the dowels from it using an appropriate puller.

27. Position the eccentric shaft as required and lift the intermediate housing off. If any rotor seals stick to it, put them back into their original position.

28. Remove the front rotor housing and remove the seals and segregate them.

29. Lift the eccentric shaft out, then remove the front rotor.

COMPONENT INSPECTION & REPLACEMENT

Front, Intermediate and Rear Housings

1. Check the housing for signs of gas or water leakage.

2. Remove the sealing compound from the housing surface with a cloth or brush soaked in solvent or thinner.

3. Remove the carbon deposits from the front housing with extra fine emery cloth.

4. Check for distortion by placing a straight-edge on the surface of the housing. Measure the clearance between the straight-edge and the housing with a feeler gauge. If the clearance is greater than 0.0016 in. (0.04mm) at any point, replace the housing.

5. Use a dial indicator to check for wear on the rotor contact surfaces of the housing. Replace the housing if any of the following measurements are not within specification:

1 Side seal wear: 0.0039 (0.10mm) max.

2 Side seal wear, overlapping oil seal wear: 0.0004 in. (0.01mm) max.

3 Side seal wear, outside oil seal wear: 0.0039 in. (0.10mm) max.

4 Oil seal wear: 0.0008 in. (0.02mm) max.

Front Stationary Gear and Main Bearing

1. Examine the teeth of the stationary gear for wear or damage.

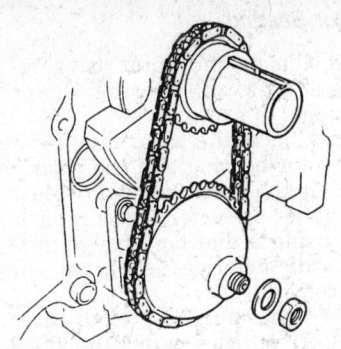

Oil pump drive gear, driven gear and chain — rotary engine

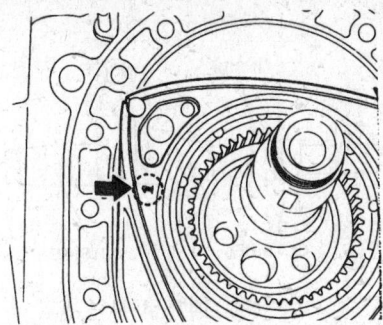

Seal groove numbers on the rotor face.

2. Be sure the main bearing shows no signs of excessive wear, scoring or flaking.

3. Check the main bearing to eccentric journal clearance by measuring the shaft journal diameter with a micrometer and the bearing inside diameter with a dial bore gauge.

4. On 1990-91 vehicles, the specified clearance is 0.0016-0.0039 in. (0.04-0.10mm). On 1993-94 vehicles, the inside and outside specifications of the journals differ. The specified clearance is 0.0023-0.0043 in. (0.06-0.11mm) for the inside and 0.0031-0.0051 in. (0.08-0.13mm) for the outside.

5. If the main bearing is damaged or the clearance is incorrect and main bearing replacement is necessary, proceed to Step 6.

6. Remove the attaching bolts and press the stationary gear and main bearing assembly out of the housing.

7. On 1993-94 vehicles, remove the screw from the stationary gear.

8. Press the main bearing from the stationary gear.

9. Press a new main bearing into the stationary gear. On 1990-91 vehicles, make sure the bearing lug is in-line with the slot in the stationary gear. On 1993-94 vehicles, make sure the small hole in the bearing is in-line with the screw hole in the stationary gear.

10. On 1993-94 vehicles, remove the old thread-locking compound from the screw and screw hole threads. Apply new thread-locking compound to the screw and tighten the screw to 41 inch lbs. (4.7 Nm).

Rear Stationary Gear and Main Bearing

Inspect the rear stationary gear and main bearing in a similar manner to the front. In addition, examine the O-ring, which is located in the stationary gear, for signs of wear or damage. To replace the stationary gear, use the following procedure.

1. Remove the rear stationary gear attaching bolts.

2. Drive the stationary gear from the rear housing with a brass drift.

3. Apply a light coating of grease to a new O-ring and fit it into the groove on the stationary gear.

4. Apply sealer to the flange of the stationary gear.

5. Install the stationary gear on the housing so the slot on its flange aligns with the dowel on the rear housing. Use care not to damage the O-ring during installation.

6. Tighten the stationary gear bolts, evenly, in several stages, to 16 ft. lbs. (22 Nm).

Rotor Housings

1. Examine the inner margin of both housings for signs of gas or water leakage.

2. Wipe the inner surface of each housing with a clean cloth to remove the carbon deposits.

3. Clean all of the rust deposits out of the cooling passages of each rotor housing.

4. Remove the old sealer using the proper removal solvent.

5. Examine the chromium plated inner surfaces for scoring, flaking or other signs of damage. If any are present, the housing must be replaced.

6. Check the widths of both rotor housings, at points **A**, **B**, **C** and **D**, using a micrometer.

7. If the difference between the thickness at point **A** and the minimum thickness at the other points exceeds 0.0024 in. (0.06mm), replace the rotor housing.

Rotors

1. Check the rotor for signs of blowby around the side and corner seal areas.

2. Remove the carbon from the rotor with a non-abrasive sponge and

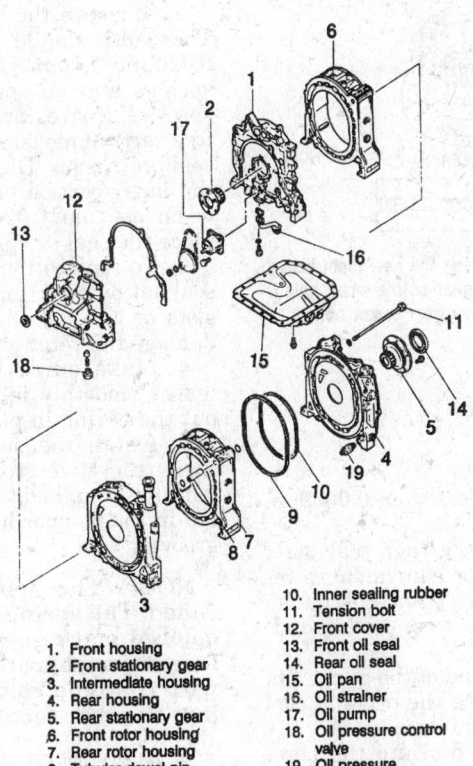

1. Front housing	10. Inner sealing rubber
2. Front stationary gear	11. Tension bolt
3. Intermediate housing	12. Front cover
4. Rear housing	13. Front oil seal
5. Rear stationary gear	14. Rear oil seal
6. Front rotor housing	15. Oil pan
7. Rear rotor housing	16. Oil strainer
8. Tubular dowel pin	17. Oil pump
9. Outer sealing rubber	18. Oil pressure control valve
	19. Oil pressure regulator valve

Engine housing components — rotary engine

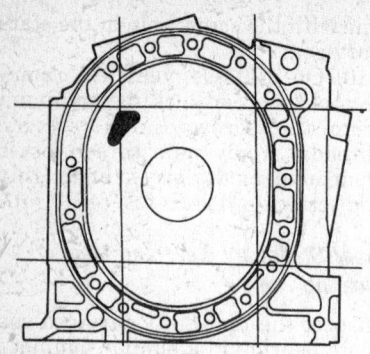

Measure housing distortion in these 4 directions

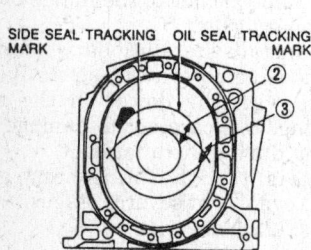

SIDE SEAL TRACKING MARK   OIL SEAL TRACKING MARK

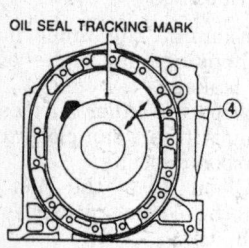

OIL SEAL TRACKING MARK

Check the housing contact surface in these areas

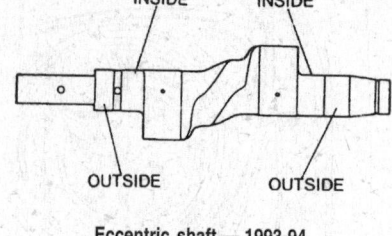

Eccentric shaft — 1993-94

On 1990-91 engines, press the new main bearing into the stationary gear so the bearing lug is in line with the stationary gear slot

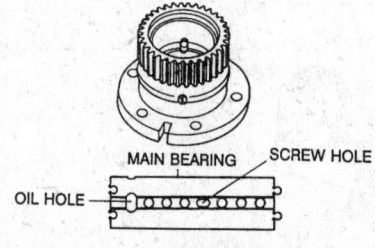

MAIN BEARING   SCREW HOLE

OIL HOLE

On 1993-94 engines, press the new main bearing into the stationary gear so the small hole is in line with the stationary gear screw hole.

carbon cleaner. Be careful not to remove the surface coating, especially around the seal grooves.

3. Wash the rotor in solvent and blow it dry with compressed air.

4. Examine the internal gear for cracks or damaged teeth. If the internal gear is damaged, the rotor and gear must be replaced as a single assembly.

5. Measure the rotor width at 3 points, with a micrometer. Compare the rotor width against the width of the rotor housing at point **A**, which was measured above. Replace the rotor if the difference between both

measurements is less than 0.0039 in. (0.10mm).

6. To check the corner seal bore, tool 49 0839 165 or equivalent is required. This is a "go-no-go" gauge used to check the wear and roundness of the bore.

   a. If neither end of the gauge fits into the bore, use the original corner seal over again.

   b. If one end fits into the bore, replace the corner seal.

   c. If both ends fit into the bore, replace the rotor.

Rotor Bearing

1. Check the rotor bearing for wear, flaking, scoring or other damage.

2. Check the clearance between the rotor bearing and the rotor journal on the eccentric shaft. Measure the inner diameter of the rotor bearing using a dial bore gauge and the outer diameter of the journal using a micrometer.

3. The specified clearance on 1990-91 vehicles is 0.0016-0.0039 in. (0.04-0.10mm). The clearance on 1993-94 vehicles should be 0.0016-0.0043 in. (0.04-0.11mm).

4. If the bearing is damaged or the clearance is incorrect and it is necessary to replace the bearing, proceed to Step 5.

5. The bearing must be pressed out of the rotor past internal gear, being careful not to damage the gear.

6. Place the rotor on the press support with internal gear faced upward. Press the new rotor bearing into the rotor so the bearing lug is aligned with the slot of the rotor bore. Press the new bearing until it is flush with the rotor boss.

Oil Seal

1. Inspect the seal for wear or damage and replace, if necessary.

2. Measure the oil seal lip width. The width should be no more than 0.020 in. (0.5mm). Install the oil seal springs and oil seals into their respective grooves and check them for free vertical movement. Check the oil seal protrusion. The protrusion above the inner portion of the rotor should be no less than 0.020 in. (0.5mm). Replace the seal or spring, if necessary.

3. To replace the seal, pry the old seal out by inserting the tool into the slots on the rotor. Be careful not to damage the rotor.

4. Make sure the new oil seal moves smoothly in the groove without the O-ring in place.

5. Install the oil seal springs in their respective grooves on the rotor with the round edge of the spring fitted in the stopper hole of the oil seal grooves.

NOTE: The springs are color coded. The spring with the cream colored mark goes into the front face of each rotor. The spring with the blue colored mark goes into the rear face of each rotor.

6. Apply clean engine oil to the new O-ring and install in the oil seal.

7. Place the inner oil seal in the oil seal groove so the square edge of the

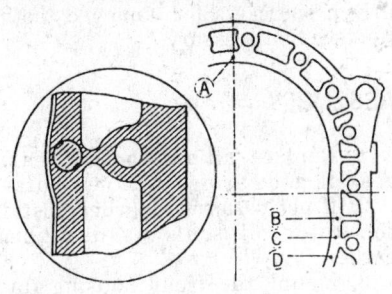

Measure the rotor housing width at the indicated points

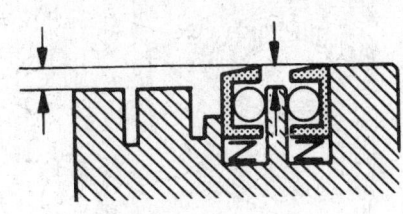

Measuring oil seal protrusion

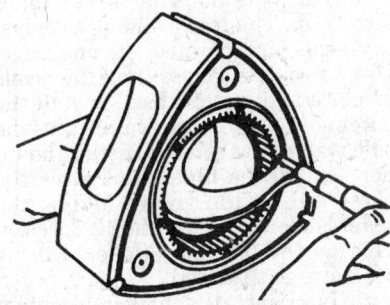

Measure the rotor width at points A, B and C.

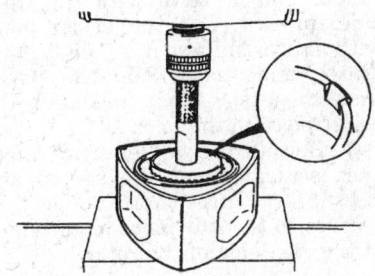

Install the bearing so the lug is in line with the slot of the rotor bore

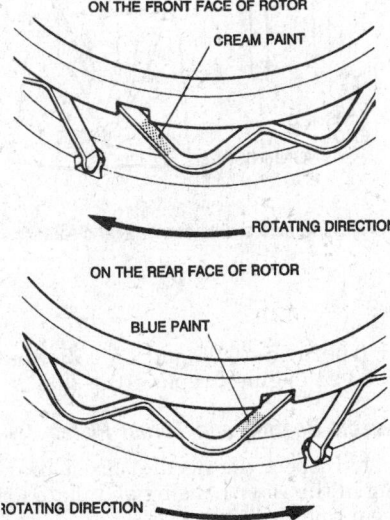

ON THE FRONT FACE OF ROTOR

CREAM PAINT

ROTATING DIRECTION

ON THE REAR FACE OF ROTOR

BLUE PAINT

ROTATING DIRECTION

The oil seal springs are identified by paint marks: cream color on the front face of each rotor, blue on the rear face

middle touches, the seals are still good. Do this with all 3 seals.

4. Using a feeler gauge, check the side clearance between the apex seal and the groove in the rotor. Install the seal into its proper groove and insert the gauge until its tip contacts the bottom of the groove.

   a. Non-turbocharged engine apex seal-to-rotor standard clearance: 0.0024-0.0040 in. (0.062-0.102mm).

   b. Turbocharged engine apex seal-to-rotor standard clearance: 0.0020-0.0040 in. (0.051-0.101mm).

   c. Maximum clearance, both engines: 0.0059 in. (0.15mm)

5. With the spring on a flat surface, measure the free height with a vernier caliper. The long spring should be 0.181 in. (4.6mm) high, the short spring should be 0.067 in. (1.7mm). Replace the short seal spring if the combined apex seal height is less than 0.295 in. (7.5mm).

Side Seals

1. Remove the carbon deposits from the side seals and their springs. Check the side seals for cracks and wear.

2. Install the side seals and springs and make sure the seal moves freely against the spring in the groove. The seal should protrude from the groove a minimum of 0.020 in. (0.5mm).

3. Check the clearance between the side seals and their grooves with a feeler gauge. Standard clearance is 0.0011-0.0031 in. (0.028-0.078mm). Maximum clearance is 0.0039 in. (0.10mm).

4. Check the clearance between the side seals and the corner seals with all installed in the rotor. The standard clearance is 0.0020-0.0059 in. (0.05-0.15mm). The maximum clearance is 0.016 in. (0.40mm).

5. If the side seal must be replaced, adjust the side seal-to-corner seal standard clearance by lapping the flat (non-finished) end of the side seal.

Corner Seals

1. Clean the carbon deposits and carefully examine the corner seals, springs and soft seals.

2. Install the corner seal assemblies and make sure each seal moves freely against the spring in the groove.

3. Corner seal clearance is measured by measuring seal protrusion above the rotor. The protrusion should be a minimum of 0.020 in. (0.5mm).

spring fits into the notch of the oil seal.

8. Using finger pressure only, press the new oil seal in, using a used oil seal, until the lip of the new seal is approximately 0.016 in. (0.4mm) below the surface of the rotor.

9. After installation, push the oil seal slowly, by hand, and make sure it moves freely.

Apex Seals

1. Wash the seals and the springs in cleaning solution. Be careful not to

damage the finish. Check the apex seals for cracks or wear.

2. Measure the combined height of the upper and lower seals at 2 points. The standard height is 0.315 in. (8mm), minimum is 0.256 in. (6.5mm). Replace the short seal spring if the combined height is less than 0.295 in. (7.5mm).

3. Put the 2 seals together, top-to-top, and measure the gap between them to check for warping. If the ends of the seals touch and there is a gap in the middle, replace the seals. If there is a gap at the ends and the

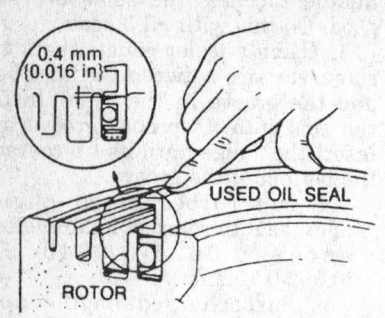

Use the old oil seal to install the new one

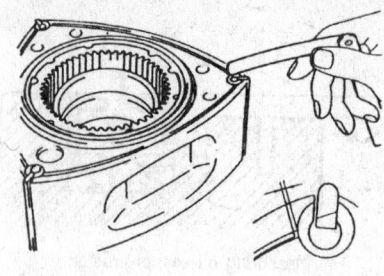

Measuring side seal-to-corner seal clearance

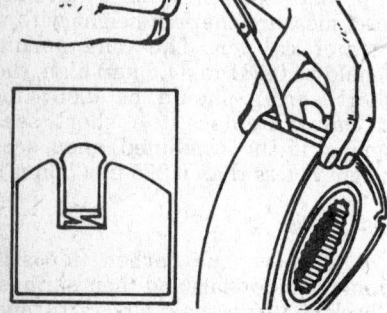

Check the gap between the apex seal and groove with a feeler gauge

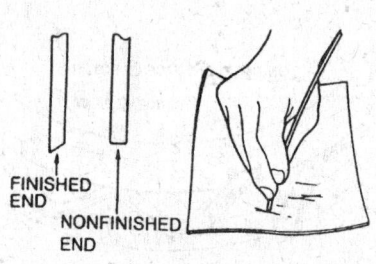

Adjusting side seal-to-corner seal clearance

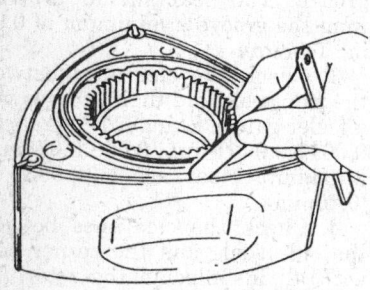

Measuring side seal-to-groove clearance

Eccentric Shaft

1. Wash the eccentric shaft in solvent and blow out the oil passages with compressed air. Check the shaft for wear, cracks or other signs of damage; remove the oil jet and check the spring and ball for free movement.

2. To make sure the shaft is straight, check eccentric shaft runout at the end of the shaft. Rotate the shaft slowly and note the dial indicator reading. If run-out is greater than 0.0047 in. (0.12mm) on 1990 engines

or 0.0024 in. (0.06mm) on 1991 and 1993-94 engines, replace the shaft.

Needle Bearing and Thrust Plate

1. Inspect the needle thrust bearing in the rotor housing end plate for wear and damage.

2. Inspect the bearing housing and the thrust plate for wear and damage.

Oil Pump Drive Chain and Sprocket

1. Lay the chain on a flat surface and check the entire length for broken links.

Checking eccentric shaft runout

2. Check the oil pump drive and driven sprockets for damaged teeth. Replace as necessary.

ASSEMBLY

1. Replace all oil control seals, gaskets and O-rings with new parts.

2. If not performed earlier, install the rotor oil seals as described earlier.

3. Mount the front housing into the engine stand and install the thrust plate with the chamfer facing the housing. Install the bearing and plate and torque the bolts to 16 ft. lbs. (22 Nm).

4. Turn the housing so the inner face is up. The inner and outer housing seals are painted on one edge. Use petroleum jelly to hold the seals in place and install them. Install the outer seal so the white paint faces the side wall of the groove. Install the inner seal so the blue paint faces the outer wall of the groove and so the seam is placed within the 12-3 o'clock area on the housing. Make sure the seals are not twisted.

5. Lubricate the housing contact surfaces, stationary gear and main bearing with engine oil. Do not oil the housing seals just installed.

6. Place the front rotor on a clean rubber pad or cloth with the front side upward. Cut the assist piece with a razor knife so it is 0.08-0.11 in. (2.0-2.8mm) long. Peel the paper from the assist piece and stick the assist piece to the apex seal.

7. Install the upper and lower apex seals without the spring and side piece into their respective grooves so the side piece mounting is at the rear side of the rotor.

NOTE: If the apex seals are installed incorrectly, poor gas sealing may result.

8. Install the new soft seals, corner seal springs and corner seals into their respective grooves. Make sure the chamfer faces the bottom of the groove.

9. Install the side seal springs and side seals into their respective grooves. Make sure the paint mark faces the bottom of the groove. Make sure there is smooth movement of the corner seals and side seals by lightly pressing them. Apply petroleum jelly to the side seals.

10. Apply clean engine oil to the rotor oil seal, rotor bearing and internal gear.

11. Hold the apex seals in place with a rubber band or used O-ring and place the rotor on the front hous-

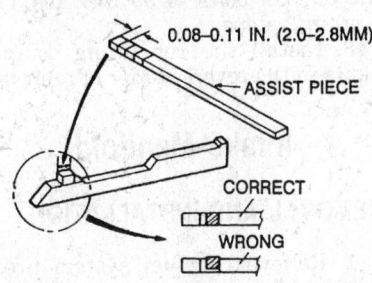

0.08–0.11 IN. (2.0–2.8MM)

ASSIST PIECE

CORRECT

WRONG

Installing the assist piece on the apex seal

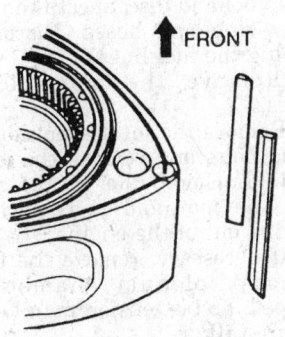

FRONT

Apex seal installation

ing. Mesh the internal and stationary gears so one of the rotor apexes is at the 3 o'clock, 6 o'clock, 9 o'clock or 12 o'clock positions. Be careful not to place the rotor on the sealing rubber.

12. Make sure the pilot bearing in the eccentric shaft is properly installed and greased. Oil the shaft and rotor journal and carefully install the shaft through the rotor and housing.

13. Use petroleum jelly to hold the new O-ring in place on the housing and apply a silicone sealer to the 2 outer "legs" on the bottom of the housing. Lubricate the walls of the

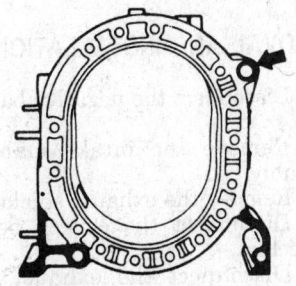

Apply sealer to the legs on the bottom and install a new O-ring at the top right

housing with clean engine oil and carefully slip it over the rotor.

14. Lubricate the dowels with clean engine oil and insert them through the front rotor housing holes and into the front housing.

15. Remove the rubber band or O-ring from the installed rotor and slide the apex seal springs into place, small spring first. Fit each side piece into its original position and confirm that the springs are set correctly on the side piece. Make sure each seal moves smoothly by pressing its head.

16. Install the new soft seals into the corner seals and install the corner seal springs and corner seals so the chamfered surfaces face the bottom of the groove.

17. Install the side seal springs and side seals so the paint mark faces the bottom of the groove. Make sure the corner seals and side seals move smoothly by lightly pressing them.

18. Apply petroleum jelly to the new outer and inner sealing rubbers. Install the outer sealing rubber to the front side so the white paint faces the side wall of the groove. Install the inner sealing rubber to the front side so the blue paint faces the outer wall of the groove and the seam is placed between the 9-12 o'clock positions. Make sure the inner and outer sealing rubbers are not twisted.

19. Apply clean engine oil to the contact surfaces of the intermediate housing and to the rotor oil seal on the rear side of the front rotor. Do not get oil on the sealing rubber. Install a new O-ring and apply sealer to the housing legs as before.

20. Turn the eccentric shaft so the rear rotor journal faces the intake and exhaust port side. Lift the shaft about 1 in. (25mm) and install the intermediate housing over the shaft and onto the front housing. Be careful not to lift the shaft more than 1.4 in. (35mm).

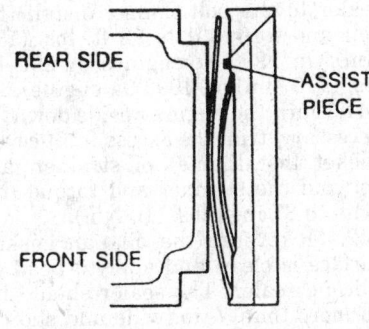

REAR SIDE

ASSIST PIECE

FRONT SIDE

Apex seal spring installation

21. Install the outer and inner sealing rubber to the rear side of the intermediate housing using the same procedure as for the front side of the intermediate housing. Apply clean engine oil to the rear contact surfaces, but do not get oil on the sealing rubber.

22. Assemble the rear rotor and housing in the same procedure as the front. Remember the side piece on the apex seal goes towards the rear housing.

23. Apply clean engine oil to a new rear oil seal and the groove of the rear stationary gear. Install the seal into the stationary gear.

24. Install the oil regulator valve and tighten to 57 ft. lbs. (78 Nm).

25. Apply petroleum jelly to the new outer and inner sealing rubbers. Install the outer sealing rubber so the white paint faces the side wall of the groove. Install the inner sealing rubber so the blue paint faces the outer wall of the groove and the seam is placed between the 9-12 o'clock positions. Make sure the inner and outer sealing rubbers are not twisted.

26. Apply clean engine oil to the contact surfaces, stationary gear and main bearing and to the rotor oil seal of the rear rotor's rear side. Do not get oil on the sealing rubber. Install a new O-ring and apply sealer to the housing legs as before.

27. Install the rear housing onto the rear rotor housing. Check that the side pieces of the apex seals are not wedged between the rotor housing and side housing.

28. Install a new washer on each tension bolt, and lubricate the threads and sealing washer of each bolt with engine oil. Start the bolts in the holes and tighten them finger-tight, making sure to install them into their original position.

29. Torque the bolts in 3 steps, in sequence, to 28 ft. lbs. (39 Nm). After the bolts are torqued, make sure the eccentric shaft turns smoothly and easily.

30. Lubricate the oil seal in the rear housing.

31. If equipped with a manual transmission:

  a. Fit the key into place on the eccentric shaft and install the flywheel.

  b. Apply thread locking compound to the eccentric shaft and sealer to the contact surface of the nut.

  c. Install the flywheel locknut. Hold the flywheel securely and tighten the nut to 360 ft. lbs. (490 Nm).

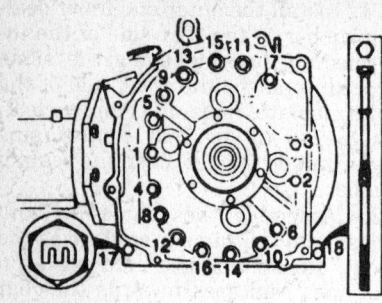

Tension bolt torque sequence; make sure the marked bolt is in position 17 and the bolt with the tube in position 18

32. If equipped with an automatic transmission:

a. Install the key and counterweight onto the eccentric shaft.

b. Apply thread locking compound to the eccentric shaft threads and sealer to the contact surface of the nut.

c. Install and torque the nut to 360 ft. lbs. (490 Nm).

NOTE: If equipped with automatic transmission, do not hold the driveplate to hold the eccentric shaft when removing or installing the large nut. The torque on the nut is over 300 ft. lbs. (400 Nm) and the driveplate is not designed to withstand that much torque.

d. Install the driveplate on the counterweight and torque the nuts to 44 ft. lbs. (60 Nm). On 1990-91 engines, the driveplate must be properly positioned. On 1993-94 vehicles, the driveplate bolts must be tightened in sequence.

33. Turn the engine so the front faces up. Install the end-play spacer, needle bearing, thrust washer, balance weight, oil pump drive sprocket

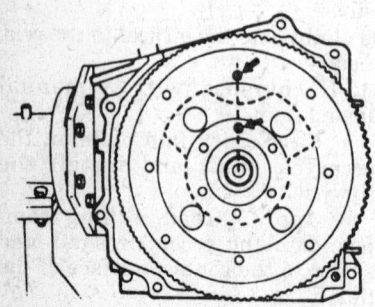

Install the drive plate in this position relative to the counterweight — 1990-91 vehicles with automatic transmission

and drive gear onto the front of the eccentric shaft.

NOTE: When installing the needle bearing, make sure it is not caught by the spacer.

34. Install the eccentric shaft pulley boss and bolt and torque to 98 ft. lbs. (132 Nm).

35. Use a dial indicator to check the eccentric shaft end-play. Standard end-play is 0.0016-0.0028 in. (0.040-0.070mm); maximum is 0.0035 in. (0.009mm). Different thickness spacers are available from the manufacturer to correct excessive or insufficient end-play.

36. After checking or setting the end-play, remove the pulley and install the oil pump. Torque the bolts to 87 in. lbs. (9.8 Nm). Install the key, sprockets and drive chain and the lock washer and nut. Torque the nut to 33 ft. lbs. (46 Nm) and bend the lock washer tab.

37. Install the drive gear with the chamfered surface facing the housing.

38. If removed, install the oil pressure control valve in the front cover and torque to 36 ft. lbs. (49 Nm). Install a new front oil seal, new O-ring and backup ring, and a new gasket on the front cover. Install the front cover to the engine. Torque the bolts to 17 ft. lbs. (22 Nm).

39. Install the eccentric shaft pulley boss with the old lock bolt and tighten it by hand. Without pushing the eccentric shaft, remove the bolt and measure the shaft depth inside the pulley boss. If there is more than 0.096 in. (2.44mm) between the end of the shaft and the face of the pulley, the thrust bearing is caught behind the spacer and must be installed correctly.

40. When the front cover is properly installed and the shaft depth in the pulley boss is correct, install the bypass valve and spring into the end of the eccentric shaft and install a new O-ring onto a new lock bolt. Apply a sealer to the bolt flange, install the bolt and torque it to 98 ft. lbs. (132 Nm) On 1990-91 engines or 200 ft. lbs. (270 Nm) on 1993-94 engines.

41. Turn the engine upside down. If necessary, trim the excess front cover gasket. Install a new oil strainer gasket and the strainer and torque the bolts to 87 inch lbs. (10 Nm).

42. Make sure the oil pan gasket surface is clean and apply a bead of silicone sealer. The sealer should be no more than ¼ in. wide and should be inside the bolt holes. Install the gasket, apply a second bead to the

gasket and install the oil pan. Torque the oil pan bolts to 95 inch lbs. (11 Nm) in 2 steps.

43. Install the remaining components in the reverse order of removal.

Intake Manifold

REMOVAL AND INSTALLATION

1. Relieve the fuel system pressure and disconnect the negative battery cable.

2. Drain the cooling system.

3. Remove the air inlet ducting and disconnect the accelerator cable.

4. Label and disconnect the necessary wiring and hoses. Disconnect and plug the fuel lines.

5. Remove the manifold oil nozzles.

6. Remove the intake manifold retaining bolts and remove the intake manifold. Cover the intake ports while the manifold is removed to keep dirt out of the engine.

7. If necessary, remove the throttle body, plenum chamber, if equipped, and extension manifold.

To install:

8. Make sure all gasket mating surfaces are clean.

9. Install a new manifold-to-engine gasket and install the intake manifold assembly with the retaining bolts.

10. Tighten the intake manifold-to-engine bolts to 19 ft. lbs. (25 Nm).

11. Install the manifold oil nozzles.

12. Connect the fuel lines and all hoses and wiring.

13. Connect the accelerator cable and the air intake ducting.

14. Connect the negative battery cable. Fill and bleed the cooling system.

15. Start the engine and bring to normal operating temperature. Check for leaks. Check the idle speed.

Exhaust Manifold

REMOVAL AND INSTALLATION

1. Disconnect the negative battery cable.

2. Remove the intake manifold assembly.

3. Remove the exhaust shields.

4. Disconnect the oxygen sensor connector.

5. Disconnect the exhaust pipe from the manifold or turbocharger.

6. On turbocharged engines, remove the turbocharger and wastegate assembly and cover the air,

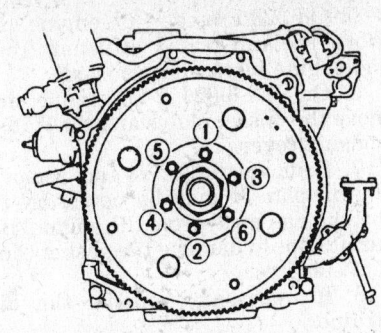

Drive plate bolt torque sequence — 1993-94 vehicles with automatic transmission

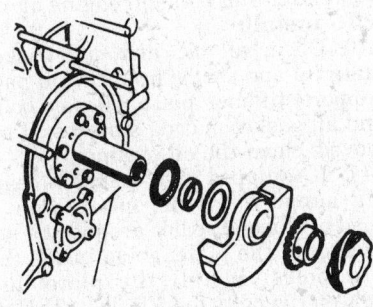

Front balance weight and thrust bearing assembly installation

water and oil openings to keet them clean.

7. Remove the nuts to remove the exhaust manifold from the engine. Cover the exhaust ports to keep dirt out of the engine.

To install:

8. Clean all gasket mating surfaces.

9. Using a new gasket, install the exhaust manifold to the engine.

10. Install the nuts and tighten to 34 ft. lbs. (46 Nm) on 1990-91 vehicles or 57 ft. lbs. (78 Nm) on 1993-94 vehicles.

11. If equipped, install the turbocharger.

12. Connect the exhaust pipe to the manifold or turbocharger. Tighten the nuts to 59 ft. lbs. (80 Nm) on non-turbocharged engines or 38 ft. lbs. (51 Nm) on turbocharged engines.

13. Connect the oxygen sensor connector and install the exhaust shields.

14. Install the intake manifold assembly.

15. Connect the negative battery cable. Start the engine and bring to normal operating temperature. Check for leaks.

Turbocharger

REMOVAL AND INSTALLATION

1990-91

1. Disconnect the negative battery cable. Drain the cooling system.

2. Disconnect the air hoses from the air pump and remove the air pump from the engine.

3. Remove the air ducting from the turbocharger.

4. Disconnect the connector from the air control valve and remove the valve from the engine.

5. Disconnect the split air pipe from the engine and remove the pipe along with the gasket.

6. Disconnect the water hose and the water pipe from the engine and remove them.

7. Disconnect the supply and return oil pipes from the turbocharger and cover the openings.

8. Remove the shields and disconnect the exhaust system from the turbocharger. Remove the gasket and discard it.

9. Unstake the retainer tabs from the retainer plate with a small prying tool. Remove the nuts and washers that secure the turbocharger to the exhaust manifold studs and remove the turbocharger from the engine. Cover all the turbocharger openings to prevent the entry of dirt and foreign matter. Remove the turbocharger gasket and discard it.

To install:

10. Thoroughly clean the exhaust manifold and turbocharger contact surfaces and check the exhaust manifold for warpage using a feeler gauge and straight-edge.

11. Install a new turbocharger gasket onto the exhaust manifold and carefully guide the turbocharger over the mounting studs and onto the gasket. Install the nuts and new lock washers. Torque the nuts to 40 ft. lbs. (54 Nm). Once the nuts are torqued, crimp the tabs on the nut retaining plate to prevent the nuts from loosening. Remove the protective covers from the turbocharger openings.

12. Connect the exhaust pipe with a new gasket. Torque the nuts to 38 ft. lbs. (51 Nm).

13. Install the remaining components in reverse of the removal procedure. Use new gaskets:

   a. Oil pipes.
   b. Water pipe and water hose.
   c. Air pump and air hoses.
   d. Split air pipe.
   e. Air control valve.
   f. Air ducting.

   g. Heat shields.

14. Fill the cooling system and connect the negative battery cable. Start the engine and check for leaks.

1993-94

1. Disconnect the negative battery cable. Raise and safely support the vehicle.

2. Remove the engine undercover and drain the cooling system.

3. Remove the bolts from the converter support bracket. Remove the nuts and remove the main converter.

4. Remove the exhaust pipe/turbocharger shields. Disconnect the connector and remove the oxygen sensor.

5. Remove the nuts and remove the front exhaust pipe/secondary converter assembly.

6. Remove the fresh air duct, air intake hoses and air cleaner assembly.

7. Disconnect the accelerator cable. Label and disconnect the hoses, remove the mounting bolt and remove the pressure chamber.

8. Remove the hose and intercooler air pipe from the turbocharger outlet pipe.

9. Disconnect the drive belt and remove the air pump.

10. Remove the outlet pipe from between the primary and secondary turbocharger outlets. Cover the outlet openings to prevent the entrance of dirt or foreign material.

11. Disconnect the hoses and connectors and remove the charge control valve assembly.

12. Remove the primary and secondary air intake pipes. Cover the turbocharger intake openings to prevent the entrance of dirt or foreign material.

13. Disconnect the coolant hose. Disconnect the oil supply and return lines. Cover the line and turbocharger openings to prevent the entrance of dirt or foreign material.

14. Remove the mounting nuts and remove the turbocharger assembly. Remove the turbocharger control actuator.

NOTE: Do not hold the actuator rod or hose when carrying the turbocharger.

To install:

15. Make sure the turbocharger compressor wheel assembly turns smoothly. If there is excessive drag or noise, replace the turbocharger.

16. Clean all gasket mating surfaces.

17. Make sure the paint mark on the actuator rod is aligned with the

actuator bracket. If they are not aligned, loosen the locknut and adjust the actuator rod length.

18. Remove the turbocharger mounting studs on the exhaust manifold and replace with new. Tighten stud bolts **A** to 17 ft. lbs. (24 Nm) and stud bolt **B** to 8.7 ft. lbs. (12 Nm).

19. Using new gaskets, install the turbocharger assembly on the exhaust manifold. Tighten nuts **A** to 38 ft. lbs. (51 Nm), nuts **B** to 21 ft. lbs. (29 Nm) and nuts **C** to 42 ft. lbs. (57 Nm).

20. Connect the coolant hose. Connect the return lines using new gaskets. Tighten the nuts to 95 inch lbs. (10.7 Nm).

21. Connect the oil inlet pipe and tighten the connection using a backup wrench.

22. Install the turbocharger control actuator and tighten the bolts to 16 ft. lbs. (22 Nm). Connect the air hoses and install a new clip on the actuator rod.

23. Install the primary and secondary intake pipes, using new gaskets. Tighten the nuts to 95 inch lbs. (11 Nm). Connect the hoses.

24. Install the charge control valve assembly.

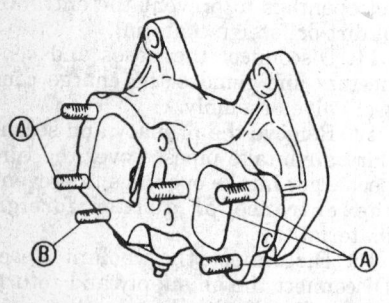

Exhaust manifold stud identification — 1993-94

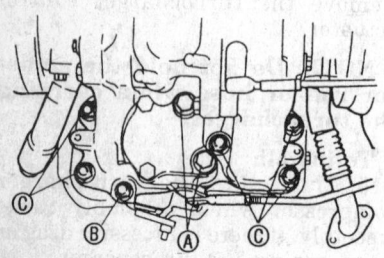

Turbocharger mounting nut identification — 1993-94

25. Install the turbocharger outlet pipe to the turbocharger, using new gaskets. Tighten the nuts to 95 inch lbs. (11 Nm). Install the air hose and air pipe connecting the outlet pipe to the intercooler. Tighten the air pipe mounting bolts to 95 inch lbs. (11 Nm).

26. Install the air pump. Install the drive belt and adjust the tension.

27. Install the pressure chamber and tighten the bolt to 95 inch lbs. (11 Nm). Connect the hoses.

28. Connect the accelerator cable.

29. Install the air cleaner assembly, air hoses and fresh air duct.

30. Install the front exhaust pipe/converter assembly to the turbocharger using a new gasket. Tighten the nuts to 38 ft. lbs. (51 Nm).

31. Install the oxygen sensor and tighten to 36 ft. lbs. (49 Nm). Connect the electrical connector.

32. Install the exhaust pipe/turbocharger shields.

33. Install the main converter assembly using new gaskets. Tighten the nuts to 66 ft. lbs. (89 Nm). Install the bracket bolts and tighten to 19 ft. lbs. (26 Nm).

34. Install the engine undercover and lower the vehicle.

35. Connect the negative battery cable. Fill and bleed the cooling system.

36. Start the engine and check for leaks and proper operation.

ENGINE LUBRICATION

Oil Pan

REMOVAL AND INSTALLATION

323, Protege, MX-3, MX-6 and 626

1. Disconnect the negative battery cable. Raise and safely support the vehicle.

2. Remove the engine undercover, if equipped. Position a suitable container under the oil pan. Remove the drain plug and drain the oil.

3. Remove the exhaust pipe from the exhaust manifold and from the catalytic converter. If necessary, remove the exhaust pipe bracket from the engine block.

4. On MX-3 1.8L and MX-6/626 2.5L engines, remove the transverse member from under the oil pan.

5. On 323/Protege 1.6L engine, remove the integrated stiffener from the engine block and transaxle.

6. On MX-6/626 2.2L engine, remove the gusset plates and the clutch housing cover.

7. Remove the bolts and remove the oil pan. It may be necessary to pry the pan away from the engine. Be careful not to damage the gasket contact surfaces.

8. If necessary remove the oil strainer.

9. On 323/Protege, MX-3 1.6L engine and MX-6/626 2.2L engines, remove the main bearing support/stiffener plate that is installed between the oil pan and engine block.

To install:

10. Clean all oil, dirt, old gasket material and sealer from the oil pan, support/stiffener plate, oil pan bolts and all gasket mating surfaces. If removed, clean the oil strainer.

11. If equipped with the main bearing support/stiffener plate, run a bead of silicone sealer around the perimeter of the plate, going inside the bolt holes. Install the plate and tighten the bolts to 15 ft. lbs. (21 Nm) on 323/Protege/MX-3 or 104 inch lbs. (12 Nm) on MX-6/626.

NOTE: Make sure all old sealer is removed from the bolts prior to installation. Installing a bolt coated with old sealer could result in cracking of the bolts holes.

12. If removed, install the oil strainer using a new gasket. Tighten the bolts to 95 inch lbs. (11 Nm).

13. If used, apply silicone sealer to new rubber end gaskets and press them into place on the engine.

14. Apply a bead of silicone to the perimeter of the oil pan, going around the inside of the bolt holes and install the pan to the engine. Install the oil pan bolts finger-tight.

15. On 323/Protege 1.6L and MX-6/626 2.2L engines, tighten the oil pan bolts to 95 inch lbs. (11 Nm). On MX-6/626 2.0L engine, tighten the oil pan bolts to 18 ft. lbs. (25 Nm). On 323/Protege 1.8L and MX-3 1.6L engines, tighten bolts **A** to 95 inch lbs. (11 Nm) and bolts **B** to 38 ft. lbs. (52 Nm). On MX-3 1.8L and MX-6/626 2.5L engines, tighten bolts **A** to 95 inch lbs. (11 Nm) and bolts **B** to 18 ft. lbs. (25 Nm).

NOTE: Make sure all old sealer is removed from the bolts prior to installation. Installing a bolt coated with old sealer could result in cracking of the bolts holes.

16. On MX-6/626 2.2L engine, install the clutch housing cover and

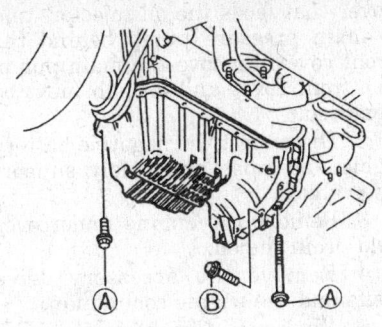

Oil pan bolt identification — 323/Protege 1.8L and MX-3 1.6L engines

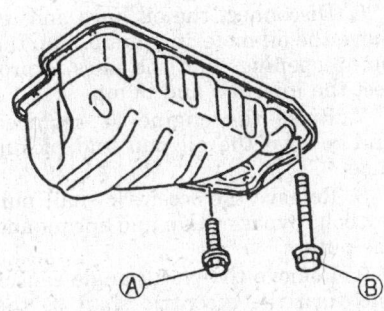

Oil pan bolt identification — MX-3 1.8L and MX-6/626 2.5L engines

tighten the bolts to 95 inch lbs. (11 Nm). Install the gusset plates and tighten the bolts to 38 ft. lbs. (52 Nm).

17. On 323/Protege 1.6L engine, install the integrated stiffener to the engine block and transaxle. Tighten the bolts to 38 ft. lbs. (52 Nm).

18. On MX-3 1.8L and MX-6/626 2.5L engines, install the transverse member. Tighten the bolts to 93 ft. lbs. (126 Nm).

19. Install the front exhaust pipe bracket, if equipped. Install the front exhaust pipe, using new gaskets. Tighten the exhaust manifold flange nuts to 34 ft. lbs. (46 Nm).

20. Install the oil pan drain plug using a new gasket. Tighten the drain plug to 30 ft. lbs. (41 Nm) on all except 2.2L engine, where the torque is 15 ft. lbs. (20 Nm).

21. Install the engine undercover and lower the vehicle.

22. Fill the engine with the proper type and quantity of oil.

23. Connect the negative battery cable. Start the engine and bring to normal operating temperature. Check for leaks.

Miata

1. Disconnect the negative battery cable and raise and safely support the vehicle.

2. Remove the engine undercover and drain the oil. Remove the dipstick and tube.

3. Remove both lower engine mount nuts and disconnect the steering shaft joint at the steering rack.

4. Attach lifting equipment and lift the engine slightly.

5. Support the crossmember with a jack and remove the nuts and bolts on each side. Lower the crossmember until the clearance between the oil pan and steering gear is 4 in. (100mm) or more.

6. Remove the oil pan bolts and lower the pan enough to remove the oil strainer bolts. If prying the pan is necessary, pry at the pan-to-transmission face. Be careful not to damage the block sealing surfaces.

7. Remove the oil pan and carefully pry the baffle off the block.

To install:

8. Make sure all the old sealer is cleaned off the pan, baffle, block and bolts. Make sure all surfaces are clean and dry.

9. Apply a bead of silicone sealer to the baffle, making sure the bead is inside the bolt holes. Install the baffle with a few of the pan bolts and allow the sealer to set up long enough to hold the baffle in place when the bolts are removed.

10. Apply silicone sealer to each end of the block and press the rubber end gaskets into place. Make sure the notches on the gaskets face the front and rear of the engine block.

11. Install the oil pickup tube with a new gasket and torque the bolts and nut to 95 inch lbs. (11 Nm).

12. Apply a bead of silicone sealer to the oil pan, making sure the bead is inside the bolt holes. Fit the pan into place and torque the pan-to-engine bolts to 95 inch lbs. (11 Nm). Start at the center and work out. Torque the pan-to-transmission bolts to 66 ft. lbs. (89 Nm).

13. Raise the crossmember and set the engine into place. Torque the crossmember nuts to 87 ft. lbs. (118 Nm) and the bolts to 61 ft. lbs. (83 Nm).

14. Torque the engine mount nuts to 58 ft. lbs. (78 Nm).

15. Connect the steering shaft to the rack and install the dipstick. Install the engine undercover and lower the vehicle.

16. Connect the negative battery cable. Fill the engine with the proper type and quantity of oil.

17. Start the engine and bring to normal operating temperature. Check for leaks.

929

1. Disconnect the negative battery cable and raise and safely support the vehicle.

2. Remove the engine undercover and drain the oil.

3. Remove the bolts and carefully pry the oil pan from the engine. Be careful not to damage the gasket surfaces.

To install:

4. Clean the old sealer from the engine and pan bolts. Thoroughly clean the oil, dirt and old sealer from the oil pan.

5. Apply a bead of silicone sealer to the pan, making sure it is inside the bolt holes.

6. Install the pan and torque the bolts to 87 inch lbs. (10 Nm). Install the drain plug, using a new gasket, and tighten to 30 ft. lbs. (41 Nm).

7. Install the engine undercover and lower the vehicle.

8. Fill the engine with the proper type and quantity of engine oil. Connect the negative battery cable, start the engine and bring to normal operating temperature. Check for leaks.

RX-7

1990-91

1. Disconnect the negative battery cable and raise and safely support the vehicle.

2. Remove the undercover and drain the oil. Disconnect the oil level and temperature sensor wires, if equipped.

3. Attach engine lifting equipment and remove the fan from the front of the engine.

4. Remove the engine mount nuts and raise the engine slightly. Remove the right side mount from the vehicle.

5. Remove the oil pan bolts and carefully pry the pan off the engine. Be careful not to damage the sealing surfaces.

To install:

6. Clean the old sealer off the engine and bolts. Thoroughly clean the oil, dirt and old sealer from the oil pan.

7. The pan can be installed with or without a gasket. In either case, apply a bead of silicone sealer to the gasket and/or the pan. Make sure the bead is inside the bolt holes.

8. Install the pan and torque the bolts to 95 inch lbs. (11 Nm).

9. Install the engine mount and torque the bolt to 69 ft. lbs. (93 Nm).

10. Lower the engine into place and torque the mounting nuts to 34 ft. lbs. (46 Nm). Torque fan nuts to 104 inch lbs. (12 Nm).

11. Connect the electrical connectors to the sensors. Install the engine undercover and lower the vehicle.

12. Fill the engine with the proper type and quantity of engine oil. Connect the negative battery cable, start the engine and bring to normal operating temperature. Check for leaks.

1993-94

1. Disconnect the negative battery cable. Raise and safely support the vehicle.

2. Remove the engine undercover. Remove the drain plug from the oil pan and drain the oil into a suitable container.

3. Remove the stabilizer bar.

4. Install engine support tool 49 G017 5A0 or equivalent. Remove the engine mount nuts and take the weight from the mounts with the engine support tool.

5. Disconnect the steering gear from the crossmember.

6. Support the crossmember with a jack. Remove the power steering hose bracket and the mounting bolts/nuts from the crossmember. Lower the crossmember from the vehicle.

7. Remove the engine mount brackets from the engine. Disconnect the oil level sensor connector and remove it from the harness bracket.

8. Remove the oil pan bolts and the oil pan. If necessary, pry the oil pan from the engine, using the prying tool only at the rear of the engine and being careful not to damage the contact surfaces.

To install:

9. Thoroughly clean the oil, dirt and old sealer from the oil pan. Clean the old sealer and any foreign material from the contact surfaces on the engine and from the oil pan bolts.

10. Apply silicone sealer to the contact surfaces of the oil pan and the engine side of the new gasket.

11. Install the oil pan and tighten the bolts to 104 inch lbs. (12 Nm).

12. Connect the oil level sensor connector. Install the engine mount brackets and tighten the bolts to 68 ft. lbs. (93 Nm).

13. Raise the crossmember into position. Install the bolts/nuts and tighten to 86 ft. lbs. (117 Nm). Install the power steering hose bracket.

14. Install the steering gear to the crossmember and tighten the bolts to 38 ft. lbs. (51 Nm).

15. Remove the engine support tool. Install the mount nuts and tighten to 49 ft. lbs. (68 Nm).

16. Install the stabilizer bar. Tighten the stabilizer bar bracket bolts to 19 ft. lbs. (25 Nm).

17. Install the drain plug, using a new gasket, and tighten to 30 ft. lbs. (41 Nm). Install the engine undercover and lower the vehicle.

18. Fill the engine with the proper type and quantity of engine oil. Connect the negative battery cable, start the engine and bring to normal operating temperature. Check for leaks.

Oil Pump

REMOVAL AND INSTALLATION

Except RX-7 and 1992-94 929

1. Disconnect the negative battery cable.

2. Remove the timing belt and crankshaft sprocket. On 929, drain the cooling system and remove the thermostat housing.

3. Raise and safely support the vehicle.

4. Remove the oil pan and oil strainer.

5. Remove the mounting bolts and remove the oil pump. If necessary, pry out the old oil seal being careful not to damage the seal housing area.

To install:

6. Clean all gasket mating surfaces. If necessary, lubricate the lip of a new oil seal and install the seal in the pump, using a seal installer.

7. Install the oil pump, using a new gasket. Tighten the mounting bolts to 19 ft. lbs. (25 Nm) on all except 2.2L engine. On 2.2L engine, tighten the 8mm bolts to 19 ft. lbs. (25 Nm) and the 10mm mounting bolts to 38 ft. lbs. (52 Nm).

8. Install the oil strainer and oil pan. Lower the vehicle.

9. On 929, install the thermostat housing using a new gasket. Tighten the bolts to 19 ft. lbs. (25 Nm).

10. Install the crankshaft sprocket and timing belt.

11. Fill the engine with the proper type and quantity of engine oil. Fill and bleed the cooling system, as necessary. Connect the negative battery cable, start the engine and bring to normal operating temperature. Check for leaks.

RX-7

1990-91

1. This engine uses 2 oil pumps; a metering pump bolted to the front cover that feeds the oil injectors and a main pressure pump behind the front cover. Remove the main pump, the front cover and oil pan must be removed.

2. Disconnect the negative battery cable and raise and safely support the vehicle.

3. Remove the engine undercover and drain the oil.

4. Remove the accessory drive belts and the engine cooling fan.

5. Without disconnecting the hoses, remove the power steering pump and the air conditioner compressor and secure them aside. Remove the pump/compressor bracket.

6. Disconnect the oil lines and remove the oil metering pump. Cap the pump openings and the lines to protect the injectors and pump.

7. Raise the engine as required and remove the oil pan and pickup tube.

8. Remove the eccentric shaft pulley bolt, bypass valve and spring and the pulley.

9. Remove the crank angle sensor and turn the eccentric shaft so the balance weight is at the bottom. Remove the front cover.

10. Remove the distributor drive gear. Bend the lock tab away from the nut and remove the nut and washer from the front of the oil pump.

11. Slide the pump sprocket and drive sprocket with the chain off the engine. Remove the bolts to remove the pump.

To install:

12. Remove the balance weight and make sure the thrust bearing and spacer are properly positioned. Pull out on the eccentric shaft when sliding the balance weight back on so the thrust bearing does not fall behind the spacer.

13. Install the oil pump and torque the bolts to 87 inch lbs. (10 Nm).

14. Install the sprockets and chain. Torque the nut to 34 ft. lbs. (46 Nm) and bend the lock washer tab. When installing the distributor drive gear, the chamfer faces the front cover.

15. It is recommended that the front cover oil seal be replaced. Press the old seal out, lubricate the new seal and press it in with a seal tool or socket.

16. If removed, install the oil pressure control valve into the front cover and torque to 36 ft. lbs. (49 Nm). Install a new O-ring and gasket and install the front cover to the engine. Torque the bolts to 17 ft. lbs. (23 Nm).

17. Temporarily install the pulley with the old lock bolt and tighten it by hand. Without pushing the eccentric shaft, remove the bolt and measure the shaft depth inside the pulley. If there is more than 0.096 in. (2.44mm) between the end of the shaft and the face of the pulley, the thrust bearing is caught behind the spacer and must be installed correctly.

18. A new pulley lock bolt is recommended. Install the bypass valve and spring into the end of the eccentric shaft and install a new O-ring onto the lock bolt. Apply a sealer to the bolt flange, install the bolt and torque it to 98 ft. lbs. (132 Nm).

19. At the oil pan sealing surface, trim the excess front cover gasket. Install a new oil strainer gasket and the strainer and torque the bolts to 87 inch lbs. (10 Nm).

20. Install the oil pan and engine mount and lower the engine onto the mounts.

21. The remaining accessory parts can be installed in the reverse order of removal. Observe the following torque values:

Metering oil pump — 95 inch lbs. (11 Nm)

Oil pipe fittings — 15 ft. lbs. (20 Nm) with new gaskets

Water pump assembly — 20 ft. lbs. (26 Nm) in a crisscross pattern, remember to shim studs that don't contact the gasket

Fan nuts — 104 inch lbs. (12 Nm).

1993-94

The engine must be removed from the vehicle and disassembled to remove and install the main oil pump.

1992-94 929

1. Remove the engine from the vehicle and position on a suitable workstand.

2. Remove the timing belt covers, timing belt and crankshaft sprocket.

3. Remove the A/C compressor mounting bracket.

4. Remove the oil pan, oil strainer and baffle plate.

5. Remove the oil pan block assembly.

6. Remove the thermostat housing assembly.

7. Remove the oil pump mounting bolts and remove the oil pump. If necessary, pry out the old oil seal being careful not to damage the seal housing area.

To install:

8. Clean all gasket mating surfaces. If necessary, lubricate the lip of a new oil seal and install the seal in the pump, using a seal installer.

9. Install the oil pump, using a new gasket, and tighten the bolts to 19 ft. lbs. (25 Nm).

10. Install the thermostat housing using a new gasket. Tighten the bolts to 19 ft. lbs. (25 Nm).

11. Cut away any portion of the oil pan gasket that projects toward the oil pan.

12. Install the baffle plate to the oil pan block assembly and tighten the bolts to 26 inch lbs. (3 Nm).

13. Apply a bead of silicone sealer to the perimeter of the oil pan block assembly and install it on the cylinder block. Tighten the bolts, in 2-3 steps, to 95 inch lbs. (11 Nm).

14. Install the oil strainer and oil pan.

15. Install the remaining components in the reverse order of removal.

Rear Main Bearing Oil Seal

REMOVAL AND INSTALLATION

Except RX-7

1. Disconnect the negative battery cable. Raise and safely support the vehicle.

2. Remove the transaxle or transmission.

3. If equipped with manual transaxle or transmission, remove the clutch pressure plate and disc.

4. Remove the flywheel.

5. Cut the oil seal lip with a razor knife. Pry the oil seal from the housing using a small prybar. Be careful not to damage the crankshaft or seal housing surfaces.

To install:

6. Apply a small amount of clean engine oil to the lip of the new seal and push the seal in slightly by hand.

7. Tap the seal in evenly using a seal installer. The seal must be installed so it is flush with the edge of the rear cover on all except 1.8L and 2.5L 6-cylinder engines. On the 1.8L engine, the seal must protrude 0.020 in. (0.5mm). On the 2.5L engine, the seal must protrude 0.030 in. (0.7mm).

8. Install the flywheel. Tighten the bolts to 76 ft. lbs. (103 Nm) on all except 1.8L, 2.5L and 3.0L 6-cylinder engines. On 1.8L and 2.5L engines, tighten the bolts to 49 ft. lbs. (67 Nm). On 3.0L engine, tighten the bolts to 81 ft. lbs. (110 Nm).

NOTE: Tighten the flywheel bolts in 2-3 steps, in a crisscross pattern.

9. If equipped with manual transaxle or transmission, install the clutch disc and pressure plate.

10. Install the transaxle or transmission and lower the vehicle. Connect the negative battery cable.

RX-7

1. Disconnect the negative battery cable. Raise and safely support the vehicle.

2. Remove the transmission.

3. If equipped with manual transmission, remove the clutch pressure plate and disc.

4. If equipped with manual transmission, remove the flywheel as follows:

a. Keep the flywheel from turning by installing flywheel holder tool 49 F011 101 or equivalent.

b. Remove the flywheel locknut.

c. Remove the flywheel using a suitable puller. Remove the key.

5. If equipped with automatic transmission, remove the driveplate and counterweight as follows:

a. Install counterweight holder tool 49 1881 055 or equivalent.

b. Remove the driveplate.

c. Remove the locknut.

d. Remove the counterweight using a suitable puller. Remove the key.

6. Cut the oil seal lip with a razor knife. Pry the oil seal from the stationary gear using a small prybar. Be careful not to damage the stationary gear or eccentric shaft surfaces.

To install:

7. Apply a small amount of clean engine oil to the lip of the new seal and push the seal in slightly by hand.

8. Tap the seal in evenly using a seal installer. The seal must be installed so it is flush with the edge of the rear cover.

9. If equipped with manual transmission, proceed as follows:

a. Install the key in the eccentric shaft and install the flywheel.

b. Install the flywheel holder tool.

c. Apply thread-locking compound to the eccentric shaft threads.

d. Install the locknut and tighten to 360 ft. lbs. (490 Nm).

e. Remove the holder tool.

10. If equipped with automatic transaxle, proceed as follows:

a. Install the key in the eccentric shaft and install the counterweight.

b. Install the counterweight holder tool.

c. Apply thread-locking compound to the eccentric shaft threads.

d. Install the locknut and tighten to 360 ft. lbs. (490 Nm).

e. Install the driveplate and tighten the bolts to 44 ft. lbs. (60 Nm). On 1990-91 vehicles, the driveplate must be installed so the holes in the counterweight and driveplate align.

f. Remove the holder tool.

11. If equipped with manual transmission, install the clutch pressure plate and disc.

12. Install the transmission and lower the vehicle. Connect the negative battery cable.

ENGINE COOLING

Radiator

REMOVAL AND INSTALLATION

Except RX-7 and 929

1. Disconnect the negative battery cable.

2. Remove the engine undercover, if equipped and drain the cooling system.

3. Remove the necessary air ducts.

4. Disconnect the electric cooling fan connector and, if equipped, temperature sensor connector.

5. Disconnect the coolant reservoir and upper and lower radiator hoses. If equipped with automatic transaxle or transmission, disconnect the oil cooler lines and plug the hoses.

6. On all except MX-3 and Miata, remove the upper radiator mounting brackets. On MX-3, remove the upper shroud panel.

7. Lift the radiator/cooling fan(s) assembly from the vehicle. On Miata, support the radiator and remove the mounting bolts.

8. Remove the radiator/cooling fans assembly.

9. If necessary, remove the cooling fan(s)/shroud assembly from the radiator.

10. Installation is the reverse of removal. Fill the cooling system, start the engine and bring to normal operating temperature. Check for leaks.

929

1. Disconnect the negative battery cable and drain the coolant.

2. Disconnect the vacuum lines, if equipped, and remove the air inlet duct.

3. Remove the upper and lower radiator hoses and the coolant reservoir hose. If equipped with an automatic transmission, disconnect and plug the cooling hoses.

4. Remove the fasteners for the fan and shroud and lift them out together. It may be easier to remove the shroud and move it back towards the engine to access the nuts holding the fan/clutch assembly.

5. Remove the bolts and lift the radiator out of the vehicle.

6. Installation is the reverse of removal. After installation, make sure the fan turns without contacting the shroud. Fill the cooling system, start the engine and bring to normal operating temperature. Check for leaks.

RX-7

1990-91

1. Disconnect the negative battery cable. Drain the cooling system.

2. Remove the mounting nuts and remove the cooling fan. Remove the air intake duct.

3. Remove the battery and battery tray.

4. Disconnect the upper and lower radiator hoses and the heater hose from the radiator.

5. Disconnect the coolant level sensor connector.

6. If equipped with automatic transmission, disconnect and plug the oil cooler hoses.

7. Remove the mounting bolts and remove the radiator/shroud assembly. If necessary remove the shroud and coolant filler neck from the radiator.

8. Installation is the reverse of the removal procedure. Fill the cooling system, start the engine and bring to normal operating temperature. Check for leaks.

1993-94

1. Disconnect the negative battery cable. Raise and safely support the vehicle.

2. Drain the cooling system.

3. Remove the fresh air duct and the air cleaner assembly.

4. Remove the battery box, battery and battery tray.

5. Remove the upper radiator hose.

6. Remove the relay box and position aside, leaving the wiring connected.

7. Disconnect the cooling fan electrical connectors.

8. Remove the engine undercover.

9. Remove the stabilizer bar and brackets assembly.

10. Remove the lower radiator hose and the air separation hose.

11. If equipped with automatic transmission, disconnect and plug the oil cooler hoses.

12. Remove the A/C condenser mounting bolts, position the condenser away from the radiator and secure it with wire. Do not disconnect the A/C lines.

13. Remove the power steering oil line bracket and the A/C high pressure line bracket.

14. Remove the radiator brackets and radiator mounting bolts and remove the radiator/cooling fans assembly. Be careful not to damage the condenser during radiator removal.

15. If necessary, remove the cooling fans/shroud assembly from the radiator.

To install:

16. Install the cooling fans/shroud assembly to the radiator, if removed.

17. Install the radiator/cooling fans assembly into the vehicle and tighten the radiator bracket mounting bolts.

18. Install the power steering and A/C line brackets.

19. Install the A/C condenser and secure with the mounting bolts.

20. If equipped with automatic transmission, unplug and connect the oil cooler hoses.

21. Install the air separation and lower radiator hoses.

22. Install the stabilizer bar/brackets assembly. Tighten the stabilizer bar end nuts to 39 ft. lbs. (53 Nm) and the bracket bolts to 19 ft. lbs. (25 Nm).

23. Install the engine undercover.

24. Connect the cooling fan electrical connectors.

25. Install the relay box and tighten the mounting bolt to 95 inch lbs. (11 Nm).

26. Install the upper radiator hose.

27. Install the battery tray, battery and battery box.

28. Install the air cleaner assembly and connect the ducts.

29. Connect the battery cables. Fill the cooling system, start the engine and bring to normal operating temperature. Check for leaks.

Heater Core

REMOVAL AND INSTALLATION

CAUTION

If equipped with an air bag system, the air bag must be disarmed and removed before removing the steering wheel. Accidental deployment of the air bag could cause severe personal injury.

---

1. If equipped with an air bag, properly disarm it.
2. On all except 929, the dashboard must be removed to remove the heater core assembly. Disconnect the negative battery cable and drain the coolant.
3. Disconnect the heater hoses at the engine firewall.
4. Remove the shift lever knob and the center console.
5. Remove the steering wheel and upper and lower column covers.
6. Remove the instrument cluster.
7. Remove the heater ducts and the glove compartment assembly.
8. Remove the trim pieces as required and remove the heater controls and radio.
9. Loosen the steering column bolts as required and lower the column.
10. Pry out the defroster grille or the center caps between the grille sections and remove the screws or bolts.
11. With all wires and control cables disconnected, remove the bolts and remove the dashboard from the vehicle.
12. Remove the screws and remove the heater unit from the firewall.
13. Remove the screws to split the case and remove the heater core from the housing. Take notice of how the air control doors fit together.
    To install:
14. Install the heater core and air control doors and fit the halves of the housing together.
15. Install the housing and connect the ducts.
16. Install the dashboard and connect the wiring and control cables.
17. Install the gauge panel and connect the wiring.
18. Assemble the steering column and install the steering wheel.
19. Fill the cooling system and test the heater.

Water Pump

REMOVAL AND INSTALLATION

Except RX-7

1. Disconnect the negative battery cable. Drain the cooling system.
2. Remove the timing belt covers and remove the timing belt.
3. On Miata, remove the power steering pump and position aside, without disconnecting the hoses.
4. On 1.6L and 1.8L 4-cylinder engines, disconnect the coolant bypass pipe and remove the coolant inlet pipe from the water pump.
5. On 2.0L engine, remove the power steering pump belt adjuster.
6. On 1.8L and 2.5L 6-cylinder engines, remove the right side engine mount bracket.
7. Remove any timing belt idler pulley(s) still attached to the water pump.
8. Remove the water pump mounting bolts and water pump.
   To install:
9. Clean all gasket mating surfaces.
10. If equipped, install new rubber seal(s) on the water pump.
11. Using a new gasket, install the water pump on the engine. Tighten the mounting bolts to 19 ft. lbs. (25 Nm).
12. Install any timing belt idler pulleys that were removed and tighten the bolt(s) to 38 ft. lbs. (52 Nm).
13. On 1.8L and 2.5L 6-cylinder engines, install the engine mount bracket and tighten the bolts to 44 ft. lbs. (60 Nm).
14. On 2.0L engine, install the power steering pump adjuster and tighten the bolts to 16 ft. lbs. (22 Nm).
15. On 1.6L and 1.8L 4-cylinder engines, install the coolant inlet pipe, using a new gasket. Tighten the bolts to 19 ft. lbs. (25 Nm). Connect the coolant bypass pipe using a new O-ring.
16. On Miata, install the power steering pump and tighten the bolts to 40 ft. lbs. (54 Nm).
17. Install the timing belt and the timing belt covers.
18. Fill the cooling system. Connect the negative battery cable, start the engine and bring to normal operating temperature. Check for leaks.

RX-7

1990-91

1. Disconnect the negative battery cable and drain the cooling system.

2. Turn the eccentric shaft so the pulley mark lines up with the indicator pin.
3. Remove the fan, accessory drive belts, air pump and bracket, alternator and bracket and water pump pulley. Remove the belt drive pulley from the eccentric shaft.
4. Disconnect the coolant hoses and the sensor wiring from the water pump.
5. Remove the nuts and slide the water pump assembly off the studs.
   To install:
6. Clean all gasket mating surfaces.
7. Install the water pump using a new gasket. Tighten the nuts to 20 ft. lbs. (26 Nm).
8. Connect the hoses and sensor wiring.
9. Install the eccentric shaft and water pump pulleys and tighten the bolts to 95 inch lbs. (11 Nm).
10. Install the brackets and the alternator and air pump. Install the accessory drive belts and adjust the belt tension.
11. Install the fan and tighten the nuts to 104 inch lbs. (12 Nm). Make sure there is ⅝-15/16 in. (16-24mm) clearance between the fan and shroud after installation. Reposition the shroud, if necessary for clearance.
12. Fill the cooling system. Connect the negative battery cable, start the engine and bring to normal operating temperature. Check for leaks.

1993-94

1. Disconnect the battery cables and remove the battery box, battery and battery tray. Drain the cooling system.
2. Remove the fresh air duct and the air cleaner assembly. Remove the intercooler-to-throttle body hose and funnel.
3. Disconnect the accelerator cable. Disconnect the filler port coolant hose from the water pump.
4. Remove the turbocharger-to-intercooler pipe and hose. Remove the water pump pulley and drive belt.
5. Remove the water pump body coolant hose from the rear of the water pump. Label and disconnect the electrical connectors and remove the alternator and alternator bracket.
6. Remove the air pump and air pump bracket. Remove the upper radiator hose.
7. Remove the intercooler and air separation tank, but do not remove the air duct from the body.
8. Remove the subframe at the front of the vehicle. Remove the lower radiator hose.

9. Remove the remaining coolant hoses from the water pump. Disconnect the metering oil lines.

10. Remove the metering oil pump connector from the engine hanger. Remove bolt **A**, then position the metering oil line and metering oil pump harness under the lower radiator hose.

11. Remove nuts **B** and remove the water pump.

To install:

12. Clean all gasket mating surfaces.

13. Install the water pump, using a new gasket. Tighten the nuts to 19 ft. lbs. (25 Nm).

14. Reposition the metering oil pump harness and line and install the bolt in the water pump. Tighten to 19 ft. lbs. (25 Nm).

15. Install the metering oil pump connector to the engine hanger. Connect the metering oil lines, using new gaskets, and tighten the bolts to 10 ft. lbs. (13 Nm).

16. Install the coolant hose at the rear of the water pump and connect the heater hose. Install the lower radiator hose.

17. Install the subframe at the front of the vehicle and tighten the bolts to 95 inch lbs. (11 Nm).

18. Install the intercooler and air separation tank. Tighten the bolts to 95 inch lbs. (11 Nm).

19. Install the upper radiator hose. Install the air pump and alternator with the brackets.

20. Connect the remaining coolant hose at the rear of the water pump. Install the water pump pulley and drive belt. Tighten the pulley bolts to 95 inch lbs. (11 Nm).

21. Install the turbocharger-to-intercooler hose and pipe.

22. Connect the filler port coolant hose at the water pump. Install the air cleaner assembly and fresh air duct.

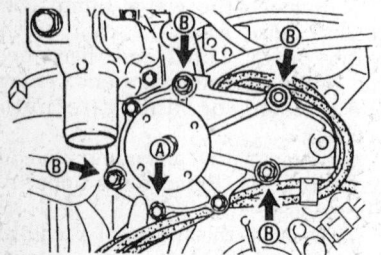

Water pump nut/bolt identification — 1993-94 rotary engine

23. Connect the accelerator cable. Install the intercooler-to-throttle body hose and funnel.

24. Install the battery tray, battery and battery box. Connect the battery cable.

25. Fill the cooling system. Start the engine and bring to normal operating temperature. Check for leaks and check the coolant level.

Thermostat

REMOVAL AND INSTALLATION

Except 1992-94 929 and 1993-94 RX-7

1. Disconnect the negative battery cable. Drain the cooling system.

2. On all except 1.8L and 2.5L 6-cylinder engines, disconnect the radiator hose from the thermostat housing cover. On 1.8L and 2.5L engines, remove the water inlet pipe from the thermostat housing cover and remove the engine harness bracket.

3. If equipped, disconnect the water thermoswitch electrical connector from the thermostat housing cover. Remove the bolts or nuts and remove the cover.

4. Remove the thermostat.

To install:

5. Clean the thermostat housing and thermostat housing cover contact surfaces.

6. On all except 929, install the thermostat. On 323/Protege, MX-3 and 1990-92 MX-6/626, install the thermostat with the jiggle pin facing the thermostat housing cover and toward the top of the cylinder head. On Miata and RX-7, make sure the jiggle pin is facing upward. On 1993-94 MX-6/626, install the thermostat so the projection and left jiggle pin are at the top and facing the thermostat housing cover.

7. If equipped with a separate thermostat housing gasket (some thermostats are equipped with integral O-rings), install it with the printed side facing the thermostat. On RX-7, make sure the gasket notch and thermostat jiggle pin align.

8. Install the thermostat housing cover. On 929, install the thermostat into the cover and install the cover with the mark facing the front of the engine.

9. Install the thermostat housing cover bolts and tighten to 19 ft. lbs. (25 Nm) on all except RX-7 and 1990-92 MX-6/626. On RX-7, tighten the bolts to 87 inch lbs. (10 Nm). On

1990-92 MX-6/626, tighten the nuts to 22 ft. lbs. (30 Nm).

10. If equipped, connect the water thermoswitch electrical connector.

11. On all except 1.8L and 2.5L 6-cylinder engines, connect the radiator hose and tighten the clamp. On 1.8L and 2.5L engines, install the engine harness bracket and tighten the bolt to 19 ft. lbs. (25 Nm). Connect the water inlet pipe, using a new O-ring and tighten the pipe bracket bolt to 19 ft. lbs. (25 Nm).

12. Fill the cooling system. Connect the negative battery cable, start the engine and bring to normal operating temperature. Check for leaks and the coolant level.

1992-94 929

1. Disconnect the negative battery cable. Raise and safely support the vehicle and remove the engine undercover.

2. Drain the cooling system.

3. Remove the fresh air duct and the air cleaner assembly. Remove the upper radiator hose.

4. Remove the cooling fan and shroud. Remove the alternator belt and the water pump pulley.

5. Remove the water bypass hose and the lower radiator hose.

6. Remove the thermostat housing from the engine. Remove the housing cover and thermostat.

To install:

7. Make sure the cover, housing and cylinder block contact surfaces are clean. If the integral thermostat gasket is damaged, replace the thermostat.

8. Install the thermostat in the cover with the spring facing the thermostat housing. Install the cover on the housing and tighten the bolts to 19 ft. lbs. (25 Nm).

9. Using a new gasket, install the thermostat housing on the engine. Tighten the bolts to 19 ft. lbs. (25 Nm).

10. Install the lower radiator hose and water bypass hose to the thermostat housing.

11. Install the water pump pulley and alternator belt. Adjust the belt tension.

12. Install the cooling fan and shroud. Tighten the fan nuts to 95 inch lbs. (11 Nm).

13. Install the air cleaner assembly and fresh air duct. Install the engine undercover and lower the vehicle.

14. Fill the cooling system. Connect the negative battery cable, start the engine and bring to normal operating temperature. Check for leaks and coolant level.

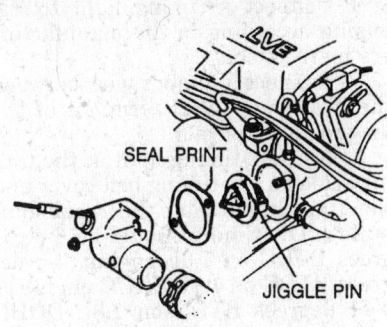

Thermostat installation — 2.2L engine

1993-94 RX-7

1. Disconnect the negative battery cable and drain the cooling system.
2. Remove the fresh air duct and the air cleaner assembly.
3. Remove the coolant hose from the thermostat cover.
4. Remove the drive belt and remove the air pump.
5. Remove the upper radiator hose.
6. Disconnect the coolant level sensor connector.
7. Remove the thermostat cover and remove the thermostat.

   To install:
8. Make sure the thermostat cover and engine contact surfaces are clean. Replace the thermostat if the gasket is damaged.
9. Install the thermostat in the engine with the spring toward the engine and the jiggle pin at the top.
10. Install the thermostat cover and tighten the bolts to 95 inch lbs. (11 Nm).
11. Connect the coolant level sensor connector and the upper radiator hose.
12. Install the air pump and the drive belt. Adjust the belt tension.
13. Connect the coolant hose to the thermostat cover.
14. Install the air cleaner assembly and the fresh air duct.
15. Fill the cooling system. Connect the negative battery cable, start the engine and bring to normal operating temperature. Check for leaks and coolant level.

Cooling System Bleeding

1. Fill the radiator up to the filler neck with a 50/50 mixture of water and anti-freeze. Fill the coolant reservoir to the **F** mark with the same water/anti-freeze mixture.

2. Install the radiator cap and reservoir cap securely and start the engine. Run the engine at idle until it reaches normal operating temperature.

NOTE: If the coolant temperature increases beyond normal, there is excessive air in the system. Stop the engine and allow it to cool, then repeat Steps 1 and 2.

3. Run the engine at 2200-2800 rpm for 5 minutes.
4. Stop the engine and let it cool. Repeat Steps 1-3, then go to Step 5.

———— **CAUTION** ————
Do not remove the radiator cap until the engine is cool, or personal injury from hot coolant or steam may result.

5. Remove the reservoir cap and radiator cap slowly, using a thick rag, Verify that the engine coolant level is near the filler neck. If not repeat Steps 1-5.
6. Fill the reservoir to the **F** with the 50/50 water and anti-freeze mixture.

ENGINE ELECTRICAL

NOTE: Disconnecting the negative battery cable on some vehicles may interfere with the functions of the on board computer systems and may require the computer to undergo a relearning process, once the negative battery cable is reconnected.

Distributor

REMOVAL

1. Disconnect the negative battery cable.
2. Turn the crankshaft pulley, in the normal direction of rotation, until the No. 1 cylinder piston is at Top Dead Center (TDC) on the compression stroke. The mark on the crankshaft pulley should be aligned with the **T** on the timing belt cover.
3. Label and remove the spark plug wires from the distributor cap. Remove the distributor cap.
4. Disconnect the wiring harness from the distributor. Disconnect the vacuum hoses, if equipped.

5. Mark the position of the distributor housing on the cylinder head.
6. Remove the distributor mounting bolt(s) and remove the distributor. Remove and discard the distributor O-ring.

INSTALLATION

Timing Not Disturbed

1. Apply clean engine oil to a new O-ring and install it on the distributor.
2. Install the distributor in the cylinder head. Make sure the distributor rotor is pointing toward the No. 1 spark plug tower position on the distributor cap.
3. Install the distributor mounting bolts. Align the marks made on the distributor housing and cylinder head during removal and loosely tighten the bolts.
4. Connect the distributor wiring and, if equipped, vacuum hoses.
5. Install the distributor cap and secure the screws.
6. Connect the spark plug wires to the distributor cap in their original locations.
7. Connect the negative battery cable. Check and adjust the ignition timing.

Timing Disturbed

1. Disconnect the spark plug wire and remove the spark plug from the No. 1 cylinder. Place a finger over the spark plug hole.
2. Turn the crankshaft pulley in the normal direction of rotation until compression is felt; the piston is approaching TDC on the compression stroke. Continue rotating the crankshaft pulley until the pulley mark aligns with the **T** mark on the timing belt cover.
3. Apply clean engine oil to a new O-ring and install it on the distributor.
4. Install the distributor in the cylinder head. Make sure the distributor rotor is pointing toward the No. 1 spark plug tower position on the distributor cap.
5. Install the distributor mounting bolts. Align the marks made on the distributor housing and cylinder head during removal and loosely tighten the bolts.
6. Connect the distributor wiring and, if equipped, vacuum hoses.
7. Install the distributor cap and secure the screws.
8. Install the spark plug in the No. 1 cylinder and connect the spark plug wire.

9. Connect the spark plug wires to the distributor cap in their original locations.

10. Connect the negative battery cable. Check and adjust the ignition timing.

Distributorless Ignition

REMOVAL AND INSTALLATION

Crank Angle Sensor

1990-91 RX-7

1. Disconnect the negative battery cable.

2. Turn the eccentric shaft to position the pulley to the leading timing mark on the pulley, usually painted yellow.

3. Disconnect the crank angle sensor electrical connector and remove the crank angle sensor lock bolt.

4. Slowly pull up on the crank angle sensor and remove it from the vehicle.

To install:

5. Align the matching marks on the crank angle sensor housing and the driven gear.

6. Make sure the eccentric shaft pulley is set to the leading timing mark.

7. Install the crank angle sensor and the lock bolt.

8. Connect the negative battery cable and check the ignition timing. Tighten the lock bolt to 95 inch lbs. (11 Nm).

Miata

1. Disconnect the negative battery cable.

2. Disconnect the crank angle sensor electrical connector. Matchmark the sensor-to-housing, then remove the crank angle sensor mounting bolts.

3. Remove the crank angle sensor.

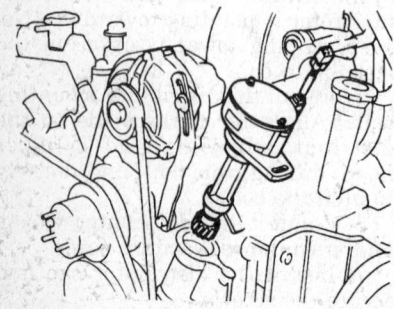

Crank angle sensor removal and Installation — 1990-91 RX-7

To install:

4. Align the matching marks on the crank angle sensor and housing. Install the sensor.

5. Torque the sensor retaining bolts 14-20 ft. lbs. (19-27 Nm).

6. Connect the negative battery cable and check the ignition timing.

Ignition Coil

1993-94 RX-7

1. Disconnect the negative battery cable.

2. Label and disconnect the vacuum hoses, remove the mounting bolts and remove the pressure chamber.

3. Disconnect the accelerator cable.

4. Label and disconnect the necessary vacuum hoses and electrical connectors from the throttle body and extension manifold assembly. Remove the mounting bolts and remove the assembly.

5. Label and disconnect the spark plug wires and electrical connectors from the coils.

6. Remove the ignition coil bracket and remove the coils from the bracket.

7. Installation is the reverse of the removal procedure. Install the extension manifold/throttle body assembly with a new gasket. Tighten the mounting bolts to 18 ft. lbs. (25 Nm).

Miata

1. Mark the position of the spark plug wires in the coil pack.

2. Disconnect the spark plug wires and the ignition coil electrical connector.

3. Remove the 3 ignition coil-to-engine bolts and the ignition coil assembly from the vehicle.

4. Installation is the reverse of the removal procedure. Torque the ignition coil mounting bolts to 19 ft. lbs. (25 Nm).

Ignition Timing

ADJUSTMENT

323/Protege

1. Apply the parking brake. If equipped with automatic transaxle, place the gearshift lever in **P**. If equipped with manual transaxle, place the gearshift lever in neutral.

2. Start the engine and bring to normal operating temperature. Make sure all electrical loads and the A/C switch are OFF.

3. Connect a timing light to the engine according to the manufacturers instructions.

4. Connect a jumper wire between the **TEN** and **GND** terminal of the diagnostic connector.

5. Aim the timing light at the timing scale on the timing belt cover and the timing mark on the crankshaft pulley. The timing should be 6-8 degrees BTDC on 1.6L engine, 4-6 degrees BTDC on 1.8L SOHC engine or 9-11 degrees BTDC on 1.8L DOHC engine.

6. If the timing is not as specified, loosen the distributor mounting bolts and turn the distributor to adjust. After adjustment, tighten the bolts to 19 ft. lbs. (25 Nm) and recheck the timing.

7. Remove the jumper wire and the test equipment.

Miata

1. Apply the parking brake. If equipped with automatic transmission, place the gearshift lever in **P**. If equipped with manual transmission, place the gearshift lever in neutral.

2. Start the engine and bring to normal operating temperature. Make sure all electrical loads are OFF.

3. Connect a tachometer and timing light to the **IG** terminal on the diagnostic connector.

NOTE: As the battery is located in the trunk, power for the timing light and tachometer is available at the blue, 1-pin power connector, located near 1 of the headlight door motors. Be careful not to ground the connector terminal as the 20A wiper fuse will be burned.

4. Connect a jumper wire between the **TEN** and **GND** terminal of the diagnostic connector.

5. Check the idle speed and adjust, if necessary. The idle speed should be 800-900 rpm.

6. Aim the timing light at the timing scale on the timing belt cover and the timing mark on the crankshaft pulley. The timing should be 9-11 degrees BTDC if equipped with manual transmission or 7-9 degrees BTDC if equipped with automatic transmission.

7. If the timing is not as specified, loosen the crank angle sensor lock bolt and turn the crank angle sensor to adjust. After adjustment, tighten the lock bolt to 19 ft. lbs. (25 Nm) and recheck the timing.

8. Remove the jumper wire and the test equipment.

MX-3

1. Apply the parking brake. If equipped with automatic transaxle, place the gearshift lever in **P**. If equipped with manual transaxle, place the gearshift lever in neutral.

2. Start the engine and bring to normal operating temperature. Make sure all electrical loads and the A/C switch are OFF.

3. Connect a timing light and tachometer to the engine according to the manufacturers instructions.

4. Connect a jumper wire between the **TEN** and **GND** terminal of the diagnostic connector.

5. Check the idle speed and adjust, if necessary. The idle speed should be 700-800 rpm if equipped with 1.6L engine or 640-700 rpm if equipped with 1.8L engine.

6. Aim the timing light at the timing scale on the timing belt cover and the timing mark on the crankshaft pulley. The timing should be 9-11 degrees BTDC.

7. If the timing is not as specified, loosen the distributor mounting bolts and turn the distributor to adjust. After adjustment, tighten the bolts to 19 ft. lbs. (25 Nm) and recheck the timing.

8. Remove the jumper wire and the test equipment.

MX-6/626

2.0L AND 2.5L ENGINES

1. Apply the parking brake. If equipped with automatic transaxle, place the gearshift lever in **P**. If equipped with manual transaxle, place the gearshift lever in neutral.

2. Start the engine and bring to normal operating temperature. Make sure all electrical loads and the A/C switch are OFF.

3. Connect a timing light and tachometer to the engine according to the manufacturers instructions.

4. Connect a jumper wire between the **TEN** and **GND** terminal of the diagnostic connector.

5. Check the idle speed and adjust, if necessary. The idle speed should be 650-750 rpm if equipped with 2.0L engine or 600-700 rpm if equipped with 2.5L engine.

6. Aim the timing light at the timing scale on the timing belt cover and the timing mark on the crankshaft pulley. The timing should be 11-13 degrees BTDC on 2.0L engine or 9-11 degrees BTDC on 2.5L engine.

7. If the timing is not as specified, loosen the distributor mounting bolts and turn the distributor to adjust. After adjustment, tighten the bolts to

19 ft. lbs. (25 Nm) and recheck the timing.

8. Remove the jumper wire and the test equipment.

2.2L ENGINE

1. Apply the parking brake. If equipped with automatic transaxle, place the gearshift lever in **P**. If equipped with manual transaxle, place the gearshift lever in neutral.

2. Start the engine and bring to normal operating temperature. Make sure all electrical loads are OFF.

3. If equipped with turbocharger, ground the test connector, located above the left-hand strut tower, with a jumper wire.

4. Connect a timing light to the engine according to the manufacturers instructions.

5. On non-turbocharged engine, disconnect and plug the hoses at the vacuum advance unit.

6. Aim the timing light at the timing scale on the timing belt cover and the timing mark on the crankshaft pulley. The timing should be 6 ± 1 degrees BTDC on non-turbocharged engines or 9 ± 1 degrees BTDC on turbocharged engines.

7. If the timing is not as specified, loosen the distributor mounting bolts and turn the distributor to adjust. After adjustment, tighten the bolts to 19 ft. lbs. (25 Nm) and recheck the timing.

8. Remove the jumper wire or connect the vacuum hoses. Remove the test equipment.

929

1990-91

1. Apply the parking brake. If equipped with automatic transmission, place the gearshift lever in **P**. If equipped with manual transmission, place the gearshift lever in neutral.

2. Start the engine and bring to normal operating temperature. Make sure all electrical loads are OFF.

3. Connect a timing light to the engine according to the manufacturers instructions.

4. Connect a jumper wire between the green, 1-pin test connector, located near the air flow meter and ground.

5. Aim the timing light at the timing scale on the timing belt cover and the timing mark on the crankshaft pulley. The timing should be 15 ± 1 degrees on SOHC engines or 8 ± 1 degrees on DOHC engines.

6. If the timing is not as specified, loosen the distributor mounting bolt and turn the distributor to adjust. Af-

ter adjustment, tighten the bolt to 19 ft. lbs. (25 Nm) and recheck the timing.

7. Remove the jumper wire and all test equipment.

1992-94

1. Apply the parking brake and place the gearshift lever in **P**.

2. Start the engine and bring to normal operating temperature. Make sure all electrical loads and the A/C switch are OFF.

3. Connect a timing light and connect a tachometer to the **IG** terminal of the diagnostic connector.

4. Connect a jumper wire between the **TEN** and **GND** terminals of the diagnostic connector.

5. Check the idle speed and adjust, if necessary. The idle speed should be 680-720 rpm.

6. Aim the timing light at the timing scale on the timing belt cover and the timing mark on the crankshaft pulley. The timing should be 11-13 degrees BTDC.

7. If the timing is not as specified, loosen the distributor mounting bolt and turn the distributor to adjust. After adjustment, tighten the bolt to 19 ft. lbs. (25 Nm) and recheck the timing.

8. Remove the jumper wire and all test equipment.

RX-7

1990-91

1. Apply the parking brake. If equipped with automatic transmission, place the gearshift lever in **P**. If equipped with manual transmission, place the gearshift lever in neutral.

2. Start the engine and bring to normal operating temperature. Make sure all electrical loads are OFF.

3. Connect a tachometer and timing light to the engine according to the manufacturers instructions.

NOTE: Self-powered timing lights may not function. Use a vehicle-powered timing light for this procedure.

4. Connect a jumper wire between the green 1-pin test connector and ground.

5. Check the idle speed and adjust, if necessary.

6. Connect the timing light to the leading spark plug wire on the front rotor and aim the timing light at the pulley and indicator pin. The yellow mark, 5 ± 1 degrees ATDC, on the pulley should align with the pin.

7. If the mark and pin do not align, remove the cap and loosen the crank angle sensor mounting bolt,

then turn the crank angle sensor to make the adjustment.

8. Connect the timing light to the trailing spark plug wire on the front rotor and aim the timing light at the pulley and indicator pin. The red mark, 20 ± 2 degrees ATDC, on the pulley should align with the pin.

9. After adjustment, tighten the crank angle sensor lock bolt to 95 inch lbs. (11 Nm) and recheck the timing.

10. Remove the jumper wire and the test equipment.

1993-94

The ignition timing is set at the factory and requires no adjustment.

Alternator

PRECAUTIONS

• Before disconnecting the battery, obtain the radio theft protection code.
• Do not reverse the battery connections or the alternator and various control computers will be damaged.
• Do not use high voltage testers when testing the rectifiers.

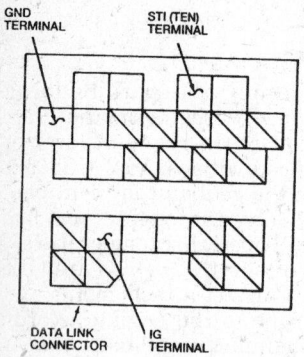

Diagnostic connector terminal locations

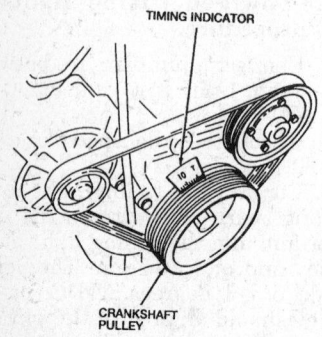

Timing scale location — 2.0L engine shown, others similar

• Do not disconnect the battery or the alternator while the engine is running. Do not start the engine with the alternator disconnected.
• Do not ground or cross any alternator connections while the engine is running.
• Remember that terminal **B** on the alternator is always the battery connection.
• Disconnect the battery cables when charging the battery with a fast charger.
• Disconnect the battery ground terminal when performing any service on electrical components.
• Disconnect the battery and control computers if electric welding is to be done anywhere on the vehicle.

BELT TENSION ADJUSTMENT

323, Protege, 1990-91 929 and RX-7, MX-3 w/1.6L Engines

1. Apply approximately 22 lbs. pressure to the belt at a point midway between the alternator and water pump pulleys on 929 or midway between the drive and alternator pulleys on 323/Protege, MX-3 and RX-7.

2. A new belt should deflect 0.31-0.35 in. (8-9mm) on 323/Protege and MX-3, 0.35-0.39 in. (9-10mm) on 929 or 0.47-0.59 in. (12-15mm) on RX-7.

3. A used belt should deflect 0.35-0.39 in. (9-10mm) on 323/Protege and MX-3, 0.39-0.47 in. (10-12mm) on 929 or 0.55-0.67 in. (14-17mm) on RX-7.

4. If the belt tension is not as specified, loosen the alternator pivot and adjusting bar bolts and lever the alternator until the tension is correct.

5. Tighten the adjusting bar bolt to 19 ft. lbs. (25 Nm) and the pivot bolt to 38 ft. lbs. (52 Nm).

Miata, 1992-94 929, 1993-94 RX-7, MX-6/626 w/2.0L and 2.2L Engines

1. Apply approximately 22 lbs. pressure to the belt at a point midway between the alternator and drive pulleys on Miata, RX-7 and MX-6/626 2.2L engine or midway between the alternator and water pump pulleys on 929 and MX-6/626 2.0L engine.

2. A new belt should deflect as follows:
Miata: 0.31-0.35 in. (8-9mm)
MX-6/626
2.0L engine: 0.26-0.27 in. (6.5-7.0mm)

2.2L engine: 0.24-0.31 in. (6-8mm)
929: 0.39-0.47 in. (10-12mm)
RX-7: 0.24-0.27 in. (6-7mm)

3. A used belt should deflect as follows:
Miata: 0.35-0.39 in. (9-10mm)
MX-6/626
2.0L engine: 0.28-0.35 in. (7-9mm)
2.2L engine: 0.27-0.35 in. (7-9mm)
929: 0.43-0.51 in. (11-13mm)
RX-7: 0.28-0.29 in. (7.0-7.5mm)

4. If the belt tension is not as specified, loosen the alternator pivot and adjusting bar bolt. Turn the adjusting bolt until the belt tension is correct.

5. Tighten the adjusting bar bolt to 19 ft. lbs. (25 Nm) and the pivot bolt to 38 ft. lbs. (52 Nm).

MX-3 1.8L and MX-6/626 2.5L Engines

1. Apply approximately 22 lbs. pressure to the belt at a point midway between the alternator and crankshaft pulleys.

2. The belt should deflect 0.24-0.27 in. (6-7mm) if it is new or 0.28-0.31 in. (7-8mm) if it is used.

3. If the deflection is not as specified, loosen the tensioner pulley locknut and turn the tensioner adjusting bolt until the tension is correct.

4. After adjustment, tighten the tensioner pulley locknut to 33 ft. lbs. (46 Nm).

REMOVAL AND INSTALLATION

Except MX-3 1.8L Engine, 1993-94 MX-6/626 and RX-7

1. Disconnect the negative battery cable. On 1993-94 929, disconnect the positive battery cable and remove the battery and battery tray.

2. On 323/Protege, disconnect the vacuum hose and remove the solenoid bracket, if equipped.

3. On Miata, disconnect the electrical connectors for the power steering pressure switch, water thermoswitch and ISC valve, then remove the air pipe.

4. Remove the alternator drive belt.

5. Label and disconnect the electrical connectors from the alternator.

6. Remove the alternator pivot and adjusting bar bolts and remove the alternator.

7. Installation is the reverse of the removal procedure. Adjust the belt tension.

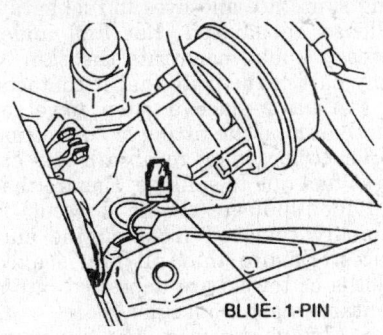

Blue, 1-pin power connector location — Miata

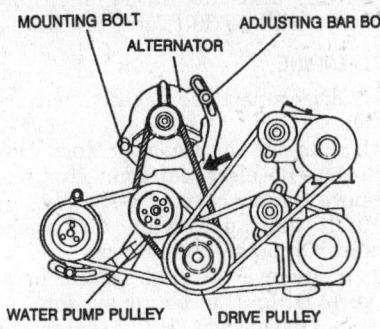

Alternator belt adjustment — 1990-91 RX-7

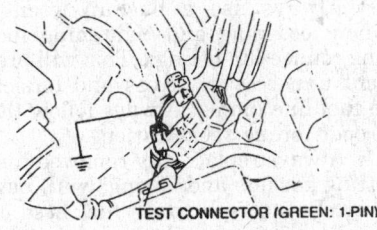

Green, 1-pin test connector location — 1990-91 929

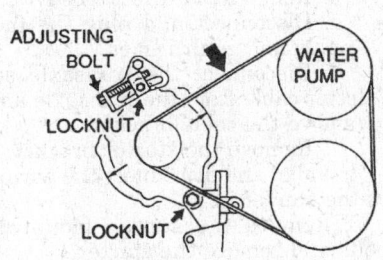

Alternator belt adjustment — 1992-94 929

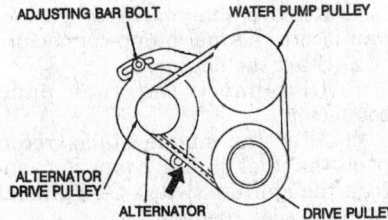

Alternator belt adjustment — 323/Protege and MX-3 with 1.6L engine

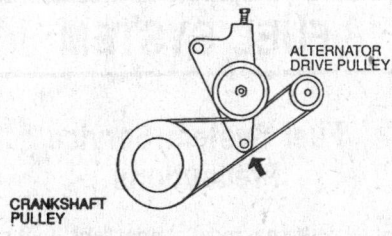

Alternator belt adjustment — MX-3 1.8L and MX-6/626 2.5L engines

MX-3 1.8L Engine

1. Disconnect the negative battery cable.
2. Remove the fresh air duct and the radiator upper bracket.
3. Disconnect the electrical connectors and remove the cooling fan/shroud assemblies.
4. Label and disconnect the electrical connectors from the alternator.
5. Raise and safely support the vehicle. Remove the engine undercover.
6. Remove the belt tensioner and remove the alternator drive belt.

7. Remove the alternator mounting bolts and remove the alternator.
8. Installation is the reverse of the removal procedure. Adjust the belt tension.

1993-94 MX-6/626

2.0L ENGINE

1. Disconnect the negative battery cable.
2. Label and disconnect the electrical connectors from the alternator.

3. Raise and safely support the vehicle.
4. Remove the transverse member.
5. Remove the front exhaust pipe.
6. Loosen the belt tension and remove the accessory drive belt.
7. Remove the pivot and adjusting bar bolts and remove the alternator.
8. Installation is the reverse of the removal procedure. Install the exhaust pipe, using new gaskets and tighten the nuts to 38 ft. lbs. (52 Nm). Tighten the transverse member bolts to 96 ft. lbs. (131 Nm). Adjust the belt tension.

2.5L ENGINE

1. Disconnect the negative battery cable.
2. Remove the fresh air duct.
3. Label and disconnect the electrical connectors from the alternator.
4. Raise and safely support the vehicle. Remove the engine undercover.
5. Remove the belt tensioner and remove the alternator drive belt.
6. Remove the A/C compressor mounting bolts and secure the compressor aside with mechanics wire, without disconnecting the refrigerant lines.
7. Remove the alternator mounting bolts and remove the alternator.
8. Installation is the reverse of the removal procedure. Tighten the alternator upper bracket bolt to 18 ft. lbs. (25 Nm) and the pivot bolt to 38 ft. lbs. (51 Nm). Tighten the A/C compressor bolts to 26 ft. lbs. (35 Nm). Adjust the belt tension.

1993-94 RX-7

1. Disconnect the negative battery cable. Partially drain the cooling system.
2. Remove the air intake hose and air relief hose.
3. Disconnect the accelerator cable.
4. Disconnect the vacuum hoses and remove the pressure chamber.
5. Remove the turbocharger-to-intercooler pipe and bracket.
6. Label and disconnect the electrical connectors from the alternator.
7. Disconnect the air pump hoses and remove the air pump.
8. Loosen the tension and remove the alternator drive belt. Remove the coolant hose at the rear of the water pump.
9. Remove the alternator mounting bolts and remove the alternator.
10. Installation is the reverse of the removal procedure. Adjust the belt tension.

Starter

REMOVAL AND INSTALLATION

Except MX-3 1.8L Engine and 1993-94 MX-6/626

1. Disconnect the negative battery cable. On 323/Protege and MX-3 1.6L engine, disconnect the positive battery cable and remove the battery and battery tray.
2. Raise and safely support the vehicle. Remove the engine undercover.
3. On 323/Protege, MX-3 with 1.6L engine and MX-6/626 2.2L engine, remove the intake manifold bracket.
4. Remove the starter bracket, if equipped.
5. Label and disconnect the wiring from the starter.
6. Remove the starter mounting bolts and remove the starter.
7. Installation is the reverse of the removal procedure. Tighten the starter mounting bolts to 34 ft. lbs. (46 Nm).

MX-3 1.8L Engine

1. Disconnect the negative battery cable.
2. Remove the nuts and the upper strut bar from between the strut towers.
3. Remove the intake air hose from between the air cleaner and throttle body.
4. Label and disconnect the wiring from the starter.
5. Remove the mounting bolts and remove the starter.
6. Installation is the reverse of the removal procedure. Tighten the starter mounting bolts to 38 ft. lbs. (52 Nm).

1993-94 MX-6/626

2.0L ENGINE

1. Disconnect the negative battery cable.
2. Remove the fresh air duct and resonance chamber.
3. Label and disconnect the electrical connectors and remove the air cleaner assembly.
4. Remove the intake manifold bracket.
5. Label and disconnect the wiring at the starter.
6. Remove the starter mounting bolts and remove the starter.
7. Installation is the reverse of the removal procedure. Tighten the starter mounting bolts to 33 ft. lbs.

(46 Nm) and the intake manifold bracket bolts to 38 ft. lbs. (51 Nm).

2.5L ENGINE

1. Disconnect the negative battery cable.
2. Remove the fresh air duct. Disconnect the electrical connector and remove the air cleaner assembly.
3. If equipped with automatic transaxle, proceed as follows:
   a. Relieve the fuel system pressure. Drain the cooling system.
   b. Disconnect the accelerator cable from the throttle body. Label and disconnect the electrical connectors, vacuum hoses and coolant hoses from the throttle body.
   c. Remove the throttle body.
   d. Disconnect and plug the fuel supply and return lines.
   e. Disconnect the transaxle selector cable from the transaxle and remove the cable bracket.
   f. Remove the starter bracket.
4. Label and disconnect the wiring at the starter.
5. Remove the starter mounting bolts and remove the starter.
6. Installation is the reverse of the removal procedure. Tighten the starter mounting bolts to 38 ft. lbs. (51 Nm).

FUEL SYSTEM

Fuel System Service Precautions

Safety is the most important factor when performing not only fuel system maintenance, but any type of maintenance. Failure to conduct maintenance and repairs in a safe manner may result in serious personal injury or death. Maintenance and testing of the vehicle's fuel system components can be accomplished safely and effectively by adhering to the following rules and guidelines.

• To reduce the possibility of fire and personal injury, always disconnect the negative battery cable unless the repair or test procedure requires that battery voltage be applied.

• Always relieve the fuel system pressure prior to disconnecting any fuel system component (injector, fuel rail, pressure regulator, etc.), fitting or fuel line connection. Exercise extreme caution whenever relieving fuel system pressure to avoid expos-

ing skin, face and eyes to fuel spray. Please be advised that fuel under pressure may penetrate the skin or any part of the body that it contacts.

• Always place a shop towel or cloth around the fitting or connection prior to loosening to absorb any excess fuel due to spillage. Ensure that all fuel spillage (should it occur) is quickly removed from engine surfaces. Ensure that all fuel soaked cloths or towels are deposited into a suitable waste container.

• Always keep a dry chemical (Class B) fire extinguisher near the work area.

• Do not allow fuel spray or fuel vapors to come into contact with a spark or open flame.

• Always use a backup wrench when loosening and tightening fuel line connection fittings. This will prevent unnecessary stress and torsion to fuel line piping. Always follow the proper torque specifications.

• Always replace any removed fuel fitting gaskets and O-rings with new ones. Do not substitute fuel hose or equivalent where fuel pipe is installed.

RELIEVING FUEL SYSTEM PRESSURE

323, Protege and MX-3

1. Remove the rear seat cushion and locate the fuel pump connector.
2. Start the engine.
3. Disconnect the fuel pump connector.
4. After the engine stalls, reconnect the fuel pump connector and turn the ignition switch **OFF**. Install the rear seat cushion.

Miata

1. Start the engine.
2. Disconnect the circuit opening relay connector, located under the left side of the instrument panel.
3. After the engine stalls, reconnect the circuit opening relay and turn the ignition switch **OFF**.

MX-6/626

2.0L AND 2.5L ENGINES

1. Start the engine.
2. Remove the fuel pump relay from the relay box, located in the left side of the engine compartment.
3. After the engine stalls, reinstall the relay and turn the ignition switch **OFF**.

2.2L ENGINE

1. Start the engine.

2. Disconnect the circuit opening relay connector, located under the left side of the instrument panel.

3. After the engine stalls, reconnect the circuit opening relay and turn the ignition switch **OFF**.

929

1990-91

1. Start the engine.

2. Disconnect the fuel pump connector, located in the right-hand side of the trunk.

3. After the engine stalls, reconnect the fuel pump connector and turn the ignition switch **OFF**.

1992-94

1. Start the engine.

2. Remove the circuit opening relay connector from the relay box, located in the right side of the engine compartment.

3. After the engine stalls, reinstall the relay connector and turn the ignition switch **OFF**.

RX-7

1990-91

1. Raise the hatch and lift the floor mat. Locate the fuel pump connector.

2. Start the engine.

3. Disconnect the fuel pump connector.

4. After the engine stalls, reconnect the fuel pump connector and turn the ignition switch **OFF**. Reinstall the mat and lower the hatch.

1993-94

1. Start the engine.

2. Remove the circuit opening relay from the relay box, located in the left side of the engine compartment.

3. After the engine stalls, reinstall the relay and turn the ignition switch **OFF**.

Fuel Tank

REMOVAL AND INSTALLATION

323, Protege and MX-3

1. Remove the rear seat cushion. Relieve the fuel system pressure and remove the fuel pump cover. Disconnect the negative battery cable.

2. Disconnect the fuel supply and return hose.

3. Raise and safely support the vehicle. Drain the fuel tank into a suitable container.

4. If equipped with 4WD, proceed as follows:

    a. Remove the rear exhaust pipe and muffler assembly.

    b. Mark the position of the driveshaft on the flanges and remove the driveshaft.

    c. Disconnect the electrical connector and fuel lines and remove the transfer pump.

5. Support the fuel tank with a jack. Label and disconnect the evaporative hoses and fuel filler hose.

6. Remove the insulator at the front of the tank.

7. Remove the mounting bolts from the retaining straps and let the straps swing forward. Remove the fuel tank.

To install:

8. Install the tank and mounting bolts to the retaining straps.

9. Install the insulator at the front of the tank.

10. Connect the evaporative hoses and fuel filler hose.

11. If equipped with 4WD, proceed as follows:

    a. Install the transfer pump connect the electrical connectors.

    b. Install the driveshaft.

    c. Install the rear exhaust pipe and muffler assembly.

12. Refill the fuel tank.

13. Install the fuel pump cover and rear seat cushion. Connect the negative battery cable, start the engine and check for leaks.

Miata

1. Relieve the fuel system pressure and disconnect the negative battery cable.

2. Raise and safely support the vehicle. Drain the fuel tank into a suitable container.

3. Remove the rear exhaust pipe and muffler assembly.

4. Remove the power plant frame member as follows:

    a. Mark the position of the driveshaft on the axle flange and remove the driveshaft.

    b. Disconnect the wire harness from the power plant frame member.

    c. Remove the bracket from between the frame member and transmission.

    d. Remove the differential side bolts and pry out the spacer from between the bottom of the differential and the frame member.

    e. Remove the differential mounting spacer from the underside of the differential.

    f. Insert a M14 **x** 1.5 bolt through the bottom of the frame

member and into the sleeve in the differential. Twist and pull the bolt downward.

    g. Install a M6 **x** 1 bolt into the hole in the side of the sleeve block to hold the sleeve, then remove the M14 **x** 1.5 bolt.

    h. Remove the M6 **x** 1 bolt.

    i. Remove the transmission side bolts and remove the power plant frame member.

NOTE: Do not remove the spacers from the top rear of the power plant frame member. If the are removed, the entire frame member must be replaced.

5. Label and disconnect the fuel filler hoses, fuel lines and evaporative hoses. Disconnect the fuel pump connector.

6. Remove the fuel filter cover and remove the fuel filter bolts or nuts. Remove the fuel filter with the hoses attached.

7. Remove the brake line junction nuts and remove the brake line junction with the line and hose still connected.

8. Remove the battery cable clamp and remove the battery cable.

9. Support the rear crossmember with a jack and remove the rear crossmember mounting bolts and nuts.

10. Lower the rear crossmember assembly, being careful not to damage the brake hose, brake line or fuel lines.

11. Support the fuel tank with a jack and remove the mounting bolts. Lower the fuel tank from the vehicle.

To install:

12. Raise the fuel tank into position and install the mounting bolts. Tighten to 22 ft. lbs. (30 Nm).

13. Install the rear crossmember assembly and tighten the bolts/nuts to 86 ft. lbs. (117 Nm).

14. Install the battery cable with the clamp.

15. Install the brake line junction and secure with the nuts.

16. Install the fuel filter and tighten the nuts/bolts to 95 inch lbs. (11 Nm). Install the fuel filter cover.

17. Connect the fuel pump connector, evaporative hoses, fuel lines and fuel filler hoses.

18. Install the power plant frame as follows:

    a. Install the differential mounting spacer to the underside of the differential and tighten the bolts to 38 ft. lbs. (52 Nm).

    b. Support the transmission with a jack so it is level.

    c. Position the power plant frame member and snugly tighten

the transmission side bolts by hand.

d. Make sure the sleeve is installed into the block.

e. Install the spacer and bolts, then snugly tighten them. The reamer bolt is installed in the forward hole.

f. Snugly install the power plant frame bracket.

g. Tighten the transmission side bolts to 91 ft. lbs. (124 Nm), then tighten the differential side bolts to the same specification.

h. Tighten the power plant frame bracket-to-frame member bolt to 91 ft. lbs. (124 Nm) and the power plant frame bracket-to-transmission bolts to 40 ft. lbs. (54 Nm).

i. Measure the distance between the bottom of the power plant frame member and a straightedge laid between the floor pan channels. The distance should be 2.403-2.797 in. (61-71mm). If the distance is not as specified, reposition the power plant frame member at the transmission.

j. Install the driveshaft, aligning the marks that were made during removal. Tighten the bolts to 22 ft. lbs. (30 Nm).

k. Connect the wire harness to the power plant frame member.

19. Install the exhaust pipe/muffler assembly, using a new gasket. Tighten the nuts to 41 ft. lbs. (55 Nm).

20. Lower the vehicle. Fill the tank and check for leaks. Start the engine and check for leaks at all fuel line connections.

MX-6/626

2.0L AND 2.5L ENGINES

1. Relieve the fuel system pressure and disconnect the negative battery cable.

2. Raise and safely support the vehicle. Drain the fuel tank into a suitable container.

3. Remove the exhaust pipe from between the catalytic converter and muffler. Remove the exhaust pipe insulator.

4. Disconnect the fuel pump connector. Label and disconnect the fuel and evaporative hoses.

5. Support the fuel tank with a jack.

6. Remove the fuel tank straps and lower the tank from the vehicle.

7. Installation is the reverse of the removal procedure. Tighten the tank strap bolts to 45 ft. lbs. (61 Nm). Install the exhaust pipe, using new gasket tighten the pipe-to-converter nuts

to 65 ft. lbs. (89 Nm) and the pipe-to-muffler nuts to 38 ft. lbs. (51 Nm). Fill the tank with fuel and check for leaks. Start the engine and check for leaks at all fuel line connections.

2.2L ENGINE

1. Relieve the fuel system pressure and disconnect the negative battery cable.

2. Remove the rear seat cushion and disconnect the electrical connectors and fuel lines.

3. Raise and safely support the vehicle. Drain the fuel from the tank into a suitable container.

4. Label and disconnect the evaporative hoses, fuel filler hose and breather hose.

5. Support the fuel tank with a jack. Remove the bolts from the fuel tank straps and let the straps swing forward.

6. Lower the fuel tank from the vehicle.

7. Installation is the reverse of the removal procedure. Tighten the tank strap bolts to 45 ft. lbs. (61 Nm). Fill the tank and check for leaks. Start the engine and check for leaks at all fuel line connections.

929

1990-91

1. Relieve the fuel system pressure and disconnect the negative battery cable.

2. Disconnect the fuel pump connector, located in the right-hand side of the trunk.

3. Lift the trunk mat and remove the fuel pump cover. Label and disconnect the fuel lines and evaporative hoses.

4. Raise and safely support the vehicle. Drain the fuel from the tank into a suitable container.

5. Support the fuel tank with a jack. Remove the fuel pump strap bolts and lower the tank from the vehicle.

6. Installation is the reverse of the removal procedure. Tighten the strap bolts to 44 ft. lbs. (61 Nm). Fill the tank with fuel and check for leaks before starting the engine. Start the engine and check for leaks at all fuel line connections.

1992-94

1. Relieve the fuel system pressure and disconnect the negative battery cable.

2. Remove the amplifier and CD changer, if equipped.

3. Lift the rear floor mat and remove the access plate. Disconnect the fuel pump connector and fuel hoses.

4. Raise and safely support the vehicle. Remove the fuel filler hose and breather hose from the fuel tank.

5. Remove the rear crossmember/axle assembly as follows:

a. Remove the wheel and tire assemblies.

b. Remove the rear lower lateral link.

c. Remove the exhaust pipe.

d. Disconnect the parking brake cables from the calipers and routing clamps.

e. Remove the brake calipers and suspend them by the coil springs.

f. Mark the position of the driveshaft on the axle flange and remove the driveshaft.

g. Loosen the upper and lower trailing link ball joint nuts. Use a suitable tool to separate the ball joints from the knuckle, then remove the nuts.

h. Remove the lower strut bolts.

i. Support the crossmember and axle assembly with a jack. Remove the nuts and lower the crossmember/axle assembly from the vehicle.

6. Label and disconnect the fuel hoses and evaporative hoses.

7. Support the fuel tank with a jack. Remove the fuel tank bracket and lower the fuel tank from the vehicle.

To install:

8. Raise the fuel tank into position and install the fuel tank bracket. Tighten the bolts to 45 ft. lbs. (61 Nm).

9. Connect the fuel hoses and evaporative hoses.

10. Install the crossmember/axle assembly as follows:

a. Raise the crossmember/axle assembly into position and install the nuts. Tighten to 86 ft. lbs. (117 Nm).

b. Install the lower strut bolts and tighten to 69 ft. lbs. (93 Nm).

c. Connect the upper and lower trailing links to the knuckles. Install the lower ball joint nuts and tighten to 116 ft. lbs. (157 Nm). Install the upper ball joint nuts and tighten to 42 ft. lbs. (57 Nm). Install new cotter pins.

d. Install the brake calipers and connect the parking brake cables.

e. Install the exhaust pipe and the rear lower lateral link.

f. Install the wheel and tire assemblies.

11. Install the fuel filler hose and breather hose. Lower the vehicle.

12. Connect the fuel lines and the fuel pump connector. Install the access plate and the floor mat.

13. Install the CD changer and amplifier, if equipped.

14. Fill the tank with fuel and check for leaks, before starting the engine. Connect the negative battery cable, start the engine and check for leaks at all fuel line connections.

RX-7

1990-91

1. Relieve the fuel system pressure and disconnect the negative battery cable.

2. Remove the fuel pump.

3. Raise and safely support the vehicle. Drain the fuel from the tank into a suitable container.

4. Label and disconnect the fuel filler hose, breather hose and evaporative hoses from the fuel tank.

5. Support the tank with a jack. Remove the fuel tank strap bolts and the fuel tank.

6. Installation is the reverse of the removal procedure. Fill the tank with fuel and check for leaks, before starting the engine. Start the engine and check for leaks at all fuel line connections.

1993-94

1. Relieve the fuel system pressure and disconnect the negative battery cable.

2. Lift the trunk carpet and disconnect the fuel pump connector. Remove the access cover.

3. Disconnect the fuel lines at the fuel pump.

4. Raise and safely support the vehicle. Drain the fuel from the tank into a suitable container.

5. Label and disconnect the fuel filler hose, breather hose and evaporative hoses.

6. Remove the tank shields.

7. Support the fuel tank with a jack. Remove the tank strap bolts and lower the fuel tank from the vehicle.

8. Installation is the reverse of the removal procedure. Tighten the tank strap bolts to 45 ft. lbs. (61 Nm). Fill the tank with fuel and check for leaks before starting the engine. Start the engine and check for leaks at all fuel line connections.

Fuel Filter

REMOVAL AND INSTALLATION

Except Miata, 1992-94 929 and 1993 RX-7

1. Relieve the fuel system pressure and disconnect the negative battery cable.

2. On 1993-94 MX-6/626 with 2.5L engine, remove the air cleaner assembly and position the wire harness aside.

3. Disconnect the fuel hoses from the fuel filter.

4. Remove the fuel filter fasteners and remove the fuel filter. On some applications, the filter is removed with the filter bracket.

5. Installation is the reverse of the removal procedure. Make sure the fuel filter is installed in the proper flow direction.

Miata, 1992-94 929 and 1993-94 RX-7

1. Relieve the fuel system pressure and disconnect the negative battery cable.

2. Raise and safely support the vehicle. The fuel filter is located at the rear of the vehicle, next to the fuel tank.

3. On RX-7, remove the splash shield. On Miata, remove the fuel filter cover.

4. Disconnect the fuel lines from the fuel filter.

5. Remove the filter mounting bolts or nuts and remove the fuel filter.

6. Installation is the reverse of the removal procedure. Make sure the fuel filter is installed in the proper flow direction.

Electric Fuel Pump

PRESSURE TESTING

1. Relieve the fuel system pressure and disconnect the negative battery cable.

2. Connect a suitable fuel pressure gauge to the fuel filter outlet or to the fuel supply line. Plug the other outlet of the fuel pressure test gauge.

3. On all except 1990-92 MX-6/626 and 1990-91 929 and RX-7, connect a jumper wire between the **FP** and **GND** terminals of the data link connector, located in the engine compartment near the battery.

4. On 1990-92 MX-6/626 and 1990-91 929 and RX-7, connect the terminals of the yellow, 2-pin test connector with a jumper wire.

5. Connect the negative battery cable and turn the ignition **ON**.

6. Read the fuel pump pressure on the gauge. Fuel pressure should be as follows:

323/Protege
1990-91: 64-85 psi.
1992-94: 64-92 psi.
Miata: 64-85 psi.
MX-3: 64-92 psi.
MX-6/626
1990-92: 64-85 psi.
1993-94
2.0L engine: 64-92 psi.
2.5L engine: 72-92 psi.
929
1990-91: 64-85 psi.
1992-94: 71-92 psi.
RX-7
1990-91: 71-92 psi.
1993-94: 71-107 psi.

REMOVAL AND INSTALLATION

323, Protege and 1990-92 MX-6/626

1. Relieve the fuel sustem pressure and disconnect the negative battery cable.

2. Remove the rear seat cushion and remove the fuel pump access cover.

3. Disconnect the electrical connector and fuel lines at the fuel pump.

4. Remove the screws and remove the fuel pump/sending unit assembly from the fuel tank.

5. If necessary, remove the fuel pump from the tank gauge sending unit.

6. Installation is the reverse of the removal procedure. Use a new seal rubber.

Miata, 929 and RX-7

1. Relieve the fuel sustem pressure and disconnect the negative battery cable.

2. Open the trunk or hatch and lift the carpet or mat. On 1992-94 929, remove the amplifier and CD changer, if equipped.

3. Remove the fuel pump access cover.

4. Disconnect the fuel pump connector and the fuel lines.

5. Remove the screws and remove the fuel pump/sending unit assembly from the fuel tank.

6. If necessary, remove the fuel pump from the tank gauge sending unit.

7. Installation is the reverse of the removal procedure. Use a new seal rubber.

1993-94 MX-6/626

1. Relieve the fuel sustem pressure and disconnect the negative battery cable.

2. Remove the fuel tank and place it on a work bench.

3. Clean any dirt from the tank in the area around the fuel pump.

4. Disconnect the fuel lines from the pump.

5. Rotate the fuel pump retaining ring counterclockwise and remove it.

6. Remove the fuel pump/sending unit assembly from the fuel tank.

7. If necessary, remove the fuel pump from the tank gauge sending unit.

8. Installation is the reverse of the removal procedure. Use a new pump gasket and rotate the retaining ring clockwise until the flange touches the stopper.

Fuel Injector

REMOVAL AND INSTALLATION

323, Protege, Miata, MX-3 1.6L and MX-6/626 2.0L and 2.2L Engines

1. Relieve the fuel system pressure and disconnect the negative battery cable.

2. On MX-6/626 2.2L engine, remove the upper intake manifold as follows:

   a. Disconnect the air intake hose from the throttle body.

   b. Disconnect the accelerator cable.

   c. Label and disconnect the vacuum hoses and electrical connectors from the throttle body and upper intake manifold.

   d. Remove the mounting bolts and remove the upper intake manifold.

3. On Miata, drain the cooling system, disconnect the hoses and remove the air valve from the upper intake manifold.

4. Disconnect the vacuum hose from the fuel pressure regulator.

5. Disconnect and plug the fuel supply and return lines.

6. Tag and disconnect the electrical connectors from the injectors.

7. Remove the fuel rail mounting bolts and remove the fuel rail with the injectors.

To install:

8. Lubricate new O-rings with clean engine oil and install on the injectors.

9. Install new insulators and install the injectors on the intake manifold.

10. Install the grommets on the injectors and install the fuel rail. Tighten the fuel rail bolts to 19 ft. lbs. (25 Nm).

11. Connect the fuel supply and return lines. Connect the vacuum hose to the fuel pressure regulator.

12. On Miata, install the air valve using a new gasket. Tighten the bolts to 69 inch lbs. (7.8 Nm). Connect the coolant hoses.

13. Install the upper intake manifold, if removed, using a new gasket. Tighten the bolts to 19 ft. lbs. (25 Nm).

14. Connect the negative battery cable and turn the ignition **ON**, to pressurize the fuel system. Check for leaks and correct, as necessary. Start the engine and check for leaks.

MX-3 1.8L and MX-6/626 2.5L Engines

1. Relieve the fuel system pressure and disconnect the negative battery cable.

2. On MX-3, remove the air intake hose. On MX-6/626, remove the air cleaner assembly.

3. Disconnect the electrical connectors from both injector injector banks.

4. Disconnect and plug the fuel supply and return lines. Disconnect the vacuum hose from the pressure regulator.

5. Disconnect the left and right fuel distributors. Remove the injector insulators.

6. Remove the accumulated connectors from the fuel distributors.

7. Remove the spacers and remove the injectors from the fuel distributor.

To install:

8. Make sure the injector holders in the fuel distributors are clean.

9. Lubricate new O-rings with clean engine oil and install them on the injectors. Install the injector into the distributor using a twisting motion. Fit the injector into the notch in the distributor.

10. Install the spacers and the accumulated connector. Tighten the connector retaining screws to 31 inch lbs. (3.5 Nm).

11. Install new insulators and the fuel distributors and tighten the bolts to 18 inch lbs. (25 Nm).

12. Connect the fuel supply and return lines. Connect the pressure regulator vacuum hose.

13. Connect the electrical connectors to the accumulated connectors.

14. Install the air cleaner housing or air hose, as necessary.

15. Connect the negative battery cable and turn the ignition **ON**, to pressurize the fuel system. Check for leaks and correct, as necessary. Start the engine and check for leaks.

929

SOHC ENGINE

1. Properly relieve the fuel system pressure.

2. Disconnect the negative battery cable and drain the cooling system.

3. Disconnect the electrical connector from the air flow meter and remove the air cleaner assembly and air ducts.

4. Disconnect the electrical connector from the air bypass valve. Label and disconnect the coolant hoses from the air bypass valve. Remove the air bypass valve.

5. Disconnect the throttle position sensor and accelerator cable from the throttle body. Remove the throttle body.

6. Label and disconnect the vacuum hoses, EGR pipe, EGR position sensor connector, coolant hose and ground wire from the air intake pipe. Remove the wiring bracket.

7. Remove the air intake pipe from the rear of the upper intake manifold.

8. Mark the position of the intake manifold runners connecting the upper and lower intake manifolds, so they can be reinstalled in their original locations. Remove the nuts and remove the intake manifold runners.

9. Label and disconnect the intake air thermosensor connector, vacuum hoses and ground wires from the upper intake manifold. Remove the upper intake manifold.

10. Label and disconnect the electrical connectors from the injectors.

11. Disconnect and plug the fuel supply and return lines. Disconnect the vacuum hose.

12. Remove the fuel rails. Remove the injectors, grommets and insulators.

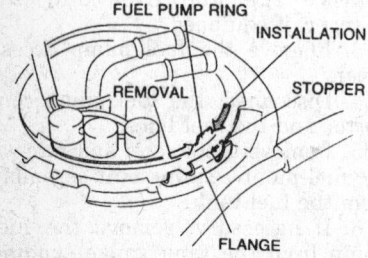

Fuel pump removal and Installation — 1993-94 MX-6/626

To install:

13. Lubricate new O-rings with clean engine oil and install them on the injectors. Install the injectors with the insulators on the lower intake manifold.

14. Install the fuel rails and tighten the retaining nuts to 19 ft. lbs. (25 Nm).

15. Connect the fuel supply and return lines and connect the vacuum hose. Connect the electrical connectors to the injectors.

16. Install a new drain hole O-ring on the lower intake manifold before installing the upper intake manifold. Install the upper intake manifold to the lower intake manifold and tighten the nuts to 19 ft. lbs. (25 Nm).

17. Connect the ground wires, vacuum hoses and intake air thermosensor connector to the upper intake manifold.

18. Install new O-rings on the intake manifold runners. Using new gaskets, install the runners, in their original locations, on the upper and lower intake manifolds. Tighten the nuts to 19 ft. lbs. (25 Nm).

19. Using a new gasket, install the air intake pipe at the rear of the upper intake manifold. Tighten the nuts to 19 ft. lbs. (25 Nm). Install the wiring bracket.

20. Connect the EGR pipe, EGR position sensor, ground wires, vacuum and coolant hoses to the air intake pipe.

21. Install the throttle body, using a new gasket. Tighten the nuts to 19 ft. lbs. (25 Nm).

22. Connect the throttle position sensor electrical connector and accelerator cable to the throttle body.

23. Install the air bypass valve and tighten the retaining bolt to 22 ft. lbs. (30 Nm). Connect the electrical connector and coolant hoses.

24. Install the air cleaner assembly and air ducts. Connect the air flow meter electrical connector.

25. Connect the negative battery cable and turn the ignition **ON** to pressurize the fuel system. Check for leaks.

26. Fill and bleed the cooling system.

27. Start the engine and bring to normal operating temperature. Check for leaks. Check the idle speed.

DOHC ENGINE

1. Properly relieve the fuel system pressure.

2. Disconnect the negative battery cable and drain the cooling system.

3. Disconnect the air intake hose from the throttle body. If necessary, disconnect the air flow meter electrical connector and remove the air cleaner assembly and air ducts.

4. Disconnect the accelerator cable. Disconnect and plug the fuel lines.

5. On 1990-91 vehicles, remove the cover from the upper intake manifold.

6. Label and disconnect the necessary hoses and electrical connectors from the throttle body. On 1990-91 vehicles, remove the cold start injector from the throttle body, leaving the fuel line connected. Remove the throttle body.

7. On 1992-94 vehicles, disconnect the electrical connector, water hoses and air hose from the air bypass valve. Remove the retaining bolts/nuts and remove the air bypass valve. Remove the air intake pipe from the upper intake manifold.

8. Label and disconnect the necessary hoses and electrical connectors from the upper intake manifold. Remove the upper intake manifold retaining bolts and the upper intake manifold.

9. Label and disconnect the electrical connectors from the fuel injectors.

10. On 1990-91 vehicles, disconnect the vacuum hose from the fuel pressure regulator and remove the fuel rail retaining nuts. Remove the fuel rail with the injectors.

11. On 1992-94 vehicles, remove the retaining bolts and cap from the top of the injector. Remove the injector by grasping the plastic part of the injector and twisting out. Disconnect the vacuum hose from the fuel pressure regulator and remove the fuel rail.

To install:

12. On 1990-91 vehicles, apply clean engine oil to new injector O-rings and install on the injectors. Install the injectors on the intake manifold and retain with the fuel rail. Tighten the fuel rail nuts to 19 ft. lbs. (25 Nm).

13. On 1992-94 vehicles, install the fuel rail. Apply a small amount of clean engine oil to new injector O-rings and install on the injectors. Install the injectors in the fuel rail using a turning motion, to prevent damaging the O-rings. Install the injector retainer caps and tighten the screws to 30 inch lbs. (3.4 Nm).

14. Connect the injector electrical connectors and connect the vacuum hose to the fuel pressure regulator. Connect the fuel lines.

15. Using a new gasket, install the upper intake manifold on the lower intake manifold. Tighten the mounting bolts to 19 ft. lbs. (25 Nm).

16. Connect the electrical connectors and hoses to the upper intake manifold.

17. On 1992-94 vehicles, install the air intake pipe on the upper intake manifold using a new gasket, and tighten the mounting bolts to 17 ft. lbs. (23 Nm). Install the air bypass valve and tighten the nuts to 19 ft. lbs. (25 Nm). Connect the coolant hoses, air hose and electrical connector to the air bypass valve.

18. Install the throttle body, using a new gasket. Tighten the nuts to 19 ft. lbs. (25 Nm). On 1990-91 vehicles, install the cold start injector on the throttle body using a new gasket. Tighten to 8 ft. lbs. (11 Nm). Connect the hoses and electrical connectors to the throttle body.

19. On 1990-91 vehicles, install the cover on the upper intake manifold. Connect the accelerator cable.

20. If removed, install the air cleaner and air ducts. Connect the air intake to the throttle body.

21. Connect the negative battery cable and turn the ignition **ON** to pressurize the fuel system. Check for leaks.

22. Fill and bleed the cooling system.

23. Start the engine and bring to normal operating temperature. Check for leaks. Check the idle speed.

RX-7

1990-91

1. Relieve the fuel system pressure and disconnect the negative battery cable. Drain the cooling system.

2. Remove the fresh air duct, air cleaner assembly and air intake hose. If equipped with turbocharger, remove the intercooler and oil filler tube.

3. Disconnect the accelerator cable and, if equipped, cruise control cable.

4. Label and disconnect the electrical connectors, vacuum hoses, coolant hoses and air hoses from the throttle body and dynamic chamber.

5. Remove the throttle body/dynamic chamber assembly.

6. Disconnect and plug the fuel lines at the secondary fuel rail. Disconnect the electrical connectors from the secondary injectors.

7. Remove the secondary fuel rail bolts and remove the secondary fuel rail, injectors, injector insulators and air bleed sockets.

8. On non-turbocharged vehicles, label and disconnect the vacuum hoses from the extension manifold. Remove the extension manifold.

9. Disconnect and plug the fuel lines at the primary fuel rail. Disconnect the electrical connectors from the primary injectors.

10. Remove the primary fuel rail bolts and remove the primary fuel rail, injectors, injector insulators, air bleed sockets and mixing plate.

To install:

11. Apply clean engine oil to new O-rings and install on the injectors.

12. Align the tabs of the mixing plate with the notches in the intermediate housing. Install the air bleed sockets and insulators, align the primary injectors and install the primary fuel rail. Tighten the fuel rail bolts to 19 ft. lbs. (25 Nm).

13. Connect the fuel lines at the primary fuel rail and connect the electrical connectors to the primary injectors.

14. On non-turbocharged engines, install the extension manifold, using a new gasket and tighten the bolts to 19 ft. lbs. (25 Nm). Connect the vacuum hoses to the extension manifold.

15. Install the air bleed sockets and insulators. Align the secondary injectors and install the secondary fuel rail. Tighten the fuel rail bolts to 19 ft. lbs. (25 Nm).

16. Connect the fuel lines at the secondary fuel rail and connect the electrical connectors to the secondary injectors.

17. Install the throttle body/dynamic chamber assembly, using a new gasket and tighten the nuts/bolts to 19 ft. lbs. (25 Nm).

18. Connect the accelerator and if equipped, cruise control cables. Connect the electrical connectors, vacuum hoses, coolant hoses and air hoses.

19. If equipped with turbocharger, install the oil filler tube and the intercooler.

20. Install the air intake duct, air cleaner assembly and fresh air duct.

21. Connect the negative battery cable, turn the ignition key **ON** to pressurize the system and check for leaks. Correct as necessary.

22. Fill and bleed the cooling system. Start the engine and check for leaks.

1993-94

1. Relieve the fuel system pressure and disconnect the negative battery cable. Drain the cooling system.

2. Remove the fresh air duct and disconnect the accelerator cable.

3. Disconnect the hoses and remove the air cleaner assembly. Remove the air cleaner-to-turbocharger hoses.

4. Disconnect the vacuum hoses and remove the pressure chamber.

5. Remove the intercooler hoses and the turbocharger-to-intercooler pipe and intercooler-to-throttle body pipe.

6. Label and disconnect the electrical connectors, vacuum and coolant hoses from the throttle body and extension manifold.

7. Remove the mounting bolts/nuts and remove the throttle body/extension manifold assembly.

8. Label and disconnect the fuel injector electrical connectors. Disconnect and plug the fuel lines.

9. Remove the primary and secondary fuel distributor assemblies.

10. Remove the screws and remove the injector covers. Remove the injectors, insulators and air bleed sockets from the fuel distributors.

To install:

11. Apply clean engine oil to new O-rings and install on the injectors. Install the injectors into the fuel distributors with a twisting motion. Install the injector caps and tighten the screws to 30 inch lbs. (3.5 Nm).

12. Align the tabs of the air bleed socket with the notches in the intermediate housing. Install the air bleed

socket, insulators and fuel distributor assemblies. Tighten the fuel distributor mounting bolts to 19 ft. lbs. (25 Nm).

13. Connect the fuel lines and the injector connectors.

14. Install the throttle body/extension manifold assembly, using a new gasket, and tighten the nuts/bolts to 19 ft. lbs. (25 Nm).

15. Connect the coolant and vacuum hoses and the electrical connectors to the throttle body and extension manifold.

16. Install the intercooler-to-throttle body and turbocharger-to-intercooler pipes and the intercooler connecting hoses.

17. Install the pressure chamber and connect the vacuum hoses.

18. Connect the accelerator cable.

19. Install the air cleaner assembly and the air hoses.

20. Connect the negative battery cable. Turn the ignition key **ON** to pressurize the system and check for leaks. Correct as necessary.

21. Fill and bleed the cooling system. Start the engine and check for leaks.

DRIVE AXLE

Halfshaft

REMOVAL AND INSTALLATION

Front

1. Raise and safely support the vehicle. Remove the wheel and tire assemblies.

2. Remove the splash shield, if equipped, and drain the transaxle.

3. Raise the staked portion of the hub locknut with a hammer and chisel. Lock the hub by applying the brakes and remove the nut.

4. Disconnect the stabilizer bar from the lower control arm.

5. Remove the cotter pin and nut from the tie rod end ball stud. Use a suitable tool to separate the tie rod end from the knuckle.

6. On 1993-94 MX-6/626, remove the transverse member.

7. Remove the lower ball joint pinch bolt and nut. Use a prybar to pry down the lower control arm and separate the ball joint from the knuckle.

8. If removing the left side shaft on MX-3 and 1993-94 MX-6/626 with

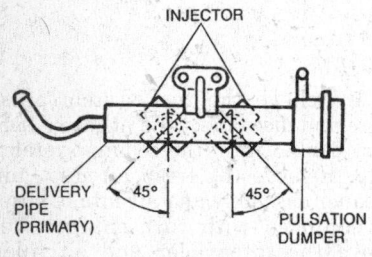

Primary injector alignment — 1990-91 non-turbocharged rotary engine

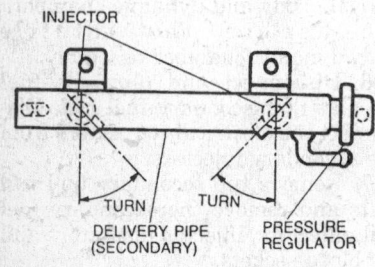

Secondary injector alignment — 1990-91 non-turbocharged rotary engine

automatic transaxle, proceed as follows:

a. Suspend the engine using engine support tool 49 G017 5A0 or equivalent.

b. Remove the bolts and nuts and remove the engine mount member.

9. Position a prybar between the inner CV-joint and transaxle case. Carefully pry the halfshaft from the transaxle being careful not damage the oil seal. If equipped with a right side intermediate shaft, insert the prybar between the halfshaft and intermediate shaft and tap on the bar to uncouple them.

10. Pull outward on the hub/knuckle assembly, push the outer CV-joint stub shaft through the hub, and remove the halfshaft. If the halfshaft is stuck in the hub, install the old hub nut to protect the stub shaft threads. Tap on the nut, with only a soft mallet, and remove the halfshaft.

NOTE: Install plug tool 49 G030 455 or equivalent, into the transaxle after removing the halfshaft, to keep the differential side gear in position. If the gear becomes mispositioned, the differential may have to be removed to realign the gear.

11. Remove the intermediate shaft, if necessary, by removing the support bearing bolts and pulling the shaft from the transaxle.

To install:

12. If removed, install a new circlip on the end of the intermediate shaft, with the end gap facing upward.

13. Install the intermediate shaft in the transaxle, being careful not to damage the oil seals. Install the support bearing bolts and tighten, in sequence, to 45 ft. lbs. (61 Nm).

14. Install a new circlip on the end of the halfshaft, with the end gap facing upward. Insert the halfshaft into the transaxle, being careful not to damage the oil seal. If equipped, push the halfshaft into the intermediate shaft.

15. Insert the other end of the halfshaft through the hub. loosely install a new locknut.

16. If installing the left side shaft on MX-3 and 1993-94 MX-6/626 with automatic transaxle, proceed as follows:

a. Install the engine mount member. Tighten the mount member-to-body nuts and bolts to 66 ft. lbs. (89 Nm).

b. On MX-3, tighten the mount-to-mount member nuts to 38 ft. lbs. (52 Nm).

c. On 1993-94 MX-6/626, tighten the front mount-to-mount member nuts to 77 ft. lbs. (104 Nm) and the side mount bolts to 44 ft. lbs. (60 Nm).

d. Remove the engine support tool.

17. Install the lower ball joint into the knuckle. Install the pinch bolt and nut and tighten to 40 ft. lbs. (54 Nm).

18. On 1993-94 MX-6/626, install the transverse member and tighten the bolts to 96 ft. lbs. (132 Nm).

19. Connect the tie rod end to the steering knuckle and tighten the nut to 42 ft. lbs. (57 Nm) on all except 1993-94 MX-6/626, where the torque is 32 ft. lbs. (44 Nm). Install a new cotter pin. Tighten the nut, if necessary, to align the ball stud hole with the nut castellation.

20. Connect the stabilizer bar to the lower control arm.

21. Install the splash shield and the wheel and tire assemblies. Lower the vehicle.

22. Lock the hub with the brakes. Tighten the new hub nut to 235 ft. lbs. (318 Nm). After torquing, stake the locknut using a hammer and dull bladed chisel.

23. Fill the transaxle with the proper type and quantity of fluid.

Rear

4WD 323/PROTEGE

1. Raise and safely support the vehicle. Remove the wheel and tire assembly.

2. Remove the wheel hub nut.

3. Mark the position of the halfshaft on the output flange and remove the nuts.

4. Remove the trailing link-to-knuckle bolt and the lateral link bolt. Pull outward on the knuckle/hub assembly and remove the halfshaft.

5. Installation is the reverse of the removal procedure. Align the half-

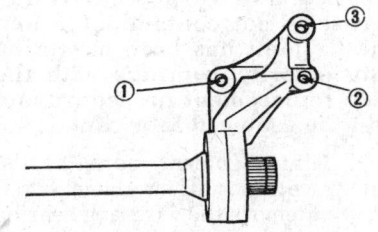

Intermediate shaft bolt torque sequence — 323/Protege

shaft on the output shaft flange. Tighten the halfshaft-to-output flange nuts to 47 ft. lbs. (64 Nm), the trailing link-to-knuckle bolt to 87 ft. lbs. (117 Nm), the lateral link bolt to 93 ft. lbs. (126 Nm) and the hub nut to 235 ft. lbs. (318 Nm).

MIATA, RX-7 AND 1990-91 929

1. Raise and safely support the vehicle. Remove the wheel and tire assembly.

2. Unstake and remove the wheel hub nut.

3. On all except 1993-94 RX-7, mark the position of the halfshaft on the output flange and remove the nuts.

4. On Miata, remove the upper control arm bolt. On 1993-94 RX-7, remove the lower control arm bolt.

5. Remove the halfshaft.

NOTE: If the halfshaft is stuck in the hub, install the used hub nut until it is flush with the end of the shaft. Tap on the nut, using only a soft mallet, to remove the halfshaft

To install:

6. On 1993-94 RX-7, install a new circlip on the inner CV-joint, with the end gap facing upward.

7. Install the halfshaft. On 1993 RX-7, be careful not to damage the oil seal. On all except 1993-94 RX-7, align the halfshaft on the output shaft flange and install the halfshaft-to-output flange nuts. Tighten the nuts to 47 ft. lbs. (64 Nm).

8. On Miata, install the upper control arm bolt and tighten to 49 ft. lbs. (69 Nm). On 1993-94 RX-7, install the lower control arm bolt and tighten to 54 ft. lbs. (73 Nm).

9. Install the wheel and tire assembly and lower the vehicle.

10. Install a new hub nut and tighten to 231 ft. lbs. (314 Nm) on all except Miata, where the torque is 217 ft. lbs. (294 Nm). Stake the hub nut, using a hammer and dull-bladed chisel.

1992-94 929

1. Raise and safely support the vehicle. Remove the wheel and tire assembly.

2. Remove the exhaust pipe.

3. Remove the cotter pin and nut and the rear lower lateral link.

4. Mark the position of the driveshaft on the axle flange and remove the driveshaft.

5. Remove the upper and lower lateral links.

6. Disconnect the stabilizer bar.

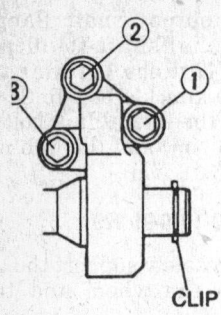

Intermediate shaft bolt torque sequence — MX-3 and MX-6/626 2.0L engine

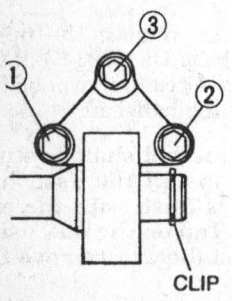

Intermediate shaft bolt torque sequence — MX-6/626 2.5L engine

7. Mark the position of the halfshaft on the output flange. Remove the halfshaft retaining nuts.

8. Unstake and remove the wheel hub nut and washer.

9. Support the subframe and differential with a jack.

10. Remove the subframe mounting nuts and washers and lower the subframe and differential approximately 4 in. (100mm). Remove the halfshaft.

NOTE: If the halfshaft is stuck in the hub, install the used hub nut until it is flush with the end of the shaft. Tap on the nut, using only a soft mallet, to remove the halfshaft

To install:

11. Align the halfshaft-to-output flange marks and install the halfshaft. Install the nuts and tighten to 47 ft. lbs. (64 Nm).

12. Raise the subframe and differential into position and install the nuts and washers.

13. Slide the halfshaft into the hub and loosely install a new hub nut and washer.

14. Connect the stabilizer bar and tighten the nut to 40 ft. lbs. (54 Nm).

15. Install the upper and lower lateral links and tighten the bolts to 86 ft. lbs. (117 Nm).

16. Install the driveshaft, aligning the marks made during removal. Tighten the nuts to 43 ft. lbs. (59 Nm).

17. Install the rear lower lateral link and tighten the nut to 47 ft. lbs. (64 Nm). Install a new cotter pin.

18. Install the exhaust pipe, using new gaskets, and tighten the nuts to 38 ft. lbs. (52 Nm).

19. Install the wheel and tire assembly and lower the vehicle.

20. Tighten the hub nut to 231 ft. lbs. (314 Nm). After torquing, stake the nut using a hammer and dull-bladed chisel.

CV-Boot

REMOVAL AND INSTALLATION

Three types of CV-joints are used. The inboard CV-joints are either double offset type or the tripot type; disassembly procedures differ accordingly. All outboard CV-joints are the Birfield type. The Birfield type CV-joint cannot be disassembled; if an outboard CV-joint boot needs replacement, the inboard CV-joint must be removed.

Double Offset CV-Joint

1. Remove the halfshaft from the vehicle and clamp it in a vise equipped with jaw caps, to prevent damage to the machined surfaces. Do not allow the vise to contact the boot or its clamps.

2. Remove the large boot clamp from the inboard CV-joint, using side cutters. After removing the clamp, roll the boot back over the shaft.

NOTE: Check the grease for contamination by rubbing it between 2 fingers. Any gritty feeling indicates a contaminated CV-joint, in which case the entire CV-joint must be disassembled, cleaned and inspected. If the grease is not contaminated and the CV-joint has been operating satisfactorily, continue with the boot replacement procedure and add the required lubricant.

3. Paint alignment marks on the outer race and shaft for assembly reference. Remove the wire ring bearing retainer and remove the outer race.

4. Paint alignment marks on the inner race and shaft for assembly reference. Remove the inner race snapring from the end of the halfshaft and

remove the inner race, cage and ball bearings from the shaft as an assembly.

NOTE: Use care to prevent damage to the bearing surfaces and cage.

5. If only the boot is being replaced, go to Step 6. If it is necessary to disassemble the CV-joint further, proceed as follows:

   a. Pry the ball bearing out of the bearing cage using a small prybar with blunted edges. Mark the inner race and the bearing cage for proper assembly.

   b. Rotate the inner race to align the bearing lands with the windows in the bearing cage. Remove the inner race through the larger end of the cage.

6. Remove the small clamp and remove the inner boot from the halfshaft. If the boot is to be reused, wrap the shaft splines with tape before removing.

7. If the outer CV-joint boot is to be replaced, remove the clamps and slide the boot off the shaft from the inboard side.

To install:

8. If the outboard boot was removed, slide the boot onto the shaft from the inboard side. Wrap tape on the splines before installing to protect the boot.

9. Install the inboard boot and remove the tape from the shaft.

10. Lubricate the inner race, bearing cage and ball bearings with high temperature CV-joint grease.

11. Position the inner race in the bearing cage and align the matchmarks.

NOTE: Install the race with the chamfered splines facing the large end of the cage.

12. Install the ball bearings in the bearing cage. The balls can be pressed into the cage windows with the heel of the hand.

13. Install the inner race, cage and balls on the halfshaft as an assembly. Make sure the chamfer on the bearing cage faces the snapring and the paint marks made during removal line up. Install the inner race snapring.

14. Lubricate the outer race with high temperature CV-joint grease. Install the outer race and add more grease to the outer race. Install the wire ring bearing retainer.

15. Position the CV-joint boot(s). Make sure the boot is fully seated in the grooves in the shaft and outer race.

16. Insert a small prybar with rounded edges between the boot and the outer bearing race to allow trapped air to escape from the boot. Install new boot clamps.

17. Wrap the clamps around the boots in a clockwise direction, pull tight with pliers and bend the locking tabs to secure in position.

18. Work the CV-joint through its full range of travel at various angles. The joint should flex, extend and compress smoothly.

19. Install the halfshaft into the vehicle.

Tripot CV-Joint

1. Remove the halfshaft from the vehicle and clamp it in a vise equipped with jaw caps, to prevent damage to the machined surfaces. Do not allow the vise to contact the boot or its clamps.

2. Remove the large boot clamp from the inboard CV-joint, using side cutters. After removing the clamp, roll the boot back over the shaft.

NOTE: Check the grease for contamination by rubbing it between 2 fingers. Any gritty feeling indicates a contaminated CV-joint, in which case the entire

CV-joint must be disassembled, cleaned and inspected. If the grease is not contaminated and the CV-joint has been operating satisfactorily, continue with the boot replacement procedure and add the required lubricant.

3. Paint alignment marks on the outer race and shaft for assembly reference. Remove the wire ring bearing retainer and remove the outer race.

4. Paint alignment marks on the tripot bearing and shaft for assembly reference. Remove the tripot bearing snapring and, using a brass drift and hammer, remove the tripot bearing from the shaft.

5. Remove the small clamp and remove the inner boot from the halfshaft. If the boot is to be reused, wrap the shaft splines with tape before removing.

6. If the outer CV-joint boot is to be replaced, remove the clamps and slide the boot off the shaft from the inboard side.

To install:

7. If the outboard boot was removed, slide the boot onto the shaft from the inboard side. Wrap tape on the splines before installing to protect the boot.

8. Install the inboard boot and remove the tape from the shaft.

9. Install the tripot assembly on the halfshaft. Tap the assembly onto the shaft using a hammer and brass drift. Install the tripot assembly retaining ring.

10. Fill the CV-joint outer race with high temperature CV-joint grease. Install the outer race over the tripot joint and install the wire ring bearing retainer.

11. Position the CV-joint boot(s). Make sure the boot is fully seated in the grooves in the shaft and outer race.

12. Insert a small prybar with rounded edges between the boot and the outer bearing race to allow trapped air to escape from the boot. Install new boot clamps.

13. Wrap the clamps around the boots in a clockwise direction, pull tight with pliers and bend the locking tabs to secure in position.

14. Work the CV-joint through its full range of travel at various angles. The joint should flex, extend and compress smoothly.

15. Install the halfshaft into the vehicle.

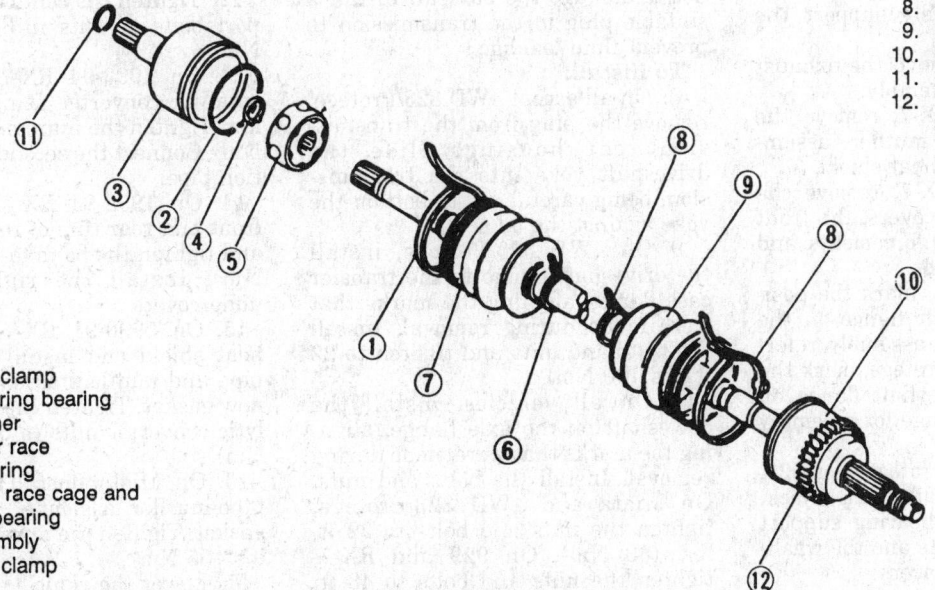

1. Boot clamp
2. Wire ring bearing retainer
3. Outer race
4. Snapring
5. Inner race cage and ball bearing assembly
6. Boot clamp
7. Boot
8. Boot clamp
9. Boot
10. Outer CV-joint
11. Circlip
12. Sensor rotor (ABS only)

Double offset CV-joint and halfshaft

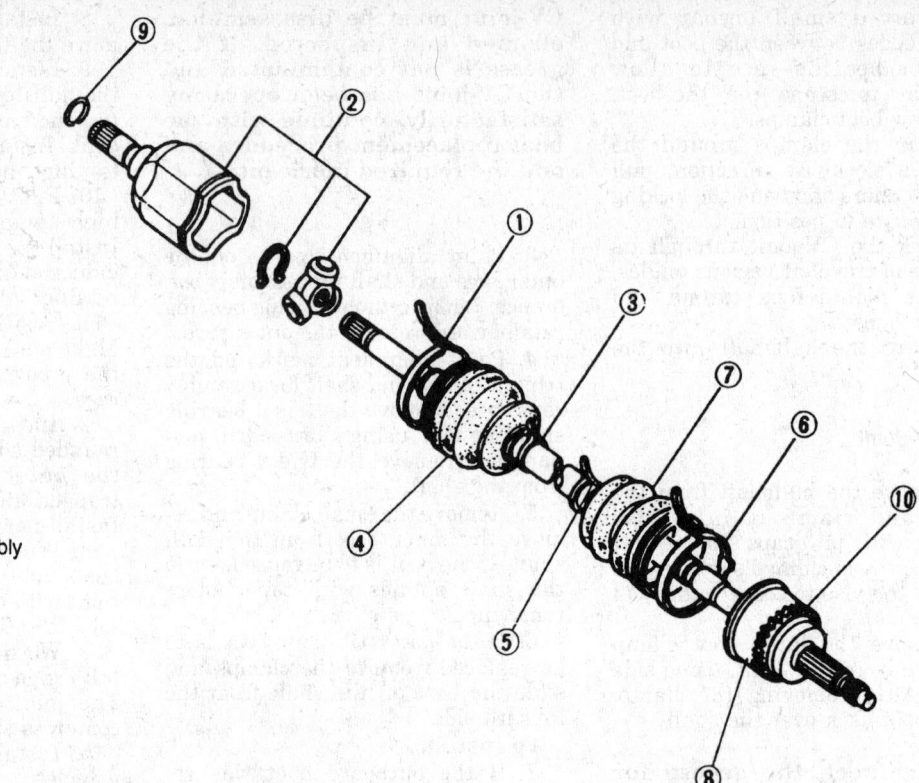

1. Boot clamp
2. Tripot joint assembly
3. Boot clamp
4. Boot
5. Boot clamp
6. Boot clamp
7. Boot
8. Outer CV-joint
9. Circlip
10. Sensor rotor (ABS only)

Tripot CV-joint and halfshaft

Driveshaft and U-Joints

REMOVAL AND INSTALLATION

1. Raise and safely support the vehicle.
2. On Miata, remove the exhaust pipe and muffler assembly.
3. On 1990-91 RX-7, remove the exhaust Y-pipe and mufflers assembly and remove the heat shield.
4. On 1993-94 RX-7, remove the right and left undercovers, the front and rear tunnel reinforcements and the catalytic converter.
5. On all vehicles, mark the position of the driveshaft flange on the rear axle flange for assembly reference. On 4WD 323/Protege, mark the position of the driveshaft flange on the transfer case flange for assembly reference.
6. On 4WD 323/Protege and 929, support the driveshaft with a jack. Remove the center bearing support assembly bolts or nuts and the washers, bushings and spacers.

NOTE: It is important that all center bearing support washers, bushings and spacers be kept in order so they can be reinstalled in their original locations.

7. Remove the driveshaft-to-flange bolts and nuts and remove the driveshaft. On all except 4WD 323/Protege, slide the driveshaft yoke from the transmission, being careful not to damage the oil seal. Install a suitable plug in the transmission to prevent fluid leakage.

To install:

8. On all except 4WD 323/Protege, remove the plug from the transmission rear housing. Slide the driveshaft yoke into the transmission, being careful not to bottom the yoke against the oil seal.
9. On 4WD 323/Protege, install the driveshaft flange to the transfer case flange, aligning the marks that were made during removal. Install the bolts and nuts and tighten to 22 ft. lbs. (30 Nm).
10. On all vehicles, install the driveshaft on the axle flange, aligning the marks that were made during removal. Install the bolts and nuts. On Miata and 4WD 323/Protege, tighten the nuts and bolts to 22 ft. lbs. (30 Nm). On 929 and RX-7, tighten the nuts and bolts to 43 ft. lbs. (59 Nm).
11. On 4WD 323/Protege and 929, support the driveshaft with a jack. Position the center bearing support

and install the retaining bolts or nuts with the bushings, washers and spacers. Make sure the bushings, washers and spacers are installed in their original locations.
12. Tighten the center bearing support bolts or nuts to 38 ft. lbs. (52 Nm).
13. On 1993-94 RX-7, install the catalytic converter using a new gasket. Tighten the nuts to 65 ft. lbs. (89 Nm). Connect the secondary air injection pipe.
14. On 1993-94 RX-7, install the front and rear tunnel reinforcements and tighten the bolts to 19 ft. lbs. (25 Nm). Install the right and left undercovers.
15. On 1990-91 RX-7, install the heat shield and install the exhaust pipe and mufflers assembly, using a new gasket. Tighten the pipe-to-catalytic converter nuts to 59 ft. lbs. (80 Nm).
16. On Miata, install the exhaust pipe/muffler assembly with a new gasket. Tighten the pipe nuts to 41 ft. lbs. (55 Nm).
17. Lower the vehicle.

Rear Axle Shaft, Bearing and Seal

REMOVAL AND INSTALLATION

4WD 323/Protege

1. Loosen the axle nut, then raise and safely support the vehicle.
2. Remove the wheel and tire assembly and the axle nut.
3. To remove just the halfshaft, matchmark the inner drive flanges so the shaft can be installed the same position. Remove the trailing link bolt and the lower control arm bolt. Remove the drive flange nuts and pull the rear strut out far enough to disengage the flanges. Slide the shaft out of the hub spline. If stuck, use a plastic hammer to avoid damaging the axle threads.
4. Remove the brake caliper assembly and hang it from the body. Do not let it hang by the hose.
5. To remove the knuckle, remove the bolts from the bottom of the strut and pull the knuckle off strut.
6. Be careful not to distort the back plate. If damaged or removed, a new one must be pressed onto the knuckle.
7. To remove the hub, remove the seal and properly support the assembly to press the hub out from the back. If the inner bearing race stays on the hub, use a chisel to move it far enough to grab it with a bearing puller.
8. Remove the snapring and press the bearing out of the knuckle.
   To install:
9. Carefully inspect all parts for wear or damage, replace as necessary. Always install a new seal and bearing.
10. When pressing the new bearing into the knuckle, make sure to press only on the outer race. Install the snapring, support the inner race and press the hub into the bearing. Failure to properly support the bearing races for pressing will ruin the bearing.
11. Install a new seal and fit the knuckle into place on the strut. Install all the bolts before tightening any of them. Torque the knuckle-to-strut and the trailing link bolts to 93 ft. lbs. (127 Nm). Torque the lower control arm bolt to 86 ft. lbs. (117 Nm).
12. Install the brake caliper and torque the bolts to 44 ft. lbs. (60 Nm).
13. If the halfshaft was removed, install it in the same position and torque the flange nuts to 47 ft. lbs. (64 Nm).

14. Install the washer and a new axle nut. With all 4 wheels on the ground, torque the nut to 235 ft. lbs. (318 Nm). Stake the nut into place.
15. Check and adjust the rear wheel alignment.

Miata

1. Loosen the axle nut, then raise and safely support the vehicle.
2. Remove the wheel and tire assembly and the axle nut.
3. To remove just the halfshaft, matchmark the inner drive flanges so the shaft can be installed the same position. Remove the nuts, pull the halfshaft flange off the differential flange and slide the shaft out of the hub spline. If stuck, use a plastic hammer to avoid damaging the axle threads.
4. Remove the brake caliper assembly and hang it from the body. Do not let it hang by the hose. Remove the disc and the ABS speed sensor.
5. Remove the lower and upper control arm bolts and remove the knuckle and hub assembly from the vehicle.
6. Be careful not to distort the back plate. If damaged or removed, a new one must be pressed onto the knuckle.
7. To remove the hub, remove the seal and properly support the assembly to press the hub out from the back. If the inner bearing race stays on the hub, use a chisel to move it far enough to grab it with a bearing puller.
8. Remove the snapring and press the bearing out of the knuckle.
   To install:
9. Carefully inspect all parts for wear or damage, replace as necessary. Always install a new seal and bearing.
10. When pressing the new bearing into the knuckle, make sure to press only on the outer race. Install the snapring, support the inner race and press the hub into the bearing. Failure to properly support the bearing races for pressing will ruin the bearing.
11. Install a new seal and fit the knuckle into place on the suspension. Torque the upper control arm bolt to 49 ft. lbs. (67 Nm) and the lower bolt to 55 ft. lbs. (75 Nm).
12. Install the brake caliper and torque the bolts to 51 ft. lbs. (69 Nm). Install the speed sensor.
13. If the halfshaft was removed, install it in the same position and torque the flange nuts to 47 ft. lbs. (64 Nm).

14. Install the washer and a new axle nut. With all 4 wheels on the ground, torque the nut to 217 ft. lbs. (294 Nm). Stake the nut into place.
15. Check and adjust the rear wheel alignment.

929

1990-91

1. Loosen the axle nut, then raise and safely support the vehicle.
2. Remove the wheel and tire assembly and the axle nut.
3. To remove just the halfshaft, matchmark the inner drive flanges so the shaft can be installed the same position. Remove the nuts, pull the halfshaft flange off the differential flange and slide the shaft out of the hub spline.
4. Remove the brake caliper assembly and hang it from the body. Do not let it hang by the hose. To disconnect the parking brake cable, loosen the back plate bolts. Remove the countersunk screws to remove the disc.
5. Remove the ABS speed sensor and the parking brake shoes.
6. Disconnect the shock absorber and the stabilizer link. Remove the cotter pins and nuts and use a ball joint press to disconnect the upper and lower control links.
7. Remove the hub knuckle assembly from the trailing arm.
8. To remove the hub, properly support the assembly to press the hub out from the back. Be careful not to distort the backplate. If the inner bearing race stays on the hub, grind a spot on the race thin enough that it can be broken off with a chisel.
9. To remove the bearing, remove the back plate. Remove the snapring and press the outer race and bearing out of the knuckle.
   To install:
10. Carefully inspect all parts for wear or damage, replace as necessary. Always install a new seal and bearing.
11. When pressing the new bearing into the knuckle, make sure to press only on the outer race. Install the snapring and back plate, support the inner race and press the hub into the bearing. Failure to properly support the bearing races for pressing will ruin the bearing.
12. Install the knuckle to the trailing arm and torque the bolts to 86 ft. lbs. (117 Nm). Connect the control links and shock absorber and torque the nuts to 55 ft. lbs. (75 Nm). Tighten as required to install new cotter pins.

13. Install the brake components and connect and adjust the parking brake cable. Torque the caliper bolts to 50 ft. lbs. (68 Nm) and the speed sensor bolt to 17 ft. lbs. (23 Nm).

14. If the halfshaft was removed, install it and torque the nuts to 47 ft. lbs. (64 Nm).

15. Install the washer and a new axle nut. With all 4 wheels on the ground, torque the nut to 231 ft. lbs. (314 Nm). Stake the nut into place.

16. Check and adjust the rear wheel alignment.

1992-94

1. Loosen the hub nut and raise and safely support the vehicle. Remove the wheel and tire assembly and the nut.

2. Remove the brake caliper and suspend it from the coil spring; do not let the caliper hang by the brake hose.

3. Remove the ABS speed sensor and the disc brake rotor. Remove the parking brake shoe assembly.

4. Disconnect the rear lower lateral link and the stabilizer bar link from the knuckle.

5. Disconnect the upper and lower lateral links and trailing links from the knuckle.

6. Remove the brake backing plate mounting bolts, remove the parking brake cable mounting bolts and remove the cable.

7. Remove the lower strut bolt and remove the hub/knuckle assembly. If the halfshaft sticks to the hub, install the old hub nut until it is flush with the end of the shaft. Tap out the shaft, using a soft mallet only.

8. Properly support the hub/knuckle assembly and press the hub from the knuckle. If the bearing race sticks to the knuckle, grind the race in 1 spot until only 0.20 in. (0.5mm) thickness remains. Cut the race with a chisel and remove it.

9. Remove the brake backing plate from the knuckle. Remove the bearing snapring.

10. Properly support the knuckle and press out the bearing.

To install:

11. Inspect the knuckle and hub for cracks or other damage. Replace parts as necessary.

12. Properly support the knuckle and press in a new bearing. Install the snapring and the brake backing plate.

13. Properly support the knuckle and press on the hub.

14. Position the hub/knuckle assembly and install the lower strut bolt. Tighten to 69 ft. lbs. (93 Nm).

15. Connect the parking brake cable and install the backing plate bolts.

16. Connect the upper trailing link and tighten the nut to 42 ft. lbs. (57 Nm). Connect the lower trailing link and tighten the nut to 116 ft. lbs. (157 Nm). Install new cotter pins.

17. Connect the upper lateral link and tighten the nut to 80 ft. lbs. (108 Nm). Connect the lower lateral link and tighten the nut to 116 ft. lbs. (157 Nm). Install new cotter pins.

18. Connect the stabilizer link and tighten the nut to 40 ft. lbs. (54 Nm). Connect the rear lower lateral link and tighten the nut to 47 ft. lbs. (64 Nm). Install a new cotter pin.

19. Install the parking brake shoe assembly and the brake rotor. Connect the ABS speed sensor and tighten the bolt to 17 ft. lbs. (23 Nm).

20. Install the brake caliper and tighten the bolts to 50 ft. lbs. (68 Nm).

21. Loosely install a new hub nut and washer. Install the wheel and tire assembly and lower the vehicle.

22. Tighten the hub nut to 231 ft. lbs. (314 Nm). After torquing, stake the nut with a hammer and dull-bladed chisel.

23. Check the wheel alignment.

RX-7

1990-91

1. Loosen the axle nut, then raise and safely support the vehicle.

2. Remove the wheel and tire assembly and the axle nut.

3. To remove just the halfshaft, matchmark the inner drive flanges so the shaft can be installed the same position. Remove the nuts, pull the halfshaft flange off the differential flange and slide the shaft out of the hub spline.

4. Remove the brake caliper assembly and hang it from the body. Do not let it hang by the hose. It may be necessary to disconnect the parking brake cable. Remove the countersunk screws to remove the disc.

5. Before removing the ABS speed sensor, measure the gap between them. Remove the speed sensor from the knuckle. Remove the 3 bolts to remove the knuckle and backplate assembly.

6. To remove the hub, properly support the assembly to press the hub out from the back. The inner bearing race will probably stay on the hub. Be careful not to distort the backplate.

7. To remove the bearing, remove the ABS sensor rotor from the hub

and use an appropriate puller to remove the inner race from the hub. Remove the snapring and press the outer race and bearing out of the knuckle.

To install:

8. Carefully inspect all parts for wear or damage, replace as necessary. Always install a new seal and bearing.

9. When pressing the new bearing into the knuckle, make sure to press only on the outer race. When pressing the hub into the bearing, support the inner race. Failure to properly support the bearing races for pressing will ruin the bearing.

10. With the knuckle assembled, install the knuckle and torque the upper and lower rear mounting bolts to 69 ft. lbs. (93 Nm). Torque the front toe control bushing bolt to 111 ft. lbs. (151 Nm).

11. Install the speed sensor and measure the gap between the sensor and rotor. The gap must be 0.016-0.039 in. (0.4-1.0mm).

12. Install the brake disc and caliper and torque the caliper mounting bolts to 40 ft. lbs. (54 Nm). Connect and adjust the parking brake cable.

13. If the halfshaft was removed, install it and torque the nuts to 47 ft. lbs. (64 Nm).

14. Install the washer and a new axle nut and begin tightening it. With the vehicle resting on all 4 wheels, torque the nut to 231 ft. lbs. (314 Nm). Stake the nut into place.

15. Check and adjust the rear wheel alignment.

1993-94

1. Loosen the hub nut and raise and safely support the vehicle. Remove the wheel and tire assembly.

2. Disconnect the ABS sensor. Remove the caliper and suspend it from the coil spring; do not let it hang by the brake hose.

3. Remove the hub nut and washer. Remove the disc brake rotor.

4. Remove the upper and lower control arm bolts and the toe control link bolt. Remove the hub/knuckle assembly.

NOTE: If the halfshaft is stuck in the hub, install the old hub nut until it is flush with the end of the shaft. Tap out the shaft, using a soft mallet only.

5. Properly support the hub/knuckle assembly and press the hub from the knuckle. If the bearing race sticks to the knuckle, grind the race in 1 spot until only 0.20 in. (0.5mm) thickness remains. Cut the race with a chisel and remove it.

6. Remove the snapring from the knuckle. Properly support the knuckle and press out the bearing.

7. Inspect the hub and knuckle for cracks or other damage and replace as necessary.

To install:

8. Properly support the knuckle and press in the new bearing. Install a new snapring.

9. Properly support the knuckle and press on the hub.

10. Install the hub knuckle assembly. Tighten the upper and lower control arm bolts to 54 ft. lbs. (73 Nm) and the toe control link bolt to 57 ft. lbs. (78 Nm).

11. Install the brake rotor and loosely install a new hub nut and washer.

12. Install the brake caliper and tighten the bolts to 49 ft. lbs. (67 Nm). Connect the ABS sensor and tighten the bolt to 18 ft. lbs. (25 Nm).

13. Install the wheel and tire assembly and lower the vehicle.

14. Tighten the wheel hub nut to 231 ft. lbs. (313 Nm). After torquing, stake the hub nut using a hammer and dull-bladed chisel.

15. Check the wheel alignment.

Front Wheel Hub, Knuckle and Bearing

REMOVAL AND INSTALLATION

323, Protege and MX-3

1. Loosen the axle nut and the lug nuts. Raise the vehicle and support it safely. Remove the wheel and tire assembly.

2. Without disconnecting the hydraulic hose, remove the brake caliper and hang it from the body. Do not let it hang by the hose. Remove the brake disc. Remove the ABS speed sensor, if equipped.

3. Remove the cotter pin and nut and separate the tie rod end from the steering knuckle.

4. Remove the pinch bolt and push the control arm down to separate the ball joint from the knuckle.

5. Remove the 2 bolts and separate the knuckle from the strut.

6. Be careful not to distort the back plate. If damaged or removed, a new one must be pressed onto the knuckle.

7. To remove the hub and bearing:

a. Remove the seal and properly support the assembly to press the hub out from the back.

b. If the inner bearing race stays on the hub, use a chisel to move it

far enough to grab it with a bearing puller.

c. Remove the snapring and press the bearing out of the knuckle.

To install:

8. Carefully inspect all parts for wear or damage, replace as necessary. Always install a new seal and bearing.

9. To install the new bearing:

a. Press the bearing into the knuckle. Make sure to press only on the outer race.

b. Install the snapring, support the inner race and press the hub into the bearing. Failure to properly support the bearing races for pressing will ruin the bearing.

c. Install a new seal.

10. Fit the knuckle onto the strut and install the bolts. Torque the bolts to 85 ft. lbs. (115 Nm).

11. Fit the lower ball joint into place, install the clamp bolt and torque it to 40 ft. lbs. (58 Nm).

12. Connect the tie rod end, torque the nut to 42 ft. lbs. (57 Nm) and tighten as required to install a new cotter pin.

13. Install the brake disc and caliper and torque the caliper bolts to 36 ft. lbs. (49 Nm). Install the ABS speed sensor, if equipped.

14. Install the washer and a new axle nut. With all 4 wheels on the ground, torque the nut to 235 ft. lbs. (318 Nm). Stake the nut into place.

15. Check and adjust the wheel alignment.

MX-6/626

1. Loosen the axle nut and the lug nuts. Raise the vehicle and support it safely. Remove the wheel and tire assembly.

2. Without disconnecting the hydraulic hose, remove the brake caliper and hang it from the body. Do not let it hang by the hose. Remove the brake disc. If equipped with ABS, remove the speed sensor.

3. Remove the cotter pin and nut and separate the tie rod end from the steering knuckle.

4. Disconnect the stabilizer bar from the lower control arm.

5. Remove the pinch bolt and push the control arm down to separate the ball joint from the knuckle.

6. Remove the 2 bolts and separate the knuckle from the strut.

7. Be careful not to distort the back plate. If damaged or removed, a new one must be pressed onto the knuckle.

8. To remove the hub and bearing:

a. Remove the seal and properly support the knuckle.

b. Press the hub out of the knuckle.

c. If the inner bearing race stays on the hub, grind a spot on the race to a thickness of approximately 0.20 in. (0.5mm). Cut the race with a chisel.

d. Remove the snapring and press the bearing out of the knuckle.

To install:

9. Carefully inspect all parts for wear or damage, replace as necessary. Always install a new seal and bearing.

10. To install the new bearing:

a. Press the knuckle onto the new bearing. Make sure to support the bearing only on the outer race.

b. Install the snapring, support the inner race and press the hub into the bearing. Failure to properly support the bearing races for pressing will ruin the bearing.

11. Install a new seal, fit the knuckle onto the strut and install the bolts. Torque the bolts to 85 ft. lbs. (115 Nm).

12. Fit the lower ball joint into place, install the clamp bolt and torque it to 40 ft. lbs. (58 Nm).

13. Connect the tie rod end, and torque the nut to 42 ft. lbs. (57 Nm) on 1990-92 vehicles or 32 ft. lbs. (44 Nm) on 1993-94 vehicles. Tighten as required to install a new cotter pin.

14. Install the brake disc and caliper and torque the caliper bolts to 72 ft. lbs. (98 Nm). Install the ABS speed sensor, if equipped, and tighten the bolts to 16 ft. lbs. (22 Nm).

15. On 1990-92 vehicles, assemble the stabilizer bar link, making sure there are 0.72-0.87 in. (18.1-22.1mm) of thread protruding from the nut. On 1993-94 vehicles, tighten the stabilizer link nut to 39 ft. lbs. (53 Nm).

16. Install the washer and a new axle nut. With all 4 wheels on the ground, torque the nut to 235 ft. lbs. (318 Nm). Stake the nut into place.

17. Check and adjust the wheel alignment.

Pinion Seal

REMOVAL AND INSTALLATION

RX-7 and 929

1. Raise and safely support the vehicle and drain the differential oil.

2. Matchmark the drive flanges and remove the driveshaft.

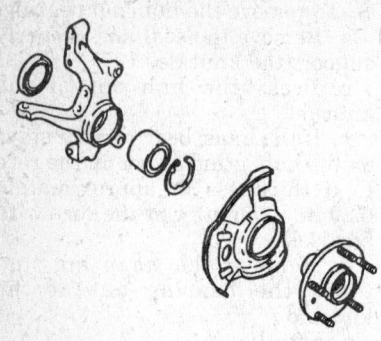

Front wheel hub, knuckle and bearing assembly — 1990-92 MX-6/626

3. Before removing the companion flange, use an inch-pound torque wrench to measure the torque required to turn the flange. This preload must the the same when the job is finished.

4. Use the special tool 49 S120 710, or equivalent, to hold the flange from turning and remove the companion flange nut.

5. Use a puller to remove the flange from the differential.

6. Carefully pry the old seal out of the housing.

To install:

7. Lightly grease the new seal and press it in with a suitable seal installation tool. Make sure the seal is flush with the housing.

8. Install the companion flange and torque the nut as required to obtain the original bearing pre-load. Be sure not to torque the nut too far or it will be necessary to disassemble the differential.

9. Install the driveshaft and refill the differential with oil.

Output Flange Oil Seal

REMOVAL AND INSTALLATION

RX-7, 929, Miata and 323 with 4WD

1. Raise and safely support the vehicle and drain the differential oil.

2. Matchmark the drive flanges and remove the halfshafts.

3. Use 2 large prybars and carefully pry the output flange out of the differential.

4. Carefully pry the old seal out.

To install:

5. Lubricate the new seal with grease and press it into place with an appropriate seal installation tool.

6. Press the output flange into the housing and tap with a soft hammer to set the clip into place in the side gear.

7. Install the halfshafts and torque the nuts to 47 ft. lbs. (64 Nm). Refill the differential with oil.

Differential Carrier

REMOVAL AND INSTALLATION

323 and Protege

1. Raise and safely support the vehicle. Remove the wheel and tire assemblies. Drain the differential oil.

2. Matchmark the flanges and remove the driveshaft.

3. Remove the lateral link and the trailing link bolts from the spindle assembly to allow the struts to move out at the bottom.

4. Disconnect the halfshafts from the differential carrier and hang them from the body with wire. Do not let them hang on the outer CV-joint.

5. Support the differential carrier, remove the mounting bolts and lower the differential from the vehicle.

6. Installation is the reverse or removal. Torque the front carrier mounting bolts to 50 ft. lbs. (68 Nm) and the rear carrier mounting bolts to 86 ft. lbs. (116 Nm). Torque the suspension bolts to 86 ft. lbs. (116 Nm). Torque the halfshaft flange nuts to 47 ft. lbs. (63 Nm) and the driveshaft bolts to 22 ft. lbs. (30 Nm).

Miata

1. Raise and safely support the vehicle and remove the wheel and tire assemblies. Drain the differential oil.

2. Disconnect the exhaust pipe at the rear catalytic converter flange and remove the pipe and muffler.

3. Matchmark the driveshaft and halfshaft flanges. Remove the driveshaft and plug the output end of the transmission. Disconnect the halfshafts and support them. Do not let them hang by the outer CV-joint.

4. Disconnect the speedometer cable from the transmission and remove the wiring harness from the transmission-to-differential frame.

5. Support the transmission and unbolt the transmission-to-differential frame from the transmission.

6. To disconnect the frame from the differential:

  a. Remove the differential mounting spacer. Mark the bolts so they can be returned to the same hole.

  b. Install a long 14 x 1.5mm bolt into the mounting spacer sleeve.

  c. Twist and pull the bolt downward.

  d. Install a small 6 x 1mm bolt into the hole in the block to hold the sleeve and remove the long bolt.

  e. Remove the small bolt.

NOTE: Do not remove the spacers from the frame. If removed, the frame and spacers must be replaced as an assembly.

7. After removing the frame, make sure the transmission is properly supported with a plate or board bolted to the frame rails of the vehicle. This will prevent damage to the crank angle sensor and the engine mounts.

8. Support the differential with a jack, remove the mounting nuts and lower the differential from the vehicle.

To install:

9. Fit the differential into place and start the mounting nuts. Install the differential mounting spacer to the differential and torque the bolts to 38 ft. lbs. (52 Nm).

10. Support the transmission so the frame can be easily installed. Start the frame-to-transmission bolts and make them finger-tight.

11. Verify that the sleeve is properly installed into the spacer block and that the shoulder bolt is in front. Install the frame to the differential and start the bolts.

12. When all mounts and bolts are started, torque the rear mount center nuts to 72 ft. lbs. (98 Nm), and the rear mount side nuts to 20 ft. lbs. (26 Nm).

13. Torque the frame-to-transmission bolts, then the frame-to-differential bolts to 91 ft. lbs. (123 Nm). On manual transmission, torque the smaller frame bracket bolts to 40 ft. lbs. (54 Nm).

14. Install the driveshaft and torque the nuts to 22 ft. lbs. (30 Nm). Attach the halfshafts and torque the nuts to 47 ft. lbs. (64 Nm).

15. Install the remaining parts in order and refill the differential with oil.

929

1990-91

1. Raise and safely support the vehicle and remove the wheel and tire assemblies. Drain the differential oil.

2. Matchmark the flanges on the driveshaft and the halfshafts. Remove the driveshaft and disconnect the halfshafts and support them. Do not let the halfshafts hang by the outer CV-joint.

3. Support the differential, remove the front and rear mounting nuts and

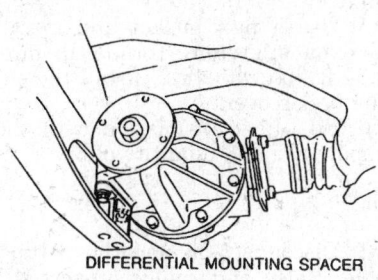

Differential mounting spacer location — Miata

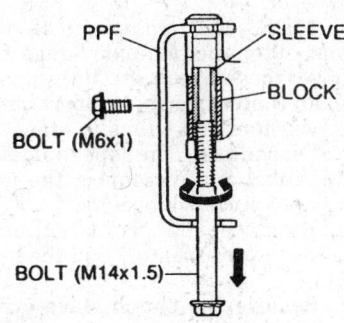

PPF

SLEEVE

BLOCK

BOLT (M6x1)

BOLT (M14x1.5)

Mounting spacer sleeve procedure — Miata

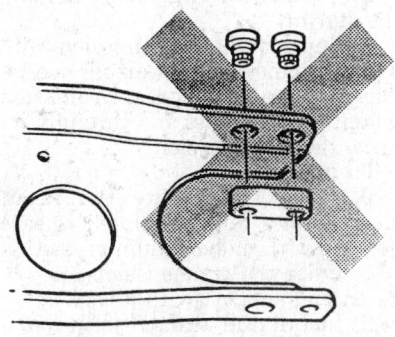

Do not remove these spacers

bolts and lower the unit from the vehicle.

4. Installation is the reverse of removal. Torque the mounting nuts and bolts to 86 ft. lbs. (117 Nm). Torque the driveshaft nuts to 43 ft. lbs. (59 Nm) and the halfshaft nuts to 47 ft. lbs. (64 Nm). Fill the differential with the proper type and quantity of oil.

1992-94

1. Disconnect the negative battery cable. Remove the wheel and tire assemblies.

2. Mark the position of the driveshaft on the axle flange and remove the driveshaft.

3. Remove the nuts and remove the exhaust pipe/muffler assembly.

4. Remove the bolts and disconnect the upper and lower lateral links from the frame member.

5. Mark the position of the halfshafts on the output shaft flanges and remove the nuts. Disconnect the halfshafts from the flanges and support them aside; do not let them hang by the outer CV-joint.

6. Support the subframe and differential with a jack. Remove the subframe mounting nuts and washers and lower the subframe and differential approximately 4 in. (100mm). Remove the mounting bolt from the front of the differential.

7. Raise the subframe and differential and install the washers and mounting nuts. Remove the mounting bolts from the rear of the differential and remove the differential.

To install:

8. Raise the differential into position and install the rear mounting bolts. Tighten to 87 ft. lbs. (118 Nm).

9. Support the subframe and differential with a jack. Remove the subframe mounting nuts and washers and lower the subframe and differential approximately 4 in. (100mm). Install the mounting bolt at the front of the differential and tighten to 76 ft. lbs. (103 Nm).

10. Raise the subframe and differential and install the washers and mounting nuts.

11. Connect the halfshafts to the output shaft flanges, aligning the marks that were made during removal. Install the nuts and tighten to 47 ft. lbs. (64 Nm).

12. Connect the upper and lower lateral links. Tighten the bolts to 86 ft. lbs. (117 Nm).

13. Install the exhaust pipe/muffler assembly, using new gaskets and tighten the nuts to 38 ft. lbs. (52 Nm).

14. Install the driveshaft on the axle flange, aligning the marks that were made during removal. Tighten the bolts to 43 ft. lbs. (59 Nm).

15. Check the differential oil level, then lower the vehicle. Check the rear wheel alignment.

RX-7

1990-91

1. Raise and safely support the vehicle and remove the rear wheel and tire assemblies. Drain the differential oil.

2. Remove the exhaust system from the Y-pipe back.

3. Matchmark the flanges for installation and remove the driveshaft.

4. Matchmark the flanges and disconnect the halfshafts at the inner end. Hang the halfshafts from the body with wire or rope. Do not let them hang by the outer CV-joint.

5. Remove the mounting nut from the left side of the differential and let the unit hang down to ease disconnecting the sub links.

6. With the links disconnected, support the differential with a jack, remove the mounting nuts and lower the unit from the vehicle.

To install:

7. Raise the differential into place and start the front and right mounting nuts or bolts.

8. Connect the sub-link assembly but don't torque any bolts yet.

9. Raise the differential to start the left mount nut. Torque the rear mount nuts to 69 ft. lbs. (93 Nm), then the front mount bolts to 77 ft. lbs. (105 Nm).

10. Torque the sub-link fasteners to 69 ft. lbs. (93 Nm).

11. Install the driveshaft and torque the nuts to 43 ft. lbs. (59 Nm). Install the halfshafts and torque the nuts to 47 ft. lbs. (64 Nm).

12. Install the exhaust system.

1993-94

1. Raise and safely support the vehicle. Remove the wheel and tire assemblies.

2. Remove the exhaust pipe.

3. Mark the position of the driveshaft on the axle flange and remove the driveshaft.

4. Remove the tunnel reinforcement bracket.

5. Support the transmission and differential with jacks and remove the transmission-to-differential frame member.

6. Remove the lower control arm-to-knuckle bolts. Pry the halfshafts from the differential and pull out on the knuckle/hub assemblies to remove the halfshafts from the differential. Support the halfshafts aside; do not let them hang by the outer CV-joint.

7. Remove the differential mounting nuts/bolts and remove the differential.

To install:

8. Raise the differential into position and install the mounting bolts/nuts. Tighten to 86 ft. lbs. (116 Nm).

9. Install new circlips on the halfshafts, with the end gaps facing upward. Install the halfshafts into the differential, being careful not to damage the oil seals.

10. Install the lower control arm-to-knuckle bolts and tighten to 54 ft. lbs. (73 Nm).

11. Install the transmission-to-differential frame as follows:

    a. Hold the differential perfectly level with the jack.

    b. Hold the frame in place with a new bolt and 8 new nuts.

    c. Tighten the frame-to-differential nuts to 130 ft. lbs. (176 Nm) and the frame-to-differential bolt to 68 ft. lbs. (93 Nm).

    d. Tighten the frame to transmission nuts to 130 ft. lbs. (176 Nm), tightening the upper nuts first.

    e. Remove the jacks from under the differential and transmission.

12. Install the tunnel reinforcement bracket and tighten the bolts to 19 ft. lbs. (26 Nm).

13. Install the driveshaft, aligning the marks that were made during removal. Tighten the bolts to 43 ft. lbs. (58 Nm).

14. Install the exhaust pipe and the wheel and tire assemblies. Check the differential oil level.

15. Lower the vehicle and check the rear wheel alignment.

MANUAL TRANSMISSION

Transmission Assembly

REMOVAL AND INSTALLATION

Miata

1. Disconnect the negative battery cable. Raise the vehicle and support safely. Drain the transmission.

2. Remove the shifter knob and the center console and remove the gearshift lever.

3. Remove the engine undercover and disconnect the exhaust pipe from the manifold. Remove the entire exhaust system as an assembly.

4. Matchmark the driveshaft flange at the rear and remove the driveshaft.

5. Without disconnecting the hydraulic hose, remove the clutch release cylinder and set it aside. Disconnect the wiring and remove the starter.

6. Disconnect the speedometer cable and remove the wiring from the frame member.

7. Support the transmission and differential with jacks. Remove the transmission-to-differential frame as follows:

    a. Remove the frame-to-transmission bracket.

    b. Remove the bolts from the underside of the frame at the differential end, noting their location. Pry out the spacer from the frame.

    c. Remove the differential mounting spacer from the underside of the differential.

    d. Insert a 14 **x** 1.5mm bolt through the frame hole and turn it into the sleeve. Twist and pull the bolt downward.

    e. Install a 6**x** 1mm bolt in the side hole to hold the sleeve and remove the long bolt. Remove the short bolt.

    f. Remove the transmission side bolts and remove the frame member.

8. Remove the bolts from the clutch housing and slide the transmission back away from the engine. Lower the transmission from the vehicle.

To install:

9. Lightly lubricate the main shaft spline and the release bearing fork contact points with molybdenum grease and install the fork. Place a wood block on a floor jack and use it to tilt the engine up in front.

10. Carefully guide the transmission into place, making sure the main shaft spline fits properly into the clutch disc. Start all the transmission-to-engine bolts, then torque them to 66 ft. lbs. (89 Nm).

11. Raise the transmission into place and install the transmission-to-differential frame and all the bolts, leaving all the bolts loose. Torque the frame-to-transmission bolts, then the frame-to-differential bolts to 91 ft. lbs. (124 Nm). Install the bracket and torque the bracket-to-transmission bolts to 40 ft. lbs. (54 Nm), the bracket-to-frame bolts to 91 ft. lbs. (124 Nm).

NOTE: After the frame installation, position a straightedge between the body frame members on each side of the vehicle. Measure the distance between the bottom of the frame to the straightedge; it should be 2.403-2.797 in. (61-71mm). If the distance is not as specified, reposition the frame member at the transmission.

12. Install the driveshaft and torque the nuts to 22 ft. lbs. (30 Nm).

13. Install the starter and connect the speedometer cable and wiring.

14. Install the clutch release cylinder.

15. Use a new gasket and install the exhaust system. Torque the nuts to 34 ft. lbs. (46 Nm). Install the engine undercover.

16. Fill the transmission with the proper type and quantity of oil.

929

1. Disconnect the negative battery cable. Raise and safely support the vehicle.

2. Drain the transmission oil.

3. Working inside the vehicle, remove the console box and the gearshift lever.

4. Mark the position of the driveshaft on the rear axle flange and remove the driveshaft. Be sure to keep all center bearing support bushings, washers and shims in order.

5. Disconnect the speedometer cable. Label and disconnect the necessary electrical connectors.

6. Remove the front exhaust pipe/converter assembly and the heat shield.

7. Remove the clutch slave cylinder shield and the clutch slave cylinder. Position aside, leaving the hydraulic line attached.

8. Label and disconnect the starter electrical connectors. Remove the starter.

9. Support the transmission with a jack. Remove the transmission-to-engine bolts and the transmission mount-to-body bolts and carefully remove the transmission.

To install:

10. Lightly lubricate the input shaft splines and the clutch release bearing with molybdenum grease.

11. Raise the transmission into position and support with a jack.

12. Install the transmission-to-engine bolts and tighten to 38 ft. lbs. (52 Nm). Install the transmission mount-to-body bolts and tighten to 42 ft. lbs. (57 Nm). Remove the jack.

13. Install the starter and tighten the bolts to 38 ft. lbs. (52 Nm). Connect the electrical connectors to the starter.

14. Install the clutch slave cylinder and shield. Tighten the bolts to 17 ft. lbs. (23 Nm).

15. Install the heat shield. Install the exhaust pipe, using new gaskets, and tighten the nuts to 34 ft. lbs. (46 Nm).

16. Connect the electrical connectors and the speedometer cable.

17. Install the driveshaft, aligning the marks that were made during removal. Tighten the axle flange bolts to 43 ft. lbs. (59 Nm). Install the

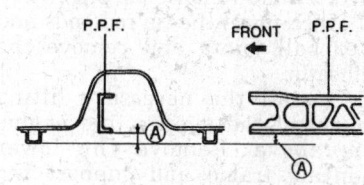

Measure distance A after installing the transmission-to-differential frame member on Miata

center bearing support bushings, washers and spacers in their original locations. Install the bolts and tighten to 38 ft. lbs. (52 Nm).

18. Fill the transmission with the proper type and quantity of oil. Lower the vehicle.

19. Install the gearshift lever and console box. Connect the negative battery cable.

RX-7

1990-91

1. Disconnect the negative battery cable. Raise the vehicle and support safely. Drain the transmission.

2. Remove the shifter knob and boot and remove the gearshift lever.

3. Unbolt the clutch release cylinder from the transmission but do not disconnect the hydraulic line. Route the assembly aside.

4. Disconnect the exhaust pipe at the manifold and at the muffler and remove the pipe and the catalytic converter. Remove the heat shield covers.

5. Matchmark the driveshaft flanges and the position of the balance washers. Remove the driveshaft and disconnect the speedometer cable and wiring.

6. Disconnect the electrical wiring and remove the starter. Remove the clutch housing inspection cover, if equipped.

7. Properly support the transmission with a transmission jack. Disconnect the rear mount and remove the mount crossmember.

8. Remove the transmission case-to-engine bolts. Slide the transmission rearward until the main shaft clears the clutch disc and carefully lower the transmission from the vehicle.

To install:

9. Lightly lubricate the main shaft spline and release bearing fork con-

tact points with molybdenum grease. Install the release bearing.

10. Install the rear mount and crossmember onto the transmission. Torque the mount-to-transmission nuts to 17 ft. lbs. (23 Nm) but do not torque the single center nut yet.

11. Fit the transmission into place, making sure the main shaft fits easily into the clutch disc spline. Push the transmission up against the engine and start all the bolts before tightening any of them. Torque the bolts to 34 ft. lbs. (46 Nm).

12. Bolt the crossmember to the body and torque the bolts to 34 ft. lbs. (46 Nm). Torque the center crossmember mount nut to 59 ft. lbs. (80 Nm).

13. Install the starter and connect the wiring. Install the clutch housing inspection plate, if equipped.

14. Connect the speedometer cable and wiring and install the exhaust heat shields.

15. Install the driveshaft, making sure to align the matchmarks and balance washers correctly.

16. When installing the exhaust pipes, use new gaskets and torque the flange nuts to 34 ft. lbs. (46 Nm).

17. Install the clutch release cylinder and shift lever and refill the transmission with the correct oil.

1993-94

1. Disconnect the negative battery cable. Raise and safely support the vehicle. Drain the transmission oil.

2. Remove the shift lever knob and the console panel assembly. Remove the insulators and the shift lever.

3. Remove the transmission undercovers.

4. Remove the clutch slave cylinder bolts and hydraulic line bracket bolt. Secure the slave cylinder aside, without disconnecting the hydraulic line.

5. Label and disconnect the electrical connectors to the starter. Remove the starter.

6. Remove the center tunnel reinforcement. Disconnect the air injection pipe and remove the catalytic converter.

7. Remove the front and rear tunnel reinforcements.

8. Remove the cover plate from under the transmission tailshaft. Mark the position of the driveshaft on the rear axle flange and remove the driveshaft.

9. Support the engine using engine support tool 49 G017 5A0 or equivalent. Support the differential with a jack.

10. Remove the transmission-to-differential frame member.

11. Label and disconnect the necessary electrical connectors. Remove the service hole covers from the transmission and remove the backup light switch.

12. Working through the service hole **A**, swing the clutch release fork so the release bearing is pushed and held toward the clutch pressure plate.

13. Insert a small prybar through service hole **B** and into the space between the wedge collar and the release bearing. Pry and separate the release bearing from the clutch pressure plate.

14. Swing the clutch release fork back and forth to make sure the release bearing and clutch pressure plate are separated.

15. If Steps 12-14 do not work, gradually loosen the 6 clutch pressure plate bolts in a crisscross pattern, working through service hole **B**. Remove the bolts and separate the pressure plate from the flywheel.

16. Support the transmission with a jack and remove the transmission-to-engine bolts. Carefully remove the transmission.

17. If the transmission was removed as per Step 15, remove the wire ring from the release bearing and separate the release bearing from the clutch pressure plate.

To install:

18. If the clutch pressure plate was removed, proceed as follows:

   a. Install a new wedge collar on the pressure plate. Apply a small amount of grease to a new wire ring and install on the wedge collar.

   b. Clean the clutch disc splines and apply a small amount of molybdenum grease to the splines.

   c. Install the clutch disc on the flywheel and install a suitable alignment tool.

   d. Install the clutch pressure plate, aligning the dowel holes with the flywheel dowels. Install the bolts and gradually tighten to 19 ft. lbs. (25 Nm), in a crisscross pattern.

   e. Remove the clutch alignment tool.

19. Coat the splines of the transmission input shaft with molybdenum grease.

20. Raise the transmission into position and install the transmission-to-engine bolts. Tighten the bolts to 38 ft. lbs. (51 Nm).

21. Working through service hole **A**, push the release cylinder end of the clutch release fork toward the transmission and connect the clutch

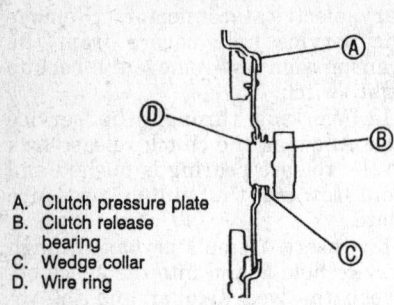

A. Clutch pressure plate
B. Clutch release bearing
C. Wedge collar
D. Wire ring

Clutch parts identification — 1993-94 RX-7

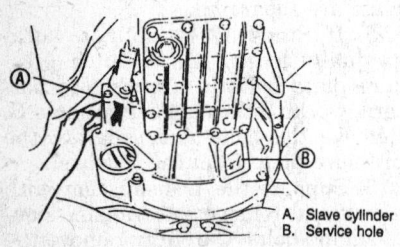

A. Slave cylinder
B. Service hole

Service hole identification — 1993-94 RX-7

release bearing to the clutch pressure plate.

22. Swing the clutch release fork back and forth to make sure the clutch release bearing is connected to the clutch pressure plate. Push the release cylinder end of the clutch release fork toward the engine and make sure it does not move past the engine-transmission mating line.

23. Install the service hole covers. Install the backup light switch and tighten to 25 ft. lbs. (34 Nm). Connect the electrical connectors.

24. Position the jack under the differential so the differential is perfectly level. Install the transmission-to-differential frame member and hold in place with a new bolt and 8 new nuts.

25. Tighten the frame-to-differential nuts to 130 ft. lbs. (176 Nm) and the frame-to-differential bolt to 68 ft. lbs. (93 Nm).

26. Tighten the frame to transmission nuts to 130 ft. lbs. (176 Nm), tightening the upper nuts first.

27. Remove the jack from under the differential. Lower the vehicle and remove the engine support tool.

28. Raise and safely support the vehicle. Position a straightedge between the right and left floorpans

and measure the distance between the bottom of the frame member and the straightedge. The distance should be 2.91 in. (74mm) minimum. If the distance is not correct, readjust the frame member.

29. Install the driveshaft, aligning the marks made during removal. Tighten the bolts to 43 ft. lbs. (58 Nm).

30. Install the cover under the transmission tailshaft. Install the front and rear tunnel reinforcements and tighten to 19 ft. lbs. (25 Nm).

31. Install the catalytic converter, using new gaskets, and tighten the nuts to 65 ft. lbs. (89 Nm). Connect the air injection pipe.

32. Install the center tunnel reinforcement and tighten the bolts to 19 ft. lbs. (25 Nm).

33. Install the starter and tighten the bolts to 38 ft. lbs. (51 Nm). Connect the starter wiring.

34. Install the clutch slave cylinder and tighten the bolts to 15 ft. lbs. (22 Nm).

35. Install the transmission undercovers. Fill the transmission with the proper type and quantity of oil and lower the vehicle.

36. Install the shift lever assembly and insulators. Install the console panel and the shift lever knob. Connect the negative battery cable.

MANUAL TRANSAXLE

Transaxle Assembly

REMOVAL AND INSTALLATION

323 and Protege

WITHOUT 4WD

1. Raise and safely support the vehicle and remove the front wheels. Remove the battery and battery box and the air cleaner and ducting.

2. Remove the splash shield and drain the transaxle oil.

3. Without disconnecting the hydraulic hose, remove the clutch release cylinder. Disconnect the speedometer cable and the wiring from the transaxle.

4. Disconnect the wiring and remove the starter.

5. Disconnect the shift linkage and the extension bar.

6. Disconnect the exhaust pipe from the manifold and the catalytic converter and remove the pipe.

7. Disconnect the tie rod ends and lower ball joints and remove the halfhsafts.

8. Install the necessary lifting equipment and support the engine from above. Remove the lower mounting frame and support the transaxle from below with a jack.

9. Remove the front and left rear mounts and allow the engine/transaxle to tilt towards the left.

10. Remove the bolts and slide the transaxle away from the engine to lower it out of the vehicle.

To install:

11. Lightly lubricate the main shaft spline and the release bearing fork contact points with molybdenum grease and install the release bearing.

12. Carefully guide the transaxle into place, making sure the main shaft spline fits properly into the clutch disc. Start all the transaxle-to-engine bolts, then torque them to 66 ft. lbs. (89 Nm).

13. Install the left rear mount but do not torque the bolts yet.

14. Install the halfshafts, making sure the inner joint is firmly seated into place. Torque the extension shaft bracket bolts to 46 ft. lbs. (62 Nm).

15. Assemble the suspension. Torque the lower ball joint pinch bolt and the tie rod end nuts to 43 ft. lbs. (59 Nm). If equipped with a stabilizer bar, adjust the link with ¾ in. (19mm) of thread showing above the locknut.

16. Install the front mount to the transaxle and torque the bolts to 38 ft. lbs. (52 Nm).

17. Install the lower mounting frame and torque the frame-to-body nuts and bolts to 66 ft. lbs. (89 Nm). Torque the mount-to-frame nuts and bolts to 38 ft. lbs. (52 Nm).

18. Connect the shift linkage and control rod.

19. Install the starter and connect the wiring. Install the clutch release cylinder.

20. connect the speedometer cable and transaxle wiring.

21. Install the splash shields and wheels.

22. Install the air cleaner and battery and fill the transaxle with oil.

WITH 4WD

1. Remove the battery and the air cleaner assembly and the ducting. Raise and support the vehicle safely and remove the undercover. Drain the transaxle and transfer case oil and remove the front wheels.

2. Disconnect the speedometer cable in the center. Remove the clutch release cylinder bolt, clip and the clutch release cylinder.

3. Disconnect the wiring from the transaxle and the starter.

4. Disconnect the shift linkage cables from the transaxle by removing the pins and cable retaining clips. Route the cables aside.

5. Matchmark the flanges and remove the driveshaft.

6. Remove the exhaust pipe and catalytic converter and the heat shield.

7. Disconnect the tie rod ends, the lower ball joints and the stabilizer rod links.

8. Remove the halfshafts and the right side extension shaft. Install special tool 40 B027 001 or equivalent into the differential to prevent the gears from becoming misaligned inside the case.

9. To remove the differential lock motor, remove the sensor switch, insert a small screwdriver into the hole and turn the rod ½ turn counterclockwise. Remove the bolts and remove the motor.

10. Remove the starter and bracket.

11. Install the necessary lifting equipment and support the engine from above. Remove the crossmember, the front mount and the mount member.

12. Remove the stiffener plate and support the transaxle with a jack.

13. Remove the bolts and separate the engine and transaxle. Carefully lower the unit out of the vehicle.

To install:

14. Lightly lubricate the main shaft spline and the release bearing fork contact points with molybdenum grease and install the release bearing.

15. Carefully guide the transaxle into place, making sure the main shaft spline fits properly into the clutch disc. Start all the transaxle-to-engine bolts, then torque the large ones to 59 ft. lbs. (80 Nm), the smaller ones to 38 ft. lbs. (52 Nm). Install the stiffener plate.

16. Install the engine mount member and all the mount bolts before tightening any of them. Torque the member-to-body bolts to 66 ft. lbs. (89 Nm) and the mount-to-frame nuts and bolts to 38 ft. lbs. (52 Nm). When all the mounts are connected, remove the lifting equipment.

17. Install the center differential lock motor and the starter and connect the wiring.

18. Install the halfshafts, making sure the inner joint is firmly seated

into place. Torque the extension shaft bracket bolts to 46 ft. lbs. (62 Nm).

19. Install the exhaust pipe with new gaskets, torque the nuts to 34 ft. lbs. (46 Nm).

20. Install the crossmember, torque the bolts to 86 ft. lbs. (117 Nm).

21. Install the driveshaft, making sure to align the marks. Torque the nuts to 22 ft. lbs. (30 Nm).

22. Assemble the suspension. Torque the lower ball joint pinch bolt and the tie rod end nuts to 43 ft. lbs. (59 Nm). If equipped with a stabilizer bar, adjust the link with ¾ in. (19mm) of thread showing above the locknut.

23. Connect the shift linkage.

24. Connect the speedometer cable and all the wiring and install the clutch release cylinder.

25. Fill the transaxle and transfer case with oil and install the undercover.

26. Install the remaining components and adjust the shift linkage as required.

MX-3

1.6L ENGINE

1. Disconnect the negative battery cable. Raise and safely support the vehicle. Drain the fluid from the transaxle.

2. Remove the wheel and tire assemblies and the splash shield.

3. Remove the resonance duct and the air cleaner assembly.

4. Disconnect the positive battery cable and remove the battery and battery tray. Label and disconnect the neutral switch and backup light connectors and the ground wire.

5. Disconnect the extension bar and shift control rod from the transaxle.

6. Remove the cotter pins and nuts and separate the tie rod ends from the knuckles. Disconnect the stabilizer links from the lower control arms.

7. Remove the halfshafts.

8. Remove the intake manifold support bracket and the starter.

9. Support the engine using engine support tool 49 G017 5A0 or equivalent. Remove the bolts/nuts and remove the engine mount member.

10. Remove the mounting bolts and line clip and position the clutch slave cylinder aside without disconnecting the hydraulic line.

11. Remove the front and left side transaxle mounts.

12. Loosen the engine support tool and lean the engine toward the transaxle. Support the transaxle with a

jack. Remove the transaxle mounting bolts and carefully remove the transaxle.

To install:

13. Raise the transaxle into position and install the transaxle-to-engine bolts. Tighten to 66 ft. lbs. (89 Nm). Install the oil pan-to-transaxle bolts and tighten to 38 ft. lbs. (52 Nm).

14. Loosely tighten the left side transaxle mount bolts. Install the front transaxle mount and tighten to 38 ft. lbs. (52 Nm).

15. Install the clutch slave cylinder and tighten the bolts to 17 ft. lbs. (23 Nm).

16. Install the engine mount member, aligning the front and rear transaxle mount stud bolts. Install the mount member-to-mount nuts and tighten to 38 ft. lbs. (52 Nm) and the mount member-to-body bolts/nuts and tighten to 66 ft. lbs. (89 Nm).

17. Tighten the left side transaxle mount-to-transaxle bolts to 69 ft. lbs. (93 Nm). Remove the engine support tool.

18. Install the starter and intake manifold support bracket. Tighten the bolts/nuts to 38 ft. lbs. (52 Nm).

19. Install the halfshafts.

20. Connect the stabilizer bar link to the lower control arm and tighten the nut to 45 ft. lbs. (61 Nm). Connect the tie rod end to the steering knuckle and tighten the nut to 42 ft. lbs. (57 Nm). Install a new cotter pin.

21. Connect the extension bar to the transaxle and tighten the bolt to 38 ft. lbs. (52 Nm). Connect the shift control rod and tighten the bolt to 17 ft. lbs. (23 Nm).

22. Remove the speedometer driven gear and add the proper type and quantity of oil. Install the driven gear and tighten the bolt to 100 inch lbs. (11 Nm). Connect the speedometer cable.

23. Connect the electrical connectors and ground wire. Install the battery tray and battery.

24. Install the air cleaner assembly and the resonance duct. Install the splash shield and the wheel and tire assemblies.

25. Lower the vehicle and connect the battery cables. Start the engine and check for leaks and proper transaxle operation.

1.8L ENGINE

1. Relieve the fuel system pressure and disconnect the negative battery cable. Raise and safely support the vehicle and drain the fluid from the transaxle.

2. Remove the wheel and tire assemblies and the splash shield.

3. Remove the resonance duct and the air cleaner assembly.

4. Disconnect the positive battery cable and remove the battery and battery tray.

5. Remove the starter and the wiring harness bracket. Disconnect the fuel lines and remove the fuel filter.

6. Label and disconnect the connectors for the neutral switch, backup light switch and speedometer sensor.

7. Remove the mounting bolts and line clip and position the clutch slave cylinder aside without disconnecting the hydraulic line.

8. Remove the transverse member and the front exhaust pipe/converter assembly.

9. Disconnect the extension bar and shift control rod from the transaxle.

10. Remove the cotter pins and nuts and separate the tie rod ends from the knuckles. Disconnect the stabilizer links from the lower control arms.

11. Remove the halfshafts and the intermediate shaft.

12. Support the engine using engine support tool 49 G017 5A0 or equivalent. Remove the bolts/nuts and remove the engine mount member.

13. Remove the left side transaxle mount and the transaxle inspection plate.

14. Loosen the engine support tool and lean the engine toward the transaxle. Support the transaxle with a jack. Remove the transaxle mounting bolts and carefully remove the transaxle.

To install:

15. Raise the transaxle into position and install the transaxle-to-engine bolts. Tighten to 73 ft. lbs. (99 Nm).

16. Install the transmission inspection plate and tighten the bolts to 38 ft. lbs. (52 Nm).

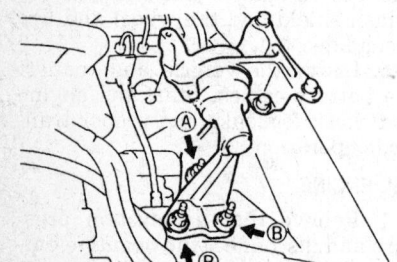

Transaxle mount-to-transaxle nut identification — MX-3 with 1.8L engine

17. Loosely tighten the left side transaxle mount bolts.

18. Install the engine mount member, aligning the front and rear transaxle mount stud bolts. Install the mount member-to-mount nuts and tighten to 38 ft. lbs. (52 Nm) and the mount member-to-body bolts/nuts and tighten to 66 ft. lbs. (89 Nm).

19. Tighten left side transaxle mount-to-transaxle nut **A** to 69 ft. lbs. (93 Nm) and nuts **B** to 30 ft. lbs. (40 Nm). Remove the engine support tool.

20. Install the halfshafts and joint shaft.

21. Connect the stabilizer bar link to the lower control arm and tighten the nut to 45 ft. lbs. (61 Nm). Connect the tie rod end to the steering knuckle and tighten the nut to 42 ft. lbs. (57 Nm). Install a new cotter pin.

22. Connect the extension bar to the transaxle and tighten the bolt to 38 ft. lbs. (52 Nm). Connect the shift control rod and tighten the bolt to 17 ft. lbs. (23 Nm).

23. Install the exhaust pipe, using new gaskets. Tighten the manifold flange nuts to 38 ft. lbs. (52 Nm).

24. Install the transverse member and tighten the bolts to 93 ft. lbs. (127 Nm).

25. Connect the electrical connectors. Install the fuel filter and connect the fuel lines.

26. Install the starter and the wiring harness bracket.

27. Install the battery tray and battery.

28. Install the air cleaner assembly and the resonance duct. Install the splash shield and the wheel and tire assemblies.

29. Fill the transaxle with the proper type and quantity of oil.

30. Lower the vehicle and connect the battery cables. Start the engine and check for leaks and proper transaxle operation.

MX-6/626

1990-92

1. Remove the battery and battery carrier.

2. Remove the air ducting and the air cleaner and air flow meter assembly.

3. Unplug the wiring and remove the fuse block.

4. Disconnect the speedometer cable and the transaxle grounds.

5. Raise and support the vehicle safely and remove the front wheels and splash shield. Drain the transaxle oil.

6. Remove the clutch release cylinder and disconnect the tie rod ends.

7. Remove the stabilizer control links. Remove the nuts and bolts from the lower control arm ball joints and pull the lower control arms downward to separate them from the steering knuckles. Be careful not to damage the ball joint dust boots.

8. Insert a small prybar between the left driveshaft and the transaxle case and tap the end of the lever to uncouple the driveshaft from the differential side gear. Pull the front hub forward and separate the driveshaft from the transaxle. Remove the left joint shaft bracket. Separate the right driveshaft and joint shaft in the same manner as the left.

NOTE: Do not insert the lever too deeply between the shaft and the case or the oil seal lip could be damaged. To avoid damage to the oil seal, hold the CV-joint at the differential and pull the driveshaft straight out.

9. Once both drive and joint shafts are removed, install differential side gear holders 49-G030-455 (turbocharged), 49-G027-003 or their equivalents, in the differential side gears to hold them in place and prevent misalignment.

10. Remove the engine-to-transaxle gusset plates and undercover. Remove the extension bar and the control rod. Remove the manifold bracket and the starter.

11. Suspend the engine from the engine hanger with a suitable lifting device or engine support fixture.

12. Remove the front and left engine mounts and bracket. Disconnect the rubber hanger from the crossmember, then remove the crossmember and left side lower control arm as an assembly.

13. Lean the engine towards the transaxle and support the transaxle with a jack. Remove the transaxle-to-engine bolts and slide the transaxle back and out from under the vehicle.

To install:

14. Lightly lubricate the main shaft spline and the release bearing fork contact points with molybdenum grease and install the release bearing.

15. Carefully guide the transaxle into place, making sure the main shaft spline fits properly into the clutch disc. Start all the transaxle-to-engine bolts, then torque them to 86 ft. lbs. (117 Nm).

16. Install the front mount and torque nuts and bolts to 66 ft. lbs. (89 Nm).

17. Install the left mount crossmember and torque the mount-to-transaxle bolts to 38 ft. lbs. (52 Nm).

Torque the crossmember bolts to 40 ft. lbs. (54 Nm), the nuts to 69 ft. lbs. (93 Nm).

18. Install the starter and bracket and torque the bolts to 38 ft. lbs. (52 Nm). Connect the wiring

19. Connect the shift linkage and the extension bar. Install the transaxle-to-engine gusset plates and torque the bolts to 38 ft. lbs. (52 Nm).

20. Install the halfshafts. When assembling the suspension pieces, torque the ball joint pinch bolts and the tie rod ends to 40 ft. lbs. (54 Nm). Install new cotter pins.

21. Assemble the stabilizer bar links and adjust them so 0.8 in. (20mm) of thread protrudes above the locknut.

22. Install the clutch release cylinder and the splash shields.

23. Connect all wiring and the speedometer cable. Install the air flow meter and air cleaner assembly and the fuse box.

24. Fill the transaxle with the proper amount of oil and install the air ducting and battery.

1993-94

1. Disconnect the battery cables and remove the battery and battery tray. Raise and safely support the vehicle. Drain the transaxle fluid.

2. Remove the ducts and the air cleaner assembly.

3. If equipped with 2.5L engine, remove the starter.

4. Label and disconnect the electrical connectors for the park/neutral switch, backup light switch and vehicle speed sensor. Disconnect the ground wires.

5. Remove the fuel filter mounting nuts and position the filter aside, leaving the fuel lines attached. Remove the wiring harness bracket.

6. Remove the mounting bolts and the hydraulic line clips, then position the clutch slave cylinder aside, leaving the hydraulic line attached.

7. Remove the wheel and tire assemblies and the splash shields. Remove the transverse member.

8. If equipped with 2.5L engine, disconnect the oxygen sensor connectors and remove the front exhaust pipe/catalytic converter assembly.

9. Disconnect the extension bar and shift control rod from the transaxle.

10. Remove the cotter pins and nuts and separate the tie rod ends from the knuckles. Disconnect the stabilizer bar from the lower control arms.

11. Remove the halfshafts and the intermediate shaft.

12. If equipped with 2.0L engine, remove the starter.

13. Remove the engine mount rubber at the right side of the engine mount member. Remove the rear transaxle mount.

14. Support the engine using engine support tool 49 G017 5A0 or equivalent. Remove the nuts and bolts and remove the engine mount member.

15. If equipped with 2.5L engine, remove the transaxle housing inspection plate.

16. Remove the left side transaxle mount.

17. Loosen the engine support tool and lean the engine toward the transaxle. Support the transaxle on a jack and remove the transaxle mounting bolts. Carefully remove the transaxle from the vehicle.

18. Remove the front transaxle mount.

To install:

19. Install the front transaxle mount and tighten the mount-to-transaxle bolts to 44 ft. lbs. (60 Nm). Loosely tighten the mount through bolt and nut.

20. Raise the transaxle into position and install the transaxle mounting bolts. If equipped with 2.5L engine, install the inspection cover. Tighten the mounting bolts to the proper torque values.

21. Loosely tighten the left side transaxle mount bolts and nuts.

22. Use the engine support tool to make sure the transaxle bolt holes and the rear transaxle mount are aligned. Install the bolts and tighten to 68 ft. lbs. (93 Nm).

23. Install the engine mount member, making sure the engine mount rubbers are properly installed. Tighten the mount member-to-body bolts/nuts to 68 ft. lbs. (93 Nm) and the front transaxle mount nuts to 77 ft. lbs. (104 Nm).

24. Tighten the front transaxle mount through bolt and nut to 86 ft. lbs. (116 Nm).

25. Tighten the left side transaxle mount bolts and nut to 68 ft. lbs. (93 Nm) and remove the engine support tool.

26. Install the engine mount rubber on the right side of the mount member and tighten the bolts to 44 ft. lbs. (60 Nm).

27. If equipped with 2.0L engine, install the starter.

28. Install the intermediate shaft and halfshafts.

29. Connect the stabilizer bar link to the lower control arm and tighten to 39 ft. lbs. (53 Nm). Install the tie rod end to the steering knuckle and tighten the nut to 32 ft. lbs. (44 Nm).

30. Connect the shift control rod to the transaxle and tighten the bolt to 18 ft. lbs. (25 Nm). Connect the extension bar and tighten the nut to 38 ft. lbs. (51 Nm).

31. If equipped with 2.5L engine, install the exhaust pipe, using new gaskets. Tighten the exhaust manifold flange nuts to 38 ft. lbs. (51 Nm). Connect the oxygen sensor connectors.

32. Install the transverse member and tighten the bolts to 96 ft. lbs. (131 Nm).

33. Install the splash shields and the wheel and tire assemblies.

34. Install the clutch slave cylinder and tighten the bolts to 16 ft. lbs. (22 Nm). Install the wiring harness bracket and tighten the bolts to 130 inch lbs. (14 Nm).

35. Install the fuel filter mounting nuts and tighten to 95 inch lbs. (11 Nm). Connect the grounds and electrical connectors.

36. If equipped with 2.5L engine, install the starter.

37. Install the air cleaner assembly and air ducts. Install the battery tray and battery.

38. Fill the transaxle with the proper type and quantity of fluid and lower the vehicle.

39. Connect the battery cables and start the engine. Check for leaks and for proper transaxle operation.

LINKAGE ADJUSTMENT

323 and Protege With 4WD

1. Set the transaxle shift lever to the neutral position.

2. On the transaxle make sure the shift and select levers are also in the neutral position.

3. Remove the shift lever console.

4. Disconnect the shift and select cables from the control levers by re-

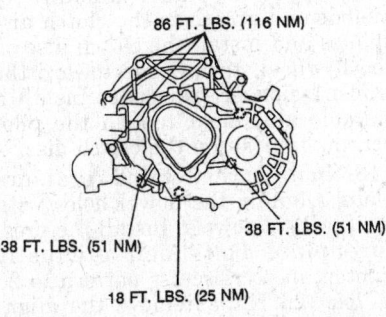

86 FT. LBS. (116 NM)

38 FT. LBS. (51 NM)

38 FT. LBS. (51 NM)

18 FT. LBS. (25 NM)

Transaxle bolt torque specifications — MX-6/626 2.0L engine

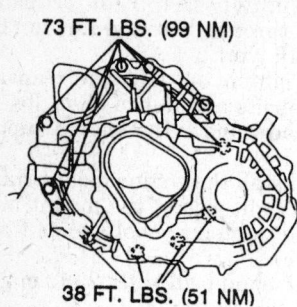

73 FT. LBS. (99 NM)

38 FT. LBS. (51 NM)

Transaxle bolt torque specifications — MX-6/626 2.5L engine

moving the pins, flat washers and spring clips. The clips must be replaced.

5. Make sure the select cable end hole aligns with the select lever pin. If not aligned, loosen cable adjusting nut and rotate the cable end until the holes are aligned.

6. Place the shift lever at the center of its front-to-rear stoke.

7. Make sure the shift cable end hole aligns with the shift lever pin. If not aligned, loosen cable adjusting nut and rotate the cable end until the holes are aligned.

8. Connect the cables.

CLUTCH

Clutch Assembly

REMOVAL AND INSTALLATION

Except 1993-94 RX-7

1. Disconnect the negative battery cable. Raise and safely support the vehicle.

2. Remove the transmission or transaxle.

3. Gradually loosen the clutch pressure plate bolts, in a crisscross pattern. Support the pressure plate and remove the bolts. Remove the pressure plate and clutch disc.

4. Inspect the pilot bearing. If it is worn or damaged and does not turn easily by hand, remove it using a puller/slide hammer.

5. Check the flywheel surface for scoring, cracks or burning and machine or replace, as necessary.

6. On all except RX-7, install holder tool 49 E011 1A0 or equivalent, to keep the flywheel from

turning. Loosen the flywheel bolts evenly and gradually in a crisscross pattern. Remove the flywheel.

7. On RX-7, install holder tool 49 F011 101 or equivalent, to keep the flywheel from turning. Remove the locknut. Remove the flywheel, using a suitable puller and remove the key from the eccentric shaft.

8. Inspect the clutch release bearing for wear. Replace it if it sticks or does not turn easily.

9. Inspect the release fork for wear or damage and replace as necessary.

To install:

10. Lubricate the release fork fingers and pivot with molybdenum grease and install in the release fork boot.

11. Install the clutch release bearing on the release fork.

12. If removed, install a new pilot bearing in the flywheel, using a suitable installation tool.

13. Make sure the flywheel mounting surface and the crankshaft or eccentric shaft mounting surfaces are clean. Remove any old sealant from the flywheel bolt hole threads and the flywheel bolts.

14. On RX-7, install the eccentric shaft key. Install the flywheel.

15. On all except RX-7, apply sealant to the flywheel bolt threads and install them hand tight. Install the flywheel holding tool. Tighten the bolts, in a crisscross pattern, to 76 ft. lbs. (102 Nm) on all except MX-3 1.8L engine and MX-6/626 2.5L engine. On MX-3 1.8L engine and MX-6/626 2.5L engine, tighten the bolts to 49 ft. lbs. (67 Nm).

16. On RX-7, apply thread locking compound to the locknut threads and the locknut and flywheel contact surfaces. Install the locknut on the eccentric shaft and install the flywheel holder tool. Tighten the locknut to 360 ft. lbs. (490 Nm).

17. Apply a small amount of molbdenum grease to the clutch disc splines and install the clutch disc on the flywheel, spring side toward the transmission or transaxle. Install a suitable alignment tool in the pilot bearing to position the clutch disc.

18. Install the clutch pressure plate, aligning the dowel holes with the flywheel dowels. Install the pressure plate bolts and gradually tighten, in a crisscross pattern to 20 ft. lbs. (26 Nm). Remove the alignment tool.

19. Install the transmission or transaxle and lower the vehicle.

1993-94 RX-7

1. Disconnect the negative battery cable. Raise and safely support the vehicle.

2. Remove the transmission.

3. Remove the clutch release fork assembly bolts and remove the release fork and bearing as an assembly. Inspect the release fork for wear or damage; make sure it swings freely without the return spring installed. Inspect the release bearing for wear, damage or sticking when it is turned. Replace parts as necessary.

4. Install flywheel holder tool 49 F011 101 or equivalent. Loosen the clutch pressure plate bolts gradually, in a crisscross pattern. Support the pressure plate, remove the bolts and remove the pressure plate and clutch disc.

5. Remove the wire ring from the wedge collar and remove the wedge collar from the pressure plate.

6. Inspect the pilot bearing for wear or damage, make sure it turns freely by hand. Remove the pilot bearing, with the oil seal, using a puller/slide hammer.

7. Inspect the flywheel for scoring, cracks or burning. Machine or replace as necessary. To remove, install holder tool 49 F011 101 or equivalent and remove the locknut. Remove the key from the eccentric shaft.

To install:

8. Install the key in the eccentric shaft and install the flywheel. Apply thread locking compound to the locknut threads and sealant to the locknut contact surface. Install the locknut.

9. Install the holder tool and tighten the locknut to 360 ft. lbs. (490 Nm).

10. Install a new pilot bearing using a suitable installer. The bearing must be installed to a depth of 0.453-0.482 in. (11.5-12.3mm). Install a new oil seal.

11. Apply a small amount of molybdenum grease to the clutch disc splines. Install the clutch disc on the flywheel, spring side toward the transmission. Install an alignment tool in the pilot bearing to position the clutch disc.

12. Install a new wedge collar on the pressure plate. Apply a small amount of grease to a new wire ring and install.

13. Align the pressure plate dowel holes with the flywheel dowels and install the flywheel. Install the pressure plate bolts and gradually tighten, in a crisscross pattern, to 19 ft. lbs. (26 Nm).

14. Lubricate the release fork and install the release fork and release bearing assembly in the transmission. Tighten the bolts to 33 ft. lbs. (46 Nm).

15. Install the transmission and lower the vehicle.

PEDAL HEIGHT ADJUSTMENT

1. Measure the distance between the upper surface of the pedal pad to the carpet.

2. The distance should be as follows:

323/Protege and MX-3   7.72-8.03 in. (196-204mm)

Miata: 6.89-7.28 in. (175-185mm)

MX-6/626

1990-92: 6.73-7.13 in. (171-181mm)

1993-94: 7.32-8.31 in. (186-211mm)

RX-7

1990-91: 7.20-7.60 in. (183-193mm)

1993-94: 6.516-6.968 in. (165.5-177mm)

3. If the distance is not as specified, loosen the locknut on the stopper bolt or switch.

4. Turn the switch or bolt until the distance is correct, then tighten the locknut.

PEDAL FREE-PLAY ADJUSTMENT

Cable Clutch

323

1. Depress the pedal lightly by hand and measure the free-play; it should be 0.35-0.59 in. (9-15mm).

2. If the free-play is not as specified, depress the clutch pedal 7 times and straighten the clutch cable in the cable bracket.

3. At the transaxle, depress the release lever by hand and pull the slack out of the cable. Measure the gap at

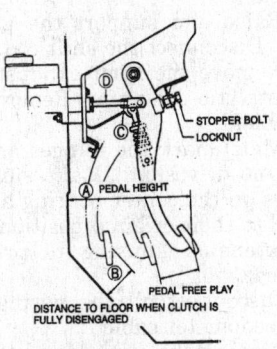

STOPPER BOLT
LOCKNUT
PEDAL HEIGHT
PEDAL FREE PLAY
DISTANCE TO FLOOR WHEN CLUTCH IS
FULLY DISENGAGED

Pedal height adjustment — vehicles with hydraulic clutch

A. Turn the adjusting nut until there is about 0.080 in. (2mm) clearance between the cable pin and the lever.

4. After adjustment, ensure that when the clutch is disengaged, the distance between the floor and the upper center of the pedal is about 3.3 in. (85mm).

5. Recheck the pedal height and adjust, if necessary.

Hydraulic Clutch

1. Depress the clutch pedal by hand until resistance is felt. The free-play should be 0.04-0.12 in. (1-3mm).

2. If the free-play is not correct, loosen the clutch master cylinder pushrod locknut and turn the pushrod to adjust.

3. After adjustment, check the disengagement height; the distance between the upper surface of the pedal pad to the floor when the clutch is fully disengaged. Disengagement height is as follows:

323/Protege: 1.61 in. (41mm)

MX-3: 2.17 in. (55mm)

Miata: 2.68 in. (68mm)

MX-6/626

1990-92: 1.54 in. (39mm)

1993-94: 2.64 in. (67mm)

RX-7

1990-91: 2.13 in. (54mm)

1993-94: 1.9 in. (48mm)

4. Tighten the locknut. Recheck the pedal height.

Clutch Cable

REMOVAL AND INSTALLATION

1. Remove the adjusting nut and pin.

2. Unbolt and remove the clutch cable bracket.

3. Disconnect the cable from the clutch pedal.

4. Withdraw the cable from the engine compartment.

5. Installation is the reverse of the removal procedure. Coat the pedal cable hook and the joint between the release lever and pin with lithium grease.

Clutch Master Cylinder

REMOVAL AND INSTALLATION

1. Disconnect the negative battery cable.

2. On 323/Protege and MX-3, remove the battery and the diagnostic connector.

3. On 1993-94 MX-6/626, remove the evaporative canister. On 1993 RX-7, remove the evaporative canister.

4. On 323/Protege, MX-3 and 1993-94 MX-6/626 and RX-7, disconnect the hose from the brake master cylinder reservoir and plug the reservoir port.

5. Remove the hydraulic line from the master cylinder using a tubing wrench.

6. Remove the mounting nuts and remove the master cylinder and gasket.

To install:

7. Install the master cylinder with a new gasket. Tighten the nuts to 18 ft. lbs. (25 Nm) on all except MX-3. On MX-3, tighten the nuts to 8.7 ft. lbs. (12 Nm).

8. Attach the hydraulic line and tighten the fitting with the tubing wrench.

9. If equipped, remove the plug from the brake master cylinder reservoir and connect the hose.

10. Install the remaining components in the reverse of removal. Bleed the air from the system.

Clutch Slave Cylinder

REMOVAL AND INSTALLATION

1. Disconnect the negative battery cable.

2. If equipped with a flexible hydraulic line connecting the slave cylinder, loosen the fitting at the hose-tube junction and remove the clip from the bracket. Remove the hose from the slave cylinder using a tubing wrench and plug the hydraulic line.

3. On all other vehicles, loosen the hydraulic line fitting at the slave cylinder. Disconnect and plug the line.

4. Remove the slave cylinder mounting bolts and remove the slave cylinder.

To install:

5. Install the slave cylinder and tighten the bolts to 16 ft. lbs. (22 Nm).

6. Connect the hydraulic line and tighten with a tubing wrench.

7. If equipped with a flexible hose, connect the hose and tighten with a tubing wrench. Attach the hose to the bracket and install the clip. Connect the hydraulic line and tighten the fitting with a tubing wrench.

8. Bleed the air from the system.

Hydraulic Clutch System Bleeding

1. Remove the rubber cap from the bleeder screw on the release cylinder.
2. Place a bleeder tube over the end of the bleeder screw.
3. Submerge the other end of the tube in a jar half filled with hydraulic brake fluid.
4. Slowly pump the clutch pedal fully and allow it to return slowly, several times.
5. While pressing the clutch pedal to the floor, loosen the bleeder screw until the fluid starts to run out. Then close the bleeder screw. Keep repeating this Step, while watching the hydraulic fluid in the jar. As soon as the air bubbles disappear, close the bleeder screw.
6. During the bleeding procedure the reservoir must be kept at least ¾ full.

AUTOMATIC TRANSMISSION

Transmission Assembly

REMOVAL AND INSTALLATION

Miata

1. Disconnect the negative battery cable. Raise and safely support the vehicle. Drain the transmission fluid.
2. Remove the engine undercover and disconnect the shift rod. Remove the complete exhaust system.
3. Mark the position of the driveshaft on the rear axle flange and remove the driveshaft.
4. Disconnect the speedometer cable and disconnect the vacuum hose from the vacuum diaphragm.
5. Label and disconnect the electrical connectors from the inhibitor switch, kickdown solenoid, overdrive cancel solenoid, oil pressure switch and lockup solenoid.
6. Remove the dipstick and dipstick tube. Disconnect the oil cooler lines.
7. Support the transmission and differential with jacks. Remove the transmission-to-differential frame as follows:
   a. Disconnect the wiring harness from the frame.

b. Remove the bolts from the underside of the frame at the differential end, noting their location. Pry out the spacer from the frame.
   c. Remove the differential mounting spacer from the underside of the differential.
   d. Insert a 14 x 1.5mm bolt through the frame hole and turn it into the sleeve. Twist and pull the bolt downward.
   e. Install a 6x 1mm bolt in the side hole to hold the sleeve and remove the long bolt. Remove the short bolt.
   f. Remove the transmission side bolts and remove the frame member.
8. Remove the torque converter bolts and the starter.
9. Remove the transmission mounting bolts and remove the transmission, being careful not to drop the torque converter.

To install:

10. Make sure the torque converter is fully installed in the transmission. The distance between 1 of the bolt hole lugs and a straightedge laid across the bellhousing should be 0.89 in. (22.5mm).
11. Raise the transmission into position and install the mounting bolts. Tighten to 66 ft. lbs. (89 Nm).
12. Install the starter. Install the torque converter bolts. Hold the flexplate with a small prybar and tighten the bolts to 27-40 ft. lbs. (36-54 Nm).
13. Install the transmission-to-frame member as follows:
   a. Install the differential mounting spacer on the underside of the differential. Tighten the mounting bolts to 38 ft. lbs. (52 Nm).
   b. Position the jack under the transmission so the transmission is level.
   c. Position the frame and install the transmission side bolts. Snug the bolts.

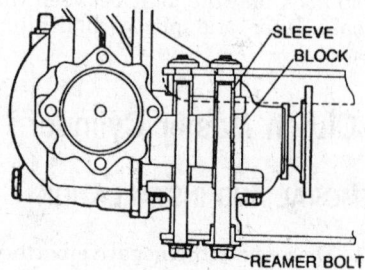

Sleeve and reamer bolt positioning — Miata

d. Make sure the sleeve is installed in the block. Install the spacer and bolts with the reamer bolt in the front hole. Snug the bolts.
   e. Tighten the transmission side bolts to 91 ft. lbs. (123 Nm), then tighten the differential bolts to the same specification.
   f. Connect the wiring harness to the frame member and remove the jacks.

NOTE: After the frame installation, position a straightedge between the body frame members on each side of the vehicle. Measure the distance between the bottom of the frame to the straightedge; it should be 2.023-2.417 in. (51.5-61.5mm). If the distance is not as specified, reposition the frame member at the transmission.

14. Connect the oil cooler lines, using new gaskets. Install the dipstick tube and dipstick.
15. Connect the electrical connectors and the vacuum hose. Connect the speedometer cable.
16. Install the driveshaft, aligning the marks made during removal. Tighten the bolts to 22 ft. lbs. (30 Nm).
17. Install the exhaust system. Connect the front pipe to the exhaust manifold, using a new gasket, and tighten the nuts to 34 ft. lbs. (46 Nm).
18. Install the engine undercover and connect the shift rod.
19. Lower the vehicle and connect the negative battery cable. Fill the transmission with the proper type and quantity of fluid. Start the engine and check for leaks and proper operation.

929

1990-91

1. Disconnect the negative battery cable. Remove the transmission oil dipstick.
2. Raise and support the vehicle safely. Disconnect the shift rod.
3. Remove the front exhaust pipe and catalytic converter. Remove the heat shield.
4. Matchmark the flanges and remove the driveshaft. Make sure the spacers on the center bearing are returned to their original position. Cap the extension housing to prevent fluid leakage.
5. Disconnect all the wiring and the speedometer cable.
6. Remove the starter and the inspection cover from the bottom of the torque converter housing.

7. Disconnect the oil pipes and the vacuum pipe. Plug the oil pipe to prevent leakage.

8. Support the engine from above as required. Place a transmission jack under the transmission and remove the crossmember assembly.

9. Remove the torque converter-to-flywheel bolts.

10. Remove the transmission-to-engine bolts and the transmission from the vehicle. Do not let the torque converter fall out.

To install:

11. Properly support the torque converter so it does not fall out. Install the rear mount and crossmember onto the transmission and torque the bolts to 21 ft. lbs. (28 Nm).

12. Fit the transmission into place and start all the bolts before tightening any of them. Torque the transmission-to-engine bolts to 38 ft. lbs. (52 Nm).

13. Install the torque converter-to-flywheel bolts and torque to 25 ft. lbs. (34 Nm). Install the inspection cover.

14. Bolt the crossmember to the body and torque the bolts to 42 ft. lbs. (57 Nm).

15. Connect the oil coolant pipes and make sure the clamps do not interfere with any other parts.

16. Install the starter and connect all wiring and vacuum lines.

17. Install the driveshaft and torque the bolts to 43 ft. lbs. (59 Nm). Make sure the center bearing spacers are properly installed and torque the bolts to 38 ft. lbs. (52 Nm).

18. Use new gaskets and install the exhaust system. Torque the flange nuts to 34 ft. lbs. (46 Nm).

19. Connect the shift rod and install the dipstick tube.

20. With everything installed, fill the transmission with the proper amount of fluid and run the engine to warm the transmission. Move the selector through all gears and check the fluid level.

1992-94

1. Disconnect the negative battery cable. Raise and safely support the vehicle. Drain the transmission fluid.

2. Remove the transmission dipstick.

3. Disconnect the oxygen sensors. Remove the exhaust system, except for the rear muffler. Remove the exhaust pipe bracket from the transmission and remove the heat shield.

4. Mark the position of the driveshaft on the axle flange and remove the driveshaft. Plug the tailshaft to prevent fluid leakage. Be sure to keep all the center bearing support bushings, washers and

spacers in order so they can be reinstalled in their original locations.

5. Remove the pinch bolts and remove the shaft connecting the rear steering gear. Disconnect the selector rod.

6. Label and disconnect the electrical connectors for the inhibitor switch, speed sensors, solenoid valve, pulse generator and knock sensor.

7. Disconnect the oil cooler lines and remove the oil filler tube.

8. Remove the starter and the transmission service hole cover. Lock the flexplate using a small prybar and remove the torque converter bolts.

9. Support the engine and transmission with jacks. Remove the transmission-to-engine bolts and the transmission mount bolts. Remove the transmission mount.

10. Carefully lower the transmission from the vehicle, being careful not to drop the torque converter.

To install:

11. Make sure the torque converter is completely installed in the transmission. Lay a straightedge across the bellhousing and measure the distance to 1 of the converter bolt hole lugs; it should be 1.161 in. (29.5mm). If the distance is less than specification, push the converter into the pump while rotating it, to properly engage the pump drive.

12. Raise the transmission into position and install the transmission-to-engine bolts. Tighten to 38 ft. lbs. (52 Nm).

13. Install the transmission mount and tighten the mount-to-body bolts to 45 ft. lbs. (61 Nm). Remove the engine and transmission jacks, then tighten the mount-to-transmission bolts/nuts to 56 ft. lbs. (77 Nm).

14. Turn the torque converter to align the bolt holes. Lock the flexplate using a small prybar and install the torque converter bolts. Tighten the bolts gradually and evenly to 25-36 ft. lbs. (34-49 Nm).

15. Install the service hole cover and the starter.

16. Install the oil filler tube using a new O-ring. Connect the oil cooler lines using new washers.

17. Connect the electrical connectors. Connect the selector rod with the washer and a new spring clip.

18. Install the rear steering gear shaft and tighten the pinch bolts to 36 ft. lbs. (49 Nm).

19. Install the driveshaft, aligning the marks made during removal. Tighten the driveshaft-to-axle flange bolts to 43 ft. lbs. (59 Nm). Install the center bearing support, making sure

all bushings, washers and spacers are installed in their original locations. Tighten the bolts to 39 ft. lbs. (53 Nm).

20. Install the heat shield and the exhaust pipe bracket. Install the exhaust system, using new gaskets, and tighten the flange nuts to 41 ft. lbs. (55 Nm). Connect the oxygen sensors.

21. Lower the vehicle and connect the negative battery cable. Fill the transmission with the proper type and quantity of fluid.

22. Start the engine and bring to normal operating temperature. Check for leaks and proper operation.

RX-7

1990-91

1. Disconnect the negative battery cable. Raise the vehicle and support safely.

2. Disconnect the exhaust pipe at the manifold and at the muffler and remove the pipe and the catalytic converter. Remove the heat shield covers.

3. Matchmark the driveshaft flanges and the position of the balance washers. Remove the driveshaft and cap the extension housing to prevent the fluid from leaking from the housing.

4. Disconnect the speedometer cable and wiring.

5. Disconnect the vacuum and oil pipes and plug the ends to prevent leakage.

6. Disconnect the electrical wiring and remove the starter.

7. Disconnect the shift rod from the transmission.

8. Remove the dipstick gauge and filler pipe.

9. Remove the inspection cover at the bottom of the torque converter housing and remove the torque converter-to-flywheel bolts.

10. Properly support the transmission with a transmission jack. Disconnect the rear mount and remove the mount crossmember.

11. Remove the transmission case-to-engine bolts. Slide the transmission rearward and carefully lower it from the vehicle. Do not let the torque converter fall out of the transmission.

To install:

12. Support the torque converter so it does not fall out of the transmission. Install the rear mount and crossmember onto the transmission. Torque the mount-to-transmission nuts to 17 ft. lbs. (23 Nm) but do not torque the single center nut yet.

13. Install the top cover onto the front of the housing and install the vacuum pipe and wiring bracket.

14. Fit the transmission into place and start all the bolts before tightening any of them. Torque the bolts to 38 ft. lbs. (52 Nm).

15. Use new gaskets and connect the oil pipes, torque to 26 ft. lbs. (35 Nm).

16. Bolt the crossmember to the body and torque the bolts to 34 ft. lbs. (46 Nm). Remove the jack and torque the center crossmember mount nut to 59 ft. lbs. (80 Nm).

17. Install the torque converter-to-flywheel bolts and torque to 25 ft. lbs. (34 Nm). Install the cover.

18. Install the starter and connect all the wiring and vacuum line.

19. Connect the speedometer cable and install the filler tube and dipstick.

20. Install the driveshaft, making sure to align the matchmarks and balance washers correctly.

21. Install the heat shields and the exhaust system. Use new gaskets and torque the flange nuts to 34 ft. lbs. (46 Nm).

22. Connect and adjust the shift rod as required.

23. Fill the transmission with the correct amount of fluid and run the engine to warm the transmission. Watch for leaks.

24. Move the selector through all gears and check for proper fluid level.

1993-94

1. Disconnect the negative battery cable. Raise and safely support the vehicle. Drain the transmission fluid.

2. Remove the transmission dipstick.

3. Remove the right and left undercovers. Remove the starter.

4. Remove the center tunnel reinforcement. Disconnect the air injection pipe and remove the catalytic converter.

5. Remove the front and rear tunnel reinforcements. Remove the cover at the front of the transmission-to-differential frame member.

6. Mark the position of the driveshaft on the axle flange and remove the driveshaft. Plug the transmission tailshaft to prevent fluid leakage.

7. Support the engine with engine support tool 49 G017 5A0 or equivalent. Support the differential with a jack. Remove the transmission-to-differential frame member.

8. Disconnect the oxygen sensor and remove the front exhaust pipe.

9. Label and disconnect the electrical connectors to the inhibitor switch, speed sensors, pulse generator and solenoid valve.

10. Disconnect the transmission selector rod and remove the torque converter cover.

11. Lock the flexplate with a small prybar and remove the torque converter bolts.

12. Remove the upper and lower oil filler tubes. Disconnect the oil cooler lines.

13. Support the transmission with a jack. Remove the transmission-to-engine bolts and carefully lower the transmission from the vehicle. Be careful not to drop the torque converter.

To install:

14. Make sure the torque converter is completely installed in the transmission. Lay a straightedge across the bellhousing and measure the distance to 1 of the converter bolt hole lugs; it should be 1.1 in. (29mm). If the distance is less than specification, push the converter into the pump while rotating it, to properly engage the pump drive.

15. Raise the transmission into position and install the transmission-to-engine bolts. Tighten to 38 ft. lbs. (51 Nm).

16. Position the jack under the differential so the differential is perfectly level. Install the transmission-to-differential frame member and hold in place with a new bolt and 8 new nuts.

17. Tighten the frame-to-differential nuts to 130 ft. lbs. (176 Nm) and the frame-to-differential bolt to 68 ft. lbs. (93 Nm).

18. Tighten the frame to transmission nuts to 130 ft. lbs. (176 Nm), tightening the upper nuts first.

19. Remove the jack from under the differential. Lower the vehicle and remove the engine support tool.

20. Raise and safely support the vehicle. Position a straightedge between the right and left floor pans and measure the distance between the bottom of the frame member and the straightedge. The distance should be 2.91 in. (74mm) minimum. If the distance is not correct, readjust the frame member.

21. Turn the torque converter to align the holes. Hold the flexplate with a small prybar and tighten the bolts, evenly and gradually, to 26-36 ft. lbs. (35-49 Nm).

22. Connect the oil cooler lines, using new washers, and tighten the banjo bolts to 26 ft. lbs. (35 Nm). Install the upper and lower oil filler tubes, using a new O-ring.

23. Install the service hole cover. Connect the selector rod, using the washer and a new spring clip.

24. Connect the electrical connectors.

25. Install the front exhaust pipe, using a new gasket, and tighten the nuts to 65 ft. lbs. (89 Nm). Connect the oxygen sensor connector.

26. Install the driveshaft, aligning the marks made during removal. Tighten the bolts to 43 ft. lbs. (58 Nm).

27. Install the cover at the front of the transmission-to-differential frame member. Install the front and rear tunnel reinforcements and tighten the bolts to 19 ft. lbs. (26 Nm).

28. Install the catalytic converter, using new gaskets. Tighten the nuts to 65 ft. lbs. (89 Nm) and connect the air injection pipe.

29. Install the center tunnel reinforcement and tighten the bolts to 19 ft. lbs. (26 Nm). Install the starter and the right and left undercovers.

30. Lower the vehicle and connect the negative battery cable. Fill the transmission with the proper type and quantity of fluid.

31. Start the engine and bring to normal operating temperature. Check for leaks and proper operation.

SHIFT LINKAGE ADJUSTMENT

1. Disconnect the negative battery cable to deactivate the shift-lock mechanism.

2. Remove the console panels and shift knob, as necessary, to gain access to the guide plate.

3. Move the selector lever to the **P** range.

4. Loosen the locknut on the adjustment lever.

5. Adjust the lever so the guide pin-to-guide plate clearance in **P** range with the push rod lightly depressed, is as specified.

6. Move the selector lever to the **N** and **D** ranges and check that there is the same guide pin-to-guide plate clearance. If not as specified, readjust the lever.

7. Reinstall the components in the reverse of their removal. Check selector lever operation.

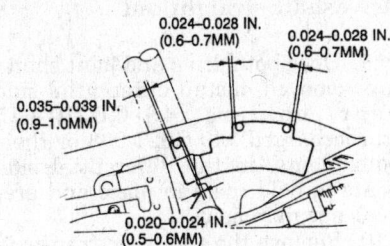

Guide pin-to-guide plate clearance specification

0.024–0.028 IN. (0.6–0.7MM)
0.024–0.028 IN. (0.6–0.7MM)
0.035–0.039 IN. (0.9–1.0MM)
0.020–0.024 IN. (0.5–0.6MM)

AUTOMATIC TRANSAXLE

Transaxle Assembly

REMOVAL AND INSTALLATION

323 and Protege

1. Raise and safely support the vehicle and remove the front wheels. Remove the battery and battery box and the air cleaner and ducting.

2. Remove the splash shield and drain the transaxle oil.

3. Disconnect the speedometer cable, throttle cable, shift cable and the wiring from the transaxle.

4. Disconnect the wiring and remove the starter.

5. On 4WD models, matchmark the flanges and remove the driveshaft.

6. Disconnect the exhaust pipe from the manifold and the catalytic converter and remove the pipe.

7. Disconnect the tie rod ends and lower ball joints and remove the halfshafts. Use special tool 49 G030 455 or equivalent to hold the differential side gears in place when the halfshafts are removed.

8. On 4WD models, to remove the differential lock motor, remove the sensor switch. Insert a small prybar into the hole and turn the rod ½ turn counterclockwise. Remove the bolts and remove the motor.

9. If equipped, remove the torque converter-to-flywheel nuts.

10. Disconnect the oil cooler hoses and plug them to prevent leakage.

11. Install the necessary lifting equipment and support the engine from above. Remove the lower mounting frame and support the transaxle from below with a jack.

12. Remove the front and left rear mounts and allow the engine/transaxle to tilt towards the left.

13. Remove the bolts and slide the transaxle away from the engine to lower it out of the vehicle. Do not let the torque converter fall out.

To install:

14. Make sure the torque converter is properly placed and carefully guide the transaxle into place. Start all the transaxle-to-engine bolts, then torque them to 59 ft. lbs. (80 Nm).

15. Install the left rear mount but do not torque the bolts yet.

16. Install the torque converter-to-flywheel nuts and torque to 25 ft. lbs. (34 Nm).

17. On 4WD models, install the differential lock motor.

18. Install the halfshafts, making sure the inner joint is firmly seated into place. Torque the extension shaft bracket bolts to 46 ft. lbs. (62 Nm).

19. Assemble the suspension. Torque the lower ball joint pinch bolt and the tie rod end nuts to 43 ft. lbs. (59 Nm). If equipped with a stabilizer bar, adjust the link with ¾ in. (19mm) of thread showing above the locknut.

20. Install the front mount to the transaxle and torque the bolts to 38 ft. lbs. (52 Nm).

21. Install the lower mounting frame and torque the frame-to-body nuts and bolts to 66 ft. lbs. (89 Nm). Torque the mount-to-frame nuts and bolts to 38 ft. lbs. (52 Nm).

22. Connect the cooler hoses, making sure the clamp does not interfere with other parts.

23. Connect the shift cable, speedometer cable, throttle cable and the wiring.

24. Install the starter and connect the wiring.

25. On 4WD models, install the driveshaft, making sure to align the matchmarks. Torque the nuts to 22 ft. lbs. (30 Nm).

26. Install the splash shields and wheels.

27. Install the air cleaner and battery.

MX-3

1. If equipped with 1.8L engine, relieve the fuel system pressure. Disconnect the negative battery cable. Raise and safely support the vehicle. Drain the transaxle fluid.

2. Remove the wheel and tire assemblies and the splash shields.

3. Disconnect the air flow meter connector and remove the resonance duct and air cleaner assembly.

4. If equipped with 1.8L engine, remove the strut bar from between the strut towers.

5. Disconnect the positive battery cable and disconnect the wiring harness from the battery tray. Remove the battery and battery tray.

6. If equipped with 1.6L engine, disconnect the speedometer cable. If equipped with 1.8L engine, disconnect the speed sensor connector.

7. Remove the clip from the cable housing and the spring clip from the transaxle lever, then remove the shift cable.

8. Label and disconnect the electrical connectors for the inhibitor switch and solenoid valve. Remove the bolt from the harness bracket and position the harness aside.

9. Remove the throttle cable at the throttle body and routing brackets. Disconnect and plug the oil cooler hoses.

10. If equipped with 1.8L engine, disconnect the oxygen sensor connectors and remove the fuel filter and the transverse member. If equipped with 1.6L engine, remove the intake manifold support bracket.

11. Remove the starter and remove the front exhaust pipe.

12. Remove the pinch bolt and separate the lower ball joint from the steering knuckle. Remove the cotter pin and nuts and separate the tie rod ends from the knuckles.

13. Disconnect the stabilizer bar from the lower control arms. Remove the brake hose and ABS sensor cable clips.

14. Support the engine using engine support tool 49 G017 5A0 or equivalent. Remove the nuts and bolt and remove the engine mount member.

15. Remove the halfshafts and intermediate shaft, if equipped. Remove the left side transaxle mount.

16. On 1.8L engine, remove the lower converter housing cover. Hold the flexplate with a small prybar and remove the torque converter nuts.

17. On 1.6L engine, insert a small prybar through the converter housing service hole and hold the flexplate. Remove the cover from the oil pan side service hole and remove the torque converter nuts.

18. Remove the front transaxle mount.

19. Loosen the engine support tool to lean the engine toward the transaxle. Support the transaxle with a jack and remove the transaxle mounting bolts. Carefully lower the transaxle from the vehicle, being

careful not to drop the torque converter.

To install:

20. Make sure the torque converter is completely installed in the transaxle. Lay a straightedge across the bellhousing and measure the distance to the torque converter (not the stud); it should be 0.535 in. (13.6mm). If the distance is less than specification, push the converter into the pump while rotating it, to properly engage the pump drive.

21. Raise the transaxle into position, making sure the converter studs align with the flexplate holes, and install the transaxle-to-engine bolts. Tighten to 59 ft. lbs. (80 Nm).

22. Install the front transaxle mount and tighten the bolt(s) to 38 ft. lbs. (52 Nm).

23. Hold the flexplate with a small prybar and tighten the converter nuts, gradually and evenly to 25-36 ft. lbs. (34-49 Nm). On 1.6L engine, install the service hole cover. On 1.8L engine, install the access plate.

24. Install the left side transaxle mount. Tighten the mount-to-body bolts to 45 ft. lbs. (61 Nm) and the mount-to-transaxle nuts to 69 ft. lbs. (93 Nm).

25. Install the halfshafts.

26. Install the engine mount member. Tighten the mount member-to-mount nuts to 38 ft. lbs. (52 Nm) and the mount member-to-body nuts/bolts to 66 ft. lbs. (89 Nm). Remove the engine support tool.

27. Attach the clip the brake hose and ABS sensor cable. Attach the stabilizer links to the lower control arms and tighten the nuts to 45 ft. lbs. (61 Nm).

28. Connect the tie rod ends to the steering knuckles and tighten the nuts to 42 ft. lbs. (57 Nm). Install new cotter pins. Connect the lower arm ball joints to the steering knuckles and install the pinch bolts and nuts. Tighten to 43 ft. lbs. (59 Nm).

29. Install the front exhaust pipe, using new gaskets. Tighten the pipe-to-converter nuts to 66 ft. lbs. (89 Nm) and the pipe-to-manifold nuts to 34 ft. lbs. (46 Nm). Connect the oxygen sensor connectors on 1.8L engine.

30. On 1.6L engine, install the intake manifold support bracket. On 1.8L engine, install the transverse member and tighten the bolts to 90 ft. lbs. (123 Nm).

31. Install the starter. On 1.8L engine, install the fuel filter and connect the fuel lines.

32. Connect the oil cooler hoses and the throttle cable. Position the harness bracket and secure with the bolt.

33. Connect the solenoid valve and inhibitor switch connectors. Connect the selector cable to the transaxle. Install the cable housing clip and a new manual lever spring clip.

34. Connect the speedometer cable or speed sensor connector, as necessary. Install the battery tray and secure the wiring harness with the bolt. Install the battery.

35. On 1.8L engine, install the strut bar and tighten the nuts to 20 ft. lbs. (26 Nm).

36. Install the air cleaner assembly and resonance duct. Connect the air flow meter connector.

37. Install the splash shields and the wheel and tire assemblies. Lower the vehicle.

38. Connect the battery cables. Fill the transaxle with the proper type and quantity of fluid. Start the engine and bring to normal operating temperature. Check for leaks and proper transaxle operation.

MX-6/626

1990-92

1. Remove the battery and battery carrier.

2. Remove the air ducting and the air cleaner and air flow meter assembly.

3. Unplug the wiring and remove the fuse block.

4. Disconnect the speedometer cable and the transaxle grounds.

5. Raise and support the vehicle safely and remove the front wheels and splash shield. Drain the transaxle fluid.

6. Disconnect the fluid cooler hoses.

7. Remove the stabilizer control links and disconnect the tie rod ends. Remove the nuts and bolts from the lower control arm ball joints and pull the lower control arms downward to separate them from the steering knuckles. Be careful not to damage the ball joint dust boots.

8. Insert a small prybar between the left driveshaft and the transaxle case and tap the end of the lever to uncouple the driveshaft from the differential side gear. Pull the front hub forward and separate the driveshaft from the transaxle. Remove the left joint shaft bracket. Separate the right driveshaft and joint shaft in the same manner as the left.

NOTE: Do not insert the lever too deeply between the shaft and the case or the oil seal lip could be damaged. To avoid damage to the oil seal, hold the CV-joint at the differential and pull the driveshaft straight out.

9. Once both drive and joint shafts are removed, install differential side gear holders 49-G030-455 (turbocharged), 49-G027-003 or their equivalents, in the differential side gears to hold them in place and prevent misalignment.

10. Remove the engine-to-transaxle gusset plates and undercover. Remove the extension bar and the control rod. Remove the manifold bracket and the starter.

11. Remove the torque converter-to-flywheel bolts.

12. Suspend the engine from the engine hanger with a suitable lifting device or engine support fixture.

13. Remove the front and left engine mounts and bracket. Disconnect the rubber hanger from the crossmember, then remove the crossmember and left side lower control arm as an assembly.

14. Lean the engine towards the transaxle and support the transaxle with a jack. Remove the transaxle-to-engine bolts and slide the transaxle back and out from under the vehicle. Do not let the torque converter fall out.

To install:

15. Carefully guide the transaxle into place, making sure the torque converter fits properly into place. Start all the transaxle-to-engine bolts, then torque them to 86 ft. lbs. (117 Nm).

16. Install the front mount and torque nuts and bolts to 66 ft. lbs. (89 Nm).

17. Install the left mount crossmember and torque the mount-to-transaxle bolts to 38 ft. lbs. (52 Nm). Torque the crossmember bolts to 40 ft. lbs. (54 Nm), the nuts to 69 ft. lbs. (93 Nm).

18. Install the torque converter-to-flywheel bolts and torque to 45 ft. lbs. (61 Nm). Connect the oil cooler hoses.

19. Install the starter and bracket and torque the bolts to 38 ft. lbs. (52 Nm). Connect the wiring

20. Connect the shift cable. Install the transaxle-to-engine gusset plates and torque the bolts to 38 ft. lbs. (52 Nm).

21. Install the halfshafts. When assembling the suspension pieces, torque the ball joint pinch bolts and the tie rod ends to 40 ft. lbs. (54 Nm). Install new cotter pins.

22. Assemble the stabilizer bar links and adjust them so 0.8 in. (20mm) of thread protrudes above

the locknut. Install the splash shields.

23. Connect all wiring and the speedometer cable. Install the air flow meter and air cleaner assembly and the fuse box.

24. Fill the transaxle with the proper amount of oil and install the air ducting and battery.

1993-94

1. Disconnect the battery cables and remove the battery and battery tray.

2. Raise and safely support the vehicle. Drain the transaxle fluid.

3. Remove the air ducts and the air cleaner assembly.

4. Remove the housing clip and remove the selector cable from the transaxle.

5. Label and disconnect the electrical connectors for the inhibitor switch, solenoid valve, oxygen sensor, vehicle speed sensor and vehicle pulse generator. Disconnect the ground wires and remove the necessary wiring harness brackets.

6. Remove the fuel filter mounting nuts and position the filter aside, leaving the fuel line attached. Remove the engine mount stay.

7. If equipped with 2.5L engine, remove the starter. Disconnect and plug the oil cooler hoses.

8. Remove the wheel and tire assemblies and the splash shields. Remove the transverse member.

9. If equipped with 2.5L engine, remove the front exhaust pipe.

10. Remove the pinch bolts from the steering knuckles. Pry the lower control arms down to separate the ball joints from the knuckles.

11. Remove the cotter pins and nuts and separate the tie rod ends from the knuckles. Remove the nuts and disconnect the stabilizer links from the lower control arms.

12. Remove the brake hose clips from the struts and remove the ABS speed sensor harness mounting nuts.

13. Separate the right side halfshaft from the intermediate shaft using a hammer and brass drift. Pry the left side shaft from the transaxle using a prybar inserted between the transaxle and the inner CV-joint. Be careful not to damage the oil seal.

14. Suspend the halfshafts with rope, in a level position. Insert plug tools 49 G030 455 or equivalent into the differential side gears to keep them from becoming mispositioned.

15. Remove the intermediate shaft.

16. If equipped with 2.0L engine, remove the intake manifold support bracket and remove the starter.

17. Remove the engine mount rubber from the right side of the engine mount member. Remove the mount-to-transaxle bolts from the rear transaxle mount.

18. Support the engine using engine support tool 49 G017 5A0 or equivalent. Remove the engine mount member nuts and bolts and remove the engine mount member.

19. If equipped with 2.5L engine, remove the torque converter access plate. On 2.0L engine, remove the seal rubber from the transaxle case near the starter mounting hole.

20. Hold the flexplate with a small prybar and remove the torque converter nuts.

21. Remove the left side transaxle mount.

22. Loosen the engine support tool and lean the engine toward the transaxle. Support the transaxle with a jack and remove the transaxle mounting bolts. Carefully lower the transaxle from the vehicle, being careful not to drop the torque converter.

23. Remove the front transaxle mount.

To install:

24. Make sure the torque converter is completely installed in the transaxle. Lay a straightedge across the bellhousing and measure the distance to the torque converter (not the stud); it should be 0.602 in. (15.3mm) on 2.0L engine or 0.551 in. (14mm) on 2.5L engine. If the distance is less than specification, push the converter into the pump while rotating it, to properly engage the pump drive.

25. Install the front transaxle mount.

26. Raise the transaxle into position, making sure the torque converter studs align with the flexplate holes, and install the transaxle mounting bolts.

27. On 2.5L engine, tighten the transaxle mounting bolts to 73 ft. lbs.

(99 Nm). On 2.0L engine, tighten bolts **A** to 73 ft. lbs. (99 Nm), bolts **B** to 38 ft. lbs. (51 Nm) and bolt **C** to 18 ft. lbs. (25 Nm).

28. Hold the flexplate with the small prybar and install the torque converter nuts. Tighten the bolts, gradually and evenly, to 45 ft. lbs. (60 Nm). On 2.5L engine, install the torque converter access plate. On 2.0L engine, install the seal rubber.

29. Install the left side transaxle mount and loosely tighten the bolts and nuts.

30. Use the engine support tool to make sure the transaxle bolt holes and the rear transaxle mount align. Install the bolts and tighten to 68 ft. lbs. (93 Nm).

31. Install the engine mount member, making sure the mount rubbers are installed properly.

32. Install the mount member-to-body bolts/nuts and tighten to 68 ft. lbs. (93 Nm). Loosely tighten the mount member-to-mount nuts.

33. Tighten the left transaxle mount mount-to-transaxle nuts and bolt to 68 ft. lbs. (93 Nm). Tighten the mount through bolt to 86 ft. lbs. (116 Nm).

34. Remove the engine support tool. Tighten the mount member-to-mount nuts to 77 ft. lbs. (104 Nm).

35. Install the mount rubber on the right side of the mount member. Tighten the bolts to 68 ft. lbs. (93 Nm).

36. If equipped with 2.0L engine, install the starter and the intake manifold support bracket.

37. Remove the plug tool from the differential side gear. Install the intermediate shaft into the transaxle. Install the support bearing to the engine and tighten the bolts, in sequence, to 45 ft. lbs. (61 Nm).

38. Remove the plug from the other differential side gear. Install a new circlip on the halfshaft with end gap facing upward. Install the halfshaft

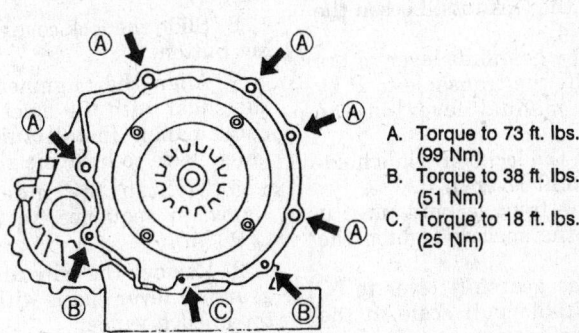

A. Torque to 73 ft. lbs. (99 Nm)
B. Torque to 38 ft. lbs. (51 Nm)
C. Torque to 18 ft. lbs. (25 Nm)

Transaxle mounting bolt identification — 2.0L engine

into the transaxle, being careful not to damage the seal. Make sure the circlip seats in the differential side gear, by pulling out on the shaft; it must not pull out.

39. Install a new circlip on the end of the other halfshaft and connect it to the intermediate shaft.

40. Connect the lower ball joints to the steering knuckles. Install the pinch bolts and tighten to 43 ft. lbs. (58 Nm).

41. Connect the stabilizer links to the lower control arms and tighten the nuts to 39 ft. lbs. (53 Nm). Connect the tie rod ends to the steering knuckles and tighten the nuts to 32 ft. lbs. (44 Nm). Install new cotter pins.

42. If equipped with 2.5L engine, install the front exhaust pipe, using new gaskets and install the starter.

43. Install the transverse member and tighten the bolts to 96 ft. lbs. (131 Nm). Install the splash shields and the wheel and tire assemblies.

44. Connect the oil cooler hoses. Install the engine mount stay.

45. Install the harness brackets and the ground wires. Connect the electrical connectors.

46. Position the fuel filter and install the mounting bolts. Install the selector cable to the cable bracket and install the clip. Connect the cable to the transaxle lever.

47. Install the air cleaner assembly and ducts. Install the battery and battery tray.

48. Connect the battery cables. Fill the transaxle with the proper type and quantity of fluid. Start the engine and bring to normal operating temperature. Check for leaks and proper transaxle operation.

SHIFT LINKAGE ADJUSTMENT

1990-92 MX-6/626

1. Remove the necessary console parts to gain access to the shift cable.
2. Loosen the locknuts. Loosen the lock bolt.
3. Move the gearshift lever to the **P** range. Shift the transaxle to **P** by moving the manual lever on the transaxle.
4. Tighten the lockbolt while holding the gearshift lever in **P**.
5. Turn the front locknut until it just touches the spacer. Tighten the rear locknut.
6. Move the gearshift lever to **N**. Attach a suitable pull scale to the gearshift lever knob.
7. With the button on the knob pressed in, push the gearshift lever

toward **R** with a force of approximately 4.4 lbs. Measure the distance the lever moves.

8. With the button on the knob pressed in, pull the gearshift lever toward **D** with a force of approximately 4.4 lbs. Measure the distance the lever moves.

9. The difference between the distances measured in Steps 7 and 8 must not exceed 0.315 in. (8mm). If the difference is greater, repeat the procedure.

10. Reinstall the console parts and check shifter operation.

323/Protege and MX-3

1. Remove the necessary console parts to gain access to the shift cable.
2. Move the gearshift lever to **P**.
3. Loosen the cable mounting bolts.
4. Push the gearshift lever against the **P** range and hold it.
5. Tighten the cable mounting bolts.
6. Reinstall the console parts and check shifter operation.

1993-94 MX-6/626

1. Remove the front console.
2. Move the gearshift lever to **P**.
3. Remove the indicator screws and lift the indicator panel.
4. Slide the lock cover and disconnect the set button.
5. Push the selector lever adjust **P** range.
6. Slide the lock cover and lock the set button.
7. Align the alignment screws in the slider with the holes in the indicator panel. Install suitable heavy gauge wire to hold the slider.
8. Tighten the indicator panel screw, in sequence, to 26 inch lbs. (2.9 Nm).
9. Remove the wire and verify the gearshift lever aligns with the indicator in each range.
10. Install the front console and check gearshift lever operation.

FRONT SUSPENSION

MacPherson Strut

REMOVAL AND INSTALLATION

Except Miata, 1992-94 929 and 1993-94 RX-7

1. Raise and safely support the vehicle. Remove the wheel and tire assembly.
2. Support the lower control arm with a jack.
3. Remove the bolt or clip attaching the brake hose and/or ABS sensor harness to the strut.
4. On 323, MX-6/626 and 929 with automatic adjusting suspension, disconnect the electrical connector and remove the actuator from the top of the strut.
5. On MX-6/626, if removing the left side strut, remove the ignition coil bracket.
6. Pain alignment marks on the strut mounting block and strut tower, so the strut can be reinstalled in the same position.
7. Remove the upper strut mounting block nuts and the strut-to-knuckle bolts and remove the strut assembly.

To install:

8. Install the strut into the strut tower, aligning the paint marks made during removal. Install the mounting nuts and tighten to 27 ft. lbs. (36 Nm) on 323, Protege and RX-7, 33 ft. lbs. (44 Nm) on 929 or 46 ft. lbs. (63 Nm) on MX-3 and MX-6/626.
9. Install the strut-to-knuckle bolts and tighten to 86 ft. lbs. (117 Nm).
10. If equipped with automatic adjusting suspension, install the actuator and connect the electrical connector.
11. Install the clip or bolt attaching the brake hose and/or ABS sensor harness.
12. Install the wheel and tire assembly and lower the vehicle. Check the front end alignment.

Miata

1. Raise and safely support the vehicle. Remove the wheel and tire assembly.
2. Remove the engine undercover. Remove the band for the wheel speed sensor harness.
3. Remove the bolt and disconnect the stabilizer bar from the link.

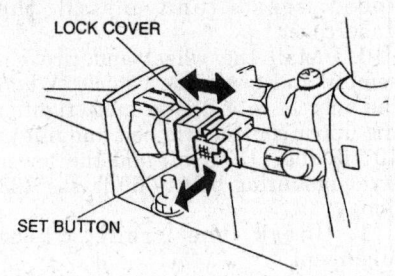

LOCK COVER

SET BUTTON

Lock cover and set button location — 1993-94 MX-6/626

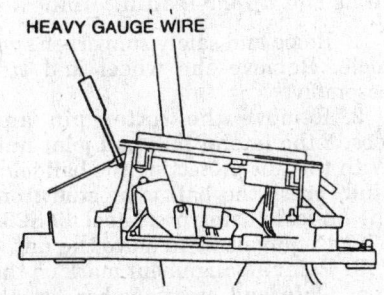

HEAVY GAUGE WIRE

Adjusting the indicator panel — 1993-94 MX-6/626

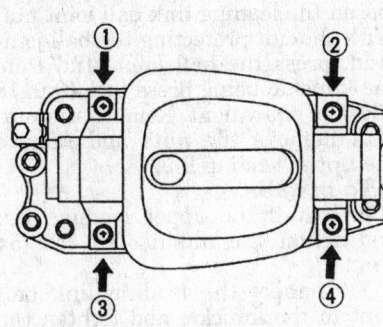

Indicator panel screw torque sequence — 1993-94 MX-6/626

4. Pain alignment marks on the upper strut mounting block and the strut tower, so the strut can be reinstalled in the same position.

5. Remove the nuts from the strut mounting block. Remove the lower strut mounting bolt and nut.

6. Loosen the lower control arm bolts and pull down on the hub/knuckle assembly. Remove the strut up through the upper control arm.

To install:

7. Position the strut and install the lower bolt and nut. Tighten to 69 ft. lbs. (93 Nm).

8. Install the strut in the strut tower, making sure the paint marks made during removal are aligned, and install the upper mounting block nuts. Tighten to 27 ft. lbs. (36 Nm).

9. Connect the stabilizer bar to the link and tighten the bolt to 40 ft. lbs. (54 Nm).

10. Tighten the lower control arm bolts and nuts to 83 ft. lbs. (113 Nm).

11. Install the engine undercover and the band for the wheel speed sensor harness. Install the wheel and tire assembly and lower the vehicle.

12. Check the front wheel alignment.

1992-94 929

1. Raise and safely support the vehicle. Remove the wheel and tire assembly.

2. Support the lower control arm with a jack.

3. Remove the clip and disconnect the brake hose from the strut. Remove the bolt and disconnect the ABS sensor harness from the strut.

4. Remove the cotter pin and loosen the nut from the upper lateral link at the spindle. Separate the upper lateral link ball joint from the spindle using tool 49 S231 575 or equivalent. Remove the nut.

5. Paint an alignment mark on the cam plate and crossmember for assembly reference, then remove the nut and bolt and the upper lateral link.

6. Remove the lower strut bolt from the lower control arm.

7. Pain alignment marks on the strut mounting block and strut tower for assembly reference. Remove the nuts and remove the strut.

To install:

8. Install the strut, making sure the brake hose bracket faces forward.

9. Install the strut into the tower, being sure to align the marks made during removal and loosely install the nuts.

10. Loosely install the lower strut mounting bolt.

11. Install the upper lateral link with the bolt and nut. Align the marks made during removal and tighten the nut to 86 ft. lbs. (117 Nm).

12. Connect the ball joint to the spindle and tighten the nut to 80 ft. lbs. (108 Nm). Install a new cotter pin.

13. Install the bolt and clip connecting the ABS harness and brake hose to the strut.

14. Install the wheel and tire assembly and lower the vehicle.

15. When the vehicle is on the ground, tighten the strut block-to-strut tower nuts to 46 ft. lbs. (63 Nm) and the lower strut bolt to 87 ft. lbs. (118 Nm).

16. Check the front wheel alignment.

1993-94 RX-7

1. Raise and safely support the vehicle. Remove the wheel and tire assembly.

2. Support the lower control arm with a jack.

3. Remove the clip and disconnect the brake hose from the strut. Remove the bolts and disconnect the ABS sensor and harness.

4. Remove the upper control arm bolts and nuts.

5. Remove the cap, nut and stopper at the top center of the strut. Pain an alignment mark on the upper strut mounting block and strut tower for assembly reference. Remove the nuts.

6. If equipped, remove the strut bar from between the strut towers.

7. Remove the lower strut mounting bolt and remove the strut.

To install:

8. Install the strut, making sure the brake hose bracket faces forward.

9. Install the strut in the strut tower, aligning the marks made during removal. If equipped, install the strut bar. Install the nuts and tighten to 46 ft. lbs. (62 Nm).

10. Install the stopper rubber and nut at the top center of the strut and tighten to 33 ft. lbs. (46 Nm). Install the cap.

11. Install the lower strut mounting bolt and tighten to 86 ft. lbs. (116 Nm).

12. Install the upper control arm bolts and nuts and tighten to 54 ft. lbs. (73 Nm).

13. Connect the ABS sensor and harness. Tighten the bolts to 16 ft. lbs. (22 Nm). Install the brake hose clip.

14. Install the wheel and tire assembly and lower the vehicle. Check the front wheel alignment.

Upper Ball Joints

INSPECTION

1. Disconnect the upper ball joint from the spindle.

2. Shake and rotate the ball stud several times.

3. Install the stud nut and measure the force required to rotate the stud in the socket, using an inch pound torque wrench.

4. Specifications for rotation torque are as follows:

Miata: 3.5-15.6 inch lbs. (0.4-1.8 Nm)

929: 4.3-13.0 inch lbs. (0.5-1.5 Nm)

RX-7: 3.5-10.4 inch lbs. (0.4-1.1 Nm)

5. If the torque is not within specification, replace the upper control arm.

REMOVAL AND INSTALLATION

The upper ball joint is an integral part of the upper control and cannot be replaced separately. If the upper ball joint is defective, the entire upper control arm must be replaced.

Lower Ball Joints

INSPECTION

1. Disconnect the lower ball joint from the knuckle or spindle.

2. Shake and rotate the ball joint stud several times.

3. Attach a suitable pull scale to the ball joint stud and measure the preload.

4. While the ball stud is rotating, the pull scale reading should be as follows:

323, Protege, MX-3, 1990-91 RX-7 and 1990-92 MX-6/626: 4.4-7.7 lbs.

Miata: 0.9-4.0 lbs.

1993-94 MX-6/626: 2.2-11.0 lbs.

1990-91 929: 1.1-2.6 lbs.

1992-94 929 and 1993-94 RX-7: 1.1-3.3 lbs.

5. If the pull scale reading is not as specified, replace the ball joint or lower control arm, as required.

REMOVAL AND INSTALLATION

Except 323, Protege, MX-3 and Miata

The lower ball joint is an integral part of the lower control and cannot be replaced separately. If the lower ball joint is defective, the entire lower control arm must be replaced.

323, Protege and MX-3

1. Raise and safely support the vehicle. Remove the wheel and tire assembly.

2. Remove the ball joint stud pinch bolt and nut from the steering

knuckle. Pry the lower control arm down from the knuckle, and separate the ball joint from the knuckle.

3. Remove the bolt and nut and remove the ball joint from the lower control arm.

4. Installation is the reverse of the removal procedure. Tighten the ball joint-to-lower control arm bolt and nut to 86 ft. lbs. (117 Nm). Tighten the ball joint pinch bolt and nut to 43 ft. lbs. (59 Nm). Check the front wheel alignment.

Miata

1. Raise and safely support the vehicle. Remove the wheel and tire assembly.

2. Remove the cotter pin and loosen the nut on the lower ball joint. With the nut protecting the ball joint stud, press the stud from the knuckle using press tool 49 0727 575 or equivalent. Remove the nut from the ball stud.

3. Remove the ball joint-to-lower control arm bolts and nut and remove the lower ball joint.

4. Installation is the reverse of the removal procedure. Tighten the ball joint-to-lower control arm bolts to 69 ft. lbs. (93 Nm). Tighten the ball joint stud nut to 57 ft. lbs. (77 Nm) and install a new cotter pin.

Upper Control Arms

REMOVAL AND INSTALLATION

Miata

1. Raise and safely support the vehicle. Remove the wheel and tire assembly.

2. Remove the undercover and remove the band for the wheel speed sensor harness. Support the lower control arm with a jack.

3. Remove the cotter pin and loosen the upper ball joint nut. Press the ball joint stud from the knuckle using press tool 49 0118 850C or equivalent. Remove the nut.

4. Remove the lower strut mounting bolt.

5. Remove the upper control arm bolt and nut and remove the upper control arm.

To install:

6. Install the upper control arm and loosely tighten the bolt and nut.

7. Loosely install the lower strut mounting bolt.

8. Connect the ball joint to the spindle and tighten to 45 ft. lbs. (61 Nm). Install a new cotter pin.

9. Install the band for the wheel speed sensor and install the undercover.

10. Install the wheel and tire assembly and lower the vehicle. When the vehicle is on the ground, tighten the upper control arm bolt and nut to 101 ft. lbs. (137 Nm) and the lower strut mounting bolt to 69 ft. lbs. (93 Nm).

11. Check the front wheel alignment.

1992-94 929

NOTE: The curved arm is referred to as the upper lateral link. The straight arm is referred to as the upper leading link.

1. Raise and safely support the vehicle. Remove the wheel and tire assembly.

2. Remove the cotter pin and loosen the lateral link ball joint nut. With the nut protecting the ball joint stud, press the ball joint stud from the knuckle using press tool 49 S231 575 or equivalent. Remove the nut.

3. Paint an alignment mark on the cam plate and crossmember for assembly reference. Remove the nut, cam plate, adjusting cam bolt and the upper lateral link.

4. Remove the cotter pin and loosen the leading link ball joint nut. With the nut protecting the ball joint stud, press the ball joint stud from the knuckle using press tool 49 0118 850C or equivalent. Remove the nut.

5. Remove the nuts and remove the upper leading link.

To install:

6. Install the upper leading link and tighten the nuts to 40 ft. lbs. (54 Nm).

7. Connect the leading link ball joint to the knuckle and tighten the nut to 42 ft. lbs. (57 Nm). Install a new cotter pin.

8. Install the upper lateral link with the adjusting cam bolt, cam plate and nut. Align the mark made during removal and tighten the nut to 86 ft. lbs. (117 Nm).

9. Connect the lateral link ball joint to the knuckle and install the nut. Tighten the nut to 80 ft. lbs. (108 Nm) and install a new cotter pin.

10. Install the wheel and tire assembly and lower the vehicle. Check the front wheel alignment.

1993-94 RX-7

1. Raise and safely support the vehicle. Remove the wheel and tire assembly.

2. Support the lower control arm with a jack.

3. Remove the brake hose clip and the brake hose from the strut. Remove the ABS sensor and the sensor harness bolts from the control arm.

4. Remove the lower strut mounting bolt and nut. Remove the upper ball joint pinch bolt.

5. Remove the upper control arm bolts and nuts and remove the upper control arm.

6. Installation is the reverse of the removal procedure. Tighten the upper control arm bolts/nuts to 54 ft. lbs. (73 Nm), the upper ball joint pinch bolt to 39 ft. lbs. (53 Nm) and the lower strut mounting bolt to 86 ft. lbs. (116 Nm). Check the front wheel alignment.

Lower Control Arms

REMOVAL AND INSTALLATION

323, Protege, MX-3, MX-6 and 626

1. Raise and safely support the vehicle. Remove the wheel and tire assembly.

2. Disconnect the stabilizer bar link from the lower control arm.

3. Remove the lower ball joint pinch bolt from the steering knuckle.

4. Remove the lower control arm bolts and nuts and remove the lower control arm.
   To install:

5. Install the lower control arm and loosely tighten the mounting nuts and bolts.

6. Connect the lower ball joint to the steering knuckle. Install the pinch bolt and tighten to 40 ft. lbs. (54 Nm).

7. On 323, Protege and 1990-92 MX-6/626, assemble the stabilizer bar link. Tighten the top nut until ¾ in. of threads are exposed.

8. On MX-3 and 1993-94 MX-6/626, connect the stabilizer link to the lower control arm and tighten the nut to 39 ft. lbs. (53 Nm).

9. Install the wheel and tire assembly and lower the vehicle. With the vehicle at normal ride height, tighten the lower control arm mounting bolts.

10. On 323, Protege and MX-3, tighten the front bushing through bolt and the rear bushing strap bolts to 93 ft. lbs. (127 Nm).

11. On 1990-92 MX-6/626, tighten the bushing through bolts to 78 ft. lbs. (106 Nm).

12. On 1993-94 MX-6/626, tighten the front bushing through bolt to 78 ft. lbs. (106 Nm) and the rear bushing strap bolts to 96 ft. lbs. (131 Nm).

13. Check the front wheel alignment.

Miata

1. Raise and safely support the vehicle. Remove the wheel and tire assembly. Remove the undercover.

2. Remove the stabilizer bar link bolt and the lower strut mounting bolt.

3. Remove the cotter pin and loosen the nut on the lower ball joint. With the nut protecting the ball joint stud, press the stud from the knuckle using press tool 49 0727 575 or equivalent. Remove the nut.

4. Paint alignment marks on the adjusting cams and the chassis for assembly reference. Remove the bolts, nuts and adjusting cams and lower control arm.
   To install:

5. Install the lower control arm and loosely tighten the bolts and nuts.

6. Connect the lower ball joint to the knuckle and tighten the nut to 57 ft. lbs. (77 Nm). Install a new cotter pin.

7. Loosely install the lower strut mounting bolt and stabilizer link bolt.

8. Install the wheel and tire assembly and the undercover. Lower the vehicle.

9. With the vehicle at normal ride height, tighten the lower control arm bolts and nuts to 83 ft. lbs. (113 Nm), being sure to align the marks on the cam plates and chassis made during removal.

10. Tighten the lower strut mounting bolt to 69 ft. lbs. (93 Nm) and the stabilizer link bolt to 40 ft. lbs. (54 Nm).

11. Check the front wheel alignment.

929

1. Raise and safely support the vehicle. Remove the wheel and tire assembly.

2. On 1990-91 vehicles, disassemble the stabilizer link and separate the stabilizer bar from the lower control arm. On 1992-94 vehicles, remove the stabilizer link bolt.

3. On 1990-91 vehicles, remove the cotter pin and nut and separate the tie rod end from the knuckle arm.

4. Remove the bolts and disconnect the tension arm from the lower control arm. On 1992-94 vehicles, remove the tension arm.

5. Remove the cotter pin and loosen the nut on the lower ball joint. With the nut protecting the ball joint stud, press the stud from the knuckle using press tool 49 S231 575 or equivalent. Remove the nut.

6. On 1992-94 vehicles, remove the lower strut mounting bolt.

7. Remove the lower control arm mounting bolt and remove the control arm.
   To install:

8. Install the lower control arm and loosely tighten the bolt.

9. On 1992-94 vehicles, loosely install the lower strut mounting bolt.

10. Install the ball joint stud in the knuckle. Install the nut and tighten to 91 ft. lbs. (124 Nm) on 1990-91 vehicles or 116 ft. lbs. (157 Nm) on 1992-94 vehicles. Install a new cotter pin.

11. Connect the tension arm to the lower control arm. Tighten the bolts to 86 ft. lbs. (117 Nm). On 1992-94 vehicles, tighten the tension arm-to-chassis bolt to 123 ft. lbs. (167 Nm).

12. On 1990-91 vehicles, connect the tie rod end to the steering knuckle arm and tighten the nut to 56 ft. lbs. (75 Nm). Install a new cotter pin.

13. On 1990-91 vehicles, assemble the stabilizer bar links so there is 0.60 in. (15mm) of thread exposed at the top. On 1992-94 vehicles, tighten the stabilizer link bolt to 40 ft. lbs. (54 Nm).

14. Install the wheel and tire assembly and lower the vehicle. With the vehicle at normal ride height, tighten the lower control arm bolt to 69 ft. lbs. (93 Nm) on 1990-91 vehicles or 86 ft. lbs. (117 Nm) on 1992-94 vehicles. On 1992-94 vehicles, tighten the lower strut mounting bolt to 87 ft. lbs. (118 Nm).

15. Check the front wheel alignment.

RX-7

1. Raise and safely support the vehicle. Remove the wheel and tire assembly.

2. Disconnect the stabilizer bar link from the lower control arm.

3. On 1993-94 vehicles, remove the lower strut mounting bolt.

4. On 1990-91 vehicles, remove the ball joint pinch bolt and separate the ball joint from the knuckle.

5. On 1993-94 vehicles, remove the cotter pin and loosen the nut on the lower ball joint. With the nut protecting the ball joint stud, press the stud from the knuckle using press tool 49 0118 850C or equivalent. Remove the nut.

6. On 1993-94 vehicles, paint alignment marks on the adjusting cams and chassis for assembly reference.

7. Remove the lower control arm bolts and remove the lower control arm.

To install:

8. Install the lower control arm and loosely tighten the bolts.

9. On 1990-91 vehicles, connect the ball joint stud to the knuckle and install the pinch bolt. Tighten to 40 ft. lbs. (54 Nm).

10. On 1993-94 vehicles, install the ball joint stud in the knuckle and install the nut. Tighten the nut to 79 ft. lbs. (107 Nm) and install a new cotter pin.

11. On 1993-94 vehicles, loosely install the lower strut mounting bolt.

12. Connect the stabilizer link to the lower control arm. Tighten the bolt to 37 ft. lbs. (50 Nm) on 1990-91 vehicles or 54 ft. lbs. (73 Nm) on 1993-94 vehicles.

13. Install the wheel and tire assembly and lower the vehicle. With the vehicle at normal ride height, tighten the lower control arm bolts. On 1990-91 vehicles, tighten the front through bolt to 69 ft. lbs. (93 Nm) and the rear bushing strap bolts to 61 ft. lbs. (83 Nm).

14. On 1993-94 vehicles, align the marks on the adjusting cams and chassis and tighten the bolts to 86 ft. lbs. (116 Nm). Tighten the lower strut bolt to 86 ft. lbs. (116 Nm).

15. Check the front wheel alignment.

Front Wheel Bearings

ADJUSTMENT

Miata, 929 and 1993-94 RX-7

The wheel bearings on these vehicles are not adjustable. To check if the bearing is serviceable, remove the wheel and tire assembly, brake caliper and disc brake rotor (the rotor and hub are 1 piece on 1990-91 929). Install a dial indicator with the indicator foot resting on the wheel hub. Try to move the hub in and out. If there is more than 0.002 in. (0.05mm) bearing play on Miata, 1990-91 929 and RX-7, or more than 0.004 in. (0.1mm) bearing play on 1992-94 929, check the wheel hub nut torque or replace the hub and bearing assembly, if necessary. On 1990-91 929, the bearing can be removed from the hub.

1990-91 RX-7

1. Raise and safely support the vehicle. Remove the wheel and tire assembly.

2. Remove the disc brake caliper and suspend it with wire from the strut.

3. Remove the grease cap, cotter pin and nut cover. Loosen the locknut.

4. Tighten the locknut to 22 ft. lbs. (29 Nm) and turn the hub 2-3 times to seat the bearings.

5. Loosen the locknut until it can be turned by hand.

6. Attach a suitable pull scale to 1 of the wheel studs and measure the frictional force.

7. Tighten the locknut until the initial turning torque reading is 2.2 lbs. Install the nut cover and a new cotter pin. Install the grease cap.

8. Install the brake caliper and wheel and tire assembly. Lower the vehicle.

REMOVAL AND INSTALLATION

Miata, 929 and 1993-94 RX-7

1. Remove the dust cap. Unstake and loosen the locknut.

2. Raise and safely support the vehicle. Remove the wheel and tire assembly.

3. Remove the brake caliper and suspend it from the coil spring.

4. On Miata, 1992-94 929 and 1993-94 Rx-7, remove the disc brake rotor. The rotor and hub are 1 piece on 1990-91 929.

5. Remove and discard the hub nut. Remove the wheel hub and bearing assembly.

6. On 1990-91 929, remove the seal and the snapring. Support the hub/rotor assembly and press out the bearing.

7. On Miata, 1992-94 929 and 1993-94 RX-7, the wheel hub and bearing cannot be disassembled.

To install:

8. On 1990-91 929, support the hub/rotor assembly and press in a new bearing. Install the snapring and press in a new wheel seal.

9. Install the hub over the spindle. Loosely install a new hub nut.

10. Install the brake rotor and the disc brake caliper. Install the wheel and tire assembly and lower the vehicle.

11. When the vehicle is on the ground, tighten the hub nut. Tighten to 130 ft. lbs. (177 Nm) on 1990-91 929, 159 ft. lbs. (216 Nm) on Miata or 173 ft. lbs. (235 Nm) on 1992-94 929 and 1993-94 RX-7.

12. Install a new dust cap.

1990-91 RX7

1. Raise and safely support the vehicle. Remove the wheel and tire assembly.

2. Remove the disc brake caliper and suspend it from the coil spring with wire.

3. Remove the disc brake rotor.

4. Remove the grease cap, cotter pin, nut cover, nut and washer.

5. Remove the hub, being careful not to drop the outer bearing.

6. Remove the outer wheel bearing. Pry the seal from the hub and remove the inner wheel bearing.

7. Clean the bearings and hub in solvent and allow to dry.

8. Examine the wheel bearings and bearing races for pits, cracks, scoring or other damage. If either a wheel bearing or bearing race is not serviceable, the bearing race will have to be removed. Wheel bearings and races are always replaced in sets.

9. If the races are to be removed, drive them out with a brass drift and hammer.

To install:

10. If the bearing races were removed, drive in new ones with a hammer and brass drift. Make sure the races are fully seated in the hub.

11. Pack the wheel bearings with high temperature wheel bearing grease. Make sure the area between the rollers and the inner race is filled.

12. Place a small amount of grease in the hub and lubricate the races.

13. Install the outer wheel bearing in the hub. Press (tap in with soft tool) in a new wheel seal and lubricate the seal lips with grease.

14. Clean all the old grease and dirt from the spindle. Install the hub over the spindle, being careful not to damage the wheel seal.

15. Install the outer wheel bearing, washer and nut.

16. Adjust the wheel bearings and install the remaining components in the reverse order of removal.

REAR SUSPENSION

MacPherson Strut

REMOVAL AND INSTALLATION

Except Miata and 1993-94 RX-7

1. As required, remove the side trim panels from the inside of the trunk or the rear seat and trim.

2. If equipped with Adjustable Shock Absorber (ASA) system, disconnect the wiring and remove the cap. Loosen and remove the top mounting nuts from the strut mounting block assembly.

3. Raise and safely support the vehicle and remove the rear wheels. The suspension will drop when the weight lifts off the wheels.

4. Unclip the brake line or wiring retainers as required and unbolt the bottom strut mount. Remove the strut.

5. Installation is the reverse of removal. Torque the following:

   a. 323, Protege, MX-3 and MX-6/626 lower strut mount bolts — 86 ft. lbs (117 Nm).

   b. 929 and RX7 lower strut mount bolt — 69 ft. lbs. (93 Nm).

   c. 323 trailing arm bolt — 50 ft. lbs. (68 Nm).

   d. 323, 1990-91 929 and RX7 upper strut mount nuts — 22 ft. lbs.(29 Nm).

   e. MX-3, MX-6 and 626 upper strut mount nuts — 46 ft. lbs. (63 Nm).

   f. 1992-94 929 upper strut mount nuts — 27 ft. lbs. (36 Nm).

Miata

1. Raise and safely support the vehicle and remove the rear wheels.

2. On the left side, remove the fuel filler pipe protector panel.

3. Remove the bolt from the lower stabilizer bar connecting link.

4. Remove the upper mount nuts and lower mount bolt and lift the spring and shock absorber out as an assembly.

5. Installation is the reverse of removal. Torque the upper mount nuts to 27 ft. lbs. (36 Nm), the lower mount bolt to 69 ft. lbs. (93 Nm) and the stabilizer link bolt to 40 ft. lbs. (54 Nm).

1993-94 RX-7

1. Raise and safely support the vehicle. Remove the rear wheel and tire assembly.

2. Remove the nut and disconnect the stabilizer bar.

3. Remove the strut upper mount nuts.

4. Remove the rear upper strut bar.

5. Remove the nut and stopper rubber at the top of the strut. Remove the strut and insulator.

To install:

6. Install the insulator on the strut so the notches face the studs.

7. Install the strut so the identification paint mark at the bottom of the strut faces rearward.

8. Install the stopper rubber and nut. Tighten to 33 ft. lbs. (46 Nm).

9. Install the upper strut bar, then install the strut upper mount nuts. Tighten to 46 ft. lbs. (62 Nm).

10. Slide the stabilizer bar link through the control arm and the strut. Install the nut and tighten the 81 ft. lbs. (110 Nm).

Rear Control Arms

REMOVAL AND INSTALLATION

323, Protege, MX-3 and 1990-92 MX6/626

1. Raise and safely support the vehicle and remove the wheels.

2. Before disconnecting the stabilizer bar link, on all except MX-3, measure the length of the threads protruding above the locknut. Remove the nuts and through bolt to disconnect the stabilizer bar.

3. Remove the nuts and bolts as required and remove the control arms.

4. Installation is the reverse of removal. Make sure to properly adjust the stabilizer bar before tightening the locknuts and check rear wheel alignment.

5. Torque the following:

   a. Inner control arm through bolt to 70 ft. lbs. (95 Nm).

   b. Outer control arm through bolt to 86 ft. lbs. (117 Nm).

   c. 323 trailing arm-to-body bolt to 69 ft. lbs. (93 Nm).

   d. Trailing arm-to-knuckle bolt to 86 ft. lbs. (117 Nm).

Miata

1. Raise and safely support the vehicle and remove the rear wheels.

2. Disconnect the stabilizer bar link and the lower shock absorber mounting bolt from the lower arm.

3. Remove the nuts and eccentric bolts and the outer through bolt and remove the lower control arm. The bushings can be replaced separately.

4. To remove the upper control arm, either re-install the lower control arm or remove the brake caliper, halfshaft and hub carrier. Do not allow the carrier to be supported only by the halfshaft.

5. Installation is the reverse of removal. Torque the upper arm through bolts ot 49 ft. lbs. (67 Nm). Torque the lower arm outer through

bolt to 55 ft. lbs. (75 Nm). After aligning the rear wheels, torque the eccentric bolts to 70 ft. lbs. (95 Nm).

1993-94 MX-6/626

1. Raise and safely support the vehicle. Remove the wheel and tire assemblies.

2. Remove the access cap from the underside of the rear crossmember.

3. Remove the bolts and nuts and remove the lateral links and trailing link. If removing the rear lateral link, paint and alignment mark on the cam plate and crossmember for assembly reference.

4. Installation is the reverse of the removal procedure. Tighten the inner and outer lateral link bolts/nuts to 86 ft. lbs. (116 Nm). Tighten the trailing link-to-body bolt to 68 ft. lbs. (93 Nm) and the trailing link-to-knuckle bolt to 86 ft. lbs. (116 Nm).

5. Do not final tighten the bolts until the vehicle is on the ground and at normal ride height.

929

1990-91

1. Raise and safely support the vehicle and remove the rear wheels.

2. Before disconnecting the stabilizer bar link, measure the length of the threads protruding above the locknut. Disconnect the stabilizer bar from the upper control arm.

3. Remove the cotter pins and nuts and use a ball joint press to disconnect the upper and lower control arms from the hub support.

4. Remove the bolts to remove the front and rear control arms from the sub-frame. The ball joint dust boots can be replaced but the joints themselves are part of the control arm and cannot be replaced separately.

5. Installation is the reverse of removal. Torque the ball joint nuts to 55 ft. lbs. (75 Nm) and tighten as required to install a new cotter pin.

6. Torque the upper arm and lower front arm-to-sub-frame bolts to 55 ft. lbs. (75 Nm). After aligning the rear wheels, torque the lower rear arm eccentric bolt to 86 ft. lbs. (117 Nm).

1992-94

1. Raise and safely support the vehicle. Remove the wheel and tire assembly.

2. Remove the cotter pin and loosen the front lower lateral link ball joint nut. With the nut protecting the ball joint stud, press out the stud with press tool 49 S231 575 or equivalent. Remove the nut.

3. Remove the bolt and remove the lower lateral link.

4. Remove the cotter pin and loosen the upper lateral link ball joint nut. With the nut protecting the ball joint stud, press out the stud with press tool 49 S231 575 or equivalent. Remove the nut.

5. Paint an alignment mark on the cam plate and crossmember for assembly reference, before removing the upper lateral link bolt. Remove the bolt and the upper lateral link.

6. Remove the cotter pin and loosen the rear lower lateral link ball joint nut. With the nut protecting the ball joint stud, press out the stud with press tool 49 0118 850C or equivalent. Remove the nut.

7. Remove the nuts and remove the rear lower lateral link.
To install:
8. Install the rear lower lateral link and tighten the nuts, in sequence, to 38 ft. lbs. (52 Nm).

9. Install the rear lower lateral link inner ball joint and tighten to 87 ft. lbs. (118 Nm).

10. Connect the rear lower lateral link outer ball joint to the knuckle and tighten the nut to 47 ft. lbs. (64 Nm). Install a new cotter pin.

11. Install the upper lateral link and loosely tighten the bolt. Connect the ball joint to the knuckle and tighten the nut to 72 ft. lbs. (98 Nm). Install a new cotter pin.

12. Install the front lower lateral link and loosely install the bolt. Connect the ball joint to the knuckle and tighten the nut to 80 ft. lbs. (108 Nm). Install a new cotter pin.

13. Install the wheel and tire assembly and lower the vehicle. With the vehicle at normal ride height, tighten the upper and front lower lateral link bolts.

14. Align the pain marks on the cam plate and crossmember and tighten the upper lateral link bolt to 86 ft. lbs. (117 Nm). Tighten the lower lateral link bolt to the same specification.

Rear Wheel Bearings

REMOVAL AND INSTALLATION

323, Protege and MX-3

1. Raise and safely support the vehicle and remove the rear wheels and the hub cap.

2. Have an assistant hold the brake or set the parking brake and loosen the axle nut.

3. If equipped, remove the brake caliper and hang it from the body. Do not let it hang by the hose. Remove the brake disc or drum.

4. Remove the axle nut and remove the hub. The bearing is part of the hub and cannot be replaced separately.
To install:
5. Install the hub with a new axle nut, do not torque the nut yet.

6. Install the brake drum or brake rotor and caliper and torque the caliper bolts to 44 ft. lbs. (60 Nm).

7. Hold the brake and torque the axle nut to 174 ft. lbs. (235 Nm). Stake the nut in place.

MX6/626

1. Raise and safely support the vehicle and remove the rear wheels.

2. Hold the brake to remove the center axle nut. If equipped with drum brakes, remove the drum.

3. Without disconnecting the hydraulic hose, remove the disc brake caliper and hang it from the body. Do not let it hang by the hose. Slide the disc and hub off the spindle.

4. On 1990-92 vehicles, the brake disc or drum and hub are 1 piece; on 1993-94 vehicles, the rotor or drum is removed separate from the hub.

5. On 1990-92 vehicles, the bearing is pressed into the hub and retained with a snapring. Remove the old seal and snapring and press the old bearing out.

6. On 1993-94 vehicles, the hub and bearing cannot be disassembled.
To install:
7. On 1990-92 vehicles, press a new bearing into the hub, install the snapring and install a new seal.

8. Install the hub and drum or rotor. If equipped, install the brake caliper.

9. Install a new spindle nut and tighten to 130 ft. lbs. (177 Nm) on 1990-92 vehicles or 173 ft. lbs. (235 Nm) on 1993-94 vehicles. Stake the nut into place.

10. Install the wheel and tire assembly and lower the vehicle.

ADJUSTMENT

1. Raise and support the vehicle safely. Remove the tire and wheel assembly.

2. Remove and properly support the caliper assembly.

3. Position a dial indicator gauge against the dust cap. Push and pull the disc brake rotor or brake drum in and out in the axial direction and measure the endplay of the wheel bearing.

4. Endplay should not exceed 0.0079 in. (0.2mm) on 1990-92 MX-6/626, but not exceed 0.002 in. (0.05mm) on all other vehicles.

5. If endplay is excessive, check the hub nut torque or replace the bearing.

Rear Axle Assembly

REMOVAL AND INSTALLATION

FWD Models with Rear Drum Brakes

1. Raise and safely support the vehicle. Remove the tire and wheel assembly.

2. Remove the locknut.

3. Remove the brake drum.

4. Remove the hub bearing assembly.

5. Remove the parking brake cable bracket. Remove the brake line clip.

6. Remove rear brake backing plate assembly. Remove the rear brake shoes if necessary.

7. Remove the hub spindle assembly (rear axle).

8. Installation is the reverse of removal procedure. Install the rear wheel bearing hub assembly or adjust the wheel bearings as necessary. Stake new locknut. Refer to the necessary service procedures.

FWD Models with Rear Disc Brakes

1. Raise and safely support the vehicle. Remove the tire and wheel assembly.

2. Remove the locknut.

3. Remove the brake caliper assembly. Do not disconnect brake line but hang rear caliper aside.

4. Remove the rear brake disc. Remove the hub bearing assembly.

5. Remove rear brake dust cover. If equipped with ABS remove the wheel speed sensor.

6. Remove the hub spindle assembly (rear axle).

7. Installation is the reverse of removal procedure. Install the rear wheel bearing hub assembly or adjust the wheel bearings as necessary. Stake new locknut. Refer to the necessary service procedures.

STEERING

Steering Wheel

—————— **CAUTION** ——————
If equipped with an air bag, the vehicle battery and the system's own back-up battery must be disconnected before removing the steering wheel. Failure to do so may result in deployment of the air bag and possible personal injury.

REMOVAL AND INSTALLATION

Without Air Bag

1. Disconnect the negative battery cable. Remove the horn pad button assembly. If equipped with a 4 spoke steering wheel, pull the center cap toward the wheel top.
2. Make matchmarks on the steering wheel and steering shaft. Never strike the steering shaft with a hammer, as damage to the column may result.
3. Remove the wheel using a suitable puller.
4. Installation is the reverse of removal. Torque the steering wheel nut to 36 ft. lbs. (49 Nm).

With Air Bag

1. Disarm the air bag.
2. At the back of the steering wheel hub, remove the nuts that hold the air bag assembly and remove the air bag. Place it in a safe place, pad side up.
3. Matchmark the wheel to the shaft and remove the nut. Use a puller to remove the wheel.
4. When installing, the clockspring must be reset.
   a. Make sure the front wheels are straight-ahead.
   b. Turn the clockspring all the way to the right.
   c. Turn the clockspring back about 2 ³/₄ turns and align the marks.
   d. Connect the wiring and install the steering wheel.
5. Torque the steering wheel nut to 36 ft. lbs. (49 Nm). Install the air bag unit.

Front Wheel Steering Rack and Pinion

REMOVAL AND INSTALLATION

323, Protege, Miata and MX-3

WITHOUT 4WD

1. Disconnect the negative battery cable. Raise and safely support the vehicle and remove the wheel and tire assemblies.
2. Remove the engine undercover.
3. Remove the cotter pins and nuts and disconnect the tie rod ends.
4. Remove the steering column universal joint bolt. Matchmark the joint to the pinion shaft.
5. If equipped with power steering, disconnect the hydraulic lines and drain the fluid into a container.
6. If equipped with manual transaxle, disconnect the extension bar and shift control rod from the transaxle.
7. Remove the bracket nuts or bolts and remove the steering rack from the vehicle.
To install:
8. When fitting the rack into place, make sure the pinion shaft and universal joint matchmarks are correctly aligned. Fit the shaft into the joint and start the steering rack bracket nuts or bolts.
9. Tighten the bracket nuts or bolts to 38 ft. lbs. (52 Nm) on 323/Protege and MX-3 or 43 ft. lbs. (59 Nm) on Miata. Install the universal joint bolt and torque it to 20 ft. lbs. (26 Nm).
10. Connect the tie rod ends and torque the nuts to 33 ft. lbs. (44 Nm) on Miata or 42 ft. lbs. (57 Nm) on 323/Protege and MX-3, then tighten as required to install a new cotter pin.
11. If equipped, connect the power steering hydraulic lines and install the undercover.
12. Install the wheel and tire assemblies and lower the vehicle. If equipped with power steering, fill the system with the proper fluid and bleed the air from the system.

WITH 4WD

1. Remove the battery and battery tray. Raise and safely support the vehicle and remove the front wheels and front crossmember.
2. Disconnect the tie rod ends and remove the bolt from the steering column universal joint. Matchmark the universal joint to the pinion shaft.
3. Disconnect the hydraulic lines and drain the fluid into a container.

4. To remove the steering rack, the front-to-rear engine mount member must be removed:
   a. Use the proper lifting equipment and support the engine from above.
   b. Disconnect the front and rear engine mounts from the mount member and remove the mount member.
   c. Remove the rear mount from the engine.
5. Remove the exhaust pipe and catalytic converter.
6. Matchmark the flanges and remove the driveshaft.
7. Lower the engine gradually until the lower left rack mounting bolt can be reached. Do not lower too far or the halfshaft joints will be damaged.
8. Remove the mount bolts and move the rack to the left to remove the steering rack.
To install:
9. When fitting the rack into place, make sure the pinion shaft and universal joint matchmarks are correctly aligned. Fit the shaft into the joint and start the steering rack bracket bolts. Torque the nuts and bolts to 38 ft. lbs. (52 Nm).
10. Use new gaskets and install the exhaust pipe. Torque the flange nuts to 34 ft. lbs. (46 Nm).
11. Install the driveshaft and torque the flange nuts to 22 ft. lbs. (30 Nm).
12. Install the engine mount and mount member. Torque the mount member nuts to 66 ft. lbs. (89 Nm), the mount-to-engine nuts to 38 ft. lbs. (52 Nm).
13. Connect the fluid lines. Install the universal joint bolt and torque it to 20 ft. lbs. (27 Nm).
14. Connect the tie rod ends and torque the nuts to 42 ft. lbs. (57 Nm) and tighten as required to install a new cotter pin.
15. Install the front crossmember and torque the bolts to 86 ft. lbs. (117 Nm).
16. Fill the pump with fluid and bleed the air from the system.

MX6/626

2-WHEEL STEERING

1. Disconnect the negative battery cable. Raise and safely support the vehicle.
2. Remove the wheel and tire assemblies. If equipped, remove the mud flaps on 1990-92 vehicles.
3. Remove the cotter pins and nuts and separate the tie rod ends from the knuckles.

4. If equipped with 2.5L engine, remove the transverse member and the front exhaust pipe. On 1993-94 vehicles, support the engine with engine support tool 49 G017 502 or equivalent, and remove the rear transaxle mount.

5. Disconnect the power steering pressure and return lines. Disconnect the oil pressure switch connector, if equipped.

6. Mark the position of the steering shaft in the column universal joint. Remove the universal joint pinch bolt.

7. Remove the mounting bolts and remove the steering gear.

To install:

8. Position the steering gear, making sure the marks made on the universal joint and steering gear shaft align, and install the mounting nuts and bolts. Tighten to 40 ft. lbs. (54 Nm). On 1993-94 vehicles, the bolts and nuts must be torqued in sequence.

9. Install the universal joint pinch bolt and tighten to 20 ft. lbs. (26 Nm).

10. Connect the power steering lines and the oil pressure switch, if equipped.

11. On 1993-94 vehicles, install the rear transaxle mount. Tighten the mounting bolts and nut to 69 ft. lbs. (93 Nm). Remove the engine support tool.

12. If equipped with 2.5L engine, install the front exhaust pipe, using new gaskets. Tighten the pipe-to-catalytic converter nuts to 66 ft. lbs. (89 Nm) and the pipe-to-exhaust manifold nuts to 38 ft. lbs. (89 Nm). Connect the oxygen sensors.

13. If equipped with 2.5L engine, install the transverse member and tighten the bolts to 97 ft. lbs. (131 Nm).

14. Connect the tie rod ends to the knuckles. On 1990-92 vehicles, tighten the nuts to 42 ft. lbs. (57 Nm). On 1993-94 vehicles, tighten the nuts

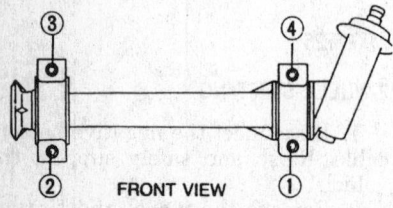

Steering gear mounting bolt torque sequence — 1993-94 MX-6/626

to 33 ft. lbs. (44 Nm). Install new cotter pins.

15. Install the wheel and tire assemblies and lower the vehicle. Fill the power steering system with the proper fluid and bleed the air from the system.

16. Check the front wheel alignment.

4-WHEEL STEERING

1. Remove the battery and battery tray. Raise and safely support the vehicle and remove the front wheels and front crossmember.

2. Disconnect the tie rod ends and remove the bolt from the steering column universal joint. Matchmark the universal joint to the pinion shaft.

3. Disconnect the hydraulic lines and drain the fluid into a container.

4. Remove the exhaust pipe and catalytic converter.

5. Disconnect the front-to-rear steering angle transfer shaft.

6. Remove the left engine mount.

7. Remove the nuts and bolts from the sub-frames and allow the frame members to hang down.

8. Remove the stabilizer bar.

9. Remove the mounting bolts and remove the steering rack.

To install:

10. When fitting the rack into place, make sure the pinion shaft and universal joint matchmarks are correctly aligned. Fit the shaft into the joint and start the steering rack bracket bolts. Torque the nuts and bolts to 38 ft. lbs. (52 Nm).

11. Install the stabilizer bar and adjust the links.

12. Attach the sub-frames and torque the bolts to 40 ft. lbs. (54 Nm).

13. Install the engine mount.

14. Connect the front-to-rear steering shaft.

15. Use new gaskets and install the exhaust pipe and catalytic converter.

16. Connect the hydraulic lines and install the front crossmember.

17. Connect the tie rod ends. Torque the nuts to 33 ft. lbs. (44 Nm) and tighten as required to install a new cotter pin.

18. With all parts installed, fill and bleed the system and adjust the rear steering angle transfer shaft.

929

1. Raise and safely support the vehicle. Remove the wheel and tire assemblies.

2. On 1990-91 vehicles, remove the lower member from under the steering gear.

3. Remove the cotter pins and nuts from the tie rod ends. Separate

the tie rod ends from the knuckles using a suitable tool.

4. Disconnect the power steering pressure and return hose.

5. Mark the position of the steering gear shaft in the column universal joint and remove the universal joint pinch bolt.

6. Remove the mounting bolts/nuts and remove the steering gear.

To install:

7. Position the steering gear in the vehicle, aligning the mark on the steering shaft with the universal joint. Install the mounting bolts/nuts and tighten to 61 ft. lbs. (83 Nm) on 1990-91 vehicles or 38 ft. lbs. (52 Nm) on 1992-94 vehicles. On 1992-93 vehicles, the bolts must be torqued in sequence.

8. Install the universal joint pinch bolt and tighten to 20 ft. lbs. (26 Nm).

9. Connect the power steering lines.

10. Connect the tie rod ends to the knuckles and tighten the nuts to 33 ft. lbs. (44 Nm) on 1990-91 vehicles or 47 ft. lbs. (64 Nm) on 1992-94 vehicles. Install new cotter pins.

11. On 1990-91 vehicles, install the lower member and tighten the bolts to 66 ft. lbs. (89 Nm).

12. Install the wheel and tire assemblies and lower the vehicle. Fill the power steering system with the proper type and quantity of fluid and bleed the air from the system.

RX-7

1990-91

1. Raise and safely support the vehicle. Remove the wheel and tire assemblies.

2. Remove the mounting nuts and bolts and remove the stabilizer bar.

3. Remove the cotter pins and nuts from the tie rod ends. Separate the tie rod ends from the knuckles using a suitable tool.

4. Mark the position of the steering gear shaft in the column universal joint and remove the universal joint pinch bolt.

5. Disconnect the power steering pressure and return hose.

6. Remove the steering gear mounting bolts and remove the steering gear.

To install:

7. Position the steering gear in the vehicle.

8. Install the steering gear mounting bolts. Tighten the bolts, in sequence, to 33 ft. lbs. (44 Nm) while pushing forward on the steering gear shaft.

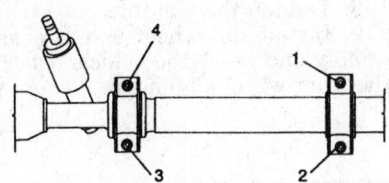

Steering gear mounting bolt torque sequence — 1992-94 929

9. Align the marks made on the steering gear shaft and universal joint and connect them. Make sure the clearance between the universal joint and the crossmember is ¼-½ in. If it is not, disconnect the intermediate shaft and repeat Step 8. Tighten the universal joint pinch bolt to 17 ft. lbs. (23 Nm).

10. Connect the power steering lines.

11. Connect the tie rod ends to the steering knuckles and tighten the nuts to 33 ft. lbs. (44 Nm). Install new cotter pin.

12. Install the stabilizer bar.

13. Install the wheel and tire assemblies and lower the vehicle. Fill the power steering system with the proper type and quantity of fluid and bleed the air from the system.

1993-94

1. Raise and safely support the vehicle. Remove the wheel and tire assemblies. Remove the undercover.

2. Remove the cotter pins and nuts from the tie rod ends. Separate the tie rod ends from the knuckles using a suitable tool.

3. Remove the stabilizer bar brackets.

4. Disconnect the power steering pressure and return lines.

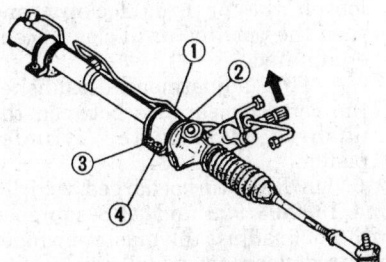

Steering gear mounting bolt torque sequence — 1990-91 RX-7

5. Mark the position of the steering gear shaft in the lower column joint and remove the bolt.

6. Remove the steering gear bracket mounting bolts.

7. Support the crossmember with a jack and remove the nuts and bolts. Slowly lower the crossmember and remove the steering gear.

To install:

8. Position the steering gear on the crossmember and raise the crossmember into position. Tighten the crossmember mounting nuts and bolts.

9. Install the steering gear mounting bracket bolts and tighten, in sequence, to 38 ft. lbs. (51 Nm).

10. Connect the column joint to the steering shaft, aligning the marks made during removal. Install the bolt and tighten to 19 ft. lbs. (26 Nm).

11. Connect the power steering lines. When connecting the pressure hose, align the pin on the hose with the hole in the steering gear.

12. Install the stabilizer bar brackets and tighten the bolts to 19 ft. lbs. (26 Nm).

13. Connect the tie rod ends to the knuckles and tighten the nuts to 32 ft. lbs. (44 Nm). Install new cotter pins.

14. Install the wheel and tire assemblies and lower the vehicle. Fill the power steering system with the proper type and quantity of fluid and bleed the air from the system.

Rear Steering Gear

REMOVAL AND INSTALLATION

MX-6/626

1. Disconnect the negative battery cable. Raise and support the vehicle safely. Remove the rear tire assemblies, as required for working clearance.

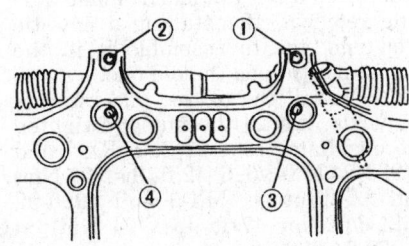

Steering gear mounting bolt torque sequence — 1993-94 RX-7

2. Disconnect the electrical connector from the steering gear assembly. Remove the electrical harness retaining bolts.

3. Remove the steering angle transfer shaft cover. Disconnect the universal joint and bolts from the steering angle transfer shaft assembly. Remove the lower cover and the brake line joint block.

4. Disconnect and cap all required fluid lines. Disconnect the lower spring link retaining bolts. Remove the solenoid valve, which is mounted on the steering gear assembly.

5. Using the proper tool, disconnect the tie rod ends from the knuckles. Remove the mounting bolts from the left and right sub-frames. Allow the components to hang freely.

6. Remove the rear steering gear bolts and the rear steering gear assembly from the vehicle.

To install:

7. Install the steering gear and torque the bolts to 34 ft. lbs. (46 Nm).

8. Connect the tie rod ends and torque the nuts to 33 ft. lbs. (44 Nm). Tighten as required to install a new cotter pin.

9. Install the solenoid valve assembly and connect the hydraulic lines and the wiring.

10. Fill and bleed the system and adjust the steering angle transfer shaft.

Power Steering Pump

REMOVAL AND INSTALLATION

1. Disconnect the negative battery cable. Disconnect and plug the hoses at the pump. If equipped, disconnect the pressure switch connector.

2. Remove the pump drive belt.

3. On all except 323, Protege, MX-3 and Miata, it is necessary to remove the pump pulley before removing the pump. Hold the pulley with tool 49 W023 585A or equivalent, or if possible, insert a small prybar through 1 of the holes in the pulley to hold it. Remove the pulley nut and pulley.

4. Support the pump, remove the mounting bolts and lift out the pump.

5. Installation is the reverse of removal. Tighten the pulley nut to 43 ft. lbs. (58 Nm). Adjust the belt tension and fill and bleed the system.

BELT ADJUSTMENT

1. Apply approximately 22 lbs. pressure to the drive belt at a point

midway between the pulleys. A new belt should deflect as follows:

323
1.6L engine: 0.31-0.35 in. (8-9mm)
Protege
1.6L engine: 0.31-0.35 in. (8-9mm)
Miata
1.6L engine: 0.31-0.35 in. (8-9mm)
MX-6/626
2.0L engine: 0.30-0.35 in. (7.5-9.0mm)
2.2L engine: 0.31-0.39 in. (8-10mm)
2.5L engine: 0.24-0.28 in. (6-7mm)
MX-3
1.6L engine: 0.31-0.35 in. (8-9mm)
1.8L engine: 0.24-0.28 in. (6-7mm)
929
1990-91: 0.28-0.35 in. (7-9mm)
1992-94: 0.31-0.37 in. (8.0-9.5mm)
RX-7
1990-91: 0.43-0.51 in. (11-13mm)
1993-94: 0.14-0.15 in. (3.5-4.0mm)

2. A used belt should deflect as follows:

323
1.6L engine: 0.35-0.39 in. (9-10mm)
Protege
1.6L engine: 0.35-0.39 in. (9-10mm)
Miata
1.6L engine: 0.35-0.39 in. (9-10mm)
MX-6/626
2.0L engine: 0.32-0.37 (8.0-9.5mm)
2.2L engine: 0.35-0.43 in. (9-11mm)
2.5L engine: 0.28-0.31 in. (7-8mm)
MX-3
1.6L engine: 0.35-0.39 in. (9-10mm)
1.8L engine: 0.28-0.31 in. (7-8mm)
929
1990-91: 0.35-0.43 in. (9-11mm)
1992-94: 0.37-0.43 in. (9.5-11.0mm)
RX-7
1990-91: 0.55-0.63 in. (14-16mm)
1993-94: 0.18-0.19 in. (4.5-5.0mm)

3. If the belt tension is not as specified, loosen the pump pivot bolt on 323, Protege, Miata, MX-3 1.6L engine and MX-6/626 2.0L engine. On all other engines the belt tension is set with a separate tensioner assembly.

4. Loosen the locknut or bolt and turn the tensioner bolt until the tension is correct. Tighten the tensioner locknut or bolt and tighten the pivot bolt, if necessary.

SYSTEM BLEEDING

1. Check the fluid level. Add fluid, as required.
2. Raise and safely support the vehicle.
3. Turn the steering wheel full cycle, in both directions, 5 times with the engine **OFF**.
4. Recheck the fluid level again and add, as required.
5. Repeat Steps 3 and 4 until the fluid level stabilizes.
6. Lower the vehicle.
7. Start the engine and allow to warm up at idle. Turn the steering wheel full cycle, in both directions, 5 times with the engine running.
8. Check that the fluid is not foamy and the level has not dropped.
9. Add fluid, if necessary and repeat Steps 7 and 8.

Tie Rod Ends

REMOVAL AND INSTALLATION

1. Raise and support the vehicle safely. Remove the wheel and tire assembly.
2. Remove the cotter pin and loosen the nut on the tie rod end ball stud. With the nut protecting the ball stud, press the stud from the knuckle using press tool 49 0118 850C or equivalent. Remove the nut and the tie rod end from the knuckle.
3. Paint a reference mark across the tie rod, jam nut and shaft.
4. Loosen the jam nut and unscrew the tie rod end from the shaft.
   To install:
5. Thread the tie rod onto the shaft and align the marks made during removal. If installing a new tie rod end, try to assemble it in the same position as the old one.
6. Install the tie rod end into the knuckle. Install the nut and tighten to on Miata, 1990-91 929, RX-7 and 1993-94 MX-6/626, 42 ft. lbs. (57 Nm) on 323/Protege, MX-3 and 1990-92 MX-6/626 or 47 ft. lbs. (64 Nm) on 1992-94 929.
7. Install a new cotter pin. If the cotter pin cannot be installed because the ball stud hole and the nut castellation do not align, tighten the nut further until the cotter pin can be installed. Never loosen the nut to install the cotter pin.
8. Tighten the jam nut.
9. Install the wheel and tire assembly and lower the vehicle. Check the front wheel alignment.

BRAKES

Master Cylinder

REMOVAL AND INSTALLATION

1. Disconnect the negative battery cable. Disconnect the fluid level sensor, if equipped.
2. Using a suitable wrench, disconnect and plug the brake fluid lines at the master cylinder. If equipped, disconnect the hose to the clutch master cylinder.
3. Remove the proportioning bypass valve attaching bolts and valve, if equipped.
4. Remove the master cylinder mounting nuts and remove the master cylinder. Remove the O-ring seal, if equipped.
   To install:
5. On all except RX-7 turbocharged vehicles and 1992-94 929 and ABS equipped MX-6/626, adjust the master cylinder pushrod clearance as follows:
   a. Install adjusting tool 49 F043 001 or equivalent on the master cylinder. Turn the bolt until it bottoms in the pushrod hole.
   b. Apply 19.7 in. Hg vacuum to the power brake booster with a vacuum pump.
   c. Invert the tool and place it on the booster.
   d. Check the clearance between the bolt and master cylinder pushrod. If there is any clearance, loosen the pushrod locknut and turn the pushrod until clearance is eliminated.
   e. This adjustment establishes the correct clearance between the pushrod and master cylinder piston.
6. On RX-7 turbocharged vehicles and 1992-94 929 and ABS equipped MX-6/626, adjust the master cylinder pushrod clearance as follows:
   a. Turn the nut on adjusting tool 49 B043 001 or equivalent, clockwise to retract the gauge rod. Install the tool on the power booster.

b. Apply 19.7 in. Hg vacuum to the power brake booster with a vacuum pump.

c. Turn the nut on the tool counterclockwise until the gauge rod just contacts the end of the master cylinder pushrod. Push lightly on the end of the gauge rod to make sure it is seated. Make sure there is no gap between the nut and the tool body.

d. Remove the tool from the booster without disturbing the adjusting nut. Invert the tool and place it on the master cylinder.

e. Push lightly on the end of the gauge rod to make sure it is bottomed in the master cylinder piston. Note any clearance between the tool body and the adjusting nut or between the body and the master cylinder. If there is no clearance at either place, the pushrod is adjusted correctly.

f. If there is clearance between the body and the adjusting nut, push lightly on the end of the gauge rod and measure the clearance between the nut and tool body. Use tools 49 B043 003 and 49 B043 004 or equivalents, to turn the master cylinder pushrod nut and lengthen the pushrod an amount equal to the measured clearance.

g. If there is clearance between the tool body and master cylinder, measure and record the height of the gauge rod. Turn the adjusting nut until the tool body sets squarely on the master cylinder. Measure and record the height of the gauge rod. Subtract the first measurement from the second, then use tools 49 B043 003 and 49 B043 004 or equivalents, to turn the nut and shorten the master cylinder pushrod an amount equal to the difference.

h. This adjustment establishes the correct clearance between the pushrod and master cylinder piston.

7. Install a new O-ring seal, if equipped.

8. Install the master cylinder on the brake booster. Install the mounting nuts and tighten to 12 ft. lbs. (16 Nm).

9. Install the proportioning bypass valve if equipped.

10. Connect the brake lines to the master cylinder. If equipped with banjo bolts, use new washers. If equipped, connect the clutch master cylinder hose.

11. Connect the fluid level sensor, if equipped, and connect the negative battery cable.

12. Fill the master cylinder reservoir and bleed the brake system.

Proportioning Valve

REMOVAL AND INSTALLATION

1. Disconnect the negative battery cable. Disconnect and plug the brake lines at the valve assembly.

2. Remove the valve bolts and the valve.

3. Installation is the reverse of the removal procedure. Bleed the system. Inspect the fluid lines for leakage.

Power Brake Booster

REMOVAL AND INSTALLATION

1. Disconnect the negative battery cable. Disconnect the vacuum hose at the booster.

2. On 1992-94 929, remove the cruise control actuator and the cruise control actuator bracket and engine hanger.

3. On 1990-92 MX-6/626, remove the steering column to gain access to the booster mounting nuts.

4. Remove the master cylinder.

5. Working inside the vehicle, remove the cotter pin and clevis pin from the clevis and brake pedal.

6. Remove the booster mounting nuts and remove the booster. Remove the booster-to-firewall gasket(s).

To install:

7. Apply sealant to a new gasket(s) and install on the booster.

8. Guide the booster studs through the firewall and install the booster. Install the nuts and tighten to 18 ft. lbs. (25 Nm).

9. Lubricate the clevis pin with grease and install through the clevis and brake pedal. Install a new cotter pin.

10. On all except RX-7 turbocharged vehicles and 1992-94 929 and ABS equipped MX-6/626, adjust the master cylinder pushrod clearance as follows:

a. Install adjusting tool 49 F043 001 or equivalent on the master cylinder. Turn the bolt until it bottoms in the pushrod hole.

b. Apply 19.7 in. Hg vacuum to the power brake booster with a vacuum pump.

c. Invert the tool and place it on the booster.

d. Check the clearance between the bolt and master cylinder pushrod. If there is any clearance, loosen the pushrod locknut and turn the pushrod until clearance is eliminated.

e. This adjustment establishes the correct clearance between the pushrod and master cylinder piston.

11. On RX-7 turbocharged vehicles and 1992-94 929 and ABS equipped MX-6/626, adjust the master cylinder pushrod clearance as follows:

a. Turn the nut on adjusting tool 49 B043 001 or equivalent, clockwise to retract the gauge rod. Install the tool on the power booster.

b. Apply 19.7 in. Hg vacuum to the power brake booster with a vacuum pump.

c. Turn the nut on the tool counterclockwise until the gauge rod just contacts the end of the master cylinder pushrod. Push lightly on the end of the gauge rod to make sure it is seated. Make sure there is no gap between the nut and the tool body.

d. Remove the tool from the booster without disturbing the adjusting nut. Invert the tool and place it on the master cylinder.

e. Push lightly on the end of the gauge rod to make sure it is bottomed in the master cylinder piston. Note any clearance between the tool body and the adjusting nut or between the body and the master cylinder. If there is no clearance at either place, the pushrod is adjusted correctly.

f. If there is clearance between the body and the adjusting nut, push lightly on the end of the gauge rod and measure the clearance between the nut and tool body. Use tools 49 B043 003 and 49 B043 004 or equivalents, to turn the master cylinder pushrod nut and lengthen the pushrod an amount equal to the measured clearance.

g. If there is clearance between the tool body and master cylinder, measure and record the height of the gauge rod. Turn the adjusting nut until the tool body sets squarely on the master cylinder. Measure and record the height of the gauge rod. Subtract the first measurement from the second, then use tools 49 B043 003 and 49 B043 004 or equivalents, to turn the nut and shorten the master cylinder pushrod an amount equal to the difference.

h. This adjustment establishes the correct clearance between the pushrod and master cylinder piston.

12. Install the master cylinder and connect the brake lines.

13. Install the remaining components in the reverse order of removal.

14. Fill the master cylinder and bleed the brake system.

Brake Caliper

REMOVAL AND INSTALLATION

1. Raise and safely support the vehicle. Remove the wheel and tire assembly.

2. Disconnect and plug the brake line at the caliper.

3. If removing a rear caliper, disconnect the parking brake cable on all except 929.

4. Remove the caliper mounting bolts and remove the caliper. On some vehicles, the caliper is retained by only 1 bolt; remove the bolt, pivot the caliper upward and slide it off the caliper support pin.

To install:

5. Install the brake caliper and tighten the bolt(s) as follows:

323, Protege and MX-3 front: 36 ft. lbs. (49 Nm)

323, Protege and MX-3 rear: 45 ft. lbs. (61 Nm)

Miata front 65 ft. lbs. (88 Nm)

Miata rear: 29 ft. lbs. (39 Nm)

1990-92 MX-6/626 front: 30 ft. lbs. (41 Nm)

1990-92 MX-6/626 rear: 17 ft. lbs. (24 Nm)

1993-94 MX-6/626 front: 36 ft. lbs. (49 Nm)

1993-94 MX-6/626 rear: 29 ft. lbs. (39 Nm)

1990-91 929 front: 69 ft. lbs. (93 Nm)

1990-91 929 rear: 17 ft. lbs. (24 Nm)

1992-94 929 front: 62 ft. lbs. (84 Nm)

1992-94 929 rear: 36 ft. lbs. (49 Nm)

RX-7 front, single piston caliper: 30 ft. lbs. (41 Nm)

RX-7 front, 4 piston caliper: 72 ft. lbs. (98 Nm)

1990-91 RX-7 rear: 17 ft. lbs. (24 Nm)

1993-94 RX-7 rear: 62 ft. lbs. (84 Nm)

6. Connect the parking brake cable, if removed.

7. Attach the brake line to the caliper. If attached with a banjo bolt, use new washers.

8. Install the wheel and tire assembly and lower the vehicle. Bleed the brake system.

Disc Brake Pads

REMOVAL AND INSTALLATION

Front

EXCEPT 323/PROTEGE, MX-3 AND RX-7 WITH 4-PISTON CALIPER

1. Remove ½ the brake fluid from the master cylinder reservoir.

2. Raise and safely support the vehicle. Remove the wheel and tire assembly.

3. If equipped with 1 caliper mounting bolt, remove the bolt and pivot the caliper upward, away from the brake pads. Secure the caliper in this position.

4. If equipped with 2 caliper mounting bolts, remove the caliper and hang it with wire from the coil spring, without disconnecting the brake hose. Do not let the caliper hang by the brake hose.

5. Remove the brake pads, noting the position of the shims and clips so they can be reassembled in the same positions.

To install:

6. Use a C-clamp or other suitable tool to push the piston back into the caliper.

7. Install the brake pads with the shims and clips.

8. Install the brake caliper and the wheel and tire assembly. Lower the vehicle.

9. Depress the brake pedal a few times to position the brake pads. Check the fluid level in the master cylinder reservoir and adjust as necessary.

323/PROTEGE, MX-3 AND RX-7 WITH 4-PISTON CALIPER

1. Remove ½ the brake fluid from the master cylinder reservoir.

2. Raise and safely support the vehicle. Remove the wheel and tire assembly.

3. Remove the spring clips and pull out the brake pad pins. Note the position of the springs so they can be reinstalled in the same positions.

4. Pull the pads and shims out the top of the caliper. Note the position of the shims so they can be reinstalled in the same positions.

To install:

5. Push the piston(s) back into the caliper using tool 49 0221 600C or equivalent.

6. Install the pads and shims.

7. Install the pins and secure with the springs.

8. Install the wheel and tire assembly and lower the vehicle.

9. Depress the brake pedal a few times to position the brake pads. Check the fluid level in the master cylinder reservoir and adjust as necessary.

Rear

1. Remove ½ the brake fluid from the master cylinder reservoir.

2. Raise and safely support the vehicle. Remove the wheel and tire assembly. Disconnect the parking brake cable.

3. If equipped with 1 caliper mounting bolt, remove the bolt and pivot the caliper upward, away from the brake pads. Secure the caliper in this position.

4. If equipped with 2 caliper mounting bolts, remove the caliper and hang it with wire from the coil spring, without disconnecting the brake hose. Do not let the caliper hang by the brake hose.

5. Remove the brake pads, noting the position of the shims and clips so they can be reassembled in the same positions.

To install:

6. On 323, Protege, Miata, MX-3 and 1993-94 MX-6/626, insert an Allen wrench into the back of the caliper. Turn the manual adjustment gear counterclockwise until it stops, to pull the caliper piston inward.

7. On RX-7, and 1990-92 MX-6/626, use tool 49 FA18 602 or equivalent to turn the caliper piston clockwise and back into the bore. Position the piston grooves at the top and bottom of the caliper.

8. On 929, use a C-clamp or other suitable tool to push the caliper piston into the bore.

9. Install the brake pads with the shims and clips. On RX-7, and 1990-92 MX-6/626, make sure the inner pad alignment pin is aligned with the piston groove.

10. Install the brake caliper. On 323, Protege, Miata, MX-3 and 1993-94 MX-6/626, use the Allen wrench to turn the manual adjustment gear clockwise until the brake pads just touch the rotor, then back off ⅓ turn.

11. Install the wheel and tire assembly and lower the vehicle.

12. Depress the brake pedal a few times to position the brake pads. Check the fluid level in the master cylinder reservoir and adjust as necessary.

Brake Rotor

REMOVAL AND INSTALLATION

1. Raise and safely support the vehicle. Remove the wheel and tire assembly.
2. Remove the brake caliper and hang it from the coil spring with wire. Do not let it hang by the brake hose. On all except 323, Protege, MX-3 and RX-7 with 4 piston caliper, remove the caliper with the support bracket attached.
3. On 1990-92 MX-6/626 rear rotor and 1990-91 929 front rotor, remove the locknut and remove the rotor, hub and bearing assembly.
4. On all other vehicles, remove the retaining screw, if equipped, and remove the rotor from the hub.
5. Installation is the reverse of the removal procedure. On 1990-92 MX-6/626 rear rotor and 1990-91 929 front rotor, tighten the hub nut to 130 ft. lbs. (177 Nm). Stake the nut.

Brake Drums

REMOVAL AND INSTALLATION

1. Raise and safely support the vehicle. Remove the wheel and tire assembly.
2. On 1990-92 MX-6/626, unstake the locknut and remove the locknut and washer.
3. On all other vehicles, remove the drum retaining screw, if equipped.
4. Remove the brake drum. If the drum is difficult to remove, push the operating lever stopper, on the backing plate, upward to release the operating lever and increase the shoe clearance.
5. Installation is the reverse of the removal procedure. On 1990-92 MX-6/626, tighten the locknut to 130 ft. lbs. (177 Nm), then stake the locknut.

Brake Shoes

REMOVAL AND INSTALLATION

1. Raise the vehicle and support safely. Remove the wheels and the brake drum. Clean the dirt from the brake components with a dry brush.
2. To ease removal of the leading shoe and Installation of the return spring later, push up on the quadrant to release the self adjuster.

3. Use brake pliers to remove the return springs. Then, use needle nose pliers to remove the holding pins from the backing plate.
4. Push the bottoms of the shoes outward in order to release them from the anchors and then unhook them at the wheel cylinder. Remove the leading shoe first. Both rear wheels should be done if either side shows excessive wear.

To install:

5. Lightly lubricate with brake grease the shoe and cylinder contact points, shoe anchor points and backing plate projections.
6. Install the shoes to the back plate, then install the springs and adjuster.
7. Install the drum and apply the brakes several times to take up the adjustment before the vehicle is driven. Also apply parking brake several times.

929

1. The parking brake on this vehicle is a drum brake inside the disc brake rotor. Raise and safely support the vehicle and remove the wheel and caliper.
2. Remove the screws to remove the disc. If necessary, insert a tool through the hole in the disc and back down the adjuster wheel.
3. Disconnect the parking brake cable.
4. Remove the return springs, then the clips and pull the shoes, adjuster and operating lever off as an assembly.
5. Installation is the reverse of removal. Screw the adjuster all the way in and make sure the threads face the front shoe on the left, rear shoe on the right.
6. To adjust, turn the adjuster until the disc will not turn, then back it down so there is no drag.

Wheel Cylinder

REMOVAL AND INSTALLATION

1. Raise and support the vehicle safely. Remove the tire and wheel assembly.
2. Remove the brake drum and brake shoes.
3. Disconnect and plug the brake lines.
4. Remove the stud nuts and bolt attaching the wheel cylinder to the backing plate and remove the wheel cylinder.

5. Installation is the reverse of removal. Be sure to bleed the system after installation.

Brake System Bleeding

1. Clean all dirt from around the master cylinder reservoir cap.
2. Remove the filler cap and fill the master cylinder reservoir to the lower edge of the filler neck.
3. Clean off the bleeder connections at all of the wheel cylinders and disc brake calipers. Attach a suitable hose to the right rear wheel cylinder or caliper bleeder screw and place the end of the hose in a suitable glass jar, submerged in clean brake fluid.
4. Have an assistant depress the brake pedal several times, then hold it in the depressed position. Loosen the bleeder screw, let the fluid drain, then retighten the screw.
5. Repeat Step 4 until bubbles cease to appear at the end of the bleeder hose, then close the bleeder valve and remove the hose. Check the level of the brake fluid in the master cylinder reservoir and add fluid, if necessary.
6. Repeat the procedure at the left rear wheel, left front wheel and right front wheel, in that order.
7. After the bleeding operation at each caliper or wheel cylinder has been completed, fill the master cylinder reservoir and replace the filler cap.

Anti-Lock Brake System Service

PRECAUTION

• Properly relieve the system pressure and disable the system before loosening any hydraulic fitting.
• Before preforming any arc welding on the vehicle, disconnect the Electronic Brake Control Module.
• When placing the vehicle in a paint drying oven, do not expose the Electronic Brake Control Module to temperatures in excess of 185°F (85°C) for longer than 2 hrs.
• Never disconnect or connect Electronic Brake Control Module or its components connectors with the ignition switch **ON**.
• Never disassemble any component of the Anti-Lock Brake System (ABS) which is designated non-serviceable; the component must be replaced as a unit.

RELIEVING ANTI-LOCK BRAKE SYSTEM PRESSURE

——————— CAUTION ———————
The Anti-Lock Brake System pressure must be properly relieved and the system disabled before loosening any hydraulic fitting. The system is capable of generating fluid pressure high enough to penetrate skin, which could be fatal.

1. With the ignition switch **OFF** and the negative battery cable disconnected, pump the brake pedal a minimum of 25 times using approximately 50 lbs. of pedal force. When a noticeable change in pedal feel occurs, the accumulator is discharged.
2. When a definite increase in pedal effort is felt, stroke the pedal a few additional times.
3. If the job requires power while the hydraulic system is open, disconnect the wiring to the ABS hydraulic unit before connecting the battery cable.

Hydraulic Unit

REMOVAL AND INSTALLATION

1. Disconnect the negative battery cable and depressurize the Anti-Lock Brake system pressure.
2. Disconnect the wiring from the hydraulic unit.
3. Disconnect and plug the brake lines and hoses from the hydraulic unit. Cap the openings.
4. Remove the hydraulic unit attaching bolts and the hydraulic unit from the vehicle.
5. Installation is the reverse of removal. Remove the caps only when ready to connect the hydraulic fittings. Bleed the system.

Wheel Speed Sensor

REMOVAL AND INSTALLATION

1. Disconnect the negative battery cable. Raise and safely support the vehicle.
2. Remove the wheel and tire assembly.
3. Disconnect the sensor electrical connector.
4. Remove the sensor mounting bolt and harness bracket bolt(s). Remove the sensor.
5. Installation is the reverse of the removal procedure. On some vehicles, the sensors cannot be interchanged between the left and right side of the vehicle. These sensors are marked **L** or **R** accordingly. Make sure the sensor is installed on the correct side.

Sensor Rotor

REMOVAL AND INSTALLATION

1. Raise and safely support the vehicle. Remove the wheel and tire assembly.
2. The sensor rotor is attached to the halfshaft on a drive axle or on the hub on a non-drive axle. Remove the halfshaft or hub accordingly.
3. Remove the sensor rotor using a puller or hammer and brass drift, as required. The sensor cannot be reused, once removed.
4. Press on a new rotor and reinstall the halfshaft or hub.

CHASSIS ELECTRICAL

Air Bag

PRECAUTIONS

• An air bag is an explosive device. Handle with extreme caution.
• Always disconnect the battery and the air bag connector before removing the steering wheel or beginning work on the air bag system.
• Air bag components must not be repaired or opened. Always use new parts, including the wiring harness.
• Always place a removed air bag unit with the horn pad facing up. Put it in a safe place where it will not be disturbed.
• The air bag unit must not be exposed to grease, fluids, or cleaning agents.
• The air bag unit must not be exposed to temperatures above 194°F (90°C) at any time. Even the heat of a soldering iron can damage or ignite the charge.
• Storage and transport of air bags is subject to rules governing explosive devices and should be done only in the original package.
• Failure to follow proper safety precautions may result in personal injury through accidental firing of the air bag, or through failure of the air bag in an accident.

DISARMING

1. Disconnect the negative battery cable.
2. On RX7, remove the panel under the left side of the dashboard.
3. On Miata, remove the bottom steering column cover.
4. Locate and unplug the blue and orange connector. Protect this connector from accidental electrical contact, including static electricity.
5. The air bag is now disarmed and the battery can be connected to perform electrical testing on other systems.
6. When ready to reconnect the air bag; disconnect the battery, connect the air bag connector, install the cover or panel and make sure no one is in the vehicle when connecting the battery.

Heater Blower Motor

REMOVAL AND INSTALLATION

1. Disconnect the negative battery cable.
2. Remove the dash undercover which is located on the passenger side of the vehicle, if equipped. Remove the glove box. Disconnect the multi-connector to the blower motor.
3. Remove the air duct in between the blower unit and the heater unit.
4. Remove the nuts and the blower unit. Disassemble the unit and remove the blower motor.
5. Installation is the reverse of removal.

Windshield Wiper Motor

REMOVAL AND INSTALLATION

Front

1. Disconnect the negative battery cable. Remove the wiper arms.
2. Remove the cowl plate screws and remove the cowl plate.
3. Disconnect the wiring and linkage from the wiper motor.
4. Unbolt and remove the motor.
5. Installation is the reverse of removal. Check the system for proper operation.

Rear

1. Disconnect the negative battery cable.
2. Remove the wiper arm and outer bushing.

3. On 323 and RX-7, remove the lower hatch trim panel. On MX-3, remove the wiper motor cover.

4. Disconnect the electrical connector and remove the wiper motor.

5. Installation is the reverse of the removal procedure.

Windshield Wiper Switch

REMOVAL AND INSTALLATION

NOTE: Refer to the Combination Switch service procedures for all vehicles except 1990-91 RX-7.

1990-91 RX-7

1. Disconnect the negative battery cable.

2. Remove the screws from the cluster switch panel.

3. Pull the panel out and disconnect the electrical connectors. Remove the cluster switch panel.

4. Remove the wiper switch from the cluster switch panel.

5. Installation is the reverse of the removal procedure.

Instrument Cluster

REMOVAL AND INSTALLATION

Except RX-7 and Miata

1. Disconnect the negative battery cable.

2. Remove the screws and remove the gauge assembly hood. Disconnect the switches as required.

3. Remove the screws and pull the gauge assembly out until the electrical connectors are visible. Disconnect the speedometer cable and all the connectors from the rear of the gauge panel and remove it.

4. Installation is the reverse of removal.

RX-7

1. Disconnect the negative battery cable and the air bag connector.

2. Remove the steering wheel.

3. Remove the 3 screws in front of the cluster glass and the 2 screws under the cluster switch panel and pull the switch panel out far enough to disconnect the switches.

4. Remove the 4 instrument cluster screws and pull the cluster out far enough to disconnect the wiring and speedometer cable.

5. Installation is the reverse of removal. Torque the steering wheel nut to 36 ft. lbs. (49 Nm).

Miata

1. Disconnect the negative battery cable and the air bag connector.

2. Remove the steering column support bolts and lower the steering column.

3. Remove the screws from the top inside and the bottom outside of the gauge hood and pull the hood off the clips.

4. Remove the screws and pull the gauge assembly out far enough to disconnect the speedometer cable and wiring.

5. Installation is the reverse of removal.

Speedometer

REMOVAL AND INSTALLATION

1. Disconnect the negative battery cable.

2. Remove the instrument cluster.

3. If equipped, remove the knob from the tripmeter reset shaft.

4. Remove the screws and remove the lens from the gauge case.

5. Remove the speedometer.

Concealed Headlights

MANUAL OPERATION

RX-7 and Miata

Under the hood, next to each headlight is the retractor motor that automatically raises and lowers the light. If the motor fails, the light can be raised or lowered manually by turning the knob on the top of each motor.

Headlight Switch

REMOVAL AND INSTALLATION

1990-91 RX-7

1. Disconnect the negative battery cable.

2. Remove the screws from the cluster switch panel.

3. Pull the panel out and disconnect the electrical connectors. Remove the cluster switch panel.

4. Remove the headlight switch from the cluster switch panel.

5. Installation is the reverse of the removal procedure.

Turn Signal Switch

REMOVAL AND INSTALLATION

1990-91 RX-7

1. Disconnect the negative battery cable.

2. Remove the screws from the cluster switch panel.

3. Pull the panel out and disconnect the electrical connectors. Remove the cluster switch panel.

4. Remove the turn signal switch from the cluster switch panel.

5. Installation is the reverse of the removal procedure.

Combination Switch

REMOVAL AND INSTALLATION

Without Air Bag

1. Disconnect the negative battery cable.

2. Remove the steering wheel.

3. Remove the steering column covers.

4. Disconnect the electrical connectors.

5. Remove the stop ring from the shaft.

6. Remove the switch retaining screws. Remove the combination switch from its mounting.

7. Installation is the reverse of the removal procedure.

With Air Bag

1. Disconnect the negative battery cable and disarm the air bag system.

2. Remove the steering wheel and the column covers.

3. Disconnect the wiring and remove the screws to remove the combination switch.

4. Installation of the switch is the reverse of removal. To install the steering wheel, the clock-spring must be reset.

   a. Make sure the front wheels are straight ahead.

   b. Turn the clock-spring all the way to the right. Don't force it.

   c. Turn the clock-spring back about 2¾ turns and align the marks.

   d. Connect the wiring and install the steering wheel.

Ignition Lock/Switch

REMOVAL AND INSTALLATION

1. Disconnect the negative battery cable.
2. Remove the steering wheel.
3. Remove the steering column covers. Remove the lower panel or air duct, if necessary.
4. Disconnect the electrical connectors.
5. Remove the switch screws and the combination switch.
6. Disconnect the ignition switch wires.
7. Use a chisel to make slots in the lock screws. Remove the screws.
8. Installation is the reverse of the removal procedure. Install the new screws until the head twists off. Make sure the lock operates properly while tightening the new locking screws.

Stoplight Switch

REMOVAL AND INSTALLATION

1. Disconnect the negative battery cable.
2. Disconnect the stoplight switch wire connector from the switch.
3. Remove the switch retainer and outer washer from the pedal pin. Slide the stoplight switch out of the brake pedal bracket and remove the switch.
4. Installation is the reverse of removal.

Clutch Switch

REMOVAL AND INSTALLATION

1. Disconnect the negative battery cable.
2. Disconnect the switch wiring.
3. Loosen the locknut and remove the switch.
4. Installation is the reverse of removal.

Neutral Safety Switch

ADJUSTMENT

Except 1993-94 MX-6/626

1. Remove the selector rod or shift cable from the manual shaft lever on the transmission.

2. Move the manual lever to **N**.
3. Loosen the switch mounting bolts. Remove the screw on the switch body, if equipped.
4. On all except 1992-94 929 and 1993-94 RX-7, align the holes of the switch and the shaft by inserting a 0.079 in. (2mm) diameter pin. On 1992-94 929 and 1993-94 RX-7, insert a 0.16 in. (4mm) pin.
5. Tighten the switch screws and remove the pin.
6. Connect the rod or cable.

1993-94 MX-6/626

1. Disconnect the negative battery cable.
2. Remove the resonance chamber, fresh air duct and air cleaner assembly.
3. Remove the spring pin and clip and disconnect the shift cable at the transmission.
4. Turn the manual shaft on the transmission to **N**.
5. Disconnect the neutral safety switch connector.
6. Loosen the switch mounting bolts.
7. Connect and ohmmeter between terminals **A** and **H**.
8. Adjust the switch so there is continuity between the terminals, then tighten the switch mounting bolts.
9. Make sure the gearshift lever range position and neutral safety switch are aligned.
10. Connect the neutral safety switch connector. Connect the shift cable and install a new spring pin and clip.
11. Install the air cleaner assembly, fresh air duct and resonance chamber. Reconnect the battery cable.

REMOVAL AND INSTALLATION

Except 1993-94 MX-6/626

1. Remove the shift cable or selector rod from the manual lever shaft on the transmission.
2. Remove the mounting bolts and remove the switch.
3. Installation is the reverse of removal procedure. Adjust the switch.

1993-94 MX-6/626

1. Disconnect the negative battery cable.
2. Remove the resonance chamber, fresh air duct and air cleaner assembly.

3. Remove the spring pin and clip and disconnect the shift cable at the transmission.
4. Disconnect the neutral safety switch connector.
5. Remove the manual shaft nut, lockwasher and lever.
6. Remove the switch mounting bolts and the switch.
   To install:
7. Rotate the manual shaft to **N**.
8. Turn the neutral safety switch so the neutral mark is in line with the flat, straight surfaces on either side of the manual shaft.
9. Loosely tighten the switch bolts and adjust the switch. Tighten the bolts to 95 inch lbs. (11 Nm).

Fuses and Circuit Breakers

Location

Fuse Panel

MIATA

The main fuse block is located on the right side of engine compartment. A second fuse block is located to the left of the steering column, just above the clutch pedal.

RX-7

The main fuse block is located in the engine compartment, near the radiator support on 1990-91 vehicles or next to the battery on 1993-94 vehicles. The fuse panel and joint box are located behind the driver's side left kick panel. On 1993-94 vehicles, there is also a relay and fuse box located in the engine compartment, near the main fuse block.

323, PROTEGE AND MX-3

The fuse blocks are located in the engine compartment, near the battery. There is also a joint box located under the left side of the dash.

626 AND MX-6

The main fuse block is located in the engine compartment, near the battery. There is also a fuse panel located under the left side of the dash.

929

The main fuse block is located in the engine compartment, near the battery. The fuse panel is located on the driver's side left kick panel, near the brake pedal. On 1992-94 vehicles, there is also a fuse and relay box located next to the battery.

Mercedes-Benz

190, 260, 300, 350, 400, 420, 500, 560, 600

12

ENGINE IDENTIFICATION

Year	Model	Engine Displacement Liters (cc)	Engine Series (ID/VIN)	Fuel System	No. of Cylinders	Engine Type
1990	190E	2.6 (2599)	M103	CIS-E	6	103.942
	300E	3.0 (2962)	M103	CIS-E	6	103.983
	300CE	3.0 (2962)	M103	CIS-E	6	104.980
	300SE	3.0 (2962)	M103	CIS-E	6	103.981
	300SL	3.0 (2962)	M104	CIS-E	6	104.981
	300TE	3.0 (2962)	M103	CIS-E	6	103.983
	300SEL	3.0 (2962)	M103	CIS-E	6	103.981
	420SEL	4.2 (4196)	M116	CIS-E	8	116.965
	500SL	5.0 (4973)	M119	CIS-E	8	119.960
	560SEC	5.6 (5547)	M117	CIS-E	8	117.968
	560SEL	5.6 (5547)	M117	CIS-E	8	117.968
1991	190E	2.3 (2298)	M102	CIS-E	4	102.985
	190E	2.6 (2597)	M103	CIS-E	6	103.942
	300D	2.5 (2497)	OM602	EDS	5	602.962
	300E	2.6 (2597)	M103	CIS-E	6	103.940
	300E	3.0 (2960)	M103	CIS-E	6	103.983
	300CE	3.0 (2960)	M104	CIS-E	6	104.980
	300TE	3.0 (2960)	M103	CIS-E	6	103.983
	300SE	3.0 (2960)	M103	CIS-E	6	103.981
	300SEL	3.0 (2960)	M103	CIS-E	6	103.981
	300SL	3.0 (2960)	M104	CIS-E	6	104.981
	350SD	3.5 (3449)	OM602	EDS	6	603.970
	350SDL	3.5 (3449)	OM602	EDS	6	603.970
	420SEL	4.2 (4196)	M116	CIS-E	8	116.965
	500E	5.0 (4972)	M119	CIS-E	8	119.960
	500SL	5.0 (4972)	M119	CIS-E	8	119.960
	560SEC	5.6 (5547)	M117	CIS-E	8	117.968
	560SEL	5.6 (5547)	M117	CIS-E	8	117.968
1992-94	190E	2.3 (2299)	M102	CIS-E	4	102.985
	190E	2.6 (2559)	M103	CIS-E	6	103.942
	300D Turbo	2.5 (2497)	OM602	EDS	5	602.962
	300E	2.6 (2559)	M103	CIS-E	6	103.940
	300E	3.0 (2960)	M103	CIS-E	6	103.983
	400E	4.2 (4196)	M119	LH	8	119.975
	500E	5.0 (4973)	M119	LH	8	119.974
	300CE	3.0 (2960)	M104	CIS-E	6	104.980
	300TE	3.0 (2960)	M103	CIS-E	6	103.983
	300E 4MATIC	3.0 (2960)	M103	CIS-E	6	103.985
	300TE 4MATIC	3.0 (2960)	M103	CIS-E	6	103.985
	300SD Turbo	3.5 (3449)	OM603	EDS	6	603.971

GENERAL ENGINE SPECIFICATIONS

Year	Engine ID/VIN	Engine Displacement Liters (cc)	Fuel System Type	Net Horsepower @ rpm	Net Torque @ rpm (ft. lbs.)	Bore × Stroke (in.)	Compression Ratio	Oil Pressure @ rpm
1990	103.942	2.6 (2599)	CIS-E	158 @ 5800	162 @ 4600	3.26 × 3.16	9.2:1	55
	103.983	3.0 (2962)	CIS-E	177 @ 5700	188 @ 4400	3.48 × 3.16	9.2:1	55
	104.980	3.0 (2962)	CIS-E	177 @ 5700	188 @ 4400	3.48 × 3.16	9.2:1	55
	103.981	3.0 (2962)	CIS-E	177 @ 5700	188 @ 4400	3.48 × 3.16	9.2:1	55
	104.981	3.0 (2962)	CIS-E	228 @ 6300	201 @ 4600	3.48 × 3.16	10.0:1	55
	103.983	3.0 (2962)	CIS-E	177 @ 5700	188 @ 4400	3.48 × 3.16	9.2:1	55
	103.981	3.0 (2962)	CIS-E	177 @ 5700	188 @ 4400	3.48 × 3.16	9.2:1	55
	116.965	4.2 (4196)	CIS-E	201 @ 5200	228 @ 3600	3.62 × 3.11	9.0:1	55
	119.960	5.0 (4973)	CIS-E	322 @ 5500	332 @ 4000	3.80 × 3.35	10.0:1	55
	117.968	5.6 (5547)	CIS-E	238 @ 4800	287 @ 3500	3.80 × 3.73	9.0:1	55
	117.968	5.6 (5547)	CIS-E	238 @ 4800	287 @ 3500	3.80 × 3.73	9.0:1	55
1991	102.985	2.3 (2298)	CIS-E	130 @ 5100	146 @ 3500	3.76 × 3.16	9.0:1	55
	103.942	2.6 (2597)	CIS-E	158 @ 5800	162 @ 4600	3.26 × 3.16	9.2:1	55
	602.962	2.5 (2497)	EDS	121 @ 4600	165 @ 2400	3.43 × 3.31	22.0:1	55
	103.940	2.6 (2597)	CIS-E	158 @ 5800	162 @ 4600	3.26 × 3.16	9.2:1	55
	103.983	3.0 (2960)	CIS-E	177 @ 5700	188 @ 4400	3.48 × 3.16	9.2:1	55
	104.980	3.0 (2960)	CIS-E	217 @ 6400	195 @ 4600	3.48 × 3.16	10.0:1	55
	103.983	3.0 (2960)	CIS-E	177 @ 5700	188 @ 4400	3.48 × 3.16	9.2:1	55
	103.981	3.0 (2960)	CIS-E	177 @ 5700	188 @ 4400	3.48 × 3.16	9.2:1	55
	103.981	3.0 (2960)	CIS-E	177 @ 5700	188 @ 4400	3.48 × 3.16	9.2:1	55
	104.981	3.0 (2960)	CIS-E	228 @ 6300	201 @ 4600	3.48 × 3.16	10.0:1	55
	603.970	3.5 (3499)	EDS	134 @ 4000	229 @ 2000	3.50 × 3.60	22.0:1	55
	603.970	3.5 (3499)	EDS	134 @ 4000	229 @ 2000	3.50 × 3.60	22.0:1	55
	116.965	4.2 (4196)	CIS-E	201 @ 5200	228 @ 3600	3.26 × 3.10	9.0:1	55
	119.960	5.0 (4972)	CIS-E	322 @ 5700	355 @ 3900	3.80 × 3.35	10.0:1	55
	119.960	5.0 (4972)	CIS-E	322 @ 5700	322 @ 4000	3.80 × 3.35	10.0:1	55
	117.968	5.6 (5547)	CIS-E	238 @ 4800	287 @ 3500	3.80 × 3.73	9.0:1	55
	117.968	5.6 (5547)	CIS-E	238 @ 4800	287 @ 3500	3.80 × 3.73	9.0:1	55
1992–94	102.985	2.3 (2299)	CIS-E	130 @ 5100	146 @ 3500	3.76 × 3.16	9.0:1	55
	103.942	2.6 (2559)	CIS-E	158 @ 5800	162 @ 4600	3.26 × 3.16	9.2:1	55
	602.962	2.5 (2497)	EDS	121 @ 4600	165 @ 2400	3.43 × 3.31	22.0:1	55
	103.940	2.6 (2559)	CIS-E	158 @ 5800	162 @ 4600	3.26 × 3.16	9.2:1	55
	103.983	3.0 (2960)	CIS-E	177 @ 5700	188 @ 4400	3.48 × 3.16	9.2:1	55
	119.975	4.2 (4196)	LH	268 @ 5700	295 @ 3900	3.62 × 3.11	10.0:1	55
	119.974	5.0 (4973)	LH	322 @ 5700	354 @ 3900	3.80 × 3.35	10.0:1	55
	104.980	3.0 (2960)	CIS-E	228 @ 6300	201 @ 4600	3.48 × 3.16	10.0:1	55
	103.983	3.0 (2960)	CIS-E	117 @ 5700	188 @ 4400	3.48 × 3.16	10.0:1	55
	103.985	3.0 (2960)	CIS-E	117 @ 5700	188 @ 4400	3.48 × 3.16	10.0:1	55
	103.985	3.0 (2960)	CIS-E	117 @ 5700	188 @ 4400	3.48 × 3.16	10.0:1	55
	603.971	3.5 (3449)	EDS	148 @ 4000	229 @ 2000	3.50 × 3.60	22.0:1	55
	104.990	3.2 (3199)	LH	228 @ 5800	229 @ 4100	3.54 × 3.30	10.0:1	55

GENERAL ENGINE SPECIFICATIONS

Year	Engine ID/VIN	Engine Displacement Liters (cc)	Fuel System Type	Net Horsepower @ rpm	Net Torque @ rpm (ft. lbs.)	Bore × Stroke (in.)	Com-pression Ratio	Oil Pressure @ rpm
	119.971	4.2 (4196)	LH	282 @ 5700	302 @ 3900	3.62 × 3.11	10.0:1	55
	119.970	5.0 (4973)	LH	322 @ 5700	354 @ 3900	3.80 × 3.35	10.0:1	55
	120.980	6.0 (5987)	LH	402 @ 5200	428 @ 3800	3.50 × 3.16	10.0:1	55
	104.981	3.0 (2960)	CIS-E	217 @ 6400	195 @ 4600	3.48 × 3.16	10.0:1	55
	119.960	5.0 (4973)	CIS-E	322 @ 5500	332 @ 4000	3.80 × 3.35	10.0:1	NA

NA—Not available
CIS-E—Electronic Continuous Injection System
EDS—Electronic Diesel System
LH—LH Jectronic Fuel Injection

GASOLINE ENGINE TUNE-UP SPECIFICATIONS

Year	Engine ID/VIN	Engine Displacement Liters (cc)	Spark Plugs Gap (in.)	Ignition Timing (deg.)		Fuel Pump (psi)	Idle Speed (rpm)		Valve Clearance	
				MT	AT		MT	AT②	In.	Ex.
1990	M103	2.6 (2588)	0.032	9B	9B	91–94	700	700	Hyd.	Hyd.
	M103	3.0 (2962)	0.032	—	TDC	91–94	—	650	Hyd.	Hyd.
	M103	3.0 (2962)	0.032	—	TDC	91–94	—	650	Hyd.	Hyd.
	M103	3.0 (2962)	0.032	—	TDC	91–94	—	650	Hyd.	Hyd.
	M104	3.0 (2962)	0.032	TDC	TDC	91–94	—	—	Hyd.	Hyd.
	M103	3.0 (2962)	0.032	—	TDC	91–94	—	650	Hyd.	Hyd.
	M103	3.0 (2962)	0.032	—	TDC	91–94	—	650	Hyd.	Hyd.
	M116	4.2 (4196)	0.032	—	TDC	91–94	—	650	Hyd.	Hyd.
	M119	5.0 (4973)	0.032	—	TDC	91–94	—	700	Hyd.	Hyd.
	M117	5.6 (5547)	0.032	—	TDC	91–94	—	650	Hyd.	Hyd.
	M117	5.6 (5547)	0.032	—	TDC	91–94	—	650	Hyd.	Hyd.
1991	M102	2.3 (2298)	0.032	5B	5B	77–80	750	750	Hyd.	Hyd.
	M103	2.6 (2597)	0.032	7–11B	7–11B	77–80	700	700	Hyd.	Hyd.
	M103	2.6 (2597)	0.032	—	7–11B	77–80	—	650	Hyd.	Hyd.
	M103	3.0 (2960)	0.032	—	6–11B	77–80	—	650	Hyd.	Hyd.
	M104	3.0 (2960)	0.032	—	NA	90–93	—	650	Hyd.	Hyd.
	M103	3.0 (2960)	0.032	—	6–11B	77–80	—	650	Hyd.	Hyd.
	M103	3.0 (2960)	0.032	—	6–11B	77–80	—	650	Hyd.	Hyd.
	M103	3.0 (2960)	0.032	—	6–11B	77–80	—	650	Hyd.	Hyd.
	M104	3.0 (2960)	0.032	NA	NA	90–93	700	650	Hyd.	Hyd.
	M116	4.2 (4196)	0.032	—	NA	90–93	—	650	Hyd.	Hyd.
	M119	5.0 (4972)	0.032	—	NA	90–93	—	650	Hyd.	Hyd.
	M119	5.0 (4972)	0.032	—	NA	90–93	—	650	Hyd.	Hyd.
	M117	5.6 (5547)	0.032	—	NA	90–93	—	650	Hyd.	Hyd.
	M117	5.6 (5547)	0.032	—	TDC	90–93	—	650	Hyd.	Hyd.
1992	M102	2.3 (2299)	0.032	8–12B	8–12B	77–80	720	720	Hyd.	Hyd.
	M103	2.6 (2599)	0.032	①	①	77–80	700	700	Hyd.	Hyd.
	M103	2.6 (2599)	0.032	①	①	77–80	NA	700	Hyd.	Hyd.
	M103	3.0 (2960)	0.032	①	①	77–80	NA	650	Hyd.	Hyd.
	M103	3.0 (2960)	0.032	①	①	77–80	NA	650	Hyd.	Hyd.
	M104	3.0 (2960)	0.032	①	①	77–80	NA	650	Hyd.	Hyd.
	M104	3.2 (3199)	—	①	①	45–55③	NA	650	Hyd.	Hyd.
	M104	3.2 (3199)	0.032	①	①	90–93	700	650	Hyd.	Hyd.
	M119	4.2 (4196)	0.032	①	①	45–55③	NA	650	Hyd.	Hyd.
	M119	4.2 (4196)	0.032	①	TDC	45–55③	NA	650	Hyd.	Hyd.
	M119	5.0 (4973)	0.032	①	①	45–55③	NA	650	Hyd.	Hyd.
	M119	5.0 (4973)	0.032	①	①.	45–55③	NA	650	Hyd.	Hyd.
	M119	5.0 (4973)	0.032	①	①	90–93	NA	650	Hyd.	Hyd.
	M120	6.0 (5987)	—	①	①	42–55③	NA	650	Hyd.	Hyd.
1993–94			REFER TO UNDERHOOD SPECIFICATIONS STICKER							

NOTE: The lowest cylinder pressure should be within 75% of the highest cylinder pressure reading. For example, if the highest cylinder is 134 psi, the lowest should be 101. Engine should be at normal operating temperature with throttle valve in the wide open position. The underhood specifications sticker often reflects tune-up specification changes in production. Sticker figures must be used if they disagree with those in this chart.

NA—Not available
B—Before Top Dead Center
Hyd.—Hydraulic
TDC—Top Dead Center

① The EZL control unit adjusts timing automatically. No adjustment is possible or necessary.
② Transmission in drive
③ After pressure regulator

DIESEL ENGINE TUNE-UP SPECIFICATIONS

Year	Engine ID/VIN	Engine Displacement Liters (cc)	Valve Clearance Intake (in.)	Exhaust (in.)	Intake Valve Opens (deg.)	Injection Pump Setting (deg.)	Injection Nozzle Pressure (psi) New	Used	Idle Speed (rpm)	Cranking Compression Pressure (psi) ①
1991	OM602	2.5 (2497) ②	Hyd.	Hyd.	12A	15A	1564–2103	1740	660–700	261–464
	OM602	3.5 (3449) ③	Hyd.	Hyd.	12A	15A	1564–2103	1740	610–650	261–464
1992–94	OM602	2.5 (2497) ④	Hyd.	Hyd.	12A	15A	1958–2103	1740	660–700	284–327
	OM603	3.5 (3449) ⑤	Hyd.	Hyd.	12A	15A	1958–2103	1740	610–650	284–327

Hyd.—Hydraulic
① Maximum difference between cylinders—
44 psi
② 300D
③ 350SD and 350SDL
④ 300D Turbo
⑤ 300SD Turbo

FIRING ORDERS

NOTE: To avoid confusion, always replace spark plug wires one at a time.

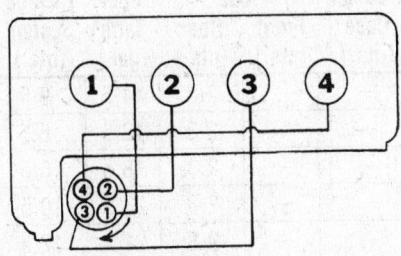

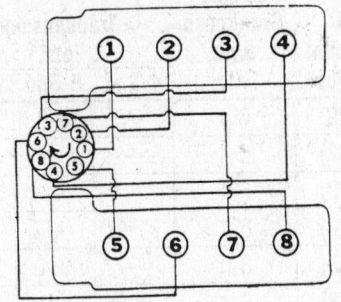

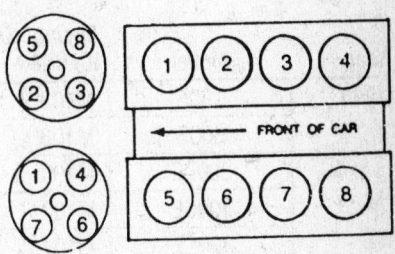

2.3L Cylinder Gasoline Engine
Engine Firing Order: 1-3-4-2
Distributor Rotation: Clockwise

5.6L SOHC Engine
Engine Firing Order: 1-5-4-8-6-3-7-2
Distributor Rotation: Clockwise

4.2L and 5.0L SOHC Engines
Engine Firing Order: 1-5-4-8-6-3-7-2
Distributor Rotation: Clockwise

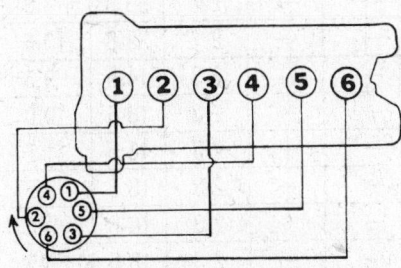

2.6L, 3.0L and 3.2L Gasoline Engines
Engine Firing Order: 1-5-3-6-2-4
Distributor Rotation: Clockwise

CAPACITIES

Year	Model	Engine ID/VIN	Engine Displacement Liters (cc)	Engine Crankcase with Filter	Transmission (pts.)			Transfer Case (pts.)	Drive Axle		Fuel Tank (gal.)	Cooling System (qts.)
					4-Spd	5-Spd	Auto.		Front (pts.)	Rear (pts.)		
1990	190E	M103	2.6 (2599)	6.4	—	3.2	12.7	—	—	2.3	14.5	9.5
	300E	M103	3.0 (2962)	6.4	—	—	13.1	—	—	2.3	18.5	8.5
	300CE	M103	3.0 (2962)	6.4	—	—	13.1	—	—	2.3	18.5	10.6
	300SE	M103	3.0 (2962)	6.4	—	—	13.1	—	—	2.3	23.8	10.6
	300SL	M104	3.0 (2962)	8.0	—	3.4	12.6	—	—	2.8	21.1	12.2
	300TE	M103	3.0 (2962)	6.4	—	—	13.1	1.5	2.0	2.3	19.0	10.6
	300SEL	M103	3.0 (2962)	6.4	—	—	13.1	—	—	2.3	23.8	10.6
	420SEL	M116	4.2 (4196)	8.5	—	—	16.2	—	—	2.7	23.8	13.8
	500SL	M119	5.0 (4973)	8.5	—	—	16.2	—	—	2.8	21.1	15.9
	560SEC	M117	5.6 (5547)	8.5	—	—	16.2	—	—	2.7	23.8	13.8
	560SEL	M117	5.6 (5547)	8.5	—	—	16.2	—	—	2.7	23.8	13.8
1991	190E	M103	2.3 (2298)	5.3	—	3.2	12.7	—	—	2.3	14.5	9.5
	190E	M103	2.6 (2597)	6.4	—	3.2	12.7	—	—	2.3	18.5	10.0
	300D	OM602	2.5 (2497)	8.0	—	—	13.1	—	—	2.3	18.5	11.7
	300E	M103	2.6 (2597)	6.9	—	—	13.1	—	—	2.3	18.5	8.5
	300E	M103	3.0 (2960)	6.9	—	—	13.1	—	—	2.3	18.5	9.5
	300CE	M104	3.0 (2960)	8.0	—	—	13.1	—	—	2.3	18.5	9.5
	300TE	M103	3.0 (2960)	6.9	—	—	13.1	1.5	2.0	2.3①	19.0	9.5
	300SE	M103	3.0 (2960)	6.9	—	—	13.1	—	—	2.3	23.8	8.5
	300SEL	M103	3.0 (2960)	6.9	—	—	13.1	—	—	2.3	23.8	11.7
	300SL	M104	3.0 (2960)	8.0	—	3.2	13.1	—	—	2.3	21.0	11.7
	350SD	OM602	3.5 (3449)	8.0	—	—	13.1	—	—	2.7	21.6	12.7
	350SDL	OM602	3.5 (3449)	8.0	—	—	13.1	—	—	2.7	21.6	12.7
	420SEL	M116	4.2 (4196)	8.5	—	—	16.2	—	—	2.7	23.8	13.8
	500E	M119	5.0 (4972)	8.5	—	—	16.2	—	—	2.7	23.8	14.3
	500SL	M119	5.0 (4972)	8.5	—	—	16.2	—	—	2.3	21.1	14.3
	560SEC	M117	5.6 (5547)	8.5	—	—	16.2	—	—	2.7	23.8	13.8
	560SEL	M117	5.6 (5547)	8.5	—	—	16.2	—	—	2.7	23.8	13.8
1992–94	190E	M102	2.3 (2299)	5.3	—	3.2	12.7	—	—	2.3	14.5	9.5
	190E	M103	2.6 (2559)	6.4	—	3.2	12.7	—	—	2.3	18.5	10.0
	300D Turbo	OM602	2.5 (2497)	8.0	—	—	13.1	—	—	2.3	18.5	11.7
	300E	M103	2.6 (2559)	6.9	—	—	13.1	—	—	2.3	18.5	8.5
	300E	M103	3.0 (2960)	6.9	—	—	13.1	—	—	2.3	18.5	9.5
	400E	M119	4.2 (4196)	6.9	—	—	13.1	—	—	2.3	18.5	9.5
	500E	M119	5.0 (4973)	6.9	—	—	13.1	—	—	2.3	18.5	9.5
	300CE	M104	3.0 (2960)	8.0	—	—	13.1	—	—	2.3	18.5	9.5
	300TE	M103	3.0 (2960)	6.9	—	—	13.1	—	—	2.3	18.5	9.5
	300E 4MATIC	M103	3.0 (2960)	6.9	—	—	13.1	1.5	2.0	2.3	18.5	9.5
	300TE 4MATIC	M103	3.0 (2960)	6.9	—	—	13.1	1.5	2.0	2.3	19.0	9.5
	300SD Turbo	OM603	3.5 (3449)	8.5	—	—	13.1	—	—	2.7	29.7	11.7

CAPACITIES

Year	Model	Engine ID/VIN	Engine Displacement Liters (cc)	Engine Crankcase with Filter	Transmission (pts.)			Transfer Case (pts.)	Drive Axle		Fuel Tank (gal.)	Cooling System (qts.)
					4-Spd	5-Spd	Auto.		Front (pts.)	Rear (pts.)		
	300SE	M104	3.2 (3199)	8.0	—	—	13.1	—	—	2.7	29.7	15.4
	400SE	M119	4.2 (4196)	8.5	—	—	16.9	—	—	2.7	29.7	17.5
	500SEL	M119	5.0 (4973)	8.5	—	—	16.9	—	—	2.7	29.7	17.5
	600SEL	M120	6.0 (5987)	10.6	—	—	16.9	—	—	2.7	29.7	21.2
	300SL	M104	3.0 (2960)	8.0	—	3.2	13.1	—	—	2.3	21.0	11.7
	500SL	M119	5.0 (4973)	8.5	—	—	16.2	—	—	2.7	21.1	14.3

① 4 Matic: 4.2
4 Matic with ASD: 11.6
Hydropneumatic Suspension: 9.9

CAMSHAFT SPECIFICATIONS

All measurements given in inches.

Year	Engine ID/VIN	Engine Displacement Liters (cc)	Journal Diameter					Elevation		Bearing Clearance	Camshaft End Play
			1	2	3	4	5	In.	Ex.		
1990	M103	2.6 (2599)	1.378	1.831	1.831	1.831	1.831	0.394	0.413	0.002	0.004
	M104	3.0 (2962)	1.378	1.831	1.831	1.831	1.831	0.394	0.413	0.002	0.004
	M116	4.2 (4196)	1.377	1.936	1.936	1.944	1.944	NA	NA	0.0016	0.004
	M117	5.6 (5547)	1.377	1.936	1.936	1.944	1.944	NA	NA	0.0016	0.004
	M119	5.0 (4973)	1.377	1.936	1.936	1.944	1.944	NA	NA	0.0016	0.004
1991	M102	2.3 (2298)	1.260	1.260	1.260	1.260	1.260	NA	NA	0.002	0.003
	OM602	2.5 (2497)	1.218	1.218	1.218	1.218	1.218	NA	NA	0.002	NA
	M103	2.6 (2597)	1.218	1.218	1.218	1.218	1.218	NA	NA	0.002	0.004
	M103	3.0 (2960)	1.218	1.218	1.218	1.218	1.218	NA	NA	0.002	0.004
	M104	3.0 (2960) ①	1.179	1.179	1.179	1.179	1.179	NA	NA	0.002	0.002–0.008
	OM602	3.5 (3449)	1.218	1.218	1.218	1.218	1.218	NA	NA	0.002	NA
	M116	4.2 (4196)	1.378	1.937	1.937	1.945	1.045	NA	NA	0.002	0.003–0.006
	M119	5.0 (4972)	1.100	1.100	1.100	1.100	1.100	NA	NA	0.002	0.002
	M117	5.6 (5547)	1.378	1.937	1.937	1.945	1.945	NA	NA	0.002	0.003–0.006
1992–94	M102	2.3 (2298)	1.260	1.260	1.260	1.260	1.260	NA	NA	0.002	0.003
	OM602	2.5 (2497)	1.218	1.218	1.218	1.218	1.218	NA	NA	0.002	NA
	M103	2.6 (2597)	1.218	1.218	1.218	1.218	1.218	NA	NA	0.002	0.004
	M103	3.0 (2960)	1.218	1.218	1.218	1.218	1.218	NA	NA	0.002	0.004
	M104	3.0 (2960) ①	1.179	1.179	1.179	1.179	1.179	NA	NA	0.002	0.002–0.008
	M104	3.2 (3199)	1.179	1.179	1.179	1.179	1.179	NA	NA	0.002–0.003	0.002–0.008
	OM603	3.5 (3449)	1.218	1.218	1.218	1.218	1.218	NA	NA	0.002	0.004
	M119	4.2 (4196)	1.100	1.100	1.100	1.100	1.100	NA	NA	0.002	0.002–0.006
	M119	5.0 (4973)	1.100	1.100	1.100	1.100	1.100	NA	NA	0.002	0.002–0.006
	M120	6.0 (5987)	1.177	1.177	1.177	1.177	1.177	NA	NA	0.002–0.003	0.002–0.008

NA—Not available
① Dual Overhead Cam

CRANKSHAFT AND CONNECTING ROD SPECIFICATIONS

All measurements are given in inches.

Year	Engine ID/VIN	Engine Displacement Liters (cc)	Crankshaft				Connecting Rod		
			Main Brg. Journal Dia.	Main Brg. Oil Clearance	Shaft End-play	Thrust on No.	Journal Diameter	Oil Clearance	Side Clearance
1990	M103	2.6 (2599)	2.360–2.361	NA	NA	①	2.031–2.032	0.001–0.002	NA
	M104	3.0 (2962)	2.360–2.361	NA	NA	①	2.031–2.032	0.001–0.002	NA
	M116	4.2 (4196)	2.517–2.518	0.002–0.003	0.004–0.009	①	1.887–1.888	0.004–0.009	0.009–0.014
	M117	5.6 (5547)	2.517–2.518	0.002–0.003	0.004–0.009	①	1.887–1.888	0.004–0.009	0.009–0.014
	M119	5.0 (4973)	2.517–2.518	0.002–0.003	0.004–0.009	①	1.887–1.888	0.004–0.009	0.009–0.014
1991	M102	2.3 (2298)	2.281–2.282	0.001–0.002	0.004–0.010	3	1.887–1.888	0.001–0.002	NA
	OM602	2.5 (2497)	2.281–2.282	0.001–0.002	0.004–0.010	4	1.887–1.888	0.001–0.002	NA
	M103	2.6 (2597)	2.360–2.361	NA	NA	①	2.031–2.032	0.001–0.002	NA
	M103	3.0 (2960)	2.360–2.361	NA	NA	①	2.031–2.032	0.001–0.002	NA
	M104	3.0 (2960)	2.360–2.361	NA	NA	①	2.031–2.032	0.001–0.002	NA
	OM602	3.5 (3449)	2.281–2.282	0.001–0.002	0.004–0.010	5	1.887–1.888	0.001–0.002	NA
	M116	4.2 (4196)	2.517–2.518	0.001–0.002	0.004–0.009	3	2.045–2.046	0.001–0.002	NA
	M119	5.0 (4972)	2.517–2.518	0.001–0.002	0.004–0.009	3	2.045–2.046	0.001–0.002	NA
	M117	5.6 (5547)	2.517–2.518	0.001–0.002	0.004–0.009	3	2.045–2.046	0.001–0.002	NA
1992–94	M102	2.3 (2298)	2.281–2.282	0.001–0.002	0.004–0.010	3	1.887–1.888	0.001–0.002	NA
	OM602	2.5 (2497)	2.281–2.282	0.001–0.002	0.004–0.010	4	1.887–1.888	0.001–0.002	NA
	M103	2.6 (2597)	2.360–2.361	0.001–0.002	0.004–0.010	①	2.031–2.032	0.001–0.002	NA
	M103	3.0 (2960)	2.360–2.361	0.001–0.002	0.004–0.010	①	2.031–2.032	0.001–0.002	NA
	M104	3.0 (2960)	2.360–2.361	0.001–0.002	0.004–0.010	①	2.031–2.032	0.001–0.002	NA
	M104	3.2 (3199)	2.360–2.361	0.001–0.002	0.004–0.010	①	2.031–2.032	0.001–0.002	NA
	OM603	3.5 (3449)	2.281–2.282	0.001–0.002	0.004–0.010	5	1.887–1.888	0.001–0.002	NA
	M119	4.2 (4196)	2.517–2.518	0.001–0.002	0.004–0.009	3	2.045–2.046	0.001–0.002	NA
	M119	5.0 (4973)	2.517–2.518	0.001–0.002	0.004–0.009	3	2.045–2.046	0.001–0.002	NA
	M120	6.0 (5987)	2.281–2.282	0.001–0.002	0.004–0.010	5	1.887–1.888	0.001–0.002	NA

NA—Not available
① Center main on 5 main bearing engines; rear main on 7 main bearing engines; 3rd from front on 300D (5 cylinder)

VALVE SPECIFICATIONS

Year	Engine ID/VIN	Engine Displacement Liters (cc)	Seat Angle (deg.)	Face Angle (deg.)	Spring Test Pressure (lbs. @ in.)	Spring Installed Height (in.)	Stem-to-Guide Clearance (in.)		Stem Diameter (in.)	
							Intake	Exhaust	Intake	Exhaust
1990	M103	2.6 (2599)	45	45	NA	NA	0.004	0.004	0.314	0.353
	M104	3.0 (2962)	45	45	NA	NA	0.004	0.004	0.314	0.352
	M116	4.2 (4196)	45	45	194	1.200	0.004	0.004	0.353	0.352
	M117	5.6 (5547)	45	45	194	1.200	0.004	0.004	0.353	0.352
	M119	5.0 (4973)	45	45	194	1.200	0.004	0.004	0.315	0.354
1991	M102	2.3 (2298)	45①	45①	191	1.929	0.004	0.004	0.314	0.353
	OM602	2.5 (2497)	45①	45①	158	2.000	0.004	0.004	0.314	0.353
	M103	2.6 (2597)	45	45	NA	NA	0.004	0.004	0.352	0.353
	M103	3.0 (2960)	45	45	NA	NA	0.004	0.004	0.314	0.353
	M104	3.0 (2960)	45	45	NA	NA	0.004	0.004	0.314	0.353
	OM602	3.5 (3449)	45	45①	158	1.062	0.004	0.004	0.314	0.352
	M116	4.2 (4196)	45	45	194	1.200	0.004	0.004	0.353	0.352
	M119	5.0 (4972)	45	45	194	1.200	0.004	0.004	0.315	0.354
	M117	5.6 (5547)	45	45	194	1.200	0.004	0.004	0.353	0.352
1992-94	M102	2.3 (2298)	45①	45①	191	1.929	0.004	0.004	0.314	0.353
	OM602	2.5 (2498)	45①	45①	160	1.063	0.004	0.004	0.313–0.314	0.352–0.353
	M103	2.6 (2597)	45	45	NA	NA	0.004	0.004	0.352	0.353
	M103	3.0 (2960)	45	45	NA	NA	0.004	0.004	0.314	0.353
	M104	3.0 (2960)	45	45	NA	NA	0.004	0.004	0.315	0.354
	M104	3.2 (3199)	45	45	NA	NA	0.004	0.004	0.276	0.315
	OM603	3.5 (3449)	45	45①	160	1.063	0.004	0.004	0.313–0.314	0.352–0.353
	M119	4.2 (4196)	45	45	194	1.200	0.004	0.004	0.353	0.352
	M119	5.0 (4973)	45	45	194	1.200	0.004	0.004	0.315	0.354
	M120	6.0 (5987)	45	45	NA	NA	0.004	0.004	0.276	0.315

NA—Not available
① Plus 15 minutes

PISTON AND RING SPECIFICATIONS

All measurements are given in inches.

Year	Engine ID/VIN	Engine Displacement Liters (cc)	Piston Clearance	Ring Gap			Ring Side Clearance		
				Top Compression	Bottom Compression	Oil Control	Top Compression	Bottom Compression	Oil Control
1990	M103	2.6 (2599)	0.001–0.002	0.008–0.016	0.008–0.016	0.010–0.016	0.004–0.005	0.003–0.004	0.001–0.002
	M104	3.0 (2962)	0.001–0.002	0.008–0.016	0.008–0.016	0.010–0.016	0.004–0.005	0.003–0.004	0.001–0.002
	M116	4.2 (4196)	0.001	0.008–0.016	0.008–0.016	0.010–0.016	0.004–0.005	0.003–0.004	0.001–0.002
	M117	5.6 (5547)	0.001	0.010–0.017	0.010–0.017	0.010–0.016	0.004–0.005	0.001–0.002	0.001–0.002
	M119	5.0 (4973)	0.001	0.010–0.017	0.010–0.017	0.010–0.016	0.004–0.005	0.001–0.002	0.001–0.002
1991	M102	2.3 (2298)	0.001	0.012–0.022	0.012–0.022	0.010–0.020	0.003–0.006	0.001–0.004	0.002–0.004
	OM602	2.5 (2497)	0.001	0.010–0.040	0.008–0.040	0.008–0.040	0.003–0.008	0.002–0.006	0.001–0.004
	M103	2.6 (2597)	0.001–0.002	0.008–0.016	0.008–0.016	0.010–0.016	0.003–0.006	0.001–0.004	0.002–0.004
	M103	3.0 (2960)	0.001–0.002	0.008–0.016	0.008–0.016	0.010–0.016	0.003–0.006	0.001–0.004	0.002–0.004
	M104	3.0 (2962)	0.001–0.002	0.008–0.016	0.008–0.016	0.010–0.016	0.003–0.006	0.001–0.004	0.002–0.004
	OM602	3.5 (3449)	0.001	0.010–0.040	0.008–0.040	0.008–0.040	0.003–0.008	0.002–0.006	0.001–0.004
	M116	4.2 (4196)	0.003	0.012–0.040	0.014–0.031	0.010–0.031	0.002–0.006	0.002–0.003	0.001–0.003
	M119	5.0 (4972)	0.003	0.014–0.040	0.014–0.031	0.010–0.031	0.002–0.006	0.002–0.003	0.001–0.003
	M117	5.6 (5547)	0.003	0.014–0.040	0.014–0.031	0.010–0.031	0.002–0.006	0.002–0.003	0.001–0.003
1992–94	M102	2.3 (2298)	0.001	0.012–0.022	0.012–0.022	0.010–0.020	0.003–0.006	0.001–0.004	0.002–0.004
	OM602	2.5 (2498)	0.001	0.010–0.040	0.008–0.040	0.008–0.040	0.003–0.008	0.002–0.006	0.001–0.004
	M103	2.6 (2597)	0.001–0.002	0.008–0.016	0.008–0.016	0.010–0.016	0.003–0.006	0.001–0.004	0.002–0.004
	M103	3.0 (2960)	0.001–0.002	0.008–0.016	0.008–0.016	0.010–0.016	0.003–0.006	0.001–0.004	0.002–0.004
	M104	3.0 (2960)	0.001–0.002	0.008–0.016	0.008–0.016	0.010–0.016	0.003–0.006	0.001–0.004	0.002–0.004
	M104	3.2 (3199)	0.001–0.002	0.008–0.016	0.008–0.016	0.010–0.016	0.003–0.006	0.001–0.004	0.002–0.004
	OM603	3.5 (3449)	0.005	0.010–0.040	0.008–0.040	0.008–0.040	0.003–0.008	0.002–0.006	0.001–0.004
	M119	4.2 (4196)	0.005–0.020	0.012–0.040	0.014–0.031	0.010–0.031	0.002–0.006	0.002–0.003	0.001–0.003
	M119	5.0 (4973)	0.005–0.020	0.012–0.040	0.014–0.031	0.010–0.031	0.002–0.006	0.002–0.003	0.001–0.003
	M120	6.0 (5987)	0.005–0.020	0.012–0.040	0.014–0.031	0.010–0.031	0.002–0.006	0.002–0.003	0.001–0.003

TORQUE SPECIFICATIONS
All readings in ft. lbs.

Year	Engine ID/VIN	Engine Displacement Liters (cc)	Cylinder Head Bolts	Main Bearing Bolts	Rod Bearing Bolts [21]	Crankshaft Damper Bolts	Flywheel Bolts	Manifold Intake	Manifold Exhaust	Spark Plugs	Lug Nut
1990	M103	2.6 (2599)	70 [8]	65	22	217	22	NA	NA	15	75
	M104	3.0 (2962)	[7]	65	33	218	[4]	NA	18	15	75
	M116	4.2 (4196)	44 [6]	[2]	33	289	[4]	NA	NA	15	75
	M117	5.6 (5547)	44 [6]	[1]	33	187	[4]	NA	20	15	75
	M119	5.0 (4973)	75 [9]	[1]	33	187	[4]	NA	20	15	75
1991	M102	2.3 (2298)	[12]	[11]	[4]	150	[10]	NA	NA	15	75
	OM602	2.5 (2497)	[14]	[11]	[4]	236	[10]	18	18	—	75
	M103	2.6 (2597)	[13]	[11]	[4]	218	[3]	NA	NA	15	75
	M103	3.0 (2960)	[13]	[11]	[4]	218	[3]	NA	NA	15	75
	M104	3.0 (2960)	[13]	[11]	[4]	218	[3]	NA	NA	15	75
	OM602	3.5 (3449)	[14]	[11]	[4]	236	[3]	18	18	—	75
	M116	4.2 (4196)	[15]	[2]	[16]	218	[3]	NA	NA	15	75
	M119	5.0 (4972)	[12]	[2]	[16]	295	[3]	NA	NA	15	75
	M117	5.6 (5547)	[15]	[2]	[16]	218	[3]	NA	NA	15	75
1992-94	M102	2.3 (2298)	[12]	[11]	[4]	150	[10]	NA	NA	15	75
	OM602	2.5 (2448)	[22]	[11]	22	235	[10]	18	18	—	75
	M103	2.6 (2597)	[13]	[11]	[4]	218	[3]	NA	NA	15	75
	M103	3.0 (2960)	[13]	[11]	[4]	218	[3]	NA	NA	15	75
	M104	3.0 (2960)	[12]	[11]	[5]	295	[10]	18	18	15	75
	M104	3.2 (3199)	[12]	[11]	[5]	295	[10]	18	18	15	75
	OM603	3.5 (3449)	[22]	[11]	22	235	[10]	18	18	—	75
	M119	4.2 (4196)	[12]	[20]	[19]	295	[10]	18	NA	15	75
	M119	5.0 (4973)	[12]	[20]	[19]	295	[10]	18	NA	15	75
	M120	6.0 (5987)	[12]	[18]	[17]	295	[10]	18	NA	15	75

NA—Not available

① M 10 bolts—37 ft. lbs.
M 12 bolts—72 ft. lbs.
② M 10 bolts—43 ft. lbs.
M 12 bolts—58 ft. lbs.
③ 1st step—22-25 ft. lbs.
2nd step—90-100 degrees torquing angle
④ 1st step—22-25 ft. lbs.
2nd step—90-100 degrees torquing angle
⑤ 1st step—22 ft. lbs.
2nd step—90-100 degrees torquing angle
⑥ 1st step—22 ft. lbs.
2nd step—44 ft. lbs., setting time 10 minutes
3rd step—Loosen bolts and retighten to 44 ft. lbs.
⑦ 1st step—29 ft. lbs.
2nd step—51 ft. lbs., setting time 10 minutes
3rd step—90 degrees torquing angle
4th step—90 degrees torquing angle
⑧ 1st step—70 ft. lbs.
2nd step—90 degrees torquing angle
3rd step—90 degrees torquing angle

⑨ 1st step—75 ft. lbs.
2nd step—90 degrees torquing angle
3rd step—90 degrees torquing angle
⑩ Automatic transmission:
1st step—22 ft. lbs.
2nd step—90 degrees torquing angle
Manual transmission:
1st step—37 ft. lbs.
2nd step—90 degrees torquing angle
⑪ 1st step—40 ft. lbs.
2nd step—90 degrees torquing angle
⑫ 1st step—40 ft. lbs.
2nd step—90 degrees torquing angle
3rd step—90 degrees torquing angle
⑬ 1st step—52 ft. lbs.
2nd step—90 degrees torquing angle
3rd step—90 degrees torquing angle
⑭ Allen head bolts
1st step—11 ft. lbs.
2nd step—26 ft. lbs.
3rd step—90 degrees torquing angle and wait 10 minutes
4th step—90 degrees torquing angle

⑮ 1st step—22 ft. lbs.
2nd step—44 ft. lbs.
3rd step—warm engine to 176°F (80°C) and retorque to 44 ft. lbs.
⑯ 1st step—30-40 ft. lbs.
2nd step—90-100 degrees torquing angle
⑰ 1st step—90 ft. lbs.
2nd step—90-100 degrees torquing angle
⑱ M 8 bolts—22 ft. lbs.
M 10 bolts—37 ft. lbs.
⑲ 1st step—33 ft. lbs.
2nd step—90-100 degrees torquing angle
⑳ M 10 bolts—43 ft. lbs.
M 12 bolts—58 ft. lbs.
Stud bolts—22 ft. lbs. and are not reusable
㉑ Replace stretch bolts
㉒ 1st step—11 ft. lbs.
2nd step—26 ft. lbs.
3rd step—90 degrees torquing angle
4th step—Wait 10 minutes
5th step—90 degrees torquing angle

BRAKE SPECIFICATIONS

All measurements in inches unless noted.

Year	Model	Master Cylinder Bore	Brake Disc Original Thickness	Brake Disc Minimum Thickness	Maximum Runout	Minimum Lining Thickness Front	Rear
1990	190D	[4]	0.866 [11]	0.35 [6]	0.005 [7]	0.08	0.08
	300E	[2]	0.866 [11]	[1] [5]	0.005 [7]	0.08	0.08
	300CE	[2]	0.866 [11]	[1] [5]	0.005 [7]	0.08	0.08
	300SE	[2]	1.496 [14]	[3] [5]	0.005	0.08	0.08
	300SL	[2]	1.102 [11]	[8]	0.005	0.08	0.08
	300TE	[2]	0.866 [11]	[1] [5]	0.005 [7]	0.08	0.08
	300SEL	[2]	1.496 [14]	[3] [5]	0.005	0.08	0.08
	420SEL	[2]	1.496 [14]	[3] [5]	0.005	0.08	0.08
	500SL	[2]	1.102 [11]	[8]	0.005	0.08	0.08
	560SEC	[2]	1.496 [14]	[3] [5]	0.005	0.08	0.08
	560SEL	[2]	1.496 [14]	[3] [5]	0.005	0.08	0.08
1991	190E	[4]	0.866 [11]	0.35 [6]	0.005 [7]	0.08	0.08
	190E	[4]	0.866 [11]	0.35 [6]	0.005 [7]	0.08	0.08
	300D	[2]	0.866 [11]	[1] [5]	0.005	0.08	0.08
	300E	[2]	0.866 [11]	[1] [5]	0.005	0.08	0.08
	300CE	[2]	0.866 [11]	[1] [5]	0.005	0.08	0.08
	300TE	[2]	0.866 [11]	[1] [5]	0.005	0.08	0.08
	300SE	[2]	1.496 [14]	[3] [5]	0.005	0.08	0.08
	300SEL	[2]	1.496 [14]	[3] [5]	0.005	0.08	0.08
	300SL	[2]	1.102 [11]	[8]	0.005	0.08	0.08
	300SD	[2]	1.496 [14]	[3] [5]	0.005	0.08	0.08
	300SDL	[2]	1.496 [14]	[3] [5]	0.005	0.08	0.08
	420SEL	[2]	1.496 [14]	[3] [5]	0.005	0.08	0.08
	500E	[2]	0.866 [12]	[3] [5]	0.005	0.08	0.08
	500SL	[2]	1.102 [11]	[8]	0.005	0.08	0.08
	560SEC	[2]	1.496 [14]	[3] [5]	0.005	0.08	0.08
	560SEL	[2]	1.496 [14]	[3] [5]	0.005	0.08	0.08
1992-94	190E 2.3	[4]	0.866 [10]	0.35 [6]	0.005 [7]	0.08	0.08
	190E 2.6	[4]	0.866 [11]	0.35 [6]	0.005 [7]	0.08	0.08
	300D	[2]	0.866 [11]	[1] [5]	0.005	0.08	0.08
	300E 2.6	[2]	0.866 [11]	[1] [5]	0.005	0.08	0.08
	300E	[2]	0.866 [11]	[1] [5]	0.005	0.08	0.08
	300CE	[2]	0.866 [11]	[1] [5]	0.005	0.08	0.08
	300TE	[2]	0.866 [11]	[1] [5]	0.005	0.08	0.08
	300TE 4-Matic	[2]	0.866 [11]	[1] [5]	0.005	0.08	0.08
	300SD	11/16	1.102 [9]	0.10	0.003	0.08	0.08
	300SE	11/16	1.102 [9]	0.10	0.003	0.08	0.08
	300SL	[13]	1.102 [11]	0.10	0.005	0.08	0.08
	400SEL	11/16	1.181 [10]	0.10	0.003	0.08	0.08
	500SL	[13]	1.102 [11]	0.10	0.003	0.08	0.08
	500SEL	11/16	1.181 [10]	0.10	0.003	0.08	0.08
	600SEL	11/16	1.181 [10]	0.10	0.003	0.08	0.08

[1] Caliper with 57mm piston diameter—0.44 in.
Caliper with 60mm piston diameter—0.42 in.
[2] Pushrod circuit—15/16 in.
Floating circuit—3/4 in.
[3] Caliper with 57mm piston diameter—0.81 in.
Caliper with 60mm piston diameter—0.79 in.
[4] Pushrod circuit—7/8 in.
Floating circuit—11/16 in.
[5] Rear disc—0.33 in.
[6] Rear disc—0.30 in.
[7] Rear disc—0.006 in.
[8] Front disc—1.10 in.
Rear disc—0.35 in.
[9] Rear—0.472
[10] Rear—0.866
[11] Rear—0.354
[12] Rear—0.866
[13] Pushrod circuit—1 in.
Floating circuit—3/4 in.
[14] Rear—0.394

WHEEL ALIGNMENT

Year	Model	Caster Range (deg.)	Caster Preferred Setting (deg.)	Camber Range (deg.)	Camber Preferred Setting (deg.)	Toe-in (in.)	Steering Axis Inclination (deg.)
1990	190E	10P–11P	$10\frac{1}{2}$P	$\frac{1}{2}$N–0	$\frac{3}{16}$N	$\frac{3}{32}$	NA
	300E	$9\frac{11}{16}$P–$10\frac{11}{16}$P	$10\frac{3}{16}$P	$\frac{5}{16}$N–$\frac{3}{16}$P	0	$\frac{3}{16}$	NA
	300CE	$9\frac{11}{16}$P–$10\frac{11}{16}$P	$10\frac{3}{16}$P	$\frac{5}{16}$N–$\frac{3}{16}$P	0	$\frac{3}{16}$	NA
	300SE	10P–11P	$10\frac{1}{2}$P	$\frac{1}{2}$N–0	$\frac{3}{16}$N	$\frac{3}{32}$	NA
	300SL	10P–11P	$10\frac{1}{2}$P	$\frac{1}{2}$N–0	$\frac{3}{16}$N	$\frac{3}{32}$	NA
	300SEL	10P–11P	$10\frac{1}{2}$P	$\frac{1}{2}$N–0	$\frac{3}{16}$N	$\frac{3}{32}$	NA
	300TE	$9\frac{11}{16}$P–$10\frac{11}{16}$P	$10\frac{3}{16}$P	$\frac{5}{16}$N–$\frac{3}{16}$P	0	$\frac{3}{16}$	NA
	420SEL	10P–11P	$10\frac{1}{2}$P	$\frac{1}{2}$N–0	$\frac{3}{16}$N	$\frac{3}{32}$	NA
	500SL	10P–11P	$10\frac{1}{2}$P	$\frac{1}{2}$N–0	$\frac{3}{16}$N	$\frac{3}{32}$	NA
	560SEC	10P–11P	$10\frac{1}{2}$P	$\frac{1}{2}$N–0	$\frac{3}{16}$N	$\frac{3}{32}$	NA
	560SEL	10P–11P	$10\frac{1}{2}$P	$\frac{1}{2}$N–0	$\frac{3}{16}$N	$\frac{3}{32}$	NA
1991	190E-2.3	$9\frac{11}{16}$P–$10\frac{11}{16}$P	$10\frac{3}{16}$P	$\frac{1}{2}$N–0	$\frac{5}{16}$N	$\frac{3}{32}$	NA
	190E-2.6	10P–11P	$10\frac{1}{2}$P	$\frac{11}{16}$N–$\frac{3}{16}$P	$\frac{5}{16}$N	$\frac{3}{32}$	NA
	300D	$9\frac{3}{16}$P–$10\frac{3}{16}$P	$9\frac{11}{16}$P	$\frac{5}{16}$N–$\frac{3}{16}$P	0	$\frac{3}{32}$	NA
	300E	$9\frac{3}{16}$P–$10\frac{3}{16}$P	$9\frac{11}{16}$P	$\frac{5}{16}$N–$\frac{3}{16}$P	0	$\frac{3}{32}$	NA
	300CE	$9\frac{3}{16}$P–$10\frac{3}{16}$P	$9\frac{11}{16}$P	$\frac{5}{16}$N–$\frac{3}{16}$P	0	$\frac{3}{32}$	NA
	300TE	$9\frac{3}{16}$P–$10\frac{3}{16}$P	$9\frac{11}{16}$P	$\frac{5}{16}$N–$\frac{3}{16}$P	0	$\frac{3}{32}$	NA
	300SE	$9\frac{1}{4}$P–$10\frac{1}{4}$P	$9\frac{3}{4}$P	$\frac{3}{16}$N–$\frac{3}{16}$P	0	$\frac{7}{64}$	NA
	300SEL	$9\frac{1}{4}$P–$10\frac{1}{4}$P	$9\frac{3}{4}$P	$\frac{3}{16}$N–$\frac{3}{16}$P	0	$\frac{7}{64}$	NA
	300SL	10P–11P	$10\frac{1}{2}$P	$\frac{3}{4}$N–$\frac{1}{4}$P	$\frac{1}{2}$N	$\frac{1}{4}$	NA
	350SD	$9\frac{1}{4}$P–$10\frac{1}{4}$P	$9\frac{3}{4}$P	$\frac{3}{16}$N–$\frac{3}{16}$P	0	$\frac{7}{64}$	NA
	350SDL	$9\frac{1}{4}$P–$10\frac{1}{4}$P	$9\frac{3}{4}$P	$\frac{3}{16}$N–$\frac{3}{16}$P	0	$\frac{7}{64}$	NA
	420SEL	$9\frac{1}{4}$P–$10\frac{1}{4}$P	$9\frac{3}{4}$P	$\frac{3}{16}$N–$\frac{3}{16}$P	0	$\frac{7}{64}$	NA
	500E	$9\frac{3}{16}$P–$10\frac{3}{16}$P	$9\frac{11}{16}$P	$\frac{5}{16}$N–$\frac{3}{16}$P	0	$\frac{3}{32}$	NA
	500SL	10P–11P	$10\frac{1}{2}$P	$\frac{3}{4}$N–$\frac{1}{4}$P	$\frac{1}{2}$N	$\frac{1}{4}$	NA
	560SEC	$9\frac{1}{4}$P–$10\frac{1}{4}$P	$9\frac{3}{4}$P	$\frac{3}{16}$N–$\frac{3}{16}$P	0	$\frac{7}{64}$	NA
	560SEL	$9\frac{1}{4}$P–$10\frac{1}{4}$P	$9\frac{3}{4}$P	$\frac{3}{16}$N–$\frac{3}{16}$P	0	$\frac{7}{64}$	NA
1992–94	190 2.3	$9\frac{11}{16}$P–$10\frac{11}{16}$P	$10\frac{3}{16}$P	0–$\frac{1}{2}$P	$\frac{5}{16}$P	$\frac{3}{32}$	NA
	190 2.6	$9\frac{11}{16}$P–$10\frac{11}{16}$P	$10\frac{3}{16}$P	0–$\frac{1}{2}$P	$\frac{5}{16}$P	$\frac{3}{32}$	NA
	300D	$9\frac{3}{16}$P–$10\frac{3}{16}$P	$9\frac{11}{16}$P	$\frac{5}{16}$N–$\frac{3}{16}$P	0	$\frac{3}{32}$	NA
	300E 2.6	$9\frac{3}{16}$P–$10\frac{3}{16}$P	$9\frac{11}{16}$P	$\frac{5}{16}$N–$\frac{3}{16}$P	0	$\frac{3}{32}$	NA
	300E	$9\frac{3}{16}$P–$10\frac{3}{16}$P	$9\frac{11}{16}$P	$\frac{5}{16}$N–$\frac{3}{16}$P	0	$\frac{3}{32}$	NA
	300CE	$9\frac{3}{16}$P–$10\frac{3}{16}$P	$9\frac{11}{16}$P	$\frac{5}{16}$N–$\frac{3}{16}$P	0	$\frac{3}{32}$	NA
	300TE	$9\frac{3}{16}$P–$10\frac{3}{16}$P	$9\frac{11}{16}$P	$\frac{5}{16}$N–$\frac{3}{16}$P	0	$\frac{3}{32}$	NA
	300TE 4-Matic	$9\frac{5}{8}$P–$10\frac{5}{8}$P	$10\frac{1}{8}$P	$\frac{9}{16}$N–$\frac{1}{8}$N	$\frac{1}{4}$N	$\frac{11}{64}$	NA
	300SD	$9\frac{3}{8}$P–$10\frac{3}{8}$P	$9\frac{7}{8}$P	$\frac{3}{4}$N–$\frac{1}{16}$P	$\frac{3}{16}$N	$\frac{5}{16}$	NA
	300SE	$9\frac{3}{8}$P–$10\frac{3}{8}$P	$9\frac{7}{8}$P	$\frac{3}{4}$N–$\frac{1}{16}$P	$\frac{3}{16}$N	$\frac{5}{16}$	NA
	300SL	10P–11P	$10\frac{1}{2}$P	$1\frac{3}{16}$N–$\frac{11}{16}$N	$\frac{7}{8}$N	$\frac{11}{64}$	NA
	400E	$9\frac{3}{4}$P–$10\frac{3}{4}$P	$10\frac{1}{4}$P	1N–$\frac{1}{2}$N	$\frac{11}{16}$N	$\frac{11}{64}$	NA
	400SE	$9\frac{3}{8}$P–$10\frac{3}{8}$P	$9\frac{7}{8}$P	$\frac{3}{4}$N–$\frac{1}{16}$N	$\frac{3}{16}$N	$\frac{5}{16}$	NA
	500E	$10\frac{1}{8}$P–$11\frac{1}{8}$P	$10\frac{5}{8}$P	$1\frac{3}{8}$N–$\frac{7}{8}$N	1N	$\frac{11}{64}$	NA
	500SL	10P–11P	$10\frac{1}{2}$P	$1\frac{3}{16}$N–$\frac{11}{16}$N	$\frac{7}{8}$N	$\frac{11}{64}$	NA
	500SEL	$9\frac{3}{8}$P–$10\frac{3}{8}$P	$9\frac{7}{8}$P	$\frac{3}{4}$N–$\frac{1}{16}$P	$\frac{3}{16}$N	$\frac{5}{16}$	NA
	600SEL	$9\frac{3}{8}$P–$10\frac{3}{8}$P	$9\frac{7}{8}$P	$\frac{3}{4}$N–$\frac{1}{16}$P	$\frac{3}{16}$N	$\frac{5}{16}$	NA

NA—Not available
N—Negative
P—Positive

GASOLINE ENGINE MECHANICAL

NOTE: Disconnecting the negative battery cable on some vehicles may interfere with the functions of the on board computer systems and may require the computer to undergo a relearning process, once the negative battery cable is reconnected.

Engine Assembly

— WARNING —

Care should be taken when working on Mercedes-Benz engines, since there are many aluminum parts which can be damaged, if carelessly handled.

REMOVAL AND INSTALLATION

NOTE: In all cases, Mercedes-Benz engines and transmissions are removed as a unit.

— CAUTION —

Air conditioner lines should not be indiscriminately disconnected without taking proper precautions. It is best to swing the compressor aside while still connected to its hoses. Never do any welding around the compressor- heat may cause an explosion. Also, the refrigerant, while inert at normal room temperature, breaks down under high temperature into hydrogen fluoride and phosgene (among other products), which are highly poisonous.

Except V8 and V12 Engines

1. Remove the hood, drain the cooling system and disconnect the battery. While not strictly necessary, it is better to remove the battery completely to prevent breakage by the engine as it is lifted out.
2. Remove the fan shroud and radiator.
3. Disconnect all heater hoses and oil cooler lines. Plug all openings to keep out dirt.
4. Remove the air cleaner and all fuel, vacuum and oil hoses (e.g., power steering and power brakes). Plug all openings to keep out dirt.
5. Remove the viscous coupling and fan.
6. Disconnect the accelerator linkage.

7. Disconnect all ground straps and electrical connections; it is a good idea to tag each wire for easy reassembly.
8. Detach the gearshift linkage and the exhaust pipes from the manifolds.
9. Loosen the steering relay arm and move it aside, along with the center steering rod and hydraulic steering damper.
10. The hydraulic engine shock absorber should be removed.
11. Remove the hydraulic line from the clutch housing and the oil line connectors from the automatic transmission.
12. Unbolt the clutch slave cylinder from the bellhousing after removing the return spring.
13. Remove the exhaust pipe bracket from the transmission. Support bellhousing or place a cable sling under the oil pan, to support the engine.
14. Mark the position of the rear engine support and unbolt the 2 outer bolts, remove the top bolt at the transmission and pull the support out.
15. Disconnect the speedometer cable and the front driveshaft U-joint. Push the driveshaft back and wire it aside.
16. Unbolt the engine mounts on both sides and, on 4 cylinder engines, the front limit stop.
17. Unbolt the power steering fluid reservoir and swing it aside; then, using a chain hoist and cable, lift the engine and transmission upward and outward. An angle of about 45 degrees will allow the vehicle to be pushed backward while the engine is coming up.

To install:
18. Using a chain hoist and cable, position the engine and transmission into the vehicle. An angle of about 45 degrees will allow the vehicle to be pushed backward while the engine is going in. Install the power steering reservoir.
19. Install the engine mounts on both sides and, on 4 cylinder engines, the front limit stop. Torque the bolts to 25 ft. lbs. (34 Nm).
20. Connect the speedometer cable and the front driveshaft U-joint.
21. Install the top bolt at the transmission and support.
22. Install the exhaust pipe bracket to the transmission.
23. Install the clutch slave cylinder to the bellhousing and connect the turn spring.
24. Install the hydraulic line to the clutch housing and the oil line con-

nectors to the automatic transmission.
25. Install the hydraulic engine shock absorber and torque to 30 ft. lbs. (41 Nm).
26. Tighten the steering relay arm, along with the center steering rod and hydraulic steering damper.
27. Connect the gearshift linkage and the exhaust pipes to the manifolds. Torque the manifold bolts to 20 ft. lbs. (25 Nm).
28. Connect all ground straps and electrical connections.
29. Connect the accelerator linkage.
30. Install the viscous coupling and fan.
31. Install the all fuel, vacuum and oil hoses (e.g., power steering and power brakes). Plug all openings to keep out dirt. Install the air cleaner.
32. Connect all heater hoses and oil cooler lines.
33. Install the fan shroud and radiator.
34. Install the hood, refill the cooling system and connect the battery.
35. Bleed the hydraulic clutch, power steering, power brakes and fuel system.

V8 Engines

EXCEPT 5.0L DOHC ENGINE

— CAUTION —

Removal of a V8 engine equipped with air conditioning, may require discharging the air conditioning system. Use caution; always wear safety glasses, Freon is lethal.

1. Remove the hood.
2. Drain the cooling system.
3. Remove the radiator and fan shroud.
4. Remove the cable plug from the temperature switch.
5. Remove the battery, battery frame and air filter.
6. Drain the power steering reservoir and windshield washer reservoir.
7. Disconnect and plug the high pressure and return lines on the power steering pump.
8. Detach the fuel lines from the fuel filter, pressure regulator, and pressure sensor.
9. If equipped, loosen the line to the supply and anti-freeze tanks. If equipped, disconnect the lines to the hydro-pneumatic suspension.
10. Disconnect the cables from the ignition coil and transistor ignition switchbox.
11. Disconnect the brake vacuum lines.

12. Detach the cable connections for the following:
   a. Venturi control unit
   b. Temperature sensor
   c. Distributor
   d. Temperature switch
   e. Cold start valve

13. Remove the regulating shaft by pushing it in the direction of the firewall.

14. Disconnect the thrust and pullrods.

15. Disconnect the heater lines.

16. Detach the lines to the oil pressure and temperature gauges.

17. Remove the ground strap from the vehicle.

18. Detach the cables from the alternator, terminal bridge, and battery. Remove the battery.

19. Position a lifting sling on the engine and take up the slack in the chain.

20. Remove the left side engine mount and loosen the hex nut on the right side mount.

21. Remove the exhaust system. Remove the connecting rod chain on the rear level control valve and loosen the torsion bar slightly. Raise the vehicle slightly at the rear and remove the exhaust system in the rearward direction.

22. Disconnect the hand brake cable.

23. Remove the shield plate from the transmission tunnel.

24. Place a block of wood between the transmission and cross-yoke so the engine will not sag when the rear mount is removed.

25. Loosen the driveshaft intermediate bearing and the driveshaft slide.

26. Support the transmission.

27. Mark the installation of the crossmember and remove the crossmember. Remove the rear engine carrier with the engine mount.

28. Unbolt the front U-joint flange on the transmission and push it back. Do not loosen the clamp nut on the intermediate bearing. Support the driveshaft.

29. Disconnect the speedometer shaft, shift rod, control pressure rod, regulating linkage, for automatic transmissions, kickdown switch cable, starter lockout switch cable, and the cable for the backup light switch.

30. Remove the front engine mounting bolt and remove the engine at approximately a 45 degree angle.

31. Installation is the reverse of removal. Lower the engine until it is behind the front axle carrier. Support the transmission and lower the engine into its compartment. While lowering the engine, install the right shock mount.

32. Fill the engine with all required fluids and start the engine. Check for leaks.

To install:

33. Lower the engine until it is behind the front axle carrier. Support the transmission. While lowering the engine, install the right shock mount.

34. Install the front engine mounting bolt and torque to 40 ft. lbs. (54 Nm).

35. Connect the speedometer shaft, shift rod, control pressure rod, regulating linkage, for automatic transmissions, kickdown switch cable, starter lockout switch cable, and the cable for the backup light switch.

36. Install the front U-joint flange on the transmission.

37. Raise the transmission into place. Install the rear engine carrier, engine mount and crossmember. Torque the bolts to 35 ft. lbs. (47 Nm).

38. Tighten the driveshaft intermediate bearing and the driveshaft slide.

39. Install the shield plate to the transmission tunnel.

40. Connect the hand brake cable.

41. Install the exhaust system and torque the nuts to 25 ft. lbs. (34 Nm). Install the connecting rod chain on the rear level control valve and tighten the torsion bar slightly.

42. Install the left side engine mount and tighten the hex nut on the right side mount to 15 ft. lbs. (20 Nm).

43. Connect the cables to the alternator and terminal bridge. Install the battery.

44. Install the ground strap to the vehicle. Do not connect the battery terminals at this time.

45. Connect the lines to the oil pressure and temperature gauges.

46. Connect the heater lines.

47. Connect the thrust and pullrods.

48. Install the regulating shaft.

49. Connect the cable connections for the following:
   a. Venturi control unit
   b. Temperature sensor
   c. Distributor
   d. Temperature switch
   e. Cold start valve

50. Connect the brake vacuum lines.

51. Connect the cables to the ignition coil and transistor ignition switchbox.

52. Tighten the line to the supply and anti-freeze tanks. If equipped, connect the lines to the hydro-pneumatic suspension.

53. Connect the fuel lines to the fuel filter, pressure regulator, and pressure sensor.

54. Connect and plug the high pressure and return lines on the power steering pump.

55. Refill the power steering reservoir and windshield washer reservoir.

56. Install the battery, battery frame and air filter.

57. Install the cable plug to the temperature switch.

58. Install the radiator and fan shroud.

59. Refill the cooling system and check all engine fluids.

60. Install the hood with the help of an assistant, connect the battery cable, start the engine and check for leaks.

5.0L DOHC ENGINE

1. Disconnect the negative battery cable.

2. Mark the hood fasteners. With the help of an assistant, remove the engine hood.

3. Remove the air filter, engine compartment bottom panel and air conditioning guard plate to the condenser.

4. Drain the engine coolant and remove the radiator.

5. Disconnect the heater hoses at the firewall.

6. Remove the viscous fan coupling and fan.

7. Remove the air conditioning belt, if equipped.

8. Label and disconnect all engine wiring, vacuum lines, throttle linkage, power steering and oil cooler lines.

9. Remove the wheelhouse assembly.

10. Completely remove the exhaust system.

11. Remove the starter motor shield and air conditioning compressor.

12. Mark and disconnect the driveshaft from the transmission.

13. Label and disconnect all transmission wiring and control cables.

14. Support the transmission using a suitable jack. Disconnect the transmission mount and remove the crossmember.

15. Install engine lifting device.

16. Disconnect the engine mounts.

17. Remove the guard plate from the engine firewall.

18. Raise the engine very carefully and disconnect any connected components.

To install:

19. With the help of an assistant, lower the engine into the vehicle on a 45 degree angle.

20. Install the guard plate at the engine firewall.

21. Connect the engine mounts and torque to 25 ft. lbs. (34 Nm).

22. Support the transmission using a suitable jack. Connect the transmission mount and install the crossmember. Torque the bolts to 30 ft. lbs. (41 Nm).

23. Connect all transmission wiring and control cables.

24. Connect the driveshaft to the transmission. Use new nuts and torque to 15 ft. lbs. (20 Nm).

25. Install the starter motor shield and air conditioning compressor.

26. Install the exhaust system and torque the manifold nuts to 20 ft. lbs. (25 Nm).

27. Install the wheelhouse assembly.

28. Connect all engine wiring, vacuum lines, throttle linkage, power steering and oil cooler lines.

29. Install the air conditioning belt, if equipped.

30. Install the viscous fan coupling and fan.

31. Connect the heater hoses at the firewall.

32. Install the radiator and refill the engine coolant.

33. Install the air filter, engine compartment bottom panel and air conditioning guard plate to the condenser.

34. With the help of an assistant, install the engine hood.

35. Connect the negative battery cable, refill all fluids, start the engine and check for leaks.

12 Cylinder engine

1. Disconnect the negative battery cable, release fuel system pressure and drain the cooling system.

2. Mark the hood retaining bolts and remove with the help of an assistant.

3. Remove the air cleaner and air mass meter.

4. Remove the paneling at the bottom of the engine compartment.

5. Remove the radiator assembly and disconnect the left oil line for the automatic transmission.

6. Install a guard plate over the air conditioning condenser.

7. Disconnect the hood control cable and water hose at rear of cylinder head.

8. Remove the accessory drive belt, fan clutch and fan.

9. Label and disconnect all wiring harnesses, cables, vacuum lines, hoses and pipes from the engine and move out of the way.

10. Remove the air conditioning compressor with the hoses still attached. Wire the assembly out of the way.

11. Remove the oil cooler lines and engine mountings.

12. Completely remove the exhaust system and hang down out of the way.

13. Disconnect the driveshaft at the transmission. Replace the self-locking nuts.

14. Disconnect all cables, electrical wiring and shift rods from the transmission.

15. Disconnect the 2 front engine mounts.

16. Install a suitable engine lifting device onto the suspension eyes.

17. Remove the transmission mounts.

18. Remove the engine from the vehicle. Be careful that all components are disconnected before removing the engine from the vehicle.

To install:

19. Install the engine/transmission into the vehicle.

20. Install the engine/transmission mounts and torque the retainers. Torque the engine mount bolts to 18 ft. lbs. (25 Nm), engine carrier-to-body bolts to 30 ft. lbs. (40 Nm) and oil cooler lines to 22 ft. lbs. (30 Nm).

21. Remove the engine lifting device from the suspension eyes.

22. Connect all cables, electrical wiring and shift rods to the transmission.

23. Connect the driveshaft at the transmission. Replace the self-locking nuts.

24. Install the exhaust system.

25. Install the oil cooler lines and engine mountings. Torque the cooler lines to 22 ft. lbs. (30 Nm).

26. Install the air conditioning compressor.

27. Connect all wiring harnesses, cables, vacuum lines, hoses and pipes to the engine.

28. Install the accessory drive belt, fan clutch and fan.

29. Connect the hood control cable and water hose at rear of cylinder head.

30. Remove the guard plate over the air conditioning condenser.

31. Install the radiator assembly and connect the left oil line for the automatic transmission.

32. Install the paneling at the bottom of the engine compartment.

33. Install the air cleaner and air mass meter.

34. Install the hood with the help of an assistant.

35. Connect the negative battery cable and refill the cooling system.

36. Start the engine and check for leaks.

Engine Mounts

REMOVAL AND INSTALLATION

—— **CAUTION** ——
The engine has to be raised to take the tension off the engine mount. Make sure the engine is safely supported before attempting to remove the mount. Failure to secure the engine may result in personal injury.

1. Disconnect the negative battery cable.

2. Install the air scoops, fan cowl rings, engine compartment bottom panels or any vehicle undercovers that are in the way.

3. Place a suitable jack and a piece of wood under the engine. Do not jack under the oil pan.

4. Raise the engine far enough to take the tension off the engine mount. Use blocks of wood between the frame and engine in case the jack slips.

5. Install the engine mount retaining bolts and engine mount.

To install:

6. Install the mount and bolts. Be careful not dislodge the jack while servicing the mount.

7. Torque the bolts to 18 ft. lbs. (25 Nm).

8. Lower the jack and connect the battery cable.

Cylinder Head

REMOVAL AND INSTALLATION

4-Cylinder engine

NOTE: The cylinder head should be removed cold.

1. Disconnect the negative battery cable. Drain the radiator and remove all hoses and wires. Tag all wires to ensure easy reassembly.

2. The cylinder head cover on the 190E is removed with the spark plug cables and distributor cap still attached to it.

3. The rockers and their supports must be removed together.

4. Mark the chain, sprocket and cam for ease of assembly.

5. Using a suitable puller, remove the camshaft sprocket.

6. Remove the sprocket and chain and wire it aside.

7. Make sure the chain is securely wired so it will not slide into the engine.

8. Unbolt the manifolds and exhaust header pipe and push them aside.

9. Loosen the cylinder head hold-down bolts in the reverse order of that shown in torque diagrams for each model. It is good practice to loosen each bolt a little at a time, working around the head, until all are free. This prevents unequal stresses in the metal.

10. Reach into the engine compartment and gradually work the head loose from each end by rocking it. Never, under any circumstances, use a prybar between the head and block to pry, as the head will be scarred badly and may be ruined.

To install:

11. Clean the gasket mating surfaces and check for warpage.

12. With the help of an assistant, install the cylinder head onto the engine. Torque the head in 4 steps, in sequence. The 1st step to 18 ft. lbs. (25 Nm), 2nd step to 29 ft. lbs. (39 Nm) plus allow to set for 10 minutes, 3rd step to 90 degrees torquing angle and 4th step to 90 degrees torquing angle.

13. Install the manifolds and exhaust header pipe. Torque the pipe to 20 ft. lbs. (27 Nm).

14. Install the sprocket and timing chain. Align the timing marks.

15. Install the the rockers and their supports.

16. Install the cylinder head cover and spark plug wires.

17. Reconnect all wiring, hoses and cables to the cylinder head.

18. Connect the negative battery cable. Refill the radiator.

6-Cylinder engine

EXCEPT OHC ENGINE

NOTE: The cylinder head should be removed cold, with the camshaft, intake and exhaust manifolds attached.

1. Disconnect the negative battery cable. Remove the engine undercovers from below.

2. Drain the engine coolant. Drain the engine oil.

3. Remove the air filter.

4. Remove the distributor cap mounting bolts. Unbolt the cylinder head cover and remove it with the ignition wires and distributor cap still attached.

NOTE: Distributor cap removal will require a 5mm T-shaped Allen wrench about 80mm in length.

5. Loosen the 3 Allen screws and lift off the distributor rotor.

6. Using a 6mm Allen wrench, unscrew the distributor driver and remove it. Carefully, pry off the protective cover.

7. Remove the mounting screws for the cylinder head front cover and carefully knock the cover off with a rubber mallet.

8. Rotate the crankshaft so the No. 1 cylinder is set at TDC of the compression stroke.

9. Unscrew the timing chain tensioner plug and remove the compression spring.

10. Use a 17mm Allen-head socket and unscrew the tensioner threaded ring.

11. Insert an M8 screw into the tensioner bore, tilt it slightly and ease the tensioner from the bore. If the tensioner is difficult to remove, loosen the socket head screw above

the tensioner bore slightly; this should facilitate removal.

12. Matchmark the camshaft sprocket to the camshaft by putting a dab of paint next to the hole in the sprocket with the dowel pin.

13. Matchmark the camshaft sprocket to the timing chain.

14. Remove the mounting screws and pull off the camshaft sprocket. Secure the timing chain so it will not slip into the crankcase.

15. Remove the slide rail bolt with an impact puller.

16. Unscrew the oil dipstick guide tube bracket and pull out the dipstick and tube.

17. Unscrew the upper intake manifold mounting bolt. Loosen the lower bolt.

18. Loosen the hose clamp and remove the coolant hose at the water pump.

19. Unscrew the exhaust pipe at both flanges.

20. Disconnect the automatic transmission dipstick tube at the cylinder head and position it aside.

21. Tag and disconnect all wiring, electrical leads and vacuum hoses connected to or in the way of the cylinder head.

22. Disconnect the fuel feed and return lines, plug them and position them aside.

23. Disconnect the accelerator pedal Bowden cable.

24. Loosen the cylinder head bolts in the reverse order of the tightening sequence. Loosen each bolt, a little at a time, working around the head until all bolts are free; this will prevent unequal stress on the aluminum head.

25. Reach into the engine compartment and gradually work the head loose from the cylinder block. Never use a prybar to pry the head free.

To install:

26. Position a new cylinder head gasket on the cylinder block.

27. Connect the water pump coolant hose to the head and position the head on the block. There are 2 dowel pins for locating purposes.

28. Measure the length of the cylinder head bolts from the underside of the bolt head to the end of the bolt. If the length exceeds 108.4mm, the bolts must be replaced with new stretch bolts.

29. Install the cylinder head bolts and tighten them a little at a time, in sequence.

30. Install the camshaft sprocket and tighten the bolts to 8 ft. lbs. (11 Nm). Be sure the dowel pin is in the hole marked previously and that the

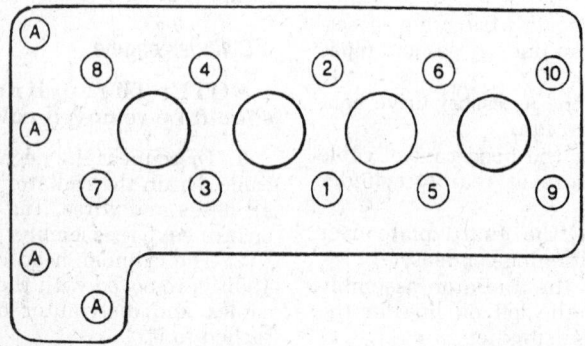

Cylinder head bolt torque sequence-4 cylinder engine, bolts (A) to 18 ft. lbs. (22 Nm)

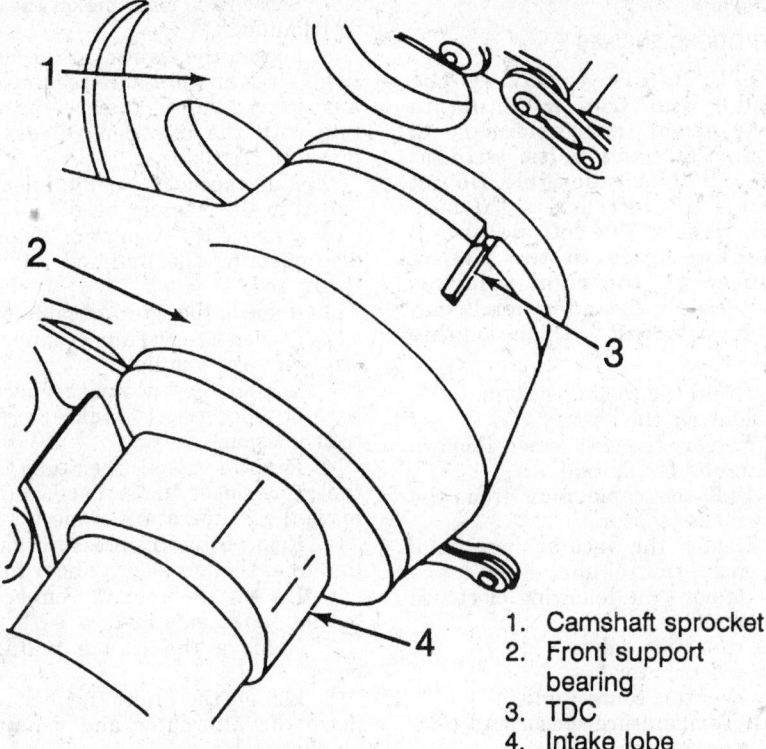

1. Camshaft sprocket
2. Front support bearing
3. TDC
4. Intake lobe

The timing marks on the camshaft bearing cap and the camshaft should be in alignment when the No. 1 cylinder is at TDC

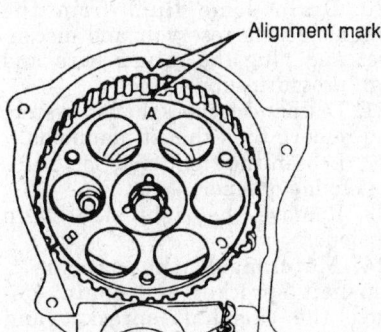

Matchmark the camshaft sprocket — 6 cylinder SOHC engine

1. Bleed shot
2. Piston
3. Metering disc
4. Check valve
5. Piston sleeve

Removing the chain tensioner — 6 cylinder SOHC engine

matchmarks on the timing chain and sprocket are aligned.

31. Slide the chain tensioner housing into the bore. Screw in the threaded ring and tighten it to 22 ft. lbs. (30 Nm). Install the thrust bolt with the detent spring. Position the compression spring and a new seal. Tighten the plug to 37 ft. lbs. (50 Nm).

32. Check the alignment of the timing marks on the camshaft bearing cap and the camshaft. When they are aligned, the engine should be at TDC of the compression stroke.

33. Install a new elastic gasket into the groove of the timing chain housing cover and mount the front cover. Tighten the 2 lower screws first. Torque all screws to 15.5 ft. lbs. (21 Nm).

34. Install the protective cover with a new seal. Install the distributor driver so the groove engages the pin on the camshaft. Tighten the screw to 15.5 ft. lbs. (21 Nm).

35. Installation of the remaining components is in the reverse order of removal.

NOTE: When refilling the coolant system on the engines, except 2.6L, always remove the hex head

plug on the left side of the cylinder head and fill the hole with coolant until it overflows. Install the plug and fill the coolant system. When filling the coolant system on the 2.6L engine, open the vent screw approximately 2 turns, start the engine and run at idle.

DOHC ENGINE

NOTE: The DOHC cylinder head should be removed cold, with the camshafts, intake and exhaust manifolds attached.

1. Disconnect the negative battery cable. Remove the engine undercovers from below.
2. Drain the engine coolant. Drain the engine oil.
3. Remove the air filter.
4. Remove the distributor cap mounting bolts. Unbolt the cylinder head cover and remove it with the ignition wires and distributor cap still attached.
5. Remove the camshaft adjuster armature for the variable valve timing.
6. Remove the upper guide track and secure the camshafts from movement.
7. Disconnect the cable from the reference value transmitter at the right wheel well (300SL).
8. Label and disconnect all electrical wiring, hoses and cables from the cylinder head assembly.
9. Disconnect the exhaust pipe from the manifold.
10. Label and remove the air injection line, dipstick guide, crankcase breather and fuel lines from the fuel distributor.
11. Remove the cylinder head bolts in the opposite sequence then torquing.
12. Tap the head with a plastic hammer. With an assistant or suitable hoist, remove the cylinder head making sure all components are disconnected.
To install:
13. Clean the gasket mating surfaces and check for warpage. Match old gasket to new for perfect match.
14. Turn the No. 1 piston to TDC.
15. Install the gasket. With a suitable hoist, lower the cylinder head onto the engine and oil and loosely install the head bolts.
16. Turn the camshafts such that the lower edges of the holes in the camshaft flange is level with the top of the cylinder head. Secure the 5mm pins.

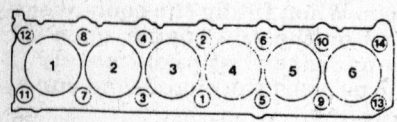

Cylinder head bolt torque sequence — 6 cylinder engines

17. Torque the cylinder head bolts in 3 steps, in sequence, to specifications.

18. Install the timing chain and remove the pins from the camshaft flange.

19. Install all wiring, hoses and cables.

20. Install the exhaust pipe and torque to 20 ft. lbs. (25 Nm).

21. Install the remaining components. Refill the engine fluids, connect the battery cable, start the engine and check for leaks.

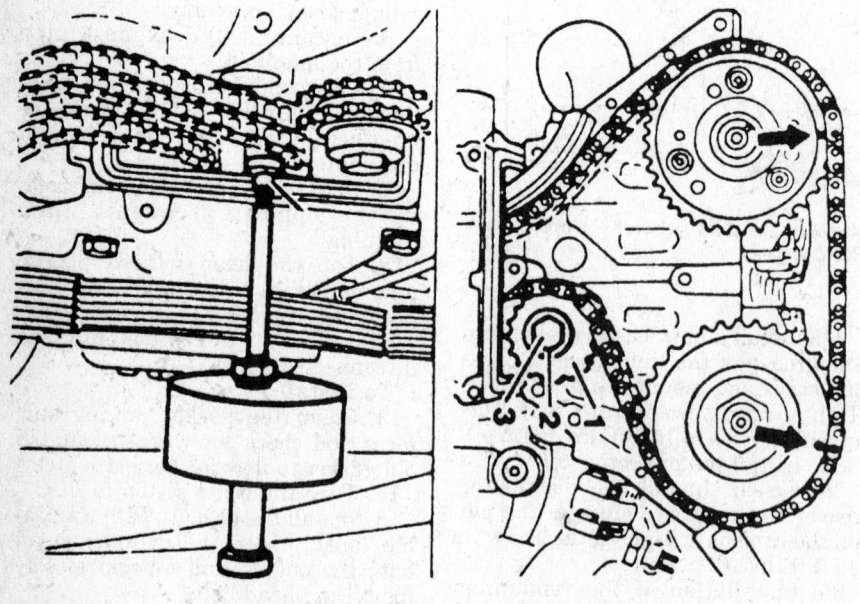

Camshaft sprocket alignment — 6 cylinder DOHC engine

V8 Engines

EXCEPT DOHC ENGINES

NOTE: Before removing the cylinder head from a V8, obtain the 4 special tools necessary to torque the head bolts; without them it will be impossible. Do not confuse the left and right side head gaskets. The left side has 2 attaching holes in the timing chain cover, the right side has only 1 hole. Cylinder heads can only be removed with the engine cold.

1. Drain the cooling system.
2. Remove the battery.
3. Remove the air cleaner. Remove the fan and fan shroud.
4. Pull the cable plug from the temperature sensor.
5. Detach the vacuum hose from the venturi control unit.
6. Remove the following electrical connections:
   a. Injection valves.
   b. Distributor
   c. Venturi control unit
   d. Temperature sensor and temperature switch
   e. Starting valve
   f. Temperature switch for the auxiliary fan.

7. Loosen the ring line on the fuel distributor.
8. Loosen the screws on the injection valves and pressure regulator or mixture regulator. Remove the ring line with the injection valves and pressure regulator.
9. Plug the holes for the injection valves in the cylinder head.
10. Remove the regulating shaft by disconnecting the pull rod and the thrust rod.
11. Remove the ignition cable plug.
12. Loosen the vacuum connection on the intake manifold.
13. Loosen the vacuum connection for the central lock at the transmission.
14. Remove the oil filler tube from the right side cylinder head and remove the temperature connector.
15. Remove the oil pressure gauge line from the left side cylinder head.
16. Loosen the coolant connection on the intake manifold.
17. Remove the intake manifold bolts.
18. Loosen the alternator belt. Remove the alternator and mounting bracket.
19. Remove the electrical connections from the distributor and electronic ignition switch gear.
20. Drain some fluid from the power steering reservoir and disconnect and plug the return hose and high pressure supply line.
21. Disconnect the exhaust system and remove the exhaust manifolds.
22. Loosen the right side holder for the engine damper.
23. Remove the right side chain tensioner.
24. Matchmark the camshaft, camshaft sprocket and chain. Remove the camshaft sprocket and chain after removing the cylinder head cover. Be sure to hang the chain and sprocket to prevent it from falling into the timing chain case.
25. Remove the upper slide rail. Remove the distributor and remove the inner slide rail on the left cylinder head. Remove the rail after the camshaft sprocket.
26. Unscrew the cylinder head bolts; this should be done with a cold engine. Unscrew the bolts in the reverse order of the torque sequences. Unscrew all the bolts, a little at a time, in the same manner, until all the bolts have been removed.
27. Remove the cylinder head; do not pry on the cylinder head.
28. Remove the cylinder head gasket.
29. Clean the cylinder head and cylinder block joint faces.

To install:

30. Position the cylinder head gasket.

31. Do not confuse the cylinder head gaskets. The left side head has 2 attaching holes in the timing chain cover while the right side has 3.

32. Install the cylinder head and torque the bolts in sequence.

33. Further installation is the reverse of removal. Insert the rear cam bearing cylinder head bolt before positioning the cylinder head. Also, install the exhaust manifold only after the cylinder head bolts have been tightened. The camshaft sprocket should be installed so the flange faces the camshaft. Check the valve clearance and fill the engine with oil. Top off the power steering tank and bleed the power steering system.

34. Run the engine and check for leaks.

DOHC ENGINE

1. Disconnect the negative battery cable and drain the engine coolant.

2. Remove the front covers.

3. Crank the No. 1 piston of the engine to 45 degrees BTDC. Look for the 4/5 on the timing indicator.

4. Mark all 4 camshaft timing gears and timing chain with colored dots at about 11 o:clock for the right outer and left inner camshaft sprocket and 1 o:clock for the right inner and left outer camshaft sprocket.

5. Lock all camshaft sprockets with special pins tool 119589001500 to prevent them from rotating.

6. Remove the timing chain tensioner and top guide rails.

7. Unscrew exhaust camshaft gears and camshaft adjuster.

8. Remove the engine cover and intake manifold.

9. Label and disconnect all electrical wiring, hoses and cables from the manifolds and cylinder head(s).

10. If equipped with an automatic transmission, remove the dipstick guide tube.

11. Disconnect the exhaust system from the head.

12. Remove the cylinder head cover very carefully.

NOTE: Make sure the engine is cold before removing cylinder head bolts.

13. Loosen the cylinder head bolts in the opposite sequence as torquing. A special Torx® like socket is needed to remove the bolts.

14. Install a suitable lifting device onto the cylinder head and remove.

To install:

15. Clean the gasket mating surfaces and check for warpage.

16. Check the head bolts for stretch. The maximum length is 6.40 in. (162.70mm). Replace if excessive.

17. Install the cylinder head gasket and head. Torque the bolts in sequence, in steps. The 1st step to 40 ft. lbs. (55 Nm), 2nd step to 90 degrees angle of rotation and 3rd step to 90 degrees angle of rotation after waiting 10 minutes. Torque the M8 bolts near the timing sprockets to 18 ft. lbs. (25 Nm).

18. Connect the exhaust pipe and torque to 20 ft. lbs. (25 Nm).

19. Install the remaining components.

20. Connect all wiring, hoses and cables.

21. Refill the engine with fluids, connect the battery cable, start the engine and check for leaks.

V12 Engine

Set the engine to TDC of No. 1 compression stroke.

1. Disconnect the negative battery cable, relieve the fuel pressure and drain the cooling system.

2. Remove the front timing cover, timing chain tensioner and timing chain guide. Remove the timing chain and secure out of the way. Keep tension on the chain so it does not fall into the crankcase.

3. Remove the vent tube guide blade bolts. Pull the guide blade out with an impact puller 116589203300 or equivalent (left cylinder head).

4. Remove the air breather, air injection and oil dipstick tube from the right cylinder head.

5. Disconnect the exhaust system.

6. Remove the automatic transmission dipstick tube.

7. Remove the intake manifold.

8. Remove the crankcase ventilation from the right cylinder head.

9. Remove the exhaust manifold from the engine.

10. Label and disconnect all electrical wiring, hoses, cables and lines from the cylinder head and related components.

11. Remove the cylinder head bolts in the opposite direction of torquing.

12. Install a camshaft holder tool 104589004000 in place of the camshaft bearing cap on the cylinder head. Install a suitable hoist on the holder tool and remove the cylinder head and gasket.

To install:

13. Clean the gasket mating surfaces and check for warpage. Match the old gasket to the new for an exact fit.

14. Install the cylinder head with the suitable hoist and camshaft holder tool 104589004000.

15. Install the cylinder head bolts and torque, in sequence, to specifications.

16. Connect all electrical wiring, hoses, cables and lines to the cylinder head and related components.

17. Install the exhaust manifold to the engine.

18. Install the crankcase ventilation to the right cylinder head.

19. Install the intake manifold.

20. Install the automatic transmission dipstick tube.

21. Connect the exhaust system.

22. Install the air breather, air injection and oil dipstick tube to the right cylinder head.

23. Install the vent tube guide blade.

24. Install the front timing cover, timing chain tensioner and timing chain guide.

25. Connect the negative battery cable and refill the cooling system.

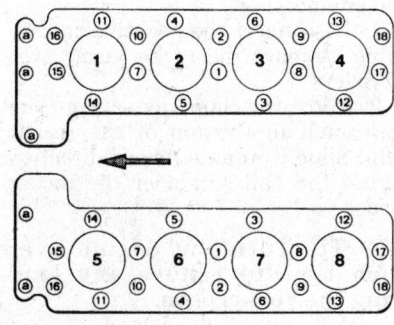

Cylinder head torque sequence — 8 Cylinder engine, except DOHC

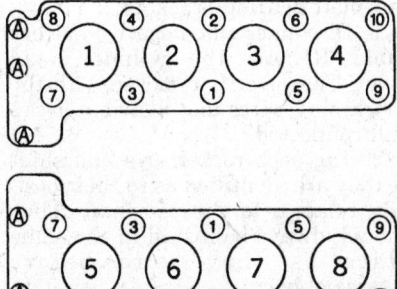

Cylinder head bolt torque sequence — 8 cylinder DOHC engine

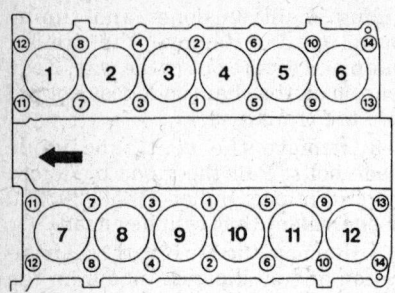

Cylinder head bolt torque sequence — 12 cylinder engine

Valve Lifters

REMOVAL AND INSTALLATION

DOHC Engines

All engines are equipped with hydraulic valve lifters. They can be checked by placing the camshaft on the base circle and use a non-metal tool to push the lifter down. If it is easier to press one lifter in comparison to the others, this one must be replaced.

Remove the cylinder head cover, camshaft and pull the lifter out with a magnetic tool.

Except DOHC Engines

Temporarily removed valve lifters must be reinstalled in their original locations. When replacing worn rocker arms, the camshaft must also be replace. If the rocker arm or hydraulic lifter is replaced, check the base setting.

Remove the rocker arm and unscrew the valve lifter with a 24mm socket.

Valve Lash

All engines are equipped with hydraulic valve clearance compensation elements (lifters) that require no periodic maintenance and adjustment.

CHECKING BASE SETTING

The base setting is the clearance between the upper edge of the cylindrical part of the plunger and the lower edge of the retaining cap (dimension A) when the cam lobe is vertical.

NOTE: A dial indicator with an extension and a measuring thrust piece (MBNA *100 589 16 63 00), 0.187 in. thick are necessary to perform this adjustment.

1. Turn the cam lobe to a vertical position, relative to the rocker arm.

2. Attach a dial indicator and tip extension and insert the extension through the bore in the rocker arm onto the head plunger. Preload the dial indicator by 0.08 in. and zero the instrument.

3. Depress the valve with a valve spring compressor. The lift on the dial indicator should be 0.028-0.075 in.

4. If the lift is excessive, the base setting can be changed by installing a new thrust piece.

5. Remove the dial indicator.

6. Remove the rocker arm.

7. Remove the thrust piece and insert the measuring disc.

8. Install the rocker arm and repeat Steps 1-3.

9. Select a thrust piece according to the table. If the measured valve was 0-0.002 in. and the 0.2146 in. thrust piece will not give the proper base setting, use the 0.2283 in. thrust piece.

10. Remove the dial indicator and the rocker arm. Install the selected thrust piece.

11. Reinstall the rocker arm and dial indicator and repeat Steps 1-3.

ADJUSTMENT

All engines use hydraulic valve clearance compensation. No adjustment is either possible or necessary.

Rocker Arms

REMOVAL AND INSTALLATION

Gasoline Engines

4 AND 6 CYLINDER SOHC ENGINES

Rocker arms on this engine are individually mounted on rocker arm shafts that fit into either side of the camshaft bearing brackets.

1. Disconnect the negative battery cable. Remove the cylinder head cover. The cover is removed with the spark plug wires and distributor cap still connected.

2. Tag each rocker arm and shaft so they are identified as to their position relative to the camshaft. They should always be install in the same place as they were before disassembly.

3. The rocker arm shaft is held axially and rotationally by a bearing bracket fastening bolt. Remove the bolt on the side of the bearing bracket

that allows access to the exposed end of the rocker shaft.

4. Thread a bolt (M8) into the end of the rocker arm shaft and slowly ease the shaft from the bearing bracket.

NOTE: Support the rocker arm/lifter assembly while removing the shaft so it will not drop onto the cylinder head. Carefully, forcing the valve down with a small prybar will remove the load on the hydraulic valve tappet and ease the removal of the shaft. Do not depress the spring too far. When the piston is up as it should be, the valve will hit the piston. As the spring goes down the thrust piece will fall into the engine.

5. Replace the bearing bracket bolt and tighten it to 11 ft. lbs. (15 Nm) until ready to replace the rocker shaft.

To install:

6. Position the rocker arm between the 2 bearing brackets and slide the shaft into place.

NOTE: The circular groove on the end of the rocker shaft must align with the mounting bolt shank to ensure proper positioning.

7. Replace the bearing bracket mounting bolt.

8. Repeat Steps 3-7 for all remaining rocker arm/shaft assemblies. Turn the engine over each time to relieve any load from the rocker arm.

9. Replace the cylinder head cover.

V8 SOHC ENGINE

Before removing the rocker arm(s), be sure they are identified as to their position relative to the camshaft lobe. They should be installed in the same place as they were before disassembly.

Be very careful removing the thrust pieces; they can easily fall into the engine.

1. Disconnect the negative battery cable. Remove the rocker arm cover or covers.

2. Force the clamping spring from the notch in the top of the rocker arm. Slide it in an outward direction across the ball socket or the rocker arm.

NOTE: Turn the engine over each time to relieve any load from the rocker arm.

3. On V8 models, the clamping spring must be forced from the adjusting screw with a small prybar.

4. Force the valve down to remove load from the rocker arm.

NOTE: Do not depress the spring too far. When the piston is up as it should be, the valve will hit the piston. As the spring goes down, the thrust piece will fall into the engine.

5. Lift the rocker arm from the ball pin and remove the rocker arm.

To install:

6. Force the rocker arm down until the rocker arm and its ball socket can be installed in the top of the pin.

7. Install the rocker arms.

8. Slide the clamping spring across the ball socket of the rocker arm until it rests in the notch of the rocker arm.

9. On V8 models, engage the clamping spring into the recess of the adjusting screw.

10. Check and, if necessary, adjust the valve clearance.

11. After completion of the adjustment, check to be sure the clamping springs are correctly seated.

12. Install the rocker arm cover and connect any hoses or lines that were disconnected.

13. Run the engine and check for leaks at the rocker arm cover.

Intake Manifold

REMOVAL AND INSTALLATION

4-Cylinder engine

1. Disconnect the negative battery cable. Remove mixture control unit with air guide housing.

2. Disconnect fuel lines.

3. Remove holder for starter cable.

4. Remove electric lines and vacuum lines.

5. Remove supporting holder for intake manifold.

6. Remove engine suspension eye.

7. Remove fastening nuts and bolt.

8. Remove intake manifold.

9. Clean and test flange surfaces with straight-edge, machine on surface plate, if required.

To install:

10. Use new gasket and reverse removal procedure. Check idle.

6-Cylinder engine

1. Disconnect the negative battery cable and drain the engine coolant.

2. Label and disconnect all vacuum, electrical and cable connectors from the intake manifold.

3. Disconnect the line support rail.

4. Remove the intake manifold mounting bolts.

5. Remove the engine compartment rear lining, if so equipped.

6. Remove the guide tube for the dipstick.

7. Remove the mounting bolts for both the manifold and supports.

8. Carefully remove the manifold and components.

To install:

9. Clean the gasket mating surfaces and check for warpage.

10. Using a new gasket that matches the old one, install the manifold and mounting hardware.

11. Evenly torque the manifold in 2 steps.

12. Reconnect all wiring, hoses and cables. Check for leakage.

13. Check and adjust the throttle linkage and idle speed.

14. Refill the engine fluids, connect the battery cable, start the engine and check for leaks.

V8 Engine

1. Disconnect the negative battery cable. Partially drain the coolant.

2. Remove the air cleaner and engine cover.

3. Disconnect the regulating linkage and remove the longitudinal regulating shaft.

4. Label and pull off all cable plug connections.

5. Disconnect and plug the fuel lines on the pressure regulator and starting valve for CIS-E engine. Disconnect the injector electrical connectors for LH engines.

6. Unscrew the nuts on the injection valves and set the injection valves aside.

7. Remove the 16 attaching bolts from the intake manifold.

8. Loosen the hose clip on the thermostat housing hose and disconnect the hose.

9. Remove the intake manifold. If a portion of the manifold must be replaced, disassembly the intake manifold. Replace the rubber connections during reassembly.

To install:

10. Install the gasket and intake manifold. Torque the bolts to specifications.

11. Tighten the hose clip on the thermostat housing hose and connect the hose.

12. Connect the fuel lines on the pressure regulator and starting valve for CIS-E engines. Connect the fuel injector and air mass meter connectors for LH engines.

13. Install all cable plug connections.

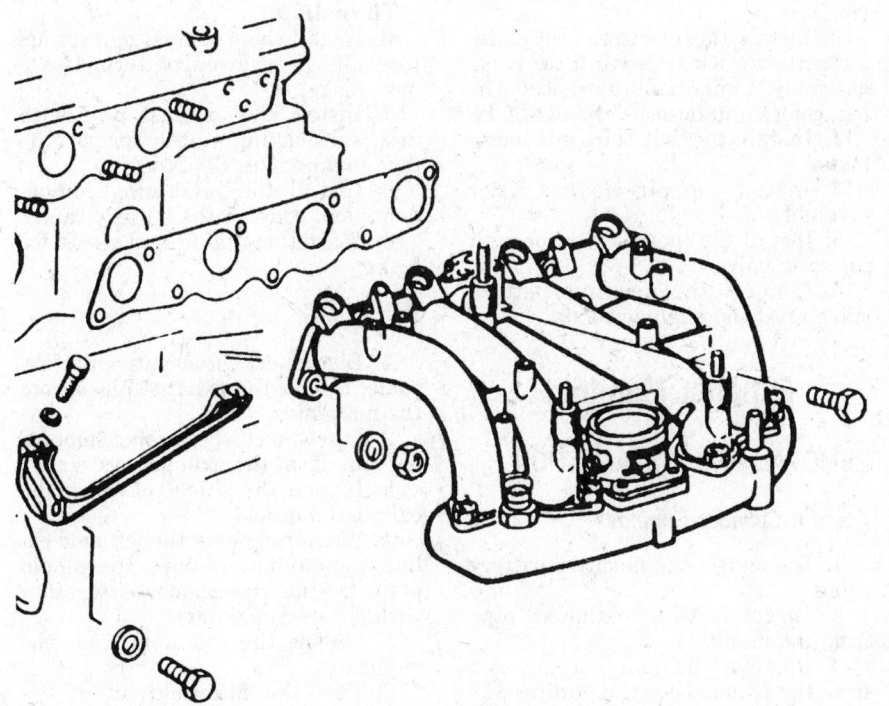

Intake manifold assembly — 4 cylinder engine, 6 cylinder similar

5. Valve connection
16. Nut
17. Washer
18. Gasket
19. Idle speed air line
20. Screw connection
21. Sealing ring
22. Upper intake manifold
23. Holder
24. Hex bolt
25. Connection
26. Sealing ring
27. Gasket
28. Screw connection
29. Sealing ring
30. Screw connection
31. Sealing ring
32. Bottom intake manifold
33. Rubber connecting piece
34. Hex bolt
35. Hex bolt
36. Sealing ring
37. Plug
38. Hose

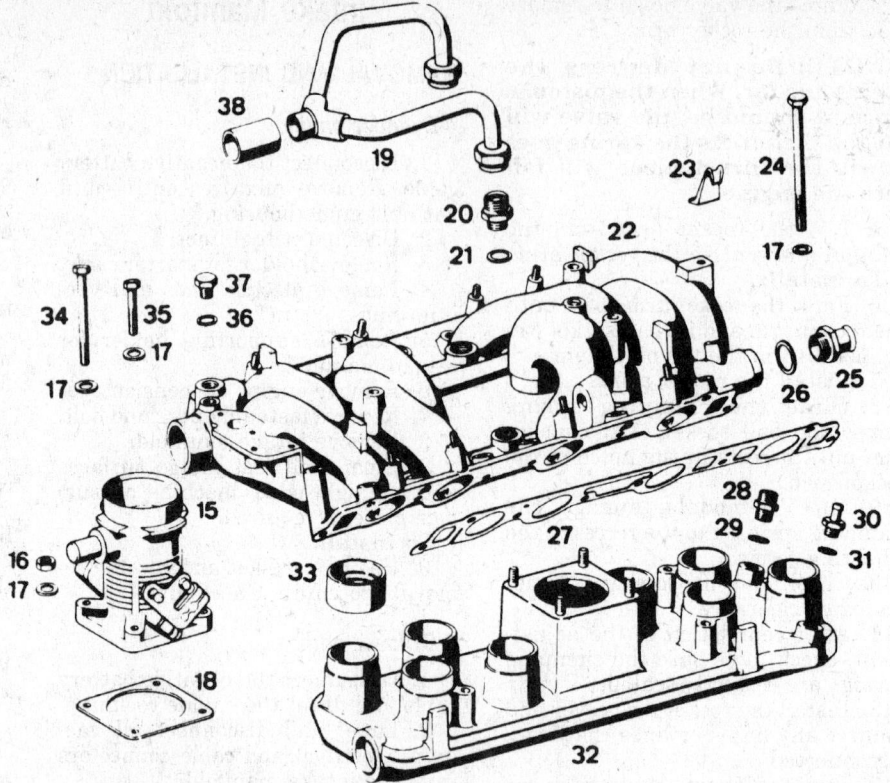

Intake manifold — 8 cylinder SOHC engine

14. Connect the regulating linkage and install the longitudinal regulating shaft, if equipped.
15. Install the air cleaner and engine cover.
16. Adjust the linkage and idle speed.
17. Connect the negative battery cable and refill the coolant.

12 Cylinder Engine

1. Disconnect the negative battery cable, relieve the fuel pressure and drain the engine coolant.
2. Remove the fuel distributor with injection valves.
3. Remove the air cleaner filter assembly.
4. Remove the hot wire air mass meter.
5. Remove the electronic accelerator actuator with the throttle valve assembly. Disconnect all electrical wiring, cables and hoses from the manifold.
6. Loosen the intake manifold bolts in an even fashion working from the middle outward.
7. Carefully remove the intake manifold and gasket.
To install:
8. Clean the gasket mating surfaces. Carefully install the intake manifold and gasket.

9. Torque the intake manifold bolts in an even fashion working from the middle outward to 18 ft. lbs. (25 Nm).
10. Install the electronic accelerator actuator with the throttle valve assembly. Connect all electrical wiring, cables and hoses to the manifold.
11. Install the hot wire air mass meter.
12. Install the air cleaner filter assembly.
13. Install the fuel distributor with injection valves.
14. Connect the negative battery cable refill the engine coolant.

Exhaust Manifold

REMOVAL AND INSTALLATION

4 and 6 Cylinder Engines

1. Disconnect the negative battery cable.
2. Disconnect the exhaust pipe from the manifold.
3. Remove the exhaust support from the transmission, if equipped.
4. Disconnect the air injection tube from the manifold, if equipped.
5. Remove the exhaust manifold retaining bolts and manifold. Be

careful with the manifold coupler tube between the 2 halves. Replace if damaged.
To install:
6. Install the manifold and torque the bolts in an even pattern. Use a new gasket.
7. Install the exhaust pipe with new self-locking nuts. Torque the pipe to 25 ft. lbs. (34 Nm).
8. Install the remaining components and connect the battery cable.
9. Start the engine and check for leaks.

V8 Engines

1. Disconnect the negative battery cable. Unbolt the exhaust pipes from the manifolds.
2. Disconnect the rubber mounting ring from the exhaust system.
3. Loosen the shield plate on the exhaust manifold.
4. When removing the left side exhaust manifold, remove the shield plate for the engine mount together with the engine damper.
5. Unbolt the manifold from the engine.
6. Pull the manifold off of the mounting.
7. Installation is the reverse of removal. Torque the manifold bolts to 18 ft. lbs. (25 Nm).

V12 Engines

RIGHT FRONT

1. Disconnect the negative battery cable.
2. Remove the serpentine belt and alternator.
3. Remove the air pump, if equipped.
4. Remove the guide tube for the oil dipstick.
5. Remove the air injection pipe and move out of the way.
6. Remove the manifold self-locking nuts and manifold.

To install:

7. Clean the gasket mating surfaces. Always use new self-locking nuts. Position the closed metal surface of the gasket facing the cylinder head.
8. Install the manifold and nuts. Torque the self-locking nuts to 20 ft. lbs. (30 Nm).
9. Install the remaining components.
10. Connect the battery cable and check for leaks.

RIGHT REAR

1. Disconnect the negative battery cable.
2. Remove the right front exhaust manifold.
3. Drain about 1 quart of transmission fluid. Remove the automatic transmission dipstick tube and move out of the way.
4. Remove the EGR valve and the bolts at the right engine mount bolt.
5. Remove the manifold retaining nuts, manifold and gasket.

To install:

6. Clean the gasket mating surfaces. Always use new self-locking nuts. Position the closed metal surface of the gasket facing the cylinder head.
7. Install the gasket, manifold and nuts. Torque the nuts to 20 ft. lbs. (30 Nm).
8. Install the engine mount bolt and EGR valve.
9. Install the dipstick tube and right front exhaust manifold.
10. Refill the transmission with fluid.
11. Connect the battery cable, start the engine and check for leaks.

LEFT FRONT

1. Disconnect the negative battery cable.
2. Remove the air injection pipe and move out of the way.
3. Remove the manifold nuts and manifold.

4. Clean the gasket mating surfaces. Always use new self-locking nuts.
5. Install the gasket, manifold and nuts. Torque the nuts to 20 ft. lbs. (30 Nm). Position the closed metal surface of the gasket facing the cylinder head.
6. Install the air injection pipe.
7. Connect the battery cable, start the engine and check for leaks.

LEFT REAR

1. Disconnect the negative battery cable.
2. Remove the left front exhaust manifold.
3. Remove the EGR valve.
4. Remove the electronic accelerator actuator with the throttle assembly.
5. Remove the bolts from the left engine mount. Install a suitable hoist and pull the engine to the right and down.
6. Remove the manifold retaining nuts, manifold and gasket.

To install:

7. Clean the gasket mating surfaces. Always use new self-locking nuts. Position the closed metal surface of the gasket facing the cylinder head.

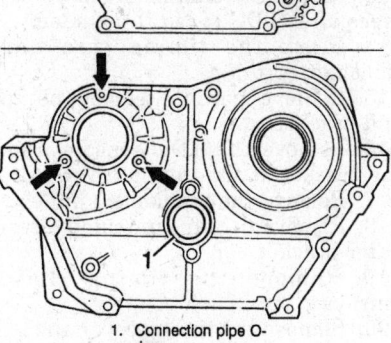

1. Connection pipe O-ring
2. Connection pipe

Front cover assembly — 6 cylinder DOHC engine

8. Install the gasket, manifold and nuts. Torque the nuts to 20 ft. lbs. (30 Nm).
9. Install the engine mount bolt and EGR valve.
10. Install the electronic accelerator actuator and throttle body.
11. Connect the battery cable, start the engine and check for leaks.

Timing Chain Front Cover

REMOVAL AND INSTALLATION

4 and 6 Cylinder engines

NOTE: The DOHC engines have a O-ring seal between the upper front cover and cylinder head, behind the water outlet. Always replace this seal when servicing the front cover or water outlet.

1. Disconnect the negative battery cable and drain the engine coolant.
2. Remove the engine cover, air cleaner and intake scoop.
3. Remove the viscous fan clutch, fan belt and mounting pulleys.
4. Disconnect all wiring and hoses from the front of the engine.
5. Remove the upper timing cover and mark the timing chain and sprockets.
6. Loosen and rotate the timing chain tensioning device.
7. Remove the power steering pump, air pump and fan bearing support.
8. Remove the TDC sensor, alternator and bracket.
9. Remove the timing covers, top and bottom.

To install:

10. Install the cover and torque the M6 bolts to 7 ft. lbs. (10 Nm) and the M8 bolts to 15 ft. lbs. (21 Nm).
11. Install the water pump and torque to 15 ft. lbs. (21 Nm).
12. Install the remaining components in reverse order.
13. Refill the engine with coolant, start the engine and check for leaks.

V8 Engines

1. Disconnect the negative battery cable and drain the radiator. Remove the air cleaner and valve cover.
2. Remove the viscous fan coupling and loosen the serpentine belt.
3. Remove the front top cover, serpentine belt and tensioner.
4. Set the engine No. 1 piston to TDC with the crankshaft pointer at the 4/5 mark on the pulley.
5. Remove the engine compartment panel.

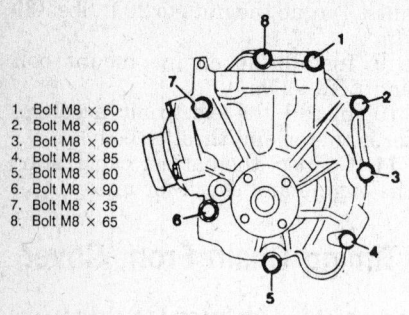

1. Bolt M8 × 60
2. Bolt M8 × 60
3. Bolt M8 × 60
4. Bolt M8 × 85
5. Bolt M8 × 60
6. Bolt M8 × 90
7. Bolt M8 × 35
8. Bolt M8 × 65

Water pump bolts — 8 cylinder DOHC engine

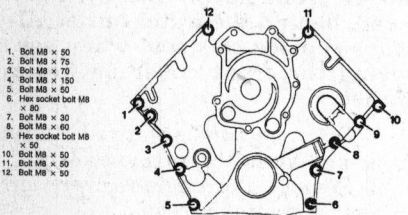

1. Bolt M8 × 50
2. Bolt M8 × 75
3. Bolt M8 × 70
4. Bolt M8 × 150
5. Bolt M8 × 50
6. Hex socket bolt M8 × 80
7. Bolt M8 × 30
8. Bolt M8 × 60
9. Hex socket bolt M8 × 50
10. Bolt M8 × 50
11. Bolt M8 × 50
12. Bolt M8 × 50

Front timing cover bolts — 8 cylinder DOHC engine, others similar

6. Remove the left exhaust pipe and cover the starter mounting opening.

7. Lock the camshafts in place using a holding pin 119589001500 or equivalent, to prevent the engine from rotating.

8. Mark all 4 camshafts sprockets and chain with colored dots, if equipped.

9. Remove the armature for the variable cam adjuster. Take off as an assembly and do not disassemble the unit.

10. Remove the alternator, bracket and timing chain tensioner.

11. Remove the top chain guide rails.

12. Remove the radiator, hoses and fan carrier.

13. Remove the thermostat housing and serpentine belt pulleys.

14. Remove the air pump and bracket. Remove the water pump cover and pump.

15. Remove the air conditioning compressor and move out of the way. Secure to the side of the vehicle with wire. Remove the compressor bracket.

16. Remove the TDC sensor.

17. Remove the oil pump and dipstick tube. Remove the top section of oil sump.

18. Remove the front cover bolts and from cover with the coil pump chain.

To install:

19. Install the front cover, new gasket and bolts. Torque the bolts to 15 ft. lbs. (20 Nm).

20. Install the water pump and torque to 15 ft. lbs. (20 Nm).

21. Install the remaining components.

22. Refill the engine with coolant and oil. Start the engine and check for leaks.

V12 Engines

1. Disconnect the negative battery cable and drain the engine coolant.

2. Place the No. 1 cylinder on TDC of the compression stroke.

3. Remove the cylinder head covers.

4. Remove the radiator, serpentine belt, idler pulley and thermostat housing.

5. Install a guard plate 120589063100 or equivalent, over the intake ports.

6. Remove the distributor, rotor, protective plate and sealing ring.

7. Remove the power steering pump reservoir with the hoses attached.

8. Remove the mounting bracket in the middle of the front cover.

9. Remove the upper front covers with the gasket and O-rings.

10. Remove the water pump.

11. Remove the air cleaner and air mass meter assembly.

12. Remove the alternator and air pump and hang out of the way.

13. Rotate the crankshaft to 30 degrees after TDC of No. 1 cylinder.

14. Mark the timing case and camshaft sprockets.

15. Remove power steering pump and bracket.

16. Remove the TDC sensors from the bracket at the timing covers.

17. Remove the crankshaft pulley.

18. Remove the air pump and alternator bracket.

19. Remove the timing chain tensioner.

20. Remove the timing cover and oil pan bolts.

21. Remove the timing cover from the engine.

To install:

22. Clean the gasket mating surfaces. Install the timing cover to the engine. Torque the bolts to 14 ft. lbs. (18 Nm).

23. Install the timing chain tensioner.

24. Install the air pump and alternator bracket.

25. Install the crankshaft pulley.

26. Install the TDC sensors to the bracket at the timing covers.

27. Install power steering pump and bracket.

28. Install the alternator and air pump.

29. Install the air cleaner and air mass meter assembly.

30. Install the water pump.

31. Install the upper front covers with the gasket and O-rings.

32. Install the mounting bracket in the middle of the front cover.

33. Install the power steering pump reservoir and hoses.

34. Install the distributor, rotor, protective plate and sealing ring.

35. Install the radiator, serpentine belt, idler pulley and thermostat housing.

36. Install the cylinder head covers.

37. Connect the negative battery cable and refill the engine coolant.

38. Start the engine and check for leaks.

Timing Chain Tensioner

REMOVAL AND INSTALLATION

4-Cylinder Engine

There are 2 kinds of timing chain tensioners. One uses an O-ring seal and the other a flat gasket. Do not install a flat gasket on a tensioner meant to be use with an O-ring.

Chain tensioners should be replaced as a unit if defective.

1. Disconnect the negative battery cable. Drain the coolant. If equipped with an air conditioner, disconnect the compressor and mounting bracket and lay it aside; do not disconnect the refrigerant lines.

2. Remove the thermostat housing.

3. Loosen and remove the chain tensioner; be careful of loose O-rings. On the 190, remove the tensioner cap nut and the tension spring; the tensioner body can be unscrewed with an Allen wrench.

4. Check the O-rings or gasket and replace, if necessary.

5. To fill the chain tensioner, place the tensioner, pressure bolt down, in a container of SAE 10 engine oil, at least up to the flat flange. Using a drill press, depress the pressure bolt slowly, about 7-10 times; be sure this is done slowly and uniformly.

6. Install the chain tensioner. Tighten the bolts evenly. Tighten the cap nut on the 190 to 51 ft. lbs. (70 Nm).

6 Cylinder and V8 Engines

EXCEPT DOHC ENGINES

The chain tensioner is connected to the engine oil circuit. Bleeding occurs once oil pressure has been established and the tensioner is filling with oil.

A venting hole has been installed in the tensioner to prevent oil foaming. If there is a lot of timing chain noise, use this type of tensioner, which is identified by a white paint dot on the cap.

Service procedures for tensioners and rails on the different V8's are similar. Arrangement and shape and size of parts however, is slightly different.

1. Disconnect the negative battery cable. On California models, disconnect the line from the tensioner.

2. Remove the bolts and the tensioner; the inside bolts will probably require a long, straight 6mm Allen key to bypass the exhaust manifold. It is a tight fit.

3. Place the tensioner vertically in a container of engine oil. Operate the pressure bolt to fill the tensioner. After filling, it should permit compression very slowly under considerable force. If not, replace the tensioner with a new unit.

4. Install the tensioner and tighten the bolts evenly.

DOHC ENGINES

1. Disconnect the negative battery cable.

2. Set the No. 1 piston on TDC with the arrow pointer near the pulley at the 4/5 mark.

3. Remove the right hand cylinder head cover. Swivel the air pump down and out of the way, if equipped.

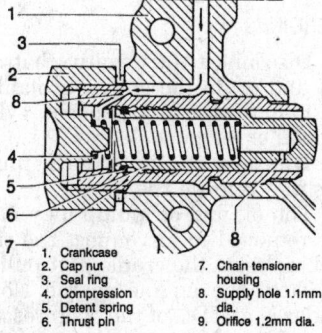

1. Crankcase
2. Cap nut
3. Seal ring
4. Compression
5. Detent spring
6. Thrust pin
7. Chain tensioner housing
8. Supply hole 1.1mm dia.
9. Orifice 1.2mm dia.

Cross section of the timing chain tensioner — 4 cylinder engine

4. Secure the right hand exhaust camshaft with a pin tool 119589001500 or equivalent, so the camshaft does not rotate.

5. Remove the serpentine belt from the alternator and remove the alternator.

6. Remove the timing chain tensioner from the right side of the engine block.

To install:

7. Install the tensioner and torque the bolts to 15 ft. lbs. (20 Nm).

8. Install the alternator and cylinder head cover.

9. Connect the battery cable, start the engine and check for abnormal noise or vibration.

V12 ENGINES

1. Disconnect the negative battery cable.

2. Remove the serpentine belt.

3. Remove the air cleaner with air quality meter, intake air scoop and air pump.

4. Turn the crankshaft to 30 degrees after TDC of No. 1 cylinder, compression stroke.

5. Loosen the plug next to the tensioner about 1 turn.

6. Remove the chain tensioner from the engine.

7. Remove the plug, fill pin and pressure spring.

To install:

8. Install the tensioner with new sealing ring. Torque the tensioner to 36 ft. lbs. (50 Nm).

9. Install the pressure spring, fill pin and plug. Torque the plug to 30 ft. lbs. (40 Nm).

10. Install the remaining components.

11. Connect the battery cable and check engine operation.

Timing Chain

REPLACEMENT

Unbroken

An endless timing chain is used on production engines but a split chain with a connecting link is used for service. The endless chain can be separated with a ""chain breaker." Only 1 master link (connecting link) should be used on a chain.

1. Disconnect the negative battery cable. Remove the spark plugs.

2. Remove the valve cover(s).

3. Clamp the chain to the camshaft gear and cover the opening of the timing chain case with rags. On 6 cylinder and V8 engines, re-

move the rocker arms from the right side camshaft.

4. Separate the chain with a chain breaker.

To install:

5. Attach a new timing chain to the old chain with a master link.

6. Using a socket wrench on the crankshaft, slowly rotate the engine in the direction of normal rotation. Simultaneously, pull the old chain through until the master link is uppermost on the camshaft sprocket; be sure to keep tension on the chain throughout this procedure.

7. Disconnect the old timing chain and connect the ends of the new chain with the master link. Insert the new connecting link from the rear so the lock washers can be seen from the front.

8. Rotate the engine until the timing marks align. Check the valve timing. Once the new chain is assembled, rotate the engine, by hand, through a least 1 complete revolution to be sure everything is OK.

Broken

4-CYLINDER ENGINE

1. Disconnect the negative battery cable and drain the engine coolant.

2. Remove engine accessories and timing chain covers.

3. Remove the cylinder head assembly.

4. Remove the tensioner blade, guiding blade and idler gear shaft with timing chain.

5. Using a puller if needed, remove the crankshaft gear.

To install:

6. Install the chain guiding blade with the open side forward. Located above the crankshaft to the right.

7. Drive the crankshaft gear with the straight pin in alignment.

8. Rivet the open roller chain with a connector link and riveting tool 000589584300 or equivalent.

9. Install a new idler gear shaft together with the chain and clip. Torque the bolt to 4 ft. lbs. (5 Nm).

10. Put the chain around the crankshaft gear and fit into the tensioner blade.

11. Fit the timing chain cover and install the TDC sensor and vibration damper.

12. Install the thermostat housing.

13. Install the cylinder head with a new gasket.

14. Fit new guiding blade in the cylinder head. Use silicone sealer.

15. Install the camshaft timing gear and torque to 59 ft. lbs. (80 Nm).

16. Recheck the TDC marking on the camshaft and vibration damper.

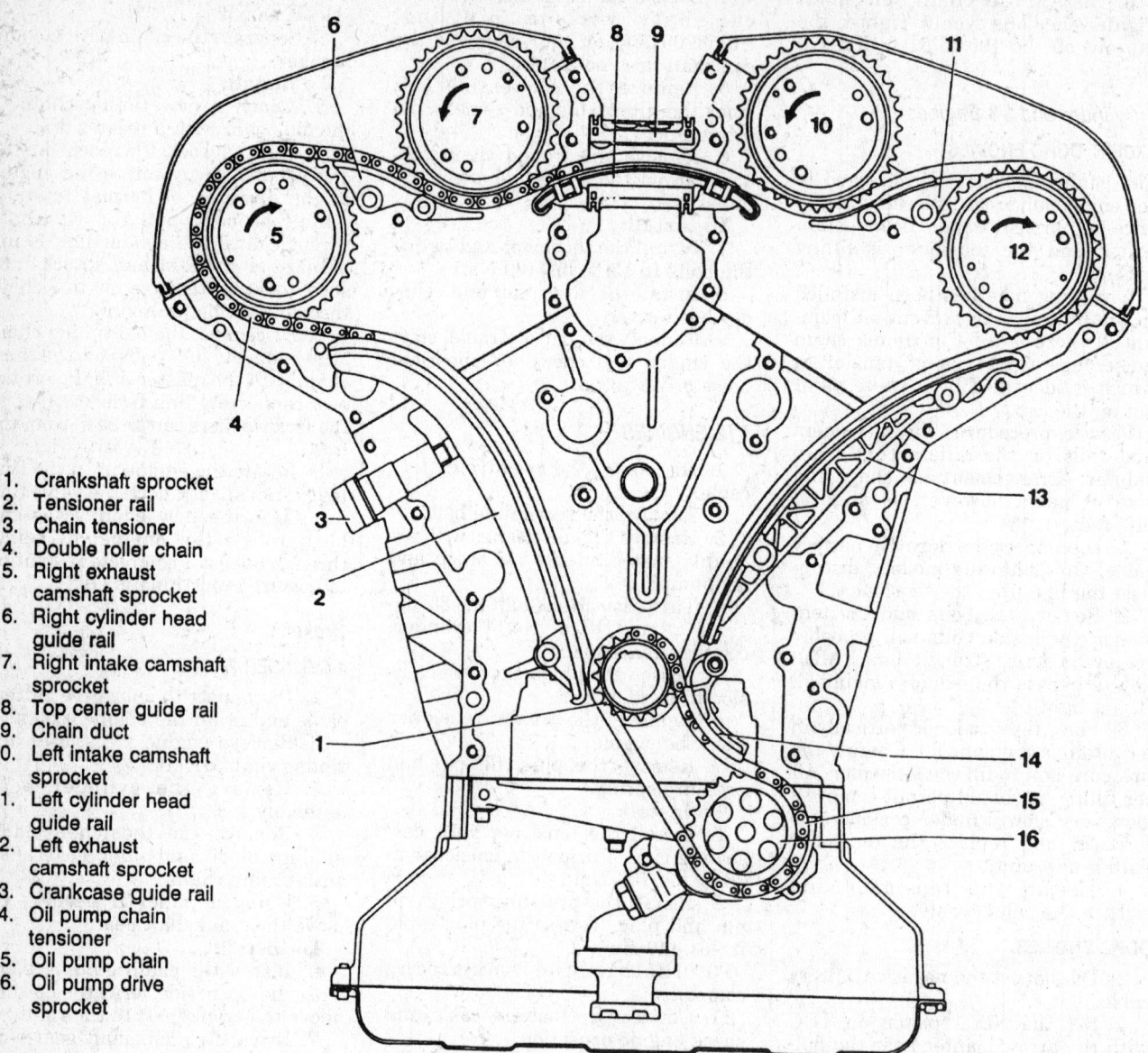

1. Crankshaft sprocket
2. Tensioner rail
3. Chain tensioner
4. Double roller chain
5. Right exhaust camshaft sprocket
6. Right cylinder head guide rail
7. Right intake camshaft sprocket
8. Top center guide rail
9. Chain duct
10. Left intake camshaft sprocket
11. Left cylinder head guide rail
12. Left exhaust camshaft sprocket
13. Crankcase guide rail
14. Oil pump chain tensioner
15. Oil pump chain
16. Oil pump drive sprocket

Timing chain components — 12 cylinder engine

It is on the right side of the camshaft, behind the sprocket.

17. Install the chain tensioner.

18. Rotate the engine to check ease of rotation.

19. Refill the engine with oil and coolant. Connect the battery cable, start the engine and check for leaks.

6 AND 8 CYLINDER ENGINES

1. Disconnect the negative battery cable and drain the engine coolant.

2. Remove the front cover, cylinder head cover and chain tensioner.

3. Disconnect the spark plugs wires and remove the plugs.

4. The oil and oil pump may have to be removed to disconnect the timing chain from the crankshaft pulley.

5. Turn the engine so the No. 1 cylinder is at TDC of the compression stroke. Line up the camshaft(s) timing mark and mark on the front camshaft journal. Remove the timing chain.

To install:

6. Install the timing chain and make sure the timing marks are lined up.

7. Install the oil pump drive chain, if removed.

8. Install the remaining components in reverse order.

9. Connect the battery cable, start the engine and check for leaks.

V12 ENGINES

1. Disconnect the negative battery cable and drain the engine coolant.

2. Remove the front covers, cylinder head covers.

3. Disconnect the spark plugs wires and remove the plugs.

4. The oil and oil pump may have to be removed to disconnect the timing chain from the crankshaft pulley.

5. Turn the engine so the No. 1 cylinder is at TDC of the compression stroke. Line up the camshaft(s) timing mark and mark on the camshaft

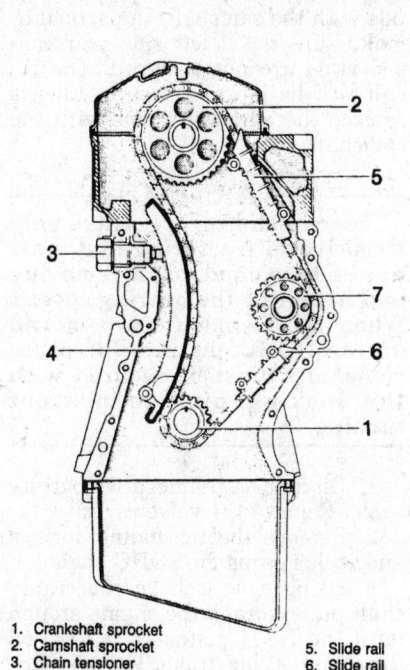

1. Crankshaft sprocket
2. Camshaft sprocket
3. Chain tensioner
4. Tensioning rail
5. Slide rail
6. Slide rail
7. Idler gear

Timing chain assembly — 4 cylinder engine

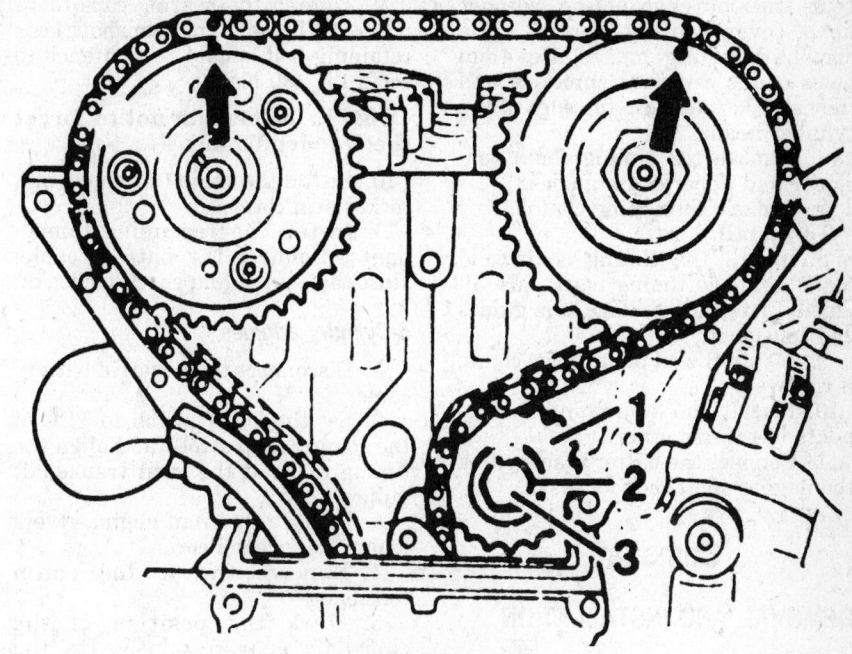

1. Timing chain idler gear
2. Idler gear washer
3. Idler gear bolt

Camshaft alignment marks — 6 cylinder DOHC engine

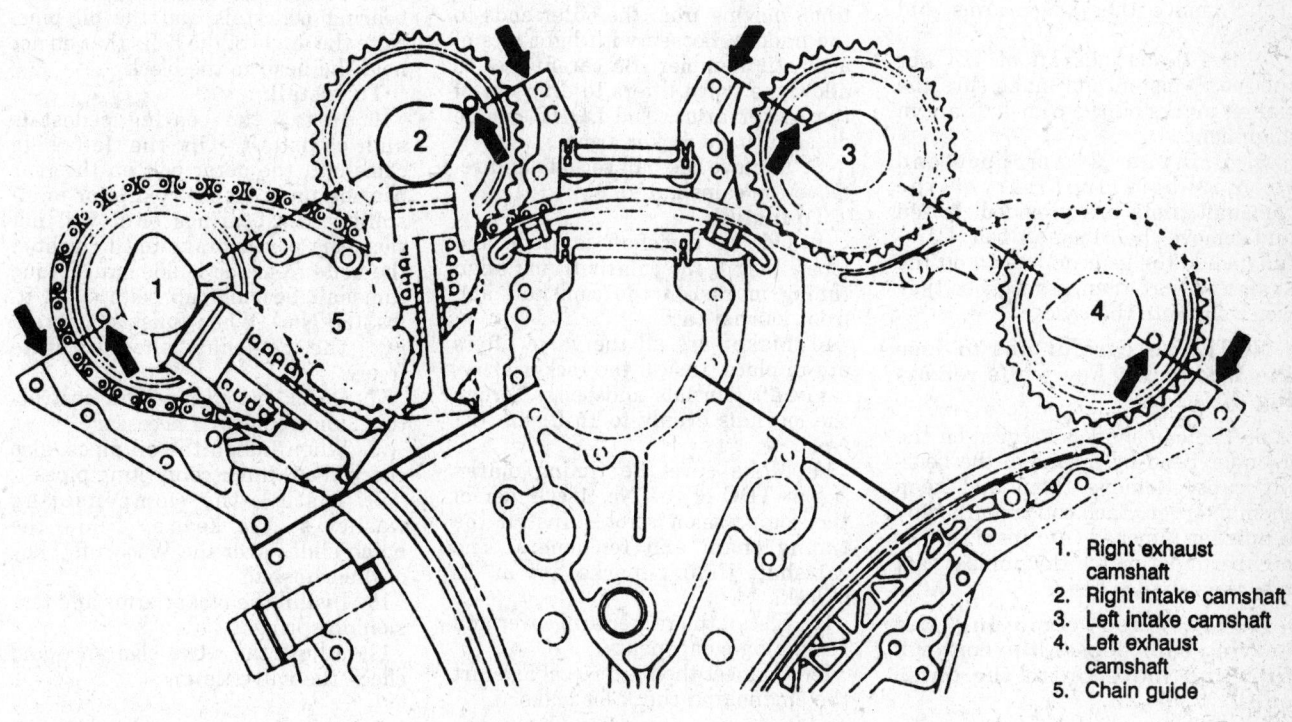

1. Right exhaust camshaft
2. Right intake camshaft
3. Left intake camshaft
4. Left exhaust camshaft
5. Chain guide

Camshaft alignment marks — 12 cylinder engine

gear and the edge of the cylinder head cover sealing surface. The camshaft timing marks are 4mm holes in the camshaft sprockets and they should touch the top edge of the cylinder heads.

6. Remove the timing chain tensioner and upper chain guides.

7. Remove the timing chain.

To install:

8. Install the timing chain and make sure the timing marks are aligned. Install the timing chain guides and tensioner.

9. Install the oil pump drive chain, if removed.

10. Install the remaining components in reverse order.

11. Connect the battery cable, start the engine and check for leaks.

Camshaft

REMOVAL AND INSTALLATION

4-Cylinder engines

NOTE: On the 190E it is always a good idea to replace the rocker arms and shafts whenever the camshaft is replaced.

1. Disconnect the negative battery cable. Remove the valve cover.

2. Remove the chain tensioner.

3. Remove the rocker arms and shafts.

4. Set the crankshaft at TDC for the No. 1 piston and make sure the timing marks on the camshaft are in alignment.

5. Using a 24mm open-end wrench, hold the rear of the camshaft, flats are provided, loosen and remove the camshaft bolt. Carefully, slide the gear and chain off the shaft and wire them securely so they won't slip into the case.

NOTE: Be careful not to lose the Woodruff® key while removing the gear.

6. The camshaft is secured on the cylinder head by means of the bearing caps. Remove them and keep them in order. Each cap is marked by a number punched into its side; this number must match the number cast into the cylinder head.

NOTE: When removing the bearing caps, loosen the center 2 first and move on to the outer ones.

7. Remove the camshaft.

To install:

8. Always make sure the No. 1 cylinder is at TDC and all timing marks are aligned.

9. Tighten the bearing caps to 15 ft. lbs. (21 Nm). The camshaft gear retaining bolt should be tightened to 58 ft. lbs. (80 Nm).

NOTE: Be certain not to forget the Woodruff® key.

10. Install the chain tensioners and rocker arm cover.

11. Install the remaining components. Connect the battery cable, start the engine and check for leaks.

6-Cylinder engines

1. Disconnect the negative battery cable.

2. Set the No. 1 piston to TDC of the compression stroke and align the timing mark at the front crankshaft pulley.

3. Remove the front engine covers and cylinder head cover.

4. Remove the timing chain tensioner.

5. Mark the position of the camshaft gear(s) relative to the camshaft using a colored marker next to the locating pin on the cam gear. The camshaft timing will change if the camshaft sprocket is turned.

6. Remove the oil pipe from the camshaft journals, noting the spray direction.

7. Starting at the ends, loosen the camshaft journal bolts one turn at a time, moving from the outer ends to the middle. Loosen with light hits of a plastic hammer. Be careful not to allow the valve lifters to drop out of the rocker arms. The DOHC engine does not have rocker arms.

8. Remove the ball sockets and remove the camshaft(s).

To install:

9. Oil the camshaft journals and lobes. Install the camshaft and align timing marks on the camshaft and front journal cap.

10. Make sure all the valve lifters are in place. Install the rocker arms, camshaft journals and bolts. Torque the journals evenly to 15 ft. lbs. (21 Nm).

11. Make sure the timing marks are at TDC of the No. 1 cylinder of the compression stroke. Install the timing chain and tensioners. The camshaft timing marks are at 12 o'clock.

12. Install the rocker arm cover and remaining components.

13. Connect the battery cable, start the engine and check for leaks.

V8 Engine

Experience shows that the right side camshaft is always the 1st one to require replacement. When the

camshaft is removed, keep the pedestals with the camshaft. In particular, make sure the 2 left side rear cam pedestals are not swapped. The result will be no oil pressure. Always replace the oil gallery pipe with the camshaft.

----------- WARNING -----------

The camshafts are extremely sensitive to fracturing and must not be tensioned when removing and installing the bearing covers. When the camshafts are moved on the DOHC engines, the other camshafts must be secured with the locking pins to prevent turning.

1. Disconnect the negative battery cable. Remove the valve cover.

2. Remove the tensioning springs and rocker arms for SOHC engines.

3. Using a wrench on the crankshaft pulley, crank the engine around until the No. 1 piston is at TDC on the compression stroke. The 4/5 mark on the crankshaft pulley for the DOHC engine. Using some stiff wire, hang the camshaft gear so the chain will not slip off the gears.

4. Remove the camshaft gear and variable valve timing device, if equipped.

5. Unbolt the camshaft, camshaft bearing pedestals and the oil pipe. Note the angle of the bolts that do not hold the head to the block.

To install:

6. Install the bearing pedestals and camshaft. On the left side camshaft, the outer bolt on the rear bearing must be inserted prior to installing the bearings or it will not clear the power brake until. Tighten the bolts from the inside out. Torque camshaft bearing cap bolts to 37 ft. lbs. (50 Nm). When finished tightening, the camshaft should rotate freely.

7. Check the oil pipes for obstructions and replace, if necessary.

8. When install the oil pipes, also check the 3 inner connecting pipes.

9. Install the compensating washer so the keyway below the notch slides over the Woodruff® key of the camshaft.

10. Install the rocker arms and tensioning springs.

11. Adjust the valve clearance and check the valve timing.

V12 Engines

The intake valve camshaft is equipped with a variable camshaft timing device. The camshaft can be removed without disassembling the timing chain.

1. Disconnect the negative battery cable and drain the engine coolant.

2. Using a wrench on the crankshaft pulley, crank the engine around until the No. 1 piston is at TDC of the compression stroke. The 4/5 mark on the crankshaft pulley for the DOHC engine. Rotate the crankshaft to 30 degree mark after TDC so the valves do not come in contact with the piston crown.

3. Remove the front covers. Remove the timing chain guide blades if removing the exhaust camshaft.

4. Remove the camshaft sprocket for exhaust camshafts only. Retain the timing chain and sprocket with wire to the engine block.

WARNING

The camshafts are extremely sensitive to fracturing and must not be tensioned when removing and installing the bearing covers.

---

5. Rotate the exhaust camshaft with the wrench 104589010100 or equivalent, until the tips of the cams on cylinders 3 or 9 are pressing centered on the bucket tappet.

6. Remove all exhaust camshaft bearing caps, except on cylinders 3 and 9.

7. Loosen the cylinder 3 and 9 bearing caps in steps of 1 turn.

8. Remove the camshaft and related components and label for exact replacement during installation.

To install:

9. The camshaft bearing caps are identified with numbers. The corresponding number is also cast into the cylinder head.

10. Check the bucket tappets for ease of movement and rotation. Oil all moving parts with clean engine oil or assembly lube.

11. Place the intake and exhaust camshafts into the bearing points. The tips of the cams on cylinders 3 and 9 must be pointing down centered.

12. Align the intake and exhaust camshafts axially at the axial bearing.

13. Install the cylinders 3 and 9 bearing caps and torque the bolts to 16 ft. lbs. (22 Nm).

14. Hold the camshafts with wrench 104589010100 when torquing on the bearing caps to cylinders 3 and 9. Install the remaining bearing caps and torque to 16 ft. lbs. (22 Nm).

15. Install the exhaust camshaft timing chain sprocket.

16. Install the timing chain and guide plates.

17. Install the front covers, cylinder head covers and remaining components.

18. Connect the battery cable and refill with engine coolant.

19. Start the engine and check for leaks and proper operation.

Valve Timing

Checking valve timing is too inaccurate at the standard tappet clearance; therefore timing values are given for an assumed tappet clearance of 0.4mm. The engines are not measured at 0.4mm but rather at 2mm.

1. To check the timing, remove the rocker arm cover and spark plugs. Remove the tensioning springs. On the 6 cylinder engine, install the testing thrust pieces. Eliminate all valve clearance.

2. Install a degree wheel.

NOTE: If the degree wheel is attached to the camshaft as shown, values read from it must be doubled.

3. A pointer must be made from a bent section of $3/16$ in. brazing rod or coat hanger wire and attached to the engine.

4. With a 22mm wrench on the crankshaft pulley, turn the engine, in the direction of rotation, until the TDC mark on the vibration damper registers with the pointer and the distributor rotor points to the No. 1 cylinder mark on the housing. The camshaft timing marks should align at this point.

NOTE: Due to the design of the chain tensioner on V8 engines, the right side of the chain travels slightly farther than the left side. This means the right side cam will be almost 7 degrees retarded compared to the left side and both marks will not simultaneously align.

5. Turn the loosened degree wheel until the pointer aligns with the 0 degree (OT) mark and tighten it in this position.

6. Continue turning the crankshaft in the direction of rotation until the camshaft lobe of the associated valve is vertical, e.g., point away from the rocker arm surface. To take up tappet clearance, insert a feeler gauge, thick enough to raise the valve slightly from its seat, between the rocker arm cone and the pressure piece.

7. Attach the indicator to the cylinder head so the feeler rests against the valve spring retainer of the No. 1 cylinder intake valve. Preload the indicator at least 0.008 in. and set to 0, make sure the feeler is exactly perpendicular on the valve spring retainer. It may be necessary to bleed down the chain tensioner at this time to facilitate readings.

8. Turn the crankshaft, in the normal direction of rotation, using a wrench on the crankshaft pulley, until the indicator reads 0.016 in. less than 0 reading.

9. Note the reading of the degree wheel at this time, remembering to double the reading, if the wheel is mounted to the camshaft sprocket.

10. Turn the crankshaft until the valve is closing and the indicator again reads 0.016 in. less than 0 reading. Make sure, at this time, that preload has remained constant, note the reading of the degree wheel. The difference between the 2 degree wheel reading is the timing angle, number of degrees the valve is open, for that valve.

11. The other valves may be checked in the same manner, comparing them against each other and the opening values. It must be remembered that turning the crankshaft contrary to the normal direction of rotation results in inaccurate readings and damage to the engine.

12. If valve timing is not to specification, the easiest way of bringing it in line, is to install an offset Woodruff® key in the camshaft sprocket. This is far simpler than replacing the entire timing chain and it is the factory-recommended way of changing valve timing provided the timing chain is not stretched too far or worn out.

13. The Woodruff® key must be installed with the offset toward the right, in the normal direction of rotation, to effect advanced valve opening; toward the left to retard.

14. Advancing the intake valve opening too much can result in piston and/or valve damage, the valve will hit the piston. To check the clearance between the valve head and the piston, the crankshaft must be positioned at 5 degrees ATDC, on intake stroke. The procedure is essentially the same as for measuring valve timing.

15. As before, the dial indicator is set to 0 after being preloaded, then the valve is depressed until it touches the top of the piston. As the normal valve head-to-piston clearance is approximately 0.035 in., the dial indicator must be preloaded at least 0.042

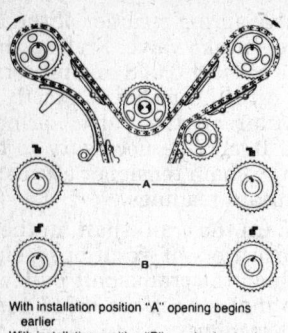

With installation position "A" opening begins earlier
With installation position "B" opening begins later

Offset Woodruff® keys — 8 cylinder SOHC engine

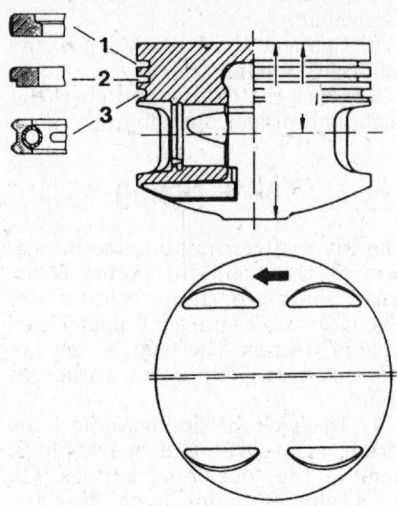

1. Rectangular compression ring with inside chamfer
2. Tapered oil scraper ring
3. Chamfered oil control ring with expander

Piston ring positioning — gasoline engine

in. so there will be enough movement for the feeler.

16. If the clearance is much less than 0.035 in., the cylinder head must be removed and checked for carbon deposits. If none exist, the valve seat must be cut deeper into the head. Always set the ignition timing after installing an offset key.

Piston and Connecting Rod

POSITIONING

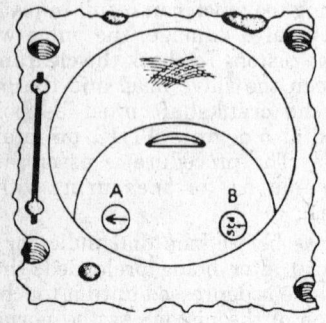

Pistons normally are marked with an arrow (a) indicating front and a weight or size marking (b).

DIESEL ENGINE MECHANICAL

NOTE: Disconnecting the negative battery cable may interfere with the functions of the on board computer systems and may require the computer to undergo a relearning process, once the negative battery cable is reconnected.

Engine Assembly

REMOVAL AND INSTALLATION

NOTE: In all cases, Mercedes-Benz engines and transmissions are removed as a unit.

——— CAUTION ———
Air conditioner lines should not be indiscriminately disconnected without taking proper precautions. It is best to swing the compressor aside while still connected to its hoses. Never do any welding around the compressor-heat may cause an explosion.

Also, the refrigerant, while inert at normal room temperature, breaks down under high temperature into hydrogen fluoride and phosgene (among other products), which are highly poisonous.

1. Remove the hood, drain the cooling system and disconnect the battery. While not strictly necessary, it is better to remove the battery completely to prevent breakage by the engine as it is lifted out.

2. Remove the fan shroud, radiator and disconnect all heater hoses and oil cooler lines.

3. Remove the air cleaner and all fuel, vacuum and oil hoses, e.g., power steering and power brakes.

4. Plug all openings to keep out dirt.

5. Remove the viscous coupling and fan.

6. Disconnect the accelerator linkage.

7. Disconnect all ground straps and electrical connections. It is a good idea to tag each wire for easy reassembly.

8. Detach the gearshift linkage and the exhaust pipes from the manifolds.

9. Loosen the steering relay arm and pull it aside, along with the center steering rod and hydraulic steering damper.

10. The hydraulic engine shock absorber should be removed.

11. Remove the hydraulic line from the clutch housing and the oil line connectors from the automatic transmission.

12. Unbolt the clutch slave cylinder from the bellhousing after removing the return spring.

13. Remove the exhaust pipe bracket from the transmission. Support the bellhousing or place a cable sling under the oil pan, to support the engine. On turbocharged models, disconnect the exhaust pipes at the turbocharger.

14. Mark the position of the rear engine support and unbolt the 2 outer bolts, then remove the top bolt at the transmission and pull the support out.

15. Disconnect the speedometer cable and the front driveshaft U-joint. Push the driveshaft back and wire it aside.

16. Unbolt the engine mounts on both sides.

17. Unbolt the power steering fluid reservoir and swing it aside; then, using a chain hoist and cable, lift the engine and transmission upward and outward. An angle of about 45 de-

grees will allow the vehicle to be pushed backward while the engine is coming up.

To install:

18. With an assistant, install the engine and transmission into the vehicle using a chain hoist and cable. Lower the engine and transmission downward at an angle of about 45 degrees.

19. Connect the engine mounts on both sides and torque the bolts to 30 ft. lbs. (40 Nm).

20. Connect the speedometer cable and the front driveshaft U-joint.

21. Install the rear engine support and bolt the 2 outer bolts.

22. Install the exhaust pipe bracket to the transmission. On turbocharged models, connect the exhaust pipes at the turbocharger. Torque the pipe bolts to 25 ft. lbs. (34 Nm).

23. Install the clutch slave cylinder to the bellhousing and install the return spring.

24. Install the hydraulic line to the clutch housing and the oil line connectors to the automatic transmission.

25. The hydraulic engine shock absorber should be installed.

26. Tighten the steering relay arm to 15 ft. lbs. (20 Nm). Connect the steering damper to the steering linkage.

27. Attach the gearshift linkage and the exhaust pipes to the manifolds. Torque the manifold bolts to 25 ft. lbs. (34 Nm).

28. Connect all ground straps and electrical connections.

29. Connect the accelerator linkage.

30. Install the viscous coupling and fan.

31. Install all fuel, vacuum and oil hoses, e.g., power steering, power brakes and air cleaner.

32. Install the radiator, fan shroud and connect all heater hoses and oil cooler lines.

33. Refill the engine coolant and install the hood.

34. Install the battery and connect.

35. Bleed the hydraulic clutch, power steering, power brakes and fuel system.

Engine Mounts

REMOVAL AND INSTALLATION

Later model diesel engines are equipped with hydraulic engine mounts. Glycol liquid is located in 2 chambers that are connected to each other. The engine mount is mainte-

nance free and requires replacement of the entire assembly due to failure.

1. Disconnect the negative battery cable, raise the vehicle and support safely.

2. Remove the air intake hose and engine stop bracket.

3. Disconnect the frame crossmember-to-mount bolts. Disconnect the engine shock absorber by unbolting the bolts at the mount and remove from the frame side.

4. Install a suitable engine hoist to the front lifting lug and raise enough to take the pressure from the mount. Place pieces of wood between the engine and frame is case of hoist failure. Be careful not to damage the fan and shroud.

5. Remove the engine supporting bracket and engine mount. A hexagon socket may have to be used for this procedure.

To install:

6. Install the mount and torque the frame bolts to 30 ft. lbs. (40 Nm), hexagon socket screw for 4-Matic to 15 ft. lbs. (20 Nm) and the engine mount to support bracket bolts to 40 ft. lbs. (55 Nm).

7. Lower the engine and check for alignment.

8. Install the remaining components.

9. Connect the battery cable, start the engine and check for vibration.

Cylinder Head

REMOVAL AND INSTALLATION

Use care to ensure that the valve timing is not disturbed.

1. Disconnect the negative battery cable. Drain the radiator and remove all hoses and wires. Tag all wires to ensure easy reassembly.

2. Remove the camshaft cover and associated throttle linkage.

3. Remove the camshaft sprocket nut.

4. Remove the rockers and their supports must be removed together.

5. Mark the chain, sprocket and cam for ease of assembly.

6. Using a suitable puller, remove the camshaft sprocket.

7. Remove the sprocket and chain and wire it aside.

NOTE: Make sure the chain is securely wired so it will not slide into the engine.

8. Unbolt the manifolds and exhaust header pipe and push them aside.

9. Loosen the cylinder head holddown bolts, in the reverse order of the torque sequence. It is good practice to loosen each bolt, a little at a time, working around the head, until all are free.

10. Reach into the engine compartment and gradually work the head loose from each end by rocking it. Never use a prybar between the head and block to pry, as the head will be scarred badly and may be ruined.

--------- WARNING ---------
All diesel engines utilize cylinder head stretch-bolts. These bolts undergo a permanent stretch each time they are tightened. When a maximum length is reached, they must be discarded and replace with new bolts. When tightening the head bolts on these engines, it is imperative that the steps listed under ""Torque Specifications" are followed exactly.

To install:

11. Clean the gasket mating surfaces. Install the cylinder head using an approved hoist.

12. Torque the cylinder head bolts in sequence as found in the Torque Specifications chart.

13. Install the manifolds and exhaust header pipe. Torque the pipe to 24 ft. lbs. (34 Nm).

14. Install the sprocket and chain.

15. Install the rockers and their supports. Torque to 15 ft. lbs. (20 Nm).

16. Install the camshaft sprocket nut.

17. Install the camshaft cover and associated throttle linkage.

18. Connect the negative battery cable. Refill the radiator and install all hoses and wires.

Valve Lash

ADJUSTMENT

The 5 and 6 cylinder diesel engines use hydraulic valve lifters. There is no need or provision for valve clearance adjustments.

Rocker Arms

The diesel engine does not use rocker arms. The camshaft acts directly on the hydraulic valve tappet.

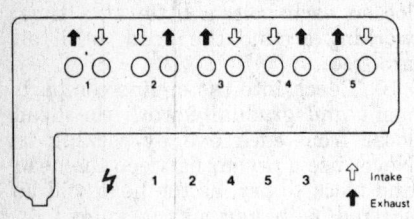

Valve arrangement — 5 cylinder diesel engine

Hydraulic Valve Tappet

Mercedes Benz call the valve tappets, hydraulic valve clearance compensating elements. These are big words for a simple component.

All diesel engines are equipped with hydraulic valve lifters. They can be checked by placing the camshaft on the base circle and use a non-metal tool to push the lifter down. If it is easier to press one lifter in comparison to the others, this one must be replaced.

REMOVAL AND INSTALLATION

Remove the cylinder head cover, camshaft and pull the lifter out with a magnetic tool.

Intake Manifold

REMOVAL AND INSTALLATION

1. Disconnect the negative battery cable.
2. Remove the engine ventilation tubes from the manifold.
3. Disconnect all electrical wiring, cables and hoses from the intake manifold.
4. Remove the manifold retaining bolts and manifold.
   To install:
5. Clean the gasket mating surfaces and install a new gasket.
6. Install the manifold and bolts. Torque the bolts to 18 ft. lbs. (25 Nm), working from the middle outward.
7. Install the remaining components and battery cable.
8. Start the engine and check for leaks.

Exhaust Manifold

REMOVAL AND INSTALLATION

1. Disconnect the negative battery cable.
2. Remove the exhaust pipe from the manifold.
3. Remove the manifold retaining bolts and manifold. It is not necessary to remove both exhaust manifolds for the 3.5L engine. Separate the gasket between cylinders 3 and 4.
   To install:
4. Clean the gasket mating surfaces and install a new gasket.
5. Install the manifold and bolts. Torque the bolts to 18 ft. lbs. (25 Nm), working from the middle outward.
6. Install the remaining components and battery cable.
7. Start the engine and check for leaks.

Turbocharger

REMOVAL AND INSTALLATION

1. Disconnect the negative battery cable. Remove the air filter.
2. Disconnect the electrical cable from the temperature switch.
3. Loosen the lower hose clamp on the air duct that connects the air filter with the compressor housing.
4. Remove the vacuum line and crankcase breather pipe.
5. Remove the air filter and air intake duct.
6. Disconnect the oil line at the turbocharger.
7. Remove the air filter mounting bracket.
8. Disconnect the turbocharger at the exhaust flange.
9. Disconnect and remove the pipe bracket on the automatic transmission.
10. Push the exhaust pipe rearward.
11. Remove the mounting bracket at the intermediate flange.
12. Unbolt and remove the turbocharger.
13. Remove the intermediate flange and oil return line at the turbocharger.
    To install:
14. Before installing the turbocharger, install the oil return line and intermediate flange.
15. Install the flange gasket between the turbocharger and exhaust manifold with the reinforcing bead

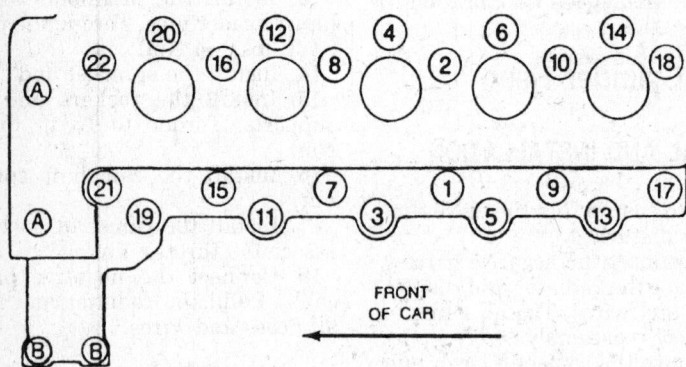

Cylinder head bolt torque sequence — 5 cylinder diesel engine

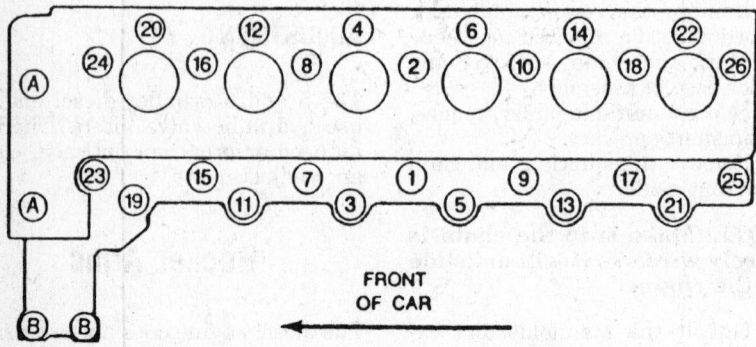

Cylinder head bolt torque sequence — 6 cylinder diesel engine

toward the exhaust manifold. Use only heat proof nuts and bolts.

16. Fill a new turbocharger with ¼ pint of engine oil through the engine oil supply bore before operating.

Timing Chain Cover

REMOVAL AND INSTALLATION

1. Disconnect the negative battery cable and drain the engine coolant.
2. Remove the engine compartment capsule, bottom section.
3. Remove the radiator, fan clutch, fan, crankshaft pulley, serpentine belt tensioner, vacuum pump, power steering pump, self-leveling suspension hydraulic pump and alternator.
4. Install a condenser guard plate.
5. Remove the cylinder head cover and charge air pipe.
6. Remove the oil dipstick tube.
7. Mark the position and remove the TDC sensor.
8. Install a suitable hoist to the engine lifting hooks. Remove the engine mounts and raise the engine.
9. Remove the timing cover-to-oil pan bolts.
10. Remove the Allen and hex bolts from the timing cover.
11. Carefully remove the cover from the engine. Be careful not to damage the oil pan and cylinder head gaskets.
   To install:
12. Use RTV sealer and a new gasket. Carefully Install the cover to the engine. Be careful not to damage the oil pan and cylinder head gaskets.
13. Install the Allen and hex bolts to the timing cover. Torque the bolts to 18 ft. lbs. (25 Nm).
14. Install the timing cover-to-oil pan bolts. Torque the small bolts to 7 ft. lbs. (10 Nm) and the large bolts to 18 ft. lbs. (25 Nm).
15. Install the engine mounts and lower the engine.

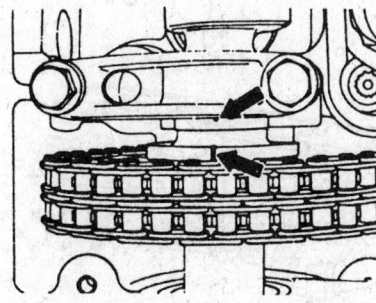

Camshaft timing marks — diesel engines

16. Install the TDC sensor.
17. Install the oil dipstick tube.
18. Install the cylinder head cover and charge air pipe.
19. Remove a condenser guard plate.
20. Install the radiator, fan clutch, fan, crankshaft pulley, serpentine belt tensioner, vacuum pump, power steering pump, self-leveling suspension hydraulic pump and alternator.
21. Install the engine compartment capsule, bottom section.
22. Connect the negative battery cable and refill the engine coolant.

Timing Chain Tensioner

FILLING WITH OIL

1. Place chain tensioner with thrust pin, in downward direction in, engine oil SAE 10 up to above collar on hex head.
2. Slowly press thrust pin 7-10 times up to stop, by means of a press or an upright drill press.
3. Upon filling, the chain tensioner should permit compressing very slowly only, uniformly and at considerable force.
4. To prevent peak pressures of chain tensioner against tensioning rail, a modified valve disk will be installed in chain tensioner.

REMOVAL AND INSTALLATION

1. Disconnect the negative battery cable.
2. Remove the timing chain tensioner from the passenger side of the engine.
   To install:
3. Renew the tensioner if there are complaints of engine noise to the timing chain.
4. Fill the tensioner with SAE 10 engine oil. Place the tensioner with the plunger bolt towards the oil and press the plunger up and down several times. It should be possible to compress the tensioner guide slowly, evenly and with little effort after filling with oil.
5. Install a new sealing ring and torque the tensioner to 48 ft. lbs. (65 Nm).

Timing Chain

REPLACEMENT

1. Disconnect the negative battery cable. Remove cylinder head cover.

2. Remove injection nozzles.
3. Remove chain tensioner.
4. Remove fan and fan cover.
5. Connect new timing chain with connecting link to old timing chain.
6. Slowly, rotate crankshaft in rotating direction of engine, while simultaneously pulling up the old timing chain until the connecting link comes to rest against uppermost point of camshaft timing gear.

NOTE: Timing chain should remain in mesh while rotating camshaft and crankshaft timing gears.

7. Take off old timing chain and connect ends of new timing chain with connecting link. For this purpose, secure chain ends with wire on camshaft timing gear.
   To install:

NOTE: Use only a rivet-type connecting link. Do not use connecting link that use a retaining spring.

8. Insert connecting link from the rear into timing chain.
9. Put separately enclosed outer flange of connecting link, with punched in IWIS identification, into pressing-on tool. The outer flange is held magnetically.
10. Place pressing-on tool on connecting link and press on flange up to stop, while holding pressing-on tool on vertical level.
11. Rearrange plunger, of assembly tool, so the notch is pointing forward.
12. Hold assembly tool on handle and rivet chain bolts individually. Tightening torque of spindle approximately 22-26 ft. lbs. (30-35 Nm).
13. Check chain bolt rivet and rivet again, if required.
14. Install chain tensioner.
15. Rotate crankshaft and check adjusting mark at TDC position of engine.

NOTE: If the adjusting mark is wrong, check timing of camshaft and begin of delivery of injection pump.

16. Install cylinder head cover and tighten to 7.5 ft. lbs. (10 Nm).
17. Install fan and fan cover.

Camshaft

REMOVAL AND INSTALLATION

1. Disconnect the negative battery cable. Remove cylinder head cover.

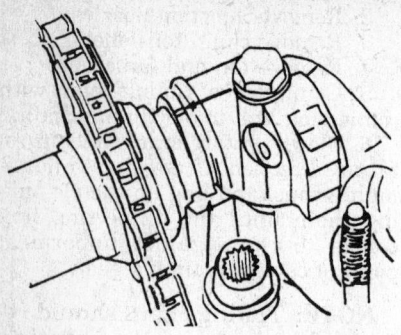

Camshaft alignment marks — 5 cylinder diesel engine

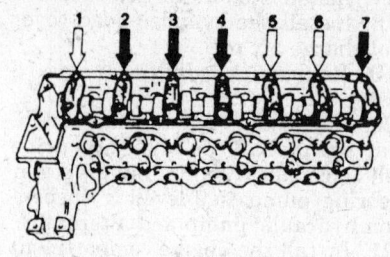

Camshaft bearing servicing sequence — 6 cylinder diesel engine

8. Remove camshaft in upward direction.

9. Remove the camshaft alignment circlip and check for misaligned condition.

10. Pull out valve tappet by means of solenoid lifter tool 102 589 03 40 00 or equivalent.

11. Check valve tappet for condition, visual checkup, and renew, if required.

To install:

NOTE: Install valve tappets only at the same spot where they were installed. If a new camshaft has been installed or if the cylinder head has been machined, check camshaft for easy operation.

12. Insert circlip for axial locating into cylinder head.

13. Lubricate camshaft and place into cylinder head, without valve tappet.

14. Tighten camshaft bearing caps uniformly to 18.5 ft. lbs. (25 Nm). Pay attention to identification of bearing caps.

15. When checking for easy operation, the camshaft can be rotated by means of a hex socket screw M10 x 30, which is screwed in through camshaft timing gear instead of fast-

2. Set crankshaft to TDC of No. 1 cylinder.

NOTE: Do not rotate the engine on the fastening screw of the camshaft timing gear; do not rotate engine in reverse.

3. Remove chain tensioner.

4. Mark the camshaft timing gear and timing chain in relation to each other.

5. Remove camshaft timing gear. To loosen screws, apply counter hold on camshaft by means of a mandrel.

6. If equipped with level control, remove pressure oil pump and place aside with lines connected.

7. To prevent damage to camshafts, be sure to apply the following sequence during assembly:

a. 2.5L engine — remove both screws on camshaft bearing 1, 2 and 6 (dark arrows). Loosen both screws on camshaft bearing 3, 4 and 5 alternately and in steps only until counter-pressure has been eliminated.

b. 3.5L engine — remove both screws on camshaft bearing 1, 5 and 6 (dark arrows). Loosen both screws for camshaft bearing 2, 3, 4 and 7 alternately and in steps only until counter-pressure has been eliminated.

1. Cylinder head
2. Center camshaft bearing brackets
3. Front camshaft bearing bracket
4. Rear camshaft bearing bracket
5. Clamping sleeve
6. Bolts (M8 × 45) — tightening torque 19 ft. lbs. (25 Nm)
7. Washer B 8,4
8. Cylinder head cover
9. Bolts (M6 × 30) — tightening torque 7 ft. lbs. (10 Nm)
10. Camshaft
11. Lock washer
12. Cylinder pin
13. Camshaft sprocket
14. Washer B 10
15. Bolt (M10 × 50) — tightening torque 48 ft. lbs. (65 Nm)
16. Timing chain
17. Chain tensioner

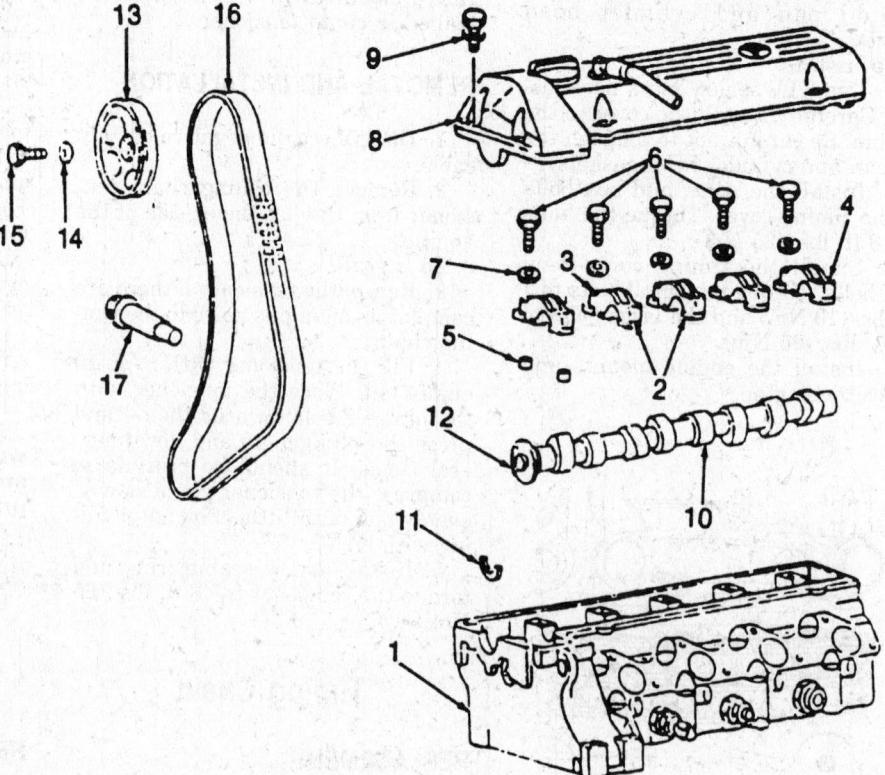

Camshaft and related components

ening screw. If the camshaft can be rotated with effort only, proceed as follows:

a. Loosen camshaft bearing caps individually. Turn camshaft, if required.

b. Repeat, until tight bearing point has been found.

c. Check camshaft for runout.

16. Lubricate valve tappets and insert. Pay attention to sequence.

17. Lubricate camshaft and place into cylinder head so the TDC mark is vertical.

18. Install camshaft bearing caps opposite of the loosening sequence. Torque the bearing caps to 18 ft. lbs. (25 Nm).

19. Mount camshaft timing gear. Pay attention to color marks. Tighten fastening screw for camshaft timing gear to 48 ft. lbs. (65 Nm). For this purpose, apply counter hold to camshaft timing gear by means of a steel pin or suitable tool.

20. Install chain tensioner.

21. If equipped with level control, mount pressure oil pump and driver.

22. Check engine for TDC marks.

23. Mount cylinder head cover.

24. Run engine, check for leaks.

Piston and Connecting Rod

POSITIONING

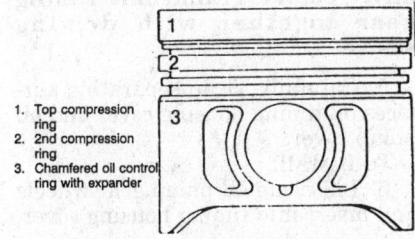

1. Top compression ring
2. 2nd compression ring
3. Chamfered oil control ring with expander

Piston ring positioning — diesel engine

ENGINE LUBRICATION

Oil Pan

REMOVAL AND INSTALLATION

4-MATIC

1. Disconnect the negative battery cable and drain the engine oil.

2. Remove the air filter assembly and bottom engine cowling.

3. Install a suitable hoist to the engine lifting hooks and take the weight off of the engine mounts.

4. Remove the engine mounts and brackets.

5. Remove the fan shroud and dipstick tube.

6. Disconnect the steering drag link with a removing tool 201589143300 or equivalent.

7. Remove the exhaust system and move out of the way.

8. Remove the front driveshaft and halfshafts.

9. Disconnect the oil level sensor.

10. Remove the oil sump bottom section and oil pump support.

11. Install a component protector plate.

12. Raise the engine.

13. Remove the left engine support at the crankcase.

14. Remove the front axle housing.

15. Remove the oil pan and pump assembly.

To install:

16. Install the oil pump assembly and torque the bolts to 18 ft. lbs. (25 Nm).

17. Install the front axle housing. Install the oil pan and torque the small bolts to 7 ft. lbs. (10 Nm) and the large bolts to 15 ft. lbs. (20 Nm).

18. Install the left engine support at the crankcase.

19. Remove the component protector plate.

20. Install the oil pan bottom section and oil pump support.

21. Connect the oil level sensor.

22. Install the front driveshaft and halfshafts.

23. Install the exhaust system.

24. Connect the steering drag link with a new self-locking nut.

25. Install the fan shroud and dipstick tube.

26. Install the engine mounts and brackets.

27. Remove the engine hoist.

28. Install the air filter assembly and bottom engine cowling.

29. Connect the negative battery cable and refill the engine oil. Start engine and check for leaks.

4 Cylinder Engine

1. Disconnect the negative battery cable and drain the engine oil.

2. Remove the air filter assembly, engine compartment fairing and suspension torsion bar.

3. Disconnect the oil level sensor.

4. Disconnect the fan shroud from the mounting and place over the fan.

5. Remove the exhaust pipe and move out of the way.

6. Remove the bolts from the transmission side.

7. Install a suitable engine hoist to the lifting hooks and raise. Disconnect the front engine mounts.

8. Remove the oil pan retaining bolts and oil pan.

To install:

9. Clean the gasket mating surfaces and install the oil pan. Torque the small bolts to 7 ft. lbs. (10 Nm) and the large bolts to 15 ft. lbs. (20 Nm).

10. Lower the engine and connect the front engine mounts.

11. Install the bolts to the transmission side.

12. Install the exhaust pipe.

13. Connect the fan shroud to the mounting.

14. Connect the oil level sensor.

15. Install the air filter assembly, engine compartment fairing and suspension torsion bar.

16. Connect the negative battery cable and refill the engine oil.

6 and 8 Cylinder, Except 4-MATIC and 500SL

NOTE: The front axle may have to be removed on 8 cylinder engines in the 107 and 126 models.

1. Disconnect the negative battery cable and drain the engine oil.

2. Remove the air filter assembly, engine compartment fairing and suspension sway bar. Remove the engine mount for model 107 and 126.

3. Disconnect the oil level sensor and automatic transmission cooler lines.

4. Disconnect the fan shroud from the mounting and place over the fan.

5. Remove the exhaust pipe and move out of the way. Disconnect the steering drag link for Models 129 and 201.

6. Remove the bolts from the transmission side, if equipped.

7. Install a suitable engine hoist to the lifting hooks and raise. Disconnect the front engine mounts.

8. Remove the oil pan retaining bolts and oil pan.

To install:

9. Clean the gasket mating surfaces and install the oil pan. Torque the small bolts to 7 ft. lbs. (10 Nm) and the large bolts to 15 ft. lbs. (20 Nm).

10. Lower the engine and connect the front engine mounts, if removed.

11. Install the bolts to the transmission side, if equipped.

12. Install the exhaust pipe.

13. Connect the fan shroud to the mounting.

14. Connect the oil level sensor.

15. Install the air filter assembly, engine compartment fairing and suspension torsion bar.

16. Install the remaining components.

17. Connect the negative battery cable and refill the engine oil.

500SL

1. Disconnect the battery cable and drain the engine oil.

2. Remove the air scoops and fan clutch.

3. Remove the fan belt and tensioner assembly.

4. Remove the air conditioning compressor and move out of the way with the hoses still connected.

5. Remove the TDC sensor at the timing cover.

6. Remove the air conditioning compressor bracket, alternator, air pump and fan carrier.

7. Disconnect the transmission fluid lines.

8. Remove the suspension sway bar.

9. Remove the bottom section of the oil pan and oil dipstick tube.

10. Install a suitable engine hoist to the lifting hooks and raise the engine enough to disconnect the front engine mounts.

11. Remove the oil pan retaining bolts, oil pan and gasket.

To install:

12. Clean the mating surfaces. Install the oil pan retaining bolts, oil pan and gasket. Torque the bolts to 8 ft. lbs. (11 Nm).

13. Lower the engine and connect the front engine mounts.

14. Install the bottom section of the oil pan and oil dipstick tube.

15. Install the suspension sway bar.

16. Connect the transmission fluid lines.

17. Install the air conditioning compressor bracket, alternator, air pump and fan carrier.

18. Install the TDC sensor at the timing cover.

19. Install the air conditioning compressor.

20. Install the fan belt and tensioner assembly.

21. Remove the air scoops and fan clutch.

22. Connect the battery cable and refill the engine oil.

12-Cylinder Engines

1. Disconnect the negative battery cable and drain the engine oil.

2. Remove the serpentine belt and air breather.

3. Remove the engine compartment paneling.

4. Disconnect the oil pressure and level sensor.

5. Disconnect the transmission fluid pipe.

6. Remove the air injection line from the oil pan.

7. Remove the front axle sway bar.

8. Remove the front springs, front axle and shock absorber.

9. Disconnect both engine mounts at the bottom.

10. Install an engine support bracket 140589016100. Attach the tool to the front and rear lifting lugs. Raise the engine slightly.

11. Remove the oil dipstick tube.

12. Remove the steering coupling cover, disconnect the steering coupling and move to the side.

13. Install a jack attachment 140589006200 to the front axle.

14. Remove the front axle retainers and lower the jack until enough clearance can be obtained to lower the oil pan.

15. Remove the alternator and oil cooler lines.

16. Remove the oil pan retaining bolts and remove the pan from the vehicle.

To install:

17. Clean the gasket mating surfaces.

18. Install the oil pan and retaining bolts. Torque the bolts to 7 ft. lbs. (10 Nm).

19. Install the alternator and oil cooler lines.

20. Install the front axle and retainers.

21. Remove the jack attachment 140589006200 from the front axle.

22. Install the steering coupling and cover.

23. Install the oil dipstick tube.

24. Connect both engine mounts at the bottom.

25. Remove the engine support bracket 140589016100 after the engine is in the mounts.

26. Install the front springs, front axle and shock absorber.

27. Install the front axle sway bar.

28. Install the air injection line to the oil pan.

29. Connect the transmission fluid pipe.

30. Connect the oil pressure and level sensor.

31. Install the engine compartment paneling.

32. Install the serpentine belt and air breather.

33. Connect the negative battery cable and refill the engine oil.

Oil Pump

REMOVAL AND INSTALLATION

4 Cylinder Engine

1. Disconnect the negative battery cable. Remove timing housing cover.

2. Remove screw and oil suction pipe with oil strainer, as well as oil pump cover.

3. Remove oil pump gear wheels from timing housing cover.

4. Check driving sleeve for damage or drive surface dents. Replace driving sleeve, if required.

NOTE: If driving sleeve cannot be pulled from crankshaft manually, remove crankshaft timing gear together with driving sleeve.

5. Carefully, clean separating surfaces on timing housing cover and oil pump cover.

To install:

6. Lubricate oil pump gear wheels and insert into timing housing cover.

NOTE: Renew oil pump gear wheels only in pairs. For this reason, they are supplied as a spare part in a set, rotor set, only.

7. Renew sealing ring on connection of oil pump cover.

8. Mount oil pump cover on timing housing cover. Position oil suction pipe with oil strainer and with new gasket on oil pump cover. Screw in fastening screws and tighten to 7.5 ft. lbs. (10 Nm).

NOTE: Pay attention to correct installation of gasket between flange of oil suction pipe and oil pump cover.

9. Check oil pump for easy operation.

10. Slip driving sleeve on crankshaft.

11. Install timing housing cover.

12. Check for leaks with engine running.

6 Cylinder Engine

1. Drain the oil and remove the oil pan and gasket.

2. Remove the oil sump.

3. Remove the pump sprocket and bolt. Remove the chain and sprocket as an assembly.

4. Remove the oil pump mounting bolts and remove the pump.

To install:

5. Install a new gasket, oil pump and torque the mounting bolts to 18 ft. lbs. (25 Nm).

6. Install the pump sprocket and torque to 24 ft. lbs. (32 Nm).

7. Install the oil pan and fill with oil.

8. Start the engine and check for leaks.

4-MATIC

1. Disconnect the negative battery cable and drain the engine oil.

2. Remove the air filter assembly and bottom engine cowling.

3. Install a suitable hoist to the engine lifting hooks and take the weight off of the engine mounts.

4. Remove the engine mounts and brackets.

5. Remove the fan shroud and dip-stick tube.

6. Disconnect the steering drag link with a removing tool 201589143300 or equivalent.

7. Remove the exhaust system and move out of the way.

8. Remove the front driveshaft and halfshafts.

9. Disconnect the oil level sensor.

10. Remove the oil sump bottom section and oil pump support.

11. Install a component protector plate.

12. Raise the engine.

13. Remove the left engine support at the crankcase.

14. Remove the front axle housing.

15. Remove the oil pump assembly.

To install:

16. Install the oil pump assembly and torque the bolts to 18 ft. lbs. (25 Nm).

17. Install the front axle housing. Torque the small bolts to 7 ft. lbs. (10 Nm) and the large bolts to 15 ft. lbs. (20 Nm).

18. Install the left engine support at the crankcase.

19. Remove the component protector plate.

20. Install the oil sump bottom section and oil pump support.

21. Connect the oil level sensor.

22. Install the front driveshaft and halfshafts.

23. Install the exhaust system.

24. Connect the steering drag link with a new self-locking nut.

25. Install the fan shroud and dipstick tube.

26. Install the engine mounts and brackets.

27. Remove the engine hoist.

28. Install the air filter assembly and bottom engine cowling.

29. Connect the negative battery cable and refill the engine oil. Start engine and check for leaks.

8-Cylinder Engine

1. Disconnect the negative battery cable. Drain engine oil.

2. Remove oil pan lower half.

3. Place compensating weight of first crankpin in horizontal position.

4. Remove screws.

5. Loosen screw on drive sprocket, tilt oil pump toward rear and remove screw.

6. Push drive sprocket away from oil pump by means of a suitable tool and remove oil pump.

To install:

7. Lift drive sprocket from drive chain.

8. Engage drive sprocket in drive chain.

9. Push oil pump on drive sprocket. Dowel sleeve in drive sprocket should enter cutout in driveshaft.

10. Tilt oil pump to rear, screw-in screw and tighten to 21 ft. lbs. (28 Nm).

11. Screw-in fastening screws and tighten to 18.5 ft. lbs. (25 Nm).

12. Install oil pan lower half with new gasket and tighten fastening screw to 7.5 ft. lbs. (10 Nm) for M6 bolts or 18.5 ft. lbs. (25 Nm) for M8 bolts.

13. Fill with engine oil.

14. Run engine and check for leaks.

12-Cylinder Engine

1. Disconnect the negative battery cable and drain the engine oil.

2. Remove the oil lever sensor and oil pan.

3. Remove the oil pump drive sprocket and oil pickup tube.

4. Remove the oil pump retaining bolts and oil pump.

To install:

NOTE: Mount sprocket so the rise points toward oil pump and the trochoid shape corresponds with that on oil pump shaft.

5. Fill the oil pump with clean engine oil. Install the pump and torque the small bolts to 80 inch lbs. (9 Nm) and the large bolts to 15 ft. lbs. (21 Nm).

6. Install the oil pickup and torque to 7 ft. lbs. (10 Nm).

7. Install oil pan.

8. Run engine, check for leaks.

Diesel Engine

1. Disconnect the negative battery cable. Remove oil pan and sump.

2. Remove the front axle housing for diesel engines.

3. Remove screw from sprocket and remove sprocket from driveshaft.

4. Remove screws and remove oil pump.

To install:

5. Position oil pump and torque screw to 18.5 ft. lbs. (25 Nm).

6. Install the drive sprocket so the curvature is facing the oil pump and torque the sprocket bolt to 18 ft. lbs. (25 Nm). On the 2.5L engine, the additional screw is torqued to 7.5 ft. lbs. (10 Nm), if equipped.

7. Install the oil sump and torque the bolts to 7 ft. lbs. (10 Nm).

NOTE: Mount sprocket so the rise points toward oil pump and the trochoid shape corresponds with that on oil pump shaft.

8. Install oil pan.

9. Run engine, check for leaks.

Rear Main Bearing Oil Seal

REMOVAL AND INSTALLATION

All engines use a 1 piece radial seal.

1. Disconnect the negative battery cable.

2. Remove the transmission and drive plate.

3. Pry out the seal with a suitable prybar rapped with a rag.

To install:

4. Use a seal installer 117589004300 or equivalent, to drive the seal into the retainer. Coat the seal with engine oil before installation.

5. The dust lip must not be resting on the crankshaft. The seal must be seated evenly, unless the seal will leak.

6. Install the driveplate and transmission.

1. Screw—tightening torque 19 ft. lbs. (25 Nm)
2. Oil pump sprocket
3. Screw—tightening torque 19 ft. lbs. (25 Nm)
4. Screw (engines 602 and 603 only)—tightening torque 7 ft. lbs. (10 Nm)
5. Oil pump (engine 601)
6. Oil pump (engine 602 and 603)

Oil pump servicing — diesel engine

1. Cylinder head cover
2. Screw—tightening torque 7 ft. lbs. (10 Nm)
3. Screw
4. Hydraulic oil pump
5. O-ring
6. Driven plate
7. Hex. head sprocket screw
8. Drive sleeve

Hydraulic oil pump servicing — diesel engine

7. Connect the battery cable, start the engine and check for leaks.

ENGINE COOLING

Radiator

REMOVAL AND INSTALLATION

Models 300D, 300TD, 300SDL, 350SD and 350SDL

NOTE: After refilling the cooling system, the system may have to be bled. Remove a cooling sensor or equivalent at the highest point in the engine's cooling system. Fill the radiator until coolant spills out of the hole. Apply thread sealing tape to the component and install. Finish filling the radiator to the proper level.

1. Disconnect the negative battery cable. If equipped with an automatic transmission, pinch oil lines from or to transmission with special tool 000 589 40 37 00 or equivalent, displacing coil spring slightly laterally and removing from radiator for this purpose.

2. Disconnect coolant hoses on radiator.

3. Pull out flat contour springs for fan cover, slightly lift fan cover and place over fan.

4. On 300D and 300TD models, remove expanding rivets for lateral radiator paneling right and left.

5. On some models, pull off holding clamps at right and left below.

6. Pull out flat contour springs for radiator and lift out radiator.

To install:

7. Reverse the removal procedure. Take note that the fastening mounts of the radiator are correctly introduced into rubber grommets of lower holders and the holders of the fan cover into holding lugs on radiator.

8. Fill with coolant, pressure test cooling system with tester and check for leaks.

Except models 300D, 300TD, 300SDL, 350SD and 350SDL

NOTE: After refilling the cooling system, the system may have to be bled. Remove a cooling sensor or equivalent, at the highest point in the engine's cooling system. Fill the radiator until coolant spills out of the hole. Apply thread sealing tape to the component and install. Finish filling the radiator to the proper level.

1. Disconnect the negative battery cable. Remove the radiator cap.

2. Unscrew the radiator drain plug and drain the coolant from the radiator. If all of the coolant in the system is to be drained, move the heater controls to WARM and open the drain cocks on the engine block.

3. If equipped with an oil cooler, drain the oil from the cooler.

4. If equipped, loosen the radiator shell.

5. Loosen the hose clips on the top and bottom radiator hoses and remove the hoses from the connections on the radiator.

6. Unscrew and plug the bottom line on the oil cooler.

7. If equipped with an automatic transmission, unscrew and plug the lines on the transmission cooler.

8. Disconnect the right and left side rubber loops and pull the radiator up and from the body.

To install:

9. Inspect and replace any hoses which have become hardened or spongy.

10. Install the radiator shell and radiator, if the shell was removed, from the top and connect the top and bottom hoses to the radiator.

11. Bolt the shell to the radiator.

12. Attach the rubber loops or position the retaining spring, as applicable.

13. Position the hose clips on the top and bottom hoses.

14. Attach the lines to the oil cooler.

15. If equipped with an automatic transmission, connect the lines to the transmission cooler.

16. Move the heater levers to the WARM position and slowly add coolant, allowing air to escape.

17. Check the oil level and fill if necessary. Run the engine for about 1 minute at idle with the filler neck open.

18. Add coolant to the specified level. Install the radiator cap and turn it until it seats in the 2nd notch. Run the engine and check for leaks.

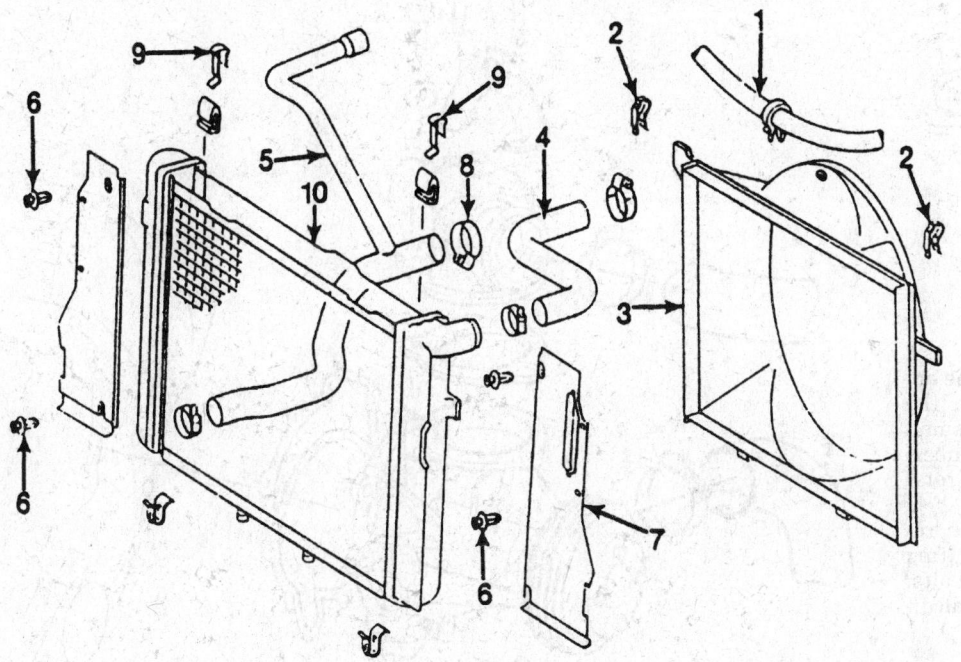

1. Clip with vent line
2. Clamps
3. Fan cover
4. Upper coolant hose
5. Lower coolant hose
6. Expanding rivet
7. Radiator cover left
8. Radiator cover right
9. Holding clamps
10. Radiator

Exploded view of the radiator assembly, other cooling systems similar

Water Pump

REMOVAL AND INSTALLATION

Gasoline Engines

4-CYLINDER ENGINE

NOTE: After refilling the cooling system, the system may have to be bleed. Remove a cooling sensor or equivalent at the highest point in the engine's cooling system. Fill the radiator until coolant spills out of the hole. Apply thread sealing tape to the component and install. Finish filling the radiator to the proper level.

1. Disconnect the negative battery cable. Drain coolant.
2. Remove air cleaner.
3. Remove radiator.
4. Loosen hose clamps and disconnect heater return line and coolant hose from coolant pump.
5. Remove fan.
6. Remove pulley of water pump.
7. Remove hex socket screws, slacken water pump V-belt and remove.
8. Pull cable from magnetic body, remove fastening screws and remove magnetic body.

9. Remove screws and place alternator with front holder aside.
10. Loosen lower hose clamp of bypass line, unscrew fastening screws and remove water pump.
11. Carefully clean sealing surfaces on water pump housing and timing housing cover.
   To install:
12. Apply gasket adhesive to gasket and pump.
13. Install pump and torque bolts to 7.5 ft. lbs. (10 Nm).
14. Complete installation by reversing removal procedure. Fill coolant system and check for leaks.

6-CYLINDER ENGINE

1. Disconnect the negative battery cable and drain the cooling system.
2. Remove the air scoop hose and viscous fan clutch.
3. Loosen and remove the serpentine belts.
4. Remove the water pump drive pulley.
5. Remove the bottom engine cover, if equipped.
6. Do not disconnect refrigerant hoses. Remove the air conditioning compressor and lay aside.
7. Remove all water and heater hoses from the pump.

8. Remove the tandom pump and move to the side. Remove the thermostat housing bolts and housing.
9. Remove the pump mounting bolts and slide the pump up and out of the engine compartment.
   To install:
10. If removed, install the thermostat so the ball valve is at the highest point. Install a new seal.
11. Install a new water pump seal and torque the retaining bolts to 18 ft. lbs. (25 Nm).
12. Install the remaining components. Torque the water pump pulley bolts to 7 ft. lbs. (10 Nm) and compressor bolts to 18 ft. lbs. (25 Nm).

8-CYLINDER ENGINE

1. Disconnect the negative battery cable. Drain the water from the radiator and block.
2. Remove the air cleaner.
3. Loosen and remove the drive belt.
4. Disconnect the upper water hose from the radiator and thermostat housing.
5. Remove the fan and coupling.
6. Remove the hose from the intake (top) connection of the water pump.
7. Set the engine at TDC. Matchmark the distributor and engine and

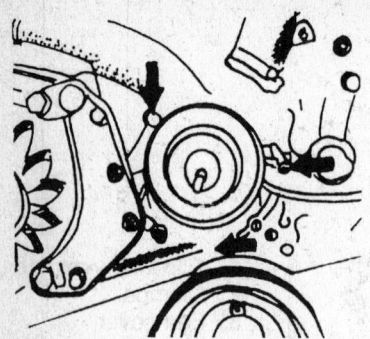

Water pump servicing — 5 cylinder diesel engine

remove the distributor. Crank the engine with a socket wrench on the crankshaft pulley bolt or with a small prybar inserted in the balancer. Crank in the normal direction of rotation only.

8. Turn the balancer so the recesses provide access to the mounting bolts. Remove the mounting bolts. Rotate the engine in the normal direction of rotation only.

9. Remove the water pump.

To install:

10. Clean the mounting surfaces of the water pump and block.

11. Installation is the reverse of removal. Always use a new gasket. Set

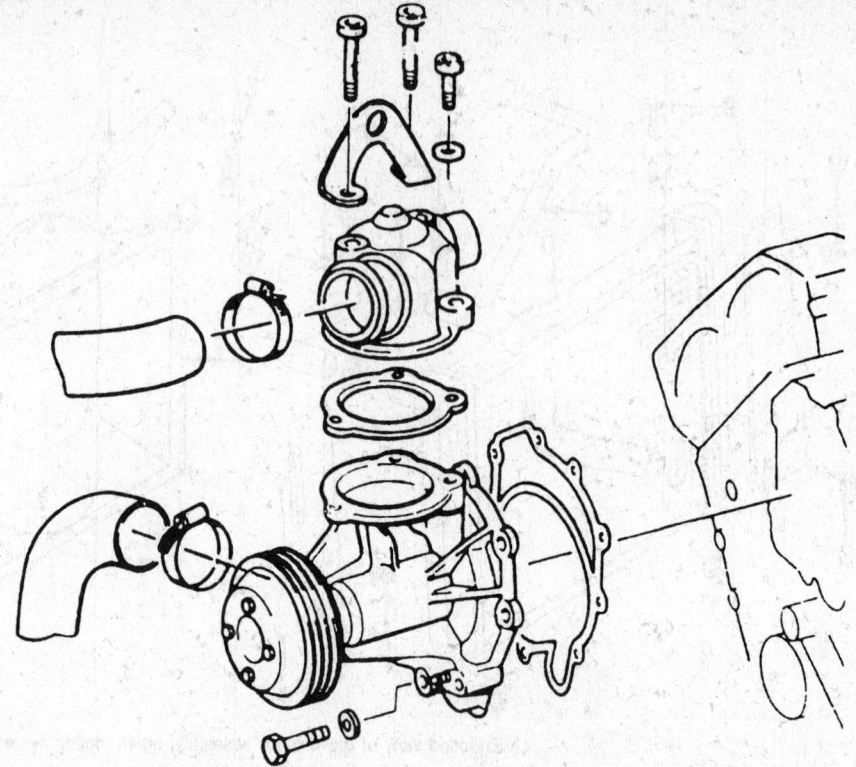

Water pump assembly — 8 cylinder DOHC engine, others similar

1. Hex head screw (engine 601) — tightening torque 19 ft. lbs. (25 Nm)
2. Fan
3. Hex head socket — tightening torque 7 ft. lbs. (10 Nm)
4. Pulley
5. Magnet, body
6. Hex head socket screw (engines 602, 603) — tightening torque 33 ft. lbs. (45 Nm)
7. Fan with visco-fan clutch
8. Hex head screw — tightening torque 7 ft. lbs. (10 Nm)
9. Pulley
10. Hex head screw — tightening torque 7 ft. lbs. (10 Nm)
11. Coolant pump
12. Gasket

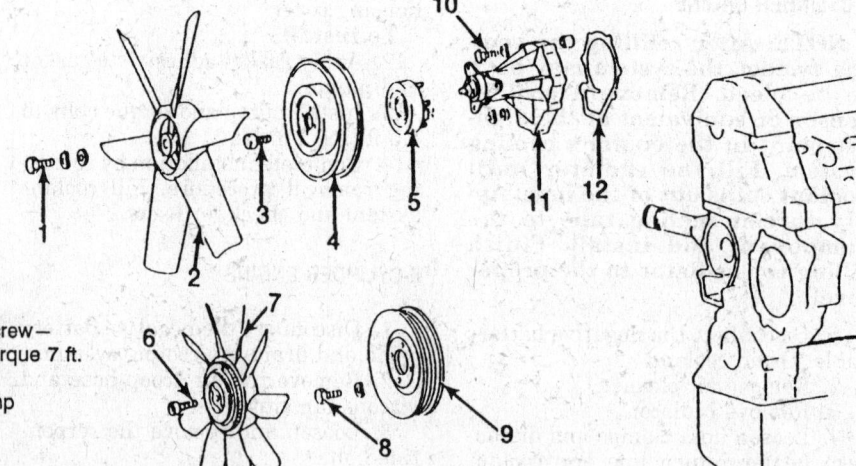

Exploded view of the water pump assembly — diesel engine

the engine at TDC and install the distributor rotor points to the notch on the distributor housing. Fill the cooling system and check and adjust the ignition timing.

12-CYLINDER ENGINE

1. Disconnect the negative battery cable and drain the engine coolant.
2. Remove the radiator and thermostat housing.
3. Loosen the bolts for the water pump pulley and fan clutch.
4. Remove the belt, fan and pulley.
5. Remove the idler pulley.
6. Disconnect the coolant hoses.

7. Remove the retaining bolts and water pump.

To install:

8. Clean the gasket mating surfaces.
9. Install the pump, gasket and bolts. Torque the bolts to 15 ft. lbs. (21 Nm).
10. Connect the coolant hoses.
11. Install the idler pulley.
12. Install the belt, fan and pulley. Torque the bolts to 7 ft. lbs. (10 Nm).
13. Install the radiator and thermostat housing.
14. Connect the negative battery cable and refill the engine coolant.

DIESEL ENGINE

NOTE: After refilling the cooling system, the system may have to be bled. Remove a cooling sensor or equivalent, at the highest point in the engine's cooling system. Fill the radiator until coolant spills out of the hole. Apply thread sealing tape to the component and install. Finish filling the radiator to the proper level.

1. Disconnect the negative battery cable. Remove fan and remove together with fan cover, if necessary.
2. Loosen fan cover and place on fan. Remove viscous fan clutch using

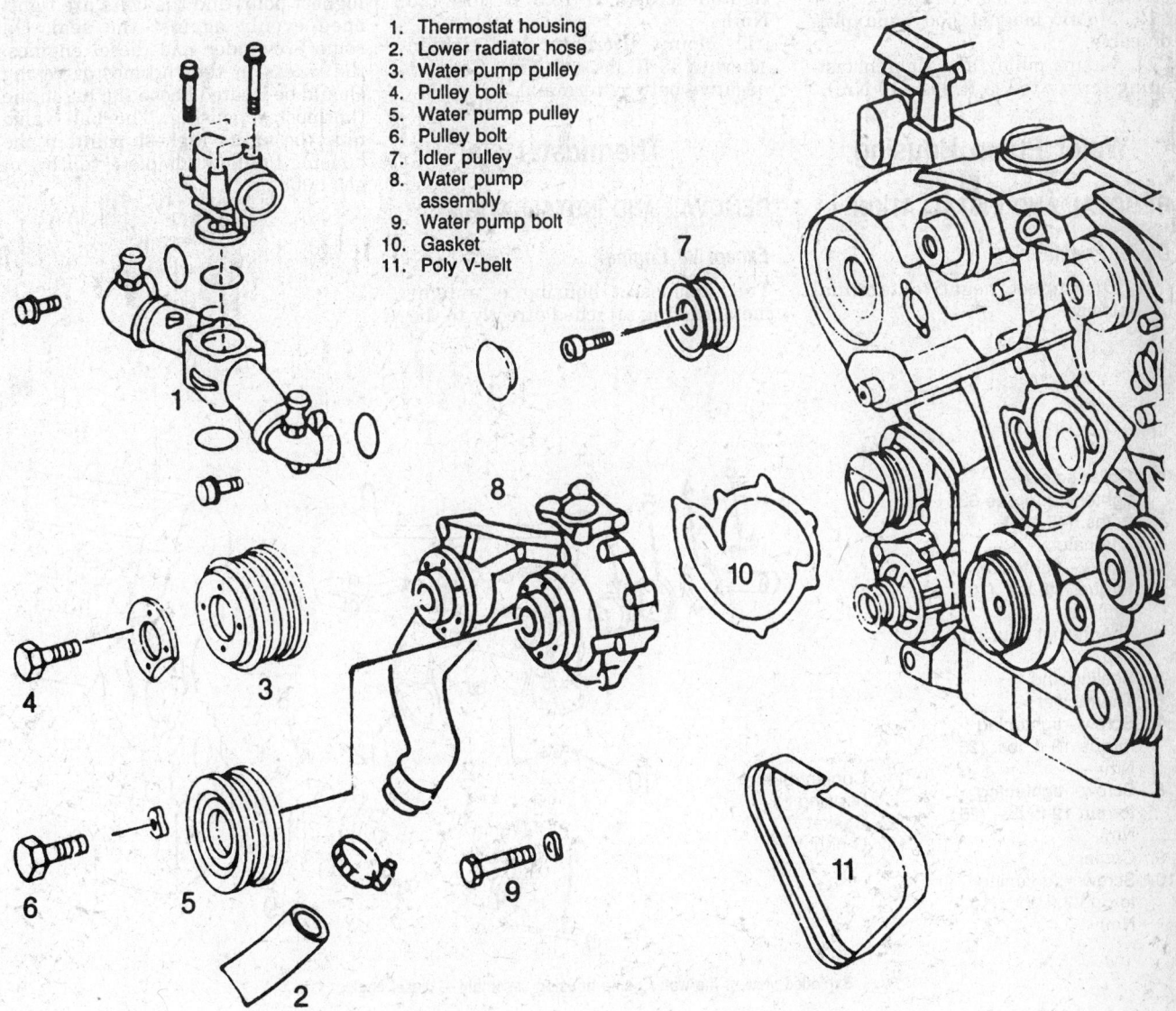

1. Thermostat housing
2. Lower radiator hose
3. Water pump pulley
4. Pulley bolt
5. Water pump pulley
6. Pulley bolt
7. Idler pulley
8. Water pump assembly
9. Water pump bolt
10. Gasket
11. Poly V-belt

Exploded view of the water pump and thermostat assembly — 12 cylinder engine

prybar element 103 589 01 09 00 or equivalent, torque wrench 001 589 72 21 00 or equivalent, and counter holder 603 589 00 40 00 or equivalent, for this purpose.

3. Remove fastening screws and pulley.

4. Remove hex nuts and magnet body.

5. The magnet carrier is glued to the water pump housing and should not be pulled off.

6. Remove water pump housing.

7. Clean sealing surfaces.

To install:

8. Insert water pump with a new gasket and tighten combination screws to 7.5 ft. lbs. (10 Nm).

9. Mount water pump with a new gasket and tighten combination screws to 7.5 ft. lbs. (10 Nm).

10. Mount magnet body and plug on cable.

11. Mount pulley and tighten fastening screws to 7.5 ft. lbs. (10 Nm).

Water Pump Housing

REMOVAL AND INSTALLATION

Diesel Engine

1. Disconnect negative terminal on battery.

2. Remove alternator and place it aside.

3. Remove alternator carrier.

4. Remove return line on crankcase and pull from water pump housing.

5. Remove water pump housing.

6. Clean sealing surfaces.

To install:

7. Renew O-ring on return line.

NOTE: Keep O-ring free of grease. For better assembly, immerse O-ring into coolant.

8. Plug coolant pump housing on return line and screw with a gasket to crankcase, tighten to 7.5 ft. lbs. (10 Nm).

9. Screw return line to crankcase.

10. Mount alternator carrier and tighten screws to 18.5 ft. lbs. (25 Nm).

11. Mount alternator and tighten screw to 33 ft. lbs. (45 Nm). Connect negative battery terminal.

Thermostat

REMOVAL AND INSTALLATION

Except V8 Engine

The thermostat housing is a light metal casting attached directly to the cylinder head. Some 6 cylinder and diesel engines have the thermostat housing attached to the side or top of the water pump housing.

1. Disconnect the negative battery cable. Open the radiator cap and depressurize the system.

2. Open the radiator drain cock and partially drain the coolant. Drain enough coolant to bring the coolant level below the level of the thermostat housing.

3. Remove the thermostat housing cover bolts and cover.

4. Note the installation position of the thermostat and remove it.

To install:

5. Installation is the reverse of removal. Be sure the thermostat is positioned with the ball valve at the highest point and the bolts are tightened evenly against the seal. On some 6 cylinder and diesel engines, the recess in the thermostat casing should be located above the lug in the thermostat housing. The ball valve must be at its highest point in the housing to allow complete venting of gas bubbles.

1. Collar screw—tightening torque 33 ft. lbs. (45 Nm)
2. Alternator
3. Screw—tightening torque 7 ft. lbs. (10 Nm)
4. Thermostat housing cap
5. Sealing ring
6. Thermostat
7. Screw—tightening torque 19 ft. lbs. (25 Nm)
8. Screw—tightening torque 19 ft. lbs. (25 Nm)
9. Carrier
10. Screw—tightening torque 7 ft. lbs. (10 Nm)
11. Coolant pump housing
12. Gasket
13. O-ring

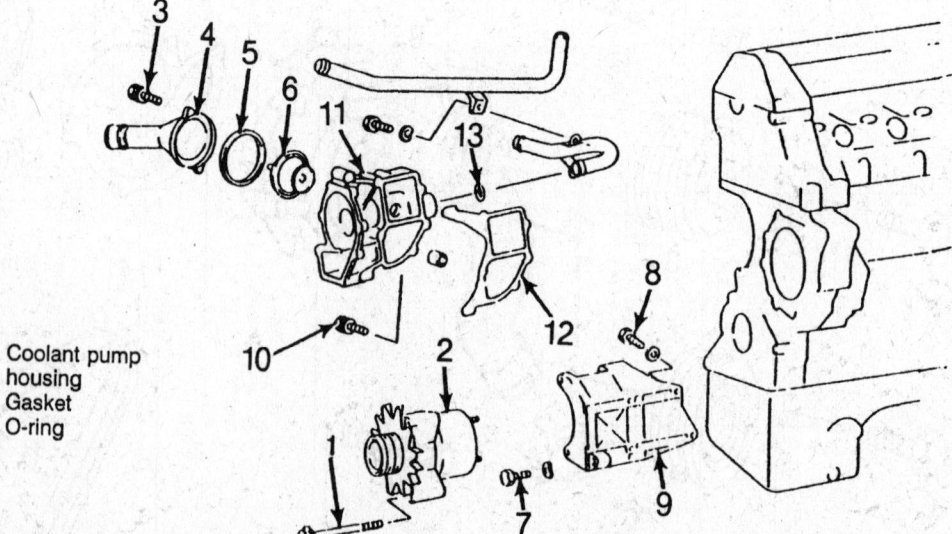

Exploded view of the water pump housing assembly — diesel engine

6. Refill the cooling system and check for leaks.

NOTE: When refilling the coolant system, always remove the hex-head plug on the left side of the cylinder head and fill the hole with coolant until it overflows. Install the plug and fill the coolant system, if equipped. Early model vehicles have a vent screw on top of the thermostat housing. Open the vent approximately 2 turns, start the engine run the engine at idle.

V8 Engine

1. Drain the coolant from the radiator and block.
2. Remove the air cleaner.
3. Disconnect the battery and remove the alternator.
4. Unscrew the housing cover on the side of the water pump and remove the thermostat.
5. If a new thermostat is to be installed, always install a new sealing ring.
   To install:
6. Install the thermostat so the ball valve is at the highest point in the housing.
7. Be sure to tighten the screws on the housing cover evenly to prevent leaks. Refill the cooling system and check of leaks.

12-Cylinder Engine

1. Disconnect the negative battery cable and drain the engine coolant.
2. Remove the fan cowl ring and lay over the fan.
3. Disconnect the cooling hoses from the thermostat housing.
4. Remove the thermostat housing and pivot 90 degrees toward the front.
5. Remove the temperature sensors.
6. Remove the housing holder 4 bolts and holder.

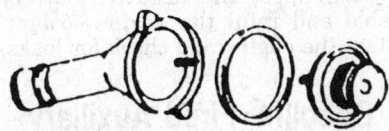

Aligning the thermostat — diesel engine shown, others similar

7. Remove the housing cover and thermostat.
   To install:
8. Install the thermostat so the ball valve is positioned at the highest point.
9. Install the cover and torque the small bolts to 80 inch lbs. (9 Nm) and the large bolts to 15 ft. lbs. (21 Nm).
10. Install the holder assembly and torque the bolts to 15 ft. lbs. (21 Nm).
11. Install the temperature sensors.
12. Install the thermostat housing and pivot 90 degrees toward the front.
13. Connect the cooling hoses to the thermostat housing.
14. Install the fan cowl ring.
15. Connect the negative battery cable, refill the engine coolant and check for air pockets and leaks.

Heater Core

REMOVAL AND INSTALLATION

Model 107

1. Disconnect the negative battery cable and drain the engine coolant.
2. Remove the grille for the air inlet on both sides.
3. Disconnect the heater hoses.
4. Remove the instrument panel assembly.
5. Disconnect the control cables, electrical connectors and vacuum hoses, if equipped.
6. Remove the left and right air duct.
7. Remove the holder between the center air duct and tunnel.
8. Loosen the nut on both connecting levers and pull connecting lever from the shaft including serrated washer.
9. Pull out center air duct with controls toward the rear. Remove the right only on vehicles with automatic transmission.
10. Remove the radio holder on the crossmember.
11. Remove the fuel injection Electronic Control Unit (ECU).
12. Remove the heater box retaining bolts.
13. Pull the heater box back until the heater pipes are disconnected from the rubber grommet in the front firewall.
14. Remove the heater box to the right under the crossmember.
15. Remove the box clips and separate the 2 halves.
16. Remove the heater core from the heater box.

To install:
17. Install the heater core to the heater box. Make sure the seal are in good condition and positioned properly.
18. Install the box clips.
19. Install the heater box to the right under the crossmember.
20. Connect to the rubber grommet in the front firewall.
21. Install the heater box retaining bolts.
22. Install the fuel injection Electronic Control Unit (ECU).
23. Install the radio holder on the crossmember.
24. Push in the center air duct with controls toward the rear.
25. Install the holder between the center air duct and tunnel.
26. Install the left and right hand air duct.
27. Connect the control cables, electrical connectors and vacuum hoses, if equipped.
28. Install the instrument panel assembly.
29. Connect the heater hoses.
30. Install the grille for the air inlet on both sides.
31. Connect the negative battery cable and refill the engine coolant.

Model 124

1. Disconnect the negative battery cable and drain the engine coolant.
2. Disconnect the heater inlet and outlet hoses. Blow the remaining coolant from the core using compressed air.
3. Remove the instrument panel assembly.
4. Remove the 6 clips and 2 screws from the upper air tube.
5. Disconnect the pipes on the heater core and swing away.
6. Remove the heater core from the top of the heater box.
   To install:
7. Install the heater core into the top of the heater box with 3 new sealing rings.
8. Connect the pipes on the heater core.
9. Install the 6 clips and 2 screws to the upper air tube.
10. Install the instrument panel assembly.
11. Connect the heater inlet and outlet hoses.
12. Connect the negative battery cable and refill the engine coolant. Check for leaks.

Model 126 and 201

1. Disconnect the negative battery cable and drain the engine coolant.

2. Push back both front seats and cover.

3. Remove the instrument panel and center console assembly.

4. Remove the ABS control unit and disconnect the heater hoses.

5. Disconnect the front and rear heating ducts from the heater box.

6. Disconnect the electronic switching unit and all other electrical connectors, hoses and cables, if equipped. Move all components out of the way and secure.

7. Remove the bracket bolts from both side of the heater box.

8. Loosen the cable straps on the housing.

9. Disconnect the air duct for fresh air nozzle.

10. Remove the heater box retainers that are accessible.

11. Pull the heater box so the heating hoses can be disconnected from the firewall.

12. Lift out the heater box over the passenger side. Hold the heater hoses upward to prevent coolant spillage.

13. Remove the clips and screws and separate the case halves. Remove the heater core from the box.

To install:

14. Install the heater core into the box and position the rubber seals. Install the brackets and other hardware.

15. Install the heater box over the passenger side.

16. Connect the heating hoses.

17. Install the heater box retainers that are accessible.

18. Connect the air duct for fresh air nozzle.

19. Loosen the cable straps on the housing.

20. Install the bracket bolts from both side of the heater box.

21. Connect the electronic switching unit and all other electrical connectors, hoses and cables, if equipped.

22. Connect the front and rear heating ducts to the heater box.

23. Install the ABS control unit.

24. Install the instrument panel and center console assembly.

25. Connect the negative battery cable and refill the engine coolant. Check for leaks and proper operation.

Model 129

1. Disconnect the negative battery cable and drain the engine coolant.

2. Discharge the air conditioning system according to state and federal CFC regulations. Always use a R-12 recycling system.

3. Remove wiper motor and linkage.

4. Remove the left and right water drain.

5. Remove the center partition wall and housing.

6. Disconnect the heater hoses from the core.

7. Remove the nut and withdraw the A/C piping from the expansion valve.

8. Remove the instrument panel and center console.

9. Label and disconnect all electrical connectors, hoses, vacuum lines and cables from the area. Move out of the way and secure.

10. Disconnect the air ducts and remove the crossmember.

11. Remove the bracket and hoses.

12. Remove the air scoop and connecting plate at the switchover valve block.

13. Remove the 4 nuts and heater box.

14. Remove the bolts and clips from the heater box. Remove the heater core from the top of the box.

To install:

15. Install the heater core into the box and position the rubber seals. Install the brackets and other hardware.

16. Install the bolts and clips to the heater box.

17. Install the 4 nuts and heater box.

18. Install the air scoop and connecting plate at the switchover valve block.

19. Install the bracket and hoses.

20. Connect the air ducts and install the crossmember.

21. Connect all electrical connectors, hoses, vacuum lines and cables.

22. Install the instrument panel and center console.

23. Install the A/C piping to the expansion valve.

24. Connect the heater hoses to the core.

25. Install the center partition wall and housing.

26. Install the left and right water drain.

27. Install wiper motor and linkage.

28. Evacuate and recharge the air conditioning system according to state and federal CFC regulations. Always use a R-12 recycling system.

29. Connect the negative battery cable and refill the engine coolant.

Model 140

1. Disconnect the negative battery cable and drain the engine coolant.

2. Remove the windshield wiper system.

3. Remove the water collector.

4. Disconnect the heater hoses from the heater core.

5. Disconnect and remove the pre-resistor group.

6. Disconnect the electrical connectors at the blower carrier.

7. Remove the instrument panel and center console.

8. Remove the insulation mat above the heater unit.

9. Remove the rear footwell air ducts.

10. Label and disconnect all electrical connectors, hoses and cables. Move out of the way and secure.

11. Remove the airbag belt control unit.

12. Remove the cross member and brackets in front and sides of the heater box.

13. Disconnect the defroster tubes.

14. Remove the heater box retaining nuts. Pull the box out to the rear. Be careful not to spill the engine coolant inside this big buck vehicle.

15. Remove the bolts and clips from the heater box. Remove the heater core from the top of the box.

To install:

16. Install the heater core into the box and position the rubber seals. Install the brackets and other hardware.

17. Install the heater box and retaining nuts.

18. Connect the defroster tubes.

19. Install the crossmember and brackets.

20. Install the airbag belt control unit.

21. Connect all electrical connectors, hoses and cables.

22. Install the rear footwell air ducts.

23. Install the insulation mat above the heater unit.

24. Install the instrument panel and center console.

25. Connect the electrical connectors at the blower carrier.

26. Connect the pre-resistor group.

27. Connect the heater hoses to the heater core.

28. Install the water collector.

29. Install the windshield wiper system.

30. Connect the negative battery cable and refill the engine coolant. Start the engine and check for leaks.

Gasoline Fired Auxiliary Heater

REMOVAL AND INSTALLATION

1. Disconnect the negative battery cable and drain the engine coolant.

2. Remove the air cleaner assembly.

3. Pinch off fuel hose and disconnect.

4. Disconnect the coolant hoses and exhaust gas line.

5. Disconnect the electrical connectors.

6. Loosen the retaining bolts for the holder and remove the heating unit with the supply unit.

To install:

7. Install the heating unit with the supply unit.

8. Connect the electrical connectors.

9. Connect the coolant hoses and exhaust gas line.

10. Install the air cleaner assembly.

11. Connect the negative battery cable and refill the engine coolant. Check the heater for proper function.

Bleeding the Cooling System

After refilling the cooling system, the system may have to be bled. Remove a cooling sensor or equivalent, at the highest point in the engine's cooling system. Fill the radiator until coolant spills out of the hole. Apply thread sealing tape to the component and install. Finish filling the radiator to the proper level.

If equipped, remove the hex-head plug on the left side of the cylinder head and fill the hole with coolant until it overflows. Install the plug and fill the coolant system. Early model vehicles have a vent screw on top of the thermostat housing. Open the vent approximately 2 turns, start the engine run the engine at idle until coolant flows from the vent.

ENGINE ELECTRICAL

NOTE: Disconnecting the negative battery cable on some vehicles may interfere with the functions of the on board computer systems and may require the computer to undergo a relearning process, once the negative battery cable is reconnected.

Distributor

REMOVAL

NOTE: The distributor is part of the cylinder head (except 116 and 117 engines). With the exception of the cap and rotor, it is not readily removable. The removal and installation procedures for all distributors on Mercedes-Benz vehicles are basically similar. Certain minor differences may exist from model-to-model.

1. The distributor is usually located on the front side or front of the engine.

2. Disconnect the negative battery cable. Remove the dust, cover, distributor cap and cable plug connections.

3. Rotate the engine in the normal direction, crank it until the distributor rotor points to the mark on the rim of the distributor housing. This indicates the No. 1 cylinder. Check the crankshaft pulley for the 0 mark.

4. The engine can be cranked with a socket wrench on the balancer bolt or with a prybar inserted in the balancer.

5. Matchmark the distributor body and the engine so the distributor can be returned to its original position.

6. Remove the distributor hold-down bolt and withdraw the distributor from the engine.

NOTE: Do not crank the engine while the distributor is removed.

INSTALLATION

Timing Not Disturbed

1. Install the distributor into the engine so the rotor is aligned with the matchmark on the housing and the housing is aligned with the matchmark on the engine. Ensure that the distributor is fully seated and the distributor shaft fully seated.

2. Install the hold-down bolts.

3. Connect the distributor electrical connectors and vacuum lines.

4. Install the distributor cap and spark plug wires.

5. Connect the battery negative cable and adjust the timing, if necessary.

Timing Disturbed

1. Position the engine so the No. 1 cylinder is at TDC of its compression stroke and the timing marks on the crankshaft pulley align.

2. Install the distributor in the engine so the rotor is aligned with the No. 1 ignition wire on the distributor cap and the housing is aligned with the matchmark on the engine. Ensure that the distributor is fully seated.

3. Install the distributor hold-down bolts.

4. Connect the distributor electrical connectors and vacuum lines.

5. Install the distributor cap and wires.

6. Connect the battery negative cable and adjust the timing.

Ignition Timing

ADJUSTMENT

Before attempting to set the timing, read the ""Ignition Timing Specifications" chart carefully and determine at what speed the timing should be set and whether the vacuum should be connected or disconnected.

NOTE: It is a good idea to paint the appropriate timing mark with dayglow or white paint to make it quickly and easily visible. On engines with transistorized coil ignition, the timing light may or may not work depending on the construction of the light.

Gasoline Engines

NOTE: Most gasoline engines utilize the new EZL electronic ignition system. Although service checking of ignition timing is possible, no adjustment is either possible or necessary. The ignition timing is controlled by the Electronic Control Unit (ECU).

1. Raise the hood and connect a tachometer.

2. Connect a timing light.

3. Run the engine at the specified speed and read the firing point on the balancing plate or vibration damper while shining the light on it.

NOTE: The balancer on some engines has 2 timing scales. If in doubt as to which scale to use, rotate the crankshaft, in the direction of rotation only, until the distributor rotor is aligned with the notch on the distributor housing (No. 1 cylinder). In this position, the timing pointer should be at TDC on the proper timing scale.

4. On 4.2L or 5.6L engines without EZL ignition, adjust the ignition timing by loosening the distributor

clamp bolt and rotating the distributor. To advance the timing, rotate the distributor in the opposite direction of normal rotation. To retard the timing, rotate the distributor in the direction of normal rotation.

5. Once the timing has been adjusted, recheck the timing once more to be sure it has not been disturbed.

6. Remove the timing light and tachometer and connect any wires that were removed.

Diesel Engines

The diesel engines do not use a distributor, so they require no ignition timing adjustment.

Alternator

PRECAUTIONS

Several precautions must be observed with alternator equipped vehicles to avoid damage to the unit.

• If the battery is removed for any reason, make sure it is reconnected with the correct polarity. Reversing the battery connections may result in damage to the one-way rectifiers.

• When utilizing a booster battery as a starting aid, always connect the positive to positive terminals and the negative terminal from the booster battery to a good engine ground on the vehicle being started.

• Never use a fast charger as a booster to start vehicles.

• Disconnect the battery cables when charging the battery with a fast charger.

• Never attempt to polarize the alternator.

• Do not use test lights of more than 12 volts when checking diode continuity.

• Do not short across or ground any of the alternator terminals.

• The polarity of the battery, alternator and regulator must be matched and considered before making any electrical connections within the system.

• Never separate the alternator on an open circuit. Make sure all connections within the circuit are clean and tight.

• Disconnect the battery ground terminal when performing any service on electrical components.

• Disconnect the battery if arc welding is to be done on the vehicle.

BELT TENSION ADJUSTMENT

Gasoline Engines

4, 6 AND 8 CYLINDER DOHC ENGINES

1. Loosen the adjusting bolt at the tensioner pulley about a half turn.

2. Turn the adjusting nut to the right until the tip of the adjustment pointer is located directly over the thick line on the adjusting scale.

3. Torque the tensioner pulley bolt to 55 ft. lbs. (75 Nm).

8-CYLINDER (SOHC) ENGINE

1. Disconnect the negative battery cable.

2. Loosen the tensioning device or accessory. Loosen the accessory mounting bolts and move to remove the belt. Loosen the tensioner pulley and adjustment bolt for the air conditioning compressor.

3. Install the belts and move the accessory to check if the belt is correct.

4. Move the accessory so the belt has about a ½ in. of deflection between the longest span. Turn the idler pulley adjusting bolt to adjust the air conditioning compressor belt.

5. Torque all mounting bolts and tensioning devices.

6. Connect the battery cable and check for proper operation.

12-CYLINDER ENGINES

The belt tension is adjusted automatically and requires no periodic maintenance. Release the poly V-belt tension with a 15mm wrench on the nut in the center of the tensioner. Move the tensioner against the stop and remove the belt.

DIESEL ENGINES

The belt tension is adjusted automatically and requires no periodic maintenance.

REMOVAL AND INSTALLATION

Viewing the engine from the front, the alternator is located on either side, usually down low. Because of the location, it is sometimes easier to remove the alternator from under the vehicle. The following is a general procedure for all models.

Gasoline Engines

4, 6 AND 8 CYLINDER DOHC ENGINES

1. Disconnect the negative battery cable.

2. Remove the fan and shroud.

3. Loosen the tensioner bolt about a half turn. Loosen the tensioning nut to the left until the belt can be removed

4. Push the setting pointer to the left and position over the thin line or 1st marking of the adjusting scale.

To install:

5. Route the belt around the pulleys and make sure the all V's are positioned on the pulleys correctly.

6. Turn the tensioner nut to the right until the tip of the setting pointer is aligned directly over the thick line or between the markings on the adjusting scale.

7. Install the fan and shroud. Connect the battery cable, start the engine and check for proper operation.

8-CYLINDER SOHC ENGINE

These engines use 4 separate V-belts, depending on installed equipment. Always replace the coolant pump and power steering belts as a pair.

1. Disconnect the negative battery cable.

2. Loosen the tensioning device or accessory. Loosen the accessory mounting bolts and move to remove the belt. Loosen the tensioner pulley and adjustment bolt for the air conditioning compressor.

3. Remove the belt and note the proper routing.

To install:

4. Install the belts and move the accessory to check if the belt is correct. Do not install belts that are too short or long. Damage to the engine and/or accessory may occur.

5. Move the accessory so the belt has about a ½ in. of deflection between the longest span. Turn the idler pulley adjusting bolt to adjust the air conditioning compressor belt.

6. Torque all mounting bolts and tensioning devices.

7. Connect the battery cable and check for proper operation.

12-CYLINDER ENGINES

1. Disconnect the negative battery cable.

2. Release the poly V-belt tension with a 15mm wrench on the nut in the center of the tensioner.

3. Move the tensioner against the stop and remove the belt.

To install:

4. Route the belt onto the pulleys. Make sure all V's are positioned properly on the pulleys.

5. Move the tensioner to the stop and install the belt. Remove the wrench from the tensioner.

6. Connect the battery cable, start the engine and check belt routing.

DIESEL ENGINES

1. Disconnect the negative battery cable.

2. Remove the fan shroud, fan and viscous clutch.

3. Remove the nut and bolt from the upper tensioner mount. Put a suitable prybar in the hole in the spring tension lever. Press the bar to the left until the bolt can be slid back in the direction of the manifold.

4. Remove the poly V-belt from the pulleys.

To install:

5. Route the belt onto the pulleys. Make sure the V's are positioned on the pulleys correctly. Damage to the belt may occur if the belt is not aligned.

6. Raise the idler pulley slightly. Turn the belt on the back, form a small loop and slide between the coolant pump and crankshaft pulley.

7. Press the belt with the left hand firmly onto the coolant pump pulley and turn this to the left until the belt has ridden up onto the idler pulley.

8. Put the belt on the idler pulley and crankshaft pulley. Rotate the free part of the belt and put on the air conditioning compressor, power steering pump, coolant pump and alternator.

9. Install the tensioner bolt and nut and torque to 18 ft. lbs. (25 Nm).

10. Install the fan clutch, fan and shroud.

11. Connect the battery cable, start the engine and check operation.

Starter

REMOVAL AND INSTALLATION

6-Cylinder in the 124 Model

1. Disconnect negative battery terminal.

2. Remove complete air cleaner.

3. Remove holder on intake manifold.

4. Remove engine compartment enclosure.

5. Disconnect electric wires for oil level and oil pressure sensor.

6. Remove starter from the bottom of the vehicle.

To install:

7. Make sure to replace all wires and washers in their original location. Install starter and torque the bolts to 40 ft. lbs. (55 Nm).

8. Connect electric wires for oil level and oil pressure sensor.

9. Install engine compartment enclosure and brackets.

10. Install holder on intake manifold.

11. Install complete air cleaner.

12. Connect negative battery terminal.

Except 6 Cylinder in 124 Model

1. Disconnect the battery cable. Remove the starter shield, if equipped. Remove the bracket at the bottom of the vehicle for the 500SL.

2. Remove all wires from the starter and tag them for location.

3. Some models use a starter shroud to protect the unit. Remove it if necessary. Unbolt the starter from the bellhousing and remove the ground cable.

4. Remove the starter from under the vehicle.

To install:

5. Install the starter motor and torque the bolts to 40 ft. lbs. (55 Nm). Be sure to replace all wires and washers in their original location.

6. Install the remaining components. Connect the battery cable and check for proper operation.

Diesel Glow Plugs

REMOVAL AND INSTALLATION

The glow plugs are located on the driver's side of the engine.

1. Disconnect the negative battery cable.

2. Disconnect the electrical connector from the glow plugs.

3. Remove the glow plug from the engine.

To install:

4. Apply anti-seize compound to the glow plug. Install the glow plug and torque to 15 ft. lbs. (20 Nm).

5. Connect the electrical connector and torque the nut to 35 inch lbs. (4 Nm).

6. Connect the battery cable and check operation.

TESTING

Without After Glowing

1. **Engine does start:** if the pre-glow indicator light fail to light when switching on the pre-glow system; disconnect the 4 or 5 pin connector from the pre-glow time-delay relay and turn the ignition key **ON**.

2. Jumper wire terminals **1** and **3** of the connector. If the glow indicator light fails to light, check and replace the indicator bulb.

3. If the bulb is OK, check the black wire from the connector termi-

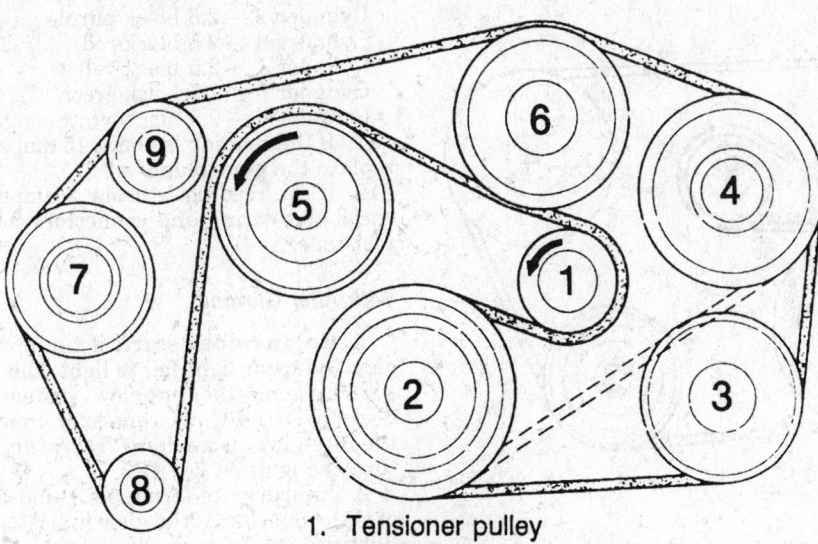

1. Tensioner pulley
2. Crankshaft
3. A/C compressor
4. Power steering pump
5. Fan
6. Water pump
7. Air pump
8. Alternator
9. Upper guide (idler) pulley

Poly V-belt routing — 3.2L engines

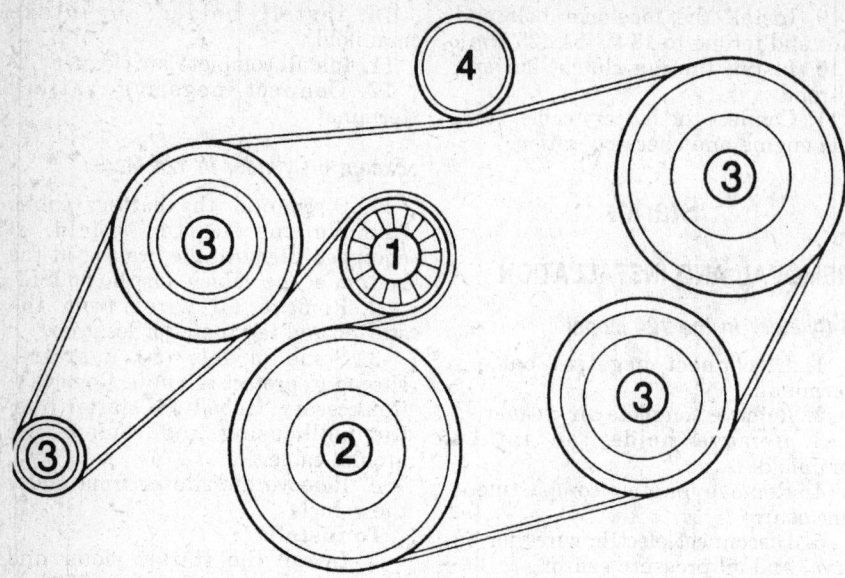

1. Tensioning roller
2. Crankshaft
3. Accessories
4. Guide pulley (only on some applications)

3.5L diesel engine Poly V-belt routing — some applications have a guide pulley installed on the cylinder head to reduce belt flap

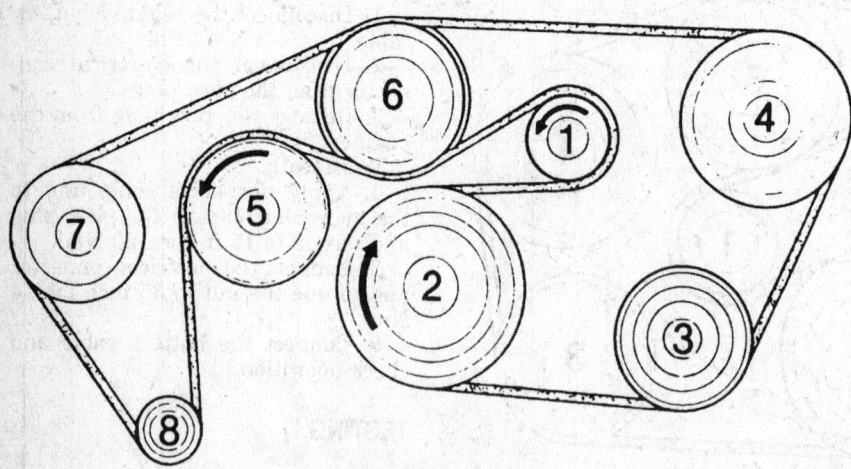

1. Tensioner pulley
2. Crankshaft
3. A/C compressor
4. Power steering pump
5. Fan
6. Water pump
7. Air pump
8. Alternator

Poly V-belt routing — 5.0L and 4.2L engines

nal **3** for continuity between the indicator light and time-delay relay.

4. If the indicator light comes ON, replace the pre-glow time-delay relay.

5. **Engine does not start:** check the voltage on terminal **30** (battery) of the pre-glow time-delay relay against ground.

6. If no voltage is present, check the red (4mm) wire from the battery terminal block to the time-delay relay terminal **30** for an interruption.

7. If voltage is present, check the 80 amp fuse for tight seat or interruption.

8. If no fault is found, check the voltage on terminal **1** of the time-delay relay connector against ground.

9. If no voltage is present when the system is switched ON, check the red/black wire from the central electric coupling jack **4** to the terminal connector for interruption. On model 124, check the pink/red wire from fuse **7** via the 12 pin connector to the time-delay relay connector.

10. Check the power consumption to the individual glow plugs at the time-delay relay. Turn the ignition switch **ON** and check the voltage after 10-20 seconds at the relay. Each plug should be 8-15 amps. The wire colors are as follows:

Cylinder 1 — 2.5 black/blue
Cylinder 2 — 2.5 black/purple
Cylinder 3 — 2.5 black/red
Cylinder 4 — 2.5 black/yellow
Cylinder 5 — 2.5 black/green
Cylinder 6 — 2.5 black/white

11. If the reading is above 15 amps, replace the glow plug.

12. If the reading is below 8 amps, check the wiring and connectors for resistance.

With After Glowing

1. **Engine does start:** if the pre-glow indicator light fail to light when switching on the pre-glow system; disconnect the 6 pin connector from the pre-glow time-delay relay and turn the ignition key **ON**.

2. Jumper wire terminals **1** and **3** of the connector. If the glow indicator light fails to light, check and replace the indicator bulb.

3. If the bulb is OK, check the black wire from the connector terminal **3** for continuity between the indicator light and time-delay relay.

4. If the indicator light comes ON, replace the pre-glow time-delay relay.

5. **Engine does not start:** check the voltage on terminal **30** (battery) of the pre-glow time-delay relay against ground.

6. If no voltage is present, check the red (4mm) wire from the battery terminal block to the time-delay relay terminal **30** for an interruption.

7. If voltage is present, check the 80 amp fuse for tight seat or interruption.

8. If no fault is found, check the voltage on terminal **1** of the time-delay relay connector against ground.

9. If no voltage is present when the system is switched ON, check the red/black wire from the central electric coupling jack **4** to the terminal connector for interruption. On model 124, check the pink/red wire from fuse **7** via the 12 pin connector to the time-delay relay connector.

10. Check the power consumption to the individual glow plugs at the time-delay relay. Turn the ignition switch **ON** and check the voltage after 10-20 seconds at the relay. Each plug should read 14-16 amps. The wire colors are as follows:

Cylinder 1 — 2.5 black/blue
Cylinder 2 — 2.5 black/purple
Cylinder 3 — 2.5 black/red
Cylinder 4 — 2.5 black/yellow
Cylinder 5 — 2.5 black/green
Cylinder 6 — 2.5 black/white

11. If the reading is above 16 amps, replace the glow plug.

12. If the reading is below 14 amps, check the wiring and connectors for resistance.

13. Check the resistance of the coolant temperature sensor and ground. The resistance should be 2272-2612 ohms at 25°C or 275-307 ohms at 80°C.

EMISSION CONTROLS

Emission Warning Lights

RESETTING

107 and 126 Models

1. The instrument cluster must be partially removed on certain models. Using a steel wire with a small hook on the end, slip the wire between the right side of the cluster and the dashboard. Turn the hook to engage the cluster and the dashboard. Turn the hook to engage the cluster and gently pull the edge of the cluster from the retaining clips.

2. Remove the oxygen sensor bulb at the extreme lower corner of the cluster. Press the cluster back into position. No reset switch is provided.

GASOLINE FUEL SYSTEM

Fuel System Service Precautions

Safety is the most important factor when performing not only fuel system maintenance but any type of maintenance. Failure to conduct maintenance and repairs in a safe manner may result in serious personal injury or death. Maintenance and testing of the vehicle's fuel system components can be accomplished safely and effectively by adhering to the following rules and guidelines.

• To avoid the possibility of fire and personal injury, always disconnect the negative battery cable unless the repair or test procedure requires that battery voltage be applied.

• Always relieve the fuel system pressure prior to disconnecting any fuel system component (injector, fuel rail, pressure regulator, etc.), fitting or fuel line connection. Exercise extreme caution whenever relieving fuel system pressure to avoid exposing skin, face and eyes to fuel spray. Please be advised that fuel under pressure may penetrate the skin or any part of the body that it contacts.

• Always place a shop towel or cloth around the fitting or connection prior to loosening to absorb any excess fuel due to spillage. Ensure that all fuel spillage (should it occur) is quickly removed from engine surfaces. Ensure that all fuel soaked cloths or towels are deposited into a suitable waste container.

• Always keep a dry chemical (Class B) fire extinguisher near the work area.

• Do not allow fuel spray or fuel vapors to come into contact with a spark or open flame.

• Always use a backup wrench when loosening and tightening fuel line connection fittings. This will prevent unnecessary stress and torsion to fuel line piping. Always follow the proper torque specifications.

• Always replace worn fuel fitting O-rings with new. Do not substitute fuel hose or equivalent where fuel pipe is installed.

RELIEVING FUEL SYSTEM PRESSURE

1. Remove the fuel filler cap and allow the vapor pressure to vent.

2. Remove the fuel pump relay, fuse or connector.

3. Start the engine and allow to run and stall. Crank 2 or 3 more times to relieve the pressure.

Fuel Tank

REMOVAL AND INSTALLATION

107, 124, 126 and 201 Model Sedans

1. Disconnect the negative battery cable.

2. Drain the fuel tank using an approved pump and container. Disconnect the fuel pump relay, remove the filler cap and start the engine until it stalls.

3. Disconnect the filler neck from the body and fuel gauge sender.

4. Remove the tank covering.

5. Disconnect all visible pressure, return and vapor lines.

6. Support the tank using an approved hoist.

7. Remove the tank retaining nuts and lower the tank far enough to disconnect any connected hoses or wiring.

To install:

8. Empty the remaining fuel from the tank.

9. Install the tank and align the cushions.

10. Install the retaining nuts and torque to 15 ft. lbs. (20 Nm).

11. Install the remaining components, connect the battery cable, fill the tank, start the engine and check for leaks.

300T Wagon

1. Disconnect the negative battery cable.

2. Drain the fuel tank using an approved pump and container. Disconnect the fuel pump relay, remove the filler cap and start the engine until it stalls.

3. Disconnect the filler neck from the body.

4. Remove the front load compartment flap or 3rd seat and back rest.

5. Disconnect the breather line and fuel gauge sender wire.

6. Disconnect any accessible hose and wiring before removal.

7. Remove the rear portion of the exhaust system.

8. Remove the splashes and bracket level pipe.

9. Remove the front retaining bolts. Push the exhaust and level pipe to the left.

10. Install a suitable hoist to the tank and remove the remaining tank retainers. Lower the tank far enough to disconnect any hoses or wiring.

To install:

11. Install a suitable hoist to the tank and install tank and retainers. Connect any hoses or wiring.

12. Install the front retaining bolts and torque to 15 ft. lbs. (20 Nm).

13. Install the splashes and bracket level pipe.

14. Install the rear portion of the exhaust system.

15. Connect any accessible hose and wiring.

16. Connect the breather line and fuel gauge sender wire.

17. Install the front load compartment flap or 3rd seat and back rest.

18. Connect the filler neck to the body.

19. Refill the fuel tank.

20. Connect the negative battery cable and check for leaks.

300 and 500SL Models

1. Disconnect the negative battery cable.

2. Drain the fuel tank using an approved pump and container. Disconnect the fuel pump relay, remove the filler cap and start the engine until it stalls.

3. Disconnect the filler neck from the body.

4. Remove the convertible partition wall.

5. Remove the cover from the filler neck.

6. Remove the control unit for the infrared remote control, if equipped.

7. Disconnect the cup seal, pressure, return and vapor hoses.

8. Place a suitable hoist under the tank and remove the retaining bolts.

9. Pull the tank back and remove far enough to disconnect any remaining hoses or wiring before removal.

To install:

10. Install the tank and connect any hoses or wiring before installation.

11. Install the retaining bolts and torque to 15 ft. lbs. (20 Nm).

12. Connect the cup seal, pressure, return and vapor hoses.

13. Install the control unit for the infrared remote control, if equipped.

14. Install the cover to the filler neck.

15. Install the convertible partition wall.

16. Connect the filler neck to the body.

17. Refill the fuel tank and check for leaks.

18. Connect the negative battery cable.

140 Model

1. Disconnect the negative battery cable and relieve the fuel pressure.

2. Release the cup seal at the filler neck and drain the tank into a suitable container.

3. Remove the fuel tank lining and right and left side trunk linings.

4. Remove the protective box for the fuel pump package.

5. Disconnect the suction and return hoses using special tool 000589710300 or equivalent.

6. Disconnect the remaining tank hoses and electrical connectors.

7. Place a suitable jack under the tank and remove the retaining nuts.

8. Lower the tank far enough to disconnect any connected components.

To install:

9. Check the tank for rust and deterioration. Remove the fuel pickup strainer, clean and install.

10. Raise the tank far enough to connect the hoses and wiring.

11. Install the retaining nuts and torque to 16 ft. lbs. (21 Nm).

12. Connect the remaining tank hoses and electrical connectors.

13. Connect the suction and return hoses.

14. Install the protective box for the fuel pump package.

15. Install the fuel tank lining and right and left side trunk linings.

16. Install the cup seal at the filler neck.

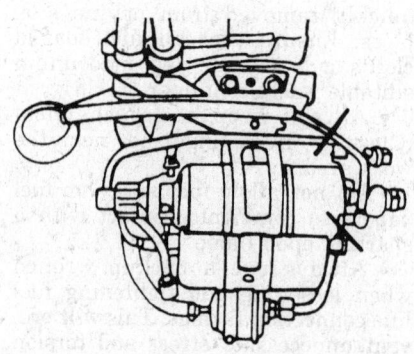

Fuel pump/filter assembly

17. Connect the negative battery cable, start the engine and check for leaks.

Fuel Filter

REMOVAL AND INSTALLATION

Two types of filters are used, depending on the vehicle. Both are located between the rear axle and the fuel tank.

1. Disconnect the negative battery cable.

2. Unscrew the cover box.

3. Remove the gas cap, fuel pump cover and pressure hoses.

4. Loosen the screws and remove the filter. Remove the connecting plug from the old filter and install it on a new filter using a new gasket.

To install:

5. Install a new filter in the direction of flow. Always replace the copper gaskets.

6. Replace the attaching screws.

7. Install the pressure hoses, pump cover and gas cap. Torque the banjo fittings to 80 inch lbs. (9 Nm).

8. Install the fuel filter in the holder by positioning it in the center of the transparent holder. Be sure the plastic sleeve between the fuel filter and fuel pump is installed. Galvanic corrosion may occur in cases of direct contact between these components.

9. Replace the cover box and check for proper sealing.

Electric Fuel Pump

NOTE: Do not confuse the electric fuel pump with the injection pump.

All Mercedes-Benz fuel injected engines are equipped with electric fuel pumps. The electric fuel pump is located under the rear floor panel. The fuel return line was also eliminated and a check ball installed in its place. The fuel pump uses a replaceable check valve on the outside of the pump which can be replaced separately. Some later model vehicles use 2 fuel pumps in the same location.

Two types of fuel pumps have been used. One, the large pump, has been replaced with a new small design which has a bypass system to prevent vapor lock.

TESTING DELIVERY VOLUME

1. Disconnect the inlet hose at the pressure regulator. Connect a fuel

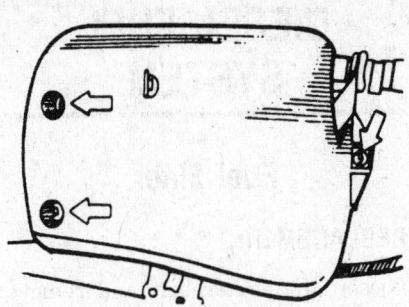

Fuel pump package cover

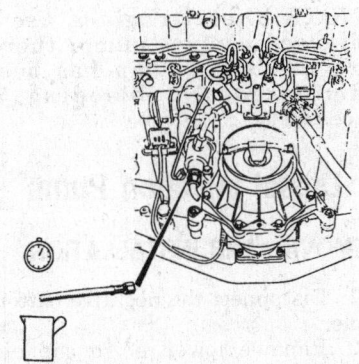

Fuel pump delivery test — CIS-E engines

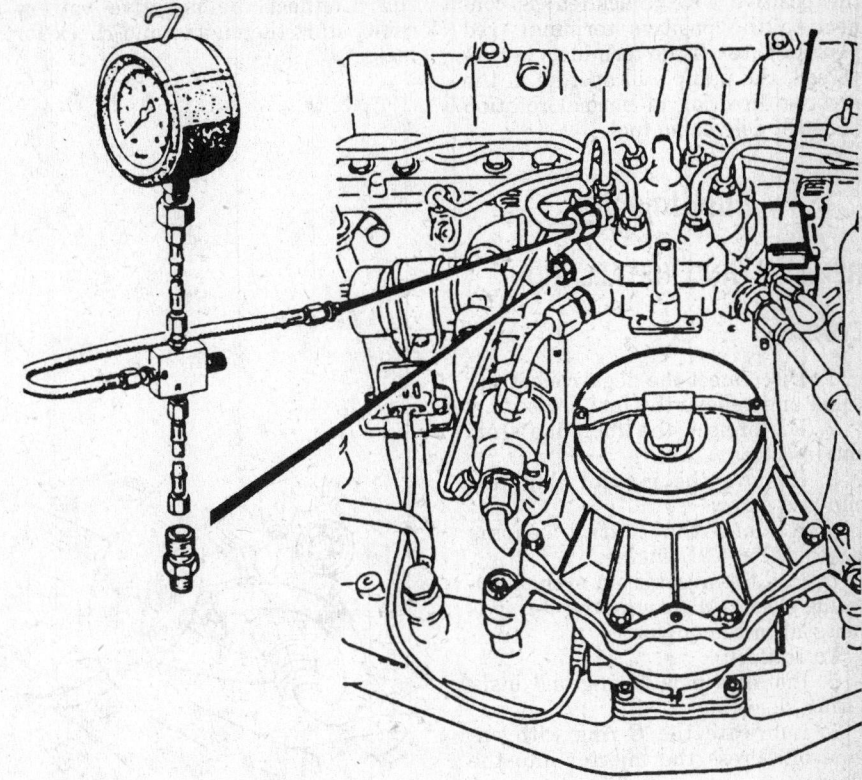

Fuel pump pressure test — CIS-E engines

hose to the fuel pressure regulator in-let hose.

2. Place the hose in an approved measuring container.

3. Turn the ignition key **ON** and measure the volume. The minimum value is 1.06 quart (1 liter) in 40 seconds.

4. Replace the fuel filter and test again. If still low, replace the fuel pump.

PRESSURE TEST

CIS-E

1. Disconnect the fuel line at the fuel distributor and connect a pressure gauge 103589002100 or equivalent, to the hose.

2. Connect an adapter 102589066300 or equivalent, to the plug fitting at the fuel distributor.

3. Jump the fuel pump relay at the manifold and check the pressure. If not within specifications, check the fuel filter and pump pressure at the pump.

4. Disconnect the pressure line at the fuel pump.

5. Connect a pressure gauge and adapter to the fuel pump outlet at the

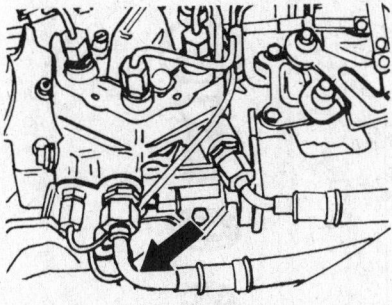

Testing fuel pump pressure — CIS-E engines

pump. The pressure should be 29-58 psi (2-4 bar).

6. Reconnect all fuel hoses and check for leaks.

LH-Jetronic

1. Disconnect the negative battery cable and bleed the fuel system.

2. Disconnect the fuel return line. Connect a pressure gauge and adapter to the shrader valve or the return fitting after the pressure regulator.

3. Connect the battery cable and start the engine.

4. The fuel pressure should be 45-55 psi with the pressure regulator connected (regulated pressure).

5. Turn the engine **OFF** and bleed the fuel system.

6. Disconnect the pressure gauge. Connect the fuel line and torque to 15 ft. lbs. (20 Nm).

REMOVAL AND INSTALLATION

1. Disconnect the negative battery cable. Raise and safely support the vehicle. The pump(s) are located at the rear of the vehicle, next to the rear axle.

2. Remove the protective cover, if equipped.

3. Remove and plug the intake, outlet and bypass lines from the pump.

4. Disconnect the electrical leads.

5. Unbolt and remove the fuel pump and vibration pads.

NOTE: The V8 and later model engines utilize 2 fuel pumps connected in series.

6. Install the fuel pump in the reverse order of removal. Be sure the electrical leads are connected to the proper terminals. The negative wire (brown) is connected to the negative terminal (brown plastic plate) and

the positive wire (black/red) is connect to the positive terminal (red plastic plate). If the terminals are reversed, the pump will operate in the reverse direction of normal rotation and will deliver no fuel.

Fuel Injector

REMOVAL AND INSTALLATION

CIS-E

1. Disconnect the negative battery cable and relieve the fuel pressure.
2. Disconnect the fuel line from the injector.
3. Remove the injector retaining clip and screw.
4. Remove the control bearing pedestal for 4.2L engine.
5. Pull the injector out of the insulating sleeve. Make sure the O-ring is not still in the engine.
To install:
6. Install a new O-ring and insulating sleeve.
7. Lubricate the O-ring with engine oil. Press the injector into the sleeve.
8. Connect the fuel line and torque to 10 ft. lbs. (15 Nm).
9. Start the engine and check for leaks.

LH-JECTRONIC

1. Disconnect the negative battery cable and relieve the fuel pressure.
2. Partially remove the cable shaft and disconnect all electrical connectors to the fuel rail assembly.
3. Disconnect the crankcase ventilation hose.
4. Disconnect the fuel pressure and return lines. Plug all open fittings.
5. Remove the fuel rail retaining screws. Carefully remove the fuel rail from the intake manifold together with the injectors.
6. Remove the injector retainers and injectors from the fuel rail.
To install:
7. Lubricate all rubber parts with clean engine oil.
8. Install the injector and retainers to the fuel rail.
9. Install the fuel rail, injectors and retaining screws.
10. Connect the fuel pressure and return lines.
11. Connect the crankcase ventilation hose.
12. Install the cable shaft and connect all electrical connectors to the fuel rail assembly.

13. Connect the negative battery cable, start the engine and check for leaks.

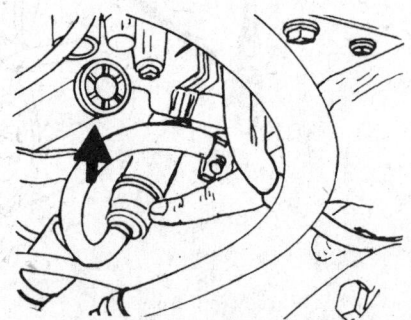

Diesel engines use a pre-filter in addition to the main fuel filter. The arrow indicates the hand operated delivery pump

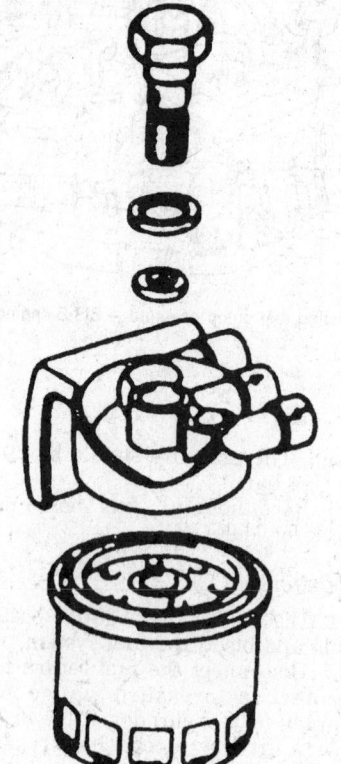

Diesel fuel filter

DIESEL FUEL SYSTEM

Fuel Filter

REPLACEMENt

Loosen the center bolt and remove the filter cartridge downward. Lubricate the new filter gasket with clean diesel fuel and install a new filter cartridge.

NOTE: Diesel engines use a self-bleeding fuel pump, therefore the hand pump has been eliminated. No bleeding is necessary.

Diesel Injection Pump

REMOVAL AND INSTALLATION

1. Disconnect the negative battery cable.
2. Remove lower noise capsule, poly V-belt tensioner, fan and shroud.
3. Remove the vacuum pump and cruise control assembly.
4. Remove the assembly cage for 1990 engines.
5. Remove the injection pump gear bolt (left hand thread).
6. Position the crankshaft pulley at 15 degrees after TDC. Fix the camshaft gear and injection pump in place with a cable strap or equivalent.
7. Remove the timing chain tensioner and control damper.
8. Press the timing chain out of the way with strips of metal and universal pliers to withdraw the chain.
9. Remove the injection pump lines and retainers using tool 000589770300.
10. Disconnect and label all cables, electrical wiring and hoses from the pump and surrounding area.
11. Remove the retaining bolts and carefully pull the pump out to the rear while holding the timing device.
To install:
12. Remove the locking bolt from the side of the injection pump.

——WARNING——
The pump will be damaged when the en gine is started if this procedure is not followed.

13. Turn the injection pump with a splined wrench on the injection pump camshaft until the lug of the gover-

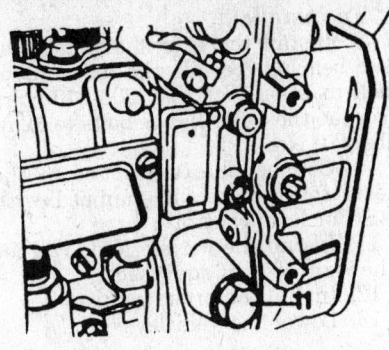

Remove the bolt in the injection pump for injection timing — diesel

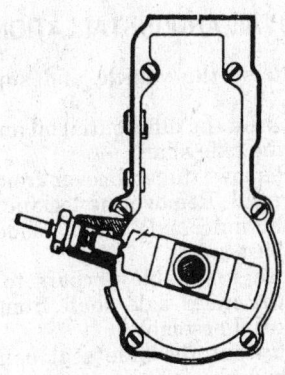

Injection pump timing mark — diesel

nor is visible in the hole, then insert the locking bolt in this position and engage in the lug.

NOTE: Always remove the locking bolt when the pump is installed to the engine. Damage to the pump will result if started with the bolt installed.

14. Install the pump and reconnect the injector lines. Torque the mounting bolts to 18 ft. lbs. (25 Nm), pump gear to 38 ft. lbs. (50 Nm) and the lines to 15 ft. lbs. (20 Nm).

15. Reconnect the timing chain and install components.

16. Install the remaining components.

17. Crank the engine 1 revolution and recheck the TDC mark of the crankshaft and camshaft. Check the start of delivery with a digital tester and adjust the pump timing, if needed.

18. Connect the battery cable and check operation.

Diesel Injection Timing

ADJUSTMENT

Position Sensor Method

1. Remove the screw plug from the side of the injection pump governor housing. Collect the lost oil.

2. Install a position sensor into the hole and connect the tester to the vehicle battery and position sensor.

3. Turn the crankshaft by hand until lamps A and B on the tester light simultaneously. Take the reading on the crankshaft pulley.

4. Loosen the injection pump and adjust until the timing pointer is at 15 degrees after TDC and both lamps are ON.

5. Install the oil and plug. Torque the plug to 22 ft. lbs. (30 Nm).

6. Recheck the oil level.

Digital Tester Method

1. Remove the timing plug from the side of the injection pump. Connect the digital tester to the timing hole and front timing pointer at the crankshaft pulley and to the battery. Refer to the tool manufacturers instructions.

2. Loosen the injection pump mountings.

3. Start the engine and run at idle and normal temperature.

4. Adjust the timing by turning the timing device to the right to retard the start of delivery and to the left to advance. The timing should be 15 degrees after TDC (ATDC).

5. Turn the engine **OFF**, remove the tools and torque the mounting bolts to 22 ft. lbs. (30 Nm).

6. Recheck the engine oil level.

Fuel Injector

REMOVAL AND INSTALLATION

— **CAUTION** —

The fuel injector is under extreme pressure. Always wear eye protection while servicing the diesel injection system. Failure to do so may cause personal injury.

1. Disconnect the negative battery cable.

2. Place shop rags around the injector. Using a flare nut and backup wrench, loosen the metal pipe slightly until the pressure is released. Remove the pipe and hoses.

3. Remove the injector using special tool 001589650900 or equivalent.

4. Install a new nozzle shim and install the injector.

5. Connect the injector pipe and torque to 15 ft. lbs. (20 Nm).

6. Replace the oil leak hose if damaged.

DRIVE AXLE

These vehicles use either 2 or 3 piece driveshaft to connect the transmission to a hypoid independent rear axle. All models covered in this book use independent rear suspension with open or enclosed driveshaft to the rear wheels.

Front Halfshaft

REMOVAL AND INSTALLATION

4-MATIC

1. Disconnect the negative battery cable, raise the vehicle and support safely.

2. Remove the engine compartment liner and front wheel.

3. Remove the halfshaft nut with a 30mm socket.

4. Remove the halfshaft-to-driveaxle flange bolts. Replace the flange bolts with new.

5. Wire the tripod joint with wire so it does not come apart. Damage to the joint will result.

6. Use a brass drift to drive the halfshaft from the hub. Be very careful not to damage the shaft threads. If the halfshaft will not dislodge, use separator tool 201589006100 to press the halfshaft from the hub.

7. Remove the halfshaft from the vehicle.

To install:

8. Install the halfshaft into the vehicle. Coat the splines with anti-seize compound.

9. Install the new halfshaft-to-driveaxle flange bolts and torque to 52 ft. lbs. (70 Nm). Replace the flange bolts with new.

10. Install the halfshaft nut and torque to 147-177 ft. lbs. (200-240 Nm) with a 30mm socket.

11. Install the engine compartment liner and front wheel.

12. Connect the negative battery cable and lower the vehicle safely.

CV-Boot

REMOVAL AND INSTALLATION

4-MATIC

1. Remove the halfshaft from the vehicle.

2. Clamp the shaft vertically in a vise with the inner (tripod) upwards.

3. Remove the boot clamp with side cutters. Mark the position of the tripod spiders in relation to the joint casing. Remove the joint casing.

4. Clean the grease off of the tripod joint and wire the rollers on the needle bearings.

5. Remove the Circlip and tripod spider from the shaft using a 3 arm puller.

6. Remove the clamps from the outer joint and slide the boot and rubber damper off of the shaft. Clean the shaft of debris before sliding the boot from the shaft.

To install:

7. Install the boot and rubber damper, if equipped. Fill the boot with CV joint grease only.

8. Install the tripod spider with the flat side towards the circlip up to the stop on the spline section. Install the circlip.

9. Install the joint casing to the matchmark.

10. Fill the joint and boot with CV-joint grease and install. Install the clamps with pliers.

11. Install the halfshaft into the vehicle.

Driveshaft and U-Joints

REMOVAL AND INSTALLATION

NOTE: Steps 1-3 apply to 4 cylinder and V8 engines. Matchmark all driveshaft connections prior to removal.

1. Raise and support the vehicle safely.

2. Fold the torsion bar down after disconnecting the level control linkage, if equipped.

3. Remove the exhaust system.

4. Remove the heat shield from the frame.

5. Support the transmission and remove the rear engine mount crossmember.

6. Without sliding the rubber sleeve back, loosen the clamp nut approximately 2 turns, the rubber sleeve will slide along.

NOTE: On 3 piece driveshafts, only the front clamp nut need be loosened. Loosen the nut with a

46mm and large open end wrenches. Torque the nut to 22-30 ft. lbs. (30-40 Nm).

7. Unscrew the U-joint mounting flange from the U-joint plate.

8. Bend back the locktabs and remove the driveshaft-to-rear axle pinion yoke bolts.

9. Remove the intermediate bearing(s)-to-frame bolts, push the driveshaft together slightly and remove it from the vehicle.

10. Try not to separate the driveshafts. If necessary, matchmark all components so they can be reassembled in the same order.

To install:

11. Always use new self-locking nuts. Torque the nuts to 33 ft. lbs. (45 Nm) and center carrier bolts to 30 ft. lbs. (40 Nm).

12. After the driveshaft is installed, rock the vehicle back and forth, several times, to settle the driveshaft.

13. Make sure neither intermediate shaft is binding against either intermediate bearing and the clearance between the intermediate bearing and the driveshaft is the same at both ends.

Rear Axle Shafts

NOTE: The rubber covered joints are filled with special oil. If they are disassembled for any reason, they must be refilled with special oil.

REMOVAL AND INSTALLATION

1. Raise and safely support the vehicle. Remove the wheel and center axle nut with 30mm socket or bolt.

2. Remove the brake caliper and suspend it from a hook.

3. Clean the dirt from the axle flange bolts. Remove the rear axle from the connection flange.

4. Remove the wiring guide rail for the right side, if equipped.

5. Disconnect the control rod from the level control unit, if equipped with ASD or level control.

6. Lift the rear axle with a jack until the axle is vertical.

7. Remove the axle shaft from the hub using a pressing tool 201589006100, or equivalent.

8. Remove the axle shaft from the vehicle. The jack may have to be lowered or raised to gain enough room to remove the shaft.

To install:

NOTE: Axle shafts are stamped R and L for right and left units. Always use new lock rings.

To install:

9. Install the axle shaft and seat the bearing. Torque the axle nut or bolt to 148-175 ft. lbs. (200-240 Nm). Torque the inner flange bolts to 52 ft. lbs. (70 Nm).

10. Connect the control rod to the level control unit, if equipped with ASD or level control

11. Install the wiring guide rail for the right side, if equipped.

12. Install the brake caliper.

13. Lower the vehicle.

Rear Axle Seal

REMOVAL AND INSTALLATION

1. Raise the vehicle and support safely.

2. Drain the differential oil and remove the axle shaft.

3. Remove the end cover from the differential. Remove the locking ring from the inner axle shaft, inside the carrier assembly.

4. Use 2 suitable prybars to dislodge the inner axle shaft from the differential assembly.

5. Pry out the axle seal using a suitable prybar.

To install:

6. Install the seal using a seal installer.

7. Install the inner axle shaft and new locking ring.

8. Install the differential cover and refill with oil. Torque the grade 8.8 bolts to 33 ft. lbs. (45 Nm) and the 10.9 bolts to 37 ft. lbs. (50 Nm).

9. Install axle shaft and torque the inner bolts to 52 ft. lbs. (70 Nm) and outer nut to 147 ft. lbs. (200 Nm).

10. Install the remaining components. Refill the differential with oil and lower the vehicle.

Front Axle Shafts

REMOVAL AND INSTALLATION

4-MATIC

1. Raise the vehicle and safely support. Remove the front wheel.

2. Remove the axle hub nut and washer and engine compartment cover.

3. Remove the self-locking bolts from the inside CV-joint.

4. Turn the steering wheel to the right. Guide the front axle shaft upwards behind the connecting flange and remove by pushing the vehicle down at the same time. Be careful not to over extend the inner CV-joint.

To install:

5. Install the axle shaft and connect with the inner joint and wheel hub.

6. Torque the hub nut and washer to 200-250 ft. lbs. (280-320 Nm) and the self-locking bolts to 51 ft. lbs. (70 Nm).

Front Axle Bearing and Seal

REMOVAL AND INSTALLATION

4-MATIC

1. Raise the vehicle and safely support.

2. Remove the front axle shaft, brake hose support, caliper and brake disc.

3. Remove the axle shaft flange using a hub puller tool 201589006100 or equivalent, with the thrust piece on the axle flange.

4. Remove the snapring from the knuckle.

5. Heat the bearing area of the knuckle and draw the bearing out of the knuckle with a removal tool 201589044300 or equivalent.

6. Using a puller, remove the bearing inner race.

To install:

7. Install the bearing using a installation tool 201589044300 or equivalent, until it contacts the inside stop.

8. Install the snapring and axle shaft flange with an installation tool 201589044300 or equivalent.

9. Install the remaining components.

10. Torque the hub nut and washer to 147-177 ft. lbs. (200-240 Nm) and the self-locking bolts to 51 ft. lbs. (70 Nm).

Front Wheel Hub and Bearings

REMOVAL AND INSTALLATION

1. Raise the vehicle and support safely.

2. Remove the front wheel, brake caliper and rotor. Hang the caliper by a piece of wire.

3. Remove the hub cap with puller 116589223300 or equivalent.

4. Remove the contact spring and loosen the internal socket head screw.

5. Remove the clamping nut and washer.

6. Remove the front hub and bearings. Use puller 201589103300, if needed.

7. Remove the grease seal and inner bearing with a wooden drift.

8. Use a bearing puller 201589003300 or equivalent, to remove the outer races from the hub.

To install:

9. Pack all moving parts and hub housing with high temperature roller bearing grease (green colored).

10. Use a bearing race install 201589014300 or equivalent, to seat the races into the hub. Make sure they are completely seated before proceeding.

11. Install the grease seal and inner bearing with a seal installer tool 201589014300 or equivalent.

12. Install the front hub and bearings.

13. Install the clamping nut and washer and adjust as follows:

   a. Torque the clamping nut to 9 ft. lbs. (12 Nm) while turn the hub.

   b. Loosen the clamping nut by approximately ⅓ of a turn.

   c. Install a dial indicator 363589022100 and adjust to 2mm preload.

   d. Check and adjust the preload by pulling and pushing the flange of the brake disc. Turn the hub several times to get a wheel bearing axial play of 0.0004-0.0008 in. (0.01-0.02mm).

14. Install the contact spring and hub cap.

15. Install the rotor, caliper and front wheel.

16. Lower the vehicle safely.

Pinion Seal

REMOVAL AND INSTALLATION

1. Raise the vehicle and support safely.

2. Disconnect the exhaust hangers and move out of the way.

3. Remove the driveshaft from the vehicle.

4. Remove the pinion nut and washer.

5. Remove the mounting flange using a gear puller.

6. Remove the pinion seal using a seal remover.

To install:

7. Install the seal with an installer. Install the flange and nut.

8. Torque the nut using a special torque wrench 001589000900 and 30mm socket to 133 ft. lbs. (180 Nm). Stake the nut with a drift.

9. Install the driveshaft into the vehicle. Torque the large 46mm driveshaft jam nut to 22-30 ft. lbs. (30-40 Nm).

10. Connect the exhaust hangers.

11. Lower the vehicle safely and check for proper operation.

Rear Axle Housing

REMOVAL AND INSTALLATION

1. Raise the vehicle and support safely.

2. Disconnect the transverse links from the frame floor.

3. Remove the exhaust system and hangers and exhaust shields if in the way.

4. Remove the driveshaft from the rear housing flange.

5. Disconnect the parking brake cables and hoses. Plug the hoses to prevent contamination.

6. Remove the roll-over switch and spring link covers (300SL and 500SL models only).

7. Disconnect the shock absorbers, torsion bar and fuel pump cover.

8. Disconnect any ADS, ASD or ABS wiring or hydraulic lines. Plug all lines to prevent leakage.

9. Drain the axle housing oil. Disconnect and remove any fuel pump components that are in the way.

10. Install a suitable jack under the axle housing.

11. Remove the housing mounting bolts and stop plate.

12. Carefully lower the axle housing and disconnect the axle shafts from the flanges.

To install:

13. Carefully raise the axle housing and connect the axle shafts to the flanges.

14. Install the housing mounting bolts and stop plate. Torque the bolts to 51 ft. lbs. (70 Nm).

15. Refill the axle housing oil. Connect any fuel pump components that are in the way.

16. Connect any ADS, ASD or ABS wiring or hydraulic lines.

17. Connect the shock absorbers, torsion bar and fuel pump cover.

18. Install the roll-over switch and spring link covers (300 and 500SL models only).

19. Connect the parking brake cables and hoses.

20. Install the driveshaft to the rear housing flange.

21. Install the exhaust system, hangers and exhaust shields.

22. Connect the transverse links to the frame floor.

23. Lower the vehicle and support safely.

MANUAL TRANSMISSION

Transmission Assembly

REMOVAL AND INSTALLATION

Models 129 and 201

1. Disconnect the battery.
2. Cover the insulation mat in the engine compartment to prevent damage.
3. Support the transmission.
4. Unbolt the rear engine mounts at the rear transmission cover.
5. Unbolt the rear engine carrier on the floor frame.
6. Unscrew the exhaust holder at the transmission. Note the number and positioning of all washers.
7. Unscrew the clamping strap and remove the exhaust pipe holder.
8. Remove the intermediate bearing shield plate.
9. Loosen the clamp nut on the driveshaft.
10. Loosen but do not remove, the intermediate bearing bolts.
11. Unbolt the driveshaft on the transmission so the companion plate remains with the driveshaft.
12. Carefully push the driveshaft as far to the rear as permitted.

NOTE: On the 190E, the fitted sleeves on the universal flange must be loosened before separating the flange from the companion plate. This will require a cylindrical mandrel.

13. Disconnect the exhaust system at the rear suspension and suspend it with wire.
14. Loosen and remove the input shaft for the tachometer.
15. Loosen and remove the tachometer driveshaft on the rear transmission case cover. Unclip the clip for the tachometer driveshaft from its holder.
16. Unscrew the holder for the line to the clutch housing. Unscrew the clutch slave cylinder and move it toward the rear until the pushrod is clear of the housing.
17. Push off the clip locks and remove the shift rods from the interme-

diate levers on the shift bracket. Note the position of the disc springs.

NOTE: When the shift rods are disconnected, do not move the shift lever into reverse or the backup light switch could be damaged.

18. Unbolt the starter and remove it.
19. Remove all transmission-to-intermediate flange screw. Remove the upper 2 last.
20. Rotate the transmission approximately 45 degrees to the left, slide it from the clutch plate and remove it downward.

NOTE: Make sure the input shaft has cleared the clutch plate before tilting the transmission.

To install:

21. Lightly grease the centering lug and splines on the transmission input shaft.

NOTE: Position the clutch slave cylinder and line above the transmission before beginning installation.

22. Move the transmission into the clutch so one gear step engages. Rotate the mainshaft back and forth until the splines on the input shaft and clutch plate are aligned.
23. Move the transmission all the way in and tighten the transmission-to-intermediate flange screws.
24. Install the starter.
25. Install the clutch slave cylinder with the proper plastic shims.
26. Installation of the remaining components is in the reverse order of removal. Please note the following:
   a. After installing the driveshaft, roll the vehicle back and forth and tighten the intermediate bearing free of tension.
   b. Tighten the driveshaft clamp nut to 22-29 ft. lbs. (30-40 Nm).
   c. Make sure of the proper positioning of all washers, spacers and shims.

LINKAGE ADJUSTMENT

NOTE: On all types of transmissions, never hammer or force a new shift knob on with the shifter installed, as the plastic bushing connected to the lever will be damaged and cause hard shifting.

Proper adjustment of the shift linkage is dependent on both the position of the shift levers at the transmission and the length of the shift rods. The shift levers, rods and bear-

ing block are all located under the floor tunnel; the driveshaft shield may have to be removed to gain access to them.

1. With the transmission in **N** and the driveshaft shield removed, if equipped, remove the clip locks and disconnect the shift rods from the intermediate shift levers under the floor shift bearing bracket.
2. With the shifter still in the **N** position, lock the 3 intermediate shift levers by inserting a 0.2156 in. rod, a No. 3 drill bit will do, or any other tool of approximately the same diameter, through the levers and the holes in the bearing bracket.
3. Check the position of the shift levers at the transmission. Adjust by loosening the clamp bolts and moving the levers.
4. With the intermediate levers locked and the shift levers adjusted properly, try hooking the shift rods back onto their respective intermediate levers. The shift rods may be adjusted by loosening the locknut and turning the ball socket on the end until they are the proper length.

NOTE: When hooking up the shift rods to the intermediate levers, be very careful not to move the transmission shift levers from their adjusted position. When reattaching the shift rods on 190 models, use only clip locks which have a radius edge. If the old style clip locks with a square edge are used, there is a possibility that the locks will pop out and the shift rods will drop.

5. Remove the locking rod from the bearing bracket, start the engine and shift through the gears a few times. Occasionally, slight binding may call for very slight further adjustments.

CLUTCH

Clutch Assembly

REMOVAL AND INSTALLATION

1. To remove the clutch, first remove the transmission.
2. Loosen the clutch pressure plate hold-down bolts, evenly, 1-1½ turns at a time, until tension is relieved. Never remove 1 bolt at a time, as damage to the pressure plate is possible.

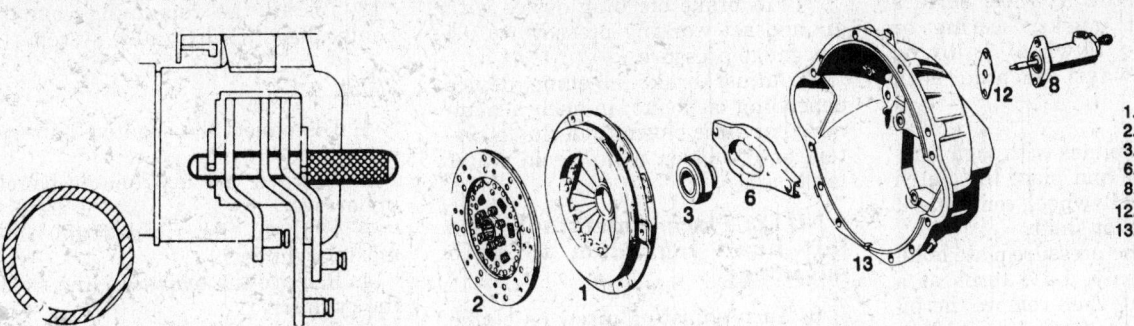

Shift cable adjustment — manual transmission

Exploded view of clutch

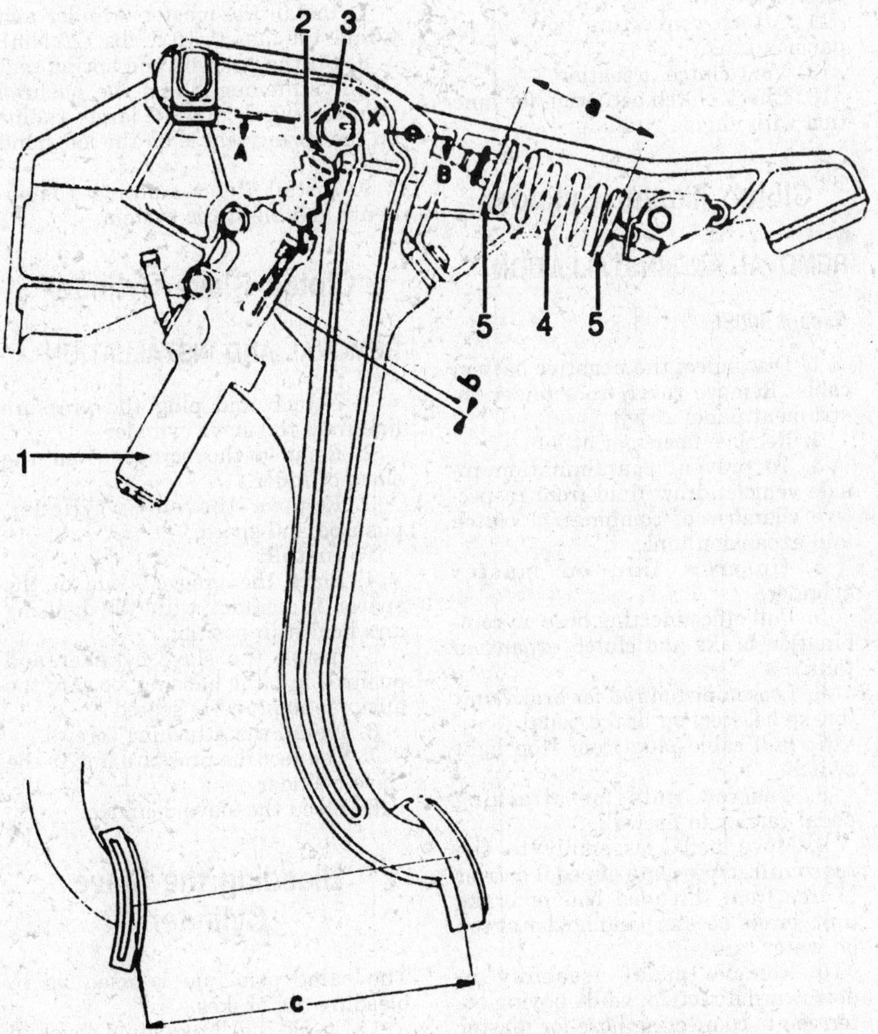

1. Plate spring clutch
2. Driven plate
3. Throwout
6. Thowout rocker
8. Slave cylinder
12. Shim
13. Clutch housing

1. Master cylinder
2. Pushrod
3. Adjusting screw
4. Off-center spring
5. Spring retainer

a. Adjusting dimension
   of off-center spring
b. Clearance between
   piston in master
   cylinder and pushrod
c. Pedal travel (lash)

Clutch adjustment

3. Examine the flywheel surface for blue heat marks, scoring or cracks. If the flywheel is to be machined, always machine both sides.

To install:

4. Coat the splines with high temperature grease and place the clutch disc against the flywheel, centering it with a clutch pilot shaft.

5. Tighten the pressure plate hold-down bolts evenly, 1-1½ turns at a time, until tight, then remove the pilot shaft. Torque the bolts to 18 ft. lbs. (25 Nm) in the same rotation as the 1-1½ turns.

NOTE: Most clutch plates have the flywheel side marked Kupplungsseite. Do not assume the pressure springs always face the transmission.

6. Apply grease to the release fork and release bearing slide before installing the transmission.

7. Install the transmission and remaining components.

8. Check the freedom of movement of the clutch by selecting reverse gear with the engine running. The transmission should shift into reverse with little or no gear noise.

ADJUSTMENTS

Without Brake Bleeding Device

1. Loosen locknut on adjusting screw on master cylinder.

2. Turn adjusting screw in such a manner that pushrod will travel the idle path **B** up to piston first when pedal is actuated. If a line mark is shown on head of adjusting screw, make sure during inspection or during adjustment that this line mark is pointing toward the rear.

Brake Bleeding Device

1. Draw brake fluid from expansion tank up to connection for clutch actuation.

2. Pull connecting hose to master cylinder from expansion tank.

3. Open venting screw on clutch sleeve cylinder and evacuate clutch system by stepping repeatedly on clutch pedal.

4. Insert plastic hose of approximately 1 meter in length, 8mm in diameter, into connecting hose and immerse other end into a container filled with water.

5. Remove the left instrument panel under cover.

6. Clamp sheet metal approximately 1.5mm thick between upper pedal stop and rubber buffer.

7. Fill brake bleeding device with air and set working pressure to 0.5 bar gauge pressure.

8. Adjust brake bleeding device depending on make, in such a manner, that air is blown from clutch system and bubbles will rise in water tank.

NOTE: Place water tank into left hand leg room to gain advantage.

9. Turn adjusting screw on clutch pedal only until airflow is interrupted and no more bubbles are rising in water tank. Tighten locknut on adjusting screw.

10. Remove sheetmetal at upper pedal stop. Bubbles should rise again in water tank. Set brake bleeding device to 0.

11. Attach connecting hose to expansion tank.

12. Vent clutch actuation.

13. Check clutch actuation for function with engine running.

Clutch Master Cylinder

REMOVAL AND INSTALLATION

Except 300SL

1. Disconnect the negative battery cable. Remove cover from under instrument panel at left.

2. Remove floor mat at left.

3. To prevent contamination inside vehicle, draw fluid from respective chamber of combination clutch and expansion tank.

4. Unscrew line on master cylinder.

5. Pull off connecting hose on combination brake and clutch expansion tank.

6. Loosen piston rod for brake unit (brake booster) on brake pedal.

7. Pull cable plug from stop light switch.

8. Unscrew nuts for attaching pedal carrier to firewall.

9. Move pedal assembly to the rear until screw plate of pedal carrier is free from threaded bolt of brake unit (brake booster) and holder at top on water tank.

10. Remove pedal assembly in downward direction, while paying attention to connecting hose for master cylinder and remove master cylinder.

To install:

11. Install any fallen rubber mounts.

12. Install the master cylinder and torque the retaining bolts to 15 ft. lbs. (20 Nm).

13. Install the remaining components. Bleed the hydraulic system.

300SL

1. Disconnect the negative battery cable.

2. Remove the instrument panel undercover.

3. Siphon the fluid from the master cylinder.

4. Remove the hydraulic line from the cylinder.

5. Remove the pedal carrier, return spring and slacken the over-center spring. Disengage the clutch and remove the circlip and pushrod, spring and spring seat.

6. Remove the master cylinder retaining nuts and master cylinder.

To install:

7. Install the master cylinder and torque the nuts to 15 ft. lbs. (20 Nm).

8. Fit the pushrod and spring seat so the stiffening rib on the pushrod points upwards and the larger radius on the spring seat is on the left hand side.

9. Install the remaining components and bleed the system.

Clutch Slave Cylinder

REMOVAL AND INSTALLATION

1. Detach and plug the pressure line from the slave cylinder.

2. Remove the screws from the slave cylinder.

3. Remove the slave cylinder, pushrod and spacer.

To install:

4. Place the grooved side of the spacer in contact with the housing and hold it in position.

5. Install the slave cylinder and pushrod into the housing; be sure the dust cap is properly seated.

6. Install the attaching screws.

7. Connect the pressure line to the slave cylinder.

8. Bleed the slave cylinder.

Bleeding the Slave Cylinder

The same principle is used as in bleeding the brakes.

1. Check the brake fluid level in the compensating tank and fill to maximum level.

2. Put a hose on the bleeder screw of the right front caliper and open the bleeder screw.

3. Have a helper depress the brake pedal until the hose is full and

there are no air bubbles. Be sure the bleeder screw is closed each time the pedal is released.

4. Put the free end of the hose on the bleeder screw of the slave cylinder and open the bleeder screw.

5. Keep stepping on the brake pedal. Close the bleeder screw on the caliper and release the brake pedal. Open the bleeder screw and repeat the process until no air bubbles show up at the mouth of the inlet line of the compensating tank. Between operations, check and, if necessary, refill the compensating tank.

6. Close the bleeder screws on the caliper and slave cylinder and remove the hose.

7. Check the clutch operation and the fluid level.

AUTOMATIC TRANSMISSION

Transmission Assembly

REMOVAL AND INSTALLATION

Models 107, 124, 126, 129 and 140

1. Disconnect negative battery terminal.
2. Remove holder for oil filler pipe on cylinder head.
3. Disengage engine longitudinal regulating shaft.
4. Force off ball socket.
5. Disconnect control wire for control pressure.
6. Pull out lock and loosen control wire.
7. Raise and safely support the vehicle.
8. Remove cross yoke center place.
9. Remove drain plug on oil pan and drain oil.
10. Remove drain plug on torque converter and drain oil.
11. Remove cover plate.
12. Remove screws for driving plate torque converter.
13. Place a fitting wooden block between engine oil pan and cross yoke.
14. Loosen exhaust system on plug connection and remove.
15. Remove crossbeam together with rear engine mount.
16. Remove cable strap and cable on kickdown solenoid valve. Remove

fastening screw for impulse transmitter and pull out impulse transmitter.

NOTE: Disconnect tachometer shaft, if equipped with a mechanical tachometer.

17. Remove exhaust support.
18. Remove exhaust shielding plate.
19. Loosen propeller shaft clamping nut and contract propeller shaft, as much as possible.
20. Remove plug for starter lock out switch.

NOTE: Starter lock out switch plug is secured by a lock, white plastic ring. Prior to pushing off plug, turn lock in upward direction. Carefully, push off plug at cable outlet and tongue, by means of 2 suitable tools.

21. Pull off plug.
22. Disconnect control rod on range selector lever.
23. Remove holder and pull off vacuum line.
24. Remove oil cooler feed line.
25. Remove oil cooler return line.
26. Remove fastening screw for oil filler pipe and push oil filler pipe in upward direction.
27. Remove all fastening screw except for 2 lateral screws.
28. Slightly, lift transmission with mount 116 589 06 62 00 or equivalent, for pit lift.
29. Remove lateral screws.
30. Push transmission to rear as far as propeller shaft permits and lower carefully.

To install:
31. Reverse removal procedure taking attention to the following:
   a. Replace sealing rings for forward and return flow lines.
   b. Torque propeller shaft clamping nuts to 22 ft. lbs. (30 Nm).
   c. Torque driveplate screw to 31 ft. lbs. (42 Nm).
   d. Screw in drain plug on oil pan and on torque converter and torque to 10.5 ft. lbs. (14 Nm).
   e. Replace self-locking screws on cross yoke center piece and torque to 33 ft. lbs. (45 Nm).
   f. Adjust cable for control pressure.

722.4 (W4A020)
MODEL 201

NOTE: Attach a 300mm square sheetmetal panel to unit compartment wall to protect insulating mat during all jobs where the transmission is lowered at the rear. Disconnect exhaust assem-

bly at rear mounting bracket and fasten by means of a wire approximately 50cm lower. If equipped with an auxiliary heater, make sure the water hose is not damaged when lowering transmission.

1. Disconnect negative cable on battery.
2. Remove holder for oil filling pipe on cylinder head and holder on valve cover.
3. If equipped with a fuel injection engine:
   a. Force off ball socket.
   b. Disconnect cable control for control pressure. Pull out lock and remove cable control.
   c. Force plastic ball socket apart by means of a prybar and pull holding bracket from slotted lever.
4. Force off ball socket. Compress holding clips and disengage cable control for control pressure.
5. Force off ball socket, remove holding clips and disengage control pressure cable control.
6. Raise and safely support the vehicle.
7. Remove drain plug on oil pan as well as torque converter and drain oil.
8. Install drain plug with new seals and tighten to 10.5 ft. lbs. (14 Nm).
9. Remove screw for driven plate torque converter.
10. Remove crossmember with rear engine mount.
11. Remove exhaust support. Remove companion plate with articulated flange-transmission.
12. Disconnect exhaust system on rear suspension.
13. Remove shielding plate.
14. Remove propeller shaft clamping nut and run together propeller shaft, as much as possible.
15. Pull off cable on kickdown solenoid valve.
16. Remove speedometer shaft. If equipped with an electronic speedometer, remove impulse transmitter.
17. Disconnect control rod on floor shift.
18. Remove fastening clip for speedometer shaft.
19. Swivel locking bracket in upward direction and pull plug from starter lockout switch.
20. Pull vacuum line form vacuum control unit.
21. Remove socket screw from oil filler pipe and pull out oil filler pipe in upward direction.
22. Remove oil cooler lines and fastening clamps.

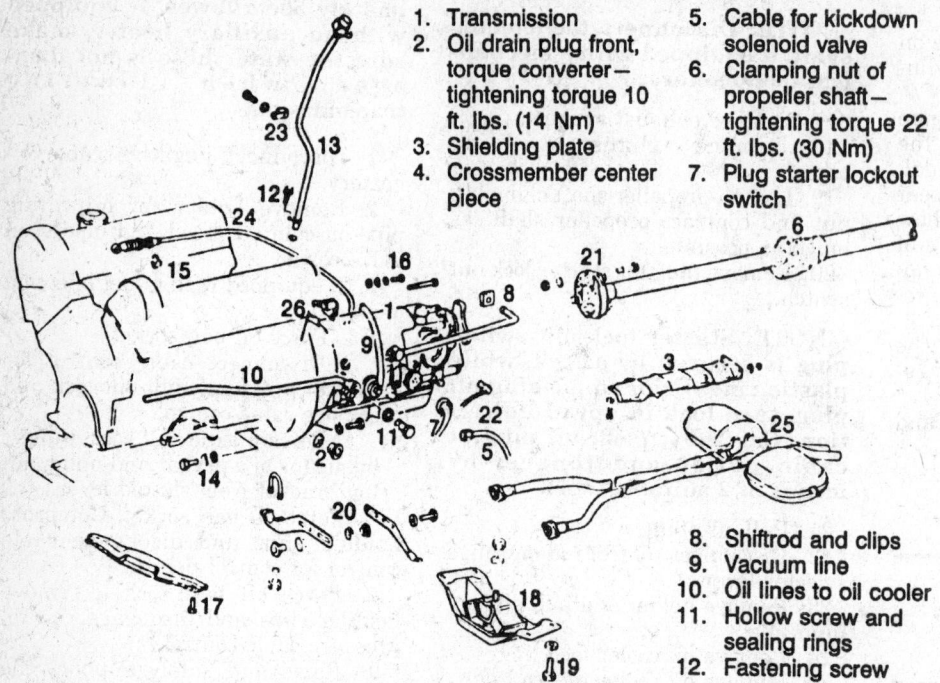

1. Transmission
2. Oil drain plug front, torque converter—tightening torque 10 ft. lbs. (14 Nm)
3. Shielding plate
4. Crossmember center piece
5. Cable for kickdown solenoid valve
6. Clamping nut of propeller shaft—tightening torque 22 ft. lbs. (30 Nm)
7. Plug starter lockout switch
8. Shiftrod and clips
9. Vacuum line
10. Oil lines to oil cooler
11. Hollow screw and sealing rings
12. Fastening screw
13. Oil filling pipe
14. Screws for fastening converter—tightening torque 31 ft. lbs. (42 Nm)
15. Fuse, control
16. Fastening screws
17. Self-locking hex head screws
18. Crossmember with rear engine mount
19. Fastening screws
20. Exhaust support
21. Unscrew companion plate on flexible flange
22. Impulse sensor, speedometer
23. Holder, oil filling pipe
24. Control pressure cable
25. Exhaust system
26. Cover position sensor EZL

Automatic transmission and related components — Models 124 and 126, others similar

23. Remove all fastening screws on transmission-to-engine except the 2 screws at left and right.

24. Insert holding device for torque converter into vent grille cutout and screw in stud until it is entering the socket of oil drain plug.

25. Slightly lift transmission with mounting for pit lift.

26. Remove remaining screws.

27. Slide transmission, to the extent propeller shaft permits, to the rear and carefully lower.

To install:

28. Install new sealing rings on oil cooler line.

29. Torque driven plate-to-converter screws to 31 ft. lbs. (42 Nm).

30. Install the transmission using a transmission jack.

31. Install remaining bolts and torque to 20 ft. lbs. (27 Nm).

32. Install the torque converter bolts.

33. Install oil cooler lines and fastening clamps.

34. Install the vacuum line form vacuum control unit.

35. Install fastening clip for speedometer shaft.

36. Connect control rod on floor shift.

37. Connect the cable on kickdown solenoid valve.

38. Install the shielding plate.

39. Connect the exhaust system on rear suspension.

40. Install the exhaust support.

41. Install the crossmember with rear engine mount.

42. Connect the cable control for control pressure. Pushing in the lock.

43. Lower the vehicle and connect negative cable on battery. Refill the transmission with fluid and road test.

4-MATIC

1. Disconnect the negative battery cable and drain the transmission fluid from the pan and torque converter.

2. Cover the insulating cover with suitable sheetmetal to prevent damage.

3. Release the pressure from the hydraulic system by switching over the lever on the service valve near the firewall. To the test position.

4. Remove the oil filler pipe at the cylinder head and remove the ball socket from the throttle control cable.

5. Remove the complete exhaust system with side support and shielding plates.

6. Disconnect the oil lines from the distributor and central lock connector.

7. Raise the transmission with a jack and remove the rear crossmember.

8. Remove the driveshafts and center bearing using a large box wrench and special tool 001589662100 or equivalent.

9. Remove the bellhousing cover plate and 6 torque converter bolts.

10. Disconnect the shift control linkage, wiring harnesses and speedometer.

11. Disconnect the oil filler tube.

12. Remove the transmission-to-engine bolts and lower the transmission. Pull the transmission/transfer case backwards and lower the transmission carefully, making sure all components are disconnected.

To install:

13. If renewing transmission, disconnect the transfer case from the transmission.

14. Raise the transmission/transfer into place and install retaining bolts. Torque the bolts to 40 ft. lbs. (55 Nm).

15. Connect the oil filler tube.

16. Connect the shift control linkage, wiring harnesses and speedometer.

17. Install the bellhousing cover plate and 6 torque converter bolts.

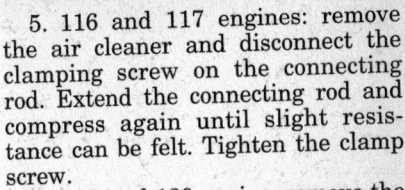

Apply Loctite® to the bolts and torque the bolts to 29 ft. lbs. (40 Nm).

18. Install the driveshafts and center bearing using a large box wrench and special tool 001589662100 or equivalent.

19. Install the rear crossmember.

20. Connect the oil lines to the distributor and central lock connector.

21. Install the complete exhaust system with side support and shielding plates.

22. Install the oil filler pipe at the cylinder head and the ball socket from the throttle control cable.

23. Remove sheetmetal from the insulating cover.

24. Connect the negative battery cable and refill the transmission fluid.

SELECTOR ROD ADJUSTMENT

NOTE: **Before performing this adjustment on any vehicle, be sure it is resting on its wheels. No part of the vehicle may be raised for this adjustment.**

NOTE: **The vehicle must be standing with the weight normally distributed on all 4 wheels.**

1. Disconnect the selector rod from the selector lever.

2. Set the selector lever in **N** and make sure there is approximately 1mm clearance between the selector lever and the **N** stop of the selector gate.

3. Adjust the length of the selector rod so it can be attached free of tension.

4. Retighten the counter nut.

CONTROL PRESSURE CABLE ADJUSTMENT

1. Make sure the throttle control cable is adjusted.

2. 102 engine: screw in adjusting far enough for the crimp nipple on the spacer sleeve to have about 1.40 in. (1mm) play. Unscrew the adjusting screw until the tip of the pointer is positioned exactly above the groove on the adjusting screw.

3. 103, 602 and 603 engines: disconnect the ball socket and pull the control cable forwards until a slight resistance can be felt. In this position, hold the ball socket over the ball head and attach and adjust by the adjusting screw if needed.

4. 104 engine: remove the air cleaner and adjust the control pressure cable by turning the adjusting screw until the tips of the needles are in alignment.

5. 116 and 117 engines: remove the air cleaner and disconnect the clamping screw on the connecting rod. Extend the connecting rod and compress again until slight resistance can be felt. Tighten the clamp screw.

6. 119 and 120 engine: remove the air cleaner and turn the adjusting screw on the cable until the pointer of the spacer sleeve aligns with the adjusting screw.

STARTER LOCKOUT SWITCH ADJUSTMENT

1. Place the transmission selector in the **N** position.

2. Insert a 5.6 in. (4mm) pin or drill through the lever into the locating hole in the switch housing.

3. If the pin will not align, loosen the switch screws and align.

4. Torque the switch screws to 72 inch lbs. (8 Nm) and remove the pin.

TRANSFER CASE

Transfer Case Assembly

REMOVAL AND INSTALLATION

4-MATIC

1. Disconnect the negative battery cable.

2. Remove the transmission and transfer case as an assembly.

3. Remove the transfer case from the rear of the transmission.

4. Install the transfer case and torque the bolts to 30 ft. lbs. (40 Nm).

5. Install the transmission/transfer case.

FRONT SUSPENSION

Shock Absorbers

REMOVAL AND INSTALLATION

Model 107

1. Raise and safely support the vehicle.

2. When removing the shock absorbers, note the position of all mounting hardware.

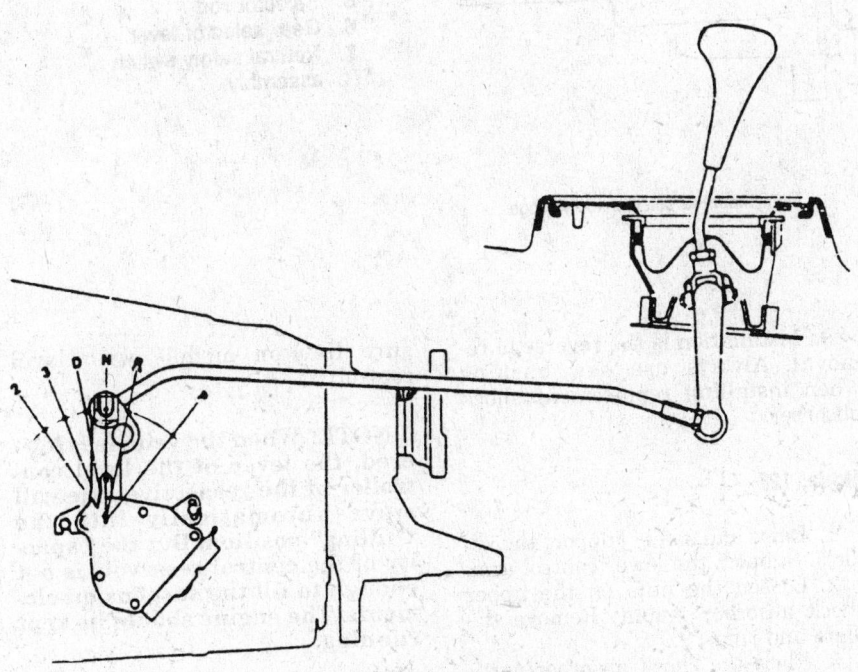

Control rod adjustment — Model 201

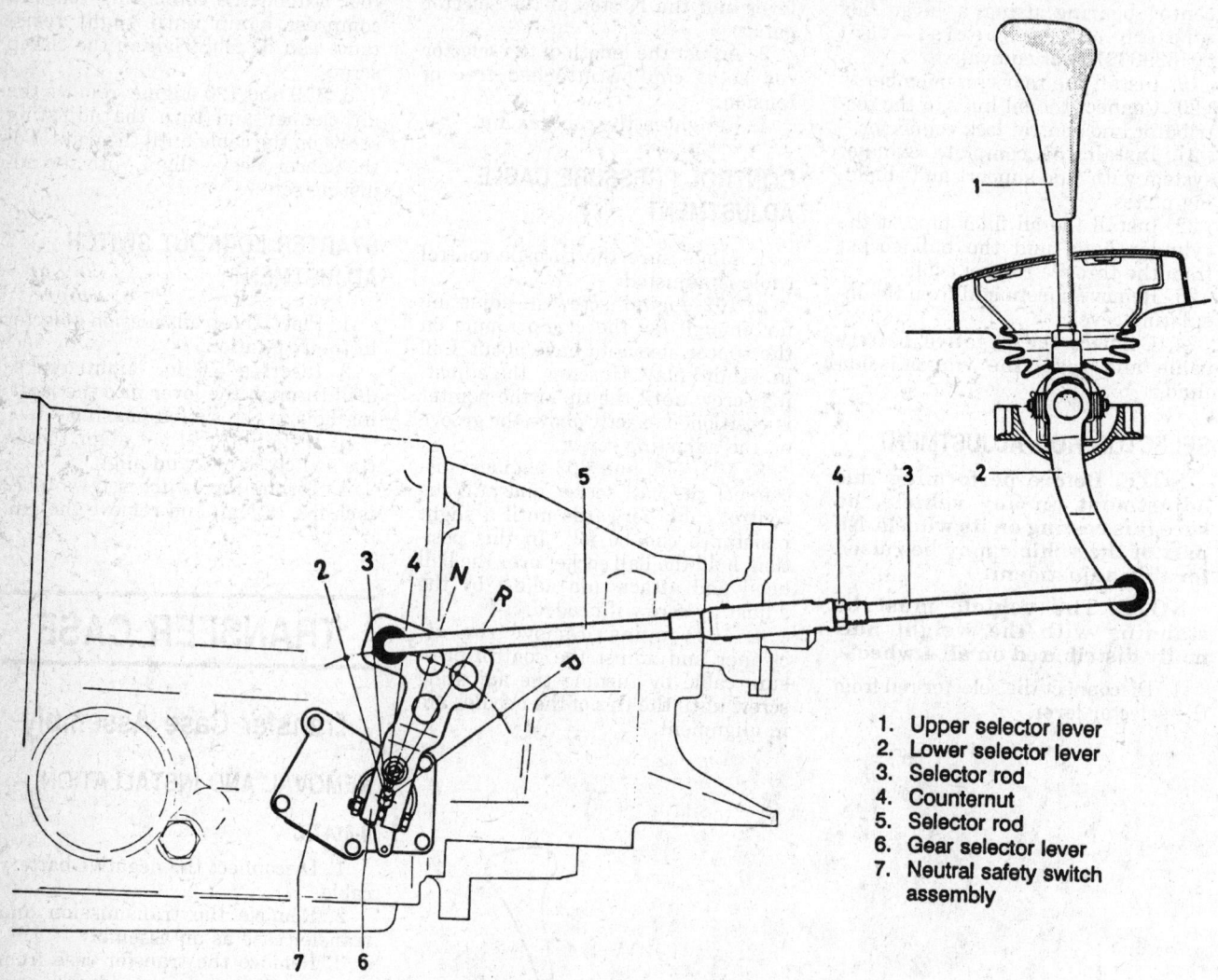

1. Upper selector lever
2. Lower selector lever
3. Selector rod
4. Counternut
5. Selector rod
6. Gear selector lever
7. Neutral safety switch assembly

Floor mounted selector rod linkage

3. Raise the hood and locate the upper shock absorber mount.

4. Support the lower control arm.

5. Unbolt the mount for the shock absorber at the top. Remove the coolant expansion tank to allow access to the right front shock absorber.

6. Remove the nuts which secure the shock absorber to the lower control arm.

7. Push the shock absorber piston rod in, install the stirrup, and remove the shock absorber.

8. Remove the stirrup, since this must be install on replacement shock absorber.

9. Installation is the reverse of removal. Always use new bushing when installing replacement shock absorber.

Model 126

1. Raise and safely support the vehicle. Support the lower control arm.

2. Loosen the nuts on the upper shock absorber mount. Remove the plate and ring.

3. Place the shock absorber vertical to the lower control arm and remove the lower mounting bolts.

4. Remove the shock absorber; be sure to disconnect and plug the pressure line on models with level control.

NOTE: When the vehicle is lowered, the lever of the level controller of the respective axle will move automatically into the ""filling" position. But the capacity of the central reservoir is not enough to fill the suspension elements. The engine should be kept running.

5. Installation is the reverse or removal. On Bilstein shocks, do not confuse the upper and lower plates. Torque the upper mounts to 18 ft. lbs.

(25 Nm) and the lower to 20 ft. lbs. (30 Nm).

MacPherson Strut

REMOVAL AND INSTALLATION

Models 124, 129, 140 AND 201

1. Raise and safely support the vehicle. Remove the wheel.
2. Using a spring compressor 124589063100 or equivalent, compress the spring until any load is removed from the lower control arm.

NOTE: When using a spring compressor, be sure a least 7½ coils are engaged before applying tension.

3. Support the lower control arm. Loosen the retaining bolt for the upper end of the damper strut by holding the inner piston rod with an Allen wrench and unscrew the nut. Never use an impact wrench on the retaining nut. Disconnect the hydraulic line from the ADS actuator, if equipped.

CAUTION

Never unscrew the nut with the axle half at full rebound the spring may fly out with considerable force, causing personal injury.

---

4. Unbolt the 2 screws and 1 nut and disconnect the lower damper strut from the steering knuckle.
5. Remove the strut down and forward. Be sure to disconnect and plug the pressure line on models with level control. Secure the steering knuckle in position so it won't tilt.
To install:
6. Note the following:
   a. When attaching the lower end of the damper strut to the steering knuckle, first position all 3 screws; next tighten the 2 lower screws to 72 ft. lbs. (100 Nm); finally, tighten the nut on the upper clamping connection screw to 54 ft. lbs. (75 Nm).
   b. Tighten the retaining nut on the upper end of the damper strut to 44 ft. lbs. (60 Nm).

Coil Springs

REMOVAL AND INSTALLATION

Models 124, 126 and 201

1. Raise and safely support the vehicle. Remove the wheel.
2. Remove the engine compartment lining under the vehicle, if equipped.

3. Install a spring compressor so at least 7½ coils are engaged.
4. Support the lower control arm and loosen the retaining nut at the upper end of the damper strut. Disconnect the ADS and ABS sensor connectors, if equipped.

CAUTION

Never loosen the damper strut retaining nut unless the wheels are on the ground, the control arm is supported or the springs have been removed; personal injury may result.

---

5. Lower the control arm slightly and remove the spring toward the front.
To install:
6. On installation, position the spring between the control arm and the upper mount so when the control arm is raised, the end of the lower coil will be seated in the impression in the control arm.
7. Raise the control arm until the spring is held securely.
8. Using a new nut, tighten the upper end of the damper strut to 44 ft. lbs. (60 Nm).
9. Slowly ease the tension on the spring compressor until the spring is seated properly and remove the compressor.
10. Installation of the remaining components is in the reverse order of removal.

Model 107

NOTE: Be extremely careful when attempting to remove the front springs as they are compressed and under considerable load.

1. Raise and safely support the vehicle. Remove the wheels.
2. Remove the front shock absorber and disconnect the sway bar.
3. Punchmark the position of the eccentric adjusters and loosen the hex bolts.
4. Support the lower control arm.
5. Knock out the eccentric pins and gradually lower the arm until spring tension is relieved.
6. The spring can now be removed.
To install:
7. For ease of installation, tape the rubber mounts to the springs.
8. Install the spring compressor and spring.
9. Install the lower control arm fasteners, but do not tighten at this time.
10. Support the lower control arm so the control arm is in the laden po-

sition and torque the bolts to 65 ft. lbs. (88 Nm).
11. Install the front shock absorber and connect the sway bar.
12. Install the wheels and lower the vehicle.

NOTE: Check caster and camber after installing a new spring.

Models 129 and 140

CAUTION

The spring is under extreme tension. Do not remove the spring unless an approved spring compressor is installed and is secure. If this caution is not followed, severe personal injury may result. Use Mercedes-Benz spring compressor 124589063100 or equivalent.

---

1. Raise the vehicle and support safely.
2. Install an approved spring compressor with the upper tensioning plate in the center of the spring and the lower tensioning plate at the bottom.
3. Turn the compressor with the tensioning cylinder far enough for about 8 windings to be covered.
4. Push the compressor cylinder through both plates and lock in the top by turning 90 degrees.
5. Compress the front spring and remove the top strut mounting only if the spring cannot be removed at this time. Disconnect the ADS sensor hydraulic pipe if equipped.
6. Place a jack under the lower control arm. Lower the front axle after disconnecting the top damper strut mounting.
7. Remove the spring with the rubber mount towards the front.
8. Place the spring in a vise and release the tension.
To install:
9. Clean the spring contact surfaces of dirt or contamination.
10. Compress the spring in the area of 8 spring windings and fit the rubber mount onto the front spring with a screwing movement.
11. Install the spring so the winding end is located in the embossed surface of the control arm. Raise the control arm and install a new damper strut nut and washer. Torque the nut to 44 ft. lbs. (60 Nm).
12. Release the tension on the spring and remove the spring compressor.
13. Connect the ADS sensor pipe, if equipped.
14. Lower the vehicle and check ride height and headlight setting.

Steering Knuckle

REMOVAL AND INSTALLATION

Models 124, 129 and 201

—————— CAUTION ——————
The spring is under extreme tension. Do not remove the spring unless an approved spring compressor is installed and is secure. If this caution is not followed, severe personal injury may result. Use Mercedes-Benz spring compressor 124589063100 or equivalent.

1. Raise and safely support the vehicle. Remove the wheel.
2. Install a spring compressor on the spring.
3. Remove the brake caliper and wire it aside; be careful not to damage the brake line.
4. Remove the brake disc and wheel hub.

NOTE: If equipped equipped with ABS, remove the speed sensor.

5. Unscrew the 3 socket-head bolts and remove the brake backing plate from the steering knuckle.
6. Tighten the spring compressor until all tension and/or lead has been removed from the lower control arm.
7. Disconnect the steering knuckle arm from the steering knuckle; this is the arm attached to the tie rod.

—————— CAUTION ——————
There must be no tension on the lower control arm; otherwise personal injury may result.

8. Unscrew the 3 bolts and disconnect the lower end of the damper strut from the steering knuckle.
9. Remove the hex-head clamp nut at the supporting joint, lower ball joint.
10. Remove the steering knuckle.
11. Installation is in the reverse order of removal. Tighten the supporting joint clamp nut to 70 ft. lbs. (125 Nm).

MODEL 107

—————— CAUTION ——————
The spring is under extreme tension. Do not remove the spring unless an approved spring compressor is installed and is secure. If this caution is not followed, severe personal injury may result.

Use Mercedes-Benz spring compressor 124589063100 or equivalent.

1. This should only be done with the front shock absorber installed. If, however, the front shock absorber has been removed, the lower control arm should be supported and the spring should be clamped with a spring tensioner. In this case, the hex nut on the guide joint should not be loosened without the spring tensioner installed.
2. Raise and safely support the vehicle.
3. Remove the wheel.
4. Remove the brake caliper.
5. Unbolt the steering relay lever from the steering knuckle. For safety, install spring clamps on the front springs.
6. Remove the hex nuts from the upper and lower ball joints.
7. Remove the ball joints from the steering knuckle with the aid of a puller.
8. Remove the steering knuckle.
To install:
9. Be sure the seats for the pins of the ball joints are free of grease. Do not torque any control arm components until the spring is in the laden position (vehicle weighted).
10. Install the steering knuckle.
11. Install the ball joints to the steering knuckle.
12. Install the hex nuts to the upper and lower ball joints. Torque the nuts to 35 ft. lbs. (48 Nm) and install new cotter pins, if equipped.
13. Install the steering relay lever to the steering knuckle.
14. Install the brake caliper.
15. Install the wheel.
16. Lower the vehicle and tighten any rubber mounted suspension components.
17. Bleed the brakes and align the front end.

MODEL 126

—————— CAUTION ——————
The spring is under extreme tension. Do not remove the spring unless an approved spring compressor is installed and is secure. If this caution is not followed, severe personal injury may result. Use Mercedes-Benz spring compressor 124589063100 or equivalent.

1. Raise and safely support the vehicle. For safety, install an approved coil spring compressor on the front spring. Support the lower control arms.

2. Remove the wheel.
3. Remove the steering knuckle arm from the steering knuckle.
4. Remove and suspend the brake caliper.
5. Remove the front wheel hub.

NOTE: If equipped equipped with ABS, disconnect the speed sensor.

6. Loosen the brake hose holder on the cover plate.
7. Loosen the guide joint nut and remove the joint from the steering knuckle.
8. Loosen the nut on the support joint.
9. Swivel the steering knuckle outward and force the ball joint from the lower control arm. Use a ball joint separator tool.
10. Remove the steering knuckle.
11. If necessary, remove the cover plate from the steering knuckle.
To install:
12. Install the steering knuckle and the cover plate.
13. Install the ball joint into the lower control arm.
14. Torque the nut on the support joint to 30 ft. lbs. (40 Nm).
15. Install the brake hose holder on the cover plate.
16. Install the front wheel hub.
17. Install the brake caliper.
18. Install the wheel.
19. Lower the vehicle.

MODEL 140

1. Raise the vehicle and support safely. Remove the front wheels.
2. Remove the caliper and hang by a wire, not the brake hose. Disconnect the ABS and ADS speed sensors, if equipped.
3. Remove the hose and cable holder with the cable.
4. Remove the rotor, hub and brake backing plate.
5. Remove the stabilizer bar linkage from the steering knuckle.

—————— CAUTION ——————
The front shock absorbers also serve as spring extension stops. Do not disconnect the shock absorber without first compressing the spring. Severe personal injury may result.

6. Install a spring compressor and compress the spring.
7. Remove the nut from the lower knuckle joint and disconnect the joint using a puller tool 140589093300 and thrust attachment 140589246300.
8. Remove the steering knuckle from the transverse link and steering knuckle.

To install:

9. Install the steering knuckle.

10. Install the nut to the lower knuckle joint and torque to 92 ft. lbs. (125 Nm).

11. Install the stabilizer bar linkage to the steering knuckle and torque to 30 ft. lbs. (40 Nm).

12. Install the rotor, hub and brake backing plate.

13. Install the hose and cable holder with the cable.

14. Install the caliper. Connect the ABS and ADS speed sensors, if equipped.

Lower Ball Joint

INSPECTION

1. Raise and safely support the vehicle. Check the steering knuckles or ball joints, by raising the front spring plate. This unloads the front suspension to allow the maximum play to be observed.

2. Late model ball joints need to be replaced only if dried out with plainly visible wear and/or play.

REMOVAL AND INSTALLATION

Models 107, 124, 129 and 201

1. Raise the vehicle and support safely. Remove the front wheel.

2. Remove the lower control arm from the vehicle. Pay attention to the front spring caution statement.

3. Place the assembly in a soft vise.

4. Use pressing tool 107589014300 or equivalent to remove the ball joint from the control arm.

To install:

5. Insert the ball joint into the tool and control arm so the mark on the ball joint corresponds with the center of the control arm. Check that the ball joint is seated correctly.

6. Install the control arm.

7. Lower the vehicle.

8. Align the front end.

Model 126

1. Raise the vehicle and support safely. Remove the front wheel.

2. Remove the brake caliper and hang with wire.

3. Support the lower control arm with a jack to retain the spring pressure during disassembly.

4. Remove the steering knuckle.

5. Use a suitable mandrel to knock out the ball joint from the steering knuckle. This will destroy the old ball joint.

To install:

6. Press the ball joint into the knuckle with the tool 116589046200 or equivalent.

7. Check the joint and boot for correct seat in the knuckle.

8. Install the remaining components. Align the front end.

Model 140

— **CAUTION** —

The lower ball joint also serve as spring extension stops. Do not disconnect the lower ball joint without first compressing the spring with an approved spring compressor. Severe personal injury may result.

1. Raise the vehicle and support safely. Remove the front wheel.

2. Remove the retaining bolt for the brake rotor and lower cover plate.

3. Support the lower control arm with a jack to retain the spring pressure during disassembly.

4. Remove the ball joint nut. Press the steering knuckle from the ball joint using a puller 140589093300.

5. Remove the transverse link by pressing out with the puller 140589093300.

6. Remove the ball joint and check the boot and joint for damage or excessive wear.

To install:

7. Install the ball joint and torque the lower nut to 103 ft. lbs. (140 Nm) and the upper to 75 ft. lbs. (100 Nm).

8. Install the transverse link.

9. Install the retaining bolt for the brake rotor and lower cover plate.

10. Install the front wheel.

11. Align the front end.

Upper Ball Joints

REMOVAL AND INSTALLATION

Model 107

1. Raise the vehicle and support safely. Remove the front wheel.

2. Place a support stand under the lower control arm to take off the spring pressure. Remove the steering knuckle-to-upper ball joint nut.

3. Disconnect the joint from the knuckle using an approved separator tool.

4. Remove the joint boot and spring.

5. Press the ball joint from the upper control using a removing tool 107589014300 or equivalent.

6. Measure the bore for the ball joint in the control arm. The mea-surement must not exceed 1.89 in. (48mm).

To install:

7. Press the ball joint into the control arm using the tool 107589014300 or equivalent.

8. Install the steering knuckle and torque the nut to 66 ft. lbs. (90 Nm).

9. Lower the vehicle and check the front end alignment.

Models 124, 129 and 201

These models do not use upper ball joints.

Models 126 and 140

The upper ball joint is an integral part of the upper control arm. They are serviced as a complete unit.

Upper Control Arm

NOTE: Models 124, 129 and 201 have no upper control arm.

REMOVAL AND INSTALLATION

Model 107

1. The front shock absorbers should remain installed. Never loosen the hex nuts of the ball joints with the shock absorber removed, unless a spring clamp is installed.

2. Raise and safely support the vehicle. Remove the wheel.

3. Support the front end.

4. Remove the steering arm from the steering knuckle.

5. Separate the brake line and brake hose from each other and plug the openings.

6. Support the lower control arm and unscrew the nuts from the ball joints.

7. Remove the ball joints from the steering knuckle.

8. Loosen the bolts on the upper control arm and remove the upper control arm.

9. Installation is the reverse of removal.

NOTE: Mount the front hex bolt from the rear in a forward direction and the rear hex bolt from the front in a rearward direction.

10. Bleed the brakes.

Model 140

1. Raise the vehicle and support safely. Remove the wheel.

2. Install a suitable jack stand under the lower control arm to support the spring tension.

3. Remove the ball joint nut and press the joint from the knuckle using a suitable prybar. Use widening tool 140589023100 if the joint is too tight to remove the ball joint.

4. Wire the steering knuckle to the suspension with wire.

5. Remove the upper bushing bolts from the frame.

6. Carefully remove the upper control arm from the vehicle.

To install:

7. Carefully Install the upper control arm to the vehicle. Do not torque the bolts until the vehicle is resting on the suspension.

8. Install the upper bushing bolts loosely.

9. Install the ball joint nut and torque to 92 ft. lbs. (125 Nm).

10. Lower the vehicle and torque the control arm-to-frame bolts to 37 ft. lbs. (50 Nm) when the vehicle is resting on the suspension.

11. Install the wheel and align the front end.

Lower Control Arm

REMOVAL AND INSTALLATION

Model 107

1. Since the front shock absorber acts as a deflection stop for the front wheels, the lower shock absorber attaching point should not be loosened unless the vehicle is resting on the wheels or unless the lower control arm is supported.

2. Raise and safely support the vehicle.

3. Support the lower control arm.

4. Loosen the lower shock absorber attachment.

5. Unscrew the steering arm from the steering knuckle.

6. Separate the brake line and brake hose and plug the openings.

7. Remove the front spring.

8. Unscrew the hex nuts on the ball joints.

9. Remove the lower ball joint and remove the lower control arm.

To install:

10. Install the lower ball joint and lower control arm. Torque the ball joint nut to 25 ft. lbs. (34 Nm).

11. Install the front spring.

12. Separate the brake line and brake hose and plug the openings.

13. Install the steering arm to the steering knuckle.

14. Torque the lower shock absorber attachment to 20 ft. lbs. (27 Nm).

15. Lower the vehicle. Bleed the brakes and check the front end alignment.

Models 124 and 201

1. Remove the engine compartment lining at the bottom of the vehicle, if equipped.

2. Raise and safely support the vehicle. Remove the wheel.

3. Support the lower control arm and disconnect the torsion bar bearing at the control arm.

4. Remove the spring.

5. Disconnect the tie rod at the steering knuckle and press out the ball joint with the proper tool.

6. Remove the brake caliper and position it aside; do not damage the brake line.

7. Remove the brake disc/wheel hub assembly.

8. Disconnect the lower end of the damper strut from the steering knuckle and remove the knuckle.

9. Mark the position of the inner eccentric pins, relative to the frame, on the bearing of the control arm.

10. Unscrew and remove the pins.

11. Remove the lower control arm.

To install:

12. Note the following:

   a. Tighten the eccentric bolts on the inner arm to 130 ft. lbs. (180 Nm).

   b. To facilitate torsion bar installation, raise the opposite side of the lower control arm.

   c. Tighten the clamp nut on the tie rod ball joint to 25 ft. lbs. (35 Nm).

   d. When installing the rear torsion bar bushing, the flats on the cone must be vertical.

Model 126

The lower control arm is the same as the front axle half. For safety install a spring compressor on the coil spring.

1. Raise and safely support the vehicle. Remove the wheels.

2. Remove the front shock absorber. Loosen the top mount first. Disconnect the ABS and ADS speed sensors and wiring connectors, if equipped.

3. Remove the front springs.

4. Separate and plug the brake lines.

5. Remove the track rod from the steering knuckle arm.

6. Matchmark the position of the eccentric bolts on the bearing of the lower control arm in relation to the crossmember.

7. Remove the shield from the cross yoke.

8. Support the front axle half.

9. Loosen the eccentric bolt on the front and rear bearing of the lower control arm and knock them out.

10. Remove the bolt from the cross yoke bearing.

11. Loosen the screw at the opposite end of the cross yoke bearing.

12. Pull the cross yoke bearing down slightly.

13. Loosen the support of the upper control arm on the torsion bar. Remove the clamp screw from the clamp.

14. Remove the upper control arm bearing on the front end.

15. Remove the front axle half.

To install:

16. Install the front axle half. Tighten the eccentric bolts on the lower control arm bearing to 35 ft. lbs. (47 Nm). with the vehicle resting on the wheels. Check the front end alignment after complete reassembly.

17. Install the upper control arm bearing on the front end.

18. Tighten the support of the upper control arm on the torsion bar to 25 ft. lbs. (34 Nm). Install the clamp screw to the clamp.

19. Tighten the screw at the opposite end of the cross yoke bearing.

20. Install the bolt to the cross yoke bearing.

21. Torque the eccentric bolt on the front and rear bearing of the lower control arm to 35 ft. lbs. (47 Nm).

22. Install the shield from the cross yoke.

23. Install the track rod to the steering knuckle arm.

24. Reconnect the brake lines. Connect the ABS and ADS speed sensors and wiring connectors, if equipped.

25. Install the front springs.

26. Install the front shock absorber.

27. Install the front wheel and lower the vehicle.

Model 129

1. Raise and safely support the vehicle.

2. Remove the lower engine compartment cover.

3. Remove the sway bar nuts and retaining bracket.

4. Using an approved spring compressor, remove the front spring.

5. Mark the control arm mounting and eccentric bolts.

6. Remove the lower control arm mounting bolts.

7. Remove the steering knuckle from the control arm by removing the clamp bolt.

To install:

8. Check the control arm support and mounting for damage.

9. Install the control arm and torque the steering knuckle to 90 ft. lbs. (125 Nm). Fill the separating slot with sealing compound to prevent contamination.

10. Insert the front eccentric bolt from the back to the front. The rear eccentric bolt from the front to the rear. Do not tighten until the vehicle weight is on the suspension.

11. Install the sway bar and torque the nuts to 15 ft. lbs. (20 Nm).

12. Install the front spring and lower the vehicle.

13. Torque the eccentric bolts to 88 ft. lbs. (120 Nm) with the vehicle weight on the suspension.

14. Adjust the front wheel alignment.

Model 140

1. Raise the vehicle and support safely. Remove the front wheel.

2. Install a suitable spring compressor. Compress the spring to take the pressure off of the suspension.

3. Disconnect the lower control arm from the steering knuckle using a separator tool 140589093300 and thrust attachment 1405896300 or equivalent.

NOTE: To attach the puller, it is necessary to remove the retaining bolt from the brake disc as well as the bottom mounting bolt for the brake backing plate.

4. Make sure the spring tension is not on the lower control arm. Disconnect the shock absorber from the control arm.

5. Mark the eccentric bolts in relation to the frame and remove.

6. Remove the lower control arm from the frame.

To install:

7. Install the lower control arm to the frame. Do not torque the bolts until the vehicle is resting on the suspension.

8. Install the eccentric bolts loosely.

9. Connect the shock absorber to the control arm and torque the nut to 75 ft. lbs. (100 Nm).

10. Connect the lower control arm to the steering knuckle and torque to 103 ft. lbs. (140 Nm).

11. Remove the spring compressor.

12. Install the front wheel, lower the vehicle and torque the eccentric bolts to 133 ft. lbs. (180 Nm) after the front end has been aligned.

Sway (Stabilizer) Bar

REMOVAL AND INSTALLATION

Model 107

1. Raise the vehicle and support safely. Remove the front wheel.

2. Disconnect the connecting linkage rods from both control arms.

3. Remove the sway bar-to-frame retainers, brackets and sway bar.

To install:

4. Check and replace any worn rubber bushing or connecting linkage. Lubricate the bushings with naphthrolene grease.

5. Install the sway bar. The rubber mounts slots should face forward. Align the sway bar before torquing the retainers.

6. Torque the frame retainers to 18 ft. lbs. (25 Nm). Tighten the connecting links to the end of the threads.

7. Bounce the front end and check for squeaks and misalignment.

8. Install the front wheel and lower the vehicle.

Models 124, 129, 140 and 201

1. Raise the vehicle and support safely. Remove the front wheel.

2. Remove the engine compartment covers.

3. Remove the mounting bracket at both control arms. Disconnect the ADS linkage from the sway bar, if equipped.

4. Remove the retaining bracket-to-leaf spring link, if equipped with 4-Matic.

5. Remove the sway bar-to-frame mounts and sway bar.

To install:

6. Check and replace any worn rubber bushings. Lubricate the bushings with naphthrolene grease.

7. Determine whether the plain bearing bushing is seated correctly. Polish the sway bar bearing bushing with fine emery paper. Insert a new snaping in the groove on the rubber bearing before installing the plain bearing, if equipped with 4-Matic.

8. Install the sway bar. The rubber mounts slots should face forward. Align the sway bar before torquing the retainers.

9. If equipped with ADS, push the clamp onto the sway bar. Fit the bushing onto the bar with the hexagon end 1st and insert into the linkage. Fit the linkage onto the sway bar so the fastening rod is facing the center of the sway bar. Push the clamp over the flat on the linkage

and torque the bolt to 7 ft. lbs. (10 Nm).

10. Torque the frame retainers to 44 ft. lbs. (60 Nm) and remaining retainers to 15 ft. lbs. (20 Nm).

11. Bounce the front end and check for squeaks and misalignment.

12. Install the front wheel and lower the vehicle.

Model 126

1. Raise the vehicle and support safely. Remove the front wheel.

2. Loosen the sway bar-to-upper control arm nut.

3. Remove the master cylinder and brake booster unit, if there is an obstruction.

4. Remove the coolant hoses and regulating linkage, if equipped.

5. Loosen the frame-to-sway bar mounting nuts and bracket.

6. Remove the covers at both ends and sway bar.

To install:

7. Check and replace any worn rubber bushings. Lubricate the bushings with naphthrolene grease.

8. Install the sway bar and mounting hardware, loosely.

9. Torque the frame-to-sway bar mounting nuts and torque to 15 ft. lbs. (20 Nm). The separating slots should face the rear of the vehicle.

10. Install the rubber end mounts so the lug of the rubber mount is seated in the recess of the upper ball joint. Torque the end bolts to 48 ft. lbs. (65 Nm).

11. Install the master cylinder and brake booster unit, if removed.

12. Lower the vehicle. Bounce the suspension and check for noise or misalignment.

Models 129 and 140

1. Raise the vehicle and support safely. Remove the front wheel.

2. Remove the engine compartment covers.

3. Remove the mounting bracket at both control arms.

4. Remove the sway bar-to-frame mounts and sway bar.

To install:

5. Check and replace any worn rubber bushings. Lubricate the bushings with naphthrolene grease.

6. Install the sway bar. The rubber mounts slots should face forward. Align the sway bar before torquing the retainers.

7. Torque the frame retainers to 44 ft. lbs. (60 Nm) and remaining retainers to 15 ft. lbs. (20 Nm).

8. Bounce the front end and check for squeaks and misalignment.

9. Install the front wheel and lower the vehicle.

Front Wheel Bearings

Refer to the Drive Axle section for 4-Matic.

ADJUSTMENT

1. Tighten the clamp nut until the hub can just be turned.
2. Slacken the clamp nut and seat the bearings on the spindle by rapping the spindle sharply with a hammer.
3. Attach a dial indicator, with the pointer indexed, onto the wheel hub.
4. Check the endplay of the hub by pushing and pulling on the flange. The endplay should be approximately 0.0004-0.0008 in.
5. Make an additional check by rotating the washer between the inner race of the outer bearing and the clamp nut. It should be able to be turned by hand.
6. Check the position of the suppressor pin in the wheel spindle and the contact spring in the dust cap.
7. Pack the dust cap with 20-25 grams of wheel bearing grease and install the cap.
8. Install the brake caliper and bleed the brakes.

REMOVAL AND INSTALLATION

If the wheel bearing play is being checked for correct setting only, it is not necessary to remove the caliper. It is only necessary to remove the brake pads.
1. Raise the vehicle and support safely. Remove the brake caliper and hang by a wire.
2. Pull the cap from the hub with a pair of channel-lock pliers. Remove the radio suppression spring, if equipped.
3. Loosen the socket screw of the clamp nut on the wheel spindle. Remove the clamp nuts and washer.
4. Remove the front wheel hub and brake disc.
5. Remove the inner race with the roller cage of the outer bearing.
6. Using a brass or aluminum drift, carefully tap the outer race of the inner bearing until it can be removed with the inner race, bearing cage and seal.
7. In the same manner, tap the outer race of the bearing off the hub.
8. Separate the front hub from the brake disc.

To install:
9. To assemble, press the outer races into the front wheel hub.
10. Pack the bearing cage with bearing grease and insert the inner race with the bearing into the wheel hub.
11. Coat the sealing ring with sealant and press it into the hub.
12. Pack the front wheel hub with 45-55 grams of wheel bearing grease. The races of the tapered bearing should be well packed and also apply grease to the front faces of the rollers. Pack the front bearings with the specified amount of grease. Too much grease will cause overheating of the lubricant and it may lose its lubricity. Too little grease will not lubricate properly.
13. Coat the contact surface of the sealing ring on the wheel spindle with Molykote paste or equivalent.
14. Press the wheel hub onto the wheel spindle.
15. Install the inner race and cage of the outer bearing.
16. Install the steel washer and the clamp nut.

REAR SUSPENSION

Shock Absorbers

REMOVAL AND INSTALLATION

Model 107

1. Remove the top and open cover flap. Remove the side cover plate to access the upper shock mount.
2. Remove the upper nuts and bushings. Use 2 wrenches for this procedure. Disconnect the hydraulic hose, if equipped with level control.
3. Remove the lower shock mounts and remove the shock through the bottom of the vehicle.

To install:
4. Install the shock. Lubricate the bushings with rubber grease.
5. Torque the lower retainers to 33 ft. lbs. (45 Nm) and the upper retaining nuts to the end of the threads. Install new copper O-rings, connect the hydraulic line and torque to 20 ft. lbs. (30 Nm), if equipped with level control.
6. Install the top and open cover flaps.

Models 124, 129, 140 and 201

1. Raise and safely support the vehicle.
2. From inside the trunk (sedans), remove the rubber cap, locknut and hex nut from the upper mount of the shock absorber.
3. Remove the control arm cover. Unbolt the mounting for the rear shock absorber at the bottom and remove the shock absorber. Be sure to disconnect and plug the pressure line, if equipped with level control (ADS).

To install:
4. Install the shock. Lubricate the bushings with rubber grease.
5. Torque the lower retainers to 44 ft. lbs. (60 Nm).
6. Install the lower mount bushing so the rounded side faces the floor and the upper faces the washer.
7. Torque the 1st nut to 10 ft. lbs. (13 Nm) and the locknut to 18 ft. lbs. (25 Nm).
8. Install new copper O-rings, connect the hydraulic line and torque to 20 ft. lbs. (30 Nm), if equipped with level control.
9. Install the top and open cover flaps.
10. Install the remaining components and lower the vehicle.

Springs

REMOVAL AND INSTALLATION

Always replace the springs in matched sets. The vehicle profile will be incorrect if only one side is installed.

Model 107

1. Raise and safely support the vehicle.
2. Remove the rear shock absorber.
3. Raise the control arm to a horizontal position. Install a spring compressor to aid in this operation.
4. Carefully, lower the control arm until it contacts the stop on the rear axle support.
5. Remove the spring and spring compressor with great care.
6. Installation is the reverse of removal. For ease of installation, attach the rubber seats to the springs with masking tape.

Models 124, 129, 140 and 201

1. Raise and safely support the vehicle. Remove the wheel.
2. Disconnect the holding clamps for the spring link cover and remove

the cover. Disconnect the ADS hydraulic pipe, if equipped.

3. Install a spring compressor and compress the spring until the spring link is free of all load.

4. Disconnect the lower end of the shock absorber.

5. Increase the tension on the spring compressor and remove the spring.

To install:

6. Note the following:

a. Position the spring so the end of the lower coil is seated in the impression of the spring seat and the upper coil seats properly in the rubber mount in the frame floor.

b. Do not release tension on the spring compressor until the lower end of the shock absorber is connected and tightened to 47 ft. lbs. (65 Nm).

7. Do not tighten the control arm bushing bolts until the vehicle weight is resting on the suspension.

8. Install the spring and lower control arm.

9. Install the shock absorber and knuckle.

10. Install the remaining components and lower the vehicle. Torque the control arm bushing bolt to 51 ft. lbs. (70 Nm) with the vehicle weight resting on the suspension. Align the rear end.

Model 126

1. Raise the vehicle and support safely. Remove the wheel. Place a jackstand under the lower control arm.

2. Remove the upper shock absorber mount from inside the trunk. Remove the shock absorber from the vehicle.

3. Install an approved spring compressor 115589003100 or equivalent, to the center of the spring. Compress about 5-6 coils together.

4. Remove the rear spring with the rubber mount.

To install:

5. Compress about 5-6 coils together with the spring compressor.

6. Install the rubber mount and position the spring so the coil end is seated in the trailing arm.

7. Loosen the spring compressor and check the spring alignment.

8. Install the shock absorber and remaining components.

9. Check the vehicle profile and correct if necessary. If the profile is not correct, the spring is probably seated incorrectly.

Lower Control Arm

REMOVAL AND INSTALLATION

1. Raise the vehicle and safely support. Remove the wheels.

2. Remove the control arm cover, if equipped.

3. Support the lower control arm using a suitable jack.

4. Disconnect the roll-over switch (Model 129) and any other pipe or wiring harness. Remove the serrated bolts from the frame transverse link and reinforcement plate.

5. Remove the rear spring using a suitable spring compressor.

6. Disconnect the shock absorber, lower ball joint and sway bar.

7. Remove the inner bushing bolt and lower control arm.

To install:

8. Install the lower control arm and loosely install the bolt and nut.

9. Connect the knuckle and torque the ball joint nut to 15 ft. lbs. (20 Nm).

10. Install the spring using a suitable spring compressor.

11. Install the spring link and sway bar. Torque the bolts to 44 ft. lbs. (60 Nm).

12. Install the remaining components and lower the vehicle.

13. Torque the inner bushing bolt to 51 ft. lbs. (70 Nm) with the vehicle weight resting on the suspension.

Upper Control Arms

REMOVAL AND INSTALLATION

1. Raise the vehicle and support safely. Remove the wheel and place a suitable jackstand under the lower control arm or rear knuckle. Be careful not to damage the suspension components.

2. Lower the vehicle to remove the spring tension from the upper control arms.

3. Remove the control arm-to-frame and knuckle nuts.

4. Remove the control arm from the vehicle.

To install:

5. Install the control arm and retainers. Do not tighten the bolts until the vehicle weight is resting on the suspension.

6. Lower the vehicle and torque the inner bolts to 52 ft. lbs. (70 Nm)

and the outer nuts to 33 ft. lbs. (45 Nm).

Rear Wheel Bearings

Refer to the Drive Axle section.

STEERING

Steering Wheel

AIRBAG PRECAUTIONS

• Most vehicles are equipped with a Supplemental Restraint System (SRS). Improper maintenance, including incorrect removal and Installation of related components, can lead to personal injury caused by unintentional activation of the Airbag.

• Testing, disassembly and assembly of the Airbag and seat belt tensioning devices must only be performed and supervised by specially trained personnel.

• The Airbag and belt tensioning devices are category T1 pyrotechnic devices. The handling, transportation and storage are subject to local, state and federal regulations under the ""Law of Explosive Substances" and must be reported to the proper trade supervisory office.

• The Airbag and seat belt devices must only be fitted when the negative battery terminal is disconnected and covered. Also, disconnect the 10-pin test connector before servicing the Airbag or seat belt tensioning device.

• If work should be interrupted, the Airbag and/or seat belt device must be returned to the storage in a sealed room. Under no circumstances should the components be left unsupervised.

• Do not test the Airbag and seat belt devices without Mercedes-Benz approved testing equipment

REMOVAL AND INSTALLATION

Without SRS

1. Disconnect the negative battery cable. On Model 107, pry the 3-pointed star trademark from the center padding. On all other models, remove the padded plate. Pull at one corner near the wheel spokes.

2. Unscrew the hex nut from the steering shaft and remove the spring washer and the steering wheel.

NOTE: All models use an Allen screw in place of the hex nut. The Allen screw must be replaced, if removed.

3. Installation is the reverse of removal. Be sure the alignment mark on the steering shaft is pointing upward and be sure the slightly curved spoke of the steering wheel is down. Torque the steering shaft nut to 25 ft. lbs. (34 Nm).

SRS

1. Turn the ignition key to the **OFF** position.
2. Disconnect the negative battery cable.
3. Remove the floor mat and passenger side kickpanel. Disconnect the red airbag test connector, if equipped.
4. From behind the steering wheel, remove the air bag retaining screws. Pull the air bag out far enough to disconnect the electrical connector.
5. Set the steering wheel in a horizontal position and lock the wheel in place.
6. Remove the countersunk nut from the steering spindle.
7. Matchmark the steering shaft and wheel. Remove the steering wheel with a suitable steering wheel puller.

To install:

8. Before installation, make sure the battery is disconnected and the key is turned to the **OFF** position.
9. Install the steering wheel and torque the shaft nut to 60 ft. lbs. (80 Nm).
10. Install the air bag and torque the screws to 53 inch lbs. (6.0 Nm).
11. Connect the red airbag test connector, install the kickpanel, connect the battery cable and check operation.

Power Steering Gear

REMOVAL AND INSTALLATION

1. Raise the vehicle and support safely. Remove the oil from the power steering reservoir using a syringe.
2. Remove the plastic cover and heat shield.
3. Detach the high-pressure hose and oil return hose from the steering assembly.
4. Cap both lines to prevent entry of dirt and remove the clamp screw

from the lower part of the coupling flange.

5. Remove the rubber plug from the cover plate and remove the U-joint socket screw. On LS90 power steering units, remove the steering spindle. Pull the steering spindle up only until the coupling is no longer engaged with the worm gear.
6. The tail pipe and left side exhaust pipe may have to be removed for access.
7. Detach the tie rod and center tie rod or drag link and track rod, from the pitman arm, using pullers or a tie rod splitter.
8. Disconnect the parameter valve connector, if equipped with speed sensitive steering.
9. Remove the hex-head bolts that hold the gearbox to the frame, press the worm shaft stub from the steering coupling and remove the gearbox from under the vehicle.

To install:

10. First install the pitman arm, if removed, aligning the matchmarks. Tighten the pitman arm nut to 110 ft. lbs. and install the cotter pin.
11. Remove the screw plug from the steering box. Turn the worm shaft until the center of the power piston is directly below the bore in the housing. Check dimension (a) which can be altered by changing the position of the pitman arm on its shaft.
12. Center the steering wheel.
13. Press the worm shaft stub into the steering shaft coupling, making sure not to damage the serrations.
14. Use new self-locking nuts to attach the gear to the frame. Torque the bolts to 37 ft. lbs. (50 Nm) plus an additional 90 degrees turning torque. Install and tighten the coupling clamp screw to 22 ft. lbs. (30 Nm).
15. Install the plug in the gearbox, using a new gasket; attach the tie rods to the pitman arm and make sure the steering knuckle arms rest against their stops at full left and right lock.
16. Connect the parameter valve connector, if equipped with speed sensitive steering.
17. Check toe-in and correct if necessary. Remove the dust covers from the fluid lines, reconnect the high and low pressure lines.
18. Fill the reservoir and connect a hose between the bleed screw on the steering and the reservoir.
19. Open the bleed screw and, with engine running, bleed the system and top up.

Power Steering Pump

REMOVAL AND INSTALLATION

Except Model 140

1. Disconnect the negative battery cable and remove the air intake hose. Remove the power steering fluid from the reservoir with an extraction syringe.
2. Remove the supply tank nut.
3. Remove the spring and damping plate.
4. Drain the oil from the tank with a syringe.
5. Loosen and remove the expanding and return hoses from the pump. Plug all connections and pump openings.
6. If necessary for clearance, loosen the radiator shell. Loosen the mounting bolts and move the pump toward the engine by using the toothed wheel. Remove the belt. Remove the pulley and the pump.
7. Loosen the plate nut and the support bolt.
8. Push the pump toward the engine and remove the belts from the pulley.
9. Unscrew the mounting bolts and remove the pump and carrier.

To install:

10. Transfer the pulley to the new pump. Install the pump and mounting bolts. Torque the bolts to 18 ft. lbs. (25 Nm).
11. Install the drive belt and adjust the tensioner.
12. Install the expanding and return hoses to the pump. Torque the fittings to 29-34 ft. lbs. (40-45 Nm).
13. Refill the oil to the tank.
14. Install the spring and damping plate.
15. Connect the negative battery cable.

Model 140

1. Disconnect the negative battery cable and remove the air intake hose. Remove the power steering fluid from the reservoir with an extraction syringe.
2. Disconnect the pressure and return hoses. Cap all open connections.
3. Loosen the belt tensioner and remove the serpentine belt. Note the belt routing before removal.
4. Remove the fan shroud ring and crossmember for the 12 cylinder engine.
5. Remove the power steering pump pulley.
6. Remove the pump retaining bolts and pump.

To install:

7. Install the pump and retaining bolts. Torque the bolts to 22 ft. lbs. (30 Nm).

8. Install the power steering pump pulley.

9. Install the fan shroud ring and crossmember for the 12 cylinder engine.

10. Install the belt and tighten the belt tensioner.

11. Connect the pressure and return hoses. Torque the large pressure hose to 37 ft. lbs. (50 Nm), small pressure line if equipped with ADS to 18 ft. lbs. (25 Nm) and return hose to 30 ft. lbs. (40 Nm).

12. Connect the negative battery cable and install the air intake hose.

13. Refill and bleed the power steering and ADS systems.

SYSTEM BLEEDING

1. The reservoir should be filled to the COLD level with power steering fluid. Remove the plastic cover for 12 cylinder engine.

2. Raise the vehicle and support it safely.

3. Turn the steering wheel fully to the right and left until no air bubbles appear in the fluid. Maintain the reservoir level.

4. Lower the vehicle and with the engine idling, turn the wheels fully to the right and left. Stop the engine.

5. Repeat the procedure until no air bubbles pass through the tube.

6. Refill the reservoir as needed and check that no further bubbles are present in the fluid. An abrupt rise in the fluid level after stopping the engine is a sign of incomplete bleeding. This will cause noise from the pump or control valve. The noise will probably subside after the vehicle sits for about an hour. Recheck the level after this time.

Tie Rod Ends

REMOVAL AND INSTALLATION

1. Remove the under cover, if equipped. Mark the tie rod and adjusting sleeve with tape.

2. Remove the self-locking nuts from the rod joint.

3. Using a tie rod separator 129589106300 or equivalent, remove the tie rod end from the steering arm.

4. Loosen the locking bolt and turn the tie rod from the adjusting sleeve.

5. Check the tie rod end for excessive backlash and damaged boots, replace if necessary.

To install:

6. Install tie rod end to the marked location. Torque the self-locking nut and adjusting sleeve nut to 34 ft. lbs. (50 Nm). Torque the collar band bolt to 15 ft. lbs. (20 Nm).

7. Have the front end aligned.

BRAKES

Master Cylinder

REMOVAL AND INSTALLATION

1. Disconnect the negative battery cable. To remove the master cylinder, first open a bleed screw at one front and one rear wheel, if equipped.

2. Pump the pedal to empty the reservoir completely. Make sure both reservoirs are completely drained.

3. Disconnect the switch connectors from the master cylinder and reservoir.

4. Remove the brake fluid reservoir from the master cylinder. Push to the side and pull to release from the rubber mounts.

5. Disconnect the brake lines at the master cylinder. Plug the ends with bleed screw caps or the equivalent.

6. Unbolt the master cylinder from the power brake unit and remove; do not loose the O-ring in the flange groove of the master cylinder.

To install:

7. Be sure to replace the O-ring between the master cylinder and the power brake unit, since this must be absolutely tight. Torque the nuts to 12-15 ft. lbs. (17-20 Nm).

8. Connect the brake lines and torque to 84 inch lbs. (10 Nm).

9. Press the brake reservoir into the rubber mounts. Make sure the reservoir is fully seated in the mounts.

10. Be sure both chambers are completely filled with brake fluid and bleed the brakes.

Power Brake Booster

REMOVAL AND INSTALLATION

Model 107

1. Disconnect the negative battery cable and disconnect the electrical connectors from the master cylinder and brake booster, if equipped.

2. Remove the master cylinder and move out of the way.

3. Disconnect the vacuum hose.

4. Remove the rubber cover from the firewall and remove the nut.

5. Remove the instrument panel undercover and pull downwards.

6. Disconnect the leg room lamp and remove the cover.

7. Remove the lock and pull out flange pin, so the pushrod is released from the pedal.

8. Remove the retaining nuts and brake booster.

To install:

9. Install the booster and retaining nuts. Torque the nuts to 12 ft. lbs. (15 Nm).

10. Install the flange pin and lock to the pushrod.

11. Connect the leg room lamp and install the cover.

12. Install the nut and rubber cover to the firewall.

13. Connect the vacuum hose.

14. Install the master cylinder.

15. Connect the negative battery cable and connect the electrical connectors to the master cylinder and brake booster, if equipped.

Model 126

1. Disconnect the negative battery cable. If equipped with a manual transmission, remove hose to master cylinder.

2. Remove master cylinder.

3. Loosen vacuum line to brake unit.

4. Remove cover under dash panel on driver's side.

5. Remove lock and remove collar bolt to release pushrod.

6. Remove nuts for fastening booster unit to front end and remove booster unit.

NOTE: Care must be taken when handling brake unit. It is made of plastic and may break.

To install:

7. Position brake unit to front end and install attaching nuts. Torque to 11 ft. lbs. (15 Nm).

8. Install collar bolt and lock to pushrod and brake pedal.

9. Install cover under dash panel.

10. Connect vacuum line to brake unit and torque nut to 22 ft. lbs. (30 Nm).

11. Install master cylinder.

12. If equipped with a manual transmission, connect hose to master cylinder on expansion tank. Bleed the brake system if hydraulic pipes were disconnected.

Models 124, 129, 140 and 201

NOTE: Care must be taken when handling brake unit. It is made of plastic and may break.

1. Disconnect the negative battery cable.

2. Remove the master cylinder and instrument panel cover.

3. Disconnect the vacuum line and disconnect the pedal return spring.

4. Remove the lock pin from the brake booster pushrod.

5. Remove the booster retaining nuts and remove the brake booster.

To install:

6. Install the booster and torque the nuts and brake lines to 11 ft. lbs. (15 Nm).

7. Connect the vacuum line and install the master cylinder.

8. Bleed the master cylinder.

Brake Caliper

REMOVAL AND INSTALLATION

Model 107

NOTE: The brake hose does not have to be disconnected if the caliper is not being serviced. Hang the assembly from a suspension component during the procedure. Do not hang by the brake hose.

1. Pump the brake fluid out of the front brake circuit through an open bleeder valve.

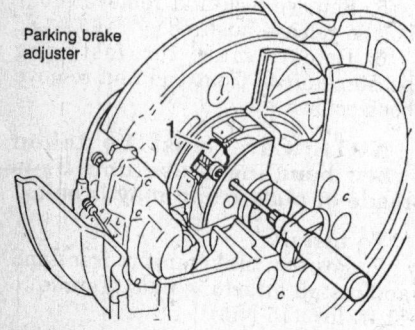

Parking brake adjuster

Power braking system — Model 126 shown, others similar

2. Remove the brake hose and plug immediately.

3. Disconnect the brake lining wear indicator out of the plug connector on fixed calipers, if equipped.

4. Unbend the locking plates from the caliper retaining bolts.

5. Remove the bolts and caliper from the steering knuckle.

To install:

6. Install the caliper and bolts. Torque the bolts to 85 ft. lbs. (115 Nm) and bend over the locking plates. Replace the locking plates if damaged.

7. Connect the brake lining wear indicator, if equipped.

8. Install the brake hose and torque to 15 ft. lbs. (20 Nm).

9. Fill the master cylinder with fluid and bleed the brake system.

Models 124, 126, 129, 140 and 201

FIXED CALIPER

NOTE: The brake hose does not have to be disconnected if the caliper is not being serviced. Hang the assembly from a suspension component during the procedure. Do not hang by the brake hose.

1. Disconnect the brake line from the caliper and plug immediately. If the system drains completely, the entire system will have to be bled.

2. Disconnect the contact sensor and plug connection from the caliper.

3. Remove the self-locking caliper-to-steering knuckle bolts and caliper. Replace with new bolts.

To install:

4. Install the caliper and torque the self-locking bolts to 85 ft. lbs. (115 Nm).

5. Install the brake hose and torque to 11 ft. lbs. (15 Nm).

6. Install the remaining components and bleed the brake system.

FLOATING CALIPER

NOTE: The brake hose does not have to be disconnected if the caliper is not being serviced. Hang the assembly from a suspension component during the procedure. Do not hang by the brake hose.

1. Disconnect the brake line from the caliper and plug immediately. If the system drains completely, the entire system will have to be bled.

2. Disconnect the contact sensor and plug connection from the caliper.

3. Remove the floating caliper bolts. Slide the caliper from the carrier.

To install:

4. Clean the floating guides and guide bolts. Lubricate with anti-seize compound or equivalent.

5. Install the caliper and torque the self-locking bolts to 50 ft. lbs. (68 Nm).

6. Install the brake hose and torque to 11 ft. lbs. (15 Nm), if removed.

7. Install the remaining components and bleed the brake system.

Disc Brake Pads

REMOVAL AND INSTALLATION

Models 124 and 201

FRONT AXLE

1. Raise and safely support the vehicle.

2. Remove the front wheel assemblies.

3. Lift the 2 holding lugs located laterally on the cover of the plug connection by means of a suitable tool and open the cover. Do not use force. Remove the cable of clip sensor from the plug connection on the floating caliper. Do not pull on the cable.

4. Remove the lower caliper bolt while applying counter hold to the sliding bolt.

5. Swing the cylinder housing upward and engage with a suitable hook to the wheel housing. Remove both brake pads from the brake carrier.

6. Pull the clip sensor from the back plate of the lining.

7. Draw some brake fluid from the expansion tank.

8. Push the piston back with resetting device 000 589 52 43 00 or equivalent.

To install:

9. Place the new brake pads into the brake carrier. Make sure the spring clamp is located in parallel with the upper edge of the lining.

10. Complete the installation by reversing the removal procedure. Torque the caliper bolt to 26 ft. lbs. (35 Nm).

11. Install the wheel assemblies and lower the vehicle. Check the brake fluid lever and replenish, if necessary.

NOTE: Prior to moving the vehicle, apply the brake pedal several times to adjust the brake pads to the brake disc.

REAR AXLE

1. Raise and safely support the vehicle.

2. Remove the rear wheel assemblies.

3. Knock the holding pin from the fixed caliper by means of a punch. Remove the cross spring.

4. Push the brake pads from the fixed caliper by means of a pushing lever.

NOTE: If the brake pads are rusted, use a puller for removal of the stuck brake pads.

5. Clean the guide surface for the brake pad in the fixed caliper with a brake caliper brush.

6. Draw some brake fluid from the expansion tank.

7. Push both the pistons back with a resetting device.

To install:

8. Place the new brake pads into the brake carrier.

9. Complete the installation by reversing the removal procedure.

10. Install the wheel assemblies and lower the vehicle. Check the brake fluid lever and replenish, if necessary.

NOTE: Prior to moving the vehicle, apply the brake pedal several times to adjust the brake pads to the brake disc.

Models 126, 129 and 140

FIXED CALIPER

1. Raise and safely support the vehicle.

2. Remove the wheel assemblies.

3. On fixed calipers with a brake lining wear indicator, pull the cables of the clip sensors from the plug connection on the fixed caliper.

4. On Teves® fixed caliper, knock the holding pin from the caliper by means of a punch.

5. On Bendix® and Girling® fixed calipers, pull both locking eyes from the holding pins and remove the holding pins.

6. Pull the clip sensor from the backing plate or brake lining. Simultaneously, remove the cross spring or spring holding lining.

NOTE: Renew the clip sensor only, when the insulating layer of the contact pin is rubbed through or in the event of damage on a part of the sensor, including the line insulation.

7. Force the brake pads from the fixed caliper by means of the forcing lever.

NOTE: If the brake pad is rusted, use a puller for removal of the stuck brake pads.

8. Clean the guide for the brake pad in the fixed caliper with a brake caliper brush.

9. Draw a slight amount of brake fluid from the expansion tank.

10. Push both the pistons back with a resetting device.

To install:

11. Place the new brake pads into the brake carrier.

12. Complete the installation by reversing the removal procedure.

13. Install the wheel assemblies and lower the vehicle. Check the brake fluid lever and replenish, if necessary.

NOTE: Prior to moving the vehicle, apply the brake pedal several times to adjust the brake pads to the brake disc.

FLOATING CALIPER

1. Raise and safely support the vehicle.

2. Remove the wheel assemblies.

3. Lift the 2 holding lugs located laterally on the cover of the plug connection by means of a suitable tool and open the cover. Do not use force. Remove the cable of clip sensor from the plug connection on the floating caliper; do not pull on the cable.

4. Remove the upper caliper bolt while applying counter hold to the sliding bolt.

5. Fold the cylinder housing in a downward direction and attach to the torsion bar by means of a suitable hook. Remove both brake pads from the brake carrier.

6. Pull the clip sensor from the lining backup plate.

NOTE: The wear indicator on the floating caliper is the inside of the brake pad only. Renew the clip sensor only, when the insulating layer of the contact pin is rubbed through or in the event of damage on a part of the sensor, including the line insulation.

7. Clean the contact surface of the brake pads in the brake carrier.

8. Draw a slight amount of brake fluid from the expansion tank.

9. Push the piston back with resetting device.

To install:

10. Place the new brake pads into the brake carrier; make sure the spring clamp is located in parallel with the upper edge of the lining.

11. Complete the installation by reversing the removal procedure. Torque the caliper bolt to 26 ft. lbs. (35 Nm).

12. Install the wheel assemblies and lower the vehicle. Check the

brake fluid lever and replenish, if necessary.

NOTE: Prior to moving the vehicle, apply the brake pedal several times to adjust the brake pads to the brake disc.

Brake Rotor

REMOVAL AND INSTALLATION

Front

MODELS 107 AND 126

1. Raise the vehicle and support safely. Remove the wheel.

2. Remove the caliper and hang from the suspension with a wire.

3. Remove the grease cap and loosen the clamp screw.

4. Remove the clamp nut, washer and outer bearing.

5. Remove the brake rotor and hub from the vehicle.

6. Place the rotor assembly in a vise.

7. Remove the 3 bolts in back of the hub.

To install:

8. Install the rotor to the hub and torque to 85 ft. lbs. (115 Nm).

9. Install the brake rotor and hub.

10. Install the outer bearing, washer and clamp nut.

11. Adjust the bearing preload.

12. Tighten the clamp screw and install the grease cap.

13. Remove the caliper and torque the bolts to 85 ft. lbs. (115 Nm).

14. Install the wheel and lower the vehicle safely.

MODELS 124, 129, 140 AND 201

1. Raise the vehicle and support safely. Remove the wheel.

2. Remove the brake caliper.

3. Remove the rotor retaining screws, if equipped. Remove the rotor from the vehicle. If stuck, strike with a rubber or plastic hammer to brake loose.

To install:

4. Remove any rust on the rotor flange and hub. Lightly lubricate the flange surface with Molykote® paste.

5. Install the rotor. Make sure the clamping sleeves are seated properly in the rotor drum. Torque the retaining screw to 82 inch lbs. (10 Nm).

6. Install the caliper and wheel. Torque the wheel lugs to 75 ft. lbs. (100 Nm).

Rear

1. Raise the vehicle and support safely. Remove the wheel.

2. Remove the brake caliper.

3. Remove the rotor retaining screws, if equipped.

4. All Models, except 107; insert a brake spoon or prybar through a hole in the rotor and backoff the parking brake shoes.

5. Remove the rotor from the vehicle. If stuck, strike with a rubber or plastic hammer to loosen.

To install:

6. Remove any rust on the rotor flange and hub. Lightly lubricate the flange surface with Molykote® paste.

7. Install the rotor. Make sure the clamping sleeves are seated properly in the rotor drum. Torque the retaining screw to 82 inch lbs. (10 Nm).

8. Turn the parking brake adjuster until the rotor will not turn. Backoff the adjusting wheel 2-3 turns or until the rotor can be turned without force for all models except 140. Turn the adjuster to the right until the rotor cannot be turned. Backoff the adjuster 5-5.5 turns until the rotor can be turned without force for Model 140.

9. Install the caliper and torque the bolts to 85 ft. lbs. (115 Nm).

10. Install the wheel. Torque the wheel lugs to 110 ft. lbs. (150 Nm).

Parking Brake Shoes

REMOVAL AND INSTALLATION

1. Raise the vehicle and support safely. Remove the wheel.

2. Loosen the parking brake shoe adjuster and remove the brake rotor.

3. Turn the rear axle shaft flange so the hole points to the shoe retaining springs. Unhook the springs with spring tool 112589096100 or equivalent.

4. Unhook the return springs with the spring tool.

5. Spread the shoes apart so they can be removed over the axle shaft flange.

6. Press out the spreader lock and remove from the brake cable.

To install:

7. Install the adjuster device so the adjusting wheel points toward the front. Lubricate all moving components with Molykote® grease, or equivalent.

8. Install the cable with the pin. Press the spreader lock against the cover ring.

9. Press out the spreader lock and remove from the brake cable.

10. Hook the return springs with the spring tool to the spring holes.

11. Install the brake rotor and adjust the parking brake.

12. Install the wheel and lower the vehicle safely.

Bleeding Brake System

WITHOUT ANTI-SKID CONTROL (ASR)

1. Carefully clean all dirt from around the master cylinder filler cap.

2. If a bleeder tank is used, follow the manufacturer's instructions.

3. Remove the filler cap and refill the master cylinder to the lower edge of the filler neck.

4. Clean off the bleeder connections at all of the disc brake calipers. Attach the bleeder hose and fixture to the right rear caliper bleeder screw and place the end of the tube in a glass jar, submerged in brake fluid.

5. Open the bleeder valve 1/2-3/4 turn. Have an assistant depress the brake pedal and allow it to return slowly. Continue this pumping action to force any air out of the system.

6. When bubbles cease to appear at the end of the bleeder hose, close the bleeder valve and remove the hose. Check the level of the brake fluid in the master cylinder and add fluid, if necessary.

7. After the bleeding operation at each caliper has been completed, refill the master cylinder reservoir and replace the filler plug.

NOTE: Never reuse brake fluid which has been removed from the lines through the bleeding process because it contains air bubbles and dirt. Do not allow the master cylinder to run dry. The entire system will have to be rebled if this happens.

ANTI-SKID CONTROL (ASR)

Except Model 140

1. Turn the ignition switch **OFF**. Remove the master cylinder cap.

2. Drain the pressure storage tank through the bleed screw labeled **SP** at the ABS/ASR unit.

3. Install a brake bleeding device according to the manufacturers instructions.

4. Bleed all 4 calipers starting with the furthest from the master cylinder.

5. Start the engine and bleed screw **SP** until clean brake fluid is free of bubbles. Allow the pressure reservoir to charge for about 30 seconds.

6. Turn the engine **OFF**

7. Fill the reservoir and install the cap.

8. Check brake operation before moving the vehicle.

Model 140

1. Turn the ignition switch **OFF**. Remove the master cylinder cap.

2. Fabricate a jumper wiring harness as shown. Disconnect the switchover valve for the master cylinder.

3. Remove fuse **28** from fuse block F1; F1 is located next to the ABS hydraulic unit.

4. Connect the flat connector from the fabricated harness to the input of fuse **28** in the fuse block.

5. Connect the alligator clip form the fabricated harness to the ground.

6. Connect the double connector to the switchover valve.

7. Install a brake bleeding device according to the manufacturers instructions.

8. Bleed all 4 calipers starting with the furthest from the master cylinder.

9. Remove the ABS hydraulic unit cover. With the ignition **OFF** open the bleed screw **SP** until clean brake fluid is free of bubbles.

10. Start the engine and open the bleed screw **SP** until clean brake fluid is free of bubbles. Allow the pressure reservoir to charge for about 30 seconds.

11. Turn the engine **OFF**. Remove the fabricated harness and reconnect all wiring.

12. Fill the reservoir and install the cap.

13. Check brake operation before moving the vehicle.

Anti-Lock Brake System Service

PRECAUTIONS

• When welding with an electric welding unit, unplug the electric control unit.

• During paint jobs, the electronic control unit may be exposed to a maximum of 203°F (95°C) for up to 2 hours or 185°F (85°C) if more time is needed.

• When removing the rear axle centerpiece, make sure the correct toothed wheel with the correct ratio for the wheel speed sensor is installed. If a wheel with the wrong number of teeth is installed, this fault will not show up when checking the system with the ABS tester. The stopping distance, however, will be increased during controlled braking.

- If work was done to non-ABS brake components, a simple operational test will be sufficient. This means that after driving about 5 mph, the yellow warning light on the instrument panel should go out if the ABS system is intact.
- If ABS components have been replaced, the entire system should be checked using the appropriate Bosch tester in combination with brake test bench or an adaptor in combination with a multimeter.

RELIEVING ANTI-LOCK BRAKE SYSTEM PRESSURE

Place a shop rag around the bleeder screw before loosening. Open the bleeder screw **SP** on the hydraulic ABS/ASR unit about 1 turn. Allow the entire contents to drain into a collection bottle.

Anti-Lock Brake (ABS) Hydraulic Unit

REMOVAL AND INSTALLATION

Models 107 and 126

1. With ignition switch **OFF**, disconnect battery negative terminal.
2. Disconnect brake lines from hydraulic unit and seal open lines with blind plugs.

NOTE: Do not loosen sealed center bolt and 2 socket screws on the hydraulic unit.

3. Remove cover fastening screw and remove cover.
4. Disconnect grounding strap from pump motor.
5. Disconnect stress relief and remove plug.

NOTE: Two relays for pump motor or for solenoid valves can be replaced.

6. Remove mounting nuts and hydraulic unit.

To install:

7. Mount hydraulic unit on mounting bracket and attach 12 terminal plug and attach stress relief.
8. Install hydraulic unit cover and screw.
9. Connect brake lines to hydraulic unit. Torque line nuts to 10 ft. lbs. (14 Nm).

NOTE: Do not interchange brake lines.

H — from master cylinder rear axle circuit
V — from master cylinder front axle circuit
l — from ABS unit to front left caliper
r — from ABS unit to front right caliper
h — from ABS unit to rear calipers
SP — pressure storage tank bleed screw

10. Connect ground terminal of battery.

Models 124, 129, 140 and 201

1. Disconnect the negative battery cable.
2. Bleed the ABS system and remove the ABS/ASR protective cover.
3. Disconnect all electrical and hydraulic lines from the hydraulic unit. Use flarenut wrenches to remove the lines. Plug all lines to prevent contamination.
4. Remove the retaining bolts and remove the unit with the mounting brackets.

To install:

5. Install the unit and torque the bolts to 15 ft. lbs. (20 Nm).
6. Connect the lines and torque to 11 ft. lbs. (15 Nm).
7. Use the following symbols for reference to the ABS hydraulic unit:
vl — front left caliper
vr — front right caliper
hl — rear left caliper
hr — rear right caliper
H — master cylinder rear axle
V — master cylinder front axle
BA — precharging pump for ASR
P — pump
E — input pressure storage tank
SP — pressure storage tank bleed screw
8. Connect all electrical wiring.
9. Bleed the ABS/ASR system.

Rear Speed Sensor

REMOVAL AND INSTALLATION

The speed sensors are located at the rear drive axle assembly.

WITHOUT ANTI-SKID CONTROL (ASR)

Except models 129 and 140

1. Disconnect the negative battery cable.
2. Remove the rear seat and backrest.
3. Remove the sensor connector and disconnect. Remove downwards

through the rubber grommet in the floor.
4. Remove the sensor retaining screw and sensor.

To install:

5. Make sure no metallic particles are located on the magnetic edge of the speed sensor. Install a new O-ring and sensor. Torque the retaining screw to 70 inch lbs. (8 Nm).
6. Connect the wiring harness.
7. Install the rear seat and backrest.
8. Connect the battery cable and check operation.

Models 129 and 140

1. Disconnect the negative battery cable.
2. Remove the sensor connector and disconnect. Open the bayonet lock by 1 notch.
3. Remove the sensor retaining screw and sensor.

To install:

4. Make sure no metallic particles are located on the magnetic edge of the speed sensor. Install a new O-ring and sensor. Torque the retaining screw to 70 inch lbs. (8 Nm).
5. Connect the wiring harness. Make sure the plug terminals are correct by aligning the letter markings.
6. Read out and erase fault memory using a Mercedes-Benz diagnostic tool, if needed.
7. Connect the battery cable and check operation.

ANTI-SKID CONTROL (ASR)

1. Disconnect the negative battery cable.
2. Remove the seat and seatback.
3. Disconnect the speed sensor connector attached to the floor.
4. Press the rubber grommet and wire through the floor.
5. Raise the vehicle and support safely.
6. Remove the exhaust system and disconnect the speed sensor connectors.
7. Remove the rear axle carrier assembly. Lower the assembly on a jack far enough to remove the speed sensors in the top of the housing.
8. Remove the retaining screw and sensor from the housing.

To install:

NOTE: The speed sensor with the straight output goes on the left and sensor with the angled output goes on the right.

9. Make sure no metallic particles are located on the magnetic edge of

the speed sensor. Install a new O-ring and sensor. Torque the retaining screw to 70 inch lbs. (8 Nm).

10. Connect the speed sensor connectors and install the exhaust system.

11. Lower the vehicle safely.

12. Press the rubber grommet and wire through the floor and connect.

13. Install the seat and seatback.

14. Connect the negative battery cable.

Front Speed Sensors

REMOVAL AND INSTALLATION

The front speed sensors are located at each wheel knuckle.

NOTE: On vehicles with ADS, the acceleration sensor is connected to the speed sensor via a sheetmetal bracket. Remove the speed sensor with the acceleration sensor bracket and pull out the right hand plug connection from the front axle distributor.

1. Disconnect the negative battery cable.

2. Raise the vehicle and support safely. Remove the wheel.

3. Remove the speed sensor wiring bracket and disconnect the coaxial plug. Always replace the O-ring.

4. Remove the rubber grommet from the wheelhouse.

5. Remove the sensor retaining screw and sensor with cable.

To install:

6. Coat the sensor bore with Molykote® grease..

7. Make sure no metallic particles are located on the magnetic edge of the speed sensor. Install a new O-ring and sensor. Torque the retaining screw to 70 inch lbs. (8 Nm).

8. Connect the speed sensor connectors.

9. Press the rubber grommet and wire through the wheelhouse and connect.

10. Install the wheel and lower the vehicle.

11. Read out and erase fault memory using a Mercedes-Benz diagnostic tool, if needed for Models 129 and 140.

12. Connect the negative battery cable.

ENGINE IDENTIFICATION

Year	Model	Engine Displacement Liters (cc)	Engine Series Identification	Fuel System	No. of Cylinders	Engine Type
1990	Precis	1.5 (1468)	4G15	MPI	4	SOHC
	Mirage	1.5 (1468)	4G15	MPI	4	SOHC
	Mirage	1.6 (1597)	4G61	MPI	4	DOHC
	Galant	2.0 (1997)	4G63	MPI	4	SOHC
	Galant	2.0 (1997)	4G63	MPI	4	DOHC
	Sigma	3.0 (2972)	6G72	MPI	6	SOHC
	Eclipse	1.8 (1755)	4G37	MPI	4	SOHC
	Eclipse	2.0 (1997)	4G63	MPI	4	DOHC
	Eclipse	2.0 (1997)	4G63	MPI	4	DOHC w/Turbo
1991	Precis	1.5 (1468)	4G15	MPI	4	SOHC
	Mirage	1.5 (1468)	4G15	MPI	4	SOHC
	Mirage	1.6 (1597)	4G61	MPI	4	DOHC
	Galant	2.0 (1997)	4G63	MPI	4	SOHC
	Galant	2.0 (1997)	4G63	MPI	4	DOHC
	Galant	2.0 (1997)	4G63	MPI	4	DOHC w/Turbo
	Eclipse	1.8 (1755)	4G37	MPI	4	SOHC
	Eclipse	2.0 (1997)	4G63	MPI	4	DOHC
	Eclipse	2.0 (1997)	4G63	MPI	4	DOHC w/Turbo
	3000GT	3.0 (2972)	6G72	MPI	6	DOHC
	3000GT	3.0 (2972)	6G72	MPI	6	DOHC w/Twin Turbo
1992	Precis	1.5 (1468)	4G15	MPI	4	SOHC
	Mirage	1.5 (1468)	4G15	MPI	4	SOHC
	Mirage	1.6 (1597)	4G61	MPI	4	DOHC
	Expo LRV	1.8 (1834)	4G93	MPI	4	SOHC
	Expo	2.4 (2351) ①	4G64	MPI	4	SOHC
	Galant	2.0 (1997)	4G63	MPI	4	SOHC
	Galant	2.0 (1997)	4G63	MPI	4	DOHC
	Galant	2.0 (1997)	4G63	MPI	4	DOHC w/Turbo
	Eclipse	1.8 (1755)	4G37	MPI	4	SOHC
	Eclipse	2.0 (1997)	4G63	MPI	4	DOHC
	Eclipse	2.0 (1997)	4G63	MPI	4	DOHC w/Turbo
	3000GT	3.0 (2972)	6G72	MPI	6	DOHC
	3000GT	3.0 (2972)	6G72	MPI	6	DOHC w/Twin Turbo
	Diamante	3.0 (2972)	6G72	MPI	6	SOHC
	Diamante	3.0 (2972)	6G72	MPI	6	DOHC

ENGINE IDENTIFICATION

Year	Model	Engine Displacement Liters (cc)	Engine Series Identification	Fuel System	No. of Cylinders	Engine Type
1993	Precis	1.5 (1468)	4G15	MPI	4	SOHC
	Mirage	1.5 (1468)	4G15	MPI	4	SOHC
	Mirage	1.8 (1834)	4G93	MPI	4	SOHC
	Expo LRV	1.8 (1834)	4G93	MPI	4	SOHC
	Expo/Expo LRV	2.4 (2351) ②	4G64	MPI	4	SOHC
	Galant	2.0 (1997)	4G63	MPI	4	SOHC
	Eclipse	1.8 (1755)	4G37	MPI	4	SOHC
	Eclipse	2.0 (1997)	4G63	MPI	4	DOHC
	Eclipse	2.0 (1997)	4G63	MPI	4	DOHC w/Turbo
	3000GT & SL	3.0 (2972)	6G72	MPI	6	DOHC
	3000GT VR-4	3.0 (2972)	6G72	MPI	6	DOHC w/Twin Turbo
	Diamante ES	3.0 (2972)	6G72	MPI	6	SOHC
	Diamante LS	3.0 (2972)	6G72	MPI	6	DOHC
1994	Precis	1.5 (1468)	4G15	MPI	4	SOHC
	Mirage	1.5 (1468)	4G15	MPI	4	SOHC
	Mirage	1.8 (1834)	4G93	MPI	4	SOHC
	Expo LRV	1.8 (1834)	4G93	MPI	4	SOHC
	Expo/Expo LRV	2.4 (2351) ②	4G64	MPI	4	SOHC
	Galant	2.0 (1997)	4G63	MPI	4	SOHC
	Eclipse	1.8 (1755)	4G37	MPI	4	SOHC
	Eclipse	2.0 (1997)	4G63	MPI	4	DOHC
	Eclipse	2.0 (1997)	4G63	MPI	4	DOHC w/Turbo
	3000GT & SL	3.0 (2972)	6G72	MPI	6	DOHC
	3000GT VR-4	3.0 (2972)	6G72	MPI	6	DOHC w/Twin Turbo
	Diamante ES	3.0 (2972)	6G72	MPI	6	SOHC
	Diamante LS	3.0 (2972)	6G72	MPI	6	DOHC

DOHC—Double Overhead Camshaft
SOHC—Single Overhead Camshaft
Carb—Carburetor
MPI—Multi-Port Injection
① 8 valve
② 16 valve

GENERAL ENGINE SPECIFICATIONS

Year	Engine Series ID	Engine Displacement Liters (cc)	Fuel System Type	Net Horsepower @ rpm	Net Torque @ rpm (ft. lbs.)	Bore × Stroke (in.)	Compression Ratio	Oil Pressure @ rpm
1990	4G15	1.5 (1468)	MPI	81 @ 5500	91 @ 3000	2.97 × 3.23	9.4:1	54 @ 2000
	4G61	1.6 (1597)	MPI	113 @ 6500	99 @ 5000	3.24 × 2.96	9.2:1	54 @ 2000
	4G37	1.8 (1755)	MPI	92 @ 5000	105 @ 3500	3.17 × 3.39	8.5:1	41 @ 2000
	4G63①	2.0 (1997)	MPI	120 @ 5000	116 @ 4500	3.35 × 3.47	8.5:1	41 @ 2000
	4G63②	2.0 (1997)	MPI	135 @ 6000	125 @ 5000	3.35 × 3.47	9.0:1	41 @ 2000
	4G63③	2.0 (1997)	Turbo	190 @ 6000	203 @ 3000	3.35 × 3.47	7.8:1	41 @ 2000
	6G72	3.0 (2972)	MPI	142 @ 5000	168 @ 2500	3.58 × 2.99	8.9:1	54 @ 2000
1991	4G15④	1.5 (1468)	MPI	81 @ 5500	91 @ 3000	2.97 × 3.23	9.4:1	54 @ 2000
	4G15⑤	1.5 (1468)	MPI	92 @ 6000	93 @ 3000	2.97 × 3.23	9.2:1	54 @ 2000
	4G61	1.6 (1597)	MPI	113 @ 6500	99 @ 5000	3.24 × 2.96	9.2:1	54 @ 2000
	4G37	1.8 (1755)	MPI	92 @ 5000	105 @ 3500	3.17 × 3.39	8.5:1	41 @ 2000
	4G63①	2.0 (1997)	MPI	120 @ 5000	116 @ 4500	3.35 × 3.47	8.5:1	41 @ 2000
	4G63②	2.0 (1997)	MPI	135 @ 6000	125 @ 5000	3.35 × 3.47	9.0:1	41 @ 2000
	4G63③	2.0 (1997)	Turbo	190 @ 6000	203 @ 3000	3.35 × 3.47	7.8:1	41 @ 2000
	6G72②	3.0 (2972)	MPI	222 @ 6000	201 @ 4500	3.58 × 2.99	10.0:1	30–80 @ 2000
	6G72③	3.0 (2972)	Twin Turbo	300 @ 6000	307 @ 2500	3.58 × 2.99	8.0:1	30–80 @ 2000
1992	4G15④	1.5 (1468)	MPI	81 @ 5500	91 @ 3000	2.97 × 3.23	9.4:1	54 @ 2000
	4G15⑤	1.5 (1468)	MPI	92 @ 6000	93 @ 3000	2.97 × 3.23	9.2:1	54 @ 2000
	4G61	1.6 (1597)	MPI	113 @ 6500	99 @ 5000	3.24 × 2.96	9.2:1	54 @ 2000
	4G93	1.8 (1834)	MPI	113 @ 6000	116 @ 4500	3.19 × 3.50	9.5:1	41 @ 2000
	4G37	1.8 (1755)	MPI	92 @ 5000	105 @ 3500	3.17 × 3.39	9.0:1	41 @ 2000
	4G63①	2.0 (1997)	MPI	120 @ 5000	116 @ 4500	3.35 × 3.47	8.5:1	41 @ 2000
	4G63②	2.0 (1997)	MPI	135 @ 6000	125 @ 5000	3.35 × 3.47	9.0:1	41 @ 2000
	4G63③	2.0 (1997)	Turbo	190 @ 6000	203 @ 3000	3.35 × 3.47	7.8:1	41 @ 2000
	4G64	2.4 (2351)⑥	MPI	116 @ 5000	136 @ 3500	3.41 × 3.94	8.5:1	41 @ 2000
	6G72②	3.0 (2972)	MPI	175 @ 5500	185 @ 3000	3.58 × 2.99	10.0:1	30–80 @ 2000
	6G72②	3.0 (2972)	MPI	202 @ 6000	199 @ 3000	3.58 × 2.99	10.0:1	30–80 @ 2000
	6G72②	3.0 (2972)	MPI	222 @ 6000	201 @ 4500	3.58 × 2.99	10.0:1	30–80 @ 2000
	6G72③	3.0 (2972)	Twin Turbo	300 @ 6000	307 @ 2500	3.58 × 2.99	8.0:1	30–80 @ 2000
1993	4G15④	1.5 (1468)	MPI	81 @ 5500	91 @ 3000	2.97 × 3.23	9.4:1	54 @ 2000
	4G15⑤	1.5 (1468)	MPI	92 @ 6000	93 @ 3000	2.97 × 3.23	9.2:1	54 @ 2000
	4G93	1.8 (1834)	MPI	113 @ 6000	116 @ 4500	3.19 × 3.50	9.5:1	41 @ 2000
	4G37	1.8 (1755)	MPI	92 @ 5000	105 @ 3500	3.17 × 3.39	9.0:1	41 @ 2000
	4G63①	2.0 (1997)	MPI	120 @ 5000	116 @ 4500	3.35 × 3.47	8.5:1	41 @ 2000
	4G63②	2.0 (1997)	MPI	135 @ 6000	125 @ 5000	3.35 × 3.47	9.0:1	41 @ 2000
	4G63③	2.0 (1997)	Turbo	190 @ 6000	203 @ 3000	3.35 × 3.47	7.8:1	41 @ 2000
	4G64	2.4 (2351)⑦	MPI	136 @ 5500	145 @ 4250	3.41 × 3.94	9.5:1	41 @ 2000
	6G72①	3.0 (2972)	MPI	175 @ 5500	185 @ 3000	3.58 × 2.99	10.0:1	30–80 @ 2000
	6G72②	3.0 (2972)	MPI	202 @ 6000	199 @ 3000	3.58 × 2.99	10.0:1	30–80 @ 2000
	6G72②	3.0 (2972)	MPI	222 @ 6000	201 @ 4500	3.58 × 2.99	10.0:1	30–80 @ 2000
	6G72③	3.0 (2972)	Twin Turbo	300 @ 6000	307 @ 2500	3.58 × 2.99	8.0:1	30–80 @ 2000

GENERAL ENGINE SPECIFICATIONS

Year	Engine Series ID	Engine Displacement Liters (cc)	Fuel System Type	Net Horsepower @ rpm	Net Torque @ rpm (ft. lbs.)	Bore × Stroke (in.)	Compression Ratio	Oil Pressure @ rpm
1994	4G15 ④	1.5 (1468)	MPI	81 @ 5500	91 @ 3000	2.97 × 3.23	9.4:1	54 @ 2000
	4G15 ⑤	1.5 (1468)	MPI	92 @ 6000	93 @ 3000	2.97 × 3.23	9.2:1	54 @ 2000
	4G93	1.8 (1834)	MPI	113 @ 6000	116 @ 4500	3.19 × 3.50	9.5:1	41 @ 2000
	4G37	1.8 (1755)	MPI	92 @ 5000	105 @ 3500	3.17 × 3.39	9.0:1	41 @ 2000
	4G63 ①	2.0 (1997)	MPI	120 @ 5000	116 @ 4500	3.35 × 3.47	8.5:1	41 @ 2000
	4G63 ②	2.0 (1997)	MPI	135 @ 6000	125 @ 5000	3.35 × 3.47	9.0:1	41 @ 2000
	4G63 ③	2.0 (1997)	Turbo	190 @ 6000	203 @ 3000	3.35 × 3.47	7.8:1	41 @ 2000
	4G64	2.4 (2351) ⑦	MPI	136 @ 5500	145 @ 4250	3.41 × 3.94	9.5:1	41 @ 2000
	6G72 ①	3.0 (2972)	MPI	175 @ 5500	185 @ 3000	3.58 × 2.99	10.0:1	30–80 @ 2000
	6G72 ②	3.0 (2972)	MPI	202 @ 6000	199 @ 3000	3.58 × 2.99	10.0:1	30–80 @ 2000
	6G72 ②	3.0 (2972)	MPI	222 @ 6000	201 @ 4500	3.58 × 2.99	10.0:1	30–80 @ 2000
	6G72 ③	3.0 (2972)	Twin Turbo	300 @ 6000	307 @ 2500	3.58 × 2.99	8.0:1	30–80 @ 2000

Carb.—Carburetor
MPI—Multi-Port Injection
① SOHC
② DOHC
③ Turbocharged
④ Precis
⑤ Mirage
⑥ 8 valve
⑦ 16 valve

ENGINE TUNE-UP SPECIFICATIONS

Year	Engine Series ID	Engine Displacement Liters (cc)	Spark Plugs Gap (in.)	Ignition Timing (deg.) MT	Ignition Timing (deg.) AT	Fuel Pump (psi)	Idle Speed (rpm) MT	Idle Speed (rpm) AT	Valve Clearance (in.) In.	Valve Clearance (in.) Ex.
1990	4G15	1.5 (1468)	0.039–0.043	5B	5B	38	750	750	0.006	0.010
	4G61	1.6 (1597)	0.039–0.043	5B	5B	38	750	750	Hyd.	Hyd.
	4G37	1.8 (1755)	0.039–0.043	5B	5B	38	750	750	Hyd.	Hyd.
	4G63 ①	2.0 (1997)	0.039–0.043	5B	5B	38	750	750	Hyd.	Hyd.
	4G63 ②	2.0 (1997)	0.039–0.043	5B	5B	38	700	700	Hyd.	Hyd.
	4G63 ③	2.0 (1997)	0.028–0.031	5B	5B	27 ④	750	750	Hyd.	Hyd.
	6G72	3.0 (2972)	0.039–0.043	—	5B	38	—	700	Hyd.	Hyd.
1991	4G15	1.5 (1468)	0.039–0.043	5B	5B	38	750	750	0.006	0.010
	4G61	1.6 (1597)	0.039–0.043	5B	5B	38	750	750	Hyd.	Hyd.
	4G37	1.8 (1755)	0.039–0.043	5B	5B	38	750	750	Hyd.	Hyd.
	4G63 ①	2.0 (1997)	0.039–0.043	5B	5B	38	750	750	Hyd.	Hyd.
	4G63 ②	2.0 (1997)	0.039–0.043	5B	5B	38	700	700	Hyd.	Hyd.
	4G63 ③	2.0 (1997)	0.028–0.031	5B	5B	27 ④	750	750	Hyd.	Hyd.
	6G72 ②	3.0 (2972)	0.039–0.043	5B	5B	38	750	750	Hyd.	Hyd.
	6G72 ③	3.0 (2972)	0.039–0.043	5B	—	34	700	—	Hyd.	Hyd.
1992	4G15	1.5 (1468)	0.039–0.043	5B	5B	38	750	750	0.006	0.010
	4G61	1.6 (1597)	0.039–0.043	5B	5B	38	750	750	Hyd.	Hyd.
	4G37	1.8 (1755)	0.039–0.043	5B	5B	38	750	750	Hyd.	Hyd.
	4G93	1.8 (1834)	0.039–0.043	5B	5B	38	750	750	0.004	0.008
	4G63 ①	2.0 (1997)	0.039–0.043	5B	5B	38	750	750	Hyd.	Hyd.
	4G63 ②	2.0 (1997)	0.039–0.043	5B	5B	38	700	700	Hyd.	Hyd.
	4G63 ③	2.0 (1997)	0.028–0.031	5B	5B	27 ④	750	750	Hyd.	Hyd.
	4G64	2.4 (2351) ⑦	0.039–0.043	5B	5B	38	750	750	Hyd.	Hyd.
	6G72 ①	3.0 (2972)	0.039–0.043	5B	5B	38	750	750	Hyd.	Hyd.
	6G72 ②	3.0 (2972)	0.039–0.043	5B	5B	38	750	750	Hyd.	Hyd.
	6G72 ③	3.0 (2972)	0.039–0.043	5B	—	34	700	—	Hyd.	Hyd.
1993	4G15	1.5 (1468)	0.039–0.043	5B	5B	38	750	750	0.006	0.010
	4G37	1.8 (1755)	0.039–0.043	5B	5B	38	750	750	Hyd.	Hyd.
	4G93	1.8 (1834)	0.039–0.043	5B	5B	38	750	750	0.004	0.008
	4G63 ①	2.0 (1997)	0.039–0.043	5B	5B	38	750	750	Hyd.	Hyd.
	4G63 ②	2.0 (1997)	0.039–0.043	5B	5B	38	700	700	Hyd.	Hyd.
	4G63 ③	2.0 (1997)	0.028–0.031	5B	5B	27 ④	750	750	Hyd.	Hyd.
	4G64	2.4 (2351) ⑧	0.039–0.043	5B	5B	38	750	750	Hyd.	Hyd.
	6G72 ①	3.0 (2972)	0.039–0.043	5B	5B	38	750	750	Hyd.	Hyd.
	6G72 ②	3.0 (2972)	0.039–0.043	5B	5B	38	750	750	Hyd.	Hyd.
	6G72 ③	3.0 (2972)	0.039–0.043	5B	—	34	700	—	Hyd.	Hyd.

ENGINE TUNE-UP SPECIFICATIONS

Year	Engine Series ID	Engine Displacement Liters (cc)	Spark Plugs Gap (in.)	Ignition Timing (deg.)		Fuel Pump (psi)	Idle Speed (rpm)		Valve Clearance (in.)	
				MT	AT		MT	AT	In.	Ex.
1994	4G15	1.5 (1468)	0.039–0.043	5B	5B	38	750	750	0.006	0.010
	4G37	1.8 (1755)	0.039–0.043	5B	5B	38	750	750	Hyd.	Hyd.
	4G93	1.8 (1834)	0.039–0.043	5B	5B	38	750	750	0.004	0.008
	4G63 ①	2.0 (1997)	0.039–0.043	5B	5B	38	750	750	Hyd.	Hyd.
	4G63 ②	2.0 (1997)	0.039–0.043	5B	5B	38	700	700	Hyd.	Hyd.
	4G63 ③	2.0 (1997)	0.028–0.031	5B	5B	27 ④	750	750	Hyd.	Hyd.
	4G64	2.4 (2351) ⑧	0.039–0.043	5B	5B	38	750	750	Hyd.	Hyd.
	6G72 ①	3.0 (2972)	0.039–0.043	5B	5B	38	750	750	Hyd.	Hyd.
	6G72 ②	3.0 (2972)	0.039–0.043	5B	5B	38	750	750	Hyd.	Hyd.
	6G72 ③	3.0 (2972)	0.039–0.043	5B	—	34	700	—	Hyd.	Hyd.

NOTE: The lowest cylinder pressure should be within 75% of the highest cylinder pressure reading. For example, if the highest cylinder is 134 psi, the lowest should be 101. Engine should be at normal operating temperature with throttle valve in the wide open position.
The underhood specifications sticker often reflects tune-up specification changes in production. Sticker figures must be used if they disagree with those in this chart.
Hyd.—Hydraulic
① SOHC
② DOHC
③ Turbocharged
④ Eclipse with automatic transaxle: 33 psi
⑤ Specification given is for hot engine. Subtract
 0.003 in. when engine is cold.
⑥ Jet valve 0.010 in.
⑦ 8 valve
⑧ 16 valve

FIRING ORDERS

NOTE: To avoid confusion, always replace spark plug wires one at a time.

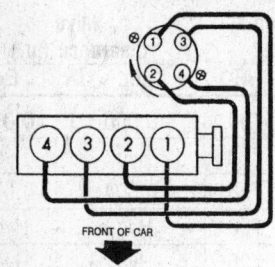

1.5L Engine (Precis and 1990 Mirage)
1.8L Engine (Eclipse)
2.0L SOHC and 2.4L Engines
Engine Firing Order: 1-3-4-2
Distributor Rotation: Clockwise

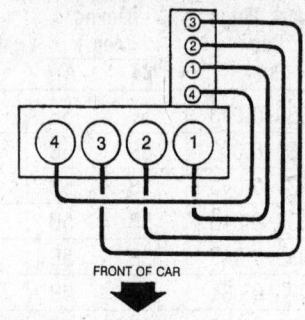

1.6L and 2.0L DOHC Engines
Engine Firing Order: 1-3-4-2
Distributorless Ignition System

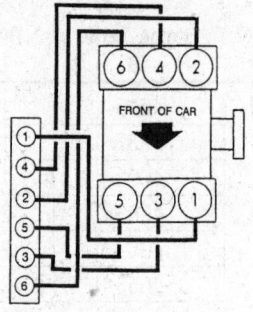

3.0L DOHC Engine
Engine Firing Order: 1-2-3-4-5-6
Distributorless Ignition System

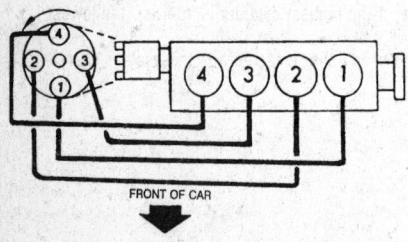

1.5L Engine (1991-94 Mirage)
1.8L Engine (Expo/Expo LRV) Engine
Firing Order: 1-3-4-2
Distributor Rotation: Counterclockwise

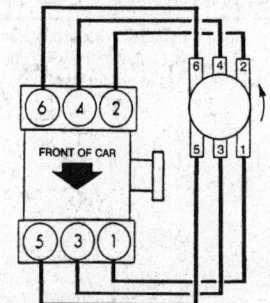

3.0L SOHC Engine
Engine Firing Order: 1-2-3-4-5-6
Distributor Rotation: Counterclockwise

CAPACITIES

Year	Model	Engine Series ID	Engine Displacement Liters (cc)	Engine Crankcase with Filter (qts.)	Transmission (pts.)			Transfer case (pts.)	Rear Drive Axle (pts.)	Fuel Tank (gal.)	Cooling System (qts.)
					4-Spd	5-Spd	Auto.				
1990	Precis	4G15	1.5 (1468)	3.5	4.4	4.4	12.2	—	—	12	5.3
	Mirage	4G15	1.5 (1468)	3.5	—	4.4	13	—	—	13	5.3
	Mirage	4G61	1.6 (1597)	4.5	—	4.4	13	—	—	13	5.3
	Galant	4G63 ①	2.0 (1997)	4	—	4	13	—	—	16	7.6
	Galant	4G63 ②	2.0 (1997)	4.5	—	4	13	—	—	16	7.6
	Sigma	6G72	3.0 (2972)	4.5	—	—	12.2	—	—	16	9.7
	Eclipse	4G37	1.8 (1755)	4	—	5	14	—	—	16	6.6
	Eclipse	4G63	2.0 (1997)	4.5	—	5	14	—	—	16	7.6
	Eclipse	4G63 ③	2.0 (1997)	4.8	—	5	14	1.25	1.5	16	7.6
1991	Precis	4G15	1.5 (1468)	3.5	4.4	4.4	12.2	—	—	12	5.3
	Mirage	4G15	1.5 (1468)	3.5	—	4.4	13	—	—	13	5.3
	Mirage	4G61	1.6 (1597)	4.5	—	4.4	13	—	—	13	5.3
	Galant	4G63 ①	2.0 (1997)	4	—	4	13	—	—	16	7.6
	Galant	4G63 ②	2.0 (1997)	4.5	—	4	13	—	—	16	7.6
	Galant	4G63 ③	2.0 (1997)	5	—	5	14	1.25	1.5	16.5	7.6
	Eclipse	4G37	1.8 (1755)	4	—	5	14	—	—	16	6.6
	Eclipse	4G63	2.0 (1997)	4.5	—	5	14	—	—	16	7.6
	Eclipse	4G63 ③	2.0 (1997)	4.8	—	5	14	1.25	1.5	16	7.6
	3000GT	6G72	3.0 (2972)	4.5	—	5	14.8	—	—	20	8.5
	3000GT	6G72 ③	3.0 (2972)	5	—	5	14.8	0.6	2.3	20	8.5
1992	Precis	4G15	1.5 (1468)	3.5	4.4	4.4	12.2	—	—	12	5.3
	Mirage	4G15	1.5 (1468)	3.5	—	4.4	13	—	—	13	5.3
	Mirage	4G61	1.6 (1597)	4.5	—	4.4	13	—	—	13	5.3
	Expo LRV	4G93	1.8 (1834)	4	—	3.8	13	1.25	1.5	14.5	6.3
	Expo	4G64	2.4 (2351) ④	4	—	4.8	13	1.25	1.5	16	7.6
	Galant	4G63 ①	2.0 (1997)	4	—	4	13	—	—	16	7.6
	Galant	4G63 ②	2.0 (1997)	4.5	—	4	13	—	—	16	7.6
	Galant	4G63 ③	2.0 (1997)	5	—	5	14	1.25	1.5	16.5	7.6
	Eclipse	4G37	1.8 (1755)	4	—	5	14	—	—	16	6.6
	Eclipse	4G63	2.0 (1997)	4.5	—	5	14	—	—	16	7.6
	Eclipse	4G63 ③	2.0 (1997)	4.8	—	5	14	1.25	1.5	16	7.6
	3000GT	6G72	3.0 (2972)	4.5	—	5	14.8	—	—	20	8.5
	3000GT	6G72 ③	3.0 (2972)	5	—	5	14.8	0.6	2.3	20	8.5
	Diamante	6G72 ①	3.0 (2972)	4.7	—	—	14.8	—	—	19	8.5
	Diamante	6G72 ②	3.0 (2972)	4.7	—	—	14.8	—	—	19	8.5

CAPACITIES

Year	Model	Engine Series ID	Engine Displacement Liters (cc)	Engine Crankcase with Filter (qts.)	Transmission (pts.) 4-Spd	5-Spd	Auto.	Transfer case (pts.)	Rear Drive Axle (pts.)	Fuel Tank (gal.)	Cooling System (qts.)
1993	Precis	4G15	1.5 (1468)	3.5	4.4	4.4	12.2	—	—	12	5.3
	Mirage Coupe	4G15	1.5 (1468)	3.5	—	4.4	13	—	—	13	5.3
	Mirage 4-Door	4G93	1.8 (1834)	4	—	4.4	13	—	—	13	5.3
	Expo LRV	4G93	1.8 (1834)	4	—	3.8	13	1.25	1.5	14.5	6.3
	Expo/Expo LRV	4G64	2.4 (2351) ⑤	4	—	4.8	13	1.25	1.5	16	7.6
	Galant	4G63 ①	2.0 (1997)	4	—	4	13	—	—	16	7.6
	Eclipse	4G37	1.8 (1755)	4	—	5	14	—	—	16	6.6
	Eclipse	4G63	2.0 (1997)	4.5	—	5	14	—	—	16	7.6
	Eclipse	4G63 ③	2.0 (1997)	4.8	—	5	14	1.25	1.5	16	7.6
	3000GT	6G72	3.0 (2972)	4.5	—	5	14.8	—	—	20	8.5
	3000GT	6G72 ③	3.0 (2972)	5	—	5	14.8	0.6	2.3	20	8.5
	Diamante	6G72 ①	3.0 (2972)	4.7	—	—	14.8	—	—	19	8.5
	Diamante	6G72 ②	3.0 (2972)	4.7	—	—	14.8	—	—	19	8.5
1994	Precis	4G15	1.5 (1468)	3.5	4.4	4.4	12.2	—	—	12	5.3
	Mirage Coupe	4G15	1.5 (1468)	3.5	—	4.4	13	—	—	13	5.3
	Mirage 4-Door	4G93	1.8 (1834)	4	—	4.4	13	—	—	13	5.3
	Expo LRV	4G93	1.8 (1834)	4	—	3.8	13	1.25	1.5	14.5	6.3
	Expo/Expo LRV	4G64	2.4 (2351) ⑤	4	—	4.8	13	1.25	1.5	16	7.6
	Galant	4G63 ①	2.0 (1997)	4	—	4	13	—	—	16	7.6
	Eclipse	4G37	1.8 (1755)	4	—	5	14	—	—	16	6.6
	Eclipse	4G63	2.0 (1997)	4.5	—	5	14	—	—	16	7.6
	Eclipse	4G63 ③	2.0 (1997)	4.8	—	5	14	1.25	1.5	16	7.6
	3000GT	6G72	3.0 (2972)	4.5	—	5	14.8	—	—	20	8.5
	3000GT	6G72 ③	3.0 (2972)	5	—	5	14.8	0.6	2.3	20	8.5
	Diamante	6G72 ①	3.0 (2972)	4.7	—	—	14.8	—	—	19	8.5
	Diamante	6G72 ②	3.0 (2972)	4.7	—	—	14.8	—	—	19	8.5

① SOHC
② DOHC
③ Turbocharged
④ 8 valve
⑤ 16 valve

CAMSHAFT SPECIFICATIONS

All measurements given in inches.

Year	Engine Series ID	Engine Displacement Liters (cc)	Journal Diameter (in.)					Elevation		Bearing Clearance (in.)	Camshaft End Play (in.)
			1	2	3	4	5	In.	Ex.		
1990	4G15	1.5 (1468)	1.811	1.811	1.811	1.811	—	1.532	1.534	0.0015–0.0031	0.002–0.008
	4G61	1.6 (1597)	1.020	1.020	1.020	1.020	1.020③	1.386	1.374	0.0020–0.0035	0.004–0.008
	4G37	1.8 (1755)	1.336	1.336	1.336	1.336	1.336	1.753	1.753	0.0020–0.0035	0.004–0.008
	4G63①	2.0 (1997)	1.336	1.336	1.336	1.336	1.336	1.753	1.753	0.0020–0.0035	0.004–0.008
	4G63②	2.0 (1997)	1.022	1.022	1.022	1.022	1.022③	1.397	1.386	0.0020–0.0035	0.004–0.008
	6G72	3.0 (2972)	1.340	1.340	1.340	1.340	—	1.604–1.624	1.604–1.624	0.0020–0.0035	0.004–0.008
1991	4G15	1.5 (1468)	1.808–1.809	1.808–1.809	1.808–1.809	1.808–1.809	—	1.506–1.526	1.520–1.540	0.0024–0.0039	0.004–0.008
	4G61	1.6 (1597)	1.020	1.020	1.020	1.020	1.020③	1.386	1.374	0.0020–0.0035	0.004–0.008
	4G37	1.8 (1755)	1.336	1.336	1.336	1.336	1.336	1.753	1.753	0.0020–0.0035	0.004–0.008
	4G63①	2.0 (1997)	1.336	1.336	1.336	1.336	1.336	1.753	1.753	0.0020–0.0035	0.004–0.008
	4G63②	2.0 (1997)	1.022	1.022	1.022	1.022	1.022③	1.397	1.386	0.0020–0.0035	0.004–0.008
	6G72	3.0 (1997)	1.020	1.020	1.020	1.020	1.020	1.377–1.397	1.366–1.386	0.0020–0.0035	0.004–0.008
1992	4G15	1.5 (1468)	1.808–1.809	1.808–1.809	1.808–1.809	1.808–1.809	—	1.506–1.526	1.520–1.540	0.0024–0.0039	0.004–0.008
	4G61	1.6 (1597)	1.020	1.020	1.020	1.020	1.020③	1.386	1.374	0.0020–0.0035	0.004–0.008
	4G37	1.8 (1755)	1.336	1.336	1.336	1.336	1.336	1.753	1.753	0.0020–0.0035	0.004–0.008
	4G93	1.8 (1834)	1.769	1.769	1.769	1.769	1.769	1.468–1.487	1.480–1.500	0.0020–0.0035	0.004–0.008
	4G63①	2.0 (1997)	1.336	1.336	1.336	1.336	1.336	1.753	1.753	0.0020–0.0035	0.004–0.008
	4G63②	2.0 (1997)	1.022	1.022	1.022	1.022	1.022③	1.397	1.386	0.0020–0.0035	0.004–0.008
	4G64④	2.4 (2351)	1.336	1.336	1.336	1.336	1.336	1.753	1.753	0.0020–0.0035	0.004–0.008
	6G72①	3.0 (2972)	1.340	1.340	1.340	1.340	—	1.604–1.624	1.604–1.624	0.0020–0.0035	0.004–0.008
	6G72②	3.0 (2972)	1.020	1.020	1.020	1.020	1.020	1.377–1.397	1.366–1.386	0.0020–0.0035	0.004–0.008

CAMSHAFT SPECIFICATIONS

All measurements given in inches.

Year	Engine Series ID	Engine Displacement Liters (cc)	Journal Diameter (in.)					Elevation		Bearing Clearance (in.)	Camshaft End Play (in.)
			1	2	3	4	5	In.	Ex.		
1993	4G15	1.5 (1468)	1.808–1.809	1.808–1.809	1.808–1.809	1.808–1.809	—	1.506–1.526	1.520–1.540	0.0024–0.0039	0.004–0.008
	4G37	1.8 (1755)	1.336	1.336	1.336	1.336	1.336	1.753	1.753	0.0020–0.0035	0.004–0.008
	4G93	1.8 (1834)	1.769	1.769	1.769	1.769	1.769	1.468–1.487	1.480–1.500	0.0020–0.0035	0.004–0.008
	4G63 ①	2.0 (1997)	1.336	1.336	1.336	1.336	1.336	1.753	1.753	0.0020–0.0035	0.004–0.008
	4G63 ②	2.0 (1997)	1.022	1.022	1.022	1.022	1.022 ③	1.397	1.386	0.0020–0.0035	0.004–0.008
	4G64 ⑤	2.4 (2351)	1.7689–1.7693	1.7689–1.7693	1.7689–1.7693	1.7689–1.7693	1.7689–1.7693	1.4720	1.4752	0.0020–0.0035	0.004–0.008
	6G72 ①	3.0 (2972)	1.340	1.340	1.340	1.340	—	1.604–1.624	1.604–1.624	0.0020–0.0035	0.004–0.008
	6G72 ②	3.0 (2972)	1.020	1.020	1.020	1.020	1.020	1.377–1.397	1.366–1.386	0.0020–0.0035	0.004–0.008
1994	4G15	1.5 (1468)	1.808–1.809	1.808–1.809	1.808–1.809	1.808–1.809	—	1.506–1.526	1.520–1.540	0.0024–0.0039	0.004–0.008
	4G37	1.8 (1755)	1.336	1.336	1.336	1.336	1.336	1.753	1.753	0.0020–0.0035	0.004–0.008
	4G93	1.8 (1834)	1.769	1.769	1.769	1.769	1.769	1.468–1.487	1.480–1.500	0.0020–0.0035	0.004–0.008
	4G63 ①	2.0 (1997)	1.336	1.336	1.336	1.336	1.336	1.753	1.753	0.0020–0.0035	0.004–0.008
	4G63 ②	2.0 (1997)	1.022	1.022	1.022	1.022	1.022 ③	1.397	1.386	0.0020–0.0035	0.004–0.008
	4G64 ⑤	2.4 (2351)	1.7689–1.7693	1.7689–1.7693	1.7689–1.7693	1.7689–1.7693	1.7689–1.7693	1.4720	1.4752	0.0020–0.0035	0.004–0.008
	6G72 ①	3.0 (2972)	1.340	1.340	1.340	1.340	—	1.604–1.624	1.604–1.624	0.0020–0.0035	0.004–0.008
	6G72 ②	3.0 (2972)	1.020	1.020	1.020	1.020	1.020	1.377–1.397	1.366–1.386	0.0020–0.0035	0.004–0.008

① SOHC
② DOHC
③ 6th journal is the same as the rest
④ 8 valve
⑤ 16 valve

CRANKSHAFT AND CONNECTING ROD SPECIFICATIONS

All measurements are given in inches.

Year	Engine Series ID	Engine Displacement Liters (cc)	Crankshaft				Connecting Rod		
			Main Brg. Journal Dia.	Main Brg. Oil Clearance	Shaft End-play	Thrust on No.	Journal Diameter	Oil Clearance	Side Clearance
1990	4G15	1.5 (1468)	1.890	0.0008–0.0018	0.0020–0.0071	3	1.6500	0.0006–0.0017	0.0039–0.0098
	4G61	1.6 (1597)	2.240	0.0008–0.0020	0.0020–0.0071	3	1.7700	0.0008–0.0020	0.0039–0.0098
	4G37	1.8 (1755)	2.240	0.0008–0.0020	0.0020–0.0071	3	1.7700	0.0008–0.0020	0.0039–0.0098
	4G63	2.0 (1997)	2.243–2.244	0.0008–0.0020	0.0020–0.0070	3	1.7709–1.7715	0.0008–0.0020	0.0040–0.0098
	6G72	3.0 (2972)	2.358	0.0008–0.0019	0.0020–0.0098	3	1.9650	0.0006–0.0018	0.0040–0.0098
1991	4G15	1.5 (1468)	1.890	0.0008–0.0028	0.0020–0.0071	3	1.6500	0.0006–0.0024	0.0039–0.0098
	4G61	1.6 (1597)	2.240	0.0008–0.0020	0.0020–0.0071	3	1.7700	0.0008–0.0020	0.0039–0.0098
	4G37	1.8 (1755)	2.240	0.0008–0.0020	0.0020–0.0071	3	1.7700	0.0008–0.0020	0.0039–0.0098
	4G63	2.0 (1997)	2.243–2.244	0.0008–0.0020	0.0020–0.0070	3	1.7709–1.7715	0.0008–0.0020	0.0040–0.0098
	6G72	3.0 (1997)	2.358	0.0008–0.0019	0.0020–0.0098	3	1.9650	0.0006–0.0018	0.0040–0.0098
1992	4G15	1.5 (1468)	1.890	0.0008–0.0028	0.0020–0.0071	3	1.6500	0.0006–0.0024	0.0039–0.0098
	4G61	1.6 (1597)	2.240	0.0008–0.0020	0.0020–0.0071	3	1.7700	0.0008–0.0020	0.0039–0.0098
	4G37	1.8 (1755)	2.240	0.0008–0.0020	0.0020–0.0071	3	1.7700	0.0008–0.0020	0.0039–0.0098
	4G93	1.8 (1834)	1.968	0.0008–0.0016	0.0020–0.0070	3	1.7709–1.7715	0.0008–0.0020	0.0040–0.0098
	4G63	2.0 (1997)	2.243–2.244	0.0008–0.0020	0.0020–0.0070	3	1.7709–1.7715	0.0008–0.0020	0.0040–0.0098
	4G64	2.4 (2351) ③	2.243–2.244	0.0008–0.0020	0.0020–0.0070	3	1.7709–1.7715	0.0008–0.0020	0.0040–0.0098
	6G72 ①	3.0 (2972)	2.358	0.0008–0.0019	0.0020–0.0098	3	1.9650	0.0006–0.0018	0.0040–0.0098
	6G72 ②	3.0 (2972)	2.358	0.0008–0.0017	0.0020–0.0098	3	1.9650	0.0006–0.0018	0.0040–0.0098

CRANKSHAFT AND CONNECTING ROD SPECIFICATIONS

All measurements are given in inches.

Year	Engine Series ID	Engine Displacement Liters (cc)	Crankshaft				Connecting Rod		
			Main Brg. Journal Dia.	Main Brg. Oil Clearance	Shaft End-play	Thrust on No.	Journal Diameter	Oil Clearance	Side Clearance
1993	4G15	1.5 (1468)	1.890	0.0008–0.0028	0.0020–0.0071	3	1.6500	0.0006–0.0024	0.0039–0.0098
	4G37	1.8 (1755)	2.240	0.0008–0.0020	0.0020–0.0071	3	1.7700	0.0008–0.0020	0.0039–0.0098
	4G93	1.8 (1834)	1.968	0.0008–0.0016	0.0020–0.0070	3	1.7709–1.7715	0.0008–0.0020	0.0040–0.0098
	4G63	2.0 (1997)	2.243–2.244	0.0008–0.0020	0.0020–0.0070	3	1.7709–1.7715	0.0008–0.0020	0.0040–0.0098
	4G64	2.4 (2351) ④	2.243–2.244	0.0008–0.0020	0.0020–0.0098	3	1.7709–1.7715	0.0008–0.0020	0.0040–0.0098
	6G72 ①	3.0 (2972)	2.358	0.0008–0.0019	0.0020–0.0098	3	1.9650	0.0006–0.0018	0.0040–0.0098
	6G72 ②	3.0 (2972)	2.358	0.0008–0.0017	0.0020–0.0098	3	1.9650	0.0006–0.0018	0.0040–0.0098
1994	4G15	1.5 (1468)	1.890	0.0008–0.0028	0.0020–0.0071	3	1.6500	0.0006–0.0024	0.0039–0.0098
	4G37	1.8 (1755)	2.240	0.0008–0.0020	0.0020–0.0071	3	1.7700	0.0008–0.0020	0.0039–0.0098
	4G93	1.8 (1834)	1.968	0.0008–0.0016	0.0020–0.0070	3	1.7709–1.7715	0.0008–0.0020	0.0040–0.0098
	4G63	2.0 (1997)	2.243–2.244	0.0008–0.0020	0.0020–0.0070	3	1.7709–1.7715	0.0008–0.0020	0.0040–0.0098
	4G64	2.4 (2351) ④	2.243–2.244	0.0008–0.0020	0.0020–0.0098	3	1.7709–1.7715	0.0008–0.0020	0.0040–0.0098
	6G72 ①	3.0 (2972)	2.358	0.0008–0.0019	0.0020–0.0098	3	1.9650	0.0006–0.0018	0.0040–0.0098
	6G72 ②	3.0 (2972)	2.358	0.0008–0.0017	0.0020–0.0098	3	1.9650	0.0006–0.0018	0.0040–0.0098

① SOHC
② DOHC
③ 8 valve
④ 16 valve

VALVE SPECIFICATIONS

Year	Engine Series ID	Engine Displacement Liters (cc)	Seat Angle (deg.)	Face Angle (deg.)	Spring Test Pressure (lbs. @ in.)③	Spring Installed Height (in.)	Stem-to-Guide Clearance (in.)		Stem Diameter (in.)	
							Intake	Exhaust	Intake	Exhaust
1990	4G15	1.5 (1468)	44–44.5	45–45.5	53	1.570	0.0008–0.0020	0.0020–0.0035	0.2600	0.2600
	4G61	1.6 (1597)	44–44.5	45–45.5	66	1.591	0.0008–0.0019	0.0020–0.0033	0.2585–0.2583	0.2571–0.2579
	4G37	1.8 (1755)	44–44.5	45–45.5	62	1.469	0.0012–0.0024	0.0020–0.0035	0.3100	0.0031
	4G63①	2.0 (1997)	44–44.5	45–45.5	66	1.591	0.0008–0.0024	0.0020–0.0035	0.3134–0.3142	0.3122–0.3130
	4G63②	2.0 (1997)	44–44.5	45–45.5	66	1.591	0.0008–0.0019	0.0020–0.0033	0.2585–0.2591	0.2571–0.2579
	6G72	3.0 (2972)	44–44.5	45–45.5	74	1.591	0.0012–0.0039	0.0020–0.0059	0.3140	0.3140
1991	4G15	1.5 (1468)	44–44.5	45–45.5	60	1.570	0.0008–0.0020	0.0020–0.0035	0.2585–0.2591	0.2571–0.2579
	4G61	1.6 (1597)	44–44.5	45–45.5	66	1.591	0.0008–0.0019	0.0020–0.0033	0.2585–0.2583	0.2571–0.2579
	4G37	1.8 (1755)	44–44.5	45–45.5	62	1.469	0.0012–0.0024	0.0020–0.0035	0.3100	0.0031
	4G63①	2.0 (1997)	44–44.5	45–45.5	66	1.591	0.0008–0.0024	0.0020–0.0035	0.3134–0.3142	0.3122–0.3130
	4G63②	2.0 (1997)	44–44.5	45–45.5	66	1.591	0.0008–0.0019	0.0020–0.0033	0.2585–0.2591	0.2571–0.2579
	6G72	3.0 (1997)	44–44.5	45–45.5	62	1.492	0.0008–0.0039	0.0020–0.0047	0.2600	0.2600
1992	4G15	1.5 (1468)	44–44.5	45–45.5	60	1.570	0.0008–0.0020	0.0020–0.0035	0.2585–0.2591	0.2571–0.2579
	4G61	1.6 (1597)	44–44.5	45–45.5	66	1.591	0.0008–0.0019	0.0020–0.0033	0.2585–0.2583	0.2571–0.2579
	4G37	1.8 (1755)	44–44.5	45–45.5	62	1.469	0.0012–0.0024	0.0020–0.0035	0.3100	0.0031
	4G93	1.8 (1834)	43.5–44	45–45.5	49	1.740	0.0008–0.0020	0.0020–0.0035	0.2350–0.2354	0.2343–0.2350
	4G63①	2.0 (1997)	44–44.5	45–45.5	66	1.591	0.0008–0.0024	0.0020–0.0035	0.3134–0.3142	0.3122–0.3130
	4G63②	2.0 (1997)	44–44.5	45–45.5	66	1.591	0.0008–0.0019	0.0020–0.0033	0.2585–0.2591	0.2571–0.2579
	4G64	2.4 (2351)④	44–44.5	45–45.5	73	1.590	0.0012–0.0024	0.0020–0.0035	0.3100	0.3100
	6G72①	3.0 (2972)	44–44.5	45–45.5	74	1.591	0.0012–0.0039	0.0020–0.0059	0.3140	0.3140
	6G72②	3.0 (2972)	44–44.5	45–45.5	62	1.492	0.0008–0.0039	0.0020–0.0047	0.2600	0.2600

VALVE SPECIFICATIONS

Year	Engine Series ID	Engine Displacement Liters (cc)	Seat Angle (deg.)	Face Angle (deg.)	Spring Test Pressure (lbs. @ in.)③	Spring Installed Height (in.)	Stem-to-Guide Clearance (in.)		Stem Diameter (in.)	
							Intake	Exhaust	Intake	Exhaust
1993	4G15	1.5 (1468)	44–44.5	45–45.5	60	1.570	0.0008–0.0020	0.0020–0.0035	0.2585–0.2591	0.2571–0.2579
	4G37	1.8 (1755)	44–44.5	45–45.5	62	1.469	0.0012–0.0024	0.0020–0.0035	0.3100	0.0031
	4G93	1.8 (1834)	43.5–44	45–45.5	49	1.740	0.0008–0.0020	0.0020–0.0035	0.2350–0.2354	0.2343–0.2350
	4G63①	2.0 (1997)	44–44.5	45–45.5	66	1.591	0.0008–0.0024	0.0020–0.0035	0.3134–0.3142	0.3122–0.3130
	4G63②	2.0 (1997)	44–44.5	45–45.5	66	1.591	0.0008–0.0019	0.0020–0.0033	0.2585–0.2591	0.2571–0.2579
	4G64	2.4 (2351)⑤	44–44.5	45–45.5	60	1.590	0.0008–0.0020	0.0012–0.0028	0.2350–0.2354	0.2343–0.2350
	6G72①	3.0 (2972)	44–44.5	45–45.5	74	1.591	0.0012–0.0039	0.0020–0.0059	0.3140	0.3140
	6G72②	3.0 (2972)	44–44.5	45–45.5	62	1.492	0.0008–0.0039	0.0020–0.0047	0.2600	0.2600
1994	4G15	1.5 (1468)	44–44.5	45–45.5	60	1.570	0.0008–0.0020	0.0020–0.0035	0.2585–0.2591	0.2571–0.2579
	4G37	1.8 (1755)	44–44.5	45–45.5	62	1.469	0.0012–0.0024	0.0020–0.0035	0.3100	0.0031
	4G93	1.8 (1834)	43.5–44	45–45.5	49	1.740	0.0008–0.0020	0.0020–0.0035	0.2350–0.2354	0.2343–0.2350
	4G63①	2.0 (1997)	44–44.5	45–45.5	66	1.591	0.0008–0.0024	0.0020–0.0035	0.3134–0.3142	0.3122–0.3130
	4G63②	2.0 (1997)	44–44.5	45–45.5	66	1.591	0.0008–0.0019	0.0020–0.0033	0.2585–0.2591	0.2571–0.2579
	4G64	2.4 (2351)⑤	44–44.5	45–45.5	60	1.590	0.0008–0.0020	0.0012–0.0028	0.2350–0.2354	0.2343–0.2350
	6G72①	3.0 (2972)	44–44.5	45–45.5	74	1.591	0.0012–0.0039	0.0020–0.0059	0.3140	0.3140
	6G72②	3.0 (2972)	44–44.5	45–45.5	62	1.492	0.0008–0.0039	0.0020–0.0047	0.2600	0.2600

① SOHC
② DOHC
③ At installed height
④ 8 valve
⑤ 16 valve

PISTON AND RING SPECIFICATIONS

All measurements are given in inches.

| Year | Engine Series ID | Engine Displacement Liters (cc) | Piston Clearance | Ring Gap | | | Ring Side Clearance | | |
				Top Compression	Bottom Compression	Oil Control	Top Compression	Bottom Compression	Oil Control
1990	4G15	1.5 (1468)	0.0008–0.0016	0.0079–0.0138	0.0079–0.0138	0.0079–0.0276	0.0012–0.0028	0.0008–0.0024	NA
	4G61	1.6 (1597)	0.0008–0.0016	0.0098–0.0157	0.0138–0.0197	0.0079–0.0276	0.0012–0.0028	0.0012–0.0028	NA
	4G37	1.8 (1755)	0.0004–0.0012	0.0118–0.0177	0.0079–0.0138	0.0080–0.0280	0.0018–0.0033	0.0008–0.0024	NA
	4G63	2.0 (1997)	0.0010–0.0020	0.0098–0.0177	0.0138–0.0197	0.0079–0.0276	0.0012–0.0028	0.0012–0.0028	NA
	6G72	3.0 (2972)	0.0012–0.0020	0.0118–0.0177	0.0098–0.0157	0.0118–0.0154	0.0020–0.0035	0.0008–0.0024	NA
1991	4G15	1.5 (1468)	0.0008–0.0016	0.0079–0.0138	0.0079–0.0138	0.0079–0.0276	0.0012–0.0028	0.0008–0.0024	NA
	4G61	1.6 (1597)	0.0008–0.0016	0.0098–0.0157	0.0138–0.0197	0.0079–0.0276	0.0012–0.0028	0.0012–0.0028	NA
	4G37	1.8 (1755)	0.0004–0.0012	0.0118–0.0177	0.0079–0.0138	0.0080–0.0280	0.0018–0.0033	0.0008–0.0024	NA
	4G63	2.0 (1997)	0.0010–0.0020	0.0098–0.0177	0.0138–0.0197	0.0079–0.0276	0.0012–0.0028	0.0012–0.0028	NA
	6G72	3.0 (1997)	0.0012–0.0020	0.0118–0.0177	0.0177–0.0236	0.0079–0.0236	0.0012–0.0028	0.0008–0.0024	NA
1992	4G15	1.5 (1468)	0.0008–0.0016	0.0079–0.0138	0.0079–0.0138	0.0079–0.0276	0.0012–0.0028	0.0008–0.0024	NA
	4G61	1.6 (1597)	0.0008–0.0016	0.0098–0.0157	0.0138–0.0197	0.0079–0.0276	0.0012–0.0028	0.0012–0.0028	NA
	4G37	1.8 (1755)	0.0004–0.0012	0.0118–0.0177	0.0079–0.0138	0.0080–0.0280	0.0018–0.0033	0.0008–0.0024	NA
	4G93	1.8 (1834)	0.0008–0.0016	0.0098–0.0157	0.0157–0.0217	0.0079–0.0236	0.0012–0.0028	0.0008–0.0024	NA
	4G63	2.0 (1997)	0.0010–0.0020	0.0098–0.0177	0.0138–0.0197	0.0079–0.0276	0.0012–0.0028	0.0012–0.0028	NA
	4G64	2.4 (2351) ③	0.0004–0.0012	0.0098–0.0177	0.0079–0.0157	0.0079–0.0276	0.0012–0.0028	0.0008–0.0024	NA
	6G72 ①	3.0 (2972)	0.0012–0.0020	0.0118–0.0177	0.0098–0.0157	0.0118–0.0154	0.0020–0.0035	0.0008–0.0024	NA
	6G72 ②	3.0 (1997)	0.0012–0.0020	0.0118–0.0177	0.0177–0.0236	0.0079–0.0236	0.0012–0.0028	0.0008–0.0024	NA

PISTON AND RING SPECIFICATIONS

All measurements are given in inches.

| Year | Engine Series ID | Engine Displacement Liters (cc) | Piston Clearance | Ring Gap | | | Ring Side Clearance | | |
				Top Compression	Bottom Compression	Oil Control	Top Compression	Bottom Compression	Oil Control
1993	4G15	1.5 (1468)	0.0008–0.0016	0.0079–0.0138	0.0079–0.0138	0.0079–0.0276	0.0012–0.0028	0.0008–0.0024	NA
	4G37	1.8 (1755)	0.0004–0.0012	0.0118–0.0177	0.0079–0.0138	0.0080–0.0280	0.0018–0.0033	0.0008–0.0024	NA
	4G93	1.8 (1834)	0.0008–0.0016	0.0098–0.0157	0.0157–0.0217	0.0079–0.0236	0.0012–0.0028	0.0008–0.0024	NA
	4G63	2.0 (1997)	0.0010–0.0020	0.0098–0.0177	0.0138–0.0197	0.0079–0.0276	0.0012–0.0028	0.0012–0.0028	NA
	4G64	2.4 (2351)④	0.0008–0.0016	0.0098–0.0138	0.0157–0.0217	0.0039–0.0157	0.0012–0.0028	0.0008–0.0024	NA
	6G72①	3.0 (2972)	0.0012–0.0020	0.0118–0.0177	0.0098–0.0157	0.0118–0.0154	0.0020–0.0035	0.0008–0.0024	NA
	6G72②	3.0 (1997)	0.0012–0.0020	0.0118–0.0177	0.0177–0.0236	0.0079–0.0236	0.0012–0.0028	0.0008–0.0024	NA
1994	4G15	1.5 (1468)	0.0008–0.0016	0.0079–0.0138	0.0079–0.0138	0.0079–0.0276	0.0012–0.0028	0.0008–0.0024	NA
	4G37	1.8 (1755)	0.0004–0.0012	0.0118–0.0177	0.0079–0.0138	0.0080–0.0280	0.0018–0.0033	0.0008–0.0024	NA
	4G93	1.8 (1834)	0.0008–0.0016	0.0098–0.0157	0.0157–0.0217	0.0079–0.0236	0.0012–0.0028	0.0008–0.0024	NA
	4G63	2.0 (1997)	0.0010–0.0020	0.0098–0.0177	0.0138–0.0197	0.0079–0.0276	0.0012–0.0028	0.0012–0.0028	NA
	4G64	2.4 (2351)④	0.0008–0.0016	0.0098–0.0138	0.0157–0.0217	0.0039–0.0157	0.0012–0.0028	0.0008–0.0024	NA
	6G72①	3.0 (2972)	0.0012–0.0020	0.0118–0.0177	0.0098–0.0157	0.0118–0.0154	0.0020–0.0035	0.0008–0.0024	NA
	6G72②	3.0 (1997)	0.0012–0.0020	0.0118–0.0177	0.0177–0.0236	0.0079–0.0236	0.0012–0.0028	0.0008–0.0024	NA

NA—Not available
① SOHC
② DOHC
③ 8 valve
④ 16 valve

TORQUE SPECIFICATIONS

All readings in ft. lbs.

Year	Engine Series ID	Engine Displacement Liters (cc)	Cylinder Head Bolts	Main Bearing Nuts	Rod Bearing Bolts	Crankshaft Damper Bolts	Flywheel Bolts	Manifold Intake	Manifold Exhaust	Spark Plugs	Lug Nut
1990	4G15	1.5 (1468)	51–54 ①	36–40	23–25	51–72 ③	94–101	11–14	11–14	18	80
	4G61	1.6 (1597)	65–72 ②	47–51	36–38	80–94 ④	94–101	18–22	18–22	18	80
	4G37	1.8 (1755)	51–54	37–39	24–25	80–94	94–101	13–18	13–18	18	100
	4G63 ⑥	2.0 (1997)	65–72	38	38	87 ④	98	13	13	18	80
	4G63 ⑦	2.0 (1997)	65–72	47–51	36–38	80–94	94–101	18–22	18–22	18	⑤
	6G72	3.0 (2972)	76–83	58	38	108–116	55	13	13	18	75
1991	4G15	1.5 (1468)	51–54 ①	47–51	36–38	51–72 ③	94–101	11–14	11–14	18	80
	4G61	1.6 (1597)	65–72 ②	47–51	36–38	80–94 ④	94–101	18–22	18–22	18	80
	4G37	1.8 (1755)	51–54	37–39	24–25	80–94	94–101	13–18	13–18	18	100
	4G63 ⑥	2.0 (1997)	65–72	38	38	87 ④	98	13	13	18	80
	4G63 ⑦	2.0 (1997)	65–72	47–51	36–38	80–94	94–101	18–22	18–22	18	⑤
	6G72	3.0 (1997)	87–94	58	38	130–137	55	9–11	22 ⑧	18	100
1992	4G15	1.5 (1468)	51–54 ①	47–51	36–38	51–72 ③	94–101	11–14	11–14	18	80
	4G61	1.6 (1597)	65–72	47–51	36–38	80–94 ④	94–101	18–22	18–22	18	80
	4G37	1.8 (1755)	51–54	37–39	24–25	80–94	94–101	13–18	13–18	18	100
	4G93	1.8 (1834)	⑩	⑪	⑫	134	72	13	13	18	80
	4G63 ⑥	2.0 (1997)	65–72	38	38	87 ④	98	13	13	18	80
	4G63 ⑦	2.0 (1997)	65–72	47–51	36–38	80–94	94–101	18–22	18–22	18	⑤
	4G64	2.4 (2351) ⑮	65–72	38	38	87 ④	98	13	13	18	80
	6G72 ⑥	3.0 (2972)	76–83	58	38	108–116	55	13	13	18	80
	6G72 ⑦	3.0 (1997)	87–94	58	38	130–137	55	9–11	22 ⑧	18	⑨
1993	4G15	1.5 (1468)	51–54 ①	47–51	36–38	51–72 ③	94–101	11–14	11–14	18	80
	4G37	1.8 (1755)	51–54	37–39	24–25	80–94	94–101	13–18	13–18	18	100
	4G93	1.8 (1834)	⑩	⑪	⑫	134	72	13	13	18	80
	4G63 ⑥	2.0 (1997)	65–72	38	38	87 ④	98	13	13	18	80
	4G63 ⑦	2.0 (1997)	65–72	47–51	36–38	80–94	94–101	18–22	18–22	18	⑤
	4G64	2.4 (2351) ⑯	⑬	38	⑭	87 ④	98	13	13	18	80
	6G72 ⑥	3.0 (2972)	76–83	58	38	108–116	55	13	13	18	80
	6G72 ⑦	3.0 (1997)	87–94	58	38	130–137	55	9–11	22 ⑧	18	⑨

TORQUE SPECIFICATIONS

All readings in ft. lbs.

Year	Engine Series ID	Engine Displacement Liters (cc)	Cylinder Head Bolts	Main Bearing Nuts	Rod Bearing Bolts	Crankshaft Damper Bolts	Flywheel Bolts	Manifold Intake	Manifold Exhaust	Spark Plugs	Lug Nut
1994	4G15	1.5 (1468)	51–54 ①	47–51	36–38	51–72 ③	94–101	11–14	11–14	18	80
	4G37	1.8 (1755)	51–54	37–39	24–25	80–94	94–101	13–18	13–18	18	100
	4G93	1.8 (1834)	⑩	⑪	⑫	134	72	13	13	18	80
	4G63 ⑥	2.0 (1997)	65–72	38	38	87 ④	98	13	13	18	80
	4G63 ⑦	2.0 (1997)	65–72	47–51	36–38	80–94	94–101	18–22	18–22	18	⑤
	4G64	2.4 (2351) ⑯	⑬	38	⑭	87 ④	98	13	13	18	80
	6G72 ⑥	3.0 (2972)	76–83	58	38	108–116	55	13	13	18	80
	6G72 ⑦	3.0 (1997)	87–94	58	38	130–137	55	9–11	22 ⑧	18	⑨

① Torque to 58–61 ft. lbs. when hot
② Torque to 72–80 ft. lbs. when hot
③ Pulley-to-crank sprocket bolts: 9–11 ft. lbs.
④ Pulley-to-crank sprocket bolts: 14–22 ft. lbs.
⑤ Galant: 80 ft. lbs.
  Eclipse: 100 ft. lbs.
⑥ SOHC
⑦ DOHC
⑧ See text
⑨ Diamante: 80 ft. lbs.
  3000GT: 100 ft. lbs.
⑩ Step 1: Torque to 54 ft. lbs., then loosen completely
  Step 2: Retorque to 14.5 ft. lbs.
  Step 3: Turn each an additional ¼ turn
  Step 4: Turn each another ¼ turn
⑪ 18 ft. lbs. plus ¼ turn
⑫ 14.5 ft. lbs. plus ¼ turn
⑬ Step 1: Torque to 14.5 ft. lbs.
  Step 2: Turn each an additional ¼ turn
  Step 3: Turn each another ¼ turn
⑭ Step 1: Torque to 14.5 ft. lbs.
  Step 2: Turn each an additional ¼ turn
⑮ 8 valve
⑯ 16 valve

BRAKE SPECIFICATIONS
All measurements in inches unless noted.

Year	Model	F/R	Master Cylinder Bore	Brake Disc Original Thickness	Brake Disc Minimum Thickness	Brake Disc Maximum Runout	Brake Drum Diameter Original Inside Diameter	Brake Drum Diameter Max. Wear Limit	Brake Drum Diameter Maximum Machine Diameter	Minimum Lining Thickness Front	Minimum Lining Thickness Rear
1990	Precis		0.810	0.75	0.67	0.006	7.100	7.200	7.165	0.06	0.06
	Mirage [1]		0.810	0.51	0.45	0.006	7.100	7.200	7.165	0.06	0.06
	Mirage [2]	front	0.875	0.94	0.88	0.006	—	—	—	0.06	—
		rear	—	0.39	0.33	0.006	—	—	—	—	0.06
	Galant	front	[3]	0.94	0.88	0.004	—	—	—	0.06	—
		rear	—	0.39	0.33	0.003	8.000	8.100	8.065	—	0.06
	Sigma	front	0.938	0.94	0.88	0.004	—	—	—	0.06	—
		rear	—	0.71	0.65	0.004	—	—	—	—	0.06
	Eclipse	front	[4]	0.94	0.88	0.003	—	—	—	0.06	—
		rear	—	0.39	0.33	0.003	—	—	—	—	0.06
1991	Precis		0.810	0.75	0.67	0.006	7.100	7.200	7.165	0.06	0.06
	Mirage [1][5]		0.810	0.51	0.45	0.006	7.100	7.200	7.165	0.06	0.06
	Mirage [1][6]		0.875	0.71	0.65	0.006	7.100	7.200	7.165	0.06	0.06
	Mirage [2]	front	0.938	0.94	0.88	0.006	—	—	—	0.06	—
		rear	—	0.39	0.33	0.006	—	—	—	—	0.06
	Galant	front	[7]	0.94	0.88	0.004	—	—	—	0.06	—
		rear	—	0.39	0.33	0.003	8.000	8.100	8.065	—	0.06
	Eclipse	front	[4]	0.94	0.88	0.003	—	—	—	0.06	—
		rear	—	0.39	0.33	0.003	—	—	—	—	0.06
	3000GT [8]	front	[10]	0.94	0.88	0.003	—	—	—	0.06	—
		rear	—	0.71	0.65	0.003	—	—	—	—	0.06
	3000GT [9]	front	1.063	1.18	1.12	0.003	—	—	—	0.06	—
		rear	—	0.79	0.72	0.003	—	—	—	—	0.06
1992	Precis		0.810	0.75	0.67	0.006	7.100	7.200	7.165	0.06	0.06
	Mirage [1][5]		0.810	0.51	0.45	0.006	7.100	7.200	7.165	0.06	0.06
	Mirage [1][6]		0.875	0.71	0.65	0.006	7.100	7.200	7.165	0.06	0.06
	Mirage [2]	front	0.938	0.94	0.88	0.006	—	—	—	0.06	—
		rear	—	0.39	0.33	0.006	—	—	—	—	0.06
	Expo/Expo LRV	front	[11]	0.94	0.88	0.003	—	—	—	0.06	—
		rear	—	0.39	0.33	0.003	[12]	[13]	[14]	—	0.06
	Galant	front	[7]	0.94	0.88	0.004	—	—	—	0.06	—
		rear	—	0.39	0.33	0.003	8.000	8.100	8.065	—	0.06
	Eclipse	front	[4]	0.94	0.88	0.003	—	—	—	0.06	—
		rear	—	0.39	0.33	0.003	—	—	—	—	0.06
	3000GT [8]	front	[10]	0.94	0.88	0.003	—	—	—	0.06	—
		rear	—	0.71	0.65	0.003	—	—	—	—	0.06
	3000GT [9]	front	1.063	1.18	1.12	0.003	—	—	—	0.06	—
		rear	—	0.79	0.72	0.003	—	—	—	—	0.06
	Diamante	front	1.000	0.94	0.88	0.003	—	—	—	0.06	—
		rear	—	0.71	0.65	0.003	—	—	—	—	0.06

BRAKE SPECIFICATIONS
All measurements in inches unless noted.

Year	Model	F/R	Master Cylinder Bore	Brake Disc			Brake Drum Diameter			Minimum Lining Thickness	
				Original Thickness	Minimum Thickness	Maximum Runout	Original Inside Diameter	Max. Wear Limit	Maximum Machine Diameter	Front	Rear
1993	Precis		0.810	0.75	0.67	0.006	7.100	7.200	7.165	0.06	0.06
	Mirage Coupe		0.813	⑯	⑰	0.003	7.100	7.200	7.165	0.08	⑱
	Mirage 4-Door	front	0.813⑮	⑯	⑰	0.003	—	—	—	0.08	—
		rear	—	0.04	0.33	0.003	8.000	8.100	8.065	—	⑱
	Expo/Expo LRV	front	⑪	0.94	0.88	0.003	—	—	—	0.06	—
		rear	—	0.39	0.33	0.003	⑫	⑬	⑭	—	0.06
	Galant	front	⑦	0.94	0.88	0.004	—	—	—	0.06	—
		rear	—	0.39	0.33	0.003	8.000	8.100	8.065	—	0.06
	Eclipse	front	④	0.94	0.88	0.003	—	—	—	0.06	—
		rear	—	0.39	0.33	0.003	—	—	—	—	0.06
	3000GT ⑧	front	⑩	0.94	0.88	0.003	—	—	—	0.06	—
		rear	—	0.71	0.65	0.003	—	—	—	—	0.06
	3000GT ⑨	front	1.063	1.18	1.12	0.003	—	—	—	0.06	—
		rear	—	0.79	0.72	0.003	—	—	—	—	0.06
	Diamante	front	1.000	0.94	0.88	0.003	—	—	—	0.06	—
		rear	—	0.71	0.65	0.003	—	—	—	—	0.06
1994	Precis		0.810	0.75	0.67	0.006	7.100	7.200	7.165	0.06	0.06
	Mirage Coupe		0.813	⑯	⑰	0.003	7.100	7.200	7.165	0.08	⑱
	Mirage 4-Door	front	0.813⑮	⑯	⑰	0.003	—	—	—	0.08	—
		rear	—	0.04	0.33	0.003	8.000	8.100	8.065	—	⑱
	Expo/Expo LRV	front	⑪	0.94	0.88	0.003	—	—	—	0.06	—
		rear	—	0.39	0.33	0.003	⑫	⑬	⑭	—	0.06
	Galant	front	⑦	0.94	0.88	0.004	—	—	—	0.06	—
		rear	—	0.39	0.33	0.003	8.000	8.100	8.065	—	0.06
	Eclipse	front	④	0.94	0.88	0.003	—	—	—	0.06	—
		rear	—	0.39	0.33	0.003	—	—	—	—	0.06
	3000GT ⑧	front	⑩	0.94	0.88	0.003	—	—	—	0.06	—
		rear	—	0.71	0.65	0.003	—	—	—	—	0.06
	3000GT ⑨	front	1.063	1.18	1.12	0.003	—	—	—	0.06	—
		rear	—	0.79	0.72	0.003	—	—	—	—	0.06
	Diamante	front	1.000	0.94	0.88	0.003	—	—	—	0.06	—
		rear	—	0.71	0.65	0.003	—	—	—	—	0.06

NA—Not available
① With 1.5L engine
② With 1.6L engine
③ FWD without ABS: 0.875 in.
  FWD with ABS: 0.938 in.
  AWD without ABS: 0.938 in.
  AWD with ABS: 1.00 in.
④ With non-turbocharged engine: 0.875 in.
  With turbocharged engine: 0.938 in.
⑤ Hatchback model
⑥ Sedan model
⑦ FWD with SOHC engine: 0.875 in.
  FWD with DOHC engine: 0.938 in.
  All other models: 1.00 in.
⑧ FWD
⑨ AWD

⑩ Without ABS: 1.00 in.
  With ABS: 1.063 in.
⑪ Without ABS: 0.938 in.
  With ABS: 1.00 in.
⑫ May be equipped with either 8 in. or 9 in. drums
⑬ Max. wear limit = 0.100 in. over original I/D
⑭ Max. machine diameter = 0.065 over original I/D
⑮ Vehicles with ABS—0.938
⑯ Solid type: 0.51
  Vented type: 0.71
⑰ Solid type: 0.45
  Vented type: 0.65
⑱ Shoe lining: 0.04
  Disc pads: 0.08

WHEEL ALIGNMENT

Year	Model	F/R	Caster Range (deg.)	Caster Preferred Setting (deg.)	Camber Range (deg.)	Camber Preferred Setting (deg.)	Toe-in (in.)
1990	Precis	front	④	⑤	1/2N–1/2P	0	0
		rear	—	—	NA	2/3N	1/16
	Mirage	front	2P–3P	2 1/3P	1/2N–1/2P	0	0
		rear	—	—	1N–0	2/3N	0
	Galant	front	1 1/2P–2 1/2P	2P	1/6N–5/6P	1/3P	0
		rear	—	—	⑧	⑨	⑩
	Sigma	front	1/6P–1 1/6P	2/3P	0–1P	1/2P	0
		rear	—	—	1N–1/2N	3/4N	0
	Eclipse ①	front	1 5/16P–2 5/6P	2 1/3P	1/4N–2/3P	1/4P	0
		rear	—	—	1 1/4N–1/4N	3/4N	0
	Eclipse ②	front	2P–3P	2 1/2P	1/2N–2/3P	3/32P	0
		rear	—	—	1 1/4N–1/4N	3/4N	0
	Eclipse ③	front	2P–3P	2 1/2P	1/3N–2/3P	1/6P	0
		rear	—	—	2N–1N	1 1/2N	1/8
1991	Precis	front	④	⑤	1/2N–1/2P	0	0
		rear	—	—	NA	2/3N	1/16
	Mirage	front	1 5/6P–2 5/6P	2 1/3P	1/2N–1/2P	0	0
		rear	—	—	1 1/6N–1/6N	2/3N	0
	Galant	front	1 1/2P–2 1/2P	2P	1/6N–5/6P	1/3P	0
		rear	—	—	⑧	⑨	⑩
	Eclipse ①	front	1 5/16P–2 5/6P	2 1/3P	1/4N–2/3P	1/4P	0
		rear	—	—	1 1/4N–1/4N	3/4N	0
	Eclipse ②	front	2P–3P	2 1/2P	1/2N–2/3P	3/32P	0
		rear	—	—	1 1/4N–1/4N	3/4N	0
	Eclipse ③	front	2P–3P	2 1/2P	1/3N–2/3P	1/6P	0
		rear	—	—	2N–1N	1 1/2N	1/8
	3000GT	front	3 7/16P–4 7/16P	3 15/16P	1/2N–1/2P	0	0
		rear	—	—	⑥	⑦	0
1992	Precis	front	④	⑤	1/2N–1/2P	0	0
		rear	—	—	NA	2/3N	1/16
	Mirage	front	1 5/6P–2 5/6P	2 1/3P	1/2N–1/2P	0	0
		rear	—	—	1 1/6N–1/6N	2/3N	0
	Expo/Expo LRV	front	⑪	⑫	⑬	⑭	1/8
		rear	—	—	1N–0	1/2N	1/16
	Galant	front	1 1/2P–2 1/2P	2P	1/6N–5/6P	1/3P	0
		rear	—	—	⑧	⑨	⑩
	Eclipse ①	front	1 5/16P–2 5/6P	2 1/3P	1/4N–2/3P	1/4P	0
		rear	—	—	1 1/4N–1/4N	3/4N	0
	Eclipse ②	front	2P–3P	2 1/2P	1/2N–2/3P	3/32P	0
		rear	—	—	1 1/4N–1/4N	3/4N	0

WHEEL ALIGNMENT

Year	Model	F/R	Caster Range (deg.)	Caster Preferred Setting (deg.)	Camber Range (deg.)	Camber Preferred Setting (deg.)	Toe-in (in.)
	Eclipse ③	front	2P–3P	2½P	1/3N–2/3P	1/6P	0
		rear	—	—	2N–1N	1½N	1/8
	3000GT	front	3 7/16P–4 7/16P	3 15/16P	1/2N–1/2P	0	0
		rear	—	—	⑥	⑦	0
	Diamante	front	2 1/4P–3 1/4P	2 3/4P	1/2N–1/2P	0	0
		rear	—	—	1/2N–1/2P	0	0
1993	Precis	front	④	⑤	1/2N–1/2P	0	0
		rear	—	—	NA	2/3N	1/16
	Mirage	front	—	2 1/4P	1/2N–1/2P	0	0
		rear	—	—	1 1/6N–1/6N	2/3N	0.04–0.20
	Expo/Expo LRV	front	⑪	⑫	⑬	⑭	1/8
		rear	—	—	1N–0	1/2N	1/16
	Galant	front	1 1/2P–2 1/2P	2P	1/6N–5/6P	1/3P	0
		rear	—	—	⑧	⑨	⑩
	Eclipse ①	front	1 5/16P–2 5/6P	2 1/3P	1/4N–2/3P	1/4P	0
		rear	—	—	1 1/4N–1/4N	3/4N	0
	Eclipse ②	front	2P–3P	2 1/2P	1/2N–2/3P	3/32P	0
		rear	—	—	1 1/4N–1/4N	3/4N	0
	Eclipse ③	front	2P–3P	2 1/2P	1/3N–2/3P	1/6P	0
		rear	—	—	2N–1N	1 1/2N	1/8
	3000GT	front	3 7/16P–4 7/16P	3 15/16P	1/2N–1/2P	0	0
		rear	—	—	⑥	⑦	0
	Diamante	front	2 1/4P–3 1/4P	2 3/4P	1/2N–1/2P	0	0
		rear	—	—	1/2N–1/2P	0	0
1994	Precis	front	④	⑤	1/2N–1/2P	0	0
		rear	—	—	NA	2/3N	1/16
	Mirage	front	—	2 1/4P	1/2N–1/2P	0	0
		rear	—	—	1 1/6N–1/6N	2/3N	0.04–0.20
	Expo/Expo LRV	front	⑪	⑫	⑬	⑭	1/8
		rear	—	—	1N–0	1/2N	1/16
	Galant	front	1 1/2P–2 1/2P	2P	1/6N–5/6P	1/3P	0
		rear	—	—	⑧	⑨	⑩
	Eclipse ①	front	1 5/16P–2 5/6P	2 1/3P	1/4N–2/3P	1/4P	0
		rear	—	—	1 1/4N–1/4N	3/4N	0
	Eclipse ②	front	2P–3P	2 1/2P	1/2N–2/3P	3/32P	0
		rear	—	—	1 1/4N–1/4N	3/4N	0
	Eclipse ③	front	2P–3P	2 1/2P	1/3N–2/3P	1/6P	0
		rear	—	—	2N–1N	1 1/2N	1/8
	3000GT	front	3 7/16P–4 7/16P	3 15/16P	1/2N–1/2P	0	0
		rear	—	—	⑥	⑦	0
	Diamante	front	2 1/4P–3 1/4P	2 3/4P	1/2N–1/2P	0	0
		rear	—	—	1/2N–1/2P	0	0

N—Negative
P—Positive
① With 1.8L engine
② FWD version with 2.0L engine
③ AWD version

④ Manual steering: 1/2P–1 1/2P
　 Power steering: 1 1/6P–2 1/6P
⑤ Manual steering: 1 1/32P
　 Power steering: 1 2/3P
⑥ FWD version: 1/2N–1/2P
　 AWD version: 2/3N–1/3P

⑦ FWD version: 0
　 AWD version: 1/6N
⑧ FWD version: 1 1/4N–1/4N
　 AWD version: 1 1/2N–1/2N
⑨ FWD version: 3/4N
　 AWD version: 1N

⑩ FWD version: 0
　 AWD version: 1/8
⑪ FWD version: 1 1/2P–2 5/6P
　 AWD version: 1 5/12P–2 3/4P
⑫ FWD version: 2 1/6P
　 AWD version: 2 1/12P

⑬ FWD version: 1/16N–5/16P
　 AWD version: 1/6P–1 1/16P
⑭ FWD version: 1/3P
　 AWD version: 2/3P

ENGINE MECHANICAL

NOTE: Disconnecting the negative battery cable on some vehicles may interfere with the functions of the on board computer systems and may require the computer to undergo a relearning process, once the negative battery cable is reconnected.

Engine Assembly

REMOVAL AND INSTALLATION

The following procedure can be used on all vehicles. Slight variations may occur due to extra connections, etc., but the basic procedure should cover all models.

1. Relieve fuel system pressure.
2. Remove the battery. Remove the engine undercover if equipped.
3. Matchmark the hood and hinges and remove the hood assembly. Remove the air cleaner assembly and all adjoining air intake duct work.
4. Drain the engine coolant and remove the radiator assembly, coolant reservoir, and intercooler, as equipped.
5. Remove the, transmission, transaxle and transfer case as equipped.
6. Disconnect and tag for assembly reference the connections for the accelerator cable, heater hoses, brake vacuum hose, connection for vacuum hoses, high pressure fuel line, fuel return line, oxygen sensor connection, coolant temperature gauge connection, coolant temperature sensor connector, connection for thermo switch sensor, the connection for the idle speed control, the motor position sensor connector, the throttle position sensor connector, the EGR temperature sensor connection (California vehicles), the fuel injector connectors, the power transistor connector, the ignition coil connector, the condenser and noise filter connector, the distributor and control harness, the connections for the alternator, and oil pressure switch wires.
7. Remove the air conditioner drive belt and the air conditioning compressor. Leave the hoses attached. Do not discharge the system. Wire the compressor aside.
8. Remove the power steering pump and wire aside.

9. Remove the exhaust manifold-to-head pipe nuts. Discard the gasket.
10. Attach a hoist to the engine and take up the engine weight. Remove the engine mount bracket. Remove any torque control brackets (roll stoppers). Note that some engine mount pieces have arrows on them for proper assembly. Double check that all cables, hoses, harness connectors, etc., are disconnected from the engine. Lift the engine slowly and remove from the engine compartment.

To install:

11. Install the engine and secure all control brackets.
12. Install the exhaust pipe, power steering pump and air conditioning compressor.
13. Checking the tags installed during removal, reconnect all electrical and vacuum connections.
14. Install the transmission, transaxle, and transfer case.
15. Install the radiator assembly and intercooler.
16. Install the air cleaner assembly.
17. Fill the engine with the proper amount of engine oil and coolant. Install the battery.
18. Start the engine, allow it to reach normal operating temperature. Check for leaks.
19. Check the ignition timing and adjust if necessary.
20. Install the hood.
21. Road test the vehicle and check all fluid levels and functions for proper operation.

Engine Mounts

REMOVAL AND INSTALLATION

1. Disconnect the negative battery cable. Remove the air cleaner and all necessary duct work.
2. Raise and safely support the engine so it is not resting on the engine mount. One suggested way is a block of wood between a floor jack and the oil pan. Use care not to bend or damage any components.
3. Remove the retainer bolt from the clamp securing the power steering pressure hose and the air conditioning low pressure hose.
4. Remove the coolant reservoir and bracket if they are preventing access to the engine mount bracket. It is imperative to take note of the position of the arrow on the oval shaped mounting stopper plate prior to disassembly. Remove the engine mount bracket and body connection through bolt.

5. Remove the engine mounting bracket and stopper plate.
6. Lower mounts (roll stoppers) are removed by removing the through bolt, then the frame bolts. On 3000GT, the condenser fan assembly and front catalytic converter must first be removed to gain access to the front mount.

To install:

7. Place the mount into position. Note the arrows on the stopper plates, and make sure they are installed properly; on most engines the arrows will face towards the center of the engine. When installing the lower front roll stopper, install the stopper bracket so the part of the bracket with the hole in it is facing the front of the vehicle.
8. The front lower mount through bolt nut should not be tightened until the full weight of the engine is on the mount. Torque specifications are as follows:**Expo/Expo LRV**

Upper mount to engine nuts and bolts — 42 ft. lbs. (58 Nm)

Upper mount through bolt nut — 51 ft. lbs. (70 Nm)

Lower mount through bolt nut FWD — 40 ft. lbs. (55 Nm)

Lower mount through bolt nut AWD — 38 ft. lbs. (53 Nm)**Eclipse and Galant**

Upper mount to engine nuts and bolts — 36-47 ft. lbs. (50-65 Nm)

Upper mount through bolt nut — 43-58 ft. lbs. (60-80 Nm)

Lower mount through bolt nut — 33-43 ft. lbs. (45-60 Nm)**Precis, Mirage, and Sigma**

Upper mount to engine nuts and bolts — 36-47 ft. lbs. (50-65 Nm)

Upper mount through bolt nut — 65-80 ft. lbs. (90-110 Nm)

Lower mount through bolt nut — 33-43 ft. lbs. (45-60 Nm)**Diamante and 3000GT**

Upper mount to engine nuts and bolts — 72-87 ft. lbs. (100-120 Nm)

Upper mount through bolt nut — 51 ft. lbs. (70 Nm)

Lower mount through bolt nut — 36-43 ft. lbs. (47-60 Nm)

9. Install any remaining parts that were removed.

Cylinder Head

REMOVAL AND INSTALLATION

1.5L, 2.0L SOHC Engines and 1.8L Engine (Eclipse)

1. Relieve the fuel system pressure. Disconnect the negative battery cable.
2. Drain the cooling system.

3. Remove the air intake hose and the breather hose.

4. Disconnect the accelerator cable. There will be 2 cables if equipped with cruise-control.

5. Place a shop towel around the high pressure fuel line to absorb any residual fuel remaining in the system. Disconnect the high pressure fuel line.

6. Remove the upper radiator hose, the water breather hose, the water bypass hose and the heater hose.

7. Disconnect the PCV hose.

8. Remove the spark plug cables.

9. Disconnect and plug the fuel return line.

10. Disconnect the vacuum line for the brake booster.

11. Disconnect the electrical connections for the oxygen sensor, engine coolant temperature gauge unit and the water temperature sensor.

12. Disconnect the electrical connections for the idle speed control motor, throttle position sensor, distributor, motor position sensor connector, fuel injectors, EGR temperature sensor (California vehicles), power transistor, condenser and ground cable.

13. Disconnect the engine control wiring harness.

14. Remove the clamp that holds the power steering pressure hose to the engine mounting bracket.

15. On transverse-mounted engines, place a jack and wood block under the oil pan and carefully lift just enough to take the weight off the engine mounting bracket. Then remove the bracket.

16. Remove the valve cover, gasket and half-round seal.

17. Remove the timing belt front upper cover. If possible, rotate the crankshaft clockwise until the timing marks on the cam sprocket and belt align. Remove the sprocket bolt and remove the sprocket with the timing belt attached. On 1.8L engine, place on the timing belt front lower cover. On 1.5L engine, attach a flexible cord to the hood and suspend the sprocket so it cannot turn. Remove the timing belt rear upper cover.

18. Remove the exhaust pipe self-locking nuts and separate the exhaust pipe from the exhaust manifold. Discard the gasket.

To install:

19. Thoroughly clean and dry the mating surfaces of the head and block. Check the cylinder head for cracks, damage or engine coolant leakage. Remove scale, sealing compound and carbon. Clean oil passages

thoroughly. Check the head for flatness. End to end, the head should be within 0.002 in. normally with 0.008 in. the maximum allowed out of true. The total thickness allowed to be removed from the head and block is 0.008 in. maximum.

20. Carefully install the cylinder head on the block. Using 3 even steps, torque the head bolts in sequence, to 51-54 ft. lbs. (70-75 Nm).

21. Install a new exhaust pipe gasket and connect the exhaust pipe to the manifold. Connect turbocharger lines. Install the upper rear timing cover.

22. Align the timing marks and install the cam gear or sprocket. Torque the retaining bolt to 47-54 ft. lbs. (65-75 Nm) on 1.5L engine, 58-72 ft. lbs. (80-100 Nm) on 1.8L and 2.0L engines. Check the belt tension and adjust if necessary. Install the outer timing cover. Install the distributor, if removed.

23. Apply sealer to the perimeter of the half-round seal. Install a new valve cover gasket. Install the valve cover.

24. Install the engine mount bracket. Once secure, remove the jack.

25. Install the clamp that holds the power steering pressure hose to the engine mounting bracket.

26. Connect or install all previously disconnected hoses, cables and electrical connections. Adjust the throttle cable(s).

27. Replace the O-rings and connect the fuel lines.

28. Install the air intake hose. Connect the breather hose.

29. Change the engine oil and oil filter.

30. Fill the system with coolant.

31. Connect the negative battery cable, run the vehicle until the thermostat opens, fill the radiator completely.

32. Check and adjust the idle speed and ignition timing.

33. Once the vehicle has cooled, recheck the coolant level.

1.6L and 2.0L DOHC Engines

1. Relieve fuel system pressure. Disconnect the negative battery cable.

2. Drain the cooling system.

3. Disconnect the accelerator cable. There will be 2 cables if equipped with cruise-control.

4. Remove the air cleaner with the air intake hose.

5. Disconnect the oxygen sensor, engine coolant temperature sensor, the engine coolant temperature

gauge unit and the engine coolant temperature switch on vehicles with air conditioning.

6. Disconnect the ISC motor, throttle position sensor, crankshaft angle sensor, fuel injectors, ignition coil, power transistor, noise filter, knock sensor on turbocharged engines, EGR temperature sensor (California vehicles), ground cable and engine control wiring harness.

7. Remove the upper radiator hose and the overflow tube.

8. Remove the spark plug cable center cover and remove the spark plug cables.

9. Disconnect and plug the high pressure fuel line.

10. Disconnect the small vacuum hoses.

11. Remove the heater hose and water bypass hose.

12. Remove the PCV hose.

13. If turbocharged, remove the vacuum hoses, water line and eyebolt connection for the oil line for the turbo.

14. Disconnect and plug the fuel return hose.

15. Disconnect the brake booster vacuum hose.

16. Remove the timing belt.

17. Remove the valve cover and the half-round seal.

18. On non-turbocharged engines, remove the exhaust pipe self-locking nuts and separate the exhaust pipe from the exhaust manifold. Discard the gasket.

19. On turbocharged engines, remove the sheet metal heat protector and remove the bolts that attach the turbocharger to the exhaust manifold.

20. Loosen the cylinder head mounting bolts in 3 steps, starting from the outside and working inward. Lift off the cylinder head assembly and remove the head gasket.

To install:

21. Thoroughly clean and dry the mating surfaces of the head and block. Check the cylinder head for cracks, damage or engine coolant leakage. Remove scale, sealing compound and carbon. Clean oil passages thoroughly. Check the head for flatness. End to end, the head should be within 0.002 in. normally with 0.008 in. the maximum allowed out of true. The total thickness allowed to be removed from the head and block is 0.008 in. maximum.

22. Place a new head gasket on the cylinder block with the identification marks at the front top (upward) position. Make sure the gasket has the proper identification mark for the en-

gine. Do not use sealer on the gasket. Replace the turbo gasket and ring, if equipped.

23. Carefully install the cylinder head on the block. Using 3 even steps, torque the head bolts, in sequence, to 65-72 ft. lbs. (90-100 Nm). This torque applies to a cold engine. If checking cylinder head bolt torque on hot engine, the desired specification is 72-80 ft. lbs. (100-110 Nm).

24. On turbocharged engine, install the heat shield. On non-turbocharged engine, install a new exhaust pipe gasket and connect the exhaust pipe to the manifold.

25. Apply sealer to the perimeter of the half-round seal and to the lower edges of the half-round portions of the belt-side of the new gasket. Install the valve cover.

26. Install the timing belt and all related items.

27. Connect or install all previously disconnected hoses, cables and electrical connections. Adjust the throttle cable(s).

28. Install the spark plug cable center cover.

29. Replace the O-rings and connect the fuel lines.

30. Install the air cleaner and intake hose. Connect the breather hose.

31. Change the engine oil and oil filter.

32. Fill the system with coolant.

33. Connect the negative battery cable, run the vehicle until the thermostat opens, fill the radiator completely.

34. Check and adjust the idle speed and ignition timing.

35. Once the vehicle has cooled, recheck the coolant level.

1.8L Engine (Expo LRV)

1. Relieve fuel system pressure. Disconnect the negative battery cable.

2. Drain the cooling system. Disconnect the brake booster vacuum hose and PVC valve connection.

3. Remove the upper radiator hose, overflow tube and the water hose from the thermostat to the throttle body.

4. Disconnect the air flow sensor connector. Remove the air cleaner case cover and the air intake hose.

5. Wrap the connection with a shop towel and disconnect the high pressure fuel line at the fuel rail.

6. Disconnect the fuel return hose and remove the O-ring.

7. Disconnect the accelerator cable connection from the throttle body and position aside.

8. Disconnect the electrical harnesses at the oil pressure switch, oxygen sensor, water temperature sensor connector, distributor, condenser, ISC, TPS, detonation sensor and the fuel injectors.

9. Disconnect the spark plug cables from each spark plug.

10. Unbolt the control harness assembly and position aside.

11. Remove the thermostat housing, thermostat and the thermostat case with O-ring from the engine.

12. Remove the rocker cover.

13. Remove the timing belt upper cover.

14. Rotate the crankshaft in the forward (right) direction to align the camshaft timing marks. Matchmark the camshaft sprocket and the timing belt. Tie the camshaft sprocket and the timing belt together so the sprocket will not move with respect to the timing belt.

15. While holding the camshaft sprocket in position using the appropriate wrench, remove the camshaft sprocket and with the belt attached. Wire the sprocket and belt aside making sure constant tension is maintained on the belt. Do not allow the belt to slacken or engine timing may be altered.

NOTE: When removing the camshaft sprocket, do not allow the crankshaft to rotate. If crankshaft rotation did occur, the engine timing may have been changed. Confirm proper engine timing during installation.

16. Loosen the cylinder head bolts in 2 or 3 steps in the appropriate order and remove from the cylinder head.

17. Remove the cylinder head from the engine.

--- **CAUTION** ---

When placing the removed cylinder head upside down, take care not to bend or damage the plug guide. The plug guide can not be replaced.

18. Remove the cylinder head gasket from the block.

To install:

19. Thoroughly clean and dry the mating surfaces of the head and block. Check the cylinder head for cracks, damage or engine coolant leakage. Remove scale, sealing compound and carbon. Clean oil passages thoroughly. Check the head for flatness. End to end, the head should be within 0.002 in. normally with 0.008 in. the maximum allowed out of true. The total thickness allowed to be re-

moved from the head and block is 0.008 in. maximum.

20. Place a new head gasket on the cylinder block with the identification marks facing upward. Make sure the gasket has the proper identification mark for the engine. Do not use sealer on the gasket.

21. Carefully install the cylinder head on the block. Inspect the cylinder head bolt prior to installation, the length below the head of the bolts should be below the limit of 3.795 in. (96.4mm). Apply a small amount of engine oil to the thread section and the washer of the cylinder head bolt and install so the sagging side made by tapping out the washer is facing upward. (chamfer edge faces up).

22. Tighten the cylinder head bolts in the proper order as follows:

a. In the proper tightening sequence, torque bolts to 54 ft. lbs. (75 Nm).

b. In the reverse order of the tightening sequence, fully loosen bolts.

c. In the proper tightening sequence, torque bolts to 14 ft. lbs. (20 Nm).

d. In the proper tightening sequence, tighten bolts an additional 1/4 turn (90 degrees).

e. In the proper tightening sequence, tighten bolts an additional 1/4 turn (90 degrees).

23. Install the camshaft sprocket and tighten bolt to 65 ft. lbs. (90 Nm), while holding the sprocket in place using the appropriate wrench. Confirm proper timing mark alignment.

24. Install the upper timing belt cover and rocker cover.

25. Loosen the water pipe mounting bolt.

26. Apply a thin bead of sealant MD970389 or equivalent, to the water tube connection on the thermostat case.

27. Apply a small amount of water to the O-ring of the water inlet pipe and press the thermostat case assembly onto the water inlet pipe. Install the thermostat case assembly mounting bolt tightening to 16 ft. lbs. (22 Nm).

28. Tighten the water pipe mounting bolt.

29. Install the thermostat into the housing so the jiggle valve is located at the top. Tighten the housing bolts to 10 ft. lbs. (14 Nm).

30. Connect the upper radiator hose to the thermostat housing.

31. Connect or install all previously disconnected hoses, cables and electrical connections. Adjust the throttle cable(s).

32. Replace the O-rings and reconnect the fuel lines.

33. Install the air intake hose. Connect the breather hose, air cleaner case cover and air flow sensor connector.

34. Change the engine oil and oil filter. Reconnect the brake booster and the PCV vacuum hoses.

35. Fill the system with coolant.

36. Connect the negative battery cable, run the vehicle until the thermostat opens, fill the radiator completely.

37. Check and adjust the idle speed and ignition timing.

38. Check all systems for leaks. Allow the engine to cool and recheck the coolant level.

2.4L Engine

1. Relieve fuel system pressure. Disconnect the negative battery cable.

2. Drain the cooling system.

3. Disconnect the accelerator cable.

4. Remove the radiator.

5. Disconnect the air flow sensor connector and the air intake hose. Remove the air cleaner cover.

6. Disconnect the PCV hose.

FRONT OF ENGINE ➡
INTAKE SIDE

```
o    o    o    o    o
4    6    9    7    1
2    8    10   5    3
o    o    o    o    o
```

EXHAUST SIDE

FRONT OF ENGINE ➡
INTAKE SIDE

```
o    o    o    o    o
7    5    2    4    10
9    3    1    6    8
o    o    o    o    o
```

EXHAUST SIDE

Cylinder head bolt removal (top) and Installation (bottom) sequence — all 4 cylinder engines.

7. Disconnect the water hose connection at the throttle body to water inlet pipe.

8. Disconnect the water hose connection at the throttle body to thermostat hose.

9. Wrap the connection with a shop towel and disconnect the high pressure fuel line at the fuel rail.

10. Disconnect the fuel return hose and remove the O-ring.

11. Disconnect the accelerator cable connection at the throttle body.

12. Disconnect the spark plug cables from the spark plugs.

13. Disconnect the electrical connectors from the oxygen sensor, water temperature gauge unit, engine coolant temperature sensor, TPS, power transistor connector, fuel injectors, ignition coil, distributor, and air conditioner compressor. Label prior to disconnecting to assure correct relocation on assembly.

14. Remove the bolt retaining the power steering hose and air conditioner hose clamp.

15. Remove the coolant reservoir. Remove the bolt holding the ground wire to the manifold.

16. Place a jack and wood block under the oil pan and carefully lift just enough to take the weight off the engine mounting bracket. Then remove the engine mounting bracket taking note of the position of the mount stopper.

17. Remove the valve cover, gasket and half-round seal.

18. Remove the timing belt front upper cover.

19. If possible, rotate the crankshaft clockwise until the timing marks on the cam sprocket and belt align. Matchmark the timing sprocket to the belt. Remove the sprocket bolt and remove the sprocket with the timing belt attached. Attach a flexible cord to the hood and suspend the sprocket so it cannot turn and there is no slack in the belt. Remove the timing belt rear upper cover.

20. Loosen the head bolts in the correct sequence in 2 or 3 steps. Remove the cylinder head bolts and head assembly from the block.

To install:

21. Thoroughly clean and dry the mating surfaces of the head and block. Check the cylinder head for cracks, damage or engine coolant leakage. Remove scale, sealing compound and carbon. Clean oil passages thoroughly. Check the head for flatness. End to end, the head should be within 0.002 in. normally with 0.008

in. the maximum allowed out of true. The total thickness allowed to be removed from the head and block is 0.008 in. maximum.

22. Place a new head gasket on the cylinder block with the identification marks at the top (upward) position. Make sure the gasket has the proper identification mark for the engine. Do not use sealer on the gasket. Replace the turbo gasket and ring, if equipped.

23. Carefully install the cylinder head on the block. Install the cylinder head bolts and washer. Torque to 76-83 ft. lbs. (105-115 Nm), in 3 even progressions. This torque applies to a cold engine.

NOTE: Install the head bolt washer so the sagging side made by tapping out the washer is facing upward.

24. Install the camshaft sprocket and tighten bolt to 65 ft. lbs. (90 Nm), while holding the sprocket in place using the appropriate wrench. Confirm proper timing mark alignment.

25. Apply sealer to the perimeter of the half-round seal and to the lower edges of the half-round portions of the belt-side of the new gasket. Install the valve cover.

26. Install the engine mount positioning the stopper in the same direction as it was prior to removal.

27. Install the power steering and air conditioning compressor hose clamp in position and secure with the retainer bolt. Tighten the bolt to 9 ft. lbs. (12 Nm).

28. Install the coolant reservoir tank.

29. Reconnect all electrical harness connectors disconnect during disassembly. Connect the ground wire to the manifold.

30. Connect the accelerator cables and the spark plug cables.

31. Replace the O-rings and reconnect the fuel lines.

32. Reconnect the water hoses to throttle body, thermostat and the heater assembly.

33. Install the air intake case cover, air flow sensor connector and the radiator.

34. Fill the system with coolant. Adjust the accelerator cable.

35. Firmly set the parking brake. Start the engine and allow to idle until the thermostat opens, add coolant as required to fill system to the appropriate level.

36. Check all systems for leaks. Allow the engine to cool and recheck the coolant level.

3.0L Engine

SOHC

1. Relieve fuel system pressure. Disconnect the negative battery cable.
2. Drain the cooling system.
3. Remove the air intake hose.
4. Remove the exhaust manifold.
5. Remove the air intake plenum and intake manifold.
6. Remove the timing belt.
7. Remove the camshaft sprocket and rear timing belt cover.
8. Remove the power steering pump bracket. If removing the rear (right) side head, remove the alternator brace.
9. Disconnect the water inlet pipe.
10. Remove the purge pipe assembly.
11. Remove the valve cover.
12. Loosen the cylinder head mounting bolts in 3 steps, starting from the outside and working inward. Lift off the cylinder head assembly and remove the head gasket.

To install:

13. Thoroughly clean and dry the mating surfaces of the head and block. Check the cylinder head for cracks, damage or engine coolant leakage. Remove scale, sealing com-

pound and carbon. Clean oil passages thoroughly. Check the head for flatness. End to end, the head should be within 0.002 in. normally with 0.008 in. the maximum allowed out of true. The total thickness allowed to be removed from the head and block is 0.008 in. maximum.

14. Place a new head gasket on the cylinder block making sure the identification mark on the cylinder head gasket is in the front top (upward) location. Do not use sealer on the gasket. Make sure the gasket has the proper identification mark for the engine.
15. Carefully install the cylinder head on the block. Make sure the head bolt washers are installed with the chamfered edge upward. Using 3 even steps, torque the head bolts in sequence, to 76-83 ft. lbs. (105-115 Nm). This torque specifications assumes the engine is cold.
16. Apply sealer to the lower edges of the half-round portions of the belt-side of the new gasket and install the valve cover.
17. Install the purge pipe assembly.
18. Connect the water inlet pipe.
19. Install the power steering pump bracket and alternator brace.
20. Install the rear timing belt cover and cam sprocket. Torque the retaining bolt to 65 ft. lbs. (90 Nm).
21. Install the timing belt and all related items.
22. Using all new gaskets, install the intake manifold, air intake plenum and exhaust manifold, following the proper torque sequences.
23. Install the air intake hose.
24. Change the engine oil and oil filter.
25. Fill the system with coolant.
26. Connect the negative battery cable, run the vehicle until the thermostat opens, fill the radiator completely.
27. Check and adjust the idle speed and ignition timing.

28. Once the vehicle has cooled, recheck the coolant level.

DOHC

1. Relieve fuel system pressure. Disconnect the negative battery cable.
2. Drain the cooling system.
3. Remove the air intake hoses.
4. Remove air intake plenum and intake manifold.
5. Remove the turbocharger if equipped, and exhaust manifold.
6. Remove the timing belt.
7. Remove the triple pipe assembly across the top of the engine.
8. Remove the breather hose.
9. Remove the spark plug cable center cover and remove the spark plug cables.
10. When removing the valve cover, note that bolts for the front head are black and bolts for the rear head are green. Also, all bolts are 10mm long except the 1 closest to the sprockets on the rear head which is 20mm long.
11. To remove the intake camshaft sprocket, hold the camshaft with a wrench on the hexagon near the end of the camshaft and remove the bolt.
12. Remove the center rear timing belt cover.
13. Remove the ignition coil.
14. Disconnect all water hoses from the thermostat housing and remove the housing.
15. Disconnect the water inlet from the front head.
16. Loosen the cylinder head mounting bolts in 3 steps, starting from the outside and working inward. Lift off the cylinder head assembly and remove the head gasket.

To install:

17. Thoroughly clean and dry the mating surfaces of the head and block. Check the cylinder head for cracks, damage or engine coolant leakage. Remove scale, sealing compound and carbon. Clean oil passages thoroughly. Check the head for flatness. End to end, the head should be within 0.002 in. normally with 0.008 in. the maximum allowed out of true. The total thickness allowed to be removed from the head and block is 0.008 in. maximum.
18. Place a new head gasket on the cylinder block with the identification marks in the front top (upward) position. Do not use sealer on the gasket.
19. Carefully install the cylinder head on the block. Make sure the head bolt washers are installed with the chamfered edge upward. Using 3 even steps, torque the head bolts in sequence, to 76-83 ft. lbs. (105-115 Nm) for non-turbocharged cold en-

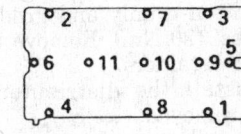

MD998051

CYLINDER HEAD
BOLT WASHER

● 6 ● 2 ● 3 ● 7   REAR BANK

● 5 ○ 1 ○ 4 ● 8

● 8 ● 4 ● 1 ● 5   FRONT BANK

● 7 ● 3 ● 2 ● 6

Cylinder head bolt tightening sequence — 3.0L engine

REAR BANK

○ 2 ○ 7 ○ 3

○ 6 ○ 11 ○ 10 ○ 9   5

○ 4 ○ 8

FRONT BANK

○ 1 ○ 8 ○ 4

○ 5 ○ 9 ○ 10 ○ 11 6

○ 3 ○ 7 ○ 2

Valve cover bolt tightening sequence — 3.0L DOHC engine

gine or 87-94 ft. lbs. (120-130 Nm) for turbocharged cold engine.

20. Connect the water inlet to the front head.

21. Replace the gaskets and install the thermostat housing and connect the hoses.

22. Install the ignition coil and center rear timing belt cover.

23. Using the same procedure as in removal, install the intake camshaft sprocket. Torque the retaining bolt to 65 ft. lbs. (90 Nm).

24. Apply sealer to the lower edges of the half-round portions of the belt-side of the new gasket and install the valve cover. Make sure green bolts are installed on the rear head and black bolts are installed on the front head. Also, make sure the longest bolt is installed in its proper location closest to the sprockets on the rear head. Tighten the bolts in the proper sequence to 26 inch lbs. Then re-tighten bolts 1-6 to 36 inch lbs.

25. Connect the spark plug cables and install the center cover.

26. Install the breather hose.

27. Install the triple pipe assembly across the top of the engine and torque the retaining bolts to 7 ft. lbs. (10 Nm).

28. Install the timing belt and all related items.

29. Using all new gaskets, install the intake manifold, air intake plenum, turbocharger and exhaust manifold, following the proper torque sequences.

30. Install the air intake hoses.

31. Change the engine oil and oil filter.

32. Fill the system with coolant.

33. Connect the negative battery cable, run the vehicle until the thermostat opens, fill the radiator completely.

34. Adjust the accelerator cable. Check and adjust the idle speed and ignition timing.

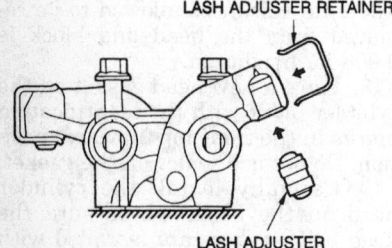

LASH ADJUSTER RETAINER

LASH ADJUSTER

Use of the hydraulic lash adjuster retaining tool

35. Once the vehicle has cooled, recheck the coolant level.

Valve Lifters

REMOVAL AND INSTALLATION

1.5L, 1.8L, 2.0L SOHC Engines

1. Disconnect the negative battery cable.

2. Remove the valve cover. In order to prevent the lash adjusters from falling out of their bores in the rocker arms, install lash adjuster retainer tools (MD998443 or equivalent) to the rocker arms.

3. Remove the distributor extension if necessary.

4. Have a helper hold the rear of the camshaft down. If not, the belt will dislodge and valve timing will be lost. Remove the rear bearing cap.

5. Loosen the remaining camshaft cap retaining bolts but don't remove them from the caps. Do not loosen the forward most camshaft bearing cap bolts.

6. At this point, the shafts can be removed as an assembly for service or service of individual components can be made by sliding component to be replaced off back end of shafts. If the later method of replacement is used, keep all parts in order or removal and install parts in same location.

7. To remove the shafts as an assembly, remove No. 2, 3 and 4 bearing caps, rocker arms, rocker shafts and bolts. It is essential that all parts are kept in the same order and orientation for reinstallation. Remove the lash adjuster tools to replace the adjuster(s) as required.

To install:

8. Apply a drop of sealant to the rear edges of the end caps.

9. Install the assembly into the front bearing cap making sure the notches in the rocker shafts are facing up. Insert the installation bolt but do not tighten at this point.

10. Install the remaining cap bolts and tighten evenly and gradually to 15 ft. lbs. (20 Nm). Remove the lash adjuster retainers.

11. Install the distributor extension, if removed.

12. Install the valve cover with a new gasket.

13. Connect the negative battery cable.

1.6L and 2.0L DOHC Engines

1. Relieve the fuel system pressure. Disconnect the negative battery cable.

2. Disconnect the accelerator cable, PCV hoses, breather hoses, spark plug cables and the remove the valve cover.

3. Rotate the crankshaft clockwise and align the timing marks so No. 1 piston will be at TDC of the compression stroke. At this time the timing marks on the camshaft sprocket and the upper surface of the cylinder head should coincide, and the dowel pin of the camshaft sprocket should be at the upper side.

NOTE: Always rotate the crankshaft in a clockwise direction. Make a mark on the back of the timing belt indicating the direction of rotation so it may be reassembled in the same direction if it is to be reused.

4. Remove the timing belt upper and lower covers.

5. Remove the timing belt.

6. Remove the crank angle sensor.

7. Remove the camshafts.

8. Visually inspect the rocker arm roller and replace if dent, damage or seizure is evident. Check the roller for smooth rotation. Replace if excess play or binding is present. Also, inspect valve contact surface for possible damage or seizure. It is recommended that all rocker arms and lash adjusters be replaced together.

To install:

9. Install the lash adjusters and rocker arms into the cylinder head. Lubricate lightly with clean oil prior to installation.

10. Apply engine oil to the lobes and journals of each camshaft. Install the camshafts into the cylinder head taking care not to confuse the intake and the exhaust camshaft; the intake camshaft has a slit on its rear end for driving the crank angle sensor. Align shafts so dowel pins on camshaft sprocket end are located on the top.

11. Install and tighten the camshaft bearing caps in the proper sequence torquing to specifications in 3 even progressions.

12. Replace the camshaft oil seals and install the sprockets.

13. Locate the dowel pin on the sprocket end of the intake camshaft at the top position, if not already done.

14. Align the punch mark on the crank angle sensor housing with the notch on the sensor plate. Install the crank angle sensor into the cylinder head.

15. Install the timing belt, covers and related components.

16. Install the valve cover using new gasket. Reconnect all related components.

17. Reconnect the negative battery cable.

3.0L DOHC Engine

1. Relieve the fuel system pressure.
2. Disconnect battery negative cable.
3. Remove the timing belt cover and timing belt.
4. Remove the center cover, breather and PCV hoses, and spark plug cables.
5. Remove the rocker cover, semi-circular packing, throttle body stay, both camshaft sprockets, and oil seals.
6. Remove the crank angle sensor and adaptor.
7. Remove the intake and exhaust camshafts.
8. Remove the rocker arms and lash adjusters from the head. It is recommended that all lash adjusters and rockers be replaced at 1 time.

To install:

9. Immerse the lash adjusters in clean diesel fuel. Using a small wire, move the plunger of the lash adjuster up and down 4 or 5 times while pushing down lightly on the check ball in order to bleed out the air. Install the lash adjusters in the cylinder head.
10. Lubricate the camshafts with heavy engine oil and position the camshafts on the cylinder head.

NOTE: Do not confuse the intake camshaft with the exhaust camshaft. On 1991 models, the intake camshaft has a V stamped on the hexagon of the shaft and the exhaust camshaft is stamped with a C. On 1992-94 models, the intake camshaft has a V or B stamped on the hexagon, and the exhaust camshaft has a D or F.

11. Make sure the dowel pin on both camshaft sprocket ends in the UP position.
12. Install the bearing caps. Tighten the caps in sequence and in 2 or 3 steps. Caps 2, 3 and 4 have a front mark. Install with the mark aligned with the front mark on the cylinder head. Intake caps have **I** stamped on the cap and exhaust caps have **E**. Also, make sure the rocker arm is correctly mounted on the lash adjuster and the valve stem end. Torque the retaining bolts to 15 ft. lbs. (20 Nm).
13. Apply a coating of engine oil to the oil seals and install.
14. Install the timing belt, valve cover and all related parts.
15. Connect the negative battery cable and check for leaks.

Valve Lash

ADJUSTMENT

Valve lash must be adjusted on all engines not equipped with automatic lash adjusters. Some engines have a small third valve called a jet valve. The jet valve must be adjusted, whether the engine uses automatic lash adjusters for the normal intake and exhaust valves or not. Thus, on some engines, there are 3 valves per cylinder that must be adjusted.

Incorrect valve clearance will cause noisy and/or unsteady engine operation, reduced engine output, and possible engine damage. Check the valve clearances and adjust as required while the engine is hot. Incorrect jet valve clearance would affect the emission levels and could also cause engine troubles, so the jet valve clearance must be correctly adjusted.

The jet valve clearance should be adjusted with the adjusting screw on the intake valve side fully loosened. The jet valve spring has very light tension, hence the adjustment is somewhat delicate. Be careful not to push in the jet valve by turning the adjusting screw in too much.

1. Warm the engine to operating temperature. Turn the engine OFF. Disconnect the negative battery cable.
2. Remove all spark plugs so engine can be easily turned by hand.
3. Remove the valve cover.
4. Turn the crankshaft clockwise until the notch on the pulley is aligned with the **T** mark on the timing belt lower cover. This brings both No. 1 and 4 cylinder pistons to Top Dead Center (TDC).
5. Wiggle the rocker arms on No. 1 and 4 cylinders up and down to determine which cylinder is at TDC on the compression stroke. Both rocker arms should move if the piston in

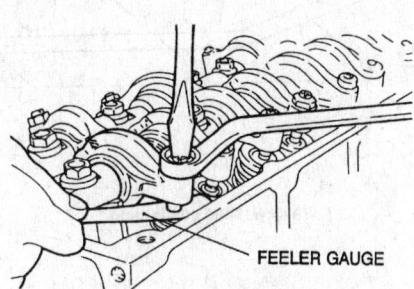

FEELER GAUGE

Tool arrangement for valve adjustment

that cylinder is at TDC on the compression stroke.

6. Measure the valve clearance with a feeler gauge. When the No. 1 piston is at TDC on the compression stroke, check No. 1 intake, jet and exhaust; No. 2 intake and jet; and No. 3 exhaust. Then turn the crankshaft clockwise 1 turn to bring No. 4 to TDC on its compression stroke. With No. 4 on TDC, compression stroke, check No. 2 exhaust; No. 3 intake and jet; and No. 4 intake, jet, and exhaust.
7. If the valve clearance is out of specification, loosen the rocker arm locknut and adjust the clearance using a feeler gauge while turning the adjusting screw. When at specification, tighten the locknut. Be sure to hold the screw tightly when tightening the locknut to prevent it from turning when tightening the locknut. Recheck the clearance and readjust.
8. After adjusting the valves, install the valve cover and spark plugs, and connect the negative battery cable.

Rocker Arms/Shafts

REMOVAL AND INSTALLATION

NOTE: The DOHC engines do not use rocker shafts. The valve are directly actuated by rocker arms. To remove the arms, the camshaft must first be removed. It is recommended that all rocker arms and lash adjusters are replaced together.

1.5L, 1.8L, 2.0L SOHC Engines Except Expo LRV With 1.5L and 1.8L Engines

1. Disconnect the negative battery cable.
2. Remove the valve cover. Install lash adjuster retainer tools MD998443 or equivalent to the rocker arms.
3. Remove the distributor extension if necessary.
4. Have a helper hold the rear of the camshaft down. If not, the belt will dislodge and valve timing will be lost.
5. Loosen the camshaft cap retaining bolts but don't remove them from the caps. Remove the rear bearing cap.
6. Loosen the remaining camshaft cap retaining bolts but don't remove them from the caps. Do not loosen the forward most camshaft bearing cap bolts.
7. At this point, the shafts can be removed as an assembly for service or

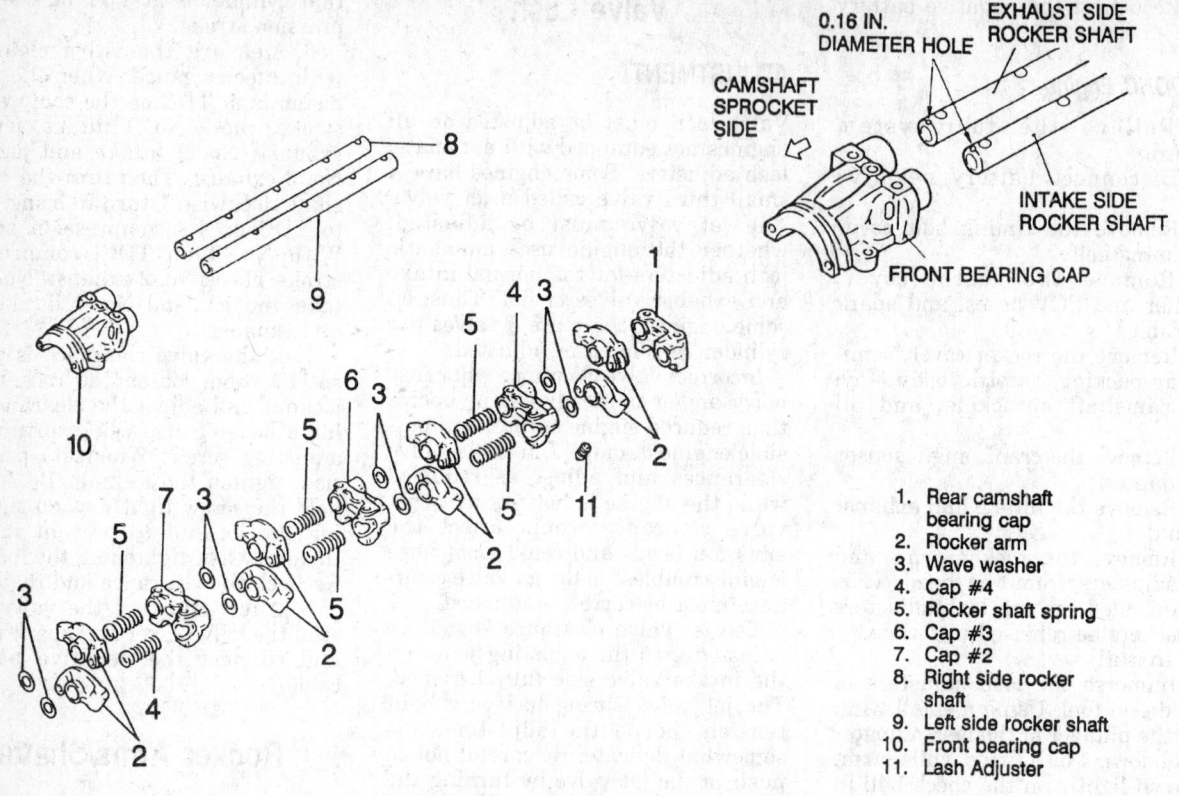

1. Rear camshaft bearing cap
2. Rocker arm
3. Wave washer
4. Cap #4
5. Rocker shaft spring
6. Cap #3
7. Cap #2
8. Right side rocker shaft
9. Left side rocker shaft
10. Front bearing cap
11. Lash Adjuster

Rocker arm and shaft assembly — 1.8L engine (Eclipse)

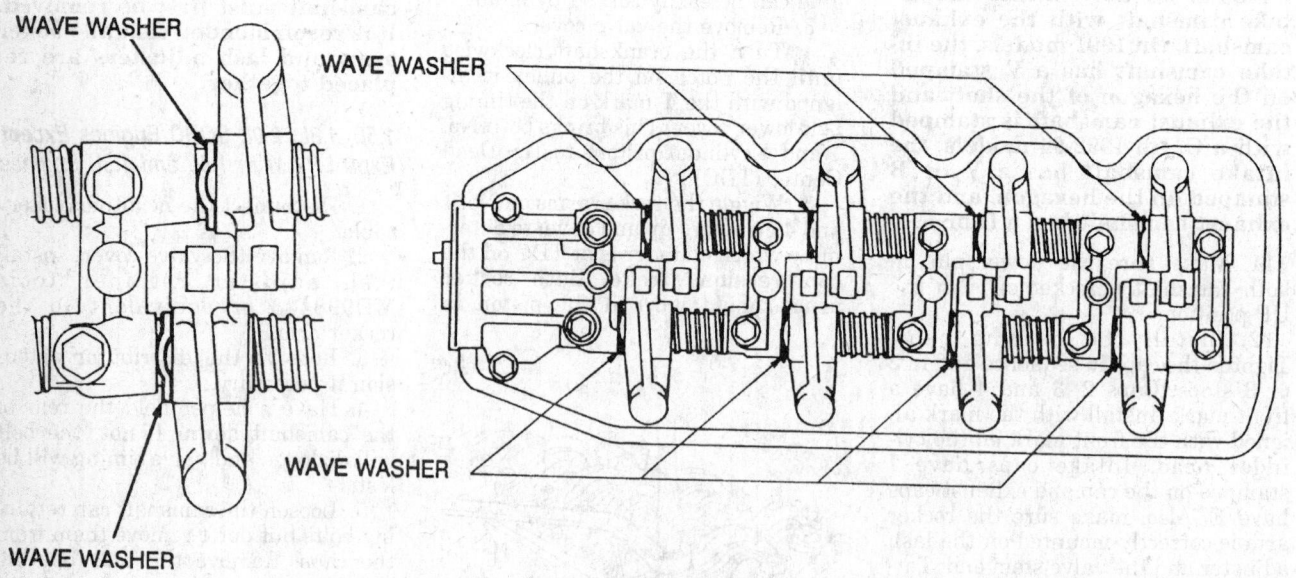

Wave washer positioning

1. Rear bearing cap
2. Rocker arm D
3. Spring
4. Rocker arm D
5. Cap #4
6. Rocker arm C
7. Rocker arm C
8. Spring
9. Cap #3
10. Rocker arm D
11. Spring
12. Rocker arm D
13. Cap #2
14. Rocker arm C
15. Rocker arm C
16. Spring
17. Wave washer
18. Right side rocker shaft
19. Left sicker shaft
20. Front bearing cap
21. Lash adjuster

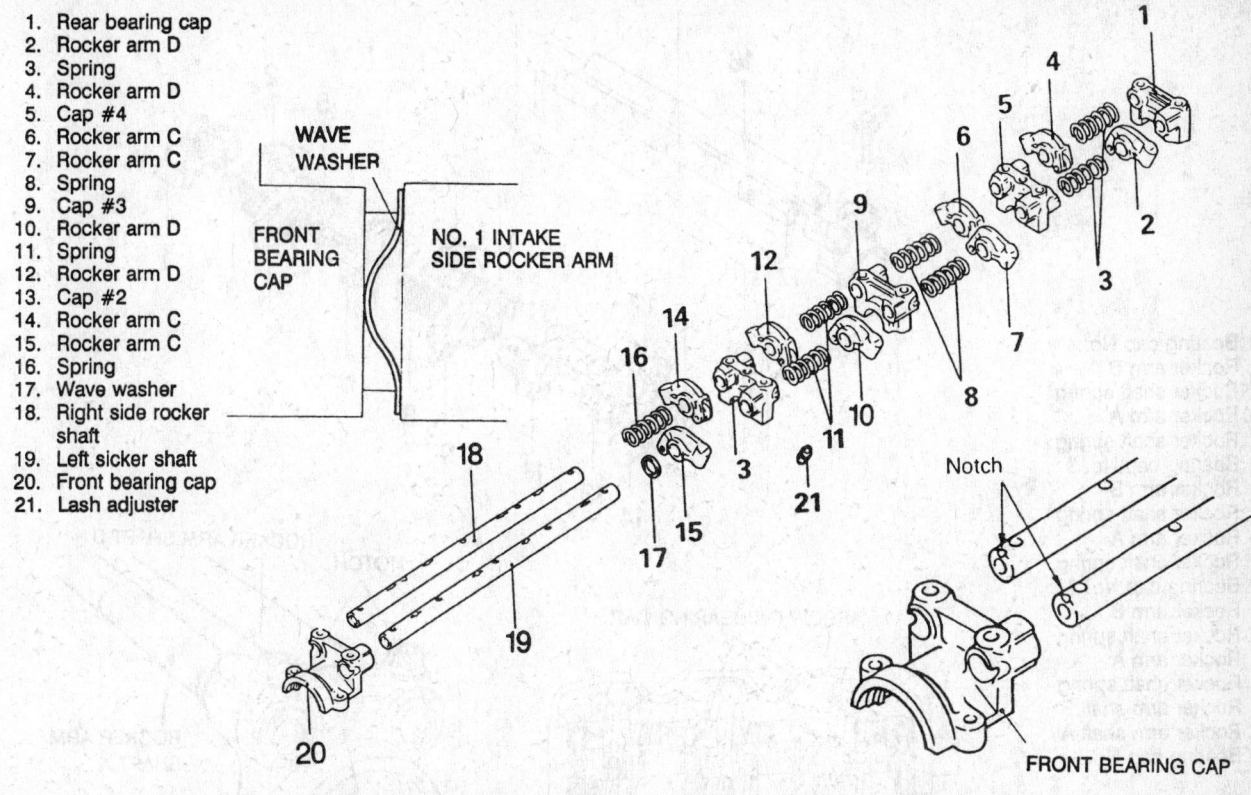

Rocker arm and shaft assembly — 2.0L engine and 2.4L SOHC engines

service of individual components can be made by sliding component to be replaced off back end of shafts. If the later method of replacement is used, only disassemble as far as needed and keep all parts in order of removal. Installation of parts in the same location and orientation is required.

8. To remove the shafts as an assembly, remove No. 2, 3 and 4 bearing caps, rocker arms, rocker shafts and bolts. It is essential that all parts be kept in the same order and orientation for reinstallation. Remove the lash adjuster tools to replace the adjuster(s), as required. Inspect the roller surfaces of the rockers. Replace if there are any signs of damage or if the roller does not turn smoothly. Check the inside bore of the rockers and lifter for wear.

To install:

9. Apply a drop of sealant to the rear edges of the end caps.

10. Install the assembly into the front bearing cap making sure the notches in the rocker shafts are facing up. Insert the installation bolt, but do not tighten at this point.

11. Install the remaining cap bolts and tighten evenly and gradually to 15 ft. lbs. (20 Nm). Remove the lash adjuster retainers.

12. Install the distributor extension, if removed.

13. Install the valve cover with a new gasket.

14. Connect the negative battery cable.

1.5L and 1.8L Engines (Expo LRV)

1. Disconnect the negative battery cable.

2. Remove the valve cover and discard the gasket.

3. Remove the rocker shaft hold-down bolts gradually and evenly and remove the rocker shaft/arm assemblies.

4. If disassembly is required, keep all parts in the exact order of removal. Inspect the roller surfaces of the rockers. Replace if there are any signs of damage or if the roller does not turn smoothly. Check the inside bore of the rockers and the adjuster tip for wear.

To install:

5. Lubricate the rocker shaft with clean engine oil and install the rockers and springs in their proper places.

6. Install the rocker shaft assemblies on the engine and tighten the bolts gradually and evenly. On 1.5L engine, torque to 14-20 ft. lbs. (20-27 Nm) on 1990 engines or 21-25 ft. lbs.

(29-35 Nm) on 1991-94 engines. On 1.8L engine, torque the rocker shaft bolts to 23 ft. lbs. (32 Nm).

7. Install the valve cover with a new gasket.

8. Connect the negative battery cable.

Intake Manifold

REMOVAL AND INSTALLATION

4-Cylinder Engines

1. Relieve the fuel system pressure.

2. Disconnect battery negative cable and drain the cooling system.

3. Disconnect the accelerator cable, breather hose and air intake hose.

4. Disconnect the upper radiator hose, heater hose and water bypass hose.

5. Remove all vacuum hoses and pipes as necessary, including the brake booster vacuum line.

6. Disconnect the high pressure fuel line, fuel return hose and remove throttle control cable brackets.

7. Tag and disconnect the electrical connectors from the coolant temperature sensor, thermo switch, idle speed control connection, EGR tem-

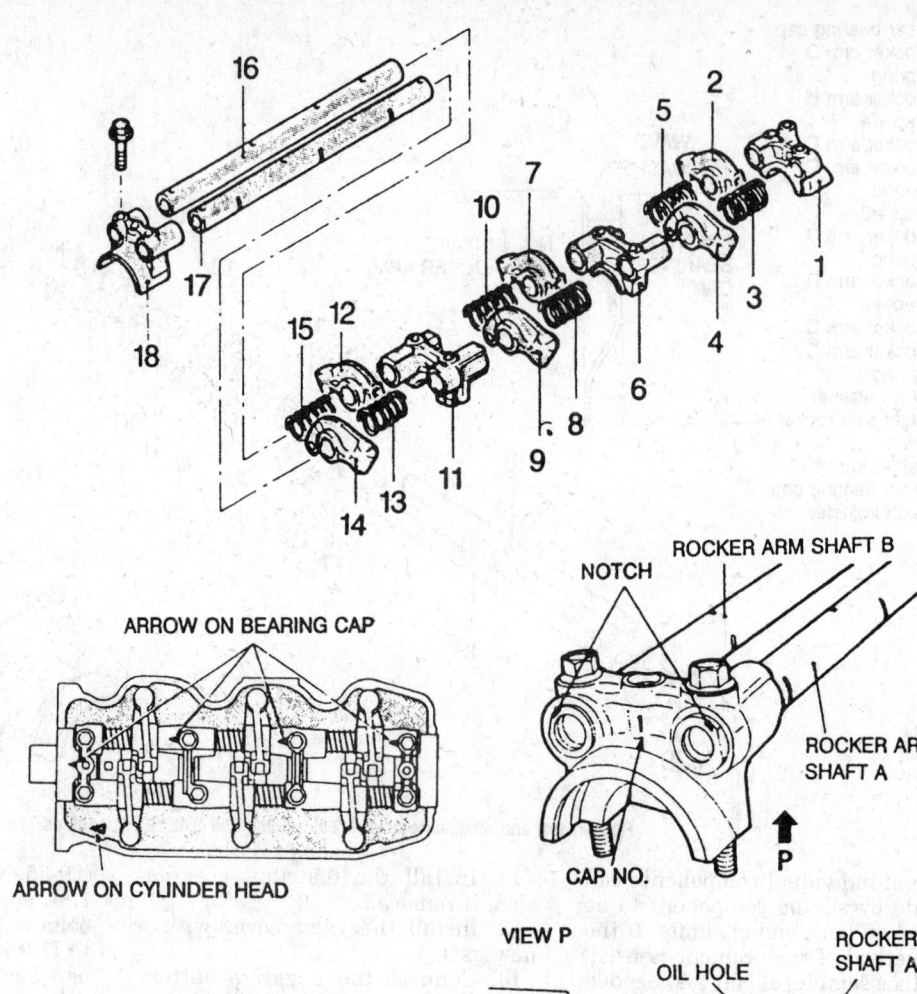

1. Bearing cap No. 4
2. Rocker arm B
3. Rocker shaft spring
4. Rocker arm A
5. Rocker shaft spring
6. Bearing cap No. 3
7. Rocker arm B
8. Rocker shaft spring
9. Rocker arm A
10. Rocker shaft spring
11. Bearing cap No. 2
12. Rocker arm B
13. Rocker shaft spring
14. Rocker arm A
15. Rocker shaft spring
16. Rocker arm shaft B
17. Rocker arm shaft A
18. Bearing cap No. 1

Rocker arm and shaft assembly — 3.0L SOHC engine

perature sensor, spark plug wires, etc. that may interfere with the manifold removal procedure.

8. Remove the fuel rail, fuel injectors, pressure regulator and insulators.

9. Remove the fuel delivery pipe, injectors and pressure regulator from the engine.

10. Remove the distributor from the engine if it passes through the manifold. Distributor removal is also necessary on the 1992-94 2.4L engine. Matchmark the distributor shaft to the housing and the housing to the head or nearest accessory prior to removal.

11. Remove the intake manifold bracket.

12. Disconnect the water hose connections at the throttle body, water inlet, and heater assembly.

13. If the thermostat housing is preventing removal of the intake manifold, remove it.

14. Disconnect the vacuum connection at the power brake booster and the PCV valve if still connected.

15. Remove the intake manifold mounting bolts and remove the intake manifold assembly. Disassemble manifold from the intake plenum on a work bench as required.

To install:

16. Assemble the intake manifold assembly using all new gaskets. Torque air intake plenum bolts to 11-14 ft. lbs. (15-19 Nm).

17. Clean all gasket material from the cylinder head intake mounting surface and intake manifold assembly. Check both surfaces for cracks or other damage. Check the intake manifold water passages and jet air passages for clogging. Clean if necessary.

18. Install a new intake manifold gasket to the head and install the manifold. Torque the manifold in a crisscross pattern, starting from the

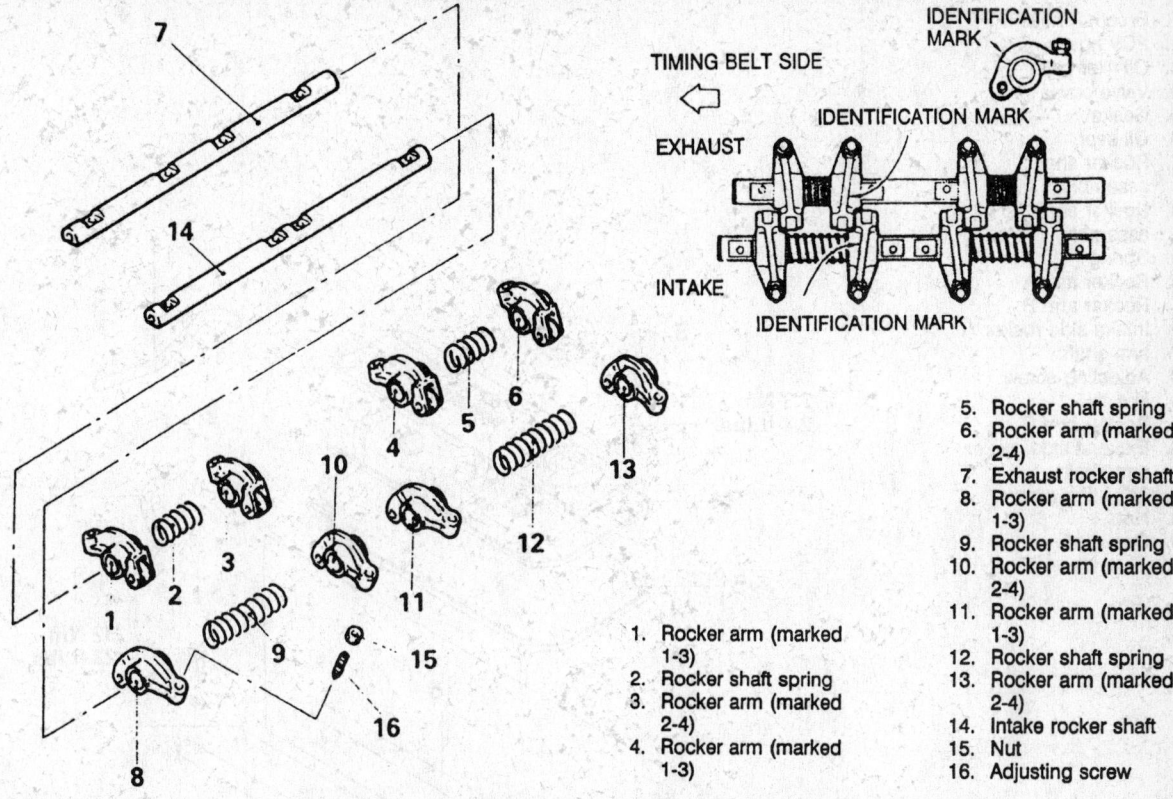

5. Rocker shaft spring
6. Rocker arm (marked 2-4)
7. Exhaust rocker shaft
8. Rocker arm (marked 1-3)
9. Rocker shaft spring
10. Rocker arm (marked 2-4)
11. Rocker arm (marked 1-3)
12. Rocker shaft spring
13. Rocker arm (marked 2-4)
14. Intake rocker shaft
15. Nut
16. Adjusting screw

1. Rocker arm (marked 1-3)
2. Rocker shaft spring
3. Rocker arm (marked 2-4)
4. Rocker arm (marked 1-3)

Rocker arm and shaft assembly — 1.5L Engine (Precis and 1990 Mirage)

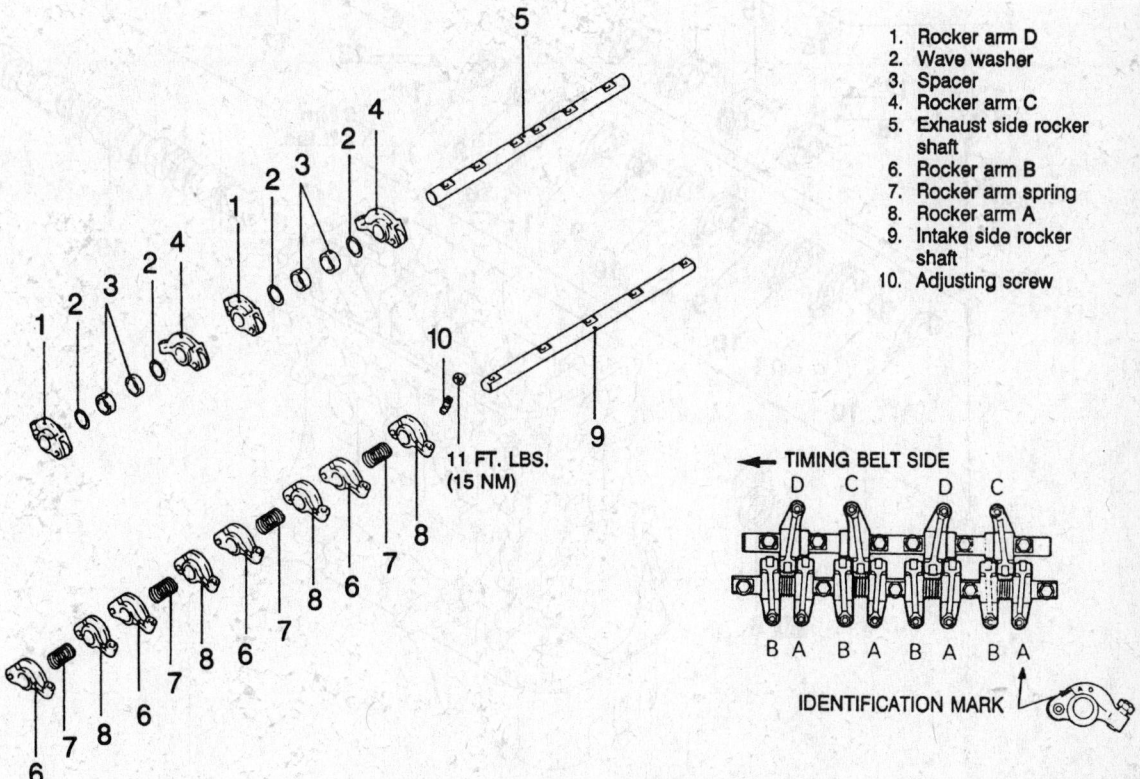

1. Rocker arm D
2. Wave washer
3. Spacer
4. Rocker arm C
5. Exhaust side rocker shaft
6. Rocker arm B
7. Rocker arm spring
8. Rocker arm A
9. Intake side rocker shaft
10. Adjusting screw

Rocker arm and shaft assembly — 1.5L Engine (1991-94 Mirage)

1. Breather hose
2. PCV hose
3. Oil filler cap
4. Valve cover
5. Gasket
6. Oil seal
7. Rocker shaft assembly
8. Rocker shaft assembly
9. Spring
10. Rocker arm A
11. Rocker arm B
12. Intake side rocker arm shaft
13. Adjusting screw
14. Nut
15. Rocker arm C
16. Exhaust side rocker arm shaft
17. Adjusting screw
18. Nut
19. Camshaft

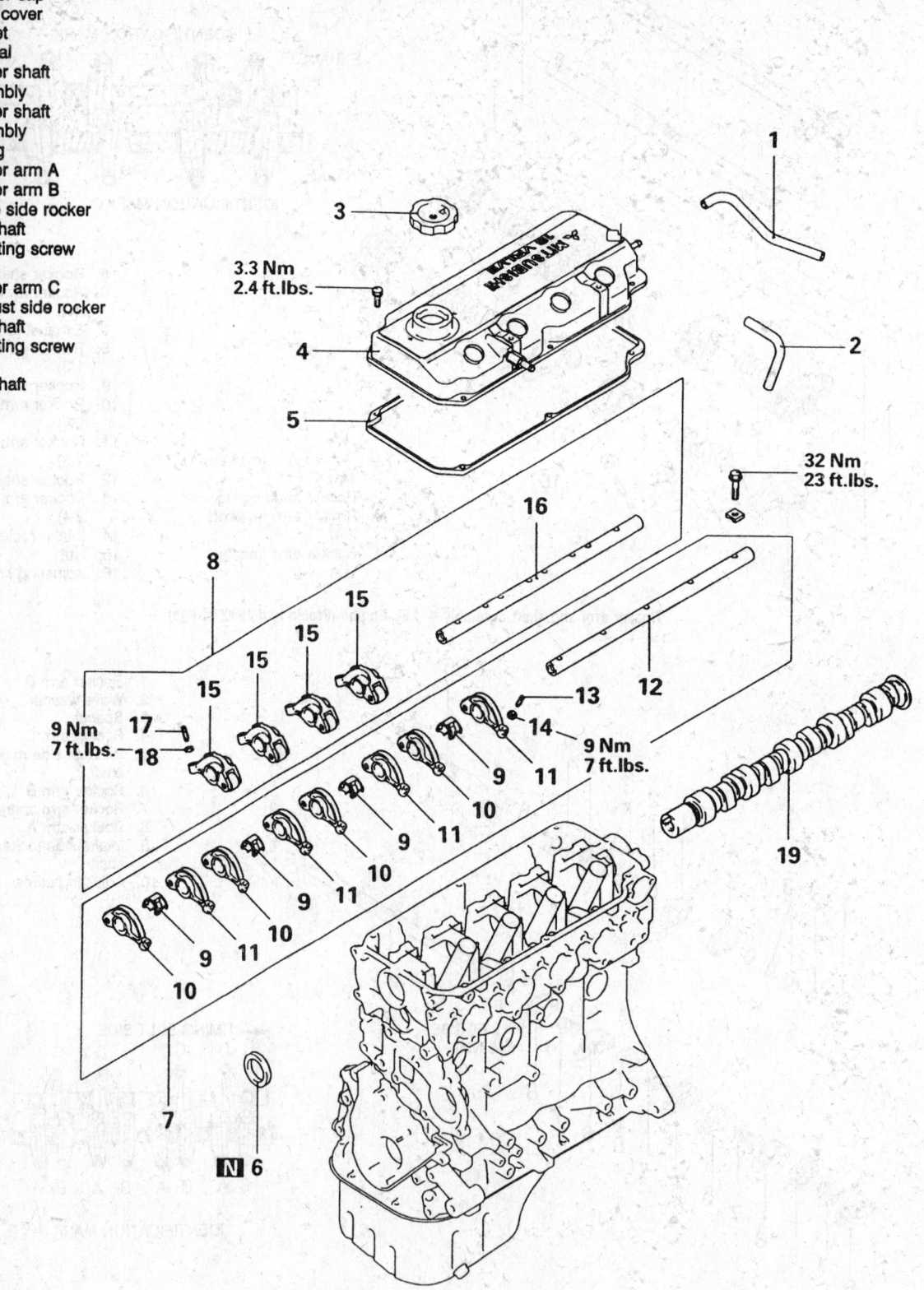

Rocker arm and shaft assembly — 1.8L Engine (Expo/Expo LRV)

1. Water hose
2. Sending unit
3. Coolant temp sensor
4. Thermo switch

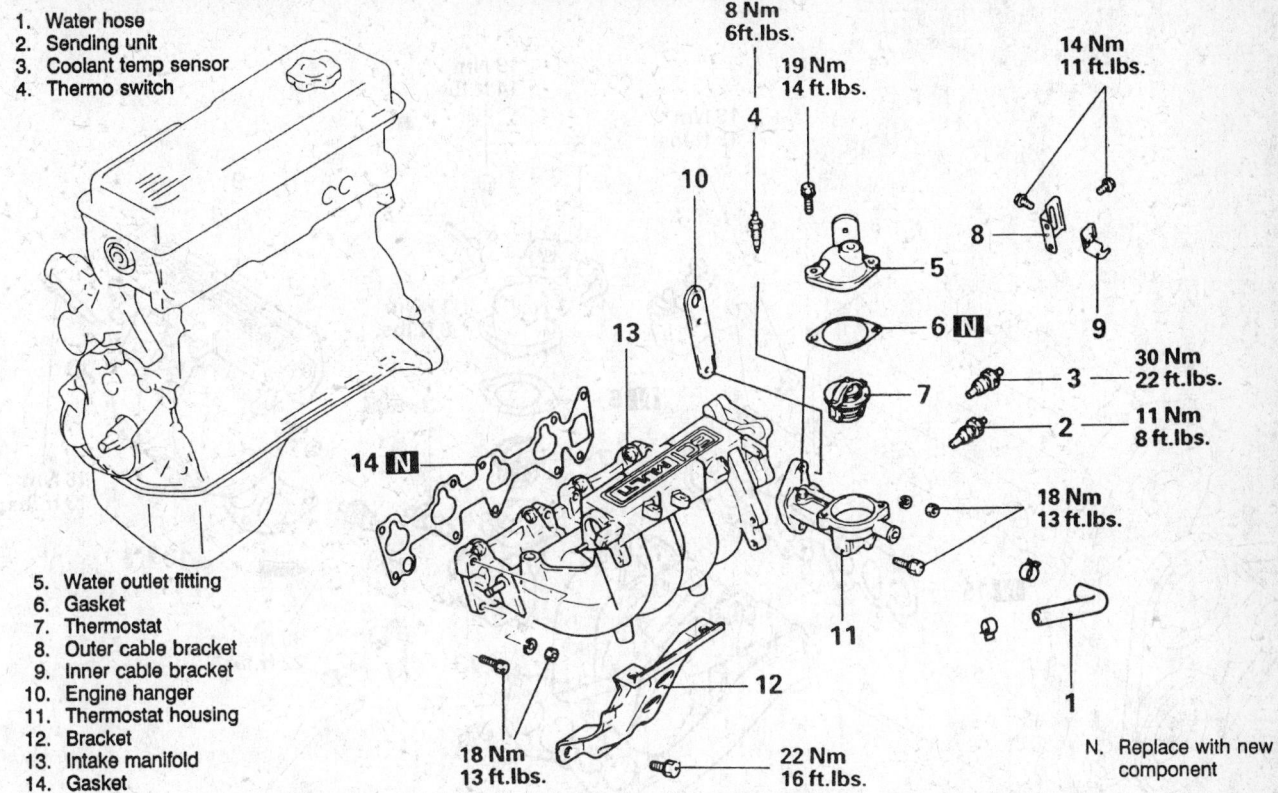

8 Nm
6ft.lbs.

19 Nm
14 ft.lbs.

14 Nm
11 ft.lbs.

30 Nm
22 ft.lbs.

11 Nm
8 ft.lbs.

18 Nm
13 ft.lbs.

5. Water outlet fitting
6. Gasket
7. Thermostat
8. Outer cable bracket
9. Inner cable bracket
10. Engine hanger
11. Thermostat housing
12. Bracket
13. Intake manifold
14. Gasket

18 Nm
13 ft.lbs.

22 Nm
16 ft.lbs.

N. Replace with new component

Intake manifold and related parts — typical of 2.0L DOHC, 1.5L, 1.6L, and 1.8L (Expo/Expo LRV) engines

inside and working outwards to 11-14 ft. lbs. (15-19 Nm).

19. Install the fuel delivery pipe, injectors and pressure regulator from the engine. Torque the retaining bolts to 7-9 ft. lbs. (10-13 Nm).

20. Install the thermostat housing, intake manifold brace bracket, distributor and throttle body stay bracket.

21. Connect or install all hoses, cables and electrical connectors that were removed or disconnected during the removal procedure.

22. Fill the system with coolant.

23. Connect the negative battery cable, run the vehicle until the thermostat opens, fill the radiator completely.

24. Adjust the accelerator cable. Check and adjust the idle speed and ignition timing.

25. Once the vehicle has cooled, recheck the coolant level.

3.0L Engine

1. Relieve the fuel system pressure.

2. Disconnect battery negative cable and drain the cooling system.

3. Remove the air intake hose(s).

4. Disconnect the accelerator control cables from the throttle body.

5. Matchmark and disconnect the vacuum hoses including the brake booster hose.

6. Disconnect the clutch booster vacuum hose connection, if equipped.

7. Disconnect all harness connectors.

8. Disconnect EGR components on California vehicles.

9. Remove the plenum retaining bracket.

10. Remove the plenum retaining nuts and bolts and remove the air intake plenum. Discard the gasket.

11. Disconnect the high pressure and return fuel hoses.

12. Matchmark and disconnect the vacuum hoses.

13. Disconnect the wire harness connectors.

14. Remove the fuel rail with the injectors attached.

15. On SOHC engines, disconnect the water hoses. On DOHC engines, remove the timing belt upper cover.

16. Remove the intake manifold mounting nuts; turbocharged engines have cone disc springs under some of the nuts which should be removed. Remove the intake manifold and discard the gaskets.

To install:

17. Check all items for cracks, clogging and warpage. Maximum

warpage is 0.008 in. (0.2mm). Replace all questionable parts.

18. Thoroughly clean and dry the mating surfaces of the heads, intake manifold and air intake plenum.

19. Install new intake manifold gaskets to the heads with the adhesive side facing up.

20. Place the manifold on the heads and install the cone disc springs and/or lock washers.

21. Lubricate the studs lightly with oil, then install the nuts following this procedure:

   a. Tighten the nuts on the front bank to 26-43 inch lbs. (3-5 Nm).

   b. Tighten the nuts on the rear bank to 9-11 ft. lbs. (12-15 Nm).

   c. Tighten the nuts on the front bank to 9-11 ft. lbs. (12-15 Nm).

   d. Repeat Steps B and C.

   e. On non-turbocharged engines only, tighten the nuts to a final torque of 13-14 ft. lbs. (18-19 Nm).

22. On SOHC engines, connect the water hoses. On DOHC engines, install the timing belt upper cover.

23. Install the fuel rail assembly.

24. Connect the harness connector and vacuum hoses.

25. Replace the O-ring and connect the fuel hoses.

26. Install a new intake air plenum gasket and install the plenum.

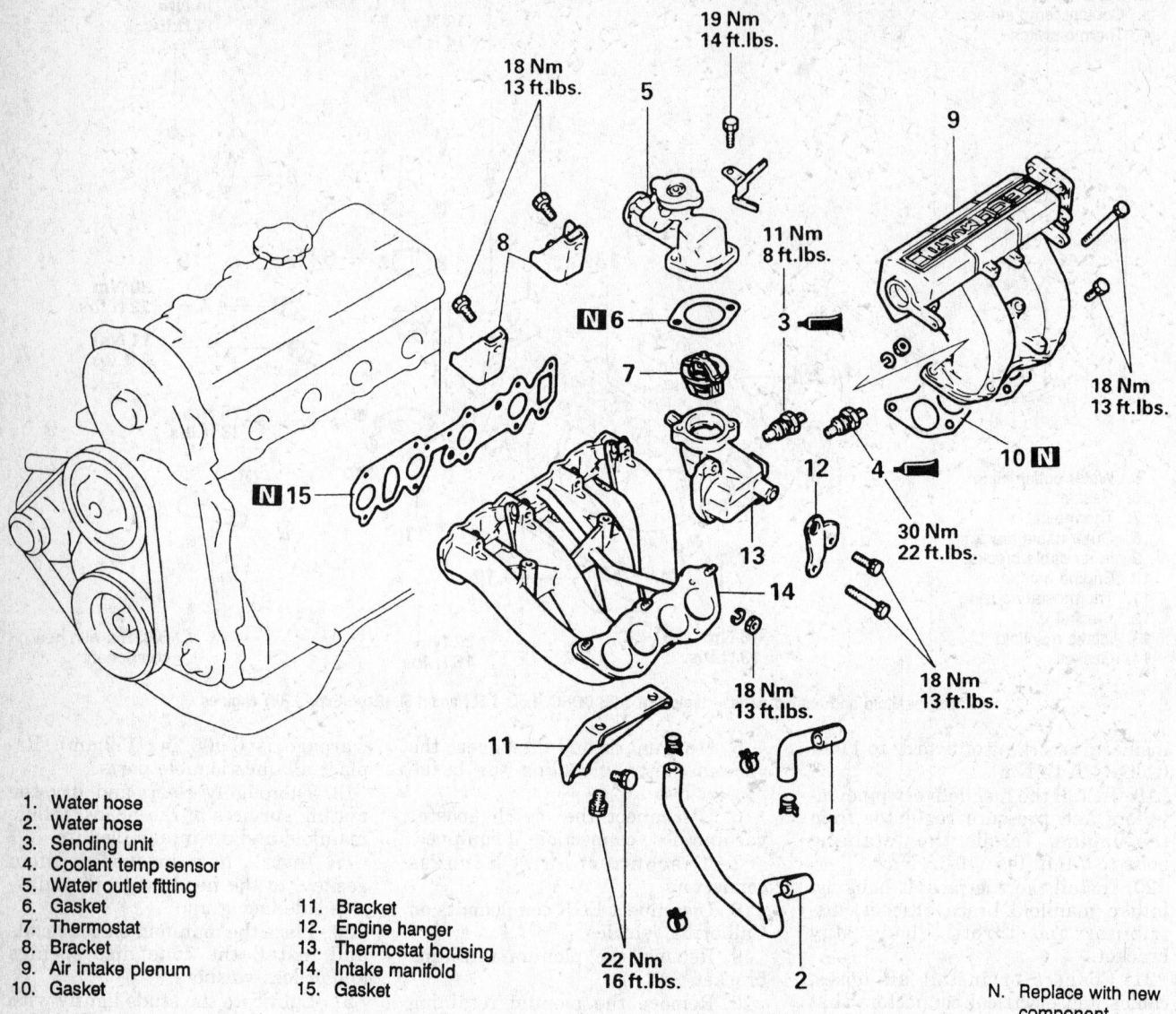

19 Nm
14 ft.lbs.

18 Nm
13 ft.lbs.

11 Nm
8 ft.lbs.

18 Nm
13 ft.lbs.

30 Nm
22 ft.lbs.

18 Nm
13 ft.lbs.

18 Nm
13 ft.lbs.

22 Nm
16 ft.lbs.

1. Water hose
2. Water hose
3. Sending unit
4. Coolant temp sensor
5. Water outlet fitting
6. Gasket
7. Thermostat
8. Bracket
9. Air intake plenum
10. Gasket
11. Bracket
12. Engine hanger
13. Thermostat housing
14. Intake manifold
15. Gasket

N. Replace with new component

Intake manifold and related parts — typical of 1.8L (Eclipse), 2.0L and 2.4L SOHC engines

Tighten the retaining nuts and bolts evenly and gradually to 13 ft. lbs. (18 Nm).

27. Install the retaining bracket.

28. Connect EGR components on California vehicles.

29. Connect the harness connectors and vacuum hoses.

30. Connect and adjust the accelerator cables.

31. Install the air intake hose(s).

32. Fill the system with coolant.

33. Connect the negative battery cable, run the vehicle until the thermostat opens, fill the radiator completely.

34. Check and adjust the idle speed and ignition timing.

35. Once the vehicle has cooled, recheck the coolant level.

Exhaust Manifold

REMOVAL AND INSTALLATION

Non-Turbocharged Engines

1. Disconnect battery negative cable.

2. Raise the vehicle and support safely.

3. Remove the exhaust pipe to exhaust manifold nuts and separate exhaust pipe. Discard gasket.

4. Lower vehicle.

5. Remove electric cooling fan assembly if necessary. If removing the front manifold on 3.0L engine, remove the dipstick tube. If removing the front manifold from 3.0L DOHC engine, remove the alternator.

6. Disconnect necessary EGR components.

7. On all except 3.0L engine, remove outer exhaust manifold heat shield and engine hanger. Disconnect the electrical connector and remove the oxygen sensor.

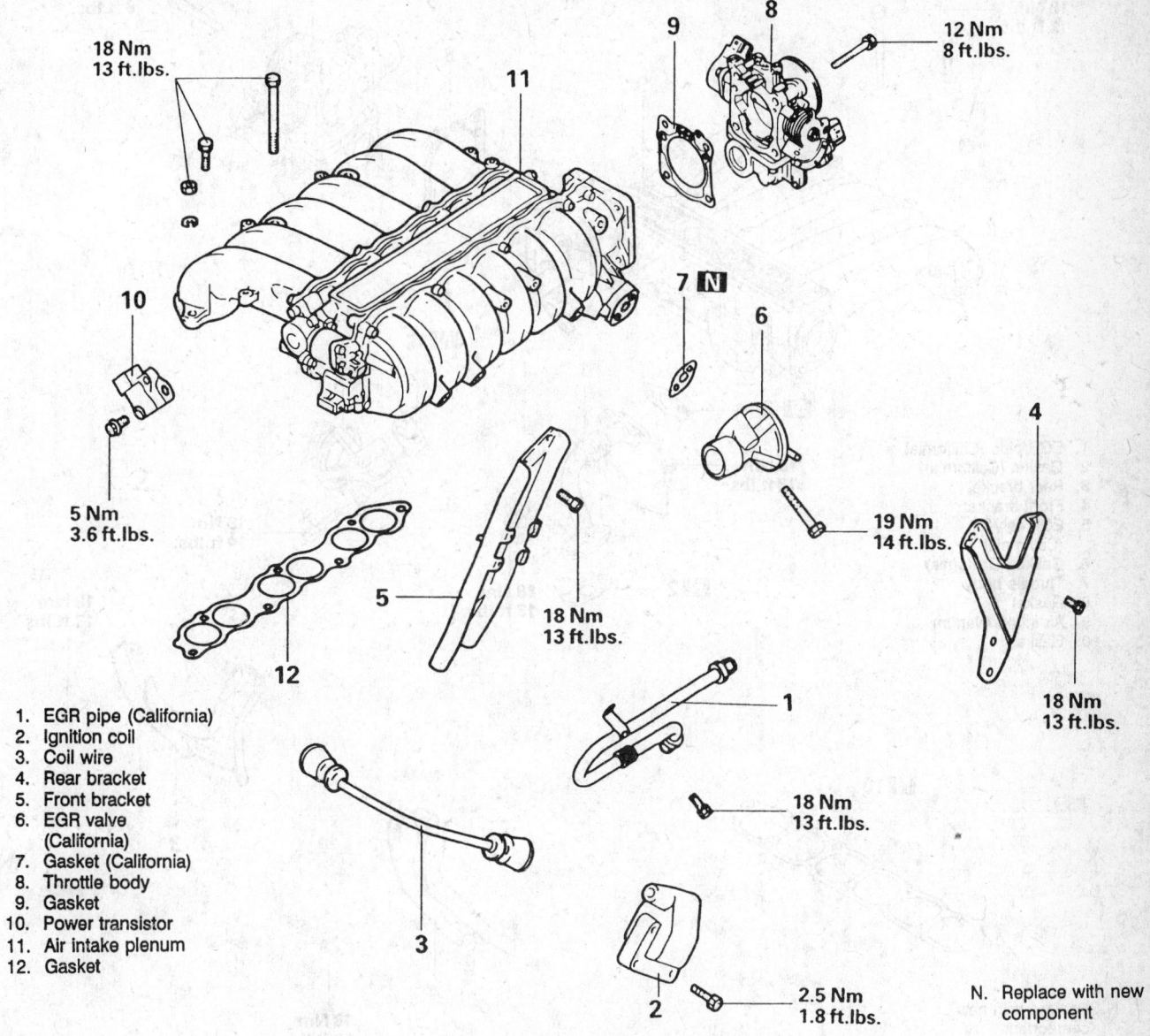

18 Nm
13 ft.lbs.

12 Nm
8 ft.lbs.

11

9

8

10

7 N

6

5 Nm
3.6 ft.lbs.

4

5

19 Nm
14 ft.lbs.

18 Nm
13 ft.lbs.

12

18 Nm
13 ft.lbs.

1

18 Nm
13 ft.lbs.

3

2

2.5 Nm
1.8 ft.lbs.

N. Replace with new component

1. EGR pipe (California)
2. Ignition coil
3. Coil wire
4. Rear bracket
5. Front bracket
6. EGR valve (California)
7. Gasket (California)
8. Throttle body
9. Gasket
10. Power transistor
11. Air intake plenum
12. Gasket

Intake air plenum and related parts — 3.0L SOHC engine

8. Remove the exhaust manifold mounting bolts, the inner heat shield and the exhaust manifold.

To install:

9. Clean all gasket material from the mating surfaces and check the manifold for damage.

10. Install a new gasket and install the manifold. Tighten the nuts, in a crisscross pattern, as follows:

SOHC engines — 11-14 ft. lbs. (15-20 Nm).

1991 3.0L DOHC engine — 33 ft. lbs. (45 Nm).

1992-94 3.0L DOHC engine — 22 ft. lbs. (30 Nm).

11. Install the heat shields.

12. Connect EGR components.

13. Install the electric cooling fan assembly, dipstick tube and alternator as required.

14. Install a new flange gasket and connect the exhaust pipe.

15. Connect the negative battery cable and check for exhaust leaks.

Turbocharged Engines

1.6L, 2.0L ENGINES

1. Disconnect the battery negative cable. Drain the cooling system.

2. Remove the condenser cooling fan and power steering pump and bracket as required.

3. Disconnect the oxygen sensor.

4. Raise the vehicle and support safely.

5. On 2.0L engine, drain the oil from the crankcase and remove the oil level indicator and tube.

6. Remove the exhaust pipe to turbocharger nuts and separate the exhaust pipe. Discard the gasket.

7. Lower vehicle. Remove air intake and vacuum hose connections.

8. Remove the upper exhaust manifold and turbocharger heat shields. Remove the exhaust manifold to turbocharger attaching bolts and nut.

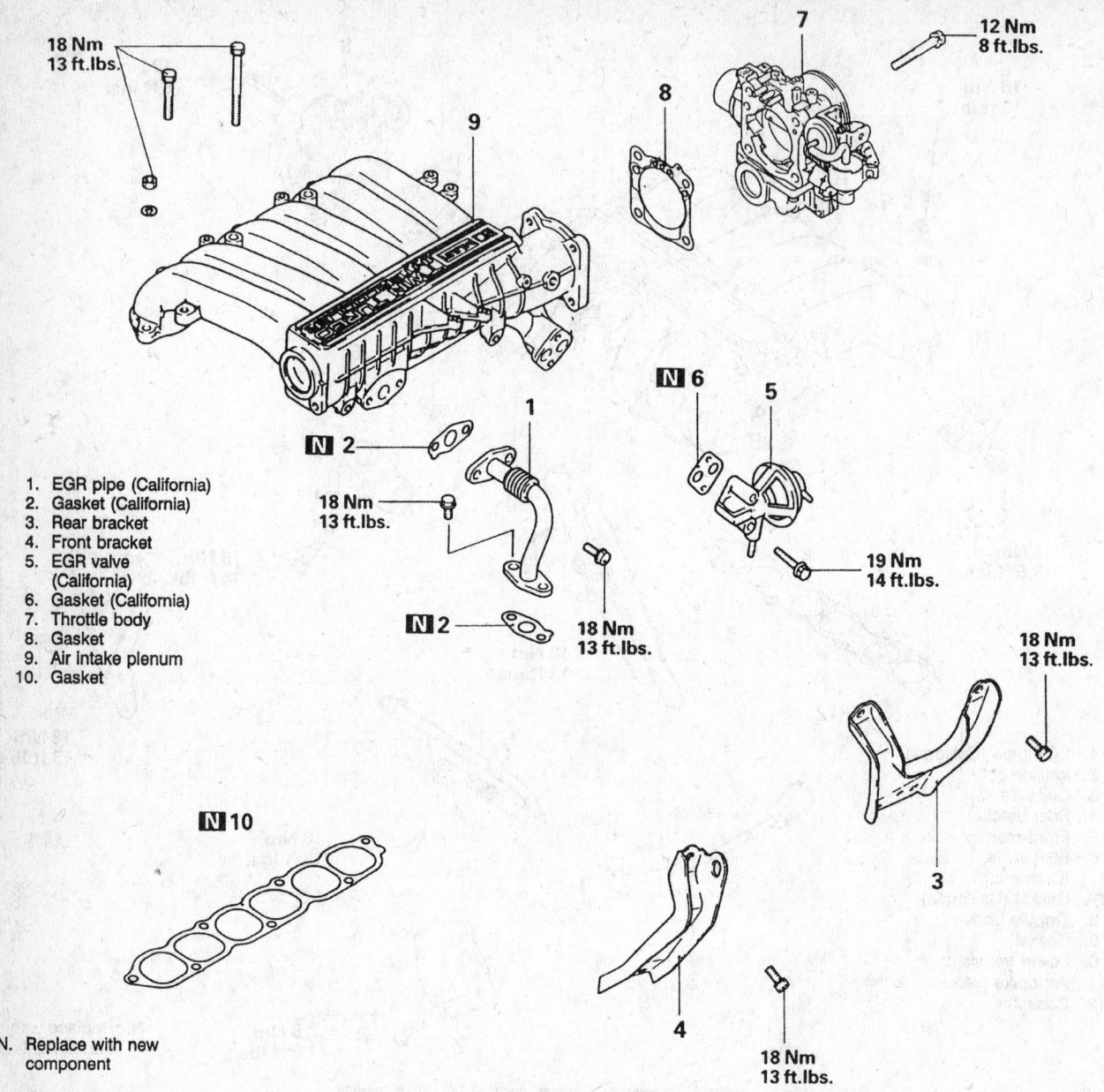

18 Nm
13 ft.lbs.

12 Nm
8 ft.lbs.

18 Nm
13 ft.lbs.

19 Nm
14 ft.lbs.

18 Nm
13 ft.lbs.

18 Nm
13 ft.lbs.

18 Nm
13 ft.lbs.

1. EGR pipe (California)
2. Gasket (California)
3. Rear bracket
4. Front bracket
5. EGR valve (California)
6. Gasket (California)
7. Throttle body
8. Gasket
9. Air intake plenum
10. Gasket

N. Replace with new component

Intake air plenum and related parts — 3.0L DOHC engine

9. Remove the engine hanger, water and oil lines from the turbo.

10. Remove the exhaust manifold mounting nuts. Remove the exhaust manifold and gasket.

To install:

11. Clean all gasket material from the mating surfaces and check the manifold for damage.

12. Install new gaskets and install the manifold. Tighten the manifold to head nuts in a crisscross pattern to 18-22 ft. lbs. (25-30 Nm). Tighten the manifold to turbo nut and bolts to 40-47 ft. lbs. (55-65 Nm).

13. Install the engine hanger, water and oil lines to the turbocharger.

14. Install the heat shields.

15. Install the new gasket and connect the exhaust pipe.

16. Install the condenser cooling fan and power steering pump. Connect the oxygen sensor harness.

17. Install the oil level indicator and tube replacing O-ring as required.

18. Fill the crankcase with clean oil and refill the cooling system.

19. Connect the negative battery cable and check for exhaust leaks.

3.0L ENGINE

1. Disconnect the negative battery cable.

2. Drain the engine coolant.

3. Remove the turbocharger assembly.

4. Remove the heat shield.

5. Remove the mounting nuts and remove the exhaust manifold. Note that cone disc springs are installed at all lower mounting points.

To install:

6. Clean all gasket material from the mating surfaces and check the manifold for damage.

7. Install new gaskets and install the manifold. Make sure all cone disc springs are in their original locations with the grooved side facing the nut.

Tighten the manifold nuts using the following procedure:

    a. Tighten all but the outer 2 nuts to 22 ft. lbs. (30 Nm).

    b. Tighten the outer 2 nuts to 34-38 ft. lbs. (47-53 Nm).

    c. Loosen the outer 2 nuts, then torque them to 22 ft. lbs. (30 Nm).

8. Install the heat shield.

9. Install the turbocharger assembly.

10. Fill the cooling system.

11. Connect the negative battery cable and check for exhaust leaks.

Turbocharger

Many turbocharger failures are due to oil supply problems. Heat soak after hot shutdown can cause the engine oil in the turbocharger and oil lines to "coke." Often the oil feed lines will become partially or completely blocked with hardened particles of carbon, blocking oil flow. Check the oil feed pipe and oil return line for clogging. Clean these tubes well. Always use new gaskets above and below the oil feed eyebolt fitting. Do not allow particles of dirt or old gasket material to enter the oil passage hole and that no portion of the new gasket blocks the passage.

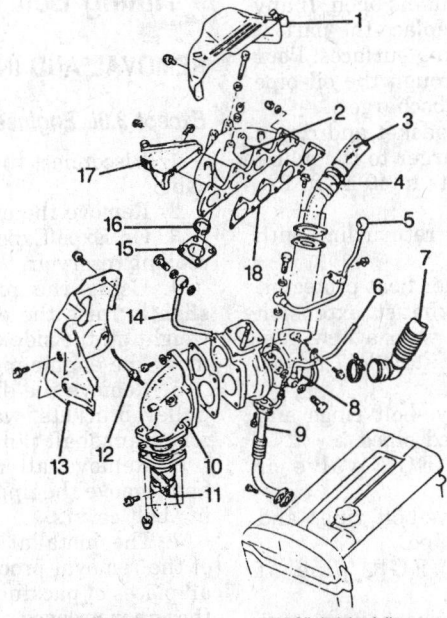

Turbocharger assembly — 1.6L and 2.0L engines

1. Upper heat shield	9. Oil drainback line
2. Exhaust manifold	10. Exhaust fitting
3. Air hose connector	11. Exhaust pipe
4. Air inlet fitting	12. Oxygen sensor
5. Oil feed pipe	13. Lower heat shield
6. Water line	14. Water line
7. Connection—air intake	15. Gasket
	16. Ring
8. Turbocharger assembly	17. Brace/bracket
	18. Manifold gasket

REMOVAL AND INSTALLATION

1.6L and 2.0L Engines

1. Disconnect the negative battery cable.

2. Drain the engine oil, cooling system, and remove the radiator. On Eclipse with air conditioning, remove the condenser fan assembly with the radiator.

3. Disconnect the oxygen sensor connector and remove the sensor.

4. Remove the oil dipstick and tube on Eclipse and Galant.

5. Remove the air intake bellows hose, the wastegate vacuum hose, the connections for the air outlet hose, and the upper and lower heat shields.

6. On Eclipse and Galant, unbolt the power steering pump and bracket assembly and leaving the hoses connected, wire it aside.

7. Remove the self-locking exhaust manifold nuts, the triangular engine hanger bracket, the eyebolt and gaskets that connect the oil feed line to the turbo center section, and the water cooling lines. The water line under the turbo has a threaded connection.

8. Remove the exhaust pipe nuts and gasket and lift off the exhaust manifold. Discard the gasket.

9. Remove the 2 through bolts and 2 nuts that hold the exhaust manifold to the turbocharger.

10. Remove the 2 capscrews from the oil return line (under the turbo). Discard the gasket. Separate the turbo from the exhaust manifold. The 2 water pipes and oil feed line can still be attached.

11. Visually check the turbine wheel (hot side) and compressor wheel (cold side) for cracking or other damage. Check whether the turbine wheel and the compressor wheel can be easily turned by hand. Check for oil leakage. Check whether or not the wastegate valve remains open. If any problem is found, replace the part. Inspect oil passages for restriction or deposits and clean as required.

12. The wastegate can be checked with a pressure tester. Apply approximately 9 psi to the actuator and make sure the rod moves. Do not apply more than 10.3 psi or the diaphragm in the wastegate may be damaged. Vacuum applied to the wastegate actuator should be maintained, replace if leaks vacuum. Do not attempt to adjust the wastegate valve.

To install:

13. Prime the oil return line with clean engine oil. Replace all locking nuts. Before installing the threaded connection for the water inlet pipe, apply light oil to the inner surface of the pipe flange. Assemble the turbocharger and exhaust manifold.

14. Install the exhaust manifold using a new gasket.

15. Connect the water cooling lines, oil feed line and engine hanger.

16. If removed, install the power steering pump and bracket.

17. Install the heat shields, air outlet hose, wastegate hose and air intake bellows.

18. Install the oil dipstick tube and dipstick. Install the oxygen sensor.

19. Install the radiator assembly.

20. Fill the engine with oil, fill the cooling system and reconnect the negative battery cable.

3.0L Engine

RIGHT SIDE (FRONT) TURBOCHARGER

1. Disconnect the negative battery cable.

2. Remove the radiator.

3. Remove the right side transaxle bracket.

4. Remove the front exhaust pipe.

5. Carefully matchmark, diagram or photograph all air intake hoses and pipes along the front of the engine. It is imperative that all of these pieces are installed in the exact same

positions when assembling. Remove the hoses and pipes and keep covered in a clean area.

6. Remove the alternator.
7. Remove the oil dipstick tube.
8. Remove the turbocharger heat protector.
9. Remove the water feed pipes.
10. Remove the oxygen sensor.
11. Remove the oil return line.
12. Remove the exhaust extension fitting and bracket.
13. Remove all air conditioning components preventing removal of the turbocharger.
14. Remove the oil feed tube.
15. Remove the turbocharger to exhaust manifold bolts and remove the turbocharger assembly.

To install:
16. Visually check the turbine wheel (hot side) and compressor wheel (cold side) for cracking or other damage. Check whether the turbine wheel and the compressor wheel can be easily turned by hand. Check for oil leakage. Check whether or not the wastegate valve remains open. If any problem is found, replace the part.
17. Clean all mating surfaces. Pour clean engine oil through the oil pipe feed hole in the turbocharger.
18. Install a new gasket and ring a install the turbocharger to the manifold. Torque the bolts to 40-47 ft. lbs. (55-65 Nm).
19. Replace the eye-bolt rings and install the oil feed pipe.
20. Install the removed air conditioning components.
21. Install the exhaust extension fitting and bracket with a new gasket. Torque the nuts to 40-47 ft. lbs. (55-65 Nm).
22. Install the oil return line with new gaskets.
23. Install the oxygen sensor.
24. Replace the eye-bolt rings and install the water feed pipes.
25. Install the turbocharger heat protector.
26. Install the dipstick tube.
27. Install the alternator.
28. Install all air intake hoses and pipes along the front of the engine. Make sure all are in their proper positions.
29. Install a new gasket and connect the front exhaust pipe.
30. Install the right side transaxle bracket.
31. Install the radiator.
32. Fill the system with coolant.
33. Connect the negative battery cable and check for exhaust leaks.

LEFT SIDE (REAR) TURBOCHARGER
1. Remove the battery.
2. Drain the coolant.

3. Remove the front exhaust pipe.
4. Disconnect the accelerator cable from the throttle body.
5. Remove the intake air hose, the air pipe across the top of the engine and its heat shield.
6. Remove the clutch booster vacuum hose and disconnect the accelerator cable from the pedal.
7. Remove the air intake hoses coming from the air cleaner box.
8. Remove the oxygen sensor and the turbocharger heat protector.
9. Remove the EGR pipe if equipped.
10. Remove the oil feed pipe.
11. Remove the EGR valve if equipped.
12. Remove the water feed pipes.
13. Remove the exhaust extension fitting and bracket.
14. Remove the inner heat protector.
15. Remove the oil return tube.
16. Remove the turbocharger to exhaust manifold nuts and remove the turbocharger assembly.

To install:
17. Visually check the turbine wheel (hot side) and compressor wheel (cold side) for cracking or other damage. Check whether the turbine wheel and the compressor wheel can be easily turned by hand. Check for oil leakage. Check whether or not the wastegate valve remains open. If any problem is found, replace the part.
18. Clean all mating surfaces. Pour clean engine oil through the oil pipe feed hole in the turbocharger.
19. Install a new gasket and ring a install the turbocharger to the manifold. Torque the nuts to 40-47 ft. lbs. (55-65 Nm).
20. Install the oil return line with new gaskets.
21. Install the inner heat protector.
22. Install the exhaust extension fitting and bracket with a new gasket. Torque the nuts to 40-47 ft. lbs. (55-65 Nm).
23. Replace the eye-bolt rings and install the water feed pipes.
24. Install the EGR valve if equipped.
25. Replace the eye-bolt rings and install the oil feed pipe.
26. Install the EGR pipe if equipped.
27. Install the turbocharger heat protector and oxygen sensor.
28. Install the air intake hoses coming from the air cleaner box. Make sure the triangular aligning marks are engaged.
29. Connect the accelerator cable to from the pedal and install the clutch booster vacuum hose.

30. Install the heat shield, the air pipe across the top of the engine and the air intake hose.
31. Connect the accelerator cable to the throttle body.
32. Install a new gasket and connect the front exhaust pipe.
33. Fill the system with coolant.
34. Install the battery.
35. Connect the negative battery cable and check for exhaust leaks.

Front Cover Oil Seal

REPLACEMENT

1. Disconnect the negative battery cable.
2. Remove the accessory drive belts.
3. Remove the crankshaft pulley.
4. Carefully pry the seal from the cover without scratching its bore.
5. Install a new seal squarely into the cover opening.
6. Install the crankshaft pulley. Thoroughly clean and dry the crankshaft pulley bolt and apply a very thin bead of thread locking compound to the threads. Torque the bolt to 87 ft. lbs. (118 Nm).
7. Install the belts.

Timing Belt Front Cover

REMOVAL AND INSTALLATION

Except 3.0L Engines

1. Disconnect the negative battery cable.
2. Remove the engine undercover.
3. On Expo/Expo LRV, remove the coolant reservoir.
4. Using the proper equipment, slightly raise the engine to take the weight off the side engine mount. Remove the engine mount bracket.
5. Remove the drive belts, tension pulley brackets, water pump pulley and crankshaft pulley.
6. Remove all attaching screws and remove the upper and lower timing belt covers.
7. The installation is the reverse of the removal procedure. Make sure all pieces of packing are positioned in the inner grooves of the covers when installing.

3.0L Engine

SOHC

1. Disconnect the negative battery cable.
2. Remove the engine undercover.

3. Remove the cruise control actuator.

4. Remove the accessory drive belts.

5. Remove the air conditioner compressor tension pulley assembly.

6. Remove the tension pulley bracket.

7. Using the proper equipment, slightly raise the engine to take the weight off the side engine mount. Remove the engine mounting bracket.

8. Disconnect the power steering pump pressure switch connector. Remove the power steering pump and wire aside.

9. Remove the engine support bracket.

10. Remove the crankshaft pulley.

11. Remove the timing belt cover cap.

12. Remove the timing belt upper and lower covers.

To install:

13. Install the timing covers. Make sure all pieces of packing are positioned in the inner grooves of the covers when installing.

14. Install the crankshaft pulley. Torque the bolt to 108-116 ft. lbs. (150-160 Nm).

15. Install the engine support bracket.

16. Install the power steering pump and reconnect wire harness at the power steering pump pressure switch.

17. Install the engine mounting bracket and remove the engine support fixture.

18. Install the tension pulleys and drive belts.

19. Install the cruise control actuator.

20. Install the engine undercover.

21. Connect the negative battery cable.

DOHC

1. Disconnect the negative battery cable.

2. Remove the engine undercover.

3. Remove the cruise control actuator.

4. Remove the alternator. Remove the air hose and pipe.

5. Remove the belt tensioner assembly and the power steering belt.

6. Remove the crankshaft pulley.

7. Disconnect the brake fluid level sensor.

8. Remove the timing belt upper cover.

9. Using the proper equipment, slightly raise the engine to take the weight off the side engine mount. Remove the engine mount bracket.

10. Remove the alternator/air conditioner idler pulley.

11. Remove the engine support bracket. The mounting bolts are different lengths; mark them for proper installation.

12. Remove the timing belt lower cover. Timing bolt cover mounting bolts are different in length, note their position during removal.

To install:

13. Make sure all pieces of packing are positioned in the inner grooves of the lower cover, position cover on engine and install mounting bolts in their original location.

14. Install the engine support bracket and secure using mounting bolts in their original location. Lubricate the reaming area of the reamer bolt and tighten slowly.

15. Install the idler pulley.

16. Install the engine mount bracket. Remove the engine support fixture.

17. Make sure all pieces of packing are positioned in the inner grooves of the upper cover and install.

18. Connect the brake fluid level sensor.

19. Install the crankshaft pulley. Torque the bolt to 130-137 ft. lbs. (180-190 Nm).

20. Install the belt tensioner assembly and the power steering belt.

21. Install the air hose and pipe.

22. Install the alternator.

23. Install the cruise control actuator.

24. Install the engine undercover.

25. Connect the negative battery cable.

Timing Belt and Tensioner

ADJUSTMENT

1.5L and 1.8L Engines (Eclipse) and 2.0L SOHC Engine

1. Disconnect the negative battery cable.

2. Remove the timing belt covers.

3. On 1.8L engine, adjust the silent shaft (inner) belt tension first. Loosen the idler pulley center bolt so the pulley can be moved.

4. Move the pulley by hand so the long side of the belt deflects about ¼ in.

5. Hold the pulley tightly so the pulley cannot rotate when the bolt is tightened. Tighten the bolt to 15 ft. lbs. (20 Nm) and recheck the deflection amount.

6. To adjust the timing (outer) belt, first loosen the pivot side tensioner bolt and then the slot side bolt. Allow the spring to take up the slack.

7. Tighten the slot side tensioner bolt and then the pivot side bolt. If the pivot side bolt is tightened first, the tensioner could turn with bolt, causing over tension.

8. Turn the crankshaft clockwise. Loosen the pivot side tensioner bolt and then the slot side bolt. Tighten the slot bolt and then the pivot side bolt.

9. Check the belt tension on 1.5L engine by holding the tensioner and timing belt together by hand and give the belt a slight thumb pressure at a point level with tensioner center. Make sure the belt cog crest comes as deep as about ¼ of the width of the slot side tensioner bolt head. On 1.8L engine, the deflection of the longest span of the belt should be about 0.40 in. Do not manually overtighten the belt or it will howl.

10. Install the timing belt covers and all related items.

11. Connect the negative battery cable.

1.8L and 2.4L Engines (Expo/Expo LRV)

1. Disconnect negative battery cable.

2. Remove the timing belt covers.

3. On 2.4L engine, adjust the silent shaft (inner) belt tension first as follows:

   a. Loosen the idler pulley center bolt so the pulley can be moved.

   b. Move the pulley by hand so the long side of the belt deflects about ¼ in.

   c. Hold the pulley tightly so the pulley cannot rotate when the bolt is tightened. Tighten the bolt to 15 ft. lbs. (20 Nm) and recheck the deflection amount.

4. To adjust the timing (outer) belt, first loosen the pivot side tensioner bolt and then the slot side bolt. Allow the spring to take up the slack.

5. Check to make sure the timing marks on each sprocket are aligned. Turn the crankshaft in normal direction (clockwise), by 2 teeth of the crankshaft sprocket.

NOTE: The purpose of Step 5 is to apply the proper amount of tension to the tension side of the timing belt, be sure not to turn the crankshaft in the opposite direction (counterclockwise).

6. Tighten the slot side tensioner bolt and then the pivot side bolt. If the pivot side bolt is tightened first, the tensioner could turn with bolt, causing over tension.

7. Lightly clamp the center of the span between the camshaft sprocket

and the water pump sprocket on the belt tension side with your thumb and fore-finger. Check to be sure the clearance between the reverse surface of the belt and the inside of the undercover seal line is at the standard value.

   a. 1.8L engine — 1.18 in. (30mm).

   b. 2.4L engine — 0.55 in. (14mm).

8. Install the timing belt covers and all related items.

9. Connect the negative battery cable.

1.6L and 2.0L DOHC Engines

1. Disconnect the negative battery cable.

2. Remove the timing belt covers.

3. Adjust the silent shaft (inner) belt tension first. Loosen the idler pulley center bolt so the pulley can be moved.

4. Move the pulley by hand so the long side of the belt deflects about ¼ in.

5. Hold the pulley tightly so the pulley cannot rotate when the bolt is tightened. Tighten the bolt to 15 ft. lbs. (20 Nm) and recheck the deflection amount.

6. To adjust the timing (outer) belt, turn the crankshaft ¼ turn counterclockwise, then turn it clockwise to move No. 1 cylinder to TDC.

7. Loosen the center bolt. Using tool MD998752 or equivalent and a torque wrench, apply a torque of 1.88-2.03 ft. lbs. (2.6-2.8 Nm). If the body of the vehicle interferes with the special tool and the torque wrench, use a jack and slightly raise the engine assembly. Holding the tensioner pulley, tighten the center bolt.

8. Screw special tool MD998738 or equivalent, into the engine left support bracket until its end makes contact with the tensioner arm. At this point, screw the special tool in some more and remove the set wire attached to the auto tensioner, if wire was not previously removed. Then remove the special tool.

9. Rotate the crankshaft 2 complete turns clockwise and let it sit for approximately 15 minutes. Then, measure the auto tensioner protrusion (the distance between the tensioner arm and auto tensioner body) to ensure that it is within 0.15-0.18 in. (3.8-4.5mm). If out of specification, repeat Steps 1-4 until the specified value is obtained.

10. If the timing belt tension adjustment is being performed with the engine mounted in the vehicle, and clearance between the tensioner arm

and the auto tensioner body cannot be measured, the following alternative method can be used:

   a. Screw in special tool MD998738 or equivalent, until its end makes contact with the tensioner arm.

   b. After the special tool makes contact with the arm, screw it in some more to retract the auto tensioner pushrod while counting the number of turns the tool makes until the tensioner arm is brought into contact with the auto tensioner body. Make sure the number of turns the special tool makes conforms with the standard value of 2½-3 turns.

   c. Install the rubber plug to the timing belt rear cover.

11. Install the timing belt covers and all related items.

12. Connect the negative battery cable.

3.0L Engine

SOHC

1. Disconnect the negative battery cable.

2. Remove the timing belt covers.

3. Loosen the bolt that holds the tensioner in place and allow the spring to automatically apply tension to the belt.

4. Rotate the crankshaft smoothly, 2 engine revolutions clockwise. Tighten the tensioner bolt to 20 ft. lbs. (25 Nm). Do not turn the engine counterclockwise.

5. Measure the belt tension between the rear camshaft sprocket and the crankshaft with belt tension gauge. The specification is 46-68 lbs. (210-310 N).

6. Install the timing belt covers and all related items.

7. Connect the negative battery cable.

DOHC

1. Disconnect the negative battery cable.

2. Remove the timing belt covers.

3. Turn the crankshaft ¼ turn counterclockwise, then turn it clockwise until all timing marks are aligned.

4. Loosen the center bolt on the tensioner pulley. Using tool MD998767 or equivalent and a torque wrench, apply a torque of 7.2 ft. lbs. (10 Nm). Tighten the tensioner bolt; make sure the tensioner doesn't rotate with the bolt.

5. Remove the set wire attached to the auto tensioner, if wire was not previously removed.

6. Rotate the crankshaft 2 complete turns clockwise and let it sit for approximately 5 minutes. Then, check that the set pin can easily be inserted and removed from the hole in the auto tensioner.

NOTE: Even if the set pin cannot be easily inserted, the auto tensioner is normal if its rod protrusion is within specification.

7. Measure the auto tensioner protrusion (the distance between the tensioner arm and auto tensioner body) to ensure that it is within 0.15-0.18 in. (3.8-4.5mm). If out of specification, repeat Steps 1-4 until the specified value is obtained.

8. Check again that the timing marks on all sprockets are in proper alignment.

9. Install the timing belt covers and all related items.

10. Connect the negative battery cable.

REMOVAL AND INSTALLATION

1.5L and 1.8L Engines (Expo LRV)

1. Disconnect the negative battery cable. Remove the engine under cover.

2. Raise and safely support the weight of the engine using the appropriate equipment. Remove the front engine mount bracket and accessory drive belts.

3. On Expo, remove the coolant reservoir tank.

4. Remove timing belt upper and lower covers.

5. Make a mark on the back of the timing belt indicating the direction of rotation so it may be reassembled in the same direction if it is to be reused. Loosen the timing belt tensioner and remove the timing belt.

NOTE: If coolant or engine oil comes in contact with the timing belt, they will drastically shorten its life. Also, do not allow engine oil or coolant to contact the timing belt sprockets or tensioner assembly.

6. Remove the tensioner spacer, tensioner spring and tensioner assembly.

7. Inspect the timing belt for cracks on back surface, sides, bottom and check for separated canvas. Check the tensioner pulley for smooth rotation.

To install:

8. Position the tensioner, tensioner spring and tensioner spacer on engine block.

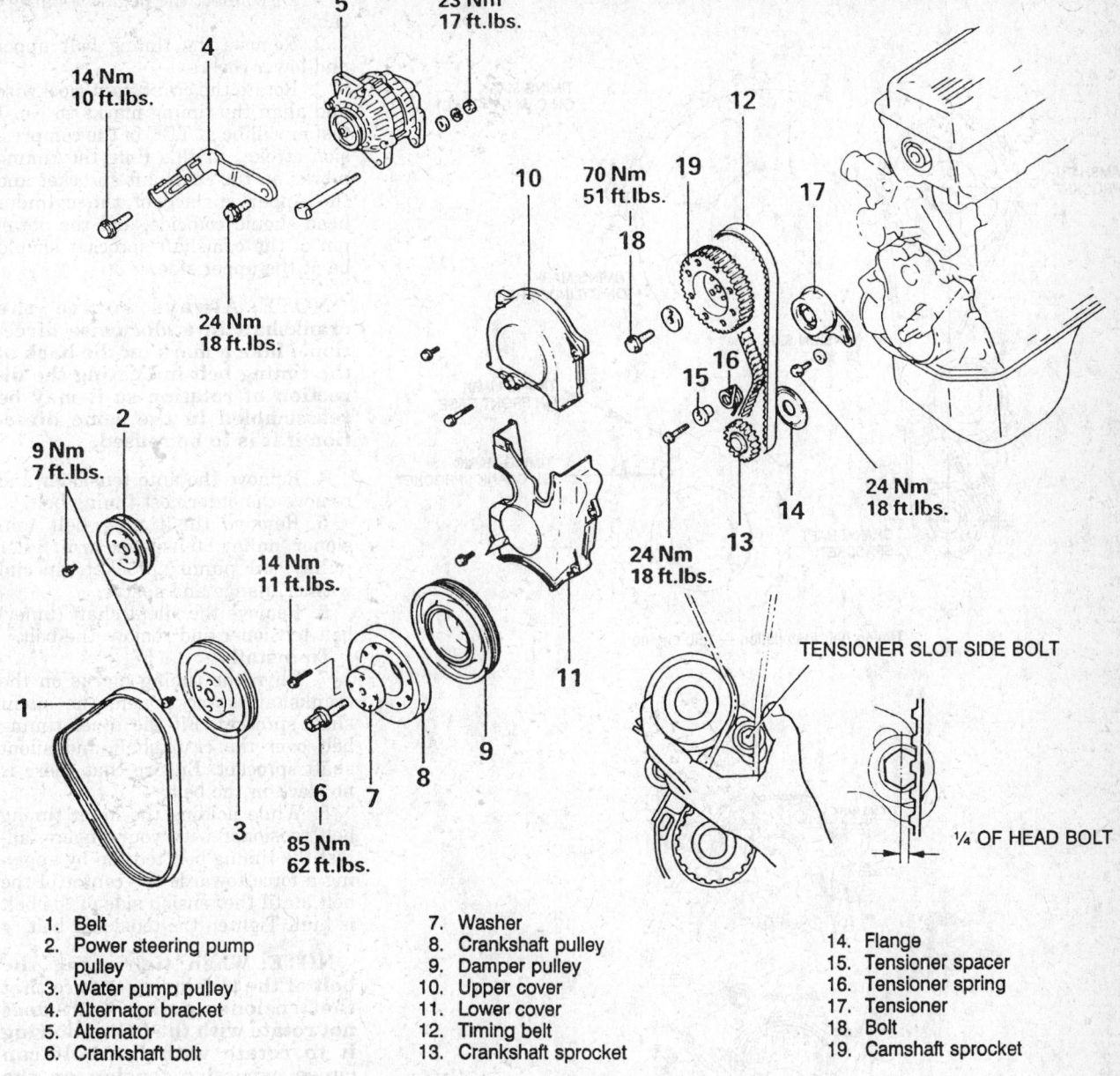

1. Belt
2. Power steering pump pulley
3. Water pump pulley
4. Alternator bracket
5. Alternator
6. Crankshaft bolt
7. Washer
8. Crankshaft pulley
9. Damper pulley
10. Upper cover
11. Lower cover
12. Timing belt
13. Crankshaft sprocket
14. Flange
15. Tensioner spacer
16. Tensioner spring
17. Tensioner
18. Bolt
19. Camshaft sprocket

Timing belt covers, timing belt and related parts — 1.5L engine

9. Align the timing marks on the camshaft sprocket and crankshaft sprocket. This will position No. 1 piston on TDC on the compression stroke.

10. Position the timing belt on the crankshaft sprocket and keeping the tension side of the belt tight, set it on the camshaft sprocket.

11. Apply counterclockwise force to the camshaft sprocket to give tension to the belt and make sure all timing marks are aligned.

12. Loosen the pivot side tensioner bolt and the slot side bolt. Allow the spring to take up the slack.

13. Tighten the slot side tensioner bolt and then the pivot side bolt. If the pivot side bolt is tightened first, the tensioner could turn with bolt, causing over tension.

14. Turn the crankshaft clockwise. Loosen the pivot side tensioner bolt and then the slot side bolt to allow the spring to take up any remaining slack. On 1.8L engine, tighten the adjuster bolt to 18 ft. lbs. (24 Nm). On 1.5L engine, tighten the slot bolt and then the pivot side bolt to 14-20 ft. lbs. (20-27 Nm).

15. Check the belt tension by holding the tensioner and timing belt together by hand and give the belt a slight thumb pressure at a point level with tensioner center. Make sure the belt cog crest comes as deep as about ¼ of the width of the slot side tensioner bolt head. Do not manually overtighten the belt or it will howl.

16. Install the timing belt covers and all related items.

17. Connect the negative battery cable.

1.6L and 2.0L DOHC Engines

NOTE: The 1.6L engine is not equipped with silent shafts. Disregard all instructions pertaining to silent shafts if working on that engine.

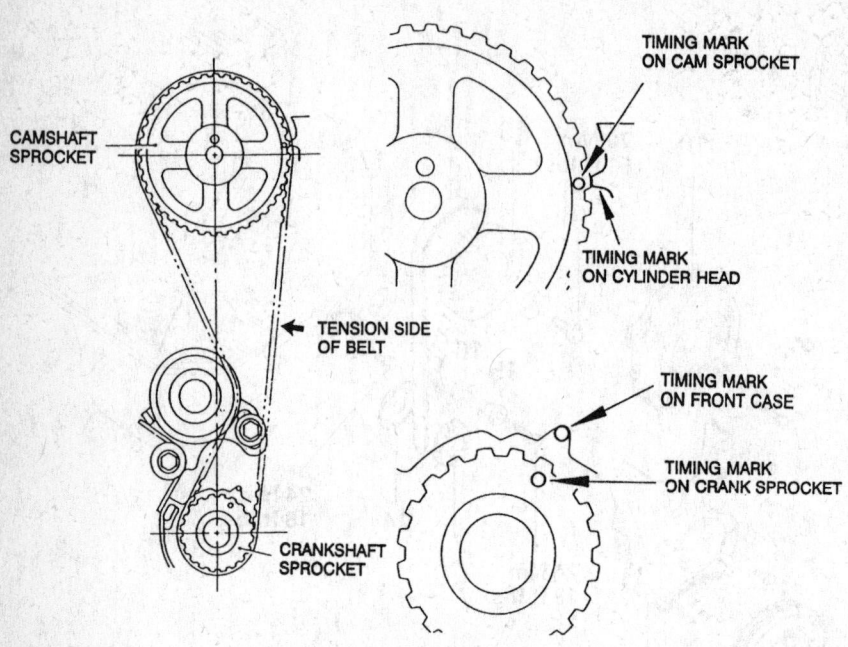

Timing belt installation — 1.5L engine

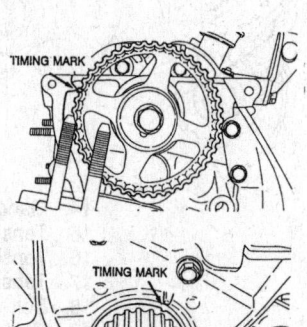

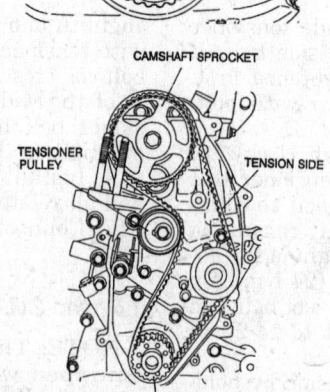

Timing belt installation — 1.8L (Expo/Expo LRV) engine

1. Disconnect the negative battery cable.

2. Remove the timing belt upper and lower covers.

3. Rotate the crankshaft clockwise and align the timing marks so No. 1 piston will be at TDC of the compression stroke. At this time the timing marks on the camshaft sprocket and the upper surface of the cylinder head should coincide, and the dowel pin of the camshaft sprocket should be at the upper side.

NOTE: Always rotate the crankshaft in a clockwise direction. Make a mark on the back of the timing belt indicating the direction of rotation so it may be reassembled in the same direction if it is to be reused.

4. Remove the auto tensioner and remove the outermost timing belt.

5. Remove the timing belt tensioner pulley, tensioner arm, idler pulley, oil pump sprocket, special washer, flange and spacer.

6. Remove the silent shaft (inner) belt tensioner and remove the belt.

To install:

7. Align the timing marks on the crankshaft sprocket and the silent shaft sprocket. Fit the inner timing belt over the crankshaft and silent shaft sprocket. Ensure that there is no slack in the belt.

8. While holding the inner timing belt tensioner with your fingers, adjust the timing belt tension by applying a force towards the center of the belt, until the tension side of the belt is taut. Tighten the tensioner bolt.

NOTE: When tightening the bolt of the tensioner, ensure that the tensioner pulley shaft does not rotate with the bolt. Allowing it to rotate with the bolt can cause excessive tension on the belt.

9. Check belt for proper tension by depressing the belt on its' long side with your finger and noting the belt deflection. The desired reading is 0.20-0.28 in. (5-7mm). If tension is not correct, readjust and check belt deflection.

10. Install the flange, crankshaft and washer to the crankshaft. The flange on the crankshaft sprocket must be installed towards the inner timing belt sprocket. Tighten bolt to 80-94 ft. lbs. (110-130 Nm).

11. To install the oil pump sprocket, insert a Phillips screwdriver with a shaft 0.31 in. (8mm) in diameter into the plug hole in the left side of the cylinder block to hold the

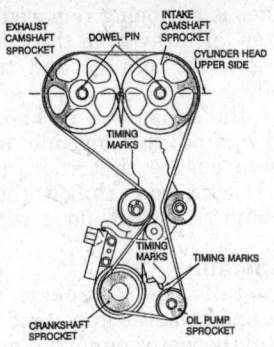

Timing belt installation — 1.6L and 2.0L DOHC engines

left silent shaft. Tighten the nut to 36-43 ft. lbs. (50-60 Nm).

12. Using a wrench, hold the camshaft at its' hexagon between journal No. 2 and 3 and tighten bolt to 58-72 ft. lbs. (80-100 Nm). If no hexagon is present between journal No. 2 and 3, hold the sprocket stationary with a spanner wrench while tightening the retainer bolt.

13. Carefully push the auto tensioner rod in until the set hole in the rod aligned up with the hole in the cylinder. Place a wire into the hole to retain the rod.

14. Install the tensioner pulley onto the tensioner arm. Locate the pinhole in the tensioner pulley shaft to the left of the center bolt. Then, tighten the center bolt finger-tight.

15. When installing the timing belt, turn the 2 camshaft sprockets so their dowel pins are located on top. Align the timing marks facing each other with the top surface of the cylinder head. When you let go of the exhaust camshaft sprocket, it will rotate 1 tooth in the counterclockwise direction. This should be taken into account when installing the timing belts on the sprocket.

NOTE: Both camshaft sprockets are used for the intake and exhaust camshafts and are provided with 2 timing marks. When the sprocket is mounted on the exhaust camshaft, use the timing mark on the right with the dowel pin hole on top. For the intake camshaft sprocket, use the 1 on the left with the dowel pin hole on top.

16. Align the crankshaft sprocket and oil pump sprocket timing marks.

17. After alignment of the oil pump sprocket timing marks, remove the plug on the cylinder block and insert a Phillips screw driver with a shaft diameter of 0.31 in. (8mm) through the hole. If the shaft can be inserted 2.4 in. deep, the silent shaft is in the

correct position. If the shaft of the tool can only be inserted 0.8-1.0 in. (20-25mm) deep, turn the oil pump sprocket 1 turn and realign the marks. Reinsert the tool making sure it is inserted 2.4 in. deep. Keep the tool inserted in hole for the remainder of this procedure.

NOTE: The above step assures that the oil pump socket is in correct orientation to the silent shafts. This step must not be skipped or a vibration may develop during engine operation.

18. Install the timing belt as follows:

a. Install the timing belt around the intake camshaft sprocket and retain it with 2 spring clips or binder clips.

b. Install the timing belt around the exhaust sprocket, aligning the timing marks with the cylinder head top surface using 2 wrenches. Retain the belt with 2 spring clips.

c. Install the timing belt around the idler pulley, oil pump sprocket, crankshaft sprocket and the tensioner pulley. Remove the 2 spring clips.

d. Lift upward on the tensioner pulley in a clockwise direction and tighten the center bolt. Make sure all timing marks are aligned.

e. Rotate the crankshaft ¼ turn counterclockwise. Then, turn in clockwise until the timing marks are aligned again.

19. To adjust the timing (outer) belt, turn the crankshaft ¼ turn counterclockwise, then turn it clockwise to move No. 1 cylinder to TDC.

20. Loosen the center bolt. Using tool MD998738 or equivalent and a torque wrench, apply a torque of 1.88-2.03 ft. lbs. (2.6-2.8 Nm). Tighten the center bolt.

21. Screw the special tool into the engine left support bracket until its end makes contact with the tensioner arm. At this point, screw the special tool in some more and remove the set wire attached to the auto tensioner, if the wire was not previously removed. Then remove the special tool.

22. Rotate the crankshaft 2 complete turns clockwise and let it sit for approximately 15 minutes. Then, measure the auto tensioner protrusion (the distance between the tensioner arm and auto tensioner body) to ensure that it is within 0.15-0.18 in. (3.8-4.5mm). If out of specification, repeat Step 1-4 until the specified value is obtained.

23. If the timing belt tension adjustment is being performed with the engine mounted in the vehicle, and

clearance between the tensioner arm and the auto tensioner body cannot be measured, the following alternative method can be used:

a. Screw in special tool MD998738 or equivalent, until its end makes contact with the tensioner arm.

b. After the special tool makes contact with the arm, screw it in some more to retract the auto tensioner pushrod while counting the number of turns the tool makes until the tensioner arm is brought into contact with the auto tensioner body. Make sure the number of turns the special tool makes conforms with the standard value of 2½-3 turns.

c. Install the rubber plug to the timing belt rear cover.

24. Install the timing belt covers and all related items.

25. Connect the negative battery cable.

1.8L Engine (Eclipse) and 2.0L and 2.4L SOHC Engines

1. If possible, position the engine so the No. 1 piston is at TDC of the compression stroke.

2. Disconnect the negative battery cable. On Expo with 2.4L engine, remove the coolant reservoir and the power steering and air conditioner hose clamp bolt.

3. Remove the timing belt covers.

4. Remove the timing (outer) belt tensioner and remove the outer timing belt.

5. Remove the outer crankshaft sprocket and flange.

6. Remove the silent shaft (inner) belt tensioner and remove the belt.

To install:

7. Align the timing marks of the silent shaft sprockets and the crankshaft sprocket with the timing marks on the front case. Wrap the timing belt around the sprockets so there is no slack in the upper span of the belt and the timing marks are still aligned.

8. Install the tensioner pulley and move the pulley by hand so the long side of the belt deflects about ¼ in.

9. Hold the pulley tightly so the pulley cannot rotate when the bolt is tightened. Tighten the bolt to 15 ft. lbs. (20 Nm) and recheck the deflection amount.

10. Install the timing belt tensioner fully toward the water pump and tighten the bolts. Place the upper end of the spring against the water pump body.

11. Align the timing marks of the camshaft, crankshaft and oil pump

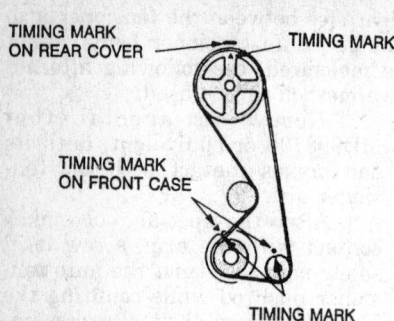

Timing belt installation — 1.8L (Eclipse), 2.0L and 2.4L SOHC engines

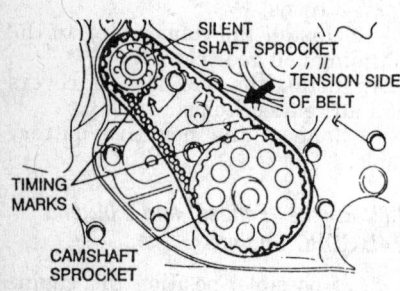

Silent shaft belt installation

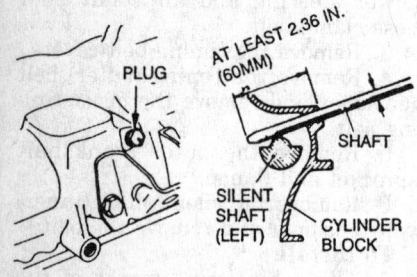

Checking the rear silent shaft for proper positioning

sprockets with their corresponding marks on the front case or rear cover.

NOTE: There is a possibility to align all timing marks and have the oil pump sprocket and silent shaft out of time, causing an engine vibration during operation. If the following step is not followed exactly, there is a 50 percent chance that the silent shaft alignment will be 180 degrees off.

12. Before installing the timing belt, ensure that the left side (rear) silent shaft (oil pump sprocket) is in the correct position as follows:

a. Remove the plug from the rear side of the block and insert a tool with shaft diameter of 0.31 in. (8mm) into the hole.

b. With the timing marks still aligned, the shaft of the tool must be able to go in at least 2⅓ in. If the tool can only go in about 1 in., the shaft is not in the correct orientation and will cause a vibration during engine operation. Remove the tool from the hole and turn the oil pump sprocket 1 complete revolution. Realign the timing marks and insert the tool. The shaft of the tool must go in at least 2⅓ in.

c. Recheck and realign the timing marks.

d. Leave the tool in place to hold the silent shaft while continuing.

13. Install the belt to the crankshaft sprocket, oil pump sprocket, then camshaft sprocket, in that order. While doing so, make sure there is no slack between the sprocket except where the tensioner is installed.

14. Recheck the timing marks' alignment. If all are aligned, loosen the tensioner mounting bolt and allow the tensioner to apply tension to the belt.

15. Remove the tool that is holding the silent shaft and rotate the crankshaft a distance equal to 2 teeth on the camshaft sprocket. This will allow the tensioner to automatically apply the proper tension on the belt. Do not manually overtighten the belt or it will howl.

16. Tighten the lower mounting bolt first, then the upper spacer bolt.

17. To verify correct belt tension, check that the deflection at the longest span of the belt is about ½ in.

18. Install the timing belt covers and all related items.

19. Connect the negative battery cable.

3.0L SOHC Engine

1. If possible, position the engine so the No. 1 cylinder is at TDC of its compression stroke. Disconnect the negative battery cable. Remove the timing covers from the engine.

2. If the same timing belt will be reused, mark the direction of the timing belt's rotation for installation in the same direction. Make sure the engine is positioned so the No. 1 cylinder is at the TDC of its compression stroke and the sprockets' timing marks are aligned with the engine's timing mark indicators.

3. Loosen the timing belt tensioner bolt and remove the belt. If the tensioner is not being removed, position it as far away from the center of the engine as possible and tighten the bolt.

4. If the tensioner is being removed, paint the outside of the spring to ensure that it is not installed backwards. Unbolt the tensioner and remove it along with the spring.

To install:

5. Install the tensioner, if removed, and hook the upper end of the spring to the water pump pin and the lower end to the tensioner in exactly the same position as originally installed. If not already done, position both camshafts so the marks align with those on the rear. Rotate the crankshaft so the timing mark aligns with the mark on the oil pump.

6. Install the timing belt on the crankshaft sprocket and while keeping the belt tight on the tension side, install the belt on the front camshaft sprocket.

7. Install the belt on the water pump pulley, then the rear camshaft sprocket and the tensioner.

8. Rotate the front camshaft counterclockwise to tension the belt between the front camshaft and the crankshaft. If the timing marks became misaligned, repeat the procedure.

9. Install the crankshaft sprocket flange.

10. Loosen the tensioner bolt and allow the spring to apply tension to the belt.

11. Turn the crankshaft 2 full turns in the clockwise direction until the timing marks align again. Now that the belt is properly tensioned, torque the tensioner lock bolt to 21 ft. lbs. (29 Nm). Measure the belt tension between the rear camshaft sprocket and the crankshaft with belt tension gauge. The specification is 46-68 lbs. (210-310 N).

12. Install the timing belt covers and all related parts.

13. Connect the negative battery cable and road test the vehicle.

3.0L DOHC Engine

1. If possible, position the engine so the No. 1 cylinder is at TDC of its compression stroke. Disconnect the negative battery cable. Remove the timing covers from the engine.

2. If the same timing belt will be reused, mark the direction of the timing belt's rotation for installation in the same direction. Make sure the engine is positioned so the No. 1 cylinder is at the TDC of its compression stroke and the sprockets' timing

1. Engine support bracket
2. Bolt
3. Washer
4. Crankshaft pulley
5. Access cover
6. Right side upper front cover
7. Cap
8. Left side upper front cover
9. Front lower cover
10. Flange

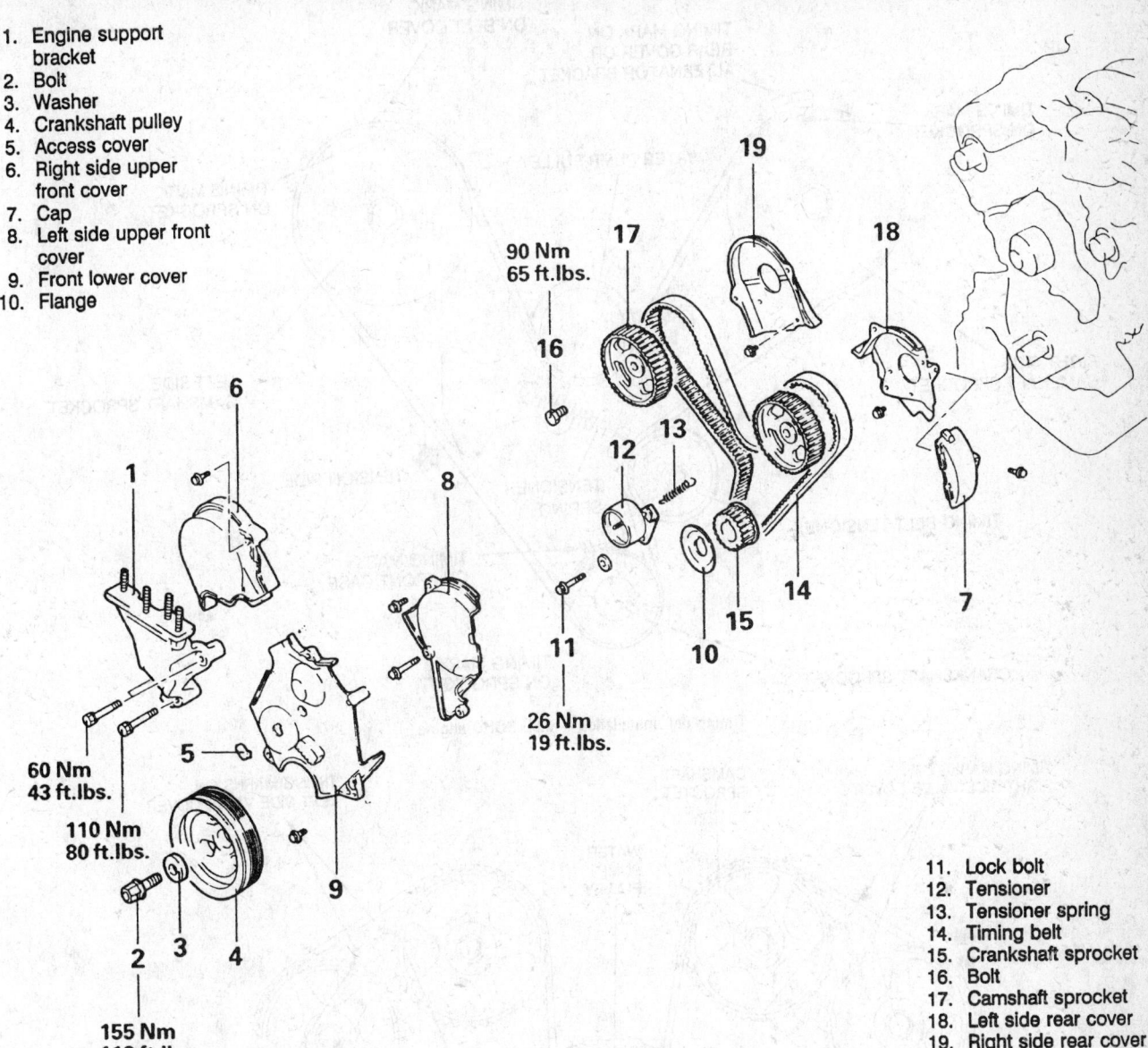

90 Nm 65 ft.lbs.

60 Nm 43 ft.lbs.

110 Nm 80 ft.lbs.

155 Nm 112 ft.lbs.

26 Nm 19 ft.lbs.

11. Lock bolt
12. Tensioner
13. Tensioner spring
14. Timing belt
15. Crankshaft sprocket
16. Bolt
17. Camshaft sprocket
18. Left side rear cover
19. Right side rear cover

Timing belt covers, timing belt and related parts — 3.0L SOHC engine

marks are aligned with the engine's timing mark indicators on the valve covers or head.

3. Loosen the timing belt tensioner bolt and remove the belt.

4. Remove the tensioner assembly.

To install:

5. If the auto tensioner rod is fully extended, reset it as follows:

   a. Clamp the tensioner in a soft-jaw vice in level position.

   b. Slowly push the rod in with the vice until the set hole in the rod is aligned with the hole in the cylinder.

   c. Insert a stiff wire into the set holes to retain the position.

   d. Remove the assembly from the vice.

6. Leave the retaining wire in the tension and install to the engine.

NOTE: On 1991 DOHC 3.0L engines, clean and inspect both auto tensioner mounting bolts. Coat the threads of the old bolts with thread sealer. If new bolts are installed, inspect the heads of the new bolts. If there is white paint on the bolt head, no sealer is required. If there is no paint on the head of the bolt, apply a coat of thread sealer to the bolt. Install both bolts and torque to 17 ft. lbs. (24 Nm).

7. If the timing marks of the camshaft sprockets and crankshaft sprocket are not aligned at this point, proceed as follows:

NOTE: Keep fingers out from between the camshaft sprockets. The sprockets may move unexpectedly because of valve spring pressure and could pinch fingers.

   a. Align the mark on the crankshaft sprocket with the mark on the front case. Then move the sprocket 2 teeth clockwise to lower the piston so the valve can't touch the piston when the camshafts are being moved.

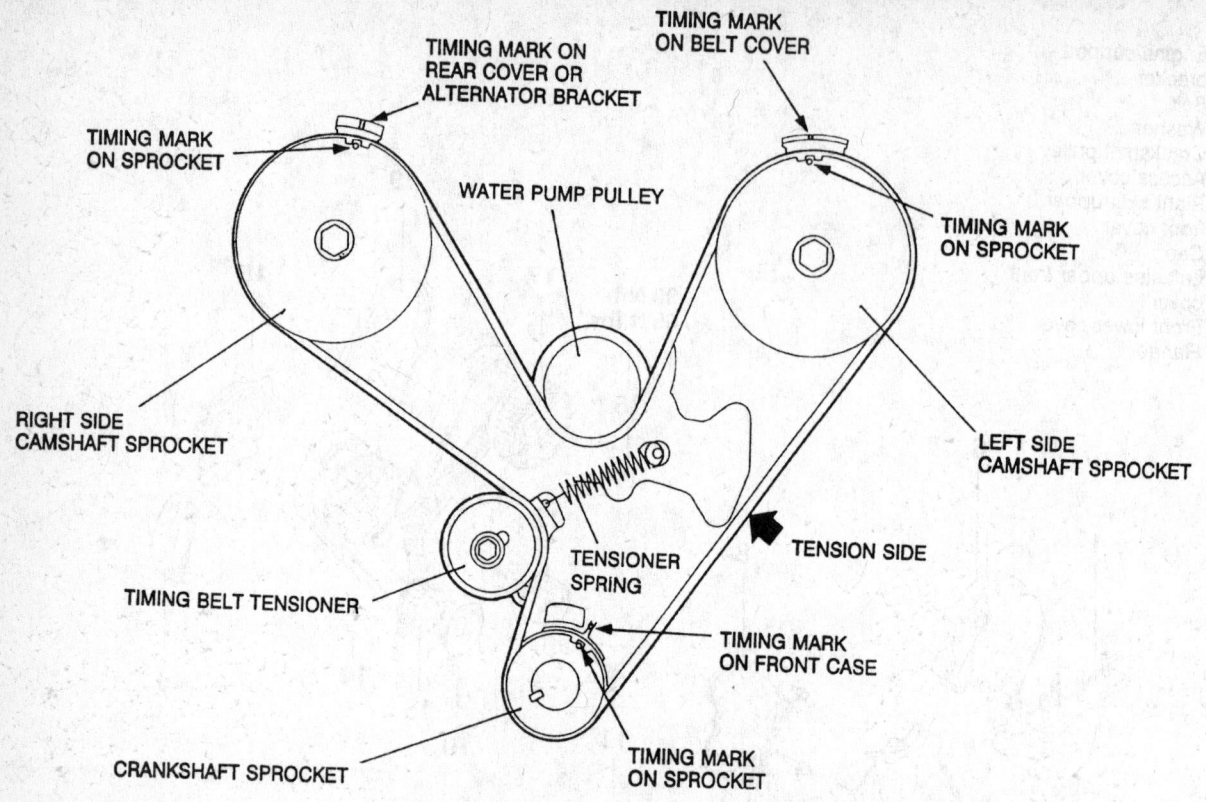

TIMING MARK ON REAR COVER OR ALTERNATOR BRACKET

TIMING MARK ON BELT COVER

TIMING MARK ON SPROCKET

WATER PUMP PULLEY

TIMING MARK ON SPROCKET

RIGHT SIDE CAMSHAFT SPROCKET

LEFT SIDE CAMSHAFT SPROCKET

TIMING BELT TENSIONER

TENSIONER SPRING

TENSION SIDE

TIMING MARK ON FRONT CASE

CRANKSHAFT SPROCKET

TIMING MARK ON SPROCKET

Timing belt installation — 3.0L SOHC engine

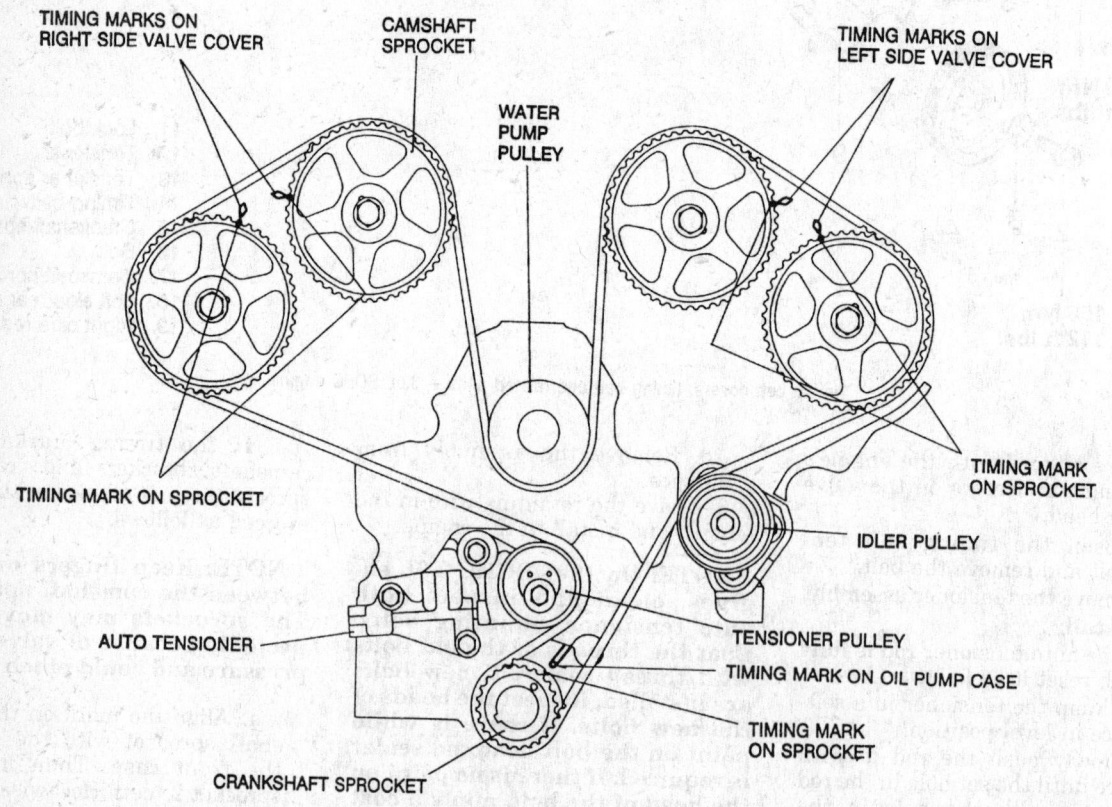

TIMING MARKS ON RIGHT SIDE VALVE COVER

CAMSHAFT SPROCKET

WATER PUMP PULLEY

TIMING MARKS ON LEFT SIDE VALVE COVER

TIMING MARK ON SPROCKET

TIMING MARK ON SPROCKET

IDLER PULLEY

AUTO TENSIONER

TENSIONER PULLEY

TIMING MARK ON OIL PUMP CASE

TIMING MARK ON SPROCKET

CRANKSHAFT SPROCKET

Timing belt installation — 3.0L DOHC engine

b. Turn each camshaft sprocket 1 at a time to align the timing marks with the mark on the valve cover or head. If the intake and exhaust valves of the same cylinder are opened simultaneously, they could interfere with each other. Therefore, if any resistance is felt, turn the other camshaft to move the valve.

c. Align the timing mark of the crankshaft sprocket, then continue 1 tooth farther in the counterclockwise direction to facilitate belt installation.

8. Using 4 spring loaded paper clips to hold the belt on the cam sprockets, install the belt to the sprockets in the following order:

1st — exhaust camshaft sprocket for the front head

2nd — intake camshaft sprocket for the front head

3rd — water pump pulley

4th — intake camshaft sprocket for the rear head

5th — exhaust camshaft sprocket for the rear head

6th — idler pulley

7th — crankshaft sprocket

8th — tensioner pulley

9. Turn the tensioner pulley so its pin holes are located above the center bolt. Then press the tensioner pulley against the timing belt and simultaneously tighten the center bolt.

10. Make certain that all timing marks are still aligned. If so, remove the 4 clips.

11. Turn the crankshaft ¼ turn counterclockwise, then turn it clockwise until all timing marks are aligned.

12. Loosen the center bolt on the tensioner pulley. Using tool MD998767 or equivalent and a torque wrench, apply a torque of 7.2 ft. lbs. (10 Nm). Tighten the tensioner bolt; make sure the tensioner doesn't rotate with the bolt.

13. Remove the set wire attached to the auto tensioner, if the wire was not previously removed.

14. Rotate the crankshaft 2 complete turns clockwise and let it sit for approximately 5 minutes. Then, make sure the set pin can easily be inserted and removed from the hole in the tensioner.

15. Measure the auto tensioner protrusion (the distance between the tensioner arm and auto tensioner body) to ensure that it is within 0.15-0.18 in. (3.8-4.5mm). If out of specification, repeat Steps 1-4 until the specified value is obtained.

16. Install the timing belt covers and all related items.

17. Connect the negative battery cable.

Timing Sprockets and Oil Seals

REMOVAL AND INSTALLATION

1. Disconnect the negative battery cable.

2. Remove the valve cover(s) and timing belt(s).

3. Remove the crankshaft pulley retainer bolts and remove the pulley.

4. Remove the crankshaft sprocket retainer bolt and washer from the sprocket, if used, and remove sprocket. If sprocket is difficult to remove, the appropriate puller may be used. If no bolts are used on the sprocket, use the appropriate puller to remove.

5. Hold the camshaft stationary using the hexagon cast between journals No. 2 and 3 and remove the retainer bolt. Remove the sprocket from the camshaft. If the camshaft does not have a hexagon cast between journals No. 2 and 3, use the appropriate spanner wrench to hold the shaft in position while removing the bolt.

6. Pry the seals from the bores and replace using the proper installation tools.

7. Install the sprockets to their shafts. Install the retainer bolts and torque the camshaft sprocket bolt to 47-54 ft. lbs. (65-75 Nm) on 1.5L engine, 65 ft. lbs. (90 Nm) on Expo/Expo LRV and 1992-94 3000GT or 58-72 ft. lbs. (80-100 Nm) on the remaining engines.

8. Torque the crankshaft sprocket retaining bolt to 80-94 ft. lbs. (110-130 Nm) on 1.6L, 1.8L, 2.0L and 2.4L engines or 51-72 ft. lbs. (70-100 Nm) on 1.5L engine.

9. Install the timing belt(s) and valve cover(s).

10. Connect the negative battery cable and check for leaks.

Camshaft

REMOVAL AND INSTALLATION

1.5L, 1.8L, 2.0L SOHC Engines, Except 1.5L and 1.8L Engines (Expo LRV)

1. Disconnect the negative battery cable. Remove the valve covers and timing belt.

2. Install auto lash adjuster retainer tools MD998443 or equivalent, on the rocker arms.

3. If removing the right side (front) camshaft on 3.0L engine, remove the distributor extension.

4. Remove the camshaft bearing caps but do not remove the bolts from the caps.

5. Remove the rocker arms, rocker shafts and bearing caps, as an assembly.

6. Remove the camshaft from the cylinder head.

7. Inspect the bearing journals on the camshaft, cylinder head, and bearing caps.

To install:

8. Lubricate the camshaft journals and camshaft with clean engine oil and install the camshaft in the cylinder head.

9. Align the camshaft bearing caps with the arrow mark depending on cylinder numbers and install in numerical order.

10. Apply sealer at the ends of the bearing caps and install the assembly.

11. Torque the bearing cap bolts in the following sequence: No. 3, No. 2, No. 1 and No. 4 to 85 inch lbs. (10 Nm).

12. Repeat the sequence increasing the torque to 15 ft. lbs. (20 Nm).

13. Install the distributor extension, if removed.

14. Install the timing belt or timing chain parts, valve cover and all other related parts.

15. Connect the negative battery cable and check for leaks.

1.5L and 1.8L Engines (Expo LRV)

1. Disconnect the negative battery cable.

2. Rotate the engine to bring No. 1 piston to TDC of its compression stroke. Remove the timing belt and valve cover.

3. Remove the camshaft sprocket and oil seal.

4. Loosen both rocker arm assemblies gradually and evenly and remove.

5. On 1990 engines, remove the camshaft rear cover, rear cover gasket, thrust plate and camshaft thrust case.

6. Remove the camshaft from the head.

7. Carefully check all parts for damage and wear.

To install:

8. Lubricate the camshaft with heavy engine oil and slide it into the head.

9. If equipped, insert the camshaft thrust case in cylinder head with the threaded hole facing upward and align the threaded hole with the bolt hole in the cylinder head. Install and firmly tighten the attaching bolt.

10. Check the camshaft end-play between the thrust case and camshaft. The camshaft end-play should be 0.0020-0.0080 in. (0.5-0.20mm). If the end-play is not within specification, replace the camshaft thrust bearing.

11. Install the rocker shaft assemblies. Torque the bolts gradually and evenly to 14-20 ft. lbs. (20-27 Nm) on 1990 engines or 21-25 ft. lbs. (29-35 Nm) on 1991-94 engines.

12. When installing the oil seal, coat the external surface with engine oil. Position the seal on the camshaft end and drive it into place.

13. Install the camshaft sprocket, timing belt and valve cover with new gasket.

14. Connect the negative battery cable and check for leaks.

1.6L and 2.0L DOHC Engines

1. Relieve the fuel system pressure.
2. Disconnect battery negative cable.
3. Disconnect the accelerator cable.
4. Remove the timing belt cover and timing belt.
5. Remove the center cover, breather and PCV hoses, and spark plug cables.
6. Remove the rocker cover, semicircular packing, throttle body stay, crankshaft angle sensor, both camshaft sprockets, and oil seals.
7. Loosen the bearing cap bolts in 2-3 steps. Label and remove all camshaft bearing caps.

NOTE: If the bearing caps are difficult to remove, use a plastic hammer to gently tap the rear part of the camshaft.

8. Remove the intake and exhaust camshafts.
9. Check the camshaft journals for wear or damage. Check the cam lobes for damage. Also, check the cylinder head oil holes for clogging.
To install:
10. Lubricate the camshafts with heavy engine oil and position the camshafts on the cylinder head.

NOTE: Do not confuse the intake camshaft with the exhaust camshaft. The intake camshaft has a split on its rear end for driving the crank angle sensor.

11. Make sure the dowel pin on both camshaft sprocket ends are located on the top.
12. Install the bearing caps. Tighten the caps in sequence and in 2 or 3 steps. No. 2 and 5 caps are of the same shape. Check the markings on the caps to identify the cap number and intake/exhaust symbol. Only **L** (intake) or **R** (exhaust) is stamped on No. 1 bearing cap. Also, make sure the rocker arm is correctly mounted on the lash adjuster and the valve stem end. Torque the retaining bolts to 15 ft. lbs. (20 Nm).
13. Apply a coating of engine oil to the oil seal. Using tool MD998307 or equivalent, press-fit the seal into the cylinder head.
14. Align the punch mark on the crank angle sensor housing with the notch in the plate. With the dowel pin on the sprocket side of the intake camshaft at top, install the crank angle sensor on the cylinder head.

NOTE: Do not position the crank angle sensor with the punch mark positioned opposite the notch; this position will result in incorrect fuel injection and ignition timing.

15. Install the timing belt, valve cover and all related parts.
16. Connect the negative battery cable and check for leaks.

3.0L DOHC Engine

1. Relieve the fuel system pressure.
2. Disconnect battery negative cable.
3. Remove the timing belt cover and timing belt.
4. Remove the center cover, breather and PCV hoses, and spark plug cables.
5. Remove the rocker cover, semicircular packing, throttle body stay, crankshaft angle sensor, both camshaft sprockets, and oil seals.
6. Remove the crank angle sensor and adaptor.
7. Loosen the bearing cap bolts in 2-3 steps. Label and remove all camshaft bearing caps.

NOTE: If the bearing caps are difficult to remove, use a plastic hammer to gently tap the rear part of the camshaft.

8. Remove the intake and exhaust camshafts.
9. Check the camshaft journals for wear or damage. Check the cam lobes for damage. Also, check the cylinder head oil holes for clogging.

To install:
10. Lubricate the camshafts with heavy engine oil and position the camshafts on the cylinder head.

NOTE: Do not confuse the intake camshaft with the exhaust camshaft. The intake camshaft has a V or B stamped on the hexagon depending on the application. The exhaust camshaft has a C, D or F stamped on the hexagon depending on application.

11. Make sure the dowel pin on both camshaft sprocket ends are located as shown.
12. Install the bearing caps. Tighten the caps in sequence and in 2 or 3 steps. Caps 2, 3 and 4 have a front mark. Install with the mark aligned with the front mark on the cylinder head. Intake caps have **I** stamped on the cap and exhaust caps have an **E**. Also, make sure the rocker arm is correctly mounted on the lash adjuster and the valve stem end. Torque the retaining bolts to 15 ft. lbs. (20 Nm).
13. Apply a coating of engine oil to the oil seals and install.
14. Install the timing belt, valve cover and all related parts.
15. Connect the negative battery cable and check for leaks.

Intermediate Shaft

REMOVAL AND INSTALLATION

1.8L Engine (Eclipse)

1. Disconnect the negative battery cable.
2. Remove the oil filter, oil pressure switch, oil gauge sending unit and oil filter bracket and gasket.
3. Drain engine oil. Remove engine oil pan, oil screen and gasket.
4. Remove the front engine cover which is also the oil pump cover. Different length bolts are used. Take note of their locations. If the cover sticks to the block, look for a special slot provided and pry with a suitable tool. Discard the shaft seal and gasket.
5. Remove the oil pump driven gear flange bolt. When loosening this bolt, first insert a suitable tool approximately 3/8 in. diameter into the plug hole on the left side of the cylinder block to hold the silent shaft. Remove the oil pump gears and remove the front case assembly. Remove the threaded plug, the oil pressure relief spring and plunger.

1. Rear bearing cap
2. Front bearing cap
3. Oil seal
4. Cap #5
5. Cap #2
6. Cap #4
7. Cap #3
8. Camshaft
9. Rocker arm
10. Lash adjuster
11. Oil delivery body

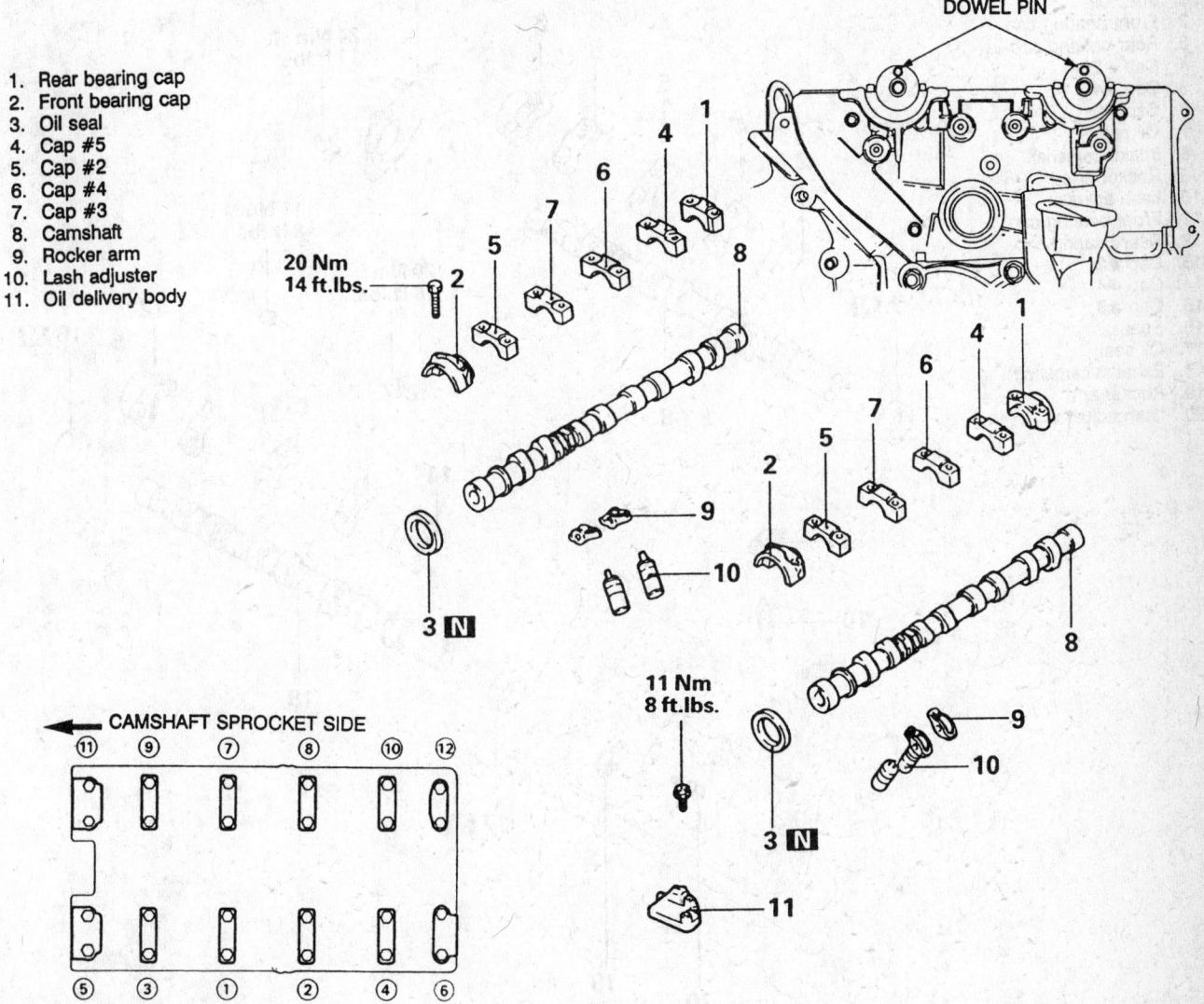

Camshaft, rocker arms and lash adjusters with bearing cap tightening sequence and camshaft installation positioning — 1.6L and 2.0L DOHC engines

6. Remove the silent shaft oil seals, the crankshaft oil seal and front case gasket.

7. Remove the silent shafts.

To install:

8. Installation is the reverse of the removal procedure. Use new gaskets and seals. Clean all mating surfaces well.

9. Use care to get the proper length bolt in the correct location on the timing cover as well as the oil pump cover.

10. Refill with engine oil. Install new filter. Check for leaks.

Silent Shafts

REMOVAL AND INSTALLATION

4-Cylinder Engines

NOTE: A special oil seal guide MD998285 or equivalent, is needed to complete this operation.

1. Disconnect the negative battery cable.

2. Remove the oil filter, oil pressure switch, oil gauge sending unit, oil filter mounting bracket and gasket.

3. Raise and safely support the vehicle. Drain engine oil. Remove engine oil pan, oil screen and gasket.

4. Lower the vehicle. Remove the timing belts.

5. Remove the front engine cover which is also the oil pump cover. Different length bolts are used. Take note of their locations. On 1.8L engine, if the cover sticks to the block, look for a special slot provided and pry with a flat bladed tool. Discard the shaft seal and gasket.

6. Remove the oil pump driven gear flange bolt. When loosening this bolt, first insert a tool approximately 3/8 in. diameter into the plug hole on

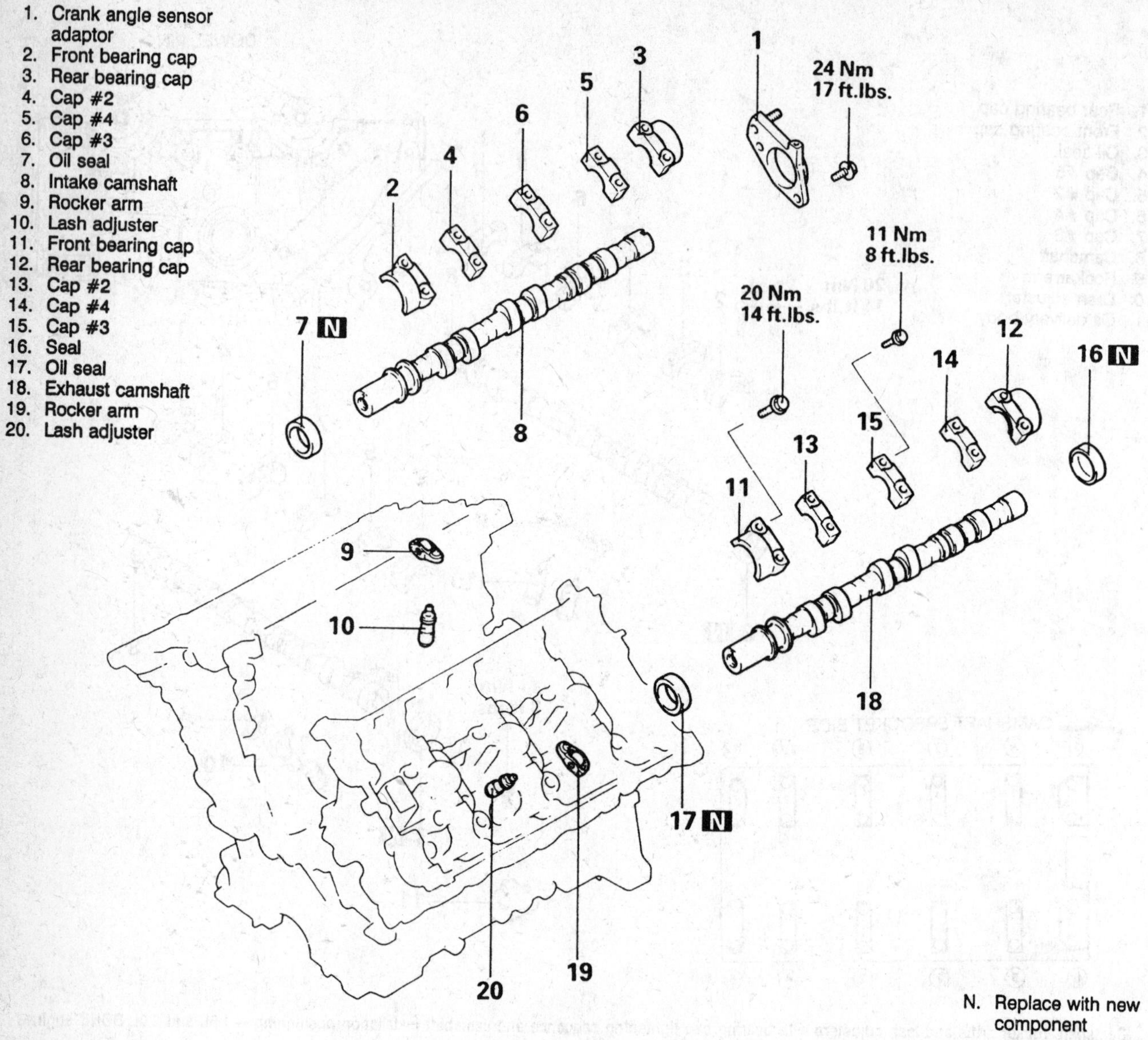

1. Crank angle sensor adaptor
2. Front bearing cap
3. Rear bearing cap
4. Cap #2
5. Cap #4
6. Cap #3
7. Oil seal
8. Intake camshaft
9. Rocker arm
10. Lash adjuster
11. Front bearing cap
12. Rear bearing cap
13. Cap #2
14. Cap #4
15. Cap #3
16. Seal
17. Oil seal
18. Exhaust camshaft
19. Rocker arm
20. Lash adjuster

24 Nm 17 ft.lbs.

11 Nm 8 ft.lbs.

20 Nm 14 ft.lbs.

N. Replace with new component

Camshaft, rocker arms and lash adjusters — 3.0L DOHC engine

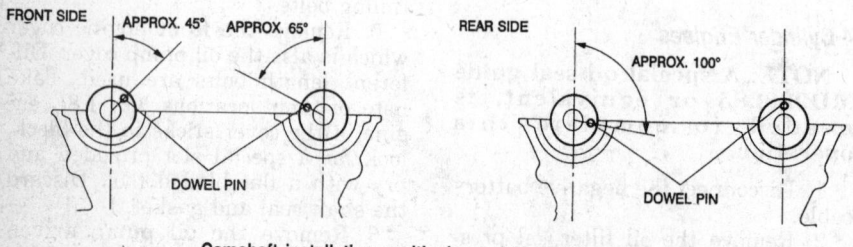

Camshaft installation positioning — 3.0L DOHC engine

FRONT SIDE APPROX. 45° APPROX. 65° DOWEL PIN

REAR SIDE APPROX. 100° DOWEL PIN

the left side of the cylinder block to hold the silent shaft. Remove the oil pump gears and remove the front case assembly. Remove the threaded plug, the oil pressure relief spring and plunger.

7. Remove the silent shaft oil seals, the crankshaft oil seal and front case gasket.

8. Remove the silent shafts.

To install:

9. Carefully install the silent shafts to the block.

10. Install the oil pump components.

11. Install new seals and install the front case with a new gasket.

12. Install the timing belts and all related items. Make sure the orientation of the silent shafts is correct using alignment tool as specified in the timing belt section of this chapter.

NOTE: The timing of the oil pump sprocket and connected silent shaft can be incorrect, even with the timing mark aligned. Incorrect orientation of the silent shaft will result in engine vibration during operation. Follow the alignment procedure in the timing belt section of this chapter.

13. Install the oil pan, oil filter mounting bracket, oil switches oil filter and oil.

14. Connect the negative battery cable and check for leaks.

Piston and Connecting Rod

POSITIONING

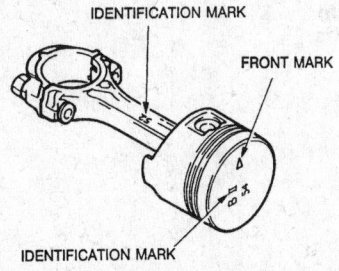

Piston positioning and identification marks. Note that some 3.0L pistons may have an "R" (which goes forward for cylinders 1-3-5) and an "L" (which goes forward for cylinders 2-4-6) on the piston top.

ENGINE LUBRICATION

Oil Pan

REMOVAL AND INSTALLATION

Except Expo/Expo LRV

1. Disconnect the negative battery cable.
2. Raise the vehicle and support safely.
3. Remove the oil pan drain plug and drain the engine oil. On 1.6L engine equipped with turbocharger, remove the oil return pipe and gasket.
4. On 1.8L engine, disconnect and lower the exhaust pipe.

5. On 3000GT equipped with AWD, remove the transfer assembly.
6. On some 2.0L engine applications, remove the crossmember, disconnect and lower the exhaust pipe and on turbocharged engines, disconnect the return pipe for the turbocharger from the side of the oil pan.
7. Remove the oil pan mounting bolts, separate and remove the engine oil pan.
To install:
8. Thoroughly clean and dry the oil pan, cylinder block bolts and bolt holes.
9. Apply a thin bead of sealer around the surface of the oil pan.
10. Assemble the oil pan to the cylinder block within 15 minutes after applying the sealant.
11. Install the oil pan mounting bolts and torque to 4-6 ft. lbs. (6-8 Nm). On 1.6L engine equipped with turbocharger, install the oil return pipe using a new gasket.
12. Fill the engine with the proper amount of oil.
13. Connect the negative battery cable and check for leaks.

Expo/Expo LRV

1. Disconnect negative battery cable.
2. Raise and safely support the vehicle.
3. Remove the front exhaust pipe and gasket.
4. If equipped with AWD, remove the transfer assembly with the propeller shaft still installed.
5. Remove the bellhousing cover.
6. If equipped with 2.4L engine and FWD, remove the front left driveshaft from the transaxle.
7. Remove the oil pan mounting bolts and nuts. Remove the oil pan using tool MD998727 or equivalent, and a brass bar. Take care not to deform the pan flange during removal.
To install:
8. Thoroughly clean and dry the oil pan, cylinder block bolts and bolt holes.
9. Apply a thin bead of sealer around the flange surface of the oil pan. Make sure the bead of sealer is on the area between the bolt holes and the inside of the pan, and in the shallow groove around the flange of the oil pan.
10. Assemble the oil pan to the cylinder block within 15 minutes after applying the sealant.
11. Install the oil pan mounting bolts and nuts and tighten to 5 ft. lbs. (7 Nm).
12. Install the bellhousing cover.
13. Install the front driveshaft.

14. Install the transfer assembly.
15. Install the front exhaust pipe.
16. Lower the vehicle and add clean engine oil to the correct level. Reconnect the negative battery cable and check for leaks.

Oil Pump

REMOVAL AND INSTALLATION

NOTE: Whenever the oil pump is disassembled or the cover removed, the gear cavity must be filled with petroleum jelly for priming purposes. Do not use grease.

1. Disconnect the negative battery cable.
2. Remove the front engine mount bracket and accessory drive belts.
3. Remove timing belt upper and lower covers.
4. Remove the timing belt and crankshaft sprocket.
5. Remove the oil pan.
6. Remove the oil screen and gasket.
7. Remove and tag the front cover mounting bolts. Note the lengths of the mounting bolts as they are removed for proper installation.
8. On 1.6L engine, remove the plug cap using tool MD998162 or equivalent, and remove the oil pressure switch.
9. Remove the front case cover and oil pump assembly. If necessary, the silent shaft can come out with the assembly. Disassemble as required.

NOTE: On 1.5L engine, the outer gear may not have any marks indicating its installed direction. Make a mark on the reverse side of the outer gear so it can be reinstalled in its proper position.

To install:
10. Thoroughly clean all gasket material from all mounting surfaces.
11. Apply engine oil to the entire surface of the gears or rotors. On 1.5L engine, make sure the outer gear is installed in the same direction as before according to the mark made at the time of removal.
12. On engines with silent shafts, install the drive/driven gears with the 2 timing marks aligned.
13. Assemble the front case cover and oil pump assembly to the engine block using a new gasket. On 1.6L engine, assemble the front case cover and oil pump assembly using tool MD998285 or equivalent, on the front end of the crankshaft.

1. Oil filter
2. Drain plug
3. Gasket
4. Oil pan
5. Oil screen
6. Gasket
7. Relief plug
8. Gasket
9. Relief spring
10. Relief plunger
11. Oil seal
12. Front case
13. Gasket
14. Oil pump cover
15. Outer rotor
16. Inner rotor

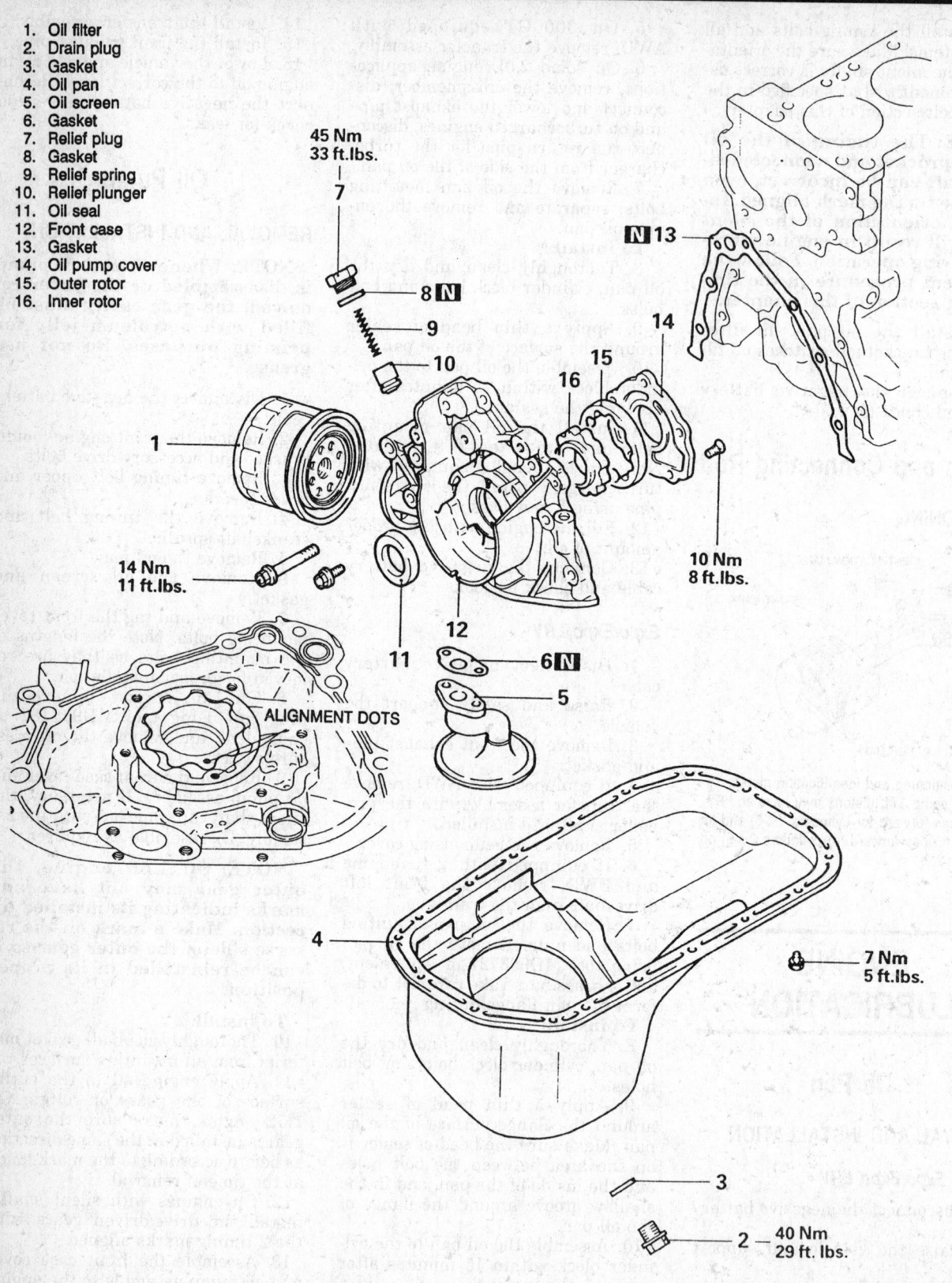

45 Nm
33 ft.lbs.
7

8 N

9

10

14 Nm
11 ft.lbs.

1

11

12

ALIGNMENT DOTS

N 13

14

15

16

10 Nm
8 ft.lbs.

6 N

5

4

7 Nm
5 ft.lbs.

3

2 — 40 Nm
29 ft. lbs.

N. Replace with new component

Oil pump components — typical of 1.5L, 1.8L (Expo/Expo LRV) and 3.0L engines

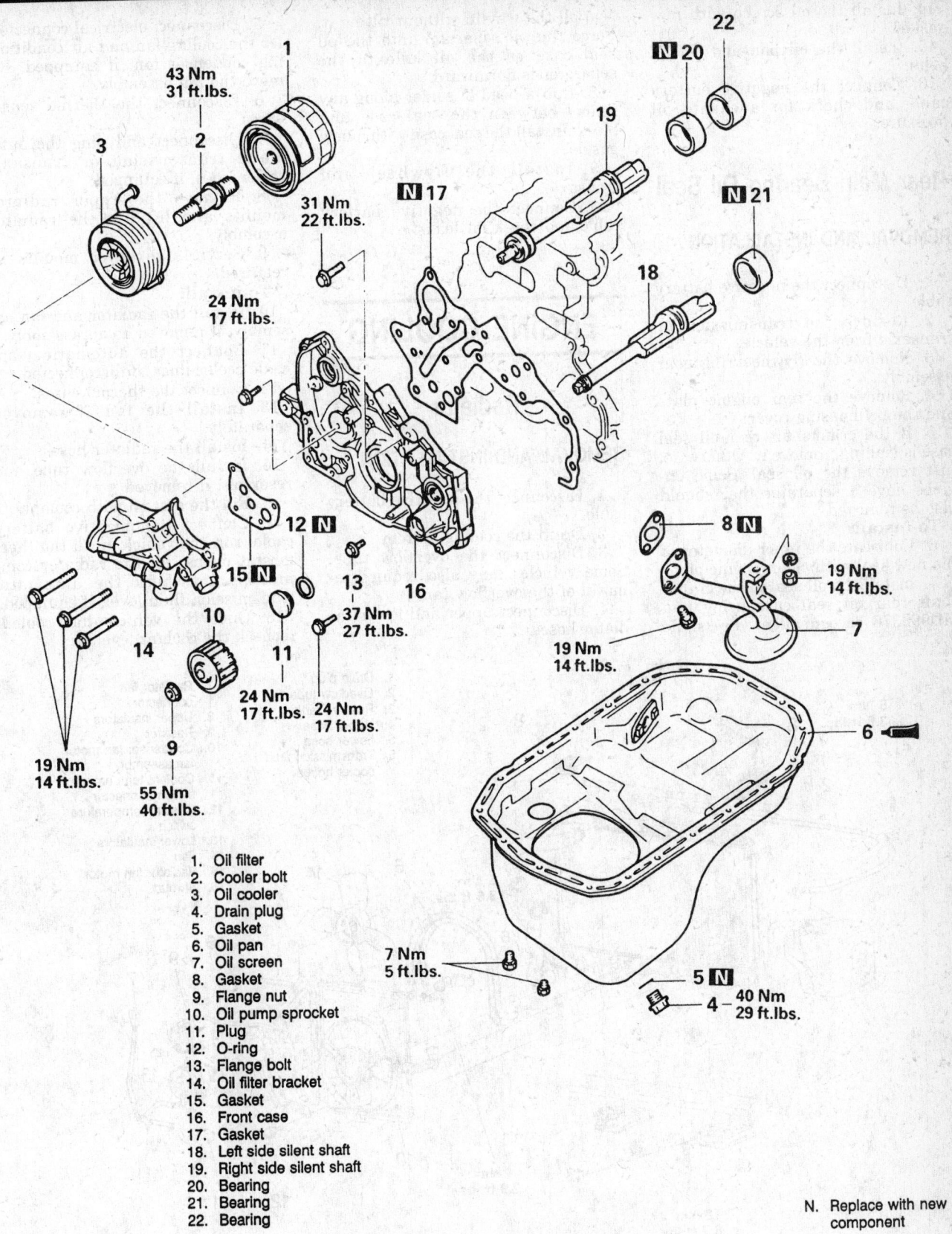

1. Oil filter
2. Cooler bolt
3. Oil cooler
4. Drain plug
5. Gasket
6. Oil pan
7. Oil screen
8. Gasket
9. Flange nut
10. Oil pump sprocket
11. Plug
12. O-ring
13. Flange bolt
14. Oil filter bracket
15. Gasket
16. Front case
17. Gasket
18. Left side silent shaft
19. Right side silent shaft
20. Bearing
21. Bearing
22. Bearing

N. Replace with new component

Oil pump and silent shafts — typical of all 4 cylinder engines

14. Install the oil screen with new gasket.

15. Install the oil pan and timing belts.

16. Connect the negative battery cable and check for adequate oil pressure.

Rear Main Bearing Oil Seal

REMOVAL AND INSTALLATION

1. Disconnect the negative battery cable.

2. Remove the transmission or transaxle from the vehicle.

3. Remove the flywheel/ring gear assembly.

4. Remove the rear engine plate and the bellhousing cover.

5. If the crankshaft rear oil seal case is leaking, remove it. Otherwise, just remove the oil seal. Some engines have a separator that should also be removed.

To install:

6. Lubricate the inner diameter of the new seal with clean engine oil.

7. Install the oil seal in the crankshaft rear oil seal case using tool MD998376 or equivalent. Press the

seal all the way in without tilting it. Force the oil separator into the oil seal case so the oil hole in the separator is downward.

8. Run a bead of sealer along any seams between the seal case and block. Install the seal case with a new gasket.

9. Install the flywheel and transaxle.

10. Connect the negative battery cable and check for leaks.

ENGINE COOLING

Radiator

REMOVAL AND INSTALLATION

1. Disconnect the negative battery cable.

2. Drain the cooling system.

3. Disconnect the overflow tube. Some vehicles may also require removal of the overflow tank.

4. Disconnect upper and lower radiator hoses.

5. Disconnect electrical connectors for the cooling fan and air conditioning condenser fan, if equipped. Remove the fan assembly.

6. Disconnect the thermo sensor wires.

7. Disconnect and plug the automatic transmission or transaxle cooler lines, if equipped.

8. Remove the upper radiator mounts and lift out the radiator assembly.

9. Service the lower mounts as required.

To install:

10. Install the radiator and fan assembly, if removed as an assembly.

11. Connect the automatic transaxle cooler lines, if disconnected.

12. Connect the thermo wires.

13. Install the fan if removed separately.

14. Install the radiator hoses.

15. Install the overflow tube and reservoir, if removed.

16. Fill the system with coolant.

17. Connect the negative battery cable, run the vehicle until the thermostat opens, fill the radiator completely and check the automatic transmission fluid level, if equipped.

18. Once the vehicle has cooled, recheck the coolant level.

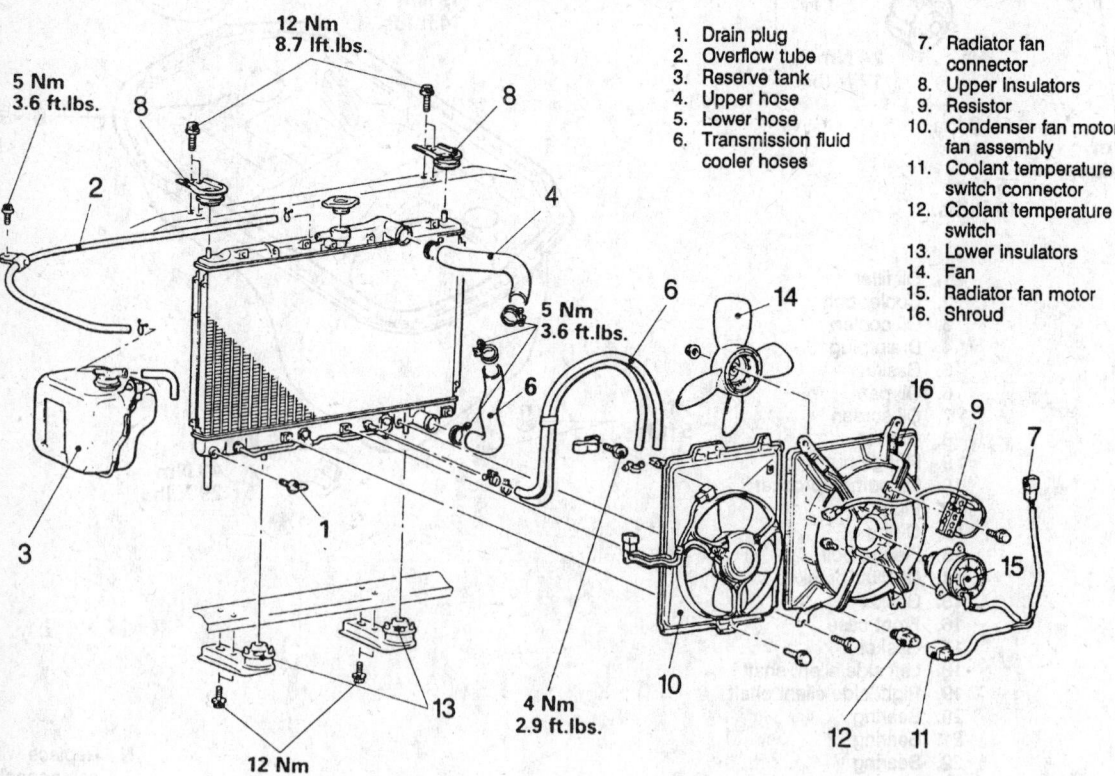

1. Drain plug
2. Overflow tube
3. Reserve tank
4. Upper hose
5. Lower hose
6. Transmission fluid cooler hoses
7. Radiator fan connector
8. Upper Insulators
9. Resistor
10. Condenser fan motor fan assembly
11. Coolant temperature switch connector
12. Coolant temperature switch
13. Lower insulators
14. Fan
15. Radiator fan motor
16. Shroud

Arrangement of radiator and fans

Heater Core

REMOVAL AND INSTALLATION

Diamante

1. Disarm the air bag as follows:

a. Position the front wheels in the straight-ahead position and place the key in the **LOCK** position. Remove the key from the ignition lock cylinder.

b. Disconnect the negative battery cable and insulate the cable end with high-quality electrical tape or similar non-conductive wrapping.

c. Wait at least 1 minute before working on the vehicle. The air bag system is designed to retain enough voltage to deploy the air bag for a short period of time even after the battery has been disconnected.

2. Drain the cooling system and disconnect the heater hoses from the core tubes. Plug the hoses.

3. Remove the passenger side under cover.

4. Remove the right side foot shower duct.

5. To remove the console, remove the ashtray and remove the revealed screw. Then remove the 4 screws from the sides of the assembly and remove.

6. Remove the decorative plugs from the driver's knee protector. Remove the revealed screws, the knee protector assembly and the protector support bracket.

7. Remove the steering column covers.

8. Remove the glove box striker, glove box, glove box outer casing and the screw below the assembly.

9. Remove the radio bezel and the stereo entertainment system.

10. Remove the climate control system control head.

11. Remove the cup holder.

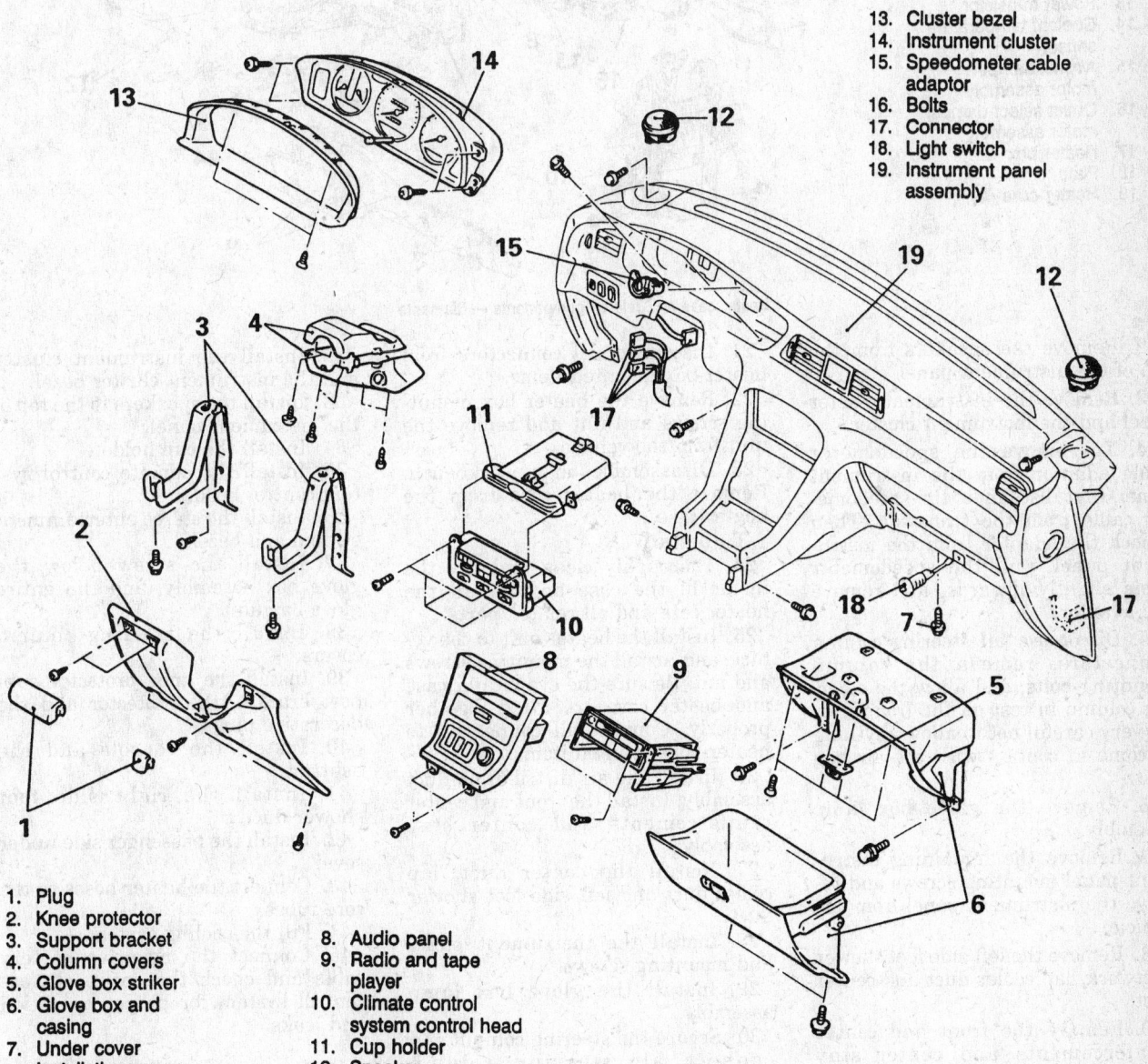

13. Cluster bezel
14. Instrument cluster
15. Speedometer cable adaptor
16. Bolts
17. Connector
18. Light switch
19. Instrument panel assembly

1. Plug
2. Knee protector
3. Support bracket
4. Column covers
5. Glove box striker
6. Glove box and casing
7. Under cover installation screw
8. Audio panel
9. Radio and tape player
10. Climate control system control head
11. Cup holder
12. Speaker

Instrument panel and related components — Diamante

1. Heater hoses
2. Under cover
3. Right side foot shower duct
4. Instrument panel
5. Foot shower nozzle
6. Lap cooler duct
7. Center duct assembly
8. Left side foot shower duct
9. Reinforcement panel
10. Center stay
11. Distribution duct assembly
12. Mounting hardware
13. Power transistor
14. Coolant temperature sensor
15. Air mix damper motor assembly
16. Outlet select damper motor assembly
17. Heater box
18. Plate
19. Heater core

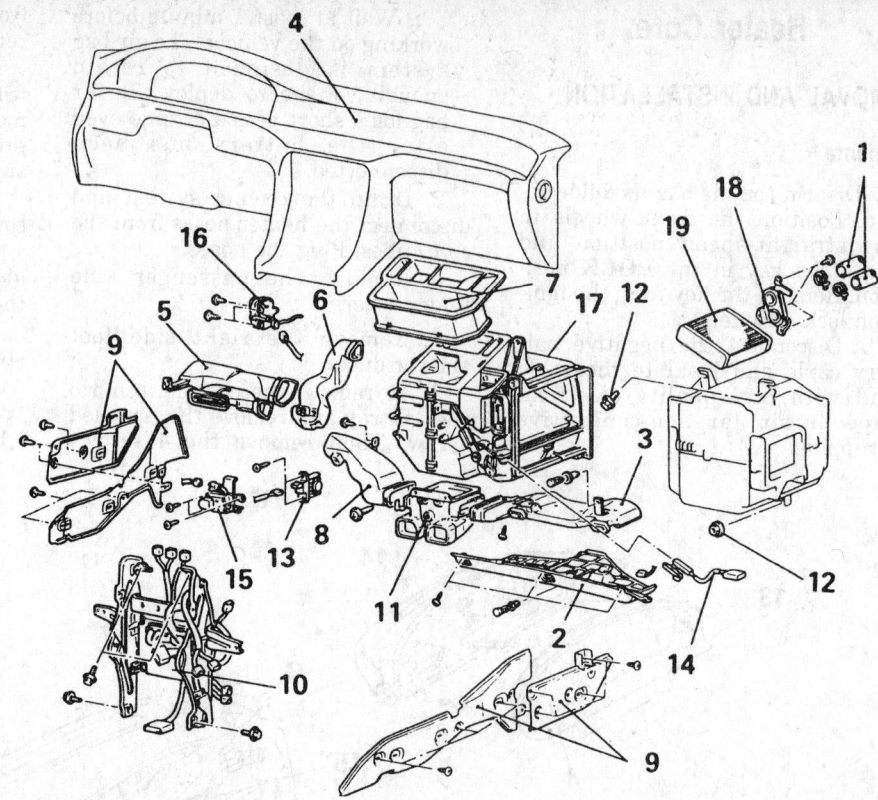

Heater case and related components — Diamante

12. Remove the speakers from the top of the instrument panel.

13. Remove the instrument cluster bezel and the instrument cluster.

14. To remove the speedometer cable adaptor from the instrument panel, first disconnect the speedometer cable from the transaxle. Then unlock the adaptor from the instrument panel, pull the speedometer cable slightly inwards, and remove the adaptor.

15. Disconnect all steering column connectors, remove the column mounting bolts, and allow the steering column to rest on the front seat. Be very careful not to allow anything to come in contact with the air bag unit.

16. Remove the glove box lamp assembly.

17. Remove the remaining instrument panel mounting screws and remove the instrument panel from the vehicle.

18. Remove the left side foot shower ductwork, lap cooler duct and center duct.

19. Remove the front and center reinforcements and center stay assembly.

20. Remove the air distribution duct assembly.

21. Disconnect all connectors from heater-box-mounted items.

22. Remove the heater box mounting screws and nut and remove the unit from the vehicle.

23. Disassemble on a workbench. Remove the heater core from the heater case.

To install:

24. Thoroughly clean and dry the inside of the case and install the heater core and all related parts.

25. Install the heater unit to the vehicle and install the mounting screws and nut. Be sure the evaporator case and heater case are fitted together properly. Connect all connectors to heater-box-mounted items.

26. Install the air distribution duct assembly. Install the front and center reinforcements and center stay assembly.

27. Install the center duct, lap cooler duct and left side foot shower duct.

28. Install the instrument panel and mounting screws.

29. Install the glove box lamp assembly.

30. Secure the steering column and connect all steering column connectors.

31. Install the speedometer cable adaptor to the instrument panel.

32. Install the instrument cluster and the instrument cluster bezel.

33. Install the speakers to the top of the instrument panel.

34. Install the cup holder.

35. Install the climate control system control head.

36. Install the stereo entertainment system and bezel.

37. Install the screw below the glove box assembly, and the entire glove box unit.

38. Install the steering column covers.

39. Install the knee protector support bracket, the protector and the decorative plugs.

40. Install the console and the ashtray.

41. Install the right side foot shower duct.

42. Install the passenger side under cover.

43. Connect the heater hoses to the core tubes.

44. Fill the cooling system.

45. Connect the negative battery cable and check the entire climate control system for proper operation and leaks.

Eclipse

1. Disconnect the negative battery cable.

1. Plug
2. Knee protector
3. Hood lock release handle
4. Lower cover
5. Upper cover
6. Cover
7. Outer cluster bezel
8. Radio bezel
9. Radio assembly
10. Center air outlet
11. Dial knobs
12. Inner cluster bezel
13. Stopper
14. Glove box assembly
15. Instrument cluster
16. Speedometer cable adaptor
17. Speaker garnish
18. Bracket
19. Screw
20. Lap duct
21. Shower duct
22. Steering shaft mounting bolt
23. Instrument panel mounting screw
24. Instrument panel mounting bolt
25. Instrument panel

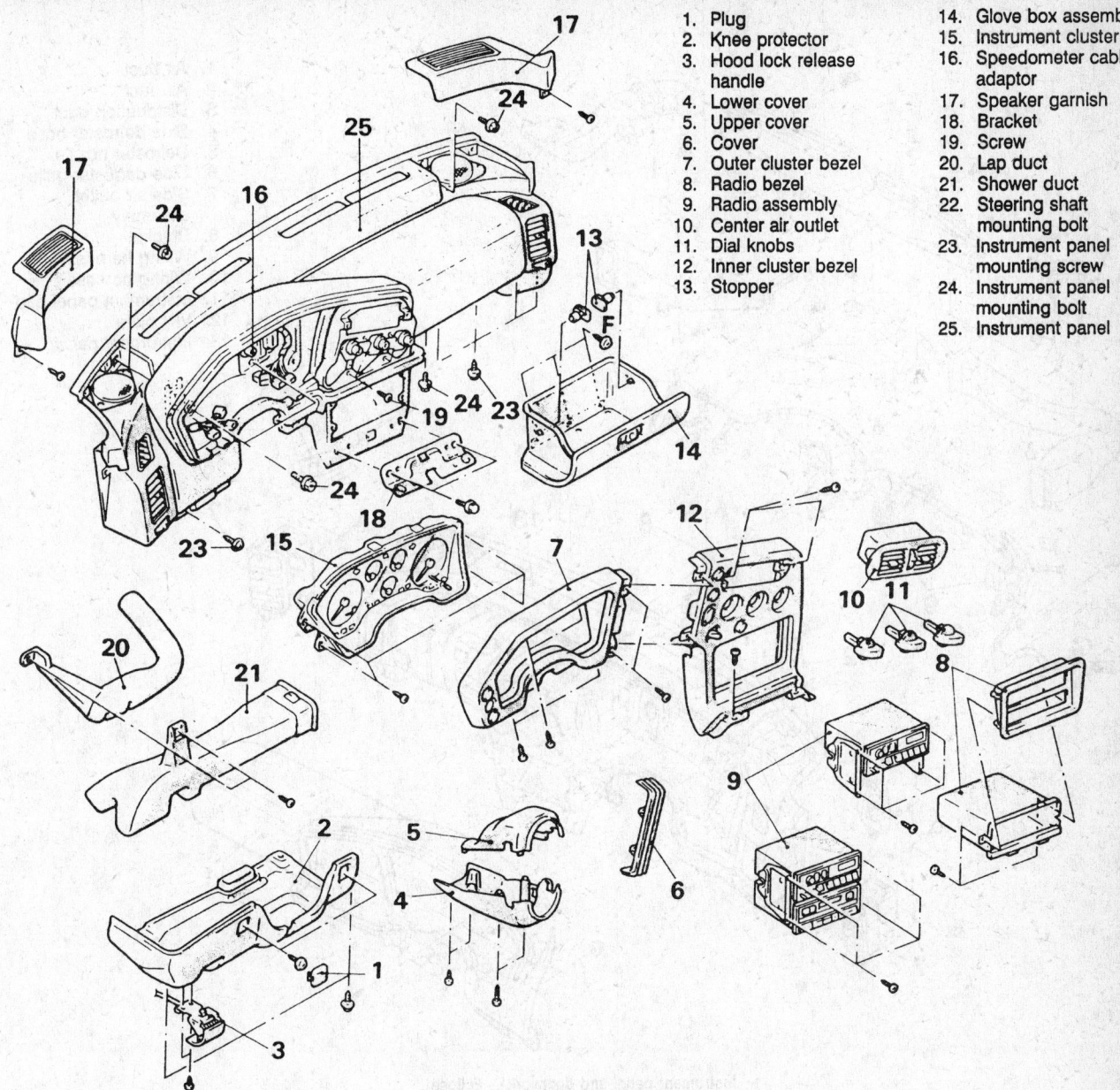

Instrument panel and related components — Eclipse

2. Drain the cooling system and properly discharge the air conditioning system and disconnect the refrigerant lines from the evaporator, if equipped. Cover the exposed ends of the lines to minimize contamination.

3. Remove the floor console by first removing the plugs, then the screws retaining the side covers and the small cover piece in front of the shifter. Remove the shifter knob, manual transmission, and the cup holder. Remove both small pieces of upholstery to gain access to retainer screws. Disconnect both electrical connectors at the front of the console.

Remove the shoulder harness guide plates and the console assembly.

4. Locate the rectangular plugs in the knee protector on either side of the steering column. Pry these plugs out and remove the screws. Remove the screws from the hood lock release lever and the knee protector.

5. Remove the upper and lower column covers.

6. Remove the narrow panel covering the instrument cluster cover screws, and remove the cover.

7. Remove the radio panel and remove the radio.

8. Remove the center air outlet assembly by reaching through the grille

and pushing the side clips out with a small flat-tipped tool while carefully prying the outlet free.

9. Pull the heater control knobs off and remove the heater control panel assembly.

10. Open the glove box, remove the plugs from the sides and the glove box assembly.

11. Remove the instrument gauge cluster and the speedometer adapter by disconnecting the speedometer cable at the transaxle, pulling the cable sightly towards the vehicle interior, then giving a slight twist on the adapter to release it.

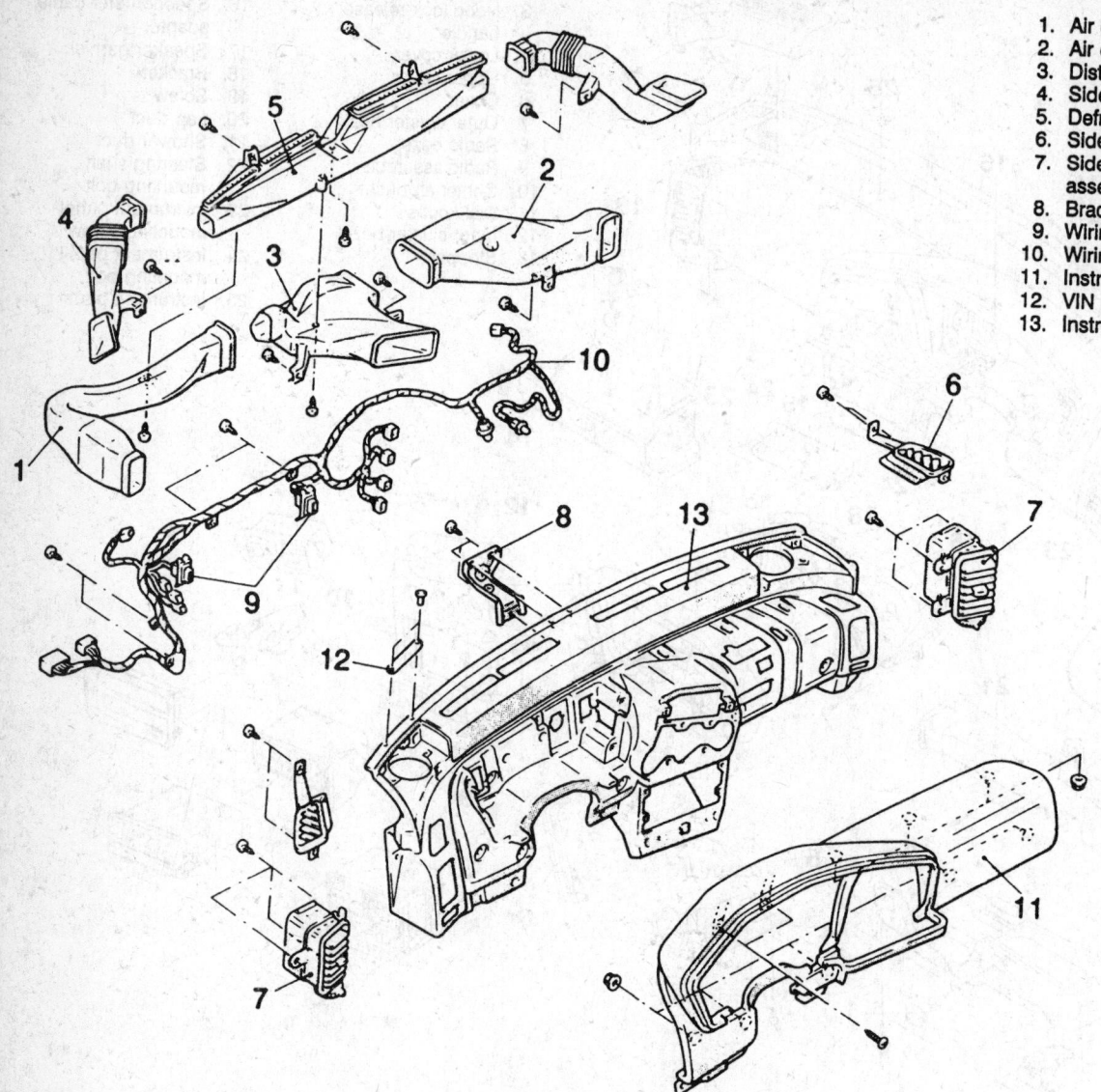

1. Air duct
2. Air duct
3. Distribution duct
4. Side defroster hose
5. Defroster nozzle
6. Side defroster grille
7. Side air outlet assembly
8. Bracket
9. Wiring harness
10. Wiring harness
11. Instrument panel pad
12. VIN plate
13. Instrument panel

Instrument panel and ductwork — Eclipse

12. Remove the left and right speaker covers from the top of the instrument panel.

13. Remove the center plate below the heater controls.

14. Remove the heater control assembly installation screws.

15. Remove the lower air ducts.

16. Drop the steering column by removing the bolts.

17. Remove the instrument panel mounting screws, bolts and the instrument panel assembly.

18. Remove both stamped steel reinforcement pieces.

19. Remove the lower ductwork from the heater box.

20. Remove the upper center duct.

21. Vehicles without air conditioning will have a square duct in place of the evaporator; remove this duct if present. If equipped with air conditioning, remove the evaporator assembly:

   a. Remove the wiring harness connectors and the electronic control unit.

   b. Remove the drain hose and lift out the evaporator unit.

   c. If servicing the assembly, disassemble the housing and remove the expansion valve and evaporator.

22. With the evaporator removed, remove the heater unit. To prevent bolts from falling inside the blower assembly, set the inside/outside air-selection damper to the position that permits outside air introduction.

23. Remove the cover plate around the heater tubes and remove the core fastener clips. Pull the heater core from the heater box, being careful not to damage the fins or tank ends.

To install:

24. Thoroughly clean and dry the inside of the case. Install the heater core to the heater box. Install the clips and cover.

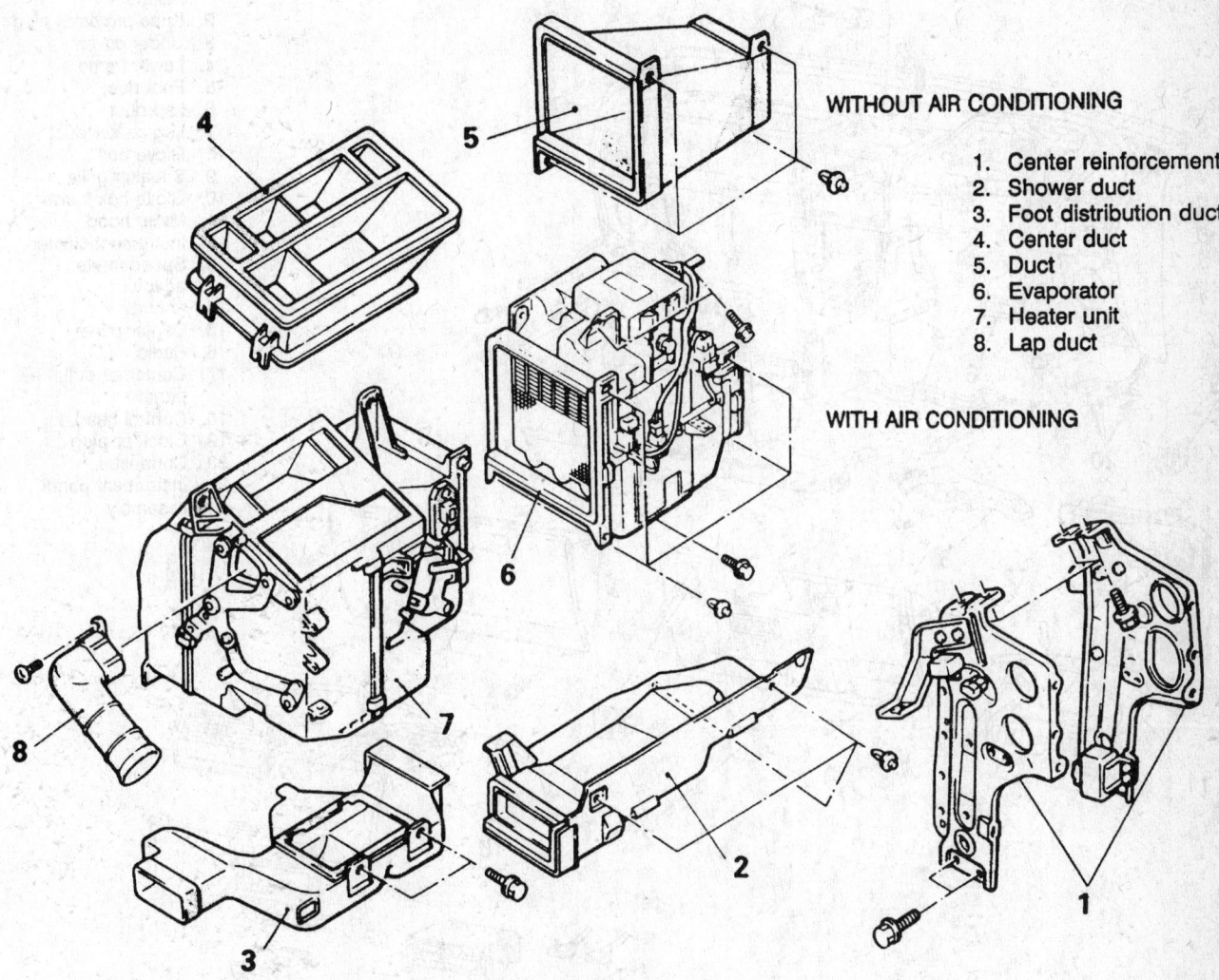

WITHOUT AIR CONDITIONING

1. Center reinforcement
2. Shower duct
3. Foot distribution duct
4. Center duct
5. Duct
6. Evaporator
7. Heater unit
8. Lap duct

WITH AIR CONDITIONING

Heater case and related components — Eclipse

25. Install the heater box and connect the duct work.

26. Assemble the housing, evaporator and expansion valve, making sure the gaskets are in good condition. Install the evaporator housing.

27. Using new lubricated O-rings, connect the refrigerant lines to the evaporator.

28. Install the electronic transmission ELC box. Connect all wires and control cables.

29. Install the instrument panel assembly and the console by reversing their removal procedures.

30. Evacuate and recharge the air conditioning system. If the evapora-tor was replaced, add 2 oz. of refrigerant oil during the recharge.

31. Connect the negative battery cable and check the entire climate control system for proper operation. Check the system for leaks.

Expo/Expo LRV

1. Disconnect negative battery cable.

2. Drain the engine coolant.

3. Remove the hood lock release handle, instrument panel under cover, lower frame, foot duct, lap duct and the lap heater duct.

4. Remove the glove box, speaker harness and the glove box frame.

5. Remove the meter hood and combination meter from the instrument panel. Remove the adapter lock and pull the speedometer cable into the passenger compartment slightly. Remove the rear of the adapter from the cable. Next, turn the adapter so the notched section is aligned with the tab on the cable section and slide adapter outward to remove.

6. Remove the ash tray from the center panel. Remove the mounting screws, radio and the center panel from the vehicle.

7. Remove the center air outlet from instrument panel by removing the clip on the lower section of the

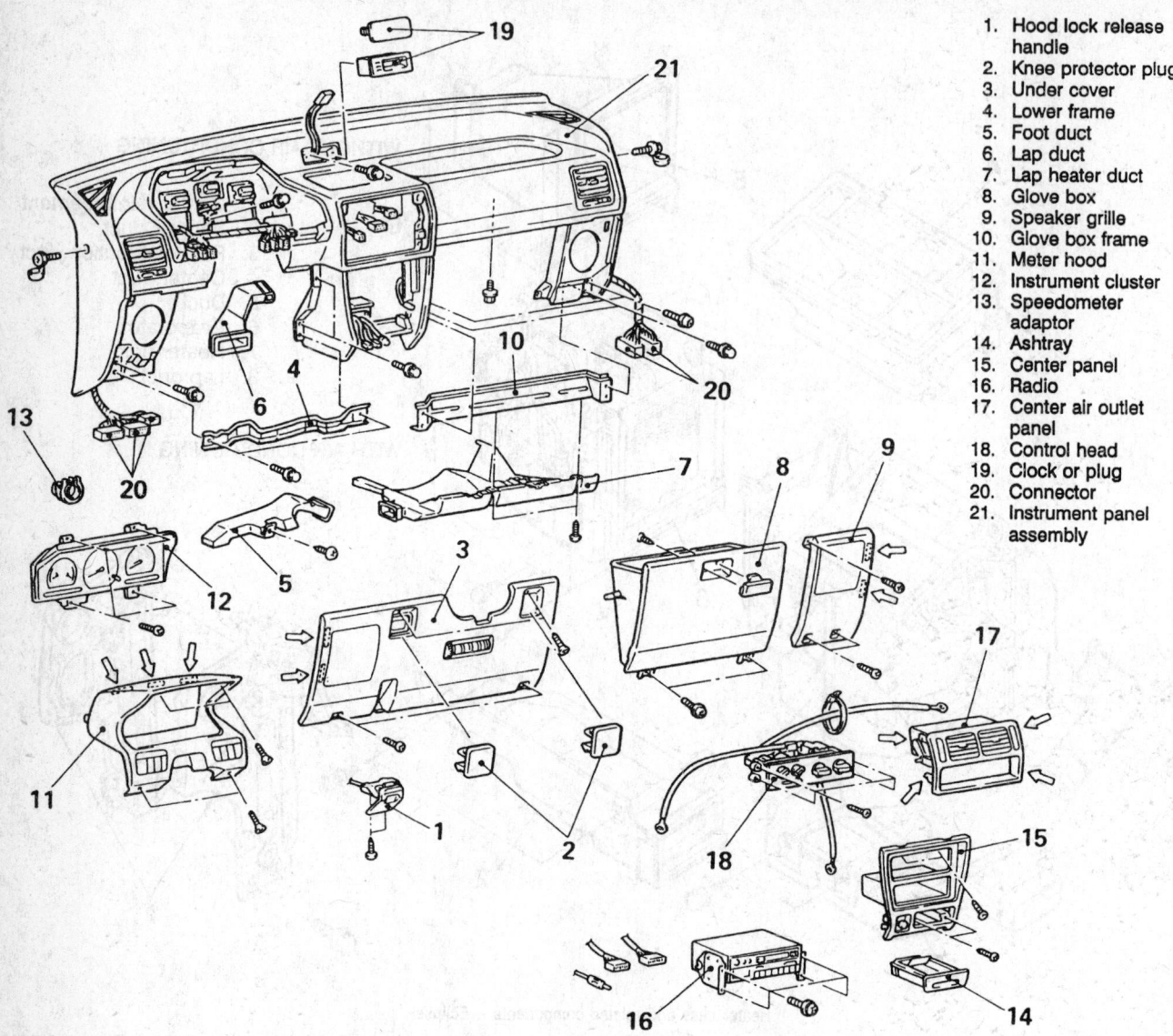

1. Hood lock release handle
2. Knee protector plug
3. Under cover
4. Lower frame
5. Foot duct
6. Lap duct
7. Lap heater duct
8. Glove box
9. Speaker grille
10. Glove box frame
11. Meter hood
12. Instrument cluster
13. Speedometer adaptor
14. Ashtray
15. Center panel
16. Radio
17. Center air outlet panel
18. Control head
19. Clock or plug
20. Connector
21. Instrument panel assembly

Instrument panel and related components — Expo/Expo LRV

outlet. Next insert a flat tipped tool in between the fins and remove the clip on the top section while pulling the lock spring toward the inside. Remove the center air outlet assembly.

8. Disconnect the air selection, temperature and mode selection control cables from the heater box and remove the heater control assembly.

9. Remove the clock or plug from the upper instrument panel. Remove the instrument panel retaining bolt under the plug.

10. Lower the steering column by removing the bolt and nut under the column.

11. Remove the floor console side covers. If equipped with manual transaxle, remove the shifter knob.

12. Remove the floor console switch panel, mounting bolts and the floor console from the vehicle.

13. Remove the instrument panel retainer bolts and the instrument panel.

14. Disconnect the heater hoses at the heater box.

15. Remove the heater joint duct by first removing the pin type retainer clips on the duct using the following procedure:

a. This type of clip is removed by pressing down on the center pin with a blunt pointed tool. Press down a little more than $1/16$ in. (2mm); this releases the clip. Pull the clip outward to remove it.

b. Do not push the pin inward more than necessary because it may damage the grommet or the pin may fall in if pushed in too far. Once the clips are removed, use a plastic trim stick to pry the piece loose.

16. Remove the center reinforcement. Remove the cooling unit mounting nut if equipped with air conditioning.

17. Disconnect and remove the ABS control unit and the automatic transmission ELC control unit.

18. Remove the foot distribution duct and disconnect the rear heater duct connection.

19. Remove both stamped steel instrument panel supports.

20. Remove the mounting bolts and the heater unit from the vehicle. Be careful not to damage the heater tubes or to spill coolant inside the vehicle.

21. Remove the cover plate around the heater tubes and the core fastener clips. Pull the heater core from the heater box, being careful not to damage the fins or tank ends.

To install:

22. Thoroughly clean and dry the inside of the case. Install the heater core to the heater box. Install the clips and cover.

23. Install the heater unit into position on the vehicle and install the evaporator and heater unit mounting nuts and clips.

24. Install the automatic transaxle ELC box and the ABS control unit.

25. Connect the air selection, temperature and mode selection control cables from the heater box and install the heater control assembly.

26. Install both stamped steel instrument panel supports. Connect the connector for the ECI control relay.

27. Install the remaining instrument panel components reversing the removal procedure.

28. Install the center console as follows:

    a. Install the front console box assembly.

    b. Install the shift lever knob on manual transaxle vehicles.

    c. Install the rear console box assembly.

    d. Install the floor console switch panel

    e. Install the coin holder and the console box tray.

29. Refill the cooling system.

30. Evacuate and recharge the air conditioning system. Add 2 oz. of refrigerant oil during the recharge if the evaporator was replaced.

31. Connect the negative battery cable and check the entire climate control system for proper operation. Check the system for leaks.

Galant and Sigma

1. Disconnect the negative battery cable.

NOTE: If equipped with an air bag, wait for 1 minute to elapse before working inside the vehi- cle. **The air bag system is set to deploy for a short period of time after the battery is disconnected.**

2. With the engine cold, set the temperature control lever to the **FULL HOT** position. Drain the engine coolant.

3. Disconnect the coolant hoses running to the heater pipes at the firewall.

4. Remove the center console.

5. Remove the heater cover.

6. Remove the steering wheel.

7. Remove the small steering column panel.

8. Remove the under cover.

9. Remove the upper and lower steering column covers and disconnect the wiring connectors.

10. Remove the instrument cluster hood.

11. Remove the mounting screws for the instrument cluster.

12. Pull the cluster out and disconnect the speedometer adaptor behind the cluster. Remove the cluster.

13. Remove the floor console and the under frame.

14. Disconnect and remove the air duct, lap heater duct, side defroster duct and the vertical defroster duct.

15. Remove the glove box.

16. Remove the ashtray and its mount. Disconnect the light wiring before removing.

17. Remove the heater control faceplate.

18. Remove the heater control panel and disconnect its harness.

19. Remove the right side under cover from the instrument panel and remove the under frame.

20. On the left side of the instrument panel, remove the fuse box cover and unbolt the fusebox from the instrument panel.

21. Remove the front pillar (windshield pillar trim) from each pillar.

22. Remove the kick panel trim from each side.

23. Loosen the defroster garnish, disconnect the photo sensor wiring and remove the garnish and defroster grille.

24. Remove the grille for the center air outlet.

25. Remove the bolts holding the steering column bracket to the instrument panel.

26. Remove the center reinforcement bracket.

27. On the left side, remove the retaining nuts holding the instrument panel under frame to the body.

28. On the right side, remove the under frame retaining bolts. Take note that the bolts are different; the flanged bolt must be correctly reinstalled.

29. Remove the remaining nuts and bolts holding the instrument panel. As the instrument panel comes loose, label and disconnect the wiring harnesses. Carefully remove the instrument panel.

30. If equipped with automatic climate control, remove the power control unit on the lower front of the heater unit.

31. Remove the duct joint between the heater unit and evaporator case (with air conditioning) or blower assembly (heater only).

32. Carefully separate the vacuum hose harness at the connector.

33. Remove the heater unit from the vehicle.

34. To remove the heater core, first remove the cover from the water valve. Disconnect the links and remove the vacuum actuator.

35. Remove the clamps and slide the heater core out of the case. Remove the water valve after the core is removed.

36. With the case removed, the heater core may be changed after the water valve is removed. Remove the plastic cover, remove the clamps and hose and remove the water valve.

To install:

37. Thoroughly clean and dry the inside of the case. Install the core and the water valve, using new hose or clamps.

38. Install the vacuum actuator and the connecting link. Put the cover on the water valve.

39. Install the heater unit and tighten the mounting bolts.

40. Carefully attach the vacuum hose connector to the vacuum harness. Make certain the hoses mate firmly and securely.

41. Install the heater cover, then install the center console.

42. Install the duct joint between heater and evaporator or blower.

43. Install the power control unit and carefully connect the links and rods.

44. Install the heater hoses under the hood.

45. Install the instrument panel by reversing its removal procedure.

46. Install the center console.

47. Install the upper and lower steering column covers.

48. Install the center panel under cover.

49. Install the small column panel.

50. Install the steering wheel.

51. Fill the cooling system.

52. Connect the negative battery cable and check the entire climate

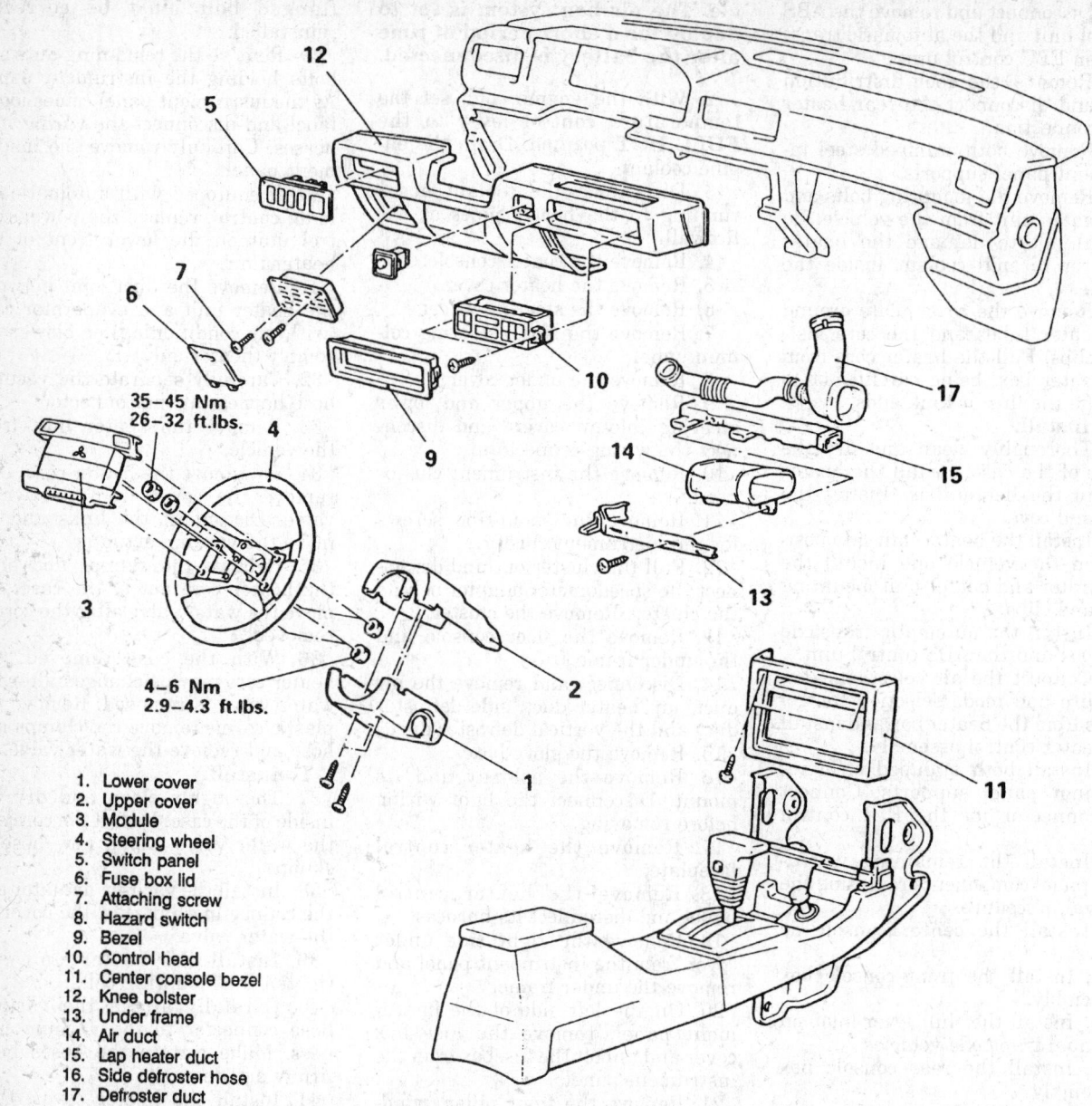

35–45 Nm
26–32 ft.lbs.

4–6 Nm
2.9–4.3 ft.lbs.

1. Lower cover
2. Upper cover
3. Module
4. Steering wheel
5. Switch panel
6. Fuse box lid
7. Attaching screw
8. Hazard switch
9. Bezel
10. Control head
11. Center console bezel
12. Knee bolster
13. Under frame
14. Air duct
15. Lap heater duct
16. Side defroster hose
17. Defroster duct

Instrument panel and related components — Sigma shown

control system for proper operation and leaks.

Mirage

1. Disconnect the negative battery cable.

2. Drain the cooling system and disconnect the heater hoses.

3. Remove the front seats by removing the covers over the anchor bolts, the underseat tray, the seat belt guide ring, the seat mounting nuts and bolts and disconnect the seat belt switch wiring harness from under the seat. Then lift out the seats.

4. Remove the floor console by first taking out the coin holder and the console box tray. Remove the remote control mirror switch or cover. All of these items require only a plastic trim tool to carefully pry them out.

5. Remove the rear half of the console.

6. Remove the shift lever knob on manual transmission vehicles.

7. Remove the front console box assembly.

8. A number of the instrument panel pieces may be retained by pin type fasteners. They may be removed using the following procedure:

a. This type of clip is removed by pressing down on the center pin with a suitable blunt pointed tool. Press down a little more than $1/16$ in. (2mm); this releases the clip. Pull the clip outward to remove it.

b. Do not push the pin inward more than necessary because it may damage the grommet or the pin may fall in if pushed in too far. Once the clips are removed, use a plastic trim stick to pry the piece loose.

9. Remove both lower cowl trim panels (kick panels).

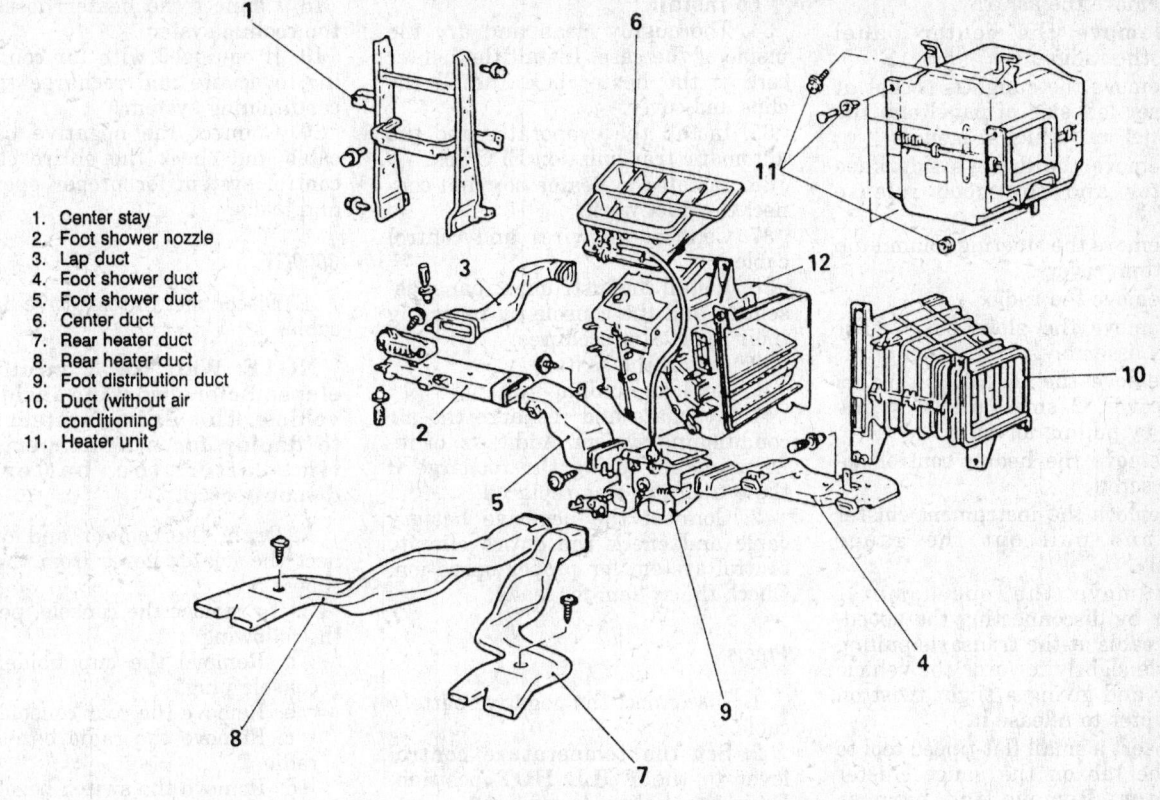

1. Center stay
2. Foot shower nozzle
3. Lap duct
4. Foot shower duct
5. Foot shower duct
6. Center duct
7. Rear heater duct
8. Rear heater duct
9. Foot distribution duct
10. Duct (without air conditioning
11. Heater unit

Heater case and related components — Galant and Sigma

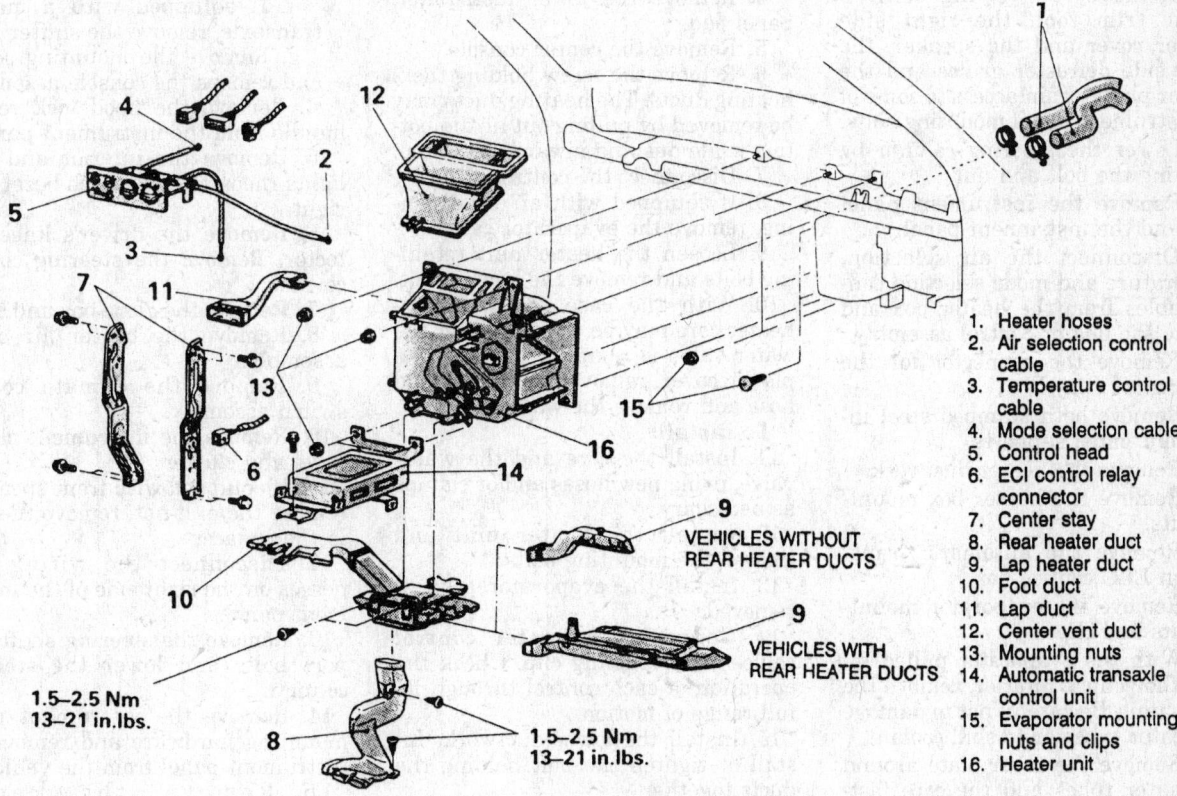

1.5–2.5 Nm
13–21 in.lbs.

VEHICLES WITHOUT
REAR HEATER DUCTS

VEHICLES WITH
REAR HEATER DUCTS

1.5–2.5 Nm
13–21 in.lbs.

1. Heater hoses
2. Air selection control cable
3. Temperature control cable
4. Mode selection cable
5. Control head
6. ECI control relay connector
7. Center stay
8. Rear heater duct
9. Lap heater duct
10. Foot duct
11. Lap duct
12. Center vent duct
13. Mounting nuts
14. Automatic transaxle control unit
15. Evaporator mounting nuts and clips
16. Heater unit

Heater case and related components — Mirage

10. Remove the ashtray.

11. Remove the center panel around the radio.

12. Remove the sunglass pocket at the upper left side of panel and the side panel into which it mounts.

13. Remove the driver's side knee protector and the hood release handle.

14. Remove the steering column top and bottom covers.

15. Remove the radio.

16. Remove the glove box striker and box assembly.

17. Remove the instrument panel lower cover, 2 small pieces in the center, by pulling forward.

18. Remove the heater control assembly screw.

19. Remove the instrument cluster bezel and pull out the gauge assembly.

20. Remove the speedometer adapter by disconnecting the speedometer cable at the transaxle pulling the cable sightly towards the vehicle interior and giving a slight twist on the adapter to release it.

21. Insert a small flat-tipped tool to open the tab on the gauge cluster connector. Remove the harness connectors.

22. Remove, by prying with a plastic trim tool, the right side speaker cover and the speaker, the upper side defroster grilles and the clock or plug to gain access to some of the instrument panel mounting bolts.

23. Lower the steering column by removing the bolt and nut.

24. Remove the instrument panel bolts and the instrument panel.

25. Disconnect the air selection, temperature and mode selection control cables from the heater box and remove the heater control assembly.

26. Remove the connector for the ECI control relay.

27. Remove both stamped steel instrument panel supports.

28. Remove the heater ductwork.

29. Remove the heater box mounting nuts.

30. Remove the automatic transmission ELC control box.

31. Remove the evaporator mounting nuts and clips.

32. With the evaporator pulled toward the vehicle interior, remove the heater unit. Be careful not to damage the heater tubes or to spill coolant.

33. Remove the cover plate around the heater tubes and the core fastener clips. Pull the heater core from the heater box, being careful not to damage the fins or tank ends.

To install:

34. Thoroughly clean and dry the inside of the case. Install the heater core to the heater box. Install the clips and cover.

35. Install the evaporator and the automatic transmission ELC box.

36. Install the heater box and connect the duct work.

37. Connect all wires and control cables.

38. Install the instrument panel assembly and the console by reversing their removal procedures.

39. Install the seats.

40. Refill the cooling system.

41. Evaporate and recharge the air conditioning system. Add 2 oz. of refrigerant oil during the recharge if the evaporator was replaced.

42. Connect the negative battery cable and check the entire climate control system for proper operation. Check the system for leaks.

Precis

1. Disconnect the negative battery cable.

2. Set the temperature control lever to the **FULL HOT** position. Drain the cooling system.

3. Disconnect the heater hoses.

4. Remove the lower instrument panel pad.

5. Remove the center console.

6. Remove the screw holding the 2 heating ducts. The heating ducts may be removed by pulling out at the bottom while pushing inward at the top.

7. Disconnect the control cables.

8. If equipped with air conditioning, remove the evaporator case.

9. Loosen the heater unit retaining bolts and remove the heater unit.

10. With the case removed, the heater core may be changed after the water valve is removed. Remove the plastic cover, remove the clamps and hose and remove the water valve.

To install:

11. Install the core and the water valve, using new hoses and/or clamps as necessary.

12. Install the heater unit and tighten the mounting bolts.

13. Install the evaporator case, if removed.

14. Connect the heater control cables and retaining clip. Check the operation of each control through its full range of motion.

15. Install the lower ductwork. Install or tighten the bolt holding the ducts together.

16. Install the center console.

17. Install the lower instrument panel pad.

18. Connect the heater hoses. Fill the cooling system.

19. If equipped with air conditioning, evacuate and recharge the air conditioning system.

20. Connect the negative battery cable and check the entire climate control system for proper operation and leaks.

3000GT

1. Disconnect the negative battery cable.

NOTE: Wait for 1 minute to elapse before working inside the vehicle. The air bag system is set to deploy for a short period of time after the battery is disconnected.

2. Drain the coolant and disconnect the heater hoses from the core tubes.

3. To remove the console, perform the following:

a. Remove the cup holder and console plug.

b. Remove the rear console.

c. Remove the radio bezels and radio.

d. Remove the switch bezel.

e. Remove the side covers and front console garnish.

f. If equipped with a manual transaxle, remove the shifter knob.

g. Remove the mounting screws and remove the console assembly.

4. Remove the hood lock release handle from the instrument panel.

5. Remove the interior and dash lights rheostat and switch bezel to its right.

6. Remove the driver's knee protector. Remove the steering column covers.

7. Remove the glove box and cover.

8. Remove the center air outlet assembly.

9. Remove the climate control switch assembly.

10. Remove the instrument cluster bezel and cluster.

11. If equipped with front speakers, remove them. If not, remove the plug in their place.

12. Disconnect the wiring harnesses on the right side of the instrument panel.

13. Remove the steering shaft support bolts and lower the steering column.

14. Remove the instrument panel mounting hardware and remove the instrument panel from the vehicle.

15. Remove the center reinforcement.

16. Remove the foot warmer ducts and lap duct.

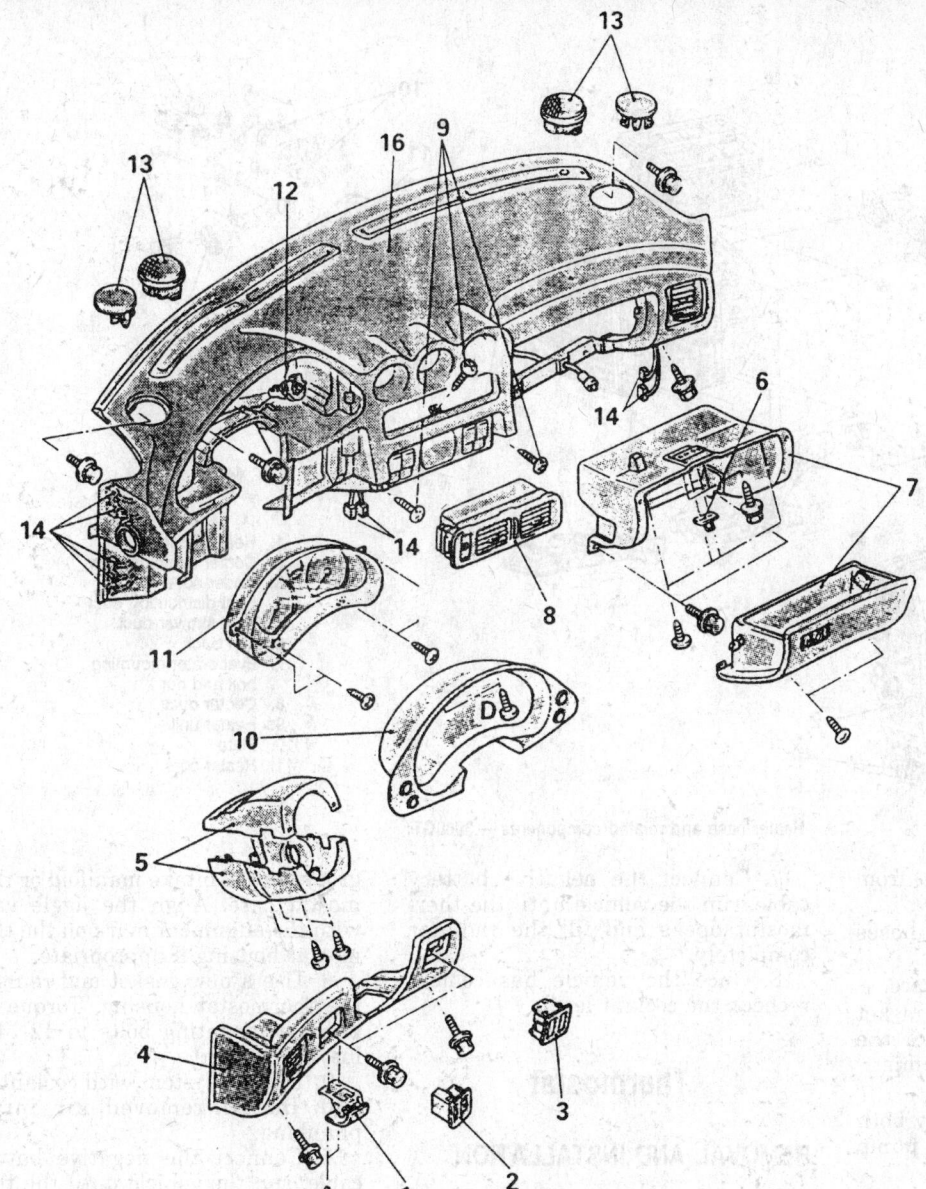

1. Hood lock release handle
2. Rheostat
3. Switch garnish
4. Knee protector
5. Column cover
6. Glove box striker
7. Glove box assembly
8. Center air outlet
9. Screws
10. Cluster bezel
11. Instrument cluster
12. Speedometer cable adaptor
13. Speaker or plug
14. Wiring harnesses
15. Bolts
16. Instrument panel

Instrument panel and related components — 3000GT

17. If equipped with air conditioning, remove the evaporator case mounting bolt and nut to allow clearance for heater unit removal.

18. Remove the center duct above the heater unit.

19. Remove the heater unit and disassemble on a workbench. Remove the heater core from the heater case.

To install:

20. Thoroughly clean and dry the inside of the case and install the heater core and all related parts.

21. Install the heater unit to the vehicle and install the mounting screws.

22. Install the center duct above the unit.

23. Secure the evaporator case with the bolt and nut.

24. Install the lap duct and foot warmer ducts.

25. Install the center reinforcement.

26. Install the instrument panel by reversing its removal procedure.

27. Install the hood lock release cable handle.

28. Install the console.

29. Fill the cooling system.

30. Connect the negative battery cable and check the entire climate control system for proper operation and leaks.

Water Pump

REMOVAL AND INSTALLATION

1. Disconnect the negative battery cable.

2. Drain the cooling system.

3. Remove the engine undercover.

4. Disconnect the clamp bolt from the power steering hose.

5. Support the engine with the appropriate equipment and remove the engine mount bracket.

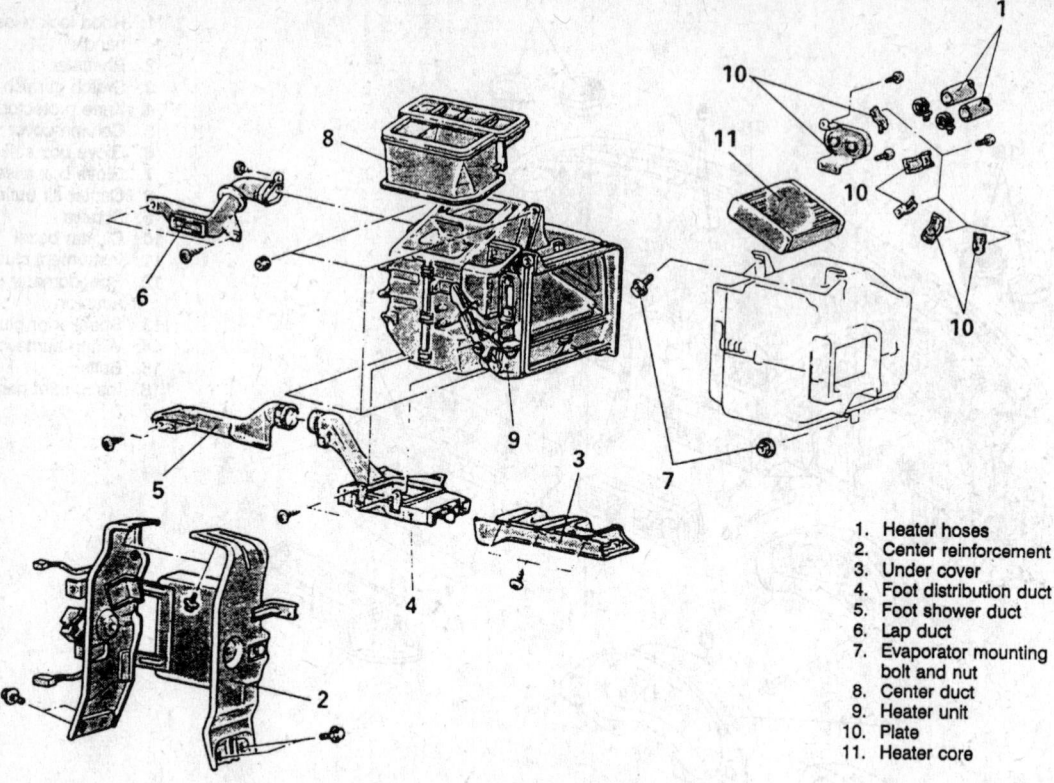

1. Heater hoses
2. Center reinforcement
3. Under cover
4. Foot distribution duct
5. Foot shower duct
6. Lap duct
7. Evaporator mounting bolt and nut
8. Center duct
9. Heater unit
10. Plate
11. Heater core

Heater case and related components — 3000GT

6. Remove the timing belt(s) from the front of the engine.

7. Disconnect the coolant hoses from the pump, if equipped.

8. Remove the alternator brace.

9. Remove the water pump, gasket if equipped, and O-ring where the water inlet pipe(s) joins the pump.

To install:

10. Thoroughly clean and dry both gasket surfaces of the water pump and block.

11. Install a new O-ring into the groove on the front end of the water inlet pipe. Do not apply oils or grease to the O-ring. Wet with water only.

12. Install the gasket and pump assembly and tighten the bolts. If the water pump does not use a gasket, apply a small bead of sealer around the pump body; be sure to go around all bolt holes. Note the marks on the bolt heads. Those marked **4** should be torqued to 9-11 ft. lbs. Those bolts marked **7** should be torqued from 14-20 ft. lbs.

13. Connect the hoses to the pump.

14. Reinstall the timing belt and related parts.

15. Install the engine undercover.

16. Fill the system with coolant.

17. Connect the negative battery cable, run the vehicle until the thermostat opens and fill the radiator completely.

18. Once the vehicle has cooled, recheck the coolant level.

Thermostat

REMOVAL AND INSTALLATION

1. Disconnect the negative battery cable.

2. Drain the cooling system.

3. Remove necessary air intake plumbing.

4. Disconnect the upper radiator hose and overflow hose from the thermostat housing.

5. Remove the thermostat housing cover and gasket if equipped.

6. Remove the thermostat, taking note of its original positioning in the housing or intake manifold. Some have an alignment mark that should align with the thermostat's jiggle valve.

To install:

7. Install the thermostat so its flange seats tightly in the machined groove in the intake manifold or thermostat case. Align the jiggle valve with the alignment mark on the thermostat housing if appropriate.

8. Use a new gasket and reinstall the thermostat housing. Torque the housing mounting bolts to 12-14 ft. lbs. (17-20 Nm).

9. Fill the system with coolant.

10. Install removed air intake plumbing.

11. Connect the negative battery cable, run the vehicle until the thermostat opens and fill the radiator completely.

12. Once the vehicle has cooled, recheck the coolant level.

Cooling System Bleeding

All vehicles are equipped with a self-bleeding thermostat. Slowly fill the cooling system in the conventional manner; air will vent through the jiggle valve in the thermostat. Run the vehicle until the thermostat has opened and continue filling the radiator. Recheck the coolant level after the vehicle has cooled.

ENGINE ELECTRICAL

NOTE: Disconnecting the negative battery cable on some vehicles may interfere with the functions of the on-board computer systems and may require the computer to undergo a relearning process, once the negative battery cable is reconnected.

Distributor

REMOVAL

1. Disconnect the negative battery cable. Remove the ignition wire cover, if equipped.
2. Disconnect the distributor harness electrical connectors.
3. Unscrew the distributor cap hold-down screws or release the clips, and lift off the distributor cap with all ignition wires still connected. Remove the coil wire, if necessary.
4. Matchmark the rotor to the distributor housing and the distributor housing to the engine.

NOTE: Do not crank the engine during this procedure. If the engine is cranked, the matchmark must be disregarded.

5. Remove the hold-down nut.
6. Carefully remove the distributor from the engine.

INSTALLATION

NOTE: Some engines may be sensitive to the routing of the distributor sensor wires. If routed near the high-voltage coil wire or the spark plug wires, the electromagnetic field surrounding the high voltage wires could generate an occasional disruption of the ignition system operation.

Timing Not Disturbed

1. Install a new distributor housing O-ring and lubricate with clean oil.
2. Install the distributor in the engine so the rotor is aligned with the matchmark on the housing and the housing is aligned with the matchmark on the engine. Make sure the distributor is fully seated and the distributor shaft is fully engaged.
3. Install the hold-down nut.

4. Connect the distributor harness connectors.
5. Make sure the sealing O-ring is in place, install the distributor cap and tighten the screws or secure the clips.
6. Connect the negative battery cable.
7. Adjust the ignition timing and tighten the hold-down nut.

Timing Disturbed

1. Install a new distributor housing O-ring and lubricate with clean oil.
2. Position the engine so the No. 1 piston is at TDC of its compression stroke and the mark on the vibration damper is aligned with **0** on the timing indicator.
3. Align the distributor housing and gear mating marks. Install the distributor in engine so the slot or groove of the distributor's installation flange aligns with the distributor installation stud in the engine block. Make sure the distributor is fully seated. Inspect alignment of the distributor rotor making sure the rotor is aligned with the position of the No. 1 ignition wire in the distributor cap.

NOTE: Make sure the rotor is pointing where No. 1 runner originates inside the cap, if equipped, and not where the No. 1 ignition wire plugs into the cap.

4. Install the hold-down nut.
5. Connect the distributor harness connectors.
6. Make sure the sealing O-ring is in place, install the distributor cap and tighten the screws or secure the clips.
7. Connect the negative battery cable.
8. Adjust the ignition timing and tighten the hold-down bolt.

Distributorless Ignition System

REMOVAL AND INSTALLATION

Crank Angle Sensor

1. Disconnect the negative battery cable.
2. Disconnect the sensor harness connector.
3. Unscrew the cap hold-down screws and lift off the cap.

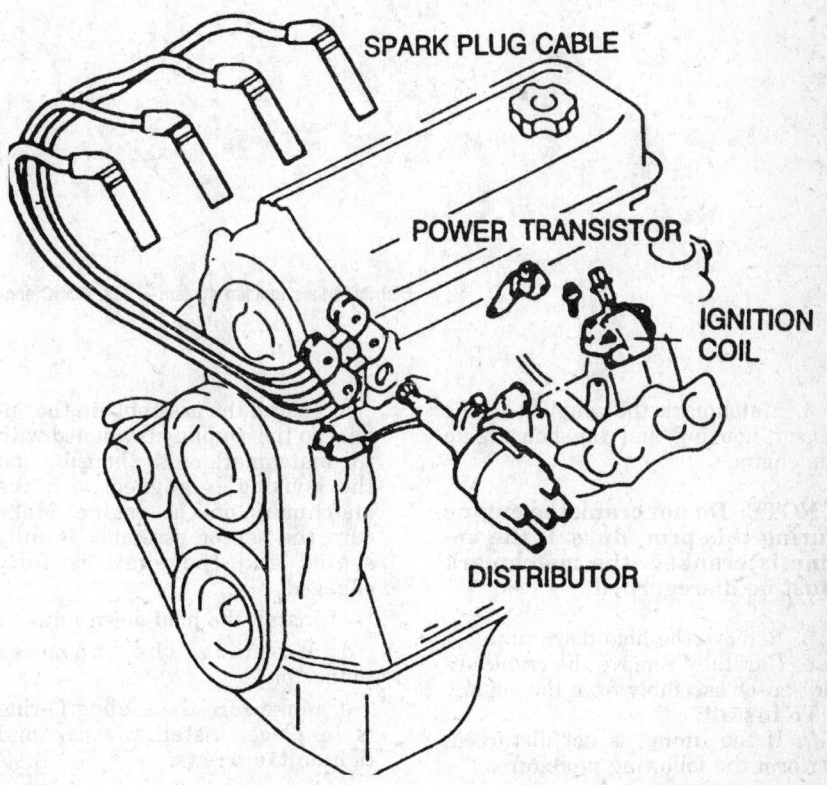

Ignition system — SOHC 4 cylinder engines, except 1991-94 1.5L (Mirage) and 1.8L (Expo LRV) engines

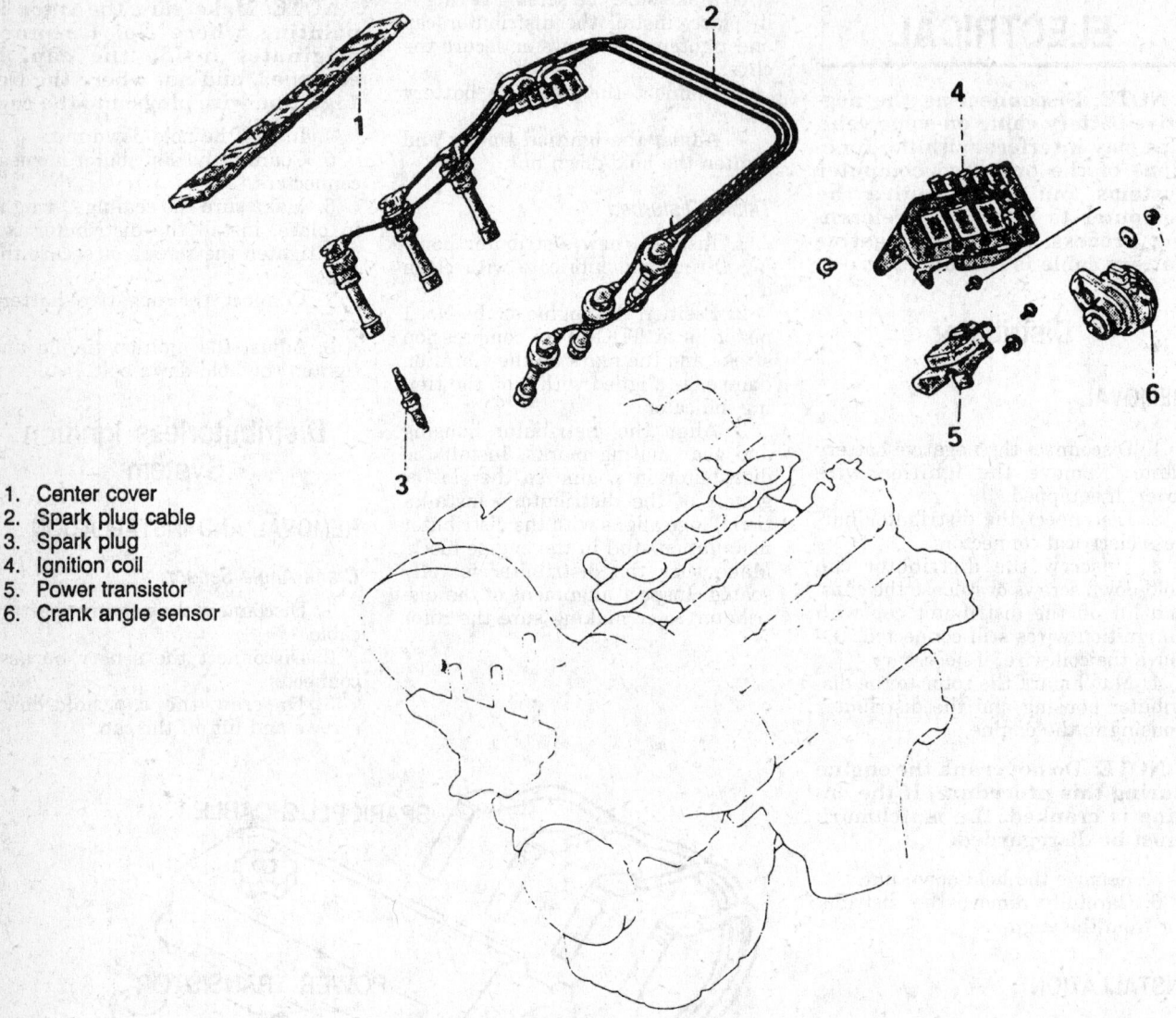

1. Center cover
2. Spark plug cable
3. Spark plug
4. Ignition coil
5. Power transistor
6. Crank angle sensor

Distributorless ignition system — 3.0L DOHC engine

4. Matchmark the coupling to the sensor housing and the housing to the engine.

NOTE: Do not crank the engine during this procedure. If the engine is cranked, the matchmark must be disregarded.

5. Remove the hold-down nut.
6. Carefully remove the crank angle sensor assembly from the engine.
To install:
7. If the timing is not disturbed, perform the following procedures:
    a. Install a new housing O-ring and lubricate with clean oil.

    b. Install the assembly in the engine so the coupling is aligned with the matchmark on the housing and the housing is aligned with the matchmark on the engine. Make sure the sensor assembly is fully seated and the shaft is fully engaged.

    c. Install the hold-down nut.

    d. Connect the harness connector.

    e. Make sure the sealing O-ring is in place, install the cap and tighten the screws.

    f. Connect the negative battery cable.

    g. Adjust the ignition timing, if applicable, and tighten the hold-down nut.

8. If the timing is disturbed, perform the following procedures:
    a. Install a new housing O-ring and lubricate with clean oil.

    b. Position the engine so the No. 1 piston is at TDC of its compression stroke and the mark on the vibration damper is aligned with **0** on the timing indicator.

    c. Install the sensor in the engine so the factory matchmark on the coupling (notch) is aligned with the matchmark on the housing (punch mark) and the housing is

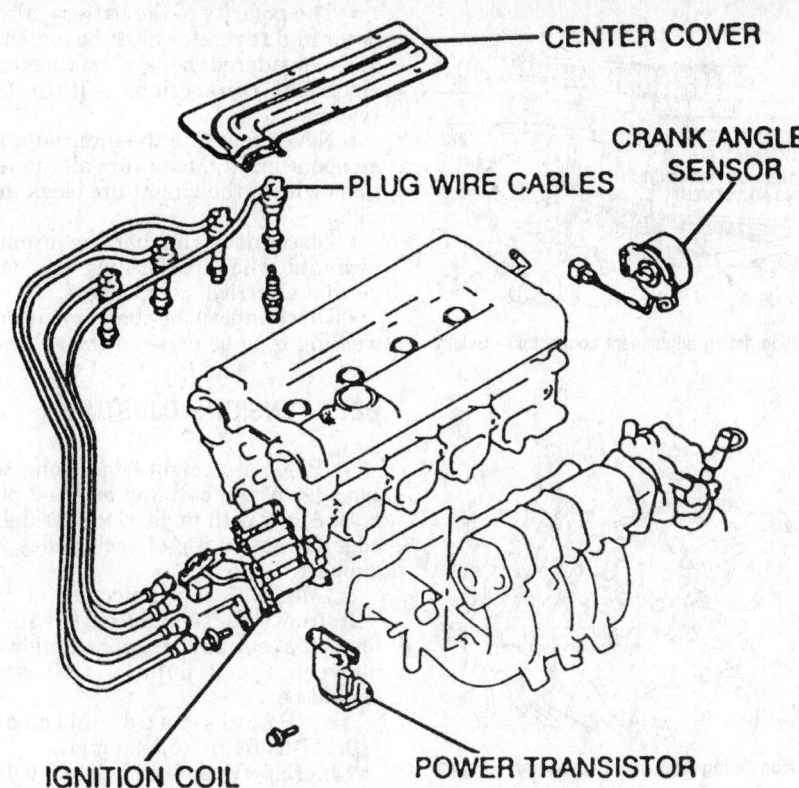

Distributorless ignition system — 1.6L and 2.0L DOHC engines

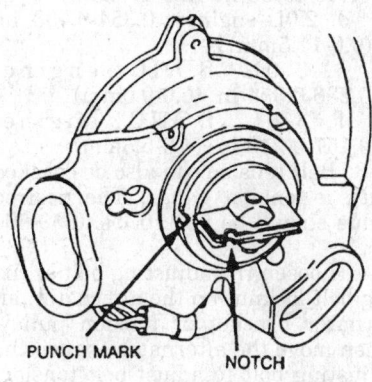

Crank angle sensor alignment marks

aligned with the matchmark on the engine. Make sure the sensor assembly is fully seated and the shaft is fully engaged.

d. Install the hold-down nut.

e. Connect the harness connector.

f. Make sure the sealing O-ring is in place, install the cap and tighten the screws.

g. Connect the negative battery cable.

h. Adjust the ignition timing, if applicable, and tighten the hold-down nut.

Ignition Coil

1. Disconnect the negative battery cable.

2. Tag and remove the spark plug wires from the ignition coil by gripping the boot and not the cable.

3. Remove the mounting screws and coil from engine.

4. Installation is the reverse of the removal procedure.

Power Transistor

1. Disconnect the negative battery cable.

2. Tag and disconnect the wires from the power transistor.

3. Remove the retaining screw and lift the power transistor from the engine.

4. Installation is the reverse of the removal procedure.

Ignition Timing

ADJUSTMENT

1. Set the parking brake, start and run the engine until normal operating temperature is obtained. Keep all lights and accessories OFF and the front wheels straight-ahead. Place the transaxle in **P** for automatic transaxle or Neutral for manual transaxle.

2. If not at specification, set the idle speed to the correct level.

3. Turn the engine **OFF**. Remove the water-proof cover from the ignition timing adjusting connector, and connect a jumper wire from this terminal to a good ground. This connector is located:

Precis: near the positive battery terminal.

Mirage: near the center of the firewall.

Galant: near of the center of the firewall.

Sigma: near the ignition coil on the left side of the engine compartment.

Eclipse: on the firewall just behind the battery.

Expo/Expo LRV: on the firewall near the left strut tower.

3000GT: on the firewall just behind the battery.

Diamante: slightly left of center on the firewall.

4. Connect a conventional power timing light to the No. 1 cylinder spark plug wire. Start the engine and run at idle.

5. Aim the timing light at the timing scale located near the crankshaft pulley.

6. Loosen the distributor or crank angle sensor hold-down nut just enough so the housing can be rotated.

7. Turn the housing in the proper direction until the specified timing is reached. Tighten the hold-down nut and recheck the timing. Turn the engine **OFF**.

8. Remove the jumper wire from the ignition timing adjusting terminal and install the water-proof cover.

9. Start the engine and check the actual timing (the timing without the terminal grounded). This reading should be approximately 5 degrees more than the basic timing. Actual timing may increase according to altitude. Also, actual timing may fluctuate because of slight variation accomplished by the ECU. As long as the basic timing is correct, the engine is timed correctly.

10. Turn the engine **OFF**. Disconnect the timing apparatus and tachometer.

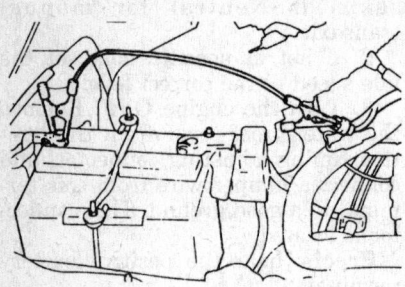

Ignition timing adjustment connector — Precis

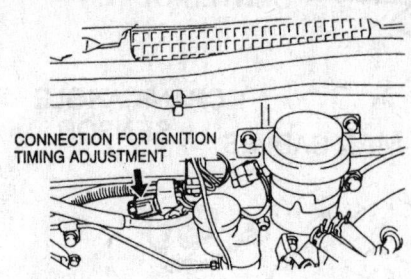

Ignition timing adjustment connector — Galant

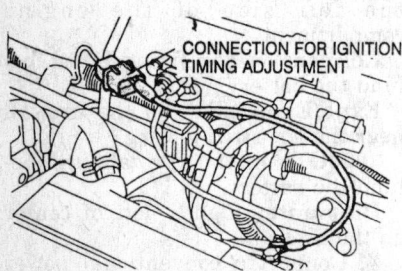

Ignition timing adjustment connector — Mirage with 1.5L engine

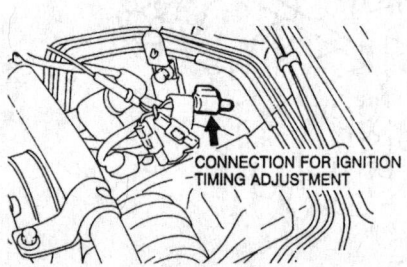

Ignition timing adjustment connector — Sigma

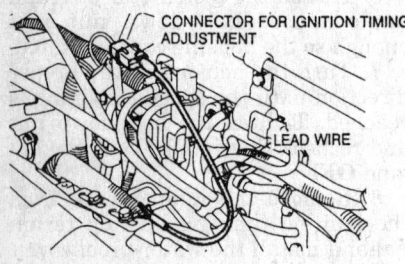

Ignition timing adjustment connector — Mirage with 1.6L engine

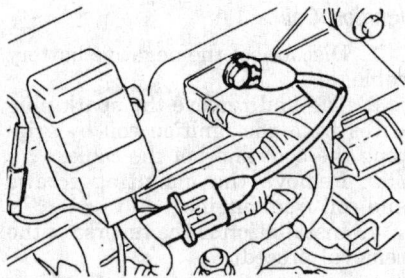

Ignition timing adjustment connector — Eclipse

Alternator

PRECAUTIONS

• If the battery is removed for any reason, make sure it is reconnected with the correct polarity. Reversing the battery connections may result in damage to the 1-way rectifiers.

• When utilizing a booster battery as a starting aid, always connect the positive to positive terminals and the negative terminal from the booster battery to a good engine ground on the vehicle being started.

• Never use a fast charger as a booster to start vehicles.

• Disconnect the battery cables when charging the battery with a fast charger.

• Never attempt to polarize the alternator.

• Do not use test lamps of more than 12 volts when checking diode continuity.

• Do not short across or ground any of the alternator terminals.

• The polarity of the battery, alternator and regulator must be matched and considered before making any electrical connections within the system.

• Never separate the alternator on an open circuit. Make sure all connections within the circuit are clean and tight.

• Disconnect the battery ground terminal when performing any service on electrical components.

• Disconnect the battery if arc welding is to be done on the vehicle.

BELT TENSION ADJUSTMENT

1. Place a straight-edge along the top edge of the belt and across 2 pulleys. Allow both ends of the straight-edge to rest on top of each pulley for support.

2. Measure the deflection of the belt from the straight-edge with a force of about 22 lbs. applied midway between the 2 pulleys. Deflection should be:

   a. Precis and Mirage: 0.217-0.354 in. (5.5-9.0mm)

   b. Expo/Expo LRV: 0.340-0.470 in.(8.5 — 12 mm).

   c. Eclipse with 1.8L engine: 0.315-0.433 in. (8.0-11.0mm)

   d. 2.0L engines: 0.354-0.453 in. (9.0-11.5mm)

   e. 3.0L SOHC engine: 0.236-0.354 in. (6.0-9.0mm)

   f. 3.0L DOHC engine: 0.157-0.216 in. (4.0-5.5mm)

3. Belt tension can also be checked with a tension gauge. The desired value should be 55-110 lbs. (250-500 N).

4. Loosen the adjusting bolt or fixing bolt locknut on the alternator, alternator bracket or tension pulley. Then move the alternator or turn the adjusting bolt to adjust belt tension. Secure the bolt or locknut when finished.

REMOVAL AND INSTALLATION

1.5L and 2.4L Engines

1. Disconnect the negative battery cable.

2. On Mirage, remove the left side cover panel under the vehicle.

3. Remove the drive belts.

4. Remove both water pump pulleys.

5. Remove the alternator upper bracket/brace.

6. Disconnect the alternator electrical connectors and remove alternator.

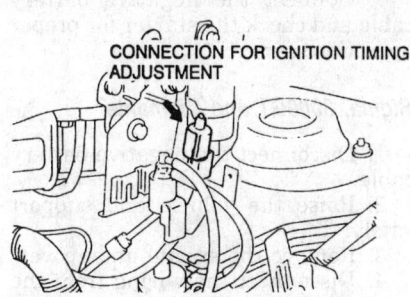

Ignition timing adjustment connector — Expo/Expo LRV

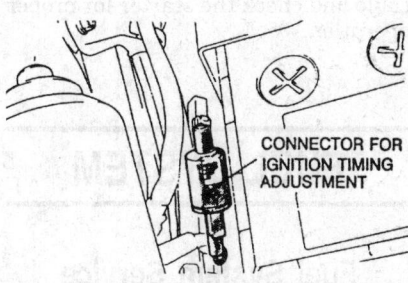

Ignition timing adjustment connector — 3000GT

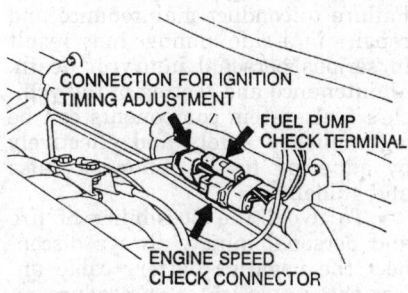

Ignition timing adjustment connector — Diamante

To install:
7. Position the alternator on the lower mounting fixture and install the lower mounting bolt and nut. Tighten nut just enough to allow for movement of the alternator.
8. Install the alternator upper bracket/brace and connect the alternator electrical harness.
9. Install the water pump pulleys.
10. Install the drive belts and adjust to the proper tension.
11. Install the left side cover panel under the vehicle as required.

12. Connect the negative battery cable and check for proper operation.

1.6L Engine

1. Disconnect the negative battery cable.
2. Remove the left side cover panel under the vehicle.
3. Remove the alternator and power steering drive belts and both water pump pulleys.
4. Remove the alternator adjuster brace.
5. Disconnect the alternator electrical connection.
6. Remove the battery, windshield washer tank and battery tray.
7. Remove the attaching bolts at the top of the radiator and lift up the radiator. Do not disconnect the radiator hoses.
8. Remove the alternator from the vehicle.
To install:
9. While lifting the radiator, position the alternator on the engine mounting fixture. Lower the radiator and reinstall the upper attaching bolts.
10. Install the lower mounting bolt and nut. Tighten nut just enough to allow movement of the alternator.
11. Install the battery, windshield washer tank and battery tray.
12. Connect the alternator electrical connections.
13. Install the alternator adjuster brace.
14. Install both water pump pulleys and tighten mounting bolts to 6-7 ft. lbs. (8-10 Nm).
15. Install the alternator and power steering drive belts and adjust to the proper tension.
16. Install the left side cover panel under the vehicle.
17. Connect the negative battery cable and check for proper operation.

1.8L Engine (Expo LRV)

1. Disconnect negative battery cable.
2. Remove the accessory drive belts.
3. Disconnect the electrical harness from the alternator.
4. Remove the alternator mounting nut, bolt and upper brace assembly from the vehicle.
To install:
5. Install the alternator and secure using mounting nuts. Make sure the upper brace assembly is in place.
6. Install and adjust drive belts to the proper tension. Secure all mounting hardware.
7. Reconnect the negative battery cable and check system operation.

1.8L and 2.0L Engines(Eclipse and Galant)

1. Disconnect the negative battery cable. Remove the left side undercover from the vehicle.
2. If equipped with air conditioning, remove the condenser electric fan motor and shroud assembly.
3. Remove alternator, water pump and air conditioner compressor drive belts.
4. Remove both water pump pulleys and the alternator top brace.
5. Disconnect the alternator wiring and remove the alternator from the vehicle.
6. The installation is the reverse of the removal procedure.

3.0L SOHC Engine

1. Disconnect the negative battery cable. Remove the air cleaner assembly.
2. Loosen the tensioner pulley and remove the alternator drive belt.
3. Remove the accelerator cable from the intake plenum extension.
4. Remove the brake booster vacuum hose.
5. If equipped with an EGR valve, remove it.
6. Disconnect the alternator connectors and remove the mounting bolts. Remove the alternator from behind the surge tank at the center of the vehicle.
To install:
7. Position the alternator on the lower mounting fixture and install bolts. Tighten the lower mounting bolt to 14-18 ft. lbs. (20-25 Nm) and the upper bolt to 8-11 ft. lbs. (12-15 Nm).
8. Connect the alternator electrical connectors to the alternator.
9. Install the EGR valve, if removed. Connect the vacuum hose connection at the brake booster.
10. Install the accelerator cable to the intake plenum extension. Check the accelerator cable adjustment as follows:
   a. Turn the ignition key **ON** but do not start the engine. With the ignition left in this condition wait 15 seconds.
   b. Check to ensure that the throttle lever is in contact with the fixed Speed Adjusting Screw (SAS).
   c. Check that the inner cable play is within specifications. For manual transaxle, the desired value is 0.04-0.08 in. (1-2mm). If equipped with automatic transaxle, the desired value is 0.12-0.20 in. (3-5mm).

d. If not within the desired value, loosen the adjusting bolts and slide plate so play at the inner cable will fall within the desired value. Retighten the adjusting bolts.

11. Reinstall the drive belt and adjust the tensioner until the proper belt tension is achieved.

12. Install the air cleaner and connect the negative battery cable. Check the charging system for proper operation.

3.0L DOHC Engine

1. Disconnect the negative battery cable. Remove the surge tank.

2. Remove the necessary air delivery hoses to gain access to the alternator.

3. If equipped with air conditioning, remove the clamp nut, raise the suction hose and suspend it from the engine hood.

4. Loosen the tensioner pulley and remove the alternator drive belt.

5. Disconnect the oxygen sensor connector.

6. Disconnect the alternator wiring, remove the alternator bracket mounting bolts and remove the bracket and alternator as an assembly. Separate on a workbench.

SOHC ENGINE

A. Crankshaft pulley
B. Power steering pump pulley
C. Tensioner pulley
D. Alternator pulley
E. Idler pulley
F. Air conditioner compressor pulley

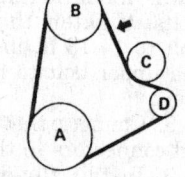

DOHC ENGINE WITHOUT AIR CONDITIONING

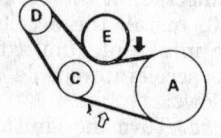

DOHC ENGINE WITH AIR CONDITIONING

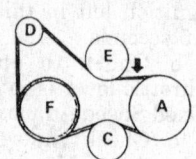

Serpentine belt arrangement — 3.0L engines

To install:

7. Install the alternator onto the bracket and install bracket assembly to the engine.

8. Connect the oxygen sensor connector.

9. Install the drive belt and adjust to proper tension using the tensioner pulley.

10. Install air conditioning suction hose to its original position and secure using clamp nut.

11. Install the air delivery hose(s) and the surge tank.

12. Reconnect the negative battery cable and check the charging system for proper operation.

Starter

REMOVAL AND INSTALLATION

Precis, Mirage and Expo/Expo LRV

1. Disconnect the negative battery cable.

2. Disconnect the air-flow sensor assembly connector and remove the breather hose. Remove the resonator retaining nuts and remove the air intake hose and resonator assembly as required.

NOTE: Use care when removing the air cleaner cover because the air-flow sensor is attached and is a sensitive component.

3. Remove the heat shield from beneath the intake manifold on the 1.5L engine.

4. Disconnect the starter motor electrical connections.

5. Remove the starter motor mounting bolts and remove the starter.

6. The installation is the reverse of the removal procedure.

7. Connect the negative battery cable and check the starter for proper operation.

Eclipse and Galant

1. Remove the battery and battery tray from the engine compartment.

2. Disconnect the speedometer cable connector at the transaxle end.

3. If equipped with 1.8L engine, remove the bracket on the lower side if the intake manifold.

4. Disconnect the starter motor electrical connections.

5. Remove the starter motor mounting bolts and remove the starter.

6. The installation is the reverse of the removal procedure.

7. Connect the negative battery cable and check the starter for proper operation.

Sigma, 3000GT and Diamante

1. Disconnect the negative battery cable.

2. Raise the vehicle and support safely.

3. Remove the engine undercover.

4. Disconnect the wiring from the starter.

5. Remove the mounting bolts and starter from the vehicle.

6. The installation is the reverse of the removal procedure.

7. Connect the negative battery cable and check the starter for proper operation.

FUEL SYSTEM

Fuel System Service Precaution

Safety is the most important factor when performing fuel system service. Failure to conduct maintenance and repairs in a safe manner may result in serious personal injury or death. Maintenance and testing of the vehicle's fuel system components can be accomplished safely and effectively by adhering to the following rules and guidelines.

• To avoid the possibility of fire and personal injury, always disconnect the negative battery cable unless the repair or test procedure requires that battery voltage be applied.

• Always relieve the fuel system pressure prior to disconnecting any fuel system component (injector, fuel rail, pressure regulator, etc.), fitting or fuel line connection. Exercise extreme caution whenever relieving fuel system pressure to avoid exposing skin, face and eyes to fuel spray. Please be advised that fuel under pressure may penetrate the skin or any part of the body that it contacts.

• Always place a shop towel or cloth around the fitting or connection prior to loosening to absorb any excess fuel due to spillage. Ensure that all fuel spillage (should it occur) is quickly removed from engine surfaces. Ensure that all fuel soaked cloths or towels are deposited into a suitable waste container.

- Always keep a dry chemical (Class B) fire extinguisher near the work area.
- Do not allow fuel spray or fuel vapors to come into contact with a spark or open flame.
- Always use a backup wrench when loosening and tightening fuel line connection fittings. This will prevent unnecessary stress and torsion to fuel line piping. Always follow the proper torque specifications.
- Always replace worn fuel fitting O-rings with new. Do not substitute fuel hose or equivalent, where fuel pipe is installed.

RELIEVING FUEL SYSTEM PRESSURE

Fuel Injected Engines

1. Loosen the fuel filler cap to release fuel tank pressure.
2. Disconnect the fuel pump harness connector:

Diamante: the connector is located at the rear of the fuel tank.
Eclipse: the connector is located at the rear of the fuel tank.
Expo/Expo LRV: remove the rubber grommet on the underside of the floor panel, in front of the fuel tank, to gain access to the connector.
Galant: the connector is located at the rear of the fuel tank.
Mirage: remove the rear seat cushion to gain access to the connector.
Precis: the connector is located in front of the fuel tank.
Sigma: the connector is located at the rear of the fuel tank.
3000GT: remove the fuel system access cover in the luggage compartment to gain access to the connector.

3. Start the vehicle and allow it to run until it stalls from lack of fuel. Turn the key to the **OFF** position.
4. Disconnect the negative battery cable, then reconnect the fuel pump connector and reinstall the fuel filler cap.
5. Wrap shop towels around the fitting that is being disconnected to absorb residual fuel in the lines.

Fuel Tank

REMOVAL AND INSTALLATION

1. Relieve fuel system pressure.
2. Disconnect the negative battery cable.
3. Raise the vehicle and support safely.

4. Drain the fuel from the fuel tank into an approved container.
5. Remove AWD and 4WS components as required in order to gain access to the fuel tank.
6. Disconnect the return hose, high pressure hose and all other hoses and connectors connected to the pump/sending unit.

— **CAUTION** —
Cover all fuel hose connections with a shop towel, prior to disconnecting, to prevent splash of fuel that could be caused by residual pressure remaining in the fuel line.

7. Disconnect the filler and vent hoses. Place a support under the tank and remove the retaining nuts.
8. Lower the tank from the vehicle.
To install:
9. Install the fuel tank and connect the filler and vent hoses. Tighten the tank retaining nuts to 17-22 ft. lbs. (24-31 Nm).
10. Connect the return hose, high pressure hose and all other hoses and connectors connected to the pump/sending unit.
11. Install removed AWD and 4WS components.
12. Lower the vehicle and return fuel to the gas tank.
13. Connect the negative battery cable and check the entire system for proper operation and leaks.

Fuel Filter

REMOVAL AND INSTALLATION

— **CAUTION** —
Do not use conventional fuel filters, hoses or clamps when servicing fuel injection systems. They are not compatible with the injection system and could fail, causing personal injury or damage to the vehicle. Use only hoses and clamps specifically designed for fuel injection.

1. First relieve the fuel pressure. Disconnect the negative battery cable.
2. The filter is located in the engine compartment, mounted either on the firewall or inner fender panel. On 3000GT, remove the battery and battery tray with washer tank.
3. If necessary, remove the air cleaner assembly with intake hoses. On Galant, remove the compressor for the electronically controlled suspension, if equipped.

4. Hold the fuel filter nut securely with a backup or spanner wrench. Cover the hoses with shop towels and remove the eye bolt. Discard the gaskets.
5. If the high pressure hose connection is accomplished with another eye bolt connection; first separate the flare nut connection at the line, then repeat Step 5. Otherwise, separate the flare nut connection at the filter. Discard the gaskets.
6. Remove the mounting bolts and remove the fuel filter from the vehicle.
To install:
7. If equipped with flare fitting, install a new O-ring and tighten the fitting by hand before installing the filter to the vehicle.
8. Install the filter to its bracket only finger-tight. Movement of the filter will ease attachment of the fuel lines.
9. Install new O-rings and connect the high pressure hose and eye bolt, then the main pipe and eye bolt. While holding the fuel filter nut, tighten the eye bolts to 22 ft. lbs. (30 Nm). Tighten the flare nut to 25 ft. lbs. (35 Nm).
10. Tighten the mounting bolts fully.
11. Install the air cleaner assembly, battery and battery tray with washer tank, if removed. Install the suspension compressor on Galant.
12. Connect the negative battery cable, install the fuel filler cap, turn the key to the **ON** position to pressurize the fuel system and check for leaks. Release the fuel pressure and repair leaks as required.

Electric Fuel Pump

PRESSURE TESTING

1. Relieve fuel system pressure. Disconnect the battery negative cable.
2. Disconnect the fuel high pressure hose at the delivery pipe side.
3. Connect a fuel pressure gauge to tools MD998709 and MD998742 or exact equivalent, with appropriate adaptors, seals and/or gaskets to prevent leaks during the test. Install the gauge and adapter between the delivery pipe and high pressure hose. Install carefully to prevent leaks.
4. Connect the negative battery cable.
5. Apply battery voltage to the terminal for fuel pump activation located in the engine compartment to

1. Fuel tank cap
2. Drain plug
3. Return hose
4. Vapor hose
5. Sending unit connector
6. Fuel pump connector
7. High pressure hose
8. Filler tube
9. Vapor hose
10. Nut
11. Tank band bracket
12. Tank band

13. Fuel tank
14. Vapor hose
15. Overfill limiter
16. Fuel gauge sending unit
17. Electric fuel pump
18. Fuel filler neck

N. Replace with new component

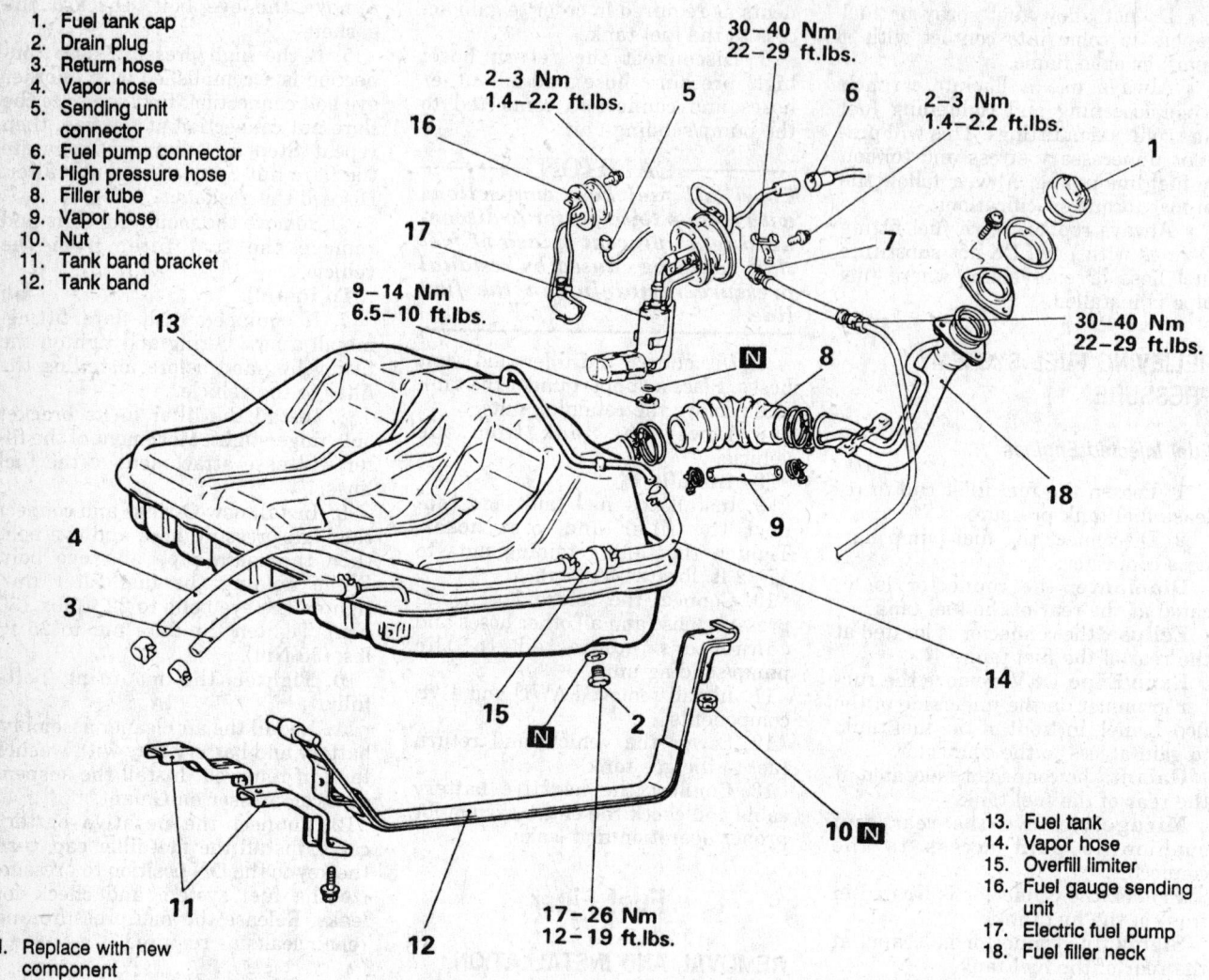

Typical fuel tank and related components

run the fuel pump, and check for leaks.

6. Start the engine and run at curb idle speed.

7. Measure the fuel pressure and compare to specifications.

8. Locate and disconnect the vacuum hose running to the fuel pressure regulator. Plug the end of the hose and record the fuel pressure again. The fuel pressure should have increased approximately 10 psi.

9. Reconnect the vacuum hose the fuel pressure regulator. After the fuel pressure stabilizes, race the engine 2-3 times and check that the fuel

pressure does not fall when the engine is running at idle.

10. Check to be sure there is fuel pressure in the return hose by gently pressing the fuel return hose with fingers while racing the engine. There will be no fuel pressure in the return hose when the volume of fuel flow is low.

11. If fuel pressure is too low, check for a clogged fuel filter, a defective fuel pressure regulator or a defective fuel pump, any of which will require replacement.

12. If fuel pressure is too high, the fuel pressure regulator is defective and will have to be replaced or the

fuel return is bent or clogged. If the fuel pressure reading does not change when the vacuum hose is disconnected, the hose is clogged or the valve is stuck in the fuel pressure regulator and it will have to be replaced.

13. Stop the engine and check for changes in the fuel pressure gauge. It should not drop. If the gauge reading does drop, watch the rate of drop. If fuel pressure drops slowly, the likely cause is a leaking injector which will require replacement. If the fuel pressure drops immediately after the engine is stopped, the check valve in the

N. Replace with new component

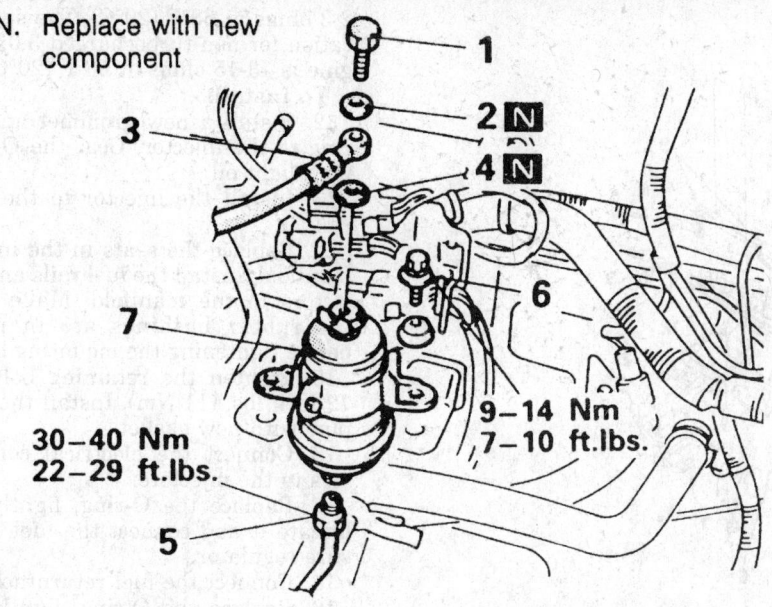

30–40 Nm
22–29 ft.lbs.

9–14 Nm
7–10 ft.lbs.

1. Eye bolt
2. O-ring
3. High pressure fuel hose
4. O-ring
5. Main fuel pipe
6. Mounting bolt
7. Fuel filter

Fuel filter, fuel lines, and mounting hardware

fuel pump isn't closing and the fuel pump will have to be replaced.

14. Relieve fuel system pressure.

15. Disconnect the high pressure hose and remove the fuel pressure gauge from the delivery pipe.

16. Install a new O-ring in the groove of the high pressure hose. Connect the hose to the delivery pipe and tighten the screws. After installation, apply battery voltage to the terminal for fuel pump activation to run the fuel pump. Check for leaks.

REMOVAL AND INSTALLATION

1. Relieve fuel system pressure.

2. Disconnect the negative battery cable.

3. Raise the vehicle and support safely.

4. Drain the fuel from the fuel tank.

5. Disconnect the return hose, high pressure hose and all other hoses and connectors connected to the pump/sending unit.

6. Disconnect the filler and vent hoses. Place a suitable support under the tank and remove the retaining nuts. Lower the tank from the vehicle.

7. Remove the fuel pump cover (if equipped), retaining nuts and fuel pump/sending unit assembly from the tank.

To install:

8. Install the replacement pump using a new gasket. Be certain the pump is installed in the same location, facing the same direction as before.

9. Install the fuel tank and all related items to the vehicle. Secure all tank retaining nuts.

10. Connect the negative battery cable and check the entire system for proper operation and leaks.

Fuel Injector

REMOVAL AND INSTALLATION

1.5L and 1.8L Engines (Eclipse)and 2.0 SOHC Engine

1. Relieve the fuel system pressure.

2. Disconnect the negative battery cable. Remove the air breather hose, as required.

3. Disconnect the vacuum connections and the fuel return hose. Cover the connection with shop cloths in case of any residual pressure and to avoid fuel spillage.

4. Remove the fuel pressure regulator and O-ring.

5. Wrap the connection with a shop towel and disconnect the high pressure fuel line at the fuel rail.

6. Remove the accelerator cable clamp as required. Remove the connection for the control harness.

7. Disconnect the electrical harness from each injector connector.

8. Remove the injector rail retaining bolts. Make sure the rubber mounting bushings do not get lost.

9. Lift the rail assembly up and away from engine.

10. Remove the injectors from the rail by pulling gently. Discard the lower insulator. Check the resistance through the injector. The specification is 13-16 ohms at 70°F (20°C).

To install:

11. Install a new grommet and O-ring to the injector. Coat the O-ring with light weight oil.

12. Install the injector to the fuel rail.

13. Install the fuel rail and injectors to the manifold. Make sure the rubber bushings are in place before tightening the mounting bolts.

14. Tighten the retaining bolts to 72 inch lbs. (11 Nm).

15. Connect the electrical connectors to the injectors.

16. Replace the O-ring on the fuel pressure regulator, lightly lubricate and insert on delivery pipe.

17. Connect the fuel return hose.

18. Replace the O-ring on high pressure fuel line, lightly lubricate it and connect to delivery pipe.

19. Connect the negative battery cable and check the entire system for proper operation and leaks.

1.6L and 2.0L DOHC Engines

1. Relieve the fuel system pressure.

2. Disconnect the negative battery cable.

3. Wrap the connection with a shop towel and disconnect the high pressure fuel line at the fuel rail.

4. Disconnect the fuel return hose and remove the O-ring.

5. Disconnect the vacuum hose from the fuel pressure regulator. Remove the fuel pressure regulator and O-ring.

6. Disconnect the PCV hose. On 2.0L engine, remove the center cover.

7. Label and disconnect the electrical connectors from each injector.

8. Remove the injector rail retaining bolts. Make sure the rubber mounting bushings do not get lost.

9. Lift the rail assembly up and away from the engine.

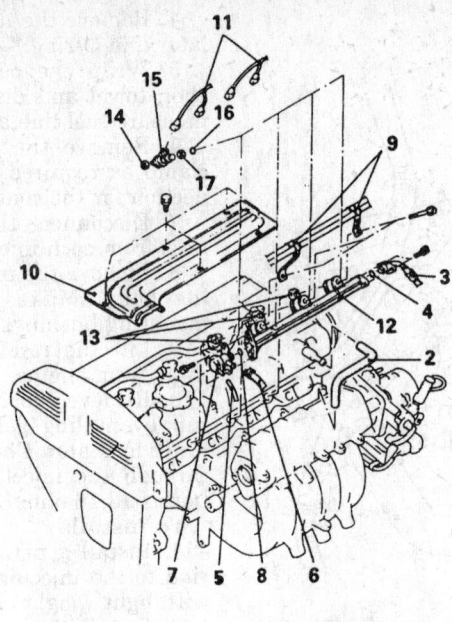

1. Breather hose
2. PCV hose
3. High pressure fuel hose
4. O-ring
5. Vacuum hose
6. Fuel return hose
7. Fuel pressure regulator
8. O-ring
9. Accelerator cable clamp
10. Center cover
11. Wire harness
12. Fuel rail
13. Insulator
14. Insulator
15. Injector
16. O-ring
17. Grommet

Fuel rail, injectors and related parts — 1.6L and 2.0L DOHC engines

10. Remove the injectors from the rail by pulling gently. Discard the lower insulator. Check the resistance through the injector. The specification for 2.0L turbocharged engine is 2-3 ohms at 70°F (20°C). The specification for the others is 13-15 ohms at 70°F (20°C).

To install:

11. Install a new grommet and O-ring to the injector. Coat the O-ring with light oil.

12. Install the injector to the fuel rail.

13. Replace the seats in the intake manifold. Install the fuel rail and injectors to the manifold. Make sure the rubber bushings are in place before tightening the mounting bolts.

14. Tighten the retaining bolts to 72 inch lbs. (11 Nm).

15. Connect the connectors to the injectors and install the center cover. Connect the PCV hose.

16. Replace the O-ring, lightly lubricate it and connect the fuel pressure regulator.

17. Connect the fuel return hose.

18. Replace the O-ring, lightly lubricate it and connect the high pressure fuel line.

19. Connect the negative battery cable and check the entire system for proper operation and leaks.

3.0L Engine

1. Relieve the fuel system pressure.

2. Disconnect the negative battery cable.

3. Drain the cooling system.

4. Disconnect all components from the air intake plenum and remove the plenum from the intake manifold. Discard the gaskets.

5. Wrap the connection with a shop towel and disconnect the high pressure fuel line at the fuel rail.

6. Disconnect the fuel return hose and remove the O-ring.

7. Disconnect the vacuum hose from the fuel pressure regulator. Remove the fuel pressure regulator and O-ring.

8. Disconnect the electrical connectors from each injector.

9. Remove the fuel pipe connecting the fuel rails. Remove the injector rail retaining bolts. Make sure the rubber mounting bushings do not get lost.

10. Lift the rail assemblies up and away from the engine.

11. Remove the injectors from the rail by pulling gently. Discard the lower insulator. Check the resistance through the injector. The specification for 3.0L turbocharged engine is

2-3 ohms at 68°F (20°C). The specification for non-turbocharged 3.0L engine is 13-15 ohms at 68°F (20°C).

To install:

12. Install a new grommet and O-ring to the injector. Coat the O-ring with light oil.

13. Install the injector to the fuel rail.

14. Replace the seats in the intake manifold. Install the fuel rails and injectors to the manifold. Make sure the rubber bushings are in place before tightening the mounting bolts.

15. Tighten the retaining bolts to 72 inch lbs. (11 Nm). Install the fuel pipe with new gasket.

16. Connect the electrical connectors to the injectors.

17. Replace the O-ring, lightly lubricate it and connect the fuel pressure regulator.

18. Connect the fuel return hose.

19. Replace the O-ring, lightly lubricate it and connect the high pressure fuel line.

20. Using new gaskets, install the intake plenum and all related items. Torque the plenum mounting bolts to 13 ft. lbs. (18 Nm).

21. Fill the cooling system.

22. Connect the negative battery cable and check the entire system for proper operation and leaks.

1.8L and 2.4L Engines (Expo/Expo LRV)

1. Relieve the fuel system pressure.

2. Disconnect the negative battery cable.

3. Disconnect and remove the air intake hoses as required.

4. Wrap the connection with a shop towel and disconnect the high pressure fuel line at the fuel rail.

5. Disconnect the fuel return hose and remove the O-ring.

6. Disconnect the accelerator cable connection from the throttle body and position aside.

7. Disconnect the vacuum connection from the fuel pressure regulator.

8. Disconnect the electrical harness connector from each fuel injector.

9. Remove the injector rail retaining bolts. Make sure the rubber mounting insulators do not get lost.

10. Lift the rail assembly up and away from engine.

11. Remove the injectors from the rail by pulling gently. Discard the lower insulator. Check the resistance through the injector. The specification is 13-16 ohms at 70°F (20°C).

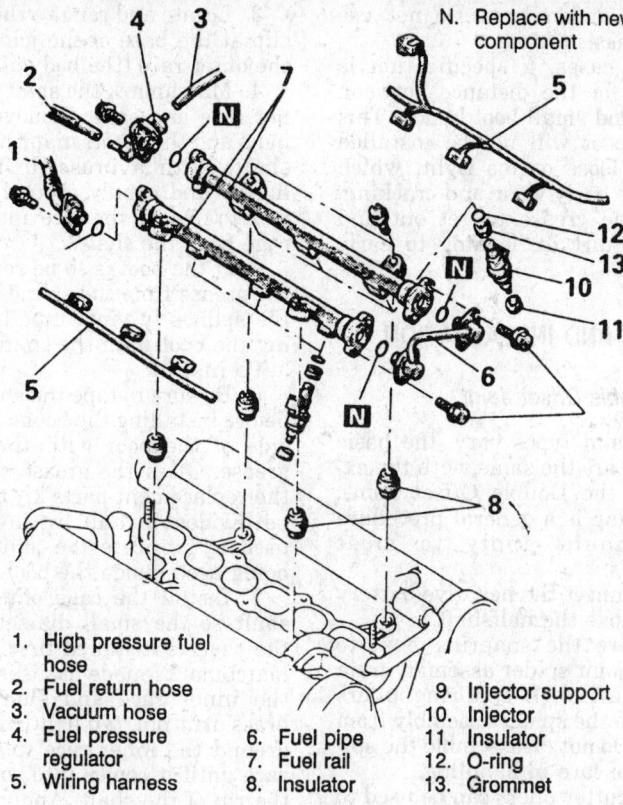

N. Replace with new component

1. High pressure fuel hose
2. Fuel return hose
3. Vacuum hose
4. Fuel pressure regulator
5. Wiring harness
6. Fuel pipe
7. Fuel rail
8. Insulator
9. Injector support
10. Injector
11. Insulator
12. O-ring
13. Grommet

Fuel rail, injectors and related parts — 3.0L engines

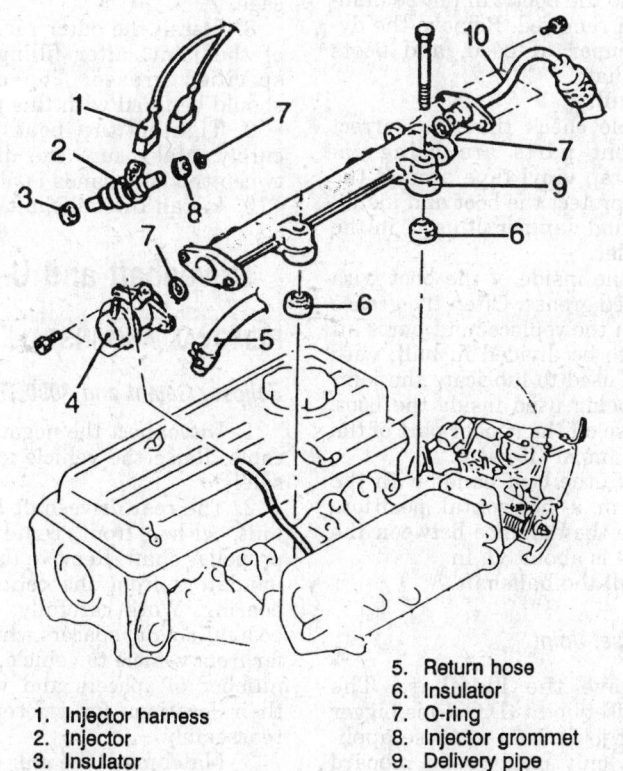

1. Injector harness
2. Injector
3. Insulator
4. Pressure regulator
5. Return hose
6. Insulator
7. O-ring
8. Injector grommet
9. Delivery pipe
10. Pressure line

Fuel rail, injectors and related parts — typical of SOHC 4 cylinder engines

To install:

12. Install a new grommet and O-ring to the injector. Coat the O-ring with light weight oil.

13. Install the injector to the fuel rail.

14. Install the fuel rail and injectors to the manifold. Make sure the rubber bushings are in place before tightening the mounting bolts.

15. Tighten the retaining bolts to 8.7 ft. lbs. (12 Nm).

16. Connect the electrical connectors to the injectors.

17. Replace the O-ring on the fuel pressure regulator, lightly lubricate and install on the delivery pipe. Connect the vacuum hose to the fuel pressure regulator.

18. Connect the fuel return hose.

19. Replace the O-ring on high pressure fuel line, lightly lubricate it and connect to delivery pipe.

20. Reconnect the accelerator cable to the throttler body and adjust to specifications.

21. Connect the negative battery cable and check the entire system for proper operation and leaks.

DRIVE AXLE

Halfshaft

REMOVAL AND INSTALLATION

NOTE: If the vehicle is going to be rolled while the halfshafts are out of the vehicle, obtain 2 outer CV-joints or proper equivalent tools and install to the hubs. If the vehicle is rolled without the proper torque applied to the front wheel bearings, the bearings will no longer be usable.

1. Disconnect the negative battery cable.

2. Remove the cotter pin, halfshaft nut and washer.

3. Raise the vehicle and support safely. If equipped with ABS, remove the front wheel speed sensor. If equipped with Active Electronic Control Suspension, disconnect the front height sensor from the lower control arm. Remove the lower ball joint and the tie rod end from the steering knuckle.

4. On vehicles with an inner shaft, remove the center support bearing bracket bolts and washers.

5. On vehicles with an inner shaft, remove the halfshaft by setting up a

puller on the outside wheel hub and pushing the halfshaft from the front hub. Then tap the shaft union at the joint case with a plastic hammer to remove the halfshaft and inner shaft from the transaxle.

6. On vehicles without an inner shaft, remove the halfshaft by setting up a puller on the outside wheel hub and pushing the halfshaft from the front hub. After pressing the outer shaft, insert a prybar between the transaxle case and the halfshaft and pry the shaft from the transaxle. Do not pull on the shaft; doing so damages the inboard joint. Do not insert the prybar too far or the oil seal in the case may be damaged.

To install:

7. Inspect the halfshaft boot for damage or deterioration. Check the ball joints and splines for wear.

8. Replace the circlips on the ends of the halfshafts.

9. Insert the halfshaft into the transaxle. Make sure it is fully seated.

10. Pull the strut assembly out and install the other end to the hub.

11. Install the center bearing bracket bolts and tighten to 33 ft. lbs. (45 Nm).

12. Install the washer so the chamfered edge faces outward. Install the nut and tighten temporarily.

13. Install the tie rod end and ball joint.

14. Install the wheel and lower the vehicle to the floor. Tighten the axle nut with the brakes applied. Tighten the nut to a maximum torque of 188 ft. lbs. (260 Nm). Install the cotter pin and bend to secure.

CV-Boot

These vehicles use several different types of joints. Engine size, transaxle type, whether the joint is an inboard or outboard joint, even which side of the vehicle is being serviced could make a difference in joint type. Be sure to properly identify the joint before attempting joint or boot replacement. Look for identification numbers at the large end of the boots and/or on the end of the metal retainer bands.

The 4 types of joints used are the Birfield Joint, (B.J.), the Tripod Joint (T.J.), the Double Offset Joint (D.O.J.) and the Rzeppa Joint (R.J.). In addition, some left side shafts will have a round dynamic damper installed on the shaft. Special grease is generally used with these joints and is often supplied with the replace-

ment joint and/or boot. Do not use regular chassis grease.

In most cases, a specification is called out for the distance between the large and small boot bands. This is so the boot will not be installed either too loose or too tight, which could cause early wear and cracking, allowing the grease to get out and water and dirt in, leading to early joint failure.

REMOVAL AND INSTALLATION

Except Double-Offset Joint

Although joint types vary, the basic procedures are the same, with the exception of the Double Offset Joint. The following is a general procedure which should apply to most applications.

1. Disconnect the negative battery cable. Remove the halfshaft.

2. Remove the snapring next to the tripod joint spider assembly from the halfshaft with snapring pliers and remove the spider assembly from the shaft. Do not disassemble the spider and use care in handling.

3. Side cutter pliers can be used to cut the metal retaining bands.

4. If the boot is be reused, wrap vinyl tape around the spline part of the shaft so the boot will not be damaged when removed. Remove the dynamic damper, if used, and boots from the shaft.

To install:

5. Double check that the correct replacement parts are being installed. Wrap vinyl tape around the splines to protect the boot and install the boots and damper, if used, in the correct order.

6. Fill the inside of the boot with the specified grease. Often the grease supplied in the replacement parts kit is meant to be divided in half, with half being used to lubricate the joint and half being used inside the boot. Keep grease off the rubber part of the dynamic damper (if used).

7. Secure the boot bands with the halfshaft in a horizontal position. Make sure the distance between the boot bands is about 3¼ in.

8. Install the halfshaft.

Double-Offset Joint

1. Remove the halfshaft. The Double Offset Joint (D.O.J.) is bigger than other joints and in these applications, is only used as an inboard joint.

2. Side cutter pliers can be used to cut the metal retaining bands.

3. Locate and remove the large circlip at the base of the joint. Remove the outer race (the body of the joint).

4. Matchmark the shaft, D.O.J. inner race and cage. Remove the joint balls and the small snapring from the shaft. With a brass drift pin, tap lightly and evenly around the inner race to remove the race and the inner cage from the shaft.

5. If the boot is to be reused, wipe the grease from the splines and wrap the splines in vinyl tape before sliding the boot from the shaft.

To install:

6. Be sure to tape the shaft splines before installing the boots. Fill the inside of the boot with the specified grease. Often the grease supplied in the replacement parts kit is meant to be divided in half, with half being used to lubricate the joint and half being used inside the boot.

7. Install the cage onto the halfshaft so the small diameter side of the cage is installed first. Align the matchmarks made at disassembly on the inner race and shaft. With a brass drift pin, tap lightly and evenly around the inner race to install the race until it comes into contact with the rib of the shaft. Apply the specified grease to the inner race and cage and fit them together aligning the matchmarks. Insert the balls into the cage.

8. Install the outer race (the body of the joint) after filling with the specified grease. The outer race should be filled with this grease.

9. Tighten the boot bands securely. Make sure the distance between the boot bands is about 3¼ in.

10. Install the halfshaft.

Driveshaft and U-Joints

REMOVAL AND INSTALLATION

Eclipse, Galant and 3000GT w/AWD

1. Disconnect the negative battery cable. Raise the vehicle and support safely.

2. The rear driveshaft is a 3-piece unit, with a front, center and rear propeller shaft. Remove the nuts and insulators from the center support bearing. Work carefully. There will be a number of spacers which will differ from vehicle to vehicle. Check the number of spacers and write down their locations for reference during reassembly.

3. Matchmark the rear differential companion flange and the rear driveshaft flange yoke. Remove the companion shaft bolts and remove

the driveshaft, keeping it as straight as possible so as to ensure that the boot is not damaged or pinched. Use care to keep from damaging the oil seal in the output housing of the transfer case.

NOTE: Damage to the boot can be avoided and work will be easier if a piece of cloth or similar material is inserted in the boot.

4. Do not lower the rear of the vehicle or oil will flow from the transfer case. Cover the opening to keep dirt out.

To install:

5. Install the driveshaft to the vehicle and align the matchmarks at the rear yoke. Install the bolts and torque to 22-25 ft. lbs. (30-35 Nm) on Galant and Eclipse or 36-43 ft. lbs. (50-60 Nm) on 3000GT.

6. Install the center support bearing with all spacers in place. Torque the retaining nuts to 22-25 ft. lbs. (30-35 Nm).

7. Check the fluid levels in the transfer case and rear differential case.

Expo/Expo LRV

1. Disconnect the battery negative cable.

2. Raise the vehicle and support safely. Drain the oil from the transfer assembly.

3. Disconnect the front exhaust pipe.

4. Make mating marks on the differential companion flange and the flange yoke. Remove the locking nut from the center support and remove the propeller shaft. Make note of washers and spacers used so they can be reinstalled in their original location.

NOTE: Remove the propeller shaft in a straight and level manner so as to ensure that the boot is not damaged through pinching. Damage can be avoided if a piece of cloth or similar material is inserted into the boot. Cover the opening of the transfer assembly to prevent dirt from entering the transfer assembly.

5. Installation is the reverse of the removal procedure. Tighten the rear flange bolts and nuts to 22-25 ft. lbs. (30-35 Nm), the locking nuts on the center support to 22 ft. lbs. (30 Nm), refill the transfer assembly and check the fluid level in the transaxle assembly.

Rear Axle Shaft, Bearing and Seal

REMOVAL AND INSTALLATION

Eclipse, Galant, and 3000GT w/AWD

1. Disconnect the negative battery cable. Raise the vehicle and support safely.

2. Remove the bolts that attach the rear halfshaft to the companion flange.

3. Use a prybar to pry the inner shaft out of the differential case. Don't insert the prybar too far or the seal could be damage.

4. Remove the rear halfshaft from the vehicle.

5. If equipped with ABS, remove the rear wheel speed sensor.

6. Remove the caliper, pads and brake rotor.

7. Hold the axle shaft stationary and remove the axle shaft self-locking nut and washer.

8. Using a slide hammer, separate the axle shaft from the companion flange and remove.

9. Use a vice and gear puller tool to disassemble the axle shaft and companion flange assemblies.

To install:

10. Assemble the axle shaft and companion shaft assemblies using new parts as required.

11. Install the axle shaft to the housing and slide the axle shaft over it. Install the washer and new self-locking nut. Hold the axle shaft stationary and torque the nut to 116-159 ft. lbs. (160-220 Nm) for Galant, Eclipse and 1991 non-turbocharged 3000GT. Torque to 217 ft. lbs. (300 Nm) 1992-94 3000GT.

12. Install the brake rotor, pads and caliper.

13. Install the ABS rear wheel speed sensor.

14. Replace the circlip and install the rear halfshaft to the differential case. Make sure it snaps in place. Torque the companion flange bolts to 40-47 ft. lbs. (55-65 Nm).

15. Check the fluid level in the rear differential.

Expo/Expo LRV w/AWD

1. Disconnect the negative battery cable. Raise the vehicle and support safely.

2. Remove the bolts that attach the rear halfshaft to the rear carrier.

3. Remove the cotter pin, driveshaft nut cover and nut from the rear driveshaft.

NOTE: Do not apply the vehicle weight to the wheel bearing while loosening the driveshaft nut or bearing damage may occur.

4. Separate the shaft from the hub using a puller. Remove the shaft from the flange and lift from the vehicle.

5. Installation is the reverse of the removal procedure. Torque the retainers on the rear carrier to 40-47 ft. lbs. (55-65 Nm) and the shaft end nut to 145-188 ft. lbs. (200-260 Nm).

Front Wheel Hub, Knuckle and Bearing

REMOVAL AND INSTALLATION

1. Disconnect the negative battery cable.

2. Remove the cotter pin, halfshaft nut and washer.

3. Raise the vehicle and support safely. If equipped with ABS, remove the front wheel speed sensor. If the vehicle is equipped with Active Electronic Control Suspension, disconnect the front height sensor from the lower control arm. Remove the ball joint and tie rod end from the steering knuckle.

4. Remove the caliper and brake pads and suspend with a wire.

5. On vehicles with an inner shaft, remove the center support bearing bracket bolts and washers. Remove the halfshaft by setting up a puller on the outside wheel hub and pushing the halfshaft from the front hub. Then tap the joint case with a plastic hammer to remove the halfshaft shaft and inner shaft from the transaxle.

6. On vehicles without an inner shaft, remove the halfshaft by setting up a puller on the outside wheel hub and pushing the halfshaft from the front hub. After pressing the outer shaft, insert a prybar between the transaxle case and the halfshaft and pry the shaft from the transaxle.

7. On 3000GT with AWD, the front hub/bearing assembly can be serviced at this point as a unit. If the knuckle is being removed, proceed. All others models require knuckle removal for service.

8. Unbolt the lower end of the strut and remove the hub and steering knuckle assembly.

9. Set up a puller with the knuckle/hub in a vise and pull the

hub from the knuckle. Do not use a hammer to accomplish this or the bearing will be damaged.

10. Once the hub and outer bearing inner race are removed with a puller, the bearing outer races can be removed by tapping out with a brass drift pin and a hammer.

To install:

11. Assemble the hub/knuckle assembly with pressing tools, using new parts as required.

12. Install the knuckle assembly to the vehicle and install the strut bolts.

13. On AWD 3000GT, torque the front hub/bearing assembly nuts to 76 ft. lbs. (105 Nm).

14. Apply a thin coat of grease to the outside of the outer races and install into the hub with a bearing driver.

15. Apply multi-purpose grease to the bearings, inside surface of the hub and the lip of the grease seal. Place the outside bearing into the knuckle and install the seal with a driver.

16. The hub is assembled to the knuckle with a puller. Draw the parts together firmly to seat the bearings. Use a small torque wrench to check the bearing turning torque. It should be 16 inch lbs. or less for all applications except Mirage and Precis. On those, turning torque should be 11 lbs. or less. Check that the bearings feel smooth when rotated.

17. Apply a thin coat of grease to the lip of the halfshaft side axle seal and drive into place until it contacts the inner bearing outer race.

18. Replace the circlips on the ends of the halfshafts.

19. Insert the halfshaft into the transaxle. Make sure it is fully seated.

20. Pull the strut assembly out and install the other end to the hub.

21. Install the center bearing bracket bolts and tighten to 33 ft. lbs. (45 Nm).

22. Install the washer so the chamfered edge faces outward. Install the nut and tighten temporarily.

23. Install the tie rod end and ball joint.

24. Install the wheel and lower the vehicle to the floor. Tighten the axle nut with the brakes applied. Tighten the nut to a torque of 145-188 ft. lbs. (200-260 Nm). Install the cotter pin and bend to secure.

Pinion Seal

REMOVAL AND INSTALLATION

Front Differential

1. Disconnect the negative battery cable.
2. Remove the front halfshaft.
3. Using a suitable puller or prying tool, remove the seal from the case.

To install:

4. Apply a thin coat of multi-purpose grease to the seal lip and the seal contact surface.
5. Install the new seal with an appropriate driver.
6. Install the front halfshaft.

Rear Differential

1. Raise the vehicle and support safely.
2. Matchmark the rear propeller shaft and companion flange and remove the shaft. Don't let it hang from the transaxle. Tie it up to the underbody.
3. Hold the companion flange stationary and remove the large self-locking nut in the center of the companion flange.
4. Using a puller, remove the flange. Pry the old seal out.

To install:

5. Apply a thin coat of multi-purpose grease to the seal lip and the companion flange seal contacting surface. Install the new seal with an appropriate driver.
6. Install the companion flange. Install a new locknut and torque to 137 ft. lbs. (190 Nm) on Expo/Expo LRV and 160 ft. lbs. (220 Nm) on the remaining models. The rotation torque of the drive pinion should be about 2-3 inch lbs.

Differential Carrier

REMOVAL AND INSTALLATION

Eclipse, Galant and 3000GT w/AWD

1. Raise the vehicle and support safely.
2. Drain the differential gear oil. Remove exhaust parts as required.
3. Matchmark and remove the rear driveshaft.
4. Remove the rear halfshafts.

5. On 3000GT and Galant, remove or disconnect the 4 wheel steering oil pump.
6. The large mounting bolts that hold the differential carrier support plate to the underbody may use self-locking nuts. Before removing them, support the rear axle assembly in the middle with a transmission jack. Remove the nuts, then remove the support plate(s) and the square dynamic damper from the rear of the carrier.
7. Lower the differential carrier and remove from the vehicle.

To install:

8. Install the unit and all mounting brackets. Replace all locknuts. Install or connect the 4 wheel steering oil pump.
9. Use new circlips on the inboard joints and install.
10. Install the torque tube and rear driveshaft, matching up the marks made at disassembly.
11. With the vehicle level, fill the rear differential.

Expo/Expo LRV

1. Raise the vehicle and support safely.
2. Drain the differential gear oil and remove the center exhaust pipe.
3. Remove the rear halfshafts from the carrier and support out of the way.
4. Matchmark the differential companion flange and flange yoke for reference during installation and disconnect the propeller shaft from the carrier. Support shaft out of the way leaving attached to the transfer assembly.
5. Support the rear carrier assembly using the appropriate equipment. Remove the carrier mounting bolts and lower carrier from the vehicle.

To install:

6. Raise the rear carrier into position and torque the side retaining bolts to 72-87 ft. lbs. (100-120 Nm). Tighten the retainer bolts through the rear support member to 69 ft. lbs. (95 Nm).
7. Install the propeller shaft, with matchmarks aligned, and the rear halfshafts to the carrier. Tighten the halfshaft flange nuts to 40-47 ft. lbs. (55-65 Nm).
8. Install the center exhaust pipe using new gasket.
9. With the vehicle level, fill the rear differential.

MANUAL TRANSMISSION

Transmission Assembly

REMOVAL AND INSTALLATION

1. Disconnect the negative battery cable. From inside the vehicle, remove the gearshift lever assembly.
2. Remove the driveshaft.
3. Raise the vehicle and safely support. Drain the transmission. Disconnect the reverse light switch connector and speedometer cable.
4. Remove the clutch slave cylinder.
5. Remove the bellhousing cover and starter.
6. Using the proper equipment, support the weight of the transmission, then and remove the rear mount.
7. Remove the bellhousing bolts and remove the transmission assembly from the vehicle.

To install:

8. Lift the transmission into position and push forward until the input shaft splines engage. Install the bellhousing bolts and torque to 30 ft. lbs. (41 Nm).
9. Install the rear mount.
10. Install the starter and bellhousing cover.
11. Install the clutch slave cylinder.
12. Connect the reverse light switch connector and speedometer cable.
13. Install the driveshaft. Fill the transmission with gear oil.
14. From inside the vehicle, seal the the gearshift lever assembly gasket and install.
15. Connect the negative battery cable and road test. Check the reverse light switch for proper opera-

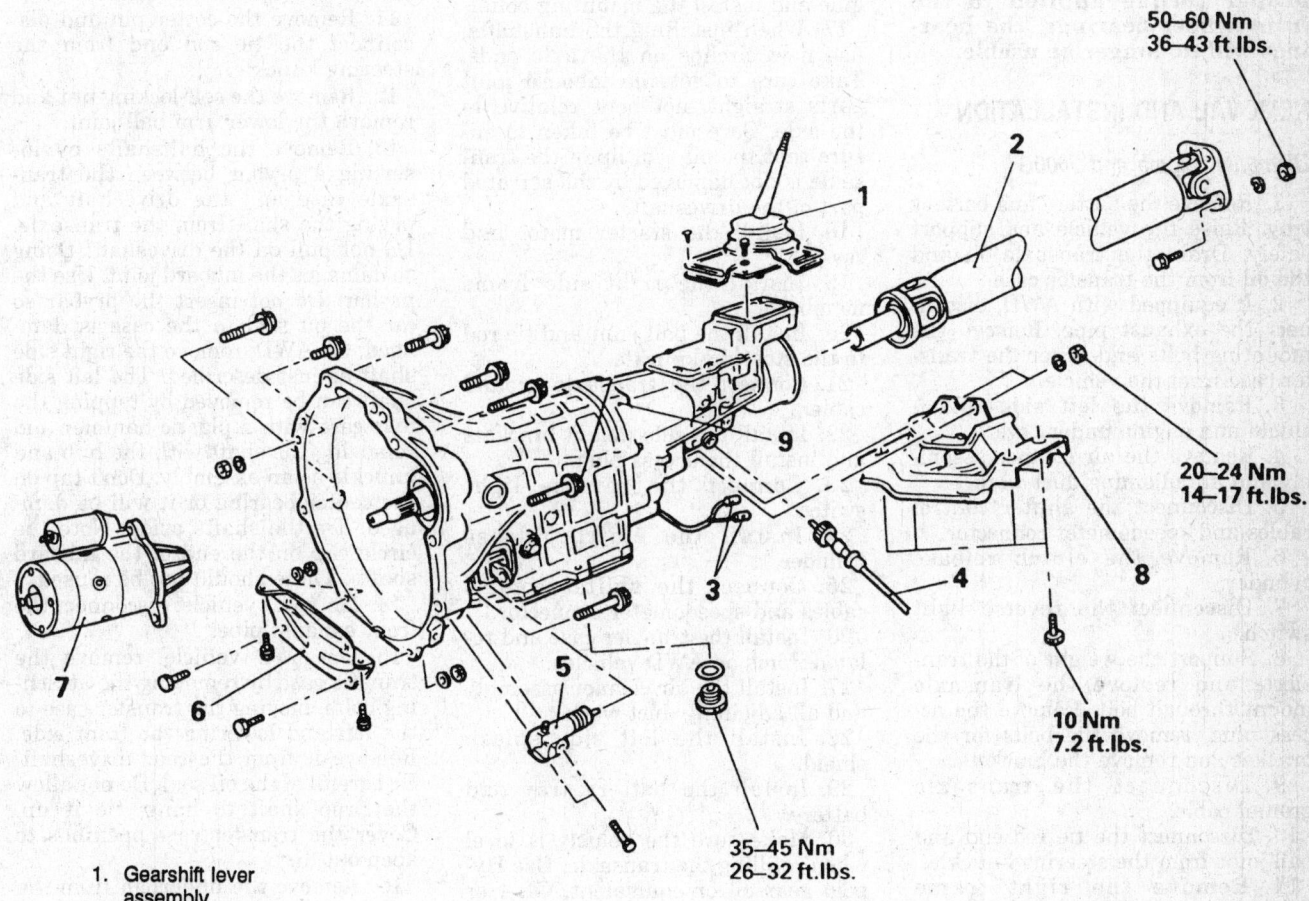

50–60 Nm
36–43 ft.lbs.

20–24 Nm
14–17 ft.lbs.

10 Nm
7.2 ft.lbs.

35–45 Nm
26–32 ft.lbs.

1. Gearshift lever assembly
2. Driveshaft
3. Reverse light switch connector
4. Speedometer cable
5. Slave cylinder
6. Bellhousing cover
7. Starter
8. Rear mount
9. Transmission assembly

Manual transmission assembly

tion. Since this is a direct actuating shifter, there is no adjustment.

MANUAL TRANSAXLE

Transaxle Assembly

NOTE: If the vehicle is going to be rolled while the halfshafts are out of the vehicle, obtain 2 outer CV-joints or proper equivalent tools and install to the hubs. If the vehicle is rolled without the proper torque applied to the front wheel bearings, the bearings will no longer be usable.

REMOVAL AND INSTALLATION

Diamante, Sigma and 3000GT

1. Remove the battery and battery tray. Raise the vehicle and support safely. Drain the transaxle oil and the oil from the transfer case.
2. If equipped with AWD, disconnect the exhaust pipe. Remove the mounting bolts and lower the transfer case from the vehicle.
3. Remove the left side splash shield and engine under cover.
4. Remove the air cleaner assembly and all adjoining duct work.
5. Disconnect the shifter control cables and speedometer connector.
6. Remove the clutch release cylinder.
7. Disconnect the reverse light switch.
8. Support the weight of the transaxle and remove the transaxle mount through bolt. Remove the access plug, remove the bolts for the bracket and remove the brackets.
9. Disconnect the transaxle ground cable.
10. Disconnect the tie rod end and ball joint from the steering knuckle.
11. Remove the right frame member.
12. Remove the starter motor.
13. Remove the halfshafts by inserting a prybar between the transaxle case and the driveshaft and prying the shaft from the transaxle. Do not pull on the driveshaft. Doing so damages the inboard joint. Use the prybar. Do not insert the prybar so far the oil seal in the case is damaged. On AWD, remove the right side shaft as just described. The left side shaft can be removed by tapping with

a plastic hammer. Remove the shaft with the hub and knuckle as an assembly. Don't tap on the center bearing or it will be damaged. Tie the shafts aside. Note the circle clip on the end of the inboard shafts. These should not be reused.
14. Remove the transaxle brackets.
15. Remove the transaxle assembly. On turbocharged vehicles, take care to prevent damaging the lower radiator hose with the transaxle housing. Wind tape around the lower hose and put tape on the transaxle housing. Support the transaxle assembly using the proper jack, move the transaxle away from the engine and lower it.

To install:

16. Install the transaxle to the engine and install the mounting bolts.
17. When installing the halfshafts, use new circlips on the axle ends. Take care to get the inboard joint parts straight, not bent relative to the axle. Care must be taken to ensure that the oil seal lip of the transaxle is not damaged by the serrated part of the driveshaft.
18. Install the starter motor and cover.
19. Install the right side frame member.
20. Install the ball joint and tie rod to the steering knuckle.
21. Connect the transaxle ground cable.
22. Install the side mount brackets and install the access plug.
23. Connect the reverse light switch.
24. Install the clutch release cylinder.
25. Connect the shifter control cables and speedometer connector.
26. Install the transfer case and related items on AWD vehicles.
27. Install the air cleaner assembly and all adjoining duct work.
28. Install the left side splash shield.
29. Install the battery tray and battery.
30. Make sure the vehicle is level when refilling the transaxle. Use Hypoid gear oil or equivalent, GL-4 or higher.
31. Connect the negative battery cable and check the transaxle and transfer case for proper operation. Make sure the reverse lamps come ON when in reverse.

Eclipse and Galant

1. Remove the battery.
2. Remove the auto-cruise actuator and bracket underhood, on the passenger side inner fender wall.

3. Drain the transaxle and transfer case.
4. Remove the air intake hose.
5. Remove the cotter pin securing the select and shift cables and remove the cable ends from the transaxle.
6. Remove the connection for the clutch release cylinder and without disconnecting the hydraulic line, secure aside.
7. Disconnect the backup light switch and the speedometer cable.
8. Disconnect the starter electrical connections and remove the starter motor.
9. Remove the transaxle mount bracket.
10. Raise the vehicle and support safely. Remove the undercover.
11. Remove the cotter pin and disconnect the tie rod end from the steering knuckle.
12. Remove the self-locking nut and remove the lower arm ball joint.
13. Remove the halfshafts by inserting a prybar between the transaxle case and the driveshaft and prying the shaft from the transaxle. Do not pull on the driveshaft. Doing so damages the inboard joint. Use the prybar. Do not insert the prybar so far the oil seal in the case is damaged. On AWD, remove the right side shaft as just described. The left side shaft can be removed by tapping the axle case with a plastic hammer and removing the shaft with the hub and knuckle as an assembly. Don't tap on the center bearing or it will be damaged. Tie the shafts aside. Note the circle clip on the end of the inboard shafts. These should not be reused.
14. On AWD vehicle, disconnect the front exhaust pipe.
15. On AWD vehicle, remove the transfer case by removing the attaching bolts, moving the transfer case to the left and lowering the front axle. Remove it from the rear driveshaft. Be careful of the oil seal. Do not allow the prop shaft to hang; tie it up. Cover the transfer case openings to keep out dirt.
16. Remove the underpan from the transaxle bellhousing. On AWD, also remove the crossmember and the triangular gusset.
17. Remove the transaxle lower coupling bolt. It is just above the halfshaft opening on 2WD or transfer case opening on AWD.
18. Remove the transaxle assembly. On turbocharged vehicle, take care to prevent damaging the lower radiator hose with the transaxle housing. Wind tape around the lower hose and put tape on the transaxle housing.

Support the transaxle assembly using the proper jack, move the transaxle to the right and lower it.

To install:

19. Install the transaxle to the engine and install the mounting bolts.

20. Install the transaxle lower coupling bolt.

21. Install the underpan, crossmember and the triangular gusset.

22. Install the transfer case on AWD vehicles and connect the exhaust pipe.

23. When installing the halfshafts, use new circlips on the axle ends. Take care to get the inboard joint parts straight, not bent relative to the axle. Care must be taken to ensure that the oil seal lip of the transaxle is not damaged by the serrated part of the driveshaft.

24. Connect the tie rod and ball joint to the steering knuckle.

25. Install the transaxle mount bracket.

26. Install the starter motor.

27. Connect the backup light switch and the speedometer cable.

28. Install the clutch release cylinder.

29. Connect the select and shift cables and install new cotter pins.

30. Install the air intake hose.

31. Install the auto-cruise actuator and bracket underhood, on the passenger side inner fender wall.

32. Install the battery.

33. Make sure the vehicle is level when refilling the transaxle. Use Hypoid gear oil or equivalent, GL-4 or higher.

34. Connect the negative battery cable and check the transaxle and transfer case for proper operation. Make sure the reverse lights come ON when in reverse.

Expo/Expo LRV

1. Disconnect negative battery cable. Support the weight of the engine using the appropriate fixture.

2. Remove the air cleaner assembly. Remove the transaxle upper coupling bolts.

3. Raise and safely support the vehicle.

4. Disconnect the control cable connections from the transaxle.

5. Disconnect the reverse light switch connection.

6. Disconnect the speedometer cable from the transaxle.

7. Remove the starter motor leaving the harness connected and secure aside.

8. Disconnect the tie rod end from the steering knuckle. Disconnect the stabilizer bar.

9. Remove the right side under cover. Drain the transaxle fluid.

10. Insert a prybar between the transaxle case and the driveshaft and pry the shaft from the transaxle. Turn the driveshaft and suspend with a wire so there are no sharp bends in any of the joints. Turn the right side shaft 90 degrees towards the front of the vehicle so it will not be a hindrance.

NOTE: When removing the shaft, use a prybar. Do not pull on the driveshaft; doing so will damage the inboard joint. Do not insert the prybar so deep as to damage the oil seal.

11. Remove the clutch oil line bracket bolt and remove the release cylinder. Suspend the cylinder out of the way leaving the oil lines connected.

12. On AWD models, remove the front exhaust pipe and transfer assembly.

13. Remove the center support member.

14. Remove the bellhousing cover. Support the transaxle using a transmission jack.

15. Remove the transaxle mount bolt.

16. Remove the transaxle assembly lower part coupling bolts.

17. Slide the transaxle assembly away from the engine and remove from the vehicle.

To install:

18. Position the transaxle assembly against the engine. Install the transaxle assembly lower part coupling bolts.

19. Install the transaxle mount bolt and tighten nut to 51 ft. lbs. (70 Nm).

20. On 1.8L engine, install the center support member.

21. Remove the transaxle jack. Install the bellhousing cover.

22. Install the clutch oil line bracket bolt and release cylinder.

23. Install the front driveshafts so the inboard joint part of the shaft is straight in relation to the transaxle. Care must be taken to ensure that the oil seal lip part of the transaxle is not damaged by the serrated part of the driveshaft.

24. Connect the tie rod end from the steering knuckle. Disconnect the stabilizer bar.

25. Install the right side under cover. Install the starter motor.

26. Connect the tie rod ends to the steering knuckle and secure using new cotter pin.

27. Reconnect the speedometer cable, backup switch connector and the control cable connector.

28. Refill the transaxle assembly with Hypoid gear oil or equivalent, GL-4 or higher. Install the air cleaner assembly.

29. Connect the negative battery cable and check the transaxle and transfer case for proper operation. Make sure the reverse lights come ON when in reverse.

Mirage and Precis

1. Disconnect the negative battery cable.

2. Remove the battery and battery tray.

3. Remove the air cleaner assembly and air hoses.

4. Raise the vehicle and support safely.

5. Drain the transaxle oil.

6. If equipped with 1.6L engine, remove the tension rod.

7. Disconnect the shifter cables.

8. Remove the clutch release cylinder and clutch oil line bracket and secure to the body. Do not disconnect the fluid lines. Disconnect the clutch cable, if equipped with cable controlled clutch system.

9. Disconnect the backup lamp switch connector, speedometer cable connection and remove the starter motor.

10. Remove the transaxle mounting bolts and bracket.

11. Remove the sheet metal undercover.

12. Disconnect the tie rod ends and the lower ball joint connections.

13. Remove the halfshafts by inserting a prybar between the transaxle case and the driveshaft and prying the shaft from the transaxle. Do not pull on the driveshaft. Doing so damages the inboard joint. Use the prybar. Do not insert the prybar so far the oil seal in the case is damaged. Remove the right side shaft as just described. The left side shaft can be removed by tapping with a plastic hammer. Remove the shaft with the hub and knuckle as an assembly. Don't tap on the center bearing or it will be damaged. Tie the shafts aside. Note the circle clip on the end of the inboard shafts. These should not be reused.

14. Remove the bellhousing lower cover. Remove the transaxle to engine bolts and lower the transaxle from the vehicle.

To install:

15. Install the transaxle to the engine and install the mounting bolts.

16. When installing the halfshafts, use new circlips on the axle ends. Take care to get the inboard joint parts straight, not bent relative to

the axle. Care must be taken to ensure that the oil seal lip of the transaxle is not damaged by the serrated part of the driveshaft.

17. Install the undercover.

18. Install the mounting brackets.

19. Install the starter making sure to fasten the ground wire with the upper fastener and the harness fastener with the lower fastener.

20. Connect the backup light switch connector and speedometer cable.

21. Install the clutch and shifter actuation components. If the hydraulic system was opened, it should be bled after installation.

22. Install the tension rod.

23. Install the air cleaner and battery.

24. Make sure the vehicle is level when refilling the transaxle. Use Hypoid gear oil or equivalent, GL-4 or higher.

25. Connect the negative battery cable and check the transaxle for proper operation. Make sure the reverse lights come ON when in reverse.

LINKAGE ADJUSTMENT

There are 2 cables: the select cable and the shift cable.

1. On the transaxle, put the select lever in **N** and move the transaxle shift lever to put it in **4th** gear. Depress the clutch, if necessary, to shift.

2. Move the shift lever in the vehicle to the **4th** gear position until it contacts the stop.

3. Turn the adjuster turn buckle so the shift cable eye aligns with the eye in the gear shift lever. When installing the cable eye, make sure the flange side of the plastic bushing at the shift cable end is on the cotter pin side.

4. The cables should be adjusted so the clearance between the shift lever and both stoppers are equal when the shift lever is moved to 3rd and 4th gear. Move the shift lever to each position and check that the shifting is smooth.

CLUTCH

Clutch Assembly

REMOVAL AND INSTALLATION

1. Disconnect the negative battery cable. Raise and safely support the vehicle.

2. Remove the transaxle assembly from the vehicle.

3. Remove the pressure plate attaching bolts. If the pressure plate is to be reused, loosen the bolts in succession, 1 or 2 turns at a time to prevent warping the the cover flange.

4. Remove the pressure plate release bearing assembly and the clutch disc. Do not use solvent to clean the bearing.

5. Inspect the condition of the clutch components and replace any worn parts.

To install:

6. Inspect the flywheel for heat damage or cracks. Resurface or replace the flywheel as required, using new bolts.

7. Using the proper alignment tool, install the clutch disc to the flywheel. Install the pressure plate assembly and tighten the pressure plate bolts evenly to 14-16 ft. lbs. (19-22 Nm). Remove the alignment tool.

8. Apply a very light coat of high temperature grease to the clutch fork at the ball pivot and where the fork contacts the bearing. Also a little bit of grease can be applied to end of the release cylinder's pushrod and to the pushrod hole on the fork. Apply a light coat of grease on the transaxle input shaft splines.

9. Install a new clutch release bearing. Pack its inner surface with grease.

10. Install the transaxle assembly and check for proper clutch operation.

PEDAL HEIGHT/FREE-PLAY ADJUSTMENT

1. Measure the clutch pedal height from the face of the pedal pad to the firewall. The desired distances are as follows:

   a. Precis and Mirage — 6.61-6.8 in. (168-171mm)

   b. Galant and Eclipse — 6.93-7.17 in. (176-182mm)

   c. 3000GT with FWD — 6.93-7.17 in. (176-182mm)

   d. 3000GT with AWD — 7.2-7.4 in. (183-188mm)

   e. Expo/Expo LRV — 7.68-7.87 in. (195-200mm)

2. Measure the clutch pedal clevis pin play at the face of the pedal pad. The standard values are as follows:

   a. Precis and Mirage — 0.04-0.12 in. (1-3mm)

   b. Galant and Eclipse — 0.04-0.12 in. (1-3mm)

   c. 3000GT with FWD — 0.24-0.51 in. (6-13mm)

   d. 3000GT with AWD — 0.49-0.79 in. (12-20mm)

   e. Expo/Expo LRV — 0.04-0.12 in. (1-3mm)

3. If the clutch pedal height or clevis pin play are not within the standard values, adjust as follows:

   a. For vehicles without cruise control, turn and adjust the bolt so the pedal height is the standard value, then tighten the locknut.

   b. Vehicles with auto-cruise control system, disconnect the clutch switch connector and turn the switch to obtain the standard clutch pedal height. Then, lock with the locknut.

   c. Turn the pushrod to adjust the clutch pedal clevis pin play to agree with the standard value and secure the pushrod with the locknut.

NOTE: When adjusting the clutch pedal height or the clutch pedal clevis pin play, be careful not to push the pushrod toward the master cylinder.

   d. Check that when the clutch pedal is depressed all the way, the interlock switch switches over from **ON** to **OFF**.

Clutch Cable

ADJUSTMENT

To adjust the clutch cable, turn the adjusting wheel at the firewall to obtain the proper free-play of about 1 inch.

REMOVAL AND INSTALLATION

1. Disconnect the negative battery cable.

2. Remove the cable retaining clamps.

3. Remove the cotter pin from the clutch actuating arm at the transaxle and disconnect the cable.

4. Rotate the adjusting wheel counterclockwise to loosen the cable.

Disconnect the cable at the pedal and remove the cable from the vehicle.

5. The installation is the reverse of the removal procedure.

6. Lubricate all pivot points. Adjust the cable to achieve proper free-play.

Clutch Master Cylinder

REMOVAL AND INSTALLATION

1. Disconnect the negative battery cable.

2. Remove necessary underhood components in order to gain access to the clutch master cylinder.

3. Loosen the line at the cylinder and allow the fluid to drain. Use care; brake fluid damages paint.

4. On all but AWD 3000GT, remove the clevis pin retainer at the clutch pedal and remove the washer and clevis pin. AWD 3000GT has a clutch pedal booster which directly activates the master cylinder.

5. Remove the 2 nuts and pull the cylinder from the firewall. A seal should be between the mounting flange and firewall. This seal should be replaced.

6. The installation is the reverse of the removal procedure.

7. Lubricate all pivot points with grease.

8. Bleed the system at the slave cylinder using DOT 3 brake fluid and check the adjustment of the clutch pedal.

Clutch Slave Cylinder

REMOVAL AND INSTALLATION

1. Disconnect the negative battery cable. Remove necessary underhood components in order to gain access to the clutch release cylinder.

2. Remove the hydraulic line and allow the system to drain.

3. Remove the bolts and pull the cylinder from the transaxle housing. On some 1.5L engines, instead of a pushrod bearing against the clutch arm, a clevis pin and yoke is used. Simply remove the circlip, pull out the clevis pin and remove the cylinder.

4. The installation is the reverse of the removal procedure.

5. Lubricate all pivot points with grease.

6. Bleed the system using DOT 3 brake fluid.

Hydraulic Clutch System Bleeding

1. Fill the reservoir with brake fluid.

2. Loosen the bleed screw, have the clutch pedal pressed to the floor.

3. Tighten the bleed screw and release the clutch pedal.

4. Repeat the bleeding operation until the fluid is free of air bubbles.

NOTE: It is suggested to attach a hose to the bleeder and place the other end into a container at least ½ full of brake fluid during the bleeding operation. Do not allow the reservoir to run out of fluid during the bleeding operation.

AUTOMATIC TRANSMISSION

Transmission Assembly

REMOVAL AND INSTALLATION

1. Disconnect the negative battery cable. Raise and support the vehicle safely. Loosen the oil pan screws, tap the oil pan at one corner to break it loose and then allow the fluid to drain out one side. Remove the pan and remove the remaining fluid.

2. Remove its attaching bolt and then remove the transaxle pan filler tube by pulling it upward and out of the transaxle case.

3. Remove both top transaxle attaching bolts from the converter housing.

4. Disconnect the starter wiring and remove the starter.

5. Disconnect the oil cooler hoses at the metal tubes near the engine block. Then, unbolt and remove the tubes and their mountings from the block.

6. Remove the 4 bolts and remove the converter housing cover. Remove the torque converter bolts.

7. Disconnect the speedometer cable. Disconnect the transaxle control rod and the connection lever at the cross shaft assembly.

8. Disconnect the transaxle ground cable. Remove the driveshaft.

9. Support the rear of the transaxle with a floor jack. Unbolt the transaxle rear support bracket by removing 2 bolts on either side. Then, unbolt the bracket from the transaxle.

10. Remove the remaining bolts from the area of the converter housing. Separate the transaxle from the engine and remove it.

To install:

11. Prior to installation, check the distance between the front of the bellhousing and the torque converter driveplate bolts with a straightedge and ruler. The distance must be at least 1.38 in. Install the transmission pan.

12. Lift the transmission into position and install the attaching bolts. Install the transmission rear support and the driveshaft. Connect the transmission ground strap.

13. Install the speedometer cable, transmission control rod and connection lever. Install the oil cooler hoses and install the converter cover.

14. Install the starter. Fill the transmission with fluid and lower the vehicle.

15. Check that the transmission will start only in **N** and **P** positions and that the reverse lights light up in **R** position.

CONTROL ROD ADJUSTMENT

1. Place the transmission in **N**.

2. Raise the vehicle and safely support.

3. Remove the adjustment screw from the inhibitor switch. This screw is located just below the rod attaching nut.

4. Loosen the switch mounting bolts.

5. Using a small punch, move the switch until the pin fits into the aligning hole. Hold the position and tighten the mounting screws.

6. The control rod should now be adjusted. Check it and the inhibitor switch for proper operation.

AUTOMATIC TRANSAXLE

Transaxle Assembly

NOTE: If the vehicle is going to be rolled while the halfshafts are out of the vehicle, obtain 2 outer CV-joints or proper equivalent tools and install to the hubs. If the vehicle is rolled without the proper torque applied to the front wheel bearings, the bearings will no longer be usable.

REMOVAL AND INSTALLATION

Diamante, Sigma and 3000GT

1. Disarm the air bag, if equipped. Remove the battery, battery tray and washer tank.
2. Remove the air cleaner assembly and adjoining duct work.
3. Disconnect the shifter control cable.
4. Disconnect and plug the oil cooler hoses.
5. Disconnect the inhibitor switch, kickdown servo switch, pulse generator, oil temperature sensor, shift control solenoid valve, and ground cable.
6. Disconnect the speedometer cable.
7. Raise the vehicle and support it safely. Remove the undercovers. On Diamante with 4 wheel steering, remove the rear power steering pump heat protector and disconnect the lines from the pump. Plug the lines to prevent dirt intrusion.
8. Support the weight of the transaxle and remove the mount bracket. Remove the upper bellhousing bolts.
9. Disconnect the tie rod end and ball joint from the steering knuckle.
10. Remove the right frame member.
11. Remove the starter.
12. Remove the halfshafts by inserting a prybar between the transaxle case and the driveshaft and prying the shaft from the transaxle. Do not pull on the driveshaft. Doing so damages the inboard joint. Use the prybar. Do not insert the prybar so far the oil seal in the case is damaged. Tie the halfshafts aside.
13. Remove the remaining mounting brackets.
14. Remove the bellhousing cover plate.
15. Remove the special bolts holding the flexplate to the torque converter.

16. After removing the bolts, push the torque converter toward the transaxle so it doesn't stay on the engine side and allow oil to pour out the converter hub.
17. Remove the lower transaxle to engine bolts and remove the transaxle assembly.

To install:

18. After the torque converter has been mounted on the transaxle, install the transaxle assembly on the engine. Tighten the driveplate bolts to 34-38 ft. lbs. (46-53 Nm). Install the bellhousing cover.
19. Install the mounting brackets.
20. Replace the circlips and install the halfshafts to the transaxle.
21. Install the starter and frame member.
22. Install the tie rods and ball joint to the steering arm.
23. Install the upper bellhousing bolts.
24. Install the transaxle mounting bracket.
25. Install the undercovers.
26. Connect the speedometer cable.
27. Connect the inhibitor switch, kickdown servo switch, pulse generator, oil temperature sensor, shift control solenoid valve, and ground cable.
28. Connect the oil cooler hoses.
29. Connect the shifter control cable.
30. Install the air cleaner assembly and adjoining duct work.
31. Install the washer tank, battery tray and battery.
32. Refill with Dexron® II.
33. Start the engine and allow to idle for 2 minutes. Apply parking brake and move selector through each gear position, ending in **N**. Recheck fluid level and add if necessary. Fluid level should be between the marks in the **HOT** range.

Eclipse and Galant

1. Remove the battery and battery tray.
2. On 1990-91 equipped with auto-cruise, remove the control actuator and bracket.
3. Drain the transaxle fluid.
4. Remove the air cleaner assembly, intercooler and air hose.
5. Remove the adjusting nut and disconnect the shift cable.
6. Disconnect and tag the electrical connectors for the solenoid, neutral safety switch (inhibitor switch), the pulse generator kickdown servo switch and oil temperature sensor.
7. Disconnect the speedometer cable and oil cooler lines.
8. Disconnect the wires to the starter motor and remove the starter.

9. Remove the upper transaxle to engine bolts.
10. Support the transaxle and remove the transaxle mounting bracket.
11. Raise the vehicle and support safely. Remove the sheet metal under guard.
12. Remove the tie rod ends and the ball joints from the steering knuckle.
13. Remove the halfshafts by inserting a prybar between the transaxle case and the driveshaft and prying the shaft from the transaxle. Do not pull on the driveshaft. Doing so damages the inboard joint. Use the prybar. Do not insert the prybar so far the oil seal in the case is damaged. Tie the halfshafts aside.
14. On AWD, disconnect the exhaust pipe, remove the frame pieces, and remove the transfer case.
15. Remove the lower bellhousing cover and remove the special bolts holding the flexplate to the torque converter. To remove, turn the engine crankshaft with a box wrench and bring the bolts into position appropriate for removal, 1 at a time. After removing the bolts, push the torque converter toward the transaxle so it doesn't stay on the engine allowing oil to pour out the converter hub or cause damage to the converter.
16. Remove the lower transaxle to engine bolts and remove the transaxle assembly.

To install:

17. After the torque converter has been mounted on the transaxle, install the transaxle assembly on the engine. Tighten the driveplate bolts to 34-38 ft. lbs. (46-53 Nm). Install the bellhousing cover.
18. On AWD, install the transfer case and frame pieces. Connect the exhaust pipe using a new gasket.
19. Replace the circlips and install the halfshafts to the transaxle.
20. Install the tie rods and ball joint to the steering arm.
21. Install the transaxle mounting bracket.
22. Install the under guard.
23. Install the starter.
24. Connect the speedometer cable and oil cooler lines.
25. Connect the solenoid, neutral safety switch (inhibitor switch), the pulse generator kickdown servo switch and oil temperature sensor.
26. Install the shift control cable.
27. Install the air hose, intercooler and air cleaner assembly.
28. If equipped with auto-cruise, install the control actuator and bracket.

29. Refill with Dexron® II.
30. Start the engine and allow to idle for 2 minutes. Apply parking brake and move selector through each gear position, ending in **N**. Recheck fluid level and add if necessary. Fluid level should be between the marks in the **HOT** range.

Expo/Expo LRV

1. Disconnect negative battery cable.
2. Remove the air cleaner assembly.
3. Disconnect the transaxle control lever. Disconnect and plug the oil cooler lines.
4. Disconnect the pulse generator connector, oil temperature connector, kickdown servo switch connector, inhibitor switch connector and solenoid valve connection.
5. Disconnect the speedometer cable connection. Remove the oil level dipstick and tube.
6. Install holding fixture to the top of the engine to support engine weight.
7. Remove the top transaxle upper coupling bolts.
8. Raise and safely support the vehicle.
9. Remove the starter motor leaving wire harness attached.
10. Remove the right side under cover. Drain the transaxle fluid.
11. Disconnect the tie rod ends, stabilizer bar and lower ball joints. If equipped with AWD, it will be necessary to remove the right driveshaft from the vehicle.
12. Except AWD, remove the driveshafts from the transfer case, insert a prybar between the driveshaft and the transaxle case and pry the shaft from the transaxle housing. Swing the shafts out of the way keeping the joints straight, and suspend using wire. Turn the right shaft 90 degrees toward the front of the vehicle so it will not be a hindrance.

NOTE: Do not pull on the shaft during removal from the transaxle; doing so will damage the inboard joint. Do not insert the prybar so deep as to damage the oil seal.

13. Remove the lower bellhousing cover. Scribe a mark on the driveplate and transaxle converter face using chalk. Remove the driveplate connecting bolts while turning the crankshaft.

14. Support the transaxle using a transmission jack. Remove the center support.
15. Remove the transaxle mount bolt and bracket.
16. If equipped with AWD, disconnect the front exhaust pipe and remove the transfer assembly.
17. Remove the lower transaxle case coupling bolts, press the torque converter towards the transfer case to prevent separation during removal and lower the transfer case from the vehicle.

To install:
18. Install the transaxle into the vehicle and secure using the lower case coupling bolts.
19. Install the transaxle mount bolt and bracket, torque through bolt nut to 51 ft. lbs. (70 Nm).
20. Align the scribe marks on the converter and the driveplate. Install the driveplate connecting bolts torqueing to 33-38 ft. lbs. (46-53 Nm).
21. Install the transfer assembly and the center cross member. Remove the transmission jack.
22. Install the center exhaust pipe.
23. Install the drive axles into the transfer case taking care not to damage the oil seal lip part of the transaxle with the serrated part of the driveshaft.
24. Connect the tie rod ends, stabilizer bar and lower ball joints.
25. Install the right side under cover.
26. Lower the vehicle. Install the upper transaxle coupling bolts.
27. Connect the speedometer cable, and the electrical harness connectors disconnected during the removal procedure.
28. Install the starter motor torqueing the retainer bolts to 35 ft. lbs. (49 Nm).
29. Connect the transaxle cooler hoses and the connections for the manual controls.
30. Install the air cleaner assembly and the oil level dipstick and tube.
31. Refill with Dexron® II.
32. Start the engine and allow to idle for 2 minutes. Apply parking brake and move selector through each gear position, ending in **N**. Recheck fluid level and add if necessary. Fluid level should be between the marks in the **HOT** range. Check operation of all gauges and meters.

Mirage and Precis

1. Disconnect the negative battery cable.
2. Remove the battery and battery tray.

3. Remove the air pipe and air hose.
4. Raise the vehicle and support safely.
5. Drain the transaxle oil.
6. If equipped with 1.6L engine, remove the tension rod.
7. Disconnect the control cable and cooler lines.
8. Disconnect the throttle control cable on 3 speed transaxle.
9. Disconnect the shift control solenoid valve connector on 4 speed transaxle.
10. Disconnect the inhibitor switch and kickdown servo switch on 4 speed transaxle.
11. Disconnect the pulse generator and oil temperature sensor on 4 speed transaxle.
12. Disconnect the speedometer cable and remove the starter.
13. Remove the transaxle mounting bolts and bracket.
14. Remove the under guard pan.
15. Disconnect the steering tie rod end and the ball joint from the steering arm.
16. Remove the halfshafts at the inboard side from the transaxle. Tie the joint assembly aside.
17. Remove the bellhousing cover and remove the driveplate bolts.
18. Remove the transaxle assembly lower connecting bolt, located just over the halfshaft opening.
19. Properly support the transaxle assembly and lower it moving it to the right for clearance.

To install:
20. After the torque converter has been mounted on the transaxle, install the transaxle assembly on the engine. Tighten the driveplate bolts to 34-38 ft. lbs. (46-53 Nm). Install the bellhousing cover.
21. Replace the circlips and install the halfshafts to the transaxle.
22. Install the tie rods and ball joint to the steering arm.
23. Install the underguard and the mounting brackets.
24. Install the starter.
25. Connect the speedometer cable.
26. Connect the control cables, oil cooler lines and electrical connections.
27. Install the tension rod.
28. Install the air pipe and hose, battery tray and battery.
29. Refill with Dexron® II.
30. Start the engine and allow to idle for 2 minutes. Apply parking brake and move selector through each gear position, ending in **N**. Recheck fluid level and add if necessary. Fluid level should be between the marks in the **HOT** range.

SHIFTER CONTROL CABLE ADJUSTMENT

1. The shifter cable adjustment is done at the neutral safety switch (inhibitor switch). Locate the switch on the transaxle and note the alignment holes in the arm and the body of the switch. Place the selector lever in **N**. Place the manual lever of the transaxle in the neutral position.

2. Check alignment of the hole in the manual control lever to the hole in the inhibitor switch body. If the holes do not align, adjustment is required.

3. To adjust, loosen the nut on the cable end and pull the cable end by hand until the alignment holes match. Tighten the nut. Check that the transaxle shifts and conforms to the positions of the selector lever.

THROTTLE CONTROL CABLE ADJUSTMENT

Most vehicles do not use a throttle linkage. Instead, the throttle position sensor provides an electric signal to the transaxle, so no adjustment is required.

1. Check that the throttle lever is in the CURB IDLE position, with the engine **OFF** but at normal operating temperature.

2. At the lower cable bracket, raise the cone shaped cover to uncover a small fitting on the cable. By loosening the locknut and adjuster nut, make the distance between the fitting on the cable and the lower collar is 0.020-0.060 in.

3. With the throttle in the wide open position, check that the cable does not bind.

TRANSFER CASE

Transfer Case

REMOVAL AND INSTALLATION

Eclipse, Galant and 3000GT

1. Disconnect the battery negative cable.

2. Raise the vehicle and support safely. Drain the transfer oil.

3. On 3000GT, remove necessary front bumper components.

4. Disconnect the front exhaust pipe.

5. Unbolt the transfer case assembly and remove by sliding it off the rear driveshaft. Be careful not to damage the oil seal in the transfer case output housing. Do not let the rear driveshaft hang; suspend it from a frame piece. Cover the opening in the transaxle and transfer case to keep oil from dripping and to keep dirt out.

To install:

6. Lubricate the driveshaft sleeve yoke and oil seal lip on the transfer extension housing. Install the transfer case assembly to the transaxle. Use care when installing the rear driveshaft to the transfer case output shaft.

7. Tighten the transfer case to transaxle bolts to 40-43 ft. lbs. (55-60 Nm) on Eclipse with manual transaxle; 43-58 ft. lbs. (60-80 Nm) on Eclipse with automatic transaxle or 64 ft. lbs. (88 Nm) on 3000GT.

8. Install the exhaust pipe using a new gasket. Install removed bumper components.

9. Refill the transfer case and check oil levels in transaxle and transfer case.

Expo/Expo LRV

1. Disconnect the battery negative cable.

2. Raise the vehicle and support safely. Drain the oil from the transfer assembly.

3. Disconnect the front exhaust pipe.

4. Make mating marks on the differential companion flange and the flange yoke. Remove the propeller shaft.

NOTE: Remove the propeller shaft in a straight and level manner so as to ensure that the boot is not damaged through pinching. Damage can be avoided if a piece of cloth or similar material is inserted into the boot. Cover the opening of the transfer assembly to prevent dirt from entering the transfer assembly.

5. Remove the transfer assembly mounting bolts and the transfer assembly from the vehicle.

To install:

6. Position the transfer assembly into the vehicle and secure using the mounting bolts, tightened to 51 ft. lbs. (70 Nm).

7. Align the mating marks and install propeller shaft.

8. Attach the front exhaust pipe using new gasket.

9. Reconnect the negative battery and lower the vehicle. Refill the transfer case and check oil levels in transaxle and transfer case.

FRONT SUSPENSION

MacPherson Strut

REMOVAL AND INSTALLATION

1. Disconnect the negative battery cable.

2. If removing the right front strut:

   a. On Expo/Expo LRV, remove the auto-cruise control actuator.

   b. On vehicles with Electronic Control Suspension, disconnect the front height sensor rod from the control arm.

3. On Expo/Expo LRV, disconnect and remove the daytime running lamp delay and control unit from the mounting bracket located on top of the left strut tower.

4. Raise and safely support vehicle.

5. Remove the brake hose and tube bracket. Do not pry the brake hose and tube clamp away when removing it.

6. If equipped with ABS, disconnect the front speed sensor mounting clamp from the strut. Support the lower arm and remove the strut to knuckle bolts. Use a piece of wire to suspend the knuckle to keep the weight off the brake hose.

7. Remove the dust cover from the top of the strut. On Sigma with ECS, disconnect the air lines from the strut and remove the O-rings. On other vehicles with ECS, disconnect the air line and remove the bushing and O-ring, then disconnect the electrical connector and remove the actuator from the top of the strut.

8. Before removing the top bolts, make matchmarks on the body and the strut insulator for proper reassembly. If this plate is installed improperly, the wheel alignment will be wrong. Remove the strut upper bolts and remove the strut assembly from the vehicle.

To install:

9. Install the strut to the vehicle and install the top bolts.

10. Install or connect ECS components. Rubber parts should be replaced if damaged and lubricated prior to installation.

11. Install to the knuckle and install the bolts.

12. Install the brake hose bracket and the ABS clamp.

13. Install the daytime running lamp delay and control unit to the mounting bracket located on top of the left strut tower.

14. Install the auto-cruise control actuator. Connect the front height sensor rod from the control arm.

15. Install the wheel and tire assembly. Perform a front end alignment and check the ECS system for proper operation and air leaks.

Ball Joints

NOTE: The lower ball joints are not serviceable. If defective, the entire lower arm must be replaced. The ball joints can be check using the procedure below.

INSPECTION

1. Remove the control arm. Wiggle the ball joint a few times to make sure it is free.

2. Double-nut the stud and use a torque wrench to measure how much torque is required to turn it. Starting torque should be:

    a. Diamante and 3000GT: 86-191 inch lbs. (10-22 Nm).

    b. Eclipse, Galant, Sigma: 26-87 inch lbs. (3-10 Nm).

    c. Expo/Expo LRV: 17-78 inch lbs. (2-9 Nm).

    d. Mirage and Precis: 48 inch lbs. (5.5 Nm) or less.

3. If the stud has more resistance than specified, replace the lower arm assembly. If the resistance is less, it may still be reused unless it has excessive play.

4. A new grease boot can be installed using a large socket for a driver.

Lower Control Arm

REMOVAL AND INSTALLATION

1. Disconnect the negative battery cable.

2. Raise the vehicle and support safely. On vehicles with Electronic Control Suspension, disconnect the front height sensor rod from the control arm.

3. Remove sway bar links from lower control arm.

4. Disconnect the ball joint stud from the steering knuckle.

5. Remove the inner mounting frame-through bolt and nut.

6. Remove the rear mount bolts. Remove the clamp if equipped.

7. Remove the rear rod bushing if servicing.

To install:

8. Assemble the control arm and bushing.

9. Install the control arm to the vehicle and install the through bolt. Replace the nut and snug temporarily.

10. Install the rear mount clamp, bolts and replacement nuts. Torque the bolts to:

    a. Precis and Mirage: 43-58 ft. lbs. (60-80 Nm)

    b. Expo/Expo LRV: 51 ft. lbs. (70 Nm)

    c. Except above vehicles: 70 ft. lbs. (95 Nm).

11. Torque the nuts, if equipped, to 30 ft. lbs. (41 Nm). Connect the ball joint stud to the knuckle. Install a new nut and torque to 43-52 ft. lbs. (60-72 Nm).

12. Install the sway bar and links.

13. Lower the vehicle to the floor for the final torquing of the frame mount through bolt.

14. Once the full weight of the vehicle is on the floor, torque the frame mount through bolt nuts to 75-90 ft. lbs. (102-122 Nm).

15. Connect the negative battery cable.

Sway Bar

REMOVAL AND INSTALLATION

Except Diamante, Expo/Expo LRV, and 3000GT

1. Disconnect the negative battery cable.

2. Raise and safely support vehicle. Remove the front exhaust pipe if necessary.

3. If necessary, remove the tie rod end from the steering knuckle.

4. Remove the center cross-member rear installation bolts.

5. Remove the stabilizer link bolts. On the ball stud type, hold ball stud with a hex wrench and remove the self-locking nut with a box wrench.

6. Remove the stabilizer bar mounts and remove the bar from the vehicle.

7. The installation is the reverse of the removal procedure. Lubricate all rubber parts when installing. Note that the bar brackets are marked left and right.

8. Tighten the link bolts with rubber bushings just until the bushings are squashed to the width of the washer.

Diamante and 3000GT

1. Disconnect the negative battery cable.

2. Raise the vehicle and support safely.

3. Remove the front exhaust pipe and engine undercover.

4. Remove the left and right frame members.

5. On AWD vehicles with automatic transaxle, remove the transfer case bracket and transfer case.

6. Remove the sway bar link.

7. Remove the sway bar brackets and remove the sway bar from the vehicle.

To install:

8. Note that the bar brackets are marked left and right. Lubricate all rubber parts and install the bushings, the sway bar and brackets.

9. Install the sway bar link.

10. Install the transfer case and bracket.

11. Install the frame members.

12. Install the engine undercover and exhaust pipe.

13. Connect the negative battery cable.

Expo/Expo LRV

1. Disconnect the negative battery cable.

2. Raise and safely support vehicle. Remove the front exhaust pipe.

3. Remove the stabilizer bar mounting nuts.

4. Remove the bolts from the stabilizer bar mounting fixtures and remove the bar, bushings and fixtures from the vehicle.

5. Installation is the reverse of the removal procedure. Torque the stabilizer fixture mounting fixtures to 16 ft. lbs. (22 Nm), the stabilizer bar link nuts to 29 ft. lbs. (40 Nm) and the exhaust flange nuts to 33 ft. lbs. (45 Nm).

Front Wheel Bearings

NOTE: This section pertains to Rear Wheel Drive vehicles only. For Front Wheel Drive and/or All Wheel Drive vehicles, please refer to the Drive Axle section.

ADJUSTMENT

1. Remove the wheel and grease cap. Remove the cotter pin and locking cap from the nut.

2. Torque the wheel bearing nut to 14.5 ft. lbs. and then loosen the nut. Retorque the nut to 3.6 ft. lbs. and install the lock cap and cotter a new cotter pin. Tighten the nut to clear

the hole for cotter pin installation; don't loosen it.

3. Install the grease seal and the wheel.

REMOVAL AND INSTALLATION

1. Raise and support the vehicle safely. Remove the tire and wheel. Remove the caliper.

2. Remove the grease cap. Remove the cotter pin and locking cap from the nut.

3. Being careful not to drop the outer bearing, pull off the brake disc and wheel hub.

4. Remove the grease inside the wheel hub.

5. Using a brass drift, carefully drive the outer bearing race out of the hub.

6. Remove the inner bearing seal and bearing.

To install:

7. Check the bearings for wear or damage and replace them, if necessary.

8. Coat the inner surface of the hub with grease.

9. Grease the outer surface of the bearing race and drift it into place in the hub.

10. Pack the inner and outer wheel bearings with grease. If the brake disc has been removed and/or replaced, tighten the retaining bolts to specification.

11. Install the inner bearing in the hub. Being careful not to distort it, install the oil seal with its lip facing the bearing. Drive the seal on until its outer edge is even with the edge of the hub.

12. Install the hub/disc assembly on the spindle, being careful not to damage the oil seal.

13. Install the outer bearing, washer and spindle nut. Adjust the bearing.

REAR SUSPENSION

Shock Absorber Assembly

REMOVAL AND INSTALLATION

Expo/Expo LRV

1. Disconnect the negative battery cable.

2. Remove the trim cover inside the hatch area for access to the top mounting nuts.

3. Support the lower arm with a jack and compress the coil spring. Remove the lower mounting nut.

4. Remove the cap from the upper end of the shock.

5. Remove the upper mounting nut and the shock from the vehicle.

To install:

6. Install the shock absorber to the lower arm so the flat mounting boss on the shock absorber is against the lower control arm. Install the lower nut and tighten to 72 ft. lbs. (100 Nm).

7. Install the upper nut and torque to 33 ft. lbs. (45 Nm).

8. Install the cap and trim cover.

9. Lower the arm and remove the jack.

MacPherson Strut

REMOVAL AND INSTALLATION

1. Disconnect the negative battery cable. Remove the trim panel inside the trunk or hatch area for access to the top mounting nuts. On Sigma, remove the rear seat.

2. Remove the top cap. On Sigma with ECS, disconnect the air tubes and O-rings from the actuator, then carefully matchmark the actuator bracket and remove the actuator bracket and actuator from the piston rod. Use a wrench on the rod to prevent rotation. Remove the mounting nuts. Disconnect the ECS connector if equipped.

3. Remove the brake tube bracket bolt if necessary.

4. Raise and safely support torsion axle and arm assembly slightly. Make sure the jack does not contact the lateral rod.

5. Remove the strut lower mounting nut or bolts, and remove strut from the vehicle.

To install:

6. Install the strut assembly and install the mounting nuts or bolts.

7. Remove the brake tube bracket bolt if necessary.

8. On Sigma with ECS, install the actuator and actuator bracket to the strut, using the matchmarks made earlier. Use a wrench on the rod to prevent rotation. Connect the air tubes with new lubricated O-rings to the actuator. Connect the ECS connector if equipped.

9. Install the mounting nuts and top cap.

10. Install removed the trim panel inside the trunk or hatch area for access to the top mounting nuts. On Sigma, install the rear seat.

11. Connect the negative battery cable. Check the ECS system for proper operation and leaks on Sigma.

Coil Springs

REMOVAL AND INSTALLATION

Expo/Expo LRV

1. Remove the rear stabilizer bar.

2. Using a jack, support the lower arm. Remove the rear shock absorber.

3. If equipped with AWD, remove the rear driveshaft mounting bolts at the carrier flange and hang the driveshaft from the vehicle body using wire.

4. If equipped with ABS, remove the speed sensor clamp bolt and relocate out of the way. Do not apply tension to the wire harness of the connector.

5. Scribe mating marks on the lower arm shaft assembly and the crossmember. To remove the coil spring, loosen the shaft assembly nut and slowly lower the rear end of the lower arm. It is not necessary to remove the nut, only to loosen it.

To install:

6. Install the coil spring into the seats making sure both ends of the spring are correctly aligned with the spring seat groove.

7. Slowly raise the rear the rear end of the lower arm and align the scribe marks made during disassembly. Tighten shaft assembly nut to 69 ft. lbs. (95 Nm).

8. Install the speed sensor clamp to it's original location and secure the wire harness making.

9. Install the rear driveshaft to the flange and secure tightening mounting bolts to 40-47 ft. lbs. (55-65 Nm).

10. Reconnect the lower portion of the shock and tighten the retaining bolt to 72 ft. lbs. (100 Nm).

11. Lower the arm and remove the jack.

Rear Control Arms

REMOVAL AND INSTALLATION

Expo/Expo LRV

1. Disconnect negative battery cable.

2. Remove the rear stabilizer bar.

3. If equipped with AWD, remove the rear axle shaft.

4. Remove the rear brake drum.

5. If equipped with ABS, remove the rear caliper assembly and brake disc.

6. Remove the rear hub assembly. If equipped with ABS, take care not to damage the rotor teeth during hub removal.

7. Disconnect the parking brake cable from the rear brake shoe.

8. If equipped with ABS, disconnect and remove the rear wheel sensor.

NOTE: The speed sensor has a pole piece projecting from it. This exposed tip must be protected from impact or scratches. Do not allow the pole piece to contact the toothed wheel during removal or installation.

9. Remove the rear shock and coil spring.

10. Remove the brake line and parking brake mounting bolts from the lower control arm.

11. Matchmark and remove the inboard lower arm pivot bolt. Remove the flange bolt and the arm from the vehicle.

To install:

12. Install the arm on the vehicle and secure with the flange bolt, temporarily tighten the nut. Install the arm pivot bolt and temporarily tighten the nut.

13. Install the rear shock and coil spring.

14. Install the brake line and parking brake mounting bolts to the lower control arm.

15. Connect the parking brake cable to the rear brake shoe.

16. Install the rear hub assembly.

17. Install the rear brake drum or, if equipped with ABS, install the rear caliper assembly and brake disc.

18. Install the rear axle shaft.

19. Install and connect the rear wheel speed sensor. Use a brass or other non-magnetic feeler gauge to check the air gap between the tip of the pole piece and the toothed wheel. Correct gap is 0.012-0.035 in. (0.3-0.9mm). Tighten the 2 sensor bracket bolts to 10 ft. lbs. (14 Nm) with the sensor located so the gap is the same at several points on the toothed wheel. If the gap is incorrect, it is likely that the toothed wheel is worn or improperly installed.

20. Lower the vehicle and tighten the lower arm flange bolt nut and the arm pivot bolt to 69 ft. lbs. (95 Nm).

21. Install the rear stabilizer bar and reconnect the negative battery cable.

22. Bleed the brake system if any lines where opened. Adjust the parking brake and perform a rear wheel alignment.

Galant and Eclipse w/AWD, 3000GT and Diamante

1. Disconnect the negative battery cable. On FWD 3000GT, remove the rear strut assembly. Raise and safely support vehicle. Remove the brake line clamp bolt.

2. Remove the ball joint(s) from the rear trailing arm/steering knuckle.

3. If removing the lower arm, disconnect the sway bar link from the arm.

4. Matchmark and remove the inboard lower arm pivot bolt, if necessary, and remove the arm from the vehicle.

5. Installation is the reverse of the removal procedure. Replace all self-locking nuts. Do not torque the inboard pivot nuts until the full weight of the vehicle is on the ground.

6. On Eclipse, torque the lower arm installation nut to 65-80 ft. lbs. (90-110 Nm) and the upper arm installation nut to 101-116 ft. lbs. (140-160 Nm). On 3000GT, torque the lower and the upper arm installation nuts to 101-116 ft. lbs. (140-160 Nm).

7. Perform a rear wheel alignment.

Rear Trailing Arm

REMOVAL AND INSTALLATION

Galant and Eclipse w/AWD, 3000GT and Diamante

1. Disconnect the negative battery cable. Raise and safely support vehicle.

2. Remove the rear caliper from the brake disc and suspend with a wire. Remove the brake disc. Disconnect the parking brake cable and remove the mounting bolts along the trailing arm.

3. Remove the bolt(s) holding the speed sensor bracket to the knuckle and remove the assembly from the vehicle.

NOTE: The speed sensor has a pole piece projecting from it. This exposed tip must be protected from impact or scratches. Do not allow the pole piece to contact the toothed wheel during removal or installation.

4. On AWD, remove the rear axle to companion flange bolts and nuts and separate the axle from the companion flange. Remove the self-locking nut and remove the axle hub and companion flange. Remove the dust shield.

5. On FWD 3000GT, remove the axle hub unit, parking brake shoes and backing plate. Remove the sway bar link bolt.

6. Remove the lower strut mounting bolt.

7. Remove the control arms from the trailing arm.

8. Remove the trailing arm front mounting nuts and bolts and remove the trailing arm from the vehicle. On AWD, remove the connecting rod at the front of the arm using tool MB991254 or equivalent.

To install:

9. Assemble the trailing arm and connecting rod. Install the trailing arm to the vehicle and install the front mounting nuts and bolts. Complete the final tightening of these when the full weight of the vehicle is on the ground.

10. Install the control arms to the trailing arm, using new self-locking nuts.

11. Install the lower strut bolt.

12. On FWD 3000GT, install the sway bar link. Install the parking brake parts and axle hub unit.

13. On AWD, install the dust shield, axle hub and companion flange with a new self-locking nut. Connect the rear axle to the companion flange.

14. Temporarily install the speed sensor to the knuckle; tighten the bolts only finger-tight.

15. Route the cable correctly and loosely install the clips and retainers. All clips must be in their original position and the sensor cable must not be twisted. Improper installation may cause cable damage and system failure.

NOTE: The wiring in the harness is easily damaged by twisting and flexing. Use the white stripe on the outer insulation to keep the sensor harness properly placed.

16. Use a brass or other non-magnetic feeler gauge to check the air gap between the tip of the pole piece and the toothed wheel. Correct gap is 0.012-0.035 inch (0.3-0.9mm). Tighten the 2 sensor bracket bolts to 10 ft. lbs. (14 Nm) with the sensor located so the gap is the same at several points on the toothed wheel. If the gap is incorrect, it is likely that the toothed wheel is worn or improperly installed.

17. Install the brake disc, caliper and connect the parking brake cable,

if not already done. Install the mounting clamps bolts.

18. Double check everything for correct routing and Installation. Lower the vehicle so its full weight is on the floor.

19. On Eclipse and FWD 3000GT, torque the front trailing arm/spindle assembly mount nuts to 101-116 ft. lbs. (140-160 Nm). On AWD 3000GT, tighten front trailing arm/spindle assembly mount nuts to 145-174 ft. lbs. (200-240 Nm).

20. Perform a rear wheel alignment.

Rear Wheel Bearings

NOTE: This section pertains to Front Wheel Drive vehicles only. For Rear Wheel Drive and/or All Wheel Drive vehicles, please refer to the Drive Axle section.

REMOVAL AND INSTALLATION

Except Expo/Expo LRV, Mirage and Precis

1. Raise the vehicle and support safely.
2. Remove the tire and wheel assembly.
3. Remove the bolt(s) holding the speed sensor bracket to the knuckle and remove the assembly from the vehicle.

NOTE: The speed sensor has a pole piece projecting from it. This exposed tip must be protected from impact or scratches. Do not allow the pole piece to contact the toothed wheel during removal or installation.

4. Remove the caliper from the brake disc and suspend with a wire.
5. Remove the brake disc.
6. Remove the grease cap, self-locking nut and tongued washer.
7. Remove the rear hub assembly.

NOTE: The rear hub assembly can not be disassembled. If bearing replacement is required, replace the assembly as a unit.

To install:
8. Install the hub assembly.
9. Install the tongued washer and a new self-locking nut. Torque the nut to 144-188 ft. lbs. (200-260 Nm), align with the indentation in the spindle, and crimp.
10. Set up a dial indicator and measure the end-play while moving the hub in and out. If the end-play exceeds 0.004 in. (0.01mm) for Eclipse

or 0.002 in. (0.005mm) for 3000GT, retorque the nut. If still beyond the limit, replace the hub unit.

11. Install the grease cap and brake parts.

12. Temporarily install the speed sensor to the knuckle; tighten the bolts only finger-tight.

13. Route the cable correctly and loosely install the clips and retainers. All clips must be in their original position and the sensor cable must not be twisted. Improper installation may cause cable damage and system failure.

NOTE: The wiring in the harness is easily damaged by twisting and flexing. Use the white stripe on the outer insulation to keep the sensor harness properly placed.

14. Use a brass or other non-magnetic feeler gauge to check the air gap between the tip of the pole piece and the toothed wheel. Correct gap is 0.012-0.035 in. (0.3-0.9mm). Tighten the 2 sensor bracket bolts to 10 ft. lbs. (14 Nm) with the sensor located so the gap is the same at several points on the toothed wheel. If the gap is incorrect, it is likely that the toothed wheel is worn or improperly installed.

15. Install the wheel.

Expo/Expo LRV

1. Raise the vehicle and support safely. Remove the tire and wheel assembly.

2. If equipped with ABS, remove the caliper assembly, brake disc and rear wheel speed sensor from the adapter. If not equipped with ABS, remove the brake drum.

NOTE: The speed sensor has a pole piece projecting from it. This exposed tip must be protected from impact or scratches. Do not allow the pole piece to contact the toothed wheel during removal or installation.

3. Remove the dust cap, nut and tongued washer. Do not use an air gun to remove the nut.

4. Remove the rear hub assembly taking care not to scrape or damage the teeth of the speed rotor, if equipped.

5. Inspect the hub unit bearing for wear or damage. If replacement of the bearing is required, the hub assembly and bearing is to be replaced as a unit. The rear hub unit bearing assembly should should not be dismantled.

6. Installation is the reverse of the removal procedure.

Mirage and Precis

1. Raise the vehicle and support safely.
2. Remove the tire and wheel assembly.
3. If equipped with rear disc brakes, remove the caliper from the disc and remove the brake disc.
4. Remove the dust cap and bearing nut. Do not use an air gun to remove the nut.
5. Remove the outer wheel bearing.
6. Remove the drum and/or axle hub with the inner wheel bearing and the grease seal.
7. Remove the grease seal and remove the inner bearing.

To install:
8. Lubricate the inner bearing and install to the drum or hub.
9. Install a new grease seal.
10. To determine if the self-locking nut is reusable:

a. Screw in the self-locking nut until about 1/16 in. of the spindle is showing.

b. Measure the torque required to turn the self-locking nut counterclockwise.

c. The lowest allowable torque is 48 inch lbs. (5.5 Nm). If the measured torque is less than the specification, replace the nut.

11. Install the drum and/or hub to the vehicle.

12. Lubricate and install the outer wheel bearing to the spindle.

13. Torque the self-locking nut to 108-145 ft. lbs. (150-200 Nm).

14. Set up a dial indicator and measure the end-play while moving the hub or drum in and out. If the end-play exceeds 0.008 in. (0.002mm), retorque the nut. If still beyond the limit, replace the bearings.

15. Install the grease cap and wheel assembly.

Rear Axle Assembly

REMOVAL AND INSTALLATION

1. Raise the vehicle and support safely.
2. Remove the tire and wheel assembly.
3. Disconnect the ECS height sensing rod if equipped. If equipped with ABS, remove the bolts holding the speed sensor bracket to the trail-

ing arm and remove the sensor assembly from the vehicle.

NOTE: The speed sensor has a pole piece projecting from it. This exposed tip must be protected from impact or scratches. Do not allow the pole piece to contact the toothed wheel during removal or installation.

4. If equipped with rear disc brakes, remove the caliper from the disc and remove the brake disc.

5. Remove the dust cap and bearing nut. Do not use an air gun to remove the nut.

6. Remove the outer wheel bearing.

7. Remove the drum and/or axle hub with the inner wheel bearing and the grease seal.

8. Remove the parking brake cable, brake hose, tube bracket and brake shoes with backing plate from the axle.

9. Remove the lateral rod mounting bolt and nut and secure the lateral rod to the axle beam with a piece of wire.

10. Using the proper equipment, slightly raise the torsion axle and arm assembly. Remove lower strut mounting bolt.

11. Remove the front trailing arm mount bolts and remove the rear axle assembly.

To install:

12. Install the rear axle assembly to the vehicle and install the strut mounting bolts. Install the front mount bolts and lateral rod bolts. Do not tighten these until the full weight of the vehicle is on the ground.

13. Install the backing plate, brake shoes, cable and hose.

14. On Mirage, to determine if the self-locking nut is reusable:

a. Screw in the self-locking nut until about 1/16 in. of the spindle nut is showing.

b. Measure the torque required to turn the self-locking nut counterclockwise.

c. The lowest allowable torque is 48 inch lbs. (5.5 Nm). If the measured torque is less than the specification, replace the nut.

15. Install the drum and/or axle hub. On Mirage, lubricate and install the outer wheel bearing to the spindle. Torque the self-locking nut to 108-145 ft. lbs. (150-200 Nm).

16. On Eclipse, install the tongued washer and a new self-locking nut. Torque the nut to 144-188 ft. lbs. (200-260 Nm), align with the indentation in the spindle, and crimp.

17. Install the grease cap and brake parts.

18. Temporarily install the speed sensor to the knuckle; tighten the bolts only finger-tight.

19. Route the cable correctly and loosely install the clips and retainers. All clips must be in their original position and the sensor cable must not be twisted. Improper installation may cause cable damage and system failure.

NOTE: The wiring in the harness is easily damaged by twisting and flexing. Use the white stripe on the outer insulation to keep the sensor harness properly placed.

20. Use a brass or other non-magnetic feeler gauge to check the air gap between the tip of the pole piece and the toothed wheel. Correct gap is 0.012-0.035 in. (0.3-0.9mm). Tighten the 2 sensor bracket bolts to 10 ft. lbs. (14 Nm) with the sensor located so the gap is the same at several points on the toothed wheel. If the gap is incorrect, it is likely that the toothed wheel is worn or improperly installed.

21. Install the wheel.

22. Lower the vehicle so the full weight of the vehicle is on the floor.

23. On Mirage, torque the front trailing arm bolt to 94-108 ft. lbs. (130-150 Nm). On Eclipse, torque the trailing arm bolt to 72-87 ft. lbs. (100-120 Nm).

24. Torque the axle side lateral rod nut to 58-72 ft. lbs. (80-100 Nm) on Mirage or 72-87 ft. lbs. (100-120 Nm) on Eclipse.

STEERING

Steering Wheel

NOTE: If equipped with an air bag, be sure to disarm it before entering the vehicle.

REMOVAL AND INSTALLATION

Without Air Bag

1. Disconnect the negative battery cable.

2. Remove the horn pad and disconnect horn button connector.

3. Remove steering wheel retaining nut.

4. Matchmark the steering wheel to the shaft.

5. Use a steering wheel puller to remove the steering wheel. Do not

hammer on steering wheel to remove it. The collapsible column mechanism may be damaged.

To install:

6. Line up the matchmarks and install the steering wheel. Torque the retaining nut to 29 ft. lbs. (40 Nm).

7. Install the steering wheel attaching nut and torque to 33 ft. lbs. (45 Nm).

8. Reconnect the horn connector and install the horn pad.

Air Bag

1. To disarm the airbag system:

a. Position the front wheels in the straight-ahead position and place the key in the **LOCK** position. Remove the key from the ignition lock cylinder.

b. Disconnect the negative battery cable and insulate the cable end with high-quality electrical tape or similar non-conductive wrapping.

c. Wait at least 1 minute before working on the vehicle. The air bag system is designed to retain enough voltage to deploy the air bag for a short period of time even after the battery has been disconnected.

d. If necessary, enter the vehicle from the passenger side and turn the key to unlock the steering column.

2. Remove the air bag module mounting nut from behind the steering wheel. Matchmark the steering wheel.

3. Disconnect the connector of the clockspring from the air bag module, press the air bag's lock towards the module to spread the lock open. While holding lock in this position, use a small tipped prying tool to gently pry the connector from the module.

4. Store the air bag module in a clean, dry place with the pad cover facing up.

5. Remove the steering wheel retaining nut. Matchmark the steering wheel to the shaft. Use a steering wheel puller to remove the wheel. Do not use a hammer or the collapsible mechanism in the column could be damaged.

To install:

6. Confirm that the front wheels are in a straight-ahead position. Center the clockspring by aligning the **NEUTRAL** mark on the clockspring with the mating mark on the casing.

7. Line up and install the steering wheel. Torque the retaining nut to 29 ft. lbs. (40 Nm).

Manual Steering Rack

REMOVAL AND INSTALLATION

Eclipse

1. Disconnect the negative battery cable. Raise and safely support vehicle.

2. Remove the bolt holding lower steering column joint to the rack and pinion input shaft.

3. Remove the cotter pins and disconnect the tie rod ends.

4. Locate the triangular brace near the stabilizer bar brackets on the crossmember and remove both the brace and the stabilizer bar brackets.

5. Remove the through bolt from the round roll stopper and remove the rear bolts from the center crossmember.

6. Disconnect the front exhaust pipe.

7. Remove the rack and pinion steering assembly and its rubber mounts. Move the rack to the right to remove from the crossmember. Use caution to avoid damaging the boots.

To install:

8. Install the rack and mounting bolts, torquing bolts to 43-58 ft. lbs. (60-80 Nm). When installing the rubber rack mounts, align the projection of the mounting rubber with the indentation in the crossmember. Install the pinch bolt.

9. Connect the exhaust pipe.

10. Install the center member mounting bolts and roll stopper through bolt.

11. Install the stabilizer bar brackets and brace.

12. Connect the tie rod ends.

13. Perform a front end alignment.

Mirage

1. Disconnect the battery negative cable. Raise the vehicle and support safely.

2. Remove the pinch bolt holding the lower steering column joint to the rack and pinion input shaft.

3. Remove the cotter pins and disconnect the tie rod ends.

4. Remove the rack and pinion steering assembly and its rubber mounts.

5. The installation is the reverse of the removal procedure.

6. Perform a front end alignment.

Precis

1. Raise and support the vehicle safely. Remove the bolt which secures the universal joint in the steering shaft to the gearbox; inside the vehicle where the steering linkage passes through the toe board.

2. Remove the cotter pin from the tie rod end ball stud and loosen the nut. Press the ball stud out of the steering knuckle with a vise like tool such as MB991113 or equivalent; then remove the nut. Do the same on the other side.

3. Cut the band off the steering joint rubber boot.

4. Remove both attaching bolts from the gearbox housing clamp on either side and pull the gearbox out the left side of the vehicle. Work slowly to keep the unit from being damaged.

To install:

5. Install the unit in reverse order.

6. There are rubber tabs on the inside and outside of the sleeve. The larger tab must go on the inside.

7. Use a new band for the steering joint rubber boot. Adjust toe-in.

8. Use the following torques: bracket attaching bolts, 43-58 ft. lbs.; ball stud nut, 17 ft. lbs., then turn farther to align castellations with the cotter pin hole and install a new cotter pin.

9. Turn the steering wheel back and forth to test steering and support the vehicle safely.

Power Steering Rack

REMOVAL AND INSTALLATION

Diamante and 3000GT

NOTE: Prior to removal of the steering gear box, center the front wheels and remove the ignition key. Failure to do so may damage the SRS clockspring and render SRS system inoperative, risking serious driver injury.

1. Disconnect the negative battery cable. Disarm the air bag.

2. Disconnect the front exhaust pipe.

3. If equipped with AWD, remove the transfer case assembly.

4. Remove the bolt holding lower steering column joint to the rack and pinion input shaft.

5. Remove the cotter pins and disconnect the tie rod ends.

6. Remove the left and right frame members.

7. Remove the stabilizer bar bracket.

8. If equipped with 4 wheel steering, disconnect the lines going to the rear pump.

9. Remove the rack and pinion steering assembly and its rubber mounts. Move the rack to the right to remove from the crossmember. Use caution to avoid damaging the boots.

To install:

10. Install the rack and install the mounting bolts, tightening bolts to 51 ft. lbs. (70 Nm). When installing the rubber rack mounts, align the projection of the mounting rubber with the indentation in the crossmember. Install the pinch bolt.

11. Connect the lines going to the 4 wheel steering rear pump and to the rack itself.

12. Install the frame members and torque the bolts to 50 ft. lbs. (68 Nm).

13. Connect the tie rods and Install new cotter pins.

14. Install the transfer case and front exhaust pipe.

15. Refill the reservoir and bleed the system.

16. Perform front end alignment.

Eclipse, Galant and Sigma

NOTE: If equipped with an air bag, prior to removal of the steering gear box, center the front wheels and remove the ignition key. Failure to do so may damage the SRS clockspring and render SRS system inoperative, risking serious driver injury.

1. Disconnect the negative battery cable. Raise the vehicle and support safely.

2. Remove the bolt holding lower steering column joint to the rack and pinion input shaft.

3. Remove the transfer case, if equipped.

4. Remove the cotter pins and disconnect the tie rod ends.

5. Locate the triangular brace near the stabilizer bar brackets on the crossmember and remove both the brace and the stabilizer bar brackets.

6. Remove the through bolt from the round roll stopper and remove the rear bolts from the center crossmember.

7. Disconnect the front exhaust pipe.

8. Disconnect the power steering fluid pressure pipe and return hose from the rack fittings. If equipped with 4 wheel steering, disconnect the lines going to the rear pump.

9. Remove the rack and pinion steering assembly and its rubber mounts. Move the rack to the right to remove from the crossmember. Use caution to avoid damaging the boots.

To install:

10. Install the rack and install the mounting bolts. Torque the mounting bolts to 43-58 ft. lbs. (60-80 Nm). When installing the rubber rack mounts, align the projection of the mounting rubber with the indentation in the crossmember. Install the pinch bolt.

11. Connect the power steering fluid lines to the rack.

12. Connect the exhaust pipe.

13. Install the center member mounting bolts and roll stopper through bolt.

14. Install the stabilizer bar brackets and brace.

15. Connect the tie rod ends.

16. Install the transfer case.

17. Refill the reservoir and bleed the system.

18. Perform a front end alignment.

Expo/Expo LRV, Mirage and Precis

1. Disconnect the battery negative cable. Raise the vehicle and support safely.

2. Remove the pinch bolt holding the lower steering column joint to the rack and pinion input shaft.

3. Remove the cotter pins and disconnect the tie rod ends from the steering knuckle.

4. On Expo/Expo LRV equipped with AWD, remove the transfer case rear bracket.

5. On Expo/Expo LRV equipped with 2.4L engine and FWD, disconnect the stabilizer bar and remove as required.

6. Disconnect the power steering fluid pressure pipe and return hose from the rack fittings.

7. Remove the rack and pinion steering assembly and its rubber mounts.

To install:

8. Install the steering gear into the vehicle and secure using the retainer clamps and bolts.

9. Connect the power steering fluid lines to the rack fittings.

10. Install the stabilizer bar and rear transaxle bracket.

11. Connect the tie rod ends to the steering knuckles.

12. Connect the negative battery cable. Refill the reservoir and bleed the system.

13. Perform a front end alignment.

Rear Steering Gear

REMOVAL AND INSTALLATION

1. Disconnect the negative battery cable. Raise the vehicle and support safely.

2. Drain the power steering fluid.

3. Remove the main muffler assembly.

4. Remove the rear shock absorber lower mounting bolts.

5. Using the proper equipment, support the weight of the rear differential. Remove the 2 small crossmember brackets.

6. Remove the large self-locking crossmember mounting nuts on the differential side.

7. Remove the oil line clamp bolts.

8. Remove the pressure tubes.

9. Hold the tie rod ends stationary and remove the tie rod end nuts. Remove the tie rod ends from the trailing arms.

10. Remove the mounting bolts and remove the rear steering gear.

To install:

11. Secure the unit to the crossmember. Move the power cylinder piston rod over its full stroke to determine its neutral position.

12. Align the tie rod ends with the holes in the trailing arms and install the nuts. Adjust the length of the tie rods with the nuts if necessary. The difference in length between the 2 tie rod ends should not exceed 0.04 in. (1mm). The nuts' torque specification is 42 ft. lbs. (58 Nm).

13. Replace the O-rings and install the pressure tubes. Clamp in place.

14. Install the large self-locking crossmember mounting nuts on the differential side. Torque to 80-94 ft. lbs. (110-130 Nm). Remove the support equipment.

15. Install the 2 small crossmember brackets.

16. Install the shock mounting bolts.

17. Install the muffler assembly.

18. Refill the reservoir and bleed the system.

19. To check and see if the system is functioning:

  a. Raise the vehicle safely so all 4 wheels turn freely.

  b. Run the vehicle at 50 mph.

  c. Turn the steering wheel quickly to the left and right and make sure the rear wheels steer in the same direction as the front wheels.

20. Perform a rear alignment.

Power Steering Pump

REMOVAL AND INSTALLATION

Front

1. Disconnect the battery negative cable.

2. Remove the pressure switch connector from the side of the pump.

3. If the alternator is located under the oil pump, cover it with a shop towel to protect it from oil.

4. Disconnect the return fluid line. Remove the reservoir cap and allow the return line to drain the fluid from the reservoir. If the fluid is contaminated, disconnect the ignition high tension cable and crank the engine several times to drain the fluid from the gearbox.

5. On Expo/Expo LRV equipped with 2.4L engine, remove the alternator drive belt and the heat protector.

6. Disconnect the pressure line.

7. Remove the pump drive belt and unbolt the pump from its bracket.

To install:

8. Install the pump, wrap the belt around the pulley and tighten the bolts.

9. Replace the O-rings and connect the pressure line. Connect the pressure line so the notch in the fitting aligns and contacts the pump's guide bracket.

10. Connect the return line.

11. Connect the pressure switch connector.

12. Adjust the belt tension and tighten the adjusting bolts.

13. Refill the reservoir and bleed the system.

Rear

GALANT AND 3000GT

1. Disconnect the negative battery cable. Raise the vehicle and support safely.

2. Drain the power steering fluid.

3. Remove the main muffler assembly.

4. Remove the rear shock absorber lower mounting bolts.

5. Remove the 2 small crossmember brackets.

6. Using the proper equipment, support the weight of the rear differential. Remove the large self-locking crossmember mounting nuts on the differential side.

7. Disconnect the pressure and suction hoses from the fittings on the pump.

8. Remove the pump retaining bolt and remove the pump from the rear

differential assembly. Do not attempt to disassemble the pump; it is not serviceable.

To install:

9. Replace the O-ring and install the pump assembly to the differential. Make sure the housing is fully seated and the gear is fully engaged. Install the retaining bolt.

10. Replace the O-ring and connect the fluid lines to the pump.

11. Install the large self-locking crossmember mounting nuts on the differential side. Torque to 80-94 ft. lbs. (110-130 Nm). Remove the support equipment.

12. Install the 2 small crossmember brackets.

13. Install the shock mounting bolts.

14. Install the muffler assembly.

15. Refill the reservoir and bleed the system.

--- CAUTION ---

Extreme caution should be taken when testing the rear steering pump. Ensure that the vehicle is supported safely and that all components are torqued to specification prior be testing.

16. To check and see if the system is functioning:

a. Raise the vehicle safely so all 4 wheels turn freely.

b. Run the vehicle at 50 mph.

c. Turn the steering wheel quickly to the left and right and make sure the rear wheels steer in the same direction as the front wheels.

DIAMANTE

1. Disconnect the negative battery cable. Drain the system.

2. Remove the rear power steering pump heat protector, located on the engine side of the differential on the transaxle.

3. Disconnect the pressure line from the pump.

4. Disconnect the suction hose from the pump.

5. Remove the mounting bolts and remove the pump from the transaxle.

6. The installation is the reverse of the removal procedure. Torque the mounting bolts to 17 ft. lbs. (24 Nm).

7. Refill the reservoir and bleed the system.

--- CAUTION ---

Extreme caution should be taken when testing the rear steering pump. Ensure that the vehicle is supported safely and that all components are torqued to specification prior be testing.

8. To check and see if the system is functioning:

a. Raise the vehicle safely so all 4 wheels turn freely.

b. Run the vehicle at 50 mph.

c. Turn the steering wheel quickly to the left and right and make sure the rear wheels steer in the same direction as the front wheels.

BELT ADJUSTMENT

1. Press the belt in about the center between the power steering pump pulley and the pulley it shares, usually the water pump pulley. With reasonable pressure applied, about 22 lbs., the belt should deflect about $^{1}/_{4}$-$^{3}/_{8}$ in.

2. Adjustment can be made by loosening the 3 bolts that hold the pump. Place a suitable bar or lever between the body of the pump and gently pry to get the desired tension.

3. Retighten the 3 bolts and check again.

SYSTEM BLEEDING

Front

1. Raise the vehicle and support safely.

2. Manually turn the pump pulley a few times.

3. Turn the steering wheel all the way to the left and to the right 5 or 6 times.

4. Disconnect the ignition high tension cable and, while operating the starter motor intermittently, turn the steering wheel all the way to the left and right 5-6 times for 15-20 seconds. During bleeding, make sure the fluid in the reservoir never falls below the lower position of the filter. If bleeding is attempted with the engine running, the air will be absorbed in the fluid. Bleed only while cranking.

5. Connect ignition high tension cable, start engine and allow to idle.

6. Turn the steering wheel left and right until there are no air bubbles in the reservoir. Confirm that the fluid is not milky and the level is up to the specified position on the gauge. Confirm that there is is very little change in the fluid level when the steering wheel is turned. If the fluid level changes more than 0.2 in. the air has not been completely bled. Repeat the process.

Rear

1. Bleed the front steering system.

2. Start the engine and let it idle.

3. Loosen the bleeder screw on the left side of the control valve and install special tool MB991230 to the bleeder.

4. Turn the steering wheel all the way to the left, then immediately turn it half way back. Confirm that air has discharged with the fluid.

5. Repeat Step 4 two or three times as required, to remove all air from the rear system. Stop the engine.

6. Loosen the power cylinder (rear steering gear) bleeder screw about $^{1}/_{8}$ turn and install the same special tool with the rotation prevention metal fixtures to prevent the bleeder from opening more.

7. Start the engine and run to 50 mph to circulate the fluid.

8. Maintain a speed of 20 mph and turn the steering wheel back and forth. Air should be discharged through the tube of the special tool and into the oil reservoir.

9. Repeat until all air is removed from the power cylinder.

Tie Rod Ends

REMOVAL AND INSTALLATION

1. Disconnect the battery negative cable.

2. Raise the vehicle and support safely.

3. Wire brush the threads on the tie rod shaft and lubricate with penetrating oil. Loosen the locknut.

4. Remove the cotter pin and nut and press the tie rod end from the steering knuckle.

5. Hold the tie rod shaft with locking pliers and turn the tie rod end off, counting the number of turns for installation purposes.

6. The installation is the reverse of the removal procedure. Install the tie rod end the same number of turns that it took to remove the old one.

7. Perform a front end alignment.

BRAKES

Master Cylinder

REMOVAL AND INSTALLATION

1. Disconnect the negative battery cable.

2. Disconnect the fluid level sensor connector.

3. Disconnect the brake lines from the master cylinder. If a separate fluid reservoir is used, plug the lines to prevent drainage.

4. On 3000GT, disconnect the low pressure hose.

5. Remove the 2 nuts securing the master cylinder and lift off. On Expo/Expo LRV, slide the proportioning valve assembly off the master cylinder mounting studs prior to master cylinder removal.

To install:

6. Bench bleed the master cylinder.

7. Install master cylinder and proportioning valve to the studs and install the nuts.

8. Install the brake lines to the master cylinder. Bleed brake system starting at the master cylinder. If air remains in the system continue bleeding the entire system.

9. Connect the negative battery cable and check the brakes for proper operation.

Proportioning Valve

REMOVAL AND INSTALLATION

1. Disconnect the negative battery cable.

2. Locate the proportioning valve, usually below the master cylinder.

3. Tag and disconnect the brake lines from the valve.

4. Remove the proportioning valve from the engine compartment. On Expo/Expo LRV, remove the master cylinder retainer nuts to remove the proportioning valve assembly.

5. The installation is the reverse of the removal procedure.

6. Bleed the brakes in the following order: **Diamante, Eclipse, Sigma, and 3000GT**
   a. Right rear caliper
   b. Left front caliper
   c. Left rear caliper
   d. Right front caliper

7. Bleed the brakes in the following order: **Expo/Expo LRV, Mirage and Precis**
   a. Left rear wheel cylinder or caliper
   b. Right front cylinder
   c. Right rear wheel cylinder or caliper
   d. Left front caliper

8. Connect the negative battery cable and check the brakes for proper operation.

Power Brake Booster

REMOVAL AND INSTALLATION

1. Disconnect the negative battery cable. If necessary, relocate the relay box and the solenoid valve located at the power brake unit.

2. Disconnect the vacuum hose from the booster. Pull it straight off. Prying off the vacuum hose could damage the check valve installed in the brake booster.

3. Disconnect the brake level sensor connector.

4. Remove the nuts attaching the master cylinder to the booster and remove the master cylinder.

5. From inside the passenger compartment, remove the cotter pin and clevis pin that secures the booster pushrod to the brake pedal.

6. Remove the nuts that attach the booster to the dash panel and remove it from the vehicle.

7. The installation is the reverse of the removal procedure.

8. Connect the negative battery cable, bleed the brakes and check for proper operation.

Brake Caliper

REMOVAL AND INSTALLATION

Front

1. Disconnect the negative battery cable.

2. Raise the vehicle and support safely. Remove appropriate wheel assembly.

3. To disconnect the front brake hose, hold the nut on the brake hose side and loosen the flared brake line nut.

4. Remove the caliper lock pins and remove the caliper.

5. The installation is the reverse of the removal procedure. Make sure the brake hose is not twisted after installation. Refill the brake fluid as required and bleed the brakes.

Rear

PARKING BRAKE MECHANISM IN CALIPER

1. Disconnect the negative battery cable.

2. Raise the vehicle and support safely. Remove appropriate wheel assembly.

3. Disconnect the parking brake cable from the actuator on the caliper.

4. To disconnect the brake hose, hold the nut on the brake hose side and loosen the flared brake line nut.

5. Remove the retaining bolts and remove rear caliper assembly.

6. The installation is the reverse of the removal procedure. Make sure the brake hose is not twisted after installation.

7. Refill the brake fluid as required and bleed the brakes.

PARKING BRAKE SHOES

1. Disconnect the negative battery cable.

2. Raise the vehicle and support safely. Remove appropriate wheel assembly.

3. To disconnect the brake hose, hold the nut on the brake hose side and loosen the flared brake line nut.

4. Remove the caliper lock pins and remove the caliper.

5. The installation is the reverse of the removal procedure. Make sure the brake hose is not twisted after installation. Refill the brake fluid as required and bleed the brakes.

Disc Brake Pads

REMOVAL AND INSTALLATION

1. Disconnect the battery negative cable.

2. Raise the vehicle and support safely.

3. Remove appropriate wheel assembly.

4. On the front of AWD 3000GT, remove the pad retaining pins and pull the pads out of the caliper body.

5. On others, remove the caliper from its adaptor. Do not allow the caliper to hang by the brake line. On some vehicles, the caliper can be flipped up by leaving the upper pin in place and using it as a pivot point. Take note of the clips, pins, antisqueal shims and other parts for reference at assembly.

6. On vehicles with rear disc brakes, it may help to loosen the parking brake cable from inside the vehicle and disconnect the parking brake end from the rear caliper.

To install:

7. Use a large C-clamp to compress the piston(s) back into the caliper bore. On rear disc brakes with the parking brake mechanism incorporated into the caliper, a special tool is needed to turn the piston back into the bore.

8. Install the pads and all other small parts. Note that rear disc pads on calipers with the parking brake

mechanism incorporated into the caliper should have a projection on the back side of the shoe that fits into the rear caliper piston.

9. Install the caliper. Make sure the brake hose is not twisted after installation. Connect the parking brake cable if disconnected.

10. Install the tire and wheel assembly and connect the negative battery cable. Pump the brake pedal until firm before putting transaxle in gear or moving vehicle.

Brake Rotor

REMOVAL AND INSTALLATION

Except Mirage and Precis Front Rotor

1. Raise the vehicle and support safely. Remove appropriate wheel assembly.

2. Remove the caliper and brake pads.

3. The rotor on most models is held to the hub by 2 small threaded screws. Remove screws, if equipped, and pull off the rotor.

4. Installation is the reverse of the removal process.

Mirage and Precis Front Rotor

1. Loosen the large driveshaft nut while the vehicle is still on the ground with the brakes applied. Then raise and safely support vehicle. Remove appropriate wheel assembly.

2. Remove the axle end nut and lock washer.

3. Remove the caliper from its bracket. Do not allow the caliper to hang by the brake line. Remove the brake pads.

4. Remove the ball joint and tie rod end from the lower control arm.

5. Use and puller to push the half-shaft through the rotor/hub assembly.

6. Remove the lower strut bolts and remove the assembly from the vehicle.

7. To separate the rotor from the hub assembly, remove the rotor retainer bolts and separate using tool MB991001 or equivalent.

To install:

8. Assemble the rotor and hub. Tighten the nuts to 40 ft. lbs. (54 Nm) and install the assembly to the vehicle.

9. Install the washer so the chamfered edge faces outward. Install the nut and tighten temporarily.

10. Install the ball joint and tie rod end.

11. Install the brake components.

12. Install the wheel and lower the vehicle to the floor. Tighten the axle nut with the brakes applied to a maximum torque of 188 ft. lbs. (260 Nm). Install the cotter pin and bend to secure.

Brake Drums

REMOVAL AND INSTALLATION

Rear Hub Assembly

1. Raise the vehicle and support it safely.

2. Remove the wheel and tire assembly.

3. Remove the brake drum from the vehicle.

4. The installation is the reverse of the removal procedure.

Without Rear Hub Assembly

1. Raise the vehicle and support it safely.

2. Remove the wheel and tire assembly.

3. Remove the dust cap.

4. Remove the self-locking nut.

5. Remove the outer wheel bearing.

6. Remove the drum with the inner wheel bearing from the spindle. Remove the grease seal.

To install:

7. To determine if the self-locking nut is reusable:

   a. Screw in the self-locking nut until about 1/16 in. of the spindle is showing.

   b. Measure the torque required to turn the self-locking nut counterclockwise.

   c. The lowest allowable torque is 48 inch lbs. (5.5 Nm). If the measured torque is less than the specification, replace the nut.

8. Lubricate and install the inner wheel bearing. Install a new grease seal.

9. Install the drum to the spindle.

10. Lubricate and install the outer wheel bearing.

11. Torque the self-locking nut to 108-145 ft. lbs. (150-200 Nm).

12. Install the grease cap.

Brake Shoes

REMOVAL AND INSTALLATION

1. Raise the vehicle and support safely. Remove appropriate wheel assembly.

2. Remove the brake drum. Remove the shoe to shoe spring.

3. Take note of the springs and clips for proper reassembly. Remove the shoe hold-down clips and remove the shoes.

To install:

4. Thoroughly clean and dry the backing plate. To prepare the backing plate, lubricate the bosses, anchor pin and parking brake actuating lever pivot surface lightly with lithium-based grease.

5. Remove, clean and dry all parts still on the old shoes. Lubricate the star wheel shaft threads with anti-seize lubricant and transfer all parts to their proper locations on the new shoes.

6. Install shoes to the vehicle.

7. Connect the parking brake cable.

8. Adjust the star wheel.

9. To determine if the self-locking nut is reusable:

   a. Screw in the self-locking nut until about 1/16 in. of the spindle is showing.

   b. Measure the torque required to turn the self-locking nut counterclockwise.

   c. The lowest allowable torque is 48 inch lbs. (5.5 Nm). If the measured torque is less than the specification, replace the nut.

10. Remove any grease from the linings and install the drum to the spindle.

11. Lubricate and install the outer wheel bearing.

12. Torque the self-locking nut to 108-145 ft. lbs. (150-200 Nm).

13. Install the grease cap.

Wheel Cylinder

REMOVAL AND INSTALLATION

1. Raise the vehicle and support safely. Remove appropriate wheel assembly.

2. Remove the brake drum. Remove the shoe to shoe spring.

3. Remove the shoe to lever spring and remove the adjuster assembly.

4. Take note of the springs and clips for proper reassembly. Remove the shoe hold-down clips and remove the shoes. Separate the parking brake cable from the rear brake shoe during removal.

To install:

5. Thoroughly clean and dry the backing plate. To prepare the backing plate, lubricate the bosses, anchor pin and parking brake actuating lever pivot surface lightly with lithium-based grease.

6. Remove, clean and dry all parts still on the old shoes. Lubricate the star wheel shaft threads with anti-seize lubricant and transfer all parts to their proper locations on the new shoes.

7. Install shoes to the vehicle.

8. Connect the parking brake cable.

9. Adjust the star wheel.

10. To determine if the self-locking nut is reusable:

a. Screw in the self-locking nut until about 1/16 in. of the spindle is showing.

b. Measure the torque required to turn the self-locking nut counterclockwise.

c. The lowest allowable torque is 48 inch lbs. (5.5 Nm). If the measured torque is less than the specification, replace the nut.

11. Remove any grease from the brake linings and install the drum to the spindle.

12. Lubricate and install the outer wheel bearing.

13. Torque the self-locking nut to 108-145 ft. lbs. (150-200 Nm).

14. Install the grease cap.

Brake System Bleeding

NOTE: If using a pressure bleeder, follow the instructions furnished with the unit and choose the correct adaptor for the application. Do not substitute an adapter that "almost fits" as it will not work and could be dangerous.

MASTER CYLINDER

If the master cylinder is off the vehicle it can be bench bled.

1. Connect 2 short pieces of brake line to the outlet fittings, bend them until the free end is below the fluid level in the master cylinder reservoir.

2. Fill the reservoir with fresh brake fluid. Pump the piston slowly until no more air bubbles appear in the reservoirs.

3. Disconnect the 2 short lines, refill the master cylinder and securely install the cylinder caps.

4. If the master cylinder is on the vehicle, it can still be bled, using a flare nut wrench.

5. Open the brake lines slightly with the flare nut wrench while pressure is applied to the brake pedal by a helper inside the vehicle.

6. Be sure to tighten the line before the brake pedal is released.

7. Repeat the process with both lines until no air bubbles come out.

CALIPERS AND WHEEL CYLINDERS

1. Fill the master cylinder with fresh brake fluid. Check the level often during the procedure.

2. Starting with the wheel farthest from the master cylinder, remove the protective cap from the bleeder and place where it will not be lost. Clean the bleeder screw.

—— **CAUTION** ——

When bleeding the brakes, keep face away from the brake area. Spewing fluid may cause facial and/or visual damage. Do not allow brake fluid to spill on the car's finish; it will remove the paint.

3. If the system is empty, the most efficient way to get fluid down to the wheel is to loosen the bleeder about 1/2-3/4 turn, place a finger firmly over the bleeder and have a helper pump the brakes slowly until fluid comes out the bleeder. Once fluid is at the bleeder, close it before the pedal is released inside the vehicle.

NOTE: If the pedal is pumped rapidly, the fluid will churn and create small air bubbles, which are almost impossible to remove from the system. These air bubbles will accumulate and a spongy pedal will result.

4. Once fluid has been pumped to the caliper or wheel cylinder, open the bleed screw again, have the helper press the brake pedal to the floor, lock the bleeder and have the helper slowly release the pedal. Wait 15 seconds and repeat the procedure (including the 15 second wait) until no more air comes out of the bleeder upon application of the brake pedal. Remember to close the bleeder before the pedal is released inside the vehicle each time the bleeder is opened. If not, air will be introduced into the system.

5. If a helper is not available, connect a small hose to the bleeder, place the end in a container of brake fluid and proceed to pump the pedal from inside the vehicle until no more air comes out the bleeder. The hose will prevent air from entering the system.

6. Repeat the procedure on remaining wheel cylinders in the following order: **Diamante, Eclipse, Sigma, and 3000GT**

a. Right rear caliper

b. Left front caliper

c. Left rear caliper

d. Right front caliper

7. Repeat the procedure on remaining wheel cylinders in the following order: **Expo/Expo LRVP, Mirage and Precis**

a. Left rear wheel cylinder or caliper

b. Right front cylinder

c. Right rear wheel cylinder or caliper

d. Left front caliper

8. Hydraulic brake systems must be totally flushed if the fluid becomes contaminated with water, dirt or other corrosive chemicals. To flush, bleed the entire system until all fluid has been replaced with the correct type of new fluid.

9. Install the bleeder cap on the bleeder to keep dirt out. Always road test the vehicle after brake work of any kind is done.

Anti-Lock System Brake Service

PRECAUTIONS

• Certain components within the ABS system are not intended to be serviced or repaired individually. Only those components with removal and Installation procedures should be serviced.

• Do not use rubber hoses or other parts not specifically specified for the ABS system. When using repair kits, replace all parts included in the kit. Partial or incorrect repair may lead to functional problems and require the replacement of components.

• Lubricate rubber parts with clean, fresh brake fluid to ease assembly. Do not use lubricated shop air to clean parts; damage to rubber components may result.

• Use only DOT 3 brake fluid from an unopened container.

• If any hydraulic component or line is removed or replaced, it may be necessary to bleed the entire system.

• A clean repair area is essential. Always clean the reservoir and cap thoroughly before removing the cap. The slightest amount of dirt in the fluid may plug an orifice and impair the system function. Perform repairs after components have been thoroughly cleaned; use only denatured alcohol to clean components. Do not allow ABS components to come into contact with any substance containing mineral oil; this includes used shop rags.

• The Anti-Lock control unit is a microprocessor similar to other computer units in the vehicle. Ensure that the ignition switch is **OFF** before removing or installing controller harnesses. Avoid static electricity discharge at or near the controller.

• If any arc welding is to be done on the vehicle, the ABS control unit connectors should be disconnected before welding operations begin.

FILLING THE SYSTEM

The brake fluid reservoir is part of the normal brake system and is filled or checked in the usual manner. Always clean the reservoir cap and surrounding area thoroughly before removing the cap. Fill the reservoir only to the **FULL** or **MAX** mark; do not overfill. Use only fresh DOT 3 brake fluid from unopened containers. Do not use any fluid containing a petroleum base. Do not use any fluid which has been exposed to water or moisture. Failure to use the correct fluid will affect system function and component life.

BLEEDING THE SYSTEM

Diamante, Eclipse and 3000GT

LINES AND CALIPERS

The brake system must be bled any time a line, hose or component is loosened or removed. Any air trapped within the lines can affect pedal feel and system function. Bleeding the system is performed in the usual manner with an assistant in the vehicle to pump the brake pedal. Make certain the fluid level in the reservoir is maintained at or near correct levels during bleeding operations.

With the ignition **OFF**, depress the brake pedal several times until pedal feel changes to a noticeably stiffer resistance. Slowly pump the pedal a few more times; with the pedal depressed, loosen the bleeder screw 1/3-1/2 turn. Tighten the bleeder screw before the fluid pressure is gone. Release the pedal, pump again slowly, hold the pedal depressed and repeat the bleeding process until no air bubbles are seen in the fluid.

If bleeding is necessary at all wheels, begin at the right rear, then the left front, left rear and right front wheels.

MASTER CYLINDER

If the master cylinder has been emptied of fluid, it must be bled separately from the rest of the system. Since the cylinder has no check valve, air can become trapped within it. To bleed the brake master cylinder after it has been drained:

1. Disconnect the 2 brake lines from the master cylinder. Plug the lines immediately. The brake fluid reservoir must be in place and connected to the master cylinder. Check the fluid level before beginning.

2. An assistant should slowly depress and hold the brake pedal.

3. With the pedal held down, use fingers to plug each outlet port on the master cylinder; release the brake pedal.

4. Repeat Steps 2 and 3 three or four times. The air will be bled from the cylinder.

5. Connect the brake lines to the master cylinder and tighten the fittings to 10 ft. lbs. (13.5 Nm).

6. Start the engine, allowing the system to pressurize and self-check. Shut the ignition **OFF** and bleed the brake lines at the wheels.

Galant and Sigma

The complete brake system must be bled any time a line, hose or component is loosened or removed. Any air trapped within the lines can affect pedal feel and system function. Bleeding the system is performed in the usual manner with an assistant in the car to pump the brake pedal, but these systems require bleeding of several ports in addition to the usual wheel locations. Make certain the fluid level in the reservoir is maintained at or near correct levels during bleeding operations.

Use of a box-end or brake bleeder wrench is recommended to avoid damage to bleeder port fittings; a socket and ratchet will be needed to bleed the delay valve on Sigma with V6 engine.

With the ignition **OFF**, depress the brake pedal several times until pedal feel changes to a noticeably stiffer resistance. Slowly pump the pedal a few more times; with the pedal depressed, loosen the bleeder screw 1/3-1/2 turn. Tighten the bleeder screw before the fluid pressure is gone. Release the pedal, pump again slowly, hold the pedal depressed and repeat the bleeding process until no air bubbles are seen in the fluid.

NOTE: The brake pedal will develop an unusually heavy or hard feel during bleeding of the rear brake on FWD vehicles. This results from fluid constriction within the delay valve and is not a sign of malfunction.

Correct bleeding order for Sigma with V6 engine is: left rear wheel, left rear delay valve, right front wheel, outboard bleeder port on hydraulic unit, right rear wheel, right rear delay valve, left front wheel and inboard bleeder port on hydraulic unit.

Bleeding order for Galant FWD vehicles is: right rear wheel, right rear delay valve, left front wheel, inboard bleeder port on hydraulic unit, left rear wheel, left rear delay valve, right front wheel and outboard bleeder port on the hydraulic unit.

Bleed Galant AWD brakes in this order: right rear wheel, left front wheel, inboard bleeder port on the hydraulic unit, left rear wheel, right front wheel and outboard bleeder port on the hydraulic unit.

Hydraulic Unit

REMOVAL AND INSTALLATION

Diamante and 3000GT

1. Disconnect the negative battery cable. Remove the splash shield from beneath the vehicle.

2. Use a syringe or similar device to remove as much fluid as possible from the reservoir. Some fluid will be spilled from lines during removal of the hydraulic unit; protect adjacent painted surfaces.

3. Lift the relay box with the harness attached and position it aside.

4. Remove the air intake duct.

5. Disconnect the brake lines from the hydraulic unit. Correct reassembly is critical. Label or identify the lines before removal. Plug each line immediately after removal. It will be necessary to hold the relay box aside to allow wrench access.

6. Disconnect the wiring harness connections at the hydraulic unit.

7. Disconnect the hydraulic unit ground strap from the chassis.

8. Remove the 3 bolts holding the hydraulic unit bracket. Remove the unit and the bracket.

NOTE: The hydraulic unit is heavy; use care when removing it. The unit must remain in the upright position at all times and be protected from impact and shock.

9. Set the unit upright supported by blocks on the workbench. The hydraulic unit must not be tilted or turned upside down. No component of the hydraulic unit should be loosened or disassembled.

10. Loosen the nut holding the bracket to the hydraulic unit and remove the bracket.

11. Disconnect the external ground wire from the bracket.

To install:

12. Install the bracket if removed. Connect the ground wire to the bracket.

13. Install the hydraulic unit into the vehicle, keeping it upright at all times.

14. Install the retaining nuts and tighten.

15. Connect the hydraulic unit wiring harness.

16. Connect each brake line loosely to the correct port and double check the placement. Tighten each line to 11 ft. lbs. (15 Nm).

17. Fill the reservoir to the MAX line with brake fluid.

18. Bleed the master cylinder, then bleed the brake lines.

19. Secure the relay box in position and install the air duct.

20. Install the splash shield.

Eclipse

1. Disconnect the negative battery cable. Use a syringe or similar device to remove as much fluid as possible from the reservoir. Some fluid will be spilled from lines during removal of the hydraulic unit; protect adjacent painted surfaces.

2. On turbocharged engine, remove the center intercooler duct. Loosen the clamps and remove the bolts holding the duct to the air cleaner.

3. Disconnect the brake lines from the hydraulic unit. Correct reassembly is critical. Label or identify the lines before removal. Plug each line immediately after removal.

4. Remove the cover from the relay box. Disconnect the electrical harness to the hydraulic unit.

5. Disconnect the hydraulic unit ground strap from the chassis.

6. Remove the 3 nuts holding the hydraulic unit. Remove the unit upwards.

NOTE: The hydraulic unit is heavy; use care when removing it. The unit must remain in the upright position at all times and be protected from impact and shock.

7. Set the unit upright supported by blocks on the workbench. The hydraulic unit must not be tilted or turned upside down. No component of the hydraulic unit should be loosened or disassembled.

8. The bracket assemblies and relays may be removed if desired.

To install:

9. Install the relays and brackets if removed.

10. Install the hydraulic unit into the vehicle, keeping it upright at all times.

11. Install the retaining nuts and tighten.

12. Connect the ground strap to the chassis bracket. Connect the hydraulic unit wiring harness.

13. Install the cover on the relay box.

14. Connect each brake line loosely to the correct port and double check the placement. Tighten each line to 10 ft. lbs. (13.5 Nm).

15. Fill the reservoir to the MAX line with brake fluid.

16. Bleed the master cylinder, then bleed the brake lines.

17. If equipped, install the intercooler air duct.

Expo/Expo LRV

1. Disconnect the negative battery cable. Remove the splash shield from beneath the vehicle.

2. Use a syringe or similar device to remove as much fluid as possible from the reservoir. Some fluid will be spilled from lines during removal of the hydraulic unit; protect adjacent painted surfaces.

3. Remove the dust cover and the oil reservoir.

4. Disconnect the brake lines from the hydraulic unit. Correct reassembly is critical. Label or identify the lines before removal. Plug each line immediately after removal.

5. Disconnect the HYDRAULIC unit electrical harness connectors.

6. Disconnect the hydraulic unit ground strap from the chassis.

7. Remove the 3 nuts holding the hydraulic unit. Remove the unit upwards.

NOTE: The hydraulic unit is heavy; use care when removing it. The unit must remain in the upright position at all times and be protected from impact and shock.

8. Set the unit upright supported by blocks on the workbench. The hydraulic unit must not be tilted or turned upside down. No component of the hydraulic unit should be loosened or disassembled.

9. The bracket assemblies and relays may be removed if desired.

To install:

10. Install the relays and brackets if removed.

11. Install the hydraulic unit into the vehicle, keeping it upright at all times.

12. Install the retaining nuts and tighten.

13. Connect the ground strap to the chassis bracket. Connect the hydraulic unit wiring harness.

14. Connect the hydraulic unit electrical harness connectors.

15. Install the dust cover and the oil reservoir.

16. Connect each brake line loosely to the correct port and double check the placement. Tighten each line to 10 ft. lbs. (13.5 Nm).

17. Fill the reservoir to the MAX line with brake fluid.

18. Bleed the master cylinder, then bleed the brake lines. Refill the master cylinder and check for proper operation.

Galant and Sigma

1. Use a syringe or similar device to remove as much fluid as possible from the reservoir. Some fluid will be spilled from lines during removal of the hydraulic unit; protect adjacent painted surfaces.

2. Remove the splash shield from the left front wheel house or fender area.

3. Remove the coolant reserve tank. On Galant, remove the coolant reservoir bracket.

4. Remove the dust shield from below the hydraulic unit.

5. Disconnect the brake hoses and lines from the hydraulic unit. Correct reassembly is critical. Label or identify the lines before removal. Plug each line and each port immediately after removal.

6. Remove the cover from the relay box. Disconnect the electrical harness to the hydraulic unit.

7. Remove the bolts holding the 3 mounting brackets to the vehicle; remove the unit downward and out of the vehicle.

NOTE: The hydraulic unit is heavy; use care when removing it. The unit must remain in the upright position at all times and be protected from impact and shock.

8. Set the unit upright supported by blocks on the workbench. The hydraulic unit must not be tilted or turned upside down. No component of the hydraulic unit should be loosened or disassembled.

9. The brackets and relays may be removed if desired.

To install:

10. Install the brackets and relays if they were removed. Tighten the bracket bolts to 16 ft. lbs. (22 Nm).

11. Install the hydraulic unit into the vehicle, keeping it upright at all times.

12. Install the retaining bolts holding the brackets to the vehicle. Tighten the bolts to 16 ft. lbs. (22 Nm).

13. Connect the hydraulic unit wiring harness.

14. Install the cover on the relay box.

15. Connect each brake line loosely to the correct port and double check the placement. Tighten each line to 10 ft. lbs. (13.5 Nm).

16. Fill the reservoir to the **MAX** line with brake fluid.

17. Bleed the brake system.

18. Install the dust shield and the coolant reserve tank with its bracket.

19. Install the fender splash shield.

20. Check ABS system function by turning the ignition **ON** and observing the dashboard warning lamp. Test drive the vehicle and confirm system operation.

Anti-Lock Control Unit

REMOVAL AND INSTALLATION

Except Expo/Expo LRV

1. Ensure that the ignition switch is **OFF** throughout the procedure.

2. For Eclipse and 3000 GT, remove the interior right rear quarter trim panel. Depending on the model, removal of the rear seat back and/or cushion may be required. For Sigma, Galant and Diamante, remove the left side luggage compartment trim panel.

3. Release the lock on the bottom of the connector; disconnect the multi-pin connector from the control unit. On Eclipse, access may be easier if the external ground is disconnected from the bracket.

4. Remove the retaining nuts and remove the control unit from its bracket. The bracket may be removed if desired.

To install:

5. Place the bracket in position if it was removed. Install the controller and tighten the retaining nuts.

6. Connect the ground wire to the bracket, if removed. Insure a proper, tight connection. The ground must be connected before the multi-pin harness is connected.

7. Connect the multi-pin connector and secure the lock.

8. Install the rear quarter trim panel or the luggage compartment trim.

Expo/Expo LRV

1. Ensure that the ignition switch is **OFF** throughout the procedure.

2. Remove the cup holder in front of the center console.

3. Remove the console side covers.

4. Disconnect the electrical harness from the control unit.

5. Remove the fasteners and the control unit from the vehicle.

6. Installation is the reverse of the removal procedure.

G-Sensor

REMOVAL AND INSTALLATION

Eclipse

1. Ensure that the ignition switch is **OFF** throughout the procedure.

2. Remove the rear seat cushion.

3. Disconnect the wiring harness to G-sensor.

4. Remove the retaining bolts and remove the sensor.

5. To install, position the sensor, tighten the retaining bolts and connect the harness.

6. Install the rear seat cushion.

Expo/Expo LRV

1. Disconnect negative battery cable.

2. Remove the floor console.

3. Disconnect the wiring harness connector from the sensor.

4. Remove the retaining screw and G-sensor from the mounting bracket.

5. Installation is the reverse of the removal procedure.

Galant

1. For the front sensor, remove the console assembly.

2. For the rear sensor, remove the trunk floor mat.

3. Disconnect the G-sensor wiring harness.

4. Remove the cover from the rear sensor. Remove the sensor from the bracket. Remove the bracket if desired.

To install:

5. Reinstall the bracket if it was removed.

6. Install the G-sensor and connect the wiring harness. Tighten the retaining bolts to 8 ft. lbs. (11 Nm)

7. Install the cover on the rear G-sensor.

8. Install the console and/or the trunk floor mat or carpet.

3000GT

1. Disconnect the negative battery cable. Remove the rearmost console assembly.

NOTE: If equipped with SRS, when removing the floor console, don't allow any impact or shock to the SRS diagnostic unit.

2. Remove the front console assembly.

3. Disconnect the G-sensor wiring harness.

4. Remove the G-sensor from the bracket. Remove the bracket if desired.

To install:

5. Reinstall the bracket. Tighten the bolts to 4 ft. lbs. (5 Nm).

6. Install the G-sensor and connect the wiring harness.

7. Install the front and rear console assemblies.

Wheel Speed Sensors

REMOVAL AND INSTALLATION

— CAUTION —
Vehicles equipped with air bag systems will have wiring and system components in the fender or wheel well area. The ABS components must be correctly identified before beginning repairs. Improper work procedures may cause impaired function of the ABS and/or SRS systems

1. Raise and safely support the vehicle.

2. Remove the wheel and tire.

3. Remove the inner fender or splash shield.

4. Beginning at the sensor end, carefully disconnect or release each clip and retainer along the sensor wire. Take careful note of the exact position of each clip; they must be reinstalled in the identical position. Rear wheel sensor harnesses will be held by plastic wire ties; these may be cut away but must be replaced at reassembly.

5. Disconnect the sensor connector at the end of the harness.

6. Remove the 2 bolts holding the speed sensor bracket to the knuckle

and remove the assembly from the vehicle.

NOTE: The speed sensor has a pole piece projecting from it. This exposed tip must be protected from impact or scratches. Do not allow the pole piece to contact the toothed wheel during removal or installation.

7. Remove the sensor from the bracket.

To install:

8. Assemble the sensor onto the bracket and tighten the bolt to 10 ft. lbs. (14 Nm). Note that the brackets are different for the left and right front wheels. Each bracket has identifying letters stamped on it.

9. Temporarily install the speed sensor to the knuckle; tighten the bolts only finger-tight.

10. Route the cable correctly and loosely install the clips and retainers. All clips must be in their original position and the sensor cable must not be twisted. Improper installation may cause cable damage and system failure.

NOTE: The wiring in the harness is easily damaged by twisting and flexing. Use the white stripe on the outer insulation to keep the sensor harness properly placed.

11. Use a brass or other non-magnetic feeler gauge to check the air gap between the tip of the pole piece and the toothed wheel. Correct gap is 0.012-0.035 inch (0.3-0.9mm). Tighten the 2 sensor bracket bolts to 10 ft. lbs. (14 Nm) with the sensor located so the gap is the same at several points on the toothed wheel. If the gap is incorrect, it is likely that the toothed wheel is worn or improperly installed.

12. Tighten the screws and bolts for the cable retaining clips.

13. Install the inner fender or splash shield.

14. Install the wheel and tire. Lower the vehicle to the ground.

Front Toothed Wheel Rings

REMOVAL AND INSTALLATION

1. Raise and safely support the vehicle.

2. Remove the wheel and tire.

3. Remove the wheel speed sensor and disconnect sufficient harness clips to allow the sensor and wiring to be moved out of the work area.

NOTE: The speed sensor has a pole piece projecting from it. This exposed tip must be protected from impact or scratches. Do not allow the pole piece to contact the toothed wheel during removal or installation.

4. Remove the front hub and knuckle assembly.

5. Remove the hub from the knuckle.

6. Support the hub in a vise with protected jaws. Remove the retaining bolts from the toothed wheel and remove the toothed wheel.

To install:

7. Fit the new toothed wheel onto the hub and tighten the retaining bolts to 7 ft. lbs. (10 Nm).

8. Assemble the hub to the knuckle

9. Install the hub and knuckle assembly to the vehicle.

10. Install the wheel speed sensor.

11. Install the wheel and tire.

12. Lower the vehicle to the ground.

Rear Toothed Wheel Rings

REMOVAL AND INSTALLATION

Front Wheel Drive

1. Raise and safely support the vehicle.

2. Remove the wheel and tire.

3. Remove the wheel speed sensor and disconnect sufficient harness clips to allow the sensor and wiring to be moved out of the work area.

NOTE: The speed sensor has a pole piece projecting from it. This exposed tip must be protected from impact or scratches. Do not allow the pole piece to contact the toothed wheel during removal or installation.

4. Remove the hub assembly.

5. Support the hub in a vise with protected jaws. Remove the retaining bolts from the toothed wheel and remove the toothed wheel.

To install:

6. Fit the new toothed wheel onto the hub and tighten the retaining bolts to 7 ft. lbs. (10 Nm).

7. For all ABS equipped vehicles except Sigma with V6 engine, install the hub assembly to the vehicle. The center hub nut is not reusable. The new nut must be tightened to 144-188 ft. lbs. (200-260 Nm). After the nut is tightened, align the nut

with the spindle indentation and crimp the nut in place.

8. On Sigma with V6 engine, assemble and install the hub, outer bearing, tongued washer and locknut. To set the wheel bearing end-play:

a. Tighten the locknut to 14 ft. lbs. (20 Nm).

b. Rotate the hub 180 degrees or more counterclockwise, then return it to the original position. Repeat the rotation and return at least 3 more times. Temporarily fitting the brake disc will make the hub easier to turn.

c. Loosen the locknut to 0 ft. lbs., then retighten it to 7 ft. lbs. (10 Nm).

d. Again rotate the hub at least 180 degrees counterclockwise and return it to its original position.

e. Reset the locknut to 7 ft. lbs. (10 Nm).

f. Install the lock cap and cotter pin. If the cotter pin will not align with the holes in the lock cap, reposition the cap. If no alignment is possible, loosen the locknut by no more than 15 degrees.

g. Once the cotter pin is in place, rotate the hub at least 180 degrees counterclockwise and return it to its original position.

9. Install the wheel speed sensor.

10. Install the wheel and tire.

11. Lower the vehicle to the ground.

All Wheel Drive

EXCEPT EXPO/EXPO LRV

1. Raise and safely support the vehicle.

2. Remove the wheel and tire.

3. Disconnect the parking brake cable from the caliper.

4. Remove the speed sensor and its O-ring. Disconnect sufficient clamps and wire ties to allow the sensor to be moved well out of the work area.

NOTE: The speed sensor has a pole piece projecting from it. This exposed tip must be protected from impact or scratches. Do not allow the pole piece to contact the toothed wheel during removal or installation.

5. Remove the brake caliper and brake disc.

6. Remove the 3 retaining nuts and bolts holding the outer end of the driveshaft to the companion flange. Swing the axle shaft away and support it with stiff wire. Do not overextend the joint in the axle; do not allow it to hang of its own weight.

7. Remove the retaining nut and washer on the back of the driveshaft. Use special tool MB 990767 or equivalent to counterhold the hub.

8. Remove the companion flange from the knuckle.

9. Using an axle puller which bolts to the wheel lugs, remove the axle shaft assembly.

10. Fit the shaft assembly in a press with the toothed wheel completely supported by a bearing plate such as special tool MB 990560 or its equivalent.

11. Press the toothed wheel off the axle shaft.

To install:

12. Press the new toothed wheel onto the shaft with the groove facing the axle shaft flange.

13. Install the axle shaft to the knuckle and fit the companion flange in place.

14. Install the lock washer and a new self-locking nut on the axle shaft. Tighten the nut to 116-159 ft. lbs. (160-220 Nm).

15. Swing the axle assembly into place and install the 3 nuts and bolts. Tighten each to 45 ft. lbs. (61 Nm).

16. Install the brake disc and caliper.

17. Install the wheel speed sensor. Always use a new O-ring.

18. Connect the parking brake cable to the caliper.

19. Install the wheel and tire; lower the vehicle to the ground.

EXPO/EXPO LRV

1. Disconnect negative battery cable.

2. Raise and safely support the vehicle. Remove the tire and wheel assembly.

3. Remove the cotter pin, cover and driveshaft nut.

4. Remove the speed sensor and its O-ring. Disconnect sufficient clamps and wire ties to allow the sensor to be moved well out of the work area.

NOTE: The speed sensor has a pole piece projecting from it. This exposed tip must be protected from impact or scratches. Do not allow the pole piece to contact the toothed wheel during removal or installation.

5. Remove the rear driveshaft from the vehicle.

6. Fit the shaft assembly in a press with the toothed wheel completely supported by a bearing plate such as special tool MB990560 or equivalent.

7. Press the toothed wheel off the axle shaft.

To install:

8. Press the new toothed wheel onto the shaft with the groove facing the axle shaft flange.

9. Install the axle on vehicle. Tighten the inner flange retainers to 40-47 ft. lbs. (55-65 Nm).

10. Install the driveshaft nut and torque to 145-188 ft. lbs. (200-260 Nm). Secure using new cotter pin.

11. Install the speed sensor and secure the wiring harness in its' original location. Always use a new O-ring.

12. Install the tire and wheel assembly.

CHASSIS ELECTRICAL

Air Bag

DISARMING

1. Position the front wheels in the straight-ahead position and place the key in the **LOCK** position.

2. Disconnect the negative battery cable and insulate the cable end with high-quality electrical tape or similar non-conductive wrapping.

3. Wait at least 1 minute before working on the vehicle. The air bag system is designed to retain enough voltage to deploy for a short period of time even after the battery has been disconnected.

4. If necessary, enter the vehicle from the passenger side and turn the key to unlock the steering column.

Heater Blower Motor

REMOVAL AND INSTALLATION

Precis and Sigma

1. Disconnect the negative battery cable.

2. Remove the instrument panel under cover and glove box assembly(s).

3. On Precis, disconnect the resistor and blower motor wire connectors.

4. Remove the motor cooling tube.

5. Remove the attaching screws and remove the blower assembly from the blower case and disassemble.

To install:

6. Position the blower motor onto the blower case and install the attaching screws.

7. Install the absorber bracket, if removed. Install the cooling tube.

8. On Precis, connect the resistor and blower motor wire connector.

9. Install the glove box(s) and instrument panel under cover.

10. Connect the negative battery cable and check the blower for proper operation.

Eclipse, 3000GT and Diamante

1. Disconnect battery negative cable.

2. On Eclipse, remove the right side duct. On 3000GT, remove the instrument panel under cover.

3. Remove the molded hose from the blower assembly.

4. Remove the blower motor assembly.

5. Remove the packing seal.

6. Remove the fan retaining nut and fan in order to replace the motor.

To install:

7. Check that the blower motor shaft is not bent and that the packing is in good condition. Clean all parts of dust, etc.

8. Assemble the motor and fan. Install the blower motor then connect the connector.

9. Install the molded hose. Install the duct or under cover.

10. Connect the negative battery cable and check the entire climate control system for proper operation.

Mirage

1. Disconnect the negative battery cable.

2. Remove the glove box assembly and pry off the speaker cover to the lower right of the glove box.

3. Remove the passenger side lower cowl side trim kick panel.

4. Remove the passenger side knee protector, which is the panel surrounding the glove box opening.

5. Remove the glove frame along the top of glove box opening.

6. Remove the lap heater duct. This is a small piece on vehicles without a rear heater or much larger piece on vehicles with a rear heater.

7. Disconnect the electrical connector from the blower motor.

8. Remove the cooling tube from the blower assembly.

9. Remove the MPI computer from the lower side of the cowl.

10. Remove the blower motor assembly and disassemble on a workbench.

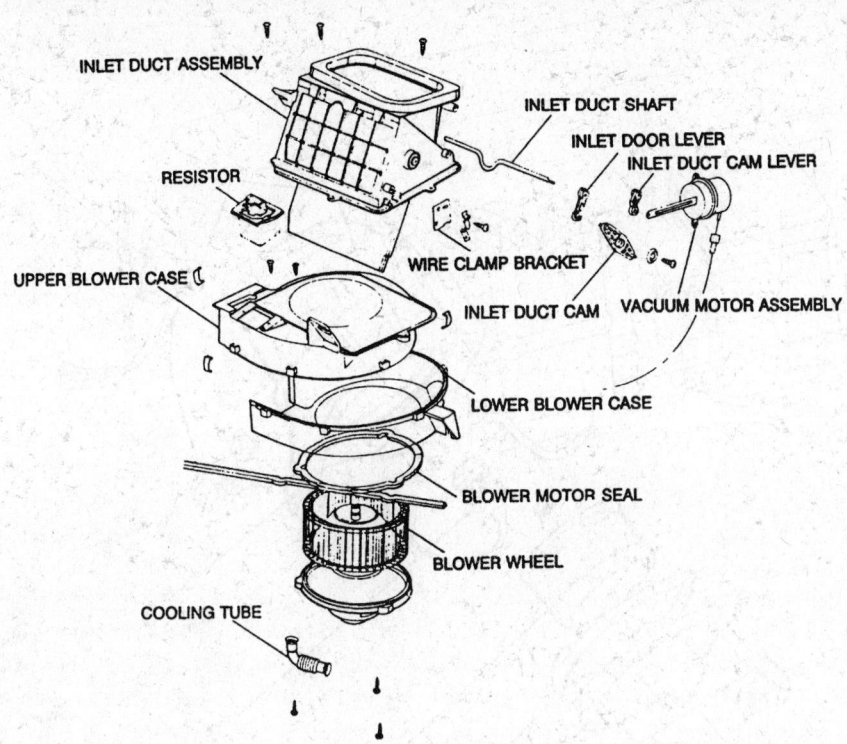

Exploded view of the blower case — Precis

To install:

11. Assemble the motor and fan. Install the blower motor assembly and connect the wiring and cooling tube.
12. Install the MPI computer.
13. Install the lap heater duct.
14. Install the glove box frame, interior trim pieces and glove box assembly.
15. Connect the negative battery cable and check the entire climate control system for proper operation.

Galant

1. Disconnect the negative battery cable.
2. Remove the glove box assembly and under cover.
3. Remove the foot heater duct.
4. Disconnect the MPI relay and glove box switch.
5. Remove the glove box frame.
6. Remove the cowl side trim.
7. Remove the motor cooling tube and disconnect the motor connector.
8. Remove the screws and remove the blower assembly from the blower case. Disassemble on a workbench.
To install:
9. Assemble the unit and install the blower assembly to the case.
10. Install the cooling tube and connect the connector.

11. Install the cowl side trim and glove box frame.
12. Connect the MPI relay and glove box switch.
13. Install the foot heater duct.
14. Install the glove box assembly and under cover.
15. Connect the negative battery cable and check the entire climate control system for proper operation and leaks.

Windshield Wiper Motor

REMOVAL AND INSTALLATION

Precis, Mirage and Expo/Expo LRV
FRONT

1. Disconnect the negative battery cable.
2. Remove the windshield wiper arms by unscrewing the cap nuts and lifting the arms from the linkage posts.
3. Remove the front deck garnish panel.
4. Remove both windshield holders.
5. Remove the clips that hold the deck cover. If they are the pin type,

they may be removed using the following procedure:

   a. Remove the clip by pressing down on the center pin with a suitable blunt pointed tool. Press down a little more than 1/16 in. (2mm). This releases the clip. Pull the clip outward to remove it.
   b. Do not push the pin inward more than necessary because it may damage the grommet, or if pushed too far, the pin may fall in. Once the clips are removed, use a plastic trim stick to pry the deck cover loose.
6. On Mirage, remove the air intake screen.
7. Loosen the wiper motor assembly mounting bolts and remove the windshield wiper motor. Disconnect the linkage from the motor assembly. If necessary, remove the linkage from the vehicle.

NOTE: The installation angle of the crank arm and motor has been factory set, do not remove them unless it is necessary to do so. If arm must be removed, remove them only after marking their mounting positions.

To install:
8. Install the windshield wiper motor and connect the linkage. Connect the electrical harness to the motor.
9. When installing the trim and garnish pieces and reusing pin type clips, use the following procedure:
   a. With the pin pulled out, insert the trim clip into the hole in the trim.
   b. Push the pin inward until the pin's head is flush with the grommet.
   c. Check that the trim is secure.
10. Install the wiper arms and tighten nuts to 17 ft. lbs. (24 Nm).
11. Connect the negative battery cable and check the wiper system for proper operation.

REAR

1. Disconnect the negative battery cable.
2. Remove the rear wiper arm by removing the cap nut cover, unscrewing the cap nut and lifting the arm from the linkage post.
3. Remove the large interior trim panel. Use a plastic trim stick to unhook the trim clips of the liftgate trim. There will be a row of metal liftgate clips across the top. There will be 2 rows of trim clips that retain the rest of the panel.
4. Disconnect the electrical harness at the wiper motor. Remove the

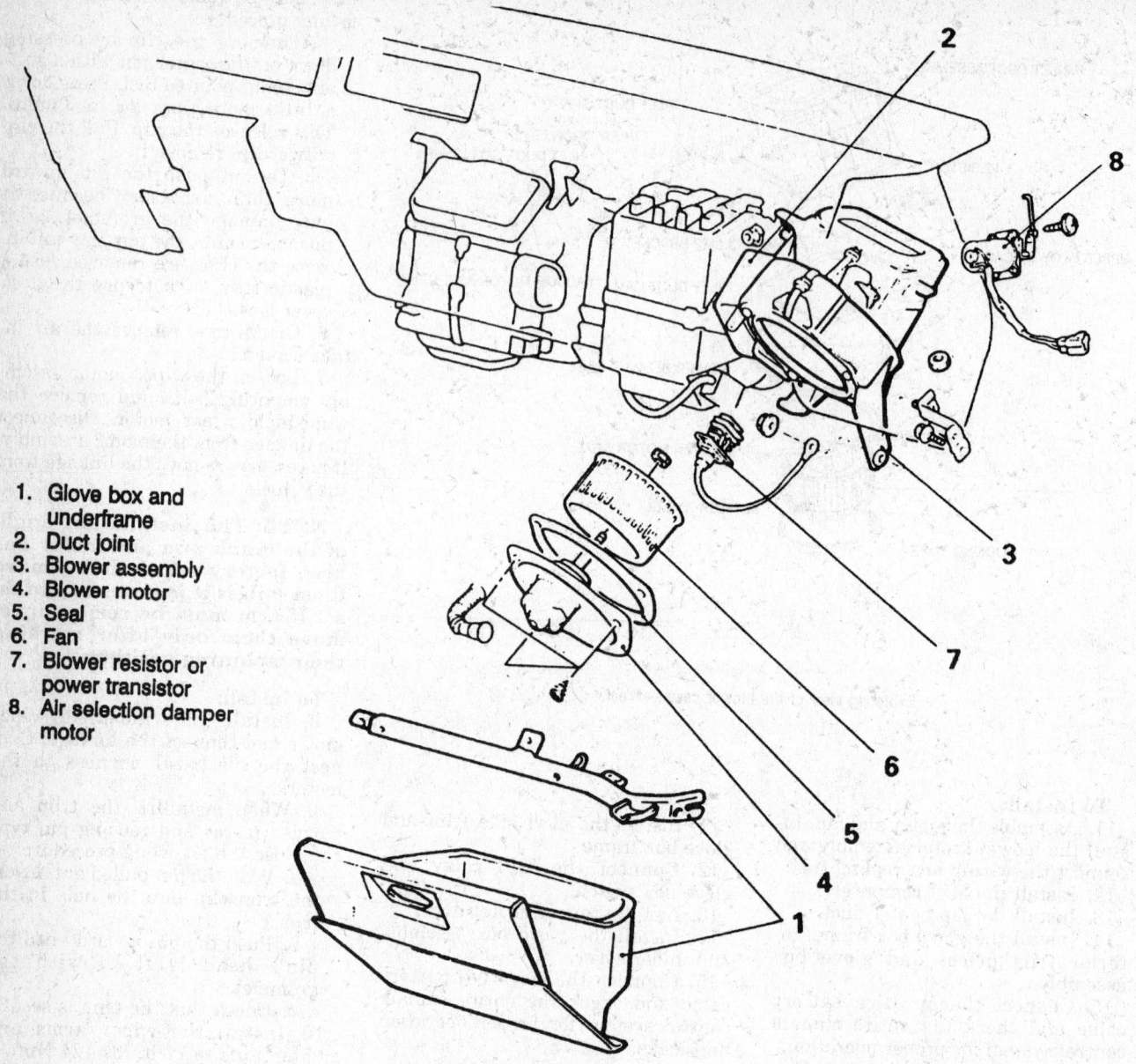

1. Glove box and underframe
2. Duct joint
3. Blower assembly
4. Blower motor
5. Seal
6. Fan
7. Blower resistor or power transistor
8. Air selection damper motor

Blower motor and related parts — Sigma

rear wiper assembly. Do not loosen the grommet for the wiper post.

To install:

5. Install the motor and grommet. Mount the grommet so the arrow on the grommet is pointing downward.
6. Install the wiper arm.
7. Connect the negative battery cable and check rear wiper system for proper operation.
8. If operation is satisfactory, fit the tabs on the upper part of the liftgate trim into the liftgate clips and secure the liftgate trim.

Galant, Eclipse, Sigma

FRONT

1. Disconnect the negative battery cable.
2. Remove the windshield wiper arms by unscrewing the cap nuts and lifting the arms from the linkage posts.
3. Remove the front garnish panel.
4. Remove the air inlet trim pieces.
5. Remove the hole cover.
6. Remove the wiper motor by loosening the mounting bolts, remov-

ing the motor assembly, then disconnecting the linkage.

NOTE: The installation angle of the crank arm and motor has been factory set; do not remove them unless it is necessary to do so. If they must be removed, remove them only after marking their mounting positions.

To install:

7. Install the windshield wiper motor and connect the linkage.
8. Reinstall all trim pieces.
9. Reinstall the wiper blades. Note that the driver's side wiper arm should be marked **D** or **Dr** and the

1. Right side undercover
2. Foot shower duct
3. Glove box frame
4. Evaporator mounting bolt and nut
5. Air changeover motor
6. MPI control relay
7. MPI computer
8. Instrument panel lower bracket
9. Blower assembly
10. Blower motor assembly
11. Blower case

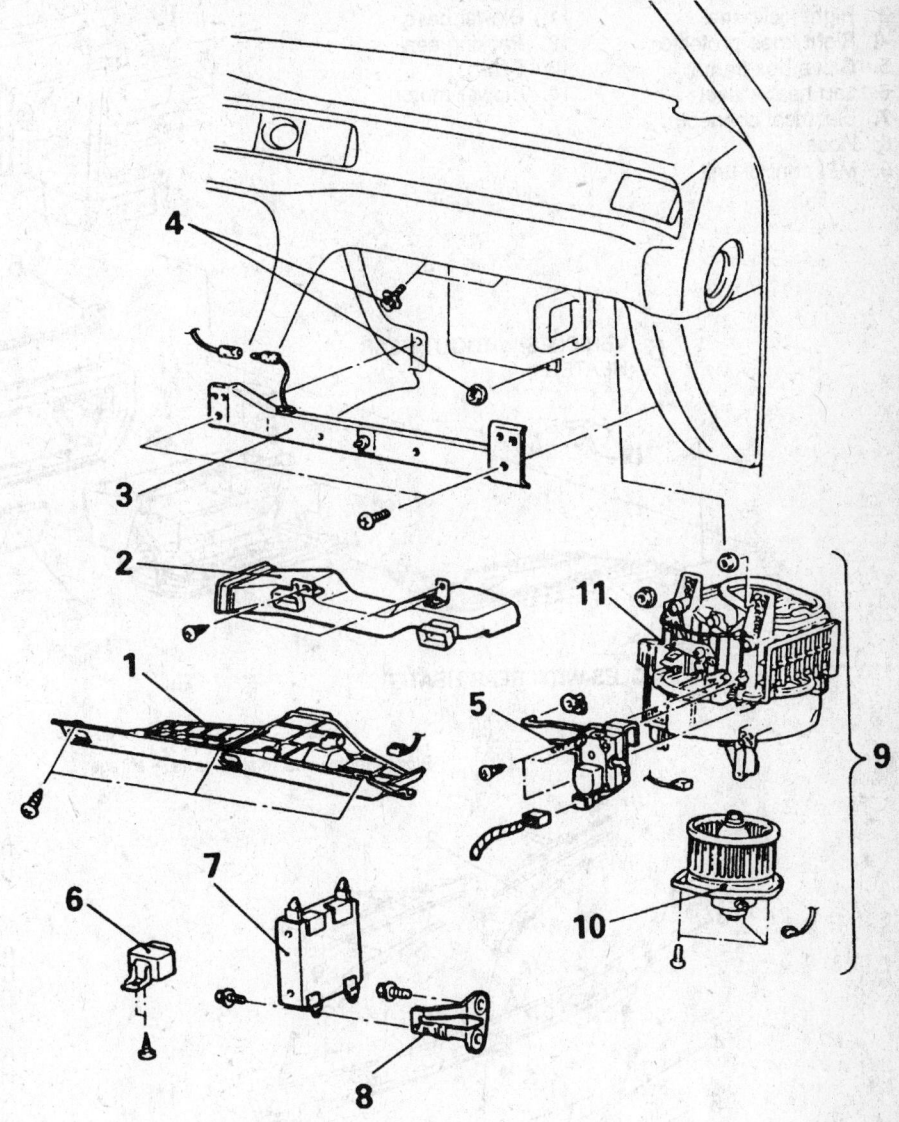

Blower motor and related parts — Diamante

passenger's side wiper arm should be marked **A** or **As**. The identification marks should be located at the base of the arm, near the pivot. Install the arms so the blades are 1 inch from the garnish molding when parked.

10. Connect the negative battery cable and check the wiper system for proper operation.

REAR

1. Disconnect the negative battery cable.

2. Remove the rear wiper arm by removing the cover, unscrewing the nut and lifting the arm from the linkage post.

3. Remove the large interior trim panel. Use a plastic trim stick to unhook the trim clips of the liftgate trim.

4. If equipped with rear air spoiler, remove the wiper grommet.

5. Remove the rear wiper assembly. Do not loosen the grommet for the wiper post.

To install:

6. Install the motor and grommet. Mount the grommet so the arrow on the grommet is pointing upward.

7. Install the wiper arm.

8. Connect the negative battery cable and check the rear wiper for proper operation.

9. If operation is satisfactory, fit the tabs on the upper part of the liftgate trim into the liftgate clips and secure the liftgate trim.

3000GT and Diamante

FRONT

1. Disconnect the negative battery cable.

2. Remove the windshield wiper arms by unscrewing the cap nuts and lifting the arms from the linkage posts.

3. Remove the access hole cover.

4. Remove the wiper motor mounting bolts.

1. Glove box assembly
2. Speaker cover
3. Right kickpanel
4. Right knee protector
5. Glove box frame
6. Lap heater duct
7. Electrical connector
8. Hose
9. MPI control unit
10. Blower motor assembly
11. Blower case
12. Packing seal
13. Fan
14. Blower motor

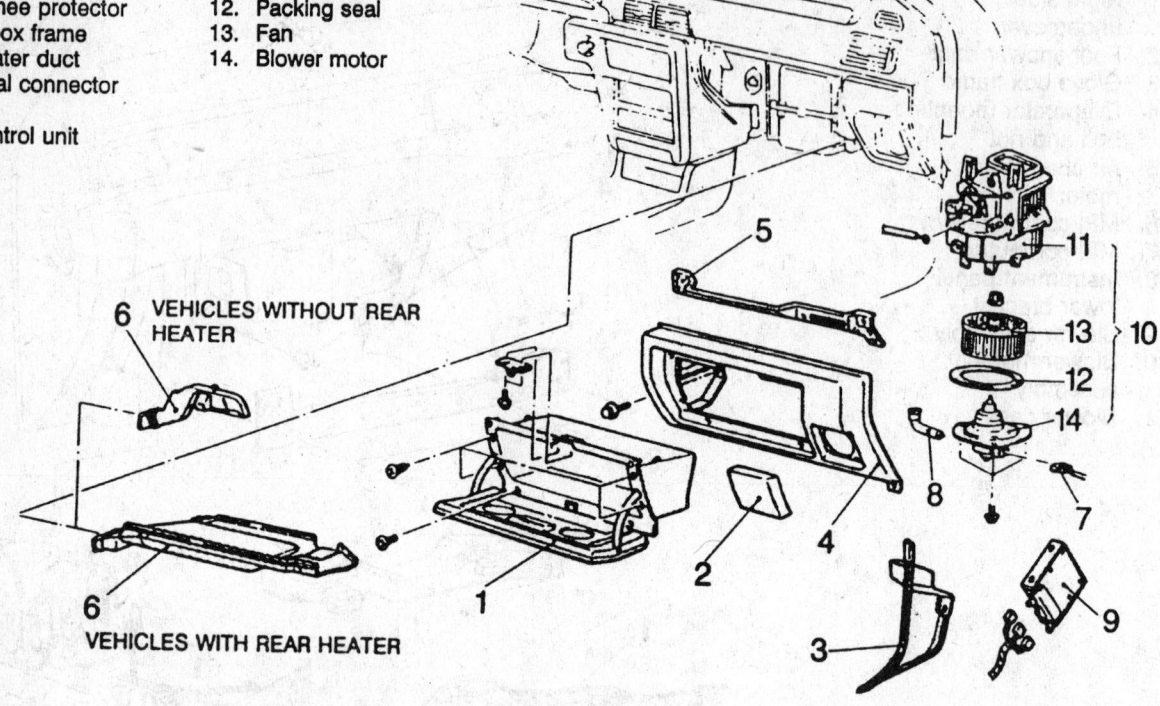

Blower motor and related parts — Mirage

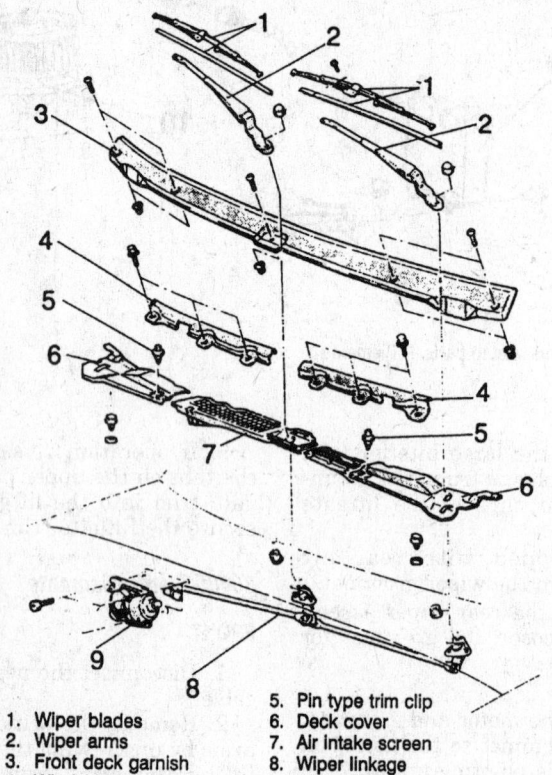

1. Wiper blades
2. Wiper arms
3. Front deck garnish
4. Windshield holder
5. Pin type trim clip
6. Deck cover
7. Air intake screen
8. Wiper linkage
9. Wiper motor

Windshield wiper assembly — Mirage

5. Detach the motor crank arm from the wiper linkage and remove the motor.

NOTE: The installation angle of the crank arm and motor has been factory set; do not remove them unless it is necessary to do so. If they must be removed, remove them only after marking their mounting positions.

To install:

6. Install the windshield wiper motor and connect the linkage.

7. Install the access hole cover.

8. Reinstall the wiper blades. Note that the driver's side wiper arm should be marked **D** and the passenger's side wiper arm should be marked **A**. The identification marks should be located at the base of the arm, near the pivot. Install the arms so the blades are parallel to the garnish molding when parked.

9. Connect the negative battery cable and check the wiper system for proper operation.

REAR

1. Disconnect the negative battery cable.

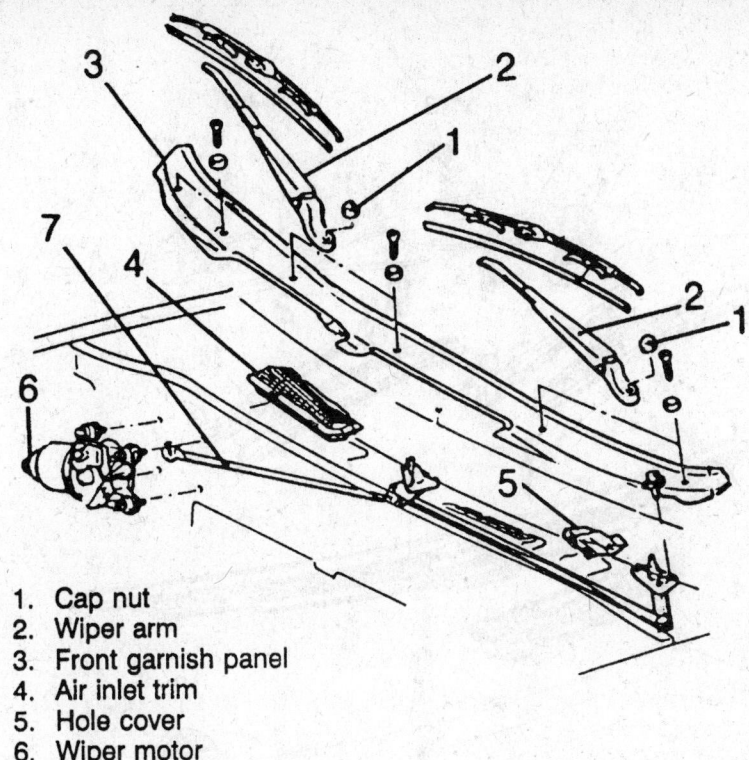

1. Cap nut
2. Wiper arm
3. Front garnish panel
4. Air inlet trim
5. Hole cover
6. Wiper motor
7. Wiper linkage

Windshield wiper assembly — Eclipse

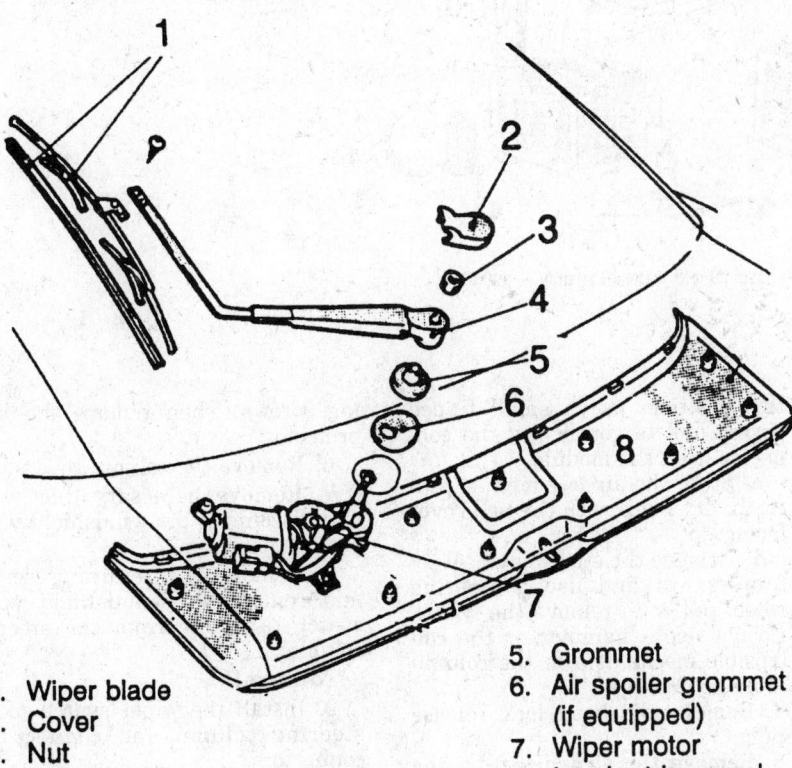

1. Wiper blade
2. Cover
3. Nut
4. Wiper arm
5. Grommet
6. Air spoiler grommet (if equipped)
7. Wiper motor
8. Interior trim panel

Liftgate wiper assembly — Eclipse

2. Remove the liftgate lower trim. Remove the clips that hold the trim by using the following procedure:

a. Remove the clip by pressing down on the center pin with a blunt pointed tool. Press down a little more than 1/16 in. (2mm). This releases the clip. Pull the clip outward to remove it.

b. Do not push the pin inward more than necessary because it may damage the grommet, or if pushed too far, the pin may fall in. Once the clips are removed, use a plastic trim stick to pry the trim cover loose.

3. Remove the rear spoiler, center brace and center brake light.

4. Lift the small cover, remove the retaining nut and remove the wiper arm and spacer.

5. Remove the mounting bolts and remove the wiper motor.

To install:

6. Install the motor and install the retaining bolts.

7. Install the spacer, wiper arm and retaining nut. The arm should be positioned so the upper tip points to the upper left corner of the rear window when parked. Connect the battery and check the operation of the motor before proceeding. If satisfactory, disconnect the cable and proceed.

8. Install the rear spoiler and related parts.

9. Install the interior trim piece.

10. Connect the negative battery cable and recheck the system for proper operation.

Windshield Wiper Switch

REMOVAL AND INSTALLATION

NOTE: On vehicles not covered here, the windshield wiper switch is incorporated into the combination switch and is not separately serviceable.

Sigma, 3000GT and Diamante

1. Disconnect the negative battery cable.

2. If equipped with an air bag, disarm as follows:

a. Position the front wheels in the straight-ahead position and place the key in the **LOCK** position. Remove the key from the ignition lock cylinder.

b. Disconnect the negative battery cable and insulate the cable end with high-quality electrical tape or similar non-conductive wrapping.

1. Wiper blade
2. Wiper arm
3. Deck garnish
4. Right side air inlet garnish
5. Hole cover
6. Wiper cover
7. Linkage
8. Battery
9. Battery tray
10. Washer tank
11. Washer motor
12. Level sensor
13. Washer nozzle
14. Washer tube

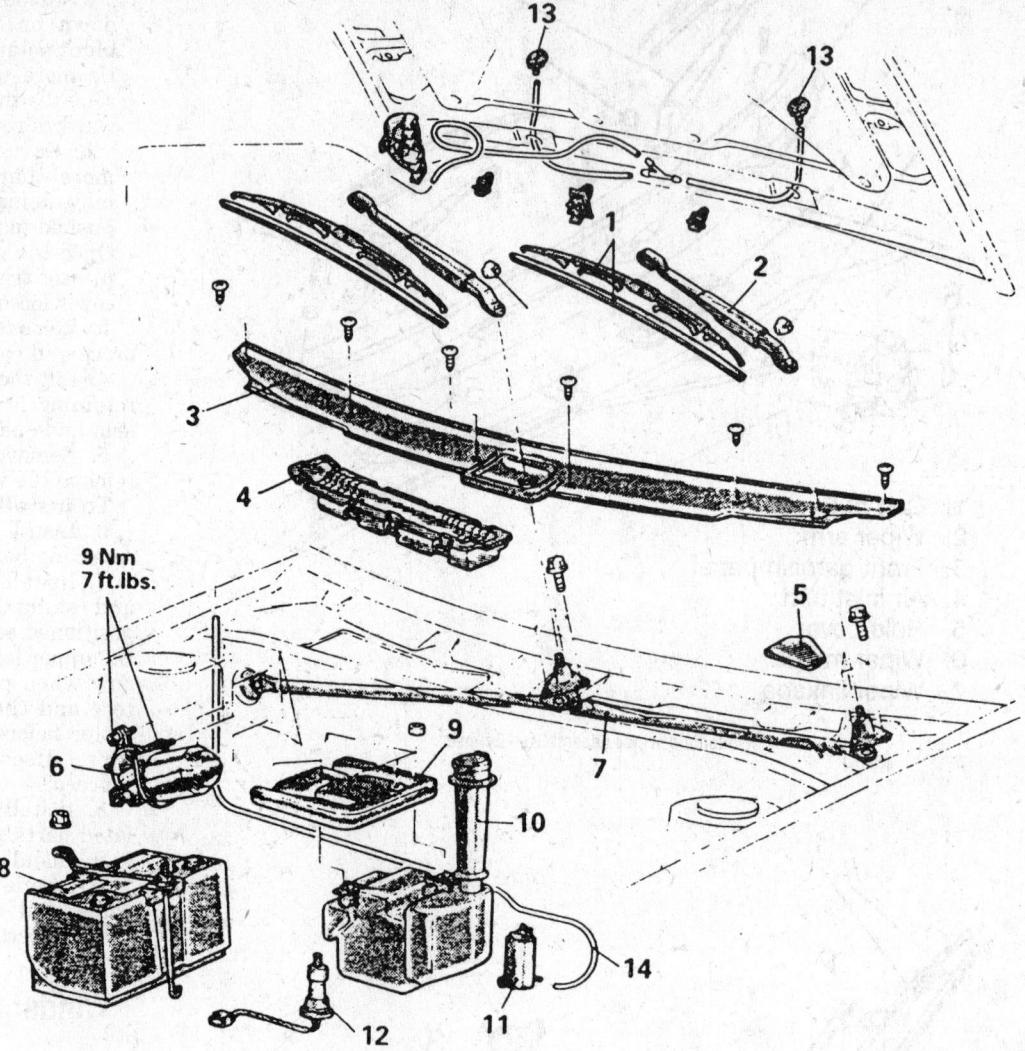

Windshield wiper assembly — 3000GT

c. Wait at least 1 minute before working on the vehicle. The air bag system is designed to retain enough voltage to deploy the air bag for a short period of time even after the battery has been disconnected.

3. Remove the steering wheel as follows:

a. Remove the air bag module mounting nut from behind the steering wheel.

b. To disconnect the connector of the clockspring from the air bag module, press the air bag's lock towards the module to spread the lock open. While holding lock in this position, use a small tipped prying tool to gently pry the connector from the module.

c. Store the air bag module in a clean, dry place with the pad cover facing up.

d. Remove the steering wheel retaining nut and use a steering wheel puller to remove the wheel. Do not use a hammer or the collapsible mechanism in the column could be damaged.

4. Remove the hood lock release handle.

5. Remove the switches from the knee protector below the steering column and remove the exposed retaining screws. Then remove the knee protector.

6. Remove the column covers.

7. Remove necessary duct work and disconnect the windshield wiper switch connectors.

8. Remove the retaining screws and remove the windshield wiper switch assembly from the steering column.

To install:

9. Install the wiper switch to the steering column and connect the connectors.

10. Install any removed duct work.

11. Install the column covers.

12. Install the knee protector and switches.

13. Install the hood release handle.

14. Confirm that the front wheels are in a straight-ahead position. Center the clockspring by aligning the **NEUTRAL** mark on the clockspring with the mating mark on the casing. Then install the steering wheel and torque the retaining nut to 29 ft. lbs. (40 Nm).

15. Connect the negative battery cable and check the windshield wiper and washer for proper operation.

Instrument Cluster

REMOVAL AND INSTALLATION

Precis and Mirage

1. Disconnect the negative battery cable. Remove the center trim panel.

2. Remove the knee protector. If pin type clips are used, they may be removed using the following procedure:

   a. This type of clip is removed by pressing down on the center pin with a suitable blunt pointed tool. Press down a little more than 1/16 in. (2mm). This releases the clip. Pull the clip outward to remove it.

b. Do not push the pin inward more than necessary because it may damage the grommet or the pin may fall in, if pushed in too far. Once the clips are removed, use a plastic trim stick if necessary to pry the knee protector loose.

3. Remove the instrument cluster bezel.

4. Remove the instrument cluster. Disassemble and remove gauges or the speedometer as required.

NOTE: If the speedometer cable adapter requires service, disconnect the cable at the transaxle end. Pull the cable slightly toward the vehicle interior, release the lock by turning the adapter to the right or left and remove the adapter.

5. The installation is the reverse of the removal procedure. Use care not to damage the printed circuit board or any gauge components.

6. Connect the negative battery cable and check all cluster-related items for proper operation.

Galant, Sigma, and Expo/Expo LRV

1. Disconnect negative battery cable.

2. Remove the 2 retainer screws on the lower surface of the meter hood.

3. Remove the retainer screws from the under side top portion of the meter hood.

4. Carefully remove the meter hood from the face of the combination meter.

5. Remove the 4 retainer screws and the combination meter assembly with the bezel attached. Remove the front bezel and remove gauges or the speedometer as required.

NOTE: If the speedometer cable adapter requires service, disconnect the cable at the transaxle end. Pull the cable slightly toward the vehicle interior, release the lock by turning the adapter to the right or left and remove the adapter.

6. The installation is the reverse of the removal procedure. Use care not to damage the printed circuit board or any gauge components.

7. Connect the negative battery cable and check all cluster-related items for proper operation.

Eclipse

1. Disconnect the negative battery cable.

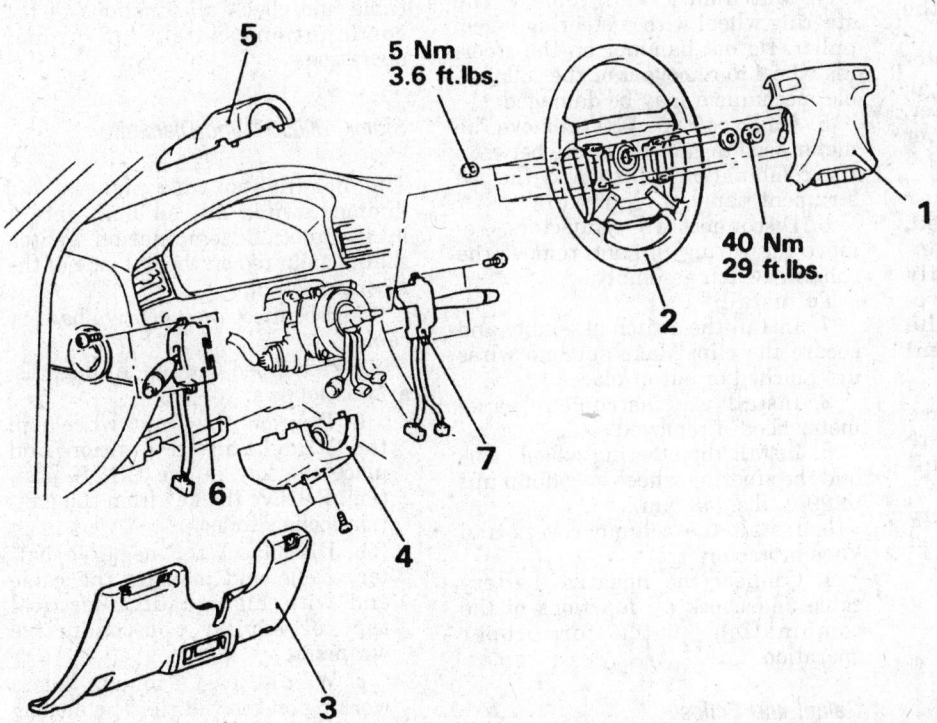

1. Air bag module
2. Steering wheel
3. Knee protector assembly
4. Lower column cover
5. Upper column cover
6. Lighting switch
7. Windshield wiper switch

5 Nm
3.6 ft.lbs.

40 Nm
29 ft.lbs.

Combination switch and related parts — Diamante; Sigma and 3000GT similar

2. Remove the screw cover on the side of the cluster panel assembly.

3. Remove the front instrument cluster bezel.

4. Remove the instrument cluster. Disassemble and remove gauges or the speedometer as required.

NOTE: If the speedometer cable adapter requires service, disconnect the cable at the transaxle end. Pull the cable slightly toward the vehicle interior, release the lock by turning the adapter to the right or left and remove the adapter.

5. The installation is the reverse of the removal procedure. Use care not to damage the printed circuit board or any gauge components.

6. Connect the negative battery cable and check all cluster-related items for proper operation.

3000GT and Diamante

1. Disconnect the negative battery cable.

NOTE: If equipped with an air bag, be sure to disarm it before entering the vehicle.

2. Remove the hood lock release handle and switches from the knee protector below the steering column. Then remove the exposed retaining screws and remove the knee protector.

3. Remove the upper and the lower steering column covers.

4. Remove the instrument cluster bezel.

5. Remove the instrument cluster. Disassemble and remove gauges or the speedometer as required.

NOTE: If the speedometer cable adapter must be serviced, disconnect the cable at the transaxle end. Pull the cable slightly toward the vehicle interior, release the lock by turning the adapter to the right or left and remove the adapter.

6. The installation is the reverse of the removal procedure. Use care not to damage the printed circuit board or any gauge components.

7. Connect the negative battery cable and check all cluster-related items for proper operation.

Concealed Headlights

MANUAL OPERATION

If the headlight covers will not raise electrically, remove the fusible link

from the relay box, then remove the boot on the rear area of the pop-up motor and turn the manual knob clockwise until the cover is open. Perform this procedure on both the left and right sides.

Combination Switch

NOTE: On all except Sigma, 3000GT and Diamante, the headlights, turn signals, dimmer switch, horn switch, windshield wiper/washer, intermittent wiper switch and on some models, the cruise control function are all built into 1 multi-function combination switch that is mounted on the steering column. On the aforementioned vehicles, the combination switch is really a lighting-function switch.

REMOVAL AND INSTALLATION

Precis, Mirage and Expo/Expo LRV

1. Disconnect the negative battery cable.

2. Remove the knee protector panel under the steering column, then the upper and lower column covers. On Expo/Expo LRV, remove the instrument panel under cover.

3. Remove the horn pad by pulling the lower end outward.

4. Matchmark and remove the steering wheel with a steering wheel puller. Do not hammer on the steering wheel to remove it or the collapsible mechanism may be damaged.

5. On Expo/Expo LRV, remove the meter hood to gain clearance between the combination switch and the instrument panel, if required.

6. Disconnect all connectors, remove the wiring clip and remove the column switch assembly.

   To install:

7. Install the switch assembly and secure the clip. Make sure no wires are pinched or out of place.

8. Install the instrument panel meter hood if removed.

9. Install the steering wheel. Torque the steering wheel-to-column nut to 29 ft. lbs. (40 Nm).

10. Install the column covers and knee protector.

11. Connect the negative battery cable and check all functions of the combination switch for proper operation.

Galant and Eclipse

1. Disconnect the negative battery cable.

2. Remove the knee protector panel under the steering column.

3. Remove the horn pad attaching screw on the under side of the steering wheel and remove the horn pad by pushing the pad upward.

4. Matchmark and remove the steering wheel with a steering wheel puller. Do not hammer on the steering wheel to remove it or the collapsible mechanism may be damaged.

5. Locate the rectangular plugs in the knee protector on either side of the steering column. Pry these plugs out and remove the screws. Remove the screws from the hood lock release lever and remove the knee protector.

6. Remove the upper and lower column covers.

7. Remove the lap cooler ducts.

8. Remove the band retaining the switch wiring.

9. Disconnect all connectors, remove the wiring clip and remove the column switch assembly.

   To install:

10. Install the switch assembly and secure the clip. Make sure no wires are pinched or out of place.

11. Install the lap cooler ducts.

12. Install the column covers and knee protector.

13. Install the steering wheel. Torque the steering wheel-to-column nut to 29 ft. lbs. (40 Nm).

14. Connect the negative battery cable and check all functions of the combination switch for proper operation.

Sigma, 3000GT and Diamante

The headlights, turn signals and dimmer switch are all built into 1 multi-function combination switch that is mounted on the left side of the steering column.

1. Disconnect the negative battery cable.

2. If equipped with an air bag, disarm as follows:

   a. Position the front wheels in the straight-ahead position and place the key in the **LOCK** position. Remove the key from the ignition lock cylinder.

   b. Disconnect the negative battery cable and insulate the cable end with high-quality electrical tape or similar non-conductive wrapping.

   c. Wait at least 1 minute before working on the vehicle. The air bag system is designed to retain enough voltage to deploy the air bag for a short period of time even

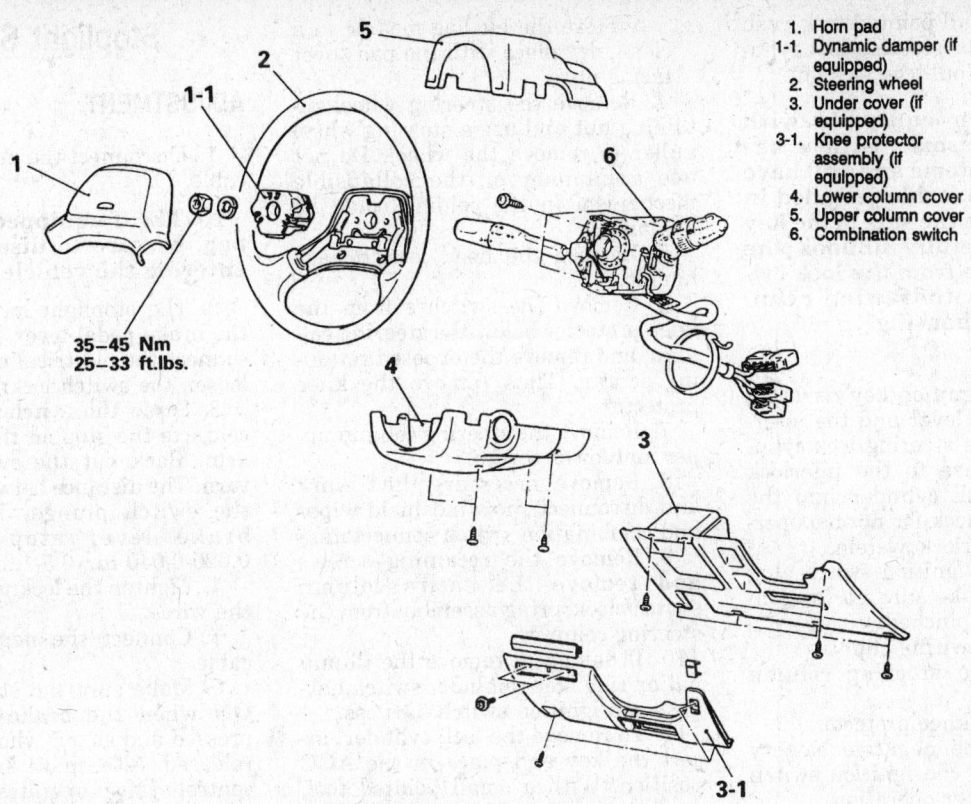

1. Horn pad
1-1. Dynamic damper (if equipped)
2. Steering wheel
3. Under cover (if equipped)
3-1. Knee protector assembly (if equipped)
4. Lower column cover
5. Upper column cover
6. Combination switch

35–45 Nm
25–33 ft.lbs.

Combination switch and related parts — Galant shown

after the battery has been disconnected.

NOTE: If equipped with an air bag, be sure to disarm it before entering the vehicle. Failure to do so could result in personal injury or death.

3. Remove the steering wheel as follows:

a. Remove the air bag module mounting nut from behind the steering wheel.

b. To disconnect the connector of the clockspring from the air bag module, press the air bag's lock towards the module to spread the lock open. While holding lock in this position, use a small tipped prying tool to gently pry the connector from the module.

c. Store the air bag module in a clean, dry place with the pad cover facing up.

d. Remove the steering wheel retaining nut and use a steering wheel puller to remove the wheel. Do not use a hammer or the collapsible mechanism in the column could be damaged.

4. Remove the hood lock release handle.

5. Remove the switches from the knee protector below the steering column, and remove the exposed retaining screws. Then remove the knee protector.

6. Remove the column covers.

7. Remove necessary duct work and disconnect the combination switch connectors.

8. Remove the retaining screws and remove the combination switch assembly from the steering column.

To install:

9. Install the switch to the steering column and connect the connectors.

10. Install any removed duct work.

11. Install the column covers.

12. Install the knee protector and switches.

13. Install the hood release handle.

14. Confirm that the front wheels are in a straight-ahead position. Center the clockspring by aligning the **NEUTRAL** mark on the clockspring with the mating mark on the casing. Then install the steering

wheel and torque the retaining nut to 29 ft. lbs. (40 Nm).

15. Connect the negative battery cable and check all functions of the combination switch for proper operation.

Ignition Switch

REMOVAL AND INSTALLATION

Except Sigma, 3000GT and Diamante

1. Disconnect the negative battery cable. Remove the hood lock release lever from the lower panel.

2. Remove the lower instrument panel knee protector.

3. Remove the lower steering column cover. On Expo/Expo LRV, remove the meter hood.

4. Remove the clip that holds the wiring against the steering column.

5. Remove the key reminder switch if equipped. Unplug the ignition switch from the steering lock cylinder and remove.

6. Insert the key into the steering lock cylinder and turn to the **ACC** position.

7. With a small pointed tool, push the lock pin of the steering lock cylinder inward and pull the lock out.

NOTE: When equipped with automatic transaxle, Eclipse has safety-lock systems and will have a key interlock cable installed in a slide lever on the side of the key cylinder. Carefully unhook the interlock cable from the lock cylinder while withdrawing cylinder from lock housing.

To install:

8. With the ignition key removed, install the slide lever and the interlock cable to the steering lock cylinder. Apply grease to the interlock cable and install cylinder into the lock housing. Check for normal operation of the interlock system.

9. Install the ignition switch plug carefully and make sure no wires in the harness are pinched.

10. Install the wiring clip.

11. Install the steering column covers.

12. Install the knee protector.

13. Connect the negative battery cable and check the ignition switch and lock for proper operation.

Sigma, 3000GT and Diamante

1. Disconnect the negative battery cable.

2. If equipped with an air bag, disarm as follows:

a. Position the front wheels in the straight-ahead position and place the key in the **LOCK** position. Remove the key from the ignition lock cylinder.

b. Disconnect the negative battery cable and insulate the cable end with high-quality electrical tape or similar non-conductive wrapping.

c. Wait at least 1 minute before working on the vehicle. The air bag system is designed to retain enough voltage to deploy the air bag for a short period of time even after the battery has been disconnected.

3. If equipped with an air bag, remove the air bag module as follows:

a. Remove the air bag module mounting nut from behind the steering wheel.

b. To disconnect the connector of the clockspring from the air bag module, press the air bag's lock towards the module to spread the lock open. While holding lock in this position, use a small tipped prying tool to gently pry the connector from the module.

c. Store the air bag module in a clean, dry place with the pad cover facing up.

4. Remove the steering wheel retaining nut and use a steering wheel puller to remove the wheel. Do not use a hammer or the collapsible mechanism in the column could be damaged.

5. Remove the hood lock release handle.

6. Remove the switches from the knee protector below the steering column, and remove the exposed retaining screws. Then remove the knee protector.

7. Remove the steering column upper and lower covers.

8. Remove necessary duct work and disconnect the windshield wiper and combination switch connectors.

9. Remove the retaining screws and remove the entire column switch/clockspring assembly from the steering column.

10. If damaged, remove the illumination ring, key reminder switch harness and ignition switch harness.

11. To remove the lock cylinder, insert the key and place in the **ACC** position. With a small pointed tool, push the lock pin of the steering lock cylinder inward and pull the lock out.

To install:

12. Install the lock cylinder; make sure the lock pin snaps into place.

13. Install any other removed items, making sure no wires are pinched.

14. Install the column switch/clockspring assembly to the steering column and connect the connectors.

15. Install any removed duct work.

16. Install the column covers.

17. Install the knee protector and switches.

18. Install the hood release handle.

19. Center the clockspring by aligning the **NEUTRAL** mark on the clockspring with the mating mark on the casing. Then install the steering wheel and torque the retaining nut to 29 ft. lbs. (40 Nm).

20. Connect the negative battery cable and check all functions of column-mounted switches and the ignition switch for proper operation.

Stoplight Switch

ADJUSTMENT

1. Disconnect the negative battery cable.

NOTE: If equipped with an air bag, be sure to disarm it before entering the vehicle.

2. The stoplight switch works off the brake pedal lever. To adjust, disconnect the electrical connection and loosen the switch locknut.

3. Screw the switch inward until it contacts the stop on the brake pedal arm. Back out the switch ½-1 full turn. The distance between the end of the switch plunger bore and the brake lever stop should be 0.020-0.040 in. (0.5-1.0mm).

4. Tighten the locknut and connect the wires.

5. Connect the negative battery cable.

6. Make sure the stoplights come **ON** when the brake pedal is depressed and go out when the pedal is released. Also, make sure the cruise control system operates properly.

REMOVAL AND INSTALLATION

1. Disconnect the negative battery cable.

NOTE: If equipped with an air bag, be sure to disarm it before starting any repairs on the vehicle.

2. Locate the stoplight switch above the brake pedal lever.

3. Disconnect the wiring connectors from the switch and unscrew the switch.

To install:

4. Thread the stoplight switch into the switch holding bracket. Adjust the switch to achieve correct operation.

5. Connect the stoplight wires.

6. Connect the negative battery cable.

7. Make sure the stoplights come **ON** when the brake pedal is depressed and go out when the pedal is released. Also, make sure the cruise control system operates properly.

Clutch Switch

ADJUSTMENT

The clutch interlock switch is located at the top of the clutch pedal arm. Note that there may be 2 switches;

one will be a cruise control cut-out switch.

1. Clutch interlock switch adjustment is made with the pedal fully depressed.

2. Measure the gap between the switch plunger and the arm stop. The gap should be 0.140 in. (3.5mm).

3. If adjustment is necessary, loosen the locknut and rotate the switch until the desired clearance is obtained. Tighten locknut to lock switch in place.

4. After completing the adjustment, check that the pedal free-play, measured at the face of the pedal pad is 0.240-0.510 in. (6-13mm). The distance between the pedal pad and the firewall when the clutch is disengaged (applied) should be as follows:

   a. Precis, Mirage and 3000GT — 2.20 in. or greater.

   b. Expo/Expo LRV — 1.77 in. or greater.

   c. Eclipse Expo/Expo LRV — 2.80 in. or greater.

5. If these dimensions are not right, the hydraulic clutch system may need further servicing.

REMOVAL AND INSTALLATION

1. Disconnect the negative battery cable.

NOTE: If equipped with an air bag, be sure to disarm it before starting any repairs on the vehicle.

2. Locate the interlock switch above the clutch pedal lever.

3. Disconnect the wiring connectors from the switch and unscrew the switch.

To install:

4. Thread the switch into the mounting bracket and adjust to 0.140 in. (3.5mm) clearance.

5. Reconnect the interlock wires.

6. Make sure the engine will not start unless the clutch pedal is depressed. Also, make sure the cruise control system operates properly.

Neutral Safety Switch

ADJUSTMENT

1. Locate the neutral safety switch on the top of the transaxle. Note that several different cable attaching methods have been used. The procedure here can be used as a general guide for all.

2. Place the selector lever in **N**.

3. Loosen the 2 adjusting nuts to free up the cable and lever.

4. Place the safety switch manual control lever in **N**.

5. Note that 1 end of the safety switch manual control lever has a 12mm wide square end. There is also a 12mm wide tab on the switch body flange. Loosen both retaining bolts and turn the safety switch until these portions align. Tighten the bolts, making sure the switch doesn't move.

6. Loosen the adjuster nuts and gently pull the cable to remove any slack. Gently tighten adjusting nut until it just starts to contact the adjuster. Secure adjusting nut with its locknut then turn nut to lock.

7. Verify that the switch lever moves to positions corresponding to each position of the selector lever.

8. Make sure the engine only starts in **P** and **N**. Also make sure the reverse lights come ON in **R**.

REMOVAL AND INSTALLATION

1. Disconnect the negative battery cable.

2. Disconnect the selector cable from the lever.

3. Remove the 2 retaining screws and lift off the switch.

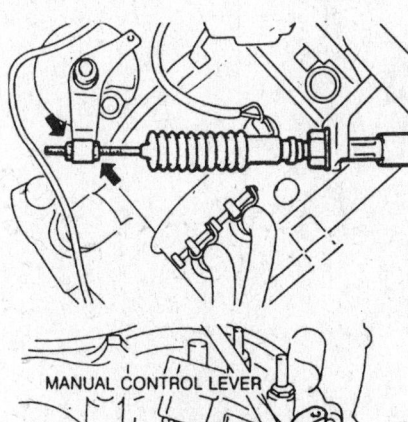

MANUAL CONTROL LEVER

INHIBITOR SWITCH

MOUNTING BOLTS

Automatic transaxle neutral safety (inhibitor) switch and adjustment

4. The installation is the reverse of the removal procedure. Do not tighten the bolts until the switch is adjusted.

5. Make sure the engine only starts in **P** and **N**. Also make sure the reverse lights come ON in **R**.

Fuses and Fusible Links

LOCATION

3000GT, Galant, Sigma and Diamante

One fuse panel is located on the passenger side, under the hood, just forward of the air flow box. It shares the panel with a bank of relays. This panel also contains several fusible links. On 3000GT, Galant and Sigma, another fuse panel is the multi-purpose fuse block located under the instrument panel, on the left side behind the driver's knee protector. On Diamante, 3 additional fuse boxes are located under the instrument panel, on the left side behind the driver's knee protector.

Eclipse

There are 3 main fusible links the MPI circuit — 20 amp, the radiator fan motor circuit — 30 amp and the ignition switch circuit — 30 amp. They are found under the hood in a centralized junction with the battery positive cable clamp. Another fuse panel is located on the passenger side, under the hood, just forward of the strut tower. It shares the panel with a bank of relays. This panel contains fuses and several fusible links. Another fuse panel is on the driver's side, under the hood, back against the firewall. A fourth fuse panel is the multi-purpose fuse block located inside the vehicle, on the left side behind the driver's knee protector.

Mirage and Expo/Expo LRV

The Mirage and Expo/Expo LRV have several fuse panels. One fuse panel is located on the passenger side, under the hood, just behind the battery. It shares the panel with a bank of relays. This panel also contains several fusible links. Another fuse panel is on the driver's side, under the hood, up front behind the headlight. It controls air conditioning functions. A third fuse panel is the multi-purpose fuse block located inside the vehicle, on the left side behind the driver's knee protector.

Precis

Fuses are located in the fuse box at the left kick panel and the relay box under the left side of the dash.

Fusible links are located in a holder next to the battery or in a holder at the left front of the engine compartment.

Flashers

LOCATION

3000GT

Hazard Flasher/Turn Signal Unit — located at the left kick panel.

Diamante

Turn Signal and Hazard Flasher Unit — located in the Relay box under the left side of the instrument panel.

Mirage, Expo/Expo LRV and Precis

Fuse Box Relay (red) — located in the fusible link box, at the battery.

Fuse Box — located in the left kick panel.

Hazard Flasher — located in the relay box under the left side of the dash.

Main Fuse Box — located on the side of the battery.

Main-Fusible Link Box — located at the battery.

Sub-Fusible Link Box — located at the left front of the engine compartment.

Sigma

Turn Signal/Hazard Flasher Unit — located at under the left side of the dash in the relay box.

ENGINE IDENTIFICATION

Year	Model	Engine Displacement Liters (cc)	Engine Series (ID/VIN)	Fuel System	No. of Cylinders	Engine Type
1990	240SX	2.4L (2389)	KA24E	EFI	4	SOHC
	300ZX	3.0L (2960)	VG30DE	EFI	6	DOHC
		3.0L (2960)	VG30DETT (Twin Turbo)	EFI	6	DOHC
	Maxima	3.0L (2960)	VG30E	EFI	6	SOHC
	Pulsar	1.6L (1597)	GA16i	EFI	4	SOHC
	Sentra	1.6L (1597)	GA16i	EFI	4	SOHC
	Stanza	2.4L (2389)	KA24E	EFI	4	SOHC
1991	240SX	2.4L (2389)	KA24DE	EFI	4	DOHC
	300ZX	3.0L (2960)	VG30DE	EFI	6	DOHC
		3.0L (2960)	VG30DETT (Twin Turbo)	EFI	6	DOHC
	Maxima	3.0L (2960)	VG30E	EFI	6	SOHC
	Sentra/NX	1.6L (1597)	GA16DE	EFI	4	DOHC
		2.0L (1998)	SR20DE	EFI	4	DOHC
	Stanza	2.4L (2389)	KA24E	EFI	4	SOHC
1992	240SX	2.4L (2389)	KA24DE	EFI	4	DOHC
	300ZX	3.0L (2960)	VG30DE	EFI	6	DOHC
		3.0L (2960)	VG30DETT (Twin Turbo)	EFI	6	DOHC
	Maxima	3.0L (2960)	VG30E	EFI	6	SOHC
		3.0L (2960)	VE30DE	EFI	6	DOHC
	Sentra/NX	1.6L (1597)	GA16DE	EFI	4	DOHC
		2.0L (1998)	SR20DE	EFI	4	DOHC
	Stanza	2.4L (2389)	KA24E	EFI	4	SOHC
1993	240SX	2.4L (2389)	KA24DE	EFI	4	DOHC
	300ZX	3.0L (2960)	VG30DE	EFI	6	DOHC
		3.0L (2960)	VG30DETT (Twin Turbo)	EFI	6	DOHC
	Altima	2.4L (2389)	KA24DE	EFI	4	DOHC
	Maxima	3.0L (2960)	VG30E	EFI	6	SOHC
		3.0L (2960)	VE30DE	EFI	6	DOHC
	Sentra/NX	1.6L (1597)	GA16DE	EFI	4	DOHC
		2.0L (1998)	SR20DE	EFI	4	DOHC
1994	240SX	2.4L (2389)	KA24DE	EFI	4	DOHC
	300ZX	3.0L (2960)	VG30DE	EFI	6	DOHC
		3.0L (2960)	VG30DETT (Twin Turbo)	EFI	6	DOHC
	Altima	2.4L (2389)	KA24DE	EFI	4	DOHC
	Maxima	3.0L (2960)	VG30E	EFI	6	SOHC
		3.0L (2960)	VE30DE	EFI	6	DOHC
	Sentra/NX	1.6L (1597)	GA16DE	EFI	4	DOHC
		2.0L (1998)	SR20DE	EFI	4	DOHC

EFI—Electronic Fuel Injection
DOHC—Double Overhead Camshaft
SOHC—Single Overhead Camshaft

GENERAL ENGINE SPECIFICATIONS

Year	Engine ID/VIN	Engine Displacement Liters (cc)	Fuel System Type	Net Horsepower @ rpm	Net Torque @ rpm (ft. lbs.)	Bore × Stroke (in.)	Compression Ratio	Oil Pressure @ rpm
1990	KA24E	2.4L (2389)	EFI	140 @ 5600	152 @ 4400	3.50 × 3.78	8.6:1	60–70 @ 3000
	VG30DE	3.0L (2960)	EFI	222 @ 6400	198 @ 4800	3.43 × 3.27	10.5:1	51–65 @ 3000
	VG30DETT	3.0L (2960) ①	EFI	②	283 @ 3600	3.43 × 3.27	8.1:1	51–65 @ 3000
	VG30E	3.0L (2960)	EFI	160 @ 5200	181 @ 2800	3.43 × 3.27	9.0:1	53–65 @ 3200
	GA16i	1.6L (1597)	EFI	90 @ 6000	96 @ 3200	2.99 × 3.47	9.4:1	57–71 @ 3000
	KA24E	2.4L (2389)	EFI	138 @ 5600	148 @ 3200	3.50 × 3.78	8.6:1	60–70 @ 3000
1991	KA24DE	2.4L (2389)	EFI	155 @ 5600	160 @ 4400	3.50 × 3.78	8.6:1	60–70 @ 3000
	VG30DE	3.0L (2960)	EFI	222 @ 6400	198 @ 4800	3.43 × 3.27	10.5:1	51–65 @ 3000
	VG30DETT	3.0L (2960) ①	EFI	②	283 @ 3600	3.43 × 3.27	8.5:1	51–65 @ 3000
	VG30E	3.0L (2960)	EFI	160 @ 5200	181 @ 2800	3.43 × 3.27	9.0:1	53–65 @ 3200
	GA16DE	1.6L (1597)	EFI	110 @ 6000	108 @ 4000	2.99 × 3.46	9.5:1	50–64 @ 3000
	SR20DE	2.0L (1998)	EFI	140 @ 6400	132 @ 4800	3.39 × 3.39	9.5:1	46–57 @ 3200
	KA24E	2.4L (2389)	EFI	138 @ 5600	148 @ 4400	3.50 × 3.78	8.6:1	60–70 @ 3000
1992	KA24DE	2.4L (2389)	EFI	155 @ 5600	160 @ 4400	3.50 × 3.78	9.5:1	60–70 @ 3000
	VG30DE	3.0L (2960)	EFI	222 @ 6400	198 @ 4800	3.43 × 3.27	10.5:1	51–65 @ 3000
	VG30DETT	3.0L (2960) ①	EFI	②	283 @ 3600	3.43 × 3.27	8.5:1	51–65 @ 3000
	VG30E	3.0L (2960)	EFI	160 @ 5200	181 @ 2800	3.43 × 3.27	9.0:1	53–65 @ 3200
	VE30DE	3.0L (2960)	EFI	190 @ 5600	190 @ 4000	3.43 × 3.27	10.0:1	60–74 @ 3000
	GA16DE	1.6L (1597)	EFI	110 @ 6000	108 @ 4000	2.99 × 3.46	9.5:1	50–64 @ 3000
	SR20DE	2.0L (1998)	EFI	140 @ 6400	132 @ 4800	3.39 × 3.39	9.5:1	46–57 @ 3200
	KA24E	2.4L (2389)	EFI	138 @ 5600	148 @ 4400	3.50 × 3.78	8.6:1	60–70 @ 3000
1993	KA24DE ③	2.4L (2389)	EFI	155 @ 5600	160 @ 4400	3.50 × 3.78	9.5:1	60–70 @ 3000
	VG30DE	3.0L (2960)	EFI	222 @ 6400	198 @ 4800	3.43 × 3.27	10.5:1	51–65 @ 3000
	VG30DETT	3.0L (2960) ①	EFI	②	283 @ 3600	3.43 × 3.27	8.5:1	51–65 @ 3000
	VG30E	3.0L (2960)	EFI	160 @ 5200	181 @ 2800	3.43 × 3.27	9.0:1	53–65 @ 3200
	VE30DE	3.0L (2960)	EFI	190 @ 5600	190 @ 4000	3.43 × 3.27	10.0:1	60–74 @ 3000
	GA16DE	1.6L (1597)	EFI	110 @ 6000	108 @ 4000	2.99 × 3.46	9.5:1	50–64 @ 3000
	SR20DE	2.0L (1998)	EFI	140 @ 6400	132 @ 4800	3.39 × 3.39	9.5:1	46–57 @ 3200
1994	KA24DE ③	2.4L (2389)	Fuel	155 @ 5600	160 @ 4400	3.50 × 3.78	9.5:1	60–70 @ 3000
	VG30DE	3.0L (2960)	EFI	222 @ 6400	198 @ 4800	3.43 × 3.27	10.5:1	51–65 @ 3000
	VG30DETT	3.0L (2960) ①	EFI	②	283 @ 3600	3.43 × 3.27	8.5:1	51–65 @ 3000
	VG30E	3.0L (2960)	EFI	160 @ 5200	181 @ 2800	3.43 × 3.27	9.0:1	53–65 @ 3200
	VE30DE	3.0L (2960)	EFI	190 @ 5600	190 @ 4000	3.43 × 3.27	10.0:1	60–74 @ 3000
	GA16DE	1.6L (1597)	EFI	110 @ 6000	108 @ 4000	2.99 × 3.46	9.5:1	50–64 @ 3000
	SR20DE	2.0L (1998)	EFI	140 @ 6400	132 @ 4800	3.39 × 3.39	9.5:1	46–57 @ 3200

NOTE: Horsepower and torque are SAE net figures. They are measured at the rear of the transmission with all accessories installed and operating. Since the figures vary when a given engine is installed in different models, some are representative rather than exact.

EFI—Electronic Fuel Injection
① Twin Turbocharger
② MT: 300 @ 6400
   AT: 280 @ 6400
③ 240SX Application—9.2:1 compression ratio
   on (1993) Altima Application

GASOLINE ENGINE TUNE-UP SPECIFICATIONS

Year	Engine ID/VIN	Engine Displacement Liters (cc)	Spark Plugs Gap (in.)	Ignition Timing (deg.) MT	AT	Fuel Pump (psi)	Idle Speed (rpm) MT	AT	Valve Clearance In.	Ex.
1990	KA24E	2.4L (2389)	0.039–0.043	15B	15B	②	750	750	Hyd.	Hyd.
	VG30DE	3.0L (2960)	0.039–0.043	15B	15B	②	770	750	Hyd.	Hyd.
	VG30DETT	3.0L (2960)	0.039–0.043	15B	15B	②	770	750	Hyd.	Hyd.
	VG30E	3.0L (2960)	0.039–0.043	15B	15B	②	750	700	Hyd.	Hyd.
	GA16i	1.6L (1597)	0.039–0.043	①	①	②	800	900	Hyd.	Hyd.
1991	KA24DE	2.4L (2389)	0.039–0.043	20B	20B	②	750	750	0.012–0.015	0.013–0.016
	VG30DE	3.0L (2960)	0.039–0.043	15B	15B	②	700	770	Hyd.	Hyd.
	VG30DETT	3.0L (2960)	0.039–0.043	15B	15B	②	700	750	Hyd.	Hyd.
	VG30E	3.0L (2960)	0.039–0.043	15B	15B	②	750	700	Hyd.	Hyd.
	GA16DE	1.6L (1597)	0.039–0.043	10B	10B	②	800	800	0.015	0.016
	SR20DE	2.0L (1998)	0.031–0.035	15B	15B	②	800	800	Hyd.	Hyd.
	KA24E	2.4L (2389)	0.039–0.043	15B	15B	②	750	750	Hyd.	Hyd.
1992	KA24DE	2.4L (2389)	0.039–0.043	20B	20B	②	750	750	0.012–0.015	0.013–0.016
	VG30DE	3.0L (2960)	0.039–0.043	15B	15B	②	700	770	Hyd.	Hyd.
	VG30DETT	3.0L (2960)	0.039–0.043	15B	15B	②	700	750	Hyd.	Hyd.
	VG30E	3.0L (2960)	0.039–0.043	15B	15B	②	750	700	Hyd.	Hyd.
	VE30DE	3.0L (2960)	0.039–0.043	15B	15B	②	750	750	Hyd.	Hyd.
	GA16DE	1.6L (1597)	0.039–0.043	10B	10B	②	800	800	0.015	0.016
	SR20DE	2.0L (1998)	0.031–0.035	15B	15B	②	800	800	Hyd.	Hyd.
	KA24E	2.4L (2389)	0.039–0.043	15B	15B	②	750	750	Hyd.	Hyd.
1993	KA24DE	2.4L (2389)	0.039–0.043	20B	20B	②	750	750	0.012–0.015	0.013–0.016
	VG30DE	3.0L (2960)	0.039–0.043	15B	15B	②	700	770	Hyd.	Hyd.
	VG30DETT	3.0L (2960)	0.039–0.043	15B	15B	②	700	750	Hyd.	Hyd.
	VG30E	3.0L (2960)	0.039–0.043	15B	15B	②	750	700	Hyd.	Hyd.
	VE30DE	3.0L (2960)	0.039–0.043	15B	15B	②	750	750	Hyd.	Hyd.
	GA16DE	1.6L (1597)	0.039–0.043	10B	10B	②	800	800	0.015	0.016
	SR20DE	2.0L (1998)	0.031–0.035	15B	15B	②	800	800	Hyd.	Hyd.
1994	KA24DE	2.4L (2389)	0.039–0.043	20B	20B	②	750	750	0.012–0.015	0.013–0.016
	VG30DE	3.0L (2960)	0.039–0.043	15B	15B	②	700	770	Hyd.	Hyd.
	VG30DETT	3.0L (2960)	0.039–0.043	15B	15B	②	700	750	Hyd.	Hyd.
	VG30E	3.0L (2960)	0.039–0.043	15B	15B	②	750	700	Hyd.	Hyd.
	VE30DE	3.0L (2960)	0.039–0.043	15B	15B	②	750	750	Hyd.	Hyd.
	GA16DE	1.6L (1597)	0.039–0.043	10B	10B	②	800	800	0.015	0.016
	SR20DE	2.0L (1998)	0.031–0.035	15B	15B	②	800	800	Hyd.	Hyd.

NOTE: The underhood specifications sticker often reflects tune-up specification changes in production. Sticker figures must be used if they disagree with those in this chart.

MT—Manual transmission
AT—Automatic transmission
NA—Not adjustable
B—Before Top Dead Center
Hyd.—Hydraulic valve lash adjusters

① With throttle sensor harness connected—7° BTDC ±5°
② Fuel pressure is measured at idle speed between the fuel filter and fuel pipe (engine) side

36.3 psi—with pressure regulator vacuum hose connected
43.4 psi—with pressure regulator vacuum hose disconnected

FIRING ORDERS

NOTE: To avoid confusion, always replace spark plug wires one at a time.

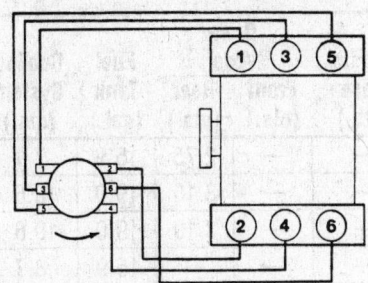

VG30E Engines
 Engine Firing Order: 1-2-3-4-5-6
 Distributor Rotation: Counterclockwise

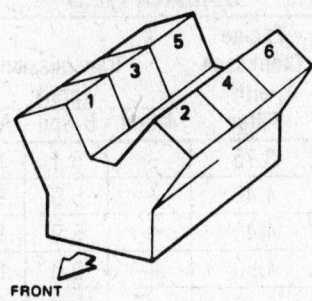

FRONT

VG30DE, VG30DETT and VE30DE Engines
 Engine Firing Order: 1-2-3-4-5-6
 Distributorless Ignition System

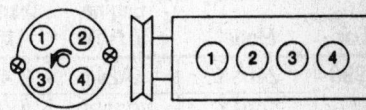

KA24E, KA24DE, SR20DE, GA16i and GA16DE Engines
 Engine Firing Order: 1-3-4-2
 Distributor Rotation: Counterclockwise

CAPACITIES

Year	Model	Engine ID/VIN	Engine Displacement Liters (cc)	Engine Crankcase with Filter	Transmission (pts.) 4-Spd	Transmission (pts.) 5-Spd	Transmission (pts.) Auto.■	Transfer Case (pts.)	Drive Axle Front (pts.)	Drive Axle Rear (pts.)	Fuel Tank (gal.)	Cooling System (qts.)
1990	240SX	KA24E	2.4L (2389)	3.75	—	5.1	17.5	—	—	2.75	15.9	7.1
	300ZX	VG30DE	3.0L (2960)	4.40	—	5.9	16.2	—	—	3.10	19.0	10.6
		VG30DETT	3.0L (2960)	4.40	—	5.9	16.2	—	—	3.10	19.0	10.6
	Maxima	VG30E	3.0L (2960)	4.50	—	10.0	15.5	—	—	—	15.9	8.7
	Pulsar	GA16i	1.6L (1597)	3.40	—	5.9	13.2	—	—	—	13.3	6.3
	Sentra	GA16i	1.6L (1597)	3.40	5.75	5.9	13.2	2.2	—	2.10	13.3	6.0
	Stanza	KA24E	2.4L (2389)	3.75	—	10.0	15.8	—	—	—	16.4	7.9
1991	240SX	KA24DE	2.4L (2389)	3.75	—	5.1	17.5	—	—	2.75	15.9	7.1
	300ZX	VG30DE	3.0L (2960)	4.10	—	5.9	16.2	—	—	3.10	19.0	10.6
		VG30DETT	3.0L (2960)	4.10	—	5.9	16.2	—	—	3.10	19.0	10.6
	Maxima	VG30E	3.0L (2960)	4.10	—	10.0	15.5	—	—	—	18.5	8.7
	Sentra/NX	GA16DE	1.6L (1597)	3.40	—	6.2	15.0	—	—	—	13.2	5.5
		SR20DE	2.0L (1998)	3.70	—	7.5	15.0	—	—	—	13.2	6.2
	Stanza	KA24E	2.4L (2389)	3.70	—	10.0	15.8	—	—	—	16.4	7.9
1992	240SX	KA24DE	2.4L (2389)	3.75	—	5.1	17.5	—	—	2.75	15.9	7.1
	300ZX	VG30DE	3.0L (2960)	4.10	—	5.9	16.2	—	—	3.10	19.0	10.6
		VG30DETT	3.0L (2960)	4.10	—	5.9	16.2	—	—	3.10	19.0	10.6
	Maxima	VG30E	3.0L (2960)	4.10	—	10.0	15.5	—	—	—	18.5	8.7
		VE30DE	3.0L (2960)	4.00	—	10.0	20.0	—	—	—	18.5	11.0
	Sentra/NX	GA16DE	1.6L (1597)	3.40	—	6.2	15.0	—	—	—	13.2	5.5
		SR20DE	2.0L (1998)	3.70	—	7.5	15.0	—	—	—	13.2	6.2
	Stanza	KA24E	2.4L (2389)	3.70	—	10.0	15.8	—	—	—	16.4	7.9
1993	240SX	KA24DE	2.4L (2389)	3.75	—	5.1	17.5	—	—	2.75	15.9	7.1
	300ZX	VG30DE	3.0L (2960)	4.10	—	5.9	16.2	—	—	3.10	19.0	10.6
		VG30DETT	3.0L (2960)	4.10	—	5.9	16.2	—	—	3.10	19.0	10.6
	Altima	KA24DE	2.4L (2389)	3.90	—	10.0	20.0	—	—	—	15.9	8.2
	Maxima	VG30E	3.0L (2960)	4.10	—	10.0	15.5	—	—	—	18.5	8.7
		VE30DE	3.0L (2960)	4.00	—	10.0	20.0	—	—	—	18.5	11.0
	Sentra/NX	GA16DE	1.6L (1597)	3.40	—	6.2	15.0	—	—	—	13.2	5.5
		SR20DE	2.0L (1998)	3.70	—	7.5	15.0	—	—	—	13.2	6.2
1994	240SX	KA24DE	2.4L (2389)	3.75	—	5.1	17.5	—	—	2.75	15.9	7.1
	300ZX	VG30DE	3.0L (2960)	4.10	—	5.9	16.2	—	—	3.10	19.0	10.6
		VG30DETT	3.0L (2960)	4.10	—	5.9	16.2	—	—	3.10	19.0	10.6
	Altima	KA24DE	2.4L (2389)	3.90	—	10.0	20.0	—	—	—	15.9	8.2
	Maxima	VG30E	3.0L (2960)	4.10	—	10.0	15.5	—	—	—	18.5	8.7
		VE30DE	3.0L (2960)	4.00	—	10.0	20.0	—	—	—	18.5	11.0
	Sentra/NX	GA16DE	1.6L (1597)	3.40	—	6.2	15.0	—	—	—	13.2	5.5
		SR20DE	2.0L (1998)	3.70	—	7.5	15.0	—	—	—	13.2	6.2

NOTE: Use specifications as a guide for refill process.
■ Figure is for drain and refill

CAMSHAFT SPECIFICATIONS

All measurements given in inches.

Year	Engine ID/VIN	Engine Displacement Liters (cc)	Journal Diameter					Elevation		Bearing Clearance	Camshaft End Play
			1	2	3	4	5	In.	Ex.		
1990	GA16i	1.6L (1597)	1.6510–1.6518	1.6510–1.6518	1.6510–1.6518	1.6510–1.6518	1.6510–1.6518	NA	NA	0.0018–0.0035	0.0012–0.0051
	KA24E	2.4L (2389)	1.2967–1.2974	1.2967–1.2974	1.2967–1.2974	1.2967–1.2974	1.2967–1.2974	0.409	0.409	0.0018–0.0035	0.0028–0.0059
	VG30DE	3.0L (2960)	1.0998–1.1006	1.0998–1.1006	1.0998–1.1006	1.0998–1.1006	1.0998–1.1006	NA	NA	0.0018–0.0035	0.0018–0.0035
	VG30DETT	3.0L (2960)	1.0998–1.1006	1.0998–1.1006	1.0998–1.1006	1.0998–1.1006	1.0998–1.1006	NA	NA	0.0018–0.0035	0.0018–0.0035
	VG30E	3.0L (2960)	1.8866–1.8874 ①	1.8472–1.8480	1.8472–1.8480	1.8472–1.8480	1.6732–1.6742	NA	NA	0.0024–0.0041	0.0012–0.0024
1991	KA24DE	2.4L (2389)	1.0998–1.1006	0.9423–0.9431	0.9423–0.9431	0.9423–0.9431	0.9423–0.9431	NA	NA	0.0018–0.0035	0.0028–0.0059
	VG30DE	3.0L (2960)	1.0998–1.1006	1.0998–1.1006	1.0998–1.1006	1.0998–1.1006	1.0998–1.1006	NA	NA	0.0018–0.0034	0.0012–0.0031
	VG30DETT	3.0L (2960)	1.0998–1.1006	1.0998–1.1006	1.0998–1.1006	1.0998–1.1006	1.0998–1.1006	NA	NA	0.0018–0.0034	0.0012–0.0031
	VG30E	3.0L (2960)	1.8866–1.8874 ①	1.8472–1.8480	1.8472–1.8480	1.8472–1.8480	1.6701–1.6709	NA	NA	0.0018–0.0035	0.0012–0.0024
	GA16DE	1.6L (1597)	1.0998–1.1006	0.9423–0.9431	0.9423–0.9431	0.9423–0.9431	0.9423–0.9431	NA	NA	0.0018–0.0034	0.0045–0.0074
	SR20DE	2.0L (1998)	1.0998–1.1006	1.0998–1.1006	1.0998–1.1006	1.0998–1.1006	1.0998–1.1006	0.394	0.362	0.0018–0.0034	0.0022–0.0055
	KA24E	2.4L (2389)	1.2967–1.2974	1.2967–1.2974	1.2967–1.2974	1.2967–1.2974	1.2967–1.2974	0.409	0.409	0.0018–0.0035	0.0028–0.0059
1992	KA24DE	2.4L (2389)	1.0998–1.1006	0.9423–0.9431	0.9423–0.9431	0.9423–0.9431	0.9423–0.9431	NA	NA	0.0018–0.0035	0.0028–0.0059
	VG30DE	3.0L (2960)	1.0998–1.1006	1.0998–1.1006	1.0998–1.1006	1.0998–1.1006	1.0998–1.1006	NA	NA	0.0018–0.0034	0.0012–0.0031
	VG30DETT	3.0L (2960)	1.0998–1.1006	1.0998–1.1006	1.0998–1.1006	1.0998–1.1006	1.0998–1.1006	NA	NA	0.0018–0.0034	0.0012–0.0031
	VG30E	3.0L (2960)	1.8866–1.8874 ①	1.8472–1.8480	1.8472–1.8480	1.8472–1.8480	1.6701–1.6709	NA	NA	0.0018–0.0035	0.0012–0.0024
	VE30DE	3.0L (2960)	1.0211–1.0218	1.0211–1.0218	1.0211–1.0218	1.0211–1.0218	1.0211–1.0218	NA	NA	0.0018–0.0034	0.0028–0.0058
	GA16DE	1.6L (1597)	1.0998–1.1006	0.9423–0.9431	0.9423–0.9431	0.9423–0.9431	0.9423–0.9431	NA	NA	0.0018–0.0034	0.0045–0.0074
	SR20DE	2.0L (1998)	1.0998–1.1006	1.0998–1.1006	1.0998–1.1006	1.0998–1.1006	1.0998–1.1006	0.394	0.362	0.0018–0.0034	0.0022–0.0055
	KA24E	2.4L (2389)	1.2967–1.2974	1.2967–1.2974	1.2967–1.2974	1.2967–1.2974	1.2967–1.2974	0.409	0.409	0.0018–0.0035	0.0028–0.0059

All measurements given in inches.

Year	Engine ID/VIN	Engine Displacement Liters (cc)	Journal Diameter					Elevation		Bearing Clearance	Camshaft End Play
			1	2	3	4	5	In.	Ex.		
1993	KA24DE	2.4L (2389)	1.0998– 1.1006	0.9423– 0.9431	0.9423– 0.9431	0.9423– 0.9431	0.9423– 0.9431	NA	NA	0.0018– 0.0035	0.0028– 0.0059
	VG30DE	3.0L (2960)	1.0998– 1.1006	1.0998– 1.1006	1.0998– 1.1006	1.0998– 1.1006	1.0998– 1.1006	NA	NA	0.0018– 0.0034	0.0012– 0.0031
	VG30DETT	3.0L (2960)	1.0998– 1.1006	1.0998– 1.1006	1.0998– 1.1006	1.0998– 1.1006	1.0998– 1.1006	NA	NA	0.0018– 0.0034	0.0012– 0.0031
	VG30E	3.0L (2960)	1.8866– 1.8874 ①	1.8472– 1.8480	1.8472– 1.8480	1.8472– 1.8480	1.6701– 1.6709	NA	NA	0.0018– 0.0035	0.0012– 0.0024
	VE30DE	3.0L (2960)	1.0211– 1.0218	1.0211– 1.0218	1.0211– 1.0218	1.0211– 1.0218	1.0211– 1.0218	NA	NA	0.0018– 0.0034	0.0028– 0.0058
	GA16DE	1.6L (1597)	1.0998– 1.1006	0.9423– 0.9431	0.9423– 0.9431	0.9423– 0.9431	0.9423– 0.9431	NA	NA	0.0018– 0.0034	0.0045– 0.0074
	SR20DE	2.0L (1998)	1.0998– 1.1006	1.0998– 1.1006	1.0998– 1.1006	1.0998– 1.1006	1.0998– 1.1006	0.394	0.362	0.0018– 0.0034	0.0022– 0.0055
1994	KA24DE	2.4L (2389)	1.0998– 1.1006	0.9423– 0.9431	0.9423– 0.9431	0.9423– 0.9431	0.9423– 0.9431	NA	NA	0.0018– 0.0035	0.0028– 0.0059
	VG30DE	3.0L (2960)	1.0998– 1.1006	1.0998– 1.1006	1.0998– 1.1006	1.0998– 1.1006	1.0998– 1.1006	NA	NA	0.0018– 0.0034	0.0012– 0.0031
	VG30DETT	3.0L (2960)	1.0998– 1.1006	1.0998– 1.1006	1.0998– 1.1006	1.0998– 1.1006	1.0998– 1.1006	NA	NA	0.0018– 0.0034	0.0012– 0.0031
	VG30E	3.0L (2960)	1.8866– 1.8874 ①	1.8472– 1.8480	1.8472– 1.8480	1.8472– 1.8480	1.6701– 1.6709	NA	NA	0.0018– 0.0035	0.0012– 0.0024
	VE30DE	3.0L (2960)	1.0211– 1.0218	1.0211– 1.0218	1.0211– 1.0218	1.0211– 1.0218	1.0211– 1.0218	NA	NA	0.0018– 0.0034	0.0028– 0.0058
	GA16DE	1.6L (1597)	1.0998– 1.1006	0.9423– 0.9431	0.9423– 0.9431	0.9423– 0.9431	0.9423– 0.9431	NA	NA	0.0018– 0.0034	0.0045– 0.0074
	SR20DE	2.0L (1998)	1.0998– 1.1006	1.0998– 1.1006	1.0998– 1.1006	1.0998– 1.1006	1.0998– 1.1006	0.394	0.362	0.0018– 0.0034	0.0022– 0.0055

NA—Not available
① Front of engine, left hand camshaft only

CRANKSHAFT AND CONNECTING ROD SPECIFICATIONS

All measurements are given in inches.

Year	Engine ID/VIN	Engine Displacement Liters (cc)	Crankshaft				Connecting Rod		
			Main Brg. Journal Dia.	Main Brg. Oil Clearance	Shaft End-play	Thrust on No.	Journal Diameter	Oil Clearance	Side Clearance
1990	GA16i	1.6L (1597)	1.9668–1.9671	0.0008–0.0017	0.0024–0.0071	3	1.5731–1.5738	0.0004–0.0014	0.0079–0.0185
	KA24E	2.4L (2389)	2.3609–2.3612	0.0008–0.0019	0.0020–0.0071	3	1.7701–1.7706	0.0004–0.0014	0.0080–0.0120
	VG30DE	3.0L (2960)	2.4790–2.4793	0.0011–0.0022	0.0020–0.0071	4	1.9672–1.9675	0.0011–0.0019	0.0079–0.0138
	VG30DETT	3.0L (2960)	2.4790–2.4793	0.0011–0.0022	0.0020–0.0071	4	1.9672–1.9675	0.0011–0.0019	0.0079–0.0138
	VG30E	3.0L (2960)	2.4790–2.4793	0.0011–0.0022	0.0020–0.0067	4	1.9667–1.9675	0.0006–0.0021	0.0079–0.0138
1991	KA24DE	2.4L (2389)	2.3609–2.3612	0.0008–0.0019	0.0020–0.0071	3	1.9672–1.9675	0.0004–0.0014	0.0080–0.0160
	VG30DE	3.0L (2960)	2.4790–2.4793	0.0011–0.0022	0.0020–0.0071	4	1.9672–1.9675	0.0011–0.0019	0.0079–0.0138
	VG30DETT	3.0L (2960)	2.4790–2.4793	0.0011–0.0022	0.0020–0.0071	4	1.9672–1.9675	0.0011–0.0019	0.0079–0.0138
	VG30E	3.0L (2960)	2.4790–2.4793	0.0011–0.0022	0.0020–0.0071	4	1.9667–1.9675	0.0006–0.0021	0.0079–0.0138
	GA16DE	1.6L (1597)	1.9668–1.9671	0.0007–0.0017	0.0024–0.0071	3	1.5735–1.5738	0.0004–0.0014	0.0079–0.0185
	SR20DE	2.0L (1998)	2.1643–2.1646	0.0002–0.0009	0.0039–0.0102	3	1.8885–1.8887	0.0008–0.0018	0.0079–0.0138
	KA24E	2.4L (2389)	2.3609–2.3612	0.0008–0.0019	0.0020–0.0071	3	1.7701–1.7706	0.0004–0.0014	0.0080–0.0160
1992	KA24DE	2.4L (2389)	2.3609–2.3612	0.0008–0.0019	0.0020–0.0071	3	1.9672–1.9675	0.0004–0.0014	0.0080–0.0160
	VG30DE	3.0L (2960)	2.4790–2.4793	0.0011–0.0022	0.0020–0.0071	4	1.9672–1.9675	0.0011–0.0019	0.0079–0.0138
	VG30DETT	3.0L (2960)	2.4790–2.4793	0.0011–0.0022	0.0020–0.0071	4	1.9672–1.9675	0.0011–0.0019	0.0079–0.0138
	VG30E	3.0L (2960)	2.4790–2.4793	0.0011–0.0022	0.0020–0.0071	4	1.9667–1.9675	0.0006–0.0021	0.0079–0.0138
	VE30DE	3.0L (2960)	2.4790–2.4793	0.0011–0.0022	0.0020–0.0067	4	1.9672–1.9675	0.0011–0.0019	0.0079–0.0138
	GA16DE	1.6L (1597)	1.9668–1.9671	0.0007–0.0017	0.0024–0.0071	3	1.5735–1.5738	0.0004–0.0014	0.0079–0.0185
	SR20DE	2.0L (1998)	2.1643–2.1646	0.0002–0.0009	0.0039–0.0102	3	1.8885–1.8887	0.0008–0.0018	0.0079–0.0138
	KA24E	2.4L (2389)	2.3609–2.3612	0.0008–0.0019	0.0020–0.0071	3	1.7701–1.7706	0.0004–0.0014	0.0080–0.0160

CRANKSHAFT AND CONNECTING ROD SPECIFICATIONS

All measurements are given in inches.

Year	Engine ID/VIN	Engine Displacement Liters (cc)	Crankshaft				Connecting Rod		
			Main Brg. Journal Dia.	Main Brg. Oil Clearance	Shaft End-play	Thrust on No.	Journal Diameter	Oil Clearance	Side Clearance
1993	KA24DE	2.4L (2389)	2.3609–2.3612	0.0008–0.0019	0.0020–0.0071	3	1.9672–1.9675	0.0004–0.0014	0.0080–0.0160
	VG30DE	3.0L (2960)	2.4790–2.4793	0.0011–0.0022	0.0020–0.0071	4	1.9672–1.9675	0.0011–0.0019	0.0079–0.0138
	VG30DETT	3.0L (2960)	2.4790–2.4793	0.0011–0.0022	0.0020–0.0071	4	1.9672–1.9675	0.0011–0.0019	0.0079–0.0138
	VG30E	3.0L (2960)	2.4790–2.4793	0.0011–0.0022	0.0020–0.0071	4	1.9667–1.9675	0.0006–0.0021	0.0079–0.0138
	VE30DE	3.0L (2960)	2.4790–2.4793	0.0011–0.0022	0.0020–0.0067	4	1.9672–1.9675	0.0011–0.0019	0.0079–0.0138
	GA16DE	1.6L (1597)	1.9668–1.9671	0.0007–0.0017	0.0024–0.0071	3	1.5735–1.5738	0.0004–0.0014	0.0079–0.0185
	SR20DE	2.0L (1998)	2.1643–2.1646	0.0002–0.0009	0.0039–0.0102	3	1.8885–1.8887	0.0008–0.0018	0.0079–0.0138
	KA24E	2.4L (2389)	2.3609–2.3612	0.0008–0.0019	0.0020–0.0071	3	1.7701–1.7706	0.0004–0.0014	0.0080–0.0160
1994	KA24DE	2.4L (2389)	2.3609–2.3612	0.0008–0.0019	0.0020–0.0071	3	1.9672–1.9675	0.0004–0.0014	0.0080–0.0160
	VG30DE	3.0L (2960)	2.4790–2.4793	0.0011–0.0022	0.0020–0.0071	4	1.9672–1.9675	0.0011–0.0019	0.0079–0.0138
	VG30DETT	3.0L (2960)	2.4790–2.4793	0.0011–0.0022	0.0020–0.0071	4	1.9672–1.9675	0.0011–0.0019	0.0079–0.0138
	VG30E	3.0L (2960)	2.4790–2.4793	0.0011–0.0022	0.0020–0.0071	4	1.9667–1.9675	0.0006–0.0021	0.0079–0.0138
	VE30DE	3.0L (2960)	2.4790–2.4793	0.0011–0.0022	0.0020–0.0067	4	1.9672–1.9675	0.0011–0.0019	0.0079–0.0138
	GA16DE	1.6L (1597)	1.9668–1.9671	0.0007–0.0017	0.0024–0.0071	3	1.5735–1.5738	0.0004–0.0014	0.0079–0.0185
	SR20DE	2.0L (1998)	2.1643–2.1646	0.0002–0.0009	0.0039–0.0102	3	1.8885–1.8887	0.0008–0.0018	0.0079–0.0138
	KA24E	2.4L (2389)	2.3609–2.3612	0.0008–0.0019	0.0020–0.0071	3	1.7701–1.7706	0.0004–0.0014	0.0080–0.0160

VALVE SPECIFICATIONS

Year	Engine ID/VIN	Engine Displacement Liters (cc)	Seat Angle (deg.)	Face Angle (deg.)	Spring Test Pressure (lbs. @ in.)	Spring Installed Height (in.)	Stem-to-Guide Clearance (in.)		Stem Diameter (in.)	
							Intake	Exhaust	Intake	Exhaust
1990	GA16i	1.6L (1597)	45	45	③	⑦	0.0008–0.0020	0.0008–0.0020	0.2348–0.2354	0.2582–0.2587
	KA24E	2.4L (2389)	45	45	①	②	0.0008–0.0021	0.0016–0.0028	0.2742–0.2748	0.3129–0.3134
	VG30DE	3.0L (2960)	45	45	⑨	⑧	0.0008–0.0021	0.0016–0.0028	0.2348–0.2354	0.2341–0.2346
	VG30DETT	3.0L (2960)	45	45	⑨	⑧	0.0008–0.0021	0.0016–0.0028	0.2348–0.2354	0.2341–0.2346
	VG30E	3.0L (2960)	45	45	⑩	⑪	0.0008–0.0021	0.0016–0.0029	0.2742–0.2748	0.3136–0.3138
1991	KA24DE	2.4L (2389)	45	45	123 @ 1.024	⑫	0.0008–0.0021	0.0016–0.0029	0.2742–0.2748	0.2734–0.2740
	VG30DE	3.0L (2960)	45	45	120 @ 1.043	⑧	0.0008–0.0021	0.0016–0.0029	0.2348–0.2354	0.2341–0.2346
	VG30DETT	3.0L (2960)	45	45	120 @ 1.043	⑧	0.0008–0.0021	0.0016–0.0029	0.2348–0.2354	0.2341–0.2346
	VG30E	3.0L (2960)	45	45	④	⑪	0.0008–0.0021	0.0016–0.0029	0.2742–0.2748	0.3136–0.3138
	GA16DE	1.6L (1597)	45	45	NA	⑤	0.0008–0.0020	0.0008–0.0028	0.2152–0.2157	0.2144–0.2150
	SR20DE	2.0L (1998)	45	45	130 @ 1.181	⑥	0.0008–0.0021	0.0016–0.0029	0.2348–0.2354	0.2341–0.2346
	KA24E	2.4L (2389)	45	45	①	②	0.0008–0.0021	0.0016–0.0028	0.2742–0.2748	0.3129–0.3134
1992	KA24DE	2.4L (2389)	45	45	123 @ 1.024	⑫	0.0008–0.0021	0.0016–0.0029	0.2742–0.2748	0.2734–0.2740
	VG30DE	3.0L (2960)	45	45	120 @ 1.043	⑧	0.0008–0.0021	0.0016–0.0029	0.2348–0.2354	0.2341–0.2346
	VG30DETT	3.0L (2960)	45	45	120 @ 1.043	⑧	0.0008–0.0021	0.0016–0.0029	0.2348–0.2354	0.2341–0.2346
	VG30E	3.0L (2960)	45	45	④	⑪	0.0008–0.0021	0.0016–0.0029	0.2742–0.2748	0.3136–0.3138
	VE30DE	3.0L (2960)	45	45	120 @ 1.043	NA	0.0008–0.0017	0.0016–0.0025	0.2352–0.2354	0.2344–0.2346
	GA16DE	1.6L (1597)	45	45	NA	⑤	0.0008–0.0020	0.0016–0.0028	0.2152–0.2157	0.2144–0.2150
	SR20DE	2.0L (1998)	45	45	130 @ 1.181	⑥	0.0008–0.0021	0.0016–0.0029	0.2348–0.2354	0.2341–0.2346
	KA24E	2.4L (2389)	45	45	①	②	0.0008–0.0021	0.0016–0.0028	0.2742–0.2748	0.3129–0.3134

VALVE SPECIFICATIONS

Year	Engine ID/VIN	Engine Displacement Liters (cc)	Seat Angle (deg.)	Face Angle (deg.)	Spring Test Pressure (lbs. @ in.)	Spring Installed Height (in.)	Stem-to-Guide Clearance (in.)		Stem Diameter (in.)	
							Intake	Exhaust	Intake	Exhaust
1993	KA24DE	2.4L (2389)	45	45	123 @ 1.024	⑫	0.0008–0.0021	0.0016–0.0029	0.2742–0.2748	0.2734–0.2740
	VG30DE	3.0L (2960)	45	45	120 @ 1.043	⑧	0.0008–0.0021	0.0016–0.0029	0.2348–0.2354	0.2341–0.2346
	VG30DETT	3.0L (2960)	45	45	120 @ 1.043	⑧	0.0008–0.0021	0.0016–0.0029	0.2348–0.2354	0.2341–0.2346
	VG30E	3.0L (2960)	45	45	④	⑪	0.0008–0.0021	0.0016–0.0029	0.2742–0.2748	0.3136–0.3138
	VE30DE	3.0L (2960)	45	45	120 @ 1.043	NA	0.0008–0.0017	0.0016–0.0025	0.2352–0.2354	0.2344–0.2346
	GA16DE	1.6L (1597)	45	45	NA	⑤	0.0008–0.0020	0.0016–0.0028	0.2152–0.2157	0.2144–0.2150
	SR20DE	2.0L (1998)	45	45	130 @ 1.181	⑥	0.0008–0.0021	0.0016–0.0029	0.2348–0.2354	0.2341–0.2346
1994	KA24DE	2.4L (2389)	45	45	123 @ 1.024	⑫	0.0008–0.0021	0.0016–0.0029	0.2742–0.2748	0.2734–0.2740
	VG30DE	3.0L (2960)	45	45	120 @ 1.043	⑧	0.0008–0.0021	0.0016–0.0029	0.2348–0.2354	0.2341–0.2346
	VG30DETT	3.0L (2960)	45	45	120 @ 1.043	⑧	0.0008–0.0021	0.0016–0.0029	0.2348–0.2354	0.2341–0.2346
	VG30E	3.0L (2960)	45	45	④	⑪	0.0008–0.0021	0.0016–0.0029	0.2742–0.2748	0.3136–0.3138
	VE30DE	3.0L (2960)	45	45	120 @ 1.043	NA	0.0008–0.0017	0.0016–0.0025	0.2352–0.2354	0.2344–0.2346
	GA16DE	1.6L (1597)	45	45	NA	⑤	0.0008–0.0020	0.0016–0.0028	0.2152–0.2157	0.2144–0.2150
	SR20DE	2.0L (1998)	45	45	130 @ 1.181	⑥	0.0008–0.0021	0.0016–0.0029	0.2348–0.2354	0.2341–0.2346

① Intake:
    Outer—135.8 @ 1.480
    Inner—63.9 @ 1.283
  Exhaust:
    Outer—144 @ 1.343
    Inner—73.9 @ 1.146
② Free height:
    Intake—outer: 2.261; inner: 2.100
    Exhaust—outer: 1.343; inner: 1.887
③ Intake—110.0 @ 1.331
    Exhaust—122.6 @ 1.346

④ Outer—117 lbs. @ 1.181
    Inner—57 lbs. @ 0.984
⑤ Free height:
    Intake—2.071
    Exhaust—2.154
⑥ 1.9433—Free height
⑦ Free height:
    Intake: 2.071
    Exhaust: 2.154

⑧ 1.697 in. free height
⑨ 26.5 @ 1.043
⑩ 25 @ 0.984
⑪ Free height:
    Outer—2.016
    Inner—1.736
⑫ 1.756—Free height

PISTON AND RING SPECIFICATIONS

All measurements are given in inches.

Year	Engine ID/VIN	Engine Displacement Liters (cc)	Piston Clearance	Ring Gap			Ring Side Clearance		
				Top Compression	Bottom Compression	Oil Control	Top Compression	Bottom Compression	Oil Control
1990	GA16i	1.6L (1597)	0.0006–0.0014	0.0079–0.0138	0.0146–0.0205	0.0079–0.0236	0.0016–0.0031	0.0012–0.0028	—
	KA24E	2.4L (2389)	0.0008–0.0016	0.0110–0.0169	①	0.0079–0.0236	0.0016–0.0031	0.0012–0.0028	—
	VG30DE	3.0L (2960)	0.0006–0.0014	0.0083–0.0157	0.0197–0.0299	0.0079–0.0299	0.0016–0.0029	0.0012–0.0025	—
	VG30DETT	3.0L (2960)	0.0010–0.0018	0.0083–0.0157	0.0197–0.0299	0.0079–0.0299	0.0016–0.0029	0.0012–0.0025	—
	VG30E	3.0L (2960)	0.0006–0.0014	0.0083–0.0173	0.0071–0.0173	0.0079–0.0299	0.0016–0.0029	0.0012–0.0025	—
1991	KA24E	2.4L (2389)	0.0008–0.0016	0.0110–0.0205	0.0177–0.0272	0.0079–0.0272	0.0016–0.0031	0.0012–0.0028	—
	VG30DE	3.0L (2960)	0.0006–0.0010	0.0083–0.0157	0.0197–0.0299	0.0079–0.0299	0.0016–0.0029	0.0012–0.0025	0.0006–0.0075
	VG30DETT	3.0L (2960)	0.0010–0.0018	0.0083–0.0157	0.0197–0.0299	0.0079–0.0299	0.0016–0.0029	0.0012–0.0025	0.0006–0.0075
	VG30E	3.0L (2960)	0.0006–0.0014	0.0083–0.0173	0.0071–0.0173	0.0079–0.0299	0.0016–0.0029	0.0012–0.0025	0.0006–0.0075
	GA16DE	1.6L (1597)	0.0006–0.0014	0.0079–0.0138	0.0146–0.0205	0.0079–0.0236	0.0016–0.0031	0.0012–0.0028	—
	SR20DE	2.0L (1998)	0.0004–0.0012	0.0079–0.0118	0.0138–0.0197	0.0079–0.0236	0.0018–0.0031	0.0012–0.0026	—
	KA24E	2.4L (2389)	0.0008–0.0016	0.0110–0.0205	①	0.0079–0.0272	0.0016–0.0031	0.0012–0.0028	—
1992	KA24DE	2.4L (2389)	0.0008–0.0016	0.0110–0.0205	0.0177–0.0272	0.0079–0.0272	0.0016–0.0031	0.0012–0.0028	—
	VG30DE	3.0L (2960)	0.0006–0.0010	0.0083–0.0157	0.0197–0.0299	0.0079–0.0299	0.0016–0.0029	0.0012–0.0025	0.0006–0.0075
	VG30DETT	3.0L (2960)	0.0010–0.0018	0.0083–0.0157	0.0197–0.0299	0.0079–0.0299	0.0016–0.0029	0.0012–0.0025	0.0006–0.0075
	VG30E	3.0L (2960)	0.0006–0.0014	0.0083–0.0173	0.0071–0.0173	0.0079–0.0299	0.0016–0.0029	0.0012–0.0025	0.0006–0.0075
	VE30DE	3.0L (2960)	0.0006–0.0014	0.0080–0.0150	0.0190–0.0270	0.0080–0.0270	0.0016–0.0031	0.0012–0.0025	—
	GA16DE	1.6L (1597)	0.0006–0.0014	0.0079–0.0138	0.0146–0.0205	0.0079–0.0236	0.0016–0.0031	0.0012–0.0028	—
	SR20DE	2.0L (1998)	0.0004–0.0012	0.0079–0.0118	0.0138–0.0197	0.0079–0.0236	0.0018–0.0031	0.0012–0.0026	—
	KA24E	2.4L (2389)	0.0008–0.0016	0.0110–0.0205	①	0.0079–0.0272	0.0016–0.0031	0.0012–0.0028	—

PISTON AND RING SPECIFICATIONS

All measurements are given in inches.

Year	Engine ID/VIN	Engine Displacement Liters (cc)	Piston Clearance	Ring Gap Top Compression	Ring Gap Bottom Compression	Ring Gap Oil Control	Ring Side Clearance Top Compression	Ring Side Clearance Bottom Compression	Ring Side Clearance Oil Control
1993	KA24DE	2.4L (2389)	0.0008–0.0016	0.0110–0.0205	0.0177–0.0272	0.0079–0.0272	0.0016–0.0031	0.0012–0.0028	—
	VG30DE	3.0L (2960)	0.0006–0.0010	0.0083–0.0157	0.0197–0.0299	0.0079–0.0299	0.0016–0.0029	0.0012–0.0025	0.0006–0.0075
	VG30DETT	3.0L (2960)	0.0010–0.0018	0.0083–0.0157	0.0197–0.0299	0.0079–0.0299	0.0016–0.0029	0.0012–0.0025	0.0006–0.0075
	VG30E	3.0L (2960)	0.0006–0.0014	0.0083–0.0173	0.0071–0.0173	0.0079–0.0299	0.0016–0.0029	0.0012–0.0025	0.0006–0.0075
	VE30DE	3.0L (2960)	0.0006–0.0014	0.0080–0.0150	0.0190–0.0270	0.0080–0.0270	0.0016–0.0031	0.0012–0.0025	—
	GA16DE	1.6L (1597)	0.0006–0.0014	0.0079–0.0138	0.0146–0.0205	0.0079–0.0236	0.0016–0.0031	0.0012–0.0028	—
	SR20DE	2.0L (1998)	0.0004–0.0012	0.0079–0.0118	0.0138–0.0197	0.0079–0.0236	0.0018–0.0031	0.0012–0.0026	—
1994	KA24DE	2.4L (2389)	0.0008–0.0016	0.0110–0.0205	0.0177–0.0272	0.0079–0.0272	0.0016–0.0031	0.0012–0.0028	—
	VG30DE	3.0L (2960)	0.0006–0.0010	0.0083–0.0157	0.0197–0.0299	0.0079–0.0299	0.0016–0.0029	0.0012–0.0025	0.0006–0.0075
	VG30DETT	3.0L (2960)	0.0010–0.0018	0.0083–0.0157	0.0197–0.0299	0.0079–0.0299	0.0016–0.0029	0.0012–0.0025	0.0006–0.0075
	VG30E	3.0L (2960)	0.0006–0.0014	0.0083–0.0173	0.0071–0.0173	0.0079–0.0299	0.0016–0.0029	0.0012–0.0025	0.0006–0.0075
	VE30DE	3.0L (2960)	0.0006–0.0014	0.0080–0.0150	0.0190–0.0270	0.0080–0.0270	0.0016–0.0031	0.0012–0.0025	—
	GA16DE	1.6L (1597)	0.0006–0.0014	0.0079–0.0138	0.0146–0.0205	0.0079–0.0236	0.0016–0.0031	0.0012–0.0028	—
	SR20DE	2.0L (1998)	0.0004–0.0012	0.0079–0.0118	0.0138–0.0197	0.0079–0.0236	0.0018–0.0031	0.0012–0.0026	—

① For rings punched with R or T—0.0177–0.0236
For rings punched with N—0.0217–0.0276

TORQUE SPECIFICATIONS

All readings in ft. lbs.

Year	Engine ID/VIN	Engine Displacement Liters (cc)	Cylinder Head Bolts	Main Bearing Bolts	Rod Bearing Bolts	Crankshaft Damper Bolts	Flywheel Bolts	Manifold		Spark Plugs
								Intake	Exhaust	
1990	GA16i	1.6L (1597)	④	34–38	⑤	98–112	⑦	12–15	12–15	14–22
	KA24E	2.4L (2389)	①	34–38	②	87–116	⑧	12–15	12–15	14–22
	VG30DE	3.0L (2960)	④	67–74	②	159–174	61–69	⑨	17–20	14–22
	VG30DETT	3.0L (2960)	④	67–74	②	159–174	61–69	⑨	20–23	14–22
	VG30E	3.0L (2960)	④	67–74	②	90–98	61–69③	⑨	13–16	14–22
1991	KA24DE	2.4L (2389)	④	34–38	②	105–112	⑧	12–14	27–35	14–22
	VG30DE	3.0L (2960)	④	67–74	②	159–174	61–69	⑨	17–20	14–22
	VG30DETT	3.0L (2960)	④	67–74	②	159–174	61–69	⑨	20–23	14–22
	VG30E	3.0L (2960)	④	67–74	②	90–98	61–69③	⑨	13–16	14–22
	GA16DE	1.6L (1597)	④	34–38	⑤	98–112	⑦	12–15	16–21	14–22
	SR20DE	2.0L (1998)	④	54–61	⑥	105–112	61–69	13–15	27–35	14–22
	KA24E	2.4L (2389)	①	34–38	②	87–116	⑧	12–15	12–15	14–22
1992	KA24DE	2.4L (2389)	④	34–38	②	105–112	⑧	12–14	27–35	14–22
	VG30DE	3.0L (2960)	④	67–74	②	159–174	61–69	⑨	17–20	14–22
	VG30DETT	3.0L (2960)	④	67–74	②	159–174	61–69	⑨	20–23	14–22
	VG30E	3.0L (2960)	④	67–74	②	90–98	61–69③	⑨	13–16	14–22
	VE30DE	3.0L (2960)	④	67–74	43–48	123–130	61–69	17–20	17–20	14–22
	GA16DE	1.6L (1597)	④	34–38	⑤	98–112	⑦	12–15	16–21	14–22
	SR20DE	2.0L (1998)	④	54–61	⑥	105–112	61–69	13–15	27–35	14–22
	KA24E	2.4L (2389)	①	34–38	②	87–116	⑧	12–15	12–15	14–22
1993	KA24DE	2.4L (2389)	④	34–38	②	105–112	⑧	12–14	27–35	14–22
	VG30DE	3.0L (2960)	④	67–74	②	159–174	61–69	⑨	17–20	14–22
	VG30DETT	3.0L (2960)	④	67–74	②	159–174	61–69	⑨	20–23	14–22
	VG30E	3.0L (2960)	④	67–74	②	90–98	61–69③	⑨	13–16	14–22
	VE30DE	3.0L (2960)	④	67–74	43–48	123–130	61–69	17–20	17–20	14–22
	GA16DE	1.6L (1597)	④	34–38	⑤	98–112	⑦	12–15	16–21	14–22
	SR20DE	2.0L (1998)	④	54–61	⑥	105–112	61–69	13–15	27–35	14–22
1994	KA24DE	2.4L (2389)	④	34–38	②	105–112	⑧	12–14	27–35	14–22
	VG30DE	3.0L (2960)	④	67–74	②	159–174	61–69	⑨	17–20	14–22
	VG30DETT	3.0L (2960)	④	67–74	②	159–174	61–69	⑨	20–23	14–22
	VG30E	3.0L (2960)	④	67–74	②	90–98	61–69③	⑨	13–16	14–22
	VE30DE	3.0L (2960)	④	67–74	43–48	123–130	61–69	17–20	17–20	14–22
	GA16DE	1.6L (1597)	④	34–38	⑤	98–112	⑦	12–15	16–21	14–22
	SR20DE	2.0L (1998)	④	54–61	⑥	105–112	61–69	13–15	27–35	14–22

① Tighten in 2 steps:
　1st—22 ft. lbs.
　2nd—58 ft. lbs.
　Then loosen all bolts completely.
　Final torque is in 2 steps:
　　1st—22 ft. lbs.
　　2nd—54–61 ft. lbs.
　(If angle torquing in 2nd step, turn all bolts 80 to 85 degrees clockwise with an angle torque wrench.)
② Tighten in 2 steps:
　1st—10–12 ft. lbs.
　2nd—28–33 ft. lbs.
　(If angle torquing, tighten bolts to 60–65 degrees clockwise.)

③ Flywheel (M/T) or driveplate (A/T)
④ See text
⑤ Tighten in 2 steps:
　　1st—10 to 12 ft. lbs.
　　2nd—17–21 ft. lbs.
　(If angle torquing in 2nd step, turn all nuts 35–40 degrees with an angle torque wrench.)
⑥ Tighten in 2 steps:
　　1st—10–12 ft. lbs.
　　2nd—30–33 ft. lbs.
　(If angle torquing in 2nd step, turn all nuts 60 to 65 degrees with an angle torque wrench.)

⑦ M/T flywheel—61–69
⑧ M/T flywheel—105–112
　　A/T driveplate—69–76
⑨ Tighten intake nut in two steps:
　　1st—2.2–3.6 ft. lbs.
　　2nd—17–20 ft. lbs.
　Tighten in take bolt in two steps:
　　1st—2.2–3.6 ft. lbs.
　　2nd—12–14 ft. lbs.

BRAKE SPECIFICATIONS
All measurements in inches unless noted.

Year	Model	Master Cylinder Bore	Brake Disc Original Thickness	Brake Disc Minimum Thickness	Maximum Runout	Brake Drum Diameter Original Inside Diameter	Brake Drum Diameter Max. Wear Limit	Brake Drum Diameter Maximum Machine Diameter	Minimum Lining Thickness Front	Minimum Lining Thickness Rear
1990	240SX	0.937	—	0.709①	0.0028	—	—	—	0.079	0.059
	300ZX	0.941	—	0.945④	0.0028	—	—	—	0.079	0.079
	Maxima	1.000	—	0.787⑤	0.0028	9.000	9.090	9.060	0.079	0.059
	Pulsar	1.000	—	0.394②	0.0028	8.000	8.090	8.060	0.079	0.059
	Sentra	1.000	—	0.394③	0.0028	8.000	8.090	8.050	0.079	0.059
	Stanza	1.000	—	0.787⑤	0.0028	9.000	9.090	9.060	0.079	0.059
1991	240SX	0.937	—	0.709①	0.0028	—	—	—	0.079	0.059
	300ZX	0.941	—	1.102	0.0028	—	—	—	0.079	0.079
	Maxima	1.000	—	0.787⑤	0.0028	9.000	9.090	9.060	0.079	0.059
	Sentra/NX	1.000	—	0.954	0.0028	7.000	7.090	7.060	0.079	0.059
	Stanza	1.000	—	0.787⑤	0.0028	9.000	9.090	9.060	0.079	0.059
1992	240SX	0.937	—	0.709①	0.0028	—	—	—	0.079	0.059
	300ZX	0.941	—	1.102	0.0028	—	—	—	0.079	0.079
	Maxima	1.000	—	0.787⑤	0.0028	9.000	9.090	9.060	0.079	0.059
	Sentra/NX	1.000	—	0.954	0.0028	7.000	7.090	7.060	0.079	0.059
	Stanza	1.000	—	0.787⑤	0.0028	9.000	9.090	9.060	0.079	0.059
1993	240SX	0.937	—	0.709①	0.0028	—	—	—	0.079	0.059
	300ZX	0.941	—	1.102	0.0028	—	—	—	0.079	0.079
	Altima	1.000	—	0.787⑤	0.0028	9.000	9.090	9.060	0.079	0.059
	Maxima	1.000	—	0.787⑤	0.0028	9.000	9.090	9.060	0.079	0.059
	Sentra/NX	1.000	—	0.954	0.0028	7.000	7.090	7.060	0.079	0.059
1994	240SX	0.937	—	0.709①	0.0028	—	—	—	0.079	0.059
	300ZX	0.941	—	1.102	0.0028	—	—	—	0.079	0.079
	Altima	1.000	—	0.787⑤	0.0028	9.000	9.090	9.060	0.079	0.059
	Maxima	1.000	—	0.787⑤	0.0028	9.000	9.090	9.060	0.079	0.059
	Sentra/NX	1.000	—	0.954	0.0028	7.000	7.090	7.060	0.079	0.059

NOTE: Minimum lining thickness is as recommended by the manufacturer. Due to variation in state inspection regulations, the minimum allowable thickness may be different than recommended.
① 0.315 Rear brake disc application
② 0.630 Front brake disc: SE Model
③ 0.630 Front brake disc: Wagon 4x2 and
   Wagon 4x4
④ 0.630 Rear brake disc: 300ZX all
⑤ 0.354 Rear brake disc application

WHEEL ALIGNMENT

		Caster		Camber			
Year	Model	Range (deg.)	Preferred Setting (deg.)	Range (deg.)	Preferred Setting (deg.)	Toe-in (in.)	Steering Axis Inclination (deg.)
1990	240SX (Front)	6P–7 1/2P	—	1 1/2N–0	—	1/32–3/32	13 1/4
	(Rear)	—	—	1 5/8N–5/8N	—	1/32–3/16	—
	300ZX (Front)	9P–10 1/2P	—	1 9/16N–1/16N	—	0–3/32	12 15/16
	(Rear)	—	—	1 5/8N–5/8N	—	1/64–3/16	—
	Maxima (Front)	1/2P–2P	—	1N–1/2P	—	1/32–1/8	14 3/8
	(Rear)	—	—	1 5/16N–3/16P	—	0–5/32P	—
	Pulsar (Front)	1 3/16P–2 11/16P	—	1 1/4N–1/4P	—	①	14 13/16
	(Rear)	—	—	2N–1/2N	—	⑥	—
	Sentra 2WD (Front—Cpe)	7/8P–2 3/8P	—	1 1/16N–7/16P	—	④	14 3/4
	(Rear Cpe)	—	—	2N–1/2N	—	⑥	—
	(Front exc Cpe)	3/4P–2 1/4P	—	15/16N–9/16P	—	②	14 1/2
	(Rear exc Cpe)	—	—	1 7/8N–3/8N	—	0–3/16P	—
	Sentra 4WD (Front)	1/8P–1 5/8P	—	7/8N–5/8P	—	④	13 15/16
	(Rear)	—	—	7/8N–5/8P	—	0–3/16	—
	Stanza (Front)	5/8P–2 1/16P	—	1/2N–1P	—	1/16–1/8	14 1/2
	(Rear)	—	—	1 7/16N–3/16P	—	0–5/16	—
1991	240SX (Front)	6P–7 1/2P	—	1 1/2N–0	—	1/32–3/32	13 1/4
	(Rear)	—	—	1 5/8N–5/8N	—	1/32–3/16	—
	300ZX (Front)	9P–10 1/2P	—	1 9/16N–1/16N	—	0–3/32	12 15/16
	(Rear)	—	—	1 5/8N–5/8N	—	1/64–3/16	—
	Maxima (Front)	1/2P–2P	—	1N–1/2P	—	1/32–1/8	14 3/8
	(Rear)	—	—	1 5/16N–3/16P	—	0–5/32P	—
	Sentra/NX (Front)	7/8P–2 3/8P	—	1 1/16N–7/16P	—	④	14 3/4
	(Rear)	—	—	2N–1/2N	—	⑥	—
	Stanza (Front)	5/8P–2 1/16P	—	1/2N–1P	—	1/16–1/8	14 1/2
	(Rear)	—	—	1 7/16N–3/16P	—	0–5/16	—
1992	240SX (Front)	6P–7 1/2P	—	1 1/2N–0	—	1/32–3/32	13 1/4
	(Rear)	—	—	1 5/8N–5/8N	—	1/32–3/16	—
	300ZX (Front)	9P–10 1/2P	—	1 9/16N–1/16N	—	0–3/32	12 15/16
	(Rear)	—	—	1 5/8N–5/8N	—	1/64–3/16	—
	Maxima (Front)	1/2P–2P	—	1N–1/2P	—	1/32–1/8	14 3/8
	(Rear)	—	—	1 5/16N–3/16P	—	0–5/32P	—
	Sentra/NX (Front)	7/8P–2 3/8P	—	1 1/16N–7/16P	—	④	14 3/4
	(Rear)	—	—	2N–1/2N	—	⑥	—
	Stanza (Front)	5/8P–2 1/16P	—	1/2N–1P	—	1/16–1/8	14 1/2
	(Rear)	—	—	1 7/16N–3/16P	—	0–5/16	—

WHEEL ALIGNMENT

Year	Model	Caster Range (deg.)	Caster Preferred Setting (deg.)	Camber Range (deg.)	Camber Preferred Setting (deg.)	Toe-in (in.)	Steering Axis Inclination (deg.)
1993	240SX (Front)	6P–7½P	—	1½N–0	—	1/32–3/32	13¼
	(Rear)	—	—	1⅝N–⅝N	—	1/32–3/16	—
	300ZX (Front)	9P–10½P	—	1 9/16N–1/16N	—	0–3/32	12 15/16
	(Rear)	—	—	1⅝N–⅝N	—	1/64–3/16	—
	Altima (Front)	1P–3P	—	½N–½P	—	0–⅛	14⅞
	(Rear)	—	—	2N–0	—	1/16–⅛	—
	Maxima (Front)	½P–2P	—	1N–½P	—	1/32–⅛	14⅜
	(Rear)	—	—	1 5/16N–3/16P	—	0–5/32P	—
	Sentra/NX (Front)	⅞P–2⅜P	—	1 1/16N–7/16P	—	④	14¾
	(Rear)	—	—	2N–½N	—	⑥	—
1994	240SX (Front)	6P–7½P	—	1½N–0	—	1/32–3/32	13¼
	(Rear)	—	—	1⅝N–⅝N	—	1/32–3/16	—
	300ZX (Front)	9P–10½P	—	1 9/16N–1/16N	—	0–3/32	12 15/16
	(Rear)	—	—	1⅝N–⅝N	—	1/64–3/16	—
	Altima (Front)	1P–3P	—	½N–½P	—	0–⅛	14⅞
	(Rear)	—	—	2N–0	—	1/16–⅛	—
	Maxima (Front)	½P–2P	—	1N–½P	—	1/32–⅛	14⅜
	(Rear)	—	—	1 5/16N–3/16P	—	0–5/32P	—
	Sentra/NX (Front)	⅞P–2⅜P	—	1 1/16N–7/16P	—	④	14¾
	(Rear)	—	—	2N–½N	—	⑥	—

N—Negative
P—Positive
① 1/16 Toe Out—1/16 Toe In
② 1/32 Toe Out—1/16 Toe In
③ 1/32 Toe Out—⅛ Toe In
④ 1/32 Toe Out—1/16 Toe In
⑤ 3/32 Toe Out—5/16 Toe In
⑥ 1/16 Toe Out—3/32 Toe In

SERIAL NUMBER IDENTIFICATION

Vehicle Identification Plate

On all models, the vehicle identification plate is attached to the hood ledge or the firewall. The VIN plate is mounted on the radiator core on 300ZX. The identification plate gives the vehicle type, model, engine displacement in cc, SAE horsepower rating, wheelbase, engine number and chassis number.

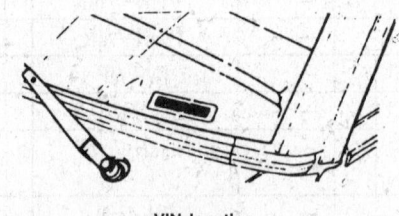

VIN location

Engine Number

On most vehicles, the engine number is stamped on the right side top edge of the cylinder block. On 240SX, the number is stamped on the block just below the valve cover looking from the driver's seat. On the 300ZX, the number is stamped on the right rear edge of the right cylinder bank, looking from driver seat. On the Maxima, the number can be found on the driver's side edge of the front cylinder bank, looking from driver's seat. On the 1990-92 Stanza and Altima, the number is stamped on the cylinder block just below the valve cover looking down at the front of the engine.

The engine serial number is preceded by the engine model code.

Chassis Number

The chassis number is on the firewall under the hood on all models. On the 240SX, the chassis number plate is affixed to the firewall next to the wiper motor on the passenger's side of the engine compartment. All vehicles also have the Vehicle Identification Number (VIN) on a plate attached to the top of the instrument

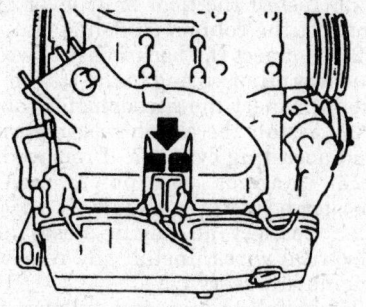

Engine serial number location on 240SX, Altima and 1990-92 Stanza

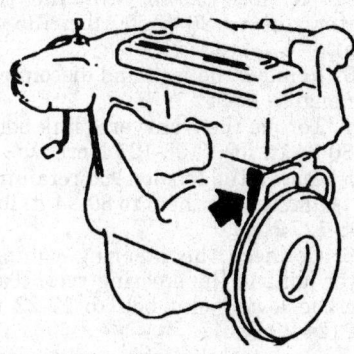

Engine serial and code number location

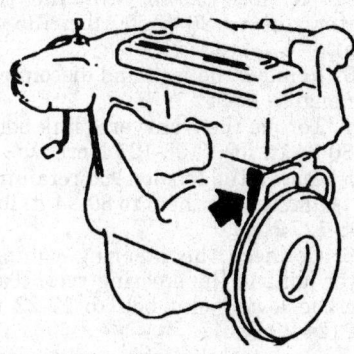

Engine serial and code number location

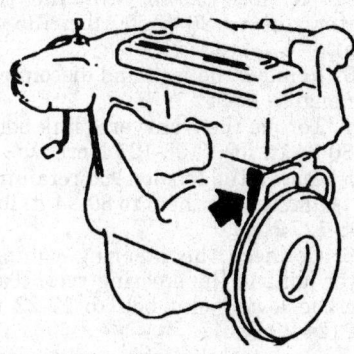

Engine identification number location — most engines

panel on the driver's side, visible through the windshield. The chassis serial number is preceded by the model designation. All models have an Emission Control information label affixed to the firewall or on the underside of the hood.

Transmission/Transaxle Number

The transmission/transaxle identification number tag is attached to the upper area or side area of the unit.

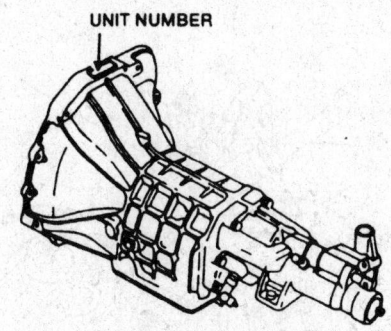

UNIT NUMBER

Location of the manual transmission serial number

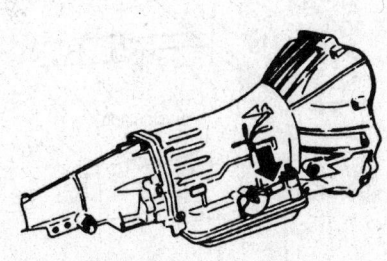

Location of the automatic transmission serial number

ENGINE MECHANICAL

NOTE: Disconnecting the negative battery cable on some vehicles may interfere with the functions of the on-board computer systems and may require the computer to undergo a relearning process, once the negative battery cable is reconnected.

Engine Assembly

REMOVAL AND INSTALLATION

240SX

1. Mark the hood hinge relationship and remove the hood.
2. Release the fuel system pressure and disconnect the negative battery cable.
3. Drain the cooling system and transmission fluid.
4. Remove the radiator after disconnecting the automatic transmission coolant tubes, if equipped.
5. Remove the air cleaner.
6. Remove the fan and pulley.
7. Disconnect or remove following:
Water temperature gauge wire
Oil pressure sending unit wire
Ignition distributor primary wire
Starter motor connections
Fuel hose
Alternator leads
Heater hoses
Throttle and choke connections
Engine ground cable and all wiring harnesses
Any interfering engine accessories

— **CAUTION** —
On vehicles with air conditioning, it is necessary to remove the compressor and the condenser from their mounts. Do not attempt to disconnect any of the air conditioner hoses.

8. Disconnect the power brake booster hose from the engine.
9. Remove the clutch operating cylinder and return spring, if equipped.
10. Disconnect the speedometer cable from the transmission. Disconnect the backup light switch and any other wiring or attachments to the transmission.
11. Disconnect the column shift linkage. Remove the floor shift lever.

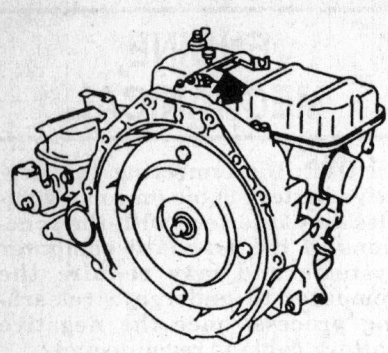

Transaxle serial number location automatic

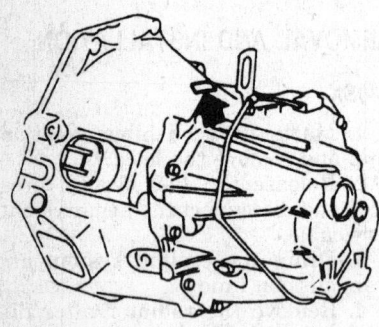

Transaxle serial number location manual

12. Raise and safely support the vehicle. Detach the exhaust pipe from the exhaust manifold. Remove the front section of the exhaust system.

13. Mark the relationship of the flanges and disconnect the driveshaft.

14. Support the transmission with a jack. Remove the rear cross member, if required.

15. Attach a hoist to the lifting hooks on the engine at either end of the cylinder head. Support the engine with a suitable jack.

16. Unbolt the front engine mount brackets from the block. Tilt and remove the engine by lowering the jack under the transmission and raising the hoist.

To install:

17. Lower the engine into the vehicle and align the block with with the front mount brackets. On the 300ZX, torque the engine gusset bolts in 6 stages to 22-29 ft. lbs. (29-39 Nm). Torque the engine mount bolts to 32-41 ft. lbs. (43-55 Nm).

18. Install the rear crossmember, if removed.

19. Connect the driveshaft. Make sure the driveshaft flanges are aligned properly.

20. Install the floor shift lever and connect the column shift linkage.

21. Connect the backup light switch and any other wiring to the transmission. Connect the speedometer cable.

22. Install the clutch return spring and operating cylinder, if removed.

23. Connect the power brake booster hose to the engine.

24. Connect all engine hoses and electrical wires. Install any removed engine accessory.

25. Install the fan and pulley.

26. Install the air cleaner.

27. Install the radiator and connect the transmission cooling lines, if equipped.

28. Fill the transmission and cooling system to the proper levels.

29. Install the hood and connect the negative battery cable.

30. Make all the necessary engine adjustments. Road test the vehicle for proper operation.

300ZX

WITH MANUAL TRANSMISSION

1. Mark the hood hinge relationship and remove the hood.

2. Release the fuel system pressure, disconnect the negative battery cable and raise and safely support the vehicle.

3. Remove the undercover.

Steering column, tension rod and transverse link attachment points

4. Drain the coolant from both sides of the block and from the radiator.

5. Drain the oil pan.

6. Disconnect and label all engine vacuum hoses, fuel piping, harnesses and connectors.

7. Disconnect and remove the front exhaust tube sections.

8. Mark the relationship of the flanges and disconnect the driveshaft.

9. Remove the radiator.

10. Remove the drive belts.

11. Remove the cooling fan and coupling.

12. Remove the power steering pump, alternator, starter and clutch operating cylinder.

13. Discharge the air conditioning system and remove the compressor from the engine. Disconnect the air conditioning tube clamps.

14. Disconnect the steering column lower joint from the steering rack.

15. Remove the tension rod retaining bolts on both sides.

16. Loosen the transverse link bolts on both sides.

17. Support the rear suspension member using the proper equipment.

18. Install engine slingers to the block and connect a suitable lifting device to the slingers. Tension the lifting device slightly.

19. Remove the rear suspension member retaining bolts and center nut.

20. Remove the engine mount bracket bolts from both sides and slowly lower the transmission jack. Lift the engine and transmission from the vehicle.

To install:

21. Lower the engine and transmission into the vehicle and slowly raise the transmission jack. Install the engine mount bracket bolts. Torque the bolts to 30-38 ft. lbs. (40-42 Nm).

22. Install the rear suspension bolts and center nut. Torque the bolts to 38-48 ft. lbs. (51-65 Nm) and the center nut to 26-33 ft. lbs. (35-45 Nm).

23. Remove the jack and disconnect the engine hoist.

24. Torque the transverse link bolts to 80-94 ft. lbs. (108-127 Nm).

25. Install the tension rod retaining bolts and torque them to 80-94 ft. lbs. (108-127 Nm).

26. Connect the steering column lower joint to the steering rack. Torque the lower joint bolt to 17-22 ft. lbs. (24-29 Nm).

27. Connect the air conditioning tube clamps and mount the air conditioning compressor on the engine.

28. Install the clutch operating cylinder, starter, alternator and power steering pump.

29. Install the cooling fan and coupling.

30. Install the drive belts.

31. Install the radiator.

32. Install the driveshaft. Make sure the flanges are aligned properly. On non-turbo models, torque the flange bolts to 29-33 ft. lbs. (39-45 Nm) or 40-47 ft. lbs. (54-64 Nm) on turbocharged models.

33. Connect and install the front exhaust tube sections.

34. Connect the engine connectors, harnesses, fuel piping and vacuum hoses.

35. Install the undercover.

36. Fill the transmission and cooling system to the proper levels.

37. Install the hood and connect the negative battery cable.

38. Make all the necessary engine adjustments. Charge the air conditioning system.

WITH AUTOMATIC TRANSMISSION

1. Mark the hood hinge relationship and remove the hood.

2. Relieve the fuel system pressure, disconnect the negative battery cable and raise and support the vehicle safely.

3. Remove the undercover.

4. Drain the coolant from both sides of the block and from the radiator.

5. Drain the oil pan.

6. Disconnect and label all engine vacuum hoses, fuel piping, harnesses and connectors.

7. Disconnect and remove the front exhaust tube sections.

8. Mark the relationship of the flanges and disconnect the driveshaft.

9. Remove the radiator.

10. Remove the drive belts.

11. Remove the cooling fan and coupling.

12. Remove the power steering pump, alternator and starter.

13. Remove or disconnect the transmission mounting bolts.

14. Connect an engine hoist to the engine lifting brackets and tension the hoist.

15. Remove the engine mount bracket bolts and slowly lift the engine from the vehicle.

   To install:

16. Lower the engine into the vehicle and install the engine mount bracket bolts. Torque the bolts to 30-38 ft. lbs. (40-42 Nm).

17. Install the starter, alternator and power steering pump.

18. Install the cooling fan and coupling.

19. Install the drive belts.

20. Install the radiator.

21. Install the driveshaft. Make sure the flanges are aligned properly. On non-turbo models, torque the flange bolts to 29-33 ft. lbs. (39-45 Nm) or 40-47 ft. lbs. (54-64 Nm) on turbocharged models.

22. Connect and install the front exhaust tube sections.

23. Connect the engine connectors, harnesses, fuel piping and vacuum hoses.

24. Install the undercover.

25. Fill the transmission and cooling system to the proper levels.

26. Install the hood and connect the negative battery cable.

27. Make all the necessary engine adjustments. Charge the air conditioning system. Road test the vehicle for proper operation.

Altima, Maxima, Pulsar, Sentra and Stanza

It is recommended that the engine and transaxle be removed as a unit. If need be, the units may be separated after removal.

NOTE: On the Sentra (GA16i and GA16DE engines), the engine cannot be removed separately from the transaxle. Remove the engine and the transaxle as a unit. If equipped with 4WD, remove the engine, transaxle and transfer case together.

1. Mark the hood hinge relationship and remove the hood.

2. Release the fuel system pressure, disconnect the negative battery cable and raise and support the vehicle safely.

3. Drain the cooling system and the oil pan.

4. Remove the air cleaner and disconnect the throttle cable.

5. Disconnect or remove the following:
   Drive belts
   Ignition wire from the coil to the distributor
   Ignition coil ground wire and the engine ground cable
   Block connector from the distributor
   Fusible links
   Engine harness connectors
   Fuel and fuel return hoses
   Upper and lower radiator hoses
   Heater inlet and outlet hoses
   Engine vacuum hoses
   Carbon canister hoses and the air pump air cleaner hose

Any interfering engine accessories: power steering pump, air conditioning compressor or alternator

Driveshaft from transfer unit for 4WD vehicles. Make sure to match-mark flanges

6. Remove the air pump air cleaner.

7. Remove the carbon canister.

8. Remove the auxiliary fan, washer tank, grille and radiator (with fan assembly).

9. Remove the clutch cylinder from the clutch housing for manual transaxles.

10. Remove both buffer rods without altering the length of the rods. Disconnect the speedometer cable.

11. Remove the spring pins from the transaxle gear selector rods.

12. Install engine slingers to the block and connect a suitable lifting device to the slingers. Do not tension the lifting device at this point.

13. Disconnect the exhaust pipe at both the manifold connection and the clamp holding the pipe to the engine.

14. On the Sentra, Pulsar and Stanza, remove the lower ball joint.

15. Drain the transaxle gear oil.

16. Disconnect the right and left side halfshafts from their side flanges and remove the bolt holding the radius link support.

NOTE: When drawing out the halfshafts on the Sentra, Pulsar and Stanza, it is necessary to loosen the strut head bolts.

17. Lower the shifter and selector rods and remove the bolts from the motor mount brackets. Remove the nuts holding the front and rear motor mounts to the frame. On the Sentra, Stanza and Pulsar, disconnect the clutch and accelerator wires and remove the speedometer cable with its pinion from the transaxle.

18. Lift the engine/transaxle assembly up and away from the vehicle.

   To install:

19. Lower the engine/transaxle assembly into the vehicle. When lowering the engine onto the frame, make sure to keep it as level as possible.

20. Check the clearance between the frame and clutch housing and make sure the engine mount bolts are seated in the groove of the mounting bracket.

21. After installing the motor mounts, adjust and install the buffer rods. On the 1990 Pulsar with GA16i engine, Maxima and Sentra: front should be 3.50-3.58 in. (89-91mm), and the rear, 3.90-3.98 in. (99-101mm).

22. On the Stanza, tighten the engine mount bolts first, then apply a

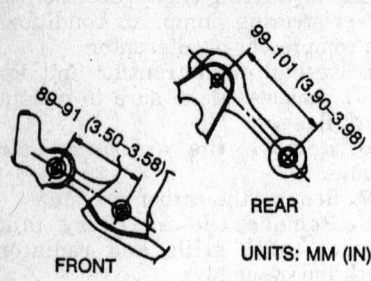

99–101 (3.90–3.98)

89–91 (3.50–3.58)

REAR

FRONT

UNITS: MM (IN)

Front and rear buffer rod length adjustment on Maxima and Sentra

load to the mounting insulators before tightening the buffer rod and sub-mounting bolts.

23. On the Sentra, Stanza and Pulsar connect the clutch and accelerator wires and install the speedometer cable with its pinion to the transaxle.

24. Raise the shifter and selector rods to their normal operating positions.

25. Connect the halfshafts.

26. On the Sentra and Pulsar connect the lower ball joint and install new cotter pins.

27. Connect the exhaust pipe to the manifold connection and the clamp holding the pipe to the engine.

28. Disconnect the lifting device and remove the engine slingers.

29. Insert the spring pins into the transaxle gear selector rods.

30. Connect the speedometer cable.

31. Mount the clutch cylinder onto the clutch housing.

32. Install the auxiliary fan, washer tank, grille and radiator (with fan assembly).

33. Install the carbon canister.

34. Install the air pump air cleaner.

35. Install or connect all hoses, belts, harnesses, connectors and components that were necessary to remove the engine.

36. Connect the throttle cable and install the air cleaner.

37. Fill the transaxle and cooling system to the proper levels.

38. Install the hood and connect the negative battery cable.

39. Make all the necessary engine adjustments. Charge the air conditioning system. Road test the vehicle for proper operation.

Engine Mounts

REMOVAL AND INSTALLATION

1. Raise and support the vehicle safely.

2. Attach a hoist to the engine and lift until the slack in the chain is taken up.

3. Inspect all mounts to determine which is defective. A defective mount will have the rubber portion of the mount separated from the metal backing or stud.

4. Remove the nuts from the engine mounts.

NOTE: Inspect the engine compartment for components that may bind when the engine is raised. Disconnect these components.

5. Lift the engine the exact amount needed to remove the engine mount. Do not lift any higher.

6. Remove the engine mounts.

To install:

7. Install the engine mounts.

8. Lower the engine and tighten the engine mount-to-engine nuts to 32-41 ft. lbs. (43-55 Nm). Tighten the engine mount-to-frame nuts to 41-49 ft. lbs. (55-67 Nm).

9. Remove the engine hoist and lower the vehicle.

Cylinder Head

REMOVAL AND INSTALLATION

NOTE: To prevent distortion or warping of the cylinder head, allow the engine to cool completely before removing the head bolts.

GA16i Engine

1. Disconnect the negative battery cable, drain the cooling system and relieve the fuel system pressure.

2. Disconnect the exhaust tube from the exhaust manifold.

3. Remove the intake manifold support bracket.

4. Remove the air cleaner assembly.

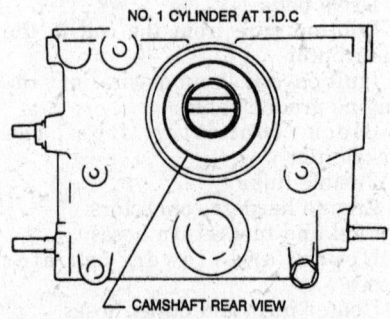

NO. 1 CYLINDER AT T.D.C

CAMSHAFT REAR VIEW

When camshaft is aligned as shown, the No. 1 piston is at TDC — GA16i engine

5. Disconnect the center wire from the distributor cap.

6. Remove the rocker arm cover.

7. Mark and remove the distributor.

8. Remove the spark plugs.

9. Set the No. 1 cylinder at TDC of the compression stroke by rotating the engine until the cut out machined in the rear of the camshaft is horizontally aligned with the cylinder head.

10. Hold the camshaft sprocket stationary with the proper tool and loosen the sprocket bolt. Place highly visible and accurate paint or chalk alignment marks on the camshaft sprocket and the timing chain, then slide the sprocket from the camshaft and lift the timing chain from the sprocket. Remove the sprocket. The timing chain will not fall off the crankshaft sprocket unless the front cover is removed. This is due to the cast portion of the front cover located on the lower side of the crankshaft sprocket which acts a stopper mechanism. For this reason a chain stopper (wedge) is not required to remove the cylinder head.

11. Loosen the cylinder bolts in 2-3 stages to prevent warpage and cracking of the head. One of the cylinder head bolts is longer than the rest. Mark this bolt and make a note of its location.

12. Carefully remove the cylinder head from the block, pulling the head up evenly from both ends. If the head seems stuck, do not pry it off. Tap lightly around the lower perimeter of the head with a rubber mallet to help break the seal. The cylinder head and the intake and exhaust manifolds are removed together. Remove the cylinder head gasket.

To install:

13. Thoroughly clean both the cylinder block and head mating surfaces. Avoid scratching either.

14. Turn the crankshaft and set the No. 1 cylinder at TDC on its compression stroke. This is done by aligning the timing pointer with the appropriate timing mark on the pulley. To ensure that the No. 1 piston is at TDC, verify that the knock pin in the front of the camshaft is set at the top.

15. Place a new gasket on the block and lower the head onto the gasket.

NOTE: These engines use 2 different length cylinder head bolts. Bolt (1) is 5.24 in. (133mm) while bolts (2) thru (10) are 4.33 in. (110mm). Do not confuse the location of these bolts.

16. Coat the threads and the seating surface of the head bolts with clean engine oil and use a new set of

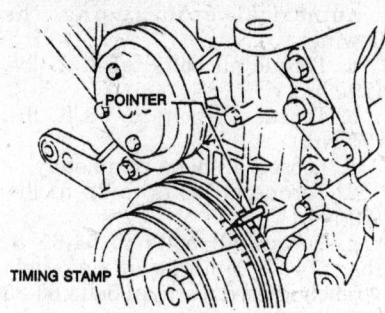

When the crankshaft pulley marks are aligned as shown, the No. 1 piston is at TDC

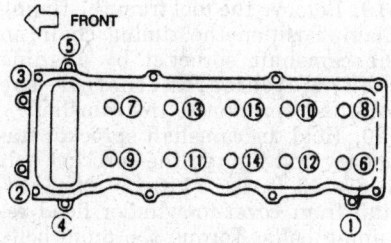

Loosen the cylinder head bolts in several stages in the order shown — GA16i and GA16DE engines

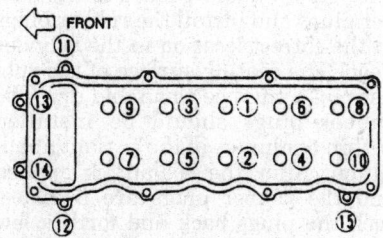

Cylinder head bolt tightening sequence — GA16i and GA16DE engines. Bolt (1) is the longest bolt

washers. Install the cylinder head bolts in their proper locations and tighten as follows:

a. Tighten all the bolts in sequence to 22 ft. lbs. (30 Nm).

b. Tighten all bolts in sequence to 47 ft. lbs.(64 Nm).

c. Loosen all bolts in reverse of the tightening sequence.

d. Tighten all bolts again to 22 ft. lbs. (30 Nm).

e. If an angle torque wrench is not available, torque the bolts in sequence to 43-51 ft. lbs. (58-59 Nm). If using an angle torque wrench for this step, tighten bolt

(1) 80-85 degrees clockwise and bolts (2) thru (10) 60-65 degrees clockwise.

f. Finally, tighten bolts (11) thru (15) to 4.6-6.1 ft. lbs. (6.3-8.3 Nm).

17. Place the timing chain on the camshaft sprocket using the alignment marks. Slide the sprocket and timing chain onto the camshaft and install the center bolt.

18. At this point, check the hydraulic valve lifters for proper operation pushing hard on each lifter hard with finger-tip pressure. Make sure the rocker arm is not on the camshaft lobe when making this check. If the valve lifter moves more than 0.04 in. (1mm), air may be inside it.

19. Install the spark plugs.

20. Install the distributor.

21. Install the rocker arm cover.

22. Connect the center wire to the distributor cap.

23. Install the air cleaner assembly.

24. Install the intake manifold support bracket.

25. Fill the cooling system to the proper level and connect the negative battery cable.

26. Make all the necessary engine adjustments. If there was air in the lifters, bleed the air by running the engine at 1000 rpm for 10 minutes. Road test the vehicle for proper operation.

GA16DE Engine

1. Disconnect the negative battery cable, drain the cooling system and relieve the fuel system pressure.

2. Remove all drive belts. Disconnect the exhaust tube from the exhaust manifold.

3. Remove the power steering bracket.

4. Remove the air duct to intake manifold collector.

5. Remove the front right side wheel, splash cover and front undercovers.

6. Remove the front exhaust pipe and engine front mounting bracket.

7. Remove the rocker arm cover.

8. Remove the distributor cap. Remove the spark plugs.

9. Set the No. 1 cylinder at TDC of the compression stroke.

10. Mark and remove the distributor assembly.

11. Remove the camshaft sprocket cover and gusset. Remove the water pump pulley. Remove the thermostat housing.

12. Remove the chain tensioner and chain guide. Loosen idler sprocket bolt.

13. Remove the camshaft sprocket bolts, camshaft sprocket, camshaft

brackets and camshafts. Remove the idler sprocket bolt. These parts should be reassembled in their original position.

14. Loosen the cylinder bolts in 2-3 stages to prevent warpage and cracking of the cylinder head assembly and note location of all head bolts.

15. Carefully remove the cylinder head from the block, pulling the head up evenly from both ends. If the head seems stuck, do not pry it off. Tap lightly around the lower perimeter of the head with a rubber mallet to help break the seal. The cylinder head and the intake and exhaust manifolds are removed together. Remove the cylinder head gasket.

To install:

16. Thoroughly clean both the cylinder block and head mating surfaces. Avoid scratching either.

17. Coat the threads and the seating surface of the head bolts with clean engine oil and use a new set of washers as necessary. Install the cylinder head assembly (always replace the head gasket). Install head bolts (with washers) in their proper locations and tighten as follows:

a. Tighten all the bolts in sequence to 22 ft. lbs. (29 Nm).

b. Tighten all bolts in sequence to 43 ft. lbs. (59 Nm).

c. Loosen all bolts in reverse of the tightening sequence.

d. Tighten all bolts again in sequence to 22 ft. lbs. (29 Nm).

e. Tighten bolts to 50-55 degrees clockwise in sequence or if angle wrench is not available, tighten bolts to 40-46 ft. lbs. (54 — 62 Nm) in sequence.

f. Finally, tighten bolts (11) thru (15) to 4.6-6.1 ft. lbs. (6.3-8.3 Nm).

18. Install the upper timing chain assembly.

19. Install all other components in the reverse order of the removal procedure. Refill and check all fluid levels. Road test the vehicle for proper operation.

KA24E Engine

NOTE: After completing this procedure, allow the rocker cover to cylinder head rubber plugs to dry for 30 minutes before starting the engine. This will allow the liquid gasket sealer to cure properly.

1. Release the fuel system pressure.

2. Disconnect the negative battery cable and drain the cooling system.

3. On 240SX, remove the power steering drive belt, power steering

pump, idler pulley and power steering brackets.

4. Tag and disconnect all the vacuum hoses, water hoses, fuel tubes and wiring harnesses necessary to gain access to cylinder head.

5. Disconnect the air induction hose from the collector assembly.

6. Detach the accelerator bracket. If necessary mark the position and remove the accelerator cable wire end from the throttle drum.

7. Unbolt the intake manifold collector from the intake manifold.

8. Remove the intake manifold.

9. Unplug the exhaust gas sensor and remove the exhaust cover and exhaust pipe at exhaust manifold connection. Remove the exhaust manifold from the cylinder head.

10. Remove the rocker cover. If cover sticks to the cylinder head, tap it with a rubber hammer. Be careful not to strike the rocker arms when removing the rocker arm cover.

NOTE: After removing the rocker cover matchmark the timing chain with the camshaft sprocket with paint or equivalent.

11. Set No. 1 cylinder piston at TDC on its compression stroke. The No. 1 piston will be at TDC when the timing pointer is aligned with the red

timing mark on the crankshaft pulley.

12. Loosen the camshaft sprocket bolt. Do not turn engine when removing the bolt.

13. Support the timing chain with the proper tool.

14. Remove the camshaft sprocket.

15. Remove the front cover-to-cylinder head retaining bolts.

NOTE: The cylinder head bolts should be loosened in 2-3 steps in the correct order to prevent head warpage or cracking.

16. Remove the cylinder head bolts in the correct sequence. Lift the cylinder head off the engine block. It may be necessary to tap the head lightly with a rubber mallet to loosen it.

To install:

17. Confirm that the No. 1 piston is at TDC on its compression stroke as follows. Align timing mark with the red (0 degree) mark on the crankshaft pulley. Make sure the distributor rotor head is set at No. 1 on the distributor cap. Confirm that the knock pin on the camshaft is set at the top position.

18. Install the cylinder head with a new gasket and torque the head bolts

in numerical order using the following:

 a. Torque all bolts to 22 ft. lbs. (29 Nm).

 b. Torque all bolts to 58 ft. lbs. (78 Nm).

 c. Loosen all bolts completely.

 d. Torque all bolts to 22 ft. lbs. (29 Nm).

 e. Torque all bolts to 54-61 ft. lbs. (74-83 Nm), or if an angle wrench is used, turn all bolts 80-85 degrees clockwise.

NOTE: Do not rotate crankshaft and camshaft separately, or valves will hit the tops of the pistons.

19. Remove the tool from the timing chain. Position the timing chain on the camshaft sprocket by aligning each matchmark. Install the camshaft sprocket to the camshaft.

20. Hold the camshaft sprocket stationary and tighten the sprocket bolt to 87-116 ft. lbs. (118-157 Nm). Install front cover-to-cylinder head retaining bolts. Torque the 6mm bolts to 5-6 ft. lbs. (7-8 Nm) and the 8mm bolts to 12-15 ft. lbs. (16-21 Nm).

21. Install the intake manifold and collector assembly with new gaskets.

22. Install the exhaust manifold with new gaskets.

23. Apply liquid gasket to the rubber plugs and install the rubber plugs in the correct location in the cylinder head. The seating surface of the rubber plugs must be clean and dry. The rubber plugs should be installed within 5 minutes of the sealant application. After the sealant is applied and the rubber plugs are in place, rock the plugs back and forth a few times to distribute the sealant evenly. Wipe the excess sealant from the cylinder head with a clean rag.

24. Install the rocker cover with new gasket.

25. Attach the accelerator bracket and cable if removed.

26. Connect all the vacuum hoses, water hoses, fuel tubes and electrical connections that were removed to gain access to cylinder head.

27. Reconnect the air induction hose to collector assembly.

28. Install the spark plugs and spark plug wires in the correct location.

29. On 240SX, install the power steering brackets, idler pulley and power steering pump.

30. Install the drive belts.

31. Fill the cooling system and connect the negative battery cable.

32. Make all the necessary engine adjustments. Road test the vehicle for proper operation.

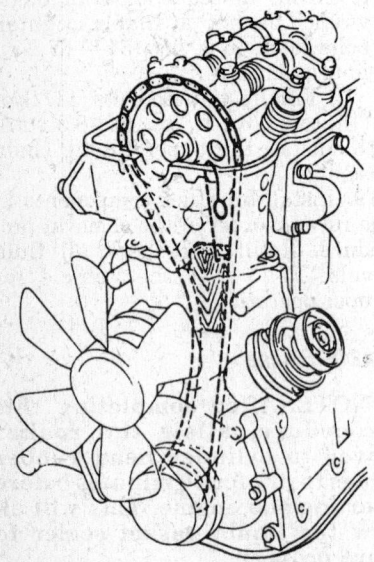

On KA24E engine, support the timing chain with a special tool when removing the cylinder head

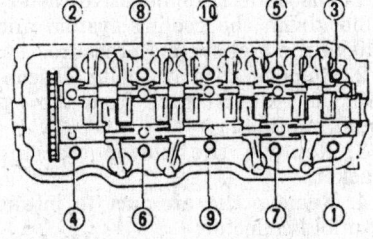

Cylinder head bolt loosening sequence — KA24E and KA24DE engines

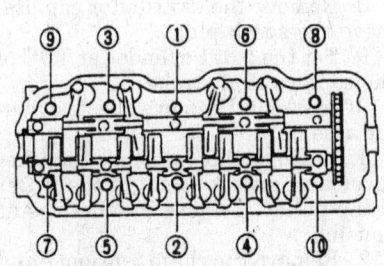

Cylinder head bolt tightening sequence — KA24E and KA24DE engines

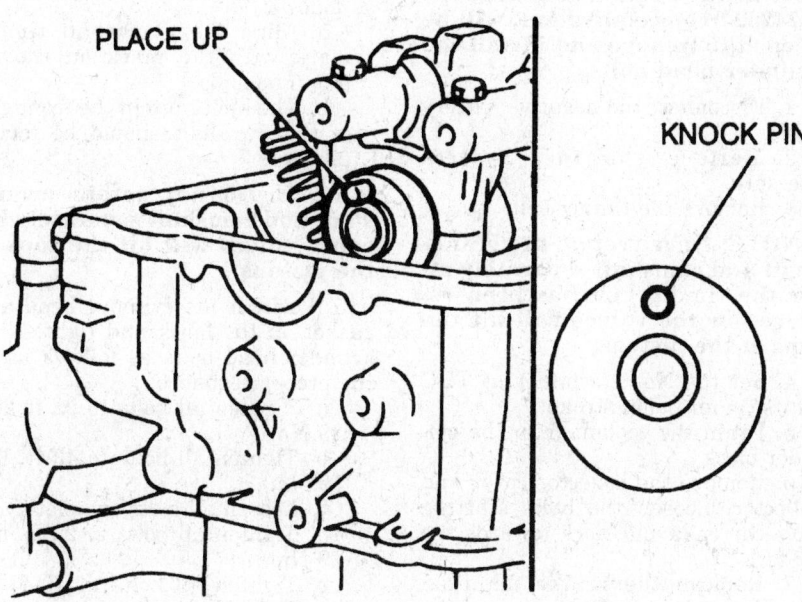

When the camshaft knock pin is at the top No. 1 piston is at TDC — KA24E engine

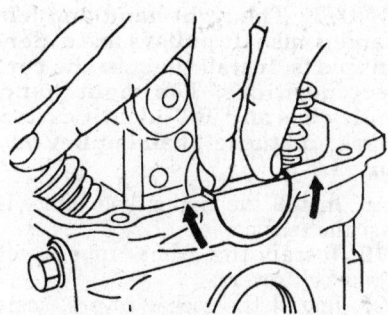

Rubber plug installation — KA24E engine

KA24DE Engine

1. Release the fuel system pressure.

2. Disconnect the negative battery cable and drain the cooling system. Drain the engine oil.

3. Remove all vacuum hoses, fuel lines, wires, electrical connections as necessary.

4. Remove the front exhaust pipe and A.I.V. pipe, if necessary.

5. Remove the air duct, cooling fan with coupling and radiator shroud.

6. Remove the the fuel injector tube assembly with injectors.

7. Disconnect and mark spark plug wires. Remove the spark plugs.

8. Set No. 1 piston at TDC on compression stroke. Remove the rocker cover assembly.

9. Mark and remove the distributor assembly.

10. Remove the camshaft sprocket, brackets and camshafts. These parts should be reassembled in their original position. Bolts should be loosened in 2-3 steps.

11. Loosen cylinder head bolts in 2 or 3 steps in sequence.

12. Remove the camshaft sprocket cover. Remove the upper chain tensioner and upper chain guides.

13. Remove the upper timing chain and idler sprocket bolt. Lower timing chain will not disengaged from the crankshaft sprocket.

14. Remove the cylinder head with the intake manifold, collector and exhaust manifold assembly.

To install:

15. Check all components for wear. Replace as necessary. Clean all mating surfaces and replace the cylinder head gasket.

16. Install cylinder head. Tighten cylinder head in the following sequence:

   a. Tighten all bolts in sequence to 22 ft. lbs. (30 Nm).

   b. Tighten all bolts in sequence to 59 ft. lbs. (80 Nm).

   c. Loosen all bolts in sequence completely.

   d. Tighten all bolts in sequence to 18-25 ft. lbs. (24-34 Nm).

   e. Tighten all bolts to 86 to 91 degrees clockwise, or if an angle wrench is not available, tighten all bolts in sequence to 55-62 ft. lbs. (74-84 Nm).

17. Install upper timing chain assemble in the correct position. Align all timing marks.

18. Install all other components in the reverse order of the removal procedure. Refill and check all fluid levels. Road test the vehicle for proper operation.

SR20DE Engine

1. Release the fuel pressure. Disconnect the negative battery cable.

2. Raise and safely support the vehicle. Remove the engine undercovers.

3. Remove the front right wheel and engine side cover.

4. Drain the cooling system. Remove the radiator assembly.

5. Remove the air duct to intake manifold.

6. Remove the drive belts and water pump pulley.

7. Remove the alternator and power steering pump.

8. Remove all vacuum hoses, fuel hoses, wires, electrical connections.

9. Remove all spark plugs.

10. Remove the A.I.V. valve and resonator.

11. Remove the rocker cover and oil separator.

12. Remove the intake manifold supports, oil filter bracket and power steering bracket.

13. Set No. 1 at TDC on the compression stroke. Rotate crankshaft until mating marks on camshaft sprockets are in the correct position.

14. Remove the timing chain tensioner.

15. Mark and remove the distributor assembly. Remove the timing chain guide and camshaft sprockets.

16. Remove the camshafts, camshaft brackets, oil tubes and baffle plate. Keep all parts in order for correct installation.

17. Remove the water hose from the cylinder block and water hose from the heater.

18. Remove the starter motor. Remove the water pipe bolt.

19. Remove the cylinder outside bolts. Remove the cylinder head bolts in 2 or 3 steps. Remove the cylinder

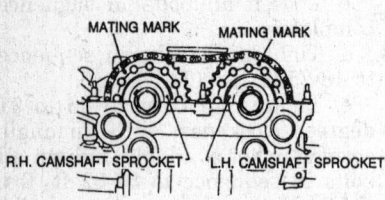

Camshaft sprocket correct position — SR20DE engine

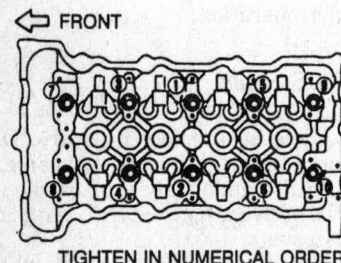

TIGHTEN IN NUMERICAL ORDER

Cylinder head torque sequence — SR20DE engine

head completely with manifolds attached.

To install:

20. Check all components for wear. Replace as necessary. Clean all mating surfaces and replace the cylinder head gasket.

21. Install cylinder head. Tighten cylinder head in the following sequence:

a. Tighten all bolts in sequence to 29 ft. lbs. (39 Nm).

b. Tighten all bolts in sequence to 58 ft. lbs. (78 Nm).

c. Loosen all bolts in sequence completely.

d. Tighten all bolts in sequence to 25-33 ft. lbs. (34-44 Nm).

e. Tighten all bolts to 90-100 degrees clockwise in sequence

f. Tighten all bolts additional 90-100 degrees clockwise in sequence. Do not turn any bolt 180-200 degrees clockwise all at once.

22. Install all other components in the reverse order of the removal procedure. Refill and check all fluid levels. Road test the vehicle for proper operation.

VG30E Engines

NOTE: On all models, a special hex head wrench ST10120000 (J24239-01) or equivalent, will be needed to remove and install the cylinder head bolts.

1. Disconnect the negative battery cable.

2. Relieve the fuel system pressure.

3. Remove the timing belt.

NOTE: Never rotate the crankshaft and camshaft separately after the timing belt has been removed or the valves will hit the tops of the pistons.

4. Set the No. 1 cylinder at TDC on its compression stroke.

5. Drain the coolant from the cylinder block.

6. Remove the collector cover and collector. Loosen the bolts starting from the ends and work towards the center.

7. Remove the intake manifold with fuel tube assembly. Loosen the intake manifold bolts starting from the front of the engine and proceed in criss-cross pattern.

8. Remove the power steering pump bracket.

9. Remove the exhaust collector bracket.

10. Disconnect the exhaust manifold balance and connecting tubes.

11. Remove the bolts securing the camshaft pulleys and rear timing cover.

12. Discharge the air conditioning system and remove the compressor and compressor bracket. Remove the rocker covers and plug all lines.

13. Loosen the cylinder head bolts in the proper sequence. Remove the cylinder head with the exhaust manifolds attached. It may be necessary to tap the head lightly with a rubber mallet to loosen it.

To install:

14. Make sure the No. 1 cylinder is set at TDC on its compression stroke as follows:

a. Align the crankshaft timing mark with the mark on the oil pump housing.

b. The knock pin in the front end of the camshaft should be facing upward.

NOTE: Do not rotate crankshaft and camshaft separately because valves will hit the tops of the pistons.

15. Position the cylinder head and gasket on the block and tighten the cylinder head bolts as follows using the proper sequence:

a. Tighten all bolts to 22 ft. lbs. (29 Nm).

b. Tighten all bolts to 43 ft. lbs. (59 Nm).

c. Loosen all bolts completely.

d. Tighten all bolts to 22 ft. lbs. (29 Nm).

e. Tighten all bolts to 40-47 ft. lbs. (54-64 Nm) or if using an angle wrench, turn all bolts 60-65 degrees clockwise.

16. Tighten the rear timing belt cover.

17. Install the camshaft pulley and tighten to 58-65 ft. lbs. (79-88 Nm).

NOTE: The right hand and left hand camshaft pulleys are different parts. Install them in the correct positions. The right hand pulley has an ""R3" identification mark and the left hand pulley has an ""L3".

18. Install the timing belt and adjust the tension.

19. Install the front upper and lower belt covers.

20. Install the rocker covers, compressor bracket and air conditioning compressor.

21. Install the intake manifold and fuel tube and tighten both the nuts and bolts as follows: first to 2-4 ft.

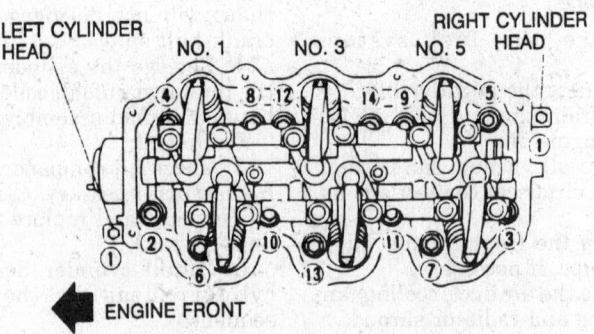

Cylinder head loosening sequence VG30E

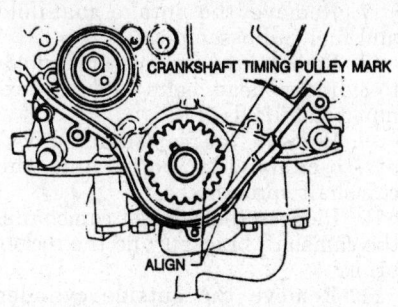

Aligning timing mark and mark oil pump housing — V6 engine

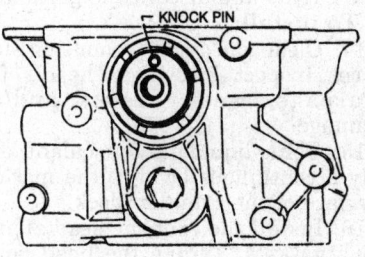

Knock pin of camshaft facing upward — V6 engine

lbs. (3-5 Nm), then to 17-20 ft. lbs. (24-27 Nm).

22. Connect the exhaust manifold balance and connecting tubes. Tighten the exhaust manifold connecting tube and tighten to 16-20 ft. lbs. (22-27 Nm).

23. Install the exhaust collector bracket.

24. Install the power steering pump bracket.

25. Install the intake manifold and fuel tube assembly. Make sure to tighten the bolts in 2-3 stages using the proper torque sequence.

26. Install the collector and collector cover. When installing the collector cover, always use a new gasket. Tighten the throttle chamber-to-collector bolts in 2 stages; 6.5-8 ft. lbs. (9-11 Nm) and then to 13-16 ft. lbs. (18-22 Nm).

27. Install and tension the drive belts.

28. Fill the cooling system to the proper level and connect the negative battery cable.

29. Make all the necessary engine adjustments. Charge the air conditioning system.

VG30E (MAXIMA) Engine

NOTE: A special hex head wrench ST10120000 (J24239-01) or equivalent will be needed to remove and install the cylinder head bolts.

1. Relieve the fuel system pressure and disconnect the negative battery cable.

2. Drain the cooling system. There are 2 cylinder block drain plugs. The left side drain plug is located beside the oil level gauge and the right side drain plug is located behind the right hand halfshaft boot.

3. Remove the timing belt.

NOTE: Do not rotate either the crankshaft or camshaft from this point onward, or the valves could be bent by hitting the tops of the pistons.

4. Disconnect and tag all vacuum and water hoses connected to the intake collector.

5. Mark and remove the distributor, ignition wires and disconnect the accelerator and cruise control (ASCD) cables from the intake manifold collector.

6. Remove the collector cover and the collector from the intake manifold, there are upper and lower collector covers. Disconnect and tag all harness connectors and vacuum lines to gain access to the cover retaining bolts.

7. Remove the intake manifold and fuel tube assembly. Loosen the intake manifold bolts starting from the front of the engine and proceed in criss-cross pattern towards the center.

8. Remove the exhaust collector bracket.

9. Remove the exhaust manifold covers.

10. Disconnect the exhaust manifold from the exhaust pipe.

11. Remove the camshaft pulleys and the rear timing cover securing bolts. Remove the rocker arm covers.

12. Remove the air conditioning compressor and alternator from the their mounting brackets. Remove the mounting brackets. Do not disconnect the refrigerant lines from the compressor and plug.

13. Remove the cylinder head bolts in the correct sequence. Lift the cylinder head off the engine block with the exhaust manifolds attached. It may be necessary to tap the head lightly with a rubber mallet to loosen it.

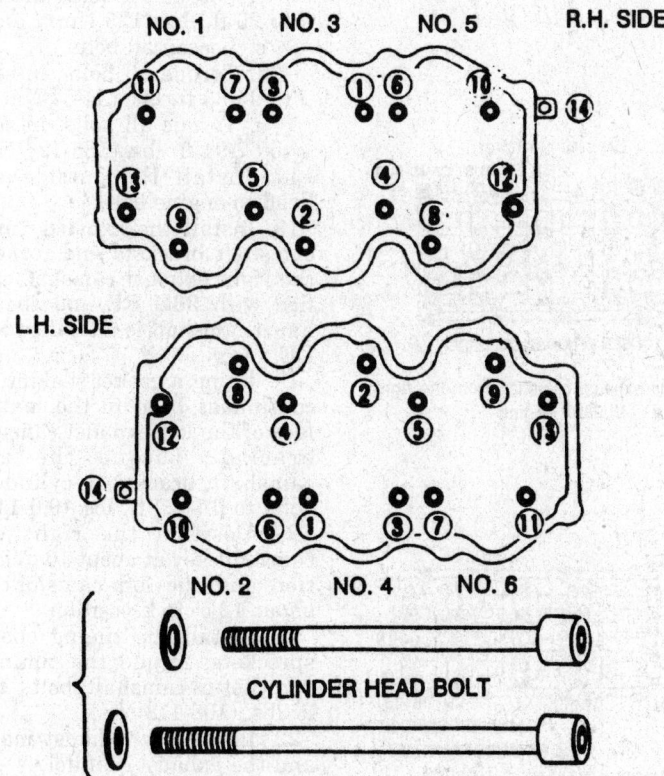

Cylinder head torque sequence — VG30E

To install:

14. Make sure the No. 1 cylinder is set at TDC on its compression stroke as follows:

  a. Align the crankshaft timing mark with the mark on the oil pump housing.

  b. The knock pin in the front end of the camshaft should be facing upward.

NOTE: Do not rotate crankshaft and camshaft separately because valves will hit piston head.

15. Install the cylinder head with a new gasket. Apply clean engine oil to the threads and seats of the bolts and install the bolts with washers in the correct position. Note that bolts 4, 5, 12, and 13 are 4.95 in. (127mm) long. The other bolts are 4.13 in. (106mm) long.

16. Torque the bolts in the proper sequence as follows:

  a. Torque all bolts, in sequence, to 22 ft. lbs. (29 Nm).

  b. Torque all bolts, in sequence, to 43 ft. lbs. (58 Nm).

  c. Loosen all bolts completely.

  d. Torque all bolts, in sequence, to 22 ft. lbs. (29 Nm).

  e. Torque all bolts, in sequence, to 40-47 ft. lbs. (54-64 Nm). If using an angle torque wrench, torque them 60-65 degrees tighter rather than going to 40-47 ft. lbs. (54-64 Nm).

17. Install the alternator and air conditioner compressor mounting brackets. Mount the compressor and alternator.

18. Install the rear timing cover bolts. Install the camshaft pulleys. Make sure the pulley marked R3 goes on the right and that marked L3 goes on the left. Align the timing marks if necessary and then install the timing belt and adjust the belt tension.

19. Connect the exhaust manifold to the exhaust pipe.

20. Install the exhaust manifold covers.

21. Install the exhaust collector bracket.

22. Install the intake manifold and fuel tube assembly.

23. Install the intake manifold collector cover.

24. Connect the accelerator and cruise control cables to the intake manifold and install the distributor and ignition wires.

25. Connect the vacuum and water hoses to the intake collector.

26. Install and tension the timing belt.

27. Fill the cooling system and connect the negative battery cable.

28. Make all the necessary engine adjustments. Road test the vehicle for proper operation.

VE30DE (MAXIMA) Engine

NOTE: To remove or install the cylinder head, you'll need a cylinder head bolt wrench ST10120000 (J24239-01) or equivalent.

1. Release the fuel pressure. Disconnect the negative battery cable.

2. Rotate the crankshaft to position the No. 1 piston on TDC of it's compression stroke.

3. Drain the cooling system. Disconnect all the electrical connectors, vacuum hoses and water hoses connected to the intake manifold collector.

4. The crank angle sensor is located in the rear of the left cylinder head, mark it's position, disconnect the electrical connector from it and remove.

5. Remove the timing chain.

NOTE: Do not rotate either the crankshaft or camshaft from this point onward or the valves could be bent by hitting the pistons.

6. Remove the intake manifold collector.

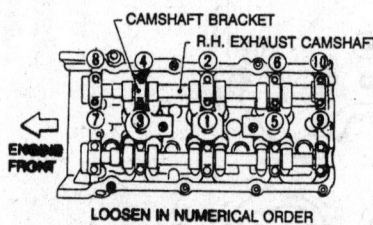

Removing the exhaust camshaft from the right cylinder head — VE30DE engine

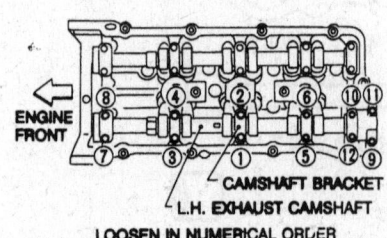

Removing the exhaust camshaft from the left cylinder head — VE30DE engine

7. Remove the intake manifold and fuel rail assembly.

8. Remove the exhaust manifold-to-cylinder head bolts and the exhaust manifolds.

9. Remove the camshaft sprockets-to-camshafts bolts and the camshaft sprockets.

10. Remove the exhaust camshafts, the camshaft brackets and the rocker arms.

11. Remove the outside cylinder head bolts.

12. Loosen the cylinder head-to-engine bolts, in sequence, using 2-3 steps.

13. Lift the cylinder head(s) from the engine and discard the gasket(s).

To install:

14. Clean the gasket mounting surfaces. Inspect the cylinder head(s) for warpage, wear, cracks and/or damage.

15. Using liquid gasket sealant, apply a continuous bead to the mating surface of the cylinder block.

16. Install the cylinder head(s) and new gaskets. Torque the head bolts by performing the following procedures:

  a. Torque all bolts, in sequence, to 29 ft. lbs. (39 Nm).

  b. Torque all bolts, in sequence, to 90 ft. lbs. (123 Nm).

  c. Loosen all bolts.

  d. Torque all bolts, in sequence, to 25-33 ft. lbs. (34-44 Nm).

  e. Torque all bolts, in sequence, to 87-94 ft. lbs. (188-127 Nm).

17. Install the outside cylinder head-to-engine bolts.

18. Install the exhaust camshafts, camshaft brackets and rocker arms; the right exhaust camshaft is identified with **96E RE** and the left exhaust camshaft is identified with **96E LE**.

19. Using a gasket sealant, apply a continuous bead to the mating surface of the left exhaust camshaft end bracket. Torque the exhaust camshaft bracket-to-cylinder head bolts to 6.7-8.7 ft. lbs. (9.0-11.0 Nm).

20. Position the right exhaust camshaft key at about 10 o'clock position and the left camshaft key at about 12 o'clock position.

21. Install the timing chains and sprockets; torque the timing chain sprocket-to-camshaft bolts to 80-87 ft. lbs. (108-118 Nm).

22. Install the exhaust manifold(s) and the exhaust manifold(s)-to-cylinder head(s) bolts.

23. Install the intake manifold and fuel rail assembly.

24. Install the intake manifold collector.

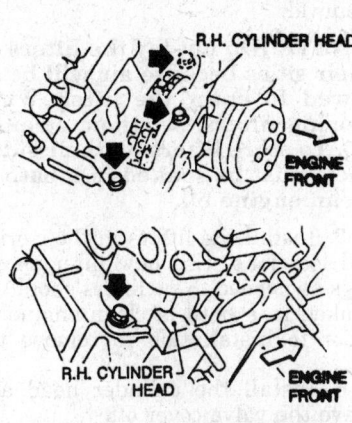

Removing the outside cylinder head-to-engine bolts — VE30DE engine

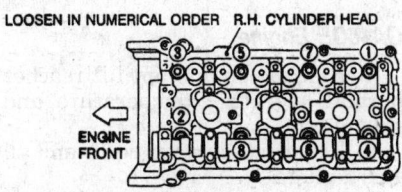

Removing the cylinder head bolts from the right cylinder head — VE30DE engine

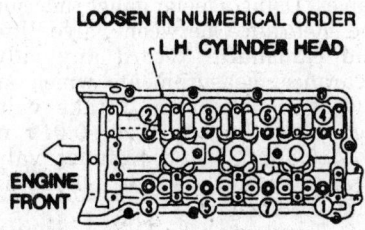

Removing the cylinder head bolts from the left cylinder head — VE30DE engine

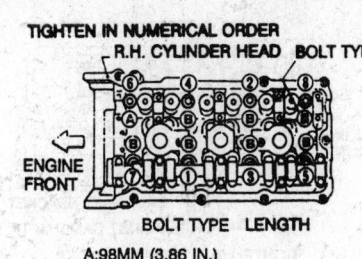

TIGHTEN IN NUMERICAL ORDER
R.H. CYLINDER HEAD — BOLT TYPE

ENGINE FRONT

BOLT TYPE LENGTH
A:98MM (3.86 IN.)
B:112.5MM (4.43 IN.)

Torquing procedure for the right cylinder head — VE30DE engine

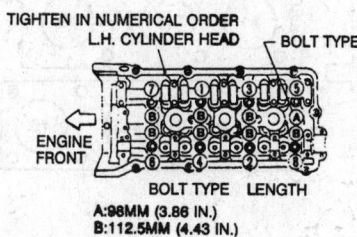

TIGHTEN IN NUMERICAL ORDER
L.H. CYLINDER HEAD — BOLT TYPE

ENGINE FRONT

BOLT TYPE LENGTH
A:98MM (3.86 IN.)
B:112.5MM (4.43 IN.)

Torquing procedure for the left cylinder head — VE30DE engine

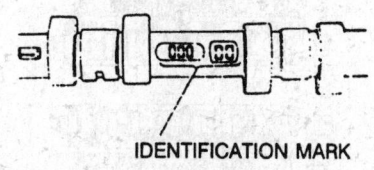

IDENTIFICATION MARK

View of the camshaft identification marks — VE30DE engine

25. Align and install the crank angle sensor to the rear of the left cylinder head, connect the electrical connector to it.

26. Connect all the electrical connectors, vacuum hoses and water hoses to the intake manifold collector. Refill the cooling system.

27. Connect the negative battery cable. Start the engine check the engine timing. After the engine reaches the normal operating temperature check for the correct coolant level.

28. Road test the vehicle for proper operation.

VG30DE and VG30DETT (300ZX) Engines

1. Relieve the fuel system pressure and disconnect the negative battery cable.

2. Drain the cooling system.

3. Remove the intake manifold collector.

4. Remove the injector pipe assembly.

5. Remove the valve covers.

6. Remove the timing belt.

7. Remove the idler pulley and idler pulley stud bolt.

8. Remove the intake manifold.

9. Disconnect the exhaust tube from the exhaust manifold.

10. Loosen the cylinder head bolts (in reverse order of installation sequence) in 2-3 stages. Lift the cylinder head off the engine block wih the exhaust manifolds attached. It may be necessary to tap the head lightly with a rubber mallet to loosen it.

To install:

11. Make sure the No. 1 cylinder is set at TDC on its compression stroke as follows:

    a. Align the crankshaft timing mark with the mark on the oil pump housing.

    b. Align camshaft sprocket timing mark with the mark on the rear timing belt cover.

12. Install the cylinder head with a new gasket. Apply clean engine oil to the threads and seats of the bolts and install the bolts with washers in the correct position.

13. Torque the bolts in the proper sequence as follows:

    a. Torque all bolts, in sequence, to 29 ft. lbs. (39 Nm).

    b. Torque all bolts, in sequence, to 90 ft. lbs. (123 Nm).

    c. Loosen all bolts completely.

    d. Torque all bolts, in sequence, to 25-33 ft. lbs. (34-44 Nm).

    e. Torque all bolts, in sequence, to 90 ft. lbs. (123 Nm). If using an angle torque wrench, torque them 60-70 degrees tighter rather than going to 90 ft. lbs. (123 Nm).

    f. Torque the 6mm ""X" bolts to 7-9 ft. lbs. (10-12 Nm). There is one of these bolts per head.

14. Connect the exhaust tube to the exhaust manifold.

15. Install the intake manifold.

16. Install the idler pulley and stud bolt.

17. Install and tension the timing belt.

18. Install the valve covers. Use sealant on the exhaust side valve cover.

19. Install the injector pipe assembly.

Positioning the exhaust camshafts — VE30DE engine

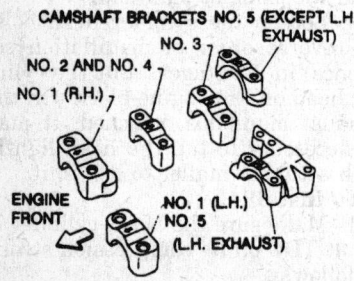

View of the exhaust camshaft brackets — VE30DE engine

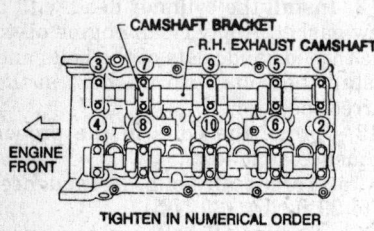

Torquing procedure for the right exhaust camshaft brackets — VE30DE engine

20. Install the intake manifold collector.

21. Fill the cooling system to the proper level and connect the negative battery cable.

22. Make all the necessary engine adjustments. Road test the vehicle for proper operation.

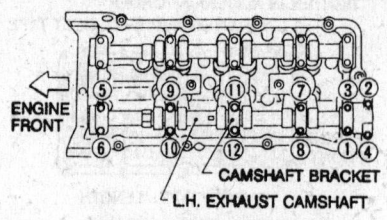

Torquing procedure for the left exhaust camshaft brackets — VE30DE engine

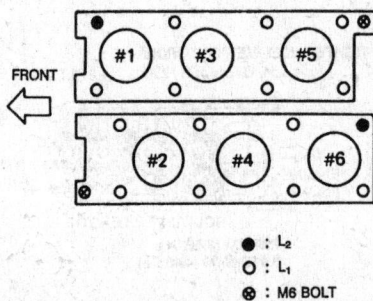

Torque the 6mm ""X"" bolts to 7-9 ft. lbs. (10-12 Nm)

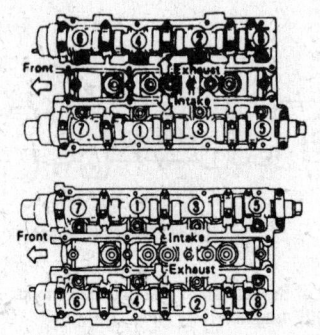

Cylinder head torque sequence — VG30DE and VG30DETT engines

Valve Lifters

REMOVAL AND INSTALLATION

1. Disconnect the negative battery cable.

2. Remove the rocker arms and shafts.

3. Remove the cylinder head assembly, if required.

4. Withdraw the lifters from the head or from the bore in the rocker. Tag each lifter to the corresponding cylinder head opening or rocker. If the lifter is installed in the rocker,

remove the snapring first. Be careful not to bend the snapring during removal.

NOTE: Do not lay the lifters on their sides because air will be allowed to enter the lifter. When storing lifters, set them straight up. To store lifters on their sides, they must be soaked in a bath of clean engine oil.

5. Install the lifters in their original locations. Use new lifter snaprings as needed. New lifters should be soaked in a bath of clean engine oil prior to installation to remove the air.

6. Install the cylinder head and leave the valve cover off.

7. Install the rocker arms and shafts.

8. Check the lifters for proper operation by pushing hard on each lifter with finger-tip pressure. If the valve lifter moves more than 0.04 in. (1mm), air may be inside it. Make sure the rocker arm is not on the camshaft lobe when making this check. If there was air in the lifters, bleed the air by running the engine at 1000 rpm for 10 minutes.

Valve Lash

ADJUSTMENT

GA16DE Engine

1. Run the engine until it reaches normal operating temperature and shut if off.

2. Remove the rocker cover and all spark plugs.

3. Set No. 1 cylinder at TDC on compression stroke. Align pointer with TDC mark on crankshaft pulley. Check that the valve lifters on No. 1 cylinder are loose and valve lifters on No. 4 are tight. If not, turn crankshaft one revolution (360 degrees) and align as above.

4. Check both No. 1 intake and both No. 1 exhaust valves, both No. 2 intake valves and both No. 3 exhaust valves. Using a feeler gauge, measure the clearance between valve lifter and camshaft. Record any valve clearance measurements which are out of specification. Intake valve clearance (hot) is 0.008-0.019 in. (0.21-0.49mm) and exhaust valve clearance (hot) is 0.012-0.023 in. (0.30-0.58mm).

5. Turn crankshaft one revolution (360 degrees) and align mark on crankshaft pulley with pointer. Check both No. 2 exhaust valves, both No. 3 intake valves, both No. 4

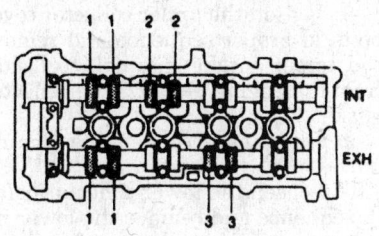

Valve adjustment step No. 1 — GA16DE and KA24DE engines

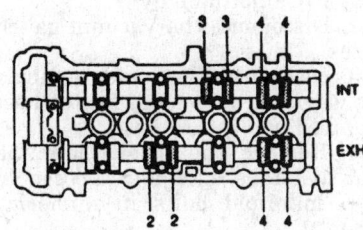

Valve adjustment step No. 2 — GA16DE and KA24DE engines

intake valves and both No. 4 exhaust valves. Using a feeler gauge, measure the clearance between valve lifter and camshaft. Record any valve clearance measurements which are out of specification. Intake valve clearance (hot) is 0.008-0.019 in. (0.21-0.49mm) and exhaust valve clearance (hot) is 0.012-0.023 in. (0.30-0.58mm).

6. If all valve clearances are within specification, install all related parts as necessary.

7. If adjustement is necessary, adjust valve clearance while engine is cold by removing adjusting shim. Determine replacement adjusting shim size using formula. Using a micrometer determine thickness of removed shim. Calculate thickness of new adjusting shim so valve clearance comes within specified valves. R = thickness of removed shim, N = thickness of new shim, M = measured valve clearance.

INTAKE: N = R + (M - 0.0146 in. or 0.37mm)

EXHAUST: N = R + (M - 0.0157 in. or 0.40mm)

8. Shims are available in 50 sizes (thickness is stamped on shim, this side always installed down), select

new shims with thickness as close as possible to calculated valve.

KA24DE Engine

1. Run the engine until it reaches normal operating temperature and shut if off.

2. Remove the rocker cover and all spark plugs.

3. Set No. 1 cylinder at TDC on compression stroke. Align pointer with TDC mark on crankshaft pulley. Check that the valve lifters on No. 1 cylinder are loose and valve lifters on No. 4 are tight. If not turn crankshaft one revolution 360 degrees and align as above.

4. Check both No. 1 intake and both No.1 exhaust valves, both No. 2 intake valves and both No. 3 exhaust valves. Using a feeler gauge, measure the clearance between valve lifter and camshaft. Record any valve clearance measurements which are out of specification. Intake valve clearance (hot) is 0.012-0.015 in. (0.31-0.39mm) and exhaust valve clearance (hot) is 0.013-0.016 in. (0.33-0.41mm).

5. Turn crankshaft one revolution (360 degrees) and align mark on crankshaft pulley with pointer. Check both No. 2 exhaust valves, both No. 3 intake valves and both No. 4 exhaust valves. Using a feeler gauge, measure the clearance between valve lifter and camshaft. Record any valve clearance measurements which are out of specification. Intake valve clearance (hot) is 0.012-0.015 in. (0.31-0.39mm) and exhaust valve clearance (hot) is 0.013-0.016 in. (0.33-0.41mm).

6. If all valve clearances are within specification, install all related parts as necessary.

7. If adjustement is necessary, adjust valve clearance while engine is cold by removing adjusting shim. Determine replacement adjusting shim size using formula. Using a micrometer determine thickness of removed shim. Calculate thickness of new adjusting shim so valve clearance comes within specified valves. R = thickness of removed shim, N = thickness of new shim, M = measured valve clearance.

INTAKE: N = R + (M - 0.0138 in. or 0.35mm)

EXHAUST: N = R + (M - 0.0146 in. or 0.0146mm)

8. Shims are available in 37 sizes (thickness is stamped on shim-this side always installed down), select new shims with thickness as close as possible to calculated value.

Rocker Arms/Shaft

REMOVAL AND INSTALLATION

NOTE: All rocker shaft REMOVAL AND INSTALLATION procedures are given in the Camshaft section.

Intake Manifold

REMOVAL AND INSTALLATION

Pulsar and Sentra

1. Relieve the fuel system pressure, disconnect the negative battery cable and drain the cooling system.

2. Remove the air cleaner assembly.

3. Disconnect the throttle linkage, electrical connections, fuel and vacuum lines from the throttle body or throttle chamber.

4. The throttle body/throttle chamber can be removed from the manifold at this point or can be removed as an assembly with the intake manifold.

5. On all engines, remove the manifold support stays.

6. Loosen the intake manifold retaining bolts in the the proper sequence and separate the manifold from the cylinder head.

7. Remove the intake manifold gasket and clean all the gasket contact surfaces thoroughly with a gasket scraper and suitable solvent. All traces of old gasket material must be removed to ensure proper sealing. Inspect the intake manifold for cracks. Using a metal straightedge, check the surface of the intake manifold for warpage.

To install:

8. Lay the new intake manifold gasket onto the cylinder head and position the intake manifold over the mounting studs and onto the gasket. Install the mounting nuts and torque them to specification in the proper sequence.

9. On all engines, install the manifold support stays.

10. If removed, install the throttle body or throttle chamber.

11. Connect the throttle linkage, electrical connections, fuel and vacuum lines.

12. Install the air cleaner.

13. Fill the cooling system to the proper level and connect the negative battery cable.

14. Road test the vehicle for proper operation.

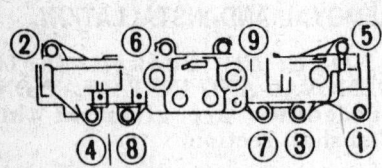

Intake manifold nut loosening sequence — GA16i, GA16DE and SR20DE engines

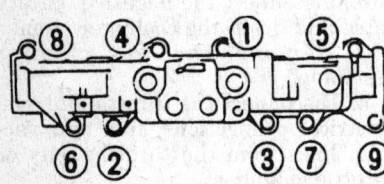

Intake manifold nut tightening sequence — GA16i, GA16DE and SR20DE engines

300ZX

1. Relieve the fuel system pressure, disconnect the negative battery cable and drain the cooling system.
2. Disconnect the air inlet hoses from both throttle chambers.
3. Disconnect the throttle cable from the accelerator drum located in the middle of the throttle chambers.
4. Disconnect the electrical connectors and vacuum lines from both throttle chambers.
5. Disconnect and tag the electrical wire connectors and vacuum lines from the intake manifold collector.

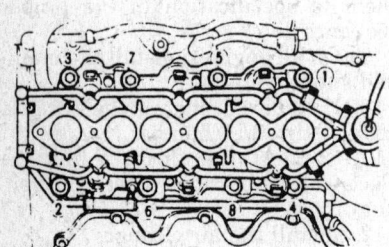

Intake manifold removal and installation — 300ZX

6. Unbolt and remove the intake manifold collector with the throttle chambers attached. Remove the collector gasket.
7. Disconnect the fuel supply and return lines from the injector assembly. Plug the lines to prevent leakage.
8. Remove the injector assembly from the intake manifold.
9. Remove the intake manifold and gaskets.

To install:
10. Install the intake manifold with a new gasket. Tighten the intake manifold bolts evenly in steps to specification.
11. Install the fuel injectors with new insulators and O-rings.
12. Connect the injector supply and return lines.
13. Install the intake manifold collector with a new gasket. Torque the collector bolts to 12-15 ft. lbs. (16-21 Nm).
14. Connect the vacuum lines and electrical connectors to the collector.
15. Connect the vacuum lines and electrical connectors to the throttle chambers.
16. Connect the throttle cable to the center drum.
17. Connect the air inlet hoses to the the throttle chambers.
18. Fill the cooling system to the proper level and connect the negative battery cable.
19. Make all the necessary engine adjustments. Road test the vehicle for proper operation.

Maxima

VG30E ENGINE

The Maxima has a slightly different collector/intake manifold assembly. The previous single collector is replaced by upper and lower collectors. Each collector has its own bolt REMOVAL AND INSTALLATION sequence.
1. Relieve the fuel system pressure, disconnect the negative battery cable and drain the cooling system.
2. Remove the distributor and the ignition wires.
3. Disconnect the Automatic Speed Control Device (ASCD) and accelerator wires from the intake manifold collector.
4. Disconnect the harness connectors for the AAC valve, throttle sensor and idle switch.
5. Disconnect the air cut out valve water hose.
6. Disconnect the PCV valve hoses.
7. Disconnect the vacuum hoses from the vacuum gallery, swirl control valve, master brake cylinder,

EGR control valve and EGR flare tube.
8. Loosen the upper collector cover bolts in proper sequence and remove the upper intake manifold collector from the engine. Remove the collector gasket.
9. Disconnect the engine ground harness.
10. Loosen the lower collector bolts, in sequence and remove the lower intake manifold collector from the engine.
11. Disconnect the harness connectors for all injectors, engine temperature switch and sensor, power valve control solenoid valve, EGR control solenoid valve, EGR temperature sensor (California only).
12. Disconnect the vacuum gallery hoses.
13. Disconnect the pressure regulator valve vacuum hose, heater hose, fuel feed and return hose.
14. Remove the intake manifold and fuel tube assembly. Loosen intake manifold bolts in numerical order.

To install:
15. Install the intake manifold and fuel tube assembly with a new gasket. Tighten the manifold bolts and nuts in 2-3 stages in sequence.
16. Connect the hoses and electrical wires to the intake manifold and fuel tube.
17. Install the upper and lower collector and collector cover with new gaskets. Tighten collector to intake manifold bolts in 2-3 stages by reversing the removal sequence.
18. Connect the vacuum lines, hoses, cables and brackets to the collector cover and collector assembly.
19. Install the distributor and ignition wires.
20. Fill the cooling system to the proper level and connect the negative battrey cable.
21. Make all the necessary engine adjustments. Road test the vehicle for proper operation.

1992-94 VE30DE ENGINE

1. Disconnect the negative battery cable.
2. Disconnect the electrical connectors from the throttle position sensor, the exhaust gas temperature sensor and/or etc.
3. Label and disconnect the hoses from the throttle body, the EGR valve, the EGR control solenoid valve, the intake manifold collector, the power valve control solenoid valve (if equipped with a manual transaxle) and the power valve actuator (if equipped with a manual transaxle).

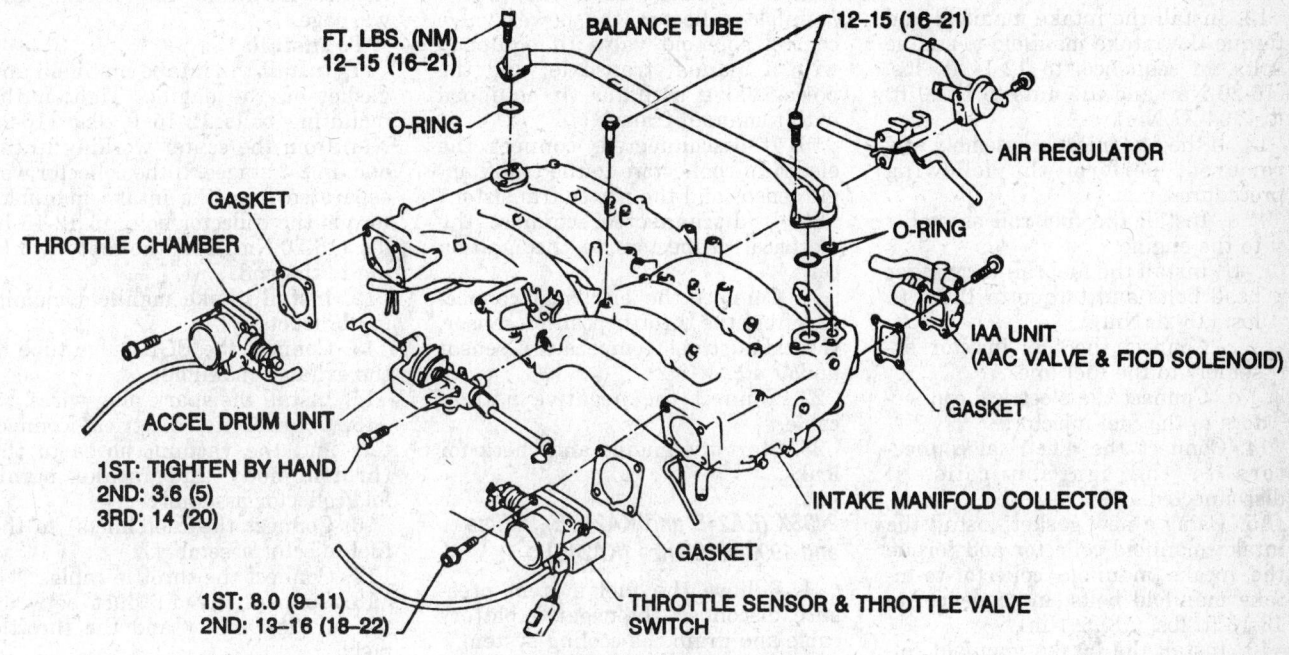

Intake manifold collector assembly — 300ZX

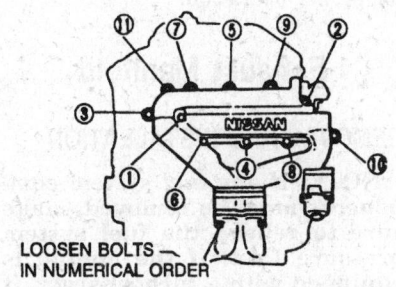

Loosening the upper intake manifold collector bolts in sequence — VG30E engine

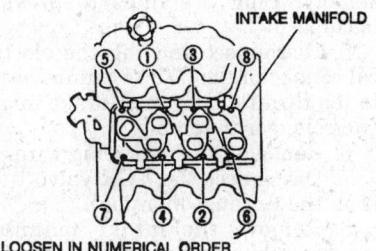

Loosening the intake manifold to engine bolts in sequence — VG30E engine

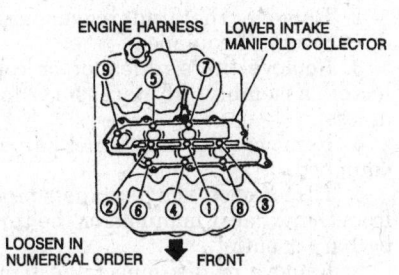

Loosening the lower intake manifold collector bolts in sequence — VG30E engine

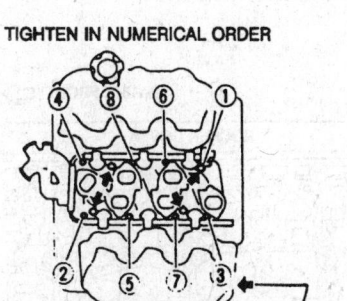

Torquing the intake manifold to engine bolts in sequence in steps — 1990-92 VG30E engine

4. Disconnect the accelerator cable from the throttle body.

5. Remove the intake manifold collector support-to-intake manifold collector and the intake manifold collector support-to-cylinder head bolts and the supports.

6. Remove the intake manifold collector-to-intake manifold bolts and the intake manifold collector.

7. If necessary, disconnect the electrical connectors from the ignition coils.

8. If necessary, disconnect the electrical connector from the crank angle sensor and the power transistor.

9. If the fuel injector assembly is in the way, perform the following procedures:

a. Disconnect the electrical connectors from the fuel injectors.

b. Disconnect the fuel injector assembly from the fuel lines.

c. Remove the fuel rail-to-cylinder head bolts.

d. Remove the fuel rail assembly from the engine.

10. Remove the intake manifold-to-engine bolts, in sequence, by reversing the torquing sequence. Lift the intake manifold from the engine and discard the gasket.

To install:

11. Clean the gasket mounting surfaces.

12. Install the intake manifold and torque the intake manifold-to-engine bolts, in sequence, to 12-14 ft. lbs. (16-20 Nm) and the nuts to 17-20 ft. lbs. (24-27 Nm).

13. If the fuel injector assembly was removed, perform the following procedures:

   a. Install the fuel rail assembly to the engine.

   b. Install the fuel rail-to-cylinder head bolts and torque to 12-14 ft. lbs. (16-20 Nm).

   c. Connect the fuel injector assembly to the fuel lines.

   d. Connect the electrical connectors to the fuel injectors.

14. Connect the electrical connectors to the ignition coils, if disconnected.

15. Using a new gasket, install the intake manifold collector and torque the intake manifold collector-to-intake manifold bolts, in sequence, to 13-16 ft. lbs. (18-22 Nm).

16. Install the intake manifold collector support and torque the bolts to 12-15 ft. lbs. (16-21 Nm).

17. Connect the accelerator cable to the throttle body.

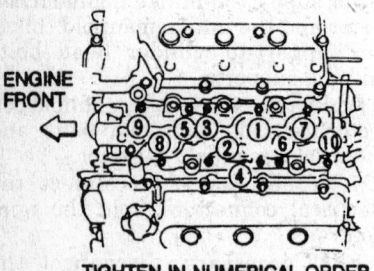

TIGHTEN IN NUMERICAL ORDER

Torquing the intake manifold to engine bolts in sequence in steps — VE30DE engine

TIGHTEN IN NUMERICAL ORDER

Intake manifold collector torque sequence — VE30DE engine

18. Connect the hoses to the throttle body, the EGR valve, the EGR control solenoid valve, the intake manifold collector, the power valve control solenoid valve (if equipped with a manual transaxle) and the power valve actuator (if equipped with a manual transaxle).

19. If disconnected, connect the electrical connectors to the crank angle sensor and the power transistor.

20. If disconnected, connect the electrical connectors to the ignition coils.

21. Connect the electrical connectors from the throttle position sensor, the exhaust gas temperature sensor and/or etc.

22. Connect the negative battery cable.

23. Start the engine and check for leaks.

240SX (KA24E and KA24DE), Altima and 1990-92 Stanza (KA24E)

1. Relieve the fuel system pressure, disconnect the negative battery cable and drain the cooling system.

2. Remove the air duct between the air flow meter and the throttle body.

3. Disconnect the throttle cable.

4. Disconnect the fuel supply and return lines from the fuel injector assembly. Plug the lines to prevent leakage.

5. Disconnect and tag the electrical connectors and the vacuum hoses to the throttle body and intake manifold/collector assembly.

6. Remove the spark plug wires.

7. Disconnect the EGR valve tube from the exhaust manifold.

8. Remove the intake manifold mounting brackets.

9. Unbolt the intake manifold collector/throttle body from the intake manifold or just remove the mounting bolts and separate the intake manifold from the cylinder head with the collector attached.

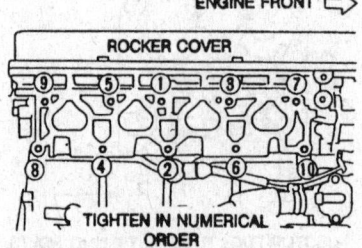

TIGHTEN IN NUMERICAL ORDER

Intake manifold torque sequence — KA24E and KA24DE engines

10. Using a putty knife, clean the gasket mounting surfaces. Check the intake manifold for cracks and warpage.

To install:

11. Install the intake manifold and gasket on the engine. Tighten the mounting bolts 12-15 ft. lbs. (16-20 Nm) from the center working to the end, in 2-3 stages. If the collector was separated from the intake manifold, torque the collector bolts to 12-15 ft. lbs. (16-20 Nm) from the center working to the end.

12. Install intake manifold mounting brackets.

13. Connect the EGR valve tube to the exhaust manifold.

14. Install the spark plug wires.

15. Connect the electrical connectors and the vacuum hoses to the throttle body and intake manifold/collector assembly.

16. Connect the fuel line(s) to the fuel injector assembly.

17. Connect the throttle cable.

18. Connect the air duct between the air flow meter and the throttle body.

19. Fill the cooling system to the proper level and connect the negative battery cable.

20. Make all the necessary engine adjustments. Road test the vehicle for proper operation.

Exhaust Manifold

REMOVAL AND INSTALLATION

NOTE: If any fuel system components must be removed, make sure to relieve the fuel system pressure first. If the engine is equipped with a turbocharger, it may be easier to remove the exhaust manifolds, with the turbochargers(s) atttached.

1. Disconnect the negative battery cable. Raise and support the vehicle safely.

2. Remove the undercover and dust covers, if equipped.

3. Remove the air cleaner or collector assembly, if necessary for access.

4. Remove the heat shield(s), if equipped.

5. Disconnect the exhaust pipe from the exhaust manifold or the turbocharger outlet.

6. Remove or disconnect the temperature sensors, oxygen sensors, air induction pipes, brackets and other attachments from the manifold.

7. Disconnect the EAI and EGR tubes from their fittings, if equipped.

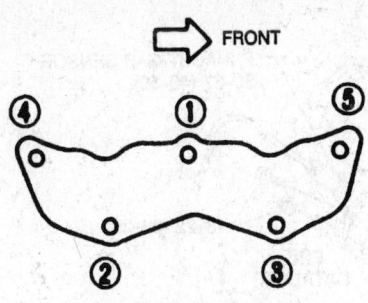

Intake manifold collector bolt torque sequence — 240SX, Altima and 1990-92 Stanza

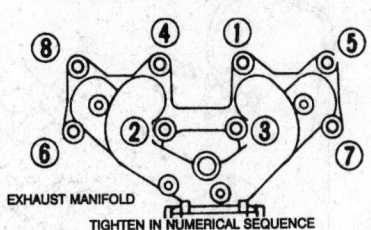

Exhaust manifold torque sequence — GA16i

8. Loosen and remove the exhaust manifold attaching nuts (loosen each bolt/nuts in steps) and remove the manifold(s) from the block. Discard the exhaust manifold gaskets and replace with new gaskets.

9. Clean the gasket surfaces and check the manifold for cracks and warpage.

To install:

10. Install the exhaust manifold with a new gasket. Torque the manifold fasteners from the center outward in several stages to specifications.

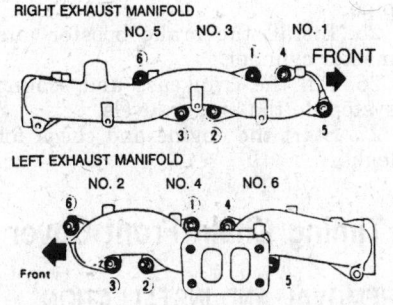

Exhaust manifold torque sequence — V-Series engines

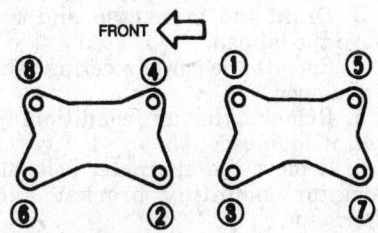

Exhaust manifold torque sequence — 240SX, Altima and 1990-92 Stanza

11. Connect the EAI and EGR tubes to the connections on the manifold as necessary.

12. Install or connect the temperature sensors, oxygen sensors, air induction pipes, brackets and other attachments to the manifold.

13. Connect the exhust pipe to the manifold or turbocharger outlet using a new gasket.

14. Install the heat shields.

15. Install the air cleaner or collector assembly.

16. Install the undercovers and dust covers.

17. Connect the negative battery cable.

Turbocharger

REMOVAL AND INSTALLATION

NOTE: If the turbocharger is being replaced, always drain the crankcase and replace the oil and filter to ensure a clean oil supply. This is especially true in cases of complete turbocharger failure where there is the possibility of metal particles entering the engine's lubricating system and damaging the new turbocharger assembly.

Right Side

1. Drain the cooling system and the oil pan.

2. Remove the right portion of the cowl top.

3. Remove the battery.

4. Remove the air inlet hose and pipe.

5. Disconnect the lower pipe from the turbo.

6. Remove the Automatic Speed Control Device (ASCD) bracket with wiper motor and solenoid valves.

7. Unplug the exhaust gas harness connector.

8. Disconnect the turbocharger water hoses and oil supply tube. Plug the ends to prevent leakage.

9. Remove the 2 bolts that attach the pre-catalyst to the turbocharger.

10. Remove the oil pressure switch.

11. Remove the oil filter.

12. Disconnect the oil return tube. Plug the end to prevent leakage.

13. Disconnect the front exhaust tube and pre-catalyst.

14. Disconnect the oil hose from the oil filter bracket. Plug the end to prevent leakage.

15. Disconnect the remaining water tubes from the turbocharger. Plug the ends to prevent leakage.

16. Remove the cotter pin from the wastegate actuating rod.

17. Remove the oil filter bracket.

18. Relieve the tabs on the turbocharger attaching nut locking plates. There are 2 locking plates.

19. Remove the 4 nuts and separate the turbocharger from the exhaust manifold. Clean the gasket surfaces.

To install:

20. Mount the turbocharger onto the exhaust manifold with a new gasket. Install the 4 attaching nuts and torque them to 32-40 ft. lbs. (43-54 Nm) in a criss-cross pattern.

21. Once the nuts are torqued, bend the tabs of the locking plates firmly around the flats of each nut.

22. Install the oil filter bracket.

23. Connect the wastegate actuating rod and insert the cotter pin.

24. Connect the water tubes to the turbo. Use new metal crush washers on the banjo fittings.

25. Connect the oil hose to the oil filter bracket.

26. Connect the front exhaust tube and pre-catalyst. Use new gaskets.

27. Connect the oil return tube. Use new metal crush washers on the banjo fitting.

28. Install a new oil filter.

29. Install the oil pressure switch.

30. Attach the pre-catalyst to the turbocharger. Use a new gasket.

31. Connect the oil supply tube and remaining water hoses. Use new metal crush washers on the banjo fittings.

32. Plug in the exhaust gas harness connector.

33. Mount the solenoid valves, wiper motor and Automatic Speed Control Device (ASCD) bracket.

34. Connect the lower pipe to the turbo.

35. Install the air inlet hose and pipe.

36. Install the battery.

37. Install the right portion of the top cowl.

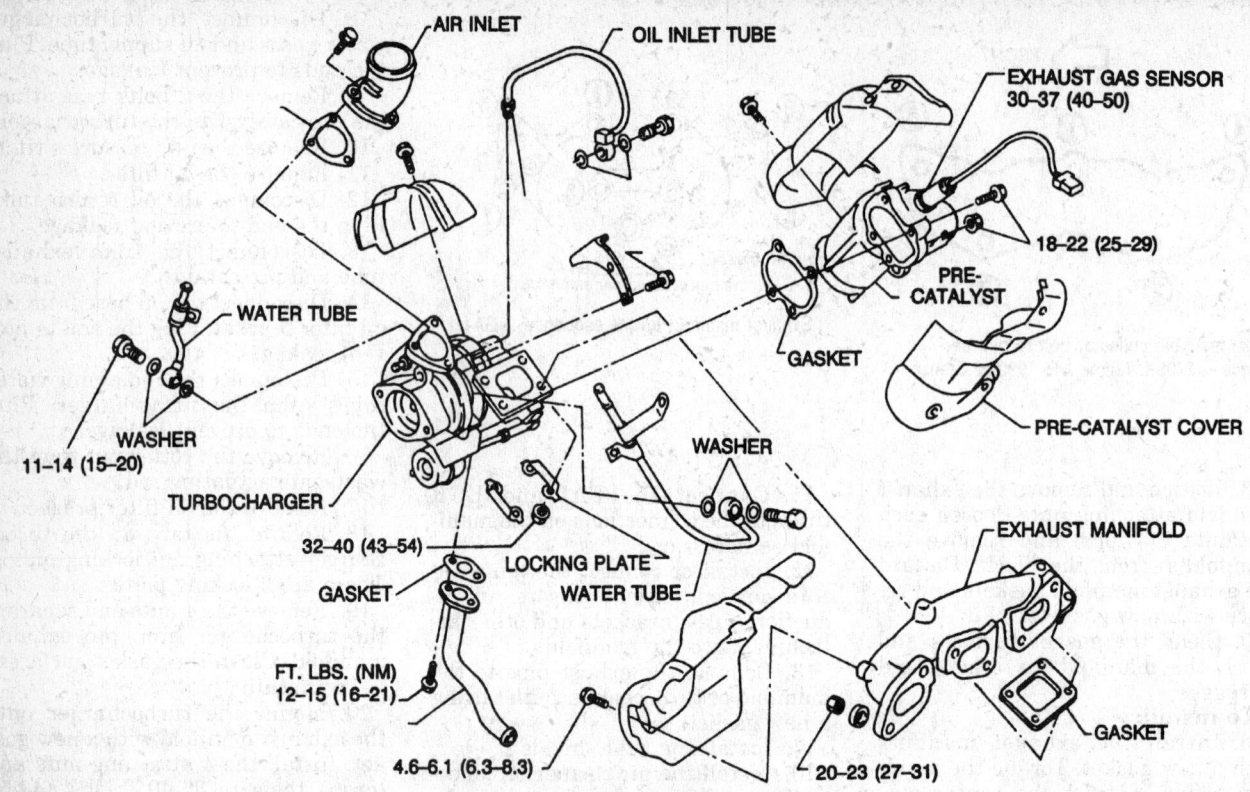

Right side turbocharger assembly — 300ZX

38. Fill the crankcase and cooling system to the proper levels.

39. Start the engine and check for leaks.

LEFT SIDE

1. Drain the cooling system and the oil pan.

2. Remove the brake master cylinder and brake booster.

3. Remove the air inlet hose and pipe.

4. Disconnect the lower pipe from the turbocharger.

5. Disconnect the water tubes. Plug the the tube ends to prevent leakage.

6. Remove the 2 bolts that attach the pre-catalyst to the turbocharger.

7. Remove the front exhaust tube and pre-catalyst.

8. Disconnect the steering column lower joint from the steering rack.

9. Disconnect the oil return tube and remaining water tubes. Plug the tube ends to prevent leakage.

10. Disconnect the EGR tube and remove the wastegate valve actuator bracket.

11. Remove the exhaust manifold cover.

12. Remove the exhaust manifold attaching nuts. Remove the turbocharger and exhaust manifold to-

gether as one unit. Release the tabs on the attaching nut locking plates. There are 2 locking plates. Remove the 4 nuts and separate the turbocharger from the exhaust manifold. Clean the gasket surfaces.

To install:

13. Mount the turbocharger onto the exhaust manifold with a new gasket. Install the 4 attaching nuts and torque them to 32-40 ft. lbs. (43-54 Nm) in a criss-cross pattern.

14. Once the nuts are torqued, bend the tabs of the locking plates firmly around the flats of each nut.

15. Install the exhaust manifold/turbocharger assembly with new gaskets. Torque the exhaust manifold nuts to 20-23 ft. lbs. (27-31 Nm).

16. Install the exhaust manifold cover.

17. Install the wastegate valve actuator bracket and connect the EGR tube.

18. Connect the water tubes and oil return tube. Use new metal crush gaskets on the banjo fittings.

19. Connect the steering column lower joint from the steering rack.

20. Install the front exhaust tube and pre-catalyst.

21. Attach the pre-catalyst to the turbocharger.

22. Connect the remaining water tubes.

23. Connect the lower pipe to the turbocharger.

24. Install the air inlet hose and pipe.

25. Install the brake booster and master cylinder.

26. Fill the crankcase and cooling system to the proper levels.

27. Start the engine and check for leaks.

Timing Chain Front Cover

REMOVAL AND INSTALLATION

1990 Pulsar and Sentra (GA16i)

1. Disconnect the negative battery cable.

2. Drain the cooling system.

3. Drain the crankcase and remove the oil pan.

4. Remove the power steering belt, if equipped.

5. Remove the air conditioning belt, if equipped.

6. Remove the alternator belt, alternator mounting bracket and alternator.

7. Remove the air cleaner.

8. Connect a suitable lifting device to the front side lifting bracket and tension the hoist to support the engine. Remove the front engine mount-

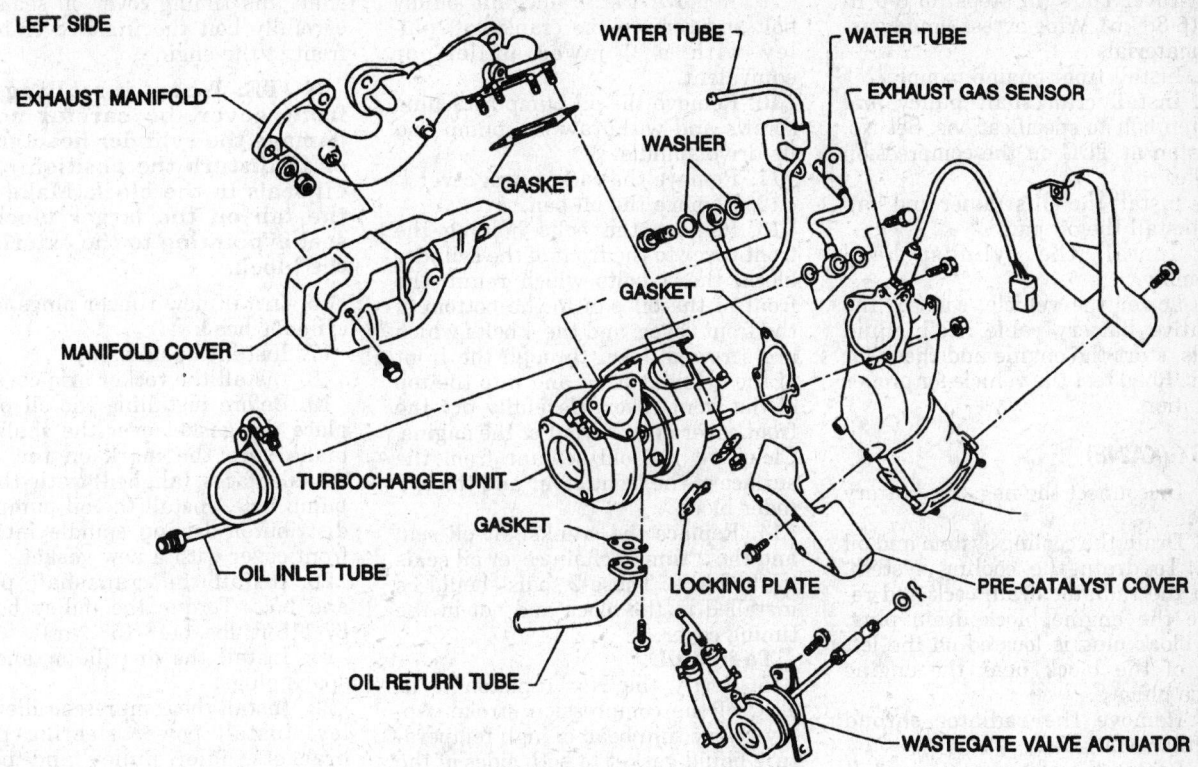

Left side turbocharger assembly — 300ZX

ing bracket from the block and keep the hoist tensioned to support the weight of the engine.

9. Disconnect the thermo switch connector wire from the thermostat housing and remove the water pump.

10. Loosen the timing chain tensioner mounting bolt and remove the timing chain tensioner and gasket from the front cover.

11. Remove the rocker arm cover and cover gasket.

12. Remove the spark plugs and set the No. 1 piston to TDC of the compression stroke. When the No. 1 piston is at TDC the crankshaft and camshaft keyways will be in the 12 o'clock position or the distributor rotor will point to the No. 1 cylinder. Do not disturb the engine once in this position.

13. Remove crankshaft pulley. Be careful not to lose the Woodruff key.

14. Loosen the retaining bolts and remove the front cover from the cylinder block. There are 6mm and 8mm size bolts. Note and record the location of each size bolt.

15. Clean all the old sealant from the surface of the front cover and the cylinder block.

16. Replace the front cover oil seal.
To install:

17. Verify the No. 1 piston is at TDC. Apply a bead of high tempera-

ture liquid gasket to both sides of the front cover. Place the front cover onto the cylinder block and install the retaining bolts. Torque the 6mm bolts to 5-6 ft. lbs. (6-8 Nm) and the 8mm bolts to 12-15 ft. lbs. (16-21 Nm).

NOTE: When installing the front cover, be careful not to damage the cylinder head gasket.

18. Mount the crankshaft pulley with the Woodruff key. Torque the pulley bolt to 98-112 ft. lbs. (132-152 Nm).

19. Install the spark plugs and connect the spark plug wires.

20. Install the rocker arm cover with a new gasket.

21. Install the timing chain tensioner onto the front cover with a new gasket. Torque the timing chain tensioner bolt to 9-14 ft. lbs. (13-19 Nm).

22. Install the water pump and connect the thermo-switch wire to the thermostat housing. Torque the water pump mounting bolts evenly to 5-6 ft. lbs. (6-8 Nm).

23. Slowly lower the engine and align the holes in the front engine mount bracket with the holes in the block. Install the bracket mounting bolts and torque them to 29-40 ft. lbs. (39-54 Nm).

24. Install the air cleaner.

25. Install the accessories, drive belts and adjust the tension.

26. Fill the crankcase and the cooling system to the proper levels.

27. Connect the negative battery cable.

1991-94 Sentra (GA16DE and SR20DE)1991-94 240SX (KA24DE) Altima (KA24DE)

1. Remove the negative battery cable.

2. Drain the engine oil and coolant.

3. Remove the cylinder head assembly.

4. Raise and support the vehicle safely. Remove the oil pan, oil strainer and baffle plate.

5. Remove the crankshaft pulley using a suitable puller. Removal of the radiator may be necessary to gain clearance.

6. Support the engine and remove the front engine mount.

7. Loosen the front cover bolts in 2 or 3 steps and remove the front cover.
To install:

8. Clean all mating surfaces of liquid gasket material.

9. Apply a continious bead of liquid gasket to the mating surface of the timing cover. Install the oil pump drive spacer and front cover. Tighten

front cover bolts (in steps) to 5-6 ft. lbs. (6-8 Nm). Wipe excess liquid gasket material.

10. Install front engine mount.

11. Install crankshaft pulley and tighten bolt to specifications. Set No. 1 piston at TDC on the compression stroke.

12. Install the oil strainer and baffle. Install the oil pan.

13. Install the cylinder head assembly.

14. Lower the vehicle, connect the negative battery cable, Refill fluid levels, start the engine and check for leaks. Road test the vehicle for proper operation.

240SX (KA24E)

1. Disconnect the negative battery cable.

2. Drain the cooling system and oil pan. To drain the cooling system, open the radiator drain cock and remove the engine block drain plug. The block plug is located on the left side of the block near the engine freeze plugs.

3. Remove the radiator shroud and the cooling fan.

4. Loosen the alternator drive belt adjusting screw and remove the drive belt.

5. Remove the power steering and air conditioning drive belts.

6. Remove the spark plugs and the distributor cap. Set the No. 1 piston to TDC of the compression stroke. Carefully remove the the distributor. Before removal, scribe alignment marks in the timing cover and flat portion of the oil pump/distributor drive spindle. This alignment is critical and if not done properly, it could cause difficulty is aligning the distributor and setting the timing.

7. Remove the power steering pump, idler pulley and the power steering brackets.

8. Remove the air conditioning compressor idler pulley.

9. Remove the crankshaft pulley bolt and remove the crankshaft pulley with a 2 jawed puller, or equivalent.

10. Remove the oil pump attaching screws and withdraw the pump and its drive spindle.

11. Remove the rocker arm cover.

12. Remove the oil pan.

13. Remove the bolts holding the front cover to the front of the cylinder block, the 4 bolts which retain the front of the oil pan to the bottom of the front cover, and the 4 bolts which are screwed down through the front of the cylinder head and into the top of the front cover. Carefully pry the front cover off the front of the engine. Clean all the old sealant from the surface of the front cover and the cylinder block.

14. Replace the crankshaft oil seal and the 2 timing chain cover oil seals in the block. These 2 seals should be installed in the block and not in the timing cover.

To install:

15. Verify the No. 1 piston is at TDC of the compression stroke. Apply a very thin bead of high temperature liquid gasket to both sides of the front cover and to where the cover mates with the cylinder head. Apply a light coating of grease to the crankshaft and timing cover oil seals and carefully bolt the front cover to the front of the engine.

NOTE: When installing the front cover, be careful not to damage the cylinder head gasket or to disturb the position of the oil seals in the block. Make sure the tab on the larger block oil seal is pointing to the exterior of the block.

16. Install new rubber plugs in the cylinder head.

17. Install the oil pan.

18. Install the rocker arm cover.

19. Before installing the oil pump, place the gasket over the shaft and make sure the mark on the drive spindle faces (aligned) with the oil pump hole. Install the oil pump and distributor driving spindle into the front cover with a new gasket.

20. Install the crankshaft pulley and bolt. Torque the pulley bolt to 87-116 ft. lbs. (118-157 Nm).

21. Install the distributor and the spark plugs.

22. Install the compressor idler pulley. Install power steering pump brackets, idler pulley and power steering pump. Install the drive belts and adjust the tension.

23. Install the radiator shroud and the cooling fan.

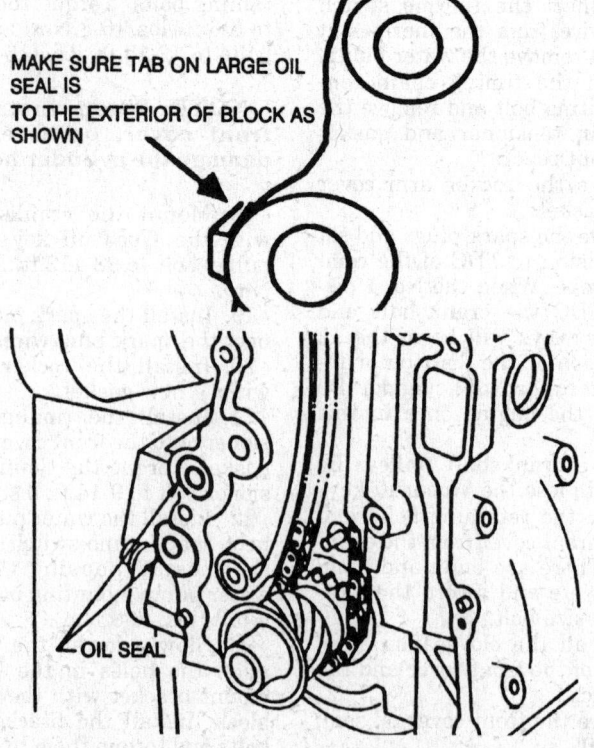

MAKE SURE TAB ON LARGE OIL SEAL IS TO THE EXTERIOR OF BLOCK AS SHOWN

OIL SEAL

Cylinder block timing chain cover seals on KA24E engine. Make sure tab on larger seal is positioned as shown

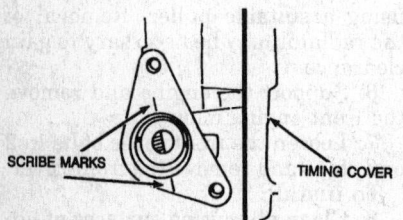

SCRIBE MARKS   TIMING COVER

Aligning the timing cover and distributor/oil pump drive spindle — KA24E engine

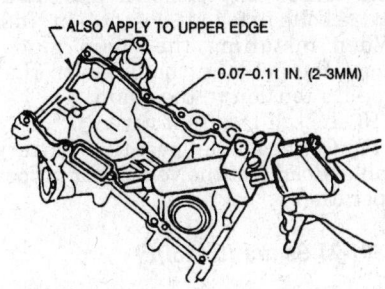

— ALSO APPLY TO UPPER EDGE

0.07–0.11 IN. (2–3MM)

Applying sealant to front cover — KA24E engine

24. Refill the cooling system and crankcase to the proper levels.

25. Connect the negative battery cable.

26. Start the engine, check/set the ignition timing and check for engine leaks. Road test the vehicle for proper operation.

1990-92 Stanza (KA24E)

1. Disconnect the negative battery cable.

2. Raise the front of the vehicle and support safely.

3. Remove the right front wheel.

4. Remove the dust cover and undercover.

5. Drain the oil pan.

6. Set the No. 1 piston at TDC of the compression stroke.

7. Remove the alternator and air conditioning compressor drive belts.

8. Remove the alternator and adjusting bar.

9. Remove the oil separator.

10. Remove the power steering pump pulley, pump stay and mounting bracket.

11. Discharge the air conditioning system and remove the compressor and mounting bracket.

12. Remove the crankshaft pulley and oil pump drive boss.

13. Remove the oil pan.

14. Remove the oil strainer mounting bolt.

15. Remove the bolts that attach the front cover to the head and the block.

16. Remove the rocker cover.

17. Support the engine with a suitable lifting device.

18. Unbolt the right side engine mount bracket from the block and lower the engine.

19. Remove the front cover.

20. Clean all the old sealant from the surface of the front cover and the cylinder block.

21. Replace the crankshaft oil seal and the 2 timing chain cover oil seals

in the block. These 2 seals should be installed in the block and not in the timing cover.

To install:

22. Verify the No. 1 piston is at TDC. Apply a very thin bead of high temperature liquid gasket to both sides of the front cover and to where the cover mates with the cylinder head. Apply a light coating of grease to the crankshaft and timing cover oil seals and carefully mount the front cover to the front of the engine.

NOTE: When installing the front cover, be careful not to damage the cylinder head gasket or to disturb the position of the oil seals in the block. Make sure the tab on the larger block oil seal is pointing to the exterior of the block.

23. Install new rubber plugs in the cylinder head.

24. Raise the engine and install the right engine mount bracket bolts. Torque the bolts to 58-65 ft. lbs. (78-88 Nm).

25. Install the rocker arm cover.

26. Install the front cover bolts.

27. Install the oil strainer mounting bolt.

28. Install the oil pan.

29. Install the oil pump drive boss and the crankshaft pulley. Torque the pulley bolt to 87-116 ft. lbs. (118-157 Nm).

30. Install the air conditioning compressor bracket and mount the compressor.

31. Install the power steering bracket, pump stay and power steering pump.

32. Install the oil separator.

33. Install the dust cover and undercover.

34. Mount the right front wheel and lower the vehicle.

35. Fill the crankcase to the proper level and charge the air conditioning system.

36. Make all the necessary engine adjustments.

1992-94 Maxima (VE30DE)

The oil pump is an integral part of the front cover.

1. Remove all accessory drive belts and the alternator.

2. Remove the cylinder heads.

3. Unbolt the engine from its mounts and raise the engine up from the body.

4. Remove the crankshaft damper-to-crankshaft bolt and the damper.

5. Drain the engine oil and remove the oil pan.

6. Remove the oil strainer-to-engine bolt, oil strainer-to-oil pump bolts and the strainer.

7. Remove the front cover-to-engine bolts and the front cover.

8. Remove the oil pump assembly-to-engine bolts, along with the oil strainer and remove the assembly from the engine.

9. Clean the gasket mating surfaces.

To Install:

10. Pack the oil pump full of petroleum jelly to prevent the pump from cavitating when the engine is started.

11. Apply a bead of liquid sealant to the front cover mating surfaces.

12. Install the front cover and torque the front cover-to-engine bolts to 4.6-6.1 ft. lbs. (6.3-8.3 Nm) except for bolt above oil filter housing and 12-15 ft. lbs. (16-21 Nm) for bolt above oil filter housing.

13. Using a new gasket, install the strainer and torque the strainer-to-front cover bolts to 12-15 ft. lbs. (16-21 Nm) and the strainer-to-engine bolt to 4.6-6.1 ft. lbs. (6.3-8.3 Nm).

14. Install the oil pan.

15. Install the cylinder heads.

16. Install the alternator and all drive belts. Reconnect the negative battery cable.

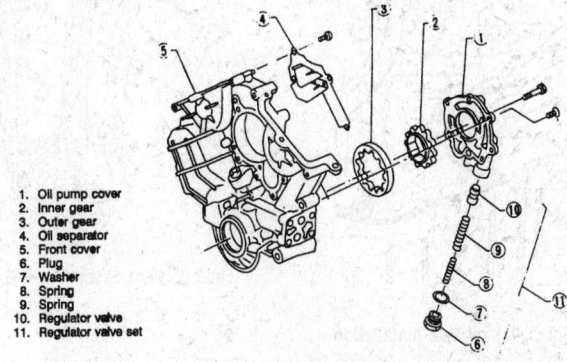

1. Oil pump cover
2. Inner gear
3. Outer gear
4. Oil separator
5. Front cover
6. Plug
7. Washer
8. Spring
9. Spring
10. Regulator valve
11. Regulator valve set

Exploded view of the oil pump assembly — VE30DE engine

17. Start engine, check ignition timing and check for oil leaks.

Front Cover Oil Seal

REPLACEMENT

1. Disconnect the negative battery cable.
2. Remove the crankshaft pulley.
3. Using a suitable tool, pry the oil seal from the front cover.

NOTE: When removing the oil seal, be careful not the gouge or scratch the seal bore or crankshaft surfaces.

4. Wipe the seal bore with a clean rag.
5. Lubricate the lip of the new seal with clean engine oil.
6. Install the seal into the front cover with a suitable seal installer.
7. Install the crankshaft pulley.
8. Connect the negative battery cable.

Timing Chain and Sprockets

REMOVAL AND INSTALLATION

1990 Pulsar and Sentra (GA16i)

1. Disconnect the negative battery cable.
2. Set the No. 1 piston at TDC of the compression stroke.
3. Remove the front cover.
4. If necessary, define the timing marks with chalk or paint to ensure proper alignment.
5. Hold the camshaft sprocket stationary with a spanner wrench or similar tool and remove the camshaft sprocket bolt.
6. Remove the chain guides.
7. Remove the camshaft sprocket.

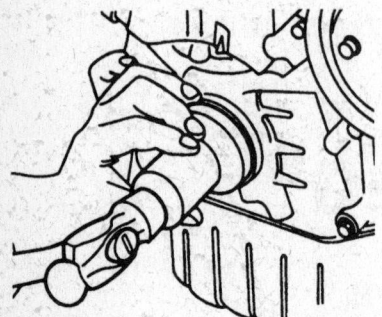

Timing chain front cover oil seal installation

8. Remove the oil pump spacer.
9. Remove the crankshaft sprocket and timing chain.

To install:
10. Verify that the No. 1 piston is at TDC of the compression stroke. The crankshaft keyways should be at the 12 o'clock position.
11. Install the camshaft sprocket, bolt and washer. The alignment mark must face towards the front. When installing the washer, place the non-chamfered side of the washer towards the face of camshaft sprocket. Tighten the bolt just enough to hold the sprocket in place.
12. Install the crankshaft sprocket making sure the alignment mark is facing the front.
13. Install the timing chain by aligning the silver links at the 12 o'clock and 6 o'clock positions on the chain with the timing marks on the crankshaft and camshaft sprockets. The number of links between the 2 silver links are the same for the left and the right sides of the chain, so either side of the chain may be used to align the sprocket timing marks.
14. Torque the camshaft sprocket bolt to 72-94 ft. lbs. (98-128 Nm) once the chain is in place and aligned.
15. Install the chain guides and tensioner. Use a new tensioner gasket

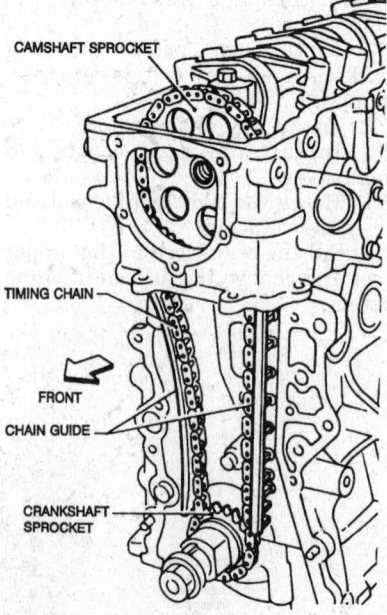

Timing chain assembly — GA16i engine

and torque the tensioner and chain guide bolts to 9-14 ft. lbs. (13-19 Nm). When installing the chain guide, move the guide in the direction that applies tension to the chain.
16. Install the front cover.
17. Connect the negative battery cable. Road test the vehicle for proper operation.

1991-94 Sentra (GA16DE)

1. Disconnect the negative battery cable. Relieve the fuel pressure.
2. Remove the cylinder head assembly.
3. Remove the idle sprocket shaft from the rear side.
4. Remove the upper timing chain assembly.
5. Remove the center member.
6. Remove the oil pan assembly, oil strainer and crankshaft pulley.
7. Support engine and remove the engine front mounting bracket.
8. Remove the front cover. One retaining bolt for the front cover assembly is located on the water pump.
9. Remove the idler sprocket.
10. Remove the lower timing chain assembly, oil pump drive spacer, chain guide, crankshaft sprocket.

To install:
11. Confirm that No. 1 piston is set at TDC on compression stroke. Install the chain guide.
12. Install crankshaft sprocket and lower timing chain. Set timing chain by aligning its mating mark with the one on the crankshaft sprocket. Make sure sprocket's mating mark faces engine front. The number of links between the alignment marks are the same for the left and right side.
13. Install the front cover assembly.
14. Install engine front mounting.
15. Install oil strainer, oil pan assembly and crankshaft pulley.
16. Install center member.
17. Set idler sprocket by aligning the mating mark on the larger sprocket with the silver mating mark on the lower timing chain.
18. Install upper timing chain and set it by aligning the mating mark on the smaller sprocket with the silver mating marks on the upper timing chain. Make sure sprocket marks face engine front.
19. Install idler sprocket shaft.
20. Install the cylinder head assembly.
21. Install all remaining components in reverse order of removal.
22. Connect the negative battery cable. Refill all fluid levels. Road test the vehicle for proper operation.

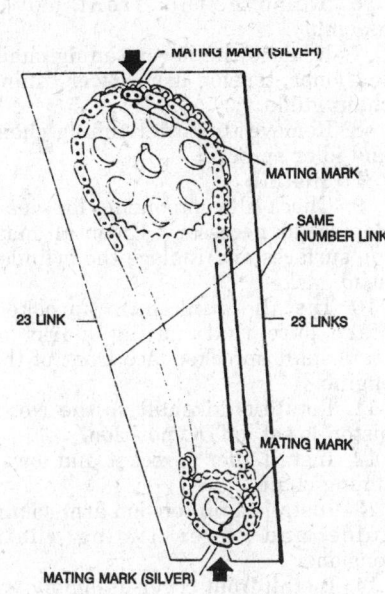

Timing chain and sprocket alignment marks — GA16i engine

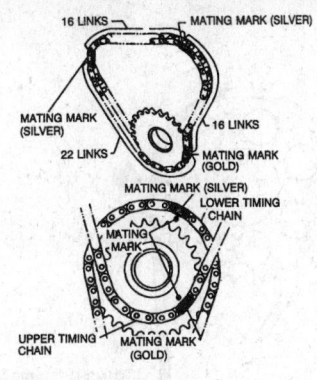

Timing chain installation — GA16DE engine

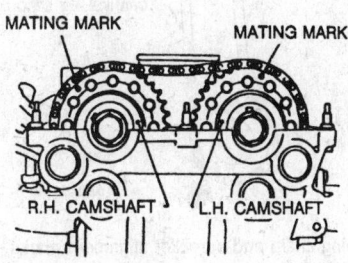

Timing chain installation — SR20DE engine

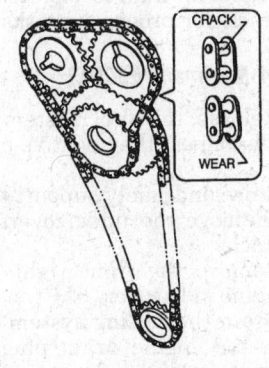

Timing chain assembly — GA16DE engine

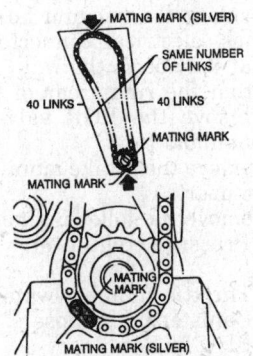

Timing chain installation — GA16DE engine

so the mating mark is inline with mating mark on crankshaft sprocket. The mating marks on timing chain for the camshaft sprockets should be silver. The mating mark on the timing chain for the crankshaft sprocket should be gold.

14. Install the timing chain and timing chain guides.

15. Install front engine mount.

16. Install the crankshaft pulley and set No. 1 piston at TDC on the compression stroke.

17. Install the oil strainer, baffle plate and oil pan.

18. Install the cylinder head, camshafts, oil tubes and baffles. Position the left camshaft keyway at 12 o'clock and the right camshaft keyway at 10 o'clock.

19. Install the camshaft sprockets by lining up the mating marks on the timing chain with the mating marks on the camshaft sprockets. Tighten the camshaft bolts to 101-116 ft. lbs. (137-157 Nm).

20. Install the timing chain guide and distributor. Ensure rotor is at 5 o'clock position.

21. Install the chain tensioner. Press the camshaft stopper down and the press-in sleeve until the hook can be engaged on the pin. When tensioner is bolted in position the hook will release automatically. Ensure the arrow on the outside faces the front of the engine.

22. Install all other components in reverse order of removal.

23. Connect the negative battery cable. Refill all fluid levels. Road test the vehicle for proper operation.

1991-94 Sentra (SR20DE)

1. Relieve the fuel system pressure and remove the negative battery cable.

2. Drain the coolant from the radiator and engine block. Remove the radiator.

3. Remove the right front wheel and engine side cover.

4. Remove the drive belts, water pump pulley, alternator and power steering pump.

5. Label and remove the vacuum hoses, fuel hoses and wire harness connectors.

6. Remove the cylinder head.

7. Raise and support the vehicle safely.

8. Remove the oil pan.

9. Remove the crankshaft pulley using a suitable puller.

10. Remove the engine front mount.

11. Remove the front cover.

12. Remove the timing chain guides and timing chain. Check the timing chain for excessive wear at the roller links. Replace the chain if necessary.

To install:

13. Install the crankshaft sprocket. Position the crankshaft so that No. 1 piston is set at TDC (keyway at 12 o'clock, mating mark at 4 o'clock) fit timing chain to crankshaft sprocket

1990 240SX and 1990-92 Stanza (KA24E)

1. Disconnect the negative battery cable.

2. Set the No. 1 piston at TDC of the compression stroke.

3. Remove the front cover.

4. If necessary, define the timing marks with chalk or paint to ensure proper alignment.

5. Hold the camshaft sprocket stationary with a spanner wrench or similar tool and remove the camshaft sprocket bolt.

6. Remove chain tensioner.

7. Remove the chain guides.

8. Remove the timing chain.

9. Remove the sprocket oil slinger, oil pump drive gear and crankshaft gear.

To install:

10. Install the crankshaft sprocket, oil pump drive gear and oil slinger onto the end of the crankshaft. Make

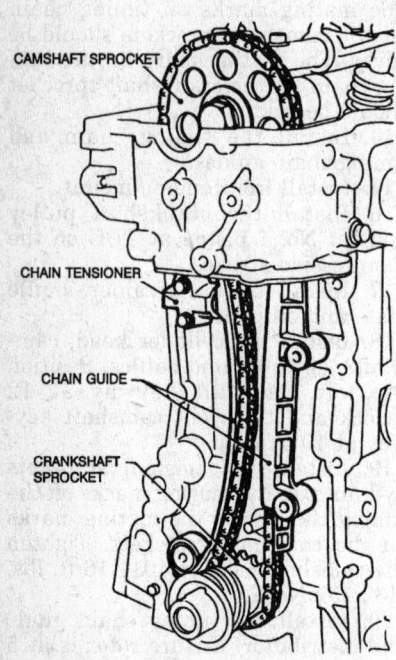

Timing chain installation — SR20DE engine

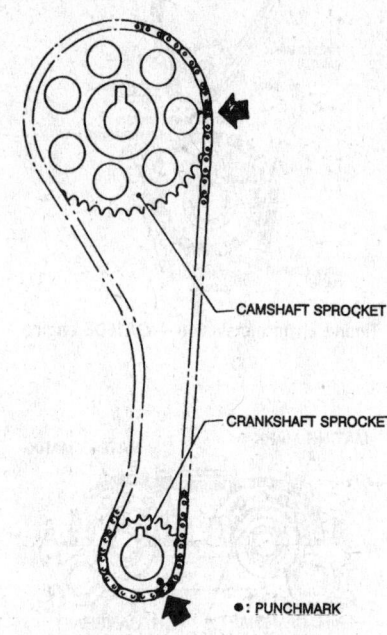

Timing chain and sprocket alignment marks — KA24E engine

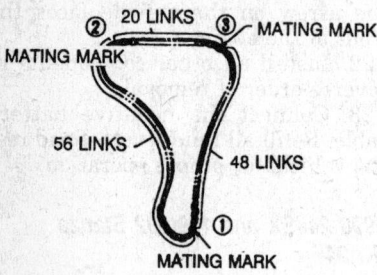

Timing chain assembly — KA24E engine

sure the crankshaft sprocket timing marks face toward the front.

11. Install the camshaft sprocket, bolt and washer. The alignment mark must face towards the front. Tighten the bolt just enough to hold the sprocket in place.

12. Verify that the No. 1 piston is at TDC of the compression stroke. The crankshaft keyways should be at the 12 o'clock position.

13. Install the timing chain by aligning the marks on the chain with the marks on the crankshaft and camshaft sprockets. Torque the camshaft sprocket bolt to 87-116 ft.

lbs. (118-157 Nm) once the timing chain is in place and aligned.

14. Install the chain tensioner and chain guide.

15. Install the front cover.

16. Connect the negative battery cable.

Altima and 1991-94 240SX (KA24DE)

1. Release the fuel system pressure.

2. Disconnect the negative battery cable and drain the cooling system. Drain engine oil.

3. Remove the cylinder head assembly.

4. Remove the oil pan.

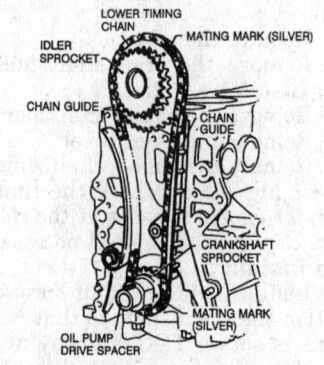

Timing chain installation — KA24DE engine

5. Remove the oil strainer, crankshaft pulley.

6. Remove the front cover assembly.

7. Remove the lower timing chain tensioner, tension arm, lower timing chain guide.

8. Remove the lower timing chain and idler sprocket.

To install:

9. Check all components for wear. Replace as necessary. Clean all mating surfaces and replace the cylinder head gasket.

10. Install crankshaft sprocket. Make sure that mating marks of crankshaft sprocket face front of the engine.

11. Rotate crankshaft so the No. 1 piston is set a TDC position.

12. Install idler sprocket and lower timing chain.

13. Install chain tension arm, chain guide and lower timing chain tensioner.

14. Install front cover assembly.

15. Install crankshaft pulley, oil strainer and oil pan.

16. Install the cylinder head assembly.

17. Install all remaining components in reverse order of removal.

18. Connect the negative battery cable. Refill all fluid levels. Road test the vehicle for proper operation.

1992-94 Maxima (VE30DE)

1. Release the fuel system pressure. Disconnect the negative battery cable.

2. Raise and safely support the vehicle. Remove the undercovers from the vehicle.

3. Remove the front right wheel and engine side cover.

4. Drain the cooling system by removing the engine drain plugs and opening the radiator drain cock.

5. Remove the radiator.

6. Remove the air duct from the intake manifold.

7. Remove the blow-by pipe.

8. Remove the vacuum hoses, the fuel lines, electrical connectors and etc., that may be in the way.

9. From the right rear of the engine, remove the EGR valve-to-exhaust manifold tube.

10. Remove the intake manifold collector supports.

11. Remove the following hoses:

   a. Pressure regulator vacuum hose

   b. Throttle chamber water hoses

   c. Canister purge hose

   d. Blow-by hose

12. Remove the intake manifold collector.

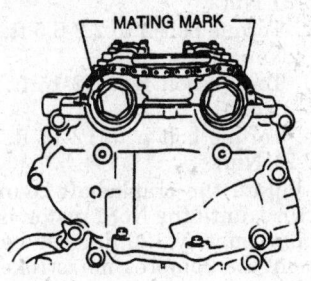

Timing chain installation — KA24DE engine

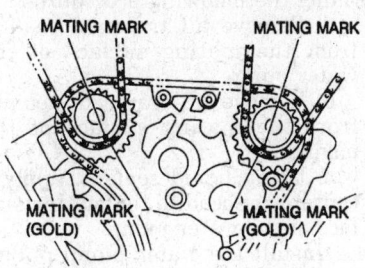

Timing chain installation — VE30DE engine

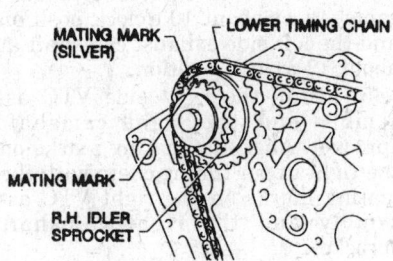

Timing chain installation — VE30DE engine

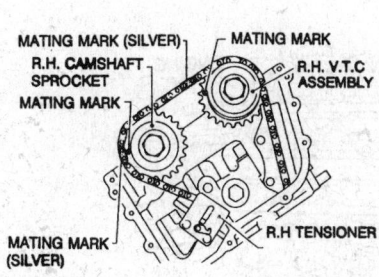

Timing chain installation — VE30DE engine

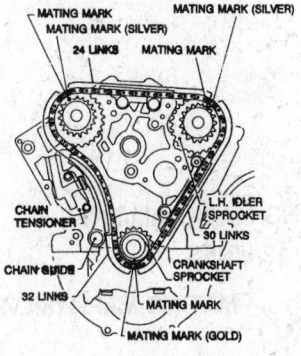

Timing chain installation — VE30DE engine

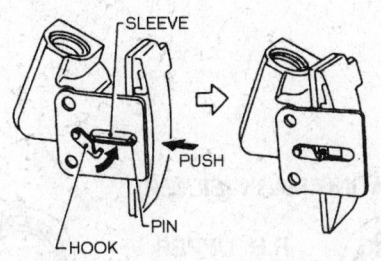

Timing chain tensioner installation — VE30DE engine

24. Remove the crank angle sensor. Remove the timing chain tensioners from each upper timing chain.

25. Using a backup wrench to secure the intake camshaft, remove the intake camshaft sprocket-to-camshaft bolts, the VTC assemblies and the intake camshaft sprockets.

26. Remove the both cylinder heads. Remove the water pipe.

27. Remove the water pump pulley and the water pump.

28. Remove the oil pan, the crankshaft pulley, the oil strainer and the oil filter bracket.

29. Remove the front cover, the alternator adjusting bar and the upper timing chains.

30. Remove the lower timing chain guides, the idler sprockets and the lower timing chain.

31. Inspect the timing chains for cracks and/or excessive wear at the roller links; if necessary, replace the timing chain(s).

To install:

32. Install the crankshaft sprocket on the crankshaft. Make sure the No. 1 cylinder is at the TDC of it's compression stroke.

33. Install the right idler sprocket and timing chain guides.

34. Position the lower timing chain on the right idler sprocket by aligning the mating mark on the right idler sprocket with the silver mating mark on the lower timing chain.

35. Install the left idler sprocket with the lower timing chain; align the mating marks on the lower timing chain with the mating marks on the left idler sprocket and crankshaft sprocket. Install the chain guide and the chain tensioner.

36. Position the upper timing chains on the idler sprockets by aligning the mating marks on the idler sprockets with the gold mating marks on the upper timing chains.

37. Install the oil pump drive spacer, the front cover and the alternator adjusting bar by performing the following procedures:

  a. Remove all traces of sealant from the mating surfaces of the front cover and the engine block.

  b. Using liquid sealant, apply a continuous bead to the mating surface of the front cover.

  c. Wipe excessive sealant from the cylinder head mounting surfaces.

38. Install the oil filter bracket, the oil strainer, the crankshaft pulley and the oil pan.

39. Make sure the No. 1 cylinder is on the TDC of it's compression stroke.

13. Remove the ignition coils and the spark plugs.

14. Remove the IAA unit and heater pipe. Remove the fuel injector rail assembly.

15. From the front of the intake manifold, remove the right VTC solenoid valve.

16. Remove the intake manifold.

17. Remove the drive belts, the air conditioning compressor and the alternator.

18. Remove the air conditioning compressor bracket and the alternator bracket.

19. Remove the idler pulley bracket and the dipstick tube.

20. Remove the left exhaust manifold. Remove the power steering pump and it's bracket.

21. Remove the right exhaust manifold. Remove the rocker arm covers.

22. Working between the intake and exhaust camshafts, of each cylinder head, remove the upper timing chain guides.

23. Rotate the crankshaft to position the No. 1 cylinder on TDC of it's compression stroke.

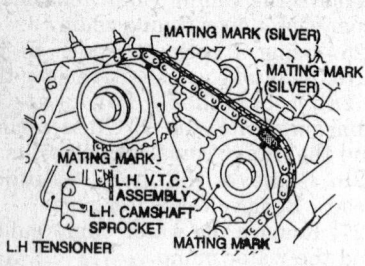

Timing chain installation — VE30DE engine

Water pipe bolts tightening procedure:

1. Tighten A and B bolts to finger tight
2. Tighten C bolts to 12–15 ft. lbs. (16–21 Nm)
3. Tighten A bolts to 2.2–6.5 ft. lbs. (3–9 Nm)
4. Tighten B bolts to 12–15 ft. lbs. (16–21 Nm)
5. Tighten A bolts to 12–15 ft. lbs. (16–21 Nm)

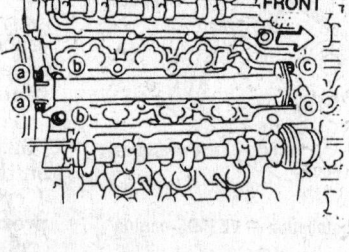

Water pipe torque procedure — VE30DE engine

40. Install the water pump by performing the following procedures:

a. Remove all traces of sealant from the mating surface of the water pump.

b. Remove all traces of sealant from the mating surface of the engine.

c. Using liquid sealant, apply a continuous bead to the mating surface of the water pump.

41. Install the water pump pulley. Install the water pipe by performing the following procedures:

a. Torque bolt **a** and **b** finger-tight.

b. Torque bolt **c** to 12–15 ft. lbs. (16–21 Nm).

c. Torque bolt **a** to 2.2–6.5 ft. lbs. (3–9 Nm).

d. Torque bolt **b** to 12–15 ft. lbs. (16–21 Nm).

e. Torque bolt **a** to 12–15 ft. lbs. (16–21 Nm).

42. Rotate the crankshaft counterclockwise, until the No. 1 piston is set at approximately 120 degrees before TDC on the compression stroke, to prevent interference of the valves and pistons.

43. Install the cylinder heads.

44. Install the camshafts, the camshaft brackets and the rocker arms. Position the right side exhaust camshaft at about 10 o'clock position and the left side exhaust camshaft at about 12 o'clock position.

45. Install the right side VTC assembly and the right camshaft sprocket. Align the mating marks on the right upper timing chain with the mating marks on the right VTC assembly and the right camshaft sprocket.

46. Install the right timing chain tensionser. Before installing the chain tensioner, press in sleeve until the hook can be engaged on the pin;

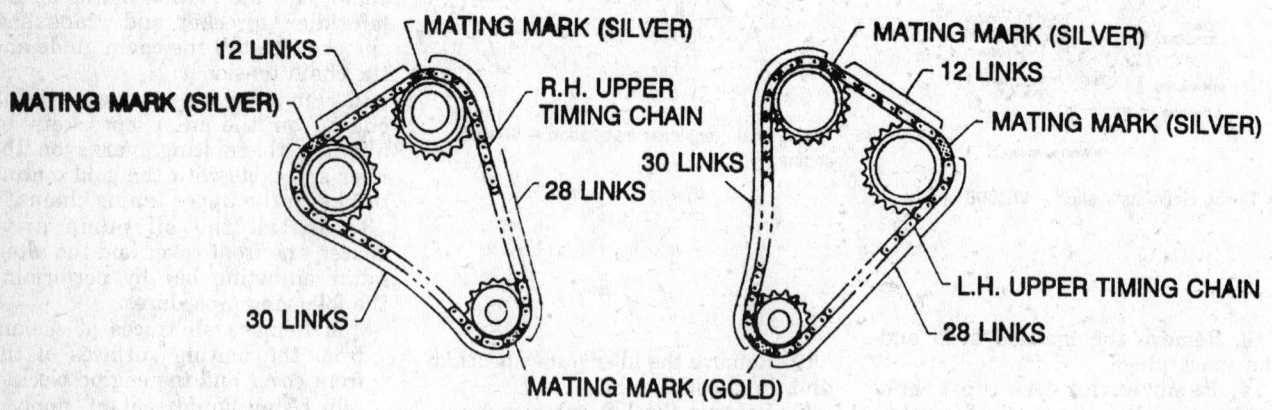

Timing chain alignment — VE30DE engine

make sure the hook used to retain the chain tensioner is released.

NOTE: There are 2 types of chain tensioners; be careful not to install the left chain tensioner onto the right cylinder head.

47. Rotate the crankshaft clockwise to set the No. 1 piston at the TDC of it's compression stroke.

48. Install the left side VTC assembly and the left camshaft sprocket. Align the mating marks on the left upper timing chain with the mating marks on the left VTC assembly and the left camshaft sprocket.

49. Install the left chain tensioner; make sure the upper timing chains are in the correct positions.

50. Install the crank angle sensor; make sure the position of the camshaft and rotor position of the crank angle sensor are aligned.

51. Install the upper front covers. Install the upper chain guides on both cylinder heads. Install the rocker arm covers.

52. Install any parts removed in the reverse order of removal. When installing the VTC solenoid valve, always use new O-rings and lubricate the O-rings with engine oil.

Timing Belt Front Cover

REMOVAL AND INSTALLATION

VG30E Engines

1. Disconnect the negative battery cable.
2. Drain the cooling system.
3. Remove the engine undercovers.
4. Remove the radiator shroud and fan.
5. Remove the power steering, alternator and air conditioning compressor drive belts.
6. Remove the suction pipe bracket and disconnect the lower coolant hose from the suction pipe.
7. Remove compressor drive belt idler bracket.
8. Set No. 1 cylinder at TDC of the compression stroke (necessary for timing belt removal).
9. Remove the crankshaft pulley.
10. Remove the front upper and lower belt covers and gaskets.
To install:
11. Install the upper and lower timing belt covers with new gaskets. Torque the covers bolts to 2-4 ft. lbs. (3-5 Nm).
12. Install the crankshaft pulley. Torque the pully bolt to 90-98 ft. lbs. (123-132 Nm).

13. Install the compressor drive belt idler bracket.
14. Connect the lower coolant hose to the suction pipe and install the suction pipe bracket.
15. Install and tension the drive belts.
16. Install the radiator fan and shroud.
17. Install the engine undercovers.
18. Fill the cooling system to the proper level.
19. Connect the negative battery.

VG30DE and VG30DETT Engines

1. Disconnect the negative battery cable.
2. Remove the engine undercover.
3. Drain the cooling system.
4. Remove the radiator.
5. Remove the drive belts.
6. Remove the cooling fan and cooling fan coupling.
7. Remove the crankshaft pulley bolt.
8. Remove the starter and lock the flywheel ring gear using a suitable locking device. This is done to prevent the crankshaft gear from turning during REMOVAL AND INSTALLATION.
9. Remove the crankshaft pulley using a suitable puller.
10. Remove the water inlet and outlet housings.
11. Remove the timing belt covers and gaskets.
To install:
12. Install the timing belt covers with new gaskets. Torque the cover bolts to 2-4 ft. lbs. (3-5 Nm).
13. Install the water inlet and outlet housings with new gaskets.
14. Install the crankshaft pulley. Torque the pulley bolt to 159-174 ft. lbs. (21-235 Nm).
15. Remove the flywheel locking device and install the starter.
16. Install the cooling fan and cooling fan coupling.
17. Install and tension the drive belts.
18. Install the radiator.
19. Fill the cooling system to the proper level.
20. Connect the negative battery cable.

VG30E (1990-92 MAXIMA) Engine

1. Disconnect the negative battery cable.
2. Raise and support the front of the vehicle safely.
3. Remove the engine undercovers.
4. Drain the cooling system.
5. Remove the right front wheel.
6. Remove the engine side cover.

7. Remove the alternator, power steering and air conditioning compressor drive belts from the engine. When removing the power steering drive belt and loosen the idler pulley from the right side wheel housing.
8. Remove the upper radiator and water inlet hoses.
9. Remove the water pump pulley.
10. Remove the idler bracket of the compressor drive belt.
11. Remove the crankshaft pulley with a suitable puller.
12. Remove the upper and lower timing belt covers and gaskets.
To install:
13. Install the upper and lower timing belt covers with new gaskets.
14. Install the crankshaft pulley. Torque the pulley bolt to 90-98 ft. lbs. (123-132 Nm).
15. Install the compressor drive belt idler bracket.
16. Install the water pump pulley and install the upper radiator and water inlet hoses.
17. Install the drive belts.
18. Install the engine side cover.
19. Mount the front right wheel.
20. Install the engine undercovers.
21. Lower the vehicle.
22. Fill the cooling system and connect the negative battery cable.

Timing Belt and Tensioner

REMOVAL AND INSTALLATION

VG30E Engines

1. Disconnect the negative battery cable.
2. Drain the cooling system.
3. Remove the engine undercovers.
4. Remove the radiator shroud and fan.
5. Remove the power steering, alternator and air conditioning compressor drive belts.
6. Remove the suction pipe bracket and disconnect the lower coolant hose from the suction pipe.
7. Remove the spark plugs.
8. Set No. 1 cylinder at TDC of the compression stroke.
9. Remove the crankshaft pulley.
10. Remove the front upper and lower belt covers and gaskets.
11. Using chalk or paint, mark the relationship of the timing belt to the camshaft and the camshaft sprockets. Also mark the timing belt's direction of rotation. Align the punch mark on the left hand camshaft pulley with the mark on the upper rear timing belt cover. Align the punchmark on the crankshaft with

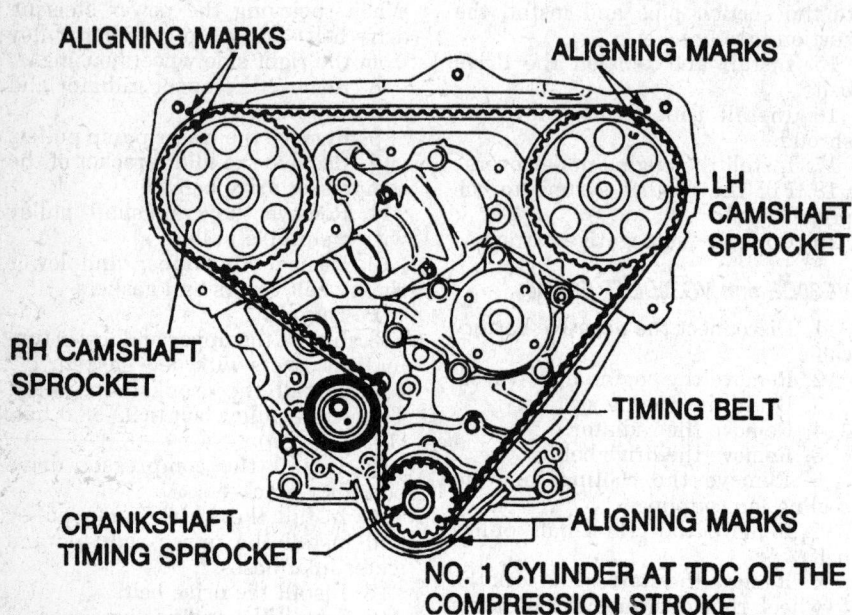

ALIGNING MARKS

ALIGNING MARKS

LH CAMSHAFT SPROCKET

RH CAMSHAFT SPROCKET

TIMING BELT

CRANKSHAFT TIMING SPROCKET

ALIGNING MARKS

NO. 1 CYLINDER AT TDC OF THE COMPRESSION STROKE

Timing belt installation and timing mark alignment — VG30E engines

the notch on the oil pump housing. Temporarily install the crankshaft pulley bolt to allow for crankshaft rotation.

12. Loosen the timing belt tensioner and return spring then remove the timing belt. Check that the tensioner spring turns smoothly and check the tensioner spring for wear.

To install:

13. Before installing the timing belt confirm that No. 1 cylinder is at TDC on its compression stroke. Install tensioner and tensioner spring. If stud is removed, apply locking sealant to threads before installing.

14. Swing the tensioner fully clockwise with hexagon wrench and temporarily tighten locknut.

15. Point the arrow on the timing belt toward the front belt cover. Align the white lines on the timing belt with the punch marks on all 3 pulleys.

NOTE: There are 133 total timing belt teeth. If timing belt is installed correctly, there will be 40 teeth between left hand and right hand camshaft sprocket timing marks. There will be 43 teeth between left hand camshaft sprocket and crankshaft sprocket timing marks.

16. Loosen tensioner locknut, keeping tensioner steady with an Allen wrench.

17. Swing tensioner 70-80 degrees clockwise with the Allen wrench and temporarily tighten locknut.

18. Install the spark plugs. Turn crankshaft clockwise 2-3 times, then slowly set No. 1 cylinder at TDC on its compression stroke.

19. Push middle of timing belt between right hand camshaft sprocket and tensioner pulley with a force of 22 ft. lbs.

20. Loosen tensioner locknut, keeping tensioner steady with the Allen wrench.

21. Insert a 0.138 in. (0.35mm) thick and 0.5 in. (12.7mm) wide feeler gauge between the bottom of tensioner pulley and timing belt. Turn crankshaft clockwise and position gauge completely between tensioner pulley and timing belt. The timing belt will move about 2.5 teeth.

22. Tighten tensioner locknut, keeping tensioner steady with the Allen wrench.

23. Turn crankshaft clockwise or counterclockwise and remove the gauge.

24. Rotate the engine 3 times, then set No. 1 at TDC on its compression stroke.

25. Timing belt deflection is 0.512-0.571 in. (13.0-14.5mm) at 22 lbs. of pressure. If it is out of specified range, readjust the timing belt.

26. Install the upper and lower timing belt covers and complete the remainder of the installation in reverse of the removal procedure.

VG30DE and VG30DETT Engines

1. Disconnect the negative battery cable.

2. Remove the engine undercover.

3. Drain the cooling system.

4. Remove the radiator.

5. Remove the drive belts.

6. Remove the cooling fan and cooling fan coupling.

7. Remove the crankshaft pulley bolt.

8. Remove the starter and lock the flywheel ring gear using a suitable locking device. This is done to prevent the crankshaft gear from turning during REMOVAL AND INSTALLATION.

9. Remove the crankshaft pulley using a suitable puller, then remove the locking device.

10. Remove the water inlet and outlet housings.

11. Remove the timing belt covers and gaskets.

12. Install a suitable 6mm stopper bolt in the tenioner arm of the auto tensioner so the length of the pusher does not change.

13. Set the No. 1 piston at TDC of the compression stroke.

14. Remove the auto-tensioner and the timing belt.

To install:

15. Check the auto-tensioner for oil leaks in the pusher rod and diaphragm. If oil is evident, replace the auto-tensioner assembly.

16. Verify that the No. 1 piston is at TDC of the compression stroke.

17. Align the timing marks on the camshaft and crankshaft sprockets with the timing marks on the rear timing belt cover and the oil pump housing.

18. Remove all the spark plugs.

19. With a feeler gauge, check the clearance between the tensioner arm and the pusher of the auto-tensioner. The clearance should be 0.16 in. (4mm) with a slight drag on the feeler gauge. If the clearance is not as specified, mount the tensioner in a vise and adjust the clearance. When the clearance is set, insert the stop-

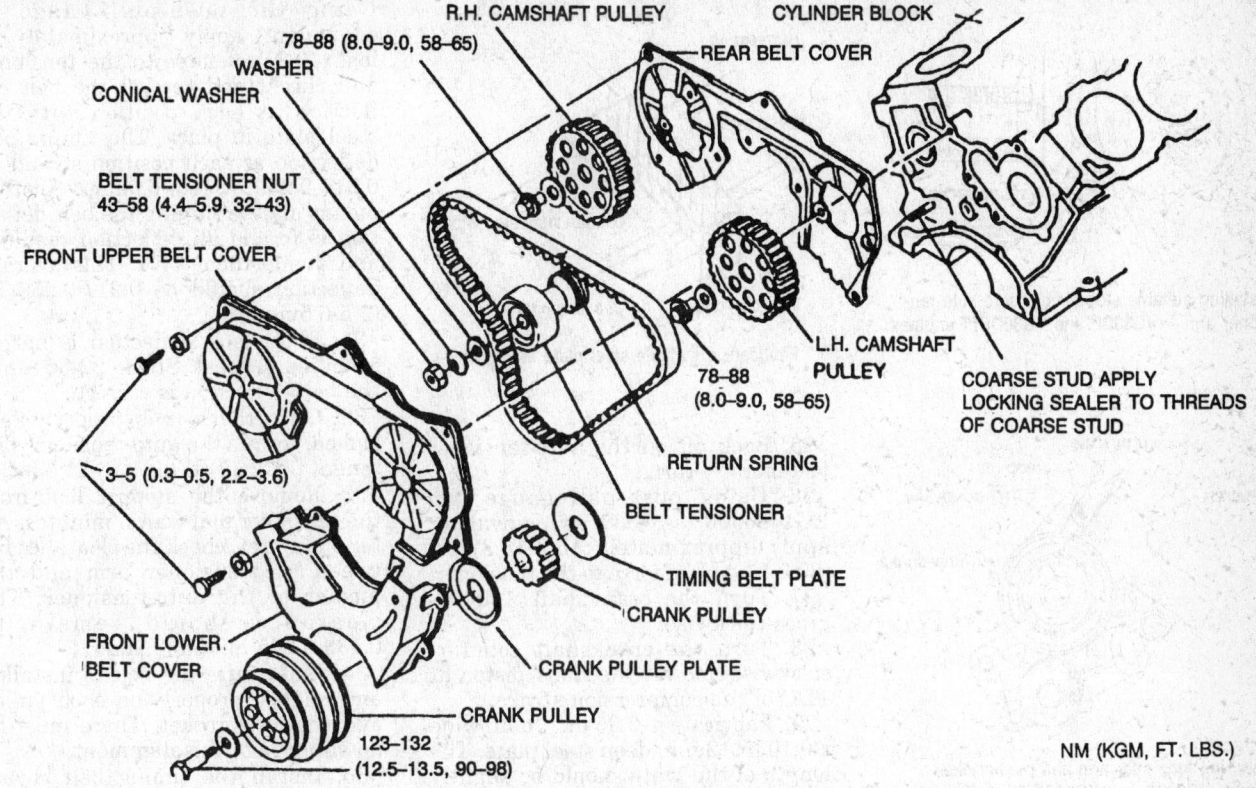

R.H. CAMSHAFT PULLEY

CYLINDER BLOCK

REAR BELT COVER

78–88 (8.0–9.0, 58–65)

WASHER

CONICAL WASHER

BELT TENSIONER NUT
43–58 (4.4–5.9, 32–43)

FRONT UPPER BELT COVER

L.H. CAMSHAFT PULLEY

78–88
(8.0–9.0, 58–65)

COARSE STUD APPLY
LOCKING SEALER TO THREADS
OF COARSE STUD

3–5 (0.3–0.5, 2.2–3.6)

RETURN SPRING

BELT TENSIONER

TIMING BELT PLATE

CRANK PULLEY

FRONT LOWER
BELT COVER

CRANK PULLEY PLATE

CRANK PULLEY

123–132
(12.5–13.5, 90–98)

NM (KGM, FT. LBS.)

Timing belt assembly — VG30E engines

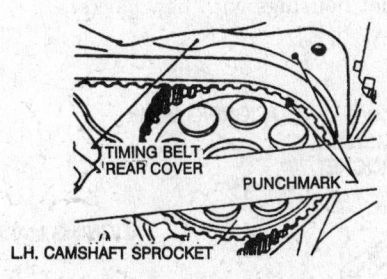

TIMING BELT
REAR COVER

PUNCHMARK

L.H. CAMSHAFT SPROCKET

LH camshaft sprocket timing belt alignment
marks — VG30E engines

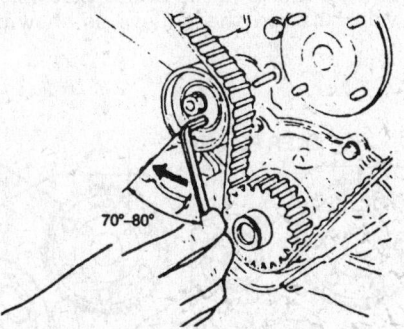

70°–80°

Swing the tensioner 70-80 degrees clockwise

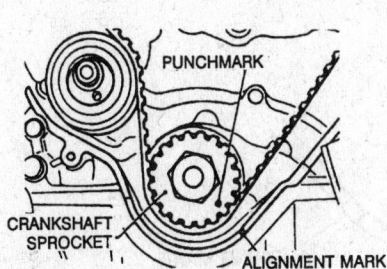

PUNCHMARK

CRANKSHAFT
SPROCKET

ALIGNMENT MARK

Crankshaft sprocket timing belt alignment
marks — VG30E engines

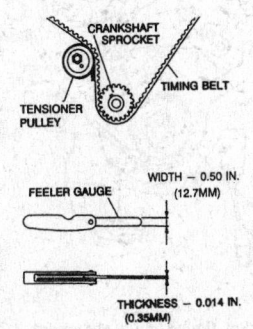

CRANKSHAFT
SPROCKET

TIMING BELT

TENSIONER
PULLEY

FEELER GAUGE

WIDTH – 0.50 IN.
(12.7MM)

THICKNESS – 0.014 IN.
(0.35MM)

Checking timing belt adjustment with a feeler
gauge

per bolt into the tensioner arm to retain the adjustment.

NOTE: When adjusting the clearance, do not push the tensioner arm with the stopper bolt fitted, because damage to the threaded portion of the bolt will result.

20. Mount the auto-tensioner and tighten nuts and bolts by hand.
21. Install the timing belt. Ensure the timing sprockets are free of oil and water. Do not bend or twist the timing belt. Align the white lines on the belt with the timing marks on the camshaft and crankshaft sprockets. Point the arrow on the belt towards the front.
22. Push the auto-tensioner slightly towards the timing belt to prevent the belt from slipping. At the same time, turn the crankshaft 10 degrees clockwise and torque the tensioner fasteners to 12-15 ft. lbs. (16-21 Nm).

NOTE: Do not push the tensioner too hard because it will create excessive tension on the belt.

23. Turn the crankshaft 120 degrees counterclockwise.
24. Turn the crankshaft clockwise and set the No. 1 piston at TDC of the compression stroke.

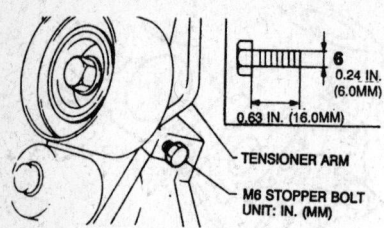

Installing suitable stopper bolt into auto ten-sioner arm — VG30DE and VG30DETT engines

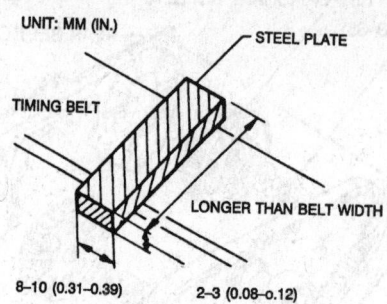

Fabricate a suitable steel plate as shown

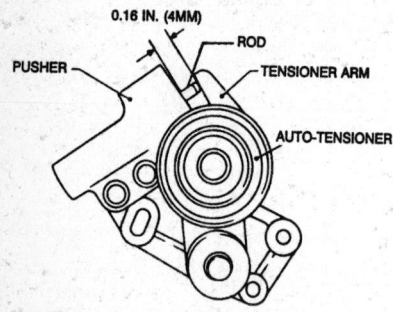

Checking tensioner arm and pusher clear-ance — VG30DE and VG30DETT engines

25. Back off on the auto-tensioner fasteners ½ turn.

26. Using push-pull gauge No. EG1486000 (J-38387) or equivalent, apply approximately 15.2-18.3 lbs. (67.7-81.4 N) of force to the tensioner.

27. Turn the crankshaft 120 degrees clockwise.

28. Turn the crankshaft counterclockwise and set the No. 1 piston at TDC of the compression stroke.

29. Fabricate a 0.35 in. (9mm) wide x 0.10 in. (2mm) deep steel plate. The length of the plate should be slightly longer than the width of the belt.

30. Set the steel plate at positions **A**, **B**, **C** and **D** of the timing belt midway between the pulleys as shown.

Using the push-pull gauge or equivalent, apply approximately 11 lbs. (49 N) of force to the tensioner and check (and record) the belt deflection at each position with the steel plate in place. The timing belt deflection at each position should be 0.217-0.256 in. (5.5-6.5mm). Another means of determining the belt deflection is to add all deflection readings and divide them by 4. This average deflection should be 0.217-0.256 in. (5.5-6.5mm).

31. If the belt deflection is not as specified, repeat Steps 22-30 until the belt deflection is correct.

32. Once the belt is properly tensioned, torque the auto-tensioner fasteners to 12-15 ft. lbs. (16-21 Nm).

33. Remove the stopper bolt from the tensioner and wait 5 minutes. After 5 minutes, check the clearance between the tensioner arm and the pusher of the auto-tensioner. The clearance should remain at 0.138-0.205 in. (3.5-5.2mm).

34. Make sure the belt is installed and aligned properly on each pulley and timing sprocket. There must be no slippage or misalignment.

35. Install the timing belt covers with new gaskets. Torque the covers bolts to 2-4 ft. lbs. (3-5 Nm).

36. Install the water inlet and outlet housings with new gaskets.

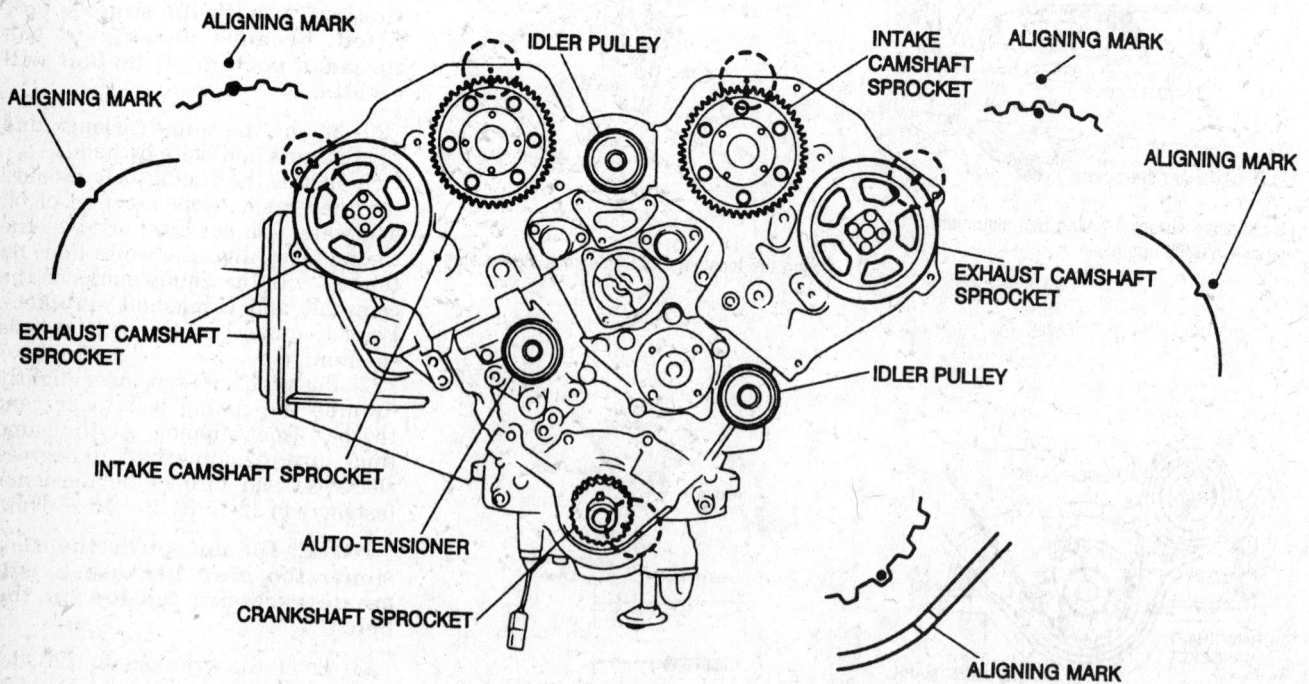

Camshaft and crankshaft sprocket timing mark alignment — VG30DE and VG30DETT engines

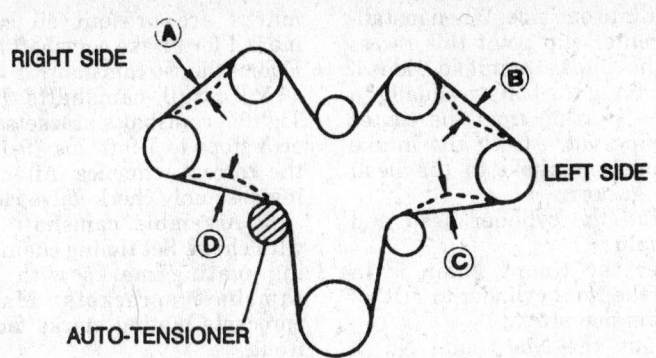

Set the steel plate at each position on the belt

37. Install the crankshaft pulley. Torque the pulley bolt to 159-174 ft. lbs. (21-235 Nm).

38. Remove the flywheel locking device and install the starter.

39. Install the cooling fan and cooling fan coupling.

40. Install and tension the drive belts.

41. Install the radiator.

42. Fill the cooling system to the proper level.

43. Connect the negative battery cable.

VG30E (1990-92 MAXIMA) Engine

1. Disconnect the negative battery cable.

2. Raise and support the front of the vehicle safely.

3. Remove the engine undercovers.

4. Drain the cooling system.

5. Remove the front right side wheel.

6. Remove the engine side cover.

7. Remove the alternator, power steering and air conditioning compressor drive belts from the engine. When removing the power steering drive belt, loosen the idler pulley from the right side wheel housing.

8. Remove the upper radiator and water inlet hoses.

9. Remove the water pump pulley.

10. Remove the idler bracket of the compressor drive belt.

11. Remove the crankshaft pulley with a suitable puller.

12. Remove the upper and lower timing belt covers and gaskets.

13. Rotate the engine with a socket wrench on the crankshaft pulley bolt to align the punchmark on the left hand camshaft pulley with the mark on the upper rear timing belt cover; align the punchmark on the crankshaft with the notch on the oil pump housing; temporarily install the crankshaft pulley bolt to allow for crankshaft rotation.

14. Use a hex wrench to turn the belt tensioner clockwise and tighten the tensioner locknut just enough to hold the tensioner in position. Then, remove the timing belt.

To install:

15. Before installing the timing belt, confirm that No. 1 cylinder is at TDC on its compression stroke. Install tensioner and tensioner spring. If stud is removed apply locking sealant to threads before installing.

16. Swing tensioner fully clockwise with hexagon wrench and temporarily tighten locknut.

17. Point the arrow on the timing belt toward the front belt cover. Align the white lines on the timing belt with the punch marks on all 3 pulleys.

NOTE: There are 133 total timing belt teeth. If timing belt is installed correctly there will be 40 teeth between left hand and right hand camshaft sprocket timing marks. There will be 43 teeth between left hand camshaft sprocket and crankshaft sprocket timing marks.

18. Loosen tensioner locknut, keeping tensioner steady with a hexagon wrench.

19. Swing tensioner 70-80 degrees clockwise with hexagon wrench and temporarily tighten locknut.

20. Turn crankshaft clockwise 2-3 times, then slowly set No. 1 cylinder at TDC of the compression stroke.

21. Push middle of timing belt between right hand camshaft sprocket and tensioner pulley with a force of 22 lbs. (10 Kg).

22. Loosen tensioner locknut, keeping tensioner steady with a hexagon wrench.

23. Insert a 0.138 in. (0.35mm) thick and 0.5 in. (12.7mm) wide feeler gauge between the bottom of tensioner pulley and timing belt. Turn crankshaft clockwise and position gauge completely between ten-

sioner pulley and timing belt. The timing belt will move about 2.5 teeth.

24. Tighten tensioner locknut, keeping tensioner steady with a hexagon wrench.

25. Turn crankshaft clockwise or counterclockwise and remove the gauge.

26. Rotate the engine 3 times, then set No. 1 at TDC on its compression stroke. Check timing belt tension, the reference valve is 0.51-0.059 in. (13-15mm) deflection with a 22 lbs. (10 Kg) force applied.

27. Install the upper and lower timing belt covers with new gaskets.

28. Install the crankshaft pulley. Torque the pulley bolt to 90-98 ft. lbs. (123-132 Nm).

29. Install the compressor drive belt idler bracket.

30. Install the water pump pulley and torque the nuts to 12-15 ft. lbs. (16-21 Nm). Install the upper radiator and water inlet hoses.

31. Install the drive belts.

32. Install the engine side cover.

33. Mount the front right wheel.

34. Install the engine undercovers.

35. Lower the vehicle.

36. Fill the cooling system and connect the negative battery cable.

Timing Sprockets

REMOVAL AND INSTALLATION

1. Disconect the negative battery cable.

2. Set the No. 1 piston to TDC of the compression stroke.

3. Remove the timing belt covers.

4. Remove the timing belt.

5. Using a suitable spanner wrench and a socket wrench, remove the camshaft pulley bolt and washer.

6. Using a suitable puller, remove the crankshaft gear and timing belt plates from the crankshaft. Be careful not to gouge or scratch the surface of the crankshaft when removing the gear.

7. Inspect the timing gear teeth for wear and replace as necessary.

To install:

8. Install the crankshaft gear with new Woodruff key.

9. Install the camshaft sprockets.

NOTE: On VG30E engines, the right hand and left hand camshaft pulleys are different. Install them in their correct positions. The right hand pulley has an R3 identification mark and the left hand pulley has an L3.

10. Install the timing belt.

11. Install the timing belt covers.
12. Connect the negative battery cable.

Camshaft

REMOVAL AND INSTALLATION

GA16i (1990 Pulsar and 1990 Sentra) Engine

1. Disconnect the negative battery cable.
2. Remove the timing chain.
3. Remove the cylinder head with manifolds attached.
4. Remove the intake and exhaust manifolds from the cylinder head. Loosen the bolts in 2-3 stages in the proper sequence.
5. Loosen the rocker arm shaft bolts in 2-3 stages and lift the rocker arm/shaft assembly from the cylinder head. The rocker arm shaft is marked with an **F** to indicate that it faces towards the front of the engine. Place a similar mark on the cylinder head for your own reference.
6. Loosen the thrust plate retaining bolt.
7. Withdraw the camshaft and the thrust plate from the front of the cylinder head. The thrust plate is located to the camshaft with a key. Retain this key.
To install:
8. Clean all cylinder head, intake and exhaust manifold gasket surfaces. Lubricate the camshaft and rocker arm/shaft assemblies with a liberal coating of clean engine oil. Then, slide the camshaft and thrust plate into the front of the cylinder head. Don't forget to install the thrust plate key.
9. Install the rocker shafts and rocker arms making sure the **F** on the rocker shaft points toward the front of the engine. Install the rocker shaft retaining bolts, spring clips and washers. The center spring clip has a

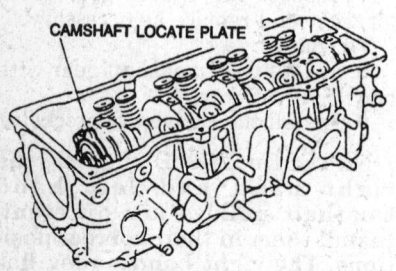

Rocker arm shaft positioning — GA16i engine

recess cut into one side. When installing the center clip point this recess toward the intake manifold side of the head. Snug the bolts gradually in 2-3 stages starting from the center and working out. Attach the intake and exhaust manifold to the head with new gaskets.
10. Install the cylinder head and timing chain.
11. After the timing chain is in place, set the No. 1 cylinder to TDC of the compression stroke.
12. Torque the No. 1 and No. 2 rocker shaft bolts to 27-30 ft. lbs. (37-41 Nm). Then, set the No. 4 cylinder to TDC and torque the No. 3 and No. 4 rocker shaft bolts to 27-30 ft. lbs. (37-41 Nm).
13. Connect the negative battery cable.

GA16DE (1991-92 Sentra) Engine

NOTE: Modify service steps as necessary. This is a complete disassembly repair procedure. Review the complete procedure before starting this repair.

1. Disconnect the negative battery cable, drain the cooling system and relieve the fuel system pressure.
2. Remove all drive belts. Disconnect the exhaust tube from the exhaust manifold.
3. Remove the power steering bracket.
4. Remove the air duct to intake manifold collector.
5. Remove the front right side wheel, splash cover and front undercovers.
6. Remove the front exhaust pipe and engine front mounting bracket.
7. Remove the rocker arm cover.
8. Remove the distributor cap. Remove the spark plugs.
9. Set the No. 1 cylinder at TDC of the compression stroke.
10. Mark and remove the distributor assembly.
11. Remove the camshaft sprocket cover and gusset. Remove the water pump pulley. Remove the thermostat housing.
12. Remove the chain tensioner, chain guide. Loosen idler sprocket bolt.
13. Remove the camshaft sprocket bolts, camshaft sprockets, camshaft brackets and camshafts. These parts should be reassembled in their original position. Bolts should be loosen in 2 or 3 steps (loosen bolts in the reverse of the tightening order).
To install:
14. Install camshafts. Make sure the camshafts are installed in the correct position. Note identification

marks are present on camshafts mark I for intake camshaft and mark E for exhaust camshaft.
15. Install camshafts brackets. Tighten camshafts brackets bolts in 2 or 3 steps to 7-9 ft. lbs. (9-12 Nm) in the correct sequence. After completing assembly check valve clearance.
16. Assemble camshaft sprocket with chain. Set timing chain by aligning mating marks with those of camshaft sprockets. Make sure sprockets mating marks face engine front.
17. Install camshaft sprocket bolts. Install upper chain tensioner and chain guide.
18. Install lower chain tensioner (make sure that the gasket is installed properly). Check that no problems occur when engine is rotated. Make sure that No. 1 piston is set to TDC on compression stroke.
19. Install thermostat housing, water pump pulley. Install the distributor assembly.
20. Install camshaft sprocket cover and rocker cover.
21. Install all remaining components in reverse order of removal.
22. Connect the negative battery cable. Refill all fluid levels. Road test the vehicle for proper operation.

KA24E (1990 240SX and 1990-92 Stanza) Engine

1. Disconnect the negative battery cable.
2. Remove the timing chain.
3. Remove the cylinder head. Do not remove the camshaft sprocket at this time.
4. Loosen the rocker shaft bolt evenly in proper sequence. Start from the outside and work toward the center.
5. Mount a dial indicator to the cylinder head and set the stylus of the indicator on the head of the camshaft sprocket bolt. Zero the indicator and measure the camshaft endplay by moving the camshaft back and forth. Endplay should be within specifications.
6. Remove the camshaft brackets and lift the camshaft with sprocket from the cylinder head.
To install:
7. Clean all cylinder head, intake and exhaust manifold gasket surfaces. Lubricate the camshaft and rocker arm/shaft assemblies with a liberal coating of clean engine oil. Lay the camshaft and sprocket into the cylinder head so the knock pin is at the front of the head at the 12 o'clock postion. Install the camshaft brackets. The camshaft bracket direc-

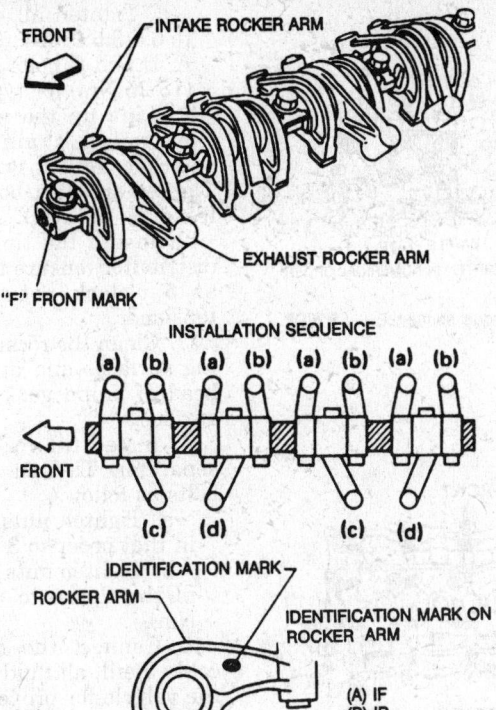

INSTALLATION SEQUENCE

IDENTIFICATION MARK
ROCKER ARM

IDENTIFICATION MARK ON
ROCKER ARM

(A) IF
(B) IR
(C) E24
(D) E13

Rocker arm shaft identification — GA16i engine

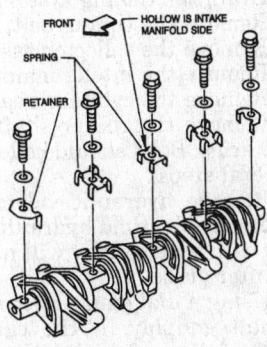

Rocker arm shaft bolt retainer positioning —
GA16i engine

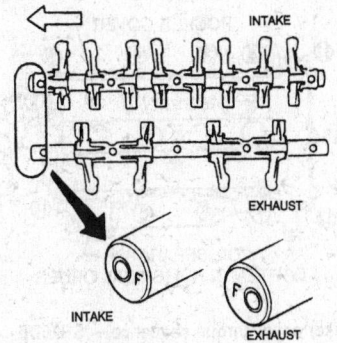

Rocker arm shaft positioning — KA24E engine

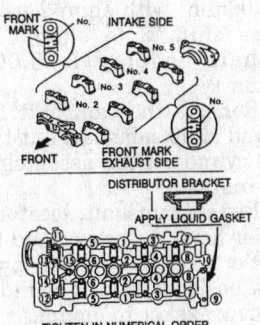

TIGHTEN IN NUMERICAL ORDER

Camshaft bearing caps and torque sequence —
GA16DE engine

tional arrows must face the toward the front of the engine.

8. Install the rocker shaft and rocker arms. Both intake and exhaust rocker shafts are stamped with an **F** mark. This mark must face the front of the engine during installation. Install the rocker arm bolts and spring clips so the cut outs are facing as shown. Torque the rocker arm bolts in the proper sequence to 27-30 ft. lbs. (37-41 Nm).

9. Install the timing chain.

10. Install the cylinder head. Use new rubber plugs when installing the cylinder head.

11. Connect the negative battery cable.

KA24DE Engine

NOTE: Modify service steps as necessary. This is a complete disassembly repair procedure. Review the complete procedure before starting this repair.

1. Release the fuel system pressure.

2. Disconnect the negative battery cable and drain the cooling system. Drain the engine oil.

3. Remove all vacuum hoses, fuel lines, wires, electrical connections as necessary.

4. Remove the front exhaust pipe and A.I.V. pipe.

5. Remove the air duct, cooling fan with coupling and radiator shroud.

6. Remove the the fuel injector tube assembly with injectors.

7. Disconnect and mark spark plug wires. Remove the spark plugs.

8. Set No. 1 piston at TDC on compression stroke. Remove the rocker cover assembly.

9. Mark and remove the distributor assembly.

10. Remove the camshaft sprocket, brackets and camshafts. These parts should be reassembled in their original position. Bolts should be loosened in 2 or 3 steps (loosen all bolts in the reverse of the tightening order).

To install:

11. Install camshafts and camshafts brackets. Torque camshaft brackets in 2 or 3 steps in sequence to 9 ft. lbs. (12 Nm) After completing assembly check valve clearance.

12. Install camshaft sprockets.

13. Install chain guide between both camshaft sprockets and distributor assembly.

14. Install all remaining components in reverse order of removal.

15. Connect the negative battery cable. Refill all fluid levels. Road test the vehicle for proper operation.

SR20DE Engine

1. Disconnect the negative battery cable. Remove the rocker cover and oil separator.

2. Rotate the crankshaft until the No.1 piston is at TDC on the compression stroke. Then rotate the crankshaft until the mating marks on the camshaft sprockets line up with the mating marks on the timing chain.

3. Remove the timing chain tensioner.

4. Remove the distributor.

5. Remove the timing chain guide.

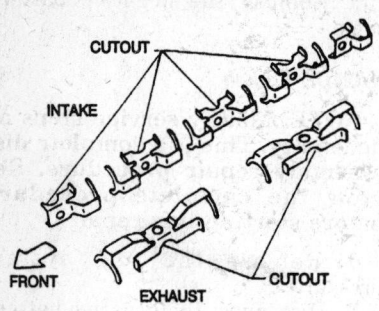

Spring clip installation — KA24E engine

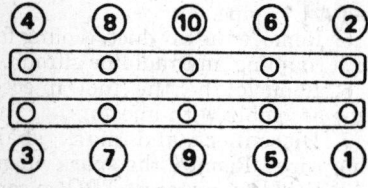

Rocker shaft bolt loosening sequence — KA24E engine. Tighten in reverse of loosening sequence

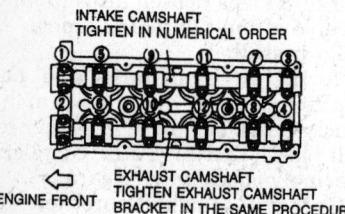

Camshaft bracket torque sequence — KA24DE engine

6. Remove the camshaft sprockets. Use a wrench to hold the camshaft while loosening the sprocket bolt.

7. Loosen the camshaft bracket bolts in the opposite order of the torquing sequence.

8. Remove the camshaft.

To install:

9. Clean the left hand camshaft end bracket and coat the mating surface with liquid gasket. Install the camshafts, camshaft brackets, oil tubes and baffle plate. Ensure the left camshaft key is at 12 o'clock and the right camshaft key is at 10 o'clock.

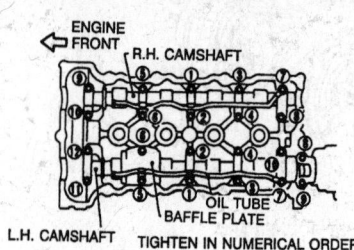

Camshaft bracket torque sequence — SR20DE engine

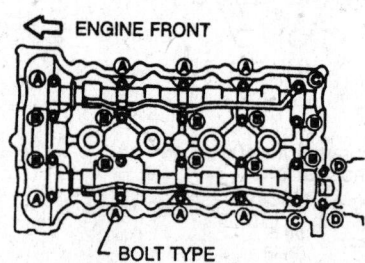

Camshaft bolt location — SR20DE engine

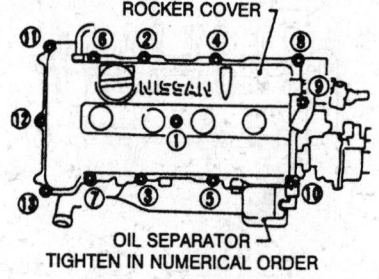

Rocker cover torque sequence — SR20DE engine

10. The procedure for tightening camshaft bolts must be followed exactly to prevent camshaft damage. Tighten bolts as follows:

a. Tighten right camshaft bolts 9 and 10 (in that order) to 1.5 ft. lbs. (2 Nm), then tighten bolts 1-8 (in that order) to the same specification.

b. Tighten left camshaft bolts 11 and 12 (in that order) to 1.5 ft. lbs. (2 Nm), then tighten bolts 1-10 (in that order) to the same specification.

c. Tighten all bolts in sequence to 4.5 ft. lbs. (6 Nm).

d. Tighten all bolts in sequence to 6.5-8.5 ft. lbs. (9-12 Nm) for type A, B and C bolts and 13-19 ft. lbs. (18-25 Nm) for type D bolts.

11. Line up the mating marks on the timing chain and camshaft sprockets and install the sprockets. Tighten sprocket bolts to 101-116 ft. lbs. (137-157 Nm).

12. Install the timing chain guide, distributor (ensure that rotor head is at 5 o'clock position) and chain tensioner.

13. Clean the rocker cover and mating surfaces and apply a continious bead of liquid gasket to the mating surface.

14. Install the rocker cover and oil separator. Tighten the rocker cover bolts as follows:

a. Tighten nuts 1, 10, 11 and 8, in that order to 3 ft. lbs. (4 Nm).

b. Tighten nuts 1-13 as indicated in the figure to 6-7 ft. lbs. (8-10 Nm).

15. Connect the negative battery cable. Refill all fluid levels. Road test the vehicle for proper operation.

VG30E Engines

1. Disconnect the negative battery cable.

2. Drain the cooling system.

3. Remove the timing belt.

4. Remove the collector assembly.

5. Remove the intake manifold.

6. Remove the cylinder head.

7. Remove the rocker shafts with rocker arms. Bolts should be loosened in several steps.

8. Remove hydraulic valve lifters and lifter guide. Hold hydraulic valve lifters with wire so they will not drop from lifter guide.

9. Using a dial gauge measure the camshaft endplay. If the camshaft endplay exceeds the limit of 0.0012-0.0024 in. (0.030-0.0061mm), select the thickness of a camshaft locate plate so the endplay is within specification. For example, if camshaft endplay measures 0.0031 in. (0.08mm) with shim 2 used, then change shim 2 to shim 3 so the camshaft endplay is 0.0020 in. (0.05mm).

10. Remove the camshaft front oil seal and slide camshaft out the front of the cylinder head assembly.

To install:

11. Install camshaft, locater plates, cylinder head rear cover and front oil seal. Set camshaft knock pin at 12 o'clock position. Install cylinder head with new gasket to engine.

12. Install valve lifter guide assembly. Assemble valve lifters in their original position. After installing

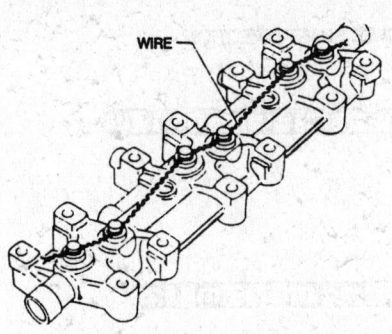

Holding the V6 valve lifters in place

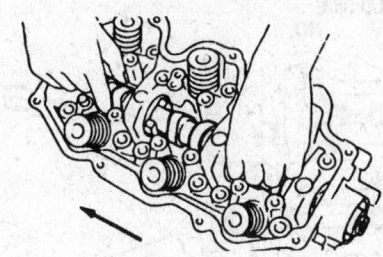

Remove the V6 camshaft in the direction of the arrow

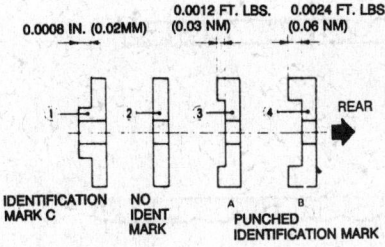

Select shim thickness so that camshaft thickness is within specifications

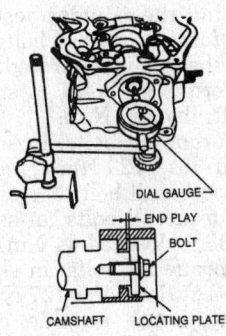

Using a dial indicator to measure camshaft endplay — V6 engine

them in the correct location remove the wire holding them in lifter guide.

13. Install rocker shafts in correct position with rocker arms. Tighten bolts in 2-3 stages to 13-16 ft. lbs. (18-22 Nm). Before tightening, be sure to set camshaft lobe at the position where lobe is not lifted or the valve closed. Set each cylinder 1 at a time or follow the procedure below. The cylinder head, intake manifold,

collector and timing belt must be installed:

a. Set No. 1 piston at TDC of the compression stroke and tighten rocker shaft bolts for No. 2, No. 4 and No. 6 cylinders.

b. Set No. 4 piston at TDC of the compression stroke and tighten rocker shaft bolts for No. 1, No. 3 and No. 5 cylinders.

c. Torque specification for the rocker shaft retaining bolts are 13-16 ft. lbs. (18-22 Nm).

14. Fill the cooling system to the proper level.

15. Connect the negative battery cable.

VG30DE AND VG30DETT ENGINES

1. Disconnect the negative battery cable.

2. Drain the cooling system.

3. Remove the the timing belt.

4. Remove the cylinder head with the exhaust manifold.

5. Separate the exhaust manifold from the cylinder head.

6. Remove the camshaft sprockets. Remove the front plate, O-ring and spring from the right (intake) camshaft to gain access to the sprocket bolt. The left camshaft sprocket is held in place by plate and 4 bolts.

7. Remove the rear timing belt cover.

8. Mount a dial indicator and set the stylus of the indicator on the end of the camshaft. Zero the indicator and measure the camshaft endplay by moving the camshaft back and forth. Endplay should be within 0.0012-0.0031 in. (0.03-0.08mm).

9. Remove the camshaft brackets. Loosen the bolts in the proper sequence (reverse the installation torque sequence) gradually in 2-3 stages.

10. Gently pry the camshaft oil seals from the cylinder head.

11. Remove the timing control solenoid valves.

12. Remove the camshafts.

To install:

13. Install the camshafts so the knock pins are aligned properly. The exhaust side camshaft (left side) has a spline that accepts the crank angle sensor.

14. Install the timing control solenoid valves. Torque the bracket bolts to 12-18 ft. lbs. (16-25 Nm). Apply liquid gasket to the valve seating surface before installation.

15. Install the camshaft brackets. Torque the bracket bolts in sequence to 7-9 ft. lbs. (9-12 Nm). Tighten the bolts gradually in 2-3 stages. When installing the front camshaft brackets, apply liquid gasket to the bracket seating surface.

16. Coat the lips of the new camshaft seals with clean engine oil and install the seals into the cylinder head.

17. Install the rear timing belt covers. Torque the cover bolts to 5-6 ft. lbs. (6-8 Nm).

18. Install the camshaft sprockets. Torque the right side (intake) sprocket bolt 90-98 ft. lbs. (123-132 Nm) and the left side (exhaust) sprocket retainer bolts to 10-14 ft. lbs. (14-19 Nm). When tightening the sprocket fasteners, make sure to hold the camshafts stationary.

19. Mount the exhaust manifold to the head with new gaskets.

20. Install the cylinder head.

21. Install the timing belt.

22. Fill the cooling system to the proper level.

23. Connect the negative battery cable.

VE30DE Engine

NOTE: Modify service steps as necessary. This is a complete disassembly repair procedure. Review the complete procedure before starting this repair.

1. Release the fuel pressure. Disconnect the negative battery cable.

2. Rotate the crankshaft to position the No. 1 piston on TDC of it's compression stroke.

3. Drain the cooling system. Disconnect all the electrical connectors, vacuum hoses and water hoses connected to the intake manifold collector.

4. The crank angle sensor is located in the rear of the left cylinder head, mark it's position, disconnect the electrical connector from it and remove it.

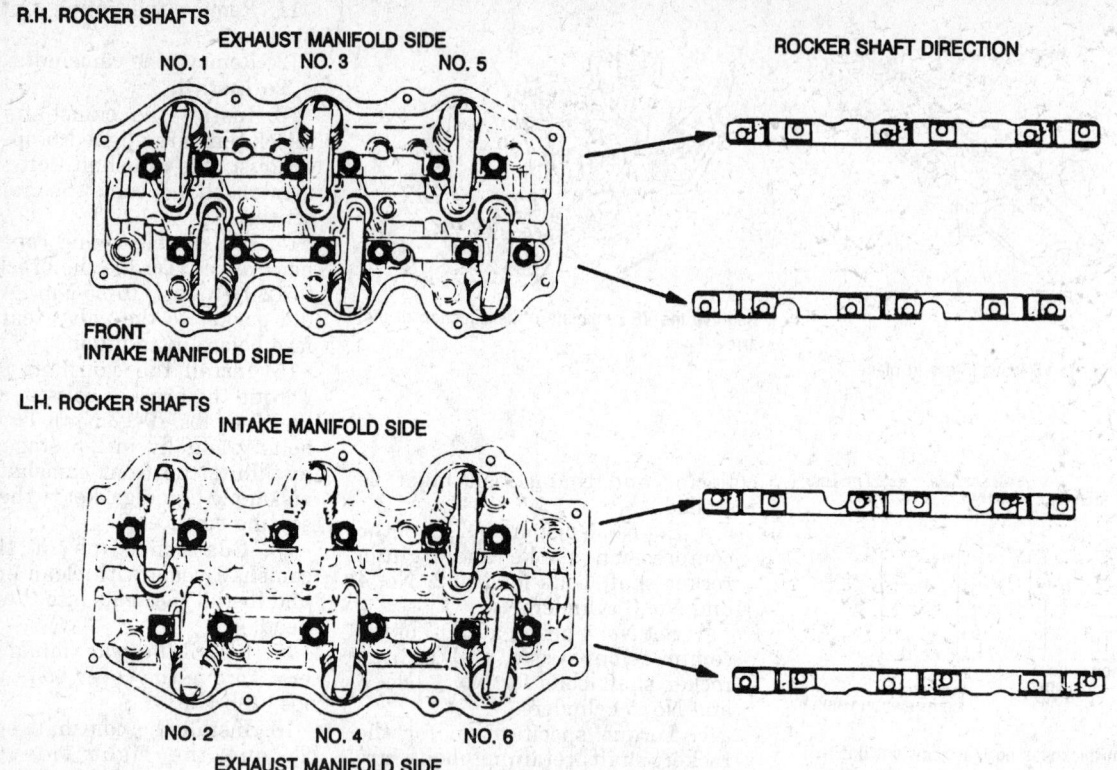

R.H. ROCKER SHAFTS

EXHAUST MANIFOLD SIDE
NO. 1   NO. 3   NO. 5

ROCKER SHAFT DIRECTION

FRONT
INTAKE MANIFOLD SIDE

L.H. ROCKER SHAFTS

INTAKE MANIFOLD SIDE

NO. 2   NO. 4   NO. 6
EXHAUST MANIFOLD SIDE

Rocker shaft/arm installation procedure — VG30E engines

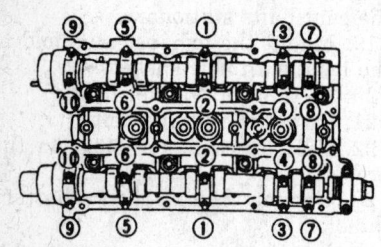

Camshaft bracket torque sequence — VG30DE and VG30DETT engines

⟨ FRONT

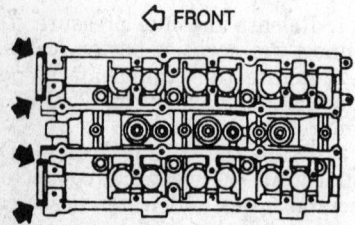

When installing front side camshaft bracket, apply liquid gasket as shown — VG30DE and VG30DETT engines

5. Remove the timing chain.

NOTE: Do not rotate either the crankshaft or camshaft from this point onward or the valves could be bent by hitting the pistons.

6. Remove the intake manifold collector.

7. Remove the intake manifold and fuel rail assembly.

8. Remove the exhaust manifold(s)-to-cylinder head(s) bolts and the exhaust manifolds.

9. Remove the camshaft sprockets-to-camshafts bolts and the camshaft sprockets.

10. Remove the exhaust camshafts, the camshaft brackets and the rocker arms.

11. Remove the outside cylinder head bolts.

12. Loosen the cylinder head-to-engine bolts, in sequence, using 2-3 steps.

13. Lift the cylinder head(s) from the engine and discard the gasket(s).

   To install:

14. Clean the gasket mounting surfaces. Inspect the cylinder head(s) for warpage, wear, cracks and/or damage.

15. Using liquid gasket sealant, apply a continuous bead to the mating surface of the cylinder block.

16. Install the cylinder head(s) and gaskets, torque the head bolts by performing the following procedures:

   a. Torque all bolts, in sequence, to 29 ft. lbs. (39 Nm).

   b. Torque all bolts, in sequence, to 90 ft. lbs. (123 Nm).

   c. Loosen all bolts.

   d. Torque all bolts, in sequence, to 25-33 ft. lbs. (34-44 Nm).

   e. Torque all bolts, in sequence, to 87-94 ft. lbs. (188-127 Nm).

17. Install the outside cylinder head-to-engine bolts.

18. Install the exhaust camshafts, camshaft brackets and rocker arms; the right exhaust camshaft is identified with **96E RE** and the left exhaust camshaft is identified with **96E LE**.

19. Using a gasket sealant, apply a continuous bead to the mating surface of the left exhaust camshaft end bracket. Torque the exhaust camshaft bracket-to-cylinder head bolts to 6.7-8.7 ft. lbs. (9.0-11.0 Nm).

20. Position the right exhaust camshaft key at about 10 o'clock position and the left camshaft key at about 12 o'clock position.

21. Install the timing chains and sprockets; torque the timing chain sprocket-to-camshaft bolts to 80-87 ft. lbs. (108-118 Nm).

22. Install the exhaust manifold(s) and the exhaust manifold(s)-to-cylinder head(s) bolts.

23. Install the intake manifold and fuel rail assembly.

24. Install the intake manifold collector.

25. Align and install the crank angle sensor to the rear of the left cylinder head and connect the electrical connector to it.

26. Connect all the electrical connectors, vacuum hoses and water hoses to the intake manifold collector. Refill the cooling system.

27. Connect the negative battery cable. Start the engine check the engine timing. After the engine reaches the normal operating temperature check for the correct coolant level.

28. Road test the vehicle for proper operation.

Piston and Connecting Rod

POSITIONING

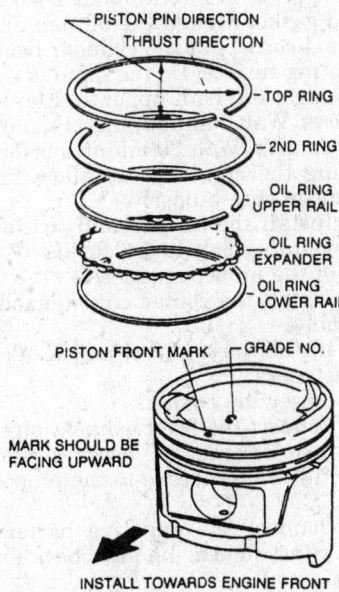

Piston ring identification and positioning — all engines

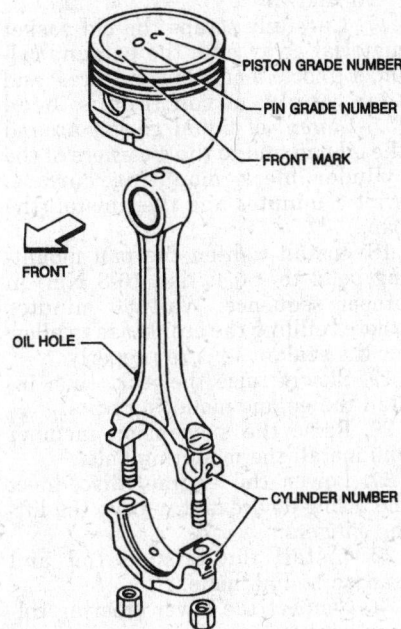

Piston and connection rod positioning — all engines

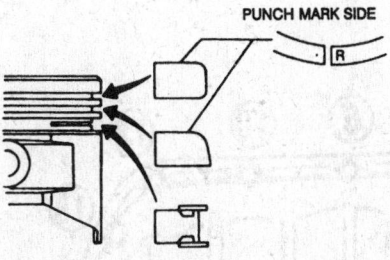

Piston ring installation — all engines

ENGINE LUBRICATION

Oil Pan

REMOVAL AND INSTALLATION

240SX

1. Disconnect the negative battery cable.

2. Raise the front of the vehicle and support safely.

3. Drain the oil pan.

4. Separate the front stabilizer bar from the side member.

5. Position a block of wood between a floor jack and the engine and then raise the engine slightly in its mounts.

6. Remove the oil pan retaining bolts in the proper sequence.

7. Insert a seal cutter between the oil pan and the cylinder block.

8. Tapping the cutter with a hammer, slide it around the entire edge of the oil pan. Do not drive the seal cutter into the oil pump or rear seal retainer portion or the aluminum mating surface will be deformed.

9. Lower the oil pan from the cylinder block and remove it from the front side of the engine.

To install:

10. To install, carefully scrape the old gasket material away from the pan and cylinder block mounting surfaces and then apply a continuous bead (3.5-4.5mm) of liquid gasket around the oil pan to the 4 corners of the cylinder block mounting surface. Wait 5 minutes and then install the pan.

11. Install the oil pan and tighten the mounting bolts to 3.6-5.1 ft. lbs. (5-7 Nm) in proper sequence (reverse removal sequence). Wait 30 minutes before refilling the crankcase to allow for the sealant to cure properly.

12. Connect the front stabilizer to the side bar.

13. Lower the vehicle.

14. Fill the crankcase to the proper level.

15. Connect the negative battery cable. Start the engine and check for leaks.

300ZX

1. Disconnect the negative battery cable.

2. Raise the front of the vehicle and support safely.

3. Remove the engine undercover.

4. Drain the oil pan.

5. Remove the oil filter and bracket.

6. Remove the rear engine gussets from both sides.

7. Disconnect the air conditioning tube clamps.

8. Disconnect the lower steering column joint from the steering rack.

9. Remove the tension rod and transverse link bolts from both sides.

10. Support the suspension member with a suitable jack. Install engine lifting slingers, connect a lifting

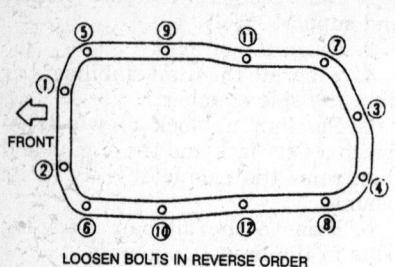

Oil pan bolt removal sequence on 240SX.
Tighten bolts in reverse order

device to the slingers and lift the engine.

11. Remove the suspension member bolts and lower the suspension member.

12. Remove the engine mounting bolts from both sides and slowly lower the transmission jack.

13. Remove the oil pan bolts in the proper sequence.

14. Insert a seal cutter between the oil pan and the cylinder block.

15. Tapping the cutter with a hammer, slide it around the entire edge of the oil pan. Do not drive the seal cutter into the oil pump or rear seal retainer portion or the aluminum mating surface will be deformed.

16. Lower the oil pan from the cylinder block and remove it.

To install:

17. Carefully scrape the old gasket material away from the pan and cylinder block mounting surfaces and then apply a continuous bead (3.5-4.5mm) of liquid gasket around the oil pan and to the 4 corners of the cylinder block mounting surface. Wait 5 minutes and then install the pan.

18. Install tighten the pan mounting bolts to 4-6 ft. lbs. (6-8 Nm) in proper sequence. Wait 30 minutes before refilling the crankcase to allow for the sealant to cure properly.

19. Slowly raise the jack, then install the engine mounting bolts.

20. Raise the suspension member and install the mounting bolts.

21. Lower the engine, disconnect the lifting device and remove the lifting slingers.

22. Install the tension rod and transverse link bolts.

23. Connect the lower steering column joint to the steering rack.

24. Install the air conditioning tube clamps.

25. Install the rear engine gussets.

26. Install the oil filter bracket with a new oil filter.

27. Install the engine undercover.

28. Lower the vehicle.

29. Fill the crankcase to the proper level.

30. Connect the negative battery cable. Start the engine and check for leaks.

Maxima

1. Disconnect the negative battery cable.

2. Raise the front of the vehicle and support safely.

3. Drain the oil pan.

4. Remove the engine lower covers.

5. Using a suitable jack and block of wood, support the engine in the area of the crank pulley area.

6. Remove the engine mounting insulator fasteners.

7. Remove the center crossmember.

8. Remove the oil pan bolts in the proper sequence.

9. Insert a seal cutter between the oil pan and the cylinder block.

10. Tapping the cutter with a hammer, slide it around the entire edge of the oil pan. Do not drive the seal cutter into the oil pump or rear seal retainer portion or the aluminum mating surface will be deformed.

11. Lower the oil pan from the cylinder block and remove it.

To install:

12. Carefully scrape the old gasket material away from the pan and cylinder block mounting surfaces and then apply a thin continuous bead of liquid gasket around the oil pan and to the 4 corners of the cylinder block mounting surface. Do the same to the oil pan gasket; both upper and lower surfaces. Wait 5 minutes and then install the pan. Wait 30 minutes before refilling the crankcase to allow the sealant to cure properly.

13. Install the oil pan and tighten the mounting bolt to 5-6 ft. lbs. (7-8 Nm) in the proper sequence.

14. Install the center crossmember assembly.

15. Install the engine mount insulator fasteners.

16. Lower the engine.

17. Connect the front exhaust pipe.

18. Install the engine lower covers.

19. Fill the crankcase to the proper level.

20. Connect the negative battery cable. Start the engine and check for leaks.

Pulsar, Sentra and 1990-92 Stanza

EXCEPT SR20DE ENGINE

1. Disconnect the negative battery cable.

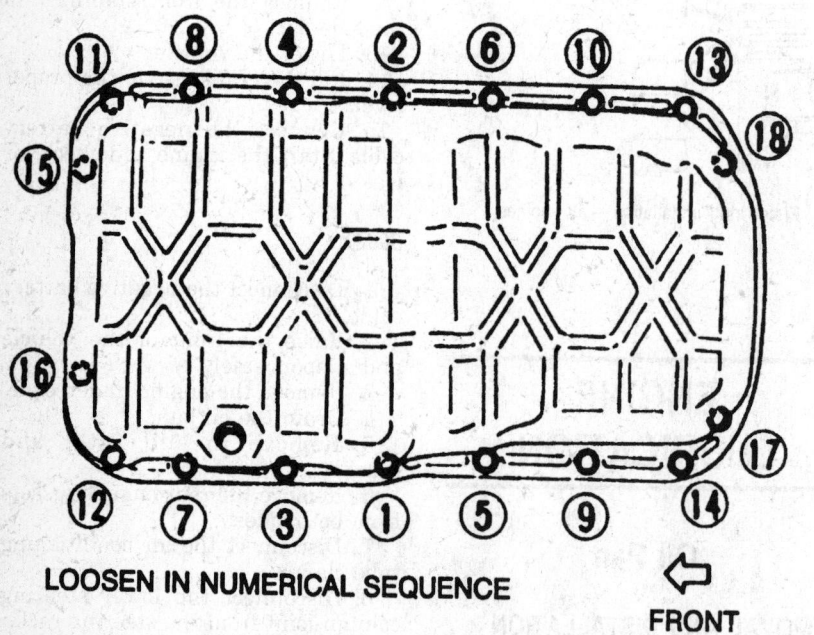

LOOSEN IN NUMERICAL SEQUENCE

FRONT

Oil pan bolt tightening sequence on 300ZX. Loosen bolts in reverse order

2. Raise the vehicle and support safely.

3. Drain the oil pan.

4. Remove the right side splash cover.

5. Remove the right side undercover.

6. Remove the center member (2WD vehicles only).

7. Remove the forward section of the exhaust pipe.

8. Remove the oil pan bolts.

9. Insert a seal cutter between the oil pan and the cylinder block.

10. Tapping the cutter with a hammer, slide it around the entire edge of the oil pan. Do not drive the seal cutter into the oil pump or rear seal retainer portion or the aluminum mating surface will be deformed.

11. Lower the oil pan from the cylinder block and remove it.

To install:

12. Carefully scrape the old gasket material away from the pan and cylinder block mounting surfaces and then apply a thin continuous bead of liquid gasket around the oil pan and to the 4 corners of the cylinder block mounting surface. Do the same to the oil pan gasket (upper and lower area). Wait 5 minutes and then install the pan. Wait 30 minutes before refilling the crankcase to allow the sealant to cure properly.

13. Install the oil pan and tighten the mounting bolts to 5-6 ft. lbs. (7-8 Nm), working from the center bolt outward.

14. Install the forward section of the exhaust pipe using new gaskets.

15. Install the center member (2WD vehicles only).

16. Install the right side undercover.

17. Install the right side splash cover.

18. Lower the vehicle.

19. Fill the crankcase to the proper level.

20. Connect the negative battery cable. Start the engine and check for leaks.

SR20DE Engine

1. Raise and support the vehicle safely. Remove the engine undercover and drain the oil.

2. Remove the steel oil pan bolts in the proper sequence (reverse installation sequence). Remove the steel oil pan. Insert tool KV10111100 or equivalent, between steel oil pan and aluminum oil pan to pry apart.

3. Remove the oil baffle bolts and oil baffle. Remove the front tube.

4. Set a suitable jack under the transaxle and raise the engine with and engine hoist.

5. If equipped with an automatic transaxle, remove the transaxle shift control cable.

6. Remove the compressor gussets, the rear cover plate and all aluminum oil pan bolts. Loosen aluminum oil pan bolts in the proper sequence (reverse installation sequence).

7. Remove the 2 engine-to-transaxle bolts and refit the them into vacant holes at the bottom of the oil pan. Remove the aluminum oil pan. Use tool KV10111100 or equivalent, to pry oil pan from block. Remove the engine to transaxle bolts.

To install:

8. Clean the oil pan rail of all liquid gasket and apply a new bead of ⅛ inch thickness to the aluminum oil pan rail.

9. Install the aluminum oil pan and torque bolts 1-16 to 12-14 ft. lbs. (16-19 Nm) and bolts 17-18 to 5-6 ft. lbs. (6-8 Nm) in the opposite order of removal.

10. Install the 2 engine to transaxle bolts, rear cover plate, compressor gussets, automatic transmission shift control cable (if equipped), center member, front tube and baffle plate.

11. Clean the steel oil pan rail of all liquid gasket and apply a new bead of ⅛ inch thickness to the steel oil pan rail.

12. Install the steel oil pan and install bolts until snug. Tighten bolts in the reverse order of removal and wait 30 minuites before refilling crankcase with oil.

Altima (KA24DE Engine)

1. Raise and support the vehicle safely. Remove the engine undercover and drain the oil.

2. Remove the steel oil pan bolts in the proper sequence (reverse installation sequence). Remove the steel oil pan. Insert tool KV10111100 or equivalent, between steel oil pan and aluminum oil pan to pry apart.

3. Remove the oil baffle bolts and oil baffle. Remove the front exhaust pipe.

4. Set a suitable jack under the transaxle and raise the engine with and engine hoist.

5. Remove the center member.

6. Remove the compressor gussets, the rear cover plate and all aluminum oil pan bolts. Loosen aluminum oil pan bolts in the proper sequence (reverse installation sequence).

7. Remove the aluminum oil pan. Use tool KV10111100 or equivalent, to pry oil pan from block.

To install:

8. Clean the aluminum oil pan rail of all liquid gasket and apply a new bead of ⅛ inch thickness to the aluminum oil pan rail.

9. Install the aluminum oil pan and torque bolts 1-16 to 12-14 ft. lbs. (16-19 Nm) and bolts 17-18 to 5-6 ft. lbs. (6-8 Nm) in the opposite order of removal.

10. Install the rear cover plate, compressor gussets, center member, front exhaust pipe, oil strainer and baffle plate.

11. Clean the steel oil pan rail of all liquid gasket and apply a new bead of ⅛ inch thickness to the steel oil pan rail.

12. Install the steel oil pan and install bolts until snug. Tighten bolts in the reverse order of removal and wait 30 minutes before refilling crankcase with oil.

Oil Pump

REMOVAL AND INSTALLATION

GA16i and KA24E (1990-92 Stanza) Engines

The oil pump consists of an inner and outer gear located in the front cover.

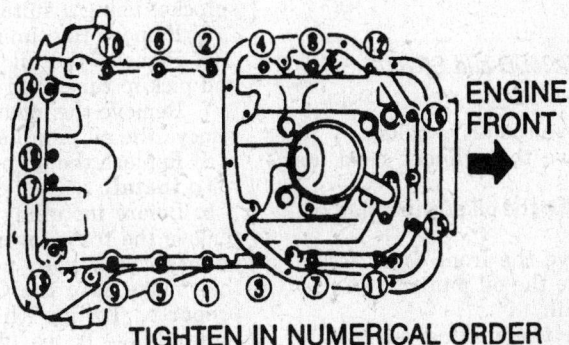

TIGHTEN IN NUMERICAL ORDER

Aluminum oil pan installation torque sequence — SR20DE and KA24DE engines

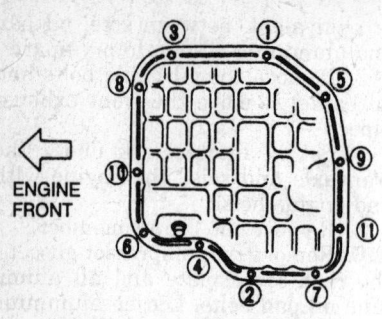

ENGINE
FRONT

TIGHTEN IN NUMERICAL ORDER

Steel oil pan installation torque sequence —
SR20DE and KA24DE engines

Removal of the front cover is necessary to gain access to the oil pump.

1. Disconnect the negative battery cable.
2. Remove the front cover with the strainer tube.
3. Loosen the oil pump cover retaining screw and mounting bolts and separate the oil pump cover from the front cover.
4. Remove the oil pump inner and outer gears.

To install:

5. Thoroughly clean the oil pump cover mating surfaces and the gear cavity.
6. Install the outer gear into the cavity.
7. Install the inner gear so the grooved side is facing up (towards the oil pump cover). Make sure the gears mesh properly and pack the pump cavity with petroleum jelly.
8. Install the oil pump cover. On GA16i engines, torque the retaining screws to 2.2-3.6 ft. lbs. (3-5 Nm) and the bolts to 3.6-5.1 ft. lbs. (5-7 Nm). On KA24E engine, torque the cover screws to 2.2-3.6 ft. lbs. (3-5 Nm) and the bolts to 12-15 ft. lbs. (16-21 Nm).
9. Install the front cover with a new seal.
10. Connect the negative battery cable. Start the engine and check for leaks.

GA16DE, KA24DE and SR20DE Engines

1. Remove the drive belts.
2. Remove the cylinder head and oil pan.
3. Remove the oil strainer and baffle plate.
4. Remove the front cover assembly. Remove the oil pump.

To install:

5. Clean the mating surfaces of liquid gasket and apply a fresh bead of 1/8 in. thickness.

6. Coat the oil pump gears with oil. Using a new oil seal and O-ring, install the front cover assembly.
7. Install the oil strainer, baffle plate, oil pan, cylinder head and drive belts.

KA24E (240SX) Engine

1. Disconnect the negative battery cable.
2. Drain the oil pan.
3. Turn the crankshaft so No. 1 piston is at TDC on its compression stroke.
4. Remove the distributor cap and mark the position of the distributor rotor in relation to the distributor base with a piece of chalk.
5. Remove the splash shield.
6. Remove the oil pump body with the drive spindle assembly.

To install:

7. To install, fill the pump housing with engine oil, align the punch mark on the spindle with the hole in the pump. No. 1 piston should be at TDC on its compression stroke.
8. With a new gasket and seal placed over the drive spindle, install the oil pump and drive spindle assembly. Make sure the tip of the drive spindle fits into the distributor shaft notch securely. The distributor rotor should be pointing to the matchmark made earlier.
9. Install the splash shield.
10. Install the distributor cap.
11. Fill the crankcase to the proper level.
12. Connect the negative battery cable. Start the engine and check for leaks. Check the ignition timing.

VG30E, VG30DE and VG30DETT Engines

1. Disconnect the negative battery cable.
2. Remove the oil pan.
3. Remove the timing belt.
4. Remove the crankshaft timing sprocket using a suitable puller.
5. Remove the timing belt plate.
6. Remove the oil pump strainer and pickup tube from the oil pump.
7. Remove the mounting bolts and remove the oil pump and gasket.
8. Replace the oil pump seal.

To install:

9. Before installing the oil pump, remove the front cover and pack the pump's cavity with petroleum jelly, then make sure the O-ring is fitted properly. Torque the front cover screws to 3-4 ft. lbs. (4-5 Nm).
10. Mount the oil pump with a new gasket. Torque the 8mm retaining

bolts to 16-22 ft. lbs. (22-29 Nm) and the 6mm bolts to 5-6 ft. lbs. (6-8 Nm).
11. Install the oil pump strainer and pickup tube with a new O-ring. Torque the pickup tube mounting bolts to 12-15 ft. lbs. (16-21 Nm).
12. Install the timing belt plate.
13. Install the crankshaft timing sprocket.
14. Install the timing belt.
15. Install the oil pan.
16. Connect the negative battery cable. Start the engine and check for leaks.

VE30DE Engine

NOTE: The oil pump is an integral part of the front cover assembly.

1. Remove all accessory drive belts and the alternator.
2. Remove the cylinder heads.
3. Unbolt the engine from its mounts and raise the engine up from the unibody.
4. Remove the crankshaft damper-to-crankshaft bolt and the damper.
5. Drain the engine oil and remove the oil pan.
6. Remove the oil strainer-to-engine bolt, oil strainer-to-oil pump bolts and the strainer.
7. Remove the front cover-to-engine bolts and the front cover.
8. Remove the oil pump assembly-to-engine bolts, along with the oil strainer, and remove the assembly from the engine.
9. Clean the gasket mating surfaces.

To install:

10. Pack the oil pump full of petroleum jelly to prevent the pump from cavitating when the engine is started.
11. Apply a bead of liquid sealant to the front cover mating surfaces.
12. Install the front cover and torque the front cover-to-engine bolts to 4.6-6.1 ft. lbs. (6.3-8.3 Nm) except for bolt above oil filter housing and 12-15 ft. lbs. (16-21 Nm) for bolt above oil filter housing.
13. Using a new gasket, install the strainer and torque the strainer-to-front cover bolts to 12-15 ft. lbs. (16-21 Nm) and the strainer-to-engine bolt to 4.6-6.1 ft. lbs. (6.3-8.3 Nm).
14. Install the oil pan.
15. Install the cylinder heads.
16. Install the alternator and all drive belts. Reconnect the negative battery cable.
17. Start engine, check ignition timing and check for oil leaks.

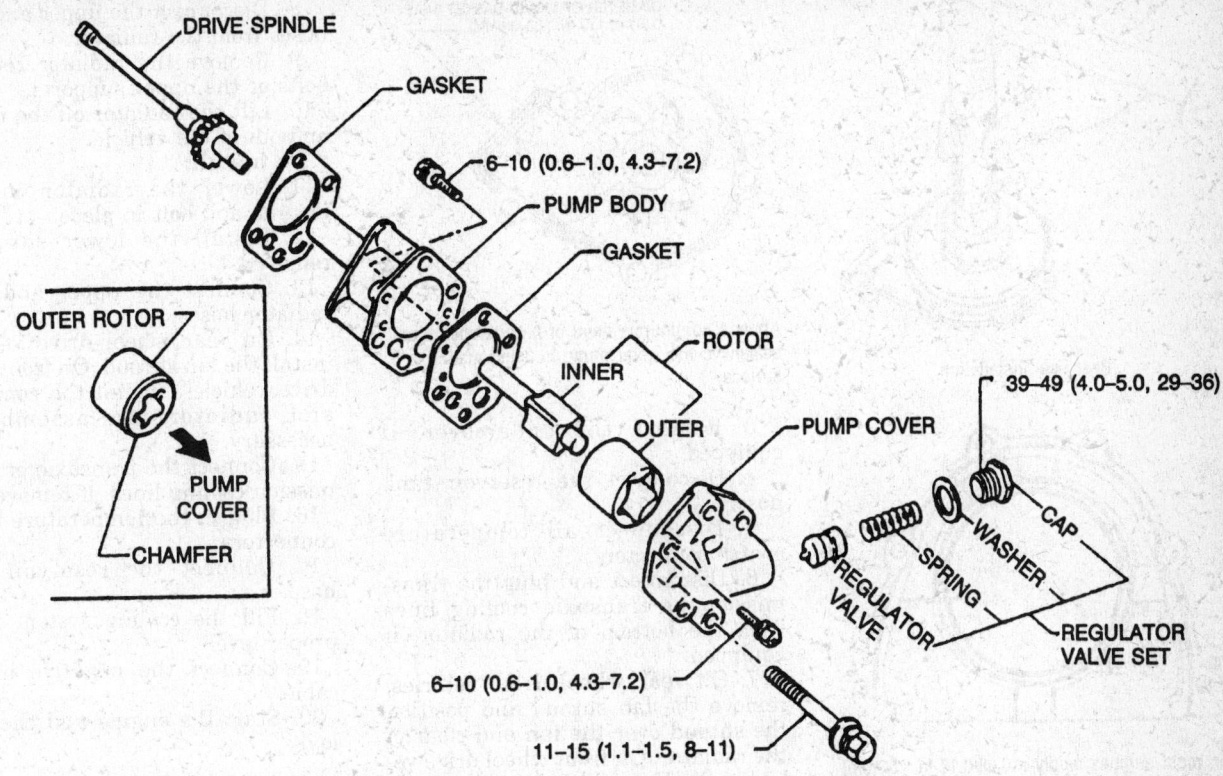

Align the punch mark on the drive spindle with the oil hole — 240SX

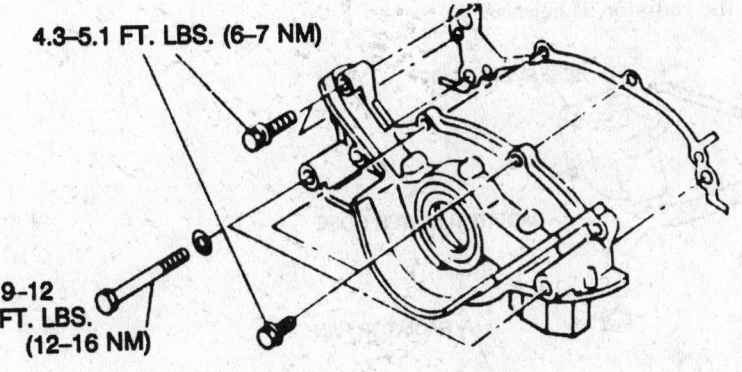

Oil pump installation — V6 engine

Rear Main Bearing Oil Seal

REMOVAL AND INSTALLATION

1. Remove the transmission or transaxle.
2. Remove the flywheel or driveplate.
3. Remove the rear oil seal retainer from the block.
4. Using a suitable prying tool, remove the oil seal from the retainer.
   To install:
5. Thoroughly scrape the surface of the retainer to remove any traces

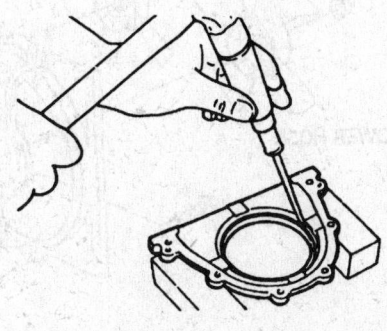

Rear seal removal

of the existing sealant or gasket material.
6. Wipe the seal bore with a clean rag.
7. Apply clean engine oil to the new oil seal and carefully install it into the retainer using the proper seal installation tool.
8. Install the rear oil seal retainer into the engine, along with a new gasket. Apply a 0.08-0.12 in. (2-3mm) bead of liquid gasket to the rear oil seal retainer prior to installation. Torque the bolts to 3-6 ft. lbs. (4-8 Nm).
9. Install the flywheel or driveplate.
10. Install the transmission or transaxle.

ENGINE COOLING

Radiator

REMOVAL AND INSTALLATION

1. Disconnect the negative battery cable.
2. Drain the cooling system.

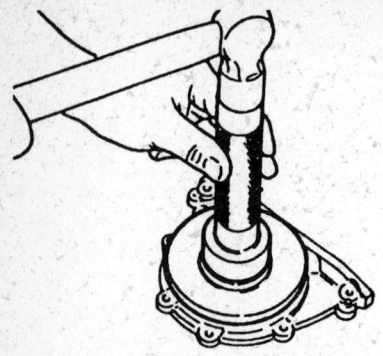

Rear seal installation

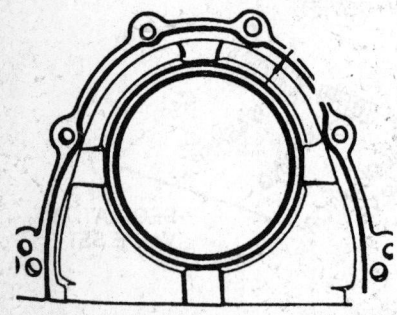

On most engines, apply a 0.08-0.12 in. (2-3mm) of liquid gasket to the rear oil seal retainer

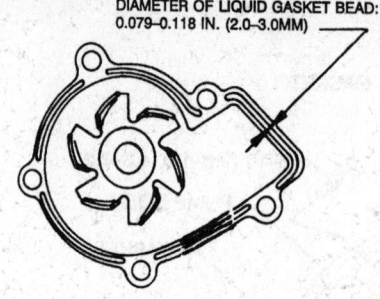

DIAMETER OF LIQUID GASKET BEAD: 0.079-0.118 IN. (2.0-3.0MM)

Apply a continuous bead of high temperature sealant to the water pump housing mating surface

3. Remove the undercover, if equipped.

4. Disconnect the reservoir tank hose.

5. Disconnect all temperature switch connectors.

6. Disconnect and plug the transmission or transaxle cooling lines from the bottom of the radiator, if equipped.

7. On rear wheel drive vehicles, remove the fan shroud and position the shroud over the fan and clear of the radiator. On front wheel drive vehicles, discharge the air conditioning system, then unbolt and remove the condenser and radiator fan assembly from the radiator, if necessary.

8. Disconnect the upper and lower hoses from the radiator.

9. Remove the radiator retaining bolts or the upper supports.

10. Lift the radiator off the mounts and out of the vehicle.

To install:

11. Lower the radiator onto the mounts and bolt in place.

12. Install the lower shroud, if removed.

13. Connect the upper and lower radiator hoses.

14. On rear wheel drive vehicles, install the fan shroud. On front wheel drive vehicles, install the condenser and radiator fan assembly as necessary.

15. Connect the transaxle or transmission cooling lines, if removed.

16. Plug in the temperature switch connectors.

17. Connect the reservoir tank hose.

18. Fill the cooling system to the proper level.

19. Connect the negative battery cable.

20. Start the engine and check for leaks.

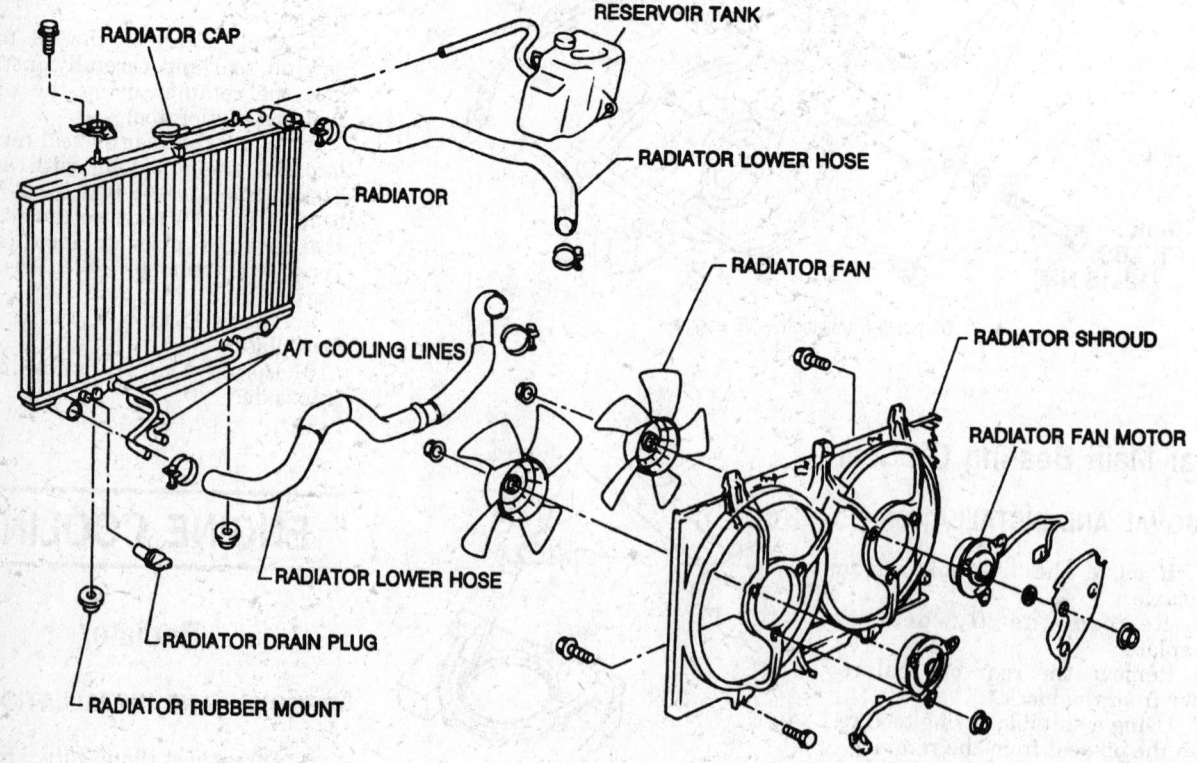

Radiator assembly

Heater Core

REMOVAL AND INSTALLATION

240SX, 300ZX and Altima

1. Disconnect the negative battery cable.
2. Drain the cooling system.
3. Remove the instrument panel and any necessary trim panels.
4. Remove the heater unit assembly and heater core hoses. Remove the heater core from the heater unit box.
5. Installation is the reverse of removal. Clean heater case housing of all debris before installation. Check system for proper operation.

Maxima

1. Disconnect the negative battery cable.
2. Set the TEMP lever to the HOT position.
3. Drain the cooling system.
4. Disconnect the heater hoses from the heater unit.
5. Remove the front floor mats.
6. Remove the instrument panel lower covers.
7. Remove the ventilator duct.
8. Remove the instrument panel.
9. Remove the rear heater duct from the floor of the vehicle.
10. Disconnect the wiring harness connectors.
11. Separate the heating unit from the cooling unit. Remove the 2 screws at the bottom sides of the heater unit and the 1 screw from the top of the unit. Lift out the heater together with the heater control assembly.
12. Remove the center vent cover and heater control assembly, loosening the clips and screws.
13. Remove the screws securing the door shafts.
14. Remove the clips from the case and split the case. Remove the core.
15. Separate the heater case halves and slide the core from the case.
   To install:
16. Install the heater core and assemble the heater case halves. Use new gaskets and seals as required.
17. Install the door shaft retaining screws.
18. Install the heater control assembly and center vent cover.
19. Mount the heater unit/control assembly and install the upper and lower attaching screws.
20. Plug in the wiring harness connectors.
21. Install the rear heater duct.
22. Install the instrument panel.
23. Install the ventilator duct.

24. Install the instrument panel lower covers.
25. Install the floor mats.
26. Connect the heater hoses. Use new grommets as required.
27. Fill the cooling system to the proper level.
28. Connect the negative battery cable.

Pulsar and Sentra

1. Disconnect the negative battery cable.
2. Set the TEMP lever to the maximum HOT position and drain the engine coolant.
3. Disconnect the heater hoses at the engine compartment.
4. Remove the instrument panel assembly.
5. Remove the heater control assembly.
6. If equipped with air conditioning, separate the heating unit from the cooling unit.
7. Remove the heater unit assembly.
8. Remove the case clips and split the case. Remove the core.
   To install:
9. Install the heater core and assemble the heater case halves. Use new gaskets and seals as required. Always check the operation of the air mix door when re-attaching the heater case halves.
10. Mount the heater unit and connect it the cooling unit, if equipped.
11. Install the heater control assembly.
12. Install the instrument panel.
13. Connect the heater hoses. Use new grommets as required.
14. Fill and bleed the cooling system.
15. Connect the negative battery cable.

Stanza

1. Disconnect the negative battery cable.
2. Set the TEMP lever to the maximum HOT position and drain the engine coolant.
3. Disconnect the heater hoses at the engine compartment.
4. Remove the instrument panel assembly.
5. Remove the heater control assembly.
6. Remove pedal bracket mounting bolts, steering column mounting bolts, brake and clutch pedal cotter pins.
7. Move the pedal bracket and steering column to the left.

8. Disconnect the air mix door control cable and heater valve control lever, then remove the control lever.
9. Remove the core cover and remove the core.
   To install:
10. Install the core and cover. Use new seals and gaskets as required.
11. Install the control and heater valve levers. Connect the air mix door control cable.
12. Move the steering column and brake pedal bracket to the right. Install the clutch and brake pedal cotter pins and steering column and brake pedal bolts.
13. Install the heater control assembly.
14. Install the instrument panel.
15. Connect the heater hoses to the core. Use new grommets as required.
16. Fill and bleed the cooling system.
17. Connect the negative battery cable.

Water Pump

REMOVAL AND INSTALLATION

4-Cylinder

1. Disconnect the negative battery cable.
2. Drain the coolant from the radiator and cylinder block.
3. Remove all the drive belts.
4. Unbolt the water pump pulley and the water pump attaching bolts.
5. Separate the water pump with the gasket, if installed, from the cylinder block.
6. Remove all gasket material or sealant from the water pump mating surfaces. All sealant must be removed from the groove in the water pump surface also.
   To install:
7. Apply a continuous bead of high temperature liquid gasket to the water pump housing mating surface. The housing must be attached to the cylinder block within 5 minutes after the sealant is applied. After the pump housing is bolted to the block, wait at least 30 minutes for the sealant to cure before starting the engine.
8. Position the water pump (and gasket) onto the block and install the attaching bolts. Torque the small retaining bolts to about 5 ft. lbs. (6.8 Nm) and large retaining bolts 12-14 ft. lbs. (16-19 Nm).
9. Install the water pump pulley.
10. Install the drive belts and adjust the tension.
11. Fill the cooling system to the proper level.

12. Connect the negative battery cable.

6-Cylinder

1. Disconnect the negative battery cable and drain the coolant from the radiator and the cylinder block.
2. On 300ZX, remove the undercover and the radiator.
3. Remove the radiator shroud.
4. Remove the power steering, compressor and alternator drive belts.
5. Remove the cooling fan and coupling.
6. Disconnect the water pump hoses.
7. On 300ZX, unbolt and remove the inlet and outlet pipes from the block.
8. Remove the water pump pulley, then the upper and lower timing covers.

NOTE: Be careful not to get coolant on the timing belt and to avoid deforming the timing cover, make sure there is enough clearance between the timing cover and the hose clamp.

9. Remove the water pump retaining bolts, note different lengths and remove the pump.
10. Make sure the gasket sealing surfaces are clean and free of all the old gasket material.

To install:
11. Mount the water pump and gasket onto the cylinder block. Torque the retaining bolts evenly to 12-15 ft. lbs. (16-21 Nm).
12. Install the upper and lower timing belt covers and crankshaft pulley.
13. On 300ZX, install the inlet and outlet pipes and torque the nuts and bolts to 12-14 ft. lbs. (16-19 Nm).
14. Connect the water pump hoses.
15. Install the cooling fan and coupling.
16. Install and tension the drive belts.
17. Install the radiator shroud.
18. On 300ZX, install the undercover and radiator.
19. Fill the cooling system and connect the negative battery cable.

Thermostat

REMOVAL AND INSTALLATION

1. Disconnect the negative battery cable and drain the coolant from the radiator and the cylinder block. On Maxima and 300ZX, there are 2 cylinder block drain plugs.

2. On 300ZX, remove the undercover.
3. On GA16i engines, disconnect the water temperature switch connector from the thermostat housing.
4. Remove the radiator hose from the water outlet side and remove the bolts securing the water outlet to the cylinder head.
5. On 300ZX, remove the radiator shroud, drive belts for cooling fan and coupling and water inlet pipe.
6. Remove the thermostat and clean off the old gasket or sealant from the mating surfaces.

To install:
7. Install the thermostat with a new gasket. When installing the thermostat, be sure to install a new gasket or sealant and be sure the air bleed hole in the thermostat is facing the left side or upward on the engine. The jiggle valve must always face up. Also make sure the new thermostat to be installed is equipped with a air bleed hole. Some thermostats have the word TOP stamped next to the jiggle valve. Again, the word TOP and the jiggle valve must be facing up.
8. On 300ZX, install the water inlet pipe, cooling fan and coupling, drive belts and radiator shroud.
9. Install the water outlet and upper radiator hose.
10. On GA16i engines, connect the water temperature switch connector to the thermostat housing.
11. On 300ZX, install the undercover.
12. Fill the cooling system and connect the negative battery cable.

Cooling System Bleeding

1. Remove the radiator cap.
2. Fill the radiator and reservoir tank with the proper type of coolant. If equipped with an air relief plug, remove the plug and add coolant until it spills out the air relief opening. Install the plug.

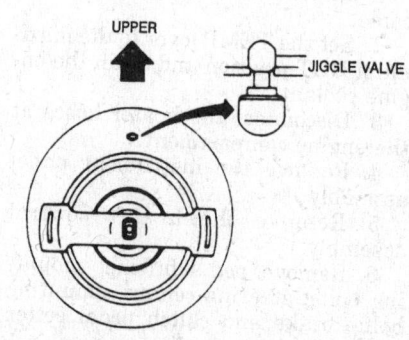

Always be sure the jiggle valve is facing upward when installing the thermostat

3. Install and tighten the radiator cap.
4. Start the engine and allow the coolant to come up to operating temperature. On 4 cylinder engine, allow the electric cooling fan to come on at least once. Run the heater at full force and with the temperature lever in the hot position. Be sure the heater control valve is functioning.
5. Shut the engine off and recheck the coolant level, refill as necessary.

ENGINE ELECTRICAL

NOTE: Disconnecting the negative battery cable on some vehicles may interfere with the functions of the on-board computer systems and may require the computer to undergo a relearning process, once the negative battery cable is reconnected.

Distributor

NOTE: The VG30DE and VG30DETT engines and VE30DE used on the 1992-94 Maxima do not use a conventional distributor and high tension wires. Instead these engines use small ignition coils fitted directly to each spark plug. The ECU controls the coils by means of a crank angle sensor and other engine management equipment.

REMOVAL

1. Disconnect the negative battery cable.
2. Release the retaining clips and lift the distributor cap straight up. It will be easier to install the distributor if the wiring is not disconnected from the cap. If the wires must be removed from the cap, label the wires according to cylinder number to aid in installation and avoid confusion.
3. Disconnect the distributor wiring harness.
4. Disconnect and label the vacuum lines, if equipped.
5. Note the position of the rotor in relation to the base. Scribe a mark on the base of the distributor and on the engine block to facilitate reinstallation. Align the marks with the direction the rotor is pointing.

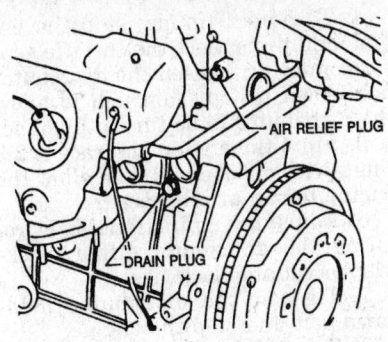

Air relief plug location for bleeding the cooling system

6. Remove the bolt(s) which hold the distributor to the engine.

7. Lift the distributor assembly from the engine.

NOTE: Once the distributor is removed, try not to disturb the position of the rotor, camshaft or crankshaft.

INSTALLATION

Timing not Disturbed

1. Insert the distributor shaft and assembly into the engine.

2. Align the distributor and engine matchmarks with the rotor. Make

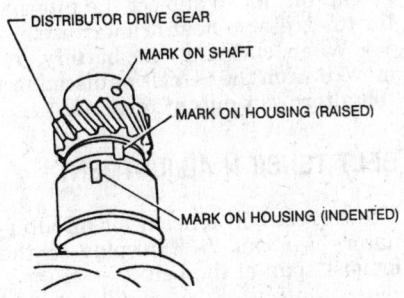

Distributor shaft and housing alignment marks — V-Series engines, except 300ZX

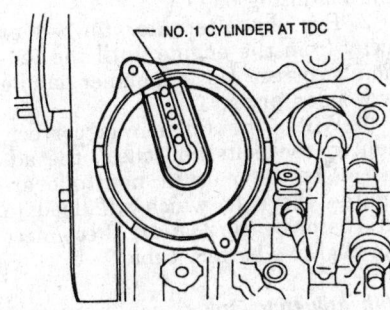

Distributor rotor at No. 1 cylinder TDC position — V-Series engines, except 300ZX

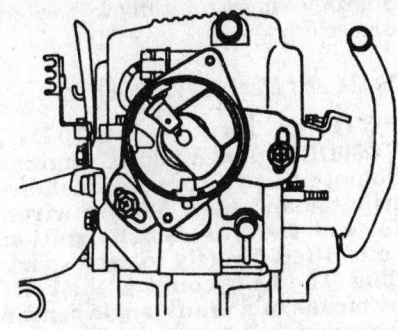

Distributor rotor at No. 1 cylinder TDC position — Stanza

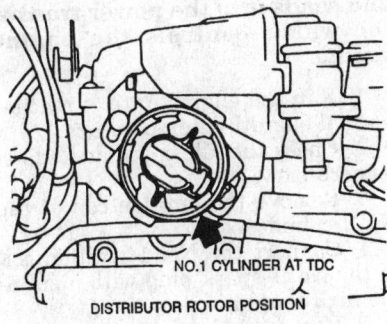

Distributor rotor at No. 1 cylinder TDC position — GA16i engine

sure the housing is pointed in the same direction as it was pointed originally. This will be done automatically if the marks on the engine and the distributor are lined up with the rotor. On 240SX, make sure the distributor driving spindle is properly aligned before inserting the distributor into the front cover.

3. Install the distributor hold-down bolt and clamp. Leave the screw loose enough so the distributor can be moved with moderate hand pressure.

4. Connect the vacuum lines, if equipped.

5. Connect the primary wire to the coil.

6. Install the distributor cap on the distributor housing. Secure the distributor cap with the spring clips.

7. Install the spark plug wires if removed. Make sure the wires are pressed all the way into the top of the distributor cap and firmly onto the spark plug.

8. Set the ignition timing.

Timing Disturbed

NOTE: If the crankshaft has been turned or the engine disturbed in any manner (i.e., disassembled and rebuilt) while the

distributor was removed or if the marks were not drawn, it will be necessary to initially time the engine. Follow the procedure given below.

1. It is necessary to place the No. 1 cylinder in the firing position to correctly install the distributor. To locate this position, the ignition timing marks on the crankshaft front pulley are used.

2. Remove the No. 1 cylinder spark plug. Turn the crankshaft until the piston in the No. 1 cylinder is moving up on the compression stroke. This can be determined by placing a thumb over the spark plug hole and feeling the air being forced out of the cylinder. Stop turning the crankshaft when the timing marks are aligned. On 240SX, the driving spindle must be properly aligned to accept the distributor.

3. Oil the distributor housing lightly where the distributor mounts to the block.

4. Install the distributor so the rotor, which is mounted on the shaft, points toward the No. 1 spark plug terminal tower position when the cap is installed. Lay the cap on top of the distributor and make a mark on the side of the distributor housing just below the No. 1 spark plug terminal. Make sure the rotor points toward that mark when installing the distributor.

5. When the distributor shaft has reached the bottom of the hole, move the rotor back and forth slightly until the driving lug on the end of the shaft enters the slots cut in the end of the oil pump shaft and the distributor assembly slides down into place.

6. When the distributor is correctly installed, the reluctor teeth should be aligned with the pickup coil. This can be accomplished by rotating the distributor body after it has been installed in the engine. Once again, line up the marks made before the distributor was removed.

7. Install the distributor hold-down bolt.

8. Install the spark plug into the No. 1 spark plug hole and continue with the remainder of the distributor installation procedure.

Ignition Timing

NOTE: Always refer to the Emission Control Information Label in the engine compartment for service procedures and specifications. The emission control label service procedures and specifications must be followed.

14-63

ADJUSTMENT

240SX, Altima, Maxima (VG30E), and Stanza

1. Locate the timing marks on the crankshaft pulley and the front of the engine.
2. Clean off the timing marks.
3. Use chalk or white paint to color the mark on the crankshaft pulley and the mark on the scale which will indicate the correct timing when aligned with the notch on the crankshaft pulley.
4. Connect a tachometer to the engine.
5. Attach a timing light to the engine, according to the manufacturer's instructions.
6. Start the engine and allow to reach normal operating temperature.
7. Check that the idle speed is set to specifications. Adjust as necessary.
8. Aim the timing light and illuminate the timing marks. If the marks on the pulley and the engine are aligned when the light flashes, the timing is correct. Turn off the engine and remove the tachometer and the timing light. If the marks are not in alignment, proceed with the following steps.
9. On 240SX, Altima and 1990-92 Stanza disconnect the throttle sensor harness connector.
10. Loosen the distributor lockbolt(s) just enough so the distributor can be turned with little effort.
11. Start the engine.
12. With the timing light aimed at pulley and the marks on the engine, turn the distributor in the direction of rotor rotation to retard the spark, and in the opposite direction of rotor rotation to advance the spark. Align the marks on the pulley and the engine with the flashes of the timing light. Tighten the hold-down bolt.
13. Disconnect the test equipment. On 240SX, Altima and 1990-92

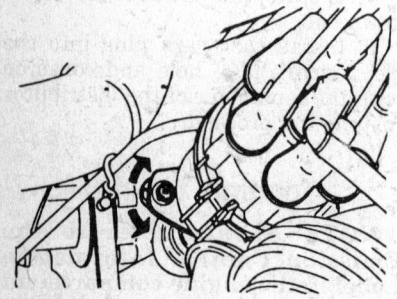

Loosen the distributor lock bolt and turn the distributor slightly to advance or retard the timing

Stanza, connect the throttle harness connector.

300ZX and Maxima (VE30DE)

NOTE: The VG30DE, VG30DETT and VE30DE engines do not utilize a conventional distributor and high tension wires. Instead they use small ignition coils fitted directly to each spark plug. The ECU controls the coils by means of a crank angle sensor from which it receives piston position and engine speed information. The ECU takes the information from the crank angle sensor and sends it to the power transistor which controls the engine timing.

1. Run the engine until it reaches normal operating temperature.
2. Check the idle speed and adjust as necessary.
3. Remove the ignition coil at the No. 1 cylinder.
4. Connect the No. 1 ignition coil to the No. 1 spark plug with a suitable high tension wire.
5. Use an inductive pickup type timing light and clamp it to the wire connected in Step 6.
6. Reconnect the air duct and hoses and then start the engine.
7. Check the ignition timing. If not to specifications, turn off the engine and loosen the 3 crank angle sensor mounting bolts slightly.

NOTE: The crank angle sensor can be found attached to the upper front cover. On the VE30DE engine, disconnect the throttle sensor harness connector and the Auxiliary Air Control (AAC) valve harness connector before adjusting the timing.

8. Restart the engine and adjust the timing by turning the sensor body slightly until the timing is within specifications. Clockwise rotation retards the timing and counterclockwise rotation advances it. Reconnect all electrical connections as necessary.

1990 Pulsar (GA16i) and Sentra (GA16i, CA16DE and SR20DE)

1. Run the engine until the water temperature indicator points to the middle of the gauge.
2. Run the engine for 1-2 minutes with no load; all electrical accessories in the off position.
3. Connect a timing light to the engine-start engine and check timing.

4. To adjust timing, stop the engine and disconnect the throttle sensor connector. Loosen the distributor hold-down bolt just enough to allow the distributor to be turned by hand.
5. Start the engine and race it 2-3 times with no load and then allow the engine to run at idle speed.
6. Adjust the ignition timing by rotating the distributor either clockwise or counterclockwise.
7. Tighten the distributor hold-down bolt and stop the engine.
8. Connect the throttle sensor connector and remove the timing light.

Alternator

PRECAUTIONS

The following precautions must be observed to prevent alternator and regulator damage:
- Be absolutely sure of correct polarity when installing a new battery or connecting a battery charger.
- Do not short across or ground any alternator or regulator terminals.
- Disconnect the battery ground cable before replacing any electrical unit.
- Never operate the alternator with any of the leads disconnected.
- When steam cleaning the engine, be careful not to subject the alternator to excessive heat or moisture.
- When charging the battery, remove it from the vehicle or disconnect the alternator output terminal.

BELT TENSION ADJUSTMENT

The correct belt tension for all alternators is about ¼-½ in. play on the longest span of the belt.

Without Adjusting Bolt

1. Disconnect the negative battery cable. Loosen the alternator pivot and mounting bolts.
2. Pry the alternator toward or away from the engine until the tension is correct. Use a hammer handle or wooden prybar.
3. When the tension is correct, tighten the bolts and check the adjustment. Be careful not to overtighten the belt, which will lead to alternator bearing failure. Reconnect the negative battery cable.

With Adjusting Bolt

1. Disconnect the negative battery cable.

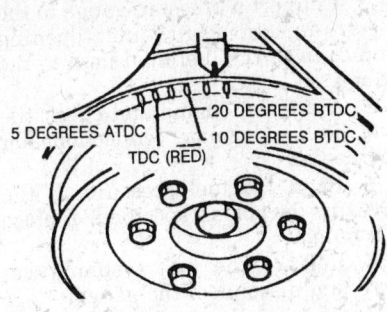

Ignition timing marks — 240SX and 1990-92 Stanza

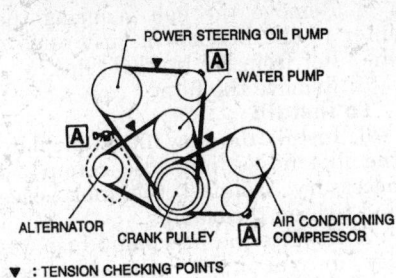

Drive belt arrangement — 240SX and 1990-92 Stanza

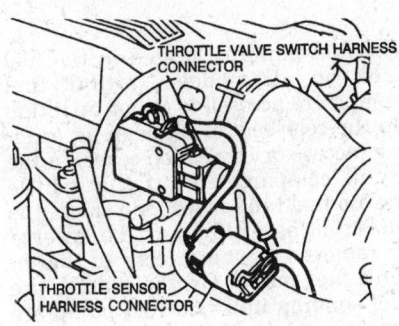

Throttle harness connector location — 240SX

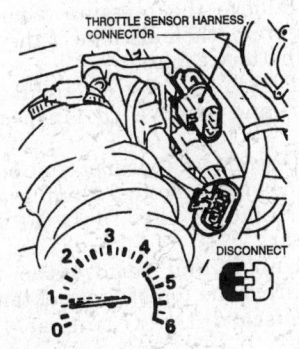

Throttle harness connector location — 1990-92 Stanza

2. Loosen the alternator adjusting bolt locknut.

3. Loosen the alternator mounting bolt(s).

4. Turn the adjusting bolt to adjust the belt tension.

5. Tighten the alternator adjusting bolt locknut.

6. Tighten the alternator mounting bolt(s).

7. Reconnect the neagative battery cable.

REMOVAL AND INSTALLATION

1. Disconnect the negative battery cable.

2. Disconnect the 2 lead wires and harness connector from the alternator.

3. Loosen the drive belt adjusting bolt and remove the belt.

4. Unscrew the alternator attaching bolts and remove the alternator from the vehicle. On 300ZX, remove the lower radiator hose bracket and pull the hose upward to gain the clearance to remove the alternator.

5. Installation is in the reverse order of removal. Adjust the drive belt tension.

Starter

REMOVAL AND INSTALLATION

1. Disconnect the negative battery cable.

2. Remove the starter heat shield (300ZX) and harness clamps, if equipped. On 1990-92 Stanza with automatic transaxle, remove the harness connectors from the harness connector bracket.

3. Disconnect and label the wires from the terminals on the solenoid.

4. Remove the 2 bolts which secure the starter to the flywheel housing and pull the starter forward and out.

5. On 1991-94 Sentra vehicles, remove the starter motor from under vehicle on SR20DE engine. On GA16DE engine (manual transaxle), remove the starter motor from the transaxle side and from the engine side on automatic transaxle applications.

6. To install, reverse the removal procedure. Check the starter for proper operation.

FUEL SYSTEM

Fuel System Service Precaution

Failure to conduct fuel system maintenance and repairs in a safe manner may result in serious personal injury. Maintenance and testing of the vehicle's fuel system components can be accomplished safely and effectively by adhering to the following rules and guidelines.

• To avoid the possibility of fire and personal injury, always disconnect the negative battery cable unless the repair or test procedure specifically requires that battery voltage be applied.

• Always relieve the fuel system pressure prior to disconnecting any fuel system component (injector, fuel rail, pressure regulator, etc.), fitting or fuel line connection. Exercise extreme caution whenever relieving fuel system pressure to avoid exposing skin, face and eyes to fuel spray. Be advised that fuel under pressure may penetrate the skin or any part of the body that it comes in contact with.

• Always place a shop towel or cloth around the fitting or connection prior to loosening to absorb any excess fuel due to spillage. Ensure that all fuel spillage (should it occur) is quickly removed from engine surfaces. Ensure that all fuel soaked cloths or towels are deposited into a suitable waste container.

• Always have a properly charged Class B dry chemical or CO2 fire extinguisher in the vicinity of the work area and always ensure work areas are adequately ventilated.

• Do not allow fuel spray or fuel vapors to come in contact with spark or open flame. Remember that smoking and fuel maintenance do not mix!

• Always use a backup wrench when loosening and tightening fuel line connection fittings. This will prevent unnecessary stress and torsion to fuel line piping. Always follow the proper torque specifications.

• Always replace worn fuel fitting O-rings with new ones. Do not substitute fuel hose or equivalent, where rigid fuel pipe is called for.

• Always use common sense.

RELIEVING FUEL SYSTEM PRESSURE

1. Remove the fuel pump fuse from the fuse block, fuel pump relay or disconnect the harness connector at the tank while engine is running.

2. It should run and then stall when the fuel in the lines is exhausted. When the engine stops, crank the starter for about 5 seconds to make sure all pressure in the fuel lines is released.

3. Install the fuel pump fuse, relay or harness connector after repair is made.

4. On some models the ""Check Engine Light" will stay on after the repair is complete. The memory code in the ECU must be erased. To erase the code disconnect the battery cables for 1 minute then reconnect.

Fuel Tank

Removal and Installation

1. Disconnect the negative battery cable.

2. Drain the fuel from the tank unit.

3. Remove the access plate from the trunk or rear seat area.

4. Disconnect all fuel lines and connections.

5. Raise and safely support the vehicle.

6. Remove the fuel tank protector, if equipped. Disconnect the fuel filler tube or filler hose at the fuel tank.

7. Remove the gas tank assembly strap retaining bolts and slowly lower the tank assembly from the vehicle.

8. Installation is the reverse of the removal procedure. Replace all line hose clamps as necessary. Always torque gas tank assembly strap retaining bolts evenly.

Fuel Filter

REMOVAL AND INSTALLATION

── CAUTION ──
Make sure to relieve the fuel system pressure before replacing the fuel filter.

1. Relieve the fuel system pressure.

2. Disconnect the negative battery cable.

3. Loosen the fuel hose clamps and disconnect the hoses from the filter.

4. Remove the bolt securing the filter to the bracket or just remove the filter from the bracket clips.

5. Remove the filter.

To install:

6. Install the new filter. Replace the fuel hoses and hose clamps, if necessary. Connect the fuel hoses and tighten the clamps.

7. Replace the fuel pump fuse, relay or reconnect the harness connector.

8. Connect the negative battery cable. Start the engine and check for leaks. On some models the ""Check Engine Light" will stay on after the repair is complete. The memory code in the ECU must be erased. To erase the code, disconnect the battery cables for 1 minute then reconnect.

Electric Fuel Pump

PRESSURE TESTING

Except Pulsar and Sentra with GA16i Engine

1. Relieve the fuel system pressure.

2. Remove the air duct, if required.

3. Connect a fuel pressure gauge between the fuel feed pipe and the fuel filter outlet.

4. Start the engine and read the fuel pressure. If the pressure is not as specified, replace the pump. If the pump output pressure is okay, go to Step 5 to check the pressure regulator.

5. Stop the engine and disconnect the fuel pressure regulator vacuum hose from the intake manifold.

6. Plug the intake manifold pressure regulator hose opening with a rubber cap.

7. Connect a vacuum pump to the fuel pressure regulator.

8. Start the engine and alternately increase and decrease the vacuum while watching the gauge. Fuel pressure should decrease as the vacuum is increased. If the pressure is incorrect, replace the pressure regulator. After replacement of the regulator, repeat the pressure test. If still incorrect, check the fuel lines for kinks or blockage and replace the pump as necessary.

Pulsar and Sentra with GA16I Engine

1. Relieve the fuel system pressure.

2. Disconnect the fuel inlet hose from the electro-injection unit.

3. Connect a pressure gauge to the electro-injection unit inlet opening and connect the fuel inlet hose to the gauge.

4. Start the engine and check the fuel line and gauge connections for fuel leaks.

5. Read the fuel pressure. If the pressure is not as specified, replace the pump.

6. Release the fuel system pressure and disconnect the gauge.

7. Connect the fuel inlet hose to the electro-injection unit.

REMOVAL AND INSTALLATION

The fuel pump is located in the fuel tank on all models. In-tank fuel pumps are accessible either by lifting up the rear seat or through an opening (access or inspection cover) in the trunk compartment. If the vehicle has no fuel tank inspection cover, the fuel tank assembly must be lowered or removed to gain access to the in-tank fuel pump. On the 300ZX, the fuel sending unit and fuel pump are separate assemblies. On the Altima, a locking ring holds the fuel pump assembly in the fuel tank unit.

1. Relieve the pressure from the fuel system, then disconnect the negative battery cable.

2. Disconnect the electrcial connector and remove the inspection cover.

3. Disconnect the inlet and outlet fuel lines from the fuel pump assembly. Remove the fuel tank if necessary.

4. Unbolt and remove the fuel pump from the top of the fuel tank.

5. Discard the O-ring seal or gasket.

To install:

6. Install the pump with a new gasket or O-ring seal. Tighten the pump retaining bolts and connect the fuel hoses. Be sure to use new clamps and that all hoses are properly seated on the fuel tank. Install fuel tank if necessary.

7. Install the fuel pump access plate.

8. Connect the pump wiring harness.

9. Connect the negative battery cable.

10. Start the engine and check for leaks. On some models, the ""Check Engine Light" will stay on after the repair is complete. The memory code in the ECU must be erased. To erase the code, disconnect the battery cables for 1 minute then reconnect.

Fuel Injector

REMOVAL AND INSTALLATION

300ZX

1. Relieve the fuel system pressure.
2. Disconnect the negative battery cable.
3. Drain coolant from the radiator.
4. Disconnect the hoses and electrical wiring from the intake manifold collector. Label each hose and wire to ensure proper placement during installation.
5. Remove the intake manifold collector assembly.
6. Remove the fuel injectors with the fuel (rail) tube as an assembly.
7. To remove the fuel injector from the fuel rail, remove the fuel injector to fuel rail bolts and the fuel injector from the fuel rail; discard the O-rings.

To install:

8. Install the fuel injector to the fuel rail, perform the following procedure:

    a. Install new O-rings onto the fuel injector.

    b. Wet the new O-rings with fuel and press the injector into the fuel rail.

    c. Install the bolts and tighten the fuel injector retainer.

9. Clean the gasket mounting surfaces if necessary.
10. Install the fuel injector and rail assembly to the intake manifold.
11. At this point of the service procedure, pressurize the fuel system and check for leaks at all fuel connections.
12. Install the intake manifold collector assembly.
13. Reconnect the hoses and electrical wiring to the intake manifold collector.
14. Refill coolant. Connect negative battery cable. Check fuel system for proper operation.

MAXIMA

VG30E ENGINE

1. Relieve the fuel system pressure.
2. Disconnect the negative battery cable.
3. Disconnect the automatic speed control device cable and accelerator cable from the intake manifold collector.
4. Disconnect the Auxiliary Air Control (AAC) valve, throttle sensor and idle switch connectors.

5. Disconnect the air cut valve water hose. Plug the end to prevent leakage.
6. Disconnect the PCV hoses.
7. Disconnect the vacuum galley, power valve actuator, master brake cylinder and EGR control valve vacuum hoses.
8. Loosen and disconnect the EGR flare tube.
9. Remove the intake upper manifold collector from the engine.
10. Disconnect the engine ground harness from the intake lower manifold collector and remove the manifold from the engine.
11. Disconnect pressure regulator vacuum hose, fuel supply and return tubes and injector electrical connectors.
12. Remove the fuel injector tube assembly.
13. Withdraw the injectors from the fuel tube.

To install:

14. Insert the fuel injector(s) into the fuel tubes with new O-rings.
15. Install the injector and fuel tube assembly.
16. Connect the injector electrical connectors, fuel supply and return tubes and pressure regulator vacuum hose. Pressurize the fuel system and check for leaks at all fuel connections.
17. Install the lower intake collector manifold and connect the engine ground harness.
18. Install the upper collector manifold.
19. Connect and tighten the EGR flare tube.
20. Connect the vacuum and PCV hoses, air cut valve water hose and electrical connectors. Install the master brake cylinder assembly and bleed system as necessary.
21. Connect the accelerator cable and automatic speed control device cable to the intake manifold collector. Adjust the cables.
22. Connect the negative battery cable.

1992-94 VE30DE Engine

1. Relieve the fuel system pressure. Disconnect the negative battery cable.
2. Disconnect the electrical connectors from the throttle position sensor, the exhaust gas temperature sensor and/or etc.
3. Label and disconnect the hoses from the throttle body, the EGR valve, the EGR control solenoid valve, the intake manifold collector, the power valve control solenoid valve (if equipped with a manual

transaxle) and the power valve actuator (if equipped with a manual transaxle).

4. Disconnect the accelerator cable from the throttle body.
5. Remove the intake manifold collector support-to-intake manifold collector and the intake manifold collector support-to-cylinder head bolts and the supports.
6. Remove the intake manifold collector-to-intake manifold bolts and the intake manifold collector.
7. If necessary, disconnect the electrical connectors from the ignition coils.
8. If necessary, disconnect the electrical connector from the crank angle sensor and the power transistor.
9. Remove the fuel injector assembly by performing the following procedures:

    a. Disconnect the electrical connectors from the fuel injectors.

    b. Disconnect the fuel injector assembly from the fuel lines.

    c. Remove the fuel rail-to-cylinder head bolts.

    d. Remove the fuel rail assembly from the engine.

10. To remove the fuel injector from the fuel rail, remove the fuel injector-to-fuel rail bolts and the fuel injector from the fuel rail; discard the O-rings.

To install:

11. To install the fuel injector to the fuel rail, perform the following procedure:

    a. Install new O-rings onto the fuel injector.

    b. Wet the new O-rings with fuel and press the injector into the fuel rail.

    c. Install the bolts and tighten the fuel injector retainer.

12. Clean the gasket mounting surfaces.
13. Install the fuel injector assembly by performing the following procedures:

    a. Install the fuel rail assembly to the engine.

    b. Install the fuel rail-to-cylinder head bolts and torque the bolts to 12-14 ft. lbs. (16-19 Nm).

    c. Connect the fuel injector assembly to the fuel lines.

    d. Connect the electrical connectors to the fuel injectors.

14. Connect the electrical connectors to the ignition coils, if disconnected.
15. Using a new gasket, install the intake manifold collector and torque the intake manifold collector-to-intake manifold bolts, from the center

to the ends in criss-cross sequence, to 13-16 ft. lbs. (18-21 Nm).

16. Install the intake manifold collector support and torque the bolts to 12-15 ft. lbs. (16-19 Nm).

17. Connect the accelerator cable to the throttle body.

18. Connect the hoses to the throttle body, the EGR valve, the EGR control solenoid valve, the intake manifold collector, the power valve control solenoid valve (if equipped with a manual transaxle) and the power valve actuator (if equipped with a manual transaxle).

19. If disconnected, connect the electrical connectors to the crank angle sensor and the power transistor.

20. If disconnected, connect the electrical connectors to the ignition coils.

21. Connect the electrical connectors from the throttle position sensor, the exhaust gas temperature sensor and/or etc.

22. Connect the negative battery cable.

23. Start the engine and check for fuel leaks.

240SX and Altima

1. Relieve the fuel system pressure.

2. Disconnect the negative battery cable.

3. Remove the related covers, harnesses, wires and tubes. Remove the BPT valve, if necessary.

4. Remove the fuel tube retaining bolts.

5. Remove the fuel tube and injector assembly from the intake manifold.

6. Withdraw the injectors from the fuel tube.

To install:

7. Clean the injector tail piece and insert the injectors into the fuel tube with new O-rings.

8. Position the injector and fuel tube assembly onto the intake manifold and install the injector tube retaining bolts.

9. Pressurize the fuel system and check for leaks at all fuel connections.

10. Install the related covers, harnesses, wires and tubes. Install the BPT valve if necessary.

11. Connect the negative battery cable.

Pulsar and Sentra (GA16i)

1. Relieve the fuel system pressure.

2. Disconnect the negative battery cable.

3. Remove the injector cover plates.

4. Using the proper tool, carefully withdraw the fuel injector straight up from the throttle body. Be careful not to damage the injector terminals during removal.

5. Remove the injector upper and lower O-rings. Install a new lower O-ring.

To install:

6. Using a 13mm socket or suitable tool, carefully push the injector into the throttle body. Make sure the injector terminals are aligned properly. Be careful not to bend the injector terminals during installation.

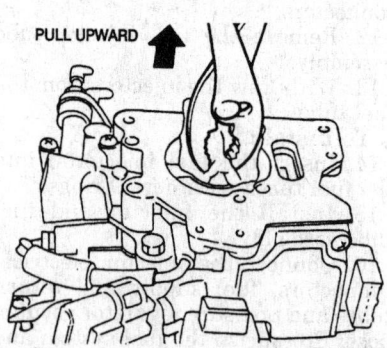

PULL UPWARD

Injector removal — GA16i engines

7. Position the new upper injector O-ring and install it with a 19mm socket or other suitable tool.

8. Install the lower (white) injector cover plate. Do not over tighten the cover screws.

9. Install the injector cover without the rubber boot. Make sure the 2 O-rings (large and small) properly seated in the cover. Make sure there is a good connection between the injector terminal and the injector cover terminal. When this connection is verified, install the cover boot.

10. Connect the negative battery cable.

11. Start the engine and check for leaks at all fuel connections.

1991-94 Sentra (GA16DE and SR20DE)

1. Relieve the fuel system pressure. Disconnect the negative battery cable.

2. Disconnect the fuel injector wiring harness connectors and vacuum line from the fuel pressure regulator.

3. Disconnect the fuel hoses from the fuel tube assembly.

4. Remove the injectors with fuel tube assembly.

5. Installation is the reverse of the removal procedure. Install injectors with fuel tube assembly to intake manifold torque all retaining bolts in

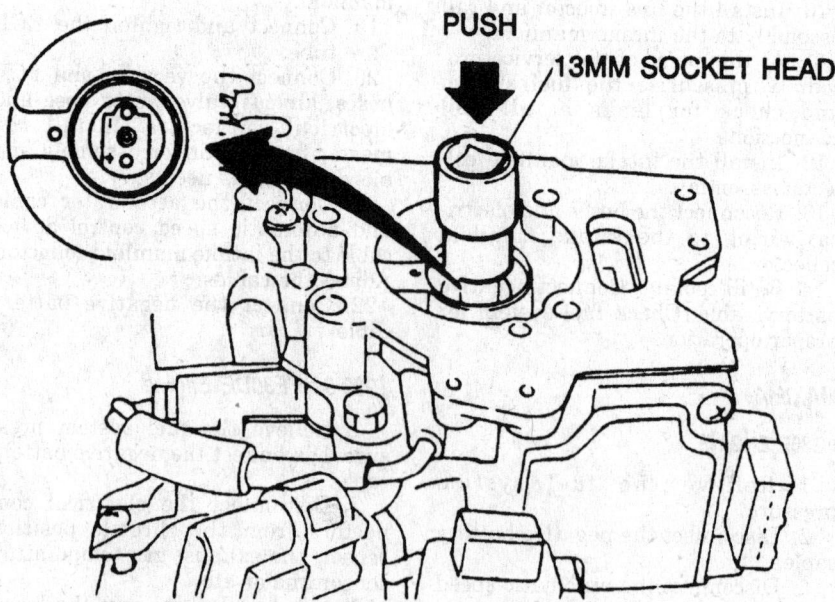

PUSH

13MM SOCKET HEAD

Injector installation — GA16i engines. Note injector terminal alignment

2 steps to 15-20 ft. lbs. (20-27 Nm). Check for fuel leaks after installation is complete.

1990-92 Stanza

1. Relieve the fuel system pressure.
2. Disconnect the negative battery cable.
3. Disconect the air duct.
4. Disconnect the supply and return hoses from the fuel tube. Plug the ends to prevent leakage.
5. Disconnect the vacuum line from the fuel pressure regulator.
6. Detach the accelerator cable bracket.
7. Disconnect the fuel injector wiring harness connectors.
8. Remove the fuel tube retaining bolts.
9. Pull the fuel tube and injector assembly from the intake manifold. Remove the injector assembly out from the No. 4 injector side.

To install:

10. Remove the O-rings and insulators and install new ones.
11. Install the injector and fuel tube assembly into the intake manifold.
12. Install the injector tube retaining bolts.
13. Connect the injector wiring harness connectors.
14. Attach the accelerator cable bracket.
15. Connect the pressure regulator vacuum line.
16. Connect the fuel supply and return hoses.
17. Connect the air duct.
18. Connect the negative battery cable.
19. Start the engine and check for leaks at all fuel connections.

DRIVE AXLE

Halfshaft

Removal and Installation

FRONT WHEEL DRIVE

This procedure applies to all 2WD drive vehicles and to the front halfshafts on 4WD vehicles. Removal and installation of the rear halfshafts on 4WD vehicles is described in this section.

NOTE: Installation of the halfshafts will require a special tool for the spline alignment of the halfshaft end and the transaxle case. Do not perform this procedure without access to this tool or suitable equivalent. The tool is J-34296, J-34297 or J-33904 depending on the vehicle.

1. Raise the vehicle and support safely.
2. Remove the wheel and tire assembly.
3. Withdraw the cotter pin from the castellated nut on the wheel hub.
4. Depress the brake pedal and remove the wheel bearing locknut.
5. Remove the brake caliper assembly without disconnecting the brake line. Support the caliper with wire.
6. Separate the halfshaft from the steering knuckle by tapping it with a block of wood and a mallet. It may be necessary to loosen (do not remove) the strut mounting bolts to gain clearance for steering knuckle removal from the halfshaft.
7. Remove the tie rod ball joint.

NOTE: Always use a new nut when replacing the tie rod ball joint.

8. Using a suitable tool, reach through the engine crossmember and carefully tap the right side inner CV-joint out of the transaxle case.
9. Using a block of wood and a suitable jack, support the engine under the oil pan.
10. Remove the support bearing bracket and bearing retainer bolts from the engine and then withdraw the right halfshaft, except Pulsar with GA16i and Sentra.
11. On vehicles with manual transaxles, carefully insert a small prybar between the left CV-joint inner flange and the transaxle case

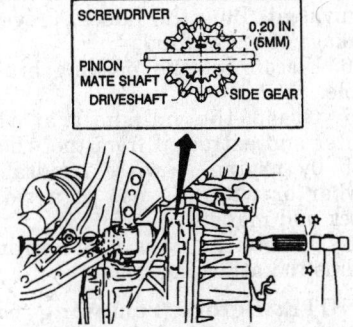

Left halfshaft removal on automatic transaxle vehicles — Maxima and Stanza

mounting surface and pry the halfshaft out of the case. Withdraw the shaft from the steering knuckle and remove it.

12. On vehicles with automatic transaxles, insert a dowel through the right side halfshaft hole and use a small mallet to tap the left halfshaft out of the transaxle case. Withdraw the shaft from the steering knuckle and remove it.

NOTE: Be careful not to damage the pinion mating shaft and the side gear while tapping the left halfshaft out of the transaxle case.

To install:

13. When installing the shafts into the transaxle, use a new oil seal and then install an alignment tool along the inner circumference of the oil seal.
14. Insert the halfshaft into the transaxle, align the serrations and then remove the alignment tool.
15. Push the halfshaft, then press-fit the circular clip on the shaft into the clip groove on the side gear.

NOTE: After insertion, attempt to pull the flange out of the side joint to make sure the circular clip is properly seated in the side gear and will not come out.

16. Install support bearing bracket retaining bolts, if equipped. Insert the driveshaft into the steering knuckle. Tighten the strut mounting bolts.
17. Connect the tie rod end ball joint and use new nut and cotter pin.
18. Mount the brake caliper assembly.
19. Install the wheel bearing locknut. Torque the nut to:
   Altima, Maxima and Stanza — 174-231 ft. lbs. (235-314 Nm)
   Sentra and 1990 Pulsar — 145-203 ft. lbs. (196-275 Nm)

NOTE: When tightening the nut, apply the brake pedal.

20. Install a new cotter pin into the wheel bearing locknut.
21. Mount the wheel and tire assembly.
22. Lower the vehicle.

Rear Wheel Drive

EXCEPT SENTRA 4WD WAGON

NOTE: When removing the rear halfshafts, cover the CV-boots with cloth to prevent damage.

1. Raise and support the rear of the vehicle safely.

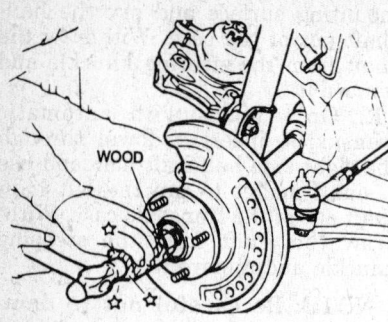

Separating the halfshaft from the steering knuckle

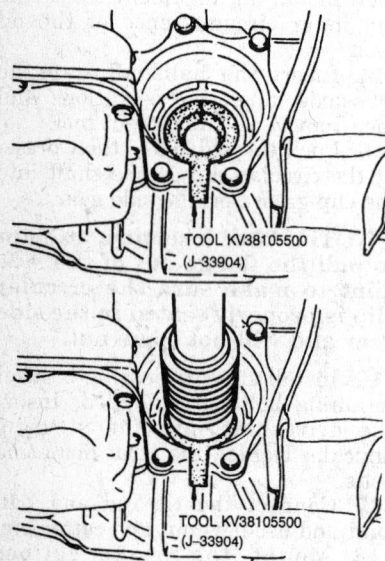

TOOL KV38105500
(J-33904)

TOOL KV38105500
(J-33904)

Halfshaft alignment tools used on front wheel drive vehicles

2. Remove the rear wheel and tire assembly.

3. Remove the adjusting cap and cotter pin from the wheel bearing locknut.

4. Apply the parking brake and remove the rear wheel locknut.

5. Disconnect the halfshaft from the differential side by removing the flange bolts.

6. Grasp the halfshaft at the center and extract if from the wheel hub by prying it with a suitable

prybar or with the use of a wood block and mallet.

NOTE: To protect the threads of the shaft, temporarily install the locknut when loosening the shaft from the wheel hub.

To install:

7. Insert the shaft into the wheel hub and temporarily install the locknut.

NOTE: Take care not to damage the oil seal or either end of the halfshaft during installation.

8. Connect the halfshaft to the differential and install the flange bolts. On 240SX and 300ZX, torque the flange bolts to 25-33 ft. lbs. (34-44 Nm).

9. Apply the parking brake and tighten the locknut. Torque the locknut to:

240SX — 174-231 ft. lbs. (236-314 Nm)

300ZX — 154-203 ft. lbs. (206-275 Nm)

10. Install a new locknut cotter pin and install the adjusting cap.

11. Mount the rear wheel and tire assembly.

12. Lower the vehicle.

SENTRA (4WD)

This procedure applies to removal and installation of the rear halfshafts only.

NOTE: When removing the rear halfshafts, cover the CV-boots with cloth to prevent damage.

1. Raise and support the rear of the vehicle safely.

2. Remove the rear wheel and tire assembly.

3. Remove the adjusting cap, insulator and cotter pin from the wheel bearing locknut.

4. Apply the parking brake and remove the rear wheel locknut.

5. Disconnect the brake line. Use a brake line wrench or suitable equivalent. Plug the line to prevent leakage of brake fluid.

6. Disconnect the parking brake cable.

7. Grasp the halfshaft at the center and extract if from the wheel hub by prying it with a suitable prybar or with the use of a wood block and mallet.

8. Remove the transverse link and radius rod attaching bolts.

NOTE: Before removing the transverse rod bolts, matchmark the toe-in adjusting bolt to the adjustment degree plate.

9. Pry the halfshaft from the differential using a small prybar.

10. Remove the knuckle attaching bolts and remove the wheel hub, baffle plate, knuckle and halfshaft as a unit. Be careful not to damage the differential drive gear oil seal during removal.

To install:

11. Mount the wheel hub, baffle plate, knuckle and driveshaft and temporarily install the wheel bearing locknut.

12. Insert the halfshaft into the transaxle and properly align the splines.

13. Push the halfshaft, then press-fit the circular clip on the shaft into the clip groove on the side gear.

NOTE: After insertion, attempt to pull the flange out of the side joint to make sure the circular clip is properly seated in the side gear and will not come out.

14. Tighten the knuckle attaching bolts.

15. Install the transverse link and radius rod attaching (fixing) bolts. Make sure the toe-in bolt matchmarks are aligned properly.

16. Connect the parking brake cable and brake line.

17. Install the rear wheel bearing nut and adjust the rear wheel bearing pre-load.

18. Install adjusting cap, insulator and a new locknut cotter pin.

19. Mount the rear wheel and tire assembly.

20. Lower the vehicle.

21. Adjust the parking brake cable and bleed the brakes.

CV-Boot

Removal and Installation

TRANSAXLE SIDE

1. Remove the halfshaft and mount in a protected jaw vise.

2. Remove the boot bands.

3. Matchmark the slide joint housing and spider assembly to the halfshaft.

4. Remove the slide joint housing from the halfshaft.

5. Remove the spider snapring.

6. Remove the spider assembly from the halfshaft.

7. Cover the driveshaft splined end with tape to protect the CV-boot.

8. Remove the CV-boot.

To install:

9. Install the CV-boot with a new boot band.

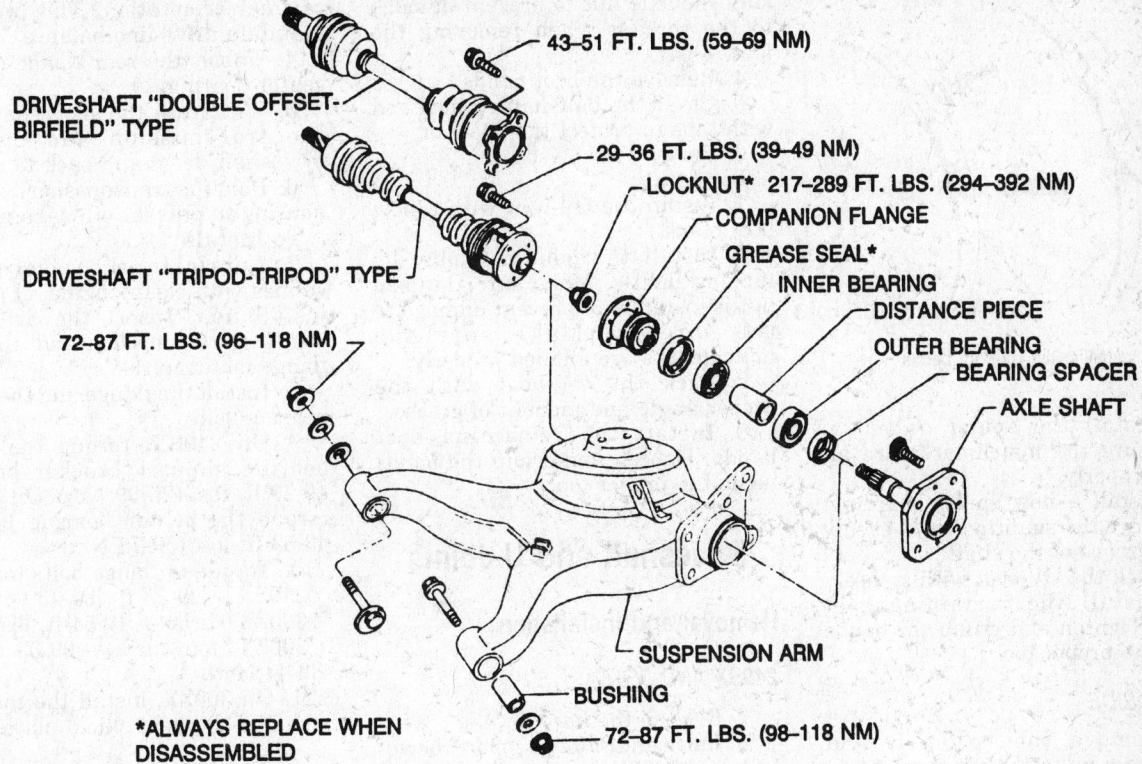

DRIVESHAFT "DOUBLE OFFSET-BIRFIELD" TYPE

43–51 FT. LBS. (59–69 NM)

DRIVESHAFT "TRIPOD-TRIPOD" TYPE

72–87 FT. LBS. (96–118 NM)

29–36 FT. LBS. (39–49 NM)

LOCKNUT* 217–289 FT. LBS. (294–392 NM)

COMPANION FLANGE

GREASE SEAL*

INNER BEARING

DISTANCE PIECE

OUTER BEARING

BEARING SPACER

AXLE SHAFT

SUSPENSION ARM

BUSHING

72–87 FT. LBS. (98–118 NM)

*ALWAYS REPLACE WHEN DISASSEMBLED

Exploded view of the rear axle shown with either the Double Off-Set Birfield type driveshaft or the Tripod type driveshaft — models with IRS

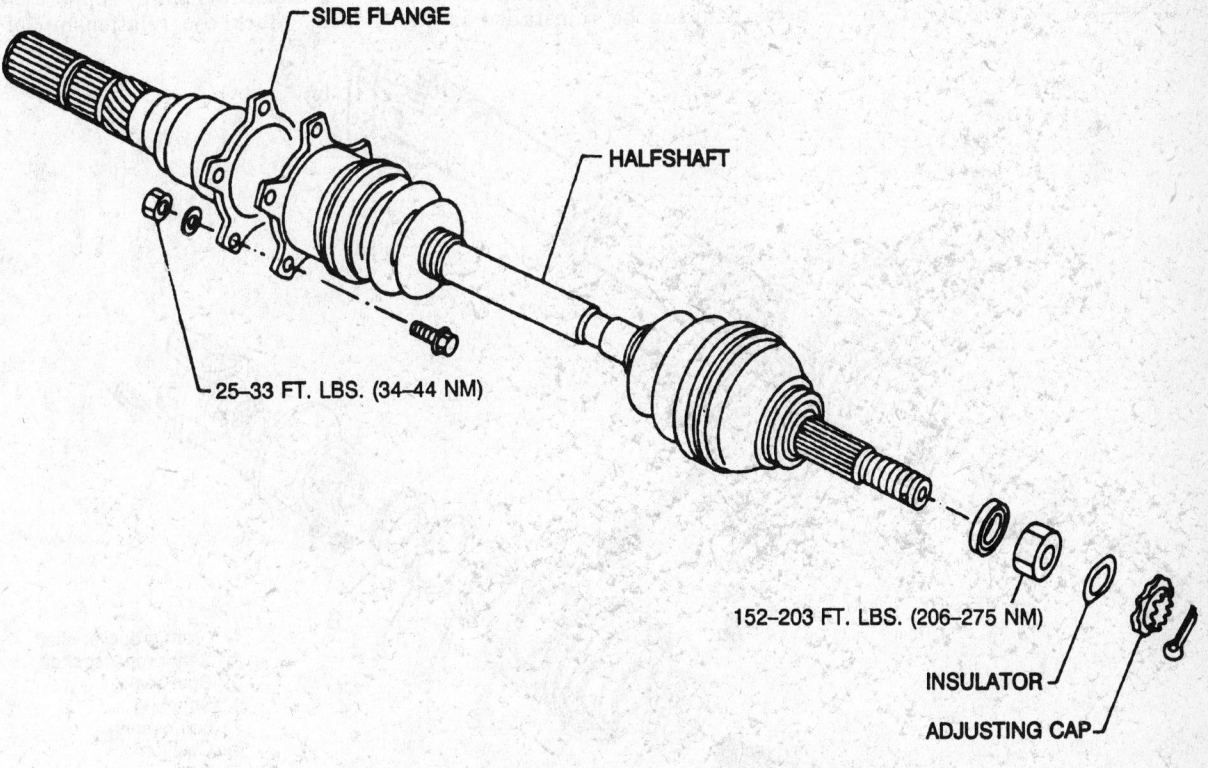

SIDE FLANGE

HALFSHAFT

25–33 FT. LBS. (34–44 NM)

152–203 FT. LBS. (206–275 NM)

INSULATOR

ADJUSTING CAP

Rear halfshaft assembly on rear wheel drive vehicles (300ZX shown)

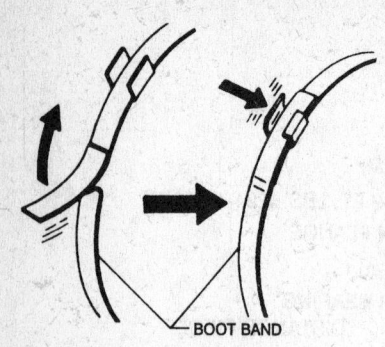

Installing the CV-boot bands

10. Install the spider assembly. Make sure the matchmarks are aligned properly.

11. Install a new spider snapring. Make sure the snapring seats evenly in the groove of the shaft.

12. Pack the CV-boot with grease.

13. Install the remaining boot bands. Tighten and crimp the bands using the proper tool.

WHEEL SIDE

1. Remove the halfshaft and mount in a protected jaw vise.

2. Matchmark the joint assembly to the shaft.

3. Remove the joint assembly from the shaft using a suitable puller. In-

stall the axle nut to prevent damage to the threads when removing the joint.

4. Remove the boot bands.

5. Cover the halfshaft splined end with tape to protect the CV-boot.

6. Remove the CV-boot.

To install:

7. Install the CV-boot with a new boot band.

8. Install the joint assembly by tapping lightly. Make sure the axle nut is installed to prevent damage to the threads. Make sure the matchmarks are aligned properly.

9. Pack the CV-boot with the proper grade and amount of grease.

10. Install the remaining boot bands. Tighten and crimp the bands using the proper tool.

Driveshaft and U-Joints

Removal and Installation

240SX AND 300ZX

1. Release the hand brake.

2. Raise and safely support the vehicle. On 300ZX, remove the the front pipe and the heat shield plate.

3. Matchmark the flanges on the driveshaft and differential so the driveshaft can be reinstalled in its

original orientation. This will help maintain drive-line balance.

4. Unbolt the rear flange and the center bearing.

5. Withdraw the driveshaft from the transmission and pull the driveshaft down and back to remove.

6. Plug the transmission extension housing to prevent oil leakage.

To install:

7. Lubricate the sleeve yoke splines with clean engine oil prior to installation. Insert the driveshaft into the transmission and align the flange matchmarks.

8. Install the flange and the center bearing bolts.

9. On 240SX, torque the center bearing support bracket bolts to 19-29 ft. lbs. (25-39 Nm). On 300ZX, torque the center bearing bolts to 43-58 ft. lbs. (59-78 Nm).

10. Torque to flange bolts to:
240SX — 29-33 ft. lbs. (39-44 Nm)
300ZX Turbo — 47-54 ft. lbs.
300ZX non-Turbo — 29-33 ft. lbs. (39-44 Nm).

11. On 300ZX, install the the front pipe and the heat shield plate.

SENTRA (4WD)

1. Raise and safely support the vehicle. Mark the relationship of the

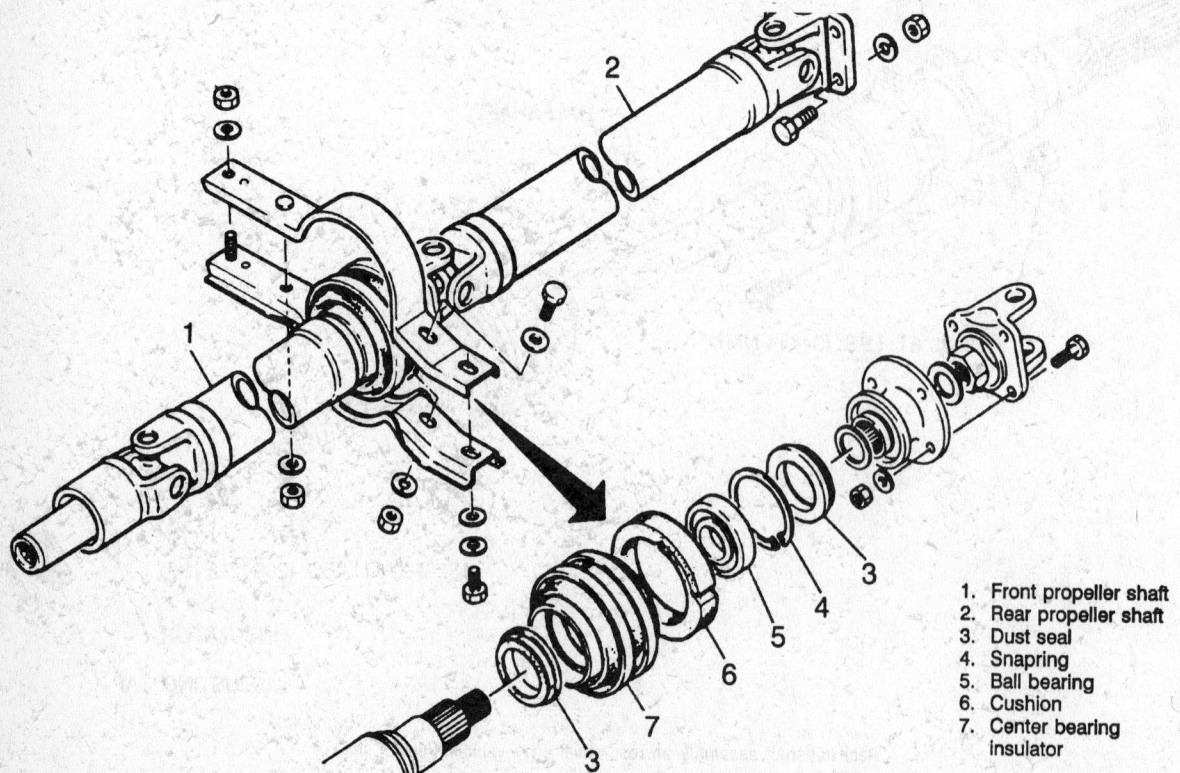

1. Front propeller shaft
2. Rear propeller shaft
3. Dust seal
4. Snapring
5. Ball bearing
6. Cushion
7. Center bearing insulator

2-piece driveshaft with center bearing assembly

driveshaft flange to the differential flange.

2. Unbolt the center bearing bracket.

3. Unbolt the driveshaft flange from the differential flange.

4. Pull the driveshaft back under the rear axle. Plug the rear of the transmission to prevent oil or fluid loss.

5. To install, align the flange matchmarks made in Step 1. Torque the front and rear flange bolts to 25-33 ft. lbs. (34-44 Nm). Torque the center bracket bolts to 19-29 ft. lbs. (25-39 Nm).

Front Axle Shaft, Bearing and Seal

Removal and Installation

300ZX

1. Raise and support the vehicle safely.

2. Remove the front wheels.

3. Unbolt the caliper and move it aside. Do not disconnect the hose from the caliper. Do not allow the caliper to hang by the hose; support the caliper with a length of wire or rest it on a suspension member.

4. Separate the tie rod and lower ball joints using the proper tool.

NOTE: The steering knuckle is made of an aluminum alloy. Be careful no to strike it when removing the ball joints.

5. Remove the kingpin lower nut and remove the steering knuckle assembly.

6. Remove the hub cap, wheel bearing locknut, sensor rotor (with ABS) or washer (without ABS).

7. Remove the wheel hub with a suitable drift.

8. Remove the wheel bearing retaining ring.

9. Press the wheel bearing from the knuckle.

10. Drive out the wheel bearing inner race to the outside of the wheel hub.

11. Remove the grease seal and splash guard (baffle plate).

To install:

12. From the outside of the knuckle, press the new wheel bearing assembly into the knuckle.

NOTE: Do not press the on the inner race of the wheel bearing assembly. Do not lubricate the surfaces of mating surfaces of the wheel bearing outer race and wheel with grease or oil. Be careful not to damage the grease seal.

13. Install the bearing retaining ring. Make sure it seats evenly in the groove of the knuckle.

14. Coat the lip of the grease seal with multi-purpose grease and install.

15. Install the splash guard.

16. Press the wheel hub into the steering knuckle.

17. Install the washer (without ABS), sensor rotor (with ABS) and wheel bearing locknut. Torque the locknut to 152-210 ft. lbs. (206-284 Nm). Stake the locknut tabs using a small cold chisel.

18. Place the hub cap onto the knuckle and tap it into place using a rubber or plastic mallet. Once the cap is seated lightly into the knuckle, install the cap retaining bolts and torque to 8-12 ft. lbs. (11-16 Nm).

19. Mount the steering knuckle assembly and tighten the lower kingpin nut.

20. Connect the tie rod and lower ball joints using the proper tool.

21. Install the brake caliper assembly.

22. Prior to checking the bearing pre-load, spin the wheel hub at least 10 revolutions in both directions to seat the bearing. Check the wheel bearing preload and axial endplay as follows:

a. Pre-load—connect a spring scale of known calibration to a wheel hub bolt and measure the turning torque. If an NSK wheel bearing is used, the turning torque should be 1.3-8.4 lbs. (5.9-37.3 N). For NTN bearings, the turning torque should be 1.8-13.0 lbs. (7.8-57.9 N).

b. Axial endplay—mount a dial indicator so the stylus of the dial rests on the face of the hub and check the wheel bearing axial endplay by attempting to rock the wheel hub in and out. The endplay should be 0.0020 in. (0.05mm) or less.

23. Mount the front wheels and lower the vehicle.

240SX

1. Raise and support the vehicle safely.

2. Remove the front wheels.

3. Work off center hub cap by using thin tool. If necessary tap around it with a soft hammer while removing. Pry off cotter pin and take out adjusting cap.

4. Apply the parking brake firmly and remove the wheel bearing nut.

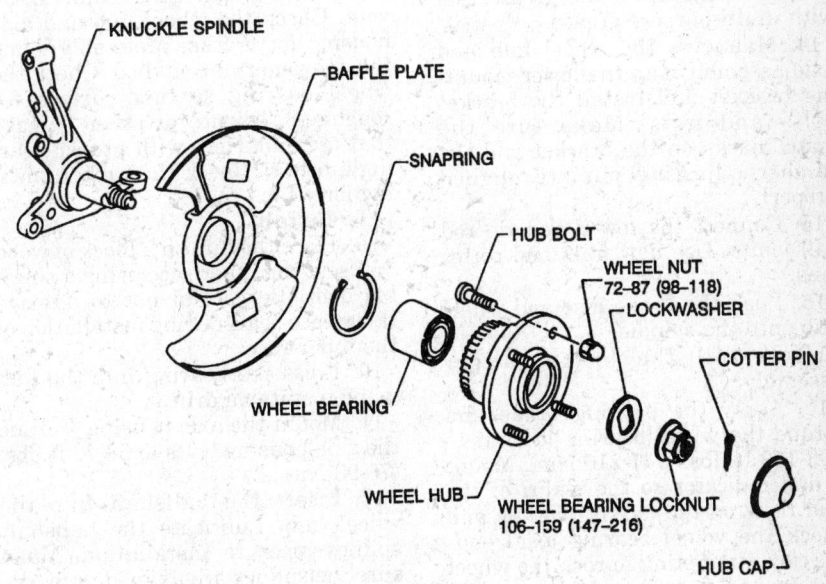

Front axle and wheel hub assembly — 240SX

The nut will require a good deal of force to remove it.

5. Unbolt the caliper and move it aside. Do not disconnect the hose from the caliper. Do not allow the caliper to hang by the hose; support the caliper with a length of wire or rest it on a suspension member.

6. Pull the brake disc and wheel hub from the spindle.

7. Separate the tie rod and lower ball joints using the proper tool.

8. Place matchmarks on the strut lower bracket and camber adjusting pin for assembly reference. Remove the lower bracket bolts and nuts. Remove the wheel hub and knuckle assembly.

9. Remove the bearing retaining ring from the wheel hub.

10. Press the bearing assembly from the wheel hub. Apply pressure from the outside of the hub to remove the bearing.

To install:

11. Press the new bearing assembly into the hub from the inside.

NOTE: Do not press the on the inner race of the wheel bearing assembly. Do not lubricate the surfaces of mating surfaces of the wheel bearing outer race and wheel with grease or oil. Be careful not to damage the grease seal.

12. Install the bearing retaining ring.

13. Coat the lip of the grease seal with multi-purpose grease.

14. Manuever the wheel hub and axle assembly onto the lower mounting bracket and install the bracket bolts and nuts. Make sure the matchmarks on the bracket and the camber adjusting pin are aligned properly.

15. Connect the lower and tie rod ball joints. Use new nuts and cotter pins.

16. Push the brake disc and wheel hub onto the spindle.

17. Install the brake caliper assembly.

18. Apply the parking brake and torque the wheel bearing locknut to 108-159 ft. lbs. (147-216 Nm). Mount a dial indicator so the stylus of the dial rests on the face of the hub and check the wheel bearing axial endplay by attempting to rock the wheel hub in and out. The endplay should be 0.0012 in. (0.03mm) or less.

19. Install a new locknut cotter pin. Install the bearing hub cap.

20. Mount the the front wheels and lower the vehicle.

Rear Axle Shaft, Bearings and Seal

Removal and Installation

240SX AND 300ZX

1. Block the front wheels.

2. Raise and support the rear of the vehicle and remove the rear wheels. Remove the cotter pin, adjusting cap and insulator.

3. Apply the parking brake firmly to hold the rear halfshaft while removing the wheel bearing locknut. Remove the wheel bearing locknut.

4. Unbolt the caliper and move it aside. Do not disconnect the hose from the caliper. Do not allow the caliper to hang by the hose; support the caliper with a length of wire or rest it on a suspension member. Remove the brake disc.

5. Separate the halfshaft from the axle housing by lightly tapping it. Cover the driveshaft boots with a shop towel to prevent damage.

6. Unbolt and remove the axle housing from the vehicle. Remove the 4 bolts that hold the wheel bearing, flange and hub to the axle housing.

7. Press the wheel bearing from the axle hub. Mount the hub in a vise and remove the inner race using a bearing replacer/puller tool. Discard the inner race. If the grease seals are being replaced, replace them as a set.

8. Clean all parts in a suitable solvent. Check the wheel hub and axle housing for cracks, preferably using the dye penetrant method. Check the wheel bearing seating surface for roughness, seizure or other damage that may interfere with proper bearing function. Check the rubber bushing for wear.

To install:

9. Place the hub on a block of wood and seat the inner race using a suitable drift. Be careful not to damage the grease seals during installation of the inner race.

10. Press the bearing into the hub using a suitable drift.

11. Mount the axle housing. Torque the axle housing bolts to 58-72 ft. lbs. (78-98 Nm).

12. Insert the halfshaft into the wheel hub. Lubricate the halfshaft splines prior to installation. Make sure the splines are aligned properly.

13. Install the caliper assembly.

14. Install the wheel bearing locknut. On 240SX, torque the nut to 174-231 ft. lbs. (235-314 Nm). On 300ZX, torque the nut to 152-203 ft. lbs. (206-275 Nm). Install the insula-

tor and fit adjusting cap. Install a new cotter pin.

15. On 300ZX, check the axial endplay as follows before mounting the rear wheels. Mount a dial indicator so the stylus of the dial rests on the face of the hub and check the wheel bearing axial endplay by attempting to rock the wheel hub in and out. The endplay should be 0.0020 in. (0.05mm) or less.

16. Mount the rear wheels and lower the vehicle.

Front Wheel Hub, Knuckle and Bearings

Removal and Installation

MAXIMA, PULSAR, SENTRA AND STANZA

1. Raise and support the vehicle safely.

2. Remove the front wheels.

3. Remove the cotter pin, adjusting cap and insulator.

4. Apply the parking brake firmly and remove the wheel bearing nut.

5. Unbolt the caliper and move it aside. Do not disconnect the hose from the caliper. Do not allow the caliper to hang by the hose; support the caliper with a length of wire or rest it on a suspension member.

6. Separate the tie rod end from the steering knuckle using the proper tool.

7. Disconnect the halfshaft from the transaxle using the proper tool or by tapping on it with a block of wood and a mallet.

NOTE: Cover the CV-boots with cloth to prevent damage when removing the halfshafts.

8. Remove the nuts and bolt that attach the knuckle to the strut. Make sure to place a visible matchmark on the adjusting pin and knuckle mounting bracket before removing these fasteners.

9. Remove the lower arm-to-ball joint bolts, if equipped.

10. Loosen the lower ball joint nut and separate the knuckle from the lower ball joint stud using the proper tool.

11. Remove the knuckle and hub assembly.

12. Drive out the hub and outside inner race with a suitable tool.

13. Withdraw the outside inner race from the wheel hub.

14. On Altima, Maxima and Stanza, remove the outer and grease

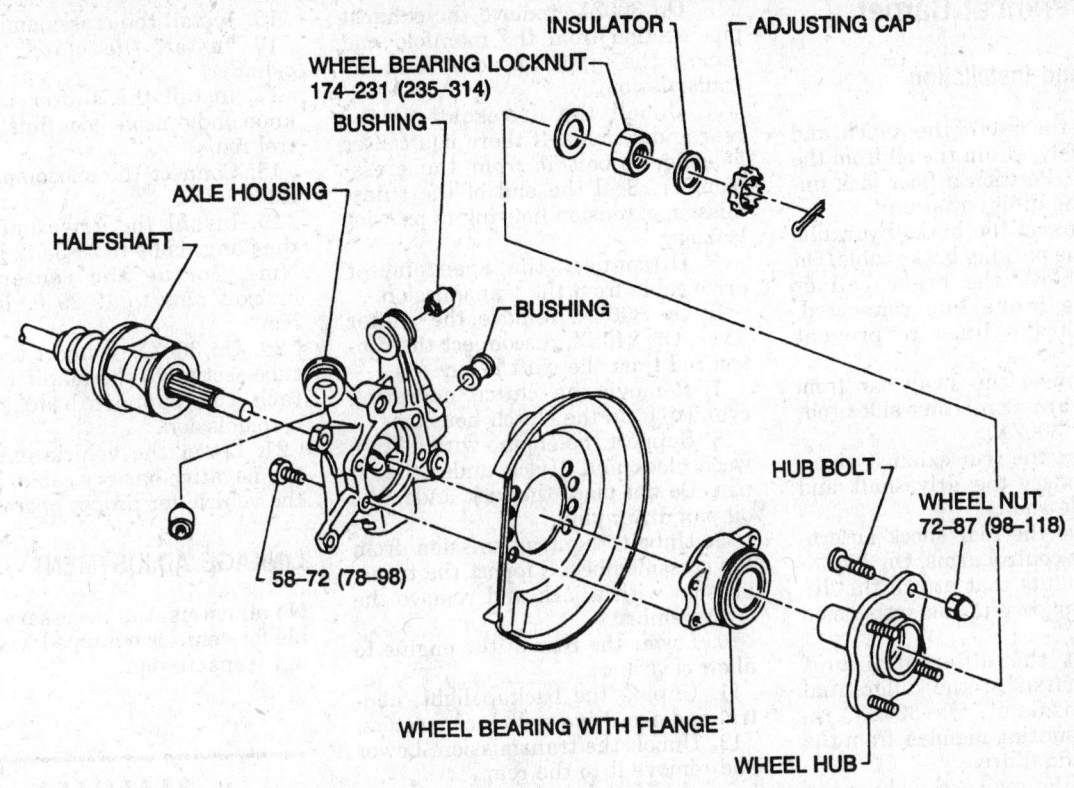

Rear axle housing assembly — 240SX shown — 300ZX similar

seals from the hub at this time, then press the outer race from the hub.

15. On Pulsar and Sentra, press the inside inner race from the hub. Set the race aside for use in removal of the wheel bearing.

16. Remove the wheel bearing retainer with the proper tool. On Altima, Maxima and Stanza, there are retainers on both sides of the hub. After both retainers are removed, the bearing can be pressed from the hub at this time.

17. On Pulsar and Sentra, place the inside inner race set aside in Step 15 on top of the wheel bearing and press the bearing out of the hub. Apply pressure to the inside of the knuckle to remove the bearing.

18. Clean all parts in a suitable solvent.

19. Check the wheel hub and axle housing for cracks, preferrably using the dye penetrant method. Check the wheel bearing seating surface for roughness, seizure or other damage that may interfere with proper bearing function.

To install:

20. On Altima, Maxima and Stanza, install the inner bearing retainer.

21. Press the new bearing into the knuckle by applying pressure to the outside of the knuckle. Do not exceed 3.3 tons of pressure.

NOTE: Do not press the on the inner race of the wheel bearing assembly. Do not lubricate the surfaces of mating surfaces of the wheel bearing outer race and wheel with grease or oil. Be careful not to damage the grease seal.

22. Install the remaining bearing retainer. Make sure it seats evenly in the groove of the knuckle.

23. Coat the lip of the seal with multi-purpose grease. On Altima, Maxima and Stanza, install the inner and outer grease seals. Make sure the lip of the seal(s) faces the inside of the hub.

24. Press the hub into the knuckle. Do not exceed 3.3 tons of pressure.

25. Clamp the knuckle portion in a vise and apply a pre-load of 3.5-5.0 tons to the outside (wheel bolt side) of the bearing with a suitable press. Spin the knuckle several turns in both directions and make sure the bearing spins freely and does not bind.

26. Mount the knuckle and hub assembly.

27. Install the lower arm-to-ball joint bolts.

28. Connect the lower ball joint to the knuckle (use new nut and cotter pin).

29. Install the knuckle-to-strut fasteners. Make sure the adjusting pin matchmarks are aligned properly.

30. Install the halfshafts.

31. Connect the tie rod end to the steering knuckle using the proper tool.

32. Install the brake caliper assembly.

33. Install the wheel bearing locknut. Torque the nut to 174-231 ft. lbs. (235-314 Nm) on Altima, Maxima and Stanza; 145-203 ft. lbs. (196-275 Nm) on Sentra and 1990 Pulsar. When tightening the nut, apply the brake pedal.

34. Install the insulator and adjusting cap. Install a new cotter pin into the wheel bearing locknut.

35. Check the axial endplay as follows: mount a dial indicator so the stylus of the dial rests on the face of the hub and check the wheel bearing axial endplay by attempting to rock the wheel hub in and out. The endplay should be 0.0020 in. (0.05mm) or less.

36. Mount the front wheels.

37. Lower the vehicle. Check front end alignment if necessary.

Differential Carrier

Removal and Installation

1. Raise the rear of the vehicle and support safely. Drain the oil from the differential. Position a floor jack underneath the differential unit.

2. Disconnect the brake hydraulic lines and the parking brake cable. On 240SX, remove the brake caliper leaving the brake line connected. Plug the brake lines to prevent leakage.

3. Disconnect the sway bar from the control arms on either sides (not required on 300ZX).

4. Remove the rear exhaust pipe.

5. Disconnect the driveshaft and the rear axle shafts.

6. Remove the rear shock absorbers from the control arms. On 300ZX, remove the nuts that attach the differential rear cove to the suspension member.

7. Unbolt the differential unit from the chassis at the differential mounting insulator. On 300ZX, remove the mounting member from the front of the final drive.

8. Lower the rear assembly out of the vehicle using the floor jack. It is best to have at least one other person helping to balance the assembly. After the final drive is removed, support the center suspension member to prevent damage to the insulators.

To install:

9. Torque the rear cover-to-insulator nuts to 72-87 ft. lbs. (98-118 Nm); mounting insulator-to-chassis bolts to 22-29 ft. lbs. (30-39 Nm); strut nuts to 51-65 ft. lbs. (69-81 Nm); sway bar-to-control arm nuts to 12-15 ft. lbs. (16-21 Nm). On 240SX and 300ZX, torque the driveshaft flange bolts to 25-33 ft. lbs. (34-44 Nm).

MANUAL TRANSMISSION

Transmission Assembly

REMOVAL AND INSTALLATION

240SX and 300ZX

1. Disconnect the negative battery cable.

2. Raise and support the vehicle safely.

3. On 300ZX, remove the exhaust pipe section from the manifold and remove the support bracket from the transmission.

4. Unbolt the driveshaft at the rear and remove. If there is a center bearing, unbolt it from the crossmember. Seal the end of the transmission extension housing to prevent leakage.

5. Disconnect the speedometer drive cable from the transmission.

6. On 300ZX, remove the shifter lever. On 240SX, disconnect the control rod from the shift lever.

7. Remove the clutch operating cylinder from the clutch housing.

8. Support the engine with a large wood block and a jack under the oil pan. Do not place the jack under the oil pan drain plug.

9. Unbolt the transmission from the crossmember. Support the transmission with a jack and remove the crossmember.

10. Lower the rear of the engine to allow clearance.

11. Unplug the backup light, neutral and overdrive switch connectors.

12. Unbolt the transmission. Lower and remove it to the rear.

NOTE: The transmission bolts are different lengths. Tagging the transmission-to-engine bolts upon removal will facilitate proper tightening during installation.

To install:

13. Raise the transmission onto the engine and install the mounting bolts. Torque the bolts as follows:

a. 240SX — tighten bolts (1), (2) and (4) to 29-36 ft. lbs. (39-49 Nm) and bolt (3) to 22-29 ft. lbs. (29-39 Nm)

b. 300ZX — tighten bolts (1), (2) and (3) to 29-36 ft. lbs. (39-49 Nm). Tighten bolts (4) and (5) to 22-29 ft. lbs. (29-39 Nm).

14. Connect the backup light, neutral and overdrive switch connectors.

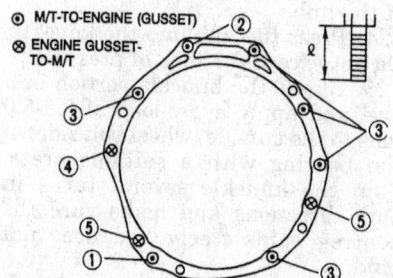

Transmission mounting bolt locations on 300ZX; bolt (1) is 100mm, bolt (2) is 65mm, bolt (3) is 60mm, bolt (4) is 55mm and bolt (5) is 25mm

15. Install the crossmember.

16. Install the clutch operating cylinder.

17. Install the shifter lever, shift knob and console boot finisher or control rod.

18. Connect the speedometer drive cable.

19. Install the driveshaft. Torque the flange bolts to 29-33 ft. lbs. (34-44 Nm). Torque the center bearing bracket nuts to 19-29 ft. lbs. (25-39 Nm).

20. On 300ZX, connect the exhaust tube section to the manifolds and attach the support bracket to the transmission.

21. Lower the vehicle and connect the negative battery cable. Road test the vehicle for proper operation.

LINKAGE ADJUSTMENT

No adjustment is necessary or possible for vehicles equipped with a manual transmission.

MANUAL TRANSAXLE

Transaxle Assembly

REMOVAL AND INSTALLATION

Except 1990-92 Stanza

1. Disconnect the negative battery cable.

2. Remove the battery and battery bracket.

3. Remove the air duct, air cleaner box and air flow meter.

4. Raise the front of the vehicle and support safely.

5. Drain the transaxle oil. Remove the starter motor assembly.

6. On Sentra (4WD) vehicles, remove the transfer case.

7. Withdraw the halfshafts from the transaxle assembly.

NOTE: When removing halfshafts, use care not to damage the lip of the oil seal. After halfshafts are removed, insert a steel bar or wooden dowel of suitable diameter to prevent the side gears from rotating and falling into the differential case.

8. On Maxima, remove the clutch operating cylinder from the transaxle.

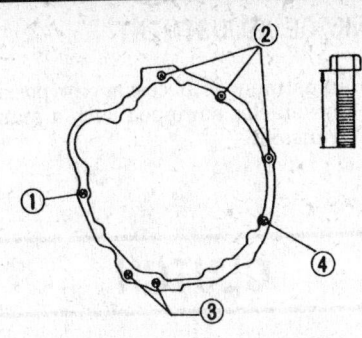

Transmission mounting bolt locations on 240SX; bolt (1) is 70mm, bolt (2) is 60mm, bolt (3) is 30mm and bolt (4) is 25mm

9. Remove the wheel well protector(s).
10. Separate the control rod and support rod from the transaxle.
11. Remove the engine gusset securing bolt and the engine mounting.
12. Remove the clutch control cable from the operating lever.
13. Disconnect speedometer cable from the transaxle.
14. Disconnect the wires from the backup, neutral and overdrive switches. On Maxima, disconnect the speed and position switch sensors from the transaxle also.
15. Support the engine by placing a jack under the oil pan, with a wooden block placed between the jack and pan for protection.
16. Support the transaxle with a hydraulic floor jack.
17. Remove the engine mounting securing bolts.

NOTE: Most of the transaxle mounting bolts are different lenghts. Tagging the bolts upon removal will facilitate proper tightening during installation.

18. Remove the bolts attaching the transaxle to the engine.
19. Using the hydraulic floor jack as a carrier, carefully lower the transaxle down and away from the engine.
To install:
20. Before installing, clean the mating surfaces on the engine rear plate and clutch housing. On Sentra (4WD), apply sealant KP510-00150 or equivalent.
21. Apply a light coat of a lithium-based grease to the spline parts of the clutch disc and the transaxle input shaft.
22. Raise the transaxle into place and bolt it to the engine. Install the engine mounts. Torque the tranasxle mounting bolts as follows:
a. Maxima — tighten bolt (1) to 12-15 ft. lbs. (16-21 Nm), bolt (2) to

22-30 ft. lbs. (30-40 Nm), bolts (3) and (4) to 32-43 ft. lbs. (43-58 Nm). Torque the front and rear gusset bolts to 22-30 ft. lbs. (30-40 Nm).
b. 1990 Pulsar and Sentra (GA16i) — tighten all bolts to 12-15 ft. lbs. (16-21 Nm).
c. 1991-94 Sentra (GA16DE) — tighten bolts (1-3) to 22-30 ft. lbs. (30-40 Nm) and tighten bolt (4) to 12-15 ft. lbs. (16-21 Nm).
d. 1991-94 Sentra (SR20DE) — tighten bolts (1-2) to 51-59 ft. lbs. (70-79 Nm) and tighten bolt (3-4) to 22-30 ft. lbs. (30-40 Nm).
e. 1990 Sentra 4WD — torque all the bolts to 22-30 ft. lbs.
23. On Maxima, connect the speed and position switch sensor wires. Connect the backup, neutral and overdrive switch wires.
24. Connect the speedometer cable to the transaxle.
25. Connect the clutch cable to the operating lever.
26. Connect the control and support rods to the transaxle. Install starter motor assembly.
27. On Maxima, install the clutch operating cylinder.
28. Install the halfshafts.

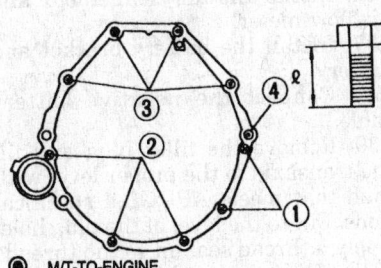

○ M/T-TO-ENGINE

⊗ ENGINE GUSSET-TO-M/T

Transaxle mounting bolt locations Maxima; bolts (1) and (2) are 25mm, bolt (3) is 55mm and bolt (4) is 65mm

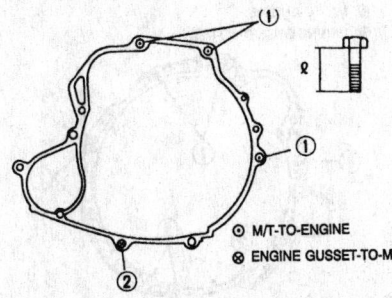

○ M/T-TO-ENGINE

⊗ ENGINE GUSSET-TO-M/T

Transaxle mounting bolt locations on 1990 Pulsar and 2WD Sentra (GA16i engine); bolt (1) is 70mm and bolt (2) is 25mm

29. On Sentra (4WD) vehicles, install the transfer case.
30. Install the wheel well protectors.
31. Lower the vehicle.
32. Install the air duct, air cleaner box and air flow meter.
33. Install the battery and battery bracket.
34. Connect the negative battery cable.
35. Remove the filler plug and fill the transaxle to the proper level with fluid that meets API GL-4 specifications. Fill to the level of the plug hole. Apply a thread sealant to the threads of the filler plug and install the plug in the transaxle case. Road test the vehicle for proper operation.

Altima and 1990-92 Stanza

1. Disconnect the negative battery cable.
2. Remove the battery and battery bracket.
3. Remove the air cleaner box with the air flow meter.
4. Remove the AIV unit on 1990-92 Stanza.
5. Remove the clutch operating cylinder from the transaxle.
6. Remove the clutch hose clamp.
7. Raise and support the vehicle safely.
8. Disconnect the speedometer cable or speed sensor from the transaxle.
9. Disconnect the position switch and all electrical connectors from the transaxle. Tag each wire.
10. Remove the breather hose clamp from the transaxle.
11. Remove the starter.
12. Disconnect the shift control rod from the transaxle.
13. Drain the transaxle fluid.
14. Remove the front exhaust pipe on 1990-92 Stanza.
15. Withdraw the halfshafts from the transaxle.

NOTE: When removing halfshafts, use care not to damage the lip of the oil seal. After shafts are removed, insert a steel bar or wooden dowel of suitable diameter to prevent the side gears from rotating and falling into the differential case.

16. Support the engine by placing a jack under the oil pan, with a wooden block placed between the jack and pan for protection.
17. Support the transaxle with a suitable floor jack.
18. Remove the rear and left engine mounts.

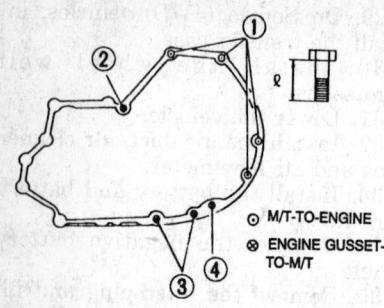

○ M/T-TO-ENGINE
⊗ ENGINE GUSSET-TO-M/T

Transaxle mounting bolt locations on Sentra 4WD; bolt (1) is 70mm, bolt (2) is 40mm, bolt (3) is 20mm and bolt (4) is 55mm

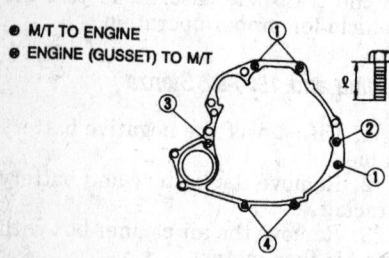

● M/T TO ENGINE
⊗ ENGINE (GUSSET) TO M/T

Transaxle mounting bolt locations on Sentra (GA16DE engine); bolt (1) is 70mm, bolt (2) is 85mm, bolt (3) is 30mm and bolt (4) is 25mm.

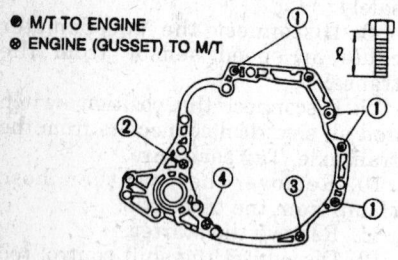

● M/T TO ENGINE
⊗ ENGINE (GUSSET) TO M/T

Transaxle mounting bolt locations on Sentra (SR20DE engine); bolt (1) is 55mm, bolt (2) is 65mm, bolt (3) is 35mm and bolt (4) is 45mm.

19. Remove the bolts attaching the transaxle to the engine.

NOTE: The transaxle mounting bolts are different lengths. Tagging the bolts upon removal will facilitate proper tightening during installation.

20. Using the jack as a carrier, carefully lower the transaxle down and away from the vehicle.

NOTE: Be careful not to strike any adjacent parts or input shaft (the shaft protruding from the

transaxle which fits into the clutch assembly) when removing the transaxle from the vehicle.

To install:

21. Before installing, clean the mating surfaces on the engine rear plate and clutch housing.

22. Apply a light coat of a lithium based grease to the spline parts of the clutch disc and the transaxle input shaft.

23. Raise the transaxle into place and install the mounting bolts. Tighten bolts (1) and (2) to 29-36 ft. lbs. (39-49 Nm). Tighten bolts (3) and (4) to 22-30 ft. lbs. (30-40 Nm).

24. Install the rear and left engine mounts.

25. Install the transaxle and engine supports.

26. Install the halfshafts.

27. Install the front exhaust pipe with new gaskets on 1990-92 Stanza.

28. Connect the shift control rod.

29. Install the starter.

30. Connect the electrical and position switch wiring.

31. Connect the speedometer cable or speed sensor.

32. Lower the vehicle.

33. Install the clutch hose clamp.

34. Install the clutch operating cylinder.

35. Install the AIV unit on the 1990-92 Stanza.

36. Install the air cleaner box and air flow meter.

37. Install the battery bracket and battery.

38. Connect the negative battery cable.

39. Remove the filler plug and fill the transaxle to the proper level with fluid that meets API GL-4 specifications. Fill to the level of the plug hole. Apply a thread sealant to the threads of the filler plug and install the plug in the transaxle. Road test the vehicle for proper operation.

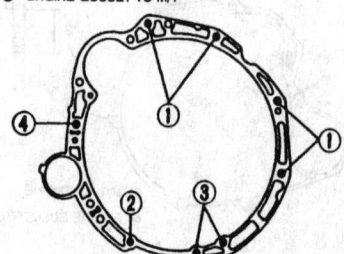

◐ M/T-TO-ENGINE
⊗ ENGINE GUSSET-TO-M/T

Transaxle mounting bolt locations on 1990-92 Stanza; bolt (1) is 45mm, bolt (2) is 25mm, bolt (3) is 30mm and bolt (4) is 40mm

LINKAGE ADJUSTMENT

No adjustment is necessary or possible for vehicles equipped with a manual transaxle.

CLUTCH

Clutch Assembly

REMOVAL AND INSTALLATION

1. Remove the transmission or transaxle assembly.

2. Insert a clutch aligning bar or similar tool all the way into the clutch disc hub. This must be done so as to support the weight of the clutch disc during removal.

3. Mark the clutch assembly-to-flywheel relationship with paint or a center punch so the clutch assembly can be assembled in the same position from which it is removed.

4. Loosen the pressure plate bolts in criss-cross fashion, a turn at a time to gradually relieve the spring pressure. Remove the bolts once the spring pressure is relieved.

5. Remove the pressure plate and clutch disc. Inspect the pressure plate or scoring for roughness, and reface or replace as necessary. Slight roughness can be smoothed with a fine emery cloth. Inspect the clutch disc for worn or oily facings, loose rivets and broken or loose springs, and replace.

6. Remove the release mechanism. On Pulsar and Sentra, the clutch lever is removed by aligning the lever retaining pins with the clutch cavity, then driving out the pins with a suitable pin punch. Inspect the release sleeve and lever contact surfaces for wear, rust or any other damage. Replace if necessary.

7. Inspect the pressure plate for wear, scoring, etc., and reface or replace as necessary. Minor imperfections or discoloration may be removed with emery cloth.

8. Inspect the release bearing. The bearing should roll freely and quietly. It should not have any cracks, pitting or wear. Replace as necessary.

To install:

9. Apply multi-purpose grease to the bearing sleeve inside groove, the contact point of the withdrawal lever and bearing sleeve, the contact surface of the lever ball pin and lever.

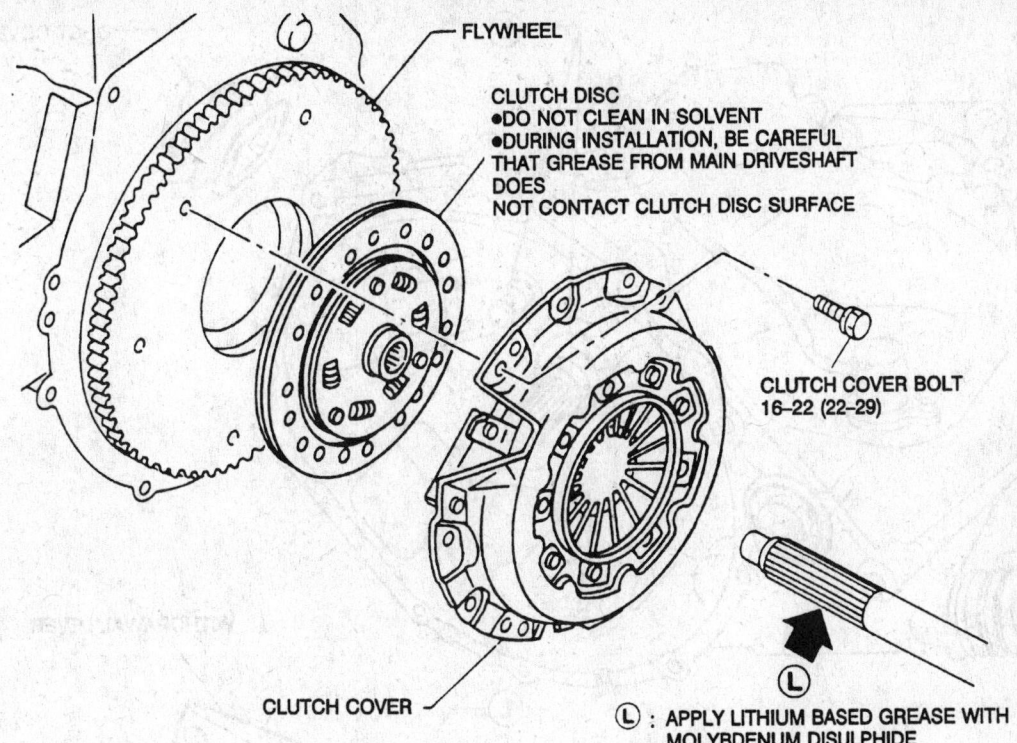

FLYWHEEL

CLUTCH DISC
● DO NOT CLEAN IN SOLVENT
● DURING INSTALLATION, BE CAREFUL THAT GREASE FROM MAIN DRIVESHAFT DOES NOT CONTACT CLUTCH DISC SURFACE

CLUTCH COVER BOLT
16–22 (22–29)

CLUTCH COVER

Ⓛ : APPLY LITHIUM BASED GREASE WITH MOLYBDENUM DISULPHIDE

Clutch assembly

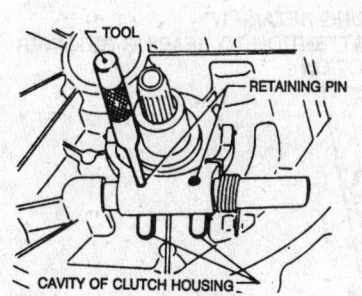

TOOL

RETAINING PIN

CAVITY OF CLUTCH HOUSING

Clutch lever retaining pin removal — Pulsar and Sentra

10. Apply a small amount of lithium based grease to the transmission/transaxle splines.

11. Install the disc on the splines and slide it back and forth a few times. Remove the disc and remove any excess grease on the hub. Be sure no grease contacts the disc or pressure plate.

NOTE: Take special care to prevent any grease or oil from getting on the clutch facing. During assembly, keep all disc facings, flywheel and pressure plate

clean and dry. Grease, oil or dirt on these parts will result in a slipping clutch when assembled.

12. Install the disc (in the correct direction), aligning it with a splined dummy shaft.

13. Install the pressure plate and torque the bolts (in steps) to 16-22 ft. lbs. (22-29 Nm) on all vehicles except 240SX and 300ZX. On 240SX and 300ZX, torque the bolts to 25-33 ft. lbs. (34-44 Nm).

14. Remove the dummy shaft.

15. Install the transmission or transaxle.

PEDAL HEIGHT/FREE-PLAY ADJUSTMENT

Hydraulic Clutch

1. Pedal height is adjusted by moving the pedal stopper or clutch switch.

2. Pedal free-play is adjusted at the clutch master cylinder pushrod by turning the locknut.

3. If the pushrod is non-adjustable, free-play is adjusted by placing shims between the master cylinder and the firewall. On some vehicles, pedal free-play can also be adjusted at the operating (slave) cylinder pushrod.

Pedal Height Above Floor
240SX: 7.32 — 7.72 in.
300ZX: 7.68 — 8.07 in.
VG30DE: 7.76 — 8.15 in.
VG30DETT: 7.20 — 7.60 in.
Altima: 6.50 — 6.89 in.
Maxima: 6.73 — 7.13 in.
Pulsar, Sentra: 6.38 — 6.77 in.
Sentra NX: 5.91 — 6.30 in.
Stanza: 6.50 — 6.89 in.
Pedal Free Play
240SX: 0.04 — 0.12 in.
300ZX: 0.04 — 0.12 in.
VG30DE: 0.04 — 0.12 in.
VG30DETT: 0.04 — 0.12 in.
Altima: 0.04 — 0.12 in.
Maxima: 0.04 — 0.12 in.
Pulsar, Sentra: 0.49 — 0.69 in.
Sentra NX: 0.43 — 0.59 in.
Stanza: 0.04 — 0.12 in.

Mechanical Clutch

1. Loosen the locknut and adjust the pedal height by means of the pedal stopper. Tighten the locknut.

2. Push the withdraw lever in by hand until resistance is felt. Adjust withdraw lever play at the lever tip end with the locknuts. Withdraw lever play should be 0.0198-0.138 in. (2.5-3.5mm).

3. Depress and release the clutch pedal several times and then recheck

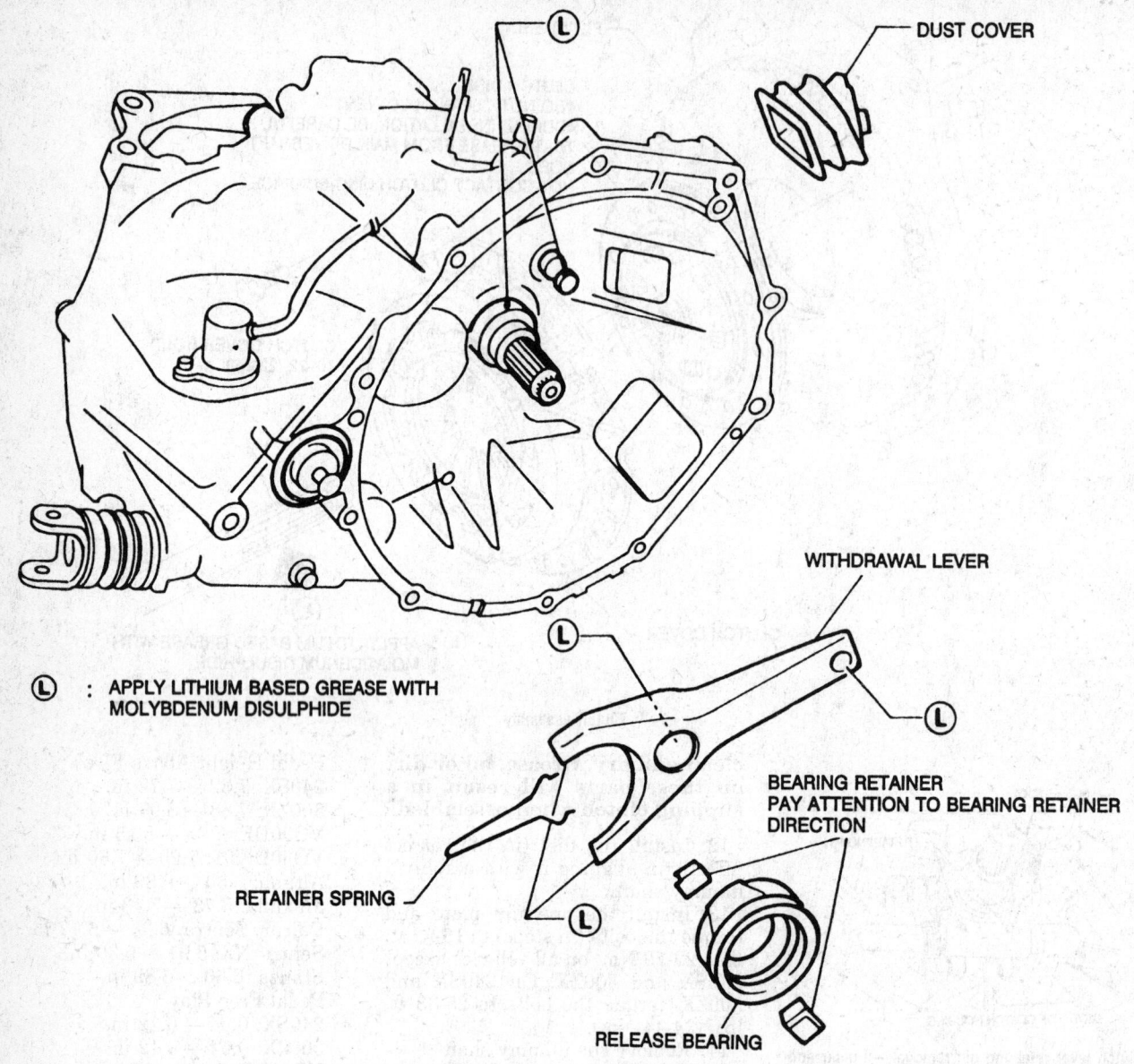

Ⓛ : APPLY LITHIUM BASED GREASE WITH MOLYBDENUM DISULPHIDE

DUST COVER

WITHDRAWAL LEVER

BEARING RETAINER
PAY ATTENTION TO BEARING RETAINER DIRECTION

RETAINER SPRING

RELEASE BEARING

Clutch release mechanism — except Pulsar and Sentra

the withdraw lever play again. Readjust if necessary.

4. Measure the pedal free travel at the center of the pedal pad.

Clutch Cable

REMOVAL AND INSTALLATION

1. Disconnect the negative battery cable.

2. Remove the floor mats.

3. Working from inside the engine compartment, loosen the adjusting nuts and locknut and disconnect the clutch cable from the withdrawal lever.

4. Working from inside the vehicle, disconnect the clutch cable from the clutch pedal.

5. Working from inside the engine compartment, remove the 2 nuts that attach the end of the cable to the fire wall.

6. From inside the engine compartment, pull the clutch cable through the firewall and remove it.

To install:

7. Route the clutch cable through the passenger compartment.

8. Position the cable end over the studs on the firewall and install the 2 mounting nuts. Torque the nuts to 6-8 ft. lbs. (9-11 Nm).

9. Connect the clutch cable to the clutch pedal.

10. Connect the clutch cable to the withdrawal lever.

11. Lubricate the pedal fulcrum pin and pivot points with lithium based grease.

12. Adjust the cable and the clutch switch.

13. Check the clutch for proper engagement.

14. Install the floor mats.

15. Connect the negative battery cable.

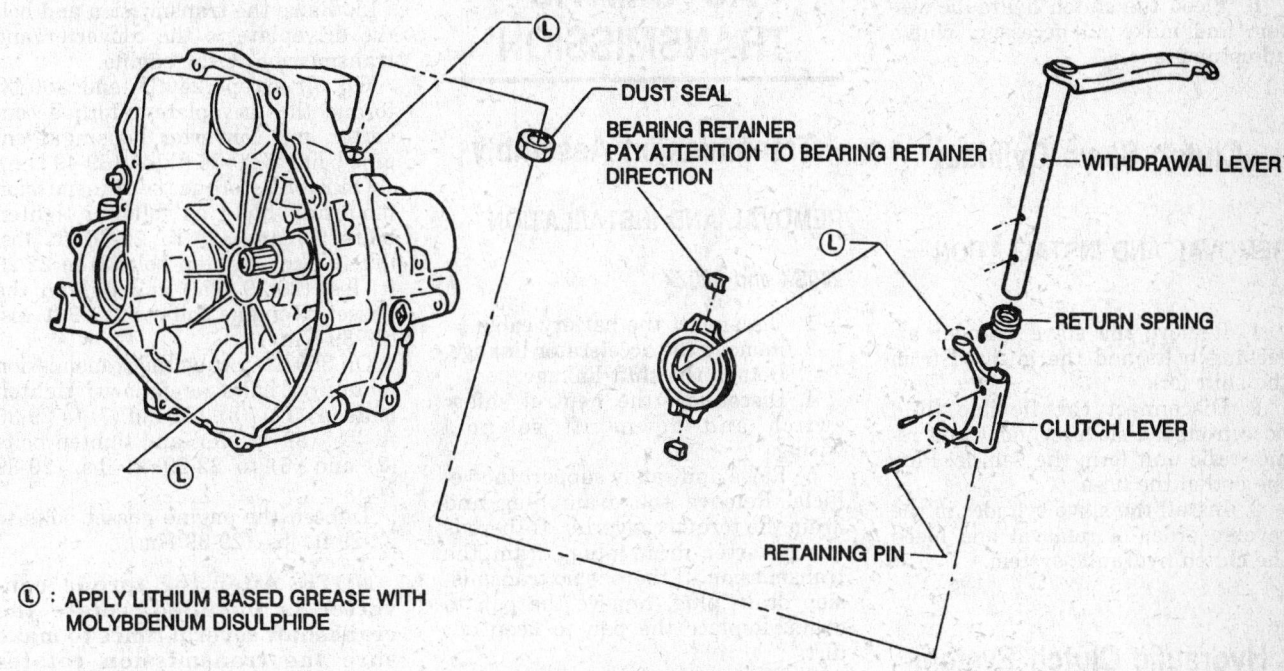

DUST SEAL

BEARING RETAINER
PAY ATTENTION TO BEARING RETAINER
DIRECTION

WITHDRAWAL LEVER

RETURN SPRING

CLUTCH LEVER

RETAINING PIN

Ⓛ : APPLY LITHIUM BASED GREASE WITH
MOLYBDENUM DISULPHIDE

Clutch release mechanism — Pulsar and Sentra

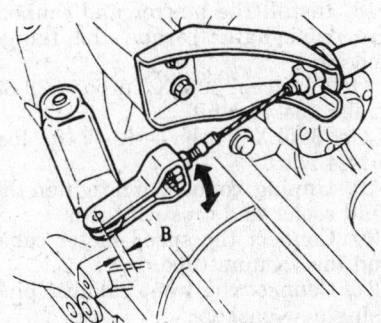

Clutch withdrawal lever adjustment on Pulsar
and Sentra. Arrow shows locknut adjustment

Clutch Master Cylinder

REMOVAL AND INSTALLATION

1. Disconnect the negative battery cable.
2. Disconnect the clutch pedal arm from the pushrod.
3. Disconnect the clutch hydraulic line from the master cylinder. Plug the end of line to prevent leakage.
4. Remove the nuts attaching the master cylinder and remove the master cylinder and pushrod toward the engine compartment side.

1. Adjust pedal height here
2. Adjust pedal free-play here
MG. Apply multi-purpose grease
H. Pedal height
h. Pedal free-play

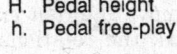
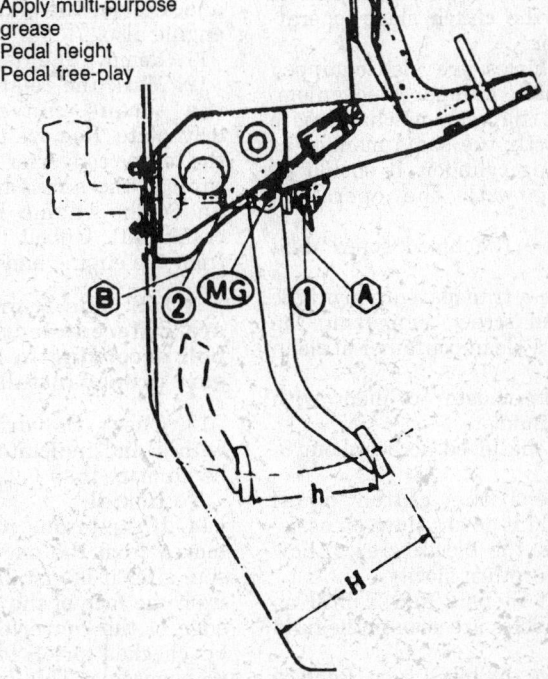

Clutch adjusting points

5. Install the master cylinder in the reverse order of removal.

6. Bleed the clutch hydraulic system and make all necessary clutch adjustments.

Clutch Slave Cylinder

REMOVAL AND INSTALLATION

1. Remove the slave cylinder attaching bolts and the pushrod from the shift fork.

2. Disconnect the flexible fluid hose from the slave cylinder and remove the unit form the vehicle. Plug the end of the hose.

3. Install the slave cylinder in the reverse order of removal and bleed the clutch hydraulic system.

Hydraulic Clutch System Bleeding

Bleeding is required to remove air trapped in the hydraulic system. This operation is necessary whenever the system has been leaking or opened for maintenance. The bleed screw is located on the clutch slave (operating) cylinder.

Some vehicles are also equipped with a clutch damper mechanism. The clutch damper mechanism is bled in exactly the same manner as the operating cylinder. It should be bled along with the operating cylinder.

1. Remove the bleed screw dust cap.

2. Attach a transparent vinyl tube to the bleed screw, immersing the free end in a clean container of clean brake fluid.

3. Fill the master cylinder with the proper fluid.

4. Open the bleed screw about ¾ turn.

5. Depress the clutch pedal quickly. Hold it down. Have an assistant tighten the bleed screw. Allow the pedal to return slowly.

6. Repeat Steps 2 and 5 until no more air bubbles are seen in the fluid container.

7. Remove the bleed tube. Replace the dust cap. Refill the master cylinder.

8. Bleed the clutch damper, if equipped.

AUTOMATIC TRANSMISSION

Transmission Assembly

REMOVAL AND INSTALLATION

240SX and 300ZX

1. Disconnect the battery cable.
2. Remove the accelerator linkage.
3. Detach the shift linkage.
4. Disconnect the neutral safety switch and downshift solenoid wiring.
5. Raise and safely support the vehicle. Remove the drain plug and drain the torque converter. If there is no converter drain plug, drain the transmission. If there is no transmission drain plug, remove the pan to drain. Replace the pan to keep out dirt.
6. Remove the front exhaust pipe.
7. Remove the vacuum tube and speedometer cable.
8. Disconnect the fluid cooler and dipstick tubes. Plug the tube ends to prevent leakage.
9. Mark and lower the driveshaft and remove the starter.
10. Support the transmission with a jack under the oil pan. Support the engine also.
11. Remove the rear crossmember.
12. Mark the relationship between the torque converter and the driveplate. Remove the bolts holding the torque converter to the driveplate through the access hole at the front, under the engine by rotating the crankshaft. Unbolt the transmission from the engine and remove it.

NOTE: The transmission bolts are different lengths. Tag each bolt according to location to ensure proper installation.

13. Check the driveplate runout with a dial indictator. Runout must be no more than 0.020 in. (0.5mm).

To install:

14. If the torque converter was removed from the engine for any reason, after it is installed, the distance from the face of the converter to the edge of the converter housing must be checked prior to installing the transmission. This is done to ensure proper installation of the torque converter. On 240SX and 300ZX (non-turbo), the dimension should be 1.02 in. (26mm) or more. On 300ZX Turbo,

the dimension should be 0.98 in. (25mm) or more.

15. Raise the transmission and bolt the driveplate to the converter and transmission to the engine.

On all except 240SX and 300ZX, torque the driveplate-to-torque converter and converter housing-to-engine bolts to 29-36 ft. lbs. (39-49 Nm).

On 240SX, torque the transmission mounting bolts as follows: tighten bolts (1) and (2) to 29-36 ft. lbs. (39-49 Nm), tighten bolt (3) to 22-29 ft. lbs. (29-39 Nm) and tighten the gusset-to-engine bolts to 22-29 ft. lbs. (29-39 Nm).

On 300ZX, torque the transmission mounting bolts as follows: tighten bolts (1), (2), (3), (6) and (7) to 29-36 ft. lbs. (39-49 Nm) and tighten bolts (2) and (5) to 22-29 ft. lbs. (29-39 Nm).

Tighten the engine gusset bolts to 22-29 ft. lbs. (29-39 Nm).

NOTE: After the torque converter is installed, rotate the crankshaft several times to make sure the transmission rotates freely and does not bind.

16. Install the rear crossmember.
17. Remove the engine and transmission supports.
18. Install the starter and connect the driveshaft. Torque the flange bolts to:

On all except 300ZX Turbo — 29-33 ft. lbs. (34-44 Nm).

On 300ZX Turbo — 40-47 ft. lbs. (54-64 Nm).

19. Unplug, connect and tighten the fluid cooler and dipstick tubes.
20. Connect the speedometer cable and the vacuum tube.
21. Connect the front exhaust pipe using new gaskets.
22. Connect the switch wiring to the transmission.
23. Connect the shift linkage.
24. Connect the negative battery cable, fill the transmission to the proper level and make any necessary adjustment.
25. Perform a road test and check the fluid level.

SHIFT LINKAGE ADJUSTMENT

240SX and 300ZX

If the detents cannot be felt or the pointer indicator is improperly aligned while shifting from **P** to **1**, the linkage should be adjusted.

1. Place the shifter in the **P**.
2. Loosen the locknuts.
3. Tighten the outer locknut X until it touches the trunnion, pulling

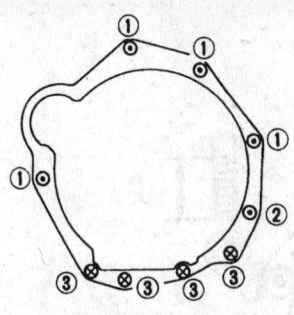

Transmission mounting bolt locations on 240SX; bolt (1) is 40mm, bolt (2) is 50mm, bolt (3) is 25mm and the gusset bolts are 20mm

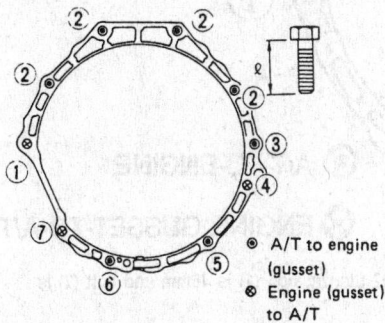

- ⊘ A/T to engine (gusset)
- ⊗ Engine (gusset) to A/T

Transmission mounting bolt locations on 300ZX (Turbo and non-turbo)

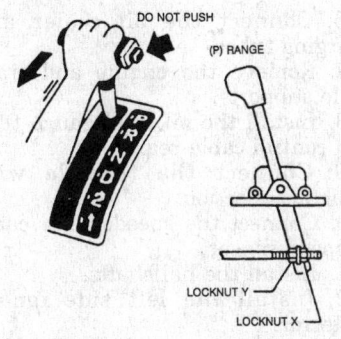

Manual control linkage adjustment — 240SX and 300ZX

the selector lever toward **R** side without pushing the button.

4. Back off the outer locknut X ¼-½ turns and then tighten the inner locknut Y to 5-11 ft. lbs. (8-15 Nm).

5. Move the selector lever from **P** to **1**. Make sure it moves smoothly.

NOTE: On some vehicles, there is an automatic transmission interlock system. This interlock system prevents the transmission selector from being shifted from the P position unless the brake pedal is depressed.

KICKDOWN SWITCH ADJUSTMENT

When the accelerator pedal is depressed, a click can be heard just before the pedal bottoms out. If the click is not heard, loosen the locknut and extend the switch until the pedal lever makes contact with the switch and the switch clicks.

On 300ZX, before adjusting the kickdown switch, make sure the accelerator cable is properly adjusted. Then, check the clearance between the stopper rubber and the threaded end of the switch with the accelerator cable fully depressed. The clearance should be 0.012-0.039 in. (0.3-1.0mm). If the clearance is not as specified, adjust by loosening the switch locknut and turning the switch in or out. Tighten the locknut and check the clearance again.

AUTOMATIC TRANSAXLE

Transaxle Assembly

REMOVAL AND INSTALLATION

Altima, Maxima, Pulsar, Sentra and Stanza

1. Disconnect the negative battery cable.
2. Raise and support the vehicle safely.
3. Remove the left front tire.
4. Drain the transaxle fluid.
5. Remove the left side fender protector.
6. Remove the halfshafts.

NOTE: Be careful not to damage the oil seals when removing the halfshafts. After removing the halfshafts, install a suitable bar so the side gears will not rotate and fall into the differential case.

7. Disconnect the speedometer cable or speed sensor.
8. Disconnect the throttle wire (cable) connection.
9. Remove the control cable rear end from the unit and remove the oil level gauge tube.
10. Place a suitable jack under the transaxle and engine. Do not place the jack under the oil pan drain plug. Support the engine with wooden

blocks placed between the engine and the center member.

11. Disconnect the oil cooler and charging tubes. Plug the tube ends to prevent leakage.
12. Remove the engine motor mount securing bolts, as required.
13. Remove the starter motor and disconnect all electrical wires from the transaxle.
14. Loosen and remove all but 3 of the bolts holding the transaxle to the engine. Leave the 3 bolts in to support the weight of the transaxle while removing the torque converter bolts.
15. Remove the driveplate or dust cover(s).
16. Remove the bolts holding the torque converter to the driveplate. Rotate the crankshaft to gain access to each bolt.
17. Before separating the torque converter, place chalk marks on 2 parts for alignment purposes during installation.

NOTE: The transaxle bolts are different lengths. Tag each bolt according to location to ensure proper installation.

18. Remove the 3 temporary bolts. Move the jack gradually until the transaxle can be lowered and removed from the vehicle through the side wheel housing.
19. Check the driveplate runout with a dial indictator. Runout must be no more than 0.020 in. (0.5mm).

To install:
20. If the torque converter was removed from the engine for any reason, after it is installed, the distance from the face of the converter to the edge of the converter housing must be checked prior to installing the transaxle. This is done to ensure proper installation of the torque converter.

Maxima — the distance should be 0.71 in. (18mm) or more.

Pulsar, Sentra and Sentra NX (GA16DE engine) with RL3F01A transaxles — it should be 0.831 in. (21mm) or more.

Sentra NX (SR20DE engine) — it should be 0.626 in. (15.9mm) or more.

Pulsar with RL4F02A transaxle — it should be 0.748 in. (19mm) or more.

Altima or Stanza — it should be 0.75 in. (19mm) or more.

21. Raise the transaxle onto the engine and install the torque coverter-to-driveplate bolts. Torque the bolts to specification. Install 3 bolts to sup-

port the transaxle while tighten the converter bolts.

NOTE: After the converter is installed, rotate the crankshaft several times to make sure the transaxle rotates freely and does not bind.

22. Install the driveplate or dust covers.

23. Install the transaxle mounting bolts torque the bolts as follows:

   a. On Maxima, tighten bolts (1) and (3) to 22-30 ft. lbs. (30-40 Nm) and bolts (2) to 29-36 ft. lbs. (39-49 Nm).

   b. On Altima and 1990-92 Stanza, tighten bolts (1) to 29-36 ft. lbs. (39-49 Nm) and bolts (2) to 22-30 ft. lbs. (30-40 Nm).

   c. On Pulsar and Sentra (GA16i engine) tighten all bolts to 14-17 ft. lbs. (19-23 Nm).

   d. On Sentra NX (GA16DE engine) tighten small bolts to 12-15 ft. lbs. (16-21 Nm) and larger bolts to 22-30 ft. lbs. (30-40 Nm).

   e. On Sentra NX (SR20DE engine) tighten bolts (1-3) to 51-59 ft. lbs. (70-79 Nm) and bolts (4-5) to 12-15 ft. lbs. (16-21 Nm).

24. Connect the transaxle wiring and install the starter.

25. Install the engine mounts, if removed.

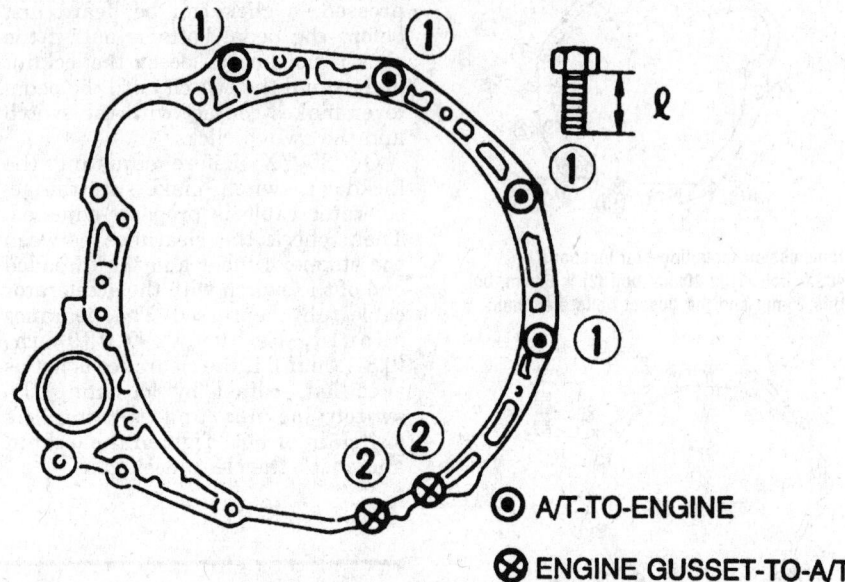

Transaxle mounting bolt locations on Altima and 1990-92 Stanza; bolt (1) is 45mm and bolt (2) is 20mm

26. Connect the oil cooler and charging tubes.

27. Remove the engine and transaxle supports.

28. Install the oil level gauge tube and control cable rear end.

29. Connect the throttle wire (cable) connection.

30. Connect the speedometer cable or speed sensor.

31. Install the halfshafts.

32. Install the left side fender protector.

33. Mount the left front tire and lower the vehicle.

34. Fill the transaxle and engine with the proper amounts of fluids.

35. Adjust the control cable and throttle wire.

36. Check the inhibitor switch for proper operation.

37. Road test the vehicle.

THROTTLE WIRE ADJUSTMENT

The throttle wire is adjusted by means of double nuts on the throttle body.

NOTE: On Altima, Maxima and 1990-92 Stanza, there is no throttle wire adjustment.

EXCEPT 1990 PULSAR

1. Loosen the adjusting nuts.

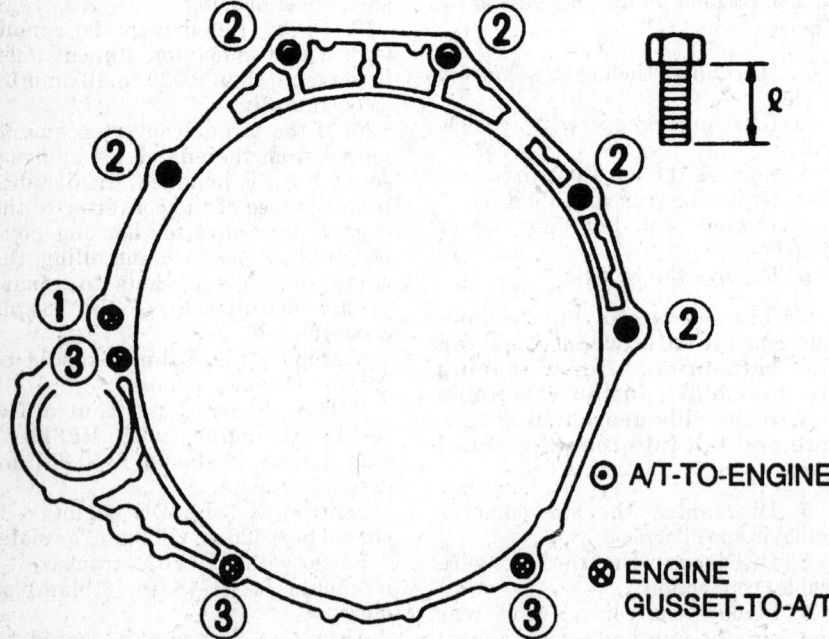

Transaxle mounting bolt locations on Maxima; bolt (1) is 60mm, bolt (2) is 45mm and bolt (3) is 25mm

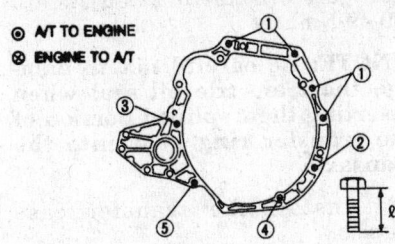

Transaxle mounting bolt locations on Sentra (SR20DE engine); bolt (1) is 55mm, bolt (2) is 50mm, bolt (3) is 65mm, bolt (4) is 35mm and bolt (5) is 45mm.

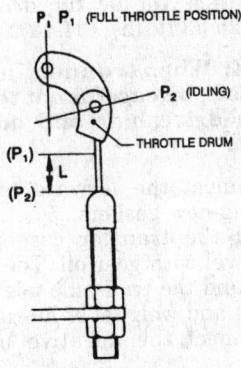

Throttle wire stroke — Sentra

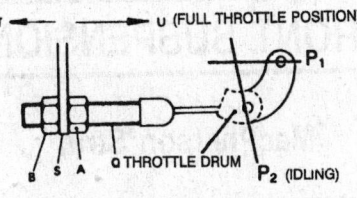

Throttle wire adjustment — Sentra

2. With the throttle fully opened, turn the threaded shaft inward as far as it will go and then tighten the first nut against the bracket.

3. Back off the nut 2¾-3¼ turns (RL4F02A transaxles) and 1-1½ turns (RL3F01A transaxles) and tighten the nut.

4. Tighten both double nuts to 5.8-7.2 ft. lbs. (8-10 Nm). The throttle drum should be held securely in the full open position.

5. On Sentra, it should be 1.079-1.236 in. (27.4-31.4mm).

1990 Pulsar

1. Remove the air cleaner cover.

2. While pressing on the lockplate, move the adjusting tube in the proper direction.

3. Return the lockplate to its original position.

4. Move the throttle drum from position P_1 to P_2 quickly.

5. Check that the throttle wire stroke (**L**) between full throttle and idling is 1.079-1.236 in. (27.4-31.4mm). Marking the throttle wire with paint dabs or a colored marker will help in measuring the throttle wire stroke.

6. Adjust the throttle wire stroke only if the throttle and accelerator wires are installed. After adjustment, make sure the parting line is straight.

CONTROL CABLE ADJUSTMENT

On all vehicles, move the selector from the **P** range through each gear to the **1** range. At each gear selection, the detent should be felt. If the detents cannot be felt or if the gear shift indicator pointer is not aligned properly, then the control cable must be adjusted.

1. Position the control lever (gear selector) in **P**.

2. Connect the control cable end to the lever in the transaxle unit and tighten the cable securing bolt.

3. Move the control lever from **P** to the **1** position. Be certain the lever works smoothly and quietly.

4. Position the lever in **P** once again. Make sure the lever locks into this position.

5. Loosen the cable adjusting locknuts.

6. While holding the select rod horizontal, tighten first locknut until it contacts the end of the rod. Then tighten second locknut.

7. Move the control lever through all of its detents again and check for smooth and quiet operation.

8. Lubricate the spring washer at the end of the cable with multi-purpose grease.

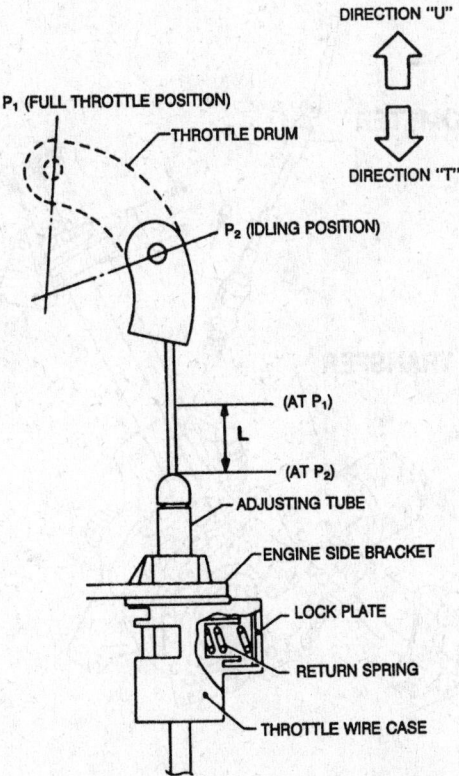

Throttle wire stroke adjustment — 1990 Pulsar

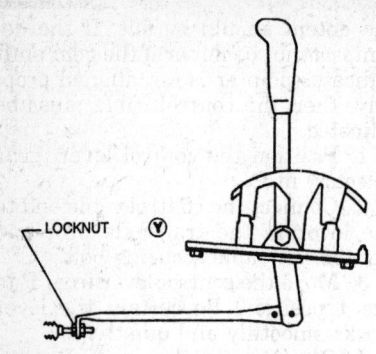

Automatic transaxle control cable adjustment — all models

TRANSFER CASE

Transfer Case Assembly

REMOVAL AND INSTALLATION

Sentra Wagon

1. Disconnect the negative battery cable.
2. Drain the gear oil from the transaxle and the transfer case.
3. Disconnect and remove the forward exhaust pipe.

4. Using chalk or paint, match-mark the flanges on the driveshaft and then unbolt the driveshaft from the transfer case.
5. Unbolt and remove the transaxle support rod from the transfer case.
6. Disconnect and remove the right side halfshaft.
7. Disconnect the speedometer gear from the transfer case.
8. Unbolt and remove the transfer case gussets (support members).
9. Use a hydraulic floor jack and a block of wood to support the transfer case.
10. Remove the transfer case-to-transaxle mounting bolts and then remove the case.

To install:
11. Lubricate the lips of the transfer side oil seal (in transaxle), adapter oil seal (in transfer) and driveshaft oil seal. Use a suitable multi-purpose grease.
12. Apply KP510-00150 or equivalent, sealant to the ring gear oil seal seating surface prior to installation of the transfer case.
13. Raise and mount the transfer case. Tighten the transfer case-to-transaxle mounting bolts to 22-30 ft. lbs. (30-40 Nm). Torque the transfer

rear gusset bolts to 29-36 ft. lbs. (39-49 Nm).

NOTE: Be careful not to damage the transaxle oil seal when inserting thew splined portion of the transfer ring gear into the transaxle.

14. Install the transfer case gussets.
15. Connect the speedometer cable.
16. Install the right side halfshaft.
17. Connect the transfer support rod to the transfer case.
18. Connect the driveshaft to the transfer case by aligning the matchmarks. Torque the driveshaft bolts to 25-33 ft. lbs. (34-44 Nm).

NOTE: When connecting the driveshaft, be careful not to damage the driveshaft and adapter oil seals.

19. Connect the forward exhaust pipe using new gaskets.
20. Fill the transfer case to the proper level with gear oil. The transfer case and the transaxle use different types and weights of lubricant.
21. Connect the negative battery cable.
22. Check the transfer case for proper operation.

FRONT SUSPENSION

MacPherson Strut

REMOVAL AND INSTALLATION

1. Raise and support the vehicle safely.
2. Remove the front wheels.
3. Disconnect and plug the brake line if it interferes with removal of the strut.
4. Support the bottom of the strut with a jack or equivalent. Place matchmarks on the strut lower bracket and camber adjusting pin if equipped, for assembly reference.
5. Unbolt the steering arm from the lower end of the strut.
6. Open the hood and remove the nuts holding the top of the strut.
7. If equipped with adjustable or Sonar suspension shocks, disconnect the electrical lead from the actuating unit.
8. Lower the jack slowly and cautiously until the strut assembly can be removed.

Transfer case assembly — Sentra 4WD

To install:

9. During installation, observing the following:

a. The self-locking nuts holding the top of the strut must be replaced.

b. Make sure the matchmarks on the bracket and the camber adjusting pin are aligned properly.

c. On vehicles with Sonar suspension, before installing the actuator ensure the output shaft on the inside of the actuating unit is aligned with the shock absorber control rod. If this is not done, the actuator will be damaged.

d. Check front end wheel alignment and bleed brake system, if necessary.

Tension Rod and Stabilizer Bar

REMOVAL AND INSTALLATION

240SX and 300ZX

1. Raise and support the vehicle safely.

2. Remove the tension rod-to-frame locknuts.

3. Remove the 2 mounting bolts at the transverse link, lower control arm and then slide out the tension rod.

4. On 240SX, to remove the tension rod, remove the bolt and nut that holds the rod to the tension rod bracket (through the bushing) and remove the tension rod-to-tranverse link bolts, nuts, bushings and washers. If the bushings are worn replace them.

5. Unbolt the stabilizer bar at each transverse link or connecting rod. On 240SX, engage the flats of stabilizer bar connecting rod with a wrench to keep the rod from moving when removing the nuts.

6. Remove the 4 stabilizer bar bracket bolts and remove the stabilizer bar.

To install:

7. During installation observe the following:

a. Tighten the stabilizer bar-to-transverse link bolts to 12-16 ft. lbs. (16-22 Nm) for 300ZX or 34-38 ft. lbs. (46-52 Nm) on 240SX.

b. Tighten the stabilizer bar bracket bolts to 22-29 ft. lbs. (29-39 Nm) for 300ZX or 29-36 ft. lbs. (39-49 Nm) on 240SX.

c. Tighten the tension rod-to-transverse link nuts to 31-43 ft. lbs. (42-59 Nm). On 240SX, torque the plain nuts to 65-80 ft. lbs.

(88-108 Nm) and the nuts with bushings and washers to 14-22 ft. lbs. (20-29 Nm). Make sure to hold the connecting rod stationary.

d. Tighten the tension rod-to-frame nut (bushing end) to 33-40 ft. lbs. (44-54 Nm). Always use a new locknut when reconnecting the tension rod to the frame.

e. Be certain the tension rod bushings are installed properly. Make sure the stabilizer bar ball joint socket is properly positioned.

NOTE: Never tighten any bolts or nuts to their final torque unless the vehicle is resting, unsupported, on the wheels (unladen).

Altima, Pulsar, Sentra, Stanza and Maxima

1. Raise and support the vehicle safely.

2. Disconnect the front exhaust pipe at the manifold and position it aside if necessary for removal of assembly.

3. Remove the stabilizer bar-to-transverse link (lower, control arm) mounting bolts. Engage the flats of stabilizer bar connecting rod with a wrench to keep the rod from moving when removing (and installing) the bolts.

4. Matchmark the stabilizer bar to the mounting clamps.

5. Remove the stabilizer bar mounting clamp bolts and then pull the bar out, around the link and exhaust pipe.

6. Installation is the reverse of the removal procedure. Never tighten the mounting bolts unless the vehicle is resting on the ground with normal weight upon the wheels. On Pulsar and Sentra, be sure the stabilizer bar ball joint socket is properly positioned.

Lower Ball Joints

INSPECTION

Dial Indicator Method

1. Raise and support the vehicle safely.

2. Clamp a dial indicator to the transverse link and place the tip of the dial on the lower edge of the brake caliper.

3. Zero the indicator.

4. Make sure the front wheels are straight ahead and the brake pedal is fully depressed.

5. Insert a long prybar between the transverse link and the inner rim of the wheel.

6. Push down and release the prybar and observe the reading (deflection) on the dial indicator. Take several readings and use the maximum dial indicator deflection as the ball joint vertical endplay. Make sure to **0** the indicator after each reading. If the reading is not within specifications, replace the transverse link or the ball joint. Ball joint vertical endplay should be 0.

Visual Approximation Method

The lower ball joint should be replaced when play becomes excessive. An effective way to visually approximate ball joint verticle endplay without the use of a dial indicator is to preform the following:

1. Raise and safely support the vehicle until the wheel is clear of the ground. Do not place the jack under the ball joint; it must be unloaded.

2. Place a long prybar under the tire and move the wheel up and down. Keep one hand on top of the tire while doing this.

3. If ¼ in. or more of play exists at the top of the tire, the ball joint should be replaced. Be sure the wheel bearings are properly adjusted before making this measurement. A double check can be made; while the tire is being moved up and down, observe the ball joint. If play is seen, replace the ball joint.

REMOVAL AND INSTALLATION

Rear Wheel Drive

NOTE: The transverse link (lower control arm) must be removed and then the ball joint must be pressed out.

1. Raise and support the vehicle safely.

2. Remove the front wheels.

3. Separate the knuckle arm from the tie rod using the proper tool.

4. Separate the knuckle arm from the strut (if equipped with a camber adjusting pin, mark assembly for correct wheel alignment).

5. Remove the stabilizer bar and tension rod.

6. Remove the transverse link and knuckle arm.

7. Separate the knuckle arm from the ball joint with a suitable press.

8. Replace the transverse link/ball joint assembly.

9. Installation is the reverse of the removal procedure. Check front end alignment if necessary.

Front Wheel Drive

1. Raise and support the vehicle safely.
2. Remove the front wheels.
3. Remove the wheel bearing locknut.
4. Separate the tie rod end ball joint from the steering knuckle with a ball joint remover, being careful not to damage the ball joint dust cover if the ball joint is to be used again.
5. On Maxima and 1990-92 Stanza, loosen, but do not remove the strut upper nuts.
6. Remove the nut that attaches the ball joint to the transverse link.
7. Separate the halfshaft from the knuckle by lightly taping the end of the shaft.
8. Separate the ball joint from the knuckle using the proper tool.
9. Installation is the reverse of the removal procedure. Use new cotter pins. Tighten the ball stud attaching nut (from ball joint-to-steering knuckle) to 22-29 ft. lbs. (30-39 Nm), and the ball joint-to-transverse link bolts to 40-47 ft. lbs. (54-64 Nm) except on Stanza. On Altima and Stanza, torque the bolts to 56-80 ft. lbs. (76-108 Nm).

Lower Control Arm (Transverse Link)

REMOVAL AND INSTALLATION

240SX and 300ZX

1. Raise and support the vehicle safely.
2. Remove the front wheels.
3. Remove the cotter pin and castle nut from the side rod (steering arm) ball joint and separate the ball joint from the side rod (tie rod) using the proper tool.
4. Separate the steering knuckle arm from the MacPherson strut (if equipped with a camber adjusting pin, mark assembly for correct wheel alignment).
5. Remove the tension rod and stabilizer bar from the lower arm.
6. Remove the nuts or bolts connecting the lower control arm (transverse link) to the suspension crossmember.
7. Remove the lower control arm (transverse link) with the suspension ball joint and knuckle arm still attached.
To install:
8. When installing the control arm, temporarily tighten the nuts

and/or bolts securing the control arm to the suspension crossmember. Tighten them fully only after the vehicle is sitting on its wheels. Check front end alignment if necessary.

Altima, Maxima and 1990-92 Stanza

1. Raise the vehicle and support it safely.
2. Unbolt and remove the stabilizer bar. The bar is removed by unfastening the clamp bolts and the bolts that hold the bar to the transverse link gusset plate. When removing the clamps, note the relationship between the clamp and paint mark on the bar.
3. Unbolt and remove the transverse link and gusset.
4. Inspect the transverse link, gusset and bushings for cracks, damage and deformation.
To install:
5. Bolt the transverse link and gusset into place. Lower the vehicle and torque the the bolts and nuts in the proper sequence as illustrated. Torque the nuts to 30-35 ft. lbs. (41-51 Nm) and the bolts to 87-108 ft. lbs. (118-147 Nm). The vehicle must be at curb weight and the tires must be on the ground. After installation is complete, check the front end alignment.

Pulsar and Sentra

1. Raise the vehicle and support it safely.
2. Remove the front wheels.
3. Remove the wheel bearing locknut.
4. Remove the tie rod ball joint with a suitable puller.
5. Remove the lower strut-to-knuckle mounting bolts and separate the strut from the knuckle.
6. Separate the outer end of the halfshaft from the steering knuckle by carefully tapping it with a rubber mallet. Be sure to cover the CV-joints with a shop rag.
7. Using a suitable ball joint removal tool, separate the lower ball joint stud from the steering knuckle.
8. Unbolt and remove the transverse link and ball joint as an assembly.
9. Installation is the reverse of the removal procedure. Make sure the tab on the transverse link clamp is pointing in the proper direction. Final tightening of all bolts should take place with the weight of the vehicle on the wheels. Check wheel alignment.

Front Wheel Bearings

ADJUSTMENT

NOTE: For wheel bearing procedures on front wheel drive vehicles, please refer to the ""Drive Axle" section.

240SX

There is no procedure for torquing the front wheel bearings due to the design of the bearing. Once the final torque is applied to the wheel bearing axle nut and the axial play is checked, no further adjustment is either necessary or possible.

Check the torque of the wheel bearing locknut. This value is 108-159 ft. lbs. (147-216 Nm). Then, mount a dial indicator to the face of the hub and check the axial play. It should not exceed 0.0012 in. (0.03mm). If the axial play is not as specified, replace the wheel bearing assembly.

300ZX

1. Raise the vehicle and support safely.
2. Remove the front wheels.
3. Prior to checking the bearing preload, spin the wheel hub at least 10 revolutions in both directions to seat the bearing.
4. To check the pre-load: connect a spring scale of known calibration to a wheel hub bolt and measure the turning torque. If an NSK wheel bearing is used, the turning torque should be 1.3-8.4 lbs. (5.9-37.3 N). For NTN bearings, the turning torque should be 1.8-13.0 lbs. (7.8-57.9 N).
5. To check the axial endplay: mount a dial indicator so the stylus of the dial rests on the face of the hub and check the wheel bearing axial endplay by attempting to rock the wheel hub in and out. The endplay should be 0.0020 in. (0.05mm) or less.
6. Mount the front wheels and lower the vehicle.

REMOVAL AND INSTALLATION

240SX

1. Raise and support the vehicle safely.
2. Remove the front wheels.
3. Work off center hub cap by using a suitable thin tool. If necessary tap around it with a soft hammer while removing. Pry off cotter pin and take out adjusting cap.
4. Apply the parking brake firmly and remove the wheel bearing nut.

The nut will require a good deal of force to remove it.

5. Unbolt the caliper and move it aside. Do not disconnect the hose from the caliper. Do not allow the caliper to hang by the hose; support the caliper with a length of wire or rest it on a suspension member.

6. Pull the brake disc and wheel hub from the spindle.

7. Separate the tie rod and lower ball joints using the proper tool.

8. Place matchmarks on the strut lower bracket and camber adjusting pin for assembly reference. Remove the lower bracket bolts and nuts. Remove the wheel hub and knuckle assembly.

9. Remove the bearing retaining ring from the wheel hub.

10. Press the bearing assembly from the wheel hub. Apply pressure from the outside of the hub to remove the bearing.

To install:

11. Press the new bearing assembly into the hub from the inside.

NOTE: Do not press the on the inner race of the wheel bearing assembly. Do not lubricate the surfaces of mating surfaces of the wheel bearing outer race and wheel with grease or oil. Be careful not to damage the grease seal.

12. Install the bearing retaining ring.

13. Coat the lip of the grease seal with multi-purpose grease.

14. Manuever the wheel hub and axle assembly onto the lower mounting bracket and install the bracket bolts and nuts. Make sure the matchmarks on the bracket and the camber adjusting pin are aligned properly.

15. Connect the lower and tie rod ball joints. Use new nuts and cotter pins.

16. Push the brake disc and wheel hub onto the spindle.

17. Install the brake caliper assembly.

18. Apply the parking brake and torque the wheel bearing locknut to 108-159 ft. lbs. (147-216 Nm). Mount a dial indicator so the stylus of the dial rests on the face of the hub and check the wheel bearing axial endplay by attempting to rock the wheel hub in and out. The endplay should be 0.0012 in. (0.03mm) or less.

19. Install a new locknut cotter pin. Install the bearing hub cap.

20. Mount the the front wheels and lower the vehicle.

300ZX

1. Raise and support the vehicle safely.

2. Remove the front wheels.

3. Unbolt the caliper and move it aside. Do not disconnect the hose from the caliper. Do not allow the caliper to hang by the hose; support the caliper with a length of wire or rest it on a suspension member.

4. Separate the tie rod and lower ball joints using the proper tool.

NOTE: The steering knuckle is made of an aluminum alloy. Be careful no to strike it when removing the ball joints.

5. Remove the kingpin lower nut and remove the steering knuckle assembly.

6. Remove the hub cap, wheel bearing locknut, sensor rotor (with ABS) or washer (without ABS).

7. Remove the wheel hub with a suitable drift.

8. Remove the wheel bearing retaining ring.

9. Press the wheel bearing from the knuckle.

10. Drive out the wheel bearing inner race to the outside of the wheel hub.

11. Remove the grease seal and splash guard (baffle plate).

To install:

12. From the outside of the knuckle, press the new wheel bearing assembly into the knuckle.

NOTE: Do not press the on the inner race of the wheel bearing assembly. Do not lubricate the surfaces of mating surfaces of the wheel bearing outer race and wheel with grease or oil. Be careful not to damage the grease seal.

13. Install the bearing retaining ring. Make sure it seats evenly in the groove of the knuckle.

14. Coat the lip of the grease seal with multi-purpose grease and install.

15. Install the splash guard.

16. Press the wheel hub into the steering knuckle.

17. Install the washer (without ABS), sensor rotor (with ABS) and wheel bearing locknut. Torque the locknut to 152-210 ft. lbs. (206-284 Nm). Stake the locknut tabs using a small cold chisel.

18. Place the hub cap onto the knuckle and tap it into place using a rubber or plastic mallet. Once the cap is seated lightly into the knuckle, install the cap retaining bolts and torque to 8-12 ft. lbs. (11-16 Nm).

19. Mount the steering knuckle assembly and tighten the lower kingpin nut.

20. Connect the tie rod and lower ball joints using the proper tool.

21. Install the brake caliper assembly.

22. Prior to checking the bearing preload, spin the wheel hub at least 10 revolutions in both directions to seat the bearing. Check the wheel bearing preload and axial end play as follows:

a. Preload — connect a spring scale of known calibration to a wheel hub bolt and measure the turning torque. If an NSK wheel bearing is used, the turning torque should be 1.3-8.4 lbs. (5.9-37.3 N). For NTN bearings, the turning torque should be 1.8-13.0 lbs. (7.8-57.9 N).

b. Axial endplay — mount a dial indicator so the stylus of the dial rests on the face of the hub and check the wheel bearing axial endplay by attempting to rock the wheel hub in and out. The endplay should be 0.0020 in. (0.05mm) or less.

23. Mount the front wheels and lower the vehicle.

REAR SUSPENSION

MacPherson Strut

REMOVAL AND INSTALLATION

240SX AND 300ZX

1. Block the front wheels.

2. Raise and support the vehicle safely.

NOTE: The vehicle should be far enough off the ground so the rear spring does not support any weight.

3. Working inside the luggage compartment, turn and remove the caps above the strut mounts. Remove the strut mounting nuts.

4. Remove the mounting bolt for the strut at the lower arm (transverse link) and then lift out the strut.

5. Installation is in the reverse order of removal. Install the upper end first and secure with the nuts snugged down, but not fully tightened. Attach the lower end of the strut to the transverse link and tighten the upper nuts to 12-14 ft. lbs. (16-19 Nm). Tighten the lower

mounting bolt to 65-80 ft. lbs. (88-108 Nm).

Pulsar and Sentra (2WD)

NOTE: Modify service steps as necessary. This is a complete disassembly repair procedure. Review the complete procedure before starting this repair.

1. Raise and support the rear of the vehicle safely.
2. Remove the rear wheels.
3. Disconnect the brake tube and parking brake cable.
4. If necessary, remove the brake assembly and wheel bearing.
5. Disconnect the parallel links and radius rod from the strut or knuckle.
6. Support the strut assembly.
7. Remove the strut upper end nuts and then remove the strut from the vehicle.
8. Installation is the reverse of the removal procedure. Tighten the:
Radius rod-to-knuckle nuts to 43-61 ft. lbs. (59-83 Nm)
Strut-to-knuckle and parallel link-to-knuckle bolts to 72-87 ft. lbs. (98-118 Nm)
Strut-to-body nuts to 18-22 ft. lbs. (25-29 Nm).

Sentra Wagon (4WD)

1. Block the front wheels.
2. Raise and support the vehicle safely.
3. Position a suitable floor jack under the transverse link on the side of the strut to be removed. Raise it just enough to support the strut.
4. Open the rear of the vehicle and remove the 3 nuts that attach the top of the strut to the body.
5. Remove the rear wheels.
6. Remove the brake line from its bracket and position it aside. Do not disconnect the brake line.
7. Remove the 2 lower strut-to-knuckle mounting bolts.
8. Carefully lower the floor jack and remove the strut.
9. Installation is the reverse order of removal. Final tightening of the strut mounting bolts should take place with the wheels on the ground and the vehicle unladen. Tighten the upper strut-to-body nuts to 33-40 ft. lbs. (45-60 Nm) and the lower strut-to-knuckle bolts to 111-120 ft. lbs. (151-163 Nm).

Altima, Maxima and 1990-92 Stanza

1. Unclip the rear brake line at the strut. Do not disconnect it.
2. Disconnect the parking brake at the equalizer.

3. Remove the parallel link mounting bolts, radius rod mounting bolts, stabilizer mounting bolts, stabilizer connecting brackets and parking brake cable mounting bracket bolts.
4. Remove the rear seat and parcel shelf.
5. Remove the 3 upper strut mounting nuts and then lift out the strut.
6. Installation is the reverse of the removal procedure. Tighten all bolts sufficiently to safely support the vehicle and then lower the vehicle to the ground so it rests on its own weight. Tighten:
Upper strut mounting nuts to 31-40 ft. lbs. (42-54 Nm)
Parallel link mounting bolts to 65-87 ft. lbs. (88-118 Nm)
Connecting rod bracket nuts to 30-35 ft. lbs. (41-47 Nm)
Stabilizer bar mounting bolts to 43-58 ft. lbs. (59-78 Nm)
Radius rod mounting bolts to 65-87 ft. lbs. (88-118 Nm) or 87-108 ft. lbs. (118-147Nm) for the lower strut mounting.

Rear Wheel Bearings

NOTE: For wheel bearing procedures on rear wheel drive models, please refer to ""Rear Axle Shaft" in the Drive Axle section.

REMOVAL AND INSTALLATION

Maxima, Pulsar, Sentra (2WD) and Stanza

1. Raise and support the vehicle safely.
2. Remove the rear wheels.
3. On rear disc brake applications, remove the brake caliper assembly and support it with wire. The brake hose need not be disconnected. Do not depress the brake pedal while the caliper is supported or the piston will pop out.
4. Work off center hub cap by using thin tool. If necessary, tap around it with a soft hammer while removing.
5. Remove the cotter pin, take out adjusting cap and wheel bearing locknut.
6. Remove drum or disc with bearing inside.

NOTE: On some applications, a circular clip holds inner wheel bearing in brake hub. On Altima, Maxima, Pulsar, Sentra and 1990-92 Stanza, the rear wheel

bearing is a sealed unit which combines the bearing, inner and outer races and grease seal.

7. Remove bearing from drum using long brass drift pin.
To install:
8. Pack the bearings.
9. Installation is the reverse of the removal procedure: During installation, observe the following:
a. On sealed type wheel bearings, the bearing must be pressed into the brake drum or brake disc.
b. Do not press the inner race of the bearing; do not coat the wheel bearing and outer hub mating surfaces with oil or grease and do not damage the grease seal.
c. On sealed type wheel bearings torque the wheel locknut to specifications.

Sentra (4WD)

1. Raise and support the vehicle safely.
2. Remove wheel bearing locknut while depressing brake pedal.
3. Disconnect brake hydraulic line and parking brake cable.
4. Separate halfshaft from knuckle by slightly tapping it with suitable tool. Cover axle boots with waste cloth so as not to damage them when removing halfshaft.
5. Remove all knuckle retaining bolts and nuts. Make a matchmark before removing adjusting pin.
6. Separate the hub from the knuckle using a suitable tool.
7. Drive out the inner (outside) race using a suitable press.
8. Remove the outer grease seal.
9. Drive the inner race (inside) from the hub. The inner grease seal will be removed with it.
10. Remove inner and outer circular clips.
11. Remove the bearings.
12. Drive out the outer race using a suitable tool.
To install:
13. Install the inner circlip in the knuckle groove.
14. Press in the new outer race from the outside of the knuckle.

NOTE: Do not apply grease the wheel bearing outer race and knuckle surfaces.

15. Pack the bearings and the grease seal lip with grease.
16. Install the outer circlip in the knuckle groove.
17. Install the inner races uisng the proper tool, then install the inner grease seal. Be careful not to damage the grease seal.
18. Press the hub into the knuckle.

19. Complete the installation of the remaining components in reverse of the removal procedure. Adjust the wheel bearings as described below.

ADJUSTMENT

Altima, Maxima, Pulsar, Sentra and 1990-92 Stanza

Due to a bearing change (later models now use a sealed type or complete hub type assembly) on these models, there is no procedure for torquing the rear wheel bearings. Once the final torque is applied to the wheel bearing axle nut and the axial play is checked, no further adjustment is either necessary or possible.

Check the torque of the wheel bearing locknut. This value is 137-188 ft. lbs. (186-255 Nm) on Altima, Maxima, Pulsar, Sentra 2WD and 1990-92 Stanza. On Sentra 4WD, the torque value is 174-231 ft. lbs. (236-314 Nm). Rotate the hub and make sure the bearing turn smoothly and quietly. Then, mount a dial indicator to the face of the hub and check the axial play. It should not exceed 0.0020 in. (0.05mm). If the axial play is not as specified, replace the necessary component.

Rear Axle Assembly

REMOVAL AND INSTALLATION

1. Raise and support the vehicle safely.
2. Remove the rear wheels.
3. Disconnect the brake line and parking brake cable.
4. Work off center hub cap by using thin tool. If necessary tap around it with a soft hammer while removing.

STEERING

Steering Wheel

———— CAUTION ————
On vehicles equipped with an air bag, turn the ignition switch to OFF position. The negative battery cable must be disconnected and wait 10 minutes after the cable is disconnected before working on the system. Failure to do so may result in deployment of the air bag and possible personal injury.

REMOVAL AND INSTALLATION

1. Position the wheels in the straight-ahead direction. The steering wheel should be right side up and level.
2. Disconnect the negative battery cable.
3. Look at the back of the steering wheel. If there are countersunk screws in the back of the steering wheel spokes, remove the screws and pull off the horn pad. Some vehicles have a horn wire running from the pad to the steering wheel. Disconnect it.

NOTE: There are other types of horn buttons or rings. The first simply pulls off. The second, which is usually a large, semi-triangular pad, must be pushed up, then pulled off. The third must be pushed in and turned clockwise.

4. Remove the rest of the horn switching mechanism, noting the relative location of the parts. Remove the mechanism only if it interferes with removal of the steering wheel.
5. Matchmark the top of the steering column shaft and the steering wheel flange.
6. Remove the attaching nut and remove the steering wheel with a puller.

NOTE: Do not strike the shaft with a hammer; which may cause the column to collapse.

To install:
7. Install the steering wheel by aligning the punch marks. Do not drive or hammer the wheel into place, or the collapsible steering column may collapse. Before installing the horn pad, apply multi-purpose grease to the surface of the cancel pin and horn contact slip-ring.
8. Tighten the steering wheel nuts to 22-29 ft. lbs. (29-39 Nm).
9. Reinstall the horn button, pad or ring.
10. Connect the negative battery cable.

Manual Steering Rack and Pinion

REMOVAL AND INSTALLATION

Sentra

1. Raise and support the vehicle safely and remove the wheels.
2. Disconnect the tie rod from the steering knuckle and loosen the steering gear attaching bolts.
3. Remove the bolt securing the lower joint to the steering gear pinion and remove the lower joint from the pinion.
4. Remove the bolts holding the steering gear housing to the body and remove the steering gear and linkage assembly from the vehicle.
5. Installation is the reverse order of the removal procedure. When fitting the lower U-joint, make sure the attaching bolt is aligned perfectly with the cut out in the splined end of the steering column shaft. Torque the steering gear mounting clamp bolts to 54-72 ft. lbs. (73-97 Nm). Torque the tie rod end nuts to 22-29 ft. lbs. (29-39 Nm).

Power Steering Rack and Pinion

REMOVAL AND INSTALLATION

NOTE: On air bag equipped vehicles, the rotation of the spiral cable is limited. If the steering gear must be removed, set the front wheels in the straight-ahead direction. Do not rotate the steering column while the steering gear is removed.

300ZX

1. Block the rear wheels. Raise and support the vehicle safely.
2. Position an oil catch pan under the power steering gear, remove the hydraulic lines from the gear and drain the oil. Plug the lines to prevent leakage.
3. Loosen the steering column lower joint shaft bolt.
4. Before disconnecting the lower ball joint set the steering gear assembly in neutral by making the wheels straight. Loosen the bolt and disconnect the lower joint. Matchmark the pinion shaft to the pinion housing to record the neutral gear position.
5. Remove the tie rod end-to-knuckle arm cotter pins and castle nuts.

6. Separate the tie rods from the knuckle arms using a suitable puller.

7. Remove the steering gear housing-to-suspension crossmember bolts.

8. Position a floor jack under the engine and raise it just enough to support the engine. Loosen the engine mounting bolts and raise the engine about ½ in. (12mm).

9. Remove the steering gear and linkage from the vehicle. **To install:**

10. Installation is the reverse of the removal procedure observing the following:

a. Tighten the gear housing mouting bracket bolts to 65-80 ft. lbs. (88-108 Nm).

b. Torque the tie rod end nuts to 22-29 ft. lbs. (29-39 Nm).

c. Torque the high pressure hydraulic line fitting to 22-26 ft. lbs. (36-40 Nm) and lower pressure fitting to 27-30 ft. lbs. (36-40 Nm).

d. When attaching the lower joint, set the left and right dust boots to equal deflection. Refill the power steering pump, start the engine and bleed the system.

NOTE: The O-ring in the lower pressure hydraulic line fitting is larger than the O-ring in the high pressure line. Make sure the O-rings are installed in the proper fittings. Observe the torque specification given for the hydraulic line fittings. Over-tightening will cause damage to the fitting threads and O-rings.

Altima, Pulsar, Sentra, Stanza, Maxima and 240SX

1. Raise and support the vehicle safely and remove the wheels.

2. Disconnect the power steering hose from the power steering gear and plug all hoses to prevent leakage.

3. Disconnect the side rod studs from the steering knuckles.

4. On Pulsar and Sentra, support the transaxle with a suitable transmission jack and remove the exhaust pipe and rear engine mounts.

5. On other vehicles, remove the lower joint assembly from the steering gear pinion. Before disconnecting the lower ball joint set the steering gear assembly in neutral by making the wheels straight. Loosen the bolt and disconnect the lower joint. Matchmark the pinion shaft to the pinion housing to record the neutral gear position.

6. Remove the steering gear and linkage assembly from the vehicle.

To install:

7. Installation is the reverse of removal procedure observing the following:

a. Make sure the pinion shaft and pinion housing are aligned properly.

b. Torque the high pressure hydraulic line fitting to 11-18 ft. lbs. (15-25 Nm) and lower pressure fitting to 20-29 ft. lbs. (27-39 Nm).

c. When attaching the lower joint, set the left and right dust boots to equal deflection.

d. On Altima, Maxima and Stanza, torque the gear housing mounting bracket bolts to 54-72 ft. lbs. (73-97 Nm) using the proper sequence. On all other models, torque the gear housing bracket bolts in criss-cross pattern to 54-72 ft. lbs. (73-97 ft. lbs.)

8. Refill the power steering pump, start the engine and bleed the system. Refill the power steering pump, start the engine and bleed the system.

NOTE: On most vehicles, the O-ring in the lower pressure hydraulic line fitting is larger than the O-ring in the high pressure line. Make sure the O-rings are installed in the proper fittings. Observe the torque specification given for the hydraulic line fittings. Over-tightening will cause damage to the fitting threads and O-rings.

Power Steering Pump

REMOVAL AND INSTALLATION

1. If necessary, remove the air cleaner duct and air cleaner.

2. Loosen power steering pump belt adjustment, if equipped:

a. Loosen the pivot and mounting bolts.

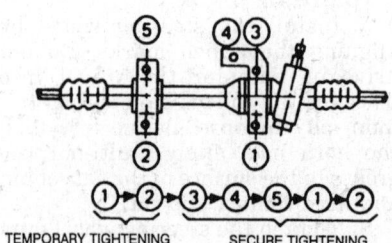

Gear housing mounting bracket bolt torque sequence — Altima, Stanza and Maxima

b. Loosen the idler pulley locknut and turn the adjusting nut counterclockwise to remove the power steering belt.

3. Remove the drive belt on the air conditioning compressor, if equipped.

4. Loosen the power steering hoses at the pump and remove the bolts holding the power steering pump to the bracket.

5. Disconnect and plug the power steering hoses and remove the pump from the vehicle.

6. Installation is the reverse of the removal procedure. Adjust power steering pump belt. Fill and bleed the power steering system.

BELT TENSION ADJUSTMENT

The correct belt tension is about ¼-½ in. play on the longest span of the belt.

Without Adjusting Bolt

1. Disconnect the negative battery cable. Loosen the power steering pump pivot and mounting bolts.

2. Pry the power steering pump toward or away from the engine until the tension is correct. Use a hammer handle or wooden prybar.

3. When the tension is correct, tighten the bolts and check the adjustment. Reconnect the negative battery cable.

With Adjusting Bolt

1. Disconnect the negative battery cable.

2. Loosen the power steering pump adjusting bolt locknut.

3. Loosen the power steering pump mounting bolt(s).

4. Turn the adjusting bolt to adjust the belt tension.

5. Tighten the power steering pump adjusting bolt locknut.

6. Tighten the power steering pump mounting bolt(s).

7. Reconnect the neagative battery cable.

Idler Pulley Adjusting Bolt Type

1. Disconnect the negative battery.

2. At the bottom of the idler pulley for the power steering pump, there is a bolt which is used to raise or lower the pulley. To free the bolt for adjustment, it is necessary to loosen the locknut in the face of the idler pulley.

3. Loosen the idler's pulley mounting bolt.

4. Turn the adjusting bolt to adjust the belt tension.

5. After adjusting the belt tension, tighten the idler's pulley mounting bolt.

6. Recconect the negative battery cable.

SYSTEM BLEEDING

1. Check the level in the power steering pump reservoir. Add fluid as necessary to the proper level.

2. Safely raise and support the vehicle until the wheels are just off the ground.

3. With the engine running, quickly turn the steering wheel all the way to the left and all the way to the right lightly touching the steering stops.

4. Stop the engine and check to see if any more fluid is required in the pump reservoir. Add fluid as necessary.

5. Repeat system bleeding procedure until fluid level no longer decreases.

Tie Rod Ends

REMOVAL AND INSTALLATION

A ball joint remover tool or equivalent, is required for this operation.

1. Raise and support the vehicle safely.

2. Locate the faulty tie rod end. It will have a lot of play in it and the dust cover will probably be torn.

3. Remove the cotter pin and nut from the tie rod stud. Note the position of the tie rod end in relation to the rest of the steering linkage.

4. Loosen the locknut.

5. Free the tie rod ball joint from either the relay rod or steering knuckle by using a ball joint remover or equivalent tool.

6. Mark the assembly, unscrew and remove the tie rod end, counting the number of turns it takes to completely free it.

To install:

7. Install the new tie rod end, turning it in exactly the same number of turns for removal. Make sure it is correctly positioned in relation to the rest of the steering linkage.

8. Fit the ball joint and nut. Torque the tie rod end to 22-36 ft. lbs. (29-39 Nm). Once the specified torque is reached, tighten further until the nut groove is aligned with the first pin hole. Install a new cotter pin.

9. Check front end wheel alignment.

BRAKES

Master Cylinder

REMOVAL AND INSTALLATION

1. Clean the outside of the cylinder thoroughly, particularly around the cap and fluid lines.

2. Disconnect the fluid lines and cap them to keep dirt out.

3. On vehicles with a fluid level gauge, disconnect the electrical connector.

4. Remove the clevis pin connecting the pushrod to the brake pedal arm inside the vehicle.

5. Unbolt the master cylinder from the firewall and remove along with gasket. If the pushrod is not adjustable, there will be shims between the cylinder and the firewall. These shims, or the adjustable pushrod, are used to adjust brake pedal free-play.

6. Installation of the master cylinder is the reverse of the removal procedure. Bleed the brakes.

Proportioning Valve

REMOVAL AND INSTALLATION

Built-in Type

On some models, the proportioning valve is incorporated into the master cylinder. Consequently, REMOVAL AND INSTALLATION procedures are limited to replacement of the master cylinder unit as a whole.

Separated Type

1. Drain brake fluid from each bleeder vavle.

2. Loosen flare nut. Remove the proportioning valve mounting bolt, then remove the flare nut.

3. Installation is the reverse of the removal procedure. Torque the valve mounting bolt to 11-13 ft. lbs. (15-18Nm). Bleed brake system.

Power Brake Booster

REMOVAL AND INSTALLATION

1. Remove the master cylinder.

2. Remove the vacuum hose at the power brake booster.

3. Remove the pushrod from the brake pedal.

4. From under the instrument panel, remove the cowl-to-booster nuts. Remove the brake booster.

5. Installation is in the reverse order of removal. Bleed the brake system.

Brake Caliper

REMOVAL AND INSTALLATION

1. Raise the vehicle and support safely.

2. Remove the front or rear wheels.

3. Disconnect the brake line from the caliper. Remove the metal gaskets from the brake hose fitting and discard them.

4. Disconnect the parking brake cable.

5. Remove the brake pads if they interfere with caliper removal.

6. Remove the brake caliper mounting bolts.

7. Remove the brake caliper assembly.

8. Installation is the reverse of the removal procedure. Torque the caliper torque member bolts to 40-72 ft. lbs. (54-98 Nm). Use new brake hose fitting gaskets. Bleed the brake system and adjust the parking brake cable.

Front Disc Brake Pads

REMOVAL AND INSTALLATION

Maxima

CL25VB BRAKES

1. Raise the vehicle and support safely.

2. Remove the front wheels.

3. Remove the pin (lower) bolt from the caliper.

4. Swing the caliper body upward on the upper bolt.

5. Remove the pad retainers and inner and outer shims.

NOTE: Do not depress the brake pedal when the cylinder body is in the raised position or the piston will pop out of the cylinder.

To install:

6. Check the level of fluid in the master cylinder. If the fluid is near the maximum level, use a clean syringe to remove fluid until the level is down well below the lip of the reservoir.

7. Use a large C-clamp or piston expansion tool to press the caliper

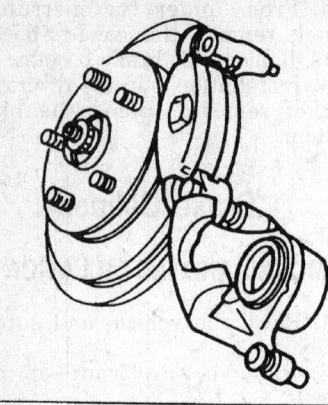

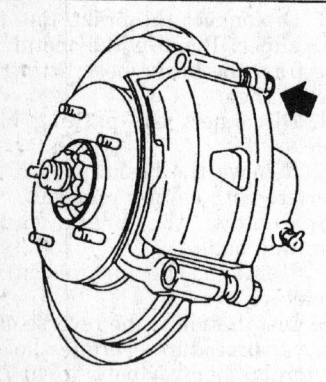

Front disc brake pad replacement

piston back into the caliper, to allow room for the installation of the new pads.

8. Install the new pads, utilizing new shims, in reverse order. Torque the lower pin bolt to 16-23 ft. lbs. (22-31 Nm).

240SX

CL22VB AND CL25VA BRAKES

CL22VB type front disc brakes are used on vehicles without ABS and CL25VA type brake are used on vehicles with ABS.

1. Raise and support the vehicle safely.
2. Remove the front wheels.
3. Remove the pin (lower) bolt from the caliper.
4. Swing the caliper body upward on the upper bolt.
5. Remove the pad retainers and inner and outer shims.

NOTE: Do not depress the brake pedal when the cylinder body is in the raised position or the piston will pop out of the cylinder.

6. Check the level of fluid in the master cylinder. If the fluid is near the maximum level, use a clean syringe to remove fluid until the level is

down well below the lip of the reservoir.

7. Use a large C-clamp or piston expansion tool to press the caliper piston back into the caliper, to allow room for the installation of the new pads.

8. Install the new pads, utilizing new shims, in reverse order. Torque the lower and main pin bolts to 16-23 ft. lbs. (22-31 Nm).

300ZX

OPZ25V AND OPZ25VA BRAKES

OPZ25VA type front disc brakes are used on turbocharged engines. OPZ25V brakes are used on non-turbocharged engines.

1. Raise the vehicle and support safely.
2. Remove the front wheels.
3. Remove the clip from the pad pin and remove the pad pin.
4. Remove the cross spring.
5. Withdraw the outer pad and insert and temporarily insert it between the lower piston and the rotor.
To install:
6. Using a suitable tool, push the upper piston back and insert the new pad so it contacts the upper piston.
7. Withdraw the old pad.
8. Push the piston back with a suitable tool to prevent it from popping out.
9. Pull out the new pad and re-install it in the correct position.
10. Repeat steps 5-9 for the inner pad.
11. Install the cross spring, pad pin and pad clip.

Altima, Pulsar, Sentra and Stanza

AD18B, AD18V, AD18VE, AD22VF, CL18B, CL18VD, CL25VA BRAKES

The CL18B, CL18VD, AD18B, AD18V, AD18VE and AD22VF type front disc brakes are used on Pulsar and Sentra depending on engine application. The Altima and Stanza uses CL25VA front disc brakes on both ABS equipped and non-ABS vehicles.

1. Raise the vehicle and support safely.
2. Remove the front wheels.
3. Remove the bottom guide pin (Altima, Stanza and Sentra) or the lock pin (Pulsar) from the caliper and swing the caliper cylinder body upward.
4. Remove the brake pad retainers and the pads.
To install:
5. Install the brake pads and caliper assembly.

6. Install the wheels and lower the vehicle.
7. Apply the brakes a few times to seat the pads. Check the master cylinder and add fluid if necessary. Bleed the brakes, if necessary.

Rear Disc Brake Pads

REMOVAL AND INSTALLATION

240SX, Altima, Maxima and 1990-92 Stanza with ABS

CL9H AND CL9HA BRAKES

The CL9H rear disc brake is used on 240SX. The CL9H and CL9HA rear disc brake are used on the Maxima on both ABS equipped and non-ABS vehicles. CL9H rear disc brakes are used on 1990-92 Stanza with ABS. The CL9HA rear disc brake are used on the Altima on both ABS equipped and non-ABS vehicles.

1. Raise and support the vehicle safely.
2. Remove the rear wheels.
3. Release the parking brake and remove the cable bracket bolt or lock spring.
4. Remove the pin bolts and lift off the caliper body.
5. Pull out the pad springs and then remove the pads and shims.
To install:
6. Clean the piston end of the caliper body and the area around the pin holes. Be careful not to get oil on the rotor.
7. Using the proper tool, carefully turn the piston clockwise back into the caliper body. Take care not to damage the piston boot.
8. Coat the pad contact area on the mounting support with a silicone based grease.
9. Install the pads, shims and the pad springs. Always use new shims.
10. Position the caliper body in the mounting support and tighten the pin bolts.
11. Mount the wheels, lower the vehicle and bleed the system if necessary.

300ZX

OPZ11VB BRAKES

1. Raise and support the vehicle safely.
2. Remove the rear wheels.
3. Disconnect the parking brake cable.
4. Remove the clip at the outside of the pad pins, if equipped.

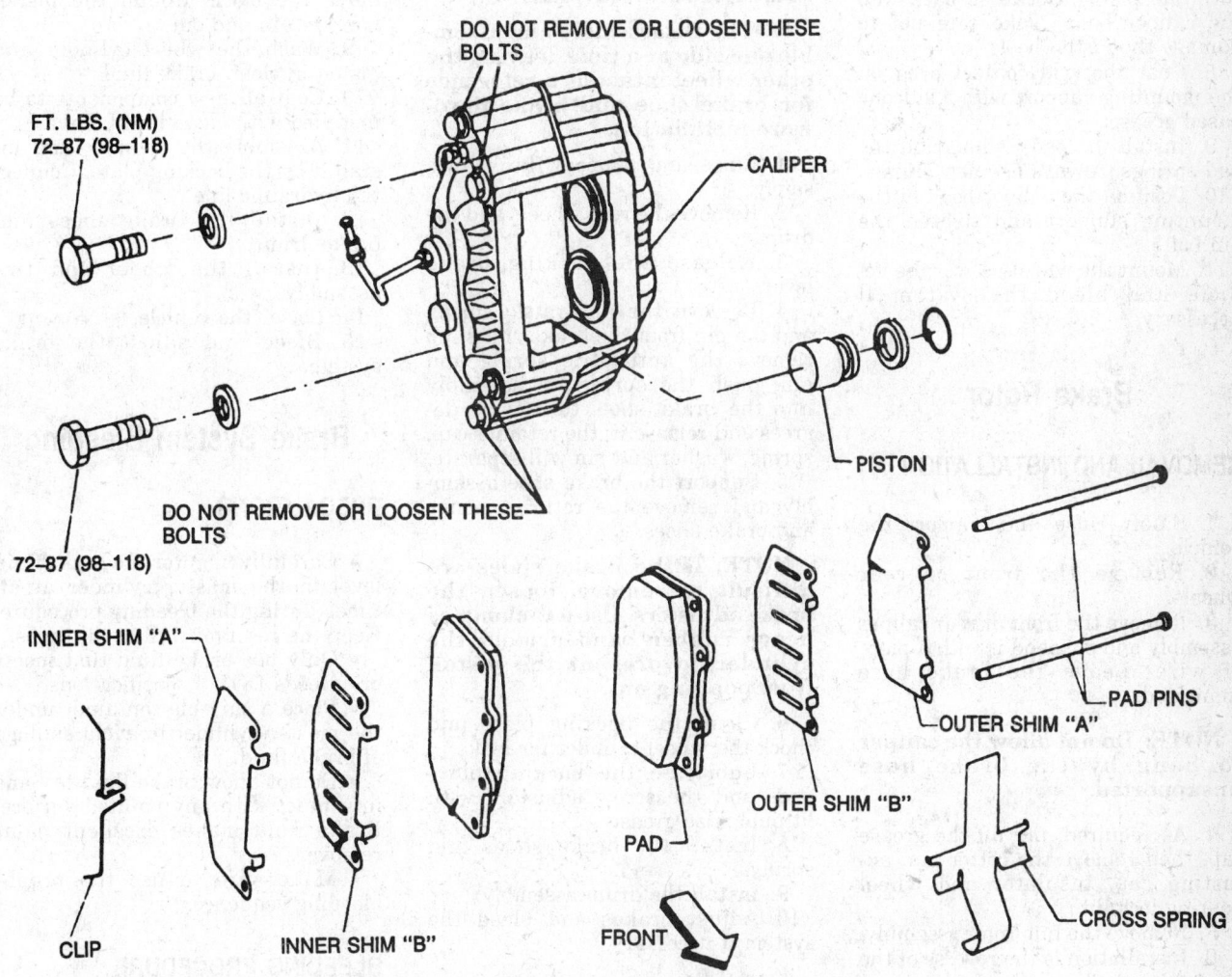

OPZ25V and OPZ25VA type front disc brake assembly — 300ZX

5. Remove the pad pin bolts. Remove the caliper assembly. Hold the anti-squeal springs in place by hand.

6. Remove the cross spring.

7. Remove the pads. When the pads are removed, do not depress the brake or else the piston will pop out.

To install:

8. Clean the end of the piston with clean brake fluid. Lightly coat the caliper-to-pad, the yoke-to-pad, the retaining pin-to-pad and the retaining pin-to-bracket surfaces with brake grease.

9. Push in on the piston while at the same time turning it clockwise into the bore. Then, with a lever between the rotor and yoke, push the yoke over until there is clearance to install the pads, equally.

10. Install the cross spring, shims, the pads, the anti-squeal springs and the pins. Install the clip. Note that the inner pad has a tab which must fit into the piston notch. Make sure the piston notch is centered to allow for proper pad installation.

11. Apply the brakes a few times to center the pads. Check the master cylinder fluid level and add fluid, if necessary.

1991-94 Sentra

AD7HA BRAKES

The AD7HA rear disc brake is used on the 1991-94 Sentra vehicles.

1. Raise and support the vehicle safely.

2. Remove the rear wheels.

3. Release the parking brake and remove the brake cable lock spring.

4. Remove the pin bolts and lift off the caliper body.

5. Pull out the pad springs and then remove the pads and shims.

To install:

6. Clean the piston end of the caliper body and the area around the pin

holes. Be careful not to get oil on the rotor.

7. Using the proper tool, carefully turn the piston clockwise back into the caliper body. Take care not to damage the piston boot.

8. Coat the pad contact area on the mounting support with a silicone based grease.

9. Install the pads, shims and the pad springs. Always use new shims.

10. Position the caliper body in the mounting support and tighten the pin bolts.

11. Mount the wheels, lower the vehicle and bleed the system if necessary.

Brake Rotor

REMOVAL AND INSTALLATION

1. Safely raise and support the vehicle.

2. Remove the front or rear wheels.

3. Remove the front or rear caliper assembly and suspend it with a piece of wire. Leave the brake hose connected.

NOTE: Do not allow the caliper to hang by the brake hose unsupported.

4. As required, pry off the grease cap, then remove the cotter pin, adjusting cap, insulator and wheel bearing locknut.

5. Remove the hub/rotor assembly.

6. Installation is the reverse of the removal procedure.

Brake Drums

REMOVAL AND INSTALLATION

1. Raise and support the vehicle safely.

2. Remove the rear wheels.

3. Release the parking brake lever fully.

4. If required, remove the wheel bearing grease cap, cotter pin and locknut.

5. Remove the brake drum. On some vehicles, there are 2 threaded service holes in each drum which accept 8mm bolts. If the drums are hard to remove, insert the bolts into the service holes and screw them in to force the drum away from the axle.

6. Installation is the reverse of the removal procedure.

Brake Shoes

REMOVAL AND INSTALLATION

NOTE: Disassemble and assemble one side at a time, leaving the other wheel intact as a reference for brake shoe and brake hardware installation.

1. Raise and support the vehicle safely.

2. Remove the rear wheels and the drums.

3. Release the parking brake lever.

4. Remove the anti-rattle spring and the pin from the brake shoes. To remove the anti-rattle spring and pin, push the spring/pin assembly into the brake shoe, turn it 90 degrees and release it; the retainer cap, spring, washer and pin will separate.

5. Support the brake shoe assembly and remove the return springs and brake shoes.

NOTE: If the brake shoes are difficult to remove, loosen the brake adjusters. Use a C-clamp or heavy rubber band around the cylinder to prevent the piston from popping out.

6. Clean the backing plate and check the wheel cylinder for leaks.

7. Lubricate the backing plate pads and the screw adjusters with lithium base grease.

8. Install the brake shoes and springs.

9. Install the drum assembly.

10. Adjust brakes and bleed the system if necessary.

Wheel Cylinder

REMOVAL AND INSTALLATION

1. Raise and support the vehicle safely.

2. Remove the tire and wheel assembly.

3. Remove the brake drum and brake shoes.

4. Disconnect the hydraulic line from the wheel cylinder. Plug the line to prevent leakage.

5. Remove the wheel cylinder from the brake backing plate.

6. Remove the dust boot and take out the piston. Discard the piston cup. The dust boot can be reused although it is best to replace it.

To install:

7. Wash all of the components in clean brake fluid.

8. Inspect the piston and piston bore. Replace any components that are severely corroded, scored or worn. The piston and piston bore may be polished lightly with crocus cloth; move the cloth around the piston bore, not in and out.

9. Wash the wheel cylinder and piston in clean brake fluid.

10. Coat all new components to be installed with clean brake fluid.

11. Assemble the cylinder and install it on the backing plate. Connect the hydraulic line.

12. Install the brake shoes and brake drum.

13. Install the wheel and tire assembly.

14. Lower the vehicle.

15. Bleed and adjust the brake system.

Brake System Bleeding

PRECAUTIONS

• Carefully monitor the brake fluid level in the master cylinder at all times during the bleeding procedure. Keep the reservoir full at all times.

• Only use brake fluid that meets or exceeds DOT 3 specifications.

• Place a suitable container under the master cylinder to avoid spillage of brake fluid.

• Do not allow brake fluid to come in contact with any painted surface. Brake fluid makes excellent paint remover.

• Make sure to use the proper bleeding sequence.

BLEEDING PROCEDURE

The brake bleeding sequence varys from vehicle to vehicle and whether the vehicle is equipped with ABS or not. Bleeding sequences are as follows:

240SX (without ABS) — left rear, right rear, right front, left front.

240SX (with ABS) and 300ZX — left rear, right rear, right front, left front, front side air bleeder on ABS actuator, rear side air bleeder on ABS actuator

Altima — right rear, left front, left rear, right front

Maxima — left rear, right front, right rear, left front

Pulsar, Sentra, Stanza — left rear, right front, right rear, left front caliper

1. If equipped with ABS, turn the ignition switch to the **OFF** position and disconnect the connectors from the ABS actuator. Wait a few minutes to allow for the system to bleed

down, then disconnect the negative battery cable.

2. Connect a transparent vinyl tube to the bleeder valve. Submerge the tube in a container half filled with clean brake fluid.

3. Fully depress the brake pedal several times.

4. With the brake pedal depressed, open the air bleeder valve to release the air.

5. Close the air bleeder valve.

6. Release the brake pedal slowly.

7. Repeat Steps 3-6 until clear fluid flows from the air bleeder valve.

8. Check the fluid level in the master cylinder reservoir and add as necessary.

Anti-Lock Brake System Service

RELIEVING ANTI-LOCK BRAKE SYSTEM PRESSURE

To relieve the pressure from the ABS system, turn the ignition switch to the **OFF** position. Disconnect the connectors from the ABS actuator. Wait a few minutes to allow for the system to bleed down, then disconnect the negative battery cable.

ABS Actuator

REMOVAL AND INSTALLATION

1. Relieve the pressure from the ABS system. Discharge air condition system and drain power steering if neceesary.

2. Disconnect the negative battery cable. Drain brake fluid.

3. Disconnect the electrical harness connectors from the actuator.

4. Disconnect the fluid lines from the actuator. Plug the ends of the lines to prevent leakage.

5. On 240SX, remove the relay bracket. Remove air condition lines and power steering lines if necessary.

6. Remove the actuator mounting bolts and nuts.

7. Remove the actuator from the mounting bracket.

To install:

8. Position the actuator onto the mounting bracket.

9. Install the actuator mounting fasteners.

10. On 240SX, install the relay bracket.

11. Connect the fluid lines and the harness connectors. Install air condi-

tion lines and power steering lines, as necessary.

12. Connect the negative battery cable. Refill all fluid levels.

13. Bleed the brake system.

ABS Front Wheel Sensor

REMOVAL AND INSTALLATION

1. Raise and support the vehicle safely.

2. Remove the front wheels.

3. Disconnect the sensor harness connector.

4. Detach the sensor mounting brackets.

5. Unbolt the sensor from the rear of the steering knuckle.

6. Withdraw the sensor from the sensor rotor. Remove the sensor mounting brackets from the sensor wiring.

NOTE: During REMOVAL AND INSTALLATION, take care not to damage the sensor or the teeth of the rotor.

To install:

7. Transfer the mounting brackets to the new sensor. Insert the sensor through the opening in the the rear of the knuckle and engage the sensor with the rotor teeth.

8. Install the sensor mounting bolts. Check and adjust the sensor-to-rotor clearance as described below. Once the clearance is set, tighten the sensor mounting bolt(s) to 8-12 ft. lbs. (11-16 Nm) on 240SX, 8-11 ft. lbs. (11-16 Nm) on 1992-94 Sentra NX and 300ZX or 13-17 ft. lbs. (18-24 Nm) on Altima, Maxima and Stanza.

9. Position and install the sensor mounting brackets. Make the sure the sensor wiring is routed properly.

10. Connect the sensor harness connector.

11. Mount the front wheels and lower the vehicle.

WHEEL SENSOR CLEARANCE ADJUSTMENT

1. Install the sensor.

2. Check the clearance between the edge of the sensor and rotor teeth using a feeler gauge. Clearances should be as follows:

    a. On 240SX, front wheel sensor clearance should be 0.0108-0.0295 in. (0.275-0.75mm).

    b. On 300ZX, front wheel sensor clearance should be 0.0087-0.0280 in. (0.22-0.71mm).

    c. On Maxima and Stanza, the clearance should be 0.008-0.039 in. (0.2-1.0mm).

    d. On Altima, the clearance should be 0.0069-0.0344 in. (0.175-0.875mm).

3. To adjust the clearance, loosen the sensor mounting bolt(s) and move the sensor back and forth until the clearance is as specified.

4. Once the clearance is set, tighten the sensor mounting bolt(s) to 8-12 ft. lbs. (11-16 Nm) on 240SX, Sentra NX and 300ZX or 13-17 ft. lbs. (18-24 Nm) on Altima, Maxima and Stanza.

ABS Rear Wheel Sensor

REMOVAL AND INSTALLATION

1. Raise and support the vehicle safely.

2. Remove the rear wheels.

3. Disconnect the sensor harness connector.

4. Detach the sensor mounting brackets.

5. Remove the sensor mounting bolts.

6. On Altima, Maxima, Stanza and Sentra NX withdraw the sensor from the rear gusset. On 240SX, the sensor is located on the side of the differential carrier near the driveshaft companion flange. On 300ZX, there are 2 sensors on the side of the differential near each halfshaft.

7. Remove the sensor mounting brackets from the sensor wiring.

To install:

8. Transfer the mounting brackets to the new sensor.

9. Install the sensor. Check and adjust the sensor-to-rotor clearance as described below. Once the clearance is set, tighten the sensor mounting bolt(s) to 13-20 ft. lbs. (18-26 Nm) except Sentra NX or 8-11 ft. lbs. (11-15 Nm) on Sentra NX.

10. Install the sensor mounting brackets. Make the sure the sensor wiring is routed properly.

11. Connect the sensor harness connector.

12. Mount the rear wheels and lower the vehicle.

WHEEL SENSOR CLEARANCE ADJUSTMENT

1. Install the rear wheel sensor.

2. Check the clearance between the edge of the sensor and rotor teeth

using a feeler gauge. Clearances should be as follows:

a. On 240SX, rear wheel sensor clearance should 0.0138-0.0246 in. (0.035-0.625mm).

b. On 300ZX, rear wheel sensor clearance should be 0.0024-0.0366 in. (0.06-0.93mm).

c. On Maxima and Stanza, the clearance should be 0.008-0.039 in. (0.2-1.0mm).

d. On Altima, the clearance should be 0.0030-0.0325 in. (0.075-0.825mm).

3. To adjust the clearance, loosen the sensor mounting bolt(s) and move the sensor back and forth until the clearance is as specified.

4. Once the clearance is set, tighten the sensor mounting bolt(s) to to 13-20 ft. lbs. (18-26 Nm) or 8-11 ft. lbs. (11-15 Nm) on Sentra NX.

CHASSIS ELECTRICAL

Air Bag

DISARMING

If equipped with an air bag, turn the ignition switch to **OFF** position. The negative battery cable must be disconnected and wait 10 minutes after the cable is disconnected before working on the system. SRS sensors must always be installed with the arrow marks facing the front of the vehicle.

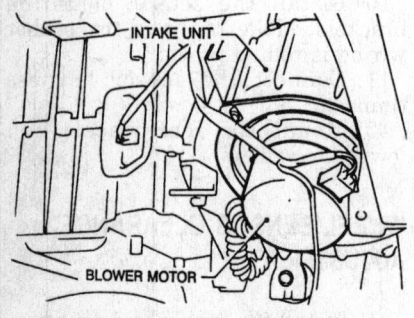

INTAKE UNIT

BLOWER MOTOR

Blower motor mounting

Heater Blower Motor

REMOVAL AND INSTALLATION

1. Disconnect the negative battery cable.

2. Remove all panels and ducting necessary to gain access to the blower motor.

3. Disconnnect the blower motor harness wiring connectors.

4. Remove the blower motor retaining screws and lower the motor/wheel from the intake housing. On some models, release the clips that attach the blower casing to the intake housing to remove the blower motor.

To install:

5. Transfer the old blower wheel to the shaft of the new motor.

6. Raise the blower/wheel assembly up and onto the intake housing. Use a new gasket, if required.

7. Install the blower motor retaining screws or lock the clips.

8. Connect the blower motor wiring.

9. Install all ducting and panels.

10. Connect the negative battery cable.

11. Check the blower for proper operation at all speeds.

Windshield Wiper Motor/Linkage

REMOVAL AND INSTALLATION

240SX, Altima and Stanza

FRONT

1. Disconnect the negative battery cable and make sure the wiper switch is in the off position.

2. Remove the wiper arm.

3. Remove the cowl cover and disconnect the wiper harness connector(s).

4. Remove the wiper motor bolts.

5. Maneuver the wiper motor so the wiper motor link exits the oblong opening in the front cowl top panel. Then, pull the motor straight out and disconnect the ball joint from the motor and wiper links.

6. Remove the wiper motor.

7. Remove the wiper link pivot blocks on the driver's and passenger's sides.

8. Withdraw the wiper link and pivot blocks as one unit from the oblong opening on the left side of the cowl top.

To install:

9. Lubricate the ball joints and pivot points with multi-purpose grease.

10. Position the wiper link and pivot block as one unit in the cowl top through the oblong hole.

11. Before installing the pivot blocks on the cowl top, hold the end of the motor side link at the hole in the front cowl top panel and insert the motor link ball pin into the wiper link hole.

12. Mount the wiper motor and install the bolt.

13. Connect the wiper motor wiring and install the cowl cover.

14. Attach the wiper arm. To reduce wiper arm looseness, prior to connecting the wiper arm, make sure the motor spline shaft and pivot area is completely free of debris and corrosion. Wire brush as necessary.

NOTE: On some vehicles, one wiper arm is longer than the other. The driver's side arm is marked with a "D" and the passenger's side with an ""A". Make sure they are installed on their respective sides.

15. Connect the negative battery cable and check the wipers for proper operation.

REAR

1. Disconnect the negative battery cable.

2. Lift up the rear hatch and remove trim panel(s).

3. Separate the rear wiper arm from the motor shaft.

4. Disconnect the wiper motor wiring harness connector.

5. Unbolt and remove the rear wiper motor from the hatch.

6. Installation is the reverse of the removal procedure. Check the wipers for proper operation.

Pulsar and Sentra

1. Disconnect negative battery cable. Detach the motor wiring plug.

2. Remove the nut connecting the linkage to the wiper motor shaft.

3. Unbolt and remove the wiper motor.

4. Installation is the reverse of the removal procedure. To reduce wiper arm looseness, prior to connecting the wiper arm, make sure the motor spline shaft and pivot area is completely free of debris and corrosion. Wire brush as necessary. Check the wipers for proper operation.

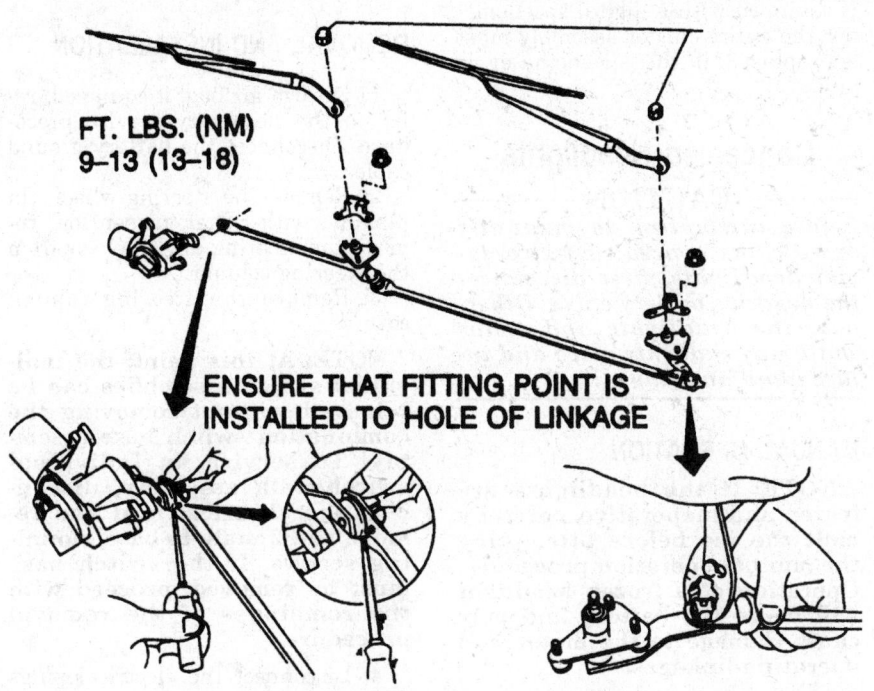

FT. LBS. (NM)
9–13 (13–18)

ENSURE THAT FITTING POINT IS INSTALLED TO HOLE OF LINKAGE

Wiper motor and arm assembly — Pulsar and Sentra

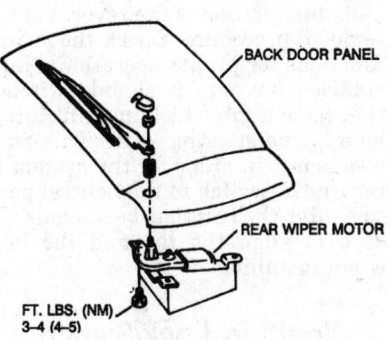

BACK DOOR PANEL

REAR WIPER MOTOR

FT. LBS. (NM)
3–4 (4–5)

Rear wiper assembly — 240SX

300ZX and Maxima

1. Disconnect the negative battery cable.
2. Lift the wiper arms. Remove the securing nuts and detach the arms.
3. Remove the air intake grille.
4. Remove the nuts holding the wiper pivots to the body.
5. Open the hood and unscrew the motor from the firewall.
6. Disconnect the wiring connector and remove the wiper motor with the linkage.

7. Installation is the reverse of the removal procedure. To reduce wiper arm looseness, prior to connecting the wiper arm, make sure the motor spline shaft and pivot area is completely free of debris and corrosion. Wire brush as necessary. Check the wipers for proper operation.

Windshield Wiper Switch

REMOVAL AND INSTALLATION

Front

The windshield wiper switch is part of the combination switch, which is mounted on the steering column.

Rear

240SX, 300ZX AND SENTRA

1. Remove the instrument cluster.
2. Remove the nut that attaches the switch to the dash.
3. Disconnect the electrical connectors from the rear of the switch, then remove it.
4. Installation is the reverse of the removal procedure. Check system for proper operation of wipers/washers.

Instrument Cluster

REMOVAL AND INSTALLATION

240SX

NOTE: When removing the Head-Up Display (HUD) finisher, be careful not to scratch the HUD's reflective surface. To prevent this, cover the finisher and reflective surface with a protective covering.

1. Disconnect the negative battery cable.
2. Remove the steering wheel and steering wheel covers, as required.
3. Remove the screws holding the cluster lid in place and remove the lid.
4. On 240SX, the cluster is held with 3 screws.
5. Carefully withdraw the cluster from the instrument panel and disconnect the speedometer cable (analog) and electrical wiring from the rear of the cluster. Make sure the wiring is labeled clearly to avoid confusion during installation.
6. Remove the cluster. Be careful not to damage the printed circuit.
7. Installation is the reverse of the removal procedure.

300ZX

1. Disconnect the negative battery cable.
2. Remove the steering wheel and steering wheel covers.
3. Remove the left and right instrument switches by removing the hooks and fasteners.
4. Remove the cluster lids and cluster retaining screws.
5. Carefully withdraw the cluster from the instrument panel and disconnect the speedometer cable and electrical wiring from the rear of the cluster. Make sure the wiring is labeled clearly to avoid confusion during installation.
6. Remove the cluster. Be careful not to damage the printed circuit.
7. Installation is the reverse of the removal procedure.

Maxima

NOTE: When removing the Head-Up Display (HUD) finisher, be careful not to scratch the HUD's reflective surface. To prevent this, cover the finisher and reflective surface with a protective covering.

1. Disconnect the negative battery cable.

2. Remove the instrument panel lower cover.

3. Remove the steering wheel and steering wheel covers.

4. Remove the cluster lids.

5. Withdraw the combination meter assembly from the instrument pad and disconnect the speedometer cable (analog).

6. Disconnect the wiring and remove the cluster. Make sure the wiring is marked clearly to avoid confusion during installation.

7. Remove the cluster. Be careful not to damage the printed circuit.

8. Installation is the reverse of the removal procedure.

Altima, Pulsar, Sentra and Stanza

NOTE: On Altima, when removing the Head-Up Display (HUD) finisher, be careful not to scratch the HUD's reflective surface. To prevent this, cover the finisher and reflective surface with a protective covering.

1. Disconnect the negative battery cable.

2. Remove the steering wheel and the steering column covers.

3. Remove the instrument cluster lid by removing its screws.

4. Remove the instrument cluster screws.

5. Gently withdraw the cluster from the instrument pad and disconnect all wiring and speedometer cable. Make sure the wires are marked clearly to avoid confusion during installation. Be careful not to damage the printed circuit.

6. Remove the cluster.

7. Installation is the reverse of removal.

Speedometer

REMOVAL AND INSTALLATION

Analog Speedometer

1. Disconnect the negative battery cable.

2. Remove the cluster. Carefully withdraw the cluster from the instrument panel and disconnect the speedometer cable and electrical wiring from the rear of the cluster.

3. Carefully remove the speedometer from the cluster. Be careful not to damage the printed circuit board.

4. Installation is the reverse of the removal procedure.

Digital Speedometer

If equipped with a digital speedometer, the entire cluster assembly must be replaced if the speedometer is faulty.

Concealed Headlights

—— CAUTION ——

Before attempting to manually operate the concealed (retractable) headlights, first disconnect the negative battery cable. Otherwise the headlights and motor shaft may suddenly move and injure hand and fingers.

MANUAL OPERATION

NOTE: If the headlights are frozen and inoperative, carefully melt the ice before attempting the manual operation procedure. Operation of a frozen headlight will drain the battery and may cause damage to the motor and operating linkages.

1. Switch the headlight and retractable headlight switches to the OFF position.

2. Disconnect the negative battery cable.

3. Remove the rubber cap from the motor shaft.

4. Manually turn the motor shaft in the counterclockwise position until the headlights are in the desired position (open or closed).

5. Install the motor shaft cap.

6. Connect the negative battery cable.

7. Check the headlights for proper operation.

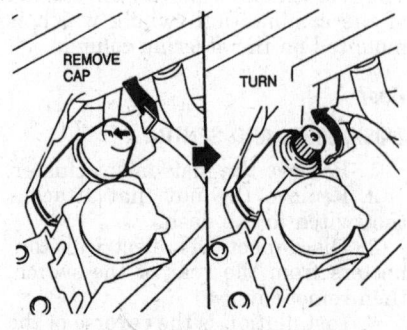

Manual operation of retractable headlights

Combination Switch

REMOVAL AND INSTALLATION

1. Disarm air bag, if equipped, refer to the necessary service procedure. Disconnect the battery ground cable.

2. Remove the steering wheel. On Maxima with Sonar suspension, remove the steering angle sensor from the steering column.

3. Remove the steering column covers.

NOTE: At this point, the individual switch assemblies can be removed without removing the combination switch base assembly. To service an individual switch/stalk assembly, disconnect the electrical lead and remove the 2 stalk-to-base mounting screws. If the switch base must be removed, proceed with the remainder of the removal procedure.

4. Disconnect the electrical plugs from the switch.

5. Remove the retaining screws, push down on the base of the switch with moderate pressure and twist the switch from the steering wheel shaft.

6. Installation is the reverse of the removal procedure. Check the switch functions for proper operation. Many vehicles have turn signal switches that have a tab which must fit into a hole in the steering shaft. This fit is necessary in order for the system to return the switch to the neutral position after the turn has been made. Be sure to align the tab and the hole when installing.

Ignition Lock/Switch

REMOVAL AND INSTALLATION

The steering lock/ignition switch/warning buzzer switch assembly is attached to the steering column by special screws or bolts whose heads shear off on installation. The screws must be drilled out to remove the assembly or removed with an appropriate tool.

1. Disarm air bag, if equipped. Disconnect the battery ground cable.

2. Remove the steering wheel, steering column covers and combination switch.

3. Disconnect the switch wiring.

4. Lower the steering column, as required.

5. Break the self-shear screws with a drill or other appropriate tool.

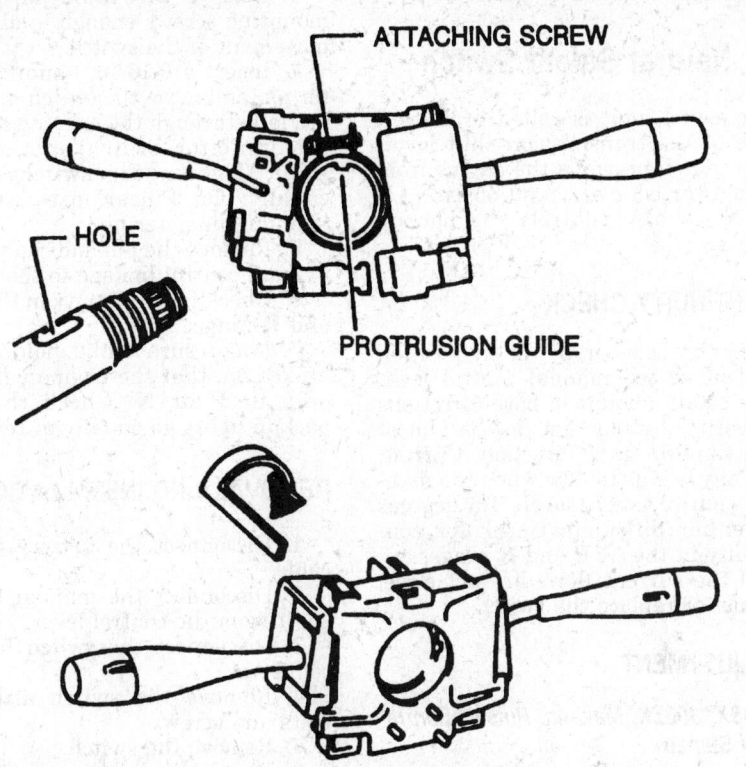

ATTACHING SCREW

HOLE

PROTRUSION GUIDE

Combination switch removal, installation and alignment

6. Remove the steering lock from the column.

To install:

7. Install the steering lock onto the column with new self-shear bolts or screws. Tighten the bolts or screws until the heads shear off.

8. Raise and secure the steering column.

9. Install the combination switch, steering column covers and steering wheel.

10. Connect the negative battery cable.

Stoplight Switch

ADJUSTMENT

1. Before adjustment, check the clearance between the pedal stopper and the threaded end of the stoplight switch. The clearance should be 0.012-0.039 in. (0.3-1.0mm) for all vehicles.

2. If the clearance is not as specified, adjust by loosening the switch locknut and moving the switch in and out as required until the clearance is as specified.

3. Tighten the locknut.

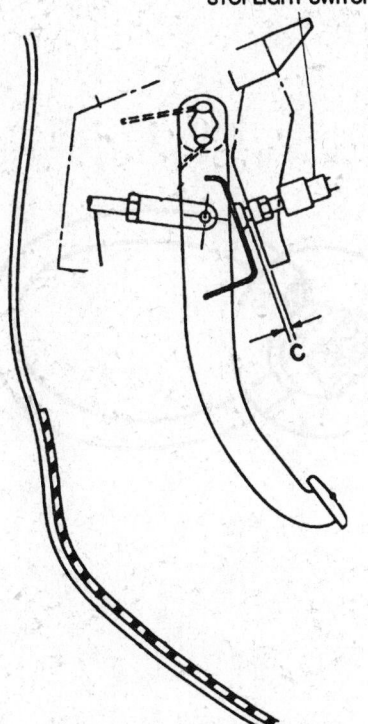

STOPLIGHT SWITCH

Stoplight switch clearance adjustment

4. Depress the brake pedal and have an assistant verify that the brake lights illuminate.

NOTE: If equipped with Automatic Speed Control Device (ASCD), the ASCD cancel switch must be adjusted with the stoplight switch.

Removal and Installation

1. Remove the floor mats.

2. Disconnect the multi-connector from the switch.

3. Note and record the amount of threads exposed on the switch.

4. Loosen the locknut and adjusting nuts and remove the switch from the mounting bracket.

To install:

5. Place the new switch in the mounting bracket.

6. Install and tighten the adjusting and locknuts so the same amount of threads is exposed as recorded in Step 3 or adjust the switch.

7. Connect the multi-connector and check that the brake lights illuminate when the brake pedal is depressed.

8. Replace the floor mats.

Clutch Switch

ADJUSTMENT

1. Before adjustment, check the clearance between the pedal stopper rubber and the threaded end of the clutch interlock switch with the clutch fully depressed. The clearance should be as follows:

240SX — 0.039-0.079 in. (1.0-2.0mm)

300ZX — 0.039-0.188 in. (1.0-3.0mm)

Altima (USA) — 0.004-0.039 in. (0.1-1.0mm)

Maxima — 0.004-0.039 in. (0.1-1.0mm)

Pulsar — 0.004-0.039 in. (0.1-1.0mm)

Sentra — 0.004-0.039 in. (0.1-1.0mm)

Stanza — 0.039-0.079 in. (1.0-2.0mm)

2. If the clearance is not as specified, adjust by loosening the switch locknut and moving the switch in and out as required until the clearance is as specified.

3. Tighten the locknut. Check operation of switch.

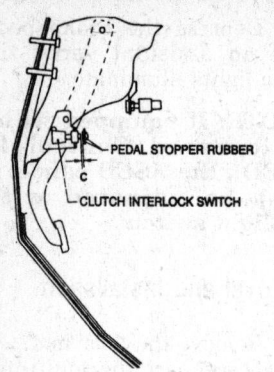

Clutch interlock switch clearance adjustment

REMOVAL AND INSTALLATION

1. Remove the floor mats.
2. Disconnect the multi-connector from the switch.
3. Note and record the amount of threads exposed on the switch.
4. Loosen the locknut and adjusting nuts and remove the switch from the mounting bracket.
   To install:
5. Place the new switch in the mounting bracket.
6. Install and tighten the adjusting and lock nuts so the same amount of threads is exposed as recorded in Step 3 or adjust the switch.
7. Connect the multi-connector.

8. Replace the floor mats.

Neutral Safety Switch

The switch unit is bolted to the left side of the transmission shift lever. The switch prevents the engine from being started in any position except **P** or **N**. It also controls the backup lights.

CONTINUITY CHECK

Hold the selector in the **N** position and move the manual control lever and equal amount in both directions to verify that current flow is almost the same in each direction. Current usually begins to flow when the manual control lever travels 1.5 degrees in either direction. Check for continuity in the **N**, **P** and **R** ranges.

If the current flows are not close, adjust or replace the switch.

ADJUSTMENT

240SX, 300ZX, Maxima, Pulsar, Sentra and Stanza

1. Disconnect the manual control linkage from the manual shaft.
2. Set the manual shaft to the **N** position.

3. Loosen the inhibitor switch mounting screws enough to allow for movement of the switch.
4. Insert a 0.16 in. (4mm) diameter pin and move the switch until the pin falls through the locating holes in the inhibitor switch and manual shaft. Tighten the switch screws equally. On Pulsar, use a 0.1 in. (2.5mm) diameter pin.
5. Remove the pin and connect the manual control linkage to the shaft.
6. Check for continuity in the **N**, **P** and **R** ranges.
7. Make sure while holding the brakes on, that the engine will start only in **P** or **N**. Check that the backup lights go on only in reverse.

REMOVAL AND INSTALLATION

1. Disconnect the battery ground cable.
2. Disconnect the manual control shaft from the control lever.
3. Disconnect the switch harness connector.
4. Remove the switch attaching bolts and screws.
5. Remove the switch.
6. Installation is the reverse of the removal procedure.
7. Adjust the switch and check for proper operation.

Fuses and Circuit Breakers

LOCATION

240SX

Fusible Links — left side engine compartment behind battery; in fuse and relay box.
Fuse Panels — (1) left side engine compartment behind battery and (2) under driver's side kick panel.
Circuit Breaker — behind driver's kick panel.

300ZX

Fusible Links — in front of negative battery cable.
Relay and Fuse Box — right side engine compartment

Altima

Fusible Links and Fuse Box — left side engine compartment.
Fuse block — under the left dash area.
Relay Box 1 — right side engine compartment.
Relay Box 2 — left side engine compartment near battery.

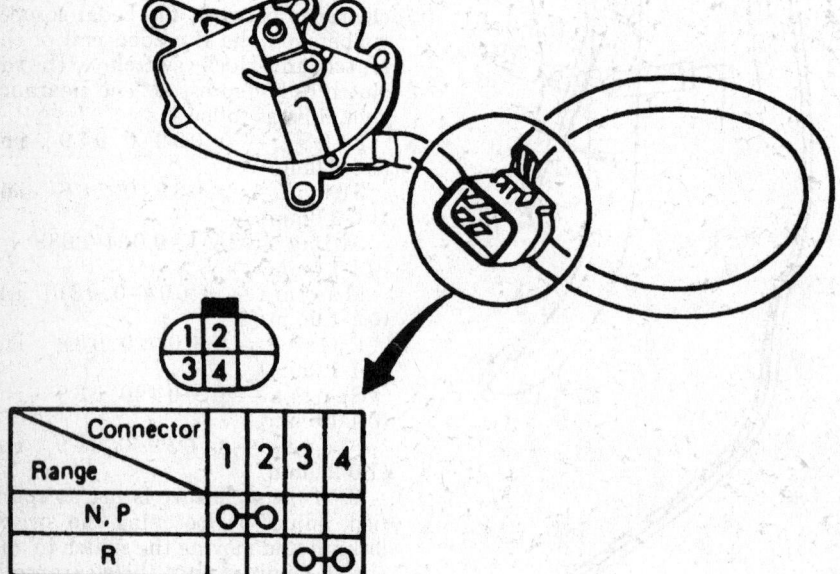

Connector Range	1	2	3	4
N, P	o—o			
R			o—o	

Checking neutral safety switch continuity — Pulsar, Sentra

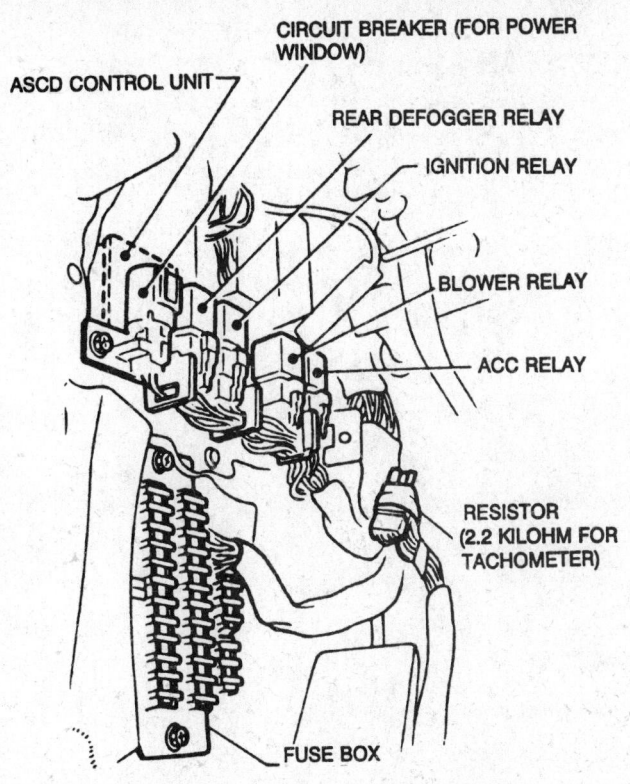

Relay box and fuse panel locations — 300ZX

ASCD CONTROL UNIT

CIRCUIT BREAKER (FOR POWER WINDOW)

REAR DEFOGGER RELAY

IGNITION RELAY

BLOWER RELAY

ACC RELAY

RESISTOR (2.2 KILOHM FOR TACHOMETER)

FUSE BOX

Maxima

Fusible Link Holder — right side engine compartment; in fuse and relay box.
Fuse Panel — behind driver's kick panel.
Relay Box — right side engine compartment; in front of battery.

Pulsar

Fusible Link Holder — off negative battery cable.
Fuse Panel — behind driver's kick panel.

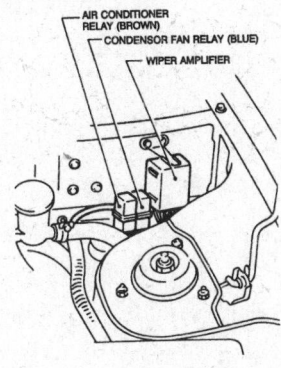

Accessory relay locations — Pulsar

AIR CONDITIONER RELAY (BROWN)

CONDENSOR FAN RELAY (BLUE)

WIPER AMPLIFIER

Sentra

Fusible Link Holder — off negative battery cable.
Fuse Panel — behind driver's kick panel.

Stanza

Fusible Link Holder — off negative battery cable.
Fuse Panel — behind driver's kick panel.

Flashers

LOCATION

240SX — behind driver's kick panel.
300ZX — behind instrument cluster to right of the steering bracket.
Altima — under the dash area to the right of the steering column.
Maxima — behind steering column next to stoplight switch.
Pulsar — behind driver's kick panel below stoplight switch.
Sentra — behind driver's kick panel below stoplight switch.
Stanza — behind driver's kick panel below stoplight switch

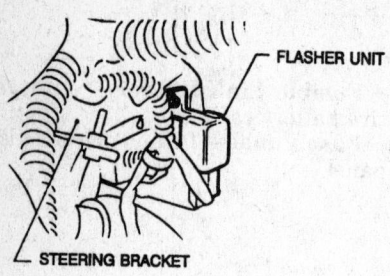

Flasher unit location — 300ZX

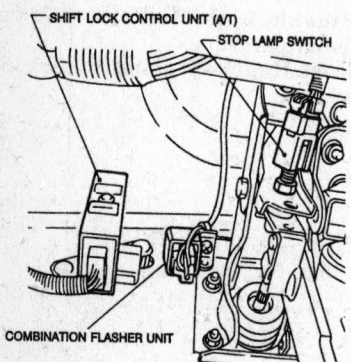

Flasher unit location — Sentra

SAAB 15

900, 9000

SPECIFICATIONS

ENGINE IDENTIFICATION

Year	Model	Engine Displacement Liters (cc)	Engine Series (ID/VIN)	Fuel System	No. of Cylinders	Engine Type
1990	900	2.0 (1985)	B202i	EFI	4	DOHC
	900	2.0 (1985)	B202L	EFI	4	DOHC, Turbo
	9000	2.0 (1985)	B202L	EFI	4	DOHC, Turbo
1991	900	2.0 (1985)	B202L	EFI	4	DOHC, Turbo
	900	2.1 (2119)	B212i	EFI	4	DOHC
	9000	2.3 (2290)	B234i	EFI	4	DOHC
	9000	2.3 (2290)	B234L	EFI	4	DOHC, Turbo
1992	900	2.0 (1985)	B202L	EFI	4	DOHC, Turbo
	900	2.1 (2119)	B212i	EFI	4	DOHC
	9000	2.3 (2290)	B234i	EFI	4	DOHC
	9000	2.3 (2290)	B234L	EFI	4	DOHC, Turbo
1993	900	2.0 (1985)	B202L	EFI	4	DOHC, Turbo
	900	2.1 (2119)	B212i	EFI	4	DOHC
	9000	2.3 (2290)	B234i	EFI	4	DOHC
	9000	2.3 (2290)	B234L	EFI	4	DOHC, Turbo
1994	900	2.0 (1985)	B202L	EFI	4	DOHC, Turbo
	900	2.1 (2119)	B212i	EFI	4	DOHC
	9000	2.3 (2290)	B234i	EFI	4	DOHC
	9000	2.3 (2290)	B234L	EFI	4	DOHC, Turbo

EFI—Electronic Fuel Injection
DOHC—Double Overhead Camshaft
TURBO—Turbocharged

GENERAL ENGINE SPECIFICATIONS

Year	Engine ID/VIN	Engine Displacement Liters (cc)	Fuel System Type	Net Horsepower @ rpm	Net Torque @ rpm (ft. lbs.)	Bore × Stroke (in.)	Compression Ratio	Oil Pressure @ 2000 rpm
1990	B202i	2.0 (1985)	EFI	125 @ 5500	123 @ 3000	3.54 × 3.07	10.1:1	51–74
	B202L	2.0 (1985)	EFI	160 @ 5500 ①	188 @ 3000 ②	3.54 × 3.07	9.0:1	54–71
1991	B202L	2.0 (1985)	EFI	160 @ 5500 ③	188 @ 3000 ②	3.54 × 3.07	9.0:1	52–75
	B212i	2.1 (2119)	EFI	140 @ 6000	133 @ 2900	3.66 × 3.07	10.1:1	52–75
	B234i	2.3 (2290)	EFI	150 @ 5500	157 @ 3800	3.54 × 3.54	10.0:1	52–75
	B234L	2.3 (2290)	EFI	200 @ 5000	244 @ 2000 ④	3.54 × 3.54	8.5:1	52–75
1992	B202L	2.0 (1985)	EFI	160 @ 5500	188 @ 3000	3.54 × 3.07	9.0:1	52–75
	B212i	2.1 (2119)	EFI	140 @ 6000	133 @ 2900	3.66 × 3.07	10.1:1	52–75
	B234i	2.3 (2290)	EFI	150 @ 5500	157 @ 3800	3.54 × 3.54	10.0:1	52–75
	B234L	2.3 (2290)	EFI	200 @ 5000	244 @ 2000 ④	3.54 × 3.54	8.5:1	52–75
1993	B202L	2.0 (1985)	EFI	160 @ 5500	188 @ 3000	3.54 × 3.07	9.0:1	52–75
	B212i	2.1 (2119)	EFI	140 @ 6000	133 @ 2900	3.66 × 3.07	10.1:1	52–75
	B234i	2.3 (2290)	EFI	150 @ 5500	157 @ 3800	3.54 × 3.54	10.0:1	52–75
	B234L	2.3 (2290)	EFI	200 @ 5000	244 @ 2000 ④	3.54 × 3.54	8.5:1	52–75
1994	B202L	2.0 (1985)	EFI	160 @ 5500	188 @ 3000	3.54 × 3.07	9.0:1	52–75
	B212i	2.1 (2119)	EFI	140 @ 6000	133 @ 2900	3.66 × 3.07	10.1:1	52–75
	B234i	2.3 (2290)	EFI	150 @ 5500	157 @ 3800	3.54 × 3.54	10.0:1	52–75
	B234L	2.3 (2290)	EFI	200 @ 5000	244 @ 2000 ④	3.54 × 3.54	8.5:1	52–75

EFI—Electronic Fuel Injection
① SPG = 165 @ 5500
② SPG = 195 @ 3000
③ SPG = 175 @ 5500
④ SPG = 222 @ 2000

GASOLINE ENGINE TUNE-UP SPECIFICATIONS

Year	Engine ID/VIN	Engine Displacement Liters (cc)	Spark Plugs Gap (in.)	Ignition Timing (deg.) MT	AT	Fuel Pump (psi)	Idle Speed (rpm) MT	AT	Valve Clearance In.	Ex.
1990	B202i	2.0 (1985)	0.024–0.028	14B	14B	①	875	875	Hyd.	Hyd.
	B202L	2.0 (1985)	0.024–0.028	16B	16B	①	875	875	Hyd.	Hyd.
1991	B202L	2.0 (1985)	0.024–0.028	16B	16B	①	850	850	Hyd.	Hyd.
	B212i	2.1 (2119)	0.024–0.028	14B	14B	①	850	850	Hyd.	Hyd.
	B234i	2.3 (2290)	0.024–0.028	14B	14B	①	850	850	Hyd.	Hyd.
	B234L	2.3 (2290)	0.024–0.028	16B	16B	①	850	850	Hyd.	Hyd.
1992	B202L	2.0 (1985)	0.024–0.028	16B	16B	①	850	850	Hyd.	Hyd.
	B212i	2.1 (2119)	0.024–0.028	14B	14B	①	850	850	Hyd.	Hyd.
	B234i	2.3 (2290)	0.024–0.028	14B	14B	①	850	850	Hyd.	Hyd.
	B234L	2.3 (2290)	0.024–0.028	16B	16B	①	850	850	Hyd.	Hyd.
1993-94				SEE UNDERHOOD SPECIFICATIONS STICKER						

NOTE: The lowest cylinder pressure should be within 75% of the highest cylinder pressure reading. For example, if the highest cylinder is 134 psi, the lowest should be 101. Engine should be at normal operating temperature with throttle valve in the wide open position.
The underhood specifications sticker often reflects tune-up specification changes in production. Sticker figures must be used if they disagree with those in this chart.
B—Before Top Dead Center
Hyd.—Hydraulic
① Fuel line pressure before the control pressure regulator is 67–70 psi (setting valve), and 48–54 psi (warm engine) after the regulator (located in the fuel distributor).

FIRING ORDERS

NOTE: To avoid confusion, always replace spark plug wires one at a time.

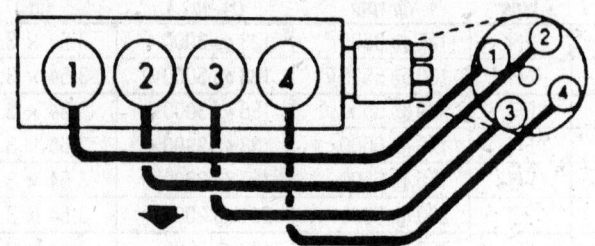

B202 (16-valve) Engine
Engine Firing Order: 1-3-4-2
Distributor Rotation: Counterclockwise
NOTE: Engines equipped with Direct Ignition (DI) system, does not use a distributor

CAPACITIES

Year	Model	Engine ID/VIN	Engine Displacement Liters (cc)	Engine Crankcase with Filter	Transmission (pts.)			Transfer case (pts.)	Drive Axle		Fuel Tank (gal.)	Cooling System (qts.)
					4-Spd	5-Spd	Auto.		Front (pts.)	Rear (pts.)		
1990	900	B202i	2.0 (1985)	4.0	5.2	6.4	17	—	2.6①	—	18.0	10.5
		B202L	2.0 (1985)	4.5	—	6.4	17	—	2.6①	—	18.0	10.5
	9000	B202L	2.0 (1985)	4.5	—	6.4	17	—	2.6①	—	18.0	10.5
1991	900	B202L	2.0 (1985)	4.5	—	6.0	17	—	2.6	—	18.0	10.5
		B212i	2.1 (2119)	4.0	5.2	6.0	17	—	2.6	—	18.0	10.5
	9000	B234i	2.3 (2290)	4.4	—	5.2	17	—	2.6	—	18.0	9.5
		B234L	2.3 (2290)	4.4	—	6.0	17	—	2.6	—	18.0	9.5
1992	900	B202L	2.0 (1985)	4.5	—	6.0	17	—	2.6	—	18.0	10.5
		B212i	2.1 (2119)	4.0	5.2	6.0	17	—	2.6	—	18.0	10.5
	9000	B234i	2.3 (2290)	4.4	—	5.2	17	—	2.6	—	18.0	9.5
		B234L	2.3 (2290)	4.4	—	6.0	17	—	2.6	—	18.0	9.5
1993	900	B202L	2.0 (1985)	4.5	—	6.0	17	—	2.6	—	18.0	10.5
		B212i	2.1 (2119)	4.0	5.2	6.0	17	—	2.6	—	18.0	10.5
	9000	B234i	2.3 (2290)	4.4	—	5.2	17	—	2.6	—	18.0	9.5
		B234L	2.3 (2290)	4.4	—	6.0	17	—	2.6	—	18.0	9.5
1994	900	B202L	2.0 (1985)	4.5	—	6.0	17	—	2.6	—	18.0	10.5
		B212i	2.1 (2119)	4.0	5.2	6.0	17	—	2.6	—	18.0	10.5
	9000	B234i	2.3 (2290)	4.4	—	5.2	17	—	2.6	—	18.0	9.5
		B234L	2.3 (2290)	4.4	—	6.0	17	—	2.6	—	18.0	9.5

① Borg Warner 37—3.0 pts.

CAMSHAFT SPECIFICATIONS

All measurements given in inches.

Year	Engine ID/VIN	Engine Displacement Liters (cc)	Journal Diameter					Elevation		Bearing Clearance	Camshaft End Play
			1	2	3	4	5	In.	Ex.		
1990	B202i	2.0 (1985)	1.1387–1.1392	1.1387–1.1392	1.1387–1.1392	1.1387–1.1392	1.1387–1.1392	0.341	0.341	NA	0.0031–0.0138
	B202L	2.0 (1985)	1.1387–1.1392	1.1387–1.1392	1.1387–1.1392	1.1387–1.1392	1.1387–1.1392	0.341	0.341	NA	0.0031–0.0138
1991	B202L	2.0 (1985)	1.1387–1.1392	1.1387–1.1392	1.1387–1.1392	1.1387–1.1392	1.1387–1.1392	0.341	0.341	NA	0.0031–0.0138
	B212i	2.1 (2119)	1.1387–1.1392	1.1387–1.1392	1.1387–1.1392	1.1387–1.1392	1.1387–1.1392	0.341	0.341	NA	0.0031–0.0138
	B234i	2.3 (2290)	1.1387–1.1392	1.1387–1.1392	1.1387–1.1392	1.1387–1.1392	1.1387–1.1392	0.341	0.341	NA	0.0031–0.0138
	B234L	2.3 (2290)	1.1387–1.1392	1.1387–1.1392	1.1387–1.1392	1.1387–1.1392	1.1387–1.1392	0.341	0.341	NA	0.0031–0.0138
1992	B202L	2.0 (1985)	1.1387–1.1392	1.1387–1.1392	1.1387–1.1392	1.1387–1.1392	1.1387–1.1392	0.341	0.341	NA	0.0031–0.0138
	B212i	2.1 (2119)	1.1387–1.1392	1.1387–1.1392	1.1387–1.1392	1.1387–1.1392	1.1387–1.1392	0.341	0.341	NA	0.0031–0.0138
	B234i	2.3 (2290)	1.1387–1.1392	1.1387–1.1392	1.1387–1.1392	1.1387–1.1392	1.1387–1.1392	0.341	0.341	NA	0.0031–0.0138
	B234L	2.3 (2290)	1.1387–1.1392	1.1387–1.1392	1.1387–1.1392	1.1387–1.1392	1.1387–1.1392	0.341	0.341	NA	0.0031–0.0138
1993	B202L	2.0 (1985)	1.1387–1.1392	1.1387–1.1392	1.1387–1.1392	1.1387–1.1392	1.1387–1.1392	0.341	0.341	NA	0.0031–0.0138
	B212i	2.1 (2119)	1.1387–1.1392	1.1387–1.1392	1.1387–1.1392	1.1387–1.1392	1.1387–1.1392	0.341	0.341	NA	0.0031–0.0138
	B234i	2.3 (2290)	1.1387–1.1392	1.1387–1.1392	1.1387–1.1392	1.1387–1.1392	1.1387–1.1392	0.341	0.341	NA	0.0031–0.0138
	B234L	2.3 (2290)	1.1387–1.1392	1.1387–1.1392	1.1387–1.1392	1.1387–1.1392	1.1387–1.1392	0.341	0.341	NA	0.0031–0.0138
1994	B202L	2.0 (1985)	1.1387–1.1392	1.1387–1.1392	1.1387–1.1392	1.1387–1.1392	1.1387–1.1392	0.341	0.341	NA	0.0031–0.0138
	B212i	2.1 (2119)	1.1387–1.1392	1.1387–1.1392	1.1387–1.1392	1.1387–1.1392	1.1387–1.1392	0.341	0.341	NA	0.0031–0.0138
	B234i	2.3 (2290)	1.1387–1.1392	1.1387–1.1392	1.1387–1.1392	1.1387–1.1392	1.1387–1.1392	0.341	0.341	NA	0.0031–0.0138
	B234L	2.3 (2290)	1.1387–1.1392	1.1387–1.1392	1.1387–1.1392	1.1387–1.1392	1.1387–1.1392	0.341	0.341	NA	0.0031–0.0138

NA—Not available

CRANKSHAFT AND CONNECTING ROD SPECIFICATIONS

All measurements are given in inches.

Year	Engine ID/VIN	Engine Displacement Liters (cc)	Crankshaft				Connecting Rod		
			Main Brg. Journal Dia.	Main Brg. Oil Clearance	Shaft End-play	Thrust on No.	Journal Diameter	Oil Clearance	Side Clearance
1990	B202i	2.0 (1985)	2.2827–2.2835	0.0008–0.0024	0.003–0.011	3	2.2047–2.2054	0.0010–0.0024	NA
	B202L	2.0 (1985)	2.2827–2.2835	0.0008–0.0024	0.003–0.011	3	2.2047–2.2054	0.0010–0.0024	NA
1991	B202L	2.0 (1985)	2.2827–2.2835	0.0008–0.0024	0.003–0.011	3	2.2047–2.2054	0.0010–0.0024	NA
	B212i	2.1 (2119)	2.2827–2.2835	0.0008–0.0024	0.003–0.011	3	2.2047–2.2054	0.0010–0.0024	NA
	B234i	2.3 (2290)	2.2827–2.2835	0.0008–0.0024	0.002–0.012	3	2.2047–2.2055	0.0010–0.0024	NA
	B234L	2.3 (2290)	2.2827–2.2835	0.0008–0.0024	0.002–0.012	3	2.2047–2.2055	0.0010–0.0024	NA
1992	B202L	2.0 (1985)	2.2827–2.2835	0.0008–0.0024	0.003–0.011	3	2.2047–2.2054	0.0010–0.0024	NA
	B212i	2.1 (2119)	2.2827–2.2835	0.0008–0.0024	0.003–0.011	3	2.2047–2.2054	0.0010–0.0024	NA
	B234i	2.3 (2290)	2.2827–2.2835	0.0008–0.0024	0.002–0.012	3	2.2047–2.2055	0.0010–0.0024	NA
	B234L	2.3 (2290)	2.2827–2.2835	0.0008–0.0024	0.002–0.012	3	2.2047–2.2055	0.0010–0.0024	NA
1993	B202L	2.0 (1985)	2.2827–2.2835	0.0008–0.0024	0.003–0.011	3	2.2047–2.2054	0.0010–0.0024	NA
	B212i	2.1 (2119)	2.2827–2.2835	0.0008–0.0024	0.003–0.011	3	2.2047–2.2054	0.0010–0.0024	NA
	B234i	2.3 (2290)	2.2827–2.2835	0.0008–0.0024	0.002–0.012	3	2.2047–2.2055	0.0010–0.0024	NA
	B234L	2.3 (2290)	2.2827–2.2835	0.0008–0.0024	0.002–0.012	3	2.2047–2.2055	0.0010–0.0024	NA
1994	B202L	2.0 (1985)	2.2827–2.2835	0.0008–0.0024	0.003–0.011	3	2.2047–2.2054	0.0010–0.0024	NA
	B212i	2.1 (2119)	2.2827–2.2835	0.0008–0.0024	0.003–0.011	3	2.2047–2.2054	0.0010–0.0024	NA
	B234i	2.3 (2290)	2.2827–2.2835	0.0008–0.0024	0.002–0.012	3	2.2047–2.2055	0.0010–0.0024	NA
	B234L	2.3 (2290)	2.2827–2.2835	0.0008–0.0024	0.002–0.012	3	2.2047–2.2055	0.0010–0.0024	NA

NA—Not available

VALVE SPECIFICATIONS

Year	Engine ID/VIN	Engine Displacement Liters (cc)	Seat Angle (deg.)	Face Angle (deg.)	Spring Test Pressure (lbs. @ in.)	Spring Installed Height (in.)	Stem-to-Guide Clearance ① (in.)		Stem Diameter (in.)	
							Intake	Exhaust	Intake	Exhaust
1990	B202i	2.0 (1985)	45	45	131–141 @ 1.12	1.46	0.020	0.020	0.2740–0.2746	0.2738–0.2748
	B202L	2.0 (1985)	45	45	131–141 @ 1.12	1.46	0.020	0.020	0.2740–0.2746	0.2738–0.2748
1991	B202L	2.0 (1985)	45	45	131–141 @ 1.12	1.46	0.020	0.020	0.2740–0.2746	0.2738–0.2748
	B212i	2.1 (2119)	45	45	131–141 @ 1.12	1.46	0.020	0.020	0.2740–0.2746	0.2738–0.2748
	B234i	2.3 (2290)	45	45	131–141 @ 1.12	1.46	0.020	0.020	0.2740–0.2746	0.2738–0.2748
	B234L	2.3 (2290)	45	45	131–141 @ 1.12	1.46	0.020	0.020	0.2740–0.2746	0.2738–0.2748
1992	B202L	2.0 (1985)	45	45	131–141 @ 1.12	1.46	0.020	0.020	0.2740–0.2746	0.2738–0.2748
	B212i	2.1 (2119)	45	45	131–141 @ 1.12	1.46	0.020	0.020	0.2740–0.2746	0.2738–0.2748
	B234i	2.3 (2290)	45	45	131–141 @ 1.12	1.46	0.020	0.020	0.2740–0.2746	0.2738–0.2748
	B234L	2.3 (2290)	45	45	131–141 @ 1.12	1.46	0.020	0.020	0.2740–0.2746	0.2738–0.2748
1993	B202L	2.0 (1985)	45	45	131–141 @ 1.12	1.46	0.020	0.020	0.2740–0.2746	0.2738–0.2748
	B212i	2.1 (2119)	45	45	131–141 @ 1.12	1.46	0.020	0.020	0.2740–0.2746	0.2738–0.2748
	B234i	2.3 (2290)	45	45	131–141 @ 1.12	1.46	0.020	0.020	0.2740–0.2746	0.2738–0.2748
	B234L	2.3 (2290)	45	45	131–141 @ 1.12	1.46	0.020	0.020	0.2740–0.2746	0.2738–0.2748
1994	B202L	2.0 (1985)	45	45	131–141 @ 1.12	1.46	0.020	0.020	0.2740–0.2746	0.2738–0.2748
	B212i	2.1 (2119)	45	45	131–141 @ 1.12	1.46	0.020	0.020	0.2740–0.2746	0.2738–0.2748
	B234i	2.3 (2290)	45	45	131–141 @ 1.12	1.46	0.020	0.020	0.2740–0.2746	0.2738–0.2748
	B234L	2.3 (2290)	45	45	131–141 @ 1.12	1.46	0.020	0.020	0.2740–0.2746	0.2738–0.2748

① Measured on the valve head; raised 0.12 in. (3mm) above the seat

PISTON AND RING SPECIFICATIONS

All measurements are given in inches.

Year	Engine ID/VIN	Engine Displacement Liters (cc)	Piston Clearance	Ring Gap Top Compression	Ring Gap Bottom Compression	Ring Gap Oil Control	Ring Side Clearance Top Compression	Ring Side Clearance Bottom Compression	Ring Side Clearance Oil Control
1990	B202i	2.0 (1985)	①	0.014–0.022	0.011–0.017	0.014–0.055	0.002–0.003	0.002–0.003	—
	B202L	2.0 (1985)	①	0.014–0.022	0.011–0.017	0.014–0.055	0.002–0.003	0.002–0.003	—
1991	B202L	2.0 (1985)	①	0.014–0.022	0.011–0.017	0.014–0.055	0.002–0.003	0.002–0.003	—
	B212i	2.1 (2119)	0.0004–0.0013	0.014–0.022	0.011–0.017	0.014–0.055	0.002–0.003	0.002–0.003	—
	B234i	2.3 (2290)	0.0003–0.0015	0.012–0.020	0.012–0.018	0.015–0.055	0.002–0.003	0.002–0.003	—
	B234L	2.3 (2290)	0.0003–0.0015	0.012–0.020	0.012–0.018	0.015–0.055	0.002–0.003	0.002–0.003	—
1992	B202L	2.0 (1985)	①	0.014–0.022	0.011–0.017	0.014–0.055	0.002–0.003	0.002–0.003	—
	B212i	2.1 (2119)	0.0004–0.0013	0.014–0.022	0.011–0.017	0.014–0.055	0.002–0.003	0.002–0.003	—
	B234i	2.3 (2290)	0.0003–0.0015	0.012–0.020	0.012–0.018	0.015–0.055	0.002–0.003	0.002–0.003	—
	B234L	2.3 (2290)	0.0003–0.0015	0.012–0.020	0.012–0.018	0.015–0.055	0.002–0.003	0.002–0.003	—
1993	B202L	2.0 (1985)	①	0.014–0.022	0.011–0.017	0.014–0.055	0.002–0.003	0.002–0.003	—
	B212i	2.1 (2119)	0.0004–0.0013	0.014–0.022	0.011–0.017	0.014–0.055	0.002–0.003	0.002–0.003	—
	B234i	2.3 (2290)	0.0003–0.0015	0.012–0.020	0.012–0.018	0.015–0.055	0.002–0.003	0.002–0.003	—
	B234L	2.3 (2290)	0.0003–0.0015	0.012–0.020	0.012–0.018	0.015–0.055	0.002–0.003	0.002–0.003	—
1994	B202L	2.0 (1985)	①	0.014–0.022	0.011–0.017	0.014–0.055	0.002–0.003	0.002–0.003	—
	B212i	2.1 (2119)	0.0004–0.0013	0.014–0.022	0.011–0.017	0.014–0.055	0.002–0.003	0.002–0.003	—
	B234i	2.3 (2290)	0.0003–0.0015	0.012–0.020	0.012–0.018	0.015–0.055	0.002–0.003	0.002–0.003	—
	B234L	2.3 (2290)	0.0003–0.0015	0.012–0.020	0.012–0.018	0.015–0.055	0.002–0.003	0.002–0.003	—

① Old Classification:
Mahle—0.0009–0.0020 in.
Schmidt—0.0005–0.0016 in.
New Classification:
Mahle/Schmidt—0.0002–0.0012 in.
Hepolite—0.0004–0.0014 in.

TORQUE SPECIFICATIONS

All readings in ft. lbs.

Year	Engine ID/VIN	Engine Displacement Liters (cc)	Cylinder Head Bolts	Main Bearing Bolts	Rod Bearing Bolts	Crankshaft Pulley Bolts	Flywheel Bolts	Manifold Intake	Manifold Exhaust	Spark Plugs	Lug Nuts
1990	B202i	2.0 (1985)	①	81	41	141	③	16	13	20	NA
	B202L	2.0 (1985)	①	81	41	141	③	16	19	20	NA
1991	B202L	2.0 (1985)	①	81	41	130	③	16	19	20	NA
	B212i	2.1 (2119)	①	81	41	130	③	16	13	20	NA
	B234i	2.3 (2290)	①	15②	15②	140	44	16	13	20	96
	B234L	2.3 (2290)	①	15②	15②	140	44	16	13	20	96
1992	B202L	2.0 (1985)	①	81	41	130	③	16	19	20	NA
	B212i	2.1 (2119)	①	81	41	130	③	16	13	20	NA
	B234i	2.3 (2290)	①	15②	15②	140	44	16	13	20	96
	B234L	2.3 (2290)	①	15②	15②	140	44	16	13	20	96
1993	B202L	2.0 (1985)	①	81	41	130	③	16	19	20	NA
	B212i	2.1 (2119)	①	81	41	130	③	16	13	20	NA
	B234i	2.3 (2290)	①	15②	15②	140	44	16	13	20	96
	B234L	2.3 (2290)	①	15②	15②	140	44	16	13	20	96
1994	B202L	2.0 (1985)	①	81	41	130	③	16	19	20	NA
	B212i	2.1 (2119)	①	81	41	130	③	16	13	20	NA
	B234i	2.3 (2290)	①	15②	15②	140	44	16	13	20	96
	B234L	2.3 (2290)	①	15②	15②	140	44	16	13	20	96

NA—Not available
① 1st Step: 44 ft. lbs.
  2nd Step: 59 ft. lbs.
  3rd Step: Turn bolt an additional ¼ turn (90°)
② Turn bolt an additional ¼ turn (90°)
③ 17mm: 44 ft. lbs.
  19mm: 63 ft. lbs.

BRAKE SPECIFICATIONS

All measurements in inches unless noted.

Year	Model	Master Cylinder Bore	Brake Disc Original Thickness	Brake Disc Minimum Thickness	Maximum Runout	Brake Drum Diameter Original Inside Diameter	Max. Wear Limit	Maximum Machine Diameter	Minimum Lining Thickness Front	Minimum Lining Thickness Rear
1990	900	0.87	0.87①	0.79②	0.003	—	—	—	0.16	0.16
	9000	0.87	0.98①	0.91②	0.003	—	—	—	0.16	0.16
1991	900	0.87	0.87①	0.79②	0.003	—	—	—	0.16	0.16
	9000	0.87	0.98①	0.91②	0.003	—	—	—	0.16	0.16
1992	900	0.87	0.87①	0.79②	0.003	—	—	—	0.16	0.16
	9000	0.87	0.98①	0.91②	0.003	—	—	—	0.16	0.16
1993	900	0.87	0.87①	0.79②	0.003	—	—	—	0.16	0.16
	9000	0.87	0.98①	0.91②	0.003	—	—	—	0.16	0.16
1994	900	0.87	0.87①	0.79②	0.003	—	—	—	0.16	0.16
	9000	0.87	0.98①	0.91②	0.003	—	—	—	0.16	0.16

① Rear Disc: 0.35 in.
② Rear Disc: 0.29 in.

WHEEL ALIGNMENT

Year	Model	F/R	Caster Range (deg.)	Caster Preferred Setting (deg.)	Camber Range (deg.)	Camber Preferred Setting (deg.)	Toe-in (in.)	Steering Axis Inclination (deg.)
1990	900	Front	1.5P–2.5P①	2P②	0–1P	0.5P	0.04–0.12	10.5–12.5
		Rear	—	—	0.75N–0.25N	0.5N	0.08–0.24	—
	9000	Front	1.15P–2.15P	1.65P	1.15N–0.15N	0.65N	0.04–0.08	10.8–11.8
		Rear	—	—	0.5N–0	0.25N	0.04–0.16	—
1991	900	Front	1.5P–2.5P①	2P②	0–1P	0.5P	0.04–0.12	10.5–12.5
		Rear	—	—	0.75N–0.25N	0.5N	0.08–0.24	—
	9000	Front	1.15P–2.15P	1.65P	1.15N–0.15N	0.65N	0.04–0.08	10.8–11.8
		Rear	—	—	0.5N–0	0.25N	0.04–0.16	—
1992	900	Front	1.5P–2.5P①	2P②	0–1P	0.5P	0.04–0.12	10.5–12.5
		Rear	—	—	0.75N–0.25N	0.5N	0.08–0.24	—
	9000	Front	1.15P–2.15P	1.65P	1.15N–0.15N	0.65N	0.04–0.08	10.8–11.8
		Rear	—	—	0.5N–0	0.25N	0.04–0.16	—
1993	900	Front	1.5P–2.5P①	2P②	0–1P	0.5P	0.04–0.12	10.5–12.5
		Rear	—	—	0.75N–0.25N	0.5N	0.08–0.24	—
	9000	Front	1.15P–2.15P	1.65P	1.15N–0.15N	0.65N	0.04–0.08	10.8–11.8
		Rear	—	—	0.5N–0	0.25N	0.04–0.16	—
1994	900	Front	1.5P–2.5P①	2P②	0–1P	0.5P	0.04–0.12	10.5–12.5
		Rear	—	—	0.75N–0.25N	0.5N	0.08–0.24	—
	9000	Front	1.15P–2.15P	1.65P	1.15N–0.15N	0.65N	0.04–0.08	10.8–11.8
		Rear	—	—	0.5N–0	0.25N	0.04–0.16	—

N—Negative
P—Positive
① w/o Power Steering: 0.5P–1.5P
② w/o Power Steering: 1P

ENGINE MECHANICAL

NOTE: Disconnecting the negative battery cable on some vehicles may interfere with the functions of the on-board computer systems and may require the computer to undergo a relearning process, once the negative battery cable is reconnected.

Engine Assembly

REMOVAL AND INSTALLATION

2.0L Engine

NOTE: The engine and transaxle assembly are removed as an assembly.

1. Raise the vehicle and support it safely.
2. Drain the cooling system. Remove the battery.
3. Remove the expansion tank retaining bolts. Disconnect the tank from the suction and remove the overflow hoses from the radiator.

4. Disconnect the upper radiator hose.
5. Loosen the drive belt for the compressor by loosening the locknut, and loosening the adjusting nut under the locknut.
6. Disconnect the upper connection on the oil cooler, loosen the pipe clip on the radiator and slide the pipe down behind the radiator.
7. Unplug the connector from the air conditioning compressor. Loosen the compressor mounting and belt tensioner.
8. Place a protective cloth over the radiator member and rest the compressor on the radiator member. Secure the compressor to the radiator member.
9. Remove the turbocharger pressure pipe, situated between the turbocharger unit and the intercooler.
10. Disconnect the Lambda probe connector leads and disconnect them from the clips.
11. From the engine compartment, unbolt the flange joint between the exhaust pipe and the exhaust manifold. Push the exhaust pipe to one side and unhook the rubber hangers from the exhaust system. Disconnect the bottom coolant hose from the water pump.

12. From under the vehicle, remove the bottom retaining bolt for the radiator fan.
13. Disconnect the speedometer drive from the transaxle.
14. Select the 4th gear and separate the rubber joint in the gear selector linkage.
15. Remove the clips and bellows at the inner universal joints.
16. Disconnect the electrical leads from the alternator and the starter motor. Unplug the connector for the oil pressure switch.
17. Remove the clips and remove the top radiator hose.
18. Disconnect the top radiator hose at the cylinder head.
19. Unscrew the junction block from the battery shelf. Remove the clamp for the fuel filter.
20. Remove the battery shelf from the engine compartment.
21. Disconnect the high tension lead from the ignition coil at the distributor cap.
22. Remove the solenoid valve from the bracket on the radiator and unplug the electrical connections.
23. Remove the bolts from the top of the radiator fan. Disconnect the wiring loom and lift out the fan.
24. Pull the connector off the air mass meter. Disconnect the air mass

meter from the air intake duct socket connector and the air cleaner. Leave the rubber socket connector attached to the turbocharger unit.

25. Remove the air intake duct by pulling it out of the opening in the wing and twisting the ends inwards.

26. Remove the air cleaner top section first, then the remaining section.

27. Disconnect the relief valve hose from the turbocharger pressure pipe and remove the pipe.

28. Disconnect the hall effect transducer, ground lead from the transaxle and electrical connector for the backup lights.

29. Disconnect the end of the throttle cable and disconnect the throttle linkage.

30. Install a clamp to the hydraulic line to the slave cylinder and pinch the line tightly. With proper wrenches, open the line to the clutch slave cylinder.

31. Remove the front wheels.

32. From both sides of the vehicle, slacken the lower bolts retaining the steering swivel member to the strut assembly. Remove the 2 upper bolts.

33. Pivot the steering swivel member outwards to pull the inboard universal joint out of the halfshaft. Position dust covers over the exposed halfshaft cups.

34. Remove the engine stay bolt.

35. Remove the steering reservoir for the servo and position it within the engine compartment. Drain the fluid from the container.

36. Disconnect the large bore hose and the delivery hose from the steering servo pump and plug the open ends.

37. Disconnect the fuel return line from the pressure regulator.

38. Remove the nut from the rear engine mounting and back off the front mount bolts a few turns.

39. Attach the lifting sling 83-92-409 or equivalent, to the rear lifting lug.

40. Lift the engine sufficiently to provide access for the removal of the components located between the engine and the firewall.

41. Disconnect the vacuum hoses from the inlet manifold.

42. Remove the coolant hoses running between the heat exchanger and the water pump pipe.

43. Separate the coupling between the fuel pipe and the fuel injection manifold. Do not allow the fuel to spill or collect.

44. Cut the clips securing the wiring looms to the oil pipe, water pipe, inlet manifold steady bar and the oil supply pipe.

45. Unclip the wiring loom to the fuel injection manifold.

46. Disconnect the grounding connections and the electrical connectors from the wiring harness.

47. Unbolt the air cooled oil cooler and place it on top of the engine. The 2 lower bolts need only be loosened.

48. Carefully remove the engine from the vehicle, taking care not to damage the radiator.

To install:

49. Carefully install the engine in the vehicle. Install the mounting bolts and tighten all engine mountings.

50. Connect the oil cooler lines to the radiator.

51. Connect all electrical connections, fuel lines, vacuum and coolant hoses and power steering lines.

52. Assemble the steering knuckle and install the halfshafts.

53. Connect the clutch master cylinder, throttle cable and ignition system wirings.

54. Connect the turbocharged system components.

55. Connect the air mass meter and radiator fan.

56. Connect the exhaust system.

57. Install all accessory drive belts and tighten to specification.

58. Fill the radiator with coolant and crankcase with engine oil.

59. Connect the negative battery cable.

60. Start the engine and allow it to reach operating temperature. Check the ignition timing and all fluid levels. Test drive the vehicle.

2.1L Engine

NOTE: The engine and transaxle assembly are removed as an assembly.

1. Remove the hood, after scribing lines around the mounting bolt positions to aid later refitting.

2. Install Saab special tool 83-93-209 or equivalent, under the right side of the upper control arm.

3. Disconnect and remove the battery.

4. Drain the engine coolant.

5. Slacken the wheel nuts on the right front wheel.

6. Raise and safely support the vehicle.

7. Put the transaxle selector into **R**.

8. Under the vehicle, remove the taper pin from the gearshift rod joint.

9. Disconnect the speedometer cable.

10. Remove the bolt securing the exhaust pipe to the clamp bracket on the transaxle.

11. Loosen the clips around the rubber boots on the CV-joints and slide the boots clear, this operation can also be done from above.

12. On the right side of the vehicle, remove the front wheel.

13. Separate the end piece from the lower control arm.

14. Separate the universal joint and position the knuckle in front of the driver. Support the end piece against the outer end of the control arm.

15. Disconnect the positive lead from the battery and free it from the clips holding it to the body. Disconnect the ground cable from the transaxle.

16. Disconnect the starter motor leads.

17. Unbolt the exhaust pipe from the exhaust manifold.

18. Disconnect the pressure pipe from the steering servo pump and have a plug handy to prevent oil escaping from the pipe. Take care not to drip oil onto the engine mounting and control arm rubbers.

19. From the left side of the vehicle, disconnect the cooling system hoses at the following connections, the heat exchanger valve, the expansion tank, the bottom of the radiator and the thermostat housing.

20. Disconnect the left fuel injection system cable harness as follows, at the air mass meter sensor, at the throttle switch, at the A.I.C. actuator, at the injectors, at the NTC resistor (thermostatic switch) and at the ground points on the front lifting lug. Use the proper tool to release the tension in the springs on the terminal blocks.

21. Disconnect the block and plug connector (ground lead). Disconnect the lead at the alternator and the green/white cable to the positive terminal on the regulator. Disconnect the ground (black) cable. Disconnect the black cable from the oil pressure switch. Disconnect the cable for the A.I.C. actuator. Disconnect the yellow/white cable from the temperature transmitter. Disconnect the gray cable from the knock detector. Release the cable harness from the clip on the fuel injection manifold, from the rear of the engine and from the coolant hose between the engine and the expansion tank.

22. Withdraw the loose cables and guide the harness unit out of the engine compartment. Place it on top of the power distribution unit.

23. Remove the adjusting bolt in the alternator bracket, remove the drive belts and lift off the alternator.

24. Disconnect the brake servo hose from the intake manifold. Disconnect the throttle cable and sheath.

25. Remove the air conditioner compressor and bracket from the block. Place them on the filter housing for the heater system. Secure the alternator so it will not drop or become damaged.

26. Disconnect the fuel lines at their connections at the front of the fuel injection manifold and on the fuel pressure regulator.

27. Remove the coil.

28. Disconnect the turbocharger pressure line from the turbocharger compressor and the intercooler/throttle housing.

29. Remove the auxiliary fan.

30. Remove the air mass meter together with the suction pipe for the turbocharger unit. Disconnect the hoses at the solenoid valve and the crankcase ventilation at the suction pipe.

31. Disconnect the cables from the hall transmitter and coil in the distributor. Free the hall transmitter cable from the clips on the clutch cover.

32. Disconnect the solenoid valve hoses from the connections on the turbocharger unit and charging pressure regulator.

33. Disconnect the hydraulic hose from the clutch slave cylinder. Plug the hose to stop fluid from escaping.

34. Remove the engine mounting bolts.

35. Attach suitable lifting equipment to the engine lifting hooks. Raise the engine until the left, inner CV-joint can be separated.

36. Raise the engine to enable the hoses on the oil cooler to be disconnected.

NOTE: When lifting the engine out of the vehicle, keep it close to the firewall to prevent the radiator and solenoid valve from being damaged by the front engine mounting.

37. Disconnect the hose to the power steering pump and drain the oil in the system.

To install:

38. Before installation, check that the inner CV-joint boots are packed with the correct grease.

39. Suspend the engine from the lifting gear. Adjust the lifting gear so the front engine mounting is slightly lower than the rear mounting.

40. Lower the engine into the engine compartment until the hoses to the oil cooler and servo pump can be connected.

41. Guide the engine into position, attending to the following items in order, the front engine mounting, left inner CV-joint and right inner CV-joint. Lower the engine until it rests on the rear engine mountings and install the mounting bolts. Unhook the lifting gear and unbolt the lifting lug from the water pump.

42. Connect the clutch master cylinder and all turbocharger unit connections.

43. Install the distributor, coil and all wiring for the electronic ignition.

44. Install the air mass meter, auxiliary fan, fuel lines, air conditioner, throttle cable and brake booster.

45. Install the alternator, drive belts, all electrical connections, cooling system hoses, exhaust system, battery and cables.

46. Assemble the steering knuckle and halfshafts.

47. Fill the radiator with coolant, the engine with oil and the transaxle with fluid. Start the engine and allow it to reach operating temperature. Check the timing and recheck all fluid levels. Test drive the vehicle.

2.3L Engine

1. Raise and support the vehicle safely. Remove the inner fender wells and right side fender. Remove the middle filler panel from under the spoiler. Lower the vehicle.

2. Drain the coolant. Disconnect the battery cables and remove the battery. Remove the brace bar for the ABS unit. Unplug the 3 connectors for the ignition system and release the clips for the leads from the bracket attached to the battery shelf.

3. Disconnect the positive battery cable from the terminal block and remove the terminal block. Disconnect the battery negative cable from the fender. Remove the battery shelf and tuck the leads out of the way.

4. Unplug the connector for the knock detector in the block. Disconnect the top radiator hose.

5. Remove the air mass meter and the brace bar for the air intake silencer. Release the toggle clips on the air cleaner and the throttle housing. Lift off the air intake complete with silencer and air mass meter.

6. Unplug the connectors for the washer fluid level sensor, remove the hose from the reservoir, remove the retaining screws and remove the reservoir.

7. Remove the clip, lift up the throttle lever and disconnect the cable from the linkage. Disconnect the fuel return hose from the fuel pressure regulator and tuck out of the way. Place a rag under the connector and disconnect the fuel supply hose from the injection rail. Pull out the end of the hose and tuck it out of the way.

8. Remove the cover over the space behind the false bulkhead panel. Remove the rubber moulding from the edge of the panel. Remove the clip securing the engine wiring loom to the bulkhead. Remove the securing bolts and lift out the bulkhead.

9. Unplug the connector in the engine wiring loom and tuck the loom away on top of the engine. Unplug the connector for the road speed sensor lead. Pull the cable out of the grommet in the bottom of the bulkhead and tuck the lead away at the top of the engine.

10. Disconnect the heater box hoses from the cylinder head and tuck them away behind the brake fluid reservoir. Unscrew the clip securing the kickdown cable to the pipe from the steering servo pump.

11. Clean the surrounding areas and disconnect the hoses from the oil cooler for the automatic transaxle. Plug the ports in the transaxle and the fittings in the hoses. Secure the hoses to the radiator crossmember.

12. Unplug the connector from the brake fluid reservoir. Remove the nut from the gear selector top linkage. Slacken the cable and tuck it behind the brake fluid reservoir.

13. Disconnect the hoses from the expansion tank. Remove the securing bolt, snip through the tie, unplug the connector and lift the tank out. Use a spanner wrench to release the tension applied by the belt tensioner and apply a hard upward pull on the belt. As the belt loosens, install locking pin 83-94-488 in the tensioner. Ease the belt off the air conditioner compressor pulley.

14. Install a protective steel panel over the oil cooler and cover the right section of the radiator crossmember with rags. Unplug the connector from the air conditioner compressor, remove the securing bolts and lift the compressor onto the radiator crossmember. Secure the compressor with a piece of wire.

15. Disconnect the top radiator hose from the water pump. Remove the clip and disconnect the bottom radiator hose from the clamp. Disconnect the oxygen sensor by unplugging the connector under the inlet manifold.

16. Snip through the ties securing the servo hoses, charcoal canister hose and wiring loom to the top tor-

que arm. Disconnect the radio suppressor lead from the torque arm and remove the arm. Disconnect the hose to the charcoal canister from the inlet manifold and tuck it out of the way.

17. Unbolt the exhaust pipe from the exhaust manifold. Unplug the connector from the oil level sensor and place the lead along the edge of the fender. Remove the top securing bolt and loosen the 2 bolts at the bottom of the oil cooler. Snip through any ties and tie the cooler to the engine.

18. Remove the securing bolt for the power steering fluid reservoir, lower the reservoir and siphon off the fluid. Disconnect the servo hose from the reservoir and tuck the end under the inlet manifold. Stand the reservoir on the bulkhead.

19. Raise and support the vehicle safely. Disconnect the steering servo delivery pipe from the pump. Use a second spanner across the flats to stop the fitting turning. Install a plug in the end of the pipe and wipe up any spills immediately. Remove the pipe clip from the support bearing rear engine mount.

20. Remove the nuts from the engine mountings on the right side. Remove the clips for the CV-boots. Loosen the bottom bolts securing the struts to the steering swivel member and remove the top bolts. Pull away the steering swivel members to separate the halfshaft joints. Lower the vehicle.

21. Unbolt the left engine mount. Disconnect the struts from the hood and install extensions 83-94-439 or equivalent, onto the ends. Attach an engine lift to the eyes on the engine. Pay particular attention to the following components when removing the engine: ABS unit, kickdown cable, cooling fan, steering servo pump, alternator pulley.

To install:
22. Install the engine assembly into the vehicle. Insert the bolt through the left engine mount prior to lowering the assembly. Pay attention that the following components are kept clear of the engine: ABS unit, kickdown cable, cooling fan, steering servo pump and the alternator pulley.

23. Tighten the engine mountings. Check that the CV-joints are greased and install the halfshafts on the transaxle. Install the struts and tighten the bolts to 58-77 ft. lbs. (78-105 Nm). Install the clips on the CV-boots.

24. Install the filler panel under the spoiler. Connect the steering servo pipe to the pump and secure the pipe

to the bearing bracket. Lower the vehicle.

25. Connect the charcoal canister, power steering fluid reservoir, oil level sensor and oil cooler, exhaust system and radiator hoses. Install the air conditioner compressor and tighten the bolts to 15 ft. lbs. (20 Nm).

26. Install the serpentine belt and release the locking pin in the tensioner. Connect the radiator hose to the expansion tank and install the tank in the vehicle.

27. Install the oxygen sensor, engine torque arm, gear selector linkage, road speed sensor, heater box hoses, throttle cable, knock detector, false bulkhead, washer hose, fuel supply and return hoses, air intake and brace bar and battery.

28. Connect the DI wiring. Install the bracket for the ABS and washer fluid reservoir. Remove the hood strut extensions.

29. Raise and support the vehicle safely. Install the right wheel well. Install the wheels and tighten the lugs to 96 ft. lbs. (130 Nm).

30. Refill the cooling system, power steering fluid, washer fluid, engine oil and transaxle fluid.

31. Start the vehicle and allow it to reach operating temperature. Check that all systems are working properly.

Engine Mounts

REMOVAL AND INSTALLATION

Front

1. Disconnect the negative battery cable.
2. Connect an engine lifting device to the engine hook and raise the engine just enough to release pressure from the engine mounts.
3. Raise the vehicle and support it on safety stands. Remove the right wheel.
4. Remove the inner fender liner.
5. Remove the bracket-to-mount bolt. Remove the mount-to-sub-frame bolts and lift out the mount.

To install:
6. Install the engine mount. Fit the bracket for the oil pipe into the groove in the mounting bracket and bolt it to the block.
7. Lower the engine until it contacts the mount and then install the lower bolt.
8. Install the fender liner and replace the wheel.
9. Lower the vehicle and connect the battery cable.

Rear

1. Disconnect the negative battery cable.
2. Cut the plastic tie holding the wire bundle, as required. Remove the torque arm.
3. Disconnect the ground wire from the bracket and remove the bracket, as required.
4. Raise the vehicle and support it on safety stands. Remove the right wheel.
5. Remove the inner fender liner.
6. Loosen the accessories drive belt tension. Loosen the alternator bolts and swivel it out of the way.
7. Remove the 4 mounting bolts and lift out the rear mount.

To install:
8. Install the mount and swivel the alternator back into position. Tighten the drive belt tension.
9. Install the fender liner and wheel. Lower the vehicle.
10. Bolt the mounting bracket to the wheel arch and connect the ground wire.
11. Install the torque arm and connect the battery cable.

Cylinder Head

REMOVAL AND INSTALLATION

900 Series

1. Remove the hood after scribing reference marks next to the mounting bolts, to aid later installation.
2. Remove the battery.
3. Drain the coolant from the radiator and cylinder block.
4. Remove the exhaust manifold and turbocharger unit.
5. Remove the tensioning pulley and drive belt from the air conditioner compressor.
6. Slacken the securing bolts for the steering pump bracket, remove the drive belt and push the pump aside.
7. Undo the wiring harness clips on the cylinder head.
8. Remove the 2 bolts in the timing cover, which are screwed into the cylinder head from underneath.
9. Remove the bolts in the right hand engine mounting which are screwed into the cylinder head, together with the spacer sleeves.
10. Disconnect the hose between the thermostat housing and the radiator at the thermostat housing.
11. Remove the fuel pressure regulator and disconnect the ground leads for the fuel injection system.

12. Remove the AIC actuator. Remove the bracket for the air conditioning compressor from the cylinder head.

13. Remove the intake manifold complete with injectors and injection manifold.

14. Disconnect the lead from the temperature transmitter.

15. Remove the lid on the valve cover and the ignition cables together with the distributor cap.

16. Remove the valve cover. Disconnect the crankcase ventilation hose and remove the semi-circular rubber plug halves from the cylinder head.

17. Remove the air conditioning compressor and put it on the air intake for the heating system.

18. Align the timing marks on the crankshaft and camshafts. To do this, remove the cover on the transaxle bell housing which reveals the timing marks on the flywheel. Turn the engine so the **0** mark on the flywheel is aligned with the mark on the housing, or the endplate if the clutch cover has been removed. This makes certain that the pistons for No. 1 and 4 cylinders are at TDC.

19. Remove the camshaft chain tensioner.

20. Block up the engine to lift the cylinder head off the block. Remove the cylinder head bolts and siphon off the oil from the cylinder head.

21. Install a guide pin in one of the bolt holes and lift off the cylinder head, making sure the pivoting guide for the camshaft chain is not damaged.

To install:

22. Align the **0** mark on the flywheel with the timing mark on the housing. Align the marks on the camshafts with their respective timing marks.

23. Install the cylinder head gasket, making sure it is held in position by the guide sleeves in the cylinder head flange.

24. Install the guide pin tool 83-92-128 or equivalent, and position the timing chain and pivoting guide.

25. Carefully install the cylinder head. Use the guide pin as a pivot for the head, which must be turned slightly to enable it to pass the pivoting guide. Thereafter, alignment will be determined by the guide sleeves.

26. Install the cylinder head bolts and tighten them in 3 stages. Stage 1, torque to 44 ft. lbs. (60 Nm) evenly. Stage 2, torque to 59 ft. lbs. (80 Nm) evenly. Stage 3, another 90 degrees (¼ turn). Retighten the bolts after the engine has reached normal oper-

ating temperature. Remember to install the 2 M8 sized bolts in the underside of the cylinder head.

27. Install the camshaft sprockets, fitting the sprocket for the exhaust camshaft first. Make sure the chain between the crankshaft sprocket and the camshaft sprocket is kept tight. Next install the intake camshaft sprocket. Keep the chain tight between the sprockets.

28. Lightly tighten the center bolts securing the camshaft sprockets. Adjust the chain tensioner and install it under tension. Tighten the bolt.

29. Release the tensioner by pressing the pivoting guide firmly against it. Thereafter, press the pivoting guide against the chain to put a basic tension on the chain.

30. Depress the pivoting guide to check that the tensioner is working. Rotate the crankshaft 2 complete turns clockwise, viewed from the transaxle end. Check that the earlier settings of the crankshaft and camshaft timings have not changed. Tighten the camshaft sprocket bolts to 49 ft. lbs. (67 Nm).

31. Continue the installation in reverse order of the removal procedure.

Camshaft gear-to-camshaft alignment

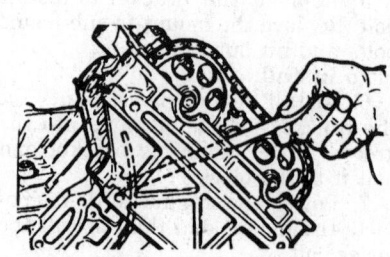

Releasing chain tensioner — 2.0L engine shown

9000 Series

1. Disconnect the negative battery cable. Raise and support the vehicle safely.

2. Remove the right front wheel assembly and the inner fender panel.

3. Drain the coolant. Remove the radiator expansion tank. Disconnect the steering servo reservoir and set aside. Leave the hoses attached.

4. Loosen the compressor drive belt and remove the belt.

5. Disconnect the electrical leads from the air compressor.

6. Unbolt the compressor from its mounting bracket. Disconnect the top pipe connecting on the air cooled oil cooler and push the pipe to one side. Rest the compressor on the radiator crossmember. Unbolt the compressor mounting bracket and remove it.

7. Unbolt the front exhaust pipe flange and unhook the rubber hangers.

8. Remove the steady bar for the turbocharger unit and the oil return pipe.

9. Disconnect the hose from the intercooler at the turbocharger unit. Disconnect the oil supply pipe from the turbocharger.

10. Disconnect the hose between the air mass meter and the turbocharger unit. Disconnect the coolant hose from the thermostat housing and the hose from the cylinder head.

11. Disconnect the oil supply hose or pipe so as not to obstruct the removal of the exhaust manifold. If necessary, remove the clip holding the pipe to the cylinder head and slave cylinder.

12. Unbolt and lift off the exhaust manifold complete with the turbocharger unit, pushing the oil supply pipe aside at the same time.

13. Disconnect the lead to the temperature transducer.

14. Remove the engine stay bracket from its attachment point on the wing.

15. Remove the bolt securing the engine stay bracket to the cylinder head. Remove the intake manifold from the cylinder head.

16. Disconnect the breather hose for the crankcase ventilation from the camshaft cover.

17. Disconnect the vacuum hose and the hall effect transducer lead from the distributor and remove the distributor cap complete with the high tension leads.

18. Unscrew and remove the spark plug inspection plate and the clips for the high tension leads.

19. Remove the camshaft cover.

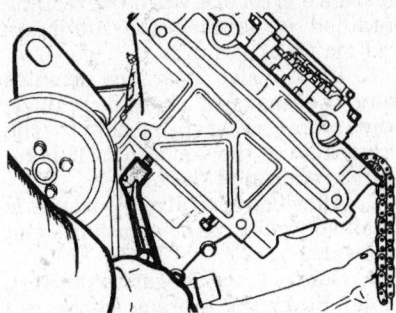

Timing cover-to-cylinder head bolts (2) — 2.0L engine shown

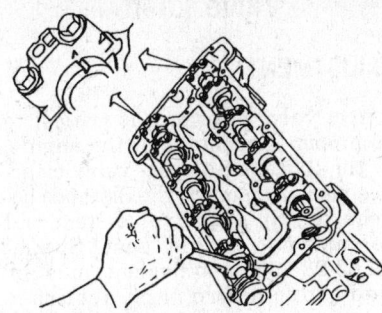

Alignment of marks on camshaft bearing caps — 2.0L engine shown

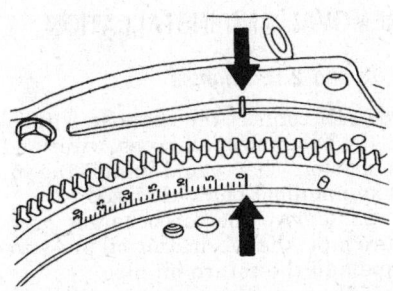

Flywheel to endplate timing marks — 2.0L engine shown

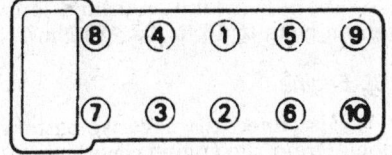

Cylinder head-bolts tightening sequence

20. Align the crankshaft with the **0** timing mark and check that the camshaft timing marks also coincide. Remove the camshaft sprockets.

21. Remove the camshaft tensioner. Remove the 2 cylinder head bolts adjacent to the timing cover, which is accessible from below.

22. Disconnect the starter motor lead from the clip on the thermostat housing.

23. Remove the Torx® type cylinder head bolts.

24. Install a guide pin in the drilled hole in the right top corner of the cyl-inder head. Make sure the timing chain is positioned such that the pivoting chain guide will not obstruct the cylinder head and carefully lift the cylinder head from the engine block.

To install:

25. Before installation, clean both the cylinder head and the engine block surfaces. Install a new gasket. Be sure the crankshaft is aligned in the **0** position and that the camshafts are align with their respective timing marks.

NOTE: When the pistons of the No. 1 and No. 4 cylinders are at TDC, the crankshaft 0 mark on the flywheel must be align with the mark on the clutch cover or the endplate, if the clutch cover has been removed. The marks on the camshafts must be align with those on the camshaft bearing caps. This indicates the exhaust valves for No. 1 and No. 4 cylinders are closed.

26. Install a guide pin in the drilled hole in the top of the right corner of the cylinder head and lower the cyl-inder head carefully into position on the engine block. Locate the cylinder head on the guide sleeves.

27. Install the cylinder head bolts, tightening them in the correct se-quence to the specified torque.

  a. Tightening sequence for the 2.0L and 2.1L engines:

    Stage 1 — 44 ft. lbs. (60 Nm).

    Stage 2 — 67 ft. lbs. (92 Nm).

    Stage 3 — run the engine to normal operating temperature and allow the engine to cool for 30 minutes.

    Stage 4 — slacken the bolts and retighten each bolt to 67 ft. lbs. (92 Nm).

    Stage 5 — tighten by turning the bolts through a further 90 de-grees (¼ turn).

  b. Tightening sequence for the 2.3L engine:

    Stage 1 — 44 ft. lbs. (60 Nm).

    Stage 2 — 59 ft. lbs. (80 Nm).

    Stage 3 — tighten by turning bolts through a further 90 degrees (¼ turn).

28. Position the inlet valve camshaft sprocket, followed by the exhaust valve camshaft sprocket. Be sure the chain is correctly positioned between the guides. Tighten the sprocket center bolts to 48 ft. lbs. (64 Nm).

29. Install the timing chain ten-sioner. Advance the tensioner before installing it. Release the tensioner and rotate the crankshaft 2 revolu-tions. Make sure the camshaft and flywheel timing marks are correctly aligned.

30. Install both halves of the split seal and the camshaft cover. Install the bolt at the distributor end and the middle bolt at the other end first. Tighten the bolts to 16 ft. lbs. (22 Nm).

31. Check that the timing marks for the distributor rotor are aligned, Install the distributor cap and con-nect the lead for the hall effect trans-ducer. Connect all vacuum hoses.

32. Connect the high tension leads to the spark plugs. Secure the leads in the clips. Install the inspection plate and tighten the retaining screws.

33. Install the clip securing the starter motor lead to the thermostat housing.

34. Install a new gasket on the inlet manifold and install the manifold in place. Install the top securing bolts first and then install the lower bolts, using an extension bar.

35. Install the bolt for the engine stay bracket to the cylinder head and position the stay bracket in place. In-stall a new gasket onto the exhaust manifold and position the exhaust manifold to the cylinder head.

36. Install the oil supply pipe. In-stall the clip and the slave cylinder bolt. Install the oil return line and the steady bar for the turbocharger unit.

37. Connect the hose between the turbocharger unit and the inter-cooler. Connect the cooler hose to the thermostat housing and the hose to the cylinder head.

38. Install the air mass meter socket connector into the turbo-charger unit and tighten the clip. Connect the hose between the inter-cooler and the turbocharger unit.

39. Install and tighten the nuts se-curing the front section of the ex-

haust pipe to the turbocharger. Bolt the air conditioning compressor mounting bracket onto the cylinder head and engine block.

40. Install the air conditioning compressor. Leave the coolant hose in the bracket when installing the compressor.

41. Connect the electrical leads and make sure the lead is clear of the compressor pulley. Install the steering servo reservoir. Install the coolant expansion tank and tighten the hose clip.

42. Connect the top pipe to the air cooled oil cooler and secure the cooler to the radiator. Install the overflow line between the expansion tank and the radiator.

43. Install the compressor belt, adjust the tension and tighten the belt tensioner bolt. Install the inner right wheel arch, and install the wheel.

44. Lower the vehicle and tighten the wheel. Connect the negative battery cable and fill the cooling system with coolant. Start the engine and test the engine operation.

Valve Lash

ADJUSTMENT

Correct valve clearance is critical to the proper functioning of the engine. On the 2.3L engine, the valve clearance measurement is the distance between the tip of the valve stem and the camshaft bearing seat. Special tool 83-93-753 or equivalent, must be used to ensure an accurate measurement.

1. Disconnect the negative battery cable.

2. Remove the camshafts and followers.

3. Place tool 83-93-753 or equivalent, across the camshaft bearing seats. Line up the instrument to read the depth to the tip of the valve stem.

4. Check that when the instrument is displaying the maximum depth reading of 0.807 in. (20.5mm) it actually reaches the tip of the valve stem. This can be verified by noting a small clearance between the tool and the bottom of the bearing bore closest to the valve.

5. Check that instrument does not touch the tip of the valve stem when showing the minimum depth reading of 0.768 in. (19.5mm). The valve

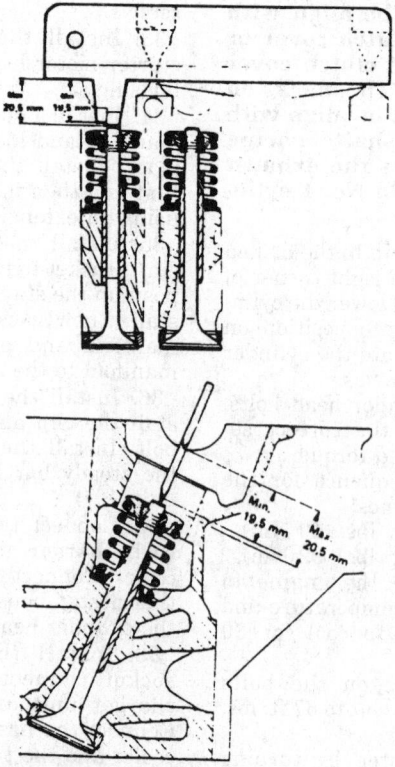

Checking valve clearance — 2.3L engine

clearance is correct when the reading obtained is between the minimum and maximum values.

6. If the valve clearance deviates from the specified checking values, adjustment must be made to the valve stem or the valve seat. This requires removal of the head.

7. After correct valve clearance is obtained, reinstall the camshafts and followers.

8. Connect the negative battery cable. Start the engine, check the timing and test drive the vehicle.

Intake Manifold

REMOVAL AND INSTALLATION

2.0L and 2.1L Engines

1. Disconnect the negative battery cable. Disconnect all hoses, wires and connectors that would inhibit the intake manifold being removed.

2. Remove the turbocharger pressure pipe, the lubricating oil pressure pipe and the return oil pipe.

3. Remove the intake manifold retaining bolts. Remove the intake manifold along with the injection manifold, injectors and the AIC regulator.

4. Installation is the reverse of the removal procedure. Be sure the proper gasket is used. A coolant leak could occur if the wrong one is used.

5. Install intake manifold and tighten bolts to 16 ft. lbs. (22 Nm).

2.3L Engine

1. Disconnect the negative battery cable. Drain the engine coolant.

2. Disconnect and remove the rubber elbow running between the throttle housing and the turbocharger.

3. Unplug the throttle position sensor. Disconnect the air conditioning hose and the coolant hoses at the throttle housing. Remove the 3 nuts and lift out the housing.

4. Unbolt the oil filler pipe bracket at the manifold and carefully position it out of the way.

5. Tag and disconnect all hoses and lines attached to the manifold.

6. Remove the A/C valve. Disconnect the fuel line from the pressure regulator.

7. Loosen the banjo fitting connecting the fuel line to the fuel rail. Cut the plastic tie and move the fuel line and pulsator out of the way. Don't lose the seals!

8. Unplug each fuel injector electrical lead and then lift off the fuel rail/injector assembly.

9. Disconnect the temperature sensor and the ground wires at the manifold.

10. Loosen the 2 screws on the cable clip underneath the manifold and move the harness assembly out of the way.

11. Disconnect the EGR pipe and all connectors.

12. Remove the mounting bolts and lift off the intake manifold.

To install:

13. Scrape off any excess gasket material, install a new gasket and install the manifold. Tighten the bolts in a crisscross pattern to 16 ft. lbs. (22 Nm).

14. Reposition the wire bundle and reconnect the EGR pipe.

15. Connect the ground wires and the temperature sensor.

16. Coat the injector O-rings with petroleum jelly and press the entire assembly into place. Reconnect all injector leads.

17. Connect the fuel line to the pressure regulator. Connect the fuel line/pulsator to the fuel rail and secure it with a plastic tie.

18. Connect the oil filler pipe bracket to the manifold and install the A/C valve.

19. Install the throttle housing and all its attachments.

20. Install the rubber elbow and refill the cooling system.

Exhaust Manifold

REMOVAL AND INSTALLATION

1. Disconnect the negative battery cable. Disconnect all necessary hoses, wires, and connectors that would inhibit the exhaust manifold from being removed.

2. Unbolt the exhaust pipe at the connecting flange.

3. If equipped with a heat shield, remove it.

4. Remove the exhaust manifold bolts. Remove the exhaust manifold from the vehicle.

To install:

5. Install the exhaust manifold. Apply an anti-seize compound to the manifold bolts and tighten to 19 ft. lbs. (26 Nm) for 2.0L turbocharged engines and 13 ft. lbs. (18 Nm) for all others. Installation is the reverse of removal.

6. Install the heat shield and connect all wires and hoses previously disconnected.

7. Connect the negative battery cable.

Turbocharger

REMOVAL AND INSTALLATION

900 Series

1. Disconnect the negative battery cable.

2. Remove the charge pressure regulator and block off the exhaust pipe.

3. Remove the battery, if required.

4. Release the tension on compressor belt.

5. Disconnect the hose between the compressor and the throttle housing.

6. Disconnect the oil supply line and the oil return line at the turbocharger unit.

7. Remove the retaining bolts securing the turbocharger to the exhaust manifold.

8. Remove the turbocharger unit from the vehicle. Plug the holes in the turbocharger unit to prevent dirt from entering.

To install:

9. Place the turbocharger unit into position and install the mounting bolts.

10. Fill the lubricating inflow of the turbocharger unit with engine oil before connecting the oil return line at the turbocharger. Connect the oil supply line and the oil return line at the turbocharger unit. Crank the engine for about 30 seconds with terminal 15 on the ignition coil disconnected. This will fill the lubricating system of the turbocharger before the engine is started.

11. Connect the hose between the compressor and the throttle housing. Adjust the belt tension.

12. Install the charged pressure regulator.

13. Install the battery, if removed. Connect the battery terminals.

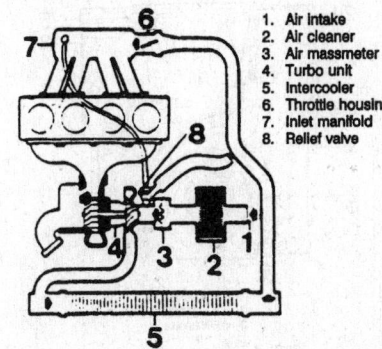

1. Air intake
2. Air cleaner
3. Air massmeter
4. Turbo unit
5. Intercooler
6. Throttle housing
7. Inlet manifold
8. Relief valve

Turbocharger assembly — 2.0L engine shown

9000 Series

1. Disconnect the negative battery cable. Release the tension on the compressor belt by slackening the belt tensioner.

2. Disconnect the top pipe coupling on the air cooled oil cooler and disconnect the clips securing the pipe to the radiator.

3. Remove the compressor mounting bolts. Insert a sheet of metal to protect the oil cooler and lift the compressor towards the expansion tank.

4. Remove the solenoid valve from its mounting on the radiator and disconnect the electrical leads.

5. Disconnect the electrical leads at the radiator fan. Unbolt and remove the fan.

6. Unplug the electrical connectors for the air mass meter. Disconnect the toggle fasteners securing the air mass meter to the air cleaner cover and pull the rubber socket connector off the turbocharger unit.

7. Disconnect the turbocharger pressure pipe from the compressor.

8. Remove the oil pipe to the turbocharger unit. Unbolt the clutch slave cylinder and remove the clip securing the oil pipe to the cylinder head. Disconnect the oil pipe banjo coupling from the block and undo the clip on the inlet manifold.

9. Disconnect the exhaust pipe from the turbocharger.

10. Disconnect the front rubber hangers for the exhaust pipe.

11. Remove the steady bar bracket between the sump and the compressor. Remove the securing bolts and loosen the oil return lines. Cap the aperture to prevent washers or nuts from the exhaust manifold dropping inside during the removal.

12. Remove the nuts securing the exhaust manifold to the cylinder head.

13. Lift the exhaust manifold from the cylinder head, along with the turbocharger unit.

14. Should further disassembly be necessary, complete as required.

To install:

15. Position the turbocharger unit to the exhaust manifold and tighten the retaining nuts. Install the new locknuts with the locking flange turned inwards.

16. Install a new gasket over the studs for the exhaust manifold and install the manifold/turbocharger unit to the cylinder head assembly. Tighten the nuts to 30 ft. lbs. (41 Nm).

17. Install the clip holding the turbocharger oil supply pipe to the inlet manifold. Connect and tighten the

banjo coupling to the engine block. Make sure the copper washers are in good condition. Secure the pipe to the turbocharger unit.

18. Install the return oil pipe and the steady bar bracket between the turbocharger unit and the crankcase. Connect the rubber hangers for the front exhaust hanger.

19. Bolt the exhaust pipe to the turbocharger. Use new locking nuts with the locking flanges turned outward. Tighten to 19 ft. lbs. (25 Nm).

20. Install the turbocharger pressure pipe to the compressor and assemble the air mass meter and rubber socket connector between the air cleaner body and the inlet side of the turbocharger.

21. Assemble the fan and solenoid valve, securing the electrical leads into their clips. Connect the return hose to the solenoid valve. Insert a piece of metal to protect the oil cooler and install the air conditioning compressor.

22. Reconnect the oil pipe to the oil cooler and secure the pipe clip to the radiator. Install the compressor belt and tighten it to specification.

Timing Chain Front Cover

REMOVAL AND INSTALLATION

2.0L and 2.1L Engines

1. Disconnect the negative battery cable.

2. Drain the engine oil and the coolant.

3. Remove the camshaft cover retaining bolts and lift off the cover.

4. Remove the bracket for the steering servo pump, complete with the pump and alternator.

5. Remove the chain tensioner.

6. Secure the flywheel and loosen the crankshaft pulley nut and remove the pulley.

7. Remove the belt tensioner and the water pump pipe.

8. Remove the oil pipes and the water pump pulley.

9. Remove the oil pump.

10. Remove the bolts and lift off the timing cover.

To install:

11. Install the timing cover and tighten the bolts to 15 ft. lbs. (20 Nm).

12. Install the oil pump pipes and water pump pulley. Install the crankshaft pulley and tighten the nut to 140 ft. lbs. (190 Nm) on the non-tur-

bocharger 2.0L engine or 130 ft. lbs. (175 Nm) on the turbocharged and 2.1L engines.

13. Install the belt tensioner, water pump pipe, chain tensioner, steering servo pump and alternator.

14. Fill the radiator with coolant and the crankcase with oil. Start the engine and check the timing.

2.3L Engine

1. Disconnect the negative battery cable.

2. Lock the flywheel using tool 83-93-993 or equivalent.

3. Raise and support the vehicle safely. Drain the coolant and the oil. Remove the right front wheel and wheel well.

4. Remove the serpentine belt and belt tensioner. Remove the tie bar between the wheel arch and the subframe.

5. Remove the steering servo pump, pump bracket and the alternator. Remove the top engine mounting bracket. Remove the torque arm.

6. Remove the engine mounting bracket, top belt tensioner bracket, air conditioner compressor and compressor bracket. Use a suitable rigid cover to prevent the oil cooler from being damaged.

7. Disconnect the coolant hoses and remove the water pump. Remove the crankshaft pulley and swivel the crankshaft sensor out of the way.

8. Move the coolant pipe aside and remove the oil pan. Remove the timing cover securing bolts. Note the locations of all bolts as they are of different lengths. Remove the bolts securing the timing cover to the cylinder head. Remove the timing cover.

To install:

9. Remove all traces of old sealant front the cover. Apply a 1mm bead of anaerobic sealant to the flanges of

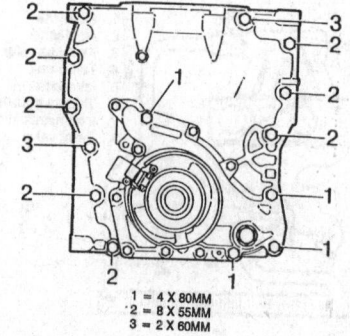

Timing chain front cover bolt positioning — 2.3L engine

the cover. Use sealant sparingly as excess sealant can get into the oilways and do serious damage to the engine.

10. Install the timing cover taking care not to damage the head gasket. Install the bolts in their correct positions and tighten to 15 ft. lbs. (20 Nm).

11. Install the oil pan and tighten bolts to 15 ft. lbs. (20 Nm). Install the coolant pipe and secure the crankshaft sensor.

12. Install the engine mountings, water pump and cooling hoses, air conditioner compressor, steering servo pump, pump bracket and the alternator. Install the top engine mounting bracket and torque arm.

13. Install the serpentine belt and belt tensioner. Remove the tie bar between the wheel arch and the subframe.

14. Install the wheel well and wheel. Fill the radiator with coolant and the engine with oil. Connect the battery. Start the engine and allow it to reach normal operating temperature. Check for leaks.

Front Cover Oil Seal

REPLACEMENT

1. Disconnect the negative battery cable. Raise and support the vehicle safely.

2. Remove the right front wheel and tire assembly. remove the inner front fender panel.

3. Loosen and remove the drive belts.

4. Remove the retaining bolt for the crankshaft pulley.

5. Remove the crankshaft pulley.

6. Using a small prybar, carefully remove the oil seal without marring the crankshaft stub end.

To install:

7. Install a new, oiled seal, using an appropriate seal installer.

8. Install the pulley and tighten the retaining bolt to 130 ft. lbs. (175 Nm) on the 2.0L turbocharger and 2.1L engines or 140 ft. lbs. (190 Nm) on the 2.0L non-turbocharger and 2.3L engines.

9. Tighten the drive belts, using a belt tension gauge. (new belt to 180 lbs. or used belt to 120 lbs.)

10. Install the forward section of the inner fender panel.

11. Replace the front wheel and lower the vehicle.

Timing Chain and Sprockets

REMOVAL AND INSTALLATION

NOTE: When removing the timing chain on the 2.3L engine, the balance shaft chain must be removed first.

1. Disconnect the negative battery cable. Remove the engine from the vehicle.

2. Remove the lid on the valve cover and remove the ignition wires. Remove the valve cover.

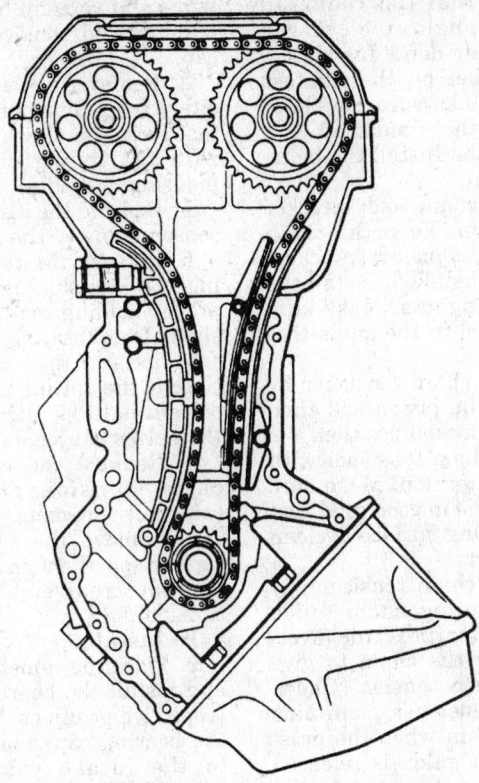

Timing chain and gears — 2.0L and 2.1L engines

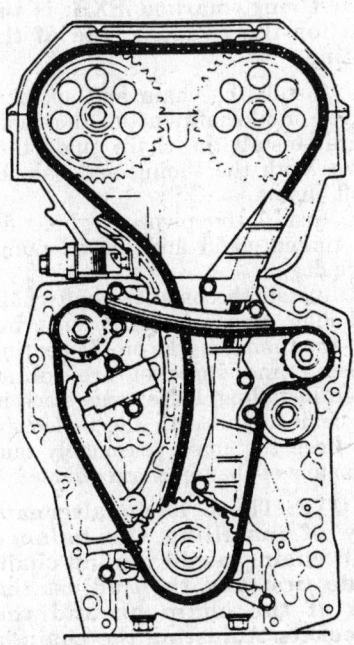

Timing chain and gears — 2.3L engine

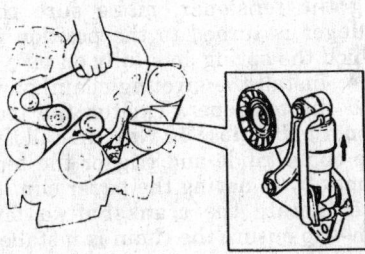

Serpentine belt adjustment — 2.3L engine

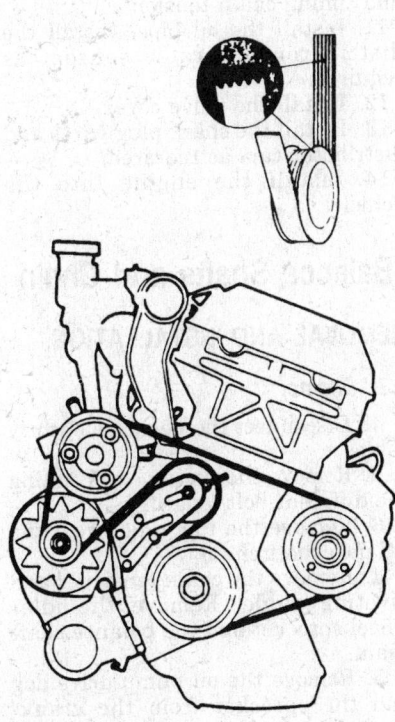

Serpentine belt adjustment — 2.0L and 2.1L engines

3. Position the crankshaft for TDC, with the **0** mark on the flywheel align with the timing mark on the transaxle end-plate. These marks must be aligned before the timing chain is removed.

4. Remove the crankshaft pulley using a puller. Remove the water pump, located behind the crankshaft pulley. Remove the timing cover, 2 bolts of which are screwed into the underside of the cylinder head.

5. The camshaft chain and crankshaft timing sprocket should now both be visible. From above, release the timing chain tensioner by pressing the pivoting guide firmly against it. Remove the chain tensioner.

6. Using a special tool to hold the camshafts, remove the center bolts securing the camshaft sprockets. Throughout this procedure, keep the camshafts in their basic correct setting. If they are rotated out of position at any stage, especially without their sprockets and chain, the valves can be damaged.

7. Disconnect the timing chain from the sprockets and remove the chain, clearing it from the crankshaft sprockets.

To install:

8. To install the timing chain, place the chain around the crank-

shaft sprocket. Run the chain up through the opening in the cylinder head if not already done. Install the chain and sprocket on the exhaust camshaft first. Make sure the chain is taut between the crankshaft and camshaft sprockets. Install the bolts, but do not tighten.

9. Install the chain and sprocket to the intake cam. Keep the chain taut between the camshaft sprockets while it is being installed. Install the bolts but do not tighten. Make sure the chain is seated in the guide tensioner grooves.

10. Tension the chain tensioner by fully depressing the piston and then rotating it to the locked position.

11. Install the chain tensioner with the piston under tension. Make sure the copper gasket is in good condition and that the sealing surface is clean and free from burrs.

12. Trigger the chain tensioner by pressing the pivoting chain guide against it, thereafter, press the pivoting guide against the chain to give the chain its basic tension. Check that the chain tensioner maintains tension on the chain when the pressure on the chain guide is released and that the basic setting stop for the tensioner holds the chain guide tight against the chain. A limited amount of play will be present until the hydraulic pressure takes over once the engine is running.

13. Check the setting by rotating the crankshaft 2 complete turns in its normal direction of rotation around to the timing mark. The basic setting of the camshafts should remain unaltered.

14. Lock the exhaust camshaft by using a wrench on the cast hex bolt and torque the sprocket bolt to 48 ft. lbs. (65 Nm). Repeat this on the intake cam.

15. Complete the procedure on the intake camshaft sprocket. When loosening or torquing the sprocket center bolts, hold the camshaft using a wrench installed over the flats on the camshaft. The accuracy of the timing chain adjustment will depend on the condition of the chain.

Camshaft

REMOVAL AND INSTALLATION

1. Disconnect the negative battery cable.
2. Remove the engine from the vehicle.
3. Remove the lid on the valve cover. Disconnect the spark plug

wires and vacuum hose from the distributor and remove the distributor cap.

4. Remove the valve cover and position the crankshaft for TDC. The **0** mark on the flywheel should align with the timing mark on the bellhousing endplate.

5. Remove the distributor or crank sensor. Remove the oil pipe.

6. Remove the center bolts securing the camshaft sprockets. Use a proper holding tool to hold the camshafts from rotating. Always keep the camshafts in their correct basic setting. If the setting of the crankshaft or camshafts is altered at this stage the valves can be damaged.

7. Remove the camshaft timing chain tensioner. Remove the camshaft sprockets.

8. Remove the camshaft bearing caps. Keep them in correct order to facilitate reassembly. Lift out the camshafts.

To install:

9. Place the camshaft into position and install the bearing caps in their respective positions. When installing, the bearing caps marked 1-5 belong to the intake cam, while those marked 6-10 go with the exhaust cam. Torque the bearing cap bolts to 11 ft. lbs. (15 Nm).

10. Install the camshaft sprockets and timing chain tensioner.

11. Install the oil pipe. Install the distributor or crank sensor, as required.

12. Install the valve cover.

13. Install the spark plug wires and distributor cap, as required.

14. Install the engine into the vehicle.

Balance Shafts and Chain

REMOVAL AND INSTALLATION

2.3L Engine

1. Disconnect the negative battery cable.
2. Remove the timing cover noting the different bolt lengths.
3. Remove the top guide from the balance shaft chain.
4. Remove the chain tensioner and pivoting guide. Remove the idler wheel sprocket and the balance shaft chain.
5. Remove the oil pump drive dog and the sprocket from the crankshaft. Remove the pivoting chain guide for the timing chain.
6. Remove the fixed chain guide for both the timing and balance shaft chains. Remove the timing chain

guard followed by the chain and sprocket.

7. Remove the balance shafts taking care not to damage the inner bearing shells.

To install:

8. Rotate the crankshaft to bring pistons No. 1 and 4 to TDC. Ensure that the timing cover flange is absolutely clean.

9. Lubricate the balance shaft journals and bearing housings. Insert the balance shafts into their respective tunnels, taking care not to damage the inner bearing shells. Tighten the bearing bolts to 9 ft. lbs. (12 Nm).

NOTE: The shaft with the smaller thrust ring, marked INL, is the one for the inlet side of the engine. The shaft with the larger thrust ring, marked EXH, is the one for the exhaust side of the engine.

10. Install the chain and sprocket on the crankshaft. Install the chain guard. Install the chain guide that serves both the timing and balance shaft chains.

11. Install the pivoting guide for the timing chain and the oil pump drive dog.

12. Install the balance shaft chain and idler wheel sprocket, ensuring that the timing marks on the bearing housing and sprocket are inline. When installing, leave some slack in the chain inline with the tensioner, and keep the chain reasonably taut by means of the top chain guide.

NOTE: There is an alternate way of installing the balance shaft chain. Install the top chain guide first and then adjust the run of the chain around the sprockets. Adjusting the chain is easier this way, although it will be more awkward to install the idler wheel sprocket.

13. Cock the chain tensioner and insert a paper clip through the hole in the cylinder to prevent the tensioner being triggered. Before installing the tensioner, make sure the plunger is turned to the position in which the spring acts fully on it.

14. Install the pivoting chain guide and the tensioner. Tighten the tensioner to 9 ft. lbs. (12 Nm). Install the top chain guide and trigger the tensioner by removing the paper clip.

15. Rotate the crankshaft a few times to ensure the chain is installed correctly.

16. Install the timing cover. Connect the negative battery cable. Start the engine, check the timing and test drive the vehicle.

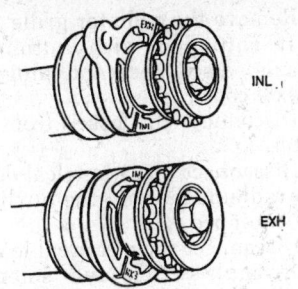

Balance shafts identification — Note the marking on the sprockets: Inlet side (smaller thrust ring) is marked INL and exhaust side (larger thrust ring) is marked EXH — 2.3L engine

Piston and Connecting Rod

POSITIONING

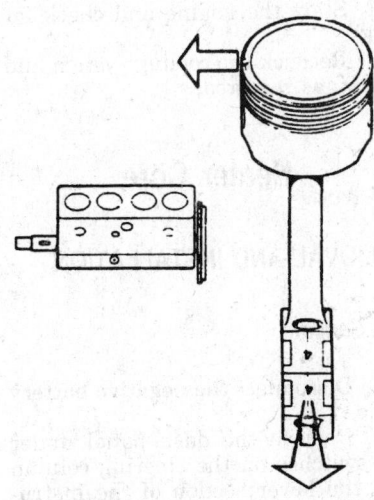

Piston positioning. The notch in the crown faces the timing cover. The numbers in the connecting rod face the exhaust side — 2.3L engine shown

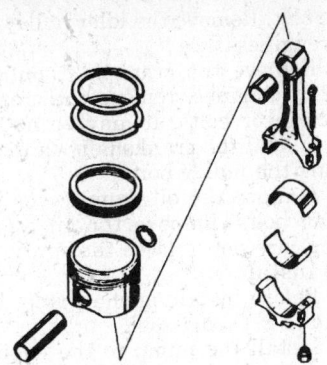

Piston and connecting rod assembly

ENGINE LUBRICATION

Oil Pan

REMOVAL AND INSTALLATION

2.0L and 2.1L Engines

1. Disconnect the negative battery cable and drain the engine oil.

2. Remove the right front wheel and fender liner, as required.

3. Remove the nut front the front and rear engine mount, and remove the bolt securing the torque arm to the top of the engine. Attach a engine lift and raise the engine off its mounts.

4. Remove the bottom bolt and the stud securing the sump to the transaxle case. Remove the bracket for the rear engine mount and brace bar, if equipped.

5. Remove the dipstick tube and unplug the oil level sensor on the pan. Remove the sensor.

6. Remove the bracket and oil return pipe for the turbocharger unit, if equipped. Fold down the edge of the splash plate and remove the 2 rubber plugs in the back of the transaxle case. Remove the 2 bolts securing the sump to the block.

7. Remove the outer filler panel on the right side. Loosen the securing bolt for the right wheel well brace bar.

8. Remove the 2 bolts in the subframe mount. Pry the sub-frame away from its front mounting and insert a block of wood about 1.0 in. (3cm) thick.

9. Remove the bolts securing the oil pan to the block and remove the pan.

To install:

10. Thoroughly clean the flanges on the pan and block. Apply Permatex® Ultra Blue Sealant or equivalent, along the groove in the edge of the sump flange.

11. Install the oil pan and bolts. Tighten the bolts, starting in the middle, to 15 ft. lbs. (20 Nm). Install the 2 rubber plugs in the transaxle case and reinstall the splash plate to its original position.

12. Remove the block of wood and install the bolts securing the subframe to the front mount. Tighten the attaching bolts for the wheel well liner brace bar.

13. Install the bracket and oil return pipe for the turbocharger unit. Make sure the seal on the pipe is in place.

14. Install the dipstick tube complete with seal. Make sure the rube is secured properly in the bracket at the top. Install the oil level sensor and plug on the connector.

15. Bolt the bracket and brace bar for the rear engine mounting into position, as required. Install the bottom bolt and stud holding the transaxle and oil pan together.

16. Lower the engine into position and install the torque arm. Install the front section of the exhaust pipe and the oxygen sensor. Install the front and rear engine mounts.

17. Install the filler panel, inner wheel well and wheel. Fill the engine with oil and run to normal operating temperature to check for leaks.

2.3L Engine

1. Disconnect the negative battery cable. Remove the oil dipstick, raise the vehicle and drain the oil.

2. Remove the right front wheel and inner wheel well. Remove the bolts in the front and rear engine mounts.

3. Remove the oxygen sensor and the front section of the exhaust pipe. Lower the vehicle.

4. Remove the tie rod between the wheel well and the sub-frame. Attach an engine crane and lift the engine slightly.

5. Remove the bottom bolt holding the transaxle to the oil pan. Unplug the connector for the oil level sensor and remove the sensor.

6. Fold down the edge of the splash plate and remove the 2 rubber plugs in the back of the transaxle case. Remove the 2 bolts securing the oil pan to the block under the plugs.

7. Remove the remaining oil pan bolts and using a drift, tap the guide

sleeve into the block. Remove the oil pan from the back first.

To install:

8. Thoroughly clean the flanges on the sump and block using solvent. Apply an even bead of Permatex® Ultra Blue sealant or equivalent, along the oil pan flange.

9. Install the rubber seal for the oil strainer in the groove on the oil pan. Install the oil pan, front edge first and then the back. Install the bolts loosely. Tighten the bolts to 15 ft. lbs. (20 Nm), starting in the middle.

NOTE: The longer bolt with washer is installed on the right side.

10. Install the 2 rubber plugs in the back of the transaxle and return the edge of the splash plate to its original position. Install the bolt securing the oil pan to the transaxle case at the bottom and install the oil level sensor.

11. Align the engine over the mounts and lower it into position. Install the tie rod between the wheel well and the sub-frame. Install the dipstick.

12. Install the bolts in the front and rear engine mounts. Install the oxygen sensor and exhaust pipe.

13. Install the inner wheel well and wheel. Lower the vehicle, fill with oil and run the engine to normal operating temperature to check for leaks.

Oil Pump

REMOVAL AND INSTALLATION

1. Raise the vehicle and support it safely.

2. Remove the right front wheel and the front inner fender panel section.

3. Loosen and remove the multi-groove belt. Loosen the compressor

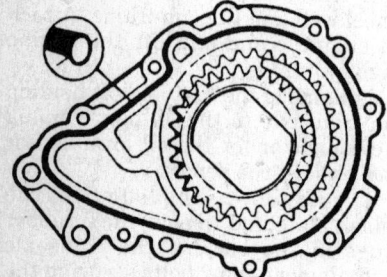

Oil pump cross-section — 2.0L engine shown

drive belt. Remove the idler pulley on 2.3L engines.

4. Remove the crankshaft pulley. On 2.3L engines, remove the crankshaft sensor bolts. It may be necessary to hold the crankshaft while removing the pulley bolt.

5. Remove the oil pump cover retaining bolts. Remove the oil pump taking care not to loose the spring.

To install:

6. Before installing the pump, install a new O-ring seal.

7. Install the pump to the engine and install the retaining bolts. Tighten the bolts to 6 ft. lbs. (8 Nm).

8. Install the pulley, crankshaft sensor, idler pulley and drive belts, as necessary. Tighten the pulley bolt to 140 ft. lbs. (190 Nm) on the 2.0L non-turbocharged and 2.3L engines or 130 ft. lbs. (175 Nm) on the 2.0L turbocharged and 2.1L engines. Tighten the new drive belt to 180 lbs. strand tension or a used belt to 120 lbs. strand tension.

9. Install the inner fender panel and the right front wheel. Lower the vehicle and check oil pump operation.

Rear Main Bearing Oil Seal

REMOVAL AND INSTALLATION

This seal is otherwise known as the crankshaft seal at the flywheel end. The seal can be changed with the engine in the vehicle, but the clutch and flywheel must first be removed.

1. Remove the transaxle and the flywheel from the vehicle.

2. Pry the old seal ring from the crankshaft, using an appropriate tool. Take care not to damage the crankshaft or sealing flange.

3. Install the new seal with the spring ring turned inwards toward the crankshaft using tool 83-92-540 or equivalent.

4. Install the flywheel and transaxle.

ENGINE COOLING

Radiator

REMOVAL AND INSTALLATION

1. Disconnect the negative battery cable.

2. Drain the cooling system.

3. Remove the radiator grille.

4. If equipped with automatic transaxle, disconnect and plug the transaxle cooler lines.

5. Disconnect the hoses from the radiator.

6. Disconnect the electrical leads to the radiator fan and the auxiliary fan, if equipped.

7. Disconnect the electrical lead to the thermal switch and solenoid valve. Remove the ignition coil and solenoid valve from the bracket. Remove the oil cooler.

8. Remove the upper radiator support.

9. Lift the radiator out of the vehicle, by pulling the top of the radiator slightly backwards.

To install:

10. Place the radiator into position in the vehicle. Install the upper radiator support.

11. Install the oil cooler. Install the ignition coil and solenoid valve to the bracket. Connect the electrical lead to the thermal switch and solenoid valve.

12. Connect the electrical leads to the radiator fan and the auxiliary fan, if equipped.

13. Connect the hoses from the radiator.

14. If equipped with automatic transaxle, connect and plug the transaxle cooler lines.

15. Install the radiator grille.

16. Fill the cooling system.

17. Connect the negative battery cable.

18. Start the engine and check for leaks.

19. Recheck the cooling system and adjust, as required.

Heater Core

REMOVAL AND INSTALLATION

900 Series

1. Disconnect the negative battery cable.

2. Remove the dash panel under the switches on the steering column and the lower section of the instrument panel.

3. Remove the air diffuser and retaining screws.

4. Remove the left defroster and speaker grille.

5. Remove the control rod from between the coolant shut off valve and the control rod by sliding the rod as far forward as it will go to free it from

the knob, then pull it rearward to free it from the shut off valve.

NOTE: The plastic joint at the control knob is accessible from underneath once the switches below the heater controls have been moved backward.

6. Remove the lower section of the heater housing.

7. Drain the coolant and disconnect the hoses. Plug the ends of the hoses to prevent coolant from leaking into the compartment.

8. Separate the heater core from the housing and guide it backward and downward. It will be necessary to disconnect the brake pedal return spring and depress the brake pedal slightly.

9. The water valve and the heater core can be separated after their removal. Do not kink or break the capillary tube.

To install:

10. Carefully guide the heater core and valve assembly into the housing.

11. Connect the heater hoses.

12. Install the lower heater housing section.

13. Install the control rod to the shut off valve.

14. Install the left defroster and speaker grille.

15. Install the air diffuser and retaining screws.

16. Install the lower instrument panel section.

17. Connect the negative battery cable.

18. Start the engine and check for leaks.

19. Recheck the cooling system and adjust, as required.

9000 Series

1. Disconnect the negative battery cable.

2. Remove the hood assembly.

3. Disconnect the wiper arms. Remove the covers on the evaporator and wiper motor. Unplug the connector for the fan control unit on vehicles with automatic climate control.

4. Remove the false fire wall panel. Drain the radiator.

5. Remove the plastic drainage tube moulding below the windshield moulding.

6. Remove the securing bolts the electronic ignition control unit and position it aside.

7. Remove the clip and unplug the connectors. Remove the complete wiper assembly.

8. Remove the rubber lead through panel for the coolant hoses.

Drain cooling system. Disconnect the quick release couplings for the coolant hoses at the heat exchanger.

9. Remove the throttle dashpot assembly.

10. Remove the vacuum pump retaining screws. Position the pump aside.

11. Remove the evaporator body retaining screws and the clips for the refrigerant hoses.

12. Remove the lock washer and disconnect the cable for the temperature valve.

13. Carefully lift the evaporator and remove the clips on either side of the fan. Remove the complete fan assembly by twisting the fan diagonally upwards.

14. Remove the screw in the center of the casing. Release the clips and the grille at the discharge duct.

15. Separate the fan housing and remove the securing screw for the fan motor.

16. Lift the cover upward and withdraw the motor complete with the impeller.

17. Release the retaining clips and disconnect the hoses from the heater core.

18. Pull the heater core from the engine side of the fire wall.

To install:

19. Install the heater core, attach the retaining clips and connect the heater hoses.

20. Install the fan housing and motor.

21. Install the evaporator and vacuum pump.

22. Connect the temperature valve cable.

23. Install the throttle dashpot assembly.

24. Install the wiper assembly and the drainage tube.

25. Install all covers, connect the wipers and connect all electrical connectors.

26. Install the hood.

27. Connect the negative battery cable.

28. Start the engine and check for leaks.

29. Recheck the cooling system and adjust, as required.

Water Pump

REMOVAL AND INSTALLATION

1. Disconnect the negative battery cable.

2. Drain the cooling system.

3. Raise and support the vehicle safely.

4. Remove the right front wheel assembly. Remove the front section of the inner fender panel.

5. Loosen the drive belts. Remove the water pump pulley and the belt tensioning pulley.

6. Remove the clips holding the oil lines at the oil cooler.

7. Remove the clips securing the water pipe to the engine block.

8. Remove the coolant hoses from the water pump.

9. Remove the bolt securing the water pump to the bracket. Remove the water pump.

To install:

10. Place the water pump into position and install the retaining bolts. Tighten the bolts to 15 ft. lbs. (20 Nm).

11. Install the coolant hoses from the water pump.

12. Install the clips holding the oil lines at the oil cooler and water pipe to the engine block.

13. Install the water pump pulley and the belt tensioning pulley. Adjust the drive belts.

14. Install the front section of the inner fender panel and the right front wheel assembly.

15. Lower the vehicle.

16. Connect the negative battery cable.

17. Start the engine and check for leaks.

18. Recheck the cooling system and adjust, as required.

Thermostat

REMOVAL AND INSTALLATION

1. Disconnect the negative battery cable.

2. Drain the cooling system.

3. Remove the thermostat housing retaining bolts and remove the housing in order to gain access to the thermostats.

4. Remove the thermostats.

5. Installation is the reverse of the removal procedure. When installing the new thermostat, always install with the spring facing down. Use sealing compound on the joining surfaces of the elbow and head. Tighten the bolts to 13 ft. lbs. (18 Nm).

Cooling System Bleeding

On 900 Series vehicles only, the bleeder nipple, located in the thermostat housing cover, should be opened when adding coolant to the system.

The nipple should not be opened when the engine is running.

9000 Series vehicles do not require a special bleeding procedure. Fill the engine with coolant, start the engine and allow it to reach operating temperature (thermostat open) and check the coolant level. Add coolant as necessary.

ENGINE ELECTRICAL

NOTE: Disconnecting the negative battery cable on some vehicles may interfere with the functions of the on-board computer systems and may require the computer to undergo a relearning process, once the negative battery cable is reconnected.

Distributor

REMOVAL

1. Rotate the engine until the No. 1 piston is at TDC of the compression stroke (crankshaft mark and timing mark aligned).
2. Disconnect the negative battery cable. Remove all necessary components in order to gain access to the distributor assembly.
3. Remove the distributor cap with the spark plug wires attached and position it out of the way.
4. Disconnect the distributor wiring connector and vacuum hoses. Be sure to tag all the wires and vacuum lines for easy installation.
5. Matchmark the distributor housing, base and the engine block for installation reference.
6. Remove the distributor base retaining nut. Remove the distributor.

NOTE: Do not rotate the engine while the distributor is removed from the engine.

INSTALLATION

Timing Not Disturbed

1. Check to ensure the crankshaft mark and timing mark are still aligned.
2. Fit the distributor into position, while aligning the matchmark on the distributor housing and the engine block.
3. Install the distributor hold-down flange and retaining bolt.
4. Connect all wiring and vacuum hoses. Reinstall distributor cap.
5. Connect the negative battery cable.
6. Start the engine. Check the ignition timing. Reset if necessary.

Timing Disturbed

1. Remove the spark plug from No. 1 cylinder. Position a finger over the plug hole. Have a helper rotate the engine. When compression pressure starts to build, it indicates the cylinder is coming up on its compression stroke. Continue rotating the engine so the timing marks align with the TDC mark.
2. Install the distributor assembly while aligning the matchmark on the distributor and engine block.
3. Connect all wiring and vacuum hoses. Reinstall distributor cap.
4. Connect the negative battery cable.
5. Start engine and set timing. Then tighten distributor mounting nut.

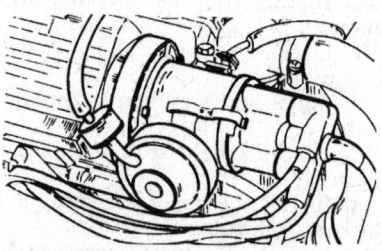

Distributor assembly location

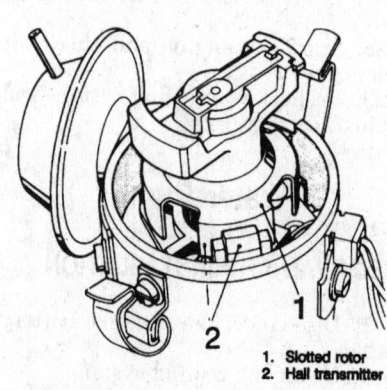

1. Slotted rotor
2. Hall transmitter

Distributor assembly with hall effect pickup

Distributorless Ignition

REMOVAL AND INSTALLATION

Crankshaft Sensor

1. Disconnect the negative battery cable.
2. Install a flywheel lock tool 83-93-993 or equivalent, to the flywheel.
3. Remove the front section of the right fender well. Remove the air conditioner belt.
4. Remove the center bolt and remove the idler wheel pulley. Remove the alternator belt.
5. Remove the crankshaft pulley. Remove the crankshaft sensor. Disconnect the electrical connector and slip through the wire tie.

To install:

6. Install the crankshaft sensor and connect the electrical connector. The crankshaft sensor bolts must be installed using Loctite® 270 or equivalent.
7. Install the crankshaft pulley.
8. Install the alternator belt, idler wheel pulley, air conditioner belt and right fender well.
9. Remove the flywheel lock and connect the negative battery cable.

Slotted Rotor

1. Disconnect the negative battery cable.
2. Install a flywheel lock tool 83-93-993 or equivalent, to the flywheel.
3. Remove the front section of the right fender well. Remove the air conditioner belt.
4. Loosen the bolt and nut on the belt tensioner. Remove the alternator belt.
5. Remove the crankshaft pulley. Remove the rotor.

To install:

6. Install the new rotor on the pulley. Install the crankshaft pulley and tighten the bolt to 140 ft. lbs. (190 Nm).
7. Install the alternator belt, idler wheel pulley, air conditioner belt and right fender well.
8. Remove the flywheel lock and connect the negative battery cable.

Ignition Coils

1. Disconnect the negative battery cable.
2. Remove the 4 bolts securing the ignition cartridge to the camshaft cover. Remove and invert the cartridge.

3. Remove the coil shroud retaining screws and remove the shroud.

4. Remove the ignition coil by lifting upward.

5. Installation is the reverse of removal. Tighten the ignition cartridge bolts to 9 ft. lbs. (12 Nm).

Ignition Timing

ADJUSTMENT

Conventional Method

1. Start the engine and allow it to reach normal operating temperature.

2. Apply the hand brake and position the gear selector in neutral for a manual transaxle or **P** for an automatic transaxle. Turn the engine and all accessories OFF.

3. Install a tachometer (connect between the negative side of the coil and ground) and check the idle speed. Adjust as necessary.

4. Disconnect and plug the vacuum advance lines at the distributor, if equipped.

5. Stop the engine and connect the timing light. Connect the power leads to the battery and the inductive pickup to the No. 1 plug wire.

6. Start the engine and allow it to idle. Point the timing light at the mark on the front cover and read the basic timing by noting the position of the groove in the front pulley in relation to the timing mark or scale on the front cover. If the timing is incorrect, loosen the distributor mounting bolt. Turn the distributor slightly to adjust timing.

7. When the reading is correct, tighten the distributor mounting bolt and turn the ignition **OFF**.

8. Reconnect the distributor advance line. Disconnect the timing light and tachometer.

Ignition Service Instrument Method

Saab ignition service instrument consists of a tachometer, camshaft angle meter, stroboscope lamp and switch for operating the starter.

The ignition service instrument is connected to the clutch cover by means of a special connector and the plug lead No. 1 cylinder by means of a terminal. The ignition service instrument is also connected to the ignition service socket at the fuse box and by means of an impulse transmitter at the plug lead for No. 1 cylinder.

The timing indicator consists of a pin in the engine flywheel and a service socket in the clutch cover.

Alternator

PRECAUTIONS

Several precautions must be observed with alternator equipped vehicles to avoid damage to the unit.

• If the battery is removed for any reason, make sure it is reconnected with the correct polarity. Reversing the battery connections may result in damage to the rectifiers.

• When utilizing a booster battery as a starting aid, always connect the positive to positive terminals and the negative terminal from the booster battery to a good engine ground on the vehicle being started.

• Never use a fast charger as a booster to start vehicles.

• Disconnect the battery cables when charging the battery with a fast charger.

• Never attempt to polarize the alternator.

• Do not use test lamps of more than 12 volts when checking diode continuity.

• Do not short across or ground any of the alternator terminals.

• The polarity of the battery, alternator and regulator must be matched and considered before making any electrical connections within the system.

• Never separate the alternator on an open circuit. Make sure all connections within the circuit are clean and tight.

• Disconnect the battery ground terminal when performing any service on electrical components.

• Disconnect the battery if arc welding is to be done on the vehicle.

BELT TENSION ADJUSTMENT

Adjust the alternator belt tension so the belt can be depressed about ½ in. at the mid-point of its longest straight run.

REMOVAL AND INSTALLATION

2.0L and 2.1L Engines

1. Disconnect the negative battery cable.

2. Raise and support the vehicle safely.

3. Remove the right front wheel assembly.

4. Remove the inner fender panel from the right fender.

5. Loosen the alternator belt and remove it from the alternator pulley.

6. Remove the alternator wire connections from the rear of the alternator.

7. Loosen the 2 securing bolts for the alternator.

8. Using a prybar, push the alternator to the left, pull the alternator forward and remove it from the vehicle.

To install:

9. Place the alternator into position and install the mounting and pivot bolts. Do not tighten at this time.

10. Connect the alternator electrical wirings.

11. Install the alternator belt and adjust the tension. Tighten the pivot bolt and mounting bolt.

12. Install the inner fender panel and right front wheel assembly.

13. Lower the vehicle.

14. Connect the negative battery cable.

2.3L Engine

1. Disconnect the negative battery cable.

2. Remove the right front wheel and inner wheel well.

3. Remove the serpentine belt.

4. Remove the brace bar from between the wheel arch and the subframe.

5. Remove the 2 securing bolts and remove the power steering pump by dropping it down and towards the rear.

6. Remove the 2 securing bolts and drop the alternator down and towards the rear. Remove the pump bracket.

7. Disconnect the electrical leads from the alternator and remove it by lifting it towards the front of the vehicle.

To install:

8. Connect the leads to the alternator and place it in position in the engine compartment.

9. Install the bracket for the power steering pump.

10. Install the top bolt in the alternator, leaving it loose. Align the alternator, secure it to the bracket and tighten the bolts.

11. Install the power steering pump, brace bar, serpentine belt, wheel well and wheel. Reconnect the negative battery cable.

Starter

REMOVAL AND INSTALLATION

Except Turbocharged and 2.3L Engines

1. Disconnect the negative battery cable.
2. Remove the flywheel cover. Remove the transaxle dipstick, if equipped with manual transaxle.
3. Remove the starter motor heat shield and the rear mounting bolts.
4. Disconnect the starter motor wires. Remove the front mounting bolts.
5. Remove the starter from the vehicle.
6. Installation is the reverse of removal.

Turbocharged Engines

1. Disconnect the negative battery cable. Remove the battery and the battery tray.
2. Remove the turbocharger suction pipe, preheater hose and the flywheel cover.
3. On manual transaxle, remove the dipstick. Remove the bracket and bolts between the turbocharger and the transaxle.
4. Disconnect the starter motor wires.
5. Loosen the oil return pipe on the turbocharger enough to allow it to be bent slightly.
6. Remove the starter motor heat shield and the rear mounting bolts.
7. Remove the front starter mounting bolts.
8. Remove the starter from the vehicle. The starter will have to be tilted downward and then lifted out forward.
To install:
9. Place the starter into position and install the mounting bolts. Connect the starter motor wires.
10. Install the starter motor heat shield and the rear mounting bolts.
11. Connect the turbocharger oil return pipe, using a new gasket.
12. If equipped with manual transaxle, install the dipstick. Install the bracket and bolts between the turbocharger and the transaxle.
13. Install the turbocharger suction pipe, preheater hose and the flywheel cover.
14. Install the battery tray and battery. Connect the battery cables, negative terminal last.

2.3L Engine

1. Disconnect the negative battery cable.
2. Remove the rubber elbow from between the air mass meter and throttle housing. Remove the top bolt in the inlet manifold brace bar.
3. Loosen the top bolt for the starter motor using an appropriate wrench and then remove the bolt using a flexible socket extension.
4. Disconnect the electrical leads and remove the lower securing bolt from below. Move the brace bar out of the way.
5. Remove the starter motor by lifting it towards the rear and up between the inlet manifold and brake master cylinder.
To install:
6. Lift the starter motor into position. Install the top bolt first, leaving it loose, and then the bottom bolt using a flexible socket extension.
7. Ensure that the starter motor is properly aligned and tighten the top bolt using an appropriate wrench.
8. Tighten the bottom bolt (with the brace bar installed) from underneath and reconnect the electrical connectors.
9. Tighten the top bolt in the inlet manifold brace bar. Install the rubber elbow. Reconnect the negative battery cable.

EMISSION CONTROLS

Emission Warning Lamps

RESETTING

EXS/EXH Warning Lamp

Some models are equipped with a mileage counter and have a dash-mounted EXS (EXH on certain models) warning light that will illuminate at approximately 30,000 mile intervals as a reminder to replace the oxygen sensor. After replacing the sensor and performing any other emission system maintenance, the warning light must be reset.

Locate the counter under the instrument panel, to the left of the steering column, next to the flasher relay. Push in the reset button and check that the warning light goes out.

NOTE: Even though the mileage counter is hard to see, there should be no problem in reaching under the instrument panel and locating it with your hand. You can also find it by reaching behind the knee panel or through the left defroster duct.

Check Engine Light

The CHECK ENGINE light will illuminate when a fault is sensed in the engine management system. The fault will be memorised by the ECU for recall later. Once the fault has been recalled and repaired, the memory must be erased.

With the jumper switch in position to recall the fault codes, switch the jumper **ON** for approximately 2.5 seconds. The light should flash 3 times quickly and then switch the jumper **OFF**. The codes are now erased.

FUEL SYSTEM

Fuel System Service Precautions

Safety is the most important factor when performing not only fuel system maintenance but any type of maintenance. Failure to conduct maintenance and repairs in a safe manner may result in serious personal injury or death. Maintenance and testing of the vehicle's fuel system components can be accomplished safely and effectively by adhering to the following rules and guidelines.

• To avoid the possibility of fire and personal injury, always disconnect the negative battery cable unless the repair or test procedure requires that battery voltage be applied.

• Always relieve the fuel system pressure prior to disconnecting any fuel system component (injector, fuel rail, pressure regulator, etc.), fitting or fuel line connection. Exercise extreme caution whenever relieving fuel system pressure to avoid exposing skin, face and eyes to fuel spray. Please be advised that fuel under pressure may penetrate the skin or any part of the body that it contacts.

• Always place a shop towel or cloth around the fitting or connection

Resetting the mileage counter

prior to loosening to absorb any excess fuel due to spillage. Ensure that all fuel spillage (should it occur) is quickly removed from engine surfaces. Ensure that all fuel soaked cloths or towels are deposited into a suitable waste container.

- Always keep a dry chemical (Class B) fire extinguisher near the work area.
- Do not allow fuel spray or fuel vapors to come into contact with a spark or open flame.
- Always use a backup wrench when loosening and tightening fuel line connection fittings. This will prevent unnecessary stress and torsion to fuel line piping. Always follow the proper torque specifications.
- Always replace worn fuel fitting O-rings with new. Do not substitute fuel hose or equivalent where fuel pipe is installed.

RELIEVING FUEL SYSTEM PRESSURE

1. Remove the luggage compartment floor and the panel over the fuel pump.
2. Disconnect the electrical connectors at the fuel pump. Remove the fuel pump fuse.
3. Crank the engine until fuel is exhausted from the system.
4. Disconnect the negative battery cable.

NOTE: Always place a shop rag into position, before loosening any fuel fittings. The shop rag will soak up any escaping fuel.

Fuel Tank

REMOVAL AND INSTALLATION

900 Series

1. Remove the luggage compartment floor, floor panel and cover over the fuel pump.
2. Drain the fuel tank, using the electrical fuel pump. Remove the fuel pump relay and operate the pump by connecting across terminals No. **30** and **27**.
3. Disconnect the negative battery cable.
4. Remove the cover from the fuel gauge sender unit and disconnect all electrical leads from the tank.
5. Remove the filler pipe and breather lines. Place a shop rag at fittings and disconnect the pressure and return fuel lines.
6. Remove the securing straps and lower the tank.
To install:
7. Check that the rubber seal is undamaged and correctly fitted to the opening of the gauge sender unit. Check that the straps are correctly fitted and plug the ends of the filler pipe and breather pipe.
8. Lift the tank into position and support by the straps. Adjust the position of the tank and then tighten the straps.
9. Reconnect all fuel lines. Ensure that the rubber grommet is in position.
10. Reconnect all electrical wiring to the fuel tank and install the covers.
11. Lower the vehicle.
12. Connect the negative battery cable.
13. Install the fuel pump relay. Add fuel and start the engine. Check for leaks.

9000 Series

1. Disconnect the negative battery cable.
2. Remove the 2 screws and lift out the luggage compartment floor. Remove the fuel tank cover and disconnect all electrical leads to the fuel tank.
3. Disconnect the fuel return line and drain the fuel tank.
4. Raise and support the vehicle safely.
5. Remove the left rear wheel.
6. Disconnect the fuel filter pipe and breather hose. Cap hoses to prevent fuel leakage and the entry of dirt.
7. Remove the parking brake cable and securing clip. Support the tank

and remove the fuel tank strap attaching nuts. Lower and remove the tank.
To install:
8. Ensure that the anti-splash device (butterfly) is vertical when installing the tank.
9. Lift the fuel tank into place and secure with the straps. Position the tank and tighten the strap attaching bolts.
10. Reconnect all fuel lines and electrical connectors.
11. Install the parking brake cable and rear wheel.
12. Lower the vehicle.
13. Install the fuel tank cover and luggage compartment floor.
14. Connect the negative battery cable.
15. Add fuel to the tank. Start the engine and check for leaks.

Fuel Filter

REMOVAL AND INSTALLATION

1. Relieve the fuel system pressure.
2. Disconnect the negative battery cable.
3. Place a shop rag into position. Loosen and remove the fuel filter fittings, using the proper wrench.
4. Remove the fuel filter assembly from the vehicle.
5. Installation is the reverse of the removal procedure. The filter is installed with arrows pointing in direction of flow.

Electric Fuel Pump

REMOVAL AND INSTALLATION

1. Disconnect the negative battery cable.
2. Relieve the fuel system pressure.
3. Remove the luggage compartment floor and pump cover.
4. Release the clip and disconnect the electrical connector to the fuel pump.
5. Disconnect the fuel lines from the pump and tie out of the way.
6. Remove the fuel pump screw top using tool 83-94-462 or equivalent. Lift the pump and transfer to a container. Tilt the pump to pour out the remaining fuel.
To install:
7. Place a new O-ring in the tank and place the pump in position. Ensure that the alignment marks are

inline. Tighten the fuel pump screw top to 40 ft. lbs. (50 Nm).

8. Place new O-rings inside the fuel line fittings and connect to the pump. Connect the electrical connector and install the safety clip.

9. Connect the negative battery cable and check that the pump is working properly. Install the pump cover and floor panel.

Fuel Injector

REMOVAL AND INSTALLATION

2.0L Engine

1. Clean the area around the injectors. Remove the false bulkhead panel.

2. Disconnect the fuel return line from the pressure regulator and the hose from the inlet manifold. Disconnect the line from the fuel filter.

3. Unplug the connectors on the injectors. Remove the fuel injection rail but leave the injectors in place.

4. Remove the O-ring seals for the injectors. Lift out the fuel rail complete with the injectors through the space between the inlet manifold and the bulkhead.

To install:

5. Release the clip to replace the injector.

6. Lubricate the injector O-ring with petroleum jelly. Install the injector in the reverse order of removal.

2.1L Engine

1. Detach the crankcase ventilation hose from the camshaft cover.

2. Unplug the electrical connectors from the injectors. Free the wiring loom by undoing the clip located at the fuel injection manifold.

3. Disconnect the banjo fittings at either end of the fuel injection manifold. Hold the injectors steady with a backup wrench.

4. Remove the bolts securing the fuel injection manifold to the inlet manifold. Lift off the fuel injection manifold complete with the injectors.

5. Slide off the clips located between the injectors and the manifold. Remove the injectors with a slight twist and a pull.

To install:

6. Prior to installation, check the O-rings on the injectors and replace any that are damaged.

7. Fit the injectors in the manifold. Check that the injectors are in the correct position and fully pushed into the inlet manifold.

8. The remainder of the installation procedure is the reverse of removal.

2.3L Engine

MULTIPORT FUEL INJECTION SYSTEM

1. Disconnect the fuel return line from the injection rail.

2. Disconnect the pulsator from the injection rail. Remove the tie and tuck the fuel line and pulsator out of the way.

3. Disconnect the vacuum hose from the pressure regulator. Unplug the connectors from the injectors.

4. Remove the bolts and lift off the injection rail complete with the injectors.

5. Remove the injector clips and then the injectors.

To install:

6. Before installing the injectors, lightly lubricate the O-rings with petroleum jelly. Fit the injection rail complete with injectors on the inlet manifold and tighten the bolts.

7. Plug the connectors into the injectors. Connect the vacuum hose to the pressure regulator. Connect the fuel hose with pulsator to the injection rail. Use a tie to secure the fuel hose.

8. Connect the fuel return line to the injection rail. Check that the system is working properly and inspect all connections for leaks.

TRIONIC ENGINE MANAGEMENT SYSTEM

1. Disconnect the negative battery cable.

2. Relieve the fuel system pressure.

3. Remove the lock mount and loosen the contact pieces for the injector.

4. Check the positions and remove the holders retaining the injector. Remove the injector.

NOTE: Before installing the injectors, lightly lubricate the O-rings with petroleum jelly.

5. Installation is the reverse of the removal procedure. Check to ensure the correct contact piece is connected to its respective injector.

DRIVE AXLE

Halfshaft

REMOVAL AND INSTALLATION

900 Series

NOTE: The entire front axle assembly must be removed in order to remove the halfshaft from the vehicle.

1. Disconnect the negative battery cable. Remove the upper shock absorber bolt.

2. Raise the vehicle and support it safely. Remove the wheel and tire assembly.

3. Remove the brake housing and position it on the wheel housing to avoid damage to the brake hose. Remove the brake disc and parking brake assembly along with the cable.

4. Remove the large clamp from the rubber bellows on the inner universal joint. To separate the inner universal joint, install the cover in the rubber bellows to stop the needle bearings from falling out and to keep dirt from entering. Install the protective cap on the inner driver.

5. Disconnect the tie rod from the steering arm using the proper tool. Remove the nut on the upper ball joint. Remove the bolts from the lower control arm bracket.

6. Remove the halfshaft through the wheel housing and remove the entire front axle assembly.

7. If the differential bearing cap is to be removed, remove the retaining bolts and remove the cap and the inner drive using the proper removal tools.

To install:

8. Install the halfshaft through the wheel housing.

9. Install the lower control arm, upper ball joint and tie rod.

10. Install the rubber bellows on the halfshafts after inserting them into the transaxle.

11. Install the brake system components previously removed. Install the wheel and tire assemblies. Lower the vehicle.

12. Install the upper shock absorber bolt and connect the negative battery. Check the alignment and test drive the vehicle.

9000 Series

1. Disconnect the negative battery cable. Remove the hubcap and loosen

the center axle nut. Raise and support the vehicle safely.

2. Remove the inner fender panel for working access.

3. Unbolt the MacPherson strut from the steering swivel member and detach the flexible brake hose from the clip on the strut.

4. Loosen the clip on the rubber boot on the inboard universal joint.

5. Separate the 2 halves of the joint. Install protective covers over the rubber boot and the drive axle.

6. Remove the hub center nut and withdraw the halfshaft from the steering swivel member.

To install:

7. Install the halfshaft and hub center nut. Tighten the hub center nut to 207-221 ft. lbs. (280-300 Nm).

8. Join the 2 halves of the joint and install the rubber boot.

9. Install the MacPherson strut and tighten the strut-to-steering swivel bolts to 58-77 ft. lbs. (78-105 Nm).

10. Install the brake hose and inner fender panel. Lower the vehicle and connect the negative battery cable. Check the alignment and test drive the vehicle.

CV-Boot

REMOVAL AND INSTALLATION

1. Place spacer tool 83-93-209 or equivalent, between the underside of the top wishbone and the body.

2. Raise and support the vehicle safely. Remove the front wheel.

3. Remove the CV-clamps and loosen CV-boot.

4. Remove the halfshaft and steering knuckle assembly. Remove the CV-boot.

To install:

5. Install the new CV-boot on the intermediate shaft. Assemble the halfshaft and steering knuckle to the intermediate shaft.

6. Pack the CV-joint and boot with grease.

7. Complete installation of the halfshaft and tighten the CV-boot clamps.

8. Install the front wheel, lower the vehicle and remove the spacer tool.

Rear Wheel Hub, Bearing and Seal

REMOVAL AND INSTALLATION

1. Raise the rear of the vehicle and support it with safety stands. Remove the wheel.

2. Unbolt and remove the brake caliper and backing plate. Position them on the rear axle without disconnecting the brake line.

3. Remove the bolt and pull off the brake disc.

4. Pry off the hub nut dust cap. Remove the hub nut and thrust washer and pull off the hub assembly.

5. Check the stub axle for damage and install the hub assembly.

6. Install the thrust washer and tighten the nut to 207-221 ft. lbs. (280-300 Nm) on 900 Series or 195-208 ft. lbs. (270-290 Nm) on 9000 Series. Stake the nut with a cold chisel and press the dust cap into place.

7. Install the brake disc. Install the caliper and tighten the bolts to 51-65 ft. lbs. (70-90 Nm).

8. Install the wheel and lower the vehicle.

Front Wheel Hub, Knuckle and Bearings

REMOVAL AND INSTALLATION

900 Series

NOTE: The entire front axle assembly must be removed from the vehicle when removing the wheel bearings.

1. Disconnect the negative battery cable. Remove the upper bolt of the shock absorber.

2. Raise the vehicle and support it safely. Remove the tire and wheel assembly.

3. Remove the brake housing and position it by the wheel housing to avoid damage to the brake hose. Remove the brake disc and parking brake assembly with the cable.

4. Remove the large clamp from the rubber bellows on the inner universal joint. To separate the inner universal joint, install the cover 73-23-736 or equivalent, in the rubber bellows to stop the needle bearing from falling out and to keep dirt from

entering. Install the protective cap 78-38-469 or equivalent, on the inner drive.

5. Disconnect the tie rod from the steering arm using the proper tool. Remove the nut on the upper ball joint. Remove the bolts from the lower control arm bracket.

6. Remove the halfshaft through the wheel housing and remove the entire front axle assembly.

7. Place the steering knuckle housing in a press and press out the halfshaft.

8. Remove the lockring and press out the bearing using a suitable drift.

To install:

9. Install the bearing and secure the lockring. Using a press, install the halfshaft.

10. Install the halfshaft through the wheel housing. Install the lower control arm, upper ball joint and tie rod.

11. Install the rubber bellows on the halfshaft after installation.

12. Install all brake system components previously removed. Install the wheel and tire, and lower the vehicle.

13. Connect the negative battery cable, install the upper shock absorber bolt and check the alignment. Test drive the vehicle.

9000 Series

The front wheel bearing are double row angular contact bearings which are permanently lubricated and maintenance free. The bearings cannot be replaced individually.

1. Loosen the hub center nut and the wheel bolts.

2. Raise the vehicle and support it safely.

3. Remove the tire and wheel assembly. Remove the hub center nut and thrust washer.

4. Remove the flexible brake hose from its support clip.

5. Unbolt the caliper and rest it upon the suspension arm.

6. Unscrew the locating stud for the disc and remove it from the hub.

7. Push in on the halfshaft. Remove the 4 bolts securing the hub to the steering swivel member.

8. Lift the hub and disc back plate from the suspension assembly. Renew the bearings or replace the hub.

9. Installation is in the reverse of the removal procedure.

10. Tighten the hub securing bolts to 37-44 ft. lbs. (50-60 Nm) and the center hub nut to 207-221 ft. lbs. (280-300 Nm).

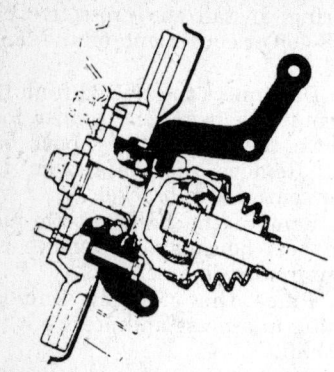

Front axle assembly — 9000 Series shown

MANUAL TRANSAXLE

Transaxle Assembly

REMOVAL AND INSTALLATION

900 Series

1. Disconnect the negative battery cable.
2. Remove the engine and transaxle from the vehicle as an assembly.
3. Position the engine and transaxle assembly in a suitable holding fixture. Drain the engine oil.
4. Remove the clutch shaft using a slide hammer and tool 87-90-529 or equivalent. Remove the slave cylinder retaining bolts.
5. Remove the transaxle-to-engine mounting bolts. Separate the transaxle from the engine assembly.
6. Installation is the reverse of the removal procedure.

9000 Series

1. Remove the battery, washer fluid container and connectors, terminal blocks, battery tray and release the stay for the hydraulic unit on ABS equipped vehicles.
2. Remove the 8 bolts for the bulkhead cover. If equipped with 2.3L engine, remove the rubber strip. Lift the cover and disconnect the washer hoses from the nozzle. Remove the cover.
3. On 2.3L equipped vehicles, separate the speedometer cable connector by first removing the washer hose and then the speedometer cable through the rubber grommet.
4. Disconnect the electrical connector from the air mass meter. On 2.3L equipped vehicles, disconnect

the connector for the intake air temperature sensor. Disconnect the hose on the delivery pipe from the bypass valve.
5. On 2.3L equipped vehicles, Remove the delivery pipe between the throttle housing and the intercooler. Also, remove the nuts retaining the starter motor. Remove the starter and place it on the steering gear.
6. Separate the selector rod universal joint and selector rod. Pinch the slave cylinder pressure hose with clamping tongs and separate the pressure line.
7. Remove the upper bolts for the stay at the wheel housing. Release the left hand engine mounting. Attach a sling to the engine lifting beam. Raise and support the vehicle safely.
8. Remove the left wheel and wheel housing liner. Disconnect the reverse light connector from the transaxle.
9. Separate the suspension arm from the ball joint. Remove the antiroll bar. Remove the lower bolt for the stay at the wheel housing and the 3 bottom bolts from the joint between the engine and the transaxle.
10. Remove the center and left skirts under the spoiler. Separate the sub-frame at the front and rear. Lower the sub-frame. Remove the universal joint and lower the vehicle.
11. Sling the transaxle from the workshop hoist and remove the top nut and bolt from the joint face. Remove the transaxle and lower to the floor.

To install:
12. Prior to installation, ensure that the halfshaft is in position and the aluminum tube is pressed into the seal.
13. Slide the transaxle into position, guiding the driver and input into place. Install the top bolt and nut into the joint face. Release the transaxle from the hoist. Raise and support the vehicle safely.
14. Fit the 3 bottom bolts into the joint face and tighten to 40-74 ft. lbs. (54-100 Nm). Install the universal joint. Raise the sub-frame into position and secure.
15. Install the anti-roll bar, suspension to the ball joint and the bracket for the wheel housing stay. Do not tighten the wheel housing stay bolt. Lower the vehicle.
16. Remove the lifting beam. Install the starter and the top mounting of the wheel housing. Now tighten all wheel housing bolts.
17. Tighten the left engine mount. Raise and support the vehicle safely.

18. Connect the negative battery cable and reverse light switch. Install the wheel housing liners, left wheel, under car skirts, selector rod universal joint, slave cylinder pressure pipe (remove the clamping tongs), speedometer cable, washer hose and the remainder of the components removed.
19. Bleed the slave cylinder, check the oil level and road test the vehicle.

LINKAGE ADJUSTMENT

900 Series

1. Engage reverse gear and turn the ignition key to the **LOCKED** position.
2. Move the gear lever back and forth. The selector rod should then move 0.12-0.16 in. (3-4mm).
3. Adjust by moving the housing longitudinally. Use special tool 87-90-370 or equivalent, to loosen the gear lever housing bolts.

9000 Series

1. Lock the gear lever in reverse by inserting a 0.16 in. (4mm) drill bit through the locating holes in the gear lever and lever housing. Remove the rubber boot for access to the holes.
2. Connect the selector rod to the selector universal joint and tighten the pinch bolt to 22-25 ft. lbs. (30-33 Nm).
3. Remove the drill bit and install the rubber boot.

CLUTCH

Clutch Assembly

REMOVAL AND INSTALLATION

900 Series

1. Disconnect the negative battery cable.
2. Remove the hood assembly. Remove the preheater hose and clutch housing cover.
3. Install the spacer 83-90-023 or equivalent, between the clutch fork and the diaphragm spring. Keep the clutch pedal depressed when the ring is being installed.
4. Unhook the spring clip and remove the cover located in front of the clutch shaft. Remove the clutch shaft plastic propeller.
5. Remove the clutch shaft by means of a M8 bolt installed in the

shaft end and tool 83-93-175 or equivalent. Withdraw the shaft as far as possible.

6. Remove the clutch slave cylinder retaining bolts.

7. Remove the clutch retaining bolts and remove the clutch, clutch disc and the slave cylinder complete with the clutch release bearing. Be sure the slave cylinder sleeve is not damaged by the clutch during the removal procedure.

To install:

8. Before re-assembling the clutch, check the condition of the clutch shaft seal located in the primary drive chain case and the condition of the support bearing in the flywheel.

9. Install the pressure plate, clutch plate and slave cylinder with release bearing as one unit onto the flywheel housing.

NOTE: Lubricate the clutch shaft splines sparingly with molybdenum disulfide paste.

10. Push the clutch shaft into engagement with the clutch plate splines and into the support bearing in the flywheel. Install 2 of the pressure plate bolts, but do not tighten them.

11. Tap in the clutch shaft so it is locked by the snapring in the primary drive sprocket.

12. Install the slave cylinder to the primary chain case. Apply thread sealing compound to the bolts.

13. Install the plastic propeller to the end of the clutch shaft. Install the seal, cover and wire clip in the front of the clutch shaft.

14. Bolt the pressure plate unit to the flywheel.

15. Have an assistant press down the clutch pedal and remove the spacer ring which was installed during removal.

NOTE: Do not depress the clutch pedal further than necessary to remove the spacer.

16. Pull the movable locking ring towards the slave cylinder housing while the clutch pedal is depressed.

17. After the clutch is installed, push the plastic sleeve against the release bearing, as required.

18. Install the flywheel housing cover and preheater hose.

19. Refit the hood. Connect the negative battery cable.

9000 Series

1. Disconnect the negative battery cable.

2. Remove the transaxle assembly.

3. Install a flywheel locking tool, if available and remove the clutch assembly from the flywheel.

To install:

4. Use a centering arbor type tool or an appropriate input shaft to center the clutch plate to the flywheel.

5. Tighten the pressure plate bolts to 10-19 ft. lbs. (13-25 Nm). Remove the flywheel lock, if used.

6. Slide the transaxle assembly over the locating dowels, engaging the transaxle input shaft into the clutch plate splines.

7. Secure the transaxle to the engine with the necessary attaching bolts. Remove the lifting sling from the transaxle.

8. Continue the installation in the reverse order of the removal procedure.

PEDAL HEIGHT/FREE-PLAY ADJUSTMENT

The clutch system in all vehicles is hydraulically operated. The slave cylinder acts directly on the release bearing and adjustment of the clutch is automatic.

Clutch Master Cylinder

REMOVAL AND INSTALLATION

1. Remove the sound baffle. Remove the clip and withdraw the clevis pin from the master cylinder pushrod.

2. Place a suitable drip tray under the pressure pipe. Pinch the supply hose with clamping tongs. Disconnect the pressure pipe from the master cylinder.

3. Remove the master cylinder mounting bolts and remove the master cylinder.

4. Release the clamping tongs and disconnect the supply hose from the master cylinder.

To install:

5. Install the supply hose and pressure pipe nipple on the master cylinder.

6. Install the master cylinder on its mounting. Tighten the pressure pipe nipple and remove the clamping tongs.

7. Install the clevis pin and the sound baffle. Bleed the system and test the operation of the clutch.

Clutch Slave Cylinder

ADJUSTMENT

The slave cylinder acts directly on the release bearing and adjustment of the clutch is automatic.

REMOVAL AND INSTALLATION

900 Series

1. Disconnect the negative battery cable.

2. Remove the clutch assembly.

3. Remove the clutch release bearing together with the clutch slave cylinder.

4. Installation is the reverse of the removal procedure.

9000 Series

1. Disconnect the negative battery cable.

2. Remove the transaxle from the vehicle.

3. Remove the clutch release bearing. Disconnect the pressure pipe. Remove the bleed nipple.

4. Remove the retaining bolts that hold the slave cylinder in place.

5. Remove the clutch slave cylinder.

6. Installation is the reverse of the removal procedure.

Hydraulic Clutch System Bleeding

1. Connect a hose to the slave cylinder bleeder valve. Place the other end of the hose in a suitable jar partially filled with brake fluid.

2. Fill the master cylinder with brake fluid.

3. Open the bleeder valve on the slave cylinder a ½ turn.

4. Place a cooling system tester gauge over the opening of the master cylinder.

5. Pump the tester until all air has been expelled from the system.

6. Close the slave cylinder bleeder valve.

7. Check that all air has been removed from the system and the clutch is operating properly. Adjust the fluid level, as required.

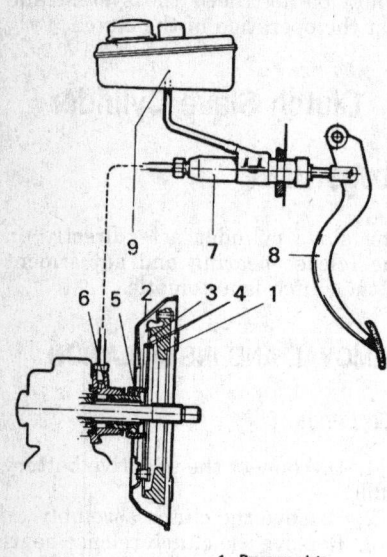

1. Pressure plate
2. Housing
3. Diaphragm spring
4. Pivot rings
5. Release bearing
6. Slave cylinder
7. Master cylinder
8. Clutch pedal
9. Clutch fluid reservoir

Clutch control — 900 Series

AUTOMATIC TRANSAXLE

Transaxle Assembly

REMOVAL AND INSTALLATION

900 Series

NOTE: The engine and transaxle must be removed as an assembly. Removal of the engine by itself is not recommended.

1. Disconnect both battery cables. Drain the engine coolant.

2. Disconnect the windshield washer hose. Mark the engine hood hinges. Remove engine hood retaining bolts then hood assembly.

3. Disconnect and remove the following items:

a. Disconnect all electrical connections from the starter motor.

b. Disconnect the upper radiator hose.

c. Disconnect all ground leads.

d. Disconnect the temperature sending unit electrical connection.

e. Remove the ignition coil.

f. Disconnect the lower radiator hose.

g. Remove the air cleaner, air intake, preheater hose, crankcase ventilation hose and intake hose.

h. Disconnect and plug the end of the fuel lines.

i. Disconnect the choke cable and the throttle cable.

j. Disconnect the hoses to the expansion tank.

k. Disconnect the oil pressure sending unit electrical connection.

l. Disconnect the alternator wiring harness.

m. Disconnect the heater hoses and the brake servo vacuum hoses.

4. Disconnect the electric wiring and fuel connections to the fuel injection system. Disconnect the flow meter and air cleaner with electrical connections.

5. If equipped with the APC system, disconnect the wiring to the solenoid valve. Remove the solenoid valve and the electrical connector to the knock sensor.

6. Remove the boot clips and rubber boots from the inner axle shafts.

7. Place special spacer tool 83-93-209 or equivalent, between the underside of the upper frame and the vehicle body from the wheel housing side. The spacer tool relieves the front suspension of load when the vehicle is raised.

8. Remove the lower end piece from the frame. Remove the steering knuckle package and support the end piece against the outer end of the frame.

9. Remove the gear selector cable retaining screw at the transaxle. Pull out the cable with the gear selector rod to its outer or **P** position. Move back the spring loaded sleeve on the gear selector rod and unhook the cable end piece.

10. Remove the exhaust pipe from the exhaust manifold.

11. Disconnect the speedometer cable from the transaxle.

12. Remove the rear engine mounting bolts.

13. Using a suitable lifting tool slightly raise the engine/transaxle assembly. Move the unit slightly to the side and remove the 2 universal joints.

14. Lift the engine transaxle assembly out of the vehicle. If equipped with power assisted steering, disconnect and plug the 2 hydraulic lines at the servo pump.

15. At this point of the procedure separate the engine from the automatic transaxle.

16. Clean the outside of the engine and automatic transaxle and drain the oil out of the engine.

17. Remove the cover over the flywheel ring gear. On turbocharged vehicles, remove the turbocharger support.

18. Remove the starter motor, if necessary.

19. Disconnect the throttle cable at the throttle housing.

20. Remove all retaining bolts between the engine and transaxle and disconnect the hydraulic hoses from the oil cooler.

21. Remove the retaining bolts securing the ring gear to the torque converter.

22. Turn the flexplate, so the plate angles will be horizontal. Carefully lift the engine off the transaxle.

23. Install the torque converter support special tool 87-90-255 or equivalent.

24. Position the transaxle assembly on suitable workstand or holding fixture.

To install:

25. Before installing the transaxle to the engine, make sure the mating surfaces are thoroughly clean.

26. Check that there are no cracks in the flexplate, particularly on turbocharged engine.

27. Remove the torque converter support. Apply anti-corrosion grease to the center pin of the torque converter and the center of the flexplate. Make sure the 2 guide sleeves are installed into the transaxle.

28. Install a new sheet metal gasket to the joint face of the transaxle. Apply Bostik silicone compound part 2680 or equivalent, into the grooves in the gasket. Install the transaxle to the engine.

29. Position the flexplate so the sheet metal angles are horizontal.

30. Take care not to damage the torque converter when lowering the engine onto the transaxle.

31. Apply thread sealing compound and tighten all retaining bolts.

32. Align the torque converter with the flexplate then gradually tighten the retaining bolts to 25-30 ft. lbs. (33-39 Nm).

33. Install the starter motor. Connect the throttle cable to the throttle housing.

34. On turbocharged vehicles, install the support for the turbocharger. Install the cover over the ring gear.

35. Refill the engine with the correct amount of engine oil.

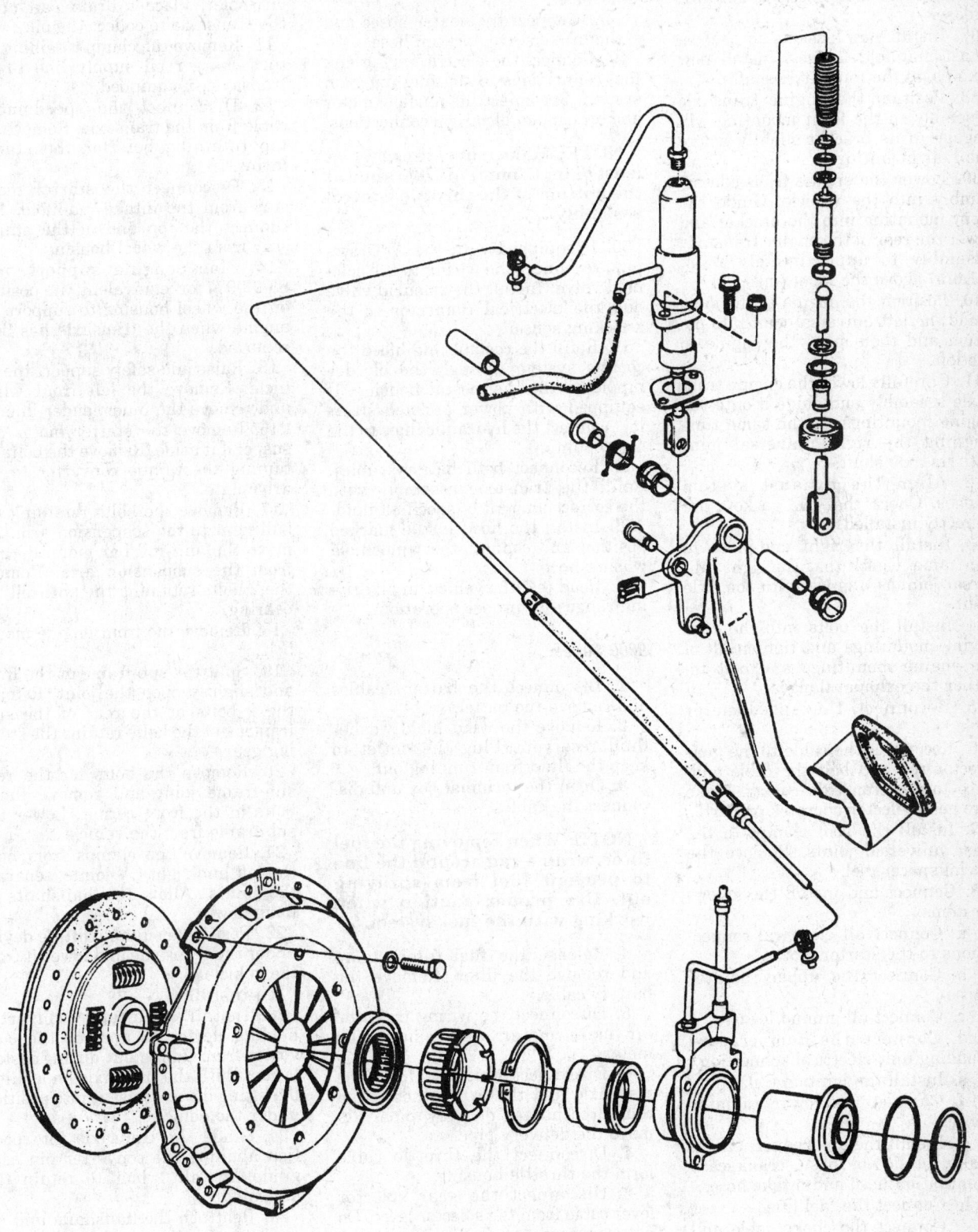

Clutch control — 9000 Series

36. Pack the inner universal joins and rubber boots with a suitable grease.

37. Install new gaskets to the exhaust manifold flanges. Install new clamps on the inner axle shafts.

38. Position the engine transaxle assembly so the front mounting will engage in its bracket slightly before the rear mountings.

39. Lower the engine transaxle assembly into the vehicle. Guide the front mounting into the bracket and lower the rear of the engine transaxle assembly to approximately 2 in. (51mm) above the mountings.

40. Position the engine to the side, guide the left universal joint into position and then move the engine to the left.

41. Carefully lower the engine transaxle assembly and guide it onto the engine mountings, at the same time aligning the right universal joint with its axle shaft.

42. Align the exhaust system flanges. Check that the gaskets are correctly installed.

43. Install the right end-piece to the frame. Check that the right universal joint is aligned with the axle shaft.

44. Install the bolts into the rear engine mountings and tighten all of the engine mountings and bolt together the exhaust flanges.

45. Reconnect the speedometer cable.

46. Reconnect the cable to the gear selector rod and bolt the cable end-piece to the transaxle casing. Make sure gear selector operates properly.

47. Install the boot clamps to the inner universal joints. Remove the special spacer tool.

48. Connect and install the following items:

a. Connect all electrical connections to the starter motor.

b. Connect the upper radiator hose.

c. Connect all ground leads.

d. Connect the temperature sending unit electrical connection.

e. Install the ignition coil.

f. Connect the lower radiator hose.

g. Install the air cleaner, air intake, preheater hose, crank case ventilation hose and intake hose.

h. Connect the fuel lines.

i. Connect the choke cable and the throttle cable.

j. Connect the hoses to the expansion tank.

k. Connect the oil pressure sending unit electrical connection.

l. Connect the alternator wiring harness.

m. Connect the heater hoses and the brake servo vacuum hoses.

49. Connect the electric wiring and fuel connections to the fuel injection system. Reconnect the air flow meter and air cleaner electrical connections.

NOTE: Make sure there is at least ½ in. (10mm) of clearance at the bottom of the throttle control assembly.

50. If equipped with the APC system, reconnect the wiring to the solenoid valve. Install the solenoid valve and the electrical connector to the knocking sensor.

51. Refill the coolant and bleed the cooling system through the bleeder nipple on the thermostat housing. If equipped with power assisted steering, connect the hydraulic lines to the servo pump.

52. Reconnect both battery cables. Refill the transaxle assembly with the correct amount of specified fluid.

53. Install the hood in the marked position and connect the windshield washer hose.

54. Road test the vehicle in all driving ranges for proper operation.

9000 Series

1. Disconnect the battery cables and remove the battery.

2. Remove the windshield washer fluid reservoir. Plug the outlet to keep the fluid from running out.

3. Open the terminal box and disconnect the cables.

NOTE: When removing the fuel filter, wrap a rag around the line to prevent fuel from spraying out. Use proper caution when working with the fuel system.

4. Release the fuel filter clamp and remove the filter. Remove the battery cable.

5. Disconnect the wiring from the air mass meter and remove the meter.

6. Disconnect the hose from the transaxle and the bypass hose from the turbocharger delivery pipe. Remove the delivery pipe.

7. Disconnect the throttle cable form the throttle housing.

8. Disconnect the gear selector lever cable from the selector lever. Do not separate the ball joint on the cable.

9. Disconnect the inlet hose from the oil cooler on top of the transaxle. Disconnect the selector lever from the transaxle.

10. Remove the return line from the oil cooler. Place a drain pan under the transaxle to collect the oil.

11. Remove the clamp retaining the turbocharger oil supply line to the transaxle, if equipped.

12. Disconnect the speedometer cable from the transaxle. Remove the top retaining bolt for the starter motor.

13. Disconnect the starter motor stay from the intake manifold. Disconnect the top end of the starter stay from the wheel housing.

14. Place engine support yoke 83-93-977 or equivalent, in position on the wheel housing to support the engine when the transaxle has been removed.

15. Raise and safely support the vehicle. Remove the left front wheel and remove the inner fender liner.

16. Remove the starter motor and suspend it aside. Remove the bolts retaining the torque converter to the driveplate.

17. Remove the bolts retaining the ball joint to the suspension arm. Remove the anti-roll bar mounting nut from the suspension arm. Remove the 2 bolts retaining the anti-roll bar bearing.

18. Remove the front engine mount bolt.

19. Split the sub-frame at the front and slightly open the joint. Remove the 2 bolts at the rear of the sub-frame, 1 of the bolts retains the steering gear.

20. Remove the bolts for the rear sub-frame joint and remove the 2 bolts in the front corner. Lower the sub-frame from the vehicle.

21. Remove the clamps from both the left and right CV-joints, separate the joints. Allow the halfshafts to hang down.

22. Position a suitable lifting device under the transaxle and lower it from the vehicle.

To install:

23. Install a suitable converter holding device to prevent the converter from falling out during installation. With the transaxle on a suitable lifting device, raise it into position under the vehicle.

24. Guide the transaxle into position aligning the converter pin as a guide. Install 1 bolt to retain the assembly.

25. Reattach the halfshafts and install the clamps over the CV-boots.

26. Install the transaxle mounting bolt through the engine mount.

27. Raise the sub-frame assembly into position. Make sure the engine mount is in position.

28. Install all sub-frame bolts and the engine mount bolt.

29. Install the anti-roll bar and bearing into the suspension arm. Install all of the suspension arm bolts.

30. Install the torque converter-to-driveplate bolts. Use Loctite® 242 or equivalent, on the bolts.

31. Install the starter and stay. Lower the vehicle.

32. Remove the engine support tool. Install the upper starter mount bolts. Connect the speedometer cable.

33. Install the turbocharger oil pipe to the engine block.

34. Reconnect the selector lever cable. The selector should be in the **N** detent. Adjust the selector as needed.

35. Reconnect the oil cooler hose to the transaxle oil cooler.

36. Reconnect the turbocharger delivery pipe. Install the air mass meter.

37. Install the battery tray. Install the fuel filter.

38. Attach the battery cable to the battery tray. Reconnect the cables to the terminal box.

39. Install the windshield washer fluid bottle and connect the electrical leads.

40. Install the battery and reconnect the cables.

41. Raise and safely support the vehicle.

42. Install the inner fender cover. Install the wheel and tire assembly.

43. Lower the vehicle, refill the fluid in the transaxle.

44. Road test the vehicle and check the operation of the transaxle. Adjust the throttle linkage as needed. Check the fluid level.

SHIFT LINKAGE ADJUSTMENT

1. Remove the gear selector lever cover.

2. Loosen the gear selector lever housing nuts with tool 83-91-23 or equivalent.

3. Lift the gear selector lever housing and turn it so the adjustment nuts of the cable will be reachable.

4. Adjust the cable longer or shorter, as required.

5. Assemble the gear selector housing and check the clearance in **N** and **D**.

6. The proper setting of the selector cable can be accomplished by adding or removing shims at the transaxle case end of the cable. A maximum of 3 shims may be used.

THROTTLE CABLE ADJUSTMENT

900 Series

1. Remove the screw for the pressure tap on the transaxle and connect a pressure gauge. Block the drive wheels and apply the parking brake.

2. Start the engine and check that the idle speed is 850 rpm in **P**.

3. Disconnect the throttle cable from the spindle lever and ensure that it is not binding. If so, clean the throttle cable thoroughly and reconnect.

4. With the gear selector in **D**, check that the cable is released and adjust the throttle cable to obtain the lowest possible pressure.

5. Readjust the cable so the pressure increases to 1.4 psi.

6. With the gear selector in **P**, check that the pressure is now 59-69 psi. Pressure should not be allowed to exceed 69 psi.

7. Tighten the cable locknuts.

9000 Series

1. With the engine idling, check the clearance between the cable stop and the end of the throttle cable. The clearance should be 0.08-0.10 in. (2.0-2.5mm).

2. If clearance is not within specification, loosen the locknuts and adjust the cable.

3. Tighten the locknuts and recheck the clearance.

FRONT SUSPENSION

Shock Absorbers

REMOVAL AND INSTALLATION

900 Series

1. Disconnect the negative battery cable. Remove the upper shock absorber nut.

2. Raise the vehicle and support it safely. Remove the tire and wheel assembly.

3. Remove the shock absorber retaining bolts. Remove the shock from the vehicle. Save all washers and rubber parts.

4. Installation is the reverse of removal. Tighten the lower shock bolts to 65 ft. lbs. (95 Nm).

MacPherson Strut

REMOVAL AND INSTALLATION

9000 Series

1. Disconnect the negative battery cable. Raise and support the vehicle safely. Remove the front tire and wheel assembly.

2. Remove the front brake hose from the retaining clip on the strut assembly.

3. Unbolt the strut from the steering swivel arm.

4. Remove the 3 retaining bolts from the top of the strut.

5. Remove the strut from the vehicle.

6. Installation is the reverse of the removal procedure. Tighten upper

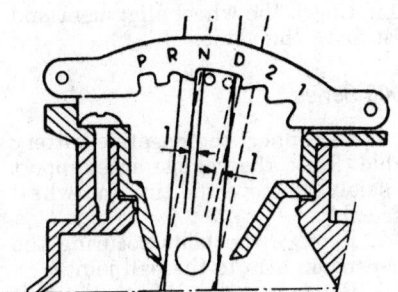

Manual linkage clearance, equal in "N" and "D"

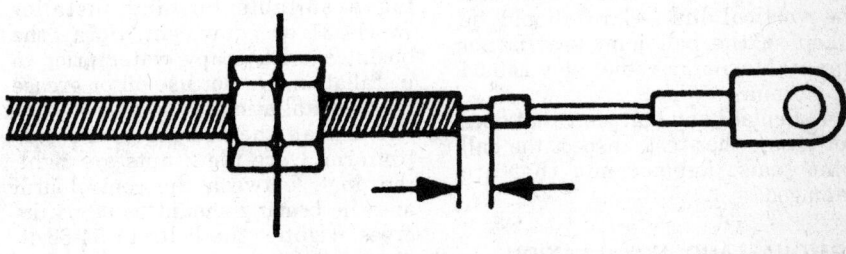

Throttle cable adjustment — 9000 Series

mounting bolts to 30-40 ft. lbs. (40-54 Nm) and lower mounting bolts to 58-77 ft. lbs. (78-105 Nm).

Coil Springs

REMOVAL AND INSTALLATION

900 Series

1. Disconnect the negative battery cable. Remove the upper shock absorber retaining nuts.
2. Raise and support the vehicle safely. Remove the tire and wheel assembly.
3. Install a spring compression tool or equivalent, engaging the upper shanks directly in the spring at the second free turn from the top of the lower shanks around the spring caps. These alignment shanks are located on the last turn of the spring with the color coded cup right beside the end of the coil.
4. Compress the spring at the top end, approximately 1½ inch. If the upper spring attachment of the steel cone is left behind in the wheel housing, remove it.
5. Remove the spring and the steel cone from the vehicle.
6. Installation is the reverse of removal.

Ball Joints

INSPECTION

NOTE: The pressure of the coil spring and shock absorber must be removed from the wishbones for correct ball joint play measurement.

1. Position spacer 83-93-209 or equivalent, under the upper wishbone.
2. Check end-play by compressing the ball joint with a pair of large pliers. Maximum end-play is 0.08 in. (2.0mm).
3. Check radial play by applying pressure between the wishbone and the vertical link. Care should be taken so the ball joint seal is not ripped. Maximum radial play is 0.04 in. (1.0mm).
4. Replace any ball joint that does not pass either test. Inspect the ball joint seals. Replace any that are damaged.

REMOVAL AND INSTALLATION

1. Disconnect the negative battery cable. Raise and support the vehicle

safely. Remove the tire and wheel assembly.
2. Remove the brake caliper and position it aside so the brake hose will not be damaged. Remove the nut that holds the ball joint bolt to the steering knuckle housing.
3. Remove the ball joint from the control arm assembly.
4. Installation is the reverse of removal. Tighten the ball joint-to-lower control arm bolts to 30-40 ft. lbs. (40-54 Nm) and the ball joint-to-steering knuckle bolts to 26-37 ft. lbs. (35-50 Nm).
5. Connect the negative battery cable.

Upper Control Arms

REMOVAL AND INSTALLATION

900 Series

NOTE: To remove the left upper control arm, the engine must first be removed from the vehicle.

1. Disconnect the negative battery cable.
2. Raise the vehicle and support it safely.
3. Remove the tire and wheel assembly. Remove the shock absorber. Compress the coil spring, using a spring compression tool.
4. Remove the 2 bolts attaching the upper ball joint and lower spring seat to the upper control arm.
5. Remove the bolts from both upper control arm bearing brackets.
6. Remove the coil spring from the vehicle.
7. Remove the control arm and bearings from the vehicle. Save the spacers under the bearings and record the number of spacers used under each bearing.
8. Remove both of the bearing nuts. Remove the bearings and bushings from the control arm.
   To install:
9. Install the rubber bushings, using a suitable bushing installer 78-41-331 or equivalent. Spray the bushings with soapy water prior to installation. Do not use oil or grease to aid installation.
10. Install the bearing to the control arm. Once the 2 nuts are tight, the angle between the control arm and the bearing should be 60-64 degrees. Tighten the bolts to 54-66 ft. lbs. (75-90 Nm).
11. Install the control arm and tighten into place. Install the upper ball joint to the control arm and in-

stall the coil spring. Check that the spring bushing is seated in the upper spring pocket.
12. Raise the outer end of the lower control arm slightly and install the shock absorber.
13. Install the wheel and lower the vehicle.
14. Connect the negative battery cable.
15. Check the wheel alignment and test drive the vehicle.

Lower Control Arms

REMOVAL AND INSTALLATION

900 Series

1. Disconnect the negative battery cable. Raise the vehicle and support it safely. Remove the tire and wheel assembly.
2. Disconnect the lower end of the shock absorber.
3. Remove the 2 bolts that attach the ball joint to the control arm.
4. Remove the lower control arm attaching bolts from under the engine compartment floor.
5. Remove the control arm and its attaching brackets from the vehicle.
6. Remove the control arm bearing nuts and remove the bearings from the control arm.
   To install:
7. Install the rubber bushings, using a suitable bushing installer 78-41-349 or equivalent. Soap the bushings prior to installation. When both nuts are tightened, the angle between the control arm and bearing should be 16-20 degrees. Tighten the bolts to 70-77 ft. lbs. (100-120 Nm).
8. Install the control arm and secure the ball joint. Raise the control arms slightly and fit the shock absorber.
9. Install the wheel and lower the vehicle.
10. Connect the negative battery cable.
11. Check the wheel alignment and test drive the vehicle.

9000 Series

1. Disconnect the negative battery cable. Raise the vehicle and support it safely. Remove the tire and wheel assembly.
2. Remove the bolts securing the suspension arm to the ball joint.
3. Remove the nut from the bolt securing the suspension arm to the anti-roll bar link. Remove the upper securing bolt for the link.

4. Press down on the suspension arm and withdraw the anti-roll bar link.

5. Remove the nuts at the front of the suspension arm from the bolts securing the arm to the frame.

6. Remove the rear bolts securing the reinforcement member to the frame.

7. Remove the bolts securing the control arm rear pivot to the frame. Remove the control arm.

To install:

8. Place the control arm into position and install the mounting bolts. Leave the nuts for the bushings in the suspension arm rear pivot loose.

9. After the arm is installed and the remaining bolts in place, tighten the rear pivot bolts. Tighten the bolts to 33-40 ft. lbs. (45-54 Nm).

10. Install the anti-roll bar link.

11. Secure the suspension arm to ball joint.

12. Install the tire and wheel assemblies.

13. Lower the vehicle. Connect the negative battery cable.

14. Jounce the vehicle several time allowing it to settle. Check the wheel alignment and adjust as required.

Anti-Roll Bars

REMOVAL AND INSTALLATION

900 Series

1. Disconnect the negative battery cable. Raise and support the vehicle safely.

2. Remove the front wheels and install the special tool 83-93-209 or equivalent, under the upper control arms, on either side of the vehicle.

3. Unbolt the anti-roll bar from the lower control arms. Unbolt the mounting at the engine compartment floor.

4. Remove the steering gear and push it forward. Remove the anti-roll bar.

To install:

5. Insert one end of the anti-roll bar and rotate it through 180 degrees. Then insert the other end and turn the bar back 180 degrees.

6. Grease the rubber bushings in the outer mountings and install them loosely.

7. Grease the rubber bushings for the mounting to the engine compartment floor. Put the mounting plate into position and slide on the bushing with the opening to the front of the car. Install the collar loosely.

8. Tighten the bolts in the outer mountings. Adjust the position of the bar.

9. Tighten the mounting at the engine compartment floor to 15-19 ft. lbs. (20-27 Nm).

10. Install the steering gear, lower the vehicle and remove the special tool.

9000 Series

1. Raise and support the vehicle safely. Remove the front wheels.

2. Remove the 2 U-clamps for the anti-roll bar. Remove the 3 bolts securing the ball joint to the suspension arm. Remove the ball joint pinch bolt, if necessary.

3. Remove the nut securing the anti-roll bar link to the suspension arm. Remove the top securing bolt for the link.

4. Push down on the suspension arm and remove the anti-roll bar link.

5. Repeat Steps 2-4 on the other side of the vehicle. Remove the anti-roll bar.

To install:

6. Position the anti-roll bar on the sub-frame. Install the anti-roll bar link with bushings and washers to the suspension arm and tighten the nuts to 15-19 ft. lbs. (20-27 Nm). Ensure that the convex side of each washer is towards the bushing.

7. Install the ball joint to the suspension arm and tighten the nuts. Use new nuts as necessary. Repeat Steps 6-7 for the other side.

8. Secure the anti-roll bar to the U-clamps. Replace the wheels and lower the vehicle.

Front Wheel Bearings

REMOVAL AND INSTALLATION

NOTE: See "Front Wheel Hub, Knuckle and Bearings" in the Drive Axle section.

REAR SUSPENSION

Shock Absorbers

REMOVAL AND INSTALLATION

1. Disconnect the negative battery cable.

2. Raise the vehicle and support it safely. Remove the tire and wheel assembly.

3. Place a service jack under the spring seat of the shock being removed.

NOTE: Always replace 1 shock at a time to prevent the rear axle from dropping and stretching the brake line.

4. Remove the shock absorber retaining nuts.

5. Remove the bolts in the spring link mounting on the rear axle anti-roll bar on the 9000 Series.

6. Lower the spring link so the shock absorber can be removed from the vehicle.

To install:

7. Place the shock absorber into position and install the retaining nuts.

8. Secure the rear axle anti-roll bar and spring link, as required.

9. After the shock absorber is completely installed, install the wheel assembly.

10. Lower the vehicle and connect the negative battery cable.

Coil Springs

REMOVAL AND INSTALLATION

1. Disconnect the negative battery cable.

2. Raise and support the vehicle safely.

3. Remove the tire and wheel assembly.

4. Position a service jack under the spring link and disconnect the lower end of the shock absorber.

5. From under the vehicle, remove the 2 locknuts that secure the front spring link bearing to the body of the vehicle.

6. Position a jackstand under the rear axle to prevent the brake lines from being damaged by the weight of the rear axle.

7. Lower the spring link so the spring(s) can be removed from the vehicle together with the upper spring support and the rubber spacer at the lower spring seating which is retained by the spring tension.

To install:

8. Place the spring(s) along with the support and rubber spacer into position.

9. Raise the rear axle, using the service jack. Secure the spring link.

10. Install the spring link bearing locknuts. Secure the shock absorber.

11. Install the tire and wheel assembly.

12. Lower the vehicle and connect the negative battery cable.

Rear Wheel Hub and Bearings

REMOVAL AND INSTALLATION

900 Series

1. Raise the vehicle and support it safely. Remove the wheel assembly.

2. Disconnect the hand brake cable from the caliper and rest the cable on the rear axle.

3. If equipped with ABS brakes, remove the wheel sensor from the hub and release the lead from the bracket on the trailing end of the spring link.

4. Remove the screw plug and unscrew the adjusting screw in the caliper.

5. Unbolt the brake caliper and wire it to the torque arm.

6. Remove the locating stud from the brake disc and remove the disc.

7. Remove the dust cap from the hub and remove the center nut. Pull the hub and bearing assembly off the stub axle.

To install:

8. Lightly lubricate the stub axle with oil. Grip the hub with both hands and apply pressure with the thumbs to the bearing race. Push the hub onto the stub axle.

9. Install a new center nut and tighten to 207-221 ft. lbs. (280-300 Nm).

10. Install the brake disc and locating stud.

11. Install the brake caliper.

12. Reconnect the parking brake cable and adjust, as required.

13. Install the wheel sensor and secure the wiring harness.

14. Install the tire and wheel assembly. Lower the vehicle.

9000 Series

1. Raise the vehicle and support it safely. Remove the wheel assembly.

2. Disconnect the hand brake cable from the lever on the brake caliper.

3. Remove the adjusting screw plug and loosen the screw slightly to allow the brake piston to slide back.

4. Unbolt the brake caliper and wire it to the torque arm.

5. If equipped with ABS brakes, remove the wheel sensor.

6. Remove the locating stud from the brake disc and remove the disc.

7. Remove the dust cap from the hub and remove the center nut. Pull the hub and bearing assembly off the stub axle.

To install:

8. Lightly lubricate the stub axle with oil. Grip the hub with both hands and apply pressure with the thumbs to the bearing race. Push the hub onto the stub axle.

9. Install a new center nut and tighten to 207-221 ft. lbs. (280-300 Nm).

10. Install the brake disc and locating stud.

11. Install the brake caliper.

12. Reconnect the parking brake cable.

13. Install the wheel sensor and secure the wiring harness.

14. Adjust the brake piston and fit the screw plug over the adjusting screw.

15. Install the tire and wheel assembly. Lower the vehicle.

Rear Axle Assembly

REMOVAL AND INSTALLATION

1. Raise and support the vehicle safely. Detach the hand brake cables from the lead through brackets on the spring links.

2. Remove the calipers and tie them out of the way. Remove the panhard rod. Position a jack under the middle of the rear axle and raise the axle sufficiently to relieve the load on it.

3. Unbolt the bottom mountings for the shocks and the anti-roll bar.

4. Lower the rear axle and remove the springs. Unbolt the front mounting for the torque arm. Remove the bolts from the trailing-end mounting for the spring link.

5. Remove the rear axle assembly.

To install:

6. Place the rear axle on a floorjack and slide it into position under the vehicle. Install the bolts in the trailing-end mounting for the spring link. Do not tighten the bolt.

7. Check that the rubbers for the coil springs are correctly positioned and seat the springs on the links. Ensure that the anti-roll bar is positioned correctly. Raise the axle and ensure that the springs are seated.

8. Install the anti-roll bar and bottom mountings for the shocks.

9. Install the spring links and tighten to 51-66 ft. lbs. (70-90 Nm). Tighten the arms and anti-roll bar bolts 30-40 ft. lbs. (40-54 Nm). Remove the floorjack and install the panhard rod.

10. Install the calipers and brakes. Secure the hand brake cables. Install the wheels and lower the vehicle.

Anti-Roll Bars

REMOVAL AND INSTALLATION

900 Series

1. Raise and support the vehicle safely.

2. Unbolt the rear mounting on the spring link. The link will now hang from the shock absorber.

3. Unbolt the front mounting nuts. Lower the rear edge of the anti roll bar.

4. Compress the mounting on the leading edge and remove the anti-roll bar.

To install:

5. Insert the anti-roll bar in the front mounting and insert the rubber bushings.

6. Insert the bolts in the rear mountings and use pliers to line up the holes in the spring link. Do not overtighten the bolts as this may damage the bushings.

7. Tighten the bolts in the front mountings. Check that the anti-roll bar is not toughing the spring link.

9000 Series

1. Raise and support the vehicle safely. Remove the rear wheels.

2. Using a suitable lifting device, relieve the load on the anti-roll bar.

3. Remove the securing bolts in the outboard mountings. Separate the anti-roll bar from the bar links and remove.

To install:

4. Install the anti-roll bar to the bar links. Install the bolts in the outboard mountings and tighten to 58-65 ft. lbs. (80-90 Nm).

5. Replace the wheels and lower the vehicle.

STEERING

Steering Wheel

—————— CAUTION ——————

Before performing any repairs, if equipped with an air bag, disconnect the negative battery cable and wait 20 minutes before working on the system. Failure to do so may result in deployment of the air bag and possible personal injury.

REMOVAL AND INSTALLATION

1. Disconnect the negative battery cable.
2. On some vehicles it will be necessary to remove the bottom cover of the steering wheel bearing.
3. Remove the steering wheel safety pad. Remove the steering wheel emblem. Remove the horn contact. Remove the steering wheel holding nut and washer.
4. Remove the steering wheel using the proper steering wheel removal tool.
5. Installation is the reverse of removal.

Manual Rack and Pinion

REMOVAL AND INSTALLATION

900 Series

1. Disconnect the negative battery cable.
2. Remove the left screen under the instrument panel and loosen the rubber bellows at the body lead through for the steering gear intermediate shaft, if required.
3. Raise and support the vehicle safely.
4. Remove the bolt holding the joint to the steering gear pinion or intermediate shaft.
5. Loosen the steering column tube from the body and separate the steering column joint from the pinion. Position the steering column so the wiring harness is not damaged.
6. Remove both tire and wheel assemblies. Remove the tie rod ends at the steering arms with the proper removal tool. Remove the 2 steering gear clamps.
7. Move the rack to the right as far as possible. Lift the steering gear to the right so the tie rod can be bent

down in the opening of the engine compartment floor.
8. Pull the rack to the left and lift the steering gear down through the opening in the engine compartment floor.

To install:

9. Carefully lift the rack assembly in through the right side wheel arch. Install and tighten the mounting bolts.
10. Secure the pinion to intermediate shaft.
11. Screw the tie-rod ends back into the track rods and measure the distance between the tie-rod end and groove in the rack to ensure that both tie-rod ends are back in the same position as before removal.
12. Tighten the nut securing each tie-rod end to the steering swivel members. Tighten the clamp bolt to 26-30 ft. lbs. (35-42 Nm); the body to steering gear bolts to 44-60 ft. lbs. (60-80 Nm); the tie rod end nuts to 37-44 ft. lbs. (50-60 Nm).
13. Install both tire and wheel assemblies.
14. Lower the vehicle.
15. Refit the left screen and rubber bellows under the instrument panel.
16. Connect the negative battery cable.

Power Rack and Pinion

REMOVAL AND INSTALLATION

900 Series

1. Disconnect the negative battery cable. Remove the left screen under the instrument panel and loosen the rubber bellows at the body lead through for the steering gear intermediate shaft, if required. Disconnect and plug the power steering fluid lines.
2. Raise and support the vehicle safely. Remove the bolt holding the joint to the steering gear pinion or intermediate shaft.
3. Loosen the steering column tube from the body and separate the steering column joint from the pinion. Position the steering column so the wiring harness is not damaged.
4. Remove both tire and wheel assemblies. Remove the tie rod ends at the steering arms with the proper removal tool. Remove the 2 steering gear clamps.
5. Move the rack to the right as far as possible. Lift the steering gear to the right so the tie rod can be bent down in the opening of the engine compartment floor.

6. Pull the rack to the left and lift the steering gear down through the opening in the engine compartment floor.

To install:

7. Carefully lift the rack assembly in through the right side wheel arch. Install and tighten the mounting bolts.
8. Secure the steering column joint to the pinion.
9. Connect the power steering fluid lines.
10. Screw the tie-rod ends back into the track rods and measure the distance between the tie-rod end and groove in the rack to ensure that both tie-rod ends are back in the same position as before removal.
11. Tighten the nut securing each tie-rod end to the steering swivel members. Tighten all other components as follow:
   a. Tighten the clamp bolt to 26-30 ft. lbs. (35-42 Nm).
   b. Tighten the body-to-steering gear bolts to 44-60 ft. lbs. (60-80 Nm).
   c. Tighten the tie rod end nuts to 37-44 ft. lbs. (50-60 Nm).
   d. Tighten the hydraulic lines to 15-25 ft. lbs. (20-34 Nm).
12. Install both tire and wheel assemblies.
13. Lower the vehicle.
14. Refit the left screen and rubber bellows under the instrument panel.
15. Connect the negative battery cable.
16. Add fluid to the steering system. Start the engine and bleed the system.
17. Check for leaks.

9000 Series

1. Disconnect the negative battery cable. Remove the padding from under the instrument panel and the trim on the left side of the center tunnel, as required. Fold back the carpet where the steering column passes through the firewall. Remove the rubber boot from the intermediate shaft.
2. Remove the pinch bolt in the lower clamp, loosen the bolt in the upper clamp and remove the intermediate shaft.
3. Remove the cover panel from the firewall. Take care not to damage the gasket, seal and plastic bushing.
4. Raise and support the vehicle safely. Remove both tire and wheel assemblies.
5. Remove the rear section of the inner fender panel under the left fender.

6. Separate the left and right tie rod ends from the steering arms.

7. Drain the power steering fluid from the pump reservoir.

8. Disconnect the hoses from the pump and reservoir. Plug the openings to prevent fluid from leaking out and dirt from entering.

9. Remove the retaining bolts from the rack and pinion assembly.

10. Remove the vertical brace between the engine sub-frame and the body.

11. Lift out the rack and pinion unit through the left fender inner panel opening. Do not damage the rubber boots or brake hose.

To install:

12. Carefully install the rack assembly in through the left fender inner panel opening. Do not damage the rubber boots or brake hose.

13. Install the vertical brace between the engine sub-frame and the body.

14. Install and tighten the rack assembly mounting bolts to 44-60 ft. lbs. (60-80 Nm).

15. Connect the hoses from the pump and reservoir.

16. Screw the tie-rod ends back into the track rods and measure the distance between the tie-rod end and groove in the rack to ensure that both tie-rod ends are back in the same position as before removal. Tighten the tie rod end nuts to 37-44 ft. lbs. (50-60 Nm).

17. Install the rear section of the inner fender panel under the left fender.

18. Install both tire and wheel assemblies. Lower the vehicle.

19. Install the cover panel to the firewall. Take care not to damage the gasket, seal and plastic bushing.

20. Install the intermediate shaft and pinch bolt. Tighten the pinch bolt to 27-32 ft. lbs. (35-42 Nm). Install the rubber boot to the intermediate shaft.

21. Refit the carpet, trim and padding inside the vehicle.

22. Connect the negative battery cable.

23. Add fluid to the steering system. Start the engine and bleed the system.

24. Check for leaks.

Power Steering Pump

REMOVAL AND INSTALLATION

900 Series

1. Disconnect the negative battery cable. Drain the fluid from the power steering pump.

2. Drain the coolant from the drain cock on the engine block and disconnect the hose from between the expansion tank and the water pump.

3. Disconnect the power steering pump hoses. Grip the hexagonal nipple on the pump when removing the delivery line.

4. Unbolt the pump unit from the bracket and the engine mounting. Remove the power steering belt. Remove the pump complete with its mounting.

5. Installation is the reverse of the removal procedure.

9000 Series

1. Disconnect the negative battery cable. Remove the fluid from the pump reservoir.

2. Raise and support the vehicle safely. Remove the right front wheel and the right inner fender panel.

3. Remove the drive belt. Remove the bracket for the engine oil filler pipe. Remove the engine stay bracket. Disconnect the hoses from the pump. Plug the openings.

4. Remove the pump retaining bolts. Remove the pump. Note that 1 bolt is located behind the pump pulley and is accessible only through the opening in the pulley.

5. Installation is the reverse of the removal procedure.

BELT ADJUSTMENT

900 Series

Tighten the belt so when finger pressure is applied to the belt at midpoint between both belt pulleys, the belt deflects not more than 0.39 in. (10mm).

9000 Series

1. After the belt has been installed, a strand tension gauge must be used to tighten the belt properly.

2. A new belt must be tightened to 170-200 lbs. (735-865 N).

3. A used belt must be tightened to 110-130 lbs. (490-580 N).

SYSTEM BLEEDING

1. Fill the power steering pump with the proper fluid.

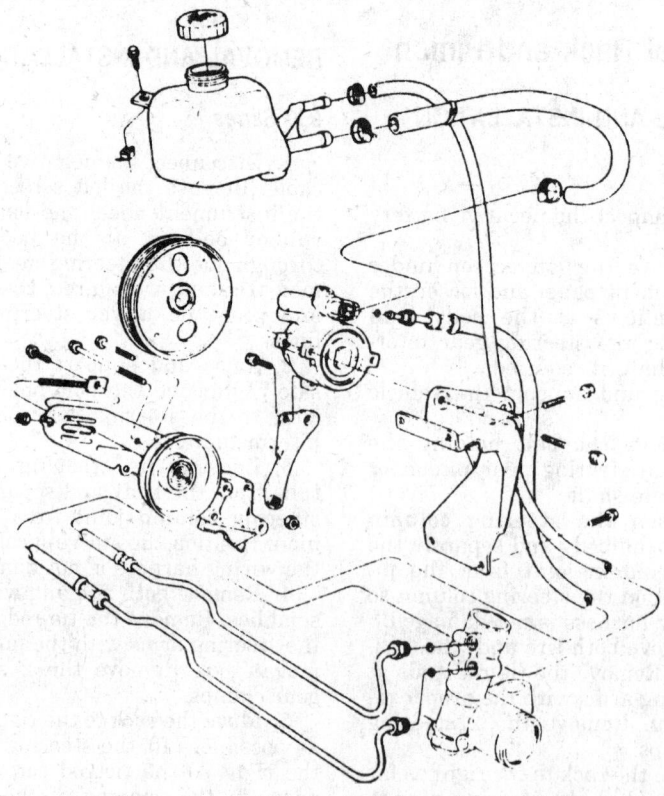

Power steering system and related components — 9000 Series

2. Start the engine and top off the level of fluid to 0.4 in. (10mm) above the bottom of the filter.

3. Turn the steering wheel from left to right several times to expel air from the system.

4. Refill the pump as needed.

5. Allow the engine to operate at idle.

Tie Rod Ends

REMOVAL AND INSTALLATION

1. Disconnect the negative battery cable. Raise and support the vehicle safely.

2. Remove the tire and wheel assembly. Remove the nut.

3. Disconnect the ball joint bolt from the steering arm using the proper removal tool. Do not knock the ball joint bolt out, as this could cause damage to the ball joint and other related parts.

4. Back off the nut that locks the end assembly to the tie rod.

5. Unscrew the end assembly from the tie rod.

6. Installation is the reverse of the removal procedure. Check and adjust the toe-in as required. Tighten the rod end locknut to 44-59 ft. lbs. (60-80 Nm).

BRAKES

Master Cylinder

REMOVAL AND INSTALLATION

1. Disconnect the negative battery cable. Disconnect the electrical connection to the brake warning switch.

2. Disconnect the hose from the clutch master cylinder to the fluid reservoir. Insert a plastic stopper in the nipple of the reservoir.

3. Disconnect the brake lines to the master cylinder.

4. Remove the nuts that hold the master cylinder to the power brake booster. Remove the master cylinder from the vehicle.

5. Installation is the reverse of removal. Bleed the brake system.

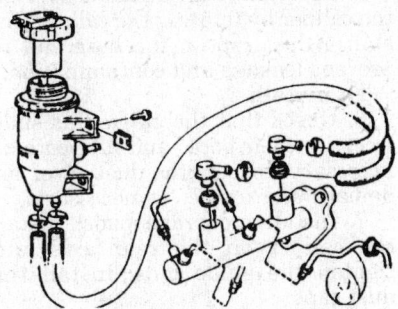

Brake master cylinder and related components — 9000 Series

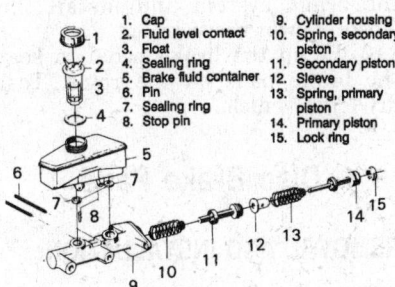

1. Cap	9. Cylinder housing
2. Fluid level contact	10. Spring, secondary piston
3. Float	
4. Sealing ring	11. Secondary piston
5. Brake fluid container	12. Sleeve
6. Pin	13. Spring, primary piston
7. Sealing ring	
8. Stop pin	14. Primary piston
	15. Lock ring

Master cylinder, exploded view — 900 Series

Power Brake Booster

REMOVAL AND INSTALLATION

1. Disconnect the negative battery cable.

2. Remove the steering column bearing cover, ashtray and safety padding screw. Remove the upper circlip on the brake pedal pushrod, if equipped.

3. Remove the 2 electrical connections on the brake light switch. Remove the safety padding screws in the engine compartment.

4. Remove the vacuum hose from the non-return valve which is located on the vacuum booster.

5. Disconnect the brake lines and the electrical connections for the brake warning switch from the master cylinder. Disconnect the line to the clutch master cylinder from the fluid reservoir. Insert stoppers in the lines to prevent loss of the brake fluid.

6. Remove the cotter pin from the servo unit pushrod at the brake pedal.

7. Remove the vacuum booster together with the master cylinder and the bracket.

NOTE: The bracket is mounted on the dash panel with 4 bolts and nuts. Three of these bolts are accessible from under the passenger's compartment after removal of the screen section and parts of the dash panel insulation felt below the instrument panel. The 4th nut is accessible from the engine compartment by the bracket.

8. Separate the master cylinder and the bracket from the vacuum booster.

To install:

9. Install the master cylinder to the vacuum booster. Install the master cylinder together with the vacuum booster into the vehicle.

10. Install the cotter pin to the servo unit pushrod at the brake pedal.

11. Connect the line from the fluid reservoir to the clutch master cylinder. Connect the brake lines and the electrical connections for the brake warning switch to the master cylinder.

12. Install the vacuum hose to the non-return valve, located on the vacuum booster.

13. Install the safety padding screws in the engine compartment and connect the 2 electrical connections on the brake light switch.

14. Install the upper circlip on the brake pedal pushrod, if equipped. Install the steering column bearing cover, ashtray and safety padding screw.

15. Connect the negative battery cable. Bleed the brake system.

Brake Caliper

REMOVAL AND INSTALLATION

900 Series

1. Raise and support the vehicle safely. Remove the appropriate wheel.

2. Remove the brake pads. Disconnect the parking brake cable from the brake housing.

3. Unscrew the brake pipes from the caliper. Insert a rubber stopper to prevent leakage and contamination.

4. Remove the bolts holding the brake caliper to the steering knuckle.

To install:

5. Check that the dust cover has not slipped out of position. Bolt the

brake assembly to the steering knuckle using a new locking plate.

6. Connect the brake lines.

7. Adjust the parking brake cable so the clearance between the lever and the yoke is 0.019 in. (0.5mm) with the parking brake in the OFF position.

8. Install the brake pads, top off the brake fluid and bleed the brake system.

9. With the engine OFF, pump the brake pedal to seat the pads. On front brakes, after pumping the pedal, pull the parking brake up 5 notches. Continue to pump the pedal until the parking brake operates after the lever has been pulled up 2-4 notches.

10. Install the wheel, lower the vehicle and test drive.

9000 Series

FRONT

1. Raise and support the vehicle safely. Remove the appropriate wheel.

2. Loosen the brake hose fitting on the caliper.

3. Remove the lower guide pin bolt and pivot the caliper up to remove the brake pads.

4. Remove the upper guide pin bolt. Disconnect the brake hose from the caliper and install a dust cap over the hose to prevent leakage and contamination. Remove the caliper assembly

To install:

5. Check that the guide pins slide freely in their bores and lubricate as necessary. Inspect the dust cover for damage and replace as necessary.

6. Reconnect the brake hose to the caliper but leave the fitting loose.

7. Install the caliper and tighten the upper guide pin bolt.

8. Install the brake pads. Tighten the lower guide pin bolt.

9. Tighten the brake hose at the caliper. Bleed the brake system.

10. Install the wheel, lower the vehicle and pump the brake pedal to seat the brake pads against the rotor.

Rear

1. Raise and support the vehicle safely. Remove the appropriate wheel.

2. Unhook the parking brake cable from the lever on the caliper. Fully depress the brake pedal and secure it in that position.

3. Loosen the brake hose fitting at the caliper. Remove the dust caps and unscrew the guide pins.

4. Remove the brake pad retaining clip and lift off the caliper body. Remove the brake pads.

5. Disconnect the brake hose from the caliper by rotating the caliper. Install a dust cap on the hose end to prevent leakage and contamination.

To install:

6. Check that the guide pins slide freely in their bores and lubricate as necessary. Inspect the dust cover for damage and replace as necessary.

7. Install the brake pads. Install the caliper on the rear axle and tighten the guide pins. Install the dust caps.

8. Install the retaining clip, tighten the brake hose fitting and reconnect the parking brake cable to the lever.

9. Adjust the parking brake, bleed the brake system and install the wheel. Lower the vehicle.

10. Pump the brake pedal to seat the brake pads on the rotor. Test drive the vehicle.

Disc Brake Pads

REMOVAL AND INSTALLATION

900

FRONT

1. Disconnect the negative battery cable.

2. Raise and support the vehicle and support it safely. Remove the wheel.

3. Remove the lower guide pin bolt.

4. Pivot the caliper upwards and remove the pads.

5. Check that the guide pins slide freely and the dust covers are in good condition.

6. Clean the surfaces between the pads and the carrier.

To install:

7. Fit the new pads and pivot the hydraulic body back to its normal position.

8. Refit and tighten the bolt in the lower guide pin to 22-26 ft. lbs. (30-35 Nm).

9. Install the wheel and tire assemblies. Lower the vehicle.

10. Pump the brake pedal to move the pads to their operating positions.

11. Connect the negative battery cable.

REAR

1. Disconnect the negative battery cable.

2. Raise the vehicle and support it with safely. Remove the wheel.

3. Release the parking brake and remove the retaining spring.

4. Slide the parking brake cable out of the slot of the lever.

5. Remove the dust caps and then use a 7mm Allen key, hexagon bit adapter, to remove the guide pins.

6. Lift off the hydraulic body and remove the pads.

To install:

7. Remove the screw plug from the parking brake adjusting screw and screw the piston into the hydraulic body by means of the adjusting screw.

8. Place the new pads into position.

9. Replace the hydraulic body and install the guide pins complete with dust caps.

10. Install the retaining spring for the parking brake lever.

11. Screw the adjusting screw fully home and then back it off approximately $1/4$-$1/2$ turn. Check that the brake disc is running freely and refit the plug.

12. Install the parking brake cable to the lever and check with a feeler gauge, that the clearance between the lever and the stop is 0.02-0.06 in. (0.5-1.5mm) Adjust as necessary by means of the adjusting screw at the parking brake lever inside the vehicle.

13. Install the tire and wheel assemblies. Lower the vehicle.

14. Connect the negative battery cable.

9000 Series

FRONT

1. Disconnect the negative battery cable.

2. Raise and support the vehicle and support it safely. Remove the tire and wheel assemblies.

3. Clean the brake housing.

4. Remove the damper spring, pin retaining clip and pad retaining pin. If the pad retaining pin is difficult to remove, use a tapping-out tool 83-90-270 or equivalent, and removal tool 89-96-175 or equivalent.

5. Remove the brake pads. If the pads are seating firmly, remove them using a pad extractor 89-95-771 or equivalent.

To install:

6. Siphon a sufficient quantity of brake fluid from the master cylinder reservoir to prevent the brake fluid from overflowing the master cylinder when installing new pads. This is necessary as the piston must be forced into the cylinder bore to provide sufficient clearance to install the pads.

7. Inspect the caliper and piston assembly for breaks, cracks or other

1. Piston
2. Seal
3. Dust cover (on piston)
4. Hydraulic body
5. Pads
6. Dust cover
7. Guide pin
8. Guide pin bolt
9. Bleed nipple
10. Dust cap

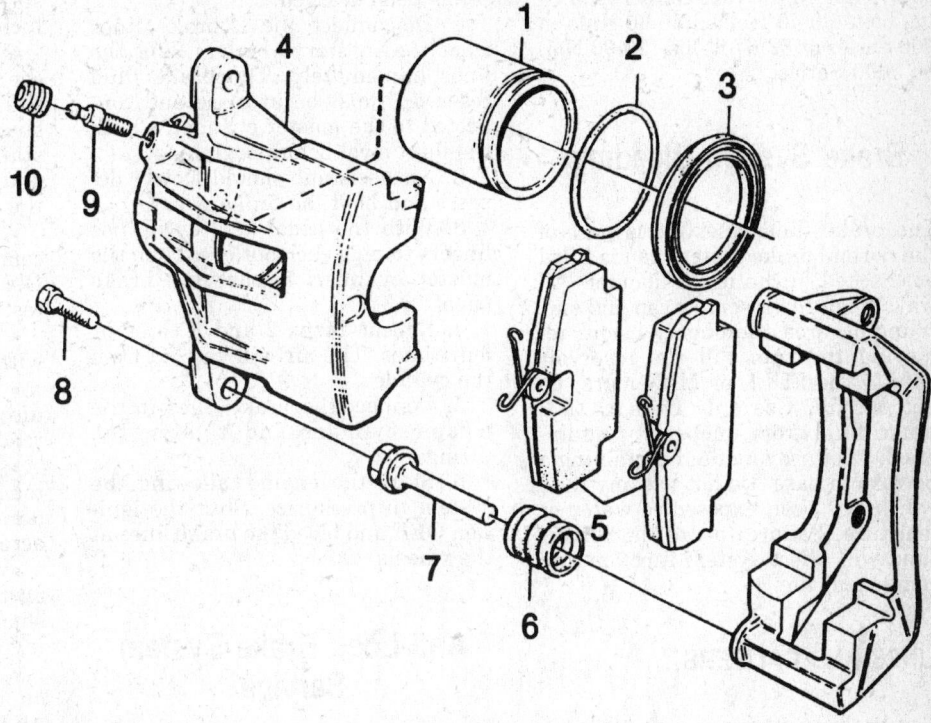

Front caliper assembly, exploded view — 1990-91 900 Series

damage. Overhaul or replace the caliper as necessary.

8. Push the piston next to the rotor back into the cylinder bore until the end of the piston is flush with the boot retaining ring. Rotate the piston using tool 89-96-043 or equivalent, while simultaneously pushing the piston back into the cylinder. The automatic parking brake is reset this way.

NOTE: If the piston is pushed further than this, the seal will be damaged and the caliper assembly will have to be overhauled. Check that the position of the piston has not displaced the dust cover and the yoke moves easily in the groove on the brake housing.

9. Fit the new brake pads together with the pad retaining pin, pin retaining clip and damper spring.
10. Refill the master cylinder with fresh brake fluid.
11. With the engine OFF, pump the brake pedal repeatedly until the foot brake starts to operate.
12. Install the tire and wheel assemblies. Pump the brake pedal several times to bring the pads into adjustment.

13. Connect the negative battery cable.
14. Road test the vehicle. If a firm pedal cannot be obtained, bleed the brakes.

REAR

1. Raise the vehicle and support it with safely. Remove the wheel.
2. Release the parking brake and remove the retaining spring.
3. Slide the parking brake cable out of the slot of the lever.
4. Remove the dust caps and then use a 7mm Allen key and hexagon bit adapter, to remove the guide pins.
5. Lift off the hydraulic body and remove the pads.
To install:
6. Remove the screw plug from the parking brake adjusting screw and screw the piston into the hydraulic body by means of the adjusting screw.
7. Place the new pads into position.
8. Replace the hydraulic body and install the guide pins complete with dust caps.
9. Install the retaining spring for the parking brake lever.
10. Screw the adjusting screw fully home and then back it off approximately ¼-½ turn. Check that the

brake disc is running freely and refit the plug.
11. Install the parking brake cable to the lever and check with a feeler gauge, that the clearance between the lever and the stop is 0.02-0.06 in. (0.5-1.5mm) Adjust as necessary by means of the adjusting screw at the parking brake lever inside the vehicle.
12. Replace the wheel and lower the vehicle.

Brake Rotor

REMOVAL AND INSTALLATION

1. Raise and support the vehicle safely. Remove the appropriate wheel.
2. Remove the brake caliper and hand out of the way using a piece of wire. Do not allow the caliper to hang by the brake hose.
3. Remove the locating stud and the servicing screw. Remove the rotor.
To install:
4. Check the rotor runout. If not within specification have the rotor ground.
5. Installation is the reverse of removal. Tighten the front caliper-to-

frame bolts to 52-81 ft. lbs. (70-110 Nm). Tighten the rear caliper mounting bolts 30-40 ft. lbs. (40-45 Nm) on 900 Series or 52-67 ft. lbs. (70-90 Nm) on 9000 Series.

Brake System Bleeding

The brake fluid reservoir is part of the normal brake system and is filled or checked in the usual manner. Always clean the reservoir cap and surrounding area thoroughly before removing the cap. Fill the reservoir only to the FULL or MAX mark; do not overfill. Use only fresh DOT 3 brake fluid from unopened containers. Do not use any fluid containing a petroleum base. Do not use any fluid which has been exposed to water or moisture. Failure to use the correct fluid will affect system function and component life.

LINES AND CALIPERS

The brake system must be bled any time a line, hose or component is loosened or removed. Any air trapped within the lines can affect pedal feel and system function. Bleeding the system is performed in the usual manner with an assistant in the car to pump the brake pedal. Make certain the fluid level in the reservoir is maintained at or near correct levels during bleeding operations.

With the ignition OFF, depress the brake pedal several times until pedal feel changes to a noticeably stiffer resistance. Slowly pump the pedal a few more times; with the pedal depressed, loosen the bleeder screw $\frac{1}{3}$-$\frac{1}{2}$ turn. Tighten the bleeder screw before the fluid pressure is gone. Release the pedal, pump again slowly, hold the pedal depressed and repeat the bleeding process until no air bubbles are seen in the fluid.

If all bleeding is necessary at all wheels, begin at the right rear, then the left front, left rear and right front wheels.

MASTER CYLINDER

If the master cylinder has been emptied of fluid, it must be bled separately from the rest of the system. Since the cylinder has no check valve, air can become trapped within it. To bleed the brake master cylinder after it has been drained:

1. Disconnect the 2 brake lines from the master cylinder. Plug the lines immediately. The brake fluid reservoir must be in place and connected to the master cylinder. Check the fluid level before beginning.

2. An assistant should slowly depress and hold the brake pedal.

3. With the pedal held down, use fingers to plug each outlet port on the master cylinder; release the brake pedal.

4. Repeat Steps 2 and 3 three or four times. The air will be bled from the cylinder.

5. Connect the brake lines to the master cylinder and tighten the fittings.

6. Start the engine, allowing the system to pressurize. Shut the ignition OFF and bleed the brake lines at the wheels.

Anti-Lock Brake System Service

PRECAUTIONS

• If the vehicle is equipped with an air bag system, always properly disable the system before commencing work on the ABS system.

• Certain components within the ABS system are not intended to be serviced or repaired individually. Only those components with removal and installation procedures should be serviced.

• Do not use rubber hoses or other parts not specifically specified for the ABS system. When using repair kits, replace all parts included in the kit. Partial or incorrect repair may lead to functional problems and require the replacement of other components.

• Lubricate rubber parts with clean, fresh brake fluid to ease assembly. Do not use lubricated shop air to clean parts; damage to rubber components may result.

• Use only brake fluid from an unopened container. Use of suspect or contaminated brake fluid can reduce system performance and/or durability.

• A clean repair area is essential. Perform repairs after components have been thoroughly cleaned; use only denatured alcohol to clean components. Do not allow ABS components to come into contact with any substance containing mineral oil; this includes used shop rags.

• The control unit is a microprocessor similar to other computer units in the vehicle. Insure that the ignition switch is OFF before removing or installing controller harnesses. Avoid static electricity discharge at or near the controller.

• Never disconnect any electrical connection with the ignition switch ON unless instructed to do so in a test.

• Avoid touching connector pins with fingers.

• Leave new components and modules in the shipping package until ready to install them.

• To avoid static discharge, always touch a vehicle ground after sliding across a vehicle seat or walking across carpeted or vinyl floors.

• If any arc welding is to be done on the vehicle, the ABS control unit should be disconnected before welding operations begin.

• Never allow welding cables to lie on, near or across any vehicle electrical wiring.

• If the vehicle is to be baked after paint repairs, disconnect and remove the control unit from the vehicle.

RELIEVING ANTI-LOCK BRAKE SYSTEM PRESSURE

The anti-lock brake system contains brake fluid under extreme pressure. Parts of the hydraulic modulator may contain brake fluid at pressures up to 3045 psi (210 bar). Extreme care must be taken when working on lines and components.

Always discharge the system pressure completely before loosening any brake line or performing any component replacement. To discharge the system pressure:

1. Turn the ignition switch OFF during the procedure.

2. Step firmly on the brake pedal at least 25-30 times. The system is not completely discharged until a distinct change is felt in the brake pedal. The effort needed to press the pedal will clearly increase when the system pressure is released.

3. Once the pedal feel changes, pump the pedal a few more times.

4. Perform tests and/or repairs as necessary with the ignition OFF at all times. If the ignition is turned

ON, the pump will run, repressurizing the system.

NOTE: A running production change was made on 9000 Series vehicles during model year 1989. Some procedures for vehicles before and after the change are different. The term early production refers to 9000 Series vehicles through VINs K1009731, K2004996 or K8000276. Late production begins with VINs K1009732, K2004997, K8000277 and covers all subsequent years and models.

Hydraulic Modulator

REMOVAL AND INSTALLATION

900 Series

1. Disconnect the negative battery cable. Depressurize the system.
2. Thoroughly clean the unit, connections and surrounding surfaces to prevent dirt from entering the hydraulics.
3. Remove the center console.
4. Remove the padded trim panel under the dash.
5. Remove the heater duct.
6. Remove the insulation from behind the pedal assembly; disconnect the left defroster hose from the heater box.
7. Remove the retaining clip and remove the pin from the hydraulic unit pushrod.
8. Remove the air intake assembly.
9. Unbolt the coolant expansion tank; move it out of the way without disconnecting the hoses.
10. Disconnect the 4 electrical connectors from the hydraulic unit.
11. Unbolt the bracket between the hydraulic unit and the front assembly. Disconnect the wiring harness to the sensor and disconnect the ground strap at the hydraulic unit. Move the bracket and wiring out of the way.
12. Use a syringe or similar tool to remove as much fluid as possible from the hydraulic unit reservoir. It will not be possible to remove all the fluid.
13. For vehicles with manual transaxles, disconnect the hose running to the clutch system from the reservoir. Immediately plug the hose end; do not allow air to enter the clutch system.
14. Label or diagram the placement of the brake lines and large-diameter return line at the hydraulic unit. Disconnect the lines together to avoid undue strain on any one line. Immediately plug the lines and the ports on the valve block to prevent dirt from entering the system.
15. Inside the vehicle, remove the 4 nuts holding the hydraulic unit to the firewall. Remove the hydraulic unit by lifting it out of the engine compartment.

To install:

NOTE: During installation, it is possible for the brake switch and/or the cruise control switch to be pressed in inadvertently. If this occurs, the switch may be reset with a pair of pliers.

16. Place the hydraulic unit in position. Make certain the pushrod is correctly aligned with the pedal assembly.
17. Connect the pushrod with the pin and clip.
18. Install the 4 retaining nuts and tighten them to 19 ft. lbs. (26 Nm).
19. Connect the brake lines and the return line.
20. For manual transaxle vehicles, connect the clutch hose to the reservoir, making sure no fluid is lost from the hose.
21. Connect the sensor connector and install the bracket at the front of the assembly. Connect the ground strap to the top bolt.
22. Connect the 4 electrical harnesses. Make sure the connectors are squarely placed and firmly fitted.
23. Install the coolant tank and reinstall the air intake.
24. Fill the hydraulic unit reservoir with clean, fresh DOT 4 brake fluid. Switch the ignition ON to confirm that the pump is working. The pump should shut off within 60-90 seconds when correct pressure is achieved. If the pump does not shut off within 120 seconds, shut the ignition OFF immediately and allow the pump at least 10 minutes to cool.
25. Inspect the system for leaks. Make certain the ABS and BRAKE warning lamps go OFF.
26. Connect the left defroster hose and reinstall the insulation at the pedals.
27. Install the heater duct; install the trim below the dash.
28. Install the center console.
29. Test drive the vehicle to confirm correct operation of the service brakes, the ABS and the clutch, if equipped.

9000 Series

NOTE: A running production change was made during model year 1989. Some procedures for vehicles before and after the change are different. The term early production refers to 9000 Series vehicles through VINs K1009731, K2004996 or K8000276. Late production begins with VINs K1009732, K2004997, K8000277 and covers all subsequent years and models.

EARLY PRODUCTION

1. Disconnect the negative battery cable. Depressurize the system.
2. Thoroughly clean the unit, connections and surrounding surfaces to prevent dirt from entering the hydraulics.
3. Remove the 5 screws holding the lower dash panel below the steering column.
4. Remove the retaining clip holding the pin to the pushrod and remove the pin.
5. Disconnect and remove the battery.
6. Gain access to the hydraulic unit by removing the following components: the clip holding the wire harness to the battery shelf, the terminal block and harness from the battery shelf, the fuel filter, the battery shelf and the rubber elbow between the throttle housing and the inlet manifold.
7. Disconnect the 4 wiring connectors from the hydraulic unit. Release the wire harness retainers. Disconnect the ground strap from the hydraulic unit.
8. Remove the bracket from the hydraulic unit.
9. Use a syringe or similar tool to remove as much fluid as possible from the hydraulic unit reservoir. It will not be possible to remove all the fluid.
10. For vehicles with manual transaxles, remove the clutch fluid hose from the hydraulic unit reservoir. Immediately plug the end of the hose; do not allow air to enter the clutch system.
11. Raise and support the vehicle safely.
12. Remove the left front wheel and the left front wheel arch liner or inner fender.
13. Disconnect the electrical connector for the pump motor at the hydraulic unit.
14. Clean the brake fittings and valve block thoroughly. Disconnect the brake lines from the valve block and immediately plug the lines and ports to prevent the entry of dirt.
15. Remove the 4 nuts holding the hydraulic unit to the firewall. Lift the hydraulic unit out of the engine compartment.

To install:

NOTE: During installation, it is possible for the brake switch and/or the cruise control switch to be pressed in inadvertently. If this occurs, the switch may be reset with a pair of pliers.

16. Place the hydraulic unit in position. Make certain the pushrod is correctly aligned with the pedal assembly.

17. Connect the pushrod with the pin and clip.

18. Install the 4 retaining nuts and tighten them to 19 ft. lbs. (26 Nm).

19. Reconnect the brake lines to the valve block.

20. Connect the pump motor harness at the hydraulic unit.

21. Install the bracket on the hydraulic unit; install the support and wire harness retainers.

22. Connect the 4 wiring harnesses to the hydraulic unit.

23. Install the rubber elbow at the throttle housing, the battery shelf, the fuel filter, the terminal block and the wire harness retainers.

24. Install the battery and connect the cables. Leave the ignition switched **OFF**.

25. If equipped with manual transaxle, reconnect the fluid hose to the reservoir.

26. Fill the reservoir with DOT 4 fluid brake fluid.

27. Switch the ignition **ON** and confirm that the pump is working. The pump should shut off within 60-90 seconds when correct pressure is achieved. If the pump does not shut off within 120 seconds, shut the ignition **OFF** immediately and allow the pump at least 10 minutes to cool.

28. Check the system for leaks. Make certain the ABS and BRAKE warning lamps are OFF.

29. Bleed the brake system.

30. Reinstall the lower dash panel.

31. Install the fender liner and wheel. Lower the vehicle to the ground.

32. Test drive the vehicle to confirm correct operation of the service brakes, the ABS and the clutch, if equipped.

LATE PRODUCTION

1. Disconnect the negative battery cable. Depressurize the system.

2. Thoroughly clean the unit, connections and surrounding surfaces to prevent dirt from entering the hydraulics.

3. Remove the 5 screws holding the lower dash panel below the steering column.

4. Remove the retaining clip holding the pin to the pushrod and remove the pin.

5. Disconnect and remove the battery.

6. Gain access to the hydraulic unit by removing the following components: the 2 clips holding the positive battery cable at the bottom of the battery shelf, the terminal block and wires at the front of the battery shelf, the bracket and connector(s) at the rear of the battery shelf and the fuel filter from the battery shelf.

7. Remove the battery shelf and move the fuel filter out of the way.

8. Use a syringe or similar tool to remove as much fluid as possible from the hydraulic unit reservoir. It will not be possible to remove all the fluid.

9. Raise and support the vehicle safely.

10. Remove the left front wheel and the left front wheel arch liner or inner fender. Remove the support between the fender and the sub-frame.

11. Disconnect the 5 wiring connectors from the hydraulic unit. Release the wire harness retainer and disconnect the ground strap from the hydraulic unit.

12. For vehicles with manual transaxle, remove the clutch fluid hose from the hydraulic unit reservoir. Immediately plug the end of the hose; do not allow air to enter the clutch system.

13. Clean the brake fittings and valve block thoroughly. Disconnect the brake lines from the valve block and immediately plug the lines and ports to prevent the entry of dirt.

14. Use an 8mm hex bit to remove the accumulator from the hydraulic unit.

15. Remove the 4 nuts holding the hydraulic unit to the firewall. Lift the hydraulic unit out of the engine compartment.

To install:

NOTE: During installation, it is possible for the brake switch and/or the cruise control switch to be pressed in inadvertently. If this occurs, the switch may be reset with a pair of pliers.

16. Place the hydraulic unit in position. Make certain the pushrod is correctly aligned with the pedal assembly.

17. Connect the pushrod with the pin and clip.

18. Install the 4 retaining nuts and tighten them to 19 ft. lbs. (26 Nm).

19. Install the accumulator. Tighten it to 28 ft. lbs. (38 Nm).

20. Reconnect the brake lines to the valve block.

21. If equipped with manual transaxle, reconnect the fluid hose to the reservoir. Make certain there is fluid in the hose before connecting it.

22. Connect the ground strap.

23. Connect the wiring harnesses to the hydraulic unit.

24. Install the fender support.

25. Reinstall the battery shelf.

26. Install the 2 clips at the bottom of the battery shelf, the terminal block and harness, the bracket and connector(s) at the rear of the shelf and the fuel filter.

27. Install the battery and connect the cables. Leave the ignition switched **OFF**.

28. Fill the reservoir with DOT 4 fluid brake fluid.

29. Turn the ignition **ON** and confirm that the pump is working. The pump should shut off within 60-90 seconds when correct pressure is achieved. If the pump does not shut off within 120 seconds, turn the ignition **OFF** immediately and allow the pump at least 10 minutes to cool.

30. Check the system for leaks. Make certain the ABS and BRAKE warning lamps are OFF.

31. Bleed the brake system.

32. Reinstall the lower dash panel.

33. Install the fender liner and wheel. Lower the vehicle.

34. Test drive the vehicle to confirm correct operation of the service brakes, the ABS and the clutch, if so equipped.

Pressure Switch

REMOVAL AND INSTALLATION

NOTE: A running production change was made on 9000 Series vehicles during model year 1989. Some procedures for vehicles before and after the change are different. The term early production refers to 9000 Series vehicles through VINs K1009731, K2004996 or K8000276. Late production begins with VINs K1009732, K2004997, K8000277 and covers all subsequent years and models.

900 Series

1. Depressurize the system.

2. Thoroughly clean the unit, connections and surrounding surfaces to prevent dirt from entering the hydraulics.

3. Remove the rubber sheath from the delivery pipe.

4. Remove the electrical connector from the pressure switch.

5. Remove the pressure switch, using a suitable socket 89-96-571 or equivalent.

To install:

6. Install a new O-ring and install the switch, tightening it to 17 ft. lbs. (23 Nm).

7. Reconnect the electrical harness to the switch.

8. Reinstall the rubber sheath on the delivery line.

9. Turn the ignition **ON**; check that the dashboard warning lamps turn OFF.

10. Inspect the brake system for leaks.

11. Test drive the vehicle, checking for the correct operation of the ABS system.

9000 Series

EARLY PRODUCTION

1. Disconnect the negative battery cable. Depressurize the system.

2. Thoroughly clean the unit, connections and surrounding surfaces to prevent dirt from entering the hydraulics.

3. Gain access to the hydraulic unit by removing the battery, fuel filter and battery shelf.

4. Disconnect the 4 wiring harnesses at the hydraulic unit.

5. Remove the bracket from the unit and disconnect the ground strap.

6. Remove the pressure switch by unscrewing it.

To install:

7. Install a new O-ring and install the switch, tightening it to 17 ft. lbs. (23 Nm).

8. Reconnect the electrical harnesses to the unit.

9. Install the support bracket and reconnect the ground strap.

10. Install the battery shelf, the fuel filter and the battery.

11. Switch the ignition **ON**; check that the dashboard warning lamps turn OFF.

12. Inspect the brake system for leaks.

13. Test drive the vehicle, checking for the correct operation of the ABS system.

LATE PRODUCTION

1. Disconnect the negative battery cable. Depressurize the system.

2. Thoroughly clean the unit, connections and surrounding surfaces to prevent dirt from entering the hydraulics.

3. Remove the rubber sheath from the delivery pipe.

4. Remove the electrical connector from the pressure switch.

5. Remove the pressure switch, using a suitable socket 89-96-571 or equivalent.

To install:

6. Install a new O-ring and install the switch, tightening it to 17 ft. lbs. (23 Nm).

7. Reconnect the electrical harness to the switch.

8. Reinstall the rubber sheath on the delivery line.

9. Switch the ignition **ON**; check that the dashboard warning lamps turn OFF.

10. Inspect the brake system for leaks.

11. Test drive the vehicle, checking for the correct operation of the ABS system.

Valve Block

REMOVAL AND INSTALLATION

900 Series Only

1. Disconnect the negative battery cable. Depressurize the system.

2. Thoroughly clean the unit, connections and surrounding surfaces to prevent dirt from entering the hydraulics.

3. Remove the air intake.

4. Remove the coolant reservoir tank and move it out of the way with the hoses connected.

5. Use a syringe or similar tool to remove as much fluid as possible from the hydraulic unit reservoir. It will not be possible to remove all the fluid.

6. Disconnect the wire harness connector at the valve block.

7. Beginning with the fitting closest to the fender, disconnect the brake lines at the underside of the valve block. For reference, the line closest to the fender is to the front left brake, the centerline is to the rear brakes and the inboard fitting, closest to the engine, is for the right front brake.

8. At the hydraulic unit, loosen the ends of the lines running to the valve block. The lines need not be disconnected, but should be loose enough to turn or flex. This will prevent strain on the lines while disconnecting the other end.

9. Disconnect the brake lines and the large diameter return line from the valve block.

10. Cut the wire tie holding the wire harness to the valve block.

11. Remove the 3 mounting nuts and remove the valve block.

To install:

12. Place the unit in position and tighten the 3 mounting nuts.

13. Connect the 3 brake lines to the bottom of the valve block. Begin with the line closest to the fender and work towards the engine. This is the same order in which they were removed.

14. Use a new cable tie to secure the wire harness to the valve block.

15. Install the brake lines from the hydraulic unit to the valve block. Tighten the fittings at both ends after the lines are correctly positioned.

16. Connect the wire harness to the valve block.

17. Install the coolant reservoir tank and install the air intake.

18. Fill the reservoir with DOT 4 fluid brake fluid.

19. Bleed the brake system.

20. Inspect the system for leaks. Switch the ignition **ON**, checking that the dash warning lamps turn OFF.

21. Test drive the vehicle to confirm correct operation of the service brakes and the ABS.

ABS Electronic Control Unit (ECU)

REMOVAL AND INSTALLATION

900 Series

1. Disconnect the negative battery cable.

2. Unbolt the ECU from the left fender in the engine compartment.

3. Lift the unit. Disconnect the wire harness and remove the unit from the vehicle.

4. Install in reverse order. When reinstalling, connect the wire harness first, fit the unit into position and secure the mounting bolts.

5. Connect the negative battery cable.

9000 Series

1. Disconnect the negative battery cable.

2. Remove the left cover on the firewall panel.

3. Loosen the clips holding the unit.

4. Lift the ECU and disconnect the wire harness.

5. Install in reverse order, making sure the clips are secure. Connect the negative battery cable.

Wheel Speed Sensors

REMOVAL AND INSTALLATION

900 Series

FRONT

1. Disconnect the sensor harness in the engine compartment. The bayonet fitting is disconnected by pushing the halves together and twisting.

2. Raise and safely support the front of the vehicle. Remove the wheel.

3. Remove the sensor harness from the guide and pull it through the grommet in the wheel arch.

4. At the wheel hub, remove the retaining screw and lift the sensor straight out. Protect the tip of the sensor from impact or damage.

NOTE: Be certain to remove the plastic sleeve from the housing. The sleeve prevents corrosion between the sensor and the housing. The sleeve must be reinstalled during reassembly.

To install:

5. Loosen the set screw on the sensor assembly and transfer the adjusting sleeve to the new sensor if one is being installed. The sleeve must slide freely; if necessary, clean surfaces with a piece of fine emery cloth.

6. Use a wire brush or similar tool to remove all traces of the fiber spacer at the tip of the sensor. Use a light solvent if necessary.

7. Remove all traces of dirt inside the housing. Check the teeth of the sensor wheel and remove any remains of the fiber spacer from the teeth of the wheel.

8. Glue a new fiber spacer to the tip of the sensor. Correct spacer thickness is 0.026 in. (0.65mm). This spacer establishes the correct air gap between the sensor and the signal wheel.

9. Install the sensor and tighten the retaining bolt.

NOTE: Do not rotate the hub once the sensor is in place; the fiber pad will the damaged.

10. Press the sensor body lightly against the signal wheel and tighten the setscrew.

11. Route the sensor harness through the grommet in the wheel arch and install the harness in the guide.

12. Connect the wiring harness in the engine compartment.

13. Install the wheel. Double check that the wire harness to the sensor is completely clear of all moving components including steering and suspension parts.

14. Lower the vehicle.

REAR

1. Remove or lift the rear seat cushion; disconnect the sensor harness. The bayonet fitting is disconnected by pushing the halves together and twisting.

2. Raise and safely support the vehicle. Remove the wheel.

3. Pull the harness through the grommet in the floor.

4. Release the clip holding the hand brake cable to the suspension arm. Take careful note of the exact placement of the clip and cable; it must be reinstalled in the exact original position.

5. Release the sensor harness from the clip on the back of the suspension arm.

6. Remove the retaining bolt and remove the sensor. Protect the tip of the sensor from damage or impact.

NOTE: Be certain to remove the plastic sleeve from the housing. The sleeve prevents corrosion between the sensor and the housing. The sleeve must be reinstalled during reassembly.

7. Loosen the set screw on the sensor assembly and transfer the adjusting sleeve to the new sensor if one is being installed. The sleeve must slide freely; if necessary, clean surfaces with a piece of fine emery cloth.

8. Use a wire brush or similar tool to remove all traces of the fiber spacer at the tip of the sensor. Use a light solvent if necessary.

9. Remove all traces of dirt inside the housing. Check the teeth of the sensor wheel and remove any remains of the fiber spacer from the teeth of the wheel.

10. Glue a new fiber spacer to the tip of the sensor. Correct spacer thickness is 0.026 in. (0.65mm). This spacer establishes the correct air gap between the sensor and the signal wheel.

11. Install the sensor and tighten the retaining bolt.

NOTE: Do not rotate the hub once the sensor is in place; the fiber pad will the damaged.

12. Press the sensor body lightly against the signal wheel and tighten the setscrew.

13. Install the clip for the hand brake cable onto the suspension arm.

14. Install the sensor harness through the floor grommet. Secure the harness in the clip on the suspension arm.

15. Install the rear wheel; lower the vehicle to the ground.

16. Connect the sensor wiring to the ABS harness and reinstall the rear seat cushion.

9000 Series

FRONT

1. Disconnect the negative battery cable. For the left sensor:
   a. Remove the left cowl cover or access panel.
   b. Lift the moulding on the panel and release the plastic clip on the panel.
   c. Disconnect the sensor harness. The bayonet fitting is disconnected by pushing the halves together and twisting.

2. For the right sensor:
   a. Remove the cover from the fresh air filter at the firewall.
   b. Lift the moulding on the panel and disconnect the plastic clip at the panel.
   c. Loosen the clips holding the air conditioning lines.
   d. Disconnect the sensor harness. The bayonet fitting is disconnected by pushing the halves together and twisting.
   e. Lift the air conditioning lines and pull the sensor lead through.

3. Loosen the retaining bolt(s) for the cowl and raise the panel enough to allow the sensor harness to pass through underneath.

4. Raise and safely support the vehicle. Remove the wheel.

5. Remove the rear part of the inner fender liner.

6. Cut the wire tie holding the sensor lead to the top bracket.

7. Pull the sensor lead through the rubber grommet in the wheel arch.

8. Remove the retaining bolt and remove the sensor.

To install:

9. Loosen the set screw on the sensor assembly and transfer the adjusting sleeve to the new sensor if one is being installed. The sleeve must slide freely; if necessary, clean surfaces with a piece of fine emery cloth.

10. Use a wire brush or similar tool to remove all traces of the fiber spacer at the tip of the sensor. Use a light solvent if necessary.

11. Remove all traces of dirt inside the housing. Check the teeth of the sensor wheel and remove any remains of the fiber spacer from the teeth of the wheel.

12. Glue a new fiber spacer to the tip of the sensor. Correct spacer thickness is 0.026 in. (0.65mm). This spacer establishes the correct air gap

between the sensor and the signal wheel.

13. Install the sensor and tighten the retaining bolt.

NOTE: Do not rotate the hub once the sensor is in place; the fiber pad will the damaged.

14. Press the sensor body lightly against the signal wheel and tighten the setscrew.

15. Feed the sensor lead through the grommet and secure the harness in the brackets. Use a wire tie at the top bracket.

16. Connect the sensor wiring to the ABS harness at the cowl.

17. Reassemble the cowl cover and/or access panels.

18. Install the rear wheel arch liner.

19. Install the wheel and lower the vehicle to the ground.

20. Turn the steering wheel lock-to-lock, checking that the speed sensor harness is completely clear of all moving parts.

REAR

1. Tilt the rear seat forward and remove the cover on either side of the floorpan.

2. Disconnect the speed sensor connector. The bayonet fitting is disconnected by pushing the halves together and twisting.

3. Raise and safely support the rear of the vehicle. Remove the wheel.

4. Release the clip and pull the sensor harness through the grommet in the floorpan.

5. Remove the retaining bolt and remove the sensor straight out of the housing.

To install:

6. Loosen the set screw on the sensor assembly and transfer the adjusting sleeve to the new sensor if one is being installed. The sleeve must slide freely; if necessary, clean surfaces with a piece of fine emery cloth.

7. Use a wire brush or similar tool to remove all traces of the fiber spacer at the tip of the sensor. Use a light solvent if necessary.

8. Remove all traces of dirt inside the housing. Check the teeth of the sensor wheel and remove any remains of the fiber spacer from the teeth of the wheel.

9. Glue a new fiber spacer to the tip of the sensor. Correct spacer thickness is 0.026 in. (0.65mm). This spacer establishes the correct air gap between the sensor and the signal wheel.

10. Install the sensor and tighten the retaining bolt.

NOTE: Do not rotate the hub once the sensor is in place; the fiber pad will the damaged.

11. Press the sensor body lightly against the signal wheel and tighten the setscrew.

12. Install the sensor harness connector through the grommet; secure the harness in the clip.

13. Install the wheel and lower the vehicle to the ground.

14. Connect the sensor harness to the ABS harness. Install the access cover.

15. Reposition the rear seat.

CHASSIS ELECTRICAL

Air Bag

DISARMING

Always disconnect the negative battery cable and wait 20 minutes prior to servicing any component that may trigger the air bag. Do not use any diagnostic instruments that are battery powered to diagnose faults in the steering wheel or electronic control unit. Using such devices may trigger the air bag.

Heater Blower Motor

REMOVAL AND INSTALLATION

Without Air Conditioning

900 SERIES

1. Disconnect the negative battery cable.

2. Remove the switch panel and the upper section of the instrument panel. The screws retaining the switch panel are of different lengths. The screws are marked with grooves. Note the position of the screws for reassembly.

3. Disconnect the electrical leads to the fan motor.

4. Remove the retaining screws for the right defroster valve housing.

5. Remove the fan retaining screws. Remove the fan from its housing.

To install:

6. Fit the fan into the housing and install the retaining screws. Connect the fan electrical lead.

7. Install the right defroster valve housing, as required.

8. Install the instrument panel and switch panel, noting the proper locations of the retaining screws.

9. Connect the negative battery cable.

9000 SERIES

1. Disconnect the negative battery cable.

2. Remove the cover from the windshield wipers.

3. Remove the fresh air filter assembly.

4. Unplug the connectors for the fan motor and fan resistors.

5. Disconnect the temperature control cable.

6. Release the clips on either side of the fan body and turn the body diagonally upwards.

7. Remove the screws in the center of the casing, release the clips and remove the grille from the discharge duct.

8. Separate the fan casing. Remove the screw securing the fan motor.

9. Lift the cover for the lead and withdraw the motor complete with impeller.

To install:

10. Install the fan assembly into the housing.

11. Install the grille to the discharge duct.

12. Install the temperature control cable.

13. Reconnect the fan resistor and fan motor connectors.

14. Install the fresh air filter assembly and windshield wiper cover.

15. Connect the negative battery cable.

With Air Conditioning

900 SERIES

1. Disconnect the negative battery cable.

2. Remove the switch panel and the upper section of the instrument panel. The screws are marked with grooves. Note the position of the screws for reassembly.

3. Disconnect the electrical leads to the fan motor.

4. Remove the retaining screws for the right defroster valve housing.

5. Remove the fan retaining screws. Remove the fan from its housing.

To install:

6. Fit the fan into the housing and install the retaining screws. Connect the fan electrical lead.

7. Install the right defroster valve housing, as required.

8. Install the instrument panel and switch panel, noting the proper locations of the retaining screws.

9. Connect the negative battery cable.

9000 SERIES

1. Disconnect the negative battery cable. Remove the hood assembly.

2. Disconnect the wiper arms. Remove the covers on the evaporator and wiper motor. Unplug the connector for the fan control unit on vehicles with automatic climate control.

3. Remove the false fire wall panel.

4. Remove the plastic drainage tube moulding below the windshield moulding.

5. Remove the electronic ignition control unit retaining bolts and position it aside.

6. Remove the clip and unplug the connectors. Remove the complete wiper assembly.

7. Remove the rubber lead through panel for the coolant hoses. Drain cooling system. Disconnect the quick release couplings for the coolant hoses at the heat exchanger.

8. Remove the throttle dashpot assembly.

9. Remove the vacuum pump retaining screws. Position the pump aside.

10. Remove the evaporator body retaining screws and the clips for the refrigerant hoses.

11. Remove the lock washer and disconnect the cable for the temperature valve.

12. Carefully lift the evaporator and remove the clips on either side of the fan. Remove the complete fan assembly by twisting the fan diagonally upwards.

13. Remove the screw in the center of the casing. Release the clips and the grille at the discharge duct.

14. Separate the fan housing and remove the securing screw for the fan motor.

15. Lift the cover upward and withdraw the motor complete with the impeller.

To install:

16. Install the fan assembly into the housing.

17. Install the grille to the discharge duct.

18. Install the temperature control cable.

19. Install the fan assembly. Secure the clips and re-fit the evaporator.

20. Install the vacuum pump and throttle dashpot assembly.

21. Connect the quick release couplings for the coolant hoses at the heat exchanger.

22. Install the wiper assembly and connect the electrical connector.

23. Install the electronic ignition control unit retaining bolts.

24. Install the false fire wall panel.

25. Install the covers on the evaporator and wiper motor. Reconnect the connector for the fan control unit on vehicles with automatic climate control.

26. Install the wiper arms.

27. Connect the negative battery cable.

Windshield Wiper Motor

REMOVAL AND INSTALLATION

900 Series

1. Disconnect the negative battery cable. Remove the wiper arms from the vehicle. Remove the rubber grommets.

2. Remove the 4 mounting screws. Disconnect the electrical lead. Remove the wiper unit from the vehicle.

3. Separate the wiper motor from the wiper assembly.

4. Installation is the reverse of the removal procedure.

9000 Series

1. Disconnect the negative battery cable.

2. Raise the covers on the wiper arms, remove the retaining nuts and lift the arms off.

3. Remove the rubber grommets from the spindles and remove the 4 bulkhead panel bolts.

4. Lift the bulkhead panel from the vehicle.

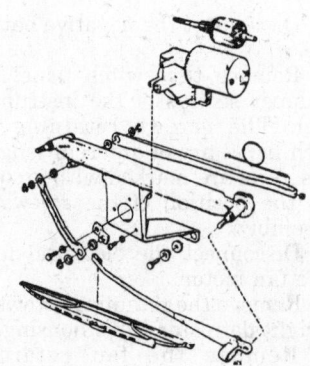

Windshield wiper and motor assembly

5. Disconnect the electrical connector from the wiper motor.

6. Remove the spindle nuts and remove the 4 retaining bolts for the wiper motor bracket.

7. Push downward and pull forward on the pushrod for the left wiper.

8. Lift out the wiper motor assembly complete with the bracket and the pushrod linkage.

To install:

9. Install the wiper motor assembly complete with the bracket and the pushrod linkage. Install the retaining bolts and spindle nuts.

10. Reconnect the wiper motor electrical connector.

11. Install the bulkhead panel.

12. Install the wiper arm and cover.

13. Connect the negative battery cable.

Windshield Wiper Switch

REMOVAL AND INSTALLATION

1. Disconnect the negative battery cable.

2. Pull the steering wheel as far forward as it will go. Remove the cover from under the steering column assembly.

3. Disconnect the electrical connector from the switch assembly.

4. Remove the switch retaining screws. Remove the switch from the vehicle.

5. Installation is the reverse of the removal procedure.

Instrument Cluster

REMOVAL AND INSTALLATION

900 Series

1. Disconnect the negative battery cable. Remove the steering wheel.

2. Remove the 4 screws in the switch panel and tilt the panel back.

3. Remove the left speaker/defroster grille. Pull apart the instrument panel connectors. Disconnect the speedometer cable.

4. Remove the instrument panel retaining screws. Carefully remove the unit from the vehicle.

5. Installation is the reverse of the removal procedure.

9000 Series

1. Disconnect the negative battery cable.

2. Remove the speaker grilles on either side of the panel.

3. Unscrew the top section of the instrument panel, which is retained by 7 screws including 1 in the glove box.

4. Lift off the top instrument panel section.

5. Remove the air duct from the opening in the top.

6. Disconnect the speedometer cable, the vacuum hoses to the turbocharger pressure gauge and unplug all connectors to the display panel.

7. Remove the 2 screws of the instrument display panel.

8. Withdraw the instrument cluster through the top of the instrument panel.

To install:

9. Place the instrument cluster into position and install the retaining screws.

10. Reconnect the speedometer cable, the vacuum hoses to the turbocharger pressure gauge and all connectors to the display panel.

11. Install the top air duct. Make sure the duct fitting is tight when reassembling the duct tubing.

12. Install the top instrument panel section.

13. Install the speaker grilles on either side of the panel.

14. Connect the negative battery cable.

Headlight Switch

REMOVAL AND INSTALLATION

1. Disconnect the negative battery cable.

2. Pull the switch from its mounting on the instrument panel assembly.

3. Disconnect the electrical connectors from the switch.

4. Remove the switch from the vehicle.

5. Installation is the reverse of the removal procedure.

Combination Switch

REMOVAL AND INSTALLATION

1. Disconnect the negative battery cable.

2. Remove the steering wheel.

3. Remove the cover under the bearing support.

4. Disconnect the combination switch electrical connections, remove the retaining bolts. Remove the switch from the vehicle.

5. Installation is the reverse of the removal procedure.

Ignition Switch

REMOVAL AND INSTALLATION

900 Series

1. Disconnect the negative battery cable.

2. Remove the center console.

3. Disconnect the electrical connections from the switch.

4. Remove the assembly from the vehicle.

5. Installation is the reverse of removal.

9000 Series

1. Disconnect the negative battery cable.

2. Remove the steering wheel assembly.

3. Remove the cover panels from the wiper/washer and direction indicator switches.

4. Remove the upper section of the instrument panel. Remove the instrument cluster assembly.

5. Remove the clip securing the wiring loom and flexible ducts to the steering column.

6. Unplug the connector for the wipers, direction signals and leads for the horn switch and ignition switch.

7. Remove the pinch bolt in the upper joint. Loosen the other bolts and withdraw the universal joint from the splines on the steering column shaft.

8. Remove the steering column wheel adjustment assembly by tapping out the roll pin and removing the nut and washer. Withdraw the shaft from the clamp and lift the upper section of the steering wheel adjustment assembly. Remove the 3 socket head bolts and lift off the holder for the directional indicator unit.

9. Remove the upper section of the steering column, removing the rubber bushing completely from the housing.

10. Remove the shake-proof washer. Remove the column bearing.

11. With the switch support out, remove the socket head screws. Remove the ignition switch.

12. To remove the cylinder, turn the ignition key to position **1**, press in on the locking tab and withdraw the cylinder.

To install:

13. Install the cylinder, socket head screws, shake-proof washer and column bearing. Install the rubber

bushing and the upper section of the column.

14. Install the steering column wheel adjustment assembly using a new roll pin. Install the directional indicator unit.

15. Install the universal joint and pinch bolt. Connect all electrical connections.

16. Install the cover panels.

17. Install the steering wheel.

18. Connect the negative battery cable.

Stoplight Switch

REMOVAL AND INSTALLATION

1. Disconnect the negative battery cable.

2. Remove the necessary trim and padding to gain access to the switch assembly.

3. Disconnect the electrical connections from the switch assembly.

4. Remove the switch from its mounting.

5. Installation is the reverse of the removal procedure.

Neutral Safety Switch

ADJUSTMENT

1. Disconnect the wires from the switch. The wide terminals are for backup lights and the narrow ones are for the starter motor.

2. Loosen the locknut and unscrew the switch 2 turns.

3. With the selector in **D**, connect a test light between the narrow terminals. The light should come on.

4. Screw the switch in until the light goes off. Mark that position on both the transaxle and the switch.

5. Move the test light to the wide terminals. Screw the switch in until the light goes off again. Record the number of turns between the 2 lights off points.

6. Turn the switch to a point halfway between the 2 lights off points.

7. Secure the locknut to 4-6 ft. lbs. (12-14 Nm). If the safety switch is locked too tight, it may be damaged.

REMOVAL AND INSTALLATION

1. Disconnect the negative battery cable.

2. Disconnect the wires from the switch and unscrew the switch.

3. Installation is the reverse of the removal procedure. After installation, adjust the switch.

Fuses and Circuit Breakers

LOCATION

900 Series

Fuses are located in the electrical distribution box on the left hand wheel housing under the hood. The oxygen sensor fuse is located on the right side of the engine compartment at the fresh air intake. The convertible top fuse is located in the engine compartment at the right side distribution block. The passive seat belt fuses are located under the left rear seat.

9000 Series

Fuses are located in a fuse box and can be reached through an access panel in the glove compartment. Fuses are also located in the electrical distribution box near the left headlight. ABS fuses are located in the engine compartment behind the firewall partition on the ABS relay and fuse board.

Fusible Links

LOCATION

Fusible links may be located at the battery, starter or alternator.

SPECIFICATIONS

ENGINE IDENTIFICATION

Year	Model	Engine Displacement Liters (cc)	Engine Series (ID/VIN)	Fuel System	No. of Cylinders	Engine Type
1990	Justy	1.2 (1189)	8	2 bbl	3	SOHC
	Justy GL	1.2 (1189)	8	MPFI	3	SOHC
	Loyale	1.8 (1781)	4	MPFI	4	SOHC
	XT	1.8 (1781)	7	MPFI	4	SOHC
	XT6	2.7 (2672)	9	MPFI	6	SOHC
	Legacy	2.2 (2212)	6	MPFI	4	SOHC
	Legacy Turbo	2.2 (2212)	6	Turbo	4	SOHC
1991	Justy GL	1.2 (1189)	7	MPFI	3	SOHC
	Justy	1.2 (1189)	7	2 bbl	3	SOHC
	Legacy	2.2 (2212)	6	MPFI	4	SOHC
	Loyale	1.8 (1781)	4	EFI	4	SOHC
	XT6	2.7 (2672)	9	MPFI	6	SOHC
	XT	1.8 (1781)	8	MPFI	4	SOHC
1992	Justy	1.2 (1189)	7	2 bbl	3	SOHC
	Justy GL	1.2 (1189)	7	MPFI	3	SOHC
	Legacy	2.2 (2212)	6	MPFI	4	SOHC
	Legacy Turbo	2.2 (2212)	6	Turbo	4	SOHC
	Loyale	1.8 (1781)	4	EFI	4	SOHC
	SVX	3.3 (3318)	3	SPFI	6	DOHC
1993	Justy	1.2 (1189)	7	MPFI	3	SOHC
	Legacy	2.2 (2212)	6	SPFI	4	SOHC
	Legacy Turbo	2.2 (2212)	6	Turbo	4	SOHC
	Loyale	1.8 (1781)	4	EFI	4	SOHC
	SVX	3.3 (3318)	3	SPFI	6	DOHC
1994	Justy	1.2 (1189)	7	MPFI	3	SOHC
	Legacy	2.2 (2212)	6	SPFI	4	SOHC
	Legacy Turbo	2.2 (2212)	6	Turbo	4	SOHC
	Loyale	1.8 (1781)	4	EFI	4	SOHC
	SVX	3.3 (3318)	3	SPFI	6	DOHC

NOTE: STD designates—4 door sedan; Station wagon; Touring wagon; 3 door wagon
OHC—Overhead Camshaft
MPFI—Multi-Point Fuel Injection
SPFI—Single-Point Fuel Injection
EFI—Electronic Fuel Injection
SOHC—Single Overhead Cam
DOHC—Dual Overhead Cam
2 bbl—2 Barrel Carburetor
OHV—Overhead Valves
Turbo—Turbocharged engine

GENERAL ENGINE SPECIFICATIONS

Year	Model	Engine ID/VIN	Engine Displacement Liters (cc)	Fuel System Type	Net Horsepower @ rpm	Net Torque @ rpm (ft. lbs.)	Bore × Stroke (in.)	Compression Ratio	Oil Pressure @ rpm
1990	XT	7	1.8 (1781)	MPFI	97 @ 5200	103 @ 3200	3.62 × 2.64	9.5:1	43 @ 5000
	XT-6	9	2.7 (2672)	MPFI	145 @ 5200	156 @ 4000	3.62 × 2.64	7.7:1	43 @ 5000
	Justy	8	1.2 (1189)	2 bbl	66 @ 5200	70 @ 3600	3.07 × 3.27	9.1:1	47 @ 3000
	Justy GL	8	1.2 (1189)	MPFI	73 @ 5600	71 @ 2800	3.07 × 3.27	9.1:1	47 @ 3000
	Loyale	4	1.8 (1781)	SPFI	90 @ 5200	101 @ 2800	3.62 × 2.64	9.5:1	43 @ 5000
	Legacy	6	2.2 (2212)	MPFI	130 @ 5600	137 @ 2400	3.82 × 2.95	9.5:1	43 @ 5000
1991	XTGL	8	1.8 (1781)	MPFI	97 @ 5200	103 @ 3200	3.62 × 2.64	9.5:1	43 @ 5000
	XT-6	9	2.7 (2672)	MPFI	145 @ 5200	156 @ 4000	3.62 × 2.64	7.7:1	43 @ 5000
	Justy	7	1.2 (1189)	2 bbl	66 @ 5200	70 @ 3600	3.07 × 3.27	9.1:1	47 @ 3000
	Justy GL	7	1.2 (1189)	MPFI	73 @ 5600	71 @ 2800	3.07 × 3.27	9.1:1	47 @ 3000
	Loyale	4	1.8 (1781)	SPFI	90 @ 5200	101 @ 2800	3.62 × 2.64	9.5:1	43 @ 5000
	Legacy	6	2.2 (2212)	MPFI	130 @ 5600	137 @ 2400	3.82 × 2.95	9.5:1	43 @ 5000
	Legacy Turbo	6	2.2 (2212)	MPFI Turbo	160 @ 5600	181 @ 2800	3.82 × 2.95	8.0:1	43 @ 5000
1992	Justy	7	1.2 (1189)	2 bbl	66 @ 5200	70 @ 3600	3.07 × 3.27	9.1:1	47 @ 3000
	Justy GL	7	1.2 (1189)	MPFI	73 @ 5600	71 @ 2800	3.07 × 3.27	9.1:1	47 @ 3000
	Loyale	4	1.8 (1781)	SPFI	90 @ 5200	101 @ 2800	3.62 × 2.64	9.5:1	43 @ 5000
	Legacy	6	2.2 (2212)	MPFI	130 @ 5600	137 @ 2400	3.82 × 2.95	9.5:1	43 @ 5000
	Legacy Turbo	6	2.2 (2212)	MPFI Turbo	160 @ 5600	181 @ 2800	3.82 × 2.95	8.0:1	43 @ 5000
	SVX	3	3.3 (3318)	MPFI	230 @ 5400	228 @ 4400	3.82 × 2.95	10.1:1	43 @ 5000
1993	Justy	7	1.2 (1189)	MPFI	73 @ 5600	71 @ 2800	3.07 × 3.27	9.1:1	47 @ 3000
	Loyale	4	1.8 (1781)	SPFI	90 @ 5200	101 @ 2800	3.62 × 2.64	9.5:1	43 @ 5000
	Legacy	6	2.2 (2212)	MPFI	130 @ 5600	137 @ 2400	3.82 × 2.95	9.5:1	43 @ 5000
	Legacy Turbo	6	2.2 (2212)	MPFI	160 @ 5600	181 @ 2800	3.82 × 2.95	8.0:1	43 @ 5000
	SVX	3	3.3 (3318)	MPFI	230 @ 5400	228 @ 4400	3.82 × 2.95	10.1:1	43 @ 5000
1994	Justy	7	1.2 (1189)	MPFI	73 @ 5600	71 @ 2800	3.07 × 3.27	9.1:1	47 @ 3000
	Loyale	4	1.8 (1781)	SPFI	90 @ 5200	101 @ 2800	3.62 × 2.64	9.5:1	43 @ 5000
	Legacy	6	2.2 (2212)	MPFI	130 @ 5600	137 @ 2400	3.82 × 2.95	9.5:1	43 @ 5000
	Legacy Turbo	6	2.2 (2212)	MPFI	160 @ 5600	181 @ 2800	3.82 × 2.95	8.0:1	43 @ 5000
	SVX	3	3.3 (3318)	MPFI	230 @ 5400	228 @ 4400	3.82 × 2.95	10.1:1	43 @ 5000

2 bbl—2 Barrel Carburetor
MPFI—Multi-Point Fuel Injection
SPFI—Sequential Fuel Injection

GASOLINE ENGINE TUNE-UP SPECIFICATIONS

Year	Model	Engine ID/VIN	Engine Displacement Liters (cc)	Spark Plugs Gap (in.)	Ignition Timing (deg.) MT	AT	Fuel Pump (psi)	Idle Speed (rpm) MT	AT	Valve Clearance In.	Ex.
1990	XT	7	1.8 (1781)	0.039–0.043	20B	20B	61–71	700	800	Hyd.	Hyd.
	XT-6	9	2.7 (2672)	0.039–0.043	20B	20B	61–71	750	750	Hyd.	Hyd.
	Justy	8	1.2 (1189)	0.039–0.043	5B	5B	1.3–2.0	800	800	0.006	0.010
	Loyale	4	1.8 (1781)	0.039–0.043	20B	20B	28–43	700	700	Hyd.	Hyd.
	Legacy	6	2.2 (2212)	0.039–0.043	20B	20B	36	700	700	Hyd.	Hyd.
	Legacy Turbo	6	2.2 (2212)	0.039–0.043	15B	15B	36	700	700	Hyd.	Hyd.
1991	XT	8	1.8 (1781)	0.039–0.043	20B	20B	61–71	700	800	Hyd.	Hyd.
	XT-6	9	2.7 (2672)	0.039–0.043	20B	20B	61–71	750	750	Hyd.	Hyd.
	Justy	7	1.2 (1189)	0.039–0.043	5B	5B	1.3–2.0	800	800	0.006	0.010
	Loyale	4	1.8 (1781)	0.039–0.043	20B	20B	28–43	700	700	Hyd.	Hyd.
	Legacy	6	2.2 (2212)	0.039–0.043	20B	20B	36	700	700	Hyd.	Hyd.
	Legacy Turbo	6	2.2 (2212)	0.039–0.043	15B	15B	36	700	700	Hyd.	Hyd.
1992	Justy	7	1.2 (1189)	0.039–0.043	5B	5B	1.3–2.0	800	800	0.006	0.010
	Loyale	4	1.8 (1781)	0.039–0.043	20B	20B	28–43	700	700	Hyd.	Hyd.
	Legacy	6	2.2 (2212)	0.039–0.043	20B	20B	36	700	700	Hyd.	Hyd.
	Legacy Turbo	6	2.2 (2212)	0.039–0.043	15B	15B	36	700	700	Hyd.	Hyd.
	SVX	3	3.3 (3318)	0.039–0.043	—	20B	43	—	610	Hyd.	Hyd.
1993	Justy	7	1.2 (1189)	0.039–0.043	5B	5B	1.3–2.0	800	800	0.006	0.010
	Loyale	4	1.8 (1781)	0.039–0.043	20B	20B	28–43	700	700	Hyd.	Hyd.
	Legacy	6	2.2 (2212)	0.039–0.043	20B	20B	36	700	700	Hyd.	Hyd.
	Legacy Turbo	6	2.2 (2212)	0.039–0.043	15B	15B	36	700	700	Hyd.	Hyd.
	SVX	3	3.3 (3318)	0.039–0.043	—	20B	43	—	610	Hyd.	Hyd.
1994	Justy	7	1.2 (1189)	0.039–0.043	5B	5B	1.3–2.0	800	800	0.006	0.010
	Loyale	4	1.8 (1781)	0.039–0.043	20B	20B	28–43	700	700	Hyd.	Hyd.
	Legacy	6	2.2 (2212)	0.039–0.043	20B	20B	36	700	700	Hyd.	Hyd.
	Legacy Turbo	6	2.2 (2212)	0.039–0.043	15B	15B	36	700	700	Hyd.	Hyd.
	SVX	3	3.3 (3318)	0.039–0.043	—	20B	43	—	610	Hyd.	Hyd.

NOTE: The lowest cylinder pressure should be within 75% of the highest cylinder pressure reading. For example, if the highest cylinder is 134 psi, the lowest should be 101. Engine should be at normal operating temperature with throttle valve in the wide open position.
The underhood specifications sticker often reflects tune-up specification changes in production. Sticker figures must be used if they disagree with those in this chart.
B—Before Top Dead Center
Hyd.—Hydraulic

FIRING ORDERS

NOTE: To avoid confusion, always replace the spark plug wires one at a time.

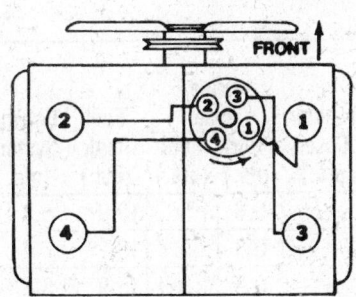

1.8L Engine
Engine Firing Order: 1-3-2-4
 Distributor Rotation: Counterclockwise

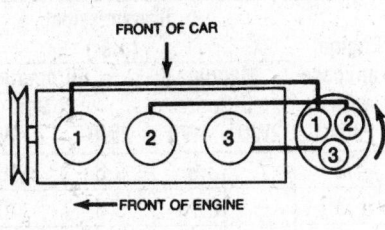

1.2L Engine
Engine Firing Order: 1-3-2
Distributor Rotation: Counterclockwise

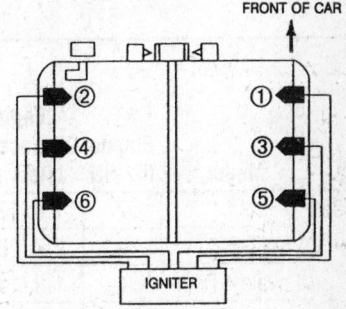

3.3 Engine
 Engine Firing Order: 1-6-3-2-5-4
 Distributorless Ignition System

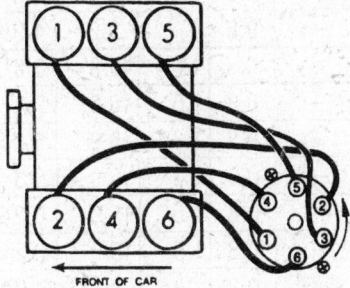

2.7L Engine
Engine Firing Order: 1-6-3-2-5-4
Distributor Rotation: Counterclockwise

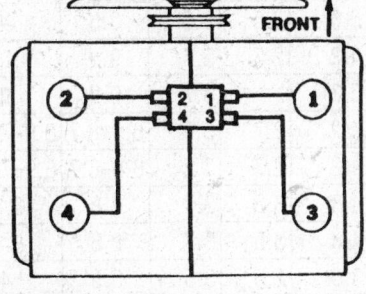

2.2L Engine
Engine Firing Order: 1-3-2-4
Distributorless Ignition System

CAPACITIES

Year	Model	Engine ID/VIN	Engine Displacement Liters (cc)	Engine Crankcase with Filter	Transmission (pts.) Manual 5-Spd 2WD	4WD	Automatic 5 Spd 2WD	4WD	Transfer Case (pts.)	Drive Axle Front (pts.)	Rear (pts.)	Fuel Tank (gal.)	Cooling System (qts.)
1990	XT	7	1.8 (1781)	4.2	2.7	3.5	9.8	10.0	—	0.8	1.5	15.9	5.8
	XT-6①	9	2.7 (2672)	5.3	—	3.7	9.8	10.0	—	0.8	1.5	15.9	7.4
	Loyale 4 Door	4	1.8 (1781)	4.2	2.7	3.5	6.5–6.7	6.9–7.1③	—	0.8	1.3⑤	15.9	5.8⑥
	Loyale Wagon	4	1.8 (1781)	4.2	2.7	3.5	6.5–6.7	6.9–7.1③	—	0.8	1.3⑤	15.9	5.8⑥
	Loyale 3 Door	4	1.8 (1781)	4.2	2.7②	2.7⑦	6.5–6.7	6.0–6.7③⑧	—	0.8	1.3⑤	15.9	5.8⑥
	Legacy 4 Door	6	2.2 (2212)	4.2	2.7	3.5	6.5–6.7	6.9–7.1③	—	0.8	1.3⑤	15.9	5.8⑥
	Legacy Wagon	6	2.2 (2212)	4.2	2.7	3.5	6.5–6.7	6.9–7.1③	—	0.8	1.3⑤	15.9	5.8⑥
	Justy	8	1.2 (1189)	3.0	2.5	3.6	3.5	4.4	—	0.8	—	9.2	4.9⑥
1991	XT	8	1.8 (1781)	4.2	2.7	3.5	9.8	10.0	—	0.8	1.5	15.9	5.8
	XT-6①	9	2.7 (2672)	5.3	—	3.7	9.8	10.0	—	0.8	1.5	15.9	7.4
	Loyale 4 Door	4	1.8 (1781)	4.2	2.7	3.5	6.5–6.7	6.9–7.1③	—	0.8	1.3⑤	15.9	5.8⑥
	Loyale Wagon	4	1.8 (1781)	4.2	2.7	3.5	6.5–6.7	6.9–7.1③	—	0.8	1.3⑤	15.9	5.8⑥
	Legacy 4 Door	6	2.2 (2212)	4.8	3.5	3.7	8.8	8.8⑨	—	0.8	1.5	15.9	6.2⑩
	Legacy Wagon	6	2.2 (2212)	4.8	3.5	3.7	8.8	8.8⑨	—	0.8	1.5	15.9	6.2⑩
	Justy	7	1.2 (1189)	3.0	2.5	3.6	3.5	4.4	—	0.8	—	9.2	4.9⑥
1992	Loyale 4 Door	4	1.8 (1781)	4.2	2.7	3.5	6.0	6.4	—	0.8	1.3	15.9	5.8
	Loyale Wagon	4	1.8 (1781)	4.2	2.7	3.5	6.0	6.4	—	0.8	1.3	15.9	5.8
	Legacy 4 Door	6	2.2 (2212)	4.8	3.5	3.7	8.8	8.8⑨	—	0.8	1.3	15.9	6.2⑩
	Legacy Wagon	6	2.2 (2212)	4.8	3.5	3.7	8.8	8.8⑨	—	0.8	1.3	15.9	6.2⑩
	Justy	7	1.2 (1189)	3.0	2.5	3.6	3.5	4.4	—	0.8	—	9.2	4.9④
	SVX	3	3.3 (3318)	6.3	—	—	10.0	10.0	—	0.8	1.3	18.2	7.4
1993	Loyale 4 Door	4	1.8 (1781)	4.2	2.7	3.5	6.0	6.4	—	0.8	1.3	15.9	5.8
	Loyale Wagon	4	1.8 (1781)	4.2	2.7	3.5	6.0	6.4	—	0.8	1.3	15.9	5.8
	Legacy 4 Door	6	2.2 (2212)	4.8	3.5	3.7	8.8	8.8⑨	—	0.8	1.3	15.9	6.2⑩
	Legacy Wagon	6	2.2 (2212)	4.8	3.5	3.7	8.8	8.8⑨	—	0.8	1.3	15.9	6.2⑩
	Justy	7	1.2 (1189)	3.0	2.5	3.6	3.5	4.4	—	0.8	—	9.2	4.9④
	SVX	3	3.3 (3318)	6.3	—	—	10.0	10.0	—	0.8	1.3	18.2	7.4
1994	Loyale 4 Door	4	1.8 (1781)	4.2	2.7	3.5	6.0	6.4	—	0.8	1.3	15.9	5.8
	Loyale Wagon	4	1.8 (1781)	4.2	2.7	3.5	6.0	6.4	—	0.8	1.3	15.9	5.8
	Legacy 4 Door	6	2.2 (2212)	4.8	3.5	3.7	8.8	8.8⑨	—	0.8	1.3	15.9	6.2⑩
	Legacy Wagon	6	2.2 (2212)	4.8	3.5	3.7	8.8	8.8⑨	—	0.8	1.3	15.9	6.2⑩
	Justy	7	1.2 (1189)	3.0	2.5	3.6	3.5	4.4	—	0.8	—	9.2	4.9④
	SVX	3	3.3 (3318)	6.3	—	—	10.0	10.0	—	0.8	1.3	18.2	7.4

① Turbo
② 3.5 w/Turbo
③ 10.0 w/Turbo
④ 5.2 w/EVCT
⑤ 1.5 w/Turbo
⑥ 6.3 w/Turbo
⑦ 3.5 w/RS
⑧ 6.9–7.1 w/RS
⑨ 9.4 w/Turbo
⑩ 7.4 w/Turbo

CAMSHAFT SPECIFICATIONS

All measurements given in inches.

Year	Engine ID/VIN	Engine Displacement Liters (cc)	Journal Diameter 1	2	3	4	5	Elevation In.	Ex.	Bearing Clearance	Camshaft End Play
1990	8	1.2 (1189)	—	—	—	—	—	1.4520–1.4528	1.4520–1.4528	—	0.0012–0.0150
	4	1.8 (1781)	1.8883–1.8890	1.9080–1.9087	1.8889–1.8890	1.5340–②1.5346	—	1.5650–1.5689	1.5650–1.5689	0.0008–0.0021	0.0012–0.0102
	7	1.8 (1781)	1.8883–1.8890	1.9080–1.9087	1.8889–1.8890	1.5340–②1.5346	—	1.5650–1.5689	1.5650–1.5689	0.0008–0.0021	0.0012–0.0102
	6	2.2 (2212)	1.4963–1.4970	1.4766–1.4774	1.2300–1.2608	—	—	1.2752–1.2791	1.2752–1.2791	0.0022–0.0035	0.0012–0.0102
	9	2.7 (2672)	1.4946–1.4953	1.9080–1.9087	1.8883–1.8890	1.9474–1.8693	1.5340–②1.5346	1.5606–1.5646	1.5606–1.5646	0.0008–0.0021	0.0012–0.0102
1991	7	1.2 (1189)	—	—	—	—	—	1.4520–1.4528	1.4520–1.4528	—	0.0012–0.0150
	4	1.8 (1781)	1.8883–1.8890	1.9080–1.9087	1.8889–1.8890	1.5340–②1.5346	—	1.5650–1.5689	1.5650–1.5689	0.0008–0.0021	0.0012–0.0102
	8	1.8 (1781)①	1.4946–1.4953	1.9080–1.9087	1.8883–1.8890	1.5340–②1.5346	—	1.5650–1.5689	1.5650–1.5689	0.0008–0.0021	0.0012–0.0102
	6	2.2 (2212)	1.4963–1.4970	1.4766–1.4774	1.2300–1.2608	—	—	1.2752–1.2791	1.2752–1.2791	0.0022–0.0035	0.0012–0.0102
	9	2.7 (2672)	1.4946–1.4953	1.9080–1.9087	1.8883–1.8890	1.9474–1.8693	1.5340–②1.5346	1.5606–1.5646	1.5606–1.5646	0.0008–0.0021	0.0012–0.0102
1992	7	1.2 (1189)	—	—	—	—	—	1.4520–1.4528	1.4520–1.4528	—	0.0012–0.0150
	4	1.8 (1781)	1.8883–1.8890	1.9080–1.9087	1.8889–1.8890	1.5340–②1.5346	—	1.5650–1.5689	1.5650–1.5689	0.0008–0.0021	0.0012–0.0102
	6	2.2 (2212)	1.4963–1.4970	1.4766–1.4774	1.2300–1.2608	—	—	1.2752–1.2791	1.2752–1.2791	0.0022–0.0035	0.0012–0.0102
	3	3.3 (3318)	1.2577–1.2584	1.1002–1.1009	1.1002–1.1009	1.1002–1.1009	—	1.5374–1.5413	1.5689–1.5728	0.0015–0.0028	③
1993	7	1.2 (1189)	—	—	—	—	—	1.4520–1.4528	1.4520–1.4528	—	0.0012–0.0150
	4	1.8 (1781)	1.8883–1.8890	1.9080–1.9087	1.8889–1.8890	1.5340–②1.5346	—	1.5650–1.5689	1.5650–1.5689	0.0008–0.0021	0.0012–0.0102
	6	2.2 (2212)	1.4693–1.4970	1.4766–1.4774	1.2300–1.2608	—	—	1.2752–1.2791	1.2752–1.2791	0.0022–0.0035	0.0012–0.0102
	3	3.3 (3318)	1.2577–1.2584	1.1002–1.1009	1.1002–1.1009	1.1002–1.1009	—	1.5374–1.5413	1.5689–1.5728	0.0015–0.0028	③
1994	7	1.2 (1189)	—	—	—	—	—	1.4520–1.4528	1.4520–1.4528	—	0.0012–0.0150
	4	1.8 (1781)	1.8883–1.8890	1.9080–1.9087	1.8889–1.8890	1.5340–②1.5346	—	1.5650–1.5689	1.5650–1.5689	0.0008–0.0021	0.0012–0.0102
	6	2.2 (2212)	1.4693–1.4970	1.4766–1.4774	1.2300–1.2608	—	—	1.2752–1.2791	1.2752–1.2791	0.0022–0.0035	0.0012–0.0102
	3	3.3 (3318)	1.2577–1.2584	1.1002–1.1009	1.1002–1.1009	1.1002–1.1009	—	1.5374–1.5413	1.5689–1.5728	0.0015–0.0028	③

① XT
② Distributor journal left-hand camshaft only
③ Exhaust: 0.0008–0.0031
  Intake: 0.0012–0.0035

CRANKSHAFT AND CONNECTING ROD SPECIFICATIONS

All measurements are given in inches.

Year	Engine ID/VIN	Engine Displacement Liters (cc)	Crankshaft				Connecting Rod		
			Main Brg. Journal Dia.	Main Brg. Oil Clearance	Shaft End-play	Thrust on No.	Journal Diameter	Oil Clearance	Side Clearance
1990	8	1.2 (1189)	1.6250–1.6290	0.0006–0.0018	0.0031–0.0070	4	0.6531–1.6535	0.0008–0.0021	0.0028–0.0118
	4	1.8 (1781)	①	②	0.0004–0.0037	2	1.7715–1.7720	0.0004–0.0021	0.0028–0.0130
	7	1.8 (1781)	①	②	0.0004–0.0037	2	1.7715–1.7720	0.0004–0.0021	0.0028–0.0130
	6	2.2 (2212)	2.3616–2.3622	④	0.0012–0.0045	3	2.0466–2.0472	0.0006–③ 0.0017	0.0028–0.0130
	9	2.7 (2672)	①	②	0.0004–0.0037	3	1.7715–1.6535	0.0004–0.0021	0.0028–0.0118
1991	7	1.2 (1189)	1.6250–1.6290	0.0006–0.0018	0.0031–0.0070	4	0.6531–1.6535	0.0008–0.0021	0.0028–0.0118
	4	1.8 (1781)	①	②	0.0004–0.0037	2	1.7715–1.7720	0.0004–0.0021	0.0028–0.0130
	8	1.8 (1781)	①	②	0.0004–0.0037	2	1.7715–1.7720	0.0004–0.0021	0.0028–0.0130
	6	2.2 (2212)	2.3616–2.3622	④	0.0012–0.0045	3	2.0466–2.0472	0.0006–③ 0.0017	0.0028–0.0130
	9	2.7 (2672)	①	②	0.0004–0.0037	3	1.7715–1.6535	0.0004–0.0021	0.0028–0.0118
1992	7	1.2 (1189)	1.6250–1.6290	0.0006–0.0018	0.0031–0.0070	4	0.6531–1.6535	0.0008–0.0021	0.0028–0.0118
	4	1.8 (1781)	①	②	0.0004–0.0037	2	1.7715–1.7720	0.0004–0.0021	0.0028–0.0130
	6	2.2 (2212)	2.3616–2.3622	④	0.0012–0.0045	3	2.0466–2.0472	0.0006–③ 0.0017	0.0028–0.0130
	3	3.3 (3318)	2.3619–2.3625	⑤	0.0012–0.0045	5	2.0466–2.0472	0.0008–0.0018	0.0028–0.0130
1993	7	1.2 (1189)	1.6250–1.6290	0.0006–0.0018	0.0031–0.0070	4	0.6531–1.6535	0.0008–0.0021	0.0028–0.0118
	4	1.8 (1781)	①	②	0.0004–0.0037	2	1.7715–1.7720	0.0004–0.0021	0.0028–0.0130
	6	2.2 (2212)	2.3616–2.3622	④	0.0012–0.0045	3	2.0466–2.0472	0.0006–③ 0.0017	0.0028–0.0130
	3	3.3 (3318)	2.3619–2.3625	⑤	0.0012–0.0045	5	2.0466–2.0472	0.0008–0.0018	0.0028–0.0130
1994	7	1.2 (1189)	1.6250–1.6290	0.0006–0.0018	0.0031–0.0070	4	0.6531–1.6535	0.0008–0.0021	0.0028–0.0118
	4	1.8 (1781)	①	②	0.0004–0.0037	2	1.7715–1.7720	0.0004–0.0021	0.0028–0.0130
	6	2.2 (2212)	2.3616–2.3622	④	0.0012–0.0045	3	2.0466–2.0472	0.0006–③ 0.0017	0.0028–0.0130
	3	3.3 (3318)	2.3619–2.3625	⑤	0.0012–0.0045	5	2.0466–2.0472	0.0008–0.0018	0.0028–0.0130

① Front: 2.1637–2.1642
  Center: 2.1635–2.1642
  Rear: 2.1636–2.1642
② Front and Rear: 0.0001–0.0014
  Center: 0.0003–0.0011
③ Turbo: 0.0010–0.0021
④ No. 1, 5: 0.0787–0.0792
  No. 2, 3, 4: 0.0787–0.0793
⑤ No. 1, 3, 7: 0.0002–0.0014
  No. 2, 4, 6: 0.0005–0.0015
  No. 5: 0.0005–0.0013
⑥ Front and Rear: 0.0004–0.0014
  Center: 0.0004–0.0012

VALVE SPECIFICATIONS

Year	Engine ID/VIN	Engine Displacement Liters (cc)	Seat Angle (deg.)	Face Angle (deg.)	Spring Test Pressure (lbs. @ in.)	Spring Installed Height (in.)	Stem-to-Guide Clearance (in.)		Stem Diameter (in.)	
							Intake	Exhaust	Intake	Exhaust
1990	8	1.2 (1189)	45	45	112–129 @ 1.248	1.248	0.0008–0.0020	0.0016–0.0028	0.2742–0.2748	0.2734–0.2740
	4	1.8 (1781)	45	45	112–129① @ 1.122	1.240	0.0014–0.0026	0.0016–0.0028	0.2736–0.2742	0.2734–0.2740
	7	1.8 (1781)	45	45	112–129① @ 1.122	1.240	0.0014–0.0026	0.0016–0.0028	0.2736–0.2742	0.2734–0.2740
	6	2.2 (2212)	45	45	92–106 @ 1.154	1.150	0.0014–0.0024	0.0016–0.0026	0.2343–0.2348	0.2341–0.2346
	9	2.7 (2672)	45	45	100–115① @ 1.122	1.240	0.0014–0.0026	0.0016–0.0028	0.2736–0.2741	0.2734–0.2740
1991	7	1.2 (1189)	45	45	112–129 @ 1.122	1.248	0.0008–0.0020	0.0016–0.0028	0.2742–0.2748	0.2734–0.2740
	4	1.8 (1781)	45	45	112–129① @ 1.122	1.240	0.0014–0.0026	0.0016–0.0028	0.2736–0.2742	0.2734–0.2740
	8	1.8 (1781)	45	45	112–129① @ 1.122	1.240	0.0014–0.0026	0.0016–0.0028	0.2736–0.2742	0.2734–0.2740
	6	2.2 (2212)	45	45	92–106 @ 1.154	1.150	0.0014–0.0024	0.0016–0.0026	0.2343–0.2348	0.2341–0.2346
	9	2.7 (2672)	45	45	100–115① @ 1.122	1.240	0.0014–0.0026	0.0016–0.0028	0.2736–0.2741	0.2734–0.2740
1992	7	1.2 (1189)	45	45	112–129 @ 1.122	1.248	0.0008–0.0020	0.0016–0.0028	0.2742–0.2748	0.2734–0.2740
	4	1.8 (1781)	45	45	112–129① @ 1.122	1.240	0.0014–0.0026	0.0016–0.0028	0.2736–0.2742	0.2734–0.2740
	6	2.2 (2212)	45	45	92–106 @ 1.154	1.150	0.0014–0.0024	0.0016–0.0026	0.2343–0.2348	0.2341–0.2346
	3	3.3 (3318)	45	45	70–80② @ 0.772	0.831	0.0012–0.0022	0.0016–0.0026	0.2344–0.2350	0.2341–0.2346
1993	7	1.2 (1189)	45	45	112–129 @ 1.122	1.248	0.0008–0.0020	0.0016–0.0028	0.2742–0.2748	0.2734–0.2740
	4	1.8 (1781)	45	45	112–129① @ 1.122	1.240	0.0014–0.0026	0.0016–0.0028	0.2736–0.2742	0.2734–0.2740
	6	2.2 (2212)	45	45	92–106 @ 1.154	1.150	0.0014–0.0024	0.0016–0.0026	0.2343–0.2348	0.2341–0.2346
	3	3.3 (3318)	45	45	70–80② @ 0.772	0.831	0.0012–0.0022	0.0016–0.0026	0.2344–0.2350	0.2341–0.2346
1994	7	1.2 (1189)	45	45	112–129 @ 1.122	1.248	0.0008–0.0020	0.0016–0.0028	0.2742–0.2748	0.2734–0.2740
	4	1.8 (1781)	45	45	112–129① @ 1.122	1.240	0.0014–0.0026	0.0016–0.0028	0.2736–0.2742	0.2734–0.2740
	6	2.2 (2212)	45	45	92–106 @ 1.154	1.150	0.0014–0.0024	0.0016–0.0026	0.2343–0.2348	0.2341–0.2346
	3	3.3 (3318)	45	45	70–80② @ 0.772	0.831	0.0012–0.0022	0.0016–0.0026	0.2344–0.2350	0.2341–0.2346

① Outer/Inner: 45–52 @ 1.122 in.
② Outer/Inner: 33–38 @ 0.772 in.

PISTON AND RING SPECIFICATIONS

All measurements are given in inches.

Year	Engine ID/VIN	Engine Displacement Liters (cc)	Piston Clearance	Ring Gap			Ring Side Clearance		
				Top Compression	Bottom Compression	Oil Control	Top Compression	Bottom Compression	Oil Control
1990	8	1.2 (1189)	0.0015–0.0028	0.0079–0.0138	0.0079–0.0138	0.0120–0.0350	0.0014–0.0030	0.0010–0.0026	0
	4	1.8 (1781)①	0.0006–②0.0014	0.0079–0.0138	0.0079–0.0138	0.0120–0.0350	0.0016–0.0031	0.0012–0.0028	0
	7	1.8 (1781)①	0.0006–②0.0014	0.0079–0.0138	0.0079–0.0138	0.0120–0.0350	0.0016–0.0031	0.0012–0.0028	0
	6	2.2 (2212)	0.0004–0.0012	0.0079–③0.0138	0.0146–0.0205	0.0079–0.0276	0.0016–0.0031	0.0012–0.0028	0
	9	2.7 (2672)	0.0006–0.0014	0.0079–0.0138	0.0079–0.0138	0.0120–0.0350	0.0016–0.0031	0.0012–0.0028	0
1991	7	1.2 (1189)	0.0015–0.0028	0.0079–0.0138	0.0079–0.0138	0.0120–0.0350	0.0014–0.0030	0.0010–0.0026	0
	4	1.8 (1781)①	0.0006–②0.0014	0.0079–0.0138	0.0079–0.0138	0.0120–0.0350	0.0016–0.0031	0.0012–0.0028	0
	8	1.8 (1781)①	0.0006–②0.0014	0.0079–0.0138	0.0079–0.0138	0.0120–0.0350	0.0016–0.0031	0.0012–0.0028	0
	6	2.2 (2212)	0.0004–0.0012	0.0079–③0.0138	0.0146–0.0205	0.0079–0.0276	0.0016–0.0031	0.0012–0.0028	0
	9	2.7 (2672)	0.0006–0.0014	0.0079–0.0138	0.0079–0.0138	0.0120–0.0350	0.0016–0.0031	0.0012–0.0028	0
1992	7	1.2 (1189)	0.0015–0.0028	0.0079–0.0138	0.0079–0.0138	0.0120–0.0350	0.0014–0.0030	0.0010–0.0026	0
	4	1.8 (1781)①	0.0006–②0.0016	0.0079–0.0138	0.0079–0.0138	0.0120–0.0350	0.0016–0.0031	0.0012–0.0028	0
	6	2.2 (2212)	0.0004–0.0012	0.0079–③0.0138	0.0146–0.0205	0.0079–0.0276	0.0016–0.0031	0.0012–0.0028	0
	3	3.3 (3318)	0.0004–0.0012	0.0079–0.0118	0.0146–0.0205	0.0079–0.0236	0.0016–0.0035	0.0012–0.0028	0
1993	7	1.2 (1189)	0.0015–0.0028	0.0079–0.0138	0.0079–0.0138	0.0120–0.0350	0.0014–0.0030	0.0010–0.0026	0
	4	1.8 (1781)①	0.0006–②0.0016	0.0079–0.0138	0.0079–0.0138	0.0120–0.0350	0.0016–0.0031	0.0012–0.0028	0
	6	2.2 (2212)	0.0004–0.0012	0.0079–③0.0138	0.0146–0.0205	0.0079–0.0276	0.0016–0.0031	0.0012–0.0028	0
	3	3.3 (3318)	0.0004–0.0012	0.0079–0.0118	0.0146–0.0205	0.0079–0.0236	0.0016–0.0035	0.0012–0.0028	0
1994	7	1.2 (1189)	0.0015–0.0028	0.0079–0.0138	0.0079–0.0138	0.0120–0.0350	0.0014–0.0030	0.0010–0.0026	0
	4	1.8 (1781)①	0.0006–②0.0016	0.0079–0.0138	0.0079–0.0138	0.0120–0.0350	0.0016–0.0031	0.0012–0.0028	0
	6	2.2 (2212)	0.0004–0.0012	0.0079–③0.0138	0.0146–0.0205	0.0079–0.0276	0.0016–0.0031	0.0012–0.0028	0
	3	3.3 (3318)	0.0004–0.0012	0.0079–0.0118	0.0146–0.0205	0.0079–0.0236	0.0016–0.0035	0.0012–0.0028	0

① XT
② TurboL 0.0004–0.0012
③ Turbo: 0.0079–0.0098

TORQUE SPECIFICATIONS

All readings in ft. lbs.

Year	Engine ID/VIN	Engine Displacement Liters (cc)	Cylinder Head Bolts	Main Bearing Bolts	Rod Bearing Bolts	Crankshaft Damper Bolts	Flywheel Bolts	Manifold Intake	Manifold Exhaust	Spark Plugs	Lug Nut
1990	8	1.2 (1189)	①	30–35	29–33	58–72	65–71	14–22	14–22	13–17	58–72
	4	1.8 (1781)	②	⑤	29–31	66–79	51–55	13–16	19–22	13–17	58–72
	6	2.2 (2212)	③	⑤	32–34	69–76	51–55	21–25	19–26	13–17	58–72
	9	2.7 (2672)	④	⑤	29–31	66–79	51–55	13–16	19–22	13–17	58–72
1991	7	1.2 (1189)	①	30–35	29–33	58–72	65–71	14–22	14–22	13–17	58–72
	4	1.8 (1781)	②	⑤	29–31	66–79	51–55	13–16	19–22	13–17	58–72
	6	2.2 (2212)	③	⑤	32–34	69–76	51–55	21–25	19–26	13–17	58–72
	9	2.7 (2672)	④	⑤	29–31	66–79	51–55	13–16	19–22	13–17	58–72
1992	7	1.2 (1189)	①	30–35	29–33	58–72	65–71	14–22	14–22	13–17	58–72
	4	1.8 (1781)	②	⑤	29–31	66–79	51–55	13–16	19–22	13–17	58–72
	6	2.2 (2212)	③	⑤	32–34	69–76	51–55	21–25	19–26	13–17	58–72
	3	3.3 (3318)	③	⑤	32–34	108–123	51–55	17–20	22–29	13–17	58–72
1993	7	1.2 (1189)	①	30–35	29–33	58–72	65–71	14–22	14–22	13–17	58–72
	4	1.8 (1781)	②	⑤	29–31	66–79	51–55	13–16	19–22	13–17	58–72
	6	2.2 (2212)	③	⑤	32–34	69–76	51–55	21–25	19–26	13–17	58–72
	3	3.3 (3318)	③	⑤	32–34	108–123	51–55	17–20	22–29	13–17	58–72
1994	7	1.2 (1189)	①	30–35	29–33	58–72	65–71	14–22	14–22	13–17	58–72
	4	1.8 (1781)	②	⑤	29–31	66–79	51–55	13–16	19–22	13–17	58–72
	6	2.2 (2212)	③	⑤	32–34	69–76	51–55	21–25	19–26	13–17	58–72
	3	3.3 (3318)	③	⑤	32–34	108–123	51–55	17–20	22–29	13–17	58–72

① Tighten all bolts in sequence to 29 ft. lbs. (39 Nm).
Tighten all bolts in sequence to 54 ft. lbs. (73 Nm).
Loosen all bolts 90° or more in the reverse order of the tightening sequence.
Tighten all bolts in sequence to 51–57 ft. lbs. (70–77 Nm).

② Tighten all bolts in sequence to 22 ft. lbs. (29 Nm).
Tighten all bolts in sequence to 43 ft. lbs. (59 Nm).
Tighten all bolts in sequence to 47 ft. lbs. (64 Nm).

③ Tighten all bolts in sequence to 22 ft. lbs. (29 Nm).
Tighten all bolts in sequence to 51 ft. lbs. (69 Nm).
Loosen all bolts by 180°, then loosen an additional 180°.
Tighten bolts 1 and 2 to 25 ft. lbs. (24 Nm) for non-turbo engines or 27 ft. lbs. (37 Nm) for turbo engines.
Tighten bolts 3, 4, 5 and 6 to 11 ft. lbs. (15 Nm) for non-turbo engines or 14 ft. lbs. (20 Nm) for turbo engines.
Tighten all bolts in sequence to 80–90°.
Tighten all bolts in sequence an additional 80–90°.

④ Tighten all bolts in sequence to 29 ft. lbs. (39 Nm).
Tighten all bolts in sequence to 47 ft. lbs. (64 Nm).
Loosen all bolts at least 90° in the reverse order of the tightening sequence.
Tighten all bolts in sequence to 44–50 ft. lbs. (60–68 Nm).

⑤ Engine is of the split case design and does not use main bearing caps. Tighten the case half bolts as follows: 3–4 ft. lbs. (6 Nm); 17–20 ft. lbs. (8 Nm); 29–35 ft. lbs. (10 Nm).

BRAKE SPECIFICATIONS

All measurements in inches unless noted.

Year	Model	Master Cylinder Bore	Brake Disc Original Thickness	Brake Disc Minimum Thickness	Maximum Runout	Brake Drum Diameter Original Inside Diameter	Brake Drum Diameter Max. Wear Limit	Brake Drum Diameter Maximum Machine Diameter	Minimum Lining Thickness Front	Minimum Lining Thickness Rear
1990	XT	0.8125	0.710⑧	0.630①	0.0039	7.09	7.17	7.17	0.295	0.256②
	XT6	0.9375	0.870⑧	0.787④	0.0039	—	—	—	0.295	0.315
	Justy	0.8125	0.709	0.610	0.0059	7.09	7.17	7.17	0.295③	0.067
	Loyale	0.8125	0.710⑧	0.630①	0.0039	7.09	7.17	7.17	0.295	0.256②
	Legacy	1.00⑤⑥	0.940⑧	0.870⑦	0.0039	—	—	—	0.295	0.256
1991	XT	0.8125	0.710⑧	0.630①	0.0039	7.09	7.17	7.17	0.295	0.256②
	XT6	0.9375	0.870⑧	0.787④	0.0039	—	—	—	0.295	0.315
	Justy	0.8125	0.709	0.610	0.0059	7.09	7.17	7.17	0.295③	0.067
	Loyale	0.8125	0.710⑧	0.630①	0.0039	7.09	7.17	7.17	0.295	0.256②
	Legacy	1.00⑤⑥	0.940⑧	0.870⑦	0.0039	—	—	—	0.295	0.256
1992	Justy	0.8125	0.709	0.610	0.0059	7.09	7.17	7.17	0.295③	0.067
	Loyale	0.8125	0.710⑧	0.630①	0.0039	7.09	7.17	7.17	0.295	0.256②
	Legacy	1.00⑤⑥	0.940⑧	0.870⑦	0.0039	—	—	—	0.295	0.256
	SVX	1.0625	1.100⑧	1.020①	0.0039	—	—	—	0.295	0.256
1993	Justy	0.8125	0.709	0.610	0.0059	7.09	7.17	7.17	0.295③	0.067
	Loyale	0.8125	0.710⑧	0.630①	0.0039	7.09	7.17	7.17	0.295	0.256②
	Legacy	1.00⑤⑥	0.940⑧	0.870⑦	0.0039	—	—	—	0.295	0.256
	SVX	1.0625	1.100⑧	1.020①	0.0039	—	—	—	0.295	0.256
1994	Justy	0.8125	0.709	0.610	0.0059	7.09	7.17	7.17	0.295③	0.067
	Loyale	0.8125	0.710⑧	0.630①	0.0039	7.09	7.17	7.17	0.295	0.256②
	Legacy	1.00⑤⑥	0.940⑧	0.870⑦	0.0039	—	—	—	0.295	0.256
	SVX	1.0625	1.100⑧	1.020①	0.0039	—	—	—	0.295	0.256

NOTE: STD. Includes 2 door, 3 door, 4 door and Wagon models
① Rear disc: 0.335 in.
② With drum brakes; 0.059 in.
③ GL Models: 0.315 in.
④ Rear disc: 0.335 in.
⑤ LX model with 4WD: 1.0625 in.
⑥ With ABS: 1.0625 in.
⑦ Rear disc: 0.335 in.
⑧ Rear disc thickness: 0.390 in.

WHEEL ALIGNMENT

Year	Model	Caster Range (deg.)	Caster Preferred Setting (deg.)	Camber Range (deg.)	Camber Preferred Setting (deg.)	Toe-in (in.)	Steering Axis Inclination (deg.)
1990	2WD XT Coupe	$3^{15}/_{16}$P–$4^{13}/_{16}$P	$4^1/_{16}$P	$3/_4$N–$3/_4$P	0	$1/_8$–$1/_8$ ①	NA
	4WD XT Coupe (4 cylinder)	$2^5/_8$P–$4^1/_8$P	$3^3/_8$P	$1/_{16}$N–$1^3/_8$P	$5/_8$P	$3/_8$ ① –$1/_8$ ①	NA
	4WD XT Coupe (6 cylinder)	$2^3/_4$P–$4^1/_4$P	$3^1/_2$P	$1/_{16}$P–$1^9/_{16}$P	$13/_{16}$P	$3/_8$ ① –$1/_8$ ①	NA
	2WD Loyale Sedan	$1^3/_4$P–$3^1/_4$P	$2^1/_2$P	0–$1^1/_2$P	$3/_4$P	$1/_4$–$1/_{16}$ ①	
	4WD Loyale Sedan without Air Susp.	$1^1/_{16}$P–$2^9/_{16}$P	$1^{13}/_{16}$P	$15/_{16}$P–$2^7/_{16}$P	$1^{11}/_{16}$P	$1/_{16}$ ① –$3/_{16}$ ①	NA
	2WD Loyale SW	$1^5/_{16}$P–$2^{13}/_{16}$P	$2^1/_{16}$P	$1/_4$P–$1^3/_4$P	1P	$1/_{16}$ ① –$3/_{16}$ ①	NA
	4WD Loyale SW	$1^3/_{16}$P–$2^5/_{16}$P	$1^9/_{16}$P	$15/_{16}$P–$2^7/_{16}$P	$1^3/_4$P	$1/_{16}$ ① –$3/_{16}$ ①	NA
	Justy	$1^1/_2$P–$3^1/_2$P	$2^1/_2$P	$5/_{16}$N–$1^{11}/_{16}$P	$11/_{16}$P	$5/_{16}$–$1/_{16}$ ①	NA
	Legacy FWD Sedan	$2^1/_{16}$P–$4^1/_{16}$P ③	$3^1/_{16}$P ④	$3/_4$N–$1/_4$P	$1/_4$N	$1/_{16}$–$1/_{16}$ ①	NA
	Legacy 4WD Sedan ②	2P–4P	3P	$1/_2$N–$1/_2$P	0	$1/_{16}$–$1/_{16}$ ①	NA
	Legacy 4WD Wagon	$1^3/_4$P–$3^3/_4$P	$2^3/_4$P	$1/_2$N–$1/_2$P	0	$1/_{16}$–$1/_{16}$ ①	NA
1991	2WD XT Coupe	$3^{15}/_{16}$P–$4^{13}/_{16}$P	$4^1/_{16}$P	$3/_4$N–$3/_4$P	0	$1/_8$–$1/_8$ ①	NA
	4WD XT Coupe (4 cylinder)	$2^5/_8$P–$4^1/_8$P	$3^3/_8$P	$1/_{16}$N–$1^3/_8$P	$5/_8$P	$3/_8$ ① –$1/_8$ ①	NA
	4WD XT Coupe (6 cylinder)	$2^3/_4$P–$4^1/_4$P	$3^1/_2$P	$1/_{16}$P–$1^9/_{16}$P	$13/_{16}$P	$3/_8$ ① –$1/_8$ ①	NA
	2WD Loyale Sedan	$1^3/_4$P–$3^1/_4$P	$2^1/_2$P	0–$1^1/_2$P	$3/_4$P	$1/_4$–$1/_{16}$ ①	
	4WD Loyale Sedan without Air Susp.	$1^1/_{16}$P–$2^9/_{16}$P	$1^{13}/_{16}$P	$15/_{16}$P–$2^7/_{16}$P	$1^{11}/_{16}$P	$1/_{16}$ ① –$3/_{16}$ ①	NA
	2WD Loyale SW	$1^5/_{16}$P–$2^{13}/_{16}$P	$2^1/_{16}$P	$1/_4$P–$1^3/_4$P	1P	$1/_{16}$ ① –$3/_{16}$ ①	NA
	4WD Loyale SW	$1^3/_{16}$P–$2^5/_{16}$P	$1^9/_{16}$P	$15/_{16}$P–$2^7/_{16}$P	$1^3/_4$P	$1/_{16}$ ① –$3/_{16}$	NA
	Justy	$1^1/_2$P–$3^1/_2$P	$2^1/_2$P	$5/_{16}$N–$1^{11}/_{16}$P	$11/_{16}$P	$5/_{16}$–$1/_{16}$ ①	NA
	Legacy FWD Sedan	$2^1/_{16}$P–$4^1/_{16}$P ③	$3^1/_{16}$P ④	$3/_4$N–$1/_4$P	$1/_4$N	$1/_{16}$–$1/_{16}$ ①	NA
	Legacy 4WD Sedan ②	2P–4P	3P	$1/_2$N–$1/_2$P	0	$1/_{16}$–$1/_{16}$ ①	NA
	Legacy 4WD Wagon	$1^3/_4$P–$3^3/_4$P	$2^3/_4$P	$1/_2$N–$1/_2$P	0	$1/_{16}$–$1/_{16}$ ①	NA
1992	2WD XT Coupe	$3^{15}/_{16}$P–$4^{13}/_{16}$P	$4^1/_{16}$P	$3/_4$N–$3/_4$P	0	$1/_8$–$1/_8$ ①	NA
	4WD XT Coupe (4 cylinder)	$2^5/_8$P–$4^1/_8$P	$3^3/_8$P	$1/_{16}$N–$1^3/_8$P	$5/_8$P	$3/_8$ ① –$1/_8$ ①	NA
	4WD XT Coupe (6 cylinder)	$2^3/_4$P–$4^1/_4$P	$3^1/_2$P	$1/_{16}$P–$1^9/_{16}$P	$13/_{16}$P	$3/_8$ ① –$1/_8$ ①	NA
	2WD Loyale Sedan	$1^3/_4$P–$3^1/_4$P	$2^1/_2$P	0–$1^1/_2$P	$3/_4$P	$1/_4$–$1/_{16}$ ①	
	4WD Loyale Sedan without Air Susp.	$1^1/_{16}$P–$2^9/_{16}$P	$1^{13}/_{16}$P	$15/_{16}$P–$2^7/_{16}$P	$1^{11}/_{16}$P	$1/_{16}$ ① –$3/_{16}$ ①	NA
	2WD Loyale SW	$1^5/_{16}$P–$2^{13}/_{16}$P	$2^1/_{16}$P	$1/_4$P–$1^3/_4$P	1P	$1/_{16}$ ① –$3/_{16}$ ①	NA
	4WD Loyale SW	$1^3/_{16}$P–$2^5/_{16}$P	$1^9/_{16}$P	$15/_{16}$P–$2^7/_{16}$P	$1^3/_4$P	$1/_{16}$ ① –$3/_{16}$ ①	NA
	Justy	$1^1/_2$P–$3^1/_2$P	$2^1/_2$P	$5/_{16}$N–$1^{11}/_{16}$P	$11/_{16}$P	$5/_{16}$–$1/_{16}$ ①	NA

WHEEL ALIGNMENT

Year	Model	Caster Range (deg.)	Caster Preferred Setting (deg.)	Camber Range (deg.)	Camber Preferred Setting (deg.)	Toe-in (in.)	Steering Axis Inclination (deg.)
	Legacy FWD Sedan	2 1/16P–4 1/16P ③	3 1/16P ④	3/4N–1/4P	1/4N	1/16–1/16 ①	NA
	Legacy 4WD Sedan ②	2P–4P	3P	1/2N–1/2P	0	1/16–1/16 ①	NA
	Legacy 4WD Wagon	1 3/4P–3 3/4P	2 3/4P	1/2N–1/2P	0	1/16–1/16 ①	NA
	SVX	1 3/4P–3 3/4P	2 3/4P	1/2N–1/2P	0	1/16–1/16 ①	NA
1993	2WD XT Coupe	3 15/16P–4 13/16P	4 1/16P	3/4N–3/4P	0	1/8–1/8 ①	NA
	4WD XT Coupe (4 cylinder)	2 5/8P–4 1/8P	3 3/8P	1/16N–1 3/8P	5/8P	3/8 ① –1/8 ①	NA
	4WD XT Coupe (6 cylinder)	2 3/4P–4 1/4P	3 1/2P	1/16P–1 9/16P	13/16P	3/8 ① –1/8 ①	NA
	2WD Loyale Sedan	1 3/4P–3 1/4P	2 1/2P	0–1 1/2P	3/4P	1/4–1/16 ①	
	4WD Loyale Sedan without Air Susp.	1 1/16P–2 9/16P	1 13/16P	15/16P–2 7/16P	1 11/16P	1/16 ① –3/16 ①	NA
	2WD Loyale SW	1 5/16P–2 13/16P	2 1/16P	1/4P–1 3/4P	1P	1/16 ① –3/16 ①	NA
	4WD Loyale SW	1 3/16P–2 5/16P	1 9/16P	15/16P–2 7/16P	1 3/4P	1/16 ① –3/16 ①	NA
	Justy	1 1/2P–3 1/2P	2 1/2P	5/16N–1 11/16P	11/16P	5/16–1/16 ①	NA
	Legacy FWD Sedan	2 1/16P–4 1/16P ③	3 1/16P ④	3/4N–1/4P	1/4N	1/16–1/16 ①	NA
	Legacy 4WD Sedan ②	2P–4P	3P	1/2N–1/2P	0	1/16–1/16 ①	NA
	Legacy 4WD Wagon	1 3/4P–3 3/4P	2 3/4P	1/2N–1/2P	0	1/16–1/16 ①	NA
	SVX	1 3/4P–3 3/4P	2 3/4P	1/2N–1/2P	0	1/16–1/16 ①	NA
1994	2WD XT Coupe	3 15/16P–4 13/16P	4 1/16P	3/4N–3/4P	0	1/8–1/8 ①	NA
	4WD XT Coupe (4 cylinder)	2 5/8P–4 1/8P	3 3/8P	1/16N–1 3/8P	5/8P	3/8 ① –1/8 ①	NA
	4WD XT Coupe (6 cylinder)	2 3/4P–4 1/4P	3 1/2P	1/16P–1 9/16P	13/16P	3/8 ① –1/8 ①	NA
	2WD Loyale Sedan	1 3/4P–3 1/4P	2 1/2P	0–1 1/2P	3/4P	1/4–1/16 ①	NA
	4WD Loyale Sedan without Air Susp.	1 1/16P–2 9/16P	1 13/16P	15/16P–2 7/16P	1 11/16P	1/16 ① –3/16 ①	NA
	2WD Loyale SW	1 5/16P–2 13/16P	2 1/16P	1/4P–1 3/4P	1P	1/16 ① –3/16 ①	NA
	4WD Loyale SW	1 3/16P–2 5/16P	1 9/16P	15/16P–2 7/16P	1 3/4P	1/16 ① –3/16 ①	NA
	Justy	1 1/2P–3 1/2P	2 1/2P	5/16N–1 11/16P	11/16P	5/16–1/16 ①	NA
	Legacy FWD Sedan	2 1/16P–4 1/16P ③	3 1/16P ④	3/4N–1/4P	1/4N	1/16–1/16 ①	NA
	Legacy 4WD Sedan ②	2P–4P	3P	1/2N–1/2P	0	1/16–1/16 ①	NA
	Legacy 4WD Wagon	1 3/4P–3 3/4P	2 3/4P	1/2N–1/2P	0	1/16–1/16 ①	NA
	SVX	1 3/4P–3 3/4P	2 3/4P	1/2N–1/2P	0	1/16–1/16 ①	NA

Air Susp.—Air suspension
N—Negative
P—Positive
SW—Station Wagon

① Toe out
② Same with air suspension
③ Legacy FWD Wagon—1 13/16P–3 13/16P
④ Legacy FWD Wagon—2 13/16P

SERIAL NUMBER IDENTIFICATION

Vehicle Identification Plate

The vehicle identification plate is located on the bulkhead in the engine compartment.

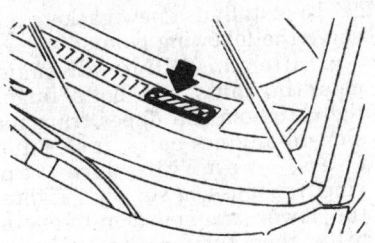

Vehicle Identification Number is located on the left side of the dash

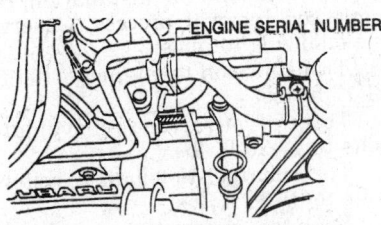

The engine number is stamped on the front right-side of the crankcase — except 1.2L engine

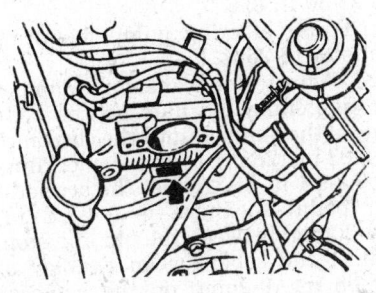

The engine number is stamped on the rear-side of the engine, below the cylinder head — 1.2L engine

Engine Number

The engine serial number is stamped on the front right side of the crankcase, on all engines except the 1.2L engine. On the 1.2L engine, the serial number is stamped at the right rear side of the engine below the cylinder head.

Vehicle Identification Number

The Vehicle Identification Number (VIN) is stamped on a plate located on the top of the dashboard on the drivers side and is visible through the windshield.

Transaxle Number

The transaxle serial number is located on a sticker fixed to the upper surface of the main case (manual transaxle) or to the converter housing (automatic transaxle).

ENGINE MECHANICAL

NOTE: Disconnecting the negative battery cable on some vehicles may interfere with the functions of the on board computer systems and may require the computer to undergo a relearning process, once the negative battery cable is reconnected.

Engine Assembly

REMOVAL AND INSTALLATION

1.2L Engine

1. Disconnect the negative battery terminal from the battery.
2. Raise and support the front of the vehicle on jackstands.
3. Raise and support the hood with the stay so it opens wider than usual.
4. Position a drain pan under the radiator, remove the drain plug and the radiator cap, then drain the cooling system.
5. Remove the bumper and the grille.
6. Disconnect the electrical connectors and the hoses from the radiator and remove the radiator.
7. Disconnect the hood release cable and remove the radiator upper member.
8. Label, then disconnect the hoses and cables from the air cleaner, the carburetor, the heater unit the brake booster, the clutch, the accelerator cable from the carburetor, the speedometer cable from the transmission and the electrical wiring harness from the distributor.
9. Disconnect the pitching stopper from the bracket.
10. Remove the engine splash covers and the exhaust pipes.
11. Disconnect the gearshift rod and stay from the transmission.
12. Remove the transverse link. Using a rod, remove the spring pin and separate the front axle shaft.
13. Remove the engine/transmission mounting brackets.
14. Using an engine hoist and a cable, attach it to the engine and lift it slightly.
15. Remove the center member and crossmember from the vehicle.
16. Lift the engine/transmission assembly carefully and remove it from the vehicle.
17. Remove the engine from the transmission, then secure the engine to a workstand.

To install:

18. Attach the engine to the transmission and attach them to an engine hoist and a cable.
19. Lower the engine/transmission slowly and carefully into the vehicle.
20. With the engine/transmission assembly slightly raised, install the center member and crossmember to the vehicle.
21. Completely lower the engine/transmission and install the mounting brackets.
22. Install the front axle shaft, spring pin and transverse link.
23. Install the gearshift rod and stay into the transmission.
24. Install the exhaust pipes and the engine splash cover.
25. Install the pitching stopper.
26. Install all removed hoses.
27. Install the hood release cable.
28. Install the radiator and connect the hoses and electrical connectors.
29. Install the grille and bumper.
30. Make sure the drain has been placed in the radiator, and fill the radiator with coolant.
31. Lower the vehicle, install the battery and close the hood.

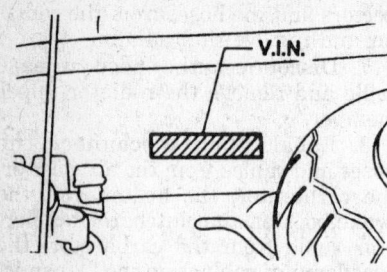

Vehicle Identification Plate is located on a plate attached to the bulkhead panel in the engine compartment

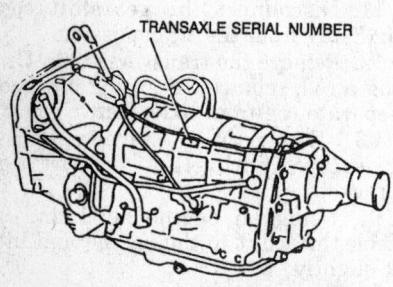

Transaxle identification plate location

1.8L Engine

1. Open the hood and prop it, securely. Remove the spare tire and the spare tire bracket.

2. If equipped with Turbo or MPFI, perform the following procedures to reduce the fuel pressure:

   a. From under the vehicle, disconnect the fuel pump electrical harness connector.

   b. Crank the engine for at least 5 seconds. If the engine starts, allow it to run until it stalls.

   c. Reconnect the fuel pump connector.

3. Remove the negative battery terminal from the battery.

4. Disconnect the air temperature sensor plug from the engine compartment.

5. Label and disconnect the fuel system hoses and the evaporative emissions system hoses.

6. Label and disconnect the vacuum hoses from the cruise control, the Master-Vac®, the air intake shutter and the heater air intake door.

7. Disconnect the electrical wiring connectors from the the alternator, the EGI, the thermoswitch, the electric fan, the A/C condenser and the ignition coil, then disconnect the main engine harness.

8. Label and disconnect the spark plug wires, the engine ground strap and the fusible link assembly.

9. Disconnect the accelerator linkage. Remove the windshield washer reservoir and position it behind the right strut tower.

10. To remove the power steering pump, perform the following procedures:

    a. Loosen the alternator pivot and mounting bolts, then shift the alternator to loosen the drive belt and remove the belt.

    b. Remove the pulley from the power steering pump.

    c. Remove the power steering pump-to-engine bolts and clamp.

    d. Remove the engine oil filler pipe brace.

    e. Remove the power steering pump and secure it to the bulkhead without disturbing the pressure lines.

11. Loosen the air intake duct hose clamps and remove the duct; seal the openings to keep dirt out of the air intake passages. Remove the upper cover.

12. Remove the air intake-to-flow meter line and cover the openings.

13. Remove the horizontal damper and clip.

14. To remove the center section of the exhaust pipe, perform the following procedures:

    a. Disconnect the temperature sensor connector.

    b. If equipped, disconnect the exhaust pipe-to-turbocharger bolts.

    c. Remove the rear cover.

    d. Remove the center exhaust section-to-transmission bolt.

    e. Remove the hanger bolts, then carefully remove the exhaust pipe (clearance is tight) to avoid damage.

    f. Slightly loosen the attaching bolts, then remove the torque converter cover.

15. If equipped, disconnect the turbocharger oil supply and drain lines. Remove the turbo-to-exhaust bolts, the turbo assembly, the lower cover and the gasket.

16. Disconnect the electrical connector from the O₂ sensor. Remove the torque converter-to-driveplate bolts.

17. Using a chain hoist, connect it to the crankshaft damper bracket and support the engine. Remove the upper engine-to-transmission bolts; leave the starter in place.

18. Drain the engine coolant, using a hose to lead coolant to a clean container. Disconnect the upper/lower radiator hoses, the oil cooler lines, the ground wire and the radiator.

19. Disconnect the oil cooler lines from the engine and drain the oil into a clean container. Disconnect the heater hoses from the side of the engine.

20. Remove the front engine mount, then the lower engine-to-transmission nuts.

21. Position a floor jack under the transmission, then raise the engine/transmission slightly. Pull the engine forward until the transmission shaft clears the clutch, then carefully raise the engine out of the engine compartment.

To install:

22. To install, use new gaskets and observe the following points:

    a. After installing all major mounting nuts and bolts finger-tight, tighten the upper transmission-to-engine bolts just snug, then, remove the engine/transmission support. Tighten the lower transmission-to-engine bolts, then tighten the engine-to-mount nuts.

    b. When torquing the turbocharger (if equipped) and the exhaust system bolts, be sure to go back and forth, tighten the bolts evenly.

23. To complete the installation, reverse the removal process. Observe the following torques:

    Transmission-to-engine bolts to 14-17 ft. lbs.

    Torque converter-to-driveplate bolts to 17-20 ft. lbs.

    Turbocharger-to-exhaust system bolts to 31-38 ft. lbs.

    Exhaust system-to-transmission bolt to 18-25 ft. lbs.

    Exhaust system hanger bolts to 7-13 ft. lbs.

    Rear exhaust pipe joint nuts to 7-13 ft. lbs.

    Power steering pump pulley bolts to 25-30 ft. lbs.

    Power steering pump mounting bolts to 18-25 ft. lbs.

24. Adjust the crankshaft damper by tightening the nuts on the body side of the damper until the clearance is 0.08 in. (2mm); torque the locknuts to 6.5-9.4 ft. lbs. Adjust the accelerator pedal so there is 0.4-1.2 in. (10-30mm) between the pin and stop. Adjust the cable for an endplay of 0-0.08 in. (0-2mm) on the actuator side. Replenish all of the fluids. Run the engine to normal operating temperatures and check for leaks in oil cooler and lines.

2.2L Engine

1. Raise and support the vehicle safely.

2. Release the fuel system pressure.

3. Disconnect the battery cables and remove the battery.

4. Drain the coolant.

5. On non-turbo engines, remove the manifold cover.

6. Remove the cooling system, radiator and fan assembly, and reservoir tank.

7. On air conditioning equipped models, discharge the air conditioning system and remove the high pressure hoses.

8. Remove the air intake system. Remove the air intake duct from non-turbo engines and the resonator chamber from turbo engines.

9. Remove the air cleaner upper cover and element.

10. On turbo engines, remove the turbocharger cooling duct and air inlet and outlet ducts.

11. Remove the evaporative canister and bracket.

12. Label and disconnect all electrical connectors, cables and vacuum hoses.

13. Remove the power steering pump.

14. On turbocharged engines, remove the turbocharger unit from the center exhaust pipe.

15. Remove the exhaust system from the engine.

16. On turbocharged engines, remove the clutch damper with bracket.

17. Remove the nut which holds the power side of the starter.

18. Remove the nuts which hold the lower side of the transmission to the engine.

19. Remove the nuts which hold the front cushion rubber to the crossmember.

20. Remove the starter.

21. On turbocharged engines, separate the clutch release fork from the release bearing.

22. On automatic transmission equipped models, separate the torque converter from the driveplate.

23. Remove the pitching stopper and bracket.

24. Disconnect the fuel delivery hose, return hose and evaporation hose.

25. Support the engine with a lifting device and the transmission with a floor jack.

26. Remove the bolt which holds the upper side of the transmission to the engine.

27. Remove the engine.

To install:

28. Install the clutch release fork and bearing onto the transmission.

29. Install the engine to the transmission and tighten the bolts which holds the right upper side of the transmission to 34-40 ft. lbs. (46-54 Nm).

30. Remove the lifting device from the engine and remove the floor jack.

31. Install the pitching stopper and tighten the body side bolt to 35-49 ft. lbs. (47-67 Nm) and the bracket side bolt to 33-40 ft. lbs. (44-54 Nm).

32. On turbocharged engines, install the clutch operating cylinder and tighten to 25-30 ft. lbs. (34-40 Nm).

33. On automatic transmission equipped vehicles, install the torque converter on the driveplate. Tighten the bolts to 17-20 ft. lbs. (23-26 Nm).

34. Install the canister and bracket. Install the power steering pump and tighten the bolts to 22-36 ft. lbs. (29-49 Nm).

35. Install the starter and tighten the bolts to 22-36 ft. lbs. (29-49 Nm).

36. Tighten the nuts which hold the lower side of the transmission to the engine to 34-40 ft. lbs. (46-54 Nm).

37. Tighten the nuts which hold the front cushion rubber to the crossmember to 40-61 ft. lbs. (54-83 Nm).

38. Install the exhaust system.

39. On turbocharged engines, install the air inlet and outlet ducts.

40. Connect all hoses, electrical connectors and cables previously disconnected.

41. On turbocharged engines, install the turbo cooling duct.

42. Install the air intake system.

43. If equipped with air conditioning, install the air conditioner high pressure hoses. Tighten to 13-23 ft. lbs. (18-31 Nm).

44. Install the cooling system. Tighten bolts to 9-11 ft. lbs. (12-15 Nm).

45. Install the manifold cover.

46. Install the battery and connect the battery cables.

47. Fill the radiator with coolant.

48. Check the level of the transmission fluid and add as necessary.

49. Check the level of the engine oil and add as necessary.

50. Start the engine and allow it to reach operating temperature. Check for leaks. Test drive the vehicle.

2.7L Engine

1. Properly relieve the fuel system pressure. Disconnect the negative battery cable. Matchmark and remove the hood.

2. Properly discharge the air conditioning system, if equipped. Drain the engine oil. Drain the cooling system.

3. Disconnect the canister hose and the hose bracket. Disconnect and plug the fuel lines.

4. Disconnect the power brake vacuum line booster. If equipped with manual transaxle and 4WD, disconnect the differential lock vacuum hose.

5. Disconnect the engine wiring harness connectors, the oxygen sensor connector, the bypass air valve control connector, the ignition coil and the distributor connector to the crank sensor.

6. Disconnect the alternator connector, the air condition compressor connector, the engine ground connector, the radiator fan motor connector and the thermo-switch electrical connector.

7. Disconnect the accelerator cable. Disconnect the cruise control cable, if equipped. Disconnect and plug the heater hoses.

8. Disconnect the hill holder cable on the clutch release fork side of the assembly, if equipped with manual transaxle.

9. Raise and support the vehicle safely. Disconnect the front exhaust pipe from the engine.

10. Disconnect the front to rear exhaust pipe connection. Disconnect the front exhaust pipe at the transaxle and hanger locations.

11. Lower the vehicle. Disconnect and plug the air conditioning compressor hoses.

12. Remove the radiator fan shroud assembly. If equipped with automatic transaxle, disconnect and plug the fluid lines. Remove the radiator.

13. Remove the timing hole plug. Remove the bolts that retain the torque converter to the driveplate, if equipped with automatic transaxle.

14. Remove the buffer rod mounting bolts. Remove the bolts that support the engine mount to the front crossmember. Remove the bolts that hold the lower side of the engine to the transaxle assembly.

15. Install the proper engine lifting equipment. Properly support the transaxle assembly.

16. Remove the bolts that retain the upper side of the engine to the transaxle.

17. Carefully remove the engine from the vehicle. If equipped with manual transaxle, move the engine in the axial direction until the mainshaft is withdrawn from the clutch cover.

To install:

18. Install the engine taking care to align the mainshaft. Install all bolts and mountings that attach the engine to the transaxle and chassis. Reconnect the torque converter to the engine flywheel (automatic transaxle).

19. Install the radiator, radiator shroud and transaxle fluid cooler lines. Install the air conditioner compressor and lines. Install the exhaust system.

20. Install the hill holder, if equipped. Reconnect all vacuum lines and hoses previously disconnected. Reconnect all electrical connections taking care to clean all connectors and ground locations.

21. Install all fuel lines. Fill the engine with oil, the transaxle with fluid and the cooling system with coolant. Start the engine and allow it to reach operating temperature. Check for leaks. Test drive the vehicle.

3.3L Engine

1. Raise and support the vehicle safely.

2. Release the fuel system pressure.

3. Disconnect the negative battery cable.

4. Remove the under body cover and drain the engine coolant.

5. Remove the radiator and all coolant hoses.

6. Discharge the air conditioning system. Disconnect and plug the air conditioning lines.

7. Remove the air intake system.

8. Disconnect the accelerator cable.

9. Disconnect the cruise control cable.

10. Label and disconnect all wiring harness connectors and cables.

11. Remove the evaporation canister, vacuum hoses and bracket.

12. Remove the exhaust system from the engine.

13. Disconnect the power steering hoses from the gear box.

14. Disconnect the automatic transmission cooler lines.

15. Remove the nuts which hold the lower side of the engine to the transmission and attach the lower side of starter.

16. Remove the nuts which attach the front cushion rubber to the subframe.

17. Separate the torque converter from the driveplate.

18. Remove the pitching stopper and bracket.

19. Disconnect the fuel delivery hose, return hose and evaporation hoses.

20. Support the engine with a lifting device and the transmission with a transmission jack.

21. Remove the bolts which hold the upper side of the engine to the transmission.

22. Remove the engine from the vehicle.

To install:

23. Install the engine to the transmission and tighten the bolts which hold the right upper side of the engine to 34-40 ft. lbs. (46-54 Nm).

24. Remove the lifting device and transmission jack.

25. Install the pitching stopper and tighten to 33-40 ft. lbs. (44-54 Nm).

26. Install the torque converter to driveplate bolts and tighten to 17-20 ft. lbs. (23-26 Nm).

27. Connect all hoses previously disconnected.

28. Install the evaporation canister and bracket.

29. Install the cooling system.

30. Install the nuts which hold the lower side of the engine to the transmission and attach the lower side of the starter. Tighten to 34-40 ft. lbs. (54-83 Nm).

31. Install the nuts which hold the front cushion rubber to the subframe. Tighten to 40-61 ft. lbs. (54-83 Nm).

32. Connect the power steering hoses to the gear box and the automatic transmission cooler lines.

33. Install the exhaust system.

34. Install the engine under cover.

35. Connect all electrical harness connectors.

36. Connect the accelerator cable.

37. Connect the cruise control cable.

38. Connect the high pressure hoses to the air conditioner compressor. Tighten to 13-23 ft. lbs. (18-31 Nm).

39. Install the air intake system

40. Connect the negative battery cable.

41. Fill the radiator with coolant.

42. Check the automatic transmission oil level and add as required.

43. Check the power steering fluid level. Add as necessary and bleed all air from the system.

44. Check the engine oil level.

45. Start the engine and allow it to reach operating temperature. Check for leaks. Test drive the vehicle.

Cylinder Head

REMOVAL AND INSTALLATION

1.2L Engine

1. Disconnect the negative battery cable. Drain the cooling system.

2. Remove the air cleaner assembly. Remove the drive belts. Remove the spark plug wires.

3. Position the engine at TDC with No. 1 cylinder on the compression stroke. Matchmark and remove the distributor assembly.

4. Remove the crankshaft pulley, using pulley removal tool 499205500 or equivalent. Remove the outer front timing belt cover.

5. Loosen the tensioner bolt and position it in the direction that loosens the belt. Tighten the tensioner bolt in that position.

6. Remove the camshaft driveplate. Mark the timing belt, in the direction of rotation, for reinstallation and than remove it from the engine.

7. Remove the tensioner and spring. Remove the camshaft pulley, using pulley removal tool 499205500 or equivalent. Remove the inner belt cover and cover mount.

8. Remove the PCV hose from the rocker arm cover. Remove the rocker arm cover retaining bolts. Remove the rocker arm cover from the engine. Remove the rocker arm assembly.

9. Remove the exhaust manifold retaining bolts. Remove the exhaust manifold from the engine. Discard the gasket.

10. Disconnect all required electrical wiring and vacuum lines. Remove the air suction valve and pipe, if equipped.

11. Disconnect the accelerator linkage. Remove the intake manifold retaining bolts. Remove the intake manifold along with the carburetor. Discard the gasket.

12. Be sure the engine is cold before removing the cylinder head bolts. Loosen, than remove the cylinder head bolts. Carefully remove the cylinder head from the engine.

To install:

13. Installation is the reverse of the removal procedure. Be sure to use new gaskets or RTV sealant, as required.

14. Install the cylinder head and tighten the bolts as follows:

   a. Step 1 — Torque all bolts in sequence to 29 ft. lbs. (39 Nm).

   b. Step 2 — Torque all bolts in sequence to 54 ft. lbs. (73 Nm).

c. Step 3 — Loosen bolts 90 degrees or more in reverse order of tightening sequence.

d. Step 4 — Torque all bolts in sequence to 54 ft. lbs. (73 Nm).

15. Adjust the valves to specification, as required. Install the camshaft pulley, timing belt, tensioner and driveplate.

16. Install the distributor and all other components previously removed. Fill the cooling system with coolant and check the engine oil.

17. Start the engine, check the ignition timing, check for leaks and test drive the vehicle.

1.8L AND 2.7L Engines

1. Disconnect the negative battery cable.

2. Remove the timing belt, belt cover and related components.

3. On turbocharged engines, remove the turbo cooling pipe together with the union screws and gaskets from the cylinder head.

4. Remove the camshaft cases, lash adjusters and related components.

5. On turbocharged engines, remove the EGR pipe.

6. Remove the accessory drive belts, alternator and air conditioner compressor if not already removed. Remove the bolt attaching the alternator bracket to the cylinder head.

7. On fuel injected engines, relieve the fuel system pressure.

8. Remove the bolts attaching the intake manifold to the cylinder head and remove the intake manifold.

9. Remove the bolt attaching the water bypass pipe bracket to the cylinder head.

10. Remove the spark plugs.

NOTE: On 2.7L engines, there are 2 types of cylinder head bolts used. Take note of cylinder head bolt arrangement as the bolts must be placed in their proper locations. Bolts number 1, 2, 9 and 13 measure 4.665 in. (118.5mm). All other bolts measure 5.217 in. (132.5mm).

11. On the 2.7L engine, loosen the cylinder head bolts in the proper sequence. Remove the cylinder heads and gaskets from the cylinder block.

To install:

12. Clean all gasket mating surfaces thoroughly. Inspect the cylinder head for warpage. Warpage should not exceed 0.0020 in. (0.05mm).

13. Install the cylinder heads using new gaskets.

14. On the 1.8L engine, tighten the cylinder head bolts as follows:

a. Tighten all bolts in sequence to 22 ft. lbs. (29 Nm).

b. Tighten all bolts in sequence to 43 ft. lbs. (59 Nm).

c. Tighten all bolts in sequence to 47 ft. lbs. (64 Nm).

15. On the 2.7L engine, tighten the cylinder head bolts as follows:

a. Tighten all bolts in sequence to 29 ft. lbs. (39 Nm).

b. Tighten all bolts in sequence to 47 ft. lbs. (64 Nm).

c. Loosen all bolts at least 90 degrees in the reverse order of the tightening sequence.

d. Tighten all bolts in sequence to 44-50 ft. lbs. (60-68 Nm).

16. Install the spark plugs. Install the water bypass pipe bracket.

17. Install the intake manifold and tighten the bolts to 13-16 ft. lbs. (18-22 Nm).

18. Install the alternator and bracket, air conditioner compressor and accessory drive belt.

19. On turbocharged engines, install the EGR pipe. Tighten the bolts to 23-27 ft. lbs. (31-37 Nm).

20. Install the camshaft cases, lash adjusters and related components.

21. On turbocharged engines, install the turbo cooling pipe. 16-18 ft. lbs. (21-24 Nm).

22. Install the timing belt, belt cover and related components.

23. Connect the negative battery cable.

24. Adjust the valve lash, as required. Start the engine and allow it to reach operating temperature. Adjust the ignition timing.

25. Check for leaks and test drive the vehicle.

NOTE: Depending on the type of cylinder heads used, retightening of the bolts may be necessary after the vehicle has be running.

2.2L Engine

1. Disconnect the negative battery cable.

2. Remove the V-belt, power steering pump, alternator and bracket.

3. Remove the valve rocker cover.

4. Disconnect the PCV hose and spark plug wires.

5. Remove the connector bracket attaching bolt.

6. Remove the crank angle sensor and cam angle sensor.

7. Disconnect the oil pressure switch. Remove the knock sensor.

8. Disconnect the blowby hose.

9. Relieve the fuel system pressure and disconnect the fuel pipes.

10. Remove the intake manifold and gasket. Remove the water pipe.

11. Remove the timing belt, camshaft sprocket and related components.

12. Remove the oil level gauge guide attaching bolt on the left cylinder head.

13. Remove the cylinder head bolts in the proper sequence. Leave bolts 1 and 3 installed loosely to prevent the cylinder head from falling.

14. While tapping the cylinder head with a plastic hammer, separate it from the cylinder block.

15. Remove bolts 1 and 3. Remove the cylinder head and gasket.

To install:

16. Clean all gasket mating surfaces thoroughly. Inspect the cylinder head for warpage. Warpage should not exceed 0.0020 in. (0.05mm).

17. Install the cylinder heads on the block using new gaskets.

18. Tighten the cylinder head bolts, after lubricating them with oil, to the following specifications:

a. Tighten all bolts in sequence to 22 ft. lbs. (29 Nm).

b. Tighten all bolts in sequence to 51 ft. lbs. (69 Nm).

c. Loosen all bolts by 180 degrees, then loosen an additional 180 degrees.

d. Tighten bolts 1 and 2 to 25 ft. lbs. (24 Nm) for non-turbo engines or 27 ft. lbs. (37 Nm) for turbo engines.

e. Tighten bolts 3, 4, 5 and 6 to 11 ft. lbs. (15 Nm) for non-turbo engines or 14 ft. lbs. (20 Nm) for turbo engines.

f. Tighten all bolts in sequence by 80-90 degrees.

g. Tighten all bolts in sequence an additional 80-90 degrees.

NOTE: Do not exceed 180 degrees total tightening.

19. Install the oil level gauge guide attaching bolt on the left cylinder head.

20. Install the timing belt, camshaft sprocket and related components.

21. Install the water pipe.

22. Install the intake manifold and tighten bolts to 21-25 ft. lbs. (28-34 Nm). Connect the fuel delivery pipes.

23. Connect the blowby hose. Install the knock sensor.

24. Connect the oil pressure switch connector.

25. Install the crank and cam angle sensors.

26. Install the connector bracket attaching bolt.

27. Connect the spark plug wires. Connect the PCV hose.

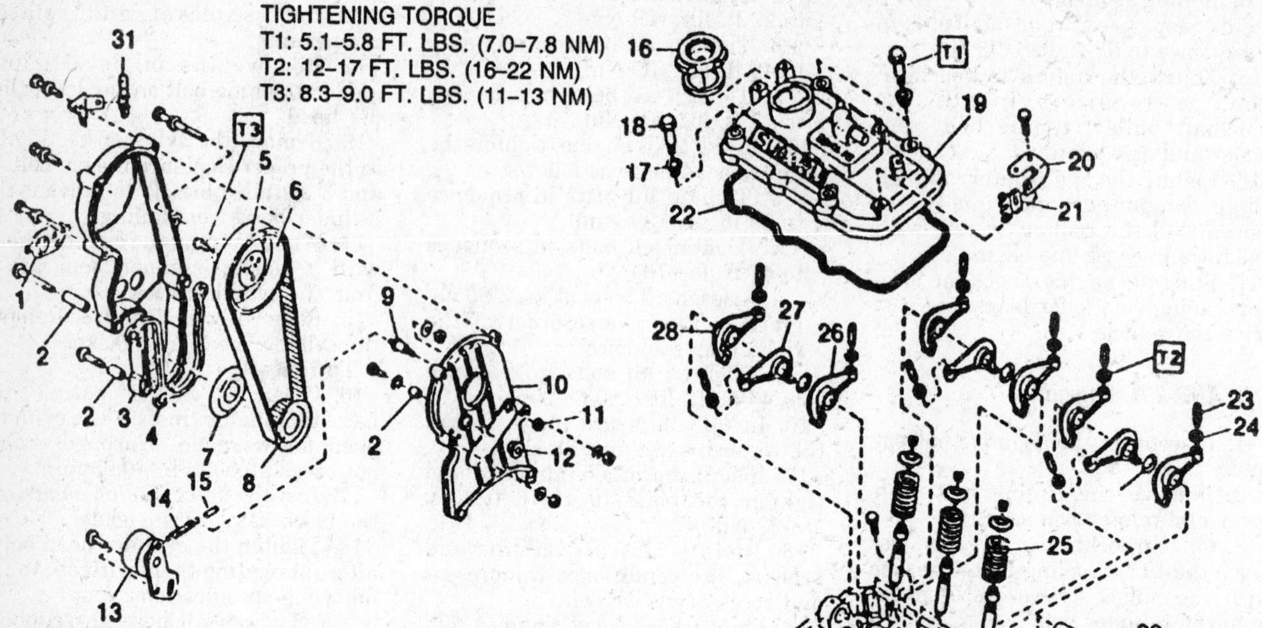

TIGHTENING TORQUE
T1: 5.1–5.8 FT. LBS. (7.0–7.8 NM)
T2: 12–17 FT. LBS. (16–22 NM)
T3: 8.3–9.0 FT. LBS. (11–13 NM)
T1
T2
T3

1. Timing belt cover plug
2. Spacer
3. Cam belt cover 2
4. Belt cover sealing 2
5. Timing belt
6. Camshaft sprocket
7. Camshaft sprocket
9. Tensioner spring bolt
10. Belt cover
11. Cam belt cover mount
12. Belt cover mount CP
13. Tensioner CP
14. Cam belt tensioner spring
15. Tensioner spring damper
16. Oil filter cap
17. Seal washer
18. Rocker cover bolt
19. Valve rocker cover CP
20. High tension cable stay
21. Vacuum hose supporter
22. Rocker cover gasket
23. Valve rocker screw
24. Nut
25. Valve Spring
26. Valve rocker arm No.
27. Valve rocker arm No. 3
28. Valve rocker arm
29. Valve rocker shaft
30. Camshaft
31. Stay

Cylinder head and related components — 1.2L engine

5
1
3
7
8
4
2
6

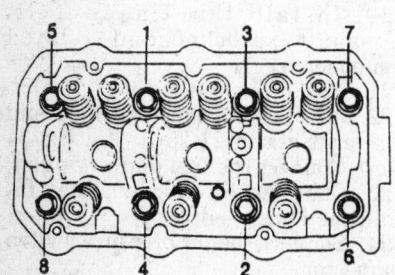

Cylinder head bolt torque sequence — 1.2L engine

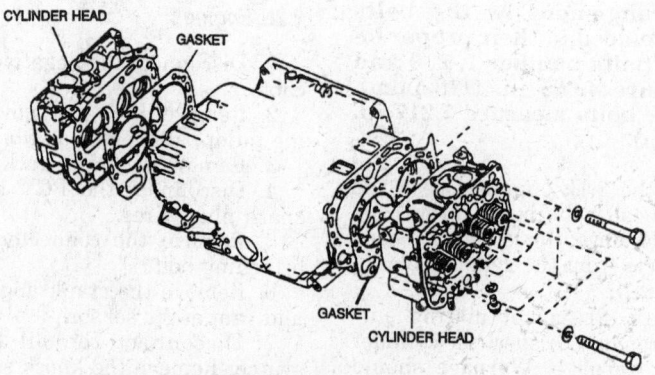

CYLINDER HEAD
GASKET
GASKET
CYLINDER HEAD

Cylinder head and related components — 1.8L engine

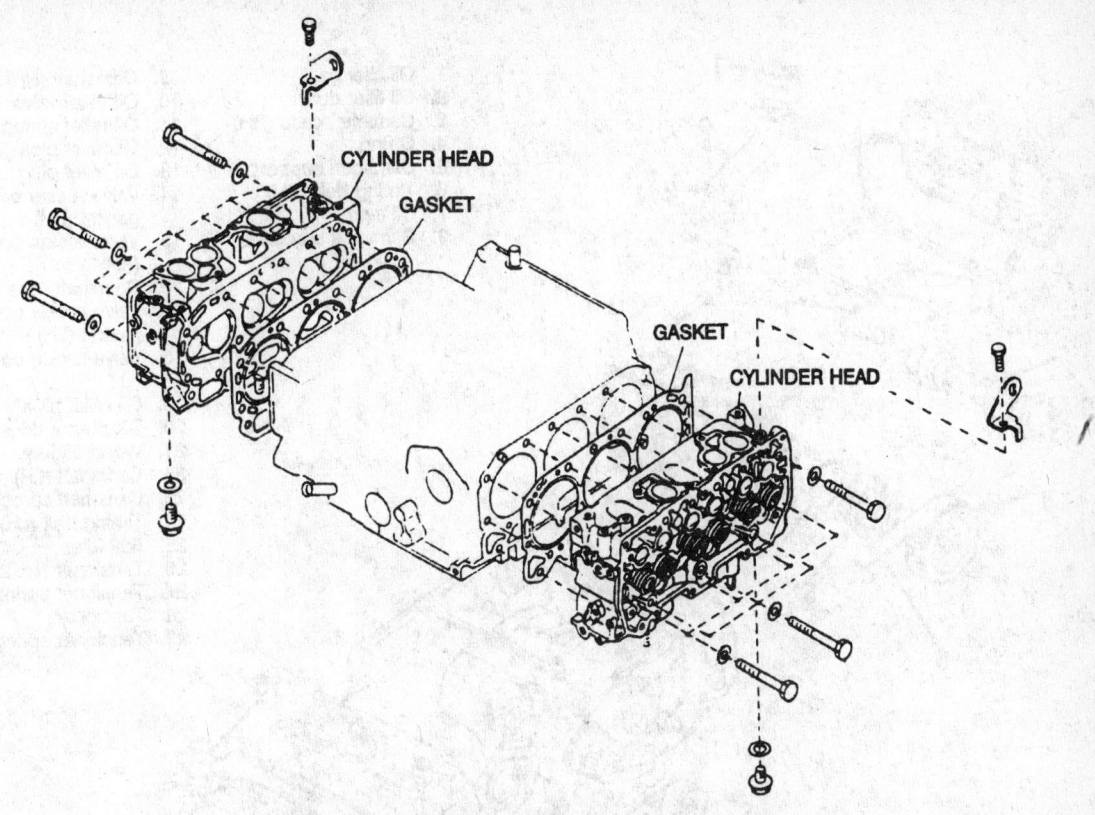

Cylinder head and related components — 2.7L engine

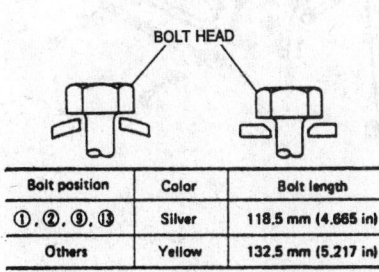

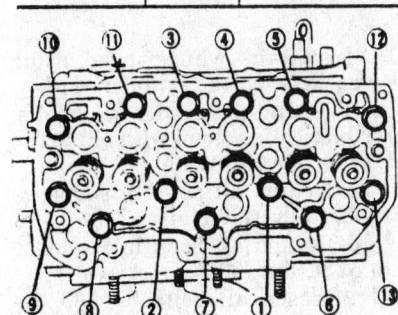

Cylinder head bolt torque sequence — 2.7L engine

Bolt position	Color	Bolt length
①, ②, ⑨, ⑬	Silver	118.5 mm (4.665 in)
Others	Yellow	132.5 mm (5.217 in)

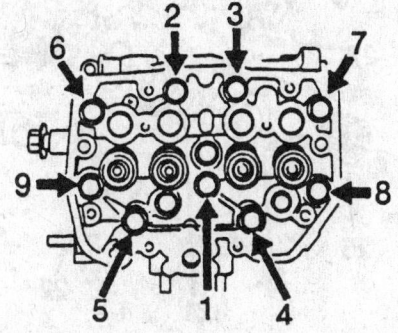

Cylinder head bolt torque sequence — 1.8L engine

28. Install the valve rocker cover and tighten bolts to 4 ft. lbs. (9 Nm).
29. Install the alternator, power steering pump and accessory drive belt.
30. Connect the negative battery cable. Start the engine and allow it to reach operating temperature. Check for leaks and test drive the vehicle.

3.3L Engine

1. Disconnect the negative battery cable.
2. Remove the timing belt, camshaft sprockets and related components.

3. Remove the EGR valve, EGR pipe and BPT.
4. Disconnect the auxiliary air control valve connector.
5. Disconnect the blowby hoses and auxiliary air valve hose.
6. Disconnect the PCV hose.
7. Disconnect the water hoses from the throttle body.
8. Relieve the fuel system pressure. Remove the collector and intake manifold assembly with the gaskets.
9. Remove the exhaust manifold and gasket.
10. Remove the cylinder head covers, camshafts and related components.
11. Remove the oil level guide and heater pipe.
12. Remove the cylinder head bolts in the proper sequence. Leave bolts 5 and 8 loosely installed to prevent the cylinder head from falling.
13. While tapping the cylinder head with a plastic hammer, separate it from the cylinder block. Remove bolts 5 and 8 to remove the cylinder head and gasket.

To install:
14. Clean all gasket mating surfaces thoroughly. Inspect the cylinder head for warpage. Warpage should not exceed 0.0020 in. (0.05mm).

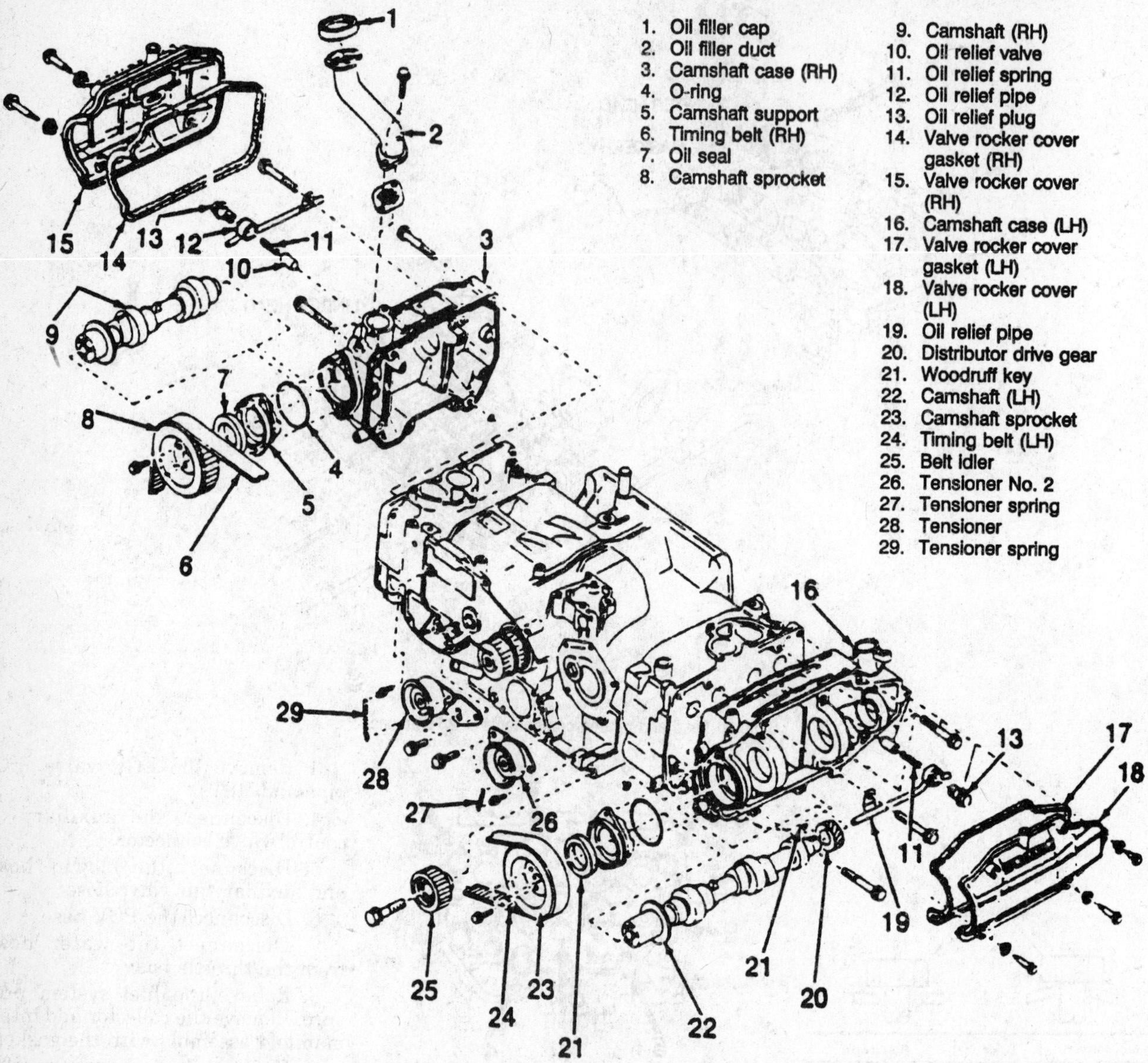

1. Oil filler cap
2. Oil filler duct
3. Camshaft case (RH)
4. O-ring
5. Camshaft support
6. Timing belt (RH)
7. Oil seal
8. Camshaft sprocket
9. Camshaft (RH)
10. Oil relief valve
11. Oil relief spring
12. Oil relief pipe
13. Oil relief plug
14. Valve rocker cover gasket (RH)
15. Valve rocker cover (RH)
16. Camshaft case (LH)
17. Valve rocker cover gasket (LH)
18. Valve rocker cover (LH)
19. Oil relief pipe
20. Distributor drive gear
21. Woodruff key
22. Camshaft (LH)
23. Camshaft sprocket
24. Timing belt (LH)
25. Belt idler
26. Tensioner No. 2
27. Tensioner spring
28. Tensioner
29. Tensioner spring

Cylinder head assembly — 1.8L engine

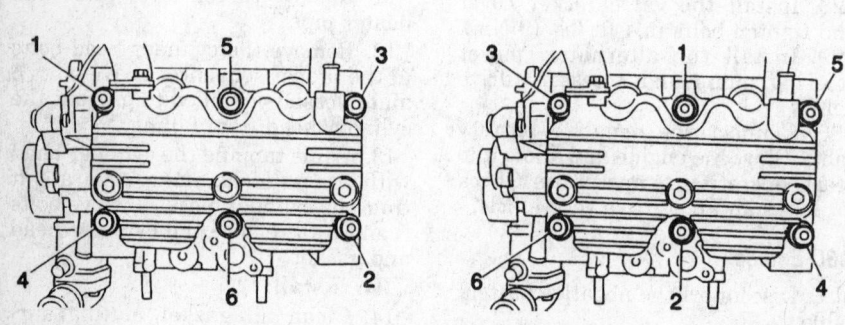

Cylinder head torque sequence — 2.2L engine

15. Install the cylinder head, using new gaskets, on the cylinder block.

16. Tighten the cylinder head bolts, after lubricating them with oil, to the following specifications:

   a. Tighten all bolts in sequence to 22 ft. lbs. (29 Nm).

   b. Tighten all bolts in sequence to 51 ft. lbs. (69 Nm).

   c. Loosen all bolts by 180 degrees, then loosen an additional 180 degrees.

   d. Tighten all bolts in sequence to 20 ft. lbs. (27 Nm).

   e. Tighten bolts 1, 2, 3 and 4 in the sequence shown by 80-90 degrees.

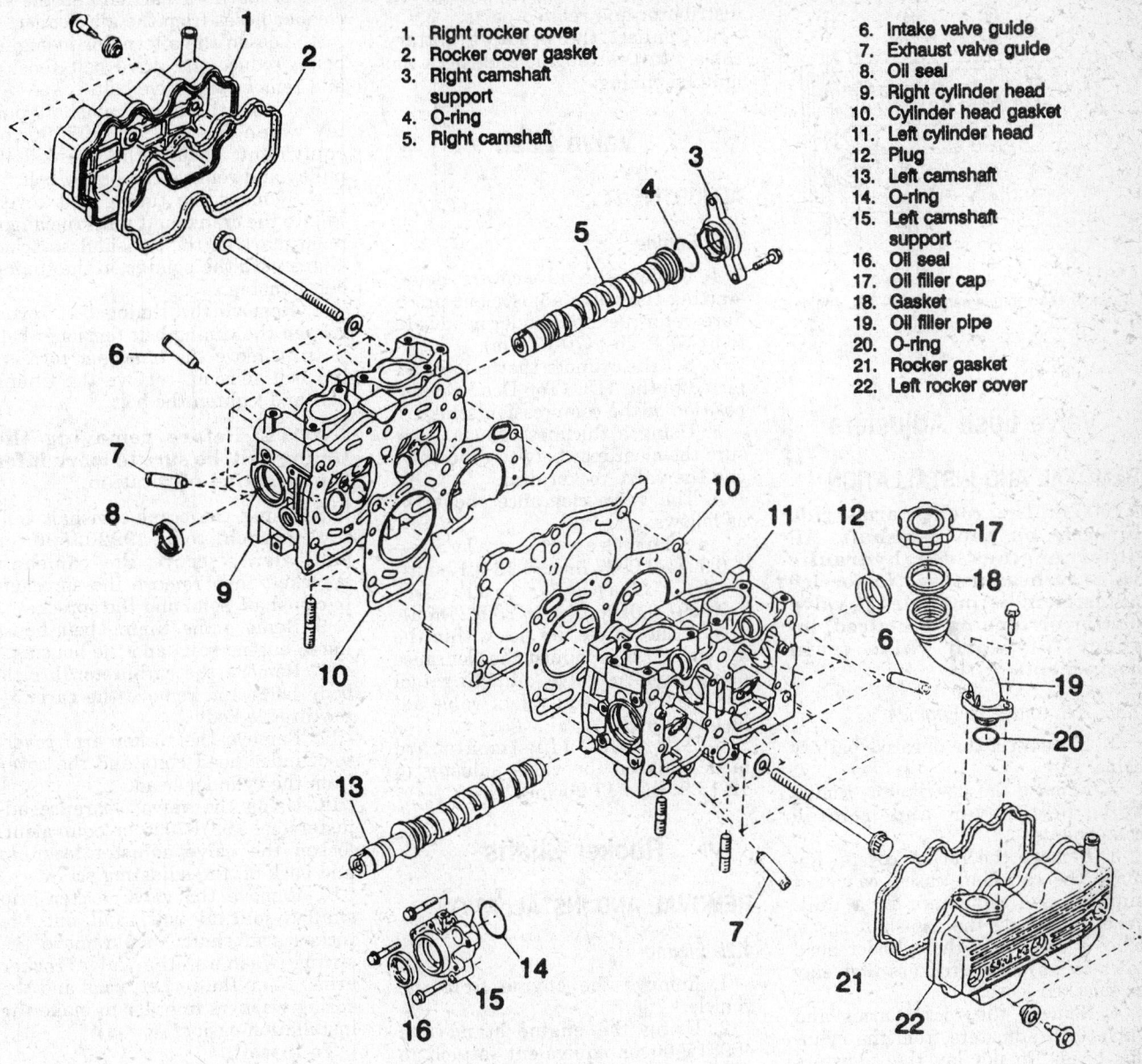

1. Right rocker cover
2. Rocker cover gasket
3. Right camshaft support
4. O-ring
5. Right camshaft
6. Intake valve guide
7. Exhaust valve guide
8. Oil seal
9. Right cylinder head
10. Cylinder head gasket
11. Left cylinder head
12. Plug
13. Left camshaft
14. O-ring
15. Left camshaft support
16. Oil seal
17. Oil filler cap
18. Gasket
19. Oil filler pipe
20. O-ring
21. Rocker gasket
22. Left rocker cover

2.2L engine cylinder head — exploded view

f. Tighten bolts 5, 6, 7 and 8 in the sequence shown to 33 ft. lbs. (44 Nm).

g. Tighten all bolts in sequence an additional 80-90 degrees.

NOTE: Do not exceed 180 degrees total tightening.

17. Install the heater pipe and oil level gauge.
18. Install the camshafts, cylinder head covers and related components.

Tighten the cylinder head cover bolts to 3-4 ft. lbs. (4-5 Nm).
19. Install the exhaust manifold using a new gasket. Tighten the bolts to 25-33 ft. lbs. (29-39 Nm).
20. Install the collector and intake manifold assembly using new gaskets. Tighten intake manifold bolts to 17-20 ft. lbs. (23-26 Nm). Connect the fuel pipes.
21. Connect the water hoses to the throttle body.

22. Connect the PCV hose, auxiliary air control valve hose, blowby hoses and auxiliary air control valve connector.
23. Install the EGR valve, EGR pipe and BPT.
24. Install the camshaft sprockets, timing belt and related components.
25. Connect the negative battery cable. Start the engine and allow it to reach operating temperature.
26. Check for leaks and test drive the vehicle.

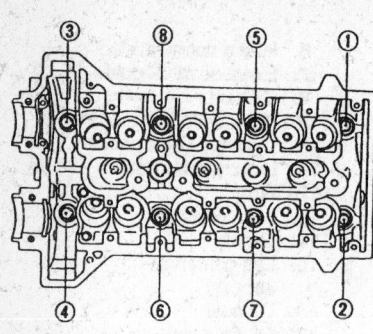

Cylinder head torque sequence — 3.3L engine

Valve Lash Adjusters

REMOVAL AND INSTALLATION

NOTE: The rocker arms ride directly on the camshaft. All other engines use hydraulic valve lash adjusters. No service adjustment is possible. If valve clatter or tapping is noticed, inspect for worn valve train components.

1.8L, 2.7L and 3.3L Engines

1. Disconnect the negative battery cable.
2. Remove the distributor, timing belt, belt cover and related components.
3. Remove the rocker covers. Remove the camshaft cases, camshaft support and camshaft as a unit. When removing the camshaft cases, place a rag under the cylinder head to catch any valve rockers that may be knocked loose.
4. Remove the rocker arms and valve lash adjusters from the cylinder head. Do not lay the adjusters down. Keep all components in the order of removal.

To install:

5. With the lash adjuster in a vertical position, push the adjuster pivot inward with a quick and hard motion. If the pivot is depressed more than 0.020 in. (0.5mm), put the adjuster in a container of oil and pump the plunger until the depression is within specification. If the lash adjuster is still not within specification, replace it.
6. Insert the lash adjusters into the cylinder head. Apply grease to the valve rocker and install the rocker on the cylinder head.
7. Install the camshaft case assembly.
8. Install the rocker covers.

9. Install timing belt, belt cover, distributor and related parts.
10. Connect the negative battery cable. Start the engine and check the ignition timing.

Valve Lash

ADJUSTMENT

1.2L Engine

1. Remove the valve covers. Before starting the valve adjustment procedure, retorque the cylinder head bolts to 51-57 ft. lbs. (70-77 Nm).
2. Set the cylinder that is to be adjusted to the TDC (Top Dead Center) position of the compression stroke.
3. Using a thickness gauge, measure the clearance between the valve and the valve rocker arm.
4. The valve clearance should be as follows:
   a. Intake valves— 0.0051-0.0067 inch (0.13-0.17mm)
   b. Exhaust valves— 0.0091-0.0106 inch (0.23-0.27mm)
5. If the valves are not within the allowable range, adjust the clearance using Subaru valve adjusting tool 49876700 or an equivalent valve adjuster wrench.
6. After the adjustments are made, tighten the valve adjuster to 12-17 ft. lbs. (17-23Nm).

Rocker Shafts

REMOVAL AND INSTALLATION

1.2L Engine

1. Remove the engine from the vehicle.
2. Using the engine stand tool 499815500 or equivalent, attach to the engine.

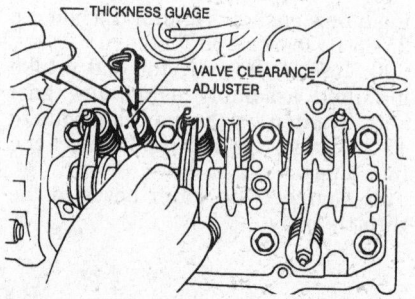

Justy 1.2L engine valve adjustment procedure

3. Remove the suction and the air cleaner hoses from the air cleaner.
4. Loosen the alternator-to-engine bolts, reduce the drive belt tension and remove the drive belt.
5. Using the crank/camshaft pulley wrench tool 499205500 or equivalent, secure the crankshaft pulley and remove the pulley bolt.
6. Remove the timing belt cover. Rotate the crankshaft until the alignment mark on the camshaft sprocket aligns with the pointer on the timing belt housing.
7. Remove the timing belt cover. Loosen the timing belt tensioner bolt ½ turn, move the tensioner to relax the belt tension, remove the timing belt and tighten the bolt.

NOTE: Before removing the timing belt, be sure to mark it for the direction of rotation.

8. Using the crank/camshaft pulley wrench tool 499205500 or equivalent, secure the camshaft sprocket, then remove the sprocket-to-camshaft bolts and the sprocket.
9. Remove the timing belt housing-to-engine bolts and the housing.
10. Remove the carburetor/throttle body bolts and remove the carburetor/throttle body.
11. Remove the rocker arm cover-to-cylinder head bolts and the cover from the cylinder head.
12. Using the valve clearance adjuster tool 498767000 or equivalent, loosen the valve adjuster locknuts and back-off the adjusting screw.
13. Remove the valve rocker arm shaft-to-journal bolt, pull out the rocker arm shaft, then remove the spring washers, the valve rocker arms. Keep the rocker arms and the spring washers in order to make the installation easier.

To install:

14. Using a putty knife, clean the gasket mounting surfaces. Inspect the rocker arm for wear; the clearance between the rocker arm and the shaft should be 0.0006-0.0022 in. (0.016-0.057mm).
15. To install, use new gaskets, sealant (where necessary) and reverse the removal procedures. Torque the camshaft sprocket-to-camshaft bolts to 8.3-9.0 ft. lbs., the crankshaft pulley-to-crankshaft bolt to 47-54 ft. lbs. Refill the cooling system and the crankcase. Operate the engine until normal operating temperature is reached and check for leaks.

2.2L Engine

1. Disconnect the PCV hose and remove the rocker cover.

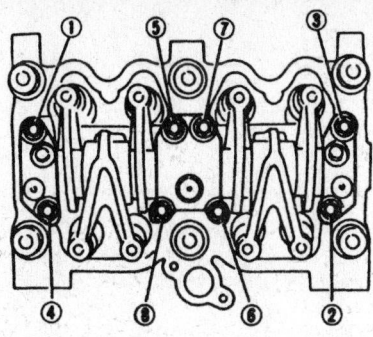

Rocker arm assembly torque sequence — 2.2L engine

2. Remove the valve rocker assembly by removing bolts 2 through 4 in numerical sequence.

3. Loosen bolt 1 but leave engaged to retain valve rocker assembly.

4. Remove bolts 5 through 8, taking care not to gouge the dowel pin.

5. Remove the valve rocker assembly.

6. Place the valve rocker assembly with the air vent on the rocker arm facing upward into clean engine oil until ready to install. This is done to prevent damaging the hydraulic lash adjuster.

To install:

7. Install the valve rocker assembly on the cylinder head.

8. Temporarily tighten bolts 1 through 4 equally.

NOTE: Do not allow the valve rocker assembly to gouge the dowel pins.

9. Tighten bolts 5 through 8 to 9 ft. lbs. (12 Nm).

10. Tighten bolts 1 through 4 to 9 ft. lbs. (12 Nm).

11. Install the rocker cover and connect the PCV hose.

Intake Manifold

REMOVAL AND INSTALLATION

1.2L Engine

1. Disconnect the negative battery cable. Drain the cooling system. Remove the air cleaner assembly. On fuel injected models, relieve the fuel system pressure.

2. Disconnect the fuel line and accelerator cable. Label and disconnect the required vacuum lines. Label and disconnect all required electrical connections. Remove the upper radiator hose.

3. Remove the necessary components in order to gain access to the intake manifold retaining bolts.

4. Remove the intake manifold retaining bolts. Remove the intake manifold and discard the gasket.

To install:

5. Clean all gasket material from the intake manifold and cylinder head.

6. Install the intake manifold using a new gasket. Tighten the intake manifold bolts to 14-22 ft. lbs. (19-30 Nm).

7. Reconnect all vacuum and electrical connections. Install all components previously removed.

8. Reconnect the radiator hose and fill the cooling system with coolant.

9. Reconnect the fuel lines and then the negative battery cable. Start the engine and check for leaks.

1.8L SPFI Engine

1. Disconnect the negative battery cable.

2. Drain the cooling system and remove the radiator hose.

3. Remove all distributor high tension wires and remove the distributor as required.

4. Label and disconnect all applicable vacuum hoses.

5. Remove the alternator as required to gain clearance.

6. Remove the silencers and silencer hoses. Remove the air cleaner assembly.

7. Remove the air suction valves and hoses.

8. Remove the EGR cover and EGR pipe.

9. Remove the PCV valve and blowby hoses.

10. Remove the air bleed from the thermostat case.

11. Label and disconnect all applicable electrical harnesses.

12. Disconnect the fuel lines and accelerator cable.

13. Remove the intake manifold bolts and carefully lift the intake manifold off the engine.

To install:

14. Clean the gasket mating surfaces thoroughly. Using a straightedge and a feeler gauge, inspect the intake manifold for flatness. Distortion should not exceed 0.020 in. (0.5mm).

15. Install the intake manifold using new gaskets and tighten the bolts to 13-16 ft. lbs. (18-22 Nm).

16. Inspect all electrical connectors for damage and replace as necessary. Connect all electrical connectors.

17. Install the air bleed on the thermostat.

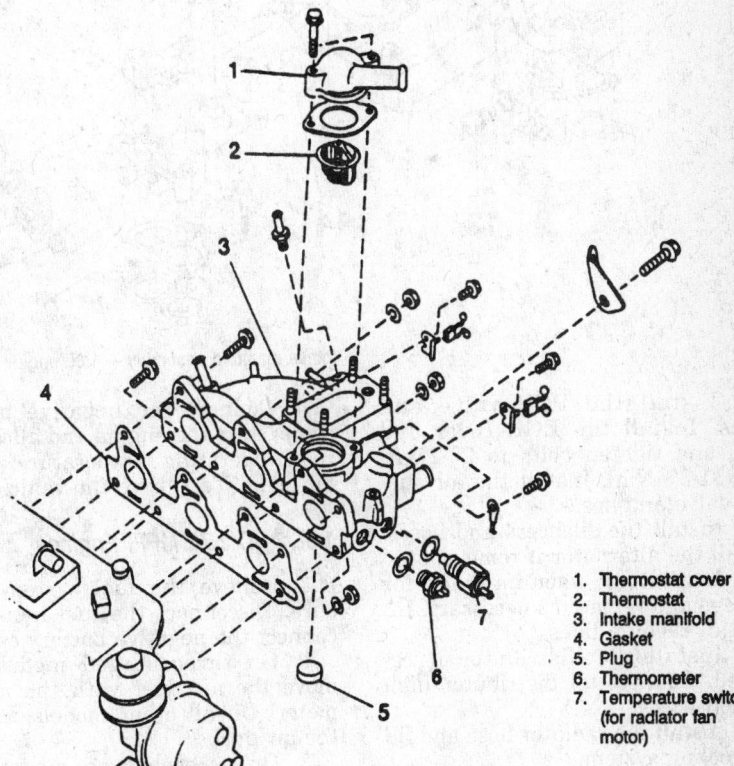

1. Thermostat cover
2. Thermostat
3. Intake manifold
4. Gasket
5. Plug
6. Thermometer
7. Temperature switch (for radiator fan motor)

Intake manifold assembly — 1.2L engine

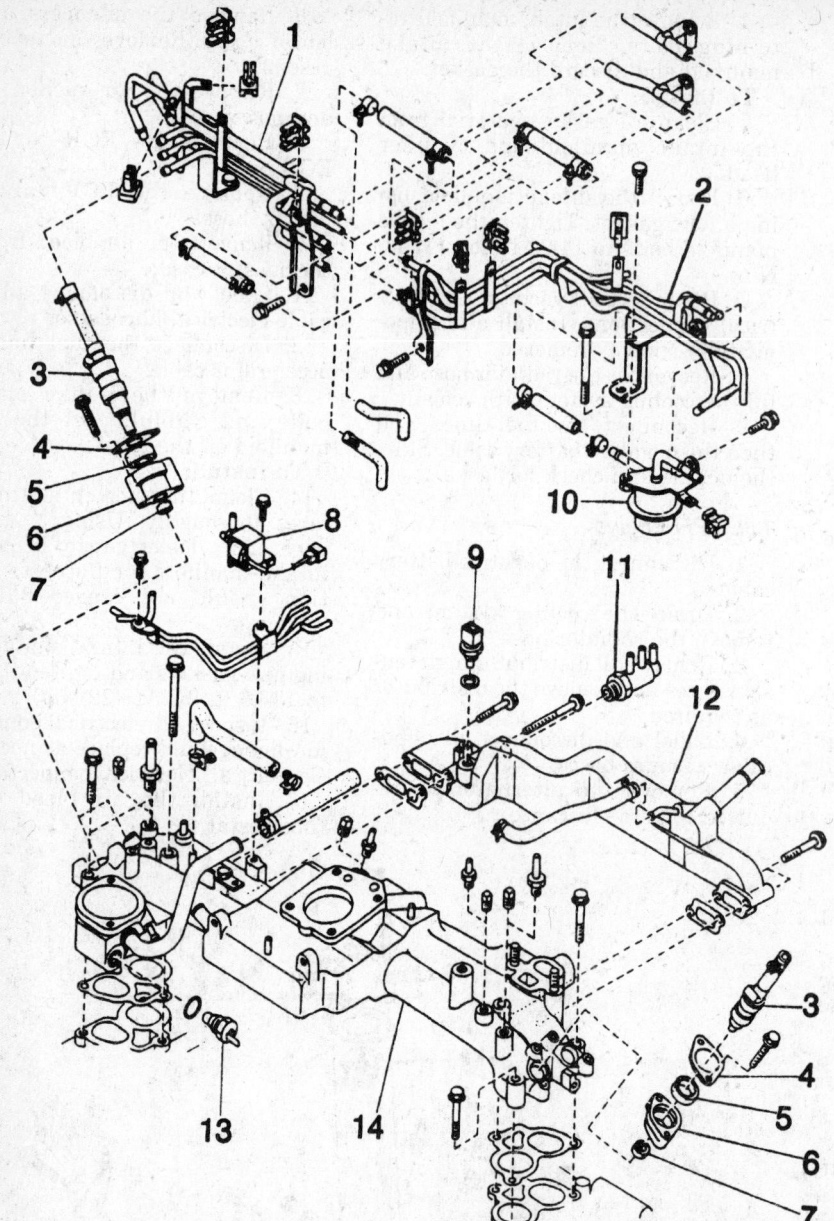

1. Fuel pipe assembly RH
2. Fuel pipe assembly LH
3. Fuel injector
4. Holder plate
5. Insulator
6. Holder
7. Seal
8. EGR solenoid valve
9. Coolant thermosensor
10. Pressure regulator
11. Thermo valve
12. Water pipe
13. Thermometer
14. Intake manifold

Intake manifold assembly — 1.8L engine with TBI

18. Install the PCV valve and hoses. Install the EGR cover and pipe, and tighten bolts to 23-27 ft. lbs. (31-37 Nm). Install the air suction valve and hoses.

19. Install the silencers and hoses. Install the alternator if removed.

20. Inspect all vacuum lines for damage and replace as necessary. Install all vacuum lines.

21. Install the distributor if removed. Connect all distributor high tension wires.

22. Install the radiator hose and fill the cooling system.

23. Connect all fuel lines and install the air cleaner assembly.

24. Connect the negative battery cable, start the engine and allow it to reach operating temperature. Check for leaks. Test drive the vehicle.

1.8L AND 2.7L MPFI Engines

1. Relieve the fuel system pressure. Disconnect the fuel lines. Disconnect the negative battery cable.

2. On turbocharged models, remove the air duct with the airflow meter. On all other models, remove the air duct.

3. On turbocharged models, remove the turbo cooling hose and turbocharger. Remove the front exhaust pipe from the cylinder head as required.

4. Remove all distributor high tension wires and remove the distributor as required.

5. Remove the alternator as required to gain clearance.

6. Label and remove all applicable electrical connectors.

7. Label and remove all applicable vacuum hoses.

8. Remove the EGR cover and pipe.

9. Disconnect the accelerator linkage. Remove the intake manifold assembly.

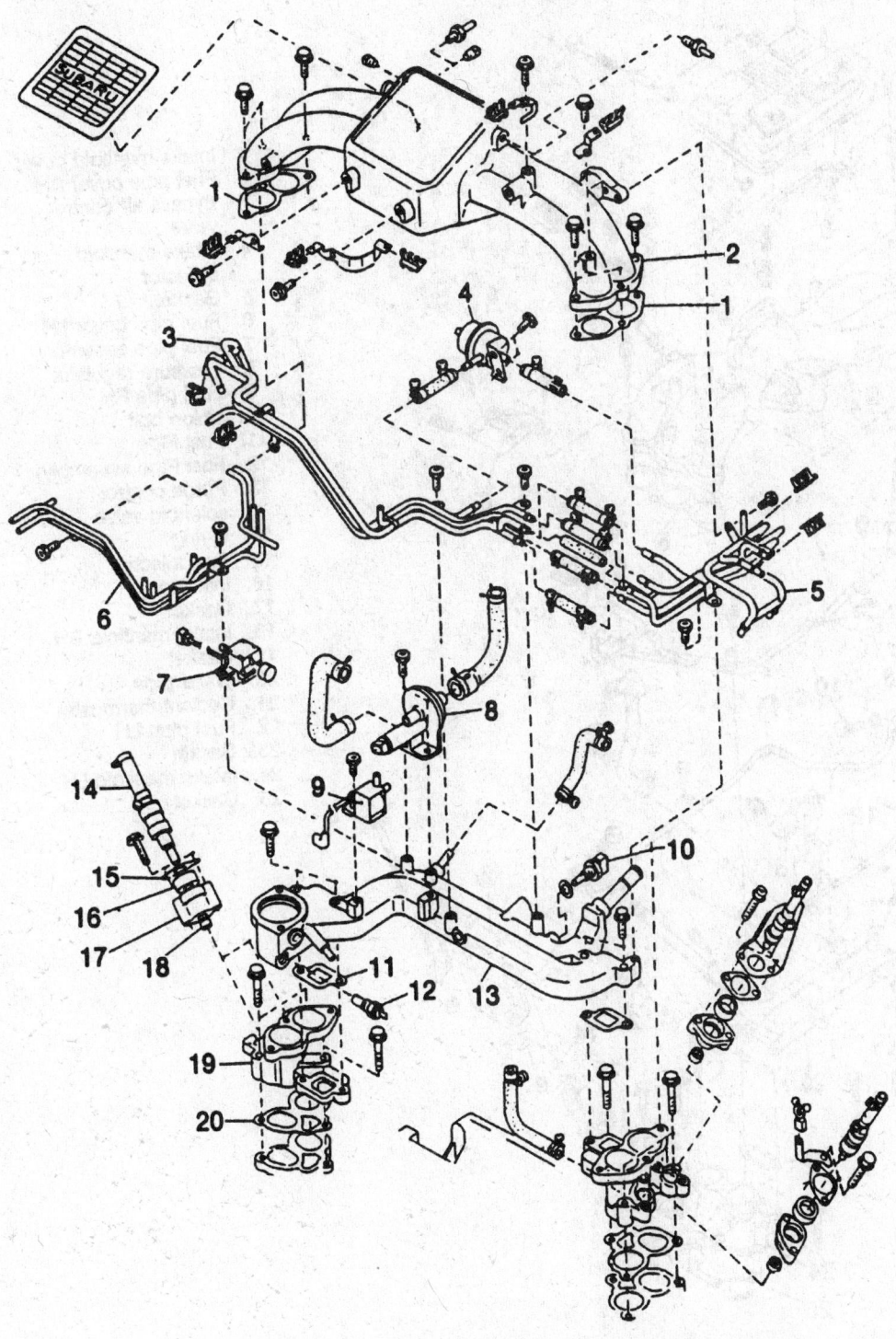

1. Gasket
2. Intake manifold collector
3. Fuel pipe RH
4. Pressure regulator
5. Fuel pipe LH
6. Vacuum pipe assembly
7. Purge control solenoid valve
8. Auxiliary air valve
9. EGR solenoid valve
10. Coolant thermosensor
11. Gasket
12. Thermometer
13. Water pipe
14. Fuel injector
15. Holder plate
16. Insulator
17. Holder
18. Seal
19. Intake manifold
20. Gasket

Intake manifold assembly — 1.8L engine with MPFI

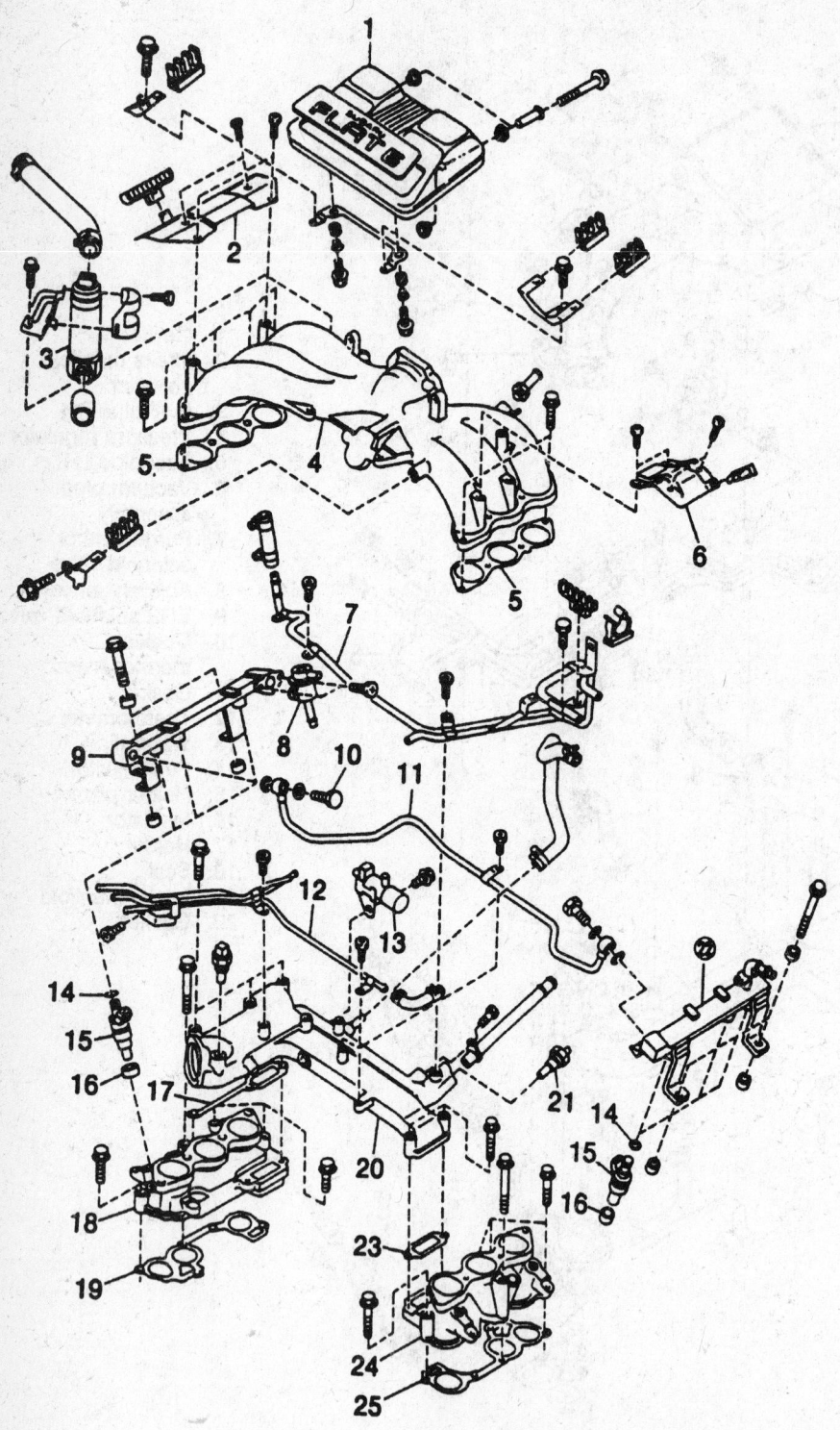

1. Intake manifold cover
2. Fuel pipe cover RH
3. Bypass air control valve
4. Intake manifold collector
5. Gasket
6. Fuel pipe cover LH
7. Fuel pipe assembly
8. Pressure regulator
9. Fuel pipe RH
10. Union bolt
11. Fuel Pipe
12. Fuel Pipe assembly
13. Purge control solenoid valve
14. O-ring
15. Fuel injector
16. Insulator
17. Gasket
18. Intake manifold RH
19. Gasket
20. Water pipe
21. Coolant thermostat
22. Fuel pipe LH
23. Gasket
24. Intake manifold LH
25. Gasket

Intake manifold assembly — 2.7L engine

To install:

10. Clean the gasket mating surfaces thoroughly. Using a straight-edge and a feeler gauge, inspect the intake manifold for flatness. Distortion should not exceed 0.020 in. (0.5mm).

11. Install the intake manifold using new gaskets and tighten the bolts to 13-16 ft. lbs. (18-22 Nm). Connect the fuel lines.

12. Install the EGR pipe and tighten to 23-27 ft. lbs. (31-37 Nm). Install the EGR cover.

13. Check all vacuum lines for deterioration and replace as necessary. Install all previously removed vacuum lines.

14. Check all electrical connectors for deterioration and replace as necessary. Install all previously disconnected electrical connectors.

15. Install the alternator if removed.

16. Inspect all distributor high tension wires and replace as necessary. Install the high tension wires and distributor.

17. On turbocharged models, install the turbo cooling hose and turbocharger. Install the front exhaust pipe from the cylinder head if removed.

18. On turbocharged models, install the air duct with the airflow meter. On all other models, install the air duct.

19. Connect the negative battery cable. Start the engine and allow it to reach operating temperature. Check for leaks and test drive the vehicle.

2.2L AND 3.3L Engines

1. Release the fuel system pressure. Disconnect the negative battery cable and remove the engine cover.

2. Drain the cooling system and remove the water pipes as required.

3. Remove power steering pump, alternator and bracket as necessary to gain clearance.

4. Label and disconnect all electrical connectors leading to the intake manifold.

5. Label and disconnect all vacuum hoses leading to the intake manifold. Disconnect the PCV and blowby hoses.

6. Label and disconnect the ignition high tension wires at the spark plugs and lay them aside.

7. Disconnect the air intake duct.

8. On turbocharged models, disconnect the turbo from the intake manifold and remove as required.

9. Disconnect the fuel supply lines and accelerator linkage.

10. Remove the intake manifold assembly.

To install:

11. Clean the gasket mating surfaces thoroughly. Using a straight edge and a feeler gauge, inspect the intake manifold for flatness. Distortion should not exceed 0.020 in. (0.5mm).

12. Install the intake manifold and tighten the bolts to specification. On the 2.2L engine tighten the short bolts to 21-25 ft. lbs. (28-34 Nm); the long bolts to 4-5 ft. lbs. (6-7 Nm). On the 3.3L engine, tighten all bolts to 17-20 ft. lbs. (23-26 Nm).

13. Install the fuel lines and accelerator linkage.

14. Install the turbocharger assembly.

15. Install the air intake duct.

16. Check the ignition high tension wires for damage and install on the spark plugs.

17. Check all vacuum lines for deterioration and replace as necessary. Install the vacuum lines.

18. Check all electrical connectors for damage and replace as necessary. Install the electrical connectors.

19. Install the PCV valve and blowby hose.

20. Install the power steering pump and alternator if removed.

21. Install the water pipes and fill the cooling system.

22. Install the engine cover.

23. Start the engine and allow it to reach operating temperature. Check for leaks and test drive the vehicle.

Exhaust Manifold

REMOVAL AND INSTALLATION

1.2L Engine

1. Disconnect the negative battery cable. Remove the air cleaner assembly.

2. Raise and support the vehicle safely. Disconnect the exhaust manifold from the exhaust pipe. Lower the vehicle.

3. Disconnect the oxygen sensor electrical connector. Remove the exhaust manifold cover plate assembly.

4. Remove the exhaust manifold retaining bolts. Remove the exhaust manifold from the engine. Discard the gasket.

To install:

5. Clean the mating surfaces of the exhaust manifold and cylinder head thoroughly. Install the exhaust manifold and tighten the bolts to 14-22 ft. lbs. (19-30 Nm).

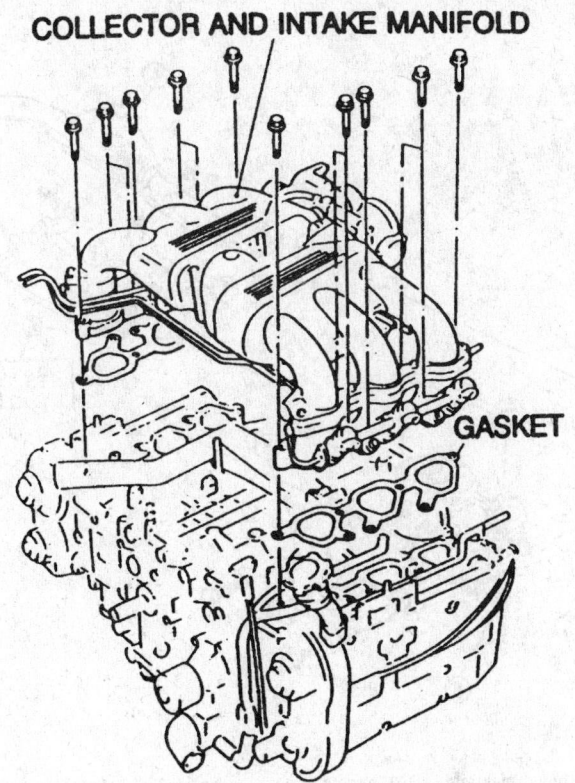

COLLECTOR AND INTAKE MANIFOLD

GASKET

Removing the intake manifold — 3.3L engine

6. Install the oxygen sensor electrical connector and manifold cover plate. Raise the vehicle and install the exhaust pipe. Lower the vehicle.

7. Install the oxygen sensor electrical connector and air cleaner. Reconnect the negative battery cable.

1.8L, 2.2L and 2.7L Engines

On these engines the front exhaust pipe bolts directly to the under side of the cylinder head. No exhaust manifold is used.

1. Disconnect the negative battery cable.

2. Raise and safely support the vehicle. Remove the engine under cover, if equipped.

3. Disconnect the electrical lead from the oxygen sensor. Remove the front exhaust pipe-to-cylinder head bolts. If equipped with a turbocharger, remove the exhaust pipe to turbocharger assembly.

4. Remove the front exhaust pipe-to-rear exhaust pipe nuts, then separate the pipes.

5. To install, reverse the removal procedures. Replace all gaskets and tighten the retaining bolts to 19-22 ft. lbs. (26-30 Nm).

3.3L Engine

1. Raise and support the vehicle safely.

2. Disconnect the oxygen sensor harness.

3. Remove the front under cover.

4. Remove the exhaust manifold covers.

5. Remove the front exhaust pipes.

6. Disconnect the EGR pipe from the right exhaust manifold.

7. Remove the exhaust manifolds.

To install:

8. Clean all gasket mating surfaces thoroughly.

9. Install the exhaust manifolds using new gaskets. Tighten the exhaust manifold-to-cylinder head nuts to 25-33 ft. lbs. (34-44 Nm) and the exhaust manifold-to-front exhaust pipe nuts to 22-29 ft. lbs. (29-39 Nm).

10. Install the exhaust manifold covers and tighten the bolts to 13-15 ft. lbs. (17-20 Nm).

11. Install the front under cover.

12. Connect the oxygen sensor harness.

13. Lower the vehicle. Start the engine and check for leaks.

Turbocharger

REMOVAL AND INSTALLATION

1. Disconnect the negative battery cable. Drain the cooling system. Remove the air cleaner.

2. Disconnect the airflow meter-to-turbocharger inlet clamp, then remove the air intake duct. Cover the airflow meter and turbocharger openings.

3. Loosen the turbocharger-to-air outlet hose clamp and the throttle body inlet to air inlet hose clamp. Remove the turbocharger-to-throttle body hose. Plug all of the openings.

4. Remove the turbocharger-to-center exhaust pipe nuts and the front exhaust pipe to turbocharger nuts.

5. Disconnect and plug the coolant lines.

6. Remove the oil feed line to turbocharger bolt and disconnect the turbocharger to oil return hose clamp and the return hose.

7. Remove the turbocharger from the exhaust manifold.

NOTE: When removing the turbocharger from the vehicle, disconnect the oil return hose.

TIGHTENING TORQUE
T1: 13–15 FT. LBS. (17–20 NM)
T2: 25–33 FT. LBS. (34–44 NM)
T3: 22–29 FT. LBS. (29–39 NM)

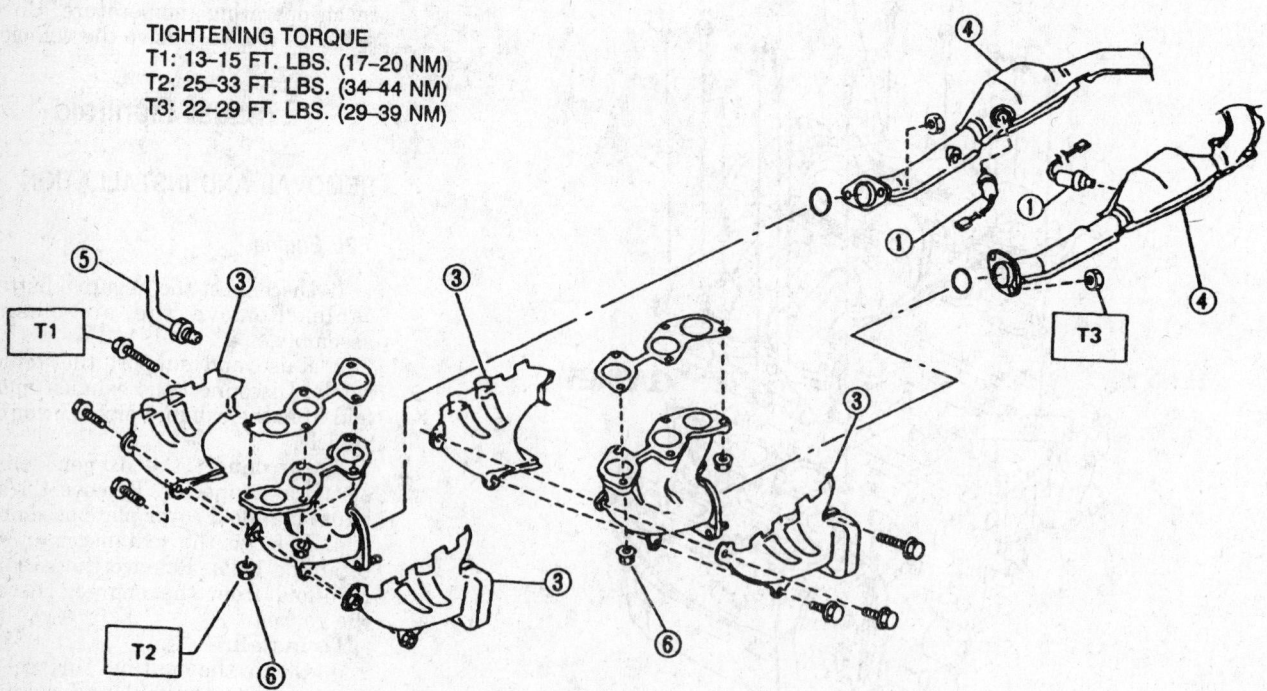

Removing the exhaust manifold — 3.3L engine

To install:

8. Installation is the reverse of the removal procedure. Be sure to fill the turbocharger assembly with clean engine oil prior to installation.

9. Be sure to use new gaskets, as required. Start the engine and check for leaks, correct as necessary.

Timing Belt Front Cover

REMOVAL AND INSTALLATION

1.2L Engine

1. Loosen the alternator-to-engine bolts, relax the drive belt tension and remove the drive belt from the front of the engine.

2. Using a socket wrench (through the hole in the right fender) and the crank/camshaft pulley wrench tool 499205500 or equivalent (to hold the crankshaft pulley), remove the crankshaft pulley-to-crankshaft bolt and the pulley from the crankshaft.

3. Remove the timing belt cover-to-engine bolts and the cover from the engine.

4. Install the timing belt cover and tighten the bolts securely.

5. Install the crankshaft pulley and tighten the bolt to 58-72 ft. lbs. (78-98 Nm).

6. Install the accessory drive belt and tighten to the proper tension.

1.8L and 2.7L Engines

1. Loosen the water pump pulley nut/bolts and the alternator-to-engine bolts, the remove the drive belt.

2. Disconnect the electrical connector from the oil pressure switch.

3. Remove the oil level gauge guide with the gauge.

4. Remove the timing hole cover from the top of the flywheel housing.

5. Using the flywheel stopper tool 498277000 or equivalent (MT), or the driveplate stopper tool 498407000 or equivalent (AT), insert it through the timing hole (in the flywheel housing) and lock the flywheel.

6. Remove the crankshaft pulley bolt and using a puller, remove the crankshaft pulley.

7. If equipped with a turbocharger, remove the belt cover plate.

8. Remove the left side, the right side and the front timing belt cover.

To install:

9. Install the timing belt covers and tighten the bolts to 3-4 ft.lbs. (4-5 Nm).

10. Install the crankshaft pulley and tighten the bolt to 66-79 ft. lbs. (89-107 Nm).

11. Remove the flywheel stopper tool.

12. Install the oil level guide and gauge.

13. Connect the oil pressure switch electrical connector.

14. Install the water pump pulley and drive belt. Tighten the drive belt to the proper tension.

2.2L and 3.3L Engines

1. Remove the accessory drive belt.

2. As required, remove the power steering pump, alternator, air conditioner compressor and associated brackets.

3. Remove the crankshaft pulley bolt and remove the crankshaft pulley.

4. Remove the belt covers.

To install:

5. Install the belt covers and tighten the bolts to 3-4 ft. lbs. (4-5 Nm).

6. Install the crankshaft pulley and tighten the bolt to 69-76 ft. lbs. (93-103 Nm) on the 2.2L engine or 108-123 ft. lbs. (147-167 Nm) on the 3.3L engine.

7. Install the power steering pump, alternator, air conditioner compressor and associated brackets.

8. Install the accessory drive belt and tension to specification.

OIL SEAL REPLACEMENT

1. Remove the timing belt cover assembly.

2. On the 1.8L engine, slide both the No. 1 and No. 2 crankshaft sprockets from the crankshaft. On the 1.2L engine, slide crankshaft sprocket from the crankshaft. When removing the crankshaft sprockets, be sure to remove the Woodruff® key from the crankshaft.

3. Using a small prybar, pry the front oil seal from the crankcase.

To install:

4. Using a new oil seal lubricated with engine oil, drive the new seal into the crankcase until it seats. When installing the new oil seal, be careful not to cut the sealing lips.

5. Reinstall the crankshaft sprockets and timing belt cover assembly.

Timing Belt and Tensioner

REMOVAL AND INSTALLATION

1.2L Engine

1. Disconnect the negative battery cable. Remove the accessory drive belt. Loosen the crankshaft pulley bolts but do not remove.

NOTE: An access hole is provided in the wheelhouse panel to loosen and then remove the crankshaft pulley bolts.

2. Position the crankshaft with No. 3 cylinder at TDC.

3. Remove the crankshaft bolts and pulley. Remove the outer front timing belt cover.

4. Loosen the tensioner bolt and position it in the direction that loosens the belt. Tighten the tensioner bolt in that position.

5. Remove the camshaft drive pulley plate. Mark the timing belt, if to be used again, in the direction of rotation for reinstallation. Remove the belt from the sprockets.

6. If necessary, remove the tensioner and spring. Remove the camshaft pulley. Remove the inner belt cover and cover mount, only as required.

To install:

7. When installing the timing belt, rotate and align the matchmark of the camshaft driven pulley 0.120 in. (3mm) diameter hole with the matchmark of the cam belt side cover.

8. Align the matchmark of the camshaft drive pulley and the crankshaft cover. Install the camshaft drive belt.

9. Ensure that each rocker arm can be moved. Loosen the tensioner bolt ½ turn.

10. Tighten the tensioner bolt below the adjusting wheel first. Tighten the other bolt. Check to be sure all sprocket and housing matching marks are in agreement.

11. Install the camshaft drive pulley plate.

12. Install the cam belt cover.

13. Install the crankshaft pulley and bolts. Tighten the crankshaft bolts to 58-72 ft. lbs. (78-98 Nm).

14. Check and adjust the valve clearance.

15. Install the accessory drive belts and tension to specification.

16. Connect the negative battery cable. Start the engine and allow it to reach operating temperature. Test drive the vehicle and check for leaks.

1.8L Engine

1. Remove the accessory drive belt, water pump pulley and pulley cover.

2. Remove the oil level gauge and guide. Disconnect the oil pressure switch electrical connector.

3. Remove the crankshaft pulley.

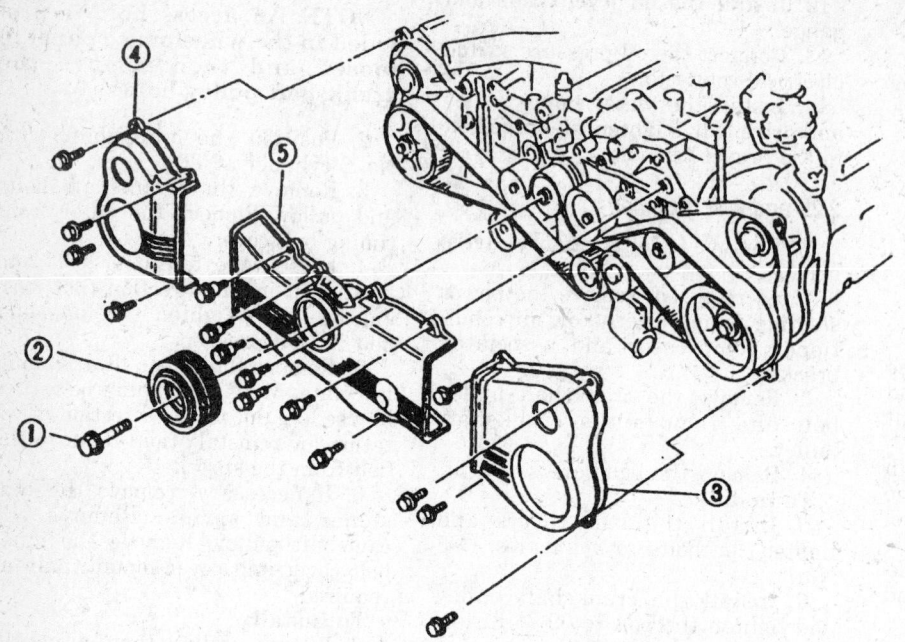

1. Water pump pulley bolt
2. Crankshaft pulley
3. Timming belt side cover
4. Timming belt side cover
5. Front timming belt cover

Removing the front engine covers — 3.3L engine

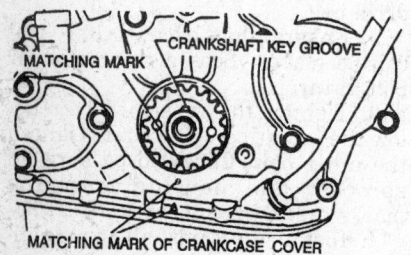

Crankshaft gear alignment — 1.2L engine

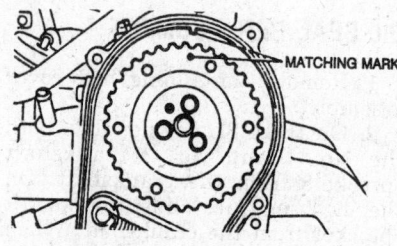

Camshaft gear alignment — 1.2L engine

4. On turbocharged engines, remove the belt cover plate.

5. Remove the timing belt covers.

6. Loosen the timing belt tensioner mounting bolts ½ turn and slacken the timing belt. Tighten the mounting bolts.

7. Mark the rotating direction of the timing belt, then remove the belt.

8. Perform the same procedure for the No. 2 timing belt. Remove the crankshaft sprockets.

9. Remove both tensioners together with the tensioner springs.

10. Remove the belt idler. Remove the camshaft sprockets.

11. Remove the No. 2 belt covers.

To install:

12. Inspect the timing belt for breaks, cracks and wear. Replace as required.

13. Check the belt tensioner and idler for smooth rotation. Replace if noisy or excessive play is noticed.

14. Install the left hand belt cover seal No. 3 to the cylinder block.

15. Install the left hand belt cover seal, left hand belt cover seal No. 4, and belt cover mount to the right rear belt cover, then install the assembly on the cylinder block. Tighten to 3-4 ft. lbs. (4-5 Nm).

16. Install the left hand belt cover seal No. 2 and belt cover mounts to left hand belt cover No. 2, then install to the cylinder head and camshaft case. Tighten to 3-4 ft. lbs. (4-5 Nm).

17. Install the right hand belt cover seal, belt cover seal No. 2 and belt cover mounts to the right hand belt cover No. 2, then install to the cylinder head and camshaft case. Tighten to 3-4 ft. lbs. (4-5 Nm).

18. Install the camshaft sprockets to the right and left camshafts. Tighten the bolts gradually in 2-3 steps to 6-7 ft. lbs. (9-10 Nm).

19. Attach the tensioner spring to the tensioner, then install to the right side of the cylinder block. Tighten the bolts temporarily by hand.

20. Attach the tensioner spring to the bolt, tighten the right side bolt and then loosen ½ turn.

21. Push down tensioner until it stops, then temporarily tighten the left bolt.

22. Install the left side tensioner in the same manner.

23. Install the belt idler to the cylinder block using care not to turn the seal. Tighten to 29-35 ft. lbs. (39-47 Nm).

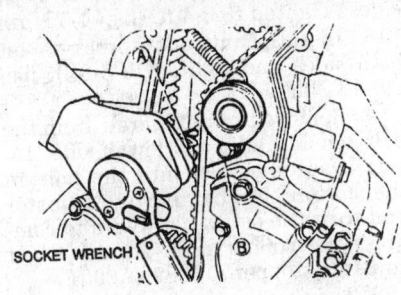

Timing belt tension adjustment — 1.2L engine

SOCKET WRENCH

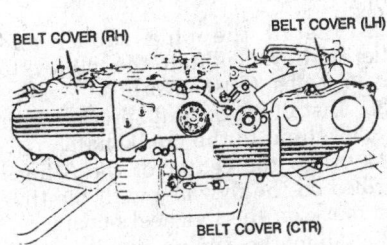

Left, center and right belt covers — typical of
1.8L, 2.2L and 2.7L engines

BELT COVER (RH)   BELT COVER (LH)

BELT COVER (CTR)

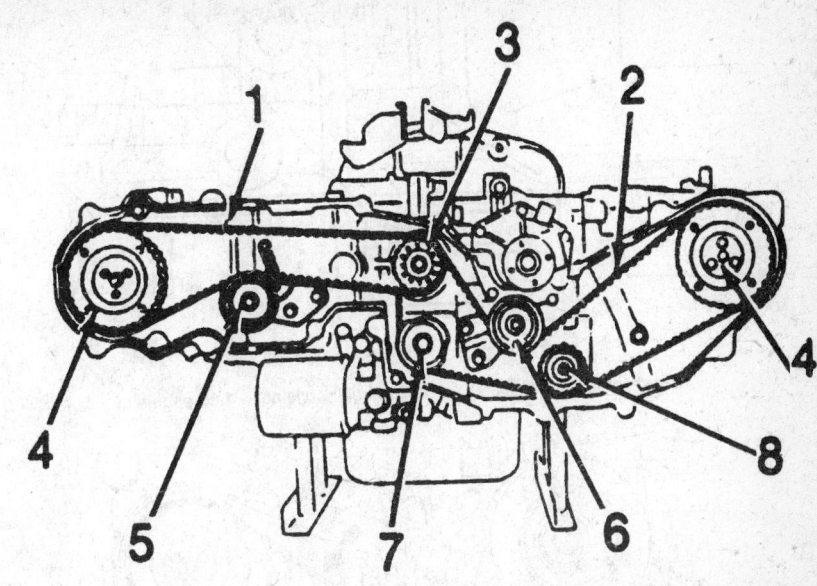

1. Right hand timing belt
2. Left hand timing belt
3. Crankshaft sprocket
4. Camshaft sprocket
5. Right hand tensioner
6. Left hand tensioner
7. Oil pump sprocket
8. Idler

Timing belt configuration — 1.8L and 2.7L engines

24. Install sprockets to the crankshaft. Install the crankshaft pulley and tighten the bolt temporarily.

25. Align the center of the three lines scribed on the flywheel with the timing mark on the flywheel housing.

26. Align the timing mark on the left hand camshaft sprocket with the notch on the belt cover.

27. Attach timing belt No. 2 to the crankshaft sprocket No. 2, oil pump sprocket, belt idler, and camshaft sprocket in that order. Avoid downward slackening of the belt.

28. Loosen tensioner No. 2 lower bolt ½ turn to apply tension. Push timing belt by hand to ensure smooth movement of tensioner.

29. Apply 25 ft. lbs. (new belt) or 18 ft. lbs. (used belt) torque to the camshaft sprocket in counterclockwise direction. While applying torque tighten tensioner No. 2 lower bolt temporarily, then tighten upper bolt temporarily.

30. Tighten the lower bolt, then the upper bolt to 13-15 ft. lbs. (17-20 Nm) in that order.

31. Check that the flywheel timing mark and left hand camshaft sprocket mark are in their proper positions.

32. Turn the crankshaft 1 turn clockwise from the position where timing belt No. 2 was installed, and align the center of the 3 lines on the flywheel with the timing mark on the flywheel housing.

33. Align the timing mark on the right hand camshaft sprocket with the notch in the belt cover.

34. Attach the timing belt to the crankshaft sprocket and camshaft sprocket, avoiding slackening of the belt on the upper side.

35. Loosen the tensioner ½ turn to apply tension to the belt. Push the belt by hand to ensure smooth operation.

36. Apply 25 ft. lbs. (new belt) or 18 ft. lbs. (used belt) torque to the camshaft sprocket in counterclockwise direction. While applying torque tighten tensioner left bolt temporarily, then tighten right bolt temporarily.

37. Tighten the left bolt, then the right bolt to 13-15 ft. lbs. (17-20 Nm) in that order.

38. Check that the flywheel timing mark and left hand camshaft sprocket mark are in their proper positions.

39. Remove the crankshaft pulley.

40. Install the right front belt cover seals and belt cover plug. Install the belt covers to the cylinder block.

41. On turbocharged engines, install the belt cover plate.

42. Install the crankshaft pulley and tighten to 66-79 ft. lbs. (89-107 Nm).

43. Install the water pump pulley and tighten to 6-7 ft. lbs. (9-10 Nm). Install the pulley cover, oil level guide and gauge and oil pressure switch connector.

44. Install and properly tension the accessory drive belt.

2.7L Engine

1. Remove the accessory drive belt, water pump pulley and pulley cover.

2. Remove the oil level gauge and guide. Disconnect the oil pressure switch electrical connector.

3. Remove the crankshaft pulley.

4. Remove the timing belt covers.

5. Loosen the timing belt tensioner mounting bolts ½ turn and slacken the timing belt. Tighten the mounting bolts.

6. Mark the rotating direction of the timing belt, then remove the right hand belt.

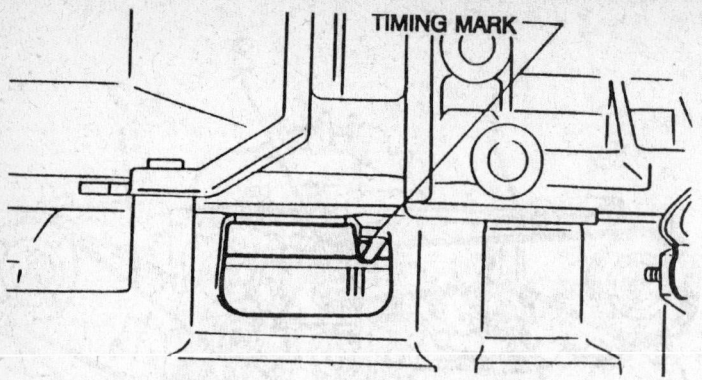

Flywheel alignment marks for timing belt servicing — 1.8L engine

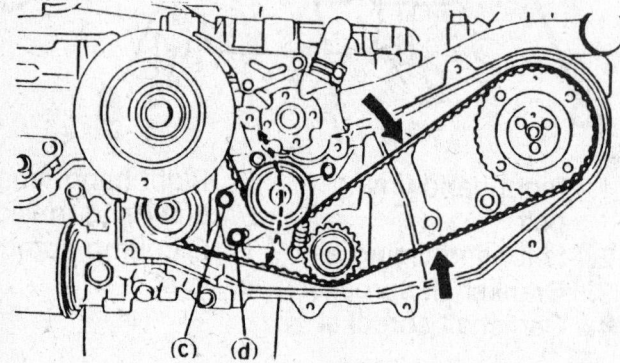

Left timing belt tensioner servicing — 1.8L engine

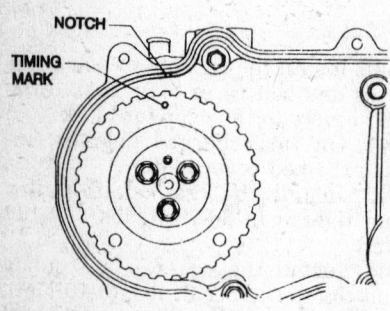

Right camshaft gear alignment — 1.8L engine — after turning engine 1 complete rotation with the left timing belt installed

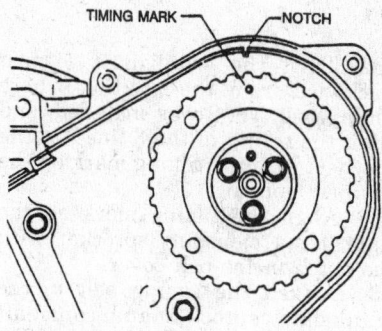

Left camshaft gear alignment — 1.8L engine

17. Install belt cover No. 2 on both sides. Tighten to 3-4 ft. lbs. (4-5 Nm).

18. Install camshaft sprockets on both sides and tighten to 8-9 ft. lbs. (11-13 Nm).

19. Remove the plug screw from the belt tension adjuster lower side. Insert a suitable tool into the hole in the bottom of the tension adjuster and turn the screw clockwise to compress the rubber boot. Install a belt adjuster stopper (13082AA000).

20. Using a syringe, add engine oil through the air vent hole on top of the rubber boot until it overflows. Install the plug screw.

21. Install the belt tension adjuster and tighten to 17-20 ft. lbs. (23-26 Nm).

22. Install the plug rubber and idler pulley. Tighten the pulley to 29-35 ft. lbs. (39-47 Nm).

23. Install crankshaft sprocket with no dowel pin to the crankshaft.

24. Align the center of the 3 lines scribed on the flywheel with the timing mark on the flywheel housing.

25. Align the timing mark on the left hand camshaft sprocket with the notch on the belt cover.

26. Install the timing belt from the crankshaft side and take care not to loosen it.

27. Install the left tensioner and check for smooth operation. Tighten the tensioner to 29-35 ft. lbs. (39-47 Nm).

28. Remove the belt adjuster stopper from the belt tension adjuster.

29. Check that the end of the left tensioner arm contacts the top of the belt tension adjuster.

30. Make sure the flywheel timing mark and left hand camshaft sprocket timing mark are in the proper positions.

31. Turn the crankshaft 1 turn clockwise from the position where the left timing belt was installed and align the center of the 3 lines scribed on the flywheel with the timing mark on the flywheel housing.

32. Align the mark on the right hand camshaft sprocket with the notch in the belt cover.

33. Temporarily tighten both belt tensioner bolts while forcing the tensioner against spring pressure (downward).

34. Install the crankshaft sprocket.

35. Install the timing belt from the crankshaft side and take care no to loosen it.

36. Loosen the left tensioner bolt by ½ turn to apply tension to the belt.

37. Apply 33-55 ft. lbs. torque to the camshaft sprocket in a counterclock-

7. Remove the right hand tensioner. Remove the crankshaft sprocket.

8. Remove the idler pulley and rubber plug.

9. Remove the plug screw from the left belt tension adjuster lower side.

10. Insert a suitable tool into the hose in the bottom of the belt tension adjuster and turn the screw clockwise to loosen the belt tension. Install a belt adjuster stopper (13082AA000). Remove the left belt tensioner.

11. Remove the left timing belt after marking the rotating direction.

12. Remove the crankshaft sprocket No. 2 and idler pulley. Remove the belt tension adjuster.

13. Remove the camshaft sprockets.

14. Remove the belt cover No. 2 from both sides.

To install:

15. Inspect the timing belt for breaks, cracks and wear. Replace as required.

16. Check the belt tensioner and idler for smooth rotation. Replace if noisy or excessive play is noticed.

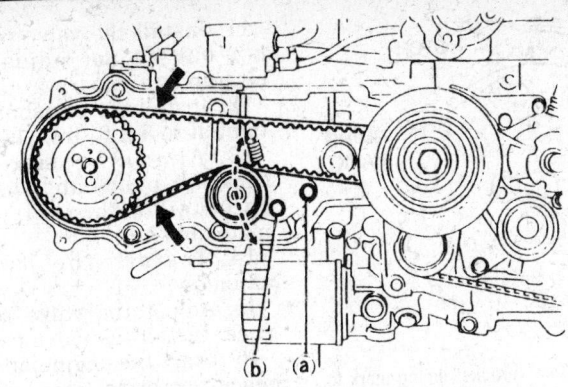

Right timing belt tensioner servicing — 1.8L engine

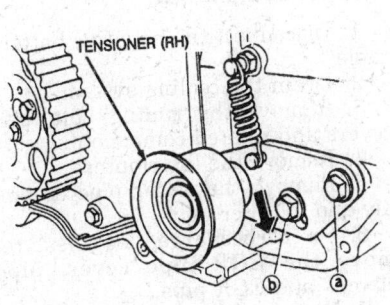

Timing belt tension adjustment — 2.7L engine

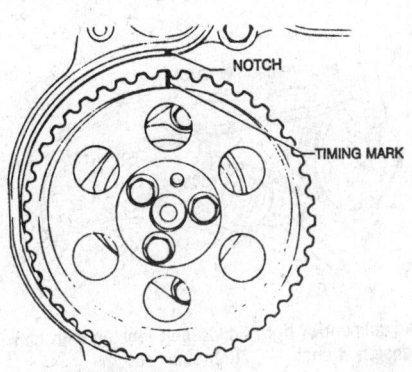

Camshaft gear alignment — 2.7L engine

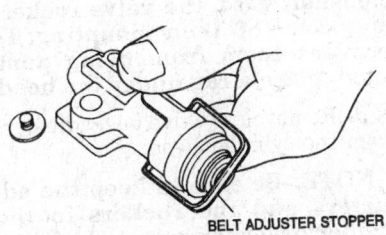

Installation of belt adjuster stopper clip — 2.7L engine

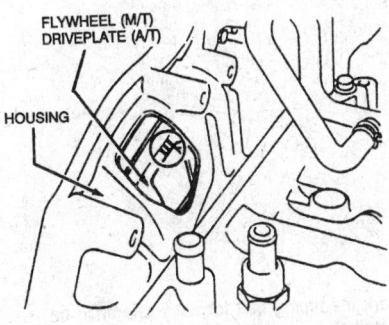

Flywheel timing mark alignment — 2.7L engine

3. Remove the cam belt covers. Align the camshaft sprockets so each sprocket notch aligns with the cam cover notches. Align the crankshaft sprocket top tooth notch, located at the rear of the tooth, with the notch on the crank angle sensor boss. Mark the 3 alignment points as well as the direction of cam belt rotation.

4. Loosen the tensioner adjusting bolts and remove the bottom 3 idlers, the cam belt and the cam belt tensioner. The cam sprockets can then be removed with a modified camshaft sprocket wrench tool.

5. If the sprockets are removed, note the reference sensor at the rear of the left cam sprocket.

To install:

6. Install the crankshaft sprocket and all of the idlers except for the lower right. Compress the hydraulic tensioner in a vise slowly and temporarily secure the plunger with a pin. Install the tensioner and the pulley.

7. After the cam belt components are installed, align the crankshaft sprocket notch on the rear sprocket tooth with the crank angle sensor boss. This places the sprocket notch in the 12 o'clock position.

8. Align the camshaft sprockets with the notches in the cam belt cover. As the directional marked belt is installed, align the marks on the belt with the crankshaft sprocket and the left camshaft sprocket. Install the lower right idler.

9. Load the tensioner by pushing it towards the crankshaft with a prybar and tighten the bolts. Remove the tensioner retention pin and the belt tension is automatically set. Rock the crankshaft back and forth 1 time to distribute the belt tension.

10. Verify the correctness of the timing by noting that the notches on the 2 cam pulleys and the notch on the crankshaft pulley all point to the 12 o'clock position when the belt is properly installed.

11. Complete the engine component assembly by installing the cam belt covers, the crankshaft pulley bolt and pulley and the remaining components.

Camshaft

REMOVAL AND INSTALLATION

1.2L Engine

1. Disconnect the negative battery cable.

2. Remove the timing belt. Remove the camshaft driven pulley.

wise direction and tighten the tensioner bolts temporarily.

38. Tighten the left, then right tensioner bolts to 17-20 ft. lbs. (23-26 Nm).

39. Make sure the flywheel timing mark and left hand camshaft sprocket timing mark are in the proper positions.

40. Install the center belt cover and crankshaft pulley. Tighten pulley bolt to 66-79 ft. lbs. (89-107 Nm).

41. Install the oil level gauge guide, water pipe, water pump pulley and belt covers.

42. Install and properly tension the accessory drive belt.

2.2L and 3.3L Engines

The 2.2L and 3.3L OHC engines use a single cam belt drive system with a serpentine type belt. The left side of the engine uses a hydraulic cam belt tensioner which is continuously self adjusting.

1. Remove the accessory drive belt.

2. Remove the crankshaft pulley bolt and crankshaft pulley.

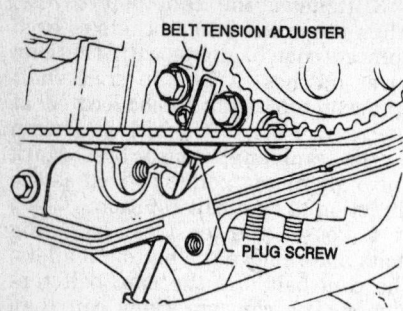

Removing the plug screw from the belt tension adjuster — 2.7L engine

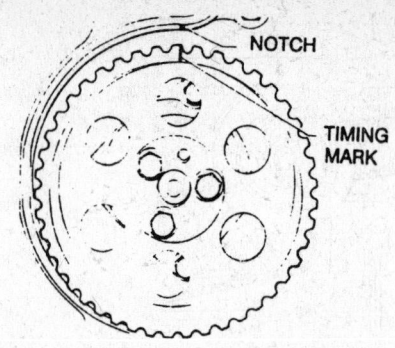

Alignment of right cam sprocket timing mark to notch in belt cover — 2.7L engine

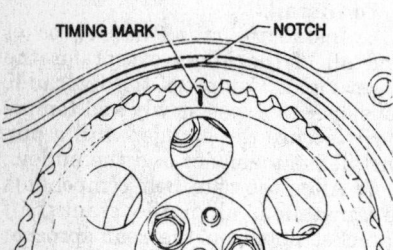

Alignment of left cam sprocket timing mark to notch in belt cover — 2.7L engine

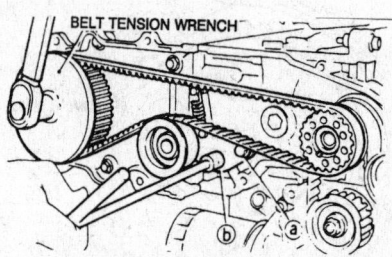

Adjustment of right timing belt tension with belt tension wrench — 2.7L engine

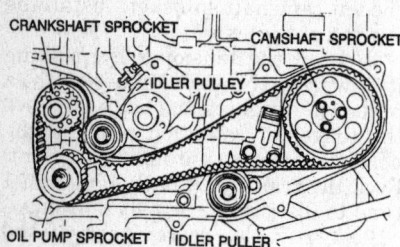

Installation of left timing belt — 2.7L engine

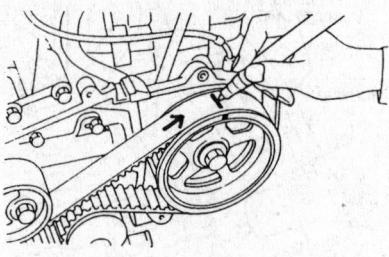

Mark the timing belt for easy reference on installation

11. Install the valve rocker assembly but do not adjust the valve clearance.

12. Install the camshaft pulley and tighten to 8-9 ft. lbs. (11-12 Nm).

13. Align the marks for the camshaft pulley and the crankshaft sprocket with their respective matchmarks.

14. Install the timing belt assembly.

15. Adjust the valve rocker clearance. Install the valve rocker cover.

16. Start the engine and allow it to reach operating temperature. Check for leaks. Set the ignition timing.

1.8L and 2.7L Engines

1. Disconnect the negative battery cable.

2. Drain the cooling system.

3. Remove the timing belt, belt covers and related components.

4. Remove the distributor.

5. Remove the water pipe assembly and oil filler duct.

6. On turbocharged engines, remove the EGR pipe cover, pipe clamps and EGR pipe.

7. Remove the valve rocker covers.

8. Remove the camshaft case, camshaft support and camshaft as a complete unit.

NOTE: When removing the camshaft case, the valve rockers may come off their mounting. To prevent them from being damaged, place a rag under the head.

9. Remove the valve lash adjusters from the cylinder head.

NOTE: Be sure to keep the adjusters and the rockers in the proper order for reinstallation.

10. Remove the camshaft support from the camshaft case. Carefully remove the camshaft from its mounting.

11. Remove an oil relief valve, relief valve spring, oil relief pipe and plug to the camshaft case.

To install:

12. Measure the camshaft runout. If runout exceeds 0.0010 in. (0.025mm), replace the camshaft.

13. Check the camshaft journals for damage or wear. If the surface of the camshaft or valve rocker is damaged or worn, repair by removing the minimum necessary amount, otherwise replace the damaged components.

14. With the valve lash adjuster in a vertical position, push the adjuster pivot quick and hard by hand. If the pivot is depressed more than 0.020 in. (0.5mm), put the adjuster in a container of light oil and move the

3. Remove the valve rocker cover and slacken the valve rocker adjustment.

4. Remove the bolt from the valve rocker shaft journal and pull the valve rocker shaft out from the cylinder head. Remove the spring washer and valve rockers.

5. Remove the camshaft taking care not to damage the bearings.

To install:

6. Clean and check the disassembled components for damage and replace as necessary.

7. Measure the rocker arm-to-shaft clearance. If clearance is greater than 0.0022 in. (0.057mm), replace the components as required.

8. Replace the rocker shaft spring if a permanent set is noted.

9. Lubricate and install the camshaft.

10. Measure the thrust clearance of the camshaft with the breaker case installed. If greater than 0.020 in. (0.5mm), grind the breaker surface of the cylinder head until the thrust clearance fall within specification.

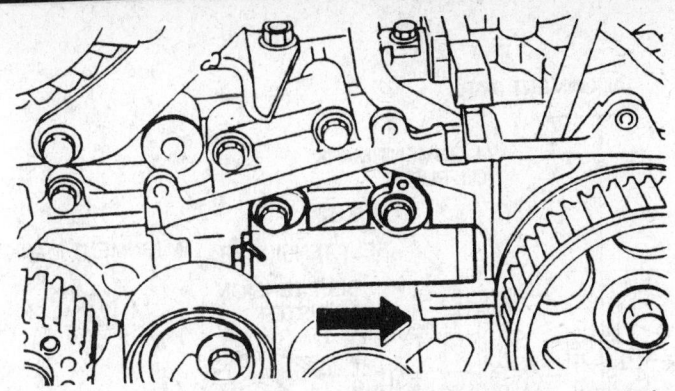

Temporarily move the tension adjuster aside with snugged bolts — 2.2L engine

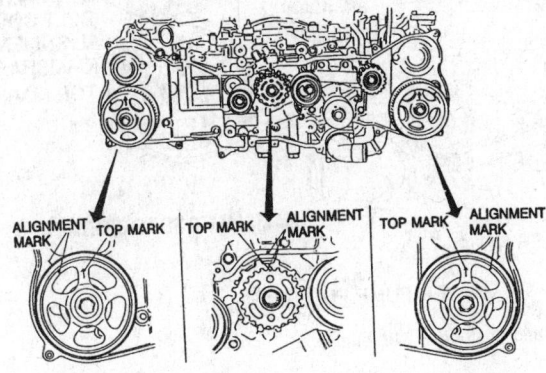

Alignment marks for timing belt installation — 3.3L engine

plunger up and down until the depression is within specification. If the adjuster will not come within specification, replace it.

15. Install an oil seal into the camshaft support, then attach the O-ring.

16. Install an oil relief valve, relief valve spring, oil relief pipe and plug to the camshaft case.

17. Install the Woodruff key on the camshaft and press fit the distributor gear. Insert the camshaft into the case and install the camshaft support. Tighten to 4-5 ft. lbs. (6-7 Nm).

18. Install the valve lash adjusters into their original positions.

19. Apply grease to the valve rockers and install.

20. Install the O-ring to the camshaft case by setting the camshaft so the cam pin is at the 12 o'clock position.

NOTE: Be sure to coat the camshaft assembly with clean engine oil prior to installation.

21. Install the camshaft case to the cylinder head, using sealing compound 1207B or equivalent. Torque the retaining bolts 17-20 ft. lbs. (23-27 Nm).

22. Install the valve rocker cover assemblies and tighten to 3-4 ft. lbs. (4-5 Nm).

23. Install the PCV hoses, and on turbocharged engines install the EGR pipe, clamps and pipe cover. Tighten the EGR pipe to 23-27 ft. lbs. (31-37 Nm).

24. Install the oil filler duct and water pipe.

25. Install the timing belt, belt cover and related parts.

26. Fill the radiator with coolant. Start the vehicle and adjust the ignition timing. Test drive the vehicle and check for leaks.

2.2L Engine

1. Remove the timing belt covers, the timing belt, camshaft sprockets and related components necessary to expose the camshaft.

2. Remove the valve rocker covers. Remove the rocker arm assemblies.

3. To remove the left camshaft, perform the following procedures:

   a. Remove the cam angle sensor.

   b. Remove the oil dipstick tube attaching bolt.

   c. Remove the camshaft support on the left side.

   d. Remove the O-ring.

   e. Remove the camshaft and oil seal (as necessary) from the left side.

4. To remove the right camshaft, perform the following procedures:

   a. Remove the camshaft support on the right side.

   b. Remove the O-ring.

   c. Remove the camshaft and seal (rear) from the right side. Remove the oil seal from the camshaft support.

To install:

5. To install the left camshaft, perform the following procedures:

   a. Lubricate the camshaft journals, install the oil seal (rear) and install the camshaft into the cylinder head.

   b. Install the O-ring into the camshaft support and install the support.

   c. Install oil seal into the camshaft support.

   d. Install the bolt into the dipstick tube and install the camshaft sensor.

6. To install the right camshaft, perform the following procedures:

   a. Lubricate the camshaft journals and install the right camshaft.

   b. Install the O-ring into the camshaft support and install the support.

   c. Install a new oil seal in the rear of the cylinder head.

7. Install the valve rocker covers and tighten to 4 ft. lbs. (5 Nm).

8. Install the timing belt covers, the timing belt, camshaft sprockets and related components.

9. Start the engine and check the ignition timing. Allow the engine to reach operating temperature and check for leaks.

3.3L ENGINE

1. Remove the timing belt, camshaft sprockets and related components necessary to gain access to the camshaft.

2. Disconnect the cam angle sensor and bracket.

3. Disconnect the ignition coil connectors and coils.

4. Disconnect the blowby hose and remove the cylinder head cover and gasket.

5. Remove the front camshaft cap.

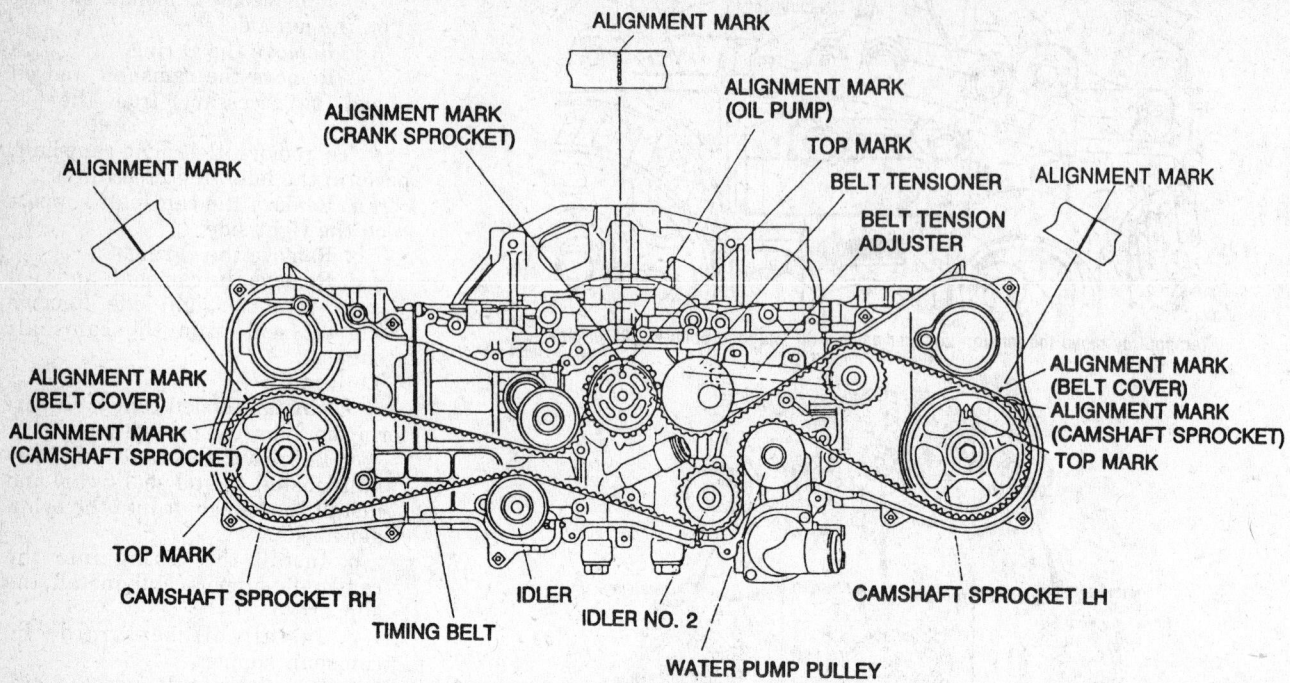

Timing belt routing and position — 3.3L engine

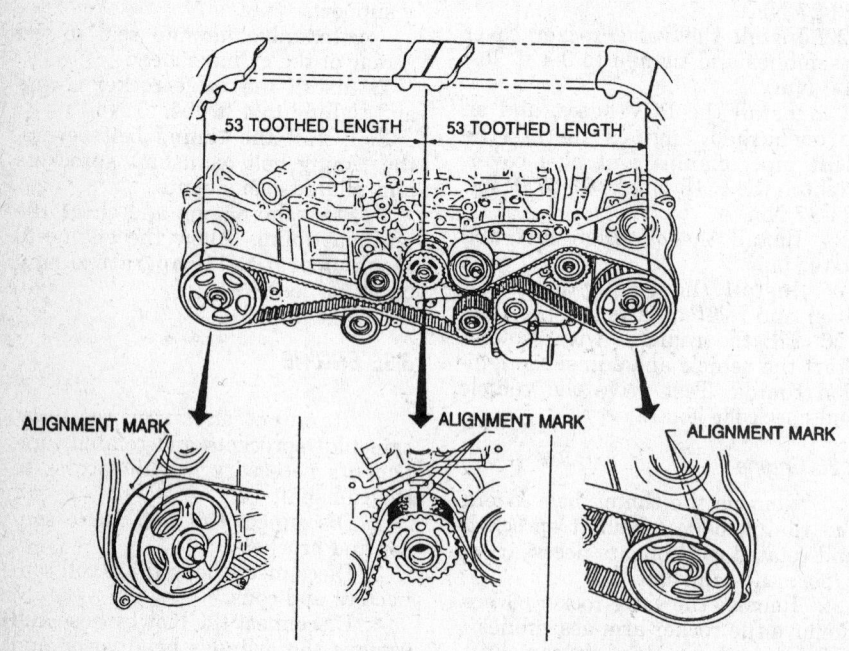

Proper installation of the timing belt — 3.3L engine

6. Remove the camshaft oil seal and plug.

NOTE: Since the camshaft thrust clearance is small, the camshaft must be removed by holding it parallel to the cylinder head. If the camshaft is not parallel to the cylinder head, the cylinder head thrust bearing portion may be damaged.

7. Remove the left cylinder camshafts as follows:

8. Rotate the intake (upper) and exhaust (lower) camshafts to that the notch at the front of the camshafts faces the 6 o'clock position on the left cylinder head and the 12 o'clock position on the right cylinder head.

9. Inspect the rear of the camshaft and check that the matchmarks on the rear gears are aligned.

10. Install a service bolt to the sub-gear mounting bolt hole of the intake camshaft gear to secure the sub-gear and driven gear.

NOTE: When removing the camshafts, ensure that the torsional spring force of the sub-gear has been eliminated.

11. Loosen the intake camshaft bolt caps in sequence. Make sure, as the bolts are turned, the clearance between the camshaft journal and the

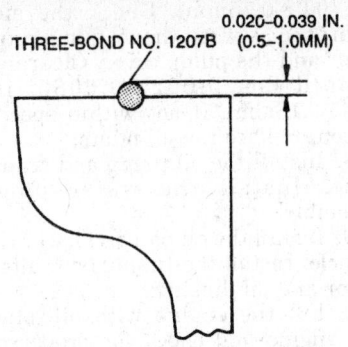

Camshaft case to cylinder head installation —
1.8L engine

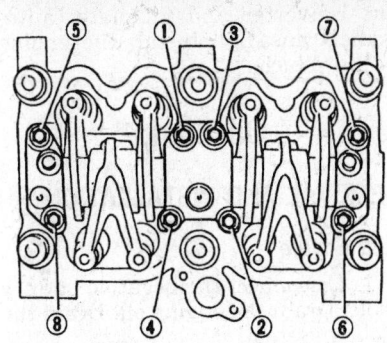

Rocker arm assembly bolt removal sequence —
2.2L engine

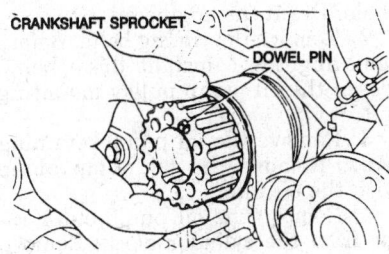

Installation of No. 1 (outer) crankshaft sprocket
with dowel pin — 2.7L engine

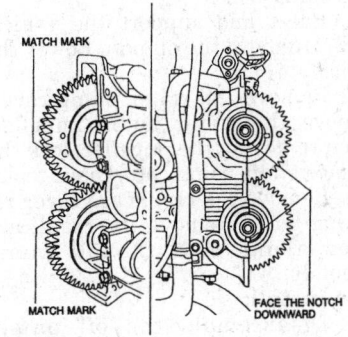

Aligning the camshafts for removal — 3.3L
engine

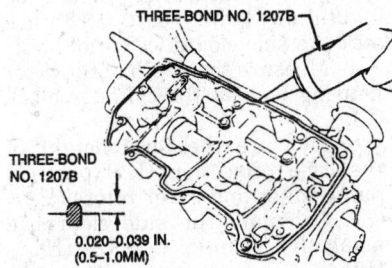

Camshaft case to cylinder head installation —
2.7L engine

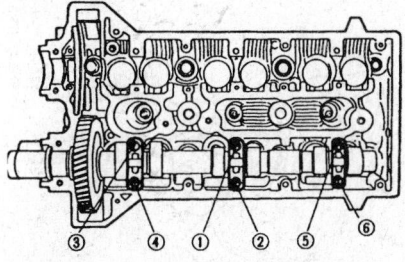

Removing and installing the camshaft retaining
caps — 3.3L engine

the camshaft runout. If it exceeds 0.0008 in. (0.02mm), replace it.

17. Measure the thrust clearance of the camshaft with the hydraulic lash adjusters not installed. If thrust clearance exceeds 0.0051 in. (0.13mm) for the intake and 0.0047 in. (0.12mm) for the exhaust, replace the camshaft caps and the cylinder head as an assembly. If necessary replace the camshaft.

18. Measure the camshaft journal oil clearance with the lash adjusters not installed. If clearance exceeds 0.0039 in. (0.10mm), replace the worn components.

19. Measure the camshaft gear backlash with the intake sub-gear not installed. If backlash exceeds 0.0118 in. (0.30mm), replace the camshafts as a set.

20. Lubricate and install the hydraulic lash adjusters.

21. Lubricate and install the camshafts with the notch on the front facing the 6 o'clock position for the left cylinder head camshafts and the 12 o'clock position for the right cylinder head camshafts. Ensure that the marks for both camshafts are facing the same position.

22. Install the camshaft caps and tighten hand-tight.

23. Tighten the bolts on the camshaft caps equally, a little at a time, in the correct sequence. Make sure, as the bolts are turned, the clearance between the camshaft journal and the cylinder head journal bearing decreases evenly at 3 places. If not, loosen the bolts and repeat the tightening procedure.

24. Tighten the camshaft cap bolts a final torque of 3-4 ft. lbs. (4-5 Nm).

25. Ensure that the matchmarks on the rear side of the camshaft gears are aligned. If not, disassemble the camshaft and perform the installation procedure again.

26. Remove the sub-gear securing bolt from the camshaft.

27. Install the front camshaft cover using fluid packing.

28. Lubricate and install new oil seals.

29. Install the camshaft plug.

30. Install the camshaft cover and connect the blowby hose.

31. Connect the ignition coil connectors and coils.

32. Connect the cam angle sensor and bracket.

33. Install the timing belt, camshaft sprockets and related components.

cylinder head journal bearing increases evenly at 3 places. If not, tighten the bolts and repeat the loosening procedure.

12. Remove the camshaft cap while holding the intake camshaft with 1 hand, then remove the camshaft. Rotate the exhaust camshaft clockwise to gain required clearance.

13. Arrange the camshaft caps in the order they were removed. They must be installed to their original positions.

14. Perform the same procedure for the exhaust camshaft.

15. Remove the hydraulic lash adjusters. Keep the lash adjusters in the order they were removed. They must be installed into their original positions.

To install:

16. Inspect the camshafts for scratches, flaking and wear. Measure

ENGINE LUBRICATION

Oil Pan

REMOVAL AND INSTALLATION

NOTE: In most cases it is not necessary to remove the engine from the vehicle to remove the oil pan.

1. Disconnect the negative battery cable. Drain the engine oil.
2. Raise and support the vehicle safely. Remove the required components in order to gain access to the oil pan retaining bolts.
3. Loosen the engine mounts and raise the engine, as necessary, to gain access to the oil pan retaining bolts.
4. Remove the oil pan retaining bolts. Remove the oil pan from the engine.

To install:

5. Clean all mating surfaces thoroughly. Using a new gasket, install the oil pan and tighten the retaining bolts to 3-4 ft. lbs (4-5 Nm).
6. Lower the engine and tighten the mounting bolts. Reinstall all components previously removed. Lower the vehicle.
7. Fill the crankcase with oil. Connect the negative battery cable. Start the engine and check for leaks.

Rear Main Bearing Oil Seal

REMOVAL AND INSTALLATION

1. Remove the engine from the vehicle and position it in a suitable holding fixture.
2. Remove the clutch assembly and the flywheel (manual transaxle) or the torque converter and flexplate (automatic transaxle) from the crankshaft.
3. Using a small prybar, pry the rear oil seal from the crankcase. Be careful not to damage the crankshaft or the crankcase housing.

To install:

4. Lubricate a new crankshaft oil seal with engine oil.
5. Using the crankshaft rear oil seal guide tool or equivalent, and the rear oil seal press tool or equivalent, drive the new oil seal into the housing until it seats.
6. Install the clutch assembly and flywheel (manual transaxle) or tor-

que converter and flexplate (automatic transaxle). Install the engine in the vehicle.

Oil Pump

REMOVAL AND INSTALLATION

1.2L Engine

1. Disconnect the negative battery cable. Drain the engine oil. Drain the cooling system.
2. Remove the oil dipstick, dipstick guide and guide sealing.
3. Remove the alternator. Remove the timing belt.
4. Raise and support the vehicle safely. Remove the oil pan. Lower the vehicle.
5. Remove the water pump cover. Remove the water pump impeller. When removing the impeller, lock the balance shaft using the proper tool.
6. Remove the crankcase cover retaining bolts. Remove the crankcase cover along with the oil pump assembly.

To install:

7. Disassemble the oil pump. Check the tip clearance of the rotors. Clearance should be 0.0008-0.0059

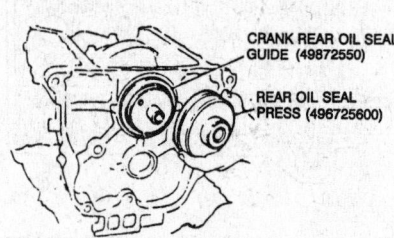

Rear main seal installation — 1.2L engine

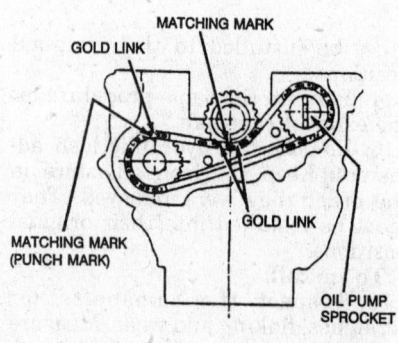

Oil pump sprocket alignment — 1.2L engine

in. (0.02-0.15mm). Check the side clearance between the oil pump inner rotor and the pump cover. Clearance should be 0.0020-0.0063 in. (0.05-0.16mm). If not within specification, replace the oil pump.

8. Install the oil pump and crankcase. Install the water pump assembly.
9. Install the oil pan and lower the vehicle. Install the timing belt, alternator and oil dipstick.
10. Fill the engine with oil, start the engine and check for proper oil pressure.

1.8L and 2.7L Engines

1. Disconnect the negative battery cable. Drain the engine oil.
2. Remove the timing belts. Before removing the camshaft drive belts, loosen the oil pump pulley mounting nut.
3. Remove the oil pump retaining bolts. Remove the oil pump along with the oil filter.
4. Remove the oil pump outer rotor from the cylinder block. Remove the oil filter from the oil pump.

To install:

5. Disassemble the oil pump. Check the case clearance by measuring the clearance between the outer rotor and the cylinder block rotor housing. The clearance should be 0.0039-0.0071 in. (0.10-0.18mm). Check the side clearance as follows:

   a. Measure the depth of the rotor housing bore in the cylinder block (L).

   b. Measure the total height of the case projection (H1) plus oil pump inner and outer rotors (H2).

   c. Calculate the side clearance using the formula: $C = L - (H1 + H2)$.

6. The clearance should be 0.05-0.16 in. (0.0020-0.0063mm). If not within specification, replace the oil pump rotors.
7. Install the oil pump assembly on the cylinder block. Install the timing belts and camshaft drive belts.
8. Fill the crankcase with oil. Start the engine and check for correct oil pressure.

2.2L Engine

1. Drain the engine oil.
2. Drain coolant from engine.
3. Remove all belt covers, drive belts and other necessary components.
4. Remove the belt tensioner bracket.
5. Remove the water pump.
6. Remove the oil pump.

To install:

7. Disassemble the oil pump and scribe alignment marks on the inner and outer rotors for ease of reassembly.

8. Measure the top clearance of the rotors. Clearance should be 0.0016-0.0055 in. (0.04-0.14mm). Measure the clearance between the outer rotor and the cylinder block housing. Clearance should be 0.0039-0.0069 in. (0.10-0.175mm). Measure the clearance between the oil pump inner rotor and the pump cover. Clearance should be 0.0008-0.0028 in. (0.02-0.07mm). If not within specification, replace the pump body or rotors.

9. Assemble the oil pump and install on the cylinder block using three bond 1215 or equivalent. Tighten bolts to specification.

10. Install the water pump, drive belts and tensioner. Fill the crankcase with oil and the radiator with coolant.

11. Start the engine and check for oil pressure and/or leaks.

3.3L

1. Disconnect the negative battery cable.

2. Drain the engine oil.

3. Remove the under cover.

4. Remove the bolts which connect the power steering oil cooler pipe assembly to the body.

NOTE: Do not remove the pipe assembly.

5. Remove the radiator fan motor assemblies.

6. Remove the drive belt cover and drive belts.

7. Remove the air conditioner belt idler assembly.

8. Remove the power steering pump bracket.

NOTE: Do not remove the power steering pump.

9. Remove the crank angle sensors and crankshaft pulley.

10. Remove the timing belt covers, timing belt and related components.

11. Remove the crankshaft sprocket, belt idlers, belt tensioner and tensioner bracket.

12. Remove the oil pump by prying it from the engine with 2 prybars.

NOTE: Take care not to scratch the gasket mating surfaces.

13. Disassemble the oil pump.

To install:

14. Measure the tip clearance of the rotors. If clearance is greater than 0.0071 in. (0.18mm), replace the rotors.

15. Measure the clearance between the outer rotor and the cylinder block rotor housing. If clearance exceeds 0.0079 in. (0.20mm), replace the rotor.

16. Measure the side clearance between the oil pump inner rotor and the pump cover. If clearance exceeds 0.0047 in. (0.12mm), replace the rotor or pump body.

17. Install a new front oil seal on the pump cover using a driver.

18. Assemble the oil pump.

19. Install the oil pump and tighten the bolts to 4-5 ft. lbs. (5-6 Nm).

20. Install the crankshaft sprocket, belt idlers, belt tensioner and tensioner bracket.

21. Install the timing belt covers, timing belt and related components.

22. Install the crank angle sensors and crankshaft pulley.

23. Install the power steering pump bracket.

24. Install the air conditioner belt idler assembly.

25. Install the drive belt cover and drive belts.

26. Install the radiator fan motor assemblies.

27. Install the bolts which connect the power steering oil cooler pipe assembly to the body.

28. Install the under cover and fill the engine with oil.

29. Connect the negative battery cable.

30. Start the engine and allow it to reach operating temperature. Check

for adequate oil pressure and check for leaks.

ENGINE COOLING

Radiator

REMOVAL AND INSTALLATION

1. Disconnect the negative battery cable. Remove the under cover as required and drain the cooling system. Drain the cooling system.

2. Loosen the hose clamps and remove the inlet (upper) and outlet (lower) hoses from the radiator. Disconnect inlet and outlet oil cooler lines (automatic transmission).

3. Remove the overflow hose and tank as required.

4. Disconnect the thermoswitch, and electric fan motor electrical connectors.

5. Remove the V-belt cover as required to gain clearance.

6. Remove the radiator attaching bolts and lift the radiator from the vehicle with the fan attached.

7. Remove the fan assembly to service the radiator.

To install:

8. Inspect the radiator cushions and replace as necessary.

9. Install the fan assembly if removed.

10. Install the radiator and tighten the attaching bolts to 9-17 ft. lbs. (13-23 Nm).

11. Install the V-belt cover, overflow hose and tank.

12. Inspect the electrical connectors for damage and replace as necessary. Install the electrical connectors.

13. Inspect the radiator hoses for deterioration and replace as necessary. Install the radiator hoses.

14. Install the transmission cooler lines on automatic transmission equipped vehicles.

15. Install the under cover if removed.

16. Fill the radiator with coolant. Start the engine and allow it to reach operating temperature.

17. Stop the engine and allow it to cool. Remove the radiator cap and add coolant as required.

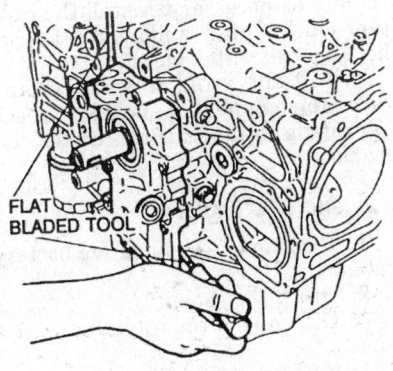

FLAT BLADED TOOL

Removing the oil pump — 3.3L engine

Heater Core

REMOVAL AND INSTALLATION

——— CAUTION ———
Properly disarm the air bag on vehicles equipped with the SRS system. Failure to do so can cause serious injury.

Except Justy

NOTE: Depending upon working clearance the air conditioning system may have to be discharged in order to service the blower motor. If this is the case, be sure to observe all the required safety precautions when discharging and recharging the air conditioning system.

1. Disconnect the negative battery cable. Drain the cooling system.
2. Disconnect the heater hoses from the heater core assembly.
3. Remove the instrument panel assembly.
4. Disconnect the electrical harness connector from the blower motor assembly. Disconnect the temperature control cable.
5. Remove the heater unit retaining bolts. Remove the heater unit from the vehicle.
6. Remove the heater core retaining connectors. Remove the heater core from its mounting.
To install:
7. Pressure test the heater core prior to installation. Install the heater core in the heater unit, and the heater unit in the vehicle.
8. Reconnect all electrical connections. Install the heater hoses.
9. Fill the cooling system with coolant. Connect the negative battery cable. Start the engine and bring to operating temperature. Check for leaks.

Justy

1. Disconnect the negative battery cable. Drain the cooling system.
2. Disconnect the heater hoses from the heater core assembly.
3. Pull off the right and left defroster ducts from the defroster nozzles. Pull the ducts from the heater unit.
4. Disconnect the electrical wires from the fan switch and the blower motor.
5. Disconnect the air mix cable from the heater unit. Disconnect the mode cable from the heater unit.

6. Remove the bolts that retain the heater unit to the instrument panel.
7. As required, for working clearance remove the glove box door assembly.
8. Disconnect the inside/outside air control cable from the blower assembly.
9. Remove the instrument panel assembly.
10. Remove the heater unit retaining bolts. Remove the heater unit from the vehicle.
11. Remove the heater core cushion. Loosen the heater core holder and than remove it. Pull the heater core from its mounting and remove it from the heater case.
To install:
12. Pressure test the new heater core prior to installation.
13. Install the heater core in the heater cushion, then install the heater core/unit assembly in the vehicle.
14. Install the instrument panel, control cables and glove box door. Connect the heater mode and control cables to the heater box. Connect all electrical connections previously disconnected.
15. Install the defroster nozzles and the heater hoses. Fill the cooling system with coolant.
16. Connect the negative battery cable, start the engine and check for leaks.

Water Pump

REMOVAL AND INSTALLATION

1.2L Engine

1. Disconnect the negative battery cable.
2. Drain the engine oil and coolant.
3. Remove the oil level gauge, oil level gauge guide and level gauge guide sealing.
4. Disconnect the connector from the alternator and remove the alternator and V-belt.
5. Remove the crankshaft pulley and camshaft belt cover.
6. Remove the camshaft belt tensioner spring and tensioner.

NOTE: Prior to removing the camshaft belt, scribe a mark indicating the drive direction of the belt for installation reference.

7. Remove the camshaft driveplate and drive belt.
8. Remove the camshaft drive pulley and driven pulley.

9. Remove the camshaft belt cover and cover mount.
10. Remove the flywheel housing.
11. Remove the oil pan and pan gasket.

NOTE: The water pump is part of the crankcase cover and must be disassembled for rebuilding.

12. Remove the crankcase cover and disassemble the water pump.
To install:
13. Clean all gasket mating surfaces thoroughly. Use new gaskets during installation.
14. Install the crankcase cover. Install the oil pan and gasket. Install the flywheel housing.
15. Install the camshaft drive belt pulleys, drive belt and drive belt covers.
16. Install the alternator and V-belt. Install the oil level gauge assembly.
17. Fill the engine with oil and the radiator with coolant.
18. Connect the negative battery cable. Start the engine and allow it to reach operating temperature. Check for leaks and test drive the vehicle.

1.8L and 2.7L Engines

1. Drain the coolant.
2. Disconnect the radiator outlet hose and water bypass hose from the water pump.
3. Loosen the pulley nuts. Loosen the alternator assembly and remove the drive belt.
4. Remove the front belt cover.
5. Remove the water pump.
To install:
6. Clean the gasket mating surfaces thoroughly. Always use new gaskets during installation.
7. Install the water pump and pulley.
8. Install the alternator, drive belt and drive belt cover. Adjust the drive belt to the proper tension. Tighten the water pump pulley bolts.
9. Inspect the coolant hoses and replace as necessary. Install the radiator outlet hose and water bypass hose on the water pump.
10. Fill the radiator with coolant. Start the engine and allow it to reach operating temperature. Check for leaks.

2.2L and 3.3L Engines

1. Disconnect the negative battery cable.
2. Drain the coolant.
3. Disconnect the radiator outlet hose.
4. Remove the radiator fan motor assembly

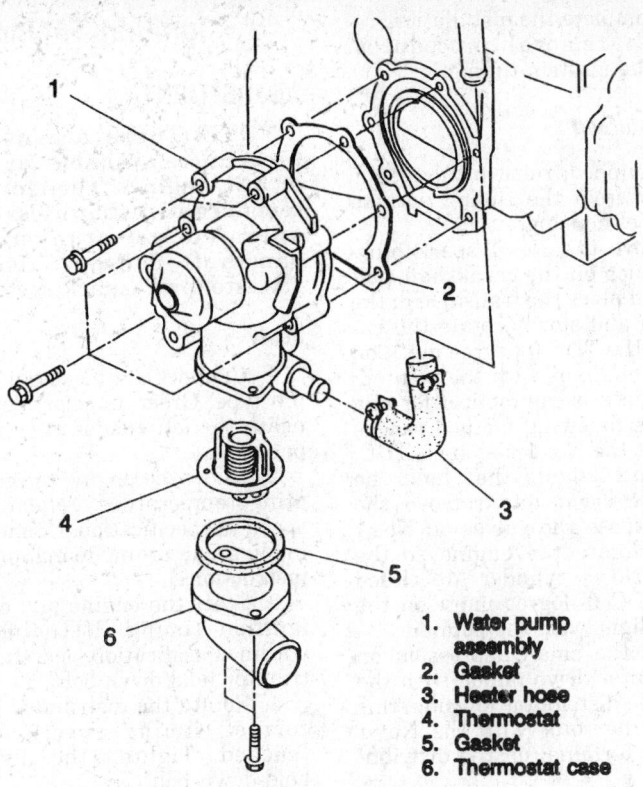

1. Water pump assembly
2. Gasket
3. Heater hose
4. Thermostat
5. Gasket
6. Thermostat case

Water pump servicing — 2.2L and 2.7L engines

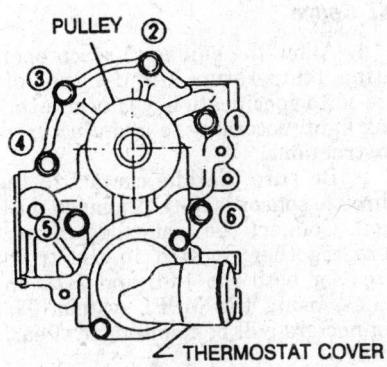

Removing the water pump — 3.3L engine

5. Remove the accessory drive belts.

6. Remove the timing belt, tensioner and camshaft angle sensor.

7. Remove the left side camshaft pulley and left side rear timing belt cover. Remove the tensioner bracket.

8. Disconnect the radiator hose and heater hose from the water pump.

9. Remove the water pump.

To install:

10. Clean the gasket mating surfaces thoroughly. Always use new gaskets during installation.

11. Install the water pump and tighten the bolts, in sequence, to 7-10 ft. lbs. (10-14 Nm). After tightening the bolts once, retighten to the same specification again.

12. Inspect the radiator hoses for deterioration and replace as necessary. Install the radiator hose and heater hose on the water pump.

13. Install the left side rear timing belt cover, left side camshaft pulley and tensioner bracket.

14. Install the camshaft angle sensor, tensioner and timing belt.

15. Install the accessory drive belts.

16. Install the radiator ran motor assembly.

17. Install the radiator outlet hose. Fill the system with coolant.

18. Connect the negative battery cable. Start the engine and allow it to reach operating temperature. Check for leaks.

Thermostat

REMOVAL AND INSTALLATION

1.2L Engine

1. Disconnect the negative battery cable. Drain the cooling system.

2. Remove the thermostat housing retaining bolts. Remove the thermostat housing and cover assembly.

3. Remove the thermostat from the intake manifold.

4. Installation is the reverse of the removal procedure. Be sure to use a new gasket or RTV sealant, as required.

1.8L and 2.7L Engines

1. Disconnect the negative battery cable. Drain the cooling system.

2. Remove the thermostat housing retaining bolts. Remove the thermostat housing and cover assembly.

3. Remove the thermostat from the intake manifold.

4. Installation is the reverse of the removal procedure. Be sure to use a new gasket or RTV sealant, as required.

2.2L and 3.3L Engines

1. Disconnect the negative battery cable. Drain the cooling system.

2. Remove the thermostat case cover and gasket. Pull out the thermostat.

To install:

3. Clean the mating surface of the thermostat case cover thoroughly.

4. Install the thermostat using a new gasket. The thermostat must be installed with the jiggle pin upward and to the front.

5. Fill the cooling system with coolant. Star the vehicle and allow it to reach operating temperature. Check the coolant level.

ENGINE ELECTRICAL

NOTE: Disconnecting the negative battery cable on some vehicles may interfere with the functions of the on board computer systems and may require the computer to undergo a relearning process, once the negative battery cable is reconnected.

Distributor

NOTE: The 1.8L and 2.7L engines with both the SPFI and MPFI systems use an LED and photodiode pulse pick-up in the distributor for cylinder and crankshaft position determination. The electronic ignition circuit operates in the same basic manner as the standard electronic distributors used on the remaining engines.

REMOVAL

1. Disconnect the negative battery cable. Remove the air cleaner assembly. If equipped, label and disconnect the hose from the distributor.
2. Disconnect the primary wire from the coil. If equipped with a breakerless ignition, disconnect the distributor electrical wiring connector from the vehicle wiring harness.
3. Disconnect the distributor cap retaining clamps or remove the screws and the cap from the distributor. Position the cap and ignition wires aside.

NOTE: If necessary to remove the ignition wires from the cap to provide room to remove the distributor, be sure to label the wires and the cap terminals for easy and accurate installation.

4. Position the engine at TDC with No. 1 cylinder on the compression stroke or using chalk, mark the distributor rotor to distributor housing and the distributor housing to engine relationships.
5. Remove the distributor to engine hold-down bolt.
6. Remove the distributor from the engine, taking care not to damage or lose the O-ring.

NOTE: Do not disturb the engine while the distributor is removed. If the engine cranked or rotated while the distributor is removed, the engine will have to be retimed.

INSTALLATION

Timing Not Disturbed

1. Position the distributor in the block, make sure the O-ring is in place, align the distributor rotor to housing marks and the distributor housing to engine marks.

NOTE: If equipped with an octane selector, install and tighten the hold-down bolt finger-tight.

2. To complete the installation, reverse the removal procedures. Recheck the ignition timing.

Timing Disturbed

1. If equipped, remove the plastic dust cover from the timing port on the flywheel housing.
2. Remove the No. 1 spark plug. Use a wrench on the crankshaft pulley bolt and place the transaxle in the **N** position and slowly rotate the engine until the TDC **0** degree mark on the flywheel aligns with the pointer.
3. If Step 2 is impractical for any reason, the following method can be used to get the No. 1 piston on TDC. Remove the 2 bolts that hold the right valve cover and remove the cover to expose the valves on No. 1 cylinder. Rotate the engine so the valves in No. 1 cylinder are closed and the TDC **0** degree mark on the flywheel aligns with the pointer.
4. Align the small depression on the distributor drive pinion with the mark on the distributor housing; this will align the rotor with the No. 1 spark plug terminal on the distributor cap.

NOTE: If equipped with an octane selector, set the pointer midway between the A and R. Make sure the O-ring is located in the proper position.

5. Align the distributor housing to engine matchmarks and install the distributor into the engine. Make sure the drive is engaged. Install the hold-down bolt finger-tight. Using a timing light, perform the ignition timing procedures.
6. To complete the installation, remove the timing light and reverse the removal procedures.

Distributorless Ignition System

REMOVAL AND INSTALLATION

Ignition Coil

2.2L AND 3.3L ENGINES

1. Disconnect the battery negative terminal.
2. Remove the intake manifold cover.
3. Disconnect the wires from the ignition coil.
4. Remove the ignition coil.
5. To install, reverse the installation procedure.

Ignition Timing

ADJUSTMENT

NOTE: There are no timing procedures available for the 2.2L or 3.3L engines. The ignition systems are distributorless and are operated via crankshaft and camshaft sensors, using the ""waste type" spark system.

Justy

1. Connect test mode connectors (2 pin type, Green in color), located beneath the left side of the instrument panel.
2. Allow the engine to reach operating temperature. Adjust the idle speed to specification. Connect a timing light, according to manufacturer's instructions.
3. Start the engine and check the ignition timing. If timing is not within specification, loosen the distributor hold-down bolt.
4. Rotate the distributor until the correct timing specification is reached. Tighten the distributor hold-down bolt.
5. Disconnect the test mode connector.

XT Coupe

1. Allow the engine to reach operating temperature. Adjust the idle speed to specification. Connect a timing light, according to manufacturers instructions.
2. Be sure the idle contact of the throttle sensor is in the engaged position. Connect the test mode connectors together, located in the trunk area for both the 1.8L and 2.7L engines, using the MPFI system. The connectors will be found near of each other.

NOTE: The check engine warning light will come ON; this does not indicate there is a problem. The ignition timing must not be adjusted and cannot be checked while the idle switch is disengaged or the test mode connectors disconnected.

3. If timing is not within specification, loosen the distributor hold-down bolt.
4. Rotate the distributor until the correct timing specification is reached. Tighten the distributor hold-down bolt.

Except Justy and XT Coupe

1. Allow the engine to reach operating temperature. Adjust the idle

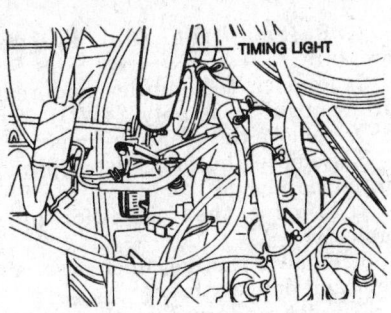

Timing mark location — except XT Coupe

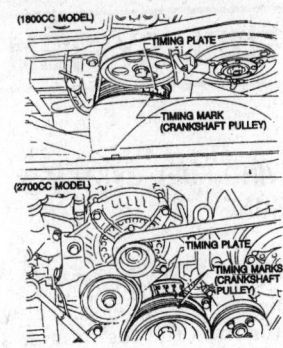

Timing mark locations — XT Coupe equipped with 1.8L and 2.7L engines

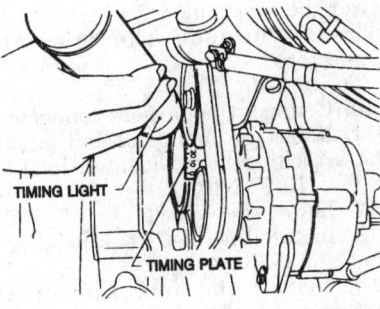

Timing mark location — 1.8L engine except XT Coupe

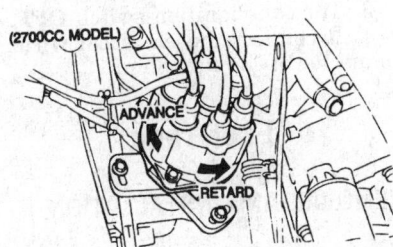

Distributor movement to change basic timing — 2.7L engine

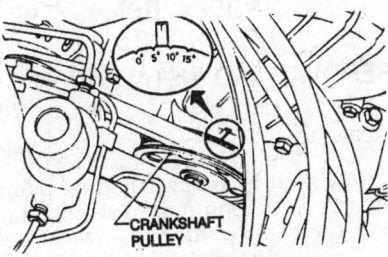

Timing mark location — 1.2L engine

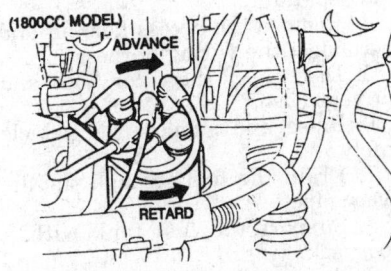

Distributor movement to change basic timing — 1.8L engine

speed to specification. Connect a timing light, according to manufacturer's instructions.

2. If the engine is equipped with a carburetor, disconnect and plug the distributor vacuum line.

3. Be sure the idle switch is in the engaged position. Connect the test mode connectors, located under the left side of the dash for the MPFI system or on the left side of the engine compartment for the SPFI system.

The connectors will be located side-by-side.

NOTE: The check engine warning light will come ON; this does not indicate that there is a problem. The ignition timing must not be adjusted and cannot be checked while the idle switch is inoperative or the test mode connectors disconnected.

4. If timing is not within specification, loosen the distributor hold-down bolt.

5. Rotate the distributor until the correct timing specification is reached. Tighten the distributor hold-down bolt.

Alternator

PRECAUTIONS

Observing these precautions will ensure safe handling of the electrical system components and will avoid damage to the vehicle's electrical system.

• Be absolutely sure of the polarity of a booster battery before making connections. Connect the cables positive to positive and negative to negative. If jump starting, connect the positive cables first and the last connection to a ground on the body of the booster vehicle, so arcing cannot ignite the hydrogen gas that may have accumulated near the battery. Even a momentary connection of a booster battery with polarity reserved may damage the alternator diodes.

• Disconnect both vehicle battery cables before attempting to charge the battery.

• Never ground the alternator output or battery terminal. Be cautious when using metal tools around a battery to avoid creating a short circuit between the terminals.

• Never run an alternator without a load unless the field circuit is disconnected.

• Never attempt to polarize an alternator.

• Never disconnect any electrical components with the ignition switch turned **ON**.

BELT TENSION ADJUSTMENT

1. To adjust the belt tension, first loosen the alternator to bracket adjusting bolt.

2. Lift the alternator to increase the tension on the belt. When it takes moderate thumb pressure to move the longest span of belt ½ in., the tension adjustment is correct.

3. Tighten the adjusting bolt so the alternator will not move in the adjusting bracket.

REMOVAL AND INSTALLATION

1. Disconnect the negative battery cable.

2. Label and disconnect the wiring from the alternator. Remove the necessary components in order to gain access to the alternator retaining bolts.

3. Remove the alternator retaining bolts.

4. Remove the drive belt. Remove the alternator from the vehicle.

5. Installation is the reverse of the removal procedure.

Starter

REMOVAL AND INSTALLATION

1. Remove the spare tire from the engine compartment, as required.

2. Disconnect the negative battery cable. As required, raise and support the vehicle safely.

3. Disconnect the wiring harness from the starter.

4. Remove the starter retaining bolts. Remove the starter from its mounting.

5. Installation is the reverse of the removal procedure.

EMISSION CONTROLS

Emission Warning Lamps

RESETTING

Some vehicles are equipped with an EGR light that illuminates when the vehicle attains 60,000 miles (96,000 km). In order to reset the light for another 60,000 mile increment, the following procedure must be done:

1. Remove the lower instrument panel cover, exposing the fuel panel.

2. Directly behind or along the side of the fuse panel, a blue 2 piece connector will be noted. Disconnect the 2 blue connectors.

3. Near the blue connectors will be a green connector that is not connected to any other wire.

4. Connect the green connector into the matching blue connector, thus resetting the emission light and recycling the system for another 60,000 mile increment.

5. Be sure the indicator light is out and reinstall the lower instrument panel cover.

FUEL SYSTEM

RELIEVING FUEL SYSTEM PRESSURE

Fuel Injected Engines

1. Disconnect the electrical wiring connector from the fuel pump.

2. Start the engine. Once the engine has stopped, crank the engine for 5 seconds or more. If the engine starts, let the engine run until it stops.

3. Turn the ignition switch **OFF**.

4. Reconnect the electrical wiring connector of the fuel pump.

Fuel Tank

REMOVAL AND INSTALLATION

Justy

1. Release the fuel system pressure.

2. Remove the rear seat and package shelf.

3. Disconnect the rollover valve and separator.

4. Remove the access hole lid and disconnect the wiring harness.

5. Disconnect the filler hose and air vent hose.

6. Raise and support the vehicle safely.

7. Drain the fuel through the delivery pipe.

8. Support the fuel tank with a floor jack.

9. Remove the parking brake cable and fuel filter bracket.

10. Disconnect the fuel hoses leading to the tank.

11. Remove the tank attaching bolts and lower the tank.

To install:

12. Raise the tank and install the attaching bolts. Tighten to 9-17 ft. lbs. (13-23 Nm).

13. Connect the fuel hoses leading to the tank.

14. Install the parking brake cable and fuel filter bracket.

15. Lower the vehicle.

16. Connect the filler hose and air vent hose.

17. Connect the wiring harness and install the access hole lid.

18. Connect the rollover valve and separator.

19. Install the rear seat and package shelf.

Except Justy

1. Release the fuel system pressure.

2. Remove the muffler and rear differential assembly (4WD). On SVX, remove the rear sub-frame.

3. Remove the fuel filler cap and drain the fuel.

4. Remove the fuel filler pipe protector.

5. Remove the fuel filler hose, air vent and delivery hose.

6. Raise and support the vehicle safely.

7. Support the fuel tank with a floor jack.

8. Loosen the attaching bolts and lower the fuel tank.

9. Disconnect the harness connector.

To install:

10. Connect the harness connector.

11. Raise the fuel tank and install the attaching bolts. Tighten to 9-17 ft. lbs. (13-23 Nm).

12. Lower the vehicle.

13. Install the fuel filler hose, air vent and delivery hose.

14. Install the fuel filler pipe protector.

15. Install the fuel filler cap.

16. Install the muffler and rear differential assembly (4WD).

Fuel Filter

REMOVAL AND INSTALLATION

Justy

1. Carefully relieve the fuel pump pressure. As required, raise and support the vehicle safely.

2. Remove the flange bolts and remove the lower fuel pump bracket assembly.

3. Disconnect and plug the fuel lines at the fuel filter.

4. Remove the fuel filter retaining bolts. Remove the fuel filter assembly from its mounting.

5. Installation is the reverse of the removal procedure.

Except Justy

The fuel filter is located inside the engine compartment on the left fender assembly.

1. Properly relieve the fuel system pressure.

2. Disconnect the fuel lines from the fuel filter.

3. Pull the fuel filter from the bracket and remove it from the vehicle.

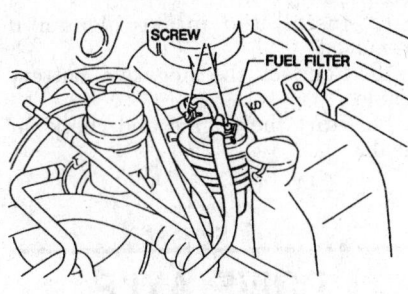

Removing the fuel filter

4. Installation is the reverse of the removal procedure. Start the engine and check for leaks.

Electric Fuel Pump

PRESSURE TESTING

1. Raise and support the vehicle safely.
2. Using a fuel pressure gauge, connect into the fuel line.
3. Turn the ignition switch to the **ON** position. Observe the fuel pressure, it should be:
2.6-3.3 psi for carburetor equipped vehicle.
61-71 psi for MPFI equipped vehicle.
36-50 psi for SPFI equipped vehicle.
4. If the fuel pump does not meet specification, replace it.
5. After testing, disconnect the pressure gauge and reconnect the fuel line.

REMOVAL AND INSTALLATION

Justy

1. Carefully relieve the fuel pump pressure. As required, raise and support the vehicle safely.
2. Remove the flange bolts and remove the lower fuel pump bracket assembly.
3. Disconnect and plug the fuel lines at the fuel pump assembly. Disconnect the fuel pump electrical connector.
4. Remove the fuel pump assembly retaining bolts. Remove the fuel pump assembly from its mounting.
5. Installation is the reverse of the removal procedure.

Except Justy

1.8L SPFI ENGINE

The pump is at the rear of the vehicle, bolted to the vehicle frame.
1. Release the fuel system pressure and disconnect the negative battery cable.
2. Keep the fuel pump harness disconnected after releasing the fuel system pressure.
3. Raise and support the vehicle safely.
4. Clamp the middle portion of the thick hose connecting the pipe and the pump to prevent fuel from flowing out of the tank.
5. Loosen the hose clamp and disconnect the hose.
6. Remove the 3 pump bracket mounting bolts and remove the pump together with the pump damper.
To install:
7. If the pump and damper have been removed from the bracket, reinstall and tighten the bolts securely.
8. Install the hose and tighten the clamp screw to 0.7-1.1 ft. lbs. (1.0-1.5 Nm).
9. Install the pump bracket in position to the vehicle body and secure it with the bolts.

NOTE: Take care to position the rubber cushion properly.

10. Connect the pump harness connector.
11. Connect the negative battery cable and test the fuel pump for proper operation.

EXCEPT 1.8L SPFI ENGINE

The fuel pump is located in the fuel tank and is part of the fuel sender assembly.
1. Relieve the fuel system pressure. Disconnect the negative battery cable.
2. Remove the floor mat or carpet from the luggage compartment.
3. Remove the access lid and disconnect the wiring connector from the sender assembly.
4. Loosen the hose clamps and disconnect the lines from the sender assembly.
5. Remove the retaining bolts and remove the pump unit from the fuel tank.
6. Use a new gasket and install the assembly in the reverse of the removal procedure. Tighten the retaining bolts to 2-4 ft. lbs. (3-6 Nm).

Carburetor

REMOVAL AND INSTALLATION

Justy

1. Disconnect the negative battery cable. Remove the air cleaner assembly.
2. Disconnect the fuel line. Disconnect the return and vent line hoses.
3. Disconnect the main diaphragm, distributor vacuum line and canister vent hose.
4. Disconnect the idle solenoid valve wires and hoses. Disconnect the harness electrical connector.
5. Disconnect the primary and secondary air bleed hoses. Disconnect the accelerator cable from the throttle lever.
6. Remove the carburetor retaining bolts. remove the carburetor from its mounting. Discard the gasket.
7. Installation is the reverse of the removal procedure. Be sure to use a new base gasket.

Fuel Injector

REMOVAL AND INSTALLATION

SPFI

1. Disconnect the negative battery cable.

NOTE: This procedure may be performed with the throttle body mounted on the intake manifold or removed. If the throttle body is mounted on the intake manifold during servicing, ensure that debris does not fall into the intake manifold through the throttle body.

2. Remove the air intake boot.
3. Remove the injector cap and gasket.
4. Disconnect the injector electrical connector.
5. Hold the injector using pliers, then pull the injector from throttle body.
6. Remove the O-ring and discard.
To install:
7. Using a new O-ring, install the injector in the throttle body.
8. Connect the injector electrical connector.
9. Install the injector cap using a new gasket.
10. Install the air intake boot.
11. Connect the negative battery cable.

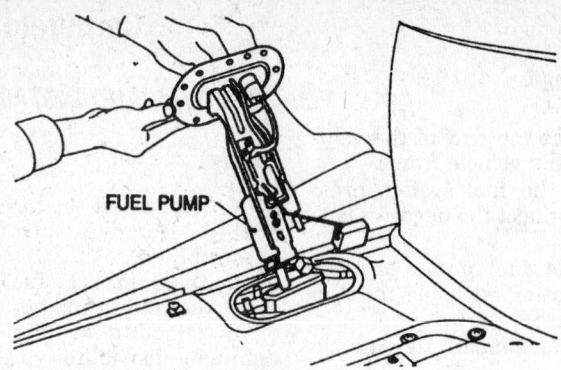

Removing the fuel sending/pump assembly from the fuel tank

MPFI

EXCEPT 1.8L AND 2.7L ENGINES

1. Relieve the fuel system pressure.
2. Disconnect the negative battery cable.
3. Label and disconnect the fuel injector electrical connectors.
4. Label and remove the hoses attached to the fuel rail.
5. Remove the fuel rail attaching bolts and gently lift the fuel rail from the engine.

NOTE: Some fuel injectors may be removed with the fuel rail while others may remain in the engine.

6. Remove the fuel injectors by pulling with a slight twist. Discard all gaskets and O-rings.

To install:

7. Install the fuel injectors using new gaskets and O-rings. Lubricate the O-rings prior to installation.
8. Install the fuel rail and tighten the attaching bolts securely.
9. Install all hoses attached to the fuel rail.
10. Install the fuel injector electrical connectors.
11. Connect the negative battery cable.

1.8L AND 2.7L ENGINES

1. Relieve the fuel system pressure.
2. Disconnect the negative battery cable.

NOTE: On some engines, it may be necessary to remove the intake plenum to gain access to the fuel lines connecting the injectors.

3. Remove the fuel lines connecting the injectors.
4. Disconnect the fuel injector electrical connectors.
5. On 2.7L engines, remove the fuel rail assembly.
6. Remove the injectors by pulling with a slight twist. Discard the gaskets and O-rings.
7. On 1.8L engines, remove the injector holder plate, insulator, holder and seal. Discard the insulator and seal.

To install:

8. Install the injectors using new gaskets, seals (insulators) and O-rings. Lubricate the O-rings prior to installation.
9. On 2.7L engines, install the fuel rail assembly.
10. Install the fuel lines connecting the injectors.

11. Connect the injector electrical connectors.
12. Install the intake plenum if removed.
13. Connect the negative battery cable.
14. Start the engine and check for leaks.

DRIVE AXLE

Halfshaft

REMOVAL AND INSTALLATION

Justy

1. Raise and support the vehicle safely. Remove the tire and wheel assembly.
2. Remove the disc brake assembly. Remove the dust cover, cotter pin, castle nut, conical spring. Remove the center piece, using the proper tools.
3. Pull the hub and disc assembly from the halfshaft. Remove the disc cover from the housing.
4. Drive out the spring pin connecting the halfshaft to the differential, using the proper tool.
5. Remove the cotter pin and the castle nut from the tie rod end ball joint.
6. Remove the tie rod end ball joint from the knuckle arm, using the proper puller.
7. Remove the bolt that retains the housing to the strut. Carefully push down the housing in order to remove it from the strut.
8. Remove the ball joint of the transverse link from the housing. Remove the housing and the halfshaft assembly as a complete unit.
9. Separate the housing from the halfshaft, using removal tools 922493000 and 921122000 or their equivalents.

To install:

10. Join the housing and halfshaft using installation tool 927210000.
11. Install housing and axle assembly to strut but do not tighten.
12. Install the dust seal on the spindle. Insert the halfshaft into the differential and install the spring pin. Lubricate the splines with grease.
13. Install the tie rod end ball joint and tighten the nut to 18-22 ft. lbs. (25-29 Nm). Tighten the housing-to-strut bolt to 25-33 ft. lbs. (34-44 Nm).

Removing the fuel injector-MPFI vehicles.

14. Install the disc cover, hub, disc brake assembly and castle nut. Install the caliper assembly.

15. Install the wheel and tire, lower the vehicle and test drive.

Except Justy

1. Release the parking brake. Raise and support the vehicle safely. Remove the tire and wheel assembly.

2. Pull out the parking brake cable outer clip from the caliper. Disconnect the parking brake cable end from the caliper lever.

3. Drive out the double offset joint spring pin, using the proper tools.

4. Loosen the 2 retaining bolts and remove the disc brake assembly from the housing. Remove the 2 bolts that connect the housing and the damper strut.

5. Remove the dust cover, cotter pin. Disconnect the tie rod end ball joint from the housing knuckle arm, using the proper puller tool.

6. Remove the halfshaft from the differential spindle along with the housing assembly.

7. Remove the housing from the halfshaft, using tool 926470000 or equivalent.

To install:

8. Install the halfshaft into the hub using installer 922431000, or

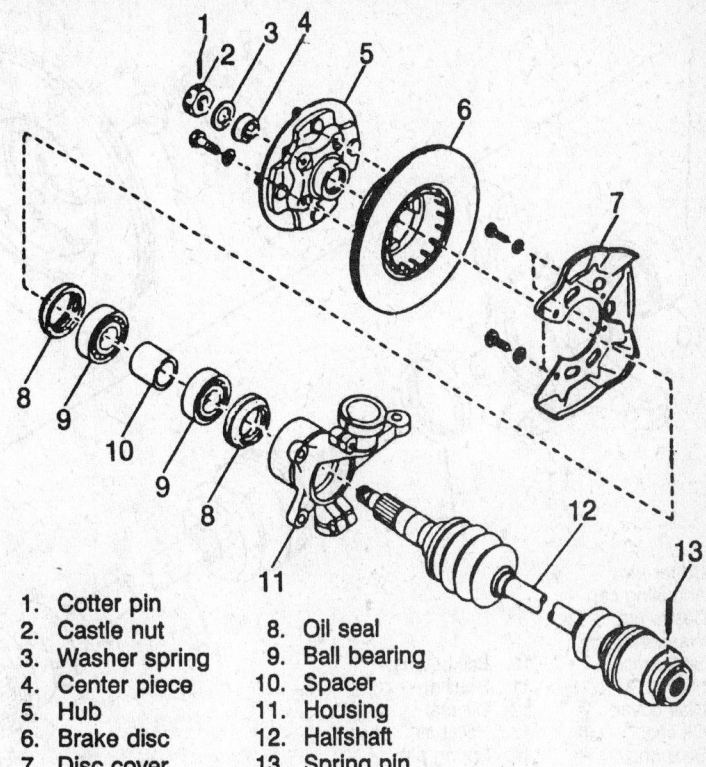

1. Cotter pin	
2. Castle nut	8. Oil seal
3. Washer spring	9. Ball bearing
4. Center piece	10. Spacer
5. Hub	11. Housing
6. Brake disc	12. Halfshaft
7. Disc cover	13. Spring pin

Front halfshaft assembly and related components — except Justy and XT Coupe with 2.7L engine

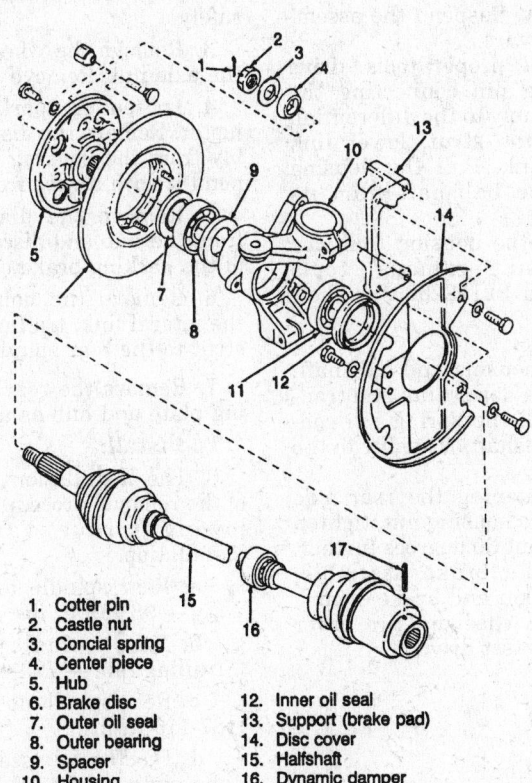

1. Cotter pin	
2. Castle nut	
3. Concial spring	
4. Center piece	
5. Hub	
6. Brake disc	12. Inner oil seal
7. Outer oil seal	13. Support (brake pad)
8. Outer bearing	14. Disc cover
9. Spacer	15. Halfshaft
10. Housing	16. Dynamic damper
11. Inner bearing	17. Spring pin

Front halfshaft assembly and related components — Justy

equivalent. Take care not to damage the inner oil seal lip. Tighten the axle nut temporarily.

9. Install the double offset joint on the spindle and drive a new spring pin into place. Install the tie rod and tighten the nut to 61-83 ft. lbs. (83-113 Nm).

10. Install the axle nut and tighten to 137 ft. lbs. (186 Nm).

11. Install the disc brake assembly and parking brake. Install the wheel and tire.

12. Lower the vehicle and test drive.

Driveshaft

REMOVAL AND INSTALLATION

4WD

1. Raise and support the vehicle safely.

2. Remove the driveshaft flange to rear differential flange bolts.

NOTE: If equipped with a center bearing, remove the center bearing to chassis bolts and lower the assembly from the vehicle.

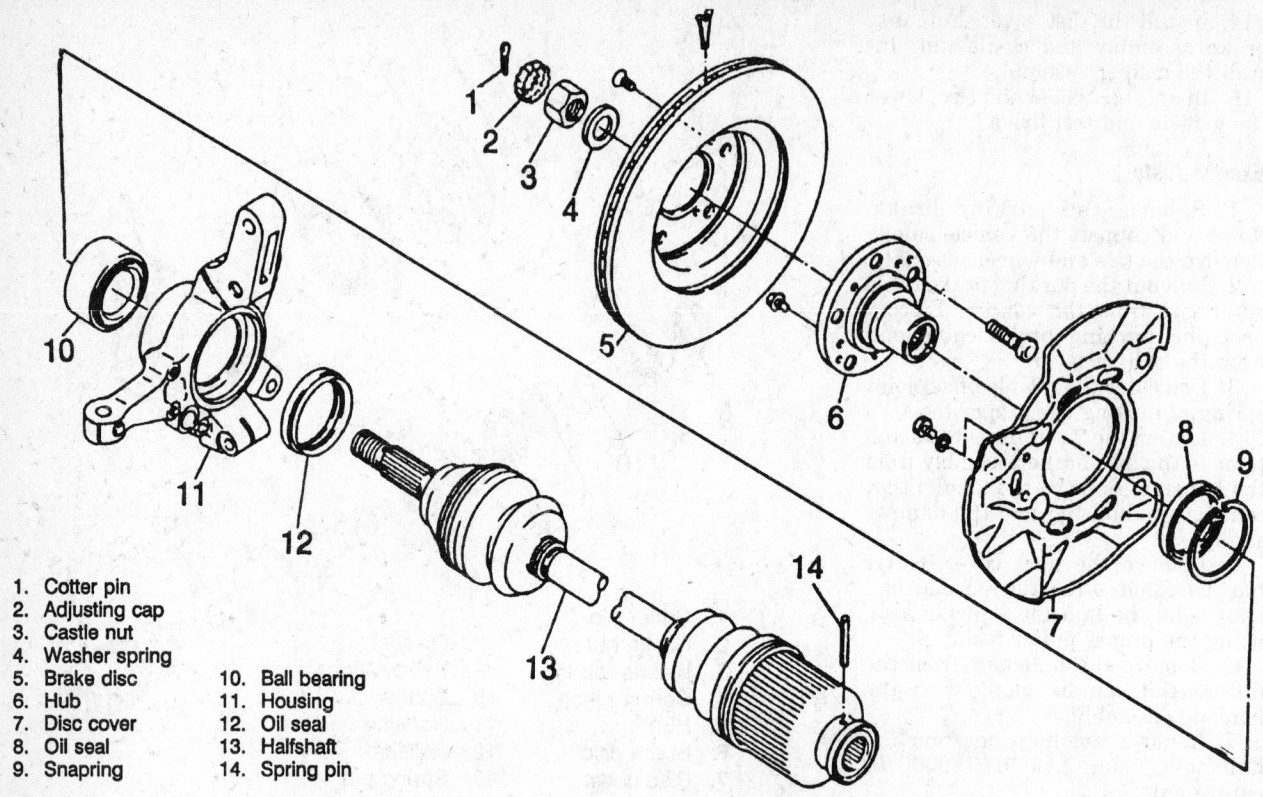

1. Cotter pin
2. Adjusting cap
3. Castle nut
4. Washer spring
5. Brake disc
6. Hub
7. Disc cover
8. Oil seal
9. Snapring
10. Ball bearing
11. Housing
12. Oil seal
13. Halfshaft
14. Spring pin

Front halfshaft assembly and related components — XT Coupe with 2.7L engine

3. Position a drain pan under the rear of the transaxle. Remove the driveshaft from the vehicle.

To install:

4. Install the driveshaft and tighten the flange bolts to 17-24 ft. lbs. (24-32 Nm).

5. If equipped with a center bearing, raise the assembly and install the center bearing bolts. Tighten to attaching bolts to 25-33 ft. lbs. (34-44 Nm).

6. Lower the vehicle, check the transaxle fluid level and test drive.

Rear Axle Shafts

REMOVAL AND INSTALLATION

Justy

2WD

1. Raise and support the vehicle safely. Remove the tire and wheel assembly.

2. Remove the dust cap. Straighten the locking washer edge. Remove the nut, lock washer and washer.

3. Remove the brake drum. Be sure not to drop the outer bearing.

4. Remove the brake line bracket from the spindle housing.

5. Loosen the bolts and remove the brake assembly. Suspend the assembly aside with wire.

6. Using the proper tools, drive out the spring pin connecting the halfshaft assembly to the differential.

7. Remove the strut, lower link and trailing link. Pull the housing along with the halfshaft from its mounting.

8. Separate the housing from the halfshaft, using removal tools 922493000 and 921122000 or their equivalent.

To install:

9. Join the housing and halfshaft. Install the strut, lower link and trailing link. Install the spring pin connecting the halfshaft assembly to the differential.

10. After tightening the rear axle halfshaft-to-axle housing nut, tighten the axle shaft nut 30 degrees further.

11. Install the brake assembly, brake line bracket and brake drum.

12. Install the wheel and tire, lower the vehicle and test drive.

Legacy and SVX

2WD LEGACY ONLY

1. Disconnect the negative battery cable.

2. Raise the vehicle and support safely.

3. Remove the wheels and unlock the axle nut. Remove the axle nut.

4. Loosen the parking brake adjuster. Remove the disc brake assembly from the backing plate and suspend it with a wire from the strut.

5. Remove the disc brake rotor from the hub and disconnect the end of the parking brake cable.

6. Remove the bolts that retain the lateral link, trailing link and the strut to the rear spindle.

7. Remove the rear spindle, backing plate and hub as a unit.

To install:

8. The installation is the reverse of the removal procedure. Use the following torque values during installation.

a. Rear spindle to strut assembly — 98-119 ft. lbs.

b. Rear spindle assembly to trailing link — 72-94 ft. lbs.

c. Rear spindle to lateral link — 87-116 ft. lbs.

d. Disc brake assembly to backing plate — 34-43 ft. lbs.

e. Axle nut — 123-152 ft. lbs.

f. Wheel nuts — 58-72 ft. lbs.

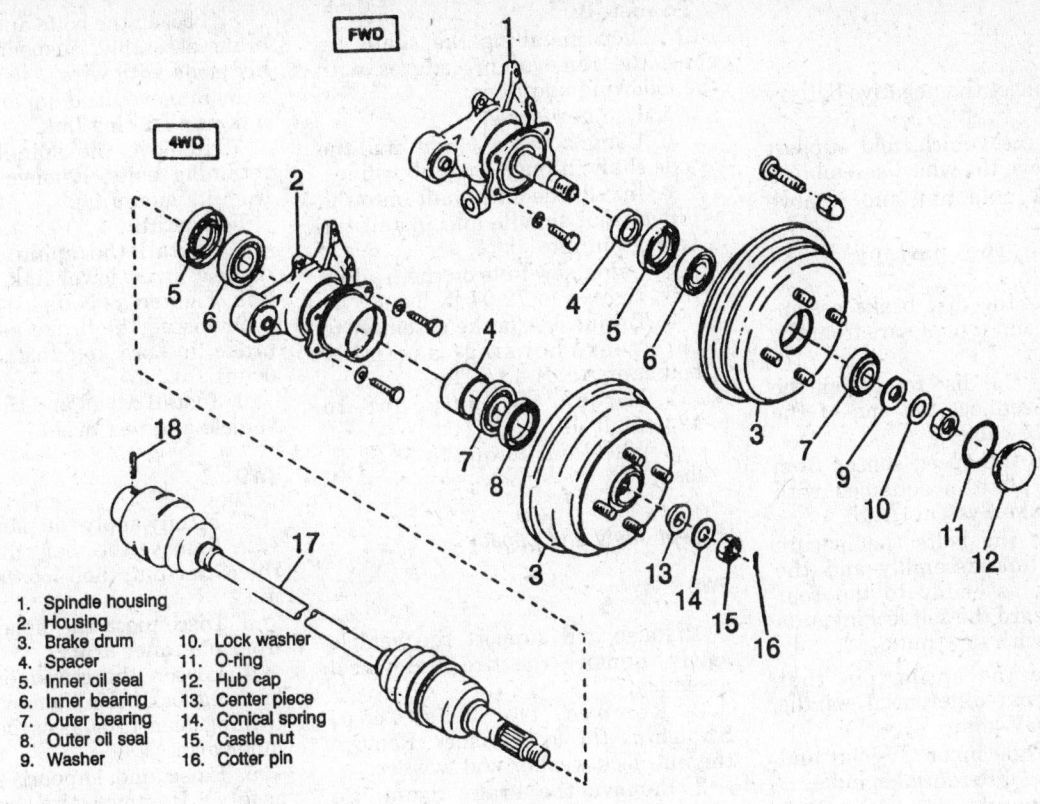

1. Spindle housing
2. Housing
3. Brake drum
4. Spacer
5. Inner oil seal
6. Inner bearing
7. Outer bearing
8. Outer oil seal
9. Washer
10. Lock washer
11. O-ring
12. Hub cap
13. Center piece
14. Conical spring
15. Castle nut
16. Cotter pin

Rear axle assembly — Justy

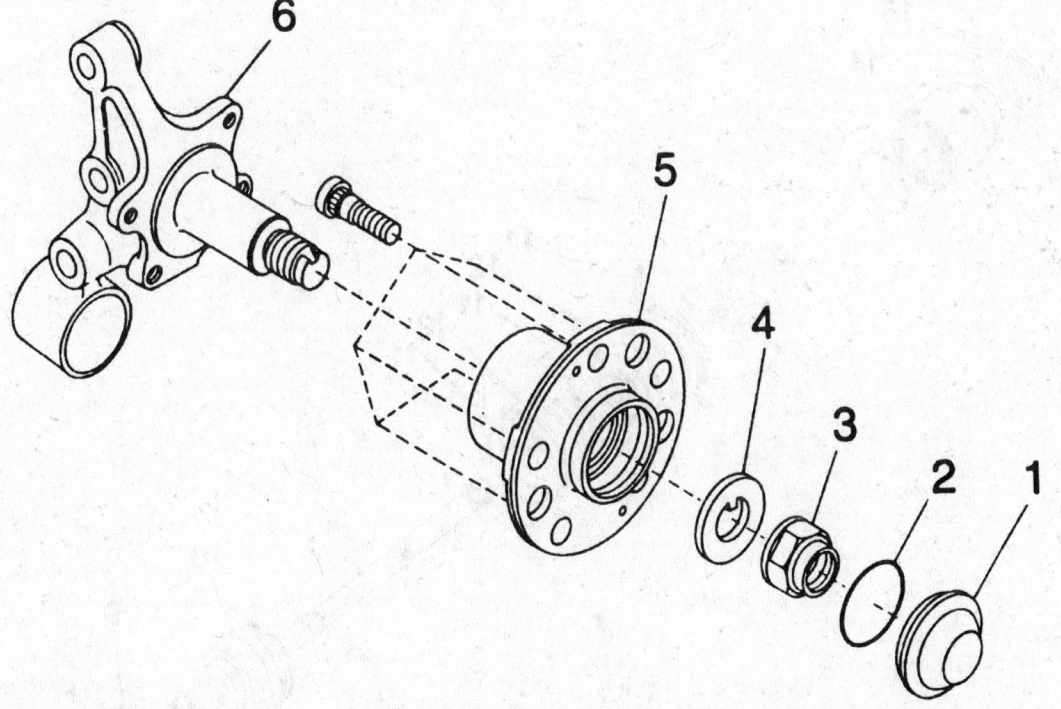

1. Hub cap
2. O-ring
3. Axle nut
4. Washer
5. Hub unit
6. Spindle

Rear axle/hub assembly — Legacy with FWD

4WD

1. Disconnect the negative battery cable.

2. Raise the vehicle and support safely. Remove the wheel assemblies.

3. Unlock axle nut and remove from axle.

4. Loosen the parking brake adjuster.

5. Remove the disc brake assembly and suspend it on a wire from the body or strut.

6. Remove the disc rotor from the hub and disconnect the end of the parking brake cable.

7. Remove the speed sensor from the backing plate, if equipped with Anti-lock Brake System (ABS).

8. Remove the bolts that secure the lateral link assembly and the trailing link assembly to the rear housing. Discard the self-locking nuts and replace with new nuts.

9. Remove the spring pin that secures the rear differential spindle to the inner CV-joint.

10. Remove the inner CV-joint and shaft from the differential spindle.

11. Disengage the rear driveshaft from the rear hub and remove the shaft.

To install:

12. When installing the shaft, reverse the removal procedures with the following additions:

   a. Use new seals.

   b. Using a new axle nut, pull the axle shaft through the hub splines.

   c. Install the axle shaft onto the differential spindle and install the spring pin into place.

   d. Using new nuts on the trailing link, tighten to 72-94 ft. lbs.

   e. Torque disc brake assembly to the rear housing assembly bolts/nuts to 34-43 ft. lbs.

   f. Torque the axle nut to 123-152 ft. lbs.

   g. Wheel nut torque to 58-72 ft. lbs.

Except Justy and Legacy

2WD

1. Raise and support the vehicle safely. Remove the tire and wheel assembly.

2. Remove the dust cap. Straighten the lock washer. Remove the nut, lock washer and washer.

3. Remove the brake drum. Be sure not to drop the outer bearing.

4. Remove the brake line bracket from the spindle housing.

5. Loosen the bolts and remove the brake assembly. Suspend the assembly aside with wire.

6. Remove the damper strut, lower link and trailing link.

7. Remove the spindle assembly retaining bolts. Remove the spindle from its mounting.

To install:

8. Install the spindle assembly, damper strut, lower link and trailing link. Tighten all bolts to specification.

9. Install the brake assembly and brake line bracket. Install the brake drum.

10. Install wheel and tire, lower the vehicle and test drive.

4WD

1. Firmly apply the parking brake.

2. Remove the rear wheel cap and the cotter pin, then loosen the castle nut.

3. Disconnect the shock absorber from the inner arm.

4. Loosen the crossmember outer bushing lock bolts. Remove the inner trailing arm to chassis bolt and the inner arm.

5. Raise and support the vehicle safely. Remove the rear wheel assemblies.

6. Using a 0.24 in. (6mm) diameter steel rod or a pin punch, drive the

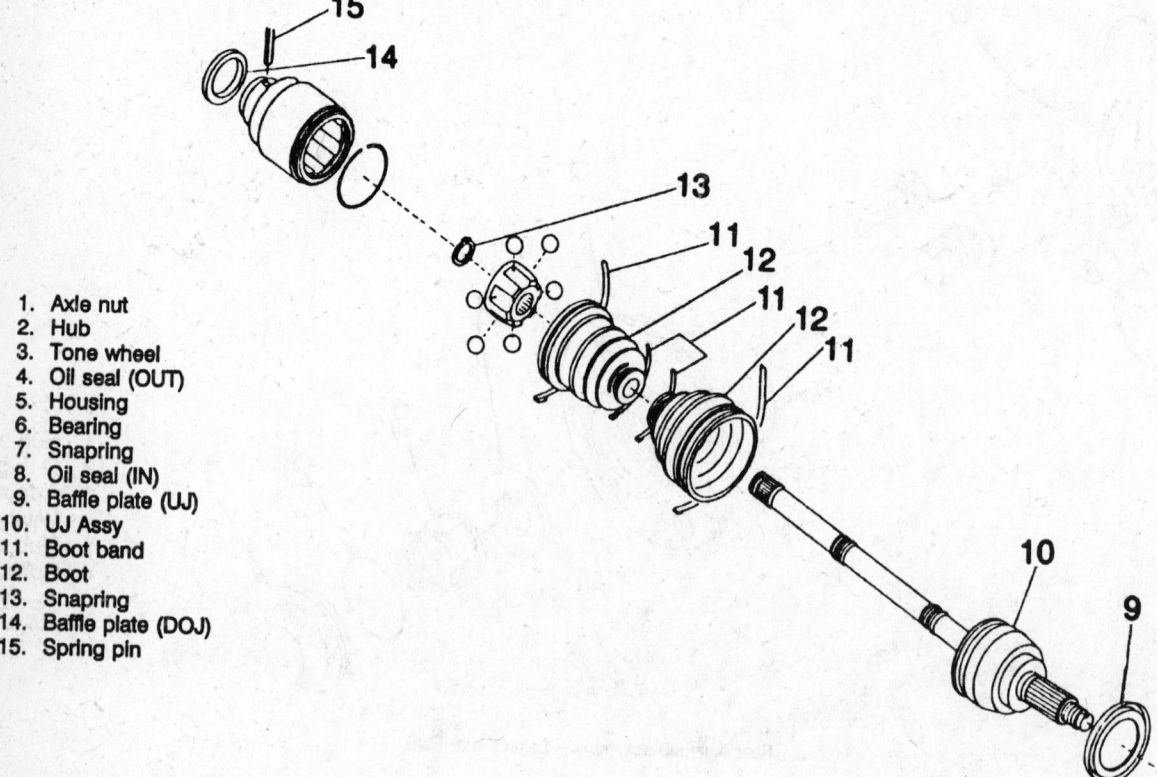

1. Axle nut
2. Hub
3. Tone wheel
4. Oil seal (OUT)
5. Housing
6. Bearing
7. Snapring
8. Oil seal (IN)
9. Baffle plate (UJ)
10. UJ Assy
11. Boot band
12. Boot
13. Snapring
14. Baffle plate (DOJ)
15. Spring pin

Front axle and hub assembly — Legacy

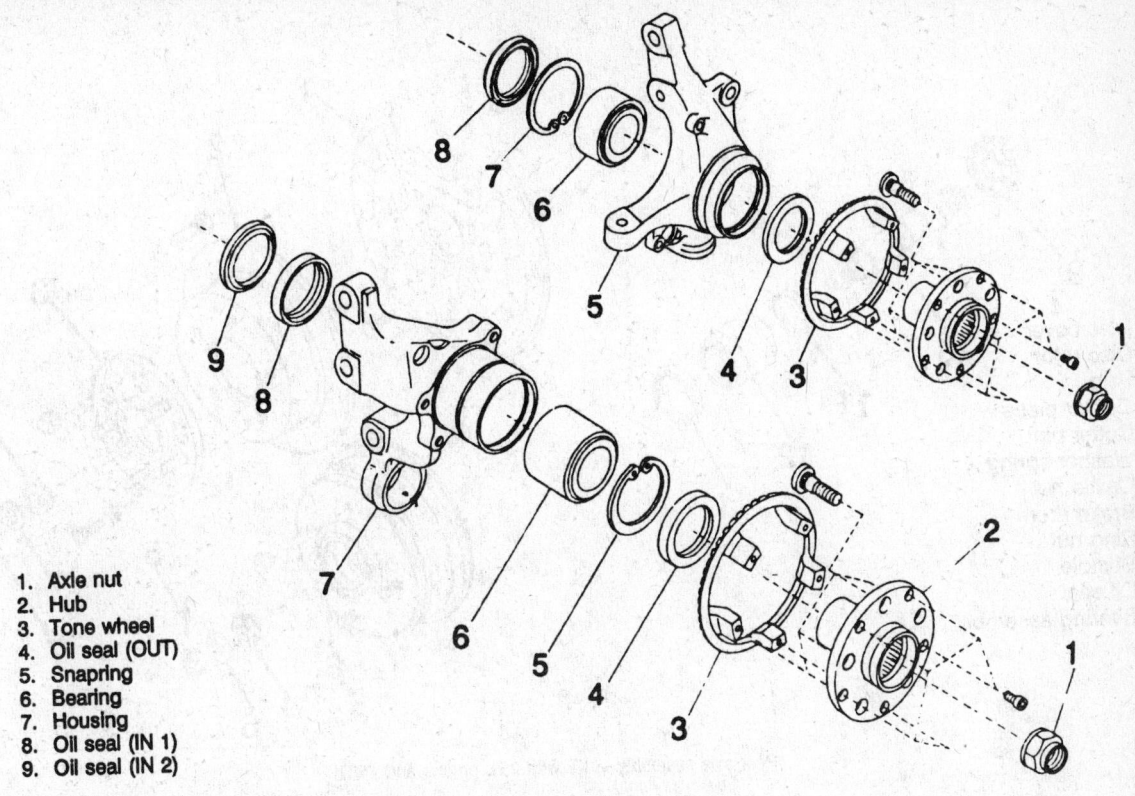

1. Axle nut
2. Hub
3. Tone wheel
4. Oil seal (OUT)
5. Snapring
6. Bearing
7. Housing
8. Oil seal (IN 1)
9. Oil seal (IN 2)

Rear hub assembly — Legacy with 4WD

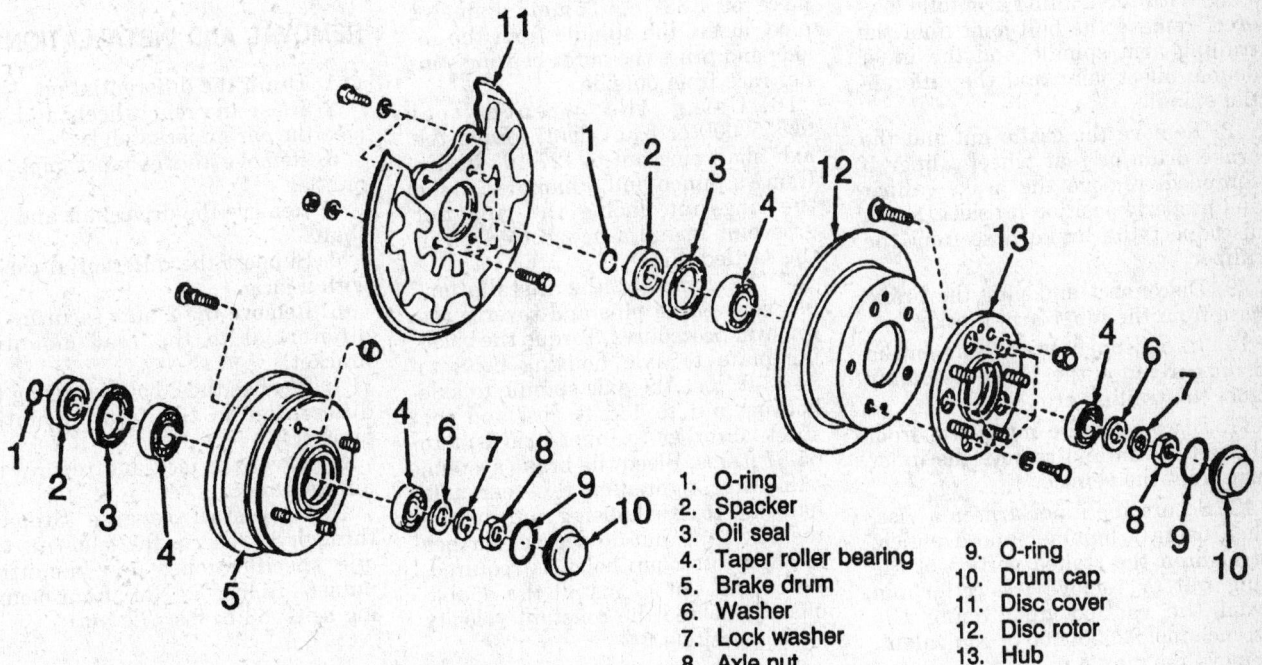

1. O-ring
2. Spacker
3. Oil seal
4. Taper roller bearing
5. Brake drum
6. Washer
7. Lock washer
8. Axle nut
9. O-ring
10. Drum cap
11. Disc cover
12. Disc rotor
13. Hub

Rear axle assembly — XT with 2.7L engine and 2WD

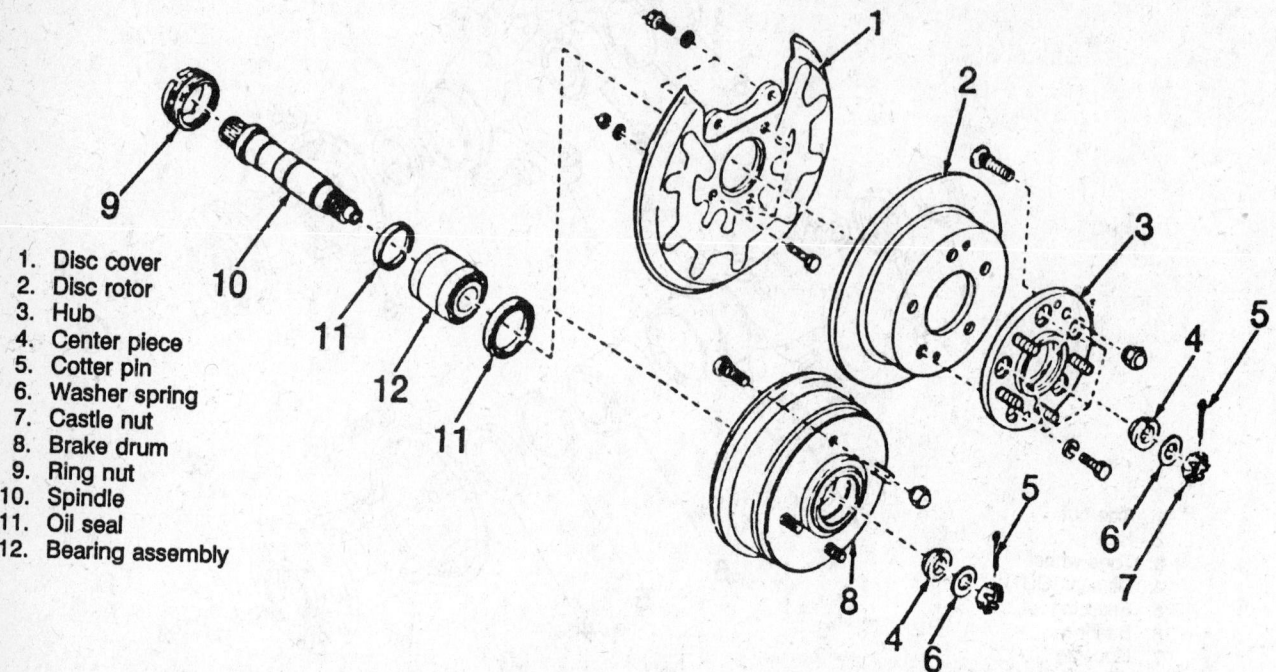

1. Disc cover
2. Disc rotor
3. Hub
4. Center piece
5. Cotter pin
6. Washer spring
7. Castle nut
8. Brake drum
9. Ring nut
10. Spindle
11. Oil seal
12. Bearing assembly

Rear axle assembly — XT with 2.7L engine and 4WD

inner/outer spring pins from the double offset joints.

7. With the trailing arm fully lowered, remove the ball joint from the trailing arm spindle and the inner double offset joint and the differential spindle.

8. Remove the castle nut and the brake drum or rear wheel caliper If equipped, remove the brake caliper and properly position it aside. Do not disconnect the brake hose from the caliper.

9. Disconnect and plug the brake hose from the inner arm bracket.

10. If equipped with rear brake drums, remove the brake assembly from the trailing arm.

11. Disconnect the inner arm from the outer arm and remove the inner arm from the vehicle.

12. Secure the inner arm in a vise, then using a hammer and a punch, straighten the staked portion of the ring nut or remove the cotter pin from the castled nut. Using the wrench tool 925550000 or equivalent, remove the ring nut.

13. Using a plastic hammer on the outside of the spindle, drive it inward to remove it.

14. Clean, inspect and replace the necessary parts.

To install:

15. Using an arbor press and a piece of 1.38 in. (35mm) diameter pipe, insert the spindle from the inside and press the outer bearing's inner race from outside.

16. Using the wrench tool 925550000 or equivalent, torque the axle shaft ring nut to 127-163 ft. lbs. Using a punch and a hammer, stake the ring nut, facing the ring nut groove or install a new cotter pin in the castled nut.

17. To complete the installation, use new spring pins and reverse the removal procedures. Torque the backing plate to axle housing bolts to 34-43 ft. lbs., the axle spindle to axle housing nut to 145 ft. lbs. and the shock absorber to inner arm bolt to 65-87 ft. lbs. Bleed the brake system.

18. After tightening the rear axle halfshaft to axle housing nut, tighten the axle shaft nut 30 degrees further to align cotter pin holes as required. Be careful not to install the double offset joint and the constant velocity joint oppositely.

Rear Differential Carrier

REMOVAL AND INSTALLATION

1. Drain the differential oil.
2. Raise the rear wheels and support the car on jackstands.
3. Remove the exhaust pipe and muffler.
4. Remove the driveshaft and axle shafts.
5. Support the differential carrier with a jack.
6. Remove the 2 nuts securing the differential to the rear mounting bracket.
7. Remove the 2 bolts securing the differential to the front mounting bracket.
8. Lower the jack and remove the differential.
9. To install reverse Steps 1 through 8. Observe the following torque specifications; rear mounting nuts: 53 ft. lbs. (72 Nm), front mounting bolts: 53 ft. lbs. (72 Nm)

Knuckle and Spindle

REMOVAL AND INSTALLATION

1. Disconnect the ground cable from the battery.

2. Apply the parking brake.

3. Remove the front wheel cap and cotter pin, and loosen the castle nut and wheel nuts.

4. Raise the vehicle, support it with jackstands and remove the front tires and wheels.

5. Release the parking brake.

6. Pull out the parking brake cable outer clip from the caliper.

7. Disconnect the parking brake cable end from the caliper lever.

8. Loosen the 2 nuts and remove the disc brake assembly from the housing.

9. Remove the 2 nuts which connect the housing and damper strut.

10. Remove the cotter pin and castle nut, and disconnect the tie rod end ball joint from the housing knuckle arm by using a puller.

11. Disconnect the strut from the housing by opening the slit of the housing and lowering the housing gradually, being careful not to damage the ball joint boot.

NOTE: Do not expand the slit of the housing more than 4mm. If the housing is hard to remove from the strut, lightly tap the hub and disc with a large rubber mallet.

12. Remove the castle nut, washer spring center piece on the axle shaft, and take out the hub and disc assembly.

13. Remove the disc cover.

14. Attach puller 926470000 to the housing and drive the axle shaft out of the housing toward the engine at the bearing location.

NOTE: If the inner bearing and/or oil seal are left on the axle shaft, remove them with a puller.

15. Disconnect the transverse link from the housing, and detach the housing.

To install:

16. Fit the housing onto the axle shaft and attach spacer installer 925130000 or 922430000, on the outer bearing inner race taking care not to damage the oil seal lip. Then, connect the rod of the installer to the thread of the axle shaft so the housing does not drop off the axle shaft.

17. Install the transverse link ball joint to the housing.

18. Turn the handle while holding the rod end, by means of a spanner, thus pushing in the housing.

19. Connect the damper strut to the housing.

20. Connect the tie rod end ball joint and housing knuckle arm. Torque the castle nut. After tightening the nut to the specified torque, fur-

ther torque the nut just enough to align the holes of the nut and ball stud. Then insert a cotter pin into the ball stud and bend it around the castle nut.

21. Install the disc cover to the housing.

22. Install the hub and disc assembly onto the axle shaft.

NOTE: Be sure to press the hub and disc assembly onto the axle shaft until the end surface of the hub contacts the ball bearing. If the assembly is hard to press, rotate it to locate the point where it is easily pressed.

23. Install the brake caliper to the housing assembly.

24. Connect the parking brake cable to the brake assembly.

25. Apply the parking brake.

26. Position the center piece, washer spring and castle nut in this order onto the axle shaft and tighten the castle nut to 145 ft. lbs. (196 Nm) on all models except the SVX and Legacy or on the SVX and Legacy tighten the castle nut to 123-152 ft. lbs. (167-206 Nm) then insert a new cotter pin and bend it around the nut.

NOTE: After tightening the nut to the specified torque, retighten it further until a slot of the castle nut is aligned to the hole in the axle shaft.

27. Install the wheel and hub cap.

28. Remove the jack stands, lower the vehicle and reconnect the negative battery cable.

Front Wheel Hub and Bearing

REMOVAL AND INSTALLATION

Justy

1. Raise and safely support the vehicle. Remove the halfshaft from the vehicle. Remove the steering knuckle from the vehicle.

2. Using a finger, move the spacer (inside the steering knuckle) in the radial direction.

3. Using a brass bar, insert it through the inner race of the outer bearing, then tap the bar with a hammer to drive out the bearing (with the oil seal); discard the bearing and the oil seal.

4. Remove the spacer and the inner bearing.

5. Position the brass bar through the outer race of the inner bearing, then using a hammer, drive the out

the bearing (with the oil seal); discard the bearing and the oil seal.

To install:

6. Clean and inspect the parts for wear, cracks and/or damage; if necessary, replace the damaged parts.

7. Using new bearings, pack them with grease.

8. Using the stand tool 922441000 or equivalent, install the steering knuckle onto the stand.

9. Using the bearing installer tool 922470000 or equivalent, and the handle tool 498477000 or equivalent, press the inner bearing into the housing until it contacts the housing stopper.

10. Using $\frac{1}{4}$ oz. of wheel bearing grease, pack the inside of the housing.

11. Invert the housing on the stand tool 922441000 or equivalent, and install the spacer.

12. Using the bearing installer tool 922470000 or equivalent, and the handle tool 498477000 or equivalent, press the outer bearing into the housing until it contacts the housing stopper.

13. Using a press and the oil seal installer tool 922450000 or equivalent, press the new outer oil seal into the steering knuckle housing, until it comes in contact with the bearing end face.

14. Invert the steering knuckle housing.

15. Using a press and the oil seal installer tool 922460000 or equivalent, press the new inner oil seal into the steering knuckle housing, until it comes in contact with the bearing end face.

16. To complete the installation, reverse the remaining removal procedures.

Except Justy

1. Raise and safely support the vehicle. Remove the halfshaft from the vehicle; be sure to remove the steering knuckle from the vehicle.

2. Using a finger, move the spacer (inside the steering knuckle) in the radial direction.

3. Using a brass bar, insert it through the inner race of the outer bearing, then tap the bar with a hammer to drive out the bearing (with the oil seal); discard the bearing and the oil seal.

4. Remove the spacer and the inner bearing.

5. Position the brass bar through the outer race of the inner bearing, then using a hammer, drive the out the bearing (with the oil seal); discard the bearing and the oil seal.

To install:

6. Clean and inspect the parts for wear, cracks and/or damage; if necessary, replace the damaged parts.

7. Using new bearings, pack them with wheel bearing grease.

8. Using the die tool 926490000 or equivalent, install the steering knuckle onto the die.

9. Using a press and the punch tool 926490000 or equivalent, press the outer bearing into the housing until it contacts the housing stopper.

10. Using ½ oz. of wheel bearing grease, pack the inside of the housing.

11. Invert the housing on the die tool 926490000 or equivalent, and install the spacer.

12. Using a press and the punch tool 926490000 or equivalent, press the inner bearing into the housing until it contacts the housing stopper.

13. Using a press and the punch tool 926490000 or equivalent, position the new outer oil seal in the punch tool so the lip faces the groove, then press it into the steering knuckle housing, until it comes in contact with the bearing end face.

14. Invert the steering knuckle housing onto the punch tool 926490000 or equivalent, so the seal lip faces the groove.

15. Using a press and the die tool 926490000 or equivalent, press the new inner oil seal into the steering knuckle housing, until it comes in contact with the bearing end face.

16. To install the steering knuckle, fit the housing onto the axle shaft and attach a spacer of the installation tool 922430000 or equivalent, on the outer bearing inner race; be careful not to damage the oil seal. Thread the axle shaft onto the installation tool, then turn the handle to draw the axle into the housing, until it is seated.

17. Install the remaining components in reverse order.

MANUAL TRANSAXLE

REMOVAL AND INSTALLATION

Justy

1. Disconnect the negative battery cable. Remove the air cleaner assembly. Raise and support the vehicle safely.

2. Disconnect the electrical wiring connectors from the starter. Remove the starter to transaxle bolts and the starter from the vehicle.

3. From the transaxle, disconnect the speedometer cable, the backup light switch connector and the ground cable. If equipped with 4WD, remove the activation hoses from the actuator.

4. Disconnect the electrical connector between the ignition coil and the distributor.

5. Disconnect the clutch cable and the bracket from the transaxle. In place of the clutch cable bracket, install the lifting hook, or equivalent.

6. Removing the pitching stopper and brackets between the transaxle and chassis.

7. Install engine supporter tool 921540000 or equivalent.

8. Install the vertical hoist to T000100 transaxle lifting hook and raise the transaxle slightly.

9. From under the vehicle, remove the under covers.

10. Disconnect the rear exhaust pipe from the front exhaust pipe and the vehicle.

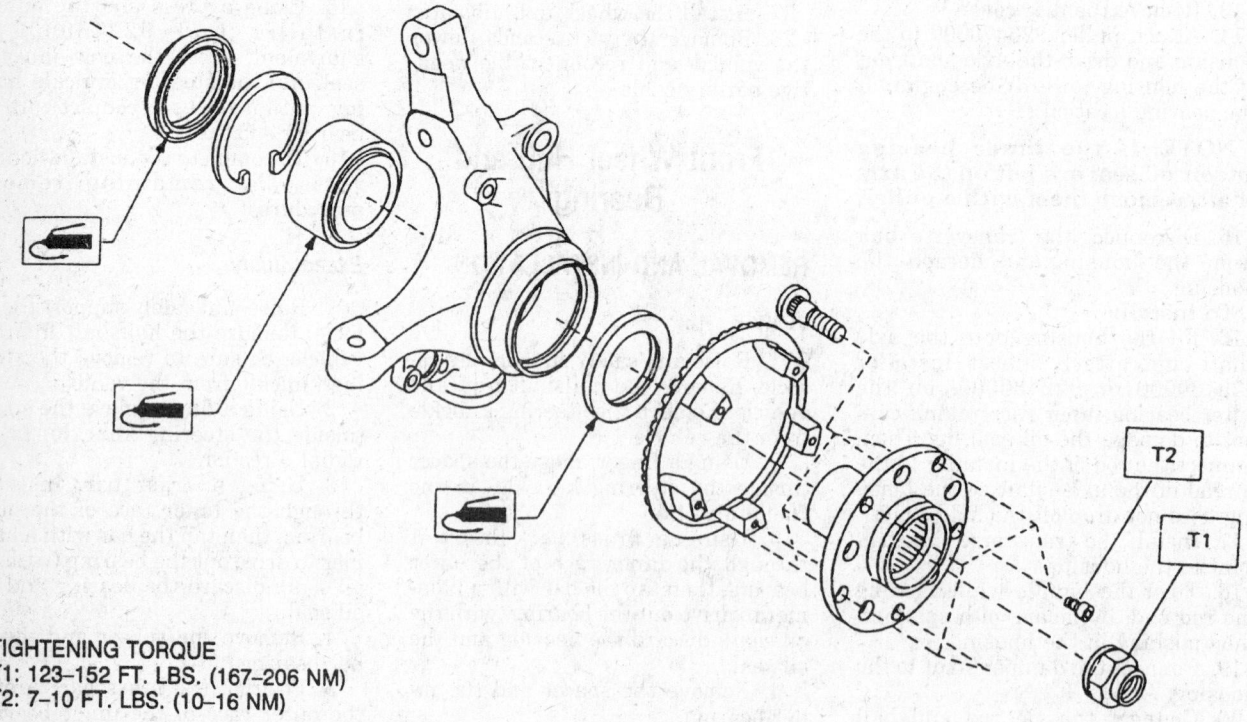

TIGHTENING TORQUE
T1: 123–152 FT. LBS. (167–206 NM)
T2: 7–10 FT. LBS. (10–16 NM)

Front knuckle and hub assembly — Legacy and SVX

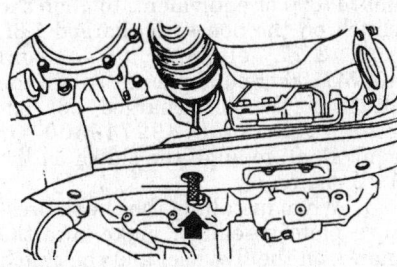

Removing the spring pin from the axle shaft — Justy

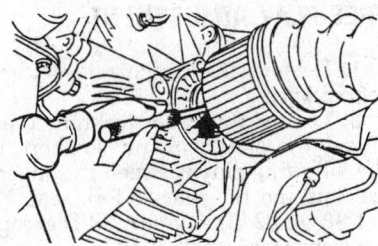

Separating the axle shaft from the driveshaft

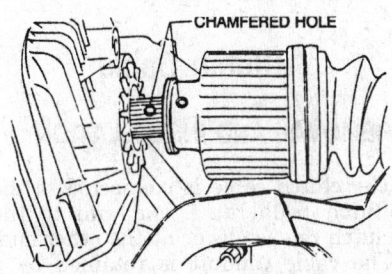

Aligning the chamfered holes of the axle shaft with the driveshaft

11. Remove the center crossmember to engine/transaxle assembly bolts.

12. Using a pin punch and a hammer, drive out the axle shaft to driveshaft spring pin. Discard the spring pin and separate the axle shaft.

13. Remove the transaxle mounting bracket.

14. Disconnect the gearshift rod and stay from the transaxle.

15. Properly support the engine assembly. Remove the transaxle to engine bolts.

16. Using the vertical hoist, lift the transaxle from the vehicle.

To install:

17. Install the transaxle assembly in the vehicle and install the transaxle-to-engine bolts. Install the gearshift rods on the transaxle.

18. Join the axle shaft and the differential. Install a new axle shaft spring pin. Install the center crossmember and tighten bolts to 27-49 ft. lbs. (37-67 Nm).

19. Install the rear exhaust pipe, engine under covers, pitching stopper and brackets, clutch cable, electrical connectors, speedometer cable, 4WD activation hoses, starter wires and starter-to-transaxle bolts.

20. Lower the vehicle, connect the negative battery cable, check the transaxle fluid and test drive the vehicle.

Legacy

1. Disconnect the negative battery cable. If equipped with a turbocharger, remove the manifold cover.

2. Remove the air intake duct. If equipped with a turbocharger, discharge the air conditioning and disconnect the air conditioner pressure hose. Remove the resonator chamber, air inlet and outlet ducts.

3. Disconnect all cables and harness connectors attached to the transaxle. Remove the starter.

4. Remove the pitching stopper rod and bracket. On turbocharged models, remove the clutch operating cylinder assembly and free the release fork. Remove the transaxle oil level gauge.

5. Remove the connector holder bracket. Remove the turbocharger cooling ducts and disconnect the center exhaust pipe from the turbocharger.

6. Remove the upper transaxle attaching bolts. Remove the driveshaft, gearshift system, front stabilizer and halfshafts.

7. Remove the nuts holding the lower side of the engine to the transaxle. Install a transaxle jack. Remove the rear cushion rubber mounting nuts and rear crossmember. Remove the transaxle.

8. On turbocharged models, remove the release bearing from the clutch cover.

To install:

9. Install the transaxle and temporarily tighten bolts. Install the clutch release assembly on Turbo models.

10. Install the rear cushion and crossmember. Tighten cushion bolts to 20-35 ft. lbs. (27-47 Nm); cross-

member front bolts to 87-116 ft. lbs. (118-157 Nm), rear 40-61 ft. lbs. (54-83 Nm). Tighten the transaxle to engine bolts to 34-40 ft. lbs. (46-54 Nm).

11. After tightening all bolts check that the release fork is in the proper position. Install the halfshafts, and temporarily install the transverse link and stabilizer.

12. Install the gear shift system and driveshaft. Lower the vehicle and tighten the transverse link to 43-51 ft. lbs. (59-69 Nm); stabilizer to 14-2 ft. lbs. (20-29 Nm).

13. Install the connector holder bracket, pitching stopper, turbocharger cooling duct, clutch operating cylinder, air conditioner hoses, resonator, air inlet and outlet.

14. Install the starter assembly. Connect all previously disconnected harnesses and connectors.

15. Connect the negative battery cable, check the transaxle fluid level and test drive the vehicle.

Except Legacy and Justy

1. Disconnect the negative battery cable. Remove the air cleaner assembly.

2. Remove the clutch cable and the hill holder cable. Remove the speedometer cable.

3. Remove the oxygen sensor electrical connector and the neutral switch connector.

4. If equipped with 4WD, remove the disconnect the electrical connections at the backup light and differential lock indicator switch assembly. Disconnect the differential lock vacuum hose.

5. Disconnect the starter electrical connections. Remove the starter retaining bolts. Remove the starter from the transaxle case.

6. Remove the air intake boot. Disconnect the pitching stopper rod from its mounting bracket. Remove the right side engine to transaxle mounting bolt.

7. Install engine support bracket 927160000 and engine support tool 927150000 or their equivalents. Remove the buffer rod from the engine and body side bracket.

NOTE: Before attaching the special engine support tools, connect the adjuster to the buffer rod assembly on the right side of the engine.

8. Raise and support the vehicle safely.

9. Disconnect the exhaust pipes at the exhaust manifold flange. Remove

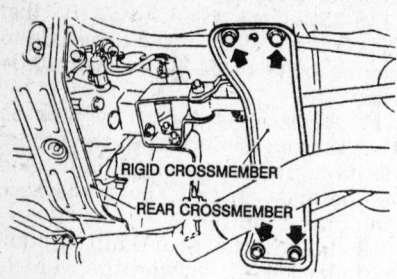

View of the rigid and rear crossmembers — XT Coupe

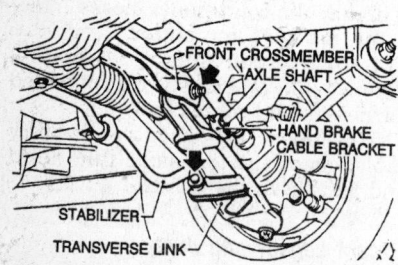

View of the front suspension assembly — XT Coupe

the exhaust system up to the rear exhaust pipe assembly.

10. If equipped with 4WD, match-mark and remove the driveshaft. Remove the complete gear shift assembly.

11. Loosen the upper bolt and nut from the plate that secures the transverse link to the stabilizer. Remove the lower bolt and separate the link from the stabilizer.

12. Remove the right brake cable bracket from the transverse link. Remove the bolt retaining the link to the crossmember on each side.

13. Lower the transverse link. Using tool 398791700 or equivalent, remove the spring pin and separate the axle shaft from the driveshaft on each side of the assembly by pushing the rear of the tire outward.

14. Remove the engine to transaxle mounting bolts. Position the proper transaxle jack under the transaxle assembly.

15. Remove the rear cushion rubber mounting bolts. Remove the rear crossmember assembly.

16. Turn the engine support tool adjuster counterclockwise in order to slightly raise the engine.

17. Move the transaxle jack toward the rear of the vehicle until the mainshaft is withdrawn from the clutch cover.

18. Carefully remove the transaxle assembly from the vehicle.

To install:

19. Carefully raise the transaxle until the mainshaft is aligned with the clutch side. Install the engine to the transaxle and temporarily tight the mounting bolts.

20. Install the rear crossmember rubber cushion and tighten nuts to 20-35 ft. lbs. (27-47 Nm). Install the rear crossmember and tighten front bolts to 65-87 ft. lbs. (88-118 Nm); rear bolts to 27-49 ft. lbs. (37-67 Nm).

21. Tighten the engine to transaxle nuts to 34-40 ft. lbs. (46-54 Nm). Remove the transaxle jack.

22. Install the halfshaft into the differential and spring pin into place. Install the transverse link and stabilizer temporarily to the front crossmember. Install the brake cable bracket. Lower the vehicle and tighten transverse link bolt to 43-51 ft. lbs. (59-69 Nm); stabilizer bolts to 14-22 ft. lbs. (20-29 Nm).

23. Install the gearshift system. Install the driveshaft (4WD vehicles). Install the starter, pitching stopper, timing hole plug, air intake boot and speedometer cable. Reconnect all electrical and vacuum connectors.

24. Connect the clutch cable and hill holder. Install the front exhaust pipe.

25. Connect the negative battery cable, check the transaxle fluid level and test drive the vehicle.

CLUTCH

REMOVAL AND INSTALLATION

1. Remove the transaxle from the vehicle.

2. Gradually loosen the pressure plate to flywheel assembly bolts. Loosen the bolts 1 turn at a time, working around the pressure plate.

3. Remove the clutch plate and the disc from the vehicle.

To install:

4. Inspect the parts for wear or damage and replace any parts, as necessary.

5. Installation is the reverse of the removal procedure.

6. Use clutch disc guide tool 499747000 or equivalent, to align the clutch on the non-turbocharged 1.8L and 2.7L engines. Use tool 499747100 or equivalent, to align the clutch on the turbocharged 1.8L engine. Use tool 499745500 or equivalent, to align the clutch on the 1.2L engine.

7. When installing the clutch pressure plate assembly, make sure the marks on the flywheel and the clutch pressure plate assembly are at least 120 degrees apart. This is for purposes of balance. Also, make sure the clutch disc is installed properly, noting the **FRONT** and **REAR** markings.

FREE-PLAY ADJUSTMENT

1. Remove the clutch release fork return spring.

2. Loosen the cable locknut, then adjust the spherical nut so there is the following play between the spherical nut and the release fork seat.

1.8L and 2.7L engines, 2WD except turbocharger — 0.08-0.12 in.

2WD/4WD turbocharged, 1.8L engine and the 4WD 2.7L engine — 0.12-0.16 in.

1.2L engine — 0.08-0.16 in.

3. Tighten the locknut and reconnect the release spring.

Clutch Cable

REMOVAL AND INSTALLATION

The clutch cable is connected to the clutch pedal at 1 end and to the clutch release lever at the other end. The cable conduit is retained by a bolt and clamp on a bracket mounted on the flywheel housing.

1. If necessary, raise and support the vehicle safely.

2. Disconnect both ends of the cable and the conduit, then remove the assembly from under the vehicle.

3. Using engine oil, lubricate the clutch cable. If the cable is defective, replace it.

4. Installation is the reverse the removal procedure.

ADJUSTMENT

The clutch cable can be adjusted at the cable bracket where the cable is attached to the side of the transaxle housing.

1. Remove the circlip and clamp.

2. Slide the cable end in the direction desired and then replace the cir-

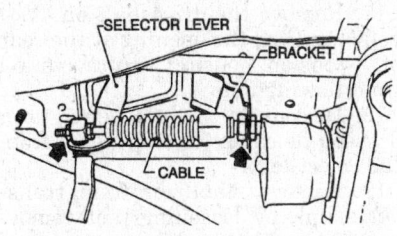

View of the selector cable and the selector cable bracket — XT Coupe

clip and clamp into the nearest gutters on the cable end.

NOTE: The cable should not be stretched out straight nor should it have right angle kinks in it. Any straightening should be gradual.

3. Check the clutch for proper operation.

AUTOMATIC TRANSAXLE

Transaxle

REMOVAL AND INSTALLATION

Justy

WITH ECVT

NOTE: When removing and installing ECVT transaxle, always remove and install the engine and transaxle as an assembly.

1. Disconnect the negative battery cable. Drain the coolant by removing drain plug from radiator.
2. Remove the grille. Disconnect hoses and electric wiring from radiator and remove the radiator.
3. Remove front hood release cable and remove radiator upper support member. Disconnect horn and remove the air cleaner assembly.
4. Disconnect the following hoses and cables:
   a. Hoses from carburetor
   b. Hoses from the heater unit
   c. Hose for brake booster
   d. Clutch cable
   e. Accelerator cable
   f. Choke cable from carburetor, if equipped

g. Speedometer cable
h. Distributor wiring
5. Disconnect selector cable. Set selector lever at **N** position. Remove clip and detach selector cable from bracket. Remove snap pin, clevis pin and separate selector cable from transaxle.
6. Remove the pitching stopper from the bracket.
7. Disconnect the starter cable, engine wiring harness connectors, ground lead terminals and brush holder harness connector.
8. Remove the hanger from the rear of transaxle.
9. Remove under covers and remove the exhaust system.
10. Remove the driveshaft from transaxle.
11. Remove transverse link.
12. Remove the spring pin retaining the axle shaft by using a suitable tool and separate front axle shaft from the transaxle.
13. Remove engine and transaxle mounting brackets.
14. Raise the engine and remove center member and crossmember.
15. Lift the engine/transaxle assembly carefully and remove it from the vehicle.
   To install:
16. Position the engine/transaxle assembly in the vehicle. Install engine and transaxle mounting brackets.
17. Install center member and crossmember.
18. Install the axle shaft to transaxle with new spring pin.
19. Install gearshift rod and stay to transaxle.
20. Install the exhaust system. Connect driveshaft to transaxle.
21. Install transverse link and under covers to the vehicle.
22. Reconnect the pitching stopper to bracket.
23. Reconnect the following hoses and cables:
   a. Hoses to carburetor
   b. Hoses to the heater unit
   c. Hose to brake booster
   d. Clutch cable to transaxle
   e. Accelerator cable
   f. Choke cable from carburetor, if equipped
   g. Speedometer cable
   h. Distributor wiring
24. Reconnect the starter cable, engine wiring harness connectors, ground lead terminals and brush holder harness connector. Install the air cleaner assembly.
25. Install radiator upper member and connect hood release cable to lock assembly. Reconnect the horn.

26. Install the radiator and connect hoses and electric wiring. Attach grille to the vehicle.
27. Refill the coolant. Reconnect the battery cable.
28. Check all fluid levels. Road test vehicles for proper operation in all driving ranges.

XT COUPE

1.8L AND 2.7L ENGINES

1. Disconnect the negative battery cable. Remove the air cleaner assembly.
2. Remove the clutch cable and the hill holder cable. Remove the speedometer cable. Remove the torque converter from the driveplate.
3. Remove the oxygen sensor electrical connector and the neutral switch connector.
4. If equipped with 4WD, remove the disconnect the electrical connections at the backup light and differential lock indicator switch assembly. Disconnect the differential lock vacuum hose.
5. Disconnect the starter electrical connections. Remove the starter retaining bolts. Remove the starter from the transaxle case.
6. Remove the air intake boot. Disconnect the pitching stopper rod from its mounting bracket. Remove the right side engine to transaxle mounting bolt.
7. Install engine support bracket 927160000 and engine support tool 927150000 or their equivalents. Remove the buffer rod from the engine and body side bracket.

NOTE: Before attaching the special engine support tools, connect the adjuster to the buffer rod assembly on the right side of the engine.

8. Raise and support the vehicle safely.
9. Disconnect the exhaust pipes at the exhaust manifold flange. Remove the exhaust system up to the rear exhaust pipe assembly.
10. If equipped with 4WD, matchmark and remove the driveshaft. Remove the complete gear shift assembly.
11. Loosen the upper bolt and nut from the plate that secures the transverse link to the stabilizer. Remove the lower bolt and separate the link from the stabilizer.
12. Remove the right brake cable bracket from the transverse link. Remove the bolt retaining the link to the crossmember on each side.
13. Lower the transverse link. Using tool 398791700 or equivalent, re-

move the spring pin and separate the axle shaft from the driveshaft on each side of the assembly by pushing the rear of the tire outward.

14. Remove the engine to transaxle mounting bolts. Position the proper transaxle jack under the transaxle assembly. Disconnect the transaxle cooler lines.

15. Remove the rear cushion rubber mounting bolts. Remove the rear crossmember assembly.

16. Turn the engine support tool adjuster counterclockwise in order to slightly raise the engine.

17. Move the transaxle jack toward the rear of the vehicle until the mainshaft is withdrawn from the clutch cover.

18. Carefully remove the transaxle assembly from the vehicle.

To install:

19. Carefully raise the transaxle until the mainshaft is aligned with the clutch side. Install the engine to the transaxle and temporarily tighten the mounting bolts.

20. Install the rear crossmember rubber cushion and tighten nuts to 20-35 ft. lbs. (27-47 Nm). Install the rear crossmember and tighten front bolts to 65-87 ft. lbs. (88-118 Nm); rear bolts to 27-49 ft. lbs. (37-67 Nm).

21. Tighten the engine-to-transaxle nuts to 34-40 ft. lbs. (46-54 Nm). Remove the transaxle jack.

22. Install the halfshaft into the differential and spring pin into place. Install the transverse link and stabilizer temporarily to the front crossmember. Install the brake cable bracket. Lower the vehicle and tighten transverse link bolt to 43-51 ft. lbs. (59-69 Nm); stabilizer bolts to 14-22 ft. lbs. (20-29 Nm).

23. Install the gearshift system. Install the driveshaft (4WD vehicles). Install the starter, pitching stopper, timing hole plug, air intake boot and speedometer cable. Reconnect all electrical and vacuum connectors.

24. Connect the clutch cable and hill holder. Install the front exhaust pipe. Connect the oil cooler lines. Install and tighten the torque converter mounting bolts to 17-20 ft. lbs. (23-26 Nm).

25. Connect the negative battery cable, check the transaxle fluid level and test drive the vehicle.

1800 Sedan/Station Wagon, Loyale and XT Coupe

2WD AND 4WD NON-ELECTRONIC 3 AND 4-SPEED TRANSAXLES

1. Disconnect the negative battery cable.

2. Remove clamp from spare tire supporter and remove the spare tire.

NOTE: Use care when removing spare tire assembly from the vehicle.

3. Remove spare tire supporter and battery clamp.

4. Remove speedometer cable and retaining clip. Before disconnecting speedometer cable, remove front exhaust pipe on 4 speed automatic transaxle.

5. Disconnect the following electrical harness connections on the 3 speed automatic transaxle:
    a. Oxygen sensor connector
    b. ATF temperature switch connector
    c. Kickdown solenoid valve connector
    d. 4WD solenoid valve connector on 4WD equipped vehicles

6. Disconnect the following electrical harness connections on the 4 speed automatic transaxle:
    a. Oxygen sensor connector
    b. Transaxle harness connector
    c. Inhibitor switch connector
    d. Revolution sensor connector on 4WD equipped vehicles

7. Disconnect the diaphragm vacuum hose on 3 speed automatic transaxle and 4WD vacuum hose on 4WD equipped vehicles.

8. Remove clip band which secures air breather hose to pitching stopper.

9. Remove the pitching stopper rod. Remove the starter.

10. Remove timing hole inspection plug and remove the 4 bolts which hold torque converter to driveplate.

11. Support the engine assembly with special engine support tool 926610000 or equivalent.

12. Remove engine-to-transaxle mounting nut and bolt on the right side.

13. Remove the exhaust system.

NOTE: Apply a penetrating oil or equivalent to all exhaust retaining nuts in advance to facilitate removal.

14. On turbocharged vehicles, remove accelerator cable cover and upper and lower turbocharger covers. Remove the center exhaust pipe at turbocharger location and at rear exhaust pipe. Remove any exhaust brackets or hangers that attach to the transaxle, as necessary.

15. On non-turbocharged vehicles, disconnect front exhaust pipe from the engine and from the rear exhaust pipe. Remove any exhaust brackets or hangers that attach to the transaxle as necessary.

16. Drain all transaxle fluid from the oil pan.

17. Remove the driveshaft on 4WD vehicles. Plug the opening at the rear of extension housing to prevent oil from flowing out.

18. Disconnect the linkage rod for a 3 speed or cable for a 4 speed. from the select lever.

19. Remove stabilizer from transverse link by loosening (not removing) nut and bolt on the lower side of plate.

20. Remove parking brake cable bracket from transverse link and bolt holding transverse link to crossmember on each side. Lower the transverse link.

21. Remove spring pin and separate axle shaft from transaxle on each side.

NOTE: Use a suitable tool to remove spring pin. Discard old spring pin and always install a new pin.

22. Disconnect the axle shaft from transaxle on each side. Be sure to remove axle shaft from transaxle by pushing the rear of tire outward.

23. Remove engine-to-transaxle mounting nuts.

24. Disconnect oil cooler hoses and oil supply pipe. Be careful not to damage the oil supply pipe O-ring.

25. Place transaxle jack or equivalent under transaxle. Always support transaxle case with a transaxle jack.

NOTE: Do not place jack under oil pan otherwise oil pan may be damaged.

26. Remove rear cushion rubber mounting nuts and rear crossmember. Move torque converter and transaxle as a unit away from the engine. Remove the transaxle.

To install:

27. Install transaxle to engine and temporarily tighten engine-to-transaxle mounting nuts.

28. Install rear crossmember to rear cushion rubber mounts. Align rear cushion guide with rear crossmember guide hole and tighten nuts.

29. Install rear crossmember to chassis. Be careful not to damage threads. Torque rear crossmember bolts to 39-49 ft. lbs.

30. Tighten engine to transaxle nuts on the lower side to 34-40 ft. lbs. Remove transaxle jack from the vehicle.

31. Install axle shaft to transaxle and install spring pin into place.

NOTE: Always use new spring pin. Be sure to align the halfshaft and shaft from the transaxle at chamfered holes and engage shaft splines correctly.

32. Install transverse link temporarily to front crossmember by using bolt and self-locking nut. Do not complete final torque at this point.

33. Install stabilizer temporarily to transverse link. Install parking brake cable bracket to transverse link.

34. Connect the linkage rod for a 3 speed or cable for a 4 speed to the select lever. Make sure the lever operates smoothly all across the operating range.

35. Install propeller shaft on 4WD vehicles. Torque propeller shaft to rear differential retaining bolts to 13-20 ft. lbs. and center bearing location retaining bolts to 25-33 ft. lbs.

36. Connect oil cooler hoses and oil supply pipe. Lower vehicle to floor.

37. Tighten transverse link to front crossmember mounting bolts and transverse link to stabilizer mounting bolts with the tires placed on the ground when the vehicle is not loaded. Tightening torque for transverse link to front crossmember (self-locking nuts) 43-51 ft. lbs. and transverse link to stabilizer 14-22 ft. lbs.

38. Tighten engine to transaxle nuts on the upper side to 34-40 ft. lbs.

39. Raise vehicle and safely support. Install exhaust system.

NOTE: Before installing exhaust system, connect speedometer cable on 4 speed vehicles.

40. On turbocharged vehicles, install the center exhaust pipe at turbocharger location and at rear exhaust pipe. Install any exhaust brackets or hangers that attach to the transaxle as necessary. Install upper and lower turbocharger covers and accelerator cable cover.

41. On non-turbocharged vehicles, connect front exhaust pipe to the engine and rear exhaust pipe. Install any exhaust brackets or hangers that attach to the transaxle as necessary.

42. Remove the special engine support tool. Install and tighten torque converter to driveplate mounting bolts to 17-20 ft. lbs.

43. Install timing hole inspection plug.

44. Install starter.

45. Install pitching stopper. Be sure to tighten the bolt for the body side first and then the 1 for engine or transaxle side. Tightening torque for

chassis side is 27-49 ft. lbs. and for engine or transaxle side is 33-40 ft. lbs.

46. Reconnect the following electrical harness connections on the 3 speed automatic transaxle:

   a. Oxygen sensor connector
   b. ATF temperature switch connector
   c. Kickdown solenoid valve connector
   d. 4WD solenoid valve connector on 4WD equipped vehicles

47. Reconnect the following electrical harness connections on the 4 speed automatic transaxle:

   a. Oxygen sensor connector
   b. Transaxle harness connector
   c. Inhibitor switch connector
   d. Revolution sensor connector on 4WD equipped vehicles

48. Reconnect the diaphragm vacuum hose on 3 speed automatic transaxle and 4WD vacuum hose on 4WD equipped vehicles.

49. Secure air breather hose to pitching stopper with a clip band.

50. Reconnect the speedometer cable. Manually tighten cable nut all the way and then turn it approximately 30 degrees more with a tool.

51. Connect the battery ground cable. Refill and check transaxle oil level.

52. Install spare tire supporter and battery clamp. Install spare tire.

53. Road test vehicle for proper operation across all operating ranges.

XT Coupe, Legacy and SVX

4-SPEED ELECTRONIC TRANSAXLE

1. Disconnect the negative battery cable.

2. Remove speedometer cable or electronic wiring connector from speed sensor.

3. Disconnect the following electrical harness connections on the automatic transaxle:

   a. Oxygen sensor connector
   b. Transaxle harness connector
   c. Inhibitor switch connector
   d. Revolution sensor connector on 4WD equipped vehicles
   e. Crankshaft and camshaft angle sensor connector on Legacy vehicles
   f. Knock sensor connectors and transaxle ground terminal on Legacy vehicles

4. Remove clip band which secures air breather hose to pitching stopper.

5. Remove the starter and air intake boot.

6. Remove timing hole inspection plug and remove the 4 bolts which hold torque converter to driveplate.

7. Disconnect pitching stopper rod from bracket.

8. Remove engine to transaxle mounting nut and bolt on the right side.

9. Remove the buffer rod from the vehicle. Support the engine assembly with special engine support tool or equivalent.

10. Remove the exhaust system. Remove exhaust brackets or hangers that attach to the transaxle, as necessary.

11. Matchmark and remove the driveshaft on 4WD vehicles. Plug the opening at the rear of extension housing to prevent oil from flowing out.

12. Disconnect the gear shift cable from the transaxle select lever.

13. Remove stabilizer from transverse link.

14. Remove parking brake cable bracket from transverse link and bolt holding transverse link to crossmember on each side. Lower the transverse link.

15. Remove spring pin and separate halfshaft from transaxle on each side.

NOTE: Use a suitable tool to remove spring pin. Discard old spring pin and always install a new pin.

16. Disconnect the halfshaft from transaxle on each side. Be sure to remove axle shaft from transaxle by pushing the rear of tire outward.

17. Remove engine to transaxle mounting nuts.

18. Disconnect oil cooler hoses.

19. Place transaxle jack or equivalent, under transaxle. Always support transaxle case with a transmission jack.

NOTE: Do not place jack under oil pan otherwise oil pan may be damaged.

20. Remove rear cushion rubber mounting nuts and rear crossmember.

21. Move torque converter and transaxle as a unit away from the engine. Remove the transaxle.

To install:

22. Install transaxle to engine and temporarily tighten engine to transaxle mounting nuts.

23. Install rear crossmember to rear cushion rubber mounts. Align rear cushion guide with rear crossmember guide hole and tighten nuts.

24. Install rear crossmember to chassis; be careful not to damage threads. Torque rear crossmember bolts to 39-49 ft. lbs.

25. Tighten engine to transaxle retaining nuts to 34-40 ft. lbs. Remove transaxle jack from the vehicle.

26. Remove the engine support tool and install buffer rod.

27. Install axle shaft to transaxle and install spring pin into place.

NOTE: Always use new spring pin. Be sure to align the axle shaft and shaft from the transaxle at chamfered holes and install shaft splines correctly.

28. Install transverse link temporarily to front crossmember by using bolt and self locking nut. Do not complete final torque at this point.

29. Install stabilizer temporarily to transverse link. Install parking brake cable bracket to transverse link.

30. Lower vehicle to floor. Tighten transverse link to front crossmember mounting bolts and transverse link to stabilizer mounting bolts with the tires placed on the ground when the vehicle is not loaded. Tightening torque for transverse link to front crossmember (self locking nuts) 43-51 ft. lbs. and transverse link to stabilizer 14-22 ft. lbs.

31. Raise and safely support the vehicle. Reconnect the gear shift cable to the select lever. Make sure the lever operates smoothly all across the operating range.

32. Install propeller shaft on 4WD vehicles. Torque propeller shaft-to-rear differential retaining bolts to 17-24 ft. lbs. and center bearing location retaining bolts to 25-33 ft. lbs.

33. Connect oil cooler hoses.

34. Tighten engine to transaxle bolts to 34-40 ft. lbs.

35. Install starter.

36. Install pitching stopper. Be sure to tighten the bolt for the body side first and then the 1 for engine or transaxle side. Tightening torque for chassis side is 27-49 ft. lbs. and for engine or transaxle side is 33-40 ft. lbs.

37. Install and tighten torque converter-to-driveplate mounting bolts to 17-20 ft. lbs.

38. Install timing hole inspection plug, air intake boot and air breather hose to pitching stopper.

39. Reconnect the following electrical harness connections on the automatic transaxle:

   a. Oxygen sensor connector
   b. Transaxle harness connector
   c. Inhibitor switch connector
   d. Revolution sensor connector on 4WD equipped vehicles
   e. Crankshaft and camshaft angle sensor connector on Legacy
   f. Knock sensor connectors and transaxle ground terminal on Legacy

40. Reconnect the speedometer cable. Manually tighten cable nut all the way and then turn it approximately 30 degrees more with a tool.

41. Install exhaust system and exhaust brackets or hangers that attach to the transaxle, as necessary.

42. Connect the battery ground cable. Refill and check transaxle oil level.

43. Road test vehicle for proper operation across all operating ranges.

SHIFT LINKAGE ADJUSTMENT

1. Loosen the clamp nuts on the shifting rod at the bottom of the shift lever on the transaxle.

2. Place the selector lever in **N** and hold it forward against the detent.

3. Check that the transaxle shift lever is in the **N** position by pulling it all the way back into **P** and then pushing it forward 2 positions.

4. Tighten the clamp nuts.

KICKDOWN SOLENOID ADJUSTMENT

If used, an audible click should be heard from the solenoid on the right side of the transaxle, when the accelerator pedal is pushed down all the way with the engine OFF and the ignition switch in the **ON** position. The switch is operated by the upper part of the accelerator lever inside the vehicle. The position of the switch can be varied to give quicker or slower kickdown response.

TRANSFER CASE

REMOVAL AND INSTALLATION

1. Disconnect the negative battery cable.

2. Raise and support the vehicle safely.

3. Remove the transaxle assembly from the vehicle.

4. Position the assembly in a suitable holding fixture.

5. Disassemble the transfer case from the transaxle.

6. Installation is the reverse of the removal procedure. Tighten the transfer case-to-transaxle nuts to 35-40 ft. lbs.

FRONT SUSPENSION

MacPherson Strut

REMOVAL AND INSTALLATION

Justy

1. Disconnect the negative battery cable. Remove the bolts that retain the strut assembly to the body.

2. Raise and support the vehicle safely. Remove the tire and wheel assembly.

3. Remove the brake hose from the brake hose bracket on the strut assembly. Remove the retaining bolt that retains the brake hose bracket to the strut.

4. Properly support the hub and disc assembly. Remove the retaining bolt from the strut to the housing.

5. Fit the proper tool into the housing slit and pull the strut assembly from the housing.

6. Remove the strut from the vehicle.

   To install:

7. Install the strut and tighten the upper attaching nuts to 29-43 ft. lbs. (39-59 Nm); lower attaching bolts to 25-40 ft. lbs. (34-54 Nm).

8. Install the brake hose and bracket assembly. Install the wheel and lower the vehicle.

Except Justy

1. Disconnect the negative battery cable. If equipped with air suspension, remove the cover and the air line assembly.

2. Remove the bolts that retain the strut assembly to the body.

3. Raise and support the vehicle safely. Remove the tire and wheel assembly.

4. Disconnect the brake hose from the caliper body. Pull the brake hose retaining clip and remove the brake hose from the damper strut bracket.

5. Remove the bolt that retains the damper strut to the housing. Remove the bolt that retains the damper strut bracket to the housing.

6. Pull the strut assembly from the housing gradually and carefully, with the housing assembly in the downward position.

7. Remove the strut assembly from the vehicle.

   To install:

8. Install the strut assembly on the vehicle. Tighten the strut attaching bolts to 28-37 ft. lbs. (38-50 Nm).

9. Install the brake hose on the caliper and bleed the brake system. If equipped with air suspension, install the air line assembly.

10. Install the wheel and tire. Lower the vehicle, connect the negative battery cable and test drive the vehicle.

Ball Joints

INSPECTION

1. Raise and support the vehicle safely.

2. Using a prybar, position it under the wheel, then pry upward on the wheel several times. If more than 0.012 in. (3mm) of movement is noticed at the ball joint it should be replaced.

3. Inspect the dust seal, if damaged it should be replaced.

REMOVAL AND INSTALLATION

1. Raise and support the vehicle safely. Remove the tire and wheel assembly.

2. Properly support the lower control arm assembly. Remove the cotter pin and castle nut from the ball joint.

3. Disconnect the ball joint from the lower control arm assembly.

4. Remove the bolt retaining the ball joint to the housing. Remove the ball joint from the housing.

To install:

5. Install the ball joint into the housing and tighten the nut to 28-37 ft. lbs. (38-50 Nm).

6. Connect ball joint to the transverse link and tighten the castle nut to 29 ft. lbs. (39 Nm). Install the cotter pin in the castle nut.

7. Install the front wheels and lower the vehicle.

Lower Control Arm

REMOVAL AND INSTALLATION

Justy

1. Raise and support the vehicle safely. Remove the tire and wheel assembly.

2. Properly support the lower control arm. Remove the brake hoses as necessary. Remove the bolt that retains the lower control arm to the crossmember.

3. Remove the ball joint retaining bolt and the stabilizer tension rods. Remove the ball joint, if required.

4. Remove the lower control arm from the vehicle.

To install:

5. Install the ball joint, if removed. Install the lower control arm. Tighten the crossmember-to-control arm bolt to 43-58 ft. lbs. (59-78 Nm) only after the vehicle is on the ground with the chassis loaded.

6. Install the castle nut on the ball joint and tighten to 29 ft. lbs. (39 Nm).

7. Temporarily install the tension rod-to-control arm bolt. Then, install the tension rod-to-bracket bolt and tighten to 40-54 ft. lbs. (54-74 Nm). Now, tighten the tension rod-to-control arm bolt to 54-69 ft. lbs. (74-93 Nm).

NOTE: It is very important that the tension rod bolts be tightened in the order given in the text. If the tightening sequence is reversed, the tension rod will interfere with the bracket causing unusual noise.

8. Install the wheels. If components were replaced, have the alignment checked.

Loyale and XT

1. Raise and support the vehicle safely. Remove the tire and wheel assembly.

2. As required, remove the parking brake cable from the lower control arm assembly.

3. Remove the bolt that retains the stabilizer assembly to the lower control arm.

4. Remove the front exhaust pipe, as necessary to gain working clearance.

5. Properly support the lower control arm assembly. Remove the ball joint from its mounting.

6. Remove the lower control arm to crossmember retaining bolt. Remove the lower control arm from the vehicle.

To install:

7. Install the lower control arm. Tighten the retaining bolt to 43-51 ft. lbs. (59-69 Nm) only after the vehicle is on the ground with the chassis loaded.

8. Install the ball joint and tighten the castle nut to 18-22 ft. lbs. (25-29 Nm). Install any exhaust system components previously removed.

9. Install the stabilizer assembly and tighten the bolts to 14-22 ft. lbs. (20-29 Nm). Install the parking brake cable bracket.

10. Install the wheels, lower the vehicle and check the alignment.

Legacy

1. Raise and safely support the front of the vehicle.

2. Remove the wheel and tire assembly.

3. Disconnect the stabilizer link and the transverse link.

4. Remove the ball joint-to-housing retaining bolt and remove the ball joint end from the housing.

5. Remove the nuts (not the bolts) that retain the transverse link to the crossmember.

6. Remove the 2 bolts securing the rear of the transverse link to the chassis.

7. Remove the bolts from the transverse link and lower it from the vehicle.

To install:

8. Install the transverse link into position and loosely install the 2 bolts that retain the link to the chassis.

──────── **CAUTION** ────────
All of the retaining nuts used are of the self-locking type and must be replaced when they are removed. Failure to replace the bolts may cause the retaining bolts to work loose and cause loss of vehicle control and personal injury

9. Install the bolts used to retain the transverse link to the crossmember and loosely install the nuts.

10. Install the ball joint into the housing. Tighten the ball joint pinch bolt to 29-43 ft. lbs. (39-59 Nm).

11. Connect the stabilizer link to the transverse link and loosely install the bolts.

12. The suspension bolts must be tightened in the following order:

a. Transverse link-to-stabilizer: 14-22 ft. lbs. (20-29 Nm).

b. Transverse link-to-crossmember: 61-83 ft. lbs. (83-113 Nm).

c. Transverse link rear bushing-to-chassis: 145-217 ft. lbs. (196-294 Nm).

13. Move the transverse link back and forth until the clearance between the link and bushing is 1-1.5mm. The torque for the transverse link end bushing is 152-195 ft. lbs. (206-265 Nm).

14. Install the wheel and lower the vehicle.

SVX

1. Raise and safely support the front of the vehicle.

2. Remove the front wheel.

3. Separate the ball joint from the housing.

4. Remove the rear control arm support bolts.

5. Remove the left and right retaining bolts and lower the arm from the vehicle.

To install:

——————— CAUTION ———————

All of the retaining nuts used are of the self-locking type and must be replaced when they are removed. Failure to replace the bolts may cause the retaining bolts to work loose and cause loss of vehicle control and personal injury

6. Install the lower control arm assembly and the rear support bolts. Keep all of the bolts loose.

7. Install the ball joint to the housing and loosely install the retaining bolt.

NOTE: The suspension bolts must be tightened with the vehicle on the ground and the weight of the vehicle on the suspension.

8. Install the wheel and lower the vehicle to the ground.

9. Tighten the ball joint retaining bolt to 33-43 ft. lbs. (45-59 Nm). Tighten the rear support-to-sub frame bolts to 93-123 ft. lbs. (127-167 Nm). Tighten the lower arm rear retaining bolts to 56-73 ft. lbs. (76-100 Nm).

Stabilizer Bar

REMOVAL AND INSTALLATION

1. Raise and safely support the front of the vehicle.

2. Remove the wheels.

3. Mark the location and direction of the stabilizer mountings. This will ensure proper installation. Remove the right side ABS sensor clamp, if equipped.

4. Remove the stabilizer-to-crossmember bolts. On the SVX, remove the 2 stabilizer link bolts and remove the stabilizer link.

5. Remove the bolts that secure the stabilizer to the front transverse link.

6. Remove the jack-up plate from the crossmember and remove the stabilizer from the vehicle. On the SVX it will have to be removed from the right side.

To install:

7. Check all of the bushings for deformity or tears. Replace any bushing that shows signs of deterioration.

8. Install the bushings and housings on the stabilizer, aligning any marks before removal.

9. Install the stabilizer into position and install the retaining bolts. Tighten bolts to the following torque:

Except SVX:

Jack-up plate-to-crossmember — 17-31 ft. lbs. (23-42 Nm).

Stabilizer link-to-transverse link — 18-25 ft. lbs. (25-34 Nm).

Stabilizer-to-crossmember — 15-21 ft. lbs. (21-28 Nm).

SVX:

Stabilizer link-to-stabilizer lever — 23-31 ft. lbs. (32-42 Nm).

Stabilizer bar-to-stabilizer lever — 33-43 ft. lbs. (45-59 Nm).

Stabilizer bar-to-crossmember — 15-21 ft. lbs. (21-28 Nm).

10. Install the right side ABS sensor clamp, if removed.

11. Install the wheels and lower the vehicle.

REAR SUSPENSION

Shock Absorbers

REMOVAL AND INSTALLATION

1. Raise and support the vehicle safely. Remove the tire and wheel assembly.

2. Properly support the rear axle assembly. Loosen the upper shock absorber to chassis nuts.

3. Remove the washer and the bushing, being sure to note their correct assembly sequence for installation.

4. Remove the shock absorber to trailing arm retaining bolt. Remove the shock absorber from its mounting.

To install:

5. Install the shock absorber and tighten the bolts to specification. Be sure to properly install the washers.

6. Do not fully tighten the upper mounting nuts until the lower shock nut has been installed with the washer and the pin shoulder contracting each other.

7. Install the wheels and lower the vehicle.

MacPherson Strut

REMOVAL AND INSTALLATION

Justy

1. Raise and support the vehicle safely. Remove the tire and wheel assembly. Properly support the rear axle assembly.

2. From the upper portion of the strut mount, remove the trim cover.

3. Remove the strut to body retaining nut. Push the lower arm downward, and remove the coil spring.

4. Remove the strut to axle housing bolts. Remove the strut from the vehicle.

To install:

5. When installing coil spring, fit the lower rubber seat and coil spring end face in the coil spring seat mounting recess of the lower control arm.

6. Install the strut-to-housing bolt and tighten to 25-40 ft. lbs.

7. Install the wheels and remove the supports from under the rear axle. Lower the vehicle and test drive.

Except Justy

1. Raise and support the vehicle safely. Remove the tire and wheel assembly.

2. If equipped with air suspension, remove the cover and disconnect the air line.

3. Properly support the rear axle assembly. On Loyale and XT, remove the upper strut retaining bracket mounting bolts. On Legacy and SVX models, remove the upper strut mounting nut.

4. Remove the lower strut retaining bolts.

5. Remove the strut assembly from the vehicle.

To install:

6. On Loyale and XT, install the strut assembly and tighten the lower attaching bolts to 51-87 ft. lbs. (69-118 Nm), tighten the upper retaining bolts to 65-94 ft. lbs. (88-127 Nm). On Legacy, tighten the lower mounting bolts to 137-174 ft. lbs. (186-235 Nm) and the upper nut to 36-51 ft. lbs. (49-69 Nm). On SVX, tighten the lower mounting bolts to 98-127 ft. lbs. (132-172 Nm).

7. If equipped with air suspension, reconnect the air line. Install the wheel and tire assembly and remove the supports under the rear axle.

8. Lower the vehicle and test drive.

Springs

REMOVAL AND INSTALLATION

Justy

1. Raise and support the vehicle safely. Remove the tire and wheel assembly. Properly support the rear axle assembly.

2. Remove the strut bolt trim cover and remove the strut upper bolts.

NOTE: The rear spring is under extreme tension. Serious injury can result if the spring should fly out of the vehicle.

3. Place a floorjack under the control arm to prevent the spring from expanding. Remove the rear spindle to control arm bolt. Slowly lower the control arm until all spring pressure is released. Push the control arm downward, and remove the coil spring.

To install:

4. Place the spring in the holder cups. Ensure that the spring insulators are installed. Using a floor jack, lift up on the lower control arm to compress the spring. Install the control arm bolts and tighten to 54-69 ft. lbs. (74-93 Nm).

5. Install the rear strut and tighten the lower bolts to 72-87 ft. lbs. (98-118 Nm) and the upper nuts to 40-54 ft. lbs. (54-74 Nm).

6. Remove the rear axle supports and lower the vehicle.

Rear Control Arms

REMOVAL AND INSTALLATION

Justy

1. Raise and support the vehicle safely. Remove the tire and wheel assembly.

2. Properly support the rear axle assembly. Remove the coil spring assembly.

3. Remove the control arm to crossmember bolt. Separate the control arm from the crossmember.

4. Remove the control arm to axle housing bolt Separate the control arm from the axle housing.

5. Remove the assembly from the vehicle.

To install:

6. Install the control arm on the axle housing and tighten the bolts to 54-69 ft. lbs. (74-93 Nm).

7. Install the control arm to crossmember bolt and tighten to 43-58 ft. lbs. (59-78 Nm).

8. Install the coil spring. Install the wheels, remove the rear axle supports and lower the vehicle.

Legacy

TRAILING LINK

1. Loosen the rear wheel lugs, raise and safely support the vehicle and remove the wheel assemblies.

2. Remove the rear parking brake clamps and the ABS sensors, as required.

3. Remove the bolts retaining the trailing link to the body.

4. Remove the bolts retaining the trailing link to the rear housing.

5. Remove the trailing link from the vehicle.

6. To install the trailing link, place in position and install the bolts at each end.

7. Torque the bolts to 72-94 ft. lbs.

8. Complete the assembly.

LATERAL LINK

1. Remove the stabilizer from the lateral link.

2. Remove the parking brake cable and the ABS sensor clamp from the trailing link, as required.

3. Loosen the bolts that secure the trailing link to the bracket and remove the bolts that retain the trailing link to the rear housing.

4. If equipped with 4WD, remove the Double Offset Joint (DOJ) pin and axle shaft to provide working space.

5. Remove the front lateral link from the rear crossmember.

6. Temporarily install front lateral link to the rear crossmember and remove the rear lateral link from the crossmember.

7. To install the link, reverse the removal procedure. Torque the bolts to the following specifications:
   a. 4WD — 61-83 ft. lbs.
   b. FWD — 87-116 ft. lbs.

Loyale and XT

1. Raise and support the vehicle safely. Remove the tire and wheel assembly.

2. Properly support the rear axle assembly.

3. Remove the strut to lower control arm bolt and separate the strut from the lower control arm.

4. If equipped with 4WD, use a 0.24 in. (6mm) pin punch and drive the spring pins from the halfshaft-to-axle shaft and the halfshaft to differential assembly. While pushing downward on the inner arm, separate the halfshaft from the axle shaft. Pull the halfshaft from the differential and position it aside.

5. Disconnect and plug the brake hose from the brake line at the lower control arm.

6. Remove the outer arm-to-lower control arm bolts, then separate the lower control arm from the outer arm. Properly support the inner arm.

7. Remove the inner arm-to-crossmember bolt. Remove the lower control arm from the vehicle.

To install:

8. Install the inner arm and tighten the inner arm to crossmember bolt to 51-65 ft. lbs. (69-88 Nm). Install the outer arm and tighten the attaching bolts to 94-108 ft. lbs. (127-147 Nm).

9. Install the brake hose and line. If equipped with 4WD, reassemble the halfshaft to differential assembly using new spring pins.

10. Install the strut, remove the rear axle supports and lower the vehicle. As required, bleed the brake system.

SVX

TRAILING LINK

1. Loosen the rear wheel lugs, raise and safely support the vehicle and remove the wheel assemblies.

2. Remove the rear parking brake clamps and the ABS sensors, as required.

3. Remove the bolts retaining the trailing link to the body.

4. Remove the bolts retaining the trailing link to the rear housing.

5. Remove the trailing link from the vehicle.

To install:

6. To install the trailing link, place in position and install the bolts at each end.

7. Torque the rear link-to-housing through bolt to 80-101 ft. lbs. (137-177 Nm) and the front link through bolt to 101-130 ft. lbs. (137-177 Nm).

8. Complete the assembly by connecting the remaining components, installing the wheel and lowering the vehicle.

LATERAL LINK

1. Raise and safely support the vehicle.

2. Remove the wheel and tire assemblies. Remove the rear exhaust pipe.

3. Remove the stabilizer bar from the rear suspension.

4. Remove the parking brake cable and ABS sensor harness brackets.

5. Disconnect the parking brake cable clamp.

6. Disconnect the trailing link at the housing.

7. Disconnect the lateral links at the housing assembly.

8. Using a suitable halfshaft removing tool, carefully pry the halfshaft from the rear differential and support it with a wire from the body.

9. Place an alignment mark on the lateral link-to-crossmember bolt. This bolt must be installed in the same position or rear wheel alignment will be incorrect.

10. Remove the later link-to-rear crossmember bolts and remove the link.

To install:

11. Install the lateral link to the crossmember and loosely install the bolts.

NOTE: All of the fasteners must be tightened with the weight of the vehicle on the suspension. Be sure to align the marks made during removal on the rear lateral link bolts.

12. Connect the lateral link at the housing assembly. Loosely install the bolts.

13. Connect The trailing link at the housing and loosely install the bolts.

14. Reposition the ABS harness and the parking brake cable clips.

15. Install the rear exhaust pipe and the rear tire assemblies.

16. Lower the vehicle to the ground and tighten all fasteners to the following torques:

    a. Front lateral link-to-sub frame through bolt (bolt without cap for the end) — 72-101 ft. lbs. (98-137 Nm).

    b. Rear lateral link-to-sub frame through bolt (bolt with cap, closest to the differential) — 61-83 ft. lbs. (83-113 Nm).

    c. Trailing link-to-housing bolt — 80-101 ft. lbs. (108-137 Nm).

    d. Stabilizer link nut — 12-17 ft. lbs. (16-14 Nm).

Rear Wheel Bearings

ADJUSTMENT

2WD

1. Raise and support the vehicle safely. Remove the rear wheel assembly.

2. Temporarily tighten the axle nut to 36 ft. lbs. on all vehicles except Justy or to 29 ft. lbs. for Justy.

3. Turn the drum or disc back and forth several times to ensure that bearings are properly seated.

4. Turn the nut backwards 1/8-1/4 turn in order to obtain the correct starting point.

5. Using a spring gauge at 90 degrees to the wheel lug, check the rotating force. Specifications should be 1.9-3.2 lbs. for all vehicles except Justy or for Justy are 3.1-4.4 lbs.

6. After the adjustment is completed, bend the lock washer. After installing a new O-ring to the grease cap, install the cap.

REMOVAL AND INSTALLATION

1. Raise and support the vehicle safely. Remove the rear tire and wheel assembly.

2. If equipped with rear disc brakes, remove the caliper and properly support it.

3. Using a small prybar, remove the rear wheel grease cap.

4. Using a hammer and a punch, flatten the lock washer and loosen the axle nut. Remove the lock washer and the thrust plate. When removing the drum or disc, be careful not to drop the inner race from the outer bearing.

NOTE: If the brake drum on the Justy is difficult to remove, use wheel puller tool 9224930000 or equivalent, to remove the brake drum.

5. Using a gear puller, remove the spacer and the inner race of the inner bearing.

6. Using a brass drift and a hammer, drive the outer race of the inner bearing from the drum or disc.

7. Using a brass drift and a hammer, drive the outer race of the outer bearing from the drum or disc.

To install:

8. Clean and inspect the parts for damage, replace defective parts, if necessary.

9. Using bearing installation tool 925220000 or equivalent, for all vehicles except Justy or tool 922111000 or equivalent, for Justy, press the outer race of the inner bearing into the drum or disc until it seats against the shoulder.

10. When pressing the bearing, be sure not to exceed the load to the bearing, so as not to damage it.

11. Apply a small amount of grease to the oil seal lips, then install the oil seal until it is flush with the drum or disc.

12. Using bearing installation tool 921130000 or equivalent, for all vehicles except Justy or tool 922111000 or equivalent, for Justy, press the outer

race of the outer bearing into the drum or disc until it seats against the shoulder.

13. Apply approximately 1/8 oz. of wheel bearing grease to the inner and the outer bearings. Fill the disc or drum hub with 1 oz. of wheel bearing grease.

14. Install a new spacer O-ring, the spacer and the inner race of the inner bearing onto the trailing arm spindle.

15. When installing the spacer, be sure to face the stepped surface toward the bearing. Use a new thrust plate and lock washer.

16. To complete the installation, reverse the removal procedure. Adjust the wheel bearing.

STEERING

CAUTION

Properly disarm the air bag on vehicles equipped with the SRS system. Failure to do so can cause serious injury.

Steering Wheel

REMOVAL AND INSTALLATION

Except legacy and SVX

1. Disconnect the negative battery cable.

2. Disconnect the horn lead from the wiring harness, located beneath the instrument panel. On the XT Coupe, remove the horn pad.

NOTE: If equipped with telescopic steering wheel, remove the telescopic lever assembly.

3. Working behind the steering wheel, remove the steering wheel cover to steering wheel screws. It may be necessary to lower the column from the dash by removing the screws.

4. Lift the crash pad assembly from the front of the wheel.

5. Matchmark the steering wheel and the column for installation.

6. Remove the steering wheel retaining nut. Using a steering wheel puller tool, remove the steering wheel from the column.

To install:

7. Install the steering wheel on the column in the same position as removed. Tighten the center nut to 36-43 ft. lbs. (49-59 Nm) on Justy and

22-29 ft. lbs. (29-39 Nm) on Loyale and XT.

NOTE: Do not hammer on the steering wheel or the steering column, as damage to the collapsible column could result.

8. Install the crash pad assembly and wheel cover.

9. If the column was lowered, tighten the steering column-to-dash screws.

10. Install the telescopic lever, if removed. Connect the horn lead and install the horn pad, if removed.

Legacy and SVX

— **CAUTION** —
Properly disarm the air bag on vehicles equipped with the SRS system. Failure to do so can cause serious injury.

1. Properly disarm the air bag system, on models equipped. Disconnect the negative battery cable.

— **CAUTION** —
Wait at least 10 minutes after disarming the air bag to avoid accidental deployment.

2. Disconnect the horn lead from the wiring harness, located beneath the instrument panel. On models without air bag, remove the horn pad by pulling it off.

NOTE: If equipped with telescopic steering wheel, remove the telescopic lever assembly.

3. On models with an air bag, working behind the steering wheel, remove the steering column covers. Use a No. 30 Torx® bit and remove the air bag module retaining bolts.

4. Disconnect the air bag module connector and remove the module from the steering wheel. Place the module face up on a flat surface.

5. Matchmark the steering wheel and the column for installation.

6. Remove the steering wheel retaining nut. Using a steering wheel puller tool, remove the steering wheel from the column.

To install:

7. Install the steering wheel on the column in the same position as removed. Tighten the center nut to 22-29 ft. lbs. (29-39 Nm).

NOTE: Do not hammer on the steering wheel or the steering column, as damage to the collapsible column could result.

8. Install the crash pad or air bag assembly and the column covers.

9. Install the telescopic lever, if removed. Connect all of the electrical leads. Re-arm the air bag.

Manual Steering Rack

REMOVAL AND INSTALLATION

Justy

1. Disconnect the negative battery cable. Raise and support the vehicle safely. Remove the front tire and wheel assemblies.

2. Disconnect the universal joint coupling bolts. Remove the dust seal.

3. Using the proper tools, disconnect the tie rod ends from the knuckle arms.

4. Remove the steering rack retaining bolts. Lower the assembly and pull the pinion from the dust seal toward the engine compartment.

5. Remove the steering rack from the vehicle.

To install:

6. Installation is the reverse of the removal procedure. Tighten the rack mounting bolts to 33-43 ft. lbs. (44-59 Nm).

7. Adjust the toe-in and the turning angles to specifications.

8. Tighten the tie rod end to 18-22 ft. lbs. (25-29 Nm).

XT Coupe

1. Be sure the parking brake lever is in the released position. Disconnect the negative battery cable.

2. Raise and support the vehicle safely. Remove the front tire and wheel assemblies.

3. Remove the outer tie rod end cotter pin. Remove the castle nut. Using the proper tool, remove the tie rod end from the steering knuckle.

4. Remove the pinch bolt from the torque rod universal joint.

NOTE: Do not attempt to remove the steering rack assembly or crossmember with the pinch bolt installed to the torque rod universal joint.

5. Loosen the exhaust manifold retaining bolts. Lower the exhaust pipe.

6. Remove the steering rack retaining bolts.

7. Move the assembly toward the pinion. As the pinion shafts comes off the torque rod, rotate the steering rack rearward and remove it from the vehicle, toward the pinion.

To install:

8. Installation is the reverse of the removal procedure. Tighten the rack retaining bolts to 33-43 ft. lbs. (44-59 Nm).

9. Adjust the toe-in and the turning angles to specifications.

10. Tighten the tie rod end to steering knuckle nuts to 18-22 ft. lbs. (25-29 Nm).

Except Justy and XT Coupe

1. Disconnect the negative battery cable.

2. Raise and support the vehicle safely. Remove the front tire and wheel assemblies.

3. Remove the tie rod end cotter pin and loosen the castle nut. Using a ball joint puller, separate the tie rod ends from the housing knuckle arm.

4. If necessary, disconnect the hand brake cable hanger from the tie rod.

5. Remove the pinch bolt from the torque rod universal joint. Disconnect the pinion with the gearbox from the steering column.

6. If equipped with an hot air pipe, disconnect it.

7. Disconnect the exhaust manifold to engine bolts, pull downward on the exhaust manifold.

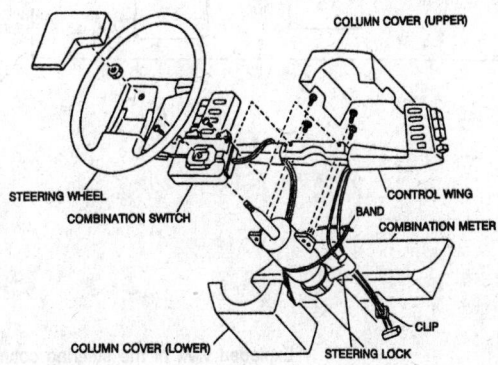

Typical steering wheel and related components

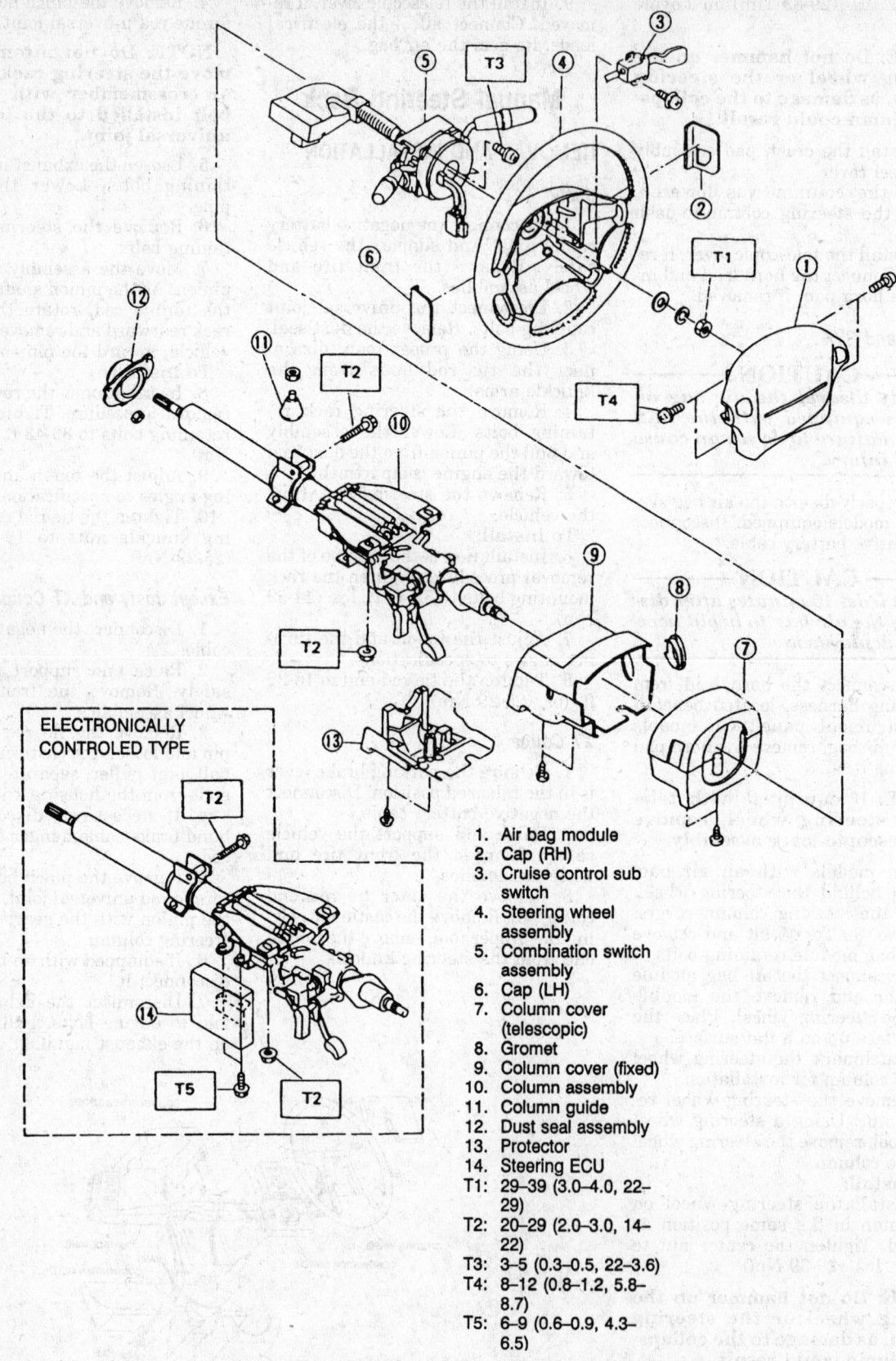

1. Air bag module
2. Cap (RH)
3. Cruise control sub switch
4. Steering wheel assembly
5. Combination switch assembly
6. Cap (LH)
7. Column cover (telescopic)
8. Gromet
9. Column cover (fixed)
10. Column assembly
11. Column guide
12. Dust seal assembly
13. Protector
14. Steering ECU
T1: 29–39 (3.0–4.0, 22–29)
T2: 20–29 (2.0–3.0, 14–22)
T3: 3–5 (0.3–0.5, 22–3.6)
T4: 8–12 (0.8–1.2, 5.8–8.7)
T5: 6–9 (0.6–0.9, 4.3–6.5)

ELECTRONICALLY CONTROLED TYPE

Exploded view of the steering column — SVX — Legacy similar

8. Remove the boot from the steering rack.

9. Remove the steering rack to crossmember bolts, pull downward on the steering rack to disconnect the pinion flange. Turn the gearbox rearward and remove it toward the left side.

10. When removing the gearbox, be careful not to damage the gearbox boot. Inspect the removed parts for wear or damage and if necessary, replace the parts.

To install:

11. To install, reverse the removal procedures. Torque the steering gearbox to crossmember bolts to 35-52 ft. lbs. (48-66 Nm).

12. Torque the pinch bolt to universal joint to 15-20 ft. lbs.

13. Torque the exhaust manifold to engine bolts to 19-22 ft. lbs. (25-29 Nm).

14. Torque the rubber coupling to steering rack bolts to 7-14 ft. lbs. (10-20 Nm).

15. Torque the tie rod end to steering knuckle nut to 18-22 ft. lbs. (26-29 Nm).

16. Adjust the toe-in and the turning angles to specifications.

17. When torquing the tie rod end to steering knuckle nuts, torque the nut 60 degrees turn further, after torquing to specification.

Power Steering Rack

REMOVAL AND INSTALLATION

1. Disconnect the negative battery cable. Remove the spare tire. If equipped with a turbocharger, remove the spare tire support.

2. If necessary, disconnect the thermo-sensor connector.

3. Raise and support the vehicle safely. Remove the front tire and wheel assemblies.

4. Disconnect the electrical connector from the oxygen sensor. Remove the front exhaust pipe assembly. If equipped with an air stove, remove it.

5. Remove the tie rod end cotter pin and loosen the castle nut. Using a ball joint puller, separate the tie rod ends from the steering knuckle arm.

6. As required, remove the jack up plate and the clamp.

7. From the power steering rack, remove the center pressure pipe, connect a vinyl hose to the pipe and

joint, then turn the steering wheel to discharge the fluid into a container.

NOTE: When discharging the power steering fluid, turn the steering wheel fully, left and right. Be sure to disconnect the other pipe and drain the fluid in the same manner.

8. Make alignment marks on the steering shaft universal joint assembly to power steering unit and the steering shaft to universal joint assembly. Remove the lower and upper universal joint to shaft bolts. Lift the universal joint assembly upward and secure it aside.

9. From the control valve of the gearbox assembly, remove the power steering **C** and **D** pressure pipes. Remove pipe **D** first and pipe **C** second.

10. From the control valve of the gearbox assembly, remove the power steering **A** and **B** pressure pipes. Remove pipe **A** first and pipe **B** second.

11. Remove the power steering gearbox to crossmember assembly bolts. Remove the gearbox assembly from the vehicle.

To install:

12. Installation is the reverse of the removal procedure. When installing the universal joint assembly, be sure to align the matchmarks.

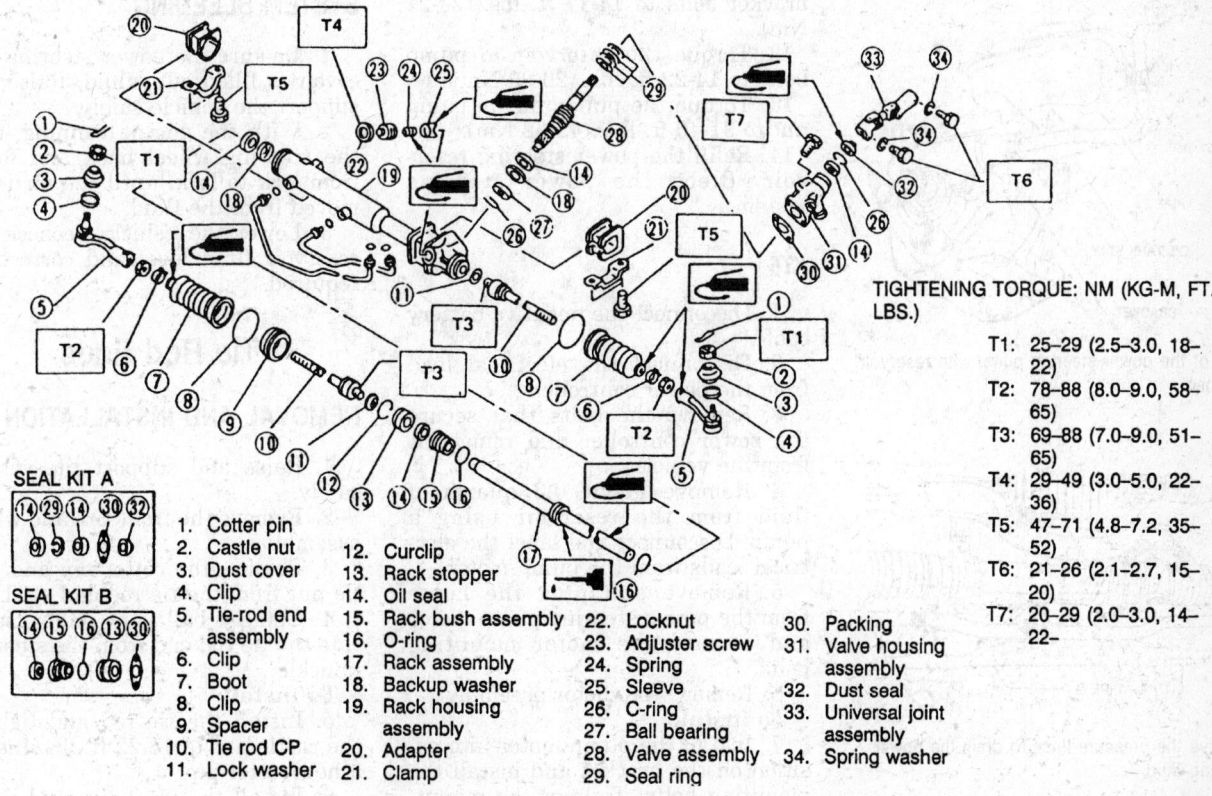

SEAL KIT A

SEAL KIT B

1. Cotter pin
2. Castle nut
3. Dust cover
4. Clip
5. Tie-rod end assembly
6. Clip
7. Boot
8. Clip
9. Spacer
10. Tie rod CP
11. Lock washer
12. Curclip
13. Rack stopper
14. Oil seal
15. Rack bush assembly
16. O-ring
17. Rack assembly
18. Backup washer
19. Rack housing assembly
20. Adapter
21. Clamp
22. Locknut
23. Adjuster screw
24. Spring
25. Sleeve
26. C-ring
27. Ball bearing
28. Valve assembly
29. Seal ring
30. Packing
31. Valve housing assembly
32. Dust seal
33. Universal joint assembly
34. Spring washer

TIGHTENING TORQUE: NM (KG-M, FT. LBS.)

T1: 25–29 (2.5–3.0, 18–22)
T2: 78–88 (8.0–9.0, 58–65)
T3: 69–88 (7.0–9.0, 51–65)
T4: 29–49 (3.0–5.0, 22–36)
T5: 47–71 (4.8–7.2, 35–52)
T6: 21–26 (2.1–2.7, 15–20)
T7: 20–29 (2.0–3.0, 14–22)

Exploded view of the steering rack — Legacy, Loyale and XT

13. Torque the power steering gearbox to crossmember bolts to 35-52 ft. lbs.

14. Torque the power steering pressure pipes 7-12 ft. lbs., the universal joint assembly to power steering gearbox bolts 16-19 ft. lbs. and the universal joint assembly to steering shaft bolts 16-19 ft. lbs.

15. Torque the tie rod end to steering knuckle nut 18-22 ft. lbs. After torquing this nut, turn it 60 degrees further.

16. Torque the wheel lug nuts to specification. Refill and bleed the power steering system. Check and adjust the toe-in and the steering angle.

Power Steering Pump

REMOVAL AND INSTALLATION

Except XT6

1. Disconnect the negative battery cable.

2. Using a siphon, drain the power steering fluid from the reservoir.

3. Loosen, but do not remove the power steering pump pulley nut. Loosen the pulley drive belts.

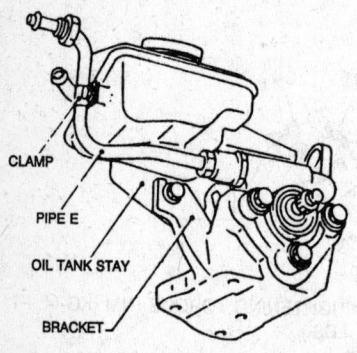

CLAMP

PIPE E

OIL TANK STAY

BRACKET

View of the power steering pump with reservoir attached

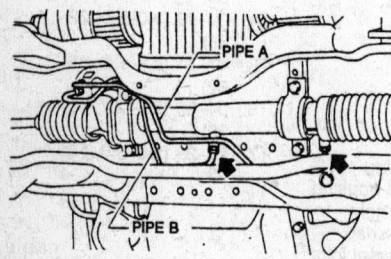

PIPE A

PIPE B

Remove the pressure lines to drain the power steering fluid

4. Remove the power steering pump pulley nut and the pulley.

5. Disconnect and plug the **A** pressure hose from the **E** pipe. Disconnect the **B** pressure hose from the oil tank.

6. When disconnecting the **A** hose, use wrenches to prevent the **E** pipe from twisting.

7. Remove the **E** hose to reservoir clamp. Loosen the reservoir to bracket bolt, then remove the **A** and **B** bolts on the upper part of the reservoir, this will allow the fluid to run out.

NOTE: To minimize the fluid loss from the reservoir, remove both bolts while the reservoir is pressed against the oil pump, then quickly remove the reservoir. It is a good idea to remove the pump and the reservoir as a unit, then separate the reservoir from the pump on a bench.

8. Remove the power steering pump to bracket bolts. Remove the pump from the vehicle.

To install:

9. Installation is the reverse of the removal procedure; be sure to use new O-rings.

10. Torque the power steering pump to bracket bolts to 22-36 ft. lbs. (29-49 Nm).

11. Torque the reservoir stay to bracket bolts to 14-17 ft. lbs. (20-24 Nm).

12. Torque the reservoir to pump bolts to 14-22 ft. lbs. (20-29 Nm).

13. Torque the pulley nut to pump nut to 31-46 ft. lbs. (42-62 Nm).

14. Refill the power steering reservoir. Bleed the power steering system.

XT6

1. Disconnect the negative battery cable.

2. Disconnect the electrical lead from the power controller.

3. Remove the bolts that secure the power controller and remove it from the vehicle.

4. Remove about 0.3 quarts of fluid from the reservoir using a pump. Disconnect and label the electrical leads from the pump motor.

5. Remove and plug the hoses from the power steering pump motor and remove the motor mounting bolts.

6. Remove the motor assembly.

To install:

7. Install the pump motor into position on the bracket and install the mounting bolts. Tighten the mounting bolts to 17-31 ft. lbs. (23-42 Nm).

8. Connect the fluid lines to the pump motor assembly and tighten the high pressure hose to 7-14 ft. lbs. (10-20 Nm). Tighten the low pressure hose to 1.4-2.2 ft. lbs. (2-3 Nm).

9. Reconnect the electrical leads to the pump motor.

10. Install the power controller. Refill the power steering fluid reservoir to the correct level.

11. Bleed the system. Check the operation of the system.

DRIVE BELT ADJUSTMENT

1. Using a pair of adjustable jawed pliers, with a piece of rag between the jaws, remove the idler cover cap by turning and pulling.

2. Turn the adjusting bolt until the correct belt tension is obtained. If removing the belt, loosen the adjusting bolt until the drive belt can be removed.

NOTE: The correct belt tension is obtained when the belt can be flexed 6-8 mm by applying finger pressure to the midpoint of the longest span.

3. After a new belt is installed and the correct tension obtained, replace the idler cap cover by pushing in and turning.

SYSTEM BLEEDING

1. Be sure the power steering reservoir is filled with fluid. Raise and support the vehicle safely.

2. With the engine running, turn the steering wheel back and forth, from lock to lock, until the air is removed from the fluid.

3. Lower the vehicle, recheck the reservoir fluid level and correct, as required.

Tie Rod Ends

REMOVAL AND INSTALLATION

1. Raise and support the vehicle safely.

2. Remove the front tire and wheel assemblies.

3. Remove the cotter pin and castle nut from the tie rod end stud.

4. Using a ball joint puller, separate the tie rod end from the steering knuckle.

To install:

5. Install the tie rod and tighten the castle nut to 18-22 ft. lbs. Install a new cotter pin.

6. Install the front tire and lower the vehicle.

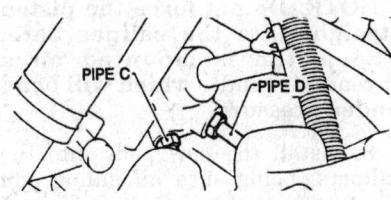

View of the power steering gear pressure lines

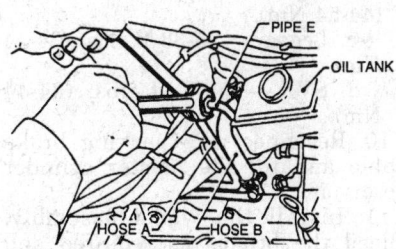

Disconnect the power steering pump hoses from the pressure lines

BRAKES

Master Cylinder

REMOVAL AND INSTALLATION

1. Disconnect the negative battery cable. Disconnect and plug the brake lines at the master cylinder.
2. It is advised to thoroughly drain the fluid from the master cylinder before performing any removal procedures.
3. If equipped with fluid level indicator, disconnect the electrical harness connector from the master cylinder.
4. Remove the master cylinder to power brake booster retaining nuts. Remove the master cylinder from its mounting.
   To install:
5. Bench bleed the master cylinder prior to installtion.
6. Install the master cylinder on the power booster and tighten the nuts to 7-13 ft. lbs. (10-18 Nm).
7. Connect the fluid level indicator. Connect the brake lines and

tighten the flarenut to 9-13 ft. lbs. (13-18 Nm).
8. Bleed the brake system as required.

Proportioning Valve

The proportioning valve is attached to a bracket and is located directly under the master cylinder. It's purpose is to provide even braking pressure to all of the wheels.

REMOVAL AND INSTALLATION

1. Disconnect the negative battery cable. Disconnect and plug the brake tubes from the proportioning valve. If equipped with an electrical connector, disconnect it.
2. Remove the proportioning valve-to-bracket bolts. Remove the valve from the vehicle.
3. Installation is the reverse of the removal procedure. Tighten the flarenuts to 9-13 ft. lbs. (13-18 Nm); the proportioning valve attaching nuts to 15-21 ft. lbs. (20-29 Nm).

Power Brake Booster

REMOVAL AND INSTALLATION

Except SVX

1. Disconnect the negative battery cable. Disconnect the vacuum hose from the power brake booster. If equipped, disconnect the connector for the brake fluid level indicator.
2. Remove the master cylinder from the brake booster. Depending upon the vehicle, it may not be necessary to completely remove the master cylinder. It may be possible to remove the retaining bolts and position the assembly aside.
3. Remove the brake pedal pushrod to power booster spring pin and clevis pin, then disconnect the pushrod from the brake pedal.
4. From under the dash, remove the power booster to firewall bolts.
5. Remove the brake booster assembly from the vehicle.
6. Installation is the reverse of the removal procedure. Tighten the attaching nuts to 9-17 ft. lbs. (13-23 Nm). Bleed the brake system, as required.

SVX

1. Disconnect the negative battery cable. Properly discharge the air conditioning system.

2. Raise and safely support the vehicle. Remove the performance rod from beneath the transaxle. It is bolted to the sub frame assembly.
3. Drain about 1 quart of transaxle fluid from the transaxle.
4. Remove the upper transaxle dipstick housing bolt and remove the lower bolt.
5. Lower the vehicle slightly and remove the cruise control actuator from the firewall.
6. Disconnect the positive battery wire from the starter.
7. Disconnect and plug the low pressure air conditioning line.
8. Disconnect the vacuum hose from the brake booster.
9. Remove the master cylinder from the booster. Inside of the vehicle, remove the snap pin and the clevis from the actuator rod.
10. Inside of the vehicle, remove the 4 nuts that secure the booster. Remove the brake booster from the engine compartment.
    To install:
11. Install the brake booster in position and install the mounting nuts. Tighten the mounting bolts to 7-13 ft. lbs. (13-18 Nm).
12. Reconnect the actuator rod at the pedal assembly. Install the master cylinder onto the booster.
13. Connect the vacuum hose at the booster. Connect the refrigerant low pressure line.
14. Connect the positive battery cable at the starter. Install the cruise control actuator.
15. Raise and safely support the vehicle. Install the transaxle dipstick housing. Install the performance rod.
16. Lower the vehicle. Properly recharge the air conditioning system.
17. Fill the transaxle to the proper level. Connect the negative battery cable.

Brake Caliper

REMOVAL AND INSTALLATION

Front

1. Raise and support the vehicle safely. Remove the front wheels.
2. Remove the brake hose from the caliper body and plug the hose to prevent the entrance of dirt or moisture.
3. Remove the hand brake cable and brake pads. Remove the caliper assembly by pulling it out of the support. Do not remove the guide pin unless it it damaged.

To install:

4. Rotate the piston until the notch at the head of the piston is vertical.

5. Install the hand brake cable and brake pads. Install the caliper assembly on the support and tighten the support bolt to 36-51 ft. lbs. (49-69 Nm).

6. Connect the brake hose and tighten the fitting to 11-15 ft. lbs. (15-21 Nm).

7. Bleed the brake system. Install the wheels and lower the vehicle. Check the fluid level in the master cylinder.

Rear

1. Raise and support the vehicle safely. Remove the rear wheels.

2. Disconnect and plug the brake hose from the caliper body.

3. Remove the bolts securing the caliper to the support and remove the caliper.

To install:

4. Install the caliper and tighten the attaching bolts to 34-43 ft. lbs. (46-58 Nm).

5. Connect the brake hose and tighten the fitting to 12-14 ft. lbs. (16-20 Nm).

6. Bleed the brake system. Install the rear wheels and lower the vehicle. Check the fluid level in the master cylinder.

Disc Brake Pads

REMOVAL AND INSTALLATION

Front

1. Raise and support the vehicle safely. Remove the wheel assemblies.

2. Release the parking brake and disconnect the cable from the caliper lever.

3. Remove the lock pin bolts from the lower front of the caliper.

4. Rotate the caliper on the support, swinging it upward and aside.

5. Remove the brake disc pads, noting the position of the shim pads and pad clips.

To install:

6. Inspect the brake rotor, calipers and retaining components. Correct as necessary.

7. Remove a small portion of brake fluid from the master cylinder reservoir. With an appropriate tool, turn the caliper piston clockwise into the cylinder bore and align the notches.

Be sure the boot is not twisted or pinched.

NOTE: Do not force the piston straight into the caliper bore. The piston is mounted on a threaded spindle which will bend under pressure.

8. Install the new pads into the calipers, being sure all shims and clips are in their original positions.

9. Swing the calipers down into position and install the lock pin bolts. Tighten the lock pin bolt to the following specifications:

   a. Justy — 16-23 ft. lbs. (22-31 Nm).

   b. Loyale and XT — 33-40 ft. lbs. (44-54 Nm).

   c. Legacy — 25-33 ft. lbs. (34-44 Nm).

   d. SVX — 25-33 ft. lbs. (34-44 Nm).

10. Reconnect the parking brake cable and fill the master cylinder reservoir.

11. Install the wheel assembly. Bleed the brakes as required and lower the vehicle. Road test the vehicle.

Rear

1. Raise and safely support the vehicle. Remove the wheel assemblies.

2. Disconnect the brake pad lining wear indicator, if equipped. Remove any anti-rattle springs or clips, if equipped.

3. Pull the caliper away from the center of the vehicle to push piston into caliper bore. Remove the caliper guide pins and remove the caliper from the rotor. Hang the caliper from the body with a support wire.

4. Slide the disc pads from the caliper, noting any shims or shields behind the pad.

NOTE: If equipped with parking brake, use a suitable tool to rotate the piston back into the caliper bore. If not equipped with parking brake, the piston can be pushed straight back into the bore.

5. Push the piston into the caliper bore. To install the pads, position any shims or shields in place and reverse the removal procedure.

6. Tighten the lower caliper bolt to the following torque:

   a. Loyale and XT — 16-23 ft. lbs. (22-31 Nm).

   b. Legacy — 12-17 ft. lbs. (16-24 Nm).

   c. SVX — 12-17 ft. lbs. (16-24 Nm).

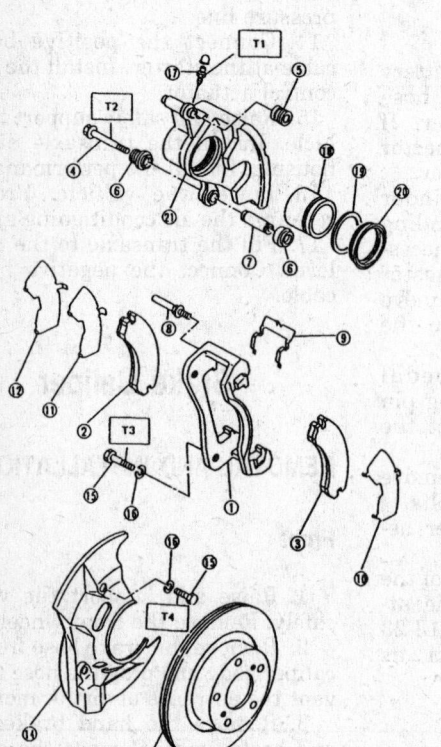

1. Support
2. Pad compl. (inside)
3. Pad compl. (outside)
4. Lock pin
5. Guide pin boot
6. Lock pin boot
7. Lock pin sleeve
8. Guide pin
9. Pad clip
10. Outer shim
11. Inner shim
12. Shim
13. Front brake disc
14. Front disc cover
15. Bolt
16. Washer
17. Air bleeder screw
18. Piston
19. Piston seal
20. Piston boot
21. Caliper body

TIGHTENING TORQUE: NM (KG-M, FT. LBS.)

T1: 7-9 (0.7-0.9, 5.1-6.5)

T2: 34-44 (3.5-4.5, 25-33)

T3: 69-88 (7-9, 51-65)

T4: 10-18 (1.0-1.8, 7.2-13.0)

Exploded view of the front disc brake assembly

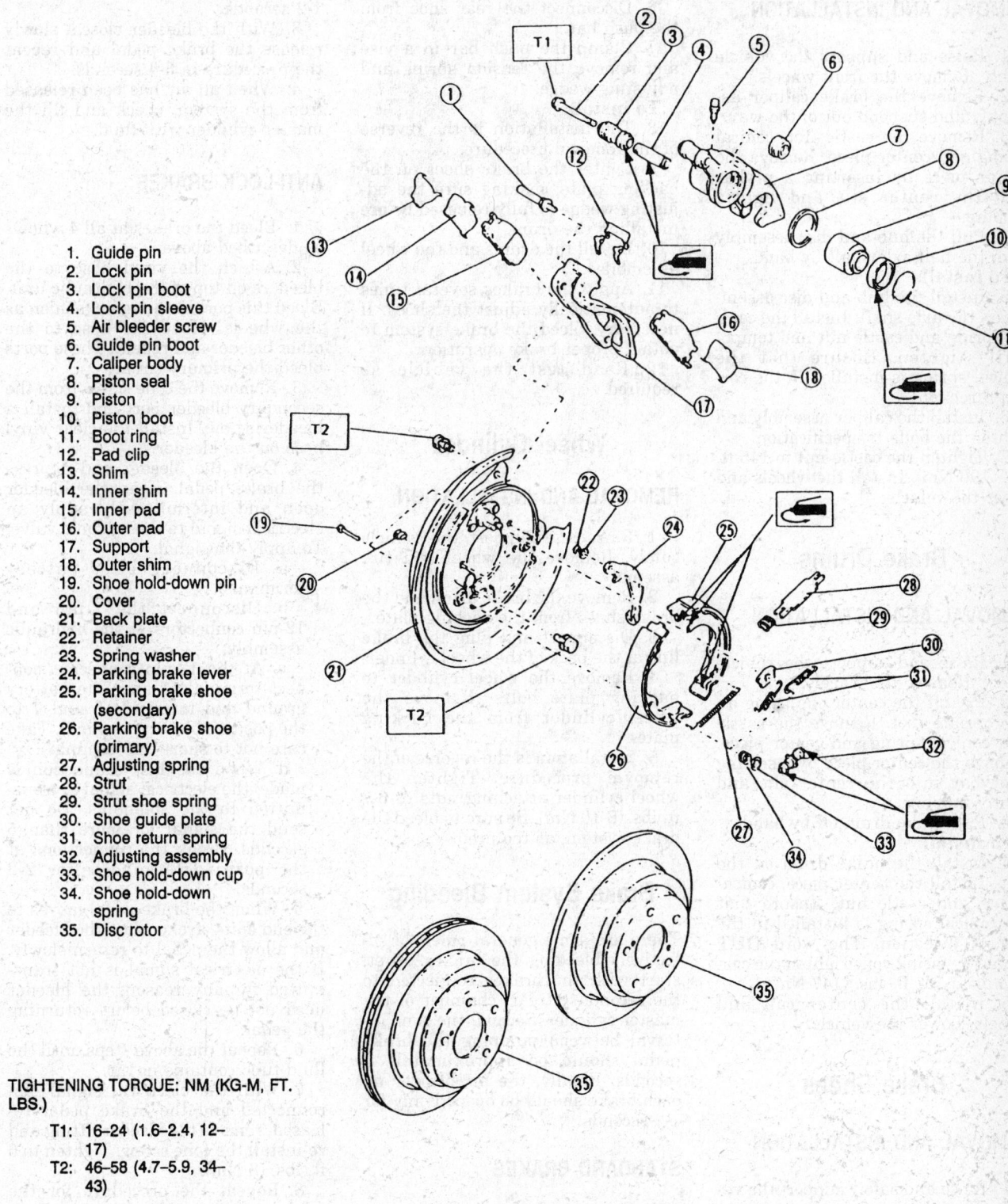

1. Guide pin
2. Lock pin
3. Lock pin boot
4. Lock pin sleeve
5. Air bleeder screw
6. Guide pin boot
7. Caliper body
8. Piston seal
9. Piston
10. Piston boot
11. Boot ring
12. Pad clip
13. Shim
14. Inner shim
15. Inner pad
16. Outer pad
17. Support
18. Outer shim
19. Shoe hold-down pin
20. Cover
21. Back plate
22. Retainer
23. Spring washer
24. Parking brake lever
25. Parking brake shoe (secondary)
26. Parking brake shoe (primary)
27. Adjusting spring
28. Strut
29. Strut shoe spring
30. Shoe guide plate
31. Shoe return spring
32. Adjusting assembly
33. Shoe hold-down cup
34. Shoe hold-down spring
35. Disc rotor

TIGHTENING TORQUE: NM (KG-M, FT. LBS.)

T1: 16–24 (1.6–2.4, 12–17)

T2: 46–58 (4.7–5.9, 34–43)

Exploded view of the rear disc brake assembly

Brake Rotor

REMOVAL AND INSTALLATION

1. Raise and support the vehicle safely. Remove the front wheels.
2. Remove the brake caliper assembly and suspend out of the way.
3. Remove the castle nut, conical spring and center piece. Remove the center piece by inserting a prybar into the center slit and lightly tapping.
4. Pull the hub and disc assembly from the half axle shaft by hand.
To install:
5. Install the hub and disc assembly on the axle shaft. Install the conical spring and castle nut and temporarily tighten. Ensure that the conical spring is installed in the correct direction.
6. Install the caliper assembly and tighten the bolts to specification.
7. Tighten the castle nut to 145 ft. lbs. (196 Nm). Install the wheels and lower the vehicle.

Brake Drums

REMOVAL AND INSTALLATION

1. Raise and support the vehicle safely. Remove the wheels.
2. Pry off the center cap using an appropriate tool. Remove the castle nut, conical spring and center piece. Remove the center piece by inserting a prybar into the center slit and lightly tapping.
3. Pull brake drum off by hand.
To install:
4. Install the brake drum on the axle. Install the center piece, conical spring and castle nut. Ensure that the conical spring is installed in the correct direction. The word **OUT** should be facing you. Tighten the castle nut to 108 ft. lbs. (147 Nm).
5. Install the center cap and wheels. Lower the vehicle.

Brake Shoes

REMOVAL AND INSTALLATION

1. Raise and safely support the vehicle. Remove the rear wheels.
2. Remove the brake drums.
3. Remove the adjusting wedge spring and the upper and lower return springs.
4. Remove the hold-down springs.

5. Lift the brake shoes from the backing plate and disconnect the parking brake, if equipped.
6. Disconnect the rear shoe from the push bar.
7. Clamp the push bar in a vise and remove the tension spring and adjusting wedge.
To install:
8. The installation is the reverse of the removal procedure.
9. Center the brake shoes on the backing plate, making sure the adjusting wedge is fully released before installing the drum.
10. Install the drums and the wheel assemblies.
11. Apply the brakes several times to automatically adjust the shoes. If necessary, bleed the brake system to obtain proper brake operation.
12. Road test the vehicle as required.

Wheel Cylinder

REMOVAL AND INSTALLATION

1. Raise and support the vehicle safely. Remove the wheel and tire assembly.
2. Remove the brake drum and the brake shoes from the backing plate.
3. Disconnect and plug the brake line at the back of the wheel cylinder.
4. Remove the wheel cylinder to backing plate bolts. Remove the wheel cylinder from the backing plate.
5. Installation is the reverse of the removal procedure. Tighten the wheel cylinder attaching nuts to 6-7 ft. lbs. (8-10 Nm). Be sure to bleed the brake system, as required.

Brake System Bleeding

There are some general rules for effectively bleeding the brakes. First, start with the brakes connected to the secondary (rear) chamber of the master cylinder. Second, the time interval between pumping the brake pedal should be approximately 3 seconds. Finally, the air bleeder on each brake should be opened only for 1-2 seconds.

STANDARD BRAKES

1. Fit one end of a vinyl tube into the air bleeder and put the other end into a brake fluid container.
2. Starting with the wheel that is farthest from the master cylinder, slowly depress the brake pedal and

keep it depressed. Then, open the air bleeder to discharge air together with the fluid. Keep the bleeder open only 1-2 seconds.
3. With the bleeder closed, slowly release the brake pedal and repeat the procedure in 3-4 seconds.
4. When all air has been released from the system, check and fill the master cylinder with fluid.

ANTI-LOCK BRAKES

1. Bleed the brakes at all 4 wheels as described above.
2. Attach the vinyl hose to the bleeders on top of the hydraulic unit. Bleed this port in the same fashion as the wheels. Move the hose to the other bleeder and repeat. These ports bleed the primary circuit.
3. Remove the cone screw from the secondary bleeder port and install a bleeder screw. Install the clear vinyl hose on the bleeder.
4. Open the bleeder and depress the brake pedal. Keep the bleeder open and intermittently apply an electrical signal to the solenoid valve. To apply the signal:
   a. Disconnect both battery terminals.
   b. Disconnect the 2-pin and 12-pin connectors at the hydraulic assembly.
   c. At the 12-pin connector, connect terminals 1 and 3 to battery ground and terminals 5 and 7 to the positive battery terminal. Take care not to short the terminals.
   d. When the last connection is made, the electrical signal is transmitted to the solenoids. Do not send the signal for more than 5 seconds. Break the connections at the positive terminal after 2-3 seconds.
5. When the brake pedal moves to the end of its stroke, close the bleeder and allow the pedal to return slowly. If the electrical signal is not transmitted for any reason, the bleeder need not be closed before returning the pedal.
6. Repeat the above steps until the fluid tube contains no air.
7. With the electrical signal disconnected and the brake pedal released, remove the bleeder fitting and re-install the cone screw. Tighten to 6 ft. lbs. (8 Nm).
8. Repeat the procedure for the other secondary bleeder port. Both secondary ports must be bled.
9. Carefully remove the jumper wires and reconnect the connectors to the hydraulic unit. Connect the battery cables with the ignition **OFF**.

Anti-Lock System Brake Service

PRECAUTIONS

• Certain components within the ABS system are not intended to be serviced or repaired individually. Only those components with removal and Installation procedures should be serviced.

• Do not use rubber hoses or other parts not specifically specified for the ABS system. When using repair kits, replace all parts included in the kit. Partial or incorrect repair may lead to functional problems and require the replacement of components.

• Lubricate rubber parts with clean, fresh brake fluid to ease assembly. Do not use lubricated shop air to clean parts; damage to rubber components may result.

• Use only DOT 3 brake fluid from an unopened container.

• If any hydraulic component or line is removed or replaced, it may be necessary to bleed the entire system.

• A clean repair area is essential. Always clean the reservoir and cap thoroughly before removing the cap. The slightest amount of dirt in the fluid may plug an orifice and impair the system function. Perform repairs after components have been thoroughly cleaned; use only denatured alcohol to clean components. Do not allow ABS components to come into contact with any substance containing mineral oil; this includes used shop rags.

• The Anti-Lock control unit is a microprocessor similar to other computer units in the vehicle. Ensure that the ignition switch is **OFF** before removing or installing controller harnesses. Avoid static electricity discharge at or near the controller.

• If any arc welding is to be done on the vehicle, the Anti-Lock Control Unit (ALCU) connectors should be disconnected before welding operations begin.

Hydraulic Unit

REMOVAL AND INSTALLATION

1. Disconnect the negative battery cable. Disconnect the harness connectors at the hydraulic unit.

2. Remove the emission canister from the engine compartment.

3. Disconnect the inlet and outlet lines from the top of the actuator. Label the lines for installation. Immediately plug the lines and ports to prevent the entry of dirt.

4. Remove the screw holding the ABS relay cover and remove the cover. Remove the bolts holding the hydraulic unit bracket to the body. Note that one of these bolts has the pump motor ground attached.

5. Lift the actuator and bracket clear of the vehicle. Keep the unit upright at all times. The brackets and relays may be removed for transfer to a replacement unit.

6. Except for the 2 relays, the hydraulic unit contains no replaceable components. Never attempt to disassemble the unit.

   To install:

7. Install the relays and brackets. The nuts on the bushing bolts holding the hydraulic unit to the brackets should be tightened to 6 ft. lbs. (8 Nm).

8. Install the hydraulic unit and brackets and tighten the nuts to 25 ft. lbs. (34 Nm). Make sure the ground is attached.

9. Check that the relays are firmly seated and install the relay cover. Connect the brake lines and tighten to 11 ft. lbs. (15 Nm).

10. Install the canister in the engine compartment. Bleed all 4 wheels, then bleed the hydraulic ac-

TIGHTENING TORQUE: NM (KG-M, FT. LBS.)

T1: 1.2–1.5 (0.12–0.15, 0.9–1.1)
T2: 13–18 (1.3–1.8, 9–13)
T3: 23–42 (2.3–4.3, 17–31)
T4: 7–9 (0.7–0.9, 5.1–6.5)
T5: 15–20 (1.5–2.0, 11–14)
T6: 2–3 (0.2–0.3, 1.4–2.2)

1. Hydraulic control unit assembly
2. Motor relay
3. Valve relay
4. Hydraulic control unit bracket (A)
5. Clamp
6. Inlet joint RH
7. Inlet joint LH
8. Joint bracket
9. Rear LH outlet
10. Front RH outlet
11. Front LH outlet
12. Rear RH outlet
13. Hydraulic control unit bracket (B)
14. Connector

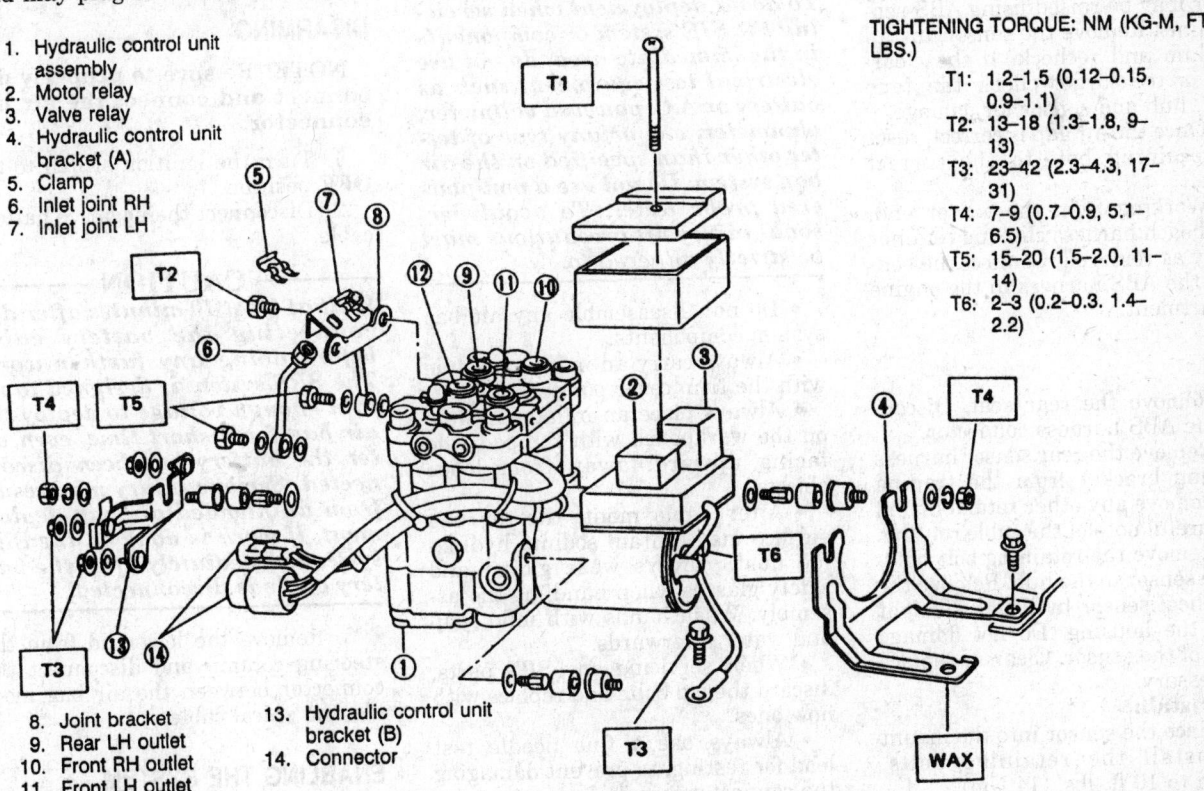

Removing the ABS hydraulic unit

tuator primary and secondary circuits.

Wheel Speed Sensor

REMOVAL AND INSTALLATION

Front

1. Disconnect the negative battery cable. Disconnect the speed sensor harness in the engine compartment.
2. Remove the bolts holding the sensor harness brackets. Take careful note of placement and location of the harness retainers.
3. Remove the sensor retaining bolt at the front hub. Remove the front wheel speed sensor by lifting it straight out of the housing. Do not damage the tip of the sensor. Clean or replace as necessary.

To install:
4. Place the sensor into the mount and install the retaining bolts. Tighten to 10 ft. lbs. (14 Nm).
5. Remove the caliper and brake disc. Use a non-ferrous feeler gauge to check the clearance between the top of the sensor and the tone wheel. Check the clearance at several locations on the hub. Clearance should be 0.039-0.059 in. (1.0-1.5mm).
6. If the air gap is too small, the sensor may be raised using ABS sensor shims. Remove the sensor, install the shim and recheck. If the clearance is too large, check the tone wheel, hub and sensor for damage.
7. Once the air gap is correct, reset the retaining bolt to the correct torque.
8. Working from the sensor end, install each harness clip and retainer exactly as removed. Connect the sensor to the ABS harness in the engine compartment.

Rear

1. Remove the rear seat. Disconnect the ABS harness connector.
2. Remove the rear sensor harness retaining bracket from the trailing link. Remove any other retainers and take careful note of the cable routing.
3. Remove the retaining bolt holding the sensor to the hub. Remove the rear wheel sensor by lifting straight out of the housing. Do not damage the tip of the sensor. Clean or replace as necessary.

To install:
4. Place the sensor into the mount and install the retaining bolts. Tighten to 10 ft. lbs. (14 Nm).
5. Remove the caliper and brake disc. Use a non-ferrous feeler gauge

to check the clearance between the top of the sensor and the tone wheel. Check the clearance at several locations on the hub. Clearance should be 0.031-0.051 in. (0.8-1.3mm).
6. If the air gap is too small, the sensor may be raised using ABS sensor shims. Remove the sensor, install the shim and recheck. If the clearance is too large, check the tone wheel, hub and sensor for damage.
7. Once the air gap is correct, reset the retaining bolt to the correct torque.
8. Working from the sensor end, install each harness clip and retainer exactly as removed. Connect the sensor to the ABS harness in the engine compartment.

CHASSIS ELECTRICAL

Air Bag

PRECAUTIONS

—— **CAUTION** ——
To avoid deployment when servicing the SIR system or components in the immediate area, do not use electrical test equipment such as battery or A.C. powered voltmeter, ohmmeter, etc. or any type of tester other than specified on the air bag system. Do not use a non-powered probe tester. To avoid personal injury all precautions must be strictly adhered to.

• Do not disassemble any air bag system components.
• Always carry an inflator module with the trim cover pointed away.
• Always place an inflator module on the workbench with the pad side facing upward, away from loose objects.
• After deployment, the air bag surface may contain sodium hydroxide dust. Always wear gloves and safety glasses when handling the assembly. Wash hands with mild soap and water afterwards.
• When servicing any SRS parts, discard the old bolts and replace with new ones.
• Always use a fine needle test lead for testing, to prevent damaging the connector terminals.
• Never disconnect any electrical connection with the ignition switch

ON unless instructed to do so in a test.
• Before disconnecting the negative battery cable, make a record of the contents memorized by each memory system like the clock, audio, etc., when service or repairs are completed make certain to reset these memory systems.
• Always wear a grounded wrist static strap when servicing any control module or component labeled with a Electrostatic Discharge (ESD) sensitive device symbol.
• Avoid touching module connector pins.
• Leave new components and modules in the shipping package until ready to install them.
• Always touch a vehicle ground after sliding across a vehicle seat or walking across vinyl or carpeted floors to avoid static charge damage.
• All sensors are specifically calibrated to a particular series. The sensors, mounting brackets and wiring harness must never be modified from original design.
• Never strike or jar a sensor, or deployment could happen.
• The inflator module must be deployed before it is scrapped.
• Any visible damage to sensors requires component replacement.

DISARMING

NOTE: Be sure to properly disconnect and connect the air bag connector.

1. Turn the ignition switch to the **OFF** position.
2. Disconnect the negative battery cable.

—— **CAUTION** ——
Wait at least 10 minutes after disconnecting the battery cable before doing any further work. The SRS system is designed to retain enough voltage to deploy the air bag for a short time, even after the battery has been disconnected. Serious injury may result from unintended air bag deployment, if work is done on the SRS system immediately after the battery cable is disconnected.

3. Remove the lower lid from the steering column and disconnect the connector between the air bag module and spiral cable.

ENABLING THE SYSTEM

1. Reconnect the connector between the air bag module and spiral

cable. Then install the lower steering column lid.

2. Reconnect the negative battery cable.

3. Turn the ignition switch to the **ON** position and observe the SRS warning light. The SRS warning light should illuminate for approximately 7 seconds, turn OFF and remain OFF for at least 45 seconds.

4. If the SRS warning light function as indicated in Step 3, the SRS system is functioning properly.

Blower Motor

REMOVAL AND INSTALLATION

Justy

1. Disconnect the negative battery cable.

2. Remove the coupler that connects the instrument panel harness to the blower motor.

3. Remove the coupler that connects the resistor to the instrument panel harness.

4. Detach the blower assembly. Remove the screws retaining the blower motor to the blower assembly.

5. Remove the motor assembly. Remove the nut retaining the fan to the motor assembly.

To install:

6. Install the motor assembly and tighten the nuts to specification.

7. Install the couplers that connect the resistor to the instrument panel and the instrument panel to the blower motor.

8. Connect the negative battery cable.

XT Coupe, Legacy and SVX

NOTE: Depending upon working clearance the air conditioning system may have to be discharged in order to service the blower motor. If this is the case, be sure to observe all the required safety precautions when discharging and recharging the air conditioning system.

1. Disconnect the negative battery cable.

2. Remove the lower instrument panel cover on the passenger side of the vehicle.

3. Remove the glove box assembly, as required for working clearance.

4. Remove the heater duct, if not equipped with air conditioning.

5. If equipped with air conditioning, separate the evaporator from the blower assembly.

6. Disconnect the blower motor harness and the resistor electrical harness connector.

7. Remove the blower motor retaining bolts. Remove the blower motor assembly from its mounting.

To install:

8. Install the blower motor retaining bolts and tighten to 4-7 ft. lbs. Connect the blower motor harness and the resistor electrical harness connector.

9. Install the evaporator to the blower assembly as required. Install the heater duct as required. Install the glove box.

10. Install the lower instrument panel cover and connect the negative battery cable.

Loyale

NOTE: Depending upon working clearance the air conditioning system may have to be discharged in order to service the blower motor. If this is the case, be sure to observe all the required safety precautions when discharging and recharging the air conditioning system.

1. Disconnect the negative battery cable.

2. Remove the lower instrument panel cover on the passenger side of the vehicle. Remove the glove box assembly, as required for working clearance.

3. If equipped with a vacuum actuator, set the control lever to the **CIRC** position and disconnect the vacuum hose from the assembly. Remove the actuator from its mounting.

4. Remove the heater duct, if not equipped with air conditioning.

5. If equipped with air conditioning, separate the evaporator from the blower assembly.

6. Disconnect the blower motor harness and the resistor electrical harness connector.

7. Remove the blower motor retaining bolts. Remove the blower motor assembly from its mounting. As required, separate the fan from the blower motor.

To install:

8. Install the blower motor and tighten the retaining bolts to specification. Connect the blower motor harness and the resistor electrical harness connector.

9. Install the evaporator to the blower assembly as required. Install the heater duct as required. Install the glove box.

10. Install the vacuum actuator and connect the vacuum line. Install the lower instrument panel cover and connect the negative battery cable.

Windshield Wiper Motor

REMOVAL AND INSTALLATION

Justy

1. Disconnect the negative battery cable.

2. At the wiper motor, disconnect the electrical connector.

3. Remove the wiper motor to cowl bolts.

4. Separate the wiper link from the motor.

5. If necessary, replace the wiper motor.

To install:

6. Install the wiper motor and tighten the cowl bolts. Install the wiper link on the motor. Tighten the bolts to 65 inch lbs. (7.4 Nm).

7. Connect the electrical connector and the negative battery cable. Check for proper operation.

Except Justy

1. Disconnect the negative battery cable.

2. Remove the wiper blades from the wiper arms by pulling the retaining lever up and sliding the blade away from the arm.

3. Slide the covering boot up the wiper arm.

4. Remove the wiper arms to linkage nuts and the arms.

5. Disconnect the electrical wiring connectors from the wiper motor.

6. Remove the cowl to body screws and the cowl from the vehicle.

7. Find or fabricate a ring which has the same diameter as the outer diameter of the plastic joint that retains the linkage to the wiper motor. Force the ring down over the joint to force the 4 plastic retaining jaws inward, then disconnect and remove the linkage.

8. Remove the wiper motor to firewall bolts and the motor.

To install:

9. Install the wiper motor and tighten the attaching bolts. Tighten the bolts to 65 inch lbs. (7.4 Nm).

10. Install the wiper linkage. Install the cowl. Connect the wiper electrical wiring harness.

11. Connect the negative battery cable and install the wiper arms after the ignition switch has been on for a few seconds to put the linkage in the parked position.

Rear Window Wiper Motor

REMOVAL AND INSTALLATION

1. At the rear window, pull the wiper blade outward from the arm and press down on the clip, then remove the blade from the arm.

2. Remove the wiper arm cover.

3. Loosen the wiper arm-to-wiper assembly nut, then remove the nut and the arm from the assembly.

4. Remove the wiper assembly-to-rear gate cap, nut and cushion.

5. From inside of the rear gate, remove the wiper motor assembly trim panel.

6. Disconnect the electrical connector from the wiper motor assembly.

7. Remove the wiper motor assembly-to-rear gate bolts and the motor assembly from the rear gate.

8. If necessary, replace the wiper motor.

9. To install, reverse the above procedures. Tighten the wiper motor bolts to 65 inch lbs. (7.4 Nm). With the rear wiper motor switch in the OFF position, install the wiper arm blade so it is positioned 25mm above the rear glass molding.

Instrument Cluster

REMOVAL AND INSTALLATION

Justy

1. Disconnect the negative battery cable. Remove the steering wheel.

2. Remove the defroster duct assembly.

3. Disconnect the heater control cable from the inside/outside air selector rod at the heater unit.

4. Disconnect the speedometer cable. Disconnect the electrical harness connectors.

5. Remove the covers for the instrument cluster retaining bolts.

6. Remove the instrument cluster retaining bolts. Remove the instrument cluster from its mounting.

To install:

7. Install the instrument cluster and tighten the retaining bolts securely. Install the screw covers.

8. Connect the speedometer cable and electrical harness.

9. Install the heater control cable and the defroster duct assembly.

10. Install the steering wheel and connect the negative battery cable.

XT Coupe

1. Disconnect the negative battery cable. Remove the lower cover on the driver's side. Remove the side ventilation duct.

2. Open the fuse box lid. Remove the fuse box to instrument panel screws and the fuse box.

3. Remove the lower cover on the passenger's side. Using a medium prybar, pry the upper cover, at 3 points, from the instrument panel.

4. Remove the console. Remove the steering column assembly, the combination meter and the control wing as a unit.

5. Disconnect the electrical harness connectors from the radio and other necessary components.

6. Remove the instrument panel to chassis bolts and the instrument panel from the vehicle.

To install:

7. Install the instrument panel and tighten the bolts securely. Connect the electrical harness connector.

8. Install the steering column and console. Install the lower and upper instrument panel covers.

9. Install the fuse box, the side ventilation duct and the lower instrument panel cover on the drivers side. Connect the negative battery cable.

Legacy, Loyale

1. Disconnect the negative battery cable.

2. Remove the bolts securing the steering column and pull it down.

3. Disconnect the electrical wiring connectors, then remove the cluster visor screws and the visor.

4. Remove the cluster retaining screws, then pull the cluster out far enough to disconnect the speedometer cable and electrical connectors from behind, then remove the cluster assembly from the vehicle.

To install:

5. Install the instrument cluster. Connect all electrical connectors and the speedometer cable. Tighten the attaching screws securely.

6. Install the cluster visor screws and the visor. Lift the steering column and tighten the bolts to specification. Connect the negative battery cable.

SVX

1. Disconnect the negative battery cable. Properly disarm the air bag.

2. Move the steering wheel to its lowest tilt position. Remove the lower steering column cover.

3. Remove the lower cluster cover and the screws that retain the cluster visor.

4. Disconnect the clock while pulling the visor away from the cluster.

5. Remove the screws that retain the cluster and tilt the cluster forward. Disconnect the electrical leads.

6. Remove the cluster from the vehicle.

To install:

7. Install the cluster in position and connect the electrical leads.

8. Install the cluster retaining screws and install the cluster visor. Be sure to connect the clock.

9. Install the lower cluster cover panel and the lower steering column cover.

10. Connect the negative battery cable.

Gauges and Printed Circuit Board

REMOVAL AND INSTALLATION

The individual gauges and the printed circuit board can be removed after the removal of the instrument cluster. The circuit board is retained

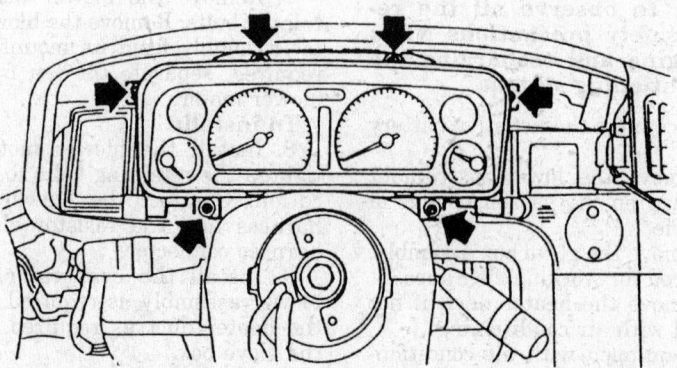

Removing the instrument cluster — SVX

by nuts and the individual gauges are retained by screws.

Headlight Switch

REMOVAL AND INSTALLATION

XT

The headlight switch is a part of a lighting switch assembly, installed on a control wing at the left side of the steering wheel.

1. Disconnect the negative battery terminal from the battery.
2. Remove the lower steering column (upper/lower) cover screws and the upper/lower covers from the column.
3. Remove the steering wheel center cover, the steering wheel-to-shaft nut and the steering wheel from the steering column.
4. Disconnect the electrical harness-to-steering column clip and band.
5. Remove the combination switch-to-steering column screws and the switch assembly from the steering wheel.
6. Remove the left control wing-to-steering column bolts and the left control wing from the steering column.
7. Remove the control wing case screws and separate the cases from each other; this will provide access to the headlight switch.
8. To replace the headlight switch knob, perform the following procedures:

   a. Using a pin rod, lightly push the pawl (inside the switch knob) inward and pull the knob outward.

NOTE: When removing the switch knob, be careful not to damage the switch brush.

   b. To install the knob onto the switch, place the knob on the switch, place a finger on the back side of the switch and squeeze the knob onto the switch.
9. If necessary, replace the headlight switch.
10. To install, reverse the removal procedure.

NOTE: When reassembling the control wing cases; be careful not to get the electrical harness caught between the cases.

Combination Switch

REMOVAL AND INSTALLATION

On all models except the XT, the combination switch contains the switches for the turn signal, lighting and wiper/washer functions of the vehicle. The XT models do not control the headlights from this switch, but retain the other functions. The stalk assemblies are mounted to a main switch body located on the steering column. Once the assembly is removed the individual switches can be removed. On all models except the SVX there are 2 stalk controls, on the SVX there are 3 stalk controls.

1. Disarm the air bag, if equipped. Disconnect the negative battery cable. Remove the lower cover to instrument panel screws and the lower cover.
2. Remove the covers to steering column screws and the upper and lower column covers.
3. Remove the steering wheel cover and the nut. Using a steering wheel puller tool, remove the steering wheel from the steering column.
4. Remove the electrical harness to steering column clip and band fitting, then disconnect the electrical connectors.
5. Remove the combination switch to control wing bracket screws on XT, on other models remove the switch mounting screws. Remove the switch assembly from its mounting.

   To install:
6. Install the combination switch and tighten the bracket screws securely. Connect the electrical harness.
7. Install the steering wheel assembly and tighten the center nut to specification. Install the steering column covers and the lower instrument panel cover.
8. Connect the negative battery cable. Check for proper operation.

Ignition Switch

REMOVAL AND INSTALLATION

NOTE: The ignition switch is mounted to the steering column using shear bolts. These bolts are constructed so the heads shear off when the bolt is torqued.

1. Disconnect the negative battery cable. Remove the steering wheel.
2. Remove the upper and lower steering column covers from the steering column.

3. Remove the hazard knob.
4. Drill a pilot hole into the shear bolts, then using a screw extractor, remove the screws from the steering column.
5. Remove the ignition switch from the steering column.

   To install:
6. Install the ignition switch using new shear bolts.
7. Install the hazard knob, steering column covers and the steering wheel.
8. Connect the negative battery cable and check the switch for proper operation.

Stoplight Switch

REMOVAL AND INSTALLATION

The stoplight switch is located on the brake pedal bracket, under the instrument panel. The switch is held in place by 2 locknuts, by which all adjustment is accomplished. To replace the switch, the wiring is disconnected, the locknuts are loosened and the switch removed.

After installation, the travel to operate the switch plunger should be adjusted to 0.071-0.130 in. (1.8-3.3mm).

Neutral Safety Switch

ADJUSTMENT

This switch is mounted on the transaxle shift lever shaft, bolted to the transaxle. It also operates the backup lights.

1. Remove the shift lever shaft nut.
2. Remove the shift lever from the shaft.
3. Make sure the slot in the shaft is vertical, **N** position.
4. Remove the switch mounting bolts but leave the switch in place.
5. Remove the setscrew from the lower face of the switch.
6. Insert a 0.059 in. drill bit through the setscrew hole. Turn the switch slightly so the bit passes through into the back part of the switch.
7. Bolt the switch down.
8. Remove the drill bit and replace the set screw.
9. Install the lever and tighten the shaft nut.
10. Make sure the engine can start only in **P** or **N** and that the backup lights turn functioning in **R**. Adjust the shift linkage, if necessary.

Fusible Links

LEGACY

The main fusible link is located in the underhood fuse box.

LOYALE

The fusible links are located in a box on the left fender apron, ahead of the shock tower.

JUSTY

The 30 and 60 amp main fuses are located in a holder on the left front shock tower, near the brake master cylinder.

XT

The fusible links are located in a box at the left side of the engine compartment, near the battery.

SVX

The main fusible link is located under the hood next to the battery in a holder near the sidewall.

Fuses and Circuit Breakers

EXCEPT SVX

There are fuses for all of the vehicle electrical systems located in the main and sub fuse boxes. The fuse rating and circuit it protects are indicated on the fuse box cover. The power window circuit breakers are located under the front seat.

SVX

The main fuse box is located under the hood while the sub fuse box is located under the left side of the instrument panel.

Toyota 17

Camry, Celica, Corolla, Cressida, MR2, Paseo, Supra, Tercel

SERIAL NUMBER IDENTIFICATION

Identification Plate

All vehicles have the Vehicle Identification Number (VIN) stamped on a plate which is attached to the left side of the instrument panel. This plate is visible through the windshield.

The serial number consists of a series identification number followed by a 6-digit production number. It should be noted, however, that there is no 1990 MR2. It was reintroduced mid-year. If the VIN information should indicate that the vehicle is a 1990, use the 1991 specifications and repair procedures.

Engine Number

Basically, Toyota uses 5 types of engines:

    A-Series:
        4A-FE, 4A-GE, 7A-FE
    E-Series:
        3E, 3E-E, 5E-FE
    M-Series:
        7M-GE, 7M-GTE
    S-Series:
        3S-FE, 3S-GTE, 5S-FE
    Z-Series:
        2VZ-FE, 3VZ-FE

Engines within each series are similar, as the cylinder block designs are the same. Variances within each series may be due to ignition types, displacements and cylinder head design.

Serial numbers of the engines may be found on the following locations:

A-Series engines — stamped vertically on the left side rear of the engine block.

E-Series engines — stamped on the left side rear of the engine block.

M-Series engines — stamped horizontally on the passenger side of the engine block, behind the alternator.

S-Series engines — the serial number can be found on the rear left side of the block, under the thermostat housing.

Z-Series engines — stamped on the front, right (passenger) side of the cylinder block.

ENGINE IDENTIFICATION

Year	Model	Engine Displacement Liters (cc)	Engine Series (ID/VIN)	Fuel System	No. of Cylinders	Engine Type
1990	Tercel	1.5 (1457)	3E	1 bbl	4	SOHC
		1.5 (1457)	3E-E	EFI	4	SOHC
	Corolla	1.6 (1587)	4A-FE	EFI	4	DOHC
		1.6 (1587)	4A-GE	EFI	4	DOHC
	Camry	2.0 (1998)	3S-FE	EFI	4	DOHC
		2.5 (2507)	2VZ-FE	EFI	6	DOHC
	Celica	1.6 (1587)	4A-FE	EFI	4	DOHC
		2.0 (1998)	3S-GTE	EFI	4	DOHC, TURBO
		2.2 (2164)	5S-FE	EFI	4	DOHC
	Supra	3.0 (2954)	7M-GE	EFI	6	DOHC
		3.0 (2954)	7M-GTE	EFI	6	DOHC, TURBO
	Cressida	3.0 (2954)	7M-GE	EFI	6	DOHC
1991	Tercel	1.5 (1457)	3E-E	EFI	4	SOHC
	Corolla	1.6 (1587)	4A-FE	EFI	4	DOHC
		1.6 (1587)	4A-GE	EFI	4	DOHC
	Camry	2.0 (1998)	3S-FE	EFI	4	DOHC
		2.5 (2507)	2VZ-FE	EFI	6	DOHC
	Celica	1.6 (1587)	4A-FE	EFI	4	DOHC
		2.0 (1998)	3S-GTE	EFI	4	DOHC, TURBO
		2.2 (2164)	5S-FE	EFI	4	DOHC
	Supra	3.0 (2954)	7M-GE	EFI	6	DOHC
		3.0 (2954)	7M-GTE	EFI	6	DOHC, TURBO
	MR2	2.0 (1998)	3S-GTE	EFI	4	DOHC, TURBO
		2.2 (2164)	5S-FE	EFI	4	DOHC
	Cressida	3.0 (2954)	7M-GE	EFI	6	DOHC
1992	Tercel	1.5 (1457)	3E-E	EFI	4	SOHC
	Paseo	1.5 (1495)	5E-FE	EFI	4	DOHC
	Corolla	1.6 (1587)	4A-FE	EFI	4	DOHC
	Camry	2.2 (2164)	5S-FE	EFI	4	DOHC
		3.0 (2952)	3VZ-FE	EFI	6	DOHC
	Celica	1.6 (1587)	4A-FE	EFI	4	DOHC
		2.0 (1998)	3S-GTE	EFI	4	DOHC, TURBO
		2.2 (2164)	5S-FE	EFI	4	DOHC
	Supra	3.0 (2954)	7M-GE	EFI	6	DOHC
		3.0 (2954)	7M-GTE	EFI	6	DOHC, TURBO
	MR2	2.0 (1998)	3S-GTE	EFI	4	DOHC, TURBO
		2.2 (2164)	5S-FE	EFI	4	DOHC
	Cressida	3.0 (2954)	7M-GE	EFI	6	DOHC

ENGINE IDENTIFICATION

Year	Model	Engine Displacement Liters (cc)	Engine Series (ID/VIN)	Fuel System	No. of Cylinders	Engine Type
1993	Tercel	1.5 (1457)	3E-E	EFI	4	SOHC
	Paseo	1.5 (1495)	5E-FE	EFI	4	DOHC
	Corolla	1.6 (1587)	4A-FE	EFI	4	DOHC
		1.8 (1762)	7A-FE	EFI	4	DOHC
	Camry	2.2 (2164)	5S-FE	EFI	4	DOHC
		3.0 (2952)	3VZ-FE	EFI	6	DOHC
	Celica	1.6 (1587)	4A-FE	EFI	4	DOHC
		2.0 (1998)	3S-GTE	EFI	4	DOHC, TURBO
		2.2 (2164)	5S-FE	EFI	4	DOHC
	MR2	2.0 (1998)	3S-GTE	EFI	4	DOHC, TURBO
		2.2 (2164)	5S-FE	EFI	4	DOHC
1994	Tercel	1.5 (1457)	3E-E	EFI	4	SOHC
	Paseo	1.5 (1495)	5E-FE	EFI	4	DOHC
	Corolla	1.6 (1587)	4A-FE	EFI	4	DOHC
		1.8 (1762)	7A-FE	EFI	4	DOHC
	Camry	2.2 (2164)	5S-FE	EFI	4	DOHC
		3.0 (2952)	3VZ-FE	EFI	6	DOHC
	Celica	1.6 (1587)	4A-FE	EFI	4	DOHC
		2.0 (1998)	3S-GTE	EFI	4	DOHC, TURBO
		2.2 (2164)	5S-FE	EFI	4	DOHC
	MR2	2.0 (1998)	3S-GTE	EFI	4	DOHC, TURBO
		2.2 (2164)	5S-FE	EFI	4	DOHC

1 bbl—1 barrel carburetor
2 bbl—2 barrel carburetor
EFI—Electronic Fuel Injection
DOHC—Double Overhead Camshaft
SOHC—Single Overhead Camshaft
TURBO—Turbocharged

GENERAL ENGINE SPECIFICATIONS

Year	Engine ID/VIN	Engine Displacement Liters (cc)	Fuel System Type	Net Horsepower @ rpm	Net Torque @ rpm (ft. lbs.)	Bore × Stroke (in.)	Compression Ratio	Oil Pressure (psi) ①
1990	3E	1.5 (1457)	1 bbl	78 @ 6000	87 @ 4000	2.87 × 3.43	9.3:1	4.3
	3E-E	1.5 (1457)	EFI	82 @ 5200	89 @ 4400	2.87 × 3.43	9.3:1	4.3
	4A-GE	1.6 (1587)	EFI	130 @ 6800	102 @ 5800	3.19 × 3.03	9.5:1	4.3
	3S-FE	2.0 (1998)	EFI	115 @ 5200	124 @ 4400	3.39 × 3.39	9.3:1	4.3
	2VZ-FE	2.5 (2507)	EFI	156 @ 5600	160 @ 4400	3.44 × 2.74	9.0:1	4.3
	4A-FE	1.6 (1587)	EFI	103 @ 6000 ②	102 @ 3200 ③	3.19 × 3.03	9.5:1	4.3
	3S-GTE	2.0 (1998)	EFI	200 @ 6000	200 @ 3200	3.39 × 3.39	9.5:1	4.3
	5S-FE	2.2 (2164)	EFI	130 @ 5400	140 @ 4400	3.43 × 3.58	9.5:1	4.3
	7M-GE	3.0 (2956)	EFI	200 @ 6000	188 @ 3600	3.27 × 3.58	9.2:1	4.3
	7M-GTE	3.0 (2956)	EFI	232 @ 5600	254 @ 3200	3.27 × 3.58	8.4:1	4.3
1991	3E-E	1.5 (1457)	EFI	82 @ 5200	90 @ 4400	2.88 × 3.43	9.3:1	4.3
	4A-GE	1.6 (1587)	EFI	130 @ 6800	105 @ 6000	3.19 × 3.03	10.3:1	4.3
	3S-FE	2.0 (1998)	EFI	115 @ 5200	124 @ 4400	3.39 × 3.39	9.3:1	4.3
	2VZ-FE	2.5 (2507)	EFI	156 @ 5600	160 @ 4400	3.44 × 2.74	9.0:1	4.3
	4A-FE	1.6 (1587)	EFI	103 @ 6000 ②	102 @ 3200 ③	3.19 × 3.10	9.5:1	4.3
	3S-GTE	2.0 (1998)	EFI	200 @ 6000	200 @ 3200	3.39 × 3.39	8.8:1	4.3
	5S-FE	2.2 (2164)	EFI	130 @ 5400	140 @ 4400	3.43 × 3.58	9.5:1	4.3
	7M-GE	3.0 (2956)	EFI	200 @ 6000	188 @ 3600	3.27 × 3.58	9.2:1	4.3
	7M-GTE	3.0 (2956)	EFI	232 @ 5600	254 @ 3200	3.27 × 3.58	8.4:1	4.3
1992	3E-E	1.5 (1457)	EFI	82 @ 5200	89 @ 4400	2.88 × 3.43	9.3:1	4.3
	5E-FE	1.5 (1495)	EFI	100 @ 6400	91 @ 3200	2.91 × 3.43	9.4:1	4.3
	5S-FE	2.2 (2164)	EFI	135 @ 5400	145 @ 4400	3.43 × 3.58	9.5:1	4.3
	3VZ-FE	3.0 (2952)	EFI	185 @ 5200	195 @ 4400	3.44 × 3.23	9.6:1	4.3
	4A-FE	1.6 (1587)	EFI	103 @ 6000 ②	102 @ 3200 ③	3.19 × 3.03	9.5:1	4.3
	3S-GTE	2.0 (1998)	EFI	200 @ 6000	200 @ 3200	3.39 × 3.39	8.8:1	4.3
	7M-GE	3.0 (2956)	EFI	200 @ 6000	188 @ 3600	3.27 × 3.58	9.2:1	4.3
	7M-GTE	3.0 (2956)	EFI	232 @ 5600	254 @ 3200	3.27 × 3.58	8.4:1	4.3
1993	3E-E	1.5 (1457)	EFI	82 @ 5200	89 @ 4400	2.88 × 3.43	9.3:1	4.3
	5E-FE	1.5 (1495)	EFI	100 @ 6400	91 @ 3200	2.91 × 3.43	9.4:1	4.3
	5S-FE	2.2 (2164)	EFI	135 @ 5400	145 @ 4400	3.43 × 3.58	9.5:1	4.3
	3VZ-FE	3.0 (2952)	EFI	185 @ 5200	195 @ 4400	3.44 × 3.23	9.6:1	4.3
	4A-FE	1.6 (1587)	EFI	103 @ 6000 ②	102 @ 3200 ③	3.19 × 3.03	9.5:1	4.3
	7A-FE	1.8 (1762)	EFI	115 @ 5600	115 @ 2800	3.19 × 3.37	9.5:1	4.3
	3S-GTE	2.0 (1998)	EFI	200 @ 6000	200 @ 3200	3.39 × 3.39	8.8:1	4.3
1994	3E-E	1.5 (1457)	EFI	82 @ 5200	89 @ 4400	2.88 × 3.43	9.3:1	4.3
	5E-FE	1.5 (1495)	EFI	100 @ 6400	91 @ 3200	2.91 × 3.43	9.4:1	4.3
	5S-FE	2.2 (2164)	EFI	135 @ 5400	145 @ 4400	3.43 × 3.58	9.5:1	4.3
	3VZ-FE	3.0 (2952)	EFI	185 @ 5200	195 @ 4400	3.44 × 3.23	9.6:1	4.3
	4A-FE	1.6 (1587)	EFI	103 @ 6000 ②	102 @ 3200 ③	3.19 × 3.03	9.5:1	4.3
	7A-FE	1.8 (1762)	EFI	115 @ 5600	115 @ 2800	3.19 × 3.37	9.5:1	4.3
	3S-GTE	2.0 (1998)	EFI	200 @ 6000	200 @ 3200	3.39 × 3.39	8.8:1	4.3

1 bbl—1 barrel carburetor
2 bbl—2 barrel carburetor
EFI—Electronic Fuel Injection

① Values given are at idle
② In California, 102 @ 5800
③ In California, 101 @ 4800

GASOLINE ENGINE TUNE-UP SPECIFICATIONS

Year	Engine ID/VIN	Engine Displacement Liters (cc)	Spark Plugs Gap (in.)	Ignition Timing (deg.) MT	AT	Fuel Pump (psi)	Idle Speed (rpm) MT	AT	Valve Clearance (in.) In.	Ex.
1990	3E	1.5 (1457) ①	0.043	3B	3B	2.6–3.5	700	900	0.008	0.008
	3E-E	1.5 (1457)	0.043	10B	10B	38–44	800	800	0.008	0.008
	4A-FE	1.6 (1587)	0.031	10B	10B	38–44	②	②	0.006–0.010	0.008–0.012
	4A-GE	1.6 (1587)	0.031	10B	10B	38–44	800	800	0.006–0.010	0.008–0.012
	3S-FE	2.0 (1998)	0.043	10B	10B	38–44	650–750	650–750	0.007–0.011	0.011–0.015
	2VZ-FE	2.5 (2507)	0.043	10B	10B	38–44	650–750	650–750	0.005–0.009	0.011–0.015
	5S-FE	2.2 (2164)	0.043	10B	10B	38–44	650–⑤ 750③	650–750④	0.007–0.011	0.011–0.015
	7M-GE	3.0 (2956)	0.043	10B	10B	38–44	700	700	0.006–0.010	0.008–0.012
	7M-GTE	3.0 (2956)	0.031	10B	10B	33–40	650	650	0.006–0.010	0.006–0.010
	3S-GTE	2.0 (1998)	0.031	10B	10B	33–38	750–850	800	0.006–0.010	0.008–0.012
1991	3E-E	1.5 (1457)	0.043	10B	10B	33–37	750	800	0.008	0.008
	4A-FE	1.6 (1587)	0.031	10B	10B	38–44	⑥	⑥	0.006–0.010	0.008–0.012
	4A-GE	1.6 (1587)	0.031	10B	10B	38–44	800	800	0.006–0.010	0.008–0.012
	3S-FE	2.0 (1998)	0.043	10B	10B	38–44	650	650	0.007–0.011	0.011–0.015
	2VZ-FE	2.5 (2507)	0.043	10B	10B	38–44	700	700	0.005–0.009	0.011–0.015
	3S-GTE	2.0 (1998)	0.031	10B	10B	34–38	800	800	0.006–0.010	0.008–0.012
	5S-FE	2.2 (2164)	0.043	10B	10B	38–44	700⑦⑧	750⑦⑧	0.007–0.011	0.011–0.015
	7M-GE	3.0 (2956)	0.043	10B	10B	38–44	700	700	0.006–0.010	0.008–0.012
	7M-GTE	3.0 (2956)	0.031	10B	10B	33–40	650	650	0.006–0.010	0.008–0.012
1992	3E-E	1.5 (1457)	0.043	10B	10B	40.8–44.7	750	800	0.008	0.008
	5S-FE	2.2 (2164)	0.043	10B	10B	38–44	700–⑪ 800⑩⑧	700–⑪ 800⑩⑧	0.007–0.011	0.011–0.015
	3VZ-FE	3.0 (2952)	0.043	10B	10B	38–44	650–750	650–750	0.005–0.009	0.011–0.015
	4A-FE	1.6 (1587)	0.031	10B	10B	38–44	800⑦⑨	800⑦⑨	0.006–0.010	0.008–0.012
	3S-GTE	2.0 (1998)	0.031	10B	10B	33–38	750–850	750–850	0.006–0.010	0.011–0.015⑦
	7M-GE	3.0 (2956)	0.043	10B	10B	38–44	700	700	0.006–0.010	0.008–0.012

GASOLINE ENGINE TUNE-UP SPECIFICATIONS

Year	Engine ID/VIN	Engine Displacement Liters (cc)	Spark Plugs Gap (in.)	Ignition Timing (deg.)		Fuel Pump (psi)	Idle Speed (rpm)		Valve Clearance (in.)	
				MT	AT		MT	AT	In.	Ex.
	7M-GTE	3.0 (2956)	0.031	10B	10B	33–40	650	650	0.006–0.010	0.008–0.012
	3S-GTE	2.0 (1998)	0.031	10B	10B	33–38	650–850	750–850	0.006–0.010	0.008–0.012
1993	3E-E	1.5 (1457)	0.043	10B	10B	40.8–44.7	750	800	0.008	0.008
	7A-FE	1.8 (1762)	0.031	10B	10B	38–44	800	800	0.006–0.010	0.008–0.012
	5S-FE	2.2 (2164)	0.043	10B	10B	38–44	700–⑪ 800⑩⑧	700–⑪ 800⑩⑧	0.007–0.011	0.011–0.015
	3VZ-FE	3.0 (2952)	0.043	10B	10B	38–44	650–750	650–750	0.005–0.009	0.011–0.015
	4A-FE	1.6 (1587)	0.031	10B	10B	38–44	800⑦⑨	800⑦⑨	0.006–0.010	0.008–0.012
	3S-GTE	2.0 (1998)	0.031	10B	10B	33–38	750–850	750–850	0.006–0.010	0.011–0.015⑦
	3S-GTE	2.0 (1998)	0.031	10B	10B	33–38	650–850	750–850	0.006–0.010	0.008–0.012
1994	3E-E	1.5 (1457)	0.043	10B	10B	40.8–44.7	750	800	0.008	0.008
	7A-FE	1.8 (1762)	0.031	10B	10B	38–44	800	800	0.006–0.010	0.008–0.012
	5S-FE	2.2 (2164)	0.043	10B	10B	38–44	700–⑪ 800⑩⑧	700–⑪ 800⑩⑧	0.007–0.011	0.011–0.015
	3VZ-FE	3.0 (2952)	0.043	10B	10B	38–44	650–750	650–750	0.005–0.009	0.011–0.015
	4A-FE	1.6 (1587)	0.031	10B	10B	38–44	800⑦⑨	800⑦⑨	0.006–0.010	0.008–0.012
	3S-GTE	2.0 (1998)	0.031	10B	10B	33–38	750–850	750–850	0.006–0.010	0.011–0.015⑦
	3S-GTE	2.0 (1998)	0.031	10B	10B	33–38	650–850	750–850	0.006–0.010	0.008–0.012

NOTE: The lowest cylinder pressure should be within 75% of the highest cylinder pressure reading. For example, if the highest cylinder is 134 psi, the lowest should be 101. Engine should be at normal operating temperature with throttle valve in the wide open position.
The underhood specifications sticker often reflects tune-up specification changes in production. Sticker figures must be used if they disagree with those in this chart.
MT—Manual Transmission
AT—Automatic Transmission
B—Before Top Dead Center
① Carburetor used on this model
② 2WD: 700
   4WD: 800
③ Celica Canada: 750–850
④ Canada: 700–800

⑤ MR2 Canada: 800–900
⑥ 2WD Federal and Canada: 700
   2WD California and 4WD: 800
⑦ Celica
⑧ MR2 (USA M/T, Canada A/T): 750
   (USA A/T): 700
   (Canada M/T): 850

⑨ 2WD (Canada and except California): 700
   2WD (California): 800
   4WD: 800
⑩ Camry
⑪ Celica (USA): 650–750
   (Canada): 700–800

FIRING ORDERS

NOTE: To avoid confusion, always replace spark plug wires one at a time.

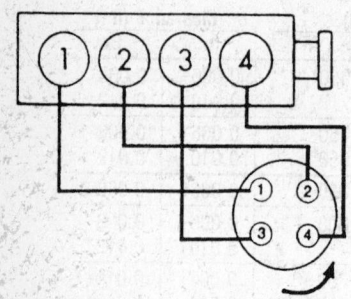

3E and 3E-E Engines
Engine Firing Order: 1-3-4-2
Distributor Rotation: Counterclockwise

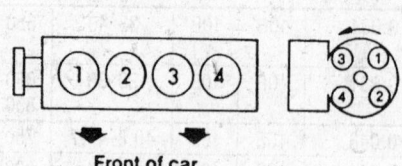

Front of car

4A-F, 4A-FE and 7A-FE Engines
Engine Firing Order: 1-3-4-2
Distributor Rotation: Counterclockwise

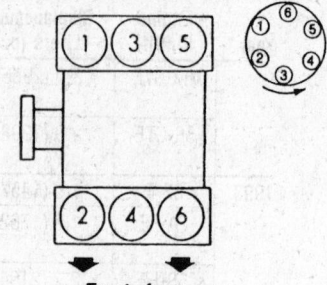

Front of car

2VZ-FE and 3VZ-FE Engines
Engine Firing Order: 1-2-3-4-5-6
Distributor Rotation: Counterclockwise

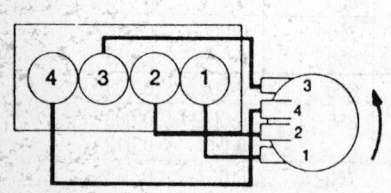

3S-FE, 3S-GE, 3S-GTE and 5S-FE Engines
Engine Firing Order: 1-3-4-2
Distributor Rotation: Counterclockwise

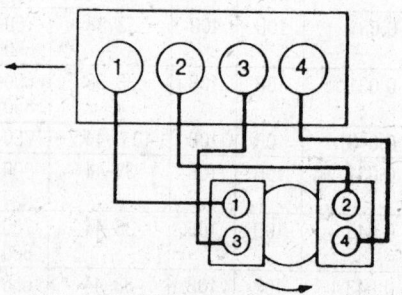

4A-GE and 4A-GZE Engines
Engine Firing Order: 1-3-4-2
Distributor Rotation: Counterclockwise

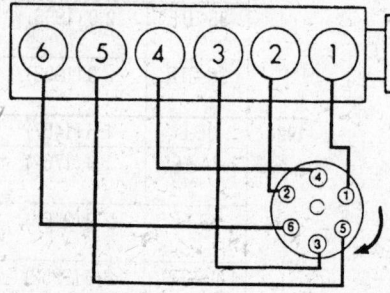

7M-GE Engine
Engine Firing Order: 1-5-3-6-2-4
Distributor Rotation: Clockwise

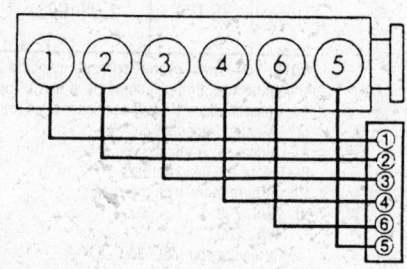

7M-GTE Engine
Engine Firing Order: 1-5-3-6-2-4
Distributorless Ignition System

CAPACITIES

Year	Model	Engine ID/VIN	Engine Displacement Liters (cc)	Engine Crankcase with Filter (qts.)	Transmission (pts.)			Transfer case (pts.)	Drive Axle		Fuel Tank (gal.)	Cooling System (qts.)
					4-Spd	5-Spd	Auto. [26]		Front (pts.)	Rear (pts.)		
1990	Tercel	3E	1.5 (1456)	3.4	5.0	5.0	5.2	—	3.0	—	11.9	5.5
		3E-E	1.5 (1457)	3.4	—	5.0	4.6	—	3.0	—	11.9	5.9
	Corolla	4A-FE	1.6 (1587)	3.3	—	10.6	[1]	[2]	3.0[3]	2.4	13.2	6.1
		4A-GE	1.6 (1587)	3.4	—	5.4	—	—	—	—	13.2	6.2
	Camry	3S-FE	2.0 (1998)	4.1	—	[4]	[7]	1.5	3.4[6]	2.4	15.9	[5]
		2VZ-FE	2.5 (2508)	4.1	—	8.8	5.2	—	2.2[6]	—	15.9	10.0
	Celica	4A-FE	1.6 (1587)	3.3	—	5.4	7.0	—	3.0	—	15.9[9]	6.8
		3S-GTE	2.0 (1998)	3.8	—	11.0	—	[21]	—	2.4[8]	15.9[9]	6.8
		5S-FE	2.2 (2164)	[10]	—	5.4	7.0	—	3.0	—	15.9[9]	[13]
	Supra	7M-GE	3.0 (2954)	4.7	—	5.0	3.4	—	—	2.8	18.5	8.6
		7M-GTE	3.0 (2954)	4.7	—	6.4	3.4	—	—	2.8	18.5	8.7
	Cressida	7M-GE	3.0 (2954)	4.3	—	—	3.4	—	—	2.8	18.5	8.8
1991	Tercel	3E-E	1.5 (1457)	3.4	—	5.0	5.2	—	3.0	—	11.9	5.2[14]
	Corolla	4A-FE	1.6 (1587)	3.3	—	[11]	[1]	1.6	3.0[3]	2.4	13.2	6.3
		4A-GE	1.6 (1587)	3.9	—	[11]	[1]	1.6	3.0	2.4	13.2	6.4
	Camry	3S-FE	2.0 (1998)	4.3	—	5.4	[15]	1.4	—	2.4	15.9	[5]
		2VZ-FE	2.5 (2507)	4.1	—	8.8	5.2	—	[16]	—	15.9	10.0
	Celica	4A-FE	1.6 (1587)	3.3	—	5.4	5.4	—	3.0	—	15.9	[12]
		3S-GTE	2.0 (1998)	4.1	—	11.0	7.0	[21]	—	2.4[8]	15.9[9]	6.9
		5S-FE	2.2 (2164)	[10]	—	5.4	5.4	—	3.0	—	15.9	[13]
	Supra	7M-GE	3.0 (2954)	4.7	—	5.0	3.4	—	—	2.8	18.5	8.6
		7M-GTE	3.0 (2954)	5.0	—	6.4	3.4	—	—	2.8	18.5	8.6
	MR2	3S-GTE	2.0 (1998)	4.1	—	8.8	5.4	—	—	3.0	14.3	14.4
		5S-FE	2.2 (2164)	4.4	—	5.4	5.4	—	—	3.0	14.3	13.7
	Cressida	7M-GE	3.0 (2954)	4.7	—	—	3.4	—	—	2.2	18.5	8.8
1992	Tercel	3E-E	1.5 (1457)	3.4	—	5.0	5.2	—	3.0	—	11.9	5.2[14]
	Paseo	5E-FE	1.5 (1495)	3.4	—	5.0	6.6	—	3.0	—	11.9	5.3[21]
	Corolla	4A-FE	1.6 (1587)	3.4	—	[18]	[1]	[19]	—	2.4	13.2	6.5
	Camry	5S-FE	2.2 (2164)	4.3	—	5.4	5.2	—	3.4	—	18.5	6.7
		3VZ-FE	3.0 (2952)	4.5	—	8.8	6.2	—	3.4	—	18.5	9.0
	Celica	4A-FE	1.6 (1587)	3.4	—	5.4	5.2	—	3.4	—	15.9[9]	[20]
		3S-GTE	2.0 (1998)	4.1	—	5.4	5.2	[21]	3.4	2.4[8]	15.9	[20]
		5S-FE	2.2 (2164)	[10]	—	11.0	—	—	3.4	—	15.9	6.9
	Supra	7M-GE	3.0 (2954)	4.7	—	5.2	3.4	—	—	2.8	18.5	8.6
		7M-GTE	3.0 (2954)	5.0	—	6.4	3.4	—	—	2.8	18.5	8.6
	MR2	3S-GTE	2.0 (1998)	4.1	—	8.8	7.0	—	—	3.4	14.3	14.4
		5S-FE	2.2 (2164)	4.5	—	5.4	7.0	—	—	3.4	14.3	13.7
	Cressida	7M-GE	3.0 (2954)	4.7	—	—	3.4	—	—	2.8	18.5	8.8

CAPACITIES

Year	Model	Engine ID/VIN	Engine Displacement Liters (cc)	Engine Crankcase with Filter (qts.)	Transmission (pts.)			Transfer case (pts.)	Drive Axle		Fuel Tank (gal.)	Cooling System (qts.)
					4-Spd	5-Spd	Auto.㉖		Front (pts.)	Rear (pts.)		
1993	Tercel	3E-E	1.5 (1457)	3.4	—	5.0	5.2	—	3.0	—	11.9	5.2⑭
	Paseo	5E-FE	1.5 (1495)	3.4	—	5.0	6.6	—	3.0	—	11.9	5.3⑰
	Corolla	4A-FE	1.6 (1587)	3.4	—	5.4	5.2	—	—	—	13.2	6.5
		7A-FE	1.8 (1762)	3.4	—	5.4	5.2	—	—	—	13.2	6.6
	Camry	5S-FE	2.2 (2164)	4.3	—	5.4	5.2	—	3.4	—	18.5	6.7
		3VZ-FE	3.0 (2952)	4.5	—	8.8	6.2	—	3.4	—	18.5	9.0
	Celica	4A-FE	1.6 (1587)	3.4	—	5.4	5.2	—	3.4	—	15.9⑨	⑳
		3S-GTE	2.0 (1998)	4.1	—	5.4	5.2	㉑	3.4	2.4⑧	15.9	⑳
		5S-FE	2.2 (2164)	⑩	—	11.0	—	—	3.4	—	15.9	6.9
	MR2	3S-GTE	2.0 (1998)	4.1	—	8.8	7.0	—	—	3.4	14.3	14.4
		5S-FE	2.2 (2164)	4.5	—	5.4	7.0	—	—	3.4	14.3	13.7
1994	Tercel	3E-E	1.5 (1457)	3.4	—	5.0	5.2	—	3.0	—	11.9	5.2⑭
	Paseo	5E-FE	1.5 (1495)	3.4	—	5.0	6.6	—	3.0	—	11.9	5.3⑰
	Corolla	4A-FE	1.6 (1587)	3.4	—	5.4	5.2	—	—	—	13.2	6.5
		7A-FE	1.8 (1762)	3.4	—	5.4	5.2	—	—	—	13.2	6.6
	Camry	5S-FE	2.2 (2164)	4.3	—	5.4	5.2	—	3.4	—	18.5	6.7
		3VZ-FE	3.0 (2952)	4.5	—	8.8	6.2	—	3.4	—	18.5	9.0
	Celica	4A-FE	1.6 (1587)	3.4	—	5.4	5.2	—	3.4	—	15.9⑨	⑳
		3S-GTE	2.0 (1998)	4.1	—	5.4	5.2	㉑	3.4	2.4⑧	15.9	⑳
		5S-FE	2.2 (2164)	⑩	—	11.0	—	—	3.4	—	15.9	6.9
	MR2	3S-GTE	2.0 (1998)	4.1	—	8.8	7.0	—	—	3.4	14.3	14.4
		5S-FE	2.2 (2164)	4.5	—	5.4	7.0	—	—	3.4	14.3	13.7

① 2WD with 3-SP: 5.2 pts.
  2WD with 4-SP: 6.6 pts.
  4WD: 6.6 pts.
② 4WD-M/T: included with transmission
  4WD-A/T: 1.4 pts.
③ 3-SP automatic
④ 2WD: 5.4 pts.
  4WD: 10.6 pts. (including transfer case)
⑤ M/T: 6.8 pts.
  A/T (2WD): 6.7 qts.
  A/T (4WD): 7.2 qts.
⑥ 2WD automatic

⑦ 2WD: 5.2 pts.
  4WD: 7.4 pts.
⑧ 4WD
⑨ 4WD: 18.0 gal.
⑩ w/oil cooler: 4.4 qts.
  w/out oil cooler: 4.3 qts.
⑪ M/T, 2WD: 5.4 pts.
  M/T, 4WD: 10.6 pts.
⑫ M/T: 5.5 qts.
  A/T: 5.8 qts.
⑬ M/T: 6.6 qts.
  A/T: 6.4 qts.
⑭ M/T: 5.2 qts.
  A/T: 5.7 qts.
⑮ 2WD: 5.4 pts.
  4WD: 12.4 pts.

⑯ 4 cyl. automatic, 2WD: 2.2 pts.
  6 cyl. automatic, 2WD: 3.4 pts.
⑰ M/T: 5.3 qts.
  A/T: 5.7 qts.
⑱ 2WD: 5.4 qts.
  4WD: 10.6 qts.
⑲ M/T: Included with transaxle
  A/T: 1.4 pts. additional
⑳ 4A-FE engine—
    M/T: 5.5 qts.
    A/T: 5.9 qts.
  5S-FE engine—
    M/T: 6.6 qts.
    A/T: 7.0 qts.
㉑ Included with transmission
㉒ Drain and refill

CAMSHAFT SPECIFICATIONS

All measurements given in inches.

Year	Engine ID/VIN	Engine Displacement Liters (cc)	Journal Diameter							Elevation		Bearing Clearance	Camshaft End Play
			1	2	3	4	5	6	7	In.	Ex.		
1990	3E, 3E-E	1.5 (1456)	1.0622–1.0628	1.0622–1.0628	1.0622–1.0628	1.0622–1.0628	—	—	—	1.3917–1.3957 ⑥	1.4106–1.4146	0.0015–0.0029	0.0031–0.0071
	4A-FE	1.6 (1587)	0.9035–0.9041 ③	0.9035–0.9041	0.9035–0.9041	0.9035–0.9041	—	—	—	1.3862–1.3902	1.3744–1.3783	0.0015–0.0028	②
	4A-GE	1.6 (1587)	1.0610–1.0616	1.0610–1.0616	1.0610–1.0616	1.0610–1.0616	—	—	—	1.3823–1.3980	1.3823–1.3980	0.0014–0.0028	0.0031–0.0075
	3S-FE	2.0 (1998)	1.0614–1.0620	1.0614–1.0620	1.0614–1.0620	1.0614–1.0620	—	—	—	1.3902–1.3941	1.4000–1.4039	0.0010–0.0024	⑤
	3S-GTE	2.0 (1998)	1.0614–1.0620	1.0614–1.0620	1.0614–1.0620	1.0614–1.0620	—	—	—	1.6146–1.6185 ⑩	1.6146–1.6185 ⑩	0.0010–0.0024	0.0047–0.0114
	5S-FE	2.2 (2164)	1.0614–1.0620	1.0614–1.0620	1.0614–1.0620	1.0614–1.0620	—	—	—	1.3902–1.3941	1.4000–1.4039	0.0010–0.0024	⑤
	2VZ-FE	2.5 (2507)	1.0610–1.0616	1.0610–1.0616	1.0610–1.0616	1.0610–1.0616	1.0610–1.0616	—	—	1.5555–1.5594	1.5339–1.5378	0.0014–0.0028	0.0012–0.0031
	7M-GE, 7M-GTE	3.0 (2954)	1.0610–1.0616	1.0586–1.0620	1.0586–1.0620	1.0586–1.0620	1.0586–1.0620	1.0586–1.0620	1.0586–1.0620	1.5024 ⑪	1.5098	0.0010–0.0037 ①	0.0031–0.0075
1991	3E-E	1.5 (1456)	1.0622–1.0628	1.0622–1.0628	1.0622–1.0628	1.0622–1.0628	—	—	—	1.3917–1.3957 ⑥	1.4106–1.4146	0.0015–0.0029	0.0031–0.0071
	4A-FE	1.6 (1587)	0.9035–0.9041 ③	0.9035–0.9041	0.9035–0.9041	0.9035–0.9041	—	—	—	1.3862–1.3902	1.3744–1.3783	0.0015–0.0028	②
	4A-GE	1.6 (1587)	1.0610–1.0616	1.0610–1.0616	1.0610–1.0616	1.0610–1.0616	—	—	—	1.3823–1.3980	1.3823–1.3980	0.0014–0.0028	0.0031–0.0071
	3S-FE	2.0 (1998)	1.0614–1.0620	1.0614–1.0620	1.0614–1.0620	1.0614–1.0620	—	—	—	1.3744–1.3783	1.4000–1.4039	0.0010–0.0024	⑤
	3S-GTE	2.0 (1998)	1.0614–1.0620	1.0614–1.0620	1.0614–1.0620	1.0614–1.0620	—	—	—	1.6146–1.6185	1.6146–1.6185	0.0010–0.0024	0.0047–0.0114
	5S-FE	2.2 (2164)	1.0614–1.0620	1.0614–1.0620	1.0614–1.0620	1.0614–1.0620	—	—	—	1.3902–1.3941	1.4000–1.4039	0.0010–0.0024	⑤
	2VZ-FE	2.5 (2507)	1.0610–1.0616	1.0610–1.0616	1.0610–1.0616	1.0610–1.0616	1.0610–1.0616	—	—	1.5555–1.5594	1.5339–1.5378	0.0014–0.0028	0.0012–0.0031
	7M-GE, 7M-GTE	3.0 (2954)	1.0610–1.0616	1.0586–1.0620	1.0586–1.0620	1.0586–1.0620	1.0586–1.0620	1.0586–1.0620	1.0586–1.0620	1.5024 ⑪	1.5098	0.0010–0.0037 ①	0.0031–0.0075
1992	3E-E	1.5 (1457)	1.0622–1.0628	1.0622–1.0628	1.0622–1.0628	1.0622–1.0628	—	—	—	1.3917–1.3957 ⑥	1.4106–1.4146	0.0015–0.0029	0.0031–0.0071
	5E-FE	1.5 (1495)	0.9035–0.9041 ③	0.9035–0.9041	0.9035–0.9041	0.9035–0.9041	0.9035–0.9041	—	—	1.6343–1.6382	1.6264–1.6303	0.0014–0.0028	0.0018–0.0039
	4A-FE	1.6 (1587)	0.9035–0.9041 ③	0.9035–0.9041	0.9035–0.9041	0.9035–0.9041	—	—	—	1.3862–1.3902	1.3744–1.3783	0.0014–0.0028	②
	5S-FE ⑧	2.2 (2164)	1.0614–1.0620	1.0614–1.0620	1.0614–1.0620	1.0614–1.0620	1.0614–1.0620	—	—	1.6539–1.6579	1.5772–1.5811	0.0010–0.0024	⑤
	3VZ-FE	3.0 (2952)	1.0610–1.0616	1.0610–1.0616	1.0610–1.0616	1.0610–1.0616	1.0610–1.0616	—	—	1.6598–1.6638	1.6520–1.6559	0.0014–0.0028	0.0013–0.0031
	3S-GTE	2.0 (1998)	1.0614–1.0620	1.0614–1.0620	1.0614–1.0620	1.0614–1.0620	1.0614–1.0620	—	—	1.6146–1.6185	1.6177–1.6217	0.0010–0.0024	0.0047–0.0094

CAMSHAFT SPECIFICATIONS
All measurements given in inches.

Year	Engine ID/VIN	Engine Displacement Liters (cc)	Journal Diameter							Elevation		Bearing Clearance	Camshaft End Play
			1	2	3	4	5	6	7	In.	Ex.		
	7M-GE	3.0 (2954)	1.0610–1.0616	1.0586–1.0620	1.0586–1.0620	1.0586–1.0620	1.0586–1.0620	1.0586–1.0620	1.0586–1.0620	1.5024	1.5098	⑦	0.0031–0.0075
	7M-GTE	3.0 (2954)	1.0610–1.0616	1.0586–1.0620	1.0586–1.0620	1.0586–1.0620	1.0586–1.0620	1.0586–1.0620	1.0586–1.0620	1.5098	1.5098	⑦	0.0031–0.0075
	5S-FE ⑨	2.2 (2164)	1.0614–1.0620	1.0614–1.0620	1.0614–1.0620	1.0614–1.0620	1.0614–1.0620	—	—	1.3902–1.3941	1.4000–1.4039	0.0010–0.0024	⑤
1993	3E-E	1.5 (1457)	1.0622–1.0628	1.0622–1.0628	1.0622–1.0628	1.0622–1.0628	—	—	—	1.3917–1.3957 ⑥	1.4106–1.4146	0.0015–0.0029	0.0031–0.0071
	5E-FE	1.5 (1495)	0.9035–0.9041 ③	0.9035–0.9041	0.9035–0.9041	0.9035–0.9041	0.9035–0.9041	—	—	1.6343–1.6382	1.6264–1.6303	0.0014–0.0028	0.0018–0.0039
	4A-FE	1.6 (1587)	0.9822–0.9829	0.9822–0.9829	0.9822–0.9829	0.9822–0.9829	—	—	—	1.6450–1.6539	1.6520–1.6560	0.0014–0.0028	②
	7A-FE	1.8 (1762)	0.9822–0.9829	0.9822–0.9829	0.9822–0.9829	0.9822–0.9829	—	—	—	1.6450–1.6539	1.6520–1.6560	0.0014–0.0028	②
	5S-FE ⑧	2.2 (2164)	1.0614–1.0620	1.0614–1.0620	1.0614–1.0620	1.0614–1.0620	1.0614–1.0620	—	—	1.6539–1.6579	1.5772–1.5811	0.0010–0.0024	⑤
	3VZ-FE	3.0 (2952)	1.0610–1.0616	1.0610–1.0616	1.0610–1.0616	1.0610–1.0616	1.0610–1.0616	—	—	1.6598–1.6638	1.6520–1.6559	0.0014–0.0028	0.0013–0.0031
	3S-GTE	2.0 (1998)	1.0614–1.0620	1.0614–1.0620	1.0614–1.0620	1.0614–1.0620	1.0614–1.0620	—	—	1.6146–1.6185	1.6177–1.6217	0.0010–0.0024	0.0047–0.0094
	5S-FE ⑨	2.2 (2164)	1.0614–1.0620	1.0614–1.0620	1.0614–1.0620	1.0614–1.0620	1.0614–1.0620	—	—	1.3902–1.3941	1.4000–1.4039	0.0010–0.0024	⑤
1994	3E-E	1.5 (1457)	1.0622–1.0628	1.0622–1.0628	1.0622–1.0628	1.0622–1.0628	—	—	—	1.3917–1.3957 ⑥	1.4106–1.4146	0.0015–0.0029	0.0031–0.0071
	5E-FE	1.5 (1495)	0.9035–0.9041 ③	0.9035–0.9041	0.9035–0.9041	0.9035–0.9041	0.9035–0.9041	—	—	1.6343–1.6382	1.6264–1.6303	0.0014–0.0028	0.0018–0.0039
	4A-FE	1.6 (1587)	0.9822–0.9829	0.9822–0.9829	0.9822–0.9829	0.9822–0.9829	—	—	—	1.6450–1.6539	1.6520–1.6560	0.0014–0.0028	②
	7A-FE	1.8 (1762)	0.9822–0.9829	0.9822–0.9829	0.9822–0.9829	0.9822–0.9829	—	—	—	1.6450–1.6539	1.6520–1.6560	0.0014–0.0028	②
	5S-FE ⑧	2.2 (2164)	1.0614–1.0620	1.0614–1.0620	1.0614–1.0620	1.0614–1.0620	1.0614–1.0620	—	—	1.6539–1.6579	1.5772–1.5811	0.0010–0.0024	⑤
	3VZ-FE	3.0 (2952)	1.0610–1.0616	1.0610–1.0616	1.0610–1.0616	1.0610–1.0616	1.0610–1.0616	—	—	1.6598–1.6638	1.6520–1.6559	0.0014–0.0028	0.0013–0.0031
	3S-GTE	2.0 (1998)	1.0614–1.0620	1.0614–1.0620	1.0614–1.0620	1.0614–1.0620	1.0614–1.0620	—	—	1.6146–1.6185	1.6177–1.6217	0.0010–0.0024	0.0047–0.0094
	5S-FE ⑨	2.2 (2164)	1.0614–1.0620	1.0614–1.0620	1.0614–1.0620	1.0614–1.0620	1.0614–1.0620	—	—	1.3902–1.3941	1.4000–1.4039	0.0010–0.0024	⑤

① No. 1: 0.0014–0.0028
② Intake: 0.0012–0.0033
  Exhaust: 0.0014–0.0035
③ Exhaust No. 1: 0.9822–0.9829
④ 3S-GTE: 0.0039–0.0094
⑤ Intake: 0.0018–0.0039
  Exhaust: 0.0012–0.0033
⑥ Intake Sub-lobes: 1.3744–1.3783
⑦ No. 1 Journal: 0.0014–0.0028
  No. 2–No. 7 Journals: 0.0010–0.0037
⑧ Camry
⑨ Celica
⑩ 3S-GTE: 1.3961–1.4000
⑪ 7M-GTE: 1.5098

CRANKSHAFT AND CONNECTING ROD SPECIFICATIONS

All measurements are given in inches.

Year	Engine ID/VIN	Engine Displacement Liters (cc)	Crankshaft				Connecting Rod		
			Main Brg. Journal Dia.	Main Brg. Oil Clearance	Shaft End-play	Thrust on No.	Journal Diameter	Oil Clearance	Side Clearance
1990	3E, 3E-E	1.5 (1457)	1.9683–1.9685	0.0006–0.0014	0.0008–0.0087	3	1.6923–1.6929	0.0006–0.0019	0.0059–0.0138
	4A-FE	1.6 (1587)	1.8891–1.8898	0.0006–0.0013	0.0008–0.0087	3	1.5742–1.5748	0.0008–0.0020	0.0059–0.0098
	4A-GE	1.6 (1587)	1.8891–1.8898	0.0006–0.0013	0.0008–0.0087	3	1.6529–1.6535	0.0008–0.0020	0.0059–0.0098
	3S-FE	2.0 (1998)	2.1649–2.1655	0.0010–0.0017	0.0008–0.0087	3	1.8892–1.8898	0.0009–0.0022	0.0063–0.0123
	3S-GTE	2.0 (1998)	2.1653–2.1655	0.0006–0.0013①	0.0008–0.0087	3	1.8892–1.8898	0.0009–0.0022	0.0063–0.0123
	5S-FE	2.2 (2164)	2.1653–2.1655	0.0006–0.0013①	0.0008–0.0087	3	2.0466–2.0472	0.0009–0.0022	0.0063–0.0123
	2VZ-FE	2.5 (2507)	2.5191–2.5197	0.0011–0.0022	0.0008–0.0087	3	1.8892–1.8898	0.0011–0.0026	0.0059–0.0123
	7M-GE, 7M-GTE	3.0 (2954)	2.3625–2.3627	0.0012–0.0019	0.0020–0.0098	4	2.0470–2.0472	0.0008–0.0021	0.0063–0.0117
1991	3E-E	1.5 (1457)	1.9683–1.9685	0.0006–0.0013	0.0008–0.0087	3	1.6923–1.6929	0.0006–0.0019	0.0059–0.0138
	4A-FE	1.6 (1587)	1.8891–1.8898	0.0006–0.0013	0.0008–0.0087	3	1.5742–1.5748	0.0008–0.0020	0.0059–0.0098
	4A-GE	1.6 (1587)	1.8891–1.8898	0.0006–0.0013	0.0008–0.0087	3	1.6529–1.6535	0.0008–0.0020	0.0059–0.0098
	3S-FE	2.0 (1998)	2.1649–2.1655	0.0010–0.0017	0.0008–0.0087	3	1.8892–1.8898	0.0009–0.0022	0.0063–0.0123
	3S-GTE	2.0 (1998)	2.1653–2.1655	0.0006–0.0013①	0.0008–0.0087	3	1.8892–1.8898	0.0009–0.0022	0.0063–0.0123
	5S-FE	2.2 (2164)	2.1653–2.1655	0.0006–0.0013①	0.0008–0.0087	3	2.0466–2.0472	0.0009–0.0022	0.0063–0.0123
	2VZ-FE	2.5 (2507)	2.5191–2.5197	0.0011–0.0022	0.0008–0.0087	3	1.8892–1.8898	0.0011–0.0026	0.0059–0.0123
	7M-GE, 7M-GTE	3.0 (2954)	2.3625–2.3627	0.0012–0.0019	0.0020–0.0098	4	2.0470–2.0472	0.0008–0.0021	0.0063–0.0117
1992	3E-E	1.5 (1457)	1.9683–1.9685	0.0006–0.0014	0.0008–0.0079	3	1.6923–1.6929	0.0006–0.0019	0.0059–0.0138
	4A-FE	1.6 (1587)	1.8891–1.8898	0.0006–0.0013	0.0008–0.0087	3	1.5742–1.5748	0.0008–0.0020	0.0059–0.0098
	5E-FE	1.5 (1495)	1.9683–1.9685	0.0006–0.0014	0.0008–0.0079	3	1.6923–1.6929	0.0006–0.0019	0.0059–0.0138
	3VZ-FE	3.0 (2952)	2.5191–2.5197	0.0011–0.0022	0.0008–0.0087	3	2.1648–2.1654	0.0011–0.0026	0.0059–0.0130
	3S-GTE	2.0 (1998)	2.1653–2.1655	0.0006–0.0013①	0.0008–0.0087	3	1.8892–1.8898	0.0009–0.0022	0.0063–0.0123
	5S-FE	2.2 (2164)	2.1653–2.1655	0.0006–0.0013①	0.0008–0.0087	3	2.0466–2.0472	0.0009–0.0022	0.0063–0.0123
	7M-GE, 7M-GTE	3.0 (2954)	2.3625–2.3627	0.0012–0.0019	0.0020–0.0098	4	2.0470–2.0472	0.0008–0.0021	0.0063–0.0117

CRANKSHAFT AND CONNECTING ROD SPECIFICATIONS

All measurements are given in inches.

Year	Engine ID/VIN	Engine Displacement Liters (cc)	Crankshaft Main Brg. Journal Dia.	Crankshaft Main Brg. Oil Clearance	Crankshaft Shaft End-play	Crankshaft Thrust on No.	Connecting Rod Journal Diameter	Connecting Rod Oil Clearance	Connecting Rod Side Clearance
1993	3E-E	1.5 (1457)	1.9683–1.9685	0.0006–0.0014	0.0008–0.0079	3	1.6923–1.6929	0.0006–0.0019	0.0059–0.0138
	4A-FE	1.6 (1587)	1.8891–1.8898	0.0006–0.0013	0.0008–0.0087	3	1.5742–1.5748	0.0008–0.0020	0.0059–0.0098
	7A-FE	1.8 (1762)	1.8891–1.8898	0.0006–0.0013	0.0008–0.0087	3	1.8891–1.8898	0.0008–0.0017	0.0059–0.0098
	5E-FE	1.5 (1495)	1.9683–1.9685	0.0006–0.0014	0.0008–0.0079	3	1.6923–1.6929	0.0006–0.0019	0.0059–0.0138
	3VZ-FE	3.0 (2952)	2.5191–2.5197	0.0011–0.0022	0.0008–0.0087	3	2.1648–2.1654	0.0011–0.0026	0.0059–0.0130
	3S-GTE	2.0 (1998)	2.1653–2.1655	0.0006–0.0013 ①	0.0008–0.0087	3	1.8892–1.8898	0.0009–0.0022	0.0063–0.0123
	5S-FE	2.2 (2164)	2.1653–2.1655	0.0006–0.0013 ①	0.0008–0.0087	3	2.0466–2.0472	0.0009–0.0022	0.0063–0.0123
1994	3E-E	1.5 (1457)	1.9683–1.9685	0.0006–0.0014	0.0008–0.0079	3	1.6923–1.6929	0.0006–0.0019	0.0059–0.0138
	4A-FE	1.6 (1587)	1.8891–1.8898	0.0006–0.0013	0.0008–0.0087	3	1.5742–1.5748	0.0008–0.0020	0.0059–0.0098
	7A-FE	1.8 (1762)	1.8891–1.8898	0.0006–0.0013	0.0008–0.0087	3	1.8891–1.8898	0.0008–0.0017	0.0059–0.0098
	5E-FE	1.5 (1495)	1.9683–1.9685	0.0006–0.0014	0.0008–0.0079	3	1.6923–1.6929	0.0006–0.0019	0.0059–0.0138
	3VZ-FE	3.0 (2952)	2.5191–2.5197	0.0011–0.0022	0.0008–0.0087	3	2.1648–2.1654	0.0011–0.0026	0.0059–0.0130
	3S-GTE	2.0 (1998)	2.1653–2.1655	0.0006–0.0013 ①	0.0008–0.0087	3	1.8892–1.8898	0.0009–0.0022	0.0063–0.0123
	5S-FE	2.2 (2164)	2.1653–2.1655	0.0006–0.0013 ①	0.0008–0.0087	3	2.0466–2.0472	0.0009–0.0022	0.0063–0.0123

① No. 3 journal: 0.0010–0.0017

VALVE SPECIFICATIONS

Year	Engine ID/VIN	Engine Displacement Liters (cc)	Seat Angle (deg.)	Face Angle (deg.)	Spring Test Pressure (lbs. @ in.)	Spring Installed Height (in.)	Stem-to-Guide Clearance (in.)		Stem Diameter (in.)	
							Intake	Exhaust	Intake	Exhaust
1990	3E, 3E-E	1.5 (1457)	45	44.5	35.1	1.384	0.0010–0.0024	0.0012–0.0026	0.2350–0.2356	0.2348–0.2354
	4A-FE	1.6 (1587)	45	44.5	34.8	1.366	0.0010–0.0024	0.0012–0.0026	0.2350–0.2356	0.2348–0.2354
	4A-GE	1.6 (1587)	45	44.5	35.9	1.366	0.0010–0.0024	0.0012–0.0026	0.2350–0.2356	0.2348–0.2354
	3S-FE	2.0 (1998)	45	45.5	42.5	1.366	0.0010–0.0024	0.0012–0.0026	0.2350–0.2356	0.2348–0.2354
	3S-GTE	2.0 (1998)	45	45.5	53.1	1.354	0.0010–0.0023	0.0012–0.0025	0.2346–0.2352	0.2344–0.2350
	5S-FE	2.2 (2164)	45	45.5	42.5	1.366	0.0010–0.0024	0.0012–0.0026	0.2350–0.2356	0.2348–0.2354
	2VZ-FE	2.5 (2507)	45	45.5	47.2	1.331	0.0010–0.0024	0.0012–0.0026	0.2350–0.2356	0.2348–0.2354
	7M-GE, 7M-GTE	3.0 (2954)	45	45.5	35.0	1.378	0.0010–0.0024	0.0012–0.0026	0.2350–0.2356	0.2348–0.2354
1991	3E-E	1.5 (1457)	45	44.5	35.1	1.384	0.0010–0.0024	0.0012–0.0026	0.2350–0.2356	0.2348–0.2354
	4A-FE	1.6 (1587)	45	44.5	34.8	1.366	0.0010–0.0024	0.0012–0.0026	0.2350–0.2356	0.2348–0.2354
	4A-GE	1.6 (1587)	45	44.5	35.9	1.366	0.0010–0.0024	0.0012–0.0026	0.2350–0.2356	0.2348–0.2354
	3S-FE	2.0 (1998)	45	45.5	42.5	1.366	0.0010–0.0024	0.0012–0.0026	0.2350–0.2356	0.2348–0.2354
	3S-GTE	2.0 (1998)	45	45.5	53.1	1.354	0.0010–0.0023	0.0012–0.0025	0.2346–0.2352	0.2344–0.2350
	5S-FE	2.2 (2164)	45	45.5	42.5	1.366	0.0010–0.0023	0.0012–0.0026	0.2350–0.2356	0.2348–0.2354
	2VZ-FE	2.5 (2507)	45	45.5	47.2	1.331	0.0010–0.0024	0.0012–0.0026	0.2350–0.2356	0.2348–0.2354
	7M-GE, 7M-GTE	3.0 (2954)	45	44.5	35.0	1.378	0.0010–0.0024	0.0012–0.0026	0.2350–0.2356	0.2348–0.2354
1992	3E-E	1.5 (1457)	45	44.5	35.1	1.384	0.0010–0.0024	0.0012–0.0026	0.2350–0.2356	0.2348–0.2354
	5E-FE	1.5 (1495)	45	44.5	33.3–36.8	1.252	0.0010–0.0024	0.0012–0.0026	0.2350–0.2356	0.2348–0.2354
	4A-FE	1.6 (1587)	45	44.5	34.8	1.366	0.0010–0.0024	0.0012–0.0026	0.2350–0.2356	0.2348–0.2354
	5S-FE	2.2 (2164)	45	45.5	36.8–42.5	1.366	0.0010–0.0024	0.0012–0.0026	0.2350–0.2356	0.2348–0.2354
	3VZ-FE	3.0 (2952)	45	44.5	38.4–42.4	1.311	0.0010–0.0024	0.0012–0.0026	0.2350–0.2356	0.2348–0.2354
	3S-GTE	2.0 (1998)	45	44.5	45.2–53.1	1.354	0.0010–0.0023	0.0012–0.0025	0.2346–0.2352	0.2344–0.2350

VALVE SPECIFICATIONS

Year	Engine ID/VIN	Engine Displacement Liters (cc)	Seat Angle (deg.)	Face Angle (deg.)	Spring Test Pressure (lbs. @ in.)	Spring Installed Height (in.)	Stem-to-Guide Clearance (in.)		Stem Diameter (in.)	
							Intake	Exhaust	Intake	Exhaust
	7M-GE	3.0 (2954)	45	44.5	35.0	1.378	0.0010–0.0024	0.0012–0.0026	0.2350–0.2356	0.2348–0.2354
	7M-GTE	3.0 (2954)	45	44.5	35.0	1.378	0.0010–0.0024	0.0012–0.0026	0.2350–0.2356	0.2348–0.2354
1993	3E-E	1.5 (1457)	45	44.5	35.1	1.384	0.0010–0.0024	0.0012–0.0026	0.2350–0.2356	0.2348–0.2354
	5E-FE	1.5 (1495)	45	44.5	33.3–36.8	1.252	0.0010–0.0024	0.0012–0.0026	0.2350–0.2356	0.2348–0.2354
	4A-FE	1.6 (1587)	45	44.5	37.3	1.248	0.0010–0.0024	0.0012–0.0026	0.2350–0.2356	0.2348–0.2354
	7A-FE	1.8 (1762)	45	44.5	37.3	1.248	0.0010–0.0024	0.0012–0.0026	0.2350–0.2356	0.2348–0.2354
	5S-FE	2.2 (2164)	45	45.5	36.8–42.5	1.366	0.0010–0.0024	0.0012–0.0026	0.2350–0.2356	0.2348–0.2354
	3VZ-FE	3.0 (2952)	45	44.5	38.4–42.4	1.311	0.0010–0.0024	0.0012–0.0026	0.2350–0.2356	0.2348–0.2354
	3S-GTE	2.0 (1998)	45	44.5	45.2–53.1	1.354	0.0010–0.0023	0.0012–0.0025	0.2346–0.2352	0.2344–0.2350
1994	3E-E	1.5 (1457)	45	44.5	35.1	1.384	0.0010–0.0024	0.0012–0.0026	0.2350–0.2356	0.2348–0.2354
	5E-FE	1.5 (1495)	45	44.5	33.3–36.8	1.252	0.0010–0.0024	0.0012–0.0026	0.2350–0.2356	0.2348–0.2354
	4A-FE	1.6 (1587)	45	44.5	37.3	1.248	0.0010–0.0024	0.0012–0.0026	0.2350–0.2356	0.2348–0.2354
	7A-FE	1.8 (1762)	45	44.5	37.3	1.248	0.0010–0.0024	0.0012–0.0026	0.2350–0.2356	0.2348–0.2354
	5S-FE	2.2 (2164)	45	45.5	36.8–42.5	1.366	0.0010–0.0024	0.0012–0.0026	0.2350–0.2356	0.2348–0.2354
	3VZ-FE	3.0 (2952)	45	44.5	38.4–42.4	1.311	0.0010–0.0024	0.0012–0.0026	0.2350–0.2356	0.2348–0.2354
	3S-GTE	2.0 (1998)	45	44.5	45.2–53.1	1.354	0.0010–0.0023	0.0012–0.0025	0.2346–0.2352	0.2344–0.2350

PISTON AND RING SPECIFICATIONS

All measurements are given in inches.

| Year | Engine ID/VIN | Engine Displacement Liters (cc) | Piston Clearance | Ring Gap | | | Ring Side Clearance | | |
				Top Compression	Bottom Compression	Oil Control	Top Compression	Bottom Compression	Oil Control
1990	3E, 3E-E	1.5 (1457)	0.0028–0.0035	0.0102–0.0189	0.0118–0.0224	0.0059–0.0205	0.0016–0.0031	0.0012–0.0028	Snug
	4A-FE	1.6 (1587)	0.0024–0.0031	0.0098–0.0177	0.0059–0.0157	0.0039–0.0276	0.0016–0.0031	0.0012–0.0028	Snug
	4A-GE	1.6 (1587)	0.0039–0.0047	0.0098–0.0185	0.0079–0.0165	0.0059–0.0205	0.0012–0.0031	0.0012–0.0028	Snug
	3S-FE	2.0 (1998)	0.0018–0.0026	0.0118–0.0205	0.0138–0.0236	0.0079–0.0217	0.0004–0.0031	0.0012–0.0028	Snug
	3S-GTE	2.0 (1998)	0.0028–0.0035	0.0130–0.0217	0.0177–0.0264	0.0079–0.0236	0.0016–0.0031	0.0012–0.0028	Snug
	5S-FE	2.2 (2164)	0.0031–0.0039	0.0106–0.0197	0.0138–0.0234	0.0079–0.0217	0.0012–0.0028	0.0012–0.0028	Snug
	2VZ-FE	2.5 (2507)	0.0018–0.0026	0.0118–0.0205	0.0138–0.0236	0.0079–0.0217	0.0004–0.0031	0.0012–0.0028	Snug
	7M-GE	3.0 (2954)	0.0031–0.0039	0.0091–0.0150	0.0098–0.0209	0.0039–0.0157	0.0012–0.0028	0.0008–0.0024	Snug
	7M-GTE	3.0 (2954)	0.0028–0.0035	0.0114–0.0173	0.0098–0.0209	0.0039–0.0173	0.0008–0.0024	0.0008–0.0024	Snug
1991	3E-E	1.5 (1457)	0.0028–0.0035	0.0102–0.0189	0.0118–0.0224	0.0059–0.0205	0.0016–0.0031	0.0012–0.0028	Snug
	4A-FE	1.6 (1587)	0.0024–0.0031	0.0098–0.0177	0.0059–0.0157	0.0039–0.0276	0.0016–0.0031	0.0012–0.0028	Snug
	4A-GE	1.6 (1587)	0.0039–0.0047	0.0098–0.0185	0.0079–0.0165	0.0059–0.0205	0.0012–0.0031	0.0012–0.0028	Snug
	3S-FE	2.0 (1998)	0.0018–0.0026	0.0118–0.0205	0.0138–0.0236	0.0079–0.0217	0.0004–0.0031	0.0012–0.0028	Snug
	3S-GTE	2.0 (1998)	0.0028–0.0035	0.0130–0.0217	0.0177–0.0264	0.0079–0.0236	0.0016–0.0031	0.0012–0.0028	Snug
	5S-FE	2.2 (2164)	0.0031–0.0039	0.0106–0.0197	0.0138–0.0234	0.0079–0.0217	0.0012–0.0028	0.0012–0.0028	Snug
	2VZ-FE	2.5 (2507)	0.0018–0.0026	0.0118–0.0205	0.0138–0.0236	0.0079–0.0217	0.0004–0.0031	0.0012–0.0028	Snug
	7M-GE	3.0 (2954)	0.0031–0.0039	0.0091–0.0150	0.0098–0.0209	0.0039–0.0157	0.0012–0.0028	0.0008–0.0024	Snug
	7M-GTE	3.0 (2954)	0.0028–0.0035	0.0114–0.0173	0.0098–0.0209	0.0039–0.0173	0.0008–0.0024	0.0008–0.0024	Snug
1992	3E-E	1.5 (1457)	0.0028–0.0035	0.0102–0.0189	0.0118–0.0224	0.0059–0.0205	0.0016–0.0031	0.0012–0.0028	Snug
	4A-FE	1.6 (1587)	0.0024–0.0031	0.0098–0.0177	0.0059–0.0157	0.0039–0.0276	0.0020–0.0031	0.0012–0.0028	Snug
	5E-FE	1.5 (1495)	0.0035–0.0043	0.0102–0.0189	0.0118–0.0224	0.0059–0.0197	0.0016–0.0031	0.0012–0.0028	Snug
	3S-GTE	2.0 (1998)	0.0028–0.0035	0.0130–0.0217	0.0177–0.0264	0.0079–0.0236	0.0016–0.0031	0.0012–0.0028	Snug
	5S-FE	2.2 (2164)	0.0055–0.0063	0.0106–0.0197	0.0138–0.0234	0.0079–0.0217	0.0016–0.0031	0.0012–0.0028	Snug

PISTON AND RING SPECIFICATIONS

All measurements are given in inches.

Year	Engine ID/VIN	Engine Displacement Liters (cc)	Piston Clearance	Ring Gap			Ring Side Clearance		
				Top Compression	Bottom Compression	Oil Control	Top Compression	Bottom Compression	Oil Control
	3VZ-FE	3.0 (2952)	0.0051–0.0059	0.0110–0.0197	0.0150–0.0236	0.0059–0.0234	0.0004–0.0031	0.0012–0.0028	Snug
	7M-GE	3.0 (2954)	0.0031–0.0039	0.0091–0.0150	0.0098–0.0209	0.0039–0.0157	0.0012–0.0028	0.0008–0.0024	Snug
	7M-GTE	3.0 (2954)	0.0028–0.0035	0.0114–0.0173	0.0098–0.0209	0.0039–0.0173	0.0012–0.0024	0.0008–0.0024	Snug
1993	3E-E	1.5 (1457)	0.0028–0.0035	0.0102–0.0189	0.0118–0.0224	0.0059–0.0205	0.0016–0.0031	0.0012–0.0028	Snug
	4A-FE	1.6 (1587)	0.0033–0.0041	0.0098–0.0177	0.0138–0.0197	0.0059–0.0177	0.0018–0.0033	0.0012–0.0028	—
	7A-FE	1.8 (1762)	0.0033–0.0041	0.0098–0.0177	0.0138–0.0197	0.0059–0.0177	0.0018–0.0033	0.0012–0.0028	—
	5E-FE	1.5 (1495)	0.0035–0.0043	0.0102–0.0189	0.0118–0.0224	0.0059–0.0197	0.0016–0.0031	0.0012–0.0028	Snug
	3S-GTE	2.0 (1998)	0.0028–0.0035	0.0130–0.0217	0.0177–0.0264	0.0079–0.0236	0.0016–0.0031	0.0012–0.0028	Snug
	5S-FE	2.2 (2164)	0.0055–0.0063	0.0106–0.0197	0.0138–0.0234	0.0079–0.0217	0.0016–0.0031	0.0012–0.0028	Snug
	3VZ-FE	3.0 (2952)	0.0051–0.0059	0.0110–0.0197	0.0150–0.0236	0.0059–0.0234	0.0004–0.0031	0.0012–0.0028	Snug
1994	3E-E	1.5 (1457)	0.0028–0.0035	0.0102–0.0189	0.0118–0.0224	0.0059–0.0205	0.0016–0.0031	0.0012–0.0028	Snug
	4A-FE	1.6 (1587)	0.0033–0.0041	0.0098–0.0177	0.0138–0.0197	0.0059–0.0177	0.0018–0.0033	0.0012–0.0028	—
	7A-FE	1.8 (1762)	0.0033–0.0041	0.0098–0.0177	0.0138–0.0197	0.0059–0.0177	0.0018–0.0033	0.0012–0.0028	—
	5E-FE	1.5 (1495)	0.0035–0.0043	0.0102–0.0189	0.0118–0.0224	0.0059–0.0197	0.0016–0.0031	0.0012–0.0028	Snug
	3S-GTE	2.0 (1998)	0.0028–0.0035	0.0130–0.0217	0.0177–0.0264	0.0079–0.0236	0.0016–0.0031	0.0012–0.0028	Snug
	5S-FE	2.2 (2164)	0.0055–0.0063	0.0106–0.0197	0.0138–0.0234	0.0079–0.0217	0.0016–0.0031	0.0012–0.0028	Snug
	3VZ-FE	3.0 (2952)	0.0051–0.0059	0.0110–0.0197	0.0150–0.0236	0.0059–0.0234	0.0004–0.0031	0.0012–0.0028	Snug

TORQUE SPECIFICATIONS

All readings in ft. lbs.

Year	Engine ID/VIN	Engine Displacement Liters (cc)	Cylinder Head Bolts	Main Bearing Bolts	Rod Bearing Bolts	Crankshaft Damper Bolts	Flywheel Bolts	Manifold Intake	Manifold Exhaust	Spark Plugs	Lug Nut
1990	3E, 3E-E	1.5 (1457)	⑥	42	29	112	88	14	38	13	76
	4A-FE	1.6 (1587)	44⑦	44	36	87	58	14	18	13	76
	4A-GE	1.6 (1587)	⑧	44	①	101	54	20	29	13	76
	3S-FE	2.0 (1998)	③	43	36	80	65	14	36	13	76
	3S-GTE	2.0 (1998)	③	43	49	80	80	14	38	13	76
	5S-FE	2.2 (2164)	③	43	④	80	②	14	36	13	76
	2VZ-FE	2.5 (2507)	⑩	⑤	④	181	61	13	13	13	76
	7M-GE, 7M-GTE	3.0 (2954)	58⑦	75	47	195	54	13	29	13	76
1991	3E-E	1.5 (1457)	⑥	42	29	112	65	14	35	13	76
	4A-FE	1.6 (1587)	44⑦	44	36	87	58	14	18	13	76
	4A-GE	1.6 (1587)	⑧	44	⑨	101	54	20	29	13	76
	3S-FE	2.0 (1998)	③	43	36	80	65	14	36	13	76
	3S-GTE	2.0 (1998)	③	43	49	80	80	14	38	13	76
	5S-FE	2.2 (2164)	③	43	④	80	65	14	36	13	76
	2VZ-FE	2.5 (2507)	⑩	⑤	④	181	61	13	29	13	76
	7M-GE, 7M-GTE	3.0 (2954)	58⑦	75	47	195	54	13	29	13	76
1992	3E-E	1.5 (1457)	⑥	42	29	112	65	14	38	13	76
	4A-FE	1.6 (1587)	44⑦	44	36	87	58⑪	14	18	13	76
	5E-FE	1.5 (1495)	③	42	29	112	65	14	35	13	76
	3S-GTE	2.0 (1998)	③	43	49	80	80	14	38	13	76
	5S-FE	2.2 (2164)	③	43	④	80	②	14	36	13	76
	3VZ-FE	3.0 (2952)	⑩⑫	⑤	④	181	61	13	29	13	76
	7M-GE, 7M-GTE	3.0 (2954)	58⑦	75	47	195	54	13	29	13	76
1993	3E-E	1.5 (1457)	⑥	42	29	112	65	14	38	13	76
	4A-FE	1.6 (1587)	⑧	44	⑬	87	58⑪	14	29	13	76
	5E-FE	1.5 (1495)	③	42	29	112	65	14	35	13	76
	7A-FE	1.8 (1762)	⑧	44	⑬	87	58⑪	14	29	13	76
	3S-GTE	2.0 (1998)	③	43	49	80	80	14	38	13	76
	5S-FE	2.2 (2164)	③	43	④	80	②	14	36	13	76
	3VZ-FE	3.0 (2952)	⑩⑫	⑤	④	181	61	13	29	13	76
1994	3E-E	1.5 (1457)	⑥	42	29	112	65	14	38	13	76
	4A-FE	1.6 (1587)	⑧	44	⑬	87	58⑪	14	29	13	76
	5E-FE	1.5 (1495)	③	42	29	112	65	14	35	13	76
	7A-FE	1.8 (1762)	⑧	44	⑬	87	58⑪	14	29	13	76
	3S-GTE	2.0 (1998)	③	43	49	80	80	14	38	13	76
	5S-FE	2.2 (2164)	③	43	④	80	②	14	36	13	76
	3VZ-FE	3.0 (2952)	⑩⑫	⑤	④	181	61	13	29	13	76

① 29 ft. lbs. and an additional 90 degree turn
② M/T: 65
   A/T: 61
③ 36 ft. lbs. and an additional 90 degree turn
④ 18 ft. lbs. and an additional 90 degree turn
⑤ 45 ft. lbs. and an additional 90 degree turn
⑥ 22 ft. lbs., 36 ft. lbs. and an additional 90 degree turn

⑦ Torque in sequence, in 3 steps
⑧ 22 ft. lbs., an additional 90 degree turn plus an additional 90 degree turn
⑨ 29 ft. lbs. plus an additional 90 degree turn
⑩ 25 ft. lbs., an additional 90 degree turn plus an additional 90 degree turn
⑪ A/T: 47 ft. lbs.

⑫ Torque in sequence in 3 steps. Recessed head bolt: 13 ft. lbs.
⑬ 22 ft. lbs. plus an additional 90 degree turn

BRAKE SPECIFICATIONS

All measurements in inches unless noted.

Year	Model	Master Cylinder Bore	Brake Disc			Brake Drum Diameter			Minimum Lining Thickness	
			Original Thickness	Minimum Thickness	Maximum Runout	Original Inside Diameter	Max. Wear Limit	Maximum Machine Diameter	Front	Rear
1990	Tercel	①	0.433	0.394	0.0059	7.087	7.126	7.126	0.039	0.039
	Corolla	①	③	③	④	7.874	7.913	7.913	0.039	0.039
	Camry	①	⑤	⑤	⑥	9.000 ⑰	0.079 ⑱	9.079 ⑱	0.039	0.039
	Celica	①	0.866 ⑭	⑦	⑥	7.874 ⑰	7.913 ⑱	7.913 ⑱	0.039	0.039
	Supra	①	0.866 ⑲	0.827	0.0051	7.48 ⑳	7.52 ⑳	7.52 ⑳	0.039	0.039
	Cressida	①	0.866 ⑲	⑩	⑪	6.93 ⑳	6.97 ⑳	6.97 ⑳	0.039	0.039
1991	Tercel	①	0.709	0.669	0.0035	7.087	7.126	7.126	0.039	0.039
	Corolla	①	③	④	④	7.874	7.913	7.913	0.039	0.039
	Camry	①	⑤	⑤	⑥	9.000 ⑰	0.079 ⑱	9.079 ⑱	0.039	0.039
	Celica	①	0.866 ⑭	⑦	⑥	7.874 ⑰	7.913 ⑱	7.913 ⑱	0.039	0.039
	Supra	①	0.866 ㉕	⑩	0.0051	7.48 ⑳	7.52 ⑳	7.52 ⑳	0.040	0.040
	MR2	①	⑬	⑧	⑨	—	—	—	0.039	0.039
	Cressida	①	0.866 ⑲	⑩	⑪	—	—	—	0.039	0.039
1992	Tercel	①	0.709	0.669	0.0035	7.087	7.126	7.126	0.039	0.039
	Paseo	①	0.709	0.669	0.0035	7.087	7.126	7.126	0.039	0.039
	Corolla	①	0.709	0.669	0.0035	7.874	7.913	7.013	0.039	0.039
	Camry	①	1.102 ⑭	1.124 ⑮	0.0020 ⑯	9.000 ⑲	9.079 ⑱	9.079 ⑱	0.039	0.039
	Celica	①	0.984 ⑭	0.906 ⑮	0.0028 ⑯	7.874 ⑰	7.913 ⑱	7.913 ⑱	0.039	0.039
	Supra	①	0.866 ⑲	0.827 ②	0.0051	7.48 ⑳	7.52 ⑳	7.52 ⑳	0.039	0.039
	MR2	①	⑬	⑧	⑨	—	—	—	0.039	0.039
	Cressida	①	0.866 ⑲	0.827 ②	0.0028 ㉑	6.93 ⑳	6.97 ⑳	6.97 ㉑	0.039	0.039
1993	Tercel	①	0.709	0.669	0.0035	7.087	7.126	7.126	0.039	0.039
	Paseo	①	0.709	0.669	0.0035	7.087	7.126	7.126	0.039	0.039
	Corolla	①	0.709	0.669	0.0035	7.874	7.913	7.013	0.039	0.039
	Camry	①	1.102 ⑭	1.124 ⑮	0.0020 ⑯	9.000 ⑰	9.079 ⑱	9.079 ⑱	0.039	0.039
	Celica	①	0.984 ⑭	0.906 ⑮	0.0028 ⑯	7.874 ⑰	7.913 ⑱	7.913 ⑱	0.039	0.039
	MR2	①	⑬	⑧	⑩	—	—	—	0.039	0.039

① Not specified by the manufacturer
② Rear: 0.669
③ Original Thickness—Front
    4A-GE engine: 0.866
    4A-FE engine: 0.709
  Minimum Thickness—Front
    4A-GE engine: 0.827
    4A-FE engine: 0.669
  Original Thickness—Rear: 0.354
  Minimum Thickness—Rear: 0.315
④ Front disc: 0.0035
  Rear disc: 0.0039
⑤ Original Thickness
  Front: 0.984
  Rear: 0.394
  Minimum Thickness
  Front: 0.045
  Rear: 0.354

⑥ Front: 0.0028
  Rear: 0.0059
⑦ Front: 0.787
  Rear: 0.354
⑧ Front: 0.945
  Rear: 0.591
⑨ Front: 0.0028
  Rear: 0.0039
⑩ Front: 0.827
  Rear: 0.669
⑪ Front: 0.0028
  Rear: 0.0051
⑫ Rear: 0.669
⑬ Front: 0.984
  Rear: 0.630

⑭ Rear: 0.394
⑮ Rear: 0.354
⑯ Rear: 0.0059
⑰ Parking brake: 6.69
⑱ Parking brake: 6.73
⑲ Rear: 0.709
⑳ Parking brake
㉑ Rear: 0.0051

WHEEL ALIGNMENT

Year	Model	Caster Range (deg.)	Caster Preferred Setting (deg.)	Camber Range (deg.)	Camber Preferred Setting (deg.)	Toe-in (in.)	Steering Axis Inclination (deg.)
1990	Tercel	①	②	3/4N–3/4P	0	0.08 out–0.08 in	11½
	Corolla (2WD)	9/16P–2 1/16P	1 5/16P	1N–1/2P	1/4N	0–5/32	12 13/16
	Corolla (4WD)	3/4P–1 3/4P	1 1/4P	5/16N–11/16P	3/16P	0–5/32	12
	Camry (Sedan)	1 3/16P–2 3/16P	1 11/16P	1/16N–1 1/16P	9/16P	0.04 out–0.04 in	12 3/4
	Camry (Wagon)	1/2P–1 1/2P	1P	0–1P	1/2P	0.04 out–0.04 in	12 13/16
	Celica	1/4P–1 3/4P	1P	15/16N–9/16P	3/16N	1/16–1/8	14 3/16
	Supra	7 3/16P–8 3/16P	7 11/16P	11/16N–5/16P	3/16N	3/64 out–3/64 in	10 15/16
	Cressida	6 9/16P–8 1/16P	7 5/16P	0–1P	1/2P	3/32–1/4	13 3/16
1991	Tercel	1 3/4P–3 1/4P	2 1/2P	3/4N–3/4P	0	3/64 out–3/64 in	11½
	Corolla (2WD)	9/16P–2 1/16P	1 5/16P	1N–1/2P	1/4N	0–5/64	12 5/8
	Corolla (4WD)	3/4P–1 3/4P	1 1/4P	5/16N–11/16P	3/16P	0–5/64	12
	Camry (Sedan)	1 3/16P–2 3/16P	1 11/16P	1/16N–1 1/16P	9/16P	0.04 out–0.04 in	12 3/4
	Camry (Wagon)	1/2P–1 1/2P	1P	0–1P	1/2P	0.04 out–0.04 in	12 13/16
	Celica	1/4P–1 3/4P	1P	15/16N–9/16P	3/16P	1/16–1/8	14 3/16
	Supra	7 3/16P–8 3/16P	7 11/16P	11/16N–5/16P	3/16N	3/64 out–3/64 in	10 15/16
	MR2	2P–3 1/4P	2 3/4P	1 13/32N–13/32N	1N	0.04 out–0.04 in	13
	Cressida	6 9/16P–8 1/16P	7 5/16P	0–1P	1/2P	3/32–1/4	13 3/16
1992	Tercel	1P–2 1/2P	1 3/4P	1 1/16N–1/3P	5/12N	0.04 out–0.12 in	12 1/4 ± 3/4
	Paseo	2/3P–2 1/6P	1 5/12P	1 1/6N–1/3P	5/12N	0.04 out–0.12 in	12 1/4 ± 3/4
	Corolla (2WD)	2/3P–2 1/6P	1 5/12P	11/12N–7/12P	1/6N	0.04 out–0.12 in	12 2/3 ± 3/4
	Corolla (4WD)	3/4P–2P	1 1/4P	1/3N–2/3P	1/6P	0.04 out–0.12 in	12 1/12 ± 1/2
	Camry	5/12P–1 11/12P	1 1/6P	1 1/3N–1/6P	7/12N	0.08 out–0.08 in	13 1/12 ± 3/4
	Celica (2WD)	1/6P–1 2/3P	1 1/12P	11/12N–7/12P	1/6N	0.08 out–0.08 in	14 1/6 ± 3/4
	Celica (4WD)	1/12P–1 7/12P	5/6P	11/12N–7/12P	1/6N	0.08 out–0.08 in	14 1/6 ± 3/4
	Supra	6 5/6P–8 1/3P	7 7/12P	11/16N–7/12P	1/6N	0.08 out–0.08 in	10 11/12 ± 3/4
	MR2	2P–3 1/2P	2 3/4P	1 2/3N–2/3P	11/12N	0.04 out–0.04 in	13 1/2 ± 3/4
	Cressida	6 7/16P–8 1/12P	7 1/3P	1/4N–1 1/4P	1/2P	0–0.16 in	13 1/6 ± 3/4

WHEEL ALIGNMENT

		Caster		Camber			Steering
Year	Model	Range (deg.)	Preferred Setting (deg.)	Range (deg.)	Preferred Setting (deg.)	Toe-in (in.)	Axis Inclination (deg.)
1993	Tercel	1P-2 1/2P	1 3/4P	1 1/16N-1/3P	5/12N	0.04 out-0.12 in	12 1/4 ± 3/4
	Paseo	2/3P-2 1/6P	1 5/12P	1 1/6N-1/3P	5/12N	0.04 out-0.12 in	12 1/4 ± 3/4
	Corolla (2WD)	2/3P-2 1/6P	1 5/12P	11/12N-7/12P	1/6N	0.04 out-0.12 in	12 2/3 ± 3/4
	Camry	5/12P-1 11/12P	1 1/6P	1 1/3N-1/6P	7/12N	0.08 out-0.08 in	13 1/12 ± 3/4
	Celica (2WD)	1/6P-1 2/3P	11/12P	11/12N-7/12P	1/6N	0.08 out-0.08 in	14 1/6 ± 3/4
	Celica (4WD)	1/12P-1 7/12P	5/6P	11/12N-7/12P	1/6N	0.08 out-0.08 in	14 1/6 ± 3/4
	MR2	2P-3 1/2P	2 3/4P	1 2/3N-2/3P	11/12N	0.04 out-0.04 in	13 1/2 ± 3/4
1994	Tercel	1P-2 1/2P	1 3/4P	1 1/16N-1/3P	5/12N	0.04 out-0.12 in	12 1/4 ± 3/4
	Paseo	2/3P-2 1/6P	1 5/12P	1 1/6N-1/3P	5/12N	0.04 out-0.12 in	12 1/4 ± 3/4
	Corolla (2WD)	2/3P-2 1/6P	1 5/12P	11/12N-7/12P	1/6N	0.04 out-0.12 in	12 2/3 ± 3/4
	Camry	5/12P-1 11/12P	1 1/6P	1 1/3N-1/6P	7/12N	0.08 out-0.08 in	13 1/12 ± 3/4
	Celica (2WD)	1/6P-1 2/3P	11/12P	11/12N-7/12P	1/6N	0.08 out-0.08 in	14 1/6 ± 3/4
	Celica (4WD)	1/12P-1 7/12P	5/6P	11/12N-7/12P	1/6N	0.08 out-0.08 in	14 1/6 ± 3/4
	MR2	2P-3 1/2P	2 3/4P	1 2/3N-2/3P	11/12N	0.04 out-0.04 in	13 1/2 ± 3/4

N—Negative
P—Positive
① Manual Steering Gear: 1/4P-1 3/4P
Power Steering Gear: 1 3/4-3 1/4P
② Manual Steering Gear: 1P
Power Steering Gear: 2 1/2P

ENGINE MECHANICAL

CAUTION

To avoid personal injury and accidental deployment of the air bag, work must be started after about 90 seconds or longer from the time the ignition switch is turned to the LOCK position and the battery cable is disconnected from the battery.

NOTE: Disconnecting the negative battery cable on some vehicles may interfere with the functions of the on-board computer systems and may require the computer to undergo a relearning process, once the negative battery cable is reconnected.

Engine Assembly

REMOVAL AND INSTALLATION

2VZ-FE Engine

1. Disconnect the negative battery cable.
2. Remove the battery.
3. Drain the cooling system and engine oil.
4. Remove the hood.
5. Remove the ignition coil, igniter and bracket assembly.
6. Remove the radiator.
7. Remove the and coolant reservoir tank.
8. If equipped with automatic transaxle, disconnect the throttle cable from the throttle body.
9. If equipped with cruise control, remove the cruise control actuator and vacuum pump.
10. Remove the air cleaner assembly.
11. If equipped with manual transaxle, remove the clutch release cylinder. Position it aside with the hydraulic line still attached.
12. Disconnect the speedometer and transaxle control cables.
13. Remove the alternator and the belt adjusting bar.
14. Remove the air conditioning compressor and position it aside. Do not disconnect the refrigerant lines.
15. Disconnect the 2 water bypass hoses and fuel lines.
16. Tag and disconnect the brake booster, air conditioning control valve and charcoal canister vacuum hoses.
17. Tag and disconnect any additional wires and lines which may interfere with engine removal.
18. Raise and support the vehicle safely.
19. Remove the engine undercovers.
20. Remove the lower suspension crossmember.
21. Remove the halfshafts.
22. Remove the power steering pump and position it aside without disconnecting the hydraulic lines.
23. Remove the front exhaust pipe.
24. Remove the engine mounting center member.
25. Remove the front, center and rear engine mount insulator and bracket assemblies.
26. Lower the vehicle. Remove the glove box and then tag and disconnect the 3 ECU connectors, the circuit opening, cowl wire and instrument wire connectors. Pull the main engine harness out through the firewall.
27. Remove the power steering reservoir tank and position it aside without disconnecting the hydraulic lines.
28. Remove the 2 right side engine mounting stays. Remove the left side engine mounting stay.
29. Connect a suitable lifting device to the 2 engine hangers. Slowly re-

move the engine/transaxle assembly as a unit.

To install:

30. When installing the engine pay close attention to the following torque specifications.

    a. Transaxle-to-engine mounting bolts — 56 ft. lbs. (77 Nm).

    b. Bracket-to-frame bolt — 40 ft. lbs. (56 Nm).

    c. Engine mount bracket-to-block — 28 ft. lbs. (39 Nm).

    d. Front and rear engine mounting through bolts and nuts — 60 ft. lbs. (84 Nm).

    e. Right hand mounting rubber on body side — 30 ft. lbs. (41 Nm). Right hand mounting rubber on engine side — 45 ft. lbs. (62 Nm).

    f. Strut-to-body nuts — 40 ft. lbs. (56 Nm).

    g. Tie rod end-to-steering knuckle ball joints — 29 ft. lbs. (40 Nm).

31. Connect a suitable lifting device to the 2 engine hangers. Slowly install the engine/transaxle assembly as a unit.

32. Install all other remaining components. Make all necessary adjustments.

33. Connect the battery cable, refill all fluids, start the engine and check for leaks.

3VZ-FE Engine

1. Disconnect the negative battery cable.

CAUTION

To avoid personal injury when working on models with an air bag, wait at least 90 seconds from the time that the ignition switch is turned to the LOCK position and the battery is disconnected before performing any further work.

2. Remove the battery and its tray.

3. Remove the hood.

4. Remove the engine undercover and then drain the engine coolant and oil.

5. Disconnect the accelerator cable from the throttle body. On models with automatic transaxle, its the throttle cable, not the accelerator.

6. Remove the air cleaner assembly, resonator and the air intake hose.

7. On models with cruise control, remove the actuator cover, unplug the connector, remove the 3 bolts and then disconnect the actuator with the bracket.

8. Disconnect the ground strap at the battery carrier.

9. Remove the radiator and then disconnect the coolant reservoir hose.

10. Remove the 3 washer tank mounting bolts, disconnect the connector and hose and then lift out the tank.

11. Tag and disconnect the:

    a. 3 connectors to the engine relay box

    b. 2 connectors from the left side fender apron

    c. Igniter connector

    d. Noise filter connector

    e. Connector at the fender apron

    f. Check connector

    g. Ground strap at the right fender apron

    h. Backup light switch and speed sensor (models with manual transaxle)

12. Disconnect the heater hoses and the fuel return hose and the fuel inlet hose.

13. On models with manual transaxle, remove the starter and clutch release cylinder. Do not disconnect the hydraulic line, simply hang the cylinder out of the way.

14. Disconnect the transaxle control cables at the transaxle.

15. Tag and disconnect all remaining vacuum hoses.

16. Remove the undercover beneath the glove box. Remove the lower instrument panel, the glove box door and the box itself. Tag and disconnect the 3 ECU connectors, the 5 cowl wire connectors and the cooling fan ECU connector. Remove the 2 nuts and then pull the engine harness into the engine compartment.

17. Without disconnecting the refrigerant lines, remove the air conditioning compressor and hang it carefully out of the way.

18. Loosen the 2 bolts and disconnect the front exhaust pipe bracket. Remove the 3 nuts attaching the front pipe to the manifold. Disconnect the pipe.

19. Remove the halfshafts.

20. Without disconnecting the hydraulic lines, remove the power steering pump and hang it aside. Disconnect the hydraulic cooling fan pressure hose.

21. Remove the 3 bolts (manual transaxle) or 4 bolts (automatic transaxle) and then disconnect the left engine mounting insulator. Pop out the plugs, remove the 4 nuts and then remove the rear engine mounting insulator. Remove the 4 bolts and remove the mount absorber. Remove the 3 bolts and disconnect the front engine mounting insulator.

22. Attach an engine lifting device to the lift hooks. Remove the 3 bolts and disconnect the control rod. Slowly and carefully, lift the engine/transaxle assembly out of the engine compartment.

To install:

23. Carefully lower the engine into the engine compartment. With the engine level and all the mounts aligned with their brackets, install the engine control rod. Tighten the 3 bolts, in the sequence shown, to 47 ft. lbs. (64 Nm). Install the right side mounting stays and tighten the small bolts to 23 ft. lbs. (31 Nm) and the larger bolts to 46 ft. lbs. (62 Nm).

24. Connect the front engine mount and tighten the bolts to 59 ft. lbs. (80 Nm). Connect the engine mount absorber and tighten the bolts to 35 ft. lbs. (48 Nm). Connect the rear mount and tighten the nuts to 48 ft. lbs. (66 Nm). Don't forget the plugs.

25. Connect the left mount and tighten the bolts (3 or 4) to 47 ft. lbs. (64 Nm).

26. Install the power steering pump and tighten the bolts to 31 ft. lbs. (43 Nm).

27. Install the halfshafts.

28. Connect the front pipe to the manifold and tighten the new nuts to 46 ft. lbs. (62 Nm) and the torque converter nuts to 32 ft. lbs. (43 Nm). Don't forget to install the bracket.

29. Install the air conditioning compressor and tighten the cylinder block bolts to 20 ft. lbs. (27 Nm) and the bracket bolts to 14 ft. lbs. (20 Nm).

30. Feed the engine harness through the cowl and reconnect it. Install the glove box.

31. Connect the vacuum hoses and the transaxle control cables.

32. Install the release cylinder and the starter.

33. Connect the fuel inlet hose and tighten it to 22 ft. lbs. (29 Nm). Connect the return hose and the 2 heater hoses.

34. Reconnect all disconnected wires.

35. Install the washer tank and connect the electrical lead and hose.

36. Install the coolant reservoir hose and the radiator.

37. Connect the ground strap to the battery carrier and then install the cruise control actuator. Install the air cleaner assembly.

38. Connect the throttle/accelerator cable and adjust it.

39. Fill the engine with oil and coolant. Connect the battery cable, start the engine and check for any leaks.

3E, 3E-E and 5E-FE Engines

1. Disconnect the negative battery cable.
2. Remove the battery and the air cleaner.
3. Scribe hinge locator marks, then remove the hood.
4. Remove the engine undercovers, if equipped.
5. Drain the cooling system and remove the radiator.
6. If equipped with automatic transaxle, disconnect and plug the transaxle fluid lines and disconnect the throttle and accelerator cables.
7. On Paseo, remove the charcoal canister and drain case.
8. Remove the windshield washer tank, disconnect the ground straps and disconnect the fuel hoses.

CAUTION

To avoid personal injury, properly release the fuel pressure on any fuel injected model before disconnecting any fuel lines.

---

9. Disconnect and tag the heater hoses.
10. If equipped with cruise control, disconnect and remove the actuator assembly.
11. If equipped with automatic transaxle, remove the accelerator cable bracket.
12. Disconnect and tag the PCV hoses and any other vacuum hoses that prevent the removal of the engine.
13. Disconnect and tag any wiring harnesses connected to the intake manifold.
14. Disconnect the brake booster hose.
15. Remove the clips and washers, then disconnect the transaxle control cables.
16. Disconnect the speedometer cable.
17. If equipped with automatic transaxle, remove the clutch release cylinder and the selecting bell crank.
18. Disconnect and label the oxygen sensor wire, the oil pressure switch wire, the coolant fan wire, the water temperature gauge wire, the backup light switch and neutral safety switch wires.
19. Disconnect and tag the starter wires.
20. Disconnect the Cold Mixture Heater (CMH) connector and the alternator electrical connector.
21. Remove the Vacuum Switching Valve (VSV).
22. If equipped with power steering, remove the power steering pump and position it aside.

23. If equipped with air conditioning, remove the air conditioning compressor and position it aside. Leave the refrigerant lines connected.
24. Disconnect the exhaust pipe at the manifold.
25. Remove the halfshafts.
26. Support the engine/transaxle assembly properly.
27. Connect a suitable lifting device to the engine lifting hooks.
28. If equipped with manual transaxle, remove the rear mounting through bolt and the rear mounting assembly. If equipped with automatic transaxle, remove the front mounting through bolt and front mounting assembly.
29. Remove the right and left side mounting bolts and brackets.
30. Carefully lift the engine assembly out of the vehicle.

To install:

31. Lower the engine into the vehicle.
32. Connect all electrical and hoses fittings to their original positions.
33. Install all necessary components in the reverse order of removal, torquing the fasteners to specifications.
34. Refill all fluids to specifications.
35. Connect the battery cable, start the engine and check for leaks.

3S-FE Engine

CAMRY (2WD)

1. Disconnect the negative battery cable.
2. Remove the hood.
3. Drain the cooling system.
4. Remove the igniter and bracket assembly.
5. Tag and disconnect all vacuum hoses, electrical wires and cables that are necessary to remove the engine.
6. Remove the radiator and coolant reservoir tank.
7. If equipped with automatic transaxle, disconnect the throttle cable and bracket from the throttle body.
8. Disconnect the accelerator cable from the throttle body.
9. If equipped with cruise control, remove the cruise control actuator and bracket.
10. Disconnect the ground wire from the alternator upper bracket.
11. Remove the air cleaner assembly, air flow meter and air cleaner hose.
12. Remove the heater hoses.
13. Disconnect and plug the fuel lines.
14. Disconnect the speedometer cable.

15. If equipped with manual transaxle, remove the clutch release cylinder and tube bracket. Do not disconnect the tube from the bracket.
16. Disconnect the transaxle control cable.
17. If equipped with air conditioning, remove the air conditioning compressor and position it aside. Do not disconnect the refrigerant lines.
18. If equipped with power steering, remove the power steering pump and position it aside. Do not disconnect the lines.
19. Raise and support the vehicle safely.
20. Drain the engine oil.
21. Remove the engine undercovers.
22. Remove the suspension lower crossmember.
23. Remove the halfshafts.
24. Disconnect the exhaust pipe from the catalytic converter.
25. Disconnect the engine mounting center crossmember member.
26. Lower the vehicle.
27. Tag and disconnect the ECU electrical connectors.
28. Connect a suitable lifting device to the engine. Raise the engine slightly and remove the engine retaining brackets and bolts.
29. Carefully remove the engine/transaxle assembly from the vehicle.

NOTE: Be careful not to hit the power steering gear housing or the neutral safety switch.

To install:

30. Lower the engine/transaxle assembly into the vehicle.
31. Connect all electrical and hoses fittings.
32. Install all necessary components.
33. During installation, observe the following torque specifications:

   a. On manual transaxles, torque the flywheel bolts to 65 ft. lbs. (88 Nm).

   b. On automatic transaxles, torque the driveplate bolts to 13 ft. lbs. (18 Nm).

   c. Left bracket and mounting insulator bolts to 35 ft. lbs. (48 Nm).

   d. Right mounting insulator and front through bolts to 47 ft. lbs. (64 Nm); rear mounting insulator-to-body bolts to 54 ft. lbs. (73 Nm).

   e. If equipped with automatic transaxle, torque the rear mounting insulator bolts to 43 ft. lbs. (58 Nm).

34. Connect the battery cable, refill all fluids, start the engine and check for leaks.

CAMRY (4WD)

1. Disconnect the negative battery cable.
2. Drain the cooling system.
3. Remove the hood.
4. Disconnect the accelerator cable from the throttle body.
5. Remove the radiator and the coolant reservoir tank.
6. Disconnect the heater hoses.
7. Disconnect the inlet hose at the fuel filter. Disconnect the return hose at the fuel return pipe.
8. Disconnect and remove the cruise control actuator.
9. Remove the air cleaner assembly.
10. Remove the clutch slave cylinder and hose bracket without disconnecting the hydraulic line. Position the assembly aside.
11. Disconnect the speedometer cable and the transaxle control cables.
12. If equipped with air conditioning, disconnect and remove the compressor with the refrigerant lines still attached. Move the compressor aside.
13. Tag and disconnect all wires, connectors and vacuum lines necessary to remove engine.
14. Raise and support the vehicle safely.
15. Drain the engine oil and remove the engine undercovers.
16. Remove the lower suspension crossmember and the halfshafts.
17. Disconnect and remove the driveshaft.
18. Remove the power steering pump with the hydraulic lines still attached and position it aside.
19. Remove the front exhaust pipe.
20. Remove the engine mounting center member and the stabilizer bar. Lower the vehicle.
21. Tag and disconnect the ECU connectors and pull them out through the firewall.
22. Remove the power steering pump reservoir tank.
23. Connect a suitable lifting device to the eyelets on the engine.
24. Remove the right side engine mount stay and then remove the insulator and bracket.
25. Remove the left side engine mount insulator and bracket.
26. Remove the engine and transaxle as an assembly.

NOTE: Be careful not to hit the power steering gear housing or the neutral safety switch.

To install:
27. Lower the engine/transaxle assembly into the vehicle.

28. Connect all electrical and hoses fittings.
29. Install all necessary components.
30. During installation, observe the following torque specifications:
  a. Right and left engine mount bracket bolts and nuts to 38 ft. lbs. (52 Nm).
  b. Right side engine mount stay bolt and nut to 54 ft. lbs. (73 Nm).
  c. Engine mounting center member: member-to-body bolts — 29 ft. lbs. (39 Nm); member-to-other bolts — 38 ft. lbs. (52 Nm).
  d. Lower crossmember bolts: outer — 153 ft. lbs. (206 Nm); inner — 29 ft. lbs. (39 Nm).
31. Connect the battery cable, refill all fluids, start the engine and check for leaks.

CELICA

1. Disconnect the negative battery cable.
2. Remove the battery.
3. Remove the hood.
4. Drain the cooling system.
5. Tag and disconnect all vacuum hoses, electrical wires and cables that are necessary to remove the engine.
6. Disconnect the ignition coil connector and high tension wire from the coil.
7. Remove the suspension upper brace.
8. Remove the radiator.
9. Remove the coolant reservoir tank.
10. If equipped with automatic transaxle, disconnect the throttle cable and bracket from the throttle body.
11. Disconnect the accelerator cable from the throttle body.
12. If equipped with cruise control, remove the cruise control actuator and bracket.
13. Remove the oxygen sensor.
14. Remove the air cleaner assembly, air flow meter, air cleaner hose and air cleaner bracket.
15. Remove the igniter.
16. Remove the heater hoses.
17. Disconnect and plug the fuel lines.
18. Disconnect the speedometer cable.
19. If equipped with manual transaxle, remove the clutch release cylinder and tube bracket. Do not disconnect the tube from the bracket.
20. Disconnect the transaxle control cable.
21. Remove the air conditioning compressor and position it aside. Do not disconnect the refrigerant lines.
22. Raise and support the vehicle safely.

23. Drain the engine oil and transaxle fluid.
24. Remove the right undercover.
25. Remove the power steering pump and position it aside. Do not disconnect the lines.
26. Remove the suspension lower crossmember.
27. Remove the halfshafts.
28. Disconnect the exhaust pipe from the catalytic converter.
29. Remove the engine rear mounting bolt. Lower the vehicle.
30. Disconnect the ECU electrical connectors.
31. Remove the power steering pump reservoir mounting bolts.
32. Connect a suitable lifting device to the engine. Raise the engine slightly and remove the engine retaining brackets and bolts.
33. Carefully remove the engine/transaxle assembly from the vehicle. Be careful not to hit the power steering gear housing or the neutral safety switch.

To install:
34. Lower the engine/transaxle assembly into the vehicle.
35. Connect all electrical and hoses fittings.
36. Install all necessary components.
37. During installation, observe the following torque specifications:
  a. Right and left engine mount bracket bolts and nuts to 38 ft. lbs. (52 Nm).
  b. Right side engine mount stay bolt and nut to 54 ft. lbs. (73 Nm).
  c. Engine mounting center member: member-to-body bolts — 29 ft. lbs. (39 Nm); member-to-other bolts — 38 ft. lbs. (52 Nm).
  d. Lower crossmember bolts: outer — 153 ft. lbs. (206 Nm); inner — 29 ft. lbs. (39 Nm).
38. Connect the battery cable, refill all fluids, start the engine and check for leaks.

3S-GTE Engine

CELICA (4WD)

1. Disconnect the negative battery cable.
2. Remove the hood.
3. Raise and support the vehicle safely.
4. Remove the engine undercovers.
5. Drain the cooling system, engine oil and transaxle fluid.
6. Remove the air cleaner assembly.
7. Disconnect the accelerator cable from the throttle body.

8. Remove the relay box from the battery. Disconnect the wires and connectors from the box.

9. Remove the air conditioning relay box from its mounting bracket.

10. Remove the injector solenoid resistor and fuel pump resistor from the engine compartment.

11. Remove the radiator and coolant overflow tank.

12. If equipped with cruise control, disconnect the wiring and remove the cruise control actuator.

13. Remove the wiper arms and outside windshield moulding. Then, remove the upper brace which is retained by 4 nuts and 2 bolts. The brace connects from the struts to the firewall.

14. Remove the ignition coil.

15. From inside the engine compartment, tag and disconnect all electrical wiring and vacuum hoses necessary to remove the engine.

16. Remove the engine wire bracket.

17. Remove the charcoal canister.

18. Disconnect the heater hoses.

19. Disconnect the speedometer cable from the transaxle.

20. Disconnect and plug the fuel hoses.

21. Remove the starter.

22. Remove the clutch release cylinder without disconnecting the hydraulic tube. Move the unit aside.

23. Disconnect the control cables from the transaxle.

24. Remove the turbocharger pressure sensor and air conditioning Air Switching Valve (ASV) from inside the engine compartment.

25. From the passenger compartment, unplug the connectors from the ECU, air conditioning amplifier and cowl wires. Pull the wiring harnesses through the firewall.

26. Remove the suspension lower crossmember.

27. Remove the front halfshafts and the driveshaft.

28. Remove the power steering pump and bracket without disconnecting the hydraulic lines. Position the pump aside.

29. Disconnect the front exhaust pipe at the manifold and tailpipe and remove it.

30. Remove the engine mounting center member and lower the vehicle. Unplug the 3 engine ECU connectors, remove the 2 screws and pull the connectors out through the firewall.

31. Remove the power steering pump reservoir tank.

32. Connect a suitable lifting device to the lifting brackets on the engine.

33. Remove the 2 bolts holding the right engine mount insulator to the mounting bracket. Remove the 4 bolts holding the left engine mount insulator to the mounting bracket.

34. Slowly and carefully, remove the engine and transaxle assembly for the top of the vehicle.

To install:

35. Lower the engine/transaxle into the vehicle.

36. Connect all electrical and hoses fittings.

37. Install all necessary components.

38. During installation, observe the following torque specifications:

a. Torque the left mounting bracket-to-transaxle case bolts to 38 ft. lbs. (52 Nm).

b. Torque the left mounting insulator through bolt to 47 ft. lbs. (63 Nm) and 4 hex head bolts to 64 ft. lbs. (87 Nm).

c. Torque the right mounting insulator nuts to 38 ft. lbs. (52 Nm) and the thru bolt to 64 ft. lbs. (87 Nm).

d. Torque the front and rear bolts to 57 ft. lbs. (77 Nm).

e. Torque the front and rear engine mounting through bolts to 64 ft. lbs. (87 Nm).

f. Torque the lower crossmember nuts and bolts to 112 ft. lbs. (152 Nm).

g. Torque the suspension upper brace nuts to 47 ft. lbs. (64 Nm) and bolts to 15 ft. lbs. (21 Nm).

39. Connect the battery cable, refill all fluids, start the engine and check for leaks.

MR2

1. Disconnect the negative battery cable.

2. Remove the hood and side panels.

3. Raise and support the vehicle safely.

4. Remove the engine undercovers.

5. Drain the cooling system, engine oil and transaxle fluid.

6. Remove the suspension upper brace that crisscrosses from the struts to the firewall.

7. Remove the air cleaner assembly.

8. Remove both air connector tubes.

9. Disconnect the accelerator cable from the throttle body.

10. If equipped with cruise control, disconnect the wiring and remove the cruise control actuator and accelerator linkage assemblies.

11. Disconnect the brake booster vacuum hose.

12. Disconnect the ground strap connector.

13. Remove the check connector and turbocharger pressure sensor.

14. Remove the injector solenoid resistor, fuel pump relay, fuel pump resistor and the air conditioning vacuum switching valve.

15. Disconnect the filler and overflow hoses from the water filler connection. Remove the water filler from the engine.

16. Remove the engine relay box. Disconnect the wires and connectors from the box.

17. Remove the ignition coil and igniter.

18. From inside the luggage compartment, disconnect the wiring harnesses for the ECU, starter relay, cooling fan and engine wires.

19. Disconnect the starter wiring.

20. Disconnect the radiator hose from the water inlet.

21. Disconnect and plug the fuel inlet and return hoses.

22. Disconnect the radiator hoses from the water outlet housing.

23. Disconnect the heater hoses.

24. Disconnect the control cables from the transaxle.

25. Remove the tailpipe and front exhaust pipe.

26. Remove the engine compartment cooling fan.

27. Remove the idler pulley bracket and unbolt the air conditioning compressor. Move the compressor aside. Leave the refrigerant lines connected.

28. Remove the intercooler.

29. Remove the rear engine mounting insulator.

30. Disconnect the speedometer cable from the transaxle.

31. Disconnect the stabilizer link from the shock absorber.

32. Remove the wire clamp bolt and remove the ABS speed sensor.

33. Remove the lower suspension arms.

34. Remove the driveshafts.

35. Remove the 4 bolts and remove the lower crossmember.

36. Remove the front engine mounting insulator.

37. Remove the nut and bolt attaching the clutch release cylinder to the transaxle. Remove the mounting bracket bolts and remove the clutch release cylinder without disconnecting the hydraulic tube.

38. Remove the right and left engine mounting stays.

39. Remove the lateral control rod and air cleaner case bracket.

40. Connect a suitable lifting device to the engine hanger brackets. Ten-

sion the lifting device to support the weight of the engine, then remove the left and right mounting insulator fasteners; 2 bolts and 3 nuts for each insulator.

41. Carefully lower then raise the engine from the vehicle.

To install:

42. Lower the engine into the vehicle.

43. Connect all electrical and hoses fittings.

44. Install all necessary components.

45. During installation, observe the following torque specifications:

a. Torque the rear engine mounting bracket-to-transaxle case bolts to 38 ft. lbs. (52 Nm) for the 14mm bolts and 57 ft. lbs. (77 Nm) for the 17mm bolts.

b. Torque the left mounting insulator through bolt to 47 ft. lbs. (63 Nm) and 4 hex head bolts to 54 ft. lbs. (73 Nm).

c. Torque the right mounting insulator nuts to 54 ft. lbs. (73 Nm) and the through bolt to 64 ft. lbs. (87 Nm).

d. Torque the front and rear bolts to 57 ft. lbs. (77 Nm).

e. Torque the front and rear engine mounting through bolts to 64 ft. lbs. (87 Nm).

f. Torque the lower crossmember nuts and bolts to 112 ft. lbs. (152 Nm).

g. Torque the suspension upper brace nuts to 47 ft. lbs. (64 Nm) and bolts to 15 ft. lbs. (21 Nm).

46. Connect the battery cable, refill all fluids, start the engine and check for leaks.

4A-GE, 4A-FE and 7A-FE Engines

COROLLA

1. Disconnect the negative battery cable.

2. Remove the battery.

3. Remove the hood.

4. Remove the engine undercovers.

5. Drain the cooling system, engine and transaxle oil.

6. Remove the air cleaner and air cleaner flexible hose.

7. Remove the coolant reservoir tank, radiator and cooling fan.

8. If equipped with automatic transaxle, disconnect the accelerator and throttle cables.

9. If equipped with cruise control, remove the cruise control actuator.

10. Disconnect the No. 2 junction block, the ground strap connector and the ground strap.

11. Disconnect the check, vacuum sensor and oxygen sensor connectors.

Disconnect the air conditioning compressor wire.

12. Disconnect the vacuum hoses at the brake booster, power steering pump, vacuum sensor, charcoal canister and vacuum switch.

13. Disconnect the fuel lines at the fuel pump.

14. Disconnect the heater hoses at the water inlet housing.

15. Remove the power steering pump and set it aside with the hydraulic lines still attached.

16. Remove the air conditioning compressor and set it aside with the refrigerant lines still attached.

17. Disconnect the speedometer cable at the transaxle.

18. If equipped with manual transaxle, remove the clutch release cylinder and position it aside with the hydraulic lines still attached.

19. Disconnect the shift control cables.

20. Raise and support the vehicle safely.

21. Disconnect the oil cooler lines and the exhaust pipe (at the manifold).

22. Disconnect the halfshafts and the driveshaft, if equipped, at the transaxle.

23. Connect a suitable lifting device to the lifting brackets on the engine and raise it just enough to relieve pressure on the mounts.

24. Pull out the hole covers and remove the 5 bolts on the front and rear engine mounts. Remove the mounts from the center crossmember. Remove the 4 center crossmember bolts and the 8 bolts from the sub-frame. Remove the front and rear mounting bolts and then remove the member.

25. Remove the engine mount stay and the mount.

26. Remove the air cleaner bracket. Disconnect the left side mounting bracket from the transaxle bracket and then lift out the engine/transaxle assembly slowly and carefully.

To install:

27. Lower the engine/transaxle into the vehicle.

28. Connect all electrical and hoses fittings.

29. Install all necessary components.

30. During installation, observe the following torque specifications:

a. Torque the right engine mount insulator bolt and nuts to 38 ft. lbs. (52 Nm). Align the insulator with the bracket on the body and tighten the bolt to 64 ft. lbs. (87 Nm).

b. Align the left engine mount insulator bracket with the tran-

saxle bracket and tighten the bolt to 35 ft. lbs. (48 Nm).

c. Install the left stay and tighten the 2 bolts to 15 ft. lbs. (21 Nm).

d. Install the engine center member and tighten the 5 bolts to 45 ft. lbs. (61 Nm).

e. Install the front and rear engine mounts and bolts. Align the bolts holes in the brackets with the center member and tighten the front mount bolts to 35 ft. lbs. (48 Nm); tighten the center and rear mounts to 42 ft. lbs. (57 Nm). Install the 8 sub-frame bolts and tighten the lower arm bolt to 152 ft. lbs. (206 Nm) and the rear bolt to 94 ft. lbs. (127 Nm).

31. Connect the battery cable, refill all fluids, start the engine and check for leaks.

CELICA

1. Disconnect the negative battery cable.

2. Remove the battery.

3. Raise the vehicle and support safely.

4. Remove the engine undercovers.

5. Drain the cooling system and engine oil.

6. Remove the air cleaner assembly along with its hose and any attachments.

7. Disconnect the accelerator and throttle cables at the bracket.

8. Remove the lower cover from the relay box. Disconnect the fusible link cassette and connectors. Remove the engine relay box.

9. Remove the air conditioning relay box from the bracket.

10. Remove the coolant reservoir tank, radiator and cooling fan.

11. Disconnect the check connector, vacuum sensor connector and ground strap from the left front fender apron. Remove the engine wiring bracket. Disconnect the noise filter assembly.

12. Remove the charcoal canister.

13. Disconnect the heater hose from the water inlet.

14. Disconnect the speedometer cable at the transaxle.

15. Disconnect the fuel hose.

16. If equipped with manual transaxle, remove the clutch release cylinder and position it aside with the hydraulic lines still attached.

17. Disconnect the shift control cables from the transaxle.

18. Tag and disconnect all vacuum hoses and electrical wires necessary to remove the engine.

19. Remove the suspension lower crossmember.

20. Disconnect the oxygen sensor connector.

21. Remove the front exhaust pipe assembly.

22. If equipped with automatic transaxle, disconnect control cable from engine mounting center member.

23. Remove the front halfshafts.

24. Unbolt the air conditioning compressor and wire it aside with the refrigerant lines still attached.

25. Remove the power steering pump assembly without disconnecting the hydraulic lines.

26. Connect a suitable lifting device to the engine lifting brackets. Tension the lifting device slightly to take the pressure off the mounts.

27. Remove the engine mounting center member.

28. Remove the front engine mounting insulator and bracket.

29. Remove the rear mounting insulator and bracket.

30. Disconnect the ground wire from the fender apron. Remove the ground strap from the transaxle.

31. Remove the right and left engine mounting stay.

32. Slowly and carefully, remove the engine and transaxle assembly from the top of the vehicle.

NOTE: Be careful not to hit the power steering gear housing or the neutral safety switch.

To install:

33. Lower the engine/transaxle into the vehicle.

34. Connect all electrical and hoses fittings.

35. Install all necessary components.

36. During installation, observe the following torque specifications:

   a. Torque the left mounting bracket-to-transaxle case bolts to 38 ft. lbs. (52 Nm).

   b. Torque the left mounting insulator-to-bracket bolts to 35 ft. lbs. (48 Nm) and the through bolt to 64 ft. lbs. (87 Nm).

   c. Torque the right engine stay bolts to 31 ft. lbs. (42 Nm) and the left engine stay bolts to 15 ft. lbs. (21 Nm).

   d. Torque the front and rear engine mounting bracket and insulator fasteners to 57 ft. lbs. (77 Nm).

   e. Torque the engine center member bolts to 38 ft. lbs. (52 Nm) and the center member-to-insulator bolts to 47 ft. lbs. (64 Nm).

   f. Torque the front and rear engine mounting through bolts to 64 ft. lbs. (87 Nm).

37. Connect the battery cable, refill all fluids, start the engine and check for leaks.

4A-GE Engine

MR2

1. Disconnect the negative battery cable.

2. Remove the battery.

3. Remove the air cleaner assembly.

4. Drain the cooling system and engine oil.

5. Remove the fuel tank protectors and the engine undercover.

6. Disconnect the accelerator cable.

7. If equipped with cruise control, disconnect the cruise control at the cable actuator. If equipped with automatic transaxle, disconnect the throttle cable.

8. Disconnect the heater hoses at the water inlet housing on the rear of the cylinder head cover. Disconnect the radiator hose and the air bleeder hose at the water inlet housing.

9. Disconnect and plug the fuel line at the fuel filter. Disconnect the fuel return hose. Tag and disconnect the vacuum hose at the charcoal canister.

10. Tag and disconnect the engine ground strap and the main wiring harness connector at the engine. Disconnect the backup light switch connector as required.

11. Disconnect the speedometer cable.

12. Remove the transaxle gravel shield.

13. Remove the ground strap from the water inlet housing.

14. Remove the radiator overflow tank.

15. Remove the air conditioning and alternator drive belts. Remove the alternator.

16. Disconnect the radiator hose at the water outlet housing.

17. Tag and disconnect the 2 connectors at the igniter, the noise filter connector, the cooling fan electrical connector, the cylinder head ground strap, the air conditioning compressor connector and the high tension leads at the ignition coil.

18. Remove the rear luggage compartment trim.

19. Tag and disconnect the circuit opening relay connector, the ball connections at the electronic control unit and the electrical lead for the cooling fan computer.

20. Pull the main wiring harness out and through the engine compartment.

21. Remove the mounting bolts and remove the air conditioning compressor. Position it aside without disconnecting the refrigerant lines.

22. If equipped with a manual transaxle, disconnect the control cables from the outer shift lever and gear shift selector lever. If equipped with automatic transaxle, disconnect the control cable at the gear shift lever.

23. If equipped with a manual transaxle, remove the control cable bracket on the transaxle. Remove the clutch release cylinder.

24. Disconnect the engine oil cooler lines, if equipped. Disconnect the automatic transaxle fluid lines if equipped.

25. Remove the exhaust pipe assembly. Remove the oxygen sensor at the exhaust manifold.

26. If equipped with automatic transaxle, remove the mounting bolts and remove the stiffener plate at the transaxle. Remove the flywheel shield.

27. Remove the right halfshaft. Disconnect the left halfshaft from the side gear shaft and position it aside.

28. Remove the front and rear engine mount bolts. Place a block of wood on a hydraulic floor jack and carefully position the jack under the engine. Raise the jack just enough to ease the engine's weight on the mounts. Remove the right and left engine mounts.

29. Make sure there are no remaining wires or hoses connected to the engine and then slowly and carefully raise the vehicle while lowering the jack supporting the engine/transaxle assembly.

To install:

30. Lower the engine into the vehicle.

31. Connect all electrical and hoses fittings.

32. Install all necessary components.

33. During installation, observe the following torque specifications:

   a. Torque the right engine mount insulator bolt and nuts to 38 ft. lbs. (52 Nm). Align the insulator with the bracket on the body and tighten the bolt to 64 ft. lbs. (87 Nm).

   b. Align the left engine mount insulator bracket with the transaxle bracket and tighten the bolt to 35 ft. lbs. (48 Nm).

   c. Install the left stay and tighten the 2 bolts to 15 ft. lbs. (21 Nm).

   d. Install the engine center member and tighten the 5 bolts to 45 ft. lbs. (61 Nm).

e. Install the front, center and rear engine mounts and bolts. Align the bolts holes in the brackets with the center member and tighten the front mount bolts to 35 ft. lbs. (48 Nm); tighten the center mounts to 38 ft. lbs. (52 Nm); and the rear mount bolts to 42 ft. lbs. (57 Nm).

f. Bounce the engine several times to unload the front and rear mounts, for automatic transmission only, and then tighten the rear bolt to 64 ft. lbs. (87 Nm). Install the front bolt and tighten it to 64 ft. lbs. (87 Nm).

34. Connect the battery cable, refill all fluids, start the engine and check for leaks.

5S-FE Engine

CAMRY

1. Disconnect the negative battery cable.

------- **CAUTION** -------

On models with an air bag, wait at least 90 seconds from the time that the ignition switch is turned to the LOCK position and the battery is disconnected before performing any further work.

2. Remove the battery and its tray.
3. Remove the hood.
4. Remove the engine undercover and then drain the engine coolant and oil.
5. Disconnect the accelerator cable from the throttle body. On models with automatic transaxle, its the throttle cable, not the accelerator.
6. Remove the air cleaner assembly, resonator and the air intake hose.
7. On models with cruise control, remove the actuator cover, unplug the connector, remove the 3 bolts and then disconnect the actuator with the bracket.
8. Disconnect the ground strap at the battery carrier.
9. Remove the radiator and then disconnect the coolant reservoir hose.
10. Remove the 3 washer tank mounting bolts, disconnect the connector and hose and then lift out the tank.
11. Tag and disconnect the:
    a. Connectors (3) to the engine relay box
    b. Connectors (2) from the left side fender apron
    c. Igniter connector
    d. Noise filter connector
    e. Connector at the fender apron
    f. Check connector

g. Air conditioner magnet switch connector, if equipped
    h. Ground strap at the right fender apron
    i. Vacuum sensor connector
    j. Backup light switch and speed sensor (models with manual transaxle)

12. Disconnect the heater hoses and the fuel return hose and the fuel inlet hose.
13. On models with manual transaxle, remove the starter and clutch release cylinder. Don't disconnect the hydraulic line, simply hang the cylinder out of the way.
14. Disconnect the transaxle control cables at the transaxle.
15. Tag and disconnect all remaining vacuum hoses.
16. Remove the undercover beneath the glove box. Remove the lower instrument panel, the glove box door and the box itself. Tag and disconnect the 2 ECU connectors and the 4 cowl wire connector. Remove the 2 nuts and then pull the engine harness into the engine compartment.
17. Without disconnecting the refrigerant lines, remove the compressor and hang it carefully out of the way.
18. Loosen the 2 bolts and disconnect the front exhaust pipe bracket. Remove the 3 nuts attaching the front pipe to the manifold. Disconnect the pipe.
19. Remove the halfshafts.
20. Without disconnecting the hydraulic lines, remove the power steering pump and hang it aside.
21. Remove the 3 bolts (manual transaxle) or 4 bolts (automatic transaxle) and then disconnect the left engine mounting insulator. Pop out the plugs, remove the 3 nuts and then remove the right engine mounting insulator. Remove the 3 bolts and disconnect the front engine mounting insulator.
22. Attach an engine lifting device to the lift hooks. Remove the 3 bolts and disconnect the control rod. Slowly and carefully, lift the engine/transaxle assembly out of the engine compartment.

To install:

23. Carefully lower the engine/transaxle into the engine compartment. With the engine level and all the mounts aligned with their brackets, install the engine control rod. Tighten the 3 bolts to 47 ft. lbs. (64 Nm).
24. Connect the front engine mount and tighten the bolts to 59 ft. lbs. (80 Nm). Connect the rear mount and

tighten the nuts to 48 ft. lbs. (66 Nm). Don't forget the plugs.
25. Connect the left mount and tighten the bolts (3 or 4) to 47 ft. lbs. (64 Nm).
26. Install the power steering pump and tighten the bolts to 31 ft. lbs. (43 Nm).
27. Install the halfshafts.
28. Connect the front pipe to the manifold and tighten the new nuts to 46 ft. lbs. (62 Nm). Don't forget to install the bracket.
29. Install the air conditioning compressor and tighten the bolts to 20 ft. lbs. (27 Nm).
30. Feed the engine harness through the cowl and reconnect it. Install the glove box.
31. Connect the vacuum hoses and the transaxle control cables.
32. Install the release cylinder and the starter.
33. Connect the fuel inlet hose and tighten to 22 ft. lbs. (29 Nm). Connect the return hose and the 2 heater hoses.
34. Reconnect all wires disconnected previously.
35. Install the washer tank and connect the electrical lead and hose.
36. Install the coolant reservoir hose and the radiator.
37. Connect the ground strap to the battery carrier and then install the cruise control actuator. Install the air cleaner assembly.
38. Connect the throttle/accelerator cable and adjust it.
39. Fill the engine with oil and coolant. Connect the battery cable, start the engine and check for any leaks.

CELICA

1. Disconnect the negative battery cable.
2. Remove the battery.
3. Remove the hood.
4. Raise the vehicle and support safely.
5. Remove the engine undercovers.
6. Drain the cooling system and engine oil.
7. Remove the air cleaner assembly along with hoses and any attachments.
8. Disconnect the accelerator and throttle cables at the bracket.
9. Remove the lower cover from the relay box. Disconnect the fusible link cassette and connectors. Remove the engine relay box.
10. Remove the air conditioning relay box from the bracket.
11. Remove the cruise control actuator assembly.
12. Remove the coolant reservoir tank, radiator and cooling fan.

13. Remove the 2 wiper arms and outside lower windshield moulding. Remove the suspension upper brace where it attaches to the struts and the firewall.

14. Remove the ignition coil assembly. Disconnect the check connector, igniter connector, vacuum sensor connector and ground strap from the left front fender apron. Remove the engine wiring bracket. Disconnect the noise filter assembly.

15. Remove the charcoal canister.

16. Disconnect the heater hose from the water inlet.

17. Disconnect the speedometer cable.

18. Disconnect the fuel hose.

19. If equipped with a manual transaxle, remove the clutch release cylinder and position it aside with the hydraulic lines still attached.

20. Disconnect the shift control cables from the transaxle.

21. Tag and disconnect the vacuum sensor hose from the gas filter on the air intake chamber, brake booster vacuum hose and air conditioning vacuum hoses on air intake chamber.

22. Disconnect 2 cowl wire connectors and engine wire clamp from engine fender apron.

23. Tag and disconnect the engine ECU connector, cowl wire connectors and air conditioning amplifier connector.

24. Remove the suspension lower crossmember.

25. Disconnect the oxygen sensor connector.

26. Remove all necessary brackets and retaining bolts.

27. Remove the front exhaust pipe assembly.

28. If equipped with automatic transaxle, disconnect control cable from engine mounting center member. Remove the front halfshafts.

29. Unbolt the air conditioning compressor and then wire it aside with the refrigerant lines still attached.

30. Remove the power steering pump assembly without disconnecting the hydraulic lines.

31. Connect a suitable lifting device to the engine lifting brackets.

32. Remove the engine mounting center member.

33. Remove the front engine mounting insulator and bracket.

34. Remove the rear mounting insulator and bracket.

35. Disconnect the ground wire from the fender apron. Remove the ground strap from the transaxle.

36. Remove the right and left engine mounting stay.

37. Slowly and carefully, remove the engine and transaxle assembly from the top of the vehicle.

NOTE: Be careful not to hit the power steering gear housing or the neutral safety switch.

To install:
38. Lower the engine/transaxle into the vehicle.

39. Connect all electrical and hoses fittings.

40. Install all necessary components.

41. During installation, observe the following torque specifications:

a. Torque the left mounting bracket-to-transaxle case bolts to 38 ft. lbs. (52 Nm).

b. Torque the left mounting insulator-to-bracket bolts to 35 ft. lbs. (48 Nm) and the through bolt to 64 ft. lbs. (87 Nm).

c. Torque the right engine stay bolts to 31 ft. lbs. (42 Nm) and the left engine stay bolts to 15 ft. lbs. (21 Nm).

d. Torque the front and rear engine mounting bracket and insulator fasteners to 57 ft. lbs. (77 Nm).

e. Torque the engine center member bolts to 38 ft. lbs. (52 Nm) and the centermember-to-insulator bolts to 47 ft. lbs. (64 Nm).

f. Torque the front and rear engine mounting through bolts to 64 ft. lbs. (87 Nm).

42. Connect the battery cable, refill all fluids, start the engine and check for leaks.

MR2

1. Disconnect the negative battery cable.

2. Remove the hood and engine side panels.

3. Raise and support the vehicle safely.

4. Remove the engine undercovers.

5. Drain the cooling system, engine oil and transaxle fluid.

6. Remove the suspension upper brace from the struts to the firewall.

7. Remove the air cleaner assembly.

8. Disconnect the accelerator cable from the throttle body.

9. If equipped with cruise control, disconnect the wiring and remove the cruise control actuator and accelerator linkage assemblies.

10. Disconnect the brake booster vacuum hose.

11. Disconnect the ground strap connector.

12. Remove the check connector and vacuum sensor.

13. Remove the the air conditioning vacuum switching valve.

14. Disconnect the filler and overflow hoses from the water filler connection. Remove the water filler from the engine.

15. Remove the engine relay box. Disconnect the wires and connectors from the box.

16. Remove the ignition coil and igniter.

17. From inside the luggage compartment, disconnect the wiring harnesses for the ECU, starter relay, cooling fan and engine wires.

18. Disconnect the starter wiring.

19. Disconnect the radiator hose from the water inlet.

20. Disconnect and plug the fuel inlet and return hoses.

21. Disconnect the radiator hoses from the water outlet housing.

22. Disconnect the heater hoses.

23. Disconnect the control cables from the transaxle.

24. If equipped with automatic transaxle, disconnect and plug the oil cooler hoses.

25. Remove the front exhaust pipe.

26. Remove the halfshafts.

27. Remove the idler pulley bracket and unbolt the air conditioning compressor. Move the compressor aside. Leave the refrigerant lines connected.

28. Remove the front and rear engine mounting insulator.

29. Disconnect the speedometer cable from the transaxle.

30. If equipped with manual transaxle, remove the nut and bolt attaching the clutch release cylinder to the transaxle. Remove the mounting bracket bolts and remove the clutch release cylinder without disconnecting the hydraulic tube. If equipped with an automatic transaxle, unbolt and remove the control cable bracket from the transaxle.

31. Remove the rear engine mounting bracket.

32. Remove the right and left engine mounting stays.

33. If equipped with manual transaxle, remove the lateral control rod and air cleaner case bracket. If equipped with automatic transaxle, unbolt the air cleaner case bracket, disconnect the charcoal canister tube and the ground strap from the transaxle.

34. Connect a suitable lifting device to the engine hanger brackets. Tension the lifting device to support the weight of the engine and remove the left and right mounting insulator fasteners.

35. Carefully lower then raise the engine from the vehicle.

To install:

36. Lower the engine into the vehicle.

37. Connect all electrical and hoses fittings.

38. Install all necessary components.

39. During installation, observe the following torque specifications:

a. Torque the left mounting bracket-to-transaxle case bolts to 38 ft. lbs. (52 Nm).

b. Torque the left mounting insulator-to-bracket bolts to 35 ft. lbs. (48 Nm) and the through bolt to 64 ft. lbs. (87 Nm).

c. Torque the right engine stay bolts to 31 ft. lbs. (42 Nm) and the left engine stay bolts to 15 ft. lbs. (21 Nm).

d. Torque the front and rear engine mounting bracket and insulator fasteners to 57 ft. lbs. (77 Nm).

e. Torque the engine center member bolts to 38 ft. lbs. (52 Nm) and the center member-to-insulator bolts to 47 ft. lbs. (64 Nm).

f. Torque the front and rear engine mounting through bolts to 64 ft. lbs. (87 Nm).

40. Connect the battery cable, refill all fluids, start the engine and check for leaks.

7M-GE and 7M-GTE Engines

SUPRA

1. Disconnect the negative battery cable.

2. Remove the hood.

3. Raise and support the vehicle safely.

4. Remove the engine undercover.

5. Drain the cooling system and engine oil.

6. Remove the radiator.

7. On 7M-GE engine, remove the air cleaner assembly. On 7M-GTE engine, remove the No. 4 air cleaner pipe along with the No. 1 and 2 air cleaner hose.

8. Remove the No. 7 air cleaner hose with the air flow meter and air cleaner cap.

9. Remove the air conditioning belt. Remove the alternator drive belt, water pump pulley and fan assembly. Remove the power steering belt.

10. Disconnect the brake booster hose, the heater valve hose, the cruise control hose and the charcoal canister hose.

11. Remove the heater hoses.

12. Tag and disconnect all electrical wire and vacuum hoses necessary to remove the engine.

13. If equipped with cruise control, disconnect the cruise control cable.

14. Disconnect the accelerator cable.

15. If equipped with automatic transmission, disconnect the throttle cable.

16. Remove the air conditioning compressor. Position the unit aside. Do not disconnect the refrigerant lines.

17. On the 7M-GTE engine, remove the No. 6 air cleaner hose and the upper radiator outlet hose.

18. Remove the power steering pump. Position the unit aside; do not disconnect the hydraulic lines.

19. If equipped with manual transmission, remove the shift lever.

20. Disconnect the ground strap from the fuel hose clamp. On the 7M-GTE engine, remove the engine mounting absorber.

21. Disconnect and plug the fuel lines.

22. Raise the vehicle and support safely.

23. Remove the exhaust pipe.

24. Remove the driveshaft.

25. Disconnect the speedometer cable.

26. If equipped with automatic transmission, remove the shift linkage. If equipped with manual transmission, remove the clutch release cylinder.

27. Properly support the engine and transmission assembly. Remove the No. 1 front crossmember. Remove the engine retaining mounts.

28. Position a piece of wood between the engine firewall and the rear of the cylinder head to prevent damage to the heater hose.

29. Make sure there are no remaining wires or hoses connected to the engine and then slowly and carefully remove the engine and transmission from the vehicle.

To install:

30. Lower the engine/transmission into the vehicle.

31. Connect all electrical and hoses fittings.

32. Install all necessary components.

33. During installation, observe the following torque specifications:

a. Torque the left mounting bracket-to-transaxle case bolts to 38 ft. lbs. (52 Nm).

b. Torque the left mounting insulator-to-bracket bolts to 35 ft. lbs. (48 Nm) and the through bolt to 64 ft. lbs. (87 Nm).

c. Torque the right engine stay bolts to 31 ft. lbs. (42 Nm) and the

left engine stay bolts to 15 ft. lbs. (21 Nm).

d. Torque the front and rear engine mounting bracket and insulator fasteners to 57 ft. lbs. (77 Nm).

e. Torque the engine center member bolts to 38 ft. lbs. (52 Nm) and the center member-to-insulator bolts to 47 ft. lbs. (64 Nm).

f. Torque the front and rear engine mounting through bolts to 64 ft. lbs. (87 Nm).

34. Connect the battery cable, refill all fluids, start the engine and check for leaks.

CRESSIDA

1. Disconnect the negative battery cable.

2. Drain the cooling system.

3. Remove the hood.

4. Remove the battery and tray.

5. Disconnect the accelerator, throttle and cruise control cables.

6. Remove the air cleaner assembly complete with the air flow meter, hoses and connector pipe.

7. Tag and disconnect all electrical wires and vacuum hoses necessary to remove the engine.

8. Remove the radiator.

9. Remove the drive belt and unbolt the air conditioning compressor. Position it aside and suspend it with wire. Do not disconnect the refrigerant lines.

10. Unbolt the power steering pump. Position it aside and suspend it with wire. Do not disconnect the hydraulic lines.

11. Remove the windshield washer fluid reservoir.

12. Remove the glove box and disconnect the 6 connectors from the main wiring harness and then pull the main wiring harness through the firewall and into the engine compartment.

13. Disconnect the heater hoses.

14. Raise the vehicle and support it safely.

15. Remove the engine undercover and drain the oil.

16. Disconnect the exhaust pipe at the manifold.

17. Disconnect the driveshaft at the transmission flange and position it aside.

18. Disconnect the speedometer cable and the transmission linkage.

19. Disconnect the starter lead and the ground lines at the stiffener plate and left side engine mount.

20. Disconnect and plug the fuel lines.

21. Remove the front wheels and then disconnect the power steering rack. Leave the hydraulic lines attached and lay the rack aside.

22. Loosen the 8 bolts and the ground strap and then remove the rear engine support.

23. Lower the vehicle and remove the 4 engine mount-to-suspension bolts. Attach an engine hoist to the 2 engine hangers and then slowly and carefully lift the engine out of the vehicle.

To install:

24. Lower the engine into the vehicle.

25. Connect all electrical and hoses fittings.

26. Install all necessary components.

27. During installation, observe the following torque specifications:

a. Torque the left mounting bracket-to-transaxle case bolts to 38 ft. lbs. (52 Nm).

b. Torque the left mounting insulator-to-bracket bolts to 35 ft. lbs. (48 Nm) and the through bolt to 64 ft. lbs. (87 Nm).

c. Torque the right engine stay bolts to 31 ft. lbs. (42 Nm) and the left engine stay bolts to 15 ft. lbs. (21 Nm).

d. Torque the front and rear engine mounting bracket and insulator fasteners to 57 ft. lbs. (77 Nm).

e. Torque the engine center member bolts to 38 ft. lbs. (52 Nm) and the center member-to-insulator bolts to 47 ft. lbs. (64 Nm).

f. Torque the front and rear engine mounting through bolts to 64 ft. lbs. (87 Nm).

28. Connect the battery cable, refill all fluids, start the engine and check for leaks.

Engine Mounts

REMOVAL AND INSTALLATION

1. Raise and safely support the vehicle.

2. Support the engine with a suitable jacking device.

3. Remove the nut and through bolt.

4. Remove the insulator. Remove the mounting bolts and bracket if necessary.

5. The installation is the reverse of the removal procedure. Torque the bolts to 57 ft. lbs. (77 Nm).

Cylinder Head

REMOVAL AND INSTALLATION

2VZ-FE and 3VZ-FE Engines

1. Disconnect the negative battery cable. Relieve the fuel pressure.

CAUTION

On models with an air bag, wait at least 90 seconds from the time that the ignition switch is turned to the LOCK position and the battery is disconnected before performing any further work.

---

2. Drain the cooling system.

3. If equipped with an automatic transmission, disconnect the throttle cable and bracket from the throttle body.

4. Disconnect the accelerator cable and bracket from the throttle body and intake chamber.

5. If equipped with cruise control, remove the actuator, vacuum pump and bracket (2VZ-FE engine).

6. Remove the air cleaner hose.

7. Remove the alternator.

8. Remove the oil pressure gauge, engine hangers and alternator upper bracket.

9. Loosen the lug nuts on the right wheel and raise and support the vehicle safely.

10. Remove the right tire and wheel assembly.

11. Remove the right undercover.

12. Remove the suspension lower crossmember (2VZ-FE engine).

13. Disconnect the exhaust pipe from the catalytic converter.

14. Separate the exhaust pipe from the catalytic converter.

15. Remove the distributor. Remove the V-bank cover on the 3VZ-FE engine.

16. Disconnect the water temperature sender gauge connector, water temperature sensor connector, cold start injector time switch connector, upper radiator hose, water hoses, and the emission control vacuum hoses. Unbolt and remove the water outlet and gaskets.

17. Remove the water bypass pipe with O-rings and gasket.

18. Remove the EGR valve and vacuum modulator. Remove the exhaust crossover pipe.

19. Remove the throttle body.

20. Remove the cold start injector pipe (2VZ-FE engine).

21. Disconnect the air chamber hose, throttle body air hose and power steering hoses, if equipped. Remove the air tube.

22. Remove the intake manifold stay and disconnect the vacuum sensing hose. Remove the intake manifold and gasket. Purchase a new gasket.

23. Remove the fuel delivery pipe and the injectors.

24. Remove the rear cylinder head plate. On the 3VZ-FE engine, remove the emission control valve set and the left side engine harness.

25. Remove the exhaust manifolds. Remove the spark plugs. On the 3VZ-FE engine, remove the oil dipstick.

26. Remove the timing belt, all camshaft timing pulleys and the No. 2 idler pulley.

27. Remove the No. 3 timing belt cover. Support the belt carefully so that the belt and pulley alignment does not shift.

28. Remove the cylinder head covers. Remove the spark plug tube gaskets on the 2VZ-FE engine.

29. Remove the intake and exhaust camshafts from each head, loosening the bolts in the proper sequence.

30. On the 3VZ-FE engine, remove the power steering pump bracket and the left side engine hanger.

31. Remove the 2 (one on each head) 8mm hex bolts. Loosen and remove the 8 head bolts evenly, in 3 passes, in the reverse order of the tightening sequence. Carefully lift the head from the engine and place it on wood blocks in a clean work area.

NOTE: If the cylinder head bolts are loosened out of sequence, warpage or cracking could result.

32. Remove the cylinder head gasket and purchase a new one (cylinder head gaskets must never be re-used). With a gasket scraper, remove all the old gasket material from the cylinder head and engine block surfaces.

To install:

33. Place the new cylinder head gasket onto the cylinder block. Place the cylinder head onto the gasket.

34. Coat the threads of the eight cylinder head bolts (12-sided) with clean engine oil and install the bolts into the cylinder head. Uniformly torque the bolts in 3 passes to an ultimate torque of 25 ft. lbs. (34 Nm), using the proper sequence. If any of the bolts does not meet the torque, replace it.

35. Mark the forward edge of each bolt with paint and then retighten each bolt an additional 90 degrees, in the proper sequence. Now repeat the process once more, for an additional 90 degrees. Check that each painted mark is now at a 180 degree angle to the front — facing the rear.

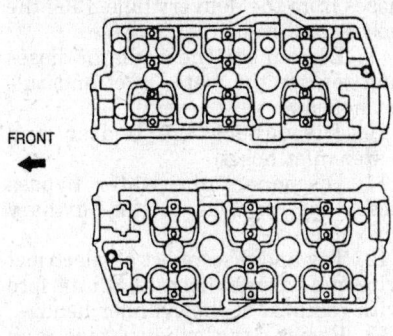

Remove the 2 hex head bolts — 2VZ-FE and 3VZ-FE engine

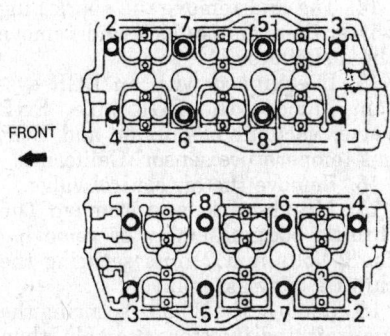

Cylinder head bolt loosening sequence — 2VZ-FE and 3VZ-FE engine

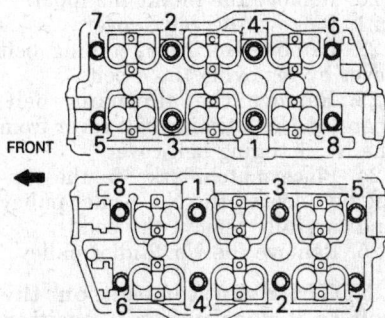

Cylinder head bolt tightening sequence — 2VZ-FE and 3VZ-FE engine

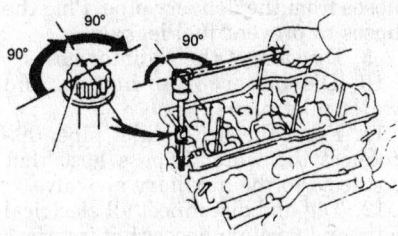

Angle torquing the cylinder head bolts — 2VZ-FE and 3VZ-FE engine

36. Coat the threads of the 2 remaining 8mm bolts with engine oil and install them. Tighten to 13 ft. lbs. (18 Nm).

37. Install the left engine hanger and tighten it to 27 ft. lbs. (37 Nm). Install the power steering pump bracket on the 3VZ-FE engine.

38. Install the camshafts, torquing the bolts in the proper sequence. On the 2VZ-FE engine, install the spark plug tube gaskets.

39. Install the cylinder head covers and tighten the bolts to 52 inch lbs. (5.9 Nm).

40. Install the No. 3 timing belt cover and tighten the 6 bolts to 65 inch lbs. (7.4 Nm). Install the No. 2 idler pulley, the camshaft timing pulleys and the timing belt.

41. Install the spark plugs.

42. Install the right and left side exhaust manifolds and tighten them to 29 ft. lbs. (39 Nm).

43. Install the intake manifold and the No. 2 idler pulley bracket. Tighten all bolts to 13 ft. lbs. (18 Nm).

44. Install the cylinder head rear plate and the oil dipstick tube.

45. Install the water bypass outlet and tighten the bolts to 14 ft. lbs. (20 Nm) on the 2VZ-FE engine or 74 inch lbs. (8.3 Nm) on the 3VZ-FE engine. On the 2VZ-FE engine, install the water outlet.

46. Install the injectors and delivery pipe. Tighten the bolts to 9 ft. lbs. (13 Nm).

47. On the 3VZ-FE engine, install the air pipe, the engine harness and the No. 1 EGR cooler. Tighten the pipe to 73 inch lbs. (8.3 Nm) and the cooler to 13 ft. lbs. (18 Nm).

48. Install the air intake chamber. Tighten the mounting bolts to 32 ft. lbs. (43 Nm), the stays to 27 ft. lbs. (37 Nm) on the 2VZ-FE engine or 29 ft. lbs. (39 Nm) on the 3VZ-FE engine.

49. Install the cold start injector. Install the distributor and the EGR assembly. Tighten the EGR bolts to 13 ft. lbs. (18 Nm).

50. On the 2VZ-FE engine, install the crossover pipe and tighten the bolts to 25 ft. lbs. (34 Nm) and the nuts to 29 ft. lbs. (39 Nm). On the 3VZ-FE engine, install the emission control valve set and tighten it to 73 inch lbs. (8.3 Nm).

51. Install the EGR pipe and tighten the bolt to 13 ft. lbs. (18 Nm) and the union nut to 58 ft. lbs. (78 Nm).

52. Install the throttle body and the ISC valve. Tighten both sets of bolts to 9 ft. lbs. (13 Nm).

53. On the 3VZ-FE engine, install the V-bank cover.

54. Install the front exhaust pipe and tighten the manifold nuts to 46 ft. lbs. (62 Nm), tighten the torque converter nuts to 32 ft. lbs. (43 Nm). Install the engine undercover on the 2VZ-FE engine.

55. Install the alternator and adjust the drive belt tension.

56. Install the air cleaner hose.

57. If equipped, install the cruise control actuator and bracket.

58. Install and adjust the accelerator cable.

59. If equipped with automatic transaxle, connect and adjust the throttle cable.

60. Fill the cooling system to the proper level with coolant.

61. Connect the negative battery cable. Start the engine and check for leaks.

62. Adjust the valves if necessary and the ignition timing.

63. Road test the vehicle and check for unusual noise, shock, slippage, correct shift points and smooth operation.

64. Recheck the coolant and engine oil levels.

3E Engine

1. Disconnect the negative battery cable.

2. Drain the cooling system.

3. Remove the air cleaner assembly.

4. Remove the right engine undercover.

5. If equipped with power steering, remove the power steering pump and bracket. If equipped with air conditioning and without power steering, remove the idler pulley bracket.

6. Disconnect the radiator hoses. Disconnect the accelerator cable. If equipped with automatic transaxle, disconnect the throttle cable from the bracket mounted to the transaxle case.

7. Remove the timing belt and camshaft timing pulley. Disconnect the heater inlet hose. Disconnect and plug the fuel lines.

8. Remove the air suction hose and valve assembly. Disconnect the brake booster hose from the intake manifold. Disconnect the water inlet hose. Disconnect the intake manifold water hose from the intake manifold.

9. Tag and disconnect all electrical wires, vacuum lines and cables that will interfere with cylinder head removal.

10. Remove the EVAP, VSV and the No. 2 cold enrichment breaker valves. Disconnect the water bypass hoses from the carburetor. Remove the valve cover.

11. Disconnect the exhaust pipe. Remove the intake manifold stay and ground strap. Remove the wire harness clamp bolt from the intake manifold.

12. Measure the cylinder head camshaft thrust clearance using a dial indicator gauge. Standard clearance should be 0.0031-0.0071 in. (0.078-0.180mm). Maximum clearance should be 0.0098 in. (0.249mm). If not within specification replace defective parts as required.

13. Loosen then remove the cylinder head bolts in 3 phases and in the proper sequence. Remove the cylinder head from the engine.

To install:

14. Installation is the reverse of the removal procedure. During installation, use a new head gasket. Torque the cylinder head bolts as follows:

   a. Tighten the cylinder head bolts in sequence to 22 ft. lbs. (29 Nm).

   b. Tighten the bolts is sequence again to 36 ft. lbs. (49 Nm).

   c. Retighten each bolt an additional 90 degree turn.

3E-E Engine

1. Disconnect the negative battery cable. Relieve the fuel pressure.

2. Remove the right engine undercover.

3. Drain the cooling system.

4. Disconnect the accelerator and throttle cables.

5. Remove the PCV hoses.

6. Remove the air cleaner and air intake collector assembly.

7. If equipped with power steering, remove the power steering pump and bracket. If equipped with air conditioning and without power steering remove the idler pulley bracket.

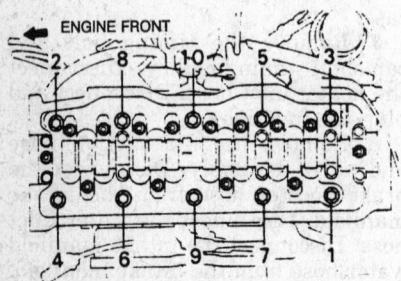

Cylinder head bolt loosening sequence — 3E and 3E-E engines

8. Remove the pulsation damper; disconnect the fuel inlet and return hoses from the delivery pipe. Plug the hoses to prevent fuel leakage.

9. Disconnect the radiator hoses.

10. Disconnect the heater and water inlet hoses.

11. From the water inlet pipe, disconnect the water bypass hose that connects to the auxiliary air valve.

12. Tag and disconnect all electrical wire and vacuum hoses that interfere with removal of the cylinder head.

13. Remove the exhaust pipe stay and disconnect the exhaust pipe from the manifold.

14. Remove the intake manifold stay.

15. Remove the timing belt and the camshaft timing pulley.

16. Remove the valve cover.

17. Loosen then remove the cylinder head bolts in 3 phases and in the proper sequence. Remove the cylinder head from the engine.

To install:

18. Clean the gasket mating surfaces. Use care not to damage the aluminum components. Lower the cylinder head onto the engine. Make sure the dowel pins are aligned and no hoses or wires are between the head and cylinder block.

19. During installation, observe the following torques:

   a. Tighten the cylinder head bolts in sequence to 22 ft. lbs. (29 Nm).

   b. Tighten the bolts in sequence again to 36 ft. lbs. (49 Nm).

   c. Retighten each bolt an additional 90 degree turn each.

20. Connect all electrical and hoses fittings.

21. Install all necessary components.

22. Connect the battery cable, refill all fluids, start the engine and check for leaks.

5E-FE Engine

1. Disconnect the negative battery cable. Relieve the fuel pressure.

2. Remove the right engine undercover.

3. Drain the cooling system.

4. Disconnect the accelerator and throttle cables.

5. Remove the PCV hoses.

6. Remove the air cleaner and air intake collector assembly.

7. If equipped with power steering, remove the power steering pump and bracket. If equipped with air conditioning and without power steering remove the idler pulley bracket.

8. Remove the pulsation damper; disconnect the fuel inlet and return

hoses from the delivery pipe. Plug the hoses to prevent fuel leakage.

9. Disconnect the radiator hoses and remove the water inlet and outlet housing.

10. Disconnect the heater and water inlet hoses.

11. Disconnect the water bypass hose that connects to the auxiliary air valve.

12. Tag and disconnect all electrical wire and vacuum hoses that interfere with removal of the cylinder head.

13. Remove the exhaust pipe stay and disconnect the exhaust pipe from the manifold, then remove the exhaust manifold.

14. Tag and remove the spark plug wires, then matchmark and remove the distributor.

15. If equipped with an EGR system, remove the EGR pipe, EGR valve, vacuum modulator and EGR gas temperature sensor (California).

16. Remove the air control valve.

17. Matchmark and remove the throttle body assembly by removing the 2 bolts and 2 nuts securing the throttle body assembly.

18. Remove the 2 bolts securing the fuel rail and injector assembly, then carefully remove it making a note of the spacer positions for reassembly.

19. Remove the air pipe.

20. Remove the intake manifold.

21. Remove the valve cover.

22. Remove the No. 2 timing belt cover by removing the 4 bolts.

23. Remove the alternator belt, then the No. 3 timing belt cover from the No. 1 timing belt cover.

24. Place matchmarks on the timing belt, loosen the No. 1 idler pulley and carefully remove the belt.

25. Remove the No. 2 idler pulley.

NOTE: Keep tension on the belt so it does not shift position and do not allow the crankshaft to rotate. This includes allowing the vehicle to roll while in gear. Do not allow anything to drop inside the belt cover, including dirt. The belt can be damaged. Do not let the belt come into contact with water, oil or grease.

26. Remove the camshaft timing pulley.

27. Remove the camshafts using the proper sequences and procedures.

28. Loosen then remove the cylinder head bolts in several passes and in the proper sequence, then remove the cylinder head from the engine.

NOTE: Failure to loosen the bolts as described can result in cylinder head warpage or cracking.

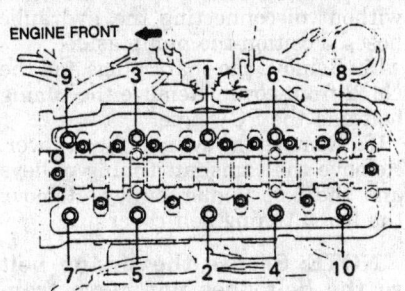

Cylinder head bolt tightening sequence — 3E and 3E-E engines

To install:

29. Clean the gasket mating surfaces using care not to damage the aluminum components, replace the gasket, then lower the cylinder head onto the engine. Make sure the dowel pins are aligned and no hoses or wires are between the head and cylinder block.

30. Lightly oil and place the 2 different size head bolts in their original positions and tighten them in several passes in the proper sequence, evenly until arriving at a torque of 33 ft. lbs. (44 Nm).

31. Mark each bolt with a reference mark and tighten each bolt in sequence an additional 90 degrees.

32. Install the camshafts using the proper sequences and procedures.

33. Install the camshaft timing pulley in its original position and torque the bolt to 37 ft. lbs. (50 Nm).

34. Install the No. 2 idler pulley, torquing the bolt to 20 ft. lbs. (27 Nm).

35. Install the timing belt on the matchmarks and tension it properly.

36. Install the No. 3 timing belt cover, the alternator belt and the No. 2 timing belt cover with its gasket and 4 bolts.

37. Install the valve cover with the proper gasket and sealer and torque the nuts to 61 inch lbs. (6.9 Nm).

38. Install the intake manifold and torque the nuts and bolts evenly to 14 ft. lbs. (19 Nm).

39. Install the particular vacuum hoses removed earlier at this location, then install the air pipe.

40. Install the fuel injector rail assembly, using new grommets and O-rings. Lightly lubricate the O-rings with gasoline and check that the injectors can be rotated smoothly once pressed in. Then install the 2 bolts and torque to 14 ft. lbs. (19 Nm).

41. Install the throttle body, using a new gasket and torquing the nuts and bolts evenly to 9 ft. lbs. (13 Nm).

42. Install the air control valve, then the exhaust manifold and torque the bolts to 35 ft. lbs. (47 Nm).

43. Reconnect all remaining electrical and hoses fittings.

44. Reinstall all remaining components.

45. Connect the battery cable, refill all fluids, start the engine and check the ignition timing and for leaks, especially fuel leaks at the injectors.

3S-FE Engine

1. Disconnect the negative battery cable. Relieve the fuel pressure.

2. Drain the cooling system.

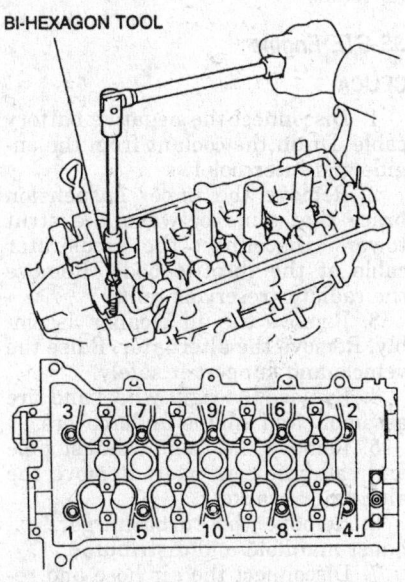

Cylinder head bolt loosening sequence — 5E-FE engine

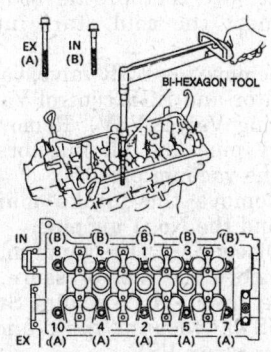

Cylinder head bolt tightening sequence — 5E-FE engine

3. If equipped with automatic transaxle, disconnect the throttle cable and bracket from the throttle body.

4. Disconnect the accelerator cable and bracket from the throttle body and intake chamber. If equipped with cruise control, remove the actuator and bracket.

5. Remove the air cleaner hose and the alternator.

6. Remove the oil pressure gauge, engine hangers and alternator upper bracket. Raise the vehicle and support safely. Remove the right wheel and tire assembly.

7. Remove the right undercover. Remove the suspension lower crossmember. Disconnect the exhaust pipe from the catalytic converter. Separate the exhaust pipe from the catalytic converter.

8. Disconnect the water temperature sender gauge connector, water temperature sensor connector, cold start injector time switch connector, upper radiator hose, water hoses and the emission control vacuum hoses.

9. Remove the water outlet and gaskets. Remove the distributor. Remove the water bypass pipe. Remove the EGR valve and modulator.

10. Remove the throttle body assembly. Remove the cold start injector pipe. Remove the air intake chamber air hose, the throttle body air hose and the power steering pump hoses, if equipped. Remove the air tube.

11. Remove the intake manifold retaining bolts. Remove the intake manifold. Remove the fuel delivery pipe and the injectors. Remove the spark plugs.

12. Remove the camshaft timing pulley. Remove the No. 1 idler pulley and tension spring. Remove the No. 3 timing belt cover. Properly support the timing belt so contact with the crankshaft timing pulley does not occur and the timing belt does not shift.

13. Remove the cylinder head cover. Arrange the grommets in order so they can be reinstalled in the correct order.

14. Remove the camshafts.

15. Loosen, then remove the cylinder head bolts in 3 phases and in the proper sequence. Remove the cylinder head from the engine.

To install:

16. Clean the gasket mating surfaces. Use care not to damage the aluminum components. Lower the cylinder head onto the engine. Make sure the dowel pins are aligned and no hoses or wires are between the head and cylinder block.

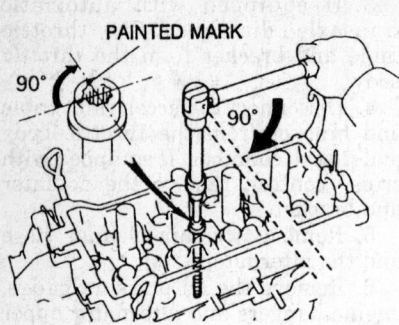

Tightening head bolts — 5E-FE engine

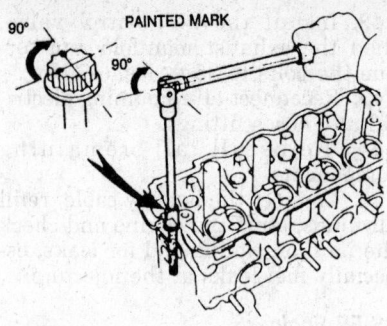

On 1990-91 3S-FE engine, torque the cylinder head bolts an additional 90 degrees in sequence.

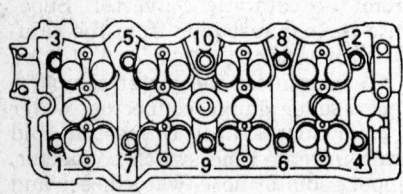

Cylinder head bolt loosening sequence — 3S-FE engines

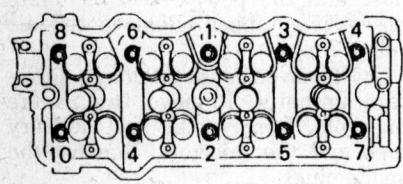

Cylinder head bolt tightening sequence — 3S-FE engines

17. During installation, observe the following torques:

a. Apply a light coat of clean engine oil to the threads of the head bolts prior to installation.

b. Torque the cylinder head to specification and in 3 phases to 36 ft. lbs. (64 Nm). Then, mark the front of each cylinder head bolt with a dab of paint. Finally, re-torque the cylinder head bolts an additional 90 degrees in the proper sequence.

18. Connect all electrical and hoses fittings.

19. Install all necessary components.

20. Connect the battery cable, refill all fluids, start the engine and check for leaks.

3S-GTE Engine

CELICA

1. Disconnect the negative battery cable. Drain the coolant from the engine and intercooler.

2. Remove the upper suspension brace that runs between the strut towers. Disconnect the accelerator cable at the throttle body. Remove the radiator reservoir tank.

3. Remove the air cleaner assembly. Remove the alternator. Raise the vehicle and support it safely.

4. Remove the right wheel and tire assembly and engine undercovers.

5. Remove the front exhaust pipe and catalytic converter. Remove the alternator brackets.

6. Remove the turbocharger, exhaust manifold and distributor.

7. Disconnect the air hose and remove the No. 2 air pipe.

8. Remove the left engine hanger along with the reservoir tank. Remove the oil pressure switch.

9. Remove the water outlet housing and the water bypass pipe.

10. Remove the throttle body and disconnect the cold start injector lead.

11. Remove the EGR valve, vacuum modulator and EGR control Vacuum Switching Valve (VSV). Remove the delivery pipe and all injectors. Remove the vacuum pipe.

12. Remove the intake manifold stays and the No. 1 air pipe.

13. Disconnect the vacuum hose and remove the fuel pressure VSV. Remove the T-VIS Vacuum Switching (VSV), vacuum tank and the turbo pressure VSV.

14. Remove the intake manifold with the air control valve. Remove

the power steering reservoir tank without disconnecting the hydraulic hoses. Position the pump aside.

15. Remove the spark plugs and the No. 2 front cover. Remove the timing belt and the PCV pipe.

16. Remove the cylinder head cover. Remove the camshaft timing pulleys and the No. 1 idler pulley. Remove the No. 3 timing belt cover.

NOTE: Secure the timing belt so the belt does not move from the crankshaft pulley.

17. Gradually loosen and remove the camshaft bearing cap bolts, in several passes, in the proper sequence. Remove the bearing caps, oil seals and lift out the camshafts.

18. Remove the right rear engine hanger. Remove the cylinder head bolts, in several stages, in the sequence and lift off the cylinder head.

To install:

19. Position the cylinder head and a new gasket on the block and torque the bolts as follows:

a. Coat the head bolts with engine oil and tighten in several passes, in sequence, to 36 ft. lbs. (54 Nm).

b. Mark the front of each bolt with a dab of paint.

c. Retighten the bolts an additional 90 degrees turn. The paint dabs should be at a 90 degree angle to the front of the head.

20. Install the right rear engine hanger and tighten it to 14 ft. lbs. (19 Nm).

21. Position the camshafts in the cylinder head with the No. 1 lobes facing outward. Coat the No. 1 bearing cap with seal packing and install all the caps over the bearing journals. Coat the bearing cap bolts with engine oil and tighten to 14 ft. lbs. (19 Nm) in several stages, in the order shown. Grease 2 new oil seals and install into the camshafts.

22. Install the No. 3 timing belt cover and the No. 1 idler pulley. Install the camshaft timing pulleys.

23. Install the cylinder head cover and the timing belt.

24. Install the remaining components, start the engine and check for leaks.

MR2

1. Disconnect the negative battery cable, then drain the coolant from the engine and intercooler.

2. Tag and disconnect all hoses, lines and wiring that interfere with removal of the turbocharger, exhaust manifold, intake manifold and cylinder head.

3. Remove the engine hood side panels.

4. Remove the upper suspension brace that runs between the strut towers.

5. Disconnect the accelerator cable at the throttle body.

6. If equipped with cruise control, remove the cruise control actuator and disconnect the accelerator linkage.

7. Remove the air cleaner cap.

8. Remove the right front engine hanger.

9. Remove the intercooler.

10. Remove the front exhaust pipe, catalytic converter and turbocharger.

11. Remove the throttle body and cold start injector.

12. Remove the exhaust manifold and distributor.

13. Remove the No. 2 air tube.

14. Remove the left engine hanger.

15. Remove the EGR vacuum modulator and Vacuum Switching Valve (VSV).

16. Remove the vacuum pipe, EGR valve and EGR pipe.

17. Remove the water outlet and housing.

18. Remove the oil pressure switch.

19. Remove the oil cooler.

20. Remove the water bypass pipe.

21. Remove the intake manifold stays and the No. 1 air pipe.

22. Remove the T-VIS Vacuum Switching (VSV), vacuum tank and the turbocharger pressure VSV.

23. Remove the intake manifold with the air control valve.

24. Remove the delivery pipe and fuel injectors.

25. Remove the cylinder head cover.

26. Remove the camshaft timing pulleys and the No. 1 idler pulley.

27. Remove the No. 3 timing belt cover.

NOTE: Secure the timing belt so the belt does not move from the crankshaft pulley.

28. Gradually loosen and remove the camshaft bearing cap bolts in several passes, in the proper sequence. Remove the bearing caps, oil seals and lift out the camshafts.

29. Remove the cylinder head bolts in several stages, in the proper sequence and lift off the cylinder head from the alignment dowels on the block.

To install:

30. Position the cylinder head and a new gasket on the block.

31. Torque the cylinder head bolts as follows:

    a. Coat the head bolts with engine oil and tighten them in several passes, in sequence to 36 ft. lbs. (49 Nm).

    b. Mark the front of each bolt with a dab of paint.

    c. Retighten the bolts an additional 90 degrees turn. The paint dabs should be at a 90 degree angle to the front of the head.

32. Position the camshafts in the cylinder head with the No. 1 lobes facing outward. Coat the No. 1 bearing cap with seal packing and install all the caps over the bearing journals. Coat the bearing cap bolts with engine oil, tighten to 14 ft. lbs. (19 Nm) in several stages, in the order shown. Grease 2 new oil seals and install the camshafts.

33. Check and adjust the valve clearance, as necessary.

34. Install the No. 3 timing belt cover, No. 1 idler pulley and camshaft timing pulleys.

35. Install the cylinder head cover with 2 new gaskets and 12 new bolt seal washers. Torque the cover bolts to 21 inch lbs. (2.5 Nm).

36. Install the remaining components, start the engine and check for leaks.

4A-FE and 7A-FE Engines

COROLLA

1. Disconnect the negative battery cable at the battery. Drain the cooling system. Relieve the fuel pressure.

2. Remove the engine undercover and then disconnect the exhaust pipe at the manifold.

3. Remove the air cleaner and hoses; disconnect the intake air temperature sensor. Disconnect the accelerator and throttle cables at the bracket on vehicles with automatic transaxle.

4. Remove the cruise control actuator cable.

5. Tag and disconnect all wires, lines and hoses that may interfere with exhaust manifold, intake manifold and cylinder head removal.

6. Disconnect the fuel lines at the fuel pump. Disconnect the heater hoses at the engine.

7. Disconnect the water hose and the bypass hose at the rear of the cylinder head. Remove the 2 bolts and pull off the water outlet pipe.

8. Remove the 2 mounting bolts and lift out the exhaust manifold stay. Remove the upper manifold insulator and exhaust manifold.

9. Remove the distributor.

10. Disconnect the 2 water hoses at the water inlet (front of head) and the inlet housing.

11. Disconnect the PCV, fuel return and vacuum sensing hoses.

12. Remove the fuel inlet pipe and the cold start injector pipe (no cold start injector is used on the 1993-94 vehicles). Disconnect the 4 vacuum hoses and then remove the EGR vacuum modulator.

13. Remove the fuel delivery pipe along with the injectors, spacers and insulators.

14. Unbolt the engine wire cover at the intake manifold and then disconnect the wire at the cylinder head.

15. Remove the intake manifold assembly.

16. Remove the drive belts and the water pump.

17. Remove the spark plugs, cylinder head cover and semi-circular plug.

18. Remove the No. 3 and No. 2 front covers. Turn the crankshaft pulley and align its groove with the **0** mark on the No. 1 front cover. Check that the camshaft pulley hole aligns with the mark on the No. 1 camshaft bearing cap (exhaust side). If not, rotate the crankshaft 360 degrees until the marks are aligned.

19. Remove the plug from the No. 1 front cover and matchmark the timing belt to the camshaft pulley. Loosen the idler pulley mounting bolt and push the pulley to the left as far as it will go; tighten the bolt. Slide the timing belt off the camshaft pulley and support it so it won't fall into the case.

20. Remove the camshaft pulley and check the camshaft thrust clearance. Remove the camshafts.

21. Gradually loosen the cylinder head mounting bolts in several passes, in the the proper sequence. Remove the cylinder head.

NOTE: The cylinder head bolts on the intake side of the cylinder head are 3.54 in. (90mm) and the bolts on the exhaust side of the head are 4.25 in. (108mm). Label the bolts to ensure proper installation.

To install:

22. Position the cylinder head on the block with a new gasket. Lightly coat the cylinder head bolts with engine oil and then install. On 1990-92, tighten the bolts in 3 stages, in the proper sequence. On the final pass, torque the bolt to 44 ft. lbs. (60 Nm). On the 1993-94 vehicles, coat the head bolts with engine oil and tighten in several passes, in the sequence shown to 22 ft. lbs. (29 Nm). Mark the front of each bolt with a dab of paint and then retighten the bolts a further 90 degree turn. The paint dabs should be at a 90 degree angle to the front of the head. Re-

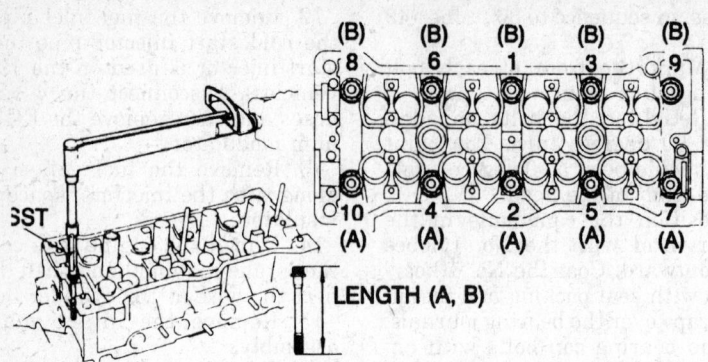

Cylinder head bolt tightening sequence — 4A-FE and 7A-FE engines (Corolla and Celica).

tighten the bolts one more time a further 90 degree turn. The paint dabs should now be pointing toward the rear of the head.

23. Position the camshafts into the cylinder head. Position the bearing caps over each journal with the arrows pointing forward.

24. Tighten each bearing cap a little at a time and in the reverse of the removal sequence. Tighten to 9 ft. lbs. (13 Nm) and recheck the camshaft end-play.

25. Install the camshaft timing pulley making sure the camshaft knock pins and the matchmarks are in alignment. Lock the camshaft and tighten the pulley bolts to 43 ft. lbs. (59 Nm).

26. Align the matchmarks made during removal and then install the timing belt on the camshaft pulley. Loosen the idler pulley set bolt. Make sure the timing belt contact at the crankshaft pulley does not shift.

27. Rotate the crankshaft clockwise 2 revolutions from TDC to TDC. Make sure each pulley aligns with the marks made previously. If the marks are not in alignment, the valve timing is wrong. Shift the timing belt contact slightly and then repeat Steps 24-26.

28. Tighten the set bolt on the timing belt idler pulley to 27 ft. lbs. (37 Nm). Measure the timing belt deflection at the SIDE span. It should deflect no more than 0.24 in. (6mm) at 4.4 lbs. of pressure. If deflection is greater, readjust by using the idler pulley.

29. Install the remaining components with new gaskets and torque all the following components in several steps from the center position to the ends: the cylinder head cover to 52 inch lbs. (8 Nm), intake manifold assembly 14 ft. lbs. (19 Nm) and exhaust manifold to 25 ft. lbs. (34 Nm).

30. Check all fluid levels and all perform all necessary adjustments.

Start the engine and check for leaks. Road test the vehicle for proper operation.

CELICA

1. Disconnect the negative battery cable. Drain the cooling system. Relieve the fuel pressure.

2. If equipped with automatic transaxle, disconnect the throttle cable and bracket from the throttle body.

3. Disconnect the accelerator cable and bracket from the throttle body.

4. Remove the air cleaner cap and hose.

5. Remove the engine undercovers. Remove the suspension lower crossmember.

6. Disconnect all lines, hoses and electrical wires that interfere with exhaust manifold, intake manifold and cylinder head removal.

7. Disconnect the front exhaust pipe, distributor and exhaust manifold.

8. Remove the water outlet and gaskets. Remove the water inlet and inlet housing.

9. Unbolt and remove the power steering pump without disconnecting hoses.

10. Remove the throttle body, cold start injector pipe, cold start injector, delivery pipe and fuel injectors.

11. Remove the Air Control Valve (ACV) assembly. Disconnect engine wiring from the timing belt cover and intake manifold.

12. Remove the vacuum pipe, EGR vacuum modulator and EGR Vacuum Switching Valve (VSV) assembly.

13. Remove the EGR valve and gasket. Remove the water inlet pipe and fuel return hose from the fuel filter.

14. Remove the intake manifold with retaining manifold stay (bracket).

15. Remove the valve cover.

16. Remove the camshaft timing pulley, No. 1 idler pulley and tension

spring and No. 3 timing belt cover. Properly support the timing belt so contact with the crankshaft timing pulley does not occur and the timing belt does not shift.

17. Remove the fan belt adjusting bar, engine hangers and power steering drive belt adjusting strut or bracket.

18. Remove the camshafts. Make sure to uniformly loosen and remove bearing cap bolts in several phases and in the proper sequence when removing the camshafts.

19. Loosen then remove the cylinder head bolts in 3 phases and in the proper sequence. Remove the cylinder head from the engine.

NOTE: The cylinder head bolts on the intake side of the cylinder head are 3.54 in. (90mm) and the bolts on the exhaust side of the head are 4.25 in. (108mm). Label the bolts to ensure proper installation.

To install:

20. Install the cylinder head on the cylinder block. Place the cylinder head in position on the cylinder head gasket.

21. Apply a light coat of clean engine oil to the threads of the head bolts before installation. Tighten the bolts in 3 stages, in the proper sequence. On the final pass, torque the bolt to 44 ft. lbs. (60 Nm).

22. Installation of the camshafts and remaining components is the reverse of the removal. Start the engine and check for leaks.

4A-GE Engine

1. Disconnect the negative battery cable. Remove the engine undercover. Drain the cooling system and engine oil.

2. Loosen the clamp and then disconnect the No. 1 air cleaner hose from the throttle body. Disconnect the actuator and accelerator cables from the bracket on the throttle body.

3. If equipped with power steering, Remove the power steering pump and its bracket. Position the pump aside with the hydraulic lines connected.

4. Loosen the water pump pulley set nuts. Remove the drive belt adjusting bolt and belt. Remove the water pump pulley.

5. Disconnect the upper radiator hose at the water outlet on the cylinder head. Disconnect the 2 heater hoses at the water bypass pipe and the cylinder head rear plate.

6. Remove the distributor. Remove the cold start injector pipe and the PCV hose from the cylinder head.

7. Remove the pulsation damper from the delivery pipe. Disconnect the fuel return hose from the pressure regulator.

8. Tag and disconnect all vacuum hoses which may interfere with cylinder head removal. Remove the wiring harness and the vacuum pipe from the No. 3 timing cover. Tag and disconnect all wires which might interfere with exhaust manifold, intake manifold and cylinder head removal.

9. Disconnect the exhaust bracket from the exhaust pipe. Disconnect the exhaust manifold from the exhaust pipe.

10. Remove the vacuum tank and the VCV valve. Remove the exhaust manifold.

11. Remove the 2 mounting bolts and remove the water outlet housing from the cylinder head with the No. 1 bypass pipe and gasket. Pull the No. 1 bypass pipe out of the housing.

12. Remove the fuel delivery pipe along with the fuel injectors.

13. Remove the intake manifold stay. Remove the intake manifold along with the air control valve.

14. Remove the cylinder head covers and their gaskets. Remove the spark plugs. Remove the No. 1 and No. 2 timing belt covers and their gaskets.

15. Rotate the crankshaft pulley until the groove is in alignment with the **0** mark on the No. 1 timing belt cover. Check that the valve lifters on the No. 1 cylinder are loose. If not, rotate the crankshaft 1 complete revolution (360 degrees).

16. Place matchmarks on the timing belt and 2 timing pulleys. Loosen the idler pulley bolts and move the pulley to the left as far as it will go and then retighten the bolt.

17. Remove the timing belt from the camshaft pulleys. When removing the timing belt, support the belt so the contact of the crankshaft timing pulley and the timing belt does not shift. Never drop anything inside the timing case cover. Be sure the timing belt does not come in contact with dust or oil.

18. Lock the camshafts and remove the timing pulleys. Remove the No. 4 timing belt cover.

19. Using a dial indicator, measure the end-play of each camshaft. If not within specification, replace the thrust bearing.

20. Loosen each camshaft bearing cap bolt a little at a time and in the correct sequence. Remove the bearing caps, camshaft and oil seal.

21. Loosen the cylinder head bolts gradually in 3 stages and in the proper order using the proper tool.

22. Remove the cylinder head.

NOTE: On 1990-91 engines, the cylinder head bolts on the right side of the cylinder head are 3.54 in. (90mm) and the bolts on the left side of the head are 4.25 in. (108mm). Label the bolts to ensure proper installation.

To install:

23. Position the cylinder head on the block with a new gasket. Lightly coat the cylinder head bolts with engine oil and then install the short head bolts on the intake side and the long ones on the exhaust side.

24. Tighten them in several passes, in the sequence shown to 22 ft. lbs. (29 Nm). Mark the front of each bolt with a dab of paint and then retighten the bolts a further 90 degree turn. The paint dabs should now all be at a 90 degree angle to the front of the head. Retighten the bolts one more time a further 90 degree turn. The paint dabs should now all be pointing toward the rear of the head.

25. Position the camshafts into the cylinder head. Position the bearing caps over each journal with the arrows pointing forward.

26. Tighten each bearing cap a little at a time and in the reverse of the removal sequence. Tighten to 9 ft. lbs. (13 Nm). Recheck the camshaft end-play.

27. Drive the camshaft oil seals onto the end of the camshafts using a suitable seal installer. Be careful not to install the oil seals crooked. Install the No. 4 timing belt cover.

28. Install the camshaft timing pulleys making sure the camshaft knock pins and the matchmarks are in alignment. Lock each camshaft and tighten the pulley bolts to 34 ft. lbs. (47 Nm).

29. Align the matchmarks made during removal and then install the timing belt on the camshaft pulley. Loosen the idler pulley set bolt. Make sure the timing belt contact at the crankshaft pulley does not shift.

30. Rotate the crankshaft clockwise 2 revolutions from TDC to TDC. Make sure each pulley aligns with the marks made previously. If the marks are not in alignment, the valve timing is wrong. Shift the timing belt contact slightly and then repeat Steps 28-30.

31. Tighten the set bolt on the timing belt idler pulley to 27 ft. lbs. (37 Nm). Measure the timing belt deflection at the top span between the 2 camshaft pulleys. It should deflect no more than 0.16 in. at 4.4 lbs. of pressure. If deflection is greater, readjust by using the idler pulley.

32. Install the remaining components, start the engine and check for leaks.

5S-FE Engine

CELICA AND MR2

1. Disconnect the negative battery cable. Drain the cooling system.

2. Tag and disconnect all lines, hoses and electrical wires that interfere with exhaust manifold, intake manifold and cylinder head removal.

3. On MR2, remove the engine undercovers, engine hood side panels and the brace that runs across the struts.

4. If equipped with automatic transaxle, disconnect the throttle cable and bracket from the throttle body.

5. Disconnect the accelerator cable and bracket from the throttle body and intake chamber.

6. If equipped with cruise control, remove the actuator and bracket.

7. Remove the air cleaner cap.

8. On Celica, remove the alternator and unbolt the air conditioning compressor from its mounting bracket. Leave the refrigerant lines connected and wire the compressor aside.

9. Remove the distributor.

10. On Celica, raise and support the vehicle safely. Remove the right tire and wheel assembly and engine undercovers.

11. Remove the suspension lower crossmember.

12. Disconnect the exhaust pipe from the catalytic converter.

13. Remove the exhaust pipe and catalytic converter.

14. Remove the water outlet and the water bypass pipe.

15. Remove the throttle body and cold start injector. On Celica, remove the cold start injector pipe.

16. Remove the EGR valve and modulator.

17. On MR2, remove the fuel pressure Vacuum Switching Valve (VSV). On Celica and MR2, remove the EGR vacuum switching valve.

18. Remove the air intake chamber air hose, the throttle body air hose, and the power steering pump hoses, if equipped. On Celica, remove the air tube.

19. Remove the intake manifold.

20. Remove the fuel delivery pipe and the injectors.

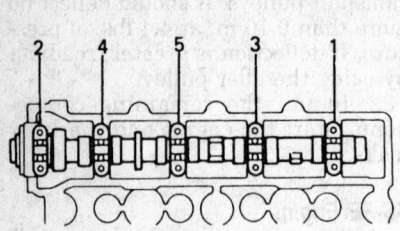

Loosen the camshaft bearing cap bolts in this order — 4A-GE engines

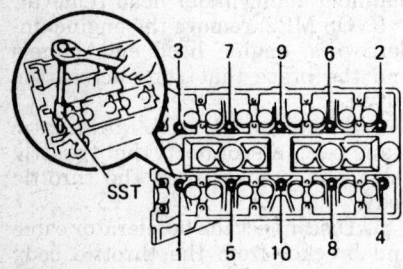

Cylinder head bolt loosening sequence — 4A-GE engines

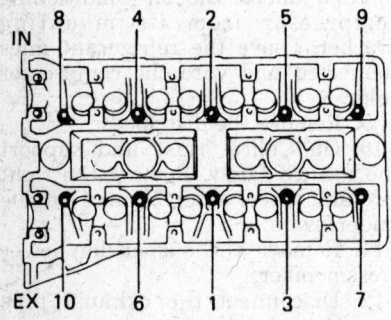

Cylinder head bolt tightening sequence — 4A-GE engines

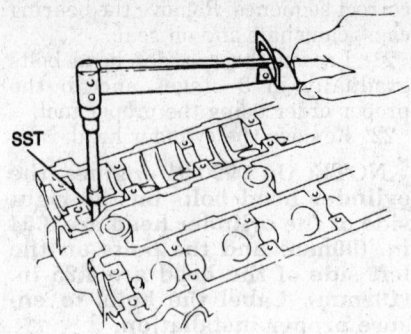

Cylinder head bolt tightening — 4A-GE engines

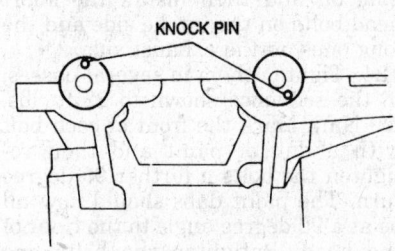

Position the camshafts into the cylinder head as shown — 4A-GE engines

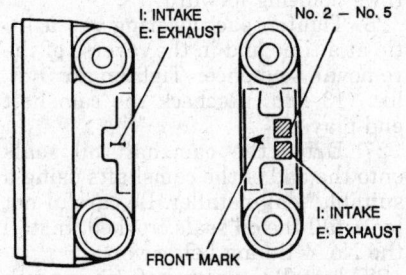

Camshaft bearing cap positioning (the arrows must always point forward) — 4A-GE engines

21. Remove the camshaft timing pulley, No. 1 idler pulley and tension spring and No. 3 timing belt cover. Properly support the timing belt so contact with the crankshaft timing pulley does not occur and the timing belt does not shift.

22. Remove the engine hangers and oil pressure switch. On Celica, remove the alternator bracket.

23. Remove the valve cover.

24. Remove the camshafts.

25. Loosen then remove the cylinder head bolts in 3 phases and in the proper sequence. Remove the cylinder head from the engine.

To install:

26. Install the cylinder head on the cylinder head block. Place the cylinder head in position on the cylinder head gasket.

27. Torque the cylinder head bolts as follows:

  a. Apply a light coat of clean engine oil to the threads of the head bolts before installation.

  b. Tighten the bolts in several passes, in the proper sequence to 36 ft. lbs. (49 Nm).

  c. Mark the front of each bolt with a dab of paint.

  d. Retighten the bolts a further 90 degree turn. The paint dabs should now be at a 90 degree angle to the front of the head.

28. Installation of the remaining components is the reverse of the removal procedure.

CAMRY

1. Disconnect the negative battery cable.

——— CAUTION ———

On models with an air bag, wait at least 90 seconds from the time that the ignition switch is turned to the LOCK position and the battery is disconnected before performing any further work.

2. Drain the cooling system.

3. If equipped with automatic transmission, disconnect the throttle cable and bracket from the throttle body.

4. Disconnect the accelerator cable and bracket from the throttle body and intake chamber.

5. If equipped with cruise control, remove the actuator and bracket.

6. Remove the air cleaner hose.

7. Remove the alternator.

8. Remove the oil pressure gauge, engine hangers and alternator upper bracket.

9. Loosen the lug nuts on the right wheel and raise and support the vehicle safely.

10. Remove the right tire and wheel assembly.

11. Remove the right undercover.

12. Apply penetrating oil to soak into the exhaust nuts and bolts.

13. Disconnect the exhaust pipe from the catalytic converter.

14. Separate the exhaust pipe from the catalytic converter.

15. Remove the distributor.

16. Disconnect the water temperature sender gauge connector, water temperature sensor connector, cold start injector time switch connector, upper radiator hose, water hoses, and the emission control vacuum hoses. Unbolt and remove the water outlet and gaskets.

17. Remove the water bypass pipe with O-rings and gasket.

18. Remove the EGR valve and vacuum modulator.

19. Remove the throttle body.

20. Disconnect the air chamber hose, throttle body air hose and power steering hoses, if equipped.

21. Remove the air tube.

22. Remove the intake manifold stay and disconnect the vacuum sens-

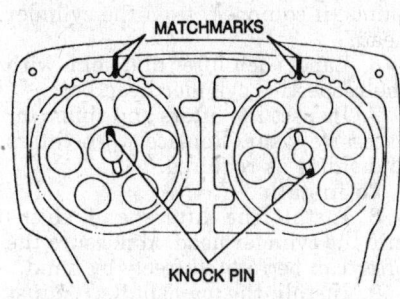

Align the camshaft knockpin with the camshaft timing pulley — 4A-GE engines

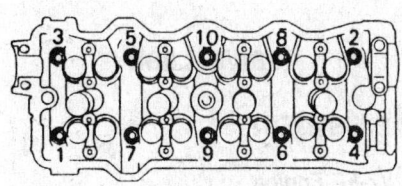

Cylinder head bolt loosening sequence — 5S-FE engine

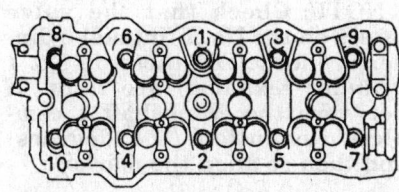

Cylinder head bolt tightening sequence — 5S-FE engine

ing hose. Remove the intake manifold and gasket. Purchase a new gasket.

23. Remove the fuel delivery pipe and the injectors.

24. Remove the spark plugs.

25. Remove the camshaft timing pulley. Remove the No. 1 idler pulley and tension spring. Remove the No. 3 timing belt cover. Properly support the timing belt so contact with the crankshaft timing pulley does not occur and the timing belt does not shift.

26. Remove the cylinder head cover. Label and arrange the grommets in order so they can be reinstalled in the

correct order. Remove the engine hangers, and the alternator bracket.

27. Remove the intake and exhaust camshafts.

28. Loosen and remove the head bolts evenly, in 3 passes, in the correct sequence. Carefully lift the head from the engine.

NOTE: If the cylinder head bolts are loosened out of sequence, warpage or cracking could result.

29. Remove the cylinder head gasket. Remove all the old gasket material from the cylinder head and engine block surfaces.

To install:

30. Place the new cylinder head gasket onto the cylinder block. Place the cylinder head onto the gasket.

31. Coat the threads of the 10 cylinder head bolts with clean engine oil and install the bolts into the cylinder head. Uniformly torque the bolts in 3 passes to an ultimate torque of 36 ft. lbs. (49 Nm), using the correct sequence. If any of the bolts does not meet the torque, replace it. Mark the forward edge of each bolt with paint and then retighten each bolt an additional 90 degrees. Check that each painted mark is now at a 90 degree angle to the front.

32. Using a 30mm socket, install the spark plug tubes and tighten to 29 ft. lbs. (39 Nm).

33. Install the intake and exhaust camshafts.

34. Install the cylinder head cover. Tighten the cover nuts to 17 ft. lbs. (23 Nm).

35. Install the No. 3 timing belt cover with the 4 cover bolts; tighten them to 69 inch lbs. (7.8 Nm). Install the hangers and alternator bracket. Tighten the hangers to 18 ft. lbs. (25 Nm) and the bracket to 31 ft. lbs. (42 Nm).

36. Install the No. 1 idler pulley and tension spring.

37. Install the camshaft timing pulley.

38. Install the spark plugs.

39. Install the injector and delivery pipe. Tighten the mounting bolts to 9 ft. lbs. (13 Nm).

40. Install the intake manifold with new gasket. Tighten the nuts and bolts to 14 ft. lbs. (19 Nm).

41. Install the air tube and connect the air intake chamber hose, throttle body air hose and power steering pump hoses, if equipped.

42. Install the cold start injector pipe, if equipped.

43. Install the throttle body.

44. Install the EGR valve and modulator with new gaskets. Tighten the

union nut to 43 ft. lbs. (59 Nm) and the bolt to 9 ft. lbs. (13 Nm).

45. Install the water bypass pipe with new O-ring and gasket. Coat the O-ring with clean engine oil after installing it into the groove in the pipe. Tighten the bolts to 78 inch lbs. (8.8 Nm). Connect the water hoses.

46. Install the water outlet with a new gasket. Torque the bolts to 11 ft. lbs. (15 Nm). Connect the upper radiator hose, water hose, emission control vacuum hoses, water temperature sender gauge connector, water temperature sensor connector and cold start injector time switch connector.

47. Install the distributer assembly.

48. Assemble the exhaust manifold and the catalytic converter with new gaskets.

49. Install the exhaust manifold and catalytic converter with new gasket to the engine. The exhaust manifold gasket should be installed so the **R** mark (most models) is toward the back.

50. Connect the exhaust pipe to the catalytic converter.

51. Install the suspension lower crossmember.

52. Install the engine right undercover.

53. Install the right front wheel and make the lug nuts snug.

54. Lower the vehicle.

55. Install the alternator.

56. Adjust the drive belt tension.

57. Install the air cleaner hose.

58. If equipped, install the cruise control actuator and bracket.

59. Install the radiator reservoir tank.

60. Install and adjust the accelerator cable.

61. If equipped with automatic transaxle, connect and adjust the throttle cable.

62. Fill the cooling system to the proper level with a good brand of ethylene glycol coolant.

63. Connect the negative battery cable.

64. Start the engine and check for leaks.

65. Adjust the valves and the ignition timing.

66. Road test the vehicle and check for unusual noise, shock, slippage, correct shift points and smooth operation.

67. Recheck the coolant and engine oil levels.

7M-GE and 7M-GTE Engines

1. Disconnect the negative battery cable. Drain the cooling system.

2. Disconnect the exhaust pipe from the exhaust manifold. Disconnect the cruise control cable, if equipped.

3. Disconnect the accelerator cable. Disconnect the throttle cable, if equipped with automatic transmission. Disconnect the engine ground strap.

4. On the 7M-GE engine, remove the No. 1 air cleaner hose along with the intake air pipe assembly. On the 7M-GTE engine, remove the No. 4 air cleaner pipe along with the No. 1 and No. 2 air cleaner hose.

5. Disconnect the cruise control vacuum hose, the charcoal canister hose and the brake booster hose.

6. Remove the radiator and heater inlet hoses. Remove the alternator.

7. On the 7M-GTE engine, remove the power steering reservoir tank. On the 7M-GTE engine, remove the cam position sensor.

8. Remove the air intake chamber with the connector. Remove the PCV pipe. Disconnect and tag all lines, hoses and electrical wires that interfere with exhaust manifold, intake manifold and cylinder head removal.

9. Remove the EGR pipe mounting bolts. Remove the manifold stay retaining bolts. On the 7M-GE engine, remove the throttle body bracket. On the 7M-GTE engine, remove the ISC pipe.

10. Remove the air intake connector mounting bolt (7M-GTE engine). On the 7M-GE engine, remove the cold start injector tube. On the 7M-GTE engine, disconnect the cold start injector. Disconnect the EGR vacuum modulator from the bracket.

11. Disconnect the engine wire from the clamps of the intake chamber. Remove the nuts and bolts, vacuum pipes and intake chamber with the connector and gasket.

12. On the 7M-GTE engine, remove the ignition coil and bracket.

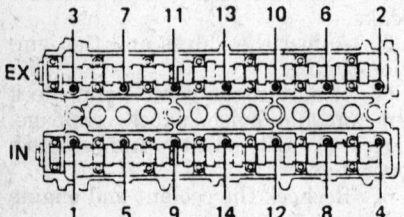

Cylinder head bolt loosening sequence — 7M-GE and 7M-GTE engines

13. Remove the pulsation damper, the VSV and the No. 1 fuel pipe. Remove the No. 2 and No. 3 fuel pipes. On the 7M-GTE engine, remove the auxiliary air pipe.

14. On the 7M-GE engine, remove the high tension wires and the distributor. Remove the oil dipstick. On the 7M-GTE engine, remove the turbocharger assembly.

15. Remove the exhaust manifold. Remove the water outlet housing. Remove the cylinder head covers. Remove the spark plugs.

16. Remove the timing belt and the camshaft timing pulleys. Remove the cylinder head retaining bolts gradually and in the proper sequence. Carefully remove the cylinder head from the engine. As the cylinder head is lifted, separate the No. 5 water by-pass line from its union.

To install:

17. Clean the gasket mating surfaces. Use care not to damage the aluminum components. Lower the cylinder head onto the engine. Make sure the dowel pins are aligned and no hoses or wires are between the head and cylinder block.

18. During installation, observe the following torques:
Cylinder head bolts:
1st step — 20 ft. lbs. (27 Nm)
2nd step — 40 ft. lbs. (54 Nm)
3rd step — 58 ft. lbs. (78 Nm)
Cam bearing caps — 8-10 ft. lbs. (11-14 Nm)
Cam sprocket — 29-39 ft. lbs. (39-53 Nm)
Crankshaft pulley — 55-61 ft. lbs. (75-83 Nm)
Manifold bolts — 15-21 ft. lbs. (20-29 Nm)
Rocker arm bolts — 17-19 ft. lbs. (23-26 Nm)
Timing gear idler bolt — 22-32 ft. lbs. (30-44 Nm)
Adjust belt tension — 0.24-0.28 in. (6-7mm)

19. Adjust the valves and connect all electrical and hoses fittings.
20. Install all necessary components.
21. Connect the battery cable, refill all fluids, start the engine and check for leaks.

Valve Lifters

REMOVAL AND INSTALLATION

1. Disconnect the negative battery cable.
2. Drain the cooling system.
3. Remove the valve cover(s).
4. Remove the camshafts.

5. Remove the valve lifters and shims, if equipped, from the cylinder head.
6. Label each lifter and shim with the respective cylinder head bore.
7. Inspect the lifters and shims for excessive wear. Replace worn lifters and shims as required.

To install:

8. Install the lifters and shims into the cylinder head. Make sure the lifter can be rotated freely by hand.
9. Install the camshafts. Adjust valve lash.
10. Install the valve cover(s) using new gaskets and sealant, as required.
11. Fill the cooling system to the proper level.
12. Connect the negative battery cable.

Valve Lash

ADJUSTMENT

2VZ-FE Engine

1. Remove the air intake chamber and the cylinder head covers.
2. Use a wrench and turn the crankshaft until the notch in the pulley aligns with the timing mark **0** of the No. 1 timing belt cover. This will ensure that No. 1 piston is at TDC of the compression stroke.

NOTE: Check that the valve lifters on the No. 1 (intake) cylinder are loose and those on No. 1 cylinder (exhaust) are tight. If not, turn the crankshaft 1 complete revolution (360 degrees) and then re-align the marks.

3. Using a flat feeler gauge measure the clearance between the camshaft lobe and the valve lifter on the first set of valves shown. This measurement should correspond to specification.

NOTE: If the measurement is within specifications, go on to the next step. If not, record the measurement taken for each individual valve.

4. Turn the crankshaft ⅔ revolution (240 degrees).
5. Measure the clearance of the second set of valves shown.

NOTE: If the measurement is within specifications, go on to the next step. If not, record the measurement taken for each individual valve.

6. Turn the crankshaft ⅔ revolution (240 degrees).

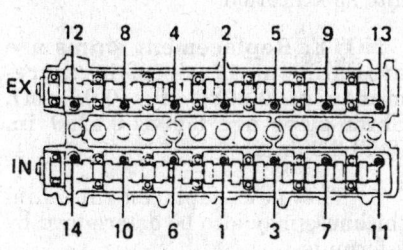

Cylinder head bolt tightening sequence — 7M-GE and 7M-GTE engines

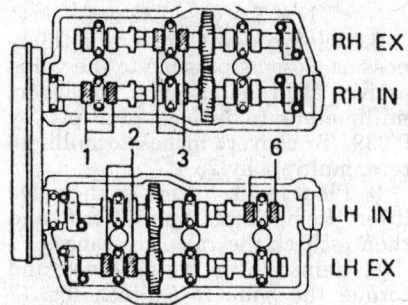

Adjust these valves first — 2VZ-FE and 3VZ-FE engines

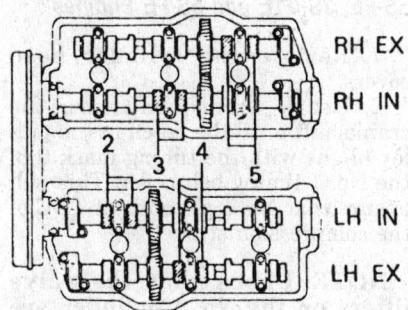

Adjust these valves second — 2VZ-FE engines

7. Measure the clearance of the third set of valves shown.

NOTE: If the measurement for this set of valves (and also the previous ones) is within specifications, go no further, the procedure is finished. If not, record the measurements and then proceed to Step 8.

8. Turn the crankshaft to position the intake camshaft lobe of the cylinder to be adjusted upward.

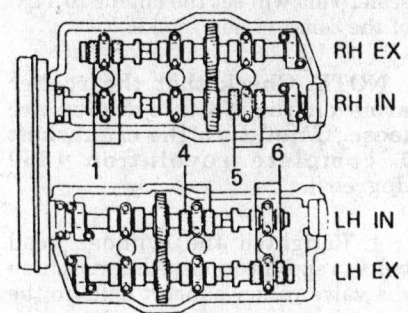

Adjust these valves third — 2VZ-FE and 3VZ-FE engines

9. Using a suitable tool, turn the valve lifter so the notch is easily accessible; it should be toward the spark plug.
10. Install tool 09248-55010 or equivalent, between the 2 camshafts lobes and then turn the handle so the tool presses down the valve lifter evenly.
11. Using a suitable tool and a magnet, remove the valve shims.
12. Measure the thickness of the old shim with a micrometer. Using this measurement and the clearance ones made earlier (from Step 3, 5 or 7), determine what size replacement shim will be required in order to bring the valve clearance into specification.

NOTE: Replacement shims are available in 17 sizes, in increments of 0.0020 in. (0.05mm), from 0.0984-0.1299 in. (2.50-3.30mm).

13. Install the new shim, remove the special tool and then recheck the valve clearances.

3VZ-FE Engine

NOTE: Adjust and inspect the valve clearance when the engine is cold.

1. Disconnect the negative battery cable.

─────── **CAUTION** ───────
On models with an air bag, wait at least 90 seconds from the time that the ignition switch is turned to the LOCK position and the battery is disconnected before performing any further work.

2. Drain the engine coolant.
3. Disconnect and remove the air intake tube.
4. Remove the cylinder head covers by removing the 6 nuts, seal washers and gaskets.

5. Use a wrench and turn the crankshaft until the notch in the pulley aligns with the timing mark **0** of the No. 1 timing belt cover. This will insure that engine is at TDC.

NOTE: Check that the valve lifters on the No. 1 (IN) cylinder are loose and that those on the No. 1 (EX) cylinder are tight. If not, turn the crankshaft one complete revolution (360 degrees) and then realign the mark.

6. Using a feeler gauge measure the clearance between the camshaft lobe and the valve lifter in the correct sequences (FIRST). This measurement should correspond to specification.

NOTE: If the measurement is within specifications, go on to the next step. If not, record the measurement taken for each individual valve. These measurements will be used later to determine the proper replacement adjusting shim.

7. Turn the crankshaft ⅔ of a revolution (240 degrees).
8. Now measure the clearance of the next set of valves (SECOND).

NOTE: If the measurement for this set of valves (and also the previous one) is within specifications, the procedure is finished. If not, record the measurements and then proceed to Step 9.

9. Turn the crankshaft a further ⅔ of a revolution (240 degrees).
10. Now measure the clearance of the next valves (THIRD).

NOTE: If the measurement for this set of valves (and also the previous 2) is within specifications, the procedure is finished. If not, record the measurements and then proceed to Step 11.

11. Turn the crankshaft to position the camshaft lobe of the valve to be adjusted faces upward.
12. Using a suitable tool, turn the valve lifter so the notch is easily accessible (toward the spark plug).
13. Install a valve lifter depressing tool between the camshaft lobe and the valve and then turn the handle so the tool presses down the valve lifter evenly.
14. Using a suitable tool and a magnet, remove the valve adjusting shim.
15. Measure the thickness of the old shim with a micrometer. Using this measurement and the clearance made earlier, determine what size replacement shim will be required in

order to bring the valve clearance into specification.

NOTE: Replacement shims are available in 17 sizes, in increments of 0.0020 in. (0.05mm). Shim sizes are 0.0984-0.1299 in. (2.50-3.30mm).

16. The new replacement shim thickness may also be determined by a formula.
- T — Thickness of used shim
- A — Measured valve clearance
- N — Thickness of new shim
- Intake:
    $$N = T + (A - 0.18mm)$$
- Exhaust:
    $$N = T + (A - 0.32mm)$$

17. Select a new shim with a thickness as close as possible to the value arrived at in the formula. To convert millimeters to inches, multiply by 0.039. To convert inches to millimeters, multiply by 25.4.

18. Place the new shim on the valve lifter. Remove the special tool and then recheck the valve clearance.

19. Install the gasket onto the cylinder head cover. Install the head cover with the seal washers and nuts. Torque the nuts to 52 inch lbs. (6 Nm).

20. Install the intake tube.

21. Refill the engine with coolant and connect the battery cable.

3E and 3E-E Engines

1. Start the engine and run it until it reaches normal operating temperature.

2. Stop the engine. Remove the air cleaner assembly and the cylinder head cover.

3. Turn the crankshaft until the point or notch on the pulley aligns with the **0** or **T** mark on the timing

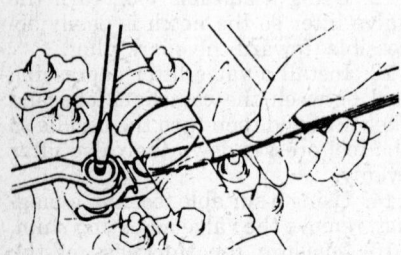

Valve lash adjustment — 3E and 3E-E engines

scale. This will set the engine to TDC of the compression stroke.

NOTE: Check that the rocker arms on the No. 1 cylinder are loose. If not, turn the crankshaft 1 complete revolution (360 degrees).

4. Retighten the cylinder head bolts to specifications. Also, retighten the valve rocker support bolts to the proper specifications.

5. Using a flat feeler gauge, check the clearance between the rocker arm and camshaft.

6. If the clearance is not within specification, the valves will require adjustment. Loosen the locknut on the end of the rocker arm and, still holding the nut with an open end wrench, turn the adjustments screw to achieve the correct clearance.

7. Once the correct valve clearance is achieved, keep the adjustment screw from turning with a suitable tool and then tighten the locknut. Recheck the valve clearances.

8. Turn the engine 1 complete revolution (360 degrees) and adjust the remaining valves.

9. Use a new gasket and install the cylinder head cover. Install the air cleaner assembly.

5E-FE Engine

NOTE: Inspect and adjust the valve clearance when the engine is cold.

1. Remove the valve cover.

2. Set the No. 1 cylinder to TDC of the compression stroke. Verify this by checking that the lifters on the No. 1 cylinder are loose and the lifters on the No. 4 cylinder are tight.

3. Check the valve clearances to be adjusted first, using a feeler gauge. Note the clearances.

4. Turn the crankshaft 1 turn and set the mark to TDC as before. Check the valve clearances to be adjusted secondly, using a feeler gauge. Note the clearances. The proper clearances should be 0.006-0.010 in. (0.15-0.25mm) for the intake side and 0.012-0.016 in. (0.31-0.41mm) for the exhaust side.

5. If out of specifications, remove the particular adjusting shim with tool 09248-55020 or equivalent.

6. Measure the thickness of the old shim with a micrometer. Using this measurement and the clearance made earlier, determine what size replacement shim will be required in

order to bring the valve clearance into specification.

NOTE: Replacement shims are available in 17 sizes, in increments of 0.0020 in. (0.05mm). Shim sizes are 0.0984-0.1299 in. (2.50-3.30mm).

7. The new replacement shim thickness may also be determined by a formula.
- T — Thickness of used shim
- A — Measured valve clearance
- N — Thickness of new shim
- Intake:
    $$N = T + (A - 0.18mm)$$
- Exhaust:
    $$N = T + (A - 0.32mm)$$

8. Select a new shim with a thickness as close as possible to the value arrived at in the formula. To convert millimeters to inches, multiply by 0.039. To convert inches to millimeters, multiply by 25.4.

9. Place the new shim on the valve lifter. Remove the special tool and then recheck the valve clearance.

10. Reinstall the valve cover and torque the bolts to 61 inch lbs. (7 Nm).

11. Start the engine and check for leaks or unusual noises.

3S-FE, 3S-GTE and 5S-FE Engines

1. Remove the cylinder head covers.

2. Use a wrench and turn the crankshaft until the notch in the pulley aligns with the timing mark **0** of the No. 1 timing belt cover. This will ensure that No. 1 piston is at TDC of the compression stroke.

NOTE: Check that the valve lifters on the No. 1 cylinder are loose and those on No. 4 cylinder are tight. If not, turn the crankshaft 1 complete revolution (360 degrees) and then realign the marks.

3. Using a flat feeler gauge measure the clearance between the camshaft lobe and the valve lifter on the first set of valves shown. This measurement should correspond to specification.

NOTE: If the measurement is within specifications, go on to the next step. If not, record the measurement taken for each individual valve.

4. Turn the crankshaft 1 complete revolution and realign the timing marks.

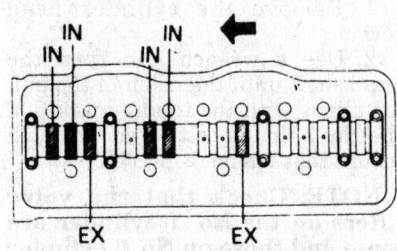

Adjust these valves first — 3E and 3E-E engines

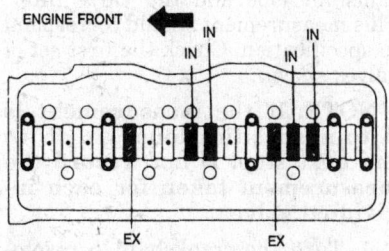

Adjust these valves second — 3E and 3E-E engines

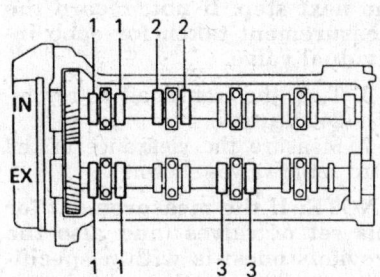

Inspecting first set of valve clearances — 5E-FE engine

5. Measure the clearance of the second set of valves.

NOTE: If the measurement for this set of valves (and also the previous one) is within specifications, go no further, the procedure is finished. If not, record the measurements and then proceed to Step 6.

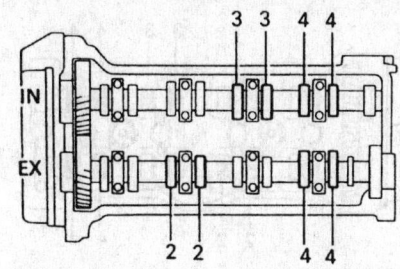

Inspecting second set of valve clearances — 5E-FE engine

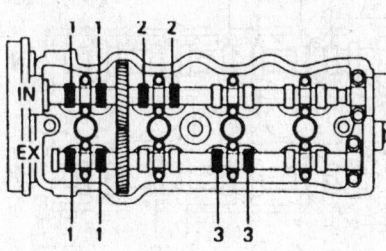

Adjust these valves first — 3S-FE engine

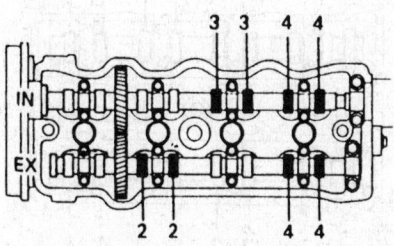

Adjust these valves second — 3S-FE engine

6. Turn the crankshaft to position the intake camshaft lobe of the cylinder to be adjusted, upward.

NOTE: Both intake and exhaust valve clearance may be adjusted at the same time, if required.

7. Using a suitable tool, turn the valve lifter so the notch is easily accessible.

8. Install tool 09248-55010 for 3S-FE, 3S-GTE and 5S-FE engines, between the 2 camshaft lobes and then turn the handle so the tool presses

down both intake and exhaust valve lifters evenly.

9. Using a suitable tool and a magnet, remove the valve shims.

10. Measure the thickness of the old shim with a micrometer. Using this measurement and the clearance ones made earlier (from Step 3 or 5), determine what size replacement shim will be required in order to bring the valve clearance into specification.

NOTE: Replacement shims are available in 27 sizes, in increments of 0.0020 in. (0.05mm). Shim sizes are 0.0787-0.1299 in. (2.00-3.30mm).

11. Install the new shim, remove the special tool and then recheck the valve clearances.

4A-FE, 7A-FE, 4A-GE Engines

1. Start the engine and run it until it reaches normal operating temperature.

2. Stop the engine. Remove the air cleaner assembly and the valve cover.

3. Use a wrench and turn the crankshaft until the notch in the pulley aligns with the timing pointer in the front cover. This will insure that engine is at TDC.

NOTE: Check that the valve lifters on the No. 1 cylinder are loose and those on No. 4 cylinder are tight. If not, turn the crankshaft 1 complete revolution (360 degrees) and then re-align the marks.

4. Using a flat feeler gauge measure the clearance between the camshaft lobe and the valve lifter. Check the first set of valves shown.

NOTE: If the measurement is within specifications, go on to the next step. If not, record the measurement taken for each individual valve.

5. Turn the crankshaft 1 complete revolution and realign the timing marks. Measure the clearance of the second set of valves shown.

NOTE: If the measurement for this set of valves (and also the previous one) is within specification, go no further, the procedure is finished. If not, record the measurements and then proceed to Step 6.

6. Turn the crankshaft to position the intake camshaft lobe of the cylinder to be adjusted, upward. Both intake and exhaust valve clearance may be adjusted at the same time, if required.

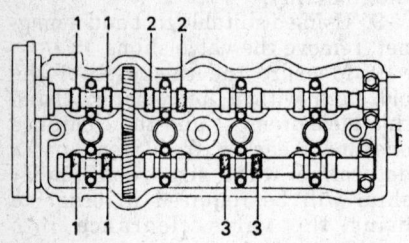

Adjust these valves first — 3S-GTE and 5S-FE engines

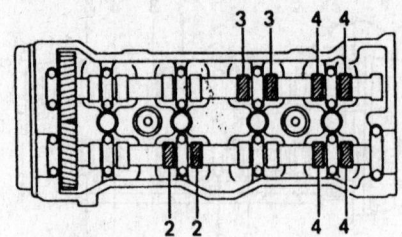

Adjust these valves second — 4A-FE and 7A-FE engines

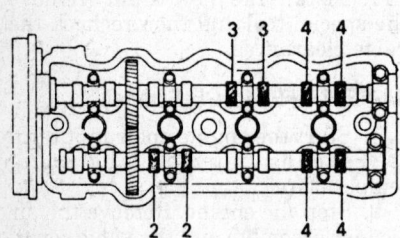

Adjust these valves second — 3S-GTE and 5S-FE engines

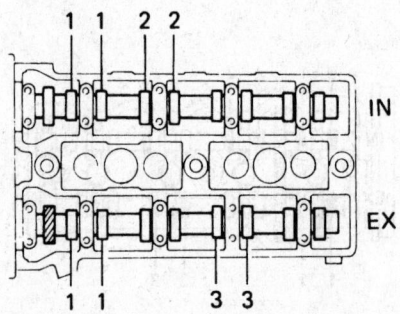

Adjust these valves first — 4A-GE (Corolla) engine

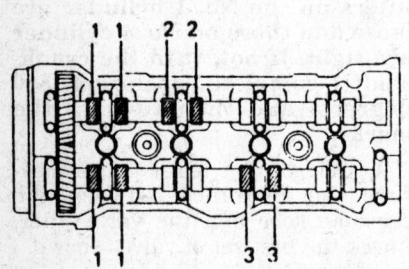

Adjust these valves first — 4A-FE and 7A-FE engines

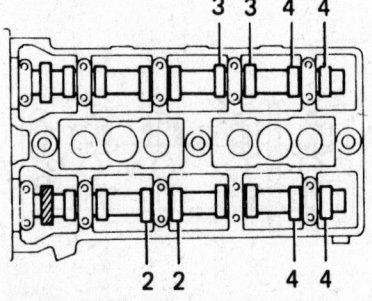

Adjust these valves second — 4A-GE (Corolla) engine

7. Using a suitable tool, turn the valve lifter so the notch is easily accessible.

8. Install tool 09248-70011 for 4A-GE engine or 09248-55010 4A-FE, 7A-FE engines between the 2 camshafts lobes and then turn the handle so the tool presses down both (intake and exhaust) valve lifters evenly. On the 4A-GE engine, the tool will work on only one valve lifter at a time.

NOTE: Position the notch toward the spark plug before pressing down the valve lifter.

9. Using a suitable tool and a magnet, remove the valve shims.

10. Measure the thickness of the old shim with a micrometer. Using this measurement and the clearance of ones made earlier, determine what size replacement shim will be required in order to bring the valve clearance into specification.

11. Install the new shim, remove the special tool and then recheck the valve clearance.

7M-GE and 7M-GTE Engines

1. Remove the cylinder head covers.

2. Use a wrench and turn the crankshaft until the notch in the pulley aligns with the timing mark **0** of the No. 1 timing belt cover. This will insure that engine is at TDC.

NOTE: Check that the valve lifters on the No. 1 cylinder are loose and those on No. 6 cylinder are tight. If not, turn the crankshaft 1 complete revolution (360 degrees) and then realign the marks.

3. Using a flat feeler gauge measure the clearance between the camshaft lobe and the valve lifter. This measurement should correspond to specification. Check the first set of valves shown.

NOTE: If the measurement is within specifications, go on to the next step. If not, record the measurement taken for each individual valve.

4. Turn the crankshaft ²/₃ revolution (240 degrees).

5. Measure the clearance of the second set of valves shown.

NOTE: If the measurement is within specifications, go on to the next step. If not, record the measurement taken for each individual valve.

6. Turn the crankshaft ²/₃ revolution (240 degrees).

7. Measure the clearance of the third set of valves shown.

NOTE: If the measurement for this set of valves (and also the previous ones) is within specifications, go no further, the procedure is finished. If not, record the measurements and then proceed to Step 8.

8. Turn the crankshaft to position the intake camshaft lobe of the cylinder to be adjusted, upward.

NOTE: Both intake and exhaust valve clearance may be adjusted at the same time.

9. Using a suitable tool, turn the valve lifter so the notch is easily accessible.

10. Install tool 09248-55010 or equivalent, between the 2 camshafts lobes and then turn the handle so the tool presses down both (intake and exhaust) valve lifters evenly.

11. Using a suitable tool and a magnet, remove the valve shims.

12. Measure the thickness of the old shim with a micrometer. Using

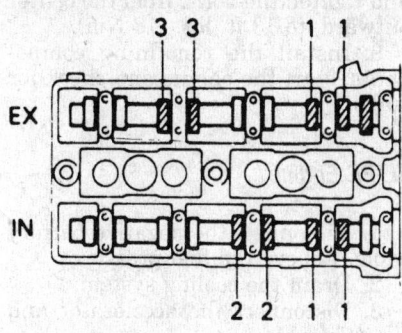

Adjust these valves first — 4A-GE engines

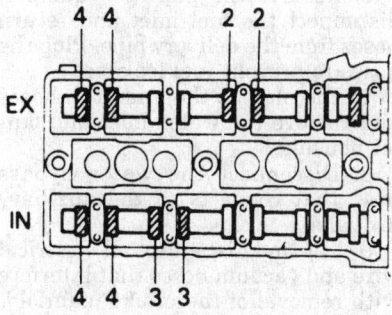

Adjust these valves second — 4A-GE engines

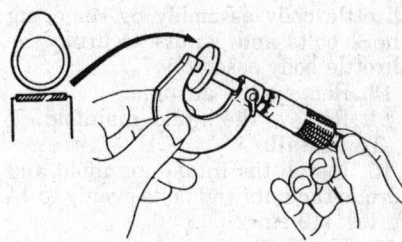

Measuring the shim size (thickness)

this measurement and the clearance made earlier (from Step 3, 5 or 7), determine what size replacement shim will be required in order to bring the valve clearance into specification.

NOTE: Replacement shims are available in 17 sizes, in increments of 0.0020 in. (0.05mm). Shim sizes are 0.0787-0.1299 in. (2.00-3.30mm).

13. Install the new shim, remove the special tool and then recheck the valve clearance.

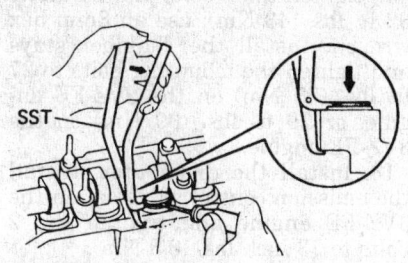

Depressing the valve lifter to remove the shim

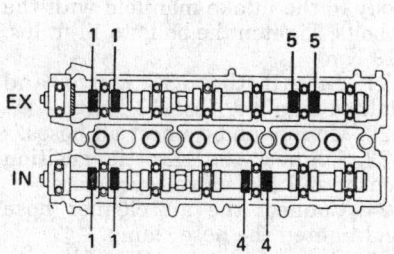

Adjust these valves first — 7M-GE and 7M-GTE engines

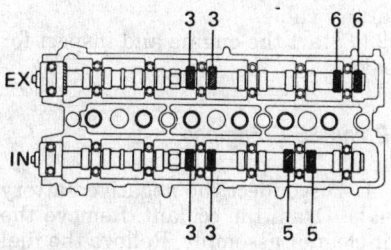

Adjust these valves second — 7M-GE and 7M-GTE engines

Rocker Arms/Shafts

REMOVAL AND INSTALLATION

3E and 3E-E Engines

1. Disconnect the negative battery cable.
2. Remove the camshaft.
3. Loosen the rocker arm adjusting screw locknuts.
4. Pull up on the top of the spring while prying the spring with a suitable tool.

5. Remove the rocker arms and arrange in order. Check the contact surface for any signs of pitting or wear.

To install:

6. Check that the adjusting screw is as shown and install a new spring to the rocker arm.
7. Press the bottom lip of the spring until it fits into the groove on the rocker arm pivot.

NOTE: Put the valve adjusting screw in the rocker arm pivot.

8. Pry the rocker spring clip onto the pivot. Pull the rocker arm up and down to check that there is spring tension and that the rocker does not rattle.

Except 3E and 3E-E Engines

The other engines do not utilize rocker arms. The valves are activated directly by the camshaft through valve adjusting shims.

Intake Manifold

REMOVAL AND INSTALLATION

2VZ-FE and 3VZ-FE Engines

1. Disconnect the negative battery cable. Drain the engine coolant. Relieve the fuel pressure.

--- **CAUTION** ---
On models with an air bag, wait at least 90 seconds from the time that the ignition switch is turned to the LOCK position and the battery is disconnected before performing any further work.

2. Disconnect the throttle/accelerator cable from the throttle body.
3. Disconnect the air cleaner hose at the air intake chamber and remove it.
4. Remove the V-bank cover on the 3VZ-FE engine.
5. Tag and disconnect all lines and hoses and then remove both the ISC valve and the throttle body.
6. Remove the EGR valve and vacuum modulator. Remove the distributor.
7. On the 3VZ-FE engine, remove the emission control valve set and then disconnect the left side engine harness.
8. Remove the cylinder head rear plate.
9. Remove the intake chamber stays, any wires and then remove the air intake chamber.

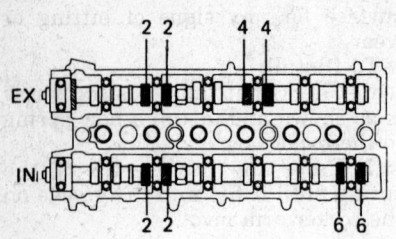

Adjust these valves third — 7M-GE and 7M-GTE engines

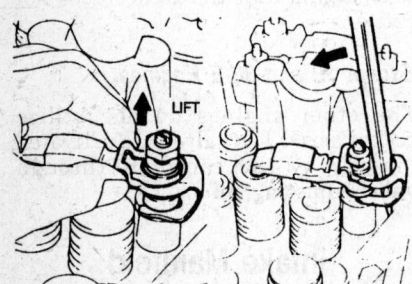

Rocker arm spring clip removal — 3E and 3E-E engines

10. Remove the fuel injection delivery pipe and the injectors.

11. Remove the water outlet and the bypass outlet.

12. Remove the 2 bolts and the No. 2 idler pulley bracket stay. Remove the 8 bolts and 4 nuts and then lift out the intake manifold.

To install:

13. Thoroughly clean the intake manifold and cylinder head surfaces. Using a machinist's straightedge and a feeler gauge, check the surface of the intake manifold for warpage. If the warpage is greater than 0.0039 in. (0.10mm), replace the intake manifold.

14. Place new gaskets onto the intake manifold and position the intake manifold between the cylinder heads. Tighten the nuts and bolts evenly (from the center to the end of the manifold) to 13 ft. lbs. (18 Nm). Tighten the No. 2 pulley bracket bolts to 13 ft. lbs. (18 Nm).

15. Install the water bypass outlet and tighten the bolts to 14 ft. lbs. (20 Nm) on the 2VZ-FE engine, or 74 inch lbs. (8.3 Nm) on the 3VZ-FE engine. Tighten the water outlet to 74 inch lbs. (8.3 Nm).

16. Install the injectors and delivery pipe.

17. Install the air intake chamber and tighten the 2 bolts and 2 nuts to 32 ft. lbs. (43 Nm); use an 8mm hex wrench. Install the chamber stays and tighten the mounting bolts to 27 ft. lbs. (37 Nm) on the 2VZ-FE engine, or 29 ft. lbs. (39 Nm) on the 3VZ-FE engine.

18. Install the distributor. Install the emission control valve set on the 3VZ-FE engine and tighten the 2 bolts to 73 inch lbs. (8.3 Nm).

19. Install the EGR valve and modulator (with new gaskets). Tighten the bolts and nuts to 13 ft. lbs. (18 Nm).

20. Place a new gasket onto the throttle body and attach the throttle body to the intake manifold with the 4 bolts. Tighten the bolts to 14 ft. lbs. (19 Nm).

21. Install the ISC valve and tighten it to 9 ft. lbs. (13 Nm).

22. Unplug and connect all hoses.

23. Connect the throttle position sensor and ISC valve connectors.

24. Connect the air cleaner hose and tighten the hose clamp.

25. Connect the throttle cable with bracket onto the throttle body. Install the return spring.

26. If equipped with automatic transaxle, connect the accelerator cable and adjust it.

27. Fill the cooling system to the proper level and connect the negative battery cable.

28. Start the engine and inspect for leaks.

3E and 3E-E Engines

1. Disconnect the negative battery cable. Drain the coolant. Remove the air cleaner assembly. Relieve the fuel pressure.

2. Tag and disconnect all wires, hoses or cables that interfere with intake manifold removal.

3. Remove the necessary components in order to gain access to the intake manifold retaining bolts.

4. Remove the carburetor or the throttle body if necessary.

5. Disconnect the intake manifold water hoses.

6. Remove the intake manifold retaining bolts. Remove the intake manifold from the vehicle.

To install:

7. Clean the gasket mating surfaces being careful not to damage the aluminum surfaces. Check the mating surfaces for warpage with a straightedge.

8. Match the old gasket with the new for an exact match. Use new gaskets when installing the manifold

and tighten the bolts, from the center outward, to 13 ft. lbs. (18 Nm).

9. Install the remaining components, start the engine and check for leaks.

5E-FE Engine

1. Disconnect the negative battery cable. Relieve the fuel pressure.

2. Drain the cooling system.

3. Disconnect the accelerator and throttle cables.

4. Remove the PCV hoses.

5. Remove the air cleaner and air intake collector assembly.

6. Remove the pulsation damper; disconnect the fuel inlet and return hoses from the delivery pipe. Plug the hoses to prevent fuel leakage.

7. Disconnect the radiator hoses and remove the water inlet and outlet housing.

8. Disconnect the water bypass hose that connects to the auxiliary air valve.

9. Tag and disconnect all electrical wire and vacuum hoses that interfere with removal of the intake manifold.

10. If equipped with an EGR system, remove the EGR pipe, EGR valve, vacuum modulator and EGR gas temperature sensor (California).

11. Remove the air control valve.

12. Matchmark and remove the throttle body assembly by removing the 2 bolts and 2 nuts securing the throttle body assembly.

13. Remove the air pipe.

14. Remove the intake manifold.

To install:

15. Install the intake manifold and torque the nuts and bolts evenly to 14 ft. lbs. (19 Nm).

16. Install the vacuum hoses, then install the air pipe.

17. Install the fuel injector rail assembly, using new grommets and O-rings. Lightly lubricate the O-rings with gasoline and check that the injectors can be rotated smoothly once pressed in. Then install the 2 bolts and torque to 14 ft. lbs. (19 Nm).

18. Install the throttle body, using a new gasket and torquing the nuts and bolts evenly to 9 ft. lbs. (13 Nm).

19. Install the air control valve, the exhaust manifold and torque the bolts to 35 ft. lbs. (47 Nm).

20. Reconnect all remaining electrical and hoses fittings.

21. Reinstall all remaining components.

22. Connect the battery cable, refill all fluids, start the engine and check the ignition timing and for leaks, especially fuel leaks at the injectors.

3S-FE and 5S-FE Engines

1. Disconnect the negative battery cable. Drain the cooling system. Remove the air cleaner assembly.

2. Tag and disconnect all wires, hoses or cables that interfere with intake manifold removal.

3. Remove the necessary components in order to gain access to the intake manifold retaining bolts.

4. Remove the throttle body and cold start injector pipe.

5. Remove the air tube assembly. If equipped with power steering, remove the hoses before removing the air tube assembly.

6. Remove the intake manifold retaining bolts. Remove the intake manifold from the vehicle.

To install:

7. Clean the gasket mating surfaces being careful not to damage the aluminum surfaces. Check the mating surfaces for warpage with a straightedge.

8. Match the old gasket with the new for an exact match. Use new gaskets when installing the manifold and tighten the bolts, from the center outward. Tighten the intake manifold mounting bolts to 14 ft. lbs. (19 Nm). Tighten the 12mm manifold stay bolt to 14 ft. lbs. (19 Nm); tighten the 14mm bolts to 31 ft. lbs. (42 Nm).

9. Install the remaining components, start the engine and check for leaks.

3S-GTE Engines

1. Disconnect the negative battery cable. Drain the cooling system. Remove the air cleaner assembly.

2. Tag and disconnect all wires, hoses or cables that interfere with intake manifold removal.

3. Remove the necessary components in order to gain access to the intake manifold retaining bolts.

4. Remove the intake manifold retaining bolts and nuts. Remove the intake manifold from the vehicle.

To install:

5. Clean the gasket mating surfaces being careful not to damage the aluminum surfaces. Check the mating surfaces for warpage with a straightedge.

6. Match the old gasket with the new for an exact match. Use new gaskets when installing the manifold and tighten the bolts, from the center outward, to 13 ft. lbs. (18 Nm).

7. Install the remaining components, start the engine and check for leaks.

4A-FE, 7A-FE, 4A-GE Engines

NOTE: On the 1993-94 4A-FE and 7A-FE engines the upper intake air chamber and intake manifold can be separated. A metal gasket is used to improve sealing performance. No cold start injector assembly is used on 1993-94 4A-FE and 7A-FE engines.

1. Relieve the fuel pressure. Disconnect the negative battery cable.

2. Remove the air cleaner assembly. Drain the coolant.

3. Tag and remove all wires, hoses or cables in the way of intake manifold removal. Remove the intake manifold stay (bracket).

4. Remove the cold start injector pipe.

5. Disconnect the electrical connectors and remove the fuel delivery pipe (fuel rail) and remove the injectors. During removal, be careful not to drop the injectors.

6. Remove the intake manifold retaining bolts. Remove the intake manifold from the vehicle.

To install:

7. Clean the gasket mating surfaces being careful not to damage the surfaces. Check the mating surfaces for warpage with a straightedge.

8. Match the old gasket with the new for an exact match. Use new gasket when installing the manifold and tighten the bolts evenly and in several passes from the center outward to the correct specifications. Install intake manifold stay (bracket).

9. Install the cold start injector pipe. Torque the cold start injector union bolt.

10. Install all necessary wires, hoses or cables. Install air cleaner assembly.

11. Refill the cooling system. Connect the negative battery cable. Start engine. Check for leaks and road test for proper operation.

7M-GE and 7M-GTE Engines

1. Disconnect the negative battery cable. Drain the cooling system.

2. Remove the air cleaner assembly.

3. Tag and disconnect all wires, hoses or cables that interfere with intake manifold removal.

4. Remove the necessary components in order to gain access to the intake manifold retaining bolts.

5. Remove the air intake connector along with the air intake chamber assembly.

6. Remove the fuel delivery pipe with the injectors still attached.

7. Remove the intake manifold retaining bolts. Remove the intake manifold from the vehicle.

To install:

8. Clean the gasket mating surfaces being careful not to damage the aluminum surfaces. Check the mating surfaces for warpage with a straightedge.

9. Match the old gasket with the new for an exact match. Use new gaskets when installing the manifold and tighten the bolts evenly from the center outward, to 13 ft. lbs. (18 Nm).

10. Install the remaining components, start the engine and check for leaks.

Exhaust Manifold

REMOVAL AND INSTALLATION

2VZ-FE Engine

1. Disconnect the negative battery cable and drain the cooling system. Relieve the fuel pressure.

2. Disconnect the throttle cable at the throttle body. If equipped with cruise control, remove the cruise control actuator and vacuum pump.

3. Remove the air cleaner hose.

4. Raise the vehicle and support safely. Remove the engine undercovers.

5. Remove the lower suspension crossmember and the front exhaust pipe.

6. Remove the alternator and the Idle Speed Control (ISC) valve.

7. Remove the throttle body, EGR pipe, EGR valve and vacuum modulator.

8. Remove the vacuum pipe and the distributor.

9. Remove the exhaust crossover pipe. Disconnect the cold start injector and then remove the injector tube.

10. Tag and disconnect all hoses leading to the air intake chamber and then remove the chamber.

11. Remove the fuel delivery pipes and the injectors.

12. Disconnect the water temperature sensor and remove the upper radiator hose. Remove the water outlet. Remove the water bypass outlet.

13. Loosen the 2 bolts and remove the cylinder head rear plate.

14. Remove the intake manifold.

15. Disconnect the oxygen sensor and then remove the outside heat insulator for the right manifold. Remove the manifold and gasket and then remove the inner heat shield.

16. Remove the left side heat shield and then remove the manifold.

To install:

17. Clean the gasket mating surfaces being careful not to damage the aluminum surfaces. Check the mating surfaces for warpage with a straightedge.

18. Match the old gasket with the new for an exact match. Use new gaskets when installing the manifold and tighten the bolts, from the center outward, to 29 ft. lbs. (39 Nm).

19. Install the remaining components, start the engine and check for leaks.

3VZ-FE Engine

1. Disconnect the negative battery cable.

------ CAUTION ------

To avoid personal injury when working on models with an air bag, wait at least 90 seconds from the time that the ignition switch is turned to the LOCK position and the battery is disconnected before performing any further work.

2. Raise the car, support it on safety stands and then remove the engine undercovers.

3. Remove the 2 front exhaust pipe stay bolts. Disconnect the front pipe from the center pipe and remove the gasket. Loosen the 3 nuts and then remove the front pipe.

4. Disconnect the O_2 sensor at the right side manifold. Remove the 3 mounting nuts and lift off the outside heat insulator.

5. Remove the 6 nuts and lift off the right side manifold and gasket.

6. Loosen the 2 nuts and bolt and lift off the left side heat insulator. Remove the 6 nuts and lift off the left side manifold and gaskets.

To install:

7. Scrape the mating surfaces of all old gasket material.

8. Install the right manifold with a new gasket. Tighten the nuts to 29 ft. lbs. (39 Nm). Install the outer insulator.

9. Use a new gasket and install the left manifold. Tighten the nuts to 29 ft. lbs. (39 Nm). Install the outer insulator.

10. Install the front exhaust pipe and tighten the manifold-to-pipe nuts to 46 ft. lbs. (62 Nm). Tighten the pipe-to-converter nuts to 32 ft. lbs. (43 Nm).

11. Connect the O_2 sensor, install the undercovers and then lower the car. Connect the battery cable.

3E and 3E-E Engines

1. Disconnect the negative battery cable. Remove the exhaust manifold heat insulator shield assembly.

2. Remove the necessary components in order to gain access to the exhaust manifold retaining bolts.

3. Disconnect the exhaust manifold bolts at the exhaust pipe. Disconnect the oxygen sensor electrical wire. It may be necessary to raise and support the vehicle safely before removing these bolts.

4. Remove the exhaust manifold retaining bolts. Remove the exhaust manifold from the vehicle.

To install:

5. Clean the gasket mating surfaces being careful not to damage the aluminum surfaces. Check the mating surfaces for warpage with a straightedge.

6. Match the old gasket with the new for an exact match. During installation, the **E** mark on the gasket must face outward. Use new gaskets when installing the manifold and tighten the bolts, from the center outward, to 38 ft. lbs. (51 Nm).

7. Install the remaining components, start the engine and check for leaks.

5E-FE Engine

1. Disconnect the negative battery cable.

2. Remove the right engine undercover.

3. Disconnect the accelerator and throttle cables.

4. Remove the PCV hoses.

5. Remove the power steering pump and bracket, if clearance is needed.

6. Tag and disconnect all electrical wire and vacuum hoses that interfere with removal of the exhaust manifold.

7. Remove the exhaust pipe stay and disconnect the exhaust pipe from

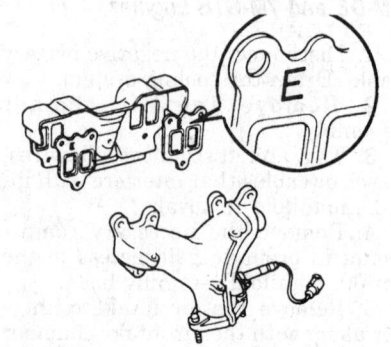

Exhaust manifold gasket installation — 3E and 3E-E engines

the manifold, then remove the exhaust manifold.

To install:

8. Clean the gasket surfaces and install the exhaust manifold, torquing the bolts to 35 ft. lbs. (47 Nm).

9. Reconnect the exhaust pipe.

10. Reconnect the cables and hoses that were disconnected.

11. Reinstall all remaining components.

12. Connect the battery cable, start the engine and check for exhaust leaks.

3S-FE and 5S-FE Engines

1. Disconnect the negative battery cable.

2. Raise and support the vehicle safely.

3. Remove the exhaust manifold heat insulator shield assembly.

4. Remove the necessary components in order to gain access to the exhaust manifold retaining bolts.

5. Disconnect the exhaust manifold bolts at the exhaust pipe or catalytic converter. It may be necessary to raise and support the vehicle safely before removing these bolts.

6. Remove the exhaust manifold retaining bolts. Remove the exhaust manifold from the vehicle. On 5S-FE engine, the exhaust manifold and catalytic converter are removed as one unit.

To install:

7. Be sure to use new gaskets. On 5S-FE engine, the **R** mark should be toward the rear. On 3S-FE engine, tighten the exhaust manifold bolts to 31 ft. lbs. (41 Nm). On 5S-FE engine, torque the exhaust manifold retaining bolts to 36 ft. lbs. (49 Nm).

3S-GTE, 4A-FE, 7A-FE4A-GE Engines

NOTE: On some 1993-94 7A-FE engine applications, the shape of the exhaust manifold was changed to adopted a manifold catalytic converter. On these applications, remove the exhaust manifold assembly then separate the catalytic converter from the manifold.

1. Disconnect the negative battery cable. Raise the vehicle and support safely. Remove the right gravel shield from under the vehicle.

2. Remove the throttle body and turbocharger.

3. Remove the exhaust pipe support stay. Unbolt the exhaust pipe from the exhaust manifold flange.

4. Disconnect the oxygen sensor connector.

5. Remove the manifold retaining nuts. Remove the exhaust manifold from the vehicle.

To install:

6. Clean the gasket mating surfaces being careful not to damage the aluminum surfaces. Check the mating surfaces for warpage with a straightedge.

7. Match the old gasket with the new for an exact match. Use new gaskets when installing the manifold and tighten the bolts, from the center outward, to the proper specification.

8. Install the remaining components, start the engine and check for leaks.

7M-GE and 7M-GTE Engines

1. Disconnect the negative battery cable. Remove the exhaust manifold heat insulator shield assembly, if equipped.

2. Remove the necessary components in order to gain access to the exhaust manifold retaining bolts.

3. Disconnect the exhaust manifold bolts at the exhaust pipe. It may be necessary to raise and support the vehicle safely before removing these bolts.

4. On 7M-GTE engine, remove the turbocharger.

5. Remove the exhaust manifold retaining bolts. Remove the exhaust manifold from the vehicle.

To install:

6. Clean the gasket mating surfaces being careful not to damage the aluminum surfaces. Check the mating surfaces for warpage with a straightedge.

7. Match the old gasket with the new for an exact match. Use new gaskets when installing the manifold and tighten the bolts, from the center outward, to 29 ft. lbs. (39 Nm).

8. Install the remaining components, start the engine and check for leaks.

Turbocharger

REMOVAL AND INSTALLATION

3S-GTE Engine

CELICA

1. Disconnect the negative battery cable. Drain the coolant from the engine and intercooler.

2. Remove the air cleaner assembly.

3. Remove the catalytic converter and the oxygen sensor.

4. Disconnect the 2 intercooler water lines and the reservoir tank

line. Loosen the clamps, disconnect the air hose and remove the intercooler.

5. Remove the alternator duct and the No. 2 alternator bracket.

6. Remove the turbocharger heat insulator and the turbocharger outlet elbow. Remove the turbocharger stay.

7. Remove the turbocharger.

8. Installation is in the reverse order of removal. Pour about 20cc of new oil into the turbocharger oil inlet and then spin the impeller to lubricate the bearing. Tighten the turbo-to-manifold bolts to 47 ft. lbs. (64 Nm).

MR2

1. Disconnect the negative battery cable.

2. Drain the coolant from the engine and the intercooler.

3. Raise and support the vehicle safely.

4. Remove the engine undercovers and engine hood side panels.

5. Tag and disconnect all water hoses, vacuum lines, air tubes, engine control cables, transaxle control cables and electrical wires that interfere with turbocharger removal.

6. Remove the brace that runs across the struts.

7. Remove the air cleaner assembly.

8. Remove the front exhaust pipe.

9. Discharge the air conditioning system. Disconnect the refrigerant hoses and electrical wiring from the compressor. Remove the compressor and idler pulley bracket from the engine.

10. Remove the front engine mounting insulator.

11. Remove the front mounting bracket and clutch release cylinder. Leave the hydraulic lines connected and position the release cylinder aside.

12. Remove the engine cooling fan.

13. Remove the catalytic converter.

14. Remove the Vacuum Transmitting Valve (VTV).

15. Remove the air bypass valve.

16. Remove the heat insulator from the turbocharger.

17. Remove the oxygen sensor.

18. Remove the heat insulators from the turbocharger outlet elbow.

19. Disconnect the oil hose from the turbocharger oil pipe.

20. Remove the turbocharger mounting stay.

21. Unbolt and remove the turbocharger oil pipe from the block.

22. Remove the 4 nuts and separate the turbocharger and gasket from the exhaust manifold.

To install:

23. Clean the turbocharger and exhaust manifold gasket surfaces.

24. Prior to installing the turbocharger, pour approximately 1.2 cubic in. (20cc) of new oil into the oil inlet and then turn the impeller wheel by hand a few times in order to lubricate the bearing.

25. Install a new gasket onto the exhaust manifold.

26. Mount the turbocharger onto the gasket and install the 4 nuts. Torque the nuts in a crisscross pattern to 47 ft. lbs. (64 Nm).

27. Installation of the remaining components is the reverse of the removal procedure. Torque the oil pipe union bolt to the block to 38 ft. lbs. (51 Nm); stay-to-turbocharger bolts to 51 ft. lbs. (69 Nm); stay-to-block bolts to 43 ft. lbs. (59 Nm) and oxygen sensor to 33 ft. lbs. (44 Nm).

7M-GTE Engine

1. Disconnect the negative battery cable and drain the cooling system.

2. Remove the No. 4 air cleaner pipe with the No. 1 and No. 2 air cleaner hoses still attached.

3. Disconnect the 3 air hoses, the PCV hose and the electrical lead at the air flow meter. Disconnect the power steering idle-up air hose and then remove the No. 7 air cleaner hose with the air flow meter and cap still attached.

4. Disconnect the oxygen sensor and remove the turbocharger heat insulator.

5. Remove the oil dipstick guide.

6. Remove the No. 1 air cleaner pipe with the No. 6 air cleaner hose.

7. Disconnect the front exhaust pipe.

8. Remove the mounting nuts and union bolt for the turbocharger oil line. Remove the turbocharger stay.

9. Remove the No. 2 turbocharger stay. Disconnect the No. 1 turbocharger water hose at the water outlet housing. Disconnect the union pipe.

10. Remove the turbocharger and its gasket.

To install:

11. Prior to installing the turbocharger, pour approximately 1.2 cubic in. (20cc) of new oil into the oil inlet and then turn the impeller wheel by hand a few times in order to lubricate the bearing.

12. Position a new gasket with the protrusion pointing toward the rear and then install the turbocharger unit. Tighten the mounting bolts to 33 ft. lbs. (44 Nm). Tighten the union bolt to 25 ft. lbs. (34 Nm) and the nut

to 9 ft. lbs. (13 Nm). The remainder of the installation is in the reverse order of removal.

Timing Belt Front Cover

REMOVAL AND INSTALLATION

3E, 3E-E and 3S-FE Engines

1. Disconnect the negative battery cable.
2. On 3E and 3E-E engines, remove the air cleaner assembly. On 3E-E engine, disconnect the accelerator and throttle cables.
3. Remove all drive belts.
4. On the 3S-FE engine remove the alternator, alternator bracket and right engine mounting stay (2WD). If equipped with cruise control remove the actuator and bracket assembly.
5. Raise and support the vehicle safely.
6. Remove the right tire and wheel assembly. Remove the right side engine undercover. Remove the right side engine mount insulator.
7. On the 3E and 3E-E engines, remove the cylinder head cover if necessary.
8. Set the No. 1 piston to TDC of the compression stroke and remove the crankshaft pulley using the proper tools.
9. Remove the engine front cover retaining bolts. Remove both front covers from the engine.
10. Installation is the reverse of the removal procedure. Use new cover seals. On 3E and 3E-E engines, torque the crankshaft pulley bolt to 112 ft. lbs. (154 Nm). On 3S-FE engine, torque the crankshaft pulley bolt to 80 ft. lbs. (108 Nm).

4A-FE, 7A-FE4A-GE Engines

1. Disconnect the negative battery cable.
2. Remove the air cleaner assembly and disconnect the accelerator and throttle cables.
3. Remove all drive belts and the washer tank.
4. On the 4A-GE engines, remove the water pump pulley.
5. Remove the alternator, alternator bracket and right engine mounting stay, if clearance is needed. If equipped with cruise control, remove the actuator and bracket assembly.
6. Raise and support the vehicle safely.
7. Remove the right tire and wheel assembly. Remove the right side en-

gine undercover. Remove the right side engine mount insulator.
8. Remove the valve cover on the 4A-FE and 7A-FE engines, if necessary.
9. Set the No. 1 piston to TDC of the compression stroke and remove the crankshaft pulley using the proper tools.
10. Remove the engine front cover retaining bolts. Remove both front covers from the engine.

To install:
11. Install front covers.
12. Install valve cover, if necessary.
13. Install right side insulator and engine undercover. Install right tire and wheel assembly.
14. Install the alternator and alternator bracket, if necessary. If equipped with cruise control, install the actuator and bracket assembly.
15. On the 4A-GE engines, install the water pump pulley.
16. Install all drive belts and the washer tank.
17. Reconnect the accelerator and throttle cables. Install air cleaner assembly. Connect the negative battery cable.

5E-FE Engine

1. Disconnect the negative battery cable.
2. Remove the right engine undercover.
3. If equipped with power steering, remove the power steering pump and bracket. If equipped with air conditioning and without power steering, remove the idler pulley bracket.
4. Tag and disconnect all electrical wire and vacuum hoses that interfere with removal of the timing belt cover.
5. Remove the No. 2 timing belt cover by removing the 4 bolts.
6. Remove the alternator belt, then the No. 3 timing belt cover from the No. 1 timing belt cover.
7. Remove the crankshaft pulley bolt and the pulley, then remove the No. 1 cover.

To install:
8. Install the crankshaft pulley bolt and the pulley, then install the No. 1 cover. Torque the crankshaft pulley bolt to 112 ft. lbs. (152 Nm).
9. Install the No. 3 timing belt cover, the alternator belt and the No. 2 timing belt cover with its gasket and 4 bolts.
10. Reinstall all remaining components.
11. Connect the battery cable, start the engine and check for unusual noises.

5S-FE Engine

1. Remove the right front wheel.
2. Remove the fender apron liner and right engine undercover.
3. Remove the drive belts.
4. Remove the cruise control actuator and bracket.
5. Remove the alternator and alternator bracket.
6. Using a wood block on the jack, raise the engine enough to relieve the weight from the engine on the right mounting side.
7. Remove the right engine mounting insulator and bracket and remove the engine moving control rod.
8. Remove the crankshaft pulley and bolt.
9. Remove the bolts and remove the upper (No. 2) timing belt cover with gasket and the lower cover.
10. Installation is the reverse of removal. Torque the crankshaft pulley bolt to 80 ft. lbs. (108 Nm).

2VZ-FE and 3VZ-FE Engines

1. Disconnect the cable from the negative battery terminal.
2. Remove the power steering pump reservoir and position it out of the way. Remove the right fender apron seal and then remove the alternator and power steering belts. On 2VZ-FE engine, remove the cruise control actuator and vacuum pump.
3. On the 3VZ-FE engine, remove the coolant reservoir hose, the washer tank and coolant overflow tank.
4. Remove the right side engine mount stays.
5. Position a piece of wood on a floor jack and then slide the jack under the oil pan. Raise the jack slightly until the pressure is off the engine mounts.
6. On the 2VZ-FE engine, remove the right side engine mount insulator. On the 3VZ-FE engine, remove the engine control rod.
7. Remove the crankshaft pulley and bolt.
8. Remove the right side engine mounting bracket.
9. Remove the bolts and lift off the upper (No. 2) cover, then the lower cover.
10. Installation is the reverse of removal. Torque the crankshaft pulley bolt to specifications.

7M-GE and 7M-GTE Engines

1. Disconnect the negative battery cable.
2. Drain the cooling system.

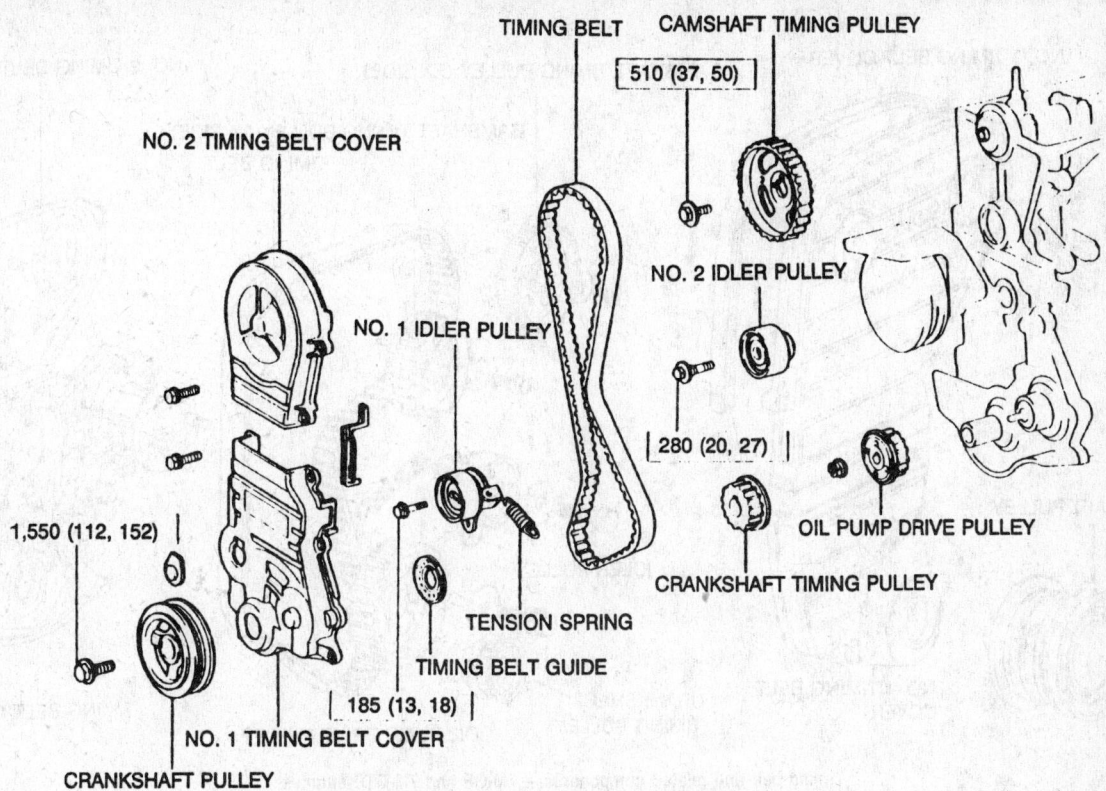

Timing belt and related components — 3E and 3E-E engines

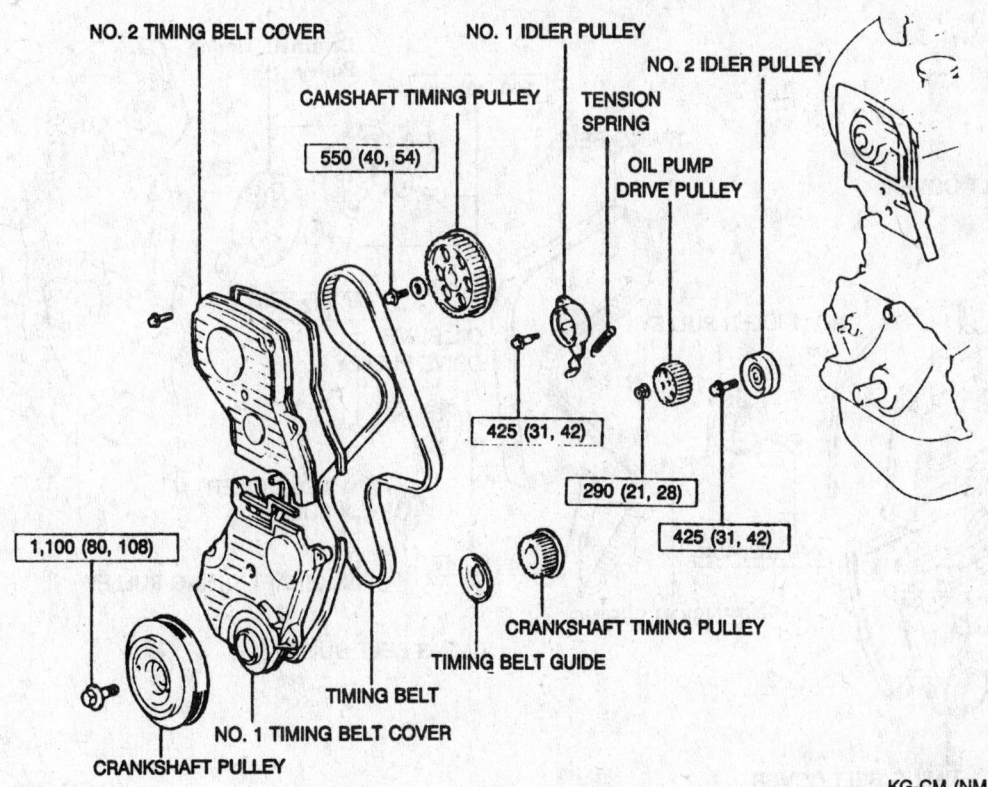

KG-CM (NM, FT. LBS.)

Timing belt and related components — 3S-FE and 5S-FE engines

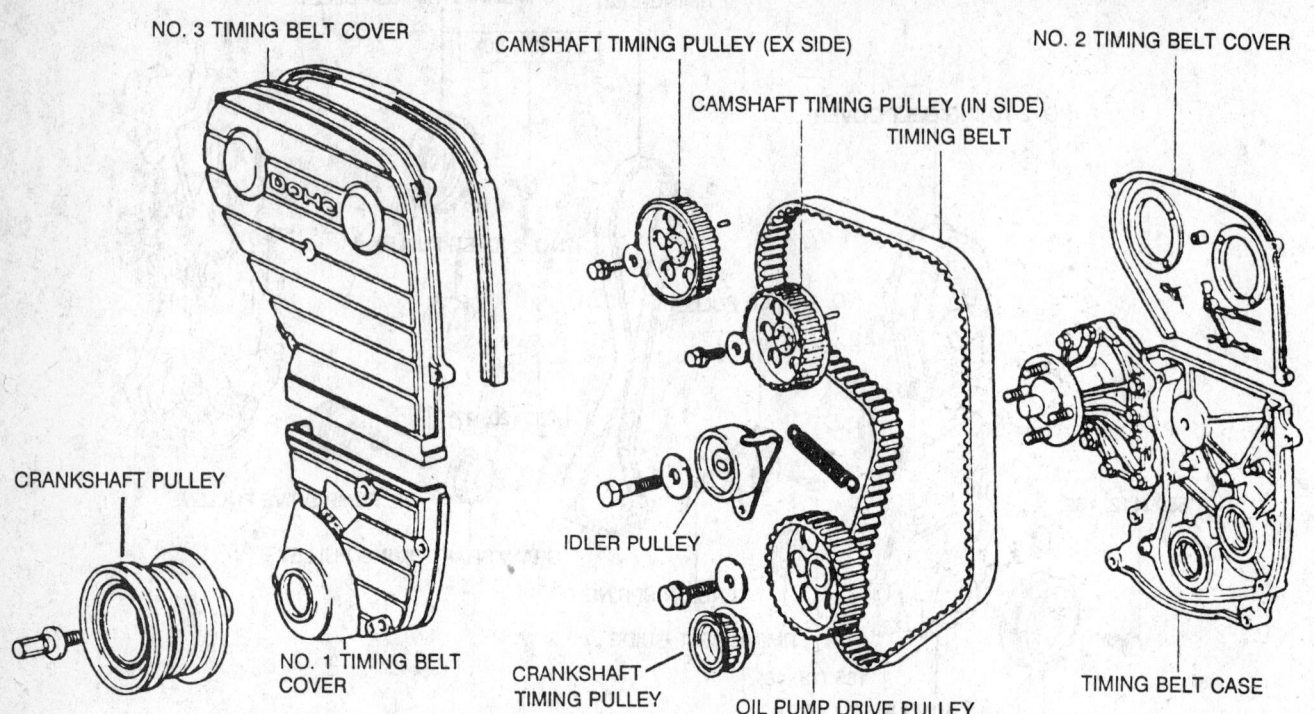

NO. 3 TIMING BELT COVER

CAMSHAFT TIMING PULLEY (EX SIDE)

CAMSHAFT TIMING PULLEY (IN SIDE)

TIMING BELT

NO. 2 TIMING BELT COVER

CRANKSHAFT PULLEY

IDLER PULLEY

NO. 1 TIMING BELT COVER

CRANKSHAFT TIMING PULLEY

OIL PUMP DRIVE PULLEY

TIMING BELT CASE

Timing belt and related components — 7M-GE and 7M-GTE engines

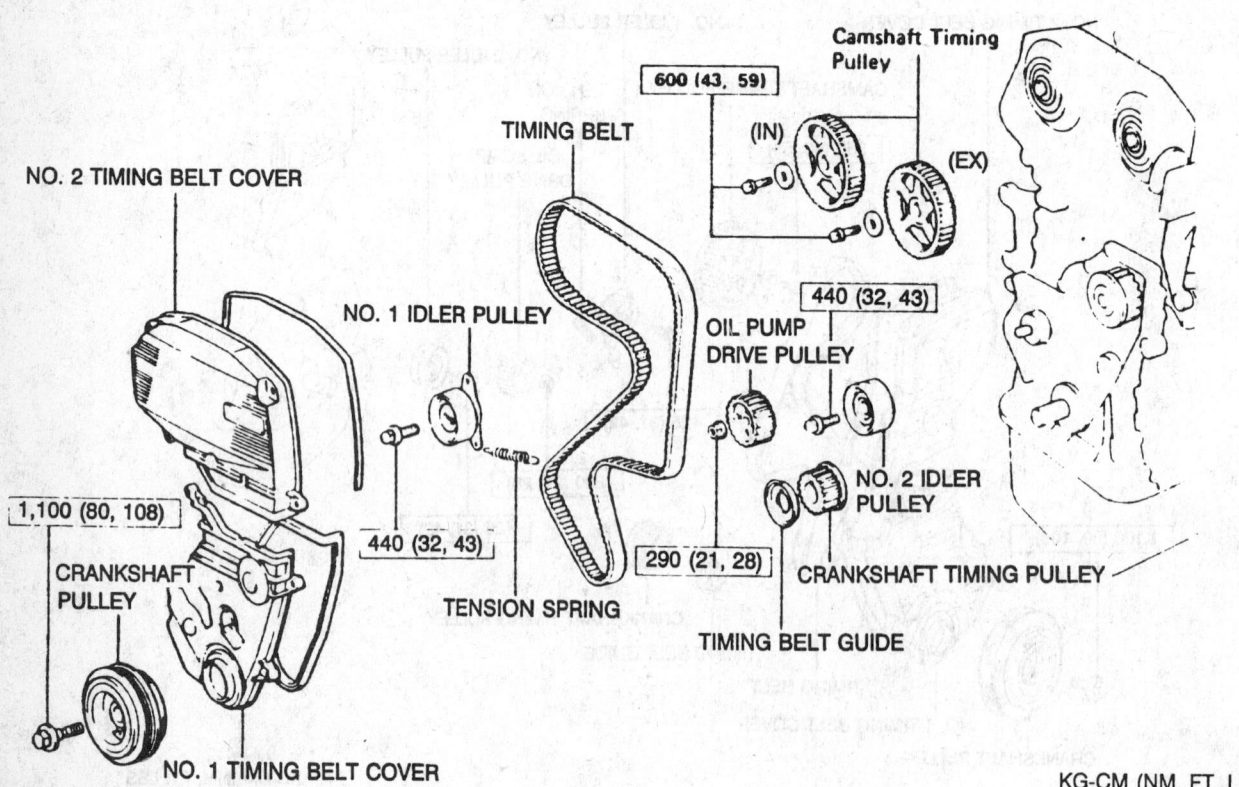

NO. 2 TIMING BELT COVER

TIMING BELT

600 (43, 59)

Camshaft Timing Pulley

(IN)

(EX)

NO. 1 IDLER PULLEY

OIL PUMP DRIVE PULLEY

440 (32, 43)

1,100 (80, 108)

CRANKSHAFT PULLEY

440 (32, 43)

TENSION SPRING

290 (21, 28)

NO. 2 IDLER PULLEY

CRANKSHAFT TIMING PULLEY

TIMING BELT GUIDE

NO. 1 TIMING BELT COVER

KG-CM (NM, FT. LBS.)

Timing belt and related components — 3S-GTE engines

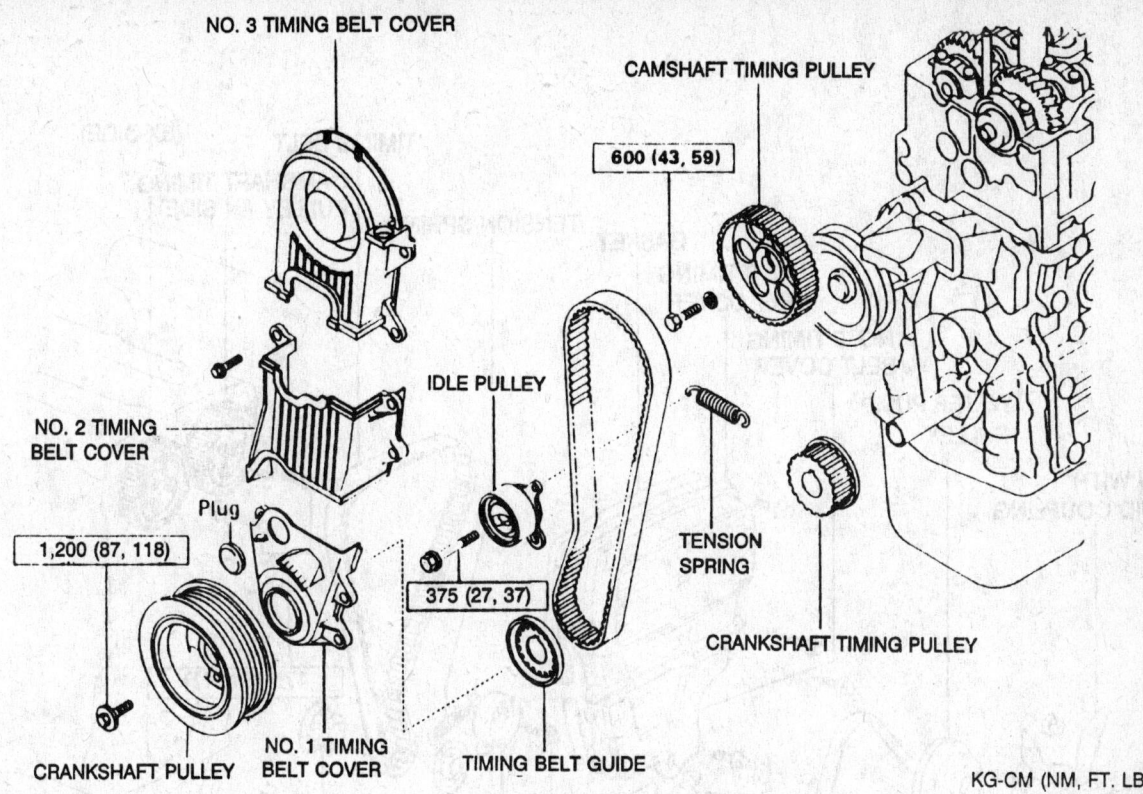

NO. 3 TIMING BELT COVER

CAMSHAFT TIMING PULLEY

600 (43, 59)

IDLE PULLEY

NO. 2 TIMING BELT COVER

Plug

1,200 (87, 118)

TENSION SPRING

375 (27, 37)

CRANKSHAFT TIMING PULLEY

CRANKSHAFT PULLEY

NO. 1 TIMING BELT COVER

TIMING BELT GUIDE

KG-CM (NM, FT. LBS.)

Timing belt and related components — 4A-FE and 7A-FE engines

3. Remove the radiator and water outlet.

4. Remove the spark plugs, drive belts and alternator.

5. Remove the upper timing belt cover and seal.

6. Set the No. 1 piston to TDC of the compression stroke.

7. Remove the timing belt from the camshaft sprockets.

8. Remove the crankshaft pulley using the proper tool.

9. Remove the lower timing belt cover and seal.

10. Installation is the reverse of the removal procedure. Use new cover seals. Torque the crankshaft pulley bolt to 195 ft. lbs. (265 Nm).

OIL SEAL REPLACEMENT

1. Remove the front covers and the timing belt.

2. Remove the crankshaft timing belt sprocket, then remove the seal.

3. Inspect the oil seal riding surface on the crankshaft for signs of wear or damage.
To install:

4. Wipe the seal bore with a clean rag.

5. Drive the oil seal into place using a suitable seal installer. Work from the front of the cover. Be extremely careful not to damage the seal.

6. Install the sprocket without disturbing the Woodruff key.

Timing Belt and Tensioner

ADJUSTMENT

The timing belt is adjusted during the installation process.

REMOVAL AND INSTALLATION

2VZ-FE Engine

1. Disconnect the negative battery cable. If equipped, remove the cruise control actuator and vacuum pump.

2. Remove the power steering oil reservoir tank and position it aside without disconnecting the hydraulic lines.

3. Raise the vehicle and support it safely. Remove the right wheel and tire assembly.

4. Remove the alternator and power steering pump drive belts.

5. Remove the right side fender apron seal.

6. Remove the right side engine mounting stays, position a floor jack under the engine and raise it just

enough to release the pressure on the mount and then remove it. If equipped with ABS, first remove the clamp bolts for the power steering oil cooler lines.

7. Remove the spark plugs.

8. Remove the upper timing belt cover and then remove the right side engine mounting bracket.

NOTE: If re-using the old timing belt, matchmark it to each of the timing pulleys and to mark it for the direction of rotation.

9. Rotate the engine until the groove in the crankshaft pulley is aligned with the **0** mark on the lower timing belt cover. Check that the marks on the camshaft timing pulleys are aligned with the ones on the inner timing belt cover; if not, rotate the engine 1 complete revolution (360 degrees).

10. Remove the timing belt tensioner and dust cover.

11. Turn the left side camshaft timing pulley clockwise slightly to release the tension on the timing belt and then slide the belt off both pulleys.

12. Remove the camshaft sprocket retaining bolts and knock pins and pull off the sprockets. Do not mix up.

13. Remove the No. 2 idler pulley.

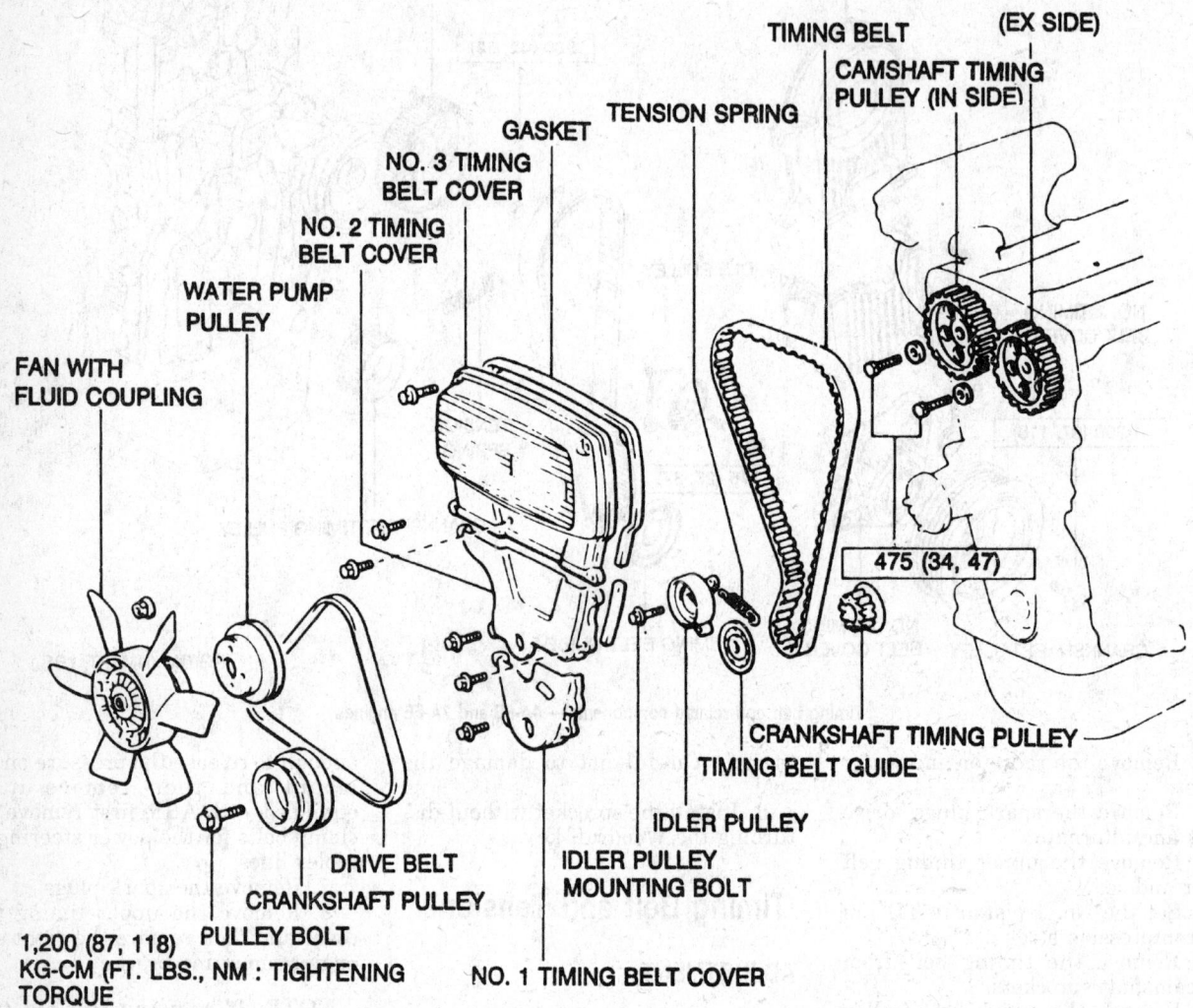

TENSION SPRING

TIMING BELT

(EX SIDE)

CAMSHAFT TIMING PULLEY (IN SIDE)

GASKET

NO. 3 TIMING BELT COVER

NO. 2 TIMING BELT COVER

WATER PUMP PULLEY

FAN WITH FLUID COUPLING

475 (34, 47)

CRANKSHAFT TIMING PULLEY

TIMING BELT GUIDE

IDLER PULLEY

IDLER PULLEY MOUNTING BOLT

DRIVE BELT

CRANKSHAFT PULLEY

PULLEY BOLT

1,200 (87, 118) KG-CM (FT. LBS., NM : TIGHTENING TORQUE

NO. 1 TIMING BELT COVER

Timing belt and related components — 4A-GE engines

14. Remove the crankshaft pulley and then remove the lower timing belt cover.

15. Remove the timing belt guide and then remove the timing belt.

To install:

16. Inspect the timing belt for any cracks, tears or other defects. Replace as required. Inspect the idler pulleys and timing sprockets; replace defective components as necessary.

17. Install the timing belt over the crankshaft sprocket so the mark on the belt aligns with the drilled mark on the sprocket. Install the belt over the No. 1 idler and water pump pulleys.

18. Install the timing belt guide so the cupped side faces outward. Install the No. 1 timing belt cover with a new gasket.

19. Install the crankshaft pulley so the set key is aligned with the groove in the shaft and then tighten the retaining bolt to 181 ft. lbs. (245 Nm).

20. Install the No. 2 idler pulley and tighten the bolt to 29 ft. lbs. (39 Nm). Check the pulley for smooth operation.

21. Install the left camshaft sprocket, flange side out, so the camshaft knock pin hole aligns with the groove in the sprocket. Install the

knock pin and tighten the sprocket bolt to 80 ft. lbs. (108 Nm).

22. Set the No. 1 piston to TDC of the compression stroke again. Rotate the right camshaft until the knock pin hole is aligned with the timing mark on the No. 3 timing belt cover. Rotate the left camshaft sprocket until the timing mark on the sprocket is aligned with the one on the No. 3 cover.

23. Check that the mark on the timing belt aligns with the edge of the No. 1 timing belt cover. Rotate the left camshaft sprocket clockwise slightly so the mark on the timing belt will align with the timing mark

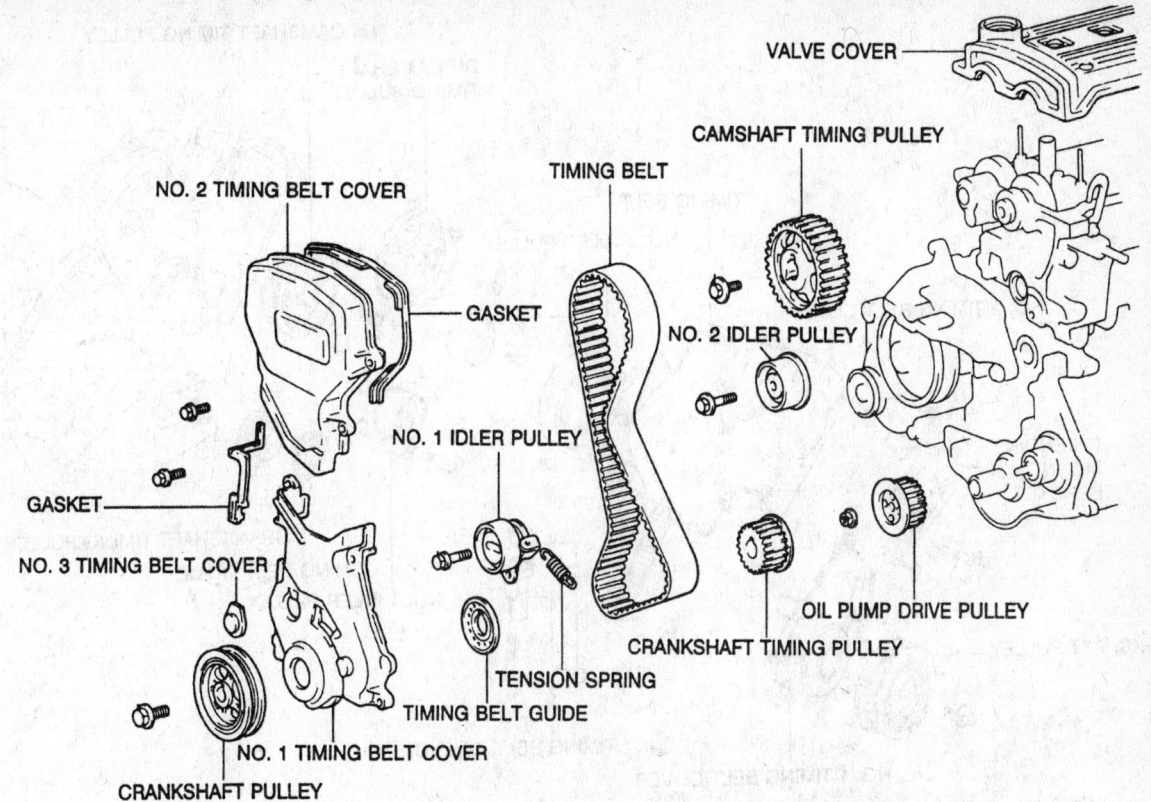

Timing belt components — 5E-FE engine

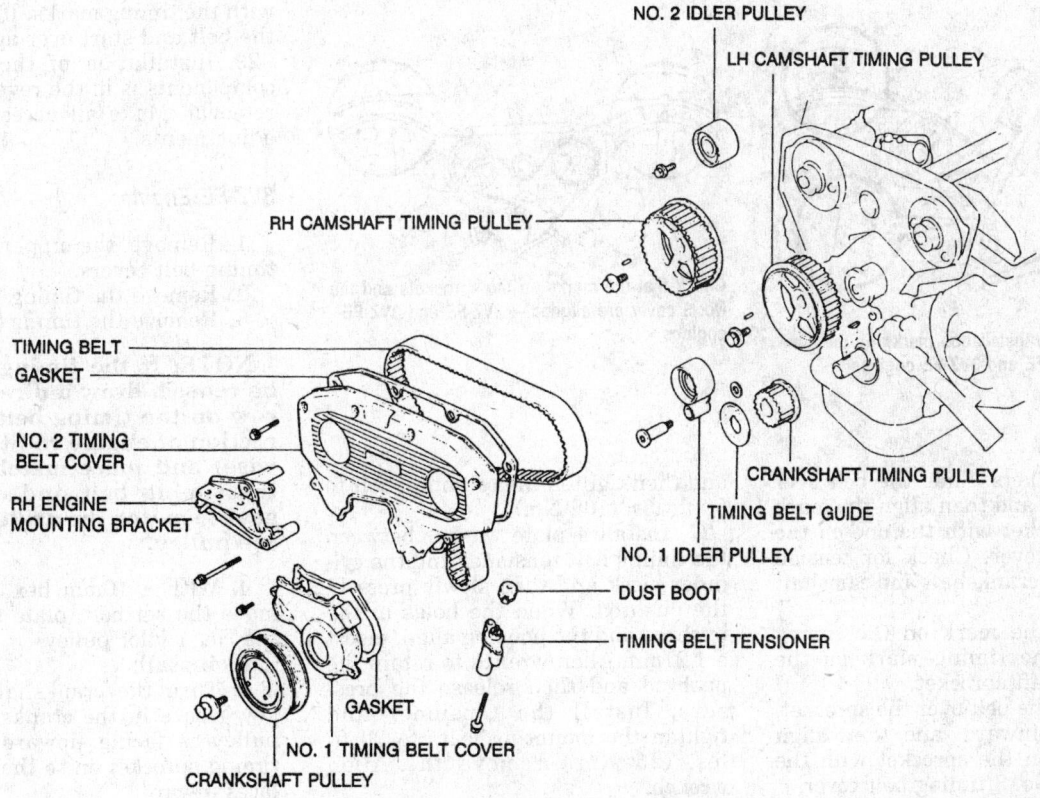

Timing belt components — 2VZ-FE engine

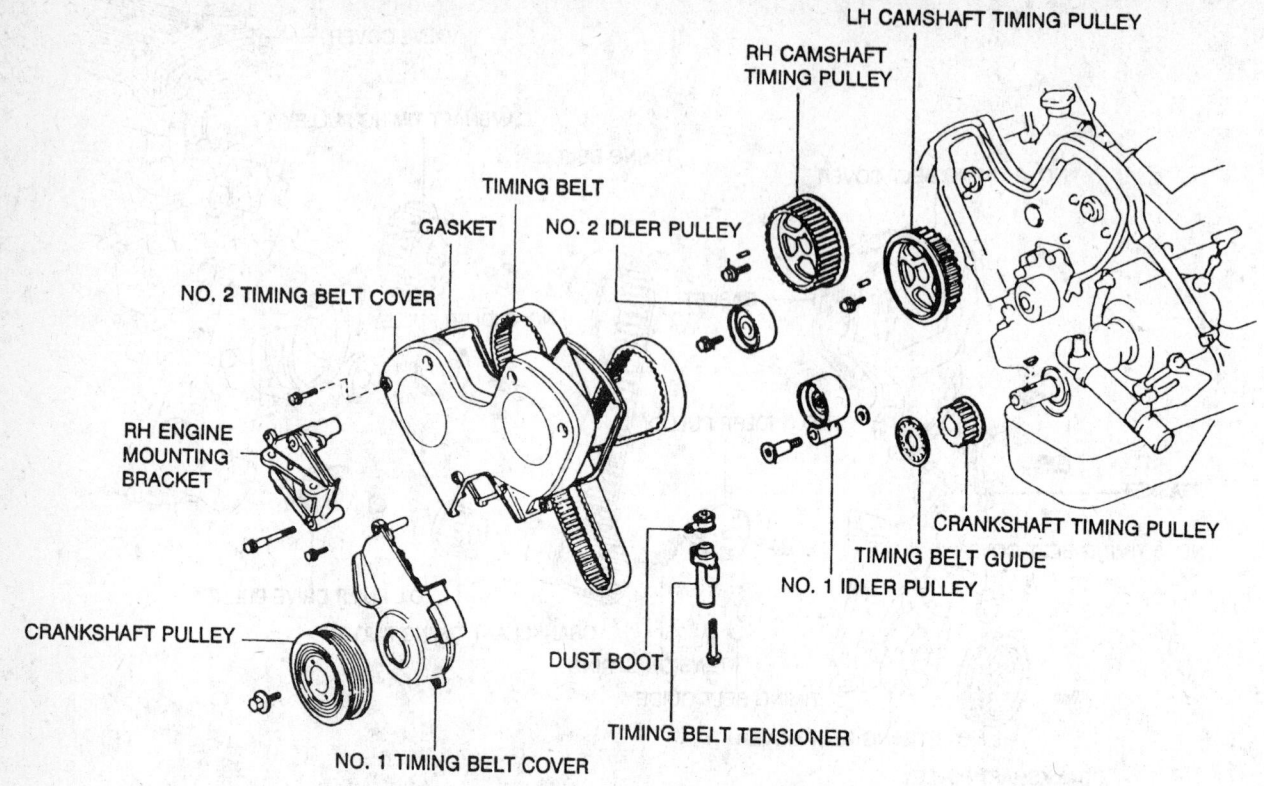

Timing belt components — 3VZ-FE engine

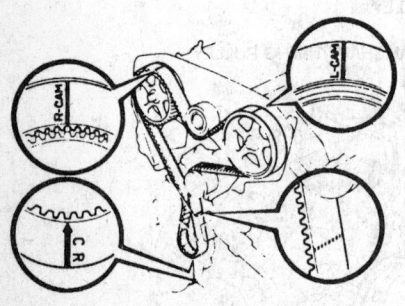

There should be installation marks on the timing belt — 2VZ-FE and 3VZ-FE engines

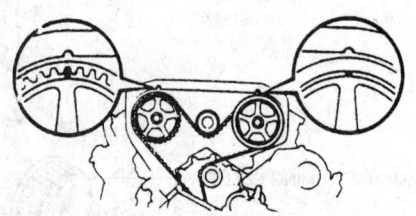

Check that the marks on the sprockets and the No. 3 cover are aligned — 2VZ-FE and 3VZ-FE engines

on the sprockets. Slide the belt over the sprocket and then align the mark on the sprocket with the one on the No. 3 belt cover. Check for tension between the crankshaft and camshaft sprockets.

24. Align the mark on the timing belt with the timing mark on the right camshaft sprocket.

25. Hang the belt over the sprocket, flange side inward, and then align the marks on the sprocket with the one on the No. 3 timing belt cover.

26. Slide the sprocket onto the camshaft so the knock pin hole and groove align. Install the knock pin

and then tighten the retaining bolt to 80 ft. lbs. (108 Nm).

27. Install a plate washer between the timing belt tensioner and the cylinder block and then slowly press in the pushrod. When the holes in the pushrod and the housing align, insert a 1.27mm Allen wrench to retain the pushrod and then release the pressure. Install the tensioner and tighten the mounting bolts to 20 ft. lbs. (26 Nm); remove the Allen wrench.

28. Rotate the crankshaft pulley 2 complete revolutions clockwise and check that each pulley is still aligned

with the timing marks. If not, remove the belt and start over again.

29. Installation of the remaining components is in the reverse order of removal. Make all necessary engine adjustments.

3VZ-FE Engine

1. Remove the upper and lower timing belt covers.
2. Remove the timing belt guide.
3. Remove the timing belt.

NOTE: If the timing belt is to be reused, draw a directional arrow on the timing belt in the direction of engine rotation (clockwise) and place matchmarks on the timing belt and crankshaft gear to match the drilled mark on the pulley.

4. With a 10mm hex wrench, remove the set bolt, plate washer and the No. 1 idler pulley.

To install:

5. Turn the crankshaft until the key groove in the crankshaft timing pulley is facing upward. Slide the timing sprocket on so the flange side faces inward.

6. Apply bolt adhesive to the first few threads of the No. 1 idler pulley set bolt, install the plate washer and

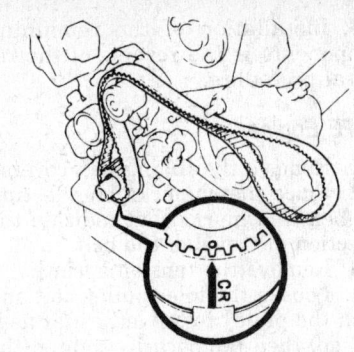

Installing the belt on the crankshaft — 2VZ-FE and 3VZ-FE engines

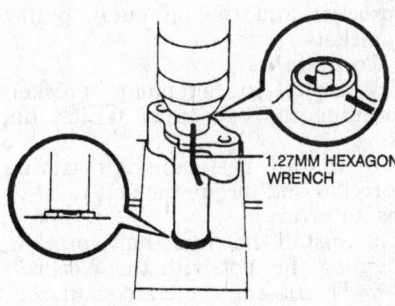

Set the timing belt tensioner — 2VZ-FE and 3VZ-FE engines

1.27MM HEXAGON WRENCH

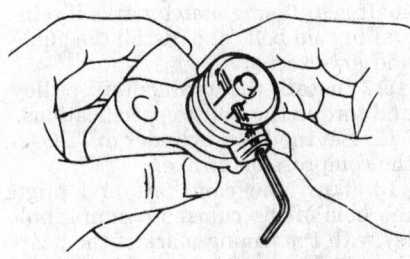

Install the hex wrench — 2VZ-FE and 3VZ-FE engines

pulley and then tighten the bolt to 25 ft. lbs. (34 Nm).

7. Install the timing belt on the crankshaft timing, No. 1 idler and water pump pulleys.

NOTE: If the old timing belt is being reinstalled, make sure the directional arrow is facing in the original direction and that the belt and crankshaft gear matchmarks are properly aligned.

8. Install the lower (No. 1) timing cover and tighten the bolts.

9. Align the crankshaft pulley set key with the key groove on the pulley and slide the pulley on. Tighten the bolt to 181 ft. lbs. (245 Nm).

10. Install the No. 2 idler pulley and tighten the bolt to 29 ft. lbs. (39 Nm). Check that the pulley moves smoothly.

11. Install the left camshaft pulley with the flange side outward. Align the knock pin hole in the camshaft with the knock pin groove on the pulley and then install the pin. Tighten the bolt to 80 ft. lbs. (108 Nm).

12. Set the No. 1 cylinder to TDC again. Turn the right camshaft until the knock pin hole is aligned with the timing mark on the No. 3 belt cover. Turn the left pulley until the marks on the pulley are aligned with the mark on the No. 3 timing cover.

13. Check that the mark on the belt matches with the edge of the lower cover. If not, shift it on the crank pulley until it does. Turn the left pulley clockwise a bit and align the mark on the timing belt with the timing mark on the pulley. Slide the belt over the left pulley. Now move the pulley until the marks on it align with the one on the No. 3 cover. There should be tension on the belt between the crankshaft pulley and the left camshaft pulley.

14. Align the installation mark on the timing belt with the mark on the right side camshaft pulley. Hang the belt over the pulley with the flange facing inward. Align the timing marks on the right pulley with the one on the No. 3 cover and slide the pulley onto the end of the camshaft. Move the pulley until the camshaft knock pin hole is aligned with the groove in the pulley and then install the knock pin. Tighten the bolt to 55 ft. lbs. (75 Nm).

15. Position a plate washer between the timing belt tensioner and the a block and then press in the pushrod until the holes are aligned between it and the housing. Slide a 1.5mm Allen wrench through the hole to keep the push rod set. Install the dust boot and then install the tensioner. Tighten the bolts to 20 ft. lbs. (26 Nm). Remove the Allen wrench.

16. Turn the crankshaft clockwise 2 complete revolutions and check that all marks are still in alignment. If not, remove the timing belt and start over again.

17. Install the right engine mount bracket and tighten to 30 ft. lbs. (39 Nm).

18. Position a new gasket and then install the upper No. 2 timing cover.

19. Install the spark plugs.
20. Install the control rod and tighten the bolts to 47 ft. lbs. (64 Nm).
21. Install the right stay and tighten to 23 ft. lbs. (31 Nm).
22. Install and adjust the drive belts.
23. Install the fender apron seal and the wheel.
24. Install the No. 2 stay and tighten the bolt to 55 ft. lbs. (75 Nm) and the nut to 46 ft. lbs. (62 Nm). Install the No. 3 stay and tighten it to 54 ft. lbs. (73 Nm).
25. Install the coolant overflow tank and the washer tank.
26. Install the power steering reservoir tank and the cruise control actuator.
27. Connect the battery cable, start the car and check for any leaks.

3E and 3E-E Engines

1. Disconnect the negative battery cable. Remove the right side engine undercover. On 3E-E engine, disconnect the accelerator and throttle cables.

2. Remove the drive belts, alternator and alternator bracket. Remove the air cleaner and air intake collector assemblies and spark plugs for the 3E-E engines.

3. Raise the engine and remove the right side engine mounting insulator assembly.

4. Remove the cylinder head cover. Set the engine to TDC on the compression stroke. Remove the crankshaft pulley using the proper removal tool.

5. Remove both timing belt covers. Remove the timing belt guide. Remove the timing belt and the No. 1 idler pulley. If using the old belt matchmark it in the direction of engine rotation. Matchmark the pulleys.

6. Remove the tension spring. Remove the No. 2 idler pulley. Remove the crankshaft pulley, camshaft pulley and oil pump pulley using the proper tools.

To install:

7. Inspect the belt for defects. Replace as required. Inspect the idler pulleys and springs. Replace defective components as required.

8. Align and install the oil pump pulley. Torque the retaining bolt to 20 ft. lbs. (26 Nm).

9. To install the camshaft timing pulley, align the camshaft knock pin with the No. 1 bearing cap mark. Align the knock pin hole on the 3E mark side with the camshaft knock

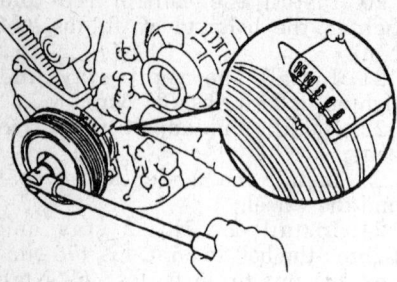

Setting No. 1 cylinder to TDC — 3VZ-FE engine

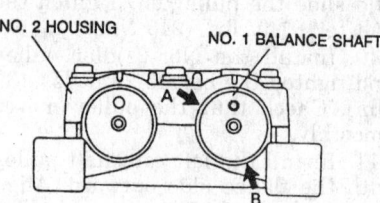

Timing sprocket installation — 3E and 3E-E engines

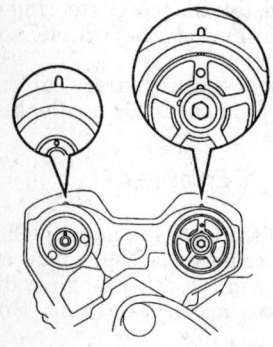

Camshaft pulley and cover marks — 3VZ-FE engine

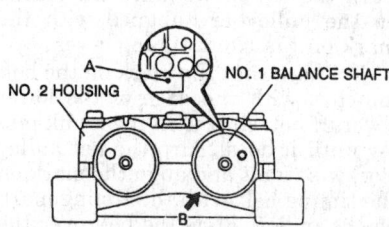

Timing sprocket alignment — 3E and 3E-E engines

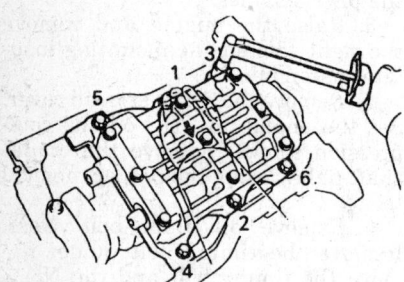

Camshaft alignment — 3E and 3E-E engines

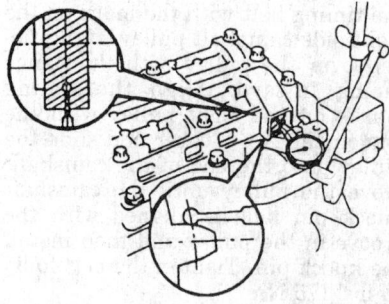

Timing belt alignment — 3E and 3E-E engines

pin hole. Torque the retaining bolt to 37 ft. lbs. (50 Nm).

10. Install the crankshaft timing pulley and align the TDC marks on the oil pump body and the crankshaft timing pulley. Install the No. 1 idler pulley. Pry the idler pulley toward the left as far as it will go and temporarily tighten the retaining bolt.

11. Install the No. 2 idler pulley and torque the retaining bolt to 20 ft. lbs. (27 Nm). Install the timing belt. If reusing the old belt, align it with the marks made during the removal procedure.

12. Inspect the valve timing and the belt tension by loosening the No. 1 idler pulley set bolt. Temporarily install the crankshaft pulley bolt and turn the crankshaft 2 complete revolutions in the clockwise direction.

13. Check that each pulley aligns with the proper markings. Torque the No. 1 idler pulley bolt to 13 ft. lbs. (18 Nm). Check for proper belt tension. Install the belt guide.

14. Install the timing belt covers. Align and install the crankshaft pulley. Torque the retaining bolt to 112 ft. lbs. (152 Nm).

15. Installation of the remaining components is the reverse of the removal procedure.

5E-FE Engine

1. Remove the timing belt covers.
2. Place matchmarks on the timing belt and marks that indicate the direction of travel of the belt.
3. Remove the tension spring.
4. Loosen the idler pulley bolt and push the pulley to the left as far as it will go, then temporarily tighten the bolt.
5. Remove the belt.
6. Remove the crankshaft timing sprocket, the camshaft timing sprocket and the oil pump pulley sprockets.

To install:
7. Install the oil pump sprocket, torquing the bolt to 27 ft. lbs. (36 Nm).
8. Install the camshaft timing sprocket and torque the bolt to 37 ft. lbs. (50 Nm).
9. Install the crankshaft sprocket, aligning the slot with the Woodruff key. Then using the crankshaft bolt, turn the crankshaft until the timing marks on the sprocket and oil pump body align. This is the setting at TDC before the marks on the belt cover can be seen.
10. Install the belt on the crankshaft gear (using matchmarks if reinstalling old belt) and install the guide and lower cover.
11. Install the crankshaft pulley and torque the bolt to specifications.
12. Set the No. 1 cylinder to TDC on the compression stroke.
13. Turn the camshaft and align the hole of the camshaft timing pulley with the timing mark of the bearing cap. The matchmarks if using the old belt should line up. Place the belt over all pulleys.
14. Loosen the adjuster pulley bolt until the pulley is moved slightly by the spring tension.
15. Turn the crankshaft pulley 2 revolutions from TDC to TDC.

NOTE: Always rotate the crankshaft clockwise.

16. Check that the pulleys align with the reference marks. If not, reinstall the belt.
17. Torque the adjuster pulley to 13 ft. lbs. (18 Nm).
18. Reinstall the remaining components, start and check for unusual noises.

3S-FE and 5S-FE Engines

1. Disconnect the negative battery cable. Raise and support the vehicle

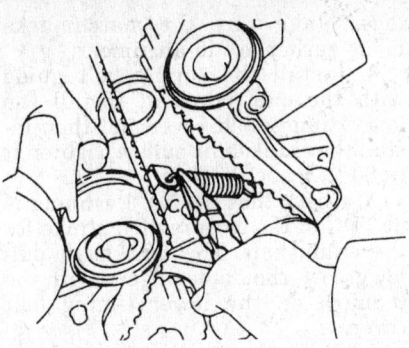

Removing timing belt tensioning spring — 5E-FE engine

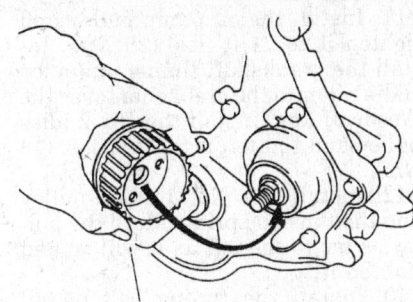

Installing oil pump pulley — 5S-FE engine

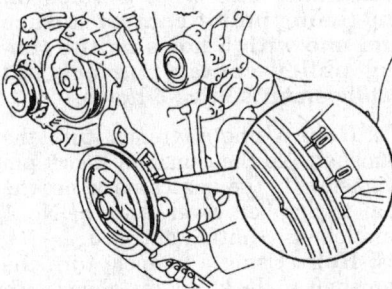

Setting No. 1 cylinder to TDC — 5E-FE engine

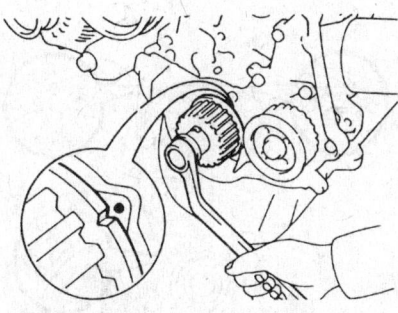

Crankshaft pulley timing mark — 5S-FE engine

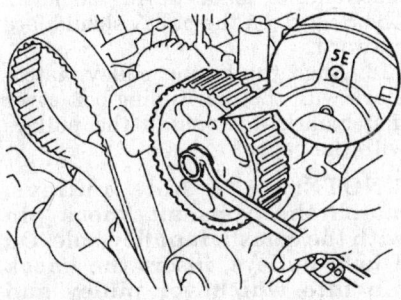

Camshaft pulley and bearing cap marks — 5E-FE engine

safely. Remove the right tire and wheel assembly.

2. If equipped, remove the cruise control actuator and bracket. Remove the drive belts.

3. Remove the alternator and alternator bracket and right engine mounting stay. Raise the engine enough to remove the right side engine mounting insulator and brackets.

4. Remove the spark plugs. Remove the upper timing cover. Position the No. 1 cylinder to TDC on the

compression stroke so the groove in the crankshaft pulley is aligned with the **0** mark in the No. 1 front cover. If the hole in the camshaft pulley is not aligned with the mark on the bearing cap, turn the crankshaft 1 complete revolution (360 degrees).

5. If reusing the belt place matchmarks on the timing belt and the camshaft pulley. Loosen the mount bolt of the No. 1 idler pulley and position the pulley toward the left as far as it will go. Tighten the bolt. Remove the belt from the camshaft pulley.

6. Remove the camshaft pulley. Remove the crankshaft pulley using the proper removal tool. Remove the lower timing cover.

7. Remove the timing belt and the belt guide. If reusing the belt mark the belt and the crankshaft pulley in the direction of engine rotation.

8. Remove the No. 1 idler pulley and the tension spring. Remove the No. 2 idler pulley. Remove the crankshaft timing pulley. Remove the oil pump pulley.

To install:

9. Inspect the belt for defects. Replace as required. Inspect the idler pulleys and springs. Replace defective components as required.

10. Align the cutouts of the oil pump pulley and shaft. Install the oil pump pulley and torque the retaining nut to 21 ft. lbs. (28 Nm).

11. To install the crankshaft pulley, align the pulley set key with the key groove of the pulley and slide it in position. Install the No. 2 idler pulley and torque the bolt to 31 ft. lbs. (42 Nm). Be sure the pulley moves freely.

12. Temporarily install the No. 1 idler pulley and tension spring. Pry the pulley toward the left as far as it will go. Tighten the bolt.

13. Temporarily install the timing belt. If reusing the old belt align the marks made during removal. Install the timing belt guide.

14. Install the No. 1 timing belt cover. Install the crankshaft pulley and tighten the bolt to 80 ft. lbs. (108 Nm).

15. Install the camshaft pulley by aligning the camshaft knock pin with the knock pin groove in the pulley. Install the washer and torque the retaining bolt to 40 ft. lbs. (54 Nm).

16. With the engine set at TDC on the compression stroke install the timing belt. If reusing the belt, align with the marks made during the removal procedure.

17. Once the belt is installed be sure there is tension between the crankshaft pulley, water pump pulley and camshaft pulley. Loosen the No. 1 idler pulley mount bolt ½ turn. Turn the crankshaft pulley 2 revolutions from TDC to TDC, in the clockwise direction. Torque the No. 1 idler pulley mount bolt to 31 ft. lbs. (42 Nm).

18. Installation the remaining components is the reverse of the removal procedure.

3S-GTE Engines

1. Disconnect the negative battery cable. Raise the vehicle and support safely. Remove the right front tire and wheel assembly. Remove the right side fender liner.

2. Remove the windshield washer and radiator reservoir tanks. Remove the cruise control actuator, if equipped.

3. Remove the power steering belt. Remove the power steering pump and position it aside with the hydraulic lines still attached.

4. Remove the alternator and support bracket. Remove the upper timing belt cover.

5. Set the No. 1 piston to TDC of the compression stroke by aligning the groove on the crankshaft pulley with the **0** mark on the lower timing belt cover. Check that the

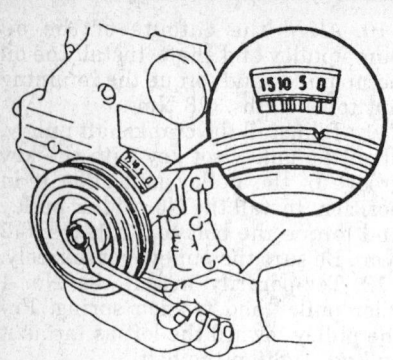

Setting No. 1 cylinder to TDC — 3S-FE and 5S-FE engines

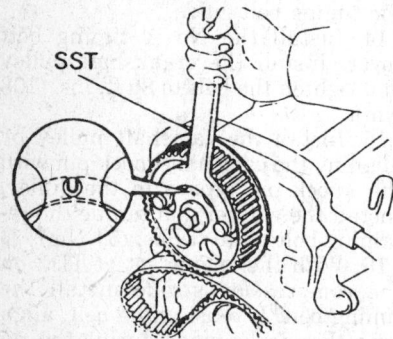

Camshaft pulley and bearing cap marks — 3S-FE and 5S-FE engines

To install:

11. Install the oil pump pulley and tighten it to 21 ft. lbs. (28 Nm). Install the crankshaft timing pulley by sliding it onto the crankshaft over the Woodruff key. Install the No. 2 idler pulley and tighten it to 32 ft. lbs. (43 Nm).

12. Install the No. 1 idler pulley and the tension spring. Move the pulley as far to the left as it will go and tighten it.

13. Install the timing belt on all pulleys except the 2 camshaft pul-

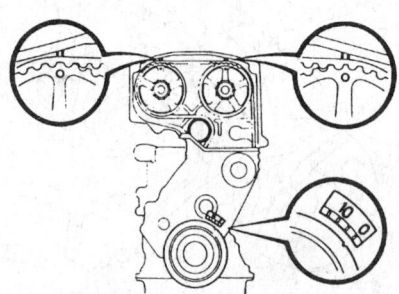

Crankshaft and camshaft pulley timing marks — 3S-GTE engines

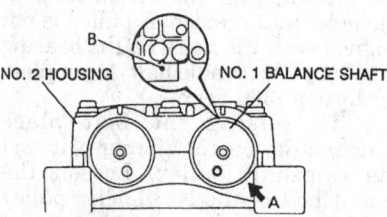

No.2 balance shaft housing groove and punch mark A — 5S-FE engine

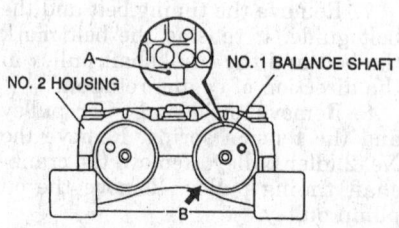

No.2 balance shaft housing groove and punch mark A — 5S-FE engine

matchmarks on the 2 camshaft timing pulleys and the rear timing belt cover are aligned. If not, turn the crankshaft 1 complete revolution clockwise (360 degrees).

6. If the timing belt is to be reused, draw a directional arrow on it and matchmark the belt to the 2 camshaft pulleys. Loosen the No. 1 idler pulley bolt and shift the pulley as far left as possible; tighten the set bolt. Remove the timing belt from the 2 camshaft pulleys. Support the belt so the contact of the belt with the remaining pulleys does not shift.

7. Carefully hold the camshafts with an adjustable wrench and remove the camshaft pulley set bolts. Remove the pulleys and their set pins.

8. Remove the crankshaft pulley. Remove the lower timing belt.

9. Remove the timing belt guide and then remove the timing belt from the remaining pulleys. Be sure to matchmark the belt to the pulleys if it is to be reused.

10. Remove the No. 1 idler pulley and the tension spring. Remove the No. 2 idler pulley, the crankshaft timing pulley and the oil pump pulley.

leys. Make sure the matchmarks made earlier are in alignment.

14. Install the timing belt guide with the cup side out. Install the lower timing belt cover and then install the crankshaft pulley. Tighten it to 80 ft. lbs. (108 Nm).

15. Check that the No. 1 cylinder is at TDC of the compression stroke for the crankshaft. The crankshaft pulley groove should be aligned with the **0** mark on the lower timing belt cover.

16. Check that the No. 1 cylinder is at TDC of the compression stroke for the camshaft.

NOTE: There are 2 types of camshafts, one with 2 holes on the timing pulley contact surface and one with 5 holes on the timing pulley contact surface. All replacements have 5 holes.

2 Hole: Using a wrench, turn the camshafts so the camshaft knock pin aligns with the matchmark on the rear timing belt cover. And the No. 1 cam lobe is pointing outward.

5 Hole: Using a wrench, turn the camshaft so the knock pin aligns with the notch in the No. 1 camshaft bearing cap.

17. Hang the timing belt on the 2 camshaft timing pulleys. Align all matchmarks made during removal. The **S** mark on the pulley should face outward.

18. Align the timing pulley matchmark with the rear timing belt cover matchmark and install the pulleys with the belt.

NOTE: On 1 hole pulleys, match the camshaft knock pin with the camshaft pulley hole. On 5 hole pulleys, insert the knock pin into whichever pulley and camshaft holes are aligned.

19. Hold the camshaft with an adjustable wrench and tighten the pulley set bolt to 43 ft. lbs. (59 Nm).

20. Rotate the engine 2 complete revolutions. Check that all marks align in the correct location. Torque the No. 1 idler pulley bolt to 32 ft. lbs. (43 Nm).

21. Installation of the remaining components is the reverse of the removal procedure. Road test the vehicle for proper operation.

4A-FE and 7A-FE Engines

1. Raise and support the vehicle safely. Remove the right wheel and undercover. Remove the air cleaner.

2. Remove the drive belts. Remove the power steering pump and the air conditioning compressor, with brack-

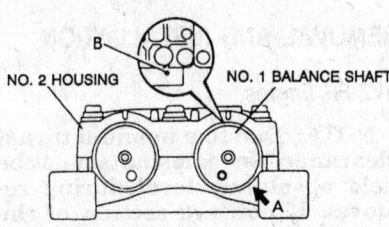

No.2 balance shaft housing groove and punch
mark A — 5S-FE engine

ets, and position them aside. Leave
the hydraulic and refrigerant lines
connected.

3. Remove the spark plugs and the
cylinder head cover. Rotate the
crankshaft pulley so the **0** mark is in
alignment with the groove in the No.
1 front cover. Check that the lifters
on the No. 1 cylinder are loose. If not,
turn the crankshaft 1 complete
revolution (360 degrees).

4. Position a floor jack under the
engine and remove the right side engine mounting insulator.

5. Remove the water pump and
crankshaft pulleys. The crankshaft
pulley will require a 2-armed puller.

6. Loosen the 9 bolts and remove
the No. 1, No. 2 and No. 3 front covers. Remove the timing belt guide.

7. Loosen the bolt on the idler pulley, push it to the left as far as it will
go and then retighten it. If reusing
the timing belt, draw an arrow in the
direction of engine revolution (clockwise) and then matchmark the belt to
the pulleys.

8. Remove the timing belt. Remove the idler pulley bolt, the pulley
and the tension spring.

9. Remove the crankshaft timing
pulley.

10. Lock the camshaft and remove
the camshaft timing pulley.

To install:

11. Install the camshaft timing pulley so it aligns with the knock pin on
the exhaust camshaft. Tighten the
pulley to 43 ft. lbs. (59 Nm). Align the
mark on the No. 1 camshaft bearing
cap with the center of the small hole
in the pulley.

12. Install the crankshaft timing
pulley so the marks on the pulley and
the oil pump body are in alignment.

13. Install the idler pulley and tension spring, move to the left as far as
it will go and tighten temporarily.

14. Align the matchmarks made
during removal and then install the
timing belt on the camshaft pulley.

Loosen the idler pulley set bolt. Make
sure the timing belt contact at the
crankshaft pulley does not shift.

15. Rotate the crankshaft clockwise
2 revolutions from TDC to TDC.
Make sure each pulley aligns with
the marks made previously. If the
marks are not in alignment, the valve
timing is wrong. Shift the timing belt
contact slightly and then repeat
Steps 14-15.

16. Tighten the set bolt on the timing belt idler pulley to 27 ft. lbs. (37
Nm). Measure the timing belt deflection at the SIDE point, looking for
0.20-0.24 in. (5-6mm) of deflection at
4.4 pounds of pressure. If the deflection is not correct, readjust the idler
pulley.

17. Installation of the remaining
components is the reverse of the removal procedure.

4A-GE Engines

1. Disconnect the negative battery
cable. Disconnect the No. 2 air
cleaner hose from the air cleaner.

2. If equipped with power steering, remove the power steering pump
and position it aside. Do not disconnect the pump hydraulic lines.

3. Loosen the water pump pulley
set nuts, loosen the drive belt adjust-

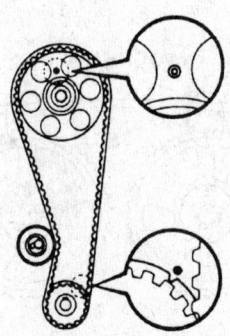

Crankshaft and camshaft pulley timing marks —
4A-FE engines

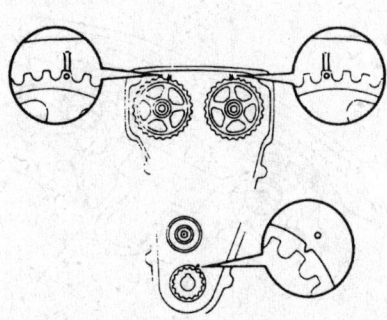

Crankshaft and camshaft pulley timing marks —
4A-GE engines

ing bolt and then remove the drive
belt. Remove the water pump pulley.

4. Remove the spark plugs. Rotate
the crankshaft pulley so the groove
on it is in alignment with the **0** mark
on the No. 1 timing belt cover. Remove the oil filler cap and check that
the cavity in the camshaft is visible.
If not, turn the camshaft 1 complete
revolution (360 degrees).

5. Remove the right side engine
mount insulator.

6. Lock the crankshaft pulley and
remove the pulley bolt. Using a gear
puller, remove the crankshaft pulley.
Remove the 3 timing belt covers and
gaskets. Remove the timing belt
guide.

7. Loosen the bolt on the idler pulley, push it to the left as far as it will
go and then retighten it. If reusing
the timing belt, draw an arrow on it
in the direction of engine revolution
(clockwise) and then matchmark the
belt to the pulleys.

8. Remove the timing belt. Remove the idler pulley bolt, the pulley
and the tension spring.

9. Remove the cylinder head covers, lock the camshaft and remove
the camshaft timing pulleys.

To install:

10. Install the camshaft timing pul-
leys and cylinder head covers.
Tighten the pulley to 34 ft. lbs. (47
Nm).

11. Install the crankshaft timing
pulley so the marks on the pulley and
the oil pump body are in alignment.

12. Install the idler pulley and its
tension spring, move it to the left as
far and tighten temporarily.

13. Install the timing belt. If the old
one is being used, align all the marks
made during removal.

14. Slowly release tension on the
idler pulley bolt and allow the idler to
take up tension on the timing belt.
Do not allow the idler to slam into the
belt; the belt may become damaged.

15. Check the tension of the timing
belt at a TOP point halfway between
the 2 camshaft sprockets. The correct
deflection is 0.18 in. (4.0mm) at 4.4
lbs. pressure. If the belt tension is
incorrect, readjust it by repeating
steps 12 and 14. If the tension is correct, tighten the idler pulley bolt to
27 ft. lbs. (37 Nm).

16. Installation of the remaining
components is the reverse order of
the removal procedure.

7M-GE and 7M-GTE Engines

1. Disconnect the negative battery
cable. Drain the cooling system. Remove the radiator. Remove the water
outlet.

2. Remove the spark plugs. Remove the drive belts. Remove the No. 3 timing belt cover.

3. Position the engine at TDC on the compression stroke. Remove the timing belt from the camshaft sprockets. If reusing the belt, matchmark the belt and the sprockets in the direction of engine rotation.

4. Remove the camshaft pulleys. Remove the crankshaft pulley using the proper removal tools. Remove the power steering air pipe, if equipped.

5. If equipped with air conditioning, remove the compressor and position it aside. Do not disconnect the refrigerant lines.

6. Remove the No. 1 timing belt cover. Remove the timing belt. Remove the idler pulley and the tension spring. Remove the oil pump drive pulley.

To install:

7. Inspect the belt for defects. Replace as required. Inspect the idler pulleys and springs. Replace defective components as required.

8. Install the oil pump drive pulley and retaining bolt. Tighten the bolt to 16 ft. lbs. (22 Nm).

9. Install the crankshaft timing pulley. Temporarily install the idler pulley and tension spring. Tighten the assembly to 36 ft. lbs. (49 Nm). Pry the idler pulley toward the left as far as it will go and temporarily tighten the bolt.

10. Temporarily install the timing belt. If reusing the old belt install it using the marks made during the removal procedure. Install the No. 1 timing belt cover.

11. Align the set key with the key groove and install the crankshaft pulley and torque the retaining bolt to 195 ft. lbs. (265 Nm).

12. Install the camshaft timing pulleys. Torque the retaining bolts to 36 ft. lbs. (49 Nm).

13. Loosen the idler pulley bolt. Install the timing belt to the Intake side and the Exhaust side. Tighten the idler pulley bolt to 36 ft. lbs. (49 Nm).

14. Make sure the timing belt tension **A** is equal to the timing belt tension **B**. If not adjust the idler pulley. Turn the engine 2 complete revolutions in the clockwise direction and check to see that everything is aligned properly.

15. Turn both the intake and exhaust camshaft pulleys inward at the same time to loosen the timing belt between the 2 sprockets. Belt deflection should be 4.4-6.6 lbs. If not adjust the idler pulley.

16. Install the remaining components, start the engine and check for leaks and proper operation.

Timing Sprockets

REMOVAL AND INSTALLATION

Timing sprocket/pulley removal and installation procedures are detailed within the individual Timing Belt sections.

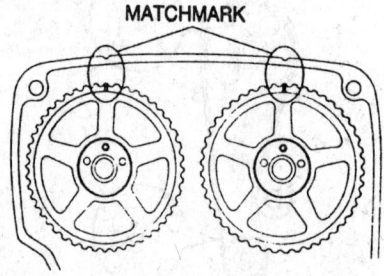

Camshaft pulley and cover marks — 7M-GE and 7M-GZE engines

Camshaft

REMOVAL AND INSTALLATION

2VZ-FE Engine

NOTE: Due to a nominal thrust clearance, the camshafts must be held absolutely level during removal. If not, the section of the cylinder head receiving the thrust may crack or be damaged, causing the camshaft to break.

1. Remove the cylinder head(s).

2. Rotate the exhaust camshaft in the right cylinder head until the 2 pointed marks on the camshaft drive and driven gears are aligned.

3. Secure the exhaust camshaft sub-gear to the driven gear with bolt. This is important as it will eliminate the torsional spring force of the sub-gear.

4. Loosen the bearing cap bolts in the proper sequence and then remove the 4 bearing caps and the right side exhaust camshaft.

5. Loosen the bearing cap bolts in the proper sequence and then remove the 5 bearing caps and the right side intake camshaft.

NOTE: Be sure to arrange all the bearing caps in their proper order.

6. Rotate the exhaust camshaft in the left cylinder head until the pointed mark on the camshaft drive and driven gears are aligned.

7. Secure the exhaust camshaft sub-gear to the driven gear with bolt. This is important as it will eliminate the torsional spring force of the sub-gear.

8. Loosen the bearing cap bolts in the proper sequence and then remove the 4 bearing caps and the left side exhaust camshaft.

9. Loosen the bearing cap bolts in the proper sequence and then remove the 5 bearing caps and the left side intake camshaft.

NOTE: Be sure to arrange all the bearing caps in their proper order.

To install:

10. Coat the thrust portion of the right side intake camshaft with suitable grease and then position the camshaft into the head so the 2 timing marks are at a 90 degree angle to the head.

11. Coat the edges of the No. 1 bearing cap with sealant and then install all 5 caps in their proper locations. Coat the bolts with engine oil

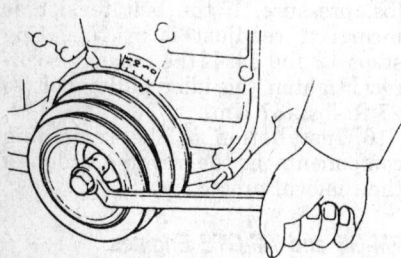

Setting No. 1 cylinder to TDC — 7M-GE and 7M-GZE engines

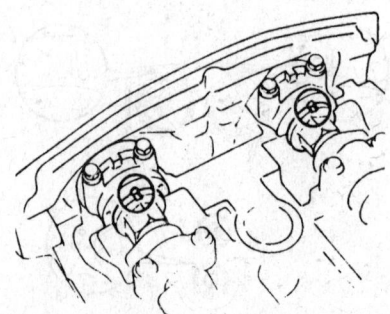

Aligning the camshaft grooves with the drilled marks in the No. 1 camshaft bearing caps — 3S-GTE engine

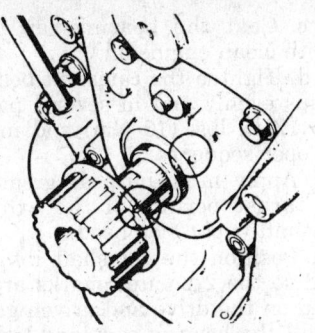

When installing the crankshaft pulley, make sure the TDC marks on the oil pump body and the pulley are in alignment — 4A-GE engine

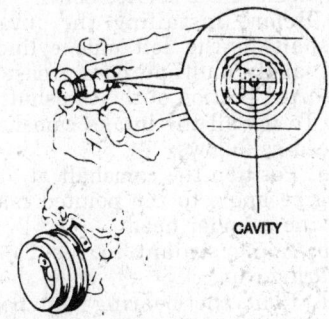

When setting the No. 1 cylinder at TDC on the 4A-GE engine, remove the oil filler cap and check that the cavity in the camshaft is visible

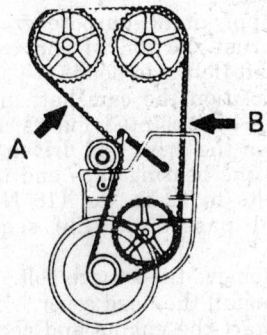

7M-GE and 7M-GTE engines timing belt tension check

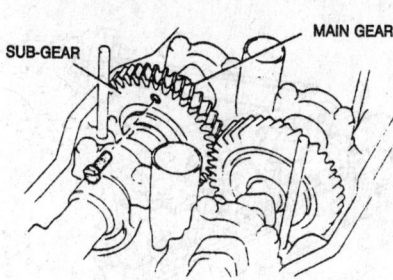

Install a service bolt in the exhaust camshaft sub-gear (right) — 2VZ-FE and 3VZ-FE engines

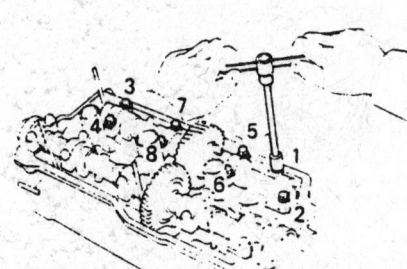

Exhaust camshaft bearing cap bolt loosening sequence (right) — 2VZ-FE and 3VZ-FE engines

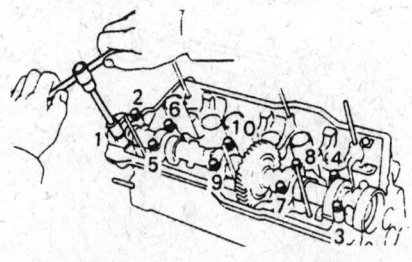

Intake camshaft bearing cap bolt loosening sequence (right) — 2VZ-FE and 3VZ-FE engines

mark aligns with the one on the intake shaft.

18. Install all 4 bearing caps in their proper locations. Coat the bolts with engine oil and then tighten them, in sequence, in several stages, to 12 ft. lbs. (16 Nm).

19. Remove the service bolt.

20. Installation of the remaining components is in the reverse order of removal.

3VZ-FE Engine

1. Remove the cylinder head covers.

NOTE: Being that the thrust clearance on both the intake and exhaust camshafts is small, the camshafts must be kept level during removal. If the camshafts are removed without being kept level, the camshaft may be caught in the cylinder head causing the head to break or the camshaft to seize.

2. To remove the exhaust camshaft from the right side cylinder head, proceed as follows:

   a. Turn the camshaft with a wrench until the 2 pointed marks on the drive and driven gears are aligned.

   b. Secure the exhaust camshaft sub-gear to the main gear using a service bolt. The manufacturer recommends a bolt 0.63-0.79 in. (16-20mm) long with a thread diameter of 6mm and a 1mm thread pitch. When removing the exhaust camshaft be sure that the torsional spring force of the sub-gear has been eliminated.

   c. Remove 8 bearing cap bolts and remove the caps. Uniformly loosen and remove bearing cap bolts in several passes and in the proper sequence.

   d. Remove the exhaust camshaft from the engine.

3. Uniformly loosen and remove the 10 bearing cap bolts in several passes, in the sequence shown. Remove the bearing caps and oil seal and then lift out the intake camshaft.

4. To remove the exhaust camshaft from the left side cylinder head, proceed as follows:

   a. Turn the camshaft with a wrench until the pointed marks on the drive and driven gears are aligned.

   b. Secure the exhaust camshaft sub-gear to the main gear using a service bolt. The manufacturer recommends a bolt 0.63-0.79 in. (16-20mm) long with a thread diameter of 6mm and a 1mm thread

and then tighten in sequence, in several stages, to 12 ft. lbs. (16 Nm).

12. Coat the thrust portion of the right side exhaust camshaft with grease and then position the camshaft into the head so the 2 timing marks align with those on the intake shaft.

13. Install all 4 bearing caps in their proper locations. Coat the bolts with engine oil and then tighten them, in sequence, in several stages, to 12 ft. lbs. (16 Nm).

14. Remove the service bolt.

15. Coat the thrust portion of the left side intake camshaft with grease and then position the camshaft into the head so the timing mark is at a 90 degree angle to the head.

16. Coat the edges of the No. 1 bearing cap with sealant and then install all 5 caps in their proper locations. Coat the bolts with engine oil and then tighten, in sequence, in several stages, to 12 ft. lbs. (16 Nm).

17. Coat the thrust portion of the left side exhaust camshaft with grease and then position the camshaft into the head so the timing

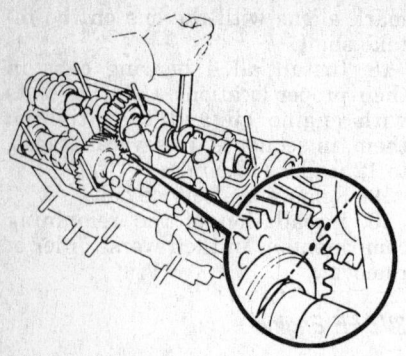

Align the single mark on the exhaust camshaft (left) — 2VZ-FE and 3VZ-FE engines

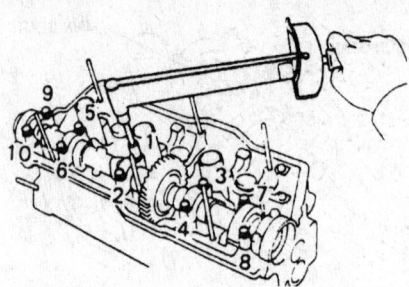

Intake camshaft bearing cap bolt tightening sequence (right) — 2VZ-FE and 3VZ-FE engines

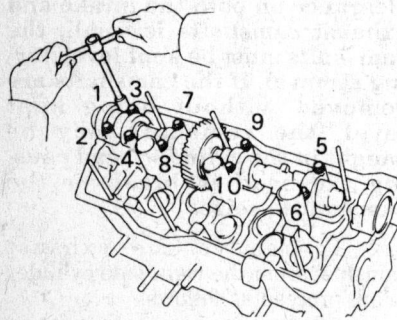

Intake camshaft bearing cap bolt loosening sequence (left) — 2VZ-FE and 3VZ-FE engines

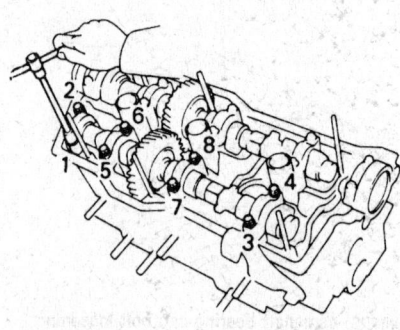

Exhaust camshaft bearing cap bolt loosening sequence (left) — 2VZ-FE and 3VZ-FE engines

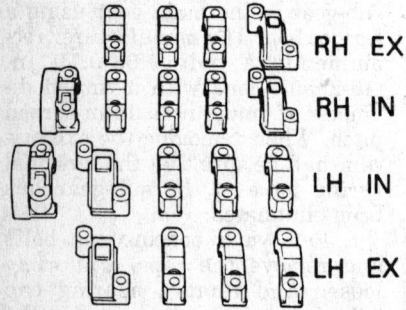

Camshaft bearing cap identification — 2VZ-FE and 3VZ-FE engines

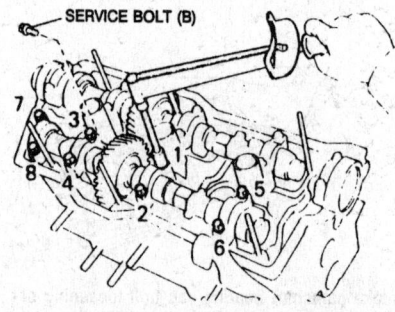

Exhaust camshaft bearing cap bolt tightening sequence (left) — 2VZ-FE and 3VZ-FE engines

pitch. When removing the exhaust camshaft be sure that the torsional spring force of the sub-gear has been eliminated.

c. Remove 8 bearing cap bolts and remove the caps. Uniformly loosen and remove bearing cap bolts in several passes and in the proper sequence.

d. Remove the exhaust camshaft from the engine.

5. Uniformly loosen and remove the 10 bearing cap bolts in several passes, in the sequence shown. Re-

move the bearing caps and oil seal and then lift out the intake camshaft.

To install:

6. Before installing the intake camshaft in the right side cylinder head, apply multi-purpose grease to the thrust portion of the camshaft.

7. To install the intake camshaft, proceed as follows:

   a. Position the camshaft at a 90 degree angle to the 2 pointed marks on the cylinder head.

   b. Apply sealant to the No. 1 bearing cap.

c. Coat the bearing cap bolts with clean engine oil.

d. Tighten the camshaft bearing caps evenly and in several passes to 12 ft. lbs. (16 Nm) and in the proper sequence.

8. Apply multi-purpose grease to the thrust portion of the exhaust camshaft (right side head).

9. Position the camshaft into the head so the 2 pointed marks are aligned on the drive and driven gears. Install the bearing caps and tighten the bolts to 12 ft. lbs. (16 Nm), in several passes, in the sequence shown.

10. Remove the service bolt.

11. Before installing the intake camshaft in the left side cylinder head, apply multi-purpose grease to the thrust portion of the camshaft.

12. To install the intake camshaft, proceed as follows:

   a. Position the camshaft at a 90 degree angle to the pointed mark on the cylinder head.

   b. Apply sealant to the No. 1 bearing cap.

   c. Coat the bearing cap bolts with clean engine oil.

   d. Tighten the camshaft bearing caps evenly and in several passes to 12 ft. lbs. (16 Nm) in the proper sequence.

13. Apply multi-purpose grease to the thrust portion of the exhaust camshaft (left side head).

14. Position the camshaft into the head so the pointed marks are aligned on the drive and driven gears. Install the bearing caps and tighten the bolts to 12 ft. lbs. (16 Nm), in several passes, in the sequence shown.

15. Remove the service bolt.

16. Install the head cover.

17. Start the engine and check for leaks.

18. Adjust the ignition timing.

3S-FE and 5S-FE Engines

1. Remove the cylinder head.

2. To remove the exhaust camshaft, set the knock pin of the exhaust camshaft at 10-45 degree BTDC of camshaft angle. This angle will help to lift the exhaust camshaft level and even by pushing No. 2 and No. 4 cylinder camshaft lobes of the exhaust camshaft toward their valve lifters.

3. Secure the exhaust camshaft sub-gear to the main gear using a service bolt. When removing the exhaust camshaft be sure the torsional spring force of the sub-gear has been eliminated.

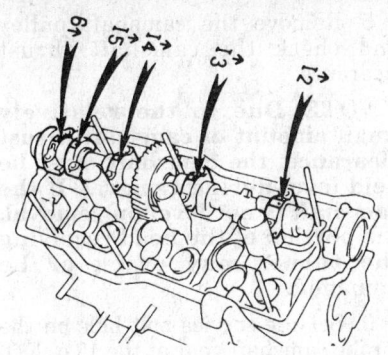

Intake camshaft bearing cap installation (left) —
2VZ-FE and 3VZ-FE engines

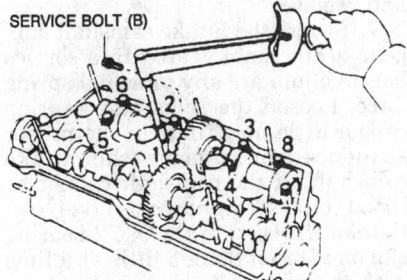

Intake camshaft bearing cap bolt tightening sequence (right) — 2VZ-FE and 3VZ-FE engines

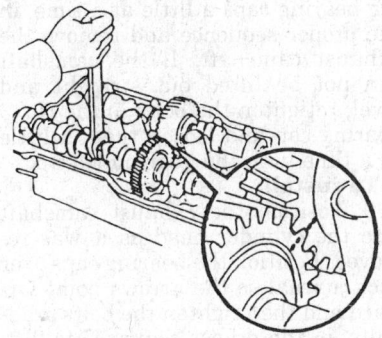

Camshaft drive and driven gear timing marks —
3VZ-FE engine

4. Remove the No. 1 and No. 2 rear bearing cap bolts and remove the cap. Uniformly loosen and remove bearing cap bolts No. 3 to No. 8 in several passes and in the proper sequence. Do not remove bearing cap bolts No. 9 and 10 at this time. Remove the No. 1, 2 and 4 bearing caps.

5. Alternately loosen and remove bearing cap bolts No. 9 and 10. As these bolts are loosened, check to see

that the camshaft is being lifted out straight and level.

NOTE: If the camshaft is not lifted out straight and level retighten No. 9 and 10 bearing cap bolts. Reverse Steps 4-1, than start over from Step 3. Do not attempt to pry the camshaft from its mounting.

6. Remove the exhaust camshaft from the engine.

7. To remove the intake camshaft, set the knock pin of the intake camshaft at 80-115 degrees BTDC of

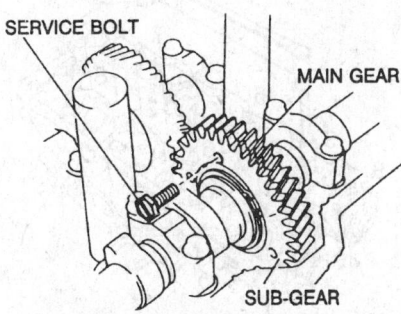

Securing exhaust camshaft sub-gear to main gear — 3S-FE and 5S-FE engines

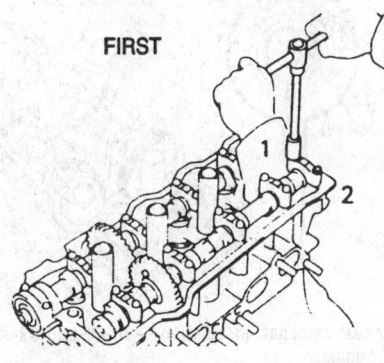

Removing exhaust camshaft — 3S-FE and 5S-FE engines

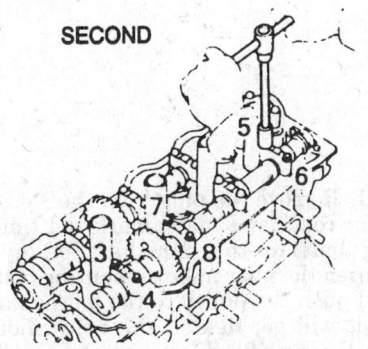

Removing exhaust camshaft — 3S-FE and 5S-FE engines

camshaft angle. This angle will help to lift the intake camshaft level and evenly by pushing No. 1 and No. 3 cylinder camshaft lobes of the intake camshaft toward their valve lifters.

8. Remove the No. 1 and No. 2 front bearing cap bolts and remove the front bearing cap and oil seal. If the cap will not come apart easily, leave it in place without the bolts.

9. Uniformly loosen and remove bearing cap bolts No. 3 to No. 8 in several phases and in the proper sequence. Do not remove bearing cap bolts No. 9 and 10 at this time. Remove No. 1, 3 and 4 bearing caps.

10. Alternately loosen and remove bearing cap bolts No. 9 and 11.

As these bolts are loosened and after breaking the adhesion on the front bearing cap, check to see that the camshaft is being lifted out straight and level.

NOTE: If the camshaft is not lifted out straight and level retighten No. 9 and 10 bearing cap bolts. Reverse Steps 10-7, then start over from Step 8. Do not attempt to pry the camshaft from its mounting.

11. Remove the intake camshaft from the engine.

To install:

12. Before installing the intake camshaft, apply multi-purpose grease to the thrust portion of the camshaft. Position the camshaft at 80 degrees BTDC of camshaft angle on the cylinder head. Apply seal packing kit 08826-00080 or equivalent and apply it to the front bearing cap. Coat the bearing cap bolts with clean engine oil. Uniformly and in several phases tighten the camshaft bearing caps to 14 ft. lbs. (19 Nm).

13. To install the exhaust camshaft, set the knock pin of the camshaft at 10 degrees BTDC of camshaft angle. Apply multi-purpose grease to the thrust portion of the camshaft. Position the exhaust camshaft gear with the intake camshaft gear so the timing marks are in alignment. Be sure to use the proper alignment marks on the gears. Do not use the assembly reference marks.

14. Turn the intake camshaft clockwise or counterclockwise little by little until the exhaust camshaft sits in the bearing journals evenly without rocking the camshaft on the bearing journals.

15. Coat the bearing cap bolts with clean engine oil. Uniformly and in several phases, tighten the camshaft bearing caps to 14 ft. lbs. (19 Nm). Remove the service bolt from the assembly.

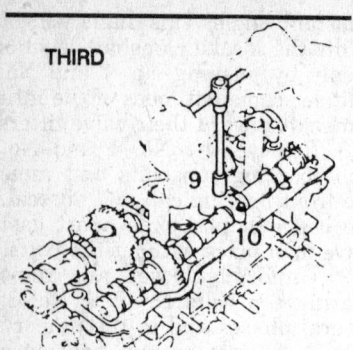

Removing exhaust camshaft — 3S-FE and 5S-FE engines

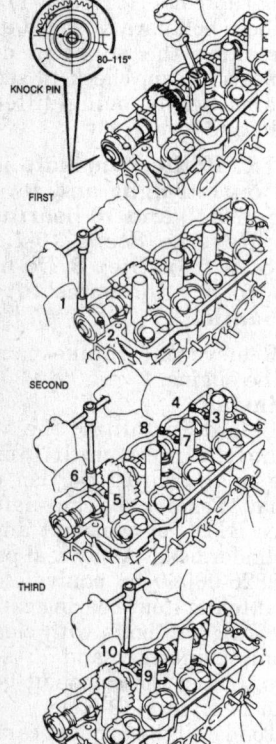

Intake camshaft removal procedure — 3S-FE and 5S-FE engines

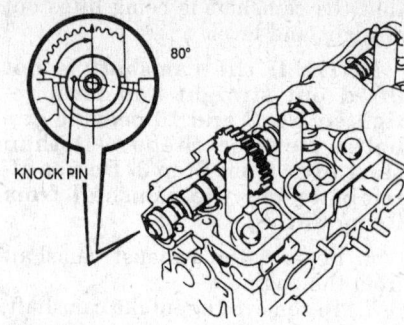

Installing the intake camshaft — 3S-FE and 5S-FE engines

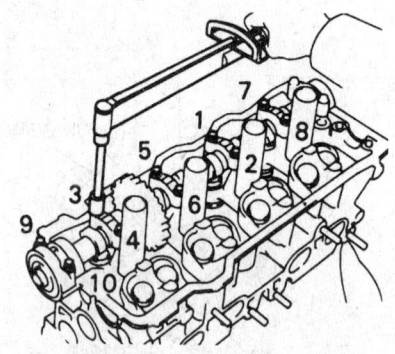

Intake camshaft bearing bolt tightening sequence — 3S-FE and 5S-FE engines

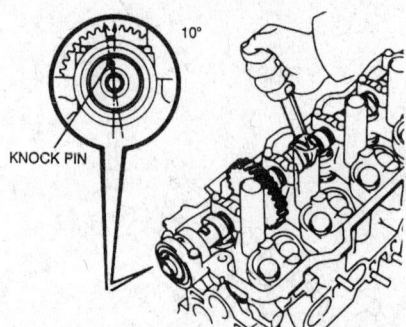

Exhaust camshaft installation — 3S-FE and 5S-FE engines

5. Remove the camshaft pulley and check the camshaft thrust clearance.

NOTE: Due to the relatively small amount of camshaft thrust clearance, the camshaft must be held level during removal. If the camshaft is not level on removal, the portion of the head receiving the thrust may crack or be damaged.

6. Set the service bolt hole on the intake camshaft gear at the 12 o'clock position so the No. 1 and 3 cylinder camshaft lobed can push their lifters evenly. Loosen the No. 1 bearing caps on each camshaft a little at a time and remove.

7. Secure the intake camshaft sub-gear to the main gear with a service bolt to eliminate any torsional spring force. Loosen the remaining bearing caps a little at a time, in the proper sequence and remove the intake camshaft. If the camshaft cannot be lifted out straight and level, re-tighten the bolts in the No. 2 bearing cap and loosen them a little at a time with the gear pulled up.

8. Turn the exhaust camshaft approximately 105 degrees so the knock pin is about 5 minutes before the 6:30 o'clock position. Loosen the remaining bearing caps a little at a time, in the proper sequence and remove the exhaust camshaft. If the camshaft can not be lifted out straight and level, retighten the bolts in the No. 3 bearing cap and loosen them a little at a time with the gear pulled up.

To install:

9. Position the exhaust camshaft into the cylinder head as it was removed. Position the bearing caps over each journal so the arrows point forward and then tighten the bolts gradually, in the proper sequence to 9 ft. lbs. (13 Nm).

10. Coat the lip of a new oil seal with grease and drive it into the camshaft.

11. Set the knock pin on the exhaust camshaft so it is just above the edge of the cylinder head and engage the intake camshaft gear to the exhaust gear so the mark on each gear is in alignment. Roll the intake camshaft down onto the bearing journals while engaging the gears with each other.

12. Position the bearing caps over each journal on the intake camshaft so the arrows point forward and then tighten the bolts gradually, in the proper sequence to 9 ft. lbs. (13 Nm).

13. Remove the service bolt and install the No. 1 intake bearing cap. If it does not fit properly, pry the

16. Installation of the remaining components is the reverse of the removal procedure.

4A-FE and 7A-FE Engines

1. Disconnect the negative battery cable. Drain the cooling system.

2. Remove the spark plugs and the cylinder head cover.

3. Remove the No. 3 and No. 2 front covers. Turn the crankshaft pulley and align its groove with the **0** mark on the No. 1 front cover. Check that the camshaft pulley hole aligns with the mark on the No. 1 camshaft bearing cap (exhaust side).

4. Remove the plug from the No. 1 front cover and matchmark the timing belt to the camshaft pulley. Loosen the idler pulley mounting bolt and push the pulley to the left as far as it will go; tighten the bolt. Slide the timing belt off the camshaft pulley and support it so it won't fall into the case.

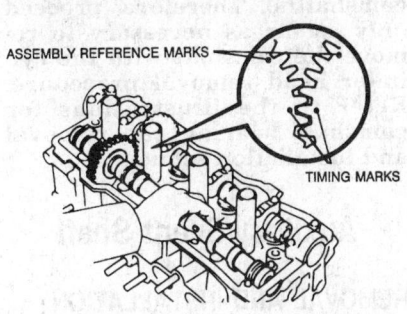

Intake and exhaust camshaft engagement — 3S-FE and 5S-FE engines

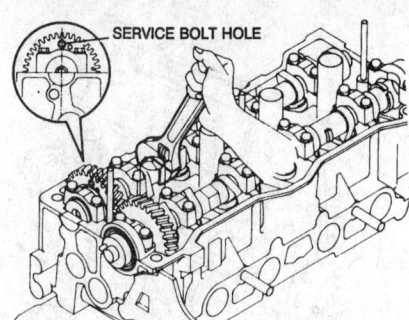

Service bolt hole positioning (intake camshaft) — 4A-FE and 7A-FE engines

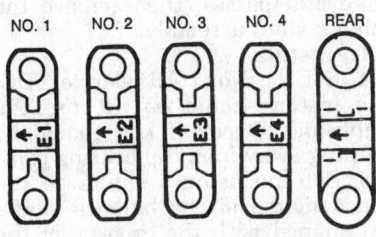

Exhaust camshaft bearing cap positioning — 3S-FE and 5S-FE engines

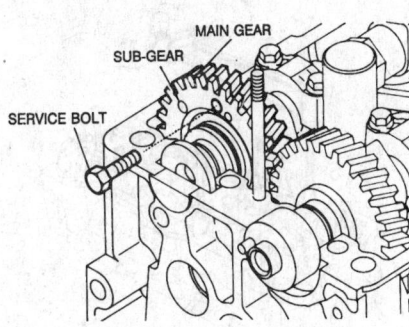

Installing the service bolt in the intake camshaft — 4A-FE and 7A-FE engines

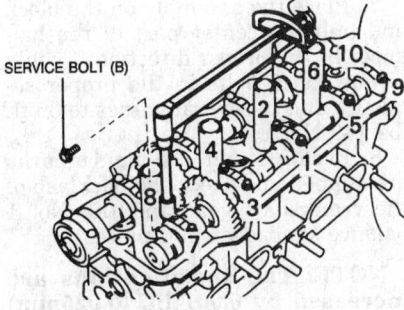

Exhaust camshaft bearing bolt tightening sequence — 3S-FE and 5S-FE engines

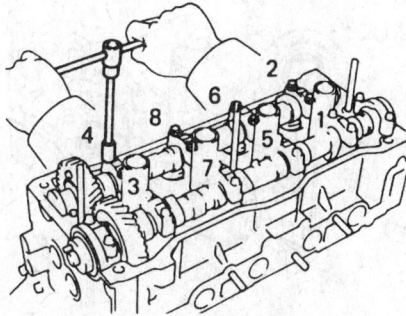

Intake camshaft bearing cap loosening sequence — 4A-FE and 7A-FE engines

camshaft gear backwards until it does. Tighten the bolts to 9 ft. lbs. (13 Nm).

14. Rotate the camshafts 1 revolution (360 degrees) from TDC to TDC and check that the marks on the 2 gears are still aligned.

15. Install the camshaft timing pulley making sure the camshaft knock pins and the matchmarks are in alignment. Lock each camshaft and tighten the pulley bolts to 43 ft. lbs. (59 Nm).

16. Align the matchmarks made during removal and then install the

timing belt on the camshaft pulley. Loosen the idler pulley set bolt. Make sure the timing belt contact at the crankshaft pulley does not shift.

17. Rotate the crankshaft clockwise 2 revolutions from TDC to TDC. Make sure each pulley aligns with the marks made previously.

18. Tighten the set bolt on the timing belt idler pulley to 27 ft. lbs. (37 Nm). Measure the timing belt deflection. If necessary, readjust by using the idler pulley.

19. Installation of the remaining components is the reverse of the removal procedure.

5E-FE Engine

1. Remove the valve cover.
2. Remove the timing belt assembly.
3. Remove the camshaft timing sprocket.

NOTE: Due to the relatively small amount of camshaft thrust clearance, the camshaft must be kept level during removal. If the camshaft is not level on removal, the portion of the head receiving the thrust may crack or be damaged.

4. Set the intake camshaft so the service bolt holes of the intake camshaft gears are directly above.
5. Remove each front bearing cap of the intake and exhaust camshafts.
6. Secure the intake camshaft sub gear to the main gear with a bolt 6mm in diameter, 16-20mm long and with a pitch of 1.0mm.
7. Evenly loosen and remove the 8 bolts of the 4 bearing caps of the exhaust camshaft and remove the exhaust camshaft. If the camshaft is not being lifted out straight, reinstall the middle bearing cap and loosen it evenly to keep the camshaft straight.
8. Evenly loosen and remove the 8 bolts of the 4 bearing caps of the intake camshaft and remove the intake camshaft. If the camshaft is not being lifted out straight, reinstall the middle bearing cap and loosen it evenly to keep the camshaft straight.
To install:
9. Apply engine oil to the thrust surface of the intake camshaft.
10. Place the intake camshaft on the cylinder head so the service bolt points directly up.
11. Install the 4 rearward bearing caps in their original order and temporarily tighten them evenly.
12. Apply engine oil to the thrust portion of the exhaust camshaft.
13. Engage the exhaust camshaft gear to the intake camshaft gear by matching the proper timing marks on each gear.

NOTE: There are other marks present for the S engine. Do not use these marks.

14. Install the 4 rearward intake bearing caps in their original order and evenly tighten temporarily.
15. Remove the service bolt.
16. Clean the mating surfaces of the No. 2 bearing cap and apply sealer. Install it temporarily tighten-

Exhaust camshaft bearing cap loosening sequence — 4A-FE and 7A-FE engines

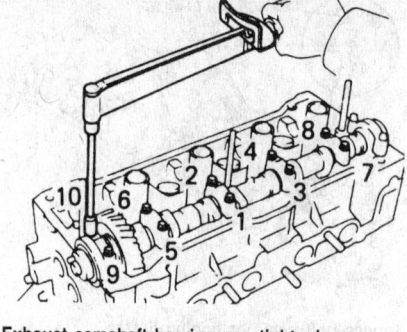

Exhaust camshaft bearing cap tightening sequence — 4A-FE and 7A-FE engines

Knockpin positioning on the exhaust camshaft — 4A-FE and 7A-FE engines

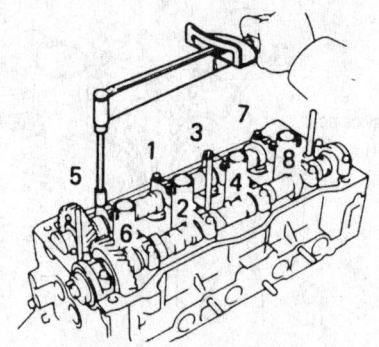

Intake camshaft bearing cap tightening sequence — 4A-FE and 7A-FE engines

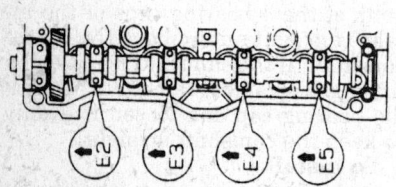

Exhaust camshaft bearing cap positioning — 4A-FE and 7A-FE engines

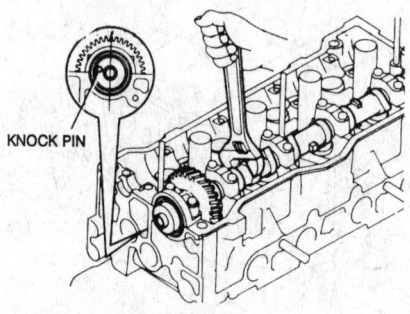

Turn the exhaust camshaft until the knockpin is here — 4A-FE and 7A-FE engines

camshaft(s). Therefore, proceed only as far as necessary to remove the camshaft with the cylinder head removal procedure. Refer to the illustrations for camshaft bearing cap removal and installation sequence.

Auxiliary/Silent Shaft

REMOVAL AND INSTALLATION

1992-94 Camry with 5S-FE Engine

1. Remove the oil pan.
2. Remove the oil pump.
3. Remove the 6 bolts evenly and in several passes, then remove the balance shaft assembly.
   To install:
4. Set the No. 1 cylinder to TDC. The piston should be up and the crankshaft Woodruff key should be pointing away from the bearing caps.
5. Set the balance shafts so the punch marks of the balance shafts are aligned with the grooves of the No. 2 housing.
6. Clean the spacer surfaces and the spacers, then install on the block. Use the thickest spacers when replacing the crankshaft or balance shaft assemblies.
7. Place the assembly on the block and pull the center part of the balancer in the proper direction. Evenly torque the 6 bolts in the proper sequence and in several passes to 36 ft. lbs. (49 Nm).
8. Recheck that the punchmarks are aligned and check the backlash of the crankshaft gear and the No. 1 balance shaft gear in 4 places.

NOTE: The specifications are increased by 0.001 in. (0.025mm) if the procedure is performed with the engine in the vehicle.

a. Rotate the crankshaft 2 or 3 times to settle the crankshaft gear and the No. 1 balance shaft gear.

b. When the No. 1 piston is at TDC, check that the punch marks of the balance shafts are aligned with the grooves of the No. 2 housing.

c. Check that punch marks A and B are at the proper positions on the No. 1 balance shaft.

d. First turn the crankshaft clockwise and align the groove of the No. 2 balance shaft housing with the punch mark A of the No. 1 balance shaft.

e. Set up a dial gauge so the needle of the dial gauge is perpendicular to the core of the No. 1 balance

ing the bolts, and install the camshaft housing plug.

17. Now torque the intake camshaft cap bolts to 9 ft. lbs. (13 Nm), in the proper sequence.

18. Apply grease to a new camshaft oil seal lip and install it as far as the deepest part of the cylinder head.

19. Install the No. 1 bearing cap and temporarily tighten the bolts.

20. Now torque the exhaust camshaft bearing cap bolts to 9 ft. lbs. (13 Nm) evenly and in the proper sequence.

21. Install the camshaft timing sprocket and torque the bolt to 37 ft. lbs. (50 Nm).

22. Reverse the remaining procedures, start the engine and check for leaks.

All Others

The procedure for removing the camshaft is given as part of the cylinder head removal procedure.

NOTE: It will not be necessary to completely remove the cylinder head in order to remove the

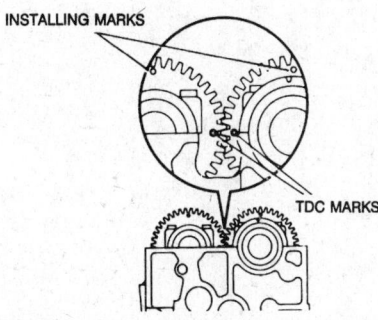

Intake camshaft bearing cap positioning — 4A-FE engines

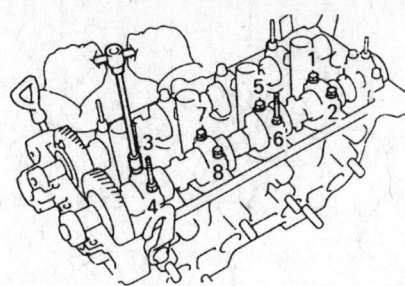

Removal sequence of exhaust camshaft bearing cap bolts — 5E-FE engine

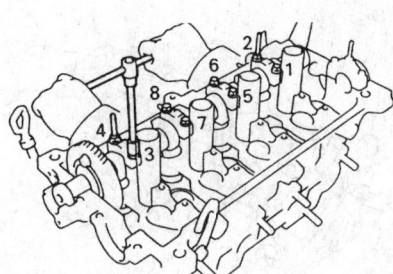

Rotate the camshaft one revolution from TDC to TDC and check that the marks are lined up — 4A-FE and 7A-FE engines

Removal sequence of intake camshaft bearing cap bolts — 5E-FE engine

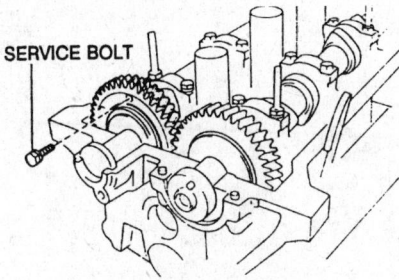

Securing intake camshaft sub-gear to main gear — 5E-FE engine

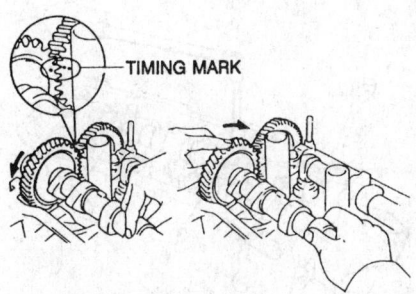

Exhaust and intake camshaft gear timing marks — 5E-FE engine

shaft and parallel with the gear tooth.

f. Turn the No. 1 balance shaft 4 or 5 times to provide a steady backlash reading.

g. Lightly turn the No. 1 balance shaft by hand and measure the backlash while pressing on the rear of the No. 1 balance shaft. The standard backlash should be 0-0.0024 in. (0-0.06mm).

h. Remove the dial gauge.

i. Turn the crankshaft clockwise to align the groove of the No. 2 housing with the punchmark B.

j. Set up the dial gauge again.

k. Measure the backlash. The standard is 0-0.0024 in. (0-0.06mm).

l. Remove the dial gauge.

m. Turn the crankshaft clockwise again to align the groove of the No. 2 housing with the punch mark A.

n. Set up the dial gauge again.

o. Measure the backlash. The standard is 0-0.0024 in. (0-0.06mm).

p. Remove the dial gauge.

q. Turn the crankshaft clockwise again to align the groove of the No. 2 housing with the punch mark B.

r. Set up the dial gauge again.

s. Measure the backlash. The standard is 0-0.0024 in. (0-0.06mm).

t. Remove the dial gauge.

9. If even 1 of the 4 points measured above exceeds the backlash specification, adjust the backlash with new spacers.

NOTE: Use the same size spacers for both the left and right sides. Varying the spacer thickness by 0.0008 in. (0.02mm) changes the backlash by about 0.0006 in. (0.014mm).

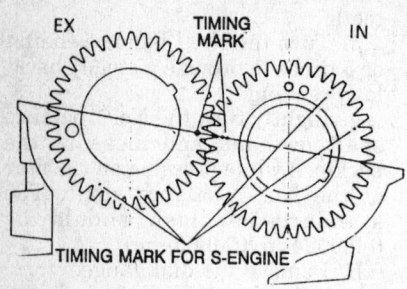

Correct exhaust and intake camshaft gear timing marks — 5E-FE engine

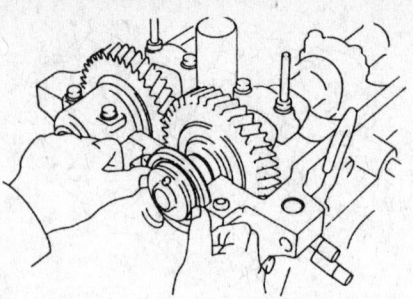

Installing exhaust camshaft oil seal — 5E-FE engine

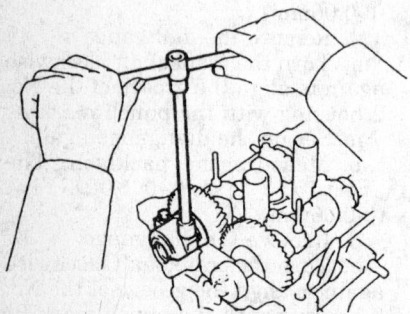

Installing No. 2 bearing cap — 5E-FE engine

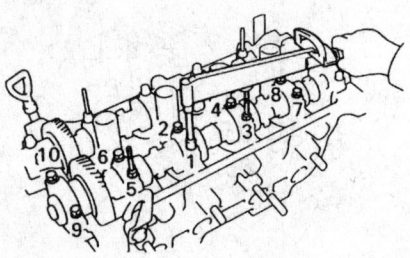

Exhaust bearing cap torque sequence — 5E-FE engine

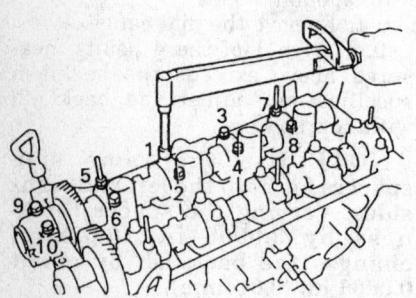

Intake bearing cap torque sequence — 5E-FE engine

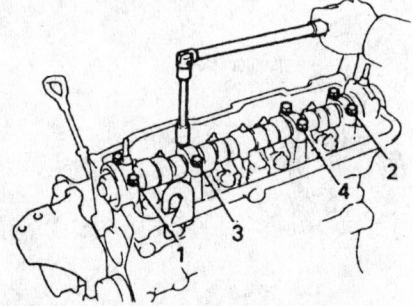

Removing the camshaft bearing caps-reverse order for installation — 3E and 3E-E engines

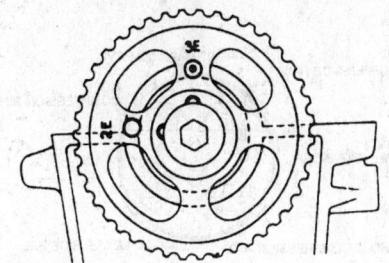

Removing the camshaft bearing caps-reverse order for installation — 7M-GE and 7M-GTE engines

Timing sprocket installation — 3E and 3E-E engines

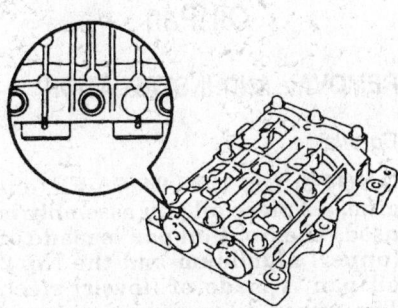

Balance shaft punchmarks — 5S-FE engine

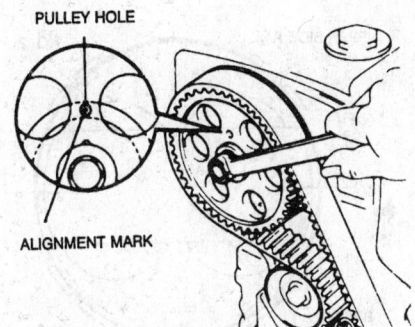

Timing sprocket alignment — 3E and 3E-E engines

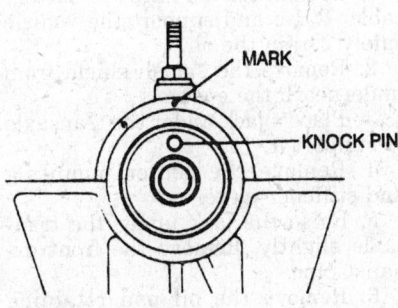

Camshaft alignment — 3E and 3E-E engines

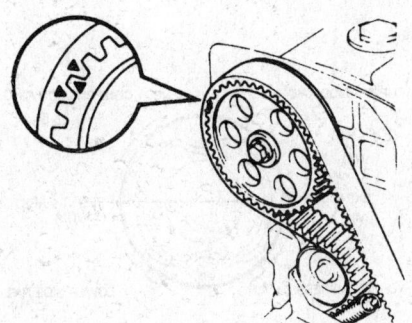

Timing belt alignment — 3E and 3E-E engines

Piston and Connecting Rod

POSITIONING

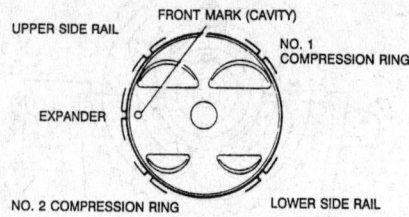

Piston ring gap positioning — 3S-GTE engines

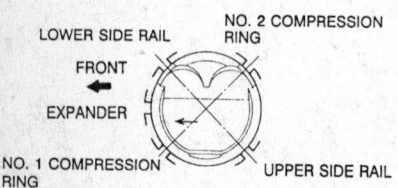

Piston ring gap positioning — 5E-FE engine

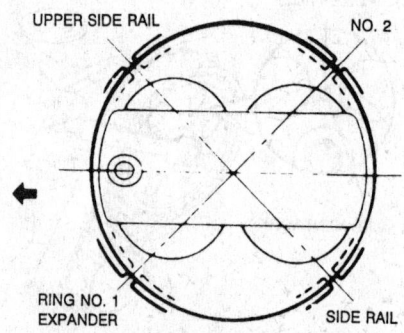

Piston ring gap positioning — 4A-FE, 4A-GE and 7A-FE engines

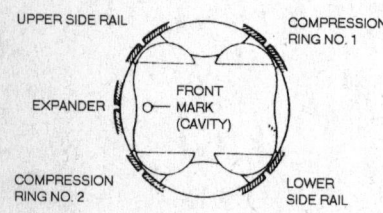

Piston ring gap positioning — 2VZ-FE and 3VZ-FE engines

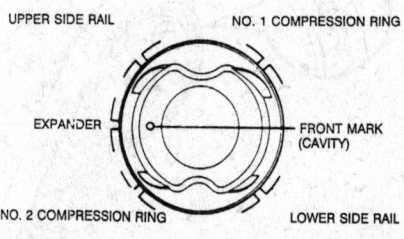

Piston ring gap positioning — 3S-FE and 5S-FE engines

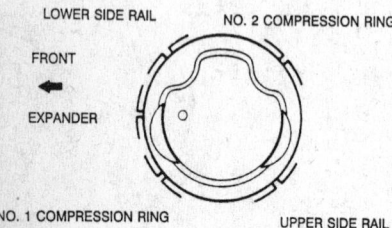

Piston ring gap positioning — 3E and 3E-E engines

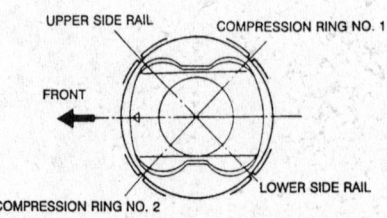

Piston ring gap positioning — 7M-GE and 7M-GTE engines

ENGINE LUBRICATION

— **CAUTION** —

To avoid personal injury and accidental deployment of the air bag, work must be started after about 90 seconds or longer from the time the ignition switch is turned to the LOCK position and the battery cable is disconnected from the battery.

Oil Pan

REMOVAL AND INSTALLATION

Corolla

NOTE: On 1993-94 7A-FE engine, a 2 piece oil pan assembly is used. The No. 1 oil pan is made of (upper) aluminum and the No. 2 oil pan is made of (lower) steel. The upper oil pan section is secured to the cylinder block and the transaxle housing, increasing rigidity.

1. Disconnect the negative battery cable. Raise and support the vehicle safely. Drain the oil.
2. Remove the splash shield from underneath the engine.
3. Place a jack under the transaxle to support it.
4. Remove the center mounting and stiffener plate.
5. Raise the jack under the transaxle slightly. Remove the front exhaust pipe.
6. Remove the oil pan retaining bolts. Remove the oil pan from the vehicle. If the oil pan does not come out easily, it may be necessary to unbolt the rear engine mounts from the crossmember. It may be necessary to remove the oil strainer and pick-up assembly to gain clearance for oil pan removal (drop oil strainer assembly right in the oil pan).
7. Installation is the reverse of the removal procedure. Tighten the oil pan bolts to 5 ft. lbs. (7.5 Nm) working from the center to the ends. Always replace the oil pan gasket and refill with engine oil. Start engine check for leaks.

Camry

1. Disconnect the negative battery cable. Raise the vehicle and support it safely. Drain the oil.

2. Remove the engine undercover. Remove the dipstick.

3. On the 3S-FE engine, disconnect the exhaust pipe. Remove the suspension lower crossmember. Remove the engine mounting center member. Remove the front engine mount insulator and bracket. On the V6 engine, remove the stiffener plate.

4. Remove the oil pan retaining bolts. Remove the oil pan.

To install:

5. Clean the gasket mating surfaces. Always use a new pan gasket. Some engines were assembled using RTV gasket material in place of a conventional gasket. In that case, apply a thin (5mm) bead of RTV material to the groove around the pan mating surface.

6. Assemble the pan within 3 minutes. Torque pan bolts to 48 inch lbs. (5.4 Nm). On the V6 engine, tighten the pan bolts to 52 inch lbs. (5.9 Nm).

7. Reverse the remaining procedures, add oil to the engine, start it and check for leaks.

Celica

EXCEPT 4A-FE ENGINE

1. Disconnect the negative battery cable. Raise the vehicle and support it safely. Drain the engine oil.

2. Remove the engine undercovers.

3. On the 5S-FE engines, disconnect the exhaust pipe from the exhaust manifold.

4. Remove the lower suspension crossmember. Remove the engine mounting center member.

5. Remove the engine stiffener plate and the oil level gauge.

6. Remove the oil pan retaining bolts. Remove the oil pan.

To install:

7. Clean all gasket mating surfaces. Take care of any rust before installation.

8. Apply a 5mm bead of RTV gasket material to the groove around the pan flange. Apply the oil within 3 minutes of application.

9. Install the oil pan and torque the oil pan bolts to 48 inch lbs. (5.4 Nm).

10. Install the remaining components, start the engine and check for leaks.

4A-FE ENGINE

1. Disconnect the negative battery cable.

2. Raise the vehicle and support it safely, then drain the engine oil.

3. Remove the engine undercovers.

4. Disconnect the front exhaust pipe.

5. Remove the lower suspension crossmember and remove the engine mounting center member.

6. Remove the oil pan retaining bolts. Remove the oil pan.

To install:

7. Clean all gasket mating surfaces.

8. Apply a 5mm bead of RTV gasket material to the groove around the pan flange. Install the oil pan within 3 minutes of application.

9. Install the oil pan and torque the 19 oil pan bolts and 2 nuts to 43 inch lbs. (4.9 Nm).

10. Install the remaining components, start the engine and check for leaks.

Supra

1. Disconnect the negative battery cable. Remove the hood if necessary.

2. Raise the vehicle and support it safely. Remove the engine undercover. Drain the engine oil.

3. If equipped with automatic transmission, remove the fluid cooler hose clamp.

4. Remove the No. 1 front suspension crossmember. Remove the front exhaust pipe bracket and stiffener plates.

5. On the 7M-GTE engine, disconnect the engine oil cooler hose from the engine oil pan.

6. Remove the brake hose brackets and clips. Disconnect the intermediate shaft. Disconnect the stabilizer bar links from the lower control arms.

7. Properly support the engine assembly. Remove the engine mounting bolts. Remove the TEMS actuator assembly.

8. Remove the shock absorbers from the body. Disconnect the front suspension member.

9. Remove the oil pan retaining bolts. Remove the oil pan from the engine.

To install:

10. Clean all gasket mating surfaces. Take care of any rust before installation.

11. Install the oil pan and torque the oil pan bolts to 9 ft. lbs. (13 Nm).

12. Install the remaining components, start the engine and check for leaks.

Cressida

1. Disconnect the negative battery cable and drain the cooling system.

2. Raise and safely support the vehicle. Remove the engine undercover and drain the oil.

3. Disconnect the front exhaust pipe at the manifold and at the main tube and remove.

4. Disconnect the automatic transmission oil cooler pipe.

5. Remove the 9 bolts, ground strap, exhaust pipe stay and the engine rear end-plate and then remove the stiffener plates.

6. Loosen the bolt and disconnect the steering intermediate shaft.

7. Disconnect the front suspension crossmember at the front engine mounts. Position a floor jack under the crossmember, remove the remaining mounting bolts and then lower the crossmember.

8. Remove the pan retaining bolts and then carefully pry the pan from the cylinder block.

To install:

9. Clean all gasket mating surfaces. Take care of any rust before installation.

10. Install the oil pan and torque the oil pan bolts to 9 ft. lbs. (13 Nm).

11. Install the remaining components, start the engine and check for leaks.

Tercel

1. Disconnect the negative battery terminal. Raise the vehicle and support it safely. Drain the oil.

2. Remove the right engine undercover. Remove the sway bar and any other necessary steering linkage parts.

3. Disconnect the exhaust pipe from the manifold. Raise the engine enough to take the weight off.

4. Remove the timing belt if necessary.

5. Continue to raise the engine enough to remove the oil pan. Remove the oil pan retaining bolts. Remove the oil pan.

To install:

6. Clean all gasket mating surfaces. Take care of any rust before installation.

7. Install the oil pan and torque the oil pan bolts to 43 inch lbs. (4.9 Nm).

8. Install the remaining components, start the engine and check for leaks.

Paseo

1. Disconnect the negative battery terminal.

2. Raise the vehicle and support it safely, then drain the oil.

3. Remove the hood.

4. Remove the oil dipstick.

5. Remove the timing belt.

6. Suspend the engine with a hoist.

NOTE: Do not raise the engine more than necessary, since wiring and other components can be damaged.

7. Remove the crankshaft timing sprocket and oil pump sprocket.

8. Remove the air conditioning compressor and mounting bracket.

9. Disconnect the oxygen sensor and disconnect the front exhaust pipe.

10. Remove the 8 oil pan bolts and 2 nuts, then remove the oil pan.

To install:

11. Clean all gasket mating surfaces.

12. Apply sealant 08826-00080, or equivalent to the oil pan.

13. Install the pan within 3 minutes and torque the nuts and bolts to 74 inch lbs. (8 Nm).

14. Install the remaining components, torquing them to specifications.

15. Add oil to the engine, start it and check for leaks.

MR2

4A-GE ENGINES

1. Disconnect the negative battery cable. Raise and support the vehicle safely. Drain the engine oil.

2. Remove the exhaust manifold pipe. Remove the timing belt. Remove the crankshaft timing pulley.

3. Support the weight of the engine with a floor jack and then remove the right side engine mount.

4. Remove the oil pan retaining bolts. Remove the oil pan.

To install:

5. Clean all gasket mating surfaces. Take care of any rust before installation.

6. Apply a 5mm bead of RTV gasket material to the groove around the pan flange. Apply the oil pan within 3 minutes of application and tighten the mounting bolts and nuts to 43 inch lbs. (6 Nm).

7. Install the remaining components, start the engine and check for leaks.

3S-GTE AND 5S-FE ENGINES

1. Disconnect the negative battery cable.

2. Drain the engine oil and remove the engine undercovers.

3. Remove the right engine hood side panel.

4. Remove the brace that runs across the struts.

5. If equipped with cruise control, remove the cruise control actuator assembly and disconnect the accelerator linkage.

6. Remove the front exhaust pipe.

7. On 3S-GTE engine with air conditioning, unbolt the compressor and move it aside. Leave the refrigerant lines connected. On 5S-FE, remove the air conditioner idler pulley.

8. On 3S-GTE engine, remove the catalytic converter and the intercooler.

9. Remove the stiffener plate.

10. On 3S-GTE engine, disconnect the turbocharger outlet hose where it connects to the oil pan.

11. Remove the dipstick.

12. Remove the oil pan 17 bolts and 2 nuts that attach the oil pan to the block.

13. Insert a suitable seal cutting tool between the oil pan and the block. Work the tool around the pan to break the sealant. Remove the oil pan.

To install:

14. Clean all gasket mating surfaces. Take care of any rust before installation.

15. Apply a 5mm bead of RTV gasket material to the groove around the pan flange. Apply the oil pan within 5 minutes of application and tighten the mounting bolts and nuts to 43 inch lbs. (6 Nm).

16. Install the remaining components, start the engine and check for leaks.

Oil Pump

REMOVAL AND INSTALLATION

2VZ-FE, 3E, 3E-E and 3S-FE Engines

1. Remove the oil pan. Remove the oil strainer. On the 3E engine, remove the dipstick.

2. Raise the engine using a chain hoist. Remove the timing belt and pulleys.

3. On the 2VZ-FE engine, remove the alternator and the air conditioning compressor and bracket. Do not disconnect the refrigerant lines.

4. Remove the oil pump from the engine.

5. Installation is the reverse of the removal procedure. Clean the gasket mating surfaces. Pack the oil pump cavities with petroleum jelly. Start the engine and check for oil pressure.

5E-FE Engine

1. Remove the oil pan.

2. Remove the 9 oil pump bolts and the tension spring bracket.

3. Using a rubber mallet, carefully tap off the oil pump and the O-ring.

To install:

4. Clean the mating surfaces of old sealer material.

5. Place the O-ring in the groove. Apply sealer 08826-00080, or equivalent, to the oil pump mating surfaces and install the pump within 5 minutes of applying the sealer.

6. Torque the bolts to 65 inch lbs. (7.4 Nm).

7. Install the oil pan.

3S-GTE (Except MR2), 4A-FE, 4A-GE Engines

1. Raise and support the vehicle safely.

2. Drain the oil.

3. Remove the oil pan and the oil strainer. Remove the oil pan baffle plate on the 4A-GE engine. Remove the crankshaft pulley and the timing belt. Remove the oil dipstick guide and dipstick.

4. Remove the mounting bolts and then use a rubber mallet to carefully tap the oil pump body from the cylinder block.

To install:

5. Position a new gasket on the cylinder block.

6. Position the oil pump on the block so the teeth on the pump drive gear are engaged with the teeth of the crankshaft gear.

7. Clean the gasket mating surfaces. Pack the oil pump cavities with petroleum jelly. Start the engine and check for oil pressure.

8. Installation of the remaining components is the reverse of the removal procedure.

3S-GTE (MR2) and 5S-FE (Except Camry) Engines

1. Disconnect the negative battery cable.

2. Drain the engine oil.

3. Remove the oil pan.

4. Remove the oil pump strainer and baffle plate.

5. Connect a suitable lifting device to the engine and raise the engine a small amount.

6. Remove the timing belt.

7. Remove the No. 2 idler pulley, crankshaft timing pulley and oil pump pulley.

8. Remove the oil pump retaining bolts.

9. Remove the oil pump and gasket by carefully tapping on the

outside of the oil pump body. Discard the gasket.

NOTE: One of the oil pump bolts is longer than the rest. Make sure this bolt is identified so it may be installed in the original location.

To install:

10. Clean the gasket mating surfaces. Pack the oil pump cavities with petroleum jelly.

11. Use a new oil pump gasket. On 3S-GTE engine, torque the oil pump bolts to 69 inch lbs. (8 Nm). On 5S-FE engine, torque the bolts to 82 inch lbs. (9.3 Nm).

12. Installation of the remaining components, start the engine and check for leaks.

3VZ-FE and 5S-FE (Camry) Engines

1. Remove the oil pan.
2. Remove the oil pan baffle plate.
3. Remove the oil strainer and O-ring.
4. Remove the timing belt. On the 3VZ-FE engine, remove the No. 1 idler and the crankshaft timing pulleys.
5. Remove the alternator and the compressor. Also, remove the compressor bracket and the power steering pump adjusting bar.
6. Remove the oil pump retaining bolts.
7. With a soft-faced hammer or rubber mallet, tap the oil pump loose from the block.
8. Remove the oil pump gasket and replace a new one.

To install:

9. Clean the cylinder block and oil pump gasket contact surfaces.
10. Place a new gasket onto the cylinder block on the 4 cylinder engine. On the V6 engine, draw a 2-3mm bead of RTV sealer. Installation of the part must be done within 5 minutes of sealant application.
11. Position the oil pump onto the block and install the bolts. On the V6 engines, insert a new O-ring and then engage the spline teeth on the drive gear with the large teeth on the end of the crankshaft.
12. Tighten the oil pump mounting bolts to 7 ft. lbs. (9 Nm) on 4 cylinder engines; the bottom 2 bolts are the long ones. On the V6, tighten the 12mm bolts to 14 ft. lbs. (20 Nm) and the 14mm bolts to 30 ft. lbs. (41 Nm).
13. On the V6 engine, install the power steering belt adjusting bar, the compressor bracket and the alternator.
14. Install the timing belt.

15. Install the baffle plate on engines, if equipped.
16. Place a new O-ring on the strainer pipe outlet and install the strainer. Tighten the 4 bolts on 4 cylinder engines to 4 ft. lbs. (5.5 Nm). On V6 engines, tighten the bolt and 2 nuts to 61 inch lbs. (7 Nm).
17. Install the oil pan and refill the engine oil.
18. Start the engine and inspect for leaks.
19. Recheck the engine oil level.

7M-GE and 7M-GZE Engines

1. Remove the oil pan.
2. Remove the oil pump bolt and loosen the union nut, then remove the oil pump.

To install:

3. Install the oil pump and torque the bolt to 16 ft. lbs. (22 Nm).
4. Torque the union nut to 25 ft. lbs. (34 Nm).
5. Stake the lockwasher.
6. Install the oil pan and the remaining components.
7. Add engine oil, start and check the engine for leaks.

Rear Main Bearing Oil Seal

The seal is a 1-piece type that is pressed into a retainer that bolts onto the rear of the block. The seal rides on the perimeter of the flywheel flange.

REMOVAL AND INSTALLATION

1. Remove the transmission or transaxle.
2. Remove the clutch cover assembly and flywheel.
3. Remove the oil seal by cutting off the lip, then using a prying tool remove the seal from the seal housing.

NOTE: Do not damage the surface of the crankshaft.

To install:

4. Lubricate the lip of the seal with multipurpose grease.
5. Install the new seal by using a seal installing tool. Tap in the seal until its surface is flush with the retainer edge.
6. The remaining installation is the reverse of removal.

ENGINE COOLING

Radiator

REMOVAL AND INSTALLATION

1. Disconnect the negative battery cable.
2. Drain the cooling system.
3. On MR2, remove the front undercovers.
4. Remove the radiator hoses.
5. If equipped with an automatic transmission or transaxle, disconnect and plug the oil cooler lines.
6. Remove the ignition coil, igniter and bracket assembly on the V6 engine.
7. Remove the hood lock from the radiator upper support, as required. It may be necessary to remove the grille in order to gain access to the hood lock/radiator support assembly.
8. Remove the fan shroud, as required. If equipped with an electric fan (2 on the MR2), disconnect the wiring harness and thermo-switch connectors.
9. Disconnect the overflow hose from the thermal expansion tank and remove the tank from its bracket.
10. Unbolt and remove the radiator upper support.
11. Remove the radiator retaining bolts. Raise the radiator and cooling fan(s) from the lower supports and remove from vehicle.

To install:

12. Lower the radiator and cooling fan(s) onto the lower supports and install the retaining bolts.
13. Install the radiator upper support.
14. Mount the thermal expansion tank and connect the overflow hose.
15. Connect the cooling fan wiring harnesses and thermo-switch connectors. Install the fan shroud, if removed.
16. Install the hood lock and grille, if removed.
17. On V6 engine, install the ignition coil, igniter and bracket assembly.

18. If equipped automatic transmission or transaxle, connect the oil cooler lines.

19. Install the radiator hoses.

20. On MR2, install the front undercovers.

21. Fill the cooling system to the proper level.

22. Connect the negative battery cable. Start the engine and check for leaks.

Heater Core

NOTE: On some vehicles, the air conditioning assembly is integral with the heater assembly (including the heater core). Therefore, the heater core removal may differ from the procedures detailed below. In some case it may be necessary to remove the air conditioning/heater housing and assembly to remove the heater core. A general heater core removal and installation procedure is outlined for each vehicle. The removal steps can be altered as required.

REMOVAL AND INSTALLATION

Tercel

1990

1. Disconnect the negative battery terminal.

2. Drain the radiator.

3. Remove the ashtray and retainer.

4. Remove the rear heater duct (optional).

5. Remove the left and right side defroster ducts.

6. Remove the under tray (optional).

7. Remove the glove box.

8. Remove the main air duct.

9. Disconnect the radio and remove it.

10. Disconnect the heater control cables and remove them. Mark each cable with the control lever that it connects to.

11. Disconnect the heater hoses.

12. Remove the front and rear air ducts.

13. Disconnect the electrical connectors and vacuum hoses going to the heater unit.

14. Remove the heater bolts and remove the heater. Slide the heater to the right side of vehicle to remove it.

15. Remove the heater core.

To install:

16. Install the heater core into the housing.

17. Fill the cooling system to the proper level. Operate the heater and check for leaks.

18. Install the remaining components, start the engine and check for proper operation.

1991-94

1. Disconnect the negative battery cable and drain the cooling system.

2. Remove the safety pad from the instrument panel.

3. If equipped with air conditioning, recover the refrigerant from the air conditioning system.

4. Disconnect and cap the evaporator hoses.

5. Remove the instrument lower finish panel and disconnect the harness from the heater and air conditioning assemblies.

6. Remove the air conditioning amplifier.

7. Remove the evaporator housing by removing the 3 screws.

8. Disconnect the heater hoses from the heater core.

9. Remove the heater/air conditioning control assembly.

10. Remove the heater register center duct, instrument panel reinforcements and remove the heater assembly.

11. Remove the screws and plates from the heater assembly case halves. Remove the core from the case.

To install:

12. Install the heater core into the case and install the retainers.

13. Install the heater case assembly and instrument panel components.

14. Install the air conditioning assembly.

15. Connect all hoses and harnesses.

16. Evacuate, recharge and leak test the air conditioning system.

17. Refill the cooling system, start the engine and check for leaks.

Celica

1. Disconnect the negative battery cable.

2. Drain the cooling system.

3. Remove the gear shift knob and console, as necessary.

4. Tag and disconnect the vacuum hoses from heater housing assembly.

5. Remove the under tray or package tray from the right side of the vehicle.

6. Release the 2 clamps and remove the blower duct from the right side of the heater housing.

7. Remove any interfering air ducts.

8. Disconnect the 2 water (heater) hoses from the rear of the heater housing.

9. Tag and disconnect all wires and cables leading from the heater housing and position them aside.

10. Remove all mounting bolts and then remove the heater housing carefully toward the rear of the vehicle.

11. Remove the heater housing assembly from the vehicle. Remove any retaining brackets or hardware that may retain the heater core to the heater housing. Grasp the heater core by the end-plate and carefully pull it out of the heater housing.

To install:

12. Install the heater core into the heater housing, make sure to clean heater housing of all dirt, leaves, etc. before heater core installation.

13. Fill the cooling system to the proper level. Operate the heater and check for leaks.

14. Install the remaining components, start the engine and check for leaks after the cooling system has pressurized.

Supra

1. Disconnect the negative battery cable.

2. Drain the cooling system.

3. Remove the charcoal canister with the bracket.

4. Tag and disconnect the vacuum hoses from heater housing assembly.

5. Recover the refrigerant from the refrigeration system.

6. Remove the glove box, its cover and reinforcement.

7. Disconnect the suction tube from the cooling unit outlet fitting and cap the opening immediately to prevent contamination.

8. Disconnect the liquid tube from the cooling unit inlet fitting and cap the opening immediately to prevent contamination.

9. Remove the fuel and anti-lock brake system computers.

10. Remove the 4 screws and 3 nuts, then remove the cooling unit with the heater core.

To install:

11. Install the heater core into the heater housing, make sure to clean heater housing of all dirt, leaves, etc., before heater core installation.

12. Reverse the removal procedures, being careful not to overtorque the air conditioning fittings.

13. Fill the cooling system.

14. Operate the heating system and check for leaks.

15. Evacuate, recharge and leak test the air conditioning system.

Paseo

1. Disconnect the negative battery cable.
2. Remove the safety pad of the instrument panel.
3. If equipped with air conditioning, remove the cooling unit.
   a. Recover the refrigerant from the refrigeration system.
   b. Disconnect the suction tube from the cooling unit outlet fitting and cap the opening immediately to prevent contamination.
   c. Disconnect the liquid tube from the cooling unit inlet fitting and cap the opening immediately to prevent contamination.
   d. Remove the instrument lower finish panel.
   e. Disconnect the cooling unit wiring and remove the air conditioning amplifier.
4. Drain the cooling system.
5. Remove the heater hoses from the heater core.
6. Remove the heater control lever assembly.
7. Remove the heater duct.
8. Remove the instrument panel reinforcement braces.
9. Remove the screw and nut, then remove the heater core unit.

To install:

10. Installation is the reverse of removal. Be careful not to overtorque the air conditioning lines.
11. Fill the cooling system and check for leaks.
12. Evacuate and recharge the air conditioning system.

Camry

1. Disconnect the negative battery cable.
2. Position a suitable drain pan under the radiator, and partially drain the cooling system.
3. Remove the heater protector by removing the screws and the 2 clips.
4. Remove the heater hoses from the heater pipes.
5. Remove the 3 screws and the 3 clamps that secure the heater core, then remove the core.

To install:

6. Install the heater core into the heater housing, make sure to clean heater housing of all dirt, leaves, etc., before heater core installation.
7. Fill the cooling system to the proper level.

8. Install the remaining components, reconnect the battery, then start and warm the engine, making sure that the cooling system stays full.
9. Stop the engine, pressurize the cooling system and check for leaks. Check the heater operation.

Cressida

1. Disconnect the negative battery cable.
2. Drain the cooling system.
3. Remove the hood release and the fuel lid release levers.
4. Remove the left instrument panel undercover and lower center pad. Remove the finish plate, then remove the radio assembly.
5. Remove the heater control knobs, heater control panel and ashtray.
6. Remove the right side instrument panel undercover, glove box door and glove box.
7. Remove the front pillar garnish, cluster finish panel and instrument cluster gauge assembly.
8. Remove the safety pad and side defroster hose. Remove the heater assembly air ducts.
9. Remove the lower pad reinforcement and remove the front seats. Remove the center console assembly and the cowl side trim panel.
10. Remove the scuff plate, then position the floor carpeting aside. Remove the rear heater duct, if equipped, and heater control assembly.
11. Disconnect the heater hoses from the heater core assembly and remove the heater core grommet.
12. Remove the blower motor duct, center duct and instrument panel brace. Remove the heater core assembly from the vehicle.
13. Remove the nuts securing the heater core to the heater core assembly and remove the heater core.

To install:

14. Install the heater core into the heater housing, make sure to clean heater housing of all dirt, leaves, etc., before heater core installation.
15. Fill the cooling system to the proper level. Operate the heater and check for leaks.
16. Install the remaining components, start the engine and check for leaks after the cooling system has pressurized.

Corolla

1. Disconnect the negative battery cable.
2. Drain the cooling system.
3. Remove the center console, scuff plate and front seats if necessary.
4. Position the floor carpet aside and remove the heater duct.
5. Remove the under tray, glove box and blower duct.
6. On the station wagon and sedan vehicles, remove the following components:
   a. Remove the heater control knobs and lens. Remove the cluster lower center panel finish, ashtray and heater control assembly.
   b. Remove the instrument cluster finish panel, radio and air ducts.
7. On the coupe and liftback vehicles, remove the following components:
   a. The instrument cluster finish panel, instrument cluster, radio trim panel and radio.
   b. Ashtray, heater control knobs, heater control panel, heater control assembly and air duct.
8. Disconnect the heater hoses from the heater core assembly and remove the heater hose grommet.
9. Remove the heater core assembly retaining screws and remove the heater core assembly from the vehicle.
10. Remove the heater core from the heater core assembly.

To install:

11. Install the heater core into the heater housing, make sure to clean heater housing of all dirt, leaves, etc., before heater core installation.
12. Fill the cooling system to the proper level. Operate the heater and check for leaks.
13. Install the remaining components, start the engine and check for leaks after the cooling system has pressurized.

MR2

1. Disconnect the negative battery cable.
2. Drain the engine cooling system. Recover the refrigerant from the air conditioning system. Plug the open refrigerant lines to prevent contamination.
3. Remove the door scuff plate and kick panels.

--- CAUTION ---

Use extreme caution when working around the SRS system. Accidental air bag deployment may occur and cause personal injury. Work must be started after approximately 90 seconds or longer from the time the ignition switch is turned to the Lock position and the negative battery terminal cable is disconnected from the battery. The air bag system is equipped with a backup power source so that if work is started within 90 seconds of disconnecting the battery cable, the air bag may be deployed.

4. Remove the steering wheels and column cover.
5. Remove the rear console box, console upper panel and console box.
6. Remove the instrument panel lower finish panel and backing plate.
7. Remove the heater duct.
8. Remove the combination switch from the steering column and remove the turn signal bracket.
9. Remove the glove box undercover and glove box assembly.
10. Remove the center cluster finish panel.
11. Remove the instrument cluster finish panel by inserting a taped suitable tool under the panel and pry outward.
12. Remove the instrument panel, pull out and disconnect any harnesses.
13. Remove the radio, heater control, ashtray retainer and clock.
14. Remove the side defroster nozzle and bracket.
15. Disconnect the steering column and remove.
16. Remove the instrument panel retainers and carefully remove the panel from the vehicle.
17. Disconnect the heater hoses.
18. Remove the heater case retainers and remove the assembly from the vehicle.
19. Remove the case half screws and clips. Separate the 2 halves and remove the heater core.
To install:
20. Install the heater core. Make sure the gaskets are in place. Assemble the case.
21. Install the heater assembly and case retainers.
22. Connect the heater hoses. Fill the cooling system and check for leaks before installing the instrument panel.
23. Install the instrument panel and retainers. Be careful not to damage the panel.

24. Connect the steering column.
25. Install the side defroster nozzle and bracket.
26. Install the radio, heater control, ashtray retainer and clock.
27. Install the instrument cluster and connect harnesses.
28. Install the instrument cluster finish panel by snapping into place.
29. Install the center cluster finish panel.
30. Install the glove box undercover and glove box assembly.
31. Install the turn signal bracket and combination switch to the steering column.
32. Install the heater duct.
33. Install the instrument panel lower finish panel and backing plate.
34. Install the rear console box, console upper panel and console box.
35. Install the steering wheel and column cover.
36. Install the door scuff plate and kick panels.
37. Evacuate, recharge and leak test the air conditioning system.
38. Connect the negative battery cable.

Water Pump

REMOVAL AND INSTALLATION

--- CAUTION ---

To avoid personal injury, do not start work until at least 90 seconds after the ignition key is turned OFF and the negative battery terminal is disconnected. This is to avoid accidental air bag deployment.

1. Disconnect the negative battery cable.
2. Drain the cooling system.
3. Remove the fan shroud retaining bolts, then remove the fan and shroud, if equipped (RWD vehicles). Loosen and remove all necessary drive belts.
4. Remove all necessary components in order to gain access to the water pump retaining bolts and nuts, or to gain access to the timing belt covers. In some cases, it may be necessary to raise the engine from the mounts.
5. On some vehicles, it will be necessary to remove the timing covers. On the Camry, Celica and MR2, remove the timing belt and pulleys.
6. Remove the oil cooler on the 3S-GTE engine.
7. As required, remove the complete air cleaner assembly.
8. Remove all hoses and inlet pipe from the water pump assembly.

9. Remove the water pump retaining bolts. Remove the water pump/fan assembly.
To install:
10. Installation is the reverse of removal. Always use a new gasket, O-ring or sealant between the pump body and its mounting.
11. Check for leaks after water pump installation is completed.

Thermostat

REMOVAL AND INSTALLATION

1. Disconnect the negative battery cable. Drain the cooling system.
2. Remove the upper radiator or water inlet hose from the thermostat housing.
3. Disconnect the electrical wire from the thermo-switch on the thermostat housing, if equipped.
4. Remove the thermostat housing retaining bolts. Remove the thermostat housing from the engine. Note location of jiggle valve.
5. Remove the thermostat.
To install:
6. Clean the gasket mating surfaces. Be sure to use a new thermostat gasket. Be sure the thermostat is installed with the spring pointing down (toward engine block) and the jiggle valve facing up. On type A thermostat, align the jiggle valve with the protrusion on the thermostat housing. The jiggle valve may be aligned within 5-10 degrees on either side of the protrusion. On type B thermostat, align the jiggle valve with the upper stud bolt in the housing.

Cooling System Bleeding

1. Fill the radiator with the proper type of coolant.
2. Loosen a fitting in a coolant passage located near the highest point on the engine. A sending unit or vacuum switching valve for example. Apply thread sealing tape or equivalent to the fitting threads. Fill the radiator until coolant comes from the hole and tighten the fitting.
3. With the radiator cap off, start the engine and allow it to run and reach normal operating temperature.
4. Run the heater at full force and with the temperature lever in the hot position. Be sure the heater control valve is functioning.
5. Shut the engine off and recheck the coolant level, refill as necessary. On 2VZ-FE engine, release the air

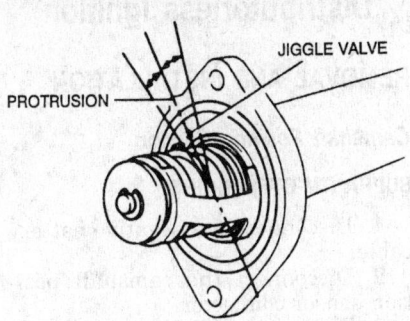

Thermostat jiggle valve alignment

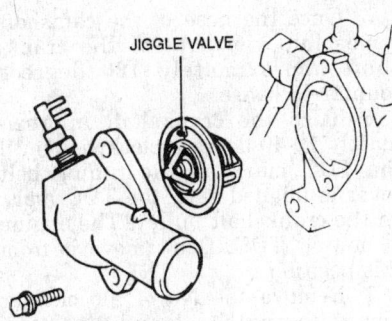

Typical thermostat assembly

from the cooling system by loosening the air relief union bolt about 4-5 turns.

ENGINE ELECTRICAL

——— CAUTION ———
To avoid personal injury, wait 90 seconds or longer after disconnecting the negative battery cable

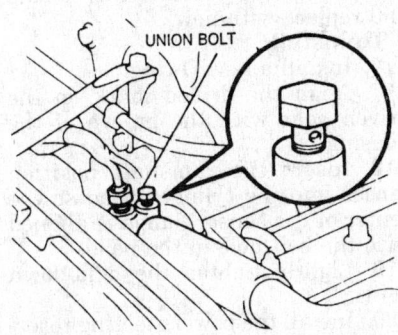

Cooling system air bleed location — 2VZ-FE engine

before attempting to remove or service any electrical component. The air bag control system is equipped with a backup power source that remains charged for a minimum of 90 seconds after the negative battery cable is disconnected. Attempting to remove or service an electrical component without allowing the time interval to elapse may result in deployment of the air bag and possible personal injury.

NOTE: Disconnecting the negative battery cable on some vehicles may interfere with the functions of the on-board computer systems and may require the computer to undergo a relearning process, once the negative battery cable is reconnected.

Distributor

REMOVAL

1. Disconnect the negative battery cable.
2. Disconnect the electrical leads and spark plug wires from the distributor.
3. Remove the waterproof cover, if installed.
4. On the Supra with the 7M-GE engine, remove the oil filler cap and rotate the crankshaft clockwise until the nose of the camshaft is visible through the hole. Turn the crankshaft counterclockwise 120 degrees. Now, turn it clockwise 10-40 degrees until the TDC marks on the front cover and the crankshaft pulley are aligned.
5. Remove the intercooler on the 3S-GTE engine.
6. Matchmark the distributor housing and the engine block and the rotor to the distributor housing; this will aid in correct positioning of the distributor during installation.
7. Remove the hold-down bolts and pull the distributor from the engine.

INSTALLATION

Timing Not Disturbed

1. Install a new distributor housing O-ring. Apply a thin coat of clean engine oil to the new O-ring before installation.
2. Insert the distributor in the block and align the matchmarks on the housing and the rotor made during removal.

3. Install the distributor hold-down bolts.
4. On 3S-GTE engine, install the intercooler.
5. Install the waterproof cover, if removed.
6. Connect the electrical leads and spark plug wires to the distributor.
7. Connect the negative battery cable.
8. Set the ignition timing.

Timing Disturbed

NOTE: Read this service procedure carefully — before starting this repair.

1. Set the engine at TDC of the No. 1 cylinder's firing stroke. This can be accomplished by removing the No. 1 spark plug and turning the engine by hand with a finger over the spark plug hole. As No. 1 is coming up on its firing stroke, pressure will be felt. Make sure the timing marks are set as follows:
   a. On the 4A-GE engine, align the groove on the crankshaft pulley with the 0 mark on the No. 1 timing cover.
   b. For all, except the Supra (7M-GE engine), Cressida, MR2, Corolla (4A-GE engine) and Camry, coat the spiral gear and governor shaft tip with clean engine oil. Align the protrusion on the distributor housing with the pin on the spiral gear drill mark side. Insert the distributor and align the center of the flange with the bolt hole on the cylinder head. Tighten the bolts.
   c. On the Supra (7M-GE engine) and Cressida, align the drilled mark on the driven gear with the groove on the distributor housing. Insert the distributor and align the stationary flange center with bolt hole in the head. Tighten the bolts.
   d. On Celica and Camry, turn the crankshaft clockwise until the slot in the forward end of the No. 1 camshaft (front of vehicle) is positioned in the vertical position. Lightly coat a new O-ring with the engine oil and slide it into position. Align the drilled mark or cut-out, on the coupling with the notch of the shaft housing. Insert the distributor into the cylinder head so the center of the flange is aligned with the bolt hole on the cylinder head.
   e. On the MR2, except 5S-FE engine, and the Corolla with 4A-GE engine, install a new O-ring. Align the drilled mark on the distributor driven gear with the cavity of the housing. On the MR2 with 5S-FE

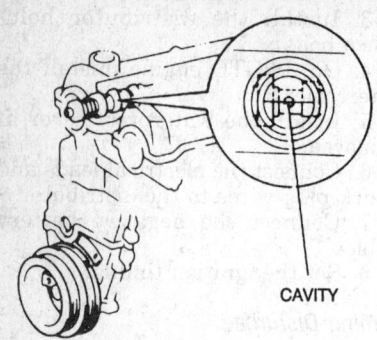

Setting the No. 1 cylinder to TDC of the compression stroke — 4A-GE engine

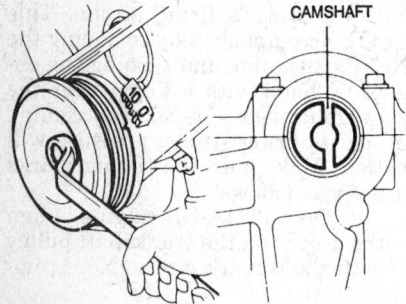

Positioning the No. 1 camshaft — 3S-FE, and 3S-GTE engines

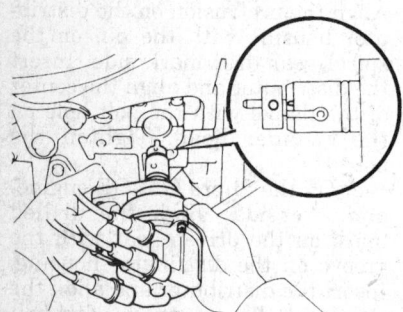

Distributor alignment — 3S-FE engines

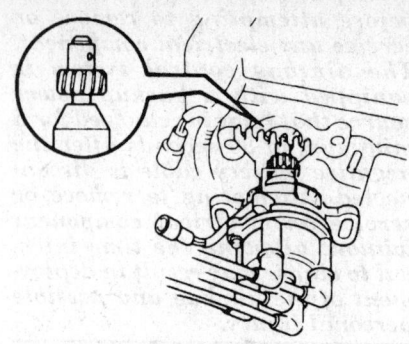

Align the drilled mark on the drive gear with the cavity of the housing — 4A-GE engine

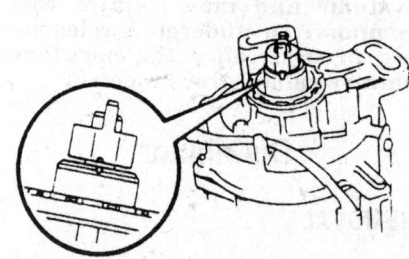

Align the marks on the coupling and the housing — 2VZ-FE engine

Distributor installation — 2VZ-FE engine

Distributorless Ignition

REMOVAL AND INSTALLATION

Camshaft Position Sensor

SUPRA (7M-GTE) ENGINE

1. Disconnect the negative battery cable.
2. Disconnect the camshaft position sensor connector.
3. Remove the oil filler cap.
4. Look into the oil filler opening and rotate the crankshaft clockwise until the the nose of the camshaft can be seen.
5. Once the nose of the camshaft comes into view, rotate the crankshaft approximately 120 degrees counterclockwise.
6. Turn the crankshaft approximately 10-40 degrees clockwise until the TDC mark on the timing belt cover is aligned with the TDC mark on the crankshaft pulley. The engine is now at TDC. Don't move it from this position.
7. Remove the No. 4 air cleaner pipe with the No. 1 and No. 2 air cleaner hoses.
8. Disconnect the 3 air hoses and the PCV hose.
9. Disconnect the air flow meter connector.
10. Disconnect the power steering idle up air hose.
11. Remove the air flow meter mounting bolt and attendant hose clamps. Remove the No. 7 air cleaner hose, air flow meter and air cleaner cap as a unit.
12. Unbolt and remove the power steering reservoir tank. Leave the hoses connected and move the tank aside.
13. Remove the camshaft position sensor hold-down bolt.
14. Withdraw the camshaft position sensor from the cylinder head.
15. Remove the camshaft position sensor O-ring. Discard the O-ring and replace with new.

To install:
16. Install a new O-ring.
17. Align the drilled mark on the driven gear with the groove of the housing.
18. Insert the camshaft position sensor into the cylinder head so the center of the sensor flange is aligned with the bolt hole in the head.
19. Lightly tighten the hold-down bolt.
20. Install the power steering reservoir tank.
21. Install the air cleaner cap, air flow meter and No. 7 air cleaner hose.

engine, turn the crankshaft clockwise until the slot in the forward end of the No. 1 camshaft, front of vehicle, is positioned in the vertical position. Then, align the cut-out portion of the coupling with the groove in the housing. Insert the distributor and align the center of the flange with the bolt hole on the cylinder head. Tighten the hold-down bolts.

f. On the Corolla (4A-FE and 7A-FE engines), install a new O-ring. Align the protrusion on the distributor housing with the groove

of the coupling side. On the 4A-FE and 7A-FE engines, align the center of the flange with the bolt hole on the cylinder head. Tighten the hold-down bolts.

g. On Camry with the V6 engine, align the cut-out marks of the coupling and the housing and then insert the distributor so the line on the housing and the cut-out on the distributor attachment cap are aligned. Tighten the hold-down bolts.

2. Connect the spark plug wires; check the idle speed and the ignition timing.

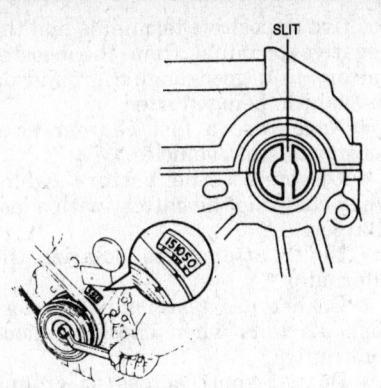

Positioning the No. 1 camshaft — 5S-FE engine

Install the mounting bolt and tighten the clamps.

22. Connect the power steering idle up air hose.

23. Connect the air flow meter connector.

24. Connect the PCV hose and 3 air hoses.

25. Install the air cleaner pip and No. 1 and No. 2 air cleaner hoses.

26. Connect the camshaft position sensor connector.

27. Start and warm the engine. Adjust the timing.

Ignition Timing

ADJUSTMENT

3E Engine

1. Disconnect the vacuum hose from the sub-diaphragm and plug it. It is the one closest to the distributor cap.

2. With the engine idling at a maximum of 950 rpm and the electric fan OFF, check the timing. It should be 3 degrees BTDC.

3. Loosen the hold-down bolt and adjust the timing, as required.

4. Retighten the hold-down bolt and recheck the ignition timing.

3E-E Engine

1. Warm the engine to normal operating temperature.

2. Open the lid on the check connector and short the connector at terminals T and E_1.

3. Check that the idle speed remains at 800 rpm.

4. Check that the ignition timing is 10 degrees BTDC at idle with the cooling fan OFF.

5. If necessary, loosen the distributor bolts so the distributor can be turned. Aim the timing light at the marks on the crankshaft pulley and slowly turn the distributor until the correct timing mark is aligned. Tighten the distributor bolts.

6. Unshort the connector.

All Remaining Engines

1. Connect a timing light to the engine.

2. Start the engine and run it at idle. Remove the rubber cap from the check connector or open the lid.

3. Short the connector at terminals T or TE_1 and E_1.

4. Make sure the engine is running at the specified idle for checking the ignition timing. The electric fan, if equipped, must be OFF and the transmission in **N**.

4A-FE engine: 800 rpm
7A-FE engine: 800 rpm
4A-GE engine: 800 rpm
5E-FE engine: 750 ± 50 rpm
7M-GE engine: 700 rpm
7M-GTE engine: 650 rpm
All remaining engines: 700 ± 50 rpm

5. Loosen the distributor pinch bolt so the distributor can be turned.

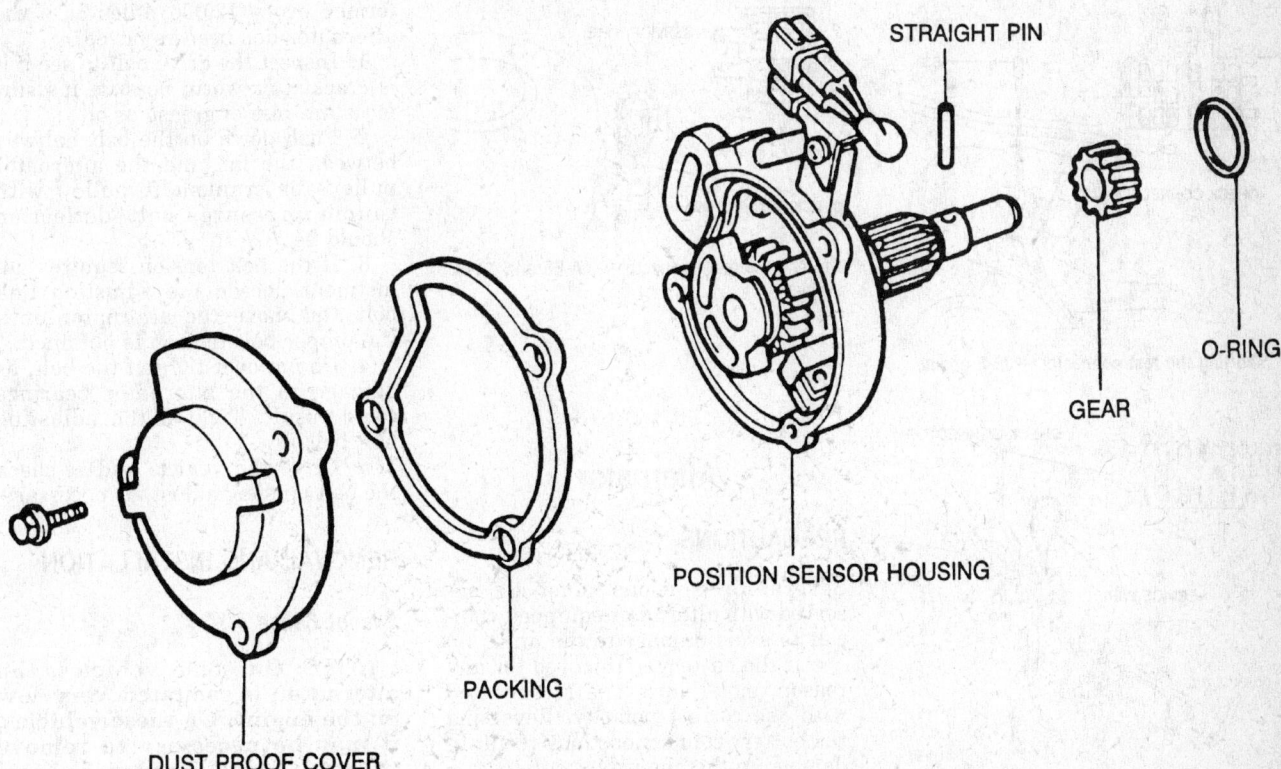

Cam position sensor exploded view — 7M-GTE engine

Set the ignition timing at 10 degrees BTDC.

NOTE: The 7M-GTE engine utilizes a cam position sensor in place of a distributor. Turn this the same as a distributor.

6. Tighten the distributor pinch bolt and unshort the connector.

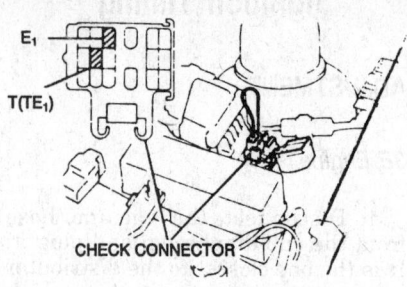

Shorting the test connector — 7M-GE and 7M-GTE (Supra) engines

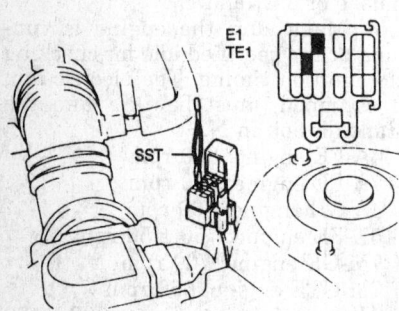

Shorting the test connector — 2VZ-FE and 3VZ-FE engines

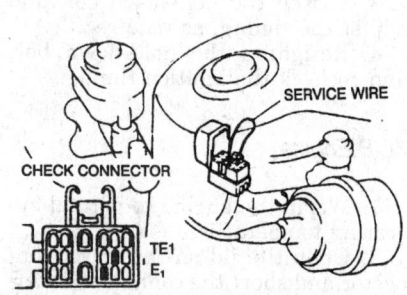

Shorting the test connector — 7M-GE engine (Cressida)

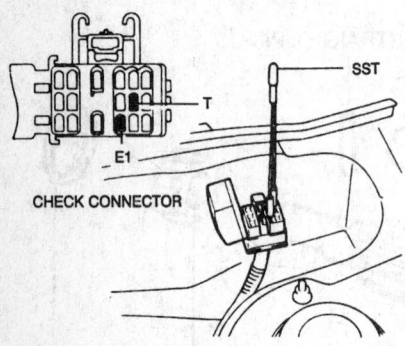

Shorting the test connector — 3E-E engine

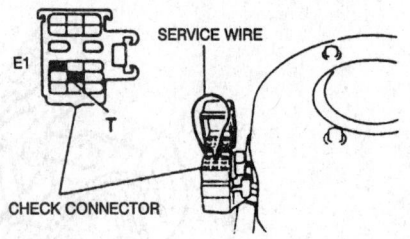

Shorting the test connector — 4A-FE and 7A-FE engines

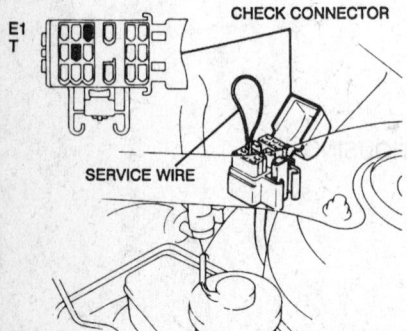

Shorting the test connector — 3S-FE and 3S-GTE engines

Alternator

PRECAUTIONS

Several precautions must be observed with alternator equipped vehicles to avoid damage to the unit.

• If the battery is removed for any reason, make sure it is reconnected with the correct polarity. Reversing the battery connections may result in damage to the one-way rectifiers.

• When utilizing a booster battery as a starting aid, always connect the positive to positive terminals and the negative terminal from the booster battery to a good engine ground on the vehicle being started.

• Never use a fast charger as a booster to start vehicles.

• Disconnect the battery cables when charging the battery with a fast charger.

• Never attempt to polarize the alternator.

• Do not use test lamps of more than 12 volts when checking diode continuity.

• Do not short across or ground any of the alternator terminals.

• The polarity of the battery, alternator and regulator must be matched and considered before making any electrical connections within the system.

• Never separate the alternator on an open circuit. Make sure all connections within the circuit are clean and tight.

• Disconnect the battery ground terminal when performing any service on electrical components.

• Disconnect the battery if arc welding is to be done on the vehicle.

BELT TENSION ADJUSTMENT

Inspection and adjustment to the alternator drive belt should be performed every 12,000 miles or if the alternator has been removed.

1. Inspect the drive belt to see if it is cracked or worn; be sure it's surfaces are free of grease or oil.

2. Push down on the belt halfway between the fan and the alternator pulleys or crankshaft pulley with thumb pressure; belt deflection should be $3/8$-$1/2$ in.

3. If the belt tension requires adjustment, loosen the adjusting link bolt and move the alternator until the proper belt tension is obtained.

4. Do not over-tighten the belt, as damage to the alternator bearings could result. Tighten the adjusting link bolt.

5. Drive the vehicle and re-check the belt tension; adjust, as necessary.

REMOVAL AND INSTALLATION

Except Celica 4WD

NOTE: On some vehicles, the alternator is mounted very low on the engine. On these vehicles, it may be necessary to remove the gravel shield and work from under the vehicle in order to gain access to the alternator.

CHECK CONNECTOR

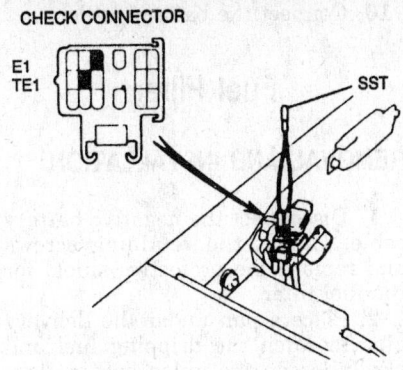

Shorting the test connector — 5S-FE engine

CHECK CONNECTOR

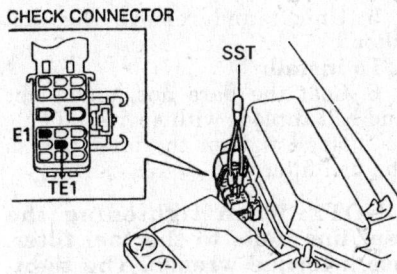

Check connector — Paseo

1. Disconnect the negative battery cable.
2. Remove the air cleaner, if necessary, to gain access to the alternator.
3. Remove the power steering or air conditioning drive belts, as required.
4. Unfasten the bolts which attach the adjusting link to the alternator. Remove the alternator drive belt.

NOTE: On the V6 engine, remove the engine mounting stays.

5. Unfasten and tag the alternator bolt and withdraw the alternator from its bracket.
6. Installation is the reverse of the removal procedure. After installing the alternator, adjust the belt tension.

Celica 4WD

1. Disconnect the negative battery cable.
2. Remove the lower alternator duct.
3. Loosen the idler pulley bolt.
4. Loosen the adjusting bolt and remove the drive belt.
5. Disconnect the alternator connectors, alternator lead wire, air conditioning compressor connector,

water temperature switch connector and oxygen sensor connector.
6. Unbolt and disconnect the ground strap and engine wire from the brackets.
7. Unbolt and remove the alternator bracket.
8. Unbolt and remove the alternator.
9. Remove the upper alternator duct and disconnect the lead wire.

To install:
10. Connect the lead wire and attach the alternator duct.
11. Install the alternator. Torque the 12mm bolt to 14 ft. lbs. (19 Nm) and the 14mm bolt to 38 ft. lbs. (52 Nm).
12. Install the alternator bracket. Torque the turbine outlet elbow bolt to 32 ft. lbs. (43 Nm) and the bracket bolt to 39 ft. lbs. (29 Nm).
13. Install the engine wire and ground strap.
14. Connect the alternator and engine wiring.
15. Install the drive belt and adjust the drive belt tension.
16. Install the lower alternator duct.
17. Connect the negative battery cable.

Starter

REMOVAL AND INSTALLATION

1. Disconnect the negative battery cable. Disconnect the cable which runs from the starter to the battery, at the battery end.
2. Remove the air cleaner assembly, if necessary, to gain access to the starter.
3. If equipped with an automatic transmission/transaxle, it may be necessary to disconnect the throttle linkage connecting rod or the transmission/transaxle oil filler tube.
4. On the Camry with a V6 engine, remove the igniter bracket. On Celica with 3S-GTE engine, remove the engine compartment relay box and the battery. On Celica with 4A-FE engine, remove the lower suspension crossmember and the air cleaner cap. On Celica with 5S-FE engine, cruise control and ABS, remove the engine compartment relay box and the cruise control actuator. On 1990-91 Corolla with 4A-GE engine, remove both engine undercovers, front exhaust pipe and electric cooling fan.
5. Remove the cruise control actuator, if equipped.
6. Label and disconnect all the wiring at the starter.

7. Remove the starter retaining bolts and remove the starter from the vehicle.
To install:
8. Install the starter. Torque the starter bolts to 29 ft. lbs. (13 Nm).
9. Reconnect all wiring. Install the cruise control actuator, if equipped.
10. Install all necessary components that were removed for starter assembly removal.
11. Reconnect the battery cable. Check starter for proper operation.

FUEL SYSTEM

— CAUTION —
To avoid personal injury and accidental deployment of the air bag, work must be started after about 90 seconds or longer from the time the ignition switch is turned to the LOCK position and the battery cable is disconnected from the battery.

Fuel System Service Precautions

Safety is the most important factor when performing not only fuel system maintenance but any type of maintenance. Failure to conduct maintenance and repairs in a safe manner may result in serious personal injury or death. Maintenance and testing of the vehicle's fuel system components can be accomplished safely and effectively by adhering to the following rules and guidelines.
• To avoid the possibility of fire and personal injury, always disconnect the negative battery cable unless the repair or test procedure requires that battery voltage be applied.
• Always relieve the fuel system pressure prior to disconnecting any fuel system component (injector, fuel rail, pressure regulator, etc.), fitting or fuel line connection. Exercise extreme caution whenever relieving fuel system pressure to avoid exposing skin, face and eyes to fuel spray. Please be advised that fuel under pressure may penetrate the skin or any part of the body that it contacts.
• Always place a shop towel or cloth around the fitting or connection prior to loosening to absorb any excess fuel due to spillage. Ensure that all fuel spillage (should it occur) is

quickly removed from engine surfaces. Ensure that all fuel soaked cloths or towels are deposited into a suitable waste container.

- Always keep a dry chemical (Class B) fire extinguisher near the work area.
- Do not allow fuel spray or fuel vapors to come into contact with a spark or open flame.
- Always use a backup wrench when loosening and tightening fuel line connection fittings. This will prevent unnecessary stress and torsion to fuel line piping. Always follow the proper torque specifications.
- Always replace worn fuel fitting O-rings with new. Do not substitute fuel hose or equivalent where fuel pipe is installed.

RELIEVING FUEL SYSTEM PRESSURE

NOTE: When disconnecting a fuel line, a large amount of fuel may leak from the connection.

1. Remove the fuel filler cap.
2. Place a container under the connection to be disconnected.
3. Place a shop towel on the connection, then slowly loosen the connection.
4. Completely disconnect the connection and plug with a rubber plug. Install the filler cap.

Fuel Tank

REMOVAL AND INSTALLATION

Carbureted Engine

1. Disconnect the negative battery cable. Relieve the fuel pressure.
2. Drain the fuel using an approved pump and container.
3. Label and disconnect the fuel filler, breather, tank-to-evaporator, filler hose and tank-to-return pipe hoses.
4. Raise the vehicle and support safely. Disconnect the tank wiring and remove the undercover, if equipped.
5. Place a floor jack under the tank, remove the retaining bolts and lower the tank far enough to disconnect any hoses and electrical connectors still connected.
To install:
6. Raise the tank with the jack and connect the hoses and electrical connectors. Install the retaining

bolts. Torque the retainer to 15 ft. lbs. (20 Nm).
7. Connect the wiring and fuel hoses.
8. Connect the breather hose and fuel filler hose.
9. Connect the battery cable, fill the tank with fuel and check for leaks.

Fuel Injected Engine

1. Disconnect the negative battery cable. Relieve the fuel system pressure.
2. Drain the tank with an approved pump and container.
3. Raise the vehicle and support safely. Remove the rear and center exhaust pipes.
4. Remove the driveshaft for 4WD and RWD vehicles. Disconnect the fuel filler and air breather hose.
5. Disconnect the feed, return and evaporative hoses.
6. Disconnect the parking brake cable bracket and return spring.
7. Disconnect the tank harness connectors.
8. Place a floor jack under the tank and remove the tank retainers. Lower the tank and disconnect any wiring or hoses.
To install:
9. Raise the tank into position and install the tank retainers. Torque the retainers to 15 ft. lbs. (20 Nm).
10. Connect the tank harnesses and hoses.
11. Connect the parking brake cable bracket and return spring.
12. Connect the feed, return and evaporative hoses.
13. Install the driveshaft, if removed. Connect the fuel filler and air breather hoses.
14. Install the rear and center exhaust pipes.
15. Refill the tank and check for leaks.

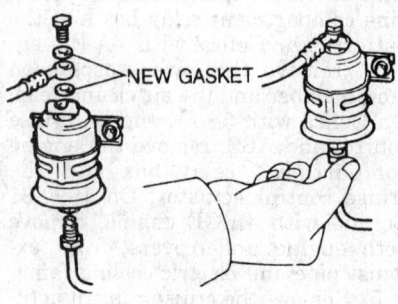

Fuel filter assembly

NEW GASKET

16. Connect the battery cable.

Fuel Filter

REMOVAL AND INSTALLATION

1. Disconnect the negative battery cable. Unbolt the retaining screws and remove the protective shield for the fuel filter.
2. Place a pan under the delivery pipe to catch the dripping fuel and slowly loosen the union bolt or flare nut to bleed off the fuel pressure.
3. Drain the remaining fuel.
4. Disconnect and plug the inlet line.
5. Unbolt and remove the fuel filter.
To install:
6. Coat the flare nut, union nut and bolt threads with engine oil.
7. Hand tighten the inlet line to the fuel filter.

NOTE: When tightening the fuel line bolts to the fuel filter, use a torque wrench. The tightening torque is very important, as under or over tightening may cause fuel leakage. Insure that there is no fuel line interference and that there is sufficient clearance between it and any other parts.

8. Install the fuel filter and then tighten the inlet bolt to 22 ft. lbs. (30 Nm).
9. Reconnect the delivery pipe using new gaskets and then tighten the union bolt to 22 ft. lbs. (30 Nm).
10. Run the engine for a few minutes and check for any fuel leaks.
11. Install the protective shield.

Mechanical Fuel Pump

The 3E engines use a mechanical type fuel pump.

PRESSURE TESTING

1. Remove the line which runs from the fuel pump to the carburetor.
2. Attach a pressure gauge to the outlet side of the pump.
3. Run the engine and check the pressure.
4. Check the pressure. It should be 2.6-3.5 psi.
5. If the pressure is below the specifications, check for restrictions or replace the pump.
6. Reconnect the carburetor line.

REMOVAL AND INSTALLATION

1. Disconnect and plug the fuel lines to the pump.
2. Remove the nuts which hold the pump to the cylinder head.
3. Remove the pump assembly.
4. Installation is the reverse of removal. Always use a new gasket when installing a fuel pump.

Electric Fuel Pump

PRESSURE TESTING

NOTE: Do not operate the fuel pump unless it is immersed in gasoline and connected to its resistor.

1. With the ignition switch in the **OFF** position, disconnect the negative battery terminal.
2. Relieve the fuel pressure and disconnect the fuel connection at the fuel filter or cold start injector, using a shop towel to catch spilled fuel.
3. Install a fuel pressure gauge, using 2 new gaskets.
4. Reconnect the negative battery terminal.
5. Using a jumper wire, connect terminals **B+** and **FP** at the check connector.

NOTE: The check connector is a small plastic box with a flip-up lid; it is found near the strut tower or battery. The box is roughly the same size and shape for every engine and terminals FP and B+ are in the same location.

6. Turn the ignition switch **ON** and read the fuel pressure gauge.
7. Turn the ignition switch **OFF** and remove the jumper wire.
8. Relieve the fuel pressure and remove the gauge, catching the spilled fuel with a shop towel.

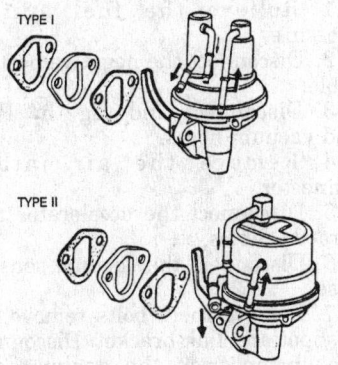

Mechanical fuel pump styles

9. Use new gaskets and connect the fuel line.
10. Reconnect the negative battery cable.

REMOVAL AND INSTALLATION

The fuel pump is mounted inside the fuel tank on all vehicles. On all vehicles except the Celica (non-turbocharged engine) and 1991-94 Tercel, removal of the fuel tank is necessary to remove the fuel pump. On Celica non-turbocharged and 1991-94 Tercel, access to the pump is

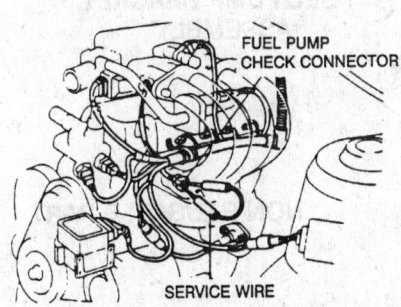

Shorting the fuel pump check connector

gained by removing the rear seat cushion.

Except Celica Non-Turbocharged, MR2 and 1991-94 Tercel

1. Disconnect the negative battery cable.
2. Drain the fuel from the tank and then remove the fuel tank.
3. Remove the bolts and then pull the fuel pump bracket up and out of the fuel tank.
4. Remove the mounting nuts then tag and disconnect the wires at the fuel pump.
5. Pull the fuel pump out of the lower side of the bracket. Disconnect the pump from the fuel hose.
6. Remove the rubber cushion and the clip. Disconnect the fuel pump filter from the pump.
7. Installation is in the reverse order of removal procedure. Use a new fuel bracket gasket.

Celica Non-Turbocharged and 1991-94 Tercel

1. Disconnect the negative battery cable.
2. Remove the rear seat cushion.
3. Remove the 5 retaining screws and floor service hole cover.

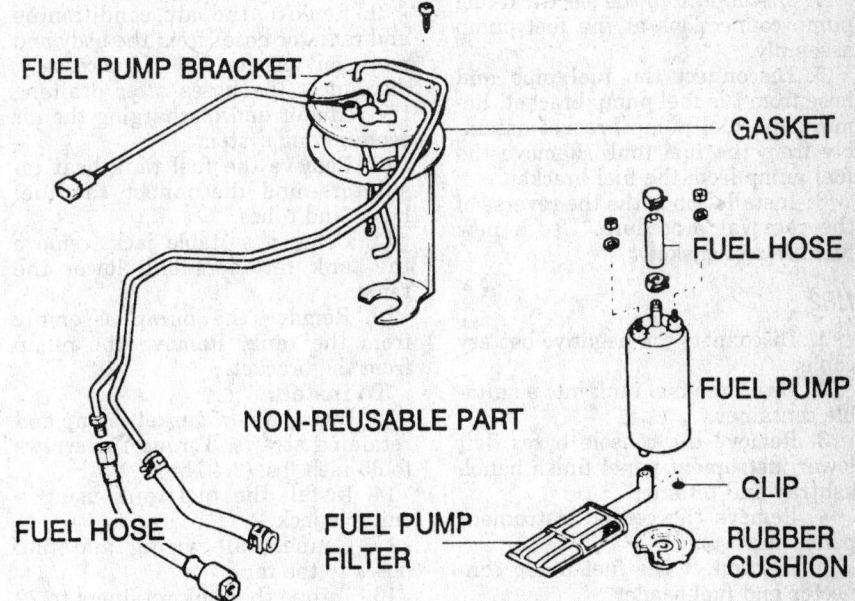

Fuel pump assembly — except Celica non-turbo

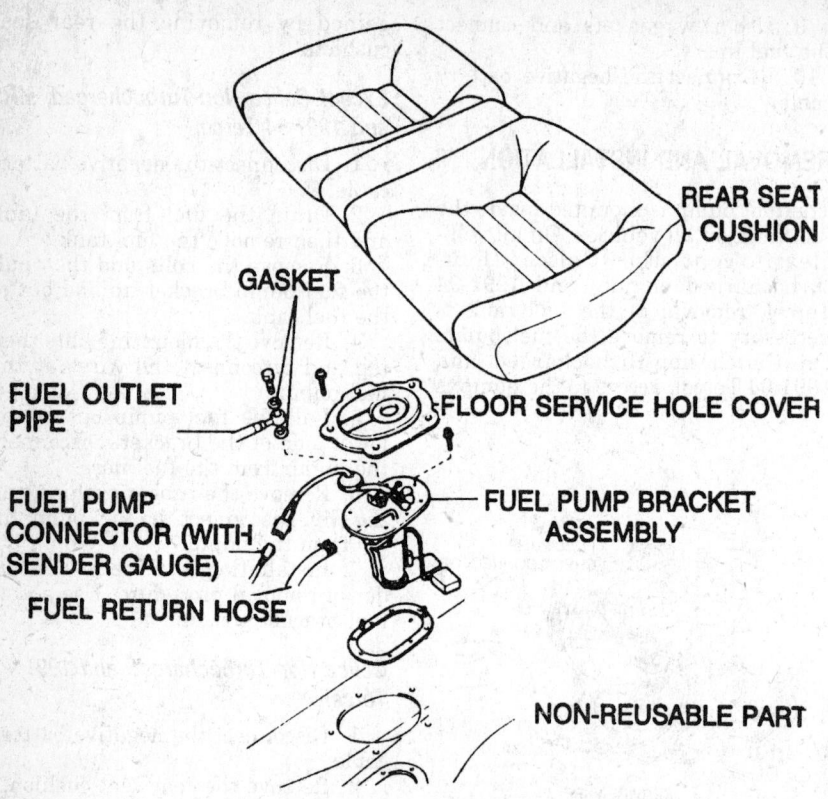

GASKET

REAR SEAT CUSHION

FUEL OUTLET PIPE

FLOOR SERVICE HOLE COVER

FUEL PUMP CONNECTOR (WITH SENDER GAUGE)

FUEL PUMP BRACKET ASSEMBLY

FUEL RETURN HOSE

NON-REUSABLE PART

Fuel pump assembly — Celica non-turbo

4. Disconnect all the electrical fuel pump connections at the fuel pump assembly.

5. Disconnect the fuel pipe and hose from the fuel pump bracket. Remove the fuel pump bracket assembly from the fuel tank. Remove the fuel pump from the fuel bracket.

6. Installation is the the reverse of the removal procedure. Use a new fuel bracket gasket.

MR2

1. Disconnect the negative battery cable.

2. Drain the fuel tank into a suitable container.

3. Remove the console boxes, left lower instrument panel finish panel, ashtray and retainer.

4. Remove the center instrument panel finish panel.

5. Disconnect the fuel pump connector and fuel sender.

6. Remove the 2 screws and floor service hole cover.

7. Remove the engine undercovers, front luggage undercover and fuel tank protectors.

8. Remove the parking brake intermediate lever and center floor crossmember.

9. Remove the air conditioning and radiator hoses from the body and move out of the way. If necessary, disconnect the hoses after draining the radiator and discharging the air conditioning system.

10. Remove the fuel tank heat insulators and disconnect the fuel hoses and tubes.

11. Using a suitable jack, remove the tank retainers and lower the tank.

12. Remove the pump assembly from the tank. Remove the pump from the bracket.

To install:

13. Install a new gasket, pump and retaining screws. Torque the screws to 35 inch lbs. (3.4 Nm).

14. Install the fuel tank using a suitable jack.

15. Connect all wiring and fuel hoses to the tank.

16. Torque the tank retainers to 22 ft. lbs. (29 Nm).

17. Install the remaining components, refill the tank and check for leaks.

18. Connect the battery cable.

Carburetor

REMOVAL AND INSTALLATION

NOTE: During carburetor removal, be sure to mark all hoses, lines and electrical connectors, etc., so these items may be properly reconnected during installation.

1. Disconnect the negative battery cable.

2. Remove the air cleaner housing and disconnect all air hoses from the air cleaner base.

3. Disconnect the fuel line, choke pipe, and distributor vacuum line.

4. Remove the accelerator linkage. With an automatic transaxle, also remove the throttle rod.

5. Label the vacuum hoses for ease of installation. Disconnect any remaining hoses, etc., from the carburetor.

6. Remove the 4 nuts that secure the carburetor to the manifold and lift off the carburetor and gasket.

7. Remove the carburetor heat insulator with 2 gaskets from the intake manifold.

8. Cover the open manifold with a clean rag to prevent small objects from dropping into the engine.

To install:

9. Use new gaskets, install the carburetor and torque the bolts evenly to 12 ft. lbs. (15 Nm).

10. Reconnect all hoses and electrical connectors.

11. After the engine is started, check for fuel leaks, idle speed and float level settings.

Fuel Injector

REMOVAL AND INSTALLATION

Tercel

1. Relieve the fuel system pressure.

2. Disconnect the negative battery cable.

3. Disconnect and tag the PCV and vacuum hoses.

4. Remove the air intake connector.

5. Disconnect the accelerator and throttle cables.

6. Disconnect the vacuum sensing hose.

7. Remove the 2 bolts remove the dashpot and link bracket. Disconnect the spring from the dashpot and throttle linkage.

8. Remove the pulsation damper and disconnect the fuel inlet hose from it.

9. Remove the clamp and disconnect the fuel return hose.

10. Remove the cold start injector pipe.

11. Disconnect the injector harness connectors.

12. Remove the 2 bolts attaching the fuel delivery pipe to the cylinder head.

13. Pull the delivery pipe and fuel injectors from the cylinder head.

NOTE: When removing the delivery pipe, be careful not to drop the injectors.

14. Remove the injectors from the delivery pipe.

15. Remove the 4 spacers and insulators from the cylinder head. Remove the grommets and O-rings from the injectors. Discard these components and replace with new.

To install:

16. Install new injector grommets and O-rings. Coat the O-rings with clean fuel prior to installation. Make sure the O-ring seats properly in the injector groove. If not, the O-ring will become pinched.

17. Install new spacers and insulators into the cylinder head. Install the injectors into the delivery pipe using a moderate back and forth twisting motion.

18. Mount the injector and delivery pipe assembly onto the cylinder head.

19. Install the delivery pipe retaining bolts and torque them to 14 ft. lbs. (19 Nm). After the bolts are tight, attempt to twist each injector back and forth a small amount by hand. The injectors should rotate smoothly. If not, the injector O-ring are probably not installed properly. Replace the O-rings as required.

20. Connect the injector harness connectors.

21. Install the cold start injector pipe.

22. Connect the fuel return hose to the delivery pipe.

23. Connect the fuel inlet hose to the delivery pipe using new gaskets. Install the pulsation damper and torque to 22 ft. lbs. (29 Nm).

24. Connect the spring to the throttle linkage and dashpot. Install the dashpot and link bracket.

25. Connect the vacuum sensing hose.

26. Connect the throttle and accelerator cables.

27. Install the air intake connector.

28. Connect the PCV hoses.

29. Connect the negative battery cable.

30. Start the engine and check for fuel leaks.

Corolla

1. Relieve the fuel system pressure.

2. Disconnect the negative battery cable.

3. Disconnect and tag the vacuum and PCV hoses.

4. Disconnect the fuel return hose from the pressure regulator.

5. Disconnect the injector harness connectors.

6. Remove the cold start injector pipe, except 1993-94 vehicles.

7. Disconnect the fuel inlet pipe.

8. Remove the delivery pipe bolts and remove the delivery pipe and fuel injectors from the cylinder head.

NOTE: When removing the delivery pipe, be careful not to drop the injectors.

9. On Corrola and MR2 with 4A-GE engine, remove the 2 spacers and 2 insulators from the cylinder head.

10. Remove the injectors from the delivery pipe. Remove the O-rings and grommets from the injectors and discard them.

To install:

11. Install new injector grommets and O-rings. Coat the O-rings with clean fuel prior to installation. Make sure the O-ring seats properly in the injector groove. If not, the O-ring will become pinched.

12. Install new spacers and insulators into the cylinder head.

13. Install the injectors into the delivery pipe using a moderate back and forth twisting motion.

14. Mount the injector and delivery pipe assembly onto the cylinder head.

15. Install the delivery pipe retaining bolts and torque them to 11-13 ft. lbs. (15-17 Nm). After the bolts are tight, attempt to twist each injector back and forth a small amount. The injectors should rotate smoothly. If not, the injector O-ring are probably not installed properly. Replace the O-ring(s) as required.

16. Connect the fuel inlet pipe using new gaskets. Torque the union bolt to 22 ft. lbs. (29 Nm).

17. Install the cold start injector pipe.

18. Connect the injector harness connectors. On 1993-94 vehicles harness and fuel injectors are color coded for correct installation).

19. Connect the fuel return hose to the fuel pressure regulator.

20. Connect the vacuum and PCV hoses.

21. Connect the negative battery cable.

22. Start the engine and check for leaks.

MR2

3S-GTE ENGINE

1. Relieve the fuel system pressure.

2. Disconnect the negative battery cable.

3. Remove the throttle body.

4. Remove the left engine hood side panel.

5. Remove the air cleaner.

6. Remove the charcoal canister.

7. Remove the EGR vacuum switching valve, vacuum modulator, EGR valve and pipe.

8. Remove the cold start injector pipe and cold start injector.

9. Remove the Idle Speed Control (ISC) water bypass hoses and air hoses.

10. Disconnect the vacuum sensing hose from the vacuum sensing pipe on the injector cover.

11. Disconnect the harness connectors from the tops of the injectors.

12. Disconnect the 2 wire clamps from the mounting bolts on the No. 2 timing cover. Disconnect the 2 wire clamps from the wire brackets on the intake manifold.

13. Disconnect the fuel inlet hose from the fuel filter.

14. Disconnect the fuel return hose from the fuel pressure regulator.

15. Remove the bolt that attaches the fuel inlet hose to the water outlet.

16. Remove the 3 bolts holding the delivery pipe to the cylinder head.

17. Disconnect the fuel inlet hose from the delivery pipe.

18. Remove the delivery pipe and fuel injectors and related components (4 insulators, 3 spacers and injector O-ring and grommets).

NOTE: When removing the delivery pipes, be careful not to drop the injectors.

19. Disconnect the vacuum sensing hose from the pressure regulator and remove the cover plate from the delivery pipe. Remove the injectors from the delivery pipe using the proper tool.

To install:

20. Insert 4 new insulators and 3 spacers into the injector openings.

21. Install the grommet and a new O-ring to the delivery pipe end of each injector.

22. Apply a thin coat of fuel to the O-ring on each injector and then press them into the delivery pipe.

Make sure the injector connectors are positioned correctly.

23. Mount the injectors together with the delivery pipes. Tighten the mounting bolts to 14 ft. lbs. (19 Nm).

24. Installation of the remaining components is the reverse of the removal procedure. The injector harness connectors are color coded. The No. 1 and No. 3 injector connectors are brown and the No. 2 and No. 4 connectors are grey. Start the engine and check for fuel leaks.

5S-FE ENGINE

1. Disconnect the negative battery cable.

2. Remove the throttle body.

3. Remove the engine hood side panels, air cleaner and cruise control actuator.

4. Remove the cold start injector pipe.

5. Disconnect the brake booster vacuum hose from the intake manifold.

6. Disconnect necessary engine wiring and remove the left and right accelerator brackets.

7. Disconnect the electrical connectors from fuel injectors.

8. Disconnect wire retaining clamps from the No. 2 timing belt cover and and intake manifold as necessary to gain access for removal/installation of fuel injectors.

9. Disconnect the fuel return hose from the return pipe.

10. Remove the delivery pipe and fuel injectors and related components (insulators, spacers, O-ring and grommet).

NOTE: When removing the delivery pipes, be careful not to drop the injectors.

11. Remove injectors from the delivery pipe.
To install:

12. Insert new insulators and spacers into the injector openings in the intake manifold.

13. Install the grommet and a new O-ring to the delivery pipe end of each injector.

14. Apply a thin coat of fuel to the O-ring on each injector and then press them into the delivery pipe.

15. Mount the injectors together with the delivery pipes onto the intake manifold. Tighten the mounting bolts to 9 ft. lbs. (13 Nm). After the bolts are tight, attempt to twist each injector back and forth a small amount. The injectors should rotate smoothly. If not, the injector O-ring are probably not installed properly. Replace the O-ring(s) as required.

16. Installation of the remaining components is the reverse of the removal procedure. Start the engine and check for leaks.

Celica

3S-FE ENGINE

1. Relieve the fuel system pressure and disconnect the negative battery cable

2. Remove the cold start injector pipe.

3. Disconnect the vacuum sensing hose from the fuel pressure regulator.

4. Disconnect the injector harness connectors.

5. Disconnect the hose from fuel return pipe.

6. Remove the fuel pressure pulsation damper.

7. Remove the 2 bolts and the delivery pipe together with the 2 injectors attached.

NOTE: When removing the delivery pipe, be careful not to drop the injectors.

8. Remove the 4 insulators and the 2 spacers from the cylinder head. Pull out the 4 injectors from the delivery pipe.
To install:

9. Insert 4 new insulators and 2 spacers into the injector holes in the cylinder head.

10. Install the grommet and a new O-ring to the delivery pipe end of each injector.

11. Apply a thin coat of fuel to the O-ring on each injector and then press them into the delivery pipe.

12. Install the injectors together with the delivery pipe into the cylinder head. Tighten the 2 mounting bolts to 9 ft. lbs. (13 Nm). After the bolts are tight, attempt to twist each injector back and forth a small amount. The injectors should rotate smoothly. If not, the injector O-ring(s) are probably not installed properly. Replace the O-ring(s) as required.

13. Install the fuel pressure pulsation damper with 2 new gaskets on the union bolt.

14. Connect the hose to the fuel return pipe.

15. Connect the injector harness connectors.

16. Connect the vacuum sensing hose to the fuel pressure regulator.

17. Install the cold start injector pipe.

18. Connect the negative battery cable.

19. Start the engine and check for leaks.

3S-GTE ENGINE

1. Relieve the fuel system pressure and disconnect the negative battery cable.

2. Remove the throttle body.

3. Remove the fuel pressure regulator.

4. Remove the EGR vacuum modulator

5. Disconnect the electrical connections from fuel injectors.

6. Remove the pulsation damper. Disconnect fuel inlet hose from the delivery pipe.

7. Disconnect the fuel return hose from the return pipe.

8. Remove the delivery pipe and fuel injectors and related components (insulators, spacers, O-ring and grommet).

NOTE: When removing the delivery pipes, be careful not to drop the injectors.

9. Remove the injectors from the delivery pipes.

10. Remove the insulators and spacers from the injector openings.
To install:

11. Insert new insulators and spacers into the injector openings in the intake manifold.

12. Install the grommet and a new O-ring to the delivery pipe end of each injector.

13. Apply a thin coat of fuel to the O-ring on each injector and then press them into the delivery pipe.

14. Mount the injectors together with the delivery pipes onto the intake manifold. Tighten the mounting bolts to 9 ft. lbs. (13 Nm). After the bolts are tight, attempt to twist each injector back and forth a small amount. The injectors should rotate smoothly. If not, the injector O-ring are probably not installed properly. Replace the O-ring(s) as required.

15. Installation of the remaining components is the reverse of the removal procedure. Start the engine and check for fuel leaks.

5S-FE ENGINE

1. Disconnect the negative battery cable.

2. Remove the throttle body.

3. Remove the air cleaner and cruise control actuator.

4. Remove the cold start injector pipe.

5. Remove the fuel pressure regulator.

6. Disconnect all necessary engine wiring.

7. Disconnect the electrical connectors from fuel injectors.

8. Disconnect wire retaining clamps from the No. 2 timing belt cover and and intake manifold as necessary to gain access for removal/installation of fuel injectors.

9. Disconnect the fuel return hose from the return pipe.

10. Remove the delivery pipe and fuel injectors and related components (insulators, spacers, O-ring and grommet).

NOTE: When removing the delivery pipes, be careful not to drop the injectors.

11. Remove injectors from the delivery pipe.

To install:

12. Insert new insulators and spacers into the injector openings in the intake manifold.

13. Install the grommet and a new O-ring to the delivery pipe end of each injector.

14. Apply a thin coat of fuel to the O-ring on each injector and then press them into the delivery pipe.

15. Mount the injectors together with the delivery pipes onto the intake manifold. Tighten the mounting bolts to 9 ft. lbs. (13 Nm). After the bolts are tight, attempt to twist each injector back and forth a small amount. The injectors should rotate smoothly. If not, the injector O-ring are probably not installed properly. Replace the O-ring(s) as required.

16. Installation of the remaining components is the reverse of the removal procedure. Start the engine and check for leaks.

Camry

3S-FE ENGINE

1. Disconnect the negative battery cable.

2. Disconnect the connector from the cold start injector.

3. Place a towel or rag under the cold start injector pipe and remove the 2 union bolts, 4 gaskets and delivery pipe.

NOTE: Loosen the union pipe bolts slowly.

4. Disconnect the vacuum sensing hose from the fuel pressure regulator.

5. Disconnect the fuel return pipe hose.

6. Remove the pulsation damper with the 2 gaskets. Discard the gaskets and purchase new ones.

7. Unbolt and remove the delivery pipe with the injectors attached.

NOTE: When removing the delivery pipe, take care not to drop the injector as damage may result.

8. Remove the 4 insulators and 2 spacers from the cylinder head.

9. Gently pull the injectors from the delivery pipe.

10. Remove the O-rings and grommets from the injectors and purchase new ones.

To install:

11. Install a new grommet and new O-ring onto each injector. Make sure that they are installed evenly, to ensure a good seat and save time from having to take the injectors out and readjust or replace the O-rings.

12. Lightly coat the O-rings with clean fuel.

13. Install the injectors into the delivery pipe. Do not cock the injector, install it straight into the opening using a light left to right twisting motion.

14. Place the 4 insulators and 2 spacers on the cylinder head.

15. Install the injectors together with the delivery pipe onto the cylinder head.

16. Go to each injector and rotate it by hand. The injector should rotate smoothly.

NOTE: If the injectors do not rotate smoothly, the O-rings are probably not installed correctly or the injectors are not installed evenly. If this is the case, pull the delivery pipe off the intake manifold and look at the O-rings to make sure they are installed correctly. Adjust the O-rings and, if damaged, replace them.

17. After the delivery pipe and injectors are properly in place, go to each injector and position the connector so that it is facing upward.

18. Install the 2 delivery pipe retaining bolts and torque them to 9 ft. lbs (13 Nm).

19. Install the pulsation damper with 2 new gaskets on both sides of the fuel hose banjo fitting. Tighten the damper.

20. Connect the fuel return hose.

21. Connect the injector connectors.

22. Connect the vacuum sensing hose.

23. Using new gaskets, connect the cold start injector pipe to the delivery pipe and cold start injector. Torque the 2 union bolts to 13 ft. lbs (18 Nm).

24. Connect the cold start injector wiring connector.

25. Connect the negative battery cable.

26. Short the **+B** and **Fp** terminals of the engine check connector with a jumper wire.

27. While the connector is shorted, pinch the fuel return hose. When the pinched, this causes the pressure in the high pressure fuel line to rise to 57 psi. At this time any leaks in any part of the system should be apparent. Carefully look at each component for leakage and check each connection.

5S-FE ENGINE

1. With the ignition in the **OFF** position, disconnect the negative battery cable.

NOTE: IF equipped with an air bag system, allow 90 seconds to pass before performing any other work.

2. Drain the engine coolant.

3. Disconnect the accelerator cable from the throttle body. If equipped with automatic transmission, disconnect the throttle cable.

4. Disconnect the air intake temperature sensor connector.

5. Disconnect the cruise control actuator cable from the clamp on the resonator.

6. Loosen the air cleaner hose clamp bolt. Disconnect the air cleaner hose from the throttle body. Release the air cleaner clips and remove the air cleaner cap with the resonator and air cleaner hose.

7. Disconnect the wiring to the throttle position sensor and the ISC valve.

8. Label and disconnect the hoses for the PCV, EGR vacuum modulator and EVAP VSV.

9. Remove the 4 bolts holding the throttle body. Label and disconnect the hoses from the throttle body.

10. Remove the throttle body with its gasket.

11. Disconnect the PS vacuum hoses.

12. Label and disconnect the hoses from the EVAP BVSV.

13. Remove the EGR valve and the vacuum modulator.

14. Disconnect the vacuum sensor hose at the air intake chamber, the brake booster vacuum hose and the vacuum sensing hose.

15. If equipped with air conditioning, disconnect the magnet switch VSV connector.

16. Disconnect the ground straps from the intake manifold.

17. Disconnect the knock sensor and EGR VSV connectors.

18. Free the engine wire harness by removing the bolt and wire clamp.

19. Remove the stays or supports holding the air intake chamber and the intake manifold.

20. Remove the intake manifold and remove the gasket.

21. Disconnect the wiring to each injector.

22. Loosen the pulsation damper and disconnect the fuel inlet pipe. Disconnect the fuel return hose.

23. Remove the retaining bolts, delivery pipe or fuel rail along with the injectors. Do not drop any injectors during removal.

24. Remove the insulators and rail spacers from the head. Remove the injectors from the fuel rail.

25. Remove the O-ring and grommet from each injector.

To install:

26. Install a new grommet on each injector. Apply a light coat of gasoline to new O-rings and install them on each injector.

27. Install the injectors into the fuel rail while turning each left and right. After installation, check that the injectors turn freely in place; if not, remove the injector and inspect the O-ring for damage or deformation.

28. Place new insulators and spacers on the head.

29. Install the fuel rail and injectors; check that the injectors still turn freely in position. Position the injector connectors upward.

30. Install the retaining bolts, tightening them to 9 ft. lbs. (13 Nm).

31. Connect the fuel return hose. Install the fuel inlet pipe and pulsation damper to the delivery pipe. Use new gaskets; tighten the union bolt to 25 ft. lbs. (34 Nm).

32. Connect the wiring to each injector.

33. Using a new gasket, install the intake manifold. Make certain all related wiring is in place before installation. Tighten the retaining nuts and bolts evenly in several passes to 14 ft. lbs. (19 Nm).

34. Install the air chamber and manifold stays. Tighten the 14mm bolt to 31 ft. lbs. (42 Nm) and the 12mm bolt to 16 ft. lbs. (22 Nm).

35. Position and secure the engine wire harness; tighten the clamp and bolt.

36. Connect the wiring to the knock sensor and the EGR VSV.

37. Connect both engine ground straps to the intake manifold.

38. Connect the air conditioning magnet switch wiring if it was removed.

39. Install the hoses for the vacuum sensor, brake booster and vacuum sensing hose.

40. Install the EGR valve and vacuum modulator. Use new gaskets. Tighten the union nut to 43 ft. lbs. (59 Nm) and the bolt to 9 ft. lbs. (13 Nm).

41. Connect the hoses to the charcoal canister and EGR VSV; connect the wiring to the EGR temperature sensor if it was removed.

42. Connect the vacuum hoses to the EVAP BVSV. Install the 2 PS vacuum hoses.

43. Connect the air and coolant hoses to the throttle body. Install a new gasket, taking note of the correct gasket placement. Install the throttle body, tightening the bolts evenly and alternately to 14 ft. lbs. (19 Nm).

NOTE: The upper mounting bolts are shorter than the lower mounting bolts. Make certain the bolts are correctly placed before tightening.

44. Connect the PCV, EGR vacuum modulator and EGR VSV hoses to the throttle body. Connect the wiring for the throttle position sensor.

45. Install the air cleaner cap, resonator and intake hose.

46. Connect the wiring to the air intake temperature sensor. Install the cruise control actuator cable.

47. Reinstall and adjust the throttle control cable if it was removed. Connect the accelerator cable.

48. Refill the engine coolant.

49. Connect the negative battery terminal.

2VZ-FE ENGINE

1. Disconnect the negative battery cable. If equipped with an air bag system, allow 90 seconds to pass before performing any other work.

2. Drain the engine coolant.

3. If equipped with automatic transmission, disconnect the throttle control cable from the throttle body and bracket. On all vehicles, disconnect the accelerator cable and bracket from the throttle body and air plenum or intake chamber.

4. Disconnect the air flow meter connector and disconnect the air hoses. Loosen the clamp bolt and disconnect the cap clips. Remove the air cleaner cover and the air flow meter with the air cleaner hose.

5. Label and disconnect the following hoses and electrical connectors: PCV hoses, vacuum sensing MAP hose, fuel pressure vacuum solenoid valve hose, emission system vacuum hoses, ISC connector, throttle position sensor and EGR temperature sensor, if equipped.

6. Remove the right upper engine stay.

7. Disconnect the cold start injector connector and fuel hose.

8. Label and disconnect the brake booster vacuum hose, PS vacuum hose and air hose, cruise control vacuum hose, wire harness clamp and fuel pressure vacuum solenoid valve hose.

9. Remove the wire harness clamp and free the wire harness. Disconnect the EGR tube.

10. Remove the 2 bolts holding the engine hanger. Disconnect and remove the air plenum stay from the air plenum.

11. Remove the air plenum or intake chamber with its gasket.

12. Disconnect the cold start injector connector, the coolant temperature sensor connector and the 6 injector connectors.

13. Disconnect the wire harness retaining clamps from the left side fuel rail.

14. Disconnect the fuel return hoses from the fuel pressure regulator and the No. 1 fuel rail. Disconnect the fuel inlet hose from the fuel filter.

15. Remove the No. 2 fuel line.

16. Remove the 2 bolts. Remove the left fuel rail together with the 3 injectors. Take great care not to drop an injector during removal.

17. Remove the 3 bolts, then remove the right fuel rail along with the injectors. Take great care not to drop an injector during removal.

18. Remove the injectors from the fuel rail. Remove the 6 insulators from the intake manifold and remove the spacers from the fuel rail mounting points.

To install:

19. Install a new grommet to each injector.

20. Lightly coat new O-rings with clean gasoline. Install the O-rings on each injector.

21. Install the injectors into the fuel rails while turning the injector left and right. Once installed, the injector should turn freely. If any binding is felt, remove the injector and inspect the O-ring for crimping or damage.

22. Place the insulators and spacers in place on the manifold.

23. Install the right and left rail assemblies in position on the intake manifold. Again check that the injectors rotate freely. Turn the injector so the electrical connector faces upward.

24. Install the retaining bolts, tightening them to 9 ft. lbs. (13 Nm).

25. Install the No. 2 fuel pipe. The gaskets at the union bolts must be replaced. Tighten the fittings to 24 ft. lbs. (32 Nm).

26. Install the inlet hose to the fuel filter and connect the return hoses to the pressure regulator and No. 1 fuel line. The washers at the union bolts must be replaced with new ones.

27. Connect the wire harness clips to the left fuel rail.

28. Attach the wiring connectors to the injectors, the cold start injector and the coolant temperature sensor.

29. Install the air intake chamber, tightening the nuts and bolts to 32 ft. lbs. (43 Nm).

30. Connect the EGR tube. Tighten it to 58 ft. lbs. (78 Nm).

31. Connect the wire harness clamp.

32. Install the intake chamber support; install the No. 1 engine hanger. Tighten the mounting bolts for both to 27 ft. lbs. (37 Nm).

33. Install the wire harness clamp, brake booster vacuum hose, PS vacuum and air hoses, cruise control vacuum hose, ground strap connector and fuel pressure vacuum solenoid valve hose.

34. Connect the cold start injector hose.

35. Install the cold start injector wiring.

36. install the upper right engine stay, tightening the bolts to 38 ft. lbs. (52 Nm).

37. Install or connect the wiring or hoses to the ISC, throttle position sensor, EGR temperature sensor, PCV, vacuum components, fuel pressure VSV and coolant bypass hoses.

38. With the air hose connected, install the air flow meter and air cleaner cover. Secure the 4 clips. Connect the air hoses and connect the wire harness to the air flow meter.

39. Reinstall the accelerator cable and bracket at the throttle body and the air plenum.

40. Install and adjust the throttle control cable, if removed.

41. Refill the cooling system.

42. Connect the negative battery cable.

3VZ-FE ENGINE

1. With the ignition switch in the **LOCK** position, disconnect the negative battery terminal. If vehicle is equipped with an air bag system, wait at least 90 seconds before performing any other work.

2. Drain the engine coolant.

3. Disconnect the accelerator cable from the throttle linkage.

4. If equipped with automatic transmission, disconnect the throttle cable from the throttle linkage.

5. Remove the air cleaner cap, air flow meter and the air cleaner hose as a unit.

6. Remove the two 5mm bolts and the V-cover.

7. Disconnect the EGR temperature connector clamp from the set of emission control valves.

8. Label and remove the hoses from the fuel pressure control VSV. Disconnect the hoses from the IACV, disconnect the VSV wiring connectors and remove the emission control valve set.

9. Label and disconnect the brake booster vacuum hose, PS air hose, PCV hose and IACV vacuum hose.

10. Disconnect the 2 ground straps.

11. Remove the wiring connector from the cold start injector. Disconnect the fuel line from the cold start injector.

12. Remove the No. 1 engine hanger and the air intake chamber support.

13. Remove the EGR pipe.

14. Remove the bolt and disconnect the hydraulic pressure pipe from the air intake chamber.

15. Disconnect the 3 hoses at the air intake plenum, disconnect the 2 coolant bypass hoses and disconnect the EGR temperature sensor connector, if equipped.

16. Disconnect the throttle position sensor connector. Detach the connector for the ISC valve and remove the air hoses from the ISC valve. Remove the PS air hose.

17. Remove the bolts and nuts holding the air plenum; remove the air plenum and gasket.

18. Disconnect the fuel return hoses from the No. 1 fuel pipe; then disconnect the fuel inlet hose from the filter.

19. Disconnect the wiring connectors from each injector.

20. Remove the No. 2 fuel pipe.

21. Remove the left delivery pipe or fuel rail; be careful not to drop the injectors during removal.

22. Remove the 3 injectors from the delivery pipe. Remove the rail spacers from the intake manifold.

23. Disconnect the 2 air hoses; remove the air pipe with the hoses attached.

24. Remove the right fuel rail and injectors. Take care not to drop an injector. Remove the injectors from the rail.

To install:

25. Install new grommets on each injector.

26. Apply a light coat of clean gasoline to new O-rings and install 2 on each injector.

27. Install each injector into the fuel rail while turning the injector left and right. Once installed, the injector should turn freely in the rail. If not, remove the injector and inspect the O-ring for damage or dislocation.

28. Place the rail spacers on the manifold. Clean the injector ports and install the right rail and injector assembly. Again check that the injectors turn freely in place.

29. Position the injector wiring connector upward. Install the bolts holding the delivery pipe and tighten them to 9 ft. lbs. (13 Nm).

30. Install the air pipe and hoses; tighten the retaining bolts only to 74 inch lbs. (8.3 Nm).

31. Repeat Steps 28 and 29 to install the left side delivery pipe and injectors.

32. Install the No. 2 fuel pipe connecting the 2 fuel rails. Use new gaskets at each union bolt. Tighten the union bolts to 25 ft. lbs. (34 Nm).

33. Connect the IACV vacuum hose.

34. Attach the wiring connectors to their proper injectors.

35. Install the inlet hose to the fuel filter using new gaskets; tighten the bolt to 22 ft. lbs. (29 Nm). Connect the return hose to the No. 1 fuel pipe.

36. Using a new gasket, install the air intake chamber. Tighten the mounting nuts to 32 ft. lbs. (43 Nm).

37. Connect the throttle position sensor harness, ISC valve wiring, ISC air hose and PS air hose.

38. Connect the EGR temperature sensor wiring.

39. Install the coolant bypass hose to the throttle body. Install the coolant bypass hose to the EGR cooler.

40. Connect the vacuum hoses to the BVSV.

41. Attach the hydraulic pressure pipe to the air intake chamber.

42. Install the EGR pipe with a new gasket and new sleeve ball. Tighten the bolts to 13 ft. lbs. (18 Nm) and the union nut to 58 ft. lbs. (78 Nm).

43. Install the No. 1 engine hanger and the air intake chamber stay. Tighten the bolts to 29 ft. lbs. (39 Nm).

44. Connect the injector pipe with new gaskets to the cold start injector. Tighten the bolts to 11 ft. lbs. (15 Nm). Attach the cold start injector wiring connector.

45. Connect the 2 ground straps.

46. Connect the brake booster vacuum hose, PS air hose, PCV hose and the IACV vacuum hose.

47. Install the emission valve set and tighten the bolts. Connect the VSV connectors and attach the 2 vacuum hoses to the IACV VSV. Install the 2 hoses to the fuel pressure VSV. Connect the EGR temperature sensor connector clamp to the valve set.

48. Install the V-bank cover on the engine.

49. Install the air cleaner cover, air flow meter and air hose as a unit. Make certain the clips are correctly engaged.

50. Connect and adjust the throttle control cable if it was removed.

51. Connect the accelerator cable and adjust it as needed.

52. Refill the engine coolant.

53. Connect the negative battery cable.

Supra

1. Relieve the fuel system pressure.

2. Disconnect the negative battery cable.

3. Drain the cooling system.

4. Tag and disconnect all hoses and wires which interfere with injector removal.

5. Disconnect accelerator connecting rod.

6. On 7M-GE engine, remove the air intake connector. On 7M-GTE engine, remove the throttle body.

7. Remove the ISC valve and gasket.

8. Disconnect the injector connectors.

9. Disconnect the cold start injector tube from the delivery pipe.

10. Remove the pulsation damper and the 2 gaskets.

11. Remove the union bolts and 2 gaskets from the fuel return pipe support.

12. Remove the clamp bolts from the No. 1 fuel pipe and Vacuum Switching Valve (VSV).

13. Remove the union bolts and 2 gaskets from the pressure regulator.

14. Disconnect the fuel hose from the No. 2 fuel pipe.

15. Remove the clamp bolt and the return fuel pipe.

16. Loosen the locknut and remove the pressure regulator.

17. Remove the 3 bolts, and then remove the delivery pipe with the injectors.

NOTE: When removing the delivery pipe, be careful not to drop the injectors.

18. Remove the 6 insulators and the 3 spacers from the cylinder head, then pull out the injectors from the delivery pipe.

To install:

19. Before installing, apply a thin coat of gasoline to the O-ring on each injector and then press them into the delivery pipe.

20. Insert 6 new insulators into the injector hole of the cylinder head.

21. Install the black rings on the upper portion of each of the 3 spacers, then install the spacers on the delivery pipe mounting hole of the cylinder head.

22. Install the 3 spacers and bolts and torque to 13 ft. lbs. (18 Nm). After the bolts are tight, attempt to twist each injector back and forth a small amount. The injectors should rotate smoothly. If not, the injector O-ring(s) are probably not installed properly. Replace the O-ring(s) as required.

23. Fully loosen the locknut of the pressure regulator. Push the pressure regulator completely into the delivery pipe by hand, then turn the regulator counterclockwise until the outlet faces outward in the correct position. Torque the locknut to 18 ft. lbs. (24 Nm).

24. Install the No. 2 fuel pipe and clamp bolt.

25. Connect the fuel hose.

26. Install the union bolt and 2 new gaskets to the pressure regulator and torque the union bolt to 18 ft. lbs. (24 Nm).

27. Install the No. 1 fuel pipe, Vacuum Switching Valve (VSV) and clamp bolt.

28. Install the union bolt and 2 new gaskets to the support pipe and torque the union bolts to 22 ft. lbs. (30 Nm).

29. Install the pulsation damper and 2 new gaskets and torque to 29 ft. lbs. (39 Nm).

30. Connect the injector connectors.

31. Install the Idle Speed Control (ISC) valve with a new gasket and torque to 9 ft. lbs. (13 Nm).

32. Install the throttle body or the air intake connector.

33. Connect the accelerator connecting rod.

34. Connect all vacuum hoses and electrical wires.

35. Refill the cooling system and connect the negative battery cable.

36. Start the engine and check for leaks.

Cressida

1. Disconnect the negative battery cable and drain the cooling system.

2. Relieve the fuel system pressure.

3. Remove the throttle body.

4. Remove the Idle Speed Control (ISC) valve.

5. Disconnect the injector harness connectors.

6. Disconnect the cold start injector from the delivery pipe.

7. Disconnect the EGR Vacuum Switching Valve (VSV) connector.

8. Remove the union bolt and 2 gaskets from the delivery pipe and fuel filter.

9. Remove the clamp bolt and remove the No. 1 fuel pipe with the vacuum switching valve.

10. Disconnect the No. 3 PCV hose.

11. Disconnect the vacuum sensing hose.

12. Disconnect the fuel hose from the No. 2 fuel pipe.

13. Remove the union bolt and 2 gaskets from the pressure regulator.

14. Remove the clamp bolts and remove the No. 2 fuel pipe.

15. Loosen the locknut and remove the fuel pressure regulator.

16. Remove the delivery pipe attaching bolts. Remove the delivery pipe with the 6 fuel injectors.

17. Remove the 6 insulators and 3 spacers from the cylinder head.

18. Remove the injectors from the delivery pipe.

To install:

19. Install new injector grommets and O-rings. Coat the O-rings with clean fuel prior to installation. Make sure the O-ring seats properly in the injector groove. If not, the O-ring will become pinched.

20. Install new insulators into the cylinder head. Install the black rings on the upper portion of each spacer. Then, install the spacers into the mounting holes in the head.

21. Install the injectors into the delivery pipe using a moderate back and forth twisting motion.

22. Mount the injector and delivery pipe assembly onto the cylinder head. Make sure the injector connectors are facing up.

23. Install the delivery pipe retaining bolts and torque them to 13 ft. lbs. (18 Nm). After the bolts are tight, attempt to twist each injector back and forth a small amount by hand. The injectors should rotate smoothly. If not, the injector O-ring are probably not installed properly. Replace the O-rings as required.

24. Install the fuel pipes and pressure regulator.

25. Connect the vacuum hoses and injector harness connectors. Install the Idle Speed Control (ISC) valve and throttle body.

26. Fill the cooling system to the proper level and connect the negative battery cable.

27. Start the engine and check for leaks.

Paseo

1. Disconnect the negative battery terminal.

2. Remove the PCV hose.

3. Disconnect the vacuum hose from the fuel pressure regulator.

4. Relieve the fuel pressure.

5. Disconnect the fuel return hose and the delivery hose and catch the spilled fuel with a shop towel.

6. Remove the accelerator cable bracket and disconnect the 4 injector connectors.

7. Remove the intake air chamber support bracket.

8. Remove the 2 delivery pipe bolts and remove the delivery pipe with the injectors, being careful not to drop the injectors. Note the positions of the spacers for installation.

To Install:

9. Install the injectors with new O-rings with the delivery pipe. Coat the new O-rings with gasoline. Make sure the injectors can be rotated by hand once they are installed.

10. Install the 2 pipe bolts and torque them to 14 ft. lbs. (19 Nm).

11. Install the air intake chamber bracket and torque to 13 ft. lbs. (17 Nm).

12. Install the injector connectors in their original positions, then install the accelerator bracket.

13. Connect the inlet hose to the delivery pipe, using new gaskets, and torque the union bolt to 22 ft. lbs. (29 Nm).

14. Connect the return hose to the return pipe.

15. Reconnect the vacuum hose to the regulator.

16. Install the PCV hose and reconnect the negative battery cable.

17. Start the engine and check for leaks.

DRIVE AXLE

── **CAUTION** ──
To avoid personal injury and accidental deployment of the air bag, work must be started after about 90 seconds or longer from the time the ignition switch is turned to the LOCK position and the battery cable is disconnected from the battery.

Halfshaft

REMOVAL AND INSTALLATION

Tercel

1. Raise the vehicle and support it safely.

2. Remove the cotter pin and locknut cap.

3. Loosen the bearing locknut.

4. Remove the brake caliper and position it aside. Remove the brake disc.

5. Remove the cotter pin and nut from the tie rod end. Using a suitable puller, disconnect the tie rod end from the steering knuckle.

6. Matchmark the lower strut mounting bracket where it attaches to the steering knuckle, remove the mounting bolts and disconnect the steering knuckle from the strut bracket.

7. Using a suitable puller, pull the axle hub off the outer halfshaft end.

8. Remove the stiffener plate from the left side of the transaxle assembly.

9. Using the proper tool, tap the halfshaft out of the transaxle casing.

To install:

NOTE: Be sure to cover the halfshaft input opening.

10. During installation, observe the following:

a. Coat the oil seal in the transaxle input opening with grease before inserting the halfshaft.

b. Tighten the tie rod end nut to 36 ft. lbs. (49 Nm).

c. Tighten the hub bearing locknut to 137 ft. lbs. (186 Nm) on 1990-91 models and to 166 ft. lbs. (226 Nm) on 1992-94 models.

d. Tighten the stiffener plate bolts to 29 ft. lbs. (39 Nm).

e. Check the front wheel alignment.

Corolla

1. Raise and safely support the vehicle.

2. Remove the cotter pin and locknut cap.

3. Loosen the bearing locknut.

4. Remove the engine undercovers.

5. Remove the cotter pin and nut from the tie rod end. Using a suitable puller, disconnect the tie rod end from the steering knuckle.

6. Remove the mounting bolts and then disconnect the steering knuckle from the lower control arm.

7. Use a rubber mallet and drive the outer end of the shaft out of the axle hub.

8. Using the proper tools, tap or pry the halfshaft out of the transaxle casing.

To install:

NOTE: Be sure to cover the halfshaft input opening.

9. During installation, observe the following:

a. Coat the oil seal in the transaxle input hole with grease before inserting the halfshaft.

b. Tighten the steering knuckle-to-lower arm bolts to 105 ft. lbs. (142 Nm).

c. Tighten the tie rod end nut to 36 ft. lbs. (49 Nm).

d. Tighten the bearing locknut to 137 ft. lbs. (186 Nm) on 1990-91 models or on 1992-94 models to 152 ft. lbs. (206 Nm).

e. Check that there is 0.08-0.12 in. (2.0-3.0mm) axial play on each shaft.

f. Check the front wheel alignment.

Celica

2WD

NOTE: The hub bearing can be damaged if it is subjected to the vehicle weight such as moving the vehicle when the halfshaft is removed. If equipped with ABS, after disconnecting halfshaft, work carefully so as not to damage the sensor rotor serrations on the halfshaft.

1. Raise and safely support the vehicle. Remove the wheels.

2. Remove the cotter pin, cap and locknut (loosen locknut while depressing brake pedal) from the hub.

3. Remove the engine undercovers.

4. Drain the transaxle fluid.

5. Remove the brake caliper and rotor disc.

6. Disconnect the tie rod end (remove cotter pin and nut) from the steering knuckle.

7. Disconnect steering knuckle from the lower arm.

8. Remove the halfshaft from the steering knuckle using a suitable puller. Cover the halfshaft boot with shop cloth or equivalent to protect it from damage.

9. Remove the left side halfshaft using the proper tool.

10. Remove the the right side half-shaft. On the 5S-FE engine, remove the 2 bolts of the center bearing bracket and pull out the halfshaft with center bearing case and center halfshaft. On the 4A-FE engine, use a suitable brass punch tap out the right side halfshaft.

To install:

11. Install the left side halfshaft. Apply grease to the transaxle oil seal lip. Position the new snapring opening side facing downward using brass punch, tap halfshaft in until it makes contact with the pinion shaft. Install the outboard joint side of the half-shaft to the axle hub.

12. Install right side halfshaft on the 5S-FE engine using the following procedure:

　　a. Apply grease to the transaxle oil seal lip.

　　b. Insert the center halfshaft with the right side to the transaxle through the bearing bracket. When inserting the halfshaft, insert so the straight pin on the center bearing case aligns with the hole on the bearing bracket.

　　c. Install retaining bolts and torque to 47 ft. lbs. (64 Nm).

　　d. Install the outboard joint side of the halfshaft to the axle hub.

13. Install right side halfshaft on the 4A-FE engine using the following procedure:

　　a. Apply grease to the transaxle oil seal lip.

　　b. Position the new snapring opening side facing downward using brass punch, tap halfshaft in until it makes contact with the pinion shaft.

　　c. Install the outboard joint side of the halfshaft to the axle hub.

14. Check that the halfshaft will not come out by trying to pull it by hand.

15. Connect the steering knuckle to the lower control arm and tighten the bolts to 94 ft. lbs. (128 Nm).

16. Connect the tie rod end to the steering knuckle and tighten the nut to 36 ft. lbs. (49 Nm). Install a new cotter pin.

17. Install all necessary brake components. Tighten the hub locknut while depressing the brake pedal. Torque to 137 ft. lbs. (186 Nm) on 1990-91 models or to 166 ft. lbs. (226 Nm) on 1992-94 models. Install the cap and use a new cotter pin.

18. Fill the transaxle to the proper level. Install the engine under cover. Check front wheel alignment.

Celica (4WD)

FRONT

NOTE: The hub bearing can be damaged if it is subjected to the vehicle weight such as moving the vehicle when the halfshaft is removed. On vehicles with ABS, after disconnecting halfshaft work carefully so as not to damage the sensor rotor serrations on the halfshaft.

1. Raise and support the vehicle safely.

2. Remove the wheels.

3. Remove the cotter pin, cap and locknut from the hub.

4. Remove the transaxle gravel shield, if equipped with manual transaxle. Remove the engine undercover and front fender apron seal.

5. Remove the cotter pin and nut from the tie rod end and then disconnect it from the steering knuckle.

6. Remove the bolt and 2 nuts and disconnect the steering knuckle from the lower control arm.

7. Loosen the 6 nuts attaching the inner end of the halfshaft to the transaxle side gear shaft.

8. Grasp the halfshaft and push the axle carrier outward until the shaft can be removed from the side gear shaft.

NOTE: Wrap the exposed end of the halfshaft in an old shop cloth to prevent damage to it.

9. Use a rubber mallet and tap the outer end of the shaft from the axle hub.

To install:

10. Press the outer end of the half-shaft into the axle hub, position the inner end and install the 6 nuts finger-tight.

11. Connect the tie rod end to the steering knuckle and tighten the nut to 36 ft. lbs. (49 Nm). Install a new cotter pin. If the cotter pin holes do not align, tighten the nut until they align. Never loosen it.

12. Connect the steering knuckle to the lower control arm and tighten to 94 ft. lbs. (127 Nm).

13. Tighten the 6 inner shaft mounting nuts to 48 ft. lbs. (65 Nm). Measure the distance between the right and left side shafts; it must be less then 27.75 in. (704.7mm).

14. With the brake pedal depressed, install the bearing locknut and tighten it to 137 ft. lbs. (186 Nm) on 1990-91 models or to 166 ft. lbs. (226 Nm) on 1992-94 models. Install the cap and a new cotter pin.

15. Install the wheels and lower the vehicle.

REAR

1. Raise and safely support the vehicle. Remove the wheels.

2. Remove the cotter pin, locknut cap and bearing nut.

3. Scribe matchmarks on the inner joint tulip and the side gear shaft flange. Loosen and remove the 4 nuts.

4. Disconnect the inner end of the shaft by punching it upward and then pull the outer end from the axle carrier. Remove the halfshaft.

To install:

5. Position the halfshaft into the axle carrier and pull the inner end down until the matchmarks are aligned.

6. Connect the halfshaft to the side gear shaft and tighten the nuts to 51 ft. lbs. (69 Nm).

7. Install the bearing nut and tighten it with the brake pedal depressed. Torque to 137 ft. lbs. (186 Nm) on 1990-91 models or to 166 ft. lbs. (226 Nm) on 1992-94 models. Install the cap and a new cotter pin.

8. Install the wheels and lower the vehicle.

Camry (2WD)

WITH 4-CYLINDER

1. Raise and support the vehicle safely.

2. Remove the front wheels.

3. Remove the cotter pin, cap and locknut from the hub.

4. Remove the engine undercovers.

5. Drain the transmission fluid if necessary.

6. Remove the transaxle gravel shield on the wagon.

7. Loosen the 6 nuts attaching the inner end of the halfshaft to transaxle, all except wagon.

NOTE: Wrap the exposed end of the halfshaft in an old shop cloth to prevent damage to it.

8. Remove the cotter pin from the tie end rod and then press the tie rod out of the steering knuckle. Remove the bolt and 2 nuts and disconnect the steering knuckle from the lower arm control.

9. On all except 4-cylinder wagon, use a 2-armed gear puller or equivalent, and press the halfshaft out of the steering knuckle.

10. On the 4-cylinder wagon, mark a spot somewhere on the left half-shaft and measure the distance between the spot and the transaxle case. Using the proper tool, pull the halfshaft out of the transaxle.

11. On the 4-cylinder wagon, use a 2-armed puller and press the outer end of the right halfshaft out of the steering knuckle. Remove the snapring at the inner end and pull the halfshaft out of the center driveshaft.

12. On all except the 4-cylinder wagon, remove the snapring on the center shaft and pull the center shaft out of the transaxle case.

To install:

13. When installing the center driveshaft on sedan, coat the transaxle oil seal with grease, insert the halfshaft through the bearing bracket and secure it with a new snapring.

14. Repeat Step 13 when installing the inner end of the right halfshaft on the 4-cylinder wagon.

15. On the right halfshaft of the 4-cylinder wagon, use a new snapring, coat the transaxle oil seal with grease and then press the inner end of the shaft into the differential housing. Check that the measurement made in Step 10 is the same. Check that there is 0.08-0.12 in. (2-3mm) of axial play. Check also that the halfshaft will not come out by trying to pull it by hand.

16. Press the outer end of each halfshaft into the steering knuckle on the 4-cylinder wagon.

17. On all except the 4-cylinder wagon, press the outer end of the halfshafts into the steering knuckle and then finger-tighten the nuts on the inner end.

18. Connect the steering knuckle to the lower control arm and tighten the bolts to 83 ft. lbs. (113 Nm).

19. Connect the tie rod end to the steering knuckle and tighten the nut to 36 ft. lbs. (49 Nm). Install a new cotter pin.

20. Tighten the hub locknut to 137 ft. lbs. (186 Nm) while depressing the brake pedal. Install the cap and use a new cotter pin.

21. On all except the 4-cylinder wagon, tighten the 6 nuts on the inner halfshaft ends to 27 ft. lbs. (36 Nm) while depressing the brake pedal.

22. Install the transaxle gravel shield on the wagon.

23. Fill the transaxle with gear oil or fluid.

24. Install the engine undercover.

1990-91 WITH 6-CYLINDER

1. Raise the front of the vehicle and use jackstands to safely secure the vehicle.

2. Remove the front wheel and remove the axle nut cotter pin, the locknut cap and the locknut, while depressing the brake pedal.

3. Remove the engine undercovers.

4. Remove the tie rod cotter pin and nut, then disconnect the tie rod end using tool 09628-62011 or equivalent.

5. Disconnect the steering knuckle from the lower arm by removing the 2 bolts.

6. Place matchmarks on the driveshaft and side gear shaft or center driveshaft, using paint and not a punch.

7. Loosen, but do not remove yet, the 6 bolts holding the driveshaft to the inner shaft.

8. Using a plastic hammer, disconnect the driveshaft from the axle hub and cover the boot with a protective cover.

NOTE: Do not subject the hub bearing to the weight of the vehicle with a driveshaft removed.

9. Remove the axle shaft.

10. To remove the left shaft, remove the 6 bolts and remove the shaft, but do not compress the inboard boot allowing the inside balls to drop out.

11. To remove the right shaft, do the following:

    a. Drain out the gear oil.

    b. Remove the bearing lock bolt.

    c. Using a suitable tool, remove the snapring, and pull out the driveshaft with the center driveshaft, tapping out the driveshaft with a brass hammer, if necessary.

To install:

12. When installing the driveshafts, pack the side gear shaft or to the center driveshaft with grease No. 90999-94029. The grease capacity is 0.09-0.12 lbs. (43-53g).

13. Place a new gasket on the inboard joint, insert and finger-tighten the 6 bolts with the 3 washers, making sure the matchmarks are aligned.

14. Reverse the remaining removal steps to complete installation, tightening fasteners to specifications.

15. Fill the transaxle with gear oil, check front end alignment and test drive.

NOTE: Do not compress the inboard boot when moving either driveshaft. If the cotter pin holes do not line up, always correct by tightening the nut until the next hole lines up. Then install a new cotter pin.

1992-94 WITH 6-CYLINDER

1. Raise the front of the vehicle and use jackstands to safely secure the vehicle.

2. Remove the front wheel and remove the axle nut cotter pin, the locknut cap and the locknut, while depressing the brake pedal.

3. Remove the front fender apron.

4. Remove the tie rod cotter pin and nut, then disconnect the tie rod end using tool 09628-62011 or equivalent.

5. Drain the gear oil.

6. Disconnect the stabilizer bar link from the lower arm.

7. Remove the bolt and the 2 nuts, then disconnect the steering knuckle from the lower ball joint.

8. Place matchmarks on the driveshaft and side gear shaft or center driveshaft, using paint and not a punch.

9. Loosen, but do not remove yet, the 6 bolts holding the driveshaft to the inner shaft.

10. Using a plastic hammer, disconnect the driveshaft from the axle hub and cover the boot with a protective cover.

NOTE: Do not subject the hub bearing to the weight of the vehicle with a driveshaft removed.

11. Using a suitable tool, pry out and remove the left axle shaft.

12. To remove the left driveshaft, remove the bearing lock bolt, remove the snapring and pull out the driveshaft.

To install:

13. To install the left driveshaft, do the following:

    a. Install a new snapring on the end of the shaft.

    b. Coat gear oil to the side gear shaft and differential case sliding surface.

    c. Using a brass bar and hammer, tap in the driveshaft until it makes contact with the pinion shaft.

NOTE: Before installing the driveshaft, set the snapring opening side facing downward. Whether or not the side gear shaft is making contact with the pinion shaft can be known by the sound or feeling when driving it inward.

    d. Check that there is 0.08-0.12 in. (2-3mm) of play in the axial direction and check that the driveshaft will not come out by trying to pull it completely out by hand.

14. To install the right driveshaft, do the following:

    a. Coat gear oil to the side gear shaft and differential case sliding surface.

b. Install the driveshaft to the transaxle through the bearing bracket, without damaging the oil seal lip.

c. Using a suitable tool, install a new snapring.

d. Install a new bearing lock bolt and tighten it to 24 ft. lbs. (32 Nm).

15. Reverse the remaining removal procedures to complete installation, tightening fasteners to specifications.

16. Fill the transaxle with gear oil, install the fender apron, check front end alignment and test drive.

NOTE: If the cotter pin holes do not line up, always correct by tightening the nut until the next hole lines up. Then install a new cotter pin.

Camry (4WD)

FRONT

1. Raise and support the vehicle safely.

2. Remove the wheels.

3. Remove the cotter pin, cap and locknut from the hub.

4. Remove the engine undercovers.

5. Disconnect the tie rod end from the steering knuckle.

6. Disconnect the lower control arm at the steering knuckle and pull it down and aside.

7. Use a plastic hammer and carefully tap the outer end of the halfshaft until it frees itself from the axle hub.

8. Cover the outer boot with a rag and then remove the inner end of the halfshaft from the transaxle. Use the proper tools.

To install:

9. Coat the lip of the oil seal with grease and then carefully drive the inner end of the shaft into the transaxle until it makes contact with the pinion shaft.

NOTE: Be careful not to damage the boots when installing the halfshafts; also, position the boot snapring so the opening is facing downward.

10. Put the outer end of each shaft into the axle hub, being careful not to damage the boots.

11. Check that there is 0.08-0.12 in. (2-3mm) of axial play. Check also that the halfshaft will not come out by hand.

12. Connect the lower control arm to the steering arm and tighten the bolt to 83 ft. lbs. (113 Nm).

13. Connect the tie rod to the steering knuckle and tighten the nut to 36

ft. lbs. (49 Nm). Use a new cotter pin to secure it.

14. Install the axle bearing locknut and tighten it to 137 ft. lbs. (186 Nm) while stepping on the brake pedal. Install the locknut cap and then a new cotter pin.

15. Fill the transaxle with gear oil or fluid, install the undercovers and wheels. Lower the vehicle and check the front end alignment.

REAR

1. Raise and support the vehicle safely. Remove the wheels.

2. Remove the cotter pin, locknut cap and bearing nut.

3. Scribe matchmarks on the inner joint tulip and the side gear shaft flange. Loosen and remove the 4 nuts.

4. Disconnect the inner end of the shaft by punching it upward and then pull the outer end from the axle carrier. Remove the halfshaft.

To install:

5. Position the halfshaft into the axle carrier and pull the inner end down until the matchmarks are aligned.

6. Connect the halfshaft to the side gear shaft and tighten the nuts to 51 ft. lbs. (69 Nm).

7. Install the bearing nut and tighten it to 137 ft. lbs. (186 Nm) on 1990-91 vehicles or 217 ft. lbs. (295 Nm) on 1992-94 vehicles, with the brake pedal depressed. Install the cap and a new cotter pin.

8. Install the wheels and lower the vehicle.

MR2

NOTE: After disconnecting halfshaft, work carefully so as not damage the sensor rotor serrations on the halfshaft.

1. Raise and support the vehicle safely.

2. Remove the wheels. Remove the speed sensor, if equipped with ABS.

3. Remove the cotter pin, cap and locknut from the hub.

4. Remove the transaxle gravel shield.

5. If the axle is retained by 6 bolts attaching the inner end of the halfshaft to transaxle, loosen them.

NOTE: Wrap the exposed end of the halfshaft in an old shop cloth to prevent damage to it.

6. If equipped with automatic transaxle, remove the 2 bolts holding the ball joint to the rear axle carrier and disconnect the lower arm from the rear axle carrier.

7. Also, if equipped with automatic transaxle, remove the cotter pin and nut using the proper tool. Disconnect the suspension arm from the rear axle carrier.

8. Remove the snapring and the bolt from the bearing bracket, if equipped.

9. If the inner joint is not retained by 6 bolts, pry the inner joint out of the transaxle.

10. While holding the halfshaft, press the outer end of the axle out of the wheel hub assembly, using a puller. Remove the halfshaft.

To install:

11. Push the outer end of the halfshaft into the wheel hub assembly.

12. Position the inner end of the halfshaft and install the 6 nuts finger-tight, if equipped. After installing a new snapring, forcefully push the inner joint into the transaxle, pull the axle by the inner joint itself to make sure it is seated.

13. Install the snapring and the bolt into the bearing bracket, if equipped. Torque the bolt to 24 ft. lbs. (32 Nm).

14. While pressing the brake pedal, tighten the wheel bearing locknut to 152 ft. lbs. (206 Nm) on models without turbocharged engine or 217 ft. lbs. (294 Nm) on models with turbocharged engine.

15. Install the locknut cap and use a new cotter pin.

16. Tighten the 6 inner end nuts to 27 ft. lbs. (36 Nm) while depressing the brake pedal. Torque the suspension arm nut to 36 ft. lbs. (49 Nm) and the lower arm to rear axle carrier to 83 ft. lbs. (113 Nm).

17. Fill the transaxle to the proper level.

18. Install the transaxle gravel shield.

Paseo

1. Raise and support the vehicle safely.

2. Remove the left engine undercover and drain the transaxle.

3. Remove the cotter pin and lock cap.

4. Apply the brake and remove the hub nut.

5. Disconnect the tie rod from the steering knuckle.

6. Disconnect the lower ball joint from the lower control arm.

7. Using a puller, remove the outer joint from the axle hub.

8. Using a brass bar and hammer, tap the inner joint out of the transaxle and remove the axleshaft.

To install:

9. Using a new snapring, push the axleshaft into the transaxle until it clicks in. Pull on the inner joint to make sure it is fully installed.

10. Push the outer joint into the axle hub.

11. Connect the lower ball joint to the lower arm and torque the fasteners to 59 ft. lbs. (80 Nm).

12. Connect the tie rod to the knuckle and torque the nut to 36 ft. lbs. (49 Nm). If the cotter pin cannot be installed, tighten to the next hole. Do not loosen the nut.

13. Install the hub nut and torque to 152 ft. lbs. (206 Nm).

14. Replace the lubricant, install the undercover and the wheel and check the front wheel alignment.

Supra and Cressida

1. Raise and support the vehicle safely. Remove the rear wheels.

2. Using a suitable jack, raise the No. 2 suspension arm until it is horizontal. Matchmarks the rear halfshaft to the side gear shaft flange.

3. Remove the 6 retaining nuts or bolts (while an assistant is depressing the brake pedal) and disconnect the rear halfshaft from the differential.

4. Remove the cotter pin and locknut cap. Loosen and remove the bearing locknut.

5. Using a suitable hammer, tap out the rear halfshaft.

6. Installation is the reverse order of the removal procedure. Tighten the bearing locknut to 203 ft. lbs. (275 Nm) and the 6 halfshaft retaining nuts or bolts to 51 ft. lbs. (69 Nm).

CV-Boot

REMOVAL AND INSTALLATION

1. Mount the halfshaft in a suitable holding fixture. Measure the length of the assembly and mark the positions of the boots.

2. Remove the inboard joint boot clamps.

3. Place matchmarks on the inboard joint tulip and tripod.

4. Remove the inboard joint tulip from the halfshaft.

5. Remove the tripod joint snapring.

6. Place matchmarks on the shaft and tripod.

7. Using a brass punch or equivalent remove the tripod joint from the halfshaft.

8. Remove inboard joint boot.

9. Remove the outboard joint boot clamps and boot.

10. Installation is the reverse of the removal procedures. Pack all CV-joints with suitable grease. Use new boot retaining clamps and snaprings as necessary. Make sure the length of the assembly equals the original length.

Driveshaft and U-Joints

REMOVAL AND INSTALLATION

1. Raise and support the rear axle housing safely.

2. Matchmark the driveshaft and companion flange. Unfasten the bolts which attach the driveshaft universal joint yoke flange to the mounting flange on the differential drive pinion.

3. If equipped with 3 universal joints, perform the following:

   a. Remove the driveshaft sub-assembly from the U-joint sleeve yoke.

   b. Remove the center support bearing from its bracket.

4. Remove the driveshaft end from the transmission.

5. Plug the transmission opening to keep the transmission oil from running out.

6. Remove the driveshaft.

To install:

7. Apply multi-purpose grease on the section of the U-joint sleeve which is to be inserted into the transmission.

8. Insert the driveshaft sleeve into the transmission.

NOTE: Be careful not to damage any of the seals.

9. If equipped with 3 U-joints and center bearings, perform the following:

   a. Adjust the center bearing clearance with no load placed on the drive line components; the top of the rubber center cushion should be 0.04 in. (1.0mm) behind the center of the elongated bolt hole.

   b. Install the center bearing assembly. Use the same number of washers on the center bearing brackets as were removed.

   c. Matchmark the arrow marks on the driveshaft and grease fittings.

10. Align the matchmarks. Secure the U-joint flange to the differential

pinion flange with the mounting bolts.

NOTE: Be sure the bolts are of the same type as those removed and that they are tightened securely.

11. Remove the axle housing supports and lower the vehicle.

12. Tighten the center bearing-to-bracket bolts to 27 ft. lbs. (37 Nm) on the Cressida or 36 ft. lbs. (49 Nm) on Supra. Tighten the flange bolts to 54 ft. lbs. (74 Nm) on the Supra and Cressida.

Camry (4WD), Celica (4WD) and Corolla (4WD),

1. Matchmark the front driveshaft flange and the front center bearing flange. Remove the 4 bolts, washers and nuts and disconnect the rear end of the front driveshaft from the front center bearing flange. Pull the shaft out of the transfer case and remove it. Plug the transfer case to prevent leakage.

2. Depress the brake pedal and loosen the cross-groove set bolts ½ turn. These bolts are at the front edge of the rear driveshaft and rear edge of the rear center bearing.

3. Matchmark the rear flange of the rear driveshaft to the differential pinion flange and then disconnect them.

4. Remove the 2 mounting bolts from the front and rear center bearings and then remove the 2 center bearings, intermediate shaft and rear driveshaft as an assembly.

5. Matchmark the universal joint and the rear center bearing flange. Remove the bolts and separate the rear driveshaft from the rear center bearing.

6. Pull the front and rear center bearings from the intermediate shaft.

To install:

7. Install the 2 center bearings onto the intermediate shaft ends and then temporarily install the assembly.

8. Align the matchmarks and connect the rear driveshaft to the differential. Tighten the bolts to 54 ft. lbs. (74 Nm) except Corolla; 27 ft. lbs. (37 Nm) on the Corolla.

9. Press the front driveshaft yoke into the transfer case, align the matchmarks at the rear of the shaft with those on the front center bearing flange and tighten the bolts to 54 ft. lbs. (74 Nm) except Corolla; 27 ft. lbs. (37 Nm) on the Corolla.

10. With the front edge of the rear driveshaft in position, depress the brake pedal and tighten the cross-

groove joint set bolts to 20 ft. lbs. (27 Nm) on all except the Celica. On the Celica, torque the bolts to 48 ft. lbs. (65 Nm).

11. With the vehicle in an unladen condition, adjust the distance between the rear edge of the boot cover and the rear driveshaft to 2.58-2.78 in. (65.5-70.5mm) on all except the Celica. On the Celica adjust the distance to 2.85-3.05 in. (72.5-77.5mm).

12. With the vehicle in an unladen condition, adjust the distance between the rear side of the center bearing housing and the rear side of the cushion to 0.45-0.53 in. (11.5-13.5mm).

13. Tighten the center bearing mounting bolts to 27 ft. lbs. (37 Nm). Make sure the center line of the bracket is at right angles to the shaft axial direction.

Rear Axle Shaft, Bearing and Seal

NOTE: These service procedures apply to rear wheel drive, 4WD vehicles and the MR2.

REMOVAL AND INSTALLATION

Corolla (4WD)

1. Raise and support the vehicle safely.
2. Drain the oil from the axle housing.
3. Remove the rear wheels.
4. Punch matchmarks on the brake drum and the axle shaft to maintain rotational balance.
5. Remove the brake drum and related components.
6. Remove the rear bearing retaining nut.
7. Remove the backing plate attachment nuts through the access holes in the rear axle shaft flange.
8. Use a slide hammer with a suitable adapter to withdraw the axle shaft from its housing.

NOTE: Use care not to damage the oil seal when removing the axle shaft.

9. Repeat the procedure for the axle shaft on the opposite side.

NOTE: Be careful not to mix the components of the 2 sides.

10. Installation is performed in the reverse order of removal. Coat the lips of the rear housing oil seal with multi-purpose grease prior to installation of the rear axle shaft. Always use new nuts, as they are the self-locking type.

Supra and Cressida

1. Raise and support the vehicle safely.
2. Remove the rear wheel and tire assembly. Remove the disc brake caliper from the rear axle carrier and suspend it with wire. Remove the rotor disc.
3. Remove the rear driveshaft. Disconnect the parking brake cable assembly.
4. Remove the bolt and nut attaching the carrier to the No. 1 suspension arm. Using the proper tool, separate the No. 1 suspension arm from the axle carrier.
5. Remove the bolt and nut attaching the carrier to the No. 2 suspension arm.
6. Disconnect the strut rod from the axle carrier. Disconnect the strut assembly from the axle carrier.
7. Disconnect the upper arm from the body and remove the axle hub assembly. Remove the upper arm mounting nut and remove the upper arm from the axle carrier.
8. Separate the backing plate and axle carrier. Using a suitable puller, remove the upper arm from the axle carrier.
9. Remove the dust deflector from the axle hub. Using a suitable puller remove the inner oil seal. Remove the hole snapring.
10. Using a suitable press, press out the bearing outer race from the axle carrier. Be sure to always replace the bearing as an assembly.
11. Remove the bearing inner race (inside) and 2 bearings from the bearing outer race.

To install:

12. Installation is the reverse of the service removal procedure. During installation, observe the following torques:

Backing plate to axle carrier nuts — 43 ft. lbs. (58 Nm).

Backing plate to axle carrier bolts — 19 ft. lbs. (26 Nm).

No. 1 suspension arm nut — 43 ft. lbs. (59 Nm) — Supra. 36 ft. lbs. (49 Nm) — Cressida.

Upper arm mounting nut — 80 ft. lbs. (108 Nm).

Strut assembly nut — 101 ft. lbs. (137 Nm).

Upper arm to body bolt — 121 ft. lbs. (164 Nm) for Supra or 119 ft. lbs. (162 Nm) for Cressida.

No. 2 suspension arm to axle carrier — 121 ft. lbs. (164 Nm) for Supra or 119 ft. lbs. (162 Nm) for Cressida.

Strut rod to axle carrier — 121 ft. lbs. (164 Nm) for Supra. 105 ft. lbs. or (142 Nm) for Cressida.

Disc brake caliper bolts — 34 ft. lbs. (47 Nm).

Camry (4WD) and Celica (4WD)

1. Raise the vehicle and support it safely.
2. Remove the rear wheel. Remove the disc brake caliper from the rear axle carrier and suspend it with wire. Remove the rotor disc.
3. Remove the rear halfshaft. Disconnect the parking brake cable assembly and remove the cable.
4. Remove the 2 axle carrier set nuts and the 2 bolts and then remove the camber adjusting cam.
5. Disconnect the strut rod at the axle carrier. Disconnect the No. 1 and No. 2 suspension arms at the axle carrier. Remove the axle carrier and hub.
6. Press the axle shaft out of the axle hub.
7. Using a 2-armed puller, remove the bearing inner race (outside) from the axle shaft. Remove the dust cover.
8. Remove the inner and outer oil seal from the axle carrier. Remove the hole snapring.
9. Using a suitable press, press out the bearing.

To install:

10. Installation is the reverse of the service removal procedure. Please observe the following notes:

Tighten the axle carrier-to-shock bolts to 188 ft. lbs. (255 Nm).

Tighten the brake caliper mounting bolts to 34 ft. lbs. (47 Nm).

With the parking brake engaged, tighten the bearing locknut to 137 ft. lbs. (186 Nm).

With the wheels resting on the ground, tighten the strut rod bolt to 83 ft. lbs. (113 Nm); tighten the 2 suspension arms to 90 ft. lbs. (123 Nm).

Check the rear wheel alignment.

MR2

1. Raise and support the vehicle safely.
2. Remove the rear wheel and tire assembly. Remove the cotter pin, bearing locknut cap and bearing locknut.
3. Disconnect the parking brake cable. Disconnect the disc brake caliper from the rear axle carrier and suspend it with wire. Remove the rotor disc.
4. Disconnect the rear axle carrier from the lower arm. Remove the cotter pin and nut from the suspension

arm. If equipped with ABS, remove the speed sensor from the axle carrier.

5. Using a suitable tool separate the suspension arm from the rear axle carrier.

6. Place matchmarks on the strut lower bracket and camber adjusting cam.

7. Remove the 2 axle carrier set nuts and 2 bolts with the camber adjusting cam. Remove the rear axle carrier and axle hub.

8. Remove the dust deflector from the axle hub. Using a suitable puller, remove the inner oil seal. Remove the hole snapring.

9. Remove the 3 bolts holding the disc brake dust cover to the rear axle carrier. Using a suitable puller remove the axle hub from the rear axle carrier.

10. Remove the bearing inner (inside) race. Using a suitable puller remove the bearing inner race (outside) from the rear axle hub.

11. Using a suitable puller remove the outer oil seal.

12. Remove the hub bearing by first placing the removed inner race (outside) in the bearing and using a suitable press, press out the bearing. Be sure to always replace the bearing as an assembly.

To install:

13. Installation is the reverse order of the removal procedure. During installation, observe the following torque specifications:

2 camber adjusting cam set bolts — 166 ft. lbs. (226 Nm).

Suspension arm nut — 36 ft. lbs. (49 Nm).

Rear axle carrier to the lower arm — 59-83 ft. lbs. (80-113 Nm).

Brake caliper — 43 ft. lbs. (59 Nm).

Bearing locknut — 137 ft. lbs. (186 Nm) all except 3S-GTE engine. On 3S-GTE engine torque the rear wheel bearing locknut to 217 ft. lbs. (294 Nm).

If equipped with ABS, torque the wheel sensor bolt to 74 inch lbs. (8.3 Nm).

Front Wheel Hub, Knuckle and Bearings

REMOVAL AND INSTALLATION

Front Wheel Drive

1. Raise and support the vehicle safely. Remove the front wheels.

2. Remove the cotter pin from the bearing locknut cap and then remove the cap.

3. Depress the brake pedal and loosen the bearing locknut.

4. Remove the brake caliper mounting nuts, position the caliper aside with the hydraulic line still attached and suspend it with a wire.

5. Remove the brake disc.

6. Remove the cotter pin and nut from the tie rod end and then, using a tie rod end removal tool, remove the tie rod.

7. Place matchmarks on the shock absorber lower mounting bracket and the camber adjustment cam, if equipped. Remove the bolts and separate the steering knuckle from the strut.

8. Remove the 2 ball joint attaching nuts and disconnect the lower control arm from the steering knuckle.

9. Carefully grasp the axle hub and knuckle assembly and pull it out from the halfshaft using the proper tool.

NOTE: Cover the halfshaft boot with a shop rag to protect it from any damage.

10. Clamp the steering knuckle in a vise and remove the dust deflector. Remove the nut holding the steering knuckle to the ball joint. Press the ball joint out of the steering knuckle.

11. Remove the dust deflector from the hub.

12. Pry out the bearing inner oil seal and then remove the hole snapring.

13. Remove the 3 bolts attaching the steering knuckle to the disc brake dust cover.

14. Remove the axle hub from the steering knuckle using the proper tool.

15. Remove the bearing inner race (inside).

16. Remove the bearing inner race (outside).

17. Remove the oil seal from the knuckle.

18. Position an old bearing inner race (outside) on the bearing and then use a hammer and a drift to carefully knock the bearing out of the knuckle.

To install:

19. Press a new bearing into the steering knuckle.

20. Using a suitable oil seal installation tool, drive a new oil seal into the knuckle.

21. Install the disc brake dust cover onto the knuckle using liquid sealant.

22. Apply grease between the oil seal lip, oil seal and the bearing and

then press the axle hub into the steering knuckle.

23. Install a new hole snapring into the knuckle.

24. Press a new oil seal onto the knuckle and coat the contact surface of the seal and the halfshaft with grease. Press a new dust deflector into the knuckle.

25. Position the ball joint on the steering knuckle and tighten the nut to specifications.

26. Connect the knuckle assembly to the lower strut bracket. Insert the mounting bolts from the rear and make sure the matchmarks made earlier are in alignment. Tighten the nuts as follows:

188 ft. lbs. (255 Nm) on the Celica.

166 ft. lbs. (226 Nm) on the Paseo and Tercel.

224 ft. lbs. (304 Nm) on the Camry.

194 ft. lbs. (263 Nm) on Corolla sedan and wagon.

27. Connect the tie rod end to the knuckle, tighten the nut to specifications and install a new cotter pin. Always tighten the nut if the hole does not line up.

28. Connect the ball joint to the lower control arm and tighten the bolt to 47 ft. lbs. (64 Nm), except on the following vehicles:

Camry — 90 ft. lbs. (123 Nm).
Celica — 94 ft. lbs. (122 Nm).
Tercel — 59 ft. lbs. (80 Nm).
Corolla sedan and wagon — 105 ft. lbs. (142 Nm).
Paseo — 59 ft. lbs. (80 Nm).

29. Install the brake disc and the caliper. Tighten the caliper mounting bolts to 65 ft. lbs. (88 Nm) on all vehicles except Camry and Celica. On Camry, torque the caliper mounting bolts to 86 ft. lbs. (117 Nm). On the Celica, torque the caliper mounting bolts to 70 ft. lbs. (95 Nm).

30. Install the bearing locknut while having someone depress the brake pedal. Tighten it to specifications. Install the adjusting nut cap and insert a new cotter pin.

31. Check the front end alignment.

Differential Front Oil Seal and Bearing

REMOVAL AND INSTALLATION

4WD

1. Unbolt and remove the rear crossmember.

2. Matchmark the differential and driveshaft flanges.

3. Remove the 4 flange bolts, nuts and washers.

4. Disconnect the driveshaft from the differential.

5. With a hammer and a cold chisel, loosen the staked part of the locking nut.

6. Using SST 09330-00021 or equivalent to hold the flange, remove the locking nut.

7. Remove the plate washer.

8. Using SST 09557-22022 or equivalent, remove the companion flange.

9. Using SST 09308-10010 or equivalent seal puller, remove the front oil seal and then remove the oil slinger.

10. Using SST 09556-22010 or equivalent bearing puller, remove the front bearing.

11. Remove the front bearing spacer. Purchase a new spacer, bearing and oil seal as required.

To install:

12. Install a new bearing spacer and bearing onto the shaft.

13. Install the oil slinger onto the shaft.

14. Using SST 09554-22010 or equivalent, drive in the new oil seal to a depth of 0.08 in. (2.0mm).

15. Coat the lip of the new oil seal with multi-purpose grease.

16. Using the removal tool, install the companion flange.

17. Install the plate washer.

18. Coat the threads of the new nut with gear oil.

19. Using the removal tool to hold the flange, torque the companion flange to 80 ft. lbs. (108 Nm).

20. Check and adjust the drive pinion preload as follows:

a. Using an inch pound torque wrench, measure the preload of the backlash between the drive pinion and the ring gear. Preload for a new bearing is 8.7-13.9 inch lbs. (1.0-1.6 Nm) and 4.3-6.9 inch lbs. (0.5-0.8 Nm) for a used bearing.

b. If the preload is greater that the specified limit, replace the bearing spacer.

c. If the preload is less than specification, re-torque the nut in 9 ft. lbs. (12 Nm) increments until the specified preload is reached. Do not exceed a maximum torque of 174 ft. lbs. (235 Nm).

d. If the maximum torque is exceeded, replace the bearing spacer and repeat the bearing preload procedure. Do not reduce the preload by backing off on the pinion nut.

21. Stake the drive pinion nut.

22. Align the driveshaft and differential flange matchmarks.

23. Install the flange bolts and torque to 54 ft. lbs. (73 Nm).

24. Install the rear crossmember and torque the retaining bolts to 53 ft. lbs. (72 Nm).

25. Remove the differential fill plug (the uppermost plug) and check the oil level. Fill the differential to the proper level with new API GL-5 hyploid gear oil.

26. Install and tighten the fill plug with a new gasket. Torque the plug to 29 ft. lbs. (39 Nm).

27. Take the vehicle for a road test and inspect for leaks.

Cressida and Supra

1. Remove the propeller shaft.

2. Drain the differential oil.

3. Matchmark and remove the companion flange, holding the flange when loosening the nut.

4. Remove the oil seal.

To install:

5. Apply grease to the seal lip and install the seal, driving it in to a depth of 0.059 in. (1.5mm).

6. Reinstall the companion flange in its original position.

7. Coat the threads of a new nut with grease and torque it to 134 ft. lbs. (181 Nm), holding the flange from moving.

8. Measure the bearing preload. For a new bearing it should be 8.7-13.9 inch lbs. (1.0-1.6 Nm) or for a reused bearing it should be 4.3-6.9 inch lbs. (0.5-0.8 Nm).

9. If the preload is greater than specified, replace the bearing spacer behind the bearing. If it is less, retighten the flange nut 9 ft. lbs. (13 Nm) at a time until the specified preload is reached.

NOTE: If the maximum torque of 250 ft. lbs. (338 Nm) is exceeded while retightening the nut, replace the bearing spacer and repeat the procedure. Do not back off the nut to reduce the preload.

Differential Carrier

REMOVAL AND INSTALLATION

4WD

COROLLA

1. Drain the differential.

2. Remove the 4 bolts on the backing plates and remove the axle shafts.

3. Matchmark and disconnect the propeller shaft from the differential.

4. Remove the differential carrier nuts and remove the carrier.

To install:

5. Install a new gasket and install the carrier.

6. Torque the 12 bolts to 23 ft. lbs. (31 Nm).

7. Install the propeller shaft to the matchmarks and torque the fasteners to 27 ft. lbs. (37 Nm).

8. Refill the differential.

EXCEPT COROLLA

1. Remove the drain plug and drain the oil from the differential into a drain pan.

2. Remove the rear driveshafts.

3. Unbolt and remove the rear crossmember.

4. Matchmark the differential and driveshaft flanges.

5. Remove the 4 flange bolts, nuts and washers.

6. Disconnect the driveshaft from the differential.

7. Raise the differential slightly with a transaxle jack and a block of wood.

8. Remove the 6 bolts and 4 mounting nuts from the differential.

9. Remove the differential from the body.

To install:

10. Position the differential into place and install the mounting bolts and nuts. Torque the group of 4 nuts and bolts to 70 ft. lbs. (95 Nm).

11. Torque the 2 bolts to 108 ft. lbs. (147 Nm).

12. Align the driveshaft and differential flange matchmarks.

13. Install the flange bolts and torque to 54 ft. lbs. (73 Nm).

14. Install the rear crossmember and torque the retaining bolts to 53 ft. lbs. (72 Nm).

15. Install the rear driveshafts.

16. Install the drain plug with a new gasket and torque the plug to 36 ft. lbs. (49 Nm).

17. Fill the differential to the proper level.

18. Install the filler plug with a new gasket and torque to 29 ft. lbs. (39 Nm).

Axle Housing

REMOVAL AND INSTALLATION

4-Wheel Drive

1. Matchmark and disconnect the driveshafts from the differential.

2. Remove the rear crossmember by removing the 4 bolts.

3. Matchmark and disconnect the propeller shaft.

4. Position a suitable jack under the differential and remove the 6

bolts securing it, then lower the differential out of the vehicle.

To install:

5. Position the differential and torque the 4 vertical bolts to 70 ft. lbs. (95 Nm), then torque the horizontal bolts to 108 ft. lbs. (147 Nm).

6. Connect the propeller shaft with the matchmarks aligned and torque the 4 bolts to 54 ft. lbs. (74 Nm).

7. Install the rear crossmember and torque the 4 bolts to 53 ft. lbs. (72 Nm).

8. Check the differential oil level.

Supra

1. Matchmark and disconnect the driveshafts.

2. Matchmark and disconnect the propeller shaft.

3. Remove the mounting bolts and remove the axle housing.

To install:

4. Position the housing and torque the rear nuts and bolts to 67 ft. lbs. (91 Nm), the front bolts to 122 ft. lbs. (166 Nm) and the stud bolts to 58 ft. lbs. (78 Nm).

5. Install the driveshafts and the propeller shaft and torque to specifications.

6. Refill the differential.

Cressida

1. Matchmark and disconnect the driveshafts.

2. Matchmark and disconnect the propeller shaft.

3. Remove the mounting bolts and remove the axle housing.

To Install:

4. Position the housing and torque the fasteners to specifications.

5. Install the driveshafts and the propeller shaft and torque to specifications.

6. Refill the differential.

MANUAL TRANSMISSION

CAUTION

To avoid personal injury and accidental deployment of the air bag, work must be started after about 90 seconds or longer from the time the ignition switch is turned to the LOCK position and the battery cable is disconnected from the battery.

Transmission Assembly

REMOVAL AND INSTALLATION

Supra

1. Disconnect the negative battery cable. Remove the center console trim panel. Remove the shift lever.

2. Raise and support the vehicle safely. Drain the transmission fluid. Remove the driveshaft.

3. Disconnect the front exhaust pipe from the tailpipe. Remove the front exhaust pipe.

4. Disconnect the speedometer cable. Disconnect the backup light switch electrical connector. If equipped with ABS, disconnect the rear speed sensor electrical connector.

5. Remove the clutch release cylinder. Remove the starter assembly.

6. Support the engine and the transmission using the proper equipment. Remove the transmission support crossmember.

7. Remove the transmission mounting bolts. Remove the flywheel housing bolts. Carefully, move the transmission rearward, down and out of the vehicle.

NOTE: On turbocharged vehicles, it will be necessary to remove the transmission with the clutch cover and disc. To do this pull the release fork through the left clutch housing hole and then remove the assembly.

8. Installation is the reverse of the removal procedure. Tighten the mounting bolts to 29 ft. lbs. (39 Nm).

LINKAGE ADJUSTMENT

Manual transmission linkage adjustments are neither possible or necessary. Damaged bushings can cause shift cable problems.

MANUAL TRANSAXLE

CAUTION

To avoid personal injury and accidental deployment of the air bag, work must be started after about 90 seconds or longer from the time the ignition switch is

turned to the LOCK position and the battery cable is disconnected from the battery.

Transaxle Assembly

REMOVAL AND INSTALLATION

Tercel

1. Disconnect the negative battery cable. If equipped with cruise control remove the battery and cruise control actuator with mounting bracket.

2. Remove the clutch release cylinder and tube clamp. Disconnect the backup light switch electrical connector.

3. Disconnect the transaxle shift control cables. Remove the selecting bellcrank along with the bracket from the transaxle case. Remove the upper transaxle-to-engine retaining bolts.

4. Raise the vehicle and support it safely. Remove the undercovers. Drain the transaxle fluid. Disconnect the speedometer cable.

5. Disconnect both halfshafts. Remove the engine rear mounting brackets. Remove the starter assembly.

6. Support the engine and transaxle assembly using the proper equipment. Disconnect the left engine mounting.

7. Remove the remaining engine-to-transaxle retaining bolts. Carefully remove the transaxle assembly from the vehicle.

8. Installation is the reverse of the removal procedure. Tighten the transaxle-to-engine bolts to 47 ft. lbs. (64 Nm) — **A**; 34 ft. lbs. (46 Nm) — **B**; and 65 inch lbs. (7.4 Nm) — **C**. Tighten the front engine mount bracket bolts to 43 ft. lbs. (58 Nm). Tighten the rear engine mount bracket bolts to 21 ft. lbs. (28 Nm). Tighten the left engine mount bolts to 35 ft. lbs. (48 Nm) and the front and rear mount bolts to 47 ft. lbs. (64 Nm).

Paseo

1. Disconnect the negative battery cable. Remove the air cleaner case assembly.

2. Remove the clutch release cylinder and ground strap. Disconnect the backup light switch electrical connector.

3. Disconnect the transaxle shift control cables. Remove the upper transaxle-to-engine retaining bolts.

4. Raise the vehicle and support it safely. Remove the undercovers.

Drain the transaxle fluid. Disconnect the speedometer cable.

5. Disconnect both halfshafts. Remove the engine rear mounting brackets. Remove the starter assembly.

6. Support the engine and transaxle assembly using the proper equipment. Disconnect the left engine mounting.

7. Remove the remaining engine-to-transaxle retaining bolts. Carefully remove the transaxle assembly from the vehicle.

8. Installation is the reverse of the removal procedure. Tighten the transaxle-to-engine bolts to 47 ft. lbs. (64 Nm) — **A**; 34 ft. lbs. (46 Nm) — **B**; and 65 inch lbs. (7.4 Nm) — **C**. Tighten the rear engine mount bracket bolts to 58 ft. lbs. (78 Nm). Tighten the left engine mount bracket bolts to 35 ft. lbs. (48 Nm).

Corolla

2WD

1. Disconnect the negative battery cable. Remove the air cleaner assembly.

2. Disconnect the backup light switch electrical connector. Remove the speedometer cable. Disconnect the transmission control cables.

3. Raise the vehicle and support safely. Remove the water inlet from the transaxle. Remove the clutch release cylinder.

4. Remove the undercover. Remove the front and rear mounting. Remove the engine mounting center member.

5. Disconnect the halfshaft from the transaxle. Disconnect the steering knuckle from the lower control arm. Pull the steering knuckle outward and remove the left halfshaft.

6. Remove the starter. Disconnect the ground strap. Remove the No. 2 engine rear plate.

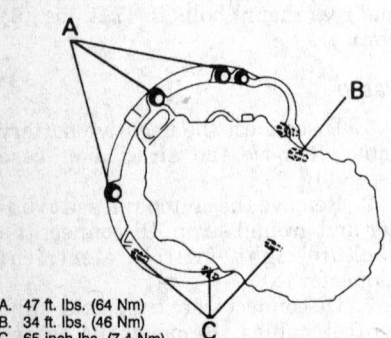

A. 47 ft. lbs. (64 Nm)
B. 34 ft. lbs. (46 Nm)
C. 65 inch lbs. (7.4 Nm)

Manual transaxle mounting bolt locations on Tercel and Paseo

7. Support the engine and the transaxle using the proper equipment. Remove the left engine mounting.

8. Remove the engine-to-transaxle retaining bolts. Carefully remove the transaxle assembly from the vehicle.

9. Installation is the reverse of the removal procedure. Tighten the 12mm engine-to-transaxle bolts to 47 ft. lbs. (64 Nm) and the 10mm bolts to 34 ft. lbs. (46 Nm). Tighten the left engine mount bolts to 38 ft. lbs. (52 Nm). Tighten the front and rear engine mount bolts and the engine mounting center member bolts to 29 ft. lbs. (39 Nm).

4WD

1. Remove the engine and transaxle as an assembly.

2. Remove the rear end-plate.

3. Disconnect the vacuum lines and then remove the transfer case vacuum actuator.

4. Remove the right and center transfer case stiffener plates.

5. Pull the transaxle out slowly until there is approximately 2.36-3.15 in. (60-80mm) clearance between the transaxle and the engine.

6. Turn the output shaft in a clockwise direction and then remove the transaxle.

To install:

7. Install the transaxle assembly to the engine and tighten the 10mm bolts to 34 ft. lbs. (46 Nm). Tighten the 12mm bolts to 47 ft. lbs. (64 Nm).

8. Tighten the 8mm stiffener plate bolts to 14 ft. lbs. (20 Nm) and the 10mm bolts to 27 ft. lbs. (37 Nm).

9. Tighten the rear end-plate mounting bolts to 17 ft. lbs. (23 Nm).

10. Install the engine/transaxle assembly.

Camry

1990-91 2WD

1. Disconnect the negative battery cable. Remove the clutch release cylinder and tube clamp. Remove the clutch tube bracket.

2. Disconnect the control cables. Disconnect the backup light switch electrical connector. Remove the ground strap.

3. Remove the starter assembly. Remove the transaxle upper mounting bolts.

4. Raise and support the vehicle safely. Remove the undercovers. Drain the transaxle fluid. Disconnect the speedometer cable.

5. Remove the suspension lower crossmember. Remove the engine mounting center member.

6. Disconnect both halfshafts. Disconnect the left steering knuckle from the lower control arm. Remove the left halfshaft. Remove the stabilizer bar.

7. Properly support the engine and remove the left engine mount.

8. Properly support the transaxle assembly. Remove the engine-to-transaxle bolts, lower the left side of the engine and carefully ease the transaxle out of the engine compartment.

To install:

9. Install the transaxle and tighten the 12mm mounting bolts to 47 ft. lbs. (64 Nm) and the 10mm bolts to 34 ft. lbs. (46 Nm).

10. Tighten the left engine mount to 38 ft. lbs. (52 Nm). Tighten the 4 center engine mount bolts to 29 ft. lbs. (39 Nm). Tighten the front and rear engine mount bolts to 32 ft. lbs. (43 Nm).

11. Tighten the lower crossmember bolts to 153 ft. lbs. (207 Nm) — 4 outer bolts; and 29 ft. lbs. (39 Nm) — 2 inner bolts.

12. Fill the transaxle with gear oil and perform road test.

1992-94 2WD

1. Disconnect the negative battery cable. Remove the air cleaner assembly and the cruise control actuator.

2. Remove the clutch release cylinder and bracket. Remove the clutch accumulator and the tube clamp.

3. Remove the starter assembly. Disconnect the backup light switch electrical connector. Remove the ground straps.

4. Disconnect the control cables.

5. Remove the upper 3 transaxle mounting bolts.

6. Disconnect the vehicle speed sensor connector.

7. Raise and support the vehicle safely. Remove the undercovers. Drain the transaxle fluid.

8. Remove the exhaust front pipe and left halfshaft.

9. Remove the steering gear housing from the front suspension member.

10. Remove the stiffener plate and the engine shock absorber.

11. Remove the engine front and rear mounting set bolts and nuts.

12. Remove the engine left mounting, the steering column set bolts, then remove the front suspension member.

13. Properly support the transaxle assembly. Remove the engine-to-transaxle bolts, lower the left side of the engine and carefully ease the transaxle out of the engine compartment.

14. Installation is the reverse of removal. Tighten all fasteners.

15. Fill the transaxle with gear oil and perform road test.

4WD

1. Remove the engine/transaxle assembly.

2. Remove the transfer case stiffener plate and the exhaust pipe front bracket.

3. Remove the left stiffener plate and the front engine mount.

4. Remove the left engine mount bracket and separate the transaxle from the engine.

5. Installation is in the reverse order of removal. Tighten the 12mm transaxle-to-engine mounting bolts to 47 ft. lbs. (64 Nm) and the 10mm bolts to 34 ft. lbs. (46 Nm).

Celica

2WD

1. Disconnect the negative battery cable. On some vehicles, it may be necessary to remove the battery. Remove the air cleaner assembly.

2. Remove the clutch tube bracket. Disconnect the backup light switch at the transaxle. Disconnect the speedometer and the engine ground strap.

3. Disconnect the transaxle control cable and position them aside.

4. Unbolt the clutch release cylinder. It may be possible to position it aside with the hydraulic line still attached.

5. Remove the upper transaxle retaining bolts. Raise the vehicle and support safely. Remove the engine undercover. Drain the transaxle fluid.

6. Disconnect the exhaust pipe from the manifold. Remove the lower suspension crossmember. Remove the starter assembly.

7. Properly support the engine and transaxle assembly. Remove the front and rear transaxle mounts. Remove the center engine mount.

8. Disconnect both halfshafts at the transaxle. Unbolt the steering knuckle from the suspension arm and pull it outward. Remove the left halfshaft.

9. On some vehicles, remove the No. 2 rear engine plate. With the engine properly supported remove the left engine mount.

10. Remove the engine-to-transaxle bolts, lower the left side of the engine and carefully ease the transaxle out of the engine compartment.

To install:

11. Install the transaxle and tighten the 12mm engine-to-tran-

saxle bolts to 47 ft. lbs. (64 Nm) and the 10mm bolts to 34 ft. lbs. (46 Nm).

12. Tighten the left engine mount bolts to 38 ft. lbs. (52 Nm).

13. Tighten the center member bolts and the front and rear engine mount bolts to 29 ft. lbs. (39 Nm).

4WD

1. Remove the engine and transaxle assembly.

2. Separate the transaxle from the engine.

3. Installation is in the reverse order of removal. Tighten the 12mm engine-to-transaxle bolts to 47 ft. lbs. (64 Nm) and the 10mm bolts to 34 ft. lbs. (46 Nm). Tighten the left engine mount bolts to 38 ft. lbs. (52 Nm). Tighten the center member bolts and the front and rear engine mount bolts to 29 ft. lbs. (39 Nm).

MR2

1. Disconnect the negative battery cable.

2. Raise the vehicle and support safely. Drain the transaxle fluid.

3. Remove the rear wheels and undercovers.

4. Disconnect the halfshafts from the knuckle and stabilizer bar from the knuckle.

5. Disconnect the exhaust pipe from the manifold.

6. Remove the air cleaner.

7. Disconnect the shift cables, clutch release cylinder and speedometer cable.

8. Remove the starter motor, rear end-plate and engine stiffener plate.

9. Install an engine holding fixture to support the engine and transaxle. Remove the engine and transaxle mounting brackets.

10. Place a suitable transaxle jack under the assembly, remove the bell housing bolts and remove the transaxle from the vehicle.

To install:

11. Place a suitable transaxle jack under the assembly, Install the transaxle bolts and torque to 47 ft. lbs. (64 Nm).

12. Install the engine and transaxle mounting brackets. Torque the engine mounts to 71 ft. lbs. (96 Nm), transaxle bolts to 47 ft. lbs. (64 Nm) and the stiffener plate bolts to 27 ft. lbs. (37 Nm).

13. Install the starter motor, rear end-plate and engine stiffener plate.

14. Connect the shift cables, clutch release cylinder and speedometer cable.

15. Install the air cleaner.

16. Connect the exhaust pipe to the manifold and torque to 46 ft. lbs. (62 Nm).

17. Connect the halfshafts to the knuckle and stabilizer bar to the knuckle.

18. Install the rear wheels and undercovers.

19. Lower the vehicle safely.

20. Connect the negative battery cable, refill the transaxle and check for leaks.

LINKAGE ADJUSTMENT

Manual transaxle linkage adjustments are neither possible or necessary. Damaged bushings can cause shift cable problems.

CLUTCH

——— CAUTION ———
To avoid personal injury and accidental deployment of the air bag, work must be started after about 90 seconds or longer from the time the ignition switch is turned to the LOCK position and the battery cable is disconnected from the battery.

Clutch Assembly

REMOVAL AND INSTALLATION

1. Disconnect the negative battery cable.

2. Remove the transmission or transaxle assembly from the vehicle.

NOTE: On the Corolla (4WD), the Camry (4WD) and Celica (4WD), the engine and transaxle are removed from the vehicle as an assembly.

3. Matchmark the clutch cover to the flywheel.

4. Remove the clutch pressure plate retaining bolts small amounts in a crisscross pattern to relieve the clutch disc spring tension.

5. Remove the clutch cover.

6. Remove the clutch disc.

7. Remove the retaining clip and withdraw the release bearing.

8. Remove the release fork and boot assembly.

To install:

9. Using a suitable clutch disc alignment tool, install the clutch disc onto the flywheel.

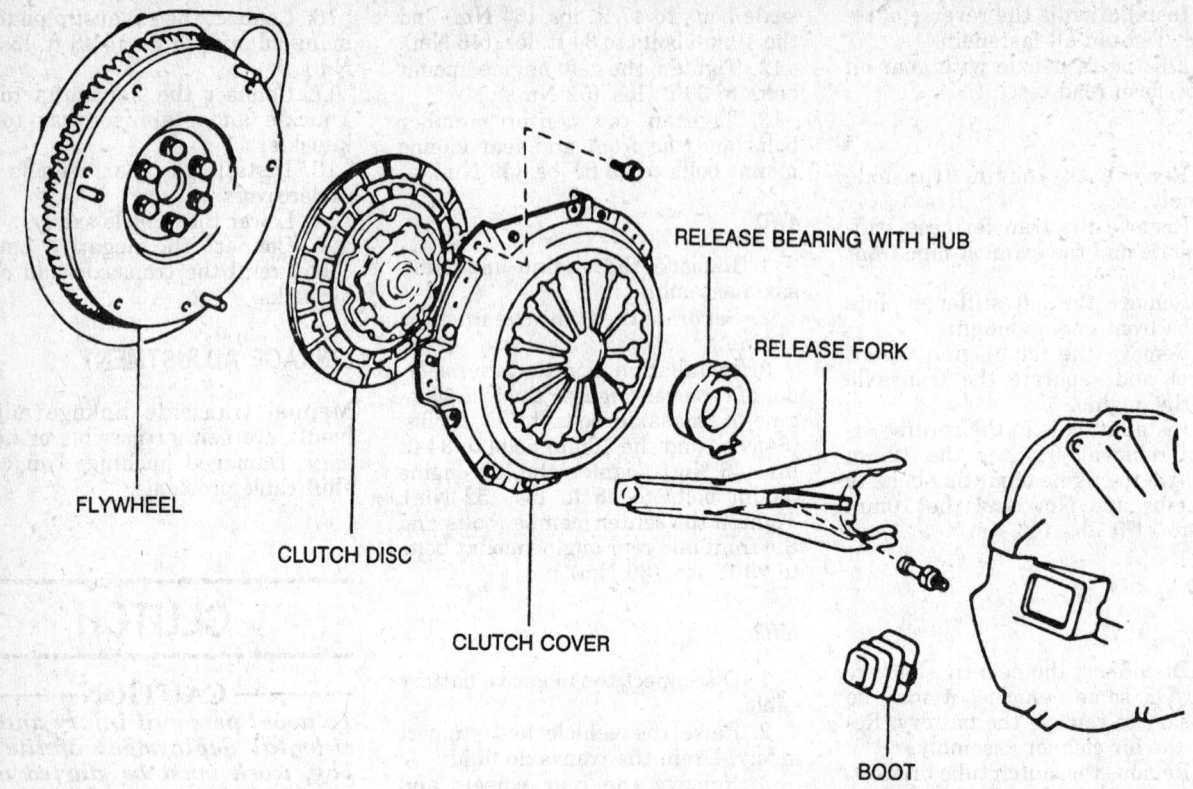

FLYWHEEL

CLUTCH DISC

CLUTCH COVER

RELEASE BEARING WITH HUB

RELEASE FORK

BOOT

Tighten the clutch cover retaining bolts in a crisscross pattern

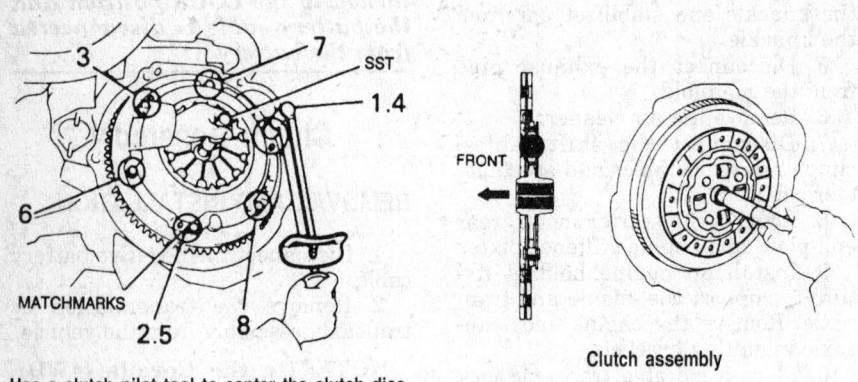

MATCHMARKS

SST

FRONT

Clutch assembly

Use a clutch pilot tool to center the clutch disc on the flywheel

10. Position the clutch cover onto the flywheel and align the matchmarks.

11. Install the clutch cover retaining bolts. Torque the bolts in a crisscross pattern to 14 ft. lbs. (19 Nm).

12. Lubricate the release fork pivot and contact points, release bearing, bearing hub and input shaft spline surfaces with a suitable molybdenum disulfide lithium based or multi-purpose grease.

13. Install the boot, release fork, hub and bearing assemblies.

14. Install the transmission or transaxle.

PEDAL HEIGHT/FREE-PLAY ADJUSTMENT

1. Adjust the clearance between the master cylinder piston and the pushrod to specification by loosening the pushrod locknut and rotating the pushrod while depressing the clutch pedal lightly.

2. Tighten the locknut when finished the adjustment.

3. Adjust the release cylinder free-play by loosening the release cylinder pushrod locknut and rotating the pushrod until proper specification is obtained.

4. Measure the clutch pedal free-play after performing the adjustments. If it fails to fall within specification, repeat the procedure. Pedal free-play specifications are as follows:

Tercel — 0.2-0.59 in. (5-15mm)
Corolla — 0.2-0.59 in. (5-15mm)
Celica — 0.2-0.59 in. (5-15mm)
Supra — 0.2-0.59 in. (5-15mm)
MR2 — 0.2-0.59 in. (5-15mm).
Paseo — 0.2-0.59 in. (5-15mm).
Camry — 0.2-0.59 in. (5-15mm).

Clutch Master Cylinder

REMOVAL AND INSTALLATION

Rear Wheel Drive

1. Disconnect the negative battery cable. Remove the pushrod clevis pin and clip.

NOTE: On some vehicles, it will be necessary to remove the under dash panel in order to gain access to the pushrod clevis pin.

2. Disconnect the fluid line.

3. Unbolts and remove the clutch master cylinder.

4. Installation is the reverse of the removal procedure. Bleed the system.

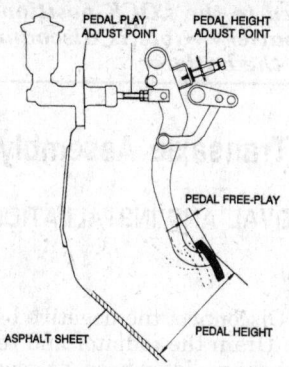

Clutch pedal adjustment points

Front Wheel Drive

1. Disconnect the negative battery cable.
2. On the Tercel, remove the reservoir tank from the clutch master cylinder.
3. On Celica with 3S-GTE engine, remove the brace that runs across the struts. On the MR2, remove the spare tire guard and luggage compartment trim cover.
4. Remove the ABS control relay, if equipped.
5. Remove the pushrod clevis pin and clip.

NOTE: On some vehicles, it will be necessary to remove the under dash panel in order to gain access to the pushrod clevis pin.

6. On the Corolla with the 4A-GE engine, remove the brake booster.
7. Disconnect the fluid line and plug the end of the line to prevent leakage.
8. Unbolt and remove the clutch master cylinder.
9. Installation is the reverse of the removal procedure. Bleed the system.

Clutch Slave Cylinder

REMOVAL AND INSTALLATION

Except MR2

1. Disconnect the negative battery cable. Raise and support the vehicle safely.
2. Remove the gravel shield, if equipped.
3. Disconnect the fluid line.
4. Remove the slave cylinder retaining bolts.
5. Remove the clutch slave cylinder from the vehicle.
6. Installation is the reverse of the removal procedure. Bleed the system.

MR2

1. Disconnect the negative battery cable.
2. Raise and support the vehicle safely.
3. Remove the engine undercover.
4. Disconnect the control cables from the transaxle.
5. Disconnect the fluid line.
6. Support the engine and transaxle.
7. From the engine side, remove the engine front mounting bracket bolts.
8. Unbolt and remove the clutch slave cylinder.
9. Installation is the reverse of the removal procedure. Bleed the system.

Hydraulic Clutch System Bleeding

1. Check and fill the clutch fluid reservoir to the specified level as necessary. During the bleeding process, continue to check and replenish the reservoir to prevent the fluid level from getting lower than ½ the specified level.
2. Remove the dust cap from the bleeder screw on the clutch slave cylinder and connect a tube to the bleeder screw and insert the other end of the tube into a clean glass or metal container.

NOTE: Take precautionary measures to prevent the brake fluid from getting on any painted surfaces.

3. Pump the clutch pedal several times, hold it down and loosen the bleeder screw slowly.
4. Tighten the bleeder screw and release the clutch pedal gradually. Repeat this operation until air bubbles disappear from the brake fluid being expelled out through the bleeder screw.

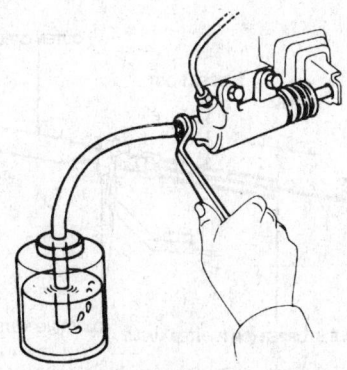

Bleeding the clutch hydraulic system

5. Repeat until all evidence of air bubbles completely disappears from the fluid being pumped out of the tube.
6. When the air is completely removed, tighten the bleeder screw and replace the dust cap.
7. Check and refill the master cylinder reservoir, as necessary.
8. Depress the clutch pedal several times to check the operation of the clutch and check for leaks.

AUTOMATIC TRANSMISSION

———— CAUTION ————
To avoid personal injury and accidental deployment of the air bag, work must be started after about 90 seconds or longer from the time the ignition switch is turned to the LOCK position and the battery cable is disconnected from the battery.

Transmission Assembly

REMOVAL AND INSTALLATION

Cressida

1. Disconnect the negative battery cable. Drain the radiator and remove the upper radiator hose. Remove the air cleaner assembly. Disconnect the transmission throttle cable.
2. Raise the vehicle and support it safely. Drain the transmission fluid. Remove the driveshaft along with the center bearing.
3. Remove the exhaust pipe together with the catalytic converter. Disconnect the manual shift linkage. Remove the speedometer cable.
4. Disconnect the oil cooler lines. As necessary, remove the transmission oil filler tube. As required, remove the starter assembly. Remove the speedometer cable.
5. Remove both stiffener plates and the catalytic converter cover from the transmission housing and cylinder block.
6. Support the engine and transmission properly. Remove the rear crossmember.
7. Remove the torque converter cover. Remove the torque converter-to-engine retaining bolts.
8. Remove the bolts retaining the transmission to the engine. carefully

remove the transmission from the vehicle.

To install:

9. Install the transmission into the vehicle and torque the bellhousing bolts to 35 ft. lbs. (48 Nm).

10. Install the exhaust pipe, starter motor and crossmember. Torque the crossmember bolts to 47 ft. lbs. (64 Nm). Torque the torque converter bolts to 20 ft. lbs. (27 Nm).

11. Install the transmission cables, linkage and driveshaft.

12. Refill the transmission with the approved fluid and check for leaks.

13. Lower the vehicle. Road test the vehicle and check operation.

Supra

1. Disconnect the negative battery cable. Remove the air cleaner assembly. Disconnect the transmission throttle cable.

2. Raise the vehicle and support it safely. Drain the transmission fluid. Disconnect the electrical connectors for the neutral safety switch and backup lights.

3. Remove the intermediate driveshaft along with the center bearing. Disconnect the exhaust pipe from the tail pipe.

4. Disconnect the transmission oil cooler lines. Plug the lines to prevent leakage. Disconnect the manual shift linkage and speedometer cable.

5. Remove the exhaust pipe bracket and torque converter cover.

6. Remove both stiffener brackets.

7. Support the engine and transmission using the proper equipment. Remove the rear crossmember.

8. Remove the engine undercover. Remove the torque converter-to-engine retaining bolts. Remove the starter.

9. Remove the bolts retaining the transmission to the engine. Carefully remove the transmission from the vehicle.

To install:

10. Install the transmission into the vehicle and torque the bellhousing bolts to 35 ft. lbs. (48 Nm).

11. Install the exhaust pipe, starter motor and crossmember. Torque the crossmember bolts to 40 ft. lbs. (54 Nm).

12. Install the transmission cables, linkage and driveshaft. Adjust the throttle cable.

13. Refill the transmission with the approved fluid and check for leaks.

14. Lower the vehicle. Road test the vehicle and check operation.

SHIFT LINKAGE ADJUSTMENT

1. Loosen the nut on the shift linkage. Push the selector lever all the way to the rear of the vehicle.

2. Return the lever 2 notches to the **N** shift position.

3. While holding the selector lever slightly toward the **R** shift position, tighten the connecting rod nut.

THROTTLE LINKAGE ADJUSTMENT

1. Remove the air cleaner.

2. Confirm that the accelerator linkage opens the throttle fully. Adjust the linkage as necessary.

3. Peel the rubber dust boot back from the throttle cable.

4. Loosen the adjustment nuts on the throttle cable bracket (cylinder head cover) just enough to allow cable housing movement.

5. Depress the accelerator pedal fully.

6. Adjust the cable housing so the gap between its end and the cable stop collar is 0.04 in. (1.0mm).

7. Tighten the adjustment nuts. Make sure the adjustment has not changed. Install the dust boot and the air cleaner.

AUTOMATIC TRANSAXLE

— CAUTION —
To avoid personal injury and accidental deployment of the air bag, work must be started after about 90 seconds or longer from the time the ignition switch is
---

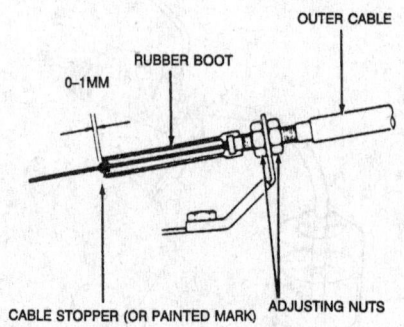

Throttle cable adjustment

turned to the LOCK position and the battery cable is disconnected from the battery.

Transaxle Assembly

REMOVAL AND INSTALLATION

Tercel

1. Disconnect the negative battery cable. Drain the radiator and remove the upper radiator hose, as required. Remove the air cleaner assembly.

2. Raise the vehicle and support it safely. Remove both halfshafts.

3. Remove the torque converter cover. Remove the bolts that retain the torque converter to the crankshaft. Remove the exhaust pipe. Remove the shift lever rod.

4. Remove the speedometer cable and backup light connector. Disconnect and remove all throttle linkage.

5. Remove the fluid lines from the transaxle. Remove the starter assembly, as required.

6. Support the engine and transaxle using a suitable jack. Remove the rear crossmember.

7. Remove the transaxle-to-engine retaining bolts. Separate the transaxle from the engine and carefully remove it from the vehicle.

To install:

8. Install the transaxle and tighten the transaxle-to-engine bolts to 47 ft. lbs. (64 Nm). Tighten the left engine mount bracket bolts to 32 ft. lbs. (43 Nm). Tighten the rear engine mount bracket bolts to 43 ft. lbs. (58 Nm). Tighten the torque converter mounting bolts to 13 ft. lbs. (18 Nm).

9. Install the transaxle cables, linkage and halfshafts.

10. Refill the transaxle if necessary with the approved fluid and check for leaks.

11. Lower the vehicle. Road test the vehicle and check operation.

Paseo

1. Disconnect the negative battery cable. Remove the air cleaner and air duct assembly.

2. Raise the vehicle and support it safely. Remove both halfshafts. Drain the fluid from the transaxle.

3. Remove the torque converter cover. Remove the torque converter bolts. Remove the exhaust pipe. Remove the shift lever rod.

4. Remove the speedometer cable and backup light connector. Disconnect and remove all linkage or cables. Disconnect the electrical connectors.

5. Remove the fluid lines from the transaxle. Remove the starter assembly.

6. Support the engine and transaxle using a suitable jack. Remove the rear crossmember.

7. Remove the transaxle-to-engine retaining bolts. Separate the transaxle from the engine and carefully remove it from the vehicle.

To install:

8. Install the transaxle and tighten the transaxle-to-engine bolts to 47 ft. lbs. (64 Nm). Tighten the left engine mount bracket bolts to 32 ft. lbs. (43 Nm). Tighten the rear engine mount bracket bolts to 43 ft. lbs. (58 Nm). Tighten the torque converter mounting bolts to 13 ft. lbs. (18 Nm).

9. Install the transaxle cables, linkage and halfshafts. Torque the starter bolt and nuts to 29 ft. lbs. (39 Nm).

10. Reinstall the removed components and refill the transaxle with the approved fluid. Check for leaks.

11. Lower the vehicle. Road test and check operation.

Corolla

1. Disconnect the negative battery cable. Remove the air cleaner.

2. Disconnect the neutral start switch. Disconnect the speedometer cable.

3. Disconnect the shift control cable and throttle linkage.

4. Disconnect the oil cooler hose. Plug the end of the hose to prevent leakage.

5. Drain the radiator and remove the water inlet pipe.

6. Raise and support the vehicle safely. Drain the transaxle fluid. As required remove the exhaust front pipe.

7. Remove the engine undercover. Remove the front and rear transaxle mounts.

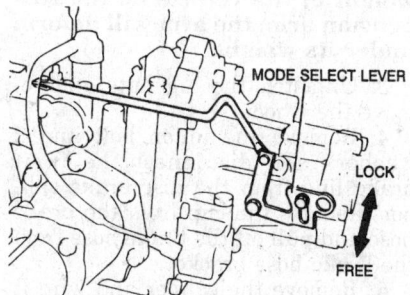

Setting the mode selector — Corolla with A241H

8. Support the engine and transaxle using the proper equipment. Remove the engine center support member.

9. Remove the halfshafts. Remove the starter assembly. Remove the steering knuckles, as required.

10. Remove the flywheel cover plate. Remove the torque converter bolts.

11. Remove the left engine mount. Remove the transaxle-to-engine bolts. Slowly and carefully back the transaxle away from the engine. Lower the assembly to the floor.

To install:

12. Install the transaxle and tighten the transaxle-to-engine bolts to 47 ft. lbs. (64 Nm). Tighten the left engine mount bracket bolts to 32 ft. lbs. (43 Nm). Tighten the rear engine mount bracket bolts to 43 ft. lbs. (58 Nm). Tighten the torque converter mounting bolts to 13 ft. lbs. (18 Nm).

13. When installing the A241H vehicle transaxle on 4WD vehicles, be sure the mode selector lever is positioned in the **FREE** mode and attach the lock bolt.

14. Install the transaxle cables, linkage and halfshafts.

15. Refill the transaxle with the approved fluid and check for leaks.

16. Lower the vehicle. Road test the vehicle and check operation.

Camry

1. Disconnect the negative battery cable. Remove the air flow meter and the air cleaner assembly.

2. Disconnect the transaxle wire connector. Disconnect the neutral safety switch electrical connector.

3. Disconnect the transaxle ground strap. Disconnect the throttle cable from the throttle linkage.

4. Remove the transaxle case protector. Disconnect the speedometer cable and control cable.

5. Disconnect the oil cooler hoses. Remove the upper starter retaining bolts, as required remove the starter assembly. Remove the upper transaxle housing bolts. Remove the engine rear mount insulator bracket set bolt.

6. Raise and support the vehicle safely. Drain the transaxle fluid.

7. Remove the left front fender apron seal. Disconnect both driveshafts.

8. Remove the suspension lower crossmember assembly. Remove the center driveshaft if equipped.

9. Remove the engine mounting center crossmember. Remove the stabilizer bar. Remove the left steering knuckle from the lower control arm.

10. Remove the torque converter cover. Remove the torque converter retaining bolts.

11. Properly support the engine and transaxle assembly. Remove the rear engine mounting bolts. Remove the remaining transaxle to engine retaining bolts.

12. Carefully remove the transaxle assembly from the vehicle.

To install:

13. Install the transaxle and tighten the 12mm transaxle housing bolts to 47 ft. lbs. (64 Nm) and the 10mm bolts to 34 ft. lbs. (46 Nm). Tighten the rear engine mount set bolts to 38 ft. lbs. (52 Nm). Tighten the torque converter mounting bolts to 20 ft. lbs. (27 Nm).

14. Install the transaxle cables, linkage and halfshafts.

15. Refill the transaxle with the approved fluid and check for leaks.

16. Lower the vehicle. Road test the vehicle and check operation.

Celica

1. Disconnect the negative battery cable. Remove the air flow meter and the air cleaner hose.

2. Disconnect the speedometer cable. Remove the starter assembly electrical connections. Disconnect the throttle cable from the throttle linkage and bracket.

3. Disconnect the ground strap. Remove the starter retaining bolts and starter assembly.

4. Remove the upper transaxle housing retaining bolts. Remove the engine rear mount insulator bracket retaining bolt.

5. Raise and support the vehicle safely. Drain the transaxle fluid. Remove the engine undercovers.

6. Remove the lower suspension crossmember. Disconnect the front and rear mounting components. Remove the engine mounting center member.

7. Remove the left halfshaft. Disconnect the right halfshaft.

8. Disconnect the exhaust pipe from the manifold. Remove the stiffener plate. Disconnect the control cable.

9. Disconnect the oil cooler hoses. Remove the torque converter cover. Remove the torque converter retaining bolts.

10. Support the engine and transaxle assembly, using the proper equipment. Remove the transaxle-to-engine retaining bolts. Disconnect the front and rear transmission mount bolts.

11. Carefully lower the transaxle assembly to the floor.

To install:

12. Install the transaxle and tighten the 12mm engine-to-transaxle bolts to 47 ft. lbs. (64 Nm) and the 10mm bolts to 34 ft. lbs. (46 Nm). Tighten the torque converter bolts to 20 ft. lbs. (27 Nm). Tighten the left engine mount bracket bolts to 32 ft. lbs. (43 Nm). Tighten the rear engine mount bracket bolts to 43 ft. lbs. (58 Nm).

13. Install the transaxle cables, linkage and halfshafts.

14. Refill the transaxle with the approved fluid and check for leaks.

15. Lower the vehicle. Road test the vehicle and check operation.

MR2

1. Disconnect the negative battery cable. Remove the air flow meter and the air cleaner hose.

2. Remove the water inlet set bolts. Disconnect the ground strap. Remove the transaxle mounting set bolt.

3. Disconnect the speedometer cable at the transaxle. Disconnect the throttle cable from the throttle linkage and the bracket.

4. Raise and support the vehicle safely. Drain the transaxle fluid. Remove the left tire.

5. Remove the transaxle gravel shield. Disconnect the speedometer cable at the transaxle assembly.

6. Disconnect the oil cooler lines at the transaxle. Remove the transaxle control cable clip and retainer and then disconnect the cable from the bracket. Remove the bracket.

7. Remove the starter assembly. Disconnect the exhaust pipe at the manifold. Remove the pipe.

8. Remove the stiffener plate. Remove the rear engine end-plate. Remove the torque converter cover. Remove the torque converter retaining bolts.

9. Disconnect both the right and left halfshafts from their side gear shafts. Depress and hold the brake pedal while removing the halfshaft retaining nuts. Properly position the halfshaft aside.

10. Disconnect the suspension arm from the rear axle carrier, using the proper tools. Disconnect the rear axle carrier from the lower control arm.

11. Disconnect the halfshaft from the side gear shaft. Properly position the driveshaft aside.

12. Support the engine and transaxle assembly, using the proper equipment. Remove the transaxle-to-engine retaining bolts. Disconnect the front and rear transmission mount bolts.

13. Carefully lower the transaxle assembly to the floor.

To install:

14. Install the transaxle and tighten the transaxle-to-engine bolts to 47 ft. lbs. (64 Nm). Tighten the left engine mount bracket bolts to 32 ft. lbs. (43 Nm). Tighten the rear engine mount bracket bolts to 43 ft. lbs. (58 Nm). Tighten the torque converter mounting bolts to 20 ft. lbs. (27 Nm).

15. Install the transaxle cables, linkage and halfshafts.

16. Refill the transaxle with the approved fluid and check for leaks.

17. Lower the vehicle. Road test the vehicle and check operation.

SHIFT LINKAGE ADJUSTMENT

1. Loosen the swivel nut on the selector lever.

2. Push the lever fully toward the right side of the vehicle.

3. Return the lever 2 notches to the **N** position.

4. Set the shift lever in the **N** position.

5. While holding the selector lever slightly toward the **R** shift position, tighten the swivel nut to 48 inch lbs. (5.4 Nm).

THROTTLE LINKAGE ADJUSTMENT

1. Remove the air cleaner.

2. Confirm that the accelerator linkage opens the throttle fully. Adjust the linkage as necessary.

3. Peel the rubber dust boot back from the throttle cable.

4. Loosen the adjustment nuts on the throttle cable bracket (cylinder head cover) just enough to allow cable housing movement.

5. Depress the accelerator pedal fully.

6. Adjust the cable housing so the distance between its end and the cable stop collar is 0.04 in. (1.0mm).

7. Tighten the adjustment nuts. Make sure the adjustment has not changed. Install the dust boot and the air cleaner.

TRANSFER CASE

—— CAUTION ——

To avoid personal injury and accidental deployment of the air bag, work must be started after about 90 seconds or longer from the time the ignition switch is turned to the LOCK position and the battery cable is disconnected from the battery.

Transfer Case Assembly

REMOVAL AND INSTALLATION

Corolla (4WD), Camry (4WD) and Celica (4WD)

1. Remove the engine/transaxle assembly.

2. Separate the transaxle from the engine.

3. Remove the 3 bolts and 5 nuts and separate the transfer case from the transaxle. Use a rubber mallet to get the 2 separated.

4. Installation is in the reverse order of removal. Remove any packing material from the transfer case mating surface. Tighten the mounting bolts and nuts to 51 ft. lbs. (69 Nm).

FRONT SUSPENSION

—— CAUTION ——

To avoid personal injury and accidental deployment of the air bag, work must be started after about 90 seconds or longer from the time the ignition switch is turned to the LOCK position and the battery cable is disconnected from the battery.

MacPherson Strut

REMOVAL AND INSTALLATION

1. Remove the hubcap and loosen the lug nuts.

2. Raise and support the vehicle safely.

NOTE: Do not support the weight of the vehicle on the suspension arm; the arm will deform under its weight.

3. Unfasten the lug nuts and remove the wheel.

4. Remove the union bolt and 2 washers and disconnect the front brake line from the disc brake caliper. Remove the clip from the brake hose and pull off the brake hose from the brake hose bracket.

5. Remove the caliper and wire it aside. Matchmark the strut lower bracket and camber adjust cam, if equipped. Remove the 2 bolts and

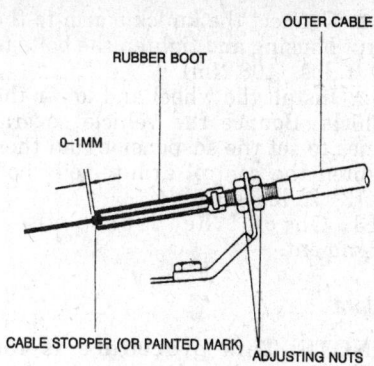

Throttle cable adjustment

nuts which attach the strut lower end to the steering knuckle lower arm.

6. Disconnect and remove the TEMS actuator from the top of the strut if equipped.

7. Remove the nuts which secure the upper strut mounting plate to the top of the wheel arch.

NOTE: Press down on the suspension lower arm, in order to remove the strut assembly. This must be done to clear the collars on the steering knuckle arm bolt holes when removing the shock/spring assembly.

To install:

8. Align the hole in the upper suspension support with the shock absorber piston or end, so they fit properly.

9. Always use a new nut and nylon washer on the shock absorber piston rod end when securing it to the upper suspension support. Torque the nut to 29-40 ft. lbs. (39-54 Nm).

NOTE: Do not use an impact wrench to tighten the nut.

10. Coat the suspension support bearing with multipurpose grease prior to installation. Pack the space in the upper support with multipurpose grease, also after installation.

11. Tighten the suspension support-to-wheel arch bolts to the following specifications:

Corolla — 29 ft. lbs. (39 Nm).
Celica — 47 ft. lbs. (64 Nm).
Camry — 47 ft. lbs. (64 Nm).
Cressida — 39 ft. lbs. (50 Nm).
Paseo — 29 ft. lbs. (39 Nm).
Tercel — 29 ft. lbs. (39 Nm).
Supra — 26 ft. lbs. (35 Nm).
MR2 — 29 ft. lbs. (39 Nm).

12. Tighten the shock absorber-to-steering knuckle arm bolts to the following specifications:

Corolla — 203 ft. lbs. (275 Nm).
1990-91 Tercel — 166 ft. lbs. (226 Nm).
1992-94 Tercel — 181 ft. lbs. (245 Nm).
Paseo — 166 ft. lbs. (226 Nm).
MR2 — 188 ft. lbs. (255 Nm).
Supra — 106 ft. lbs. (144 Nm).
Celica — 188 ft. lbs. (255 Nm).
Cressida — 80 ft. lbs. (109 Nm).
Camry — 224 ft. lbs. (304 Nm).

13. Adjust the front wheel bearing preload.

14. Bleed the brake system.

Coil Springs

REMOVAL AND INSTALLATION

1. Remove the strut assembly.
2. Compress the spring, using a spring compressor tool.
3. Remove the spring from the strut.
4. Carefully release the tension from the spring by releasing the compressor tool.

——— **CAUTION** ———
To avoid personal injury, chain or secure the spring to prevent it from being ejected. Wear eye protection. Being hit by the spring can cause severe injury.

5. Installation is the reverse of removal.

Upper Ball Joints

INSPECTION

Supra

1. Remove the front wheels and move the upper suspension arm up and down.
2. Check that the upper ball joint has no vertical play.

REMOVAL AND INSTALLATION

NOTE: If both upper and lower ball joints are to be replaced, always remove and install the lower one first.

Supra

The ball joint is an integral component of the upper control arm. Ball joint replacement requires that the entire arm assembly be replaced.

Lower Ball Joints

INSPECTION

Cressida

1. Raise the front end and position a 7 inch thick piece of wood under the tire.
2. Lower the vehicle until there is about a ½ load on the coil spring. Place jackstands for safety.
3. Make sure the wheels are straight-ahead and block the wheels with chocks.
4. Move the lower arm up and down and check that there is 0.098 in. (2.5mm) of vertical play or less.

Supra

1. Raise the front end and position a 7 inch thick piece of wood under the tire.
2. Lower the vehicle until there is about a ½ load on the coil spring. Place jackstands for safety.
3. Make sure the wheels are straight-ahead and block the wheels with chocks.
4. Move the lower arm up and down and check that there is 0.012 in. (0.3mm) of vertical play or less.

Paseo

1. Remove the lower ball joint.
2. Flip the ball joint stud back and forth 5 times, then install the nut on the stud.
3. With a needle type torque wrench, turn the nut continuously 1 turn per 3 seconds and read the torque on the 5th turn.
4. The turning torque should be 0.87-2.6 inch lbs. (1.0-2.9 Nm). Replace the ball joint if out of specifications.

Tercel, Camry, Corolla, Celica and MR2

1. Raise the vehicle and place wooden blocks under the front wheels.
2. Use jackstands for additional safety.
3. Make sure the front wheels are in a straight forward position.
4. Check the wheels.
5. Lower the jack until there is approximately ½ a load on the front springs.
6. Move the lower control arm up and down to check that there is no ball joint vertical play. Replace if any play exists.

REMOVAL AND INSTALLATION

NOTE: If replacing both upper and lower ball joints, always remove and install the lower ball joint first.

Celica

1. Raise and support the vehicle safely. Remove the wheels.
2. Disconnect the lower control arm from the steering knuckle.
3. Remove the nut and disconnect the stabilizer bar from the control arm.
4. On all but the left-side control arm, if with automatic transmissions, remove the control arm front set nut and washer. Remove the rear bracket bolts and then remove the arm.
5. On the left arm, if with automatic transmissions, remove the control arm front set nut and washer. Remove the 4 bolts and 2 nuts that attach the lower suspension crossmember to the frame and remove the crossmember. Remove the bolt and nut and lift out the lower arm with the lower arm shaft.
   To install:
6. On all but the left side control arm, if with automatic transmissions, install the lower control arm shaft washer with the tapered side toward the body. Install the lower arm with the bracket and then temporarily install the washer and nut to the lower arm shaft and bracket bolts.
7. On the left side arm, if with automatic transmissions, position the washer on the lower arm shaft and then install to the lower arm. Temporarily install the washer and nut to the shaft with the tapered side toward the body. Install the lower arm with the shaft to the body and temporarily install the rear brackets. Install the bolt and nut to the lower arm shaft and tighten to 154 ft. lbs. (208 Nm). Install the crossmember to the body and tighten the 4 bolts to 154 ft. lbs. (208 Nm). Tighten the 2 nuts to 29 ft. lbs. (39 Nm).
8. Connect the lower arm to the steering knuckle and tighten the bolt and 2 nuts to 94 ft. lbs. (127 Nm).
9. Connect the stabilizer bar to the control arm and tighten the nut to 26 ft. lbs. (35 Nm).
10. Install the wheel, lower the vehicle and bounce it several times to set the suspension.
11. Tighten the front set nut to 156 ft. lbs. (212 Nm). Tighten the rear bracket bolts to 72 ft. lbs. (98 Nm).

MR2

1. Raise the vehicle and support it safely. Remove the wheel.
2. Remove the cotter pin and castle nut and then press the lower arm out of the ball joint.
3. Press the ball joint out of the steering knuckle.
4. Remove the 2 nuts and disconnect the strut bar from the control arm.
5. Remove the lower control arm-to-body bolt and remove the arm.
   To install:
6. When installing the lower arm, position it in the strut bar and tighten the nuts finger-tight. Do the same thing with the arm-to-body bolt.
7. Connect the control arm to the ball joint and tighten the castle nut to 58 ft. lbs. (78 Nm). Install a new cotter pin.
8. Tighten the strut bar-to-arm bolts to 83 ft. lbs. (113 Nm).
9. Install the tires, lower the vehicle and bounce it several times to set the suspension.
10. Tighten the control arm-to-body bolt to 87 ft. lbs. (118 Nm). Check the wheel alignment.

Cressida

1. Raise and support the vehicle safely. Remove the wheels.
2. Remove the 2 knuckle arm-to-strut bolts. Pull down on the control arm and disconnect it and the knuckle arm from the strut.
3. Remove the cotter pin and nut and press the tie rod off the knuckle arm.
4. Remove the nut attaching the stabilizer bar to the control arm and disconnect the bar.
5. Remove the 2 nuts and then disconnect the strut bar from the control arm.
6. Disconnect the control arm from the crossmember and remove it and the rack boot protector as an assembly.
7. Remove the cotter pin and nut and then press the knuckle arm off the control arm.
   To install:
8. Press the knuckle arm into the control arm and then install the assembly into the crossmember.
9. Connect the stabilizer bar to the control arm and tighten the nut to 13 ft. lbs. (18 Nm).
10. Connect the strut bar to the control arm and tighten the nuts to 76 ft. lbs. (103 Nm).

11. Connect the knuckle arm to the strut housing and tighten the bolts to 80 ft. lbs. (108 Nm).
12. Install the wheel and lower the vehicle. Bounce the vehicle several times to set the suspension and then tighten the control arm-to-body bolt to 121 ft. lbs. (164 Nm).
13. Check the front wheel alignment.

Supra

NOTE: This procedure is for ball joint removal only.

1. Raise and support the vehicle safely.
2. Remove the wheels.
3. Remove the steering knuckle and then remove the upper control arm.
4. Remove the lower ball joint mounting nuts and the bolt. Remove the attachment plate.
5. Remove the lower ball joint.
6. Installation is in the reverse order of removal. Tighten the ball joint mounting bolt and nuts to 94 ft. lbs. (127 Nm).

Tercel

1. Raise and support the vehicle safely. Remove the wheels.
2. Remove the 2 bolts attaching the ball joint to the steering knuckle.
3. Remove the stabilizer bar nut, retainer and cushion.
4. Raise the opposite wheel until the body of the vehicle just lifts off the supports.
5. Loosen the lower control arm mounting bolt, wiggle the arm back and forth and then remove the bolt. Disconnect the lower control arm from the stabilizer bar.

NOTE: When removing the lower control arm, be careful not to lose the caster adjustment spacer.

6. Carefully mount the lower control arm in a vise and then, using a ball joint removal tool, disconnect the ball joint from the arm.
   To install:
7. Tighten the ball joint-to-control arm nut to 51-65 ft. lbs. (69-88 Nm) and use a new cotter pin.
8. Tighten the steering knuckle-to-control arm bolts to 59 ft. lbs. (80 Nm).
9. Before tightening the stabilizer bar nuts, mount the wheels and lower the vehicle. Bounce the vehicle several times to settle the suspension and then tighten the stabilizer bolts to 66-90 ft. lbs. (90-122 Nm).

10. Tighten the arm-to-body bolts to 83 ft. lbs. (113 Nm).

11. Check the front end alignment.

Paseo

1. Remove the steering knuckle with the axle hub.

2. Disconnect the lower ball joint from the knuckle.

3. Installation is the reverse of removal. Torque the ball joint to knuckle nut to 72 ft. lbs. (98 Nm). Torque the ball joint to lower arm nut to 59 ft. lbs. (80 Nm).

Corolla

1. On all vehicles, except the left side on those with automatic transaxle, perform the following:

 a. Remove the bolt and 2 nuts attaching the ball joint to the lower arm and disconnect the lower arm from the steering knuckle.

 b. On 4A-FE and 7A-FE engines, remove the nut holding the stabilizer bar to the lower arm and disconnect the bar from the arm.

 c. On 4A-GE engine, remove the lower nut on the stabilizer bar link and disconnect the link from the arm.

 d. Remove the rear bracket bolts and nut. Remove the lower arm front mounting bolt.

 e. Remove the rear bracket and the stabilizer bar bracket and lift out the lower control arm.

2. To remove the left control arm, if with automatic transaxle, perform the following:

 a. Disconnect the arm at the steering knuckle.

 b. Disconnect the stabilizer bar at the lower arm.

 c. Remove the lower arm rear brackets. Move the stabilizer bar toward the rear and remove the bracket.

 d. Remove the 6 bolts and 2 nuts and remove the suspension crossmember with the lower arm.

 e. Remove the lower arm from the crossmember.

To install:

3. To install the left control arm, if with automatic transaxle, install the lower arm on the crossmember and install the assembly to the body.

4. On all others, install the lower arm to the body, move the stabilizer bar into position and install the front mounting bolt. Install the stabilizer bar and rear brackets.

5. Connect the lower arm to the steering knuckle and tighten the bolts to 105 ft. lbs. (142 Nm).

6. On 4A-GE engine, connect the stabilizer bar link to the lower arm and tighten the nut to 26 ft. lbs. (35 Nm).

7. On vehicles except 4A-GE engine, connect the stabilizer bar to the lower arm and tighten the nut to 13 ft. lbs. (18 Nm).

8. Lower the vehicle and bounce it several times to stabilize the suspension. Tighten the lower arm front bolt to 152 ft. lbs. (206 Nm). Tighten the rear bracket bolts to 94 ft. lbs. (127 Nm) on the lower arm side, 37 ft. lbs. (50 Nm) on the stabilizer bar side and tighten the small bolt and nut to 14 ft. lbs. (19 Nm).

9. Check the front end alignment.

Camry

1. Raise and support the vehicle safely. Remove the wheels.

2. Remove the 2 bolts attaching the ball joint to the steering knuckle.

3. Remove the stabilizer bar nut, retainer and cushion.

4. Remove the nut attaching the lower arm shaft to the lower arm.

5. Remove the lower suspension crossmember (2 bolts and 4 nuts).

6. Remove the lower control arm and lower arm shaft as an assembly.

7. Grip the lower arm assembly in a vise and remove the ball joint cotter pin and retaining nut. With a ball joint removal tool, pull the ball joint out of the control arm.

To install:

8. Position the ball joint in the lower arm and tighten the nut to 90 ft. lbs. (123 Nm). Install a new cotter pin.

9. Install the lower arm to the stabilizer bar and then install the lower arm shaft to the body. Install the lower arm nut and retainer. Screw on a new stabilizer bar end nut and retainer.

10. Connect the ball joint to the steering knuckle and tighten the bolts to 83 ft. lbs. (113 Nm).

11. Install the suspension lower crossmember. Tighten the inner bolts to 32 ft. lbs. (43 Nm) and the outer bolts to 153 ft. lbs. (207 Nm).

12. Install the wheels and lower the vehicle. Bounce it several times to set the suspension.

13. Tighten the stabilizer bar end nut and the lower arm shaft-to-lower arm bolt to 156 ft. lbs. (212 Nm).

Upper Control Arm

REMOVAL AND INSTALLATION

Supra

1. Raise and support the vehicle safely. Remove the wheels.

2. Unclip the brake hose bracket at the steering knuckle, remove the retaining nut and press the upper arm out of the knuckle.

3. Remove the upper mounting bolt and nut and lift out the upper control arm.

To install:

4. Connect the upper arm to the body. Connect the arm to the steering knuckle.

5. Install the wheels and lower the vehicle. Bounce it several times to set the suspension and then tighten the arm-to-knuckle nut to 80 ft. lbs. (108 Nm). Tighten the arm-to-body bolt to 121 ft. lbs. (164 Nm).

Lower Control Arms

REMOVAL AND INSTALLATION

Tercel and Celica

1. Raise the vehicle and support safely. Remove the front wheels.

2. Disconnect the lower arm from the steering knuckle, at the ball joint.

3. Disconnect the stabilizer bar from the lower arm.

4. Remove the lower arm by loosening the front bolt. Remove the bracket bolts, stabilizer bracket and front bolt.

5. Remove the lower arm.

To install:

6. Install the lower arm assemblies. Loosely install the lower arm bushing bolts and clamp.

7. Install the ball joint bolts and torque to 59 ft. lbs. (80 Nm) for the Tercel and 94 ft. lbs. (127 Nm) for the Celica.

8. Install the stabilizer and torque to 76 ft. lbs. (103 Nm) for the Tercel and 26 ft. lbs. (34 Nm) for the Celica.

9. Install the front wheels and lower the vehicle. Bounce up and down to stabilize the suspension. With the vehicle weight on the suspension, torque the front side bolts to 105 ft. lbs. (142 Nm) for the Tercel or 156 ft. lbs. (212 Nm) for the Celica. Torque the rear bracket bolts to 94 ft. lbs. (126 Nm) for the Tercel and 72 ft. lbs. (96 Nm) for the Celica.

10. Check the front end alignment.

Paseo

1. Raise and support the vehicle safely. Remove the wheels.

2. Disconnect the lower arm from the lower ball joint.

3. Remove the lower arm by removing the 3 bolts.

To install:

4. Install lower arm and temporarily install the 3 bolts.

5. Connect the lower arm to the lower ball joint and torque the bolt and nuts to 59 ft. lbs. (80 Nm).

6. Install the wheels and stabilize the suspension by bouncing the vehicle several times.

7. Raise the vehicle and support the body with stands.

8. Support the lower arm with a floor jack.

9. Torque the front side bolts to 105 ft. lbs. (142 Nm) and the rear bolt to 94 ft. lbs. (127 Nm).

10. Lower the vehicle and check the front end alignment.

Corolla

1. Raise the vehicle and support safely. Remove the front wheels.

2. Disconnect the lower arm from the steering knuckle, at the ball joint.

3. Disconnect the stabilizer bar from the lower arm.

4. Remove the lower arm by loosening the front bolt. Remove the bracket bolts and nuts, rear and stabilizer bracket and front bolt, except left side with an automatic transaxle.

5. Remove the lower arms with the suspension crossmember with automatic transaxle. Remove the 4 left and right lower arm rear brackets, stabilizer bar bracket and 6 crossmember bolts.

To install:

6. Install the crossmember and lower arm assemblies. Loosely install the lower arm bushing bolts.

7. Install the ball joint bolts and torque to 105 ft. lbs. (142 Nm).

8. Install the stabilizer and torque to 26 ft. lbs. (35 Nm).

9. Install the front wheels and lower the vehicle. Bounce up and down to stabilize the suspension. With the vehicle weight on the suspension, torque the lower control arm bushing bolts to 174 ft. lbs. (235 Nm) for the front bolt, 94 ft. lbs. (126 Nm) for the lower arm side, 37 ft. lbs. (50 Nm) for the stabilizer bar side and 14 ft. lbs. (19 Nm) for the small bolt and nut.

10. Check the front end alignment.

Camry

1. Raise the vehicle and support safely. Remove the front wheels.

2. Disconnect the lower arm from the steering knuckle, at the ball joint.

3. Disconnect the stabilizer bar from the lower arm.

4. Remove the crossmember and lower arm as an assembly. Remove the lower suspension with the lower suspension arm shaft.

To install:

5. Install the crossmember and lower arm assemblies. Loosely install the lower arm bushing bolts. Torque the crossmember bolts to 112 ft. lbs. (152 Nm).

6. Install the ball joint bolts and torque to 90 ft. lbs. (123 Nm).

7. Install the stabilizer nut loosely.

8. Install the front wheels and lower the vehicle. Bounce up and down to stabilize the suspension. With the vehicle weight on the suspension, torque the lower control arm bushing and stabilizer nuts to 156 ft. lbs. (212 Nm).

9. Check the front end alignment.

Supra

1. Raise and support the vehicle safely. Remove the wheels.

2. Disconnect the stabilizer bar link from the lower control arm. Remove the locknut and press the ball joint out of the steering knuckle.

3. Disconnect the lower control arm at the strut. Matchmark the front and rear adjusting cams to the body. Remove the nuts and cams and then remove the lower arm.

4. Unbolt the ball joint from the control arm.

To install:

5. Install the ball joint to the arm and tighten the nuts to 94 ft. lbs. (127 Nm).

6. Position the lower control arm and install the adjusting cams and nuts finger-tight.

7. Connect the ball joint to the steering knuckle and tighten a conventional nut to 14 ft. lbs. (20 Nm). Install a locknut on top of the other and tighten it to 107 ft. lbs. (145 Nm).

8. Tighten the arm-to-strut bolt to 106 ft. lbs. (143 Nm). Tighten the stabilizer bar link nut to 47 ft. lbs. (64 Nm).

9. Install the wheels and lower the vehicle. Bounce the vehicle several times to set the suspension. Align the matchmarks on the adjusting cams and the body and tighten them to 177 ft. lbs. (240 Nm). Check the front alignment.

MR2

1. Raise the vehicle and support safely. Remove the front wheels.

2. Disconnect the lower arm from the steering knuckle, at the ball joint using a ball joint separator.

3. Disconnect the stabilizer and strut bar from the lower arm.

4. Remove the lower arm by loosening the front bolt.

To install:

5. Install the lower arm assembly. Loosely install the lower arm bushing bolt.

6. Install the ball joint bolts and torque to 58 ft. lbs. (78 Nm).

7. Install the stabilizer and torque to 47 ft. lbs. (64 Nm). Install the strut bar bolts and torque to 83 ft. lbs. (113 Nm).

8. Install the front wheels and lower the vehicle. Bounce up and down to stabilize the suspension. With the vehicle weight on the suspension, torque the lower control arm bushing bolts to 87 ft. lbs. (118 Nm).

9. Check the front end alignment.

Sway Bar

REMOVAL AND INSTALLATION

1. Raise and support the vehicle safely.

2. Carefully remove the sway bar bushing brackets.

3. Remove the sway bar link ends, making a note of the order of the bushings, spacers and washers.

4. Remove the sway bar. It may be necessary to remove additional components for clearance.

5. Installation is the reverse of removal. Do not overtighten the link ends, since the rubber bushings can be damaged.

Front Wheel Bearings

NOTE: These procedures apply to rear wheel drive vehicles only. For front wheel bearing service on front wheel drive vehicles, refer to Drive Axle.

ADJUSTMENT

The Supra, MR2 and Cressida use a hub type front wheel bearing. It is not adjustable. The bearing axial play limit is 0.0020 in. (0.05mm). If the play exceeds this limit, replace the bearing.

REMOVAL AND INSTALLATION

NOTE: Be careful not to damage any ABS parts on vehicles so equipped.

Cressida

1. Raise the vehicle and support safely. Remove the front wheel.
2. Remove the brake caliper and the rotor disc.
3. Remove the bearing cap.
4. Remove the speed sensor, if equipped with ABS.
5. Using a chisel, unstake the hub nut and remove it.
6. Remove the axle hub from the steering knuckle.
7. Remove the oil seal.
8. Remove the snapring and, using a press, remove the hub bearing.
To install:
9. Install a new bearing using a press and install the snapring.
10. Install the oil seal. Do not damage the ABS sensor rotor.
11. Install the axle hub to the steering knuckle.
12. Install a new nut and torque it to 108 ft. lbs. (147 Nm). Stake the nut.
13. Install the ABS sensor and torque the bolt to 9 ft. lbs. (12 Nm).
14. Install the grease cap, rotor and caliper. Torque the caliper bolts to 67 ft. lbs. (91 Nm).
15. Install the wheel and test drive.

MR2 and Supra

1. Raise the vehicle and support safely. Remove the front wheel.
2. Remove the brake caliper and the rotor disc.
3. Remove the bearing cap.
4. Remove the speed sensor if equipped with ABS.
5. Remove the steering knuckle with the axle hub.
6. Remove the bearing cap.
7. Using a chisel, unstake the hub nut and remove it.
8. Remove the speed sensor rotor if equipped with ABS, or remove the inner spacer.
9. Remove the axle hub from the steering knuckle or axle bearing.
10. Remove the inner race on the Supra.
11. Remove the dust cover.
12. Remove the oil seal on the Supra.
13. Remove the snapring.
14. Remove the inner race on the MR2.
15. Remove the remaining hub bearing.

To install:
16. Install a new hub bearing and the snapring.
17. Install the outer seal on the Supra.
18. Install the dust cover.
19. Install the axle hub with a press.
20. Install the spacer or sensor rotor on the MR2.
21. Install a new locknut and torque to 90 ft. lbs. (123 Nm) on the MR2 or 147 ft. lbs. (199 Nm) on the Supra. Stake the nut with a chisel.
22. Install the cap.
23. Install the knuckle with the axle hub.
24. Reassemble the other removed parts and test drive the vehicle. Check the front end alignment.

REAR SUSPENSION

--- **CAUTION** ---
To avoid personal injury and accidental deployment of the air bag, work must be started after about 90 seconds or longer from the time the ignition switch is turned to the LOCK position and the battery cable is disconnected from the battery.

Shock Absorbers

REMOVAL AND INSTALLATION

Corolla 4WD

1. Raise and support the vehicle safely. Support the rear axle.
2. Unfasten the upper shock absorber retaining nuts. It may be necessary to hold the shock absorber shaft with a suitable tool while removing the top retaining nut.

NOTE: Always remove and install the shock absorbers one at a time. Do not allow the rear axle to hang in place as this may cause damage.

3. Remove the lower shock retaining nut where it attaches to the rear axle housing.
4. Remove the shock absorber.
5. Inspect the shock for wear, leaks or other signs of damage.
6. Installation is in the reverse order of removal. During installation, observe the following:
   a. Tighten the upper retaining nuts to 18 ft. lbs. (25 Nm).

b. Tighten the lower retaining nuts to 27 ft. lbs. (37 Nm).

MacPherson Strut

REMOVAL AND INSTALLATION

Tercel

1. Working inside the vehicle, remove the shock absorber cover and package tray bracket.
2. Raise the rear of the vehicle and support safely. Remove the wheel.
3. Disconnect the brake line from the wheel cylinder, if necessary. Disconnect the brake line from the flexible hose at the mounting bracket on the strut tube. Disconnect the flexible hose from the strut.
4. Loosen the nut holding the suspension support to the shock absorber; do not remove the nut.
5. Remove the bolts and nuts mounting on the strut on the axle carrier and then disconnect the strut.
6. Remove the 2 upper strut mounting nuts and carefully remove the strut assembly.
To install:
7. Install the strut assembly into the vehicle. During installation, observe the following torque specification:
   a. Tighten the upper strut retaining nuts to 23 ft. lbs. (31 Nm) on 1990 models or 29 ft. lbs. (39 Nm) on 1991-94 models.
   b. Tighten the lower strut-to-axle carrier bolt to 50 ft. lbs. (68 Nm).
8. Bleed the brakes.

Paseo

1. Remove the rear seat, seat back and seat lock striker.
2. Remove the quarter trim.
3. Disconnect the rear seat belt.
4. Disconnect the package tray trim.
5. Remove the room partition board.
6. Raise the rear of the vehicle and support safely. Remove the wheel.
7. Remove all fasteners and remove the strut assembly.
8. Using a spring compressor, compress the spring and remove the nut and spring bumper. Remove the spring from the strut.
To install:
9. Installation is the reverse of removal. Observe the following torque specifications.
   a. Torque the spring bumper nut to 40 ft. lbs. (54 Nm).

b. Tighten the upper strut retaining nuts to 29 ft. lbs. (39 Nm).

c. Bounce the suspension before final tightening of the lower bolt and nut. Tighten the lower strut-to-axle bolt to 50 ft. lbs. (68 Nm).

Corolla (2WD) and Camry

1. On the 4-door sedan, remove the package tray and vent duct.
2. On the hatchback, remove the speaker grills.
3. Disconnect the brake line from the wheel cylinder.
4. Remove the brake line from the brake hose.
5. Disconnect the brake hose from its bracket on the strut.
6. Remove the strut suspension support cover. Loosen, but do not remove, the nut holding the suspension support to the strut.
7. Unbolt the strut from the rear arm and or axle carrier.
8. Unbolt the strut from the body.
To install:
9. Install the strut assembly. During installation, observe the following torque specifications:
   a. Tighten the strut-to-body bolts to 29 ft. lbs. (39 Nm) on the Corolla and Camry.
   b. Tighten the strut-to-axle carrier bolts 166 ft. lbs. (226 Nm) on the 1990-91 Camry, 188 ft. lbs. (255 Nm) on the 1992-94 Camry or 105 ft. lbs. (143 Nm) on Corolla.
10. Bleed and refill the brake system.

Celica

1. Raise and support the vehicle safely. Position an hydraulic jack under the rear hub assembly; raise it just enough to support the assembly.
2. On the liftback, remove the rear speaker grilles.
3. On the coupe, remove the suspension service hole cover.
4. On the ST and GT vehicles, disconnect and plug the brake line at the backing plate. Remove the clip and E-ring and then disconnect the brake hose and tube from the strut housing.
5. On the GTS, remove the union bolts and gaskets and disconnect the brake line from the brake cylinder. Remove the clip and E-ring from the strut and then disconnect the brake hose from the strut housing.
6. Loosen, but do not remove, the nut attaching the suspension support to the strut.
7. Disconnect the stabilizer bar at the lower end of the strut housing.

8. Disconnect the strut at the axle carrier.
9. Remove the 3 strut-to-body bolts and then remove the strut.
To install:
10. Tighten the upper strut-to-body nuts to 23 ft. lbs. (31 Nm) on 1990-91 models and 29 ft. lbs. (39 Nm) on 1992-94 models.
11. Tighten the lower strut-to-carrier bolts to 119 ft. lbs. (162 Nm) on 1990-91 models or 188 ft. lbs. (255 Nm) on 1992-94 models.
12. Connect the stabilizer bar to the strut.
13. Tighten the strut holding nut to 36 ft. lbs. (49 Nm). Install the dust cover onto the suspension support.
14. Reconnect the brake line and hose. Bleed the system, lower the vehicle and check the rear wheel alignment.

MR2

1. Raise and support the vehicle safely. Position a hydraulic floor jack under the rear hub assembly; raise it just enough to support the assembly.
2. Remove the union bolts and gaskets and disconnect the brake line from the brake cylinder. Remove the clip and E-ring from the strut and then disconnect the brake hose from the strut housing.
3. Matchmark the lower strut bracket and the camber adjusting cam, remove the 2 axle carrier bolts and the adjusting cam and disconnect the strut from the carrier.
4. Remove the engine hood side panel.
5. Remove the 3 upper strut-to-body nuts and then remove the strut.
To install:
6. Position the strut and tighten the upper mounting nuts to 59 ft. lbs. (80 Nm).
7. Install the engine hood side panel.
8. Connect the axle carrier to the lower strut bracket. Insert the mounting bolts from the rear and align the matchmarks made in Step 3. Tighten the nuts to 188 ft. lbs. (255 Nm).
9. Connect the brake line, bleed the system and check rear wheel alignment.

Supra and Cressida

1. Raise and support the vehicle safely. Remove the wheels.
2. Remove the speaker grille and interior quarter panel trim, if equipped with TEMS.

3. Disconnect the strut from the axle carrier.
4. Remove the strut cap. Remove the Toyota Electronic Modulated Suspension (TEMS) actuator.
5. Remove the 3 strut mounting nuts from the body and remove the strut assembly.
6. Mount the strut assembly in a vise. Using a spring compressor, compress the coil spring.
7. Remove the strut suspension support nut. Remove the strut suspension support, remove the coil spring and bumper.
To install:
8. Mount the strut in a vise. Using a spring compressor, compress the coil spring.
9. Install the bumper to the strut, align the coil spring end with the lower seat hollow and install the coil spring.
10. Align the strut suspension support hole and piston rod and install it. Align the suspension support with the strut lower bushing.
11. Install the strut suspension support nut. Connect the strut assembly with the 3 retaining nuts and torque them to 10 ft. lbs. (14 Nm).
12. Connect the strut assembly to the axle carrier and torque it to 101 ft. lbs. (137 Nm).
13. Install the TEMS actuator and strut cap. Install the quarter panel trim panel and speaker grille.

Coil Springs

REMOVAL AND INSTALLATION

Corolla 4WD

1. Raise the vehicle and support safely by the frame.
2. Jack the center of the differential far enough that the lower shock mounts can be disconnected.
3. Disconnect the lower shock absorber mounts.
4. Remove the bolt holding the stabilizer bar bushing to the rear axle housing.
5. Remove the stabilizer bar brackets.
6. Slowly lower the jack under the rear axle housing until the springs are loose. Do not allow the brake hose or cable to be pulled.
7. Withdraw the coil spring, complete with its insulator.
8. Installation is the reverse of the removal procedure.

Rear Control Arms

REMOVAL AND INSTALLATION

Upper Arms

SUPRA AND CRESSIDA

1. Raise and support the rear of the vehicle safely. Remove the wheels.

2. Unbolt the brake caliper and suspend aside. Remove the halfshaft.

3. Disconnect the parking brake cable at the equalizer. Remove the 2 cable brackets from the body and then pull the cable through the suspension member.

4. Disconnect the 2 lower arms and the strut rod at the axle carrier. Disconnect the lower strut mount.

5. Disconnect the upper arm at the body and remove the axle hub assembly.

6. Remove the upper arm mounting nut. Remove the backing plate mounting nuts and separate the plate from the carrier. Press the upper arm out of the axle carrier.

To install:

7. Connect the upper arm to the body.

8. Connect the axle hub assembly to the arm with a new nut.

9. Connect the No. 1 lower control arm with a new nut and tighten it to 43 ft. lbs. (59 Nm) on Supra and 36 ft. lbs. (49 Nm) on Cressida. Connect the No. 2 lower arm and the strut rod.

10. Tighten the upper arm mounting nut to 80 ft. lbs. (108 Nm). Tighten the strut to 101 ft. lbs. (137 Nm).

11. Reconnect the parking brake cable and install the halfshaft. Install the brake caliper and tighten the bolts to 34 ft. lbs. (47 Nm).

12. Install the wheels and lower the vehicle. Bounce it several times to set the suspension and then tighten the upper arm-to-body bolt, the No. 2 lower arm-to-carrier and the strut rod to 121 ft. lbs. (164 Nm) on Supra or 119 ft. lbs. (162 Nm) on Cressida.

COROLLA (4WD)

1. Raise and support the vehicle safely. Remove the wheels and support the rear axle safely.

2. Remove the upper control arm-to-body bolt. Remove the upper arm-to-axle bolt and lift out the upper control arm.

3. Remove the lower control arm-to-body bolt. Remove the lower arm-to-axle bolt and lift out the lower control arm.

To install:

4. Install the upper control arm with the nuts and bolts just snugged down.

5. Install the lower control arm with the nuts and bolts just snugged down.

6. Install the wheels, remove the safety stands and floor jack and then lower the vehicle.

7. Bounce the vehicle several times to stabilize the suspension and then raise the axle housing until the body is free.

8. Tighten all bolts to 72 ft. lbs. (98 Nm).

Lower Arms

MR2

1. Raise and support the vehicle safely. Remove the wheels.

2. Remove the 2 bolts and disconnect the ball joint from the rear axle carrier.

3. Remove the strut rod nut and retainer from the lower control arm.

4. Remove the bolt holding the lower control arm to the body. Remove the cushion and then disconnect the lower arm from the strut rod. Remove the lower control arm.

To install:

5. Connect the lower arm to the strut rod. Install the strut rod nut, cushion and retainer.

6. Connect the lower arm to the body and install the retaining nut finger-tight.

7. Connect the ball joint to the carrier and tighten the retaining nuts to 83 ft. lbs. (113 Nm).

8. Install the wheel and lower the vehicle. Tighten the strut rod nut to 86 ft. lbs. (117 Nm) and the arm-to-body bolt to 94 ft. lbs. (127 Nm).

CAMRY AND CELICA

1. Raise the vehicle and support safely. Remove the rear wheels.

2. Remove the nut from the axle carrier.

3. Place the matchmarks to the toe adjusting cam and suspension member.

4. Remove the service hole cover and loosen the bolt and remove the toe adjust plate No. 2.

5. Remove the bolt with toe adjusting cam and disconnect the suspension arm and remove.

To install:

6. Face the mark on the suspension arms to the rearward of the vehicle. Install the bushing with the slit side towards the rear and the small paint spot to the outside of the vehicle for the Camry.

7. Install the stamped suspension arm with the identification mark **L** for left and **R** for right. Temporarily install the suspension arms with the bolt, washer and nut. Do not tighten at this time.

8. Loosely install the bolt into the axle carrier.

9. Install the rear wheels and lower the vehicle. Bounce the suspension up and down a few times.

10. Torque suspension components with the vehicle weight loading the suspension.

11. Torque the suspension arm bolts to specifications.

12. Check the front end alignment.

COROLLA (4WD)

1. Raise and support the vehicle safely. Remove the wheels and support the rear axle safely.

2. Remove the upper control arm-to-body bolt. Remove the upper arm-to-axle bolt and lift out the upper control arm.

3. Remove the lower control arm-to-body bolt. Remove the lower arm-to-axle bolt and lift out the lower control arm.

To install:

4. Install the upper control arm with the nuts and bolts just snugged down.

5. Install the lower control arm with the nuts and bolts just snugged down.

6. Install the wheels, remove the safety stands and floor jack and then lower the vehicle.

7. Bounce the vehicle several times to stabilize the suspension and then raise the axle housing until the body is free.

8. Tighten all bolts 72 ft. lbs. (98 Nm).

SUPRA AND CRESSIDA

1. Raise and support the vehicle safely. Remove the wheels.

2. Remove the halfshaft.

3. Remove the nut and disconnect the No. 1 lower arm from the axle carrier. Matchmark the adjusting cam to the body, remove the cam and bolt and then lift out the No. 1 arm.

4. Remove the bolt and nut and disconnect the No. 2 lower arm from the axle carrier. Matchmark the adjusting cam to the body, remove the cam and bolt and then lift out the No. 2 arm.

To install:

5. Position the No. 2 arm and install the adjusting cam and bolt so the matchmarks are in alignment. Connect the arm to the axle carrier.

6. Position the No. 1 arm and install the adjusting cam and bolt so

the matchmarks are in alignment. Connect the arm to the axle carrier. Use a new nut and tighten it to 43 ft. lbs. (59 Nm).

7. Install the halfshaft.

8. Install the wheels and lower the vehicle. Bounce it several times to set the suspension and then tighten the body-to-arm bolts and nuts. Tighten the No. 2 arm-to-carrier bolt. Tighten the No. 1 arm-to-carrier nut.

9. Check the rear wheel alignment.

Rear Wheel Bearings

NOTE: These procedures apply to front wheel drive vehicles only.

REMOVAL AND INSTALLATION

Tercel and Paseo

1. Raise and support the vehicle safely.

2. Remove the rear wheels.

3. Remove the brake drums.

4. Remove the locknut cap and cotter pin. Remove the locknut.

5. Carefully pull off the axle hub along with the outer wheel bearing and thrust washer. Do not drop the bearing.

6. Pry the inner bearing oil seal out of the brake drum and then remove the inner bearing.

7. Drive out the bearing races.

To install:

8. Press new outer bearing races into the axle hub and put a liberal amount of grease in it and the bearing cap.

9. Pack the bearing with grease.

10. Position the inner bearing into the hub and then drive in a new oil seal to the original position. Lightly coat the seal with grease.

11. Position the axle hub/brake drum onto the axle shaft. Install the outer bearing and position the thrust washer. Install the bearing locknut and tighten it to 22 ft. lbs. (29 Nm) while spinning the drum.

12. Spin the axle hub several times to snug down the bearing and then loosen the bearing locknut until it can be turned by hand.

NOTE: There must be absolutely no brake drag at this time.

13. Retighten the bearing locknut until there is a bearing preload of 0.9-2.2 lbs. (3.2-9.8 N) while turning the wheel. Measure with a spring scale hooked to one of the studs.

14. Install the locknut lock, a new cotter pin and the cap. If the cotter

pin hole does not align properly, align the holes by tightening the nut to the next hole. Do not loosen the nut.

15. Lower the vehicle.

Camry, Celica and Corolla

1. Raise and support the vehicle safely.

2. Remove the rear wheel and tire assembly.

3. Remove the brake drum. On models with rear disc brakes, remove the disc brake caliper from the axle carrier and suspend it with a wire.

4. Disconnect and plug the brake line at the backing plate.

5. Remove the 4 axle hub-to-carrier bolts and slide off the hub and brake assembly. Remove the O-ring from the backing plate.

6. Remove the bolt and nut attaching the carrier to the strut rod.

7. Remove the bolt and nut attaching the carrier to the No. 1 suspension arm.

8. Remove the bolt and nut attaching the carrier to the No. 2 suspension arm.

9. Unbolt the carrier from the rear strut tube and remove the carrier.

10. Using a hammer and cold chisel, loosen the staked part of the hub nut and remove the nut.

11. Using a 2-armed puller, press the axle shaft from the hub.

12. Remove the bearing inner race (inside).

13. Using a 2-armed puller again, pull off the bearing inner race (outside) over the bearing and then press it out of the hub.

To install:

14. Position a new bearing inner race (outside) on the bearing and then press a new oil seal into the hub. Coat the lip of the seal with grease.

15. Position a new bearing inner race (inside) on the bearing and then press the inner race with the hub onto the axle shaft.

16. Install the nut and tighten it to 90 ft. lbs. (123 Nm). Stake the nut.

17. Position the axle carrier on the strut tube and tighten the nuts to specifications.

18. Install the bolt and nut attaching the carrier to the No. 2 suspension arm; finger-tighten it only.

NOTE: Make sure the lip of the nut is in the hole on the arm.

19. Repeat Step 5 for the No. 1 suspension arm.

NOTE: Make sure the lip of the nut is in the hole on the arm.

20. Install the strut rod-to-carrier bolt so the lip of the nut is in the groove on the bracket.

21. Install a new O-ring onto the axle carrier. Install the axle hub and brake backing plate. Tighten the 4 bolts to 59 ft. lbs. (80 Nm).

22. Reconnect the brake line, install the brake drum and then bleed the brakes.

23. Lower the vehicle and bounce it a few times to set the rear suspension.

24. Tighten the suspension arm bolts and the strut rod bolt to 64 ft. lbs. (87 Nm).

Rear Axle Assembly

REMOVAL AND INSTALLATION

Tercel and Paseo

1. Disconnect the parking brake cables from the backing plates.

2. Disconnect the brake lines from the backing plates.

3. Remove the lateral control rod.

4. Disconnect the lower strut mounts.

5. Remove the axle beam.

6. Installation is the reverse of removal. Torque the fasteners to specifications. Bleed the brakes and test drive the vehicle.

STEERING

Steering Wheel

—— CAUTION ——

To avoid personal injury when working on vehicles equipped with an air bag, the negative battery cable must be disconnected and at least 90 seconds must elapse before working on the system. Failure to do so may result in deployment of the air bag.

REMOVAL AND INSTALLATION

Without Air Bag

NOTE: Do not attempt to remove or install the steering wheel by hammering on it. Damage to the energy-absorbing steering column could result.

1. Disconnect the negative battery cable. Position the front wheels straight-ahead.

2. Unfasten the horn and turn signal multi-connector(s) at the base of the steering column shroud, if necessary.

3. If equipped with a 3 or 4 spoked wheel, loosen the trim pad retaining screws from the back side of the steering wheel. The 2 spoke steering wheel may be designed to be removed in the same manner as the 3 spoke, except that the trim pad may be able to be very gently pried off if not fastened by screws. Remove the pad by lifting it toward the top of the wheel to disengage the clip.

4. Lift the trim pad and disconnect or remove the horn button terminal from the wheel.

5. Remove the steering wheel hub retaining nut.

6. Scribe matchmarks on the hub and shaft to aid in correct installation.

7. Use tool 09609-20011, or equivalent, to remove the steering wheel.

8. Installation is the reverse of removal. Match the scribe marks made previously. Tighten the wheel retaining nut to 25 ft. lbs. (34 Nm).

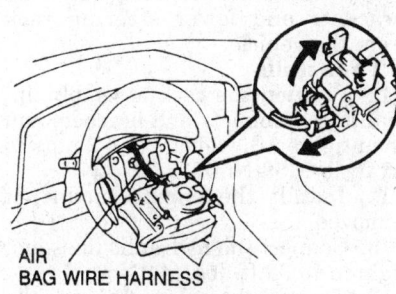

TORX® SCREW   SCREW CASE

AIR BAG WIRE HARNESS

Removing the air bag

With Air Bag

—————— CAUTION ——————

To avoid personal injury when working on air bag equipped vehicles, work must be started after 90 seconds or longer from the time the ignition switch is turned to the LOCK position and the negative battery terminal is disconnected. If the air bag system is disconnected with the ignition switch at the ON or ACC, diagnostic codes will be set. When removing the air bag, take care not to pull the air bag wire harness. When carrying the wheel pad, carry it with the upper surface facing away. When storing it, keep the upper surface of the pad facing upward.

1. Disconnect the negative battery cable.

2. Place the front wheels facing straight ahead.

3. Remove the steering wheel screw covers.

4. Using a Torx® wrench T30, loosen the screws until the groove trailing the screw circumference catches on the screw case.

5. Pull the wheel pad out from the steering wheel and disconnect the air bag connector.

6. Remove the steering wheel nut. Place matchmarks on the wheel and steering shaft.

7. Using steering wheel puller SST 09213-31021 or equivalent, remove the steering wheel.

To install:

8. Center the spiral cable.

   a. Check that the front wheels are facing straight ahead.

   b. Turn the spiral cable counterclockwise by hand until it becomes harder to turn the cable.

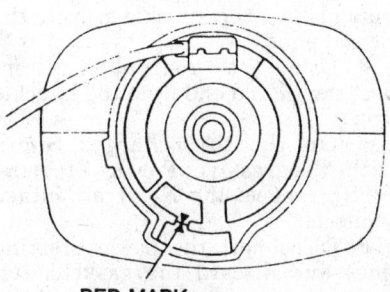

RED MARK

Centering the spiral cable

   c. Then rotate the spiral cable clockwise about 2½ turns to align the red mark.

NOTE: The spiral cable will rotate about 2½ to either left or right of center.

9. Install the steering wheel, aligning the matchmarks and torque the nut to 25 ft. lbs. (34 Nm).

10. Connect the air bag connector and install the steering pad.

11. Torque the Torx® screws to exactly 65 inch lbs. (7.4 Nm).

12. Install the screw covers.

13. Connect the battery cable and check operation.

Rack and Pinion

REMOVAL AND INSTALLATION

—————— CAUTION ——————

To avoid personal injury when working on air bag equipped vehicles, work must be started after 90 seconds or longer from the time the ignition switch is turned to the LOCK position and the negative battery terminal is disconnected.

NOTE: When disconnecting the universal joint during removal of the gear housing on air bag equipped vehicles, remove the steering wheel and perform centering of the spiral cable. Make sure the steering wheel does not rotate while performing service.

Cressida

1. Raise and support the vehicle safely and remove the front wheels. Place matchmarks on the coupling and steering column shaft. Disconnect the electrical connectors.

2. Disconnect the tie rod ends from the steering knuckles.

3. Remove the steering damper, if equipped. Matchmark and remove the power steering fluid lines.

4. Disconnect the steering rack at the coupling. Unbolt the rack and pinion from the chassis and remove. Remove the grommets from the gear housing.

To install:

5. Installation is in the reverse order of removal. Align the matchmarks and connect the steering shaft to the coupling before bolting the rack into the vehicle permanently. Torque the coupling bolt to 25 ft. lbs. (34 Nm).

6. Tighten the steering damper bolts to 20 ft. lbs. (26 Nm). Tighten

the tie rod ends to 43 ft. lbs. (59 Nm). Torque the mounting bracket bolts to 56 ft. lbs. (76 Nm) and the fluid lines to 27 ft. lbs. (36 Nm).

7. Check the fluid level, test drive and check the front end alignment.

Camry

1. Raise and support the vehicle safely. Remove the front wheels.

2. Matchmark the universal joint and shafts.

3. Remove the sliding yoke from between the steering rack housing and the steering column shaft on vehicles so equipped by loosening the upper bolt and removing the lower bolt. Slide upward and remove the intermediate shaft (rack housing side first).

4. Remove the cotter pin and nut holding the knuckle arms to the tie rod ends. Using a tie rod puller, disconnect the tie rod end from the knuckle arm.

5. Carefully remove the lower crossmember, remove the engine undercover, center engine mount member and the rear engine mount, if necessary, and supporting the engine where necessary.

6. Remove the 4 stabilizer bar set bolts on 1992-94 models. On 4WD vehicles, remove the propeller shaft. On 4WD drive vehicles and 1990-91 models with the V6 engine, disconnect the exhaust pipe.

7. Matchmark and disconnect the power steering lines, if equipped. Remove the steering gear housing brackets. Slide the gear housing to the right side and then out the left on 1990-91 2WD models, out the bottom on 4WD models and out the right on 1992-94 models.

To install:

8. Install the rack housing and torque to the following specifications.

9. Torque the rack housing mounting bolts to 43 ft. lbs. (59 Nm) on 1990-91 models or 134 ft. lbs. (181 Nm) on 1992-94 models. Torque the tie rod set nuts to 36 ft. lbs. (49 Nm). Use a new cotter pin.

10. Tighten the rear engine mounting bolts to 38 ft. lbs. (52 Nm). Tighten the center mounting member to 29 ft. lbs. (39 Nm) and the lower crossmember to 153 ft. lbs. (207 Nm).

11. On power steering-equipped vehicles, torque the lines to 33 ft. lbs. (44 Nm) on 1990-91 models or 18 ft. lbs. (25 Nm) on 1992-94 models. Be very careful not to overtighten, since the housing can crack. Bleed the power steering system and check for fluid leaks.

12. Adjust toe-in on all vehicles.

Corolla

1. Raise and support the vehicle safely. Remove the front wheels. Remove the column hole cover.

2. Remove the universal joint bolts and remove the sliding yoke from between the steering rack housing and the steering column shaft.

3. Remove the cotter pins and nuts holding the knuckle arms to the tie rod ends. Using a tie rod puller, disconnect the tie rod end from the knuckle arm.

4. Carefully remove the lower crossmember on models with power steering and remove the stabilizer bar. Remove the center crossmember and the engine mount.

5. On 4WD models with power steering, remove the propeller shaft and disconnect the exhaust pipe.

6. Label and disconnect the power steering lines, if equipped. Remove the steering gear housing brackets. Slide the gear housing to the right side and then to the left side or lower left on 4WD models to remove the housing.

To install:

7. Install the rack housing through the point of exit.

8. Torque the rack housing mounting bolts to 43 ft. lbs. (58 Nm) and the tie rod set nuts to 36 ft. lbs. (49 Nm). Use a new cotter pin.

9. Tighten all support members and mounts to specifications.

10. On power steering-equipped vehicles, torque the lines to 33 ft. lbs. (44 Nm), bleed the power steering system and check for fluid leaks.

11. Adjust toe-in on all vehicles.

Supra

1. Raise and support the vehicle safely. Remove the front wheels and the heat insulator.

2. Unbolt and remove the intermediate shaft (rack housing side first).

3. Remove the cotter pins and nuts holding the knuckle arms to the tie rod ends.

4. Using a tie rod puller, disconnect the tie rod end from the knuckle arm.

5. On the turbocharged Supra with Progressive Power Steering (PPS), remove the No. 1 air intake connector.

6. Disconnect the power steering lines and discard the gaskets. Remove the steering gear housing bolts and brackets. Slide the gear housing to the right side and then to the left side to remove the housing.

To install:

7. Install the rack housing through the point of removal.

8. Torque the rack housing mounting bolts to 56 ft. lbs. (76 Nm).

9. Connect the tie rods and torque the nuts to 36 ft. lbs. (49 Nm). Use a new cotter pin.

10. Install the intermediate shaft column side first, then rack side. Torque the clamp bolts to 24 ft. lbs. (32 Nm).

11. Torque the screw in line to 33 ft. lbs. (44 Nm), the bolt on the models without PPS to 36 ft. lbs. (49 Nm) and the bolts on models with PPS to 38 ft. lbs. (51 Nm). Bleed the power steering system and check for fluid leaks.

12. Install the intake connector.

13. Adjust toe-in on all vehicles.

Celica

1. Raise and support the vehicle safely. Remove the front wheels.

2. Remove the both engine undercovers.

3. Remove the 2 bolts that connect the steering column U-joint to the rack and then disconnect the column from the rack.

4. Remove the cotter pin and nut and then using a tie rod end removal tool, disconnect the tie rod end from the steering knuckle.

5. Remove the lower suspension crossmember.

6. Remove the mounting bolts and remove the center engine mount member.

7. On 4WD models, disconnect the exhaust pipe from the manifold and remove the propeller shaft. Also, remove the stabilizer bar and transmission control cables.

8. Tag and disconnect the 2 hydraulic lines. Position them aside and suspend on a wire.

9. Remove the charcoal canister, air cleaner and the engine mount, as required.

10. Remove the mounting bolts and brackets and lower steering rack from the vehicle.

To install:

11. Position the rack assembly, install the grommets and brackets and then tighten the 2 bolts and 2 nuts to 43 ft. lbs. (59 Nm).

12. Install the engine mount, if removed.

13. Connect the hydraulic lines and tighten to 33 ft. lbs. (44 Nm).

14. Connect the exhaust pipe to the manifold and install the propeller shaft.

15. Install the center engine mount member.

16. Install the lower crossmember and tighten the outer bolts to 112 ft. lbs. (152 Nm). Tighten the center bolt to 29 ft. lbs. (39 Nm).

17. Installation of the remaining components is in the reverse order of removal. Tighten the tie rod end nuts to 36 ft. lbs. (49 Nm) and use a new cotter pin. Tighten the steering column U-joint clamp bolts to 26 ft. lbs. (35 Nm). Fill the power steering pump to the proper level, bleed the system and check the wheel alignment.

MR2

1. Disconnect the negative battery cable.
2. Position the front wheels straight-ahead.
3. Raise the vehicle and support safely. Remove the front wheels and front luggage undercover.
4. Remove the dust cover. Matchmark the universal joint and control valve shaft for installation.
5. Disconnect the tie rod ends using a tie rod separator or equivalent.
6. If equipped with power steering, disconnect the hoses and drain the fluid into a container.
7. Remove the housing-to-frame retaining bolts and remove the assembly.
   To install:
8. Install the housing assembly and torque the strap retaining bolts to 32 ft. lbs. (43 Nm).
9. Connect the tie rods and torque to 36 ft. lbs. (49 Nm).
10. Connect the universal joint and torque to 26 ft. lbs. (35 Nm).
11. Install the dust cover and connect the power steering hoses. Torque the pressure hose bolt to 51 ft. lbs. (69 Nm).
12. Connect the battery cable. Start the engine and bleed the system.
13. Install the front wheels, lower the vehicle and check the alignment.

Tercel

1. Disconnect the negative battery cable.
2. Position the front wheels straight-ahead.
3. Raise the vehicle and support safely. Remove the front wheels.
4. Remove the column hole cover. Matchmark the universal joint and control valve shaft for installation and remove the pinch bolts.
5. Disconnect the tie rod ends using a tie rod separator or equivalent. Remove the engine mount, if equipped with power steering.

6. Disconnect the power steering hoses, if equipped, and drain the fluid into a container.
7. Disconnect the exhaust pipe and the transmission control cables, as required. Remove the housing-to-frame retaining bolts and remove the assembly.
   To install:
8. Line up the steering splines, then install the assembly and torque the retaining bolts to 32 ft. lbs. (43 Nm) on 1990 models or 43 ft. lbs. (58 Nm) on 1991-94 models.
9. Connect the universal joint and torque to 26 ft. lbs. (35 Nm) on 1990 models or 21 ft. lbs. (28 Nm) on 1991-94 models. Install the engine mount, exhaust pipe and cables.
10. Connect the tie rods and torque to 36 ft. lbs. (49 Nm).
11. Install the dust cover and connect the power steering hoses, torquing to 18 ft. lbs. (25 Nm) on 1990 models or 33 ft. lbs. (44 Nm) on 1991-94 models.
12. Connect the battery cable. Start the engine and bleed the system.
13. Install the front wheels, lower the vehicle and check the alignment.

Paseo

1. Disconnect the negative battery cable.
2. Position the front wheels straight-ahead.
3. Raise the vehicle and support safely. Remove the front wheels.
4. Remove the column hole cover. Matchmark the universal joint and control valve shaft for installation and remove the lower pinch bolt.
5. Loosen the upper bolt and slide the shaft upward and disconnect.
6. Disconnect the tie rod ends using a tie rod separator or equivalent. Remove the engine mount.
7. Remove the stabilizer bar.
8. Disconnect the power steering hoses and drain the fluid into a container.
9. Disconnect the oxygen sensor, the exhaust pipe and the transmission control cables, if equipped with manual transaxle.
10. Remove the housing-to-frame retaining bolts and remove the assembly. Slide the housing to the right first, then to the left and out.
    To install:
11. Line up the steering splines, then install the assembly and torque the retaining bolts to 43 ft. lbs. (58 Nm).
12. Connect the universal joint and torque to 21 ft. lbs. (28 Nm). Install the stabilizer bar, engine mount, ex-

haust pipe and cables. Connect the oxygen sensor.
13. Connect the tie rods and torque to 36 ft. lbs. (49 Nm).
14. Install the cover and connect the power steering hoses, torquing to 33 ft. lbs. (44 Nm).
15. Connect any remaining components and then the battery cable. Start the engine and bleed the system.
16. Install the front wheels, lower the vehicle and check the alignment.

Power Steering Pump

REMOVAL AND INSTALLATION

Camry, Celica

1. Raise and support the vehicle safely. Remove the fan shroud.
2. Remove the right front wheel and the engine undercover. Remove the lower suspension crossmember, if necessary.
3. Loosen the adjusting nut from behind the pump pulley and loosen the pivot bolt. Disconnect the vacuum hoses from the air control valve, if equipped.
4. Withdraw the drive belt. On some vehicles, it may be necessary to remove the pulley in order to remove the drive belt.
5. If equipped with an idler pulley, remove the pulley set nut. Loosen the idler pulley set nut and adjusting bolt. Remove the drive belt and loosen the drive pulley to remove the Woodruff key.
6. Remove the pulley and the Woodruff key from the pump shaft, if necessary.
7. Remove and plug the pressure and return lines from the pump and reservoir by unscrewing the fittings or removing the banjo bolt. Discard the gasket, if equipped.
8. On the 1992-94 Camry with a V6 engine, disconnect the electrical connector.

NOTE: Tie the hose ends up high so the fluid cannot flow out of them. Drain or plug the pump to prevent fluid leakage.

9. Remove the bolt from the rear mounting brace, if equipped.
10. Remove the front bracket bolts and withdraw the pump.
    To install:
11. Installation is the reverse of removal. Tighten the pump pulley mounting bolt to 25-39 ft. lbs. (34-53 Nm), if removed.

12. Connect the lines and torque the bolt to 38 ft. lbs. (51 Nm), or the line fittings to 33 ft. lbs. (44 Nm).

13. If removed, tighten the 5 outer mounting bolts on the lower crossmember to 154 ft. lbs. (209 Nm). On Celica, tighten the center bolt to 29 ft. lbs. (39 Nm).

14. Adjust the pump drive belt tension. Torque the mounting bolts to 31 ft. lbs. (42 Nm).

15. Fill the reservoir with fluid and bleed the air from the system.

MR2

The power steering pump is not driven by a conventional drive belt. Instead the pump is driven by an electric motor. The pump and motor are combined as one unit.

1. Disconnect the negative battery cable.

2. Raise and support the vehicle safely.

3. Remove the front luggage undercover.

4. Remove the pump shield and rear stay.

5. Disconnect the hydraulic lines from the pump. Plug the lines to prevent the loss of power steering fluid.

6. Disconnect the electrical wires from the top of the motor.

7. Remove the pump mounting bolts, bushings and spacers. Check the bushings for cracks and deformation. Replace as necessary.

8. Remove the pump and motor assembly.

To install:

9. Position the pump and install the mounting bolts, bushings and spacers. Torque the bolts to 19 ft. lbs. (25 Nm).

10. Connect the electrical wires to the top of the motor.

11. Connect the hydraulic lines, torquing the pressure line to 33 ft. lbs. (44 Nm).

12. Install the rear stay and pump shield.

13. Install the front luggage undercover.

14. Lower the vehicle and connect the negative battery cable.

15. Fill the power steering reservoir to the proper level and bleed the system.

Tercel and Corolla

1. Raise and support the vehicle safely. Remove the fan shroud and air cleaner, if necessary.

2. Remove the right front wheel and the engine undercover and remove the lower suspension crossmember, if necessary.

3. Remove the vacuum hoses on the Corolla, if equipped.

4. Loosen the adjusting bolt and the pivot bolt and remove the belt. On some vehicles it may be necessary to remove the pulley or idler pulley in order to remove the drive belt.

5. Remove the adjusting bracket on the Corolla.

6. Pinch the clamp and remove the return hose.

7. Remove the bolt or unscrew the pressure line and discard the gasket.

NOTE: Tie the hose ends up high so the fluid cannot flow out of them. Drain or plug the pump to prevent fluid leakage.

8. Remove the bolts from the mounting braces.

9. Remove the the pump.

To install:

10. Tighten the pulley nut to 28 ft. lbs. (38 Nm).

11. Tighten the 5 outer mounting bolts on the lower crossmember to 154 ft. lbs. (209 Nm).

12. Adjust the pump drive belt tension. Torque the mounting bolts to 32 ft. lbs. (43 Nm).

13. Install the pressure line bolt with a new gasket and torque to 34 ft. lbs. (47 Nm) on the Corolla and 1990 Tercel. Torque it to 40 ft. lbs. (54 Nm) on the 1991-94 Tercel. Torque line fittings to 33 ft. lbs. (44 Nm).

14. Install the return hose with a new clamp.

15. Fill the reservoir with fluid. Bleed the air from the system.

Paseo

1. Loosen the adjusting bolt and the pivot bolt and remove the belt.

2. Pinch the clamp and remove the return hose.

3. Remove the bolt for the pressure line and discard the gasket.

NOTE: Tie the hose ends up high so the fluid cannot flow out of them. Drain or plug the pump to prevent fluid leakage.

4. Remove the bolts from the mounting braces.

5. Remove the the pump.

To install:

6. Install the pump and related components.

7. Adjust the pump drive belt tension and torque the mounting bolts to 32 ft. lbs. (43 Nm).

8. Install the pressure line bolt with a new gasket and torque to 40 ft. lbs. (54 Nm).

9. Install the return hose with a new clamp.

10. Fill the reservoir with fluid. Bleed the air from the system.

Supra and Cressida

7M-GE ENGINE

1. Raise and support the vehicle safely. Drain the fluid from the reservoir tank.

2. Disconnect the air hose from the air control tank. Disconnect the return hose from the reservoir tank.

3. Remove the engine undercover. Disconnect and plug the pressure hose from the power steering pump.

4. Remove the power steering pump set bolt. Remove the drive belt, pulley and Woodruff key.

5. Disconnect the oil cooler hose bracket from the power steering pump, if equipped. Remove the drive belt adjust bolt and remove the brackets.

6. Remove the power steering pump.

To install:

7. Installation is the reverse order of the removal procedure. Adjust the drive belt and torque the pulley nut to 32 ft. lbs. (43 Nm), the pressure line bolt to 36 ft. lbs. (49 Nm) or the line fitting to 33 ft. lbs. (44 Nm).

8. Be sure to bleed the system upon completion of the installation procedure.

7M-GTE ENGINE

1. Raise and support the vehicle safely. Drain the fluid from the reservoir tank.

2. Remove the No. 1 and No. 2 air hoses with the No. 4 air cleaner pipe.

3. Disconnect the connector from the air flow meter. Remove the air flow meter installation bolt. Loosen the 5 clamps and disconnect the air hoses, release the 3 clips on the air cleaner case. Loosen the No. 7 air hose clamp and remove the No. 7 air cleaner hose with the air flow meter.

4. Remove the oil reservoir tank with bracket. Disconnect the 2 air hoses from the air control valve on the power steering pump.

5. Remove the adjusting strut. Remove the engine undercover.

6. Holding the power steering pump pulley, remove the pulley set nut. Remove the drive belt adjusting nut.

7. Remove the power steering pump set bolt. Remove the drive belt, pulley and Woodruff key.

8. Disconnect and plug the pressure hose from the power steering pump.

9. Remove the power steering set bolt and power steering pump.

To install:

10. Installation is the reverse order of the removal procedure. Torque the pressure line bolt to 36 ft. lbs. (49 Nm) and use a new gasket.

11. Adjust the belt, fill the reservoir and bleed the system.

BELT ADJUSTMENT

1. Inspect the power steering drive belt to see that it is not cracked or worn. Be sure its surfaces are free of grease or oil.

2. Push down on the belt halfway between the fan and the alternator pulleys (or crankshaft pulley) with thumb pressure. Belt deflection should be 3/8-1/2 in. (10-13mm).

3. If the belt tension requires adjustment, loosen the adjusting link bolt and move the power steering pump until the proper belt tension is obtained.

4. Do not over-tighten the belt, as damage to the power steering pump bearings could result. Tighten the adjusting link bolt.

5. Drive the vehicle and re-check the belt tension. Adjust as necessary.

SYSTEM BLEEDING

1. Raise and support the vehicle safely.

2. Fill the pump reservoir with the proper fluid.

3. Rotate the steering wheel from lock-to-lock several times. Add fluid if necessary.

4. With the steering wheel turned fully to one lock, crank the starter while watching the fluid level in the reservoir.

NOTE: Do not start the engine. Operate the starter with a remote starter switch or have an assistant do it from inside the vehicle. Do not run the starter for prolonged periods.

5. Repeat Step 4 with the steering wheel turned to the opposite lock.

6. Start the engine. With the engine idling, turn the steering wheel from lock-to-lock several times.

7. Lower the front of the vehicle and repeat Step 6.

8. Center the wheel at the midpoint of its travel. Stop the engine.

9. The fluid level should not have risen more than 0.2 in. (5mm). If it does, repeat Step 7.

10. Check for fluid leakage.

Tie Rod Ends

REMOVAL AND INSTALLATION

1. Scribe alignment marks on the tie rod and rack end.

2. Working at the steering knuckle arm, pull out the cotter pin and then remove the castellated nut.

3. Using a tie rod end puller, disconnect the tie rod from the steering knuckle arm.

4. Repeat the first 2 steps on the other end of the tie rod (where it attaches to the relay rod or steering rack).

To install:

5. Align the alignment marks on the tie rod and rack end.

6. Install the tie rod end.

7. Tighten the tie rod end nuts to 36 ft. lbs. (49 Nm). Install a new cotter pin.

NOTE: If the hole does not line up, always tighten the nut until the hole lines up.

8. Install the front wheels and lower the vehicle. Check the front end alignment.

BRAKES

--- **CAUTION** ---

To avoid personal injury and accidental deployment of the air bag, work must be started after about 90 seconds or longer from the time the ignition switch is turned to the LOCK position and the battery cable is disconnected from the battery.

Master Cylinder

REMOVAL AND INSTALLATION

1. Disconnect the negative battery cable. Label and disconnect the electrical connectors.

2. Remove the fluid in the master cylinder with a suitable syringe.

3. On MR2, remove the luggage compartment.

4. Disconnect the hydraulic lines from the master cylinder. Plug the ends of the lines to prevent loss of fluid.

5. Detach the hydraulic fluid pressure differential switch wiring connectors.

6. Loosen the master cylinder reservoir mounting nuts.

7. Unfasten the nuts and remove the master cylinder from the power brake unit.

To install:

8. Bench bleed the master cylinder.

9. Before tightening the master cylinder mounting nuts or bolts, screw the hydraulic line into the cylinder body a few turns.

10. Install the master cylinder or actuator. Torque the hydraulic lines to 11 ft. lbs. (15 Nm) and the master cylinder mounting nuts to 9 ft. lbs. (13 Nm).

11. After installation is completed, bleed the brake system.

Proportioning Valve

A proportioning valve is used to reduce the hydraulic pressure to the rear brakes because of weight transfer during high speed stops. This helps to keep the rear brakes from locking up by improving front to rear brake balance.

REMOVAL AND INSTALLATION

1. Disconnect the brake lines from the valve unions.

2. Remove the valve mounting bolt, if used and remove the valve.

NOTE: If the proportioning valve is defective, it must be replaced as an assembly; it cannot be rebuilt.

3. Installation is the reverse of removal. Bleed the brake system after it is completed.

Power Brake Booster

REMOVAL AND INSTALLATION

1. Disconnect the negative battery cable. Remove the master cylinder and disconnect the vacuum hose from the brake booster.

2. Remove the instrument lower finish panel, as required.

3. On the MR2, remove the wheel guard, instrument lower finish panel and air duct, if necessary.

4. Remove the brake pedal return spring.

5. Remove clip and clevis pin.

6. Remove the brake booster nuts and clevis pin.

7. Pull out the brake booster and gasket.

8. Installation is the reverse order of the removal procedure. Torque the mounting nuts to 9 ft. lbs. (13 Nm). Bleed the brake system, if necessary.

Brake Caliper

REMOVAL AND INSTALLATION

1. Raise and support the vehicle safely.
2. Remove the front or rear wheels.
3. Disconnect the brake hose from the caliper. Plug the end of the hose to prevent loss of fluid.
4. Remove the bolts that attach the caliper to the torque plate.
5. Lift up and remove the caliper assembly.
6. Installation is the reverse of the removal procedure. Grease the caliper slides and bolts with the proper lubricant. Torque the fluid line bolt to 22 ft. lbs. (30 Nm), the caliper mounting bolts to 25 ft. lbs. (34 Nm) on front disc brakes and 14 ft. lbs. (20 Nm) for rear disc brakes. Fill and bleed the system.

Disc Brake Pads

REMOVAL AND INSTALLATION

Front Disc and Rear Disc with Drum Type Parking Brake

1. Raise and support the vehicle safely.
2. Remove the wheels.
3. Siphon a sufficient quantity of brake fluid from the master cylinder reservoir to prevent any brake fluid from overflowing the master cylinder, due to improper prior fluid addition. This may be necessary as the piston must be forced into the caliper bore to provide sufficient clearance when installing the pads.
4. Grasp the caliper from behind and carefully pull it to seat the piston in its bore, if possible.
5. Loosen and remove the lower caliper slide pin (mounting bolt).
6. Swivel the caliper upward and aside, exposing the brake pads. Do not disconnect the brake line.
7. Slide out the old brake pads along with any anti-squeal shims, anti-rattle springs, pad wear indicators, pad guide plates and pad support plates. Take great care to note the position of all assorted pad hardware.
8. Check the brake disc (rotor) for thickness and run-out. Inspect the

caliper and piston assembly for breaks, cracks, fluid seepage or other damage. Overhaul or replace as necessary.

To install:
9. Install the pad support plates, anti-rattle springs or guide plates into the torque plate.
10. Install the pad wear indicators onto the inside pads. Be sure the arrow on the wear indicator plate is pointing in the rotating direction of the rotor disc.
11. Install the anti-squeal shims on the outside of each pad and then install the pad assemblies into the torque plate. If disc brake grease is applicable, do not allow it to get on the pad or rotor friction surfaces.
12. Swivel the caliper back down over the pads. If it will not fit, use a C-clamp or hammer handle and carefully force the piston into its bore. Be careful not to pinch the boot.

NOTE: On 2 piston calipers, be careful that the piston being forced in does not force the other one out.

13. Install and tighten the lower slide pin or mounting bolt.
14. Using very short strokes, pump the brake pedal until the pistons are forced tightly against the pads. The brake pedal will get hard when this happens.
15. Install the wheel and lower the vehicle. Check the brake fluid level. Adjust the parking brake, if necessary.

Rear Disc with Disc Type Parking Brake

1. Raise and support the vehicle safely.
2. Remove the wheels.
3. Siphon a sufficient quantity of brake fluid from the master cylinder reservoir to prevent any brake fluid from overflowing the master cylinder, due to improper prior fluid addition. This may be necessary as the piston must be turned into the caliper bore to provide sufficient clearance when installing the pads.
4. Loosen and remove the lower caliper mounting bolt and then rotate the caliper upward to expose the pads. Do not remove the caliper from the main pin and do not disconnect the brake line.
5. Slide out the old brake pads along with any anti-squeal shims, springs, pad wear indicators and pad support plates. Make sure to note the position of all assorted pad hardware.

To install:
6. Check the brake disc (rotor) for thickness and run-out. Inspect the caliper and piston assembly for breaks, cracks, fluid seepage or other damage. Overhaul or replace as necessary.
7. Install the anti-squeal shims to the pads.
8. Install the pads so the wear indicators are at the top. Position all hardware in its proper position.
9. Using a caliper piston tool, turn the piston in clockwise while pushing it into where it locks.
10. Position the caliper back down over the pads, fitting the pad protrusion into the piston stopper groove. Do not damage the boot.
11. Install and tighten the caliper mounting bolt to 14 ft. lbs. (20 Nm).
12. Install the wheels and lower the vehicle. Check the brake fluid level.
13. Adjust the parking brake automatic adjuster by depressing the brake pedal several times.

Brake Rotor

REMOVAL AND INSTALLATION

1. Raise and support the vehicle safely.
2. Remove the wheels.
3. Temporarily attach 2 lug nuts onto the rotor disc.
4. Unbolt the torque plate from the steering knuckle.
5. Remove the lug nuts, remove the retaining screws, if used, and pull the rotor from the wheel hub.
6. Installation is the reverse of the removal procedure.

Brake Drums

REMOVAL AND INSTALLATION

Wheel Bearing Retained

1. Remove the access cover on the backing plate.
2. Back off the adjustment by pushing on the lever with a tool and rotate the star wheel to loosen the adjustment.
3. Remove the dust cap, cotter pin, bearing retaining nut, washer and the outer wheel bearing.
4. Gently pull the drum off the spindle.
5. Installation is the reverse of removal. Adjust the wheel bearing preload and use a new cotter pin. Readjust the rear brakes.

Wheel Bearing Not Retained

1. Raise and support the vehicle safely.
2. Remove the wheels.
3. Remove the brake drum. Tap the drum lightly with a rubber mallet in order to free it. If the brake drum cannot be removed easily, insert a small prybar through the hole in the backing plate and hold the automatic adjuster lever away from the adjusting bolt. Using another prybar, relieve the brake shoe tension by rotating the adjusting bolt (star wheel) to loosen. If the drum still will not come off, use a puller.
4. Installation is the reverse of the removal procedure. Readjust the rear brakes.

Brake Shoes

REMOVAL AND INSTALLATION

With Bearing Retained Brake Drum

1. Raise and support the vehicle safely. Remove the wheels.
2. Remove the brake drums.

NOTE: Do not depress the brake pedal once the brake drum has been removed.

3. Carefully unhook the tension spring from the leading (front) brake shoe and remove the clamp, if equipped.
4. Press the hold-down spring retainer in and turn the pin.
5. Remove the hold-down spring, retainers and the pin. Pull out the brake shoe and unhook the anchor spring from the lower edge.
6. Remove the hold-down spring from the trailing (rear) shoe. Pull the shoe out with the adjuster strut, automatic adjuster assembly and springs attached and disconnect the parking brake cable. Remove the tension/return and anchor springs from the rear shoe.
7. Remove the adjusting strut. Unhook the adjusting lever spring from the rear shoe and then remove the automatic adjuster assembly by popping out the C-clip.
   To install:
8. Inspect the shoes for signs of unusual wear or scoring.
9. Check the wheel cylinder for any sign of fluid seepage or frozen pistons.
10. Clean and inspect the brake backing plate and all other components. Check that the brake drum inner diameter is within specified lim-

its. Lubricate the backing plate bosses and the anchor plate.
11. Mount the automatic adjuster assembly onto a new rear brake shoe. Make sure the C-clip fits properly. Connect the adjusting strut and install the spring.
12. Connect the parking brake cable to the rear shoe and then position the shoe so the lower end rides in the anchor plate and the upper end is against the boot in the wheel cylinder. Install the pin and the hold-down spring. Press the retainer down over the pin and rotate the pin so the crimped edge is held by the retainer. Install the anchor spring between the front and rear shoes and then stretch the spring enough so the front shoe will fit as the rear did in Step 10. Install the hold-down spring, pin and retainer. Stretch the tension/return spring between the 2 shoes and connect it so it rides freely. Do not forget the return spring clamp, if equipped.
13. Check that the automatic adjuster is operating properly. Adjust the strut as short as possible and then install the brake drum. Set and release the parking brake several times.
14. Install the wheel and lower the vehicle. Check the level of brake fluid in the master cylinder, then test drive.

Without Bearing Retained Brake Ddrum

1. Raise and support the vehicle safely. Remove the wheels.
2. Remove the brake drums.

NOTE: Do not depress the brake pedal once the brake drum has been removed.

3. Carefully unhook the return spring from the leading (front) brake shoe. Grasp the hold-down spring pin with pliers and turn it until its in line with the slot in the hold-down spring. Remove the hold-down spring and the pin. Pull out the brake shoe and unhook the anchor spring from the lower edge.
4. Remove the hold-down spring from the trailing (rear) shoe. Pull the shoe out with the adjuster strut, automatic adjuster assembly and springs attached and disconnect the parking brake cable. Unhook the return spring and then remove the adjusting strut. Remove the anchor spring.
5. Remove the adjusting strut. Unhook the adjusting lever spring from the rear shoe and then remove the automatic adjuster assembly by popping out the C-clip.

To install:
6. Inspect the shoes for signs of unusual wear or scoring.
7. Check the wheel cylinder for any sign of fluid seepage or frozen pistons.
8. Clean and inspect the brake backing plate and all other components. Check that the brake drum inner diameter is within specified limits. Lubricate the backing plate bosses and the anchor plate.
9. Mount the automatic adjuster assembly onto a new rear brake shoe. Make sure the C-clip fits properly. Connect the adjusting strut/return spring and then install the adjusting spring.
10. Connect the parking brake cable to the rear shoe and then position the shoe so the lower end rides in the anchor plate and the upper end is against the boot in the wheel cylinder. Install the pin and the hold-down spring. Rotate the pin so the crimped edge is held by the retainer.
11. Install the anchor spring between the front and rear shoes and then stretch the spring enough so the front shoe will fit as the rear did in Step 10. Install the hold-down spring and pin. Connect the return spring/adjusting strut between the 2 shoes and connect it so it rides freely.
12. Check that the automatic adjuster is operating properly. Adjust the strut as short as possible and then install the brake drum. Set and release the parking brake several times.
13. Install the wheel and lower the vehicle. Check the level of brake fluid in the master cylinder, then test drive.

Wheel Cylinder

REMOVAL AND INSTALLATION

1. Plug the master cylinder inlet to prevent hydraulic fluid from leaking.
2. Remove the brake drums and shoes.
3. Working from behind the backing plate, disconnect the hydraulic line from the wheel cylinder.
4. Unfasten the screws or the clip retaining the wheel cylinder and withdraw the cylinder.
   To install:
5. Installation is performed in the reverse order of removal. Torque the bolts to 7 ft. lbs. (10 Nm) and the line to 11 ft. lbs. (15 Nm).
6. Bleed the brake system after completing wheel cylinder, brake

shoe and drum installation. Adjust the brakes.

Brake System Bleeding

MASTER CYLINDER

1. Check the fluid level in the master cylinder. Add fluid as necessary. Never use old fluid or allow the master cylinder to run dry.
2. Disconnect the brake tubes from the master cylinder.
3. Slowly depress the brake pedal and hold it.
4. Close off the outlet opening on the master cylinder with finger pressure and release the brake pedal.
5. Repeat Steps 3 and 4 several times to bleed all the air from the master cylinder.

BRAKE LINES

1. Bleed the caliper or wheel cylinder with the longest hydraulic line. Connect a vinyl tube to the bleeder screw on the brake cylinder and submerge the other end of the tube in a transparent container half filled with clean brake fluid.
2. Pump the brake pedal several times and loosen the bleeder screw with the pedal held down.
3. When brake fluid stops coming out of the tube, tighten the bleeder screw and release the brake pedal.
4. Repeat Steps 2 and 3 until no air bubbles can be seen in the container.
5. Repeat the procedure for each wheel.
6. Check the level in the master cylinder. Add fluid as necessary.

Anti-Lock Brake System

PRECAUTIONS

• When welding with an electric welding unit, unplug the electronic control unit.
• During paint jobs, the electronic control unit may be exposed to a maximum of 203°F (95°C) for up to 2 hours or 185°F (85°C) if more time is needed.
• When removing the rear axle centerpiece, make sure the correct toothed wheel with the correct ratio for the wheel speed sensor is installed. If a wheel with the wrong number of teeth is installed, this fault will not show up when checking the system with the ABS tester. The

stopping distance, however, will be increased during controlled braking.
• If work was done to non-ABS brake components, a simple operational test will be sufficient. This means that after driving about 5 mph, the warning light on the instrument panel should go out if the ABS system is intact.
• If ABS components have been replaced, the entire system should be checked using the appropriate tester in combination with brake bench test or an adaptor in combination with a multimeter.

RELIEVING ANTI-LOCK BRAKE SYSTEM PRESSURE

Pump the brake pedal at least 20 times with the ignition key in the **OFF** position. Place a shop rag around the hydraulic line fitting and wear safety glasses when disconnecting the hydraulic lines.

Anti-Lock Brake Actuator

REMOVAL AND INSTALLATION

1. Disconnect the negative battery cable.
2. Relieve the system pressure.
3. Remove the plastic cover from the actuator.
4. Disconnect the hydraulic lines from the actuator. Plug the lines to prevent loss of fluid.
5. Disconnect the electrical connectors from the actuator.
6. Remove the actuator from the bracket.
   To install:
7. Install the actuator and torque the hydraulic lines to 11 ft. lbs. (15 Nm).
8. Connect the battery cable, fill and bleed the system, start the engine and check brake system operation before driving the vehicle.

CHASSIS ELECTRICAL

——— CAUTION ———
To avoid personal injury when working on vehicles equipped with an air bag, the negative battery cable must be disconnected and at least 90 seconds elapse before working on the system.

Failure to do so may result in deployment of the air bag and possible personal injury.

Air Bag

DISARMING

Work must be started after about 90 seconds or longer from the time the ignition switch is turned to the **LOCK** position and the battery cable is disconnected from the battery.

Heater Blower Motor

NOTE: On most vehicles, the air conditioner assembly is integral with the heater assembly (including the blower motor) and therefore the blower motor removal may differ from the procedures detailed below. In some case it may be necessary to remove the air conditioning/heater housing and assembly to remove the blower motor. A general blower motor removal and installation procedure is outlined. The removal steps can be altered, as required.

REMOVAL AND INSTALLATION

——— CAUTION ———
To avoid personal injury and accidental deployment of the air bag, work must be started after about 90 seconds or longer from the time the ignition switch is turned to the LOCK position and the battery cable is disconnected from the battery.

Celica and Supra

1. Disconnect the negative battery cable.
2. Working from under the instrument panel, unfasten the defroster hoses from the heater box.
3. Unplug the multi-connector.
4. Loosen the mounting screws and withdraw the blower assembly.
5. Installation is the reverse of the removal procedure.
6. Check the blower for proper operation at all speeds.

Cressida

1. Disconnect the negative battery cable.
2. Remove the instrument panel undercover and cowl side trim panel.
3. Remove the air duct and the glove box.

4. Disconnect the heater control cable from the blower motor and remove the blower duct.

5. Disconnect the heater relay from the heater relay electrical connector.

6. Remove the retaining screws from the blower motor assembly. Remove the assembly from the vehicle.

7. Remove the blower motor from the blower motor assembly.

8. Installation is the reverse order of the removal procedure.

9. Check the blower for proper operation at all speeds.

Corolla

1. Disconnect the negative battery cable.

2. Remove the under tray, if equipped.

3. Remove the blower duct and air duct. Before removing the air duct, remove the 2 attaching clamps.

4. Remove the glove box and the heater control cable.

5. Disconnect the electrical connector on the blower motor.

6. Remove the blower motor retaining bolts and remove the blower motor.

7. Installation is the reverse of the removal procedure.

8. Check the blower for proper operation at all speeds.

Tercel

1990-91

1. Disconnect the negative battery cable.

2. Remove the under tray, if equipped.

3. Remove the blower duct and air duct. Before removing the air duct, remove the 2 attaching clamps.

4. Remove the glove box and the heater control cable.

5. Disconnect the electrical connector on the blower motor.

6. Remove the blower motor retaining bolts and remove the blower motor.

7. Installation is the reverse of the removal procedure.

8. Check the blower for proper operation at all speeds.

1992-94

1. Disconnect the negative battery cable.

2. Remove the air conditioning amplifier with the connector connected.

3. Disconnect and remove the blower motor.

4. Installation is the reverse of removal.

MR2 and 1990-91 Camry

1. Disconnect the negative battery cable.

2. Remove the 3 screws attaching the retainer.

3. Remove the glove box. Remove the duct between the blower motor assembly and the heater assembly.

4. Disconnect the blower motor wire connector at the blower motor case.

5. Disconnect the air source selector control cable at the blower motor assembly.

6. Loosen the nuts and bolts attaching the blower motor to the blower case and remove the blower motor from the vehicle.

7. Installation is the reverse of the removal procedure.

8. Check the blower for proper operation at all speeds.

1992-94 Camry

1. Disconnect the negative battery cable.

2. Remove the glove compartment.

3. Remove the ECU and the ECU bracket.

4. Remove the connector bracket by disconnecting the connector and removing the 2 screws.

5. Disconnect the connector from the blower unit.

6. Disconnect the air inlet damper control cable.

7. Remove the 3 screws, the nut and the blower unit.

8. Installation is the reverse of removal.

Paseo

1. Disconnect the negative battery cable.

2. Remove the air conditioning amplifier.

3. Remove the blower motor.

4. Installation is the reverse of removal. Check blower motor for proper operation.

Front Windshield Wiper Motor

REMOVAL AND INSTALLATION

——————— CAUTION ———————
To avoid personal injury and accidental deployment of the air bag, work must be started after about 90 seconds or longer from the time the ignition switch is turned to the LOCK position and the battery cable is disconnected from the battery.

Paseo, Tercel and Corolla

1. Disconnect the negative battery terminal.

2. Remove the wiper arm.

3. Insert a small prybar between the linkage and the motor. Pry up to separate the linkage from the motor.

4. Disconnect the electrical connector from the motor.

5. Remove the mounting bolts and remove the motor.

6. Installation is the reverse of the removal procedure. Check for proper operation.

Celica, Supra, Camry and Cressida

1. Remove the access hole cover.

2. Separate the wiper and motor by prying gently with a small prybar.

3. Remove the left and right cowl ventilators.

4. Remove the wiper arms and the linkage mounting nuts. Push the linkage pivot ports into the ventilators.

5. Loosen the wiper link connectors at their ends and with the linkage from the cowl ventilator.

6. Start the wiper motor and turn the ignition key **OFF** when the crank is at the best position suited for removal of the motor.

NOTE: The wiper motor is difficult to remove when it is in the parked position. If the motor is turned off at the wiper switch, it will automatically return to this position.

7. Unplug the wiper motor connector.

8. Loosen the motor mounting bolts and withdraw the motor.

To install:

9. Be sure to install the wiper motor with it in the park position by connecting the multi-connector and operating the wiper control switch.

10. Assemble the crank, connect the wiring and check operation.

MR2

1. With the wiper arms in the up position and the wiper switch on low, turn the ignition switch to the **OFF** position.

2. Disconnect the negative battery cable. Disconnect the wiper motor electrical connector, then remove the light retractor relay from the wiper bracket.

3. Remove the wiper motor set bolts. Manually lower the wiper arms, then connect the wiper link hook to the dash panel service hole.

4. Disconnect the wiper motor link. Remove the wiper motor attach-

ing bolts then remove the wiper motor.

5. Installation is the reverse order of the removal procedure. Check for proper operation.

Rear Wiper Motor

REMOVAL AND INSTALLATION

1. Disconnect the negative battery cable.

2. Remove the wiper arm and rear door trim cover.

3. Disconnect the wiper motor wire connector.

4. Remove the wiper motor bracket attaching bolts and the wiper motor along with the bracket.

5. Installation is the reverse of the removal procedure. Check for proper operation.

Instrument Cluster

REMOVAL AND INSTALLATION

—————— CAUTION ——————

To avoid personal injury and accidental deployment of the air bag, work must be started after about 90 seconds or longer from the time the ignition switch is turned to the LOCK position and the battery cable is disconnected from the battery.

Cressida

1. Disconnect the negative battery cable.

2. Remove the cluster finish panel.

3. Loosen the instrument cluster retaining screws and tilt the panel forward.

4. Detach the speedometer cable and wiring connectors.

5. Remove the entire cluster assembly.

6. Remove the instruments from the panel as required.

7. Installation is the reverse of the removal procedure.

Paseo, tercel and corolla

1. Disconnect the negative battery cable.

2. Remove the steering column cover.

NOTE: Be careful not to damage the collapsible steering column mechanism.

3. On Tercel, remove the heater control knob and the center instrument cluster finish panel.

4. Remove the switches and hole cover from the cluster hood.

5. Remove the cluster hood.

6. Remove the cluster attaching screws and pull the unit forward.

7. Disconnect the speedometer and any other electrical connections that are necessary.

8. Remove the instruments from the panel as required.

9. Installation is the reverse of the removal procedure.

Camry, Celica and Supra

1. Disconnect the negative battery cable.

2. Remove the fuse box cover from under the left side of the instrument panel.

3. Remove the heater control knobs.

4. Carefully pry off the heater control panel.

5. Remove the cluster hood.

6. Unscrew the cluster finish panel retaining screws and pull out the bottom of the panel.

7. Unplug the electrical connectors and disconnect the speedometer cable.

8. Remove the instrument cluster.

9. Remove the instruments from the panel as required.

10. Installation is the reverse of the removal procedure.

MR2

1. Disconnect the negative battery cable.

2. Remove the steering column covers.

3. Pull the rheostat knob from the cluster finish panel and remove the nut from the rheostat. Remove the cluster finish panel and disconnect the rheostat multi-connector.

4. Remove the cluster hood.

5. Remove the cluster attaching screws and pull the unit forward.

6. Disconnect the speedometer and any other electrical connections that are necessary.

7. Remove the instruments from the panel as required.

8. Installation is the reverse of the removal procedure.

Concealed Headlights

—————— CAUTION ——————

To avoid personal injury before attempting to manually operate the concealed (retractable) headlights, first pull the fuse or disconnect the negative battery cable. Otherwise the headlights and motor shaft may suddenly move and catch hand and fingers. When opening and closing retractable headlights, make sure nobody is near them, otherwise personal injury may result. Also, to avoid personal injury and accidental deployment of the air bag, work must be started after about 90 seconds or longer from the time the ignition switch is turned to the LOCK position and the battery cable is disconnected from the battery.

MANUAL OPERATION

NOTE: If the headlights are frozen and inoperative, carefully melt the ice before attempting the manual operation procedure. Operation of a frozen headlight will drain the battery and may cause damage to the motor and operating linkages.

1. Switch the headlight and retractable headlight switches to the OFF position.

2. Pull the retractable headlight fuse or disconnect the negative battery cable.

3. Remove the rubber cap from the manual operation knob.

4. Manually turn the knob clockwise until the headlights are in the desired position (open or closed).

5. Install the rubber cap.

6. Install the fuse.

7. Make sure the lights work properly.

Combination Switch

REMOVAL AND INSTALLATION

—————— CAUTION ——————

To avoid personal injury and accidental deployment of the air bag, work must be started after about 90 seconds or longer from the time the ignition switch is turned to the LOCK position and the battery cable is disconnected from the battery.

1. Disconnect the negative battery cable.

2. Remove the steering column garnish.

3. Remove the upper and lower steering column covers.

4. Remove the steering wheel.

5. Trace the switch wiring harness to the multi-connector. Push in the lock levers and pull apart the connectors.

6. If equipped with Electronic Modulated Suspension (EMS), re-

move the steering sensor. On air bag equipped vehicles, disconnect the cable connectors, remove the spiral cable housing attaching screws and slide the cable assembly from the front of the combination switch.

7. Unscrew the mounting screws and slide the combination switch from the steering column.

8. Installation is the reverse of the removal procedure. Check all switch functions for proper operation.

Ignition Lock/Switch

REMOVAL AND INSTALLATION

1. Disconnect the negative battery cable.

2. Unfasten the ignition switch connector under the instrument panel.

3. Remove the screws which secure the upper and lower halves of the steering column cover.

4. Turn the lock cylinder to the **ACC** position with the ignition key.

5. Push the lock cylinder stop in with a small, round object (cotter pin, punch, etc.).

NOTE: On some vehicles, it may be necessary to remove the steering wheel and combination switch first.

6. Withdraw the lock cylinder from the lock housing while depressing the stop tab.

7. To remove the ignition switch, unfasten its securing screws and withdraw the switch from the lock housing.

To install:

8. Align the locking cam with the hole in the ignition switch and insert the switch into the lock housing.

9. Secure the switch with its screw(s).

10. Make sure both the lock cylinder and column lock are in the **ACC**

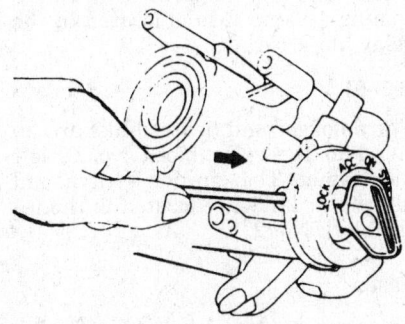

Ignition lock removal

position. Slide the cylinder into the lock housing until the stop tab engages the hole in the lock.

11. Install the steering column covers.

12. Connect the ignition switch connector.

13. Connect the negative battery cable.

Stoplight Switch

ADJUSTMENT

1. Remove the instrument lower finish panel and the air duct if required to gain access to the stoplight switch.

2. Disconnect the stoplight switch connector.

3. Loosen the switch locknut.

4. Turn the stoplight switch until the end of the switch lightly contacts the pedal stopper.

5. Hold the switch and tighten the locknut.

6. Connect the switch connector.

7. Depress the brake pedal and verify that the brake lights illuminate.

8. Install the air duct and the lower finish panel, if removed.

REMOVAL AND INSTALLATION

1. Disconnect the negative battery cable.

2. Remove the instrument lower finish panel and the air duct if required to gain access to the stoplight switch.

3. Disconnect the stoplight switch connector.

4. Remove the switch mounting nut, then slide the switch from the mounting bracket on the pedal.

To install:

5. Install the switch into the mounting bracket and adjust.

6. Connect the switch connector.

7. Depress the brake pedal and verify that the brake lights illuminate.

8. Install the air duct and the lower finish panel, if removed.

Clutch Switch

ADJUSTMENT

1. Attempt to start the engine when the clutch pedal is released. The engine should not start.

2. Depress the clutch pedal fully and attempt to start the engine. The engine should start.

3. If the engine does not start, depress the clutch pedal fully. With the clutch pedal depressed, loosen the switch locknut.

4. Use the adjusting nut to turn the switch until the tip of the switch contacts the clutch pedal stop.

5. Tighten the locknut and attempt to start the engine. Re-adjust as necessary.

6. If the switch cannot be adjusted, check the switch continuity with a suitable ohmmeter. There should be continuity between the switch terminals when the switch is on (tip pushed in) and no continuity when the switch is off (tip released). If the continuity is not as specified, replace the switch.

REMOVAL AND INSTALLATION

1. Disconnect the negative battery cable.

2. Disconnect the switch connector.

3. Remove the switch adjusting nut.

4. Withdraw the switch from the mounting bracket.

5. Installation is the reverse of the removal procedure. Adjust the switch.

Neutral Safety Switch

The shift lever is adjusted properly if the engine will not start in any position other than **N** or **P**.

ADJUSTMENT

1. Loosen the neutral start switch bolt. Position the selector in the **N** position.

2. Align the switch shaft groove with the neutral base line which is located on the switch.

3. Tighten the bolt to 48 inch lbs. (5.4 Nm) on all vehicles except Tercel wagon. On the Tercel wagon, tighten to 9 ft. lbs. (13 Nm).

REMOVAL AND INSTALLATION

1. Disconnect the negative battery cable.

2. Unplug the switch wiring connectors.

3. Disconnect the transmission control cable from the manual shift lever.

4. Remove the manual shift lever.

5. Pry the C-washer from the manual shaft nut. Discard the washer and replace with new.

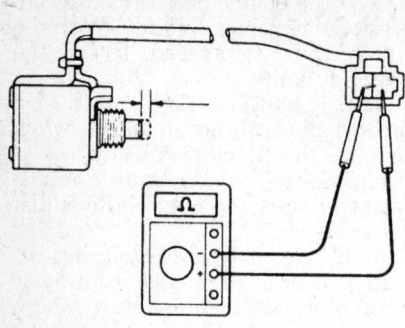

Checking clutch start switch continuity

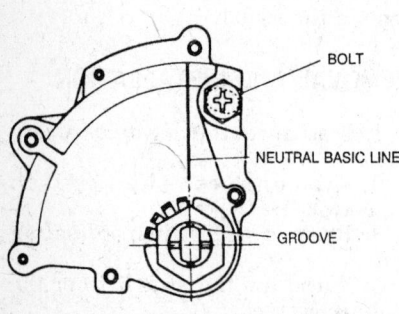

BOLT

NEUTRAL BASIC LINE

GROOVE

Neutral safety switch adjustment

6. Remove the manual shaft nut and washer.

7. Remove the manual shaft lever packing, if equipped.

8. Remove the retaining bolts and withdraw the switch from the transaxle case.

9. Installation is the reverse of the removal procedure. Adjust the switch.

Circuit Breakers

LOCATION

Camry

The automatic shoulder belt and defogger circuit breakers are located in the junction block No. 1. The heater circuit breaker is located in the relay block No. 4. The 1992-94 models are not equipped with circuit breakers.

Celica

The power and door lock circuit breakers are located in the relay block No. 1. The defogger circuit

breaker is located in the junction block No. 1. The heater circuit breaker is located in the relay block No. 4.

Corolla

The heater circuit breaker is located in the relay block No. 4. The defogger and power circuit breakers are located in the junction block No. 1, left kick panel. The air conditioning circuit breaker is behind the right kick panel on 1992-94 models.

Cressida

The heater circuit breaker is located in the relay block No. 4. The defogger and power circuit breakers are located in the junction block No. 1, left kick panel. The automatic shoulder belt and door lock circuit breakers are located in the relay block No. 3, left kick panel.

Supra

On the 1992-94 Supra, a circuit breaker is located behind the right kick panel. The heater circuit breaker is located in the relay block No. 4. The defogger and power circuit breakers are located in the junction block No. 1, left kick panel. The automatic shoulder belt and door lock circuit breakers are located in the relay block No. 3, left kick panel.

MR2

The door lock circuit breaker is located in the relay block No. 1, left kick panel, upper section. The 1992-94 models are not equipped with circuit breakers.

Tercel

The defogger circuit breaker is located in the junction block No. 1, left kick panel. The 1992-94 models are not equipped with circuit breakers.

Fusible Links

LOCATION

Camry

The condenser fan and radiator fan 30 amp fusible link is located in the relay block No. 2. The ignition, headlight and alternator fusible link is located in the fusible link box near the battery. The auto seat belt, starter relay and voltage regulator 0.5 amp

fusible link is located near the battery.

Celica

The condenser fan link is located in the relay block No. 5. The radiator fan link is located in the junction block No. 2. The ignition, starter, alternator and Anti-lock brake system links are located in the fusible link box near the battery.

Corolla

The condenser fan link is located in the relay block No. 5. The radiator fan link is located in the junction block No. 2. The air conditioning 7.5 amp fuse is located in the bottom of the relay block No. 4.

Cressida

The condenser fan, ignition switch, Anti-lock Brake System (ABS) and alternator link is located in the junction block No. 2, near the battery.

MR2

The ignition switch, heater and alternator links are located in the relay block No. 5, right side luggage compartment. The Anti-lock Brake System (ABS) link is located in the relay block No. 5, right side luggage compartment.

Supra

The ECU-battery 15 amp Fuse is located in the fuse block. The ignition switch, condenser fan, Anti-lock Brake System (ABS) and alternator link is located in the junction block No. 2, left fender.

Tercel

1990

The condenser fan and radiator fan links are located in the relay block No. 2, left inner fender. The air conditioning 10 amp fuse is located in the relay block No. 4.

1991-94

The defogger and heater links are located in the relay block No. 6, left kick panel. The ignition switch and alternator links are located in the relay block No. 2.

Paseo

The ignition and alternator fusible links are located in the fuse block No. 2 next to the battery.

Volkswagen

Cabriolet, Corrado, Fox, Golf, GTI, Jetta, Passat

SPECIFICATIONS

ENGINE IDENTIFICATION

Year	Model	Engine Displacement Liters (cc)	Engine Series (ID/VIN)	Fuel System	No. of Cylinders	Engine Type
1990	Jetta GL	1.8 (1780)	RV	Digifant II	4	SOHC
	Jetta GLI 16V	2.0 (1984)	9A	CIS-E	4	DOHC
	Jetta Carat	1.8 (1780)	PF②	Digifant II	4	SOHC
	Jetta Diesel	1.6 (1588)	ME	Bosch VE	4	SOHC
	Golf GL	1.8 (1780)	RV	Digifant II	4	SOHC
	GTI	1.8 (1780)	PF	Digifant II	4	SOHC
	GTI 16V	2.0 (1984)	9A	CIS-E	4	DOHC
	Cabriolet	1.8 (1780)	JH	CIS-E	4	SOHC
	Fox GL	1.8 (1780)	UM, JN①	CIS, CIS-E	4	SOHC
	Passat GL	2.0 (1984)	9A	CIS-E	4	DOHC
	Corrado	1.8 (1780)	PG	Digifant II	4	Supercharged
1991	Jetta GL	1.8 (1780)	RV	Digifant	4	SOHC
	Jetta GLI 16V	2.0 (1984)	9A	CIS-E	4	DOHC
	Jetta Carat	1.8 (1780)	PF②	Digifant	4	SOHC
	Jetta ECO Diesel	1.6 (1588)	1V	Bosch VE	4	Turbo
	Golf GL	1.8 (1780)	RV	Digifant	4	SOHC
	GTI	1.8 (1780)	PF	Digifant	4	SOHC
	GTI 16V	2.0 (1984)	9A	CIS-E	4	DOHC
	Cabriolet	1.8 (1780)	JH	CIS-E	4	SOHC
	Fox	1.8 (1780)	ABG	Digifant③	4	SOHC
	Passat GL	2.0 (1984)	9A	CIS-E	4	DOHC
	Corrado	1.8 (1780)	PG	Digifant	4	Supercharged
1992	Jetta GL	1.8 (1780)	PF	Digifant	4	SOHC
	Jetta GLI 16V	2.0 (1984)	9A	CIS-E	4	DOHC
	Jetta Carat	1.8 (1780)	PF②	Digifant	4	SOHC
	Jetta ECO Diesel	1.6 (1588)	1V	Bosch VE	4	Turbo
	Golf GL	1.8 (1780)	RV	Digifant	4	SOHC
	GTI	1.8 (1780)	PF	Digifant	4	SOHC
	GTI 16V	2.0 (1984)	9A	CIS-E	4	DOHC
	Cabriolet	1.8 (1780)	JH	CIS-E	4	SOHC
	Fox	1.8 (1780)	ABG	Digifant③	4	SOHC
	Passat GL	2.0 (1984)	9A	CIS-E	4	DOHC
	Passat GLS/GLX	2.8 (2860)	AAA	Motronic	6	DOHC
	Corrado	1.8 (1780)	PG	Digifant	4	Supercharged
	Corrado SLC	2.8 (2860)	AAA	Motronic	6	DOHC

ENGINE IDENTIFICATION

Year	Model	Engine Displacement Liters (cc)	Engine Series (ID/VIN)	Fuel System	No. of Cylinders	Engine Type
1993	Jetta GL	1.8 (1780)	PF	Digifant	4	SOHC
	Jetta GLI 16V	2.0 (1984)	9A	CIS-E	4	DOHC
	Jetta Carat	1.8 (1780)	PF ②	Digifant	4	SOHC
	Jetta ECO Diesel	1.6 (1588)	1V	Bosch VE	4	Turbo
	Golf GL	1.8 (1780)	RV	Digifant	4	SOHC
	GTI	1.8 (1780)	PF	Digifant	4	SOHC
	GTI 16V	2.0 (1984)	9A	CIS-E	4	DOHC
	Cabriolet	1.8 (1780)	JH	CIS-E	4	SOHC
	Fox	1.8 (1780)	ABG	Digifant ③	4	SOHC
	Passat GL	2.0 (1984)	9A	CIS-E	4	DOHC
	Passat GLS/GLX	2.8 (2860)	AAA	Motronic	6	DOHC
	Corrado	1.8 (1780)	PG	Digifant	4	Supercharged
	Corrado SLC	2.8 (2860)	AAA	Motronic	6	DOHC
1994	Jetta GL	1.8 (1780)	PF	Digifant	4	SOHC
	Jetta GLI 16V	2.0 (1984)	9A	CIS-E	4	DOHC
	Jetta Carat	1.8 (1780)	PF ②	Digifant	4	SOHC
	Jetta ECO Diesel	1.6 (1588)	1V	Bosch VE	4	Turbo
	Golf GL	1.8 (1780)	RV	Digifant	4	SOHC
	GTI	1.8 (1780)	PF	Digifant	4	SOHC
	GTI 16V	2.0 (1984)	9A	CIS-E	4	DOHC
	Cabriolet	1.8 (1780)	JH	CIS-E	4	SOHC
	Fox	1.8 (1780)	ABG	Digifant ③	4	SOHC
	Passat GL	2.0 (1984)	9A	CIS-E	4	DOHC
	Passat GLS/GLX	2.8 (2860)	AAA	Motronic	6	DOHC
	Corrado	1.8 (1780)	PG	Digifant	4	Supercharged
	Corrado SLC	2.8 (2860)	AAA	Motronic	6	DOHC

CIS-E—Continuous Injection System
Digifant—Digital Electronic Fuel Injection
① UM engine with CIS in Canada only
② RV in California
③ Digifant I in California
    Digifant II in 49 states, Canada

GENERAL ENGINE SPECIFICATIONS

Year	Engine ID/VIN	Engine Displacement Liters (cc)	Fuel System Type	Net Horsepower @ rpm	Net Torque @ rpm (ft. lbs.)	Bore × Stroke (in.)	Compression Ratio	Oil Pressure @ rpm
1990	RV	1.8 (1780)	Digifant	100 @ 5400	109 @ 3800	3.19 × 3.40	10.0:1	28 @ 2000
	9A	2.0 (1984)	CIS-E	134 @ 5800	133 @ 4400	3.25 × 3.65	10.8:1	28 @ 2000
	PF	1.8 (1780)	Digifant	105 @ 5400	114 @ 3800	3.19 × 3.40	10.0:1	28 @ 2000
	ME	1.6 (1588)	Bosch VE	52 @ 4800	72 @ 2000	3.01 × 3.40	23.0:1	28 @ 2000
	JH	1.8 (1780)	CIS-E	94 @ 5500	100 @ 3000	3.19 × 3.40	8.5:1	28 @ 2000
	UM, JN	1.8 (1780)	CIS, CIS-E	81 @ 5500	93 @ 3250	3.19 × 3.40	9.0:1	28 @ 2000
	PG	1.8 (1780)	Digifant	158 @ 5600	166 @ 4000	3.19 × 3.40	8.0:1	28 @ 2000
1991	RV	1.8 (1780)	Digifant	100 @ 5400	109 @ 3800	3.19 × 3.40	10.0:1	28 @ 2000
	9A	2.0 (1984)	CIS-E	134 @ 5800	133 @ 4400	3.25 × 3.65	10.8:1	28 @ 2000
	PF	1.8 (1780)	Digifant	105 @ 5400	114 @ 3800	3.19 × 3.40	10.0:1	28 @ 2000
	1V	1.6 (1588)	Bosch VE	52 @ 4800	71 @ 2000	3.01 × 3.40	23.0:1	28 @ 2000
	JH	1.8 (1780)	CIS-E	94 @ 5500	100 @ 3000	3.19 × 3.40	8.5:1	28 @ 2000
	PG	1.8 (1780)	Digifant	158 @ 5600	166 @ 4000	3.19 × 3.40	8.0:1	28 @ 2000
	ABG	1.8 (1780)	Digifant	81 @ 5500	93 @ 3250	3.19 × 3.40	9.0:1	28 @ 2000
1992	RV	1.8 (1780)	Digifant	100 @ 5400	109 @ 3800	3.19 × 3.40	10.0:1	28 @ 2000
	9A	2.0 (1984)	CIS-E	134 @ 5800	133 @ 4400	3.25 × 3.65	10.8:1	28 @ 2000
	PF	1.8 (1780)	Digifant	105 @ 5400	114 @ 3800	3.19 × 3.40	10.0:1	28 @ 2000
	1V	1.6 (1588)	Bosch VE	52 @ 4800	71 @ 2000	3.01 × 3.40	23.0:1	28 @ 2000
	JH	1.8 (1780)	CIS-E	94 @ 5400	100 @ 3000	3.19 × 3.40	8.5:1	28 @ 2000
	PG	1.8 (1780)	Digifant	158 @ 5600	166 @ 4000	3.19 × 3.40	8.0:1	28 @ 2000
	ABG	1.8 (1780)	Digifant	81 @ 5500	93 @ 3250	3.19 × 3.40	9.0:1	28 @ 2000
	AAA	2.8 (2860)	Motronic	178 @ 5800	177 @ 4200	3.20 × 3.52	10.0:1	28 @ 2000
1993	RV	1.8 (1780)	Digifant	100 @ 5400	109 @ 3800	3.19 × 3.40	10.0:1	28 @ 2000
	9A	2.0 (1984)	CIS-E	134 @ 5800	133 @ 4400	3.25 × 3.65	10.8:1	28 @ 2000
	PF	1.8 (1780)	Digifant	105 @ 5400	114 @ 3800	3.19 × 3.40	10.0:1	28 @ 2000
	1V	1.6 (1588)	Bosch VE	52 @ 4800	71 @ 2000	3.01 × 3.40	23.0:1	28 @ 2000
	JH	1.8 (1780)	CIS-E	94 @ 5400	100 @ 3000	3.19 × 3.40	8.5:1	28 @ 2000
	PG	1.8 (1780)	Digifant	158 @ 5600	166 @ 4000	3.19 × 3.40	8.0:1	28 @ 2000
	ABG	1.8 (1780)	Digifant	81 @ 5500	93 @ 3250	3.19 × 3.40	9.0:1	28 @ 2000
	AAA	2.8 (2860)	Motronic	178 @ 5800	177 @ 4200	3.20 × 3.52	10.0:1	28 @ 2000
1994	RV	1.8 (1780)	Digifant	100 @ 5400	109 @ 3800	3.19 × 3.40	10.0:1	28 @ 2000
	9A	2.0 (1984)	CIS-E	134 @ 5800	133 @ 4400	3.25 × 3.65	10.8:1	28 @ 2000
	PF	1.8 (1780)	Digifant	105 @ 5400	114 @ 3800	3.19 × 3.40	10.0:1	28 @ 2000
	1V	1.6 (1588)	Bosch VE	52 @ 4800	71 @ 2000	3.01 × 3.40	23.0:1	28 @ 2000
	JH	1.8 (1780)	CIS-E	94 @ 5400	100 @ 3000	3.19 × 3.40	8.5:1	28 @ 2000
	PG	1.8 (1780)	Digifant	158 @ 5600	166 @ 4000	3.19 × 3.40	8.0:1	28 @ 2000
	ABG	1.8 (1780)	Digifant	81 @ 5500	93 @ 3250	3.19 × 3.40	9.0:1	28 @ 2000
	AAA	2.8 (2860)	Motronic	178 @ 5800	177 @ 4200	3.20 × 3.52	10.0:1	28 @ 2000

GASOLINE ENGINE TUNE-UP SPECIFICATIONS

Year	Engine ID/VIN	Engine Displacement Liters (cc)	Spark Plugs Gap (in.)	Ignition Timing (deg.) MT	AT	Fuel Pump (psi)	Idle Speed (rpm) MT	AT	Valve Clearance In.	Ex.
1990	RV	1.8 (1780)	0.024–0.032	6BTDC @ Idle	6BTDC @ Idle	36②	800–900	800–900	Hyd.	Hyd.
	9A	2.0 (1984)	0.027–0.035	6BTDC @ Idle	6BTDC @ Idle	88–96②	800–900	—	Hyd.	Hyd.
	PF	1.8 (1780)	0.027–0.035	6BTDC @ Idle	6BTDC @ Idle	36②	800–900	800–900	Hyd.	Hyd.
	JH	1.8 (1780)	0.027–0.035	6BTDC @ Idle	6BTDC @ Idle	68–78②	850–1000	850–1000	Hyd.	Hyd.
	UM	1.8 (1780)	0.024–0.032	6BTDC @ Idle	6BTDC @ Idle	68–78①	800–1000	800–1000	Hyd.	Hyd.
	JN	1.8 (1780)	0.024–0.032	6BTDC @ Idle	6BTDC @ Idle	64–74①	800–1000	800–1000	Hyd.	Hyd.
	PG	1.8 (1780)	0.028–0.031	6BTDC @ Idle	—	36②	770–830		Hyd.	Hyd.
1991	RV	1.8 (1780)	0.024–0.032	6BTDC @ Idle	6BTDC @ Idle	36②	800–900	800–900	Hyd.	Hyd.
	9A	2.0 (1984)	0.027–0.035	6BTDC @ Idle	6BTDC @ Idle	88–96②	800–1000	800–1000	Hyd.	Hyd.
	PF	1.8 (1780)	0.027–0.035	6BTDC @ Idle	6BTDC @ Idle	36②	800–900	800–900	Hyd.	Hyd.
	JH	1.8 (1780)	0.027–0.035	6BTDC @ Idle	6BTDC @ Idle	36②	800–1000	800–1000	Hyd.	Hyd.
	PG	1.8 (1780)	0.028–0.031	6BTDC @ Idle	—	36②	770–830	770–830	Hyd.	Hyd.
	ABG	1.8 (1780)	0.026–0.032	6BTDC @ 2250	6BTDC @ 2250	36②	800–1000	800–1000	Hyd.	Hyd.
1992	RV	1.8 (1780)	0.024–0.032	6BTDC @ 2250	6BTDC @ 2250	36②	800–900	800–900	Hyd.	Hyd.
	9A	2.0 (1984)	0.027–0.035	6BTDC @ Idle	6BTDC @ Idle	88–96②	800–1000	800–1000	Hyd.	Hyd.
	PF	1.8 (1780)	0.027–0.035	6BTDC @ 2250	6BTDC @ 2250	36②	800–900	800–900	Hyd.	Hyd.
	JH	1.8 (1780)	0.027–0.035	6BTDC @ 2250	6BTDC @ 2250	36②	800–1000	800–1000	Hyd.	Hyd.
	PG	1.8 (1780)	0.028–0.031	6BTDC @ 2250	6BTDC @ 2250	36②	770–830	770–830	Hyd.	Hyd.
	ABG	1.8 (1780)	0.026–0.032	6BTDC @ 2250	6BTDC @ 2250	36②	800–1000	800–1000	Hyd.	Hyd.
	AAA	2.8 (2860)	0.027–0.032	NA	NA	51②	NA	NA	Hyd.	Hyd.

GASOLINE ENGINE TUNE-UP SPECIFICATIONS

Year	Engine ID/VIN	Engine Displacement Liters (cc)	Spark Plugs Gap (in.)	Ignition Timing (deg.) MT	AT	Fuel Pump (psi)	Idle Speed (rpm) MT	AT	Valve Clearance In.	Ex.
1993	RV	1.8 (1780)	0.024–0.032	6BTDC @ 2250	6BTDC @ 2250	36②	800–900	800–900	Hyd.	Hyd.
	9A	2.0 (1984)	0.027–0.035	6BTDC @ Idle	6BTDC @ Idle	88–96②	800–1000	800–1000	Hyd.	Hyd.
	PF	1.8 (1780)	0.027–0.035	6BTDC @ 2250	6BTDC @ 2250	36②	800–900	800–900	Hyd.	Hyd.
	JH	1.8 (1780)	0.027–0.035	6BTDC @ 2250	6BTDC @ 2250	36②	800–1000	800–1000	Hyd.	Hyd.
	PG	1.8 (1780)	0.028–0.031	6BTDC @ 2250	6BTDC @ 2250	36②	770–830	770–830	Hyd.	Hyd.
	ABG	1.8 (1780)	0.026–0.032	6BTDC @ 2250	6BTDC @ 2250	36②	800–1000	800–1000	Hyd.	Hyd.
	AAA	2.8 (2860)	0.027–0.032	NA	NA	51②	NA	NA	Hyd.	Hyd.
1994	RV	1.8 (1780)	0.024–0.032	6BTDC @ 2250	6BTDC @ 2250	36②	800–900	800–900	Hyd.	Hyd.
	9A	2.0 (1984)	0.027–0.035	6BTDC @ Idle	6BTDC @ Idle	88–96②	800–1000	800–1000	Hyd.	Hyd.
	PF	1.8 (1780)	0.027–0.035	6BTDC @ 2250	6BTDC @ 2250	36②	800–900	800–900	Hyd.	Hyd.
	JH	1.8 (1780)	0.027–0.035	6BTDC @ 2250	6BTDC @ 2250	36②	800–1000	800–1000	Hyd.	Hyd.
	PG	1.8 (1780)	0.028–0.031	6BTDC @ 2250	6BTDC @ 2250	36②	770–830	770–830	Hyd.	Hyd.
	ABG	1.8 (1780)	0.026–0.032	6BTDC @ 2250	6BTDC @ 2250	36②	800–1000	800–1000	Hyd.	Hyd.
	AAA	2.8 (2860)	0.027–0.032	NA	NA	51②	NA	NA	Hyd.	Hyd.

NOTE: The lowest cylinder pressure should be within 75% of the highest cylinder pressure reading. For example, if the highest cylinder is 134 psi, the lowest should be 101. Engine should be at normal operating temperature with throttle valve in the wide open position.

The underhood specifications sticker often reflects tune-up specification changes in production. Sticker figures must be used if they disagree with those in this chart.

Hyd.—Hydraulic

NA—Not available

① Engine off, pump running

② System pressure at idle

DIESEL ENGINE TUNE-UP SPECIFICATIONS

Year	Engine ID/VIN	Engine Displacement Liters (cc)	Valve Clearance		Intake Valve Opens (deg.)	Injection Pump Setting (deg.)	Injection Nozzle Pressure (psi)		Idle Speed (rpm)	Cranking Compression Pressure (psi)
			Intake (in.)	Exhaust (in.)			New	Used		
1990	ME	1.6 (1588)	0.008–① 0.012	0.016–① 0.020	NA	Align Marks	1885–③ 2001	1740③	800– 850② ④	406 min.
1991	IV⑤	1.6 (1588)	0.008–① 0.012	0.016–① 0.020	NA	Align Marks	NA	NA	800– 850	406 min.
1992	IV⑤	1.6 (1588)	0.008–① 0.012	0.016–① 0.020	NA	Align Marks	NA	NA	800– 850	406 min.
1993	IV⑤	1.6 (1588)	Hyd.	Hyd.	NA	Align Marks	NA	NA	800– 850	406 min.
1994	IV⑤	1.6 (1588)	Hyd.	Hyd.	NA	Align Marks	NA	NA	800– 850	406 min.

NA—Not available
① Engine warm
② Factory has reduced idle speed on earlier models to this specification.
③ Turbo Diesel with ME engine:
New—2306
Used—2139
④ Turbo Diesel with ME engine: 900–1000
⑤ IV Engine in ECO Diesel has a catalytic converter and is different from Turbo Diesel

FIRING ORDERS

NOTE: To avoid confusion, always replace spark plug wires one at a time.

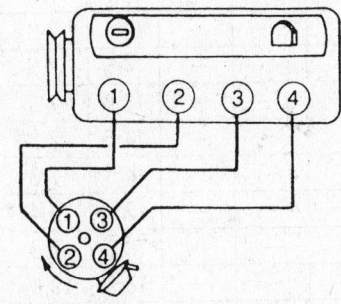

4 Cylinder Engines
Engine Firing Order: 1-3-4-2
Distributor Rotation: Counterclockwise

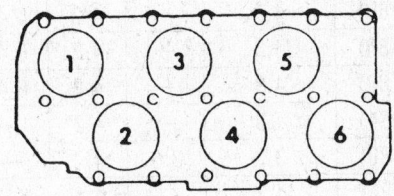

6 Cylinder Engine
Engine Firing Order: 1-5-3-6-2-4
Distributor Rotation: Counterclockwise

CAPACITIES

Year	Model	Engine ID/VIN	Engine Displacement Liters (cc)	Engine Crankcase with Filter (qts.)	Transmission (pts.) 4-Spd	5-Spd	Auto.	Transfer Case (pts.)	Drive Axle Front (pts.)	Rear (pts.)	Fuel Tank (gal.)	Cooling System (qts.)
1990	Jetta	RV & PF	1.8 (1780)	4.3	—	4.2	6.4	—	—	—	14.5	7.3
	Jetta Diesel	ME	1.6 (1588)	4.7	—	4.2	6.4	—	—	—	13.7	7.3
	Jetta GLI 16V	9A	2.0 (1984)	4.3	—	4.2	—	—	—	—	14.5	7.3
	Jetta Carat	PF	1.8 (1780)	4.3	—	4.2	6.4	—	—	—	14.5	7.3
	Cabriolet	JH	1.8 (1780)	4.3	—	4.2	6.4	—	—	—	13.8	7.3
	Golf	RV & PF	1.8 (1780)	4.3	—	4.2	6.4	—	—	—	14.5	7.3
	Golf GTI 16V	9A	2.0 (1984)	4.3	—	4.2	—	—	—	—	14.5	7.3
	Fox	UM, JN	1.8 (1780)	3.7	3.6	4.2	—	—	—	—	12.4	6.4 ①
	Passat	9A	2.0 (1984)	4.3	—	4.2	6.0	—	—	—	18.5	7.3
	Corrado	PG	1.8 (1780)	4.3	—	4.2	—	—	—	—	14.5	7.3
1991	Jetta	RV & PF	1.8 (1780)	4.3	—	4.2	6.4	—	—	—	14.5	7.3
	Jetta Diesel	1V	1.6 (1588)	4.7	—	4.2	6.4	—	—	—	13.7	7.3
	Jetta GLI 16V	9A	2.0 (1984)	4.3	—	4.2	—	—	—	—	14.5	7.3
	Jetta Carat	PF	1.8 (1780)	4.3	—	4.2	6.4	—	—	—	14.5	7.3
	Cabriolet	JH	1.8 (1780)	4.3	—	4.2	6.4	—	—	—	13.8	7.3
	Golf	RV & PF	1.8 (1780)	4.3	—	4.2	6.4	—	—	—	14.5	7.3
	Golf GTI 16V	9A	2.0 (1984)	4.3	—	4.2	—	—	—	—	14.5	7.3
	Fox	ABG	1.8 (1780)	3.7	3.6	4.2	—	—	—	—	12.4	6.4 ①
	Passat	9A	2.0 (1984)	4.3	—	4.2	6.0	—	—	—	18.5	7.3
	Corrado	PG	1.8 (1780)	4.3	—	4.2	—	—	—	—	14.5	7.3
1992	Jetta	RV & PF	1.8 (1780)	4.3	—	4.2	6.4	—	—	—	14.5	7.3
	Jetta Diesel	1V	1.6 (1588)	4.7	—	4.2	6.4	—	—	—	13.7	7.3
	Jetta GLI 16V	9A	2.0 (1984)	4.3	—	4.2	—	—	—	—	14.5	7.3
	Jetta Carat	PF	1.8 (1780)	4.3	—	4.2	6.4	—	—	—	14.5	7.3
	Cabriolet	JH	1.8 (1780)	4.3	—	4.2	6.4	—	—	—	13.8	7.3
	Golf	RV & PF	1.8 (1780)	4.3	—	4.2	6.4	—	—	—	14.5	7.3
	Golf GTI 16V	9A	2.0 (1984)	4.3	—	4.2	—	—	—	—	14.5	7.3
	Fox	ABG	1.8 (1780)	3.7	3.6	4.2	—	—	—	—	12.4	6.4 ①
	Passat	9A	2.0 (1984)	4.3	—	4.2	6.0	—	—	—	18.5	7.3
	Passat	AAA	2.8 (2860)	6.3	—	4.2	6.0	—	—	—	18.5	10.6
	Corrado	AAA	2.8 (2860)	6.3	—	4.2	6.0	—	—	—	14.5	10.6
1993	Jetta	RV & PF	1.8 (1780)	4.3	—	4.2	6.4	—	—	—	14.5	7.3
	Jetta Diesel	1V	1.6 (1588)	4.7	—	4.2	6.4	—	—	—	13.7	7.3
	Jetta GLI 16V	9A	2.0 (1984)	4.3	—	4.2	—	—	—	—	14.5	7.3
	Jetta Carat	PF	1.8 (1780)	4.3	—	4.2	6.4	—	—	—	14.5	7.3
	Cabriolet	JH	1.8 (1780)	4.3	—	4.2	6.4	—	—	—	13.8	7.3
	Golf	RV & PF	1.8 (1780)	4.3	—	4.2	6.4	—	—	—	14.5	7.3
	Golf GTI 16V	9A	2.0 (1984)	4.3	—	4.2	—	—	—	—	14.5	7.3
	Fox	ABG	1.8 (1780)	3.7	3.6	4.2	—	—	—	—	12.4	6.4 ①
	Passat	9A	2.0 (1984)	4.3	—	4.2	6.0	—	—	—	18.5	7.3
	Passat	AAA	2.8 (2860)	6.3	—	4.2	6.0	—	—	—	18.5	10.6
	Corrado	AAA	2.8 (2860)	6.3	—	4.2	6.0	—	—	—	14.5	10.6

CAPACITIES

Year	Model	Engine ID/VIN	Engine Displacement Liters (cc)	Engine Crankcase with Filter (qts.)	Transmission (pts.)			Transfer Case (pts.)	Drive Axle		Fuel Tank (gal.)	Cooling System (qts.)
					4-Spd	5-Spd	Auto.		Front (pts.)	Rear (pts.)		
1994	Jetta	RV & PF	1.8 (1780)	4.3	—	4.2	6.4	—	—	—	14.5	7.3
	Jetta Diesel	1V	1.6 (1588)	4.7	—	4.2	6.4	—	—	—	13.7	7.3
	Jetta GLI 16V	9A	2.0 (1984)	4.3	—	4.2	—	—	—	—	14.5	7.3
	Jetta Carat	PF	1.8 (1780)	4.3	—	4.2	6.4	—	—	—	14.5	7.3
	Cabriolet	JH	1.8 (1780)	4.3	—	4.2	6.4	—	—	—	13.8	7.3
	Golf	RV & PF	1.8 (1780)	4.3	—	4.2	6.4	—	—	—	14.5	7.3
	Golf GTI 16V	9A	2.0 (1984)	4.3	—	4.2	—	—	—	—	14.5	7.3
	Fox	ABG	1.8 (1780)	3.7	3.6	4.2	—	—	—	—	12.4	6.4①
	Passat	9A	2.0 (1984)	4.3	—	4.2	6.0	—	—	—	18.5	7.3
	Passat	AAA	2.8 (2860)	6.3	—	4.2	6.0	—	—	—	18.5	10.6
	Corrado	AAA	2.8 (2860)	6.3	—	4.2	6.0	—	—	—	14.5	10.6

① With A/C, 6.9 qts.

CRANKSHAFT AND CONNECTING ROD SPECIFICATIONS

All measurements are given in inches.

Year	Engine ID/VIN	Engine Displacement Liters (cc)	Crankshaft				Connecting Rod		
			Main Brg. Journal Dia.	Main Brg. Oil Clearance	Shaft End-play	Thrust on No.	Journal Diameter	Oil Clearance	Side Clearance
1990	RV, PF, PL, PG, JH, UM	1.8 (1780)	2.126	0.001–0.003	0.003–0.007	3	1.881	0.0049	0.015 max.
	9A	2.0 (1984)	2.126	0.001–0.003	0.003–0.007	3	1.881	0.0049	0.015 max.
1991	RV, PF, JH, ABG, JN, PG	1.8 (1780)	2.126	0.001–0.003	0.003–0.007	3	1.881	0.0049	0.015 max.
	1V	1.6 (1588)	2.126	0.001–0.003	0.003–0.007	3	1.881	0.0049	0.015 max.
	9A	2.0 (1984)	2.126	0.001–0.003	0.003–0.007	3	1.881	0.0049	0.015 max.
1992	RV, PF, JH, ABG, JN, PG	1.8 (1780)	2.126	0.001–0.003	0.003–0.007	3	1.881	0.0049	0.015 max.
	1V	1.6 (1588)	2.126	0.001–0.003	0.003–0.007	3	1.881	0.0049	0.015 max.
	9A	2.0 (1984)	2.126	0.001–0.003	0.003–0.007	3	1.881	0.0049	0.015 max.
	AAA	2.8 (2860)	2.325	0.001–0.002	0.003–0.007	5	2.125	0.0004–0.0020	0.012 max.
1993	RV, PF, JH, ABG, JN, PG	1.8 (1780)	2.126	0.001–0.003	0.003–0.007	3	1.881	0.0049	0.015 max.
	1V	1.6 (1588)	2.126	0.001–0.003	0.003–0.007	3	1.881	0.0049	0.015 max.
	9A	2.0 (1984)	2.126	0.001–0.003	0.003–0.007	3	1.881	0.0049	0.015 max.
	AAA	2.8 (2860)	2.325	0.001–0.002	0.003–0.007	5	2.125	0.0004–0.0020	0.012 max.
1994	RV, PF, JH, ABG, JN, PG	1.8 (1780)	2.126	0.001–0.003	0.003–0.007	3	1.881	0.0049	0.015 max.
	1V	1.6 (1588)	2.126	0.001–0.003	0.003–0.007	3	1.881	0.0049	0.015 max.
	9A	2.0 (1984)	2.126	0.001–0.003	0.003–0.007	3	1.881	0.0049	0.015 max.
	AAA	2.8 (2860)	2.325	0.001–0.002	0.003–0.007	5	2.125	0.0004–0.0020	0.012 max.

VALVE SPECIFICATIONS

Year	Engine ID/VIN	Engine Displacement Liters (cc)	Seat Angle (deg.)	Face Angle (deg.)	Spring Test Pressure (lbs. @ in.)	Spring Installed Height (in.)	Stem-to-Guide Clearance (in.)		Stem Diameter (in.)	
							Intake	Exhaust	Intake	Exhaust
1990	All	1.8 (1780)	45	45	NA	NA	0.039 ① max.	0.051 ① max.	0.314	0.313
	9A	2.0 (1984)	45	45	NA	NA	0.039 ① max.	0.051 ① max.	0.314	0.313
1991	All	1.8 (1780)	45	45	NA	NA	0.039 ① max.	0.051 ① max.	0.314	0.313
	9A	2.0 (1984)	45	45	NA	NA	0.039 ① max.	0.051 ① max.	0.314	0.313
	1V	1.6 (1588)	45	45	NA	NA	0.051 ① max.	0.051 ① max.	0.314	0.313
1992	All	1.8 (1780)	45	45	NA	NA	0.039 ① max.	0.051 ① max.	0.314	0.313
	9A	2.0 (1984)	45	45	NA	NA	0.039 ① max.	0.051 ① max.	0.314	0.313
	AAA	2.8 (2860)	45	45	NA	NA	0.039 ① max.	0.051 ① max.	0.274	0.273
	1V	1.6 (1588)	45	45	NA	NA	0.051 ① max.	0.051 ① max.	0.314	0.313
1993	All	1.8 (1780)	45	45	NA	NA	0.039 ① max.	0.051 ① max.	0.314	0.313
	9A	2.0 (1984)	45	45	NA	NA	0.039 ① max.	0.051 ① max.	0.314	0.313
	AAA	2.8 (2860)	45	45	NA	NA	0.039 ① max.	0.051 ① max.	0.274	0.273
	1V	1.6 (1588)	45	45	NA	NA	0.051 ① max.	0.051 ① max.	0.314	0.313
1994	All	1.8 (1780)	45	45	NA	NA	0.039 ① max.	0.051 ① max.	0.314	0.313
	9A	2.0 (1984)	45	45	NA	NA	0.039 ① max.	0.051 ① max.	0.314	0.313
	AAA	2.8 (2860)	45	45	NA	NA	0.039 ① max.	0.051 ① max.	0.274	0.273
	1V	1.6 (1588)	45	45	NA	NA	0.051 ① max.	0.051 ① max.	0.314	0.313

NA—Not available
① Measure with dial indicator touching valve face, camshaft end of valve stem flush with upper end of guide.

PISTON AND RING SPECIFICATIONS

All measurements are given in inches.

Year	Engine ID/VIN	Engine Displacement Liters (cc)	Piston Clearance	Ring Gap			Ring Side Clearance		
				Top Compression	Bottom Compression	Oil Control	Top Compression	Bottom Compression	Oil Control
1990	RV, PF, JH, UM, JN	1.8 (1780)	0.0010–0.0030	0.012–0.018	0.012–0.018	0.012–0.018	0.0008–0.0020	0.0008–0.0020	0.0008–0.0020
	PG	1.8 (1780)	0.0010–0.0020	0.006–0.014	0.006–0.014	0.010–0.020	0.0010–0.0030	0.0010–0.0030	0.0010–0.0030
	9A	2.0 (1984)	0.0010–0.0020	0.007–0.015	0.007–0.015	0.009–0.019	0.0008–0.0027	0.0008–0.0027	0.0008–0.0020
1991	RV, PF, JH, ABG	1.8 (1780)	0.0010–0.0030	0.012–0.018	0.012–0.018	0.012–0.018	0.0008–0.0020	0.0008–0.0020	0.0008–0.0020
	PG	1.8 (1780)	0.0010–0.0030	0.006–0.014	0.006–0.014	0.010–0.020	0.0010–0.0030	0.0010–0.0030	0.0010–0.0030
	9A	2.0 (1984)	0.0010–0.0020	0.007–0.015	0.007–0.015	0.009–0.018	0.0008–0.0027	0.0008–0.0027	0.0008–0.0020
	1V	1.6 (1588)	0.0010–0.0030	0.012–0.020	0.012–0.020	0.010–0.018	0.0020–0.0040	0.0020–0.0030	0.0010–0.0020
1992	RV, PF, JH,	1.8 (1780)	0.0010–0.0030	0.012–0.018	0.012–0.018	0.012–0.018	0.0008–0.0020	0.0008–0.0020	0.0008–0.0020
	PG	1.8 (1780)	0.0010–0.0030	0.006–0.014	0.006–0.014	0.010–0.020	0.0010–0.0030	0.0010–0.0030	0.0010–0.0030
	9A	2.0 (1984)	0.0010–0.0020	0.007–0.015	0.007–0.015	0.009–0.018	0.0008–0.0027	0.0008–0.0027	0.0008–0.0027
	AAA	2.8 (2860)	0.0010–0.0160	0.008–0.016	0.008–0.016	0.010–0.020	0.0010–0.0030	0.0010–0.0030	0.0010–0.0020
	ABG	1.8 (1780)	0.0010–0.0160	0.012–0.018	0.012–0.018	0.010–0.018	0.0010–0.0020	0.0010–0.0020	0.0010–0.0020
	1V	1.6 (1588)	0.0010–0.0030	0.012–0.020	0.012–0.020	0.010–0.018	0.0020–0.0040	0.0020–0.0030	0.0010–0.0020
1993	RV, PF, JH,	1.8 (1780)	0.0010–0.0030	0.012–0.018	0.012–0.018	0.012–0.018	0.0008–0.0020	0.0008–0.0020	0.0008–0.0020
	PG	1.8 (1780)	0.0010–0.0030	0.006–0.014	0.006–0.014	0.010–0.020	0.0010–0.0030	0.0010–0.0030	0.0010–0.0030
	9A	2.0 (1984)	0.0010–0.0020	0.007–0.015	0.007–0.015	0.009–0.018	0.0008–0.0027	0.0008–0.0027	0.0008–0.0027
	AAA	2.8 (2860)	0.0010–0.0160	0.008–0.016	0.008–0.016	0.010–0.020	0.0010–0.0030	0.0010–0.0030	0.0010–0.0020
	ABG	1.8 (1780)	0.0010–0.0160	0.012–0.018	0.012–0.018	0.010–0.018	0.0010–0.0020	0.0010–0.0020	0.0010–0.0020
	1V	1.6 (1588)	0.0010–0.0030	0.012–0.020	0.012–0.020	0.010–0.018	0.0020–0.0040	0.0020–0.0030	0.0010–0.0020

PISTON AND RING SPECIFICATIONS

All measurements are given in inches.

Year	Engine ID/VIN	Engine Displacement Liters (cc)	Piston Clearance	Ring Gap			Ring Side Clearance		
				Top Compression	Bottom Compression	Oil Control	Top Compression	Bottom Compression	Oil Control
1994	RV, PF, JH,	1.8 (1780)	0.0010–0.0030	0.012–0.018	0.012–0.018	0.012–0.018	0.0008–0.0020	0.0008–0.0020	0.0008–0.0020
	PG	1.8 (1780)	0.0010–0.0030	0.006–0.014	0.006–0.014	0.010–0.020	0.0010–0.0030	0.0010–0.0030	0.0010–0.0030
	9A	2.0 (1984)	0.0010–0.0020	0.007–0.015	0.007–0.015	0.009–0.018	0.0008–0.0027	0.0008–0.0027	0.0008–0.0027
	AAA	2.8 (2860)	0.0010–0.0160	0.008–0.016	0.008–0.016	0.010–0.020	0.0010–0.0030	0.0010–0.0030	0.0010–0.0020
	ABG	1.8 (1780)	0.0010–0.0160	0.012–0.018	0.012–0.018	0.010–0.018	0.0010–0.0020	0.0010–0.0020	0.0010–0.0020
	1V	1.6 (1588)	0.0010–0.0030	0.012–0.020	0.012–0.020	0.010–0.018	0.0020–0.0040	0.0020–0.0030	0.0010–0.0020

TORQUE SPECIFICATIONS

All readings in ft. lbs.

Year	Engine ID/VIN	Engine Displacement Liters (cc)	Cylinder Head Bolts	Main Bearing Bolts	Rod Bearing Bolts	Crankshaft Damper Bolts	Flywheel Bolts	Manifold Intake	Manifold Exhaust	Spark Plugs	Lug Nut
1990	ME	1.6 (1588)	① ②	47	33③	253	14	18	18	14	81
	RV, PF, JH, UM, JN, PL	1.8 (1780)	②	47	22③	④	14⑥	18	18	14	81
	PG	1.8 (1780)	②	47	22① ⑤	④	74	11	18	14	81
	9A	2.0 (1984)	②	47	22③	④	74	15	18	14	81
1991	RV, PF, JH, ABG, PL	1.8 (1780)	②	47	22③	④	14⑥	18	18	14	81
	PG	1.8 (1780)	②	47	22① ⑤	④	74	11	18	14	81
	9A	2.0 (1984)	②	47	22③	④	74	15	18	14	81
	1V	1.6 (1588)	① ②	47	33③	253	14	18	18	14	81
1992	RV, PF, JH, PL	1.8 (1780)	②	47	22③	④	14⑥	18	18	14	81
	PG	1.8 (1780)	②	47	22③	④	74	15	18	14	81
	9A	2.0 (1984)	②	47	22③	④	74	15	18	14	81
	1V	1.6 (1588)	① ②	47	33③	253	14	18	18	14	81
	ABG	1.8 (1780)	②	47	22③	④	14⑥	18	18	14	81
	AAA	2.8 (2860)	②	⑤	22③	328	⑦	18	18	14	81
1993	RV, PF, JH, PL	1.8 (1780)	②	47	22③	④	14⑥	18	18	14	81
	PG	1.8 (1780)	②	47	22③	④	74	15	18	14	81
	9A	2.0 (1984)	②	47	22③	④	74	15	18	14	81
	1V	1.6 (1588)	① ②	47	33③	253	14	18	18	14	81
	ABG	1.8 (1780)	②	47	22③	④	14⑥	18	18	14	81
	AAA	2.8 (2860)	②	⑤	22③	328	⑦	18	18	14	81
1994	RV, PF, JH, PL	1.8 (1780)	②	47	22③	④	14⑥	18	18	14	81
	PG	1.8 (1780)	②	47	22③	④	74	15	18	14	81
	9A	2.0 (1984)	②	47	22③	④	74	15	18	14	81
	1V	1.6 (1588)	① ②	47	33③	253	14	18	18	14	81
	ABG	1.8 (1780)	②	47	22③	④	14⑥	18	18	14	81
	AAA	2.8 (2860)	②	⑤	22③	328	⑦	18	18	14	81

① Always use new bolts
② With 12 points (polygon) head bolts
  Torque in 4 steps:
    1st step—29 ft. lbs.
    2nd step—43 ft. lbs.
    3rd step—additional ½ turn (180 degrees)
    further in one movement (two 90 degree
    turns are permissible)
    Note tightening sequence
    Do not retorque at 1000 miles
  With 6 point (hex) head bolts
    Torque in steps to 54 ft. lbs. with engine
    cold, when engine is warmed up, torque to
    61 ft. lbs. Head bolts must be retorqued
    after 1000 miles

③ Stretch bolts: 22 ft. lbs. plus ¼ (90 degree)
  turn.
④ Engine UM up to JN707651
    133 ft. lbs.
  From engine JN707652
    66 ft. lbs. plus ½ turn (180°)
⑤ Stretch bolts: 22 ft. lbs. plus ½ (80°) turn.
⑥ Auto. trans., 72 ft. lbs.
⑦ 53 ft. lbs. +90° turn.
  Always use new bolts.

BRAKE SPECIFICATIONS

All measurements in inches unless noted.

Year	Model	Master Cylinder Bore	Brake Disc Original Thickness	Brake Disc Minimum Thickness	Maximum Runout	Brake Drum Diameter Original Inside Diameter	Brake Drum Diameter Max. Wear Limit	Brake Drum Diameter Maximum Machine Diameter	Minimum Lining Thickness Front	Minimum Lining Thickness Rear
1990	Jetta	0.820	0.472 ① ②	0.393 ① ②	0.002	7.087	7.126	7.106	0.276	0.098 ③
	Jetta w/ABS	0.820	0.472 ① ②	0.393 ① ②	0.002	—	—	—	0.276	0.276
	Cabriolet	0.820	0.787 ②	0.708 ②	0.002	7.087	7.126	7.106	0.276	0.098 ③
	Golf	0.820	0.472 ① ②	0.393 ① ②	0.002	7.087	7.126	7.106	0.276	0.098 ③
	Fox	0.820	0.472 ①	0.393 ①	0.002	7.087	7.126	7.106	0.276	0.098
	Passat	0.820	0.866 ②	0.787	0.002	—	—	—	0.276	0.276
	Corrado	0.812 ④	0.866 ②	0.787	0.002	—	—	—	0.276	0.276
1991	Jetta	0.820	0.472 ① ②	0.393 ① ②	0.002	7.087	7.126	7.106	0.276	0.098 ③
	Jetta w/ABS	0.820	0.472 ① ②	0.393 ① ②	0.002	—	—	—	0.276	0.276
	Cabriolet	0.820	0.787 ②	0.708 ②	0.002	7.087	7.126	7.106	0.276	0.098 ③
	Golf	0.820	0.472 ① ②	0.393 ① ②	0.002	7.087	7.126	7.106	0.276	0.098 ③
	Fox	0.820	0.472 ①	0.393 ①	0.002	7.087	7.126	7.106	0.276	0.098
	Passat	0.820	0.866 ②	0.787	0.002	—	—	—	0.276	0.276
	Corrado	0.812 ④	0.866 ②	0.787	0.002	—	—	—	0.276	0.276
1992	Jetta	0.820	0.472 ① ②	0.393 ① ②	0.002	7.087	7.126	7.106	0.276	0.098 ③
	Jetta w/ABS	0.820	0.472 ① ②	0.393 ① ②	0.002	—	—	—	0.276	0.276
	Cabriolet	0.820	0.787 ②	0.708 ②	0.002	7.087	7.126	7.106	0.276	0.098 ③
	Golf	0.820	0.472 ① ②	0.393 ① ②	0.002	7.087	7.126	7.106	0.276	0.098 ③
	Fox	0.820	0.472 ①	0.393 ①	0.002	7.087	7.126	7.106	0.276	0.098
	Passat	0.820	0.866 ②	0.787	0.002	—	—	—	0.276	0.276
	Corrado	0.812 ④	0.866 ②	0.787	0.002	—	—	—	0.276	0.276
1993	Jetta	0.820	0.472 ① ②	0.393 ① ②	0.002	7.087	7.126	7.106	0.276	0.098 ③
	Jetta w/ABS	0.820	0.472 ① ②	0.393 ① ②	0.002	—	—	—	0.276	0.276
	Cabriolet	0.820	0.787 ②	0.708 ②	0.002	7.087	7.126	7.106	0.276	0.098 ③
	Golf	0.820	0.472 ① ②	0.393 ① ②	0.002	7.087	7.126	7.106	0.276	0.098 ③
	Fox	0.820	0.472 ①	0.393 ①	0.002	7.087	7.126	7.106	0.276	0.098
	Passat	0.820	0.866 ②	0.787	0.002	—	—	—	0.276	0.276
	Corrado	0.812 ④	0.866 ②	0.787	0.002	—	—	—	0.276	0.276
1994	Jetta	0.820	0.472 ① ②	0.393 ① ②	0.002	7.087	7.126	7.106	0.276	0.098 ③
	Jetta w/ABS	0.820	0.472 ① ②	0.393 ① ②	0.002	—	—	—	0.276	0.276
	Cabriolet	0.820	0.787 ②	0.708 ②	0.002	7.087	7.126	7.106	0.276	0.098 ③
	Golf	0.820	0.472 ① ②	0.393 ① ②	0.002	7.087	7.126	7.106	0.276	0.098 ③
	Fox	0.820	0.472 ①	0.393 ①	0.002	7.087	7.126	7.106	0.276	0.098
	Passat	0.820	0.866 ②	0.787	0.002	—	—	—	0.276	0.276
	Corrado	0.812 ④	0.866 ②	0.787	0.002	—	—	—	0.276	0.276

① Vented disc: 0.787 new, 0.708 minimum
② Rear disc: 0.394 new, 0.319 minimum
③ Rear disc pad minimum—0.276
④ With ABS—0.874

WHEEL ALIGNMENT

Year	Model	Caster ① Range (deg.)	Caster ① Preferred Setting (deg.)	Camber Range (deg.)	Camber Preferred Setting (deg.)	Toe-in (in.)	Steering Axis Inclination (deg.)
1990	Jetta GL	±30'	1°30'	±20'	−30'	0° ±10'	NA
	Jetta GLI 16V	±30'	1°35'	±20'	−40'	0° ±10'	NA
	Cabriolet	±30'	1°50'	±30'	+20'	−5' to −30'	NA
	Golf GL	±30'	1°30'	±20'	−30'	0° to ±10'	NA
	Golf GTI	±30'	1°35'	±20'	−35'	0° to ±10'	NA
	Golf GTI 16V	±30'	1°35'	±20'	−40'	0° to ±10'	NA
	Fox	±20'	2°	±20'	−30'	−20' to 0°	NA
	Fox Wagon	±20'	1°45'	±20'	−30'	−20' to 0°	NA
	Passat	±30'	+1°40'	±20'	−1°20'	0° ±10'	NA
	Corrado	±30'	+1°35'	±20'	−40'	0° ±10'	NA
1991	Jetta GL	±30'	1°30'	±20'	−30'	0° ±10'	NA
	Jetta GLI 16V	±30'	1°35'	±20'	−40'	0° ±10'	NA
	Cabriolet	±30'	1°50'	±30'	+20'	−5' to −30'	NA
	Golf GL	±30'	1°30'	±20'	−30'	0° to ±10'	NA
	Golf GTI	±30'	1°35'	±20'	−35'	0° to ±10'	NA
	GTI 16V	±30'	1°35'	±20'	−40'	0° to ±10'	NA
	Fox	±20'	2°	±20'	−30'	−20' to 0°	NA
	Fox Wagon	±20'	1°45'	±20'	−30'	−20' to 0°	NA
	Passat	±30'	+1°40'	±20'	−1°20'	0° ±10'	NA
	Corrado	±30'	+1°35'	±20'	−40'	0° ±10'	NA
1992	Jetta GL	±30'	1°30'	±20'	−30'	0° ±10'	NA
	Jetta GLI 16V	±30'	1°35'	±20'	−40'	0° ±10'	NA
	Cabriolet	±30'	1°50'	±30'	+20'	−5' to −30'	NA
	Golf GL	±30'	1°30'	±20'	−30'	0° to ±10'	NA
	Golf GTI	±30'	1°35'	±20'	−35'	0° to ±10'	NA
	GTI 16V	±30'	1°35'	±20'	−40'	0° to ±10'	NA
	Fox	±20'	2°	±20'	−30'	−10' ±10'	NA
	Fox Wagon	±20'	1°45'	±20'	−30'	−10' ±10'	NA
	Passat	±30'	+1°40'	±20'	−1°20'	0° ±10'	NA
	Corrado	±30'	+1°35'	±20'	−40'	0° ±10'	NA
	Corrado SLC	±30'	+3°25'	±20'	−1°20'	0° ±10'	NA
1993	Jetta GL	±30'	1°30'	±20'	−30'	0° ±10'	NA
	Jetta GLI 16V	±30'	1°35'	±20'	−40'	0° ±10'	NA
	Cabriolet	±30'	1°50'	±30'	+20'	−5' to −30'	NA
	Golf GL	±30'	1°30'	±20'	−30'	0° to ±10'	NA
	Golf GTI	±30'	1°35'	±20'	−35'	0° to ±10'	NA
	GTI 16V	±30'	1°35'	±20'	−40'	0° to ±10'	NA
	Fox	±20'	2°	±20'	−30'	−10' ±10'	NA
	Fox Wagon	±20'	1°45'	±20'	−30'	−10' ±10'	NA
	Passat	±30'	+1°40'	±20'	−1°20'	0° ±10'	NA
	Corrado	±30'	+1°35'	±20'	−40'	0° ±10'	NA
	Corrado SLC	±30'	+3°25'	±20'	−1°20'	0° ±10'	NA

WHEEL ALIGNMENT

Year	Model	Caster ① Range (deg.)	Caster ① Preferred Setting (deg.)	Camber Range (deg.)	Camber Preferred Setting (deg.)	Toe-in (in.)	Steering Axis Inclination (deg.)
1994	Jetta GL	± 30′	1°30′	± 20′	− 30′	0° ± 10′	NA
	Jetta GLI 16V	± 30′	1°35′	± 20′	− 40′	0° ± 10′	NA
	Cabriolet	± 30′	1°50′	± 30′	+ 20′	− 5′ to − 30′	NA
	Golf GL	± 30′	1°30′	± 20′	− 30′	0° to ± 10′	NA
	Golf GTI	± 30′	1°35′	± 20′	− 35′	0° to ± 10′	NA
	GTI 16V	± 30′	1°35′	± 20′	− 40′	0° to ± 10′	NA
	Fox	± 20′	2°	± 20′	− 30′	− 10′ ± 10′	NA
	Fox Wagon	± 20′	1°45′	± 20′	− 30′	− 10′ ± 10′	NA
	Passat	± 30′	+ 1°40′	± 20′	− 1°20′	0° ± 10′	NA
	Corrado	± 30′	+ 1°35′	± 20′	− 40′	0° ± 10′	NA
	Corrado SLC	± 30′	+ 3°25′	± 20′	− 1°20′	0° ± 10′	NA

NA—Not available
① Not adjustable

SERIAL NUMBER IDENTIFICATION

Vehicle Identification Plate

All vehicles have an identification plate bearing the chassis number on the top of the dash board at the driver's side, visible through the windshield. The VIN indicates such information as model year, type, date of manufacture, etc. This information is more easily read from the Vehicle Identification Label in the luggage compartment. That label also provides engine and transaxle code numbers, paint, interior and option code numbers. Since the manufacturer sometimes makes production changes in mid-model year, this information is sometimes required when locating parts.

Engine Number

The diesel engine number with its 2 letter code is stamped on the block between the injection pump and the vacuum pump. On 4 cylinder gasoline engines, the engine number is stamped on the block just below the cylinder head, near the No. 2 or No. 3 spark plug. On 6 cylinder engines, the engine number is stamped into the front of the block just below the cylinder head gasket.

GASOLINE ENGINE MECHANICAL

NOTE: Disconnecting the negative battery cable on some vehicles may interfere with the functions of the on-board computer or security systems and may require reprogramming when the battery cable is reconnected.

Engine Assembly

REMOVAL AND INSTALLATION

Except Fox and Corrado SLC

NOTE: The engine and transaxle are lifted as an assembly from the vehicle.

— CAUTION —
Use care when disconnecting the fuel lines. Fuel under pressure may still be in the lines and, if sprayed, may cause fire or personal injury.

1. Disconnect the battery cables and remove the battery.
2. Open the fuel filler cap to relieve tank pressure and then relieve the fuel system pressure.
3. Remove the air intake duct between the fuel distributor and the throttle body. On Corrado, remove the air tubing from the G-charger and the intercooler. At the throttle body, pull back the accelerator cable clip and disconnect the cable from the ball. Loosen the accelerator cable locknut and remove the cable from the cylinder head cover.
4. Remove the radiator cap and set the heater temperature control to full HOT. Place a pan under the thermostat housing and remove the thermostat flange to drain the coolant.
5. Remove the upper radiator hose and disconnect the wiring from the radiator fan motor and switches. Remove the mounting nuts or bolts and lift out the radiator and fan shroud as an assembly.

6. Except Corrado, at the front of the vehicle remove the apron, the trim and the grille. Disconnect the headlight electrical connectors and the hood release cable from the hood latch assembly.

7. Begin disconnecting electrical connections and vacuum lines, carefully labeling each one. Don't forget ground connections that are screwed to the body.

NOTE: If equipped with power steering, remove pump and reservoir and set them aside; do not disconnect the fluid lines. If equipped with air conditioning, remove the compressor and set it aside without disconnecting the lines.

8. On CIS fuel systems, much of the system can be removed as a unit without disconnecting fuel lines. Remove the injectors from their holes and protect them with caps. Remove the cold start injector and warm-up regulator, if equipped, and disconnect the fuel supply and return lines from the fuel distributor.

9. On vehicles with CIS fuel injection, unsnap the clips holding the air cleaner housing together and lift the fuel distributor/air sensor assembly from the vehicle with all the other fuel lines attached.

NOTE: If equipped with an automatic transaxle, place the selector lever in the P position.

10. On vehicles with cable shift linkage, disconnect the shift linkage cables and remove the clutch slave cylinder from the transaxle without disconnecting the line and set it aside.

11. On vehicles with rod shift linkage, remove the 2 rods with the plastic socket ends and unbolt the remaining linkage from the transaxle case as required. Disconnect the clutch cable, lift it from the case and set it aside.

12. Disconnect the electrical connectors from the starter, the backup light switch and the ground cable from the transaxle. Remove the speedometer cable from the transaxle and plug the hole in the case.

13. On vehicles with automatic transaxle, disconnect the cable from the actuating lever and remove it from the bracket.

14. Attach an engine sling tool VW-2024A or equivalent, to the engine and attach the sling to a suitable lifting device. On the 16V engine, remove the idle stabilizer valve and the upper intake manifold to attach the sling.

15. Unbolt the exhaust pipe from the manifold or remove the spring clamps holding the exhaust pipe to the manifold and lower the pipe.

─── **CAUTION** ───

On some models, special tools are required for removing and installing the exhaust pipe-to-manifold spring clamps; VW3140/1 and /2 or equivalent. This is a set of different sized wedges for spreading the spring clamps in steps. The installed spring clamp has considerable tension and could cause damage or injury if not properly removed. Clamps with wedges installed are also under high tension and should be handled carefully.

16. Unbolt the halfshafts from the flanges and hang them from the body with wire.

17. Make sure everything is disconnected and unbolt the mounts. Remove the starter first and the front mount with it.

18. With all mounts unbolted, slightly lower the engine/transaxle assembly and tilt it towards the transaxle side. Then carefully lift the assembly from the vehicle.

To install:

19. Carefully install the engine/transaxle assembly and make sure all mounts are securely bolted to the engine/transaxle. Start all nuts and bolts that secure the mounts to the body but don't tighten them yet.

20. With all mounts installed and the engine safely in the vehicle, allow some slack in the lifting equipment. With the vehicle safely supported, shake the engine/transaxle as a unit to settle it in the mounts. Torque all mounting bolts, starting at the rear and working forward. Torque to 33 ft. lbs. (41 Nm) for 10mm bolts or 54 ft. lbs. (73 Nm) for 12mm bolts.

21. Install the starter and torque the bolts to 33 ft. lbs. (45 Nm).

22. Connect the halfshafts to the flanges and torque the bolts to 33 ft. lbs. (45 Nm).

23. Install the exhaust pipe and use new self-locking nuts to secure the flange. Torque the nuts to 30 ft. lbs. (40 Nm). If equipped with spring clamps, the clamps can be used again.

24. Connect the shift linkage and install the clutch cable or slave cylinder. Adjust the clutch and shift linkage as required.

25. Install the fuel system components.

26. Install the air conditioning compressor and/or power steering pump,

if equipped. Install and adjust the drive belts.

27. Connect the wiring and vacuum hoses.

28. Install the radiator, fan and heater hoses. Use a new O-ring on the thermostat and torque the thermostat housing bolts to 7 ft. lbs. (10 Nm).

29. Fill and bleed the cooling system. Check the adjustment of the accelerator cable.

30. Install any body parts that were removed.

Fox

The engine is lifted from the vehicle without the transaxle.

1. Disconnect the battery ground cable and remove the battery.

2. Open the heater valve and the cap on the coolant expansion tank. Drain the coolant by removing the bottom hose. Disconnect the electrical connector from the radiator cooling fan.

3. Remove the radiator and fan as an assembly.

4. If equipped with air conditioning, remove the compressor and condenser and place them aside without disconnecting any refrigerant lines.

5. Detach and label all the electrical wires and vacuum lines connecting the engine to the body.

6. Much of the fuel system can be removed as a unit without disconnecting fuel lines. Remove the injectors from their holes and protect them with caps. Remove the cold start injector and warm-up regulator, if equipped. Disconnect the throttle cable and remove the air duct. Place these aside without disconnecting the fuel lines.

7. Disconnect the speedometer cable from the transaxle and plug the hole. Detach the clutch cable.

8. Loosen the charcoal filter clamp and move the filter to the rear of the engine compartment.

9. Remove the upper engine-to-transaxle bolts.

10. Remove the left and right engine mounting nuts.

11. Remove the front engine stop and the starter.

12. Remove the clutch cover and the 2 lower engine-to-transaxle bolts.

13. Disconnect the exhaust pipe from the manifold at the flange. Then remove the bolt from the exhaust pipe support and remove the exhaust pipe from the manifold.

14. Install transaxle support bar VW-758/1 or equivalent, with slight preload. This is to hold the transaxle in place while the engine is out.

15. Install sling US-1105, or equivalent, on the engine lifting eyes located on the left side of the cylinder head.

16. Lift the engine until its weight is taken off the engine mounts.

17. Adjust the support bar to contact the transaxle.

18. Separate the engine and transaxle.

19. Carefully lift the engine out of the engine compartment so as not to damage the transaxle main shaft, clutch and body.

To install:

20. Lubricate the clutch release bearing and transaxle main shaft splines with MOS_2 grease or equivalent; do not lubricate the guide sleeve or the clutch release bearing.

21. Carefully guide the engine into the vehicle and attach to the transaxle while keeping weight off the motor mounts.

22. Remove the transaxle support bar and lower the engine onto the engine mounts.

23. The remainder of the installation is the reverse of the removal procedure. Torque the engine mounts and subframe bolts with the engine running at idle speed. This will minimize vibration.

24. Torque the following:

Cold start valve, the radiator mount bolts and the engine-to-transaxle cover plate bolts — 7 ft. lbs. (10 Nm).

Engine-to-transaxle bolts — 42 ft. lbs. (55 Nm).

Engine mount bolts — 30 ft. lbs. (40 Nm).

Engine stop-to-body block and exhaust pipe support bolts — 18 ft. lbs. (25 Nm).

Exhaust pipe-to-manifold bolts — 22 ft. lbs. (30 Nm).

Starter bolts — 18 ft. lbs. (25 Nm).

Corrado SLC

The engine and transaxle are removed as a unit and the job requires 2 people.

1. Remove the battery; disconnect the wiring and vacuum lines as required to remove the air cleaner housing air duct.

2. Remove the front grille, headlights and hood lock support.

3. Remove the front bumper:

a. Remove the front spoiler.

b. Remove the clips between the bumper skin and the engine mount.

c. Below the bracket on each side, remove the 2 engine mount bolts that hold the bracket.

d. Pull the bumper cover forward evenly from both sides. Two people are required.

4. Drain the coolant and remove the radiator.

5. On manual transaxle, remove the clutch slave cylinder and disconnect the shift cables and support bracket.

6. On automatic transaxle, remove the clip to disconnect the shift lever cable.

7. Thread a long 8 **x** 10mm bolt into the accessory drive belt tensioner to release the tension. Move the tensioner only as required to remove the belt from the steering pump and air conditioner compressor.

8. Without disconnecting any refrigerant lines, remove the air conditioner compressor from the engine and secure it to the body. Be careful not to kink the hoses.

9. Without disconnecting any hydraulic lines, remove the power steering pump and secure it to the body. Be careful not to kink the hoses.

10. Remove the various covers from the top of the engine.

11. Remove the distributor cap, ignition wires and guides as an assembly.

12. Disconnect the accelerator cable.

13. Disconnect the 42-pin main engine wiring connector.

14. Label and disconnect the alternator, starter and transaxle wiring.

15. Disconnect the heater hoses.

16. Disconnect the main vacuum lines from the throttle body and intake manifold.

17. Disconnect the fuel supply and return lines.

18. Disconnect the oxygen sensor wire. Disconnect the exhaust pipe from the manifold.

19. Remove the bolts to disconnect the axle shafts from the drive flanges. Support the axle shafts with wire, do not let them hang by the outer CV-joint.

20. Attach a chain hoist to the lifting points on the engine.

21. Disconnect the engine and transaxle mounts and carefully lift the engine and transaxle out of the vehicle.

To install:

22. Carefully fit the engine/transaxle assembly into place.

a. Be sure the tabs on the rubber motor mounts fit properly into the mount brackets on the engine.

b. Start all the mounting bolts but do not tighten them yet.

c. With the vehicle resting on its wheels, shake the engine/transaxle assembly to settle it in the mounts.

d. Torque the bolts that fit into the upper center hole on each mount to 44 ft. lbs. (60 Nm). These procedures are important to minimize vibration.

23. Connect the axle shafts and torque the bolts to 33 ft. lbs. (45 Nm).

24. Use new gaskets and self-locking nuts to connect the exhaust pipe. Torque to 30 ft. lbs. (40 Nm) and connect the oxygen sensor wires.

25. Install the air conditioner compressor and power steering pump; install the drive belt.

26. Connect all wiring, hoses and control cables.

27. Install the clutch slave cylinder, if equipped, and adjust the shift linkage as required.

28. Install the radiator, connect the hoses and refill the cooling system.

29. Install the bumper and torque the bracket bolts to 63 ft. lbs. (85 Nm). Install the hood lock support, headlights and grille.

30. Install the battery and air cleaner assembly.

31. After testing the engine and transmission, check the headlight adjustment.

Engine Mounts

REMOVAL AND INSTALLATION

Earlier vehicles have all rubber, not hydraulic mounts. These mounts are replaceable with the same type but they must be pressed in and out.

1. With the engine properly supported from above, remove the mount carrier.

2. On non-hydraulic mounts, note the position of the mount in the carrier before pressing the old mount out. The large air gap is always at the top.

3. Reinstall the carrier and mount and center the mount in the bracket on the frame while tightening the bolts.

ENGINE ALIGNMENT

If there is excessive engine vibration, before removing mounts, an engine alignment procedure may cure the problem. Loosen all the bolts that go into the rubber mounts themselves. With the vehicle safely supported, shake the engine/transaxle as a unit to settle it in the mounts. Retorque all mounting bolts, starting at the rear and working forward. If engine vibration is not reduced, check for torn rubber mounts. The mount at the timing belt end usually fails first.

Cylinder Head

REMOVAL AND INSTALLATION

Except VR6 Engine

1. Disconnect the negative battery cable.

NOTE: On some of the 16V models, removing the battery may make the job easier.

2. Open the radiator cap and remove the thermostat housing to drain the cooling system.
3. Disconnect the throttle cable. Label and disconnect all wiring and vacuum lines from the intake manifold. On the 16V engine, remove the upper half of the intake manifold.
4. On vehicles with CIS-E fuel injection, remove the injectors and the cold start valve without disconnecting the fuel lines and cap them. Secure all the lines aside.
5. On vehicles with Digifant fuel injection, the injectors and fuel rail assembly may be left on the head. Disconnect the fuel supply and return lines and the wiring connector for the injectors.
6. Disconnect the radiator and heater hoses.
7. Disconnect and label wiring for oil pressure and temperature sensors.
8. On vehicles with CIS-E fuel injection, remove the auxiliary air regulator from the intake manifold, if equipped.
9. Remove the distributor cap and wires. On 16V engines, remove the distributor with the cap and wires as an assembly.
10. Disconnect the exhaust pipe from the exhaust manifold. If the pipe is secured to the manifold with spring clamps, insert the wedge tools to remove the spring clamps and separate the pipe from the manifold.

— CAUTION —

Special tools are required for removing and installing the clamps; VW3140/1 and /2 or equivalent. This is a set of different sized wedges for spreading the spring clamps in steps. The installed spring clamp has considerable tension and could cause damage or injury if not properly removed. Clamps with wedges in-

stalled are also under high tension and should be handled carefully.

11. Remove the EGR pipe from the exhaust manifold, if equipped.
12. Remove the accessory drive belts and any accessory that is bolted to the head. On Corrado, a special clamping tool 3191, is required to remove the spring-loaded belt tensioner.
13. Turn the engine to TDC of No. 1 cylinder, if possible, and remove the cylinder head cover, timing belt cover and belt.
14. Loosen the cylinder head bolts in the reverse of the tightening sequence.
15. Remove the bolts and lift the head straight off.

To install:

16. Before reinstalling the head, check the flatness of the head and block in both width and length, then diagonally from each corner.
17. Install the new cylinder head gasket with the word TOP or OBEN facing upward; do not use any sealing compound.
18. Carefully fit the head in place and install the bolts in positions 8 and 10 in the torque sequence. These holes are smaller and will properly locate the gasket and cylinder head.
19. Install the remaining bolts. Torque the bolts in sequence in 3 steps: 29 ft. lbs. (39 Nm), 44 ft. lbs. (60 Nm) and an additional 1/2 turn. Two 1/4 turns are allowed.
20. Install the camshaft drive belt and adjust the tension.
21. Connect the exhaust pipe to the manifold. Use new gaskets and self-locking nuts and torque to 18 ft. lbs. (25 Nm). On vehicles that use spring clamps, install the clamps and carefully remove the wedge tools.
22. Connect the EGR pipe, if equipped.

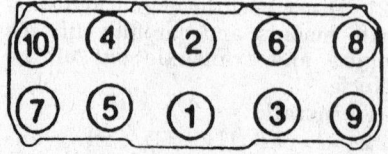

Cylinder head bolt torque sequence — 4 cylinder engine

23. On 16V engines, install the distributor. Install the distributor cap and wires.
24. On vehicles with CIS-E fuel injection, install the auxiliary air regulator to the intake manifold, if equipped.
25. Connect wiring to the oil pressure and temperature sensors.
26. Install the ignition system components.
27. Connect the radiator and heater hoses.
28. Connect the throttle cable and all wiring and vacuum lines.
29. On vehicles with Digifant fuel injection, connect the fuel supply and return lines. Connect the wiring connector for the injectors.
30. Install the thermostat with a new O-ring. Torque the housing bolts to 7 ft. lbs. (10 Nm). Refill the cooling system.
31. On vehicles with CIS-E fuel injection, install the injectors and the cold start valve.
32. Install the accessory drive belts and adjust the tension.
33. On the 16V engine, install the upper half of the intake manifold. Torque the manifold retaining bolts to 18 ft. lbs. (25 Nm).
34. Connect all wiring and vacuum lines disconnected from the intake manifold. Connect the throttle cable.
35. Install the battery, if removed. Connect the negative and positive battery cables.
36. Refill and bleed the cooling system.
37. When everything has been properly installed and connected, be sure to change the oil and filter before starting the engine.

VR6 Engine

This procedure requires special tool 3268 or equivalent. This is a setting tool that holds the camshafts in the correct position for installing the timing chains. Before removing the cylinder head, make sure new bolts are available. The cylinder head bolts are made to stretch and cannot be used again.

1. Disconnect the battery cables and remove the battery.
2. Disconnect the wiring and vacuum lines as required to remove the air cleaner, air mass sensor and duct.
3. Open the radiator cap and remove the drain plug from the coolant pipe below the intake manifold to drain the cooling system.
4. Remove the engine trim cover. Remove the distributor cap, ignition wires and wire guide as an assembly.

5. Disconnect the throttle cable. Label and disconnect the wiring and vacuum lines from the intake manifold and remove the upper manifold.

6. The injectors and fuel rail assembly may be left on the manifold. Disconnect the fuel supply and return lines and the wiring connector for the injectors.

7. Disconnect the radiator and heater hoses.

8. Thread a long 8 **x** 10mm bolt into the accessory drive belt tensioner to release the tension. Move the tensioner only as required to remove the belt.

9. Remove the alternator and the belt tensioner.

10. Remove the heatshield and the bolts to disconnect the 2 piece exhaust manifold from the engine. Note the position of the gaskets.

11. Remove the distributor and the timing chain tensioner bolt from the timing chain cover.

12. Remove the cylinder head cover, upper timing chain cover and the retaining plate.

13. If possible, rotate the crankshaft to TDC of No. 1 piston. Clean the oil off the chain and sprockets and mark the direction of rotation for assembly.

14. Hold the camshafts at the flats with a 24mm wrench and remove the bolts to remove the sprockets and chain. Note the position of the distributor drive on the short camshaft.

NOTE: Do not use the setting tool to hold the camshafts when removing or installing the sprocket bolts. The camshafts and the tool will be damaged.

15. Carefully check to make sure all necessary wires, hoses and brackets and components have been removed.

16. Loosen the cylinder head bolts in the reverse of the torque sequence. Remove and discard the bolts.

17. Remove the cylinder head.

To install:

18. Carefully clean the old gasket material from the head and the block. Before reinstalling the head, check the flatness of the head and block in both width and length, then diagonally from each corner. Maximum allowable distortion is 0.004 in. (0.1mm).

19. If the new head gasket already has sealant in the small holes at the timing chain end, remove the sealant. Apply a silicone sealer to the timing chain end and install the gasket onto the block with the word TOP or OBEN facing up.

20. Fit the cylinder head over the locating dowels and set the head onto the engine. Install new bolts and hand tighten them. Do not attempt to re-use the old bolts.

21. Torque the bolts in 3 steps:
Step 1 — 29 ft. lbs. (40 Nm)
Step 2 — 43 ft. lbs. (60 Nm)
Step 3 — an additional ½ turn. Two ¼ turns are allowed

22. Make sure the crankshaft is at TDC on No. 1 piston. Install the setting tool to lock the camshafts in place, then install the timing chain and sprockets. Make sure they are positioned to rotate in the original direction.

23. Hold the camshaft with a 24mm wrench and install the sprocket bolt. Make sure the distributor drive is correctly positioned and torque the bolts to 74 ft. lbs. (100 Nm).

24. Install the tensioner shoe and temporarily install the upper timing chain cover. Install the tensioner bolt and remove the setting tool. Rotate the crankshaft 4 full turns and stop at TDC of No. 1 piston. The setting tool should fit into the camshafts.

25. Remove the tensioner bolt and upper timing chain cover again. Apply new sealant as required, install the cover and torque the bolts to 82 inch lbs. (10 Nm). Install the tensioner bolt and torque to 15 ft. lbs. (20 Nm).

26. Install the cylinder head cover.

27. Use new gaskets and install the intake and exhaust manifolds. Torque the nuts and bolts to 18 ft. lbs. (25 Nm).

28. Install the alternator belt and adjust tension.

29. Install the accessory drive belt and adjust tension.

30. Connect the radiator and heater hoses.

31. Install the injectors, fuel rail assembly and manifold. Connect the fuel supply and return lines. Connect the wiring connector for the injectors.

32. Install the upper manifold. Torque the manifold bolts to 18 ft. lbs. (25 Nm).

33. Connect the wiring and vacuum lines disconnected from the intake manifold. Connect the throttle cable.

34. Install the distributor cap, ignition wires and wire guide as an assembly. Install the engine trim cover.

35. Disconnect the battery cables and remove the battery.

36. Refill and bleed the cooling system.

37. When everything has been properly installed and connected, be sure to change the oil and filter before starting the engine.

Valve Lifters

REMOVAL AND INSTALLATION

1. Remove the camshaft(s).

2. The valve lifters can be easily lifted out of the head by hand. Place hydraulic lifters camshaft side down on a clean surface. Keep all lifters in order so they can be installed in the same position.

To install:

3. Make sure the engine is not at TDC of any cylinder.

4. Set the lifters in place and install the camshaft. Before running the engine, allow the lifters to bleed down for 30 minutes or the valves may hit the pistons.

Intake Manifold

REMOVAL AND INSTALLATION

1. Disconnect the negative battery cable. Remove the air duct from the throttle valve body and disconnect the accelerator cable.

2. On Corrado SLC, remove the engine trim cover. Remove the distributor cap, wires and wire guide as an assembly.

3. On Digifant fuel injection systems, remove the idle stabilizer valve, fuel pump pressure switch and the fuel injector wiring harness. Disconnect the fuel supply and return lines.

4. On CIS-E fuel injection systems, remove the auxiliary air regulator. Remove the fuel injectors and the cold start valve from the cylinder head without disconnecting the fuel lines.

5. Label and disconnect the vacuum hoses as required.

6. Label and disconnect any remaining wiring as required.

7. If equipped, disconnect the EGR pipe.

8. On 16V and VR6 engines, remove the bolts to remove the upper intake manifold.

9. Remove the bolts and remove the manifold from the cylinder head.

To install:

10. On 16V and VR6 engines, install the lower intake manifold to the cylinder head with a new gasket. Torque the bolts to 18 ft. lbs. (25 Nm).

11. On the VR6 engine, if the fuel injectors were removed, examine the injector O-rings and replace as required. Install the injectors and rail.

12. Use new gaskets and fit the manifold or the upper manifold in

place. Torque the bolts to 18 ft. lbs. (25 Nm).

13. Connect fuel system hoses or install the injectors now to protect the system.

14. Connect all vacuum hoses and wiring.

15. If equipped, connect the EGR pipe.

16. Connect and adjust the throttle cable as required.

17. Install the remaining components and run the engine to check idle speed and ignition timing.

Exhaust Manifold

REMOVAL AND INSTALLATION

— CAUTION —
On some models, special tools are required for removing and installing the exhaust pipe-to-manifold spring clamps. Special tools VW3140/1 and /2, or equivalent, are a set of different sized wedges for spreading the spring clamps in steps. The installed spring clamp has considerable tension and could cause damage or injury if not properly removed. Clamps with wedges installed are under high spring pressure and should be handled carefully.

1. Disconnect the oxygen sensor wiring and remove any heatshields that may be in the way.

2. Remove the emissions sample tap and, if equipped, disconnect the EGR pipe from the exhaust manifold.

3. On models with manifold studs, remove the self-locking nuts and lower the exhaust pipe.

4. Expand the spring clamp by pushing the exhaust pipe to one side and insert the starter wedge into the clamp all the way up to the shoulder.

5. Push the pipe to the other side and install another wedge in the op-

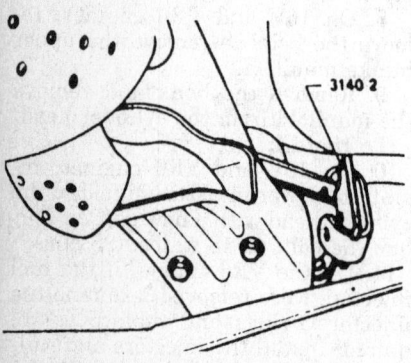

Exhaust pipe clamp removal tools

posite clamp. Continue to work the pipe side to side while pushing the wedges into the clamps until the clamps are spread far enough to lift off easily.

— CAUTION —
The removed spring clamps with wedges in them are under spring tension and, if miss-handled, could fly apart with enough force to cause serious injury. Store the removed clamps in a safe area where they won't be disturbed.

6. Remove the self-locking nuts and remove the manifold. On the VR6 engine, the exhaust manifold is 2 sections. Note the position of the gaskets.

To install:

7. Installation is the reverse of removal. Use new gaskets and self-locking nuts and torque to 18 ft. lbs. (25 Nm).

8. If the exhaust pipe is bolted to the manifold, install a new gasket and use new self-locking nuts. Torque the nuts to 30 ft. lbs. (40 Nm).

9. If equipped with spring clamps, hold the pipe in position with a new gasket and install the clamps. Carefully remove the wedge tools.

Supercharger

REMOVAL AND INSTALLATION

1990-92 Corrado

The early Corrado has a belt driven supercharger with an intercooler for supplying up to 11.6 psi (0.8 BAR) of boost. The belt is the same serpentine ribbed belt used to drive the other engine accessories. Belt tension is maintained with a spring-loaded automatic belt tensioner. Releasing the tension to remove the belt requires a special clamping tool, VW3191 or equivalent. The supercharger cannot be repaired; leaking or otherwise faulty units must be replaced.

1. Install clamping tool and compress the belt tensioner. Remove the belt from the supercharger pulley.

2. Remove the connector hose and silencer from the outlet side of the supercharger and remove the 2 upper inlet hoses.

3. Remove the front and rear mounting bolts and carefully lift the supercharger onto the top of the engine.

4. Allow the oil to drain back into the engine for a few minutes, then remove the oil lines and take the supercharger out of the vehicle.

5. Installation is the reverse of removal. Start the fittings for the oil lines but don't tighten them until the unit is bolted in place. Be sure to use new sealing rings. Torque the following:

Supercharger mounting bolts — 18 ft. lbs. (25 Nm)

Mounting bracket-to-engine bolt — 33 ft. lbs. (45 Nm)

Oil line fittings — 11 ft. lbs. (15 Nm)

Timing Chain Cover

REMOVAL AND INSTALLATION

Corrado SLC

Only the upper timing chain cover can be removed with the engine in the vehicle. The flywheel must be removed to remove the lower cover. This cover also holds the rear main oil seal.

1. Remove the engine trim cover. Remove the distributor cap and wires with the wire guide as an assembly.

2. Remove the upper intake manifold and the cylinder head cover.

3. Remove the distributor and the chain tensioner bolt.

4. Remove the bolts to remove the upper timing chain cover.

5. Installation is the reverse of removal. Use new gaskets and torque the bolts to 82 inch lbs. (10 Nm).

Timing Chain

REMOVAL AND INSTALLATION

VR6 Engine

1. Remove the distributor cap, wires and wire guide as an assembly.

2. Remove the upper intake manifold.

3. Remove the cylinder head cover.

4. Remove the timing chain tensioner bolt and the upper timing chain cover.

5. Remove the transaxle and flywheel.

6. Rotate the crankshaft to TDC of No. 1 piston.

7. Mark the direction of travel on the upper camshaft drive chain before removing. Remove the tensioner shoe and the double row chain.

8. Remove the the lower chain tensioner and remove the single row chain.

To install:

9. Check the position of the crankshaft in reference to the intermediate shaft. The ground tooth of drive gear

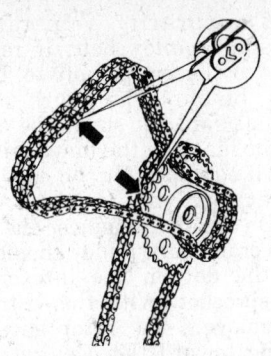

Mark the direction of the drive chains before removing — VR6 engine

A must align with the bearing split; reposition it if necessary.

10. Install the single row chain in position marked during disassembly. Install the chain tensioner and retaining bolts. Torque the bolts to 7 ft. lbs. (10 Nm).

11. Install the double row chain in position marked during disassembly. Install the chain tensioner. Torque the tensior to 15 ft. lbs. (20 Nm).

NOTE: The marking on the intermediate shaft must align with notch B or C on the thrust washer.

12. Install the upper timing chain cover. Rotate the crankshaft 4 full turns and stop at TDC of No. 1 piston and check mark again.

13. Install the flywheel and transaxle.

14. If timing marks alignment checks good, install the cylinder head cover, upper intake manifold and ignition system components.

15. Connect the negative battery cable. Start the engine a check ignition timing.

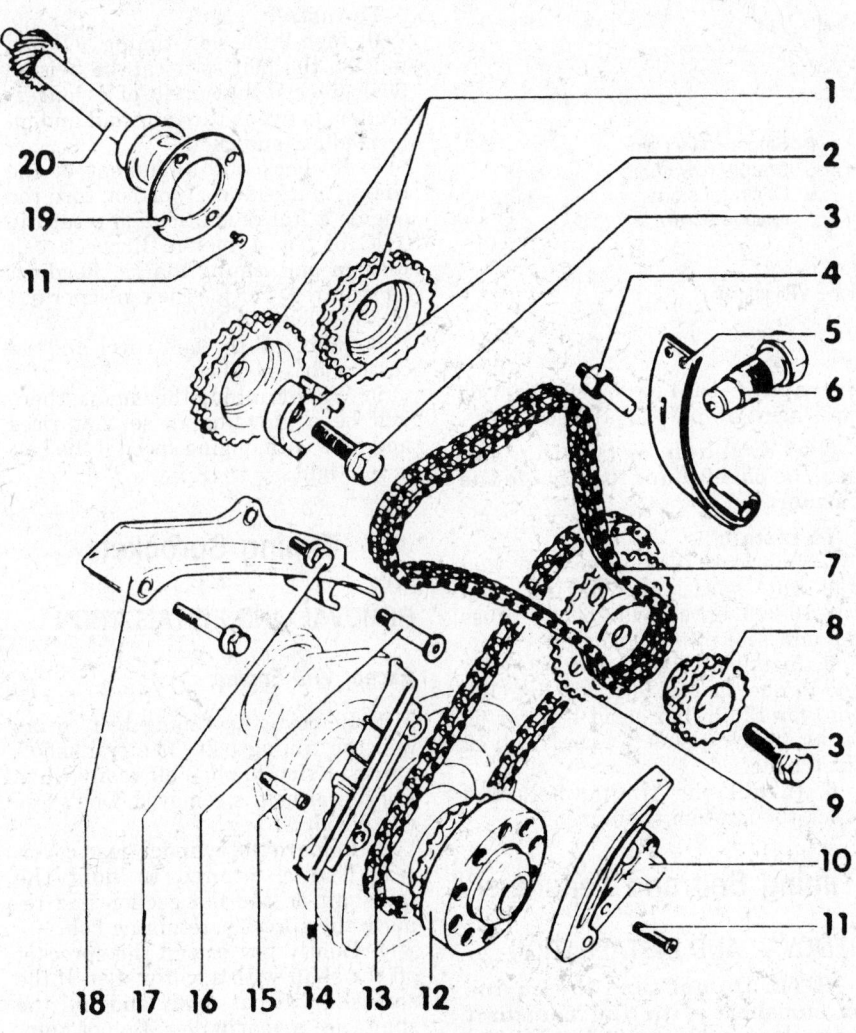

Removal and installation of the timing chains — VR6 engine

1 Camshaft chain sprocket
2 Distributor clutch
3 Bolt
4 Bearing bolt
5 Tension bar
6 Chain tensioner
7 Double row chain
8 Double row chain gear
9 Single row chain gear
10 Chain tensioner with bar
11 Bolt
12 Drive gear
13 Single row chain
14 Sliding rail
15 Bolt
16 Bearing bolt with shoulder
17 Bolt
18 Sliding rail
19 Thrust washer
20 Intermediate shaft

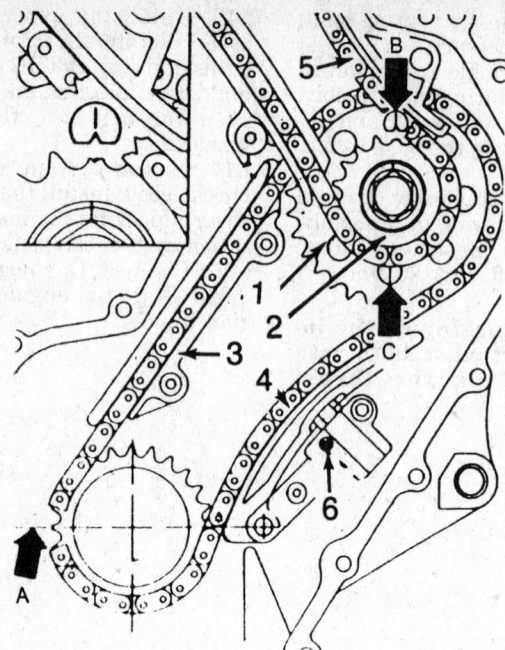

1 Single row chain gear
2 Double row chain gear
3 Sliding rail
4 Single row chain
5 Double row chain
6 Chain tensioner release screw

Timing chain chain marks — VR6 engine

Timing Belt Front Cover

REMOVAL AND INSTALLATION

Except Corrado SLC

1. Disconnect the negative battery cable.
2. Remove the accessory drive belts. On Corrado with a supercharger, install tool 3191 or equivalent, to compress the spring-loaded belt tensioner.
3. To remove the crankshaft accessory drive pulley, hold the center crankshaft sprocket bolt with a socket and loosen the pulley bolts.
4. The cover is now accessible. It comes off in 2 pieces; remove the upper ½ first. Take note of any special spacers or other hardware.
5. Installation is the reverse of removal.

FRONT OIL SEAL REPLACEMENT

1. Remove the timing belt cover and the timing belt.
2. Remove the crankshaft sprocket.
3. Using a small prybar, pry the seal from the carrier or use the seal extractor tool VW-10-219 or equivalent, to pull out the seal.

NOTE: When removing the seal, be careful not to damage the carrier.

To install:
4. Lubricate the new seal lips and use the seal installation tool VW-10-203 or equivalent, to press the new seal into the carrier.
5. Install the crankshaft sprocket and torque the bolt to 133 ft. lbs. (180 Nm) for 12mm hex head bolts or 66 ft. lbs. (90 Nm) plus ½ turn for all 12 sided bolts.
6. Install the timing belt and check the ignition timing.

Timing Belt and Tensioner

REMOVAL AND INSTALLATION

NOTE: Do not turn the engine or camshaft with the camshaft drive belt removed. The pistons will contact the valves and cause internal engine damage.

1. Disconnect the negative battery cable and remove the accessory drive belts, crankshaft pulley and the timing belt cover(s).

2. Temporarily reinstall the crankshaft pulley bolt, if removed and turn the crankshaft to TDC of No. 1 piston. The mark on the camshaft sprocket should be aligned with the mark on the inner drive belt cover, if equipped, or the edge of the cylinder head.
3. On 8-valve engines, the notch on the crankshaft pulley should align with the dot on the intermediate shaft sprocket. With the distributor cap removed, the rotor should be pointing toward the No. 1 mark on the rim of the distributor housing.
4. Loosen the locknut on the tensioner pulley and turn the tensioner counterclockwise to relieve the tension on the timing belt.
5. Slide the timing belt from the sprockets.
To install:
6. Install the new timing belt and tension the belt so it can be twisted 90 degrees at the middle of its longest section, between the camshaft and intermediate sprockets.
7. Recheck the alignment of the timing marks and, if correct, turn the engine 2 full revolutions to return to TDC of No. 1 piston. Recheck belt tension and timing marks. Readjust as required. Torque the tensioner nut to 33 ft. lbs. (45 Nm).
8. Reinstall the belt cover and accessory drive belts.
9. When running the engine, there will be a growling noise that rises and falls with engine speed if the belt is too tight.

Timing Sprockets

REMOVAL AND INSTALLATION

Except VR6 Engine

1. Remove the timing belt covers and the timing belt. The crankshaft sprocket should slide off easily when the center bolt is removed. Don't lose the Woodruff key.
2. Remove the cylinder head cover.
3. Use a wrench to hold the camshaft on the flat section and remove the sprocket retaining bolt.
4. Gently pry or tap the sprocket off the shaft with a soft mallet. If the sprocket will not easily slide off the shaft, use a gear puller. Do not hammer on the sprocket or damage to the sprocket or bearings could occur.
5. When reinstalling the sprockets, torque the camshaft sprocket bolts to 58 ft. lbs. (80 Nm) and the crankshaft sprocket bolt to 66 ft. lbs. (90 Nm) plus ½ turn.

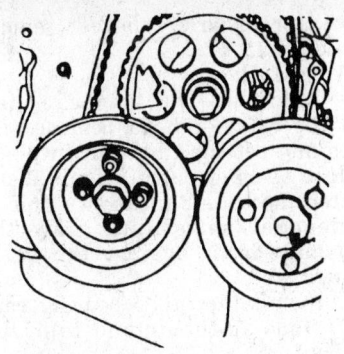

Timing marks on the crankshaft pulley and the intermediate shaft sprocket

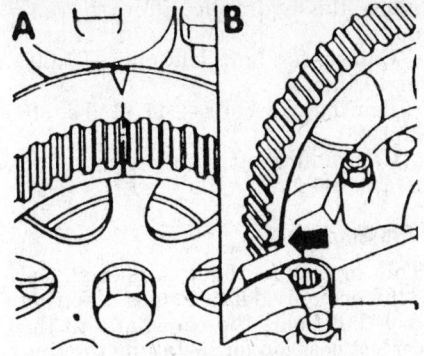

Adjusting timing belt tension

VR6 Engine

1. Disconnect the negative battery cable. Remove the distributor cap, wires and wire guide as an assembly.
2. Remove the upper intake manifold.
3. Remove the cylinder head cover.
4. Remove the timing chain tensioner bolt and the upper timing chain cover.
5. Rotate the crankshaft to TDC of No. 1 piston.
6. Mark the direction of travel on the upper camshaft drive chain. Remove the tensioner shoe and the chain.

7. Hold the camshafts at the flats with a 24mm wrench and remove the bolts to remove the sprockets. Note the position of the distributor drive on the short camshaft.

To install:

8. Hold the camshaft with a 24mm wrench and install the sprockets. Make sure the distributor drive is correctly positioned. Install the retaining bolts. Torque the bolts to 74 ft. lbs. (100 Nm).
9. Install the camshaft drive chain so the marks on the chain sprockets are matched at the base of the cylinder head, directly across from each other.

10. Install the timing chain tensioner. Install the tensioner bolt and torque to 15 ft. lbs. (20 Nm).
11. Install the upper timing chain cover and torque the bolts to 82 inch lbs. (10 Nm).
12. Install the cylinder head cover, upper intake manifold and ignition system components.

Camshaft

REMOVAL AND INSTALLATION

8-Valve Engine

1. Disconnect the negative battery cable. Remove the timing belt cover(s), the timing belt, camshaft sprocket and cylinder head cover.
2. Number the bearing caps from front to back. If the cap does not already have one, scribe an arrow pointing towards the front of the engine. The caps are offset and must be installed correctly. Factory numbers on the caps are not always on the same side.
3. Remove the front and rear bearing caps. Loosen the remaining bearing cap nuts diagonally, in several steps, starting from the outside caps near the ends of the head and working toward the center.
4. Remove the bearing caps and the camshaft.

To install:

5. Install a new oil seal and end plug in the cylinder head. Lubricate the camshaft bearing journals and lobes and set the camshaft in place.
6. Install the bearing caps in the correct position with the arrow pointing towards the front of the engine. Tighten the cap nuts diagonally and in several steps until they are torqued to 15 ft. lbs. (20 Nm). Do not over-torque.
7. Install the drive sprocket and torque the bolt to 58 ft. lbs. (80 Nm).
8. Align the timing marks, install the timing belt and adjust the tension.
9. On engines with hydraulic lifters, wait at least ½ hour after installing the camshaft before starting the engine to allow the lifters to leak down. Observe the following torques:

Camshaft shaft end-play — 0.006 in. (0.15mm)

Bearing cap bolts — 15 ft. lbs. (20 Nm)

Camshaft sprocket bolt — 58 ft. lbs. (80 Nm)

16-Valve Engine

1. Remove the timing belt cover.

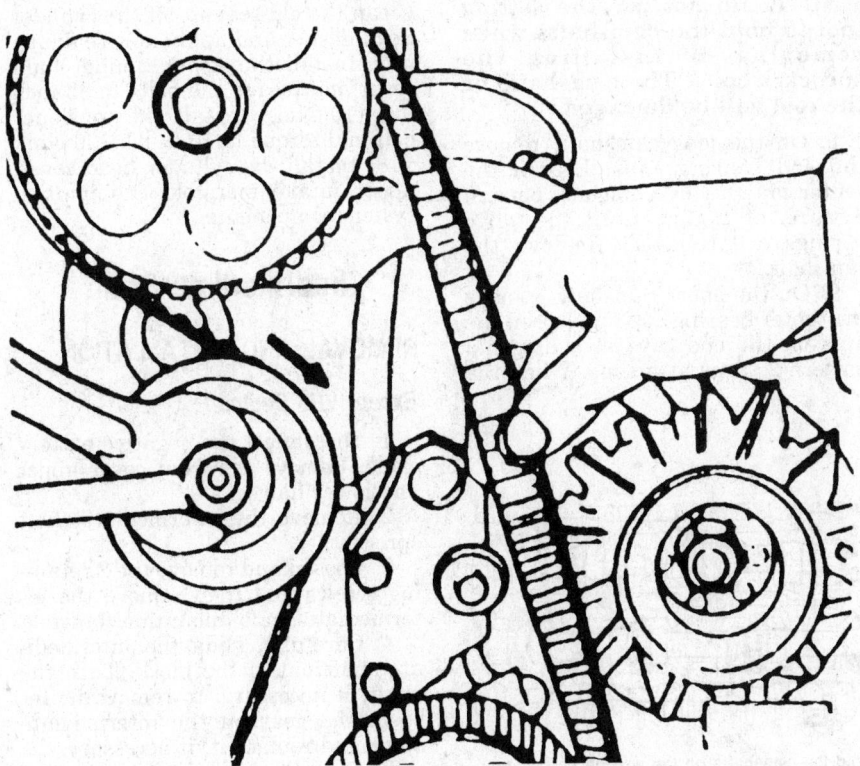

Timing marks on camshaft sprockets: A — 16-valve engine, B — 8-valve engine

2. Remove the upper intake manifold and cylinder head cover.

3. Turn the engine to TDC on cylinder No. 1, then slacken and remove the timing belt and camshaft sprocket.

4. With a felt marker only, match-mark the timing chain to the camshafts for reinstallation.

5. Remove the camshaft chain.

6. On the intake camshaft, remove bearing caps No. 5 and 7 and the chain end cap. Then loosen bearing caps No. 6 and 8 alternately and diagonally.

7. On the exhaust camshaft, remove bearing caps No. 1 and 3 and the end caps. Then loosen bearing caps No. 2 and 4 alternately and diagonally.

8. Remove the remaining bearing cap bolts and remove the camshafts.

To install:

9. Lubricate the camshaft bearing journals and lobes and set the camshafts in place. Install the camshaft drive chain so the marks on the chain sprockets are matched at the base of the cylinder head, directly across from each other.

NOTE: When installing the bearing caps, make sure the notch points towards the intake side of the head.

10. On the intake camshaft, install and torque bearing caps No. 6 and 8 alternately and diagonally.

11. Install and torque the remaining intake camshaft bearing caps.

12. On the exhaust camshaft, torque bearing caps No. 2 and 4 alternately and diagonally.

13. Install and torque the remaining exhaust camshaft bearing caps.

14. Install the drive sprocket and timing belt.

15. Install remaining parts in reverse order of removal. Wait at least ½ hour after installing camshaft shafts before starting the engine to

allow the hydraulic lifters to leak down.

Camshaft shaft end-play — 0.006 in. (0.15mm)

Bearing cap bolts — 11 ft. lbs. (15 Nm)

Camshaft shaft sprocket bolt — 48 ft. lbs. (65 Nm)

VR6 Engine

This procedure requires special tool 3268 or equivalent. This is a setting tool that holds the camshafts in the correct position for installing the timing chains.

1. Remove the distributor cap, wires and wire guide as an assembly.

2. Remove the upper intake manifold.

3. Remove the cylinder head cover.

4. Remove the timing chain tensioner bolt and the upper timing chain cover.

5. Rotate the crankshaft to TDC of No. 1 piston.

6. Mark the direction of travel on the upper camshaft drive chain. Remove the tensioner shoe and the chain.

7. Hold the camshafts at the flats with a 24mm wrench and remove the bolts to remove the sprockets. Note the position of the distributor drive on the short camshaft.

NOTE: Do not use the setting tool to hold the camshafts when removing or installing the sprocket bolts. The camshafts or the tool will be damaged.

8. On the long camshaft, remove the end bearing caps. Loosen the center cap nuts in a diagonal pattern 2 turns at a time until the valve springs are relieved. Remove the camshaft.

9. On the short camshaft, remove the center bearing cap and loosen the nuts on the end caps in a diagonal pattern 2 turns at a time. When the

valve springs are relieved, remove the camshaft.

To install:

10. Lubricate the long camshaft and the cylinder head bearing surfaces and set the camshaft in place. Install bearing caps 3 and 5 and tighten the bolts 2 turns at a time in a diagonal pattern to draw the camshaft down against the valve springs.

11. Install the other bearing caps and torque all the nuts to 15 ft. lbs. (20 Nm).

12. Repeat the process with the short camshaft, using bearing caps 2 and 6 to draw the camshaft down against the springs.

13. Hold the camshaft with a 24mm wrench and install the sprockets. Make sure the distributor drive is correctly positioned and torque the bolts to 74 ft. lbs. (100 Nm).

14. Make sure the crankshaft is at TDC on No. 1 piston. Install the setting tool and install the timing chain.

15. Install the tensioner shoe and temporarily install the upper timing chain cover. Install the tensioner bolt and remove the setting tool. Rotate the crankshaft 4 full turns and stop at TDC of No. 1 piston. The setting tool should fit into the camshafts.

16. Remove the tensioner bolt and upper timing chain cover again. Clean the old sealant off the cylinder head gasket and apply new sealant.

17. Install the upper timing chain cover and torque the bolts to 82 inch lbs. (10 Nm). Install the tensioner bolt and torque to 15 ft. lbs. (20 Nm).

18. Install the cylinder head cover, upper intake manifold and ignition system components.

Intermediate Shaft

REMOVAL AND INSTALLATION

Except VR6 Engine

1. Disconnect the negative battery cable. Remove the front cover upper and lower halves.

2. Remove the intermediate shaft sprocket.

3. Loosen and remove the 2 retaining screws and then remove the intermediate shaft mounting flange.

4. Carefully, slide the intermediate shaft out of the block. Turn the shaft, if necessary, to remove it. Inspect the gear on the intermediate shaft and replace it, if necessary.

To install:

5. Install the intermediate shaft to the block. Install new oil seal and O-ring in the mounting flange.

16-valve engine camshaft shaft alignment

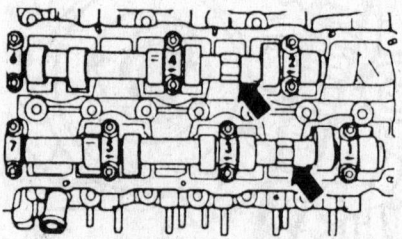

Hold the camshafts on the wrench flats to remove and install the sprocket bolts

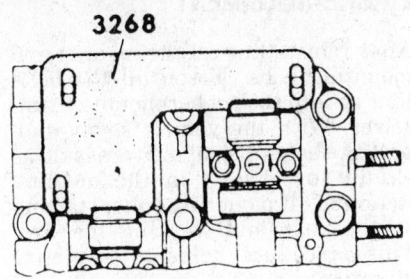

3268

Camshaft setting tool holds the camshafts in place when installing the chain: do not use this tool to loosen or tighten the sprocket bolts

6. Install the mounting flange and retaining bolts. When installing the mounting flange be sure the oil return hole is at the bottom. Torque the retaining bolts to 18 ft. lbs. (25 Nm).

7. Install the front cover. Connect the negative battery cable.

VR6 Engine

1. Disconnect the negative battery cable. Remove the distributor cap, wires and wire guide as an assembly.

2. Remove the upper intake manifold.

3. Remove the cylinder head cover.

4. Remove the timing chain tensioner bolt and the upper timing chain cover.

5. Rotate the crankshaft to TDC of No. 1 piston.

6. Mark the direction of travel on the upper camshaft drive chain. Remove the tensioner shoe and the chain.

7. Hold the camshafts at the flats with a 24mm wrench and remove the bolts to remove the sprockets. Note the position of the distributor drive on the short camshaft.

8. With the intermediate shaft gear removed, remove the thrust washer retaining bolts. Pull the shaft out from the engine.

To install:

9. Install the intermediate shaft in the engine until the oil pump gear is completely engaged with the intermediate shaft gear.

10. Install the thrust washer and the retaining bolts. Torque the bolts to 7 ft. lbs. (10 Nm).

11. Hold the camshaft with a 24mm wrench and install the sprockets. Make sure the distributor drive is correctly positioned. Install the retaining bolts. Torque the bolts to 74 ft. lbs. (100 Nm).

12. Install the camshaft drive chain so the marks on the chain sprockets are matched at the base of the cylin-

der head, directly across from each other.

13. Install the timing chain tensioner. Install the tensioner bolt and torque to 15 ft. lbs. (20 Nm).

14. Install the upper timing chain cover and torque the bolts to 82 inch lbs. (10 Nm).

15. Install the cylinder head cover, upper intake manifold and ignition system components. Connect the negative battery cable.

Piston and Connecting Rod

POSITIONING

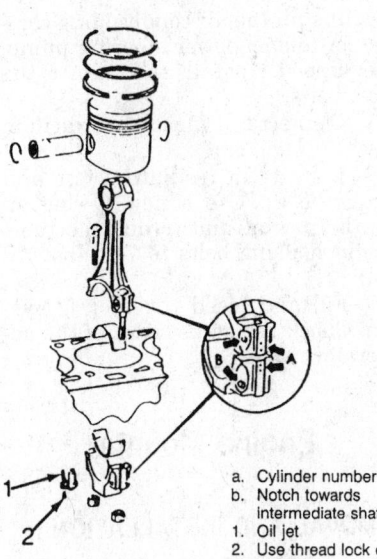

a. Cylinder number
b. Notch towards intermediate shaft
1. Oil jet
2. Use thread lock on the screw

On all 4 cylinder engines, arrow on piston points towards the camshaft drive belt

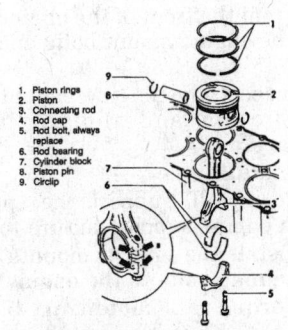

1. Piston rings
2. Piston
3. Connecting rod
4. Rod cap
5. Rod bolt, always replace
6. Rod bearing
7. Cylinder block
8. Piston pin
9. Circlip

On VR6 engine, highest side of piston crown is toward center of engine block, connecting rod number is opposite the crown

DIESEL ENGINE MECHANICAL

NOTE: Disconnecting the negative battery cable on some vehicles may interfere with the functions of the on-board computer or security systems and may require reprogramming when the battery cable is reconnected.

Engine Assembly

REMOVAL AND INSTALLATION

1. The engine and transaxle are lifted from the vehicle as an assembly. Disconnect the battery cables and remove the battery.

2. Open the fuel filler cap to relieve tank pressure, then loosen the fuel filter fitting to relieve system pressure. Be sure to take the appropriate fire safety precautions.

3. Remove the air filter and disconnect the accelerator cable from the injection pump.

4. Remove the radiator cap. Turn the heater temperature control all the way towards warm and remove the thermostat housing to drain the coolant.

5. Remove the upper radiator hose and disconnect the wiring from the radiator fan motor and switches. Remove the mounting nuts or bolts and lift out the radiator and fan shroud as an assembly.

6. Begin disconnecting electrical connections and vacuum lines, carefully labeling each one. Don't forget ground connections that are screwed to the body.

7. If equipped with power steering, remove pump and secure it to the body. Do not disconnect the hydraulic lines. If equipped with air conditioning, remove the compressor and secure it aside without disconnecting the lines.

8. Disconnect the fuel inlet and outlet lines from the injection pump and plug the holes to keep the pump clean. Note the outlet fitting has a special orifice.

9. On turbocharged engines, disconnect the exhaust pipe and the oil lines from the turbocharger and cap the oil line fittings on the turbocharger. Unbolt the turbocharger and lift it out of the engine.

10. If equipped with an automatic transaxle, place the selector lever in

P and disconnect the selector cable at the transaxle.

11. On manual transaxle shift linkage, remove the 2 rods with the plastic socket ends and unbolt the remaining linkage from the case as required. Disconnect the clutch cable, lift it out of the case and set it aside.

12. Disconnect the wiring from the starter, the backup light switch and the ground cable from the transaxle. Remove the speedometer cable from the transaxle and plug the hole in the case.

13. Attach an engine sling tool VW-2024A or equivalent, to the engine and attach the sling to a suitable lifting device.

14. Remove the nuts or spring clamps holding the exhaust pipe to the manifold or turbocharger.

------ **CAUTION** ------

On some models, special tools are required for removing and installing the exhaust pipe-to-manifold spring clamps; VW3140/1 and /2 or equivalent. This is a set of different sized wedges for spreading the spring clamps in steps. The installed spring clamp has considerable tension and could cause damage or injury if not properly removed. Clamps with wedges installed are also under high tension and should be handled carefully.

15. Unbolt the halfshafts from the flanges and hang them from the body with wire.

16. Make sure everything is disconnected and unbolt the mounts. Remove the starter first and the front mount with it.

17. With all mounts unbolted, slightly lower the engine/transaxle assembly and tilt it towards the transaxle side. Then carefully lift the assembly out of the vehicle.

To install:

18. Carefully install the engine/transaxle assembly and make sure all mounts are securely bolted to the engine/transaxle. Start all nuts and bolts that secure the mounts to the body but don't tighten them yet.

19. With all mounts installed and the engine safely in the vehicle, allow some slack in the lifting equipment. With the vehicle safely supported, shake the engine/transaxle as a unit to settle it in the mounts. Torque all mounting bolts, starting at the rear and working forward. Torque to 33 ft. lbs. (41 Nm) for 10mm bolts or 54 ft. lbs. (73 Nm) for 12mm bolts.

20. Install the starter and torque the bolts to 33 ft. lbs. (45 Nm).

21. Connect the halfshafts to the flanges and torque the bolts to 33 ft. lbs. (45 Nm).

22. Install the exhaust pipe and use new self-locking nuts to secure the flange. Torque the nuts to 30 ft. lbs. (40 Nm). If equipped with spring clamps, the clamps can be used again.

23. Connect the shift linkage and the clutch cable, if equipped. Make any necessary adjustments.

24. Install the fuel injector lines and torque to 18 ft. lbs. (25 Nm). Be careful not to over torque the line nuts. If a line is damaged or clogged, replace all lines as a set.

25. Connect the inlet and outlet lines to the injector pump. Note the special outlet fitting has the word "OUT" printed on the top. Use new gaskets.

26. Install the air conditioning compressor and/or power steering pump, if equipped. Install and adjust the drive belts.

27. Connect the wiring and vacuum hoses.

28. Install the radiator, fan and heater hoses. Use a new O-ring on the thermostat and torque the thermostat housing bolts to 7 ft. lbs. (10 Nm).

29. Fill and bleed the cooling system. Check the adjustment of the accelerator cable.

Engine Mounts

REMOVAL AND INSTALLATION

1. Disconnect the negative battery cable.

2. Using an engine support fixture tool, center it on the cowl and attach it to the engine. Raise the engine slightly to take the weight off of the engine mounts.

3. From the front of the engine, remove the engine mount bolts and the mount.

4. Inspect the engine mount for deterioration and replace it, if necessary.

To install:

5. To install, support the engine using a engine support fixture tool.

6. Install the engine mounts and the retaining bolts to the engine.

7. Torque all mounting bolts, starting at the rear and working forward. Torque to 33 ft. lbs. (41 Nm) for 10mm bolts or 54 ft. lbs. (73 Nm) for 12mm bolts.

ENGINE ALIGNMENT

After reinstalling all the mounts and mounting bolts, loosen all the bolts that go into the rubber mounts themselves. With the vehicle safely supported, shake the engine/transaxle as a unit to settle it in the mounts. Retorque all mounting bolts, starting at the rear and working forward. This procedure helps to minimize vibration.

Cylinder Head

REMOVAL AND INSTALLATION

NOTE: The cylinder head bolts on all diesel vehicles are stretch bolts and must be replaced when removed.

1. Disconnect the battery ground cable.

2. Remove the thermostat and drain the cooling system.

3. Remove the fuel lines from the injectors and the pump as an assembly. Put the lines where they will stay clean; protect the injector and pump fittings with caps.

4. Disconnect the radiator and heater hoses.

5. Disconnect all vacuum and electrical connections and carefully label for installation.

6. On turbocharged vehicles, unbolt the exhaust pipe and oil lines from the turbocharger and remove the turbocharger.

7. On non-turbocharged vehicles, remove the air cleaner and disconnect the exhaust pipe from the manifold.

------ **CAUTION** ------

On some models, special tools are required for removing and installing the exhaust pipe-to-manifold spring clamps; VW3140/1 and /2 or equivalent. This is a set of different sized wedges for spreading the spring clamps in steps. The installed spring clamp has considerable tension and could cause damage or injury if not properly removed. Clamps with wedges installed are also under high tension and should be handled carefully.

8. Remove the cylinder head cover and camshaft drive belt cover.

9. Turn the engine to TDC of No. 1 cylinder, if possible, and remove the camshaft drive belt.

10. Remove the head bolts in the reverse order of installation sequence and lift the head out of the vehicle.

The torque sequence is the same as for gasoline engines.

To install:

11. On these engines, the pistons actually project above the deck of the block. If the crankshaft and pistons are not to be removed, examine the old head gasket to see how many notches are on the edge near the oil return hole, between No. 2 and 3 cylinders. Replace the gasket with the same thickness.

12. If the pistons were removed or if the old gasket in not available, the piston height (pop up) must be measured to select the proper head gasket. Use a dial indicator or caliper to obtain the measurement.

Pop-up on engines with solid lifters:

0.026-0.031 in. (0.67-0.80mm) — 1 notch

0.032-0.035 in. (0.81-0.90mm) — 2 notches

0.036-0.040 in. (0.91-1.02mm) — 3 notches

Pop-up on engines with hydraulic lifters:

0.026-0.034 in. (0.66-0.86mm) — 1 notch

0.034-0.035 in. (0.87-0.90mm) — 2 notches

0.036-0.040 in. (0.91-1.02mm) — 3 notches

13. Install the new cylinder head gasket with the word TOP or OBEN facing upward. Do not use any sealing compound.

14. Turn the crankshaft to TDC of No. 1 cylinder, then back about 1/4 turn to bring all pistons about even.

15. Carefully lower the head on and install new head bolts into No. 8 and 10 first. These holes are smaller and will properly locate the gasket and cylinder head.

16. Install the remaining bolts and torque in the proper sequence in 3 steps: 29 ft. lbs. (40 Nm), 44 ft. lbs. (60 Nm), then a full 1/2 turn more. Two quarter turns are allowed.

Measure piston pop-up to determine required head gasket thickness — diesel engine

17. Installation of the remaining parts is the reverse of removal, be sure to change the oil and filter. Install the camshaft drive belt and set injection pump timing.

18. Install the fuel injector lines and torque to 18 ft. lbs. (25 Nm). Be careful not to over torque the line nuts. If a line is damaged or clogged, replace all lines as a set.

19. After the engine has be run about 1000 miles, the cylinder head bolts must be re-torqued. Remove the cylinder head cover and turn each head bolt, in sequence, an additional 1/4 turn in 1 movement. This can be done on a cold or warm engine.

Valve Lifters

REMOVAL AND INSTALLATION

1. Remove the camshaft.
2. The valve lifters can be easily lifted out of the head by hand. Place hydraulic lifters camshaft side down on a clean surface. Keep all lifters in order so they can be installed in the same position.

To install:

3. Make sure the engine is not at TDC of any cylinder.
4. Set the lifters in place and carefully install the camshaft. Allow the lifters to bleed down for 30 minutes before turning the engine or the valves may hit the pistons.
5. Install the camshaft drive belt and adjust the belt tension and valve lash.

Valve Lash

ADJUSTMENT

All vehicles have hydraulic valve lifters and require no adjustment. On these vehicles there will be a sticker under the hood indicating hydraulic lifters.

Intake Manifold

REMOVAL AND INSTALLATION

1. Disconnect the hose and wiring from the blow-off valve.
2. Disconnect the air inlet hose.
3. Remove the bolts to remove the intake manifold.
4. Installation is the reverse of removal. Use a new gasket and torque the bolts to 18 ft. lbs. (25 Nm).

Exhaust Manifold

REMOVAL AND INSTALLATION

— **CAUTION** —

On some models, special tools are required for removing and installing the exhaust pipe-to-manifold spring clamps; VW3140/1 and /2 or equivalent. This is a set of different sized wedges for spreading the spring clamps in steps. The installed spring clamp has considerable tension and could cause damage or injury if not properly removed. Clamps with wedges installed are also under high tension and should be handled carefully.

1. Disconnect the negative battery cable and remove any heatshields that may be in the way.
2. On turbocharged engines, unbolt the exhaust pipe from the turbocharger outlet.
3. On non-turbocharged engines, expand the spring clamp by pushing the exhaust pipe to one side and insert the starter wedge into the clamp all the way up to the shoulder.
4. Push the pipe to the other side and install another wedge in the opposite clamp. Continue to work the pipe side to side while pushing the wedges into the clamps until the clamps are spread far enough to lift off easily.

— **CAUTION** —

The removed spring clamps with wedges in them are under spring pressure and, if miss handled, could fly apart with enough force to cause serious injury. Store the removed clamps in a safe area where they won't be disturbed.

5. On turbocharged engines, remove the turbocharger oil lines and the turbocharger.
6. Remove the manifold locking nuts and lift the manifold off the head.
7. Installation is the reverse of removal. Use new gaskets and locking nuts and torque to 18 ft. lbs. (25 Nm).

Turbocharger

REMOVAL AND INSTALLATION

1. Disconnect the negative battery cable.
2. Remove the exhaust pipe from the turbocharger outlet.

3. Clean the oil supply fitting on the top of the turbocharger and remove the supply line and bracket.

4. Remove the inlet air hose.

5. Under the vehicle, remove the oil return line and the turbocharger mounting bracket.

6. Still underneath, remove the turbo-to-manifold bolts. Lift the turbocharger out from the top.

To install:

7. Installation is the reverse of removal. Before installing the oil supply line, fill the connection on the turbocharger with engine oil. Torque the following:

Turbocharger-to-exhaust manifold — 33 ft. lbs. (45 Nm)

Mounting bracket nuts — 18 ft. lbs. (25 Nm)

Turbocharger outlet nuts — 18 ft. lbs. (25 Nm)

Oil return line — 22 ft. lbs. (30 Nm)

Timing Belt Cover

REMOVAL AND INSTALLATION

1. Remove the accessory drive belts.

2. To remove the crankshaft accessory drive pulley, hold the center crankshaft sprocket bolt with a socket and loosen the pulley bolts.

3. The cover is now accessible. It comes off in 2 pieces, remove the upper half first. Take note of any special spacers or other hardware.

4. Installation is the reverse of removal. Torque the cover bolts to 87 inch lbs. (10 Nm).

Timing Belt and Tensioner

Timing belts are designed to last 60,000-75,000 miles. If the vehicle has been stored for long periods (2 years or more), the belt should be

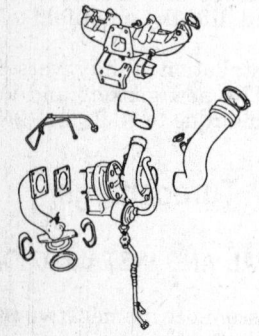

Diesel engine turbocharger and exhaust manifold

changed before returning the vehicle to service.

ADJUSTMENT

1. Disconnect the negative battery cable.

2. Remove the upper drive belt cover.

3. Strike the drive belt 1 time with a rubber hammer between the camshaft gear and injection pump gear.

4. Install and suitable belt tension gauge. Measure the belt tension between the camshaft and injection pump gear. Record the reading.

5. Turn the crankshaft 1 complete turn and measure the tension again. Compare the average of the 2 readings with specifications.

6. The belt tension specified value is 12-13.

7. If the belt tension is below specifications, turn the tensioner to the right. If belt tension is above specifications, turn the tensioner to the left.

8. Install the upper drive belt cover. Connect the negative battery cable.

REMOVAL AND INSTALLATION

Some special tools are required. A flat bar, VW tool 2065A or equivalent, is used to secure the camshaft in position. A pin, VW tool 2064 or equivalent, is used to fix the pump position while the timing belt is removed. The camshaft and pump work against spring pressure and will move out of position when the timing belt is removed. It is not difficult to find substitutes but do not remove the timing belt without these tools.

NOTE: Do not turn the engine or camshaft with the timing belt removed. The pistons will contact the valves and cause internal engine damage.

1. Disconnect the negative battery cable and remove the accessory drive belts, crankshaft pulley and the timing belt cover(s). Remove the camshaft cover and rubber plug at the back end of the camshaft.

2. Temporarily reinstall the crankshaft pulley bolt and turn the crankshaft to TDC of No. 1 piston. The mark on the camshaft sprocket should be aligned with the mark on the inner timing belt cover or the edge of the cylinder head.

3. With the engine at TDC, insert the bar into the slot at the back of the

camshaft. The bar rests on the cylinder head to will hold the camshaft in position.

4. Insert the pin into the injection pump drive sprocket to hold the pump in position.

5. Loosen the locknut on the tensioner pulley and turn the tensioner counterclockwise to relieve the tension on the timing belt. Slide the timing belt from the sprockets.

To install:

6. Install the new timing belt and adjust the tension so the belt can be twisted 45 degrees at a point between the camshaft and pump sprockets. Torque the tensioner nut to 33 ft. (45 Nm).

7. Remove the holding tools.

8. Turn the engine 2 full revolutions to return to TDC of No. 1 piston. Recheck belt tension and timing mark alignment, readjust as required.

9. Install the belt cover and accessory drive belts.

10. If the belt is too tight, there will be a growling noise that rises and falls with engine speed.

Timing Sprockets

REMOVAL AND INSTALLATION

NOTE: The 12-point crankshaft sprocket bolt is meant to be used 1 time only and must be replaced when removed.

1. Remove the timing belt covers and the timing belt. The crankshaft sprocket should slide off easily when the center bolt is removed. Don't lose the Woodruff key.

2. Remove the cylinder head cover.

3. Use a wrench to hold the camshaft on the flat section and remove the sprocket retaining bolt.

4. Gently pry or tap the sprocket off the shaft with a soft mallet. If the sprocket will not easily slide off the shaft, use a gear puller. Do not hammer on the sprocket or damage to the sprocket or bearings could occur.

5. Installation is the reverse of removal. On crankshaft sprocket bolts, oil the threads before installing the bolt. Torque the bolts as follows:

a. Camshaft sprocket — 33 ft. lbs. (45 Nm).

b. Crankshaft sprocket 12-point bolt — 66 ft. lbs. (90 Nm) plus ½ turn.

6. Install the timing belt, check valve timing, adjust the belt tension and install the covers.

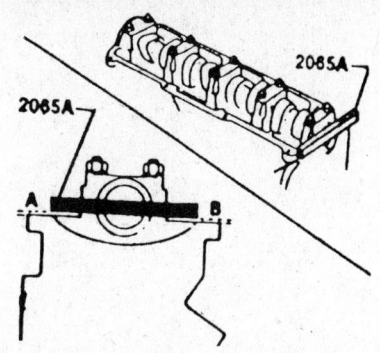

Locking the camshaft in TDC position using a special tool — diesel engine

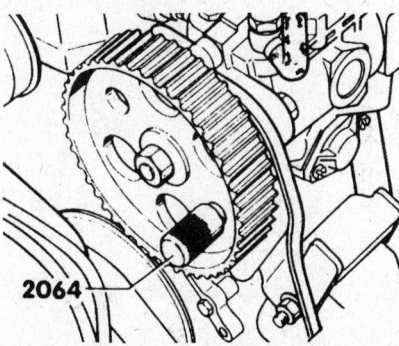

Locking the camshaft sprocket in TDC position using a special tool — diesel engine

Camshaft

REMOVAL AND INSTALLATION

1. Disconnect the negative battery cable. Remove the timing belt cover(s), the timing belt, cylinder head cover and the camshaft sprocket.

2. Number the bearing caps from front to back. If the cap does not already have one, scribe an arrow pointing towards the front of the engine. The caps are offset and must be installed correctly. Factory numbers on the caps are not always on the same side.

3. Remove the front and rear bearing caps. Loosen the remaining bearing cap nuts a little at a time to avoid bending the camshaft. Start from the outside caps near the ends of the head and work toward the center.

4. Remove the bearing caps and the camshaft.

To install:

5. Install a new oil seal and end plug in the cylinder head. Lubricate the camshaft bearing journals and lobes and set the camshaft in place.

6. Install the bearing caps in the correct position with the arrow pointing towards the front of the engine. Tighten the cap nuts diagonally and in several steps until they are torqued to 15 ft. lbs. (20 Nm). Do not over torque. Camshaft shaft end-play should be about 0.006 in. (0.15mm).

7. Install the drive sprocket and timing belt. Wait at least ½ hour after installing the camshaft before starting the engine to allow the lifters to leak down.

Intermediate Shaft

REMOVAL AND INSTALLATION

1. Disconnect the negative battery cable. Remove the front cover upper and lower halves.

2. Remove the intermediate shaft sprocket.

3. Loosen and remove the 2 retaining screws and then remove the intermediate shaft mounting flange.

4. Carefully, slide the intermediate shaft out of the block. Turn the shaft, if necessary, to remove it. Inspect the gear on the intermediate shaft and replace it, if necessary.

To install:

5. Install the intermediate shaft to the block. Install new oil seal and O-ring in the mounting flange.

6. Install the mounting flange and retaining bolts. When installing the mounting flange be sure the oil return hole is at the bottom. Torque the retaining bolts to 18 ft. lbs. (25 Nm).

7. Install the front cover. Connect the negative battery cable.

Pistons and Connecting Rods

POSITIONING

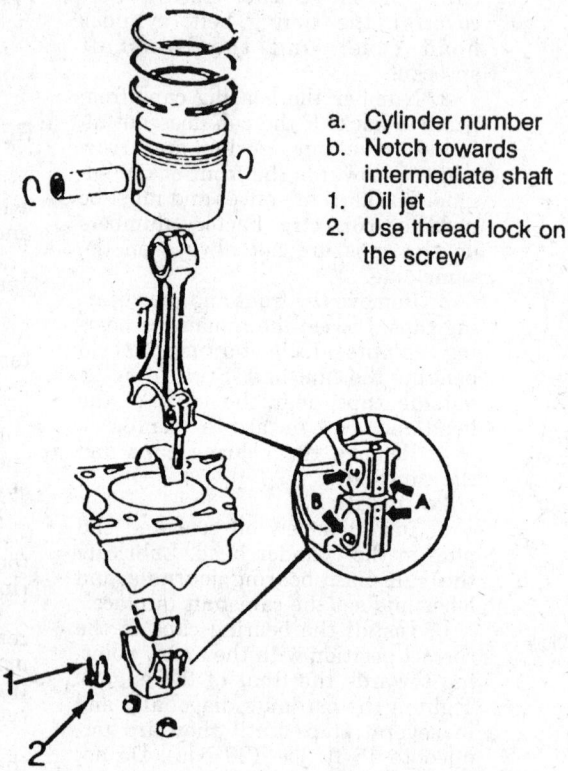

a. Cylinder number
b. Notch towards intermediate shaft
1. Oil jet
2. Use thread lock on the screw

Piston and connecting rod positioning — diesel engine

ENGINE LUBRICATION

Oil Pan

REMOVAL AND INSTALLATION

Except Fox

The oil pan can be removed with the engine in the vehicle.

1. Raise and safely support the vehicle and drain the oil.
2. Loosen and remove the bolts retaining the oil pan.
3. Lower the pan from the engine.
   To install:
4. Make sure the gasket surface is flat and install the pan with a new gasket.
5. Torque the retaining bolts in a crisscross pattern to 14 ft. lbs. (20 Nm). Do not over-torque.

6. Refill the engine with oil. Start the engine and check for leaks.

Fox

1. Raise and safely support the vehicle and drain the oil.
2. Support and slightly raise the engine from overhead with a suitable lifting device.
3. Gradually loosen the engine crossmember mounting bolts. Remove the left and right side engine mounts.
4. Carefully lower the crossmember from the vehicle.
5. Remove the oil pan retaining bolts and lower the pan from the vehicle.
   To install:
6. Make sure the gasket surface is flat and install the pan and new gasket.
7. Torque the retaining bolts in a crisscross pattern to 14 ft. lbs. (20 Nm).
8. Install the crossmember and torque the crossmember-to-frame bolts to 42 ft. lbs. (57 Nm) and the

engine mount bolts to 32 ft. lbs. (43 Nm).

9. Refill the engine with oil. Start the engine and check for leaks.

Oil Pump

REMOVAL AND INSTALLATION

1. Raise and safely support the vehicle and remove the oil pan.
2. Remove the mounting bolts and lower the pump from the engine.
3. Remove the bottom cover and disassemble the pump. The pressure relief valve is in the bottom cover.
4. Clean and inspect all parts for wear and replace as needed.
5. After reassembling the pump, prime it with oil and install in the reverse order of removal.
6. Observe the following torques:
   Oil pump bottom cover bolts — 7 ft. lbs. (10 Nm)
   Oil pump suction foot bolts — 7 ft. lbs. (10 Nm)
   Oil pump retaining bolts — 18 ft. lbs. (25 Nm)

Rear Main Bearing Oil Seal

REMOVAL AND INSTALLATION

The rear main oil seal is located in a housing on the rear of the cylinder block. To replace the seal on all vehicles it is necessary to remove the transaxle and flywheel.

1. Remove the transaxle and flywheel.

2. Using a small prybar, pry the old seal out of the support ring.

3. To install, lightly oil the new seal and press it into place using tool VW-2003/2A or equivalent, to start the seal and tool VW-2003/1 or equivalent, to seat the seal. Be careful not to damage the seal or score the crankshaft.

4. Install the flywheel and transaxle.

ENGINE COOLING

Radiator

REMOVAL AND INSTALLATION

Except Corrado SLC

NOTE: When replacing coolant/antifreeze, only a phosphate-free product must be used to help prevent damage to the water jacket sealing surfaces of the cylinder head. Other types of coolant may cause corrosion of the cooling system, thus leading to engine overheating and damage.

1. To drain the cooling system, remove the thermostat housing from under the water pump housing.

2. Disconnect the wiring on the radiator for the thermostatic switch and electric fan(s).

3. Remove the upper and lower hoses and the overflow hose.

4. There will be 1 or 2 bolted clips holding the top of the radiator. Remove these clips and carefully lift the radiator and fan assembly up and out

of the vehicle. Be careful not to lose the rubber washers on the bottom locating studs.

5. The fan and shroud can be unbolted and removed as an assembly.

6. Installation is the reverse of removal. Torque the clip bolts to 7 ft. lbs. (10 Nm).

Corrado SLC

1. Read this entire procedure before starting work. Remove the battery.

2. Remove the front grille, headlights and hood lock support.

3. Remove the front bumper:

   a. Remove the front spoiler.

   b. Remove the clips between the bumper skin and the engine mount.

   c. Below the bracket on each side, remove the 2 engine mount bolts that hold the bracket.

   d. Pull the bumper cover forward evenly from both sides. Two people are required.

4. To drain the coolant, remove the drain plug from the coolant pipe below the intake manifold.

5. If equipped with air conditioning, remove the refrigerant hose clamps and pull the condenser forward as far as possible.

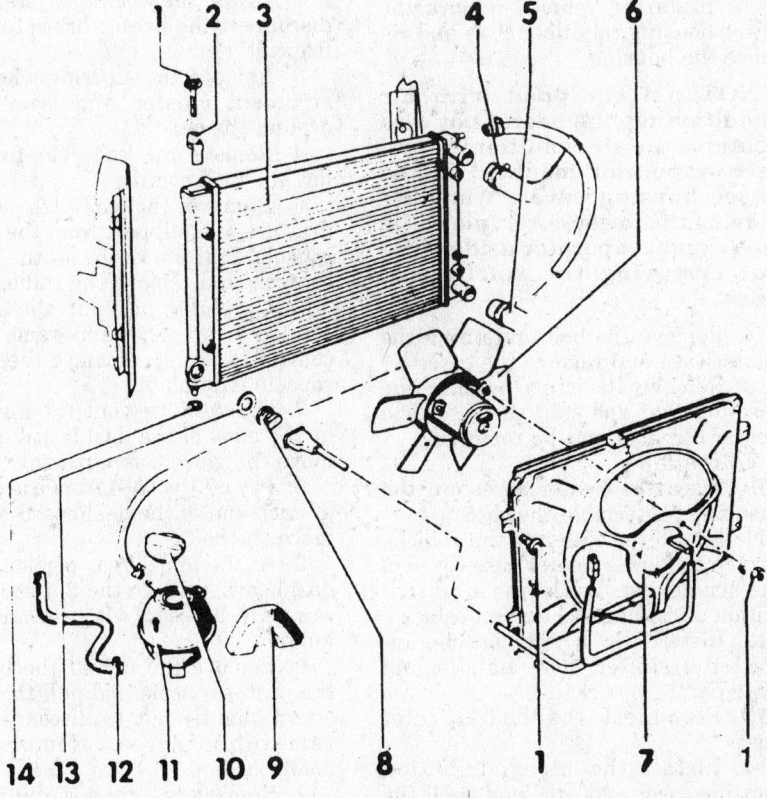

1. Bolt
2. Upper radiator mount
3. Radiator
4. Upper hose
5. Lower hose
6. Electric cooling fan
7. Fan shroud
8. Radiator fan thermoswitch
9. Cover
10. Pressure cap
11. Coolant expansion tank
12. To coolant hose
13. Sealing washer
14. Sealing washer

Radiator and fan assembly — Jetta, GTI and Cabriolet

6. Remove the upper mount brackets and remove the radiator from the top.

To install:

7. Fit the radiator and fan assembly into place and install the brackets.

8. Secure the condenser in place and connect the fan wiring.

9. Connect the hoses and install the drain plug.

10. Before installing the body parts, fill the cooling system and make sure it does not leak.

11. Install the bumper and torque the bracket bolts to 63 ft. lbs. (85 Nm).

12. Install the remaining body parts and adjust the headlight aim as required.

Auxiliary Coolant Pump Switch

TESTING

Corrado SLC

At the thermostat housing, 2 switches and a plug, or on air conditioned vehicles, 3 switches are mounted in a row. The center yellow switch operates the cooling fans and the auxiliary electric coolant pump. When the ignition switch is **OFF** and the coolant temperature in the radiator is below about 145°F (63°C), but the coolant in the engine is above 215°F (101°C), this switch will close and the fan and pump will run.

TESTING

1. Turn the ignition switch **ON**, then **OFF** again.

2. At the thermostat housing, disconnect the wiring from the center yellow temperature switch.

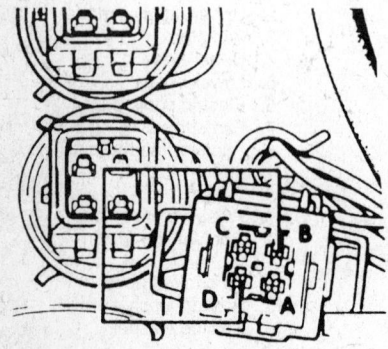

Jumper terminals B and D to run fans and auxiliary coolant pump — Corrado SLC

3. Use a jumper wire to connect terminals **B** and **D**. The fan and the electric water pump should both run.

Heater Core

REMOVAL AND INSTALLATION

The heater core is contained in the fresh air/heater box located in the center of the dashboard. On air conditioned vehicles, the evaporator is also located in the heater box.

Fox

1. The entire dashboard and heater assembly must be removed. Disconnect the negative battery cable.

2. Drain the engine coolant or clamp the heater hoses.

3. Disconnect the heater hoses at the firewall and plug the core fittings.

4. Inside the vehicle, remove the knee bar, if equipped, the shifter handle and boot. Remove the center console and the temperature controls from the dash.

5. Remove the left and right air distribution ducts.

6. In the engine compartment, remove the cowl cover and remove the air distribution housing cover.

7. Inside the vehicle, remove the lower housing retaining clips and remove the housing.

NOTE: If equipped with air conditioning, the heater box also contains the air conditioning system evaporator mounted in the lower housing cover. When removing the lower cover, place the cover and evaporator aside without removing the refrigerant lines.

8. Remove the bolts retaining the heater case and remove the case.

9. Remove the clips holding the case together and split the case. The heater core can now be removed.

To install:

10. Place the heater core into the case and reassemble the case.

11. Install the case into the vehicle. Attach the lower heater case cover to the heater case. Install the air distribution ducts and the control cables.

12. Install the center console. Install the shifter boot, handle and knee bar.

13. Reconnect the heater inlet hoses.

14. Install the air distribution housing cover and cowl and refill the cooling system.

Cabriolet

1. Disconnect the negative battery cable.

2. Drain the cooling system or clamp the heater hoses.

3. Disconnect the heater hoses at the firewall and plug the core fittings to prevent coolant leakage inside the vehicle.

4. Inside the vehicle, remove the center console side panels and all ducting from the heater box. Locate the heater core cover on the side of the case and remove the retaining clips and the cover.

5. The heater core can now be removed from the case.

To install:

6. Insert the heater core into the case. Install the heater core cover, making sure the gasket on the cover is properly fitted.

7. Connect the ducting and assemble the console.

8. Connect the heater hoses at the firewall. Fill and bleed the cooling system.

Passat and Corrado

1. This procedure requires removal of the dashboard and air distribution assembly. Disconnect the negative battery cable.

2. Drain the cooling system and disconnect the heater hoses from the firewall.

3. Remove the steering wheel, instrument cluster and trim panel around the cluster.

4. Remove the knee bar from below the dashboard.

5. Remove the cassette storage drawers, if equipped, from the center console. Pull the knobs off the heater controls and remove the radio.

6. Carefully pry out the heater control trim plate and remove the control assembly. Remove the center console trim plate.

7. Carefully pry out the air vents at the ends of the dashboard and remove the glove compartment.

8. Pry off the caps from the screws at each end of the dashboard and remove the bolts.

9. At the upper rear portion of the dashboard, remove the 2 nuts. These can only be seen with the aid of a mirror.

10. Remove the nut at the back of the center console and pull the dashboard slightly out to disconnect the remaining wires. Remove the dashboard.

11. Remove the air distribution assembly and remove the heater core.

To install:

12. If the retaining lugs are broken off, the heater core can be secured in place with screws. Install the heater core and the air distribution assembly. Make sure the seal is in good condition, replace, if necessary.

13. Prior to installing the dashboard, connect all wiring behind it.

14. Install the dashboard and secure it in place with the rear retaining nut.

15. At the upper rear portion of the dashboard, install the 2 retaining nuts.

16. Finally, secure the dash with screws at each end of the dashboard.

17. Install the air vents at the ends of the dashboard and install the glove compartment.

18. Install the center console trim plate. Install the control assembly and the heater control trim plate.

19. Install the cassette storage drawers, if equipped, in the center console.

20. Install the radio, the heater knobs and heater controls.

21. Install the knee bar under the dashboard.

22. Install the steering wheel, instrument cluster and trim panel around the cluster.

23. Connect the heater hoses to the firewall. Fill and bleed the cooling system.

Golf, Jetta and GTI

1. This procedure requires removal of the dashboard and air distribution assembly. Disconnect the negative battery cable.

2. Drain the cooling system and disconnect the heater hoses from the firewall.

3. Properly discharge the air conditioning system using freon recovery equipment.

4. Remove the gear shift knob and boot and remove the center console.

5. Remove the steering wheel.

6. Remove the knee bar from below the dashboard.

7. Remove the steering column support bracket and lower the column.

8. Pull the knobs off the heater controls and remove the control assembly and the radio.

9. Remove the headlight switch and switch blanks to gain access to the screws. Remove the instrument cluster and trim panel around the cluster.

10. Remove the glove compartment.

11. At the firewall, remove the plastic tray and remove the 2 nuts holding the top of the dashboard.

12. Remove the main fuse panel and disconnect the plugs at the back. Disconnect the ground wires.

13. Disconnect any remaining wiring from the dashboard and remove the 4 last screws. Remove the dashboard.

14. Disconnect the ducts and remove the heater housing. Remove the screws and slide the heater core out of the housing.

To install:

15. Install the heater core and make sure the housing seals and gaskets are in good condition. Replace as necessary.

16. Connect the ducts to the heater housing.

17. Connect the wiring to the dashboard. Secure the dashboard in place with the 4 retaining screws; 1 at each end and 1 at each end of the instrument cluster area.

18. Connect the plugs at rear of the main fuse panel and secure it in place. Connect the ground wires.

19. At the firewall, install the plastic tray and install the 2 nuts securing the dashboard at the top.

20. Install the glove compartment.

21. Install the instrument cluster and trim panel around the cluster. Install the headlight switch and switch blanks.

22. Install the radio and control assembly. Install the knobs on the heater controls.

23. Install the steering column support bracket and lower the column.

24. Install the knee bar under the dashboard.

25. Install the steering wheel.

26. Install the center console. Install the gear shift boot and knob.

27. Evacuate and recharge the air conditioner. Fill and bleed the cooling system.

Water Pump

REMOVAL AND INSTALLATION

Except Corrado and Jetta Diesel

1. To drain the cooling system, remove the thermostat housing from under the water pump housing.

2. Raise and safely support the vehicle. Loosen but don't remove the bolts holding the pulley to the water pump.

3. Remove the timing belt cover.

4. Loosen the alternator and/or steering pump as required to remove the water pump drive belt.

5. Remove the water pump pulley. On some vehicles, the crankshaft pulley must also be removed by removing the bolts holding the pulley to the timing belt sprocket.

6. All the bolts are now accessible and the water pump can be removed from its housing.

To install:

7. Be sure to clean the housing before installing the new gasket. Install the pump into the housing and torque the pump-to-housing bolts to 7 ft. lbs. (10 Nm).

8. Install the water pump drive pulley and torque the bolts to 15 ft. lbs. (20 Nm). If the crankshaft drive pulley was removed, install it and torque the bolts to 15 ft. lbs. (20 Nm).

9. Adjust drive belt tension and install the thermostat and housing. Torque the bolts to 7 ft. lbs. (10 Nm).

Corrado

WITHOUT AIR CONDITIONING

The water pump is driven by the same belt that drives the alternator and supercharger. On vehicles with air conditioning, the water pump and steering pump use the same V-belt.

1. To drain the cooling system, remove the thermostat housing from under the water pump housing.

2. Loosen the water pump pulley bolts but don't remove the pulley yet.

3. Install the belt tensioner holding tool VW3191 or equivalent, to compress the tensioner and loosen the belt.

4. Loosen the power steering pump and remove its drive belt.

5. With the water pump pulley removed, the pump bolts are now accessible. Remove the pump.

To install:

6. Clean the housing and use a new gasket when installing the pump. Torque the bolts to 7 ft. lbs. (10 Nm).

7. The water pump and crankshaft pulleys must be aligned. Loosen the outer section bolts and turn the outer section relative to the inner section until the 2 pulleys are aligned; water pump pulley moves in and out. Torque the bolts to 18 ft. lbs. (25 Nm).

8. Remove the belt tensioner tool and complete the reassembly. Torque the thermostat housing bolts to 7 ft. lbs. (10 Nm) and fill the cooling system.

WITH AIR CONDITIONING

1. To drain the cooling system, remove the thermostat housing from under the water pump housing.

2. Raise and safely support the vehicle.

3. Working under the vehicle, loosen but don't remove the bolts holding the pulley to the water pump.

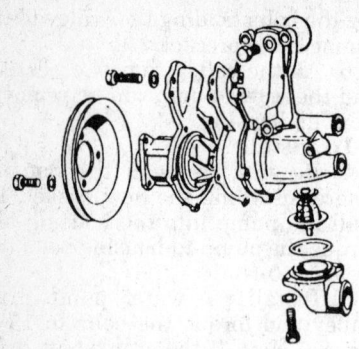

Water pump and thermostat housing — all except Corrado and Jetta Diesel

LOOSEN BOLTS (A) TURN INNER PART (B) TO ALIGN PULLEYS (C)

Water pump pulley alignment — Corrado without air conditioning

4. Loosen the power steering pump and remove the drive belt.

5. Remove the water pump pulley and remove the pump.

To install:

6. Installation is the reverse of removal. Be sure to clean the pump housing before installing the pump with a new gasket. Torque the following:

Water pump-to-housing — 7 ft. lbs. (10 Nm)

Water pump drive pulley — 15 ft. lbs. (20 Nm)

Thermostat housing — 7 ft. lbs. (10 Nm)

Steering pump bolts — 18 ft. lbs. (25 Nm)

Corrado SLC

To remove the main coolant pump, the engine mounts must be unbolted and the engine must be lifted slightly. Do not jack the engine from below, use a hoist and lift from above. Also, a special wrench is required to remove the pump, tool VAG 1590.

1. Disconnect the negative battery cable and remove the plug in the coolant pipe below the intake manifold to drain the cooling system.

2. Disconnect the front exhaust pipe from the catalytic converter.

3. Thread a long 8 x 10mm bolt into the top of the belt tensioner. Tighten the bolt just enough to loosen and remove the accessory drive belt.

4. Remove the distributor cap and wires and the wire guide as an assembly. Attach a lifting yoke to the lifting eyes on the engine.

5. Remove the center bolt from each of the 3 engine mounts and lift the engine as required to gain access to the pump.

6. Use the special tool VAG 1590 to remove the coolant pump pulley bolts and remove the pulley.

7. Remove the bolts and push the engine slightly to the left to remove the pump and O-ring.

To install:

8. Install the pump with a new O-ring and torque the bolts to 15 ft. lbs. (20 Nm). Install the pulley.

9. Set the engine down on the mounts. Make sure the tabs on the front and rear engine mounts fit into the slot in the brackets on the engine. Start all the mount bolts but do not tighten them yet.

10. Shake the engine to settle it in the mounts, then torque the bolts to 44 ft. lbs. (60 Nm).

11. Install the accessory drive belt and remove the bolt from the tensioner.

12. Use new gaskets and nuts and connect the exhaust pipe to the catalytic converter. Torque the nuts to 18 ft. lbs. (25 Nm).

13. Install the drain plug and refill the cooling system. The system holds 10.6 qts. (10L).

14. Connect the battery and run the engine to check for leaks.

Jetta Diesel

On some diesel engines, the belt tension is adjusted with shims between the outer and inner halves of the pulley. On others, the alternator swivels to adjust belt tension.

1. To drain the cooling system, remove the thermostat housing from under the water pump housing.

2. Raise and safely support the vehicle.

3. Working under the vehicle, loosen but don't remove the bolts holding the pulley to the water pump.

4. On vehicles with a movable alternator, loosen the alternator and remove the drive belt.

5. Remove the water pump pulley and remove the pump.

To install:

6. Installation is the reverse of removal. Be sure to clean the pump

housing before installing the new gasket. Torque the following:

Water pump-to-housing — 7 ft. lbs. (10 Nm)

Water pump drive pulley — 15 ft. lbs. (20 Nm)

Thermostat housing — 7 ft. lbs. (10 Nm)

Alternator mounting bolts — 18 ft. lbs. (25 Nm)

Thermostat

REMOVAL AND INSTALLATION

Except Corrado SLC

The thermostat is the lowest point in the cooling system and is on the bottom of the water pump housing. Removing the thermostat is the only way to completely drain the coolant.

1. With a catch pan under the vehicle, loosen the bolts on the thermostat housing.

2. Remove the cap from the overflow bottle and allow the coolant to drain completely.

3. When the coolant is drained, remove the thermostat housing and clean both mating surfaces.

4. When installing, the thermostat spring goes up into the water pump housing and the new O-ring goes onto the thermostat. Torque the bolts to 7 ft. lbs. (10 Nm).

5. Refill the cooling system and check for leaks.

Corrado SLC

The thermostat housing is bolted to the flywheel end of the engine and includes the temperature sensor and 1 or 2 thermo-switches. The switches can be removed by removing the mounting clips. The cooling system drain plug is on the pipe leading from the housing to the other end of the engine. When removing any part from the thermostat housing, always replace the O-ring.

Cooling System Bleeding

WITH BLEEDER SCREW

Set the heat valve in the **WARM** position, start the engine and bring it to normal operating temperature. Run the engine at fast idle and open the venting screw on the thermostat housing until the coolant comes out free of air bubbles. Close the bleeder screw and refill the cooling system.

WITHOUT BLEEDER SCREW

Fill the cooling system, place the heater valve in the **WARM** position, close the pressure cap to the second (fully closed) position. Start the engine and bring to normal operating temperature. Carefully release the pressure cap to the first position and squeeze the upper and lower radiator hoses in a pumping action to allow trapped air to escape through the radiator. Recheck the coolant level and close the pressure cap to its second position.

ENGINE ELECTRICAL

Distributor

REMOVAL

1. Disconnect the coil high tension wire and the connector plug at the distributor. Disconnect vacuum lines, if equipped.
2. Unsnap the cap retainer clips, and remove the cap and static shield as a unit.
3. At the front crankshaft pulley bolt, turn the engine to Top Dead Center (TDC) on No. 1 piston. Make a chalk or paint mark where the rotor points to the rim of the distributor; some vehicles already have a notch there. Also matchmark the distributor to the engine block or head.
4. Remove the bolt and distributor clamp and lift the distributor straight out.

INSTALLATION

Timing Not Disturbed

1. On some vehicles, the distributor engages its drive with an offset slot and is easy to reinstall in the reverse order of removal, even if the crankshaft or camshaft has been turned. Gently rotate the rotor while pushing the distributor into place. Install the hold-down bolt and adjust the ignition timing.
2. On engines with the drive gear on the distributor, make sure the engine is still at TDC and insert the distributor with the matchmarks aligned.

3. Install the hold-down clamp and bolt, connector plug, cap and static shield, and high tension wires.
4. Check and adjust the ignition timing.

Timing Disturbed

1. Rotate the crankshaft to TDC of No. 1 piston.
2. With a suitable tool, turn the oil pump drive so it is parallel with the crankshaft.
3. Install the rotor onto the distributor and align it with the No. 1 mark on the rim of the body.
4. Install the distributor, making sure the rotor still aligns with the mark when the distributor is all the way in.
5. With the distributor installed, install the hold-down clamp and bolt, connector plug, cap and static shield, and high tension wires.
6. Check and adjust the ignition timing.

Ignition Timing

ADJUSTMENT

NOTE: The manufacturer specifies timing, idle speed and CO value all be adjusted together. On some vehicles with Digifant engine management systems, these items are not adjustable. See the underhood sticker for details. There are 2 methods of checking ignition timing. One method is the use of a timing light, the other is the use of diagnostic tool VAG 1367 or equivalent.

1. Run the engine to normal operating temperature, stop engine and connect a tachometer. Using either a timing light or diagnostic tool VAG 1367 or equivalent, connect according to manufacturer's instructions.
2. If equipped, disconnect both plugs from the idle stabilizer and

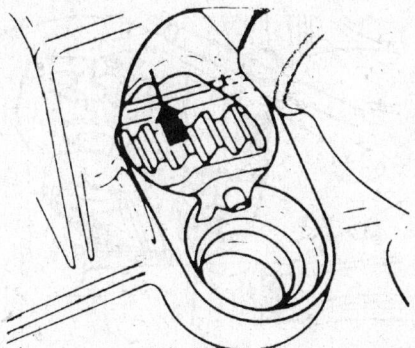

Ignition timing marks located on the flywheel

plug them together. On engines with Digifant engine management systems, with the ignition **ON** but the engine not running, verify that the idle stabilizer valve hums or buzzes. Do not disconnect any vacuum lines from the distributor.
3. Start the engine. On vehicles with Digifant engine management systems, disconnect the blue coolant temperature sensor plug.
4. Turn OFF all electrical equipment and set the idle speed.
5. If using a timing light, remove the timing mark cover from the top of the bell housing and, with the engine running, shine the timing light at the marks on the flywheel.
6. If using the diagnostic tool VAG 1367 or equivalent, observe the analog reading.
7. If adjustment is required, loosen the distributor clamp bolt and rotate the distributor as needed to set the correct timing degree. Stop the engine and reconnect plugs.

Alternator

PRECAUTIONS

• Before doing any work on any electrical system, always stop the engine and disconnect the battery cables.
• Disconnect the battery, engine control unit and ABS control unit, if equipped, before using electric welding equipment on the vehicle.
• Electronic parts and systems can be easily and permanently damaged through careless use of electric welding, charging, soldering or test equipment. Carefully follow manufacturer's instructions when using such equipment.
• If equipped with electronically theft-protected radios, obtain the security code before disconnecting the battery.

BELT TENSION ADJUSTMENT

Except Corrado

1. Loosen both upper alternator bracket bolts.
2. Loosen the lower alternator pivot bolt. This is a long bolt with a 6mm socket head which should be accessible with the proper tool without removing the timing belt shield.
3. Do not use a prybar to tighten the belt. It is easy to gain enough tension pulling the alternator by hand against the belt. Some vehicles have

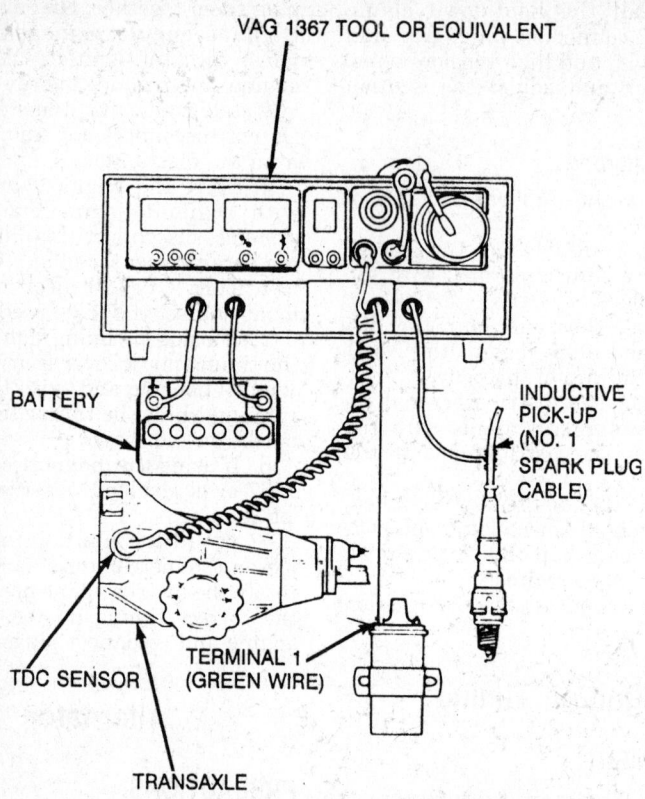

Using diagnostic tool VAG 1367 or equivalent to check ignition timing

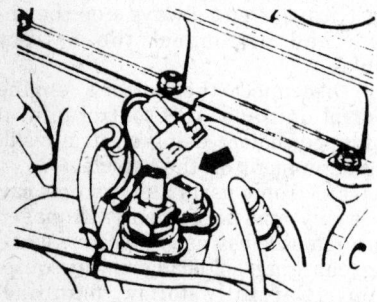

For vehicles equipped with Digifant engine management systems, disconnect the blue coolant temperature sensor plug prior to checking ignition timing

a toothed rack for setting belt tension.

4. Proper belt tension is attained when moderate finger pressure deflects the belt midway between the pulleys about 0.200 in. (5mm).

5. Securely tighten the mounting bolts.

Corrado

This vehicle is equipped with a serpentine ribbed belt which drives all accessories. On models without air conditioning, this belt drives the water pump also. Belt tension is maintained with a spring-loaded belt tension damper and idler pulley. Tension adjustment is maintained automatically by spring force. Before installing the damper onto its mounting bolts, it must be compressed 5 times to evacuate air, using VAG tool 3191 or equivalent.

Corrado SLC

This vehicle is equipped with a serpentine ribbed belt which drives

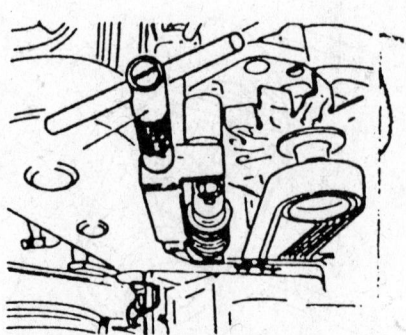

Belt tensioner compressing tool used — Corrado with supercharger

all accessories. Belt tension is maintained with a spring-loaded idler pulley. Tension adjustment is maintained automatically by spring force. To loosen the tension, install a long 8 x 10mm bolt into the hole in the top of the tensioner. Tighten the bolt only as required to remove the belt from the alternator.

REMOVAL AND INSTALLATION

Except Corrado

1. Disconnect the battery cables.
2. Remove the multi-connector plug and/or wires from the alternator and tag them for correct reinstallation.
3. Remove both upper alternator mounting bolts and bracket.
4. Remove the lower alternator pivot bolt. This is a long bolt with a 6mm socket head which should be accessible with the proper tool without removing the timing belt shield. Remove the alternator.
5. Installation is the reverse of removal. When reinstalling the belt, with moderate finger pressure the belt should deflect about 0.200 in. (5mm).

Corrado

1. Disconnect the battery cables.
2. Remove the multi-connector plug and/or wires from the alternator and tag them for correct reinstallation.
3. On supercharged models, remove the belt cover and install the clamping tool 3191 or equivalent, to collapse the automatic belt tensioner.
4. On SLC, install the bolt to move the spring tensioner and relieve the belt tension.
5. Remove the alternator bolts to lift the alternator from the vehicle.
6. Installation is the reverse of removal.

Voltage Regulator

REMOVAL AND INSTALLATION

The voltage regulator on all vehicles is mounted externally on the rear of the alternator. It can be removed without removal or disassembly of the alternator. The alternator field brushes are a part of the regulator and should project no less than 0.200 in. (5mm) from the regulator. If the brushes are not within specification, replace the regulator.

Install 8x10mm bolt to loosen the belt tension — Corrado SLC

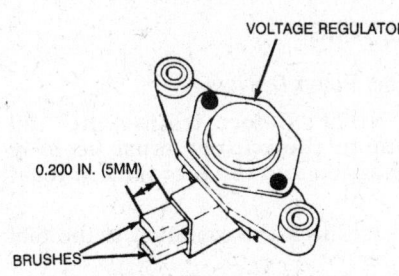

Checking brush protrusion

Starter

REMOVAL AND INSTALLATION

Bosch Starters

NOTE: On some vehicles, the same bolts hold an engine mount and the starter. Additionally some starter bolts hold the engine and transaxle together. Always support the weight of the engine when removing the starter.

1. Disconnect the battery ground cable.
2. Raise and safely support the vehicle.
3. Support the weight of the engine with tool 10-222 or equivalent. Do not jack up the oil pan.
4. Tag and disconnect the wires from the starter.
5. Remove starter mounting bolts and remove the starter.
6. Installation is the reverse of removal. Torque the mounting bolts to 33 ft. lbs. (45 Nm).

Mitsubishi Starters

1. Disconnect the battery ground cable.

2. Raise and safely support the vehicle.
3. Support the weight of the engine with tool 10-222 or equivalent. Do not jack up the oil pan.
4. Remove the engine/transaxle cover plate.
5. Unbolt and remove the starter side motor mount and carrier.
6. Disconnect and mark the starter wiring.
7. Remove starter mounting bolts and the starter.
8. Installation is the reverse of removal. Torque the mounting bolts to 33 ft. lbs. (45 Nm).

Diesel Glow Plugs

REMOVAL AND INSTALLATION

1. Remove the busbar connecting the glow plugs and determine which plugs need replacement.
2. Remove the defective plugs.
3. When installing new plugs, torque to 22 ft. lbs. (30 Nm).

NOTE: Diesel glow plugs have an air gap much like a spark plug to prevent overheating of the plug. Over-torquing the glow plug will close the gap and cause the plug to burn out.

TESTING

1. Disconnect the engine temperature sensor.
2. Connect a test light between No. 4 cylinder glow plug and ground. The glow plugs are connected by a flat, coated busbar, located near the bottom of the cylinder head.
3. Turn the ignition key **ON**; the test light should light, then go out after 10-30 seconds.
4. If there is no voltage, possible problems include a blown fuse, lack of power to or from the glow plug relay (check wiring) or the relay itself.
5. To test each plug individually, disconnect the wire and remove the busbar from the glow plugs.
6. Connect an ohmmeter to each glow plug connection or use a test light. Each plug must have continuity to ground. The engine will probably start with one defective glow plug, but it will produce excessive smoke.

EMISSION CONTROLS

Emission Warning Lamps

RESETTING

On models so equipped, the OXS warning light on the dash will turn on when it is time to replace the oxygen sensor. This is usually at 30,000 mile intervals. Under the hood near the wiper motor, is a black box with the speedometer cable connected to it. The mileage counter turns on the warning light. To reset the counter, find the white button on the box and push it in with a pen, listening (feeling) for the click.

GASOLINE FUEL SYSTEM

Fuel System Service Precautions

- Do not allow fuel spray or fuel vapors to come into contact with a heating element or open flame. Do not smoke while working on the fuel system.
- Always disconnect the negative battery cable unless the repair or test procedure requires that battery voltage be applied.
- Always relieve the fuel system pressure prior to disconnecting any fitting or fuel line connection.
- To control fuel spray when relieving system pressure, place a shop towel around the fitting prior to loosening to catch the spray. Ensure that all fuel spillage is quickly wiped up and that all fuel soaked rags are deposited into a proper fire safety container.
- Always keep a dry chemical (Class B) fire extinguisher near the work area.
- Always use a backup wrench when loosening and tightening fuel line fittings. Always follow the proper torque specifications.
- Do not re-use fuel system gaskets and O-rings, replace with new ones. Do not substitute fuel hose where fuel pipe is installed.

RELIEVING FUEL SYSTEM PRESSURE

On CIS systems, fuel pressure can be vented at the cold start injector line, either at the fuel distributor end or the injector end. Lay a rag over the fitting and use a socket or line wrench to crack the fitting.

On Digifant systems, pressure can be vented at the fuel pump switch in front of the throttle body. Lay a rag over the switch and loosen the clamp.

Fuel Tank

REMOVAL AND INSTALLATION

Except Fox

1. Disconnect the negative battery cable. Remove the access panel under the rear seat or in the luggage compartment and disconnect the gauge sending unit wiring and hoses.
2. Raise and safely support the vehicle and drain the fuel tank.
3. On Cabriolet, remove the right rear inner fender and disconnect the breather hose from the filler. Remove but do not disconnect the gravity valve.
4. Detach the fuel pump bracket from the body and lower the pump enough to disconnect the fuel hoses from the tank.
5. On Cabriolet, the rear axle must be dropped out of the way. Disconnect the brake hydraulic hoses at both sides of the rear axle.
6. Detach the rear axle from the body on both sides and let it hang on the parking brake cable guides.
7. Unhook the muffler supports and pull the large hose from the filler neck.
8. Support the tank, loosen the straps and carefully lower the tank out of the vehicle.
   To install:
9. If a new tank is being installed, glue new foam strips to the tank in the same location as the old ones. Position the tank and connect the wiring and hoses to the sending unit.
10. Secure the tank in place with the straps and connect all hoses. Position the clamps so they do not contact the body.
11. Coat the tank with a rust protector or undercoating.
12. Install the rear axle, connect the hydraulic lines and bleed the brakes. Tighten the tank strap bolts to 17 ft. lbs. (23 Nm).

Fox

1. Disconnect the negative battery cable. Remove the access panel under the rear seat or in the luggage compartment and disconnect the gauge sending unit wiring and hoses.
2. Raise and safely support the vehicle; drain the fuel tank.
3. Disconnect the fuel filler hose.
4. Support the tank, loosen the straps and carefully lower the tank out of the vehicle.
5. Installation is the reverse of removal. Tighten the tank strap bolts to 17 ft. lbs. (23 Nm).

Fuel Filter

REMOVAL AND INSTALLATION

On the Digifant system, the fuel filter is a lifetime unit and only needs to be changed in the event of contamination. It is mounted under the vehicle, near the rear axle. The pump, accumulator, filter and reservoir are all part of a single assembly, but the filter can be removed separately.

On the CIS system, the fuel filter is mounted under the hood, sometimes on the fuel distributor. To make the job easier, open the clips holding the

air filter housing and lift the whole assembly.

1. Disconnect the negative battery cable.
2. On vehicles with the Digifant system, raise and safely support the vehicle.
3. Relieve the fuel system pressure.
4. Remove the fuel lines, the mounting bracket nut and the filter.
5. Installation is the reverse of removal. Be sure to use the new sealing rings and torque the fuel lines to the filter to 14 ft. lbs. (20 Nm).

Electric Fuel Pump

TESTING

Fuel Pump Delivery

NOTE: Before testing the fuel pump, the battery must be fully charged and the fuel tank at least ¼ full.

1. Check the condition of the fuel filter.
2. Disconnect the high tension terminal from the ignition coil at the distributor and securely ground it.
3. Disconnect the fuel return fuel line and hold it in a measuring

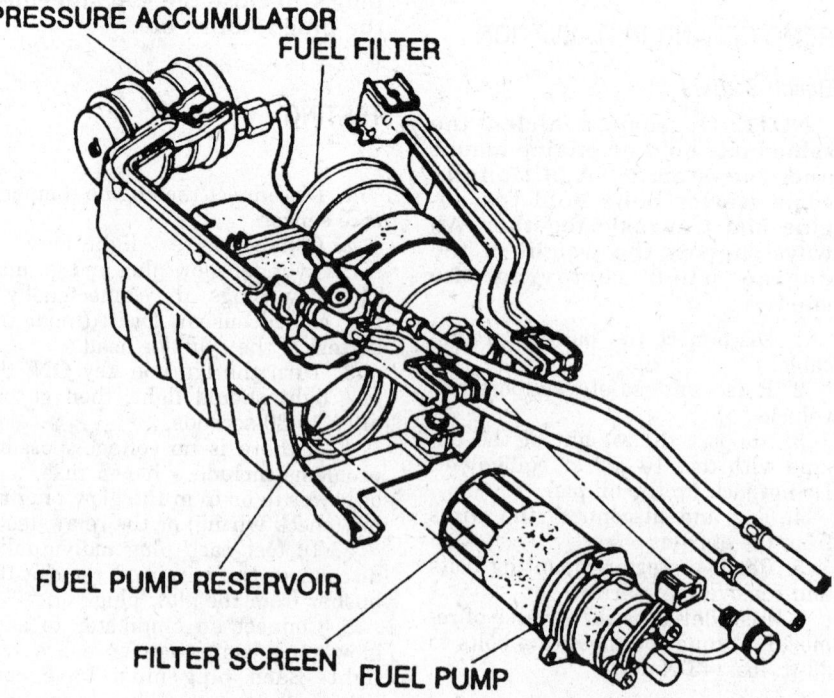

Fuel pump and reservoir assembly — Digifant system

PRESSURE ACCUMULATOR
FUEL FILTER
FUEL PUMP RESERVOIR
FILTER SCREEN
FUEL PUMP

container with a capacity of 1 qt. (1000cc).

4. Have an assistant run the starter for 30 seconds while watching the quantity of fuel delivered. The minimum allowable flow is $9/16$ qt. (760cc) in 30 seconds.

5. If the flow is below specification, check the delivery of the fuel transfer pump, which is mounted with the gauge sending unit in the tank.

6. Under the rear seat or under the luggage compartment, remove the cover to expose the hoses and wires to the pump/sending unit.

7. Disconnect the output hose from the tank unit and plug it. Install a temporary fuel line and put the other end into the measuring container.

8. Have an assistant operate the starter for 10 seconds and measure the fuel delivered. The specification is about 10 oz. (300cc).

9. If the transfer pump is good, check for a dirty fuel filter, blocked lines or blocked fuel tank strainer, if equipped. If all of these are in good condition but the quantity measured is Step 4 is low, replace the main pump.

REMOVAL AND INSTALLATION

Except Corrado SLC

1. The main fuel pump is located under the vehicle in front of the rear axle or in front of the tank on the right side. Disconnect the negative battery cable.

2. Raise and safely support the vehicle.

3. Disconnect the electrical connector.

4. Relieve the fuel system pressure.

5. Remove the mounting bolts and the fuel pump.

6. Installation is the reverse of removal. Be sure to use new sealing rings and/or gaskets.

Corrado SLC

1. The fuel pump and gauge sending unit are all one assembly. They are mounted inside the fuel tank and are accessible from inside the vehicle. Disconnect the negative battery cable.

2. Remove the luggage compartment carpet and remove the access plate in the floor.

3. Label and disconnect the wiring and hoses.

4. Loosen and remove the flange nut and the O-ring.

5. Turn the pump counterclockwise to remove the pump and gauge sending unit.

6. Installation is the reverse of removal. Make sure the marks on the flange and fuel tank are aligned.

Transfer Pump

REMOVAL AND INSTALLATION

Except Corrado SLC

1. Disconnect the negative battery cable.

2. Under the rear seat or in the rear of the vehicle, pull back the carpet and remove the access plate from the floor (3 screws).

3. Disconnect the electrical connector and remove the fuel hoses from the sending unit.

4. Unscrew the cap and carefully lift the sending unit from the fuel tank. Note the orientation of the float in the tank.

5. Remove the transfer pump from the sending unit.

6. Installation is the reverse of removal. Be sure the float points the same way and use a new O-ring at the sending unit cap.

Fuel Injector

REMOVAL AND INSTALLATION

CIS-E

1. Relieve the pressure from the system.

2. Using a fuel injector removal tool, pry the injectors up out of the head. A spray lubricant can help release stuck injectors.

3. Hold the fuel line fitting with a line wrench and unscrew the injector.

4. Installation is the reverse of removal. Lightly lubricate the rubber rings.

Digifant

The electric injectors are held in place by the rail and cannot be removed separately.

Except Corrado SLC

1. Disconnect the negative battery cable.

2. Relieve the pressure from the fuel system.

3. Dismount the idle stabilizer valve and lay it aside.

4. Remove the intake manifold supports and cylinder head cover.

5. Unplug the wiring harness end connector and pry wiring guide away from the fuel distributor retainers.

6. Remove the fuel distributor retaining bolts and remove the rail, wiring guide and injectors as an assembly.

7. Installation is the reverse of removal.

Corrado SLC

1. Remove the ignition cap, wires and wire guide as an assembly.

2. Label and disconnect the wiring and hoses and remove the air intake duct with the mass air sensor.

3. Label and disconnect the wiring and hoses as required to remove the upper intake manifold.

4. Disconnect the wiring and the fuel supply and return hoses from the fuel rail. Disconnect the vacuum line from the pressure regulator.

5. Remove the bolts and remove the fuel rail and injectors as an assembly. It may be necessary to gently pry the injectors out of the ports.

To install:

6. Lightly lubricate the O-rings and fit the injectors into the ports. Secure the rail with the bolts.

7. Connect the wiring, fuel hoses and vacuum line.

8. Install the intake manifold with a new gasket and torque the bolts to 18 ft. lbs. (25 Nm).

9. Connect the wiring, hoses and control cables and install the air duct with the air mass sensor.

10. Install the ignition components and run the engine to check for leaks.

DRIVE AXLE

Halfshaft

REMOVAL AND INSTALLATION

NOTE: When loosening or tightening axle nuts, make sure the vehicle is on the ground. Axle nut torque is high enough that attempting to loosen it may cause the vehicle to fall off the jackstands.

1. With the vehicle on the ground, remove the front axle nut.

2. Raise and safely support vehicle and remove the front wheels.

3. Remove the socket head bolts retaining the halfshaft to the transaxle flange.

4. Separate the strut from the control arm:

a. On Fox, matchmark the ball joint to the control arm and remove the nuts to disconnect the ball joint from the control arm.

b. On Passat and Corrado, remove the bolts securing the ball joint to the control arm.

c. On all other vehicles, remove the ball joint clamping bolt and push the control arm down, away from the ball joint.

5. Remove the transaxle side of the halfshaft from the drive flange and secure it out of the way. Do not let it hang unsupported.

6. Push the halfshaft out of the hub. A wheel puller may be required.

To install:

7. Fit the halfshaft to the drive flange and install the bolts. It is not necessary to torque them yet.

8. Apply a thread locking compound to the outer ¼ in. of the spline. Slip the spline through the hub and loosely install a new axle nut.

9. Assemble the front suspension, being careful to align the matchmarks.

a. On Fox, torque the ball joint-to-control arm nuts to 47 ft. lbs. (65 Nm).

b. On Passat and Corrado, torque the ball joint bolts to 26 ft. lbs. (35 Nm).

c. On all other models, torque the ball joint clamping bolt to 37 ft. lbs. (50 Nm).

10. Install the wheel and hold it to keep the axle from turning. Torque the inner axle bolts to 33 ft. lbs. (45 Nm).

11. With the vehicle on the ground, torque the axle nut:

Fox and Cabriolet — 175 ft. lbs. (240 Nm)

Golf, Jetta and Passat — 195 ft. lbs. (265 Nm)

Corrado with supercharger — 195 ft. lbs. (265 Nm)

Corrado SLC — 66 ft. lbs. (90 Nm) plus 45 degrees

12. Check and adjust the front wheel alignment.

CV-Joint/Boot

REMOVAL AND INSTALLATION

1. Raise and safely support the vehicle and remove the halfshaft.

2. Pry open and remove the boot clamps with a pair of wire cutters.

3. With the halfshaft securely clamped in a vise, the outer CV-joint and boot can be removed by sharply

rapping out on the joint with a plastic hammer. The joint will snap off the circlip and slide off the axle.

4. To remove the inner joint, remove the circlip from the center and slide the joint and boot off the axle.

To install:

5. Always replace both circlips and make sure the CV-joint is clean before installation. Wrap a piece of black electrical tape around the shaft splines and slip the inner clamp and the boot onto the shaft.

6. Remove the tape and install the dished washer with the concave side out. On the outer joint, install the thrust washer and a new circlip.

7. To install the outer joint, place it onto the spline and carefully tap straight in on the end with a plastic hammer. The joint will click into place over the circlip.

8. To install the inner joint, slide it onto the spline and push in enough to allow the circlip to fit into the groove in the axle shaft.

9. Install the inner clamp on the boot and fill the boot with special CV-joint grease. Do not use any other type of grease.

10. On the inner joint, stick the gasket to the joint before installing the halfshaft into the vehicle. Install the outer boot clamp and install the halfshaft.

Front Steering Knuckle

REMOVAL AND INSTALLATION

On Fox, the strut must be removed but a spring compressor is not needed. On all models, the hub and bearing are pressed into the knuckle and the bearing cannot be reused once the hub has been removed.

NOTE: When loosening or tightening axle nuts, make sure the vehicle is on the ground. Axle nut torque is high enough that attempting to loosen it may cause the vehicle to fall off the jack stands.

1. With the vehicle on the ground, remove the front axle nut.

2. Raise and safely support the vehicle and remove the front wheels. On Fox, remove the strut.

3. Detach the brake line from the strut and remove the caliper. Hang it from the body with wire.

4. Remove the caliper carrier and brake rotor.

5. Remove the cotter pin and nut and press out the tie rod end. A small puller is required.

6. Remove the ball joint clamp bolt and push the control arm down to disengage the ball joint.

7. Front wheel camber is set with eccentric washers on the bolts holding the bearing housing to the strut. Clean and mark the position of these washers so they can be reinstalled in the same position.

8. Remove the bolts and take the knuckle and bearing housing off the strut.

To install:

9. Fit the knuckle to the strut and install the bolts. Align the marks and torque the nuts to 70 ft. lbs. (95 Nm).

10. Make sure the axle splines are clean and apply a bead of thread locking compound to the outer portion. Slide the axle into the hub and install a new axle nut. Do not torque it yet.

11. Fit the lower ball joint in place and install the clamp bolt. Torque it to 37 ft. lbs. (50 Nm).

12. Connect the tie rod and torque the nut to 26 ft. lbs. (35 Nm), then tighten as required to install a new cotter pin.

13. Install the brake disc and caliper. Torque the carrier bolts to 92 ft. lbs. (125 Nm) and the caliper guide bolts to 26 ft. lbs. (35 Nm). Secure the brake line in place.

14. With the wheel installed and the vehicle on the ground, torque the axle nut:

Cabriolet and Fox — 175 ft. lbs. (237 Nm)

Passat, Corrado, Golf and Jetta — 195 ft. lbs. (265 Nm)

Front Wheel Bearing

REMOVAL AND INSTALLATION

1. Raise and safely support the vehicle and remove the strut or steering knuckle.

2. To remove the hub, support the strut or knuckle assembly in an arbor press with the hub facing down.

3. Use a proper size arbor that will fit through the bearing and press the hub out.

4. If the inner bearing race stayed on the hub, clamp the hub in a vise and use a bearing puller to remove it.

5. On the knuckle, remove the splash shield and internal snaprings from the bearing housing.

6. With the knuckle in the same pressing position, press the bearing out.

7. Clean the bearing housing and hub with a wire brush and inspect all parts. Replace parts that have been distorted or discolored from heat. If

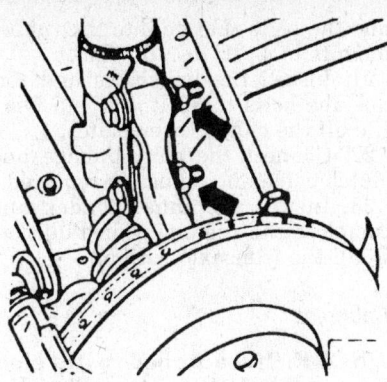

Camber adjusting eccentric washers

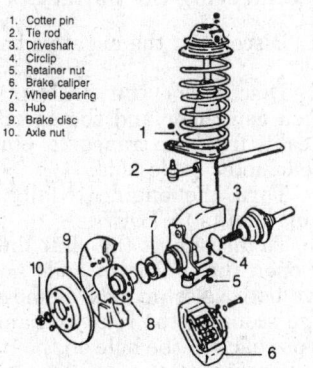

1. Cotter pin
2. Tie rod
3. Driveshaft
4. Circlip
5. Retainer nut
6. Brake caliper
7. Wheel bearing
8. Hub
9. Brake disc
10. Axle nut

Front suspension components — Fox

the hub is not absolutely perfect where it contacts the inner bearing race, the new bearing will fail quickly.

To install:

8. The new bearing is pressed in from the hub side. Install the snapring and support the bearing housing on the press.

9. Using the old bearing as a press tool, press the new bearing into the housing up against the snapring. Make sure the press tool contacts only the outer race of the bearing.

10. Install the outer snapring and splash shield.

11. Support the inner race on the press and press the hub into the bearing. Make sure the inner race is supported or the bearing fail quickly.

12. Install the strut or knuckle and be sure to torque the axle nut before allowing the vehicle to roll.

Rear Axle Shafts/Stub Axles

REMOVAL AND INSTALLATION

1. Raise and safely support the vehicle and remove the rear wheels.

2. On drum brakes, insert a small pry tool through one of the wheel bolt holes and push the adjusting wedge up. On disc brakes, remove the caliper and carrier. Hang the caliper from the spring with wire.

3. Remove the grease cap, cotter pin, locknut, adjusting nut, thrust washer, wheel bearing and brake drum or disc.

4. On drum brakes, disconnect and plug the brake line.

5. Remove the brake backing plate, with the brakes attached and the stub axle.

To install:

6. Install the back plate and stub axle and torque the bolts:

Stub axle/back plate on Golf and Jetta — 52 ft. lbs. (70 Nm)

Stub axle/back plate on all others — 44 ft. lbs. (60 Nm)

7. When reinstalling the wheel bearing nut, the thrust washer must still move with a small pry tool. Don't forget to bleed the drum brakes.

8. On vehicles with rear disc brakes, torque the caliper bolts to 48 ft. lbs. (65 Nm).

MANUAL TRANSAXLE

Transaxle Assembly

REMOVAL AND INSTALLATION

Passat and Corrado

NOTE: If equipped with electronically theft-protected radio, obtain the security code before disconnecting the battery.

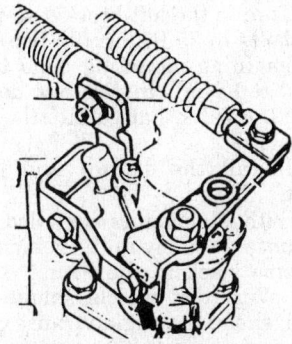

Cable shift linkage — Passat and Corrado transaxle; the relay lever is on the left

1. Disconnect the negative battery cable.

2. On Corrado with supercharger, remove the intercooler tubing.

3. Disconnect the backup light switch connector and the speedometer cable from the transaxle, plug the speedometer cable hole.

4. Remove the clutch slave cylinder without disconnecting the hydraulic line. Hang the cylinder from the body with wire.

5. On the cable shift linkage, remove the backup light switch bracket. Disconnect the cable from the relay lever but remove the gearshift lever with the cable still attached. Remove the cable support and set the cables aside.

6. If necessary, remove the intake hose from the air flow sensor.

7. Remove the upper transaxle-to-engine bolts.

8. Raise and safely support the vehicle and remove the front wheels. Connect the engine sling tool VW-10-222A or equivalent, to the loop in the cylinder head and just take the weight of the engine off the mounts. On 16V engine, the idle stabilizer valve must be removed to attach the tool. Do not try to support the engine from below.

9. Remove the drain plug and drain the oil from the transaxle. Dispose of the oil properly.

10. Remove the starter and front mount.

11. Remove the 3 bolts from the right side mount, between engine and firewall.

12. Remove the large center bolt from the left side transaxle mount. On vehicles with ABS, this bolt can be reached by removing the cooling system overflow bottle.

13. Remove the radiator fan shroud and fan as an assembly.

14. Remove the long transaxle support bracket which connects the front and rear mounts on the left side.

15. Remove the heatshield for the right side inner CV-joint.

16. Disconnect the halfshafts from the output flanges and hang them from the body.

17. Remove the left rear transaxle mount. It may be necessary to push the engine/transaxle rearward to get the lower bolt out.

18. Lower the transaxle slightly.

19. Remove the bell housing cover and position a jack under the transaxle.

20. Remove the last transaxle-to-engine bolts and gently pry the transaxle away from the engine. Lower it carefully from the vehicle.

To install:

21. Press the clutch release lever towards the transaxle housing and secure it with a pin or 8mm bolt.

22. Coat the input shaft lightly with molybdenum grease and carefully fit the transaxle in place. If necessary, put the transaxle in any gear and turn an output flange to align the input shaft spline with the clutch spline.

23. Install the engine-to-transaxle bolts and torque to 59 ft. lbs. (80 Nm).

24. When installing the mounts to the transaxle, torque the left and rear bracket-to-transaxle bolts to 18 ft. lbs. (25 Nm). Torque the remaining mount-to-transaxle bolts to 44 ft. lbs. (60 Nm). Don't forget the balance weight. Install but do not torque the bolts that go into the rubber mounts.

25. Install the starter and front mount.

26. With all mounts installed and the transaxle safely in the vehicle, allow some slack in the lifting equipment. With the vehicle safely supported, shake the engine/transaxle as a unit to settle it in the mounts. Torque all mounting bolts, starting at the rear and working forward. Torque the bolts that go into the rubber transaxle mounts to 44 ft. lbs. (60 Nm).

27. Install the halfshafts and torque the bolts to 33 ft. lbs. (45 Nm). Install the heatshield.

28. Remove the pin or bolt from the release lever and install the clutch slave cylinder. Torque the bolts to 18 ft. lbs. (25 Nm).

29. Lubricate the shift linkage lightly with molybdenum grease and install it. Torque the bolts to 18 ft. lbs. (25 Nm). Adjust the linkage as required.

30. Install the radiator fan assembly and connect the wiring.

31. Complete the installation and refill the transaxle with oil.

Jetta and Golf

NOTE: If equipped with electronically theft-protected radio, obtain the security code before disconnecting the battery.

1. Disconnect the negative battery cable.

2. Disconnect the backup light switch connector and the speedometer cable from the transaxle; plug the speedometer cable hole.

3. Remove the upper engine-to-transaxle bolts.

4. Remove the 3 right side engine mount bolts, between engine and firewall.

5. To disconnect the shift linkage, pry open the ball joint ends and remove the shift and relay shaft rods.

6. Remove the center bolt from the left transaxle mount.

7. Raise and safely support the vehicle and remove the front wheels. Connect the engine sling tool VW-10-222A or equivalent, to the loop in the cylinder head and just take the weight of the engine off the mounts. On 16V engine, the idle stabilizer valve must be removed to attach the tool. Do not try to support the engine from below.

8. Remove the drain plug and drain the oil from the transaxle. Dispose of the oil properly.

9. Remove the left inner fender liner.

10. Disconnect the halfshafts from the inner drive flanges and hang them from the body.

11. Remove the clutch cover plate and the small plate behind the right halfshaft flange.

12. Remove the starter and front engine mount.

13. Disconnect the clutch cable and remove it from the transaxle housing.

14. Remove the remaining transaxle mount bolts and mounts.

15. Place a jack under the transaxle and remove the last bolts holding it to the engine. Carefully pry the transaxle away from the engine and lower it from the vehicle.

To install:

16. Coat the input shaft lightly with molybdenum grease and carefully fit the transaxle in place. If necessary, put the transaxle in any gear and turn an output flange to align the input shaft spline with the clutch spline.

17. Install the engine-to-transaxle bolts and torque to 55 ft. lbs. (75 Nm).

18. When installing the mounts to the transaxle, torque the rear bracket-to-engine bolts and the transaxle support bolts to 18 ft. lbs. (25 Nm). Torque the left bracket-to-transaxle bolts to 25 ft. lbs. (35 Nm) and the remaining mounting bolts to 44 ft. lbs. (60 Nm). Install but do not torque the bolts that go into the rubber mounts.

19. Install the starter and front mount.

20. With all mounts installed and the transaxle safely in the vehicle, allow some slack in the lifting equipment. With the vehicle safely supported, shake the engine/transaxle as a unit to settle it in the mounts. Torque all mounting bolts, starting at the rear and working forward. Tor-

que the bolts that go into the rubber mounts to 44 ft. lbs. (60 Nm).

21. Install the halfshafts and torque the bolts to 33 ft. lbs. (45 Nm). Install the clutch cover plates.

22. Connect the shift linkage and clutch cable and adjust as required.

23. Install the inner fender and complete the remaining installation. Refill the transaxle with oil.

Cabriolet

NOTE: If equipped with electronically theft-protected radio, obtain the security code before disconnecting the battery.

1. Disconnect the negative battery cable.

2. Disconnect the backup light switch connector and the speedometer cable from the transaxle, plug the speedometer cable hole.

3. Turn the engine to align the timing marks to TDC.

4. To disconnect the shift linkage, pry open the ball joint ends and remove both selector rods. Remove the pin, disconnect the relay rod and put the pin back in the hole on the rod for safe keeping.

5. Raise and safely support the vehicle and remove the front wheels. Connect the engine sling tool VW-10-222A or equivalent, to the loop in the cylinder head and just take the weight of the engine off the mounts. On 16V engine, the idle stabilizer valve must be removed to attach the tool. Do not try to support the engine from below.

6. Remove the drain plug and drain the oil from the transaxle. Dispose of the oil properly.

7. Detach the clutch cable from the linkage and remove it from the transaxle case.

8. Remove the starter and front engine mount.

9. Remove the small cover behind the right halfshaft flange and remove the clutch cover plate.

10. Disconnect the halfshafts from the drive flanges and hang them up with wire.

11. Remove the long center bolt from the left side transaxle mount.

12. Remove the entire rear mount assembly from the body and differential housing.

13. Lower the engine hoist enough to let the left mount free of the body and remove the mount from the transaxle.

14. Place a transaxle support jack under the transaxle, remove all the transaxle-to-engine bolts and carefully pry the transaxle away from the

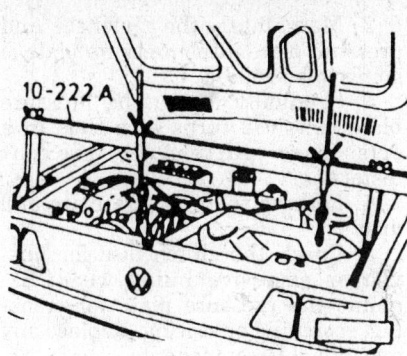

Supporting the engine to remove the transaxle

engine. Lower the transaxle from under the vehicle.

To install:

15. Coat the input shaft lightly with molybdenum grease and carefully fit the transaxle in place. If necessary, put the transaxle in any gear and turn an output flange to align the input shaft spline with the clutch spline.

16. Install the engine-to-transaxle bolts and torque to 55 ft. lbs. (75 Nm).

17. When installing the mounts to the transaxle, torque the bolts to 33 ft. lbs. (45 Nm). Install but do not torque the bolts that go into the rubber mounts.

18. Install the starter and front mount.

19. With all mounts installed and the transaxle safely in the vehicle, allow some slack in the lifting equipment. With the vehicle safely supported, shake the engine/transaxle as a unit to settle it in the mounts. Torque all mounting bolts, starting at the rear and working forward. Torque the bolts that go into the rubber mounts to 25 ft. lbs. (35 Nm). Torque the front mount bolts to 38 ft. lbs. (52 Nm).

20. Install the halfshafts and torque the bolts to 33 ft. lbs. (45 Nm). Install the clutch cover plates.

21. Connect the shift linkage and clutch cable and adjust as required.

22. Complete the remaining installation and refill the transaxle with oil.

Fox

NOTE: If equipped with electronically theft-protected radio, obtain the security code before disconnecting the battery.

1. Raise and safely support the vehicle and remove the front wheels.

2. Remove the drain plug and drain the oil from the transaxle. Dispose of the oil properly.

3. Disconnect the battery ground cable.

4. Disconnect the clutch cable.

5. Disconnect the exhaust pipe from the manifold.

6. Disconnect the speedometer cable and backup light switch.

7. Remove the bolt on the shift linkage, pry the control rod joint off and push the shift linkage coupling off the transaxle.

8. Detach the halfshafts from the transaxle.

9. Remove the starter and clutch cover plate.

10. Remove the exhaust pipe bracket from the transaxle and remove the pipe at the catalytic converter.

11. Support the transaxle with a jack.

12. Remove the transaxle crossmember and front mount bolts.

13. Remove the engine-to-transaxle bolts.

14. Carefully pry the transaxle away from the engine and lower it from the vehicle.

To install:

15. Coat the input shaft lightly with molybdenum grease and carefully fit the transaxle in place. If necessary, put the transaxle in any gear and turn an output flange to align the input shaft spline with the clutch spline.

16. Install the engine-to-transaxle bolts and torque to 40 ft. lbs. (55 Nm).

17. Torque the crossmember-to-body bolts to 47 ft. lbs. (65 Nm).

18. Install the rubber mount and torque the bracket bolts to 18 ft. lbs. (25 Nm) and the mount-to-body bolts to 80 ft. lbs. (110 Nm).

19. Connect the halfshafts to the drive flanges and torque the bolts to 33 ft. lbs. (45 Nm).

20. Install the remaining parts and adjust the clutch and shift linkage as required. Refill the transaxle with oil.

SHIFT LINKAGE ADJUSTMENT

Passat and Corrado

This procedure requires special tools VW 3193 and VW3192/1 or equivalent.

1. Put the transaxle in neutral, remove the shift knob and boot.

2. Loosen the nut and bolt connecting the cables to the shift levers so the cables move freely.

3. Loosen bolt **C** and install the adjusting tool.

4. Pivot the locating pin for the tool under the bearing plate and tighten nut **D**.

5. Push the shifter into the detent and all the way to the left and tighten the slide with bolt **E**.

6. Push the shifter all the way to the right, into the detent, and tighten bolt **C**.

7. At the other end of the cables, install the special wedge and pin so there is no play in the lever but the lever is not raised.

8. The linkage is now set in place. Tighten the cables to the levers and remove the tools to check shifter operation.

Golf and Jetta

This procedure requires special tool VW 3104 or equivalent.

1. Put the transaxle in neutral.

2. Under the vehicle, loosen the clamp on the shifter rod so the shifter moves freely on the rod.

3. Remove the shifter knob and the boot.

4. Position the gauge alignment tool VW-3104 or equivalent, on the shifting mechanism and lock it in place.

5. Align the shift rod with the selector lever and torque the clamp to 19 ft. lbs. (26 Nm). The shifter linkage must not be under load during the adjustment.

6. Check shifter operation.

Cabriolet

1. Remove the shifter knob and boot.

2. Align the holes of the lever housing plate with the holes of the lever bearing plate. Check shifter operation.

3. If further adjustment is required, working under the vehicle remove the boot and loosen the shift rod clamp so the shifter moves easily on the rod.

4. Center the shift finger (fore and aft) in the lockout plate and move the shifter so the finger is disengaged from the lock out by {169}/16 in. (15mm).

5. Tighten the rod clamp to 14 ft. lbs. (20 Nm) and check shifter operation. If operation is spongy or binding, readjust the lock out finger to 1/2 in. (13mm).

Fox

1. Shift into neutral.

2. Remove the gear shift lever knob and shift boot.

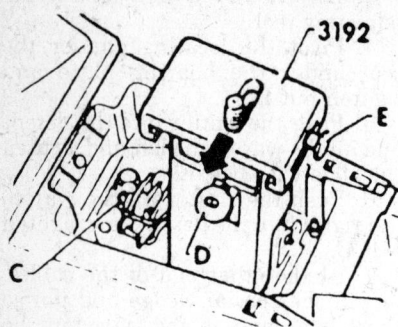

Passat and Corrado shifter adjustment

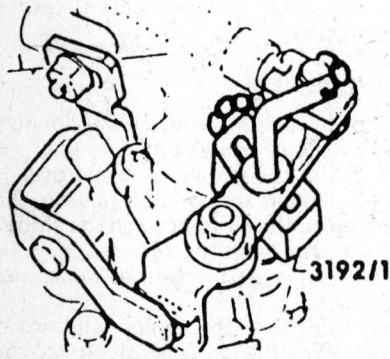

Passat and Corrado adjusting wedge in place

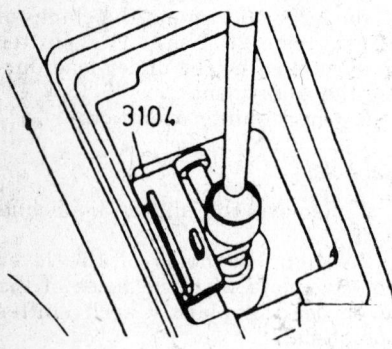

Golf and Jetta shifter adjusting tool

CLUTCH

Clutch Assembly

REMOVAL AND INSTALLATION

Jetta, Golf and Cabriolet

1. Raise and safely support the vehicle and remove the transaxle.
2. Attach a toothed flywheel holder tool VW-558 or equivalent, to the flywheel and gradually loosen the flywheel-to-pressure plate bolts a few turns at a time. Use a crisscross pattern to prevent distortion.
3. Remove the flywheel and the clutch disc.
4. Use a small prybar to remove the release plate retaining ring. Remove the release plate.

To install:

5. Use new bolts to attach the pressure plate to the crankshaft. Use a thread locking compound and torque the bolts in a diagonal pattern to 72 ft. lbs. (100 Nm).
6. Lightly lubricate the clutch disc splines, release plate contact surface and pushrod socket with multi-purpose grease. Install the release plate, retaining ring and clutch disc.
7. Install a centering tool VW-547 or equivalent, to align the clutch disc.
8. Install the flywheel, tightening the bolts 1-2 turns at a time in a crisscross pattern to prevent distortion. Torque the bolts to 14 ft. lbs. (20 Nm).
9. Remove the alignment tool, reinstall the transaxle and adjust the clutch cable.

Fox, Passat and Corrado

1. Raise and safely support the vehicle and remove the transaxle.

2. Matchmark the flywheel and pressure plate if the pressure plate is going to be reused.
3. Gradually loosen the pressure plate bolts 1-2 turns at a time in a crisscross pattern to prevent distortion.
4. Remove the pressure plate and disc.
5. Check the clutch disc for uneven or excessive lining wear. Examine the pressure plate for cracking, scorching or scoring. Replace any questionable components.

To install:

6. Install the clutch disc and pressure plate with the springs on the disc towards the plate. Use an alignment tool to keep the clutch disc centered.
7. Gradually tighten the pressure plate-to-flywheel bolts in a crisscross pattern. Tighten the bolts to 18 ft. lbs. (24 Nm).
8. Install the clutch release bearing.
9. Install the transaxle.

PEDAL HEIGHT/FREE-PLAY ADJUSTMENT

Hydraulic Clutch

If equipped with hydraulic clutch linkage, the slave cylinder has a bleeder screw to purge air from the system. The clutch pedal linkage rod is adjustable to maintain proper pedal height of ⅜in. (10mm) above brake pedal.

Adjustable Clutch

On cable operated clutches with an adjustable cable, special tool US5043 or equivalent, is available to make it easier to determine proper adjustment. The tool is a simple go or no-go gauge, but proper adjustment can be accomplished without it.

1. Depress the clutch pedal several times.

3. Loosen the clamp nuts and check that shift finger slides freely on the shift rod.
4. Move the gear shift lever to the right side, between 3rd and 4th gear position. The gear shift lever should remain perpendicular to the ball housing.
5. With the inner shift lever in neutral and the gear shift lever between 3rd and 4th gear, tighten the clamp nut.
6. Check the engagement of all gears, including reverse and make sure the gear shift lever moves freely.

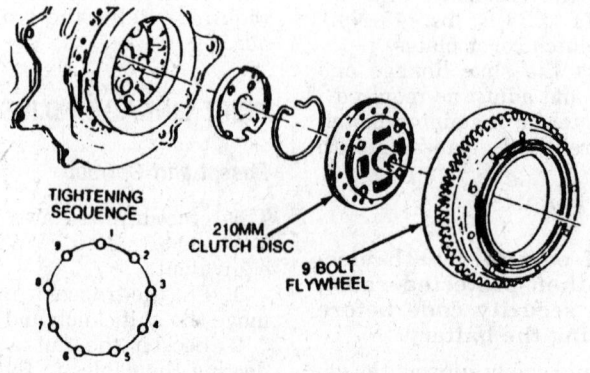

TIGHTENING SEQUENCE **210MM CLUTCH DISC** **9 BOLT FLYWHEEL**

Clutch assembly — Golf, Jetta and Cabriolet

2. Pull the cable adjusting sleeve up at the transaxle until resistance is felt and insert the gauge or measure the clearance.

3. Loosen the locknut and turn the adjusting sleeve until there is no free play at the gauge. Without the gauge, this distance should be 0.472 in. (12mm).

4. Tighten the locknut and operate the pedal several times. Recheck the adjustment.

Self-Adjusting Cables

1. If the original cable is being reinstalled, compress the spring and

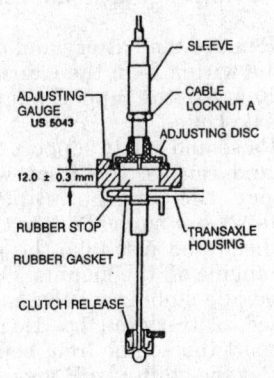

Clutch cable adjustment using gauge

hold the cable in place on the transaxle. Another person is required to attach the cable to the clutch lever.

2. If a new cable is being installed, there is a strap holding the spring in place. Remove the strap after the cable is in place.

3. Operate the pedal several times to adjust the cable.

Clutch Cable

REMOVAL AND INSTALLATION

Adjustable Cable

1. Loosen the adjustment.
2. Disengage the cable at the lever arm, noting the placement of the parts.
3. Unhook the cable from the pedal and pull the cable from the firewall.

To install:
4. Grease the pedal end and install and connect the new cable. Adjust the pedal free-play.

Self-Adjusting Cable

1. Depress the pedal several times.
2. Compress the spring located under the boot at the top of the ad-

juster mechanism and remove the cable at the release lever, noting the placement of the parts.

3. Unhook the cable from the pedal and pull the cable from the firewall.

To install:
4. Grease the pedal end and install the new cable onto the pedal. Compress the spring and have a helper pull the cable down and install to the release lever.

5. If the adjuster spring is retained by a strap, remove the strap after cable installation.

6. Depress the clutch pedal several times to adjust the cable.

Clutch Master Cylinder

REMOVAL AND INSTALLATION

The clutch master cylinder is located on the firewall below the brake master cylinder. The clutch slave cylinder is located on top of the transaxle. The clutch master cylinder is supplied fluid from the brake fluid reservoir. Whenever any part of the system is removed or replaced the system must be bled to remove any air that may be in the lines.

1. Remove the windshield washer bottle.
2. Remove the pressure line from the rear of the clutch master cylinder and plug the fitting.
3. Disconnect the fluid supply hose from the brake fluid reservoir.
4. Inside the vehicle, disconnect the pushrod from the clutch pedal by removing the clip on the retaining pin.
5. Remove the 2 mounting nuts and remove the clutch master cylinder from the vehicle.

To install:
6. Insert the pushrod through the firewall, install new nuts and torque to 5 ft. lbs. (7 Nm). Pin the rod to the pedal and install the clip.

7. Connect the supply line to the brake master cylinder and install the pressure line to the rear of the clutch master cylinder.

8. Fill the brake reservoir and bleed the clutch system.

Clutch Slave Cylinder

REMOVAL AND INSTALLATION

1. Raise and safely support the vehicle.
2. Disconnect and plug the pressure line to the slave cylinder.

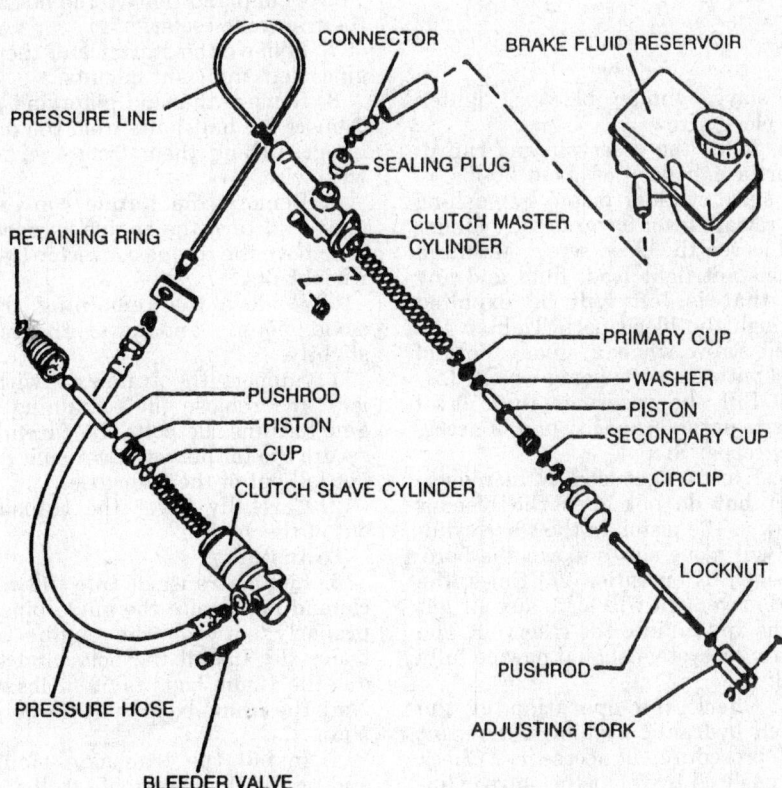

Hydraulic clutch components

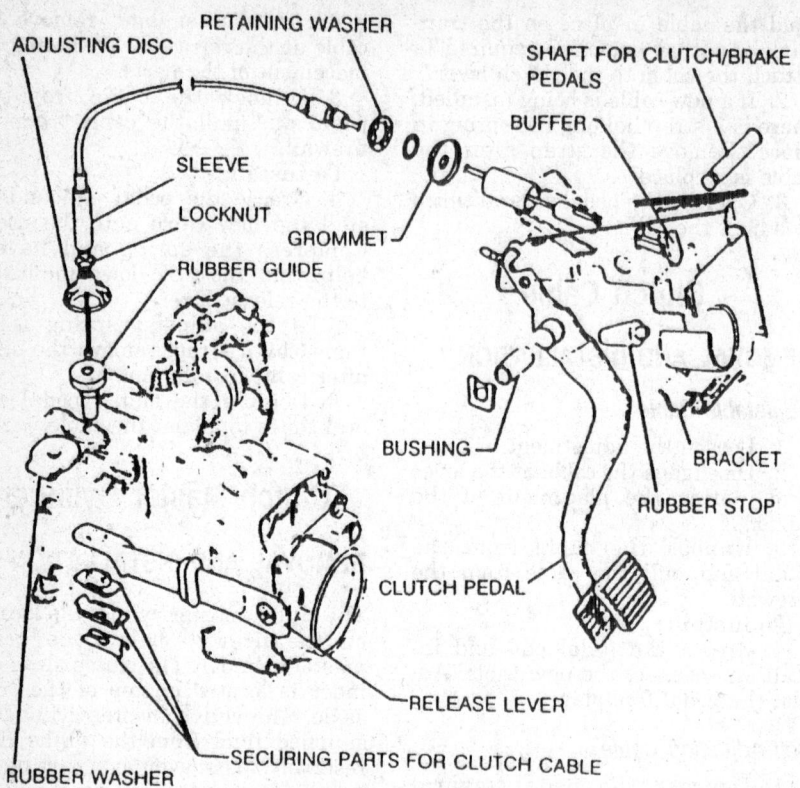

RETAINING WASHER

ADJUSTING DISC

SHAFT FOR CLUTCH/BRAKE PEDALS

BUFFER

SLEEVE

LOCKNUT

GROMMET

RUBBER GUIDE

BUSHING

BRACKET

RUBBER STOP

CLUTCH PEDAL

RELEASE LEVER

SECURING PARTS FOR CLUTCH CABLE

RUBBER WASHER

Clutch pedal and cable assembly

AUTOMATIC TRANSAXLE

Transaxle Assembly

REMOVAL AND INSTALLATION

Passat

1. If equipped with electronically theft-protected radio, obtain the security code before disconnecting the battery.
2. Remove the battery and disconnect the wiring from the transaxle.
3. Remove the upper engine-to-transaxle bolts.
4. Raise and safely support the vehicle and remove the front wheels. Connect the engine sling tool VW-10-222A or equivalent, to the cylinder head and just take the weight of the engine off the mounts. On Passat, the idle stabilizer valve must be removed to attach the tool. Do not try to support the engine from below.
5. Put the shifter in **P** and disconnect the shift cable.
6. Clamp and remove the hoses at the transaxle cooler.
7. Remove the starter and the engine's left and right mounts.
8. Remove the skid plate and disconnect the halfshafts from the drive flanges. Hang them from the body with wire.
9. Remove the torque converter plate and turn the engine as needed to remove the torque converter-to-flywheel bolts.
10. Remove the remaining transaxle mounts and lower the hoist slightly.
11. Support the transaxle with a jack and remove the remaining engine-to-transaxle bolts. Be careful to secure the torque converter so it does not fall out of the transaxle.
12. Carefully lower the transaxle out of the vehicle.
   To install:
13. Fit the transaxle into the vehicle and make sure the guide pins fit properly between the engine and transaxle. Install the bolts and torque the 12mm bolts to 59 ft. lbs. (80 Nm), the 10mm bolts to 44 ft. lbs. (60 Nm).
14. Install the transaxle mounts and torque the bolts to 44 ft. lbs. (60 Nm). Torque the left side bracket-to-transaxle bolts to 18 ft. lbs. (25 Nm).

3. Remove the slave cylinder by removing the spring pin and clip from the transaxle.
   To install:
4. Align the slave cylinder on the transaxle housing and insert the spring pin and clip. Bolt the cylinder in place.
5. Connect the pressure line and lower the vehicle.
6. Fill the brake reservoir and bleed the system.

Hydraulic Clutch System Bleeding

1. The clutch and brakes share the same reservoir. Clean all dirt and grease from the cap to make sure no foreign substances enter the system.
2. Remove the cap and diaphragm and fill the reservoir to the top with the approved DOT 3 or 4 brake fluid. Fully loosen the bleed screw which is in the slave cylinder body next to the inlet connection.
3. At this point bubbles of air will appear at the bleed screw outlet. When the slave cylinder is full and a steady stream of fluid comes out of the slave cylinder bleeder, tighten the bleed screw.
4. Refill the reservoir and cap it. Exert a light load of about 20 lbs. to the slave cylinder piston by pushing the release lever towards the cylinder and loosen the bleed screw. Maintain a constant light load; fluid and any air that is left will be expelled through the bleed port. Tighten the bleed screw when a steady flow of fluid with no air is being expelled.
5. Fill the reservoir fluid level back to normal capacity and, if necessary repeat Step 4.
6. Exert a light load to the release lever but do not open the bleeder screw as the piston in the slave cylinder will move slowly down the bore. Repeat this operation 2-3 times; the fluid movement will force any air left in the system into the reservoir. The hydraulic system should now be fully bled.
7. Check the operation of the clutch hydraulic system and repeat this procedure, if necessary. Check the pushrod travel at the slave cylinder to insure the minimum travel is 0.57 in. (15mm).

15. Install the torque converter bolts and torque to 44 ft. lbs. (60 Nm).

16. Connect the halfshafts and torque the bolts to 33 ft. lbs. (45 Nm).

17. Connect and adjust the shift linkage as required.

18. Install the remaining parts and check the fluid level in the transaxle.

Corrado

NOTE: When loosening or tightening axle nuts, make sure the vehicle is on the ground. Axle nut torque is high enough that attempting to loosen it may cause the vehicle to fall off the support.

1. This vehicle is equipped with a theft protected radio. Obtain the security code and remove the battery.

2. With the vehicle on the ground, loosen the front axle nuts.

3. On supercharged models, remove the intercooler ducting. It may be necessary to remove the ducting for the brakes.

4. Disconnect the wiring from the transaxle.

5. Clamp the coolant hoses and disconnect them from the transaxle fluid intercooler.

6. Raise and safely support the vehicle and remove the front wheels. Connect the engine sling tool VW-10-222A or equivalent, to the cylinder head and just take the weight of the engine off the mounts. Do not try to support the engine from below.

7. Make sure the gear selector is in **P** and disconnect the shift cable from the transaxle.

8. Remove the starter and the left transaxle mount.

9. At the bottom of the left strut, matchmark the position of the steering knuckle to the strut. Remove the bolts to swing the steering knuckle down.

10. Disconnect the halfshafts from the drive flanges and remove them.

11. Remove the cover plate and the torque converter-to-flywheel bolts.

12. With all mounts disconnected, lower the sling tool and move the engine/transaxle to the right. Place a jack under the transaxle and remove the engine-to-transaxle bolts.

13. When lowering the transaxle out of the vehicle, make sure the torque converter does not fall out.

To install:

14. Fit the transaxle in place and make sure the torque converter is properly positioned when installing the bolts. Torque the 10mm bolts to 44 ft. lbs. (60 Nm) and the 12mm bolts to 59 ft. lbs. (80 Nm).

15. Install the mounts using the same torque values. Torque the left side bracket-to-transaxle bolts to 18 ft. lbs. (25 Nm). Remove the lifting equipment.

16. Attach the torque converter to the flywheel and torque the bolts to 44 ft. lbs. (60 Nm). Install the cover plate.

17. Make sure the splines on the halfshafts are clean and install the halfshafts. Torque the bolts to 33 ft. lbs. (45 Nm) and install new nuts on the axles. Do not torque the nuts until the vehicle is on the ground.

18. Reassemble the left steering knuckle to the strut, making sure to align the matchmarks. Torque the bolts to 70 ft. lbs. (95 Nm). It will probably still be necessary to align the front wheels.

19. Install the remaining parts and adjust the shift cable as required.

20. When the vehicle is on the ground, torque the axle nut to 195 ft. lbs. (265 Nm).

Golf, Jetta and Cabriolet

1. If equipped with electronically theft-protected radio, obtain the security code before disconnecting the battery.

2. Disconnect the battery and the speedometer drive and plug the hole in the transaxle.

3. On Golf and Jetta, with the vehicle on the ground, remove the front axle nuts.

NOTE: When loosening or tightening an axle nut, make sure the vehicle is on the ground. Axle nut torque is high enough that attempting to loosen it may cause the vehicle to fall.

4. Raise and safely support the vehicle and remove the front wheels. Connect the engine sling tool VW-10-222A or equivalent, to the cylinder head and just take the weight of the engine off the mounts. On 16V engine, the idle stabilizer valve must be removed to attach the tool. Do not try to support the engine from below.

5. Remove the driver's side rear transaxle mount and support bracket.

6. On Golf and Jetta, remove the front mount bolts from the transaxle and from the body and remove the mount as a complete assembly.

7. Remove the selector and accelerator cables from the transaxle lever but leave them attached to the bracket. Remove the bracket assembly to save the adjustment.

8. Unbolt the halfshafts from the drive flanges. On Golf and Jetta, the shafts must be removed, which may require separating the ball joints from the wheel bearing housing to gain the necessary clearance. Remove the ball joint clamping bolt.

9. Remove the heatshield and brackets and remove the starter. On Cabriolet, the front mount comes off with the starter.

10. Turn the engine as needed to remove the torque converter-to-flywheel bolts.

11. Remove the remaining transaxle mounts and, on Golf and Jetta, the subframe bolts and allow the subframe to hang free.

12. Support the transaxle with a jack and remove the remaining engine-to-transaxle bolts. Be careful to secure the torque converter so it does not fall out of the transaxle.

13. Carefully lower the transaxle from the vehicle.

To install:

14. When reinstalling, make sure the torque converter is fully seated on the pump shaft splines. The converter should be recessed into the bell housing and turn by hand. Keep checking that it still turns while drawing the engine and transaxle together with the bolts.

15. Install the engine-to-transaxle bolts and torque to 55 ft. lbs. (75 Nm).

16. Install all mount and subframe bolts before tightening any on them. Tighten the bolts starting at the rear and work forward. Torque the smaller bolts to 25 ft. lbs. (34 Nm) and the larger bolts to 58 ft. lbs. (80 Nm). Remove the lifting equipment when all mounts are installed.

17. Install the torque converter-to-flywheel bolts and torque them to 26 ft. lbs. (35 Nm).

18. Install the starter and torque the bolts to 14 ft. lbs. (20 Nm). Install the heatshields.

19. If the halfshafts were removed, make sure the splines are clean and apply a thread locking compound to the splines before sliding it into the hub. Connect the halfshafts to the drive flanges and torque the bolts to 37 ft. lbs. (50 Nm). Install new axle nuts but do not fully torque them until the vehicle is on the ground.

20. If removed, fit the ball joints to the control arm and torque the clamping bolt to 37 ft. lbs. (50 Nm).

21. Connect and adjust the shift linkage as required.

22. When assembly is complete and the vehicle is on its wheels, torque the axle nuts to 195 ft. lbs. (265 Nm).

SHIFT/THROTTLE LINKAGE ADJUSTMENT

1. With the engine warm and the gear selector in **P**, loosen the adjusting nut and disconnect the accelerator pedal cable from the transaxle.

2. On the intake plenum, loosen the nuts on the cable bracket and move the sleeve away from the throttle to take up any play. The throttle must remain closed.

3. Turn the nut on the throttle side of the bracket up to the bracket and tighten the other nut against the bracket. Be sure the throttle is still against its stop.

4. Reconnect the cable to the transaxle and have an assistant push the gas pedal to the floor.

5. Push the transaxle lever against the stop and turn the adjusting nut to remove all slack from the cable. Tighten the locknut, release the pedal and push it again to check adjustment.

FRONT SUSPENSION

MacPherson Strut

REMOVAL AND INSTALLATION

Except Fox

NOTE: When loosening or tightening axle nuts, make sure the vehicle is on the ground. Axle nut torque is high enough that attempting to loosen it may cause the vehicle to fall off the support.

1. With the vehicle on the ground, remove the front axle nut.

2. Raise and safely support the vehicle and remove the front wheels.

3. Detach the brake line from the strut and remove the caliper. Hang it from the body with wire.

4. Clean and matchmark the position of the strut to the wheel bearing housing for reassembly.

5. Remove the bolts and push the steering knuckle down away from the strut.

— **CAUTION** —
On Cabriolet, do not remove the large nut in the center of the top bearing. The spring will be released while still compressed.

6. On Cabriolet, remove the nuts holding the rubber strut bearing and lower the strut from the vehicle. On other vehicles, remove the large center nut to lower the strut from the vehicle.

To install:

7. Place the strut into the fender and install the nuts. On Cabriolet, torque the 3 nuts to 14 ft. lbs. (20 Nm). On all other models, torque the center nut to 44 ft. lbs. (60 Nm).

8. Fit the wheel bearing housing into the strut and torque the bolts to 70 ft. lbs. (95 Nm).

9. Install the brake caliper and torque the bolts to 44 ft. lbs. (60 Nm).

10. When assembly is complete and the vehicle is on the ground, torque the axle nut to 145 ft. lbs. (196 Nm) for M18 nut or 175 ft. lbs. (237 Nm) for M20 nut.

Fox

NOTE: When loosening or tightening axle nuts, make sure the vehicle is on the ground. Axle nut torque is high enough that attempting to loosen it may cause the vehicle to fall off the support.

1. With the vehicle on the ground, remove the front axle nut.

2. Raise and safely support the vehicle and remove the wheels.

3. Remove the brake caliper from the strut and hang from the body it with wire. Detach the brake line from the strut and remove the rotor.

4. At the tie rod end, remove the cotter pin and the castellated nut and remove the end from the strut with a puller.

5. Loosen the stabilizer bar bushings and detach the end from the strut being removed.

6. Remove the ball joint clamp bolt and push the control arm down to disengage the ball joint from the strut.

7. On some vehicles, the halfshaft spline is secured in the hub with thread sealer. The best way to remove it is to push it out with a wheel puller. Do not use heat; this will ruin the bearing. Pull the strut away from the halfshaft.

8. Remove the upper strut-to-fender retaining nut and lower the strut assembly down and out of the vehicle.

To install:

9. Install the upper end of the strut and torque the nut to 44 ft. lbs. (60 Nm).

10. Make sure the axle splines are clean and apply fresh thread sealer to the outer end. Insert the axle through

the hub and install a new axle nut. Do not torque the nut until the vehicle is on the ground.

11. Fit the ball joint into the strut and torque the clamping bolt to 44 ft. lbs. (60 Nm).

12. Lightly lubricate the stabilizer arm bushings with silicone and install them. Torque the bolts to 15 ft. lbs. (20 Nm).

13. Install the brake calipers and torque the bolts to 44 ft. lbs. (60 Nm).

14. When the assembly is complete and the vehicle is on the ground, torque the axle nut to 170 ft. lbs. (230 Nm).

Lower Ball Joints

INSPECTION

1. To check the ball joint, raise and safely support the vehicle. Let the front wheels hang free.

2. Insert a prybar between the control arm and the ball joint clamping bolt. Be careful to not damage the ball joint boot.

3. Measure the play between the bottom of the ball joint and the clamping bolt with a caliper. Total must not exceed 0.100 in. (2.5mm).

REMOVAL AND INSTALLATION

1. Raise and safely support the vehicle, allowing the front wheels to hang. Remove the front wheels.

2. Matchmark the ball joint-to-control arm position.

3. Remove the ball joint clamping bolt.

4. Pry the lower control arm down to remove the ball joint from the strut.

5. Remove the ball joint-to-lower control arm retaining nuts and bolts or drill out the rivets with a ¼ in. (6mm) drill.

6. Remove the ball joint assembly.

To install:

7. Install the ball joint in the reverse order of removal. If no parts were installed other than the ball joint, align the matchmarks. No camber adjustment is necessary if this is done. Pull the ball joint into alignment with pliers. Tighten the 2 control arm-to-ball joint bolts to 47 ft. lbs. (64 Nm) and the ball joint clamping bolt to 44 ft. lbs. (60 Nm).

8. On all other vehicles, bolt the new ball joint in place. Torque the bolts to 18 ft. lbs. (25 Nm) and ball joint clamping bolt to 37 ft. lbs. (50 Nm).

Lower Control Arm

REMOVAL AND INSTALLATION

NOTE: When removing the driver's side control arm on Cabriolet equipped with an automatic transaxle, it may be necessary to lift the engine/transaxle. First support the engine from above or below. Remove the front left engine mounting nut and bolt, remove the rear mount and raise the engine to expose the front control arm bolt.

1. Raise and safely support the vehicle and remove the wheels.
2. Remove the ball joint clamping bolt and pry the control arm down.
3. Remove the rubber bushings to unfasten the stabilizer bar.
4. Remove the control arm mounting bolts and remove the control arm.
To install:
5. Installation is the reverse of removal. Torque the following components:
Fox control arm bushing bolts — 40 ft. lbs. (55 Nm)
Cabriolet control arm bushing bolts — 50 ft. lbs. (68 Nm)
All others: front bushing bolts — 96 ft. lbs. (130 Nm), rear bolts: 59 ft. lbs. (80 Nm)
Stabilizer bar link rods — 18 ft. lbs. (25 Nm)
Stabilizer bar bushing clamp bolts — 32 ft. lbs. (43 Nm)
Ball joint clamping bolt — 37 ft. lbs. (50 Nm) for 8mm bolt or 44 ft. lbs. (60 Nm) for 10mm bolt

Sway Bar

REMOVAL AND INSTALLATION

1. Raise and safely support the vehicle.
2. Remove the front wheel and tire assemblies.
3. Disconnect the sway bar ends links from both lower control arms.
4. Remove the bolts retaining the sway bar mounting bushing brackets.
5. Remove the sway bar.
6. Installation is the reverse of the removal procedure. Torque the mounting bracket bolts and the end link nuts to 18 ft. lbs. (25 Nm).

REAR SUSPENSION

Shock Absorbers

REMOVAL AND INSTALLATION

NOTE: Do not remove both suspension struts at the same time or the axle beam will be hanging on the brake lines.

1. Working inside the vehicle, remove the cap from the top shock mount and note the way the washers and bushings installed.
2. Remove the upper strut-to-body bolts.
3. Slowly lift the vehicle until the wheels are slightly off the ground.
4. Unbolt the strut from the axle and carefully remove the strut from the vehicle. It may be necessary to press the axle down slightly when removing the strut.
5. Installation is the reverse of removal. Torque the strut-to-body bolts to 26 ft. lbs. (35 Nm) and the strut-to-axle bolts to 77 ft. lbs. (105 Nm).

Rear Wheel Bearings

REMOVAL AND INSTALLATION

Drum

1. Raise and safely support the vehicle and remove the rear wheels.
2. On drum brakes, insert a small pry tool through a wheel bolt hole and push up on the adjusting wedge to slacken the rear brake adjustment.
3. Remove the grease cap, cotter pin, locking ring, axle nut and thrust washer. Carefully remove the bearing and put all these parts where they will stay clean.
4. Before installing, pack the bearing. If any brake dust has fallen onto the axle, wipe off all the axle grease and put on new high temperature bearing grease.
5. Installation is reverse of removal.

Rotor

1. Raise and safely support the vehicle and remove the rear wheels.
2. Remove the brake caliper without disconnecting the hydraulic hose. Support the caliper so it does not hang by the hose.
3. Remove the brake disc.
4. Remove the hub cap and the nut and washer. The torque on the

nut is very high, make sure the vehicle is firmly supported and will not fall.
5. Remove the hub/bearing unit from the spindle. The bearing is a sealed unit pressed into the hub.
6. Installation is the reverse of the removal procedure. Torque the hub nut to 170 ft. lbs. (230 Nm).

ADJUSTMENT

1. When adjusting the bearing nut, the thrust washer must still be movable with light effort with a small pry tool.
2. When installing the locking ring, keep trying different positions of the ring on the nut until the cotter pin goes into the hole. Don't turn the nut to align the locking ring with the hole in the axle. Use a new cotter pin. Install the grease cap with a rubber hammer.

Rear Axle Assembly

REMOVAL AND INSTALLATION

1. Raise and safely support the vehicle and remove the rear wheels.
2. Remove the rear brake caliper or drum.
3. Disconnect the brake line and remove the caliper or back plate (with brakes attached) from the vehicle.
4. Disconnect the other end of the brake line; unclip the brake line and parking brake cable from the axle. Unhook the brake pressure regulator spring from the bracket.
5. Support one side of the axle beam so it does not fall and remove the lower shock mount bolts from both sides.
6. Unless it is the part being repaired, avoid removing the axle bushing brackets. Removing these will mean aligning the rear bushings upon reassembly.
7. Remove the bolt from the center of each bushing and lower the axle from the vehicle.
To install:
8. Install the axle but do not torque the bushing bolts yet. They should be torqued with the vehicle on the ground to properly align the bushings.
9. Install the brakes, connect the hydraulic line and bleed the brakes.
10. With the vehicle on the ground, torque the right side axle bushing bolt first, then pry the left side bushing slightly towards the center of the vehicle and torque the left side.

11. Torque the following:

Passat axle bushing bolts — 52 ft. lbs. (70 Nm)

All other axle bushing bolts — 44 ft. lbs. (60 Nm)

Passat lower shock bolt — 77 ft. lbs. (105 Nm)

Golf/Jetta and Corrado shock mount — 52 ft. lbs. (70 Nm)

Cabriolet shock mount — 32 ft. lbs. (45 Nm)

Fox shock mount — 52 ft. lbs. (70 Nm)

12. Connect the brake line at the axle side. Secure the brake line and parking brake cable at the axle.

13. Connect the brake pressure regulator spring to the bracket.

14. If equipped with disc brakes, install the caliper or back plate, with brakes attached. Connect the brake line to the caliper.

15. If equipped with drum brakes, install the brake drum.

16. Install the wheel assemblies.

STEERING

Steering Wheel

The air bag system is equipped with a backup power supply. The battery must be disconnected for more than 20 minutes before the power supply is fully discharged and the system is considered disarmed. A memory saver device will keep the power supply charged.

— CAUTION —

Failure to properly disarm the air bag system may result in accidental deployment of the air bag and possible personal injury.

REMOVAL AND INSTALLATION

With Air Bag

1. Disconnect battery, wait more than 20 minutes.
2. Remove the Torx head screws at the back of the steering wheel.
3. Carefully detach the air bag unit from the wheel and disconnect the wire at the center.
4. Place unit in a safe place, horn pad up.
5. Point the front wheels straight-ahead, remove the ignition key to lock the steering column and remove the nut and spring washer.

6. Mark the position of the wheel to the spline and pull the wheel straight off.
7. Installation is the reverse of removal. Torque the steering wheel nut to 30 ft. lbs. (40 Nm). When installing the air bag, use new Torx screws and tighten to 7.5 ft. lbs. (10 Nm). Do not over torque or the air bag may not function properly.

Without Air Bag

1. Remove the horn pad.
2. Remove the ignition key and turn the wheel until it locks.
3. Remove the center nut and matchmark the wheel to the splines.
4. Pull the wheel straight off.
5. Installation is the reverse of removal. Torque the center nut to 30 ft. lbs. (40 Nm).

Manual Steering Rack

ADJUSTMENT

On some vehicles, there is a rack and pinion free-play adjustment screw and locknut; however, this is not always accessible with the rack installed in the vehicle. Loosen the locknut and adjust the screw to allow smooth, non-binding movement of the rack.

REMOVAL AND INSTALLATION

1. Raise and safely support the vehicle.
2. Remove both front wheels and disengage both tie rod ends.
3. At the steering column, remove the boot clamp, push the boot towards the body and remove the clamp bolt from the universal joint.
4. Remove the rack mounting nuts and remove the rack from its mounts.
5. At this point on some vehicles, the rack cannot be removed from the body. Support the engine/transaxle and remove the subframe bolts or the rear transaxle mount and bracket to allow the rack to move towards the rear.
6. Installation is the reverse of removal. Torque the subframe bolts to 96 ft. lbs. (130 Nm).

Power Steering Rack

REMOVAL AND INSTALLATION

1. Raise and safely support the vehicle.

2. Remove both front wheels and disengage both tie rod ends.
3. Remove the low pressure (suction) hose from the pump and drain the system into a catch pan. Properly discard the fluid.
4. At the steering column, remove the boot clamp, push the boot towards the body and remove the clamp bolt from the universal joint.
5. On Cabriolet, remove the exhaust manifold and shift linkage bracket.
6. Remove the rack mounting clamp nuts and remove the clamps.
7. At this point on some vehicles, the rack cannot be removed from the body. Support the engine/transaxle and remove the subframe bolts to allow the rack to move towards the rear. On Cabriolet, remove the transaxle mount and bracket.
8. Disconnect the power steering hydraulic lines and remove the rack.

To install:

9. Make sure the mounting bushings are in good condition. Fit the rack assembly into place and torque the clamp nuts to 22 ft. lbs. (32 Nm).
10. Install any subframe bolts that were removed.
11. Connect the hydraulic lines and install the steering column universal joint bolt.
12. Fill the system with new fluid and run the engine to check for leaks and bleed the system.

Power Steering Pump

REMOVAL AND INSTALLATION

1. Remove the suction hose and the pressure line from the pump, drain the fluid into a catch pan. Properly discard the fluid.
2. Loosen the tensioning bolt at the front of the tensioning bracket and remove the drive belt from the pump drive pulley.
3. Remove the pump mounting bolts and lift the pump from the vehicle.
4. To install, reverse the removal procedures. Torque the mounting bolts to 15 ft. lbs. (20 Nm). Tension the drive belt. Fill the reservoir with approved power steering fluid and bleed the system.

BELT ADJUSTMENT

To tension the drive belt, adjust the tensioner bolt so the belt will flex ½ in. (13.0mm) under light thumb pressure.

SYSTEM BLEEDING

1. With the wheels turned all the way to the left, add power steering fluid to the **COLD** mark on the fluid level indicator.

2. Start the engine and run at fast idle momentarily. Shut the engine OFF and recheck fluid level. If necessary; add fluid to bring level to the **COLD** mark.

3. Start the engine and bleed the system by turning the wheels from side to side without hitting the stops.

NOTE: Fluid with air in it has a light tan or red appearance.

4. Return the wheels to the center position and keep the engine running for 2-3 minutes.

5. Road test the vehicle and recheck the fluid level making sure it is at the **HOT** mark.

Tie Rod Ends

REMOVAL AND INSTALLATION

1. Raise and safely support the vehicle and remove the front wheels.

2. Remove the cotter pin and nut and press out the tie rod end. A small puller is required.

3. Hold the tie rod with a small pipe wrench or locking pliers and loosen the locking nut.

4. Back the nut away from the rod end far enough to mark the threads at the rod end with a crayon or chalk, then unscrew the end from the tie rod.

To install:

5. When installing the new tie rod end, screw it onto the rod up to the mark on the threads. When tightening the locknut, hold the tie rod end and tighten the nut securely against it.

6. Reinstall the tie rod end into the steering knuckle and install the nut. Torque the nut to 22 ft. lbs. (30 Nm), then tighten as required to install a new cotter pin.

7. With the wheels on, lower the vehicle and roll it back and forth to settle the suspension. Check toe adjustment.

NOTE: On some vehicles, only the right tie rod is adjustable.

BRAKES

———— CAUTION ————
Vehicles equipped with anti-lock brakes have extremely high fluid pressure in the system at all times. Do not disconnect any hydraulic fittings or open a bleeder without properly relieving the system pressure. Failure to properly discharge the system pressure may result in severe personal injury.

Master Cylinder

REMOVAL AND INSTALLATION

Without ABS

1. Disconnect and plug the brake lines.

2. Disconnect the electrical plug from the sending unit for the low fluid switch.

3. Remove the 2 master cylinder mounting nuts and remove the master cylinder and reservoir.

4. The reservoir is held into the master cylinder by a press fit into rubber sealing plugs and can easily be pulled off. To reinstall, moisten the plugs with brake fluid and press it on.

To install:

5. Position the master cylinder and reservoir assembly onto the mounting studs on the booster and install the washers and nuts. Tighten the nuts to 15 ft. lbs. (20 Nm).

6. Remove the plugs and connect the brake lines.

7. Fill the reservoir and bleed the entire brake system.

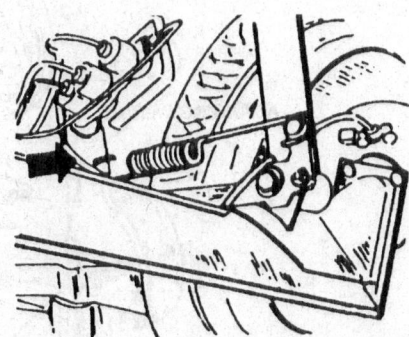

Relieving pressure at the proportioning valve — push the lever toward the axle

---

Proportioning Valve

REMOVAL AND INSTALLATION

1. Raise and safely support the vehicle.

2. Disconnect the spring and relieve the pressure by pushing the lever towards the axle.

3. Using a line wrench, loosen the lines to the proportioning valve.

4. Remove the retaining nuts and remove the proportioning valve from the frame.

5. Installation is the reverse of removal. Bleed the brake system.

Power Brake Booster

REMOVAL AND INSTALLATION

Without ABS

1. Remove the master cylinder from the booster.

2. At the pedals, remove the clevis pin on the end of the booster pushrod by unclipping it and pulling it from the clevis.

3. Disconnect the vacuum hose from the booster.

4. Unbolt the booster; remove the 2 nuts under the dashboard or the 4 nuts holding the booster to its bracket. Remove the booster.

5. Installation is the reverse of removal. Install the master cylinder and bleed the system.

Brake Caliper

REMOVAL AND INSTALLATION

Front

1. Disconnect the negative battery cable. Draw off brake fluid with a suitable syringe.

2. Disconnect the hydraulic brake lines.

3. Raise and safely support the vehicle. Remove the front tire and wheel assembly.

4. Disconnect the hose union at the caliper. Plug the hose to prevent dirt from entering.

5. Remove the caliper mounting bolts and remove the caliper.

6. The installation is the reverse of the removal procedure. Bleed the brake system.

7. Torque the caliper bolts to 26 ft. lbs. (35 Nm).

Rear

1. Disconnect the negative battery cable. Draw off brake fluid with a suitable syringe.
2. Disconnect the hydraulic brake lines.
3. Raise and safely support the vehicle. Remove the rear tire and wheel assembly.
4. Remove the caliper mounting bolts and disconnect the brake pad wear indicator plug.
5. Remove the caliper assembly by pulling to the rear.
6. The installation is the reverse of the removal procedure. Bleed the brake system.
7. Torque the caliper bolts to 26 ft. lbs. (35 Nm).

Disc Brake Pads

REMOVAL AND INSTALLATION

Front

1. Raise and safely support the vehicle.
2. Remove the tire and wheel assembly.
3. Remove the caliper guide bolts and the spring clamp.
4. Turn up the caliper and remove the brake pads. The inner pad is located with a spring in the piston.

NOTE: The brake pads on both calipers on 1 axle should be replaced at the same time.

5. Lubricate the mounting pads with a suitable grease.
6. The installation is the reverse of the removal procedure. Bleed the brake system.

Rear

1. Raise and safely support the vehicle.
2. Remove the tire and wheel assembly.
3. Remove the caliper guide bolts and the spring clamp.
4. Turn up the caliper and remove the brake pads. The inner pad is located with a spring in the piston.

NOTE: The brake pads on both calipers on 1 axle should be replaced at the same time.

5. Lubricate the mounting pads with a suitable grease.
6. The installation is the reverse of the removal procedure. Bleed the brake system.

Brake Rotor

REMOVAL AND INSTALLATION

Front

1. Raise and safely support the vehicle. Remove the front tire and wheel assembly.
2. Disconnect the rubber grommet from the bracket, if equipped.
3. Disconnect and support the caliper, using a piece of wire.
4. Remove the mounting bolts and remove the brake rotor with the proper tool.
5. The installation is the reverse of the removal procedure.

Rear

1. Raise and safely support the vehicle. Remove the tire and wheel assembly.
2. Disconnect and support the caliper, using a piece of wire.
3. Remove the mounting bolts from the caliper support and remove the brake rotor.
4. Always replace both discs of the same axle.
5. The installation is the reverse of the removal procedure. Adjust the parking brake.

6. Torque the caliper support mounting bolts to 53 ft. lbs. (70 Nm).

Brake Drums

REMOVAL AND INSTALLATION

1. Raise and safely support vehicle and remove the rear wheels. Make certain the parking brake is released.
2. Insert a small pry tool through a wheel bolt hole and push up on the adjusting wedge to slacken the rear brake adjustment.
3. Remove the grease cap, cotter pin, locking ring, axle nut and thrust washer. Carefully remove the bearing and put all these parts where they will stay clean.
4. Carefully remove the drum.
5. Before installing, if any brake dust has fallen onto the axle, wipe off all the axle grease and apply a coat of new high temperature bearing grease. Install the parts in the reverse order of removal.

NOTE: When tightening the axle nut, the thrust washer must still be movable with a small pry tool. Spin the drum and check that the thrust washer can still be moved.

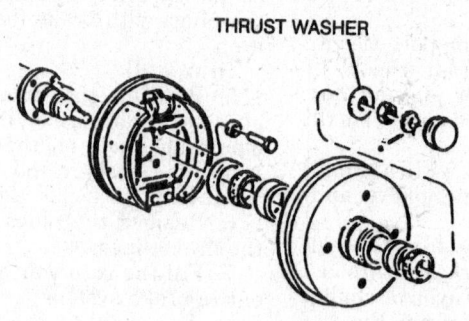

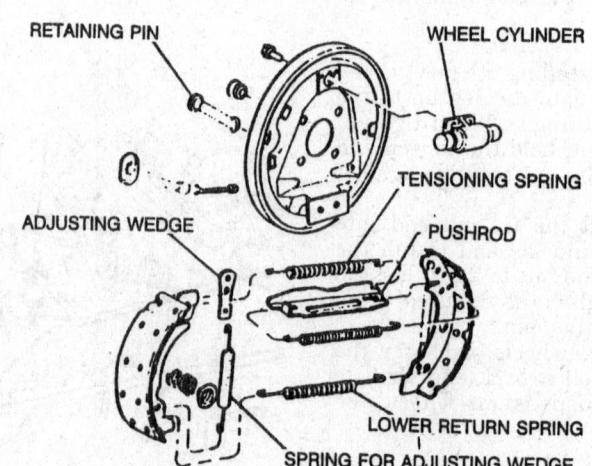

Rear brake assembly on drum brakes

6. When installing the locking ring, keep trying different positions of the ring on the nut until the cotter pin goes into the hole. Don't turn the nut to align the locking ring with the hole in the axle. Use a new cotter pin. Install the grease cap with a rubber hammer.

Brake Shoes

REMOVAL AND INSTALLATION

1. Raise and safely support the vehicle and remove the rear wheels. Make certain the parking brake is released.

2. Remove the rear brake drum.

3. Remove the spring retainers by holding the pin behind the back plate, push in on the retainer and turn it 1/4 turn.

4. Remove the shoes from the back plate by pulling first 1 shoe, then the other against the upper spring and from its wheel cylinder slot. Detach the parking brake cable from the brake lever. The entire shoe assembly should now be free of the vehicle.

5. Carefully note the position of each spring, as spring shapes and positions have varied from vehicle to vehicle and year to year.

6. Clamp the pushrod in a vise and begin removing the springs, starting with the lower return spring, adjusting wedge spring, upper return spring and then the tensioning spring and adjusting wedge.

7. On most vehicles, the parking brake lever must be removed from the old shoes and reused. When new parts are purchased, don't forget the clip that holds the parking brake lever pin in place.

To install:

8. Check the wheel cylinder for frozen pistons or leaks. If any defects are found, replace the wheel cylinder.

9. Inspect the springs. If the springs are damaged or show signs of overheating they should be replaced. Indications of overheated springs are discoloration and distortion.

10. Inspect the brake drum and recondition or replace as necessary.

11. Clean the back plate and lubricate the shoe contact points with brake lubricant.

12. With the push rod clamped in a vise, attach the front brake shoe and tensioning spring.

13. Insert the adjusting wedge between the front shoe and pushrod so its lug is pointing toward the backing plate.

14. Remove the parking brake lever from the old shoe and attach it onto the new rear brake shoe.

15. Put the rear brake shoe and parking brake lever assembly onto the pushrod and hook up the spring.

16. Connect the parking brake cable to the lever and place the whole assembly onto the backing plate.

17. Install the hold-down springs.

18. Install the upper and lower return springs.

19. Install the adjusting wedge spring.

20. Center the brake shoes on the backing plate making sure the adjusting wedge is fully released (all the way up) before installing the drum.

21. Install the drum and wheel assembly.

22. Apply the brake pedal a few times to bring the brake shoe into adjustment.

23. If the wheel cylinder was replaced, bleed the system.

24. Road test the vehicle.

Wheel Cylinder

REMOVAL AND INSTALLATION

1. Raise and safely support the vehicle and remove the wheel, drum and brake shoes.

2. Loosen the brake line on the rear of the cylinder but do not pull the line away from the cylinder or it may bend.

3. Remove the bolts and lockwashers that attach the wheel cylinder to the backing plate and remove the cylinder.

4. Position the new wheel cylinder on the backing plate and install the cylinder attaching bolts and lockwashers. Torque to 6 ft. lbs. (8 Nm).

5. Attach the brake line.

6. Install the brakes and bleed the system.

7. Road test the vehicle.

Brake System Bleeding

The same procedure for bleeding the brake system may be used for vehicles with or without ABS brakes.

NOTE: Use only new DOT 4 brake fluid in all Volkswagen vehicles. Do not use silicone (DOT 5) fluid. Even the smallest traces can cause severe corrosion to the hydraulic system. All brake fluids are corrosive to paint.

1. On vehicles with power brakes, bleed brakes with the engine OFF and booster vacuum discharged; pump the pedal with the bleeders closed about 20 times until the pedal effort gets stiff.

2. Fill the fluid reservoir.

3. On vehicles with a rear brake pressure regulator at the rear axle, press the lever towards the rear axle when bleeding the brakes.

4. Connect a clear plastic tube to the bleeder valve at the right rear wheel, with the other end in a clean container.

5. Using either a power bleeder or an assistant pumping the pedal, open the bleeder valve until there are no air bubbles in the fluid stream. Be careful not to let the reservoir run out.

6. Repeat the procedure in sequence at the left rear, right front, left front: working farthest from the master cylinder to the nearest.

Anti-Lock Brake System Service

Vehicles with Anti-lock Brake Systems (ABS) have an electronic fault memory and an indicator light on the instrument panel. When the engine is first started, the light will go on to indicate the system is pressurizing and performing a self diagnostic check. After the system is at full pressure, the light will go out. If it remains lit, there is a fault in the system. The fault memory can only be accessed with the VW testers VAG 1551 or VAG 1598, or equivalent. Be sure to unplug the ABS control unit connector and ground before doing any electric welding on the vehicle.

— **CAUTION** —
The ABS modulator assembly is capable of self-pressurizing to more than 3000 psi. Serious injury may result if the brake service is attempted without disabling and depressurizing the system.

RELIEVING ANTI-LOCK BRAKE SYSTEM PRESSURE

With the ignition **OFF**, pump the brake pedal 25-35 times to depressurize the system. The system will recharge itself via the electric pump as soon as the ignition is turned **ON**. Disconnect the pump or the battery to prevent unintended pressurization. The system can then be bled normally.

Modulator Assembly

REMOVAL AND INSTALLATION

1. Turn the ignition **OFF** and depress the brake pedal 25-35 times to depressurize the modulator assembly. Disconnect the pump or battery to prevent unintended pressurization.

2. Inside the vehicle, under the left rear seat for Passat, or behind the left kick panel for Corrado or near the right tail light for Golf and Jetta, locate and disconnect the ABS control unit and the ground connection.

3. Remove the brake fluid from the reservoir with a suction pump.

4. Disconnect the brake lines from the modulator assembly and protect its connections from contamination with suitable plugs.

5. Working inside the vehicle, remove the left shelf under the dash to gain access to the brake pedal linkage. Remove the clevis bolt and disconnect the pedal.

6. Remove the locknuts and remove the pressure modulator.

7. Installation is the reverse of removal. Use new locknuts and torque to 18 ft. lbs. (25 Nm). Refill the reservoir with new brake fluid and bleed the system.

Wheel Sensor

In addition to the pressure modulator and electronic control unit, the ABS system includes a wheel speed sensor. These sensors feed a speed signal to the control unit, which compares all the speed signals. Brake fluid pressure is modified as needed to prevent wheel lockup.

REMOVAL AND INSTALLATION

1. Raise and safely support the vehicle.

2. Remove the wheel and unbolt and remove the sensor from the wheel bearing housing.

3. The rotor portion of the sensor assembly is secured to the inside of the wheel hub. To remove the front rotor, the hub must be pressed out of the front wheel bearing.

4. On the rear wheels, the sensor is bolted to the stub axle just above the axle beam mounting pad. The sensor rotor is pressed into the brake disc. To remove it:

 a. Remove the wheel bearing and the brake rotor.

 b. Insert a drift pin through the wheel bolt holes and gently tap the speed sensor rotor out a little bit at each hole, much like removing an inner wheel bearing race.

To install:

5. When reinstalling, use a suitable sleeve to drive the speed sensor rotor into the disc evenly. When the cover ring is installed, the distance from the ring to the splash shield should be 0.375 in. (9.5mm).

6. When reinstalling the sensor, use a dry lubricant on the sides of the sensor and torque the bolt to 7 ft. lbs. (10 Nm).

CONTROL UNIT

The ABS electronic control unit is located under the rear seat on the left side.

1. Disconnect the negative battery cable.

2. Remove the lower seat cushion.

3. Remove the control unit retaining screws. Disconnect the harness connector and remove the control unit.

4. Installation is the reverse order of the removal procedure.

5. Connect the negative battery cable.

CHASSIS ELECTRICAL

Air Bag

DISARMING

To disarm the air bag system, disconnect the negative battery cable for more than 20 minutes. This will allow the backup power supply capacitor to discharge. Do not use a memory-saver device or the power supply will remain charged. The air bag can then be removed and the battery connected for other electrical test work. Before installing the air bag, disconnect the battery and allow the power supply to discharge for more than 20 minutes.

PRECAUTIONS

- An air bag is an explosive device. Handle with extreme caution.
- Always disconnect the battery before beginning work on the air bag system and wait 20 minutes for the backup power supply to discharge.
- Do not use a computer memory-saver device. It will keep the backup power supply charged.
- Air bag components must not be repaired or opened. Always use new parts.
- Always place a removed air bag unit with the horn pad facing up. Put it in a safe place where it will not be disturbed.
- The air bag unit must not be exposed to grease, fluids, or cleaning agents.
- The air bag unit must not be exposed to temperatures above 194°F (90°C) at any time. Even the heat of a soldering iron can damage or ignite the charge.
- Any testing on the air bag system must be done with the air bag installed in the vehicle. Use only Volkswagen approved test equipment and procedures specified with that equipment's instruction manual.
- Storage and transport of air bags is subject to rules governing explosive devices and should be done only in the original package.
- Failure to follow proper safety precautions may result in personal injury through accidental firing of the air bag, or through failure of the air bag in an accident.

Heater Blower Motor

REMOVAL AND INSTALLATION

Except Cabriolet and Fox

The blower motor is located behind the glove box and it may be easier to remove the glove box to gain access to the motor. The series resistor is mounted on the motor.

1. Disconnect the wires at the blower motor.

2. At the blower motor flange near the cowl, disengage the retaining lug; pull down on the lug.

3. Turn the motor assembly clockwise to release it from its mount, then lower it from the plenum.

4. Installation is the reverse of removal.

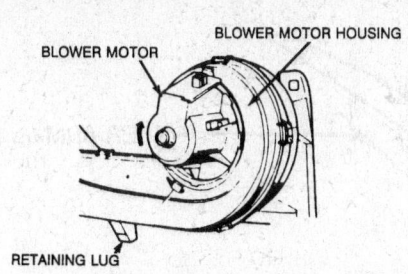

BLOWER MOTOR
BLOWER MOTOR HOUSING
RETAINING LUG

Removal and installation of the blower motor — except Cabriolet and Fox

Cabriolet and Fox

The blower motor and series resistor are reached from under the hood, just in front of the windshield.

1. Disconnect the negative battery cable.
2. Remove the clips and gasket holding the water deflector in place and remove the deflector.
3. To remove the plastic cover that is now visible. Some vehicles have fasteners which are accessed from both under the hood and under the dash. If after removing all screws, bolts or clips visible from above, the cover still won't lift off, check under the dash for more screws.
4. On vehicles with air conditioning, disconnect the linkage for the air distribution flaps. Remove the remaining plastic cover.
5. The blower and series resistor are now accessible. Remove the screws and the motor.
6. Installation is the reverse of removal. Be sure the seal around the motor is properly reinstalled.

Windshield Wiper Motor

REMOVAL AND INSTALLATION

When removing the wiper motor, leave the mounting frame in place. If possible, do not remove the wiper drive crank from the motor shaft.

1. Disconnect the negative battery cable and unplug the multi-connector from the wiper motor.
2. Disconnect the crank arm from the wiper arm assembly.
3. Remove the retaining nut and the crank arm from the wiper motor shaft.
4. Remove the motor mounting bolts and the motor from the vehicle.
To install:
5. Temporarily connect the multi-connector and run the motor. Turn the switch OFF and disconnect the

power after the motor stops; it will stop in the park position.
6. Connect the crank arm to the wiper assembly and reverse the removal procedures.

Instrument Cluster

REMOVAL AND INSTALLATION

Except Corrado and Passat

1. Disconnect the negative battery cable and pull off the temperature control knobs and levers.
2. Unclip the heater control trim plate, separate the electrical connectors and remove the plate.
3. Remove the retaining screws and the instrument panel trim plate.
4. Remove the retaining screws and pull out the instrument panel.
5. Squeeze the clips on the speedometer cable head and remove the cable from the instrument cluster.
6. Disconnect all of the vacuum hose and the electrical connections.
7. Installation is the reverse of removal.

Corrado and Passat

1. Disconnect negative battery cable.
2. Peel off the horn button cover, starting at the bottom and remove the steering wheel.
3. Remove the screw trim caps, trim screws and cluster trim.
4. Unscrew the trip odometer reset button.
5. Remove the cover screws (1) and cover, then remove the cluster screws (2) and cluster.
6. Carefully disconnect the vacuum line and multi-point connector.
7. Installation is the reverse of removal.

Speedometer

REMOVAL AND INSTALLATION

1. Disconnect the negative battery cable.
2. Remove the instrument cluster from the instrument panel.
3. Remove the cluster lens and retainer from the cluster.
4. Remove the speedometer retaining screws from the rear of the cluster.
5. Remove the speedometer/odometer from the cluster.
6. Installation is the reverse order of the removal procedure. Connect battery negative cable.

Headlight Switch

REMOVAL AND INSTALLATION

1. Disconnect the negative battery cable.
2. Carefully pry on one side of the switch, then the other, to walk the switch from its position; be careful not to damage the dash padding.
3. To reinstall, reconnect the wires and push the switch back into its position.

Combination Switch

REMOVAL AND INSTALLATION

——— CAUTION ———
If equipped with an air bag, the negative battery cable must be disconnected for 20 minutes before working on the system. Failure to do so may result in deployment of the air bag and possible personal injury.

1. Disconnect the negative battery cable and remove the steering wheel.
2. Remove the screws securing the steering column covers and remove the covers.
3. Remove the 3 retaining screws and remove the turn signal switch.
4. Remove the screws to remove windshield wiper/washer switch and carefully disconnect the wires.
5. Installation is the reverse of the removal procedure.

Ignition Lock/Switch

REMOVAL AND INSTALLATION

——— CAUTION ———
If equipped with an air bag, the negative battery cable must be disconnected for 20 minutes before working on the system. Failure to do so may result in deployment of the air bag and possible personal injury.

1. Disconnect the negative battery cable and remove steering wheel.
2. Remove bottom switch cover, turn signal and wiper switches.
3. Some vehicles have a locking ring and spring below the switches. To remove, place a thin tube or pipe over the splines and push lightly against the spring. Remove the locking ring with snapring pliers and allow the spring to push the locking ring and spacer up. Lift out the remaining parts.

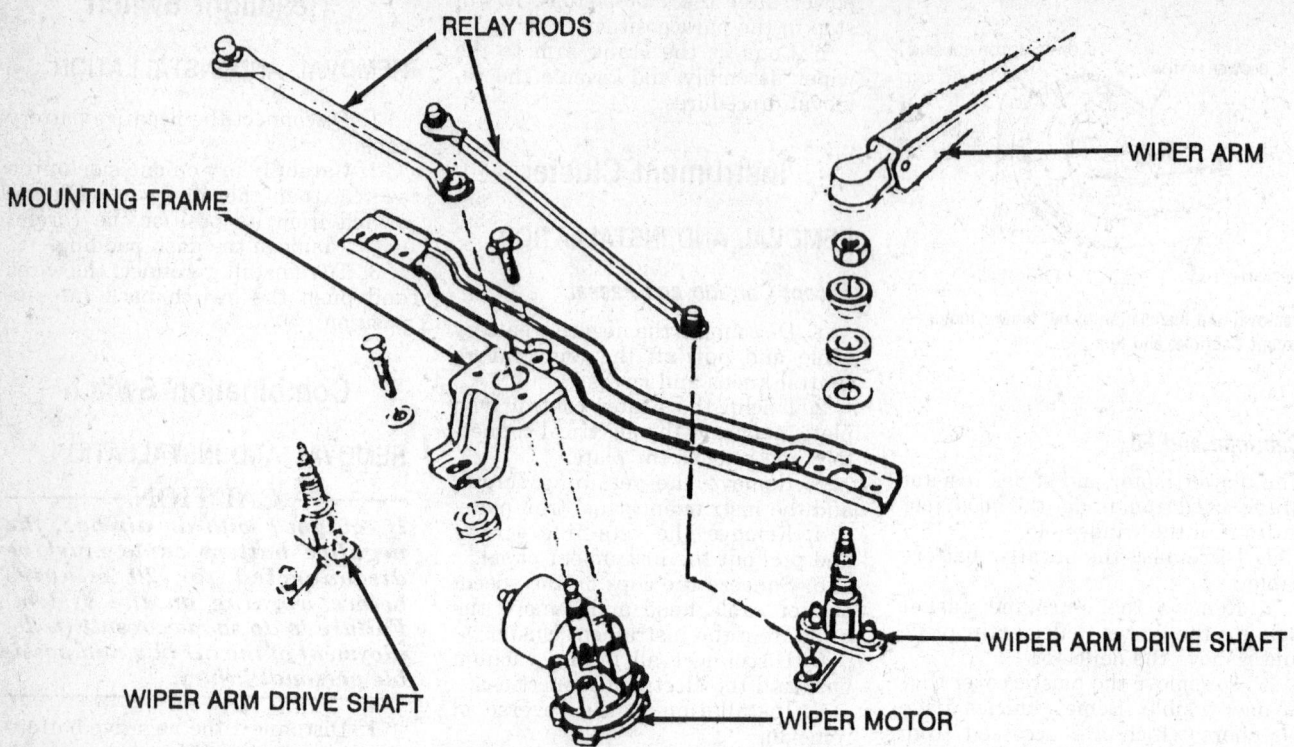

Removal and installation of the wiper motor

Programming the radio security code — proper security code is accepted

4. Unplug the ignition switch, remove the socket-head screw and remove the entire lock and support ring housing.

5. To remove the lock cylinder, carefully drill a ⅛in. (3.2mm) hole into the housing at the spot indicated, insert a key into the lock and remove the key and cylinder.

To install:

6. Insert the ignition key in the switch cylinder. The cylinder is held in place with a spring-loaded detent that automatically clicks into the drilled hole when the cylinder is pushed into the housing. Push the ignition switch into the steering column housing until it is seated.

7. Install the lock and support ring housing. Secure it with the retaining screw.

8. Connect the ignition switch harness connector.

9. For vehicles with a locking ring, install the spacer and locking ring.

10. Install the turn signal and wiper switches. Install the bottom switch cover.

11. Install the steering wheel. On Cabriolet, install the air bag assembly.

Stoplight Switch

ADJUSTMENT

1. Loosen the stoplight switch locknut and back off the stoplight switch until it does not touch the brake pedal.

2. If required, adjust the pedal height.

3. Screw in the stoplight switch until the plunger is fully depressed; threaded end touching the pad on the pedal arm.

4. Back off the switch ½ turn and tighten the locknut.

REMOVAL AND INSTALLATION

1. Disconnect the negative battery cable. Disconnect the stoplight switch electrical connectors.

2. Loosen the stoplight switch locknut and back off the stoplight switch until it is removed from the brake pedal.

3. Installation is the reverse order of the removal procedure.

Clutch Switch

ADJUSTMENT

On vehicles with cruise control, the system is deactivated by a vacuum switch connected to the clutch linkage. The cruise control is disabled when the clutch pedal is pushed. There is no adjustment or repair possible. If the switch malfunctions, it must be replaced.

REMOVAL AND INSTALLATION

1. Disconnect the negative battery cable.

2. Disconnect the switch wiring.

3. Loosen the locknut and remove the switch.

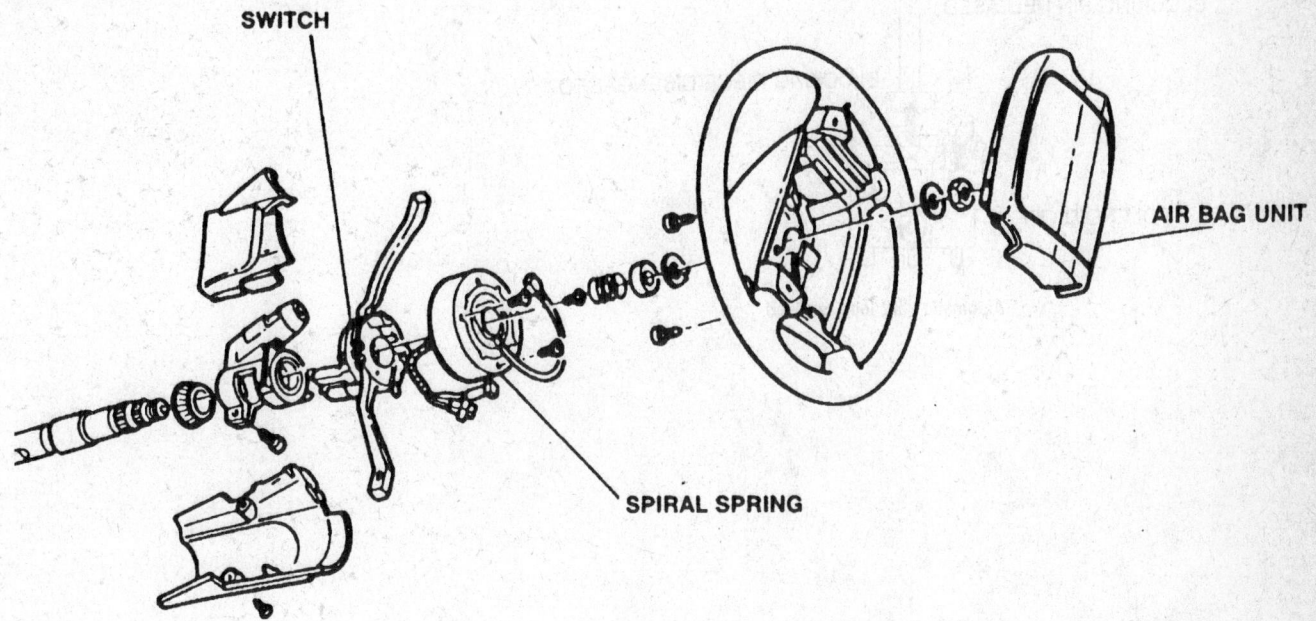

SWITCH

AIR BAG UNIT

SPIRAL SPRING

Steering wheel and wiper switch removal with air bag system

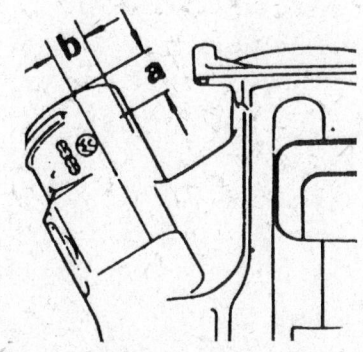

Dimension A — 0.470 in. (12mm) Dimension B — 0.390 in. (10mm)

4. Installation is the reverse of removal.

Neutral Safety Switch

ADJUSTMENT

Neutral safety switches, in all vehicles, are at the shifter inside the vehicle. Adjustment is accomplished by moving the switch on the slots so the starter will operate only in **P** or **N**.

All newer vehicles have an automatic shift lock that prevents the shifter from moving out of **P** or **N** with the engine running unless the brake pedal is pushed. If the vehicle speed is over 3 mph, the locking system will not activate. There is also a 1 second delay when shifting into **N**.

With the ignition **ON** and the shifter in **P** or **N**, a solenoid is activated and a blocking piece prevents the locking pin from moving when the shifter button is pushed. When the brake pedal is pushed, the solenoid is deactivated and the spring-loaded blocking piece moves away, allowing the shifter button to be pushed in.

1. Put the shifter in **P**.
2. With the cable screw loose at the gear lever shaft, move the shaft into the park detent.
3. Rock the vehicle to make sure the transaxle is really in **P** and tighten the shift lever screw to 18 ft. lbs. (25 Nm).
4. Remove the detent assembly to adjust the solenoid switch. With the solenoid off there should be a gap of 0.012 in. (0.3mm) between the pushrod and blocking piece.

5. With 12 volts supplied to the solenoid, the shift lever should be held in **P** or **N** until the brake pedal is pushed.

Fuses, Circuit Breakers and Relays

LOCATION

The fuse/relay panel is located to the left of the steering column. The function of each fuse is listed on the shelf or panel cover. The entire panel can be removed as a unit by removing the single screw or the locking clips and lifting the panel out. The large plugs on the back of the panel are keyed and cannot be installed incorrectly.

Flashers

LOCATION

The flasher is always on the relay assembly but its location varies from year-to-year, even on the same vehicle. It is always one of the corner locations.

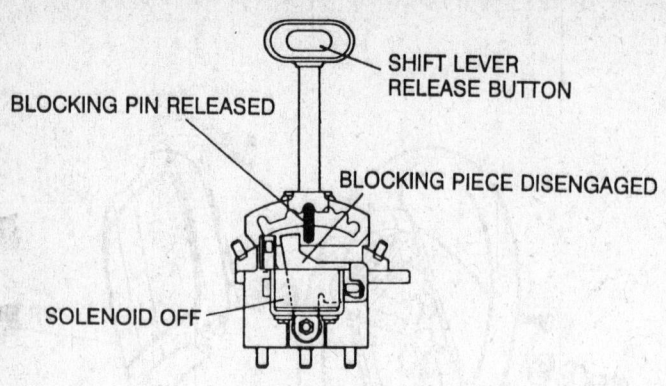

Automatic shift lock released

ENGINE IDENTIFICATION

Year	Model	Engine Displacement Liters (cc)	Engine Series (ID/VIN)	Fuel System	No. of Cylinders	Engine Type
1990	240	2.3 (2316)	B-230F	LH2.4	4	SOHC
	240DL	2.3 (2316)	B-230F	⑧	4	SOHC
	740	2.3 (2316)	B-230F	⑨	4	SOHC
	740GL	2.3 (2316)	B-230F	⑨	4	SOHC
	740GLE	2.3 (2316)	B-234F	LH2.4	4	DOHC ①
	740 Turbo	2.3 (2316)	B-230FT ②	LH2.4	4	SOHC
	760GLE	2.8 (2849)	B-280F	LH2.2	6	SOHC
	760 Turbo	2.3 (2316)	B-230FT ②	LH2.4	4	SOHC
	780	2.8 (2849)	B-280F	LH2.2	6	SOHC
	780 Turbo	2.3 (2316)	B-230FT ②	LH2.4	4	SOHC
1991	240	2.3 (2316)	B-230F	⑧	4	SOHC
	740	2.3 (2316)	B-230F	Regina	4	SOHC
	740GL	2.3 (2316)	B-230F	Regina	4	SOHC
	740 Turbo	2.3 (2316)	B-230FT ②	LH2.4	4	SOHC
	940GLE	2.3 (2316)	B-230F	LH2.4	4	DOHC ①
	940SE	2.3 (2316)	B-230FT ②	LH2.4	4	SOHC
	940 Turbo	2.3 (2316)	B-230FT ②	LH2.4	4	SOHC
	Coupe	2.3 (2316)	B-230FT ②	LH2.4	4	SOHC
1992	240	2.3 (2316)	B-230F	⑤	4	SOHC
	240GL	2.3 (2316)	B-230F	⑥	4	SOHC
	740	2.3 (2316)	B-230F	⑦	4	SOHC
	740 Turbo	2.3 (2316)	B-230FT ②	LH2.4	4	SOHC
	940GL	2.3 (2316)	B-230F	Regina	4	SOHC
	940 Turbo	2.3 (2316)	B-230FT ②	LH2.4	4	SOHC
	960	2.9 (2922)	B-6304F ④	Motronic 1.8	6	DOHC ③
1993	240	2.3 (2316)	B-230F	⑤	4	SOHC
	240GL	2.3 (2316)	B-230F	⑥	4	SOHC
	740	2.3 (2316)	B-230F	⑦	4	SOHC
	740 Turbo	2.3 (2316)	B-230FT ②	LH2.4	4	SOHC
	850 FWD	2.4 (2435)	B-5254F	LH3.2	5	DOHC ⑩
	940GL	2.3 (2316)	B-230F	Regina	4	SOHC
	940 Turbo	2.3 (2316)	B-230FT ②	LH2.4	4	SOHC
	960	2.9 (2922)	B-6304F ④	Motronic 1.8	6	DOHC ③
1994	240	2.3 (2316)	B-230F	⑤	4	SOHC
	240GL	2.3 (2316)	B-230F	⑥	4	SOHC
	740	2.3 (2316)	B-230F	⑦	4	SOHC
	740 Turbo	2.3 (2316)	B-230FT ②	LH2.4	4	SOHC
	850 FWD	2.4 (2435)	B-5254F	LH3.2	5	DOHC ⑩
	940GL	2.3 (2316)	B-230F	Regina	4	SOHC
	940 Turbo	2.3 (2316)	B-230FT ②	LH2.4	4	SOHC
	960	2.9 (2922)	B-6304F ④	Motronic 1.8	6	DOHC ③

LH—Bosch LH Fuel Injection
DOHC—Double Overhead Camshaft
SOHC—Single Overhead Camshaft
① 16 valve
② Turbocharged engine
③ 24 valve
④ B6304F—Fuel Injected w/Catalytic Converter
B6304G—Fuel Injected w/o Catalytic Converter

⑤ Vehicle Identification Code (VIC)
244-8201-131 LH3.1
244-8801-171 LH2.4
⑥ Vehicle Identification Code (VIC)
244-8202-231 LH3.1
244-8802-271 LH2.4
⑦ With EGR—LH 2.4
Without EGR—Regina

⑧ USA Federal and Canada, without EGR, fuel system LH2.4:
Manual transmission—1289368
Automatic transmission—1289369
USA Federal, without EGR, fuel system LH3.1:
Manual transmission—1289338
⑨ California—LH2.4
Except California—Regina

⑩ 20 valve

GENERAL ENGINE SPECIFICATIONS

Year	Engine ID/VIN	Engine Displacement Liters (cc)	Fuel System Type	Net Horsepower @ rpm	Net Torque @ rpm (ft. lbs.)	Bore × Stroke (in.)	Compression Ratio	Oil Pressure @ rpm
1990	B-230F	2.3 (2316)	④	114 @ 5400	136 @ 2750	3.78 × 3.15	9.8:1	35–85 @ 2000
	B-230FT	2.3 (2316)	④	①	②	3.78 × 3.15	8.7:1	35–85 @ 2000
	B-234F	2.3 (2316)	LH2.4	153 @ 5700	150 @ 4450	3.78 × 3.15	10.0:1	35–85 @ 2000
	B-280F	2.8 (2849)	LH2.2	144 @ 5100	173 @ 3750	3.58 × 2.87	9.5:1	⑤
1991	B-230F	2.3 (2316)	④	114 @ 5400	136 @ 2750	3.78 × 3.15	9.8:1	35–85 @ 2000
	B-230FT	2.3 (2316)	④	162 @ 4800	195 @ 3450	3.78 × 3.15	8.7:1	35–85 @ 2000
	B-234F	2.3 (2316)	LH2.4	153 @ 5700	150 @ 4450	3.78 × 3.15	10.0:1	35–85 @ 2000
1992	B-230F	2.3 (2316)	③	114 @ 5400	136 @ 2750	3.78 × 3.15	9.8:1	35–85 @ 2000
	B-230FT	2.3 (2316)	LH2.4	162 @ 4800	195 @ 3450	3.78 × 3.15	8.7:1	35–85 @ 2000
	B-6304F	2.9 (2922)	Motronic	204 @ 6000	197 @ 4300	3.27 × 3.54	10.7:1	36 @ 2000
1993	B-230F	2.3 (2316)	③	114 @ 5400	136 @ 2750	3.78 × 3.15	9.8:1	35–85 @ 2000
	B-230FT	2.3 (2316)	LH2.4	162 @ 4800	195 @ 3450	3.78 × 3.15	8.7:1	35–85 @ 2000
	B-5254F	2.4 (2435)	LH3.2	168 @ 6200	162 @ 3300	3.27 × 3.54	10.5:1	NA
	B-6304F	2.9 (2922)	Motronic	204 @ 6000	197 @ 4300	3.27 × 3.54	10.7:1	36 @ 2000
1994	B-230F	2.3 (2316)	③	114 @ 5400	136 @ 2750	3.78 × 3.15	9.8:1	35–85 @ 2000
	B-230FT	2.3 (2316)	LH2.4	162 @ 4800	195 @ 3450	3.78 × 3.15	8.7:1	35–85 @ 2000
	B-5254F	2.4 (2435)	LH3.2	168 @ 6200	162 @ 3300	3.27 × 3.54	10.5:1	NA
	B-6304F	2.9 (2922)	Motronic	204 @ 6000	197 @ 4300	3.27 × 3.54	10.7:1	36 @ 2000

NOTE: Horsepower and torque are SAE net figures. They are measured at the rear of the transmission with all accessories installed and operating. Since the figures vary when a given engine is installed in different models, some are representative rather than exact.

NA—Not available

① 740 Turbo—162 @ 4800
   760 Turbo—162 @ 4000
   780 Turbo—188 @ 5100
② 740 Turbo and 760 Turbo—195 @ 3450
   780 Turbo—206 @ 3900
③ 240—LH
   740 and 940GL—Regina
④ Refer to "Engine Identification Chart"
⑤ Engine warm:
     14.2 psi @ 900 rpm
     56.8 psi @ 3000 rpm

GASOLINE ENGINE TUNE-UP SPECIFICATIONS

Year	Engine ID/VIN	Engine Displacement Liters (cc)	Spark Plugs Gap (in.)	Ignition Timing (deg.)		Fuel Pump (psi)	Idle Speed (rpm)		Valve Clearance	
				MT	AT		MT	AT	In.	Ex.
1990	B-230F	2.3 (2316)	0.028	12B②	12B②	43	775	775	0.016①	0.016①
	B-230FT	2.3 (2316)	0.028–0.032	12B	12B	43	750	750	0.016–0.018	0.016–0.018
	B-234F	2.3 (2316)	0.028	15B	15B	42	850	850	—	—
	B-280F	2.8 (2849)	0.024–0.028	—	16B	36	—	750	0.006–0.008	0.012–0.014
1991	B-230F	2.3 (2316)	0.028	12B②	12B②	43	775	775	0.016①	0.016①
	B-230FT	2.3 (2316)	0.028–0.032	12B	12B	43	750	750	0.016–0.018	0.016–0.018
	B-234F	2.3 (2316)	0.028	15B	15B	42	—	850	—	—
1992	B-230F	2.3 (2316)	0.028	—	12B②	43	—	775	0.014–0.018	0.014–0.018
	B-230FT	2.3 (2316)	0.028–0.032	—	12B	43	—	775	0.014–0.018	0.014–0.018
	B-6304F	2.9 (2922)	0.024–0.028	—	14–18B	43	—	700–800	NA	NA
1993–94	REFER TO UNDERHOOD SPECIFICATIONS STICKER									

NOTE: The lowest cylinder pressure should be within 75% of the highest cylinder pressure reading. For example, if the highest cylinder is 134 psi, the lowest should be 101. Engine should be at normal operating temperature with throttle valve in the wide open position.
The underhood specifications sticker often reflects tune-up specification changes in production. Sticker figures must be used if they disagree with those in this chart.
NA—Not available
B—Before Top Dead Center
① Engine warm
② Rex 1: 10°/775

FIRING ORDERS

NOTE: To avoid confusion, always replace spark plug wires one at a time.

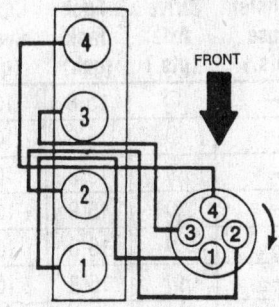

FRONT

B230F and B234F — 4 Cylinder Engine
Engine Firing Order: 1-3-4-2
Distributor Rotation: Clockwise

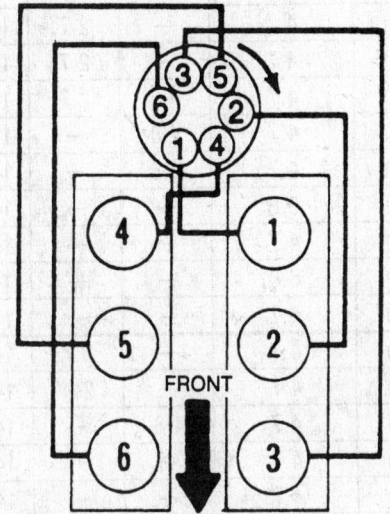

FRONT

B280F — 6 Cylinder Engine
Engine Firing Order: 1-6-3-5-2-4
Distributor Rotation: Clockwise

CAPACITIES

Year	Model	Engine ID/VIN	Engine Displacement Liters (cc)	Engine Crankcase with Filter (qts.)	Transmission (pts.) 4-Spd	5-Spd	Auto.	Transfer Case (pts.)	Drive Axle (pts.)	Fuel Tank (gal.)	Cooling System (qts.)
1990	240	B-230F	2.3 (2316)	4.7	—	2.7	14.0③	—	②	15.8	10.0
	240DL	B-230F	2.3 (2316)	4.7	—	2.7	14.0③	—	②	15.8	10.0
	740	B-230F	2.3 (2316)	4.7	—	2.7	14.0③	—	②	15.8	10.0
	740GL	B-230F	2.3 (2316)	4.7	—	2.7	14.0③	—	②	15.8	10.0
	740GLE	B-234F	2.3 (2316)	4.7	4.8	—	14.0③	—	②	15.8	10.0
	740 Turbo	B-230FT	2.3 (2316)	4.7	4.8	—	14.0③	—	②	15.8	10.0
	760GLE	B-280F	2.8 (2849)	6.8	—	—	14.0③	—	②	21.0	10.5
	760 Turbo	B-230FT	2.3 (2316)	4.7	—	—	14.0③	—	②	①	10.0
	780	B-280F	2.8 (2849)	6.8	—	—	14.0③	—	②	21.0	10.5
	780 Turbo	B-230FT	2.3 (2316)	4.7	—	—	14.0③	—	②	21.0	10.5
1991	240	B-230F	2.3 (2316)	4.7	—	2.7	14.0③	—	②	15.8	10.0
	740	B-230F	2.3 (2316)	4.7	—	2.7	14.0③	—	②	15.8	10.0
	740 Turbo	B-230FT	2.3 (2316)	4.7	4.8	—	14.0③	—	②	15.8	10.0
	940GLE	B-230F	2.3 (2316)	4.7	—	—	14.0③	—	②	15.8	10.0
	940SE	B-230FT	2.3 (2316)	4.7	—	—	14.0③	—	②	①	10.0
	940 Turbo	B-230FT	2.3 (2316)	4.7	—	—	14.0③	—	②	15.8	10.0
	Coupe	B-230FT	2.3 (2316)	4.7	—	—	14.0③	—	②	21.0	10.5
1992	240	B-230F	2.3 (2316)	4.7	—	2.7	14.0③	—	②	15.8	10.0
	240GL	B-230F	2.3 (2361)	4.7	—	2.7	14.0③	—	②	15.8	10.0
	740	B-230F	2.3 (2316)	4.7	—	—	14.0③	—	②	15.8	10.0
	740 Turbo	B-230FT	2.3 (2316)	4.7	—	—	14.0③	—	②	15.8	10.0
	940GL	B-230F	2.3 (2316)	4.7	—	—	14.0③	—	②	15.8	10.0
	940 Turbo	B-230FT	2.3 (2316)	4.7	—	—	14.0③	—	②	15.8	10.0
	960	B-6304F	2.9 (2922)	6.0	—	—	NA	—	②	①	11.3
1993	240	B-230F	2.3 (2316)	4.7	—	2.7	14.0③	—	②	15.8	10.0
	240GL	B-230F	2.3 (2316)	4.7	—	2.7	14.0③	—	②	15.8	10.0
	740	B-230F	2.3 (2316)	4.7	—	—	14.0③	—	②	15.8	10.0
	740 Turbo	B-230FT	2.3 (2316)	4.7	—	—	14.0③	—	②	15.8	10.0
	850 FWD	B-5254F	2.4 (2435)	—	—	—	NA	—	—	19.3	—
	940GL	B-230F	2.3 (2316)	4.7	—	—	14.0③	—	②	15.8	10.0
	940 Turbo	B-230FT	2.3 (2316)	4.7	—	—	14.0③	—	②	15.8	10.0
	960	B-6304F	2.9 (2922)	6.0	—	—	NA	—	②	①	11.3
1994	240	B-230F	2.3 (2316)	4.7	—	2.7	14.0③	—	②	15.8	10.0
	240GL	B-230F	2.3 (2316)	4.7	—	2.7	14.0③	—	②	15.8	10.0
	740	B-230F	2.3 (2316)	4.7	—	—	14.0③	—	②	15.8	10.0
	740 Turbo	B-230FT	2.3 (2316)	4.7	—	—	14.0③	—	②	15.8	10.0
	850 FWD	B-5254F	2.4 (2435)	—	—	—	NA	—	—	19.3	—
	940GL	B-230F	2.3 (2316)	4.7	—	—	14.0③	—	②	15.8	10.0
	940 Turbo	B-230FT	2.3 (2316)	4.7	—	—	14.0③	—	②	15.8	10.0
	960	B-6304F	2.9 (2922)	6.0	—	—	NA	—	②	①	11.3

NA—Not available
① 4-door—21.0
  5-door—15.8
② 1030 axle—2.8
  1031 axle—3.4
③ Approximately 5 pts. in torque converter

CAMSHAFT SPECIFICATIONS

All measurements given in inches.

Year	Engine ID/VIN	Engine Displacement Liters (cc)	Journal Diameter					Elevation		Bearing Clearance	Camshaft End Play
			1	2	3	4	5	In.	Ex.		
1990	B-230F	2.3 (2316)	1.179–1.180	1.179–1.180	1.179–1.180	1.179–1.180	—	0.374	0.414	0.0012–0.0028	0.004–0.016
	B-230FT	2.3 (2316)	1.179–1.180	1.179–1.180	1.179–1.180	1.179–1.180	—	0.374	0.414	0.0012–0.0028	0.004–0.016
	B-234F	2.3 (2316)	NA	NA	NA	NA	—	0.370	0.370	0.0012–0.0028	0.004–0.016
	B-280F	2.8 (2849)	1.592–1.593	1.616–1.617	1.639–1.640	0.664–1.665	—	0.235	0.214	0.0014–0.0034	NA
1991	B-230F	2.3 (2316)	1.179–1.180	1.179–1.180	1.179–1.180	1.179–1.180	—	0.374	0.414	0.0012–0.0028	0.004–0.016
	B-230FT	2.3 (2316)	1.179–1.180	1.179–1.180	1.179–1.180	1.179–1.180	—	0.374	0.414	0.0012–0.0028	0.004–0.016
	B-234F	2.3 (2316)	NA	NA	NA	NA	—	0.370	0.370	0.0012–0.0028	0.004–0.016
1992	B-230F	2.3 (2316)	1.179–1.180	1.179–1.180	1.179–1.180	1.179–1.180	—	0.374	0.414	0.0012–0.0028	0.004–0.016
	B-230FT	2.3 (2316)	1.179–1.180	1.179–1.180	1.179–1.180	1.179–1.180	—	0.374	0.414	0.0012–0.0028	0.004–0.016
	B-6304F	2.9 (2922)	NA	NA	NA	NA	—	0.354	0.354	NA	0.002–0.008
1993	B-230F	2.3 (2316)	1.179–1.180	1.179–1.180	1.179–1.180	1.179–1.180	—	0.374	0.414	0.0012–0.0028	0.004–0.016
	B-230FT	2.3 (2316)	1.179–1.180	1.179–1.180	1.179–1.180	1.179–1.180	—	0.374	0.414	0.0012–0.0028	0.004–0.016
	B-6304F	2.9 (2922)	NA	NA	NA	NA	—	0.354	0.354	NA	0.002–0.008
1994	B-230F	2.3 (2316)	1.179–1.180	1.179–1.180	1.179–1.180	1.179–1.180	—	0.374	0.414	0.0012–0.0028	0.004–0.016
	B-230FT	2.3 (2316)	1.179–1.180	1.179–1.180	1.179–1.180	1.179–1.180	—	0.374	0.414	0.0012–0.0028	0.004–0.016
	B-6304F	2.9 (2922)	NA	NA	NA	NA	—	0.354	0.354	NA	0.002–0.008

NA—Not available

CRANKSHAFT AND CONNECTING ROD SPECIFICATIONS

All measurements are given in inches.

Year	Engine ID/VIN	Engine Displacement Liters (cc)	Crankshaft				Connecting Rod		
			Main Brg. Journal Dia.	Main Brg. Oil Clearance	Shaft End-play	Thrust on No.	Journal Diameter	Oil Clearance	Side Clearance
1990	B-230F	2.3 (2316)	2.4981–2.4986	0.0011–0.0033	0.0015–0.0058	5	2.1255–2.1260	0.0009–0.0028	0.006–0.014
	B-230FT	2.3 (2316)	2.4981–2.4986	0.0011–0.0033	0.0015–0.0058	5	2.1255–2.1260	0.0009–0.0028	0.006–0.014
	B-234F	2.3 (2316)	1.9640–1.9648	0.0011–0.0033	0.0015–0.0058	5	2.0472–2.0476	0.0009–0.0028	0.006–0.018
	B-280F	2.8 (2849)	2.7576–2.7583	0.0035	0.0028–0.0106	4	2.3611–2.3618	0.0008–0.0015	0.007–0.013
1991	B-230F	2.3 (2316)	2.4981–2.4986	0.0011–0.0033	0.0015–0.0058	5	2.1255–2.1260	0.0009–0.0028	0.006–0.014
	B-230FT	2.3 (2316)	2.4981–2.4986	0.0011–0.0033	0.0015–0.0058	5	2.1255–2.1260	0.0009–0.0028	0.006–0.014
	B-234F	2.3 (2316)	1.9640–1.9648	0.0011–0.0033	0.0015–0.0058	5	2.0472–2.0476	0.0009–0.0028	0.006–0.018
1992	B-230F	2.3 (2316)	2.4981–2.4986	0.0011–0.0033	0.0015–0.0058	5	2.1255–2.1260	0.0009–0.0028	0.006–0.014
	B-230FT	2.3 (2316)	2.4981–2.4986	0.0011–0.0033	0.0015–0.0058	5	2.1255–2.1260	0.0009–0.0028	0.006–0.014
	B-6304F	2.9 (2922)	2.5590	0.0009–0.0019	NA	NA	1.9690	NA	0.005–0.017
1993	B-230F	2.3 (2316)	2.4981–2.4986	0.0011–0.0033	0.0015–0.0058	5	2.1255–2.1260	0.0009–0.0028	0.006–0.014
	B-230FT	2.3 (2316)	2.4981–2.4986	0.0011–0.0033	0.0015–0.0058	5	2.1255–2.1260	0.0009–0.0028	0.006–0.014
	B-6304F	2.9 (2922)	2.5590	0.0009–0.0019	NA	NA	1.9690	NA	0.005–0.017
1994	B-230F	2.3 (2316)	2.4981–2.4986	0.0011–0.0033	0.0015–0.0058	5	2.1255–2.1260	0.0009–0.0028	0.006–0.014
	B-230FT	2.3 (2316)	2.4981–2.4986	0.0011–0.0033	0.0015–0.0058	5	2.1255–2.1260	0.0009–0.0028	0.006–0.014
	B-6304F	2.9 (2922)	2.5590	0.0009–0.0019	NA	NA	1.9690	NA	0.005–0.017

VALVE SPECIFICATIONS

Year	Engine ID/VIN	Engine Displacement Liters (cc)	Seat Angle (deg.)	Face Angle (deg.)	Spring Test Pressure (lbs. @ in.)	Spring Installed Height (in.)	Stem-to-Guide Clearance (in.)		Stem Diameter (in.)	
							Intake	Exhaust	Intake	Exhaust
1990	B-230F	2.3 (2316)	45	44.5	158 @ 1.08	1.79	0.0012–0.0024	0.0024–0.0036	0.3132–0.3138	0.3128–0.3134
	B-230FT	2.3 (2316)	45	44.5	158 @ 1.08	1.79	0.0012–0.0024	0.0024–0.0036	0.3132–0.3138	0.3128–0.3134
	B-234F	2.3 (2316)	45	44.5	144 @ 1.04	1.69	0.0012–0.0024	0.0016–0.0028	NA	NA
	B-280F	2.8 (2849)	45	44.5	143 @ 1.18	1.85	①	①	②	②
1991	B-230F	2.3 (2316)	45	44.5	158 @ 1.08	1.79	0.0012–0.0024	0.0024–0.0036	0.3132–0.3138	0.3128–0.3134
	B-230FT	2.3 (2316)	45	44.5	158 @ 1.08	1.79	0.0012–0.0024	0.0024–0.0036	0.3132–0.3138	0.3128–0.3134
	B-234F	2.3 (2316)	45	44.5	144 @ 1.04	1.69	0.0012–0.0024	0.0016–0.0028	NA	NA
1992	B-230F	2.3 (2316)	45	44.5	158 @ 1.08	1.79	0.0012–0.0024	0.0024–0.0036	0.3132–0.3138	0.3128–0.3134
	B-230FT	2.3 (2316)	45	44.5	158 @ 1.08	1.79	0.0012–0.0024	0.0024–0.0036	0.3132–0.3138	0.3128–0.3134
	B-6304F	2.9 (2922)	45.25	45.5	270 @ 1.34	NA	0.0012–0.0024	0.0012–0.0024	NA	NA
1993	B-230F	2.3 (2316)	45	44.5	158 @ 1.08	1.79	0.0012–0.0024	0.0024–0.0036	0.3132–0.3138	0.3128–0.3134
	B-230FT	2.3 (2316)	45	44.5	158 @ 1.08	1.79	0.0012–0.0024	0.0024–0.0036	0.3132–0.3138	0.3128–0.3134
	B-6304F	2.9 (2922)	45.25	45.5	270 @ 1.34	NA	0.0012–0.0024	0.0012–0.0024	NA	NA
1994	B-230F	2.3 (2316)	45	44.5	158 @ 1.08	1.79	0.0012–0.0024	0.0024–0.0036	0.3132–0.3138	0.3128–0.3134
	B-230FT	2.3 (2316)	45	44.5	158 @ 1.08	1.79	0.0012–0.0024	0.0024–0.0036	0.3132–0.3138	0.3128–0.3134
	B-6304F	2.9 (2922)	45.25	45.5	270 @ 1.34	NA	0.0012–0.0024	0.0012–0.0024	NA	NA

NOTE: Exhaust valves for turbo engines are stellite coated and must not be machined. They may be ground against the valve seat.
NA—Not available
① Tapered valve guide ID—0.3150–0.3158 in.
② Tapered valve stem
    Intake
        Base—0.3135–0.3141 in.
        Top—0.3139–0.3145 in.
    Exhaust
        Base—0.3127–0.3133 in.
        Top—0.3136–0.3141 in.

PISTON AND RING SPECIFICATIONS

All measurements are given in inches.

Year	Engine ID/VIN	Engine Displacement Liters (cc)	Piston Clearance	Ring Gap			Ring Side Clearance		
				Top Compression	Bottom Compression	Oil Control	Top Compression	Bottom Compression	Oil Control
1990	B-230F	2.3 (2316)	0.0004–0.0012	0.0118–0.0217	0.0118–0.0217	0.0118–0.0256	0.0024–0.0036	0.0016–0.0028	0.0012–0.0026
	B-230FT	2.3 (2316)	0.0004–0.0012	0.0118–0.0217	0.0118–0.0217	0.0118–0.0256	0.0024–0.0036	0.0016–0.0028	0.0012–0.0026
	B-234F	2.3 (2316)	0.0004–0.0012	0.0118–0.0217	0.0118–0.0217	0.0118–0.0256	0.0024–0.0036	0.0016–0.0028	0.0012–0.0026
	B-280F	2.8 (2849)	0.0007–0.0015	0.0158–0.0236	0.0158–0.0236	0.0158–0.0571	0.0021–0.0029	0.0010–0.0021	0.0004–0.0092
1991	B-230F	2.3 (2316)	0.0004–0.0012	0.0118–0.0217	0.0118–0.0217	0.0118–0.0256	0.0024–0.0036	0.0016–0.0028	0.0012–0.0026
	B-230FT	2.3 (2316)	0.0004–0.0012	0.0118–0.0217	0.0118–0.0217	0.0118–0.0256	0.0024–0.0036	0.0016–0.0028	0.0012–0.0026
	B-234F	2.3 (2316)	0.0004–0.0012	0.0118–0.0217	0.0118–0.0217	0.0118–0.0256	0.0024–0.0036	0.0016–0.0028	0.0012–0.0026
1992	B-230F	2.3 (2316)	0.0004–0.0012	0.0118–0.0217	0.0118–0.0217	0.0118–0.0256	0.0024–0.0036	0.0016–0.0028	0.0012–0.0026
	B-230FT	2.3 (2316)	0.0004–0.0012	0.0118–0.0217	0.0118–0.0217	0.0118–0.0256	0.0024–0.0036	0.0016–0.0028	0.0012–0.0026
	B-6304F	2.9 (2922)	NA	0.0080–0.0160	0.0080–0.0160	0.0090–0.0200	0.0020–0.0033	0.0012–0.0026	0.0008–0.0022
1993	B-230F	2.3 (2316)	0.0004–0.0012	0.0118–0.0217	0.0118–0.0217	0.0118–0.0256	0.0024–0.0036	0.0016–0.0028	0.0012–0.0026
	B-230FT	2.3 (2316)	0.0004–0.0012	0.0118–0.0217	0.0118–0.0217	0.0118–0.0256	0.0024–0.0036	0.0016–0.0028	0.0012–0.0026
	B-6304F	2.9 (2922)	NA	0.0080–0.0160	0.0080–0.0160	0.0090–0.0200	0.0020–0.0033	0.0012–0.0026	0.0008–0.0022
1994	B-230F	2.3 (2316)	0.0004–0.0012	0.0118–0.0217	0.0118–0.0217	0.0118–0.0256	0.0024–0.0036	0.0016–0.0028	0.0012–0.0026
	B-230FT	2.3 (2316)	0.0004–0.0012	0.0118–0.0217	0.0118–0.0217	0.0118–0.0256	0.0024–0.0036	0.0016–0.0028	0.0012–0.0026
	B-6304F	2.9 (2922)	NA	0.0080–0.0160	0.0080–0.0160	0.0090–0.0200	0.0020–0.0033	0.0012–0.0026	0.0008–0.0022

NA—Not available

TORQUE SPECIFICATIONS

All readings in ft. lbs.

Year	Engine ID/VIN	Engine Displacement Liters (cc)	Cylinder Head Bolts	Main Bearing Bolts	Rod Bearing Bolts	Crankshaft Damper Bolts	Flywheel Bolts	Manifold		Spark Plugs	Lug Nut
								Intake	Exhaust		
1990	B-230F	2.3 (2316)	④	80	②	③	51	12	12	18	NA
	B-230FT	2.3 (2316)	④	80	②	③	51	12	12	18	NA
	B-234	2.3 (2316)	⑤	80	②	③	51	12	12	18	NA
	B-280F	2.8 (2849)	⑥	⑦	⑧	177–206	33–37	7–11	7–11	8–10	NA
1991	B-230F	2.3 (2316)	④	80	②	③	51	12	12	18	NA
	B-230FT	2.3 (2316)	④	80	②	③	51	12	12	18	NA
	B-234F	2.3 (2316)	⑤	80	②	③	51	12	12	18	NA
1992	B-230F	2.3 (2316)	④	80	②	③	51	12	12	18	NA
	B-230FT	2.3 (2316)	④	80	②	③	51	12	12	18	NA
	B-6304F	2.9 (2922)	⑨	NA	⑩	221	①	15	18	19	NA
1993	B-230F	2.3 (2316)	④	80	②	③	51	12	12	18	NA
	B-230FT	2.3 (2316)	④	80	②	③	51	12	12	18	NA
	B-6304F	2.9 (2922)	⑨	NA	⑩	221	①	15	18	19	NA
1994	B-230F	2.3 (2316)	④	80	②	③	51	12	12	18	NA
	B-230FT	2.3 (2316)	④	80	②	③	51	12	12	18	NA
	B-6304F	2.9 (2922)	⑨	NA	⑩	221	①	15	18	19	NA

NA—Not available

① 51 ft. lbs. ex. B280
 B280—33–37 ft. lbs.
 B6304F—33 + 50 degrees

② Torque in stages:
 1st step—14 ft. lbs.
 2nd step—angle-tighten 90°

③ Torque in stages:
 1st step—43 ft. lbs.
 2nd step—angle-tighten 90°

④ Torque in stages:
 1st step—14 ft. lbs.
 2nd step—43 ft. lbs.
 3rd step—angle-tighten 90°

⑤ Torque in stages:
 1st step—15 ft. lbs.
 2nd step—30 ft. lbs.
 3rd step—angle-tighten 115°

⑥ Tighten all bolts in stages:
 1. Tighten bolts to 43 ft. lbs.
 2. a. Loosen bolt 1, tighten it to 15 ft. lbs.
 b. Angle-tighten to 106 degrees using special tool 5098.
 c. Repeat this for remaining bolts using sequence shown in text.
 d. Loosen and tighten each bolt in turn.
On 1990 models using fixed washer bolts:
Tighten all bolts in stages:
 1. Tighten bolts to 44 ft. lbs.
 2. a. Loosen bolts
 b. Tighten bolts to 30 ft. lbs.
 c. Angle-tighten bolts 160°–180°
 3. Adjust valves

⑦ Tighten all nuts in stages:
 1. 22 ft. lbs.
 2. Slacken nut 1
 3. Tighten nut 1 22–26 ft. lbs.
 4. Angle-tighten nut 1 to 73°–77°
 5. Slacken and retighten the other nuts in the order specified in stages 2–4.

The 4 fasteners which hold No. 2 and 3 main bearings to engine block should be tightened to 15–18 ft. lbs. after the main bearing nuts have been tightened to the specified torque.

⑧ 1. Oil threads
 2. Tighten No. 1 bolt to 18 ft. lbs.
 3. Tighten No. 2 bolt to 18 ft. lbs. + angle-tighten 75°
 4. Angle-tighten No. 1 bolt 75°
 5. Check/tighten both bolts 37 ft. lbs.

⑨ Cylinder head: stage 1—15 ft. lbs.
 stage 2—44 ft. lbs.
 stage 3 angle tightening—150°
Bolts should be tightened in sequence from center towards ends.

⑩ Tighten in stages:
 1st step—15 ft. lbs.
 2nd step—angle-tighten 90°

BRAKE SPECIFICATIONS
All measurements in inches unless noted.

Year	Model	Master Cylinder Bore	Brake Disc			Brake Drum Diameter			Minimum Lining Thickness	
			Original Thickness	Minimum Thickness	Maximum Runout	Original Inside Diameter	Max. Wear Limit	Maximum Machine Diameter	Front	Rear
1990	240	①	0.870	0.790	0.0024	0.393	0.314	0.003	0.120	0.078
	240DL	①	0.870	0.790	0.0024	0.393	0.314	0.003	0.120	0.078
	740	NA②	0.870	0.790	0.0024	0.378	0.330	0.004	0.120	0.078
	740GL	NA②	0.870	0.790	0.0024	0.378	0.330	0.004	0.120	0.078
	740GLE	NA	0.870	0.790	0.0024	0.378	0.330	0.004	0.120	0.078
	740 Turbo	NA	0.870	0.790	0.0024	0.378	0.330	0.004	0.120	0.078
	760GLE	NA	0.870	0.790	0.0024	0.393	0.314	0.003	0.120	0.078
	760 Turbo	NA	0.870	0.790	0.0024	③	④	⑤	0.120	0.078
	780 Coupe	NA	0.870	0.790	0.0024	0.393	0.314	0.003	0.120	0.078
	780 Turbo	NA	0.870	0.790	0.0024	0.393	0.314	0.003	0.120	0.078
1991	240	NA	0.870	0.790	0.0024	0.393	0.314	0.003	0.120	0.078
	740	NA	1.020	0.910	0.0024	0.378	0.330	0.004	0.120	0.078
	740GL	NA②	0.870	0.790	0.0024	0.378	0.330	0.004	0.120	0.078
	740 Turbo	NA	0.870	0.790	0.0024	0.378	0.330	0.004	0.120	0.078
	940GLE	NA	1.020	0.910	0.0024	0.378	0.330	0.004	0.120	0.078
	940SE	NA	1.020	0.910	0.0024	③	④	⑤	0.120	0.078
	940 Turbo	NA	1.020	0.910	0.0024	0.378	0.330	0.004	0.120	0.078
	940 Coupe	NA	1.020	0.910	0.0024	0.378	0.330	0.004	0.120	0.078
1992	240	①	0.870	0.790	0.0024	0.393	0.314	0.003	0.120	0.078
	240GL	①	0.870	0.790	0.0024	0.393	0.314	0.003	0.120	0.078
	740	NA	1.020	0.910	0.0024	0.378	0.330	0.004	0.120	0.078
	740 Turbo	NA	1.020	0.910	0.0024	0.378	0.330	0.004	0.120	0.078
	940GL	NA	1.020	0.910	0.0024	0.378	0.330	0.004	0.120	0.078
	940 Turbo	NA	1.020	0.910	0.0024	0.378	0.330	0.004	0.120	0.078
	960	NA	1.020	0.910	0.0024	③	④	⑤	0.120	0.078
1993	240	①	0.870	0.790	0.0024	0.393	0.314	0.003	0.120	0.078
	240GL	①	0.870	0.790	0.0024	0.393	0.314	0.003	0.120	0.078
	740	NA	1.020	0.910	0.0024	0.378	0.330	0.004	0.120	0.078
	740 Turbo	NA	1.020	0.910	0.0024	0.378	0.330	0.004	0.120	0.078
	940GL	NA	1.020	0.910	0.0024	0.378	0.330	0.004	0.120	0.078
	940 Turbo	NA	1.020	0.910	0.0024	0.378	0.330	0.004	0.120	0.078
	960	NA	1.020	0.910	0.0024	③	④	⑤	0.120	0.078
1994	240	①	0.870	0.790	0.0024	0.393	0.314	0.003	0.120	0.078
	240GL	①	0.870	0.790	0.0024	0.393	0.314	0.003	0.120	0.078
	740	NA	1.020	0.910	0.0024	0.378	0.330	0.004	0.120	0.078
	740 Turbo	NA	1.020	0.910	0.0024	0.378	0.330	0.004	0.120	0.078
	940GL	NA	1.020	0.910	0.0024	0.378	0.330	0.004	0.120	0.078
	940 Turbo	NA	1.020	0.910	0.0024	0.378	0.330	0.004	0.120	0.078
	960	NA	1.020	0.910	0.0024	③	④	⑤	0.120	0.078

NA—Not available
① Stepped bore—0.620/0.878
② Stepped bore
③ 4-door—0.393
  5-door—0.378
④ 4-door—0.314
  5-door—0.330
⑤ 4-door—0.003
  5-door—0.004

WHEEL ALIGNMENT

Year	Model	Caster Range (deg.)	Caster Preferred Setting (deg.)	Camber Range (deg.)	Camber Preferred Setting (deg.)	Toe-in (in.)	Steering Axis Inclination (deg.)
1990	240DL	3P–4P	3.5P	0.25P–0.75P	0.5P	1/8	12
	240DL	3P–4P	3.5P	0.25P–0.75P	0.5P	1/8	12
	740	4.5P–5.5P	5P	0.2N–0.8P	0.3P	1/32	NA
	740GL	4.5P–5.5P	5P	0.2N–0.8P	0.3P	1/32	NA
	740GLE	4.5P–5.5P	5P	0.2N–0.8P	0.3P	1/32	NA
	740 Turbo	4.5P–5.5P	5P	0.2N–0.8P	0.3P	1/32	NA
	760GLE	4.5P–5.5P	5P	0.2N–0.8P	0.3P	9/64	NA
	760 Turbo	4.5P–5.5P	5P	0.2N–0.8P	0.3P	9/64	NA
	780	4.5P–5.5P	5P	0.2N–0.8P	0.3P	9/64	NA
	780 Turbo	4.5P–5.5P	5P	0.2N–0.8P	0.3P	9/64	NA
1991	240	3P–4P	3.5P	0.25P–0.75P	0.5P	1/8	12
	740	4.5P–5.5P	5P	0.2N–0.8P	0.3P	1/32	NA
	740GL	4.5P–5.5P	5P	0.2N–0.8P	0.3P	1/32	NA
	740 Turbo	4.5P–5.5P	5P	0.2N–0.8P	0.3P	1/32	NA
	940GLE	4.5P–5.5P	5P	0.2N–0.8P	0.3P	1/32	NA
	940SE	4.5P–5.5P	5P	0.2N–0.8P	0.3P	1/32	NA
	940 Turbo	4.5P–5.5P	5P	0.2N–0.8P	0.3P	1/32	NA
	Coupe	4.5P–5.5P	5P	0.2N–0.8P	0.3P	9/64	NA
1992	240	3P–4P	3.5P	0.25P–0.75P	0.5P	1/8	12
	240GL	3P–4P	3.5P	0.25P–0.75P	0.5P	1/8	12
	740	4.5P–5.5P	5P	0.2N–0.8P	0.3P	1/32	NA
	740 Turbo	4.5P–5.5P	5P	0.2N–0.8P	0.3P	1/32	NA
	940GL	4.5P–5.5P	5P	0.2N–0.8P	0.3P	1/32	NA
	940 Turbo	4.5P–5.5P	5P	0.2N–0.8P	0.3P	1/32	NA
	960	4.5P–5.5P	5P	0.2N–0.8P	0.3P	1/32	NA
1993	240	3P–4P	3.5P	0.25P–0.75P	0.5P	1/8	12
	240GL	3P–4P	3.5P	0.25P–0.75P	0.5P	1/8	12
	740	4.5P–5.5P	5P	0.2N–0.8P	0.3P	1/32	NA
	740 Turbo	4.5P–5.5P	5P	0.2N–0.8P	0.3P	1/32	NA
	940GL	4.5P–5.5P	5P	0.2N–0.8P	0.3P	1/32	NA
	940 Turbo	4.5P–5.5P	5P	0.2N–0.8P	0.3P	1/32	NA
	960	4.5P–5.5P	5P	0.2N–0.8P	0.3P	1/32	NA
1994	240	3P–4P	3.5P	0.25P–0.75P	0.5P	1/8	12
	240GL	3P–4P	3.5P	0.25P–0.75P	0.5P	1/8	12
	740	4.5P–5.5P	5P	0.2N–0.8P	0.3P	1/32	NA
	740 Turbo	4.5P–5.5P	5P	0.2N–0.8P	0.3P	1/32	NA
	940GL	4.5P–5.5P	5P	0.2N–0.8P	0.3P	1/32	NA
	940 Turbo	4.5P–5.5P	5P	0.2N–0.8P	0.3P	1/32	NA
	960	4.5P–5.5P	5P	0.2N–0.8P	0.3P	1/32	NA

NOTE: Camber must always be adjusted before Toe-in. All measurements to be carried out on an empty vehicle.
NA—Not available
N—Negative
P—Positive

SERIAL NUMBER IDENTIFICATION

Vehicle Identification Plate

The VIN plate on all vehicles is located on the top left surface of the dash and is also stamped on the right door pillar. Emission control information is on a label located on the left shock tower, under the hood. There is also a vehicle plate on the right shock tower that includes the VIN number, engine type, emission equipment, vehicle weights and color codes.

Engine Number

B230F AND B234F

Engine type designation, part number and serial number identification, stamped into the left side of the block just below the head. An information tag is also affixed to the timing cover.

B280F

Engine type designation, part number and serial number identification is stamp on the cylinder block.
Early type: between the cylinder banks, to rear.
Late type: right front, between the inlet manifold and water pump.

B6304F

Engine type designation, part number and serial number identification is punched in the left-hand side of the cylinder block. An identification label is also affixed to the timing cover.

Transmission Number

The transmission type designation, serial number and part number appear on a metal plate riveted to the underside of the transmission. The final drive reduction ratio, part number and serial number are found on a metal plate riveted to the left side of the differential.

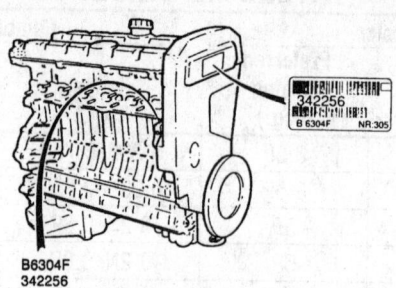

B6304F engine identification location

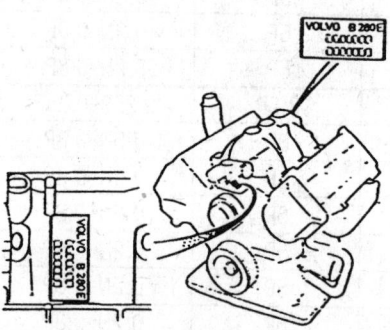

B280F engine identification location

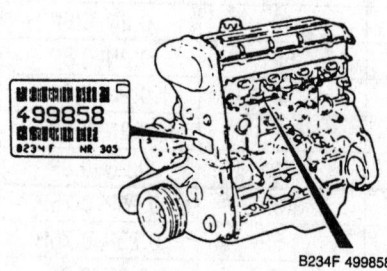

B234F, B230F and B230F turbocharged engine identification location

ENGINE MECHANICAL

NOTE: Disconnecting the negative battery cable on some vehicles may interfere with the functions of the on-board computer systems and may require the computer to undergo a relearning process, once the negative battery cable is reconnected.

Engine Assembly

REMOVAL AND INSTALLATION

B230F Engine

1. If equipped with manual transmission, remove the 4 retaining clips and lift up the shifter boot. Then, remove the snapring from the shifter.
2. Remove the battery.
3. Disconnect the windshield washer hose and engine compartment light wire. Scribe marks around the hood mount brackets on the underside of the hood for later alignment. Remove the hood.
4. Remove the overflow tank cap. Drain the cooling system.
5. Remove the upper and lower radiator hoses. Disconnect the overflow hoses at the radiator. Disconnect the PCV hose at the cylinder head.
6. If equipped with automatic transmission, disconnect the oil cooler lines at the radiator.
7. Remove the radiator and fan shroud.
8. Remove the air cleaner assembly and hoses.
9. Disconnect the hoses at the air pump. Remove the air pump and drive belt, if equipped.
10. Disconnect the vacuum pump hoses and remove the vacuum pump. Disconnect the power brake booster vacuum hose.
11. Remove the power steering pump, drive belt and bracket. Position aside.
12. If equipped with air conditioning, remove the crankshaft pulley and compressor drive belt. Then, install the pulley again for reference. Remove the air conditioning wire connector and the compressor from its bracket and position aside. Remove the bracket.
13. Disconnect the vacuum hoses from the engine. Disconnect the carbon canister hoses.
14. Disconnect the distributor wire connector, high tension lead, starter cables and the clutch cable clamp.
15. Disconnect the wiring harness at the voltage regulator. Disconnect the throttle cable at the pulley and the wire for the air conditioning at the manifold solenoid.
16. Remove the gas cap. Disconnect the fuel lines at the filter and return pipe.
17. At the firewall, disconnect the electrical connectors for the ballast resistor and relays. Disconnect the heater hoses.
18. Disconnect the micro-switch connectors at the intake manifold

and all remaining harness connectors to the engine.

19. Drain the crankcase.

20. Remove the exhaust manifold flange retaining nuts. Loosen the exhaust pipe clamp bolts and remove the bracket for the front exhaust pipe mount.

21. From underneath, remove the front motor mount bolts.

22. If equipped with automatic transmission, place the gear selector lever in **P** and disconnect the gear shift control rod from the transmission.

23. On manual transmission vehicles, disconnect the clutch cable. Then, loosen the set screw, drive out the pivot pin and remove the shifter from the control rod.

24. Disconnect the speedometer and the driveshaft from the transmission.

25. On overdrive equipped vehicles, disconnect the control wire from the shifter.

26. Raise and support the vehicle safely. Then, using a floor jack and a wooden block, support the weight of the engine beneath the transmission.

27. Remove the bolts for the rear transmission mount. Remove the transmission support crossmember.

28. Lift out the engine using the proper lifting equipment.

To install:

29. If detached, join the engine and transmission. Install the engine assembly in the vehicle and tighten all engine mounting bolts. Install the transmission crossmember and remove the floor jack.

30. Install the driveshaft, speedometer cable, clutch cable (manual transmission) and gear selector mechanism.

31. Install the exhaust system. On turbocharger equipped vehicles, install the turbocharger and related exhaust pipes.

32. Install the air conditioner compressor and related accessory drive units. Install all accessory drive belts and tighten to the proper tension. Install the vacuum pump.

33. Install the radiator and shroud. Install all vacuum, coolant and fuel lines and hoses. Connect all electrical connectors previously disconnected.

34. Install the hood, windshield wipers, battery and any other component previously removed.

35. Fill the engine with oil, the radiator with coolant and the transmission with fluid.

36. Adjust the reversing lock clamp and the gear selector. Adjust the throttle valve/pulley, automatic transmission kick-down cable and link rod.

37. Start the engine and allow it to reach operating temperature. Check and adjust the engine idle. Check for leaks.

B234F Engine

1. Disconnect the negative battery cable.

2. Disconnect the ground connection at the top of the side frame rail.

3. Release the bolted joint at the exhaust manifold front bracket.

4. Attach the sling or lifting equipment to the rear of the motor and support the motor from above. Release any wiring harnesses from their clips and place the wiring aside of the lifting gear.

5. Remove the splash guard under the engine, drain the engine oil and remove the air intake duct.

6. Remove the wiring clips on the front crossmember and right frame rail. Release the battery from the clips and work the wiring free of the roll bar.

7. If equipped with air conditioning, remove the compressor from its mount and position it aside. Do not disconnect any lines or hoses from the compressor.

8. Remove the bottom nut on the left engine mount.

9. On manual transmission vehicles, remove the clutch slave cylinder and position aside. Be careful of the rubber boot; it retains the piston within the cylinder.

10. Separate the front and rear universal joints. Unbolt the center support bearing and withdraw the driveshaft toward the rear of the vehicle.

11. Cut the rear cable tie holding the transmission wiring and separate the connectors.

12. For vehicles with manual transmission, the gear lever is removed by removing the locking bolt, removing

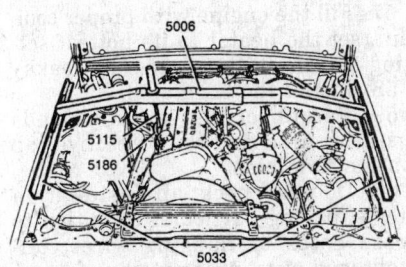

Engine replacement tooling — B234F engine shown, other similar

the pivot pin between the lever and the selector rod and removing the circlip from the lever sleeve. Push the shift lever up and remove the bushings. For vehicles with automatic transmissions, the selector lever is disconnected by removing the clips from the joints between the lever and the selector rod. Withdraw the arm from the mounting.

13. Release the bolted joint at the front of the catalytic converter and release the oxygen sensor wire from the rear clip.

14. Remove the front exhaust pipe by removing the bolts at its joint to the exhaust manifold.

15. If equipped with automatic transmission, disconnect the oil lines at the transmission and plug the lines.

16. Remove the transmission crossmember. As soon as it is removed, position a floor jack below the transmission to support it.

NOTE: The following steps are in the upper engine area. It may be helpful to temporarily remove the hoist equipment for access. The hoist will need to be reinstalled later in the removal procedure.

17. Remove the upper heat shield from the exhaust manifold. Remove the air hose from the lower heat shield.

18. Remove the top nut from the right motor mount.

19. Open the draincock on the right side of the engine block and drain the coolant into a container.

20. Label and remove the wiring from the distributor cap. Remove the cap and rotor and disconnect the braided engine ground wire.

21. Disconnect the wire to terminal 1 on the coil. Separate the wiring connectors on the right shock tower and release the cable clips on the firewall. Free the wiring from the clips.

22. Disconnect the heater hoses on the left firewall.

23. Release the fuel line connection at the left firewall and attend to any fuel spillage immediately. Plug the fuel lines.

24. Disconnect the wiring connector on the left side of the firewall and free the wires from the clips.

25. Disconnect the air mass meter, its wiring and the hoses connected to the air intake.

26. Release the throttle cable from the pulley.

27. Remove the vacuum hose to the brake booster from the intake manifold. Remove the evaporation hose

from the intake manifold and the return line from the fuel distributor.

28. At the left shock tower, release the engine wiring harness from its clips and disconnect the wiring connectors. Remove the power steering reservoir from its clips.

29. Disconnect the coolant hoses at the thermostat housing and at the water pump.

30. Remove the drive belts.

31. Remove the radiator fan, the fan shroud and the drive pulley.

32. Remove the power steering pump from its mount. Place the pump on paper or rags on top of the left shock tower. Do not disconnect any hoses from the pump.

33. If the lifting equipment was removed earlier, reconnect it.

34. Check the surroundings of the engine and transmission unit. With the exception of the jack and the motor mounts, there should be nothing connecting the engine/transmission assembly to the body of the vehicle. Take slight tension on the hoist and check that the engine is balanced. Reposition the lift points if the engine is not balanced.

35. Lift out the engine and transmission, being very careful of the radiator and surrounding components. Support the engine on appropriate stand.

To install:

36. When reinstalling, check the position and security of the hoist equipment. Lift the engine and transmission into place in the vehicle.

37. Guide the engine mounts into place and support the transmission on the floor jack.

38. Replace the transmission crossmember and make sure the wiring for the oxygen sensor runs above the crossmember. Remove the floor jack when the crossmember is secure. The engine hoisting equipment may also be removed.

39. Use a new gasket and attach the exhaust pipe to the manifold. Attach the wire to the oxygen sensor.

40. Reconnect the shifting mechanism to the transmission.

41. Reconnect the transmission wiring and secure the harness with new wire ties.

42. Install the driveshaft. Tighten the front and rear universal joints and attach the center support bearing.

43. On manual transmission vehicle, connect the clutch slave cylinder. On automatic transmissions, connect the oil cooler lines.

44. Install the lower nut for the left motor mount. On vehicles with air

conditioning, remount the compressor on its brackets.

45. Track the wiring between the anti-roll bar and the front crossmember. Install the cable clips on the crossmember and right side frame rail. Install the splash guard under the vehicle. Reconnect the wiring to the ground connection on the right frame rail.

46. Install the nut on the top of the right engine mount. Install the upper heat shield on the manifold and the air tube to the lower heat shield.

47. Reconnect the coolant hoses. The bottom hose connects to the water pump and the upper hose to the thermostat housing.

NOTE: Note the marking on the upper hose. The hose must run at least 1 inch away from the alternator belt.

48. Remount the power steering pump. Install its belt and the air conditioning belt, if equipped, and adjust to the correct tension.

49. Install the fan, pulley and shroud. Secure the wiring below the fan with new wire ties. Install the drive belt and adjust to the correct tension.

50. Reconnect the rear wiring harnesses on the firewall. Plug all connectors carefully and secure harnesses within the clips.

51. Reinstall the distributor rotor, cap and wires. Connect the braided engine ground cable.

52. Reconnect the wiring at the left shock tower. Make sure the wiring is secure in its clips. Install the power steering reservoir.

53. At the intake manifold, connect the vacuum line to the brake booster, the evaporation line and the return line for the fuel distributor.

54. At the left side of the firewall, attach the heater hoses and connect the fuel line.

55. Reattach the throttle cable to the pulley.

56. Install the air mass meter with its hoses and connections.

57. Fill the engine with proper coolant, set the heater to its hottest setting and check the system for leaks.

58. Install the engine oil.

59. Reconnect the battery leads (positive first) and the protective cap on the terminals.

60. Double check all installation items, paying particular attention to loose hoses or hanging wires, untightened nuts, poor routing of hoses and wires (too tight or rubbing) and tools left in the engine area.

61. Start the engine and check for leaks. This engine may be somewhat

noisy when started; the noise will disappear as the tappets fill with oil.

B280F Engine

1. If equipped with manual transmission, remove the shifter assembly. From underneath, loosen the set screw, drive out the pivot pin and pull up the boot. Remove the reverse pawl bracket, shifter snapring and lift out the shifter.

2. Remove the battery.

3. Disconnect the windshield washer hose and engine compartment light wire. Scribe marks around the hood mount brackets on the underside of the hood for later hood alignment. Remove the hood.

4. Remove the air cleaner assembly.

5. Remove the splash guard under the engine.

6. Drain the cooling system.

7. Remove the overflow tank cap. Remove the upper and lower radiator hoses and disconnect the overflow hoses at the radiator.

8. If equipped with automatic transmission, disconnect the transmission cooler lines at the radiator.

9. Remove the radiator and fan shroud.

10. Disconnect the heater hoses, power brake hose at the intake manifold and the vacuum pump hose at the pump. Remove the vacuum pump and O-ring in the valve cover. Remove the gas cap.

11. At the firewall, disconnect the fuel lines at the filter and return pipe. Disconnect the relay connectors and all other wire connectors. Disconnect the distributor wires.

--- **CAUTION** ---
Use caution when disconnecting the fuel lines. The fuel lines may be under high pressure.

12. Disconnect the evaporative control carbon canister hoses and the vacuum hose at the EGR valve.

13. Disconnect the voltage regulator wire connector.

14. Disconnect the throttle cable and kickdown cable, on automatic transmission vehicles, the vacuum amplifier hose at the T-pipe and the hoses at the thermostat.

15. Disconnect the air pump hose at the backfire valve, the solenoid valve wire and the micro-switch wire.

16. Remove the exhaust manifold flange retaining nuts (both sides).

17. If equipped with air conditioning, remove the compressor and drive belt and place it aside. Do not disconnect the refrigerant hoses.

18. Drain the crankcase.

19. Remove the power steering pump, drive belt and bracket. Position aside.

20. From underneath, remove the retaining nuts for the front motor mounts.

21. Remove the front exhaust pipe, if needed.

22. On 49 states vehicles, remove the front exhaust pipe hangers and clamps and allow the system to hang.

23. If equipped with automatic transmission, place the shift lever in **P**. Disconnect the shift control lever at the transmission.

24. On manual transmission vehicles, disconnect the clutch cylinder from the bell housing. Leave the cylinder connected; secure it to the vehicle.

25. Disconnect the speedometer cable and driveshaft at the transmission.

26. Raise and safely support the vehicle. Place jackstands under the reinforced box member area to the rear of each front jacking attachment. Then, using a floor jack and a thick, wide wooden block, support the weight of the engine under the oil pan.

27. Remove the bolts for the rear transmission mount. Remove the transmission support crossmember.

28. Lift out the engine and transmission as a unit.

To install:

29. If separated, join the engine and transmission. Install the engine assembly in the vehicle and tighten all mounting bolts to specification. Install the transmission crossmember.

30. Install the driveshaft and speedometer cable. On manual transmission vehicles, install the clutch assembly and gear shift assembly. On automatic transmission vehicles install the gear selector assembly.

31. Install the exhaust system. Install all air conditioning compressor, power steering pump, air pump and alternator. Install and tighten all accessory drive belts to specification.

32. Connect the throttle and kickdown cables. Connect the charcoal canister and evaporative emissions control hoses.

33. Install the fuel lines and filter. Install the heater hoses and vacuum pump hoses.

34. Install the radiator, shroud and radiator hoses. Connect all other hoses or lines previously disconnected. Connect all electrical connections.

35. Install the hood, battery and gear selector.

36. Fill the cooling system with coolant, the engine with oil and the transmission with fluid. Start the engine and bring it to operating temperature. Check the idle speed. Check for leaks.

B6304F Engine

1. Disconnect the negative battery cable.

2. Disconnect the wiring connected to the positive terminal, battery positive lead, ground lead connection to the body at top of side member and clip on the side member.

3. Remove the battery.

4. Remove the auxiliary drive belt.

5. Remove the cooling fan.

6. Release the upper bolts and disconnect the connector at the relay in front of the battery. Disconnect the ground lead at the right side ground terminal.

7. Drain the cooling system.

8. Remove the upper and lower radiator hoses from the engine. Remove the radiator overflow hose.

9. Remove the transmission cooler lines from the radiator.

10. Remove the top nut on both left and right side engine mountings.

11. Disconnect and remove the large and small crankcase ventilation hoses, idling hose and idling valve lead.

12. Disconnect and remove the EVAP valve hoses (2) at the intake manifold. Disconnect the air mass meter connector, air preheater hose and throttle pulley cover.

13. Remove the servo pump mounting bolts (3 bolts at front and 2 at rear).

14. Disconnect and remove the fuel return line at the regulator and fuel line at bulkhead. Remove the throttle cable, cruise control vacuum hose and fuel line snap catches.

15. Remove the engine wiring harness cover and disconnect the harness connector. Disconnect the relay connector. Remove the harness duct retaining nuts.

16. Disconnect the heater hoses at bulkhead, ECC hoses at intake manifold and brake servo vacuum hose. Disconnect the timing pickup and camshaft sensor connectors.

17. Support the engine at rear, using the engine removal tool assembly (5033, 5006, 5115, 5428 and 5429 or equivalent).

18. Remove the splash guard and air baffle under the engine.

19. Remove the radiator mounting bolts.

20. Drain the engine oil.

21. Disconnect the hose at the oil thermostat in cylinder block.

22. Disconnect the air conditioning compressor lead. Remove the air conditioning compressor mounting bolts. Support the compressor aside.

23. Remove the exhaust pipe flanges at the manifold. Remove the lower section of the air preheater pipe and remove the exhaust pipe shield.

24. Remove the oil pipe connections at the transmission. Plug the openings.

25. Remove the clips between the gear selector lever and control rod/reaction arm. Withdraw the rods from mounting.

26. Disconnect and remove the oxygen sensor wiring.

NOTE: Before separating the driveshaft, mark the coupling halves for reassembly.

27. Disconnect the driveshaft and remove the transmission support member.

28. Place a jack under the transmission. Remove the lifting tools.

29. Remove the radiator upper attachments and lift out the radiator assembly.

30. Install the engine lifting tool 2810 or equivalent, and adjust the lifting yoke to ensure the engine is balanced.

NOTE: Position the wiring harnesses so as to avoid damage when lifting.

31. Remove the jack from under the transmission.

32. Remove the engine and transmission assembly from the vehicle.

33. Mount the engine in the stand and fixture tool 2520 and 5297 or equivalent.

To install:

34. Install the lifting tools to the engine assembly.

35. Install the engine into the vehicle, guiding the engine mounting into position.

36. Install the mounting nuts and torque to 37 ft. lbs. (50 Nm).

37. Position a jack to support the transmission. Remove the lifting tool.

38. Support the rear of the engine, using the 2 support rails and lifting beam assembly. Remove the jack from beneath the transmission.

39. Using the transmission lifting tool 5972 or equivalent, raise the transmission. Tighten the bolted joints between the support member and side members. Tighten the transmission bump stop nut 37 ft. lbs. (50 Nm).

40. Attach the control rod and reaction arm to the gear selector lever mounting. Install the locking clip.

41. Connect the oxygen sensor lead.

42. Install the driveshaft. Tighten the front and rear couplings, noting the marks made during removal.

43. Inspect the preheater pipe O-ring. Connect the preheater pipe to the exhaust pipe. Tighten the sump bolts.

44. Install the air conditioning compressor.

45. Reconnect the hoses to the oil cooler and torque to 22 ft. lbs. (30 Nm)

46. Remove the lifting tools from rear of engine.

47. Install the heater hoses.

48. Install the timing pickup and camshaft position sensor connectors.

49. Connect the engine connector to the wiring harness connector at left side wheel housing. Connect the relay and install the wiring duct retaining nuts.

50. Connect the fuel hoses, vacuum hoses and electrical connectors.

51. Install the throttle cable and throttle pulley cover.

52. Install the servo pump. Install the auxiliary drive belt.

53. Connect the radiator hoses and transmission oil pipes.

54. Install the cooling fan. Connect the cooling fan lead.

55. Connect the battery leads in holders. Install the battery. Connect the lead at the right side wheel housing and battery positive leads.

56. Raise the vehicle and support it safely.

57. Install the transmission lines. Install the exhaust pipe and heat shield.

NOTE: Loosen the catalytic convertor bolts, then re-tighten. This will prevent stress in the system.

58. Install the radiator mounting bolts, air baffle and splash guard.

59. Fill the cooling system.

60. Connect the negative battery cable. Start the engine and check for leaks.

Engine Mounts

REMOVAL AND INSTALLATION

B230F Engine

1. Disconnect the negative battery lead.

2. Assemble the engine lifting tools and raise the engine slightly.

3. Remove the engine mount retaining nuts.

4. When replacing the left side engine mount, cut the strap for the power steering hose.

To install:

5. Place the engine mounts into position. On left side engine mount, attach the bracket at the intake manifold and engine mount. Install the strap for the power steering.

6. Install the lower engine mounts on the front axle member. Lower the engine and remove the lifting tools.

7. Connect the negative battery lead.

B234F Engine

LEFT SIDE

1. Disconnect the negative battery lead.

2. Remove the air mass meter and air inlet hose.

3. Remove the engine mounting bottom nut. If necessary, remove the front splash guard.

4. Assemble the engine lifting tools and raise the engine slightly.

NOTE: Be careful not to damage the fan blades by contact with the shroud.

5. Remove the 3 bolts securing the mounting to the cylinder block. Remove the engine mount.

To install:

6. Place the engine mount into position with the cable clip and support at the top bolt.

7. Lower the engine, while guiding the bottom bolt of the mounting into the bracket. Install the retaining nut.

8. If removed, install the front splash guard.

9. Install the air mass meter and air inlet hose.

10. Connect the negative battery lead.

RIGHT SIDE

1. Disconnect the negative battery lead.

2. Remove the air preheating hose from the bottom heat shield.

3. Remove the 4 nuts securing the bottom mounting plate.

4. Disconnect the air inlet hose from the throttle housing.

5. Assemble the engine lifting tools and raise the engine slightly.

NOTE: Be careful not to damage the fan blades by contact with the shroud.

6. Remove the engine mounting and bottom mounting plate.

To install:

7. Place the engine mounting and bottom mounting plate into position.

8. Lower the engine, while guiding the mounting plate and mounting into position. Remove the lifting tools.

9. Install the 4 nuts securing the engine mounting and bottom mounting plate.

10. Install the air preheating hose and air inlet hose.

11. Connect the negative battery lead.

B280F Engine

FRONT MOUNT

1. Disconnect the negative battery lead.

2. Assemble the engine lifting tools and raise the engine slightly.

NOTE: Be careful not to damage the fan blades by contact with the shroud.

3. Raise and support the vehicle safely. Remove the engine splash guard.

4. Remove the nuts and bolts securing the engine mounts, remove the engine mounts.

To install:

5. Place the engine mounts into position and install the mounting nuts and bolts.

NOTE: When installing the bolts, make certain the battery negative lead is fastened under 1 of them.

6. Lower the engine and remove the lifting tools.

7. Connect the negative battery lead.

REAR MOUNT

1. Disconnect the negative battery lead.

2. Raise and support the vehicle safely.

3. Position a service jack beneath the transmission and raise the engine slightly.

4. Remove the engine mounting bushings, using a mandrel tool 5225 or equivalent.

To install:

5. Install the bushings, using the mandrel.

NOTE: When installing the bushings, note the position of the arrows on the bushings. The arrows must point to mark on the bracket.

6. Remove the service jack and lower the vehicle.

7. Connect the negative battery lead.

B6304F Engine

1. Disconnect the negative battery cable.

2. Remove the engine mounting top nut.

3. Assemble the engine lifting tools and raise the engine slightly.

NOTE: Be careful not to damage the fan blades by contact with the shroud.

4. Raise the vehicle and support it safely. Remove the splash guard under the engine.

5. Remove the mounting nuts and bolts.

6. On left side engine mount, remove the mount and bracket towards the front.

7. On right side engine mount, remove the mount and bracket towards the rear.

To install:

8. Assemble the new mounting on the bracket. Install the mounting and bracket.

9. Install the splash guard. Lower the vehicle and remove the lifting tools.

10. Connect the negative battery lead.

Cylinder Head

REMOVAL AND INSTALLATION

B230F Engine

1. Disconnect the battery.

2. Remove the overflow tank cap and drain the coolant. Disconnect the upper radiator hose.

3. Remove the distributor cap and wires.

4. Remove the PCV hoses.

5. Remove the EGR valve and vacuum pump.

6. Remove the air pump, if equipped, and air injection manifold. Disconnect and remove all hoses to the turbocharger, if equipped. Plug all open hoses and holes immediately.

7. Remove the exhaust manifold and header pipe bracket.

8. Remove the intake manifold. Disconnect the manifold brace and the hose clamp to the bellows for the fuel injection air flow unit. Disconnect the throttle cable and all vacuum hoses and electrical connectors to the fuel injection unit.

9. Remove the fuel injectors.

10. Remove the valve cover.

11. Loosen the fan shroud and remove the fan. Remove the shroud. Remove the upper belts and pulleys.

12. Remove the timing belt cover. Remove the timing belt.

13. Remove the camshaft, if necessary.

14. Loosen the cylinder head bolts by reversing the torque sequence. Remove the cylinder head.

To install:

15. Check the position of the crankshaft. No. 1 piston should be at TDC. Check the position of the camshaft for cylinder No. 1. Both lobes should be in such a position that if the head were installed, the valves would be closed.

16. Install the cylinder head gasket and the cylinder head. Ensure that the O-ring for the water pump is in place. Apply a light coat of oil to the head bolts and install.

17. Tighten the head bolts in 3 stages using the proper sequence.
   a. Stage 1 — tighten all bolts to 14 ft. lbs. (20 Nm).
   b. Stage 2 — tighten all bolts to 43 ft. lbs. (60 Nm).
   c. Stage 3 — angle tighten all bolts an additional 90 degrees.

18. Install the camshaft, camshaft gear and spacer, as required. Do not allow the camshaft to turn during installation. Set the timing belt tensioner and install the timing belt. Remove the tool from the belt tensioner to tension the belt.

19. Rotate the engine 1 full turn. Loosen the tensioner bolt 1 full turn and re-tighten to set the tensioner. Adjust the valve lash.

20. Install the fan shroud and fan. Install the accessory drive belts and pulleys.

21. Install the intake manifold, fuel injection system, throttle cable and valve covers.

22. Install the exhaust manifold and header pipe. Install the air pump assembly. If equipped with a turbo-

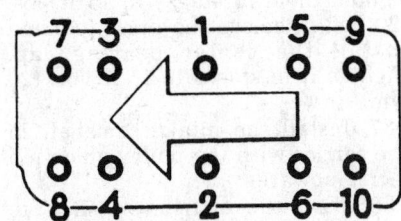

Head bolt tightening sequence for B230F and B234F. When removing, loosen the bolts in reverse order.

charger, install the turbocharger and related parts.

23. Install the EGR valve, vacuum pump, PCV hoses, distributor cap and wires, overflow tank and battery.

24. Fill the radiator with coolant, check the engine oil and transmission fluid. Start the engine and allow it to reach operating temperature. Check for leaks.

B234F Engine

NOTE: The use of the correct special tools or their equivalent, as required for this procedure.

1. Disconnect the negative battery cable.

2. Remove the heat shield over the exhaust manifold.

3. Remove the cap from the expansion tank and open the draincock on the right side of the motor. Collect the drained coolant in a suitable container.

4. Unbolt the exhaust pipe from the bracket, remove the manifold nuts and remove the manifold from the head.

5. On the left side of the engine, remove the support under the intake manifold and remove the bottom bolt in the cylinder block.

6. Remove the manifold intact and tie it or support it safely.

7. Disconnect the temperature sensor connectors, the heating hose under cylinders No. 3 and 4 and the upper radiator hose at the thermostat.

8. Remove the upper and lower timing belt covers.

9. Align the camshaft and crankshaft marks. Turn the engine to TDC, of the compression stroke, on cylinder No. 1 and make sure the pulley marks and the crank marks align.

10. Remove the protective cap over the timing belt tensioner locknut. Loosen the locknut, compress the tensioner, to release tension on the belts and retighten the locknut, holding the tensioner in place.

11. Remove the timing belt from the camshafts. Do not crease or fold the belt.

NOTE: The camshafts and the crankshaft must not be moved when the belt is removed.

12. Remove the timing belt idler pulleys.

13. Remove the camshaft drive pulleys. Use a counterhold wrench to prevent the camshaft from turning.

14. Remove the plate or panel behind the pulleys. Remove the cover plate for the ignition wires. Label and disconnect the ignition wiring from

the spark plugs and the distributor cap. Remove the coil wire from the distributor cap.

15. Remove the valve cover and gasket. Clean the surfaces of any gasket remains.

16. Remove the distributor housing from the camshaft carrier. Remove the ignition wire clip next to the left bolt.

17. Plug the spark plug holes with suitable material. Remove the center bearing cap for each camshaft. Remove the third nut in the center. Mark the camshaft bearing caps for proper reinstallation.

18. Install a camshaft press tool 5021 or equivalent, on the exhaust side camshaft in place of the removed bearing cap. When it is securely in place, remove the remaining bearing caps and nuts. Remove the tool and remove the exhaust camshaft.

19. Remove the intake camshaft in identical fashion.

NOTE: Label or identify each camshaft and its bearing caps. All removed components should be kept in order.

20. Using a magnet or a small suction cup, remove the tappets. Store them upside down, to prevent oil drainage and keep them in order. They are not interchangeable.

21. Remove the remaining 4 nuts in the center of the camshaft carrier and detach the carrier from the head. If it is stuck, tap it very gently with a plastic mallet. Remove the O-rings around the spark plug holes.

22. Wipe the remaining oil off the cylinder head and remove the bolts in order. When all the bolts are removed, the cylinder head may be lifted free of the vehicle.

NOTE: The head is aluminum. Support it on clean wood blocks or similar to avoid scoring the face.

23. Clean the camshaft carrier and the head assembly of all gasket material and sealer. Carefully scrape the joint surfaces with a plastic scraper. Do not use metal tools to scrape or clean. Wash the surfaces with a degreasing compound and blow the surfaces completely dry. Inspect the head bolts for any sign of stretching or elongation in the mid-section. If this is observed or suspected, discard the bolt. Bolts may not be used more than 5 times.

To install:

24. Install the new head gasket and a new O-ring for the water pump. Carefully place the cylinder head into position. Do not damage the gasket.

25. Clean the head bolts and apply a light coat of oil. Install them and tighten, in sequence, in 3 steps to 15 ft. lbs. (20 Nm), then all bolts to 30 ft. lbs. (41 Nm) and tighten each bolt through 115 degree of arc in 1 continuous motion. The use of protractor fitting tool 5098 or equivalent, is strongly recommended for this task.

26. Install the exhaust manifold with a new gasket. Attach the front exhaust pipe to its bracket and install the heat shields.

27. On the left side of the motor, connect the temperature sensors, the heating hose under cylinders 3 and 4 and the upper coolant hose to the thermostat.

28. Fill the cooling system and check carefully for leaks, particularly around the head to block joint.

29. Install the intake manifold with a new gasket. Tighten the bottom bolts a few turns and place the manifold in position. Tighten all the bolts from the center outwards.

30. Reattach the support under the intake manifold and the cable clip. Double check all connections on and around the intake manifold.

31. Apply liquid sealing compound to the camshaft carrier. Use a small paint roller or similar and evenly coat the surfaces which match to the head and the bearing cap joint faces.

32. Install the camshaft carrier on the head and secure it with 4 of the 5 center nuts tightened to 15 ft. lbs. (20 Nm). Do not install the middle nut.

33. Oil all matching surfaces on the camshaft carrier, bearing caps and tappets.

34. Insert the tappets. They must be inserted in their original order and place.

35. Install the exhaust side camshaft by placing it in the carrier with the pulley guide pin facing up. Using the rear bearing cap as a guide, press the camshaft into place with the press tool. Install the bearing caps in the original order.

36. Install the bearing cap nuts and tighten them in stages to 15 ft. lbs. (20 Nm). Remove the press tool and install the center bearing cap. Tighten it in stages to 15 ft. lbs. (20 Nm).

37. Install the intake camshaft in the carrier with the pulley guide pin facing upwards.

38. Turn the distributor shaft to align the driver with the markings on the distributor housing. Install new O-rings on the housing and rotor shaft.

39. Using the rear bearing cap as a guide, press the camshaft into place with the press tool. Install the bearing caps in the original order.

40. Install the bearing cap nuts and tighten them in stages to 15 ft. lbs. (20 Nm). Remove the press tool and install the center bearing cap. Tighten it in stages to 15 ft. lbs. (20 Nm).

41. Install the center nut in the camshaft carrier and tighten it to 15 ft. lbs. (20 Nm).

42. Double check the tightness of all the camshaft carrier nuts and the bearing cap nuts. All should be 15 ft. lbs. (20 Nm). Do not overtighten.

43. Reinstall the distributor, connect the coil wire and install the ignition wire clip at the left bolt. Remove the paper plugs from the spark plug holes.

44. Use a silicone sealer and apply to the front and rear camshaft bearing caps. Install new gaskets for the valve cover and the spark plug wells. Install the spark plug gasket with the arrow pointing towards the front of the vehicle and the word **UP** facing up. Make sure the valve cover gasket is correctly positioned and install the valve cover.

45. Reconnect the ground wire at the distributor.

46. Install the ignition wires and the cover plate.

47. Using a compression seal driver tool 5025 or similar, install the oil seals for the front of each camshaft. Camshafts must not be allowed to turn during this operation.

48. Install the upper backing plate over the ends of the camshafts and adjust the plate so the camshafts are centered in the holes.

49. Replace the idler pulleys and tighten their mounts to 18.5 ft. lbs. (25 Nm).

50. Install the camshaft drive pulleys, using a counterhold to prevent the camshafts from turning.

51. Making sure the camshaft pulleys are properly aligned with the marks on the backing plate, position the timing belt so the double mark on the belt coincides exactly with the top mark on the belt guide plate, at the top of the crankshaft. Place the belt onto the camshaft pulleys and make sure the single marks on the belt line up exactly with the marks on the pulleys. Fit the belt over the idler pulleys right side idler first, then the left.

52. Double check that the engine is on TDC of the compression stroke, for cylinder No. 1 and that all the belt markings line up as they should.

53. Loosen the tensioner locknut. Rotate the crankshaft clockwise 1 full

turn until the belt markings again coincide with the pulley markings.

NOTE: The engine must not be rotated counterclockwise while the tensioner is loose.

54. Turn the crankshaft smoothly clockwise until the pulley marks are 1½ teeth beyond the marks on the backing plate.

55. Tighten the tensioner locknut. Install the lower timing belt cover.

56. Install the radiator fan and pulley, the alternator drive belt and the negative battery cable.

57. Double check all installation items, paying particular attention to loose hoses or hanging wires, untightened nuts, poor routing of hoses and wires (too tight or rubbing) and tools left in the engine area.

58. Start the engine and allow it to run until the thermostat opens. Use extreme caution since the timing belt is exposed.

NOTE: This engine may be somewhat noisy when started. The noise will subside as oil reaches the tappets. Do not exceed 2500 rpm while the tappets are noisy.

59. Shut the engine OFF, rotate the crankshaft to bring the engine to TDC of the compression stroke of cylinder No. 1 and use tool 998 8500 or equivalent, to check the belt tension. Correct deflection is 5.5 ± 0.2 units when measured between the exhaust camshaft pulley and the idler. If the tension is not correct, repeat Steps 51-54.

60. Install the upper timing belt cover. Start the engine and final check all functions.

B280F Engine

1. Disconnect the battery. Drain the coolant.

2. Remove the air cleaner assembly and all attaching hoses.

3. Disconnect the throttle cable. On automatic transmission equipped vehicles, disconnect the kickdown cable.

4. Disconnect the EGR vacuum hose and remove the pipe between the EGR valve and manifold.

5. Remove the oil filler cap and cover the hole with a rag. Disconnect the PCV pipe(s) from the intake manifold.

6. Remove the front section of the intake manifold.

7. Disconnect the electrical connector and fuel line at the cold start injector. Disconnect the vacuum hose, both fuel lines. and the electrical connector from the control pressure regulator.

8. Disconnect the hose, pipe and electrical connector from the auxiliary air valve. Remove the auxiliary air valve.

9. Disconnect the electrical connector from the fuel distributor. Remove the wire loom from the intake manifolds. Disconnect the spark plug wires.

10. Disconnect the fuel injectors from their holders.

11. Disconnect the distributor vacuum hose, carbon filter hose and diverter valve hose from the intake manifold. Also, disconnect the power brake hose and heater hose at the intake manifold.

12. Disconnect the throttle control link from it pulley.

13. If equipped with an EGR vacuum amplifier, disconnect the wires from the throttle micro-switch and solenoid valve.

14. At the firewall, disconnect the fuel lines from the fuel filter and return line.

15. Remove the 2 attaching screws and lift out the fuel distributor and throttle housing assembly.

16. If not equipped with an EGR vacuum amplifier, disconnect the EGR valve hose from under the throttle housing.

17. Remove the cold start injector, rubber ring and pipe.

18. Remove the 4 retaining bolts and lift off the intake manifold. Remove the rubber rings.

19. Remove the splash guard under the engine.

20. If removing the left cylinder head, remove the air pump from its bracket.

21. Remove the vacuum pump and O-ring in the valve cover. Remove the vacuum hose from the wax thermostat.

22. If removing the right cylinder head, disconnect the upper radiator hose.

23. On air conditioned vehicles, remove the air conditioning compressor and secure it aside. Do not disconnect the refrigerant lines.

24. Disconnect the distributor leads and remove the distributor. Remove

the EGR valve, bracket and pipe. At the firewall, disconnect the electrical connectors at the relays.

25. On air conditioned vehicles, remove the rear compressor bracket.

26. Disconnect the coolant hose(s) from the water pump to the cylinder head(s). If removing the left cylinder head, disconnect the lower radiator hose at the water pump.

27. Disconnect the air injection system supply hose from the applicable cylinder head. Separate the air manifold at the rear of the engine. If removing the left cylinder head, remove the backfire valve and air hose.

28. Remove the valve cover(s).

29. On the left cylinder head, remove the Allen head screw and 4 upper bolts to the timing gear cover. On the right cylinder head, remove the 4 upper bolts to the timing gear cover and the front cover plate.

30. From under the vehicle, remove the exhaust pipe clamps for both header pipes.

31. If removing the right cylinder head, remove the retainer bracket bolts and pull the dipstick tube out of the crankcase.

32. Remove the applicable exhaust manifold(s).

33. Remove the cover plate at the rear of the cylinder head.

34. Rotate the camshaft sprocket for the applicable cylinder head, into position so the large sprocket hole aligns with the rocker arm shaft. With the camshaft in this position, loosen the cylinder head bolts, in sequence, same sequence as tightening, and remove the rocker arm and shaft assembly.

35. Loosen the camshaft retaining fork bolt, directly in back of sprocket and slide the fork away from the camshaft.

36. Next, it is necessary to hold the camshaft chain stretched during camshaft removal. Otherwise, the chain tensioner will automatically take up the slack, making it impossible to reinstall the sprocket on the camshaft without removing the timing chain cover to loosen the tensioner device. To accomplish this, a sprocket retainer tool 999 5104 is installed over the sprocket with 2 bolts in the top of the timing chain cover. A bolt is then screwed into the sprocket to hold it in place.

37. Remove the camshaft sprocket center bolt and push the camshaft to the rear, so it clears the sprocket.

38. Remove the cylinder head.

NOTE: Do not remove the cylinder head by pulling straight up. Instead, lever the head off by inserting 2 spare head bolts into the front and rear inboard cylinder head bolt holes and pulling toward the applicable wheel housing. Otherwise, the cylinder liners may be pulled up, breaking the lower liner seal and leaking coolant into the crankcase. If any do pull up, new liner seals must be used and the crankcase completely drained. If the head(s) seem stuck, gently tap around the edges of the head(s) with a rubber mallet, to break the joint.

39. Remove the head gasket. Clean the contact surfaces with a plastic scraper and lacquer thinner using all applicable cautions when working with flammable solvents.

40. If the head is going to be off for any length of time, install liner holders tool 999 5093 or 2 strips of thick stock steel with holes for the head bolts, so the liners stay pressed down against their seals. Install the holders width-wise between the middle 4 head bolt holes.

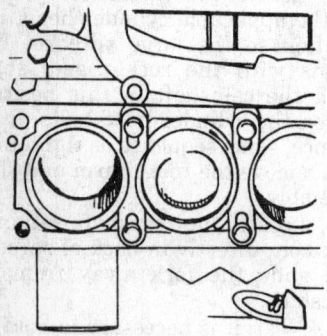

Cylinder liner holders installed on the B280F engine

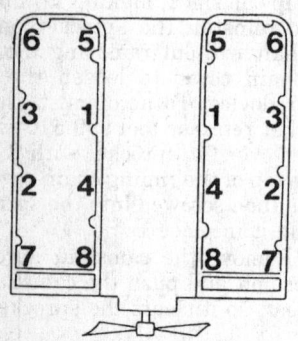

Tightening sequence for cylinder head bolts — B280F engine

To install:

41. If the dowels at the outboard corners of the block have slipped down, use needle-nose pliers to retrieve them. Remember to keep the timing chain taunt during cylinder head installation.

42. Remove the liner holders and install the head gaskets. The left and right head gaskets are different, ensure the correct one is installed. Install the cylinder head.

43. Except 1990 asbestos-free gasket, with fixed-washer bolts — Install the camshaft and remove the timing chain retainer tool. Install the head bolts finger-tight after lubricating with oil. Tighten all bolts in stages as follows:

　　a. Tighten all bolts to 43 ft. lbs. (60 Nm).

　　b. Loosen 1 bolt and retorque it to 15 ft. lbs. (20 Nm). Angle-tighten this bolt to 106 degrees, using special tool 5098 or equivalent.

　　c. Repeat this exact same procedure for the remaining bolts in sequence shown. Loosen and tighten each bolt in turn.

NOTE: After the engine has been warmed to operating temperature, let the engine cool for 2 hours then angle-tighten each bolt a further 45 degrees.

44. 1990 asbestos-free gasket, with fixed-washer bolts — Install the camshaft and remove the timing chain retainer tool. Install the head bolts finger-tight after lubricating with oil. Tighten all bolts in stages as follows:

　　a. Tighten bolts to 44 ft. lbs. (60 Nm).

　　b. Loosen bolts, tighten to 30 ft. lbs. (40 Nm).

　　c. Angle-tighten to 160-180 degrees.

45. Install the camshaft center bolt and tighten to 52-66 ft. lbs. (70-90 Nm). Install the timing gear case and rear cylinder head covers. Check and adjust the valve lash. After adjusting valve lash, turn the engine to TDC on No. 1 piston.

46. Install the valve covers, air injection system, exhaust pipes and manifolds.

47. Install all coolant hoses, install the air conditioner compressor brackets, distributor, EGR valve, cold start injector and intake manifold.

48. Install the vacuum pump and lower splash shield. Connect all electrical connections previously disconnected.

49. Install the throttle linkage, fuel injectors and all fuel injection system

hoses, lines and electrical connections.

50. Connect the battery. Fill the radiator with coolant, check the engine and transmission oil. Start the engine and allow it to reach operating temperature. Check for leaks.

51. Allow the engine to cool for 2 hours then angle-tighten each cylinder head bolt a further 45 degrees.

B6304F Engine

1. Disconnect the negative battery cable.

2. Position a suitable drain pan and drain the cooling system.

3. Remove the front exhaust pipe, heat shield and exhaust manifold(s).

4. Remove the coolant pipe bolts.

5. Remove the timing belt and tensioner assembly.

6. Remove the transmission mounting plate bolt.

7. Remove the air mass meter and intake hose.

8. Remove the throttle pulley cover, throttle cable and cable bracket.

9. Disconnect the throttle switch lead and vacuum hoses at throttle housing and cruise control servo.

10. Remove the intake manifold (outer section).

11. Mark the positions and remove the ignition coils.

12. Mark the camshaft pulleys (intake and exhaust sides) and remove the pulleys, using tool 5199 or equivalent.

13. Remove the camshaft sensor, ground terminals and temperature sensor connector. Remove the coolant hose at rear.

14. Carefully tap the top half of the cylinder head upwards, using a copper mallet.

15. Tap the joint lugs and camshaft front ends. Remove the camshafts.

16. Remove the cylinder head bolts, starting at the outside and working inwards. Lift the cylinder head from the engine. Remove the gasket.

17. Clean and inspect the cylinder head and block mating surface.

　To install:

18. Align the crankshaft timing mark, by removing the starter motor and installing the crankshaft locking tool 5451 or equivalent. Turn the crankshaft until it is stopped by the tool.

19. Fit a new cylinder head gasket and install the bottom half of the cylinder head. Oil the cylinder head bolts; install and torque in sequence. Torque in 3 stages:

　　a. Tighten in sequence to 15 ft. lbs. (20 Nm).

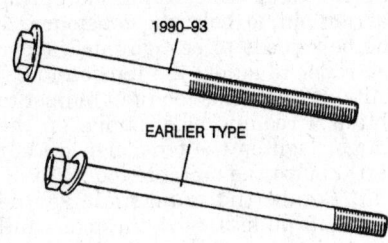

1990-93

EARLIER TYPE

Cylinder head bolt identification — B280F engine

b. Tighten in sequence to 44 ft. lbs. (60 Nm).

c. Tighten in sequence an additional 130 degrees.

20. Install new O-rings in the spark plug wells and oil the camshaft bearing seats.

21. Apply sealing compound part 1161059-9 or equivalent, to the upper section of the cylinder head.

NOTE: Do not allow any compound to penetrate the coolant or oil passages.

22. Oil the camshaft bearing seats and install the camshaft.

23. Place the upper section of the cylinder head into position. Install the press tools 5454 or equivalent, and tighten against the lower section. Install the bolts and working from the inside outwards, tighten to 13 ft. lbs. (17 Nm). Remove the tools.

24. Grease the camshaft front seal and tap the seal into place.

25. Place the upper timing cover into position. Install the camshaft pulleys while aligning the timing marks.

26. Install and tighten the pulley mounting bolts.

27. Remove the timing cover and install the mounting plate bolt.

28. Place the timing belt around the camshaft and right side idler. Place the belt over the camshaft pulleys, around the water pump and press over the tensioner pulley.

29. Install the belt tensioner. Tighten the tensioner mounting bolts to 18 ft. lbs. (25 Nm).

30. Slacken the camshaft pulley bolts and withdraw the tensioner locking pin. Insert the remaining camshaft pulley bolt. Hold the pulley, using the counterhold tool 5199 or equivalent, and tighten all bolts alternately to 15 ft. lbs. (20 Nm).

31. Remove the crankshaft locking tool. Install the protective plug and install the starter motor.

32. Install the upper timing cover.

33. Check that the timing marks on the crankshaft and camshaft pulleys are correctly aligned.

34. Grease the camshaft front seal and press the seal into place.

35. Install the camshaft sensor, ground terminals and temperature sensor connector. Install the coolant hose at rear.

36. Install the ignition coils, spark plug cover and auxiliary drive belt.

37. Install the damper guard and splash guard.

38. Install the intake manifold.

39. Install the exhaust manifold, using a new gasket. Install the heat shield and front exhaust pipe.

40. Connect the temperature sensor and coolant hose to the thermostat.

41. Loosen the catalytic convertor bolts and re-tighten to 18 ft. lbs. (25 Nm). This is necessary to prevent stress in the system.

42. Change the engine oil. Fill the cooling system.

43. Connect the negative battery lead. Start the engine and check for leaks.

44. Recheck the cooling system.

Valve Lifters

REMOVAL AND INSTALLATION

B234F Engine

NOTE: The use of the correct special tools or their equivalent is required for this procedure.

1. Disconnect the negative battery cable.

2. Remove the alternator drive belt, the radiator fan and its pulley.

3. Remove the upper and lower timing belt covers.

4. Align the camshaft and crankshaft marks. Turn the engine to TDC of the compression stroke on cylinder No. 1 and make sure the pulley

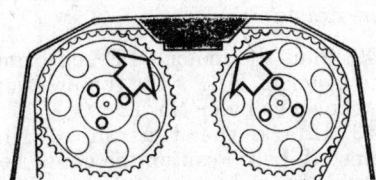

Double-check the alignment of the camshaft gear marks after installing timing belt — B6304F engine

marks and the crankshaft marks align with their matchmarks on either the backing plate (camshaft pulleys) or the belt guide plate (crankshaft).

5. Remove the protective cap over the timing belt tensioner locknut. Loosen the locknut, compress the tensioner to release tension on the belts and retighten the locknut, holding the tensioner in place.

6. Remove the timing belt from the camshafts; do not crease or fold the belt.

NOTE: The camshafts and the crankshaft must not be moved when the belt is removed.

7. Remove the timing belt idler pulleys.

8. Remove the camshaft drive pulleys. Use a counterhold wrench to prevent the camshaft from turning.

9. Remove the plate or panel behind the pulleys. Remove the cover plate for the ignition wires. Label and disconnect the ignition wiring from the spark plugs and the distributor cap; remove the coil wire from the distributor cap.

10. Remove the valve cover and gasket. Clean the surfaces of any gasket remains.

11. Remove the distributor housing from the camshaft carrier. Remove the ignition wire clip next to the left bolt.

12. Plug the spark plug holes with suitable material. Remove the center bearing cap for each camshaft. Mark the camshaft bearing caps for proper reinstallation.

13. Install a camshaft press tool 5021 or similar, on the exhaust side camshaft in place of the removed bearing cap. When it is securely in place, remove the remaining bearing caps and nuts. Remove the tool and remove the exhaust camshaft.

14. Remove the intake camshaft in identical fashion.

NOTE: Label or identify each camshaft and its bearing caps. All removed components should be kept in order.

15. Using a magnet or a small suction cup, remove the tappets. Store them upside down, to prevent oil drainage and keep them in order. They are not interchangeable.

To install:

16. Clean and inspect the camshaft carrier and tappet bores for any sign of wear or scoring.

17. Oil all matching surfaces on the camshaft carrier, bearing caps and tappets.

18. Insert the tappets. They must be inserted in their original order and place.

19. Install the exhaust side camshaft by placing it in the carrier with the pulley guide pin facing up. Using the rear bearing cap as a guide, press the camshaft into place with the press tool. Install the bearing caps in the original order.

20. Install the bearing cap nuts and tighten them in stages to 15 ft. lbs. (20 Nm). Remove the press tool and install the center bearing cap; tighten it in stages to 15 ft. lbs. (20 Nm).

21. Install the intake camshaft in the carrier with the pulley guide pin facing upwards.

22. Turn the distributor shaft to align the driver with the markings on the distributor housing. Install new O-rings on the housing and rotor shaft.

23. Using the rear bearing cap as a guide, press the camshaft into place with the press tool. Install the bearing caps in the original order.

24. Install the bearing cap nuts and tighten them in stages to 15 ft. lbs. (20 Nm).

25. Double check the tightness of all the camshaft bearing cap nuts. All should be 15 ft. lbs. (20 Nm). Do not overtighten.

26. Reinstall the distributor, connect the coil wire and install the ignition wire clip at the left bolt. Remove the protective covers from the spark plug holes.

27. Use a silicone sealer and apply to the front and rear camshaft bearing caps. Install new gaskets for the valve cover and the spark plug wells. Install the spark plug gasket with the arrow pointing towards the front of the vehicle and the word **UP** facing up. Make sure the valve cover gasket is correctly positioned and install the valve cover.

28. Reconnect the ground wire at the distributor.

29. Install the ignition wires and the cover plate.

30. Using a compression seal driver tool 5025 or similar, install the oil seals for the front of each camshaft. Camshafts must not be allowed to turn during this operation.

31. Install the upper backing plate over the ends of the camshafts and adjust the plate so the camshafts are centered in the holes.

32. Replace the idler pulleys and tighten their mounts to 18.5 ft. lbs. (25 Nm).

33. Install the camshaft drive pulleys, using a counterhold to prevent the camshafts from turning.

34. Reinstall the camshaft belt by aligning the double line marking on the belt with the top marking on the belt guide plate at the top of the crankshaft. Stretch the belt around the crank pulley and place it over the tensioner and the right side idler. Place the belt on the camshaft pulleys. The single line marks on the belt should align exactly with the pulley markings. Route the belt around the oil pump drive pulley and press the belt onto the left side idler.

35. Check that all the markings align and that the engine is still positioned at TDC, of the compression stroke, for cylinder No. 1.

36. Loosen the tensioner locknut.

37. Turn the crankshaft clockwise. The camshaft pulleys should rotate 1 full turn until the marks again align with the marks on the backing plate.

NOTE: The engine must not be rotated counterclockwise during this procedure.

38. Smoothly rotate the crankshaft further clockwise until the camshaft pulley markings are 1½ teeth beyond the marks on the backing plate. Tighten the tensioner locknut.

39. Reinstall the fan pulley and fan. Install all the drive belts and connect the battery cable.

40. Double check all installation items, paying particular attention to loose hoses or hanging wires, untightened nuts, poor routing of hoses and wires (too tight or rubbing) and tools left in the engine area.

41. Start the engine and allow it to run until the thermostat opens.

--- **CAUTION** ---
Use care, the upper and lower timing belt covers are still removed. The belt and pulleys are exposed and moving at high speed.

NOTE: This engine may be somewhat noisy when started. The noise will subside as oil reaches the tappets. Do not exceed 2500 rpm while the tappets are noisy.

42. Shut the motor OFF and bring the motor to TDC of the compression stroke on cylinder No. 1.

43. Check the tension of the camshaft belt. Position the gauge between the right (exhaust) camshaft pulley and the idler. Belt tension must be 5.5 ± 0.2 units on a suitable belt tension gauge. If the belt needs adjustment, remove the rubber cap over the tensioner locknut and loosen the locknut.

44. Insert a suitable tool between the tensioner wheel and the spring carrier pin to hold the tensioner. If the belt needs to be tightened, move the roller to adjust the tension to 6.0 units. If the belt is too tight, adjust to obtain a reading of 5.0 units on the gauge. Tighten the tensioner locknut and remove the suitable tool.

45. Rotate the crankshaft so the camshaft pulleys move through 1 full revolution and recheck the tension on the camshaft belt. It should now be 5.5 ± 0.2 units. Install the plastic plug over the tensioner bolt.

46. Reinstall the remaining belt covers. Start the engine and final check performance.

Valve Lash

NOTE: The B234F engine uses hydraulic lash adjusters which do not require adjustment.

ADJUSTMENT

B230F Engines

1. Remove the valve cover. Scribe chalk marks on the distributor body indicating each of the 4 spark plug wire leads in the cap. Remove the distributor cap.

2. Crank over the engine with a remote starter switch or with a wrench on the crankshaft pulley center bolt (22mm hex) until the engine is in the firing position for No. 1 cylinder. At this point, the **0** degree or TDC mark on the crankshaft pulley is aligned with the timing pointer, the rotor is pointing at the No. 1 spark plug wire cap position and the camshaft lobes for No. 1 cylinder are pointing at the 10 o'clock and 2 o'clock positions. At this point, the clearance between the camshaft lobe and valve depressor (tappet) may be checked for the intake and exhaust valve of cylinder No. 1, using a feeler gauge. When checking clearance, the wear limit is 0.012-0.018 in. (0.3-0.4mm) for a cold engine and 0.012-0.020 in. (0.3-0.5mm) for a hot engine at 176°F (80°C).

3. Repeat Step 2 for cylinders No. 3, 4 and 2, in that order. Each time, rotate the crankshaft pulley 180 degrees so the rotor is pointing to the spark plug wire cap position for that cylinder and the camshaft lobes are pointing at the 10 and 2 o'clock positions for the valves of that cylinder.

4. If any of the valve clearance measurements are outside the wear limit, remove the old valve adjusting disc and install a new one to bring

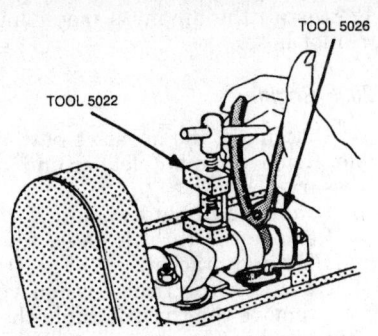

B230F valve adjustment tools — tappet depressor (5022) and shim pliers (5026)

the clearance within specifications. First, rotate the valve depressors (tappets) until their notches are at a right angle to the engine center line. Attach valve depressor tool 999 5022 or equivalent, to the camshaft and screw down the tool spindle until the depressor (tappet) groove is just above the edge of its bore and still accessible with the special pliers tool 999 5026.

5. Remove the valve adjusting disc and measure with a micrometer. The valve clearance should be set to these tolerances: 0.014-0.016 in. (0.35-0.40mm) for a cold engine and 0.016-0.018 in. (0.40-0.45mm) for a hot engine. So, if the measured clearance had been 0.019 in. (0.48mm) and the desired clearance 0.016 in. (0.40mm), for a net difference of 0.003 in. (0.076mm), then the new valve adjusting disc should be 0.003 in. (0.076mm) thicker than the old one to take up the clearance. Valve adjusting discs are available in sizes 0.130-0.180 in. (3.3-4.6mm), in 0.002 in. (0.050mm) increments. Always oil the new disc and install it with the marks facing down.

6. Remove the valve tappet depressor tool. Rotate the engine a few times and recheck clearance. Install the valve cover with a new gasket.

B280F Engine

1. In order to gain access to the valve covers, disconnect or remove the following:

    a. Air conditioning compressor from bracket; do not disconnect refrigerant hoses

    b. EGR valve and hoses

    c. Air conditioning compressor bracket

    d. Fuel injection control pressure regulator

    e. Air pump

    f. Vacuum pump

    g. Hoses and wires from solenoid valve, California only

2. Using a 36mm hex socket on the crankshaft pulley bolt, rotate the crankshaft to the No. 1 cylinder TDC position, of the compression stroke. At this point the **0** mark on the timing plate aligns with the crankshaft pulley notch, the distributor rotor is pointing to the No. 1 cylinder spark plug wire cap position and both valves for No. 1 cylinder have clearance. At this position, adjust the intake valves of cylinders No. 1, 2 and 4; the exhaust valves of cylinders No. 1, 3 and 6. Insert a feeler gauge between the rocker arm and valve stem. Loosen the locknut and turn the adjusting screw in the required direction. Tighten the locknut and recheck clearance. The clearance should be.

• Cold engine Intake — 0.004-0.006 in. (0.10-0.15mm) Exhaust — 0.010-0.012 in. (0.25-0.30mm)

• Hot engine Intake — 0.006-0.008 in. (0.15-0.20mm) Exhaust — 0.012-0.014 in. (0.30-0.35mm)

3. Rotate the crankshaft pulley 1 full 360 degrees turn to adjust the remaining valves. At this point, the **0** mark will again align with the pulley notch, the rotor is pointing 180 degrees opposite its former position and

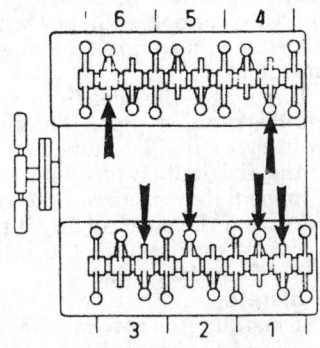

Adjust these valves (arrow) with the No. 1 cylinder at TDC — B280F engine

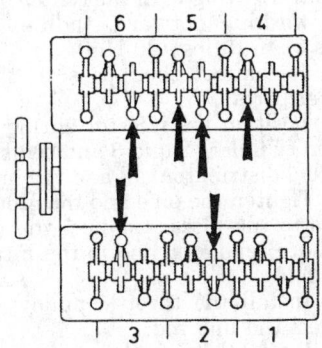

Adjust these valves (arrow) after rotating the crankshaft 360 degrees — B280F engine

the No. 1 cylinder rockers contact the ramps of the camshaft. At this position, adjust the intake valves of cylinders No. 3, 5 and 6; the exhaust valves of cylinders No. 2, 4 and 5.

4. Install the valve covers with new gaskets. Connect all disconnected equipment.

Rocker Arms/Shafts

REMOVAL AND INSTALLATION

B280F Engine

1. Disconnect the negative battery cable.

2. Remove the air cleaner assembly.

3. Disconnect the air pump bracket.

4. Remove the left valve cover, if necessary.

5. Tie the upper radiator hose aside and remove the oil filler cap and carbon canister hose.

6. On air conditioned vehicles, remove the air conditioning compressor from the bracket. Do not disconnect the hoses.

7. Remove the EGR valve.

8. Remove the air conditioning compressor rear bracket.

9. Remove the control pressure regulator.

10. Disconnect any hoses or wires in the way. Remove the right valve cover, if necessary.

NOTE: Do not jar the head while the rocker and bolts are loose, as the cylinder liner O-ring seals may break, requiring engine disassemble.

11. The rocker arm bolts double as cylinder head bolts. Loosen the head bolts by reversing the torque sequence. If removing both rocker shafts, mark them left and right.

    To install:

12. Install the rocker shafts. Follow cylinder head installation procedure for proper torque specification and sequence. Adjust the valve lash.

13. Install the valve covers, EGR valve, control pressure regulator, air conditioning compressor and bracket and air pump.

14. Connect all fuel, coolant and vacuum lines previously disconnected. Connect all electrical connections previously disconnected. Connect the battery.

15. Start the engine and allow it to reach operating temperature. Check for leaks.

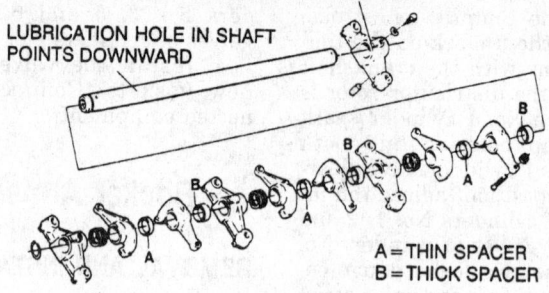

THE FLAT FACE ON THE SHAFT
SUPPORT MUST BE TURNED TOWARDS
THE SNAPRING GROOVE

LUBRICATION HOLE IN SHAFT
POINTS DOWNWARD

A = THIN SPACER
B = THICK SPACER

Rocker arm shaft assembly — B280F engine

Intake Manifold

REMOVAL AND INSTALLATION

B230 Engine

1. Disconnect the negative battery cable. Remove the air cleaner and all necessary hoses.
2. Remove the PCV valve.
3. Remove the connector at the cold start injector.
4. Remove the fuel hose from the cold start injector.
5. Remove the cold start injector.
6. Remove the connector on the auxiliary valve.
7. Disconnect the hoses at the auxiliary valve.
8. Remove the auxiliary valve.
9. On turbocharged engines, disconnect the turbocharger inlet hose, between turbo unit and intake manifold. Plug the hose immediately.
10. Remove the intake manifold brace.
11. Disconnect the distributor vacuum hose at the intake manifold.
12. Loosen the clamp for the rubber connecting pipe on the air-fuel control unit.
13. Remove the manifold bolts and remove the manifold.
To install:
14. Clean the gasket mating surfaces thoroughly. Install the intake manifold, using new gaskets, and tighten the bolts to 15 ft. lbs. (20 Nm).
15. Install the intake manifold brace, air-fuel control unit connecting pipe, turbocharger inlet hose (if equipped), auxiliary valve, cold start injector, fuel hose and PCV valve.
16. Connect all vacuum, fuel and coolant hoses previously disconnected. Connect all electrical connectors previously disconnected.
17. Connect the negative battery cable, start the engine and bring it to operating temperature. Adjust the timing and check for leaks.

B234F Engine

1. Remove the air mass meter and the air intake hose.
2. Detach the throttle pulley from the intake manifold and remove the link rod from the throttle lever.
3. Separate the throttle housing from the intake manifold and cut the cable tie holding the wiring to the vacuum hose connections.
4. Disconnect the lines and hoses from the manifold, including the brake booster vacuum hose, the evaporation line, the oil trap, the fuel pressure regulator line and the air control valve line. If equipped with a vacuum tank, disconnect its line at the manifold.
5. Disconnect the fuel return line at the distribution pipe. Disconnect the wiring to the injectors and remove the distribution pipe and injectors. Immediately protect these components from the entry of any dirt.
6. Unbolt and remove the intake manifold from the engine.
To install:
7. If installing a new manifold, it is necessary to transfer the various hose nipples and plugs to the new part. Install the manifold with a new gasket. Starting with the center bolts and working outward, tighten the bolts to 15 ft. lbs. (20 Nm).
8. Reconnect the hoses to their proper ports.
9. Position the injector wiring between cylinders 2 and 3 and reinstall the fuel distributor rail and the injectors. Tighten the pipe and the ground wires to the block. Connect the fuel pressure regulator line to the intake manifold.
10. Install the throttle pulley and connect the link rod.
11. Install the throttle housing with a new gasket. Check the operation of the throttle stops and switches.

12. Install the air mass meter and air inlet hose.

B280F Engine

1. Disconnect the negative battery cable. Remove the air cleaner and all necessary hoses.
2. Drain the radiator coolant.
3. Remove the throttle cable from the pulley and bracket.
4. On automatic transmission vehicles, remove the throttle cable that is connected to the transmission.
5. Remove the EGR pipe from the EGR valve to the manifold.
6. Disconnect the EGR vacuum line.
7. Remove the oil filler cap and PCV valve.

NOTE: Cover the oil cap opening with a rag to keep dirt out.

8. Remove the front manifold bolts and remove the front section of the manifold.
9. Disconnect the cold start connector, fuel line and injector.
10. Disconnect the pressure control regulator vacuum lines, fuel lines and the connector.
11. Remove the auxiliary valve and its necessary piping.
12. Disconnect the electrical connections at the air fuel control unit.
13. Remove all 6 spark plug wires.
14. Remove all 6 injectors.
15. Move the wiring harness to the outside of the manifold.
16. Disconnect the vacuum hose at the distributor and the intake manifold.
17. Disconnect the heater hose at the intake manifold.
18. Disconnect the hose to the diverter valve.
19. Disconnect the vacuum hose to the power brake booster.
20. Disconnect the throttle cable link.
21. Disconnect the wires to the micro-switch.
22. Pull the wires away from the intake manifold.
23. Remove the fuel filter line and the return line.
24. Remove the air control unit.
25. Disconnect the vacuum hose from the throttle valve housing.
26. Remove the pipe and cold start injector assembly.
27. Remove the intake manifold from the vehicle.
To install:
28. Clean all gasket mating surfaces thoroughly. Install the intake manifold using new gaskets and tighten the bolts to 7-11 ft. lbs. (10-15 Nm).

29. Install the cold start injector assembly, air control unit, fuel filter and return line, throttle cable, EGR valve, diverter valve, heater hose, injectors and spark plug wires.

30. Install all vacuum, fuel and coolant hoses previously removed. Connect all electrical connections previously disconnected.

31. Fill the radiator with coolant and check the engine and transmission oil. Connect the negative battery cable. Start the engine and bring to operating temperature. Check for leaks.

B6304F Engine

1. Disconnect the negative battery lead.

2. Disconnect the connector at the air mass meter.

3. Disconnect the idling valve lead and air hose. Remove the flame trap holder and remove the intake hose.

4. Remove the throttle pulley cover.

5. Disconnect and remove the throttle switch lead, throttle cable and bracket, cruise control vacuum servo and vacuum hoses at throttle housing.

6. Remove the injector cover plate and distribution manifold retaining bolts (3).

7. Disconnect the pressure regulator vacuum hose and fuel line bracket.

8. Carefully lift out the injector and distribution manifold assembly.

9. Remove the air preheater hose. Remove left and right side power stage connectors on the bottom of the manifold. Remove the manifold bottom mounting.

10. Disconnect the brake servo hose and vacuum hoses under the manifold.

11. Cut away the clamps securing the rubber sleeves between the manifold sections and lift out the outer manifold section.

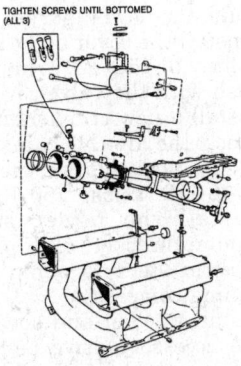

TIGHTEN SCREWS UNTIL BOTTOMED (ALL 3)

Intake manifold assembly — B280F engine

12. Remove the upper bolts and loosen the lower bolts. Remove the inner section of the manifold.

To install:

13. Install the inner section of the manifold, using a new gasket. Install the rubber sleeves on the inner section and lubricate the free ends with petroleum jelly. Install the mounting bolts and torque to 15 ft. lbs. (20 Nm).

14. Route the wiring between the 2nd and 3rd branches of the outer manifold section. Place the manifold against the lower section and connect the crankcase ventilation hoses.

15. Insert the manifold branches in the rubber sleeves. Secure with new Oetiker clamps.

16. Tighten the manifold lower mounting. Reconnect the vacuum hoses, brake servo hose, power stage connectors and air preheater hose.

17. Inspect the injector O-rings. Lubricate with petroleum jelly.

18. Reconnect the fuel pressure regulator vacuum hose.

19. Press the fuel distribution manifold into position. Tighten the manifold.

20. Reconnect the injector connectors, EGR vacuum hoses. Install the injector cover.

21. Install the throttle cable, throttle pulley cover and vacuum hoses (cruise control and throttle housing).

22. Install the cable bracket at the throttle pulley. Reconnect the PCV, idling valve lead, air hose, air mass meter and throttle housing connector.

23. Connect the negative battery lead. Start the engine and check operation.

Exhaust Manifold

REMOVAL AND INSTALLATION

B230F Engine

1. Disconnect the negative battery cable. Remove the air cleaner and all necessary hoses.

2. Remove the EGR valve pipe from the manifold.

3. Remove the exhaust pipe from the exhaust manifold.

4. Remove the manifold bolts and remove the manifold.

NOTE: Remember to install new manifold gaskets before installing the manifold.

5. Installation is the reverse of removal.

6. Torque the manifold bolts to 10-20 ft. lbs. (14-27 Nm).

B234F Engine

1. Disconnect the front exhaust pipe from the manifold. Disconnect the catalytic converter from the front muffler.

2. Remove the heat shields (top and bottom) from the manifold and remove the air preheat hose.

3. Disconnect the front exhaust pipe from the bracket on the bell housing.

4. Unbolt the exhaust manifold and remove it from the vehicle.

To install:

5. Install the manifold with a new gasket and tighten the bolts to 15 ft. lbs. (20 Nm).

6. Install the front exhaust pipe with a new gasket; tighten the joint to the manifold to 20 ft. lbs. (27 Nm). Reattach the catalytic converter to the front muffler.

7. Install the heat shields and the preheat hose.

B280F Engine

1. Raise and support the vehicle safely.

2. Unbolt the crossover pipe from the left and right side of the exhaust manifolds, if equipped.

NOTE: If the vehicle has the Y-type exhaust pipe, disconnect this pipe at the left and right manifolds.

3. Remove any other necessary hardware.

4. Remove the left and right side manifolds.

5. Installation is the reverse of removal.

NOTE: Always use new gaskets when reinstalling the manifolds.

6. Torque the manifold bolts to 7-11 ft. lbs. (10-15 Nm).

B6304F Engine

1. Disconnect the negative battery cable.

2. Remove the exhaust pipe mounting nuts at the manifold joints.

3. Remove the heat shield retaining bolts and remove the heat shield.

4. Remove the exhaust manifold mounting nuts. Remove the exhaust manifold and gasket.

To install:

5. Before installation, clean the manifold and cylinder head mating surfaces.

6. Fit a new gasket and place the exhaust manifold into position. Install the mount lifting lug on studs between 3rd and 4th exhaust branches. Torque the studs to 15 ft.

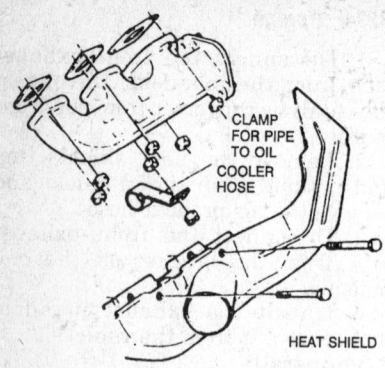

CLAMP FOR PIPE TO OIL COOLER HOSE

HEAT SHIELD

Exhaust manifold assembly — B280F engine

lbs. (20 Nm) and mounting nuts to 18 ft. lbs. (25 Nm).

7. Install the heat shield to rear manifold. Torque to 11 ft. lbs. (15 Nm).

8. Install the front exhaust pipe to manifold. Using thread locking compound, torque to 44 ft. lbs. (60 Nm).

NOTE: Loosen the joint at the catalytic convertor and re-tighten to 18 ft. lbs. (25 Nm). This is necessary to prevent stresses in the system.

9. Connect the negative battery lead. Start the engine and check for leaks.

Turbocharger

REMOVAL AND INSTALLATION

B230F Turbocharged Engine

1. Disconnect the battery ground cable.

2. Disconnect expansion tank from retainer. Remove expansion tank retainer.

3. Remove preheater hose to the air cleaner. Remove the pipe and rub-

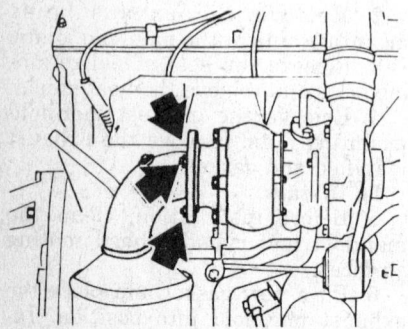

Disconnect the turbocharger unit from the exhaust manifold — B230F turbocharged engine

ber bellows between the air/fuel control unit and the turbocharger unit. Pull out the crankcase ventilation hose from the pipe.

4. Remove the pipe and pipe connector between the turbocharger unit and the intake manifold.

NOTE: Cover the turbocharger intake and outlet ports to keep dirt out of the system.

5. Disconnect the exhaust pipe and secure it aside.

6. Disconnect the spark plug wires at the plugs.

7. Remove the upper heat shield. Remove the brace between the turbocharger unit and the manifold.

8. Remove the lower heat shield by removing the 1 retaining screw under the manifold.

9. Remove the oil pipe clamp, retaining screws on the turbocharger and the pipe connection screw in the cylinder block under the manifold. Do not allow any dirt to enter the oil passages.

10. Remove the manifold retaining screws and washers. Let 1 nut remain in position to keep the manifold in position.

11. Remove the oil delivery pipe. Cover the opening on the turbocharger.

12. Disconnect the air/fuel control unit by loosening the clamps. Move the unit with the lower section of the air cleaner up to the right side wheel housing. Place a cover over the wheel housing as protection.

13. Remove the air cleaner filter.

14. Remove the remaining nut and washer on the manifold. Lift the assembly forward and up. Remove the manifold gaskets. Disconnect the return oil pipe O-ring from the cylinder block.

15. Disconnect the turbocharger unit from the manifold.

To install:

16. Be sure to use a new gasket for the exhaust manifold and a new O-ring to the return oil pipe. Keep everything clean during assembly and use extreme care in keeping dirt out of the various turbocharger inlet and outlet pipes and hoses.

17. Install the turbocharger on the exhaust manifold and tighten the bolts as follows:

    a. Step 1 to 0.7 ft. lbs. (3.0 Nm)

    b. Step 2 to 30 ft. lbs. (133 Nm)

    c. Step 3, tighten all bolts an additional 120 degrees (⅓ turn).

18. Install the exhaust manifold and turbocharger assembly on the

engine. Connect all oil pipes from and to the turbocharger using new O-rings.

19. Install the air/fuel control unit and air cleaner. Install the heat shields, spark plug wires, exhaust pipes, preheater assembly and expansion tank. Connect the negative battery cable.

20. Disconnect the wire at terminal 15 (brown) of the ignition coil. Use the ignition key to turn the engine over for about 30 seconds. This circulates oil to the turbocharger, providing start-up lubrication.

21. Turn the ignition **OFF**, reconnect the coil wire, start the engine and allow it to idle for a few minutes prior to test driving.

Timing Chain Front Cover

REMOVAL AND INSTALLATION

B280F Engine

1. Disconnect the negative battery cable. Remove the air cleaner and valve covers.

2. Loosen the fan shroud and remove the fan. Remove the shroud.

3. Loosen the alternator, air pump, power steering pump, air conditioning compressor and remove the drive belts.

4. Block the flywheel from turning, remove the crankshaft pulley nut (36mm) and the pulley.

NOTE: Do not drop the pulley key into the crankcase.

5. Remove the power steering pump and place aside. Remove the pump bracket.

6. Remove the timing chain cover retaining bolts, 25-11mm hex bolts, tap and remove the cover.

To install:

7. Clean the gasket contact surfaces. Place the upper gasket on the cover and the lower gasket on the block. Install the cover and tighten to 7-11 ft. lbs. (10-15 Nm). Trim the gaskets flush with the valve cover.

8. Install a new crankshaft seal.

9. Block the flywheel, install the pulley, key and tighten the 36mm nut to 118-132 ft. lbs. (160-180 Nm).

10. Install the power steering pump, pump bracket, alternator, air pump, power steering pump and air conditioning compressor.

11. Install the fan and shroud. Install the accessory drive belts. Connect the negative battery cable. Start the engine and check for leaks.

Front Cover Oil Seal

REMOVAL AND INSTALLATION

B280F Engine

1. Disconnect the negative battery cable. Remove the air cleaner and valve covers.
2. Loosen the fan shroud and remove the fan. Remove the shroud.
3. Loosen the alternator, air pump, power steering pump, air conditioning compressor and remove the drive belts.
4. Block the flywheel from turning, remove the crankshaft pulley nut (36mm) and the pulley.

NOTE: Do not drop the pulley key into the crankcase.

5. Remove the seal, using a suitable puller tool 9 995 069-3 or equivalent.

NOTE: Be careful not to damage the timing chain cover contact surface.

To install:

6. Fill the space between the seal lips with grease and install the new seal, using tool 5103 or equivalent.
7. Block the flywheel, install the pulley, key and tighten the 36mm nut to 118-132 ft. lbs. (160-180 Nm).
8. Install the power steering pump, pump bracket, alternator, air pump, power steering pump and air conditioning compressor.
9. Install the fan and shroud. Install the accessory drive belts. Connect the negative battery cable. Start the engine and check for leaks.

Timing Chain and Sprockets

REMOVAL AND INSTALLATION

B280F Engine

1. Remove the timing chain cover.
2. Remove the oil pump sprocket and drive chain.
3. Slacken the tension in both camshaft timing chains by rotating each tensioner lock ¼ turn counterclockwise and pushing the rubbing block piston.
4. Remove both chain tensioners. Remove the 2 curved and the 2 straight chain damper/runners.
5. Remove the camshaft sprocket retaining bolt, 10mm Allen head and the sprocket and chain assembly. Repeat for the other side.

To install:

6. Install the chain tensioners and tighten to 5 ft. lbs. (7 Nm). Install the curved chain damper/runners and tighten to 7-11 ft. lbs. (10-15 Nm). Install the straight chain damper/runners and torque to 5 ft. lbs. (7 Nm).
7. First install the left side camshaft sprocket and chain:

   a. Rotate the crankshaft, using crankshaft nut, if necessary, until the crankshaft key is pointing directly to the left side camshaft and

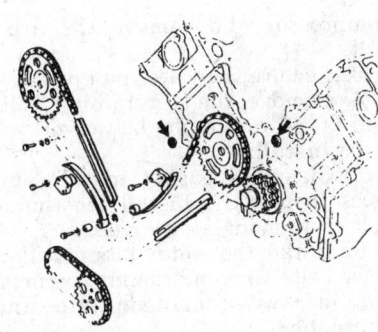

Timing chain tensioner and chain assembly — B280F engine

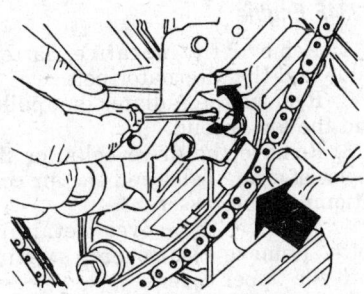

Relieving chain tension — B280F engine

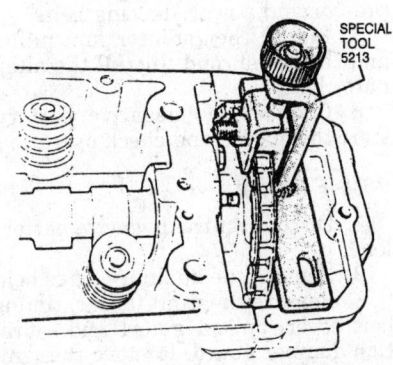

Timing chain holding tool 5213 — B280F engine

the left side camshaft key groove is pointing straight up (12 o'clock).

   b. Place the chain on the left side sprocket so the sprocket notchmark is centered precisely between the 2 white lines on the chain.

   c. Position the chain on the crankshaft sprocket (inner), making sure the other white line on the chain aligns with the crankshaft sprocket notch.

   d. While holding the left side chain and sprockets in this position, install the sprocket and chain on the left side camshaft, chain stretched on tension side, so the sprocket pin fits into the camshaft recess.

   e. Tighten the sprocket center bolt to 51-59 ft. lbs. (69-80 Nm); use a suitable tool to keep camshaft from turning.

8. To install the right side camshaft sprocket and chain:

   a. Rotate the crankshaft clockwise until the crankshaft key points straight down (6 o'clock).

   b. Align the camshaft key groove so it is pointing halfway between the 8 and 9 o'clock positions; at this position, the No. 6 cylinder rocker arms will rock.

   c. Place the chain on the right side sprocket so the sprocket notchmark is centered precisely between the 2 white lines on the chain.

   d. Then, position the chain on the middle crankshaft sprocket, making sure the other white line aligns with the crankshaft sprocket notch.

   e. Install the sprocket and chain on the camshaft so the sprocket notch fits into the camshaft recess.

   f. Tighten the sprocket nut to 51-59 ft. lbs. (69-80 Nm).

9. Rotate the chain tensioners ¼ turn clockwise each. The chains are tensioned by rotating the crankshaft 2 full turns clockwise. Recheck to make sure the alignment marks coincide.
10. Install the oil pump sprocket and chain.
11. Install the timing chain cover.

Timing Belt Front Cover

REMOVAL AND INSTALLATION

B230F Engine

1. Disconnect the negative battery cable. Loosen the fan shroud and remove the fan. Remove the shroud.
2. Loosen the alternator, power steering pump and air conditioning

Left side camshaft timing chain installation sequence — B280F engine

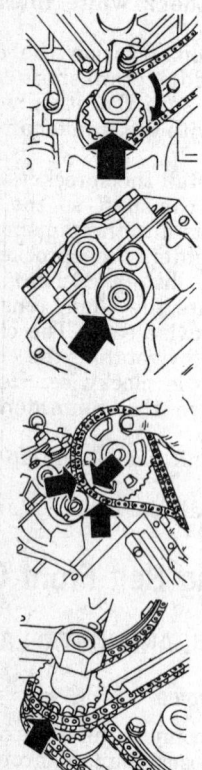

Right side camshaft timing chain installation sequence — B280F engine

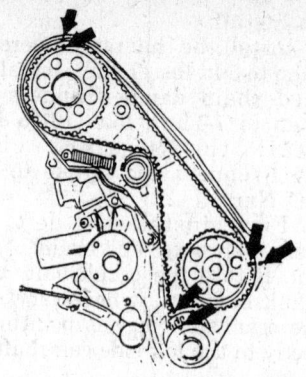

Timing belt alignment — B230F engine

compressor and remove the drive belts.

3. Remove the water pump pulley.

4. Remove the 4 retaining bolts and lift off the timing belt cover.

To install:

5. Clean all gasket mating surfaces thoroughly. Install the timing belt cover using a new gasket.

6. Install the water pump pulley, drive belts, air conditioning compressor, power steering pump and alternator.

7. Install the fan and shroud. Install the accessory drive belts. Connect the negative battery cable. Start the engine and check for leaks.

B234F Engine

1. Remove the negative battery cable and the alternator belt.

2. Remove the radiator fan, pulley and the fan shroud.

3. Remove the drive belts for the power steering belts and the air conditioning compressor.

4. Remove the cover retaining bolts. Remove the covers, starting with the upper cover.

To install:

5. Install the lower; then upper timing belt cover.

6. Install the air conditioning compressor and power steering belts.

7. Install the radiator fan, pulley and the fan shroud. Install the alternator belt.

8. Connect the negative battery, start the engine and check operation.

B6304F Engine

1. Disconnect the negative battery lead.

2. Remove the auxiliary drive belt.

3. Remove the front (lower) timing belt cover, splash guard and vibration damper guard. Remove the ignition coil cover.

4. Remove the upper timing cover.

To install:

5. Install the upper timing belt cover. Install the ignition coil cover.

6. Install the front (lower) timing belt cover, splash guard and vibration damper guard.

7. Install the auxiliary drive belt.

8. Connect the negative battery lead.

OIL SEAL REPLACEMENT

B234F Engine

1. Disconnect the negative battery cable.

2. Remove the timing/balance shaft belts.

3. Remove the timing belt right side idler.

4. Remove the crankshaft pulley, using a counterhold and guide tools 5284 and 5872 or equivalent, between the cylinder head, in right-hand idler bolt hole.

5. Carefully pry out the seal. Avoid damaging the sealing faces on the shaft and in seating flange.

To install:

6. Before installing the new seal, thoroughly clean the crankshaft end and seating flange.

7. Lubricate the new seal and tap the seal into the seating flange.

NOTE: Face of seal should normally be flush with the chamfered edge in the housing; however, if the shaft end shows sign of wear, seal may be located approximately 0.12 in. (3mm) further in.

8. Install the balance shaft drive pulley. Guide must face outwards.

9. Install the timing belt pulley and guides.

10. Install the crankshaft damper/pulley. Tighten the crankshaft bolt in 2 stages. First tighten to 44 ft. lbs. (60 Nm); then tighten an additional 60 degrees.

11. Turn the crankshaft to TDC on No. 1 cylinder.

12. Install the right-hand idler. Tighten to 18.5 ft. lbs. (25 Nm).

13. Install the timing/balance shaft belts as described in this section.

14. Connect the negative battery cable.

B6304F Engine

1. Disconnect the negative battery cable.

2. Remove the timing belt as described in this section.

3. Remove the crankshaft pulley, using a suitable puller.

4. Carefully pry out the old seal.

To install:

5. Before installing the new seal, thoroughly clean the crankshaft face.

6. Lubricate the new seal and tap the seal into place, using tool 5455 or equivalent.

7. Install the timing belt as described in this section.

8. Connect the negative battery cable.

Timing Belt and Tensioner

REMOVAL AND INSTALLATION

B230F Engine

1. Remove the timing belt cover.

2. To remove the tension from the belt, loosen the nut for the tensioner and press the idler roller back. The tension spring can be locked in this position by inserting the shank end of a 3mm drill through the pusher rod.

3. Remove the 6 retaining bolts and the crankshaft pulley.

4. Remove the belt, taking care not to bend it at any sharp angles. The belt should be replaced at 45,000 mile intervals, if it becomes oil soaked or frayed or if on a vehicle that has not been operated for any length of time.

To install:

5. If the crankshaft, idler shaft or camshaft were disturbed while the belt was out, align each shaft with its corresponding index mark to assure proper valve timing and ignition timing, as follows:

   a. Rotate the crankshaft so the notch in the convex crankshaft gear belt guide aligns with the embossed mark on the front cover (12 o'clock position).

   b. Rotate the idler shaft so the dot on the idler shaft drive sprocket aligns with the notch on the timing belt rear cover (4 o'clock position).

   c. Rotate the camshaft so the notch in the camshaft sprocket inner belt guide aligns with the notch in the forward edge of the valve cover (12 o'clock position).

6. Install the timing belt (don't use any sharp tools) over the sprockets and then over the tensioner roller. New belts have yellow marks. The 2 lines on the drive belt should fit toward the crankshaft marks. The next mark should then fit toward the intermediate shaft marks, etc. Loosen the tensioner nut and let the spring tension automatically take up the slack. Tighten the tensioner nut to 37 ft. lbs. (51 Nm).

7. Rotate the crankshaft 1 full revolution clockwise and make sure the timing marks still align.

8. Install the drive belts, radiator fan and shroud. Connect the negative battery cable.

B234F Engine

NOTE: The B234F engine has 2 belts, one driving the camshafts and one driving the balance shafts. The camshaft belt may be removed separately. The balance shaft belt requires removal of the camshaft belt. During reassembly, the exact placement of the belts and pulleys must be observed.

1. Remove the negative battery cable and the alternator belt.

2. Remove the radiator fan, its pulley and the fan shroud.

3. Remove the drive belts for the power steering belts and the air conditioning compressor.

4. Beginning with the top cover, remove the retaining bolts and remove the timing belt covers.

5. Turn the engine to TDC, of the compression stroke, on cylinder No. 1. Make sure the marks on the camshaft pulleys align with the marks on the backing plate and that the marking on the belt guide plate (on the crankshaft) is opposite the TDC mark on the engine block.

6. Remove the protective cap over the timing belt tensioner locknut. Loosen the locknut, compress the tensioner to release tension on the belts and re-tighten the locknut, holding the tensioner in place.

7. Remove the timing belt from the camshafts. Do not crease or fold the belt.

NOTE: The camshafts and the crankshaft must not be moved when the belt is removed.

8. Check the tensioner by spinning it counterclockwise and listening for any bearing noise within. Check also that the belt contact surface is clean and smooth. In the same fashion, check the timing belt idler pulleys. Make sure the are tightened to 18.5 ft. lbs. (25 Nm).

9. If the balance shaft belt is to be removed:

   a. Remove the balance shaft belt idler pulley from the engine.

   b. Loosen the locknut on the tensioner and remove the belt. Slide the belt under the crankshaft pulley assembly. Check the tensioner and idler wheels carefully for any sign of contamination. Check the ends of the shafts for any sign of oil leakage.

   c. Check the position of the balance shafts and the crankshaft after belt removal. The balance shaft markings on the pulleys should align with the markings on the backing plate and the crankshaft marking should still be aligned with the TDC mark on the engine block.

   d. When refitting the balance shaft belt, observe that the belt has colored dots on it. These marks assist in the critical placement of the belt. The yellow dot will align the right lower shaft, the blue dot will align on the crank and the other yellow dot will match to the upper left balance shaft.

   e. Carefully work the belt in under the crankshaft pulley. Make sure the blue dot is opposite the bottom (TDC) marking on the belt guide plate at the bottom of the crankshaft. Fit the belt around the left upper balance shaft pulley, making sure the yellow mark is opposite the mark on the pulley. Install the belt around the right lower balance shaft pulley and again check that the mark on the belt aligns with the mark on the pulley.

   f. Work the belt around the tensioner. Double check that all the markings are still aligned.

   g. Set the belt tension by inserting an Allen key into the adjusting hole in the tensioner. Turn the crankshaft carefully through a few degrees on either side of TDC to check that the belt has properly engaged the pulleys. Return the crank to the TDC position and set the adjusting hole just below the 3 o'clock position when tightening the adjusting bolt. Use the Allen wrench, in the adjusting hole, as a counter hold and tighten the locking bolt to 29.5 ft. lbs. (40 Nm).

   h. Use tool 998 8500 or equivalent to check the tension of the belt. Install the gauge over the position of the removed idler pulley. The tension must be 1-4 units on the scale or the belt must be readjusted.

To install:

10. Reinstall the camshaft belt by aligning the double line marking on the belt with the top marking on the belt guide plate at the top of the crankshaft. Stretch the belt around the crank pulley and place it over the tensioner and the right side idler. Place the belt on the camshaft pulleys. The single line marks on the

belt should align exactly with the pulley markings. Route the belt around the oil pump drive pulley and press the belt onto the left side idler.

11. Check that all the markings align and that the engine is still positioned at TDC, of the compression stroke, for cylinder No. 1.

12. Loosen the tensioner locknut.

13. Turn the crankshaft clockwise. The camshaft pulleys should rotate 1 full turn until the marks again align with the marks on the backing plate.

NOTE: The engine must not be rotated counterclockwise during this procedure.

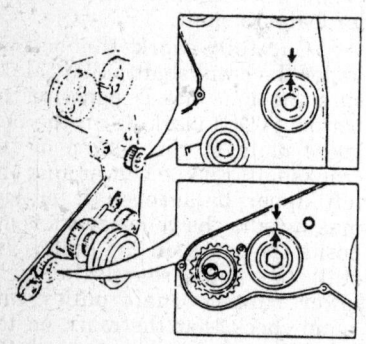

Balance shaft alignment — B234F engine

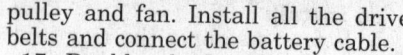
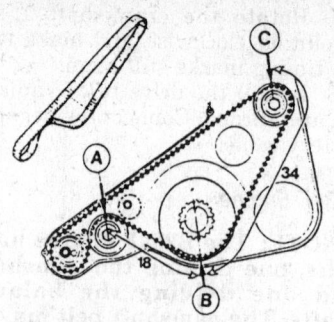

Balance shaft belt markings. There should be 18 teeth between A and B, 34 teeth between B and C — B234F engine

14. Smoothly rotate the crankshaft further clockwise until the camshaft pulley markings are 1½ teeth beyond the marks on the backing plate. Tighten the tensioner locknut.

15. Check the tension on the balance shaft belt; it should now be 3.8 units on a suitable belt tension gauge. If the tension is too low, adjust the tensioner clockwise. If the tension is too high, repeat Step 9g.

16. Check the belt guide for the balance shaft belt and make sure it is properly seated. Install the center timing belt cover, the one that covers the tensioner, the fan shroud, fan

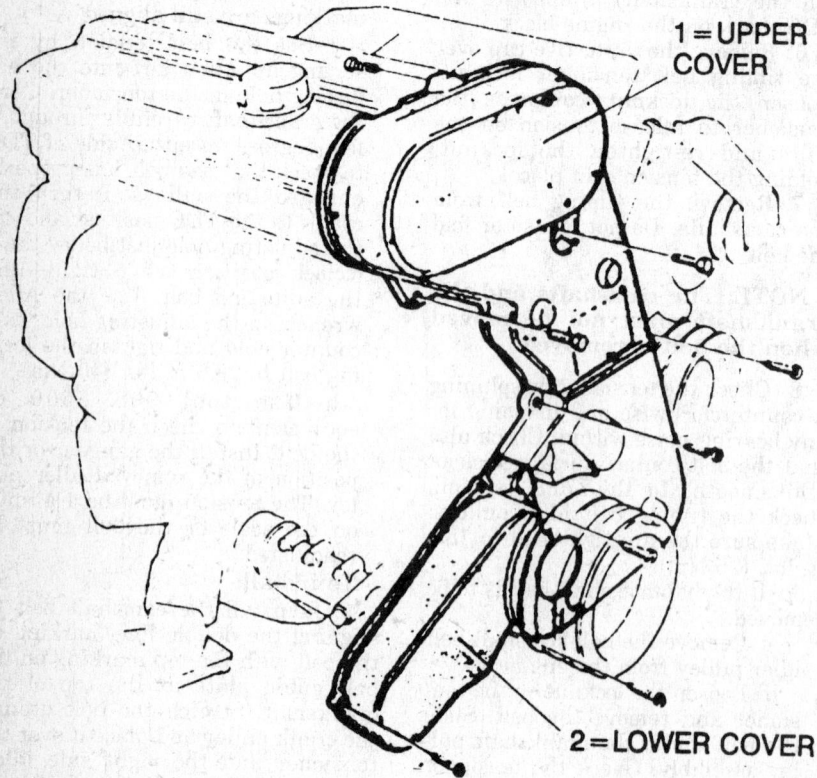

1 = UPPER COVER

2 = LOWER COVER

Timing belt upper cover (1) and lower cover (2) — B234F engine

pulley and fan. Install all the drive belts and connect the battery cable.

17. Double check all installation items, paying particular attention to loose hoses or hanging wires, untightened nuts, poor routing of hoses and wires (too tight or rubbing) and tools left in the engine area.

18. Start the engine and allow it to run until the thermostat opens.

CAUTION
The upper and lower timing belt covers are still removed. The belt and pulleys are exposed and moving at high speed.

19. Shut the engine OFF and bring the motor to TDC, of the compression stroke, on cylinder No. 1.

20. Check the tension of the camshaft belt. Position the gauge between the right (exhaust) camshaft pulley and the idler. Belt tension must be 5.5 ± 0.2 units on a suitable belt tension gauge. If the belt needs adjustment, remove the rubber cap over the tensioner locknut, cap is located on the timing belt cover, and loosen the locknut.

21. Insert a suitable tool between the tensioner wheel and the spring carrier pin to hold the tensioner. If the belt needs to be tightened, move the roller to adjust the tension to 6.0 units. If the belt is too tight, adjust to obtain a reading of 5.0 units on the gauge. Tighten the tensioner locknut.

22. Rotate the crankshaft so the camshaft pulleys move through 1 full revolution and recheck the tension on the camshaft belt. It should now be 5.5 ± 0.2 units. Install the plastic plug over the tensioner bolt.

23. Final check the tension on the balance shaft belt by fitting the gauge and turning the tensioner clockwise. Only small movements are needed. After any needed readjustments, rotate the crankshaft clockwise through 1 full revolution and recheck the balance shaft belt. The tension should now be on the final specification of 4.9 ± 0.2 units.

24. Install the idler pulley for the balance shaft belt. Reinstall the upper and lower timing belt covers.

25. Start the engine and final check performance.

B6304F Engine

1. Disconnect the negative battery cable.

2. Remove the auxiliary drive belts.

3. Remove the front timing belt cover.

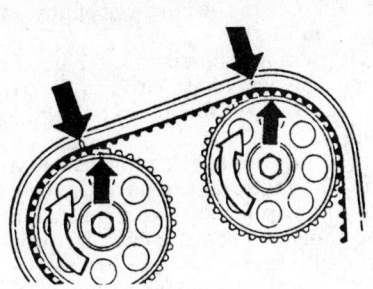

Rotate the engine 1½ teeth — B234F engine

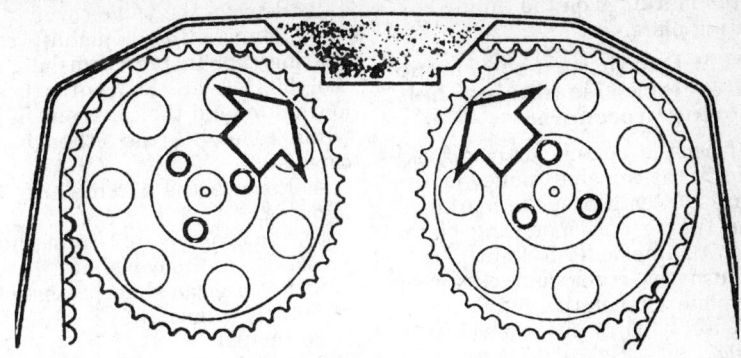

Aligning camshafts/crankshaft timing marks — B6304F engine

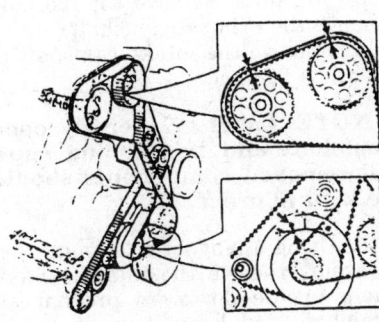

Timing mark alignment — B234F engine

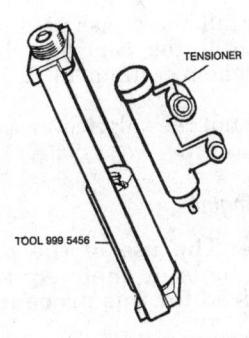

TOOL 999 5456

Volvo recommends that this special tool be used to compress the tensioner to avoid damage

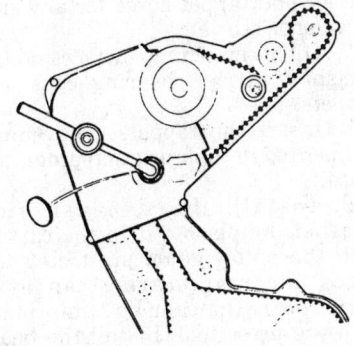

Timing belt tensioner adjustment — B234F engine

4. Remove the splash guard, vibration damper guard and ignition coil cover.

5. Rotate the crankshaft clockwise, until the timing marks on the camshaft pulleys and timing belt mounting plate and crankshaft pulley/oil pump housing are aligned. Remove the upper timing belt cover.

6. Check the belt tensioner. Replace the tensioner, if required.

7. Remove the tensioner upper mounting bolts. Loosen the tensioner lower mounting bolt and twist the

tensioner to free the plunger. Remove the lower mounting bolt and remove the tensioner.

8. Remove the timing belt.

NOTE: Do not rotate the crankshaft while the timing belt is removed.

9. Check the tensioner and idler pulleys, as follows:

a. Spin the pulleys and listen for bearing noise.

b. Check that the pulley surfaces in contact with the belt are clean and smooth.

c. Check the tensioner pulley arm and idler pulley mountings.

d. Torque the tensioner pulley arm to 30 ft. lbs. (40 Nm) and the idler pulley to 18 ft. lbs. (25 Nm).

To install:

10. Place the belt around the crankshaft pulley and right side idler. Place the belt over the camshaft pulleys. Position the belt around water pump and press over tensioner pulley.

11. Insert the tensioner mounting bolts. Torque to 18 ft. lbs. (25 Nm).

12. Remove the locking pin. Install the front timing belt cover.

13. Turn the crankshaft through 2 revolutions and check that the timing marks on the crankshaft and camshaft pulleys are correctly aligned.

14. Install the ignition coil, front timing belt cover, auxiliary drive belts, vibration damper guard and splash guard.

15. Connect the negative battery lead, start and check the engine operation.

NOTE: The lever bushing, on the B234F and B6304F engines, must be greased everytime the belt is replace or the tensioner pulley removed. This is necessary to help prevent seizure of the bushing, with the possible risk of incorrect belt tension. Service the bushing, using the following procedure:

• Remove the lever mounting bolt, tensioner pulley and sleeve behind the bolt.

• Grease the surfaces of the bushing, bolt and sleeve, using part 1161246-2 or equivalent.

• Install the sleeve, tensioner pulley and lever mounting bolt.

• Tighten the bolt 30 ft. lbs. (40 Nm).

ADJUSTMENT

B234F Engine

1. Place a tension gauge 9988500 or equivalent, between the exhaust camshaft drive pulley and tensioner.

2. Read the gauge. If the belt tension is correct, the gauge should read between 3.2-4.2 units.

3. If the reading is incorrect, remove the protective rubber cap in the timing belt cover. Slacken the locknut.

4. Turn the crankshaft clockwise through 1 revolution. Camshaft pulley markings should again coincide

with the markings on the timing belt mounting plate.

NOTE: Do not turn the engine counterclockwise during belt tensioning procedure.

5. Turn the engine further clockwise until the camshaft pulley markings are 1½ teeth past the markings on the timing belt mounting plate. Tighten the tensioner locknut.

6. Turn the crankshaft clockwise to complete 1 revolution (TDC).

7. Check that all markings coincide.

8. Recheck the belt tension.

9. If the reading is still not correct, proceed as follows:
   a. Slacken the tensioner locknut.
   b. Install the measuring gauge. Insert a suitable prybar between the tensioner pulley and the end of the spring carrier pin.
   c. Re-adjust the belt to obtain the specified tension. Tighten the tensioner locknut 37 ft. lbs. (50 Nm).

10. Install the protective rubber cap over the tensioner locknut. Install the upper timing belt cover.

B6304F Engine

1. Place a tension gauge (9988500 or equivalent) between the exhaust camshaft drive pulley and water pump.

2. Read the gauge. If the belt tension is correct, the gauge should read between 3.5-4.6 units.

3. If the reading is incorrect, replace the tensioner.

Camshaft

REMOVAL AND INSTALLATION

B230F Engine

1. Remove the timing belt cover.

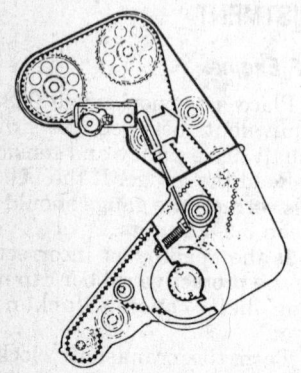

Adjusting timing belt — B234F engine

2. Remove the valve cover.

3. Remove the camshaft center bearing cap. Install camshaft press tool 5021 over the center bearing journal to hold the camshaft in place while removing the other bearing caps.

4. Remove the 4 remaining bearing caps.

5. Remove the seal from the forward edge of the camshaft.

6. Release camshaft press tool and lift out the camshaft.

   To install:

7. Install the camshaft after lubricating with oil. Install the camshaft seal.

8. Install the camshaft press tool and install the camshaft bearing caps. Tighten bolts to 14 ft. lbs. (20 Nm).

9. Install the valve cover and timing belt cover.

B234F Engine

NOTE: The use of the correct special tools or their equivalent is required for this procedure.

1. Disconnect the negative battery cable.

2. Remove the alternator drive belt, the radiator fan and its pulley.

3. Remove the upper and lower timing belt covers.

4. Align the camshaft and crankshaft marks. Turn the engine to TDC of the compression stroke on cylinder No. 1 and make sure the pulley marks and the crankshaft marks align with their matchmarks on either the backing plate (cam pulleys) or the belt guide plate (crankshaft).

5. Remove the protective cap over the timing belt tensioner locknut. Loosen the locknut, compress the tensioner to release tension on the belts and re-tighten the locknut, holding the tensioner in place.

6. Remove the timing belt from the camshafts; do not crease or fold the belt.

NOTE: The camshafts and the crankshaft must not be moved when the belt is removed.

7. Remove the timing belt idler pulleys.

8. Remove the camshaft drive pulleys. Use a counterhold wrench to prevent the camshaft from turning.

9. Remove the plate or panel behind the pulleys. Remove the cover plate for the ignition wires. Label and disconnect the ignition wiring from the spark plugs and the distributor cap; remove the coil wire from the distributor cap.

10. Remove the valve cover and gasket. Clean the surfaces of any gasket remains.

11. Remove the distributor housing from the camshaft carrier. Remove the ignition wire clip next to the left bolt.

12. Plug the spark plug holes with suitable material. Remove the center bearing cap for each camshaft. Mark the camshaft bearing caps for proper reinstallation.

13. Install a camshaft press tool 5021 or similar, on the exhaust side camshaft, in place of the removed bearing cap. When it is securely in place, remove the remaining bearing caps and nuts. Remove the tool and remove the exhaust camshaft.

14. Remove the intake camshaft in identical fashion.

NOTE: Label or identify each camshaft and its bearing caps. All removed components should be kept in order.

15. Using a magnet or a small suction cup, remove the tappets. Store them upside down, to prevent oil drainage, and keep them in order. They are not interchangeable.

   To install:

16. Clean and inspect the camshaft carrier and tappet bores for any sign of wear or scoring.

17. Oil all matching surfaces on the camshaft carrier, bearing caps and tappets.

18. Insert the tappets. They must be inserted in their original order and place.

19. Install the exhaust side camshaft by placing it in the carrier with the pulley guide pin facing up. Using the rear bearing cap as a guide, press the camshaft into place with the press tool. Install the bearing caps in the original order.

20. Install the bearing cap nuts and tighten them in stages to 15 ft. lbs. (20 Nm). Remove the press tool and install the center bearing cap; tighten it in stages to 15 ft. lbs. (20 Nm).

21. Install the intake camshaft in the carrier with the pulley guide pin facing upwards.

22. Turn the distributor shaft to align the driver with the markings on the distributor housing. Install new O-rings on the housing and rotor shaft.

23. Using the rear bearing cap as a guide, press the camshaft into place with the press tool. Install the bearing caps in the original order.

24. Install the bearing cap nuts and tighten them in stages to 15 ft. lbs. (20 Nm).

25. Double check the tightness of all the camshaft bearing cap nuts. All should be 15 ft. lbs. (20 Nm). Do not overtighten.

26. Reinstall the distributor, connect the coil wire and install the ignition wire clip at the left bolt. Remove the protective covers from the spark plug holes.

27. Use a silicone sealer and apply to the front and rear camshaft bearing caps. Install new gaskets for the valve cover and the spark plug wells. Install the spark plug gasket with the arrow pointing towards the front of the vehicle and the word **UP** facing up. Make sure the valve cover gasket is correctly positioned and install the valve cover.

28. Reconnect the ground wire at the distributor.

29. Install the ignition wires and the cover plate.

30. Using a compression seal driver tool 5025 or similar, install the oil seals for the front of each camshaft. Camshafts must not be allowed to turn during this operation.

31. Install the upper backing plate over the ends of the camshafts and adjust the plate so the camshafts are centered in the holes.

32. Replace the idler pulleys and tighten their mounts to 18.5 ft. lbs. (25 Nm).

33. Install the camshaft drive pulleys, using a counterhold to prevent the camshafts from turning.

34. Reinstall the camshaft belt by aligning the double line marking on the belt with the top marking on the belt guide plate at the top of the crankshaft. Stretch the belt around the crank pulley and place it over the tensioner and the right side idler. Place the belt on the camshaft pulleys. The single line marks on the belt should align exactly with the pulley markings. Route the belt around the oil pump drive pulley and press the belt onto the left side idler.

35. Check that all the markings align and that the engine is still positioned at TDC, of the compression stroke, for cylinder No. 1.

36. Loosen the tensioner locknut.

37. Turn the crankshaft clockwise. The camshaft pulleys should rotate 1 full turn until the marks again align with the marks on the backing plate.

NOTE: The engine must not be rotated counterclockwise during this procedure.

38. Smoothly rotate the crankshaft further clockwise until the camshaft pulley markings are 1½ teeth beyond the marks on the backing plate. Tighten the tensioner locknut.

39. Reinstall the fan pulley and fan. Install all the drive belts and connect the battery cable.

40. Double check all installation items, paying particular attention to loose hoses or hanging wires, untightened nuts, poor routing of hoses and wires (too tight or rubbing) and tools left in the engine area.

41. Start the engine and allow it to run until the thermostat opens.

CAUTION

Use care. The upper and lower timing belt covers are still removed. The belt and pulleys are exposed and moving at high speed.

NOTE: This engine may be somewhat noisy when started. The noise will subside as oil reaches the tappets. Do not exceed 2500 rpm while the tappets are noisy.

42. Shut the motor off and bring the motor to TDC of the compression stroke on cylinder No. 1.

43. Check the tension of the camshaft belt. Position the gauge between the right (exhaust) camshaft pulley and the idler. Belt tension must be 5.5 ± 0.2 units on a suitable belt tension gauge. If the belt needs adjustment, remove the rubber cap over the tensioner locknut and loosen the locknut.

44. Insert a suitable tool between the tensioner wheel and the spring carrier pin to hold the tensioner. If the belt needs to be tightened, move the roller to adjust the tension to 6.0 units. If the belt is too tight, adjust to obtain a reading of 5.0 units on the gauge. Tighten the tensioner locknut and remove the suitable tool.

45. Rotate the crankshaft so the camshaft pulleys move through 1 full revolution and recheck the tension on the camshaft belt. It should now be 5.5 ± 0.2 units. Install the plastic plug over the tensioner bolt.

46. Reinstall the remaining belt covers. Start the engine and final check performance.

B280F Engine

1. Remove the cylinder head.
2. Remove the camshaft rear cover plate.
3. Remove the camshaft retaining fork at the front of the cylinder head.
4. Pull the camshaft out the rear of the head.
To install:
5. Oil the camshaft and followers and install. Tighten the camshaft re-

taining bolt to 7-11 ft. lbs. (10-15 Nm).

6. Install the camshaft retaining fork, install the rear cover plate and install the cylinder head.

Balance Shafts

REMOVAL AND INSTALLATION

B234F Engine

NOTE: The use of the correct special tools or their equivalent is required for this procedure.

LEFT SHAFT AND HOUSING

1. Remove the timing and balance shaft belts.
2. Use a counterhold tool 5362 and remove the left side balance shaft pulley.
3. Remove the air mass meter and inlet hose.
4. Unfasten the bracket under the intake manifold and remove the bracket holding the alternator and power steering pump. These may be moved aside and tied with wire to the left shock tower.
5. Remove the bolts securing the balance shaft housing to the block. Using an extractor tool 5376 or similar, carefully separate the housing from the block. The housing must be removed evenly from both its front and rear mounts.
To install:
6. Clean the joint faces on the cylinder block. Place new O-rings in the grooves around the oil passages on the housing. The rings can be held in place with a light coating of grease.
7. Install the balance shaft housing. Make absolutely sure the housing is evenly mounted on the front and rear mountings. Tighten the bolts alternately in a diagonal pattern. Tighten each bolt ½ turn at a time; tighten them to 15 ft. lbs. (20 Nm). When all the bolts are at 15 ft. lbs. (20 Nm), loosen them individually and tighten each one to 7.5 ft. lbs. (10 Nm), plus 90 degrees of rotation.

NOTE: Make certain the shaft does not seize within the housing during installation.

8. If the halves of the housing were split apart during the repair, tighten the joint bolts to 6 ft. lbs. (8 Nm).
9. Install the drive pulley. Use a counterholding tool. Note that the pulley has a slot which will align with the guide on the shaft. The shallow side of the pulley faces inward,

toward the engine. Tighten the center bolt for the pulley to 37 ft. lbs. (50 Nm).

10. Install the bracket for the alternator and power steering pump. Double check their connections and hoses. Attach the support under the intake manifold and don't forget the wire clamp on the bottom bolt.

11. Install the air mass meter and its intake hose.

12. Install the balance shaft belt and camshaft belt.

RIGHT SHAFT AND HOUSING

1. Remove the timing and balance shaft belts.

2. Use a counterhold tool 5362 and remove the left side balance shaft pulley.

3. Remove the balance shaft belt tensioner and remove the bolt running through the backing plate to the balance shaft housing.

4. Remove the air mass meter and its air inlet hose.

5. Remove the air preheat hose from the bottom heat shield at the exhaust manifold. Remove the nuts holding the right engine mount to the crossmember.

6. Connect a hoist or engine lift apparatus to the top of the engine. Lift the engine at the right side, be-

ing careful to maintain clearance between the brake master cylinder and the intake manifold.

7. Remove the complete motor mount from the block, including the pad and lower mounting plate.

8. Remove the bolts securing the balance shaft housing to the block. Using a extractor tool 5376 or similar, carefully separate the housing from the block. The housing must be removed evenly from both its front and rear mounts.

To install:

9. Clean the joint faces on the cylinder block. Place new O-rings in the grooves around the oil passages on the housing. The rings can be held in place with a light coating of grease.

10. Install the balance shaft housing. Make absolutely sure the housing is evenly mounted on the front and rear mountings. Tighten the bolts alternately in a diagonal pattern. Tighten each bolt ½ turn at a time; tighten them to 15 ft. lbs. (20 Nm). When all the bolts are at 15 ft. lbs. (20 Nm), loosen them individually and tighten each one to 7.5 ft. lbs. (10 Nm), plus 90 degrees of rotation.

NOTE: Make certain the shaft does not seize within the housing during installation.

11. If the halves of the housing were split apart during the repair, tighten the joint bolts to 6 ft. lbs. (8 Nm).

12. Install the drive pulley. Use a counterholding tool. Note that the pulley has a slot which will align with the guide on the shaft. The shallow side of the pulley faces inward, toward the engine. Tighten the center bolt for the pulley to 37 ft. lbs. (50 Nm).

13. Install the engine mount onto the block.

14. Using the studs on the crossmember as a guide, lower the engine into place on the front crossmember. When the engine is correctly seated, the lifting apparatus may be removed.

15. Reinstall the air mass meter and its air intake hose.

16. Reinstall the motor mount bolts and the air preheat tube at the lower part of the exhaust manifold.

17. Install the bolt through the backing plate and into the balance shaft housing. Reinstall the belt tensioner, tightening the bolt so the pulley is movable when the belt is in position.

18. Reinstall the balance shaft and camshaft belts.

Piston and Connecting Rod

POSITIONING

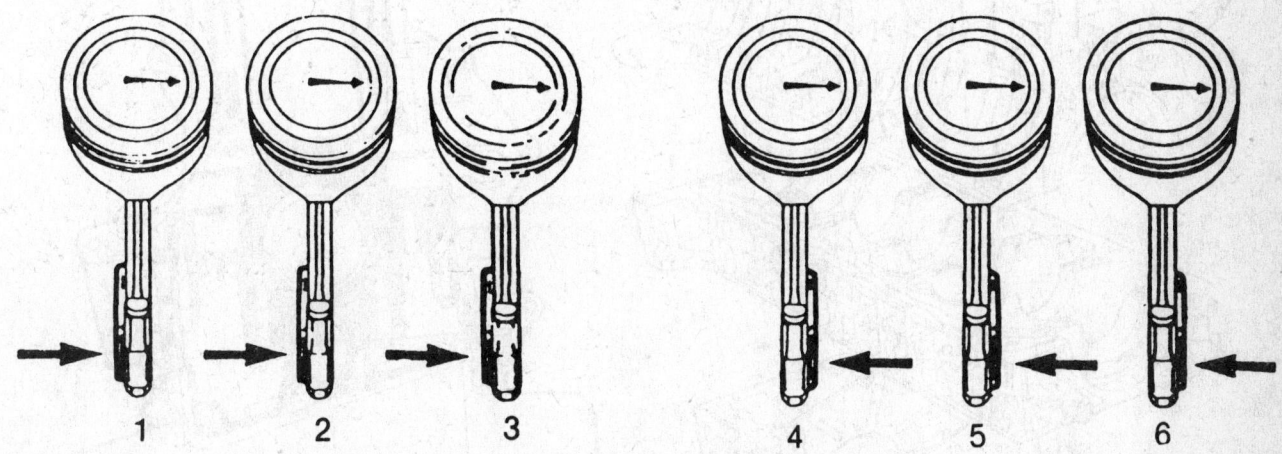

Piston and connecting rod position — B280F engine shown

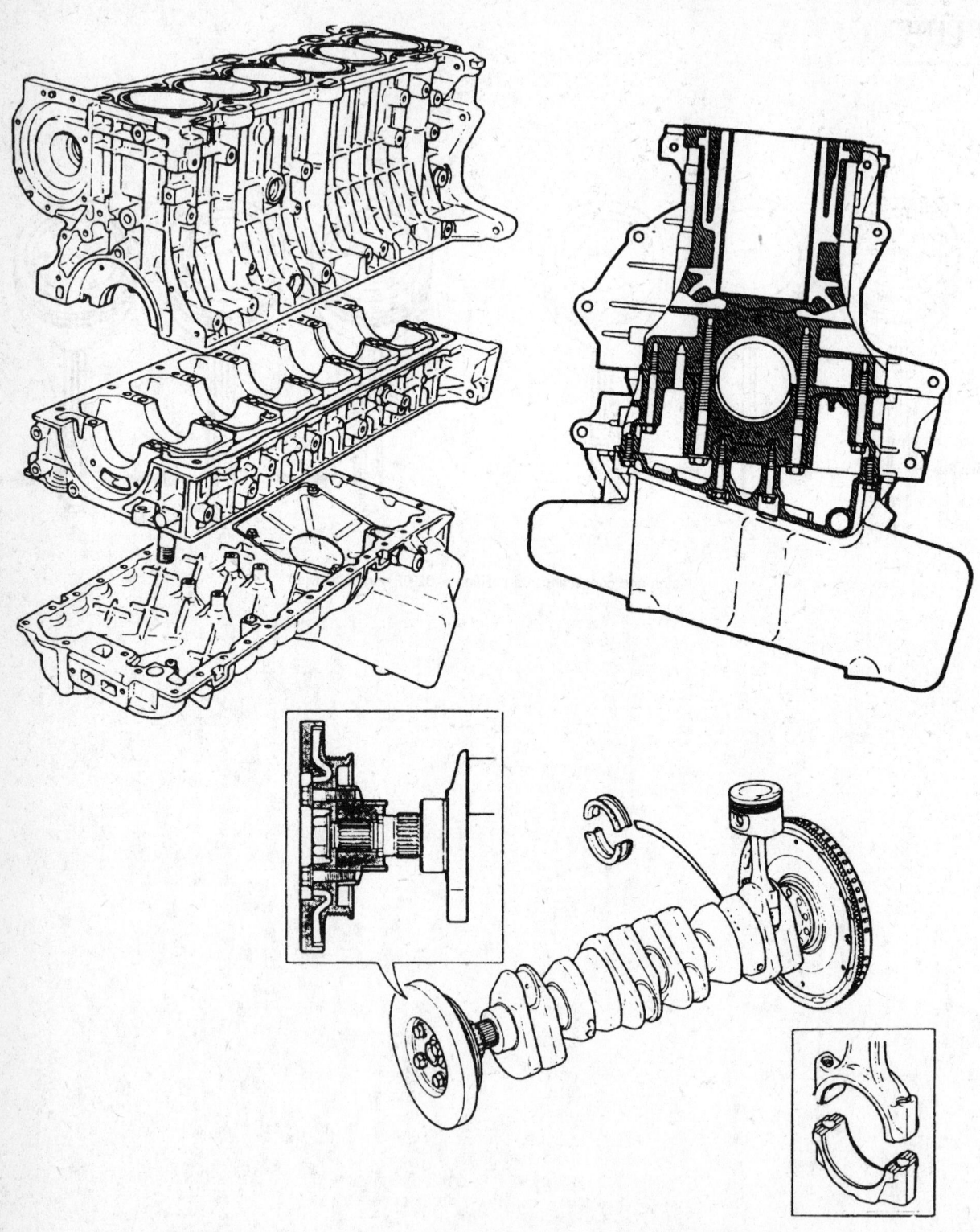

Aluminum block with cast iron liners equipped with 1-piece 7 main bearing girdle — B6304F engine

ENGINE LUBRICATION

Oil Pan

REMOVAL AND INSTALLATION

B230F Engine

1. Disconnect the negative battery cable. Raise and support the vehicle safely.
2. Drain the engine oil.
3. Remove the splash guard.
4. Remove the engine mount retaining nuts.
5. Remove the lower bolt and loosen the top bolt on the steering column yoke.
6. Slide the yoke assembly up on the steering shaft.
7. Raise and safely support the front of the engine.
8. Remove the retaining bolts for the front axle crossmember.
9. Remove the crossmember.
10. Remove the left engine mount.
11. Remove the pan support bracket.
12. Remove the pan bolts and remove the pan.
To install:
13. Clean the gasket mating surfaces thoroughly. Install the oil pan and using new gaskets, tighten the bolts to 8 ft. lbs. (11 Nm).
14. Lower the engine and install all engine mounts. Install the front crossmember and install the bolts.
15. Install the yoke assembly on the steering shaft and tighten the bolts to 18 ft. lbs. (24 Nm).
16. Install the splash guard, lower the vehicle and connect the negative battery cable. Fill the engine with oil.

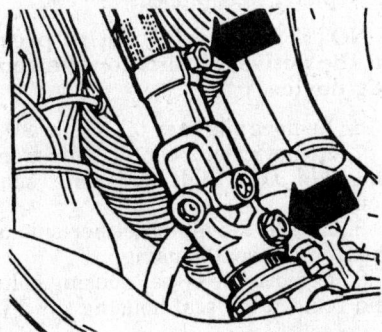

Steering yoke removal. Arrows indicate the retaining nuts

17. Start the engine and allow it to reach operating temperature. Check for leaks.

B234F Engine

1. Raise and safely support the vehicle. Disconnect the negative battery cable and remove the engine oil dipstick.
2. Remove the air mass meter and air inlet hose. Loosen the fan shroud.
3. Remove the bolts at both ends of the crossmember.
4. Fit a chain hoist or lifting apparatus to the top of the engine and relieve the weight of the engine by lifting the at the front.
5. At the right motor mount, unbolt the bottom mounting plate from the crossmember. At the left motor mount, unbolt the upper mounting plate from the cylinder block.
6. Drain the engine oil and replace the drain bolt when the pan is empty. Use a new washer and tighten the bolt to 44 ft. lbs. (60 Nm).
7. Remove the splash guard from under the engine, the bottom nut for the left motor mount and the wiring harness bracket from the transmission cover.
8. At the steering shaft, remove the lower clamping bolt and loosen the upper bolt. Matchmark the position of the splined joint and slide the fitting up the steering shaft.
9. Remove the rubber bump-stop on the front crossmember and remove the reinforcing bracket between the engine and transmission.
10. Disassemble the bolted joint at the front of the catalytic converter.
11. Carefully elevate the engine with the hoist. Make very certain that no hoses or wires are strained and that clearance is maintained at the firewall. Raise the motor only enough to perform the next Steps of the procedure.
12. Remove the left motor mount.
13. Unbolt and remove the oil pan. It will need to be lifted and turned during removal.
To install:
14. Clean the gasket surfaces and install the new gasket so the small tab on the gasket is on the same side as the starter. Lift the pan into place, install the retaining bolts and tighten them to 8 ft. lbs. (11 Nm).
15. Install the reinforcing bracket between the engine and transmission. Attach it first to the transmission and then to the engine block. Tighten the bracket in stages so all the bolts pull up evenly.

16. Install the bump-stop on the front crossmember. Lift the crossmember into position against the side rails, install the bolts and tighten only a few turns to hold it in place.
17. When all the bolts are installed, tighten the crossmember bolts to 70 ft. lbs. (95 Nm). Install the left motor mount and secure the plate to the cylinder block. Don't forget to attach the cable clip on the upper bolt.
18. Paying close attention to the placement of the motor mounts, lower the engine into position. When the engine is correctly seated, the lifting equipment may be removed from the vehicle.
19. At the right motor mount, tighten the plate onto the crossmember. Check the connection of the air preheat tube at the exhaust manifold.
20. Tighten the fan shroud. Adjust the position of the bottom bracket as needed.
21. Reconnect the wiring harness bracket at the transmission, the bolted joint at the front of the catalytic converter and install the splash guard under the engine.
22. Tighten the left motor mount.
23. Observing the markings made earlier, reassemble the steering shafts. Insert and tighten the bottom bolt to 15 ft. lbs. (20 Nm). Tighten the upper bolt the same. Don't forget to install the small spring clips on the bolts.
24. Install the air mass meter and its hoses and connectors.
25. Fill the engine with the correct amount of oil and reinstall the dipstick.
26. Lower the vehicle, reconnect the battery cable and start the engine. Check for leaks.

B280F Engine

1. Disconnect the negative battery cable. Raise and support the vehicle safely. Remove the splash guard.
2. Drain the crankcase.
3. Remove the oil pan retaining bolts. Swivel the pan past the stabilizer bar and remove.
To install:
4. Clean the gasket mating surfaces thoroughly. Install the oil pan, using a new gasket, and tighten the bolts to 6-8 ft. lbs. (8-11 Nm).
5. Install the splash guard, lower the vehicle and fill the crankcase with oil. Connect the negative battery cable. Start the engine and allow it to reach operating temperature. Check for leaks.

Oil Pump

REMOVAL AND INSTALLATION

B230F Engine

1. Remove the oil pan.
2. Remove the 2 oil pump retaining bolts. Remove the oil pump and pull the delivery tube from the block.

To install:

3. When installing, use new sealing rings at either end of the delivery tube.
4. Install the pump with the delivery tube attached. Align the pipe to the block so the seal does not become damaged. Tighten the 2 oil pump retaining bolts.
5. Attach the clamp for the oil trap drain hose to the oil pump bolts. Make sure the hose is securely clamped behind the oil pump shoulder. Do not shorten the hose.

B234F Engine

1. Remove the timing belt.
2. Using a counterholding tool 5039 or similar, remove the oil pump drive pulley.
3. Thoroughly clean the area around the oil pump. Place sheets of newspaper or a container on the splash guard to contain any spillage and remove the oil pump mounting bolts. Remove the pump from the engine.
4. Remove the seal from the groove in the block. Clean the area with solvent, making certain there are no particles of dirt trapped in the pump area.

To install:

5. Install the new seal in the groove and install the new oil pump. Lubricate the pump with clean engine oil before installation. Tighten the mounting bolts to 7 ft. lbs. (10 Nm).
6. Using the counterhold, install the drive pulley and tighten the center bolt to 15 ft. lbs. (20 Nm), plug 60 degrees of rotation.
7. Clean the area of any oil spillage. Remove the paper or container from the splash guard.
8. Install the timing belt.

B280F Engine

The oil pump body is cast integrally with the cylinder block. It is chain driven by a separate sprocket on the crankshaft and is located behind the timing chain cover. The pickup screen and tube are serviced by removing the oil pan. To check the pump gears or remove the oil pump cover:

1. Disconnect the negative battery cable. Remove the air cleaner and valve covers.
2. Loosen the fan shroud and remove the fan. Remove the shroud.
3. Loosen the alternator, air pump, power steering pump, air conditioning compressor, if equipped, and remove their drive belts.
4. Block the flywheel from turning and remove the 36mm bolt and the crankshaft pulley.

NOTE: Do not drop the key into crankcase.

5. Remove the timing gear cover (25 bolts).
6. Remove the oil pump drive sprocket and chain.
7. Remove the oil pump cover and gears.

To install:

8. Prime the pump, remove all air by filling it with clean engine oil and operating the pump by hands, before installation. Install the oil pump gears and cover. Install the oil pump drive sprocket and chain.
9. Install the timing gear cover, crankshaft pulley, alternator, air pump, power steering pump, air conditioning compressor and all accessory drive belts.
10. Remove the flywheel block and install the valve covers. Connect the negative battery cable.

B6304F Engine

1. Disconnect the negative battery cable.
2. Drain the cooling system.
3. Remove the auxiliary drive belt, front timing belt cover, cooling fan and splash guard. Remove the radiator.
4. Turn the crankshaft until the timing marks on the camshaft pulleys/timing belt cover mounting plate and crankshaft pulley/oil pump housing are aligned. Remove the upper timing belt cover.
5. Remove the vibration damper.
6. Remove the timing belt.
7. Remove the crankshaft pulley, using a suitable puller.
8. Remove the oil pump mounting bolts and remove the oil pump.

To install:

9. Before installing the oil pump, thoroughly clean the mating surfaces.
10. Transfer the shield.
11. Place a new gasket into position. Then install the oil pump, using tool 5455 or equivalent. Use the mounting bolts as a guide. Pull in the pump using the crankshaft center nut.
12. Apply thread locking compound to the pump mounting bolts and install the bolts. Tighten alternately to 7 ft. lbs. (10 Nm).
13. Install the crankshaft pulley, using the center bolt and spacer.
14. Install the timing belt.
15. Install the vibration damper. Tighten the center nut to 221 ft. lbs. (300 Nm).
16. Install the tensioner. Align the timing marks and install the ignition coil cover.
17. Install the radiator.
18. Install the front timing belt cover, cooling fan and splash guard. Install the auxiliary drive belt.

Rear Main Bearing Oil Seal

REMOVAL AND INSTALLATION

B230F and B234F Engines

1. Disconnect the negative battery terminal.
2. Remove the transmission.
3. Remove the clutch and pressure plate, if equipped.
4. Remove the pilot bearing snapring and remove the bearing.
5. Remove the flywheel or driveplate, as equipped.

NOTE: Be careful not to press in the activator pins for the timing device.

6. Remove the rear oil pan brace.
7. Remove the 2 center bolts from the pan that bolt into the seal housing.
8. Loosen 2 bolts on either side of the 2 in the seal housing.
9. Remove the 6 seal housing bolts and remove the seal housing.

NOTE: Be careful not to damage the oil pan gasket when removing the seal housing.

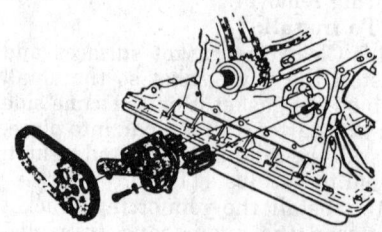

Oil pump installation — B280F engine

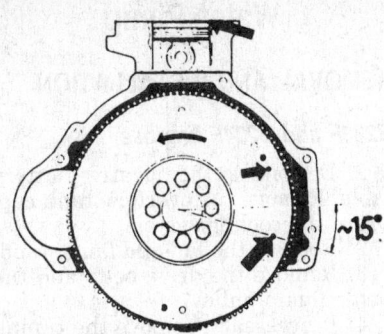

Flywheel installation — B230F and B234F engines

10. Remove the seal using special tool 2817 or a suitable replacement.

To install:

11. Use a new gasket on the seal housing and coat the seal with oil prior to installation. Install the seal.

12. Install the seal housing.

13. Install the rear oil pan brace and flywheel. Torque the flywheel bolts to 47-54 ft. lbs. (64-73 Nm). When installing the flywheel turn the crankshaft to bring the No. 1 piston to TDC. The lower flywheel pin should be installed approximately 15 degrees from the horizontal and opposite the starter.

14. Install the pilot bearing. Install the clutch assembly and transmission, as required.

15. Connect the negative battery cable. Fill the transmission with fluid. Start the engine and allow it to reach operating temperature. Check for leaks.

B280F Engine

1. Disconnect the negative battery terminal.

2. Remove the transmission.

3. Remove the clutch and pressure plate, if equipped.

4. Remove the flywheel or driveplate, on automatic transmissions.

NOTE: On automatic transmissions remove the crankshaft spacer.

5. Remove the 2 rear pan bolts.

6. Remove the bolts in the seal housing and then the housing.

NOTE: Gently remove the housing so as not to damage the oil pan gasket.

7. Using tool 5107, remove the old seal.

To install:

8. Using the seal tool, install the new seal. Install the seal housing and

tighten the seal housing bolts to 7-11 ft. lbs. (10-15 Nm).

9. Install the rear oil pan bolts. Install the flywheel and clutch assembly, as required. Tighten the flywheel bolts to 33-37 ft. lbs. (45-50 Nm).

10. Install the transmission and connect the negative battery cable. Fill the transmission with oil. Start the engine and allow it to reach operating temperature. Check for leaks.

B6304F Engine

1. Disconnect the negative battery cable.

2. Remove the transmission from the vehicle.

3. Remove the flexplate.

4. Carefully pry out the seal, taking care not to damage the sealing faces on the shaft and in seat.

To install:

5. Before installing the seal, thoroughly clean the seat and inspect for signs of wear.

6. Lubricate the mating surface between the seat and seal. Oil the seal lips and press the new seal into place, using a suitable seal installer tool 5430 and 1801 or equivalent.

7. Install the flexplate. Use new bolts and thread locking compound. Tighten the bolts in 2 stages: first to 33 ft. lbs. (45 Nm); then tighten an additional 50 degree turn.

8. Install the transmission.

9. Connect the negative battery cable.

ENGINE COOLING

Radiator

REMOVAL AND INSTALLATION

1. Drain the cooling system.

2. Remove the upper and lower radiator hoses. Remove the expansion tank. If equipped with automatic transmission, remove the transmission cooler lines.

3. Disconnect the electrical connectors for the coolant sensor and the electric cooling fan.

4. Remove the retaining bolts for the radiator shroud and remove the radiator.

To install:

5. Install the radiator and tighten the bolts for the radiator shroud. Ensure that the radiator is positioned for maximum air flow. Connect the electrical connectors.

6. Install the radiator hoses, expansion tank and transmission cooler lines.

7. Fill the radiator with coolant and check the transmission fluid. Start the engine and allow it to reach operating temperature. Check the coolant level and transmission fluid.

Heater Core

REMOVAL AND INSTALLATION

Without Air Conditioning

1. Disconnect the negative battery cable. Pinch the heater hoses near the firewall to prevent coolant from escaping. Remove the heater unit.

2. Place the unit on its side with the control valve facing upward. Remove the spring clips and separate the housing halves.

3. Disconnect the capillary tube from the heater core and then lift out the core.

To install:

4. Install the heater core. Take care to transfer the foam plastic packing to the new heater core. Install the fragile capillary tube carefully on the core.

5. Join the housing halves and install the spring clips. Install the heater unit.

6. Connect the negative battery cable. Start the engine and check the coolant level after it has reached operating temperature.

With Air Conditioning

240 SERIES

— **CAUTION** —
Do not disconnect the refrigerant lines from the air conditioning system.

1. Disconnect the negative battery cable. Pinch the heater hoses near the firewall to prevent coolant from escaping. Remove the combination heater-air conditioner unit.

2. Remove the left outer end of the central unit. Remove the locking retainer and the blower wheel.

3. Remove the 2 retaining screws for the left transmission tunnel bracket.

4. Remove the lockring for the left intake shutter shaft.

5. Remove the 3 retaining screws and lift off the inner end.

6. Remove the 3 retaining screws for the fan motor retainer.

7. Disconnect the heater hoses at the heater core.

8. Remove the clamps which retain the central unit halves together, lift off the left half and remove the heater core.

To install:

9. Install the heater core. Take care to transfer the foam plastic packing to the new heater core. Join the heater unit halves and install the spring clips.

10. Install the fan motor, inner end and intake shutter shaft. Install the outer end of the central unit, locking retainer and blower wheel.

11. Install the combination heater/air conditioner unit. Connect the heater hoses at the heater core.

12. Connect the negative battery cable. Start the engine and allow it to reach operating temperature. Check the coolant level and for leaks.

EXCEPT 240 SERIES

1. Disconnect the negative battery cable.

2. Pinch the hoses to the heater core near the firewall in the engine compartment. Use locking pliers. Make sure the hoses are pinched sufficiently so the hose is completely blocked off. Remove the hose clamps on the engine compartment side of the hoses, close to the firewall.

3. Press down the clip under the ashtray and pull the tray out. Remove the cigarette lighter and the storage compartment.

4. Remove the engine console around the shift lever and parking brake. Unplug the connector.

5. Remove the panel under the driver's side dashboard and remove the air duct to the steering column outlet.

6. Pull down the driver's side floor mat and remove the front and rear edge side panel screws. Remove the panels.

7. On the passenger's side, remove the 3 clips that fasten the panel under the glove compartment and remove the panel. Remove the glove compartment and light.

8. Pull down the floor mat on the right side and remove the front and rear edge side panel screws.

9. Remove the radio compartment by pressing forward on the inner wall and removing the screw.

10. Remove the screws inside the center console and remove the side panel screws and the panels.

11. Remove the panel around the heater control. Remove the radio compartment console and remove the control panel. Free the central electrical unit and remove the mounting.

12. Remove the center panel vent and the screw holding the distribution unit. Mark all air ducts to the panel vents and to the distribution unit with tape for later installation and remove the ducts.

13. Remove the vacuum hoses from the vacuum motors.

14. Remove the distribution unit. Remove the heater core retaining clips and remove the heater core.

To install:

15. Install the heater core and fasten using the retaining clips. Install the distribution unit and connect the vacuum hoses to the motors. On climate control unit-equipped vehicles, connect the red hose to the upper shutter for the panel vents and the light brown hose to the lower shutter. Connect the yellow and blue hoses to the floor/defrost shutter, the yellow to the lower one. On automatic climate control-equipped vehicles, connect the red hose to the upper shutter for the panel vent and the blue hose to the defrost vent. Connect the light brown hose to the lower shutter for the panel unit.

16. Install all ducts in their marked positions. Install the center panel vent, heater control panel and radio compartment console.

17. Install the center console and replace the floor mat. Install the glove compartment and clip the under dash panel into place. Install the front and rear edge side panels. Install the engine console around the shift lever and parking brake.

18. Install the ashtray. From the engine side, connect the heater hoses to the heater core. Connect the negative battery cable.

19. Start the engine, allow it to reach operating temperature, check the coolant level and check for leaks.

Water Pump

REMOVAL AND INSTALLATION

B230F and B234F Engines

1. Disconnect the negative battery cable. Remove the overflow tank cap. Drain the cooling system.

2. Remove the fan and fan shroud.

3. Remove the drive belts and the water pump pulley.

4. If necessary, remove the timing belt cover.

5. Remove the lower radiator hose.

6. Remove the retaining bolt for the coolant pipe, beneath exhaust manifold, and pull the pipe rearward.

7. Remove the 6 retaining bolts and lift off the water pump.

To install:

8. Clean the gasket contact surfaces thoroughly and use a new gasket and O-rings, especially between the cylinder head and top of water pump.

9. Install the water pump and tighten the bolts to 11-15 ft. lbs. (15-20 Nm). Install the coolant pipe, lower radiator hose, timing belt cover (as necessary), accessory drive belts and water pump pulley.

10. Install the fan and fan shroud. Fill the coolant system with coolant. Start the engine and allow it to reach operating temperature. Check for leaks. Add coolant as necessary.

B280F Engine

1. Disconnect the negative battery cable. On some versions of this engine it may be necessary to remove the front and main sections of the intake manifold.

2. Remove the overflow tank cap and drain the cooling system.

3. Disconnect both radiator hoses. On automatic transmission vehicles, disconnect the transmission cooler lines at the radiator. Disconnect the fan shroud. Remove the radiator and fan shroud.

4. Remove the fan.

5. Remove the hoses from the water pump to each cylinder head.

6. Remove the fan belts. Remove the water pump pulley.

7. Loosen the hose clamps at the rear of the water pump.

8. Remove the water pump from the block (3 bolts).

To install:

9. Transfer the thermal time sender and temperature sensor to the new water pump.

10. Transfer the thermostat cover, thermostat and rear pump cover to the new pump.

Check that the O-ring around the lower lip of the water pump is in good condition. Replace if there is any damage.

11. Install the new pump and tighten the bolts to 11-15 ft. lbs. (15-20 Nm). Install the clamps, water pump pulley and fan belts.

12. Install the hoses that reach to each cylinder head. Install the fan, shroud and radiator. If equipped with an automatic transmission, connect the transmission cooler lines. Install the intake manifold, as necessary.

13. Connect the negative battery cable and fill the radiator with coolant. Start the engine and allow it to reach operating temperature. Check for leaks.

B6304F Engine

1. Disconnect the negative battery cable.

2. Drain the cooling system, by opening the drain cock on the right side of the cylinder block. Re-install the drain cock.

3. Remove the timing belt.

4. Remove the water pump retaining bolts (7) and remove the water pump.

To install:

5. Before installing the water pump, clean the mating surfaces.

6. Install the water pump, using a new gasket. Tighten and torque the mounting bolts 15 ft. lbs. (20 Nm).

7. Install the timing belt.

8. Fill the cooling system.

9. Start the engine and check for leaks.

Thermostat

REMOVAL AND INSTALLATION

1. Disconnect the negative battery cable.

2. Drain the cooling system. On the B6304F engine, drain the system by opening the drain cock on the right side of the cylinder block. Re-install the drain cock.

3. Remove the thermostat housing retaining bolts. Remove the thermostat housing, thermostat and gasket.

To install:

4. Before installing the thermostat, thoroughly clean the mating surfaces.

5. Fit a new gasket and place the thermostat into position.

6. Install the thermostat housing.

7. Fill the cooling system.

8. Connect the negative battery lead, start the engine and check for leaks.

Cooling System Bleeding

1. Fill the radiator with the proper type of coolant.

2. With the radiator cap off, start the engine and allow it to reach normal operating temperature.

3. Run the heater at full force and with the temperature lever in the HOT position. Be sure the heater control valve is functioning.

4. Shut the engine OFF and recheck the coolant level, refill as necessary.

ENGINE ELECTRICAL

NOTE: Disconnecting the negative battery cable on some vehicles may interfere with the functions of the on-board computer systems and may require the computer to undergo a relearning process when the negative battery cable is reconnected.

Volvo uses several different ignition systems. Bosch LH Series engine management systems are used on most models. The designation for these ignition systems is: EZ115K and EZ116K. In addition, a few models use the Bendix Regina engine management system and this ignition system is designated REX-1. In 1992, the 960 models were equipped with the Bosch Motronic 1.8 engine management system

The EZ115K, EZ116K and REX-1 ignition systems used on 240, 700 and 940 Series are like most engine management systems currently in use. The ignition and fuel control functions are closely integrated. Sensors feed information to an on-board computer which makes necessary adjustments. Some self-diagnostic capabilities are built into the computer to help troubleshooting.

The Bosch Motronic 1.8 system, used on the model 960 with the 2.9L B6304F engine, is a totally integrated engine management system. The fuel and ignition functions are controlled by the same on-board computer in the Electronic Control Unit (ECU). This particular system uses a Distributorless Ignition System (DIS) where individual coil assemblies are mounted right on the spark plugs eliminating the distributor and associated wiring.

Distributor

The only function of the distributor is to distribute voltage to the spark plugs. There are no advance functions built into the distributor. It is no longer possible to adjust ignition timing through the distributor.

REMOVAL AND INSTALLATION

There is no conventional distributor. A distributor cap is mounted to the rear of the camshaft drive housing and contains only a rotor. The distributor cap may be removed and replaced. If the rotor is to be replaced, use care. In some cases, the rotor must be destroyed to be removed.

Ignition system components are interrelated with fuel system components. For most components the removal is straight forward, just the removal of the retaining screws. Use care to make sure any ground connections are clean and tight and handle sensors with care.

Distributorless Ignition

The B6304F engine, fitted on the 960, is equipped with the Motronic 1.8 combined fuel/ignition system. This system is equipped with a powerful control unit which controls the ignition and fuel injection functions in the cylinders by means of individual ignition coils and injectors.

The Electronic Control Unit (ECU) computes the instant at which each ignition coil must deliver its pulse. There are 6 coils controlled by 2 power units. The ECU uses information from many sensors to compute timing. The ignition coils are mounted directly on the spark plugs. The 2 power units which control the coils are mounted on the intake manifold, 1 on the front and 1 on the rear, for cooling. The front power unit is connected to cylinders 1, 3 and 5 while the rear unit serves cylinders 2, 4 and 6. Firing order is 1-5-3-6-2-4. Each power unit has 3 stages, each connected to an individual coil. The ignition voltage is extremely high, upwards of 40,000 volts to aid cold starts and to fire the lean mixtures required by emission laws.

The control unit is provided with adaptive Lambda control (oxygen sensor) and idling control functions and with a timing retardation function to eliminate knock. The service requirement is minimal, since neither the CO level nor the idling speed requires adjustment.

For the Motronic 1.8 system Distributorless Ignition System, the following procedures may be used.

REMOVAL AND INSTALLATION

Camshaft Sensor

1. The camshaft sensor is mounted at the rear of the cylinder head on the exhaust side. Disconnect the negative battery cable.
2. Remove any ducting or hoses that may be in the way, matchmarking for assembly.
3. Disconnect the electrical connector taking care not to damage the connector or pins. Ground connections are secured with electrical eyelets and small screws. Use care when disconnecting these pieces.
4. Remove the hold-down bolts for the sensor body.
5. Pull the camshaft sensor away from the cylinder head, noting the drive slots in the camshaft for reassembly.
   To install:
6. Make sure the drive slots in the camshaft properly mesh with the camshaft sensor drive.
7. Install the hold-down bolts and make sure the electrical connection is secure.

Ignition Coils

This system uses 6 individual coils, 1 on each spark plug.

1. Disconnect the negative battery cable.
2. Remove the large coil cover on top of the engine that is secured to the camshaft cover. Use care not to drop any of the small retaining screws.
3. Remove any ducting or hoses that may be in the way, matchmarking for reassembly.
4. Remove the hold-down capscrews from the coil top.
5. Disconnect the electrical connector from the coil top assembly.
6. Carefully pull the coil from the spark plug, pulling straight up while turning slightly to disengage from the top of the spark plug.
   To install:
7. Press the coil straight down onto the spark plug. There should be a slight click as the coil seats on the spark plug top.
8. Install the hold-down capscrews and make sure the electrical connection is secure.
9. Install the coil cover and make sure any hose connections that were removed are now secure.

Ignition Amplifiers

There are 2 ignition amplifiers. They are mounted on the intake manifold. One feeds odd number cylinder coils, the other, even numbers.

1. Remove any ducting or hoses that may be in the way, matchmarking for reassembly.
2. Remove the hold-down capscrews from the amplifier being serviced.
3. Carefully disengage the electrical connector and lift the amplifier from the vehicle.
   To install:
4. Install the ignition amplifier. Use care to make sure the hold-down capscrews are firmly in place, but use caution not to over-torque when working around light alloy parts.
5. Make sure the electrical connection is secure.

Ignition Timing

ADJUSTMENT

The EZ115K, EZ116K and REX-1 ignition systems, used on 240, 700 and 900 Series (except 1992 960 model), incorporates an anti-knock and ignition setting control. These 2 controls are integrated and require no adjustments.

The ignition timing on these vehicles may be checked with a conventional timing light. The timing, however, cannot be adjusted. If the ignition setting is wrong, use the following procedure:

1. Check the throttle switch.
2. Check that the wiring to the crank sensor is correctly connected at the firewall.
3. Open the cover of the test connector and connect the cable to terminal **6**.
4. Turn the ignition to the **ON** position. Select test function 1 by pushing the button once for more than 1 second and count the number of blinks. Note the number and press again in case there are more fault codes (up to 3). Note the fault codes to begin troubleshooting.
   a. Code 1-1-1 — No fault codes in memory.
   b. Code 1-4-2 — Fault in control unit. Engine runs with safety-retarded ignition timing (approximately 10 degrees).
   c. Code 1-4-3 — Knock sensor faulty. Engine runs with safety-retarded ignition timing (approximately 10 degrees).
   d. Code 1-4-4 — Load signal missing from fuel system control

unit. Control unit selects full-load ignition.
   e. Code 2-1-4 — Engine speed sensor faulty.
   f. Code 2-2-4 — Coolant temperature sensor faulty.
   g. Code 2-3-4 — Throttle switch for idling faulty. Engine runs with safety-retarded ignition timing (does not apply to REX-1 ignition system).
   h. Code 3-3-4 — Throttle switch in idle position (REX-1 ignition only).
5. If fault Code 1-1-1 (no fault in memory) appears, check the fuel system.
6. If the LED does not light when the button is pressed or no code is blinked out, check the connection at the ECU.

Alternator

PRECAUTIONS

Several precautions must be observed when working on the alternator system to avoid damage to the unit.

- If the battery is removed for any reason, make sure it is reconnected with the correct polarity. Reversing the battery connections may result in damage to the 1-way rectifiers.
- When utilizing a booster battery as a starting aid, always connect the positive to positive terminals and the negative terminal from the booster battery to a good engine ground on the vehicle being started.
- Never use a fast charger as a booster to start vehicles.
- Disconnect the battery cables when charging the battery with a fast charger.
- Never attempt to polarize the alternator.
- Do not use test lamps of more than 12 volts when checking diode continuity.
- Do not short across or ground any of the alternator terminals.
- The polarity of the battery, alternator and regulator must be matched and considered before making any electrical connections within the system.
- Never separate the alternator on an open circuit. Make sure all connections within the circuit are clean and tight.
- Disconnect the battery ground terminal when performing any service on electrical components.
- Disconnect the battery if arc welding is to be done on the vehicle.

BELT TENSION ADJUSTMENT

Accessory drive belt tension is correct when the deflection made with light finger pressure on the belt at a midway point is about ½ in. Any belt that is glazed, frayed or stretched so it cannot be tightened sufficiently, must be replaced.

Incorrect belt tension is corrected by moving the driven accessory (alternator, air pump, power steering pump or air conditioning compressor) away from or toward the driving pulley. Loosen the mounting and adjusting bolts on the respective accessory and tighten them, once the belt tension is correct. Never position a metal prybar on the rear end of the alternator, air pump or power steering pump housing. They can be deformed easily.

REMOVAL AND INSTALLATION

1. Disconnect the negative battery cable. Raise the vehicle and support safely, if needed.
2. Disconnect the electrical leads to the alternator. Remove all necessary components in order to gain access to the alternator retaining bolts.
3. Remove the adjusting arm-to-alternator bolt and the adjusting arm-to-engine bolt.
4. Remove the alternator mounting bolt.
5. Remove the fan belt and lift the alternator forward and out.
   To install:
6. Install the alternator and belt. Tension the belt to specifications.
7. Connect the electrical leads to the alternator and install all other previously removed components.
8. Connect the negative battery cable, start the vehicle and test the charging system.

Starter

REMOVAL AND INSTALLATION

1. Disconnect the negative battery cable.
2. Disconnect the leads from the starter motor. Remove the necessary components in order to gain access to the starter retaining bolts. Raise and safely support the vehicle.
3. Remove the bolts retaining the starter motor to the flywheel housing and lift it off.
   To install:
4. Position the starter motor to the flywheel housing and install the retaining bolts finger-tight. Apply lock-

ing compound to the threads and tighten the bolts to approximately 25 ft. lbs. (34 Nm).
5. Connect the starter motor leads and the negative battery cable.

EMISSION CONTROLS

Emission Warning Lamps

RESETTING

On most vehicles, there is an Engine Service or a Lamda Sond light on the instrument panel that lights up at specific intervals or if the on-board computer detects a fault. Re-setting this lamp is a simple procedure. Remove the sound proofing on the firewall above the pedals and remove the screws and catches at the base of the instrument panel. Tilt the panel out and locate the red reset button.

FUEL SYSTEM

Fuel System Service Precautions

Safety is the most important factor when performing not only fuel system maintenance but any type of maintenance. Failure to conduct maintenance and repairs in a safe manner may result in serious personal injury or death. Maintenance and testing of the vehicle's fuel system components can be accomplished safely and effectively by adhering to the following rules and guidelines.
• To avoid the possibility of fire and personal injury, always disconnect the negative battery cable unless the repair or test procedure requires that battery voltage be applied.
• Always relieve the fuel system pressure prior to disconnecting any fuel system component (injector, fuel rail, pressure regulator, etc.), fitting or fuel line connection. Exercise extreme caution whenever relieving fuel system pressure to avoid exposing skin, face and eyes to fuel spray. Please be advised that fuel under

pressure may penetrate the skin or any part of the body that it contacts.
• Always place a shop towel or cloth around the fitting or connection prior to loosening to absorb any excess fuel due to spillage. Ensure that all fuel spillage (should it occur) is quickly removed from engine surfaces. Ensure that all fuel soaked cloths or towels are deposited into a suitable waste container.
• Always keep a dry chemical (Class B) fire extinguisher near the work area.
• Do not allow fuel spray or fuel vapors to come into contact with a spark or open flame.
• Always use a backup wrench when loosening and tightening fuel line connection fittings. This will prevent unnecessary stress and torsion to fuel line piping. Always follow the proper torque specifications.
• Always replace worn fuel fitting O-rings with new. Do not substitute fuel hose or equivalent, where fuel pipe is installed.

RELIEVING FUEL SYSTEM PRESSURE

1. Remove the fuel pump relay.
   a. On 240 Series, the relay is located next to the control unit.
   b. On 700 and 900 Series, the relay is in the fuse box, behind the ashtray. The relay is furthest to the left, on the second row.
2. Start the engine repeatedly until the engine will no longer start, indicating that the fuel pressure is relieved.

NOTE: Before disconnecting any fuel fittings, always place a shop rag in position to catch any fuel spill.

Fuel Tank

REMOVAL AND INSTALLATION

1. Disconnect the negative battery cable. Raise and support the vehicle safely.
2. Release the fuel system pressure. Drain the fuel tank completely.

——— CAUTION ———
When performing this procedure, always have a dry-chemical fire extinguisher handy. Fuel vapors are extremely explosive.

3. In the trunk, remove the panels which cover the filler hose. It may be necessary to remove the spare tire on

some vehicles. Roll back the carpet and remove the access panel cover.

4. Disconnect the fuel filler pipe connection. Label and disconnect all fuel lines leading to the fuel tank. Label and disconnect all electrical connectors at the fuel tank.

5. Position a floor jack under the tank, using a large piece of wood as a cushion between the fuel tank and the floor jack. Raise the jack so it just contacts the tank.

6. If equipped with a saddle type fuel tank (driveshaft runs through a tunnel in the fuel tank), matchmark the driveshaft and remove.

7. Remove any shields or protective covers on the tank. Loosen and remove the tank retaining bolts. Lower the jack slowly and inspect for any obstructions.

8. Once on the ground, remove the fuel sender unit by unscrewing the lock-ring at the top of the tank. Drain the remaining fuel from the tank.

To install:

9. Install the fuel sender unit and tighten the lock-ring. Install the protective shields and raise the fuel tank into position. Install and tighten the attaching bolts.

10. Remove the floor jack. Install the driveshafts. Connect all fuel and electrical lines leading to the fuel tank.

11. Install the protective panel in the trunk and replace the spare tire (as required) and the carpet.

12. Lower the vehicle, connect the negative battery cable, turn the ignition key **ON** and check for leaks.

Fuel Filter

REMOVAL AND INSTALLATION

1. Disconnect the negative battery cable.
2. Relieve the fuel system pressure.
3. Raise and safely support the vehicle safely.
4. Remove the fuel lines, mounting bracket nut and the filter. Place a container under the filter to catch the excess fuel.

To install:

NOTE: Fuel flow direction arrow is marked on the new (and old) filter. Arrow follows direction from fuel tank to engine.

5. Install the new filter in the proper direction. Be sure to use the new sealing rings and torque the fuel lines to the filter to 14 ft. lbs. (20 Nm).

6. Connect the negative battery cable, turn the ignition **ON** and check for leaks.

Electric Fuel Pump

All vehicles are equipped with an electric impeller pump (feed pump or pre-pump) located in the fuel tank. The feed pump is used to maintain the pressure in the feed pipes to the main fuel pump.

The fuel pump (main pump) is an electric roller pump, cooled by the fuel which flows through it. It has a non-return valve which opens if the pressure gets to high.

Both the tank pump and fuel pump operates when either the starter motor or the engine is running.

PRESSURE TESTING

1. Relieve the fuel pressure.
2. Connect a fuel pressure gauge 5011 or equivalent, between the fuel line and distribution manifold.

NOTE: Position a shop towel in place to catch any spilled fuel when the fuel line connections are removed.

3. On 700 and 900 Series, remove the seat belt reminder, since this makes the test more easily performed. It is located in the middle of the top row in the fuse box.

4. Start the fuel pump (fuel pump relay removed) by connecting a jumper lead between terminals 30 and 87/2 on the relay socket. Verify the pump operation by removing the fuel cap and listening.

5. Note the gauge reading. The fuel pressure should be approximately 43.5 psi (300 kPa).

6. Remove the jumper lead. Relieve the fuel system pressure and remove the pressure gauge.

7. Re-install the fuel pump relay.

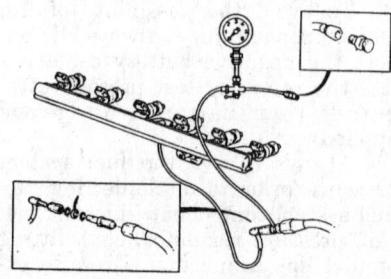

Checking fuel system pressure — B6304F engine shown

REMOVAL AND INSTALLATION

Main Pump

1. Disconnect the negative battery cable.
2. Raise and safely support the vehicle.
3. Disconnect the electrical connector.
4. Relieve the fuel system pressure.

— **CAUTION** —
When relieving the pressure in the fuel system, place a container under the fuel pump to catch the excess fuel.

5. Remove the mounting bolts and the fuel pump.

6. Installation is the reverse of removal. When installing, be sure to use new sealing rings and/or gaskets.

In-Tank Fuel Pump (Feed Pump or Pre-Pump)

1. Disconnect the negative battery cable. Raise and support the vehicle safely. Relieve the fuel system pressure.

2. Remove the fuel tank.

3. Loosen the lockring at the top of the fuel tank and remove the sending unit with the transfer pump attached. Note the direction of the float in the tank.

4. Remove the transfer pump from the sending unit.

To install:

5. Install the transfer pump on the sending unit. Install the sending unit in the fuel tank. Do not overtighten the lock-ring as the plastic threads on some fuel tanks are easily stripped.

6. Install the fuel tank in the vehicle.

7. Lower the vehicle. Connect the negative battery cable, start the engine and check for leaks. Check the system fuel pressure.

Fuel Injector

REMOVAL AND INSTALLATION

1. Relieve the fuel system pressure. Disconnect all fuel and vacuum connections.

2. Loosen the attaching bolts and remove the fuel distribution rail and injectors as an assembly.

3. Remove the injector by pulling it from the injection rail.

To install:

4. When installing injectors, check the rubber O-rings for damage and replace as necessary. Lubricate the

O-rings with petroleum jelly prior to installation.

5. Install the fuel rail assembly and tighten all attaching bolts. Connect all fuel and vacuum lines.

DRIVE AXLE

Halfshaft

REMOVAL AND INSTALLATION

Multi-Link Suspension

1. Raise and support the vehicle safely.

2. Remove the rear wheels and loosen the halfshaft retaining nut in the center of the wheel bearing housing.

3. Remove the bolts holding the lower section of the differential. Remove the lower section with the trailing links attached.

4. Remove the bolts holding the halfshaft to the differential and remove the shaft from the wheel bearing housing. Inspect the CV-boots for damage and replace as necessary.

To install:

5. Install the wheel end of the halfshaft first, then install the differential end. Using new bolts, tighten to 70 ft. lbs. (94 Nm).

6. Temporarily install 2 long 12mm bolts in the center holes of the lower differential section. The bolts will hold the lower section in place for alignment. Alignment of the panel is critical to proper rear wheel alignment.

7. Once aligned, install the 8 attaching bolts and tighten to 52 ft. lbs. (70 Nm), plus 30 degrees of rotation.

8. Install a new halfshaft retaining nut and tighten to 103 ft. lbs. (139 Nm), plus 60 degrees of rotation.

9. Install the wheel and lower the vehicle.

Driveshaft and U-Joints

REMOVAL AND INSTALLATION

1. Raise and safely support the vehicle.

2. Mark the relative positions of the driveshaft yokes and transmission and differential housing flanges for purposes of assembly. Remove the nuts and bolts which retain the front and rear driveshaft sections to the

transmission and differential housing flanges, respectively. Remove the support bearing housing from the driveshaft tunnel and lower the driveshaft and universal joint assembly as a unit.

3. Pry up the lock washer and remove the support bearing retaining nut. Pull off the rear section of the driveshaft with the intermediate universal joint and splined shaft of the front section. The support bearing may now be pressed off the driveshaft.

4. Remove the support from it housing.

5. Inspect the driveshaft sections for straightness. Using a dial indicator or rolling the shafts along a flat surface, make sure the driveshaft out-of-round does not exceed 0.010 in. (0.25mm). Do not attempt to straighten a damaged shaft. Any shaft exceeding 0.010 in. (0.25mm) out-of-round will cause substantial vibration and must be replaced. Also, inspect the support bearing by pressing the races against each other by hand and turning them in opposite directions. If the bearing binds at any point, it must be discarded and replaced.

To install:

6. Install the support bearing into its housing.

7. Press the support bearing and housing onto the front driveshaft section. Push the splined shaft of the front section, with the intermediate universal joint and rear driveshaft section, into the splined sleeve of the front section. Install the retaining nut and lock washer for the support bearing.

8. Taking note of the alignment marks made prior to removal, position the driveshaft and universal joint assembly to its flange connections and install but do not tighten its retaining nuts and bolts. Position the support bearing housing to the driveshaft tunnel and install the retaining nut. Tighten the nuts which retain the driveshaft sections to the transmission and differential housing flanges to a torque of 25-30 ft. lbs. (34-40 Nm).

9. Lower the vehicle. Road test the vehicle and check for driveline vibrations and noise.

Rear Axle Shaft, Bearing and Seal

REMOVAL AND INSTALLATION

Except Multi-Link Rear Suspension

1. Raise and safely support the vehicle.

2. Remove the applicable wheel and tire assembly.

3. Place a wooden block under the brake pedal, plug the master cylinder reservoir vent hole. Remove and plug the brake line from the caliper. Be careful not to allow any brake fluid to spill onto the disc or pads. Remove the 2 bolts which retain brake caliper to the axle housing and lift off the caliper. Lift off the brake disc.

4. Remove the thrust washer bolts through the holes in the axle shaft flange. Using a slide hammer, remove the axle shaft, bearing and oil seal assembly. If possible, pull out the shaft by temporarily reinstalling the brake disc and using this to grab on to while pulling out the axle shaft.

5. Using an arbor press, remove the axle shaft bearing and its locking ring from the axle shaft. Remove and discard the old oil seal.

To install:

6. Fill the space between the lips of the new oil seal with wheel bearing grease. Position the new seal on the axle shaft. Using an arbor press, install the bearing with a new locking ring, onto the axle shaft.

7. Thoroughly pack the bearing with wheel bearing grease. Install the axle shaft into the housing, rotating it so it indexes with the differential. Install the bolts for the thrust washer and tighten to 36 ft. lbs. (50 Nm).

8. Install the brake disc. Position the brake caliper to its retainer on the axle housing and install the 2 retaining bolts. Torque the caliper retaining bolts to 45-50 ft. lbs. (61-68 Nm).

9. Unplug the brake line and connect it to the caliper. Bleed the caliper of all air trapped in the system.

10. Position the wheel and tire assembly on its lugs and hand-tighten the lug nuts. Remove the jack stands and lower the vehicle. Torque the lug nuts to 70-100 ft. lbs. (95-135 Nm).

Multi-Link Rear Suspension

1. Raise and support the vehicle safely.

2. Remove the wheel, brake caliper, rotor and parking brake cable. Hang the caliper out of the way on a

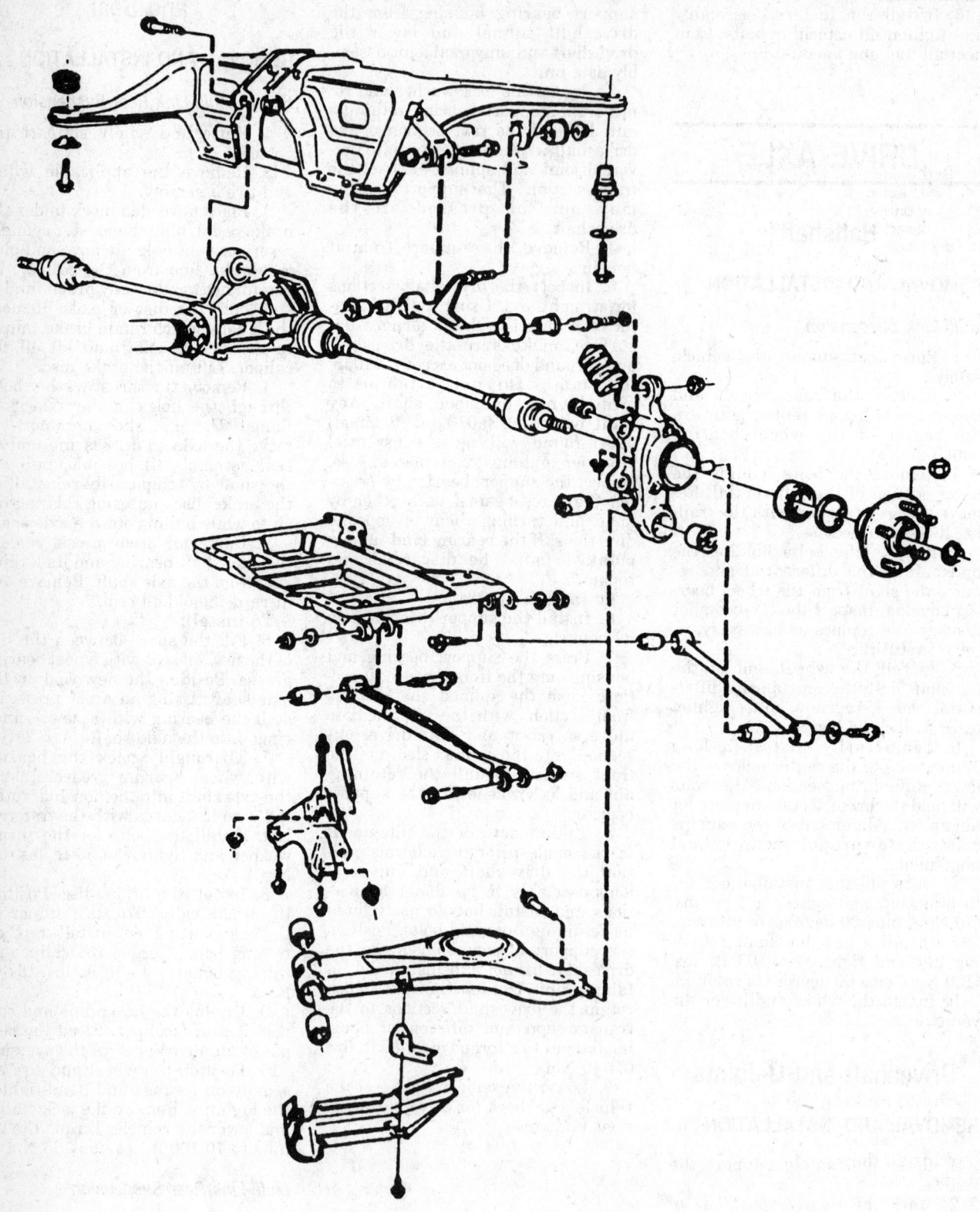

Multi-link differential — 940 and Coupe vehicles shown

1. Flange on transmission
2. Front universal joint
3. Front section of driveshaft
4. Support bearing
5. Intermediate universal joint
6. Rear section of driveshaft
7. Rear universal joint
8. Flange on rear axle

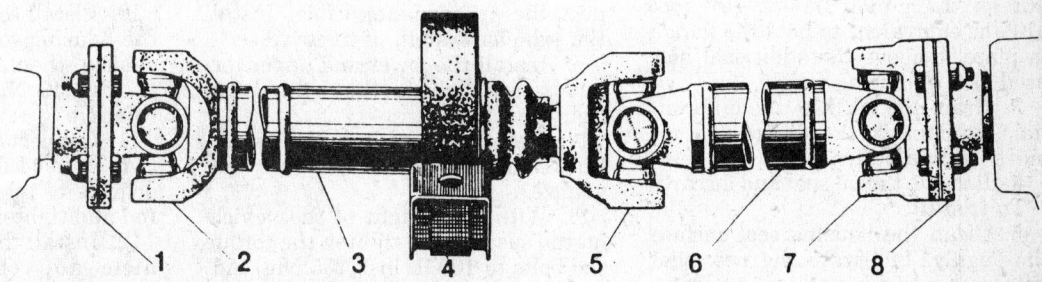

Driveshaft with support bearing

piece of wire. Mark the position of the rotor prior to removal.

3. Remove the support arm, lower link arm and track rod. Use a puller to remove the track rod.

4. Remove the upper link. The wheel bearing housing can now be removed. There are shims between the bearing housing and the upper link arm. Collect them when the housing is removed.

5. Mount the housing in a vise and using tool 5340 or equivalent, apply a counter hold to the bearing housing. Press out the hub with a proper sized drift.

6. Remove the circlip holding the bearing and press the bearing out. Using tools 2722 and 5310 or equivalent, pull the inner ring off the hub.

To install:

7. Press in the bearing and install the circlip. Press on the inner ring. A counter hold must be used to avoid damaging the bearing.

8. Install the wheel bearing housing on the halfshaft. Install the shims between the upper link. Install the retaining nut.

9. Pull the wheel bearing housing outward at the top and tighten the upper link arm nut to 85 ft. lbs. (115

Nm). Pulling the housing outward insures proper alignment.

10. Tilt the bearing housing outward and install the lower link. Push the bottom of the bearing housing inwards and tighten the bolt to 36 ft. lbs. (48 Nm), plus 90 degrees of rotation.

11. Install the support arm and tighten to 44 ft. lbs. (59 Nm), plus 90 degrees of rotation. Install the track rod and tighten to 63 ft. lbs. (85 Nm).

12. Install the parking brake cable. Install the rotor and caliper. Tighten the caliper bolts to 44 ft. lbs. (59 Nm).

13. Tighten the center halfshaft nut to 103 ft. lbs. (139 Nm), plus 60 degrees of rotation. Install the wheel and lower the vehicle.

14. Perform a rear wheel alignment.

Pinion Seal

REMOVAL AND INSTALLATION

Except Multi-Link Rear Suspension

1. Raise and support the vehicle safely.

2. Disconnect the driveshaft at the differential. Using tool 5149 or

equivalent, loosen and remove the large center nut in the center of the pinion flange.

3. Using a puller, remove the flange from the housing. Remove the old seal and discard.

To install:

4. Clean the housing seal surface thoroughly. Lubricate the new seal with grease and install using a suitable driver. Install the flange using tool 5156 or equivalent.

5. Check the serial number of the rear axle. If it begins with an **S** prefix, follow Step a. If it does not begin with an **S** prefix, follow Step b.

a. Axles denoted by the **S** prefix contain a compression sleeve in the differential housing. On these vehicles, install the center nut and carefully tighten to 1.3 ft. lbs. (1.7 Nm) or finger-tight. Make sure the brakes are not applied and turn the flange at about 1 revolution per second to tighten the nut. An alternate method is to tighten the nut to 130 ft. lbs. (176 Nm) using a torque wrench.

b. On axles that do not begin with an **S** prefix, simply install the center nut and tighten to 145-180 ft. lbs. (196-244 Nm) using a fixture to hold the flange in place.

6. Install the driveshaft and check the oil level in the differential. Lower the vehicle.

Multi-Link Rear Suspension

1. Raise and support the vehicle safely. Matchmark the driveshaft and remove.

2. Loosen and remove the center nut on the pinion flange. Use tool 5149 or equivalent to hold the flange in place. Remove the additional bolt used as a balancing weight.

3. Drain the oil from the differential. Matchmark the flange and remove using a puller.

4. Remove the oil seal and discard.

To install:

5. Clean the housing seal surface thoroughly. Lubricate the new seal with grease and install using a suitable driver. Install the flange using tool 5156 or equivalent.

6. Install the center nut and tighten to 132-145 ft. lbs. (179-196 Nm). Do not overtighten the center nut.

7. Install the driveshaft paying attention to the matchmarks. Install the weight bolt. Tighten the bolts to 36 ft. lbs. (48 Nm). Fill the differential with oil and lower the vehicle.

Axle Housing

REMOVAL AND INSTALLATION

Except Multi-Link Rear Suspension

1. Raise and support the vehicle safely. Remove the brake calipers and hang them out of the way using a piece of wire. Remove the rotors and parking brake assembly.

2. Remove the thrust washer bolts through the holes in the rear axle flanges. Using a slide hammer puller, remove the rear axle shaft, bearing and oil seal assembly.

3. Support the rear axle housing using a floor jack. Disconnect the lower torque rod. Disconnect or remove any exhaust system component, as required. Remove the speedometer connector.

4. Remove the driveshaft. Remove the upper torque rod and shock absorbers.

5. Remove the front brackets for the support arms and pry them loose. Remove the rear axle. Once the axle is clear of the vehicle, remove the sway bar. Mark the support arms for left and right side, and remove.

To install:

6. Install the left and right support arms. Fit the bushings within the clamps and tighten the clamps in a crisscross pattern to 33 ft. lbs. (48 Nm). Install the sway bar.

7. Raise the axle assembly into position and install the support arm bolts. Tighten the support arm bracket bolts to 35 ft. lbs. (47 Nm) and the through bolt to 62 ft. lbs. (84 Nm).

8. Install the driveshaft and connect the speedometer cable. Install the exhaust system, if removed.

9. Install the lower and upper torque rods. Tighten the bolts hand tight.

10. Install the axles, brake assemblies and rear wheels. Lower the vehicle.

11. With the weight of the vehicle on the suspension, tighten the torque rod bolts to 100 ft. lbs. (135 Nm). Adjust the parking brake cable and check the oil level in the differential.

Multi-Link Rear Suspension

1. Raise and support the vehicle safely.

2. On 1 side only, remove the bolt holding the support arm to the wheel bearing housing and drive out the support arm. Remove the bolt holding the lower link arm to the wheel bearing housing.

3. Remove the bolts holding the track rod to the wheel bearing housing. Use a puller and a long bolt to move the rod away from the housing.

4. Remove the 8 bolts joining the upper and lower sections of the rear axle housing. Swing the lower part of the wheel bearing housing outward and swing down the lower part of the axle housing. It will still have the 2 arms attached to it and will be attached to the vehicle by the arms on the opposite side.

5. Matchmark and disconnect the rear flange of the driveshaft. Place a floor jack under the center of the differential for support. Remove the 3 bolts holding the differential to the upper housing.

6. Lower the differential and remove the wiring to the impulse sender. Remove the bolts holding the axles to the differential. Remove the differential from the vehicle.

To install:

7. Raise the differential into position and connect the impulse sender connector. Install the 3 bolts to the upper housing. Tighten the bolts to 117 ft. lbs. (158 Nm). When the bolts are secure, the floor jack may be removed.

8. Attach the halfshafts and tighten the bolts to 22 ft. lbs. (29 Nm), plus 90 degrees rotation. Install the driveshaft and tighten the bolts to 36 ft. lbs. (48 Nm). Ensure that the matchmarks are positioned correctly.

9. Raise the lower section of the axle housing and loosely install the 8 bolts. Align the panel by placing long 12mm bolts in the centering holes. Once aligned, tighten the lower housing bolts to 52 ft. lbs. (70 Nm), plus 90 degrees of rotation.

10. Install the lower link arm. Push the housing toward the center of the vehicle, then tighten the bolts to 36 ft. lbs. (49 Nm), plus 90 degrees of rotation.

11. Connect the support arm and tighten to 44 ft. lbs. (59 Nm), plus 90 degrees of rotation. Install the track rod and tighten to 62 ft. lbs. (84 Nm).

12. Install the wheels, lower the vehicle and check the oil in the differential.

MANUAL TRANSMISSION

Transmission Assembly

REMOVAL AND INSTALLATION

The transmission or the transmission overdrive assembly may be removed with the engine installed in the vehicle.

240 Series

1. Disconnect the negative battery cable. Disconnect the backup light connector at the firewall.

2. Raise and safely support the vehicle. Loosen the set screw and drive out the pin for the shifter rod. Disconnect the shift lever from the rod.

3. Inside the vehicle, pull up the shift boot. Remove the fork for the reverse gear detent. Remove the snapring and lift up the shifter.

4. Disconnect the clutch cable and return spring at the throw-out fork and flywheel housing.

5. Disconnect the exhaust pipe bracket(s) from the flywheel cover. Remove the oil pan splash guard.

6. Using a floor jack and a block of wood, support the engine under the oil pan. Remove the transmission support crossmember.

7. Disconnect the driveshaft. Disconnect the speedometer cable. If equipped, disconnect the overdrive wire.

8. Remove the starter retaining bolts and pull free of the flywheel housing.

9. Support the transmission using another floor jack. Remove the flywheel bellhousing-to-engine bolts and remove the transmission.

To install:

10. Install the transmission in the vehicle and tighten the flywheel housing-to-engine bolts to 25-35 ft. lbs. (34-47 Nm).

11. Install the starter, driveshaft, speedometer cable and overdrive wire, if equipped.

12. Install the transmission crossmember and remove the floor jack. Install the oil pan splash guard and exhaust pipe brackets.

13. Connect the clutch cable and return spring. Assemble the gear shift lever.

14. Lower the vehicle. Connect the backup light connector and negative battery cable.

15. Check the transmission oil level. Adjust the clutch as required.

Except 240 series

1. Disconnect the negative battery cable.

2. Attach lifting beam tool 5006 or equivalent, to the rear of the engine. This will support the engine once the transmission is removed.

3. Raise and support the vehicle safely.

4. Disconnect the driveshaft at the transmission flange.

5. Disconnect the support bearing for the driveshaft at the crossmember.

6. Remove the driveshaft from the vehicle.

7. Disconnect the exhaust system at the muffler.

8. Loosen the lock screw at the shifter assembly. Remove the pin through the gear shift lever. Remove the lock pin ring. Push the gear shift lever up.

9. Remove the transmission crossmember and bracket. Cut the wire straps and disconnect the wires at the transmission.

10. Disconnect the clutch cable at the clutch slave cylinder.

11. Disconnect the exhaust system attachment at the transmission cover.

12. Position a suitable jack under the transmission assembly. Remove the transmission to engine retaining bolts. Remove the transmission from the vehicle.

To install:

13. Install the transmission in the vehicle and tighten 30 ft. lbs. (41 Nm).

14. Install the exhaust system attachment, clutch cable and slave cylinder.

15. Install the crossmember and bracket. Connect all electrical connections.

16. Install the shifter assembly. Install the remainder of the exhaust system.

17. Install the driveshaft. Lower the vehicle and disconnect the lifting beam.

18. Connect the negative battery cable, check the transmission oil level and test drive the vehicle. Adjust the clutch as required.

LINKAGE ADJUSTMENT

Reverse gear detent clearance is the only adjustment that can be made to the shift linkage. Remove the shift lever cover, trim frame and ashtray assembly. Engage 1st gear and adjust the clearance between the detent plate and the gear shift lever. Also check clearance should be 0.004-0.06 in. (0.1-1.5mm).

CLUTCH

Clutch Assembly

REMOVAL AND INSTALLATION

1. Remove the transmission.

2. Scribe alignment marks on the clutch and flywheel. In order to prevent warpage, slowly loosen the bolts which retain the clutch to the flywheel diagonally in rotation. Remove

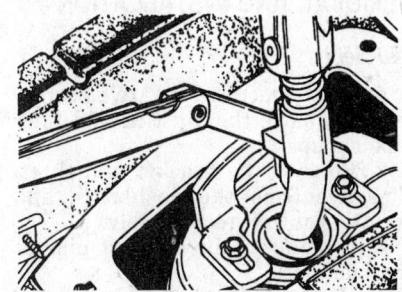

Reverse gear detent clearance adjustment — manual transmission

the bolts and lift off the clutch and pressure plate.

3. Inspect the clutch assembly.

4. Clean the pressure plate and flywheel thoroughly with solvent prior to installation.

To install:

5. Position the clutch assembly, the longest side of the hub facing backwards, to the flywheel and align the bolt holes. Insert a pilot shaft (centering mandrel or drift) or an input shaft from an old transmission of the same type, through the clutch assembly and flywheel so the flywheel pilot bearing is centered.

6. Install the 6 bolts which retain the clutch assembly to the flywheel and tighten them diagonally in rotation, a few turns at a time. After all the bolts are tightened, remove the pilot shaft (centering mandrel).

7. Install the transmission.

8. If equipped with a hydraulic clutch, bleed the clutch.

Clutch Cable

REMOVAL AND INSTALLATION

1. Raise and support the vehicle safely.

2. Disconnect the clutch cable from the clutch fork. Some vehicles are equipped with a release bearing that rotates. These vehicles will have a clutch return spring at the pedal assembly.

3. Disconnect the cable at the pedal assembly. Remove the cable. On some early vehicles, the clutch cable is fitted with a weight. Do not replace the weight when installing the new cable.

To install:

4. Install the cable in the vehicle.

5. Connect the clutch cable at the clutch fork and the pedal assembly.

6. Adjust the clutch cable.

CLUTCH ADJUSTMENT

1. Clutch play is adjusted under the vehicle at the clutch fork.

2. Loosen the locknut on the fork side of the cable bracket and turn the adjust nut until the proper play is achieved. Tighten the locknut.

NOTE: Vehicles equipped with hydraulic clutch assemblies are not adjustable.

3. Clutch play for all engines except turbocharged is 0.12-0.20 in. (3-5mm). Turbocharged engine clutch play (free movement rearward) is 0.04-0.12 in. (1-3mm).

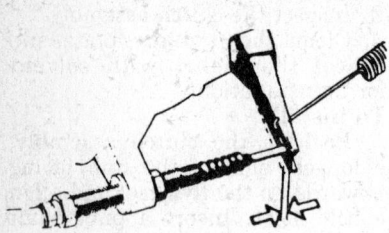

Adjusting the cable operated clutch

Clutch Master Cylinder

REMOVAL AND INSTALLATION

1. Remove the panel under the instrument panel. Remove the locking spring and pin from the clutch pedal assembly.
2. Disconnect the hose from the clutch fluid reservoir.
3. Unscrew the nipple from the cylinder housing. Place a container under the cylinder to catch the fluid that will spill out. Unbolt and remove the cylinder housing.
4. Installation is the reverse of removal. Make sure there is 0.04 in. (1mm) clearance between the pushrod and the pistons and adjust, if necessary. Fill the reservoir with DOT 4 brake fluid and bleed the system.

Clutch Slave Cylinder

REMOVAL AND INSTALLATION

1. Raise and support the vehicle safely.
2. Disconnect the fluid line a the cylinder.

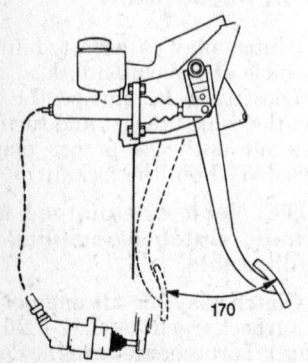

Checking the hydraulic clutch travel

3. Unbolt the cylinder from the flywheel housing.
4. Installation is the reverse of removal.
5. Bleed the hydraulic clutch system.

Hydraulic Clutch System Bleeding

The hydraulic clutch system should be bled any time the hoses have been loosened or any component replaced. The bleeding process is similar to bleeding the brake system. The purpose is to remove any air trapped within the lines.

Add brake fluid to the reservoir. Attach a length of hose to the bleeder nipple on the slave cylinder (at the transmission) and put the other end in a clear glass jar. Put enough brake fluid in the jar to cover the end of the hose.

Have an assistant press the clutch pedal to the floor. Open the bleeder screw on the slave cylinder. Close the bleeder while the pedal is still depressed and repeat the process. As the bleeder is released each time, note the fluid in the jar. When no bubbles are seen, the system is bled. Tighten the bleeder fitting and remove the hose.

During bleeding, note the amount of fluid remaining in the reservoir. If the fluid level drops below the minimum level of the reservoir, refill with fluid before proceeding.

AUTOMATIC TRANSMISSION

Transmission Assembly

REMOVAL AND INSTALLATION

240 Series

1. Disconnect the negative battery cable. Remove the dipstick and filler pipe clamp.
2. Remove the bracket and throttle cable from the dashboard and throttle control, respectively.
3. Disconnect the exhaust pipe at the manifold.
4. Raise and safely support the vehicle.
5. Drain the fluid into a clean container.

6. Disconnect the driveshaft from the transmission flange.
7. Disconnect the selector lever controls and remove the reinforcing bracket from the pan.
8. Remove the torque converter attaching bolts.
9. Support the transmission with a jack equipped with a holding fixture.
10. Remove the crossmember.
11. Disconnect the exhaust pipe brackets and remove the speedometer cable from the case.
12. Remove the filler pipe.
13. Place a wooden block between the engine and firewall and lower the jack until the engine is against the block.

NOTE: If the battery cable appears to stretch too much, remove it.

14. Disconnect the starter wires, remove the converter housing bolts and pull the transmission backwards to clear the guide pins. Remove the transmission assembly.
To install:
15. Install the transmission assembly and tighten 14mm bolts to 35 ft. lbs. (47 Nm). Connect the starter wires.
16. Install the battery cable, if removed. Install the filler pipe, exhaust system, speedometer cable and transmission crossmember.
17. Install the torque converter attaching bolts. Install the selector lever controls and bracket.
18. Install the driveshaft and lower the vehicle. Install the throttle control and bracket. Connect the negative battery cable.
19. Fill the transmission with fluid, start the engine and check for leaks. Recheck the transmission fluid level after the vehicle reaches operating temperature.

Except 240 Series

1. Disconnect the negative battery cable. Place the gear selector in the **P** position.
2. Disconnect the kickdown cable at the throttle pulley on the engine. Disconnect the battery ground cable.
3. Disconnect the oil filler tube at the oil pan and drain the transmission oil.
4. Disconnect the control rod at the transmission lever and disconnect the reaction rod at the transmission housing.
5. On AW 71 transmissions, disconnect the wire at the solenoid, slightly to the rear of the transmission-to-driveshaft flange.

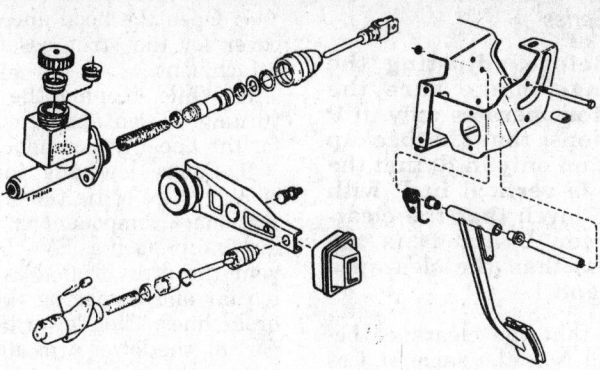

Hydraulic clutch assembly

6. Matchmark the transmission-to-driveshaft flange and unbolt the driveshaft.

7. Remove the transmission cross-member assembly.

8. Disconnect the exhaust pipe at the joint and remove the exhaust pipe bracket from the exhaust pipe. Remove the rear engine mount with the exhaust pipe bracket.

9. On B280F equipped vehicles, remove the bolts retaining the starter motor.

10. Remove the cover for the alternate starter motor location and the cover plate at the torque converter housing bottom on B280F equipped vehicles.

11. Disconnect the oil cooler lines at the transmission.

12. Remove the 2 upper screws at the torque converter cover. Remove the oil filler tube.

13. Place a suitable jack under the transmission.

14. Remove the screws retaining the torque converter to the driveplate. Pry the torque converter back from the driveplate with a small prybar.

15. Slowly lower the transmission when pulling it back to clear the input shaft. Do not tilt the transmission forward or the torque converter may slide off.

To install:

16. Install the transmission and tighten the attaching bolts. Install the torque converter bolts. Install the torque converter cover and filler tube.

17. Connect the oil cooler lines. On B280F equipped vehicles, install the alternate starter and converter housing cover.

18. On B280F equipped vehicles, install the starter motor. Install the exhaust pipe along with the rear engine mount.

19. Install the exhaust pipe and bracket along with the rear engine mount.

20. Install the driveshaft, connect the solenoid wire (AW71 transmission), the control rod and reaction rod. Move the gear selector to the **P** position before attaching the control rod.

21. Install the oil filler tube, kickdown cable and connect the negative battery cable. Adjust the gear shift linkage and the kickdown cable.

22. Fill the transmission with fluid, start the engine and check for leaks. Recheck the transmission fluid level after the vehicle reaches operating temperature.

B6304F Engine

1. Disconnect the negative battery cable.

2. Support the engine, using the special tools 5006, 5033, 5115, 5429 and 5186 or their equivalent.

3. Remove the preheater pipe under the engine. Be careful not to damage the O-ring.

4. Disconnect the front section of the exhaust pipe.

5. Disconnect the transmission cooler lines. Plug the openings.

6. Disconnect the transmission connectors (3). Release the oxygen sensor lead from the transmission unit and support member.

7. Matchmark the driveshaft coupling halves to aid during re-assemble. Disconnect the driveshaft.

8. Remove the clips between the gear selector lever and control rod/reaction arm. Withdraw the rods from the mounting.

9. Disconnect the transmission support member from the transmission bump-stop and side members. Carefully lower the transmission.

10. Remove the torque converter-to-flexplate retaining bolts.

11. Position a suitable jack beneath the transmission. Remove the trans-

mission housing bolts. Separate the torque convertor from the flexplate and lower the transmission.

12. Lift the transmission into position, while aligning the torque convertor with the flexplate.

13. Install the transmission housing mounting bolts.

14. Install the torque convertor retaining bolts. Tighten alternately to 22 ft. lbs. (30 Nm).

15. Raise the transmission and secure the support member. Torque to 37 ft. lbs. (50 Nm).

16. Install the gear selector lever. Install the locking clips.

17. Connect the transmission oil cooler lines.

18. Connect the transmission connectors and oxygen sensor lead.

19. Connect the driveshaft. Check to ensure the matchmarks are aligned.

20. Lubricate the O-ring and install the preheater pipe.

21. Install the front exhaust pipe.

22. Remove the engine support tools.

23. Check and adjust all fluids.

24. Connect the negative battery lead, start the engine and check for leaks.

SHIFT LINKAGE ADJUSTMENT

240 Series

EXCEPT BW55 TRANSMISSION

NOTE: On AW70/AW71 transmissions, the gear selector shift console has been moved forward and the shift linkage has been shortened.

1. Disconnect the shift rod from the transmission lever. Place both the transmission lever and the gear selector lever in the **2** position.

2. Adjust the length of the shift control rod so a small clearance of 0.040 in. (1mm) is obtained between the gear selector lever inhibitor and the inhibitor plate, when the shift control rod is connected to the transmission lever.

3. Position the gear selector lever in **D** and make sure a similar small clearance of 0.04 in. (1mm) exists between the lever inhibitor and the inhibitor plate. Disconnect the shift control rod from the transmission lever and adjust if necessary.

4. Lock the control rod bolt with its safety clasp and tighten the locknut. Make sure the control rod lug follows with the transmission lever.

5. After moving the transmission lever to the **P** and **1** positions, make sure the clearances remain the same. In addition, make sure the output shaft is locked with the selector lever in the **P** position.

WITH BW55 TRANSMISSION

1. With the engine off, check that the distance between the **D** position and its forward stop is equal to the distance between the **2** position and its rearward stop, when the gear selector is moved. If not sure, remove the gear quadrant cover and measure.

2. If adjustment is necessary, a rough setting is made by loosening the locknut and rotating the clevis on the control rod to the transmission. A fine adjustment can be made by rotating the knurled sleeve between the control rod locknut and the pivot for the gear selector lever. Increasing the rod length will decrease clearance between the **D** position and its forward stop and vice-versa. Maximum permissible length of exposed thread between the locknut and the control rod is 1.1 in. (28mm).

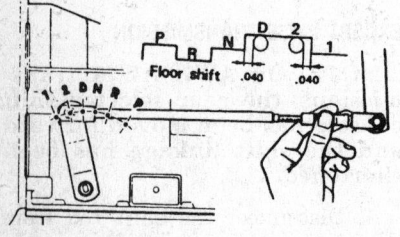

Adjust the shift linkage using the adjusting nut at the bottom of the gear selector

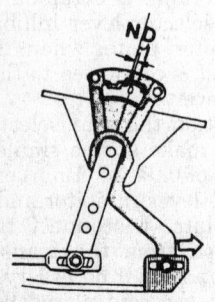

The clearance between the D and N position on the gear selector should be the same or less than the clearance between the 2 and 1 position

Except 240 Series

NOTE: Before adjusting the shift linkage, make sure the starter motor operates only in P or N positions; that the backup lights light up only in R; that the shift lever is vertical in P with the vehicle level; that the clearance between D and N is the same or less than the clearance between 2 and 1.

1. Check that the clearance between **D** and **N** is the same or less than the clearance between **2** and **1** on the shift lever. If clearance is correct, tighten the locknut to 12-17 ft. lbs. 16-23 Nm). If clearance is not correct, adjust as follows:

2. If no clearance is felt in **D**, move the reaction rod arm rearwards about 0.08 in. (2mm).

3. If no clearance is felt in position **2**, move the reaction rod arm forwards about 0.12 in. (3mm). Tighten the locknut.

4. After adjustment, check that the vehicle starts only in **P** or **N** and that the backup light does not light in **R**, reduce clearance in **D** by moving the rod arm forward slightly.

FRONT SUSPENSION

MacPherson Strut

REMOVAL AND INSTALLATION

1. Remove the hub cap and loosen the lug nuts a few turns.

2. Firmly apply the parking brake and blocks in back of the rear wheels.

3. Raise and safely support the vehicle or using a floor jack at the center of the front crossmember. When the wheels are 2-3 in. (50-76mm) off the ground, the vehicle is high enough. Place jackstands under the front jacking points. Then, remove the floor jack from the crossmember, if used, and reposition it under the applicable lower control arm to provide support at the outer end. Remove the wheel and tire assembly.

4. Using a ball joint puller, disconnect the steering rod from the steering arm.

5. Disconnect the stabilizer bar at the link upper attachment.

6. Remove the bolt retaining the brake line bracket to the fender well.

7. Open the hood and remove the cover for the strut assembly upper attachment.

8. While keeping the strut from turning, loosen and remove the nut for the upper attachment.

9. Before lowering the strut assembly, wire or tie the strut to some stationary component or use a holding fixture such as SVO 5045, to prevent the strut from traveling down too far and damaging the hydraulic brake lines. Then lower the jack supporting the lower arm and allow the strut to tilt out to about a 60 degree angle. At this angle, the top of the strut assembly should just protrude past the wheel well, allowing removal of the strut from the top.

To install:

10. Carefully lift and guide the strut assembly into its upper attachment in the spring tower. Connect the stabilizer bar to the stabilizer link. Guide the shock absorber spindle into the upper attachment and raise the jack under the lower control arm. Install the washer and nut on top of the shock absorber spindle. While holding the spindle from turning, tighten the nut to 15-25 ft. lbs. (20-34 Nm). Install the cover.

11. Attach the brake line bracket to its mount. Tighten the nut retaining the stabilizer bar to the link. Connect the steering rod at the steering arm.

12. Install the wheel and tire assembly. Lower the vehicle. Jounce the suspension a few times and then road test.

Lower Ball Joints

INSPECTION

Maximum axial play with normally loaded front end is 0.12 in. (3mm). Maximum radial play is 0.02 in. (0.5mm).

REMOVAL AND INSTALLATION

240 Series

1. Raise and safely support the vehicle.

2. Remove the tire and wheel assembly.

3. Reach in between the spring coils and loosen the shock absorber cap nut a few turns.

4. Remove the 4 bolts (12mm) retaining the ball joint seat to the bottom of the strut.

5. Remove the 3 nuts (19mm) retaining the ball joint to the lower control arm.

6. Place the ball joint and attachment assembly in a vise and remove the 19mm nut from the ball joint stud. Then, drive out the old ball joint.

To install:

7. Install the new ball joint in the attachment and tighten the stud nut to 35-50 ft. lbs. (47-68 Nm).

NOTE: On vehicles with power steering, the ball joints are different for the left and right side. Compared to previous years, the ball joint is 0.393 in. (1mm) forward in control rod attachment. It is therefore most important that these ball joints are installed on the correct side.

8. Attach the ball joint assembly to the strut. Tighten to 15-20 ft. lbs. (20-27 Nm).

9. Attach the ball joint assembly to the control arm. Tighten to 70-95 ft. lbs. (95-130 Nm).

10. Tighten the shock absorber cap nut. Install the wheel and tire. Lower the vehicle and road-test.

Except 240 Series

1. Raise and safely support the vehicle. Remove the wheel.

2. Remove the bolt connecting the anti-roll bar link to the control arm.

3. Remove the cotter pin for the ball joint stud and remove the nut.

4. Using a ball joint press, remove the ball joint from the control arm. Make sure the press is aligned directly with the stud and that the rubber grease boot is not damaged by the puller.

5. Remove the bolts holding the ball joint to the spring strut. Press the control arm down and remove the ball joint.

To install:

6. When installing the new ball joint, always use new bolts and coat all threads with a liquid thread sealer. Torque bolts to 22 ft. lbs. (30 Nm), checking that the bolt heads sit flat on the ball joint, then angle-tighten (protractor-torque) 90 degrees torque the nut holding the control arm ball joint stud to 44 ft. lbs. (60 Nm). Use a new cotter pin on the ball joint stud and install the anti-roll bar link.

7. Install the nut holding the control arm ball joint stud and tighten to 44 ft. lbs. (59 Nm). Always use a new cotter pin on the ball joint stud.

8. Install the anti-roll bar and wheel. Lower the vehicle and check the alignment.

Lower Control Arms

REMOVAL AND INSTALLATION

240 Series

1. Raise and support the vehicle safely. Remove the front wheel.

2. Disconnect the stabilizer link at the control arm. Remove the ball joint.

3. Remove the control arm rear attachment plate, then remove the front retaining bolt.

4. Remove the control arm.

To install:

5. If the bushings are to be replaced, note that the right and left bushings are not interchangeable. The right side bushing should be turned so the small slots point horizontally when installed. Torque the retaining bolt to 55 ft. lbs. (75 Nm), the rear bushing to 4 ft. lbs. (5.5 Nm) and the rear attachment bolts to 30 ft. lbs. (40 Nm).

6. Install the bracket onto the control arm and tighten it finger-tight. Install the control arm and tighten the bolts a few turns. Install the stabilizer link and tighten the nuts loosely.

7. Install the ball joint and tighten the attaching bolts to 25-35 ft. lbs. (34-47 Nm). Tighten the stabilizer link.

8. Install the wheels and lower the vehicle. Roll the vehicle backward and forward while bouncing the front end. This normalizes the suspension.

9. Tighten the rear mount to 38-44 ft. lbs. (51-60 Nm) and the front mount to 55 ft. lbs. (75 Nm).

Except 240 Series

1. Raise and support the vehicle safely. Remove the front wheels.

2. Remove the ball joint nut. Disconnect the stabilizer link and strut bolt. Remove the front bushing.

3. Remove the ball joint. Unbolt the control arm at the crossmember and remove.

To install:

4. If the bushings are to be replaced, use an appropriate press and install the bushings from the front side of the arm.

5. Install the control arm over the end of the strut rod but do not tighten into place.

6. Install the ball joint and tighten to 44 ft. lbs. (60 Nm). Install the bushing, washer and bolt for the strut rod. Tighten to 70 ft. lbs. (94 Nm).

7. Install the stabilizer link and tighten to 63 ft. lbs. (85 Nm).

8. Install the wheels and lower the vehicle. Roll the vehicle backward and forward while bouncing the front end. This normalizes the suspension.

9. Tighten the control arm bolts to 63 ft. lbs. (85 Nm).

Stabilizer Bar

REMOVAL AND INSTALLATION

1. Raise and support the vehicle safely. Remove the front wheels. Remove the splash guard, if equipped.

2. Remove the nut holding the upper sway bar link.

3. Remove the bolts for the retaining brackets and remove the sway bar.

To install:

4. Replace the link bushings if worn. Reconnect the lower link to the sway bar.

5. Install the sway bar and tighten the retaining brackets. Install the links and tighten the upper link nut until 1.65 in. (42mm) remains between the upper and lower surfaces of the washers.

6. Install the splash guard, if equipped. Install the wheels and lower the vehicle.

Front Wheel Bearings

Removal, Installation and Adjustment

1. Remove the hub cap and loosen the lug nuts a few turns.

2. Firmly apply the parking brake. Raise and safely support the vehicle. Support the lower control arms. Remove the wheel and tire assembly.

3. Remove the front caliper.

4. Pry off the grease cap from the hub. Remove the cotter pin and castle nut. Use a hub puller to pull off the hub. On the 760 model, remove the brake disc. If the inner bearing remains lodged on the stub axle, remove it with a puller.

5. Using a drift, remove the inner and outer bearing rings.

To install:

6. Thoroughly clean the hub, brake disc and grease cap.

7. Press in the new inner and outer bearing rings with a drift.

8. Press grease into both bearing with a bearing packer. If one is not available, pack the bearings with as much wheel bearing grease as possible by hand. Also coat the outsides of the bearings and the outer rings pressed into the hub. Fill the recess

in the hub with grease up to the smallest diameter on the outer ring for the outer bearing. Place the inner bearing in position in the hub and press its seal in with a drift. The felt ring should be thoroughly coated with light engine oil.

9. Place the hub onto the stub axle. Install the outer bearing washer and castle nut.

10. Adjust the front wheel bearings by tightening the castle nut to 45 ft. lbs. (60 Nm) to seat the bearings. Then, back off the nut 1/3 of a turn counterclockwise. Torque the nut to 12 inch lbs. (1.36 Nm). If the nut slot does not align with the hole in the stub axle, tighten the nut until the cotter pin may be installed. Make sure the wheel spins freely without any side-play.

11. Fill the grease cap halfway with wheel bearing grease and install it on the hub.

12. Install the front caliper.

13. Install the wheel and tire assembly. Lower the vehicle. Tighten the lug nut to 70-100 ft. lbs. (95-135 Nm) and install the hub cap.

REAR SUSPENSION

Shock Absorbers

REMOVAL AND INSTALLATION

1. Remove the hub cap and loosen the lug nuts a few turns. Raise and safely support the vehicle to unload the shock absorbers. Remove the wheel and tire assembly.

2. Remove the nuts and bolts which retain the shock absorber to its upper and lower attachments and remove the shock absorber. Make sure the spacing sleeve, inside the axle support arm for the lower attachment, is not misplaced.

3. The damping effect of the shock absorber may be tested by securing the lower attachment in a vise and extending and compressing it. A properly operating shock absorber should offer approximately 3 times as much resistance to extending the unit as compressing it. Replace the shock absorber if it does not function as above or if the fixed rubber bushings are damaged. Replace any leaking shock absorber.

To install:

4. Position the shock absorber to its upper and lower attachments. Make sure the spacing sleeve is installed inside the axle support (trailing) arm and is aligned with the lower attachment bolt hole.

5. Install the retaining nuts and bolts and torque to 63 ft. lbs. (85 Nm). On some vehicles, the shock fits inside the support arm.

6. Install the wheel and tire assembly. Lower the vehicle. Tighten the lug nuts to 70-100 ft. lbs. (95-135 Nm) and install the hub cap.

Coil Springs

REMOVAL AND INSTALLATION

Except Multi-Link Suspension

1. Remove the hub cap and loosen the lug nuts a few turns. Raise and safely support the vehicle. Remove the wheel and tire assembly.

2. Place a hydraulic jack under the rear axle housing and raise the housing sufficiently to compress the spring. Loosen the nuts for the upper and lower spring attachments.

——— CAUTION ———
It is imperative that the axle housing be lowered with extreme care until the spring is fully extended. As an added safety measure, a chain may be attached to the lower spring coil and secured to the axle housing.

3. Disconnect the shock absorber at its upper attachment. Carefully lower the jack and axle housing until the spring is fully extended. Remove the spring.

To install:

4. Position the retaining bolt and inner washer, for the upper attachment, inside the spring and then, while holding the outer washer and rubber spacer to the upper body attachment, install the spring and inner washer to the upper attachment (sandwiching the rubber spacer) and tighten the retaining bolt.

5. Raise the jack and secure the bottom of the spring to its lower attachment with the washer and retaining bolt.

6. Connect the shock absorber to its upper attachment. Install the wheel and tire assembly.

7. Lower the vehicle. Tighten the lug nuts to 70-100 ft. lbs. (95-135 Nm) and install the hub cap.

Multi-Link Suspension

NOTE: To properly remove and install the rear coil springs the rear support arm assembly must be removed.

1. Raise and support the vehicle safely. Remove the rear wheels and support arm guards.

2. Remove the retaining bolts at the front and rear of the support arm. Separate the rear end of the support arm from the wheel bearing housing.

3. Place a jack with fixture 5972 or equivalent, under the support arm and clamp into place.

4. Remove the retaining bolt at the top of the damper and lower the support arm complete with the spring and damper.

To install:

5. Lift the assembly into place and tighten the upper damper bolt to 62 ft. lbs. (85 Nm).

6. Replace the mounting bolt and nut at the front of the support arm. Tighten the large nut to 51 ft. lbs. (70 Nm), plus 90 degrees of rotation. Tighten the other bolts to 35 ft. lbs. (48 Nm).

7. Tap the support arm in at the rear and tighten the bolt to 44 ft. lbs. (60 Nm), plus 90 degrees rotation.

8. Replace the control arm guard and wheels. Lower the vehicle.

Rear Control Arm

REMOVAL AND INSTALLATION

Except Multi-Link Suspension

1. Raise and support the vehicle safely. Remove the rear wheels.

2. Matchmark and disconnect the driveshaft.

3. Remove the rear axle housing assembly.

4. Unbolt the rear control arm from the axle housing.

To install:

5. Install the control arm on the axle housing and tighten the bolt finger-tight.

6. Raise the assembly into position and install the axle-to-frame bolts finger-tight.

7. Install all other components and lower the vehicle. Tighten all control arm bolts to 85 ft. lbs. (115 Nm).

Multi-Link Suspension

1. Raise and support the vehicle safely. Remove the rear wheels.

2. Remove the brake caliper and tie it out of the way. Remove the bolt

holding the rear support arm to the wheel housing and tap the support arm loose.

3. Remove the nut and bolt holding the lower control arm to the wheel bearing housing. Remove the track rod.

4. Remove the upper control arm from the wheel bearing housing. Note the number of shims between the upper control arm and the bearing housing.

5. Remove the nuts and bolts holding the upper control arm to the rear axle member. Remove the control arm from the vehicle.

To install:

6. Install the control arm and hand tighten the nuts and bolts attaching it to the rear axle. Install the spacers at the wheel bearing housing, position the arm and install the nut holding the arm to the housing.

7. Tighten the rear most nut at the axle support to 62 ft. lbs. (84 Nm). Tighten the front nut and bolt to 51 ft. lbs. (69 Nm), plus 60 degrees of rotation.

8. Pull the top of the wheel bearing housing outward and tighten upper control arm nut to 84 ft. lbs. (113 Nm). Pull the wheel bearing housing out and install the lower control arm. Do not tighten at this time.

9. Pull the wheel bearing housing inward and tighten the control arm nut to 37 ft. lbs. (50 Nm), plus 90 degrees of rotation.

10. Install the support arm and tighten to 44 ft. lbs. (59 Nm), plus 90 degrees of rotation. Install the track rod and tighten to 62 ft. lbs. (84 Nm).

11. Install the brake caliper and wheel. Lower the vehicle. Perform a rear wheel alignment.

STEERING

Steering Wheel

CAUTION

If equipped with an air bag, the negative battery cable must be disconnected, before working on the system. Failure to do so may result in deployment of the air bag and possible personal injury.

REMOVAL AND INSTALLATION

NOTE: The use of a knock-off type steering wheel puller or the use of a hammer may damage the collapsible column and is not recommended.

240 Series

1. Disconnect the negative battery cable.

2. Remove the retaining screws for the upper half of the molded turn signal housing and lift off the housing.

3. Pry off the steering wheel impact pad.

4. Disconnect the horn plug contact.

5. Remove the steering wheel nut.

6. With the front wheels pointing straight-ahead and the steering wheel centered, install a steering wheel puller. Use a universal type puller, such as SVO 2263 or equivalent.

To install:

7. Make sure the front wheels are pointing straight-ahead, then place the centered steering wheel on the column with the plug contact to the left. Install the nut and tighten to 20-30 ft. lbs. (27-40 Nm).

8. Connect the horn plug contact and install the impact pad.

9. Install the upper turn signal housing half.

10. Connect the negative battery cable and test the operation of the horn.

Except 240 Series

1. Disconnect the negative battery cable.

2. Gently pry up the lower edge of the steering wheel center pad and remove it.

3. Unscrew the steering wheel center nut and remove the wheel using a suitable puller.

4. When installing, torque the center nut to 26 ft. lbs. (35 Nm).

Manual Rack and Pinion

REMOVAL AND INSTALLATION

1. Disconnect the negative battery cable. Remove the lock bolt and nut from the column flange, at the steering gear. Bend apart the flange slightly with a suitable tool.

2. Raise and safely support the vehicle. Remove the front wheels.

3. Disconnect the steering rods from the steering arms, using a ball joint puller.

4. Remove the splash guard.

5. Disconnect the steering gear from the front axle member.

6. Disconnect the steering gear from the steering gear flange. Remove steering gear.

To install:

7. Install rubber spacers and plates for the steering gear attachment points.

8. Position the steering gear and guide the pinion shaft into the steering shaft flange. The recess on the pinion shaft should be aligned towards the lock bolt opening in the flange.

9. Attach the steering gear to the front axle member. Check that the U-bolts are aligned in the plate slots. Install flat washers and nuts.

10. Install the splash guard.

11. Connect the steering rods to the steering arms.

12. Install the front wheels and lower the vehicle.

13. Install the lock bolt for the steering shaft flange.

Power Rack and Pinion

REMOVAL AND INSTALLATION

1. Disconnect the negative battery cable. Loosen the steering column shaft flange from the pinion shaft. Remove the lock bolt and bend apart the flange slightly.

2. Raise and safely support the vehicle. Remove the front wheels.

3. Disconnect the steering rods from the steering arms, with a ball joint puller.

4. Remove the splash guard.

5. Disconnect the hoses at the steering gear. Install protective plugs in the hose connections.

6. Remove the steering gear from the front axle member.

7. Remove the steering gear by pulling down until it is free from the steering shaft flange. On the 740 and 760 GLE models, disconnect the lower steering shaft from the steering gear by removing the snaprings from the clamps. Loosen the upper clamp bolt, remove the lower clamp bolt and slide the joint up on the shaft. Then remove the unit on the left side of the vehicle.

To install:

8. Position the steering gear and attach the pinion shaft to the steering shaft flange.

9. Install right side U-bolt and bracket but do not tighten the nuts.

10. Install left side retaining bolts and tighten. Tighten the U-bolt nuts.

11. Connect the steering rods to the steering arms.

12. Install the lock bolt on the steering column flange.

13. Connect the return and pressure hoses to the steering gear.

Power Steering Pump

REMOVAL AND INSTALLATION

1. Disconnect the negative battery cable. Remove all dirt and grease from around the suction line connections and from around the delivery line of the pump housing.

2. Using a container to catch any power steering fluid that might run out, disconnect the lines and plug them to prevent dirt from entering the system.

3. Remove the tensioning bolt and the attaching bolts.

4. Clear the pump free of the fan belt and lift it out.

To install:

5. If a new pump is to be used, the old brackets, fitting and pulley must be transferred from the old unit. The pulley may be removed with a puller and pressed on the pump shaft with a press tool. Under no circumstances should the pulley be hammered on, as this will damage the pump bearings.

6. To install, place the pump in position and loosely fit the attaching bolts. Connect the lines to the pump with new seals.

7. Place the fan belt onto the pulley and adjust the fan belt tension.

8. Tighten the tensioning bolt and the attaching bolts.

9. Fill the reservoir with Type A automatic transmission fluid and bleed the system.

SYSTEM BLEEDING

1. Fill the reservoir up to the edge with Automatic Transmission Fluid Type A. Raise and safely support the vehicle. Place the transmission in **N** and apply the parking brake.

2. Start the engine and fill the reservoir as the level drops.

3. When the reservoir level has stopped dropping, slowly turn the steering wheel from lock to lock several times. Add fluid to the reservoir, if necessary.

4. Locate the bleeder screw on the power steering gear. Open the bleeder screw ½-1 turn and close it when oil starts flowing out.

5. Continue to turn the steering wheel slowly until the fluid in the reservoir is free of air bubbles.

6. Stop the engine and observe the oil level in the reservoir. If the oil level rises more than ¼ in. (6.35mm) past the level mark, air still remains the system. Continue bleeding until the level rise is correct.

7. Lower the vehicle.

Tie Rod Ends

REMOVAL AND INSTALLATION

1. The ball joints of the tie rod may be replaced individually.

2. Remove the tie rod locking nut and use a suitable tool to press the tie rod stud from the steering arm.

3. After the ball joint is disconnected, loosen the locknut on the tie rod and release the clamp bolt.

4. Unscrew the ball joint out of the tie rod, taking note of the number of turns.

To install:

5. Install the replacement tie rod end ball joint and thread onto the tie rod the same number of turns counted at removal. Tighten the clamp bolt locknut-to-tie rod to 55-65 ft. lbs. (75-88 Nm). The new ball joint is pressed into its connection and the ball stud nut tightened to 23-27 ft. lbs. (31-37 Nm).

6. After reconditioning of the rods and joints, the wheel alignment must be checked and adjusted.

BRAKES

Master Cylinder

REMOVAL AND INSTALLATION

1. Disconnect the negative battery cable. To prevent brake fluid from spilling onto and damaging the paint, place a protective cover over the fender apron and rags under the master cylinder.

2. Disconnect and plug the brake lines from the master cylinder.

3. Remove the nuts which retain the master cylinder and reservoir assembly to the vacuum booster and lift the assembly forward, being careful not to spill any fluid on the fender. Empty out and discard the brake fluid.

To install:

NOTE: Do not depress the brake pedal while the master cylinder is removed.

4. In order for the master cylinder to function properly when installed to the vacuum booster, the adjusting nut for the thrust rod of the booster must not prevent the primary piston of the master cylinder from returning to its resting position. A clearance (C) of 0.004-0.04 in. (0.1-1.0mm) is required between the thrust rod and primary piston with the master cylinder installed. The clearance may be adjusted by rotating the adjusting nut for the booster thrust rod in the required direction. To determine what the clearance (C) will be when the master cylinder and booster are connected, first measure the distance (A) between the face of the attaching flange and the center of the primary piston on the master cylinder, then measure the distance (B) that the thrust rod protrudes from the fixed surface of the booster, making sure the thrust rod is depressed fully with a partial vacuum existing in the booster. When the measurement is subtracted from measurement (A), clearance (C) should be obtained. If not, adjust the length of the thrust rod by turning the adjusting screw to suit. After the final adjustment is obtained apply a few drops of locking compound, such as Loctite®, to the adjusting nut.

5. Position the master cylinder and reservoir assembly onto the studs for the booster and install the washers and nuts. Tighten the nuts to 17 ft. lbs. (23 Nm).

6. Remove the plugs and connect the brake lines.

7. Bleed the entire brake system.

Proportioning Valve

REMOVAL AND INSTALLATION

1. Remove and plug the brake pipe from the master cylinder, at the valve connection.

2. Loosen the connection for the flexible brake hose to the rear wheel a maximum of ¼ turn.

3. Remove the bolt(s) which retain the valve to the underbody and unscrew the valve from the rear brake hose.

To install:

4. Install the valve. Place a new seal on it and screw the valve onto the rear brake hose and hand

tighten. Secure the valve to the underbody with the retaining bolt(s).

5. Connect the brake pipe and tighten both connections, making sure there is no tension on the flexible rear hose.

6. Bleed the brake system.

Brake System Warning Valve

VALVE RESETTING

1. Disconnect the plug contact and screw out the warning switch so the pistons inside the valve may return to their normal position.

2. Repair and bleed the faulty hydraulic circuit.

3. Screw in the warning switch and tighten it to a torque of 10-14 ft. lbs. (14-19 Nm). Connect the plug contact.

REMOVAL AND INSTALLATION

1. Placing a rag under the valve to catch the brake fluid, loosen the pipe connections and disconnect the brake lines. Disconnect the electrical plug contact and lift out the valve.

2. Connect the new warning valve in the reverse order of removal. Connect the plug contact.

3. Bleed the entire brake system.

Power Brake Booster

REMOVAL AND INSTALLATION

1. Disconnect the negative battery cable.

2. Remove the master cylinder to power booster retaining bolts and position the master cylinder aside. Be careful not to damage the brake lines.

3. Disconnect the vacuum assist hose, from the booster.

4. From inside the vehicle, disconnect the brake pedal rod.

5. Remove the power booster retaining bolts. Remove the power booster from the vehicle.

6. Installation is the reverse of the removal procedure.

Brake Caliper

REMOVAL AND INSTALLATION

1. Raise and support the vehicle safely. Remove the wheels.

2. Plug the reservoir cap vent hole. Label and disconnect the brake

lines at the caliper. Plug the lines to prevent the entry of dirt.

NOTE: On rear brake calipers, disconnect the brake hose at the frame, remove the caliper and then disconnect the hose from the caliper.

3. Remove the 2 caliper attaching bolts and lift the unit off the retainer.

To install:

4. Check the mating surfaces of the caliper and retainer to ensure they are clean. Always use new retaining bolts and lightly coat them with locking compound.

5. Install the brake pads making sure the caliper is parallel to the disc and that the disc can rotate freely. Position the caliper to its retainer over the disc and install the 2 retaining bolts. Tighten the bolts to 65-70 ft. lbs. (88-95 Nm) on the 240 Series or 25 ft. lbs. (34 Nm) on all other vehicles.

6. Connect the brake lines to the caliper. Unplug the reservoir cap vent hole.

7. Install the wheels and lower the vehicle. Bleed the brake system.

Brake Rotor

REMOVAL AND INSTALLATION

Front Rotors

240 SERIES

1. Raise and support the vehicle safely. Remove the wheels.

2. Remove the brake caliper but do not disconnect the brake hose. Hang the caliper out of the way.

3. Loosen and remove the small retaining screws on the face of the disc. Some vehicles may also have a guide pin which locates the road wheel. Remove this pin, if equipped. Remove the rotor from the hub.

To install:

4. Ensure that the disc is sitting squarely on the mount and install the retaining screws and locating pin as required.

5. Install the caliper and pads. Check that the disc can turn freely and that the caliper is seated.

6. Install the wheel and lower the vehicle.

EXCEPT 240 SERIES

1. Raise and support the vehicle safely. Remove the wheels.

2. Remove the caliper and pads. Do not disconnect the brake hose. Place caliper on the control arm or hang it out of the way.

3. Remove the hub grease cap, the cotter pin and castle nut. Remove the outer wheel bearing. Take off the brake rotor and hub assembly.

To install:

4. Clean the disc well if it is to be reused. Remove the old grease seal. Clean the grease from the inner hub and take out the inner bearing. In some cases, the bearing may remain on the spindle. A suitable puller should be used for removal.

5. Pack the wheel bearings with a quality high-temperature grease, filling the voids between the bearings and fill the recesses in the hub with grease. Install a new grease seal.

6. Install the brake rotor, outer bearing and castle nut. Adjust the front wheel bearing by turning the rotor while tightening the nut to about 45 ft. lbs. (60 Nm). Unscrew the nut ½ turn. Tighten the nut to only 12 inch lbs. (1.36 Nm) of torque which is just finger-tight and install the cotter pin. If the holes are not in line, tighten to the nearest hole.

7. Fill the grease cap half full with grease.

8. Install the caliper and brake pad. Road test to check braking action.

Rear Rotors

240 SERIES

1. Raise and support the vehicle safely. If there are no guide pins, mark the position of the wheel on the hub. Remove the wheels.

2. Remove the caliper and pads. Do not disconnect the brake hose, hang it out of the way. Some vehicles may have a small stud threaded into the disc. While helping to locate the wheel, this stud also retains the disc to the hub. Remove the pin, if equipped.

3. The brake rotor should pull off the hub. Note that the parking brake shoes are inside the rotor. Make sure the parking brake is off before trying to remove the rotors.

To install:

4. Clean the hub/rotor seating area well. Install the hub and hold in place with the threaded guide pin, if used.

5. Install the caliper and brake pads. Install wheels and road test to check braking action.

EXCEPT 240 SERIES

1. Raise and support the vehicle safely. If there are no guide pins, mark the position of the wheel on the hub. Remove the wheels.

2. Remove the caliper and pads. Do not disconnect the brake hose, hang it out of the way.

3. If the rotor is to be reused make matchmarks on the rotor and hub so the rotor can be reassembled in the same relationship to the hub. Remove the brake rotor. If necessary, tap the inside of the disc with a plastic-faced mallet.

To install:

4. If equipped with ABS, use a soft brush to remove dirt from the pickup and toothed wheel. Make sure the mating surfaces on the hub and disc are clean.

5. Install the rotor. If the original is being reused, align the matchmarks made at disassembly. If a new replacement rotor is being installed, look for an alignment mark on the rotor and install the rotor with the marking as close as possible to a factory mark on the hub, as permitted by the wheel studs.

6. Install the guide pin.

7. Install the brake caliper. Use new attaching bolts and tighten them to 72 ft. lbs. (97 Nm). Install the brake pads.

8. Install the wheel and lower the vehicle. Test drive and check braking action.

Disc Brake Pads

REMOVAL AND INSTALLATION

NOTE: The brake pads should be replaced when there is approximately 0.12 in. (3.0mm) of the lining left. The linings should under no circumstances be less than 0.06 in. (1.5mm).

Front Brakes

ATE TYPE

1. Raise the vehicle and support safely.

2. Mark the position of the wheels on the hubs and remove the front wheels.

3. Remove the retaining pins using a punch.

4. Remove the retaining spring.

5. Remove the brake pads and identify the pads, if they are to be reused.

To install:

6. Compress the pistons using a pair of pliers of special tool 2809 or equivalent.

7. Install the brake pads.

8. Install 1 retaining pin and a new retaining spring.

9. Install the other retaining pin.

10. Check the brake fluid level and pump the brake pedal.

11. Install the front wheel assemblies and lower the vehicle.

——————— CAUTION ———————
Check the brake pedal operation prior to driving the vehicle.

GIRLING TYPE

1. Raise the vehicle and support safely.

2. Mark the position of the wheels on the hubs and remove the front wheels.

3. Remove the spring clips.

4. Remove the retaining pins.

5. Remove the retaining springs.

6. Remove the brake pads and identify the pads if they are to be reused.

To install:

7. Compress the pistons using a pair of pliers of special tool 2809 or equivalent.

8. Install the brake pads.

9. Install the retaining springs.

10. Install the retaining pins.

11. Install the spring clips.

12. Check the brake fluid level and pump the brake pedal.

13. Install the front wheel assemblies and lower the vehicle.

——————— CAUTION ———————
Check the brake pedal operation prior to driving the vehicle.

Rear Brakes

ATE TYPE

1. Raise the vehicle and support safely.

2. Mark the position of the wheels on the hubs and remove the rear wheels.

3. Remove the retaining pins using a punch.

4. Remove the retaining spring.

5. Remove the brake pads and identify the pads if they are to be reused.

To install:

6. Compress the pistons using service tool 2809 or equivalent.

7. Install the brake pads.

8. Install 1 retaining pin and a new retaining spring.

9. Install the other retaining pin.

10. Check the brake fluid level and pump the brake pedal.

11. Install the rear wheel assemblies and lower the vehicle.

——————— CAUTION ———————
Check the brake pedal operation prior to driving the vehicle.

GIRLING TYPE

1. Raise the vehicle and support safely.

2. Mark the position of the wheels on the hubs and remove the rear wheels.

3. Remove the retaining spring.

4. Remove the spring clips.

5. Remove the retaining pins.

6. Remove the retaining springs.

7. Remove the brake pads and identify the pads if they are to be reused.

8. Remove any shims or damper washers fitted between the pads and the caliper pistons.

To install:

9. Compress the pistons using service tool 2809 or equivalent.

10. Install any shims or damper washers.

11. Install the brake pads.

12. Install the springs.

13. Install the retaining pins.

14. Install the spring clips.

15. Install the retaining spring.

NOTE: If damper washers have been fitted, make sure the large flat side faces the piston. A feeler gauge can be used to fit the washers.

16. Check the brake fluid level and pump the brake pedal.

17. Install the rear wheel assemblies and lower the vehicle.

——————— CAUTION ———————
Check the brake pedal operation prior to driving the vehicle.

ADJUSTMENT

1. Remove the rear ashtray, between the front seat backs, or the rear of the center console.

2. Tighten the parking brake cable adjusting screw so the brake is fully applied when pulled up 2-3 notches.

3. If one cable is stretched more than the other, they can be individually adjusted by removing the parking brake cover (2 screws) and turning the individual cable adjusting nut at the front of each yoke pivot.

4. Install the ashtray and parking brake cover, if equipped.

REMOVAL AND INSTALLATION

240 Series

1. Apply the parking brake. Remove the hub caps for the rear wheels and loosen the lug nuts a few turns.

2. Raise and safely support the vehicle. Remove the wheel and tire assembly. Release the parking brake.

3. Remove the bolt and the wheel from the pulley.

4. Remove the rubber cover for the front attachment of the cable sleeve and nut, as well as the attachment for the rubber suspension ring on the frame. Remove the cable from the other side of the attachment in the same manner.

5. Hold the return spring in position. Pry up the lock and remove the lock pin so the cable releases from the lever.

6. Remove the return spring with washers. Loosen the nut for the rear attachment of the cable sleeve. Lift the cable forward after loosening both side of the attachments and remove it.

To install:

7. Adjust the rear brake shoes of the parking brake by removing the rear ashtray between the front seat backs.

8. Tighten the parking brake cable adjusting screw so the brake is fully applied when pulled up 2-3 notches.

9. If one cable is stretched more than the other, they can be individually adjusted by removing the parking brake cover (2 screws) and turning the individual cable adjusting nut at the front of each yoke pivot.

10. Install the ashtray and parking brake cover, if equipped.

11. Install new rubber cable guides for the cable suspension. Place the cable in position in the rear attachment and tighten the nut. Install the washers and return spring. Oil the lock pin and install it, together with the cable, on the lever. Install the attachment and rubber cable guide on the frame.

12. Install the cable in the same manner on the side of the vehicle.

13. Place the cable sleeve in position in the front attachments and install the rubber covers.

14. Lubricate and install the pulley on the pull rod. Adjust the pulley so the parking brake is fully engaged with the lever at the 3rd or 4th notch.

15. Install the wheel and tire assemblies. Lower the vehicle. Tighten the lug nut to 70-100 ft. lbs. (95-135 Nm) and install the hub caps.

Except 240 Series

SHORT CABLE; RIGHT SIDE

1. Raise and safely support the vehicle.

2. Remove the right brake caliper rear wheel. Remove the right brake caliper and hang it from the coil spring with a wire. Remove the brake disc. Unhook the rear return spring and remove the brake shoes.

3. Push out the pin holding the cable to the brake lever. Remove the rubber bellows (boot) from the backing plate and remove the bellows from the cable.

4. Remove the spring clip, pin and cable from the back of the differential housing. Remove the cable guide on the differential by removing the top bolt from the housing cover. Remove the cable.

To install:

5. Install the cable guide on the new cable. Check the rubber bellows for wear or damage and replace if necessary. Install the bellows and position it through the hole in the backing plate. Make sure the bellows sits correctly on the backing plate.

6. Smear the contact surfaces of the brake levers with a thin layer of heat resistant graphite grease. Connect the cable to the lever and install the pin.

NOTE: The arrow stamped on the lever should point upward and outwards.

7. Push the cable through and place the lever in position behind the rear axle flange.

8. Install the cable guide on the axle. Connect the cable to the equalizer using the pin and spring clip.

9. Install the brake shoes and rear return spring. Install the brake disc and caliper. Use new bolts. and torque to 43 ft. lbs. (58 Nm). Make sure the disc rotates freely. Adjust parking brake. Install the wheel and lower the vehicle.

LONG CABLE; LEFT SIDE

1. Remove the center console.

2. Slacken the parking brake adjusting screw. Remove the cable lock ring and remove the cable. Pull out the cable from the spring sleeve.

3. Raise and safely support the vehicle. Remove the left rear wheel.

4. Remove the left rear brake caliper and hang it from the coil spring with a piece of wire. Remove the brake disc and rear return spring. Remove the brake shoes.

5. Push out the pin holding the cable to the lever. Remove the rubber bellows from the backing plate and remove the bellows from the cable.

6. Pull out the cable from the backing plate and the equalizer on top of the rear axle.

7. Remove the cable clamp on the sub-frame, above the driveshaft, and the cable.

To install:

8. Install the new cable through the grommet in the floor; check that the grommet sits correctly. Clamp the cable to the sub-frame.

9. Smear the contact surfaces of the brake levers with a thin layer of heat resistant graphite grease. Connect the cable to the lever and install the pin.

NOTE: The arrow stamped on the lever should point upward and outwards.

10. Push the cable through and place the lever in position behind the rear axle flange.

11. Install the cable guide on the axle. Connect the cable to the equalizer using the pin and spring clip.

12. Install the brake shoes and rear return spring. Install the brake disc and caliper. Use new bolts and torque to 43 ft. lbs. (58 Nm). Make sure the disc rotates freely. Adjust the parking brake. Install the wheel and lower the vehicle.

Brake System Bleeding

Whenever a spongy brake pedal indicates that there is air in the system, or when any part of the hydraulic system has been removed for service, the system must be bled. In addition, if the level in the master cylinder reservoir is allowed to drop below the minimum mark for too long a period of time, air may enter the system, necessitating bleeding.

If only one caliper is removed for servicing, it is usually necessary to bleed only that unit. If, however, the master cylinder, warning valve, or any of the main system lines are removed, the entire system must be bled.

Be careful not to spill any brake fluid onto the brake surfaces or the paint. When bleeding the entire system, the rear of the car should be raised higher than the front. Only use brake fluid bearing the designation DOT 4.

NOTE: The following procedure is acceptable for use on vehicles with and without ABS.

1. Check to make sure floor mats are not obstructing pedal travel. Full pedal travel should be 6 in. (150mm).

2. Clean the cap and top of the master cylinder reservoir, and make sure the vent hole in the cap is open. Fill the reservoir to the maximum mark. Never allow the level to drop below the minimum mark during bleeding.

3. If only one brake caliper or line was removed, it will usually suffice to bleed only that wheel. Otherwise, prepare to bleed the entire system beginning at the left front wheel.

4. Remove the protective cap for the bleeder and fit a suitable line wrench on the nipple. Install a tight plastic hose onto the nipple and insert the other end of the hose into a glass bottle containing clean brake fluid. The hose must hang down below the surface of the fluid or air will be sucked into the system when the brake pedal is released.

5. Open the bleeder screw a maximum of ½ turn. Have a helper slowly depress the pedal until it bottoms, pause a second, and then quickly release the pedal. This should be repeated until the fluid flowing into the bottle is completely free of air bubbles. During this procedure, check the master cylinder reservoir frequently. When completed, press the pedal to the bottom of its stroke and tighten the bleeder screw. Install the protective cap.

NOTE: The front calipers, on some vehicles, are equipped with 2-3 bleeder screws. Attach one hose to each screw and submerge in brake fluid.

6. If the entire system is to be bled, use the same procedure for the remaining bleeder screws at the right front, left rear and right rear wheel. Follow this order specifically. If the pedal still feels spongy after bleeding the entire system, repeat the bleeding sequence.

7. Fill the reservoir to the maximum line. Turn the ignition **ON** but do not start the engine. Apply moderate force to the brake pedal. The pedal must travel no more than 2.40 in. (61mm) without ABS or 2.17 in. (55mm) with ABS. The brake warning and/or ABS warning lights must not be ON.

Anti-Lock Brake System Service

SYSTEM PRECAUTIONS

• If equipped with an air bag system, always properly disable the system before commencing work on the ABS system.

• Certain components within the ABS system are not intended to be serviced or repaired individually. Only those components with REMOVAL AND INSTALLATION procedures should be serviced.

• Do not use rubber hoses or other parts not specifically specified for the ABS system. When using repair kits, replace all parts included in the kit. Partial or incorrect repair may lead to functional problems and require the replacement of other components.

• Lubricate rubber parts with clean, fresh brake fluid to ease assembly. Do not use lubricated shop air to clean parts; damage to rubber components may result.

• Use only brake fluid from an unopened container. Use of suspect or contaminated brake fluid can reduce system performance and/or durability.

• A clean repair area is essential. Perform repairs after components have been thoroughly cleaned. Do not allow ABS components to come into contact with any substance containing mineral oil; this includes used shop rags.

• The control unit is a microprocessor similar to other computer units in the vehicle. Insure that the ignition switch is **OFF** before removing or installing controller harnesses. Avoid static electricity discharge at or near the controller.

• Never disconnect any electrical connection with the ignition switch **ON** unless instructed to do so in a test.

• Avoid touching connector pins with fingers.

• Leave new components and modules in the shipping package until ready to install them.

• To avoid static discharge, always touch a vehicle ground after sliding across a vehicle seat or walking across carpeted or vinyl floors.

• If any arc welding is to be done on the vehicle, the ABS control unit should be disconnected before welding operations begin.

• Never allow welding cables to lie on, near or across any vehicle electrical wiring.

• If the vehicle is to be baked after paint repairs, disconnect and remove the control unit from the vehicle.

Hydraulic Modulator

REMOVAL AND INSTALLATION

1. Disconnect the negative battery cable.
2. Remove the cover from the hydraulic modulator.
3. Remove both relays from the top of the unit; disconnect the wiring connector at the unit.

4. Disconnect the ground strap from the hydraulic modulator.
5. Place rags or towels around the unit to absorb brake fluid which will be spilled.
6. Clean the line connections thoroughly. Label each line using the letters marked on the hydraulic modulator (V, H, l, r, h).
7. Remove the brake lines from the modulator. Remove the bolt from the modulator support and push the support to the right. Remove the hydraulic modulator.

To install:
8. If a new modulator is being installed, remove the hexagonal plugs from the old unit and install on the new unit. Check that the rubber pads are not damaged; install the rubber pads onto the hexagonal plugs.
9. Install the modulator and tighten the support. If installing a new unit, remove the plugs from the brake line ports.
10. Reconnect the brake lines according to the labels made at removal. The lines must be in their exact original positions.
11. Remove the rags from the work area and dispose of them properly.
12. Install the relays on the hydraulic modulator.
13. Connect the wiring harness and the ground strap.
14. Install the cover on the unit.
15. Bleed the brake system. Vehicles with hydraulic clutches may require bleeding of the clutch system as well.
16. When bleeding is complete, test the brake system by having an assistant press hard on the brake pedal. Keep it depressed for 30 seconds. During the 30 second period, check that no leakage occurs at the brake line connections on the hydraulic modulator.
17. Connect the negative battery cable. Test drive the vehicle, confirming system function.

Control Unit

REMOVAL AND INSTALLATION

1. Disconnect the negative battery cable.
2. Remove the soundproofing under the left dashboard.
3. Loosen or remove the clips and retainers holding the control unit. Lift the unit out.
4. Remove the electrical harness from the unit.
5. Reinstall in reverse order. Connect the negative battery cable.

Wheel Speed Sensors

REMOVAL AND INSTALLATION

Front

1. Raise and safely support the front of the vehicle.
2. Remove the tire and wheel.
3. With the ignition switch **OFF**, disconnect the wheel speed sensor lead from the ABS harness. Remove any retaining bolts or clips holding the harness in place.

NOTE: Clips and retainers must be reinstalled in their exact original location. Take careful note of the position of each retainer and of the correct harness routing during removal.

4. Remove the single bolt holding the speed sensor.
5. Carefully remove the sensor straight out of its mount. Do not subject the sensor to shock or vibration. Protect the tip of the sensor at all times.
To install:
6. Fit the sensor into position. Make certain the sensor sits flush against the mounting surface. It must not be crooked.
7. Install the retaining bolt.
8. Route the sensor cable correctly and install the harness clips and retainers. The cable must be in its original position and completely clear of moving components.
9. Connect the sensor cable to the ABS harness.
10. Install the wheel and tire.
11. Lower the vehicle to the ground.

Rear

WITHOUT MULTI-LINK SUSPENSION

1. Raise and safely support the vehicle.
2. Disconnect the sensor connector from the harness.
3. Remove the clips and retainers holding the sensor wire to the axle. Take note of the routing of the sensor wire; exact reinstallation is required.
4. Remove the retaining bolt holding the sensor to the differential housing.
5. Remove the sensor straight out of the housing; protect the tip from impact.
6. Reinstall in reverse order.

WITH MULTI-LINK SUSPENSION

1. Remove the spare tire and fold back the trunk carpet to expose the fuel filler pipe. Remove the cover(s) from the filler pipe.
2. Break the seal on the speed sensor harness connector and disconnect the sensor from the ABS harness.
3. Press the rubber grommet free of the bodywork and feed the sensor harness to the outside of the vehicle.
4. Raise and safely support the vehicle.
5. Install a jack with support fixture 5972 or its equivalent under the rear axle.
6. Remove the 2 bolts on each side of the rear axle assembly which hold the member to the body. Lower the rear axle slightly, but do not allow the driveshaft to press against the fuel tank.
7. Disconnect the right brake wire from its attachment.
8. Remove the sensor cable from the retaining clips and clamps. Take note of the routing of the cable; it must be reinstalled in its exact original position.
9. Clean the sensor area; remove the retaining bolts and remove the sensor. Protect the tip from damage or impact.
To install:
10. Apply a light coat of oil to the O-ring on the new sensor. Fit the sensor into place without damaging the tip. Tighten the retaining bolts to 7.5 ft. lbs. (10 Nm).
11. Install the sensor harness into the cable retainers, making certain it is routed correctly and out of the way of all moving parts.
12. Feed the cable through the body and secure the grommet.
13. Connect the right brake wire.
14. Raise the rear axle assembly and install the 4 bolts. Tighten each bolt to 52 ft. lbs. (70 Nm), then angle tighten each an additional 60 degrees.
15. Lower the vehicle to the ground.
16. Connect the sensor wiring harness to the ABS harness in the trunk and reseal the connector. Clamp the cable to the filler pipe.
17. Install the filler covers, reposition the carpet and install the spare tire.
18. Test drive the vehicle, confirming correct function of the ABS system and the dashboard warning lamp.

CHASSIS ELECTRICAL

Air Bag

DISARMING

─── CAUTION ───

Vehicles equipped with an air bag must be disarmed prior to performing service on the air bag or related systems. Disconnect the negative battery cable and keep the ignition in the OFF position before attempting to service these components. Failure to do so may result in deployment of the air bag and possible personal injury.

REMOVAL AND INSTALLATION

240 Series

WITHOUT AIR CONDITIONING

1. Disconnect the negative battery cable.
2. Remove the heater unit.
3. Place the unit on its side with the control valve facing upward. Remove the spring clips and separate the housing halves.
4. Lift out the fan motor and replace it with a new unit, making sure the support leg without the foot points to the output for the defroster channel.
To install:
5. Assemble the heater housing halves with new spring clips and seal the joint without clips with soft sealing compound.
6. Install the heater unit.

WITH AIR CONDITIONING

In order to remove the blower motor, both the right and left blower wheels must first be removed. The heater unit does not have to be removed.

1. Disconnect the negative battery cable.
2. Lift the carpet and remove the central unit side panels.
3. Remove the retaining screws for the control panel and move the panel as far back on the transmission tunnel as the electrical cables will permit.
4. Remove the attaching screws for the rear seat heater ducts and disconnect the ducts from the central unit.
5. Remove the instrument cluster.

6. Remove the glovebox by unscrewing the 4 attaching screws, removing the glovebox door stop and disconnecting the wires from the glovebox courtesy light. Remove the molded dashboard padding from under the glovebox.

7. Disconnect the vacuum hoses to the left and right defroster nozzle vacuum motors, then remove the nozzles and the left and right air ducts.

8. Remove the air hoses between the left and right inside air vents.

9. Remove the clamps on the central unit outer ends and remove the ends.

10. Pry off the locking retainer for the blower wheels and remove both left and right blower wheels.

11. Position the heater control valve capillary tube aside.

12. Remove the left inner end (blower housing) from the central unit.

13. Unscrew the 3 retaining screws and remove the fan motor retainer.

14. Disconnect the plug contact from the fan motor control panel. Release the tabs of electric cables from the plug contact, remove the rubber grommet and pull the electrical cables down through the central unit right opening.

15. Remove the fan motor from the left opening.

To install:

16. Install the fan motor and connect all electrical connectors. Install the fan motor retainer. Install the left end (blower housing) on the central unit.

17. Install the heater control valve capillary tube. Install the left and right blower wheels and lock in place with the retainer. Install the central unit outer ends and clamps. Install the air hoses.

18. Install the vacuum hoses to the defroster nozzles and air ducts. Install the instrument cluster. Install the rear seat heater ducts.

19. Install the control panel and install the retaining screws. Install the central unit side covers. Install the carpet.

20. Connect the negative battery cable. Test the operation of all functions.

Except 240 Series

1. Disconnect the negative battery cable. Remove the panel under the glove compartment.

2. Unfasten the screws securing the fan motor and lower the motor. Disconnect the hose for air cooling on the motor and disconnect the wiring.

3. Remove the motor and fan.

To install:

4. Reconnect the wiring to the fan motor.

5. Spread sealer around the mounting face of the fan mounting flange and install the fan motor.

6. Reconnect the hose for cooling and check fan operation. Reinstall the panel under the glove compartment.

7. Connect the negative battery cable.

Windshield Wiper Motor and/or Linkage

REMOVAL AND INSTALLATION

1. Disconnect the negative battery cable.

2. Lift the wiper arm and unscrew the nut. Remove the wiper arm.

3. Remove the rubber seals from the wiper well cover panel.

4. Open the hood fully.

5. Disconnect the water tubes from the clips.

6. Remove the wiper well cover bolts or clips, as required.

7. Position the hood in its normal raised position and remove the wiper well cover panel. Close the hood.

8. If removing the linkage, remove the linkage retaining bolts.

9. Remove the wiper motor cover and disconnect the electrical connector.

10. Lift the wiper unit and remove the spindle nut (or bolt) and bolts retaining the wiper motor in position. Remove the wiper motor.

To install:

11. Fit the wiper motor into position. Install the retaining bolts and spindle nut (or bolt).

12. Reconnect the electrical connector and install the wiper motor cover.

13. Install the wiper linkage, if removed.

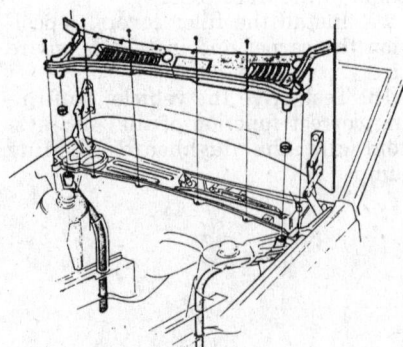

Removing wiper well cover

14. Check that the wipers are in PARK position, then install the wiper well cover panel. Connect the wiper/washer tubes.

15. Install the wiper arms.

16. Connect the negative battery cable.

Tailgate Wiper Motor

REMOVAL AND INSTALLATION

1. Disconnect the negative battery cable.

2. Remove the trim panel from the tailgate.

3. Remove the link nut on the motor.

4. Remove the wiper motor retaining bolts and lift out the motor.

5. Check to ensure the motor is in PARK position before installing it.

6. Reassemble in the reverse order.

Headlight Wiper Motor

REMOVAL AND INSTALLATION

1. Disconnect the negative battery cable.

2. Pull the wiper arm away from the headlight and lift the spindle cover. Remove the nut and remove the headlight wiper arm.

3. Disconnect the headlight wiper motor electrical leads.

4. Remove the nuts from the motor. Slide off the plastic tubing, as required. Remove the motor.

5. Check to ensure the motor is in PARK position before installing it.

6. Reassemble in the reverse order.

Instrument Cluster

REMOVAL AND INSTALLATION

1. Disconnect the negative battery cable.

2. Remove the trim moldings and switch panels, as required.

3. Remove the ventilation grilles by turning the grille to MAX position upwards and prying out the lower part with fingers.

4. Remove the casing retaining screws and lift out the combined instrument cluster.

To install:

5. Place the instrument cluster into position and install the retaining screws.

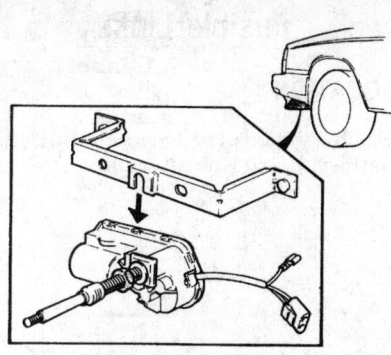

Headlight wiper motor replacement

6. Install the ventilation grilles, as required.
7. Install switch panels and trim moldings, as required.
8. Connect the negative battery cable.

Combination Switch

REMOVAL AND INSTALLATION

1. Turn the steering wheel to straight-ahead position.
2. Disconnect the negative battery cable.
3. On vehicles equipped with air bag assembly, detach the air bag assembly by removing the 2 Torx screws on the back of the steering wheel.
4. Remove the steering wheel center bolt and remove the steering wheel assembly.

NOTE: The steering wheel can be left in position when removing the column switches for 760 Series.

5. Remove the steering column height adjuster, as required.
6. Remove the steering column casings.

7. Remove the screws from the appropriate switch.
8. Disconnect the electrical connector and remove the appropriate switch.

To install:

9. Install the switch and secure the electrical connector.
10. Install the steering column casings. Install the steering column height adjuster, as required.
11. Install the steering wheel assembly.
12. Install the air bag assembly, if equipped.
13. Connect the negative battery cable.

Ignition Lock/Switch

REMOVAL AND INSTALLATION

240 Series

1. Disconnect the negative battery cable.
2. Remove noise insulation panel and center side panel.
3. Disconnect the wires from the switch.
4. Pry out the switch with a suitable tool.
5. Install in reverse of removal.

Except 240 Series

1. Remove the sound proofing under the instrument panel.
2. Disconnect the connector from the ignition switch.
3. Remove the upper steering column casing and the panel around the ignition switch.
4. Loosen the mounting screw for the switch.
5. Insert the key and turn it to the **START** position. Through the hole under the holder, press in the catch and remove the ignition switch.

To install:

6. Insert the key, turn and depress the locking tab. Remove the key.
7. Position the switch and release the locking tab by inserting the key. Tighten the mounting screw.
8. Install the steering column casing and the panel around the ignition switch. Connect the electrical connector. Install the sound proofing.

Stoplight Switch

ADJUSTMENT

The stoplight switch should be adjusted so the brake lights come on when the brake pedal is depressed by $1/8$-$1/2$ inch. Loosen the locknut and adjust the switch. Tighten the locknut and check the operation of the switch.

REMOVAL AND INSTALLATION

1. Disconnect the negative battery cable.
2. Disconnect the electrical wiring on the switch.
3. Loosen the locknut and unscrew the switch.
4. Installation is the reverse of removal. Adjust the switch to specification.

Neutral Safety Switch

ADJUSTMENT

All vehicles have an adjustable switch, located under the shifter quadrant on the tunnel.

1. Remove the shifter quadrant cover.
2. Place the shifter lever in **P**. Check that the round switch contact centers over the indicating line for **P**. If not, loosen the 2 switch mounting screws and align the switch.
3. Place the shifter lever in **N**. Repeat the check and adjust as necessary.
4. Finally check that the engine starts only in **P** or **N** and check that the backup lights work only in **R**.

Fuses and Circuit Breakers

LOCATION

240 Series

Fuses are located at the left side kick panel. An inline fuse serving the Jetronic fuel injection system is located on the left hand wheel housing, by

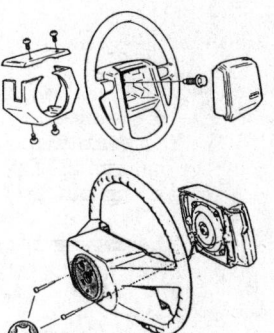

TORX
T30

Removing air bag assembly

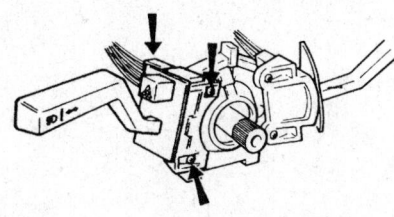

Steering column switches removal — 700 Series shown

the ignition coil. An inline fuse serving the EZ-116-K ignition system is located at the left hand wheel housing by the ignition coil.

700 and 900 Series

Fuses are located under the center of the dash attached to the side of the relay box or at the left kick panel.

Fusible Links

LOCATION

Fusible links may be located at the battery, starter or alternator.